# 2017
# Harris
# Illinois
# Industrial Directory

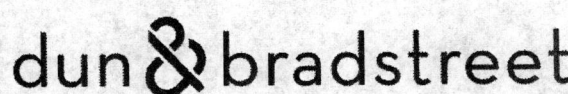

 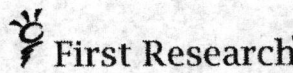 

Published September 2017 next update September 2018

**WARNING: Purchasers and users of this directory may not use this directory to compile mailing lists, other marketing aids and other types of data, which are sold or otherwise provided to third parties. Such use is wrongful, illegal and a violation of the federal copyright laws.**

**CAUTION**: Because of the many thousands of establishment listings contained in this directory and the possibilities of both human and mechanical error in processing this information, Mergent Inc. cannot assume liability for the correctness of the listings or information on which they are based. Hence, no information contained in this work should be relied upon in any instance where there is a possibility of any loss or damage as a consequence of any error or omission in this volume.

*Publisher*
Mergent Inc.
444 Madison Ave
New York, NY 10022

©Mergent Inc All Rights Reserved
2017 Mergent Business Press
ISSN 1080-2614
ISBN 978-1-68200-360-2

# TABLE OF CONTENTS

Summary of Contents & Explanatory Notes ................................................................................................ 4
User's Guide to Listings ............................................................................................................................... 6

### Geographic Section
County/City Cross-Reference Index .......................................................................................................... 9
Firms Listed by Location City ................................................................................................................... 13

### Standard Industrial Classification (SIC) Section
SIC Alphabetical Index ............................................................................................................................ 899
SIC Numerical Index ............................................................................................................................... 903
Firms Listed by SIC ................................................................................................................................. 907

### Alphabetic Section
Firms Listed by Firm Name .................................................................................................................... 1145

### Product Section
Product Index ........................................................................................................................................ 1433
Firms Listed by Product Category ......................................................................................................... 1461

# SUMMARY OF CONTENTS

Number of Companies ................................................. 22,701
Number of Decision Makers ..................................... 55,059
Minimum Number of Employees ........................................ 3

# EXPLANATORY NOTES

### How to Cross-Reference in This Directory
**Sequential Entry Numbers.** Each establishment in the Geographic Section is numbered sequentially (G-0000). The number assigned to each establishment is referred to as its "entry number." To make cross-referencing easier, each listing in the Geographic, SIC, Alphabetic and Product Sections includes the establishment's entry number. To facilitate locating an entry in the Geographic Section, the entry numbers for the first listing on the left page and the last listing on the right page are printed at the top of the page next to the city name.

### Source Suggestions Welcome
Although all known sources were used to compile this directory, it is possible that companies were inadvertently omitted. Your assistance in calling attention to such omissions would be greatly appreciated. A special form on the facing page will help you in the reporting process.

### Analysis
Every effort has been made to contact all firms to verify their information. The one exception to this rule is the annual sales figure, which is considered by many companies to be confidential information. Therefore, estimated sales have been calculated by multiplying the nationwide average sales per employee for the firm's major SIC/NAICS code by the firm's number of employees. Nationwide averages for sales per employee by SIC/NAICS codes are provided by the U.S. Department of Commerce and are updated annually. All sales—sales (est)—have been estimated by this method. The exceptions are parent companies (PA), division headquarters (DH) and headquarter locations (HQ) which may include an actual corporate sales figure—sales (corporate-wide) if available.

### Types of Companies
Descriptive and statistical data are included for companies in the entire state. These comprise manufacturers, machine shops, fabricators, assemblers and printers. Also identified are corporate offices in the state.

### Employment Data
The employment figure shown in the Geographic Section includes male and female employees and embraces all levels of the company: administrative, clerical, sales and maintenance. This figure is for the facility listed and does not include other plants or offices. It should be recognized that these figures represent an approximate year-round average. These employment figures are broken into codes A through G and used in the Product and SIC Sections to further help you in qualifying a company. Be sure to check the footnotes on the bottom of pages for the code breakdowns.

## Standard Industrial Classification (SIC)

The Standard Industrial Classification (SIC) system used in this directory was developed by the federal government for use in classifying establishments by the type of activity they are engaged in. The SIC classifications used in this directory are from the 1987 edition published by the U.S. Government's Office of Management and Budget. The SIC system separates all activities into broad industrial divisions (e.g., manufacturing, mining, retail trade). It further subdivides each division. The range of manufacturing industry classes extends from two-digit codes (major industry group) to four-digit codes (product).

For example:

| Industry Breakdown | Code | Industry, Product, etc. |
| --- | --- | --- |
| *Major industry group | 20 | Food and kindred products |
| Industry group | 203 | Canned and frozen foods |
| *Industry | 2033 | Fruits and vegetables, etc. |

*Classifications used in this directory

Only two-digit and four-digit codes are used in this directory.

## Arrangement

1. The **Geographic Section** contains complete in-depth corporate data. This section is sorted by cities listed in alphabetical order and companies listed alphabetically within each city. A County/City Index for referencing cities within counties precedes this section.

> IMPORTANT NOTICE: It is a violation of both federal and state law to transmit an unsolicited advertisement to a facsimile machine. Any user of this product that violates such laws may be subject to civil and criminal penalties, which may exceed $500 for each transmission of an unsolicited facsimile. Mergent Inc. provides fax numbers for lawful purposes only and expressly forbids the use of these numbers in any unlawful manner.

2. The **Standard Industrial Classification (SIC) Section** lists companies under approximately 500 four-digit SIC codes. An alphabetical and a numerical index precedes this section. A company can be listed under several codes. The codes are in numerical order with companies listed alphabetically under each code.

3. The **Alphabetic Section** lists all companies with their full physical or mailing addresses and telephone number.

4. The **Product Section** lists companies under unique Harris categories. An index preceding this section lists all product categories in alphabetical order. Companies can be listed under several categories.

# USER'S GUIDE TO LISTINGS

## GEOGRAPHIC SECTION

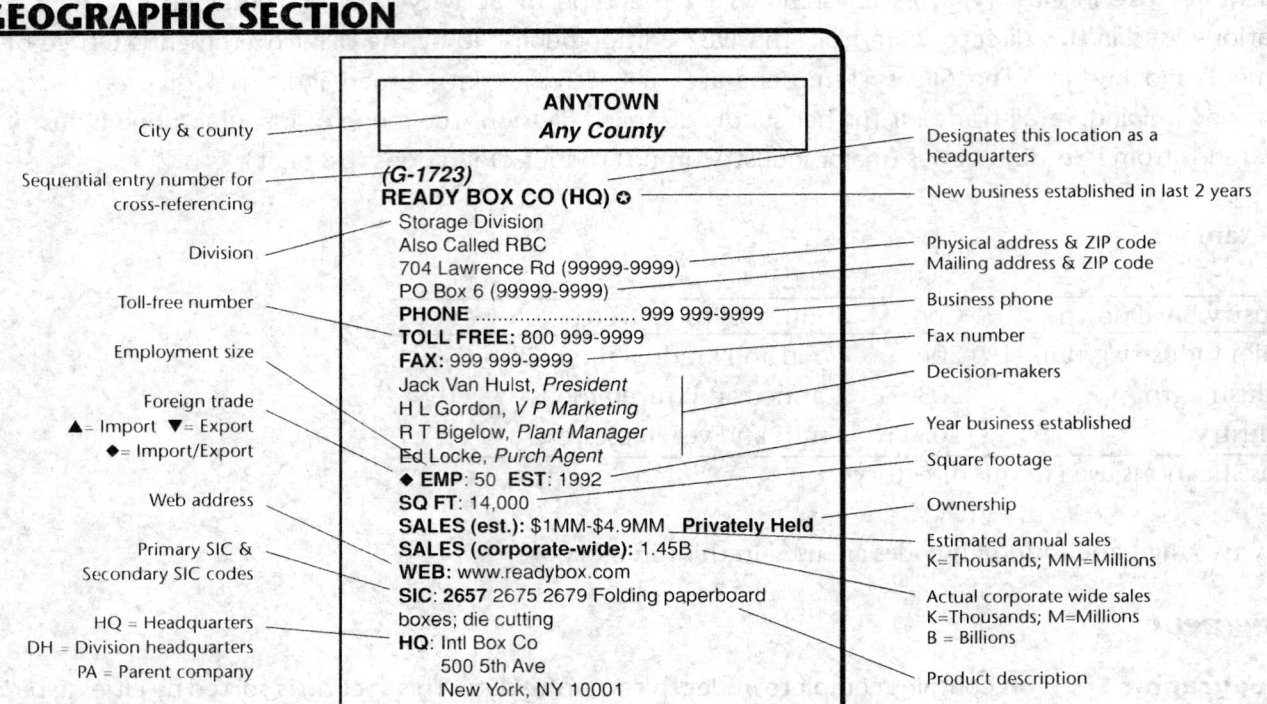

## SIC SECTION

## ALPHABETIC SECTION

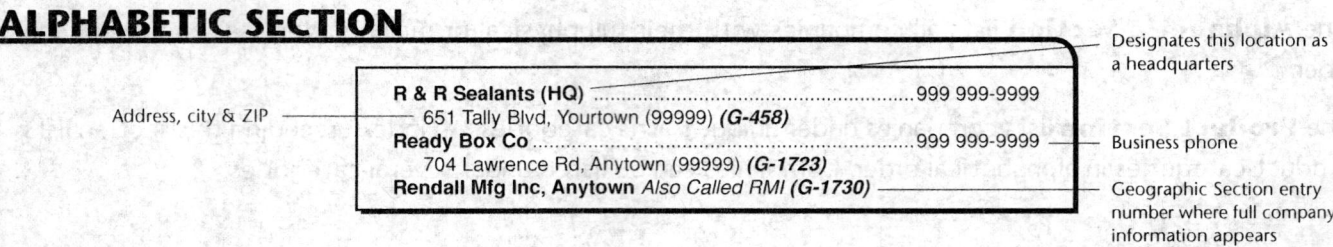

## PRODUCT SECTION

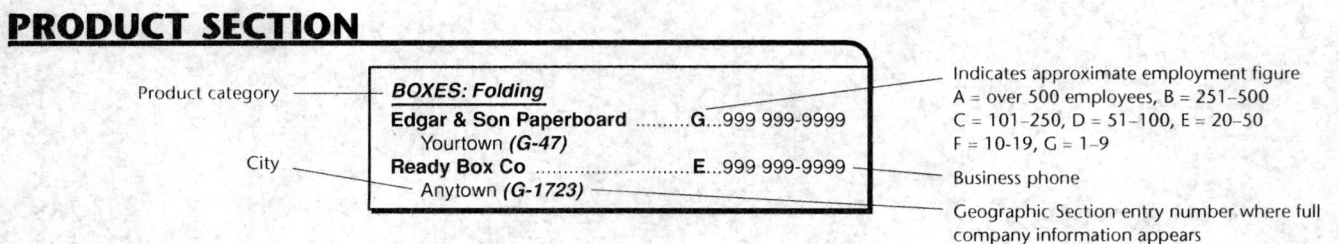

# GEOGRAPHIC SECTION
Companies sorted by city in alphabetical order
In-depth company data listed

# STANDARD INDUSTRIAL CLASSIFICATIONS
Alphabetical index of classifcation descriptions
Numerical index of classifcation descriptions
Companies sorted by SIC product groupings

# ALPHABETIC SECTION
Company listings in alphabetical order

# PRODUCT INDEX
Product categories listed in alphabetical order

# PRODUCT SECTION
Companies sorted by product and manufacturing service classifications

# Illinois
## County Map

# COUNTY/CITY CROSS-REFERENCE INDEX

**Adams**
- Camp Point .............. (G-2971)
- Clayton ..................... (G-7269)
- Coatsburg ................. (G-7300)
- Fowler ..................... (G-10272)
- Liberty .................... (G-13295)
- Payson .................... (G-17246)
- Plainville ................. (G-17662)
- Quincy .................... (G-17789)
- Ursa ........................ (G-21105)

**Alexander**
- Cairo ....................... (G-2927)
- Tamms .................... (G-20826)

**Bond**
- Greenville ................ (G-11387)
- Mulberry Grove ........ (G-15459)
- Pocahontas .............. (G-17683)

**Boone**
- Belvidere ................. (G-1726)
- Caledonia ................ (G-2930)
- Capron .................... (G-2994)
- Garden Prairie ......... (G-10793)
- Poplar Grove ........... (G-17713)

**Brown**
- Mount Sterling ......... (G-15390)
- Timewell ................. (G-20884)

**Bureau**
- Buda ....................... (G-2648)
- Depue ..................... (G-8134)
- Ladd ....................... (G-12792)
- Malden .................... (G-14164)
- Neponset ................. (G-15859)
- Ohio ........................ (G-16753)
- Princeton ................. (G-17740)
- Spring Valley ........... (G-20374)
- Tiskilwa .................. (G-20958)
- Walnut .................... (G-21329)

**Calhoun**
- Batchtown ............... (G-1517)
- Hamburg ................. (G-11526)
- Hardin ..................... (G-11593)

**Carroll**
- Chadwick ................ (G-3440)
- Lanark ..................... (G-13149)
- Milledgeville ........... (G-14816)
- Mount Carroll .......... (G-15290)
- Savanna .................. (G-19396)
- Shannon .................. (G-19899)
- Thomson ................. (G-20864)

**Cass**
- Arenzville ............... (G-688)
- Ashland ................... (G-926)
- Beardstown ............. (G-1520)
- Virginia ................... (G-21304)

**Champaign**
- Broadlands .............. (G-2550)
- Champaign .............. (G-3444)
- Dewey ..................... (G-8310)
- Fisher ..................... (G-10191)
- Foosland ................. (G-10232)
- Gifford .................... (G-10910)
- Homer ..................... (G-12073)
- Ivesdale .................. (G-12377)
- Mahomet ................. (G-14157)
- Ogden ..................... (G-16743)
- Pesotum .................. (G-17533)
- Philo ....................... (G-17539)
- Rantoul ................... (G-17917)
- Sadorus ................... (G-19117)
- Saint Joseph ............ (G-19316)
- Savoy ...................... (G-19408)
- Seymour .................. (G-19897)
- Sidney .................... (G-19936)
- Thomasboro ............ (G-20859)
- Tolono .................... (G-20971)
- Urbana .................... (G-21068)

**Christian**
- Assumption .............. (G-930)
- Morrisonville ........... (G-15150)
- Moweaqua ............... (G-15458)
- Pana ........................ (G-17135)
- Taylorville .............. (G-20831)

**Clark**
- Casey ...................... (G-3380)
- Marshall .................. (G-14318)
- Martinsville ............. (G-14332)
- West Union ............. (G-21826)

**Clay**
- Clay City ................. (G-7261)
- Flora ....................... (G-10200)
- Ingraham ................. (G-12199)
- Louisville ................ (G-13909)
- Xenia ...................... (G-22643)

**Clinton**
- Albers ..................... (G-353)
- Aviston ................... (G-1243)
- Bartelso ................... (G-1314)
- Breese ..................... (G-2437)
- Carlyle .................... (G-3052)
- Damiansville ............ (G-7700)
- Germantown ............ (G-10892)
- Hoffman .................. (G-11988)
- Keyesport ................ (G-12696)
- New Baden .............. (G-15862)
- Trenton ................... (G-20989)

**Coles**
- Ashmore .................. (G-928)
- Charleston ............... (G-3589)
- Humboldt ................ (G-12128)
- Lerna ...................... (G-13287)
- Mattoon ................... (G-14382)
- Oakland .................. (G-16724)

**Cook**
- Alsip ....................... (G-426)
- Argo ....................... (G-693)
- Arlington Heights .... (G-699)
- Bartlett .................... (G-1315)
- Bedford Park ........... (G-1528)
- Bellwood ................. (G-1692)
- Berkeley .................. (G-2043)
- Berwyn .................... (G-2054)
- Blue Island .............. (G-2237)
- Bridgeview .............. (G-2457)
- Broadview ............... (G-2551)
- Brookfield ............... (G-2621)
- Burbank ................... (G-2806)
- Burnham .................. (G-2815)
- Calumet City ........... (G-2935)
- Calumet Park ........... (G-2956)
- Chicago ................... (G-3661)
- Chicago Heights ...... (G-7077)
- Chicago Ridge ......... (G-7138)
- Cicero ..................... (G-7175)
- Country Club Hills ... (G-7403)
- Countryside ............. (G-7411)
- Crestwood ............... (G-7473)
- Des Plaines ............. (G-8135)
- Dixmoor .................. (G-8319)
- Dolton ..................... (G-8362)
- East Hazel Crest ...... (G-8663)
- Elk Grove Village .... (G-9247)
- Elmwood Park ......... (G-9966)
- Evanston ................. (G-10001)
- Evergreen Park ........ (G-10109)
- Flossmoor ................ (G-10223)
- Ford Heights ........... (G-10233)
- Forest Park .............. (G-10234)
- Forest View ............. (G-10258)
- Franklin Park ........... (G-10380)
- Glencoe ................... (G-10998)
- Glenview ................. (G-11094)
- Glenwood ................ (G-11215)
- Hanover Park ........... (G-11574)
- Harvey .................... (G-11649)
- Harwood Heights ..... (G-11681)
- Hazel Crest .............. (G-11706)
- Hickory Hills ........... (G-11767)
- Hillside ................... (G-11907)
- Hodgkins ................. (G-11970)
- Hoffman Estates ...... (G-11989)
- Homewood .............. (G-12090)
- Inverness ................. (G-12200)
- Justice ..................... (G-12594)
- Kenilworth .............. (G-12662)
- La Grange ............... (G-12724)
- La Grange Highlands (G-12749)
- La Grange Park ........ (G-12751)
- Lansing ................... (G-13156)
- Lemont .................... (G-13221)
- Lincolnwood ............ (G-13499)
- Lynwood ................. (G-14017)
- Lyons ...................... (G-14028)
- Markham ................. (G-14301)
- Matteson ................. (G-14368)
- Maywood ................ (G-14414)
- Mc Cook ................. (G-14443)
- Melrose Park ........... (G-14577)
- Merrionette Park ..... (G-14736)
- Midlothian ............... (G-14765)
- Morton Grove .......... (G-15186)
- Mount Prospect ....... (G-15308)
- Niles ....................... (G-15952)
- Norridge .................. (G-16094)
- Northbrook .............. (G-16194)
- Northfield ................ (G-16390)
- Northlake ................ (G-16424)
- Oak Forest ............... (G-16571)
- Oak Lawn ................ (G-16594)
- Oak Park ................. (G-16648)
- Olympia Fields ........ (G-16803)
- Orland Park ............. (G-16836)
- Palatine ................... (G-16994)
- Palos Heights .......... (G-17098)
- Palos Hills .............. (G-17114)
- Palos Park ............... (G-17126)
- Park Forest .............. (G-17168)
- Park Ridge .............. (G-17177)
- Phoenix ................... (G-17540)
- Posen ...................... (G-17726)
- Prospect Heights ...... (G-17772)
- Richton Park ........... (G-17975)
- River Forest ............ (G-17996)
- River Grove ............. (G-18004)
- Riverdale ................. (G-18014)
- Riverside ................. (G-18028)
- Rolling Meadows ..... (G-18705)
- Rosemont ................ (G-18989)
- S Chicago Hts .......... (G-19098)
- Sauk Village ............ (G-19391)
- Schaumburg ............. (G-19417)
- Schiller Park ............ (G-19796)
- Skokie ..................... (G-19942)
- South Holland .......... (G-20237)
- Steger ...................... (G-20565)
- Stickney .................. (G-20624)
- Stone Park ............... (G-20632)
- Streamwood ............. (G-20638)
- Summit Argo ........... (G-20759)
- Thornton .................. (G-20866)
- Tinley Park .............. (G-20886)
- Westchester ............. (G-21827)
- Western Springs ....... (G-21862)
- Wheeling ................. (G-21991)
- Willow Springs ........ (G-22193)
- Wilmette .................. (G-22241)
- Winnetka ................. (G-22300)
- Worth ...................... (G-22631)

**Crawford**
- Annapolis ................ (G-609)
- Flat Rock ................. (G-10195)
- Oblong .................... (G-16729)
- Palestine ................. (G-17093)
- Robinson ................. (G-18055)

**Cumberland**
- Greenup .................. (G-11381)
- Neoga ..................... (G-15857)
- Toledo .................... (G-20961)

**De Witt**
- Clinton .................... (G-7276)
- Farmer City ............. (G-10178)
- Kenney .................... (G-12664)

**Dekalb**
- Cortland .................. (G-7383)
- De Kalb .................. (G-7817)
- Dekalb .................... (G-8071)
- Genoa ..................... (G-10875)
- Hinckley .................. (G-11934)
- Kingston ................. (G-12706)
- Kirkland .................. (G-12711)
- Malta ...................... (G-14165)
- Sandwich ................ (G-19360)
- Somonauk ............... (G-20124)
- Sycamore ................. (G-20784)
- Waterman ................ (G-21407)

**Douglas**
- Arcola ..................... (G-665)
- Arthur ..................... (G-880)
- Atwood ................... (G-947)
- Tuscola ................... (G-21014)
- Villa Grove ............. (G-21227)

**Dupage**
- Addison .................. (G-14)
- Aurora .................... (G-952)
- Bartlett .................... (G-1327)
- Bensenville ............. (G-1808)
- Bloomingdale .......... (G-2091)
- Burr Ridge .............. (G-2818)
- Carol Stream ........... (G-3086)
- Clarendon Hills ....... (G-7257)
- Darien ..................... (G-7786)
- Downers Grove ....... (G-8384)
- Elmhurst ................. (G-9828)
- Eola ........................ (G-9988)
- Glen Ellyn .............. (G-10956)
- Glendale Heights ..... (G-11006)
- Hinsdale .................. (G-11938)
- Itasca ...................... (G-12222)
- Lisle ....................... (G-13552)
- Lombard .................. (G-13756)
- Medinah .................. (G-14576)
- Naperville ............... (G-15587)
- Oak Brook ............... (G-16483)
- Oakbrook Terrace .... (G-16693)
- Roselle .................... (G-18926)
- Villa Park ................ (G-21231)
- Warrenville ............. (G-21340)
- West Chicago .......... (G-21650)
- Westmont ................ (G-21875)
- Wheaton .................. (G-21932)
- Willowbrook ........... (G-22199)
- Winfield .................. (G-22283)
- Wood Dale .............. (G-22326)
- Woodridge ............... (G-22447)

**Edgar**
- Chrisman ................. (G-7173)
- Kansas .................... (G-12659)
- Paris ....................... (G-17139)

**Edwards**
- Albion ..................... (G-355)
- West Salem ............. (G-21824)

**Effingham**
- Altamont ................. (G-548)
- Dieterich ................. (G-8312)
- Effingham ............... (G-8820)
- Mason ..................... (G-14361)
- Montrose ................. (G-15089)
- Shumway ................ (G-19932)
- Teutopolis ............... (G-20847)
- Watson .................... (G-21433)

**Fayette**
- Farina ..................... (G-10172)
- Ramsey ................... (G-17913)
- Saint Elmo .............. (G-19303)
- Saint Peter .............. (G-19320)
- Shobonier ................ (G-19921)
- Vandalia .................. (G-21113)

# COUNTY/CITY CROSS-REFERENCE

### Ford
| City | Entry # |
|---|---|
| Gibson City | (G-10897) |
| Kempton | (G-12661) |
| Paxton | (G-17236) |
| Piper City | (G-17558) |

### Franklin
| City | Entry # |
|---|---|
| Benton | (G-2020) |
| Buckner | (G-2647) |
| Christopher | (G-7174) |
| Ewing | (G-10120) |
| Logan | (G-13755) |
| Sesser | (G-19894) |
| Thompsonville | (G-20861) |
| West Frankfort | (G-21804) |
| Whittington | (G-22186) |

### Fulton
| City | Entry # |
|---|---|
| Astoria | (G-934) |
| Canton | (G-2980) |
| Cuba | (G-7679) |
| Fairview | (G-10165) |
| Farmington | (G-10185) |
| Lewistown | (G-13289) |
| Smithfield | (G-20119) |
| Vermont | (G-21138) |

### Gallatin
| City | Entry # |
|---|---|
| Equality | (G-9989) |
| Junction | (G-12593) |
| Omaha | (G-16807) |
| Ridgway | (G-17983) |
| Shawneetown | (G-19904) |

### Greene
| City | Entry # |
|---|---|
| Carrollton | (G-3307) |
| Eldred | (G-8927) |
| Rockbridge | (G-18212) |
| Roodhouse | (G-18882) |
| White Hall | (G-22183) |

### Grundy
| City | Entry # |
|---|---|
| Braceville | (G-2410) |
| Coal City | (G-7291) |
| Mazon | (G-14438) |
| Minooka | (G-14836) |
| Morris | (G-15090) |

### Hamilton
| City | Entry # |
|---|---|
| Dahlgren | (G-7689) |
| Macedonia | (G-14047) |
| Mc Leansboro | (G-14464) |

### Hancock
| City | Entry # |
|---|---|
| Augusta | (G-951) |
| Burnside | (G-2817) |
| Carthage | (G-3312) |
| Dallas City | (G-7695) |
| Hamilton | (G-11530) |
| Nauvoo | (G-15852) |
| Plymouth | (G-17682) |
| Warsaw | (G-21370) |

### Hardin
| City | Entry # |
|---|---|
| Cave In Rock | (G-3402) |
| Elizabethtown | (G-9245) |
| Rosiclare | (G-19047) |

### Henderson
| City | Entry # |
|---|---|
| Oquawka | (G-16812) |
| Stronghurst | (G-20712) |

### Henry
| City | Entry # |
|---|---|
| Alpha | (G-425) |
| Annawan | (G-610) |
| Atkinson | (G-943) |
| Cambridge | (G-2965) |
| Cleveland | (G-7271) |
| Colona | (G-7343) |
| Galva | (G-10782) |
| Geneseo | (G-10796) |
| Kewanee | (G-12667) |
| Lynn Center | (G-14015) |
| Orion | (G-16835) |
| Osco | (G-16899) |

### Iroquois
| City | Entry # |
|---|---|
| Ashkum | (G-925) |
| Chebanse | (G-3630) |
| Cissna Park | (G-7253) |
| Clifton | (G-7272) |
| Crescent City | (G-7455) |
| Gilman | (G-10942) |
| Loda | (G-13751) |
| Milford | (G-14811) |
| Onarga | (G-16808) |
| Watseka | (G-21413) |

### Jackson
| City | Entry # |
|---|---|
| Ava | (G-1237) |
| Campbell Hill | (G-2974) |
| Carbondale | (G-2999) |
| De Soto | (G-7818) |
| Gorham | (G-11254) |
| Makanda | (G-14162) |
| Murphysboro | (G-15570) |
| Pomona | (G-17693) |

### Jasper
| City | Entry # |
|---|---|
| Newton | (G-15936) |
| Sainte Marie | (G-19323) |
| Willow Hill | (G-22192) |

### Jefferson
| City | Entry # |
|---|---|
| Belle Rive | (G-1605) |
| Dix | (G-8317) |
| INA | (G-12184) |
| Mount Vernon | (G-15396) |
| Opdyke | (G-16810) |

### Jersey
| City | Entry # |
|---|---|
| Dow | (G-8382) |
| Elsah | (G-9976) |
| Grafton | (G-11255) |
| Jerseyville | (G-12416) |

### Jo Daviess
| City | Entry # |
|---|---|
| East Dubuque | (G-8616) |
| Elizabeth | (G-9241) |
| Galena | (G-10714) |
| Hanover | (G-11571) |
| Scales Mound | (G-19415) |
| Stockton | (G-20630) |
| Warren | (G-21335) |

### Johnson
| City | Entry # |
|---|---|
| Buncombe | (G-2799) |
| Goreville | (G-11250) |
| Ozark | (G-16993) |
| Vienna | (G-21222) |

### Kane
| City | Entry # |
|---|---|
| Aurora | (G-1101) |
| Batavia | (G-1401) |
| Big Rock | (G-2086) |
| Burlington | (G-2811) |
| Carpentersville | (G-3270) |
| Dundee | (G-8559) |
| East Dundee | (G-8627) |
| Elburn | (G-8872) |
| Elgin | (G-8928) |
| Geneva | (G-10807) |
| Gilberts | (G-10911) |
| Hampshire | (G-11542) |
| Kaneville | (G-12599) |
| Lafox | (G-12793) |
| Maple Park | (G-14196) |
| North Aurora | (G-16117) |
| Pingree Grove | (G-17555) |
| Saint Charles | (G-19129) |
| Sleepy Hollow | (G-20117) |
| South Elgin | (G-20179) |
| Sugar Grove | (G-20716) |
| Virgil | (G-21302) |
| Wasco | (G-21372) |
| West Dundee | (G-21794) |

### Kankakee
| City | Entry # |
|---|---|
| Aroma Park | (G-878) |
| Bonfield | (G-2385) |
| Bourbonnais | (G-2386) |
| Bradley | (G-2412) |
| Grant Park | (G-11312) |
| Herscher | (G-11759) |
| Kankakee | (G-12601) |
| Manteno | (G-14179) |
| Momence | (G-14978) |
| Reddick | (G-17952) |
| Saint Anne | (G-19118) |
| Union Hill | (G-21039) |

### Kendall
| City | Entry # |
|---|---|
| Bristol | (G-2549) |
| Millington | (G-14819) |
| Montgomery | (G-15026) |
| Newark | (G-15932) |
| Oswego | (G-16901) |
| Plano | (G-17663) |
| Yorkville | (G-22647) |

### Knox
| City | Entry # |
|---|---|
| Abingdon | (G-9) |
| Dahinda | (G-7688) |
| Galesburg | (G-10737) |
| Knoxville | (G-12721) |
| Maquon | (G-14215) |
| Saint Augustine | (G-19128) |
| Wataga | (G-21398) |
| Williamsfield | (G-22189) |
| Yates City | (G-22646) |

### Lake
| City | Entry # |
|---|---|
| Abbott Park | (G-1) |
| Antioch | (G-612) |
| Bannockburn | (G-1253) |
| Barrington | (G-1268) |
| Beach Park | (G-1518) |
| Buffalo Grove | (G-2650) |
| Deer Park | (G-7969) |
| Deerfield | (G-7974) |
| Fox Lake | (G-10273) |
| Grayslake | (G-11320) |
| Gurnee | (G-11416) |
| Hainesville | (G-11522) |
| Hawthorn Woods | (G-11701) |
| Highland Park | (G-11820) |
| Highwood | (G-11884) |
| Hoffman Estates | (G-12071) |
| Indian Creek | (G-12185) |
| Ingleside | (G-12186) |
| Inverness | (G-12207) |
| Island Lake | (G-12212) |
| Kildeer | (G-12699) |
| Lake Barrington | (G-12798) |
| Lake Bluff | (G-12827) |
| Lake Forest | (G-12874) |
| Lake Villa | (G-13010) |
| Lake Zurich | (G-13032) |
| Libertyville | (G-13297) |
| Lincolnshire | (G-13422) |
| Lindenhurst | (G-13545) |
| Long Grove | (G-13886) |
| Mettawa | (G-14762) |
| Mundelein | (G-15460) |
| North Barrington | (G-16151) |
| North Chicago | (G-16157) |
| Old Mill Creek | (G-16756) |
| Park City | (G-17166) |
| Port Barrington | (G-17718) |
| Riverwoods | (G-18037) |
| Round Lake | (G-19051) |
| Round Lake Beach | (G-19072) |
| Round Lake Heights | (G-19081) |
| Round Lake Park | (G-19083) |
| Russell | (G-19097) |
| South Barrington | (G-20131) |
| Third Lake | (G-20858) |
| Vernon Hills | (G-21141) |
| Volo | (G-21308) |
| Wadsworth | (G-21321) |
| Wauconda | (G-21434) |
| Waukegan | (G-21516) |
| Winthrop Harbor | (G-22319) |
| Zion | (G-22678) |

### Lasalle
| City | Entry # |
|---|---|
| Earlville | (G-8593) |
| Grand Ridge | (G-11257) |
| La Salle | (G-12760) |
| Leland | (G-13218) |
| Leonore | (G-13285) |
| Lostant | (G-13906) |
| Marseilles | (G-14308) |
| Mendota | (G-14714) |
| Oglesby | (G-16746) |
| Ottawa | (G-16944) |
| Peru | (G-17498) |
| Ransom | (G-17916) |
| Seneca | (G-19886) |
| Serena | (G-19892) |
| Sheridan | (G-19918) |
| Streator | (G-20682) |
| Tonica | (G-20973) |
| Troy Grove | (G-21012) |
| Utica | (G-21106) |
| Wedron | (G-21646) |

### Lawrence
| City | Entry # |
|---|---|
| Bridgeport | (G-2449) |
| Lawrenceville | (G-13194) |
| Saint Francisville | (G-19312) |
| Sumner | (G-20770) |

### Lee
| City | Entry # |
|---|---|
| Amboy | (G-596) |
| Ashton | (G-929) |
| Compton | (G-7366) |
| Dixon | (G-8321) |
| Harmon | (G-11595) |
| Lee | (G-13217) |
| Paw Paw | (G-17233) |
| Steward | (G-20623) |
| Sublette | (G-20714) |

### Livingston
| City | Entry # |
|---|---|
| Blackstone | (G-2087) |
| Chatsworth | (G-3626) |
| Cornell | (G-7381) |
| Cullom | (G-7681) |
| Dwight | (G-8588) |
| Fairbury | (G-10121) |
| Flanagan | (G-10194) |
| Forrest | (G-10260) |
| Pontiac | (G-17696) |
| Saunemin | (G-19395) |

### Logan
| City | Entry # |
|---|---|
| Atlanta | (G-946) |
| Elkhart | (G-9825) |
| Emden | (G-9983) |
| Lincoln | (G-13404) |
| Mount Pulaski | (G-15388) |

### Macon
| City | Entry # |
|---|---|
| Argenta | (G-689) |
| Blue Mound | (G-2274) |
| Decatur | (G-7819) |
| Elwin | (G-9977) |
| Forsyth | (G-10271) |
| Harristown | (G-11607) |
| Maroa | (G-14305) |
| Mount Zion | (G-15450) |
| Oreana | (G-16816) |
| Warrensburg | (G-21338) |

### Macoupin
| City | Entry # |
|---|---|
| Benld | (G-1804) |
| Brighton | (G-2540) |
| Bunker Hill | (G-2803) |
| Carlinville | (G-3030) |
| Gillespie | (G-10941) |
| Girard | (G-10945) |
| Mount Olive | (G-15301) |
| Palmyra | (G-17097) |
| Piasa | (G-17543) |
| Staunton | (G-20553) |
| Virden | (G-21296) |

### Madison
| City | Entry # |
|---|---|
| Alhambra | (G-418) |
| Alton | (G-557) |
| Bethalto | (G-2080) |
| Collinsville | (G-7312) |
| Cottage Hills | (G-7397) |
| Dorsey | (G-8380) |
| East Alton | (G-8598) |
| Edwardsville | (G-8787) |
| Glen Carbon | (G-10952) |
| Godfrey | (G-11221) |
| Granite City | (G-11258) |
| Hamel | (G-11528) |
| Hartford | (G-11609) |
| Highland | (G-11775) |
| Madison | (G-14139) |
| Marine | (G-14246) |
| Maryville | (G-14340) |
| Roxana | (G-19084) |
| Saint Jacob | (G-19315) |
| South Roxana | (G-20312) |
| Troy | (G-21002) |
| Venice | (G-21137) |
| Wood River | (G-22440) |

### Marion
| City | Entry # |
|---|---|
| Alma | (G-422) |
| Centralia | (G-3404) |
| Kinmundy | (G-12709) |

# COUNTY/CITY CROSS-REFERENCE

| | ENTRY # | | ENTRY # | | ENTRY # | | ENTRY # | | ENTRY # |
|---|---|---|---|---|---|---|---|---|---|
| Odin | (G-16738) | Mc Lean | (G-14463) | Chillicothe | (G-7160) | **Rock Island** | | **Stark** | |
| Patoka | (G-17230) | Normal | (G-16063) | Dunlap | (G-8566) | Buffalo Prairie | (G-2797) | Bradford | (G-2411) |
| Salem | (G-19326) | Saybrook | (G-19413) | East Peoria | (G-8699) | Coal Valley | (G-7294) | Toulon | (G-20976) |
| Sandoval | (G-19355) | Shirley | (G-19920) | Edelstein | (G-8779) | Cordova | (G-7374) | Wyoming | (G-22636) |
| Vernon | (G-21139) | Stanford | (G-20551) | Edwards | (G-8781) | East Moline | (G-8669) | **Stephenson** | |
| Walnut Hill | (G-21334) | Towanda | (G-20978) | Elmwood | (G-9963) | Hillsdale | (G-11901) | Dakota | (G-7694) |
| **Marshall** | | **Menard** | | Glasford | (G-10951) | Milan | (G-14772) | Davis | (G-7805) |
| Henry | (G-11739) | Athens | (G-937) | Hanna City | (G-11567) | Moline | (G-14916) | Freeport | (G-10644) |
| Lacon | (G-12785) | Greenview | (G-11386) | Mapleton | (G-14205) | Port Byron | (G-17719) | German Valley | (G-10890) |
| Sparland | (G-20315) | Petersburg | (G-17534) | Mossville | (G-15248) | Reynolds | (G-17953) | Kent | (G-12665) |
| Toluca | (G-20972) | **Mercer** | | Peoria | (G-17297) | Rock Island | (G-18157) | Lena | (G-13272) |
| Varna | (G-21132) | Aledo | (G-367) | Princeville | (G-17763) | Silvis | (G-19939) | Mc Connell | (G-14442) |
| Washburn | (G-21374) | Alexis | (G-375) | Trivoli | (G-20999) | Taylor Ridge | (G-20830) | Orangeville | (G-16814) |
| Wenona | (G-21647) | Joy | (G-12592) | West Peoria | (G-21822) | **Saline** | | Pearl City | (G-17248) |
| **Mason** | | Matherville | (G-14367) | **Perry** | | Carrier Mills | (G-3305) | Rock City | (G-18124) |
| Easton | (G-8777) | New Boston | (G-15867) | Cutler | (G-7687) | Eldorado | (G-8917) | Winslow | (G-22317) |
| Havana | (G-11694) | New Windsor | (G-15929) | Du Quoin | (G-8550) | Galatia | (G-10711) | **Tazewell** | |
| Kilbourne | (G-12697) | Viola | (G-21292) | Pinckneyville | (G-17544) | Harrisburg | (G-11596) | Deer Creek | (G-7961) |
| Manito | (G-14172) | **Monroe** | | **Piatt** | | Raleigh | (G-17908) | Delavan | (G-8133) |
| Mason City | (G-14362) | Columbia | (G-7350) | Bement | (G-1800) | Stonefort | (G-20637) | East Peoria | (G-8700) |
| **Massac** | | Fults | (G-10709) | Cerro Gordo | (G-3439) | **Sangamon** | | Green Valley | (G-11378) |
| Metropolis | (G-14752) | Hecker | (G-11732) | Cisco | (G-7249) | Auburn | (G-948) | Groveland | (G-11415) |
| **Mcdonough** | | Valmeyer | (G-21112) | Mansfield | (G-14178) | Buffalo | (G-2649) | Hopedale | (G-12121) |
| Adair | (G-11) | Waterloo | (G-21400) | Monticello | (G-15074) | Chatham | (G-3617) | Mackinaw | (G-14118) |
| Bushnell | (G-2897) | **Montgomery** | | **Pike** | | Dawson | (G-7816) | Minier | (G-14833) |
| Colchester | (G-7307) | Butler | (G-2910) | Barry | (G-1311) | Divernon | (G-8316) | Morton | (G-15152) |
| Good Hope | (G-11243) | Coffeen | (G-7306) | Chambersburg | (G-3443) | Glenarm | (G-10996) | North Pekin | (G-16192) |
| Macomb | (G-14121) | Farmersville | (G-10183) | Detroit | (G-8309) | Mechanicsburg | (G-14574) | Pekin | (G-17253) |
| **Mchenry** | | Fillmore | (G-10189) | Griggsville | (G-11412) | New Berlin | (G-15866) | Peoria | (G-17483) |
| Algonquin | (G-376) | Hillsboro | (G-11888) | New Canton | (G-15868) | Pawnee | (G-17234) | Tremont | (G-20981) |
| Bull Valley | (G-2798) | Litchfield | (G-13680) | Pearl | (G-17247) | Pleasant Plains | (G-17681) | Washington | (G-21377) |
| Cary | (G-3320) | Nokomis | (G-16055) | Perry | (G-17497) | Riverton | (G-18034) | **Union** | |
| Crystal Lake | (G-7524) | Raymond | (G-17938) | Pittsfield | (G-17560) | Rochester | (G-18114) | Alto Pass | (G-556) |
| Fox River Grove | (G-10285) | **Morgan** | | Pleasant Hill | (G-17680) | Springfield | (G-20383) | Anna | (G-600) |
| Harvard | (G-11615) | Alexander | (G-374) | **Pope** | | Williamsville | (G-22190) | Cobden | (G-7301) |
| Hebron | (G-11715) | Chapin | (G-3588) | Golconda | (G-11239) | **Schuyler** | | Dongola | (G-8379) |
| Huntley | (G-12131) | Concord | (G-7368) | Herod | (G-11747) | Rushville | (G-19090) | Jonesboro | (G-12591) |
| Johnsburg | (G-12430) | Franklin | (G-10378) | **Pulaski** | | **Scott** | | **Vermilion** | |
| Lake In The Hills | (G-12981) | Jacksonville | (G-12378) | Grand Chain | (G-11256) | Winchester | (G-22278) | Allerton | (G-421) |
| Lakemoor | (G-13143) | Meredosia | (G-14734) | Mound City | (G-15256) | **Shelby** | | Catlin | (G-3401) |
| Marengo | (G-14217) | South Jacksonville | (G-20311) | Mounds | (G-15258) | Cowden | (G-7452) | Danville | (G-7702) |
| Mc Henry | (G-14462) | Waverly | (G-21645) | Olmsted | (G-16757) | Mode | (G-14849) | East Lynn | (G-8668) |
| McCullom Lake | (G-14471) | Woodson | (G-22530) | Ullin | (G-21031) | Shelbyville | (G-19905) | Fairmount | (G-10162) |
| McHenry | (G-14473) | **Moultrie** | | **Putnam** | | Sigel | (G-19938) | Fithian | (G-10193) |
| Oakwood Hills | (G-16727) | Bethany | (G-2084) | Granville | (G-11317) | Tower Hill | (G-20980) | Georgetown | (G-10886) |
| Richmond | (G-17954) | Dalton City | (G-7699) | Hennepin | (G-11733) | Windsor | (G-22282) | Henning | (G-11737) |
| Ringwood | (G-17986) | Lovington | (G-14012) | Mark | (G-14298) | **St. Clair** | | Hoopeston | (G-12107) |
| Spring Grove | (G-20323) | Sullivan | (G-20739) | Putnam | (G-17788) | Belleville | (G-1606) | Oakwood | (G-16725) |
| Trout Valley | (G-21001) | **Ogle** | | **Randolph** | | Cahokia | (G-2923) | Potomac | (G-17738) |
| Union | (G-21033) | Byron | (G-2911) | Baldwin | (G-1250) | Caseyville | (G-3393) | Rossville | (G-19050) |
| Village of Lakewood | (G-21290) | Creston | (G-7471) | Chester | (G-3650) | Centreville | (G-3438) | Tilton | (G-20878) |
| Wonder Lake | (G-22321) | Davis Junction | (G-7810) | Coulterville | (G-7398) | Dupo | (G-8569) | Westville | (G-21928) |
| Woodstock | (G-22532) | Forreston | (G-10268) | Ellis Grove | (G-9826) | East Carondelet | (G-8613) | **Wabash** | |
| **Mclean** | | Kings | (G-12705) | Evansville | (G-10108) | East Saint Louis | (G-8739) | Allendale | (G-420) |
| Bloomington | (G-2142) | Leaf River | (G-13210) | Percy | (G-17495) | Fairview Heights | (G-10166) | Keensburg | (G-12660) |
| Carlock | (G-3049) | Lindenwood | (G-13551) | Prairie Du Rocher | (G-17739) | Freeburg | (G-10633) | Mount Carmel | (G-15260) |
| Chenoa | (G-3633) | Monroe Center | (G-15025) | Red Bud | (G-17940) | Lebanon | (G-13212) | **Warren** | |
| Colfax | (G-7311) | Mount Morris | (G-15295) | Rockwood | (G-18704) | Marissa | (G-14296) | Cameron | (G-2970) |
| Cooksville | (G-7372) | Oregon | (G-16818) | Ruma | (G-19088) | Mascoutah | (G-14348) | Monmouth | (G-15010) |
| Danvers | (G-7701) | Polo | (G-17687) | Sparta | (G-20316) | Millstadt | (G-14820) | Roseville | (G-19045) |
| Downs | (G-8547) | Rochelle | (G-18076) | Steeleville | (G-20560) | National Stock Yards | (G-15849) | **Washington** | |
| Ellsworth | (G-9827) | Stillman Valley | (G-20625) | Tilden | (G-20877) | New Athens | (G-15860) | Addieville | (G-13) |
| Gridley | (G-11404) | Woosung | (G-22630) | **Richland** | | O Fallon | (G-16459) | Ashley | (G-927) |
| Heyworth | (G-11764) | **Peoria** | | Claremont | (G-7256) | Sauget | (G-19381) | Nashville | (G-15833) |
| Hudson | (G-12123) | Bartonville | (G-1390) | Noble | (G-16049) | Scott Air Force Base | (G-19885) | Okawville | (G-16754) |
| Le Roy | (G-13207) | Brimfield | (G-2547) | Olney | (G-16758) | Smithton | (G-20120) | Richview | (G-17981) |
| Lexington | (G-13291) | | | | | Swansea | (G-20774) | Venedy | (G-21136) |

## COUNTY/CITY CROSS-REFERENCE

### Wayne
- Cisne ............... (G-7250)
- Fairfield ............ (G-10135)
- Mount Erie ......... (G-15294)
- Sims ................ (G-19941)

### White
- Carmi ............... (G-3062)
- Crossville .......... (G-7521)
- Enfield ............. (G-9987)
- Grayville ........... (G-11369)
- Norris City ......... (G-16111)
- Springerton ........ (G-20382)

### Whiteside
- Albany ............. (G-352)
- Coleta .............. (G-7310)
- Deer Grove ........ (G-7967)
- Erie ................. (G-9991)
- Fulton .............. (G-10700)
- Galt ................ (G-10781)
- Lyndon ............. (G-14013)
- Morrison ........... (G-15141)
- Prophetstown ..... (G-17767)
- Rock Falls ......... (G-18126)
- Sterling ............ (G-20582)
- Tampico ........... (G-20828)

### Will
- Beecher ........... (G-1596)
- Bolingbrook ....... (G-2275)
- Channahon ....... (G-3564)
- Crest Hill .......... (G-7457)
- Crete ............... (G-7508)
- Custer Park ....... (G-7686)
- Elwood ............. (G-9978)
- Frankfort .......... (G-10290)
- Homer Glen ...... (G-12076)
- Joliet ............... (G-12449)
- Lockport ........... (G-13700)
- Manhattan ........ (G-14167)
- Mokena ........... (G-14850)
- Monee ............. (G-14990)
- Naperville ......... (G-15789)
- New Lenox ....... (G-15869)
- Park Forest ....... (G-17176)
- Peotone ........... (G-17484)
- Plainfield .......... (G-17575)
- Rockdale .......... (G-18213)
- Romeoville ....... (G-18790)
- Shorewood ....... (G-19923)
- University Park ... (G-21041)
- Wilmington ....... (G-22268)

### Williamson
- Carterville ........ (G-3309)
- Creal Springs .... (G-7453)
- Energy ............. (G-9984)
- Herrin .............. (G-11748)
- Johnston City .... (G-12445)
- Marion ............. (G-14247)
- Pittsburg .......... (G-17559)

### Winnebago
- Cherry Valley .... (G-3637)
- Durand ............ (G-8585)
- Loves Park ....... (G-13911)
- Machesney Park (G-14048)
- Pecatonica ....... (G-17250)
- Rockford .......... (G-18235)
- Rockton ........... (G-18691)
- Roscoe ............ (G-18887)
- Seward ............ (G-19896)
- South Beloit ...... (G-20135)
- Winnebago ....... (G-22294)

### Woodford
- Congerville ....... (G-7369)
- El Paso ............ (G-8865)
- Eureka ............. (G-9994)
- Germantown Hills (G-10895)
- Goodfield ......... (G-11244)
- Metamora ........ (G-14739)
- Minonk ............ (G-14834)
- Roanoke .......... (G-18047)

# GEOGRAPHIC SECTION

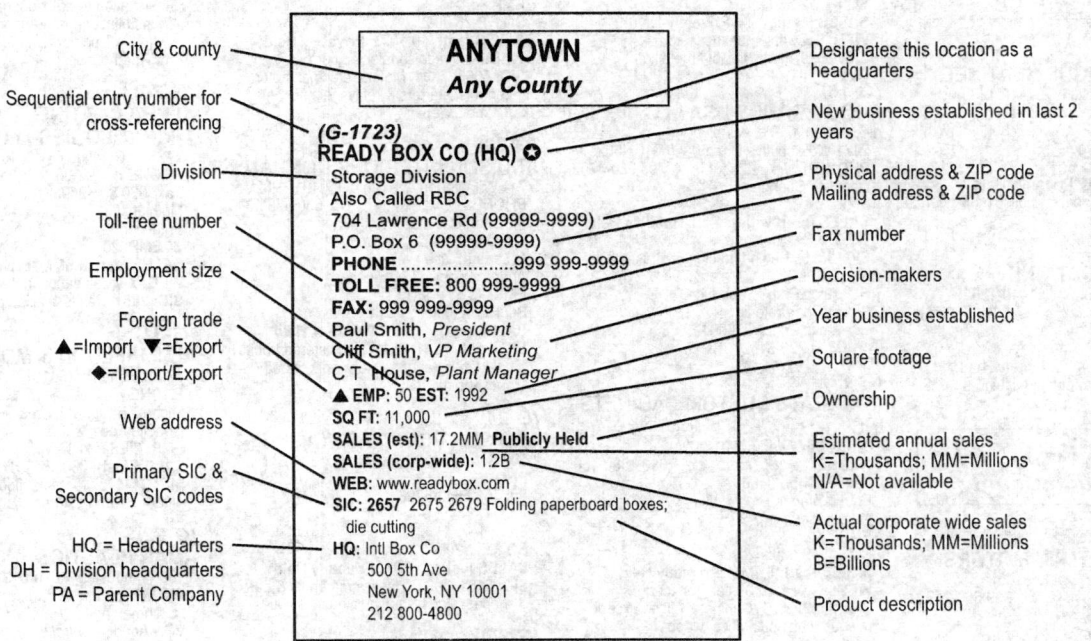

*See footnotes for symbols and codes identification.*
- This section is in alphabetical order by city.
- Companies are sorted alphabetically under their respective cities.
- To locate cities within a county refer to the County/City Cross Reference Index.

**IMPORTANT NOTICE:** It is a violation of both federal and state law to transmit an unsolicited advertisement to a facsimile machine. Any user of this product that violates such laws may be subject to civil and criminal penalties which may exceed $500 for each transmission of an unsolicited facsimile. Harris InfoSource provides fax numbers for lawful purposes only and expressly forbids the use of these numbers in any unlawful manner.

## Abbott Park
### Lake County

**(G-1)**
**ABBOTT LABORATORIES (PA)**
Also Called: CURATE SNACKS
100 Abbott Park Rd (60064-3500)
PHONE.................224 667-6100
Fax: 847 938-3076
Miles D White, *Ch of Bd*
Michael T Rousseau, *President*
Hubert L Allen, *Exec VP*
Brian J Blaser, *Exec VP*
John M Capek, *Exec VP*
▲ **EMP:** 12284 **EST:** 1900
**SALES:** 20.8B **Publicly Held**
**WEB:** www.abbott.com
**SIC: 2834** 2835 3841 3826 Pharmaceutical preparations; druggists' preparations (pharmaceuticals); vitamin, nutrient & hematinic preparations for human use; vitamin preparations; in vitro & in vivo diagnostic substances; blood derivative diagnostic agents; hemotology diagnostic agents; microbiology & virology diagnostic products; diagnostic apparatus, medical; medical instruments & equipment, blood & bone work; IV transfusion apparatus; blood testing apparatus

**(G-2)**
**ABBOTT LABORATORIES**
Abbott Diagnostic Division
100 Abbott Park Rd (60064-3500)
PHONE.....................847 937-6100
Lawrence Blyn PHD, *Branch Mgr*
**EMP:** 19

**SALES (corp-wide):** 20.8B **Publicly Held**
**SIC: 2835** 2899 In vitro & in vivo diagnostic substances; chemical preparations
**PA:** Abbott Laboratories
  100 Abbott Park Rd
  Abbott Park IL 60064
  224 667-6100

**(G-3)**
**ABBOTT LABORATORIES**
200 Abbott Park Rd (60064-3537)
PHONE.....................847 937-6100
Barry Dowell, *Sales & Mktg St*
Mark Weishaar, *Sales & Mktg St*
Maija Bentley, *Branch Mgr*
William King, *Manager*
Thomas Boyle, *Director*
**EMP:** 617
**SALES (corp-wide):** 20.8B **Publicly Held**
**SIC: 2834** 3841 Pharmaceutical preparations; diagnostic apparatus, medical
**PA:** Abbott Laboratories
  100 Abbott Park Rd
  Abbott Park IL 60064
  224 667-6100

**(G-4)**
**ABBOTT LABORATORIES INC**
200 Abbott Park Rd (60064-3537)
PHONE.....................224 668-2076
Fax: 847 935-0618
Miles D White, *CEO*
Steven Lewis, *Vice Pres*
Sam Bsaibes, *Project Mgr*
Dan Novak, *Engineer*
Matt Mittino, *Mktg Dir*
◆ **EMP:** 574
**SALES (est):** 228.8MM
**SALES (corp-wide):** 20.8B **Publicly Held**
**SIC: 2834** 3841 Pharmaceutical preparations; diagnostic apparatus, medical

**PA:** Abbott Laboratories
  100 Abbott Park Rd
  Abbott Park IL 60064
  224 667-6100

**(G-5)**
**ABBOTT NUTRITION MFG INC**
200 Abbott Park Rd (60064-3503)
PHONE.....................614 624-6083
**EMP:** 7
**SALES (corp-wide):** 20.8B **Publicly Held**
**SIC: 2834** Pharmaceutical preparations
**HQ:** Abbott Nutrition Manufacturing Inc.
  2351 N Watney Way Ste C
  Fairfield CA 94533
  707 399-1100

**(G-6)**
**ABBOTT POINT OF CARE INC**
Also Called: Apoc
100 Abbott Park Rd (60064-3502)
PHONE.....................847 937-6100
Fax: 847 937-2013
Sharon Bracken, *Vice Pres*
**EMP:** 180
**SALES (corp-wide):** 20.8B **Publicly Held**
**SIC: 3841** Surgical & medical instruments; diagnostic apparatus, medical
**HQ:** Abbott Point Of Care Inc.
  400 College Rd E
  Princeton NJ 08540
  609 454-9000

**(G-7)**
**ABBOTT PRODUCTS INC (DH)**
100 Abbott Park Rd (60064-3502)
PHONE.....................847 937-6100
Miles D White, *Chairman*
Gail Auerbach, *Vice Pres*
Chris Offen, *Vice Pres*
Virginia Hubert, *Warehouse Mgr*

J Keeshen, *Manager*
▲ **EMP:** 260 **EST:** 1964
**SQ FT:** 67,000
**SALES (est):** 43.1MM
**SALES (corp-wide):** 20.8B **Publicly Held**
**WEB:** www.mytestosterone.com
**SIC: 2834** 8731 Antihistamine preparations; hormone preparations; cough medicines; cold remedies; commercial physical research

**(G-8)**
**ABBVIE HOLDINGS INC**
Also Called: Abbott Pharmaceutical Corp
100 Abbott Park Rd (60064-3502)
PHONE.....................847 937-7632
Gordon R Solway, *Ch of Bd*
Richard A Gonzalez, *President*
Brian Richmond, *Exec VP*
James E Morrow, *Vice Pres*
Steves H Koehler, *Treasurer*
**EMP:** 95
**SQ FT:** 43,000
**SALES (est):** 14MM
**SALES (corp-wide):** 25.6B **Publicly Held**
**WEB:** www.abbott.com
**SIC: 2834** Thyroid preparations
**PA:** Abbvie Inc.
  1 N Waukegan Rd
  North Chicago IL 60064
  847 932-7900

## Abingdon
### Knox County

**(G-9)**
**ABINGTON ARGUS-SENTINEL**
507 N Monroe St Ste 3 (61410-1285)
P.O. Box 143, Avon (61415-0143)
PHONE..................................309 462-3189
Deb Fowlks, *Manager*
EMP: 3
SALES (est): 112K **Privately Held**
SIC: 2711 Newspapers, publishing & printing

**(G-10)**
**EAGLE PUBLICATIONS**
507 N Monroe St Ste 3 (61410-1285)
PHONE..................................309 462-5758
Lynne Campbell, *Manager*
EMP: 4
SALES (est): 133.7K **Privately Held**
SIC: 2711 Newspapers, publishing & printing

## Adair
### Mcdonough County

**(G-11)**
**AL COOK ELECTRIC MOTORS**
21845 N 850th Rd (61411-9265)
PHONE..................................309 653-2337
Fax: 309 653-2426
Albert Cook, *Owner*
Linda Cook, *Co-Owner*
EMP: 2
SALES (est): 200K **Privately Held**
SIC: 1731 7694 5063 5084 Electrical work; electric motor repair; electrical apparatus & equipment; motors, electric; motor controls, starters & relays: electric; industrial machinery & equipment; motors & generators

**(G-12)**
**BIN LONG & ELECTRIC**
6240 E 2100th St (61411-9367)
PHONE..................................309 758-5407
George Long, *Executive*
EMP: 2
SALES (est): 264.9K **Privately Held**
SIC: 3699 Electrical equipment & supplies

## Addieville
### Washington County

**(G-13)**
**OTTEN CONSTRUCTION CO INC**
786 Old Saint Louis Rd (62214-1608)
PHONE..................................618 768-4310
EMP: 6
SALES: 200K **Privately Held**
SIC: 1521 2452 Single-Family House Construction Mfg Prefabricated Wood Buildings

## Addison
### Dupage County

**(G-14)**
**A & H MANUFACTURING INC**
200 W Laura Dr (60101-5014)
PHONE..................................630 543-5900
Habib Abbas, *President*
Fatima Abbas, *Admin Sec*
EMP: 11
SALES (est): 1.7MM **Privately Held**
SIC: 2844 2841 Toilet preparations; soap & other detergents

**(G-15)**
**ABLE METAL HOSE INC**
15 W Laura Dr (60101-5187)
PHONE..................................630 543-9620
Fax: 630 543-0906
James C Nevara Jr, *President*
Francis A Fitzgerald, *Vice Pres*
Anthony J Nevara, *Vice Pres*
EMP: 12
SQ FT: 17,500
SALES (est): 2MM **Privately Held**
WEB: www.ablemetalhose.com
SIC: 3599 Hose, flexible metallic

**(G-16)**
**ACCO BRANDS USA LLC**
Also Called: G B C Velobind
2171 W Executive Dr # 500 (60101-5625)
PHONE..................................708 280-4702
Dennis L Chandler,
EMP: 35
SALES (corp-wide): 1.5B **Publicly Held**
WEB: www.gbc.com
SIC: 3579 Binding machines, plastic & adhesive
HQ: Acco Brands Usa Llc
4 Corporate Dr
Lake Zurich IL 60047
800 222-6462

**(G-17)**
**ACCURATE CUSTOM CABINETS INC**
115 W Fay Ave (60101-5091)
PHONE..................................630 458-0460
Fax: 630 458-0466
Paul F Steger, *President*
Gary Keller, *Corp Secy*
EMP: 20
SQ FT: 12,000
SALES (est): 3.4MM **Privately Held**
WEB: www.accuratecabinets.com
SIC: 2522 2521 Cabinets, office: except wood; cabinets, office: wood

**(G-18)**
**ACCURATE FINISHERS**
1433 W Fullerton Ave B (60101-4366)
PHONE..................................630 543-8575
Guillermo Aleman, *Principal*
EMP: 9
SALES (est): 926.2K **Privately Held**
SIC: 3399 Powder, metal

**(G-19)**
**ACI PLASTICS MANUFACTURING**
1430 W Bernard Dr (60101-4330)
PHONE..................................630 629-0400
Rich Brook, *Manager*
EMP: 3 EST: 2011
SALES (est): 269.2K **Privately Held**
SIC: 3999 Manufacturing industries

**(G-20)**
**ACRYLIC SERVICE INC**
1060 W Republic Dr (60101-3133)
PHONE..................................630 543-0336
Fax: 630 543-0719
Dale Damitz, *President*
EMP: 1
SQ FT: 7,200
SALES: 400K **Privately Held**
SIC: 3993 2542 3089 Displays & cutouts, window & lobby; signs, not made in custom sign painting shops; office & store showcases & display fixtures; plastic processing

**(G-21)**
**ACTION ROTARY DIE INC**
1208 W National Ave (60101-3131)
PHONE..................................630 628-6830
Fax: 630 628-6832
Scott Curtin, *President*
Nancy Curtin, *Corp Secy*
Seth Albert, *Opers Mgr*
Andre McClinton, *Purchasing*
Josh Mattson, *Sales Staff*
EMP: 40
SQ FT: 18,000
SALES (est): 5.9MM **Privately Held**
WEB: www.actionrotary.com
SIC: 3544 Special dies & tools

**(G-22)**
**ADDISON ELECTRIC INC**
502 W Factory Rd (60101-4411)
PHONE..................................800 517-4871
Fax: 630 628-8097
Jay Patel, *President*
Ali Mohammed, *Human Res Mgr*
Tom Oliversen, *Sales Engr*
Jim Cartensen, *Sales Staff*
Bill Janus, *Sales Associate*
EMP: 20
SQ FT: 26,000
SALES (est): 19.1MM **Privately Held**
WEB: www.addisonelectric.com
SIC: 5063 7694 Motors, electric; motor controls, starters & relays: electric; electric motor repair

**(G-23)**
**ADDISON INTERIORS COMPANY**
711 W Fullerton Ave Ste A (60101-3282)
PHONE..................................630 628-1345
Fax: 630 628-1245
Giovanni Lanera, *President*
G Lanera, *Vice Pres*
Andree Lanera, *Bookkeeper*
EMP: 15
SQ FT: 12,000
SALES (est): 1.9MM **Privately Held**
SIC: 2512 7641 2511 Upholstered household furniture; upholstery work; wood household furniture

**(G-24)**
**ADDISON PRO PLASTICS INC**
503 S Westgate St Ste D (60101-4531)
PHONE..................................630 543-6770
Fax: 630 543-6798
Andy Creasor, *President*
EMP: 1
SQ FT: 1,200
SALES (est): 318.9K **Privately Held**
SIC: 5162 3993 Plastics materials & basic shapes; signs & advertising specialties

**(G-25)**
**ADVANCED WEIGHING SYSTEMS INC**
1433 W Fullerton Ave H (60101-4366)
PHONE..................................630 916-6179
Arthur W Guest, *President*
David Arnold, *Treasurer*
Matt Wade, *Admin Sec*
EMP: 9
SQ FT: 1,500
SALES (est): 1.5MM **Privately Held**
SIC: 3596 5046 Industrial scales; scales, except laboratory

**(G-26)**
**ADVANCED WELDING LTD**
760 W Factory Rd (60101-4309)
PHONE..................................708 205-4559
William Meyers, *Managing Prtnr*
Skip Meyers, *Partner*
EMP: 17
SQ FT: 2,000
SALES: 3.5MM **Privately Held**
SIC: 3441 Fabricated structural metal

**(G-27)**
**AIF INC**
Also Called: Absolute Indus Fabricators
1393 W Jeffrey Dr (60101-4331)
PHONE..................................630 495-0077
Ronda Musuraca, *President*
Joseph F Musuraca, *Admin Sec*
EMP: 32
SALES (est): 7.9MM **Privately Held**
SIC: 3315 Wire & fabricated wire products

**(G-28)**
**AIR DUCT MANUFACTURING INC**
1515 W Fullerton Ave B (60101-3000)
PHONE..................................630 620-9866
Fax: 630 628-9585
Amir Sharify, *President*
EMP: 8
SALES (est): 964.8K **Privately Held**
SIC: 3585 1611 Parts for heating, cooling & refrigerating equipment; general contractor, highway & street construction

**(G-29)**
**ALLIED GARAGE DOOR INC**
310 W Gerri Ln (60101-5012)
P.O. Box 817, Lombard (60148-0817)
PHONE..................................630 279-0795
Lawrence Parise, *President*
Will Tortoriello, *General Mgr*
John Franco, *Info Tech Mgr*
EMP: 40
SALES (est): 2.6MM **Privately Held**
WEB: www.alliedgaragedoor.com
SIC: 1751 5211 2431 3442 Garage door, installation or erection; garage doors, sale & installation; garage doors, overhead: wood; rolling doors for industrial buildings or warehouses, metal

**(G-30)**
**ALPHA COATING TECHNOLOGIES LLC**
1735 W Cortland Ct (60101-4208)
PHONE..................................630 268-8787
Fax: 630 806-9593
Muthiah Jeno,
Anita Jeno,
▲ EMP: 20
SALES (est): 4.9MM **Privately Held**
WEB: www.alphacoatingtech.com
SIC: 2851 Paints & allied products

**(G-31)**
**ALUMAFLOOR & MORE INC**
870 S Fiene Dr (60101-5110)
PHONE..................................630 628-0226
Michael Strugalski, *President*
Isabelle Paez, *Agent*
EMP: 2 EST: 2013
SALES (est): 330.4K **Privately Held**
SIC: 3444 5713 Metal flooring & siding; floor covering stores

**(G-32)**
**AMAR PLASTICS INC**
100 W Industrial Rd (60101-4508)
PHONE..................................630 627-4105
Lakshman Agadi, *President*
Vijay Agadi, *Controller*
Gene Barry, *Sales Staff*
Ada Spahija, *Sales Staff*
John Weber, *Marketing Staff*
EMP: 12
SQ FT: 20,000
SALES (est): 1.3MM **Privately Held**
SIC: 3841 Surgical & medical instruments

**(G-33)**
**AMERICAN CIRCUIT SYSTEMS INC**
712 S Westgate St (60101-5024)
PHONE..................................630 543-4450
Fax: 630 543-4452
Ashok Sheth, *President*
Pam Shah, *Bookkeeper*
George Jankovsky, *Sales Staff*
EMP: 40
SQ FT: 10,000
SALES (est): 1.8MM **Privately Held**
SIC: 3672 Printed circuit boards

**(G-34)**
**AMERICAN CNC MACHINE CO INC**
749 W Fullerton Ave (60101-3258)
PHONE..................................630 628-6490
Fax: 630 628-6882
Mandy Lanute, *President*
EMP: 34
SQ FT: 20,000
SALES (est): 5.4MM **Privately Held**
SIC: 3599 Machine shop, jobbing & repair

**(G-35)**
**AMERICAN DIESEL TUBE CORP**
1240 W Capitol Dr (60101-5375)
PHONE..................................630 628-1830
Fax: 630 628-1970
Jeffrey Mandala, *President*
Juergen Guido, *Chairman*
▲ EMP: 10 EST: 1981
SQ FT: 6,000
SALES (est): 1.6MM **Privately Held**
SIC: 3714 3498 3317 5084 Fuel systems & parts, motor vehicle; fabricated pipe & fittings; steel pipe & tubes
PA: Ditefras Holding Ag
C/O Urs Heer
Glarus GL
556 401-250

**(G-36)**
**AMERICAN GASKET TECH INC**
Also Called: Agt Products
10 W Laura Dr (60101-5112)
PHONE..................................630 543-1510

Fax: 630 543-1595
Nicholas Kalouris, *President*
Jimmy Roussakis, *General Mgr*
Dimitris Poulokefalos, *Vice Pres*
Alex Nakos, *Sales Mgr*
Joanne Gugliuzza, *Manager*
▲ **EMP:** 58
**SQ FT:** 110,000
**SALES (est):** 13.5MM **Privately Held**
**WEB:** www.advancedgenerator.com
**SIC:** 3053 3089 Gaskets, all materials; injection molding of plastics; extruded finished plastic products; blister or bubble formed packaging, plastic

*(G-37)*
### AMERICAN PRGRSSIVE CRCUITS INC
1772 W Armitage Ct (60101-4207)
**PHONE** ............................. 630 495-6900
Fax: 630 495-6901
Shailesh Patel, *President*
Sal C Patel, *VP Opers*
**EMP:** 25
**SQ FT:** 17,000
**SALES (est):** 1.8MM **Privately Held**
**SIC:** 3672 Wiring boards; circuit boards, television & radio printed

*(G-38)*
### AMERICAN YEAST CORP TENNESSEE
1417 S Jeffrey Dr (60101)
**PHONE** ............................. 630 932-1290
Mona Legal, *Vice Pres*
**EMP:** 3
**SALES (corp-wide):** 12.3MM **Privately Held**
**SIC:** 2099 Yeast
**HQ:** American Yeast Corporation Tennessee
251 Stiles Dr
Memphis TN 38127
901 358-4788

*(G-39)*
### AMERIGRAPHICS CORP
Also Called: AGC
1010 W National Ave (60101-3127)
**PHONE** ............................. 630 543-9790
Keith Urness, *CEO*
**EMP:** 8
**SALES (est):** 1MM **Privately Held**
**SIC:** 3479 Coating of metals with plastic or resins

*(G-40)*
### ANCHOR PRODUCTS COMPANY
52 W Official Rd (60101-4589)
**PHONE** ............................. 630 543-9124
Fax: 630 543-9131
Robert Thrun, *President*
Gary S Thrun, *Vice Pres*
Gary Hampson, *Plant Mgr*
Alexandra Thrun, *QC Mgr*
Evelyn Felbab, *Office Mgr*
**EMP:** 50 **EST:** 1925
**SQ FT:** 15,000
**SALES (est):** 12.9MM **Privately Held**
**WEB:** www.anchorsurgical.com
**SIC:** 3841 Surgical instruments & apparatus; needles, suture

*(G-41)*
### APPLE PRINTING CENTER
1433 W Fullerton Ave E (60101-4366)
P.O. Box 1555, Lombard (60148-8555)
**PHONE** ............................. 630 932-9494
Fax: 630 932-9088
Craig Drummond, *President*
Jacqueline Drummond, *Corp Secy*
**EMP:** 1
**SQ FT:** 3,000
**SALES (est):** 370.2K **Privately Held**
**WEB:** www.appleprintingcenter.com
**SIC:** 2752 2791 2789 Lithographing on metal; typesetting; bookbinding & related work

*(G-42)*
### APSER LABORATORY INC
Also Called: Apser Labs
625 W Factory Rd Ste B (60101-4412)
**PHONE** ............................. 630 543-3333
Ansar M Ahmed, *President*
Soofia Ahmed, *Admin Sec*

**EMP:** 75
**SQ FT:** 250,000
**SALES:** 22MM **Privately Held**
**SIC:** 2834 9999 Pharmaceutical preparations; nonclassifiable establishments

*(G-43)*
### AR INDUSTRIES
1405 W Bernard Dr Ste C (60101-4341)
**PHONE** ............................. 630 543-0282
Anthony Romano, *Owner*
**EMP:** 3
**SALES (est):** 261.2K **Privately Held**
**SIC:** 3999 Manufacturing industries

*(G-44)*
### ARI INDUSTRIES INC
381 S Ari Ct (60101-4353)
**PHONE** ............................. 630 953-9100
Fax: 630 953-0590
Kazuo Okazaki, *Ch of Bd*
Daniel Malcolm, *President*
Mark Bolen, *Vice Pres*
Maryjane Banta, *Admin Sec*
Nancy Grizzle, *Admin Sec*
▲ **EMP:** 60
**SQ FT:** 52,000
**SALES (est):** 15.8MM
**SALES (corp-wide):** 113.8MM **Privately Held**
**WEB:** www.ariindustries.com
**SIC:** 3823 3357 Industrial process control instruments; nonferrous wiredrawing & insulating
**PA:** Okazaki Manufacturing Company
3-1-3, Gokodori, Chuo-Ku
Kobe HYO 651-0
782 518-200

*(G-45)*
### ARNEL INDUSTRIES INC
57 W Interstate Rd (60101-4509)
**PHONE** ............................. 630 543-6500
Edward H Green Jr, *President*
Deborah Green, *Treasurer*
**EMP:** 30 **EST:** 1958
**SQ FT:** 75,000
**SALES (est):** 3.8MM **Privately Held**
**SIC:** 3089 3494 Injection molding of plastics; valves & pipe fittings

*(G-46)*
### ASPEN MANUFACTURING COMPANY
1001 W Republic Dr Ste 6 (60101-3106)
**PHONE** ............................. 630 495-0922
Fax: 630 495-0924
Gary Kukla, *President*
**EMP:** 9
**SQ FT:** 7,500
**SALES (est):** 994.1K **Privately Held**
**SIC:** 3452 Bolts, nuts, rivets & washers

*(G-47)*
### AT&L RESOURCES LLC (HQ) ✪
Also Called: Midwest Label Resorces
444 W Interstate Rd (60101-4518)
**PHONE** ............................. 918 925-0154
Allen Cameron, *President*
Shirley Sminth, *CFO*
Carline Harvey, *Human Resources*
Jeffrey Pelcher, *Admin Sec*
**EMP:** 3 **EST:** 2016
**SALES:** 500K
**SALES (corp-wide):** 107.2MM **Privately Held**
**SIC:** 2759 Labels & seals: printing
**PA:** Worldwide Printing And Distribution, Inc.
2900 E Apache St
Tulsa OK 74110
918 295-0112

*(G-48)*
### AUTOMATIC MACHINERY RESOURCES
Also Called: A M R
1001 W Republic Dr Ste 8 (60101-3106)
**PHONE** ............................. 630 543-4944
Juan Guemez, *President*
**EMP:** 3
**SQ FT:** 2,000

**SALES (est):** 432.9K **Privately Held**
**SIC:** 7699 7694 Industrial machinery & equipment repair; printing trades machinery & equipment repair; rebuilding motors, except automotive

*(G-49)*
### AUTOMATIC SWISS CORPORATION
1130 W National Ave Ste A (60101-3166)
**PHONE** ............................. 630 543-3888
Fax: 630 543-1486
James Rupprecht, *President*
Peter Witt, *Vice Pres*
Linda West, *Manager*
David Witt, *Administration*
**EMP:** 25 **EST:** 1965
**SQ FT:** 22,500
**SALES (est):** 5.2MM **Privately Held**
**WEB:** www.automaticswiss.com
**SIC:** 3451 Screw machine products

*(G-50)*
### B C DIE & MOLD INC
1046 W Republic Dr (60101-3133)
**PHONE** ............................. 630 543-5090
William Chesrow Jr, *President*
**EMP:** 4
**SQ FT:** 3,600
**SALES (est):** 240K **Privately Held**
**SIC:** 3544 Dies & die holders for metal cutting, forming, die casting

*(G-51)*
### BALDWIN OXY-DRY CORPORATION (DH)
1210 N Swift Rd (60101-6104)
**PHONE** ............................. 630 595-3651
Fax: 630 595-5433
Edward T Mc Loughlin, *Chairman*
Mary Ellen Cahill, *Vice Pres*
Don Gustafson, *Vice Pres*
Martin Haver, *CFO*
▲ **EMP:** 70 **EST:** 1941
**SQ FT:** 35,000
**SALES (est):** 12.3MM **Privately Held**
**WEB:** www.oxydry.com
**SIC:** 3555 Printing trades machinery
**HQ:** Baldwin Technology Company, Inc.
8040 Forsyth Blvd
Saint Louis MO 63105
314 726-2152

*(G-52)*
### BELFORD ELECTRONICS INC
1460 W Jeffrey Dr (60101-4343)
**PHONE** ............................. 630 705-3020
Fax: 630 691-1118
Gary Belford, *Ch of Bd*
Richard Belford, *President*
Michael Belford, *Vice Pres*
Kristin Belford, *Accounts Mgr*
Eric Terez, *Cust Mgr*
▲ **EMP:** 30
**SQ FT:** 15,000
**SALES (est):** 9.7MM **Privately Held**
**WEB:** www.belfordelect.com
**SIC:** 5065 3357 Electronic parts & equipment; fiber optic cable (insulated)

*(G-53)*
### BERGST SPECIAL TOOLS INC
Also Called: Bergst Engineering
723 W Annoreno Dr (60101-4315)
**PHONE** ............................. 630 543-1020
Laneta Bergst, *President*
Allen Bergst, *COO*
**EMP:** 6
**SQ FT:** 10,000
**SALES (est):** 750K **Privately Held**
**SIC:** 3544 3449 Special dies, tools, jigs & fixtures; miscellaneous metalwork

*(G-54)*
### BERNDT & THACKER INC
761 W Racquet Club Dr B (60101-4317)
**PHONE** ............................. 630 628-1934
Fax: 630 628-1375
Don Berndt, *President*
**EMP:** 10
**SALES:** 500K **Privately Held**
**SIC:** 3599 Machine shop, jobbing & repair

*(G-55)*
### BIBLE TRUTH PUBLISHERS INC
59 W Industrial Rd (60101-4582)
P.O. Box 649 (60101-0649)
**PHONE** ............................. 630 543-1441
Fax: 630 543-1476
Donald F Rule, *President*
Stephen Rule, *Publisher*
▲ **EMP:** 9 **EST:** 1947
**SQ FT:** 19,000
**SALES:** 539K **Privately Held**
**SIC:** 5961 2721 Religious merchandise, mail order; magazines: publishing only, not printed on site

*(G-56)*
### BIROM CABINETRY LLC
1433 W Fullerton Ave L (60101-4366)
**PHONE** ............................. 312 286-7132
Roman Birev, *Principal*
**EMP:** 4
**SALES (est):** 430K **Privately Held**
**SIC:** 2434 Wood kitchen cabinets

*(G-57)*
### BLACK & DECKER CORPORATION
901 S Rohlwing Rd Ste A (60101-4217)
**PHONE** ............................. 630 521-1097
Dennis Dallaglio, *General Mgr*
Jeff Persic, *Manager*
**EMP:** 12
**SALES (corp-wide):** 11.4B **Publicly Held**
**WEB:** www.blackanddecker.com
**SIC:** 3546 Power-driven handtools
**HQ:** The Black & Decker Corporation
701 E Joppa Rd
Towson MD 21286
410 716-3900

*(G-58)*
### BLACKHAWK MOLDING CO INC (PA)
120 W Interstate Rd (60101-4564)
**PHONE** ............................. 630 628-6218
Fax: 630 543-7994
Douglas Hidding, *President*
Dale Berg, *General Mgr*
Robert Hidding, *Vice Pres*
Clarence Fellows, *Plant Mgr*
Dick Hogan, *CFO*
◆ **EMP:** 80 **EST:** 1950
**SQ FT:** 73,000
**SALES:** 23.1MM **Privately Held**
**WEB:** www.blackhawkcollection.com
**SIC:** 3089 Caps, plastic

*(G-59)*
### BRADLEY MACHINING INC
753 W Annoreno Dr (60101-4315)
**PHONE** ............................. 630 543-2875
Fax: 630 543-3742
Edward Youngerman, *President*
John Ernie, *Manager*
Colleen Youngerman, *Admin Sec*
**EMP:** 10
**SQ FT:** 7,800
**SALES (est):** 1.6MM **Privately Held**
**WEB:** www.bradleymachining.com
**SIC:** 3545 3599 3451 Micrometers; machine shop, jobbing & repair; screw machine products

*(G-60)*
### BRAND X-RAY COMPANY
910 S Westwood Ave (60101-4917)
**PHONE** ............................. 630 543-5331
Fax: 630 543-8551
Jerry Kastic, *President*
Daniel Cestic, *General Mgr*
Joseph Farley, *Design Engr*
David Kassmier, *Admin Sec*
**EMP:** 16
**SQ FT:** 3,800
**SALES (est):** 3.1MM **Privately Held**
**WEB:** www.brandx-ray.com
**SIC:** 3844 X-ray apparatus & tubes

*(G-61)*
### BROMINE SYSTEMS INC
1001 W Republic Dr Ste 9 (60101-3106)
**PHONE** ............................. 630 624-3303
Gregory Johnson, *President*
**EMP:** 3

# Addison - Dupage County (G-62)  GEOGRAPHIC SECTION

SALES (est): 556.6K **Privately Held**
SIC: 2899 Water treating compounds

### (G-62)
### BRUNOS AUTOMOTIVE PRODUCTS
14 W Industrial Rd Ste A (60101-4538)
PHONE.................................630 458-0043
Bruno Massel, *President*
EMP: 5
SALES (est): 822.4K **Privately Held**
WEB: www.brunosauto.com
SIC: 3711 3714 Automobile assembly, including specialty automobiles; motor vehicle parts & accessories

### (G-63)
### C & C TOOLING INC (PA)
344 W Interstate Rd (60101-4516)
PHONE.................................630 543-5523
Jack Corsello, *President*
EMP: 11
SALES (est): 1.8MM **Privately Held**
SIC: 3545 Machine tool accessories

### (G-64)
### C CN CHICAGO CORP
421 S Irmen Dr Ste B (60101-4307)
PHONE.................................847 671-3319
Sally Jackson, *President*
Sara Wilson, *Exec VP*
EMP: 3
SQ FT: 5,000
SALES (est): 567K **Privately Held**
SIC: 3555 Printing trades machinery

### (G-65)
### C D TOOLS MACHINING INC
33 W Fullerton Ave (60101-3711)
PHONE.................................773 859-2028
Cecylia Dworzynski, *Owner*
Agnieszka K Mendocha, *Administration*
EMP: 5
SALES: 200K **Privately Held**
SIC: 3599 Machine & other job shop work

### (G-66)
### C&R DIRECTIONAL BORING
880 S Fiene Dr (60101-5110)
PHONE.................................630 458-0055
Russell Cooper, *Owner*
EMP: 2
SALES (est): 362.5K **Privately Held**
SIC: 1381 Directional drilling oil & gas wells

### (G-67)
### CABOT MCRLECTRONICS POLSG CORP
39 W Official Rd (60101-4532)
PHONE.................................630 543-6682
Mark Drzewiecki, *President*
Jose Camacho, *General Mgr*
Michael Teplan, *Plant Mgr*
Sonja Sliwa, *Manager*
Frances Henderson, *Admin Sec*
EMP: 20
SQ FT: 16,000
SALES (est): 3.4MM
SALES (corp-wide): 430.4MM **Publicly Held**
WEB: www.surfacefinishes.com
SIC: 3827 3544 3829 Optical instruments & lenses; special dies, tools, jigs & fixtures; measuring & controlling devices
PA: Cabot Microelectronics Corporation
  870 N Commons Dr
  Aurora IL 60504
  630 375-6631

### (G-68)
### CADILLAC TANK MET FBRCTORS INC
225 W Gerri Ln (60101-5009)
P.O. Box 247 (60101-0247)
PHONE.................................630 543-2600
Fax: 630 543-9849
Betty Arnold, *President*
Jack Arnold, *Vice Pres*
Susan McField, *Manager*
EMP: 22 EST: 1947
SQ FT: 17,000
SALES (est): 3.9MM **Privately Held**
WEB: www.cadillactank.com
SIC: 3599 Machine shop, jobbing & repair

### (G-69)
### CARDON MOLD FINISHING INC
703 W Annoreno Dr Ste 4 (60101-4323)
PHONE.................................630 543-5431
Fax: 630 543-5410
Donald Musial, *President*
Carol Musial, *Corp Secy*
EMP: 4
SQ FT: 1,600
SALES (est): 300K **Privately Held**
SIC: 3544 3471 Special dies, tools, jigs & fixtures; plating & polishing

### (G-70)
### CDL TECHNOLOGY INC
Also Called: Crown Machine
511 S Vista Ave (60101-4422)
P.O. Box 1127 (60101-8127)
PHONE.................................630 543-5240
Fax: 630 543-4656
George Holmes, *Principal*
Joe Goliak, *Sales Engr*
Katrina Bailey, *Manager*
Barbara Holmes, *Admin Sec*
Janice Ganz, *Administration*
◆ EMP: 22
SQ FT: 55,000
SALES (est): 5MM **Privately Held**
WEB: www.cdli.com
SIC: 3559 5084 Plastics working machinery; industrial machinery & equipment

### (G-71)
### CEF INDUSTRIES LLC (DH)
320 S Church St (60101-3750)
PHONE.................................630 628-2299
Fax: 630 628-1386
Karin Nelson, *CEO*
Steve Murphy, *Business Mgr*
Joe Kubicki, *Warehouse Mgr*
Katie Falbo, *Buyer*
Jim King, *Engineer*
EMP: 114 EST: 1946
SQ FT: 83,000
SALES (est): 23.6MM
SALES (corp-wide): 3.1B **Publicly Held**
WEB: www.cefind.com
SIC: 3728 3812 Governors, aircraft propeller feathering; landing skis & tracks, aircraft; search & navigation equipment
HQ: Transdigm, Inc.
  4223 Monticello Blvd
  Cleveland OH 44121
  216 706-2939

### (G-72)
### CENTRAL TOOL SPECIALTIES CO
325 W Factory Rd Ste A (60101-5027)
PHONE.................................630 543-6351
Fax: 630 543-6392
Ron Nisson, *President*
Ben Gananski, *Plant Mgr*
Brennan Peckhart, *Sales Associate*
EMP: 8 EST: 1962
SQ FT: 7,500
SALES (est): 1.1MM **Privately Held**
WEB: www.centraltoolspecialties.com
SIC: 3544 3469 3354 Special dies, tools, jigs & fixtures; metal stampings; aluminum extruded products

### (G-73)
### CHICAGO BREAD COMPANY (DH)
Also Called: Boudin Bakery
1405 W Fullerton Ave (60101-4321)
PHONE.................................630 620-1849
Fax: 630 620-5242
Louis J Giraudo, *Ch of Bd*
David Wolsgram, *President*
Gayle Debrosse, *Vice Pres*
Rick Rodrick, *Plant Mgr*
Ron Maccarone, *CFO*
EMP: 19
SQ FT: 12,000
SALES (est): 5.1MM **Privately Held**
SIC: 2051 Bakery: wholesale or wholesale/retail combined
HQ: Andre-Boudin Bakeries, Inc.
  50 Francisco St Ste 200
  San Francisco CA 94133
  415 882-1849

### (G-74)
### CHICAGO PRINT PARTNERS LLC
120 W Laura Dr (60101-5114)
PHONE.................................312 525-2015
Paul Lawless,
EMP: 10
SALES (est): 2MM **Privately Held**
SIC: 2759 Commercial printing

### (G-75)
### CHICAGO PRINTING AND EMB INC
777 W Factory Rd (60101-4308)
PHONE.................................630 628-1777
Yousuf Razzak, *President*
Don Starck, *Vice Pres*
Jaaved Razzak, *Admin Sec*
EMP: 12
SQ FT: 30,000
SALES (est): 2.2MM **Privately Held**
WEB: www.yourshirtstore.com
SIC: 7336 2395 2759 Silk screen design; embroidery & art needlework; promotional printing

### (G-76)
### CHRISTENSEN PRECISION PRODUCTS
1056 W Republic Dr (60101-3133)
PHONE.................................630 543-6525
Karen Palicka, *President*
Ronald Palicka, *Vice Pres*
EMP: 8
SQ FT: 2,600
SALES (est): 500K **Privately Held**
SIC: 3444 Sheet metalwork

### (G-77)
### CIRRUS PRODUCTS
711 W Racquet Club Dr (60101-4317)
PHONE.................................630 501-1881
Ben Kirchhoff, *Owner*
EMP: 4
SALES (est): 170K **Privately Held**
SIC: 2741 Miscellaneous publishing

### (G-78)
### CNC SWISS INC
761 W Racquet Club Dr A (60101-4317)
PHONE.................................630 543-9595
Jay Borysca, *President*
Boguslaw Siembab, *Principal*
EMP: 5
SALES (est): 838.4K **Privately Held**
SIC: 3451 Screw machine products

### (G-79)
### COMPONENT SALES INCORPORATED
130 S Fairbank St (60101-3120)
PHONE.................................630 543-9666
Fax: 630 543-9616
James R Lovelace III, *President*
James R Lovelace Jr, *Founder*
Tom Lovelace, *Corp Secy*
Mark Lovelace, *Vice Pres*
Brian Lovelace, *Treasurer*
EMP: 12
SQ FT: 2,500
SALES: 1.4MM **Privately Held**
SIC: 2752 5065 Commercial printing, offset; semiconductor devices

### (G-80)
### COMPUTERIZED FLEET ANALYSIS
Also Called: Cfa Software
1020 W Fullerton Ave A (60101-4335)
P.O. Box 1309 (60101-8309)
PHONE.................................630 543-1410
Fax: 630 543-1904
Jim Magee, *President*
Michael Ohlinger, *President*
James Magee, *Vice Pres*
David Magee, *CFO*
Nels Olson, *Director*
EMP: 8
SQ FT: 2,800
SALES (est): 881.4K **Privately Held**
WEB: www.cfasoftware.com
SIC: 7372 Business oriented computer software

### (G-81)
### CONDOR TOOL & MANUFACTURING
321 W Gerri Ln (60101-5011)
PHONE.................................630 628-8200
Fax: 630 628-8205
Larry Miller, *President*
EMP: 10
SQ FT: 7,500
SALES: 1MM **Privately Held**
SIC: 3089 3364 3544 Injection molding of plastics; zinc & zinc-base alloy die-castings; special dies, tools, jigs & fixtures

### (G-82)
### COSMO FILMS INC (HQ)
775 W Belden Ave Ste D (60101-4944)
PHONE.................................630 458-5200
Sandeep Dutta, *Acting Pres*
Charles Bohmer, *Business Mgr*
N More, *Engineer*
Rajeev Joshi, *Human Resources*
Murali RAO, *Manager*
◆ EMP: 25 EST: 2007
SQ FT: 28,000
SALES (est): 14.7MM
SALES (corp-wide): 211.9MM **Privately Held**
SIC: 3081 Polypropylene film & sheet
PA: Cosmo Films Limited
  1008, Dlf Tower-A,
  New Delhi DEL 11002
  112 686-3968

### (G-83)
### CRANE DORRAY CORPORATION
320 S Lombard Rd (60101-3024)
P.O. Box 1465, Elmhurst (60126-8465)
PHONE.................................630 893-7553
Ron Jaeger, *President*
EMP: 8
SQ FT: 3,500
SALES (est): 713.7K **Privately Held**
WEB: www.cranedorray.com
SIC: 3625 Switches, electric power

### (G-84)
### CRW FINISHING INC (PA)
1470 W Jeffrey Dr (60101-4356)
PHONE.................................630 495-4994
Charles W Calbeck Sr, *President*
Melanie Calbeck, *Corp Secy*
Chuck Calbeck Jr, *Vice Pres*
James Popek, *Plant Mgr*
Joseph Hubbert, *Regl Sales Mgr*
EMP: 20 EST: 1977
SQ FT: 18,000
SALES: 4.6MM **Privately Held**
WEB: www.crwfinishing.com
SIC: 3541 3559 Deburring machines; metal finishing equipment for plating, etc.

### (G-85)
### CUT - TO - SIZE TECHNOLOGY INC
345 S Fairbank St (60101-3137)
PHONE.................................630 543-8328
Fax: 630 543-3918
Mark Karkos, *President*
Maria Karkos, *Admin Sec*
EMP: 20
SQ FT: 31,000
SALES (est): 4.4MM **Privately Held**
WEB: www.cuttosizetechnology.com
SIC: 2541 Store & office display cases & fixtures

### (G-86)
### DAGGER TOOL CO INC
501 W Interstate Rd (60101-4414)
PHONE.................................630 279-5050
Fax: 630 279-5066
Arthur Tessman Sr, *President*
Mildred Tessman, *Admin Sec*
EMP: 6 EST: 1967
SQ FT: 3,000
SALES: 800K **Privately Held**
SIC: 3599 3544 Machine shop, jobbing & repair; special dies, tools, jigs & fixtures

### (G-87)
### DFT INC
423 W Interstate Rd (60101-4517)
PHONE.................................630 628-8352
Leon Thill, *President*

## Addison - Dupage County (G-114)

EMP: 6
SQ FT: 5,000
SALES (est): 869.5K  Privately Held
WEB: www.dfttrikes.com
SIC: 8742 3751 Manufacturing management consultant; motorcycles, bicycles & parts

**(G-88)**
**DIAL TOOL INDUSTRIES INC**
201 S Church St (60101-3747)
PHONE...................630 543-3600
Fax: 630 543-3630
Steven Pagliuzza, *President*
Bill Klicka, *Opers Mgr*
Rick Raskow, *Mfg Mgr*
Mario Pagliuzza, *Admin Sec*
EMP: 100 EST: 1955
SQ FT: 40,000
SALES (est): 21.1MM  Privately Held
WEB: www.dialtool.com
SIC: 3469 3544 Stamping metal for the trade; special dies, tools, jigs & fixtures

**(G-89)**
**DIAMOND EDGE MANUFACTORING**
644 W Winthrop Ave (60101-4436)
PHONE...................630 458-1630
Louis Papamihail, *President*
Roman Buchacz, *Admin Sec*
EMP: 4
SQ FT: 3,500
SALES (est): 673.7K  Privately Held
SIC: 3541 7699 Machine tools, metal cutting type; industrial tool grinding

**(G-90)**
**DIAMOND TOOL & MOLD INC**
1212 W National Ave (60101-3131)
PHONE...................630 543-7011
Larry Sieber, *President*
Mark Cooper, *Admin Sec*
EMP: 9
SALES: 750K  Privately Held
SIC: 3069 Molded rubber products

**(G-91)**
**DICIANNI GRAPHICS INCORPORATED**
421 S Addison Rd (60101-4650)
PHONE...................630 833-5100
Fax: 630 833-5180
Peter P Dicianni III, *President*
Ben Goetz, *Vice Pres*
Mike Vassolo, *Vice Pres*
Steve Caswell, *Prdtn Mgr*
Mary Dicianni, *Office Mgr*
EMP: 12
SQ FT: 2,700
SALES (est): 2MM  Privately Held
WEB: www.dicianni.com
SIC: 2752 7336 Commercial printing, offset; graphic arts & related design

**(G-92)**
**DICKSON/UNIGAGE INC**
Also Called: Dickson Company, The
930 S Westwood Ave (60101-4997)
PHONE...................630 543-3747
Fax: 630 543-0498
Michael Unger, *President*
James F Foley, *Chairman*
Mark T Kohlmeier, *Corp Secy*
Jimmy Springer, *Production*
Denise Dumian, *Purch Mgr*
▲ EMP: 45
SQ FT: 200,000
SALES (est): 12.6MM  Privately Held
WEB: www.dicksonweb.com
SIC: 3823 5084 3822 3572 Temperature instruments: industrial process type; pressure measurement instruments, industrial; humidity instruments, industrial process type; measuring & testing equipment, electrical; auto controls regulating residntl & coml environmt & applncs; computer storage devices

**(G-93)**
**DIE PROS INC**
1233 W Capitol Dr Ste B (60101-3170)
PHONE...................630 543-2025
Fax: 630 543-5062
Dennis M Lee, *President*
EMP: 4

SQ FT: 2,500
SALES (est): 240K  Privately Held
SIC: 3544 Dies, steel rule; dies & die holders for metal cutting, forming, die casting

**(G-94)**
**DIMENSION MOLDING CORPORATION**
777 W Annoreno Dr (60101-4383)
PHONE...................630 628-0777
Fax: 630 628-0780
Michael Siclianses, *President*
Michael Degrenier, *Vice Pres*
▲ EMP: 40
SALES (est): 7.1MM  Privately Held
WEB: www.dimensionmold.com
SIC: 3089 Injection molded finished plastic products

**(G-95)**
**DNP ENTERPRISES INC (PA)**
1213 W Capitol Dr (60101-5301)
PHONE...................630 628-7210
Mark Poulopoulos, *President*
Deborah Poulopoulos, *Admin Sec*
EMP: 4
SQ FT: 6,000
SALES (est): 454K  Privately Held
SIC: 3599 Machine & other job shop work

**(G-96)**
**DOBAKE BAKERIES INC**
1405 W Fullerton Ave (60101-4321)
PHONE...................630 620-1849
Daniel W Giraudo, *CEO*
EMP: 10
SQ FT: 13,000
SALES: 3MM  Privately Held
SIC: 2052 5812 Bakery products, dry; American restaurant

**(G-97)**
**DORAL INC**
Also Called: J & F Engineering
344 W Interstate Rd (60101-4516)
PHONE...................630 543-5523
James A Turus, *Owner*
EMP: 3
SQ FT: 5,000
SALES (est): 175.9K  Privately Held
SIC: 3544 Special dies, tools, jigs & fixtures

**(G-98)**
**DOYLE SIGNS INC (PA)**
232 W Interstate Rd (60101-4563)
P.O. Box 1068 (60101-8068)
PHONE...................630 543-9490
Fax: 630 543-9493
Terrence J Doyle, *President*
Joseph T Doyle, *Vice Pres*
Margaret Neander, *Vice Pres*
Patrick Doyle, *VP Mfg*
Joe Carroll, *Purch Mgr*
EMP: 75
SQ FT: 36,800
SALES (est): 17.7MM  Privately Held
WEB: www.doylesigns.com
SIC: 3993 Electric signs

**(G-99)**
**DSI SPACEFRAMES INC**
509 S Westgate St (60101-4530)
PHONE...................630 607-0045
Thomas Rj Chambers, *President*
▲ EMP: 30
SQ FT: 12,000
SALES: 8.8MM  Privately Held
SIC: 3446 3441 Architectural metalwork; fabricated structural metal

**(G-100)**
**DTI MOLDING TECHNOLOGIES INC**
201 S Church St (60101-3747)
PHONE...................630 543-3600
Mario Pagliuzza, *President*
Judy Grein, *Administration*
▲ EMP: 54
SQ FT: 40,000
SALES: 2.5MM  Privately Held
SIC: 3089 Molding primary plastic

**(G-101)**
**DU-KANE ASPHALT CO**
600 S Lombard Rd (60101-4206)
P.O. Box 1129 (60101-8159)
PHONE...................630 953-1500
Fax: 630 932-0994
Paul J Dunteman Sr, *President*
Allan L Dunteman, *Vice Pres*
EMP: 5 EST: 1963
SQ FT: 10,000
SALES (est): 919.3K  Privately Held
SIC: 2951 Road materials, bituminous (not from refineries)

**(G-102)**
**DYNAMAC INC**
1229 W Capitol Dr (60101-3116)
PHONE...................630 543-0033
Kent Higgins, *President*
Paul Flauter, *Prdtn Mgr*
Imam Quraishi, *QA Dir*
Martin J Keane Sr, *Sales Mgr*
Rita Rokos, *Office Mgr*
EMP: 32
SQ FT: 15,000
SALES (est): 6.4MM  Privately Held
WEB: www.dynamac-usa.com
SIC: 3599 Machine shop, jobbing & repair

**(G-103)**
**E & T PLASTIC MFG CO INC**
Also Called: E & T Plastics of Illinois
140 S Fairbank St (60101-3120)
PHONE...................630 628-9048
Al Bennett, *Manager*
EMP: 15
SALES (corp-wide): 25.4MM  Privately Held
SIC: 3089 Extruded finished plastic products
PA: E & T Plastic Manufacturing Co., Inc.
  4545 37th St
  Long Island City NY 11101
  718 729-6226

**(G-104)**
**E-JAY PLASTICS CO**
115 W Laura Dr (60101-5113)
PHONE...................630 543-4000
Fax: 630 543-4077
Robert Tyler, *President*
Joan Tyler, *Treasurer*
EMP: 10
SQ FT: 13,000
SALES (est): 890K  Privately Held
SIC: 3089 3083 Molding primary plastic; laminated plastics plate & sheet

**(G-105)**
**EAGLE CARPET SERVICES LTD**
135 S Fairbank St (60101-3119)
PHONE...................956 971-8560
William C Kotlow, *Principal*
Joe Baker, *Principal*
Jim Price, *Principal*
Martin Somen, *Principal*
Charles P Pytlarz, *Admin Sec*
▲ EMP: 5
SQ FT: 3,000
SALES (est): 249.4K  Privately Held
SIC: 2273 Carpets & rugs

**(G-106)**
**EAGLE GEAR & MANUFACTURING CO**
740 W Racquet Club Dr (60101-4318)
PHONE...................630 628-6100
Marek Tyrka, *President*
EMP: 7
SALES: 1MM  Privately Held
SIC: 3462 Gear & chain forgings

**(G-107)**
**ELCAST MANUFACTURING INC**
Also Called: Elcast Lighting
815 S Kay Ave Ste B (60101-4938)
PHONE...................630 628-1992
Fax: 630 543-5392
Peter Biedermann, *President*
Gary Landow, *Manager*
Christine Lurski, *Admin Sec*
▲ EMP: 20
SALES (est): 3.1MM  Privately Held
WEB: www.elcastltg.com
SIC: 3648 3645 Lighting equipment; residential lighting fixtures

**(G-108)**
**ELECTRONIC DISPLAYS INC**
135 S Church St (60101-3746)
PHONE...................630 628-0658
Fax: 630 628-0936
Judith Holmberg, *President*
James Holmberg, *Principal*
Bob Holmberg, *Sales Mgr*
▲ EMP: 18
SQ FT: 25,000
SALES (est): 3.2MM  Privately Held
WEB: www.electronicdisplays.com
SIC: 3993 Scoreboards, electric

**(G-109)**
**ELK GROVE RUBBER & PLASTIC CO**
99 W Commercial Ave (60101-4501)
PHONE...................630 543-5656
Fax: 630 543-5696
Brian Lovitsch, *President*
Joseph Sabatino, *Vice Pres*
Jean Lovitsch, *Office Mgr*
EMP: 15
SQ FT: 8,000
SALES: 1.3MM  Privately Held
SIC: 3061 Mechanical rubber goods

**(G-110)**
**ELLIOTT MACHINE & TOOL CORP**
511 W Interstate Rd (60101-4414)
PHONE...................630 543-6755
Jimmy C Mc Namer, *President*
Barbara Mc Namer, *Admin Sec*
EMP: 3
SQ FT: 3,000
SALES (est): 230K  Privately Held
SIC: 3599 Machine shop, jobbing & repair

**(G-111)**
**ENCON ENVIRONMENTAL CONCEPTS**
643 W Winthrop Ave (60101-4435)
PHONE...................630 543-1583
Fax: 630 543-1523
Robert Rusteberg, *President*
EMP: 17
SQ FT: 10,000
SALES (est): 3.7MM  Privately Held
WEB: www.encon.tv
SIC: 5712 2434 Cabinet work, custom; wood kitchen cabinets

**(G-112)**
**ESSEX GROUP INC**
758 W Racquet Club Dr (60101-4318)
PHONE...................630 628-7841
Jessica Utterback, *Manager*
EMP: 69
SALES (corp-wide): 70.4MM  Privately Held
SIC: 3357 Building wire & cable, nonferrous
HQ: Essex Group, Inc.
  1601 Wall St
  Fort Wayne IN 46802
  260 461-4000

**(G-113)**
**EUROPEAN ORNAMENTAL IRON WORKS**
1786 W Armitage Ct (60101-4207)
PHONE...................630 705-9300
Michael Pietanza, *President*
EMP: 8
SQ FT: 2,400
SALES (est): 800K  Privately Held
SIC: 1799 3496 3446 3441 Ornamental metal work; miscellaneous fabricated wire products; architectural metalwork; fabricated structural metal; metal household furniture

**(G-114)**
**EXO FABRICATION INC**
1140 W Fullerton Ave (60101-4304)
PHONE...................630 501-1136
Leslie E Smiling, *President*
EMP: 6
SALES: 500K  Privately Held
SIC: 3441 Fabricated structural metal

## Addison - Dupage County (G-115)

**(G-115)**
**FDF ARMATURE INC**
220 W Gerri Ln (60101-5010)
PHONE .................................. 630 458-0452
Fax: 630 458-0887
Frank Defrenza, *President*
▲ **EMP:** 8 **EST:** 1998
**SQ FT:** 7,400
**SALES (est):** 710K **Privately Held**
**SIC:** 7694 Rebuilding motors, except automotive

**(G-116)**
**FIBERGLASS SOLUTIONS CORP**
436 W Belden Ave (60101-4903)
PHONE .................................. 630 458-0756
Emily A Quiniff, *President*
Gregory Quiniff, *Corp Secy*
Paul Quiniff, *Vice Pres*
**EMP:** 9
**SQ FT:** 5,000
**SALES:** 500K **Privately Held**
**WEB:** www.mannequinco.com
**SIC:** 2221 Fiberglass fabrics

**(G-117)**
**FINISHING COMPANY**
136 W Commercial Ave (60101-4504)
PHONE .................................. 630 559-0808
JW Carlson, *President*
Brian Bedford, *Manager*
Mark Griego, *Manager*
Peter Hurley, *Manager*
Connie Vrenios, *Manager*
**EMP:** 155
**SALES (est):** 17.2MM **Privately Held**
**WEB:** www.finishingcompany.com
**SIC:** 3471 3479 2851 Anodizing (plating) of metals or formed products; aluminum coating of metal products; colors in oil, except artists'

**(G-118)**
**FLAVORFOCUS LLC**
1210 N Swift Rd (60101-6104)
PHONE .................................. 630 520-9060
David Peterson, *Mng Member*
Larry J Wadsworth,
**EMP:** 80
**SALES (est):** 19.9MM **Privately Held**
**SIC:** 2869 Perfumes, flavorings & food additives

**(G-119)**
**FLEXTRON INC**
130 W Fay Ave (60101-5108)
PHONE .................................. 630 543-5995
Fax: 630 543-5996
Mike Dwyer, *President*
**EMP:** 14
**SQ FT:** 13,000
**SALES:** 1MM **Privately Held**
**WEB:** www.flextron.com
**SIC:** 3599 Hose, flexible metallic

**(G-120)**
**FLOWSERVE CORPORATION**
409 S Vista Ave (60101-4420)
PHONE .................................. 630 543-4240
Mark A Blinn, *Branch Mgr*
**EMP:** 30
**SALES (corp-wide):** 3.9B **Publicly Held**
**SIC:** 3568 Power transmission equipment
**PA:** Flowserve Corporation
5215 N Oconnor Blvd Connor
Irving TX 75039
972 443-6500

**(G-121)**
**FONTELA ELECTRIC INCORPORATED (PA)**
1406 W Jeffrey Dr (60101-4356)
PHONE .................................. 630 932-1600
Fax: 630 932-1642
Antonio Fontela, *President*
Debra C Fontela, *Admin Sec*
**EMP:** 15
**SQ FT:** 6,000
**SALES (est):** 1.1MM **Privately Held**
**WEB:** www.fontelaelectric.com
**SIC:** 7694 Rebuilding motors, except automotive

**(G-122)**
**FORMAR INC**
Also Called: True Dimension
1049 W Republic Dr (60101-3132)
PHONE .................................. 630 543-1151
Fax: 630 543-0155
Mark Boryscka, *President*
Randolph Boryscka, *Corp Secy*
Scott Toms, *QC Mgr*
Jay Boryscka, *Engineer*
Linda Boryscka, *Persnl Mgr*
**EMP:** 12
**SQ FT:** 12,700
**SALES (est):** 2.2MM **Privately Held**
**WEB:** www.true-dimension.com
**SIC:** 3599 Machine shop, jobbing & repair

**(G-123)**
**FRANCH & SONS TRNSP INC**
329 N Mill Rd Unit 108 (60101)
PHONE .................................. 630 392-3307
Paul M Franch, *President*
**EMP:** 3
**SALES (est):** 400K **Privately Held**
**SIC:** 2679 7389 Papier mache articles, except statuary & art goods;

**(G-124)**
**FURNEL INC (PA)**
350 S Stewart Ave (60101-3310)
PHONE .................................. 630 543-0885
Fax: 630 543-1963
John P Murzanski, *President*
**EMP:** 26
**SQ FT:** 10,000
**SALES (est):** 3.5MM **Privately Held**
**SIC:** 3089 3544 Injection molding of plastics; industrial molds

**(G-125)**
**G BRANCH CORP**
409 S Vista Ave Unit B (60101-4420)
PHONE .................................. 630 458-1909
Grant Branch, *Owner*
**EMP:** 52
**SALES (est):** 4.6MM **Privately Held**
**SIC:** 3444 Sheet metalwork

**(G-126)**
**G L TOOL AND MANUFACTURING CO**
815 S Kay Ave Ste A (60101-4938)
PHONE .................................. 630 628-1992
Fax: 630 628-1994
Robert Lurski, *President*
Sue Zielinski, *Manager*
Christine Lurski, *Admin Sec*
▲ **EMP:** 16
**SQ FT:** 11,000
**SALES (est):** 1.8MM **Privately Held**
**SIC:** 3471 Finishing, metals or formed products

**(G-127)**
**GALLON INDUSTRIES INC**
Also Called: Bm Welding
341 W Factory Rd (60101-5003)
PHONE .................................. 630 628-1020
Neville Gallon, *President*
Joy Gallon, *Admin Sec*
**EMP:** 22
**SALES (est):** 3.3MM **Privately Held**
**SIC:** 3441 Fabricated structural metal

**(G-128)**
**GARRATT-CALLAHAN COMPANY**
340 S La Londe Ave (60101-3394)
PHONE .................................. 630 543-4411
Fax: 630 543-8382
John Keating, *Branch Mgr*
**EMP:** 7
**SALES (corp-wide):** 65MM **Privately Held**
**WEB:** www.g-c.com
**SIC:** 2899 Water treating compounds
**PA:** Garratt-Callahan Company
50 Ingold Rd
Burlingame CA 94010
650 697-5811

**(G-129)**
**GE BETZ INC**
Also Called: Hercules Industrial Division
333 S Lombard Rd (60101-3023)
PHONE .................................. 630 543-8480
Rich Johnson, *General Mgr*
Joseph Catanese, *Safety Dir*
Brian Vannoni, *Opers-Prdtn-Mfg*
Donald Wallenberg, *Purch Mgr*
Darren Vitosh, *Manager*
**EMP:** 21
**SALES (corp-wide):** 123.6B **Publicly Held**
**SIC:** 2899 Water treating compounds
**HQ:** Ge Betz, Inc.
4636 Somerton Rd
Trevose PA 19053
215 355-3300

**(G-130)**
**GEM MANUFACTURING CORPORATION**
367 S Rohlwing Rd Ste Q (60101-3064)
PHONE .................................. 630 458-0014
Kirit Dave, *President*
**EMP:** 4
**SQ FT:** 4,400
**SALES (est):** 350K **Privately Held**
**SIC:** 3714 Motor vehicle parts & accessories

**(G-131)**
**GENERAL ENGINEERING WORKS**
1515 W Wrightwood Ct (60101-3034)
PHONE .................................. 630 543-8000
Fax: 630 543-8005
Sue Peters, *President*
John Gassensmith, *Vice Pres*
**EMP:** 40
**SQ FT:** 25,000
**SALES (est):** 8.1MM **Privately Held**
**WEB:** www.gewinc.com
**SIC:** 3451 Screw machine products

**(G-132)**
**GENERAL GRINDING CO**
1514 W Wrightwood Ct (60101-3071)
PHONE .................................. 630 543-9088
Fax: 630 543-6881
Ariel Monsivais, *President*
**EMP:** 7 **EST:** 1950
**SQ FT:** 5,000
**SALES (est):** 938.9K **Privately Held**
**SIC:** 3599 Machine shop, jobbing & repair

**(G-133)**
**GENERAL PLATING CO INC**
303 W Fay Ave (60101-5007)
PHONE .................................. 630 543-0088
Fax: 630 543-3546
Josephine Maleski, *President*
Dave Maleski, *Principal*
Jim Maleski, *Vice Pres*
Lisa Maleski, *Admin Sec*
**EMP:** 7
**SQ FT:** 5,000
**SALES (est):** 845.1K **Privately Held**
**SIC:** 3471 Electroplating of metals or formed products; finishing, metals or formed products

**(G-134)**
**GEORGE HANSEN & CO INC**
50 W Laura Dr (60101-5115)
PHONE .................................. 630 628-8700
Fax: 630 678-8716
William Hansen, *CEO*
Susan Hansen, *CFO*
**EMP:** 11 **EST:** 1953
**SQ FT:** 14,000
**SALES (est):** 940K **Privately Held**
**WEB:** www.georgehansenco.com
**SIC:** 3544 Special dies & tools

**(G-135)**
**GLC INDUSTRIES INC**
Also Called: GLC Engineering
326 W Gerri Ln (60101-5012)
PHONE .................................. 630 628-5870
Fax: 847 233-9206
George Lambropoulos, *President*
Bill Lambropoulos, *Sales Executive*
**EMP:** 20
**SQ FT:** 12,000
**SALES (est):** 3.9MM **Privately Held**
**WEB:** www.glcinc.com
**SIC:** 3444 Sheet metalwork

**(G-136)**
**GLOBAL ABRASIVE PRODUCTS INC**
39 W Factory Rd (60101-5101)
PHONE .................................. 630 543-9466
Boris Andres, *Branch Mgr*
**EMP:** 40
**SALES (corp-wide):** 4MM **Privately Held**
**WEB:** www.preson.com
**SIC:** 2675 Paperboard die-cutting
**PA:** Global Abrasive Products, Inc.
62 Mill St
Lockport NY 14094
716 438-0047

**(G-137)**
**GOLD COAST BAKING CO**
1405 W Fullerton Ave (60101-4321)
PHONE .................................. 630 620-1849
**EMP:** 8
**SALES (est):** 901.8K **Privately Held**
**SIC:** 2051 Bread, cake & related products

**(G-138)**
**GP LIQUIDATION INC**
1427 W Jeffrey Dr (60101-4331)
PHONE .................................. 630 784-9736
Phil Gurgone, *President*
Ray Prestage, *Vice Pres*
**EMP:** 6
**SALES (est):** 1.3MM **Privately Held**
**SIC:** 3555 Printing trades machinery

**(G-139)**
**GRIND LAP SERVICES INC**
1045 W National Ave (60101-3126)
PHONE .................................. 630 458-1111
Fax: 630 458-0787
John Gallichio, *President*
Marcia Gallichio, *Corp Secy*
Bob Sove, *Prdtn Mgr*
Chuck Itzenthaler, *Foreman/Supr*
Brian Gallichio, *Engineer*
**EMP:** 27 **EST:** 1977
**SQ FT:** 27,000
**SALES (est):** 2.9MM **Privately Held**
**WEB:** www.grindlap.com
**SIC:** 7389 3599 Grinding, precision: commercial or industrial; machine shop, jobbing & repair

**(G-140)**
**HAKO MINUTEMAN INC**
111 S Rohlwing Rd (60101-3027)
PHONE .................................. 630 627-6900
Fax: 630 627-1130
Kathy Duffy, *Director*
Terry Hartsell, *Director*
Kim Rubio, *Director*
▲ **EMP:** 2 **EST:** 2012
**SALES (est):** 525.4K **Privately Held**
**SIC:** 2752 Commercial printing, offset

**(G-141)**
**HAMMOND SUZUKI USA INC**
733 W Annoreno Dr (60101-4315)
PHONE .................................. 630 543-0277
Manji Suzuki, *President*
Randy Atzman, *Purchasing*
Warren Brunsting, *Engineer*
Peter Nguyen, *CFO*
Gregg Gronowski, *Sales Dir*
▲ **EMP:** 20
**SQ FT:** 22,000
**SALES (est):** 4.2MM
**SALES (corp-wide):** 33.2MM **Privately Held**
**WEB:** www.hammondorganco.com
**SIC:** 3651 3931 Speaker systems; organs, all types: pipe, reed, hand, electronic, etc.
**PA:** Suzuki Musical Instrument Mfg.Co.,Ltd.
2-25-12, Ryoke, Naka-Ku
Hamamatsu SZO 430-0
534 612-325

**(G-142)**
**HAUSERMANN ABRADING PROCESS CO**
300 W Laura Dr (60101-5016)
PHONE .................................. 630 543-6688
Marten Hausermann, *President*
Charles Oskin, *Engineer*

## GEOGRAPHIC SECTION
### Addison - Dupage County (G-167)

Judith L Hausermann, *Treasurer*
Robert Tincu, *Sales Staff*
Belinda Croschere, *Manager*
**EMP:** 18 **EST:** 1977
**SQ FT:** 24,000
**SALES (est):** 1.4MM **Privately Held**
**SIC:** 3541 Grinding, polishing, buffing, lapping & honing machines

### (G-143)
### HAUSERMANN CONTROLS CO
Also Called: Hausermann Die & Machine
300 W Laura Dr (60101-5016)
**PHONE**..................................630 543-6688
Marten Hausermann, *President*
Kim Hausermann, *QC Dir*
Judith L Hausermann, *Treasurer*
Robert Tincu, *Sales Staff*
Kimberly Federighi, *Admin Sec*
**EMP:** 17
**SQ FT:** 24,000
**SALES (est):** 2.7MM **Privately Held**
**WEB:** www.hausermann.net
**SIC:** 3625 Numerical controls

### (G-144)
### HAUSERMANN DIE & MACHINE CO
300 W Laura Dr (60101-5016)
**PHONE**..................................630 543-6688
**Fax:** 630 543-6689
Marten Hausermann, *President*
Judith L Hausermann, *Treasurer*
Robert Tincu, *Sales Staff*
**EMP:** 16 **EST:** 1955
**SQ FT:** 24,000
**SALES (est):** 1.5MM **Privately Held**
**SIC:** 3544 3624 5084 3625 Industrial molds; electrodes, thermal & electrolytic uses: carbon, graphite; industrial machinery & equipment; relays & industrial controls; computer peripheral equipment

### (G-145)
### HERMAN SEEKAMP INC
Also Called: Clyde's Delicious Donuts
1120 W Fullerton Ave (60101-4304)
**PHONE**..................................630 628-6555
**Fax:** 630 628-6838
Kent W Bickford, *President*
Willard Bickford, *Chairman*
Mike Berman, *Manager*
Nick Tsatsafoulis, *Manager*
Mike Zdarsky, *Manager*
**EMP:** 115 **EST:** 1920
**SQ FT:** 54,000
**SALES (est):** 35.3MM **Privately Held**
**WEB:** www.clydesdonuts.com
**SIC:** 2051 2052 2053 2099 Bread, cake & related products; doughnuts, except frozen; pastries, e.g. danish: except frozen; croissants, except frozen; cookies; doughnuts, frozen; food preparations; frozen specialties

### (G-146)
### HIRE-NELSON COMPANY INC
325 W Factory Rd Ste B (60101-5090)
**PHONE**..................................630 543-9400
**Fax:** 630 543-5334
Alan Bosworth, *President*
Tony Hernandez, *General Mgr*
Daniel Fors, *Principal*
Kyle Fredrickson, *Principal*
Wayne Juda, *Principal*
**EMP:** 30 **EST:** 1977
**SQ FT:** 25,000
**SALES (est):** 5.6MM **Privately Held**
**WEB:** www.hirenelson.com
**SIC:** 2541 Office fixtures, wood; display fixtures, wood

### (G-147)
### HOEING DIE & MOLD ENGRAVING
441 W Interstate Rd (60101-4547)
**PHONE**..................................630 543-0006
**Fax:** 630 543-6633
Helmut Hoeing, *President*
Barbara Hoeing, *President*
**EMP:** 3
**SQ FT:** 3,000
**SALES:** 300K **Privately Held**
**SIC:** 3479 Engraving jewelry silverware, or metal

### (G-148)
### HOPKINS PRINTING & ENVELOPE CO
Also Called: Custom Bindery Services
120 W Laura Dr (60101-5114)
P.O. Box 389 (60101-0389)
**PHONE**..................................630 543-8227
**Fax:** 630 543-8358
James Devries, *President*
Donald Campo, *Vice Pres*
Dave Weeks, *Office Mgr*
**EMP:** 13
**SQ FT:** 15,000
**SALES:** 2MM **Privately Held**
**WEB:** www.custom-bindery.com
**SIC:** 2789 Trade binding services

### (G-149)
### HOSPITOLOGY PRODUCTS LLC
131 S Lombard Rd (60101-3019)
**PHONE**..................................630 359-5075
Sujay Kapadia, *Mng Member*
▲ **EMP:** 6
**SALES (est):** 686.3K **Privately Held**
**SIC:** 2515 Mattresses & foundations

### (G-150)
### HOT ROD CHASSIS & CYCLE INC
59 W Factory Rd (60101-5101)
**PHONE**..................................630 458-0808
Kevin Tully, *President*
Chad Hill, *Vice Pres*
Linda Reyna, *Office Mgr*
Malia Wendt, *Office Mgr*
**EMP:** 7
**SALES (est):** 941.1K **Privately Held**
**WEB:** www.hotrodchassisandcycle.com
**SIC:** 3711 Automobile bodies, passenger car, not including engine, etc.

### (G-151)
### HYDRAULICNET LLC
Also Called: Hydraulic Net
719 W Fullerton Ave A (60101-3258)
P.O. Box 801 (60101-0801)
**PHONE**..................................630 543-7630
Stephen L Smith,
▲ **EMP:** 14
**SQ FT:** 10,000
**SALES (est):** 2.7MM **Privately Held**
**WEB:** www.hydraulic.net
**SIC:** 3566 Reduction gears & gear units for turbines, except automotive

### (G-152)
### ILLINOIS SWITCHBOARD CORP
125 W Laura Dr (60101-5178)
**PHONE**..................................630 543-0910
Don Zastawny, *Ch of Bd*
William Zastawny, *President*
Patty Zastawny, *Purchasing*
Karen Williams, *CFO*
Karen L Zastawny, *Admin Sec*
**EMP:** 12
**SQ FT:** 18,000
**SALES (est):** 1.8MM **Privately Held**
**SIC:** 3613 Switchboards & parts, power; panelboards & distribution boards, electric; control panels, electric

### (G-153)
### INNOVATIVE MAG-DRIVE LLC
409 S Vista Ave (60101-4420)
**PHONE**..................................630 543-4240
Nick Rentzelos, *Principal*
**EMP:** 17 **EST:** 2014
**SALES (est):** 3.8MM **Privately Held**
**SIC:** 3568 Power transmission equipment

### (G-154)
### INTELLGENT PRCSSES AUTOMTN INC
Also Called: Ip Automation
111 S Lombard Rd Ste 7 (60101-3062)
**PHONE**..................................630 656-1215
Tom Christofilis, *CEO*
**EMP:** 5
**SALES:** 1.1MM **Privately Held**
**SIC:** 3569 General industrial machinery

### (G-155)
### ITEN INDUSTRIES INC
1545 W Wrightwood Ct (60101-3034)
**PHONE**..................................630 543-2820
**Fax:** 630 543-1463
Judy Loftus, *Principal*
Scott Humphrey, *Finance Mgr*
**EMP:** 8
**SQ FT:** 10,275
**SALES (corp-wide):** 42.8MM **Privately Held**
**WEB:** www.itenindustries.com
**SIC:** 3083 3089 2493 5113 Plastic finished products, laminated; vulcanized fiber plates, sheets, rods or tubes; hardboard, tempered; industrial & personal service paper; cellulosic manmade fibers; plastics materials & resins
**PA:** Iten Industries, Inc.
4602 Benefit Ave
Ashtabula OH 44004
440 997-6134

### (G-156)
### IVAN SCHWENKER
Also Called: Illinois Pneumatic Tool Co
1480 W Bernard Dr Ste A (60101-4334)
**PHONE**..................................630 543-7798
**Fax:** 630 543-0722
Ivan Schwenker, *Owner*
Dow Schwenker, *Manager*
**EMP:** 3
**SQ FT:** 4,000
**SALES (est):** 190K **Privately Held**
**SIC:** 3545 7699 3546 Machine tool accessories; tool repair services; power-driven handtools

### (G-157)
### J C HOSE & TUBE INC
236 S La Londe Ave Ste C (60101-3342)
**PHONE**..................................630 543-4747
Linda Chopelas, *President*
Mary Jones, *Manager*
John Chopelas, *Admin Sec*
**EMP:** 5
**SQ FT:** 5,000
**SALES (est):** 750K **Privately Held**
**SIC:** 5074 3492 Plumbing fittings & supplies; hose & tube fittings & assemblies, hydraulic/pneumatic

### (G-158)
### JASON INCORPORATED
Advance Wire Products
201 S Swift Rd (60101-5621)
**PHONE**..................................630 627-7000
**Fax:** 630 627-9826
Todd Merquith, *General Mgr*
**EMP:** 120
**SQ FT:** 48,500
**SALES (corp-wide):** 705.5MM **Publicly Held**
**WEB:** www.jasoninc.com
**SIC:** 3496 3469 3965 Miscellaneous fabricated wire products; metal stampings; fasteners, buttons, needles & pins
**HQ:** Jason Incorporated
E Michigan St Ste 900
Milwaukee WI 53202
414 277-9300

### (G-159)
### JD NORMAN INDUSTRIES INC (PA)
787 W Belden Ave (60101-4942)
**PHONE**..................................630 458-3700
**Fax:** 630 458-3701
Justin D Norman, *President*
Chey Becker-Varto, *President*
Matt Litchfield, *President*
Elizabeth Kousiakis, *Vice Pres*
Alberto Hernandez, *Plant Mgr*
▲ **EMP:** 65 **EST:** 1986
**SALES (est):** 128.5MM **Privately Held**
**WEB:** www.jamann.com
**SIC:** 3469 3496 3495 Metal stampings; miscellaneous fabricated wire products; wire springs

### (G-160)
### JET FINISHERS INC
136 W Commercial Ave (60101-4504)
**PHONE**..................................847 718-0501
**Fax:** 847 718-0502
David Allison, *President*
Evie Sitar, *Purchasing*
Mark Wilinski, *Sales Mgr*
Elois Allison, *Office Mgr*
Curtis Sell, *Admin Sec*
**EMP:** 53
**SQ FT:** 52,000
**SALES (est):** 7.3MM **Privately Held**
**WEB:** www.jetfinishers.com
**SIC:** 3479 Painting, coating & hot dipping

### (G-161)
### JVK PRECISION HARD CHROME INC
29 W Commercial Ave (60101-4501)
**PHONE**..................................630 628-0810
**Fax:** 630 628-1938
Mary Van Kollenburg, *President*
Mary Beth Van Kollenburg, *President*
James Van Kollenburg, *Treasurer*
Kim Van Kollenberg, *Admin Sec*
**EMP:** 8
**SALES (est):** 480K **Privately Held**
**SIC:** 3471 Chromium plating of metals or formed products

### (G-162)
### K & J SYNTHETIC LUBRICANTS
405 W Myrick Ave (60101-3451)
**PHONE**..................................630 628-1011
Ken Christianson, *Owner*
Joyce Christianson, *Co-Owner*
**EMP:** 6
**SALES (est):** 60K **Privately Held**
**SIC:** 2992 5172 5541 Lubricating oils & greases; lubricating oils & greases; gasoline service stations

### (G-163)
### K & P INDUSTRIES INC
Also Called: Addison Electro Polishing Div
1120 W Republic Dr Ste H (60101-3140)
**PHONE**..................................630 628-6676
**Fax:** 630 628-6696
Prahlad M Patel, *President*
Kanta P Patel, *Vice Pres*
**EMP:** 3
**SQ FT:** 1,100
**SALES (est):** 240K **Privately Held**
**SIC:** 3471 Electroplating of metals or formed products

### (G-164)
### K M I INTERNATIONAL CORP
1411 W Jeffrey Dr (60101-4331)
**PHONE**..................................630 627-6300
**Fax:** 630 627-6383
Mohammad Ibrahim, *President*
Karen S C Fann, *Admin Sec*
▲ **EMP:** 6
**SALES (est):** 587.7K **Privately Held**
**SIC:** 3999 Artificial flower arrangements

### (G-165)
### KEN MATTHEWS & ASSOCIATES INC
Also Called: Midwest Stucco-Eifs Dist
415 W Belden Ave Ste H (60101-4933)
**PHONE**..................................630 628-6470
Kenneth L Matthews, *President*
**EMP:** 3
**SQ FT:** 7,000
**SALES (est):** 280K **Privately Held**
**WEB:** www.midweststucco.com
**SIC:** 3275 Plaster & plasterboard, gypsum

### (G-166)
### KERN PRECISION
1010 W Fullerton Ave E (60101-4333)
**PHONE**..................................331 979-0954
Anton Mangold, *President*
**EMP:** 6 **EST:** 2004
**SALES (est):** 98.6K **Privately Held**
**SIC:** 3599 Industrial machinery

### (G-167)
### KIENE DIESEL ACCESSORIES INC
Also Called: Continental Cutoff Machine
325 S Fairbank St (60101-3164)
**PHONE**..................................630 543-7170
**Fax:** 708 543-5953
John F Craychee, *President*
Charles W Craychee Jr, *Vice Pres*
Alvin Mayo, *Production*
Kevin Wilson, *Marketing Staff*
Jeff Tucker, *Manager*
▲ **EMP:** 21
**SQ FT:** 19,000

## Addison - Dupage County (G-168)

SALES (est): 5.3MM **Privately Held**
WEB: www.kienediesel.com
SIC: **3541** 3829 3714 Cutoff machines (metalworking machinery); testing equipment: abrasion, shearing strength, etc.; motor vehicle parts & accessories

### (G-168)
### KIER MFG CO
1450 W Jeffrey Dr (60101-4356)
PHONE..................................630 953-9500
Daniel Kier, *President*
Jim Butkiewicz Jr, *Corp Secy*
Constance Kier, *Shareholder*
EMP: 8 EST: 1953
SQ FT: 12,000
SALES (est): 1.3MM **Privately Held**
WEB: www.kiermfg.com
SIC: **3444** 3469 Sheet metal specialties, not stamped; stamping metal for the trade

### (G-169)
### KLEER PAK MFG CO INC
320 S La Londe Ave (60101-3309)
PHONE..................................630 543-0208
Kam Patel, *President*
Gordhan Patel, *Chairman*
Ramesh Gandhi, *Vice Pres*
EMP: 20
SQ FT: 24,000
SALES: 2MM **Privately Held**
WEB: www.kleerpak.com
SIC: **2673** Food storage & frozen food bags, plastic; plastic bags: made from purchased materials

### (G-170)
### KLM TOOL COMPANY
930 S Stiles Dr (60101-4913)
PHONE..................................630 458-1700
Kazimerz Laszewicz, *President*
George Piotrowski, *General Mgr*
Mike Kazcmarczyk, *Vice Pres*
EMP: 25
SQ FT: 40,000
SALES (est): 3.2MM **Privately Held**
SIC: **3599** Machine shop, jobbing & repair

### (G-171)
### KMS INDUSTRIES LLC
923 W National Ave (60101-3125)
PHONE..................................331 225-2671
John Mitoraj, *Mng Member*
Greg Klemenswizz,
Robert Sickles,
◆ EMP: 4
SQ FT: 18,000
SALES (est): 528K **Privately Held**
SIC: **3613** Distribution cutouts

### (G-172)
### KOHOUT WOODWORK INC
759 W Factory Rd (60101-4308)
PHONE..................................630 628-6257
Steve Kohout, *President*
Esther Kohout, *Vice Pres*
EMP: 5
SALES (est): 552.2K **Privately Held**
SIC: **2499** 5031 Decorative wood & woodwork; millwork

### (G-173)
### KOPIS MACHINE CO INC
330 W Interstate Rd (60101-4559)
PHONE..................................630 543-4138
Fax: 630 543-9658
Floyd Kopis, *President*
Jo Ann Kopis, *Corp Secy*
Vincent Lombardo, *Vice Pres*
Louis Gluth, *VP Sales*
Louis Gluth, *Sales Mgr*
EMP: 28 EST: 1956
SQ FT: 9,000
SALES (est): 3.3MM **Privately Held**
WEB: www.kopismachine.com
SIC: **3599** Custom machinery

### (G-174)
### L A T ENTERPRISE INC
423 W Interstate Rd (60101-4517)
PHONE..................................630 543-5533
Fax: 630 543-5539
Leon A Thill, *President*
Charity Jibala, *Treasurer*
EMP: 3
SQ FT: 5,000
SALES (est): 408.6K **Privately Held**
SIC: **3599** Machine & other job shop work; custom machinery

### (G-175)
### LA AUTENTICA MICHOACANA NEVER
507 S Addison Rd (60101-4649)
PHONE..................................630 516-1888
EMP: 4
SALES (est): 321.1K **Privately Held**
SIC: **3421** Table & food cutlery, including butchers'

### (G-176)
### LAB TEC COSMT BY MARZENA INC
1470 W Bernard Dr (60101-4330)
PHONE..................................630 396-3970
Marzena Savas, *President*
▲ EMP: 12
SQ FT: 9,000
SALES (est): 3.4MM **Privately Held**
SIC: **2844** 7231 Concentrates, perfume; beauty shops

### (G-177)
### LACE TECHNOLOGIES INC
315 S Fairbank St (60101-3123)
PHONE..................................630 762-3865
Fax: 630 762-3856
Charles Han, *President*
EMP: 14
SQ FT: 10,000
SALES (est): 1.3MM **Privately Held**
WEB: www.leadfreeassembly.com
SIC: **3679** Electronic circuits

### (G-178)
### LAKESIDE SCREW PRODUCTS INC
1395 W Jeffrey Dr (60101-4331)
PHONE..................................630 495-1606
Fax: 630 495-1682
Zygmunt Soszko, *President*
Shanna Ramirez, *Manager*
EMP: 105 EST: 1977
SQ FT: 45,000
SALES (est): 19.3MM **Privately Held**
WEB: www.lakesidescrew.com
SIC: **3451** Screw machine products

### (G-179)
### LENROK INDUSTRIES INC
Also Called: Bramic Industries
542 W Winthrop Ave (60101-4441)
PHONE..................................630 628-1946
Fax: 630 628-0038
Jeffrey Cornell, *Director*
EMP: 6
SALES (est): 360K **Privately Held**
SIC: **3599** 8742 Machine & other job shop work; management consulting services

### (G-180)
### LEWIS ACQUISITION CORP
Also Called: Lewis Plastics
712 W Winthrop Ave (60101-4311)
PHONE..................................773 486-5660
Fax: 773 486-4287
William Lacek, *President*
David Ferdinand, *Project Engr*
Julie Banhoegarden, *Manager*
Mary Wawak, *Admin Sec*
▲ EMP: 68
SALES (est): 23.4MM **Privately Held**
SIC: **3089** Injection molding of plastics

### (G-181)
### LION WELDING SERVICE INC
729 W Fullerton Ave 4d (60101-3260)
PHONE..................................630 543-5230
Fax: 630 543-5231
Dale A Burzynski, *President*
Holly Burzynski, *Vice Pres*
EMP: 4
SQ FT: 2,800
SALES: 175K **Privately Held**
SIC: **7692** Welding repair

### (G-182)
### LOCKNUT TECHNOLOGY INC
351 S Lombard Rd (60101-3023)
PHONE..................................630 543-5330
Fax: 630 628-5331
Reinhart G Motz, *President*
Carol Motz, *Admin Sec*
▲ EMP: 10
SQ FT: 12,000
SALES (est): 1.5MM **Privately Held**
SIC: **3452** Nuts, metal

### (G-183)
### LOMBARD SWISS SCREW COMPANY
420 S Rohlwing Rd (60101-4210)
PHONE..................................630 576-5096
Fax: 630 576-5099
Bernard Seewald, *President*
Diana Konecke, *Vice Pres*
Karen Calvin, *Admin Sec*
EMP: 40
SQ FT: 27,000
SALES (est): 7.9MM **Privately Held**
WEB: www.lombardswiss.com
SIC: **3451** 5072 Screw machine products; screws

### (G-184)
### LUNDMARK INC
Also Called: Lundmark Wax Co
350 S La Londe Ave (60101-3309)
PHONE..................................630 628-1199
Fax: 630 628-1678
Timothy Burke, *President*
Mark Walters, *Purch Agent*
Bill Brennan, *VP Sales*
James N Monson, *Sales Mgr*
George Worthington, *Mktg Dir*
▼ EMP: 14
SALES (est): 2.9MM **Privately Held**
WEB: www.lundmarkwax.com
SIC: **2842** Specialty cleaning, polishes & sanitation goods

### (G-185)
### MAC-STER INC
1420 W Bernard Dr (60101-4330)
PHONE..................................847 830-7013
Andrew Sternal, *President*
Christopher Sternal, *Vice Pres*
Ann Sternal, *Admin Sec*
EMP: 10
SALES (est): 1.7MM **Privately Held**
SIC: **3444** Forming machine work, sheet metal; metal housings, enclosures, casings & other containers; hoppers, sheet metal; machine guards, sheet metal

### (G-186)
### MAGNECO INC (HQ)
223 W Interstate Rd (60101-4513)
PHONE..................................630 543-6660
Charles W Connors, *CEO*
Katie Weiner, *Accounts Mgr*
Albert Dzermcjko, *Manager*
Dominic Pautler, *Manager*
EMP: 100
SQ FT: 85,000
SALES (est): 17.5MM
SALES (corp-wide): 65.8MM **Privately Held**
SIC: **3297** Nonclay refractories
PA: Magneco/Metrel, Inc.
223 W Interstate Rd
Addison IL 60101
630 543-6660

### (G-187)
### MAGNECO INC
206 W Factory Rd (60101-5002)
PHONE..................................630 543-6660
Charles Connors, *Branch Mgr*
EMP: 8
SALES (corp-wide): 65.8MM **Privately Held**
SIC: **3297** Nonclay refractories
HQ: Magneco, Inc
223 W Interstate Rd
Addison IL 60101
630 543-6660

### (G-188)
### MAGNECO/METREL INC (PA)
223 W Interstate Rd (60101-4513)
PHONE..................................630 543-6660
Fax: 630 543-1479
Charles W Connors Jr, *President*
Dominic Pautler, *General Mgr*
Charles W Connors, *Chairman*
Madjid Soofi, *Vice Pres*
James S Irwin, *VP Sls/Mktg*
▼ EMP: 33 EST: 1981
SQ FT: 13,000
SALES: 65.8MM **Privately Held**
WEB: www.magneco-metrel.com
SIC: **3297** Nonclay refractories

### (G-189)
### MAJOR PRIME PLASTICS INC
300 S Mitchell Ct (60101-1473)
PHONE..................................630 953-4111
Reed Hadley, *Principal*
EMP: 2 EST: 2012
SALES (est): 223.4K **Privately Held**
SIC: **5169** 3081 Chemicals & allied products; unsupported plastics film & sheet

### (G-190)
### MANU-TEC OF ILLINOIS LLC
415 W Belden Ave Ste E (60101-4933)
PHONE..................................630 543-3022
Fax: 630 543-7766
Gene Marino, *CEO*
Tom Kotopka, *President*
Randall Flones, *Engineer*
Pete Mandino, *Manager*
EMP: 12
SQ FT: 7,500
SALES: 1.7MM **Privately Held**
WEB: www.manu-tec.com
SIC: **3672** 3679 Printed circuit boards; harness assemblies for electronic use: wire or cable

### (G-191)
### MARATHON MANUFACTURING INC
110 W Laura Dr (60101-5114)
PHONE..................................630 543-6262
Roy Hall, *President*
Mary Hall, *Treasurer*
▲ EMP: 30
SQ FT: 20,000
SALES (est): 6.5MM **Privately Held**
WEB: www.marathonmolding.com
SIC: **3442** Molding, trim & stripping

### (G-192)
### MATREX EXHIBITS INC
301 S Church St (60101-3749)
PHONE..................................630 628-2233
Fax: 630 628-2263
Jill D Hebert, *CEO*
Paul Vassek, *Project Mgr*
Thomas Chlebanowski, *Human Res Mgr*
Deborah Kerrigan, *Sales Staff*
Josi Smith, *Sales Staff*
EMP: 70
SQ FT: 105,000
SALES (est): 11.5MM **Privately Held**
WEB: www.matrexhibits.net
SIC: **7389** 3993 Trade show arrangement; exhibit construction by industrial contractors; signs & advertising specialties

### (G-193)
### MATRIX PACKAGING INC
1035 W Republic Dr (60101-3132)
PHONE..................................630 458-1942
Fax: 630 628-6216
Darryl Appleton, *Sales Executive*
Raj Judge, *Manager*
EMP: 4
SALES (corp-wide): 4.7B **Publicly Held**
WEB: www.matrixpackaging.com
SIC: **3089** Plastic containers, except foam
HQ: Sonoco Plastics Canada Ulc
245 Britannia Rd E
Mississauga ON L4Z 4
905 624-2337

### (G-194)
### MAXI-VAC INC
367 S Rohlwing Rd Ste F (60101-3064)
P.O. Box 668, Dundee (60118-0668)
PHONE..................................224 699-9760
Fax: 630 620-6683
Jeffrey Lichtardt, *President*
Janice Nolan, *Admin Sec*
EMP: 4
SQ FT: 4,000
SALES (est): 559.8K **Privately Held**
WEB: www.maxi-vac.com
SIC: **3452** 5084 5131 Washers, metal; industrial machinery & equipment; hair accessories

# GEOGRAPHIC SECTION
## Addison - Dupage County (G-220)

**(G-195)**
**MC DIST & MFG CO**
310 W Gerri Ln (60101-5012)
PHONE..................630 628-5180
Michael McCaleb Sr, *President*
Donna McCaleb, *Vice Pres*
William McCaleb, *Vice Pres*
Kent Tjossem, *Treasurer*
EMP: 14
SQ FT: 10,000
SALES (est): 1.6MM **Privately Held**
SIC: 3089 2431 Shutters, plastic; millwork

**(G-196)**
**MECHANICAL PRODUCTS CORP**
330 W Gerri Ln (60101-5092)
PHONE..................630 543-4842
Frank Marousek, *President*
Sharon O'Neill, *Office Mgr*
▲ EMP: 10 EST: 1963
SQ FT: 10,000
SALES (est): 1.6MM **Privately Held**
SIC: 3599 Machine shop, jobbing & repair

**(G-197)**
**MEDGYN PRODUCTS INC**
100 W Industrial Rd (60101-4508)
P.O. Box 3126, Oak Brook (60522-3126)
PHONE..................630 627-4105
Fax: 630 627-0127
Lakshman M Agadi, *President*
Ramesh Vyas, *Vice Pres*
Peters Fasas, *Opers Staff*
Rieni Muphuswamy, *Sales/Mktg Dir*
Dale Dambek, *Natl Sales Mgr*
▲ EMP: 55
SQ FT: 20,000
SALES (est): 19.1MM **Privately Held**
WEB: www.medgyn.com
SIC: 5047 3842 Medical equipment & supplies; gynecological supplies & appliances

**(G-198)**
**MEGA CIRCUIT INC**
1040 S Westgate St (60101-5022)
PHONE..................630 543-8460
Fax: 630 629-2080
Rick Savani, *President*
Kodubhai Patel, *Corp Secy*
Jim Malavia, *Vice Pres*
Paresh Patel, *Vice Pres*
Sanjay Beri, *Electrical Engi*
▲ EMP: 85
SQ FT: 23,000
SALES (est): 15.5MM **Privately Held**
SIC: 3672 Printed circuit boards

**(G-199)**
**MERKEL WOODWORKING INC**
300 S Stewart Ave (60101-3310)
PHONE..................630 458-0700
Fax: 630 458-0701
Bob Merkel, *President*
Debbie Merkel, *Corp Secy*
EMP: 15
SALES: 3MM **Privately Held**
SIC: 2431 Millwork

**(G-200)**
**METAL IMPREGNATING CORP**
121 W Official Rd (60101-4520)
P.O. Box 1067 (60101-8067)
PHONE..................630 543-3443
William Schramm, *President*
Sandee Hendricks, *Corp Secy*
Jeff Schramm, *Assistant VP*
Scott Schramm, *Assistant VP*
Yvonne Schramm, *Vice Pres*
EMP: 8 EST: 1960
SQ FT: 6,000
SALES (est): 964.9K **Privately Held**
SIC: 3479 2295 Coating of metals with plastic or resins; coated fabrics, not rubberized

**(G-201)**
**METAL IMPROVEMENT COMPANY LLC**
678 W Winthrop Ave (60101-4492)
PHONE..................630 543-4950
Fax: 630 543-8075
Leon Anderson, *Div Sub Head*
Bridget Ocallaghan, *Project Dir*
Lori Jones, *Branch Mgr*
EMP: 20
SALES (corp-wide): 2.1B **Publicly Held**
WEB: www.mic-houston.com
SIC: 3398 Shot peening (treating steel to reduce fatigue)
HQ: Metal Improvement Company, Llc
80 E State Rt 4 Ste 310
Paramus NJ 07652
201 843-7800

**(G-202)**
**METALS AND SERVICES INC**
Also Called: Ms
145 N Swift Rd (60101-1447)
PHONE..................630 627-2900
Fax: 630 627-0032
Carol Gross, *Corp Secy*
Joseph H Baessler, *Vice Pres*
John E Baessler, *Vice Pres*
Mark Baessler, *Vice Pres*
▲ EMP: 70
SQ FT: 106,000
SALES (est): 28.3MM **Privately Held**
WEB: www.metalserve.com
SIC: 3444 3449 5051 Sheet metalwork; bars, concrete reinforcing; fabricated steel; steel

**(G-203)**
**MEXACALI SILKSCREEN INC**
Also Called: M.S.I.
931 W National Ave (60101-3125)
PHONE..................630 628-9313
Fax: 630 628-9312
Tino Silva, *President*
EMP: 5
SQ FT: 10,000
SALES (est): 290K **Privately Held**
SIC: 2759 2396 Commercial printing; automotive & apparel trimmings

**(G-204)**
**MEXICALI HARD CHROME CORP**
502 W Winthrop Ave (60101-4434)
PHONE..................630 543-0646
Fax: 630 543-8271
Manuel Calvillo, *President*
Raul Calvillo, *Vice Pres*
Trinidad Calvillo, *Vice Pres*
Ed Hutchings, *Manager*
EMP: 27
SQ FT: 12,000
SALES: 1.4MM **Privately Held**
SIC: 3471 Chromium plating of metals or formed products

**(G-205)**
**MICA FURNITURE MFG INC**
Also Called: Kitchen Design Studio
1130 W Fullerton Ave (60101-4304)
PHONE..................708 430-1150
Fax: 708 430-2299
Chris Lupa, *President*
Carol Gabdawl, *Vice Pres*
EMP: 8
SQ FT: 6,000
SALES (est): 1.2MM **Privately Held**
WEB: www.mfmcabinets.com
SIC: 2434 2511 Wood kitchen cabinets; wood household furniture

**(G-206)**
**MICRO CIRCUIT INC**
1225 W National Ave (60101-3130)
PHONE..................630 628-5760
Fax: 630 628-5769
Govind Patel, *CEO*
Peter Shah, *President*
Nick Sanghani, *Vice Pres*
Mike Sanghani, *VP Sales*
EMP: 15
SQ FT: 9,000
SALES (est): 1.3MM **Privately Held**
WEB: www.microcircuit.com
SIC: 3672 Printed circuit boards

**(G-207)**
**MICRO MOLD CORPORATION**
777 W Annoreno Dr (60101-4383)
PHONE..................630 628-0777
Michael Stiglianese, *President*
EMP: 6 EST: 1963
SQ FT: 11,000
SALES (est): 884.5K **Privately Held**
WEB: www.micromoldcorp.com
SIC: 3544 Industrial molds

**(G-208)**
**MICROMATIC SPRING STAMPING INC (PA)**
45 N Church St (60101-3802)
PHONE..................630 607-0141
Fax: 847 671-3452
Theodore Prociuk, *President*
Linda Prociuk, *President*
Walter Prociuk, *President*
Dennis Prociuk, *Vice Pres*
John Giourdas, *Engineer*
EMP: 48 EST: 1936
SQ FT: 150,000
SALES (est): 9.7MM **Privately Held**
SIC: 3495 3469 Wire springs; stamping metal for the trade

**(G-209)**
**MID CITY TRUCK BDY & EQUIPMEMT**
1404 Fullerton 14th Ave Unit B 14th (60101)
PHONE..................630 628-9080
Fax: 630 628-9280
Gregg W Anderson, *President*
Rosa Aguirre, *Bookkeeper*
EMP: 10 EST: 1923
SQ FT: 19,000
SALES (est): 2.5MM **Privately Held**
SIC: 5012 7532 3715 3713 Truck bodies; body shop, trucks; truck trailers; truck & bus bodies

**(G-210)**
**MID-AMRICA PRTCTIVE CTINGS INC**
85 W Industrial Rd (60101-4505)
PHONE..................630 628-4501
Craig Martin, *President*
Leon S Martin Jr, *Vice Pres*
Christopher Baughman, *Sales Dir*
▲ EMP: 2
SQ FT: 10,000
SALES: 10MM **Privately Held**
WEB: www.midamcoat.com
SIC: 2851 Coating, air curing

**(G-211)**
**MIDWEST CORTLAND INC**
235 W Laura Dr (60101-5013)
PHONE..................847 671-0376
Fax: 847 671-0393
Roy J Urbanek, *President*
Joseph F Urbanek, *Corp Secy*
Thomas Novello Sr, *Vice Pres*
Frances Aiello, *Office Mgr*
EMP: 20 EST: 1926
SQ FT: 30,000
SALES (est): 4.1MM **Privately Held**
SIC: 2631 2675 Paperboard mills; die-cut paper & board

**(G-212)**
**MIDWEST INDEX INC**
2121 W Army Trail Rd # 105 (60101-5612)
PHONE..................847 995-8425
Fax: 630 628-7919
Michael J Gilbert, *President*
John C Eggert, *Vice Pres*
Leslie Chaeever, *Facilities Mgr*
EMP: 73
SQ FT: 29,000
SALES (est): 18MM **Privately Held**
SIC: 3555 2675 Printing trades machinery; die-cut paper & board

**(G-213)**
**MIDWEST LABELS & DECALS INC**
1001 W Republic Dr Ste 11 (60101-3106)
PHONE..................630 543-7556
Robert Schultz, *President*
EMP: 2
SALES (est): 215.5K **Privately Held**
SIC: 2759 Commercial printing

**(G-214)**
**MIDWEST MACHINE COMPANY LTD**
1001 W Republic Dr Ste 13 (60101-3106)
PHONE..................630 628-0485
Fax: 630 628-0492
Paravel Shunmugavelu, *President*
Rajkumar Nachimuthu, *MIS Mgr*
Vatsaladevi Shunmugavelu, *Admin Sec*
▲ EMP: 4
SQ FT: 2,875
SALES (est): 360K **Privately Held**
SIC: 3599 Machine shop, jobbing & repair

**(G-215)**
**MIKES MACHINERY REBUILDERS**
125 W Factory Rd (60101-5103)
PHONE..................630 543-6400
Fax: 630 543-6644
Mike Jajic, *President*
Zorica Jajic, *Vice Pres*
Nicolas Jakic, *Sales Staff*
Nick Jalic, *Sales Staff*
Nick Jajic, *Manager*
EMP: 6
SQ FT: 15,000
SALES: 750K **Privately Held**
SIC: 3542 Machine tools, metal forming type; rebuilt machine tools, metal forming types

**(G-216)**
**MILCO PRECISION MACHINING INC**
730 W Annoreno Dr (60101-4316)
PHONE..................630 628-5730
Fax: 630 628-5731
EMP: 13
SQ FT: 3,600
SALES (est): 2.3MM **Privately Held**
SIC: 3599 Industrial Machinery, Nec, Nsk

**(G-217)**
**MITSUBISHI HEAVY INDS AMER INC**
Also Called: Machine Tools Div.
1225 N Greenbriar Dr B (60101-6108)
PHONE..................630 693-4700
Fax: 630 693-4710
Jim Gifford, *Buyer*
Ray Strack, *Branch Mgr*
Koji Tanizaki, *Manager*
EMP: 11
SALES (corp-wide): 34.4B **Privately Held**
SIC: 5084 3599 Industrial machinery & equipment; machine shop, jobbing & repair
HQ: Mitsubishi Heavy Industries America, Inc.
20 Greenway Plz Ste 830
Houston TX 77046
346 308-8800

**(G-218)**
**MOFFAT WIRE & DISPLAY INC**
324 S La Londe Ave (60101-3309)
PHONE..................630 458-8560
Fax: 630 458-8556
Ramesh Gandhi, *President*
Kam Patel, *Vice Pres*
Gordhan Patel, *Admin Sec*
EMP: 13
SQ FT: 24,000
SALES (est): 2.7MM **Privately Held**
WEB: www.moffatwire.com
SIC: 3315 Wire & fabricated wire products

**(G-219)**
**MOON JUMP INC**
1750 W Armitage Ct (60101-4207)
PHONE..................630 983-0953
Edward Nunez, *Owner*
EMP: 5
SALES (est): 695.9K **Privately Held**
SIC: 3069 Life jackets, inflatable: rubberized fabric

**(G-220)**
**MOORE-ADDISON CO**
518 W Factory Rd (60101-4464)
PHONE..................630 543-6744
Jim Holland, *President*
Tom Champion, *Vice Pres*
Cindy Henrich, *Asst Office Mgr*
Dan Champion, *Information Mgr*
EMP: 29 EST: 1953
SQ FT: 14,570
SALES (est): 5.8MM **Privately Held**
WEB: www.mooreaddison.com
SIC: 3599 3089 3462 Machine shop, jobbing & repair; plastic containers, except foam; iron & steel forgings

# Addison - Dupage County (G-221)

## GEOGRAPHIC SECTION

**(G-221)**
**MORGAN OHARE INC**
701 W Factory Rd (60101-4339)
PHONE..................630 543-6780
Fax: 630 543-6792
Robert Giomi, *President*
Joan Sosinski, *Corp Secy*
Joe Talaga, *Controller*
**EMP:** 61
**SQ FT:** 70,000
**SALES (est):** 10MM **Privately Held**
**WEB:** www.morganohare.com
**SIC:** 3471 3398 Electroplating of metals or formed products; tempering of metal

**(G-222)**
**MOUNTAIN HORIZONS INC**
Also Called: Closet By Design
150 S Church St (60101-3775)
PHONE..................630 501-0190
William Taylor, *President*
**EMP:** 22
**SQ FT:** 11,700
**SALES (est):** 5.9MM **Privately Held**
**WEB:** www.closetsbydesign.net
**SIC:** 3089 Organizers for closets, drawers, etc.: plastic

**(G-223)**
**MP MOLD INC**
1480 W Bernard Dr (60101-4334)
PHONE..................630 613-8086
**EMP:** 2 **EST:** 2015
**SALES (est):** 227.9K **Privately Held**
**SIC:** 3544 Industrial molds

**(G-224)**
**N K C INC**
751 W Winthrop Ave (60101-4310)
PHONE..................630 628-9159
Diana Smith, *CEO*
**EMP:** 2 **EST:** 1999
**SQ FT:** 2,200
**SALES (est):** 209.7K **Privately Held**
**SIC:** 3599 Machine shop, jobbing & repair

**(G-225)**
**NAL WORLDWIDE HOLDINGS INC**
Also Called: Nal.syncreon Addison
1200 N Greenbriar Dr A (60101-1050)
PHONE..................630 261-3100
Chris Lennon, *Senior VP*
Christopher Lyons, *Manager*
Robert Frusolone, *Exec Dir*
Gwendolyn L Hassan, *General Counsel*
Kurt Davis, *Technician*
**EMP:** 346
**SALES (est):** 69.6MM
**SALES (corp-wide):** 91.4MM **Privately Held**
**SIC:** 3559 Automotive related machinery
**PA:** Syncreon Technology (Usa) Llc
2851 High Meadow Cir # 250
Auburn Hills MI 48326
630 261-3100

**(G-226)**
**NATURES APPEAL MFG CORP**
1788 W Whispering Ct (60101-1864)
PHONE..................630 880-6222
Ralph Jollette, *CEO*
**EMP:** 8
**SALES:** 194K **Privately Held**
**SIC:** 2869 7389 Industrial organic chemicals;

**(G-227)**
**NEUMAN BAKERY SPECIALTIES INC**
1405 W Jeffrey Dr (60101-4331)
P.O. Box 216 (60101-0216)
PHONE..................630 916-8909
Fax: 630 916-8919
George Neuman Jr, *President*
George A Neuman III, *Vice Pres*
Dan Neuman, *Manager*
**EMP:** 15 **EST:** 1928
**SQ FT:** 25,000
**SALES (est):** 2.2MM **Privately Held**
**WEB:** www.neumanbakery.biz
**SIC:** 2051 Bread, all types (white, wheat, rye, etc): fresh or frozen; cakes, pies & pastries

**(G-228)**
**NEWMAN-GREEN INC**
57 W Interstate Rd (60101-4509)
PHONE..................630 543-6500
Fax: 630 543-8523
Edward H Green, *President*
Deborah Green, *Vice Pres*
Pat Soristo, *Sales Staff*
Marc Gershon, *Technical Staff*
**EMP:** 80
**SQ FT:** 150,000
**SALES (est):** 12.8MM **Privately Held**
**WEB:** www.newman-green.com
**SIC:** 3499 3494 Aerosol valves, metal; valves & pipe fittings

**(G-229)**
**NITE LITE SIGNS & BALLOONS INC**
Also Called: Awesome Amusements Co.
506 S Westgate St (60101-4525)
P.O. Box 377, Saint Charles (60174-0377)
PHONE..................630 953-2866
Chris Manski, *President*
**EMP:** 4
**SALES (est):** 590.9K **Privately Held**
**SIC:** 7312 3993 Poster advertising, outdoor; signs & advertising specialties

**(G-230)**
**NSI SIGNS INC**
Also Called: National Sign
100-110 W Fay Ave (60101)
PHONE..................630 433-3525
Linda Menna, *President*
**EMP:** 14
**SALES (est):** 2.1MM **Privately Held**
**SIC:** 3993 Signs & advertising specialties

**(G-231)**
**NU MILL INC**
1001 W Republic Dr Ste 7 (60101-3106)
P.O. Box 5355, Glendale Heights (60139-5355)
PHONE..................630 458-8950
Kerry Garber, *President*
Sandy Garber, *Corp Secy*
**EMP:** 6
**SQ FT:** 3,000
**SALES (est):** 929.5K **Privately Held**
**SIC:** 3441 Fabricated structural metal

**(G-232)**
**OCKERLUND INDUSTRIES INC**
1555 W Wrightwood Ct (60101-3034)
P.O. Box 97, Forest Park (60130-0097)
PHONE..................630 620-1269
Fax: 708 771-0614
Guy Ockerlund, *President*
Stan Joray, *Vice Pres*
Ted Troyer, *Director*
Tracy Wyatt, *Admin Sec*
▲ **EMP:** 45
**SQ FT:** 55,000
**SALES (est):** 9.7MM **Privately Held**
**WEB:** www.ebigboxes.com
**SIC:** 2653 2441 Corrugated & solid fiber boxes; boxes, wood

**(G-233)**
**OCKERLUND WOOD PRODUCTS CO**
1555 W Wrightwood Ct (60101-3034)
PHONE..................630 620-1269
Diane Owens, *Manager*
**EMP:** 45
**SALES (est):** 4.9MM **Privately Held**
**SIC:** 2449 Boxes, wood: wirebound

**(G-234)**
**OMEGA SIGN & LIGHTING INC**
Also Called: Yesco Chicago
100 W Fay Ave (60101-5108)
PHONE..................630 237-4397
Carmela Menna, *President*
Michelle Forys, *Accounts Exec*
**EMP:** 20 **EST:** 2011
**SQ FT:** 10,000
**SALES (est):** 3.5MM **Privately Held**
**SIC:** 3993 Electric signs; neon signs; letters for signs, metal

**(G-235)**
**OMG INC**
300 S Mitchell Ct (60101-1473)
PHONE..................630 228-8377
Christine Ingersoll, *Manager*
**EMP:** 30
**SALES (corp-wide):** 828.3MM **Publicly Held**
**WEB:** www.olyfast.com
**SIC:** 3531 Roofing equipment
**HQ:** Omg, Inc.
153 Bowles Rd
Agawam MA 01001
413 789-0252

**(G-236)**
**PACKERS SUPPLIES & EQP LLC**
341 W Factory Rd (60101-5003)
PHONE..................630 543-5810
Fax: 630 543-8350
Rob Williams, *Partner*
Charles Larson, *Partner*
**EMP:** 4
**SQ FT:** 1,900
**SALES (est):** 457.8K **Privately Held**
**SIC:** 3556 5084 3423 Food products machinery; cutting, chopping, grinding, mixing & similar machinery; food industry machinery; hand & edge tools

**(G-237)**
**PARK PRODUCTS INC**
409 W Kay Ave (60101-4904)
PHONE..................630 543-2474
Fax: 630 543-2787
William Keyser, *President*
Robert Sieloff, *Admin Sec*
**EMP:** 3
**SQ FT:** 3,800
**SALES (est):** 349.5K **Privately Held**
**SIC:** 3545 3543 3544 Tools & accessories for machine tools; foundry patternmaking: special dies, tools, jigs & fixtures

**(G-238)**
**PENTEGRA SYSTEMS LLC**
780 W Belden Ave Ste A (60101-4939)
PHONE..................630 941-6000
Fax: 630 941-6060
Edward G Karl, *Mng Member*
Gregory P Augspurger, *Edward Karl*,
**EMP:** 35 **EST:** 2000
**SQ FT:** 12,500
**SALES (est):** 12.3MM **Privately Held**
**WEB:** www.pentegrasystems.com
**SIC:** 1731 3661 Sound equipment specialization; telephones & telephone apparatus

**(G-239)**
**PERFECT PASTA INC**
31 S Fairbank St Ste B (60101-3150)
PHONE..................630 543-8300
Fax: 630 543-6933
Luigi Bucaro, *President*
Vito Salamone, *Admin Sec*
▲ **EMP:** 6
**SALES (est):** 1.6MM **Privately Held**
**SIC:** 2099 Pasta, uncooked: packaged with other ingredients

**(G-240)**
**PHARMACEUTICAL LABS AND CONS I**
1010 W Fullerton Ave (60101-4333)
PHONE..................630 359-3831
Stephen R James, *Principal*
**EMP:** 3
**SALES (est):** 165.3K **Privately Held**
**SIC:** 8734 2834 Testing laboratories; pharmaceutical preparations

**(G-241)**
**PIO WOODWORKING INC**
1130 W Fullerton Ave (60101-4304)
PHONE..................630 628-6900
Andrea Faraone, *CEO*
Derek Lofgren, *Principal*
**EMP:** 2
**SALES (est):** 2.6MM **Privately Held**
**SIC:** 2431 2521 Millwork; wood office furniture

**(G-242)**
**PIONEER SERVICE INC**
542 W Factory Rd (60101-4437)
PHONE..................630 628-0249
Fax: 630 628-9343
Aneesa Shehadeh, *President*
Rose Devos, *Business Mgr*
Omar Muthana, *Vice Pres*
James Sass, *Prdtn Mgr*
Eric Smith, *Sales Dir*
**EMP:** 35
**SQ FT:** 25,000
**SALES (est):** 3.5MM **Privately Held**
**WEB:** www.pioneerserviceinc.com
**SIC:** 7389 3451 3541 Grinding, precision: commercial or industrial; screw machine products; machine tools, metal cutting type

**(G-243)**
**PLASTISOL PRODUCTS INC**
1002 W Republic Dr (60101-3133)
PHONE..................630 543-1770
Fax: 630 543-1774
Donald D Malcolm Jr, *President*
Darrah Malcolm, *Vice Pres*
Claudia Dollmeyer, *Manager*
**EMP:** 40
**SQ FT:** 42,000
**SALES (est):** 3.8MM **Privately Held**
**WEB:** www.plastisolproducts.com
**SIC:** 3479 Coating of metals & formed products

**(G-244)**
**PLATT INDUSTRIAL CONTROL INC**
3n301 Ellsworth Ave (60101-4164)
PHONE..................630 833-4388
Eileen Plahetka, *President*
**EMP:** 4
**SQ FT:** 1,500
**SALES (est):** 701.9K **Privately Held**
**SIC:** 3613 Mfg Switchgear/Switchboards

**(G-245)**
**POKORNEY MANUFACTURING CO**
45 N Church St (60101-3802)
PHONE..................630 458-0406
Fax: 630 458-0408
Carl W Erickson Jr, *President*
Eleanor Erickson, *Corp Secy*
Charles A Erickson, *Vice Pres*
Joan Deddo, *Bookkeeper*
**EMP:** 8
**SQ FT:** 15,000
**SALES (est):** 850K **Privately Held**
**SIC:** 3494 3561 Valves & pipe fittings; cylinders, pump

**(G-246)**
**POLYURETHANE PRODUCTS CORP**
31 W Industrial Rd (60101-4505)
PHONE..................630 543-6700
Fax: 630 543-0451
Govind Lakshman, *President*
Malini Lakshman, *Vice Pres*
Ajay Lakshman, *Sales Engr*
Bill Amant, *Sales Staff*
George Newman, *Technology*
▲ **EMP:** 25 **EST:** 1978
**SQ FT:** 26,000
**SALES (est):** 6.1MM **Privately Held**
**WEB:** www.polyprod.com
**SIC:** 2851 Polyurethane coatings

**(G-247)**
**PORTABLE CMMNCTONS SPCLSTS**
901 W Lake St (60101-2078)
PHONE..................630 458-1800
Fax: 630 458-9537
Nancy Phillips, *President*
Jim Baker, *Vice Pres*
Kenneth Phillips, *Vice Pres*
Russ Velky, *Manager*
**EMP:** 6
**SQ FT:** 6,000

## GEOGRAPHIC SECTION

## Addison - Dupage County (G-272)

**SALES (est):** 690K  **Privately Held**
**WEB:** www.portablecomm.com
**SIC:** 5999 7622 5064 4812 Communication equipment; intercommunication equipment repair; electrical appliances, television & radio; radio telephone communication; receiver-transmitter units (transceiver)

### (G-248)
### PORTILLOS FOOD SERVICE INC (PA)
380 S Rohlwing Rd (60101-3030)
**PHONE** ............................630 620-0460
**Fax:** 630 620-0512
Richard J Portillo, *President*
Karen Peterson, *Controller*
Dan Knipper, *Supervisor*
Sharon Portillo, *Admin Sec*
**EMP:** 30
**SQ FT:** 5,000
**SALES (est):** 26.1MM  **Privately Held**
**SIC:** 5147 2013 Meats, fresh; sausages & other prepared meats

### (G-249)
### POWER PORT PRODUCTS INC
301 W Interstate Rd (60101-4598)
**PHONE** ............................630 628-9102
**Fax:** 630 543-7614
Douglas Murphy, *President*
Christopher Murphy, *Vice Pres*
Sharon Gallo, *Treasurer*
Valeri Picchi, *Admin Sec*
▲ **EMP:** 20 **EST:** 1978
**SQ FT:** 60,000
**SALES:** 5MM  **Privately Held**
**SIC:** 3699 3052 Extension cords; air line or air brake hose, rubber or rubberized fabric

### (G-250)
### POWER-VOLT INC
300 W Factory Rd (60101-5004)
P.O. Box 383 (60101-0383)
**PHONE** ............................630 628-9999
**Fax:** 630 628-9922
Brij Lal Sharma, *President*
Vijay Sharma, *CPA*
Sam Kumar, *Marketing Mgr*
Ashish Tejpal, *Marketing Staff*
Vijay Kumari Sharma, *Admin Sec*
▲ **EMP:** 30
**SQ FT:** 26,000
**SALES (est):** 7.4MM  **Privately Held**
**WEB:** www.powervolt.com
**SIC:** 3677 Transformers power supply, electronic type

### (G-251)
### PRECISION LASER MARKING INC
900 S Kay Ave (60101-4909)
**PHONE** ............................630 628-8575
Daniel Mahazchek, *President*
Pamela Mahachek, *Admin Sec*
**EMP:** 8
**SQ FT:** 5,000
**SALES (est):** 570K  **Privately Held**
**WEB:** www.precisionlasermarking.com
**SIC:** 3599 Machine & other job shop work

### (G-252)
### PRECISION METAL PRODUCTS INC
Also Called: P M P
1209 W Capitol Dr (60101-3116)
**PHONE** ............................630 458-0100
**Fax:** 630 458-9400
Mohammed Iqbal, *President*
Richard Smith, *Vice Pres*
Rich Kloss, *QC Dir*
**EMP:** 15
**SALES (est):** 3.2MM  **Privately Held**
**SIC:** 3444 Sheet metalwork

### (G-253)
### PRECISION SERVICE MTR INC
121 W Fullerton Ave (60101-3713)
**PHONE** ............................630 628-9900
**Fax:** 630 372-9845
Kevin W Zierke, *President*
Lynn E Zierke, *Vice Pres*
Dee Yurczak, *Accounting Mgr*
Russ Bauer, *Sales Executive*
**EMP:** 15
**SQ FT:** 20,000
**SALES (est):** 3.5MM  **Privately Held**
**SIC:** 3542 Machine tools, metal forming type

### (G-254)
### PREMIER MANUFACTURING CORP
35 W Laura Dr (60101-5111)
**PHONE** ............................847 640-6644
Susan Fischer, *President*
**EMP:** 15
**SQ FT:** 10,000
**SALES (est):** 2.3MM  **Privately Held**
**SIC:** 3444 Sheet metalwork

### (G-255)
### PRESS ON INC
53 S Evergreen Ave (60101-3447)
**PHONE** ............................630 628-1630
Charles Cernock, *President*
**EMP:** 1
**SALES (est):** 250K  **Privately Held**
**SIC:** 2741 Miscellaneous publishing

### (G-256)
### PRINTING CIRCUIT BOARDS
447 S Vista Ave (60101-4420)
**PHONE** ............................630 543-3453
**Fax:** 630 543-4026
Navin Patel, *President*
Rajendra Patel, *Vice Pres*
Joan Vittorio, *Manager*
Arun M Patel, *Admin Sec*
**EMP:** 15 **EST:** 1964
**SQ FT:** 10,000
**SALES (est):** 3MM  **Privately Held**
**SIC:** 3672 Printed circuit boards

### (G-257)
### PRISM COMMERCIAL PRINTING CTRS
49 E Fullerton Ave (60101-4601)
**PHONE** ............................630 834-4443
John Mantia, *Branch Mgr*
**EMP:** 3
**SALES (corp-wide):** 2.1MM  **Privately Held**
**SIC:** 2752 Commercial printing, lithographic
**PA:** Prism Corp Commercial Printing Centers
6957 W Archer Ave
Chicago IL 60638
630 834-4443

### (G-258)
### PRO-QUA INC
305 W Laura Dr (60101-5015)
**PHONE** ............................630 543-5644
Walter Naziemiec, *President*
**EMP:** 7
**SQ FT:** 12,000
**SALES (est):** 1MM  **Privately Held**
**SIC:** 3599 Machine & other job shop work

### (G-259)
### PRODUCTIVE PORTABLE DISP INC
Also Called: Productive Displays
1460 W Bernard Dr Ste A (60101-4330)
**PHONE** ............................630 458-9100
**Fax:** 630 458-1985
Bruce Ulrich, *CEO*
Jay Volke, *Mfg Staff*
Kate Ulrich, *Admin Sec*
**EMP:** 7
**SQ FT:** 3,200
**SALES (est):** 571.2K  **Privately Held**
**WEB:** www.productivedisplays.com
**SIC:** 2759 Business forms: printing

### (G-260)
### PROTO PRODUCTIONS INC
840 S Fiene Dr (60101-5119)
**PHONE** ............................630 628-6626
**Fax:** 630 628-2232
Kenneth D Hopkins, *President*
Steven Meyer, *Marketing Staff*
Ron Craig, *Sr Project Mgr*
Deborah Ohr, *Manager*
**EMP:** 20
**SQ FT:** 13,000
**SALES:** 2MM  **Privately Held**
**WEB:** www.protoproductions.com
**SIC:** 2541 7389 2542 Display fixtures, wood; exhibit construction by industrial contractors; showcases (not refrigerated): except wood; locker boxes, postal service: except wood

### (G-261)
### QUAD-METAL INC
1345 W Fullerton Ave (60101-4319)
**PHONE** ............................630 953-0907
**Fax:** 630 953-1038
Stanley Sowa Jr, *President*
Matthew Fiore, *Corp Secy*
**EMP:** 10
**SQ FT:** 8,000
**SALES (est):** 1.5MM  **Privately Held**
**SIC:** 3444 Sheet metalwork

### (G-262)
### QUALITEK INTERNATIONAL INC
315 S Fairbank St (60101-3171)
**PHONE** ............................630 628-8083
Phodi Han, *President*
Paul Chadwick, *General Mgr*
Emily Han, *Vice Pres*
▲ **EMP:** 45 **EST:** 1980
**SQ FT:** 45,000
**SALES (est):** 9.7MM  **Privately Held**
**WEB:** www.qualitek.com
**SIC:** 2899 Fluxes: brazing, soldering, galvanizing & welding

### (G-263)
### QUALITY BAGS  INC
575 S Vista Ave (60101-4422)
**PHONE** ............................630 543-9800
**Fax:** 630 543-9812
Leopold Rivera, *CEO*
Eugene Rivera, *President*
Ron Rivera, *Vice Pres*
Glenn Rivera, *Director*
Gloria Rivera, *Admin Sec*
**EMP:** 11
**SQ FT:** 17,000
**SALES (est):** 1.5MM  **Privately Held**
**WEB:** www.qualitybags.com
**SIC:** 2671 2759 2673 Plastic film, coated or laminated for packaging; flexographic printing; plastic & pliofilm bags; cellophane bags, unprinted: made from purchased materials

### (G-264)
### QUALITY FABRICATORS  INC (PA)
1035 W Fullerton Ave (60101-3192)
**PHONE** ............................630 543-0540
**Fax:** 630 543-1064
Tom A Lovelace, *President*
James R Lovelace, *Principal*
Annette M Loveplace, *Principal*
Brian Loveplace, *Vice Pres*
Mark Loveplace, *Vice Pres*
**EMP:** 100
**SQ FT:** 110,000
**SALES (est):** 22.3MM  **Privately Held**
**WEB:** www.qfi-usa.com
**SIC:** 3444 3599 Sheet metalwork; machine shop, jobbing & repair

### (G-265)
### QUIK IMPRESSIONS GROUP INC
1385 W Jeffrey Dr (60101-4331)
**PHONE** ............................630 495-7845
**Fax:** 630 495-2534
Richard Smolke, *CEO*
Robert Spohnolz, *Vice Pres*
Daniel Caithamer, *CFO*
Frank Frasor, *Controller*
John McGray, *Sales Mgr*
**EMP:** 25 **EST:** 1995
**SALES (est):** 5.3MM  **Privately Held**
**WEB:** www.quikimpressionsgroup.com
**SIC:** 2752 Commercial printing, lithographic

### (G-266)
### R & R ENGINES AND PARTS INC
Also Called: R&R Engineering
1244 W Capitol Dr Ste 4 (60101-5373)
**PHONE** ............................630 628-1545
**Fax:** 630 628-9333
George Bronge, *Partner*
Ray Hartman, *Vice Pres*
**EMP:** 3
**SQ FT:** 6,000
**SALES (est):** 444.9K  **Privately Held**
**SIC:** 3714 Rebuilding engines & transmissions, factory basis

### (G-267)
### R-M INDUSTRIES INC
38 W Interstate Rd (60101-4510)
**PHONE** ............................630 543-3071
**Fax:** 630 543-7318
Richard A Trepanier, *President*
Marie Trepanier, *Admin Sec*
**EMP:** 10 **EST:** 1967
**SQ FT:** 3,000
**SALES (est):** 1.6MM  **Privately Held**
**SIC:** 3599 7692 3443 3398 Machine shop, jobbing & repair; welding repair; fabricated plate work (boiler shop); metal heat treating

### (G-268)
### RAIMONDE DRILLING CORP
770 W Factory Rd Ste A (60101-4300)
**PHONE** ............................630 458-0590
**Fax:** 630 583-9491
Lucille Raimonde, *President*
Anne T Leslie, *President*
Susan Oeslie, *Office Mgr*
Fran Catuto, *Admin Sec*
**EMP:** 12
**SALES (est):** 2.6MM  **Privately Held**
**WEB:** www.raimonde-drilling.com
**SIC:** 1481 1381 0711 Nonmetallic mineral services; test boring for nonmetallic minerals; mine & quarry services, nonmetallic minerals; drilling water intake wells; soil testing services

### (G-269)
### RALPH CODY GRAVROK
Also Called: Witt Disintegrating Service
729 W Fullerton Ave 6f (60101-3260)
**PHONE** ............................630 628-9570
**Fax:** 630 628-0388
Ralph Gravrok, *Owner*
**EMP:** 4
**SQ FT:** 2,000
**SALES:** 200K  **Privately Held**
**SIC:** 7699 3546 3544 Metal reshaping & replating services; power-driven handtools; special dies, tools, jigs & fixtures

### (G-270)
### RAZNY JEWELERS  LTD (PA)
1501 W Lake St Ste 1 (60101-6704)
**PHONE** ............................630 932-4900
**Fax:** 630 932-1300
Stanley Razny Jr, *President*
Ingrid Razny, *Treasurer*
Kim Rooney, *Adv Dir*
Fabiola Troncoso, *Manager*
◆ **EMP:** 35 **EST:** 1964
**SQ FT:** 8,500
**SALES (est):** 6.5MM  **Privately Held**
**WEB:** www.razny.com
**SIC:** 5944 3911 Jewelry, precious stones & precious metals; watches; rings, finger: precious metal; bracelets, precious metal; earrings, precious metal

### (G-271)
### RCL ELECTRONICS
826 S Iowa Ave (60101-4827)
**PHONE** ............................630 834-0156
Conrado Cabildo, *Owner*
**EMP:** 3
**SALES (est):** 140K  **Privately Held**
**SIC:** 3671 Electron tubes

### (G-272)
### REAL NEON INC
113 W Official Rd (60101-4520)
**PHONE** ............................630 543-0995
**Fax:** 630 543-9776
Jacek Menel, *President*
Malgorzata Kocylowska, *Admin Sec*
**EMP:** 10
**SQ FT:** 3,000
**SALES (est):** 1.1MM  **Privately Held**
**SIC:** 3993 Neon signs

## Addison - Dupage County (G-273) — GEOGRAPHIC SECTION

**(G-273)**
**REGAL MANUFACTURING CO**
Also Called: Regal Seating Company
844 S Kay Ave (60101-4907)
PHONE.................................630 628-6867
Fax: 630 921-3076
Gerald Saviano, *President*
Vince Saviano, *Vice Pres*
Dale Lund, *Opers-Prdtn-Mfg*
▲ EMP: 35
SQ FT: 35,000
SALES (est): 5.4MM **Privately Held**
WEB: www.regalseating.com
SIC: 2599 Bar furniture

**(G-274)**
**RELIABLE CONTAINER INC**
210 S Addison Rd (60101-3880)
PHONE.................................630 543-6131
Fax: 630 543-9115
James E Murphy, *President*
Robert E Murphy, *Vice Pres*
Darrel Davis, *Plant Mgr*
David Shabez, *Engineer*
Bill Vihnanek, *Sales Associate*
▲ EMP: 41
SQ FT: 65,000
SALES (est): 10.7MM **Privately Held**
SIC: 2653 Boxes, corrugated: made from purchased materials

**(G-275)**
**RELIANCE GEAR CORPORATION**
205 W Factory Rd (60101-5001)
PHONE.................................630 543-6640
Fax: 630 543-0520
Matt Mondek, *President*
Paul Campion, *General Mgr*
Harshad Gujarathi, *Plant Mgr*
Joe Heinen, *QA Dir*
Robert Shew, *Chief Engr*
▲ EMP: 56 EST: 1965
SQ FT: 22,000
SALES (est): 17.5MM
SALES (corp-wide): 27.1MM **Privately Held**
WEB: www.reliancegear.com
SIC: 3566 3568 Gears, power transmission, except automotive; power transmission equipment
PA: Ashot Ashkelon Industries Ltd.
2 Ezra Yessodi
Ashkelon 78637
867 215-87

**(G-276)**
**RESIN EXCHANGE INC**
851 S Westgate St (60101-5025)
PHONE.................................630 628-7266
Dan Donnelly, *President*
EMP: 36
SALES (est): 7.8MM **Privately Held**
SIC: 5162 2821 Resins; plastics materials & resins

**(G-277)**
**RESPA PHARMACEUTICALS INC**
625 W Factory Rd (60101-4412)
P.O. Box 88222, Carol Stream (60188-0222)
PHONE.................................630 543-3333
Paul Hennes, *CEO*
Dorothy Klays, *Principal*
Sarah Ahmed, *Project Mgr*
Tigas Gooddel, *Sales Mgr*
▲ EMP: 42
SQ FT: 300,000
SALES (est): 8.5MM **Privately Held**
WEB: www.respainc.com
SIC: 2834 Drugs acting on the respiratory system

**(G-278)**
**RF PLASTICS CO**
406 W Belden Ave (60101-4903)
PHONE.................................630 628-6033
EMP: 5
SQ FT: 6,000
SALES (est): 420K **Privately Held**
SIC: 3089 Injection Molder Of Plastics

**(G-279)**
**RICE PRECISION MACHINING**
475 W Interstate Rd (60101-4517)
PHONE.................................630 543-7220
Fax: 630 543-7279
Gladys Rice, *Owner*
EMP: 10
SQ FT: 4,800
SALES (est): 1.6MM **Privately Held**
SIC: 3599 Machine shop, jobbing & repair

**(G-280)**
**ROMTECH MACHINING INC**
755 W Factory Rd (60101-4308)
P.O. Box 233 (60101-0233)
PHONE.................................630 543-7039
Roman Szymczak, *President*
Christopher Kostecki, *Sales Mgr*
Chris Kostecki, *Manager*
EMP: 5
SQ FT: 5,000
SALES: 1MM **Privately Held**
WEB: www.romtechservice.com
SIC: 3599 Machine & other job shop work

**(G-281)**
**ROYAL BOX GROUP LLC**
Royal Group Addison, The
654 W Factory Rd (60101-4413)
PHONE.................................630 543-4464
Robert Mc Ilvane, *CEO*
Jordan Nerenberg, *Ch of Bd*
Ken Johnson, *General Mgr*
Scott Clary, *Treasurer*
EMP: 50
SALES (corp-wide): 248.1MM **Privately Held**
WEB: www.royalbox.com
SIC: 2653 Boxes, corrugated: made from purchased materials
HQ: Royal Box Group, Llc
1301 S 47th Ave
Cicero IL 60804
708 656-2020

**(G-282)**
**SCHREDER LIGHTING LLC**
2105 W Corporate Dr (60101-1466)
PHONE.................................847 621-5130
Anna Scolaro, *Finance Dir*
John W Camp Jr,
Keutgen Nicolas,
Gripp Wilson,
▲ EMP: 20
SQ FT: 7,600
SALES (est): 6.8MM
SALES (corp-wide): 23.9MM **Privately Held**
SIC: 3648 Outdoor lighting equipment
PA: Schreder Sa
Rue De Lusambo 67
Bruxelles 1190
233 201-06

**(G-283)**
**SCHULTZ BROTHERS INC**
1001 W Republic Dr Ste 11 (60101-3106)
PHONE.................................630 458-1437
Edward Schultz, *President*
EMP: 4
SQ FT: 3,000
SALES (est): 360K **Privately Held**
SIC: 2759 Labels & seals: printing

**(G-284)**
**SCHWEPPE INC**
800 S Rohlwing Rd Ste D (60101-4219)
PHONE.................................630 627-3550
Tom Nolan, *Human Resources*
Emil Goellner, *Director*
EMP: 6
SALES (est): 1MM **Privately Held**
SIC: 3089 Kitchenware, plastic

**(G-285)**
**SECURITY MOLDING INC**
255 W Factory Rd (60101-5001)
PHONE.................................630 543-8607
Fax: 630 543-2483
Lynn Ricke, *President*
Margaret Ricke, *Corp Secy*
Gayanna Weddle, *Manager*
EMP: 17
SQ FT: 8,000
SALES (est): 2.7MM **Privately Held**
WEB: www.securitymolding.com
SIC: 3089 Injection molding of plastics

**(G-286)**
**SELECTIVE PLATING INC**
240 S Lombard Rd (60101-3022)
PHONE.................................630 543-1380
Fax: 630 543-1392
Brian Snodgrass, *President*
Tanja Snodgrass, *Treasurer*
Michael Berrier, *Manager*
Judy Dafnis, *Administration*
EMP: 20
SQ FT: 10,800
SALES (est): 2.7MM **Privately Held**
WEB: www.selectiveplatinginc.com
SIC: 3471 Electroplating & plating

**(G-287)**
**SERITEX INC**
1052 W Republic Dr (60101-3133)
PHONE.................................201 755-3002
Jose Rivera, *President*
EMP: 1 EST: 1996
SALES (est): 400K **Privately Held**
SIC: 2759 Screen printing

**(G-288)**
**SERVICE METAL ENTERPRISES**
915 W National Ave (60101-3125)
PHONE.................................630 628-1444
Fax: 630 628-1472
Wyne Kruty, *President*
Barb Ott, *Office Mgr*
EMP: 5
SQ FT: 3,800
SALES (est): 165K **Privately Held**
SIC: 3444 Casings, sheet metal

**(G-289)**
**SIERRA MANUFACTURING CORP**
47 W Commercial Ave (60101-4501)
PHONE.................................630 458-8830
Fax: 630 458-8834
Darius Wozinak, *President*
Mary Kalamaris, *Admin Sec*
EMP: 6
SALES (est): 610K **Privately Held**
SIC: 3544 3546 Die sets for metal stamping (presses); cartridge-activated hand power tools

**(G-290)**
**SIGMA COATINGS INC**
150 S Church St Ste D (60101-3775)
PHONE.................................630 628-5305
Edward Eshoo, *President*
Helena Kasurinen, *Vice Pres*
Thomas Klewer, *Admin Sec*
EMP: 5
SQ FT: 17,000
SALES (est): 524.3K **Privately Held**
SIC: 2891 Adhesives & sealants

**(G-291)**
**SIKORA AUTOMATION INCORPORATED**
845 S Westgate St (60101-5025)
PHONE.................................630 833-0298
Fax: 630 833-0568
Alex Fuentes, *President*
Aiex Fuemes, *General Mgr*
EMP: 6 EST: 1973
SQ FT: 5,000
SALES (est): 1MM **Privately Held**
WEB: www.sikoraautomation.com
SIC: 3599 3829 Machine shop, jobbing & repair; measuring & controlling devices

**(G-292)**
**SIMPLEXGRINNELL LP**
91 N Mitchell Ct (60101-5608)
PHONE.................................630 268-1863
Beth Jarvis, *General Mgr*
Richard Schretter, *Project Mgr*
David Torres, *Opers Mgr*
Michael Gilson, *Engineer*
Randy Klein, *Design Engr*
EMP: 280
SALES (corp-wide): 36.8B **Privately Held**
WEB: www.simplexgrinnell.com
SIC: 3669 Emergency alarms
HQ: Simplexgrinnell Lp
4700 Exchange Ct
Boca Raton FL 33431
561 988-7200

**(G-293)**
**SIMPSON STRONG-TIE COMPANY INC**
Also Called: Simpson Anchor Systems
136 W Official Rd (60101-4521)
PHONE.................................630 613-5100
Phillip T Kingsfather, *CEO*
Roger Dankel, *President*
Bill Stuckey, *Plant Supt*
Susan Hagel, *Treasurer*
Gerald Hagel, *Manager*
▲ EMP: 25
SALES (est): 6.4MM
SALES (corp-wide): 860.6MM **Publicly Held**
WEB: www.simpsonanchors.com
SIC: 3462 5072 3452 2891 Anchors, forged; builders' hardware; bolts, nuts, rivets & washers; adhesives & sealants
HQ: Simpson Strong-Tie Company Inc.
5956 W Las Positas Blvd
Pleasanton CA 94588
925 560-9000

**(G-294)**
**SLIDECRAFT INC**
532 W Winthrop Ave (60101-4441)
P.O. Box 623, Elk Grove Village (60009-0623)
PHONE.................................630 628-1218
Fax: 630 628-1219
Robert Vieau, *President*
EMP: 2
SQ FT: 10,000
SALES (est): 288.8K **Privately Held**
SIC: 3542 Presses: forming, stamping, punching, sizing (machine tools)

**(G-295)**
**SONOCO PLASTICS INC**
1035 W Republic Dr (60101-3132)
PHONE.................................630 628-5859
Jeffrey Di Pasquale, *Branch Mgr*
EMP: 11
SALES (corp-wide): 4.7B **Publicly Held**
SIC: 3082 Unsupported plastics profile shapes
HQ: Sonoco Plastics, Inc.
1 N 2nd St
Hartsville SC 29550
843 383-7000

**(G-296)**
**SOUTHFIELD CORPORATION**
799 S Route 53 (60101-4215)
P.O. Box 1123 (60101-8123)
PHONE.................................708 563-4056
Ed Zehme, *Branch Mgr*
EMP: 57
SALES (corp-wide): 273.9MM **Privately Held**
WEB: www.prairiegroup.com
SIC: 3273 Ready-mixed concrete
PA: Southfield Corporation
8995 W 95th St
Palos Hills IL 60465
708 344-1000

**(G-297)**
**SPECIALTY NUT & BKY SUP CO INC**
1417 W Jeffrey Dr (60101-4331)
PHONE.................................630 268-8500
Pasquale Schittino, *President*
Mary Ann Schittino, *Admin Sec*
EMP: 6
SQ FT: 10,000
SALES (est): 680K **Privately Held**
WEB: www.specialtynut.com
SIC: 2068 5145 Salted & roasted nuts & seeds; nuts, salted or roasted

**(G-298)**
**SPRING R-R CORPORATION**
100 W Laura Dr (60101-5114)
PHONE.................................630 543-7445
Rick Richter, *President*
Randy Richter, *Vice Pres*
Ruth Richter, *Treasurer*
Windy Richter, *Manager*
EMP: 32

SQ FT: 24,000
SALES (est): 6.7MM  Privately Held
WEB: www.rrspring.com
SIC: 3493 Steel springs, except wire; torsion bar springs

**(G-299)**
**STYLE RITE RESTAURANT EQP CO**
578 S Vista Ave  (60101-4423)
PHONE................630 628-0940
Fax: 630 628-0977
Marilyn Loster, *President*
John Loster, *Admin Sec*
EMP: 6
SQ FT: 17,000
SALES (est): 961.4K  Privately Held
SIC: 3469  5046 Kitchen fixtures & equipment: metal, except cast aluminum; commercial cooking & food service equipment

**(G-300)**
**SUNSOURCE HOLDINGS INC**
2301 W Windsor Ct  (60101-1460)
PHONE................630 317-2700
Justin Jacobi, *CEO*
Sarah Clarin, *Human Resources*
Buck Wylie, *Sales Mgr*
Tim Brammeier, *Accounts Mgr*
Justin Schwarm, *Accounts Mgr*
EMP: 3
SALES (est): 558.7K  Privately Held
SIC: 3594 Motors: hydraulic, fluid power or air
PA: Lj2 & Co., Llc
    8 Sound Shore Dr Ste 303
    Greenwich CT 06830

**(G-301)**
**SUPERIOR SURGICAL INSTRUMEN TS**
602 W Lake Park Dr  (60101-3221)
PHONE................630 628-8437
Werner Hausner, *Principal*
EMP: 3
SALES (est): 205.9K  Privately Held
SIC: 3841 Surgical & medical instruments

**(G-302)**
**SWD INC**
910 S Stiles Dr  (60101-4913)
PHONE................630 543-3003
Fax: 630 543-3028
Richard A Delawder, *President*
Sharon Delawder, *Corp Secy*
Ashok Patel, *QC Dir*
April Elders, *Human Res Mgr*
Matthew Delawder, *Sales Mgr*
▲ EMP: 100
SQ FT: 55,000
SALES (est): 19.3MM  Privately Held
WEB: www.swdinc.com
SIC: 3471  3965 Cleaning, polishing & finishing; fasteners, buttons, needles & pins

**(G-303)**
**SYN-TECH LTD**
1550 W Fullerton Ave  (60101-3028)
PHONE................630 628-3044
Fax: 630 620-4832
Pam Shearer, *President*
Reginald Shearer, *President*
Jackie Shearer, *General Mgr*
Jeffrey Lay, *Sales Engr*
Sindy Shearer, *Office Mgr*
▲ EMP: 25
SQ FT: 25,000
SALES (est): 6.4MM  Privately Held
WEB: www.syn-techlube.com
SIC: 2992 Oils & greases, blending & compounding

**(G-304)**
**T & L SHEET METAL INC**
555 S Vista Ave  (60101-4422)
PHONE................630 628-7960
Fax: 630 628-7963
Linh Van Le, *President*
Hung Van Le, *Vice Pres*
Tien Van Tran, *Treasurer*
EMP: 10 EST: 1996
SQ FT: 30,000
SALES (est): 1.4MM  Privately Held
SIC: 3444 Sheet metalwork

**(G-305)**
**T/J FABRICATORS INC**
2150 W Executive Dr  (60101-1487)
PHONE................630 543-2293
Fax: 630 543-0538
Tom Wisniewski, *President*
Robert Wisniewski, *President*
Dave Francis, *Site Mgr*
Helen Ios, *Buyer*
Frank J Callero, *Accountant*
EMP: 65
SQ FT: 104,000
SALES (est): 12.2MM  Privately Held
WEB: www.tjfab.com
SIC: 3444  3599 Sheet metalwork; machine shop, jobbing & repair

**(G-306)**
**TACTICAL LIGHTING SYSTEMS INC**
901 S Rohlwing Rd Ste J  (60101-4229)
PHONE................800 705-0518
James P McGee, *President*
Nicholas Dedio, *General Mgr*
Rick Mills, *Vice Pres*
John Polk, *CFO*
EMP: 17
SQ FT: 20,000
SALES (est): 5MM  Privately Held
WEB: www.tacticallighting.com
SIC: 3648 Airport lighting fixtures: runway approach, taxi or ramp

**(G-307)**
**TECHNICAL TOOL ENTERPRISE**
1550 W Fullerton Ave D  (60101-3028)
PHONE................630 893-3390
EMP: 3 EST: 2007
SALES (est): 240K  Privately Held
SIC: 3546  3545  3544 Mfg Power-Driven Handtools Mfg Machine Tool Accessories Mfg Dies/Tools/Jigs/Fixtures

**(G-308)**
**TECHNY PRECISION MFG INC**
818 S Westwood Ave Ste C  (60101-4945)
PHONE................630 543-7065
Ismet Uzun, *President*
Bari Uzun, *Vice Pres*
Keven Uzun, *Opers Staff*
Lucy Uzun, *Executive Asst*
EMP: 10
SQ FT: 18,000
SALES: 750K  Privately Held
SIC: 3545 Cutting tools for machine tools

**(G-309)**
**TED HOLUM & ASSOCIATES INC**
1216 W Capitol Dr Ste C  (60101-5303)
PHONE................630 543-9355
Fax: 630 543-9387
Ted Holum, *President*
Tracy Dye, *Vice Pres*
EMP: 3
SALES: 300K  Privately Held
SIC: 2754 Fashion plates: gravure printing

**(G-310)**
**TEREX UTILITIES INC**
Also Called: Terex Services
1461 W Bernard Dr  (60101-4342)
PHONE................847 515-7030
Rick Smith, *Vice Pres*
EMP: 3
SALES (corp-wide): 4.4B  Publicly Held
WEB: www.craneamerica.com
SIC: 3625 Crane & hoist controls, including metal mill
HQ: Terex Utilities, Inc.
    12805 Sw 77th Pl
    Tigard OR 97223
    503 620-0611

**(G-311)**
**TFC GROUP LLC**
136 W Commercial Ave  (60101-4504)
Rural Route 55 W Monroe St, Chicago (60603)
PHONE................630 559-0808
Robert Salerno, *President*
Bob Butler, *VP Sales*
Samantha Butler, *Manager*
EMP: 75
SQ FT: 75,000

SALES: 6MM  Privately Held
SIC: 3471 Electroplating of metals or formed products; finishing, metals or formed products

**(G-312)**
**THOMAS ELECTRONICS INC**
330 S La Londe Ave  (60101-3309)
PHONE................315 923-2051
Fred Klingelhofer, *President*
Dennis Young, *Exec VP*
Tony Valene, *Plant Mgr*
Alex Tangora, *Purch Dir*
Rachael Castello, *Purch Mgr*
EMP: 40
SALES (corp-wide): 23.1MM  Privately Held
SIC: 3671 Cathode ray tubes, including rebuilt
PA: Thomas Electronics, Inc
    208 Davis Pkwy
    Clyde NY 14433
    315 923-2051

**(G-313)**
**THREE ANGELS PRINTING SVCS INC**
Also Called: 3 Angels
1105 S Westwood Ave  (60101-4920)
PHONE................630 333-4305
EMP: 16
SQ FT: 5,000
SALES (est): 125.6K  Privately Held
SIC: 2752 Lithographic Commercial Printing

**(G-314)**
**THYBAR CORPORATION (PA)**
Also Called: Thycurb Fabricating
913 S Kay Ave  (60101-4995)
PHONE................630 543-5300
Fax: 630 543-5309
Jeffrey Catalano, *President*
Michael Jurich, *Plant Mgr*
Ron Evitt, *Safety Mgr*
Craig Hoffman, *Purchasing*
Patricia Norris, *CFO*
EMP: 32
SQ FT: 40,000
SALES: 34MM  Privately Held
WEB: www.thybar.com
SIC: 3441  3444 Fabricated structural metal; expansion joints (structural shapes), iron or steel; sheet metalwork

**(G-315)**
**TJ TOOL INC**
1212 W National Ave  (60101-3131)
PHONE................630 543-3595
Fax: 630 543-3597
Timothy Raucci, *President*
Deborah Raucci, *Admin Sec*
EMP: 12
SQ FT: 5,000
SALES (est): 1.4MM  Privately Held
WEB: www.tjtool.com
SIC: 3312 Tool & die steel & alloys

**(G-316)**
**TJ WIRE FORMING INC**
824 S Kay Ave  (60101-4907)
PHONE................630 628-9209
Jerry Krasinski, *President*
EMP: 4
SQ FT: 6,000
SALES: 400K  Privately Held
SIC: 3312  3469 Wire products, steel or iron; metal stampings

**(G-317)**
**TOLERANCES GRINDING CO INC**
1020 W National Ave  (60101-3127)
PHONE................630 543-6066
Fax: 630 543-6067
Joseph Dernbach Jr, *President*
EMP: 20 EST: 1964
SQ FT: 8,000
SALES (est): 2.5MM  Privately Held
WEB: www.tolerancesgrinding.com
SIC: 3599 Machine shop, jobbing & repair

**(G-318)**
**TOOLEX CORPORATION**
1204 W Capitol Dr  (60101-3117)
PHONE................630 458-0001

Ron Rogalla, *President*
EMP: 8
SQ FT: 11,000
SALES: 1MM  Privately Held
SIC: 3599 Machine shop, jobbing & repair

**(G-319)**
**TOTAL ENGINEERED PRODUCTS INC**
908 S Westwood Ave  (60101-4917)
PHONE................630 543-9006
Chris Caliendo, *President*
Anthony Palumbo, *Opers Spvr*
Christine Caliendo, *Treasurer*
EMP: 3
SQ FT: 3,700
SALES (est): 490.1K  Privately Held
SIC: 3441 Fabricated structural metal

**(G-320)**
**TOYO INK INTERNATIONAL CORP**
710 W Belden Ave Ste B  (60101-4936)
PHONE................630 930-5100
James Honda, *General Counsel*
EMP: 19
SALES (corp-wide): 2.3B  Privately Held
SIC: 2893 Printing ink
HQ: Toyo Ink International Corp
    1225 N Michael Dr
    Wood Dale IL 60191
    866 969-8696

**(G-321)**
**TRANSPARENT CONTAINER CO INC (PA)**
Also Called: Tcc, Inc
325 S Lombard Rd  (60101-3023)
PHONE................708 449-8520
Fax: 630 860-3651
Scott Greiwe, *President*
Steve Fifer, *Division Mgr*
Phil Sexton, *Plant Mgr*
Cindy Anderson, *Project Mgr*
Meredith Serrano, *Project Mgr*
EMP: 50 EST: 1961
SQ FT: 72,000
SALES (est): 44.3MM  Privately Held
WEB: www.transparentcontainer.com
SIC: 3089 Plastic containers, except foam; trays, plastic

**(G-322)**
**TRANSPARENT CONTAINER CO INC**
1110 W National Ave  (60101-3129)
PHONE................630 543-1818
Rich Orton, *Safety Mgr*
EMP: 53
SALES (corp-wide): 44.3MM  Privately Held
SIC: 3089 Plastic containers, except foam; trays, plastic
PA: Transparent Container Co., Inc.
    325 S Lombard Rd
    Addison IL 60101
    708 449-8520

**(G-323)**
**TRANSPARENT CONTAINER CO INC**
325 S Lombard Rd  (60101-3023)
PHONE................708 449-8520
John Doherty, *Sales Mgr*
Steve Fifer, *Manager*
Al Carson, *IT/INT Sup*
EMP: 60
SQ FT: 90,000
SALES (corp-wide): 44.3MM  Privately Held
SIC: 3089  2671 Pallets, plastic; packaging paper & plastics film, coated & laminated
PA: Transparent Container Co., Inc.
    325 S Lombard Rd
    Addison IL 60101
    708 449-8520

**(G-324)**
**TRI-ZEE SERVICES INC**
415 W Belden Ave Ste A  (60101-4933)
PHONE................630 543-8677
John Silvestri, *President*
EMP: 3

## Addison - Dupage County (G-325)

SALES (est): 332K **Privately Held**
SIC: 1389 Construction, repair & dismantling services

### (G-325)
### TRU-NATIVE ENTERPRISES
Also Called: Tru-Native N'Genuity
50 W Commercial Ave (60101-4502)
PHONE..................630 409-3258
Valerie Littlechief, *Principal*
EMP: 2 EST: 2015
SALES (est): 279.4K **Privately Held**
SIC: 5147 2015 Meats & meat products; poultry slaughtering & processing

### (G-326)
### TRU-NATIVE ENTERPRISES
Also Called: Tru-Native N'Genuity
50 W Commercial Ave (60101-4502)
PHONE..................630 409-3258
Valerie Littlechief,
EMP: 2
SALES (est): 200K **Privately Held**
SIC: 5147 2015 Meats & meat products; poultry slaughtering & processing

### (G-327)
### TRU-TONE FINISHING INC (PA)
128 S Lombard Rd (60101-3020)
PHONE..................630 543-5520
Fax: 630 543-5624
Dennis Dlemenswicz, *President*
Lori Ard, *General Mgr*
Dennis Klemenswicz, *Founder*
Elizabeth Klemenswicz, *Corp Secy*
Greg Klemenswicz, *Vice Pres*
EMP: 35
SQ FT: 44,000
SALES (est): 7MM **Privately Held**
SIC: 3479 Painting of metal products

### (G-328)
### TRYSON METAL STAMPG & MFG INC
230 S La Londe Ave (60101-3307)
PHONE..................630 628-6570
Fax: 630 628-0016
Gursfredi Albert, *Branch Mgr*
EMP: 3
SALES (corp-wide): 5MM **Privately Held**
SIC: 3469 Stamping metal for the trade
PA: Tryson Metal Stampings And Manufacturing, Inc.
311 S Stewart Ave
Addison IL 60101
630 458-0591

### (G-329)
### TRYSON METAL STAMPG & MFG INC (PA)
311 S Stewart Ave (60101-3340)
PHONE..................630 458-0591
Albert Gursfredi, *Ch of Bd*
Felix Jarczyk, *President*
Douglas Adams, *General Mgr*
EMP: 41
SQ FT: 25,750
SALES (est): 5MM **Privately Held**
WEB: www.tryson.com
SIC: 3469 Stamping metal for the trade

### (G-330)
### TST/IMPRESO INC
450 S Lombard Rd Ste C (60101-4230)
PHONE..................630 775-9555
Fax: 847 795-9511
Bob Mladucky, *Branch Mgr*
EMP: 7
SALES (corp-wide): 83.3MM **Publicly Held**
SIC: 2621 2759 2086 2754 Paper mills; laser printing; water, pasteurized; packaged in cans, bottles, etc.; business form & card printing, gravure
HQ: Tst/Impreso, Inc.
652 Southwestern Blvd
Coppell TX 75019
972 462-0100

### (G-331)
### TURTLE WAX INC (PA)
Also Called: Turtle Wax Carwash & Car Appea
2250 W Pinehurst Blvd # 150 (60101-6103)
PHONE..................630 455-3700

Denis John Healy Jr, *CEO*
Denis J Healy Sr, *President*
Richard Capalby, *Counsel*
Thomas Kelly, *Vice Pres*
Barry Ruche, *Vice Pres*
◆ EMP: 400 EST: 1944
SQ FT: 250,000
SALES (est): 301.6MM **Privately Held**
WEB: www.turtlewax.com
SIC: 2842 Specialty cleaning, polishes & sanitation goods; automobile polish; shoe polish or cleaner; metal polish

### (G-332)
### U S TOOL & MANUFACTURING CO
1335 W Fullerton Ave (60101-4319)
PHONE..................630 953-1000
Fax: 630 953-0174
Raymond G Foreman, *President*
William Levy, *Vice Pres*
Helen Shafernack, *Office Mgr*
EMP: 20 EST: 1915
SQ FT: 13,500
SALES: 1.2MM **Privately Held**
WEB: www.ustoolandmfg.com
SIC: 3714 3429 3643 Motor vehicle engines & parts; manufactured hardware (general); current-carrying wiring devices

### (G-333)
### ULTRAMATIC EQUIPMENT CO
848 S Westgate St (60101-5087)
PHONE..................630 543-4565
Fax: 630 543-4569
Joe Astronrino, *Manager*
John Kuczko, *Manager*
EMP: 20
SALES (corp-wide): 1MM **Privately Held**
WEB: www.ultramatic.com
SIC: 3549 3541 3559 5084 Metalworking machinery; deburring machines; refinery, chemical processing & similar machinery; industrial machinery & equipment; abrasive products
PA: Ultramatic Equipment Co.
8603 E Royal Palm Rd # 260
Scottsdale AZ 85258
480 951-6000

### (G-334)
### UNISTRUT INTERNATIONAL CORP
Also Called: Unistrut Construction
2171 W Executive Dr # 100 (60101-5600)
PHONE..................630 773-3460
Joan Rasmus, *Purchasing*
Barry Catterall, *Natl Sales Mgr*
Scott Patchn, *Branch Mgr*
Sean Byrne, *Sr Project Mgr*
Patrick Urell, *Director*
EMP: 70 **Publicly Held**
WEB: www.unistrutconstruction.com
SIC: 4226 3993 3444 3443 Special warehousing & storage; signs & advertising specialties; sheet metalwork; fabricated plate work (boiler shop); fabricated structural metal; wood partitions & fixtures
HQ: Unistrut International Corporation
16100 Lathrop Ave
Harvey IL 60426
800 882-5543

### (G-335)
### V AND L POLISHING CO
341 W Interstate Rd (60101-4515)
PHONE..................630 543-5999
Dan Lavallie, *President*
Virginia Lavallie, *Vice Pres*
Richard Olsen, *Sales Staff*
EMP: 6
SQ FT: 5,000
SALES: 330K **Privately Held**
WEB: www.vlpolishing.com
SIC: 3471 Polishing, metals or formed products; cleaning, polishing & finishing

### (G-336)
### VAC-MATIC CORPORATION (PA)
2 S Lincoln Ave (60101-3519)
PHONE..................630 543-4518
Fax: 630 543-9339
Donald C Hundrieser, *President*
James Hundrieser, *Vice Pres*
Anne Hundrieser, *Admin Sec*
EMP: 5

SQ FT: 500
SALES (est): 570.3K **Privately Held**
SIC: 3089 Plastic processing

### (G-337)
### VAL-MATIC VALVE AND MFG CORP
303 S Rohlwing Rd (60101-3029)
PHONE..................630 993-4078
Joe Barnes, *Branch Mgr*
EMP: 20
SALES (corp-wide): 27.4MM **Privately Held**
SIC: 3491 Valves, automatic control; water works valves
PA: Val-Matic Valve And Manufacturing Corporation
905 S Riverside Dr
Elmhurst IL 60126
630 941-7600

### (G-338)
### VEK SCREW MACHINE PRODUCTS
777 W Winthrop Ave (60101-4310)
P.O. Box 555 (60101-0555)
PHONE..................630 543-5557
Fax: 630 543-5594
Thelma I Keyworth, *Ch of Bd*
Robert Keyworth, *President*
EMP: 8 EST: 1952
SQ FT: 7,500
SALES: 750K **Privately Held**
SIC: 3451 3599 Screw machine products; machine & other job shop work

### (G-339)
### VENUS LABORATORIES INC (PA)
Also Called: Earth Friendly Products
111 S Rohlwing Rd (60101-3027)
PHONE..................630 595-1900
Kelly Vlahakis-Hanks, *CEO*
Elli Manolas, *Ch of Bd*
Van Vlahakis, *President*
Mike Marrese, *General Mgr*
Zuliana Navarro, *General Mgr*
◆ EMP: 40
SQ FT: 40,000
SALES (est): 91MM **Privately Held**
SIC: 2842 2841 Specialty cleaning preparations; sanitation preparations; soap & other detergents

### (G-340)
### VFN FIBERGLASS INC
330 W Factory Rd (60101-5004)
PHONE..................630 543-0232
Fax: 630 543-9877
Frank Mortensen, *President*
Vic Mortensen, *Vice Pres*
Charmaine Mortensen, *Treasurer*
Gloria Mortensen, *Admin Sec*
EMP: 14
SQ FT: 8,100
SALES: 1MM **Privately Held**
WEB: www.vfnfiberglass.com
SIC: 3714 Motor vehicle parts & accessories; hoods, motor vehicle

### (G-341)
### VIS-O-GRAPHIC INC
Also Called: Vis-O-Graphic Printing
1220 W National Ave (60101-3131)
PHONE..................630 590-6100
Robert V Dahlke, *President*
Rick Ebel, *Senior VP*
John Dahlke, *Vice Pres*
Jon March, *QC Mgr*
Kellie Slovis, *Controller*
EMP: 30 EST: 1945
SQ FT: 10,000
SALES (est): 10.2MM **Privately Held**
WEB: www.visography.com
SIC: 2752 7336 Commercial printing, offset; graphic arts & related design

### (G-342)
### WESTERN PLASTICS INC
1731 W Armitage Ct (60101-4221)
PHONE..................630 629-3034
Fax: 630 629-3511
Don Edelstein, *President*
Raymond S Howard, *President*
Donald A Edelstein, *Vice Pres*

EMP: 10
SQ FT: 17,000
SALES (est): 1.5MM **Privately Held**
SIC: 3081 Polypropylene film & sheet

### (G-343)
### WIKUS SAW TECHNOLOGY CORP
700 W Belden Ave (60101-4941)
PHONE..................630 766-0960
Martin Mueller, *President*
Kellie Grengs, *Principal*
Dan Miller, *Regional Mgr*
Mark Rafalzik, *Regl Sales Mgr*
▲ EMP: 40 EST: 1999
SQ FT: 20,853
SALES (est): 6.7MM
SALES (corp-wide): 105.9MM **Privately Held**
SIC: 3425 Saw blades for hand or power saws
PA: Wikus-Sagenfabrik Wilhelm H. Kullmann GmbH & Co. Kg
Melsunger Str. 30
Spangenberg 34286
566 350-00

### (G-344)
### WIKUS TECHNOLOGY
700 W Belden Ave (60101-4941)
PHONE..................630 766-0960
EMP: 4
SALES (est): 270K **Privately Held**
SIC: 3999 Manufacturing industries

### (G-345)
### WOODLAND PLASTICS CORP
1340 W National Ave (60101-3149)
PHONE..................630 543-1144
Fax: 630 543-1525
Stephen L Sinderson, *President*
Nelson L Sinderson, *Admin Sec*
▼ EMP: 25
SQ FT: 20,000
SALES (est): 5.8MM **Privately Held**
SIC: 3089 Injection molding of plastics

### (G-346)
### WOODLAWN ENGINEERING CO INC
325 W Fay Ave (60101-5078)
PHONE..................630 543-3550
Fax: 630 543-0735
Marshall Gordon, *CEO*
Neil Gordon, *President*
Scott Gordon, *Corp Secy*
Jack Hilgenberg, *Vice Pres*
EMP: 20 EST: 1956
SQ FT: 25,000
SALES: 1MM **Privately Held**
WEB: www.woodlawnengineering.com
SIC: 3444 Sheet metalwork

### (G-347)
### WORLD WASHER & STAMPING INC
763 W Annoreno Dr (60101-4315)
PHONE..................630 543-6749
Fax: 630 628-9495
Dennis L Fielder, *President*
Chester Labno, *Vice Pres*
EMP: 13
SQ FT: 11,800
SALES (est): 1.4MM **Privately Held**
SIC: 3469 Metal stampings

### (G-348)
### XENTRIS WIRELESS LLC
1250 N Greenbriar Dr A (60101-1098)
PHONE..................630 693-9700
William Christy, *President*
Allan Bailey, *Chairman*
Paul Blevins, *CFO*
Mark Clark, *Manager*
Kim Williams, *Manager*
▲ EMP: 52
SQ FT: 82,000
SALES (est): 29.3MM **Privately Held**
WEB: www.xentrisllc.com
SIC: 3663 Cellular radio telephone

## GEOGRAPHIC SECTION

**(G-349)**
**ZABIHA HALAL MEAT PROCESSORS**
1715 W Cortland Ct (60101-4228)
PHONE.................................630 620-5000
EMP: 3
SALES (est): 245.6K **Privately Held**
SIC: 2011 Meat packing plants

**(G-350)**
**ZITROPACK LTD**
240 S La Londe Ave (60101-3307)
PHONE.................................630 543-1016
Humberto Ortiz, *President*
Ana Ortiz, *Corp Secy*
EMP: 12
SQ FT: 20,000
SALES (est): 3MM **Privately Held**
WEB: www.zitropack.com
SIC: 3565 Packaging machinery

**(G-351)**
**ZJ INDUSTRIES INC (PA)**
125 W Factory Rd (60101-5103)
PHONE.................................630 543-6400
Milos Jakic, *President*
Zorica Jajic, *COO*
Mike Jajic, *Sr Corp Ofcr*
Zorica Jakic, *Vice Pres*
Nicolas Jakic, *Sales Staff*
EMP: 18 EST: 1992
SQ FT: 36,000
SALES (est): 3.3MM **Privately Held**
WEB: www.zjindustriesinc.com
SIC: 3549 Metalworking machinery

### Albany
*Whiteside County*

**(G-352)**
**CF INDUSTRIES INC**
4 Miles W On Rte 84 (61230)
P.O. Box 446 (61230-0446)
PHONE.................................309 654-2218
Bob Wilkens, *Branch Mgr*
EMP: 100
SALES (corp-wide): 3.6B **Publicly Held**
SIC: 2873 Anhydrous ammonia
HQ: Cf Industries, Inc.
4 Parkway N Ste 400
Deerfield IL 60015
847 405-2400

### Albers
*Clinton County*

**(G-353)**
**EDS PALLET SERVICE**
409 N Commercial St (62215-1379)
P.O. Box 226 (62215-0226)
PHONE.................................618 248-5386
Fax: 618 248-5538
Ed Wittles, *Owner*
Marvin Wittles, *Owner*
EMP: 10
SALES (est): 975.4K **Privately Held**
SIC: 2448 Wood pallets & skids

**(G-354)**
**GATEWAY FUELS INC**
5260 State Route 161 (62215-1083)
P.O. Box 255 (62215-0255)
PHONE.................................618 248-5000
Brian Schrage, *Principal*
EMP: 5 EST: 2010
SALES (est): 529.5K **Privately Held**
SIC: 2869 Fuels

### Albion
*Edwards County*

**(G-355)**
**ATARAXIA LLC**
Also Called: Gold Leaf
884 Industrial St (62806-9000)
PHONE.................................618 446-3219
John Dieser, *Opers Staff*
George Archos, *Mng Member*
Ross Morreale, *Officer*
EMP: 35
SALES (est): 3.7MM **Privately Held**
SIC: 2833 Drugs & herbs: grading, grinding & milling

**(G-356)**
**CHAMPION LABORATORIES INC (DH)**
200 S 4th St (62806-1313)
PHONE.................................618 445-6011
Fax: 618 445-3107
Greg Noethlich, *President*
Teresa Schnautz, *Vice Pres*
Keith A Zar, *Vice Pres*
Kris Stanhope, *Design Engr Mgr*
Jane Hedrick, *Engineer*
◆ EMP: 1320 EST: 1936
SQ FT: 250,000
SALES: 300MM **Privately Held**
WEB: www.champlabs.com
SIC: 3714 Filters: oil, fuel & air, motor vehicle
HQ: United Components, Llc
1900 W Field Ct
Lake Forest IL 60045
812 867-4516

**(G-357)**
**CHAMPION LABORATORIES INC**
Lee Filter Division
200 S 4th St (62806-1313)
PHONE.................................618 445-6011
Lisa Matthes, *Manager*
EMP: 650 **Privately Held**
WEB: www.champlabs.com
SIC: 3569 Filters
HQ: Champion Laboratories, Inc.
200 S 4th St
Albion IL 62806
618 445-6011

**(G-358)**
**CHAMPION LABORATORIES INC**
200 S 4th St (62806-1313)
PHONE.................................803 684-3205
Rickey Gann, *Maint Spvr*
Wayne Therrell, *QC Dir*
Brenda Wilson, *Persnl Dir*
Tammy Johnson, *Personnel*
Chris Wallace, *Manager*
EMP: 300 **Privately Held**
WEB: www.champlabs.com
SIC: 3714 Motor vehicle parts & accessories
HQ: Champion Laboratories, Inc.
200 S 4th St
Albion IL 62806
618 445-6011

**(G-359)**
**CHAMPION LABORATORIES INC**
301 Industrial Dr (62806-1339)
PHONE.................................618 445-6011
Thomas Mowatt, *President*
EMP: 650 **Privately Held**
WEB: www.champlabs.com
SIC: 3714 Filters: oil, fuel & air, motor vehicle
HQ: Champion Laboratories, Inc.
200 S 4th St
Albion IL 62806
618 445-6011

**(G-360)**
**CHAMPION LABORATORIES INC**
Also Called: Fram Filtration
328 Industrial Dr (62806-1300)
PHONE.................................618 445-6011
Wade Gillard, *Manager*
EMP: 111 **Privately Held**
SIC: 3714 Filters: oil, fuel & air, motor vehicle
HQ: Champion Laboratories, Inc.
200 S 4th St
Albion IL 62806
618 445-6011

**(G-361)**
**EDWARDS COUNTY CONCRETE LLC**
327 Industrial Dr (62806-1339)
PHONE.................................618 445-2711
Rob Carter, *Office Mgr*
Jeffrey G Denny,
EMP: 4
SALES (est): 335.9K **Privately Held**
SIC: 3273 Ready-mixed concrete

**(G-362)**
**FARMERS MILL INC**
438 County Road 1500 N (62806-4125)
PHONE.................................618 445-2114
Earl Reid, *President*
Pam Reid, *Admin Sec*
EMP: 2
SQ FT: 4,800
SALES (est): 400K **Privately Held**
SIC: 5191 2041 Animal feeds; seeds: field, garden & flower; flour & other grain mill products

**(G-363)**
**FARMERS PACKING INC**
657 Illinois Route 15 (62806-4455)
PHONE.................................618 445-3822
Fax: 618 445-3829
David Seisert, *President*
EMP: 10
SALES (est): 620K **Privately Held**
SIC: 2011 Meat packing plants

**(G-364)**
**PALLET SOLUTION INC**
Hwy 130 N (62806)
PHONE.................................618 445-2316
Fax: 618 445-2316
Julie Kimbrell, *President*
Marcus Charlcraft, *Vice Pres*
Randall Kimbrell, *Manager*
EMP: 35
SQ FT: 43,000
SALES: 1.9MM **Privately Held**
SIC: 2448 Wood pallets & skids

**(G-365)**
**PREMIER TOOL & MACHINE INC**
330 Industrial Dr (62806-1300)
Rr # 4 Box 137
PHONE.................................618 445-9066
David Satava, *President*
Mary Satava, *Vice Pres*
EMP: 4
SQ FT: 6,048
SALES (est): 550K **Privately Held**
SIC: 3599 Machine shop, jobbing & repair

**(G-366)**
**T J MARCHE LTD**
11 N 5th St (62806-1021)
PHONE.................................618 445-2314
Fax: 618 445-2911
Mary Erickson, *President*
Cheryl Taylor, *Vice Pres*
EMP: 5 EST: 1974
SQ FT: 2,880
SALES (est): 751.9K **Privately Held**
SIC: 5944 7336 3993 2396 Jewelry stores; silk screen design; signs & advertising specialties; automotive & apparel trimmings

### Aledo
*Mercer County*

**(G-367)**
**ALEDO WELDING ENTERPRISES INC**
Also Called: Cokel's Welding
1802 Se 3rd St (61231-9450)
PHONE.................................309 582-2019
Fax: 309 582-2019
Don Yates, *President*
EMP: 5
SQ FT: 4,625
SALES (est): 714.1K **Privately Held**
SIC: 7692 7533 Welding repair; auto exhaust system repair shops

**(G-368)**
**GENERAL GRIND & MACHINE INC**
2103 Se 5th St (61231-9473)
P.O. Box 168 (61231-0168)
PHONE.................................309 582-5959
Fax: 309 582-2134
Mark Bieri, *President*
Steve Moreland, *General Mgr*
Mike Shull, *General Mgr*
Blake Bieri, *COO*
Schuyler Downey, *Vice Pres*
EMP: 150
SQ FT: 160,000
SALES (est): 43.5MM **Privately Held**
WEB: www.generalgrind.com
SIC: 3599 Machine shop, jobbing & repair

**(G-369)**
**HAHN READY-MIX COMPANY**
1600 Se 6th St (61231)
P.O. Box 271 (61231-0271)
PHONE.................................309 582-2436
Fax: 309 263-2204
Ralph Hill, *Branch Mgr*
EMP: 5
SALES (corp-wide): 8MM **Privately Held**
SIC: 3273 Ready-mixed concrete
PA: Hahn Ready-Mix Company
3636 W River Dr
Davenport IA 52802
563 322-1757

**(G-370)**
**HENDERSON FAMILY**
208 N College Ave (61231-1460)
PHONE.................................309 236-6783
Leo Henderson Jr, *Principal*
Jason Hessman, *Principal*
EMP: 6
SALES (est): 308K **Privately Held**
SIC: 2752 Commercial printing, lithographic

**(G-371)**
**MEMINGER METAL FINISHING INC (PA)**
2107 Se 8th St (61231-9406)
P.O. Box 225 (61231-0225)
PHONE.................................309 582-3363
Fax: 309 582-2492
Patricia Meminger, *President*
Jeremy Bigham, *Engineer*
Trent Kaufman, *Engineer*
Bruce Meminger, *Admin Sec*
EMP: 11
SALES (est): 2.7MM **Privately Held**
SIC: 3559 3471 Metal finishing equipment for plating, etc.; plating & polishing

**(G-372)**
**RODGER MURPHY**
Also Called: Goldsmith, The
103 W Main St (61231-1603)
P.O. Box 142 (61231-0142)
PHONE.................................309 582-2202
Rodger Murphy, *Owner*
Carla Murphy, *Co-Owner*
EMP: 3
SQ FT: 1,000
SALES (est): 225K **Privately Held**
SIC: 5944 7631 3911 Jewelry stores; jewelry repair services; jewelry, precious metal

**(G-373)**
**TIMES RECORD COMPANY**
219 S College Ave (61231-1734)
P.O. Box 309 (61231-0309)
PHONE.................................309 582-5112
Paul Behan, *President*
Marty Kennedy, *Vice Pres*
Marta Tucker, *Vice Pres*
Phyllis Lundquist, *Treasurer*
Susie Swearingen, *Sales Staff*
EMP: 25 EST: 1928
SQ FT: 5,000
SALES (est): 1.3MM **Privately Held**
SIC: 2711 2791 2752 Commercial printing & newspaper publishing combined; typesetting; commercial printing, lithographic

### Alexander
*Morgan County*

**(G-374)**
**RANDY WRIGHT & SON CNSTR**
901 E Old 36 (62601-7118)
PHONE.................................217 478-4171
Randy Wright, *Owner*
EMP: 5 EST: 2011
SALES (est): 246.4K **Privately Held**
SIC: 1442 Construction sand & gravel

## Alexis
*Mercer County*

**(G-375)**
**ALEXIS FIRE EQUIPMENT COMPANY**
109 E Broadway Ave (61412-5041)
P.O. Box 549 (61412-0549)
PHONE................................309 482-6121
Fax: 309 482-3235
Karl Jeffrey Morris, *President*
Dan Reese, *Business Mgr*
Daniel Don Reese, *Corp Secy*
Michael Shull, *Vice Pres*
Bob Routt, *Controller*
EMP: 70 EST: 1945
SQ FT: 42,000
SALES (est): 16.5MM **Privately Held**
WEB: www.alexisfire.com
SIC: 3711 Fire department vehicles (motor vehicles), assembly of

## Algonquin
*Mchenry County*

**(G-376)**
**A D SKYLIGHTS INC**
206 Berg St (60102-3538)
PHONE................................847 854-2900
Fax: 847 854-2902
Stefan Szefer, *President*
Jerzy Depczyk, *President*
EMP: 6
SQ FT: 8,000
SALES: 500K **Privately Held**
WEB: www.adskylightsinc.com
SIC: 3444 Skylights, sheet metal

**(G-377)**
**APAK PACKAGING GROUP INC**
208 Berg St (60102-3538)
PHONE................................630 616-7275
Peter Park, *Sales Staff*
EMP: 4
SALES (est): 347.8K **Privately Held**
SIC: 2631 Container, packaging & boxboard

**(G-378)**
**ARROW ROAD CONSTRUCTION CO**
10500 S Il Route 31 (60102-1641)
P.O. Box 334 (60102-0334)
PHONE................................847 658-1140
Fax: 847 658-1247
Terry Pyne, *Manager*
EMP: 3
SALES (corp-wide): 41.2MM **Privately Held**
WEB: www.arrowroad.com
SIC: 1611 2951 Highway & street construction; asphalt paving mixtures & blocks
PA: Arrow Road Construction Company
3401 S Busse Rd
Mount Prospect IL 60056
847 437-0700

**(G-379)**
**AVANI SPICES LLC**
1690 Stone Ridge Ln (60102-6638)
PHONE................................847 532-1075
Avani Amin Carkner, *President*
Robert Shive, *Vice Pres*
EMP: 4
SALES (est): 196.5K **Privately Held**
SIC: 2099 Food preparations

**(G-380)**
**BARTELL CORPORATION**
3671 Persimmon Dr (60102-5959)
P.O. Box 5775, Elgin (60121-5775)
PHONE................................847 854-3232
John Bartell, *President*
Barbara Bartell, *Vice Pres*
EMP: 7
SALES (est): 461.4K **Privately Held**
SIC: 8711 3549 Machine tool design; assembly machines, including robotic

**(G-381)**
**BEM WIRELESS LLC**
2654 Corporate Pkwy (60102-2560)
PHONE................................815 337-0541
Bhavita Sheth, *Controller*
Mike Nakamura, *VP Sales*
Michael Nakamura, *Mng Member*
Sheng-Huei Jou,
▲ EMP: 10
SALES: 15MM **Privately Held**
SIC: 3651 3679 Speaker systems; headphones, radio

**(G-382)**
**CANCONEX INC**
901 Armstrong St (60102-3548)
P.O. Box 7419 (60102-7419)
PHONE................................847 458-9955
Fax: 847 458-8202
James K Atkinson, *President*
EMP: 15
SQ FT: 6,000
SALES (est): 3.4MM **Privately Held**
WEB: www.canconex.com
SIC: 3535 Conveyors & conveying equipment

**(G-383)**
**CHARTER DURA-BAR INC**
2401 Huntington Dr N (60102-4400)
PHONE................................847 854-1044
Tim Heagney, *General Mgr*
EMP: 90
SALES (corp-wide): 762.9MM **Privately Held**
WEB: www.wellsmanufacturing.com
SIC: 3321 Gray iron castings
HQ: Charter Dura-Bar, Inc.
2100 W Lake Shore Dr
Woodstock IL 60098
815 338-3900

**(G-384)**
**CIGTECHS**
4069 W Algonquin Rd (60102-9401)
PHONE................................847 802-4586
EMP: 4 **Privately Held**
SIC: 2111 Cigarettes
PA: Cigtechs
173 W Irving Park Rd
Roselle IL 60172

**(G-385)**
**DAILY PROJECTS**
124 S Randall Rd (60102-9774)
PHONE................................224 209-8636
EMP: 3
SALES (est): 140.9K **Privately Held**
SIC: 2711 Newspapers, publishing & printing

**(G-386)**
**DIRECT DIMENSION INC (PA)**
8195 Pyott Rd (60156-9767)
PHONE................................815 479-1936
George Athans, *President*
Leonidas Athans, *Vice Pres*
Sue Serio, *Manager*
EMP: 4
SQ FT: 1,500
SALES (est): 1.6MM **Privately Held**
SIC: 3711 Truck & tractor truck assembly

**(G-387)**
**DISKIN SYSTEMS INC**
9550 S Il Route 31 (60102-9724)
PHONE................................815 276-7288
Troy Diskin, *President*
Pat Piercen, *Vice Pres*
EMP: 5
SALES (est): 755.9K **Privately Held**
WEB: www.diskinsystems.com
SIC: 3589 Car washing machinery

**(G-388)**
**DMJ GROUP INC**
2413 W Algonquin Rd # 227 (60102-9402)
PHONE................................847 322-7533
Denise Rognstad, *President*
Jill Rognstad, *Treasurer*
Michelle Chase, *Admin Sec*
EMP: 3
SALES (est): 173.4K **Privately Held**
SIC: 3999 Pet supplies

**(G-389)**
**FIELD WORKS INC**
1220 Armstrong St (60102-3543)
PHONE................................847 658-8200
Fax: 847 428-2587
Halina Biernat, *President*
Janusz Biernat, *Admin Sec*
EMP: 5 EST: 1996
SALES: 600K **Privately Held**
SIC: 3599 Machine shop, jobbing & repair

**(G-390)**
**FORTITUD INC**
8 Benton Ct (60102-6222)
PHONE................................312 919-4938
EMP: 6 EST: 2012
SALES (est): 460K **Privately Held**
SIC: 3699 7389 Electrical equipment & supplies;

**(G-391)**
**GAYTON ENTERPRISES LLC**
2823 Waterfront Ave (60102-6834)
P.O. Box 7277 (60102-7277)
PHONE................................847 462-4030
Thomas Gayton,
EMP: 5 EST: 2014
SALES: 500K **Privately Held**
SIC: 4959 3531 7389 Sweeping service: road, airport, parking lot, etc.; concrete plants;

**(G-392)**
**HI TEK TOOL & MACHINING INC**
2413 W Algonquin Rd (60102-9402)
PHONE................................847 836-6422
Lonnie Alford, *President*
Audrey Alford, *Vice Pres*
EMP: 5
SQ FT: 5,000
SALES: 500K **Privately Held**
SIC: 3312 Tool & die steel

**(G-393)**
**INDEPENDENT ANTIQUE RAD MFG**
200 Berg St (60102-3538)
PHONE................................847 458-7400
Peter Cook, *President*
EMP: 7 EST: 1913
SALES (est): 925.4K **Privately Held**
WEB: www.oldradman.com
SIC: 3714 3713 Radiators & radiator shells & cores, motor vehicle; heaters, motor vehicle; truck & bus bodies

**(G-394)**
**J C PRODUCTS INC**
1961 Tunbridge Ct (60102-6065)
PHONE................................847 208-9616
Jim Chmela, *President*
EMP: 5
SALES (est): 599.8K **Privately Held**
SIC: 3089 Plastic processing

**(G-395)**
**JEWEL OSCO INC**
Also Called: Jewel-Osco 3256
103 S Randall Rd (60102-9773)
PHONE................................847 854-2692
Fax: 847 854-5301
John Nile, *Manager*
David Nessler, *Manager*
EMP: 175
SALES (corp-wide): 58.8B **Privately Held**
WEB: www.jewelosco.com
SIC: 5411 2051 Supermarkets, chain; bread, cake & related products
HQ: Jewel Osco, Inc.
150 E Pierce Rd Ste 200
Itasca IL 60143
630 948-6000

**(G-396)**
**KENMODE TOOL AND ENGRG INC**
820 W Algonquin Rd (60102-2482)
PHONE................................847 658-5041
Fax: 847 658-9150
Werner Moders, *CEO*
Kurt Moders, *President*
Petra Schindler, *Vice Pres*
Kurt Gascho, *CFO*
Christa Moders, *Treasurer*
▲ EMP: 150
SQ FT: 85,000
SALES (est): 50.2MM **Privately Held**
WEB: www.kenmode.com
SIC: 3469 3544 Metal stampings; special dies & tools

**(G-397)**
**LION TOOL & DIE CO**
910 W Algonquin Rd (60102-3578)
P.O. Box 7066 (60102-7066)
PHONE................................847 658-8898
Fax: 847 658-8908
Leonard Doerrfeld, *President*
Paul Doerrfeld, *Corp Secy*
EMP: 19
SQ FT: 13,000
SALES (est): 2.2MM **Privately Held**
WEB: www.liontool.com
SIC: 3544 3599 Special dies, tools, jigs & fixtures; machine shop, jobbing & repair

**(G-398)**
**MARSHALL WOLF AUTOMATION INC (PA)**
923 S Main St (60102-2735)
PHONE................................847 658-8130
Fax: 847 658-0960
Hans J Wolf, *President*
Kathleen Wolf, *Corp Secy*
Tina Hueppe, *Vice Pres*
John Witort, *Warehouse Mgr*
Cindy Curten, *Purchasing*
◆ EMP: 20
SALES (est): 15.4MM **Privately Held**
WEB: www.wolfautomation.com
SIC: 5065 3613 Electronic parts; panelboards & distribution boards, electric

**(G-399)**
**MARTINEZ MANAGEMENT INC**
2413 W Algonquin Rd (60102-9402)
PHONE................................847 822-7202
Rich Martinez, *President*
EMP: 3
SQ FT: 2,500 **Privately Held**
SIC: 3089 Automotive parts, plastic
PA: Martinez Management, Inc.
800 Belle Terre Pkwy
Palm Coast FL 32164

**(G-400)**
**MATERIAL SERVICE CORPORATION**
Rr 31 (60102)
P.O. Box 69 (60102-0069)
PHONE................................847 658-4559
Fax: 847 658-2472
Frank Anderson, *Manager*
EMP: 27
SALES (corp-wide): 16B **Privately Held**
WEB: www.materialservice.com
SIC: 3281 1442 Stone, quarrying & processing of own stone products; construction sand & gravel
HQ: Material Service Corporation
2235 Entp Dr Ste 3504
Westchester IL 60154
708 731-2600

**(G-401)**
**NEON MOON LTD**
14 Walbridge Ct (60102-9787)
PHONE................................847 849-3200
Lisa Waitzman, *Principal*
EMP: 3
SALES (est): 157.5K **Privately Held**
SIC: 2813 Neon

**(G-402)**
**NEW LIFE PRINTING & PUBLISHING**
1508 S Main St (60102-3223)
P.O. Box 7285 (60102-7285)
PHONE................................847 658-4111
Fax: 847 658-4998
Monica Brubaker, *President*
Loren Nelson, *Vice Pres*
Diane Urias, *Office Mgr*
EMP: 6
SQ FT: 4,000
SALES: 1.5MM **Privately Held**
WEB: www.newlifeprinting.com
SIC: 2752 2721 2791 2789 Commercial printing, lithographic; periodicals; typesetting; bookbinding & related work

**GEOGRAPHIC SECTION**

**Alsip - Cook County (G-430)**

**(G-403)**
**POWERTRAIN TECHNOLOGY INC**
355 Point Ct  (60102-2228)
PHONE....................847 458-2323
Steven Fox, *President*
Vicky Fox, *Corp Secy*
▲ **EMP:** 6
**SALES (est):** 627.9K  **Privately Held**
**WEB:** www.powertraintech.com
**SIC:** 3711  Motor vehicles & car bodies

**(G-404)**
**PRO INTERCOM  LLC (PA)**
1117 Saint Andrews Ct  (60102-4129)
P.O. Box 7035  (60102-7035)
PHONE....................224 406-7108
Diana Mullis, *Principal*
▲ **EMP:** 12
**SALES (est):** 1.2MM  **Privately Held**
**SIC:** 3669  Intercommunication systems, electric

**(G-405)**
**PROGRESSIVE SOLUTIONS CORP**
2848 Corporate Pkwy  (60102-2564)
PHONE....................847 639-7272
Jayson McMahon, *President*
Jason McMahon, *Sales Mgr*
▼ **EMP:** 5
**SQ FT:** 7,000
**SALES (est):** 600K  **Privately Held**
**WEB:** www.4progressive.com
**SIC:** 2899  2841  Chemical preparations; soap & other detergents

**(G-406)**
**RAPID MANUFACTURING  INC**
1320 Chase St Ste 4  (60102-9668)
PHONE....................847 458-0888
Christine M Janikowski, *President*
Michael E Kilanski, *Corp Secy*
**EMP:** 4
**SQ FT:** 6,000
**SALES (est):** 625.6K  **Privately Held**
**SIC:** 3544  Special dies, tools, jigs & fixtures

**(G-407)**
**TOOLWELD INC**
1750 Cumberland Pkwy # 8  (60102-9517)
PHONE....................847 854-8013
Fred Hild, *President*
Eric Hild, *Treasurer*
**EMP:** 3
**SALES (est):** 320.2K  **Privately Held**
**WEB:** www.toolweldmicro.com
**SIC:** 7692  Welding repair

**(G-408)**
**USED SOLUTIONS INC**
531 Tenby Way  (60102-6513)
PHONE....................815 759-5000
Mark T Mammen, *President*
Jeff Katzbeck, *Admin Sec*
**EMP:** 3
**SALES (est):** 2MM  **Privately Held**
**WEB:** www.usedsolutions.com
**SIC:** 3549  Metalworking machinery

**(G-409)**
**V C P INC**
Also Called: V C P Printing
901 W Algonquin Rd  (60102-3573)
PHONE....................847 658-5090
Fax: 847 658-1484
Herbert Vogt, *President*
Mindy Hack, *Vice Pres*
**EMP:** 21
**SQ FT:** 12,000
**SALES (est):** 3.8MM  **Privately Held**
**WEB:** www.vcpprint.com
**SIC:** 2752  2791  7331  Commercial printing, offset; typesetting; direct mail advertising services

**(G-410)**
**VILLAGE VINTNER WINERY BREWRY**
2380 Esplanade Dr  (60102-5449)
PHONE....................847 658-4900
Joseph Condo, *Principal*
**EMP:** 7 EST: 2012

**SALES (est):** 782.2K  **Privately Held**
**SIC:** 2084  Wines, brandy & brandy spirits

**(G-411)**
**W/S PACKAGING GROUP  INC**
1310 Zange Dr  (60102-2047)
PHONE....................847 658-7363
Fax: 847 658-5584
John Gorack, *Branch Mgr*
**EMP:** 5
**SALES (corp-wide):** 778.7MM  **Privately Held**
**SIC:** 2621  5943  Wrapping & packaging papers; stationery stores
**PA:** W/S Packaging Group, Inc.
    2571 S Hemlock Rd
    Green Bay WI 54229
    920 866-6300

**(G-412)**
**WAUCONDA TOOL & ENGRG LLC (HQ)**
821 W Algonquin Rd  (60102-2480)
PHONE....................847 658-4588
Fax: 847 658-0788
Charles Burnside, *President*
Don Williams, *Vice Pres*
Edward McGinty, *Controller*
Rick Fischer, *Sales Mgr*
**EMP:** 55 EST: 1950
**SQ FT:** 45,000
**SALES (est):** 17.7MM
**SALES (corp-wide):** 833.4MM  **Publicly Held**
**WEB:** www.wauconda.com
**SIC:** 3469  3544  Stamping metal for the trade; special dies, tools, jigs & fixtures
**PA:** Nn, Inc.
    207 Mockingbird Ln Ste 10
    Johnson City TN 37604
    423 743-9151

**(G-413)**
**WAYPOINT ENTERPRISES**
2328 Stonegate Rd  (60102-6654)
PHONE....................847 551-9213
John St Pierre, *Principal*
**EMP:** 2 EST: 2010
**SALES (est):** 237.9K  **Privately Held**
**SIC:** 3732  Motorboats, inboard or outboard: building & repairing

**(G-414)**
**WEBCRAFTERS  INC**
1530 Farmhill Dr  (60102-1712)
PHONE....................847 658-6661
**EMP:** 96
**SALES (corp-wide):** 60MM  **Privately Held**
**SIC:** 2782  Memorandum books, printed
**PA:** Webcrafters, Inc.
    2211 Fordem Ave
    Madison WI 53704
    608 244-3561

**(G-415)**
**YOUNG INNOVATIONS  INC (HQ)**
2260 Wendt St  (60102-1400)
PHONE....................847 458-5400
Alfred E Brennan, *CEO*
Arthur L Herbst Jr, *President*
Richard G Richmond, *Vice Pres*
Meghan McGee, *Purchasing*
Spencer Rohn, *Marketing Staff*
▲ **EMP:** 93
**SQ FT:** 113,000
**SALES (est):** 124.6MM  **Privately Held**
**WEB:** www.yiinc.com
**SIC:** 3843  Dental equipment & supplies
**PA:** Young Innovations Holdings Llc
    111 S Wacker Dr Ste 3350
    Chicago IL 60606
    312 506-5600

**(G-416)**
**YOUNG INNOVATIONS  INC (PA)**
2260 Wendt St  (60102-1400)
PHONE....................847 458-5400
**EMP:** 57
**SALES (est):** 51.5MM  **Privately Held**
**SIC:** 3843  Mfg Dental Equipment/Supplies

**(G-417)**
**YOUNG OS  LLC**
2260 Wendt St  (60102-1400)
PHONE....................847 458-5400

Catie Pankow, *Administration*
**EMP:** 20
**SALES (est):** 2.2MM  **Privately Held**
**SIC:** 3843  Dental equipment & supplies

### Alhambra
*Madison County*

**(G-418)**
**IDEAL CABINET SOLUTIONS INC**
1105 W Main St  (62001-2175)
PHONE....................618 514-7087
Jay Kohlmiller, *President*
**EMP:** 4
**SALES (est):** 153K  **Privately Held**
**SIC:** 2434  2521  2431  Wood kitchen cabinets; wood office filing cabinets & bookcases; filing cabinets (boxes), office: wood; window trim, wood; moldings & baseboards, ornamental & trim

**(G-419)**
**JAX AMUSEMENTS**
11109 Fruit Rd  (62001-2707)
PHONE....................618 887-4761
Jack Reeves, *Owner*
**EMP:** 3 EST: 1982
**SALES (est):** 246K  **Privately Held**
**SIC:** 3581  Automatic vending machines

### Allendale
*Wabash County*

**(G-420)**
**ALLENDALE GRAVEL CO  INC (PA)**
18306 Wabash 18 Ave  (62410-2143)
PHONE....................618 263-3521
Fax: 618 263-3747
James E Litherland Jr, *President*
Sue Murphy, *Corp Secy*
**EMP:** 4 EST: 1931
**SQ FT:** 2,800
**SALES:** 3.5MM  **Privately Held**
**SIC:** 1611  1629  1442  General contractor, highway & street construction; waste water & sewage treatment plant construction; gravel mining

### Allerton
*Vermilion County*

**(G-421)**
**ELEMENT COLLECTION**
2731 County Road 100 N  (61810-9606)
P.O. Box 81, Urbana  (61803-0081)
PHONE....................217 898-5175
Theodore Gray, *Owner*
**EMP:** 2
**SALES:** 200K  **Privately Held**
**SIC:** 2741  Miscellaneous publishing

### Alma
*Marion County*

**(G-422)**
**ORCHARD VIEW WINERY**
307 2nd St  (62807-2138)
PHONE....................618 547-9911
Bradley Mazanek, *Executive Asst*
**EMP:** 4
**SALES (est):** 239K  **Privately Held**
**SIC:** 2084  Wines, brandy & brandy spirits

**(G-423)**
**SAFE SHEDS  INC**
7029 Parrill Rd  (62807-1913)
PHONE....................888 556-1531
Donald Guymon, *President*
**EMP:** 7
**SALES:** 370K  **Privately Held**
**SIC:** 3272  Concrete products

**(G-424)**
**SUMMERVLLE CONSULTING SVCS LLC**
8655 Garrett Rd  (62807-1100)
PHONE....................618 547-7142
Summerville Scott D, *Principal*
**EMP:** 3
**SALES (est):** 205.6K  **Privately Held**
**SIC:** 3421  Knife blades & blanks

### Alpha
*Henry County*

**(G-425)**
**ALL-FEED PROC & PACKG INC (PA)**
210 S 1st St  (61413-9480)
PHONE....................309 629-0001
Timothy Anderson, *President*
Deete Lyndsey, *Accountant*
▲ **EMP:** 14
**SALES (est):** 2.1MM  **Privately Held**
**WEB:** www.allfeed.com
**SIC:** 2048  Canned pet food (except dog & cat)

### Alsip
*Cook County*

**(G-426)**
**A & R MACHINE  INC**
12340 S Keeler Ave  (60803-1813)
PHONE....................708 388-4764
Fax: 708 388-4749
Roman Plewa, *President*
Jane Plewa, *Corp Secy*
Andrew Siemon, *Vice Pres*
**EMP:** 8
**SQ FT:** 8,400
**SALES (est):** 1.5MM  **Privately Held**
**WEB:** www.armachine.com
**SIC:** 3599  Machine shop, jobbing & repair

**(G-427)**
**A B S EMBROIDERY INC**
4814 W 129th St  (60803-3016)
PHONE....................708 597-7785
William Dawson, *President*
Allen Irvinsks, *Vice Pres*
Scott Parker, *Admin Sec*
**EMP:** 7
**SALES (est):** 430.1K  **Privately Held**
**SIC:** 2395  Embroidery products, except schiffli machine

**(G-428)**
**ACCORD CARTON CO**
Also Called: Accord Packaging
6155 W 115th St  (60803-5153)
PHONE....................708 272-3050
Robert S Codo, *President*
William M Codo, *Vice Pres*
Robert Mintari, *Opers Mgr*
Ruthie Keefner, *Facilities Mgr*
Jim Coen, *Sales Staff*
**EMP:** 125 EST: 1940
**SQ FT:** 120,000
**SALES (est):** 38.7MM  **Privately Held**
**WEB:** www.accordcarton.com
**SIC:** 2657  2789  2759  Folding paperboard boxes; bookbinding & related work; commercial printing

**(G-429)**
**ACCORD PACKAGING  LLC**
6155 W 115th St  (60803-5153)
PHONE....................708 272-3050
Ruthie Keefner, *Manager*
**EMP:** 35
**SALES (est):** 7.3MM  **Privately Held**
**SIC:** 2631  Container, packaging & boxboard

**(G-430)**
**ACE METAL SPINNING INC**
11630 S Mayfield Ave  (60803-6010)
PHONE....................708 389-5635
Fax: 708 389-5699
James J Baur, *President*
George Baur, *Corp Secy*

Claudia Borowski, *Manager*
**EMP:** 18
**SQ FT:** 17,000
**SALES (est):** 3.3MM **Privately Held**
**WEB:** www.acemetalspinning.com
**SIC:** 3469 3444 Spinning metal for the trade; sheet metalwork

### (G-431)
### ALL PURPOSE PRTG & BUS FORMS
12557 S Laramie Ave 2 (60803-3223)
**PHONE**.................................708 389-9192
**Fax:** 708 389-9192
Calvin R Hulford, *Owner*
**EMP:** 2 **EST:** 1963
**SQ FT:** 2,300
**SALES:** 250K **Privately Held**
**SIC:** 2752 5112 2791 Commercial printing, offset; business forms; typesetting

### (G-432)
### ALSIP MINIMILL LLC
13101 S Pulaski Rd (60803-2026)
**PHONE**.................................708 272-8700
Mike Rubinstin, *CFO*
Pat Polacek, *Controller*
John Potocsnak, *Mng Member*
**EMP:** 10
**SALES (est):** 1.4MM **Privately Held**
**SIC:** 2621 Paper mills

### (G-433)
### ANIKAM INC
Also Called: Allegra Print & Imaging
12549 S Holiday Dr (60803-3238)
**PHONE**.................................708 385-0200
Helen Makina, *Ch of Bd*
James Makina, *President*
Steve Makina, *Vice Pres*
Edward Makina, *Manager*
Ilene Moran, *Admin Sec*
**EMP:** 8 **EST:** 1986
**SQ FT:** 7,500
**SALES:** 991K **Privately Held**
**SIC:** 2752 Commercial printing, offset

### (G-434)
### ANTON-ARGIRES INC
12345 S Latrobe Ave (60803-3210)
**PHONE**.................................708 388-6250
George Argires, *CEO*
Steven Argires, *Corp Secy*
▲ **EMP:** 6 **EST:** 1949
**SQ FT:** 6,000
**SALES:** 3.7MM **Privately Held**
**WEB:** www.argires.com
**SIC:** 5145 2068 Nuts, salted or roasted; salted & roasted nuts & seeds

### (G-435)
### ARKEMA INC
Also Called: Arkema Coating Resins
12840 S Pulaski Rd (60803-1917)
**PHONE**.................................708 396-3001
Patrick E Gottschalk, *CEO*
Rory Watts, *Maintence Staff*
**EMP:** 123
**SALES (corp-wide):** 20MM **Privately Held**
**SIC:** 2812 Chlorine, compressed or liquefied; caustic soda, sodium hydroxide
**HQ:** Arkema Inc.
900 First Ave
King Of Prussia PA 19406
610 205-7000

### (G-436)
### ARKEMA INC
12840 S Pulaski Rd (60803-1917)
**PHONE**.................................708 385-2188
**EMP:** 123
**SALES (corp-wide):** 18.6MM **Privately Held**
**SIC:** 2812 Mfg Alkalies/Chlorine
**HQ:** Arkema Inc.
900 First Ave
King Of Prussia PA 19406
610 205-7000

### (G-437)
### ASAI CHICAGO
12559 S Holiday Dr Ste C (60803-3258)
**PHONE**.................................708 239-0133
**Fax:** 708 239-0117
Sam Sarcinelli, *Owner*
**EMP:** 10
**SALES (est):** 993.4K **Privately Held**
**WEB:** www.asaichicago.com
**SIC:** 3578 Automatic teller machines (ATM)

### (G-438)
### B ALLAN GRAPHICS INC
Also Called: Raised Expectations
11629 S Mayfield Ave (60803-6007)
**PHONE**.................................708 396-1704
**Fax:** 708 396-9954
Bruce Smith, *President*
Mary Snyder, *Office Mgr*
**EMP:** 12
**SALES (est):** 1.5MM **Privately Held**
**SIC:** 2752 2796 2791 2759 Commercial printing, offset; platemaking services; typesetting; commercial printing; die-cut paper & board

### (G-439)
### BBC FASTENERS INC
4210 W Shirley Ln (60803-2410)
**PHONE**.................................708 597-9100
**Fax:** 708 597-0423
Gerald E Sullivan, *President*
Eugene R Sullivan, *Principal*
James L Dion, *Vice Pres*
Stacy Foster, *Treasurer*
Kathy Sullivan, *Manager*
**EMP:** 45
**SQ FT:** 38,000
**SALES (est):** 12.8MM **Privately Held**
**WEB:** www.bbcfasteners.com
**SIC:** 3452 Bolts, metal; screws, metal; nuts, metal

### (G-440)
### BEACON INC
12223 S Laramie Ave (60803-3129)
**PHONE**.................................708 544-9900
Wayne Jagush, *President*
Jim Niemec, *General Mgr*
▼ **EMP:** 10
**SQ FT:** 11,000
**SALES (est):** 1MM **Privately Held**
**WEB:** www.beaconmetals.com
**SIC:** 3556 Food products machinery

### (G-441)
### BERRY GLOBAL INC
Also Called: Landis Plastics
5750 W 118th St (60803-6012)
**PHONE**.................................708 396-1470
Renee Alvarez, *COO*
Jennifer Bjerga, *Vice Pres*
James Torgerson, *Vice Pres*
Steve Pace, *Opers Mgr*
James Kerkstra, *Human Res Mgr*
**EMP:** 300
**SALES (corp-wide):** 6.4B **Publicly Held**
**WEB:** www.6sens.com
**SIC:** 3089 Bottle caps, molded plastic
**HQ:** Berry Global, Inc.
101 Oakley St
Evansville IN 47710
812 424-2904

### (G-442)
### BERRY GLOBAL FILMS LLC
12900 S Pulaski Rd (60803-2005)
**PHONE**.................................708 239-4619
**Fax:** 708 389-3721
Rich Przytula, *Purchasing*
Joe Oliva, *Manager*
**EMP:** 70
**SALES (corp-wide):** 6.4B **Publicly Held**
**WEB:** www.aepinc.com
**SIC:** 3081 Polyethylene film
**HQ:** Berry Global Films, Llc
95 Chestnut Ridge Rd
Montvale NJ 07645
201 641-6600

### (G-443)
### BROTHERS LEAL LLC
12007 S Cicero Ave (60803-2312)
**PHONE**.................................708 385-4400
Emmanuel Leal, *Principal*
**EMP:** 5
**SALES (est):** 675.2K **Privately Held**
**SIC:** 2541 Counter & sink tops

### (G-444)
### CAMBRIDGE-LEE INDUSTRIES LLC
12255 S Laramie Ave (60803-3129)
**PHONE**.................................708 388-0121
Bob Armon, *Manager*
**EMP:** 10
**SALES (corp-wide):** 1B **Privately Held**
**WEB:** www.united-copper.com
**SIC:** 3339 Primary nonferrous metals
**HQ:** Cambridge-Lee Industries Llc
86 Tube Dr
Reading PA 19605
610 926-4141

### (G-445)
### CHICAGO DRIVE LINE INC
11500 S Central Ave (60803-3417)
**PHONE**.................................708 385-1900
**Fax:** 708 385-2099
Roy Frestel, *President*
Rudy Krastin, *Manager*
**EMP:** 8
**SQ FT:** 10,000
**SALES (est):** 1.4MM **Privately Held**
**WEB:** www.chicagodriveline.com
**SIC:** 3714 7538 5013 Axles, motor vehicle; drive shafts, motor vehicle; general automotive repair shops; motor vehicle supplies & new parts

### (G-446)
### CHICAGO SHADE MAKERS INC
12617 S Kroll Dr (60803-3221)
**PHONE**.................................708 597-5590
**Fax:** 708 597-4649
Garry Nowiszewski, *President*
**EMP:** 3
**SALES:** 600K **Privately Held**
**SIC:** 2591 Window shades

### (G-447)
### CHICAGO WICKER & TRADING CO
Also Called: Northcape International
5625 W 115th St (60803-5125)
**PHONE**.................................708 563-2890
Thomas Murray, *President*
William Winzel, *Vice Pres*
Erin Walsh, *CFO*
Roy Sparks, *Controller*
Melissa Ruiz, *Accounts Mgr*
▲ **EMP:** 45 **EST:** 1999
**SQ FT:** 89,000
**SALES (est):** 11.5MM **Privately Held**
**WEB:** www.chicagowicker.com
**SIC:** 2511 Lawn furniture: wood

### (G-448)
### CHRISTOS WOODWORKING
5865 W 124th St (60803-3501)
**PHONE**.................................708 975-5045
**EMP:** 4
**SALES (est):** 406.5K **Privately Held**
**SIC:** 2431 Millwork

### (G-449)
### CIRCLE METAL SPECIALTIES INC
4029 W 123rd St (60803-1872)
**PHONE**.................................708 597-1700
**Fax:** 708 597-9913
Robert J Mishka, *President*
Robert M Mishka, *Vice Pres*
Michael Mishka, *Treasurer*
Susan Mishka, *Treasurer*
Maureen Fabrizio, *Admin Sec*
**EMP:** 25
**SQ FT:** 21,000
**SALES (est):** 6.4MM **Privately Held**
**WEB:** www.circlemetal.com
**SIC:** 3441 Fabricated structural metal

### (G-450)
### COCA-COLA REFRESHMENTS USA INC
5321 W 122nd St (60803-3178)
**PHONE**.................................708 597-6700
**Fax:** 708 597-0608
Jerry Ballard, *Superintendent*
Duane Hallstrom, *Vice Pres*
Jason Worby, *Training Dir*
Christine Lewandowski, *Administration*
**EMP:** 220
**SALES (corp-wide):** 41.8B **Publicly Held**
**SIC:** 2086 5149 Soft drinks: packaged in cans, bottles, etc.; groceries & related products
**HQ:** Coca-Cola Refreshments Usa, Inc.
2500 Windy Ridge Pkwy Se
Atlanta GA 30339
770 989-3000

### (G-451)
### COMET CONECTION INC
Also Called: Comet Press
5040 W 127th St (60803-3213)
P.O. Box 252, Oak Forest (60452-0252)
**PHONE**.................................312 243-5400
**Fax:** 312 243-0488
Syed Sharf Alam, *President*
**EMP:** 4
**SQ FT:** 1,450
**SALES (est):** 279.4K **Privately Held**
**SIC:** 7336 2752 7334 5045 Graphic arts & related design; commercial printing, offset; photocopying & duplicating services; computers, peripherals & software

### (G-452)
### CROWN CORK & SEAL USA INC
5555 W 115th St (60803-5178)
**PHONE**.................................708 239-5555
**Fax:** 708 239-5536
Cliff Boisvert, *Engineer*
Phil Kraft, *Engineer*
Yanze LI, *Engineer*
Jim Meyman, *Branch Mgr*
Oscar Blanco, *Manager*
**EMP:** 150
**SALES (corp-wide):** 8.2B **Publicly Held**
**WEB:** www.crowncork.com
**SIC:** 3411 Metal cans
**HQ:** Crown Cork & Seal Usa, Inc.
1 Crown Way
Philadelphia PA 19154
215 698-5100

### (G-453)
### CROWN CORK & SEAL USA INC
11535 S Central Ave (60803-3418)
**PHONE**.................................708 239-5000
**Fax:** 708 239-5010
Faroukh Dhunjisha, *Director*
**EMP:** 118
**SALES (corp-wide):** 8.2B **Publicly Held**
**WEB:** www.crowncork.com
**SIC:** 3411 Metal cans
**HQ:** Crown Cork & Seal Usa, Inc.
1 Crown Way
Philadelphia PA 19154
215 698-5100

### (G-454)
### DAMS INC
5919 W 118th St (60803-3914)
**PHONE**.................................708 385-3092
Dennis G Dams, *President*
**EMP:** 13
**SALES (est):** 3MM **Privately Held**
**SIC:** 3441 Fabricated structural metal

### (G-455)
### DART CASTINGS INC
12400 S Lombard Ln (60803-1823)
**PHONE**.................................708 388-4914
Marek Wolny, *President*
Len Janoski, *Sales Associate*
Teresa Wolny, *Admin Sec*
**EMP:** 50 **EST:** 1994
**SQ FT:** 40,000
**SALES (est):** 11.4MM **Privately Held**
**WEB:** www.dartcasting.com
**SIC:** 3363 3364 Aluminum die-castings; zinc & zinc-base alloy die-castings

### (G-456)
### DAUBERT CROMWELL LLC (PA)
12701 S Ridgeway Ave (60803-1526)
**PHONE**.................................708 293-7750
**Fax:** 708 293-7765
Martin Simpson, *CEO*
Roy Galman, *COO*
Orland Park, *Vice Pres*
Oscar Abello, *CFO*
Gary Schneider, *Regl Sales Mgr*
▲ **EMP:** 50

# GEOGRAPHIC SECTION

**Alsip - Cook County (G-480)**

SALES (est): 13MM  **Privately Held**
WEB: www.daubertcromwell.com
SIC: 2671  Packaging paper & plastics film, coated & laminated

**(G-457)**
**DONSON MACHINE COMPANY**
12416 S Kedvale Ave  (60803-1819)
PHONE..................................708 388-0880
Fax: 708 388-4308
Jim Bettinardi, *CEO*
Joseph Bettinardi, *President*
James Bettinardi, *Vice Pres*
Gina Langdon, *Bookkeeper*
Bill Busby, *Director*
▲ EMP: 80 EST: 1978
SQ FT: 20,000
SALES (est): 17MM  **Privately Held**
SIC: 3599  Machine shop, jobbing & repair

**(G-458)**
**DORALCO  INC**
Also Called: Architectural Metal Solutions
5919 W 118th St  (60803-3914)
PHONE..................................708 388-9324
Fax: 708 388-9392
Matthew Jabaay, *President*
Robert Trainor Jr, *President*
Barbara Blank, *Vice Pres*
Tom O'Malley, *Vice Pres*
Tom Trainor, *CFO*
EMP: 50
SQ FT: 18,000
SALES (est): 12MM  **Privately Held**
WEB: www.doralco.com
SIC: 1751  3231  Window & door installation & erection; doors, glass: made from purchased glass

**(G-459)**
**DURO HILEX POLY  LLC**
12245 S Central Ave  (60803-3407)
PHONE..................................708 385-8674
Tom McCombie, *Purchasing*
Rob Arnold, *Branch Mgr*
EMP: 100
SALES (corp-wide): 2.2B  **Publicly Held**
SIC: 2673  2674  Bags: plastic, laminated & coated; bags: uncoated paper & multiwall
HQ: Duro Bag Manufacturing Company
    7600 Empire Dr
    Florence KY 41042
    859 371-2150

**(G-460)**
**E2S LLC**
5120 W 125th Pl Unit A  (60803-3200)
PHONE..................................708 629-0714
Trevor Reibling, *Accounts Exec*
Michael Barnes,
EMP: 7 EST: 2012
SALES (est): 550K  **Privately Held**
SIC: 8748  3825  1731  8731  Energy conservation consultant; energy measuring equipment, electrical; energy management controls; energy research

**(G-461)**
**EDWARD F DATA**
Also Called: Jr Sons Welding
12625 S Kroll Dr  (60803-3221)
PHONE..................................708 597-0158
Edward F Data, *Owner*
EMP: 3
SALES (est): 104.5K  **Privately Held**
SIC: 7692  Welding repair

**(G-462)**
**ENGINEERED ABRASIVES  INC**
Also Called: E A
11631 S Austin Ave  (60803-6001)
PHONE..................................662 582-4143
Keith Patton, *Superintendent*
Peter Triebe, *Foreman/Supr*
Donna Walczak, *Manager*
Michael Wern, *Admin Sec*
Michael J Wern, *Admin Sec*
◆ EMP: 25
SQ FT: 50,000
SALES (est): 7.9MM  **Privately Held**
WEB: www.engineeredabrasives.com
SIC: 3629  5084  3549  3541  Blasting machines, electrical; industrial machinery & equipment; metalworking machinery; machine tools, metal cutting type

**(G-463)**
**GC AMERICA INC (HQ)**
3737 W 127th St  (60803-1542)
PHONE..................................708 597-0900
Fax: 708 371-5148
Yutaka Suzuki, *President*
M Dean Porter, *President*
Sandy Aron, *General Mgr*
Rich Lehmkuhl, *General Mgr*
Brooke Beeson, *Regional Mgr*
◆ EMP: 150 EST: 1928
SQ FT: 80,000
SALES (est): 52MM
SALES (corp-wide): 553.3MM  **Privately Held**
WEB: www.gcamerica.com
SIC: 3843  Dental equipment & supplies
PA: Gc Corporation
    3-2-14, Hongo
    Bunkyo-Ku TKY 113-0
    338 151-815

**(G-464)**
**GC MANUFACTURING AMERICA LLC**
3737 W 127th St  (60803-1532)
PHONE..................................708 597-0900
Steven Fletcher, *President*
Thomas Hawrysz, *Admin Sec*
EMP: 85
SQ FT: 95,000
SALES (est): 52MM
SALES (corp-wide): 553.3MM  **Privately Held**
SIC: 3843  Dental equipment & supplies
HQ: Gc America Inc.
    3737 W 127th St
    Alsip IL 60803
    708 597-0900

**(G-465)**
**GRASSO GRAPHICS  INC**
Also Called: Kwik Kopy Printing
5156 W 125th Pl  (60803-3200)
PHONE..................................708 489-2060
Fax: 708 489-2084
Salvatore Grasso, *President*
Bert Grasso, *Vice Pres*
Bill Bradshaw, *Sales Associate*
Patricia Grasso, *Admin Sec*
EMP: 8
SALES (est): 950K  **Privately Held**
WEB: www.grassographics.com
SIC: 2752  2791  2789  Commercial printing, lithographic; typesetting; bookbinding & related work

**(G-466)**
**GREIF  INC**
4300 W 130th St  (60803-2003)
P.O. Box 75409, Chicago  (60675-5409)
PHONE..................................708 371-4777
Fax: 708 371-9952
Andre Wooten, *Opers Mgr*
Michael Lesko, *Engineer*
Christine Trocellier, *Human Resources*
Jeff Loyd, *Manager*
Ted Bukowinski, *Technology*
EMP: 39
SALES (corp-wide): 3.3B  **Publicly Held**
WEB: www.greif.com
SIC: 2653  Corrugated & solid fiber boxes
PA: Greif, Inc.
    425 Winter Rd
    Delaware OH 43015
    740 549-6000

**(G-467)**
**GRIFFITH FOODS GROUP INC (PA)**
1 Griffith Ctr  (60803-4701)
PHONE..................................708 371-0900
D L Griffith, *President*
Michael Plichta, *President*
Shyam Mohan, *Managing Dir*
David Kim, *Counsel*
William C Frost, *Senior VP*
◆ EMP: 12 EST: 1919
SQ FT: 250,000
SALES (est): 756.3MM  **Privately Held**
WEB: www.consumerquiz.com
SIC: 2099  Seasonings: dry mixes; spices, including grinding

**(G-468)**
**GRIFFITH FOODS INC (DH)**
12200 S Central Ave  (60803-3408)
PHONE..................................708 371-0900
Dean L Griffith, *Ch of Bd*
Jennifer Convery, *President*
Joseph R Maslick, *CFO*
◆ EMP: 300
SQ FT: 250,000
SALES (est): 150MM
SALES (corp-wide): 756.3MM  **Privately Held**
SIC: 2099  Seasonings: dry mixes; spices, including grinding

**(G-469)**
**GRIFFITH FOODS WORLDWIDE INC (DH)**
Also Called: Griffith Laboratories
12200 S Central Ave  (60803-3408)
PHONE..................................708 371-0900
Dean L Griffith, *Ch of Bd*
Herve De La Vauvre, *President*
Paul Hubner, *Vice Pres*
Steve Ralson, *Production*
Neal Clute, *Purch Mgr*
EMP: 3
SQ FT: 250,000
SALES (est): 214MM
SALES (corp-wide): 756.3MM  **Privately Held**
SIC: 2099  Seasonings: dry mixes; spices, including grinding
HQ: Griffith Foods International Inc.
    1 Griffith Ctr
    Alsip IL 60803
    708 371-0900

**(G-470)**
**HANDS TO WORK RAILROADING**
12217 S Cicero Ave  (60803-2906)
PHONE..................................708 489-9776
Jim Bradley, *Owner*
EMP: 2
SALES (est): 222.7K  **Privately Held**
SIC: 2813  5945  Helium; hobbies

**(G-471)**
**HATTAN TOOL COMPANY**
4909 W 128th Pl  (60803-3011)
PHONE..................................708 597-9308
Fax: 708 597-9308
Robert Hattan, *President*
Loretta Hattan, *Admin Sec*
EMP: 9
SQ FT: 7,000
SALES (est): 1.2MM  **Privately Held**
SIC: 3599  7692  3544  Machine shop, jobbing & repair; welding repair; special dies, tools, jigs & fixtures

**(G-472)**
**HAWK FASTENER SERVICES**
12324 S Laramie Ave  (60803-3231)
PHONE..................................708 489-2000
Fax: 708 599-9943
Joe Lamantia, *Owner*
▲ EMP: 10
SALES (est): 660K  **Privately Held**
SIC: 3965  Fasteners

**(G-473)**
**INDUSTRIAL WELDER REBUILDERS**
11700 S Mayfield Ave  (60803-3565)
PHONE..................................708 371-5688
Fax: 708 371-9665
Arnold Franker, *President*
Margaret Franker, *Vice Pres*
EMP: 5 EST: 1978
SQ FT: 5,050
SALES (est): 846.2K  **Privately Held**
WEB: www.zeonz.net
SIC: 7699  5063  5084  7629  Welding equipment repair; generators; engines & parts, diesel; electrical repair shops; motors & generators; welding apparatus

**(G-474)**
**IPR SYSTEMS INC**
11651 S Mayfield Ave  (60803-6007)
PHONE..................................708 385-7500
Fax: 708 385-7515
Eugene Tylka, *President*
Caroline M Tylka, *Admin Sec*
EMP: 8
SQ FT: 10,000
SALES: 750K  **Privately Held**
WEB: www.iprsys.com
SIC: 3679  3677  3674  3612  Rectifiers, electronic; electronic transformers; semiconductors & related devices; transformers, except electric

**(G-475)**
**J & J CARBIDE & TOOL  INC**
5656 W 120th St  (60803-3410)
PHONE..................................708 489-0300
Fax: 708 489-0396
Spero Pavlopoulous, *President*
Spero Pavlopoulous, *President*
John Pavlopoulos, *Principal*
Thomas Pavlopoulos, *Vice Pres*
Agnes Tucker, *Manager*
▲ EMP: 50 EST: 1966
SQ FT: 20,000
SALES (est): 11.6MM  **Privately Held**
WEB: www.jandjcarbidetool.com
SIC: 3545  3544  Machine tool attachments & accessories; special dies & tools

**(G-476)**
**JERRYS PRO SHOP  INC**
Also Called: Hockey Warehouse
12609 S Kroll Dr  (60803-3221)
PHONE..................................708 597-1144
Fax: 708 597-9737
Jay Kucera, *Manager*
EMP: 9
SALES (corp-wide): 3.6MM  **Privately Held**
SIC: 3949  Hockey equipment & supplies, general
PA: Jerry's Pro Shop, Inc.
    501 Morse Ave Ste G
    Schaumburg IL
    847 584-0305

**(G-477)**
**K C AUDIO**
4824 W 129th St  (60803-3016)
PHONE..................................708 636-4928
Fax: 708 396-8861
Karl Cira, *Owner*
EMP: 2
SALES (est): 281.6K  **Privately Held**
SIC: 3651  Audio electronic systems

**(G-478)**
**KASTALON  INC**
Also Called: Kastalon Polyurethane Products
4100 W 124th Pl  (60803-1876)
PHONE..................................708 389-2210
Fax: 708 389-0432
R Bruce Dement, *President*
Thomas Ames, *Engineer*
Ted Burke, *Design Engr*
Darrell Johanneman, *CFO*
Michael K Dement, *Admin Sec*
▲ EMP: 75 EST: 1963
SQ FT: 50,000
SALES (est): 17.7MM  **Privately Held**
WEB: www.kastalon.com
SIC: 3089  Plastic hardware & building products

**(G-479)**
**KING METAL CO**
4200 W 122nd St  (60803-2408)
PHONE..................................708 388-3845
Fax: 708 388-3874
Douglas M Heinking, *President*
Mary Ann Heinking, *Admin Sec*
EMP: 6
SQ FT: 5,200
SALES (est): 1MM  **Privately Held**
SIC: 3446  3441  Ornamental metalwork; fabricated structural metal

**(G-480)**
**KOCSIS BROTHERS MACHINE CO (PA)**
11755 S Austin Ave  (60803-6002)
PHONE..................................708 597-8110
Louis Kocsis, *President*
Todd Peterson, *Engineer*
John Sawczenko, *Engineer*
Jason Kujak, *Design Engr*
Gerald Sullivan, *CFO*
▲ EMP: 90

# Alsip - Cook County (G-481)

SQ FT: 55,000
SALES (est): 23.3MM  **Privately Held**
WEB: www.kocsisbros.com
SIC: **3599** Machine shop, jobbing & repair

**(G-481)**
**KOCSIS TECHNOLOGIES INC (PA)**
11755 S Austin Ave  (60803-6002)
PHONE ................................... 708 597-4177
Fax: 708 371-6560
Sandra Kocsis, *President*
Tim Richards, *General Mgr*
Louis Kocsis Jr, *Vice Pres*
Richard Spence, *QC Mgr*
Todd Peterson, *Engineer*
EMP: 15
SALES (est): 15.6MM  **Privately Held**
WEB: www.kocsistech.com
SIC: **3593** 3492 Fluid power actuators, hydraulic or pneumatic; fluid power cylinders, hydraulic or pneumatic; control valves, fluid power: hydraulic & pneumatic

**(G-482)**
**KOCSIS TECHNOLOGIES INC**
Also Called: Kocisis Brothers Machine
11755 S Austin Ave  (60803-6002)
PHONE ................................... 708 597-4177
Brandon Richards, *General Mgr*
Louis Kocsis Sr, *Manager*
EMP: 5
SALES (corp-wide): 15.6MM  **Privately Held**
WEB: www.kocsistech.com
SIC: **3593** 3594 3492 Fluid power actuators, hydraulic or pneumatic; fluid power cylinders, hydraulic or pneumatic; hydrostatic drives (transmissions); control valves, fluid power: hydraulic & pneumatic
PA: Kocsis Technologies, Inc.
11755 S Austin Ave
Alsip IL 60803
708 597-4177

**(G-483)**
**LABRIOLA BAKING COMPANY LLC**
3701 W 128th Pl  (60803-1514)
PHONE ................................... 708 377-0400
Fax: 708 385-4991
Ken Cotich, *CEO*
Bret Weaver, *President*
Robert Parnow, *Chairman*
Terry Dempsey, *CFO*
Gigi Curran, *Human Res Dir*
▲ EMP: 235
SALES (est): 599.1K
SALES (corp-wide): 23.6MM  **Privately Held**
SIC: **2051** Bread, all types (white, wheat, rye, etc); fresh or frozen; bakery: wholesale or wholesale/retail combined
PA: Plaza Belmont Fund Iii, Lp
8016 State Line Rd # 215
Prairie Village KS 66208
913 381-7177

**(G-484)**
**LOMBARD INVESTMENT COMPANY (PA)**
4245 W 123rd St  (60803-1805)
PHONE ................................... 708 389-1060
George Lombard, *President*
John Lombard, *Vice Pres*
Daniel J Lombard, *Admin Sec*
EMP: 75
SQ FT: 50,000
SALES: 784.8K  **Privately Held**
SIC: **1542** 1791 3272 Commercial & office building contractors; precast concrete structural framing or panels, placing of; concrete products, precast

**(G-485)**
**LUTTRELL ENGRAVING INC**
Also Called: Lei Graphics
5000 W 128th Pl  (60803-3230)
PHONE ................................... 708 489-3800
Fax: 708 489-2202
Ravon Luttrell, *President*
Christine Luttrell, *Corp Secy*
EMP: 20
SQ FT: 9,916
SALES: 2MM  **Privately Held**
WEB: www.luttrellengraving.com
SIC: **3555** 7336 2796 Printing plates; graphic arts & related design; platemaking services

**(G-486)**
**MACHINE CONTROL SYSTEMS INC**
12549 S Laramie Ave  (60803-3223)
PHONE ................................... 708 597-1200
Fax: 708 597-1288
William Plummer, *Manager*
EMP: 6
SQ FT: 6,000
SALES (corp-wide): 680.6K  **Privately Held**
SIC: **3613** 3625 Control panels, electric; generator control & metering panels; relays & industrial controls
PA: Machine Control Systems, Inc
12424 S Austin Ave
Palos Heights IL 60463
708 389-2160

**(G-487)**
**MACHINE WORKS INC**
5621 W 120th St  (60803-3449)
PHONE ................................... 708 597-1665
Matthew Jabaay, *President*
Dottie Maltio, *Manager*
EMP: 14 EST: 1971
SQ FT: 14,000
SALES (est): 1.7MM  **Privately Held**
SIC: **3544** Special dies & tools; jigs & fixtures

**(G-488)**
**MARTIN EXPLORATION MGT CO (PA)**
Also Called: Martin Oil
4501 W 127th St  (60803-2620)
PHONE ................................... 708 385-6500
Carl C Greer, *President*
Harry Vasels, *Vice Pres*
EMP: 9
SQ FT: 3,550
SALES (est): 3.3MM  **Privately Held**
SIC: **1382** Oil & gas exploration services

**(G-489)**
**MASTERS & ALLOY LLC**
12841 S Pulaski Rd  (60803-1916)
PHONE ................................... 312 582-1880
EMP: 3
SALES (est): 273K  **Privately Held**
SIC: **3313** Alloys, additive, except copper: not made in blast furnaces

**(G-490)**
**MAUREY INSTRUMENT CORP**
5959 W 115th St  (60803-5151)
PHONE ................................... 708 388-9898
Fax: 708 581-2576
Elizabeth Petrus, *President*
Mary Kay Gadomski, *Vice Pres*
Michelle Moore, *Office Mgr*
Terrence Beverley, *Manager*
EMP: 16 EST: 1952
SQ FT: 10,000
SALES: 1MM  **Privately Held**
WEB: www.maureyinstrument.com
SIC: **3825** 3676 3625 3621 Potentiometric instruments, except industrial process type; electronic resistors; relays & industrial controls; motors & generators

**(G-491)**
**MIDWAY MACHINE & TOOL CO INC**
5828 W 117th Pl  (60803-6019)
PHONE ................................... 708 385-3450
John J Koszylko, *President*
EMP: 7
SQ FT: 9,000
SALES (est): 942.2K  **Privately Held**
WEB: www.midwaymachining.com
SIC: **3599** 7692 Machine shop, jobbing & repair; welding repair

**(G-492)**
**MIDWEST GROUP DIST & SVCS INC**
Also Called: Ewert
5801 W 117th Pl  (60803-6018)
PHONE ................................... 708 597-0059
Beth Rockouski, *President*
Michael Rockouski, *Principal*
Joe Bartosek, *Treasurer*
Demetra Delfiacco, *Admin Sec*
EMP: 7 EST: 2013
SQ FT: 5,000
SALES (est): 359.9K  **Privately Held**
SIC: **3429** Door opening & closing devices, except electrical; keys, locks & related hardware; door locks, bolts & checks; keys & key blanks

**(G-493)**
**MIDWEST LMINATING COATINGS INC**
12650 S Laramie Ave  (60803-3226)
PHONE ................................... 708 653-9500
Philip G Carollo, *President*
Jay Carollo, *Vice Pres*
John Watkins, *Treasurer*
Jo Ann Miller, *Admin Sec*
EMP: 25
SQ FT: 100,000
SALES (est): 6.6MM  **Privately Held**
WEB: www.midwestlaminating.com
SIC: **2671** 3353 3081 2672 Paper coated or laminated for packaging; plastic film, coated or laminated for packaging; foil, aluminum; unsupported plastics film & sheet; coated & laminated paper

**(G-494)**
**MIDWEST MACHINE SERVICE INC**
5632 Pleasant Blvd  (60803)
PHONE ................................... 708 229-1122
Fax: 708 636-0022
Ronald Zima, *President*
Jeff Eddington, *Vice Pres*
Mark Larson, *Regl Sales Mgr*
EMP: 15
SQ FT: 2,000
SALES (est): 2MM  **Privately Held**
SIC: **3599** 7629 Machine shop, jobbing & repair; electrical repair shops

**(G-495)**
**MOBILOC LLC**
5800 W 117th Pl  (60803-6019)
PHONE ................................... 773 742-1329
Charles Morrissey, *Chairman*
EMP: 9
SALES (est): 831.1K  **Privately Held**
SIC: **3699** Security devices

**(G-496)**
**NAEGELE INC**
5661 W 120th St  (60803-3449)
PHONE ................................... 708 388-7766
Fax: 708 388-7799
Richard Naegele, *President*
Mike Philip, *Sales Mgr*
▲ EMP: 6
SALES (est): 500K  **Privately Held**
WEB: www.naegele-inc.com
SIC: **2499** Applicators, wood

**(G-497)**
**NATIONAL DIRECT LIGHTING**
4101 W 123rd St  (60803-1803)
PHONE ................................... 708 371-4950
Robert Sorensen, *President*
Kevin Krantz, *COO*
Jim Ouellette, *Vice Pres*
EMP: 25 EST: 1975
SALES (est): 1.7MM  **Privately Held**
SIC: **3641** Electric lamps

**(G-498)**
**NELSON SASH SYSTEMS INC**
Also Called: Nss Exteriors
4650 W 120th St  (60803-2317)
PHONE ................................... 708 385-5815
Paul Mitoraj, *President*
Charise Mitoraj, *Admin Sec*
EMP: 8
SQ FT: 12,000
SALES: 1.3MM  **Privately Held**
SIC: **3442** Window & door frames; sash, door or window: metal

**(G-499)**
**NEW PROCESS STEEL LP**
5761 W 118th St  (60803-6011)
PHONE ................................... 708 389-3482
Fax: 708 389-9835
Mark Neumann, *Purchasing*
Tom Claes, *Branch Mgr*
EMP: 75
SALES (corp-wide): 305.4MM  **Privately Held**
SIC: **5051** 3469 Sheets, metal; steel; sheets, galvanized or other coated; stamping metal for the trade
PA: New Process Steel, L.P.
1322 N Post Oak Rd
Houston TX 77055
713 686-9631

**(G-500)**
**NORTHERN PRODUCTS COMPANY**
11536 S Central Ave  (60803-3417)
PHONE ................................... 708 597-8501
Fax: 708 597-3056
John M Carmody, *President*
Kathy Mashin, *COO*
Dan Mallek, *Vice Pres*
Dave Gibson, *Opers Mgr*
Jennifer Fox, *Director*
EMP: 65
SQ FT: 20,000
SALES (est): 11.6MM  **Privately Held**
WEB: www.northernproducts.net
SIC: **3086** Packaging & shipping materials, foamed plastic

**(G-501)**
**NUFARM AMERICAS INC (HQ)**
Also Called: Nufarm North American Office
11901 S Austin Ave Ste A  (60803-6013)
PHONE ................................... 708 377-1330
Fax: 630 455-2001
Brendan Deck, *President*
Dale Mellody, *General Mgr*
Kim Bedard, *Business Mgr*
Keith Moon, *Vice Pres*
Thomas Lyons, *VP Opers*
◆ EMP: 60
SQ FT: 15,000
SALES: 653.9MM
SALES (corp-wide): 2B  **Privately Held**
WEB: www.nufarm.com
SIC: **2869** 2879 Industrial organic chemicals; agricultural chemicals
PA: Nufarm Limited
103-105 Pipe Rd
Laverton North VIC 3026
392 821-000

**(G-502)**
**NUMERICAL CONTROL INCORPORATED**
12325 S Keeler Ave  (60803-1812)
PHONE ................................... 708 389-8140
Fax: 708 389-8156
Timothy Gorham, *President*
Douglas Buchler, *President*
EMP: 9
SQ FT: 6,000
SALES (est): 1.6MM  **Privately Held**
SIC: **3569** 7699 3613 Assembly machines, non-metalworking; professional instrument repair services; switchgear & switchboard apparatus

**(G-503)**
**OM PRINTING CORPORATION**
Also Called: Endpoint Graphics
12250 S Ccero Ave Ste 110  (60803)
P.O. Box 1147, Westmont  (60559-8347)
PHONE ................................... 708 482-4750
Nag Sripada, *President*
Kameswar Sripada, *Vice Pres*
EMP: 6
SQ FT: 3,000
SALES (est): 667.2K  **Privately Held**
SIC: **2752** Commercial printing, offset

## Alsip - Cook County (G-530)

**(G-504)**
**OZINGA CHICAGO READY MIX CON**
12660 S Laramie Ave (60803-3226)
PHONE..................708 479-9050
EMP: 43
SALES (corp-wide): 221.8MM **Privately Held**
SIC: 3273 Ready-mixed concrete
HQ: Ozinga Chicago Ready Mix Concrete, Inc
2255 S Lumber St
Chicago IL 60616

**(G-505)**
**PC MARBLE INC**
5859 W 117th Pl (60803-6018)
PHONE..................708 385-3360
Attila Suto, *President*
EMP: 23
SQ FT: 1,500
SALES (est): 2.4MM **Privately Held**
SIC: 1411 Marble, dimension-quarrying

**(G-506)**
**PENNANT FOODS**
11746 S Austin Ave (60803-6003)
PHONE..................708 752-8730
EMP: 4 EST: 2008
SALES (est): 365.6K **Privately Held**
SIC: 5141 2099 Groceries, general line; food preparations

**(G-507)**
**PETERSON ELCTR-MSICAL PDTS INC**
11601 S Mayfield Ave (60803-6007)
PHONE..................708 388-3311
Fax: 708 388-3341
Scott Peterson, *President*
Richard Peterson, *Chairman*
Patrick Bovenizer, *Vice Pres*
Peter Borsa, *Purch Agent*
Bob Dommer, *Engineer*
▲ EMP: 38
SQ FT: 18,000
SALES (est): 7.6MM **Privately Held**
WEB: www.petersonemp.com
SIC: 3679 3931 Electronic switches; musical instruments

**(G-508)**
**PHOENIX BUSINESS SOLUTIONS LLC**
12543 S Laramie Ave (60803-3223)
PHONE..................708 388-1330
Jim Kapustiak, *Superintendent*
Brian Richardson, *Foreman/Supr*
Peggy Hrindak, *Sales Mgr*
Janousek Gerard, *Mng Member*
Mike Janousek, *Sr Project Mgr*
EMP: 41
SQ FT: 5,000
SALES (est): 9.5MM **Privately Held**
WEB: www.phoenixbs.com
SIC: 1731 2752 General electrical contractor; advertising posters, lithographed

**(G-509)**
**PINTAS CULTURED MARBLE**
5859 W 117th Pl (60803-6018)
PHONE..................708 385-3360
Fax: 847 385-5918
John A Pinta, *President*
Gerald Pinta, *Vice Pres*
James Pinta, *Vice Pres*
Mike Manion, *Controller*
Roy Botello, *Manager*
EMP: 26
SQ FT: 42,000
SALES (est): 1.7MM **Privately Held**
SIC: 3281 2434 2821 Marble, building: cut & shaped; wood kitchen cabinets; plastics materials & resins

**(G-510)**
**PLASTIPAK PACKAGING INC**
12325 S Laramie Ave (60803-3206)
PHONE..................708 385-0721
Fax: 708 385-1421
Brian Hopf, *Plant Mgr*
Perry Dailey, *Branch Mgr*
Tricia Kennedy, *Manager*
EMP: 105

SALES (corp-wide): 36.3MM **Privately Held**
WEB: www.plastipak.com
SIC: 3089 3085 Pallets, plastic; plastics bottles
HQ: Plastipak Packaging, Inc.
41605 Ann Arbor Rd E
Plymouth MI 48170
734 455-3600

**(G-511)**
**POLMAX LLC**
Also Called: Experior Transport
12161 S Central Ave (60803-3405)
PHONE..................708 843-8300
Tom Dulian, *CEO*
Norbert Loszewski, *President*
Konrad Szczepaniec, *Assoc VP*
Conrad Szccetaniez, *Controller*
Lynn Koclanis,
EMP: 250
SQ FT: 2,000
SALES (est): 62.8MM **Privately Held**
SIC: 4212 3829 4111 Local trucking, without storage; transits, surveyors'; local & suburban transit

**(G-512)**
**PPG INDUSTRIES INC**
Also Called: PPG 5524
5151 W 122nd St (60803-3102)
PHONE..................708 597-7044
Fax: 708 597-1492
Chris Gallus, *Branch Mgr*
Brian Bulger, *Manager*
EMP: 4
SALES (corp-wide): 14.7B **Publicly Held**
WEB: www.ppg.com
SIC: 2851 Paints & allied products
PA: Ppg Industries, Inc.
1 Ppg Pl
Pittsburgh PA 15272
412 434-3131

**(G-513)**
**PRESTONE PRODUCTS CORPORATION**
Also Called: Honeywell
13160 S Pulaski Rd (60803-2009)
PHONE..................708 371-3000
Rob Salas, *Plant Mgr*
Donald Hampton, *Plant Mgr*
Tom Hedges, *Purch Mgr*
Daniel Pintar, *Research*
Dave Thompson, *Controller*
EMP: 65
SALES (corp-wide): 496.1K **Privately Held**
WEB: www.honeywell.com
SIC: 2899 Antifreeze compounds
HQ: Prestone Products Corporation
1900 W Field Ct
Lake Forest IL 60045

**(G-514)**
**PROCESS AND CONTROL SYSTEMS**
5836 W 117th Pl (60803-6019)
PHONE..................708 293-0557
Fax: 708 293-0589
John Wojcik, *President*
Jeff Koehler, *Vice Pres*
Karl Kurgvel, *Vice Pres*
Sandy Farenga, *Purch Agent*
John Frederick, *Admin Sec*
EMP: 17
SQ FT: 10,000
SALES: 3.8MM **Privately Held**
WEB: www.pacs-inc.com
SIC: 7371 3625 Custom computer programming services; control equipment, electric

**(G-515)**
**QUALITY SNACK FOODS INC**
Also Called: Q S F
3750 W 131st St (60803-1503)
PHONE..................708 377-7120
Fax: 773 285-8662
Victor L Sharp Jr, *President*
Gary S Trepina, *Exec VP*
Tom Musil, *Site Mgr*
Deborah L Trepina, *Treasurer*
Victor Mendoza, *Manager*
◆ EMP: 70
SQ FT: 25,000

SALES (est): 12.5MM **Privately Held**
WEB: www.qualitysnackfoods.com
SIC: 2096 Potato chips & similar snacks

**(G-516)**
**R K PRECISION MACHINE INC**
12512 S Springfield Ave (60803-1409)
PHONE..................574 293-0231
Tom Rosinski, *President*
EMP: 3 EST: 1957
SQ FT: 5,500
SALES (est): 210K **Privately Held**
SIC: 3599 Machine shop, jobbing & repair

**(G-517)**
**RAE PRODUCTS AND CHEM CORP (PA)**
11638 S Mayfield Ave (60803-6010)
PHONE..................708 396-1984
Donna Gruenberg, *President*
Samantha Zickus, *Treasurer*
Kurt Gruenberg, *Manager*
Samantha Morek, *Admin Sec*
EMP: 6
SQ FT: 46,000
SALES (est): 7MM **Privately Held**
SIC: 5169 3542 Sealants; marking machines

**(G-518)**
**RELIANCE DENTAL MFG CO**
5805 W 117th Pl (60803-6018)
P.O. Box 38, Worth (60482-0038)
PHONE..................708 597-6694
Fax: 708 597-7560
Robert Faxel, *President*
Richard Faxel, *Vice Pres*
EMP: 7
SQ FT: 7,500
SALES (est): 840K **Privately Held**
WEB: www.stcglobal.net
SIC: 3843 Dental materials

**(G-519)**
**RESOURCE PLASTICS INC**
5623 W 115th St (60803-5125)
PHONE..................708 389-3558
Fax: 708 389-3592
Bill Steinhaus, *President*
Bob Murphy, *President*
Kimberly McCormies, *Manager*
EMP: 70
SQ FT: 170,563
SALES: 23.2MM **Privately Held**
WEB: www.resource-plastics.com
SIC: 5085 3089 Industrial supplies; plastic processing

**(G-520)**
**RICHARDS COMPANY II INC**
3555 W 123rd St (60803-4125)
PHONE..................708 385-6633
William F Abel, *Manager*
EMP: 10
SALES (corp-wide): 4.5MM **Privately Held**
WEB: www.wcrichards.com
SIC: 2851 5198 Paints & allied products; paints
PA: The Richards Company Ii Inc
3555 W 123rd St
Alsip IL
708 385-6633

**(G-521)**
**RJL INC**
Also Called: Labriola
3701 W 128th Pl (60803-1514)
PHONE..................708 385-4884
◆ EMP: 235
SQ FT: 62,000
SALES (est): 65.7MM **Privately Held**
WEB: www.labriolabaking.com
SIC: 2051 Bread, Cake, And Related Products

**(G-522)**
**RM LUCAS CO (PA)**
Also Called: Lucas Coatings
12400 S Laramie Ave (60803-3209)
PHONE..................773 523-4300
Fax: 773 523-3290
Robert Barry, *President*
Brandon Applegate, *Controller*
Barbara Zahorik, *Accounting Mgr*
Joe Murphy, *Sales Dir*

Tom Nelson, *Sales Staff*
▼ EMP: 35 EST: 1935
SQ FT: 92,000
SALES (est): 15.6MM **Privately Held**
SIC: 2952 2891 1761 Asphalt felts & coatings; adhesives & sealants; roofing contractor

**(G-523)**
**ROOSEVELT PAPER COMPANY**
5100 W 123rd St (60803-3106)
PHONE..................708 653-5121
Roger Jackman, *Maint Spvr*
Bob Tureck, *Branch Mgr*
EMP: 25
SALES (corp-wide): 198.7MM **Privately Held**
SIC: 2679 Paper products, converted
PA: Roosevelt Paper Company
1 Roosevelt Dr
Mount Laurel NJ 08054
856 303-4100

**(G-524)**
**RPI EXTRUSION CO**
5623 W 115th St (60803-5125)
PHONE..................708 389-2584
Robert Murphy, *Owner*
EMP: 5
SALES (est): 583.4K **Privately Held**
SIC: 3089 Extruded finished plastic products

**(G-525)**
**RUSSO WHOLESALE MEAT INC**
12306 S Cicero Ave (60803-2908)
PHONE..................708 385-0500
Frank Russo, *President*
Joseph Russo, *Admin Sec*
EMP: 5 EST: 1995
SQ FT: 2,700
SALES (est): 729K **Privately Held**
SIC: 2013 5147 2045 2033 Sausages & related products, from purchased meat; meats & meat products; pizza mixes: from purchased flour; pizza doughs, prepared: from purchased flour; pizza sauce: packaged in cans, jars, etc.; pizza supplies

**(G-526)**
**S & W MACHINE WORKS INC**
12623 S Kroll Dr (60803-3221)
PHONE..................708 597-6043
Fax: 708 597-9974
Phillip Wisniewski, *President*
William Shalloo, *Admin Sec*
EMP: 6
SQ FT: 3,600
SALES (est): 852.8K **Privately Held**
SIC: 3599 Machine shop, jobbing & repair

**(G-527)**
**SEALMASTER/ALSIP**
5844 W 117th Pl (60803-6019)
PHONE..................708 489-0900
Kyle Arlen, *Principal*
EMP: 3
SALES (est): 226.9K **Privately Held**
SIC: 2951 Asphalt paving mixtures & blocks

**(G-528)**
**SIGN OUTLET INC**
5516 W Cal Sag Rd (60803-3309)
PHONE..................708 824-2222
Darren Rust, *President*
EMP: 4
SQ FT: 3,000
SALES (est): 639.9K **Privately Held**
SIC: 3993 Neon signs

**(G-529)**
**SOTIROS FOODS INC**
12560 S Holiday Dr Ste B (60803-3248)
PHONE..................708 371-0002
Glynn Searl, *President*
EMP: 4
SALES (est): 878.8K **Privately Held**
SIC: 5141 2099 5149 Groceries, general line; food preparations; groceries & related products

**(G-530)**
**SOUTHWEST PRINTING CO**
12003 S Pulaski Rd (60803-1221)
PHONE..................708 389-0800

## Alsip - Cook County (G-531)

Fax: 708 389-0802
Paul Krueger, *President*
Neva C Krueger, *Treasurer*
Tina McGreevy, *Office Mgr*
EMP: 5
SQ FT: 8,472
SALES (est): 544.5K **Privately Held**
SIC: **2752** 2759 Commercial printing, offset; commercial printing

### (G-531)
**SUBURBAN INDUS TL & MFG CO**
11606 S Mayfield Ave (60803-6010)
PHONE ............................. 708 597-7788
Fax: 708 371-5795
Richard Kovach, *President*
Irene Kovach, *Corp Secy*
Mike Kovach, *Vice Pres*
Maryann Blaha, *Manager*
EMP: 10
SQ FT: 8,000
SALES (est): 1.4MM **Privately Held**
SIC: **3599** Machine shop, jobbing & repair

### (G-532)
**T J METAL CO**
4631 W 120th St (60803-2316)
PHONE ............................. 708 388-6191
Tom Penkala, *Owner*
EMP: 5
SQ FT: 50,000
SALES (est): 480K **Privately Held**
SIC: **5093** 3341 Metal scrap & waste materials; secondary nonferrous metals

### (G-533)
**TAYCORP INC (PA)**
Also Called: Taylor Spring Mfg. Co.
5700 W 120th St (60803-3710)
PHONE ............................. 708 629-0921
Fax: 708 422-3877
John M Tyrakowski, *President*
Henry Tyrakowski, *Chairman*
Steven C Tyrakowski, *Corp Secy*
Rick Melody, *Research*
Steve Noyes, *Sales Mgr*
▲ EMP: 22
SQ FT: 16,000
SALES (est): 2.7MM **Privately Held**
WEB: www.taylorspring.com
SIC: **3495** 3677 Wire springs; electronic coils, transformers & other inductors

### (G-534)
**TAYLORS CANDY INC**
4855 W 115th St (60803-2864)
PHONE ............................. 708 371-0332
Douglas R Taylor, *President*
Gregory D Taylor, *Vice Pres*
Jeanne McMohan, *Manager*
EMP: 28
SQ FT: 28,000
SALES (est): 4.3MM **Privately Held**
SIC: **7389** 2064 Packaging & labeling services; candy & other confectionery products; popcorn balls or other treated popcorn products

### (G-535)
**TMS MANUFACTURING CO**
Also Called: Tms Mfg / Wc Richards Co
3555 W 123rd St (60803-4125)
PHONE ............................. 847 353-8000
Gerard Garcia, *Buyer*
EMP: 3 EST: 2014
SALES (est): 289.4K **Privately Held**
SIC: **2851** Paints & allied products

### (G-536)
**UESCO INDUSTRIES INC**
Also Called: Service Center
5908 W 118th St (60803-6037)
P.O. Box 489, Worth (60482-0489)
PHONE ............................. 708 385-7700
John Parson, *Agent*
EMP: 8
SALES (corp-wide): 8.4MM **Privately Held**
WEB: www.uescocranes.com
SIC: **3531** 3536 5084 Cranes; hoists, cranes & monorails; industrial machinery & equipment

PA: Uesco Industries, Inc.
 5908 W 118th St
 Alsip IL 60803
 800 325-8372

### (G-537)
**UESCO INDUSTRIES INC (PA)**
Also Called: Uesco Crane
5908 W 118th St (60803-6037)
P.O. Box 489, Worth (60482-0489)
PHONE ............................. 800 325-8372
Fax: 708 385-6889
Donald Marks, *President*
Warren Marks, *President*
Jeanette Marks, *Vice Pres*
Mike Jemilo, *Purch Dir*
Ryan Marks, *Sales Staff*
EMP: 40
SQ FT: 20,000
SALES (est): 8.4MM **Privately Held**
WEB: www.uescocranes.com
SIC: **3536** 7699 5063 Cranes, overhead traveling; industrial machinery & equipment repair; electrical supplies

### (G-538)
**UNION CARBIDE CORPORATION**
12840 S Pulaski Rd (60803-1999)
PHONE ............................. 708 396-3000
Fax: 708 396-3051
Bill Paterson, *Purch Mgr*
Patrick E Gottschalk, *Branch Mgr*
EMP: 57
SALES (corp-wide): 48.1B **Publicly Held**
SIC: **2869** Ethylene oxide
HQ: Union Carbide Corporation
 1254 Enclave Pkwy
 Houston TX 77077
 281 966-2727

### (G-539)
**VAN LEER CONTAINERS INC (HQ)**
4300 W 130th St (60803-2094)
PHONE ............................. 708 371-4777
Fax: 708 371-2047
Tony A Riley, *President*
Dian Toczek, *Human Res Mgr*
Linda Deady, *Admin Sec*
◆ EMP: 150
SQ FT: 415,000
SALES (est): 47.8MM
SALES (corp-wide): 3.3B **Publicly Held**
SIC: **3412** Metal barrels, drums & pails
PA: Greif, Inc.
 425 Winter Rd
 Delaware OH 43015
 740 549-6000

### (G-540)
**VENTUREDYNE LTD**
Scientific Dust Collectors
4101 W 126th St (60803-1901)
PHONE ............................. 708 597-7090
Michael Gerardi, *General Mgr*
Donald Marshall, *Materials Mgr*
John Lampos, *Engineer*
Brian Mathews, *Engineer*
Dale Purdy, *Marketing Staff*
EMP: 30
SALES (corp-wide): 110MM **Privately Held**
SIC: **3829** Measuring & controlling devices
PA: Venturedyne, Ltd.
 600 College Ave
 Pewaukee WI 53072
 262 691-9900

### (G-541)
**VERSATILITY TL WORKS MFG INC**
Also Called: Vtw
11532 S Mayfield Ave (60803-6009)
PHONE ............................. 708 389-8909
Fax: 708 389-8955
Edward Freimuth Jr, *President*
Margarete Freimuth, *Admin Sec*
EMP: 17 EST: 1972
SQ FT: 20,000
SALES (est): 4MM **Privately Held**
WEB: www.versatilitytool.com
SIC: **3541** 5013 Machine tool replacement & repair parts, metal cutting types; automotive stampings

### (G-542)
**W & K MACHINING INC**
4711 W 120th St (60803-2318)
PHONE ............................. 708 430-9000
Krzysztof Labedzki, *President*
EMP: 5
SALES (est): 772.8K **Privately Held**
SIC: **3599** Machine shop, jobbing & repair

### (G-543)
**WEMCO INC**
11721 S Austin Ave (60803-6002)
PHONE ............................. 708 388-1980
Fax: 708 388-1982
Brandon Goodwin, *President*
William Kuhn, *Vice Pres*
EMP: 17
SQ FT: 12,000
SALES (est): 1.5MM **Privately Held**
SIC: **3556** 7699 7692 Food products machinery; industrial machinery & equipment repair; welding repair

### (G-544)
**WINDY CITY GOLD POPCORN INC**
4855 W 115th St (60803-2864)
PHONE ............................. 708 596-9940
Gregory Taylor, *President*
Doug R Taylor, *Vice Pres*
Ken Taylor, *Vice Pres*
Douglas L Taylor, *Admin Sec*
EMP: 7 EST: 2011
SQ FT: 15,000
SALES (est): 493.3K **Privately Held**
SIC: **2064** Popcorn balls or other treated popcorn products

### (G-545)
**WORLDWIDE TILES LTD INC**
11708 S Mayfield Ave (60803-3565)
PHONE ............................. 708 389-2992
EMP: 3 EST: 2004
SALES (est): 180K **Privately Held**
SIC: **3281** 5032 Mfg Cut Stone/Products Whol Brick/Stone Material

### (G-546)
**WORTH STEEL AND MACHINE CO**
4001 W 123rd St (60803-1801)
PHONE ............................. 708 388-6300
William Bender, *President*
Vita Bender, *President*
Jim Degrado, *General Mgr*
Marge Acevedo, *Principal*
Robert Bender, *Principal*
▲ EMP: 25
SQ FT: 45,000
SALES (est): 10.2MM **Privately Held**
WEB: www.worthsteel.com
SIC: **3547** 3316 Rolling mill machinery; bars, steel, cold finished, from purchased hot-rolled

### (G-547)
**WRAP-ON COMPANY LLC**
11756 S Austin Ave (60803-6003)
PHONE ............................. 708 496-2150
Fax: 708 496-2154
David McArdle, *President*
Allan Dudycha, *Manager*
Jerome J Trakszelis, *Manager*
Rodney Welty, *Admin Sec*
▲ EMP: 25
SQ FT: 50,000
SALES: 3.8MM
SALES (corp-wide): 42.3MM **Privately Held**
WEB: www.wrapon.com
SIC: **3494** Plumbing & heating valves; pipe fittings
PA: Mcardle Ltd.
 1600 E Main St Ste B
 Saint Charles IL 60174
 630 584-6580

## Altamont
### Effingham County

### (G-548)
**ALTAMONT NEWS**
7 Do It Dr (62411-1135)
P.O. Box 315 (62411-0315)
PHONE ............................. 618 483-6176
Omer Siebert, *Partner*
Norma Siebert, *Partner*
Joe Baker, *Publisher*
EMP: 6
SQ FT: 2,100
SALES (est): 100K **Privately Held**
SIC: **2711** Newspapers: publishing only, not printed on site

### (G-549)
**ARCHER-DANIELS-MIDLAND COMPANY**
Also Called: ADM
601 W Division St (62411-1145)
P.O. Box 247 (62411-0247)
PHONE ............................. 618 483-6171
Fax: 618 483-5655
Dennis Schall, *Manager*
EMP: 6
SALES (corp-wide): 62.3B **Publicly Held**
WEB: www.admworld.com
SIC: **5153** 5191 2875 Grain elevators; farm supplies; fertilizers, mixing only
PA: Archer-Daniels-Midland Company
 77 W Wacker Dr Ste 4600
 Chicago IL 60601
 312 634-8100

### (G-550)
**BETTER NEWS PAPERS INC**
Also Called: Altonat
118 N Main St (62411-1448)
P.O. Box 315 (62411-0315)
PHONE ............................. 618 483-6176
Mark Hoskins, *Manager*
EMP: 6
SALES (corp-wide): 3MM **Privately Held**
SIC: **2711** Newspapers; newspapers, publishing & printing
PA: Better News Papers, Inc
 314 E Church St Ste 1
 Mascoutah IL 62258
 618 566-8282

### (G-551)
**FREDERKING CONSTRUCTION CO**
8595 N 300th St (62411-3503)
PHONE ............................. 618 483-5031
Fax: 618 483-5125
David W Frederking, *President*
Shane Frederking, *Vice Pres*
Sandy Heyden, *Admin Sec*
EMP: 9
SQ FT: 2,000
SALES (est): 582.1K **Privately Held**
SIC: **1521** 1522 1542 2452 Single-family housing construction; multi-family dwelling construction; nonresidential construction; prefabricated buildings, wood

### (G-552)
**H & D MOTOR SERVICE**
901 W Cumberland Rd (62411-1000)
PHONE ............................. 217 342-3262
Robert L Hardiek, *Owner*
EMP: 3 EST: 1945
SQ FT: 2,400
SALES: 110K **Privately Held**
SIC: **3599** 5013 Machine shop, jobbing & repair; automotive supplies & parts; automotive supplies

### (G-553)
**IRWIN SEATING COMPANY**
610 E Cumberland Rd (62411-1640)
P.O. Box 320 (62411-0320)
PHONE ............................. 618 483-6157
Win Irwin, *CEO*
Michael Antrim, *Engineer*
EMP: 120
SALES (corp-wide): 143.5MM **Privately Held**
SIC: **2531** Stadium furniture

# GEOGRAPHIC SECTION
## Alton - Madison County (G-580)

HQ: Irwin Seating Company
3251 Fruit Ridge Ave Nw
Grand Rapids MI 49544
616 784-2621

**(G-554)**
**PROMARK ADVERTISING SPECIALTIE**
4 N Frontage Rd (62411-3563)
P.O. Box 285 (62411-0285)
**PHONE**..................618 483-6025
Dawn Burrow, *Principal*
**EMP:** 5
**SALES (est):** 420.4K **Privately Held**
**SIC:** 2759 5941 7311 Screen printing; sporting goods & bicycle shops; advertising agencies

**(G-555)**
**RAMSEY WELDING INC**
5360 E 900th Ave (62411-2446)
**PHONE**..................618 483-6248
Russell Ramsey, *President*
Rosemary Holland, *Admin Asst*
**EMP:** 20
**SALES:** 6MM **Privately Held**
**SIC:** 7692 Cracked casting repair

## Alto Pass
### Union County

**(G-556)**
**ALTO VINYARDS INC (PA)**
8515 Highway 127 (62905-2033)
**PHONE**..................618 893-4898
**Fax:** 618 893-4935
Paul Renzaglia, *President*
Leon Dangbar, *Manager*
**EMP:** 13
**SQ FT:** 5,000
**SALES (est):** 2.9MM **Privately Held**
**WEB:** www.altovineyards.net
**SIC:** 5182 2084 Liquor; wines, brandy & brandy spirits

## Alton
### Madison County

**(G-557)**
**ABBOTT MACHINE CO (PA)**
700 W Broadway (62002-6104)
P.O. Box 149 (62002-0149)
**PHONE**..................618 465-1898
**Fax:** 618 465-2495
Rick Abbott, *President*
Robert W Abbott, *Principal*
Michael St Peters, *Corp Secy*
▲ **EMP:** 19
**SQ FT:** 46,000
**SALES:** 6MM **Privately Held**
**WEB:** www.abbottmachineco.com
**SIC:** 5084 3599 Machine tools & accessories; machine shop, jobbing & repair

**(G-558)**
**AEP INC**
1225 Cabin Club Dr (62002-7415)
**PHONE**..................618 466-7668
Peter Kuhn, *Principal*
**EMP:** 5
**SALES (est):** 325K **Privately Held**
**SIC:** 3089 5099 Plastics products; durable goods

**(G-559)**
**ALTON SHEET METAL CORP**
801 E Broadway (62002-6404)
P.O. Box 557 (62002-0557)
**PHONE**..................618 462-0609
**Fax:** 618 462-6170
William N Knetzer, *President*
Marlene Knetzer, *Controller*
**EMP:** 13
**SQ FT:** 8,000
**SALES (est):** 3MM **Privately Held**
**SIC:** 1711 3441 Warm air heating & air conditioning contractor; fabricated structural metal

**(G-560)**
**ALTON STEEL INC**
5 Cut St (62002-1776)
**PHONE**..................618 463-4490
**Fax:** 618 463-3789
John Simmons, *Ch of Bd*
Terry Laird, *General Mgr*
Jim Hrusovsky, *Principal*
Micheal Cook, *Vice Pres*
Steven Vaughan, *Safety Mgr*
▲ **EMP:** 259
**SALES (est):** 121.1MM **Privately Held**
**WEB:** www.altonsteel.com
**SIC:** 3312 Blast furnaces & steel mills

**(G-561)**
**ARDENT MILLS LLC**
Also Called: Food Group
145 W Broadway (62002-6222)
**PHONE**..................618 463-4411
**Fax:** 618 463-4419
Jason Watt, *Sales Executive*
Alan Mersnick, *Branch Mgr*
**EMP:** 105
**SALES (corp-wide):** 30.3B **Publicly Held**
**WEB:** www.conagra.com
**SIC:** 2041 Flour
HQ: Ardent Mills Llc
1875 Lawrence St Ste 1400
Denver CO 80202
800 851-9618

**(G-562)**
**B & B CUSTOM TS & GIFTS**
2714 Corner Ct (62002-5328)
**PHONE**..................618 463-0443
**Fax:** 618 463-0448
Marsha Bennett, *Owner*
Kevan Bennett, *Owner*
**EMP:** 4
**SQ FT:** 2,400
**SALES (est):** 250K **Privately Held**
**SIC:** 2396 2395 Screen printing on fabric articles; embroidery & art needlework

**(G-563)**
**B D ENTERPRISES**
Also Called: B D Sport Photos and Trophies
655 E Broadway (62002)
**PHONE**..................618 462-5861
**Fax:** 618 465-6850
William Daniels, *Owner*
**EMP:** 3
**SQ FT:** 1,600
**SALES:** 80K **Privately Held**
**SIC:** 7335 5094 2759 Commercial photography; trophies; screen printing

**(G-564)**
**BERGESCH HEATING & COOLING**
8116 Wolf Rd (62002-7930)
**PHONE**..................618 259-4620
Robert Bergesch, *Owner*
**EMP:** 3
**SALES (est):** 183.7K **Privately Held**
**SIC:** 1711 3585 Warm air heating & air conditioning contractor; refrigeration & heating equipment

**(G-565)**
**C & L MANUFACTURING ENTPS**
Also Called: Industrial Processs and Sensor
2109 Holland St (62002-3339)
**PHONE**..................618 465-7623
Thomas Lehnen, *President*
Jesse Lehnen, *General Mgr*
**EMP:** 3 **EST:** 1923
**SQ FT:** 1,500
**SALES:** 100K **Privately Held**
**WEB:** www.ipscustom.com
**SIC:** 3269 3829 3357 3315 Pyrometer tubes; thermocouples; nonferrous wire-drawing & insulating; steel wire & related products

**(G-566)**
**CLODFELTER ENGRAVING INC**
2109 Holland St (62002-3339)
**PHONE**..................314 968-8418
Marvin Clodfelter, *President*
Dirk Clodfelter, *Vice Pres*
Teena Schtad, *Vice Pres*
**EMP:** 8
**SQ FT:** 4,000

**SALES (est):** 660K **Privately Held**
**WEB:** www.clodfelterengraving.net
**SIC:** 2796 Engraving on copper, steel, wood or rubber; printing plates; photoengraving plates, linecuts or halftones

**(G-567)**
**COPE & SONS ASPHALT**
3510 Thomas Ave (62002-4119)
**PHONE**..................618 462-2207
Joanne Cope, *Owner*
**EMP:** 3
**SALES (est):** 154.9K **Privately Held**
**SIC:** 1771 2951 Concrete work; asphalt paving mixtures & blocks

**(G-568)**
**COPE PLASTICS INC (PA)**
4441 Indl Dr (62002)
P.O. Box 129, Godfrey (62035-0129)
**PHONE**..................618 466-0221
**Fax:** 618 466-7975
Jane Saale, *CEO*
P Jane Saale, *President*
Dean Bryson, *Regional Mgr*
Jeff Maynard, *COO*
Gene A Appal, *Vice Pres*
**EMP:** 100 **EST:** 1946
**SQ FT:** 165,000
**SALES (est):** 239.4MM **Privately Held**
**WEB:** www.copeplastics.com
**SIC:** 5162 3599 Plastics sheets & rods; resins, synthetic; plastics products; machine & other job shop work

**(G-569)**
**D & R MACHINE COMPANY INC (PA)**
4131 Alby St (62002-4484)
**PHONE**..................618 465-5611
David Gotter, *CEO*
Rene A Gotter, *Vice Pres*
Debie Droege, *Manager*
Mark Lang, *Manager*
**EMP:** 7 **EST:** 1997
**SQ FT:** 7,000
**SALES (est):** 2.4MM **Privately Held**
**SIC:** 3599 Machine shop, jobbing & repair

**(G-570)**
**D W TERRY WELDING COMPANY**
1860 E Broadway (62002-6664)
**PHONE**..................618 433-9722
Erick Terry, *Principal*
**EMP:** 3
**SALES (est):** 192.5K **Privately Held**
**SIC:** 7692 1799 3812 3444 Welding repair; welding on site; search & navigation equipment; sheet metalwork

**(G-571)**
**DORAS SPINNING WHEEL INC**
96 Northport Dr (62002-5940)
**PHONE**..................618 466-1900
Dora Vinson, *President*
Jeffrey S Vinson, *Corp Secy*
Margaret Engemann, *Vice Pres*
**EMP:** 3
**SALES:** 60K **Privately Held**
**WEB:** www.dorasspinningwheel.com
**SIC:** 2395 Embroidery & art needlework

**(G-572)**
**EAGLE FORUM (PA)**
322 State St Ste 301 (62002-6135)
**PHONE**..................618 462-5415
**Fax:** 618 462-8909
Phyllis Schlafly, *President*
Ann Longon, *Vice Pres*
Eunie Smith, *Vice Pres*
Ruth Carlson, *Exec Dir*
**EMP:** 6
**SALES:** 1MM **Privately Held**
**SIC:** 2731 2721 Pamphlets: publishing only, not printed on site; periodicals

**(G-573)**
**EAGLE TUBULAR PRODUCTS INC**
105 Chessen Ln (62002-2050)
**PHONE**..................618 463-1702
**Fax:** 618 463-1755
Jeffrey Fleming, *President*
Tara Fiala, *Manager*

Kat Buescher, *Administration*
Jodi Warren, *Administration*
**EMP:** 25
**SQ FT:** 10,000
**SALES (est):** 10.2MM **Privately Held**
**WEB:** www.eagletubular.com
**SIC:** 3317 Steel pipe & tubes

**(G-574)**
**ELECTRONICS BOUTIQUE AMER INC**
128 Alton Sq (62002-5917)
**PHONE**..................618 465-3125
David Heasner, *Manager*
**EMP:** 5
**SALES (corp-wide):** 8.6B **Publicly Held**
**SIC:** 7372 Prepackaged software
HQ: Electronics Boutique Of America Inc.
625 Westport Pkwy
Grapevine TX 76051
817 424-2000

**(G-575)**
**ENERGY SOLUTIONS INC**
1520 Worden Ave (62002-4069)
**PHONE**..................618 465-5404
Bill Stoutenborough, *President*
Fay Stoutenborough, *Admin Sec*
**EMP:** 2
**SQ FT:** 4,000
**SALES (est):** 206.1K **Privately Held**
**SIC:** 1799 3443 Window treatment installation; heat exchangers: coolers (after, inter), condensers, etc.

**(G-576)**
**GREEN INVESTMENT GROUP INC**
601 E 3rd St Ste 215 (62002-6318)
**PHONE**..................618 465-7277
Raymond Stillwell, *President*
**EMP:** 6
**SALES (est):** 654.7K **Privately Held**
**SIC:** 3533 Oil & gas field machinery

**(G-577)**
**HANLEY INDUSTRIES INC**
3640 Seminary St (62002-5730)
P.O. Box 1058 (62002-1058)
**PHONE**..................618 465-8892
**Fax:** 618 465-3195
T Gaynor Blake, *President*
Danny Stahl, *Vice Pres*
Don Elik, *Project Mgr*
Jim Klug, *Prdtn Mgr*
Hubert Presley, *Prdtn Mgr*
**EMP:** 48
**SQ FT:** 75,000
**SALES (est):** 11.9MM **Privately Held**
**WEB:** www.hanleyindustries.com
**SIC:** 2892 Explosives; detonators & detonating caps; detonators, high explosives; squibbs, electric

**(G-578)**
**IMPERIAL MFG GROUP INC**
1450 Discovery Pkwy (62002-6504)
**PHONE**..................618 465-3133
**Fax:** 618 633-1973
Richard Hayes, *Branch Mgr*
**EMP:** 11
**SALES (corp-wide):** 35.2MM **Privately Held**
**SIC:** 5074 3444 Plumbing & hydronic heating supplies; metal ventilating equipment; ducts, sheet metal
**PA:** Imperial Manufacturing Group Inc
40 Rue Industrial
Richibucto NB E4W 4
506 523-9117

**(G-579)**
**JADE SCREEN PRINTING**
220 Main St (62002-1742)
**PHONE**..................618 463-2325
Ruth Ann Hellemeyer, *Owner*
**EMP:** 5
**SALES (est):** 386.9K **Privately Held**
**SIC:** 2752 Commercial printing, lithographic

**(G-580)**
**JBL - ALTON**
2345 State St (62002-4320)
**PHONE**..................618 466-0411
Rhonda Hausman, *Manager*

# Alton - Madison County (G-581)

EMP: 3
SALES (est): 214.1K  Privately Held
SIC: 1311  Crude petroleum & natural gas

### (G-581)
### LANGA RESOURCE GROUP INC
Also Called: Girl's Gear
705 Belle St (62002-2306)
PHONE..........................618 462-1899
Fax: 618 462-1898
Janice Melzer Langa, *President*
Scott Langa, *Admin Sec*
EMP: 7
SALES (est): 582.3K  Privately Held
WEB: www.langaresourcegroup.com
SIC: 2395  Embroidery & art needlework

### (G-582)
### LENHARDT TOOL AND DIE COMPANY
3400 Bloomer Dr (62002-1999)
PHONE..........................618 462-1075
Fax: 618 462-1075
Jack E Lenhardt, *President*
Jean Webb, *Corp Secy*
Diana Lenhardt, *Shareholder*
EMP: 60 EST: 1960
SQ FT: 48,000
SALES (est): 11.7MM  Privately Held
WEB: www.lenhardttool.com
SIC: 3544  3621  Special dies, tools, jigs & fixtures; motors & generators

### (G-583)
### LYNNS PRINTING CO
3050 Homer M Adams Pkwy (62002-4859)
PHONE..........................618 465-7701
Fax: 618 465-9225
Barbara Lynn, *Owner*
Rick Lynn, *Manager*
EMP: 6
SALES (est): 460K  Privately Held
WEB: www.lynnsprinting.com
SIC: 2752  2791  2789  Commercial printing, offset; typesetting; bookbinding & related work

### (G-584)
### MARCAL ROPE & RIGGING INC (PA)
1862 E Broadway (62002-6664)
P.O. Box 477 (62002-0477)
PHONE..........................618 462-0172
Fax: 618 462-1368
Richard Miller, *CEO*
Thomas R Miller, *President*
Tom Horstman, *Opers Mgr*
Kristy Crawford, *Purchasing*
Mary Capps, *Accounts Mgr*
EMP: 26
SQ FT: 24,000
SALES (est): 8.4MM  Privately Held
WEB: www.marcalrigging.com
SIC: 3496  Slings, lifting: made from purchased wire; chain, welded; cable, uninsulated wire: made from purchased wire

### (G-585)
### MATRIX SERVICE INC
3403 E Broadway (62002-2043)
PHONE..........................618 466-4862
Fax: 618 462-6420
Brian Mans, *Manager*
EMP: 12
SALES (corp-wide): 1.3B  Publicly Held
WEB: www.matrixservice.com
SIC: 1791  3443  7699  Storage tanks, metal: erection; tanks standard or custom fabricated: metal plate; tank repair & cleaning services
HQ: Matrix Service Inc.
5100 E Skelly Dr Ste 700
Tulsa OK 74135
918 838-8200

### (G-586)
### OLIVE OIL MARKETPLACE INC (PA)
108 W 3rd St (62002-6207)
PHONE..........................618 304-3769
Timothy Meeks, *President*
EMP: 4
SQ FT: 1,600
SALES (est): 15.1MM  Privately Held
SIC: 2079  5411  Olive oil; grocery stores, independent

### (G-587)
### QUALITY DRILLING SERVICE LLP (PA)
1715 Liberty St (62002-4515)
PHONE..........................937 663-4715
Mari-Lynn Slayton, *General Ptnr*
EMP: 1
SQ FT: 120
SALES: 1.4MM  Privately Held
SIC: 1381  Drilling oil & gas wells

### (G-588)
### RONEY MACHINE WORKS INC
412 Pearl St (62002-6675)
PHONE..........................618 462-4113
Fax: 618 462-3713
Marianne Roney, *President*
Lee Roney, *Vice Pres*
Dennis Banks, *Office Mgr*
EMP: 20 EST: 1950
SQ FT: 52,000
SALES (est): 4.1MM  Privately Held
SIC: 3443  Heat exchangers: coolers (after, inter), condensers, etc.

### (G-589)
### SCHWARTZKOPF PRINTING INC
4121 Humbert Rd (62002-7116)
PHONE..........................618 463-0747
James M Schwartzkopf, *President*
Teresa Dressel, *Corp Secy*
Donna Schwartzkopf, *Vice Pres*
EMP: 16
SQ FT: 15,000
SALES: 2.1MM  Privately Held
WEB: www.schwprinting.com
SIC: 2752  Commercial printing, offset

### (G-590)
### SOFTHAUS LTD
Also Called: Vic Cook System
518 Beacon St (62002-6119)
PHONE..........................618 463-1140
Victor Cook, *Partner*
EMP: 3
SALES (est): 230K  Privately Held
SIC: 7372  7371  Prepackaged software; computer software systems analysis & design, custom

### (G-591)
### SURFACE MINING RECLAMATION OFF
501 Belle St Ste 216 (62002-6169)
PHONE..........................618 463-6460
Al Clayeborn, *Manager*
EMP: 29  Publicly Held
WEB: www.osmre.gov
SIC: 1241  Coal mining services
HQ: Office Of Surface Mining Reclamation & Enforcement
1951 Constitution Ave N
Washington DC 20240

### (G-592)
### SWI ENERGY LLC
601 E 3rd St Ste 302 (62002-6318)
P.O. Box 249 (62002-0249)
PHONE..........................618 465-7277
Andrew Stillwell,
EMP: 3
SALES (est): 215.9K  Privately Held
SIC: 2869  Industrial organic chemicals

### (G-593)
### TODAYS ADVANTAGE INC
192 Alton Square Mall Dr A (62002-5258)
P.O. Box 867 (62002-0867)
PHONE..........................618 463-0612
Fax: 618 463-0733
James Seibold, *President*
Sharon McRoy, *Publisher*
Jim Seibold, *Publisher*
Fred Pollard, *Editor*
Phillis Bierman, *Accounts Exec*
EMP: 11
SALES (est): 720K  Privately Held
WEB: www.todaysadvantage.com
SIC: 2711  Newspapers; newspapers, publishing & printing

### (G-594)
### U WASH EQUIPMENT CO
116 Northport Dr (62002-5904)
P.O. Box 877 (62002-0877)
PHONE..........................618 466-9442
Fax: 618 466-6018
C Rick Meeks, *President*
Ruth Meeks, *Vice Pres*
EMP: 5
SQ FT: 7,300
SALES (est): 510K  Privately Held
SIC: 3589  Car washing machinery

### (G-595)
### ZIEMER USA INC
620 E 3rd St (62002-6317)
PHONE..........................618 462-9301
David Bragg, *President*
Angela Braida, *Treasurer*
Beth Pratt, *Bookkeeper*
Pam Kaizer, *Marketing Staff*
EMP: 16
SQ FT: 24,000
SALES (est): 2.6MM  Privately Held
SIC: 3851  Ophthalmic goods
HQ: Ziemer Group Ag
Allmendstrasse 11
Port BE
323 327-070

## Amboy
### Lee County

### (G-596)
### ADDISON PRECISION PRODUCTS
200 E Kellen Dr (61310-1831)
P.O. Box 144 (61310-0144)
PHONE..........................815 857-4466
Fax: 815 857-3355
John T Smith, *President*
Steven Counihan, *Vice Pres*
EMP: 11
SQ FT: 17,000
SALES: 1.5MM  Privately Held
WEB: www.addisonprecision.com
SIC: 3599  Machine & other job shop work

### (G-597)
### AMBOY NEWS
245 E Main St (61310-1439)
P.O. Box 162 (61310-0162)
PHONE..........................815 857-2311
Fax: 815 857-2517
Jhon Shank, *Principal*
Tonja Greenfield, *Adv Dir*
Monetta Young, *Relations*
EMP: 3
SALES (est): 163.5K  Privately Held
WEB: www.amboynews.com
SIC: 2711  2791  2752  Newspapers, publishing & printing; typesetting; commercial printing, lithographic

### (G-598)
### EQUITY LIFESTYLE PRPTS INC
970 Green Wing Rd (61310-9446)
PHONE..........................815 857-3333
Daniel E Connell, *Branch Mgr*
EMP: 4
SALES (corp-wide): 870.4MM  Publicly Held
SIC: 3799  Recreational vehicles
PA: Equity Lifestyle Properties, Inc.
2 N Riverside Plz Ste 800
Chicago IL 60606
312 279-1400

### (G-599)
### SENSIENT FLAVORS LLC
25 E Main St (61310-1661)
PHONE..........................815 857-3691
Bridget Hindert, *Purch Mgr*
Mark Allen, *Branch Mgr*
Rich Bartlett, *Supervisor*
John Phelps, *Maintence Staff*
EMP: 12
SALES (corp-wide): 1.3B  Publicly Held
SIC: 2087  Flavoring extracts & syrups
HQ: Sensient Flavors Llc
2800 W Higgins Rd Ste 900
Hoffman Estates IL 60169
317 243-3521

## Anna
### Union County

### (G-600)
### ANNA QUARRIES INC
1000 Quarry Rd (62906)
P.O. Box 180 (62906-0180)
PHONE..........................618 833-5121
Fax: 618 833-4584
Edward T Simonds, *President*
William Pyatt, *Vice Pres*
Paul Jany, *Plant Supt*
Laura Wilson, *Human Res Mgr*
Ralph Isom, *Manager*
EMP: 32
SQ FT: 1,800
SALES (est): 4.8MM  Privately Held
SIC: 1411  1422  Limestone, dimension-quarrying; crushed & broken limestone

### (G-601)
### ANNA-JONESBORO MOTOR CO INC
Also Called: John Deere Authorized Dealer
100 S Green St (62906)
P.O. Box 400 (62906-0400)
PHONE..........................618 833-4486
Fax: 618 833-2111
Kent Keller, *Manager*
EMP: 8
SALES (corp-wide): 6.1MM  Privately Held
SIC: 7694  5082  Motor repair services; construction & mining machinery
PA: Anna-Jonesboro Motor Co Inc
Hwy 146 E
Anna IL 62906
618 833-3673

### (G-602)
### CUNNINGHAM ELECTRONICS CORP
120 N Main St (62906-1617)
PHONE..........................618 833-7775
Fax: 618 833-8447
Shirley Cunningham, *President*
William R Cunningham, *President*
Doug Devore, *Manager*
A John Bigler, *Director*
EMP: 7
SQ FT: 2,500
SALES (est): 788.6K  Privately Held
WEB: www.cunninghamcouponsystem.com
SIC: 7372  Prepackaged software

### (G-603)
### GAZETTE DEMOCRAT
Also Called: Repperts Warehouse Office Furn
108 Lafayette St 112 (62906-1544)
P.O. Box 529 (62906-0529)
PHONE..........................618 833-2150
Fax: 618 833-5813
Jerry L Reppert, *Owner*
EMP: 40
SQ FT: 6,300
SALES (est): 3MM  Privately Held
SIC: 2711  5712  5943  Newspapers, publishing & printing; office furniture; office forms & supplies

### (G-604)
### GAZETTE-DEMOCRAT
Also Called: Mondays Pub
112 Lafayette St (62906-1544)
P.O. Box 529 (62906-0529)
PHONE..........................618 833-2158
Jerry Repert, *Owner*
Geof Skinner, *Advt Staff*
EMP: 25
SALES (est): 920K  Privately Held
WEB: www.annanews.com
SIC: 2711  Newspapers

### (G-605)
### ILLINI READY MIX INC
Also Called: Anna Plant
300 Mckinley St (62906-1830)
PHONE..........................618 833-7321
Fax: 618 734-0294
Perry Wright, *Manager*
EMP: 7

**SALES (corp-wide):** 2.8MM **Privately Held**
**WEB:** www.etsimonds.com
**SIC:** 3273 Ready-mixed concrete
**PA:** Illini Ready Mix, Inc
  801 W Industrial Park Rd
  Carbondale IL 62901
  618 734-0287

**(G-606)**
### J W REYNOLDS MONUMENT CO INC
517 E Vienna St Ste A (62906-2047)
**PHONE** .................. 618 833-6014
Kurt Swinford, *Principal*
Kurt Swinsford, *Principal*
**EMP:** 6
**SALES (est):** 227.7K
**SALES (corp-wide):** 72.2K **Privately Held**
**WEB:** www.rockofages.com
**SIC:** 3281 5999 6553 Cut stone & stone products; monuments, cut stone (not finishing or lettering only); monuments, finished to custom order; mausoleum operation
**HQ:** Rock Of Ages Corporation
  560 Graniteville Rd
  Graniteville VT 05654
  802 476-3115

**(G-607)**
### LEWIS BROTHERS BAKERIES INC
Also Called: Bunny Bread
101 Springfield Ave Ste I (62906-2154)
**PHONE** .................. 618 833-5185
John Pickle, *General Mgr*
**EMP:** 6
**SALES (corp-wide):** 647.6MM **Privately Held**
**WEB:** www.lewisbakeries.net
**SIC:** 2051 Bread, all types (white, wheat, rye, etc): fresh or frozen
**PA:** Lewis Brothers Bakeries Inc
  500 N Fulton Ave
  Evansville IN 47710
  812 425-4642

**(G-608)**
### REHABILITATION AND VOCATIONAL
214 S Davie St (62906-1237)
**PHONE** .................. 618 833-5344
Gary Griffith, *CEO*
Robert Neely, *Controller*
**EMP:** 40
**SALES (corp-wide):** 2.4MM **Privately Held**
**WEB:** www.rave.com
**SIC:** 5112 8331 2394 Office supplies; job training & vocational rehabilitation services; canvas & related products
**PA:** Rehabilitation And Vocational Education Program, Inc.
  1390 State Route 127 S
  Jonesboro IL 62952
  618 833-5344

## Annapolis
### Crawford County

**(G-609)**
### WERNZE FARMS INC
20563 N 400th St (62413-2205)
**PHONE** .................. 618 569-4820
Scotty Davidson, *Owner*
**EMP:** 2
**SALES (est):** 268.7K **Privately Held**
**SIC:** 3523 Driers (farm): grain, hay & seed

## Annawan
### Henry County

**(G-610)**
### PATRIOT FUELS BIODIESEL LLC
101 Patriot Way (61234-9753)
**PHONE** .................. 309 935-5700
Cash Colbert, *Treasurer*
Deb Enger, *Accountant*
Gene A Griffith,
Richard Vondra,
▲ **EMP:** 10
**SQ FT:** 1,000
**SALES (est):** 2.2MM **Privately Held**
**SIC:** 2911 Diesel fuels

**(G-611)**
### PATRIOT RENEWABLE FUELS LLC
Also Called: CHS Annawan
101 Patriot Way (61234-9753)
P.O. Box 560 (61234-0560)
**PHONE** .................. 309 935-5700
Gary Anderson, *President*
Patty Greteman, *Controller*
Tom Malecha, *Admin Sec*
**EMP:** 65
**SALES (est):** 21.5MM
**SALES (corp-wide):** 30.3B **Publicly Held**
**SIC:** 2869 Ethyl alcohol, ethanol
**HQ:** Patriot Holdings, Llc
  101 Patriot Way
  Annawan IL 61234
  309 935-5700

## Antioch
### Lake County

**(G-612)**
### A & S ARMS INC
847 Forest View Way (60002-6216)
**PHONE** .................. 224 267-5670
Shaun Unell, *Principal*
**EMP:** 6
**SALES (est):** 208.4K **Privately Held**
**SIC:** 3482 3484 7389 Small arms ammunition; guns (firearms) or gun parts, 30 mm. & below;

**(G-613)**
### ADVENT TOOL & MFG INC
710 Anita Ave (60002-1857)
**PHONE** .................. 847 395-9707
**Fax:** 847 549-9714
James Hartford, *President*
Kathy Krieps, *Controller*
▲ **EMP:** 18 **EST:** 1974
**SQ FT:** 20,000
**SALES (est):** 4.4MM **Privately Held**
**WEB:** www.advent-threadmill.com
**SIC:** 3545 2284 Machine tool accessories; thread mills

**(G-614)**
### AJS PREMIER PRINTING INC
893 Main St (60002-1508)
**PHONE** .................. 847 838-6350
**EMP:** 6
**SALES (est):** 560K **Privately Held**
**SIC:** 2759 2752 Commercial Printing Lithographic Commercial Printing

**(G-615)**
### AKERUE INDUSTRIES LLC (PA)
Also Called: Kay Home Products
90 Mcmillen Rd (60002-1845)
**PHONE** .................. 847 395-3300
**Fax:** 847 395-3305
Murray John J, *Principal*
K M Borre, *Principal*
Ralph Hoekstra, *Design Engr*
David D Bornstein, *Controller*
Geraldine Ellis,
▲ **EMP:** 40
**SQ FT:** 355,000
**SALES (est):** 7.9MM **Privately Held**
**WEB:** www.kayhomeproducts.com
**SIC:** 2599 Factory furniture & fixtures

**(G-616)**
### ALL WEST PLASTICS INC
Also Called: Mgs Manufacturing Group
606 Drom Ct (60002-1825)
**PHONE** .................. 847 395-8730
**Fax:** 847 395-9227
Chris Navratil, *General Mgr*
Randell M Hanson, *Program Mgr*
◆ **EMP:** 60
**SQ FT:** 36,000
**SALES (est):** 11.5MM
**SALES (corp-wide):** 258.6MM **Privately Held**
**WEB:** www.allwestplasticsinc.com
**SIC:** 3089 Injection molding of plastics
**HQ:** Mgs Group North America, Inc.
  W190n11701 Moldmakers Way
  Germantown WI 53022
  262 250-2950

**(G-617)**
### ANTIOCH FINE ARTS FOUNDATION
41380 N Il Route 83 (60002-1907)
**PHONE** .................. 847 838-2274
Gayle Monde, *President*
Lisa Clark, *Vice Pres*
Roger Shule, *Vice Pres*
Richard A Ellinghusen, *Treasurer*
Kagie Diorio, *Admin Sec*
**EMP:** 7
**SALES (est):** 561.7K **Privately Held**
**WEB:** www.antiochfinearts.org
**SIC:** 3263 8412 Whiteware, fine type semivitreous table or kitchen articles; museums & art galleries

**(G-618)**
### ANTIOCH PACKING HOUSE
510 Main St (60002-1396)
**PHONE** .................. 847 838-6800
**Fax:** 847 838-6803
Frank E Beranek, *President*
**EMP:** 7
**SALES (est):** 200K **Privately Held**
**SIC:** 5421 2011 Meat markets, including freezer provisioners; meat packing plants

**(G-619)**
### ART NEWVO INCORPORATED
25819 W Grail Lk Rd Ste 1 (60002)
**PHONE** .................. 847 838-0304
**Fax:** 847 838-0305
Tina Rengel, *President*
Lance Rengel, *Vice Pres*
**EMP:** 4
**SQ FT:** 1,500
**SALES (est):** 100K **Privately Held**
**WEB:** www.artnewvo.com
**SIC:** 2752 2396 Commercial printing, lithographic; automotive & apparel trimmings

**(G-620)**
### ASH PALLET MANAGEMENT INC (PA)
61 Mcmillen Rd (60002-1844)
P.O. Box 8582, Gurnee (60031-7018)
**PHONE** .................. 847 473-5700
Anthony James Ash, *President*
Judy Haapasaari, *Accountant*
**EMP:** 55 **EST:** 2012
**SQ FT:** 150,000
**SALES (est):** 9.5MM **Privately Held**
**SIC:** 2448 Pallets, wood & wood with metal

**(G-621)**
### ASSOCIATED PRINTERS INC
43215 N Grandview Ter (60002-8958)
**PHONE** .................. 847 548-8929
Melissa Hettlinger, *President*
**EMP:** 3
**SALES (est):** 293.4K **Privately Held**
**WEB:** www.associatedprinters.com
**SIC:** 2752 Commercial printing, lithographic

**(G-622)**
### BESCO AWARDS & EMBROIDERY
Also Called: Besco Marketing
43085 N Crawford Rd (60002-9573)
**PHONE** .................. 847 395-4862
**Fax:** 847 395-4878
Elgin Southgate, *Partner*
Barbara Southgate, *Partner*
**EMP:** 4
**SALES (est):** 280K **Privately Held**
**SIC:** 7699 3231 China firing & decorating to individual order; ornamental glass: cut, engraved or otherwise decorated; decorated glassware: chipped, engraved, etched, etc.

**(G-623)**
### BILLER PRESS & MANUFACTURING
966 Victoria St (60002-1519)
**PHONE** .................. 847 395-4111
**Fax:** 847 395-4232
Raymond Nordling, *President*
David Plumb, *Corp Secy*
Norman E Biller, *Vice Pres*
**EMP:** 7 **EST:** 1956
**SQ FT:** 3,500
**SALES (est):** 690K **Privately Held**
**SIC:** 2752 2791 2789 2759 Commercial printing, offset; lithographing on metal; typesetting; bookbinding & related work; commercial printing

**(G-624)**
### BLACKWING FOR PETS INC
17618 W Edwards Rd (60002-7206)
**PHONE** .................. 203 762-8620
Anthony Bennie, *President*
**EMP:** 4
**SALES (est):** 100K **Privately Held**
**SIC:** 2048 Prepared feeds

**(G-625)**
### BMI PRODUCTS NORTHERN ILL INC
Also Called: Maxit
28919 W Il Route 173 (60002-9115)
**PHONE** .................. 847 395-7110
Arnold Germann, *President*
Bernd Stern, *CFO*
Andrea Smith, *Manager*
Steven Gnorski, *Admin Sec*
▲ **EMP:** 20
**SQ FT:** 50,000
**SALES (est):** 4MM **Privately Held**
**WEB:** www.maxit-usa.com
**SIC:** 3273 3255 2899 Ready-mixed concrete; clay refractories; chemical preparations

**(G-626)**
### BRAESIDE LLC
Also Called: Braeside Displays
945 Anita Ave (60002-1867)
**PHONE** .................. 847 395-8500
Nathan Kelly, *CEO*
**EMP:** 25 **EST:** 2015
**SQ FT:** 38,000
**SALES (est):** 917.2K **Privately Held**
**SIC:** 3993 Displays & cutouts, window & lobby

**(G-627)**
### CABINETS DOORS AND MORE LLC
25819 W Grass Lake Rd (60002-8502)
**PHONE** .................. 847 395-6334
Justin Lauterbach,
**EMP:** 4
**SQ FT:** 2,800
**SALES (est):** 225K **Privately Held**
**WEB:** www.cabinetdoordepot.com
**SIC:** 2511 5712 2434 2431 Lawn furniture: wood; outdoor & garden furniture; wood kitchen cabinets; millwork

**(G-628)**
### CHICAGO INK & RESEARCH CO INC
97 Ida Ave (60002-1887)
**PHONE** .................. 847 395-1078
**Fax:** 847 395-3568
Charles Doty, *President*
Arthur Doty, *Treasurer*
Joan Pettavino, *Office Mgr*
**EMP:** 5
**SQ FT:** 9,900
**SALES (est):** 682.5K **Privately Held**
**WEB:** www.chicagoink.com
**SIC:** 3953 3952 Marking devices; lead pencils & art goods

**(G-629)**
### DIGITAL EDGE SIGNS INC
248 W Depot St A (60002-3200)
**PHONE** .................. 847 838-4760
Don Decks, *President*
**EMP:** 3
**SALES (est):** 276.2K **Privately Held**
**SIC:** 3993 Signs & advertising specialties

## Antioch - Lake County (G-630) — GEOGRAPHIC SECTION

### (G-630) DOMS INCORPORATED
940 Anita Ave (60002-1816)
PHONE.............................847 838-6723
Fax: 847 838-6725
Mark Stevens, *President*
Martin J Stevens, *President*
Paul Stevens, *Vice Pres*
Matthew Wilhite, *Opers Staff*
**EMP:** 20 **EST:** 1960
**SALES:** 500K **Privately Held**
**WEB:** www.domsoutdoor.com
**SIC: 3569** Filter elements, fluid, hydraulic line

### (G-631) FINAL FINISH BOAT WORKS
811 Pickard Ave (60002-1308)
PHONE.............................847 603-1345
Steven Mika, *President*
**EMP:** 4
**SALES (est):** 345.6K **Privately Held**
**SIC: 3732** Boat building & repairing

### (G-632) FISCHER PAPER PRODUCTS INC (PA)
179 Ida Ave (60002-1838)
PHONE.............................847 395-6060
Fax: 847 395-8619
Benno Fischer, *President*
Joshua M Fischer, *Exec VP*
William C Fischer, *Vice Pres*
Ruthann Alter, *Purchasing*
Thomas Mann, *CFO*
▲ **EMP:** 75
**SQ FT:** 65,000
**SALES (est):** 16.3MM **Privately Held**
**WEB:** www.fppi.net
**SIC: 2674** 2673 Paper bags: made from purchased materials; garment & wardrobe bags, (plastic film)

### (G-633) FORBIDDEN SWEETS INC
471 Main St Ste 4 (60002-3011)
PHONE.............................847 838-9692
Roxanne Abbeduto, *President*
Cheryl Schroeder, *Vice Pres*
**EMP:** 6
**SQ FT:** 3,000
**SALES:** 500K **Privately Held**
**SIC: 2064** Candy bars, including chocolate covered bars

### (G-634) GFI INNOVATIONS LLC
861 Anita Ave (60002-1813)
PHONE.............................847 263-9000
Jeff Baron, *Mng Member*
Lorraine Warner, *Manager*
John Borkovec,
Robert Lerson,
Derek Pedreza,
**EMP:** 9
**SALES (est):** 1.6MM **Privately Held**
**WEB:** www.gfiinnovations.com
**SIC: 3586** Measuring & dispensing pumps

### (G-635) GILDAY SERVICES
Also Called: Gilday Service Company
25870 W Hermann Ave (60002-9639)
PHONE.............................847 395-0853
Fax: 847 395-1222
Mark Gilday, *Owner*
**EMP:** 4
**SQ FT:** 1,500
**SALES:** 1MM **Privately Held**
**SIC: 2299** 7359 7699 Polishing felts; floor maintenance equipment rental; industrial machinery & equipment repair

### (G-636) GLK ENTERPRISES INC
Also Called: Alston Race Cars
248 E Depot St Unit 2 (60002)
PHONE.............................847 395-7368
Larry Lichter, *President*
Mike Ruth, *Manager*
**EMP:** 6
**SQ FT:** 10,000
**SALES (est):** 600K **Privately Held**
**SIC: 3714** Motor vehicle parts & accessories

### (G-637) GREENBRIER COMPANIES INC
23858 W Sarah Ct (60002-9355)
PHONE.............................847 838-1435
William Furman, *President*
**EMP:** 4
**SALES (corp-wide):** 2.6B **Publicly Held**
**WEB:** www.gbrx.com
**SIC: 3743** Railroad equipment
**PA:** The Greenbrier Companies Inc
1 Centerpointe Dr Ste 200
Lake Oswego OR 97035
503 684-7000

### (G-638) JANIS PLASTICS INC
330 North Ave (60002-1858)
PHONE.............................847 838-5500
Fax: 847 838-0200
Manu Graditor, *President*
Mike Pighini, *Treasurer*
John Shaffer, *Sales Staff*
Ken Penge, *Manager*
Darline Populorum, *Manager*
▼ **EMP:** 100 **EST:** 1946
**SQ FT:** 180,000
**SALES (est):** 12.7MM **Privately Held**
**WEB:** www.janisplastics.com
**SIC: 3993** Signs, not made in custom sign painting shops; displays & cutouts, window & lobby; advertising artwork

### (G-639) LAKES REG PRTG & GRAPHICS LLC
25325 W Hickory St (60002-8899)
PHONE.............................847 838-5838
Balsanek Edward F, *Principal*
**EMP:** 2
**SALES (est):** 205.6K **Privately Held**
**SIC: 2752** Commercial printing, lithographic

### (G-640) LAKEVIEW METALS INC (PA)
905 Anita Ave (60002-1815)
PHONE.............................847 838-9800
Kevin C Looby, *President*
▲ **EMP:** 38
**SQ FT:** 3,000
**SALES (est):** 10.7MM **Privately Held**
**SIC: 3469** Metal stampings

### (G-641) LEGEND DYNAMIX INC
Also Called: Legend Engraving Company
77 Mcmillen Rd Ste 106 (60002-1820)
PHONE.............................847 789-7007
Robert Linco, *President*
**EMP:** 4
**SALES (est):** 427.2K **Privately Held**
**SIC: 3479** 3231 Metal coating & allied service; products of purchased glass

### (G-642) M C STEEL INC
43160 N Crawford Rd (60002-9572)
PHONE.............................847 350-9618
Thomas McClanahan, *President*
Marilyn Grace, *General Mgr*
**EMP:** 41 **EST:** 1974
**SQ FT:** 54,000
**SALES (est):** 6.2MM **Privately Held**
**WEB:** www.mcsteelonline.com
**SIC: 5051** 3317 Metals service centers & offices; steel; steel pipe & tubes

### (G-643) MARSHALL FURNITURE INC
999 Anita Ave (60002-1817)
PHONE.............................847 395-9350
Fax: 847 223-3331
Richard Mangione, *President*
Timothy Ryter, *Vice Pres*
James Hassett, *Engineer*
Michelle Wille, *VP Sls/Mktg*
Colleen Coia, *Controller*
**EMP:** 20
**SQ FT:** 26,750
**SALES (est):** 3.8MM **Privately Held**
**WEB:** www.marshallfurniture.com
**SIC: 2599** Factory furniture & fixtures

### (G-644) MCARTHUR MACHINING INC
303 Main St Ste 100a (60002-3027)
PHONE.............................847 838-6998
Rich McArthur, *President*
**EMP:** 2
**SALES (est):** 248.7K **Privately Held**
**SIC: 3599** Machine shop, jobbing & repair

### (G-645) MEYER MACHINE & EQUIPMENT INC (PA)
Also Called: Pro-Air Service, Co.
351 Main St (60002-3012)
PHONE.............................847 395-2970
James W Meyer, *President*
Dan Meyer, *Project Mgr*
Louis Erenberg, *Sales Mgr*
Kim Mrkonich, *Agent*
Judy Wesword, *Admin Sec*
▲ **EMP:** 12
**SQ FT:** 18,000
**SALES (est):** 3.8MM **Privately Held**
**WEB:** www.meyermachine.com
**SIC: 7699** 3589 Industrial equipment services; commercial cleaning equipment

### (G-646) MIDWEST SCREENS LLC
Also Called: Chicago Retractable Awnings
303 Main St Ste 111 (60002-3027)
PHONE.............................847 557-5015
**EMP:** 3
**SALES (est):** 257.2K **Privately Held**
**SIC: 3442** Screen doors, metal

### (G-647) MODERN HOME PRODUCTS CORP (PA)
150 S Ram Rd (60002-1901)
PHONE.............................847 395-6556
Fax: 847 395-9121
Thomas Koziol, *President*
Tom Nitz, *Vice Pres*
Dale Davis, *Manager*
Sue Webber, *Manager*
George Koziol, *Admin Sec*
▲ **EMP:** 25
**SQ FT:** 50,000
**SALES (est):** 3.2MM **Privately Held**
**WEB:** www.mhpgrills.com
**SIC: 3648** Gas lighting fixtures

### (G-648) PAULMAR INDUSTRIES INC
39804 N Stonebridge Ct (60002-2342)
PHONE.............................847 395-2520
Fax: 847 395-2475
Robert Menary, *President*
Paula Menary, *Vice Pres*
**EMP:** 10
**SALES:** 720K **Privately Held**
**WEB:** www.paulmar.com
**SIC: 3861** 7371 Photographic equipment & supplies; computer software development

### (G-649) PETER LEHMAN INC
40126 N Il Route 83 (60002-1903)
P.O. Box 298 (60002-0298)
PHONE.............................847 395-7997
Peter Lehman, *President*
Jeanne Lehman, *Vice Pres*
**EMP:** 5
**SQ FT:** 2,600
**SALES (est):** 250K **Privately Held**
**SIC: 3444** Sheet metalwork

### (G-650) PICKARD INCORPORATED
782 Pickard Ave (60002-1574)
PHONE.............................847 395-3800
Fax: 847 395-3827
Andrew Pickard Morgan, *President*
Andrews Pickard Morgan, *President*
Sandra Parisi, *Sales Mgr*
Mike Ater, *Sales Staff*
▲ **EMP:** 73 **EST:** 1895
**SQ FT:** 65,000
**SALES (est):** 10.1MM **Privately Held**
**WEB:** www.pickardchina.com
**SIC: 3262** Vitreous china table & kitchenware; dishes, commercial or household: vitreous china; tableware, vitreous china

### (G-651) POEM LIGHTING COMPANY
144 Oakwood Dr (60002-1660)
PHONE.............................847 395-1768
Daniel F Hanrahan, *President*
Betty J Hanrahan, *Vice Pres*
**EMP:** 5
**SALES:** 150K **Privately Held**
**SIC: 3648** Lighting equipment

### (G-652) PRO TOOLS & EQUIPMENT INC
Also Called: Technocure
23529 Eagles Nest Rd (60002-8725)
PHONE.............................847 838-6666
James B Weinstein, *President*
**EMP:** 2
**SALES:** 1.5MM **Privately Held**
**SIC: 3559** Automotive maintenance equipment

### (G-653) RON & PATS PIZZA SHACK
40338 N Deep Lake Rd (60002-7201)
PHONE.............................847 395-5005
Ron Ramig, *Owner*
**EMP:** 4
**SALES (est):** 160K **Privately Held**
**SIC: 2041** 5812 Flour & other grain mill products; eating places

### (G-654) SE STEEL INC (PA)
43160 N Crawford Rd (60002-9572)
PHONE.............................847 350-9618
Thomas McClanahan, *President*
Marilyn Grace, *Admin Sec*
**EMP:** 3
**SQ FT:** 40,000
**SALES (est):** 1.1MM **Privately Held**
**SIC: 3312** 5051 Tubes, steel & iron; steel

### (G-655) SKACH MANUFACTURING CO INC
950 Anita Ave (60002-2447)
PHONE.............................847 395-3560
Fax: 847 395-9123
Will H Shineflug, *President*
Robert Shineflug, *Vice Pres*
David Keller, *Plant Mgr*
Connie Fisher, *Admin Sec*
**EMP:** 22 **EST:** 1953
**SQ FT:** 18,000
**SALES (est):** 4.4MM **Privately Held**
**WEB:** www.skachcoldform.com
**SIC: 3452** 3643 3316 Bolts, nuts, rivets & washers; rivets, metal; current-carrying wiring devices; contacts, electrical; cold finishing of steel shapes

### (G-656) THELEN SAND & GRAVEL INC (PA)
Also Called: Westosha Airport
28955 W Il Route 173 # 1 (60002-9116)
PHONE.............................847 838-8800
Fax: 847 395-3452
Steve Thelen, *President*
Dan Shepard, *Exec VP*
Tom Thelen, *Vice Pres*
Jeff Bychowski, *Opers Mgr*
Mary Varak, *Sls & Mktg Exec*
**EMP:** 68
**SQ FT:** 10,000
**SALES (est):** 31.4MM **Privately Held**
**WEB:** www.thelensg.com
**SIC: 1442** 4581 3273 4212 Construction sand & gravel; hangar operation; ready-mixed concrete; dump truck haulage; grading

### (G-657) THOMAS-ZIENTZ GROUP INC
925 Carney Ct (60002-2461)
PHONE.............................847 395-2363
**EMP:** 5
**SQ FT:** 2,500
**SALES (est):** 510K **Privately Held**
**SIC: 3545** Mfg Machine Tool Accessories

### (G-658) TRANSCEND CORP
90 Mcmillen Rd (60002-1845)
PHONE.............................847 395-6630

▲ = Import ▼ = Export ◆ = Import/Export

EMP: 3 EST: 2010
SALES (est): 130K **Privately Held**
SIC: 3471 Plating/Polishing Service

**(G-659)**
**TRI COUNTY LIFT TRUCKS INC**
Also Called: Tricounty
1020 Anita Ave (60002-1818)
P.O. Box 967, Lake Villa (60046-0967)
PHONE..............................847 838-0183
Fax: 847 838-1146
Joseph Gonzalez, *President*
John Norys, *Treasurer*
Tim Sheilds, *Admin Sec*
EMP: 5
SQ FT: 4,500
SALES: 500K **Privately Held**
SIC: 3537 Forklift trucks

**(G-660)**
**TRIFAB INC**
606 Longview Dr (60002-1843)
PHONE..............................847 838-2083
Fax: 847 395-7957
William Crutchfield Jr, *Principal*
Al Ruck Jr, *Corp Secy*
Greg Crutchfield, *Vice Pres*
EMP: 4
SALES (est): 460K **Privately Held**
SIC: 3441 Fabricated structural metal

**(G-661)**
**UNITED CANVAS INC**
Also Called: United Awning
25434 W Il Route 173 (60002-8356)
PHONE..............................847 395-1470
John Hauser, *President*
Steven Gundelach, *Corp Secy*
EMP: 23
SQ FT: 8,000
SALES: 1.2MM **Privately Held**
WEB: www.unitedawning.com
SIC: 2394 7641 3444 Convertible tops, canvas or boat: from purchased materials; awnings, fabric: made from purchased materials; reupholstery & furniture repair; reupholstery; sheet metalwork

**(G-662)**
**VEHICLE IMPROVEMENT PDTS INC**
151 S Ram Rd (60002-1937)
PHONE..............................847 395-7250
Fax: 847 395-9460
Cate Brusenbach, *Purch Agent*
Dan Klugiewicz, *Engineer*
Kathy Adams, *Bookkeeper*
◆ EMP: 3
SQ FT: 50,000
SALES (est): 6.6MM
SALES (corp-wide): 231.3MM **Privately Held**
WEB: www.vipwheels.com
SIC: 3714 Motor vehicle parts & accessories
PA: Indiana Mills & Manufacturing Inc
18881 Immi Way
Westfield IN 46074
317 896-9531

**(G-663)**
**WEX DISTRIBUTORS INC**
40471 N Bluff Dr (60002-7921)
PHONE..............................847 691-5823
David G Wechselberger, *President*
Marcia Wechselberger, *Vice Pres*
EMP: 4
SALES (est): 383.7K **Privately Held**
SIC: 2052 Cookies

**(G-664)**
**WILLIAM DAVIS & CO**
488 Donin Dr (60002-2510)
PHONE..............................847 395-6860
Fax: 847 395-9548
William C Davis, *Owner*
Judith Davis, *Owner*
EMP: 2
SALES: 2MM **Privately Held**
SIC: 3599 Machine shop, jobbing & repair

## Arcola
### Douglas County

**(G-665)**
**ARCOLA RECORD HERALD**
Also Called: Arcola Rcord Hrld-Rankin Publr
118 E Main St (61910-1435)
P.O. Box 217 (61910-0217)
PHONE..............................217 268-4950
Chris Slack, *Owner*
EMP: 4
SALES (est): 14.2K **Privately Held**
SIC: 2711 Newspapers

**(G-666)**
**CENTRAL WOOD LLC**
226 E County Road 200n (61910-3739)
PHONE..............................217 543-2662
Willard A Miller,
Kathryn Miller,
Lorene Miller,
Noah Miller,
Omer A Miller,
EMP: 7
SQ FT: 19,352
SALES: 4MM **Privately Held**
SIC: 2431 2439 Moldings, wood: unfinished & prefinished; doors, wood; door frames, wood; window sashes, wood; structural wood members

**(G-667)**
**DOUGLAS COUNTY MIL MOLDINGS**
Also Called: Douglas County Molding
326 E County Road 100n (61910-3746)
PHONE..............................217 268-4689
William Otto, *Owner*
Rhoda Otto, *Manager*
EMP: 6
SALES (est): 505.8K **Privately Held**
SIC: 2431 Moldings, wood: unfinished & prefinished

**(G-668)**
**EFFINGHAM EQUITY INC**
912 E County Road 600n (61910-3574)
PHONE..............................217 268-5128
Greg Taylor, *Branch Mgr*
EMP: 15
SALES (corp-wide): 322.5MM **Privately Held**
SIC: 5191 5153 2048 5171 Farm supplies; grain & field beans; prepared feeds; petroleum bulk stations & terminals; lumber & other building materials
PA: Effingham Equity, Inc.
201 W Roadway Ave
Effingham IL 62401
217 342-4101

**(G-669)**
**G L DOEMELT**
Also Called: Cnc Machining
299 Egyptian Trl (61910-1904)
P.O. Box 157 (61910-0157)
PHONE..............................217 268-4243
Fax: 217 268-3615
Gary L Doemelt, *President*
Clay Domelt, *Vice Pres*
EMP: 11
SQ FT: 20,000
SALES: 1.8MM **Privately Held**
WEB: www.cncmachining.com
SIC: 3599 Machine shop, jobbing & repair

**(G-670)**
**HERFF JONES LLC**
Collegiate Cap & Gown
901 Bob King Dr (61910-1905)
PHONE..............................217 268-4543
Fax: 217 268-4855
Marty Clapp, *Purch Agent*
Terry Hayden, *Manager*
EMP: 180
SALES (corp-wide): 1.1B **Privately Held**
WEB: www.herffjones.com
SIC: 2389 Academic vestments (caps & gowns)
HQ: Herff Jones, Llc
4501 W 62nd St
Indianapolis IN 46268
800 419-5462

**(G-671)**
**HUMBOLDT BROOM COMPANY**
901 E County Road 300n (61910-3711)
P.O. Box 165 (61910-0165)
PHONE..............................217 268-3718
Carol Turner, *Principal*
EMP: 5
SALES (est): 500K **Privately Held**
SIC: 3991 Brooms

**(G-672)**
**J & M REPRESENTATIVES INC**
Also Called: Simply Amish
401 E County Road 200n (61910-3750)
P.O. Box 67 (61910-0067)
PHONE..............................217 268-4504
Fax: 217 268-4316
Kevin Kauffman, *President*
Paula Murray, *Engineer*
Preston Owen, *CFO*
Adlai J Mast, *Treasurer*
Treston Owen, *Comptroller*
▲ EMP: 54
SQ FT: 115,000
SALES: 18.5MM **Privately Held**
SIC: 2511 Wood household furniture; wood bedroom furniture; kitchen & dining room furniture; breakfast sets (furniture): wood

**(G-673)**
**KAUFMANS CUSTOM CABINETS**
363 E County Road 200n (61910-3749)
PHONE..............................217 268-4330
Reuben Kaufman, *Owner*
EMP: 16
SALES (est): 730K **Privately Held**
SIC: 2434 2511 5712 2499 Wood kitchen cabinets; vanities, bathroom: wood; wood household furniture; furniture stores; decorative wood & woodwork

**(G-674)**
**LAVERNS WOOD ITEMS**
421 E County Road 200n (61910-3750)
PHONE..............................217 268-4544
Lavern Yoder, *Owner*
EMP: 6
SALES: 210K **Privately Held**
SIC: 2511 Wood household furniture

**(G-675)**
**LIBMAN COMPANY**
220 N Sheldon St (61910-1616)
PHONE..............................217 268-4200
Fax: 217 268-4168
Robert Libman, *President*
William Libman, *Corp Secy*
Keena King, *Production*
Jeff Sloan, *Purch Mgr*
Jan Ziebka, *Senior Buyer*
◆ EMP: 250 EST: 1898
SQ FT: 800,000
SALES (est): 83.6MM **Privately Held**
WEB: www.libman.com
SIC: 3991 2392 Brooms & brushes; mops, floor & dust

**(G-676)**
**MID-STATE INDUSTRIES OPER INC (PA)**
908 Bob King Dr (61910-1906)
PHONE..............................217 268-3900
Fax: 217 268-3906
Kevin S Corely, *President*
Ralph Becker, *CFO*
EMP: 35
SQ FT: 70,000
SALES (est): 17.2MM **Privately Held**
WEB: www.midstate.org
SIC: 3316 5051 Cold finishing of steel shapes; metals service centers & offices

**(G-677)**
**MONAHAN FILAMENTS LLC (HQ)**
Also Called: Specialty Filaments
215 Egyptian Trl (61910-1904)
P.O. Box 250 (61910-0250)
PHONE..............................217 268-4957
Mike Arsenalut, *Plant Mgr*
Craig Desautels, *Maint Spvr*
Jason Weber, *QC Mgr*
Linda Oldenburg, *HR Admin*
Jon Monahan, *Sales Staff*
▲ EMP: 53

SQ FT: 82,000
SALES (est): 19.3MM
SALES (corp-wide): 20.9MM **Privately Held**
WEB: www.monahanfilaments.com
SIC: 3089 Molding primary plastic
PA: The Thomas Monahan Company
202 N Oak St
Arcola IL 61910
217 268-5771

**(G-678)**
**MONAHAN PARTNERS INC**
200 N Oak St (61910-1425)
P.O. Box 248 (61910-0248)
PHONE..............................217 268-5758
Patrick Monahan, *President*
Kevin Monahan, *Vice Pres*
EMP: 13
SALES (est): 1.5MM **Privately Held**
SIC: 3751 Mopeds & parts

**(G-679)**
**MORNINGSIDE WOODCRAFT**
545 E County Road 200n (61910-3754)
PHONE..............................217 268-4313
Marcus L Mast, *Principal*
EMP: 3
SALES (est): 215.1K **Privately Held**
SIC: 2511 Wood household furniture

**(G-680)**
**OLD HERITAGE CREAMERY LLC**
222 N County Road 575e (61910-3784)
PHONE..............................217 268-4355
Samuel L Gingerich, *Principal*
EMP: 3
SALES (est): 156.4K **Privately Held**
SIC: 2021 Creamery butter

**(G-681)**
**PLANKS APPLE BUTTER**
175 N County Road 525e (61910-3782)
PHONE..............................217 268-4933
Robert Hochstetler, *Owner*
EMP: 3
SALES (est): 186.6K **Privately Held**
SIC: 2033 Apple sauce: packaged in cans, jars, etc.

**(G-682)**
**PRINTER CONNECTION**
319 S Elm St (61910-1731)
P.O. Box 153 (61910-0153)
PHONE..............................217 268-3252
Derek Sitz, *Owner*
EMP: 4
SALES: 160K **Privately Held**
SIC: 2759 Commercial printing

**(G-683)**
**RANKIN PUBLISHING INC**
Also Called: Business Magazine
204 E Main St (61910-1416)
P.O. Box 130 (61910-0130)
PHONE..............................217 268-4959
Fax: 217 268-4815
Donald Rankin, *President*
Linda Rankin, *Admin Sec*
EMP: 12 EST: 1867
SQ FT: 1,625
SALES (est): 610K **Privately Held**
SIC: 2711 2721 Job printing & newspaper publishing combined; magazines: publishing & printing

**(G-684)**
**SCHROCKS SAWMILL**
59 N County Road 450e (61910-3757)
PHONE..............................217 268-3632
Allen Schrock, *Partner*
Jonas Schrock, *Partner*
EMP: 3
SALES (est): 249.5K **Privately Held**
SIC: 2421 Sawmills & planing mills, general

**(G-685)**
**SLACK PUBLICATIONS**
736 Dogwood Dr (61910-1604)
PHONE..............................217 268-4950
Chris Slack, *Owner*
Cindy Slack, *Co-Owner*
EMP: 5

Arcola - Douglas County (G-686)

SALES (est): 237K **Privately Held**
SIC: 2711 Newspapers, publishing & printing

**(G-686)**
**THOMAS MONAHAN COMPANY (PA)**
202 N Oak St (61910-1425)
P.O. Box 250 (61910-0250)
PHONE .................................. 217 268-5771
Thomas Monahan, *President*
Tom Monahan, *COO*
James Monahan, *Vice Pres*
Layne Sutherland, *Purch Agent*
Brian Warfel, *Controller*
▲ **EMP:** 13 **EST:** 1922
**SQ FT:** 2,400
**SALES (est):** 20.9MM **Privately Held**
SIC: 2519 5159 Furniture, household: glass, fiberglass & plastic; broomcorn

**(G-687)**
**WALNUT GROVE PACKAGING**
578 E County Road 200n (61910-3754)
PHONE .................................. 217 268-5112
Dennis K Yoder, *Owner*
**EMP:** 2 **EST:** 1999
**SALES (est):** 220.3K **Privately Held**
SIC: 2448 Pallets, wood

## Arenzville
### Cass County

**(G-688)**
**COON RUN DRAINAGE & LEVEE DST**
826 Arenzville Rd (62611-3007)
PHONE .................................. 217 248-5511
Thomas Burrus, *Principal*
Robert Fitzsimmons, *Principal*
**EMP:** 4
**SALES (est):** 146.9K **Privately Held**
SIC: 3259 Clay sewer & drainage pipe & tile

## Argenta
### Macon County

**(G-689)**
**AUTUMN MILL**
13014 Cemetery Rd (62501-8040)
PHONE .................................. 217 795-3399
Tammy Allen, *Owner*
**EMP:** 5
**SALES (est):** 298.2K **Privately Held**
SIC: 2421 5211 Sawmills & planing mills, general; lumber products

**(G-690)**
**MICHAEL GOSS CUSTOM CABINETS**
11760 Cemetery Rd (62501-8264)
PHONE .................................. 217 864-4600
Michael Goss, *President*
**EMP:** 5
**SALES (est):** 527.1K **Privately Held**
SIC: 2599 Cabinets, factory

**(G-691)**
**OSBORNES MCH WELD FABRICATION**
8269 Dunbar Rd (62501-8117)
PHONE .................................. 217 795-4716
Fax: 217 795-4716
Roger P Osbourne, *President*
Charles R Osborne, *Treasurer*
Carol Osborne, *Admin Sec*
**EMP:** 3
**SQ FT:** 4,000
**SALES:** 100K **Privately Held**
SIC: 3599 7692 3444 3443 Machine shop, jobbing & repair; welding repair; sheet metalwork; fabricated plate work (boiler shop); fabricated structural metal

**(G-692)**
**ROBERTS AND DOWNEY CHAPEL EQP**
101 S North St (62501-8234)
P.O. Box 198 (62501-0198)
PHONE .................................. 217 795-2391
Rick Roberts, *President*
Elizabeth Roberts, *Corp Secy*
**EMP:** 6
**SALES (est):** 761.4K **Privately Held**
WEB: www.robertsanddowney.com
SIC: 2531 Church furniture

## Argo
### Cook County

**(G-693)**
**INGREDION INCORPORATED**
6400 S Archer Rd Bldg 90 (60501-1935)
P.O. Box 345 (60501-0345)
PHONE .................................. 708 563-2400
Tom Siil, *Engineer*
Marek Siczek, *Finance Mgr*
Shale Susin, *Manager*
**EMP:** 153
**SALES (corp-wide):** 5.7B **Publicly Held**
SIC: 2046 Wet corn milling; corn starch; corn oil products; corn sugars & syrups
PA: Ingredion Incorporated
5 Westbrook Corporate Ctr # 500
Westchester IL 60154
708 551-2600

**(G-694)**
**OWENS CORNING SALES LLC**
5824 S Archer Rd (60501-1410)
PHONE .................................. 708 594-6911
Fax: 708 496-1684
Jerry Moore, *Principal*
**EMP:** 350
**SALES (corp-wide):** 5.6B **Publicly Held**
WEB: www.owenscorning.com
SIC: 3296 2952 Roofing mats, mineral wool; asphalt felts & coatings
HQ: Owens Corning Sales, Llc
1 Owens Corning Pkwy
Toledo OH 43659
419 248-8000

**(G-695)**
**OWENS CORNING SALES LLC**
7800 W 59th St (60501-1434)
PHONE .................................. 708 594-6935
Fax: 708 594-6981
Russell K Snyder, *Exec VP*
Mark Schulte, *Manager*
**EMP:** 40
**SALES (corp-wide):** 5.6B **Publicly Held**
WEB: www.owenscorning.com
SIC: 3996 2951 2952 2891 Asphalted-felt-base floor coverings: linoleum, carpet; asphalt paving mixtures & blocks; asphalt felts & coatings; adhesives & sealants; paints & allied products
HQ: Owens Corning Sales, Llc
1 Owens Corning Pkwy
Toledo OH 43659
419 248-8000

**(G-696)**
**OWENS-CORNING FIBERGLASS TECH**
7734 W 59th St (60501-1428)
PHONE .................................. 708 563-9091
Dave Brown, *President*
Liz Reid, *Vice Pres*
Steven Cowan, *Manager*
**EMP:** 5
**SALES (est):** 827.3K
**SALES (corp-wide):** 5.6B **Publicly Held**
WEB: www.owenscorning.com
SIC: 3296 Fiberglass insulation
HQ: Owens Corning Sales, Llc
1 Owens Corning Pkwy
Toledo OH 43659
419 248-8000

**(G-697)**
**WELDBEND CORPORATION**
6600 S Harlem Ave (60501-1930)
PHONE .................................. 708 594-1700
Fax: 773 582-7621
James J Coulas Jr, *President*
David Shulman, *General Mgr*
Epitacio Torres, *Engineer*
James Coulas, *CIO*
Mildred Hynes, *Admin Sec*
▲ **EMP:** 200
**SQ FT:** 420,000
**SALES (est):** 86.8MM **Privately Held**
WEB: www.weldbend.com
SIC: 3462 Flange, valve & pipe fitting forgings, ferrous

**(G-698)**
**WILLIMS-HYWARD INTL CTINGS INC**
7400 W Archer Ave (60501-1218)
PHONE .................................. 708 458-0015
Henry Jostock, *Treasurer*
Ed Kurcz, *Manager*
**EMP:** 15
**SALES (corp-wide):** 10.8MM **Privately Held**
SIC: 8051 3743 2851 8731 Skilled nursing care facilities; railroad equipment; paints & allied products; commercial physical research
PA: Williams-Hayward International Coatings, Inc.
7425 W 59th St
Summit Argo IL 60501
708 563-5182

## Arlington Heights
### Cook County

**(G-699)**
**4EVER PRINTING INC**
Also Called: 4ever Design Studio
3401b N Kennicott Ave (60004)
PHONE .................................. 847 222-1525
Maksim Vaurysh, *President*
**EMP:** 3
**SALES (est):** 200.4K **Privately Held**
SIC: 7372 7389 Publishers' computer software; design services

**(G-700)**
**A G MITCHELLS JEWELERS LTD**
10 N Dunton Ave (60005-1426)
PHONE .................................. 847 394-0820
Fax: 847 394-3829
James Mitchell, *President*
Alfred Mitchell, *Principal*
Esther H Mitchell, *Exec VP*
Doug Mitchell, *Vice Pres*
**EMP:** 10
**SQ FT:** 6,500
**SALES (est):** 1.2MM **Privately Held**
WEB: www.mjltd.com
SIC: 3911 7631 5944 Jewelry apparel; watch repair; jewelry stores

**(G-701)**
**AAA PRESS SPECIALISTS INC**
Also Called: AAA Press International
3160 N Kennicott Ave (60004-1426)
PHONE .................................. 847 818-1100
Fax: 847 818-0071
Jack Ludwig, *President*
Sharon Ludwig, *Treasurer*
Mark Hahn, *VP Sales*
John Denten, *Marketing Staff*
Mike Wardynski, *Administration*
▲ **EMP:** 18
**SQ FT:** 20,000
**SALES (est):** 4MM **Privately Held**
WEB: www.aaapress.com
SIC: 3641 5084 7699 Ultraviolet lamps; printing trades machinery, equipment & supplies; industrial equipment services

**(G-702)**
**ADHES TAPE TECHNOLOGY INC**
3339 N Ridge Ave (60004-1411)
PHONE .................................. 847 496-7949
Jiliang Chen, *President*
Hong Qian, *Director*
**EMP:** 5
**SQ FT:** 2,400
**SALES (est):** 443.5K **Privately Held**
SIC: 2241 3069 5085 Fabric tapes; rubber tape; adhesives, tape & plasters

**(G-703)**
**AFS INC**
3232 Nordic Rd (60005-4729)
PHONE .................................. 847 437-2345
Gary Murino, *President*
Jon Pfeifer, *Branch Mgr*
Harry Sayre, *Branch Mgr*
**EMP:** 12
**SALES (est):** 896.2K **Privately Held**
SIC: 2869 Fuels

**(G-704)**
**AGILENT TECHNOLOGIES INC**
720 W Algonquin Rd (60005-4416)
PHONE .................................. 847 690-0431
**EMP:** 3275
**SALES (corp-wide):** 4.2B **Publicly Held**
SIC: 3825 Instruments to measure electricity
PA: Agilent Technologies, Inc.
5301 Stevens Creek Blvd
Santa Clara CA 95051
408 345-8886

**(G-705)**
**ALCON COMPONENTS**
716 N Arlington Hts Rd (60004-5664)
P.O. Box 2057 (60006-2057)
PHONE .................................. 847 788-0901
Phil Stubbs, *President*
**EMP:** 6
**SALES (est):** 530K **Privately Held**
SIC: 3711 Motor vehicles & car bodies

**(G-706)**
**ALDEN & OTT PRINTING INKS CO (DH)**
616 E Brook Dr (60005-4622)
PHONE .................................. 847 956-6830
Fax: 847 956-6906
Thomas G Alden, *President*
Arek Curylo, *General Mgr*
Marisela Moctezuma, *Purch Dir*
Keith Baumann, *Finance*
Chris Hedlund, *Sales Mgr*
▲ **EMP:** 70 **EST:** 1957
**SQ FT:** 30,000
**SALES (est):** 17MM
**SALES (corp-wide):** 879.3MM **Privately Held**
WEB: www.aldenottink.com
SIC: 2893 Printing ink
HQ: Hubergroup Usa, Inc.
2850 Festival Dr
Kankakee IL 60901
815 929-9293

**(G-707)**
**ALLTEMATED INC (PA)**
3353 N Ridge Ave (60004-1411)
PHONE .................................. 847 394-5800
Randall J Temple, *President*
Steve Hall, *Vice Pres*
Bridgette Riley, *Human Res Dir*
Ann Annese, *Director*
**EMP:** 40
**SQ FT:** 10,500
**SALES (est):** 5.4MM **Privately Held**
WEB: www.alltemated.com
SIC: 3661 7389 Telephone & telegraph apparatus; packaging & labeling services

**(G-708)**
**ALPHA ACRYLIC DESIGN**
3359 N Ridge Ave Ste A (60004-7812)
PHONE .................................. 847 818-8178
Phillip Liu, *General Ptnr*
Jeffrey Rockenbach, *Manager*
**EMP:** 3
**SALES (est):** 290K **Privately Held**
WEB: www.alphaacrylic.com
SIC: 3089 5199 Plastic kitchenware, tableware & houseware; gifts & novelties

**(G-709)**
**AMERICAN COLLOID MINERALS CO**
1500 W Shure Dr Fl 7 (60004-1477)
P.O. Box 95411, Hoffman Estates (60195-0411)
PHONE .................................. 800 527-9948
Fax: 847 506-6195
Bruce J Birney, *Principal*
Tena Heartsill, *Safety Dir*
Craig Havlick, *Transptn Dir*

Chuck McAulay, *Plant Mgr*
Greg Haak, *Opers Spvr*
▼ **EMP:** 30
**SALES (est):** 2.9MM **Privately Held**
**SIC:** 1459 Clay & related minerals

**(G-710)**
**AMERICAN SOC PLASTIC SURGEONS (PA)**
444 E Algonquin Rd # 100 (60005-4666)
**PHONE** .................................. 847 228-9900
**Fax:** 847 228-9131
Malcom Roth MD, *President*
John Canady, *Sr Corp Ofcr*
Michael Castello, *Exec VP*
Robert Micek, *CFO*
Russ Holbrook, *Human Res Dir*
**EMP:** 80 **EST:** 1931
**SQ FT:** 31,000
**SALES (est):** 21.4MM **Privately Held**
**SIC:** 8621 8322 2721 Medical field-related associations; individual & family services; periodicals

**(G-711)**
**AMPCO METAL INCORPORATED (PA)**
Also Called: Ampco Aquisition
1117 E Algonquin Rd (60005-4791)
**PHONE** .................................. 847 437-6000
Michael Fishers, *CEO*
J F Dalin, *President*
Wilko Beukers, *Vice Pres*
Gary Recinella, *CFO*
Andrew Sobol, *Sales Mgr*
◆ **EMP:** 27 **EST:** 2003
**SQ FT:** 30,000
**SALES (est):** 10.9MM **Privately Held**
**WEB:** www.ampcometal.com
**SIC:** 3366 3331 3351 5085 Copper foundries; bronze foundry; bars (primary), copper; bars & bar shapes, copper & copper alloy; welding supplies

**(G-712)**
**AMPEX SCREW MFG INC**
2936 Malmo Dr (60005-4726)
**PHONE** .................................. 847 228-1202
**Fax:** 847 228-1257
Herta Mueller, *President*
Charles Mueller, *Vice Pres*
**EMP:** 7
**SQ FT:** 10,000
**SALES (est):** 930K **Privately Held**
**SIC:** 3452 3451 Bolts, metal; rivets, metal; screw machine products

**(G-713)**
**ANDERSON & VREELAND-ILLINOIS**
525 W University Dr (60004-1815)
**PHONE** .................................. 847 255-2110
**Fax:** 847 255-2231
Howard Vreeland Sr, *President*
Wesley Anderson, *Vice Pres*
Ray Bucher, *Controller*
Phil Novak, *Office Mgr*
Rosemary Russo, *Services*
▲ **EMP:** 10
**SQ FT:** 24,000
**SALES (est):** 2.4MM
**SALES (corp-wide):** 51.4MM **Privately Held**
**WEB:** www.andersonvreeland.com
**SIC:** 5084 3555 Printing trades machinery, equipment & supplies; printing plates
**PA:** Anderson & Vreeland, Inc.
 8 Evans St
 Fairfield NJ 07004
 973 227-2270

**(G-714)**
**ANGLE PRESS INC**
415 E Golf Rd Ste 101 (60005-4049)
**PHONE** .................................. 847 439-6388
Fujio Nakagawa, *President*
**EMP:** 9
**SALES (est):** 812.4K **Privately Held**
**SIC:** 2741 Miscellaneous publishing

**(G-715)**
**ARENS CONTROLS COMPANY LLC**
3602 N Kennicott Ave (60004-1467)
**PHONE** .................................. 847 844-4700
Brian Krause, *Business Mgr*
George Anderson, *Facilities Mgr*
John Saunders, *Purch Mgr*
Joe Heinisch, *Buyer*
Sue Lorusso, *QC Mgr*
▲ **EMP:** 90
**SQ FT:** 97,000
**SALES (est):** 23.7MM
**SALES (corp-wide):** 2.1B **Publicly Held**
**WEB:** www.arenscontrols.com
**SIC:** 3568 Power transmission equipment
**PA:** Curtiss-Wright Corporation
 13925 Balntyn Corp Pl
 Charlotte NC 28277
 704 869-4600

**(G-716)**
**ARLINGTON STRL STL CO INC**
1727 E Davis St (60005-2811)
**PHONE** .................................. 847 577-2200
**Fax:** 847 259-1727
Richard Clarbour, *President*
S Daniel Clarbour, *Vice Pres*
Ray Tomczak, *Opers Mgr*
Lee Clarbour, *Treasurer*
**EMP:** 28
**SQ FT:** 11,000
**SALES (est):** 10.6MM **Privately Held**
**WEB:** www.arlingtonsteel.com
**SIC:** 3441 Fabricated structural metal

**(G-717)**
**ARROWS UP INC**
3 W College Dr Rear 1 (60004-1991)
**PHONE** .................................. 847 305-2550
**Fax:** 847 305-2582
John Allegretti, *President*
**EMP:** 5
**SALES (est):** 995.8K **Privately Held**
**SIC:** 3523 3412 2448 5039 Crop storage bins; pails, shipping: metal; cargo containers, wood & wood with metal; grain storage bins; bins & containers, storage

**(G-718)**
**ASCO VALVE INC**
443 S Banbury Rd (60005-2001)
**PHONE** .................................. 630 789-2082
Scott Manminato, *Manager*
**EMP:** 12
**SALES (corp-wide):** 14.5B **Publicly Held**
**WEB:** www.rapcoassoc.com
**SIC:** 3491 Solenoid valves
**HQ:** Asco Valve, Inc.
 50-60 Hanover Rd
 Florham Park NJ 07932
 973 966-2437

**(G-719)**
**AUTOMTIC LQUID PCKG SLTONS LLC**
2445 E Oakton St (60005-4819)
**PHONE** .................................. 847 372-3336
Arjun Ramrajhyani, *President*
**EMP:** 20
**SQ FT:** 100,000
**SALES (est):** 2.1MM **Privately Held**
**SIC:** 3565 Packaging machinery

**(G-720)**
**AVANT TECNO USA INC**
3020 Malmo Dr (60005-4728)
**PHONE** .................................. 847 380-9822
▲ **EMP:** 23
**SALES:** 4.8MM **Privately Held**
**SIC:** 3523 Loaders, farm type: manure, general utility

**(G-721)**
**BACT PROCESS SYSTEMS INC**
3345 N Arlington Hts B (60004-1591)
**PHONE** .................................. 847 577-0950
N S Balakrishnan, *President*
Jerry Kabat, *Manager*
**EMP:** 6
**SQ FT:** 2,000
**SALES (est):** 1.6MM **Privately Held**
**SIC:** 3564 Air cleaning systems

**(G-722)**
**BAKERY CRESCENT CORPORATION**
270 E Algonquin Rd (60005-4662)
**PHONE** .................................. 847 956-6470
Shin Azumaya, *President*
Shibata Yoshi, *Info Tech Dir*
Yoshi Shibata, *Webmaster*
**EMP:** 4
**SALES (est):** 260K **Privately Held**
**SIC:** 2051 Bread, cake & related products

**(G-723)**
**BAPTIST GENERAL CONFERENCE (PA)**
Also Called: Harvest Publications Div
2002 S Arlington Hts Rd (60005-4193)
**PHONE** .................................. 800 323-4215
**Fax:** 847 228-5376
Jerry Sheveland, *President*
Ray Swatkowski, *Exec VP*
Stephen Doggett, *Vice Pres*
Lewis Petrie, *Vice Pres*
Larson Ron, *Vice Pres*
**EMP:** 75
**SQ FT:** 28,500
**SALES (est):** 9.9MM **Privately Held**
**WEB:** www.mbcworld.org
**SIC:** 8661 8221 2731 2721 Non-church religious organizations; theological seminary; books; publishing only; periodicals publishing only

**(G-724)**
**BE MCGONAGLE INC**
Also Called: Somebody's Pub & Grille
858 S Arthur Ave (60005-2828)
**PHONE** .................................. 847 394-0413
Beth McGonagle, *President*
**EMP:** 4
**SALES (est):** 243.6K **Privately Held**
**SIC:** 2599 Bar, restaurant & cafeteria furniture

**(G-725)**
**BIZSTARTERSCOM LLC**
126 E Wing St Ste 321 (60004-6064)
**PHONE** .................................. 847 305-4626
Jeff Williams, *Principal*
**EMP:** 3
**SALES (est):** 272.4K **Privately Held**
**SIC:** 3812 Defense systems & equipment

**(G-726)**
**BLACK ROCK MILLING AND PAV CO**
2400 Terminal Dr (60005)
**PHONE** .................................. 847 952-0700
Danielle Peterson, *Owner*
**EMP:** 10
**SALES (est):** 710.3K **Privately Held**
**SIC:** 2952 Asphalt felts & coatings

**(G-727)**
**BOX OF RAIN LTD**
Also Called: EDR ELECTRONICS INC.
1504 E Algonquin Rd (60005-4718)
**PHONE** .................................. 847 640-6996
**Fax:** 847 640-9717
Donald Boe, *President*
**EMP:** 4
**SQ FT:** 1,750
**SALES:** 179.7K **Privately Held**
**WEB:** www.edrelectronics.com
**SIC:** 3625 Electric controls & control accessories, industrial

**(G-728)**
**BRAN-ZAN HOLDINGS LLC (PA)**
Also Called: Chef M J Brando
1655 N Arlington Heights (60004-3958)
**PHONE** .................................. 847 342-0000
Steven Marlowe, *Principal*
**EMP:** 15
**SQ FT:** 10,000
**SALES (est):** 50MM **Privately Held**
**WEB:** www.branzan.com
**SIC:** 2034 Potato products, dried & dehydrated

**(G-729)**
**BREX-ARLINGTON INCORPORATED**
714 E Kensington Rd (60004-6201)
**PHONE** .................................. 847 255-6284
Richard Brex, *President*
Tom Zolandek, *Vice Pres*
**EMP:** 15 **EST:** 1971
**SQ FT:** 3,100
**SALES (est):** 2.1MM **Privately Held**
**WEB:** www.brexarlingtoninc.com
**SIC:** 1711 3444 Warm air heating & air conditioning contractor; sheet metalwork

**(G-730)**
**BRITE-O-MATIC MFG INC**
527 W Algonquin Rd (60005-4411)
**PHONE** .................................. 847 956-1100
**Fax:** 847 956-1225
Lynne Mohr, *President*
William J Gasser, *Chairman*
David Hamaker, *Plant Mgr*
Paul Hamaker, *Facilities Mgr*
Jim Salyers, *Design Engr*
**EMP:** 52
**SQ FT:** 25,000
**SALES (est):** 10.9MM **Privately Held**
**SIC:** 3589 Car washing machinery

**(G-731)**
**BRITT INDUSTRIES INC**
Also Called: Metal Finishers
3010 Malmo Dr (60005-4728)
**PHONE** .................................. 847 640-1177
**Fax:** 847 640-7465
Caroline M Schroll, *President*
William R Schroll, *Vice Pres*
Karen Tourtellott, *Office Mgr*
**EMP:** 20
**SQ FT:** 30,000
**SALES (est):** 2.4MM **Privately Held**
**SIC:** 3479 Coating of metals with plastic or resins; painting of metal products

**(G-732)**
**BUHRKE INDUSTRIES LLC (HQ)**
Also Called: IMS Buhrke-Olson
511 W Algonquin Rd (60005-4499)
**PHONE** .................................. 847 981-7550
**Fax:** 847 981-0485
Mark Simanton, *CEO*
Keith Krutz, *President*
James Talarek, *COO*
Richard Tile, *Purchasing*
Bill Smith, *VP Engrg*
▲ **EMP:** 450
**SQ FT:** 400,000
**SALES (est):** 40MM
**SALES (corp-wide):** 607.5MM **Privately Held**
**WEB:** www.buhrke.com
**SIC:** 3469 Metal stampings
**PA:** Ims Companies, Llc
 1 Innovation Dr
 Des Plaines IL 60016
 847 391-8100

**(G-733)**
**C L GREENSLADE SALES INC (PA)**
505 E Golf Rd Ste H (60005-4000)
**PHONE** .................................. 847 593-3450
**Fax:** 847 593-3468
John Brennan, *President*
**EMP:** 5
**SQ FT:** 2,000
**SALES (est):** 730.3K **Privately Held**
**WEB:** www.gsi-sales.com
**SIC:** 3679 Electronic circuits

**(G-734)**
**CHICAGO NEWS LLC**
415 E Golf Rd Ste 106 (60005-4049)
Sauchanka Vera, *Principal*
**EMP:** 5
**SALES (est):** 166.1K **Privately Held**
**SIC:** 2711 Newspapers

**(G-735)**
**CHINO WORKS AMERICA INC**
121 S Wilke Rd Ste 226 (60005-1530)
**PHONE** .................................. 630 328-0014
George Bartosiak, *Branch Mgr*
**EMP:** 5
**SALES (corp-wide):** 163.4MM **Privately Held**
**SIC:** 3823 Industrial instrmnts msrmnt display/control process variable
**HQ:** Chino Works America, Inc
 22301 S Wstn Ave Ste 105
 Torrance CA 90501
 310 787-8899

## Arlington Heights - Cook County (G-736)

**(G-736)**
**COLOR SIGNS**
3110 N Arlington Hts Rd  (60004-1532)
PHONE ................................ 847 368-0101
Jay Brown, *Owner*
**EMP:** 5
**SALES (est):** 320.3K **Privately Held**
**SIC:** 3993  Signs & advertising specialties

**(G-737)**
**COMMERCIAL DYNAMICS INC**
2025 S Arlington Hts Rd  (60005-4152)
PHONE ................................ 847 439-5300
**EMP:** 4 **EST:** 2006
**SALES (est):** 260K **Privately Held**
**SIC:** 3599  Mfg Industrial Machinery

**(G-738)**
**COMPUTER INDUSTRY ALMANAC INC**
Also Called: Internet Industry Almanac
1013 S Belmont Ave  (60005-3201)
PHONE ................................ 847 758-1926
Karen Petska, *President*
Karen Tepska, *President*
**EMP:** 3
**SALES:** 125K **Privately Held**
**WEB:** www.c-i-a.com
**SIC:** 7379  2731  Computer related consulting services; books: publishing only

**(G-739)**
**CONTOUR SCREW PRODUCTS INC**
3014 Malmo Dr  (60005-4728)
PHONE ................................ 847 357-1190
**Fax:** 847 357-1192
Richard Tignino, *President*
Mary Tignino, *Corp Secy*
Albert Kupstys, *Sr Corp Ofcr*
Laura Cooke, *Human Res Mgr*
**EMP:** 35
**SQ FT:** 28,000
**SALES:** 2.5MM **Privately Held**
**WEB:** www.contourscrew.com
**SIC:** 3599  3451  Machine shop, jobbing & repair; screw machine products

**(G-740)**
**COUNTRYSIDE PURE WATER SOLUTIO**
3 W College Dr Rear 1  (60004-1991)
PHONE ................................ 847 255-5524
Ray Schwarz, *Owner*
**EMP:** 3
**SALES (est):** 264.1K **Privately Held**
**WEB:** www.countrysideecowater.com
**SIC:** 3589  Water purification equipment, household type

**(G-741)**
**CUSTOM RODS BY GRANDT LTD**
Also Called: Grandt's Custom Fishing Rods
203 S Highland Ave  (60005-1828)
PHONE ................................ 847 577-0848
James A Grandt, *President*
**EMP:** 2
**SALES (est):** 297.6K **Privately Held**
**WEB:** www.grandtrods.com
**SIC:** 3949  5941  Rods & rod parts, fishing; sporting goods & bicycle shops

**(G-742)**
**CUT RITE DIE CO**
732 N Dryden Ave  (60004-5730)
PHONE ................................ 847 394-0492
Theodore E Smith, *Partner*
**EMP:** 3
**SALES (est):** 199.1K **Privately Held**
**SIC:** 3544  Special dies & tools

**(G-743)**
**D&J ARLINGTON HEIGHTS INC**
Also Called: Fastsigns
1814 N Arlington Hts Rd  (60004-3910)
PHONE ................................ 847 577-8200
**Fax:** 847 577-7853
Gerald A Becker, *President*
David Becker, *Admin Sec*
**EMP:** 3
**SQ FT:** 2,000
**SALES (est):** 455.3K **Privately Held**
**SIC:** 3993  Signs & advertising specialties

**(G-744)**
**DANA PLASTIC CONTAINER CORP (HQ)**
6 N Hickory Ave  (60004-6205)
PHONE ................................ 847 670-0650
Daniel Hidding, *CEO*
David Hidding, *President*
Mike Haber, *CFO*
▲ **EMP:** 2
**SQ FT:** 45,000
**SALES (est):** 3.8MM
**SALES (corp-wide):** 11.7MM **Privately Held**
**WEB:** www.danaplastic.com
**SIC:** 3085  Plastics bottles
**PA:** Dana Molded Products, Inc.
     810 Commerce Pkwy
     Carpentersville IL 60110
     847 783-1800

**(G-745)**
**DAWES LLC (PA)**
Also Called: Dawe's Laboratories
3355 N Arlington Hts Rd  (60004-7706)
PHONE ................................ 847 577-2020
**Fax:** 847 577-1898
Charles R Dawe,
Cameron Gillingham,
▼ **EMP:** 10 **EST:** 1926
**SQ FT:** 6,000
**SALES (est):** 3.7MM **Privately Held**
**SIC:** 2048  8731  2833  Prepared feeds; commercial physical research; medicinals & botanicals

**(G-746)**
**DIAMOND MACHINE WERKS INC**
Also Called: Automtic Lquid Packg Solutions
2445 E Oakton St  (60005-4879)
PHONE ................................ 847 437-0665
Ted Geiselman, *President*
Brad Farrell, *Project Mgr*
Steve Karnatz, *Engineer*
Margaret Brock, *Executive*
Siegfried Weiler, *Admin Sec*
▲ **EMP:** 50
**SQ FT:** 65,000
**SALES (est):** 12.5MM **Privately Held**
**SIC:** 3569  3565  Assembly machines, non-metalworking; bottling machinery: filling, capping, labeling

**(G-747)**
**DJW MACHINING INC**
2912 Malmo Dr  (60005-4726)
PHONE ................................ 847 956-5330
Tedd Wosny, *President*
**EMP:** 9
**SALES (est):** 1.5MM **Privately Held**
**SIC:** 3599  Machine shop, jobbing & repair

**(G-748)**
**DURACLEAN INTERNATIONAL INC**
220 W Campus Dr Ste A  (60004-1498)
PHONE ................................ 847 704-7100
Vincent Caffarello, *President*
Wilbur Gage, *Exec VP*
Bill Ondratschek, *Vice Pres*
**EMP:** 10
**SQ FT:** 12,000
**SALES (est):** 3.2MM **Privately Held**
**WEB:** www.duraclean.com
**SIC:** 6794  7217  2842  Franchises, selling or licensing; carpet & upholstery cleaning; cleaning or polishing preparations

**(G-749)**
**ELMHURST ENTERPRISE GROUP INC**
Also Called: Kwik Kopy Printing
11 E Golf Rd  (60005-4001)
PHONE ................................ 847 228-5945
**Fax:** 847 228-1777
Robert Vollmer, *President*
Courtney R Vollmer, *Vice Pres*
**EMP:** 6
**SQ FT:** 1,150
**SALES (est):** 694.7K **Privately Held**
**SIC:** 2752  2791  2789  Commercial printing, lithographic; typesetting; bookbinding & related work

**(G-750)**
**ERGO HELP INC**
Also Called: Ergo Automatics
2466 E Oakton St  (60005-4820)
PHONE ................................ 847 593-0722
**Fax:** 847 593-0797
Gene Vatel, *President*
**EMP:** 4
**SALES (est):** 2.2MM **Privately Held**
**SIC:** 3593  3423  5084  Fluid power cylinders & actuators; hand & edge tools; materials handling machinery

**(G-751)**
**EROWA TECHNOLOGY INC**
2535 S Clearbrook Dr  (60005-4623)
PHONE ................................ 847 290-0295
**Fax:** 847 290-0298
Hans Hediger, *President*
Nils Fagerman, *Regional Mgr*
Robert Byers, *Vice Pres*
Thomas Lanz, *Engineer*
Kathy Gresens, *Bookkeeper*
▲ **EMP:** 17
**SQ FT:** 10,000
**SALES (est):** 8.3MM **Privately Held**
**WEB:** www.erowatech.com
**SIC:** 5084  3544  7699  Machine tools & accessories; special dies, tools, jigs & fixtures; industrial equipment services
**HQ:** Erowa Ag
     Winkelstrasse 8
     Reinach AG
     627 650-707

**(G-752)**
**FASPRO TECHNOLOGIES INC (PA)**
500 W Campus Dr  (60004-1408)
PHONE ................................ 847 392-9500
Igor Shkarovsky, *CEO*
Nikita Postovalov, *General Mgr*
Molly Morrison, *Regl Sales Mgr*
Yury Persits, *Director*
**EMP:** 95
**SQ FT:** 40,000
**SALES (est):** 20.3MM **Privately Held**
**SIC:** 3443  Plate work for the metalworking trade

**(G-753)**
**FAUSTOS BAKERY**
Also Called: Fausto's Bread Bakery
16 S Evergreen Ave  (60005-1428)
PHONE ................................ 847 255-9049
**Fax:** 847 255-1608
Fausto Bonica, *Owner*
**EMP:** 4
**SALES (est):** 190.2K **Privately Held**
**SIC:** 2051  Bread, cake & related products

**(G-754)**
**FEDEX OFFICE & PRINT SVCS INC**
205 W Rand Rd  (60004-3144)
PHONE ................................ 847 670-4100
Jeff Szdenski, *Manager*
**EMP:** 20
**SALES (corp-wide):** 50.3B **Publicly Held**
**WEB:** www.kinkos.com
**SIC:** 7334  3993  2789  Photocopying & duplicating services; signs & advertising specialties; bookbinding & related work
**HQ:** Fedex Office And Print Services, Inc.
     7900 Legacy Dr
     Plano TX 75024
     214 550-7000

**(G-755)**
**FONTANA ASSOCIATES INC**
Also Called: Breachers Tape
2605 S Clearbrook Dr  (60005-4625)
P.O. Box 962, Lake Zurich  (60047-0962)
PHONE ................................ 888 707-8273
Nicholas Caradonna Jr, *President*
**EMP:** 1
**SALES (est):** 500K **Privately Held**
**SIC:** 2891  5085  Adhesives & sealants; adhesives, tape & plasters

**(G-756)**
**G & J ASSOCIATES INC**
Also Called: Signs By Tomorrow
1315 E Davis St  (60005-2132)
PHONE ................................ 847 255-0123
**Fax:** 847 255-0183
Gerd K Loof, *President*
Joe Loof, *Manager*
**EMP:** 4
**SALES (est):** 369.6K **Privately Held**
**SIC:** 3993  Signs & advertising specialties

**(G-757)**
**G AND D ENTERPRISES INC**
Also Called: Shockwaves Promotional Apparel
1425 E Algonquin Rd  (60005-4715)
PHONE ................................ 847 981-8661
**Fax:** 773 981-8662
Doreen Gaardbo, *President*
Greg Gaardbo, *Vice Pres*
**EMP:** 30
**SQ FT:** 70,000
**SALES (est):** 4.7MM **Privately Held**
**WEB:** www.shockwavesapparel.com
**SIC:** 2759  3993  2396  2395  Screen printing; signs & advertising specialties; automotive & apparel trimmings; pleating & stitching

**(G-758)**
**G R LEONARD & CO INC (PA)**
Also Called: Leonard's Guide
115 E University Dr  (60004-1803)
PHONE ................................ 847 797-8101
**Fax:** 847 797-9016
David Ercolani, *CEO*
Elizabeth Stern, *Corp Secy*
Ahmed Hawari, *Vice Pres*
Josephine Worman, *Director*
▲ **EMP:** 20 **EST:** 1912
**SQ FT:** 30,000
**SALES (est):** 1.6MM **Privately Held**
**WEB:** www.leonardsguide.com
**SIC:** 2741  Directories: publishing only, not printed on site; guides: publishing only, not printed on site

**(G-759)**
**GE HEALTHCARE HOLDINGS INC**
3350 N Ridge Ave  (60004-1412)
PHONE ................................ 847 398-8400
Daniel Peters, *President*
William Clarke MD, *Exec VP*
Russel P Mayer, *Vice Pres*
J E Reller, *Vice Pres*
Jack Waterman, *Vice Pres*
▲ **EMP:** 1498
**SQ FT:** 126,000
**SALES (est):** 185.2MM **Privately Held**
**WEB:** www.amersham.co.uk
**SIC:** 2835  2833  5169  5122  In vitro & in vivo diagnostic substances; radioactive diagnostic substances; medicinals & botanicals; chemicals & allied products; medicinals & botanicals
**HQ:** Ge Healthcare Limited
     White Lion Rd
     Amersham BUCKS HP7 9
     149 454-4000

**(G-760)**
**GRAND FORMS & SYSTEMS INC**
204 N Kennicott Ave  (60005-1258)
P.O. Box 1128  (60006-1128)
PHONE ................................ 847 259-4600
**Fax:** 847 259-9727
Gregory G Grana, *President*
Rita Grana, *Admin Sec*
**EMP:** 10
**SALES (est):** 670K **Privately Held**
**WEB:** www.grandeduindiana.org
**SIC:** 2759  5112  2761  2752  Business forms: printing; business forms; manifold business forms; commercial printing, lithographic

**(G-761)**
**H FIELD & SONS INC**
2605 S Clearbrook Dr  (60005-4625)
PHONE ................................ 847 434-0970
**Fax:** 847 434-0980
Lew Field, *President*
Joe Field, *Chairman*
Charles Field, *Vice Pres*
Chuck Field, *Vice Pres*
Cindy Yokum, *CFO*
**EMP:** 10 **EST:** 1933
**SQ FT:** 48,000

SALES (est): 2.1MM  Privately Held
WEB: www.fieldbox.com
SIC: 2653  5113  2657  Boxes, corrugated: made from purchased materials; boxes & containers; folding paperboard boxes

### (G-762)
### HAAKER MOLD CO INC
628 N Salem Ave  (60004-5332)
PHONE.................................847 253-8103
Ronald Haaker, *President*
Linda Steiner, *Office Mgr*
EMP: 3
SALES (est): 180K  Privately Held
SIC: 3544  Industrial molds

### (G-763)
### HEARING SCREENING ASSOC LLC
Also Called: Hsa
3333 N Kennicott Ave  (60004-1429)
PHONE.................................855 550-9427
Thomas Larsen, *President*
Leigh Heinen, *Admin Asst*
EMP: 9  EST: 2015
SALES (est): 420.1K  Privately Held
SIC: 3841  5047  Surgical & medical instruments; instruments, surgical & medical
HQ: William Demant Holding A/S
    Kongebakken 9
    SmOrum  2765
    391 771-00

### (G-764)
### HEART PRINTING INC
Also Called: Heart Printing & Form Service
1624 W Northwest Hwy  (60004-5254)
PHONE.................................847 259-2100
Fax: 847 259-1117
Mark A Poe, *President*
Poe Lyndy, *Vice Pres*
Lyn Poe, *Vice Pres*
EMP: 4
SQ FT: 1,200
SALES (est): 390K  Privately Held
SIC: 2752  2791  2789  2759  Commercial printing, offset; typesetting; bookbinding & related work; commercial printing

### (G-765)
### HIGH-5 PRINTWEAR INC
3311 N Ridge Ave  (60004-1411)
PHONE.................................847 818-0081
Fax: 847 818-0082
John Schram, *CEO*
Kristie Schram, *President*
EMP: 5
SALES (est): 495.9K  Privately Held
SIC: 5699  2759  T-shirts, custom printed; screen printing

### (G-766)
### HITACHI METALS AMERICA  LLC
85 W Algonquin Rd Ste 400  (60005-4429)
PHONE.................................847 364-7200
Harry Tanakca, *Branch Mgr*
EMP: 10
SALES (corp-wide): 80.6B  Privately Held
SIC: 3264  Magnets, permanent: ceramic or ferrite
HQ: Hitachi Metals America, Ltd.
    2 Manhattanville Rd # 301
    Purchase NY 10577
    914 694-9200

### (G-767)
### HOLLINGSWORTH & VOSE COMPANY
4256 N Arlington Hts Rd  (60004-1300)
PHONE.................................847 222-9228
Donna Kasper, *Manager*
EMP: 3
SALES (corp-wide): 776.8MM  Privately Held
SIC: 2621  Paper mills
PA: Hollingsworth & Vose Company
    112 Washington St
    East Walpole MA 02032
    508 850-2000

### (G-768)
### HONEYWELL INTERNATIONAL INC
1460 1500 W Dundee Rd  (60004)
PHONE.................................847 797-4000
Fax: 847 797-3666
Bill Lagrotta, *Area Mgr*
Robert Dittrich, *Engineer*
Patrick Holleran, *Accounting Mgr*
William Lagrotta, *Manager*
Jimmy Douglas, *Supervisor*
EMP: 60
SALES (corp-wide): 39.3B  Publicly Held
WEB: www.honeywell.com
SIC: 8711  3585  8731  7382  Heating & ventilation engineering; air conditioning units, complete: domestic or industrial; heating equipment, complete; commercial physical research; security systems services
PA: Honeywell International Inc.
    115 Tabor Rd
    Morris Plains NJ 07950
    973 455-2000

### (G-769)
### HOUSE OF DOOLITTLE  LTD (PA)
3001 Malmo Dr  (60005-4727)
PHONE.................................847 593-3417
Fax: 847 228-9051
Bailey W Blethen, *President*
Bill Blethen, *General Mgr*
James Hutchison, *Opers Mgr*
Amy Svoboda, *Webmaster*
Ronald Stavoe, *Admin Sec*
EMP: 40
SQ FT: 62,000
SALES (est): 7.4MM  Privately Held
WEB: www.houseofdoolittle.com
SIC: 2752  3993  2678  Calendars, lithographed; signs & advertising specialties; memorandum books, except printed: purchased materials; desk pads, paper: made from purchased materials

### (G-770)
### IBBOTSON HEATING CO
514 S Arthur Ave  (60005-2141)
PHONE.................................847 253-0866
Fax: 847 577-3409
Ralph Ibbotson, *President*
John R Kelly, *President*
Marjorie Kelly, *Treasurer*
Mary Jane Ibbotson, *Admin Sec*
EMP: 32
SQ FT: 5,000
SALES (est): 5MM  Privately Held
WEB: www.ibbotsonheating.com
SIC: 1711  3444  Warm air heating & air conditioning contractor; sheet metalwork

### (G-771)
### ID3 INC
768 W Algonquin Rd  (60005-4416)
PHONE.................................847 734-9781
Steven L Begor, *President*
EMP: 11
SQ FT: 3,000
SALES (est): 735K  Privately Held
WEB: www.id3logos.com
SIC: 3089  Identification cards, plastic

### (G-772)
### IGAR BRIDAL INC
723 E Dundee Rd  (60004-1542)
PHONE.................................224 318-2337
Elzbieta Giezycka, *President*
EMP: 3  EST: 2015
SQ FT: 1,500
SALES: 200K  Privately Held
SIC: 2335  7219  Wedding gowns & dresses; garment making, alteration & repair

### (G-773)
### IGT TESTING SYSTEMS INC
543 W Golf Rd  (60005-3904)
PHONE.................................847 952-2448
Fred Kooy, *President*
Thomas Klepper, *Technical Staff*
EMP: 4
SQ FT: 2,037
SALES: 500K  Privately Held
SIC: 3826  8748  Analytical instruments; systems analysis & engineering consulting services
PA: Reprotest Produktie B.V.
    Randstad 22 2
    Almere
    204 099-300

### (G-774)
### ILLINOIS HAND & UPPER EXTREMIT
515 W Algonquin Rd  (60005-4439)
PHONE.................................847 956-0099
Michael I Vender, *Principal*
EMP: 4
SALES (est): 415.7K  Privately Held
SIC: 3131  Uppers

### (G-775)
### IMPREX INTERNATIONAL  INC
2916 Malmo Dr  (60005-4726)
PHONE.................................847 364-4930
Jerry K Gantz, *President*
Erica Mason, *Corp Secy*
Lucas Mason, *Manager*
EMP: 3
SQ FT: 1,500
SALES (est): 986.6K  Privately Held
WEB: www.imprex.net
SIC: 5085  3545  Industrial tools; machine tool accessories

### (G-776)
### IMPRO INTERNATIONAL INC
Also Called: Impro Graphics
3110 N Arlington Hts Rd  (60004-1532)
PHONE.................................847 398-3870
Fax: 847 506-7390
Richard Saetre, *President*
Tim Grew, *Executive*
EMP: 4  EST: 1996
SQ FT: 2,500
SALES (est): 521.8K  Privately Held
WEB: www.impro.com
SIC: 2759  Commercial printing

### (G-777)
### INFINITE CNVRGNCE SLUTIONS INC (PA)
3231 N Wilke Rd  (60004-1437)
PHONE.................................224 764-3400
Anne Taylorsmith, *Accounting Mgr*
Frank Rindos, *Sales Dir*
Candace Turner, *Manager*
Alex Sander, *Software Engr*
Nakul Saunshi, *Software Engr*
EMP: 4
SQ FT: 15,000
SALES (est): 1.4MM  Privately Held
SIC: 7372  7373  8999  Prepackaged software; computer integrated systems design; communication services

### (G-778)
### INNOVATIVE HESS PRODUCTS LLC
Also Called: Milmour Products
2605 S Clearbrook Dr  (60005-4625)
PHONE.................................847 676-3260
Fax: 847 676-0193
Kevin Hess, *Mng Member*
▲ EMP: 406
SALES (est): 54.5MM  Privately Held
SIC: 2821  Plastics materials & resins

### (G-779)
### INTOWN ELECTRIC
900 E Euclid Ave  (60004-5742)
PHONE.................................847 305-4816
Tom Hucthison, *President*
EMP: 7
SALES (est): 1.1MM  Privately Held
SIC: 3699  Electrical equipment & supplies

### (G-780)
### ITUS CORPORATION LLC
2130 S Goebbert Rd # 104  (60005-5263)
PHONE.................................888 537-5661
Naveen Sharma, *Principal*
EMP: 3
SALES (est): 157.9K  Privately Held
SIC: 3842  Bulletproof vests

### (G-781)
### J F SCHROEDER COMPANY  INC
2616 S Clearbrook Dr  (60005-4626)
PHONE.................................847 357-8600
John R Schroeder, *President*
Elaine Schroeder, *Treasurer*
EMP: 20  EST: 1955
SQ FT: 15,000
SALES (est): 3.3MM  Privately Held
SIC: 3544  3469  3444  Die sets for metal stamping (presses); stamping metal for the trade; sheet metalwork

### (G-782)
### JEFFREY JAE INC (PA)
907 E Brookwood Dr  (60004-2615)
PHONE.................................847 394-1313
Jae Bersch, *President*
Max Parker, *Purch Mgr*
▲ EMP: 30
SALES: 11MM  Privately Held
SIC: 3089  3452  Hardware, plastic; bolts, nuts, rivets & washers

### (G-783)
### JET GRINDING & MANUFACTURING
2309 E Oakton St Ste A  (60005-4809)
PHONE.................................847 956-8646
Fax: 847 956-0142
Jerry Nosek, *President*
Ann Leenheer, *Info Tech Mgr*
EMP: 10  EST: 1966
SALES (est): 1.6MM  Privately Held
WEB: www.jetgrinding.com
SIC: 3599  Grinding castings for the trade

### (G-784)
### JO-ANN STORES  LLC
Also Called: Jo-Ann Fabrics & Crafts
373 E Palatine Rd  (60004-3938)
PHONE.................................847 394-9742
Joe Dinatale, *Branch Mgr*
EMP: 16
SALES (corp-wide): 3.2B  Privately Held
WEB: www.joann.com
SIC: 2211  Canvas & other heavy coarse fabrics: cotton
HQ: Jo-Ann Stores, Llc
    5555 Darrow Rd
    Hudson OH 44236
    330 656-2600

### (G-785)
### JOHNSON CONTROLS  INC
3007 Malmo Dr  (60005-4781)
PHONE.................................847 364-1500
Fax: 847 364-1536
Mike Wolpert, *President*
Greg Schackle, *Engineer*
Jim Ahern, *Manager*
Chip Loeb, *Network Enginr*
EMP: 40
SALES (corp-wide): 36.8B  Privately Held
SIC: 2531  Seats, automobile
PA: Johnson Controls, Inc.
    5757 N Green Bay Ave
    Milwaukee WI 53209
    414 524-1200

### (G-786)
### JTEKT TOYODA AMERICAS CORP (DH)
Also Called: Toyoda Machinery USA Corp
316 W University Dr  (60004-1812)
P.O. Box 74053, Chicago  (60690-8053)
PHONE.................................847 253-0340
Fax: 847 253-0540
Kent Nakamura, *Ch of Bd*
Howard W Michael, *President*
Hiroyuki Kaijima, *Exec VP*
William Vejnovic, *Engineer*
Clyde Chaffee, *Controller*
◆ EMP: 140  EST: 1977
SQ FT: 100,000
SALES (est): 44MM
SALES (corp-wide): 11.6B  Privately Held
WEB: www.toyodausa.com
SIC: 3541  3625  5084  Machine tools, metal cutting type; grinding machines, metalworking; electric controls & control accessories, industrial; machine tools & metalworking machinery; machine tools & accessories; controlling instruments & accessories
HQ: Jtekt North America Corporation
    29570 Clemens Rd
    Westlake OH 44145
    440 835-1000

### (G-787)
### JTH ENTERPRISES INC
311 W University Dr  (60004-1811)
PHONE.................................847 394-3355

# Arlington Heights - Cook County (G-788) — GEOGRAPHIC SECTION

James Hommer, *President*
Mike Smith, *Controller*
**EMP:** 42
**SALES (est):** 5MM **Privately Held**
**WEB:** www.jthenterprises.com
**SIC:** 3089 Molding primary plastic

### (G-788)
### KEONIX CORPORATION
922 N Chicago Ave (60004-4425)
P.O. Box 87 (60006-0087)
**PHONE** ............................ 847 259-9430
Michael McKee, *President*
**EMP:** 5
**SQ FT:** 1,000
**SALES:** 500K **Privately Held**
**WEB:** www.keonix.com
**SIC:** 3625 3545 Relays & industrial controls; machine tool accessories

### (G-789)
### KNIPEX TOOLS LP
2035 S Arlington Heights (60005-4522)
**PHONE** ............................ 847 398-8520
Alan Sipe, *General Mgr*
Todd Shumate, *Exec VP*
Helen Mills, *Controller*
Ilona Dovidaitiene, *Finance*
Michelle Devenny, *Sales Staff*
▲ **EMP:** 15
**SQ FT:** 3,000
**SALES (est):** 3.4MM
**SALES (corp-wide):** 157MM **Privately Held**
**SIC:** 3423 Hand & edge tools
**PA:** Knipex-Werk C. Gustav Putsch Kg
Oberkamper Str. 13
Wuppertal 42349
202 479-40

### (G-790)
### KRAVET INC
3441 N Ridge Ave (60004-1413)
**PHONE** ............................ 847 870-1414
**Fax:** 847 870-8741
Anna Marks, *Manager*
**EMP:** 9
**SALES (corp-wide):** 400.9MM **Privately Held**
**WEB:** www.kfi.net
**SIC:** 3448 Prefabricated metal buildings
**PA:** Kravet Inc.
225 Cent Ave S
Bethpage NY 11714
516 293-2000

### (G-791)
### LAWLOR MARKETING
2035 S Arlington Hts Rd (60005-4515)
**PHONE** ............................ 847 357-1080
Dan Lawlor, *Principal*
**EMP:** 4
**SALES (est):** 190.3K **Privately Held**
**SIC:** 2037 Frozen fruits & vegetables

### (G-792)
### LAWRENCE MADDOCK
Also Called: Morton Grove Auto Electric
500 S Arthur Ave (60005-2141)
**PHONE** ............................ 847 394-1698
**Fax:** 847 637-1199
Lawrence Maddock, *Owner*
**EMP:** 11
**SQ FT:** 2,600
**SALES (est):** 666.3K **Privately Held**
**SIC:** 7539 7694 Alternators & generators, rebuilding & repair; armature rewinding shops

### (G-793)
### LINE GROUP INC (PA)
Also Called: Line Tool & Stamping Co
539 W Algonquin Rd (60005-4411)
**PHONE** ............................ 847 593-6810
**Fax:** 847 593-0363
Al G Panico, *President*
Joseph A Katalak, *Admin Sec*
**EMP:** 43
**SQ FT:** 40,000
**SALES (est):** 8.8MM **Privately Held**
**WEB:** www.thelinegroup.com
**SIC:** 3469 3544 3423 3824 Stamping metal for the trade; special dies & tools; hand & edge tools; electromechanical counters

### (G-794)
### LIVE WIRE & CABLE CO
409 W University Dr (60004-1813)
**PHONE** ............................ 847 577-5483
Perry Stein, *President*
Sean Ohara, *Sales Executive*
Elisha M Prero, *Admin Sec*
**EMP:** 7
**SQ FT:** 20,000
**SALES (est):** 1.2MM **Privately Held**
**WEB:** www.livew-c.com
**SIC:** 3357 Communication wire

### (G-795)
### LODAN ELECTRONICS INC
3311 N Kennicott Ave (60004-1429)
**PHONE** ............................ 847 398-5311
**Fax:** 847 398-5340
Raymond A Kedzior, *President*
Thomas Cornhoff, *President*
Brett Kedzior, *Vice Pres*
Patricia Bonner, *CFO*
Andrew Longhinl, *Director*
**EMP:** 200
**SQ FT:** 100,000
**SALES (est):** 47.8MM **Privately Held**
**WEB:** www.lodan.com
**SIC:** 3496 Miscellaneous fabricated wire products

### (G-796)
### LUCKY YUPPY PUPPY CO INC
533 W Golf Rd (60005-3904)
**PHONE** ............................ 847 437-7879
Terry Gold, *President*
Larry Glick, *Vice Pres*
▲ **EMP:** 6
**SALES (est):** 623.7K **Privately Held**
**WEB:** www.lypcproducts.com
**SIC:** 3999 5199 Pet supplies; pet supplies

### (G-797)
### MAG-DRIVE LLC
2225 E Oakton St (60004-4815)
**PHONE** ............................ 847 690-0871
Anthony Baroud,
**EMP:** 3
**SALES (est):** 268.2K **Privately Held**
**SIC:** 3511 Turbines & turbine generator sets

### (G-798)
### MANHATTAN EYELASH EXT SEW ON
8 S Dunton Ave (60005-1402)
**PHONE** ............................ 847 818-8774
Kyoung Jun, *Owner*
**EMP:** 3
**SALES (est):** 102.2K **Privately Held**
**SIC:** 3999 Eyelashes, artificial

### (G-799)
### MASON CHEMICAL COMPANY (HQ)
721 W Algonquin Rd Ste A (60005-4408)
**PHONE** ............................ 847 290-1621
**Fax:** 847 290-1625
Jean E Mason, *President*
Gregg H Mason, *Admin Sec*
▲ **EMP:** 14
**SALES (est):** 2.1MM
**SALES (corp-wide):** 81.9MM **Privately Held**
**WEB:** www.maquat.com
**SIC:** 2819 Industrial inorganic chemicals
**PA:** Pilot Chemical Company Of Ohio
2744 E Kemper Rd
Cincinnati OH 45241
513 326-0600

### (G-800)
### MCCORMICKS ENTERPRISES INC
216 W Campus Dr Ste 101 (60004-1442)
P.O. Box 577 (60006-0577)
**PHONE** ............................ 847 398-8680
**Fax:** 847 398-8625
Ernest Webb, *President*
Jean Cozier, *Vice Pres*
David Dombeck, *Purchasing*
Brian Anderson, *Sales Mgr*
Amy Buckbee, *Sales Mgr*
**EMP:** 20
**SQ FT:** 7,000
**SALES (est):** 2.6MM **Privately Held**
**WEB:** www.mccormicksnet.com
**SIC:** 5736 2399 5734 5961 Brass instruments; drums & related percussion instruments; flags, fabric; software, business & non-game; catalog & mail-order houses; record & prerecorded tape stores

### (G-801)
### MECHANICAL MUSIC CORP
Also Called: Advantage Worldwide Wholesale
3319 N Ridge Ave (60004-1411)
**PHONE** ............................ 847 398-5444
**Fax:** 847 398-5441
William A Walzak, *President*
David Hall, *VP Sales*
Arley Canterbury, *Info Tech Dir*
**EMP:** 11
**SQ FT:** 5,000
**SALES (est):** 1.7MM **Privately Held**
**WEB:** www.dealsmusic.com
**SIC:** 5099 3161 3931 3651 Musical instruments; musical instruments parts & accessories; musical instrument cases; musical instruments; household audio & video equipment

### (G-802)
### MILLENNIUM PRINTING INC
434 S Reuter Dr (60005-2232)
**PHONE** ............................ 847 590-8182
Amy Hofeld, *President*
**EMP:** 2
**SALES (est):** 540K **Privately Held**
**SIC:** 2621 Business form paper

### (G-803)
### MINUTEMAN PRESS INC
1324 W Algonquin Rd (60005-3401)
**PHONE** ............................ 847 577-2411
**Fax:** 847 577-2501
Scott Clemetsen, *President*
**EMP:** 4
**SQ FT:** 1,500
**SALES (est):** 405.2K **Privately Held**
**SIC:** 2752 2789 2759 Commercial printing, lithographic; bookbinding & related work; commercial printing

### (G-804)
### MONTANA MINERALS DEV CO
1500 W Shure Dr (60004-1443)
**PHONE** ............................ 800 426-5564
Ryan F McKendrick, *CEO*
**EMP:** 4
**SALES (est):** 192.9K
**SALES (corp-wide):** 1.6B **Publicly Held**
**SIC:** 1481 Nonmetallic minerals development & test boring
**HQ:** Amcol International Corp
2870 Forbs Ave
Hoffman Estates IL 60192
847 851-1500

### (G-805)
### MONTCLARE SCIENTIFIC GLASS
25 N Hickory Ave (60004-6204)
**PHONE** ............................ 847 255-6870
Peter Calandra, *President*
Kathleen Calandra, *Vice Pres*
**EMP:** 8
**SQ FT:** 3,000
**SALES:** 700K **Privately Held**
**SIC:** 3229 3231 Glassware, industrial; bulbs for electric lights; products of purchased glass

### (G-806)
### MORITEQ RUBBER CO
Also Called: Moriteq USA Contacts
710 W Algonquin Rd (60005-4416)
**PHONE** ............................ 847 734-0970
Hidenori Tanabe, *President*
Naoko Alborz, *Manager*
Yoshihiro Mori, *Admin Sec*
**EMP:** 11
**SALES (est):** 1.6MM **Privately Held**
**WEB:** www.moritequsa.com
**SIC:** 2822 Synthetic rubber

### (G-807)
### MOTOROLA SOLUTIONS INC
1155 W Dundee Rd (60004-1421)
**PHONE** ............................ 847 540-8815
Allen Dickson, *Principal*
**EMP:** 142
**SALES (corp-wide):** 6B **Publicly Held**
**WEB:** www.motorola.com
**SIC:** 3663 Radio & TV communications equipment
**PA:** Motorola Solutions, Inc.
500 W Monroe St Ste 4400
Chicago IL 60661
847 576-5000

### (G-808)
### NATIONAL COMPONENT SALES INC
Also Called: World Wide Broach
1229 E Algonquin Rd Jk (60005-4761)
**PHONE** ............................ 847 439-0333
**Fax:** 847 439-0359
Patricia L Reff, *Principal*
Terry Kyner, *Vice Pres*
Peter Reff, *Vice Pres*
**EMP:** 10
**SQ FT:** 5,000
**SALES (est):** 590K **Privately Held**
**SIC:** 3599 3544 Machine shop, jobbing & repair; special dies, tools, jigs & fixtures

### (G-809)
### NOKIA SLUTIONS NETWORKS US LLC
1455 W Shure Dr (60004-7810)
**PHONE** ............................ 224 248-8204
Irene Short, *Safety Mgr*
**EMP:** 12
**SALES (corp-wide):** 13.4B **Privately Held**
**SIC:** 3663 Radio & TV communications equipment
**HQ:** Nokia Solutions And Networks Us Llc
6000 Connection Dr
Irving TX 75039
972 374-3000

### (G-810)
### OBERWEIS DAIRY INC
Also Called: Oberweis Ice Cream and Dar Str
9 E Dundee Rd (60004-1539)
**PHONE** ............................ 847 368-9060
**Fax:** 847 368-9062
Elaine Oberweis, *Manager*
**EMP:** 12
**SALES (corp-wide):** 202.6MM **Privately Held**
**WEB:** www.webfc.net
**SIC:** 2026 5963 5451 Milk processing (pasteurizing, homogenizing, bottling); milk delivery; milk; ice cream (packaged)
**PA:** Oberweis Dairy, Inc.
951 Ice Cream Dr
North Aurora IL 60542
630 801-6100

### (G-811)
### OHARE PRECISION METALS LLC
2404 Hamilton Rd (60005-4812)
**PHONE** ............................ 847 640-6050
Ahmed Salem, *Owner*
Mike Delgado, *Sales Mgr*
Tom Knowles,
**EMP:** 24
**SQ FT:** 12,000
**SALES (est):** 4.5MM **Privately Held**
**SIC:** 3599 Grinding castings for the trade

### (G-812)
### OLSON METAL PRODUCTS LLC (HQ)
Also Called: IMS Buhrke-Olson
511 W Algonquin Rd (60005-4411)
**PHONE** ............................ 847 981-7550
Mark Simanton, *CEO*
**EMP:** 15 **EST:** 2008
**SALES (est):** 75.7MM
**SALES (corp-wide):** 607.5MM **Privately Held**
**SIC:** 3469 Metal stampings
**PA:** Ims Companies, Llc
1 Innovation Dr
Des Plaines IL 60016
847 391-8100

### (G-813)
### OLYMPIC BINDERY INC
1105 N Chestnut Ave (60004-4615)
**PHONE** ............................ 847 577-8132
**Fax:** 708 344-4265

Dan Mooney, *President*
John A Welacha, *Vice Pres*
Linda Castino, *Manager*
Eddie Shamo, *Manager*
**EMP:** 97
**SQ FT:** 60,000
**SALES (est):** 8.9MM  Privately Held
**WEB:** www.olympicbindery.com
**SIC:** 2789  Paper cutting

### (G-814)
### OPTIMAL ENERGY LLC
507 W Golf Rd  (60005-3904)
P.O. Box 59082, Schaumburg  (60159-0082)
Sanjiv Pillai, *President*
Jinen Adenwala, *CTO*
**EMP:** 6
**SALES (est):** 731.7K  Privately Held
**SIC:** 3585  Parts for heating, cooling & refrigerating equipment

### (G-815)
### PADDOCK PUBLICATIONS INC (PA)
Also Called: Daily Herald
155 E Algonquin Rd  (60005-4617)
P.O. Box 280  (60006-0280)
**PHONE** .................. 847 427-4300
**Fax:** 847 427-1550
Doug Ray, *President*
Caroline Linden, *Editor*
Susan Stark, *Editor*
Daniel E Baumann, *Chairman*
Bob Finch, *Vice Pres*
**EMP:** 450 EST: 1872
**SQ FT:** 145,000
**SALES (est):** 122.6MM  Privately Held
**WEB:** www.dailyherald.com
**SIC:** 2711  Newspapers, publishing & printing

### (G-816)
### PAN PAC INTERNATIONAL INC
3456 N Ridge Ave Ste 300  (60004-7817)
**PHONE** .................. 847 222-9077
**Fax:** 847 222-9078
▲ **EMP:** 7
**SQ FT:** 12,000
**SALES (est):** 730K  Privately Held
**SIC:** 3562  Mfg Ball & Roller Bearings & Casters

### (G-817)
### PAYLOCITY HOLDING CORPORATION (PA)
3850 N Wilke Rd  (60004-1269)
**PHONE** .................. 847 463-3200
Steven I Sarowitz, *Ch of Bd*
Steven R Beauchamp, *President*
Jennifer Blair, *District Mgr*
John Mason-Smith, *District Mgr*
Daniel Mayer, *District Mgr*
**EMP:** 24
**SQ FT:** 135,000
**SALES (est):** 230.7MM  Publicly Held
**SIC:** 7372  Prepackaged software; business oriented computer software

### (G-818)
### PLASTIC SERVICES GROUP
115 S Wilke Rd Ste 206e  (60005-1519)
**PHONE** .................. 847 368-1444
Dan Bendixon, *President*
**EMP:** 5
**SALES (est):** 448.7K  Privately Held
**WEB:** www.plasticservicesgroup.com
**SIC:** 3089  8711  Extruded finished plastic products; engineering services

### (G-819)
### PRECISION-TEK MFG INC
Also Called: Precision-Tek Mfg
3206 Nordic Rd  (60005-4729)
**PHONE** .................. 847 364-7800
**Fax:** 847 364-7882
Keith Pflum, *President*
James Rewis, *General Mgr*
Alfredo Gudas, *Buyer*
Terry Anderson, *Manager*
**EMP:** 36
**SQ FT:** 16,000
**SALES (est):** 7.4MM  Privately Held
**WEB:** www.precision-tek.com
**SIC:** 3451  Screw machine products

### (G-820)
### PRESTIGE WEDDING DECORATION
3405 N Ridge Ave  (60004-1413)
**PHONE** .................. 847 845-0901
Evgeni Pritsker, *Principal*
▲ **EMP:** 4 EST: 2010
**SALES (est):** 277.2K  Privately Held
**SIC:** 2335  Wedding gowns & dresses

### (G-821)
### PRIME TIME SPORTS LLC
220 W Campus Dr Ste C  (60004-1479)
**PHONE** .................. 847 637-3500
Janice Stephens, *Marketing Staff*
Debra Bell, *Office Mgr*
Christy Commiso, *Office Mgr*
Chance Fuller, *Director*
Robert Densmore, *Asst Director*
**EMP:** 14
**SQ FT:** 1,500
**SALES (est):** 2.5MM  Privately Held
**SIC:** 3663  Satellites, communications

### (G-822)
### PRINT TURNAROUND INC
3025 Malmo Dr  (60005-4727)
**PHONE** .................. 847 228-1762
**Fax:** 847 228-1912
Bruce Johnson, *President*
Pam McKeown, *Opers Staff*
Dominick De Micco, *Shareholder*
**EMP:** 17
**SQ FT:** 3,600
**SALES (est):** 2.2MM  Privately Held
**WEB:** www.printturnaround.com
**SIC:** 2752  2791  2789  Commercial printing, offset; typesetting; bookbinding & related work

### (G-823)
### PRINTING DIMENSIONS
1515 S Highland Ave  (60005-3663)
**PHONE** .................. 847 439-7521
Richard M Bilek, *Principal*
**EMP:** 3
**SALES (est):** 234.4K  Privately Held
**WEB:** www.printingdimensions.com
**SIC:** 2752  Commercial printing, lithographic

### (G-824)
### QUICKSILVER MECHANICAL INC
3361 N Ridge Ave  (60004-1411)
**PHONE** .................. 847 577-1564
Michael Scanlan, *President*
**EMP:** 6
**SALES (est):** 932.2K  Privately Held
**SIC:** 3444  Sheet metalwork

### (G-825)
### R & D CLARK LTD
1918 N Eastwood Dr  (60004-3203)
**PHONE** .................. 847 749-2061
**Fax:** 847 392-4908
Donald B Clark, *President*
Elizabeth Clark, *Vice Pres*
**EMP:** 3
**SALES:** 300K  Privately Held
**SIC:** 5169  8731  3829  5085  Chemicals & allied products; commercial physical research; measuring & controlling devices; thermometers, liquid-in-glass & bimetal type; industrial supplies

### (G-826)
### R L KOLBI COMPANY
Also Called: Kolbi Pipe Marker Co
416 W Campus Dr  (60004-1406)
**PHONE** .................. 847 506-1440
Rob Sietz, *President*
Rob Seitz, *Sales Mgr*
Tom Antontlli, *Sales Executive*
**EMP:** 18
**SQ FT:** 5,200
**SALES (est):** 4.7MM  Privately Held
**WEB:** www.kolbipipemarkers.com
**SIC:** 3821  Pi tapes (metal periphery direct reading diameter tapes)

### (G-827)
### RADOVENT ILLINOIS LLC (PA)
766 W Algonquin Rd  (60005-4416)
**PHONE** .................. 847 637-0297
Travis Jewell, *Mng Member*
**EMP:** 8
**SALES (est):** 706.4K  Privately Held
**SIC:** 3634  Air purifiers, portable

### (G-828)
### RARE BIRDS INC
321 E Rand Rd  (60004-3103)
**PHONE** .................. 847 259-7286
Ron Zick, *President*
**EMP:** 4
**SALES (est):** 238.8K  Privately Held
**WEB:** www.rarebirds.com
**SIC:** 2048  Bird food, prepared

### (G-829)
### REFLEJOS PUBLICATIONS LLC
155 E Algonquin Rd  (60005-4617)
**PHONE** .................. 847 806-1111
**Fax:** 847 806-1112
Marco Ortiz, *Assoc Editor*
Jerry Campagna,
**EMP:** 30
**SQ FT:** 2,000
**SALES (est):** 1.8MM  Privately Held
**WEB:** www.reflejos.com
**SIC:** 2711  Newspapers; newspapers: publishing only, not printed on site

### (G-830)
### REIGN PRINT SOLUTIONS INC
550 W Campus Dr  (60004-1408)
**PHONE** .................. 847 590-7091
**Fax:** 847 590-7099
William G Jourdan III, *President*
Cheryl Linskey, *Accountant*
Lynn Galizia, *Admin Sec*
**EMP:** 7
**SQ FT:** 3,000
**SALES (est):** 1.7MM  Privately Held
**WEB:** www.reignprintsolutions.com
**SIC:** 5112  7379  2752  5943  Business forms; office supplies; computer & photocopying supplies; computer related consulting services; commercial printing, lithographic; office forms & supplies

### (G-831)
### REILLY COMMUNICATION GROUP
3030 W Salt Creek Ln # 201  (60005-5002)
**PHONE** .................. 630 756-1225
John F Reilly, *Owner*
Sean Reilly, *Publisher*
Eleanor M Goss, *Controller*
Kristine Minnich, *Manager*
Mary B Massat, *Director*
**EMP:** 15
**SALES (est):** 992K  Privately Held
**WEB:** www.rcgpubs.com
**SIC:** 2721  Magazines: publishing & printing

### (G-832)
### RW WELDING INC
1511 S Princeton Ave  (60005-3414)
**PHONE** .................. 847 541-5508
Robert O'Keith, *President*
**EMP:** 3
**SALES (est):** 185.2K  Privately Held
**SIC:** 7692  Welding repair

### (G-833)
### RYAN PRODUCTS INC
319 S Burton Pl  (60005-2063)
**PHONE** .................. 847 670-9071
Diane Crawford, *President*
Ronald Crawford, *Vice Pres*
**EMP:** 4
**SALES (est):** 443.2K  Privately Held
**SIC:** 2385  2393  Bibs, waterproof: made from purchased materials; bags & containers, except sleeping bags: textile

### (G-834)
### S C C PUMPS INC
708 W Algonquin Rd  (60005-4416)
**PHONE** .................. 847 593-8495
**Fax:** 847 593-8204
Kenneth Porter, *President*
Diane Nakis, *Vice Pres*
Eric Porter, *Vice Pres*
Lucia A Porter, *Admin Sec*
▲ **EMP:** 7 EST: 1974
**SQ FT:** 4,000
**SALES (est):** 1.8MM  Privately Held
**WEB:** www.sccpumps.com
**SIC:** 3561  5251  3594  Cylinders, pump; pumps & pumping equipment; pumps, hydraulic power transfer

### (G-835)
### SANTEC SYSTEMS INC
2924 Malmo Dr  (60005-4726)
**PHONE** .................. 847 215-8884
**Fax:** 847 215-8847
Jaswinder Sandhu, *President*
**EMP:** 10
**SQ FT:** 2,025
**SALES (est):** 1.1MM  Privately Held
**WEB:** www.santecsystems.com
**SIC:** 3829  Ultrasonic testing equipment; aircraft & motor vehicle measurement equipment

### (G-836)
### SCRANTON GLLTTE CMMNCTIONS INC (PA)
Also Called: S G C
3030 W Salt Creek Ln # 201  (60005-5025)
**PHONE** .................. 847 391-1000
Edward S Gillette, *President*
Sean Reilly, *Publisher*
Brandon Williamson, *Publisher*
David Barista, *Publisher*
Cristen Bolan, *Editor*
◆ **EMP:** 62
**SQ FT:** 11,000
**SALES (est):** 16.1MM  Privately Held
**WEB:** www.onhort.com
**SIC:** 2721  Trade journals: publishing only, not printed on site

### (G-837)
### SEDECAL USA INC (HQ)
3190 N Kennicott Ave  (60004-1426)
**PHONE** .................. 847 394-6960
Manuel Martinez, *Principal*
Devan Moser, *Vice Pres*
Devon Moser, *Sls & Mktg Exec*
Donna Alferez, *Accounts Mgr*
Jim Lambrecht, *Manager*
▲ **EMP:** 26
**SQ FT:** 5,000
**SALES (est):** 7.1MM
**SALES (corp-wide):** 127MM  Privately Held
**WEB:** www.sedecalusa.com
**SIC:** 3844  X-ray generators
**PA:** Sociedad Espalola De Electromedicina Y Calidad Sa
Calle De La Pelaya (- Pg Industrial Rio De Janeiro) 9
Algete  28110
916 280-544

### (G-838)
### SEMPER FI PRINTING LLC
2420 E Oakton St Ste Q  (60005-4827)
**PHONE** .................. 847 640-7737
Brett Schwartz, *VP Sales*
Michael Bocskovits, *Accounts Mgr*
Craig Brunk,
**EMP:** 6 EST: 2008
**SALES (est):** 864.5K  Privately Held
**SIC:** 2752  Commercial printing, lithographic

### (G-839)
### SGC HORIZON LLC
Also Called: S G C
3030 W Salt Creek Ln  (60005-5001)
**PHONE** .................. 847 391-1000
Edward Gillette, *President*
Kevin Herda, *Info Tech Dir*
Heidi Riedl, *Education*
**EMP:** 1
**SALES (est):** 306.7K
**SALES (corp-wide):** 16.1MM  Privately Held
**SIC:** 2721  Trade journals: publishing only, not printed on site
**PA:** Scranton Gillette Communications, Inc.
3030 W Salt Creek Ln # 201
Arlington Heights IL 60005
847 391-1000

### (G-840)
### SHEET METAL WERKS INC (PA)
455 E Algonquin Rd  (60005-4620)
**PHONE** .................. 847 827-4700

Kevin Ryan, *President*
John Crne, *Superintendent*
Patrick Ryan, *Vice Pres*
Don Dudzinski, *Project Mgr*
Greg Ivaska, *Project Mgr*
**EMP:** 51
**SQ FT:** 48,000
**SALES (est):** 4.4MM **Privately Held**
**WEB:** www.sheetmetalwerks.com
**SIC:** 3444 Sheet metalwork

*(G-841)*
**SONOCO PROTECTIVE SOLUTIONS**
Also Called: Thermal Safe Brands
3930 N Ventura Dr Ste 450 (60004-7432)
**PHONE**...................................847 398-0110
**EMP:** 30
**SALES (corp-wide):** 5B **Publicly Held**
**SIC:** 3086 Mfg Expandable Polystyrene Foam
**HQ:** Sonoco Protective Solutions, Inc.
1 N 2nd St
Hartsville SC 29550
843 383-7000

*(G-842)*
**SONOCO PRTECTIVE SOLUTIONS INC**
Also Called: Sca Thermosafe
3930 N Ventura Dr Ste 450 (60004-7432)
**PHONE**...................................847 398-0110
Richard Smith, *Manager*
Jennifer Mee, *Administration*
**EMP:** 55
**SALES (corp-wide):** 4.7B **Publicly Held**
**WEB:** www.tuscarora.com
**SIC:** 2631 Container, packaging & boxboard
**HQ:** Sonoco Protective Solutions, Inc.
1 N 2nd St
Hartsville SC 29550
843 383-7000

*(G-843)*
**STELMONT INC**
Also Called: Arlington Signs & Banners
818 W Northwest Hwy (60004-5344)
**PHONE**...................................847 870-0300
**Fax:** 847 870-0300
Monte Sellers, *President*
Stella Sellers, *Corp Secy*
**EMP:** 5 **EST:** 1998
**SQ FT:** 6,000
**SALES (est):** 539K **Privately Held**
**WEB:** www.arlingtonsigns.com
**SIC:** 3993 Signs & advertising specialties

*(G-844)*
**STICKON ADHESIVE INDS INC**
Also Called: Stickon Packaging Systems
2605 S Clearbrook Dr (60005-4625)
**PHONE**...................................847 593-5959
**Fax:** 847 593-4253
Nicholas M Caradonna, *President*
Nicholas A Caradonna, *General Mgr*
**EMP:** 27
**SQ FT:** 10,000
**SALES (est):** 7.4MM **Privately Held**
**WEB:** www.stickon.com
**SIC:** 5199 7699 5084 2295 Packaging materials; industrial equipment services; processing & packaging equipment; packaging machinery & equipment; coated fabrics, not rubberized; tape, varnished: plastic & other coated (except magnetic)

*(G-845)*
**STONE FABRICATORS COMPANY**
1604 N Clarence Ave (60004-4024)
**PHONE**...................................847 788-8296
Kerry Kremer, *Partner*
**EMP:** 3
**SALES (est):** 206.5K **Privately Held**
**SIC:** 2541 Counter & sink tops

*(G-846)*
**SU ENTERPRISE INC**
403 N Reuter Dr (60005-1127)
**PHONE**...................................847 394-1656
**Fax:** 847 394-8699
Neichung Su, *President*
Neiming Su, *Vice Pres*
**EMP:** 6 **EST:** 1993

**SALES (est):** 517.9K **Privately Held**
**WEB:** www.suenterprise.com
**SIC:** 7372 Prepackaged software

*(G-847)*
**SUBURBAN PRESS INC**
Also Called: Universal Printing
3650 N Wilke Rd (60004-1273)
**PHONE**...................................847 255-2240
**Fax:** 847 255-2319
Gary McGrath, *President*
**EMP:** 20
**SQ FT:** 14,000
**SALES (est):** 3.2MM **Privately Held**
**WEB:** www.suburbanpress.net
**SIC:** 2752 Commercial printing, offset

*(G-848)*
**SUMMIT SIGNWORKS INC**
2265 E Ashbury Ct (60004-4363)
**PHONE**...................................847 870-0937
**EMP:** 3
**SALES (est):** 200K **Privately Held**
**SIC:** 3993 Mfg Signs/Advertising Specialties

*(G-849)*
**SWAGATH GROUP INC**
Also Called: Manpasand Restaurant
644 E Golf Rd (60005-4061)
**PHONE**...................................847 640-6446
Srinivas Nelavelli, *President*
Eswar Balasubla, *Admin Sec*
**EMP:** 5
**SALES (est):** 1.5MM **Privately Held**
**SIC:** 2499 Food handling & processing products, wood

*(G-850)*
**T K O QUALITY OFFSET PRINTING**
4141 N Yale Ave (60004-7924)
**PHONE**...................................847 709-0455
Vincent Kunicki, *President*
Jennie Osgoodby, *Corp Secy*
**EMP:** 5
**SQ FT:** 5,000
**SALES (est):** 700K **Privately Held**
**SIC:** 2752 Commercial printing, offset

*(G-851)*
**TAGORE TECHNOLOGY INC**
5 E College Dr Ste 200 (60004-1963)
**PHONE**...................................847 790-3799
Amitava Das, *President*
**EMP:** 7
**SALES (est):** 747.3K **Privately Held**
**SIC:** 3674 8731 Semiconductors & related devices; commercial physical research

*(G-852)*
**TECHNIC INC**
3265 N Ridge Ave (60004-1490)
**PHONE**...................................773 262-2662
**Fax:** 847 398-1825
Jim Sincell, *Manager*
**EMP:** 8
**SALES (corp-wide):** 135.1MM **Privately Held**
**WEB:** www.technic.com
**SIC:** 2899 Metal treating compounds
**PA:** Technic, Inc.
47 Molter St
Cranston RI 02910
401 781-6100

*(G-853)*
**TELEFLEX INCORPORATED**
900 W University Dr (60004-1824)
**PHONE**...................................847 259-7400
Robert Turoff, *Plant Mgr*
Ken Chandler, *Materials Mgr*
Scott Thode, *Facilities Mgr*
Jeremy Oliphant, *QA Dir*
Meena Saujani, *Engineer*
**EMP:** 100
**SALES (corp-wide):** 1.8B **Publicly Held**
**WEB:** www.teleflex.com
**SIC:** 3842 3841 Surgical appliances & supplies; surgical & medical instruments
**PA:** Teleflex Incorporated
550 E Swedesford Rd # 400
Wayne PA 19087
610 225-6800

*(G-854)*
**TELLURIAN TECHNOLOGIES INC**
3455 W Salt Creek Ln # 500 (60005-1090)
**PHONE**...................................847 934-4141
**Fax:** 847 934-4175
William B Deutschmann, *President*
Debbie Pavlick, *Director*
◆ **EMP:** 103
**SQ FT:** 2,500
**SALES (est):** 12.6MM **Privately Held**
**WEB:** www.telluriantech.com
**SIC:** 3679 5065 3873 3825 Quartz crystals, for electronic application; oscillators; electronic parts & equipment; watches, clocks, watchcases & parts; instruments to measure electricity

*(G-855)*
**THOMPSON & WALSH LLC**
Also Called: Admiral Graphics
547 W Golf Rd (60005-3904)
**PHONE**...................................847 734-1770
Kathy Harlow, *Office Mgr*
Troy Thompson,
Nathan Walsh,
**EMP:** 7 **EST:** 1994
**SALES (est):** 656.6K **Privately Held**
**SIC:** 7389 2752 Printers' services: folding, collating; commercial printing, lithographic

*(G-856)*
**TOWN SQUARE PUBLICATIONS LLC**
155 E Arlington Hts Rd (60005)
**PHONE**...................................847 427-4633
Dan Nugara, *President*
**EMP:** 1
**SALES (est):** 1.5MM
**SALES (corp-wide):** 122.6MM **Privately Held**
**SIC:** 2759 Publication printing
**PA:** Paddock Publications, Inc.
155 E Algonquin Rd
Arlington Heights IL 60005
847 427-4300

*(G-857)*
**TRIBEAM INC**
1323 S Fernandez Ave (60005-3543)
**PHONE**...................................847 409-9497
Michael Kazecki, *CEO*
James Baker, *Treasurer*
▲ **EMP:** 9
**SQ FT:** 1,000
**SALES (est):** 1.1MM **Privately Held**
**WEB:** www.tribeam.com
**SIC:** 3663 Mobile communication equipment

*(G-858)*
**TRICK PERCUSSION PRODUCTS INC**
17 E University Dr (60004-1801)
**PHONE**...................................847 342-2019
Michael R Dorfman, *President*
Bill Borenstein, *Admin Sec*
**EMP:** 3
**SQ FT:** 13,000
**SALES (est):** 1MM **Privately Held**
**WEB:** www.trickdrums.com
**SIC:** 3931 Percussion instruments & parts; drums, parts & accessories (musical instruments)

*(G-859)*
**TRU-VU MONITORS INC**
925 E Rand Rd Ste 200 (60004-4078)
**PHONE**...................................847 259-2344
Herb Ruterschmidt, *President*
Alan Cook, *Sales Engr*
**EMP:** 3
**SALES (est):** 339.2K **Privately Held**
**SIC:** 3599 Industrial machinery

*(G-860)*
**ULTRAMARK INC**
2420 E Oakton St Ste I (60005-4827)
P.O. Box 308, Mount Prospect (60056-0308)
**PHONE**...................................847 981-0400
Howard Peck, *President*
Mike McNeill, *Vice Pres*
Mary Condon, *Manager*
▲ **EMP:** 7

**SQ FT:** 5,000
**SALES (est):** 1.2MM **Privately Held**
**SIC:** 3578 Point-of-sale devices

*(G-861)*
**UNIFIED SOLUTIONS CORP**
Also Called: Unified Distributors
3456 N Ridge Ave Ste 200 (60004-7817)
**PHONE**...................................847 478-9100
Yan Bolotin, *CEO*
Dmitry Shraybman, *COO*
Joel Geller, *Buyer*
Debbie Antkowiak, *Controller*
Kevin Hickman, *Natl Sales Mgr*
**EMP:** 30
**SQ FT:** 30,000
**SALES:** 12MM **Privately Held**
**SIC:** 7629 5999 3661 7389 Telecommunication equipment repair (except telephones); mobile telephones & equipment; telephone & telegraph apparatus; packaging & labeling services; testing laboratories; electronic parts & equipment

*(G-862)*
**VANITIES INC**
212 W University Dr (60004-1810)
**PHONE**...................................847 483-0240
**Fax:** 847 483-0250
James Stubing, *President*
Barbara Stubing, *Corp Secy*
**EMP:** 6
**SQ FT:** 12,000
**SALES:** 600K **Privately Held**
**WEB:** www.vanities.com
**SIC:** 2434 Vanities, bathroom: wood

*(G-863)*
**VIBGYOR OPTICAL SYSTEMS CORP**
1140 N Phelps Ave (60004-5030)
**PHONE**...................................847 818-0788
Bharat Verma, *President*
**EMP:** 45
**SQ FT:** 3,200
**SALES (est):** 5.1MM **Privately Held**
**SIC:** 3827 Optical instruments & lenses

*(G-864)*
**VIBGYOR OPTICS INC**
Also Called: Optical Systems
1140 N Phelps Ave (60004-5030)
**PHONE**...................................847 818-0788
**Fax:** 847 818-0799
Bharat S Verma, *President*
Anuradha Verma, *Vice Pres*
Sonia Gill, *Admin Sec*
**EMP:** 40
**SQ FT:** 5,400
**SALES:** 2MM **Privately Held**
**SIC:** 5049 3827 Optical goods; optical instruments & lenses

*(G-865)*
**VISCO TECHNOLOGIES USA INC**
511 W Golf Rd (60005-3904)
**PHONE**...................................847 993-3047
Hideyuki Adachi, *CEO*
Ichiro Sugimoto, *Vice Pres*
**EMP:** 4 **EST:** 2014
**SALES (est):** 322.1K
**SALES (corp-wide):** 18.9MM **Privately Held**
**SIC:** 3674 Integrated circuits, semiconductor networks, etc.
**PA:** Visco Technologies Corporation
1-11-1, Kaigan
Minato-Ku TKY 105-0
364 024-500

*(G-866)*
**VLAHOS ELECTRIC SERVICE DR**
1707 N Dale Ave (60004-4328)
**PHONE**...................................224 764-2335
**EMP:** 3 **EST:** 2010
**SALES (est):** 162.3K **Privately Held**
**SIC:** 8011 3699 Offices & clinics of medical doctors; electrical equipment & supplies

*(G-867)*
**VPNVANTAGECOM**
415 W Golf Rd Ste 5 (60005-3923)
**PHONE**...................................877 998-4678
Alex Rowley, *CEO*

EMP: 5
SALES (est): 310K Privately Held
SIC: 3669 Communications equipment

**(G-868)**
**VST AMERICA INC**
85 W Algonquin Rd 215 (60005-4422)
PHONE..................847 952-3800
Wakako Yamazaki, *Manager*
◆ EMP: 3
SALES (est): 330K Privately Held
SIC: 3559 Optical lens machinery

**(G-869)**
**W W BARTHEL & CO**
220 W Campus Dr Ste C (60004-1479)
PHONE..................847 392-5643
EMP: 6 EST: 1974
SQ FT: 2,950
SALES (est): 420K Privately Held
SIC: 2759 2752 Commercial Printing Lithographic Commercial Printing

**(G-870)**
**WEB PRINTING CONTROLS CO INC (PA)**
3350 W Salt Creek Ln # 110 (60005-1089)
PHONE..................618 842-2664
Fax: 847 382-2348
Herman Gnuechtel, *CEO*
Dean Fetherling, *Ch of Bd*
Bruce Fetherling, *Plant Mgr*
Tim Wolfe, *Purchasing*
Andy Altensey, *Engineer*
EMP: 96
SQ FT: 34,000
SALES (est): 15.7MM Privately Held
SIC: 3555 Printing trades machinery

**(G-871)**
**WEBER MARKING SYSTEMS INC (PA)**
Also Called: Weber Packaging Solutions Inc
711 W Algonquin Rd (60005-4455)
PHONE..................847 364-8500
Fax: 847 364-8575
Joseph A Weber Jr, *Ch of Bd*
Glenn C Gilly, *President*
Douglas A Weber, *Vice Pres*
John Oleary, *VP Mfg*
George Stieber, *VP Mfg*
◆ EMP: 425 EST: 1932
SQ FT: 317,000
SALES (est): 200.4MM Privately Held
WEB: www.webermarking.com
SIC: 3555 2672 2675 Printing trades machinery; labels (unprinted), gummed: made from purchased materials; die-cut paper & board

**(G-872)**
**WILL HAMMS STAINED GLASS**
628 N Highland Ave (60004-5514)
PHONE..................847 255-2230
Fax: 847 255-2230
William Hamm, *Owner*
William A Hamm, *Owner*
EMP: 10
SALES (est): 615.1K Privately Held
SIC: 3231 1793 Stained glass: made from purchased glass; glass & glazing work

**(G-873)**
**WITRON INTGRATED LOGISTICS INC**
3721 N Ventura Dr (60004-7489)
PHONE..................847 398-6130
Fax: 847 398-6140
Karl Hoegen, *CEO*
Robert Mendenhall, *Safety Dir*
Terrance Cochran, *Facilities Mgr*
Brian Farnell, *Site Mgr*
Corey Helton, *Engineer*
▲ EMP: 180
SQ FT: 25,000
SALES (est): 48.6MM
SALES (corp-wide): 185.8K Privately Held
WEB: www.witron.com
SIC: 3535 Unit handling conveying systems
HQ: Witron Logistik + Informatik Gmbh
    Neustadter Str. 21
    Parkstein 92711
    960 260-00

**(G-874)**
**WPC MACHINERY CORP**
Also Called: Web Printing Control
3350 W Salt Creek Ln (60005-5023)
PHONE..................630 231-7721
Dean Fetherling, *President*
Patricia Fetherling, *Corp Secy*
Herman Gnuechtel, *Vice Pres*
Dave McIlvaine, *Plant Mgr*
Phil Gurgone, *Opers Mgr*
EMP: 50 EST: 1976
SQ FT: 4,919
SALES (est): 3.3MM Privately Held
SIC: 7699 3555 Printing trades machinery & equipment repair; printing trades machinery

**(G-875)**
**XLOGOTECH INC**
5 E College Dr Ste 203 (60004-1963)
PHONE..................888 244-5152
Eugene Tensiper, *Principal*
EMP: 4
SALES (est): 1MM Privately Held
SIC: 5065 3572 Diskettes, computer; disk drives, computer

**(G-876)**
**XPRESSIGNS INC**
2470 E Oakton St (60005-4820)
PHONE..................888 303-0640
EMP: 3
SQ FT: 3,000
SALES (est): 177.1K Privately Held
SIC: 3993 Signs & advertising specialties

**(G-877)**
**YAMADA AMERICA INC**
955 E Algonquin Rd (60005-4301)
PHONE..................847 228-9063
Fax: 847 631-9273
Shinji Kameyama, *Principal*
Karen Chambers, *Vice Pres*
Mike Jennett, *Purchasing*
David Pressler, *Sales Mgr*
Matt Mulligan, *Sales Staff*
◆ EMP: 21
SQ FT: 30,000
SALES (est): 5.8MM
SALES (corp-wide): 81.1MM Privately Held
SIC: 3561 5084 4813 Pumps & pumping equipment; pumps & pumping equipment;
PA: Yamada Corporation
    1-1-3, Minamimagome
    Ota-Ku TKY 143-0
    337 775-101

## Aroma Park
### Kankakee County

**(G-878)**
**ANCHOR WELDING & FABRICATION**
2950 N Lowe Rd (60910-1069)
P.O. Box 26 (60910-0026)
PHONE..................815 937-1640
Janet Andreina, *President*
Nick Andreina, *Admin Sec*
EMP: 2
SQ FT: 5,200
SALES (est): 254.6K Privately Held
SIC: 3441 3442 7692 3446 Fabricated structural metal; window & door frames; welding repair; architectural metalwork; sheet metalwork; fabricated plate work (boiler shop)

**(G-879)**
**NEW DIMENSION MODELS**
Also Called: Fiberglass International
105 W Front St (60910-1058)
P.O. Box 28 (60910-0028)
PHONE..................815 935-1001
Fax: 815 935-1060
EMP: 6
SQ FT: 4,200
SALES (est): 460K Privately Held
SIC: 3469 Mfg Lawn/Garden Equipment Engineering Services Mfg Industrial Patterns

## Arthur
### Douglas County

**(G-880)**
**ARTHUR CUSTOM TANK LLC**
510 E Progress St (61911-1545)
PHONE..................217 543-4022
Bill Glawe, *General Mgr*
Edward Parker, *Corp Counsel*
Patrick Hartman,
EMP: 5
SALES (est): 1.3MM Privately Held
SIC: 3443 Tanks for tank trucks, metal plate

**(G-881)**
**ARTHUR GRAPHIC CLARION**
113 E Illinois St (61911-1331)
P.O. Box 19 (61911-0019)
PHONE..................217 543-2151
Fax: 217 543-2152
Greg Hoskins, *President*
EMP: 4 EST: 1887
SQ FT: 3,000
SALES (est): 170K Privately Held
SIC: 2711 2752 Job printing & newspaper publishing combined; commercial printing, lithographic

**(G-882)**
**BEACHYS COUNTER TOPS INC**
129 E Sr 133 (61911-6503)
PHONE..................217 543-2143
Fax: 217 543-2144
Leonard Beachy, *President*
EMP: 10 EST: 1964
SALES (est): 1.1MM Privately Held
WEB: www.illinoisamishcountry.com
SIC: 2541 Counter & sink tops

**(G-883)**
**C B M PLASTICS INC**
398 E St Rt 133 (61911-6232)
PHONE..................217 543-3870
Fred Helmuth, *President*
EMP: 10 EST: 1998
SALES (est): 1.8MM Privately Held
WEB: www.cbmplastics.com
SIC: 3442 Garage doors, overhead: metal

**(G-884)**
**C H I OVERHEAD DOORS INC**
1485 Sunrise Dr (61911-1684)
P.O. Box 260 (61911-0260)
PHONE..................217 543-2135
Timothy Miller, *CEO*
Jerry Kauffman, *Purchasing*
Howard Miller, *Purchasing*
Tisha L Pfeiffer, *CFO*
Tisha Pfeiffer, *Controller*
◆ EMP: 500
SQ FT: 13,000
SALES (est): 110.9MM
SALES (corp-wide): 1.9B Publicly Held
WEB: www.chiohd.com
SIC: 3442 Garage doors, overhead: metal
HQ: C.H.I Doors Holdings, Inc.
    1485 Sunrise Dr
    Arthur IL 61911
    217 543-2135

**(G-885)**
**CARSTIN BRANDS INC**
520 E 2nd St (61911-1129)
P.O. Box 285 (61911-0285)
PHONE..................217 543-3331
Sam S Petersheim Jr, *President*
EMP: 90
SQ FT: 37,000
SALES (est): 17MM Privately Held
WEB: www.carstinbrands.com
SIC: 3088 Bathroom fixtures, plastic; sinks, plastic; tubs (bath, shower & laundry), plastic

**(G-886)**
**CENTRAL ILLINOIS POULTRY PROC**
119 N Cr 000 E (61911-6532)
PHONE..................217 543-2937
Andy Jess, *Owner*
EMP: 15
SALES (est): 1.4MM Privately Held
SIC: 2015 Poultry slaughtering & processing

**(G-887)**
**CHI DOORS HOLDINGS INC (DH)**
Also Called: CHI Overhead Doors
1485 Sunrise Dr (61911-1684)
PHONE..................217 543-2135
Jim Overholt, *President*
Pat Knoll, *CFO*
Kathryn Hogan, *Human Res Mgr*
George Artenstein, *Regl Sales Mgr*
Dan Beckley, *Regl Sales Mgr*
◆ EMP: 2
SALES (est): 139.7MM
SALES (corp-wide): 1.9B Publicly Held
SIC: 3442 Metal doors, sash & trim
HQ: Kohlberg Kravis Roberts & Co. L.P.
    9 W 57th St Ste 4200
    New York NY 10019
    212 750-8300

**(G-888)**
**COACH HOUSE INC**
Also Called: Coach House Garages
700 E Mill St (61911-1689)
P.O. Box 320 (61911-0320)
PHONE..................217 543-3761
James Yoder, *President*
Larry Diener, *Production*
Dave Binion, *Human Res Mgr*
EMP: 41
SQ FT: 68,000
SALES (est): 8.4MM Privately Held
WEB: www.coachhousegarages.com
SIC: 2452 Prefabricated wood buildings; farm & agricultural buildings, prefabricated wood; farm buildings, prefabricated or portable: wood; panels & sections, prefabricated, wood

**(G-889)**
**CORNERSTONE BUILDING PRODUCTS**
226 E Cr 600 N (61911-6223)
PHONE..................217 543-2829
Alan Dean Miller, *Owner*
EMP: 2
SQ FT: 940
SALES (est): 255.5K Privately Held
SIC: 2952 5211 Roofing materials; doors, storm: wood or metal

**(G-890)**
**COUNTRY SIDE WOODWORKING**
550 N Cr 240 E (61911-6228)
PHONE..................217 543-4190
David L Kaufman, *Owner*
David Kaufman, *Owner*
EMP: 16
SALES (est): 2MM Privately Held
SIC: 3533 Derricks, oil or gas field

**(G-891)**
**COUNTRY WORKSHOP**
Also Called: Miller Ervin B
651 N Cr 125 E (61911-6220)
PHONE..................217 543-4094
Ervin D Miller, *Owner*
EMP: 5
SALES (est): 462.1K Privately Held
SIC: 2511 Wood household furniture

**(G-892)**
**COUNTY LINE INC**
Also Called: Douglas Knty Kreative Kitchens
750 N Cr 250 E (61911-6216)
PHONE..................217 268-5056
Fax: 217 268-5110
Ivan Gingerich, *Owner*
EMP: 27
SQ FT: 2,000
SALES (est): 2.8MM Privately Held
SIC: 2434 Wood kitchen cabinets

**(G-893)**
**CUSTOM SCREEN PRINTING**
111 N Vine St (61911-1116)
P.O. Box 144 (61911-0144)
PHONE..................217 543-3691
Alvie Jess, *Principal*
EMP: 4 EST: 1997

**Arthur - Douglas County (G-894)**

SALES (est): 303K  Privately Held
SIC: 2759  Screen printing

**(G-894)**
**DG WOOD PROCESSING**
120 E Cr 200 N  (61911-6515)
PHONE..............................217 543-2128
Fax: 217 543-2759
David Gingerich, *Owner*
EMP: 16
SALES (est): 1.7MM  Privately Held
SIC: 2448  5099  Pallets, wood; firewood

**(G-895)**
**DOEROCK INC**
Also Called: Tool World
901 E Columbia St  (61911-9737)
P.O. Box 258  (61911-0258)
PHONE..............................217 543-2101
Fax: 217 543-2529
Elmer A Schrock, *President*
Voleta Schrock, *Corp Secy*
EMP: 3
SQ FT: 2,500
SALES (est): 754.5K  Privately Held
SIC: 5072  3423  5251  Hand tools; hand & edge tools; tools, hand

**(G-896)**
**DOUGLAS COUNTY WOOD PRODUCTS**
491 N Cr 100 E  (61911-6501)
PHONE..............................217 543-2888
Steve Kaufmann, *Owner*
EMP: 7
SALES (est): 1.2MM  Privately Held
SIC: 2511  Wood bedroom furniture

**(G-897)**
**DUTCH VALLEY MEATS INC**
376 E Sr 133  (61911-6232)
PHONE..............................217 543-3354
Fax: 217 543-3358
Lorn Yoder, *President*
EMP: 6
SALES (est): 350K  Privately Held
WEB: www.chiholdings.com
SIC: 2011  Meat packing plants

**(G-898)**
**E M C INDUSTRY**
441 E Cr 400 N  (61911-6243)
PHONE..............................217 543-2894
Eldon Chutp, *Partner*
Eldon Chupp, *Partner*
EMP: 2
SALES (est): 200K  Privately Held
SIC: 2512  Upholstered household furniture

**(G-899)**
**E Z TRAIL  INC (PA)**
1050 E Columbia St  (61911-9739)
P.O. Box 168  (61911-0168)
PHONE..............................217 543-3471
Fax: 217 543-3473
Abe B Kuhns, *President*
Danny Kuhns, *Vice Pres*
Tim Kuhns, *Admin Sec*
▲ EMP: 30
SQ FT: 72,000
SALES (est): 7.1MM  Privately Held
WEB: www.e-ztrail.com
SIC: 3523  Trailers & wagons, farm

**(G-900)**
**FOUR ACRE WOOD PRODUCTS**
553 N Cr 240 E  (61911-6227)
PHONE..............................217 543-2971
Fax: 217 543-2971
David Kauffman, *Owner*
EMP: 13
SQ FT: 50,000
SALES (est): 800K  Privately Held
SIC: 2434  2431  Wood kitchen cabinets; door trim, wood

**(G-901)**
**GDS ENTERPRISES**
399 E Progress St  (61911-1431)
PHONE..............................217 543-3681
Glen Schlabach, *Owner*
EMP: 4
SQ FT: 250
SALES (est): 300K  Privately Held
SIC: 5261  3511  Garden supplies & tools; turbines & turbine generator sets

**(G-902)**
**GINGERICH CUSTOM WOODWORKING**
750 N Cr 250 E  (61911-6216)
PHONE..............................217 578-3491
Ivan Gingerich, *Owner*
EMP: 15
SALES (est): 1MM  Privately Held
SIC: 2431  Interior & ornamental woodwork & trim

**(G-903)**
**HEARTLAND MACHINE AND SUP LLC**
337 E Sr 133  (61911-6200)
PHONE..............................217 543-2678
Joseph Mast, *Mng Member*
EMP: 18
SQ FT: 4,000
SALES (est): 958K  Privately Held
SIC: 3599  Machine shop, jobbing & repair

**(G-904)**
**HELMUTH CUSTOM KITCHENS LLC**
Also Called: Family Health Foods
2004 Cr 1800e  (61911-6062)
Rr # 1 Box 129
PHONE..............................217 543-3588
Adlai L Helmuth, *Mng Member*
Edna Helmuth, *Mng Member*
Gladys Helmuth, *Mng Member*
Katie Helmuth, *Mng Member*
Paul Helmuth, *Mng Member*
EMP: 45
SQ FT: 20,000
SALES (est): 5.7MM  Privately Held
SIC: 2434  5499  Wood kitchen cabinets; health foods

**(G-905)**
**HERSCHBERGER WOOD WORKING**
145 E Cr 300 N  (61911-6541)
PHONE..............................217 543-4075
Eli Herschberger, *Owner*
EMP: 3
SALES (est): 193.4K  Privately Held
SIC: 2499  Decorative wood & woodwork

**(G-906)**
**KAUFMAN WOODWORKING**
29 E Cr 100 N  (61911-6531)
PHONE..............................217 543-3607
Lloyd Kaufman, *Owner*
EMP: 3
SALES (est): 213.3K  Privately Held
SIC: 2499  Decorative wood & woodwork

**(G-907)**
**LAMBRIGHT DISTRIBUTORS**
35 E Cr 200 N  (61911-6533)
PHONE..............................217 543-2083
Vernon Lambright, *Owner*
Elsie Lambright, *Co-Owner*
EMP: 5
SALES (est): 270K  Privately Held
SIC: 3632  5192  7623  Freezers, home & farm; books, periodicals & newspapers; refrigeration service & repair

**(G-908)**
**LITTLE CREEK WOODWORKING**
1473 Cr 1675e  (61911-6043)
PHONE..............................217 543-2815
Verna Herschberger, *Owner*
Mervin Herschberber, *Owner*
EMP: 1
SALES (est): 612K  Privately Held
SIC: 3553  2499  Furniture makers' machinery, woodworking; decorative wood & woodwork

**(G-909)**
**MASTERBRAND CABINETS  INC**
501 W Progress St  (61911-1232)
PHONE..............................217 543-3311
Bryan Barnes, *General Mgr*
Kevin Jordan, *Safety Dir*
Mick Price, *Opers-Prdtn-Mfg*
Janice Hutchcraft, *Purch Mgr*
Dave Price, *Plant Engr Mgr*
EMP: 500
SQ FT: 325,000
SALES (corp-wide): 4.9B  Publicly Held
WEB: www.mbcabinets.com
SIC: 2434  Wood kitchen cabinets
HQ: Masterbrand Cabinets, Inc.
1 Masterbrand Cabinets Dr
Jasper IN 47546
812 482-2527

**(G-910)**
**MASTERBRAND CABINETS  INC**
Also Called: Cabinet Factories Outlet
N Arthur Atwood Rd  (61911)
PHONE..............................217 543-3466
Dave Camp, *Manager*
EMP: 5
SALES (corp-wide): 4.9B  Publicly Held
WEB: www.mbcabinets.com
SIC: 2434  Wood kitchen cabinets
HQ: Masterbrand Cabinets, Inc.
1 Masterbrand Cabinets Dr
Jasper IN 47546
812 482-2527

**(G-911)**
**MASTERBRAND CABINETS  INC**
Also Called: Diy Cabinet Warehouse
100 N Vine St  (61911-1115)
PHONE..............................503 241-4964
Jim Collins, *Branch Mgr*
EMP: 5
SALES (corp-wide): 4.9B  Publicly Held
WEB: www.mbcabinets.com
SIC: 2434  Wood kitchen cabinets
HQ: Masterbrand Cabinets, Inc.
1 Masterbrand Cabinets Dr
Jasper IN 47546
812 482-2527

**(G-912)**
**MOULTRIE COUNTY HARDWOODS LLC**
Rr 1 Box 170-F  (61911)
Marion Miller,
Marlon J Miller,
EMP: 5
SQ FT: 12,000
SALES (est): 615K  Privately Held
SIC: 2426  5023  Hardwood dimension & flooring mills; wood flooring

**(G-913)**
**NELSON DOOR CO**
2245 Cr 1500e  (61911-6024)
PHONE..............................217 543-3489
Nelson Deener, *Owner*
Ruth Deener, *Co-Owner*
EMP: 5
SALES (est): 330K  Privately Held
SIC: 2431  Door frames, wood

**(G-914)**
**O & I WOODWORKING**
125 E County Rd 50 E  (61911)
PHONE..............................217 543-3155
Omer Otto, *Owner*
EMP: 4
SALES (est): 170K  Privately Held
SIC: 2511  Wood household furniture

**(G-915)**
**OKAW TRUSS  INC**
368 E Sr 133  (61911-6232)
PHONE..............................217 543-3371
Fred Helmuth, *President*
Elvin M Schrock, *General Mgr*
Tony Thomas, *Manager*
Floyd Yoder, *Admin Sec*
EMP: 425
SALES (est): 79.1MM  Privately Held
WEB: www.okawtruss.com
SIC: 2439  3441  Trusses, except roof: laminated lumber; fabricated structural metal

**(G-916)**
**OKAW VALLEY WOODWORKING LLC**
Also Called: Country Heritage Crafts
432 E Sr 133  (61911-6240)
PHONE..............................217 543-5180
Merv Yoder,
EMP: 10 EST: 2000
SQ FT: 9,000
SALES (est): 1.1MM  Privately Held
SIC: 2434  2511  5947  8412  Wood kitchen cabinets; wood household furniture; gift, novelty & souvenir shop; art gallery

**(G-917)**
**OTTOS CANVAS SHOP**
1749b State Highway 133  (61911-6111)
PHONE..............................217 543-3307
Melvin Otto, *Owner*
EMP: 5
SALES (est): 200K  Privately Held
SIC: 2394  5499  5091  Canvas & related products; health & dietetic food stores; boat accessories & parts

**(G-918)**
**PLANKS CABINET SHOP INC**
1620 State Highway 133  (61911-6015)
PHONE..............................217 543-2687
Fax: 217 543-2686
Mary Miller, *President*
Edward A Miller, *Vice Pres*
EMP: 8 EST: 1962
SQ FT: 1,000
SALES (est): 1MM  Privately Held
SIC: 2434  2511  Wood kitchen cabinets; wood household furniture

**(G-919)**
**PRAIRIE STATE MACHINE LLC**
71 E Cr 100 N  (61911-6531)
PHONE..............................217 543-3768
Glen Herschberger, *Mng Member*
EMP: 9
SQ FT: 3,780
SALES (est): 800K  Privately Held
SIC: 3553  Woodworking machinery

**(G-920)**
**RICHARD SCHROCK**
Also Called: Pineview Woodworking
41 E Cr 200 N  (61911-6533)
PHONE..............................217 543-3111
Richard Schrock, *Owner*
EMP: 6 EST: 1964
SALES (est): 850K  Privately Held
WEB: www.pineviewwoodworking.com
SIC: 2434  Wood kitchen cabinets

**(G-921)**
**SCHROCKS WOODWORKING**
135 E Cr 800 N  (61911-6211)
PHONE..............................217 578-3259
Levi Schrock, *Owner*
EMP: 4
SALES (est): 309.2K  Privately Held
SIC: 2431  Millwork

**(G-922)**
**TIMBERSIDE WOODWORKING**
715 N Cr 125 E  (61911-6209)
PHONE..............................217 578-3201
Ray L Herschberger, *Owner*
EMP: 5
SALES (est): 356.8K  Privately Held
SIC: 2517  Home entertainment unit cabinets, wood

**(G-923)**
**TRI-CUNTY WLDG FABRICATION LLC**
1031 E Columbia St  (61911-9736)
P.O. Box 137  (61911-0137)
PHONE..............................217 543-3304
Fax: 217 543-3338
Leno Otto, *Manager*
Dennis L Plank,
EMP: 40
SQ FT: 86,000
SALES (est): 6.8MM  Privately Held
SIC: 7692  1799  3441  Welding repair; welding on site; fabricated structural metal

**(G-924)**
**WILLARD R SCHORCK**
Also Called: Rocky Lane Woodworking
55 E Cr 300 N  (61911-6551)
PHONE..............................217 543-2160
Fax: 217 543-2729
Willard R Schorck, *Owner*
EMP: 12
SALES (est): 670K  Privately Held
SIC: 2431  Millwork

# GEOGRAPHIC SECTION

## Ashkum
### Iroquois County

**(G-925)**
**HEARTLAND CANDLE CO**
2739 N 700 East Rd (60911-7153)
**PHONE** ............................................. 815 698-2200
Fax: 309 463-2233
A J Wilken, *Partner*
Pam Wilken, *Partner*
Lynn Wilken, *General Ptnr*
Larry Haigh, *Manager*
**EMP:** 4
**SALES (est):** 200K **Privately Held**
**WEB:** www.heartlandcandles.com
**SIC: 3999** 5947 Candles; gift, novelty & souvenir shop

## Ashland
### Cass County

**(G-926)**
**FULTON METAL WORKS INC**
1763 Ashland Rd (62612-3456)
P.O. Box 242 (62612-0242)
**PHONE** ............................................. 217 476-8223
Stan Fulton, *President*
Dustin Fulton, *Vice Pres*
Jeanne Fulton, *Treasurer*
**EMP:** 3
**SQ FT:** 9,000
**SALES:** 220K **Privately Held**
**SIC: 3498** 3444 Tube fabricating (contract bending & shaping); sheet metalwork

## Ashley
### Washington County

**(G-927)**
**LICON INC**
23297 County Highway 7 (62808-2723)
**PHONE** ............................................. 618 485-2222
Lester Johannes, *President*
Rosemary Johannes, *Corp Secy*
Michael Johannes, *Vice Pres*
**EMP:** 3
**SQ FT:** 4,500
**SALES (est):** 330.9K **Privately Held**
**SIC: 3599** 3523 3444 Machine shop, jobbing & repair; farm machinery & equipment; sheet metalwork

## Ashmore
### Coles County

**(G-928)**
**CHARLESTON STONE COMPANY**
9709 N County Rd 2000 E (61912)
P.O. Box 260, Charleston (61920-0260)
**PHONE** ............................................. 217 345-6292
Jerald Tarble, *President*
John Tarble, *Vice Pres*
Guy Powls, *Manager*
**EMP:** 35 EST: 1937
**SQ FT:** 700
**SALES:** 5.7MM **Privately Held**
**WEB:** www.charlestonstoneco.com
**SIC: 1422** Cement rock, crushed & broken-quarrying

## Ashton
### Lee County

**(G-929)**
**N FLY CYCLE INC**
2439 Gurler Rd (61006-9509)
**PHONE** ............................................. 815 562-4620
Shawn Smith, *CEO*
▲ **EMP:** 2
**SALES (est):** 456.6K **Privately Held**
**SIC: 3751** Bicycles & related parts

## Assumption
### Christian County

**(G-930)**
**B & B EQUIPMENT**
401 S Business 5 (62510)
P.O. Box 53 (62510-0053)
**PHONE** ............................................. 217 562-2511
Joe A Burton, *Partner*
Leota Burton, *Partner*
**EMP:** 11
**SQ FT:** 800
**SALES (est):** 503.4K **Privately Held**
**SIC: 1389** Oil field services

**(G-931)**
**GOLDEN PRAIRIE NEWS**
301 S Chestnut St (62510-1299)
**PHONE** ............................................. 217 226-3721
Fax: 217 226-3579
**EMP:** 4 EST: 1959
**SQ FT:** 2,400
**SALES:** 46K **Privately Held**
**SIC: 2711** 2759 2752 Newspapers-Publishing/Printing Commercial Printing Lithographic Commercial Printing

**(G-932)**
**GSI GROUP LLC**
Gsi International
1004 E Illinois St (62510-9529)
P.O. Box 20 (62510-0020)
**PHONE** ............................................. 217 226-4401
**EMP:** 6
**SALES (corp-wide):** 7.4B **Publicly Held**
**WEB:** www.grainsystems.com
**SIC: 3523** Crop storage bins
**HQ:** The Gsi Group Llc
1004 E Illinois St
Assumption IL 62510
217 226-4421

**(G-933)**
**GSI HOLDINGS CORP (HQ)**
1004 E Illinois St (62510-9529)
**PHONE** ............................................. 217 226-4421
Scott Clawson, *CEO*
Wayne Jordan, *Credit Mgr*
Letha Frailey, *Manager*
▼ **EMP:** 1
**SALES:** 118.2MM
**SALES (corp-wide):** 7.4B **Publicly Held**
**SIC: 3523** Crop storage bins; driers (farm): grain, hay & seed; poultry brooders, feeders & waterers; hog feeding, handling & watering equipment
**PA:** Agco Corporation
4205 River Green Pkwy
Duluth GA 30096
770 813-9200

## Astoria
### Fulton County

**(G-934)**
**KK STEVENS PUBLISHING CO**
100 N Pearl St (61501-9545)
P.O. Box 590 (61501-0590)
**PHONE** ............................................. 309 329-2151
Fax: 309 329-2344
Thomas Stevens, *President*
Judy Beaird, *Editor*
Timothy Stevens, *Corp Secy*
Rose McCurdy, *Financial Exec*
Scott Wherley, *Manager*
**EMP:** 48 EST: 1959
**SQ FT:** 30,000
**SALES (est):** 4.3MM **Privately Held**
**WEB:** www.kkspc.com
**SIC: 2711** 2791 2752 2732 Job printing & newspaper publishing combined; typesetting; commercial printing, lithographic; book printing

**(G-935)**
**OIL FILTER RECYCLERS INC**
Rr 1 (61501)
**PHONE** ............................................. 309 329-2131
Donny Onken, *Owner*
**EMP:** 20 **Privately Held**
**WEB:** www.ofrinc.net
**SIC: 3533** Oil & gas drilling rigs & equipment
**PA:** Oil Filter Recyclers, Inc.
320 E Main St
Easton IL 62633

**(G-936)**
**PRAIRIELAND FS INC**
2452 N Bader Rd (61501-8817)
P.O. Box 298 (61501-0298)
**PHONE** ............................................. 309 329-2162
Fax: 309 329-2163
Keith Hufendick, *General Mgr*
Tom Trone, *Branch Mgr*
**EMP:** 7
**SALES (corp-wide):** 17.1MM **Privately Held**
**SIC: 2875** 5191 Fertilizers, mixing only; fertilizers & agricultural chemicals
**PA:** Prairieland Fs, Inc.
1132 Veterans Dr
Jacksonville IL 62650
217 243-6561

## Athens
### Menard County

**(G-937)**
**D AND I ANALYST INC (PA)**
Also Called: Ingram Soil Testing Centre
13343 Fitschen Rd (62613-7438)
**PHONE** ............................................. 217 636-7500
Fax: 217 636-7548
Dale Ingram, *President*
Rosalie Ingram, *Corp Secy*
**EMP:** 10
**SQ FT:** 1,800
**SALES (est):** 1.4MM **Privately Held**
**SIC: 2899** Soil testing kits; core wash or wax

**(G-938)**
**DONNAS HOUSE OF TYPE INC**
Also Called: Interactive Data Technologies
23267 Railsplitter Ln (62613-7613)
**PHONE** ............................................. 217 522-5050
Fax: 217 522-9673
Donna Aschenbrenner, *President*
**EMP:** 4
**SQ FT:** 2,000
**SALES (est):** 230K **Privately Held**
**WEB:** www.springfield-il.com
**SIC: 7336** 2791 7374 Commercial art & graphic design; typesetting; service bureau, computer

**(G-939)**
**MATERIAL SERVICE CORPORATION**
25142 Quarry Ave (62613-7411)
**PHONE** ............................................. 217 732-2117
Fax: 217 732-2117
Roger Brown, *Manager*
**EMP:** 20
**SALES (corp-wide):** 16B **Privately Held**
**WEB:** www.materialservice.com
**SIC: 1422** 3281 Crushed & broken limestone; cut stone & stone products
**HQ:** Material Service Corporation
2235 Entp Dr Ste 3504
Westchester IL 60154
708 731-2600

**(G-940)**
**METEER INC**
16592 Kincaid St (62613-7575)
**PHONE** ............................................. 217 636-7280
Wade E Meteer, *Principal*
**EMP:** 4
**SALES (est):** 362.5K **Privately Held**
**SIC: 3523** Farm machinery & equipment

**(G-941)**
**METEER MANUFACTURING CO**
25904 Meteer Ln (62613-7578)
**PHONE** ............................................. 217 636-8109
Fax: 217 636-8309
Patsy Meteer, *President*
Wade Meteer, *Vice Pres*
Chad Ishmael, *Buyer*
Jody Meteer, *Director*
William Meteer, *Director*
**EMP:** 7
**SALES:** 450K **Privately Held**
**WEB:** www.meteer.com
**SIC: 3599** 7692 Machine shop, jobbing & repair; welding repair

**(G-942)**
**PRECISION TANK & EQUIPMENT CO**
25203 Quarry Ave (62613-7410)
**PHONE** ............................................. 217 636-7023
Fax: 217 636-8790
Ron Swearingen, *VP Opers*
Ryan Stratton, *Bookkeeper*
Ron Lager, *Sales Mgr*
Mike Kemple, *Systems Mgr*
Harry Nichols, *Systems Staff*
**EMP:** 10
**SALES (corp-wide):** 11MM **Privately Held**
**WEB:** www.precisiontank.com
**SIC: 3443** Fabricated plate work (boiler shop)
**PA:** Precision Tank & Equipment Co.
3503 Conover Rd
Virginia IL 62691
217 452-7228

## Atkinson
### Henry County

**(G-943)**
**BROWN METAL PRODUCTS LTD**
513 N Spring (61235-7755)
P.O. Box 386 (61235-0386)
**PHONE** ............................................. 309 936-7384
Leonard Brown, *President*
Cheryl Brown, *Vice Pres*
**EMP:** 4
**SQ FT:** 6,000
**SALES (est):** 187K **Privately Held**
**SIC: 3559** Metal finishing equipment for plating, etc.

**(G-944)**
**MORTON BUILDINGS INC**
605 E Henry St (61235-9555)
P.O. Box 602 (61235-0602)
**PHONE** ............................................. 309 936-7282
Fax: 309 936-7284
Steve Hamm, *Manager*
**EMP:** 12
**SQ FT:** 5,000
**SALES (corp-wide):** 499.4MM **Privately Held**
**WEB:** www.mortonbuildings.com
**SIC: 3448** 1541 5039 1542 Buildings, portable: prefabricated metal; prefabricated building erection, industrial; prefabricated structures; agricultural building contractors
**PA:** Morton Buildings, Inc.
252 W Adams St
Morton IL 61550
800 447-7436

**(G-945)**
**TRAEYNE CORPORATION**
17982 E 2350th St (61235-9565)
**PHONE** ............................................. 309 936-7878
Tom Enyeart, *Principal*
**EMP:** 6
**SALES (est):** 241.5K **Privately Held**
**SIC: 3069** Tubes, hard rubber

## Atlanta
### Logan County

**(G-946)**
**AMY WERTHEIM (PA)**
Also Called: Rgw Candy Company
1865 2200th St Bldg 2 (61723-9125)
**PHONE** ............................................. 309 830-4361
Amy Wertheim, *Owner*
**EMP:** 3
**SQ FT:** 1,215
**SALES:** 78K **Privately Held**
**SIC: 2064** 5145 Candy & other confectionery products; candy

# Atwood
## Douglas County

**(G-947)**
**HARRIS COMPANIES INC**
521 N Illinois St (61913-9750)
P.O. Box 1108, Arkansas City KS (67005-1108)
PHONE..................217 578-2231
Roger Harris, *President*
Scott Harris, *Vice Pres*
Stan Harris, *Vice Pres*
Sandy Fiala, *Manager*
Beth Harris, *Manager*
**EMP:** 16
**SQ FT:** 25,000
**SALES (est):** 4.9MM **Privately Held**
**SIC:** 3534 Elevators & equipment

# Auburn
## Sangamon County

**(G-948)**
**BRANDT CONSOLIDATED INC**
300 W Jefferson St (62615-1424)
P.O. Box 77 (62615-0077)
PHONE..................217 438-6158
**Fax:** 217 438-9212
Josh Allen, *Branch Mgr*
Joshua Allen, *Manager*
**EMP:** 11
**SALES (corp-wide):** 180MM **Privately Held**
**WEB:** www.indresgroup.com
**SIC:** 5191 2875 Fertilizers & agricultural chemicals; fertilizers, mixing only
**PA:** Brandt Consolidated, Inc.
2935 S Koke Mill Rd
Springfield IL 62711
217 547-5800

**(G-949)**
**SOUTH COUNTY PUBLICATIONS (PA)**
Also Called: Chatham Clarion
110 N 5th St (62615-1449)
P.O. Box 50 (62615-0050)
PHONE..................217 438-6155
**Fax:** 217 438-6156
Joseph Michelich, *President*
Alan McIntire, *Treasurer*
**EMP:** 14
**SQ FT:** 2,200
**SALES (est):** 1.5MM **Privately Held**
**SIC:** 2711 Newspapers: publishing only, not printed on site

**(G-950)**
**SPRINGFIELD PLASTICS INC**
7300 W State Route 104 (62615-9259)
PHONE..................217 438-6167
**Fax:** 217 438-6949
Stephen W Baker, *President*
Fred Rice, *Treasurer*
Douglas Baker, *Manager*
Sally Kolenich, *Administration*
**EMP:** 45
**SQ FT:** 38,000
**SALES (est):** 10MM **Privately Held**
**WEB:** www.spipipe.com
**SIC:** 3082 Tubes, unsupported plastic

# Augusta
## Hancock County

**(G-951)**
**AUGUSTA EAGLE**
Also Called: Tri County Scribe
600 Main St (62311-1322)
P.O. Box 5 (62311-0005)
PHONE..................217 392-2715
**Fax:** 217 392-2619
Stacey Nicholas, *Owner*
**EMP:** 3 **EST:** 1966
**SQ FT:** 252
**SALES (est):** 95K **Privately Held**
**SIC:** 2711 Job printing & newspaper publishing combined

# Aurora
## Dupage County

**(G-952)**
**4G ANTENNA SHOP INC**
2948 Kirk Rd Ste 106 (60502-6012)
PHONE..................815 496-0444
Robert Villanueva, *Owner*
**EMP:** 4
**SALES (est):** 155.1K **Privately Held**
**SIC:** 3663 7389 Radio broadcasting & communications equipment;

**(G-953)**
**A BEADTIFUL THING**
2406 Wilton Ln (60502-6377)
PHONE..................630 236-5913
Karen Thompson, *Owner*
**EMP:** 3
**SALES (est):** 228.7K **Privately Held**
**SIC:** 3999 Beads, unassembled

**(G-954)**
**AERTRADE LLC (PA)**
1585 Beverly Ct Ste 128 (60502-8767)
PHONE..................630 428-4440
Mark Borows,
**EMP:** 8
**SALES:** 5MM **Privately Held**
**SIC:** 3728 Aircraft instruments, equipment or parts

**(G-955)**
**AIR802 LLC**
2570 Beverly Dr Ste 140 (60502-8535)
PHONE..................630 585-6383
Lilian Bryant, *General Mgr*
Anibal Martinez, *Manager*
**EMP:** 3
**SALES (est):** 172.6K **Privately Held**
**SIC:** 3568 Power transmission equipment

**(G-956)**
**AIR802 CORPORATION**
2570 Beverly Dr Ste 140 (60502-8535)
PHONE..................630 428-3108
Lilian Bryant, *CEO*
Michael Bryant, *President*
▲ **EMP:** 5
**SALES (est):** 1.2MM **Privately Held**
**WEB:** www.air802.com
**SIC:** 3679 Electronic circuits; attenuators; harness assemblies for electronic use: wire or cable

**(G-957)**
**ANGELO BRUNI**
4107 Chesapeake Dr Apt 3b (60504-5108)
PHONE..................773 754-5422
Abdulwahab Odunuga, *Partner*
Katarzyna Odunuga, *Partner*
**EMP:** 2 **EST:** 2013
**SALES (est):** 218.5K **Privately Held**
**SIC:** 5139 5122 5311 3111 Shoes; cosmetics, perfumes & hair products; department stores; leather tanning & finishing;

**(G-958)**
**APEX ENGINEERING PRODUCTS CORP**
1241 Shoreline Dr (60504-6768)
PHONE..................630 820-8888
**Fax:** 630 820-8886
Eric Ostermeier, *CEO*
Mark Bickler, *President*
Tim Fregeau, *Sales Mgr*
Michael Ostermeier, *Sales Staff*
Monica Moore, *Admin Asst*
◆ **EMP:** 12 **EST:** 1942
**SALES (est):** 3.4MM **Privately Held**
**WEB:** www.rydlyme.com
**SIC:** 2842 2899 Cleaning or polishing preparations; chemical preparations

**(G-959)**
**AR INET CORP**
2336 Pagosa Springs Dr (60503-6463)
PHONE..................603 380-3903
Anum Mirza, *President*
**EMP:** 3
**SQ FT:** 1,800

**SALES (est):** 102.7K **Privately Held**
**SIC:** 7375 7378 8748 7371 On-line data base information retrieval; computer & data processing equipment repair/maintenance; systems engineering consultant, ex. computer or professional; custom computer programming services; business oriented computer software

**(G-960)**
**AURORA CIRCUITS INC**
2250 White Oak Cir (60502-9675)
PHONE..................630 978-3830
Christopher E Kalmus, *President*
Dave Zeno, *President*
John Holmquest, *Vice Pres*
Craig Wilson, *CFO*
Thad Bartosz, *Human Res Mgr*
▲ **EMP:** 65 **EST:** 1937
**SQ FT:** 30,000
**SALES (est):** 10MM **Privately Held**
**SIC:** 3672 Printed circuit boards

**(G-961)**
**AURORA CIRCUITS LLC**
2250 White Oak Cir (60502-9675)
PHONE..................630 978-3830
Christopher Kalmus,
David Zeno,
▲ **EMP:** 64
**SQ FT:** 38,000
**SALES (est):** 6.8MM **Privately Held**
**WEB:** www.auroracircuits.com
**SIC:** 3672 Printed circuit boards

**(G-962)**
**AURORA SIGN CO**
1100 Route 34 Ste 2 (60503-9348)
PHONE..................630 898-5900
Ed Weis, *President*
Brandon Weis, *Vice Pres*
**EMP:** 8
**SALES (est):** 776K **Privately Held**
**WEB:** www.aurorasign.com
**SIC:** 3993 Electric signs; neon signs

**(G-963)**
**AUTOGENESIS LLC**
3909 75th St (60504-7920)
PHONE..................630 851-9424
Hosni Adra, *Principal*
**EMP:** 3
**SALES (est):** 249.9K **Privately Held**
**SIC:** 3465 Body parts, automobile: stamped metal

**(G-964)**
**AZTECH ENGINEERING INC**
Also Called: Aztech Locknut Company
2675 White Oak Cir Ste 1 (60502-9611)
PHONE..................630 236-3200
Mark Kaindl, *President*
Michael Kaindl, *Vice Pres*
Sara Vasicek, *Vice Pres*
Eric Bramlage, *Plant Mgr*
Bob Hoffman, *Engineer*
▲ **EMP:** 20 **EST:** 1978
**SQ FT:** 54,000
**SALES (est):** 4.6MM **Privately Held**
**WEB:** www.aztechlocknut.com
**SIC:** 3452 Nuts, metal

**(G-965)**
**B A DIE MOLD INC**
3685 Prairie Lake Ct (60504-3134)
PHONE..................630 978-4747
Alan Petrucci, *President*
Francine Petrucci, *President*
Patricia Petrucci, *Treasurer*
**EMP:** 18
**SQ FT:** 10,000
**SALES (est):** 3.8MM **Privately Held**
**WEB:** www.badiemold.com
**SIC:** 3544 Industrial molds

**(G-966)**
**B&B MACHINING INCORPORATED**
24 Gastville St (60503-9302)
PHONE..................630 898-3009
**Fax:** 630 898-5016
William Schmidt, *President*
Thomas Schmidt, *Vice Pres*
**EMP:** 16
**SQ FT:** 14,500

**SALES (est):** 1.8MM **Privately Held**
**SIC:** 3494 3599 Valves & pipe fittings; machine shop, jobbing & repair

**(G-967)**
**B-O-F CORPORATION**
801 N Commerce St (60504-7930)
PHONE..................630 585-0020
James P Knorring, *President*
Kenneth Shaw, *President*
Laura Dooley, *CFO*
Karen Shaw, *Treasurer*
Judy Muskus, *Cust Svc Dir*
**EMP:** 35
**SQ FT:** 66,000
**SALES (est):** 8.8MM **Privately Held**
**WEB:** www.bofcorp.com
**SIC:** 2542 Racks, merchandise display or storage: except wood; shelving angles or slotted bars: except wood

**(G-968)**
**BALLCO MANUFACTURING CO INC (PA)**
2375 Liberty St (60502-9442)
PHONE..................630 898-1600
**Fax:** 630 898-7367
Ozzie Van Gelderen, *President*
Dennis Krachon, *Vice Pres*
Everette Foster, *Engineer*
Andrew Stritt, *Sales Staff*
Daniel Zauner, *Sales Staff*
▲ **EMP:** 57 **EST:** 1961
**SQ FT:** 42,000
**SALES (est):** 27MM **Privately Held**
**WEB:** www.ballcomfg.com
**SIC:** 3599 Machine shop, jobbing & repair

**(G-969)**
**BERRY GLOBAL INC**
999 Bilter Rd (60502-4719)
PHONE..................630 375-0358
**EMP:** 4
**SALES (corp-wide):** 6.4B **Publicly Held**
**SIC:** 3842 Nonclassified Establishment
**HQ:** Berry Global, Inc.
101 Oakley St
Evansville IN 47710
812 424-2904

**(G-970)**
**BLUCO CORPORATION**
3500 Thayer Ct (60504-3108)
PHONE..................630 637-1820
Robert W Ellig, *President*
Todd Bennett, *Engineer*
Dave Armstrong, *Sls & Mktg Exec*
Cara Cap, *Bookkeeper*
Margy Pagone, *Human Res Mgr*
▲ **EMP:** 17
**SALES (est):** 3.9MM **Privately Held**
**WEB:** www.bluco.com
**SIC:** 3544 Special dies, tools, jigs & fixtures

**(G-971)**
**BOSE CORPORATION**
Also Called: Bose Factory Store
1650 Premium Outlet Blvd # 1257 (60502-2911)
PHONE..................630 585-6654
Jeff Anderson, *Branch Mgr*
**EMP:** 9
**SALES (corp-wide):** 3B **Privately Held**
**WEB:** www.bose.com
**SIC:** 5731 3651 Radio, television & electronic stores; household audio equipment
**PA:** Bose Corporation
100 The Mountain Rd
Framingham MA 01701
508 879-7330

**(G-972)**
**BOSTON WAREHOUSE TRADING CORP**
2600 Beverly Dr (60502-8005)
PHONE..................630 992-5604
James Wenz, *Branch Mgr*
**EMP:** 5
**SALES (corp-wide):** 17.7MM **Privately Held**
**SIC:** 3648 Decorative area lighting fixtures
**PA:** Boston Warehouse Trading Corp.
59 Davis Ave Ste 10
Norwood MA 02062
781 769-8550

## GEOGRAPHIC SECTION
### Aurora - Dupage County (G-995)

**(G-973)**
**BRAVILOR BONAMAT LLC**
1204 Bilter Rd (60502-4729)
PHONE...............................630 423-9400
Maarten Ponne, *Sales Dir*
Debora Mehlert, *Office Mgr*
▲ EMP: 10
SALES (est): 1.8MM
SALES (corp-wide): 79.2MM **Privately Held**
SIC: 3556 Roasting machinery: coffee, peanut, etc.
HQ: Bravilor Bonamat B.V.
Pascalstraat 20
Heerhugowaard
725 751-751

**(G-974)**
**BRIGHTON-BEST INTL INC**
940 Enterprise St Ste 100 (60504-4918)
PHONE...............................562 808-8000
Robert Shieh, *President*
▲ EMP: 2
SALES (est): 681.6K **Privately Held**
SIC: 5072 3965 Bolts, nuts & screws; nuts (hardware); fasteners

**(G-975)**
**BRK BRANDS INC (DH)**
Also Called: Family Gard/Brk
3901 Liberty St (60504-8122)
PHONE...............................630 851-7330
Fax: 630 851-8221
Thomas Russo, *President*
Mark Devine, *Vice Pres*
Doug Kellam, *Vice Pres*
Rich Timmons, *Vice Pres*
Edward Tyranski, *Vice Pres*
◆ EMP: 180
SQ FT: 60,000
SALES (est): 410MM
SALES (corp-wide): 13.2B **Publicly Held**
WEB: www.brkelectronics.com
SIC: 3669 Fire detection systems, electric
HQ: First Alert, Inc.
3901 Liberty St
Aurora IL 60504
630 499-3295

**(G-976)**
**CABLE MANAGEMENT PRODUCTS INC**
1005 N Commons Dr (60504-4100)
PHONE...............................630 723-0470
Julian Good, *Vice Pres*
▲ EMP: 4 EST: 2008
SALES (est): 472.9K
SALES (corp-wide): 33.8B **Privately Held**
SIC: 3644 Electric conduits & fittings
HQ: Thomas & Betts Corporation
8155 T&B Blvd
Memphis TN 38125
901 252-5000

**(G-977)**
**CABOT MICROELECTRONICS CORP (PA)**
870 N Commons Dr (60504-7963)
PHONE...............................630 375-6631
Fax: 630 375-9976
William P Noglows, *Ch of Bd*
David H Li, *President*
H Carol Bernstein, *Vice Pres*
Yumiko Damashek, *Vice Pres*
Richard Hui, *Vice Pres*
EMP: 61
SQ FT: 200,000
SALES: 430.4MM **Publicly Held**
WEB: www.cabotcmp.com
SIC: 2842 Polishing preparations & related products

**(G-978)**
**CABOT MICROELECTRONICS CORP**
845 Enterprise St (60504-7933)
PHONE...............................630 375-6631
Fax: 630 499-2606
Gary Lissy, *Branch Mgr*
EMP: 100
SALES (corp-wide): 430.4MM **Publicly Held**
WEB: www.cabotcmp.com
SIC: 3634 Heating pads, electric

PA: Cabot Microelectronics Corporation
870 N Commons Dr
Aurora IL 60504
630 375-6631

**(G-979)**
**CABOT MICROELECTRONICS CORP**
500 N Commons Dr (60504-4159)
P.O. Box 2026 (60507-2026)
PHONE...............................630 375-6631
Fax: 630 585-9976
Carlos Barros, *Engineer*
Dan Pike, *Manager*
EMP: 112
SALES (corp-wide): 430.4MM **Publicly Held**
WEB: www.cabotcmp.com
SIC: 2819 8731 Industrial inorganic chemicals; commercial physical research
PA: Cabot Microelectronics Corporation
870 N Commons Dr
Aurora IL 60504
630 375-6631

**(G-980)**
**CANO CONTAINER CORPORATION (PA)**
3920 Enterprise Ct (60504-8132)
PHONE...............................630 585-7500
Fax: 630 585-7501
Juventino Cano, *President*
Amy Ferguson, *Admin Sec*
EMP: 20
SQ FT: 60,000
SALES: 10.8MM **Privately Held**
SIC: 2653 Boxes, corrugated: made from purchased materials

**(G-981)**
**CASCADES PLASTICS INC**
Also Called: Cascades Enviropac Aurora
2300 Raddant Rd Ste B (60502-9108)
PHONE...............................450 469-3389
Fax: 630 585-1990
Randall C Mohler, *CEO*
Keith Schmidt, *Maint Spvr*
Ernie Cox, *Sales Mgr*
Beth Dunning, *Manager*
EMP: 45
SQ FT: 40,000
SALES (est): 10MM
SALES (corp-wide): 2.9B **Privately Held**
SIC: 2653 Boxes, corrugated: made from purchased materials; partitions, corrugated: made from purchased materials
HQ: Cascades Plastics Inc.
7501 S Spoede Ln
Warrenton MO 63380
636 456-9576

**(G-982)**
**CENTOR NORTH AMERICA INC**
966 Corporate Blvd # 130 (60502-9114)
PHONE...............................630 957-1000
James Thornton, *President*
▲ EMP: 30
SQ FT: 40,000
SALES (est): 6.7MM **Privately Held**
SIC: 3442 Window & door frames

**(G-983)**
**CHICAGO ADHESIVE PRODUCTS**
1105 S Frontenac St (60504-6451)
PHONE...............................630 978-7766
Raymond Kline, *Principal*
Sue Schroeder, *Director*
EMP: 4 EST: 2010
SALES (est): 455.1K **Privately Held**
SIC: 2891 Adhesives

**(G-984)**
**CONTROL SOLUTIONS LLC**
2520 Diehl Rd (60502-9497)
PHONE...............................630 806-7062
Fax: 630 806-7065
Michael McKee, *General Mgr*
Bill Glase, *VP Opers*
Curt Motisi, *Mfg Spvr*
Todd Trowbridge, *Opers Staff*
Karen Hinckley, *Senior Buyer*
▲ EMP: 89

SALES (est): 25.6MM
SALES (corp-wide): 333.4MM **Privately Held**
SIC: 3613 3625 Switchgear & switchboard apparatus; time switches, electrical switchgear apparatus; power switching equipment; relays & industrial controls; control equipment, electric; motor controls, electric; electric controls & control accessories, industrial
PA: Corinthian Capital Group, Llc
601 Lexington Ave Rm 5901
New York NY 10022
212 920-2300

**(G-985)**
**CRABTREE & EVELYN LTD**
1650 Premium Outlet Blvd # 1151 (60502-2934)
PHONE...............................630 898-3478
Fax: 630 898-3488
Felicia McCree, *Branch Mgr*
EMP: 3 **Privately Held**
WEB: www.crabtree-evelyn.com
SIC: 3499 5199 5947 Novelties & giftware, including trophies; gifts & novelties; gift shop
HQ: Crabtree & Evelyn Ltd.
102 Peake Brook Rd
Woodstock CT 06281
800 272-2873

**(G-986)**
**CRAFTSMAN TOOL & MOLD CO**
2750 Church Rd (60502-9706)
PHONE...............................630 851-8700
Fax: 630 851-3864
Wayne Sikorcin, *President*
Willy Phillips, *Counsel*
Millie Velez, *Warehouse Mgr*
Jeff Nowicki, *Program Mgr*
Scott Smith, *Manager*
EMP: 43
SQ FT: 37,000
SALES (est): 29.3MM **Privately Held**
WEB: www.craftsmanmold.com
SIC: 5084 3544 Industrial machinery & equipment; industrial molds

**(G-987)**
**CREATIVE CONTRACT PACKG LLC**
3777 Exchange Ave (60504-8102)
PHONE...............................630 851-6226
Fax: 630 851-6595
Kevin McGowen, *COO*
Dale Apold, *Vice Pres*
Mike Van Hyfte, *Plant Mgr*
Pawel Noland, *Prdtn Mgr*
Gary Smith, *Purch Agent*
EMP: 80
SQ FT: 70,800
SALES: 12.9MM
SALES (corp-wide): 9.5B **Publicly Held**
WEB: www.hormel.com
SIC: 2099 Dessert mixes & fillings; gelatin dessert preparations; desserts, ready-to-mix
PA: Hormel Foods Corporation
1 Hormel Pl
Austin MN 55912
507 437-5611

**(G-988)**
**CROCS INC**
1650 Premium Outlet Blvd # 931 (60502-2923)
PHONE...............................630 820-3572
Karen Escobar, *Branch Mgr*
EMP: 14
SALES (corp-wide): 1B **Publicly Held**
SIC: 3021 5661 Shoes, rubber or rubber soled fabric uppers; shoe stores
PA: Crocs, Inc.
7477 Dry Creek Pkwy
Niwot CO 80503
303 848-7000

**(G-989)**
**CROWN CORK & SEAL USA INC**
3737 Exchange Ave (60504-8102)
PHONE...............................630 851-7774
Fax: 630 851-7775
Philip Shaughnessy, *Plant Mgr*
Alexia Ciontea, *Research*
Vikram Trehan, *Engineer*

Tom Gaffney, *Adv Dir*
David Sieroty, *Manager*
EMP: 50
SALES (corp-wide): 8.2B **Publicly Held**
WEB: www.crowncork.com
SIC: 3411 Metal cans
HQ: Crown Cork & Seal Usa, Inc.
1 Crown Way
Philadelphia PA 19154
215 698-5100

**(G-990)**
**CUSTOM BLOW MOLDING**
2560 White Oak Cir # 140 (60502-9683)
PHONE...............................630 820-9700
EMP: 8 EST: 2014
SALES (est): 1.2MM **Privately Held**
SIC: 3089 Molding primary plastic

**(G-991)**
**CUSTOM FILTER LLC**
2300 Raddant Rd Ste A (60502-9109)
PHONE...............................630 906-2100
John Copley, *President*
Bruce Plumb, *Vice Pres*
Patrick O Brien, *CFO*
Dave Fuller,
Bill Moreland,
▲ EMP: 60
SALES (est): 16.8MM **Privately Held**
WEB: www.customfilter.com
SIC: 3564 Purification & dust collection equipment

**(G-992)**
**CYNLAR INC**
Also Called: AlphaGraphics
1585 Beverly Ct Ste 125 (60502-8764)
PHONE...............................630 820-2200
Fax: 630 820-9155
Larry Byers, *President*
Cynthia Byers, *Vice Pres*
EMP: 6
SQ FT: 2,200
SALES (est): 1MM **Privately Held**
SIC: 2752 Commercial printing, lithographic

**(G-993)**
**CYRUS SHANK COMPANY**
575 Exchange Ct (60504-8103)
PHONE...............................630 618-4732
Cyrus Shank, *Branch Mgr*
EMP: 8
SALES (corp-wide): 4.3MM **Privately Held**
SIC: 3491 Industrial valves
HQ: Cyrus Shank Company
4645 W Roosevelt Rd
Cicero IL 60804
708 652-2700

**(G-994)**
**DETROIT FORMING INC**
Also Called: D F I
2700 Church Rd (60502-8733)
PHONE...............................630 820-0500
Fax: 630 820-0076
Andrew Schrampfer, *Sales Mgr*
Joe Gibbons, *Manager*
EMP: 60
SQ FT: 35,000
SALES (corp-wide): 64.8MM **Privately Held**
WEB: www.detroitforming.net
SIC: 3089 Trays, plastic; plastic containers, except foam
PA: Detroit Forming, Inc.
19100 W 8 Mile Rd
Southfield MI 48075
248 352-8108

**(G-995)**
**DIAMOND ENVELOPE CORPORATION (PA)**
2270 White Oak Cir (60502-9675)
PHONE...............................630 499-2800
Fax: 630 499-2801
Alan J Jania, *President*
Alan W Jania, *Vice Pres*
Michael Jania, *Vice Pres*
Susan A Jania, *Vice Pres*
Rick Soderstrom, *Director*
EMP: 80
SQ FT: 100,000

## Aurora - Dupage County (G-996)

SALES (est): 21.4MM **Privately Held**
WEB: www.diamondenvelope.com
SIC: 2677 2752 Envelopes; commercial printing, lithographic

### (G-996)
**DONNA KARAN COMPANY LLC**
1650 Premium Outlet Blvd # 313 (60504-2904)
PHONE....................630 236-8900
Donna Karan, *Manager*
EMP: 157
SALES (corp-wide): 2.3B **Publicly Held**
SIC: 2335 Women's, juniors' & misses' dresses
HQ: The Donna Karan Company Llc
240 W 40th St
New York NY 10018
212 789-1500

### (G-997)
**DU PAGE PRECISION PRODUCTS CO (PA)**
3695 Darlene Ct Ste 101 (60504-6546)
PHONE....................630 849-2940
Dennis Flynn, *President*
J Michael Schroeder, *Vice Pres*
Mike Schroeder, *Vice Pres*
Michael J Flynn, *Prdtn Mgr*
Leo Breyne, *Production*
EMP: 10 EST: 1950
SQ FT: 48,000
SALES (est): 18.3MM **Privately Held**
SIC: 3599 Machine shop, jobbing & repair

### (G-998)
**DU PAGE PRECISION PRODUCTS CO**
811 Shoreline Dr (60504-6195)
PHONE....................630 849-2940
Dave Carlen, *Plant Mgr*
EMP: 75
SALES (corp-wide): 18.3MM **Privately Held**
SIC: 3599 3369 5084 3365 Machine shop, jobbing & repair; nonferrous foundries; engines & parts, diesel; aluminum foundries; steel foundries; malleable iron foundries
PA: Du Page Precision Products Co.
3695 Darlene Ct Ste 101
Aurora IL 60504
630 849-2940

### (G-999)
**DUNLEE CORPORATION**
555 N Commerce St (60504-8110)
PHONE....................630 585-2100
▲ EMP: 6
SALES (est): 1.8MM **Privately Held**
SIC: 3844 X-ray apparatus & tubes

### (G-1000)
**ECLI PRODUCTS LLC (HQ)**
Also Called: LTI
3851 Exchange Ave (60504-8106)
PHONE....................630 449-5000
Ian Rowell, *President*
Shane Nunley, *Manager*
Steven Whitt, *Info Tech Dir*
Xiaolan Huang, *Director*
EMP: 37
SALES: 28MM
SALES (corp-wide): 746.6MM **Publicly Held**
SIC: 2992 Lubricating oils & greases
PA: Quaker Chemical Corporation
901 E Hector St
Conshohocken PA 19428
610 832-4000

### (G-1001)
**ELEMECH INC**
2275 White Oak Cir Aurora (60502)
P.O. Box 1563 (60507-1563)
PHONE....................630 417-2845
Robert Gorder, *Pres*
Shelly Gorder, *Production*
Sandy Claypool, *Purch Mgr*
Matthew Sassenrath, *Engineer*
Chris Countryman, *Project Engr*
EMP: 25
SQ FT: 22,500
SALES (est): 5.5MM **Privately Held**
WEB: www.elemechinc.com
SIC: 8711 3625 7371 Electrical or electronic engineering; relays & industrial controls; computer software systems analysis & design, custom

### (G-1002)
**EMBOSSED GRAPHICS INC**
1175 S Frontenac St (60504-6451)
PHONE....................630 236-4000
Richard Pauling, *Ch of Bd*
Richard S Pauling, *President*
Ronald McCormick, *Engineer*
Philesa Stonecliffe, *Human Resources*
Paul Cervelli, *Marketing Staff*
EMP: 85
SQ FT: 120,000
SALES (est): 12.1MM **Privately Held**
WEB: www.embossed.com
SIC: 2759 Stationery: printing

### (G-1003)
**ENTAPPIA LLC**
1052 Sundew Ct (60504-6876)
PHONE....................630 546-4531
Padmanabhan Balamani,
Vijayalakshmi Kumar,
Anandtha Rajamani,
EMP: 5
SALES (est): 251.4K **Privately Held**
SIC: 7371 7379 7372 Computer software systems analysis & design, custom; software programming applications; computer related consulting services; prepackaged software; application computer software

### (G-1004)
**ENZ (USA) INC**
1585 Beverly Ct Ste 115 (60502-8731)
PHONE....................630 692-7880
Albert Enz, *President*
Dana Hicks, *Sales Mgr*
EMP: 4
SQ FT: 3,300
SALES (est): 448.5K **Privately Held**
SIC: 3999 Pipe cleaners

### (G-1005)
**EXIDE TECHNOLOGIES**
GNB Technologies
3950 Sussex Ave (60504-7932)
PHONE....................630 862-2200
Fax: 630 862-2431
Bruce Cole, *VP Mfg*
Randy Dockery, *Prdtn Mgr*
Rich Uzoras, *Warehouse Mgr*
Kenneth Scheid, *Opers Staff*
Ed Dupuis, *Mfg Staff*
EMP: 150
SALES (corp-wide): 2.5B **Privately Held**
WEB: www.exideworld.com
SIC: 3691 3692 Lead acid batteries (storage batteries); primary batteries, dry & wet
PA: Exide Technologies
13000 Deerfield Pkwy # 200
Milton GA 30004
678 566-9000

### (G-1006)
**FABRICATED PRODUCTS CO INC**
1875 Plain Ave (60502-8568)
PHONE....................630 898-6460
Fax: 630 848-3207
William W Witte, *CEO*
John Witte, *President*
Diann Witte, *Vice Pres*
EMP: 15
SQ FT: 15,000
SALES (est): 2.8MM **Privately Held**
SIC: 3443 Tanks, standard or custom fabricated: metal plate; vessels, process or storage (from boiler shops): metal plate; fuel tanks (oil, gas, etc.): metal plate; boilers: industrial, power, or marine

### (G-1007)
**FGS-IL LLC**
Also Called: Freedom Graphic Systems
780 Mcclure Rd (60502-9509)
PHONE....................630 375-8500
Fax: 630 375-8503
Tony Wang, *CEO*
Martin Liebert, *President*
William Greene, *Vice Pres*
Bruce Hawkins, *Engineer*
Terry Brady, *CFO*
EMP: 250
SALES (est): 54MM
SALES (corp-wide): 105.4MM **Privately Held**
WEB: www.fgs.com
SIC: 7331 2752 Direct mail advertising services; commercial printing, lithographic
PA: Fgs-Wi, Llc
1101 S Janesville St
Milton WI 53563
608 373-6500

### (G-1008)
**FHP-BERNER USA LP**
2188a Diehl Rd (60502)
PHONE....................630 270-1400
Francesco Burrone, *Plant Mgr*
Sherry Dray, *Director*
▲ EMP: 40
SQ FT: 120,000
SALES: 14MM **Privately Held**
SIC: 2392 Mops, floor & dust

### (G-1009)
**FIRST ALERT INC (DH)**
3901 Liberty St (60504-8122)
PHONE....................630 499-3295
Joseph Messner, *CEO*
Mark A Devine, *Vice Pres*
Edward J Tyranski, *Vice Pres*
Trisha Costello, *VP Opers*
Ed Duran, *QC Mgr*
▲ EMP: 6
SQ FT: 60,000
SALES (est): 801.2MM
SALES (corp-wide): 13.2B **Publicly Held**
SIC: 3669 3999 3446 3499 Smoke detectors; fire extinguishers, portable; stairs, fire escapes, balconies, railings & ladders; safes & vaults, metal; gas detectors; flashlights; lanterns: electric, gas, carbide, kerosene or gasoline
HQ: American Household, Inc.
2381 Nw Executive Ctr Dr
Boca Raton FL 33431
561 912-4100

### (G-1010)
**FREUDENBERG HOUSEHOLD PDTS LP**
Also Called: Freudenberg & Co
2188 Diehl Rd (60502-8775)
PHONE....................630 270-1400
Ron Tillery, *President*
Dr Wolfram Freudenberg, *Chairman*
Werner Wenning, *Chairman*
Thomas Caruso, *Business Mgr*
Alexander Kayser, *Prdtn Mgr*
◆ EMP: 134
SALES (est): 35.2MM
SALES (corp-wide): 6.9B **Privately Held**
WEB: www.ocedar.com
SIC: 2392 3991 Mops, floor & dust; brooms & brushes
HQ: Freudenberg Home And Cleaning Solutions Gmbh
Im Technologiepark 19
Weinheim
620 180-8710

### (G-1011)
**FRINGS AMERICA INC**
3015 E New York St A2-143 (60504-5162)
PHONE....................630 851-5826
Anton Enenkel, *President*
E Kenneth Wyatt Jr, *Vice Pres*
▲ EMP: 2
SQ FT: 1,000
SALES: 1.7MM
SALES (corp-wide): 11.2MM **Privately Held**
WEB: www.fringsamerica.com
SIC: 3565 Canning machinery, food
PA: Frings Verwaltungs Gmbh & Co. Kg
Jonas-Cahn-Str. 9
Bonn 53115
228 983-30

### (G-1012)
**FRONTIDA BIOPHARM INC**
2500 Molitor Rd (60502-9441)
PHONE....................215 620-3527
Tim Hanratty, *Branch Mgr*
EMP: 5
SALES (corp-wide): 32.6MM **Privately Held**
SIC: 2833 Medicinal chemicals
PA: Frontida Biopharm, Inc.
1100 Orthodox St
Philadelphia PA 19124
610 232-0112

### (G-1013)
**GANNETT STLLITE INFO NTWRK LLC**
Also Called: USA Today
495 N Commons Dr Ste 102 (60504-8221)
PHONE....................630 629-1280
Douglas McCorkindale, *CEO*
Jim Donivan, *Manager*
EMP: 117
SALES (corp-wide): 3B **Publicly Held**
SIC: 2711 Newspapers
HQ: Gannett Satellite Information Network, Llc
7950 Jones Branch Dr
Mc Lean VA 22102
703 854-6000

### (G-1014)
**GEORG-PCIFIC CORRUGATED IV LLC**
Also Called: Excel Displays & Packaging
4390 Liberty St (60504-9502)
PHONE....................630 896-3610
Keith Davis, *Accounts Mgr*
Catherine Stateman, *Admin Asst*
EMP: 119
SALES (corp-wide): 27.4B **Privately Held**
SIC: 2653 Corrugated boxes, partitions, display items, sheets & pad
HQ: Georgia-Pacific Corrugated Iv Llc
133 Peachtree St Ne
Atlanta GA 30303
404 652-4000

### (G-1015)
**GEORGIA-PACIFIC BLDG PDTS LLC**
2540 Prospect Ct (60502-9419)
PHONE....................630 449-7200
Deb Gla, *Human Res Mgr*
Deb Glass, *Personnel Exec*
Doug Dreghorn, *Marketing Mgr*
Ken Kruger, *Branch Mgr*
EMP: 5
SALES (corp-wide): 27.4B **Privately Held**
SIC: 2653 2493 2421 3275 Corrugated & solid fiber boxes; particleboard products; sawmills & planing mills, general; lumber: rough, sawed or planed; wallboard, gypsum
HQ: Georgia-Pacific Building Products Llc
133 Peachtree St Ne
Atlanta GA 30303
404 652-4000

### (G-1016)
**GLANBIA PERFORMANCE NTRTN INC**
948 Meridian Lake Dr (60504-4901)
PHONE....................630 256-7445
Juan Vega, *Manager*
EMP: 25 **Privately Held**
SIC: 2833 4225 Vitamins, natural or synthetic: bulk, uncompounded; general warehousing
HQ: Glanbia Performance Nutrition, Inc.
3500 Lacey Rd
Downers Grove IL 60515

### (G-1017)
**GLANBIA PERFORMANCE NTRTN INC**
600 N Commerce St (60504-8111)
PHONE....................630 236-3126
Tom Stucker, *Branch Mgr*
EMP: 73 **Privately Held**
SIC: 2833 Vitamins, natural or synthetic: bulk, uncompounded
HQ: Glanbia Performance Nutrition, Inc.
3500 Lacey Rd
Downers Grove IL 60515

## Aurora - Dupage County (G-1042)

**(G-1018)**
**GLOBALTECH INTERNATIONAL LLC (PA)**
Also Called: Pro-Beam USA
3909 75th St Ste 105  (60504-7934)
PHONE..................................630 327-6909
Radwan Mourad, *Mng Member*
EMP: 6
SQ FT: 1,000
SALES: 626K  **Privately Held**
SIC: 3548  7699  Electric welding equipment; welding equipment repair

**(G-1019)**
**GODIVA CHOCOLATIER INC**
1650 Premium Outlet Blvd # 1213 (60502-2901)
PHONE..................................630 820-5842
EMP: 24  **Privately Held**
SIC: 2066  Mfg Chocolate/Cocoa Prdt
HQ: Godiva Chocolatier, Inc.
   333 W 34th St Fl 6
   New York NY 10001
   212 984-5900

**(G-1020)**
**GONNELLA BAKING CO**
2435 Church Rd  (60502-9724)
PHONE..................................630 820-3433
William Smith, *Branch Mgr*
EMP: 90
SALES (corp-wide): 140.2MM  **Privately Held**
SIC: 2051  Bread, cake & related products
PA: Gonnella Baking Co.
   1117 Wiley Rd
   Schaumburg IL 60173
   312 733-2020

**(G-1021)**
**GRUNDFOS WATER UTILITY INC**
Also Called: Yeomans Pump
3905 Enterprise Ct  (60504-8132)
PHONE..................................630 236-5500
Fax: 630 236-5511
Dieter Sauer, *President*
Michael Franzen, *President*
Robert Lepera, *Vice Pres*
Larry Molinaro, *Project Mgr*
Paul Singal, *Project Mgr*
▲ EMP: 100
SQ FT: 105,000
SALES (est): 46.4MM
SALES (corp-wide): 3.5B  **Privately Held**
WEB: www.yccpump.com
SIC: 3561  Pumps, domestic: water or sump
HQ: Grundfos Arnold Ag
   Industrie Nord 12
   Schachen LU
   414 973-939

**(G-1022)**
**HANGER PROSTHETICS &**
Also Called: Hanger Clinic
4255 Westbrook Dr Ste 215  (60504-8125)
PHONE..................................630 820-5656
Sam Liang, *President*
Scott Scliski, *Branch Mgr*
EMP: 5
SALES (corp-wide): 459.1MM  **Publicly Held**
SIC: 5999  3842  Orthopedic & prosthesis applications; limbs, artificial
HQ: Hanger Prosthetics & Orthotics East, Inc.
   33 North Ave Ste 101
   Tallmadge OH 44278
   330 633-9807

**(G-1023)**
**HB FULLER CNSTR PDTS INC (HQ)**
Also Called: H.B. Fuller Construction Pdts
1105 S Frontenac St  (60504-6451)
PHONE..................................630 978-7766
Fax: 847 776-4452
Rose Mary Clyburn, *CEO*
Jeffery Burke, *Facilities Mgr*
Tammy Kring, *Accountant*
Ken Wallberg, *Manager*
Roose Jonna, *Assistant*
◆ EMP: 125
SQ FT: 190,000
SALES (est): 67.1MM
SALES (corp-wide): 2B  **Publicly Held**
WEB: www.fosterproducts.com
SIC: 2891  Adhesives
PA: H.B. Fuller Company
   1200 Willow Lake Blvd
   Saint Paul MN 55110
   651 236-5900

**(G-1024)**
**HB FULLER COMPANY**
Also Called: Adhesves Sealants Coatings Div
1105 S Frontenac St  (60504-6451)
PHONE..................................847 358-9555
Fax: 847 358-6708
Ed Dura, *Manager*
Myron Meglin, *Executive*
EMP: 5
SALES (corp-wide): 2B  **Publicly Held**
WEB: www.hbfuller.com
SIC: 2891  Glue
PA: H.B. Fuller Company
   1200 Willow Lake Blvd
   Saint Paul MN 55110
   651 236-5900

**(G-1025)**
**HEARTLAND GRANITE INC**
Also Called: CMC Granite & Marble
701 N Commerce St  (60504-8173)
PHONE..................................630 499-8000
Fax: 630 499-8045
Roy B Logan, *President*
▲ EMP: 20
SALES (est): 3.5MM  **Privately Held**
WEB: www.chicagomarble.com
SIC: 3281  Curbing, granite or stone

**(G-1026)**
**HIDROSTAL LLC**
Also Called: Hidrostal Pumps
2225 White Oak Cir  (60502-9670)
P.O. Box 3414, Oak Brook  (60522-3414)
PHONE..................................630 240-6271
John Kelly, *General Mgr*
EMP: 12
SQ FT: 3,200
SALES: 10MM  **Privately Held**
SIC: 3561  Pumps & pumping equipment

**(G-1027)**
**INDUSTRIAL MEASUREMENT SYSTEMS**
2760 Beverly Dr Ste 4  (60502-8604)
PHONE..................................630 236-5901
Donald E Yuhas, *President*
Marjorie P Yuhas, *Vice Pres*
Mark Mutton, *Engineer*
Loretta Oleksak, *Info Tech Mgr*
EMP: 6
SQ FT: 6,400
SALES (est): 560K  **Privately Held**
WEB: www.imsysinc.com
SIC: 3829  Measuring & controlling devices

**(G-1028)**
**INEOS STYROLUTION AMERICA LLC (DH)**
4245 Meridian Pkwy # 151  (60504-8018)
PHONE..................................630 820-9500
Kevin McQuade, *CEO*
Alexander Gluck, *President*
Greg Fordyce, *Vice Pres*
Tom Strifler, *Vice Pres*
Chris De La Camp, *CFO*
◆ EMP: 125
SALES (est): 162MM
SALES (corp-wide): 40B  **Privately Held**
SIC: 2869  Industrial organic chemicals
HQ: Ineos Styrolution Group Gmbh
   Mainzer Landstr. 50
   Frankfurt Am Main  60325
   695 095-5012

**(G-1029)**
**INFOPRO INC**
Also Called: Corrflow
2920 Norwalk Ct  (60502-1310)
PHONE..................................630 978-9231
John E Michelsen, *President*
Gary D Raymond, *Exec VP*
Elaine Raymond, *Admin Mgr*
EMP: 5
SALES: 330K  **Privately Held**
WEB: www.corrflow.com
SIC: 7372  7379  7371  Prepackaged software; computer related consulting services; computer software systems analysis & design, custom

**(G-1030)**
**INSIDE TRACK TRADING**
2905 Lahinch Ct  (60503-6271)
PHONE..................................630 585-9218
Eric Hadik, *Principal*
EMP: 3
SALES (est): 183.9K  **Privately Held**
SIC: 2721  Periodicals

**(G-1031)**
**INTERNATIONAL PAPER COMPANY**
2540 Prospect Ct  (60502-9419)
PHONE..................................630 449-7200
Mike Cooke, *Maintence Staff*
EMP: 8
SALES (corp-wide): 21B  **Publicly Held**
SIC: 2621  Paper mills
PA: International Paper Company
   6400 Poplar Ave
   Memphis TN 38197
   901 419-9000

**(G-1032)**
**INTERNATIONAL PAPER COMPANY**
4140 Campus Dr  (60504-4172)
PHONE..................................630 585-3300
Rick Wendorf, *Branch Mgr*
EMP: 12
SALES (corp-wide): 21B  **Publicly Held**
SIC: 2621  Paper mills
PA: International Paper Company
   6400 Poplar Ave
   Memphis TN 38197
   901 419-9000

**(G-1033)**
**INTERNATIONAL PAPER COMPANY**
4160 Campus Dr  (60504-4172)
PHONE..................................630 585-3400
Mark Hull, *General Mgr*
Lance Hileman, *Safety Mgr*
Lence Hileman, *Safety Mgr*
Chris Bianchi, *Purch Mgr*
Alan Carpenter, *Personnel*
EMP: 130
SALES (corp-wide): 21B  **Publicly Held**
WEB: www.internationalpaper.com
SIC: 2653  Corrugated & solid fiber boxes
PA: International Paper Company
   6400 Poplar Ave
   Memphis TN 38197
   901 419-9000

**(G-1034)**
**INTERNATIONAL WOOD PRODUCTS**
2812 Stuart Kaplan Ct  (60503-5774)
PHONE..................................630 530-6164
EMP: 6
SQ FT: 10,000
SALES: 500K  **Privately Held**
SIC: 3949  Manufactures Wood Playground Equipment

**(G-1035)**
**ITERNA LLC**
2600 Beverly Dr Ste 107  (60502-8004)
PHONE..................................630 585-7400
Omar Tabbara, *General Mgr*
Tamburrino Peter, *Mng Member*
▲ EMP: 20
SALES (est): 4.2MM  **Privately Held**
SIC: 3691  Batteries, rechargeable; alkaline cell storage batteries

**(G-1036)**
**JARDEN CORPORATION**
3901 Liberty St  (60504-8122)
PHONE..................................201 836-7070
Marcie Barnett, *Manager*
Richard Brand, *Business Dir*
EMP: 86
SALES (corp-wide): 13.2B  **Publicly Held**
SIC: 3089  Plastic containers, except foam
HQ: Jarden Corporation
   2381 Nw Executive Ctr Dr
   Boca Raton FL 33431
   561 447-2520

**(G-1037)**
**JCB INC**
800 Bilter Rd Ste A  (60502-4727)
PHONE..................................912 704-2995
Dustin Diplock, *Supervisor*
EMP: 4  **Privately Held**
SIC: 5082  5084  3531  3537  General construction machinery & equipment; materials handling machinery; backhoes; industrial trucks & tractors
HQ: Jcb, Inc.
   2000 Bamford Blvd
   Pooler GA 31322
   912 447-2000

**(G-1038)**
**JOHNSON CONTROLS INC**
3600 Thayer Ct Ste 300  (60504-6709)
PHONE..................................331 212-3800
EMP: 4
SALES (corp-wide): 36.8B  **Publicly Held**
SIC: 2531  Seats, automobile
PA: Johnson Controls, Inc.
   5757 N Green Bay Ave
   Milwaukee WI 53209
   414 524-1200

**(G-1039)**
**KEEBLER COMPANY**
2707 N Eola Rd Ste A  (60502-4813)
PHONE..................................630 820-9457
Dave Niestrom, *Manager*
EMP: 33
SALES (corp-wide): 13B  **Publicly Held**
WEB: www.keebler.com
SIC: 2052  Cookies
HQ: Keebler Company
   1 Kellogg Sq
   Battle Creek MI 49017
   269 961-2000

**(G-1040)**
**KELVYN PRESS INC**
Also Called: Demand One
880 Enterprise St Ste F  (60504-4923)
PHONE..................................630 585-8160
Jeff Johnson, *Branch Mgr*
EMP: 50  **Privately Held**
SIC: 2752  Commercial printing, lithographic
HQ: Kelvyn Press, Inc.
   2910 S 18th Ave
   Broadview IL 60155
   708 343-0448

**(G-1041)**
**KENDALL COUNTY CONCRETE INC**
695 Route 34  (60503-9314)
PHONE..................................630 851-9197
Fax: 630 851-0395
Thomas Schnabel, *President*
Lorraine Schnabel, *Corp Secy*
Joan Gaza, *Bookkeeper*
Wendy Leisure, *Manager*
Jon Frantz, *Traffic Dir*
EMP: 23
SQ FT: 9,000
SALES (est): 4.2MM  **Privately Held**
SIC: 3273  Ready-mixed concrete

**(G-1042)**
**KESON INDUSTRIES INC**
810 N Commerce St  (60504-7931)
PHONE..................................630 820-4200
Aaron Nosek, *President*
Jim Maurer, *Purch Mgr*
Irvin Hemmerle, *CFO*
Jeff Capstren, *VP Sales*
Shayla Grimes, *Cust Mgr*
▲ EMP: 50
SQ FT: 80,000
SALES (est): 10.4MM  **Privately Held**
WEB: www.keson.com
SIC: 3953  3545  3829  Marking devices; precision measuring tools; measuring & controlling devices

---

(PA)=Parent Co  (HQ)=Headquarters  (DH)=Div Headquarters
✪ = New Business established in last 2 years

## Aurora - Dupage County (G-1043)

**(G-1043)**
**KINDLON ENTERPRISES INC (PA)**
2300 Raddant Rd Ste B (60502-9108)
PHONE.................................708 367-4000
Randall C Mohler, *President*
Margaret Dicaro, *Admin Sec*
EMP: 1
SQ FT: 160,000
SALES (est): 29.8MM  **Privately Held**
SIC: 2653  Boxes, corrugated: made from purchased materials; pads, corrugated: made from purchased materials; partitions, corrugated: made from purchased materials

**(G-1044)**
**LABEL TEK INC**
3505 Thayer Ct Ste 200 (60504-3141)
PHONE.................................630 820-8499
Dean Hummel, *President*
EMP: 10
SQ FT: 10,000
SALES (est): 1.5MM  **Privately Held**
WEB: www.labeltekinc.com
SIC: 2754  2759  2672  Labels: gravure printing; commercial printing; coated & laminated paper

**(G-1045)**
**LEHIGH CONSUMER PRODUCTS LLC (DH)**
Also Called: Lehigh Group, The
3901 Liberty St (60504-8122)
PHONE.................................630 851-7330
Thomas Russo, *President*
Sean Moliatu, *Finance Dir*
Todd Walbert, *Director*
◆ EMP: 205
SALES (est): 151.8MM
SALES (corp-wide): 13.2B  **Publicly Held**
WEB: www.lehighgroup.com
SIC: 3965  2298  3462  3452  Fasteners, buttons, needles & pins; ropes & fiber cables; iron & steel forgings; bolts, nuts, rivets & washers; financial consultant
HQ: Jarden Corporation
2381 Nw Executive Ctr Dr
Boca Raton FL 33431
561 447-2520

**(G-1046)**
**LETTER-RITE EXPRESS  LLC**
1660 Wind Song Ln (60504-5500)
PHONE.................................847 678-1100
Russell C Brewer Jr, *Mng Member*
Robert A Brewer,
EMP: 10 EST: 2007
SQ FT: 8,000
SALES: 1.1MM  **Privately Held**
SIC: 3861  Graphic arts plates, sensitized

**(G-1047)**
**LOGICAL DESIGN SOLUTIONS INC**
562 Asbury Drive Aurora (60502)
PHONE.................................630 786-5999
Kyle Haroldsen, *CEO*
Tami Haroldsen, *Vice Pres*
EMP: 3
SALES (est): 33.8K  **Privately Held**
SIC: 7371  8748  7372  7373  Computer software systems analysis & design, custom; systems engineering consultant, ex. computer or professional; business oriented computer software; operating systems computer software; office computer automation systems integration

**(G-1048)**
**LUBRICATION TECHNOLOGY INC**
3851 Exchange Ave (60504-8106)
PHONE.................................740 574-5150
Gary D Goodan, *President*
John Christian, *Info Tech Mgr*
▲ EMP: 9
SQ FT: 5,000
SALES (est): 2.1MM  **Privately Held**
WEB: www.lubricationtechnology.com
SIC: 2992  Lubricating oils & greases

**(G-1049)**
**LULUS REAL FROYO**
1147 N Eola Rd (60502-7003)
PHONE.................................630 299-3854
Julie Collins, *Principal*
EMP: 3
SALES (est): 215.7K  **Privately Held**
SIC: 2026  Yogurt

**(G-1050)**
**LUSE THERMAL TECHNOLOGIES LLC**
3990 Enterprise Ct (60504-8132)
PHONE.................................630 862-2600
Bradford K Luse, *Principal*
EMP: 2
SALES (est): 378.4K  **Privately Held**
SIC: 3823  Thermal conductivity instruments, industrial process type

**(G-1051)**
**MAGNETROL INTERNATIONAL INC (PA)**
705 Enterprise St (60504-8149)
PHONE.................................630 723-6600
Fax: 630 969-9489
Jeffrey K Swallow, *President*
John Benway, *President*
John E Heiser, *COO*
Karolina Suda, *Project Mgr*
Steve Meier, *Mfg Mgr*
▼ EMP: 250 EST: 1979
SQ FT: 85,000
SALES (est): 104.8MM  **Privately Held**
WEB: www.sticontrols.com
SIC: 3823  3699  3643  3625  Level & bulk measuring instruments, industrial process; flow instruments, industrial process type; electrical equipment & supplies; current-carrying wiring devices; relays & industrial controls; machine tools, metal cutting type

**(G-1052)**
**MAIDENFORM LLC**
1650 Premium Outlet Blvd # 233 (60502-2902)
PHONE.................................630 898-8419
Fax: 630 898-8419
Tushbebra Crump, *Branch Mgr*
EMP: 178
SALES (corp-wide): 6B  **Publicly Held**
SIC: 2341  Women's & children's underwear
HQ: Maidenform Llc
1000 E Hanes Mill Rd
Winston Salem NC 27105
336 519-8080

**(G-1053)**
**MEDALLION PRESS  INC**
Also Called: Medallion Media Group
4222 Meridian Pkwy # 110 (60504-7947)
PHONE.................................630 513-8316
Helen A Rosburg, *CEO*
Adam C Mock, *President*
Heather Musick, *Vice Pres*
Brigitte Shepard, *Sales Staff*
Lorie Jones, *Manager*
EMP: 9
SALES (est): 827.3K  **Privately Held**
WEB: www.medallionmediagroup.com
SIC: 2741  Miscellaneous publishing

**(G-1054)**
**METTLER-TOLEDO  LLC**
Ci-Vision Division
2640 White Oak Cir Ste A (60502-4809)
PHONE.................................630 790-3355
Leverl Schoolfield, *Engineer*
Tom Mc Lean, *Manager*
Fernando Flores, *Manager*
EMP: 41
SALES (corp-wide): 2.5B  **Publicly Held**
SIC: 3823  Viscosimeters, industrial process type
HQ: Mettler-Toledo, Llc
1900 Polaris Pkwy Fl 6
Columbus OH 43240
614 438-4511

**(G-1055)**
**NASCAR CAR WASH**
3068 E New York St (60502-9204)
PHONE.................................630 236-3400
Steve Timmer, *Owner*
EMP: 9
SALES (est): 440K  **Privately Held**
SIC: 2741  Miscellaneous publishing

**(G-1056)**
**NIKE  INC**
1650 Prem Outlet Blvd # 601 (60502-2905)
PHONE.................................630 585-9568
Mark Parker, *Principal*
EMP: 38
SALES (corp-wide): 32.3B  **Publicly Held**
SIC: 3021  Rubber & plastics footwear
PA: Nike, Inc.
1 Sw Bowerman Dr
Beaverton OR 97005
503 671-6453

**(G-1057)**
**NINE WEST HOLDINGS  INC**
Also Called: Kasper
1640 Premium Outlet Blvd (60502)
PHONE.................................630 236-9258
Nancy Testin, *Branch Mgr*
EMP: 10
SALES (corp-wide): 2.1B  **Privately Held**
WEB: www.kasper.net
SIC: 2337  Women's & misses' suits & coats
PA: Nine West Holdings, Inc.
180 Rittenhouse Cir
Bristol PA 19007
215 785-4000

**(G-1058)**
**NITREX INC**
1900 Plain Ave (60504-8561)
PHONE.................................630 851-5880
Chris Morawski, *President*
Thomas G Cooper, *General Mgr*
Lenord Ngiramoai, *Manager*
EMP: 28 EST: 1991
SQ FT: 25,000
SALES: 5MM
SALES (corp-wide): 85.7K  **Privately Held**
WEB: www.nitrex.net
SIC: 3398  Metal heat treating
HQ: Nitrex Inc.
822 Kim Dr
Mason MI 48854

**(G-1059)**
**ORGANIZED NOISE INC**
Also Called: Sole Unique
231 Raintree Ct (60504-2006)
PHONE.................................630 820-9855
Anthony James Foster, *President*
EMP: 3
SALES: 60K  **Privately Held**
SIC: 3651  Audio electronic systems

**(G-1060)**
**OSI INTERNATIONAL FOODS LTD**
Also Called: Glen Oak Foods
1225 Corp Blvd Ste 300 (60504)
P.O. Box 2018 (60507-2018)
PHONE.................................630 851-6600
David G McDonald, *President*
Sheldon Lavin, *President*
George A Krzesinski, *Treasurer*
William S Lipsman, *Admin Sec*
▲ EMP: 100
SALES (est): 10.3MM
SALES (corp-wide): 18.4MM  **Privately Held**
WEB: www.osigroup.com
SIC: 2013  Sausages & other prepared meats
PA: Osi International, Inc.
1225 Corp Blvd Ste 300
Aurora IL 60505
630 851-6600

**(G-1061)**
**P DOUBLE CORPORATION**
Also Called: Auntie Anne's
1100 Fox Valley Ctr (60504-4107)
PHONE.................................630 585-7160
Fax: 630 585-7160
Bazan Savis, *Manager*
EMP: 10  **Privately Held**
SIC: 5461  2052  Pretzels; pretzels
PA: P Double Corporation
8130 Mccormick Blvd
Skokie IL 60076

**(G-1062)**
**PANASONIC CORP NORTH AMERICA**
800 Bilter Rd (60502-4726)
PHONE.................................630 801-0359
EMP: 8
SALES (corp-wide): 64.6B  **Privately Held**
SIC: 3679  Antennas, receiving
HQ: Panasonic Corporation Of North America
2 Riverfront Plz Ste 200
Newark NJ 07102
201 348-7000

**(G-1063)**
**PEERLESS INDUSTRIES  INC (PA)**
Also Called: Peerless-Av
2300 White Oak Cir (60502-9676)
PHONE.................................630 375-5100
Fax: 630 820-8537
John Potts, *President*
Walter Snodell, *Chairman*
Nick Belcore, *Exec VP*
Ken Dillion, *Vice Pres*
Keith Dutch, *Vice Pres*
▲ EMP: 260
SQ FT: 307,000
SALES (est): 43.9MM  **Privately Held**
WEB: www.peerlessindustries.com
SIC: 3429  5099  Manufactured hardware (general); video & audio equipment

**(G-1064)**
**PHILIPS ELEC N AMER CORP**
Dunlee Division
555 N Commerce St (60504-8110)
PHONE.................................630 585-2000
Pat Fitzgerald, *General Mgr*
Jim White, *Vice Pres*
Allison Hibbard, *Engineer*
Ken Schine, *Finance Mgr*
Sue Haggerty, *Human Res Mgr*
EMP: 250
SALES (corp-wide): 25.9B  **Privately Held**
WEB: www.usa.philips.com
SIC: 3844  X-ray apparatus & tubes
HQ: Philips North America Llc
3000 Minuteman Rd Ms1203
Andover MA 01810
978 659-3000

**(G-1065)**
**PHILIPS MEDICAL SYSTEMS CLEVEL**
Also Called: Dunlee Division
555 N Commerce St (60504-8110)
PHONE.................................630 585-2000
Robert Cryer, *QC Mgr*
Tim Howrey, *Sales Staff*
Edward J Richardson, *Branch Mgr*
Kelley Dixon, *Manager*
Jeffrey Kendrick, *Manager*
EMP: 5
SALES (corp-wide): 25.9B  **Privately Held**
WEB: www.usa.philips.com
SIC: 3841  Surgical & medical instruments
HQ: Philips Medical Systems (Cleveland), Inc.
595 Miner Rd
Cleveland OH 44143
440 247-2652

**(G-1066)**
**PINNAKLE TECHNOLOGIES INC**
75 Executive Dr Ste 353 (60504-8121)
PHONE.................................630 352-0070
Fax: 630 429-9091
Ajay Kshatriya, *President*
EMP: 17
SALES (est): 3.3MM  **Privately Held**
WEB: www.pinnakle.net
SIC: 5045  7371  7372  Computer software; computer software systems analysis & design, custom; prepackaged software

**(G-1067)**
**PPG ARCHITECTURAL FINISHES INC**
Also Called: Glidden Professional Paint Ctr
473 S Route 59 (60504-8167)
PHONE.................................630 820-8692
Gary Zeier, *Manager*
EMP: 6

**SALES (corp-wide):** 14.7B  **Publicly Held**
**WEB:** www.gliddenpaint.com
**SIC:** 2891  Adhesives
**HQ:** Ppg Architectural Finishes, Inc.
  1 Ppg Pl
  Pittsburgh PA 15272
  412 434-3131

### (G-1068)
### PREGIS LLC
515 Enterprise St  (60504-8143)
**PHONE**.....................................331 425-6264
**EMP:** 6
**SALES (corp-wide):** 5.6B  **Privately Held**
**SIC:** 3086  Packaging & shipping materials, foamed plastic
**HQ:** Pregis Llc
  1650 Lake Cook Rd Ste 400
  Deerfield IL 60015
  847 597-9330

### (G-1069)
### PRISM ESOLUTIONS DV ANDY FRAIN
761 Shoreline Dr  (60504-6194)
**PHONE**.....................................630 820-3820
David Clayton, *President*
Laura Grund, *Vice Pres*
Dane Vontobel, *Vice Pres*
Jan Arvesen, *Accountant*
**EMP:** 10
**SQ FT:** 5,000
**SALES:** 980K
**SALES (corp-wide):** 222.4MM  **Privately Held**
**SIC:** 7372  Prepackaged software
**PA:** Andy Frain Services, Inc.
  761 Shoreline Dr
  Aurora IL 60504
  630 820-3820

### (G-1070)
### PROCESSING TECH INTL LLC
Also Called: P T I
2655 White Oak Cir  (60502-9674)
**PHONE**.....................................630 585-5800
**Fax:** 630 585-5855
Dana Hanson, *President*
Dan Carl, *Managing Dir*
Tom Limbrunner, *Senior VP*
Colleen Messacar, *Senior VP*
Peter Lechner, *Vice Pres*
▲ **EMP:** 60
**SQ FT:** 60,000
**SALES (est):** 22.4MM  **Privately Held**
**WEB:** www.ptiextruders.com
**SIC:** 3559  Plastics working machinery

### (G-1071)
### PVH CORP
Also Called: Van Heusen
1650 Premium Outlet Blvd  (60502-2901)
**PHONE**.....................................630 898-7718
John Reinhart, *Branch Mgr*
**EMP:** 9
**SALES (corp-wide):** 8.2B  **Publicly Held**
**WEB:** www.pvh.com
**SIC:** 2321  Men's & boys' dress shirts
**PA:** Pvh Corp.
  200 Madison Ave Bsmt 1
  New York NY 10016
  212 381-3500

### (G-1072)
### RAHN USA CORP
1005 N Commons Dr  (60504-4100)
**PHONE**.....................................630 851-4220
Marcel Gatti, *President*
Steve U Lundstram, *Vice Pres*
Donato Spezzaneve, *Sales Staff*
Pola Tanner, *Manager*
W Clyde Jones III, *Admin Sec*
▲ **EMP:** 34
**SALES (est):** 7.8MM
**SALES (corp-wide):** 112.5MM  **Privately Held**
**SIC:** 2869  Industrial organic chemicals
**PA:** Rahn Ag
  Dorflistrasse 120
  ZUrich ZH 8050
  443 154-200

### (G-1073)
### REFLECTION SOFTWARE INC
900 S Frontenac St # 100  (60504-3247)
**PHONE**.....................................630 585-2300
Timothy Schorr, *President*
**EMP:** 2
**SALES (est):** 309.6K  **Privately Held**
**SIC:** 7372  Prepackaged software

### (G-1074)
### ROANOKE COMPANIES GROUP INC
2560 White Oak Cir  (60502-9681)
**PHONE**.....................................630 499-5870
William Kyte, *CEO*
**EMP:** 5
**SALES (corp-wide):** 2B  **Publicly Held**
**SIC:** 2891  3544  Caulking compounds; special dies, tools, jigs & fixtures
**HQ:** Roanoke Companies Group, Inc.
  1105 S Frontenac St
  Aurora IL 60504
  630 375-0324

### (G-1075)
### ROANOKE COMPANIES GROUP INC (DH)
1105 S Frontenac St  (60504-6451)
**PHONE**.....................................630 375-0324
Richard Tripodi, *President*
Tom Montalbano, *Controller*
Ron Loffredo, *Director*
▲ **EMP:** 90
**SQ FT:** 144,000
**SALES (est):** 14.5MM
**SALES (corp-wide):** 2B  **Publicly Held**
**SIC:** 2891  Caulking compounds; adhesives
**HQ:** H.B. Fuller Construction Products Inc.
  1105 S Frontenac St
  Aurora IL 60504
  630 978-7766

### (G-1076)
### RYANO RESINS INC
3808 Baybrook Dr  (60504-6599)
P.O. Box 47, Willow Springs, (60480-0047)
**PHONE**.....................................630 621-5677
Paul Mueller, *President*
Kimberlyu Mueller, *Admin Sec*
**EMP:** 2
**SQ FT:** 2,000
**SALES (est):** 330.8K  **Privately Held**
**SIC:** 2861  Gum & wood chemicals

### (G-1077)
### SENOPLAST USA
75 Executive Dr Ste 129  (60504-8105)
**PHONE**.....................................630 898-0731
Gunter Klepch, *Owner*
John Hayes, *Sales Mgr*
Manuel Romero, *Sales Mgr*
Wilhelm Klepsch, *Marketing Staff*
Cindy Sullivan, *Office Mgr*
**EMP:** 6  **EST:** 2001
**SQ FT:** 1,000
**SALES:** 20MM  **Privately Held**
**SIC:** 3081  Unsupported plastics film & sheet

### (G-1078)
### SIMPSON TECHNOLOGIES
Also Called: Beardsley & Piper L.L.C.
751 Shoreline Dr  (60504-3111)
**PHONE**.....................................630 978-2700
Bruce Dienst, *CEO*
David Kennedy, *President*
Scott Strobl, *Vice Pres*
Kenneth Wroblewski, *CFO*
Ed Betlinski, *Sales Staff*
**EMP:** 44
**SQ FT:** 33,000
**SALES (est):** 3.9MM
**SALES (corp-wide):** 18.2MM  **Privately Held**
**SIC:** 3542  Die casting & extruding machines; die casting machines
**PA:** Simpson Technologies Corporation
  751 Shoreline Dr
  Aurora IL 60504
  630 978-2700

### (G-1079)
### SIMPSON TECHNOLOGIES CORP (PA)
751 Shoreline Dr  (60504-3111)
**PHONE**.....................................630 978-2700
Henry W Dienst, *Ch of Bd*
Bruce Dienst, *President*
Scott Strobl, *President*
Ed Radon, *Mfg Mgr*
Diane Dannewitz, *Purch Mgr*
◆ **EMP:** 45  **EST:** 1911
**SQ FT:** 32,000
**SALES (est):** 18.2MM  **Privately Held**
**SIC:** 3559  Foundry machinery & equipment

### (G-1080)
### SMC CORPORATION OF AMERICA
858 Meridian Lake Dr F  (60504-4905)
**PHONE**.....................................630 449-0600
**Fax:** 630 449-0611
Blain Mepham, *Sales Mgr*
Mark Bakke, *Sales Staff*
Randy Ayres, *Manager*
Alan Porteous, *Manager*
**EMP:** 40
**SALES (corp-wide):** 4.2B  **Privately Held**
**WEB:** www.smcusa.com
**SIC:** 5084  3492  3491  3559  Pneumatic tools & equipment; control valves, fluid power: hydraulic & pneumatic; pressure valves & regulators, industrial; automotive related machinery; fluid power actuators, hydraulic or pneumatic; pneumatic relays, air-conditioning type; switches, pneumatic positioning remote
**HQ:** Smc Corporation Of America
  10100 Smc Blvd
  Noblesville IN 46060
  317 899-3182

### (G-1081)
### SPECIALTY CNSTR BRANDS INC (HQ)
1105 S Frontenac St  (60504-6451)
**PHONE**.....................................630 851-0782
Luis Diego Rodriguez, *General Mgr*
Geoffrey Russell, *Prdtn Mgr*
Andrew Lawrisuk, *Sales Staff*
◆ **EMP:** 15
**SALES (est):** 4MM
**SALES (corp-wide):** 2B  **Publicly Held**
**SIC:** 2891  2899  Adhesives & sealants; chemical preparations
**PA:** H.B. Fuller Company
  1200 Willow Lake Blvd
  Saint Paul MN 55110
  651 236-5900

### (G-1082)
### SPRAYING SYSTEMS CO
Also Called: Fluid Air
2580 Diehl Rd Ste E  (60502-5309)
**PHONE**.....................................630 665-5001
Michael Kenny, *Purchasing*
Martin Bender, *Branch Mgr*
Kristopher Roskos, *Manager*
**EMP:** 18
**SALES (corp-wide):** 384.3MM  **Privately Held**
**SIC:** 3499  5047  Nozzles, spray: aerosol, paint or insecticide; medical laboratory equipment
**PA:** Spraying Systems Co.
  200 W North Ave
  Glendale Heights IL 60139
  630 665-5000

### (G-1083)
### SUPERIOR TRUCK DOCK SERVICES
2431 Angela Ln  (60502-9068)
**PHONE**.....................................630 978-1697
William Meier, *President*
**EMP:** 5
**SALES (est):** 918.2K  **Privately Held**
**SIC:** 3537  Truck trailers, used in plants, docks, terminals, etc.

### (G-1084)
### SURFACE GUARD INC
515 Enterprise St  (60504-8143)
**PHONE**.....................................630 236-8250
**Fax:** 630 236-8251
Steven Malinowski, *President*
Pat Dillon, *President*
James Heimann, *Vice Pres*
John Swinarski, *Vice Pres*
Joe Graham, *Controller*
**EMP:** 79
**SALES (est):** 25.5MM
**SALES (corp-wide):** 5.6B  **Privately Held**
**WEB:** www.surfaceguard.com
**SIC:** 2671  Packaging paper & plastics film, coated & laminated
**HQ:** Pregis Llc
  1650 Lake Cook Rd Ste 400
  Deerfield IL 60015
  847 597-9330

### (G-1085)
### THOMAS PUMP COMPANY
Also Called: Liquid Lf Sprators Systems Div
2301 Liberty St  (60502-9520)
**PHONE**.....................................630 851-9393
Robert D Mc Cue Sr, *President*
Ron Mc Cue, *Corp Secy*
Robert A Mc Cue Jr, *Vice Pres*
**EMP:** 14
**SQ FT:** 12,000
**SALES:** 185K  **Privately Held**
**WEB:** www.tpcoinc.com
**SIC:** 5084  3561  Pumps & pumping equipment; pumps & pumping equipment

### (G-1086)
### TIN TREE GIFTS
2720 Stuart Kaplan Dr  (60503-5778)
**PHONE**.....................................630 935-8086
**EMP:** 3
**SALES (est):** 274.1K  **Privately Held**
**SIC:** 3356  Tin

### (G-1087)
### TINSCAPE LLC
1050 Stockton Ct  (60502-6966)
**PHONE**.....................................630 236-7236
Thomas Doyle,
▲ **EMP:** 5
**SALES (est):** 616.7K  **Privately Held**
**WEB:** www.tinscape.com
**SIC:** 3497  Metal foil & leaf

### (G-1088)
### TITAN US LLC
1585 Beverly Ct Ste 112  (60502-8725)
**PHONE**.....................................331 212-5953
Stephanie Moga, *VP Sls/Mktg*
Johann Niederberger, *Mng Member*
Robert J Van Vorrst,
**EMP:** 4
**SALES (est):** 290K  **Privately Held**
**SIC:** 8711  5085  3443  Mechanical engineering; packing, industrial; heat exchangers, condensers & components

### (G-1089)
### TRIGON INTERNATIONAL CORP
4000 Sussex Ave  (60504-7948)
**PHONE**.....................................630 978-9990
Joseph J Fenoglio, *President*
Aaron Bailey, *President*
Tom Fenoglio, *Vice Pres*
**EMP:** 35
**SQ FT:** 5,000
**SALES (est):** 9.9MM  **Privately Held**
**WEB:** www.etrigon.com
**SIC:** 3699  3541  Electron beam metal cutting, forming or welding machines; laser welding, drilling & cutting equipment; lathes

### (G-1090)
### TRINITY MACHINED PRODUCTS INC
2560 White Oak Cir  (60502-9681)
**PHONE**.....................................630 876-6992
Michael Wozniak, *President*
Charles Horn, *General Mgr*
Pawel Mikosz, *Opers Mgr*
Michael Powers, *CFO*
**EMP:** 25
**SALES (est):** 14.9K
**SALES (corp-wide):** 135MM  **Privately Held**
**SIC:** 3469  3449  3599  Metal stampings; miscellaneous metalwork; machine & other job shop work
**PA:** Wozniak Industries, Inc.
  2 Mid America Plz Ste 700
  Oakbrook Terrace IL 60181
  630 954-3400

## Aurora - Dupage County (G-1091)

**(G-1091)**
**TT TECHNOLOGIES INC**
2020 E New York St (60502-9515)
PHONE..................630 851-8200
Fax: 630 851-8299
Chris J Brahler Jr, *President*
George Mallakis, *Regional Mgr*
David Holcomb, *Vice Pres*
Joe Abell, *Project Mgr*
Craig Tholen, *Prdtn Mgr*
◆ EMP: 55
SQ FT: 10,000
SALES (est): 13MM  Privately Held
WEB: www.tttechnologies.com
SIC: 3541  5084 Drilling & boring machines; drilling equipment, excluding bits
PA: Tt Schmidt Gmbh
    Paul-Schmidt-Str. 2
    Lennestadt
    272 380-80

**(G-1092)**
**VICTAULIC COMPANY**
1207 Bilter Rd Ste 103 (60502-4725)
PHONE..................630 585-2919
Fax: 630 585-7043
Michael Infanger, *Sales Staff*
John Malloy, *Manager*
EMP: 260
SALES (corp-wide): 767.9MM  Privately Held
SIC: 3494  Couplings, except pressure & soil pipe
PA: Victaulic Company
    4901 Kesslersville Rd
    Easton PA 18040
    610 559-3300

**(G-1093)**
**W L ENGLER DISTRIBUTING INC**
Scott Wood & Metal
4 Gastville St (60503-9302)
PHONE..................630 898-5400
Fax: 630 898-8870
Scott Miller, *Manager*
EMP: 8
SALES (corp-wide): 11.2MM  Privately Held
SIC: 3444  5075 Furnace casings, sheet metal; warm air heating equipment & supplies
PA: W L. Engler Distributing, Inc.
    1035 N Throop St
    Chicago IL 60642
    773 235-4924

**(G-1094)**
**WALLFILL CO**
Also Called: Wall-Fill
2246 Kealsy Ln (60503-5651)
PHONE..................630 499-9591
Edmund Lowrie, *President*
EMP: 15
SQ FT: 8,000
SALES (est): 1.5MM  Privately Held
SIC: 3444  1761 1751 Gutters, sheet metal; siding contractor; window & door (prefabricated) installation

**(G-1095)**
**WEBSOLUTIONS TECHNOLOGY INC**
Also Called: Wsol
3817 Mccoy Dr Ste 105 (60504-4220)
PHONE..................630 375-6833
Fax: 630 654-9967
Jeff Gahn, *President*
David Hansten, *CFO*
Gail Gahn, *Admin Sec*
EMP: 27
SALES: 3.9MM  Privately Held
SIC: 7371  7372 4813 8731 Custom computer programming services; prepackaged software; ; commercial physical research

**(G-1096)**
**WESDAR TECHNOLOGIES INC**
924 Vineyard Ln (60502-8502)
PHONE..................630 761-0965
Donald Wessendorf, *President*
EMP: 4
SQ FT: 3,200

SALES: 400K  Privately Held
WEB: www.wesdar-tech.com
SIC: 7389  3089 Design services; injection molding of plastics

**(G-1097)**
**WESTELL INC (HQ)**
750 N Commons Dr (60504-7940)
PHONE..................630 898-2500
Fax: 630 898-4859
Kirk Brannock, *CEO*
Mark Tinker, *President*
Rich Cremona, *COO*
William J Noll, *Senior VP*
Chris Shaver, *Senior VP*
▲ EMP: 82
SQ FT: 173,000
SALES (est): 33.9MM  Publicly Held
WEB: www.westell.com
SIC: 3661  Telephone & telegraph apparatus

**(G-1098)**
**WESTELL TECHNOLOGIES INC (PA)**
750 N Commons Dr (60504-7940)
PHONE..................630 898-2500
Fax: 630 375-4931
Kirk R Brannock, *CEO*
Dennis O Harris, *Ch of Bd*
Richard E Good, *Senior VP*
Jarrett Smith, *Engineer*
Thomas P Minichiello, *CFO*
EMP: 21
SQ FT: 179,000
SALES: 62.9MM  Publicly Held
WEB: www.dsl-modems.com
SIC: 3661  4813 7389 Telephones & telephone apparatus; telephone communication, except radio; ; ; telephone/video communications; teleconferencing services

**(G-1099)**
**WIN TECHNOLOGIES INCORPORATED**
Also Called: Scot Electrical Products
800 S Frontenac St Unit 1 (60504-3126)
PHONE..................630 236-1020
Fax: 630 236-1030
Albert Khant, *President*
Barbara Khant, *Vice Pres*
Gerald Khant, *Vice Pres*
Glen Khant, *Vice Pres*
Neil Khant, *Vice Pres*
EMP: 35
SALES: 3.5MM  Privately Held
WEB: www.wintechimage.com
SIC: 3625  Control equipment, electric

**(G-1100)**
**WOZNIAK INDUSTRIES INC**
2560 White Oak Cir (60502-9681)
PHONE..................630 820-4052
EMP: 105
SALES (corp-wide): 150MM  Privately Held
SIC: 3469  Mfg Metal Stampings
PA: Wozniak Industries, Inc.
    2 Mid America Plz Ste 700
    Oakbrook Terrace IL 60181
    630 954-3400

### Aurora
### Kane County

**(G-1101)**
**ADVANTAGE MACHINING INC**
601 W New York St Frnt (60506-3882)
PHONE..................630 897-1220
Fax: 630 897-7344
Steve Arbizzani, *CEO*
Anthony Seidelman, *President*
Donald Johnson, *Engineer*
Sara Katzer, *Manager*
EMP: 42
SQ FT: 40,000
SALES (est): 5.6MM  Privately Held
WEB: www.researchautomation.com
SIC: 3549  3599 Assembly machines, including robotic; machine & other job shop work

**(G-1102)**
**ADVANTECH LIMITED**
601 N Russell Ave (60506-2988)
PHONE..................815 397-9133
Dennis C Freeh, *President*
EMP: 2
SQ FT: 5,000
SALES (est): 280K  Privately Held
SIC: 2899  Concrete curing & hardening compounds

**(G-1103)**
**ALL-PAK MANUFACTURING CORP**
1221 Jackson St Ste A-B (60505-5691)
PHONE..................630 851-5859
Fax: 630 851-6195
Don Smith, *President*
Thomas E Binkowski, *Admin Sec*
EMP: 60
SQ FT: 40,000
SALES (est): 13.3MM  Privately Held
WEB: www.allpakmfg.com
SIC: 2653  5199 Corrugated & solid fiber boxes; packaging materials

**(G-1104)**
**ALLEGRA NETWORK LLC**
Also Called: Allegra Print & Imaging
987 Oak Ave (60506-2422)
PHONE..................630 801-9335
EMP: 3
SALES (corp-wide): 34.2MM  Privately Held
SIC: 2752  2789 Lithographic Commercial Printing Bookbinding/Related Work
PA: Allegra Network Llc
    47585 Galleon Dr
    Plymouth MI 48170
    248 596-8600

**(G-1105)**
**ALLOY ROD PRODUCTS INC**
601 W New York St Ste 4 (60506-3888)
PHONE..................815 562-8200
EMP: 5
SALES (est): 433.4K  Privately Held
SIC: 3356  Nonferrous Rolling/Drawing

**(G-1106)**
**AMERICHEM SYSTEMS INC**
1740 Molitor Rd (60505-1346)
PHONE..................630 495-9300
Fax: 630 495-9302
Joseph A Garbarski, *President*
Michelle Kately, *Controller*
Paula Pasterski, *Manager*
EMP: 18
SQ FT: 30,000
SALES (est): 5MM
SALES (corp-wide): 45.6MM  Privately Held
WEB: www.americhemsystems.com
SIC: 3498  8711 Fabricated pipe & fittings; industrial engineers
PA: Enpro, Inc.
    121 S Lombard Rd
    Addison IL 60101
    630 629-3504

**(G-1107)**
**AMTAB MANUFACTURING CORP**
652 N Highland Ave (60506-2940)
PHONE..................630 301-7600
Fax: 630 421-3448
Doss Samikkannu, *President*
Tadeusz Hanusiak, *President*
Jerry Rivera, *President*
Jason Samikkannu, *General Mgr*
Greg Swon, *Accounting Mgr*
▲ EMP: 54 EST: 2006
SQ FT: 50,000
SALES (est): 12.1MM  Privately Held
WEB: www.amtab.com
SIC: 2521  2522 2511 Tables, office: wood; tables, office: except wood; wood household furniture

**(G-1108)**
**AMWELL**
1740 Molitor Rd (60505-1398)
PHONE..................630 898-6900
Fax: 630 898-1647
Jim McNish, *Owner*
EMP: 9 EST: 2012

SALES (est): 82.3K  Privately Held
SIC: 2086  Water, pasteurized: packaged in cans, bottles, etc.

**(G-1109)**
**ANDEL SERVICES INC**
Also Called: Bristol Blacktop
1145 S Union St (60505-5741)
PHONE..................630 566-0210
Jill Calderon, *President*
Rhonda Rodriguez, *Vice Pres*
EMP: 3
SALES (est): 250K  Privately Held
SIC: 7692  1611 1771 Services

**(G-1110)**
**ARCH PRINTING INC**
710 Morton Ave Ste N (60506-2817)
PHONE..................630 966-0235
Fax: 630 896-6685
Mary Arch, *President*
Anthony Arch, *Vice Pres*
Jessica Arch, *Officer*
EMP: 9
SQ FT: 15,000
SALES (est): 1.4MM  Privately Held
WEB: www.archprinting.com
SIC: 2752  2791 2789 Commercial printing, lithographic; typesetting; bookbinding & related work

**(G-1111)**
**ASK PRODUCTS INC**
544 N Highland Ave (60506-2986)
PHONE..................630 896-4056
Steven J Kase, *CEO*
David Paul, *CFO*
◆ EMP: 70
SQ FT: 35,000
SALES (est): 13.8MM  Privately Held
WEB: www.asklug.com
SIC: 3469  Metal stampings

**(G-1112)**
**ASTRAL POWER SYSTEMS INC**
Also Called: Zhmin Power
31 W Downer Pl Ste 408 (60506-5187)
PHONE..................630 518-1741
Min Carroll, *Principal*
EMP: 3
SALES (est): 208.5K  Privately Held
SIC: 3645  1711 3646 3672 Residential lighting fixtures; lamp & light shades; boudoir lamps; solar energy contractor; commercial indusl & institutional electric lighting fixtures; printed circuit boards

**(G-1113)**
**ATMI PRECAST INC (PA)**
960 Ridgeway Ave Fl 2 (60506-5473)
PHONE..................630 897-0577
Fax: 630 897-0747
John G Cordogan, *CEO*
James K Armbruster, *President*
Mike Pelz, *Principal*
Paul Carr, *COO*
Mike Walsh, *Vice Pres*
EMP: 25
SALES (est): 45.3MM  Privately Held
SIC: 3272  Concrete products, precast

**(G-1114)**
**ATMI PRECAST INC**
Also Called: Atmi Plant
930 Ridgeway Ave (60506-5470)
PHONE..................630 897-0577
Fax: 630 896-4871
John Armbruster, *Manager*
EMP: 48
SALES (corp-wide): 45.3MM  Privately Held
SIC: 3272  Precast terrazo or concrete products
PA: Atmi Precast, Inc.
    960 Ridgeway Ave Fl 2
    Aurora IL 60506
    630 897-0577

**(G-1115)**
**AURORA CUSTOM MACHINING INC**
1038 Sill Ave (60506-5838)
PHONE..................630 859-2638
Fax: 630 859-2895
David Lesperance, *President*
Rodney Shelton, *Safety Mgr*

# GEOGRAPHIC SECTION

## Aurora - Kane County (G-1141)

Nick Ruitenberg, *CFO*
Lisa Gronowski, *Controller*
**EMP:** 52
**SQ FT:** 32,000
**SALES (est):** 10.1MM **Privately Held**
**WEB:** www.auroracustom.com
**SIC:** 3599 Machine & other job shop work

### (G-1116)
### AURORA FASTPRINT INC
54 E Galena Blvd (60505-3314)
**PHONE**..................................630 896-5980
Kimberly A Granholm, *President*
Thomas M Bartlett, *Admin Sec*
Maggie Gibson, *Graphic Designe*
Chad Jimenez, *Graphic Designe*
**EMP:** 5
**SQ FT:** 3,500
**SALES (est):** 929.6K **Privately Held**
**WEB:** www.aurorafastprint.com
**SIC:** 2752 Commercial printing, offset

### (G-1117)
### AUTOMATION DESIGN & MFG INC
841 S River St (60506-5912)
**PHONE**..................................630 896-4206
John M Masek, *President*
Miles Masek, *General Mgr*
**EMP:** 5
**SQ FT:** 6,000
**SALES (est):** 450K **Privately Held**
**SIC:** 8711 3599 3312 3544 Designing: ship, boat, machine & product; machine shop, jobbing & repair; tool & die steel; special dies, tools, jigs & fixtures

### (G-1118)
### BAT BUSINESS SERVICES INC
Also Called: Allegra Marketing Print Web
987 Oak Ave (60506-2422)
**PHONE**..................................630 801-9335
Bart Troyer, *President*
**EMP:** 3
**SALES (est):** 500K **Privately Held**
**SIC:** 2752 Commercial printing, offset

### (G-1119)
### BENETECH INC (HQ)
2245 Sequoia Dr Ste 300 (60506-6220)
**PHONE**..................................630 844-1300
**Fax:** 630 844-0064
Ron Pircon, *President*
Robert Chmelar, *Area Mgr*
Chris Blazek, *Vice Pres*
Paul Moran, *Vice Pres*
Joe Pieters, *Vice Pres*
**EMP:** 50
**SQ FT:** 24,000
**SALES (est):** 60.3MM
**SALES (corp-wide):** 86.9MM **Privately Held**
**SIC:** 5169 5084 3823 Chemicals, industrial & heavy; chemical process equipment; combustion control instruments
**PA:** Benetech Investments Corp.
  2245 Sequoia Dr Ste 300
  Aurora IL 60506
  630 844-1300

### (G-1120)
### BENETECH (TAIWAN) LLC (DH)
2245 Sequoia Dr Ste 300 (60506-6220)
**PHONE**..................................630 844-1300
**EMP:** 3
**SALES (est):** 4MM
**SALES (corp-wide):** 86.9MM **Privately Held**
**SIC:** 5169 5084 3823 Chemicals, industrial & heavy; chemical process equipment; combustion control instruments
**HQ:** Benetech, Inc.
  2245 Sequoia Dr Ste 300
  Aurora IL 60506
  630 844-1300

### (G-1121)
### BRICKS INC (PA)
723 S Lasalle St (60505-5126)
**PHONE**..................................630 897-6926
**Fax:** 630 897-7057
Kim Schmitt, *President*
Roberto Garcia, *Traffic Dir*
Miroslaba Cruz, *Administration*
**EMP:** 6
**SALES (est):** 6.9MM **Privately Held**
**WEB:** www.bricksinc.net
**SIC:** 5032 5211 5031 5074 Brick, except refractory; concrete & cinder block; brick; concrete & cinder block; door & window products; doors, garage; windows; doors; building materials, exterior; fireplaces, prefabricated; concrete products; concrete block & brick

### (G-1122)
### BUTTERFIELD COLOR INC (PA)
625 W Illinois Ave (60506-2829)
**PHONE**..................................630 906-1980
**Fax:** 630 906-1982
Joseph G Garceau, *President*
Nick Wagner, *Purch Mgr*
Keith Boudart, *Sales Staff*
Jessica Wagner, *Manager*
▲ **EMP:** 30
**SALES (est):** 5.1MM **Privately Held**
**WEB:** www.butterfieldcolor.com
**SIC:** 2899 Core wash or wax

### (G-1123)
### C P O INC
Also Called: Century Pipe Organ Company
1500 Dearborn Ave Ofc (60505-3231)
**PHONE**..................................630 898-7733
John Hill, *President*
Sam Freedman, *Purchasing*
**EMP:** 3
**SQ FT:** 16,000
**SALES (est):** 126.1K **Privately Held**
**SIC:** 7699 3931 Organ tuning & repair; organs, all types: pipe, reed, hand, electronic, etc.

### (G-1124)
### CAPITAL PRTG & DIE CUTNG INC
Also Called: Capital Printing & Die-Cutting
303 S Highland Ave (60506-5519)
**PHONE**..................................630 896-5520
**Fax:** 630 896-8099
Jesus L Lozano, *President*
Leopoldo Lozano, *President*
Julia Lozano, *Vice Pres*
Donna Lozano, *Sales Staff*
Lorena Herrera, *Office Mgr*
**EMP:** 8
**SQ FT:** 5,000
**SALES (est):** 1.4MM **Privately Held**
**WEB:** www.capitalfinishing.com
**SIC:** 2675 2752 2759 Paper die-cutting; commercial printing, offset; embossing on paper

### (G-1125)
### CARROLL DISTRG & CNSTR SUP INC
1031 W Lake St (60506-5841)
**PHONE**..................................630 892-4855
**Fax:** 630 892-7895
Brad Hotchkiss, *Vice Pres*
Alex Xula, *Manager*
**EMP:** 6
**SALES (corp-wide):** 75.9MM **Privately Held**
**WEB:** www.carrolldistributing.com
**SIC:** 5032 3444 Concrete building products; concrete forms, sheet metal
**PA:** Carroll Distributing & Construction Supply, Inc.
  205 S Iowa Ave
  Ottumwa IA 52501
  641 683-1888

### (G-1126)
### CATERPILLAR INC
Rr 31 Box S (60507)
P.O. Box 348 (60507-0348)
**PHONE**..................................309 494-0858
Gary Alan Staupanto, *Branch Mgr*
**EMP:** 427
**SALES (corp-wide):** 38.5B **Publicly Held**
**WEB:** www.cat.com
**SIC:** 1081 Metal mining exploration & development services
**PA:** Caterpillar Inc.
  100 Ne Adams St
  Peoria IL 61629
  309 675-1000

### (G-1127)
### CHAMPION WOOD PALLETS INC
105 Hankes Ave Ste 100 (60505-6300)
**PHONE**..................................630 801-8036
**EMP:** 8
**SALES (est):** 692.9K **Privately Held**
**SIC:** 2448 Pallets, wood & wood with metal

### (G-1128)
### CHI HOME IMPROVEMENT MAG INC
Also Called: Chicago Home Improvement Mag
2031 Bryn Mawr Dr (60506-5701)
P.O. Box 547, North Aurora (60542-0139)
**PHONE**..................................630 801-7788
Sherry W Schultz, *Mng Member*
**EMP:** 4
**SALES (est):** 170K **Privately Held**
**SIC:** 2721 7389 Magazines: publishing & printing;

### (G-1129)
### CHICAGO PANEL & TRUSS INC
875 Aurora Ave Ste 1 (60505-1751)
**PHONE**..................................630 870-1300
Michael Cummings, *President*
Susan K Coleman, *Office Mgr*
**EMP:** 50
**SALES (est):** 6.7MM **Privately Held**
**WEB:** www.cptmfg.com
**SIC:** 3448 Trusses & framing: prefabricated metal

### (G-1130)
### CHICAGOLAND CLOSETS LLC
Also Called: Closets By Design
850 Ridgeway Ave Ste A (60506-5498)
**PHONE**..................................630 906-0000
Paul Ridsdale, *Mng Member*
**EMP:** 20
**SALES (est):** 1.2MM **Privately Held**
**SIC:** 2511 Storage chests, household: wood

### (G-1131)
### CIPRIANIS PASTA & SAUCE INC
1050 Northfield Dr (60505-1932)
**PHONE**..................................630 851-3086
Annette Johnson, *President*
**EMP:** 25
**SALES (est):** 3.2MM **Privately Held**
**SIC:** 2032 Italian foods: packaged in cans, jars, etc.

### (G-1132)
### CLEVELAND HDWR & FORGING CO
Fox Valley Forge
138 Pierce St (60505-2116)
**PHONE**..................................630 896-9850
**Fax:** 630 897-8635
Jorge Cruz, *General Mgr*
Todd Smith, *QC Mgr*
Vitali Basiourski, *Engineer*
Joseph Krantz, *Accounting Mgr*
Jodi Mueller, *Regl Sales Mgr*
**EMP:** 65
**SQ FT:** 60,000
**SALES (corp-wide):** 32.3MM **Privately Held**
**WEB:** www.clevelandhardware.com
**SIC:** 3462 Iron & steel forgings
**PA:** Cleveland Hardware And Forging Company
  3270 E 79th St
  Cleveland OH 44104
  216 641-5200

### (G-1133)
### CONNOR-WINFIELD CORP (PA)
2111 Comprehensive Dr (60505-1345)
**PHONE**..................................630 851-4722
Roberta A Olp, *President*
Linda Brensberger, *Opers Staff*
David Elwart, *Production*
Karen Hamby, *Purch Mgr*
Bill Beverley, *Engineer*
**EMP:** 120
**SALES (est):** 32.3MM **Privately Held**
**SIC:** 3625 3679 Timing devices, electronic; oscillators

### (G-1134)
### CORSICANA BEDDING LLC
970 S Lake St (60506-5901)
**PHONE**..................................630 264-0032
Terry Hewkin, *Principal*
**EMP:** 137
**SALES (corp-wide):** 286.1MM **Privately Held**
**SIC:** 2515 Mattresses & bedsprings
**PA:** Corsicana Bedding, Llc
  3001 S Us Highway 287
  Corsicana TX 75109
  903 872-2591

### (G-1135)
### CUSTOM CRAFT CABINETRY
605 N Broadway Ste 1 (60505-2180)
**PHONE**..................................630 897-2334
Doug Johnson, *Owner*
**EMP:** 4
**SQ FT:** 3,300
**SALES:** 200K **Privately Held**
**SIC:** 2512 1751 Upholstered household furniture; cabinet building & installation; finish & trim carpentry

### (G-1136)
### D AND D PALLETS
725 S Broadway (60505-5101)
P.O. Box 7226 (60507-7226)
**PHONE**..................................630 800-1102
Damian Diaz, *Owner*
**EMP:** 10
**SALES (est):** 492.3K **Privately Held**
**SIC:** 2448 Pallets, wood

### (G-1137)
### D R SPERRY & CO
623 Rathbone Ave (60506-5940)
**PHONE**..................................630 892-4361
**Fax:** 773 892-1664
David Murray, *President*
Benta Rasmussen, *General Mgr*
Steve Schaefer, *Prdtn Mgr*
▲ **EMP:** 55
**SQ FT:** 50,000
**SALES (est):** 11.8MM **Privately Held**
**WEB:** www.drsperry.com
**SIC:** 3589 3559 3542 3365 Water treatment equipment, industrial; chemical machinery & equipment; machine tools, metal forming type; aluminum foundries; secondary nonferrous metals; blast furnaces & steel mills

### (G-1138)
### DANS DIRT AND GRAVEL
1212 5th St (60505-5622)
**PHONE**..................................630 479-6622
Dan Schoger, *Principal*
**EMP:** 3 **EST:** 2011
**SALES (est):** 170.8K **Privately Held**
**SIC:** 1442 Construction sand & gravel

### (G-1139)
### DELTA PRODUCTS GROUP INC
1655 Eastwood Dr (60506-1121)
P.O. Box 6466 (60598-0466)
**PHONE**..................................630 357-5544
**Fax:** 630 264-9741
Mark Ostermeier, *President*
Jake Ettelbrick, *Sales Dir*
**EMP:** 10
**SQ FT:** 14,000
**SALES:** 10MM **Privately Held**
**WEB:** www.deltamedical.net
**SIC:** 2819 5169 5999 Chemicals, high purity: refined from technical grade; chemicals & allied products; cleaning equipment & supplies

### (G-1140)
### DIAZ PALLETS
760 Prairie St (60506-5512)
**PHONE**..................................630 340-3736
**EMP:** 3
**SALES (est):** 325K **Privately Held**
**SIC:** 2448 Pallets, wood & wood with metal

### (G-1141)
### DILABERTO CO INC
Also Called: Distinctive Cabinets
417 Cleveland Ave (60506-5516)
**PHONE**..................................630 892-8448
**Fax:** 630 892-8449
Michael Robbins, *President*

EMP: 4
SQ FT: 6,000
SALES (est): 300K  Privately Held
SIC: 2434  Wood kitchen cabinets

**(G-1142)**
**ECOLOTECH ASL  INC**
611 Phoenix Ct (60505-2211)
PHONE..............................630 859-0485
EMP: 5
SQ FT: 3,900
SALES (est): 440K  Privately Held
SIC: 3812  Mfg Detection Apparatus

**(G-1143)**
**ELC INDUSTRIES CORP**
325 S Union St (60505-4433)
PHONE..............................630 851-1616
Frank Heffley, *President*
Mark Berger, *Controller*
Mark Eichelberger, *Info Tech Mgr*
Augie K Fabela, *Admin Sec*
EMP: 250 EST: 1987
SALES (est): 36.4MM  Privately Held
SIC: 3647  3694  Vehicular lighting equipment; harness wiring sets, internal combustion engines

**(G-1144)**
**ELC INDUSTRIES CORP**
Also Called: Aurora Cord & Cable Company
401 Hankes Ave (60505-1716)
PHONE..............................630 851-1616
Fax: 630 851-1626
Augie Fabela, *President*
Kathy Johnson, *Purch Agent*
Tigran Shahmurabrayan, *Electrical Engi*
Rod Shrock, *CFO*
Mark Eckleberger, *Controller*
▲ EMP: 50
SQ FT: 65,000
SALES (est): 7.6MM  Privately Held
WEB: www.auroracord.com
SIC: 3647  3694  Vehicular lighting equipment; automotive electrical equipment

**(G-1145)**
**EMV WELDING INC**
850 Hearthstone Ct (60506-1900)
PHONE..............................630 853-3199
EMP: 3
SALES (est): 213.4K  Privately Held
SIC: 7692  Welding repair

**(G-1146)**
**EPIX TUBE CO  INC**
500 N Broadway (60505-2644)
PHONE..............................630 844-0960
Paul Kasperski, *Branch Mgr*
EMP: 28
SALES (corp-wide): 23.5MM  Privately Held
SIC: 3317  Steel pipe & tubes
PA: Epix Tube Co., Inc.
5800 Wolf Creek Pike
Dayton OH 45426
937 529-4858

**(G-1147)**
**EQUIPTO ELECTRONICS CORP (PA)**
351 Woodlawn Ave (60506-5575)
PHONE..............................630 897-4691
Fax: 630 897-5314
Praveen Pothapragada, *President*
Scott Beeson, *Regional Mgr*
Steven Golz, *Vice Pres*
Greg Young, *Design Engr*
Gary Michelson, *CFO*
▼ EMP: 43 EST: 1960
SQ FT: 125,000
SALES (est): 8.2MM  Privately Held
WEB: www.equiptoelec.com
SIC: 3469  Electronic enclosures, stamped or pressed metal

**(G-1148)**
**EUPHORIA CATERING AND EVENTS**
611 Pennsylvania Ave (60506-3029)
PHONE..............................630 301-4369
Rosalyn Spears, *Owner*
EMP: 4
SALES: 10K  Privately Held
SIC: 2099  Food preparations

**(G-1149)**
**EVANS TOOL & MANUFACTURING**
6s252 Hankes Rd (60506-8987)
PHONE..............................630 897-8656
Fax: 630 897-5125
James Evans, *President*
EMP: 2
SQ FT: 900
SALES: 1MM  Privately Held
SIC: 3089  Injection molding of plastics

**(G-1150)**
**EXCEL FORMS INC**
44 1/2 W Downer Pl Ste 46 (60506-5144)
P.O. Box 2906 (60507-2906)
PHONE..............................630 801-1936
Karen Heriaud, *President*
Gene Heriaud, *Corp Secy*
EMP: 3
SALES (est): 496.7K  Privately Held
SIC: 5112  2752  Stationery & office supplies; color lithography

**(G-1151)**
**FIBERBASIN  INC**
1500 Dearborn Ave Ste 13 (60505-3240)
P.O. Box 1870 (60507-1870)
PHONE..............................630 978-0705
Fax: 630 978-9771
Bradley Philo, *President*
Alex Navarro, *Co-Owner*
EMP: 14 EST: 1963
SQ FT: 35,000
SALES (est): 3.4MM  Privately Held
SIC: 3089  Plastic & fiberglass tanks

**(G-1152)**
**FLORES PRECISION PRODUCTS**
Also Called: A Flores
413 Cleveland Ave (60506-5516)
PHONE..............................630 264-2222
Fax: 630 264-2558
Angel Flores, *President*
Rose Flores, *Admin Sec*
EMP: 5
SQ FT: 4,000
SALES (est): 642.1K  Privately Held
SIC: 3544  3599  Subpresses, metalworking; machine shop, jobbing & repair

**(G-1153)**
**FM GRAPHIC IMPRESSIONS INC**
84 S Lasalle St (60505-3332)
P.O. Box 4455 (60507-4455)
PHONE..............................630 897-8788
Fax: 630 896-0665
Kaye Mason, *President*
David Thill, *Mfg Staff*
Arnold Thill, *Advt Staff*
EMP: 50
SALES (est): 4MM
SALES (corp-wide): 5.8MM  Privately Held
WEB: www.ups-psi.com
SIC: 2759  2752  3993  2791  Letterpress printing; commercial printing, offset; lithographing on metal; signs & advertising specialties; typesetting; bookbinding & related work
PA: Professional Packaging Corp
208 E Benton St
Aurora IL 60505
630 896-0574

**(G-1154)**
**FOX VALLEY HOME BREW & WINERY**
14 W Downer Pl (60506-5170)
PHONE..............................630 892-0742
Fred Harrison, *Owner*
EMP: 4
SALES (est): 313.7K  Privately Held
SIC: 2084  5149  5999  Wines; wine makers' equipment & supplies; alcoholic beverage making equipment & supplies

**(G-1155)**
**FOX VALLEY IRON & METAL CORP**
637 N Broadway (60505-2197)
PHONE..............................630 897-5907
Fax: 630 897-5707
Robert H Swickert Sr, *President*
Dolores A Swickert, *Corp Secy*
Robert H Swickert Jr, *Vice Pres*
▲ EMP: 10
SQ FT: 1,000
SALES: 2.4MM  Privately Held
SIC: 5093  3341  3312  Ferrous metal scrap & waste; metal scrap & waste materials; secondary nonferrous metals; blast furnaces & steel mills

**(G-1156)**
**FOX VALLEY LABOR NEWS INC**
726 N Edgelawn Dr (60506-1866)
P.O. Box 4155 (60507-4155)
PHONE..............................630 897-4022
Fax: 630 892-3873
Ed Richardson, *President*
Carter Crane, *Manager*
EMP: 5
SALES: 200K  Privately Held
SIC: 2711  Newspapers: publishing only, not printed on site

**(G-1157)**
**FOX VALLEY PARK DISTRICT**
Also Called: Blackberry Historical Farm
100 S Barnes Rd (60506-8118)
PHONE..............................630 892-1550
Fax: 630 892-1661
Sandy Smith, *Branch Mgr*
EMP: 100  Privately Held
WEB: www.orchardvalleygolf.com
SIC: 7996  2711  8412  Amusement parks; newspapers; museums & art galleries
PA: Fox Valley Park District
101 W Illinois Ave
Aurora IL 60506
630 897-0516

**(G-1158)**
**FOX VALLEY SIGNS INC**
219 W Galena Blvd (60506-4025)
PHONE..............................630 896-3113
Fax: 630 896-3117
Philip Libers, *President*
Donald Campbell, *Vice Pres*
EMP: 2
SQ FT: 3,000
SALES: 200K  Privately Held
SIC: 3993  7692  Signs & advertising specialties; welding repair

**(G-1159)**
**FRANKS DGTAL PRTG OFF SUPS INC**
723 Aurora Ave (60506-2156)
P.O. Box 976 (60507-0976)
PHONE..............................630 892-2511
Fax: 630 801-1990
Frank Garcia, *President*
Maria Sanchez, *Office Mgr*
EMP: 4 EST: 2007
SALES (est): 355.9K  Privately Held
SIC: 3993  Signs & advertising specialties

**(G-1160)**
**GARBE IRON WORKS INC**
Also Called: G I W
456 N Broadway (60505-2672)
PHONE..............................630 897-5100
Fax: 630 897-4090
Terry Peshia, *Ch of Bd*
Sam G Haldiman, *President*
Don Cerny, *Vice Pres*
John Peshia, *Vice Pres*
Ted Peshia, *Vice Pres*
EMP: 25
SQ FT: 45,000
SALES: 7.3MM  Privately Held
WEB: www.giwinc.com
SIC: 3441  Fabricated structural metal

**(G-1161)**
**GENGLER-LOWNEY LASER WORKS**
899 Sullivan Rd (60506-1138)
PHONE..............................630 801-4840
John M Gengler, *President*
Marie Geltz, *Treasurer*
Susan Lowney, *Admin Sec*
EMP: 10 EST: 1946
SQ FT: 10,000
SALES (est): 1.4MM  Privately Held
WEB: www.steelprecision.com
SIC: 1761  1711  7692  3444  Sheet metalwork; warm air heating & air conditioning contractor; welding repair; sheet metalwork

**(G-1162)**
**GLOBE LIFT  LLC**
101 W Illinois Ave (60506-3157)
PHONE..............................630 844-4247
Joel Schneider, *Opers Staff*
E Bradley Hahn, *Mng Member*
Doug Climenhaga,
EMP: 5
SALES (est): 410K  Privately Held
SIC: 3559  Automotive related machinery

**(G-1163)**
**GOLD SEAL CABINETS COUNTERTOPS**
1750 Eastwood Dr (60506-1153)
PHONE..............................630 906-0366
Fax: 630 906-0155
Lois A Farmer Balthazore, *President*
Thomas Balthazore, *Admin Sec*
EMP: 28
SQ FT: 10,000
SALES (est): 3.8MM  Privately Held
WEB: www.goldsealtops.com
SIC: 2434  5031  Wood kitchen cabinets; kitchen cabinets

**(G-1164)**
**GREAT LAKES PRECISION TUBE INC**
Also Called: GL Precision Tube
237 S Highland Ave (60506-5517)
PHONE..............................630 859-8940
Charles E Kuhn, *President*
Matthew Kuhn, *Purch Mgr*
Becci Rivera, *Controller*
EMP: 30
SQ FT: 32,000
SALES (est): 9.8MM  Privately Held
WEB: www.glptube.com
SIC: 3317  Steel pipe & tubes

**(G-1165)**
**GUSCO SILICONE RBR & SVCS LLC**
1500 Dearborn Ave (60505-3231)
PHONE..............................773 770-5008
Fax: 773 304-1462
Gustavo Morales, *CFO*
EMP: 9 EST: 2010
SALES (est): 1.2MM  Privately Held
SIC: 3052  3069  Rubber hose; molded rubber products; roll coverings, rubber; grommets, rubber

**(G-1166)**
**HAN-WIN PRODUCTS INC**
726 S Broadway (60505-5102)
P.O. Box 4515 (60507-4515)
PHONE..............................630 897-1591
Fax: 630 897-1642
S Richard Cherwin, *President*
Sue Morales, *Manager*
Ginette M Cherwin, *Admin Sec*
EMP: 30 EST: 1952
SQ FT: 18,000
SALES (est): 3.8MM  Privately Held
WEB: www.han-win.com
SIC: 3089  Injection molding of plastics

**(G-1167)**
**HEFKE MACHINES & MACHINING**
1060 Johnston Dr (60506-5716)
PHONE..............................630 896-6617
William Hefke, *President*
Rita Hefke, *Corp Secy*
EMP: 3
SQ FT: 3,300
SALES: 48K  Privately Held
SIC: 3599  Machine shop, jobbing & repair

**(G-1168)**
**HENRY PRATT COMPANY  LLC (DH)**
401 S Highland Ave (60506-5580)
PHONE..............................630 844-4000
Fax: 630 844-4121
Dale B Smith, *President*

Susan Snowden, *Managing Dir*
Jan Babush, *Vice Pres*
Randy Berger, *Vice Pres*
Steve Sharp, *Vice Pres*
▲ **EMP:** 210
**SQ FT:** 133,000
**SALES (est):** 120.5MM
**SALES (corp-wide):** 1.1B **Publicly Held**
**SIC: 3491** Industrial valves; water works valves; valves, nuclear
**HQ:** Mueller Co. Llc
633 Chestnut St Ste 1200
Chattanooga TN 37450
423 209-4800

**(G-1169)**
**HEVCO INDUSTRIES**
1500 Dearborn Ave Ste 10 (60505-3239)
**PHONE**.................................708 344-1342
**Fax:** 630 898-7748
Vlasta Vicenik, *President*
Henry M Vicenik II, *Vice Pres*
Tom Vicenik, *Vice Pres*
Barbara Vicenik, *Admin Sec*
**EMP:** 4
**SQ FT:** 7,500
**SALES (est):** 457.7K **Privately Held**
**SIC: 3524** Lawn & garden mowers & accessories

**(G-1170)**
**HUBBELL INCORPORATED**
1455 Sequoia Dr Ste 113 (60506-1171)
**PHONE**.................................972 756-1184
Peter G Sartori, *Branch Mgr*
**EMP:** 14
**SQ FT:** 81,200
**SALES (corp-wide):** 3.5B **Publicly Held**
**WEB:** www.hubbell.com
**SIC: 3643** Current-carrying wiring devices
**PA:** Hubbell Incorporated
40 Waterview Dr
Shelton CT 06484
475 882-4000

**(G-1171)**
**INDUSTRIAL ENCLOSURE CORP**
Also Called: I E C
619 N Loucks St Ste A (60505-2982)
P.O. Box 2817 (60507-2817)
**PHONE**.................................630 898-7499
**Fax:** 630 898-7499
John F Palmer, *President*
Dave Buddle, *General Mgr*
Mark Siegler, *Project Mgr*
Glen Levy, *Manager*
Richard Palmer, *Admin Sec*
▼ **EMP:** 50 EST: 1977
**SQ FT:** 85,000
**SALES (est):** 10.1MM **Privately Held**
**WEB:** www.industrialenclosure.com
**SIC: 2542** 3699 3469 Cabinets: show, display or storage: except wood; electrical equipment & supplies; metal stampings

**(G-1172)**
**INTERGRTED THRMFORMING SYSTEMS**
305 Hankes Ave (60505-1714)
**PHONE**.................................630 906-6895
Mike Curtis, *President*
Rina Srey, *Vice Pres*
**EMP:** 15
**SQ FT:** 12,000
**SALES:** 700K **Privately Held**
**SIC: 3089** Thermoformed finished plastic products

**(G-1173)**
**J W TODD CO**
709 Morton Ave (60506-2816)
P.O. Box 355, Batavia (60510-0355)
**PHONE**.................................630 406-5715
**Fax:** 630 897-6309
Steve Todd, *CEO*
David Todd, *Treasurer*
**EMP:** 5 EST: 1961
**SQ FT:** 2,400
**SALES (est):** 991.3K **Privately Held**
**SIC: 3535** 3537 Belt conveyor systems, general industrial use; bucket type conveyor systems; industrial trucks & tractors

**(G-1174)**
**J/B INDUSTRIES INC**
601 N Farnsworth Ave (60505-3092)
P.O. Box 1180 (60507-1180)
**PHONE**.................................630 851-9444
**Fax:** 630 851-9448
Jeff Cherif, *President*
Ron Hill Jr, *Corp Secy*
Lee Larsen, *Sr Corp Ofcr*
Jeff Bodnar, *Site Mgr*
Jim Borja, *CFO*
▲ **EMP:** 60 EST: 1967
**SQ FT:** 210,000
**SALES (est):** 30.2MM **Privately Held**
**WEB:** www.jbind.com
**SIC: 3494** 3563 Plumbing & heating valves; steam fittings & specialties; vacuum pumps, except laboratory

**(G-1175)**
**JAKES MCHNING RBILDING SVC INC**
131 2nd St (60506-5505)
**PHONE**.................................630 892-3291
**Fax:** 630 892-9622
Joseph Krippelz Sr, *President*
Jake Krippelz Jr, *Vice Pres*
Amanda Eggleston, *Purch Mgr*
Dobrilla Krippelz, *Treasurer*
Clyde Muskie, *Human Res Dir*
**EMP:** 20
**SQ FT:** 60,000
**SALES:** 5.3MM **Privately Held**
**WEB:** www.jakesinc.com
**SIC: 3599** 3541 7692 Machine shop, jobbing & repair; machine tool replacement & repair parts, metal cutting types; welding repair

**(G-1176)**
**JAMES L TRACEY CO**
1480 Sequoia Dr Ste A2 (60506-1097)
**PHONE**.................................630 907-8999
James Tracey, *Principal*
**EMP:** 13
**SALES (est):** 2.6MM **Privately Held**
**SIC: 3498** Fabricated pipe & fittings

**(G-1177)**
**JEWEL OSCO INC**
Also Called: Jewel-Osco 3252
1952 W Galena Blvd (60506-4306)
**PHONE**.................................630 859-1212
Cary Jiltey, *Manager*
**EMP:** 75
**SALES (corp-wide):** 58.8B **Privately Held**
**WEB:** www.jewelosco.com
**SIC: 5411** 2051 Supermarkets, chain; bread, cake & related products
**HQ:** Jewel Osco, Inc.
150 E Pierce Rd Ste 200
Itasca IL 60143
630 948-6000

**(G-1178)**
**JOHNOS INC (PA)**
Also Called: Main Surplus Store
1804 E New York St (60505-3262)
**PHONE**.................................630 897-6929
**Fax:** 630 897-6833
John Galles, *President*
Emilie Galles, *Vice Pres*
**EMP:** 6
**SQ FT:** 4,000
**SALES:** 520K **Privately Held**
**SIC: 5611** 5699 5094 3479 Clothing, sportswear, men's & boys'; uniforms; trophies; engraving jewelry silverware, or metal; sporting goods & bicycle shops; pleating & stitching

**(G-1179)**
**KACKERT ENTERPRISES INC**
824 2nd Ave (60505-3792)
**PHONE**.................................630 898-9339
**Fax:** 630 898-2653
Charles Kackert, *President*
Edwin Kackert, *Corp Secy*
**EMP:** 4 EST: 1956
**SALES:** 250K **Privately Held**
**SIC: 5063** 5084 3714 3625 Generators; motors, electric; switchgear; engines & transportation equipment; motor vehicle parts & accessories; relays & industrial controls; motors & generators; refrigeration & heating equipment

**(G-1180)**
**LA CHICANITA BAKERY (PA)**
700 E New York St Ste 110 (60505-3580)
**PHONE**.................................630 499-9845
Gerardo Parira, *Owner*
**EMP:** 11
**SALES (est):** 1.2MM **Privately Held**
**SIC: 2051** Bread, cake & related products

**(G-1181)**
**LABEL PRINTERS LP**
1710 Landmark Rd (60506-1192)
**PHONE**.................................630 897-6970
**Fax:** 630 897-2801
Gerald Chouinard, *Partner*
Theodore Risch, *Partner*
Donald Tade, *Partner*
Lori Campbell, *General Mgr*
Tom Erickson, *Plant Mgr*
**EMP:** 73 EST: 1967
**SQ FT:** 54,000
**SALES (est):** 15.6MM **Privately Held**
**WEB:** www.thelabelprinters.com
**SIC: 2759** Commercial printing

**(G-1182)**
**LEROYS PLASTIC CO INC**
1650 Mountain St (60505-2497)
**PHONE**.................................630 898-7006
James Leroy Frieders, *President*
Brian Frieders, *Co-Owner*
**EMP:** 10
**SQ FT:** 8,500
**SALES (est):** 2MM **Privately Held**
**SIC: 3089** Molding primary plastic

**(G-1183)**
**MAGIC MOLD REMOVAL**
689 Wood St (60505-2360)
**PHONE**.................................630 486-0912
Shane Knight, *Principal*
**EMP:** 2
**SALES (est):** 266.7K **Privately Held**
**SIC: 3544** Industrial molds

**(G-1184)**
**MCNISH CORPORATION (PA)**
Also Called: Rbc Services
840 N Russell Ave (60506-2856)
**PHONE**.................................630 892-7921
**Fax:** 630 892-7951
James A McNish, *President*
Lloyd H Cates, *Vice Pres*
Dan Harker, *COO*
Jim Barbel, *Vice Pres*
Bernard Pupino, *Mfg Mgr*
▼ **EMP:** 100 EST: 1946
**SQ FT:** 93,000
**SALES (est):** 33.2MM **Privately Held**
**WEB:** www.walker-process.com
**SIC: 3589** Water treatment equipment, industrial

**(G-1185)**
**MCS MIDWEST LLC**
85 Hankes Ave (60505-1774)
**PHONE**.................................630 393-7402
**EMP:** 4
**SALES (corp-wide):** 4.8MM **Privately Held**
**SIC: 3089** Plastic containers, except foam
**PA:** Mcs Midwest Llc
3876 Hendrickson Rd
Franklin OH 45005
513 217-0805

**(G-1186)**
**MERIDIAN INDUSTRIES INC**
Also Called: Aurora Textile Finishing Co
911 N Lake St (60506-2515)
P.O. Box 70 (60507-0070)
**PHONE**.................................630 892-7651
Ray Silva, *Vice Pres*
Robert Matz, *Plant Mgr*
Michael Skelton, *Sales Staff*
William Lucas, *Branch Mgr*
Myron Walls, *Manager*
**EMP:** 76
**SALES (corp-wide):** 374.1MM **Privately Held**
**WEB:** www.meridiancompanies.com
**SIC: 2261** 7389 Dyeing cotton broadwoven fabrics; textile & apparel services

**PA:** Meridian Industries, Inc.
735 N Water St Ste 630
Milwaukee WI 53202
414 224-0610

**(G-1187)**
**METAL ARTS FINISHING INC**
1001 S Lake St (60505-5894)
**PHONE**.................................630 892-6744
**Fax:** 630 892-8643
Steve Mayotte, *President*
**EMP:** 28
**SQ FT:** 10,000
**SALES:** 1.5MM **Privately Held**
**SIC: 3471** Electroplating of metals or formed products

**(G-1188)**
**MID-AMERICA UNDERGROUND LLC**
Also Called: Mgi Services
901 Ridgeway Ave (60506-5432)
**PHONE**.................................630 443-9999
Adam M Bosch, *President*
Benjamin J Engleson, *Mng Member*
Pablo E Guerra, *Mng Member*
**EMP:** 50
**SALES (est):** 11MM **Privately Held**
**WEB:** www.midamericaunderground.com
**SIC: 1381** 1799 1623 1794 Directional drilling oil & gas wells; boring for building construction; water, sewer & utility lines; telephone & communication line construction; pipeline construction; excavation work

**(G-1189)**
**MILLER CARBONIC INC**
Also Called: Mill Carb
1691 Landmark Rd (60506-1146)
**PHONE**.................................773 624-5651
James Rosenbaum, *President*
Scott Rosenbaum, *Vice Pres*
**EMP:** 15
**SQ FT:** 4,500
**SALES (est):** 4MM **Privately Held**
**WEB:** www.milcarb.com
**SIC: 3569** Generators: steam, liquid oxygen or nitrogen

**(G-1190)**
**MILLIKEN VALVE LLC (DH)**
Also Called: Milliken Valve Company
401 S Highland Ave (60506-5580)
**PHONE**.................................610 861-8803
Robert Jackson, *President*
Lisa Williams, *Marketing Staff*
Alex Adams, *Info Tech Mgr*
Angela Jackson, *Admin Sec*
Tonia Matyger, *Admin Asst*
▲ **EMP:** 8
**SQ FT:** 20,000
**SALES (est):** 1.4MM
**SALES (corp-wide):** 1.1B **Publicly Held**
**WEB:** www.millikenvalve.com
**SIC: 3492** Fluid power valves & hose fittings
**HQ:** Mueller Group, Llc
1200 Abernathy Rd
Atlanta GA 30328
770 206-4200

**(G-1191)**
**MINUTE MEN INC**
1725 N Frnswrth Ave Ste A (60505-1179)
**PHONE**.................................630 692-1583
**EMP:** 23
**SALES (corp-wide):** 19.8MM **Privately Held**
**SIC: 2752** Commercial printing, lithographic
**PA:** Minute Men, Inc.
3740 Carnegie Ave Ste 201
Cleveland OH 44115
216 426-2225

**(G-1192)**
**MY-LIN MANUFACTURING CO INC**
820 N Russell Ave (60506-2823)
**PHONE**.................................630 897-4100
**Fax:** 630 897-0295
Dale Myers, *President*
Sarah Passifume, *Corp Secy*
**EMP:** 20 EST: 1961
**SQ FT:** 13,000

# Aurora - Kane County (G-1193) — GEOGRAPHIC SECTION

SALES (est): 4MM Privately Held
WEB: www.lasermall.com
SIC: 3469 Metal stampings

## (G-1193)
### NANCO SALES CO INC
320 N Highland Ave (60506-3812)
P.O. Box 495 (60507-0495)
PHONE ................................. 630 892-9820
Nancy Mitchell, President
EMP: 3
SQ FT: 2,500
SALES (est): 350K Privately Held
SIC: 5113 5087 3492 Industrial & personal service paper; janitors' supplies; hose & tube fittings & assemblies, hydraulic/pneumatic

## (G-1194)
### NATIONAL METALWARES LP (PA)
900 N Russell Ave (60506-2852)
PHONE ................................. 630 892-9000
Fax: 630 892-2573
Gary C Hill, President
Steve La Fond, Partner
Jack L May Jr, Partner
Mike Sullivan, Partner
Jerry Guthke, Exec VP
▲ EMP: 250
SQ FT: 185,000
SALES (est): 52.1MM Privately Held
WEB: www.nationalmetalwares.com
SIC: 3317 3498 Steel pipe & tubes; fabricated pipe & fittings

## (G-1195)
### NOVA SYSTEMS LTD
2111 Comprehensive Dr (60505-1345)
PHONE ................................. 630 879-2296
Donald B Owen, President
EMP: 9
SQ FT: 8,000
SALES (est): 974.7K Privately Held
WEB: www.nsl1.com
SIC: 3699 8711 3829 Electrical equipment & supplies; electrical or electronic engineering; measuring & controlling devices

## (G-1196)
### NUTRIVO LLC (PA)
Also Called: Rivalus
1785 N Edgelawn Dr (60506-1078)
PHONE ................................. 630 270-1700
Lon Messenger,
EMP: 20
SQ FT: 2,000
SALES (est): 4.2MM Privately Held
SIC: 2099 Food preparations

## (G-1197)
### NUYEN AWNING CO
850 Ridgeway Ave Ste C (60506-6450)
PHONE ................................. 630 892-3995
Fred T Nuyen, President
Richard Lawrence, Vice Pres
EMP: 8 EST: 1926
SALES (est): 580K Privately Held
SIC: 2394 1799 5999 Awnings, fabric: made from purchased materials; tarpaulins, fabric: made from purchased materials; liners & covers, fabric: made from purchased materials; awning installation; awnings

## (G-1198)
### OCTAPHARMA PLASMA INC
418 Hill Ave (60505-5008)
PHONE ................................. 630 375-0028
Mindy Anderson, Director
EMP: 5
SALES (corp-wide): 1.4B Privately Held
SIC: 2836 Plasmas
HQ: Octapharma Plasma, Inc.
    10644 Westlake Dr
    Charlotte NC 28273
    704 654-4600

## (G-1199)
### ON-COR FROZEN FOODS LLC (HQ)
Also Called: On Cor
1225 Corp Blvd Ste 300 (60505)
PHONE ................................. 630 692-2283
Fax: 847 205-1070
Howard Friend, Mng Member
▲ EMP: 20 EST: 1932
SALES (est): 15.9MM
SALES (corp-wide): 2.9B Privately Held
WEB: www.on-cor.com
SIC: 2038 2099 2013 Dinners, frozen & packaged; food preparations; sausages & other prepared meats
PA: Osi Group, Llc
    1225 Corp Blvd Ste 300
    Aurora IL 60505
    630 851-6600

## (G-1200)
### ON-COR FROZEN FOODS LLC
Also Called: Production Facility
1225 Corp Blvd Ste 300 (60505)
PHONE ................................. 630 692-2283
Fax: 312 738-0228
Barney Bailey, Director
EMP: 65
SALES (corp-wide): 2.9B Privately Held
WEB: www.on-cor.com
SIC: 2038 2013 Dinners, frozen & packaged; sausages & other prepared meats
HQ: On-Cor Frozen Foods, Llc
    1225 Corp Blvd Ste 300
    Aurora IL 60505
    630 692-2283

## (G-1201)
### OSI GROUP LLC (PA)
1225 Corp Blvd Ste 300 (60505)
PHONE ................................. 630 851-6600
Fax: 630 851-6674
Sheldon Lavin, CEO
David G McDonald, President
Jim Svajgl, Division Mgr
Wade Smith, Assistant VP
Paul Carlstrom, Vice Pres
▲ EMP: 15
SALES (est): 2.9B Privately Held
SIC: 2099 Food preparations

## (G-1202)
### OSI INDUSTRIES LLC (HQ)
Also Called: Otto & Sons Div
1225 Corp Blvd Ste 105 (60505)
P.O. Box 2018 (60507-2018)
PHONE ................................. 630 851-6600
Fax: 630 892-7030
Sheldon Lavin, CEO
Michael Boccio, Vice Pres
Gerald Kolschowsky, Vice Pres
Laurel Stoltzner, QC Mgr
William Weimer, CFO
▲ EMP: 90 EST: 1918
SQ FT: 60,000
SALES (est): 1.5B
SALES (corp-wide): 2.9B Privately Held
SIC: 2099 Ready-to-eat meals, salads & sandwiches
PA: Osi Group, Llc
    1225 Corp Blvd Ste 300
    Aurora IL 60505
    630 851-6600

## (G-1203)
### PATRIOT HOME IMPROVEMENT INC (PA)
2150 Jericho Rd (60506-5757)
PHONE ................................. 630 800-1901
James King, President
Lisa Camis, Manager
EMP: 13
SQ FT: 2,000
SALES (est): 2MM Privately Held
SIC: 1389 Carpet & upholstery cleaning

## (G-1204)
### PLURIBUS GAMES LLC
725 Morton Ave (60506-2816)
PHONE ................................. 630 770-2043
Ronald McCormick,
EMP: 3
SALES (est): 183.8K Privately Held
SIC: 7371 7372 Computer software development & applications; home entertainment computer software

## (G-1205)
### PROFESSIONAL PACKAGING CORP (PA)
208 E Benton St (60504-4250)
P.O. Box 4455 (60507-4455)
PHONE ................................. 630 896-0574
Kaye Mason, President
EMP: 50
SQ FT: 20,000
SALES (est): 5.8MM Privately Held
WEB: www.ups-psi.com
SIC: 2834 Pharmaceutical preparations

## (G-1206)
### PROGRESSIVE TURNINGS INC
1680 Mountain St (60505-2439)
PHONE ................................. 630 898-3072
Fax: 630 898-0173
Lawrence S Niels, President
Clara Niels, Corp Secy
David Niels, Vice Pres
Rinda Brink, Manager
EMP: 15
SALES (est): 3.5MM Privately Held
WEB: www.progressiveturnings.com
SIC: 3451 Screw machine products

## (G-1207)
### QUALITY LOGO PRODUCTS INC
724 N Highland Ave (60506-2942)
PHONE ................................. 630 896-1627
Bret Bonnet, President
Michael Wenger, Vice Pres
▼ EMP: 48
SQ FT: 5,500
SALES (est): 14.2MM Privately Held
WEB: www.qualitylogoproducts.com
SIC: 2759 Commercial printing

## (G-1208)
### RECO OF IL INC
1669 Dearborn Ave (60505-3134)
PHONE ................................. 630 898-2010
Fax: 630 898-7590
EMP: 5 EST: 1972
SQ FT: 42,000
SALES (est): 250K Privately Held
SIC: 7692 Welding Repair

## (G-1209)
### RIVER WEST RADIATION CENTER L
1221 N Highland Ave (60506-1404)
PHONE ................................. 630 264-8580
John Potter, Principal
EMP: 1
SALES (est): 272.4K Privately Held
SIC: 3674 Radiation sensors

## (G-1210)
### ROSKUSZKA & SONS INC
Also Called: Wally's Printing
969 N Farnsworth Ave (60505-2055)
PHONE ................................. 630 851-3400
William Roskuszka, President
Greg Roskuszka, Engineer
Diane Roskuszka, Office Mgr
EMP: 14
SQ FT: 3,000
SALES (est): 1.8MM Privately Held
WEB: www.roskuszka.com
SIC: 2752 Commercial printing, offset

## (G-1211)
### RWI HOLDINGS INC (PA)
600 S Lake St (60505-5582)
PHONE ................................. 630 897-6951
Manfred Haiderer, President
Scot Patrick, Vice Pres
Richard White, Vice Pres
Kathleen Kulick, Controller
EMP: 12
SALES (est): 30MM Privately Held
SIC: 2542 5046 Partitions & fixtures, except wood; shelving, commercial & industrial

## (G-1212)
### RWI MANUFACTURING INC
Also Called: Richards-Wilcox
600 S Lake St (60505-5582)
PHONE ................................. 800 277-1699
Fax: 630 897-6994
Manfred Haiderer, Ch of Bd
Roy Koch, President
Scott Patrick, Vice Pres
Richard White, Vice Pres
Michael Nash, Project Mgr
♦ EMP: 150
SQ FT: 362,000
SALES (est): 5MM Privately Held
WEB: www.richardswilcox.com
SIC: 2522 3535 Filing boxes, cabinets & cases: except wood; overhead conveyor systems
PA: Rwi Holdings, Inc.
    600 S Lake St
    Aurora IL 60506

## (G-1213)
### S & S METAL RECYCLERS INC
Also Called: Ecology Tech
336 E Sullivan Rd (60506-9740)
PHONE ................................. 630 844-3344
Fax: 630 844-3383
Quentin Podraza, President
Thomas Zacardi, Treasurer
EMP: 15
SQ FT: 12,500
SALES (est): 2.3MM Privately Held
WEB: www.ssmetalrecyclers2.com
SIC: 4953 3341 Recycling, waste materials; secondary nonferrous metals

## (G-1214)
### SAMECWEI INC
Also Called: Sir Speedy
205 N Lake St Ste 103 (60506-4072)
PHONE ................................. 630 897-7888
Fax: 630 897-7888
John WEI, President
Bill Samec, Corp Secy
EMP: 4
SQ FT: 2,000
SALES (est): 360K Privately Held
SIC: 2752 7334 2791 2789 Commercial printing, lithographic; photocopying & duplicating services; typesetting; bookbinding & related work; commercial printing

## (G-1215)
### SHANNON & SONS WELDING
Also Called: Shannon & Sons Welding Shop
1218 E New York St (60505-3922)
PHONE ................................. 630 898-7778
Ellis Shannon, Owner
EMP: 3
SQ FT: 2,450
SALES (est): 100K Privately Held
SIC: 1799 7692 3444 Welding on site; welding repair; sheet metalwork

## (G-1216)
### SHARE MACHINE INC
2175 Rochester Dr Ste C (60506-5674)
PHONE ................................. 630 906-1810
Zekir Share, President
Zejnep Share, Admin Sec
EMP: 10
SQ FT: 18,600
SALES (est): 2MM Privately Held
SIC: 3599 Machine shop, jobbing & repair

## (G-1217)
### SICAME CORP
544 N Highland Ave (60506-2986)
PHONE ................................. 630 238-6680
Rich L Finser, Vice Pres
Kevin Simms, Opers Mgr
Kristin Van De Walle, Regl Sales Mgr
Todd Beauchamp, Manager
▲ EMP: 100
SALES (est): 14.9MM Privately Held
WEB: www.sicameusa.com
SIC: 3643 Electric connectors

## (G-1218)
### SILVACOR INC (PA)
Also Called: National Lumber
2111 Plum St Ste 274 (60506-3268)
PHONE ................................. 630 897-9211
David C Parr, President
Katherine Swanson, Admin Sec
EMP: 2
SQ FT: 80,000
SALES (est): 3.2MM Privately Held
SIC: 2426 Brush blocks, wood: turned & shaped; handle stock, sawed or planed

## (G-1219)
### SKYWIDE PUBLICITY SOLUTIONS
Also Called: Skywide PS
1006 E Galena Blvd (60505-3806)
PHONE ................................. 331 425-0341
Luz Zavala, CEO

## GEOGRAPHIC SECTION
## Aviston - Clinton County (G-1248)

EMP: 3
SALES (est): 42.7K **Privately Held**
SIC: **4841** 3993 Cable & other pay television services; signs & advertising specialties; advertising artwork

**(G-1220)**
**T & L MFG CORPORATION**
1665 Dearborn Ave (60505-3134)
P.O. Box 790 (60507-0790)
PHONE..................630 898-7100
Fax: 630 898-7268
Dorothy Wagner, *President*
Goddard Wagner, *Corp Secy*
William Wagner, *Vice Pres*
▲ EMP: 20
SQ FT: 39,000
SALES (est): 4.6MM **Privately Held**
WEB: www.tandlmfg.com
SIC: **3441** 3599 7692 Fabricated structural metal; machine shop, jobbing & repair; welding repair

**(G-1221)**
**TAG DIAMOND & LABEL**
100 Hankes Ave (60505-1747)
PHONE..................630 844-9395
Fax: 630 844-9396
Tony Oliva, *President*
EMP: 20
SALES: 1.2MM **Privately Held**
WEB: www.diamondtagandlabel.com
SIC: **7389** 2679 Printers' services: folding, collating; tags, paper (unprinted): made from purchased paper

**(G-1222)**
**TANGENT TECHNOLOGIES LLC**
1001 Sullivan Rd (60506-1065)
PHONE..................630 264-1110
Jim Aremka, *Controller*
Guy De Feo,
Francisco Morales,
Andrew Stephens,
▲ EMP: 27
SALES (est): 14.3MM **Privately Held**
WEB: www.tandeck.com
SIC: **2821** Plastics materials & resins

**(G-1223)**
**TANIC RUBBER PLATE CO**
1013 Sill Ave (60506-5837)
PHONE..................630 896-2122
Fax: 630 896-2153
Victor Dutkovich, *President*
Valentine Dutkovich, *Corp Secy*
EMP: 5 EST: 1978
SQ FT: 6,900
SALES: 250K **Privately Held**
SIC: **3555** 2796 Printing plates; plates, offset; platemaking services

**(G-1224)**
**THALES VISIONIX INC**
1444 N Farnsworth Ave # 604 (60506-1644)
PHONE..................630 375-2008
Pete Roney, *CEO*
Bob Atack, *Manager*
Heather M Acker, *Admin Sec*
EMP: 61
SALES (est): 7.6MM **Privately Held**
SIC: **3728** Aircraft parts & equipment

**(G-1225)**
**TIN MAN HEATING & COOLING INC**
Also Called: DCS Mechanical
419 Rathbone Ave (60506-5936)
PHONE..................630 267-3232
Kenneth Smith, *President*
Nicholas Cellini, *Corp Secy*
EMP: 40
SQ FT: 1,300
SALES: 9.5MM **Privately Held**
SIC: **3356** Tin

**(G-1226)**
**TOUGH ELECTRIC INC**
717 Jackson St (60505-5210)
PHONE..................630 236-8332
Rafael Fajardo, *President*
Evelyn Fajardo, *Admin Sec*
EMP: 6
SALES (est): 726.7K **Privately Held**
SIC: **3625** Relays, electric power

**(G-1227)**
**UNILOCK CHICAGO INC**
301 E Sullivan Rd (60505-9762)
PHONE..................630 892-9191
Fax: 630 892-9215
Edward J Bryant, *President*
Tony Hooper, *Vice Pres*
Joe Kerr, *Vice Pres*
Kathy Maltese, *Purch Agent*
Chris Boster, *QC Mgr*
▲ EMP: 100
SQ FT: 19,300
SALES (est): 18.8MM **Privately Held**
SIC: **3281** 1741 Paving blocks, cut stone; retaining wall construction

**(G-1228)**
**UNITY BAKING COMPANY LLC**
1130 Kenilworth Pl (60506-5457)
PHONE..................630 360-6099
Sarasin Joseph E, *Principal*
EMP: 4 EST: 2013
SALES (est): 172K **Privately Held**
SIC: **2051** Bread, cake & related products

**(G-1229)**
**VALLEY FASTENER GROUP LLC (PA)**
Also Called: V F G
1490 Mitchell Rd (60505-9582)
P.O. Box 2790 (60507-2790)
PHONE..................630 299-8910
Manny Desantis, *CEO*
Tony Coldagelli, *Controller*
Earl E Danner Jr,
Emmanuel Desantis,
Thomas Falcone,
▲ EMP: 50
SQ FT: 43,000
SALES (est): 21.6MM **Privately Held**
WEB: www.valleyrivet.com
SIC: **3452** Bolts, nuts, rivets & washers

**(G-1230)**
**VOICE**
314 N Lake St Ste 2 (60506-4086)
PHONE..................630 966-8642
Carter Crane, *President*
EMP: 7
SALES (est): 343.5K **Privately Held**
SIC: **2711** Newspapers, publishing & printing

**(G-1231)**
**WELDING COMPANY OF AMERICA**
Also Called: Upshot Putter Company
335 E Sullivan Rd (60505-9762)
PHONE..................630 806-2000
Fax: 630 806-2001
Hector Villarreal, *President*
Frank Falbo, *Engineer*
Mark Daniels, *Sales Staff*
Dawn Warren, *Office Mgr*
Don Renner, *Manager*
▼ EMP: 38
SQ FT: 17,900
SALES (est): 11.9MM **Privately Held**
WEB: www.weldcoa.com
SIC: **3499** 7692 Welding tips, heat resistant: metal; welding repair

**(G-1232)**
**WELDSTAR COMPANY (PA)**
1750 Mitchell Rd (60505-9578)
P.O. Box 1150 (60507-1150)
PHONE..................630 859-3100
Fax: 630 859-3199
John B Winkle, *CEO*
Matthew Winkle, *President*
Joseph Winkle, *Corp Secy*
Chet De King, *Vice Pres*
Steve Riva, *Controller*
▼ EMP: 32 EST: 1948
SQ FT: 22,000
SALES (est): 27.3MM **Privately Held**
WEB: www.weldstar.com
SIC: **5084** 2813 Welding machinery & equipment; industrial gases

**(G-1233)**
**WESTROCK COMPANY**
1601 Mountain St (60505-2402)
PHONE..................630 429-2400
Ed Curtis, *Manager*

EMP: 161
SALES (corp-wide): 14.1B **Publicly Held**
WEB: www.rocktenn.com
SIC: **2653** Partitions, solid fiber: made from purchased materials
HQ: Westrock Rkt Company
504 Thrasher St
Norcross GA 30071
770 448-2193

**(G-1234)**
**WORLEY MACHINING INC**
601 W New York St Ste 400 (60506-3859)
PHONE..................630 801-9198
Edward Jones, *President*
EMP: 11
SQ FT: 6,500
SALES (est): 1MM **Privately Held**
SIC: **3451** Screw machine products

**(G-1235)**
**WURST KITCHEN INC (PA)**
638 2nd Ave (60505-4418)
PHONE..................630 898-9242
Edward Schleining, *Principal*
EMP: 2 EST: 1967
SQ FT: 1,740
SALES (est): 284.6K **Privately Held**
SIC: **2013** 5421 Sausages & other prepared meats; meat markets, including freezer provisioniners

**(G-1236)**
**YETEE LLC**
110 Cross St (60506-5114)
PHONE..................630 340-0132
Michael Mancuso, *Principal*
EMP: 7
SALES (est): 317K **Privately Held**
SIC: **2253** T-shirts & tops, knit

### Ava
*Jackson County*

**(G-1237)**
**HILL TOP PALLET**
612 Bollman Rd (62907-2493)
PHONE..................618 426-9810
Howard Yoder, *Owner*
EMP: 6
SALES: 850K **Privately Held**
SIC: **2448** Wood pallets & skids

**(G-1238)**
**KUNTRY KETTLE**
178 Gordon Rd (62907-2402)
PHONE..................618 426-1600
James Yoder, *Owner*
EMP: 4
SQ FT: 5,000
SALES (est): 389.3K **Privately Held**
SIC: **2033** Jams, jellies & preserves: packaged in cans, jars, etc.

**(G-1239)**
**LONEOAK TIMBER & VENEERE CO**
45 Longhorn Trl (62907-2975)
PHONE..................618 426-3065
Mike Faults, *Owner*
EMP: 3
SALES (est): 254.1K **Privately Held**
SIC: **2411** Timber, cut at logging camp

**(G-1240)**
**MILLERS COUNTRY CRAFTS INC**
150 Millers Country Ln (62907-2094)
PHONE..................618 426-3108
Fax: 618 426-1110
Nevin Miller, *President*
Wilma Miller, *Vice Pres*
EMP: 2
SQ FT: 6,000
SALES: 700K **Privately Held**
WEB: www.millercountrydogs.com
SIC: **2033** 5149 Jams, including imitation: packaged in cans, jars, etc.; jellies, edible, including imitation: in cans, jars, etc.; honey

**(G-1241)**
**PAINTED QUARTER RIDGE**
948 Possom Rd (62907-2955)
PHONE..................618 534-9734
EMP: 3
SALES (est): 175.2K **Privately Held**
SIC: **3131** Quarters

**(G-1242)**
**RESEARCH MANNIKINS INC**
143 Lupine Ln (62907-2101)
PHONE..................618 426-3456
Fax: 618 426-3032
Greg Myers, *Editor*
Greg Hogan, *Opers Mgr*
Randy Hurst, *Branch Mgr*
Dan Beasley, *Asst Mgr*
EMP: 14
SALES (corp-wide): 7MM **Privately Held**
WEB: www.rmi-online.com
SIC: **3999** 5087 Mannequins; taxidermist tools & equipment
PA: Research Mannikins, Inc.
315 W Sherman St
Lebanon OR 97355
541 451-1538

### Aviston
*Clinton County*

**(G-1243)**
**COBRAA INC**
350 W 4th St (62216-3404)
P.O. Box 122 (62216-0122)
PHONE..................618 228-7380
Derek Sudholt, *President*
EMP: 3 EST: 2000
SALES (est): 373.8K **Privately Held**
WEB: www.cobraainc.com
SIC: **3312** Coated or plated products

**(G-1244)**
**HIDDEN LAKE WINERY LTD**
10580 Wellen Rd (62216-1019)
PHONE..................618 228-9111
Fax: 618 228-9024
Dale E Holbrook, *President*
EMP: 50
SALES (est): 1.6MM **Privately Held**
WEB: www.hiddenlakewinery.com
SIC: **7299** 2084 Banquet hall facilities; wines, brandy & brandy spirits

**(G-1245)**
**JW WELDING**
11 S Clement Dr (62216-3749)
PHONE..................618 228-7213
EMP: 8
SALES (est): 88.7K **Privately Held**
SIC: **7692** Welding repair

**(G-1246)**
**MARKUS CABINET MANUFACTURING (PA)**
601 S Clinton St (62216-3418)
PHONE..................618 228-7376
Fax: 314 436-0700
Keith Marcus, *President*
Randy Peek, *President*
Lynda Kim, *Vice Pres*
Carl Marcus, *Vice Pres*
Larry Bair, *Treasurer*
EMP: 20
SALES (est): 1.7MM **Privately Held**
SIC: **2434** Wood kitchen cabinets

**(G-1247)**
**MHWP**
Also Called: Recognitions
307 W Harrison St (62216-3547)
PHONE..................618 228-7600
Fax: 618 228-7695
Jeffrey Morgan, *Owner*
EMP: 4
SALES: 150K **Privately Held**
SIC: **2499** Wood products

**(G-1248)**
**SUDHOLT SHEET METAL INC**
350 W 4th St (62216-3404)
P.O. Box 122 (62216-0122)
PHONE..................618 228-7351
Fax: 618 228-7300

Derrik Sudholt, *President*
Amber Jansen, *Manager*
**EMP:** 9
**SQ FT:** 3,000
**SALES (est):** 1.4MM **Privately Held**
**SIC:** 1711 3444 1796 Warm air heating & air conditioning contractor; ventilation & duct work contractor; sheet metalwork; installing building equipment

**(G-1249)**
**U CAMP PRODUCTS**
449 S Spring St (62216-3412)
**PHONE**..................618 228-5080
Debbie Ludington, *Owner*
**EMP:** 5
**SALES (est):** 236.1K **Privately Held**
**SIC:** 3949 Camping equipment & supplies

## Baldwin
### Randolph County

**(G-1250)**
**FJCJ LLC**
Also Called: Grangrit
11000 Baldwin Rd (62217-1500)
P.O. Box 25 (62217-0025)
**PHONE**..................618 785-2217
**Fax:** 618 785-2414
Don Wingerter, *Plant Mgr*
Steve Bremer, *Branch Mgr*
**EMP:** 13
**SALES (corp-wide):** 7.5MM **Privately Held**
**SIC:** 1446 1241 Abrasive sand mining; coal mining services
**PA:** Fjcj, Llc
2105 Northwinds Dr
Dyer IN

**(G-1251)**
**HIGMAN LLC**
Also Called: Tillock Steel Supply and Salv
609 W Myrtle St (62217-1211)
P.O. Box 144 (62217-0144)
**PHONE**..................618 785-2545
Joel Higman, *Owner*
**EMP:** 3
**SQ FT:** 22,000
**SALES (est):** 393.8K **Privately Held**
**SIC:** 3291 3569 Abrasive metal & steel products; baling machines, for scrap metal, paper or similar material

**(G-1252)**
**US MINERALS INC**
11000 Baldwin Rd (62217-1500)
**PHONE**..................618 785-2217
Bill Hertfelder, *Manager*
Jean McMullin, *Admin Asst*
**EMP:** 15
**SALES (corp-wide):** 34.6MM **Privately Held**
**SIC:** 3291 Abrasive products
**PA:** U.S. Minerals, Inc.
18635 West Creek Dr Ste 2
Tinley Park IL 60477
219 864-0909

## Bannockburn
### Lake County

**(G-1253)**
**AVALIGN TECHNOLOGIES INC (PA)**
2275 Half Day Rd Ste 126 (60015-1274)
**PHONE**..................855 282-5446
Forrest R Whittaker, *CEO*
Berndt Fetzer, *President*
Tony O'Neill, *Senior VP*
Kim Gryzlo, *Vice Pres*
Paul Rice, *Vice Pres*
**EMP:** 29
**SALES (est):** 53.6MM **Privately Held**
**SIC:** 3829 5047 3841 Thermometers, including digital: clinical; instruments, surgical & medical; surgical & medical instruments

**(G-1254)**
**AVEXIS INC**
2275 Half Day Rd Ste 160 (60015-1221)
**PHONE**..................847 572-8280
Daniel Welch, *Ch of Bd*
Sean P Nolan, *President*
Andrew F Knudten, *Senior VP*
James J L'Italien, *Senior VP*
Ed Jelen, *Vice Pres*
**EMP:** 18 **EST:** 2010
**SQ FT:** 4,795
**SALES (est):** 2.9MM **Privately Held**
**SIC:** 2836 Biological products, except diagnostic

**(G-1255)**
**BARCOR INC**
1413 Aitken Dr (60015-1834)
P.O. Box 517, Northbrook (60065-0517)
**PHONE**..................847 940-0750
Judy Baria, *President*
Ed Baria, *Vice Pres*
**EMP:** 10
**SQ FT:** 3,000
**SALES (est):** 1MM **Privately Held**
**SIC:** 3545 3829 3823 3229 Gauges (machine tool accessories); measuring & controlling devices; industrial instrmnts msrmnt display/control process variable; pressed & blown glass

**(G-1256)**
**BAXALTA INCORPORATED (DH)**
1200 Lakeside Dr (60015-1243)
**PHONE**..................224 940-2000
Flemming Ornskov, *CEO*
Brian Goff, *President*
Jacopo Leonardi, *President*
David D Meek, *President*
Dagmar Rosa-Bjorkeson, *President*
**EMP:** 277
**SQ FT:** 260,000
**SALES:** 6.1B
**SALES (corp-wide):** 6.4B **Privately Held**
**SIC:** 2834 Pharmaceutical preparations; intravenous solutions

**(G-1257)**
**DIONEX CORPORATION**
3000 Lakeside Dr Ste 116n (60015-1279)
**PHONE**..................847 295-7500
**Fax:** 847 283-0722
Jean Free, *Research*
Peggy Benz, *Office Mgr*
Ken Larkey, *Director*
**EMP:** 6
**SALES (est):** 660K **Privately Held**
**SIC:** 3826 Chromatographic equipment, laboratory type

**(G-1258)**
**G & S MANUFACTURING INC**
2345 Waukegan Rd Ste 155 (60015-1592)
**PHONE**..................847 674-7666
**Fax:** 847 674-0158
Aron Grunfeld, *President*
Chris Salerno, *Office Mgr*
Rachel Grunfeld, *Admin Sec*
**EMP:** 10
**SQ FT:** 10,000
**SALES (est):** 920K **Privately Held**
**SIC:** 3545 Tools & accessories for machine tools

**(G-1259)**
**GCP APPLIED TECHNOLOGIES**
2051 Waukegan Rd (60015-1828)
**PHONE**..................410 531-4000
Julia Poncher, *Marketing Mgr*
Joe Bystron, *Branch Mgr*
**EMP:** 162
**SALES (corp-wide):** 1.6B **Publicly Held**
**WEB:** www.grace.com
**SIC:** 2819 Industrial inorganic chemicals
**PA:** W. R. Grace & Co.
7500 Grace Dr
Columbia MD 21044
410 531-4000

**(G-1260)**
**MARSHALL BAUER**
Also Called: M. Bauer & Associates
2000 Meadow Ln (60015-1851)
**PHONE**..................847 236-1847
Marshall Bauer, *Owner*
**EMP:** 2
**SALES (est):** 500K **Privately Held**
**SIC:** 7699 2491 Antique repair & restoration, except furniture, automobiles; wood products, creosoted

**(G-1261)**
**MEXINOX USA INC**
Also Called: Thyssenkrupp Stainless N Amer
2275 Half Day Rd Ste 300 (60015-1232)
**PHONE**..................224 533-6700
**Fax:** 847 317-1404
Stephan Lacor, *Vice Pres*
Janet Norman, *Accounts Mgr*
Steve Wasil, *Manager*
**EMP:** 55
**SQ FT:** 5,000
**SALES (est):** 8.9MM
**SALES (corp-wide):** 593.1MM **Privately Held**
**WEB:** www.mexinoxusa.com
**SIC:** 3312 Plate, sheet & strip, except coated products
**HQ:** Outokumpu Mexinox, S.A. De C.V.
Av. Industrias No. 4100
San Luis Potosi S.L.P. 78395
444 826-5118

**(G-1262)**
**MODERN SILICONE TECH INC (PA)**
2345 Waukegan Rd Ste 155 (60015-1592)
**PHONE**..................727 507-9800
Rachel Grunfeld, *CEO*
Aron Grunfeld, *President*
William McFadden, *COO*
Michelle Wasielewski, *Controller*
▲ **EMP:** 12
**SQ FT:** 60,000
**SALES (est):** 21MM **Privately Held**
**SIC:** 3053 3061 2822 Gaskets, packing & sealing devices; mechanical rubber goods; synthetic rubber

**(G-1263)**
**OUTOKUMPU STAINLESS USA LLC**
Also Called: Outokmpu High Prfmce Stainless
2275 Half Day Rd Ste 300 (60015-1232)
**PHONE**..................847 317-1400
**EMP:** 488
**SALES (corp-wide):** 593.1MM **Privately Held**
**SIC:** 3312 Stainless steel
**HQ:** Outokumpu Stainless Usa, Llc
1 Steel Dr
Calvert AL 36513
847 317-1400

**(G-1264)**
**PRINT & DESIGN SERVICES LLC**
Also Called: AlphaGraphics
2561 Waukegan Rd (60015-1569)
**PHONE**..................847 317-9001
**Fax:** 847 317-9883
Manuel Torres, *Managing Prtnr*
Ronald J Garsha, *Principal*
Uwe Trode, *Sales Staff*
Leslie Iverson, *Sales Executive*
Russell Ludwig, *Graphic Designe*
**EMP:** 5
**SQ FT:** 2,400
**SALES:** 1MM **Privately Held**
**SIC:** 2759 7334 2791 2789 Commercial printing; photocopying & duplicating services; typesetting; bookbinding & related work; commercial printing, lithographic

**(G-1265)**
**SOUTHLAND INDUSTRIES INC**
2345 Waukegan Rd Ste 155 (60015-1592)
**PHONE**..................757 543-5701
Alex Granfield, *President*
Jim Jones, *President*
Theodore L Salter, *Vice Pres*
Dixie W Moore, *Treasurer*
John Stahler, *MIS Dir*
**EMP:** 25
**SQ FT:** 108,800
**SALES (est):** 3.1MM
**SALES (corp-wide):** 13.6B **Publicly Held**
**WEB:** www.itwsouthland.com
**SIC:** 3053 3069 Gaskets & sealing devices; molded rubber products

**PA:** Illinois Tool Works Inc.
155 Harlem Ave
Glenview IL 60025
847 724-7500

**(G-1266)**
**THERMO FISHER SCIENTIFIC INC**
Also Called: Thermo Mattson
3000 Lakeside Dr Ste 116n (60015-1279)
**Fax:** 847 310-0145
John Butler, *Branch Mgr*
**EMP:** 8
**SQ FT:** 6,000
**SALES (corp-wide):** 18.2B **Publicly Held**
**SIC:** 3823 Industrial instrmnts msrmnt display/control process variable
**PA:** Thermo Fisher Scientific Inc.
168 3rd Ave
Waltham MA 02451
781 622-1000

**(G-1267)**
**WRIGHT METALS INC**
1405 Valley Rd (60015-1551)
**PHONE**..................847 267-1212
Kim A Wright, *President*
James Barkemeyer, *Corp Secy*
**EMP:** 3 **EST:** 1981
**SALES (est):** 498.7K **Privately Held**
**SIC:** 3444 Sheet metalwork

## Barrington
### Lake County

**(G-1268)**
**ASPEN CABINET DIST CORP**
364 N Bateman Cir (60010-7612)
**PHONE**..................847 381-4241
George Wray, *President*
**EMP:** 2
**SALES (est):** 209.1K **Privately Held**
**SIC:** 2434 Wood kitchen cabinets

**(G-1269)**
**B ANDREWS INC**
200 Applebee St Ste 202 (60010-3060)
**PHONE**..................847 381-7444
Dale Destree, *President*
**EMP:** 5
**SQ FT:** 2,200
**SALES (est):** 1.2MM **Privately Held**
**WEB:** www.bandrews.com
**SIC:** 5046 2542 Store fixtures & display equipment; partitions & fixtures, except wood

**(G-1270)**
**BARRINGTON CARDINAL WHSE LLC**
Also Called: Garfilds Bev Whse - Barrington
340 W Northwest Hwy (60010-3033)
**PHONE**..................847 387-3676
David Garfield, *Ch of Bd*
Adam Silvertein, *COO*
Bruce Garfield, *Mng Member*
**EMP:** 4
**SQ FT:** 10,000
**SALES (est):** 236.8K **Privately Held**
**SIC:** 2084 Wines

**(G-1271)**
**BARRINGTON CLINICAL PARTNERS**
25377 N Wagon Wheel Ct (60010-1430)
**PHONE**..................847 508-9737
Maelynn S McCrory, *Owner*
**EMP:** 4
**SALES (est):** 334K **Privately Held**
**SIC:** 3845 Electromedical equipment

**(G-1272)**
**BARRINGTON PACKAGING SYSTEMS**
Also Called: Barrington Packg Systems Group
835 Barrington Point Rd (60010-4625)
**PHONE**..................847 382-8063
George Burny, *President*
Larry Pence, *COO*
Danny Lena, *Director*
▲ **EMP:** 8

# GEOGRAPHIC SECTION
# Barrington - Lake County (G-1304)

SQ FT: 1,000
SALES (est): 2.3MM **Privately Held**
SIC: **3565** 2631 Packaging machinery; packaging board

*(G-1273)*
**BARRINGTON PRINT & COPY INC**
200 James St (60010-3328)
PHONE..................847 382-1185
Cindy Zurawski, *President*
Chris Schwartz, *Manager*
EMP: 7
SQ FT: 1,400
SALES (est): 974K **Privately Held**
SIC: **2752** Commercial printing, offset

*(G-1274)*
**BRETMAR STEEL INDUSTRY**
467 E Lake Shore Dr (60010-1466)
PHONE..................847 382-5940
Silverio Aprati, *Owner*
EMP: 2
SALES (est): 221.1K **Privately Held**
SIC: **3312** Blast furnaces & steel mills

*(G-1275)*
**CASTLEGATE PUBLISHERS INC**
25597 W Drake Rd (60010-2417)
PHONE..................847 382-6420
Michael Mercer PHD, *President*
EMP: 3 EST: 1997
SALES (est): 167.3K **Privately Held**
SIC: **2731** Book publishing

*(G-1276)*
**CEM LLC**
Also Called: Capital Engineering & Mfg Co
6000 Garlands Ln Ste 120 (60010-6029)
PHONE..................708 333-3761
John Herb, *President*
Michael Golevicz, *Vice Pres*
Suzanne Alkazar, *Human Res Mgr*
Valerie McGrath, *Manager*
Tom Herb, 
EMP: 60
SALES (est): 9MM **Privately Held**
SIC: **3441** Fabricated structural metal

*(G-1277)*
**CONTINENTAL SALES INC**
213 W Main St (60010-4205)
PHONE..................847 381-6530
Terry Wybel, *President*
▲ EMP: 5
SALES (est): 380K **Privately Held**
WEB: www.continentalsalesinc.com
SIC: **2731** Book publishing

*(G-1278)*
**COTTAGE DOOR PRESS LLC**
218 James St (60010-3328)
PHONE..................224 228-6000
Kerry Finnamore, *Manager*
Maddrell Richard, 
EMP: 10
SQ FT: 200
SALES (est): 815.8K **Privately Held**
SIC: **2741** Miscellaneous publishing

*(G-1279)*
**ECOLOCAP SOLUTIONS INC**
1250 S Grove Ave Ste 308 (60010-5066)
PHONE..................866 479-7041
Michael Siegel, *CEO*
Jeung Kwak, *Ch of Bd*
Robert Egger Jr, *COO*
Michel St-Pierre, *CFO*
EMP: 4
SALES (est): 308.9K **Privately Held**
SIC: **2869** 3691 Fuels; storage batteries

*(G-1280)*
**FORREST PRESS INC**
Also Called: Forrest Press Printing
1010 W Northwest Hwy (60010-2338)
PHONE..................847 381-1621
Fax: 847 381-1625
Nicholas R Olker, *Owner*
Char Olker, *Manager*
EMP: 4
SQ FT: 3,000
SALES: 500K **Privately Held**
SIC: **2752** 2759 Offset & photolithographic printing; commercial printing

*(G-1281)*
**FRESCO PLASTER FINISHES INC**
Also Called: Nass Fresco Finishes
228 James St Ste 2 (60010-3328)
P.O. Box 281 (60011-0281)
PHONE..................847 277-1484
Dan Nass, *President*
EMP: 8
SQ FT: 5,000
SALES: 990K **Privately Held**
SIC: **2211** Upholstery, tapestry & wall coverings: cotton

*(G-1282)*
**GRAPHIC ARTS STUDIO INC (PA)**
28 W 111 Coml Ave Commercial (60010)
PHONE..................847 381-1105
Fax: 847 381-1176
Andrew J Macchia Jr, *President*
Michele Jessup, *Project Mgr*
Robert Wise, *Production*
Thomas Langer, *CFO*
John Blackwell, *Sales Staff*
EMP: 50
SQ FT: 17,000
SALES (est): 18MM **Privately Held**
SIC: **2796** 2752 Color separations for printing; commercial printing, lithographic

*(G-1283)*
**H L M SALES INC**
618 S Northwest Hwy (60010-4618)
P.O. Box 516, Crystal Lake (60039-0516)
PHONE..................815 455-6922
George Lamping, *President*
Robert Lamping, *Vice Pres*
▲ EMP: 6
SQ FT: 1,500
SALES: 600K **Privately Held**
WEB: www.hlmsales.com
SIC: **3965** 3993 Buckles & buckle parts; signs & advertising specialties

*(G-1284)*
**HEIDELBERG USA INC**
21805 W Feld Pkwy Ste 180 (60010)
PHONE..................847 550-0915
Nick Ferris, *Branch Mgr*
EMP: 54
SALES (corp-wide): 2.6B **Privately Held**
WEB: www.karns-enterprises.net
SIC: **3555** Printing presses
HQ: Heidelberg Usa, Inc.
1000 Gutenberg Dr Nw
Kennesaw GA 30144
770 419-6500

*(G-1285)*
**LAKE COUNTY TECHNOLOGIES INC**
28w080 Coml Ave Unit 7 (60010)
PHONE..................847 658-1330
Robert Weskamp, *President*
Maryl S Weskamp, *Admin Sec*
EMP: 8
SQ FT: 2,500
SALES: 1MM **Privately Held**
SIC: **3599** Amusement park equipment

*(G-1286)*
**LINMORE PUBLISHING CO**
409 South St (60010-4546)
PHONE..................847 382-7606
Linda Mrowicki, *President*
Dan Jackson, *Vice Pres*
EMP: 2
SALES: 200K **Privately Held**
WEB: www.linmore.com
SIC: **2731** Textbooks: publishing & printing

*(G-1287)*
**LITTLE SHOP OF PAPERS LTD**
740 W Northwest Hwy (60010-2640)
PHONE..................847 382-7733
Fax: 847 382-7732
Jean A Stahr, *President*
Scott Stahr, *Admin Sec*
EMP: 6
SQ FT: 500
SALES (est): 424.7K **Privately Held**
SIC: **5947** 8999 2759 Gift shop; calligrapher; invitation & stationery printing & engraving

*(G-1288)*
**MAC AMERICAN CORPORATION**
530 Fox Glen Ct (60010-1833)
PHONE..................847 277-9450
Thomas D McAuley, *President*
▲ EMP: 6
SQ FT: 4,300
SALES (est): 12MM **Privately Held**
SIC: **2631** Paperboard mills

*(G-1289)*
**MARSHALL PUBG & PROMOTIONS**
123 S Hough St (60010-4376)
PHONE..................224 238-3530
Thomas Edinger, *Principal*
EMP: 1
SALES (est): 250K **Privately Held**
SIC: **2741** 5961 Miscellaneous publishing; record &/or tape (music or video) club, mail order

*(G-1290)*
**MERIX PHARMACEUTICAL CORP**
18 E Dundee Rd Bldg 3 (60010)
PHONE..................847 277-1111
Meryl Squires, *President*
Dori Squires, *Vice Pres*
Diann Squiers, *Sales Mgr*
Janice Lewis, *Executive Asst*
EMP: 6
SQ FT: 3,500
SALES (est): 1.5MM **Privately Held**
WEB: www.merixcorp.com
SIC: **2834** Druggists' preparations (pharmaceuticals)

*(G-1291)*
**MIDWEST WHEEL COVERS INC**
27175 W Flynn Creek Dr (60010-2306)
PHONE..................847 609-9980
Bob Palumbo, *President*
EMP: 1
SALES: 250K **Privately Held**
SIC: **3312** Wheels

*(G-1292)*
**MIYANOHITEC MACHINERY INC**
Also Called: Amt Kikai
50 Dundee Ln (60010-5106)
PHONE..................847 382-2794
Thomas Miyano, *CEO*
Steven Miyano, *President*
EMP: 4
SALES (est): 362.8K **Privately Held**
SIC: **3545** Chucks: drill, lathe or magnetic (machine tool accessories)

*(G-1293)*
**MURVIN & MEIER OIL CO**
1531 S Grove Ave Unit 203 (60010-5251)
PHONE..................847 277-8380
M Meier, *Principal*
EMP: 4
SALES (est): 322.5K **Privately Held**
SIC: **1381** Drilling oil & gas wells

*(G-1294)*
**NAUTILUS MEDICAL**
1300 S Grove Ave Ste 200 (60010-5247)
PHONE..................866 520-6477
Timothy Kelley, *Principal*
Steve Austin, *COO*
EMP: 3
SQ FT: 8,000
SALES (est): 489.2K **Privately Held**
SIC: **7372** Application computer software

*(G-1295)*
**NEW VISION SOFTWARE INC**
Also Called: 321 Learning Services
130 Kainer Ave (60010-4643)
PHONE..................847 382-1532
Fax: 847 382-1944
Randolf Hilgers, *President*
Dave Hilgers, *Vice Pres*
EMP: 3
SQ FT: 1,200
SALES (est): 220K **Privately Held**
WEB: www.nvsi.com
SIC: **7372** Prepackaged software; educational computer software

*(G-1296)*
**PACE PRINT PLUS**
1010 W Northwest Hwy (60010-2338)
PHONE..................847 381-1720
Flijah Fitzgerald, *Principal*
EMP: 4
SALES (est): 445.4K **Privately Held**
SIC: **2752** Commercial printing, lithographic

*(G-1297)*
**PJLA MUSIC**
22n159 Pepper Rd (60010)
PHONE..................847 382-3212
Peter J Laplaca, *Owner*
▲ EMP: 1
SALES: 250K **Privately Held**
SIC: **3931** 5099 Brass instruments & parts; musical instruments parts & accessories

*(G-1298)*
**PRECIOUS METAL REF SVCS INC**
Also Called: Progressive Environmental Svcs
1531 S Grove Ave Unit 104 (60010-5250)
PHONE..................847 756-2700
Sheldon B Goldner, *President*
Miguel Echeverria, *Manager*
Rob Mikel, *Manager*
EMP: 8
SALES (est): 970K **Privately Held**
SIC: **4953** 3341 Hazardous waste collection & disposal; recovery & refining of nonferrous metals

*(G-1299)*
**PRO REP SALE IL**
25560 N Countryside Dr (60010-7028)
PHONE..................847 382-1592
Jay N Thompson, *Principal*
EMP: 3
SALES (est): 147.2K **Privately Held**
SIC: **2097** Manufactured ice

*(G-1300)*
**R G CONTROLS INC**
512 Rue Chamonix (60010-3710)
PHONE..................847 438-3981
Alena Guest, *CEO*
Raymond Gust, *President*
EMP: 2
SALES: 400K **Privately Held**
SIC: **3613** Control panels, electric

*(G-1301)*
**RMB ENGINEERED PRODUCTS INC**
18-1 E Dundee Rd Ste 220 (60010-5249)
PHONE..................847 382-0100
Margaret Blomquist, *President*
Scott Blomquist, *President*
EMP: 8
SALES (est): 318.2K **Privately Held**
WEB: www.rmbengineeredproducts.com
SIC: **3443** Heat exchangers, condensers & components

*(G-1302)*
**ROMAN SIGNS**
819 W Northwest Hwy (60010-2641)
PHONE..................847 381-3425
Fax: 847 381-3497
Karen Roman, *Owner*
EMP: 9
SALES (est): 430K **Privately Held**
SIC: **3993** 7312 Signs & advertising specialties; neon signs; electric signs; signs, not made in custom sign painting shops; billboard advertising

*(G-1303)*
**ROOM DIVIDERS NOW LLC**
38 Otis Rd (60010-5120)
PHONE..................847 224-7900
Lundmark Jackson, *Mng Member*
▲ EMP: 3
SALES (est): 127.4K **Privately Held**
SIC: **2542** Pallet racks: except wood

*(G-1304)*
**SAN TELMO LTD**
330 E Main St Fl 2 (60010-3203)
PHONE..................847 842-9115
Fred Weinert, *President*

# Barrington - Lake County (G-1305)   GEOGRAPHIC SECTION

Sylvia Weinert, *Vice Pres*
**EMP:** 5
**SALES (est):** 400K **Privately Held**
**SIC:** 2844 5122 Toilet preparations; cosmetics, perfumes & hair products

### (G-1305)
### STERLING TOOL & MANUFACTURING
28080 W Coml Ave Ste 8 (60010)
**PHONE**.................................847 304-1800
**Fax:** 847 304-1806
Terry Wehrheim, *President*
Thomas Degroot, *Vice Pres*
Lee Manges, *Admin Sec*
**EMP:** 9
**SQ FT:** 3,000
**SALES:** 1MM **Privately Held**
**WEB:** www.sterlingtoolmfg.com
**SIC:** 7389 3544 3599 7699 Grinding, precision: commercial or industrial; forms (molds), for foundry & plastics working machinery; grinding castings for the trade; industrial tool grinding

### (G-1306)
### SWISS AUTOMATION INC
1020 W Northwest Hwy (60010-2338)
**PHONE**.................................847 381-4405
**Fax:** 847 381-4581
Kenneth Malo, *President*
Saul Vargas, *Opers Mgr*
Chris Sitkowski, *Purch Agent*
Kenneth Moran, *QC Mgr*
Matt Urban, *QC Mgr*
**EMP:** 99
**SQ FT:** 28,000
**SALES (est):** 24MM **Privately Held**
**WEB:** www.swissautomation.com
**SIC:** 3451 Screw machine products

### (G-1307)
### SYSTEMS INTEL
113 Brinker Rd (60010-5103)
**PHONE**.................................847 842-0120
**EMP:** 3
**SALES (est):** 189K **Privately Held**
**SIC:** 3674 Microprocessors

### (G-1308)
### TML INC
223 W Main St (60010-4205)
**PHONE**.................................847 382-1550
Andrew Loughlin, *President*
John McQuillan, *VP Sales*
▲ **EMP:** 2
**SALES (est):** 260.4K **Privately Held**
**SIC:** 3824 Mechanical & electromechanical counters & devices

### (G-1309)
### TOPVOX CORPORATION
600 Hart Rd Ste 260 (60010-2603)
**PHONE**.................................847 842-0900
Andreas Finken, *President*
Rian Appsle, *Project Mgr*
Marceline Appsle, *VP Sls/Mktg*
Marceline Absil, *Marketing Staff*
**EMP:** 500
**SQ FT:** 1,000
**SALES (est):** 491.2K **Privately Held**
**SIC:** 7372 Business oriented computer software

### (G-1310)
### TOTAL LOOK
101 Lions Dr Ste 114 (60010-3147)
**PHONE**.................................847 382-6646
Marcy Lamagnano, *Owner*
**EMP:** 3
**SALES (est):** 198.7K **Privately Held**
**SIC:** 3231 7231 Products of purchased glass; manicurist, pedicurist

## Barry
### Pike County

### (G-1311)
### DEBBIE HARSHMAN
Also Called: Paper, The
725 Bainbridge St (62312-1205)
**PHONE**.................................217 335-2112
**Fax:** 217 335-2112
Debbie Harshman, *Owner*
**EMP:** 3
**SALES (est):** 120K **Privately Held**
**SIC:** 2741 2752 2711 Business service newsletters: publishing & printing; commercial printing, lithographic; newspapers

### (G-1312)
### DYNO NOBEL INC
31879 State Highway 106 (62312-2812)
**PHONE**.................................217 285-5621
Lincoln Hirayama, *General Mgr*
Chen Rui, *General Mgr*
Blake Cecil, *Purch Agent*
Mary Knight, *Purch Agent*
John Tucker, *Technical Mgr*
**EMP:** 11
**SALES (corp-wide):** 2.5B **Privately Held**
**SIC:** 2892 Explosives
**HQ:** Dyno Nobel Inc.
2795 E Cottonwood Pkwy # 500
Salt Lake City UT 84121
801 364-4800

### (G-1313)
### GATES INC
Also Called: Gates Repair & Machine
134 Smith St (62312-1046)
P.O. Box 134 (62312-0134)
**PHONE**.................................217 335-2378
Rob Gates, *President*
Robert Gates, *President*
**EMP:** 4
**SQ FT:** 6,000
**SALES (est):** 330K **Privately Held**
**SIC:** 7537 3599 Automotive transmission repair shops; machine shop, jobbing & repair

## Bartelso
### Clinton County

### (G-1314)
### CHRISTIAN WOLF INC
12618 Pioneer Rd (62218-3003)
**PHONE**.................................618 667-9522
Deanne Norrenberns, *President*
Tim Norrenberns, *Corp Secy*
**EMP:** 7
**SALES:** 175K **Privately Held**
**SIC:** 2052 8661 2099 Cookies; religious organizations; food preparations

## Bartlett
### Cook County

### (G-1315)
### AMERI LABEL COMPANY
2015 Pennsbury Ln (60133-6712)
**PHONE**.................................847 895-8000
**Fax:** 847 895-8003
Ansar Saleem, *President*
Isaac Dean, *Vice Pres*
Syed K Rahimullah, *Vice Pres*
**EMP:** 19
**SQ FT:** 2,500
**SALES:** 1MM **Privately Held**
**SIC:** 2679 Tags & labels, paper

### (G-1316)
### CALCO LTD
960 Muirfield Dr (60133-5457)
**PHONE**.................................630 539-1800
**Fax:** 630 539-1885
Mathew Barlow, *CEO*
Michael Barlow, *President*
Ruth E Barlow, *Admin Sec*
▲ **EMP:** 10
**SQ FT:** 45,000
**SALES (est):** 2.1MM **Privately Held**
**WEB:** www.calcoltd.com
**SIC:** 3589 Water treatment equipment, industrial

### (G-1317)
### CALPORT AVIATION COMPANY
4n220 84 Ct (60133-9200)
P.O. Box 793, Bloomingdale (60108-0793)
**PHONE**.................................630 588-8091
Christopher Brown, *President*
**EMP:** 2
**SALES:** 600K **Privately Held**
**SIC:** 3728 Aircraft parts & equipment

### (G-1318)
### INFORMATION RESOURCES INC
1201 Nashua Ln (60133-5524)
**PHONE**.................................312 474-3154
Ramesh Wadhwani, *President*
**EMP:** 259
**SALES (corp-wide):** 610.8MM **Privately Held**
**SIC:** 7372 7374 Prepackaged software; data entry service
**PA:** Information Resources, Inc
150 N Clinton St
Chicago IL 60661
312 726-1221

### (G-1319)
### MIDWEST PIPE SUPPORTS INC
2171 Newport Cir (60133-5185)
**PHONE**.................................630 665-6400
Bernie Querubin, *President*
Rodrigo Querubin, *Admin Sec*
**EMP:** 4
**SQ FT:** 3,700
**SALES (est):** 422.1K **Privately Held**
**SIC:** 3498 3443 Fabricated pipe & fittings; fabricated plate work (boiler shop)

### (G-1320)
### NOOR INTERNATIONAL INC
2015 Pennsbury Ln (60133-6712)
**PHONE**.................................847 985-2300
**Fax:** 630 895-8003
Fazzu Saleem, *President*
Max Saleem, *Vice Pres*
Mohammed Saleem, *Vice Pres*
Syed Rash, *Admin Sec*
**EMP:** 7
**SQ FT:** 3,700
**SALES (est):** 685.1K **Privately Held**
**WEB:** www.noorinternational.net
**SIC:** 2759 5112 2672 2671 Business forms: printing; business forms; coated & laminated paper; packaging paper & plastics film, coated & laminated

### (G-1321)
### PENTAIR FLTRTION SOLUTIONS LLC
1040 Muirfield Dr (60133-5468)
**PHONE**.................................630 307-3000
Peter Gorr, *Mktg Dir*
Michael Madsen, *Manager*
**EMP:** 4
**SALES (corp-wide):** 14.5B **Publicly Held**
**SIC:** 3589 Water purification equipment, household type
**HQ:** Pentair Filtration Solutions, Llc
1040 Muirfield Dr
Hanover Park IL 60133
630 307-3000

### (G-1322)
### R & J SYSTEMS INC
1580 Birch Ave (60133-3704)
**PHONE**.................................630 289-3010
Richard D Stephens, *President*
**EMP:** 5
**SALES:** 100K **Privately Held**
**SIC:** 7372 Prepackaged software

### (G-1323)
### UNI ELECTRIC ENTERPRISE INC
1889 Seneca Dr (60133-6751)
**PHONE**.................................630 372-6312
Trinidad Acasio Jr, *President*
**EMP:** 3
**SALES (est):** 189.4K **Privately Held**
**SIC:** 3694 Battery cable wiring sets for internal combustion engines

### (G-1324)
### VEGA TECHNOLOGY & SYSTEMS
Also Called: Vtsi
7980 Kingsbury Dr (60133-2348)
**PHONE**.................................630 855-5068
Vincent Y Chow, *Principal*
**EMP:** 6

**SALES:** 300K **Privately Held**
**WEB:** www.sutechoptical.com
**SIC:** 3827 8742 Optical instruments & lenses; management consulting services

### (G-1325)
### WESTROCK CP LLC
965 Muirfield Dr (60133-5458)
**PHONE**.................................630 924-0104
Randy Haberman, *General Mgr*
Jim Griesbach, *Manager*
**EMP:** 50
**SALES (corp-wide):** 14.1B **Publicly Held**
**WEB:** www.smurfit-stone.com
**SIC:** 2631 Paperboard mills
**HQ:** Westrock Cp, Llc
504 Thrasher St
Norcross GA 30071

### (G-1326)
### WESTROCK CP LLC
965 Muirfield Dr (60133-5458)
**PHONE**.................................630 924-0054
**Fax:** 630 924-1338
Dan Bulich, *Plant Mgr*
Todd Carroll, *Plant Mgr*
Randy Habermann, *Manager*
Kevin O'Conner, *Maintence Staff*
Kevin O'Connor, *Maintence Staff*
**EMP:** 57
**SALES (corp-wide):** 14.1B **Publicly Held**
**SIC:** 2653 2631 Corrugated & solid fiber boxes; paperboard mills
**HQ:** Westrock Cp, Llc
504 Thrasher St
Norcross GA 30071

## Bartlett
### Dupage County

### (G-1327)
### A-B DIE MOLD INC
5n701 Meadowlark Dr (60103-2012)
**PHONE**.................................847 658-1199
Alan Kaspar, *President*
Barbara Kaspar, *Treasurer*
Deidree Spirling, *Office Mgr*
**EMP:** 13
**SQ FT:** 10,000
**SALES (est):** 1MM **Privately Held**
**SIC:** 3544 7389 Special dies, tools, jigs & fixtures; industrial molds; special dies & tools; grinding, precision: commercial or industrial

### (G-1328)
### ABRASIVE WEST LLC
1292 Humbracht Cir Ste F (60103-1688)
**PHONE**.................................630 736-0818
Kenneth L Kummer, *CEO*
**EMP:** 8
**SALES (est):** 597.6K **Privately Held**
**SIC:** 7389 3841 Grinding, precision: commercial or industrial; surgical & medical instruments; holders, surgical needle

### (G-1329)
### ALICONA CORPORATION
1261 Humbracht Cir Ste G (60103-1647)
**PHONE**.................................630 372-9900
Stefan Scherer, *President*
Mark Raleigh, *Vice Pres*
**EMP:** 3
**SALES (est):** 547.1K
**SALES (corp-wide):** 23.5MM **Privately Held**
**SIC:** 3827 Microscopes, except electron, proton & corneal
**PA:** Alicona Imaging Gmbh
Dr.-Auner-StraBe 21a
Raaba 8074
316 403-0107

### (G-1330)
### ALICONA MANUFACTURING INC
1261 Humbracht Cir Ste A (60103-1632)
**PHONE**.................................630 736-2718
Stefan Scherer, *President*
Mark Raleigh, *Principal*
**EMP:** 3
**SQ FT:** 10,000

SALES (est): 318.2K **Privately Held**
SIC: 3599 3841 Electrical discharge machining (EDM); surgical & medical instruments

### (G-1331)
### ASSURANCE TECHNOLOGIES INC
Also Called: Roentgen Industrial
1251 Humbracht Cir Ste A (60103-1693)
PHONE.................................630 550-5000
Kenneth J Losacco, *President*
Ryan Losacco, *Regl Sales Mgr*
Eric Baumler, *Sales Engr*
Ian Main, *Consultant*
Maria A Losacco, *Admin Sec*
**EMP:** 12 **EST:** 1985
**SQ FT:** 6,500
**SALES (est):** 3.3MM **Privately Held**
WEB: www.atiquality.com
SIC: 3829 3844 3545 Gauging instruments, thickness ultrasonic; X-ray apparatus & tubes; machine tool accessories

### (G-1332)
### ATI OLDCO INC (DH)
Also Called: Auto Truck
1420 Brewster Creek Blvd (60103-1695)
PHONE.................................630 860-5600
E James Dondlinger, *President*
Michael G McCotter, *Vice Pres*
Dennis Jones, *Manager*
▲ **EMP:** 115
**SQ FT:** 103,000
**SALES (est):** 67.1MM
**SALES (corp-wide):** 1.6B **Privately Held**
SIC: 3713 Truck bodies & parts
HQ: Auto Truck Group, Llc
  1420 Brewster Creek Blvd
  Bartlett IL 60103
  630 860-5600

### (G-1333)
### AUTO TRUCK GROUP LLC (DH)
Also Called: Auto Truck Grp Wyn Flt Equipme
1420 Brewster Creek Blvd (60103-1695)
PHONE.................................630 860-5600
James Dondlinger, *President*
Brad Blanco, *Vice Pres*
Joe Monteleone, *Plant Mgr*
John Smulski, *Opers Mgr*
Mike Macik, *Opers Staff*
▲ **EMP:** 200
**SQ FT:** 105,000
**SALES:** 220MM
**SALES (corp-wide):** 1.6B **Privately Held**
SIC: 3713 1541 Truck bodies & parts; truck & automobile assembly plant construction
HQ: Automotive Rentals, Inc.
  4001 Leadenhall Rd
  Mount Laurel NJ 08054
  856 778-1500

### (G-1334)
### AYLA GROUP INC
1262 Dunamon Dr (60103-1949)
PHONE.................................630 954-9432
**EMP:** 5
**SALES (est):** 11.1K **Privately Held**
SIC: 3944 8748 1731 3663 Games, toys & children's vehicles; communications consulting; communications specialization; radio broadcasting & communications equipment; antennas, transmitting & communications; fiber optics communications equipment

### (G-1335)
### BBS AUTOMATION CHICAGO INC
Also Called: Ixmation North America
1580 Hecht Ct (60103-1691)
PHONE.................................630 351-3000
Michael Macsek, *President*
Steve Vogel, *General Mgr*
Carl Tauberman, *Buyer*
Sean Richter, *Purchasing*
Marcus Ludwig, *CFO*
▲ **EMP:** 150
**SQ FT:** 79,450

**SALES (est):** 39.6MM
**SALES (corp-wide):** 274.9K **Privately Held**
WEB: www.ixmation.com
SIC: 3599 8711 Custom machinery; designing; ship, boat, machine & product
HQ: Ixmation Ag
  Industriestrasse 27
  Kestenholz SO 4703

### (G-1336)
### BEHR PROCESS CORPORATION
950 S Il Route 59 (60103-1668)
PHONE.................................630 289-6247
Tim Fisher, *Principal*
**EMP:** 59
**SALES (corp-wide):** 7.3B **Publicly Held**
SIC: 2851 Paints & paint additives
HQ: Behr Process Corporation
  3400 W Segerstrom Ave
  Santa Ana CA 92704

### (G-1337)
### BREMSKERL NORTH AMERICA INC
1291 Humbracht Cir (60103-1606)
PHONE.................................847 289-3460
Reinhard Gramatke, *President*
John Konrad, *General Mgr*
Debra Daun, *Manager*
Horst Bruhnke, *Officer*
▲ **EMP:** 5
**SQ FT:** 45,000
**SALES (est):** 1.2MM
**SALES (corp-wide):** 34.6MM **Privately Held**
SIC: 3714 Motor vehicle brake systems & parts
PA: Bremskerl-Reibbelagwerke Emmerling Gmbh & Co. Kg
  Brakenhof 7
  Estorf 31629
  502 597-80

### (G-1338)
### CHEESE MERCHANTS AMERICA LLC
1301 Schiferl Rd (60103-1701)
PHONE.................................630 221-0580
Robert Greco, *President*
Jim Smart, *Exec VP*
Brian Barrett, *CFO*
Tom Haws, *Manager*
Gene Yekelchik, *Info Tech Dir*
◆ **EMP:** 315
**SQ FT:** 277,000
**SALES (est):** 104.9MM **Privately Held**
WEB: www.cheesemerchants.com
SIC: 5143 2022 Cheese; cheese, natural & processed

### (G-1339)
### CREA AND CREA
1115 Struckman Blvd (60103-1724)
PHONE.................................630 292-5625
Scott Crea, *Principal*
**EMP:** 2
**SALES (est):** 203K **Privately Held**
SIC: 2431 Millwork

### (G-1340)
### CREATIVE WERKS LLC
1350 Munger Rd (60103-1698)
PHONE.................................630 860-2222
Brian Scott, *Branch Mgr*
**EMP:** 30
**SALES (corp-wide):** 75MM **Privately Held**
SIC: 3999 Novelties, bric-a-brac & hobby kits
PA: Creative Werks Llc
  222 Sievert Ct
  Bensenville IL 60106
  630 860-2222

### (G-1341)
### DIVERSEY INC
1564 Old Barn Rd Fl 5 (60103-2082)
PHONE.................................262 631-4001
**EMP:** 69
**SALES (corp-wide):** 6.7B **Publicly Held**
SIC: 2842 Specialty cleaning, polishes & sanitation goods

HQ: Diversey, Inc.
  2415 Cascade Pointe Blvd
  Charlotte NC 28208
  262 631-4001

### (G-1342)
### DYCO-TEC PRODUCTS LTD (PA)
29w600 Schick Rd (60103-2003)
PHONE.................................630 837-6410
John Dyer Jr, *President*
Sandy Dyer, *Vice Pres*
John W Dyer Sr, *Technical Staff*
Joan G Dyer, *Advisor*
**EMP:** 4
**SQ FT:** 2,000
**SALES (est):** 1.1MM **Privately Held**
WEB: www.dycosote.com
SIC: 5085 2851 Ink, printers'; lacquers, varnishes, enamels & other coatings

### (G-1343)
### EDM DEPT INC
Also Called: EDM Department
1261 Humbracht Cir Ste A (60103-1632)
PHONE.................................630 736-0531
Fax: 630 736-0530
Mark Raleigh, *President*
John Wank, *Vice Pres*
Susan Raleigh, *Administration*
**EMP:** 15
**SQ FT:** 3,000
**SALES (est):** 900K **Privately Held**
WEB: www.edmdept.com
SIC: 3315 Steel wire & related products

### (G-1344)
### ELGO ELECTRONIC INC
1261 Hardt Cir (60103-1690)
PHONE.................................630 626-1639
Alexander Scherr, *Principal*
**EMP:** 3 **EST:** 2010
**SALES (est):** 242.1K **Privately Held**
SIC: 3679 Electronic components

### (G-1345)
### ELITE WIREWORKS CORPORATION
Also Called: Active Wireworks
1239 Humbracht Cir (60103-1606)
PHONE.................................630 837-9100
Fax: 630 837-2751
Eugene R Kudron, *President*
Larry Steker, *Manager*
**EMP:** 10
**SQ FT:** 25,000
**SALES (est):** 1.5MM **Privately Held**
WEB: www.activewireworks.com
SIC: 3496 Miscellaneous fabricated wire products

### (G-1346)
### ENBARR LLC
431 Ford Ln (60103-6612)
PHONE.................................630 217-2101
Marvin Peplow, *Mng Member*
**EMP:** 2
**SQ FT:** 500
**SALES (est):** 1.2MM **Privately Held**
SIC: 3087 Custom compound purchased resins

### (G-1347)
### EXAMINER PUBLICATIONS INC
Also Called: Examiner, The
4n781 Gerber Rd (60103-2021)
P.O. Box 8287 (60103-8287)
PHONE.................................630 830-4145
Randall Petrik, *President*
**EMP:** 5
**SQ FT:** 1,200
**SALES (est):** 270K **Privately Held**
WEB: www.examinerpublications.com
SIC: 2711 Newspapers: publishing only, not printed on site

### (G-1348)
### FORNO PALESE BAKING COMPANY
1235 Humbracht Cir Ste 1 (60103-1683)
PHONE.................................630 595-5502
Andrew Lerario, *CEO*
Joeseph Lerario, *President*
Mark Cello Lerario, *CFO*
Daniela Cirafica, *Manager*
**EMP:** 13 **EST:** 2013

**SALES (est):** 1.3MM **Privately Held**
SIC: 2053 Croissants, frozen

### (G-1349)
### GLENWOOD TOOL & MOLD INC
1251 Humbracht Cir Ste D (60103-1693)
PHONE.................................630 289-3400
Glen Pari, *President*
Luke Turrilli, *Vice Pres*
Alicison Pari, *Admin Sec*
**EMP:** 17
**SQ FT:** 10,000
**SALES (est):** 3.8MM **Privately Held**
WEB: www.glenwoodtool.com
SIC: 3544 Industrial molds

### (G-1350)
### GLOBAL TRACK PROPERTY USA INC
Also Called: Global Track Warehouse USA
31w300 W Bartlett Rd (60103-1253)
P.O. Box 8295 (60103-8295)
PHONE.................................630 213-6863
Barry Min, *President*
Kurt Belinski, *Manager*
◆ **EMP:** 5
**SALES (est):** 1.7MM **Privately Held**
SIC: 5082 3531 Construction & mining machinery; construction machinery attachments

### (G-1351)
### GMK FINISHING
1967 Southfield Dr (60103-1332)
PHONE.................................630 837-0568
Fax: 630 837-0739
George Keith, *President*
**EMP:** 5
**SQ FT:** 4,000
**SALES (est):** 390K **Privately Held**
SIC: 7389 7641 2431 Finishing services; furniture repair & maintenance; millwork

### (G-1352)
### HERRMANN ULTRASONICS INC
1261 Hardt Cir (60103-1690)
PHONE.................................630 626-1626
Thomas Herrmann, *President*
Walter Ochs, *Principal*
Don Kuechler, *Manager*
Uwe Peregi, *Admin Sec*
**EMP:** 35
**SQ FT:** 16,000
**SALES (est):** 8MM **Privately Held**
WEB: www.herrmannultrasonics.com
SIC: 5084 3699 Welding machinery & equipment; welding machines & equipment, ultrasonic

### (G-1353)
### ILLINOIS TOOL WORKS INC
Also Called: ITW Brands
1452 Brewster Creek Blvd (60103-1695)
PHONE.................................630 372-2150
**EMP:** 104
**SALES (corp-wide):** 13.6B **Publicly Held**
SIC: 3089 3965 3499 2891 Injection molded finished plastic products; closures, plastic; synthetic resin finished products; fasteners; strapping, metal; adhesives & sealants; refrigeration & heating equipment
PA: Illinois Tool Works Inc.
  155 Harlem Ave
  Glenview IL 60025
  847 724-7500

### (G-1354)
### IMAGE CUSTOM DRAPERY
137 Amherst Dr (60103-4640)
PHONE.................................630 837-0107
William Berg, *President*
Linda Berg, *Vice Pres*
**EMP:** 3
**SALES (est):** 291.7K **Privately Held**
SIC: 2591 Drapery hardware & blinds & shades

### (G-1355)
### IMCOPEX
1271 Humbracht Cir (60103-1606)
PHONE.................................630 980-1015
Edmond Ciaglia, *Manager*
**EMP:** 8

**Bartlett - Dupage County (G-1356)**

SALES (est): 781.4K **Privately Held**
SIC: 3861 Developing machines & equipment, still or motion picture

**(G-1356)**
**INDUSTRIAL ELECTRIC SVC INC (PA)**
1055 Martingale Dr (60103-5621)
PHONE .................................. 708 997-2090
Raeesa Rahman, *President*
EMP: 1
SALES: 1.2MM **Privately Held**
SIC: 5063 3613 Panelboards; switchboards; panelboards & distribution boards, electric; switchboard apparatus, except instruments

**(G-1357)**
**INDUSTRIAL PHRM RESOURCES INC (PA)**
Also Called: I P R
1241 Hardt Cir (60103-1690)
PHONE .................................. 630 823-4700
Fax: 630 823-4701
Joseph Dougherty, *President*
Jo Ann Garcia, *Controller*
Jo A Grci, *Controller*
Juanita Gallet, *Manager*
EMP: 12
SQ FT: 20,000
SALES (est): 5.1MM **Privately Held**
WEB: www.iprinc.net
SIC: 8711 7372 5084 3559 Consulting engineer; prepackaged software; industrial machine parts; pharmaceutical machinery

**(G-1358)**
**JW SEALANTS INC**
1478 Beaumont Cir (60103-2972)
PHONE .................................. 630 398-1010
Jacek Robak, *Principal*
EMP: 4
SALES (est): 425.1K **Privately Held**
SIC: 2891 Sealants

**(G-1359)**
**KEEPER THERMAL BAG CO INC**
1006 Poplar Ln (60103-5649)
PHONE .................................. 630 213-0125
Eleanor Workman, *President*
Michael Leel, *Vice Pres*
EMP: 6
SQ FT: 2,500
SALES: 600K **Privately Held**
WEB: www.keeperthermalbags.com
SIC: 2393 Bags & containers, except sleeping bags: textile

**(G-1360)**
**M L RONGO INC**
1281 Humbracht Cir Ste A (60103-1623)
PHONE .................................. 630 540-1120
Michael L Rongo, *President*
Jeffrey D Rongo, *Vice Pres*
Greb Straumann, *CFO*
Selena Rongo, *Treasurer*
Kathleen Albrecht, *Manager*
EMP: 25 EST: 1956
SQ FT: 20,000
SALES (est): 4.6MM **Privately Held**
WEB: www.mlrongo.com
SIC: 2599 Carts, restaurant equipment; interior designer

**(G-1361)**
**MARK YOUR SPACE INC**
1235 Humbracht Cir Ste 9 (60103-1683)
PHONE .................................. 630 289-7082
Michael P Sobel, *President*
EMP: 2 EST: 2009
SALES: 300K **Privately Held**
SIC: 3993 Signs & advertising specialties

**(G-1362)**
**MEDICAL RADIATION CONCEPTS**
857 Marina Ter W (60103-4741)
P.O. Box 123, Wood Dale (60191-0123)
PHONE .................................. 630 289-1515
EMP: 4
SALES (est): 365.4K **Privately Held**
SIC: 3844 Mfg X-Ray Apparatus/Tubes

**(G-1363)**
**MIDWEST MOLDING INC**
1560 Hecht Ct (60103-1691)
PHONE .................................. 224 208-1110
Pat Patel, *President*
Hitesh Patel, *Vice Pres*
Mayur Patel, *Admin Sec*
EMP: 60
SQ FT: 120,000
SALES: 25MM **Privately Held**
WEB: www.mwmolding.com
SIC: 3089 Plastic processing

**(G-1364)**
**NU AGAIN**
494 E Thornwood Dr (60103)
PHONE .................................. 630 564-5590
Nathan Rothlisberger, *Owner*
EMP: 10
SALES (est): 693.8K **Privately Held**
WEB: www.nuagain.com
SIC: 2491 Wood preserving

**(G-1365)**
**PROMARK INTERNATIONAL INC (PA)**
Also Called: Smith-Victor
1268 Humbracht Cir (60103-1631)
PHONE .................................. 630 830-2500
Fax: 630 830-2525
Kenneth M Orlando, *President*
Keith Frisk, *Opers Mgr*
Bob Higgins, *Purch Agent*
Brad Burnett, *Electrical Engi*
Mark Prior, *CFO*
▲ EMP: 60
SALES: 14.3MM **Privately Held**
WEB: www.smithvictor.com
SIC: 3861 Tripods, camera & projector; stands, camera & projector

**(G-1366)**
**PSI SYSTEMS NORTH AMERICA INC**
1243 Humbracht Cir (60103-1606)
PHONE .................................. 630 830-9435
Matthew Wind, *President*
Elizabeth Yaksich, *Admin Sec*
▲ EMP: 5
SALES (est): 767.9K **Privately Held**
SIC: 3432 Faucets & spigots, metal & plastic

**(G-1367)**
**RANA MEAL SOLUTIONS LLC**
550 S Spitzer Rd (60103-6700)
PHONE .................................. 630 581-4100
Octavio Lopez, *Maintenance Dir*
Kevin Poore, *Mfg Staff*
EMP: 16
SALES (corp-wide): 362.9MM **Privately Held**
SIC: 2033 Spaghetti & other pasta sauce: packaged in cans, jars, etc.
HQ: Rana Meal Solutions, Llc
1400 16th St Ste 275
Oak Brook IL 60523
630 581-4100

**(G-1368)**
**RELIABLE ASPHALT CORPORATION**
2252 Southwind Blvd (60103-1304)
PHONE .................................. 630 497-8700
EMP: 3
SALES (corp-wide): 2.2MM **Privately Held**
SIC: 2951 Asphalt & asphaltic paving mixtures (not from refineries)
PA: Reliable Asphalt Corporation
3741 S Pulaski Rd
Chicago IL 60623
773 254-1121

**(G-1369)**
**ROBERT BRYSIEWICZ INCORPORATED**
Also Called: R B Engineering
956 S Bartlett Rd Ste 261 (60103-6500)
PHONE .................................. 630 289-0903
Robert Brysiewicz, *President*
EMP: 2
SALES (est): 478.8K **Privately Held**
SIC: 5084 3549 Industrial machinery & equipment; metalworking machinery

**(G-1370)**
**S & D PRODUCTS INC**
1390 Schiferl Rd (60103-1701)
PHONE .................................. 630 372-2325
David J Guanci, *President*
Cindy Flora, *Sales Mgr*
Kathleen Guanci, *Admin Sec*
EMP: 25 EST: 1957
SQ FT: 65,000
SALES (est): 5.6MM **Privately Held**
WEB: www.sdproducts.com
SIC: 3429 Manufactured hardware (general)

**(G-1371)**
**S+S INSPECTION INC**
1234 Hardt Cir (60103-1690)
PHONE .................................. 770 493-9332
Helmuth Frisch, *CEO*
Karin Campbell, *CFO*
Tracy Murphy, *Accountant*
Hans Michael Kraus, *Admin Sec*
Sandy Stillmaker, *Admin Asst*
▲ EMP: 6
SALES (est): 521.5K **Privately Held**
SALES (corp-wide): 654.5MM **Privately Held**
SIC: 3443 Separators, industrial process: metal plate
HQ: Sesotec Gmbh
Regener Str. 130
Schonberg 94513
855 430-80

**(G-1372)**
**SELECT TOOL & DIE INC**
1261 Humbracht Cir Ste F (60103-1632)
PHONE .................................. 630 372-0300
Fax: 630 543-7660
Robert Siemer, *President*
EMP: 5
SALES (est): 500.5K **Privately Held**
SIC: 3544 Special dies & tools

**(G-1373)**
**SENIOR HOLDINGS INC (HQ)**
Also Called: SEI
300 E Devon Ave (60103-4608)
PHONE .................................. 630 837-1811
Fax: 630 837-0027
Michael W Sheppard, *CEO*
Jim Mestan, *President*
Malik Shaze, *Business Mgr*
Ross Huntley, *COO*
Paul Henderson, *Vice Pres*
◆ EMP: 137
SQ FT: 350,000
SALES (est): 490.6MM
SALES (corp-wide): 1.1B **Privately Held**
WEB: www.senior-flexonics.com
SIC: 3599 2821 Hose, flexible metallic; tubing, flexible metallic; bellows, industrial: metal; polytetrafluoroethylene resins (teflon)

**(G-1374)**
**SENIOR OPERATIONS LLC**
Senior Automotives
300 E Devon Ave (60103-4608)
PHONE .................................. 630 837-1811
Ross Huntley, *Opers Staff*
Jerry Davis, *Purch Mgr*
Mike Shepherd, *Manager*
Randy Gleson, *Technology*
EMP: 600
SALES (corp-wide): 1.1B **Privately Held**
SIC: 3599 Machine shop, jobbing & repair
HQ: Senior Operations Llc
300 E Devon Ave
Bartlett IL 60103
630 837-1811

**(G-1375)**
**SENIOR OPERATIONS LLC (HQ)**
Also Called: Senior Flexonics
300 E Devon Ave (60103-4608)
PHONE .................................. 630 837-1811
Fax: 630 837-0105
David Squires, *CEO*
Mike Sheppard, *President*
Amy Legenza, *Vice Pres*
Hong Spanek, *Accounts Mgr*
▲ EMP: 400
SQ FT: 430,000
SALES: 326.9MM
SALES (corp-wide): 1.1B **Privately Held**
WEB: www.seniorplc.com
SIC: 3599 Hose, flexible metallic; tubing, flexible metallic; bellows, industrial: metal

**(G-1376)**
**SENIOR PLC**
Also Called: Senior Automotive
300 E Devon Ave (60103-4608)
PHONE .................................. 630 372-3511
Mark Rollins, *Mng Member*
Scott Swich, *Manager*
Randy Gleason, *Manager*
EMP: 5
SALES (corp-wide): 1.1B **Privately Held**
SIC: 3599 8711 Amusement park equipment; engineering services
PA: Senior Plc
59-61 High Street
Rickmansworth HERTS WD3 1

**(G-1377)**
**SIGNET SIGN COMPANY**
608 White Oak Ln (60103-2123)
PHONE .................................. 630 830-8242
Gary W Zale, *President*
EMP: 5
SALES (est): 490.4K **Privately Held**
SIC: 3993 5046 5099 1799 Electric signs; neon signs; signs, electrical; signs, except electric; sign installation & maintenance

**(G-1378)**
**SPEEDOTRON CORPORATION**
1268 Humbracht Cir (60103-1631)
PHONE .................................. 630 246-5001
Fax: 312 421-5079
Jerry B Schutt, *President*
Paul L Schutt, *Corp Secy*
Tom Schultz, *Chief Mktg Ofcr*
▲ EMP: 4
SQ FT: 20,000
SALES (est): 1.5MM **Privately Held**
WEB: www.speedotron.com
SIC: 3861 Photoflash equipment, except lamps
PA: Promark International, Inc.
1268 Humbracht Cir
Bartlett IL 60103

**(G-1379)**
**SUFFOLK BUSINESS GROUP INC**
132 N Prospect Ave (60103-4363)
PHONE .................................. 847 404-2486
Carroll McLeod, *President*
EMP: 3
SQ FT: 350
SALES: 800K **Privately Held**
WEB: www.sbgdist.com
SIC: 3825 Analog-digital converters, electronic instrumentation type

**(G-1380)**
**THERMO FISHER SCIENTIFIC INC**
Also Called: Barnant
1230 Hardt Cir (60103-1690)
PHONE .................................. 847 381-7050
Tammy Klymkowych, *Buyer*
Margie Ostrowski, *QC Mgr*
Brian Kasch, *Engineer*
Rob Rymarczyk, *Engineer*
Ian Osharow, *Finance*
EMP: 89
SALES (corp-wide): 18.2B **Publicly Held**
WEB: www.thermo.com
SIC: 3561 Pumps & pumping equipment
PA: Thermo Fisher Scientific Inc.
168 3rd Ave
Waltham MA 02451
781 622-1000

**(G-1381)**
**TROPHIES BY GEORGE**
239 Cedarfield Dr (60103-1316)
PHONE .................................. 630 497-1212
Jamie George, *Owner*
EMP: 2
SALES: 300K **Privately Held**
SIC: 3914 5999 7389 Trophies; trophies, plated (all metals); trophies & plaques; engraving service

## GEOGRAPHIC SECTION

**(G-1382)**
**TWO CONSULTING**
329 Windsor Dr (60103-5177)
PHONE..................630 830-2415
Tim Osberg, *Owner*
**EMP:** 3
**SALES (est):** 154.8K **Privately Held**
**SIC:** 8748 3999 Business consulting; advertising display products

**(G-1383)**
**UNIQUE BLISTER COMPANY**
1296 Humbracht Cir (60103-1631)
PHONE..................630 289-1232
Sue Young, *President*
**EMP:** 12
**SALES (est):** 1.2MM **Privately Held**
**WEB:** www.uniqueblister.com
**SIC:** 3081 3565 Packing materials, plastic sheet; packaging machinery

**(G-1384)**
**V AND F TRANSFORMER CORP (PA)**
Also Called: V&F Transformer
31w222 W Bartlett Rd (60103-9504)
PHONE..................630 497-8070
Fax: 630 497-8076
Dean Foderaro, *CEO*
Francis Foderaro, *President*
Leann Millar, *CFO*
Trent Hoban, *Manager*
▲ **EMP:** 85 **EST:** 1962
**SQ FT:** 30,000
**SALES (est):** 22.7MM **Privately Held**
**WEB:** www.vf-transformer.com
**SIC:** 3612 3677 5063 Specialty transformers; electronic coils, transformers & other inductors; electrical apparatus & equipment

**(G-1385)**
**VISION SALES INCORPORATED (PA)**
Also Called: Stewart S Pritikin Associates
1264 Appaloosa Way (60103-1872)
PHONE..................630 483-1900
Stewart Pritikin, *President*
Jaca-Lynn Pritikin, *Admin Sec*
▲ **EMP:** 1
**SALES (est):** 832.6K **Privately Held**
**SIC:** 5039 3315 Wire fence, gates & accessories; wire & fabricated wire products

**(G-1386)**
**WESTROCK MWV LLC**
Also Called: Westrock Healthcare
1534 Stockton Ct (60103-2938)
PHONE..................630 289-8537
**EMP:** 234
**SALES (corp-wide):** 14.1B **Publicly Held**
**WEB:** www.meadwestvaco.com
**SIC:** 2631 Linerboard
**HQ:** Westrock Mwv, Llc
501 S 5th St
Richmond VA 23219
804 444-1000

**(G-1387)**
**WINHERE BRAKE PARTS INC**
1331 Schiferl Rd (60103-1701)
PHONE..................630 307-0158
**EMP:** 3
**SALES (est):** 95.9K **Privately Held**
**SIC:** 3714 Brake drums, motor vehicle

**(G-1388)**
**WITTENSTEIN INC**
1249 Humbracht Cir (60103-1606)
PHONE..................630 540-5300
Peter Riehle, *CEO*
Dave Lax, *Engineer*
Maria Jesionowski, *Controller*
Dan Sheba, *Technology*
Brian Dunkel, *Admin Sec*
▲ **EMP:** 30
**SALES (est):** 9.2MM
**SALES (corp-wide):** 336.4MM **Privately Held**
**WEB:** www.wittenstein-us.com
**SIC:** 3566 Speed changers, drives & gears
**PA:** Wittenstein Se
Walter-Wittenstein-Str. 1
Igersheim 97999
793 149-30

**(G-1389)**
**WITTENSTEIN ARSPC SMLATION INC (PA)**
1249 Humbracht Cir (60103-1606)
PHONE..................630 540-5300
Manfred Wittenstein, *President*
Brian Dunkel, *CFO*
Annabelle Block, *Credit Mgr*
Stephanie Dzielawa, *Credit Mgr*
Jim Nivagh, *Manager*
**EMP:** 1
**SALES (est):** 957.3K **Privately Held**
**SIC:** 3728 3699 Aircraft parts & equipment; link trainers (aircraft training mechanisms); aircraft training equipment; flight simulators (training aids), electronic; electronic training devices

### Bartonville
### Peoria County

**(G-1390)**
**ALTER TRADING CORPORATION**
Also Called: Alter Recycling
7000 S Adams St Ste 2 (61607-2856)
P.O. Box 4164, Peoria (61607-0164)
PHONE..................309 697-6161
Bev Curtis, *Personnel Exec*
Chad Chatman, *Manager*
**EMP:** 18
**SALES (corp-wide):** 850.2MM **Privately Held**
**WEB:** www.altertrading.com
**SIC:** 4953 3341 Recycling, waste materials; secondary nonferrous metals
**HQ:** Alter Trading Corporation
700 Office Pkwy
Saint Louis MO 63141
314 872-2400

**(G-1391)**
**ALTORFER POWER SYSTEMS**
Also Called: Caterpillar Authorized Dealer
6315 W Fauber Rd (61607-1001)
PHONE..................309 697-1234
Fax: 309 282-2345
Bob Metzinger, *Principal*
Doug Richardson, *Vice Pres*
Ryan Roehm, *Purch Agent*
Paul Schneider, *Sales Staff*
Diane Roehm, *Supervisor*
▲ **EMP:** 2
**SALES (est):** 1MM **Privately Held**
**SIC:** 3621 7353 5082 Motors & generators; heavy construction equipment rental; construction & mining machinery

**(G-1392)**
**BARTONVILLE EQUIPMENT RENTAL**
7301 S Adams St (61607-2713)
PHONE..................309 633-0227
**EMP:** 2 **EST:** 2009
Craig S Dodd, *Owner*
**SALES (est):** 218.4K **Privately Held**
**SIC:** 3524 Lawn & garden equipment

**(G-1393)**
**CUSTOM GRAPHICS INC (PA)**
4100 Ricketts Ave (61607-2347)
PHONE..................309 633-0850
Fax: 309 633-0852
Doug Bartelmay, *President*
Doug Bartelmay, *President*
Mike Creed, *VP Sales*
Renee Lendman, *Admin Sec*
**EMP:** 22
**SQ FT:** 12,000
**SALES (est):** 3MM **Privately Held**
**SIC:** 2759 Flexographic printing

**(G-1394)**
**CUSTOM PLASTICS OF PEORIA**
4623 Enterprise Dr (61607-2760)
PHONE..................309 697-2888
Fax: 309 633-0680
Kevin Flessner, *President*
Robert Scott, *Vice Pres*
**EMP:** 4
**SQ FT:** 4,000
**SALES (est):** 400K **Privately Held**
**SIC:** 3083 5051 3082 3081 Plastic finished products, laminated; sheets, metal; aluminum bars, rods, ingots, sheets, pipes, plates, etc.; tubing, metal; unsupported plastics profile shapes; unsupported plastics film & sheet

**(G-1395)**
**J FRANCIS & ASSOC**
4603 Carol Ct (61607-1508)
PHONE..................309 697-5931
Suzanne Zircher, *President*
Jeff Zircher, *Corp Secy*
**EMP:** 3
**SALES (est):** 55K **Privately Held**
**SIC:** 3541 Electrical discharge erosion machines

**(G-1396)**
**LOYALTY PUBLISHING INC**
Also Called: Skyline Publishing
4414 Entec Dr (61607-2779)
PHONE..................309 693-0840
Rodney Lindsay, *President*
Jacy Jester, *Admin Sec*
**EMP:** 50
**SALES (est):** 3.8MM **Privately Held**
**WEB:** www.loyalty-publishing.com
**SIC:** 2741 Miscellaneous publishing

**(G-1397)**
**MIDWEST CNSTR SVCS INC PEORIA (PA)**
4200 Ricketts Ave (61607-2314)
P.O. Box 4185, Peoria (61607-0185)
PHONE..................309 697-1000
Fax: 309 697-1004
Sheila Shover, *President*
Donald D Shover, *Exec VP*
John Miller, *Vice Pres*
Daniel White II, *Vice Pres*
**EMP:** 18
**SQ FT:** 32,000
**SALES (est):** 3.5MM **Privately Held**
**SIC:** 3531 5085 7353 Construction machinery; industrial supplies; heavy construction equipment rental

**(G-1398)**
**ORBIS RPM LLC**
4428 Ricketts Ave (61607-2651)
PHONE..................309 697-1549
**EMP:** 4
**SALES (corp-wide):** 1.8B **Privately Held**
**SIC:** 3081 Polypropylene film & sheet
**HQ:** Orbis Rpm, Llc
1055 Corporate Center Dr
Oconomowoc WI 53066
262 560-5000

**(G-1399)**
**VERTICAL SOFTWARE INC**
409 Keller St (61607-2556)
PHONE..................309 633-0700
Fax: 309 633-2328
Pat Gilroy, *President*
**EMP:** 12
**SALES (est):** 1.6MM **Privately Held**
**WEB:** www.verticalsoftware.net
**SIC:** 7372 7379 Business oriented computer software; computer related consulting services
**PA:** The Paragon Corporation
3100 W Harmon Hwy
Peoria IL

**(G-1400)**
**XTREME DZIGNZ**
4001 Constitution Dr (61607-2863)
PHONE..................309 633-9311
Rhonda Condre, *Principal*
**EMP:** 3
**SALES (est):** 237.6K **Privately Held**
**SIC:** 2759 Screen printing

### Batavia
### Kane County

**(G-1401)**
**3 PENGUINS LTD**
609 Millview Dr (60510-3085)
PHONE..................630 528-7086
Tom Gorr, *Vice Pres*
**EMP:** 2
**SALES (est):** 203.2K **Privately Held**
**SIC:** 2759 Screen printing

**(G-1402)**
**ACCEL CORPORATION**
900 Douglas Rd (60510-2294)
PHONE..................630 579-6961
Fax: 630 579-6959
Dwight Morgan, *CEO*
**EMP:** 50
**SALES (corp-wide):** 228.1MM **Privately Held**
**WEB:** www.accelcolor.com
**SIC:** 2816 Color pigments
**HQ:** Accel Corporation
38620 Chester Rd
Avon OH 44011

**(G-1403)**
**ACCURIDE CORPORATION**
Also Called: Accuride Distribution Center
950 N Raddant Rd (60510-4209)
PHONE..................630 454-4299
Carl Keller, *Branch Mgr*
**EMP:** 243
**SALES (corp-wide):** 111.2MM **Privately Held**
**SIC:** 3714 Wheels, motor vehicle
**HQ:** Accuride Corporation
7140 Office Cir
Evansville IN 47715
812 962-5000

**(G-1404)**
**AGCO CORPORATION**
1500 N Raddant Rd (60510-1377)
PHONE..................630 406-3248
Fax: 630 406-3285
John Sloan, *Purch Dir*
Erwin Yee, *Purch Mgr*
Jeffery Grinnell, *Senior Buyer*
T H Harney, *Purchasing*
K Rudin, *Human Res Mgr*
**EMP:** 50
**SALES (corp-wide):** 7.4B **Publicly Held**
**WEB:** www.agcocorp.com
**SIC:** 3523 Farm machinery & equipment
**PA:** Agco Corporation
4205 River Green Pkwy
Duluth GA 30096
770 813-9200

**(G-1405)**
**AGGRESIVE MOTOR SPORTS**
Also Called: Optek
201 Oswald Ave (60510-9320)
PHONE..................630 761-1550
Nicks Sotola, *President*
**EMP:** 7
**SALES (est):** 619.1K **Privately Held**
**SIC:** 3471 Polishing, metals or formed products

**(G-1406)**
**AGGRESSIVE MOTORSPORTS INC**
Also Called: Diamond Coat
227 Oswald Ave (60510-9320)
PHONE..................847 846-7488
Nicholas Sotola, *President*
**EMP:** 5
**SALES:** 750K **Privately Held**
**SIC:** 3479 Metal coating & allied service

**(G-1407)**
**AGS TECHNOLOGY INC**
951 Douglas Rd (60510-2295)
PHONE..................847 534-6600
Fax: 847 534-6570
Christopher Racelis, *President*
Aras George Staniulis, *Vice Pres*
Ramon Racelis, *Shareholder*
Ruta Staniulis, *Admin Sec*
▲ **EMP:** 40
**SQ FT:** 79,000
**SALES (est):** 8.5MM **Privately Held**
**WEB:** www.agstechnology.com
**SIC:** 3089 Injection molding of plastics

**(G-1408)**
**ALLOYD BRANDS**
1500 Paramount Pkwy (60510-1468)
PHONE..................843 383-7000
Bruce Dusing, *Design Engr*

# Batavia - Kane County (G-1409)

**EMP:** 3 **EST:** 2010
**SALES (est):** 75.4K **Privately Held**
**SIC:** 2675 Die-cut paper & board

## (G-1409)
### ALTERNATIVE WASTEWATER SYSTEMS
1815 Phelps Dr (60510-1519)
P.O. Box 4375, Wheaton (60189-4375)
**PHONE**..................................630 761-8720
Donald Savegnago, *President*
**EMP:** 3
**SALES (corp-wide):** 1.7MM **Privately Held**
**SIC:** 3589 1711 Sewage & water treatment equipment; septic system construction
**PA:** Alternative Wastewater Systems Inc
1111 Delles Rd
Wheaton IL 60189
630 668-8584

## (G-1410)
### AMAV ENTERPRISES LTD
Also Called: Diamant Toys Unlimited
1921 W Wilson St Ste A (60510-3195)
**PHONE**..................................630 761-3077
Asher Diamant, *President*
Kovy Diamant, *Vice Pres*
Michael Sochaccevski, *Treasurer*
Rich Vreeland, *Sales Dir*
Colleen Staniszewski, *Manager*
▲ **EMP:** 1
**SQ FT:** 450
**SALES (est):** 8.6MM **Privately Held**
**WEB:** www.amav.com
**SIC:** 3944 Games, toys & children's vehicles
**PA:** Diamant Toys Ltd.
29 Hacharoshet
Ashdod

## (G-1411)
### AMCOR RIGID PLASTICS USA LLC
1300 S River St (60510-9647)
**PHONE**..................................630 406-3500
Robert Healy, *Plant Mgr*
Bob Healy, *Manager*
**EMP:** 30
**SALES (corp-wide):** 9.4B **Privately Held**
**SIC:** 3085 Plastics bottles
**HQ:** Amcor Rigid Plastics Usa, Llc
935 Technology Dr Ste 100
Ann Arbor MI 48108

## (G-1412)
### AMCOR RIGID PLASTICS USA LLC
Also Called: Ball Plastic Container Div
1300 S River St (60510-9647)
**PHONE**..................................630 406-3500
**EMP:** 14
**SALES (corp-wide):** 9.6B **Privately Held**
**SIC:** 3411 Mfg Metal Cans
**HQ:** Amcor Rigid Plastics Usa, Llc
10521 Mi State Road 52
Manchester MI 48108

## (G-1413)
### AMERICAN BOXBOARD LLC
1400 Paramount Pkwy (60510-1463)
**PHONE**..................................708 924-9810
J Clayton Shaw, *Mng Member*
Joe Bloom, *Admin Asst*
**EMP:** 40
**SALES (est):** 5.9MM **Privately Held**
**SIC:** 2653 Boxes, corrugated: made from purchased materials

## (G-1414)
### AMERICAN NATIONAL CAN CO
1300 S River St (60510-9647)
**PHONE**..................................630 406-3500
**Fax:** 630 406-3552
Cindy Ward, *Principal*
**EMP:** 7 **EST:** 2010
**SALES (est):** 859.2K **Privately Held**
**SIC:** 3085 Plastics bottles

## (G-1415)
### ANDERSON & MARTER CABINETS
Also Called: A & M Cabinets
845 E Wilson St (60510-2204)
**PHONE**..................................630 406-9840
Brad Anderson, *President*
Joel Marter, *Treasurer*
**EMP:** 4
**SQ FT:** 1,200
**SALES (est):** 430K **Privately Held**
**SIC:** 2599 2541 2517 2434 Cabinets, factory; wood partitions & fixtures; wood television & radio cabinets; wood kitchen cabinets; cabinet & finish carpentry

## (G-1416)
### APPLE GRAPHICS INC
934 Paramount Pkwy (60510-1453)
**PHONE**..................................630 389-2222
Kyle Hempel, *Sales Dir*
Roberto Ayala, *Manager*
**EMP:** 4
**SQ FT:** 4,000
**SALES (est):** 600K **Privately Held**
**SIC:** 2752 2791 2789 Commercial printing, offset; typesetting; bookbinding & related work

## (G-1417)
### ASCON CORP
472 Ridgelawn Trl (60510-8680)
**PHONE**..................................630 482-2950
Steven Rakers, *President*
Leonardo Zecchel, *Vice Pres*
Chris Rakers, *Office Mgr*
**EMP:** 3
**SALES (est):** 327.9K **Privately Held**
**WEB:** www.asconcorp.com
**SIC:** 3823 Temperature measurement instruments, industrial

## (G-1418)
### AUBREY SIGN CO INC
1847 Suncast Ln (60510-1518)
**PHONE**..................................630 482-9901
**Fax:** 630 482-9906
Michael Hoffer, *President*
Jeanne Hoffer, *Corp Secy*
**EMP:** 4
**SQ FT:** 1,800
**SALES (est):** 280K **Privately Held**
**WEB:** www.aubreysigns.com
**SIC:** 3993 Signs & advertising specialties

## (G-1419)
### BATAVIA CONTAINER INC
1400 Paramount Pkwy (60510-1463)
P.O. Box 550 (60510-0550)
**PHONE**..................................630 879-2100
**Fax:** 630 879-2494
J Clayton Shaw, *President*
Dave Widmer, *Plant Mgr*
Gabe Latham, *Project Mgr*
Charles Wasinger, *Treasurer*
Judy Gerlick, *Accountant*
**EMP:** 150
**SQ FT:** 160,000
**SALES (est):** 50.9MM **Privately Held**
**WEB:** www.bataviacontainer.com
**SIC:** 2653 Boxes, corrugated: made from purchased materials

## (G-1420)
### BATAVIA FOUNDRY AND MACHINE CO
717 First St (60510-2409)
P.O. Box 6 (60510-0006)
**PHONE**..................................630 879-1319
**Fax:** 630 879-1320
Scott Peterson, *President*
**EMP:** 5 **EST:** 1964
**SALES:** 1MM **Privately Held**
**SIC:** 3369 Nonferrous foundries

## (G-1421)
### BEVSTREAM CORP
Also Called: 1 Engineering
600 Kingsland Dr (60510-2298)
**PHONE**..................................630 761-0060
Robert Capua, *President*
Aira Capua, *Finance Mgr*
◆ **EMP:** 8

**SALES (est):** 1.8MM **Privately Held**
**SIC:** 3312 3585 Pipes & tubes; refrigeration & heating equipment

## (G-1422)
### BFC FORMS SERVICE INC
1051 N Kirk Rd (60510-1438)
**PHONE**..................................630 879-9240
Joseph Novak Jr, *President*
Matthew Novak, *Corp Secy*
Brad Novak, *Vice Pres*
Ann Weichbrodt, *Accountant*
Laura Pogwizd, *HR Admin*
**EMP:** 115 **EST:** 1975
**SQ FT:** 19,000
**SALES (est):** 33.9MM **Privately Held**
**WEB:** www.bfcprint.com
**SIC:** 2752 5112 Commercial printing, offset; business forms

## (G-1423)
### BFC PRINT
1051 N Kirk Rd (60510-1438)
**PHONE**..................................630 879-9240
Laura Pogwizd, *HR Admin*
Robin Urich, *Accounts Exec*
Steve Vogg, *Sales Executive*
Jeff Harwood, *Marketing Staff*
Keith Kanak, *Manager*
**EMP:** 11 **EST:** 2011
**SALES (est):** 1.4MM **Privately Held**
**SIC:** 2752 Commercial printing, lithographic

## (G-1424)
### BRASEL PRODUCTS INC
715 Hunter Dr (60510-1425)
P.O. Box 97 (60510-0097)
**PHONE**..................................630 879-3759
**Fax:** 630 879-6912
Melody Brasel Davoust, *President*
Mark Davoust, *Vice Pres*
Dawnmarie Griffin, *Office Mgr*
**EMP:** 9 **EST:** 1947
**SQ FT:** 9,700
**SALES (est):** 1.6MM **Privately Held**
**WEB:** www.brasel.com
**SIC:** 3842 2672 2295 Gauze, surgical; bandages: plastic, muslin, plaster of paris, etc.; coated & laminated paper; coated fabrics, not rubberized

## (G-1425)
### BYUS STEEL INC
1750 Hubbard Ave (60510-1424)
**PHONE**..................................630 879-2200
**Fax:** 630 879-2267
Bruno Gentile, *President*
Javier Huerta, *Manager*
Alisa Middendorf, *Manager*
Carol Gentile, *Admin Sec*
**EMP:** 20
**SQ FT:** 18,000
**SALES (est):** 5.9MM **Privately Held**
**SIC:** 3441 Fabricated structural metal

## (G-1426)
### CAST ALUMINUM SOLUTIONS LLC
1310 Kingsland Dr (60510-1327)
**PHONE**..................................630 482-5325
Liem McDonough, *COO*
John Bloch, *Engineer*
David Cuthbertson, *Engineer*
Jesse Mondigo, *Engineer*
James Nihei, *Design Engr*
▲ **EMP:** 60
**SALES (est):** 26.8MM **Privately Held**
**SIC:** 3363 Aluminum die-castings

## (G-1427)
### CCL LABEL (CHICAGO) INC
Also Called: Sertech
1862 Suncast Ln (60510-1516)
**PHONE**..................................630 406-9991
Jeff Adeszko, *President*
Bill McDonough, *Vice Pres*
**EMP:** 50
**SQ FT:** 23,000
**SALES:** 13.9MM
**SALES (corp-wide):** 188.4K **Privately Held**
**WEB:** www.thunder-press.com
**SIC:** 2752 Commercial printing, offset

**HQ:** Ccl Industries Inc
105 Gordon Baker Rd Suite 500
North York ON M2H 3
416 756-8500

## (G-1428)
### CFC WIRE FORMS INC
1000 Douglas Rd (60510-2278)
**PHONE**..................................630 879-7575
**Fax:** 630 879-0707
Casimir Czekajlo, *President*
Ward Brown, *Opers Mgr*
Beata Nowak, *Production*
Bernard Czekajlo, *Treasurer*
Mark Schultz, *Manager*
▲ **EMP:** 26
**SQ FT:** 60,000
**SALES (est):** 6.7MM **Privately Held**
**WEB:** www.cfcwireforms.com
**SIC:** 3312 3496 3495 Wire products, steel or iron; miscellaneous fabricated wire products; wire springs

## (G-1429)
### CHALLENGER LIGHTING CO INC
1400 Kingsland Dr (60510-1375)
**PHONE**..................................847 717-4700
**Fax:** 847 717-4720
Bonnie Proctor, *CEO*
Bruce Barna, *President*
Vicky Martin, *General Mgr*
Matt Proctor, *General Mgr*
▲ **EMP:** 42
**SQ FT:** 28,000
**SALES (est):** 10.1MM **Privately Held**
**WEB:** www.challengerlighting.com
**SIC:** 3646 Commercial indusl & institutional electric lighting fixtures; chandeliers, commercial; fluorescent lighting fixtures, commercial; ornamental lighting fixtures, commercial

## (G-1430)
### CISKE & DRESCH
1125 Paramount Pkwy Ste F (60510-4417)
**PHONE**..................................630 251-9200
Rudy Dresch, *President*
Agnes Dresch, *Corp Secy*
Victoria Dresch, *Vice Pres*
**EMP:** 3
**SQ FT:** 2,600
**SALES (est):** 199.9K **Privately Held**
**SIC:** 3471 Plating of metals or formed products; gold plating

## (G-1431)
### CLEAN SWEEP ENVIRONMENTAL INC
1805 Phelps Dr (60510-1519)
**PHONE**..................................630 879-8750
**Fax:** 630 879-3373
Bertram Hochsprung, *President*
Ryan Hochsprung, *Admin Sec*
**EMP:** 9
**SQ FT:** 10,000
**SALES (est):** 840K **Privately Held**
**SIC:** 2951 7521 Asphalt paving mixtures & blocks; composition blocks for paving; parking lots

## (G-1432)
### COMPLETE MOLD POLISHING INC
1219 Paramount Pkwy (60510-1458)
**PHONE**..................................630 406-7668
Roger A Delarche, *President*
Susan M Delarche, *Admin Sec*
**EMP:** 4
**SQ FT:** 2,000
**SALES (est):** 466.2K **Privately Held**
**SIC:** 3544 Industrial molds

## (G-1433)
### CONVEYOR INSTALLATIONS INC
1723 E Wilson St (60510-1470)
**PHONE**..................................630 859-8900
Daniel W Ross, *President*
**EMP:** 16
**SALES (est):** 4.1MM **Privately Held**
**SIC:** 3535 Conveyors & conveying equipment

## GEOGRAPHIC SECTION
## Batavia - Kane County (G-1459)

**(G-1434)**
**COSVEYOR INC**
1723 E Wilson St (60510-1470)
PHONE..................630 859-8900
Daniel Ross, *President*
EMP: 10
SALES (est): 1.5MM **Privately Held**
SIC: 3535 Conveyors & conveying equipment

**(G-1435)**
**CUSTOM CUTTINGEDGE TOOL INC**
1217 Paramount Pkwy (60510-1458)
PHONE..................847 622-0457
Fax: 847 622-0458
John Sitarz, *Owner*
Robert Mesa, *Corp Secy*
Jacki Breh, *Manager*
EMP: 4
SALES (est): 400K **Privately Held**
SIC: 3545 Machine tool accessories

**(G-1436)**
**CYBERBOND LLC**
401 N Raddant Rd (60510-4221)
PHONE..................630 761-0341
Fax: 630 761-8989
Larry Serkanic, *President*
Mark Conway, *General Mgr*
Brent Bierman, *Regional Mgr*
Joe Silvestro, *Exec VP*
Anthony Stloukal, *Opers Staff*
◆ EMP: 50
SQ FT: 20,000
SALES (est): 11.3MM **Privately Held**
WEB: www.cyberbond1.com
SIC: 2891 Adhesives

**(G-1437)**
**DAY INTERNATIONAL GROUP INC**
1333 N Kirk Rd (60510-1444)
PHONE..................630 406-6501
EMP: 65
SALES (corp-wide): 3.8B **Privately Held**
SIC: 3069 Printers' rolls & blankets: rubber or rubberized fabric
HQ: Day International Group, Inc.
14909 N Beck Rd
Plymouth MI 48170

**(G-1438)**
**DIMPLES DONUTS**
328 E Wilson St (60510-2663)
PHONE..................630 406-0303
Henry Charles, *Owner*
EMP: 4
SALES (est): 153.2K **Privately Held**
SIC: 5461 2051 Doughnuts; doughnuts, except frozen

**(G-1439)**
**DON JOHNS INC (PA)**
701 N Raddant Rd (60510-4218)
PHONE..................630 326-9650
Fax: 312 666-3384
Brian Byrne, *President*
Logan Surles, *Vice Pres*
Allan Gdalman, *Engineer*
Wayne Craig, *Branch Mgr*
Raymond A Pouse, *Director*
EMP: 23 EST: 1950
SQ FT: 12,500
SALES (est): 13.2MM **Privately Held**
WEB: www.donjohns.com
SIC: 5087 5084 3613 3625 Liquor dispensing equipment & systems; pneumatic tools & equipment; control panels, electric; control equipment, electric

**(G-1440)**
**DORAN SCALES INC**
1315 Paramount Pkwy (60510-1460)
PHONE..................630 879-1200
Mark Podl, *President*
Peter Siegrist, *Vice Pres*
Jerry Thielman, *QC Mgr*
Tom Whyte, *Design Engr*
Dorothy Pool, *Treasurer*
◆ EMP: 23
SQ FT: 20,000
SALES: 5.3MM **Privately Held**
WEB: www.doranscales.com
SIC: 3596 Weighing machines & apparatus

**(G-1441)**
**DOUBLE D PRINTING INC**
103 S Lincoln St (60510-2466)
PHONE..................630 406-8666
Fax: 630 795-0147
Mark Davis, *President*
Keith Davis, *Vice Pres*
EMP: 8
SQ FT: 5,000
SALES: 750K **Privately Held**
SIC: 2711 Newspapers, publishing & printing

**(G-1442)**
**DS CONTAINERS INC**
1789 Hubbard Ave (60510-1423)
PHONE..................630 406-9600
Fax: 630 406-1438
Isamu Yamaguchi, *President*
Sarah Howard, *President*
John Duffy, *Vice Pres*
Matt Kuehn, *Vice Pres*
Bill Smith Jr, *Vice Pres*
▲ EMP: 175
SALES (est): 63.8MM **Privately Held**
WEB: www.dscontainers.net
SIC: 3411 Metal cans

**(G-1443)**
**DU-CALL MILLER PLASTICS INC**
901 N Batavia Ave Ste 3 (60510-2195)
PHONE..................630 964-6020
Fax: 630 964-4110
William C Miller III, *President*
Linnea Miller, *Treasurer*
EMP: 10
SQ FT: 15,730
SALES (est): 840K **Privately Held**
WEB: www.du-call.com
SIC: 3089 3161 2441 Thermoformed finished plastic products; luggage; nailed wood boxes & shook

**(G-1444)**
**DYNAMESH INC**
512 Kingsland Dr (60510-2299)
PHONE..................630 293-5454
Fax: 630 293-5647
Shinya Yhamasaski, *President*
Hideaki Hayashi, *General Mgr*
Shane Waltmyer, *General Mgr*
Hiroyasu Takahashi, *Corp Secy*
Taisuke Shimosako, *Finance Dir*
▲ EMP: 25
SQ FT: 18,000
SALES (est): 4MM
SALES (corp-wide): 4.7B **Privately Held**
WEB: www.dynamesh.com
SIC: 2759 5131 5084 Screen printing; piece goods & other fabrics; industrial machinery & equipment
HQ: Nbc Meshtec Inc.
2-50-3, Toyoda
Hino TKY 191-0
425 822-411

**(G-1445)**
**E P M SALES CO INC**
280 Belleview Ln (60510-9678)
PHONE..................630 761-2051
Keith Schauer, *President*
EMP: 20
SALES (est): 2.7MM **Privately Held**
WEB: www.epmsales.com
SIC: 3559 Plastics working machinery

**(G-1446)**
**ELITE CUSTOM WOODWORKING**
219 S Water St (60510-2558)
PHONE..................630 888-4322
Jeff Schaaf, *Principal*
EMP: 4
SALES (est): 451.7K **Privately Held**
SIC: 2431 Millwork

**(G-1447)**
**FIDELITY TOOL & MOLD LTD (PA)**
1885 Suncast Ln (60510-1510)
PHONE..................630 879-2300
Fax: 630 879-2345
James Vassar, *President*
Matt Sorensen, *Plant Mgr*
Randy Vassar, *Foreman/Supr*
Lorry Vassar, *Bookkeeper*
▲ EMP: 18
SQ FT: 10,000
SALES (est): 5.8MM **Privately Held**
WEB: www.fidelitytool.com
SIC: 3544 Special dies & tools; industrial molds

**(G-1448)**
**FLEX-PAK PACKAGING PRODUCTS**
651 N Raddant Rd (60510-4219)
PHONE..................630 761-3335
Fax: 630 761-3336
William J Reimann, *President*
Joyce E Reimann, *Corp Secy*
EMP: 10 EST: 1978
SQ FT: 16,800
SALES (est): 1.9MM **Privately Held**
WEB: www.flex-pak.biz
SIC: 2673 Bags: plastic, laminated & coated

**(G-1449)**
**FLINN SCIENTIFIC INC**
770 N Raddant Rd (60510-4208)
P.O. Box 219 (60510-0219)
PHONE..................800 452-1261
Fax: 630 879-8696
Larry Flinn, *President*
Lawrence C Flinn III, *President*
Margaret Flinn, *Chairman*
Patrick J Flinn, *Vice Pres*
Gregg Dvorak, *Safety Mgr*
◆ EMP: 219
SALES (est): 96.8MM **Privately Held**
SIC: 3821 5049 Laboratory equipment: fume hoods, distillation racks, etc.; laboratory equipment, except medical or dental

**(G-1450)**
**FLINT GROUP US LLC**
1333 N Kirk Rd (60510-1444)
PHONE..................630 526-9903
Jack Ackerman, *Branch Mgr*
Bob Kopp, *Maintence Staff*
EMP: 25
SALES (corp-wide): 3.8B **Privately Held**
WEB: www.flintink.com
SIC: 2893 Printing ink
PA: Flint Group Us Llc
14909 N Beck Rd
Plymouth MI 48170
734 781-4600

**(G-1451)**
**GORDON HANN**
154 W Wilson St (60510-1945)
PHONE..................630 761-1835
Gordon Hann, *Owner*
EMP: 33
SALES (est): 2.2MM **Privately Held**
SIC: 2051 Bakery: wholesale or wholesale/retail combined

**(G-1452)**
**GREEN LADDER TECHNOLOGIES LLC**
1540 Louis Bork Dr (60510-1512)
PHONE..................630 457-1872
Ken Kubitz, *Managing Dir*
Don Bergeson, *VP Mktg*
John Konieczka, *Mng Member*
Kenneth Kubitz,
EMP: 25
SALES (est): 5.5MM **Privately Held**
SIC: 3822 Auto controls regulating residntl & coml environmt & applncs

**(G-1453)**
**GUST-JOHN FOODS & PDTS CORP**
1350 Paramount Pkwy (60510-1461)
PHONE..................630 879-8700
Gust Koutselas, *President*
John Koutselas, *Treasurer*
Leighann Blasen, *Manager*
EMP: 6 EST: 1973
SQ FT: 10,000
SALES (est): 761.6K **Privately Held**
WEB: www.northern-pines.com
SIC: 2045 2099 Pancake mixes, prepared: from purchased flour; pancake syrup, blended & mixed

**(G-1454)**
**HEMPEL GROUP INC**
934 Paramount Pkwy (60510-1453)
PHONE..................630 389-2222
Keith Hempel, *President*
Roberto Ayala, *General Mgr*
Ken Hempel, *Vice Pres*
EMP: 9
SALES (est): 1MM **Privately Held**
SIC: 2752 Commercial printing, offset

**(G-1455)**
**HENTZEN COATINGS INC**
1500 Lathem St (60510-1449)
PHONE..................414 353-4200
Joanne Coleman, *Human Res Dir*
Thomas Ellis, *Director*
EMP: 22
SALES (corp-wide): 84.3MM **Privately Held**
SIC: 2851 Lacquer: bases, dopes, thinner; enamels; polyurethane coatings; epoxy coatings
PA: Hentzen Coatings, Inc.
6937 W Mill Rd
Milwaukee WI 53218
414 353-4200

**(G-1456)**
**INCON PROCESSING LLC (HQ)**
970 Douglas Rd (60510-2294)
PHONE..................630 305-8556
John R Palmer III, *CEO*
EMP: 30
SQ FT: 30,000
SALES (est): 7.5MM
SALES (corp-wide): 390.8MM **Publicly Held**
WEB: www.incontech.com
SIC: 8734 8731 2819 Testing laboratories; commercial physical research; industrial inorganic chemicals
PA: Omega Protein Corporation
2105 City W Blvd Ste 500
Houston TX 77042
713 623-0060

**(G-1457)**
**INDUSTRIAL CONTROLS INC**
1183 Pierson Dr Ste 105 (60510-1529)
PHONE..................630 752-8100
Fax: 630 752-8110
Ken Arnold, *President*
EMP: 4
SQ FT: 4,000
SALES (est): 430K **Privately Held**
SIC: 8711 5063 3625 1622 Electrical or electronic engineering; electrical apparatus & equipment; motor control accessories, including overload relays; tunnel construction

**(G-1458)**
**INNOVATIVE PLASTECH INC**
1260 Kingsland Dr (60510-1325)
PHONE..................630 232-1808
Joanne Gustafson, *CEO*
James Gustafson, *President*
Edward Gustafson, *Exec VP*
Tracy Wolf, *Vice Pres*
Girish Raval, *Director*
EMP: 67
SQ FT: 90,000
SALES: 13MM **Privately Held**
WEB: www.inplas.com
SIC: 3089 Thermoformed finished plastic products

**(G-1459)**
**J C SCHULTZ ENTERPRISES INC**
Also Called: Flagsource
951 Swanson Dr (60510-4231)
PHONE..................800 323-9127
Fax: 630 406-5932
Janice M Christiansen, *Ch of Bd*
Jon Christiansen, *Vice Pres*
Dyana Beeh, *Credit Mgr*
Elizabeth Parmley, *Sales Staff*
Erin Charmelo, *Marketing Staff*
▲ EMP: 65 EST: 1920
SQ FT: 60,000
SALES (est): 8.4MM **Privately Held**
WEB: www.flagsource.com
SIC: 2399 5051 3446 Flags, fabric; banners, made from fabric; metals service centers & offices; architectural metalwork

**Batavia - Kane County (G-1460)**  **GEOGRAPHIC SECTION**

**(G-1460)**
**KOLORCURE CORPORATION**
1180 Lyon Rd (60510-1365)
PHONE ..................... 630 879-9050
Fax: 630 879-9449
Brian Templeman, *President*
▼ EMP: 20
SQ FT: 20,000
SALES: 6MM **Privately Held**
WEB: www.kolorcure.com
SIC: 2893 Screen process ink

**(G-1461)**
**KON PRINTING INC**
316 E Wilson St (60510-2663)
PHONE ..................... 630 879-2211
Fax: 630 879-2211
Nick Konsbruck, *President*
Mark Konsbruck, *Vice Pres*
EMP: 2
SQ FT: 4,000
SALES: 230K **Privately Held**
WEB: www.konprinting.com
SIC: 2752 2759 Commercial printing, offset; letterpress printing; business forms; printing

**(G-1462)**
**KTURBO USA INC**
1183 Pierson Dr Ste 118 (60510-1562)
PHONE ..................... 630 406-1473
Heon Seok Lee, *CEO*
Kim Woelffer, *General Mgr*
Fiona Shin, *Manager*
David Choe, *Executive*
▲ EMP: 3
SQ FT: 8,000
SALES (est): 549.2K
SALES (corp-wide): 19.2MM **Privately Held**
SIC: 3564 Turbo-blowers, industrial
PA: Kturbo Inc.
Haengjung-Ri
Chongju 28202
432 757-573

**(G-1463)**
**KWALYTI TLING MCHY RBLDING INC**
1690 E Fabyan Pkwy (60510-1492)
PHONE ..................... 630 761-8040
Fax: 630 761-8041
Gordon Erickson, *President*
Pam Cross, *Accountant*
Ed Oreilly, *Sales Associate*
▲ EMP: 18
SQ FT: 22,500
SALES: 5MM **Privately Held**
WEB: www.kwalyti.com
SIC: 5084 3542 Industrial machinery & equipment; rebuilt machine tools, metal forming types

**(G-1464)**
**LIGHTHOUSE MARKETING SERVICES**
115 Flinn St (60510-2471)
PHONE ..................... 630 482-9900
Scott Salvati, *President*
Kimberly Salvati, *Vice Pres*
EMP: 5
SALES (est): 585.5K **Privately Held**
SIC: 2759 Commercial printing

**(G-1465)**
**MAR-TEC RESEARCH INC**
1315 Paramount Pkwy (60510-1460)
PHONE ..................... 630 879-1200
William J Podl, *President*
EMP: 40
SQ FT: 1,500
SALES (est): 3.7MM **Privately Held**
SIC: 3823 8742 Industrial instrmnts msrmnt display/control process variable; industrial consultant

**(G-1466)**
**MASTERFEED CORPORATION**
1326 Hollister Dr (60510-1391)
PHONE ..................... 630 879-1133
Fax: 630 879-1185
Richard Rojic Jr, *President*
Cindy Rojic, *Admin Sec*
EMP: 3
SQ FT: 6,250
SALES: 380K **Privately Held**
SIC: 3559

**(G-1467)**
**MATERIAL CONTROL INC**
525 N River St Ste 100 (60510-2399)
PHONE ..................... 630 892-4274
Keith Clayton, *Controller*
Kurt Pfoutz, *Marketing Staff*
EMP: 15
SQ FT: 16,000
SALES (corp-wide): 69.9MM **Privately Held**
WEB: www.cotterman.com
SIC: 3844 3089 2394 5084 X-ray apparatus & tubes; plastic processing; canvas & related products; materials handling machinery
PA: Material Control Inc.
130 Seltzer Rd
Croswell MI 48422
630 892-4274

**(G-1468)**
**MATTHEW CHRISTOPHER INC**
904 Lusted Ln (60510-2796)
PHONE ..................... 212 938-6820
Matthew Christopher, *President*
EMP: 9 EST: 2015
SALES (est): 550.8K **Privately Held**
SIC: 2335 Wedding gowns & dresses

**(G-1469)**
**MAXON PLASTICS INC**
1069 Kingsland Dr (60510-2290)
PHONE ..................... 630 761-3667
Erika Meisen, *President*
Frank Dullnigg, *Vice Pres*
Sonja Bertone, *Admin Sec*
EMP: 8
SQ FT: 12,500
SALES (est): 1.2MM **Privately Held**
SIC: 3089 Injection molding of plastics

**(G-1470)**
**MIDWEST ICE CREAM COMPANY LLC**
1253 Kingsland Dr (60510-1324)
PHONE ..................... 630 879-0800
Leonard Jackson, *Branch Mgr*
EMP: 9 **Publicly Held**
SIC: 2026 Fluid milk
HQ: Midwest Ice Cream Company, Llc
630 Meadow St
Belvidere IL 61008

**(G-1471)**
**MII INC**
1380 Nagel Blvd (60510-1312)
PHONE ..................... 630 879-3000
Fax: 630 879-3900
Joseph R Kelley, *President*
Linda Kelley, *CFO*
EMP: 14
SQ FT: 14,500
SALES (est): 4.5MM **Privately Held**
WEB: www.masterimpressionsinc.com
SIC: 2621 7336 3565 Printing paper; package design; labeling machines, industrial

**(G-1472)**
**MORAN CRISTOBALIAN**
Also Called: Wimaxspot360.com
549 Peebles Ct (60510-9262)
PHONE ..................... 630 506-4777
Cristobalian Moran, *Owner*
EMP: 3
SALES (est): 144.2K **Privately Held**
SIC: 3663 7389 Antennas, transmitting & communications

**(G-1473)**
**MUSCO SPORTS LIGHTING LLC**
Also Called: Microlite
902 Paramount Pkwy Ste A (60510-4410)
PHONE ..................... 630 876-0500
Darrell Chelcun, *Vice Pres*
Jeff Messer, *Engineer*
Tom Scheu, *Manager*
EMP: 40
SALES (corp-wide): 162.5MM **Privately Held**
SIC: 3648 Lighting equipment; area & sports luminaries
HQ: Musco Sports Lighting, Llc
100 1st Ave W
Oskaloosa IA 52577
641 673-0411

**(G-1474)**
**NAPCO INC**
Also Called: Papanicholas Coffee Company
1141 N Raddant Rd (60510-4214)
P.O. Box 849 (60510-0849)
PHONE ..................... 630 406-1100
Fax: 630 406-0904
Christopher Papanicholas, *President*
Vaughn Papanicholas, *Vice Pres*
Paul Goudreault, *CFO*
James Schlicher, *Admin Sec*
▲ EMP: 24
SQ FT: 20,000
SALES (est): 6.8MM **Privately Held**
WEB: www.papanicholas.com
SIC: 2095 5812 5149 Roasted coffee; eating places; coffee, green or roasted

**(G-1475)**
**NEOMEK INCORPORATED**
Also Called: Neomek Engineering
241 Oswald Ave (60510-9320)
PHONE ..................... 630 879-5400
Bradley Johnson, *President*
David Lajoie, *General Mgr*
James Clark, *Info Tech Mgr*
EMP: 12
SQ FT: 20,000
SALES (est): 1.2MM **Privately Held**
WEB: www.neomek.com
SIC: 8711 3089 3444 Engineering services; plastic containers, except foam; sheet metalwork

**(G-1476)**
**NEON PRISM ELECTRIC SIGN CO**
1213 Paramount Pkwy (60510-1458)
PHONE ..................... 630 879-1010
Fax: 630 879-1018
Tim Phelps, *President*
Eric Smith, *Vice Pres*
EMP: 2
SQ FT: 1,650
SALES: 500K **Privately Held**
SIC: 3993 Neon signs

**(G-1477)**
**ONTARIO DIE USA**
950 Paramount Pkwy Ste 3 (60510-4412)
P.O. Box 69 (60510-0069)
PHONE ..................... 630 761-6562
Fax: 630 761-6564
Pat Kizziah, *General Mgr*
EMP: 10
SALES (est): 1.6MM **Privately Held**
WEB: www.odctooling.com
SIC: 3544 Special dies, tools, jigs & fixtures

**(G-1478)**
**P & L MARK-IT INC (PA)**
Also Called: Mark-It Company
291 Oswald Ave (60510-9394)
PHONE ..................... 630 879-7590
Fax: 630 879-7088
Lance Johnson, *President*
Philip Meere, *Chairman*
Diane Glawe, *Human Res Mgr*
Joe Caffarello, *Marketing Staff*
Mary Bossov, *Art Dir*
▲ EMP: 27
SQ FT: 21,000
SALES (est): 2.2MM **Privately Held**
WEB: www.markitco.com
SIC: 2759 3993 Decals; printing; labels & seals; printing; signs & advertising specialties

**(G-1479)**
**PAMARCO GLOBAL GRAPHICS INC**
125 Flinn St (60510-2471)
PHONE ..................... 630 879-7300
Fax: 630 879-7306
John Clinton, *Opers-Prdtn-Mfg*
Stan Hycner, *Engineer*
Joseph Trungale, *Marketing Staff*
EMP: 25 **Privately Held**
SIC: 3555 2796 Printing trades machinery; platemaking services
HQ: Pamarco Global Graphics, Inc.
235 E 11th Ave
Roselle NJ 07203
908 241-1200

**(G-1480)**
**PARTYLITE INC**
Also Called: R&D
603 Kingsland Dr (60510-4201)
PHONE ..................... 630 845-6025
Loretta Masterson, *Manager*
EMP: 25
SALES (corp-wide): 2.2B **Publicly Held**
WEB: www.blythindustries.com
SIC: 3999 Candles; potpourri
HQ: Partylite, Inc.
59 Armstrong Rd
Plymouth MA 02360
203 661-1926

**(G-1481)**
**PETAINER MANUFACTURING USA INC**
515 N River St Ste 206 (60510-2300)
PHONE ..................... 630 326-9921
Nigel Pritchard, *President*
Marc Kibbey, *Vice Pres*
Jerry Beaudion, *Director*
Mark Ellis, *Admin Sec*
EMP: 10
SQ FT: 2,000
SALES (est): 409.8K **Privately Held**
SIC: 3085 Plastics bottles

**(G-1482)**
**PICNIC TABLES INC**
222 State St (60510-2607)
PHONE ..................... 630 482-6200
Bob Runke, *President*
Andrew White, *Manager*
EMP: 6 EST: 2008
SALES (est): 597.9K **Privately Held**
SIC: 2531 Picnic tables or benches, park

**(G-1483)**
**PITTSBURGH GLASS WORKS LLC**
1020 Olympic Dr (60510-1329)
PHONE ..................... 630 879-5100
Jack Claus, *Branch Mgr*
EMP: 145
SALES (corp-wide): 457.8MM **Privately Held**
SIC: 3211 Flat glass
HQ: Pittsburgh Glass Works, Llc
30 Isabella St Ste 500
Pittsburgh PA 15212

**(G-1484)**
**PMA FRICTION PRODUCTS INC**
880 Kingsland Dr (60510-2296)
PHONE ..................... 630 406-9119
Fax: 630 406-9276
Philip Konrad, *President*
Joan Sweetman, *Controller*
Joan Konrad, *Human Res Mgr*
Paul Konrad, *Sales Mgr*
Donna Shanel, *Manager*
EMP: 60 EST: 1979
SQ FT: 60,000
SALES (est): 13.1MM **Privately Held**
WEB: www.pmautomotiveinc.com
SIC: 3499 Friction material, made from powdered metal

**(G-1485)**
**PPG INDUSTRIES INC**
1020 Olympic Dr (60510-1329)
PHONE ..................... 630 879-5100
Glenn Pulson, *Manager*
EMP: 50
SALES (corp-wide): 14.7B **Publicly Held**
WEB: www.ppg.com
SIC: 2851 Paints & allied products
PA: Ppg Industries, Inc.
1 Ppg Pl
Pittsburgh PA 15272
412 434-3131

**(G-1486)**
**PRIME LABEL GROUP LLC**
1380 Nagel Blvd (60510-1312)
PHONE ..................... 773 630-8793
EMP: 4
SALES (est): 314.4K **Privately Held**
SIC: 2671 Mfg Packaging Paper/Film

## GEOGRAPHIC SECTION
### Batavia - Kane County (G-1511)

**(G-1487)**
**PRODUCERS ENVMTL PDTS LLC**
Also Called: Environmental Solutions Intl
1261 N Raddant Dr (60510-4213)
PHONE..................630 482-5995
Kenneth Arnswald, *VP Sales*
Kent Pullen,
Peter K Whinfrey,
**EMP:** 6  **EST:** 1996
**SQ FT:** 7,000
**SALES (est):** 1.1MM  **Privately Held**
**WEB:** www.esiclean.com
**SIC:** 3589  Commercial cleaning equipment

**(G-1488)**
**QUALITY CNC INCORPORATED**
801 N Raddant Rd (60510-4217)
PHONE..................630 406-0101
**Fax:** 630 406-0102
Greg Johnson, *President*
Peggy Johnson, *Admin Sec*
**EMP:** 11
**SQ FT:** 5,000
**SALES:** 800K  **Privately Held**
**SIC:** 3599  Machine shop, jobbing & repair

**(G-1489)**
**RADCO INDUSTRIES INC (PA)**
700 Kingsland Dr (60510-2297)
P.O. Box 305, Lafox (60147-0305)
PHONE..................630 232-7966
**Fax:** 630 232-7968
Michael Damiani, *CEO*
Tony Corscadden, *VP Opers*
Marsha Barber, *Controller*
Lawrence Kendzior, *VP Finance*
Jed Seybold, *Sales Staff*
**EMP:** 21
**SQ FT:** 9,600
**SALES (est):** 1.7MM  **Privately Held**
**SIC:** 2819  Industrial inorganic chemicals

**(G-1490)**
**RANDAL WOOD DISPLAYS INC**
Also Called: Randal Retail Group
507 N Raddant Rd (60510-4220)
PHONE..................630 761-0400
**Fax:** 630 761-0404
Chris Randazzo, *President*
Chuck Bray, *Vice Pres*
Thea R Sakelaris, *Vice Pres*
Chris Breedlove, *Project Mgr*
Kurt Hermes, *Project Mgr*
▲ **EMP:** 65  **EST:** 1981
**SALES (est):** 15.6MM  **Privately Held**
**WEB:** www.randaldisplays.com
**SIC:** 2541  7389  4225  1796  Cabinets, except refrigerated: show, display, etc.: wood; counters or counter display cases, wood; shelving, office & store, wood; showcases, except refrigerated: wood; design services; general warehousing & storage; installing building equipment

**(G-1491)**
**RENU ELECTRONICS PRIVATE LTD**
336 Mckee St (60510-1920)
PHONE..................630 879-8412
Ajay Bhagwat, *President*
Wayne B Petersen, *General Mgr*
Sanjay Madkar, *Prdtn Mgr*
Shailesh Vyawahare, *VP Finance*
Girish Ghate, *Sales Mgr*
**EMP:** 2
**SQ FT:** 500
**SALES (est):** 347.9K  **Privately Held**
**WEB:** www.renuelectronics.com
**SIC:** 3559  Electronic component making machinery

**(G-1492)**
**RMF PRODUCTS INC**
1275 Paramount Pkwy (60510-1458)
P.O. Box 520 (60510-0520)
PHONE..................630 879-0020
**Fax:** 630 879-6749
Richard M Frieders, *President*
**EMP:** 2
**SQ FT:** 7,500
**SALES:** 300K  **Privately Held**
**WEB:** www.exhibitionforms.com
**SIC:** 3861  Photographic equipment & supplies

**(G-1493)**
**SCHAEFER TECHNOLOGIES LLC**
751 N Raddant Rd (60510-4218)
PHONE..................630 406-9377
Wyatt George, *Vice Pres*
Scott Rizzi, *Engineer*
Karen Lopeman, *Manager*
**EMP:** 6
**SQ FT:** 2,500
**SALES (est):** 829.9K  **Privately Held**
**SIC:** 3545  Machine tool accessories
**HQ:** Schafer Werkzeug- Und Sondermaschinenbau Gmbh
Dr.-Alfred-Weckesser-Str. 6
Bad Schonborn 76669
725 394-210

**(G-1494)**
**SCIMATCO OFFICE**
770 N Raddant Rd (60510-4208)
P.O. Box 305 (60510-0305)
PHONE..................630 879-1306
Patrick Flinn, 
Rebecca Greiner, *Purchasing*
Kevin McNulty, *Marketing Staff*
**EMP:** 50
**SALES (est):** 3.3MM  **Privately Held**
**WEB:** www.scimatco.com
**SIC:** 3999  Barber & beauty shop equipment

**(G-1495)**
**SEALY INC**
1030 E Fabyan Pkwy (60510-1410)
PHONE..................630 879-8011
**Fax:** 630 879-9105
Rick Stallman, *Safety Mgr*
Ray Pozecinski, *Manager*
Linda Vaznonis, *Administration*
Tom Krantz, *Maintence Staff*
Andrea Minton, *Clerk*
**EMP:** 220
**SQ FT:** 101,000
**SALES (corp-wide):** 3.1B  **Publicly Held**
**SIC:** 2515  Mattresses, containing felt, foam rubber, urethane, etc.; mattresses, innerspring or box spring
**HQ:** Sealy Mattress Company
1 Office Parkway Rd
Trinity NC 27370
336 861-3500

**(G-1496)**
**SITECH INC**
1101 N Raddant Rd (60510-4214)
P.O. Box 609, Geneva (60134-0609)
PHONE..................630 761-3640
**Fax:** 630 761-3644
Ramesh D Sheth, *Ch of Bd*
Sandeep Sheth, *Vice Pres*
**EMP:** 12
**SQ FT:** 13,000
**SALES (est):** 2.5MM  **Privately Held**
**WEB:** www.sitechfiber.com
**SIC:** 3357  Fiber optic cable (insulated)

**(G-1497)**
**SPECTRUM COS INTERNATIONAL**
Also Called: Marsh Products
336 Mckee St (60510-1920)
PHONE..................630 879-8008
**Fax:** 630 879-8072
Richard E Marsh, *CEO*
Doug Marsh, *President*
Ruth Marsh, *Corp Secy*
Kathlyn Marsh-Valentine, *Vice Pres*
Kim Valentine, *Vice Pres*
▲ **EMP:** 7
**SQ FT:** 17,000
**SALES (est):** 935.6K  **Privately Held**
**WEB:** www.marshproducts.com
**SIC:** 3625  3663  8731  7389  Control equipment, electric; radio & TV communications equipment; electronic research; design services

**(G-1498)**
**STEVENSON PAPER CO INC**
1775 Hubbard Ave (60510-1423)
PHONE..................630 879-5000
Elizabeth Krohn, *President*
**EMP:** 6  **EST:** 1981
**SQ FT:** 7,500
**SALES:** 1MM  **Privately Held**
**SIC:** 2675  2631  Die-cut paper & board; paperboard mills

**(G-1499)**
**STOKES SAND & GRAVEL INC**
35w160 Butterfield Rd (60510-9338)
PHONE..................815 489-0680
Danny Stokes, *President*
**EMP:** 3
**SALES (est):** 563.9K  **Privately Held**
**SIC:** 1442  Construction sand & gravel

**(G-1500)**
**SUMMIT METAL PRODUCTS INC**
1351 Nagel Blvd (60510-1313)
PHONE..................630 879-7008
**Fax:** 630 879-8068
Herbert Cozad, *President*
**EMP:** 9
**SQ FT:** 23,000
**SALES (est):** 1.1MM  **Privately Held**
**SIC:** 3441  Fabricated structural metal

**(G-1501)**
**SUNCAST CORPORATION (PA)**
701 N Kirk Rd (60510-1433)
PHONE..................630 879-2050
**Fax:** 630 879-6112
Thomas A Tisbo, *President*
Bill Sullivan, *General Mgr*
Mike Hodges, *Superintendent*
Carl Smucker, *Principal*
Michael Hamilton, *Exec VP*
◆ **EMP:** 750
**SQ FT:** 500,000
**SALES (est):** 267.4MM  **Privately Held**
**WEB:** www.suncast.com
**SIC:** 2519  3052  3432  Lawn furniture, except wood, metal, stone or concrete; garden furniture, except wood, metal, stone or concrete; rubber hose; lawn hose nozzles & sprinklers

**(G-1502)**
**SUPERIOR HEALTH LINENS LLC**
1160 Pierson Dr Ste 104 (60510-1527)
PHONE..................630 593-5091
**Fax:** 630 593-5097
Scott Reppert, *CEO*
Steve Shabat, *General Mgr*
Greg Schermerhorn, *COO*
Bill Witowski, *CFO*
Staphnie Hearns, *Office Mgr*
**EMP:** 70
**SALES (est):** 10.1MM  **Privately Held**
**SIC:** 2299  Linen fabrics

**(G-1503)**
**T N T INDUSTRIES INC**
1169 Lyon Rd (60510-1366)
PHONE..................630 879-1522
Ronald Thryselius, *President*
Shirley Thryselius, *Corp Secy*
Bob Giertz, *Accountant*
Kathy Pater, *Office Mgr*
Ed Micheal, *Manager*
**EMP:** 10
**SQ FT:** 13,800
**SALES (est):** 930K  **Privately Held**
**SIC:** 7389  3469  3544  Hand tool designers; stamping metal for the trade; special dies, tools, jigs & fixtures

**(G-1504)**
**TEAM TECHNOLOGIES INC**
1300 Nagel Blvd (60510-1312)
PHONE..................630 937-0380
**Fax:** 630 937-0381
Ashwin Patel, *Manager*
**EMP:** 60
**SALES (corp-wide):** 174.3MM  **Privately Held**
**WEB:** www.naglmfg.com
**SIC:** 3991  3089  Brushes, except paint & varnish; plastic processing
**PA:** Team Technologies, Inc.
5949 Commerce Blvd
Morristown TN 37814
423 587-2199

**(G-1505)**
**TEGRANT CORPORATION**
Also Called: Clarke Div
1500 Paramount Pkwy (60510-1468)
PHONE..................630 879-0121
William Kelly, *President*
Matthew Massett, *Info Tech Mgr*
**EMP:** 100
**SALES (corp-wide):** 4.7B  **Publicly Held**
**WEB:** www.alloyd.com
**SIC:** 2657  Paperboard backs for blister or skin packages
**HQ:** Tegrant Corporation
1401 Pleasant St
Dekalb IL 60115
815 756-8451

**(G-1506)**
**TEK PAK INC (PA)**
1336 Paramount Pkwy (60510-1461)
PHONE..................630 406-0560
**Fax:** 630 406-0577
Anthony Beyer, *President*
Gail Herni, *CFO*
Jeff McAdams, *CFO*
Scott Carter, *Treasurer*
Chad Miller, *Director*
▲ **EMP:** 55
**SQ FT:** 20,000
**SALES (est):** 15.5MM  **Privately Held**
**WEB:** www.nitro-carrier.com
**SIC:** 2672  3086  5084  3559  Tape, pressure sensitive; made from purchased materials; plastics foam products; tapping attachments; plastics working machinery

**(G-1507)**
**TIMEPILOT CORPORATION**
340 Mckee St (60510-1920)
PHONE..................630 879-6400
Douglas F Marsh, *President*
Michael C Hanlon, *Exec VP*
Sheree Womack, *Natl Sales Mgr*
Jody Mann, *Marketing Staff*
Mark Hanlon, *Manager*
**EMP:** 7
**SQ FT:** 1,500
**SALES (est):** 1MM  **Privately Held**
**WEB:** www.timepilot.com
**SIC:** 7372  Business oriented computer software

**(G-1508)**
**TOOL RITE INDUSTRIES INC**
570 S River St (60510-2675)
PHONE..................630 406-6161
Tom Peck, *President*
**EMP:** 6
**SQ FT:** 7,500
**SALES:** 460K  **Privately Held**
**SIC:** 3549  3599  Assembly machines, including robotic; machine shop, jobbing & repair

**(G-1509)**
**TREASURE KEEPER INC**
Also Called: Treasure Keeper X
1355 Paramount Pkwy (60510-1460)
PHONE..................630 761-1500
William Bradley, *President*
Brenda Bradley, *Corp Secy*
Bill Bradley, *Manager*
**EMP:** 4
**SALES (est):** 426.4K  **Privately Held**
**WEB:** www.treasurekeeper.com
**SIC:** 3544  Special dies, tools, jigs & fixtures

**(G-1510)**
**TREETOP MARKETING INC**
Also Called: Park It Bike Racks Company
717 Main St (60510-2434)
PHONE..................877 249-0479
Cyril W Matter, *President*
Emile Garneau, *Manager*
Robert H Runke, *Admin Sec*
**EMP:** 3
**SALES (est):** 319.5K  **Privately Held**
**SIC:** 3429  Bicycle racks, automotive

**(G-1511)**
**TRIANGLE DIES AND SUPPLIES INC (PA)**
1436 Louis Bork Dr (60510-1511)
PHONE..................630 454-3200
**Fax:** 630 761-9480

Joseph Marovich, *President*
Jeff Husom, *Prdtn Mgr*
Mary Polomchak, *Sales Staff*
Eric Moore, *Supervisor*
Debra L Marovich, *Admin Sec*
▲ **EMP:** 60 **EST:** 1955
**SQ FT:** 25,000
**SALES (est):** 10.5MM **Privately Held**
**WEB:** www.tridie.com
**SIC:** 3544 Dies, steel rule

**(G-1512)**
**U S COLORS & COATINGS INC**
1180 Lyon Rd (60510-1365)
**PHONE**..................................630 879-8898
Donald Templeman Sr, *President*
Brian Templeman, *Vice Pres*
**EMP:** 5
**SQ FT:** 10,000
**SALES (est):** 660K **Privately Held**
**WEB:** www.uscolors-coatings.com
**SIC:** 2893 2851 2865 Printing ink; enamels; cyclic crudes & intermediates

**(G-1513)**
**UR INC**
859 Ravinia Ct (60510-3213)
**PHONE**..................................630 450-5279
Janice Carla Hastert, *CEO*
**EMP:** 3
**SALES (est):** 250.9K **Privately Held**
**SIC:** 2087 Powders, drink

**(G-1514)**
**URBAN HOME FURNITURE & ACC INC**
Also Called: Padma's Plantation
1375 Kingsland Dr (60510-1326)
**PHONE**..................................630 761-3200
**Fax:** 630 761-3130
Renee Maria Fanjon, *President*
Brenda J Sypolt, *General Mgr*
David Sypolt, *General Mgr*
Kevin Sypolt, *COO*
▲ **EMP:** 31
**SQ FT:** 48,000
**SALES (est):** 5.8MM **Privately Held**
**WEB:** www.padmasplantation.com
**SIC:** 5021 2511 Furniture; wood lawn & garden furniture

**(G-1515)**
**VANDEVENTER MFG CO INC**
Also Called: Vandee Mfg Co Div
812 Main St (60510-2437)
P.O. Box 249 (60510-0249)
**PHONE**..................................630 879-2511
**Fax:** 630 406-1546
Ronald J Link, *President*
Leland Weaver, *Vice Pres*
**EMP:** 44
**SQ FT:** 45,000
**SALES (est):** 7.7MM **Privately Held**
**SIC:** 3451 3599 Screw machine products; machine shop, jobbing & repair

**(G-1516)**
**VARN INTERNATIONAL INC**
Also Called: Day International
1333 N Kirk Rd (60510-1444)
**PHONE**..................................630 406-6501
Grant Pieper, *VP Mfg*
Dwight Neas, *Purch Mgr*
Cesar Gonzalez, *Manager*
Marvin McNesse, *Manager*
Stacey Spivey, *Receptionist*
**EMP:** 25
**SALES (corp-wide):** 3.8B **Privately Held**
**SIC:** 5169 2899 Chemicals & allied products; chemical preparations
**HQ:** Varn International Inc
130 W 2nd St Ste 1700
Dayton OH
937 224-4000

## Batchtown
### Calhoun County

**(G-1517)**
**CALHOUN QUARRY INCORPORATED (PA)**
25 Main St (62006)
**PHONE**..................................618 396-2229

Jerome Sievers, *President*
Anthony Sievers, *Vice Pres*
Betty Sievers, *Admin Sec*
**EMP:** 11 **EST:** 1940
**SALES (est):** 1.1MM **Privately Held**
**SIC:** 1422 Limestones, ground

## Beach Park
### Lake County

**(G-1518)**
**LEPPALA MACHINING INC**
12726d W Wadsworth Rd (60087)
**PHONE**..................................847 625-0270
John Kelley, *Principal*
**EMP:** 3
**SALES (est):** 309.4K **Privately Held**
**SIC:** 3599 Machine shop, jobbing & repair

**(G-1519)**
**PRINT GRAPHICS**
37984 N Metropolitan Ave (60087-2062)
**PHONE**..................................847 249-1007
Thomas Greider, *Owner*
Jeff Michels, *Director*
**EMP:** 4
**SALES (est):** 240K **Privately Held**
**WEB:** www.pixelprintgraphics.com
**SIC:** 2759 Commercial printing

## Beardstown
### Cass County

**(G-1520)**
**BEARDSTOWN NEWSPAPERS INC**
Also Called: CASS COUNTY STAR GAZZETTE
1210 Wall St (62618-2327)
P.O. Box 79 (62618-0079)
**PHONE**..................................217 323-1010
**Fax:** 217 323-5402
Murray Cohen, *President*
Bill Mitchell, *Manager*
**EMP:** 7
**SQ FT:** 2,600
**SALES (est):** 529K **Privately Held**
**SIC:** 2711 2741 Newspapers: publishing only, not printed on site; shopping news: publishing only, not printed on site

**(G-1521)**
**CARAUSTAR INDUSTRIAL AND CON**
Also Called: Beardstown Tube Plant
100 Forest Ln (62618-7881)
**PHONE**..................................217 323-5225
Don Ervin, *Plant Mgr*
Eugene Hamilton, *Purchasing*
James E Cook, *Manager*
**EMP:** 58
**SQ FT:** 3,000
**SALES (corp-wide):** 1.5B **Privately Held**
**SIC:** 2655 Tubes, fiber or paper: made from purchased material
**HQ:** Caraustar Industrial And Consumer Products Group Inc
2031 Carolina Place Dr
Fort Mill SC 29708
803 548-5100

**(G-1522)**
**JBS USA LLC**
8295 Arenzville Rd (62618-7859)
**PHONE**..................................217 323-3774
Steve Cirkle, *COO*
Judy Paul, *Safety Mgr*
Fred Harmeyer, *QC Dir*
Patrizia Tolomelli, *QC Mgr*
Michelle White, *Human Resources*
**EMP:** 20 **Privately Held**
**WEB:** www.excelmeats.com
**SIC:** 2011 5147 Meat packing plants; meats & meat products
**HQ:** Jbs Usa Food Company
1770 Promontory Cir
Greeley CO 80634
970 506-8000

**(G-1523)**
**KENT NUTRITION GROUP INC**
8679 Kent Feed Rd (62618-8127)
P.O. Box 260 (62618-0260)
**PHONE**..................................217 323-1216
**Fax:** 217 323-1933
Mike Maberry, *Branch Mgr*
**EMP:** 10
**SALES (corp-wide):** 613.2MM **Privately Held**
**WEB:** www.kentfeeds.com
**SIC:** 2048 Livestock feeds; poultry feeds
**HQ:** Kent Nutrition Group, Inc.
1600 Oregon St
Muscatine IA 52761
866 647-1212

**(G-1524)**
**NEW LINE HARDWOODS INC**
8727 Arenzville Rd (62618-7861)
**PHONE**..................................309 657-7621
Derrick Newman, *President*
**EMP:** 65
**SQ FT:** 400,000
**SALES (est):** 4.6MM **Privately Held**
**SIC:** 2426 Furniture dimension stock, hardwood

**(G-1525)**
**OHARA AUTOGLASS INC**
7339 Drainage Rd (62618-8506)
**PHONE**..................................217 323-2300
Mark O'Hara, *Principal*
**EMP:** 2
**SALES (est):** 212.7K **Privately Held**
**SIC:** 3231 Products of purchased glass

**(G-1526)**
**PAULS MC CULLOCH SALES**
11136 Il Route 125 (62618-7808)
**PHONE**..................................217 323-2159
**Fax:** 217 323-2687
Dale Winkelman, *President*
Sherrie Winkelman, *Admin Sec*
**EMP:** 3
**SALES:** 329K **Privately Held**
**SIC:** 5531 7694 7513 Automotive accessories; automotive parts; motor repair services; truck rental & leasing, no drivers

**(G-1527)**
**RIVERSIDE MEMORIAL CO**
Also Called: Monument Company
216 W 2nd St (62618-1139)
**PHONE**..................................217 323-1280
**Fax:** 217 323-2820
Carl Hood, *Owner*
**EMP:** 3
**SQ FT:** 2,800
**SALES:** 300K **Privately Held**
**SIC:** 5999 3999 Monuments, finished to custom order; monuments & tombstones; barber & beauty shop equipment

## Bedford Park
### Cook County

**(G-1528)**
**1 HEAVY EQUIPMENT LOADING INC**
6535 S Austin Ave (60638-6108)
**PHONE**..................................773 581-7374
Inga Kevliciene, *Principal*
**EMP:** 15
**SALES (est):** 842.6K **Privately Held**
**SIC:** 1389 Construction, repair & dismantling services

**(G-1529)**
**A 2 STEEL SALES LLC**
6499 W 66th Pl (60638-5105)
**PHONE**..................................708 924-1200
Andrew Gross, *Executive*
**EMP:** 2
**SALES (est):** 210K **Privately Held**
**SIC:** 3312 Sheet or strip, steel, cold-rolled: own hot-rolled

**(G-1530)**
**A J MACHINING INC**
7229 W 66th St (60638-4701)
**PHONE**..................................708 563-2580
**Fax:** 708 563-2590

Jerry Clifford, *President*
Gene Koniecko, *Vice Pres*
**EMP:** 20
**SQ FT:** 23,000
**SALES (est):** 1.7MM **Privately Held**
**SIC:** 3599 Machine shop, jobbing & repair

**(G-1531)**
**A W ENTERPRISES INC**
Also Called: Case Guys
6543 S Laramie Ave (60638-6413)
**PHONE**..................................708 458-8989
**Fax:** 708 458-9023
Edward Otrusina, *President*
Betty F Otrusina, *Accounting Mgr*
Valerie Renteria, *Accounting Mgr*
Bridget Dynia, *Sales Staff*
**EMP:** 42 **EST:** 1962
**SQ FT:** 28,400
**SALES (est):** 6.4MM **Privately Held**
**WEB:** www.caseguys.net
**SIC:** 3172 3089 3161 Leather cases; cases, plastic; luggage

**(G-1532)**
**A2 SALES LLC (PA)**
Also Called: Alliance Steel 1, LLC
6499 W 66th Pl (60638-5105)
**PHONE**..................................708 924-1200
**Fax:** 708 924-0200
Dennis Barista, *Division Mgr*
Kevin Garcia, *General Mgr*
Eddie Moore, *General Mgr*
Ramon Lopez, *Traffic Mgr*
Michael Garvey, *CFO*
**EMP:** 55
**SQ FT:** 80,000
**SALES (est):** 56.1MM **Privately Held**
**SIC:** 5051 3399 Steel; metal powders, pastes & flakes

**(G-1533)**
**AFTON CHEMICAL CORPORATION**
7201 W 65th St (60638-4607)
**PHONE**..................................708 728-1546
**EMP:** 22
**SALES (corp-wide):** 2.1B **Publicly Held**
**SIC:** 2899 Mfg Chemical Preparations
**HQ:** Afton Chemical Corporation
500 Spring St
Richmond VA 23219
804 788-5086

**(G-1534)**
**AIRA ENTERPRISE INC**
6855 W 65th St Ste 2 (60638-4968)
**PHONE**..................................708 458-4360
**Fax:** 708 458-7976
Clarence Svehla, *President*
**EMP:** 20
**SALES (est):** 3.8MM **Privately Held**
**SIC:** 2653 Corrugated boxes, partitions, display items, sheets & pad

**(G-1535)**
**ALLIANCE STEEL CORPORATION**
6499 W 66th Pl (60638-5105)
**PHONE**..................................708 924-1200
Andrew Gross, *President*
Andy Gross, *President*
Andrew Sandberg, *Vice Pres*
Tony Villasenor, *Opers Mgr*
Mike Durby, *CFO*
▼ **EMP:** 30
**SQ FT:** 80,000
**SALES (est):** 5.2MM **Privately Held**
**SIC:** 3441 3471 Fabricated structural metal; plating & polishing

**(G-1536)**
**ALPHA PRODUCTS INC**
5570 W 70th Pl (60638-6392)
**PHONE**..................................708 594-3883
**Fax:** 708 594-6052
George Derkach, *President*
Dean Jacobson, *Info Tech Mgr*
Eric Marks, *Director*
▲ **EMP:** 37
**SQ FT:** 85,000
**SALES (est):** 10.3MM **Privately Held**
**SIC:** 3469 Metal stampings

## GEOGRAPHIC SECTION
### Bedford Park - Cook County (G-1561)

**(G-1537)**
**ARCHER WIRE INTERNATIONAL CORP (PA)**
7300 S Narragansett Ave (60638-6020)
PHONE................................708 563-1700
Fax: 708 563-1740
Leonard J Svabek, *President*
Lenn Svabek, *Vice Pres*
Don Vacco, *Vice Pres*
John Maser, *Purch Dir*
Keith Oneil, *Engineer*
▲ EMP: 110 EST: 1944
SALES (est): 40.3MM **Privately Held**
WEB: www.frybasket.com
SIC: 3496 Miscellaneous fabricated wire products

**(G-1538)**
**ART WIRE WORKS INC**
6711 S Leclaire Ave (60638-6417)
PHONE................................708 458-3993
Fax: 708 458-3008
David Collignon, *President*
Gayle Blakeslee, *Purch Agent*
Wally Kaim, *Personnel Exec*
EMP: 15
SALES (est): 2.8MM **Privately Held**
SIC: 3496 3993 3498 3444 Woven wire products; lamp frames, wire; signs & advertising specialties; fabricated pipe & fittings; sheet metalwork; partitions & fixtures, except wood

**(G-1539)**
**ASTORIA WIRE PRODUCTS INC**
Also Called: Astoria Wire & Metal Products
5303 W 74th Pl (60638-6507)
PHONE................................708 496-9950
Richard Zidek, *President*
Kevin Zidek, *Vice Pres*
Dan Candos, *Administration*
EMP: 75
SQ FT: 117,000
SALES (est): 14MM **Privately Held**
WEB: www.astoriawire.com
SIC: 2542 3496 3469 3444 Racks, merchandise display or storage: except wood; miscellaneous fabricated wire products; metal stampings; sheet metalwork

**(G-1540)**
**ASTRO PLASTIC CONTAINERS INC**
6735 S Old Harlem Ave (60638-4732)
PHONE................................708 458-7100
Fax: 708 458-7199
Magdalena Kolosa, *President*
Miroslaw Kolosa, *Shareholder*
EMP: 18
SQ FT: 30,000
SALES (est): 4.1MM **Privately Held**
SIC: 2759 Screen printing

**(G-1541)**
**BIOCARE LABS INC**
5202 W 70th Pl (60638-6320)
PHONE................................708 496-8657
Fax: 708 796-1946
Aisha R Chaudary, *President*
Curtis Davis, *General Mgr*
Betzy Martin, *Opers Mgr*
Natasha Johnson, *Office Mgr*
Sajjad Syed, *Applctn Conslt*
▼ EMP: 8
SALES (est): 1.8MM **Privately Held**
WEB: www.biocarelabs.com
SIC: 2844 Hair preparations, including shampoos; cosmetic preparations

**(G-1542)**
**BRUSIC-ROSE INC**
7300 S Central Ave (60638-6514)
PHONE................................708 458-9900
Edward A Brusic, *President*
Karen J Brusic, *Vice Pres*
Kathy Brusic, *Manager*
Jerry Cisar, *Administration*
EMP: 50
SALES (est): 5.5MM **Privately Held**
WEB: www.brusicrose.com
SIC: 2512 Upholstered household furniture

**(G-1543)**
**CENTRAL PRINTERS & GRAPHICS**
6109 W 63rd St (60638-4301)
PHONE................................773 586-3711
Fax: 773 586-9534
Edward J Osowiec, *President*
Kimberly A Osowiec, *Admin Sec*
EMP: 4
SQ FT: 1,500
SALES: 350K **Privately Held**
SIC: 2752 Commercial printing, offset

**(G-1544)**
**CLEMENT INDUSTRIES INC DEL**
Also Called: Clement Wheel
5939 W 66th St (60638-6205)
PHONE................................708 458-9141
Fax: 708 458-8481
Richard Clement, *President*
Donald Wasil, *Principal*
John Korpak, *Financial Exec*
Henry Presta, *Info Tech Dir*
EMP: 50
SQ FT: 175,000
SALES (est): 8.2MM **Privately Held**
SIC: 3714 Wheels, motor vehicle

**(G-1545)**
**CONTRACT INDUSTRIES INC**
6641 S Narragansett Ave (60638-5111)
PHONE................................708 458-8150
Fax: 708 458-8155
Mark Weitzman, *President*
Rich Rusak, *Vice Pres*
Scott Weitzman, *Vice Pres*
Carol Luberda, *Admin Sec*
EMP: 23
SQ FT: 40,000
SALES (est): 4.2MM **Privately Held**
SIC: 2541 2599 2434 2431 Office fixtures, wood; cabinets, except refrigerated: show, display, etc.: wood; restaurant furniture, wood or metal; wood kitchen cabinets; millwork; carpentry work; nonresidential construction

**(G-1546)**
**CORRUGATED SUPPLIES CO LLC (PA)**
5043 W 67th St (60638-6409)
PHONE................................708 458-5525
John Potocsnak, *COO*
Mike Rubinstein, *Vice Pres*
Jim Ryan, *Sales Mgr*
S Richard Van Horne Jr, *Mng Member*
▲ EMP: 50 EST: 1964
SQ FT: 100,000
SALES (est): 47.9MM **Privately Held**
SIC: 2653 Sheets, solid fiber: made from purchased materials

**(G-1547)**
**DAVIS ATHLETIC EQUIPMENT CO**
5021 W 66th St (60638-6403)
PHONE................................708 563-9006
Fax: 708 563-9007
Jerome Davis, *President*
Carol A Davis, *Corp Secy*
EMP: 11
SQ FT: 26,000
SALES: 1.2MM **Privately Held**
SIC: 3949 3069 Track & field athletic equipment; gymnasium equipment; football equipment & supplies, general; protective sporting equipment; pillows, sponge rubber

**(G-1548)**
**DHALIWAL LABS ILLINOIS LLC**
5202 W 70th Pl (60638-6320)
PHONE................................312 690-7734
Mina Ohearn, *Mng Member*
EMP: 60
SALES: 10.2MM
SALES (corp-wide): 74MM **Privately Held**
SIC: 2844 Toilet preparations
PA: Dhaliwal Laboratories, Llc
 11910 Shiloh Rd Ste 142
 Dallas TX 75228
 214 446-5862

**(G-1549)**
**FERTILIZER INC**
Also Called: National Liquid Fertilizer
5820 W 66th St (60638-6204)
PHONE................................708 458-8615
Bruce Nutt, *President*
EMP: 8
SALES: 950K **Privately Held**
SIC: 2873 Nitrogenous fertilizers

**(G-1550)**
**FILTER TECHNOLOGY INC**
7200 S Leamington Ave (60638-6620)
PHONE................................773 523-7200
Fax: 773 523-7672
Herman Hertsberg, *President*
Raphael Hertsberg, *Sales Engr*
EMP: 48
SQ FT: 315,000
SALES: 10MM **Privately Held**
WEB: www.filtertechnology.com
SIC: 2299 3399 Felts & felt products; laminating steel

**(G-1551)**
**GENERAL ELECTRIC COMPANY**
7337 S Mason Ave (60638-6227)
PHONE................................708 924-5055
Brod Rumer, *Manager*
Wayne D'Mura, *Manager*
EMP: 62
SALES (corp-wide): 123.6B **Publicly Held**
SIC: 3599 Machine shop, jobbing & repair
PA: General Electric Company
 41 Farnsworth St
 Boston MA 02210
 617 443-3000

**(G-1552)**
**HALLSTAR COMPANY**
5851 W 73rd St (60638-6215)
P.O. Box 910 (60499-0910)
PHONE................................708 594-5947
Thomas Seeum, *Vice Pres*
Mike Friess, *Opers Mgr*
Dan Fitzgerald, *Prdtn Mgr*
Thomas Seum, *CFO*
Scott Thompson, *Sales Staff*
EMP: 55
SALES (corp-wide): 56.9MM **Privately Held**
WEB: www.hallstar.com
SIC: 2869 2851 2822 Industrial organic chemicals; paints & allied products; synthetic rubber
PA: Hallstar Company
 120 S Riverside Plz # 1620
 Chicago IL 60606
 312 554-7400

**(G-1553)**
**HELIGEAR ACQUISITION CO (PA)**
Also Called: Northstar Aerospace Chicago
6006 W 73rd St (60638-6106)
PHONE................................708 728-2000
David McConnaughey, *CEO*
Brian Cheek, *Vice Pres*
Greg Harper, *Vice Pres*
Jason Young, *Vice Pres*
Carson Free, *Opers Staff*
EMP: 241 EST: 2012
SQ FT: 8,000
SALES: 267.3MM **Privately Held**
SIC: 3724 7699 Aircraft engines & engine parts; aircraft flight instrument repair

**(G-1554)**
**HEXION INC**
8600 W 71st St (60501-1952)
PHONE................................708 728-8834
Terry Rodeheaver, *Manager*
Bill McKay, *Manager*
EMP: 47 **Privately Held**
SIC: 2821 Plastics materials & resins
HQ: Hexion Inc.
 180 E Broad St Fl 26
 Columbus OH 43215
 614 225-4000

**(G-1555)**
**HOIST LIFTRUCK MFG INC (PA)**
6499 W 65th St (60638-5118)
PHONE................................708 458-2200
Fax: 630 458-1176
Martin Flaska, *CEO*
Steve McGinnis, *Sales Staff*
Pam Murray, *Manager*
◆ EMP: 1
SQ FT: 140,000
SALES (est): 944.1K **Privately Held**
WEB: www.hoistlift.com
SIC: 3537 5084 Forklift trucks; trucks, industrial

**(G-1556)**
**INDUSTRIAL FILTER PUMP MFG CO**
4915 W 67th St (60638-6408)
P.O. Box 1079, Mims FL (32754-1079)
PHONE................................708 656-7800
Daniel Hill, *President*
Richard Dickhaut, *Vice Pres*
EMP: 100 EST: 1927
SQ FT: 120,000
SALES (est): 18.3MM **Privately Held**
WEB: www.industrialfilter.com
SIC: 3569 3564 3561 5084 Filters, general line: industrial; blowers & fans; pumps & pumping equipment; industrial machinery & equipment

**(G-1557)**
**INTERNATIONAL PAPER COMPANY**
7333 S Lockwood Ave (60638-6523)
PHONE................................708 728-1000
David Manthe, *Project Mgr*
Mike Hammell, *Human Res Mgr*
Ed Morky, *Branch Mgr*
Bruce Albert, *Executive*
EMP: 30
SALES (corp-wide): 21B **Publicly Held**
WEB: www.internationalpaper.com
SIC: 2652 Setup paperboard boxes
PA: International Paper Company
 6400 Poplar Ave
 Memphis TN 38197
 901 419-9000

**(G-1558)**
**J K MANUFACTURING CO**
7301 W 66th St (60638-4709)
PHONE................................708 563-2500
Fax: 708 563-9500
Jozef Koniecko, *CEO*
Mark Koniecko, *President*
Bob Mader, *VP Sales*
Joann Ptaszynski, *Manager*
EMP: 58
SQ FT: 60,000
SALES (est): 12.2MM **Privately Held**
WEB: www.jkmfg.com
SIC: 3599 3444 Machine shop, jobbing & repair; sheet metalwork

**(G-1559)**
**KM4 MANUFACTURING**
7420 S Meade Ave (60638-6125)
PHONE................................708 924-5150
EMP: 8
SALES (est): 685.2K **Privately Held**
SIC: 3999 Manufacturing industries

**(G-1560)**
**L & P GUARDING LLC**
Also Called: Folding Guard
5858 W 73rd St (60638-6216)
PHONE................................708 325-0400
Alfredo Ramirez, *General Mgr*
Meraz Mary, *Opers Mgr*
Greg Miller, *Purch Agent*
Veronica Jamro, *Purchasing*
Mathew Johnson, *Engineer*
◆ EMP: 105
SALES (est): 18.7MM **Privately Held**
WEB: www.foldingguard.com
SIC: 3089 3496 Plastic hardware & building products; miscellaneous fabricated wire products

**(G-1561)**
**L LAND HARDWOODS**
6247 W 74th St (60638-6120)
PHONE................................708 496-9000
Rick Berryman, *Principal*
EMP: 5 EST: 2011
SALES (est): 764.9K **Privately Held**
SIC: 2435 Hardwood veneer & plywood

# Bedford Park - Cook County (G-1562)

## GEOGRAPHIC SECTION

**(G-1562)**
**METAL-MATIC INC**
7200 S Narragansett Ave (60638-6018)
PHONE..................708 594-7553
Fax: 708 594-7556
Dave Pratt, *Manager*
Bill Greer, *Manager*
Mark Jungclaus, *Manager*
Nancy Plung, *Personnel Assit*
**EMP:** 145
**SALES (corp-wide):** 100.6MM **Privately Held**
**WEB:** www.metal-matic.com
**SIC: 3317** 3312 Tubes, wrought: welded or lock joint; tubes, steel & iron
**PA:** Metal-Matic, Inc.
629 2nd St Se
Minneapolis MN 55414
612 378-0411

**(G-1563)**
**MIDWAY DISPLAYS INC**
6554 S Austin Ave (60638-6109)
PHONE..................708 563-2323
Wayne Lucht, *President*
Craig Gavrys, *Plant Mgr*
Rodney Lucht, *Treasurer*
Lynne Esler, *Accounts Mgr*
John Fancher, *Sales Staff*
▲ **EMP:** 25
**SALES (est):** 4.5MM **Privately Held**
**WEB:** www.midwaydisplays.com
**SIC: 3993** Signs & advertising specialties

**(G-1564)**
**MIDWEST CONVERTING INC**
6634 W 68th St (60638-4906)
PHONE..................708 924-1510
Fax: 708 924-1512
Robert Srebalus, *President*
Rose Ann Johnson, *Controller*
John Borkowski, *Admin Sec*
▲ **EMP:** 60
**SQ FT:** 256,000
**SALES (est):** 13.1MM **Privately Held**
**WEB:** www.midwestconverting.com
**SIC: 2621** Specialty papers

**(G-1565)**
**MIDWEST REMANUFACTURING LLC**
5836 W 66th St Fl 2 (60638-6204)
PHONE..................708 496-9100
Tim Mitchell, *Mng Member*
**EMP:** 7
**SQ FT:** 30,000
**SALES (est):** 665K **Privately Held**
**SIC: 3711** Automobile bodies, passenger car, not including engine, etc.; truck & tractor truck assembly; engine rebuilding: automotive

**(G-1566)**
**MODUSLINK CORPORATION**
6112 W 73rd St (60638-6115)
PHONE..................708 496-7800
Bruce Beauchamp, *Branch Mgr*
Jeff Johnson, *Technical Staff*
**EMP:** 33
**SALES (corp-wide):** 459MM **Publicly Held**
**SIC: 7372** Prepackaged software
**HQ:** Moduslink Corporation
1601 Trapelo Rd Ste 170
Waltham MA 02451
781 663-5000

**(G-1567)**
**NORTHSTAR AEROSPACE (USA) INC**
6006 W 73rd St (60638-6106)
PHONE..................708 728-2000
Bob Klemen, *Manager*
Randy White, *Technology*
Sonia Nieto-Crowther, *Executive Asst*
**EMP:** 5 EST: 2015
**SALES (est):** 126K **Privately Held**
**SIC: 3721** Aircraft

**(G-1568)**
**OLE MEXICAN FOODS INC**
5140 W 73rd St Unit A (60638-6614)
PHONE..................708 458-3296
Fax: 708 458-3507
Karen Nusser, *President*
**EMP:** 20
**SALES (corp-wide):** 269.1MM **Privately Held**
**SIC: 2032** Mexican foods: packaged in cans, jars, etc.
**PA:** Ole' Mexican Foods, Inc.
6585 Crescent Dr
Norcross GA 30071
770 582-9200

**(G-1569)**
**OMNIMAX INTERNATIONAL INC**
Amerimax Home Products
6235 W 73rd St (60638-6116)
PHONE..................770 449-7066
Mitchell B Lewis, *CEO*
**EMP:** 25
**SALES (corp-wide):** 854.7MM **Privately Held**
**WEB:** www.amerimax.com
**SIC: 3444** Sheet metalwork
**HQ:** Omnimax International, Inc.
303 Research Dr Ste 400
Norcross GA 30092
770 449-7066

**(G-1570)**
**PACKAGING CORPORATION AMERICA**
Also Called: Chicago Sheet Plant
5555 W 73rd St (60638-6505)
PHONE..................708 594-5260
**EMP:** 65
**SALES (corp-wide):** 5.7B **Publicly Held**
**SIC: 2653** Corrugated & solid fiber boxes
**PA:** Packaging Corporation Of America
1955 W Field Ct
Lake Forest IL 60045
847 482-3000

**(G-1571)**
**PACTIV LLC**
7207 S Mason Ave (60638-6225)
PHONE..................708 496-2900
Brian Anderson, *Manager*
Kathy Pahl, *Analyst*
**EMP:** 207 **Privately Held**
**SIC: 3089** 3421 Kitchenware, plastic; plates, plastic; table & food cutlery, including butchers'
**HQ:** Pactiv Llc
1900 W Field Ct
Lake Forest IL 60045
847 482-2000

**(G-1572)**
**PERKINS PRODUCTS INC**
7025 W 66th Pl (60638-4703)
PHONE..................708 458-2000
Fax: 708 458-2057
Richard Perkins, *President*
Lon Fanning, *Vice Pres*
William L Fanning, *Vice Pres*
Ralph Prestidge, *Vice Pres*
Myron Crum, *QC Mgr*
**EMP:** 48
**SQ FT:** 45,000
**SALES (est):** 16.4MM **Privately Held**
**WEB:** www.perkinsproducts.com
**SIC: 2992** Oils & greases, blending & compounding
**PA:** Dubois Chemicals, Inc.
3630 E Kemper Rd
Cincinnati OH 45241

**(G-1573)**
**POLARTECH ADDITIVES INC**
7201 S 65th St (60638-4607)
PHONE..................708 458-8450
Warren Huang, *President*
Gary Gaines, *Plant Mgr*
▲ **EMP:** 28
**SALES (est):** 6.2MM
**SALES (corp-wide):** 2B **Publicly Held**
**SIC: 2992** Lubricating oils & greases
**HQ:** Afton Chemical Corporation
500 Spring St
Richmond VA 23219
804 788-5086

**(G-1574)**
**POWER PLUS PRODUCTS INC**
6410 W 74th St Ste A (60638-6037)
PHONE..................773 788-9794
Fax: 773 788-9758
James G Eaton, *President*
Sam Urso, *Vice Pres*
Tedd Eaton, *Sales Mgr*
Richard Petty, *Sales Mgr*
▲ **EMP:** 19
**SQ FT:** 20,000
**SALES:** 5MM **Privately Held**
**SIC: 3714** Axle housings & shafts, motor vehicle

**(G-1575)**
**PRAIRIE PACKAGING INC (DH)**
7200 S Mason Ave (60638-6226)
PHONE..................708 496-1172
▼ **EMP:** 50
**SQ FT:** 100,000
**SALES (est):** 118.3MM **Privately Held**
**SIC: 3089** 3421 Kitchenware, plastic; plates, plastic; table & food cutlery, including butchers'
**HQ:** Pactiv Llc
1900 W Field Ct
Lake Forest IL 60045
847 482-2000

**(G-1576)**
**PRO WOODWORKING**
6554 S Menard Ave (60638-6208)
PHONE..................708 508-5948
Agnes Zabicki, *Owner*
Edmund Zabicki, *Owner*
**EMP:** 4
**SALES (est):** 220K **Privately Held**
**SIC: 2431** Millwork

**(G-1577)**
**RELIABLE DIE SERVICE INC**
6700 W 74th St (60638-6029)
PHONE..................708 458-5155
Fax: 708 458-5165
Robert D Shatkus, *President*
Robert A Shatkus, *Vice Pres*
Martin S Jurger, *VP Mfg*
Mary A Shatkus, *Admin Sec*
**EMP:** 10
**SQ FT:** 13,500
**SALES (est):** 1MM **Privately Held**
**SIC: 3544** 3469 Special dies, tools, jigs & fixtures; boxes: tool, lunch, mail, etc.: stamped metal

**(G-1578)**
**RIEGER PRINTING INC**
5959 S Harlem Ave (60638-3131)
PHONE..................773 229-2095
Bob Rieger, *Owner*
Gary Lorber, *Manager*
**EMP:** 5
**SALES (est):** 288.1K **Privately Held**
**SIC: 2752** Commercial printing, lithographic

**(G-1579)**
**RINGWOOD COMPANY**
Also Called: R.L. Ringwood
6715 W 73rd St (60638-6006)
PHONE..................708 458-6000
Fax: 708 458-6009
Charles J Nodus, *President*
Lisa Pratali, *Purch Mgr*
Eric Sextonson, *Sales Engr*
Bob Lantzer, *Manager*
Stephen Petrila, *Director*
▲ **EMP:** 60
**SALES (est):** 21.1MM **Privately Held**
**WEB:** www.ringwoodstarchmix.com
**SIC: 3531** 3554 Construction machinery; paper industries machinery

**(G-1580)**
**RUSCORR LLC**
5043 W 67th St (60638-6409)
PHONE..................708 458-5525
Mike Rubinstein, *Vice Pres*
John Schweiner, *Opers Staff*
WEI Xu, *CIO*
Richard Vanhorne,
Robert Larusso, *Administration*
**EMP:** 2
**SALES (est):** 544K **Privately Held**
**SIC: 2653** Sheets, solid fiber: made from purchased materials

**(G-1581)**
**S 4 GLOBAL INC**
7300 S Narragansett Ave (60638-6020)
PHONE..................708 325-1236
Lawrence J Svabek, *President*
Marv Lieberman, *Managing Dir*
**EMP:** 8 EST: 2006
**SALES (est):** 721.9K **Privately Held**
**SIC: 3312** Wire products, steel or iron

**(G-1582)**
**S A GEAR COMPANY INC**
7252 W 66th St (60638-4702)
PHONE..................708 496-0395
Fax: 708 496-1248
Sal Abdallah, *President*
Riyad Abdallah, *Vice Pres*
Robert Abdallah, *Treasurer*
Steve Tucker, *VP Sales*
▲ **EMP:** 25
**SQ FT:** 40,000
**SALES (est):** 7.7MM **Privately Held**
**WEB:** www.bstormcollectibles.com
**SIC: 3714** Gears, motor vehicle

**(G-1583)**
**SCALETTA MOLONEY ARMORING (PA)**
6755 S Belt Circle Dr (60638-4705)
PHONE..................708 924-0099
Suzanne C Scaletta, *President*
Gina Krawczyk, *COO*
Scaletta Moloney, *Vice Pres*
Dave Broche, *Opers Mgr*
Daisy Lopez, *Engineer*
▲ **EMP:** 100
**SQ FT:** 70,000
**SALES (est):** 33.6MM **Privately Held**
**SIC: 3799** Recreational vehicles

**(G-1584)**
**SEBIS DIRECT INC (PA)**
6516 W 74th St (60638-6011)
PHONE..................312 243-9300
Wes Sanders, *President*
Kathy Morrin, *Exec VP*
Dave Brady, *Senior VP*
Terrance Bockhol, *Vice Pres*
Andrew Field, *Vice Pres*
**EMP:** 35
**SQ FT:** 69,000
**SALES (est):** 5.4MM **Privately Held**
**SIC: 2759** 7374 Laser printing; data processing & preparation

**(G-1585)**
**SPECIALIZED LIFTRUCK SVCS LLC**
6650 S Narragansett Ave (60638-5112)
PHONE..................708 552-2705
Christyn Murray, *Manager*
Michael Swieter,
Martin J Flaska,
**EMP:** 12
**SALES (est):** 1.2MM **Privately Held**
**SIC: 8711** 8742 3537 Mechanical engineering; maintenance management consultant; forklift trucks

**(G-1586)**
**STAR MOULDING & TRIM COMPANY**
6606 W 74th St (60638-6013)
PHONE..................708 458-1040
Fax: 708 458-0275
David F O Keeffe, *President*
Brett Okeeffe, *Vice Pres*
Patricia O Keeffe, *Admin Sec*
**EMP:** 25 EST: 1914
**SQ FT:** 30,000
**SALES:** 4MM **Privately Held**
**WEB:** www.starmoulding.com
**SIC: 2431** Moldings, wood: unfinished & prefinished; trim, wood

**(G-1587)**
**STERLING SPRING LLC**
7171 W 65th St (60638-4605)
PHONE..................773 777-4647
John Shapiro, *Manager*
**EMP:** 43
**SALES (corp-wide):** 19.2MM **Privately Held**
**SIC: 3495** Wire springs
**PA:** Sterling Spring, L.L.C.
5432 W 54th St
Chicago IL 60638
773 582-6464

# GEOGRAPHIC SECTION
## Belleville - St. Clair County (G-1613)

**(G-1588)**
**UNITED MAINT WLDG & MCHY C**
5252 W 73rd St (60638-6616)
PHONE.................................708 458-1705
Stanley Lukanus, *President*
Stanley Strama, *Treasurer*
Mike Kusay, *Accountant*
Liz Doktor, *Office Mgr*
**EMP:** 16
**SQ FT:** 34,000
**SALES (est):** 2.2MM **Privately Held**
**SIC:** 3599 7692 Machine shop, jobbing & repair; welding repair

**(G-1589)**
**VEGETABLE JUICES INC**
Also Called: V J I
7400 S Narragansett Ave (60638-6022)
PHONE.................................708 924-9500
Elizabeth Doyle, *CEO*
Eugene J Garvy, *Chairman*
Dennis Cox, *Vice Pres*
Randy Decaire, *CFO*
Maria Arellano, *Human Res Mgr*
▲ **EMP:** 90
**SQ FT:** 175,000
**SALES (est):** 18.9MM
**SALES (corp-wide):** 123.2MM **Privately Held**
**WEB:** www.vegetablejuices.com
**SIC:** 7389 2033 Packaging & labeling services; vegetable juices: fresh
**HQ:** Naturex Inc.
375 Huyler St
South Hackensack NJ 07606
201 440-5000

**(G-1590)**
**WARNER INDUSTRIES INC**
Also Called: R & W Machine
6551 W 74th St (60638-6010)
P.O. Box 607 (60499-0607)
PHONE.................................708 458-0627
Gerald G Warner, *President*
Herb Nelson, *QC Mgr*
Cynthia West, *Treasurer*
Dee Korbel, *Sales Mgr*
Tony Giudice, *Information Mgr*
▲ **EMP:** 57 **EST:** 1946
**SQ FT:** 30,000
**SALES (est):** 11.7MM **Privately Held**
**WEB:** www.rwmachine.com
**SIC:** 3599 Machine shop, jobbing & repair

**(G-1591)**
**WASEET AMERICA**
6000 W 79th St Ste 203 (60459-3124)
P.O. Box 278, Worth (60482-0278)
PHONE.................................708 430-1950
Kaledra Ramaha, *Principal*
**EMP:** 5
**SALES (est):** 327.2K **Privately Held**
**SIC:** 2711 Newspapers

**(G-1592)**
**WELD-RITE SERVICE INC**
6715 W 73rd St (60638-6006)
PHONE.................................708 458-6000
Fax: 708 458-1051
Charles J Nodus, *President*
Lisa Pratali, *Purch Agent*
Carl W Nodus, *Admin Sec*
**EMP:** 40 **EST:** 1946
**SQ FT:** 60,000
**SALES (est):** 15.9MM **Privately Held**
**SIC:** 3441 7692 Fabricated structural metal; welding repair

**(G-1593)**
**WESTROCK CP LLC**
6131 W 74th St (60638-6118)
PHONE.................................708 458-5288
Fax: 708 458-0830
Dan Wilcher, *Safety Mgr*
Randy Haberman, *Manager*
**EMP:** 64
**SALES (corp-wide):** 14.1B **Publicly Held**
**WEB:** www.sto.com
**SIC:** 2653 2631 Sheets, corrugated: made from purchased materials; paperboard mills
**HQ:** Westrock Cp, Llc
504 Thrasher St
Norcross GA 30071

**(G-1594)**
**WORKSHOP LTD INC**
5900 W 51st St (60638-1443)
PHONE.................................708 458-3222
Guilermo Brown, *President*
**EMP:** 2
**SALES (est):** 223.4K **Privately Held**
**WEB:** www.workshop.cfgis.org
**SIC:** 2448 Pallets, wood

**(G-1595)**
**WOZNIAK INDUSTRIES INC**
Commercial Forged Products Div
5757 W 65th St (60638-5503)
PHONE.................................708 458-1220
Fax: 708 458-9346
Herbert Little, *General Mgr*
Joseph Williams, *Div Sub Head*
Marilyn Jimenez, *Production*
Robert Marovich, *Purchasing*
Michael Powers, *CFO*
**EMP:** 120
**SALES (corp-wide):** 135MM **Privately Held**
**WEB:** www.wozniakindustries.com
**SIC:** 3462 3545 3429 Iron & steel forgings; machine tool accessories; manufactured hardware (general)
**PA:** Wozniak Industries, Inc.
2 Mid America Plz Ste 700
Oakbrook Terrace IL 60181
630 954-3400

## Beecher
### Will County

**(G-1596)**
**ALUMINUM DRIVE LINE PRODUCTS**
746 Penfield St (60401-6637)
P.O. Box 539 (60401-0539)
PHONE.................................708 946-9777
Fax: 708 946-9888
Klaud Miller, *President*
**EMP:** 3
**SQ FT:** 4,000
**SALES:** 500K **Privately Held**
**SIC:** 3714 Drive shafts, motor vehicle

**(G-1597)**
**CROWN BATTERY MANUFACTURING CO**
27456 S Hickory St (60401-3497)
PHONE.................................708 946-2535
Bob Knaak, *Branch Mgr*
Gerald Zurek, *Manager*
**EMP:** 7
**SALES (corp-wide):** 222.1MM **Privately Held**
**WEB:** www.crownbattery.com
**SIC:** 3691 Storage batteries
**PA:** Crown Battery Manufacturing Company
1445 Majestic Dr
Fremont OH 43420
419 332-0563

**(G-1598)**
**JM CIRCLE ENTERPRISE INC**
28255 S Cottage Grove Ave (60401-3757)
PHONE.................................708 946-3333
Bethanie Lenting, *President*
Jacob Lenting, *Vice Pres*
Mark Wayne- Lenting, *Treasurer*
**EMP:** 3
**SALES (est):** 183.8K **Privately Held**
**SIC:** 3354 Aluminum pipe & tube

**(G-1599)**
**LACHATA DESIGN LTD**
3006 E Indiana Ave (60401-3168)
PHONE.................................708 946-2757
Robert Lachata, *President*
**EMP:** 5
**SQ FT:** 9,000
**SALES:** 500K **Privately Held**
**SIC:** 3826 Analytical instruments

**(G-1600)**
**OLDENDORF MACHINING & FABG**
3041 E Offner Rd (60401-3242)
PHONE.................................708 946-2498
Melvin Oldendorf, *Owner*
**EMP:** 8
**SALES:** 380K **Privately Held**
**SIC:** 3599 Machine shop, jobbing & repair

**(G-1601)**
**PECSON DISTRIBUTORS LLC**
27543 S Forest View Ln (60401-5021)
PHONE.................................815 342-7977
Christina E Jackson, *President*
David Wolse, *Vice Pres*
Phil Dennis, *Manager*
▲ **EMP:** 8
**SQ FT:** 5,000
**SALES:** 1MM **Privately Held**
**SIC:** 3965 Fasteners

**(G-1602)**
**SONOCO PRTECTIVE SOLUTIONS INC**
Also Called: Thermosafe
30553 S Dixie Hwy (60401-3144)
PHONE.................................708 946-3244
Chris Kluge, *Manager*
**EMP:** 49
**SALES (corp-wide):** 4.7B **Publicly Held**
**WEB:** www.tuscarora.com
**SIC:** 2676 Sanitary paper products; feminine hygiene paper products
**HQ:** Sonoco Protective Solutions, Inc.
1 N 2nd St
Hartsville SC 29550
843 383-7000

**(G-1603)**
**VALLEY RACING INC**
325 W 323rd St (60401-3518)
PHONE.................................708 946-1440
Rollie Conley, *President*
Brian Conley, *Vice Pres*
Tina Conley, *Admin Sec*
**EMP:** 4 **EST:** 1984
**SQ FT:** 5,000
**SALES (est):** 372.5K **Privately Held**
**SIC:** 7699 3751 5571 7948 Motorcycle repair service; motorcycles, bicycles & parts; motorcycle dealers; motorcycle racing

**(G-1604)**
**W L & J ENTERPRISES INC**
Also Called: Fredette Racing Products
31745 S Dixie Hwy (60401-3148)
PHONE.................................708 946-0999
Jeff Fredette, *President*
Wayne Fredette, *Vice Pres*
**EMP:** 3
**SQ FT:** 2,000
**SALES (est):** 495.1K **Privately Held**
**WEB:** www.frpoffroad.com
**SIC:** 5571 3751 Motorcycle parts & accessories; motorcycles, bicycles & parts

## Belle Rive
### Jefferson County

**(G-1605)**
**HOPKINS SAWS & KARTS INC**
Also Called: Hopkins Saws & Cart
9398 N Markham Ln (62810-2003)
PHONE.................................618 756-2778
Phillip Hopkins, *President*
Brad Hopkins, *Corp Secy*
Alta Jean Hopkins, *Vice Pres*
**EMP:** 2
**SALES (est):** 220K **Privately Held**
**SIC:** 3546 5599 Saws & sawing equipment; go-carts

## Belleville
### St. Clair County

**(G-1606)**
**ABM MARKING LTD**
Also Called: R M J Distributing
2799 S Belt W (62226-6777)
PHONE.................................618 277-3773
Fax: 618 277-3782
Barbara Merchiori, *President*
Huston Liu, *Owner*
Roger Schaefer, *COO*
Alberto Merchiori, *Senior VP*
John Bock, *Admin Sec*
▲ **EMP:** 10
**SQ FT:** 6,000
**SALES (est):** 3.7MM **Privately Held**
**WEB:** www.abmmarking.com
**SIC:** 5085 2893 2899 Industrial supplies; printing ink; chemical preparations

**(G-1607)**
**ABM MARKING SERVICES LTD**
Also Called: Rmj Distributing
2799 S Belt W (62226-6777)
PHONE.................................618 277-3773
Huston Liu, *Vice Pres*
**EMP:** 4
**SQ FT:** 4,500
**SALES (est):** 153.8K **Privately Held**
**SIC:** 3953 3825 Stencils, painting & marking; battery testers, electrical

**(G-1608)**
**ALTERNATIVE TS**
5300 N Belt W (62226-4609)
PHONE.................................618 257-0230
Fax: 618 257-0289
Andy Kinsella, *Owner*
**EMP:** 8
**SQ FT:** 2,600
**SALES:** 350K **Privately Held**
**SIC:** 3955 2396 2395 Print cartridges for laser & other computer printers; automotive & apparel trimmings; tucking, for the trade

**(G-1609)**
**ARTWEAR**
1916 Lebanon Ave (62221-2552)
PHONE.................................618 234-5522
Mary Rudman, *Owner*
**EMP:** 4
**SALES (est):** 252.6K **Privately Held**
**SIC:** 2759 Screen printing

**(G-1610)**
**BACH & ASSOCIATES**
120 N 36th St (62226-6232)
PHONE.................................618 277-1652
Gerry Bach, *Co-Owner*
Ann Bach, *Co-Owner*
**EMP:** 4
**SQ FT:** 7,000
**SALES:** 250K **Privately Held**
**SIC:** 7336 2752 Graphic arts & related design; commercial printing, lithographic

**(G-1611)**
**BELL CITY BATTERY MFG INC (PA)**
34 Empire Dr Ste 2 (62220-3585)
PHONE.................................618 233-0437
Fax: 618 234-9474
Michael Pruss, *President*
C J Hagemamm, *Vice Pres*
Cory Caywood, *Opers Mgr*
Ardell E Miller Jr, *Treasurer*
**EMP:** 5
**SQ FT:** 10,000
**SALES:** 750K **Privately Held**
**WEB:** www.bellcitybatteries.com
**SIC:** 3691 Storage batteries

**(G-1612)**
**BELLEVILLE SHOE MFG CO (PA)**
Also Called: Belleville Boot Company
100 Premier Dr (62220-3423)
PHONE.................................618 233-5600
Fax: 618 257-1112
Homer W Weidmann, *Ch of Bd*
Mark Ferguson, *President*
Yvonne Coffy, *Human Res Mgr*
Bill Tripp, *Manager*
Stu Wilson, *Manager*
◆ **EMP:** 350 **EST:** 1904
**SQ FT:** 155,000
**SALES (est):** 114.9MM **Privately Held**
**WEB:** www.bellevilleshoe.com
**SIC:** 3143 Men's footwear, except athletic; work shoes, men's

**(G-1613)**
**BENO J GUNDLACH COMPANY**
211 N 21st St (62226-6658)
PHONE.................................618 233-1781
Fax: 618 233-3636
Gregory J Gundlach, *President*

# Belleville - St. Clair County (G-1614)

Jeffrey B Gundlach, *Vice Pres*
Stephen P Gundlach, *Vice Pres*
Stephen Gundlach, *Vice Pres*
Steve Gundlach, *Vice Pres*
▲ **EMP:** 35
**SQ FT:** 60,000
**SALES (est):** 8.1MM **Privately Held**
**WEB:** www.benojgundlachco.com
**SIC:** 3423 5072 Carpet layers' hand tools; builders' hardware

## (G-1614)
### BERTCO ENTERPRISES INC
108 N Jackson St (62220-1427)
**PHONE**..................................618 234-9283
**EMP:** 3
**SQ FT:** 11,250
**SALES (est):** 250K **Privately Held**
**SIC:** 5099 3479 7389 3953 Whol Durable Goods Coating/Engraving Svcs Business Services Mfg Marking Devices Mfg Prdt-Purchased Glass

## (G-1615)
### BUILDING PRODUCTS CORP (PA)
950 Freeburg Ave (62220-2623)
P.O. Box 566 (62222-0566)
**PHONE**..................................618 233-4427
**Fax:** 618 233-2031
Paul Mueth, *President*
David Fournie, *Vice Pres*
Joan Mueth, *Vice Pres*
Aron Rauls, *Marketing Staff*
Gary Witkus, *Traffic Dir*
**EMP:** 25 **EST:** 1945
**SQ FT:** 1,000
**SALES (est):** 2.5MM **Privately Held**
**WEB:** www.buildingproductscorp.com
**SIC:** 3251 3271 Brick & structural clay tile; blocks, concrete or cinder: standard

## (G-1616)
### CALLISON DISTRIBUTING LLC
4 Premier Dr (62220-3421)
P.O. Box 463 (62222-0463)
**PHONE**..................................618 277-4300
**Fax:** 618 277-6267
Edwin H Callison Jr, 
▲ **EMP:** 60 **EST:** 1933
**SQ FT:** 52,000
**SALES (est):** 6.3MM **Privately Held**
**SIC:** 5182 2085 Liquor; distilled & blended liquors

## (G-1617)
### CAROLINE COLE INC
711 S Illinois St (62220-2141)
**PHONE**..................................618 233-0600
Torre Tribout, *Vice Pres*
**EMP:** 12
**SQ FT:** 12,000
**SALES (est):** 500K **Privately Held**
**WEB:** www.carolinecole.com
**SIC:** 3069 5712 2392 Pillows, sponge rubber; furniture stores; household furnishings

## (G-1618)
### CHELAR TOOL & DIE INC
11 N Florida Ave (62221-5498)
**PHONE**..................................618 234-6550
**Fax:** 618 234-6572
Jared Katt, *President*
Malcolm Katt, *President*
Ray Klein, *Vice Pres*
**EMP:** 60 **EST:** 1962
**SQ FT:** 38,000
**SALES (est):** 13.6MM **Privately Held**
**WEB:** www.chelar.com
**SIC:** 3544 Special dies, tools, jigs & fixtures

## (G-1619)
### CONSTRUCTION EQUIPMENT
34 Empire Dr Ste 1 (62220-3585)
**PHONE**..................................618 345-0799
Dan Feather, *Manager*
▼ **EMP:** 3
**SALES (est):** 392.4K **Privately Held**
**SIC:** 3272 Concrete products, precast

## (G-1620)
### CURRENT PLUS ELECTRIC LLC
8265 W State Route 161 (62220-2145)
**PHONE**..................................618 394-4827
**EMP:** 4
**SALES (est):** 217.2K **Privately Held**
**SIC:** 3699 1731 Electrical equipment & supplies; electric power systems contractors

## (G-1621)
### CURT SMITH SPORTING GOODS INC (PA)
213 E Main St (62220-1688)
**PHONE**..................................618 233-5177
**Fax:** 618 233-5182
Jeff Hall, *President*
John Vallero, *CFO*
George Hass, *Sales Staff*
Mike House, *Sales Staff*
Corey Muendlein, *Sales Staff*
**EMP:** 20 **EST:** 1946
**SQ FT:** 13,000
**SALES (est):** 5.5MM **Privately Held**
**SIC:** 2329 5091 Men's & boys' athletic uniforms; athletic goods

## (G-1622)
### CUSTOM CUT STENCIL COMPANY INC
132 Iowa Ave (62220-3940)
**PHONE**..................................618 277-5077
**Fax:** 618 277-1358
Carolyn Lewis, *President*
Steve Lewis, *Co-Owner*
**EMP:** 5
**SALES (est):** 360K **Privately Held**
**WEB:** www.customcutstencilco.com
**SIC:** 3953 Stencils, painting & marking

## (G-1623)
### DDK SCIENTIFIC CORPORATION
1 11th Fairway Ct (62220-4861)
**PHONE**..................................618 235-2849
Raul Duarte, *President*
**EMP:** 4
**SALES (est):** 537.3K **Privately Held**
**WEB:** www.ddkscientific.com
**SIC:** 3641 Ultraviolet lamps

## (G-1624)
### DELI STAR VENTURES INC
Also Called: King's Food Products
3 Amann Ct (62220-3461)
**PHONE**..................................618 233-0400
**Fax:** 618 233-0497
Tom Siegel, *President*
Dan Siegel, *Vice Pres*
Stephanie Siegel, *Vice Pres*
Matt Galli, *Manager*
Carole King, *Manager*
**EMP:** 15
**SQ FT:** 5,000
**SALES (est):** 7MM **Privately Held**
**WEB:** www.delistarinc.com
**SIC:** 2064 Fudge (candy)

## (G-1625)
### DELTA LABEL INC
920 Scheel St (62221-4830)
**PHONE**..................................618 233-8984
**Fax:** 618 233-5820
Mark Howell, *President*
Homer Howell, *Chairman*
Gwen Howell, *Exec VP*
**EMP:** 3
**SQ FT:** 3,500
**SALES (est):** 320.1K **Privately Held**
**SIC:** 2759 Labels & seals: printing

## (G-1626)
### DOVE INDUSTRIES INC
229 Taft St (62220-2868)
**PHONE**..................................618 234-4509
**Fax:** 618 234-6898
Eric Stephenson, *President*
Candy Stephenson, *Vice Pres*
Joyce Schauerte, *Manager*
**EMP:** 10
**SQ FT:** 24,000
**SALES (est):** 1.8MM **Privately Held**
**WEB:** www.doveindustries.com
**SIC:** 3496 Miscellaneous fabricated wire products

## (G-1627)
### DREXEL HOUSE OF DRAPES INC
Also Called: Drexel Vinisitian and Blind
3721 Lebanon Ave (62221-4490)
**PHONE**..................................618 624-5415
**Fax:** 618 624-4908
Deloris McAllister, *President*
Jack William Macallister, *Vice Pres*
Lynda Housick, *Treasurer*
**EMP:** 4 **EST:** 1954
**SALES (est):** 400K **Privately Held**
**SIC:** 5714 7349 5211 2391 Draperies; window blind cleaning; windows, storm: wood or metal; curtains & draperies

## (G-1628)
### E-LITE TOOL & MFG CO
122 Industrial Dr (62220-3432)
**PHONE**..................................618 236-1580
**Fax:** 618 236-1589
Scott Jones, *President*
Debbie Baltz, *Corp Secy*
Rick Baltz, *Vice Pres*
**EMP:** 24 **EST:** 1957
**SQ FT:** 20,500
**SALES (est):** 4.5MM **Privately Held**
**SIC:** 3544 Special dies, tools, jigs & fixtures

## (G-1629)
### EAST END EXPRESS LUBE INC
928 Carlyle Ave (62221-5510)
**PHONE**..................................618 257-1049
Paul Beeler, *President*
**EMP:** 6
**SALES (est):** 480K **Privately Held**
**SIC:** 1382 Oil & gas exploration services

## (G-1630)
### ECKERT ORCHARDS INC (PA)
951 S Green Mount Rd (62220-4814)
**PHONE**..................................618 233-0513
**Fax:** 618 235-8769
James Eckert, *President*
Larry Eckert, *Corp Secy*
Phil Climaco, *CFO*
Amanda Morgan, *Marketing Mgr*
**EMP:** 150
**SQ FT:** 500
**SALES (est):** 34MM **Privately Held**
**WEB:** www.eckerts.com
**SIC:** 2099 0175 5431 0171 Cider, nonalcoholic; peach orchard; apple orchard; fruit & vegetable markets; berry crops

## (G-1631)
### EMPIRE COMFORT SYSTEMS INC
918 Freeburg Ave (62220-2623)
P.O. Box 529 (62222-0529)
**PHONE**..................................618 233-7420
**Fax:** 618 233-7097
Don Rigney, *President*
Brian H Bauer, *Chairman*
Joe Brueggemann, *Vice Pres*
Bruce Dresner, *Vice Pres*
Judy Hurst, *Traffic Mgr*
▲ **EMP:** 200
**SQ FT:** 250,000
**SALES (est):** 42MM **Privately Held**
**WEB:** www.empirecomfort.com
**SIC:** 3949 3631 3433 Sporting & athletic goods; gas ranges, domestic; space heaters, except electric; room heaters, gas; wall heaters, except electric

## (G-1632)
### FIRE CAM LLC
321 Clearwater Dr (62220-2969)
**PHONE**..................................618 416-8390
Robert Schield, *Principal*
**EMP:** 2
**SALES (est):** 245.8K **Privately Held**
**SIC:** 3651 Video camera-audio recorders, household use

## (G-1633)
### GUNDLACH EQUIPMENT CORPORATION
1 Freedom Dr (62226-5104)
P.O. Box 385 (62222-0385)
**PHONE**..................................618 233-7208
**Fax:** 618 641-6988
Mark Kohler, *President*

Carrie Little, *Vice Pres*
Todd Ruff, *Mfg Mgr*
Alan Reuter, *Design Engr*
Carolyn Little, *HR Admin*
▲ **EMP:** 80
**SQ FT:** 63,000
**SALES (est):** 20.5MM **Publicly Held**
**WEB:** www.gundlach.us
**SIC:** 3532 Mining machinery
**PA:** Hillenbrand, Inc.
1 Batesville Blvd
Batesville IN 47006

## (G-1634)
### HEADBALL INC
Also Called: Mid America Web Solutions
41 Acorn Lake Dr (62221-4449)
**PHONE**..................................618 628-2656
Anthony Smallon, *President*
**EMP:** 3 **EST:** 1998
**SALES (est):** 252.7K **Privately Held**
**WEB:** www.headball.com
**SIC:** 3949 Soccer equipment & supplies

## (G-1635)
### I D TOGS
67 Cheshire Dr (62223-3413)
**PHONE**..................................618 235-1538
Tom Metzger, *President*
**EMP:** 3
**SALES (est):** 166.5K **Privately Held**
**SIC:** 2395 Embroidery products, except schiffli machine

## (G-1636)
### ILLINI CONCRETE INC (PA)
1300 E A St (62221-5400)
**PHONE**..................................618 235-4141
**Fax:** 618 235-7599
Amy Santen, *President*
Jeb Santen, *Vice Pres*
Don Calhoun, *Manager*
Jill Jones, *Manager*
**EMP:** 15
**SQ FT:** 5,000
**SALES (est):** 3.4MM **Privately Held**
**SIC:** 3273 Ready-mixed concrete

## (G-1637)
### INTER-TRADE GLOBAL LLC
107 W Main St (62220-1501)
**PHONE**..................................618 954-6119
Andrew Raming, *CEO*
Stephanie Pieper, *Principal*
Christoph Gertzen, *CFO*
Osama Shiha, *Manager*
**EMP:** 5
**SALES (est):** 139.9K **Privately Held**
**SIC:** 2062 0112 2063 3331 Granulated cane sugar from purchased raw sugar or syrup; rice; beet sugar; cathodes (primary), copper

## (G-1638)
### INTERNATIONAL PAPER COMPANY
3001 Otto St (62226-6711)
**PHONE**..................................618 233-5460
**Fax:** 618 233-5518
Ron Wise, *Principal*
Daniel Morris, *Opers Mgr*
Roy Taylor, *Chief Mktg Ofcr*
**EMP:** 14
**SALES (corp-wide):** 21B **Publicly Held**
**SIC:** 2621 Paper mills
**PA:** International Paper Company
6400 Poplar Ave
Memphis TN 38197
901 419-9000

## (G-1639)
### IV & RESPIRATORY CARE SERVICES
65 S 65th St Ste 1 (62223-2946)
**PHONE**..................................618 398-2720
Lori Weilmuenster, *Owner*
Tina Sonsoucie, *Manager*
Chrystal Fisher,
**EMP:** 30
**SALES (est):** 3MM **Privately Held**
**SIC:** 8093 3845 Respiratory therapy clinic; respiratory analysis equipment, electromedical

# GEOGRAPHIC SECTION
Belleville - St. Clair County (G-1667)

**(G-1640)**
**KEIL-FORNESS COMFORT SYSTEMS**
301 N Illinois St (62220-1232)
PHONE..............................618 233-3039
Fax: 618 233-3123
David C Forness, *Owner*
EMP: 5 EST: 1899
SQ FT: 3,500
SALES (est): 410K **Privately Held**
SIC: 1711 3444 Warm air heating & air conditioning contractor; sheet metalwork

**(G-1641)**
**KEMELL ENTERPRISES LLC**
612 Ganim Dr (62221-2671)
PHONE..............................618 671-1513
Candice Kemp, *Principal*
EMP: 3
SALES (est): 117.8K **Privately Held**
SIC: 3728 Refueling equipment for use in flight, airplane

**(G-1642)**
**KETTLER CASTING CO INC**
2640 Old Freeburg Rd (62220-5204)
P.O. Box 852 (62222-0852)
PHONE..............................618 234-5303
Fax: 618 234-9333
Gregg W Kettler, *President*
Jeffrey R Lutz, *President*
Judy Mallian, *Accountant*
Shelia Nunnally, *Bookkeeper*
John Bower, *Manager*
EMP: 30
SQ FT: 15,000
SALES (est): 6.3MM **Privately Held**
WEB: www.kettlercasting.com
SIC: 3321 3369 Gray iron castings; non-ferrous foundries

**(G-1643)**
**KLM COMMERCIAL SWEEPING INC**
320 Saint Sabre Dr (62226-1046)
PHONE..............................618 978-9276
Keith Kannewurf, *President*
Kevin Kannewurf, *Vice Pres*
EMP: 6
SALES: 500K **Privately Held**
SIC: 3991 Brooms & brushes; street sweeping brooms, hand or machine; whisk brooms

**(G-1644)**
**KM PRESS INCORPORATED**
120 Iowa Ave (62220-3940)
PHONE..............................618 277-1222
Kurt Matson, *President*
Carl Matson, *Treasurer*
Judy Matson, *Admin Sec*
EMP: 9
SALES (est): 1.1MM **Privately Held**
SIC: 2741 Miscellaneous publishing

**(G-1645)**
**KODERHANDT INC**
Also Called: Quality Plating Works
1651 N Charles St (62221-4928)
PHONE..............................618 233-4808
Christy Koderhandt, *President*
James R Koderhandt, *Vice Pres*
Steve Koderhandt, *Admin Sec*
EMP: 3 EST: 1927
SQ FT: 17,520
SALES (est): 282.1K **Privately Held**
SIC: 3471 Electrolizing steel

**(G-1646)**
**KOSTELAC GREASE SERVICE INC**
8105 Pecan Tree Ln (62223-7742)
PHONE..............................314 436-7166
Fax: 618 538-5444
John Kostelac III, *President*
James Kostelac, *Vice Pres*
Kay Dunn, *Systems Mgr*
EMP: 25
SQ FT: 3,000
SALES (est): 4MM **Privately Held**
WEB: www.kostelacgrease.com
SIC: 2077 4953 2992 Grease rendering, inedible; tallow rendering, inedible; refuse systems; lubricating oils & greases

**(G-1647)**
**L M C AUTOMOTIVE INC**
Also Called: Belleville Automotive
1200 W Main St (62220-1525)
PHONE..............................618 235-5242
Mark Schaefer, *President*
Linda Schaefer, *Admin Sec*
EMP: 3
SALES (est): 22.5K **Privately Held**
SIC: 3599 5013 Machine shop, jobbing & repair; automotive supplies & parts

**(G-1648)**
**LARRY RAGAN** ✪
Also Called: Ragan Kettle Corn
3809 Rolling Meadows Dr (62220-0408)
PHONE..............................618 698-1041
Larry Ragan, *Principal*
EMP: 6 EST: 2016
SALES (est): 234.8K **Privately Held**
SIC: 2064 5499 2096 Popcorn balls or other treated popcorn products; gourmet food stores; corn chips & other corn-based snacks

**(G-1649)**
**LIESE LUMBER CO INC**
2215 S Belt W (62226-6797)
P.O. Box 306 (62222-0306)
PHONE..............................618 234-0105
Lennie Colbert, *Manager*
EMP: 23
SALES (corp-wide): 10.2MM **Privately Held**
SIC: 5211 2421 Lumber & other building materials; door & window products; resawing lumber into smaller dimensions; building & structural materials, wood
PA: Liese Lumber Co., Inc.
319 E Main St
Belleville IL 62220
314 421-3652

**(G-1650)**
**MAC MEDICAL INC**
325 W Main St (62220-1505)
PHONE..............................618 719-6757
EMP: 4
SALES (est): 77.2K **Privately Held**
SIC: 5047 3999 Medical & hospital equipment; manufacturing industries

**(G-1651)**
**MARBIL ENTERPRISES INC**
Also Called: Advance Security Products
129 Wild Rose Dr (62221-3606)
PHONE..............................618 257-1810
William Douthitt, *CEO*
Mary Douthitt, *Vice Pres*
◆ EMP: 5
SQ FT: 2,000
SALES: 1.5MM **Privately Held**
WEB: www.advancesecurityproducts.com
SIC: 3699 Security control equipment & systems

**(G-1652)**
**MARTIN GLASS COMPANY (PA)**
25 Center Plz (62220-3400)
PHONE..............................618 277-1946
Fax: 618 277-6742
Martin S Kosydor, *President*
Martin J Kosydor, *Vice Pres*
Marla Wild, *Treasurer*
Kelli Kosydor, *Admin Sec*
EMP: 18
SQ FT: 9,000
SALES (est): 3.8MM **Privately Held**
WEB: www.martinglass.net
SIC: 7536 3231 5231 Automotive glass replacement shops; products of purchased glass; glass

**(G-1653)**
**MAXS ONE STOP**
1319 N 17th St (62226-6441)
PHONE..............................618 235-4005
Dennis Knoth, *Owner*
EMP: 4
SALES (est): 199.4K **Privately Held**
SIC: 2074 Cottonseed oil, cake or meal

**(G-1654)**
**MCATEERS WHOLESALE**
Also Called: McAteer's Landscape Lighting
3101 S Belt W (62226-5016)
PHONE..............................618 233-3400
Ray Mc Cateer, *Principal*
Crystal Wagner, *Cust Mgr*
EMP: 6
SALES (est): 571.5K **Privately Held**
SIC: 3645 Lamp & light shades

**(G-1655)**
**MCCLATCHY NEWSPAPERS INC**
Also Called: Belleville News Democrat
120 S Illinois St (62221-2130)
P.O. Box 427 (62222-0427)
PHONE..............................618 239-2624
Fax: 618 235-0556
Becky Pate, *Principal*
Randy Atkisson, *Controller*
Frank Duke, *VP Mktg*
Greg Edwards, *Advt Staff*
Tim Tucker, *Manager*
EMP: 275
SALES (corp-wide): 977MM **Publicly Held**
WEB: www.sacbee.com
SIC: 2711 Newspapers
HQ: Mcclatchy Newspapers, Inc.
2100 Q St
Sacramento CA 95816
916 321-1000

**(G-1656)**
**MEDIMMUNE LLC**
1668 Golf Course Dr (62220-4821)
PHONE..............................618 235-8730
Rod Woods, *Manager*
EMP: 3
SALES (corp-wide): 23B **Privately Held**
SIC: 2834 Pharmaceutical preparations
HQ: Medimmune, Llc
1 Medimmune Way
Gaithersburg MD 20878
301 398-1200

**(G-1657)**
**MESSENGER**
2620 Lebanon Ave Unit 2 (62221-3001)
PHONE..............................618 235-9601
Fax: 618 235-7416
Edward Braxton, *Owner*
EMP: 5
SALES (est): 192.4K **Privately Held**
WEB: www.bellevillemessenger.org
SIC: 2711 Newspapers

**(G-1658)**
**METRO EAST FIBERGLASS REPAIR**
1166 Heneral Ave (62220)
PHONE..............................618 235-9217
Fax: 618 235-9224
Randy G Heinlein, *President*
EMP: 5
SQ FT: 10,000
SALES: 1.7MM **Privately Held**
SIC: 3732 5551 Boats, fiberglass: building & repairing; boat dealers

**(G-1659)**
**MILLSTADT RENDERING COMPANY**
3151 Clover Leaf Schl Rd (62223-7748)
PHONE..............................618 538-5312
Robert Kostelac, *President*
Diane Rasp, *Office Mgr*
EMP: 25
SQ FT: 2,000
SALES (est): 8MM **Privately Held**
SIC: 5159 4953 2077 Farm animals; dead animal disposal; animal & marine fats & oils

**(G-1660)**
**NEWELL & HANEY INC**
6601 W Main St (62223-3025)
PHONE..............................618 277-3660
James R Linnemeier, *President*
Lisa Linnemeier, *Corp Secy*
EMP: 11
SQ FT: 1,000
SALES (est): 1.5MM **Privately Held**
SIC: 7334 2752 2791 2789 Photocopying & duplicating services; commercial printing, offset; typesetting; bookbinding & related work

**(G-1661)**
**NPT AUTOMOTIVE MACHINE SHOP**
308 N 44th St (62226-5226)
PHONE..............................618 233-1344
EMP: 2
SALES (est): 200K **Privately Held**
SIC: 3519 Mfg Internal Combustion Engines

**(G-1662)**
**OBIES TACKLE CO INC**
124 Cardinal Dr (62221-4311)
PHONE..............................618 234-5638
Fax: 618 234-6325
Pat Oberholtzer, *President*
EMP: 4
SALES: 50K **Privately Held**
WEB: www.obiestackle.com
SIC: 3949 5091 2298 Lures, fishing: artificial; sporting & recreation goods; cordage & twine

**(G-1663)**
**P T L MANUFACTURING INC**
101 Industrial Dr (62220-3412)
PHONE..............................618 277-6789
Fax: 618 233-6789
Joseph D Stock, *President*
Jane E Stock, *Corp Secy*
Brian Bert, *Engineer*
Dan Stock, *Financial Exec*
EMP: 44
SQ FT: 40,000
SALES (est): 8.6MM **Privately Held**
WEB: www.ptlmfginc.com
SIC: 3469 Stamping metal for the trade

**(G-1664)**
**PAYNE CHAUNA**
Also Called: Prima Donna Salon
6600 W Main St Ste 8 (62223-3037)
PHONE..............................618 580-2584
Chauna Payne, *Owner*
EMP: 5
SQ FT: 1,000
SALES (est): 32.7K **Privately Held**
SIC: 7231 7299 3842 Beauty Shop Misc Personal Service Mfg Surgical Appliances Mfg Surgical Appliances

**(G-1665)**
**PEAK COMPUTER SYSTEMS INC**
6400 W Main St Ste 1a (62223-3806)
PHONE..............................618 398-5612
Fax: 618 398-5618
Grant Wuller, *President*
Michele Wuller, *Vice Pres*
EMP: 11
SQ FT: 2,500
SALES (est): 1.1MM **Privately Held**
SIC: 7372 7371 Prepackaged software; computer software systems analysis & design, custom

**(G-1666)**
**PEERLESS-PREMIER APPLIANCE CO (PA)**
119 S 14th St (62220-1715)
P.O. Box 387 (62222-0387)
PHONE..............................618 233-0475
Fax: 618 235-1771
Joseph E Geary Jr, *CEO*
Gary Siburt, *President*
Alex Volansky, *President*
William T Sprague, *Chairman*
Judy Wagner, *VP Admin*
▲ EMP: 100
SQ FT: 250,000
SALES (est): 23.5MM **Privately Held**
WEB: www.premierrange.com
SIC: 3631 Gas ranges, domestic; electric ranges, domestic

**(G-1667)**
**PRUETT ENTERPRISES INC**
Also Called: Marv's Scooters
10 E Cleveland Ave (62220-2108)
PHONE..............................618 235-6184
Marvin Pruett, *President*

# Belleville - St. Clair County (G-1668)

EMP: 2
SALES (est): 215.4K  Privately Held
SIC: 3751  Motor scooters & parts

**(G-1668)**
**RAUCKMAN UTILITY PRODUCTS LLC**
33 Empire Dr  (62220-3451)
PHONE..................618 234-0001
Drew Bendick, *Sales Staff*
David Reinke, *Sales Associate*
Matt Scherbring, *Sales Associate*
James Rauckman,
▲ EMP: 3
SALES (est): 676.9K  Privately Held
SIC: 3824  Fluid meters & counting devices

**(G-1669)**
**REPLACEMENT SERVICES LLC**
15 N 1st St  (62220-1318)
PHONE..................618 398-9880
Fax: 618 398-7880
Christine Belling, *Vice Pres*
Joe Kelly, *Finance Dir*
Dow Ritter, *Human Res Dir*
Stacy Flager, *Sales Mgr*
Tom Teasdale, *Accounts Mgr*
EMP: 18
SALES (est): 2.6MM  Privately Held
WEB: www.replacementservices.com
SIC: 3961  Costume jewelry

**(G-1670)**
**ROC INDUSTRIES INC**
1218 W A St  (62220-1030)
PHONE..................618 277-6044
Fax: 618 277-2999
Robert Stock, *President*
Margaret Stock, *Corp Secy*
Greta Stock, *Treasurer*
Cheryl Smith, *Manager*
EMP: 8
SQ FT: 16,000
SALES (est): 1.6MM  Privately Held
SIC: 3559  Metal finishing equipment for plating, etc.

**(G-1671)**
**ROGER JOLLY SKATEBOARDS**
305 N Illinois St  (62220-1232)
PHONE..................618 277-7113
EMP: 4
SALES (est): 284.3K  Privately Held
SIC: 3949  Skateboards

**(G-1672)**
**ROHO INC (DH)**
100 N Florida Ave  (62221-5429)
PHONE..................618 277-9173
Tom Boucherding, *President*
Larry Jackson, *Vice Pres*
Carl Bandhold, *CFO*
Tim Richter, *VP Finance*
Chris Javillonar, *Admin Sec*
EMP: 205  EST: 2006
SQ FT: 75,000
SALES: 50MM
SALES (corp-wide): 6.7B  Privately Held
SIC: 3069  Molded rubber products
HQ: The Roho Group Inc
100 N Florida Ave
Belleville IL 62221
618 277-9173

**(G-1673)**
**ROHO INC**
1501 S 74th St  (62223-5900)
PHONE..................618 234-4899
Fax: 618 234-5917
Tom Borcherding, *President*
Johnnie Glass, *President*
Dan Wagner, *Regional Mgr*
Glenn Fournie, *Vice Pres*
Pat Meeker, *Vice Pres*
EMP: 150
SALES (corp-wide): 6.7B  Privately Held
SIC: 3069  Molded rubber products
HQ: Roho, Inc.
100 N Florida Ave
Belleville IL 62221
618 277-9173

**(G-1674)**
**RTS SENTRY INC**
4401 N Belt W  (62226-5215)
PHONE..................618 257-7100
David Hollenbeck, *President*
Brent Boyles, *Vice Pres*
EMP: 13
SQ FT: 40,000
SALES: 2MM  Privately Held
WEB: www.rtssentry.com
SIC: 3699  Security devices

**(G-1675)**
**SAFE EFFECTIVE ALTERNATIVES**
Also Called: Lice B Gone
6218 Old Saint Louis Rd  (62223-4533)
P.O. Box 528  (62222-0528)
PHONE..................618 236-2727
Jim Rompel, *President*
EMP: 10
SQ FT: 12,000
SALES (est): 2MM  Privately Held
WEB: www.s-e-a.net
SIC: 5122  2844  Hair preparations; hair preparations, including shampoos

**(G-1676)**
**SNOW PRINTING LLC**
6428 Old Saint Louis Rd  (62223-4597)
PHONE..................618 233-0712
Fax: 618 257-3331
Pam Hollenkamp, *Partner*
Barb O'Donnell, *Partner*
EMP: 5
SQ FT: 2,500
SALES (est): 570K  Privately Held
WEB: www.snowprinting.net
SIC: 2752  Commercial printing, offset

**(G-1677)**
**SWANSEA SIGN A RAMA INC**
Also Called: Sign-A-Rama
216 Frank Scott Pkwy E # 3  (62226-7612)
PHONE..................618 234-7446
Fazil Imdad, *Principal*
EMP: 3
SALES (est): 257.3K  Privately Held
SIC: 3993  Signs & advertising specialties

**(G-1678)**
**TERRASOURCE GLOBAL CORPORATION**
1 Freedom Dr  (62226-5104)
P.O. Box 385  (62222-0385)
PHONE..................618 641-6985
Todd Ruff, *Plant Mgr*
Bill Pfeifer, *Plant Mgr*
Jordan Scott, *Regl Sales Mgr*
Arlene Willmann, *Marketing Staff*
Mike Hamby, *Director*
EMP: 80  Publicly Held
SIC: 3532  Mining machinery
HQ: Terrasource Global Corporation
100 N Broadway Ste 1600
Saint Louis MO 63102
618 641-6966

**(G-1679)**
**TINNEY TOOL & MACHINE CO**
815 N Church St  (62220-4151)
PHONE..................618 236-7273
Robin Tinney, *President*
Karl Tinney, *General Mgr*
EMP: 7
SQ FT: 10,000
SALES: 550K  Privately Held
SIC: 3599  Machine shop, jobbing & repair

**(G-1680)**
**TISCH MONUMENTS INC (PA)**
Also Called: Tisch Granite & Marble
17 N 3rd St  (62220-1101)
PHONE..................618 233-3017
Fax: 618 234-0451
Donald Tisch, *President*
EMP: 3
SALES (est): 371.1K  Privately Held
SIC: 5999  3281  Monuments, finished to custom order; rock & stone specimens; cut stone & stone products

**(G-1681)**
**TOCO**
825 W Main St  (62220-1516)
PHONE..................618 257-8626
Lea Compton, *Manager*
Kim Vrooman, *Director*
EMP: 7

SALES: 50K  Privately Held
SIC: 2211  Tapestry fabrics, cotton

**(G-1682)**
**TOWN HALL SPORTS INC**
Also Called: Town Hall Archery
5901 Cool Sports Rd  (62223-6848)
PHONE..................618 235-9881
Fax: 618 235-4614
Jack Hoffarth Sr, *President*
Diana Hoffarth, *Vice Pres*
Roger Blaes, *Manager*
J Monty Hoffarth Jr, *Manager*
EMP: 11
SQ FT: 20,000
SALES: 1.5MM  Privately Held
WEB: www.townhallsports.com
SIC: 5999  2395  5941  Trophies & plaques; embroidery & art needlework; archery supplies

**(G-1683)**
**U MARK INC**
102 Iowa Ave  (62220-3940)
P.O. Box 411  (62222-0411)
PHONE..................618 235-7500
Marco Ziniti, *CEO*
Dana Wallace, *Manager*
▲ EMP: 28
SQ FT: 16,000
SALES: 2.4MM  Privately Held
WEB: www.umarkers.com
SIC: 3951  3953  Markers, soft tip (felt, fabric, plastic, etc.); stencils, painting & marking

**(G-1684)**
**UPCHURCH READY MIX CONCRETE**
950 West Blvd  (62221-4073)
PHONE..................618 235-6222
Fax: 618 322-2909
Greg Upchurch, *Manager*
EMP: 3
SALES (corp-wide): 1.1MM  Privately Held
SIC: 3273  4212  Ready-mixed concrete; local trucking, without storage
PA: Upchurch Ready Mix Concrete Inc
564 Mildred Ave
East Saint Louis IL
618 332-2954

**(G-1685)**
**VI INC**
1801 N Belt W Ste 4  (62226-8201)
PHONE..................618 277-8703
John Massen, *President*
Joe Vassen, *Admin Sec*
EMP: 2
SALES (est): 305.8K  Privately Held
SIC: 3679  Electronic loads & power supplies

**(G-1686)**
**VIDEOJET TECHNOLOGIES INC**
1 Marsh Dr  (62220-3408)
PHONE..................618 235-6804
Claire Best, *COO*
Steve H Manz, *Vice Pres*
Dennis Carron, *Opers Mgr*
John Brewer, *QC Mgr*
Brian Kauhl, *Engineer*
EMP: 150
SALES (corp-wide): 16.8B  Publicly Held
WEB: www.videojet.com
SIC: 3579  Addressing machines, plates & plate embossers
HQ: Videojet Technologies Inc.
1500 N Mittel Blvd
Wood Dale IL 60191
630 860-7300

**(G-1687)**
**VILLAGE TYPOGRAPHERS INC**
1381 Rocky Creek Ct  (62220-3082)
PHONE..................618 235-6756
Daniel D Franklin, *President*
Terry Yokota, *Vice Pres*
EMP: 2
SALES (est): 236.5K  Privately Held
WEB: www.villagetype.com
SIC: 2791  Typographic composition, for the printing trade; typesetting, computer controlled

**(G-1688)**
**VOGES INC (PA)**
100 N 24th St  (62226-6659)
P.O. Box 328  (62222-0328)
PHONE..................618 233-2760
Fax: 618 233-2288
Pauline V Voges, *President*
Debra L Voges, *Exec VP*
Mike Koenigstein, *VP Mfg*
Chris Crowell, *QC Mgr*
Julie Rutkowski, *QC Mgr*
▲ EMP: 60  EST: 1916
SQ FT: 140,000
SALES (est): 16.4MM  Privately Held
WEB: www.roeschinc.com
SIC: 3469  3585  3479  3441  Appliance parts, porcelain enameled; air conditioning equipment, complete; aluminum coating of metal products; fabricated structural metal; porcelain electrical supplies; paints & allied products

**(G-1689)**
**VOSS PATTERN WORKS INC**
123 Iowa Ave  (62220-3941)
PHONE..................618 233-4242
Fax: 618 233-4293
Leo F Voss, *President*
Mina Voss, *Treasurer*
EMP: 7  EST: 1921
SQ FT: 5,000
SALES (est): 450K  Privately Held
SIC: 3544  2796  5999  3499  Industrial molds; engraving on copper, steel, wood or rubber; printing plates; banners, flags, decals & posters; trophies, metal, except silver; industrial patterns

**(G-1690)**
**WEISS MONUMENT WORKS INC**
Also Called: Philip W Weiss Monument Works
9904 W Main St  (62223-1405)
PHONE..................618 398-1811
Philip W Weiss, *President*
Cheryl Weiss, *Treasurer*
▲ EMP: 3
SALES (est): 546.1K  Privately Held
SIC: 5999  3281  7389  Gravestones, finished; cut stone & stone products;

**(G-1691)**
**WIEMAN FUELS LP GAS COMPANY**
418 S Belt E  (62220-2652)
PHONE..................618 632-4015
David Young, *Manager*
EMP: 3
SALES (est): 178.6K  Privately Held
SIC: 2869  Fuels

## Bellwood
### Cook County

**(G-1692)**
**A R C ELECTRO REFINISHERS INC**
4113 Butterfield Rd  (60104-1798)
PHONE..................708 681-5535
Fax: 708 681-5545
Patricia Camp, *President*
Daniel Slavik, *Vice Pres*
Gary Slavik, *Treasurer*
EMP: 8  EST: 1960
SQ FT: 7,000
SALES (est): 630K  Privately Held
SIC: 3479  Painting of metal products; coating of metals with silicon

**(G-1693)**
**ALDONEX INC**
2917 Saint Charles Rd  (60104-1543)
P.O. Box 148  (60104-0148)
PHONE..................708 547-5663
Fax: 708 547-5738
Alan Miller, *President*
Wanda Miller, *Corp Secy*
Tina Oliver, *Manager*
EMP: 15
SQ FT: 27,000

SALES (est): 3.2MM  Privately Held
WEB: www.aldonex.com
SIC: 3612  5063  Specialty transformers; rectifier transformers; power & distribution transformers; transformers & transmission equipment; transformers, electric; power transmission equipment, electric

**(G-1694)**
**ASAP PALLETS INC**
2711 Washington Blvd (60104-1941)
PHONE.................................630 917-0180
Maria Rodriguez, *Principal*
EMP: 4
SALES (est): 286.2K  Privately Held
SIC: 2448  Pallets, wood & wood with metal

**(G-1695)**
**BELLWOOD DUNKIN DONUTS**
Also Called: Dunkin' Donuts
502 Mannheim Rd (60104-1750)
PHONE.................................708 401-5601
Fax: 708 544-6215
Mirga Lai, *Owner*
EMP: 10
SALES (est): 247.6K  Privately Held
SIC: 5461  2051  5812  Doughnuts; doughnuts, except frozen; ice cream, soft drink & soda fountain stands

**(G-1696)**
**BELLWOOD ELECTRIC MOTORS INC**
200 25th Ave (60104-1203)
PHONE.................................708 544-7223
Fax: 708 544-7293
Angelica Meza, *President*
Martha Meza, *Manager*
EMP: 7 EST: 1962
SQ FT: 5,000
SALES (est): 1.5MM  Privately Held
SIC: 7694  5063  Electric motor repair; motors, electric

**(G-1697)**
**BEMIS PACKAGING INC**
Bemis North America
5303 Saint Charles Rd (60104-1048)
PHONE.................................708 544-1600
Pete Mathias, *President*
Bill Lifton, *Opers Mgr*
EMP: 25
SALES (corp-wide): 4B  Publicly Held
SIC: 2671  Packaging paper & plastics film, coated & laminated
HQ: Bemis Packaging, Inc.
    3550 Moser St
    Oshkosh WI 54901
    920 527-2300

**(G-1698)**
**BERGHAUS PIPE ORGAN BUILDERS**
2151 Madison St Ste 1 (60104-1973)
PHONE.................................708 544-4052
Fax: 708 544-4058
Leonard G Berghaus, *CEO*
Brian Berghaus, *President*
Collene Berghaus, *Corp Secy*
Jean Obrien, *Office Mgr*
Judith Berghaus, *Shareholder*
EMP: 22
SQ FT: 30,000
SALES (est): 2.8MM  Privately Held
WEB: www.berghausorgan.com
SIC: 3931  7699  Organs, all types: pipe, reed, hand, electronic, etc.; organ tuning & repair

**(G-1699)**
**BORGWARNER INC**
700 25th Ave (60104-1908)
PHONE.................................248 754-9200
Darlene Baldridge, *Opers Staff*
Andy Lacy, *Electrical Engi*
Chad Cassinelli, *Human Res Mgr*
Mike Coetzee, *Manager*
EMP: 30
SALES (corp-wide): 9B  Publicly Held
SIC: 3714  Motor vehicle parts & accessories
PA: Borgwarner Inc.
    3850 Hamlin Rd
    Auburn Hills MI 48326
    248 754-9200

**(G-1700)**
**BORGWARNER TRANSM SYSTEMS**
Also Called: Borg Warner Automotive
700 25th Ave (60104-1908)
PHONE.................................708 547-2600
Fax: 708 547-3372
Patrick Johnson, *Principal*
Arshad Ansari, *Senior Engr*
Pete McDonald, *Marketing Staff*
Randy Heider, *Branch Mgr*
John Warkentien, *Supervisor*
EMP: 820
SALES (corp-wide): 9B  Publicly Held
SIC: 3714  3568  3469  3465  Transmissions, motor vehicle; power transmission equipment; metal stampings; automotive stampings
HQ: Borgwarner Transmission Systems Inc.
    3800 Automation Ave # 500
    Auburn Hills MI 48326
    248 754-9200

**(G-1701)**
**COMBINED METALS HOLDING INC**
2401 Grant Ave (60104-1660)
PHONE.................................708 547-8800
Cyrus Tang, *President*
EMP: 112
SALES (est): 8.1MM  Publicly Held
WEB: www.ketnar.org
SIC: 3312  3325  Blast furnaces & steel mills; steel foundries
HQ: Ak Steel Corporation
    9227 Centre Pointe Dr
    West Chester OH 45069
    513 425-4200

**(G-1702)**
**D A MATOT INC**
2501 Van Buren St (60104-2459)
PHONE.................................708 547-1888
Fax: 708 547-1608
Anne Matot, *President*
Anne M Kolker, *Principal*
Kathryn Matot, *Admin Sec*
▼ EMP: 60 EST: 1888
SQ FT: 40,000
SALES (est): 15.8MM  Privately Held
WEB: www.matot.com
SIC: 3534  Elevators & equipment; dumbwaiters

**(G-1703)**
**DELTROL CORP**
Also Called: Deltrol Fluid Products
3001 Grant Ave (60104-1289)
PHONE.................................708 547-0500
Fax: 708 547-6881
Paul Goc, *Plant Mgr*
Keith Pietranczyk, *Opers Staff*
Dale Radaszewski, *Production*
Ken Harner, *Purch Mgr*
Scott Pierson, *QC Mgr*
EMP: 125
SALES (corp-wide): 45.8MM  Privately Held
WEB: www.deltrol.com
SIC: 3625  3594  3494  3492  Relays, for electronic use; fluid power pumps & motors; valves & pipe fittings; fluid power valves & hose fittings; industrial valves
PA: Deltrol Corp.
    2740 S 20th St
    Milwaukee WI 53215
    414 671-6800

**(G-1704)**
**DOUGLAS PRESS INC**
2810 Madison St (60104-2295)
PHONE.................................800 323-0705
Fax: 708 547-0296
Debra Fienberg, *President*
Sherman Sotonoff, *Purchasing*
John Bednara, *Engineer*
Feinberg Sandra, *CFO*
Norene Stimburis, *VP Finance*
EMP: 250 EST: 1966
SQ FT: 17,500
SALES (est): 44.1MM  Privately Held
WEB: www.douglaspress.com
SIC: 2752  Commercial printing, offset

**(G-1705)**
**FERRARA CANDY COMPANY**
3000 Washington Blvd (60104-1946)
PHONE.................................708 432-4407
Craig Caswell, *Project Engr*
Ron Montefusco, *Branch Mgr*
EMP: 15
SALES (corp-wide): 618.9MM  Privately Held
WEB: www.ferrarapan.com
SIC: 2064  Candy & other confectionery products; chewing candy, not chewing gum; chocolate candy, except solid chocolate; jellybeans
PA: Ferrara Candy Company
    1 Tower Ln Ste 2700
    Oakbrook Terrace IL 60181
    708 366-0500

**(G-1706)**
**G J NIKOLAS & CO INC**
2800 Washington Blvd (60104-1987)
PHONE.................................708 544-0320
Fax: 708 544-9722
George J Nikolas Jr, *President*
James Koch, *Vice Pres*
Patty Jensen, *Manager*
▼ EMP: 20
SQ FT: 26,000
SALES (est): 5.3MM  Privately Held
WEB: www.finish1.com
SIC: 2851  2891  Lacquer: bases, dopes, thinner; adhesives & sealants

**(G-1707)**
**GRPHIC RICHARDS COMMUNICATIONS**
2700 Van Buren St (60104-2409)
PHONE.................................708 547-6000
Fax: 708 547-6044
Mary Lawrence, *President*
Tim Richards, *General Mgr*
Kevin Richards, *Vice Pres*
Stephen H Richards, *Vice Pres*
Steve Mueller, *Engineer*
EMP: 15 EST: 1925
SQ FT: 19,500
SALES (est): 3MM  Privately Held
WEB: www.rgcnet.com
SIC: 2752  Commercial printing, lithographic

**(G-1708)**
**H A FRAMBURG & COMPANY (PA)**
941 Cernan Dr (60104-2294)
PHONE.................................708 547-5757
Fax: 708 547-0064
Malcolm Tripp, *President*
Roberta Sikorsik, *Vice Pres*
Harry Mogadam, *CFO*
▲ EMP: 36 EST: 1905
SQ FT: 75,000
SALES (est): 4.2MM  Privately Held
SIC: 3645  3646  Residential lighting fixtures; commercial indusl & institutional electric lighting fixtures

**(G-1709)**
**INNOVTIVE DESIGN SOLUTIONS LLC**
2501 Van Buren St (60104-2459)
PHONE.................................708 547-1942
Ann Koller, *Principal*
Catherine Hartman,
John M Lane,
EMP: 3 EST: 1999
SALES: 10MM  Privately Held
SIC: 2531  Seats, miscellaneous public conveyances

**(G-1710)**
**INTRA ACTION CORP**
3719 Warren Ave (60104-2055)
PHONE.................................708 547-6644
Fax: 708 547-0687
John A Lekavich, *President*
Jeanne Weiler, *Materials Mgr*
Bob Jandeska, *Engineer*
Michael Strojny, *Manager*
Bernadette Panovich, *Admin Sec*
EMP: 32
SQ FT: 10,000

SALES (est): 6.5MM  Privately Held
WEB: www.intraaction.com
SIC: 3827  Optical instruments & apparatus

**(G-1711)**
**JAMALI KOPY KAT PRINTING INC**
2501 Saint Charles Rd (60104-1503)
PHONE.................................708 544-6164
Fax: 708 544-6569
Dawood I Burhani, *President*
EMP: 3
SQ FT: 1,000
SALES: 200K  Privately Held
SIC: 2752  7334  3993  7336  Commercial printing, offset; photocopying & duplicating services; signs & advertising specialties; graphic arts & related design

**(G-1712)**
**LEZZA SPUMONI AND DESSERTS INC**
4009 Saint Charles Rd (60104-1197)
PHONE.................................708 547-5969
Fax: 708 547-5974
Edward S Lezza, *President*
Rosemarie Lezza, *Corp Secy*
Edward S Lezza Jr, *Vice Pres*
Victor E Lezza, *Vice Pres*
Louis Lezza, *VP Sales*
EMP: 22 EST: 1905
SQ FT: 10,000
SALES: 5MM  Privately Held
WEB: www.lezza.com
SIC: 2024  2038  Ice cream & frozen desserts; frozen specialties

**(G-1713)**
**MAJESTIC ARCHTCTURAL WDWRK INC**
2150 Madison St (60104-1952)
PHONE.................................708 240-8484
Mary V Dorio, *President*
EMP: 5 EST: 2011
SALES (est): 625.5K  Privately Held
SIC: 2431  Millwork

**(G-1714)**
**MARO CARTON INC**
333 31st Ave (60104-1527)
PHONE.................................708 649-9982
Joseph J Maro III, *President*
Chris Rose, *Sales Mgr*
EMP: 2
SALES (est): 353.7K  Privately Held
WEB: www.marocarton.com
SIC: 2759  Commercial printing

**(G-1715)**
**MOBILIA INC**
1023 Cernan Dr (60104-2462)
PHONE.................................708 865-0700
Fax: 708 652-9198
Melchiore Bonfiglio, *President*
Barry Midelton, *Plant Mgr*
Rich Nona, *Engineer*
Martin Harkins, *CFO*
Marty Harkins, *CFO*
EMP: 20
SQ FT: 35,000
SALES (est): 3MM  Privately Held
WEB: www.mobiliadesignsinwood.com
SIC: 2521  2511  Wood office furniture; wood household furniture

**(G-1716)**
**QS LUXURIOUS HAIR & SHOES INC**
305 47th Ave (60104-1321)
PHONE.................................773 556-6092
Quwanna Spivery, *President*
EMP: 5 EST: 2013
SALES (est): 304.1K  Privately Held
SIC: 3999  Hair & hair-based products

**(G-1717)**
**R K J PALLETS INC**
Also Called: Kitty Pallets
1003 Cernan Dr (60104-2462)
PHONE.................................708 493-0701
Fax: 708 493-0712
Jesus Rodriguez, *President*
Nitza Anaya, *Principal*
Bill Galliger, *Principal*
Ray Rodriguez, *Vice Pres*

# Bellwood - Cook County (G-1718)

**EMP:** 10
**SQ FT:** 11,000
**SALES:** 608.7K **Privately Held**
**SIC:** 2448 Pallets, wood

### (G-1718)
### RIDER DICKERSON INC
815 25th Ave (60104-2202)
**PHONE** ................ 312 427-2926
**Fax:** 312 427-4949
William J Barta, *Principal*
Joseph Brunner, *Counsel*
Ron Rosignal, *Project Mgr*
Ron Sknerski, *Project Mgr*
Molly Hague, *Production*
**EMP:** 60
**SQ FT:** 56,000
**SALES (est):** 23.1MM **Privately Held**
**SIC:** 2752 2791 2789 Color lithography; lithographing on metal; typesetting; bookbinding & related work

### (G-1719)
### SB BORON CORPORATION
Also Called: Sb Boron
20 Davis Dr (60104-1047)
**PHONE** ................ 708 547-9002
Gary Resnick, *President*
Chris Kachiroubas, *General Mgr*
Patti Lyons, *Finance Mgr*
Joel Stone, *Admin Sec*
▲ **EMP:** 9
**SQ FT:** 11,000
**SALES (est):** 1.6MM **Privately Held**
**WEB:** www.sbboron.com
**SIC:** 2869 Industrial organic chemicals

### (G-1720)
### SHAMROCK SCIENTIFIC ◯
34 Davis Dr (60104-1247)
**PHONE** ................ 800 323-0249
**Fax:** 708 547-9021
James Kornfeld, *President*
David Klonowski, *General Mgr*
**EMP:** 80 **EST:** 2016
**SALES (est):** 836.9K
**SALES (corp-wide):** 199.9MM **Privately Held**
**SIC:** 2759 Labels & seals: printing; calendars: printing
**PA:** Pax Holdings, Llc
  758 N Broadway Ste 910
  Milwaukee WI 53202
  414 803-9983

### (G-1721)
### SKILL-DI INC
2655 Harrison St (60104-2463)
**PHONE** ................ 708 544-6080
**Fax:** 708 544-6086
Michael D Rosenquist, *President*
Richard Rosenquist, *Corp Secy*
**EMP:** 10
**SQ FT:** 23,500
**SALES (est):** 1.6MM **Privately Held**
**SIC:** 3469 Stamping metal for the trade

### (G-1722)
### SOLAB INC
2715 Grant Ave (60104-1247)
**PHONE** ................ 708 544-2200
**Fax:** 708 544-2202
Brian D Corcoran, *President*
Brian Corcoran, *Vice Pres*
Cheryl Turner, *Traffic Mgr*
▲ **EMP:** 15 **EST:** 1927
**SQ FT:** 40,000
**SALES (est):** 4.5MM **Privately Held**
**WEB:** www.sololabsinc.com
**SIC:** 2844 2841 Face creams or lotions; lipsticks; soap & other detergents

### (G-1723)
### STEELE & LOEBER LUMBER (HQ)
801 Mannheim Rd (60104-2073)
**PHONE** ................ 708 544-8383
**Fax:** 708 544-8392
Richard Loeber, *President*
**EMP:** 6
**SQ FT:** 1,500
**SALES:** 766.7K
**SALES (corp-wide):** 4MM **Privately Held**
**SIC:** 3442 Metal doors
**PA:** Steele And Loeber Lumber Co.
  801 Mannheim Rd
  Bellwood IL 60104
  708 636-5660

### (G-1724)
### SUZY CABINET COMPANY INC
2740 Washington Blvd A (60104-1957)
**PHONE** ................ 708 705-1259
Suzana Radman, *President*
Ante Marovic, *General Mgr*
**EMP:** 6
**SQ FT:** 7,500
**SALES (est):** 550K **Privately Held**
**SIC:** 2599 2431 Cabinets, factory; millwork

### (G-1725)
### TRU COAT PLATING AND FINISHING
130 Mannheim Rd (60104-1143)
**PHONE** ................ 708 544-3940
**Fax:** 708 544-3943
Carmine N Mazzone Jr, *President*
Susan Ocwieja, *Corp Secy*
Rick Mazzone, *Vice Pres*
**EMP:** 12 **EST:** 1961
**SQ FT:** 14,000
**SALES:** 1MM **Privately Held**
**SIC:** 3471 Chromium plating of metals or formed products

---

## Belvidere
### Boone County

### (G-1726)
### ACME GRINDING & MANUFACTURING
6871 Belford Indus Dr (61008-8712)
P.O. Box 509 (61008-0509)
**PHONE** ................ 815 323-1380
**Fax:** 815 323-1381
Jack Zaluckyj, *President*
Chuck Zaluckyj, *President*
Charles Zaluckyj, *Vice Pres*
Aaron Nicely, *Maintence Staff*
**EMP:** 110
**SQ FT:** 55,000
**SALES (est):** 1.3MM **Privately Held**
**WEB:** www.acmegrinding.com
**SIC:** 3599 Machine shop, jobbing & repair

### (G-1727)
### ACUMENT GLOBAL TECHOLOGIES
Also Called: Camcar
830 E Menomonie St (61008-2338)
**PHONE** ................ 815 547-7574
**EMP:** 10
**SALES (est):** 1.2MM **Privately Held**
**SIC:** 3452 Bolts, nuts, rivets & washers

### (G-1728)
### ADVANCED FINISHING
1044 Tuneberg Pkwy (61008-7933)
P.O. Box 137, Rockford (61105-0137)
**PHONE** ................ 815 964-3367
Grace Galvan, *Owner*
**EMP:** 3
**SALES (est):** 200K **Privately Held**
**SIC:** 2899 Metal treating compounds

### (G-1729)
### AIRO TOOL & MANUFACTURING INC
6823 Irene Rd (61008-8789)
**PHONE** ................ 815 547-7588
Heidi Abramat, *President*
Roy Abramat, *Vice Pres*
Andrew Abramat, *Admin Sec*
▲ **EMP:** 15
**SQ FT:** 6,000
**SALES (est):** 2.3MM **Privately Held**
**WEB:** www.airotool.com
**SIC:** 3544 3599 Special dies, tools, jigs & fixtures; machine shop, jobbing & repair

### (G-1730)
### ALLEGRA NETWORK LLC
1982 Belford North Dr (61008-8565)
**PHONE** ................ 815 877-3400
**Fax:** 815 544-0353
John Bates, *Principal*
**EMP:** 3
**SALES (est):** 291.8K **Privately Held**
**SIC:** 2752 7336 Commercial printing, lithographic; commercial art & graphic design

### (G-1731)
### AMERICAN COLLOID COMPANY
Also Called: Amcol
2786 Newburg Rd (61008-7997)
P.O. Box 37 (61008-0037)
**PHONE** ................ 815 547-5369
**Fax:** 815 544-9862
Heather Bohn, *Manager*
Craig Finnicum, *Manager*
**EMP:** 12
**SALES (corp-wide):** 1.6B **Publicly Held**
**WEB:** www.colloid.com
**SIC:** 2899 Chemical preparations
**HQ:** American Colloid Company
  2870 Forbs Ave
  Hoffman Estates IL 60192

### (G-1732)
### ANDROID INDSTRES- BLVIDERE LLC
1222 Crosslink Pkwy (61008-6310)
**PHONE** ................ 815 547-3742
Dennis Donnay, *Plant Mgr*
Gregory Nichols,
**EMP:** 220
**SALES (est):** 82.2MM
**SALES (corp-wide):** 549.9MM **Privately Held**
**SIC:** 3711 Automobile assembly, including specialty automobiles
**PA:** Android Industries, L.L.C.
  2155 Executive Hills Dr
  Auburn Hills MI 48326
  248 454-0500

### (G-1733)
### ANDROID INDUSTRIES LLC
1222 Crosslink Pkwy (61008-6310)
**PHONE** ................ 815 544-4165
**EMP:** 5
**SALES (est):** 111.5K **Privately Held**
**SIC:** 3999 Manufacturing industries

### (G-1734)
### ARROWTECH PALLET & CRATING
860 E Jackson St (61008-2332)
**PHONE** ................ 815 547-9300
John T Swenby, *President*
Ray Ridriguez, *Treasurer*
Jessica Strobbe, *Manager*
Larry W Johnson, *Admin Sec*
**EMP:** 60
**SQ FT:** 10,000
**SALES (est):** 4MM **Privately Held**
**WEB:** www.palletsales.net
**SIC:** 2448 5031 2441 Pallets, wood; skids, wood; building materials, exterior; building materials, interior; nailed wood boxes & shook

### (G-1735)
### BELROCK PRINTING INC
915 W Perry St (61008-3420)
**PHONE** ................ 815 547-1096
**Fax:** 815 547-3665
Patrick Mattison, *President*
**EMP:** 4
**SALES (est):** 97.9K **Privately Held**
**SIC:** 2752 Commercial printing, lithographic

### (G-1736)
### BELVEDERE USA LLC (PA)
1 Belvedere Blvd (61008-8594)
**PHONE** ................ 815 544-3131
**Fax:** 800 626-9750
Barry Sanders, *President*
Jerry Grossi, *General Mgr*
Horst Ackermann, *COO*
Jonathan Pugh, *Senior VP*
Chuck Jones, *Purch Dir*
◆ **EMP:** 180
**SALES (est):** 69.8MM **Privately Held**
**SIC:** 3999 Barber & beauty shop equipment; chairs, hydraulic, barber & beauty shop; furniture, barber & beauty shop; massage machines, electric; barber & beauty shops

### (G-1737)
### BELVIDERE DAILY REPUBLICAN CO
130 S State St Ste 101 (61008-3772)
**PHONE** ................ 815 547-0084
**Fax:** 815 547-3045
Keith Cruger, *President*
William Brennan, *VP Opers*
Cyndy Jenson, *Controller*
Patty Club, *Bookkeeper*
Laura Anderson, *Manager*
**EMP:** 40
**SQ FT:** 13,000
**SALES (est):** 1.6MM **Privately Held**
**SIC:** 2711 Commercial printing & newspaper publishing combined

### (G-1738)
### BIOVANTAGE FUELS LLC
1201 Crosslink Pkwy (61008-6310)
**PHONE** ................ 815 544-6028
Brian Coker, *COO*
Dawn Ness, *CFO*
Brian Toker, *Mng Member*
Kevin Madden, *Manager*
**EMP:** 15
**SQ FT:** 10,000
**SALES:** 8MM **Privately Held**
**SIC:** 2869 Fuels

### (G-1739)
### BOONE COUNTY SHOPPER INC
112 Leonard Ct (61008-3694)
**PHONE** ................ 815 544-2166
**Fax:** 815 544-5558
Ed Branom, *President*
Yvonne Branom, *President*
Shirley Ryan, *Office Mgr*
William Branom, *Manager*
**EMP:** 17 **EST:** 1948
**SQ FT:** 8,000
**SALES (est):** 1.3MM **Privately Held**
**WEB:** www.boonecountyshopper.com
**SIC:** 2741 2711 Shopping news: publishing only, not printed on site; newspapers

### (G-1740)
### BT & E CO
6877 Belford Indus Dr (61008-8712)
P.O. Box 248 (61008-0248)
**PHONE** ................ 815 544-6431
**Fax:** 815 544-2120
Robert A Buelte, *President*
Lavon Buelte, *Admin Sec*
**EMP:** 9 **EST:** 1945
**SQ FT:** 24,000
**SALES:** 1.1MM **Privately Held**
**SIC:** 7389 3544 Grinding, precision: commercial or industrial; special dies & tools

### (G-1741)
### CAISSON INC (PA)
Also Called: Interserve
720 Logistics Dr (61008-8507)
**PHONE** ................ 815 547-5925
Dana T Richardson, *President*
**EMP:** 21 **EST:** 1995
**SQ FT:** 35,000
**SALES (est):** 4.6MM **Privately Held**
**WEB:** www.interserve.com
**SIC:** 2449 2448 Rectangular boxes & crates, wood; skids, wood

### (G-1742)
### CAMCAR LLC
Also Called: Acument Tm Global Technologies
826 E Madison St (61008-2899)
**PHONE** ................ 815 547-7574
**Fax:** 815 544-7564
Bruce Swacina, *Vice Pres*
Richard Pool, *QC Mgr*
Brad Crandall, *Engineer*
Pete Varga, *Finance*
Kim Seidle, *Persnl Mgr*
**EMP:** 68 **Privately Held**
**WEB:** www.tfsi.textron.com
**SIC:** 3452 Bolts, nuts, rivets & washers
**HQ:** Camcar Llc
  4366 N Old Us Highway 31
  Rochester IN 46975
  574 223-3131

## GEOGRAPHIC SECTION

### (G-1743)
**CAMRYN INDUSTRIES LLC**
3458 Morreim Dr (61008-6308)
PHONE..................................815 544-1900
**EMP:** 150
**SALES (corp-wide):** 74K **Privately Held**
**SIC:** 2821 Molding compounds, plastics
**HQ:** Camryn Industries, Llc
  21624 Melrose Ave
  Southfield MI 48075

### (G-1744)
**CARPENTER CONTRACTORS AMER INC**
Also Called: R & D Thiel
2340 Newburg Rd Ste 200 (61008-7842)
PHONE..................................815 544-1699
**Fax:** 815 544-7132
Donald Thiel, *President*
Terry Smith, *President*
James P Jackson, *Vice Pres*
Mike Sobacki, *VP Finance*
Mark Sciortino, *Credit Mgr*
**EMP:** 300
**SALES (est):** 55.4MM
**SALES (corp-wide):** 182.9MM **Privately Held**
**WEB:** www.carpentercontractors.com
**SIC:** 1751 3441 Carpentry work; building components, structural steel
**PA:** Carpenter Contractors Of America, Inc.
  3900 Ave D Nw
  Winter Haven FL 33880
  863 294-6449

### (G-1745)
**CENTRAL RUBBER COMPANY**
844 E Jackson St (61008-2332)
PHONE..................................815 544-2191
**Fax:** 815 544-6881
J Michael Nauman, *President*
Al Maldonado, *Business Mgr*
Lawrence Korstanje, *Prdtn Mgr*
Klemens Chusin, *Manager*
Lynn Vaughan, *Executive*
▲ **EMP:** 43
**SQ FT:** 36,000
**SALES (est):** 7.1MM
**SALES (corp-wide):** 27.4B **Privately Held**
**WEB:** www.thenewjhp.com
**SIC:** 3678 3679 3643 3357 Electronic connectors; electronic switches; electronic circuits; connectors & terminals for electrical devices; communication wire; fiber optic cable (insulated)
**HQ:** Woodhead Industries, Llc
  333 Knightsbridge Pkwy # 200
  Lincolnshire IL 60069
  847 353-2500

### (G-1746)
**CHEMSCI TECHNOLOGIES INC**
6574 Revlon Dr (61008-8532)
PHONE..................................815 608-9135
Kenn Blair, *President*
▲ **EMP:** 2 **EST:** 2008
**SQ FT:** 2,800
**SALES (est):** 221.1K **Privately Held**
**SIC:** 2833 Medicinal chemicals

### (G-1747)
**CORRUGATED METALS INC**
6550 Revlon Dr (61008-8532)
PHONE..................................815 323-1310
**Fax:** 815 323-1317
Edward S Carlton Jr, *President*
Kenneth E Carlton, *Corp Secy*
Thomas J Carlton, *Vice Pres*
Brian Marinelli, *Controller*
Manny Martinez, *Accountant*
**EMP:** 18 **EST:** 1887
**SQ FT:** 35,125
**SALES (est):** 9.2MM **Privately Held**
**WEB:** www.corrugated-metals.com
**SIC:** 3444 Roof deck, sheet metal

### (G-1748)
**CURTIS WOODWORKING INC**
4820 Newburg Rd (61008-7195)
PHONE..................................815 544-3543
Curtis Sherman, *CEO*
Courtney D Sherman, *Vice Pres*
**EMP:** 2
**SALES:** 200K **Privately Held**
**SIC:** 2499 2431 Decorative wood & woodwork; millwork

### (G-1749)
**DODGE MACHINE TOOL**
204 S Main St (61008-3320)
P.O. Box 589 (61008-0589)
PHONE..................................815 544-0967
**Fax:** 815 544-5442
Gary Dodge, *President*
Charlotte Dodge, *Managing Prtnr*
Kavin Dodge, *Treasurer*
**EMP:** 4 **EST:** 1979
**SQ FT:** 3,500
**SALES (est):** 493.1K **Privately Held**
**SIC:** 3544 Special dies, tools, jigs & fixtures

### (G-1750)
**EBERSPAECHER NORTH AMERICA INC**
725 Logistics Dr (61008-8507)
PHONE..................................815 544-1421
Ronald Laing, *Manager*
**EMP:** 5
**SALES (corp-wide):** 4.6B **Privately Held**
**SIC:** 3714 Motor vehicle parts & accessories
**HQ:** Eberspaecher North America, Inc.
  29101 Haggerty Rd
  Novi MI 48377
  248 994-7010

### (G-1751)
**FAST LANE THREADS CUSTOM EMB**
1467 Mckinley Ave Ste A (61008-1360)
P.O. Box 866 (61008-0866)
PHONE..................................815 544-9898
Debora Kemp, *Owner*
**EMP:** 5
**SALES (est):** 200K **Privately Held**
**SIC:** 2395 2396 5699 Emblems, embroidered; printing & embossing on plastics fabric articles; customized clothing & apparel

### (G-1752)
**FRANKLIN DISPLAY GROUP INC (PA)**
910 E Lincoln Ave (61008-2928)
P.O. Box 127 (61008-0127)
PHONE..................................815 544-6676
George Mutert, *President*
David Lancaster, *Controller*
Jo Trevino, *Manager*
Donald Mutert Jr, *Admin Sec*
▲ **EMP:** 90 **EST:** 1978
**SQ FT:** 87,000
**SALES (est):** 24.6MM **Privately Held**
**WEB:** www.fww.com
**SIC:** 3496 Miscellaneous fabricated wire products

### (G-1753)
**FRANKLIN WIRE WORKS INC**
2519 Business Route 20 (61008-8717)
P.O. Box 127 (61008-0127)
PHONE..................................815 544-6676
**Fax:** 815 547-9239
**EMP:** 2
**SALES (est):** 300.8K **Privately Held**
**SIC:** 3496 Mfg Misc Fabricated Wire Products

### (G-1754)
**GENERAL MILLS INC**
915 E Pleasant St (61008-3350)
PHONE..................................815 544-7399
Marcia Barefield, *Safety Dir*
Gary Yonto, *Facilities Mgr*
Elton Turner, *Purch Dir*
Roger Sonnek, *QC Dir*
Mike Difford, *Engineer*
**EMP:** 50
**SALES (corp-wide):** 16.5B **Publicly Held**
**WEB:** www.generalmills.com
**SIC:** 2033 2037 2038 Vegetables: packaged in cans, jars, etc.; vegetables, quick frozen & cold pack, excl. potato products; frozen specialties
**PA:** General Mills, Inc.
  1 General Mills Blvd
  Minneapolis MN 55426
  763 764-7600

### (G-1755)
**GENERAL MILLS GREEN GIANT**
725 Landmark Dr (61008-6715)
PHONE..................................815 547-5311
Chris Masters, *Principal*
**EMP:** 3
**SALES (est):** 189.3K **Privately Held**
**SIC:** 2038 Frozen specialties

### (G-1756)
**GERDAU AMERISTEEL US INC**
Belvidere Reinforcing Steel
2595 Tripp Rd (61008-7206)
PHONE..................................815 544-9651
Mike Hand, *Manager*
**EMP:** 15 **Privately Held**
**SIC:** 3449 Bars, concrete reinforcing: fabricated steel
**HQ:** Gerdau Ameristeel Us Inc.
  4221 W Boy Scout Blvd # 600
  Tampa FL 33607
  813 286-8383

### (G-1757)
**GERDAU AMERISTEEL US INC**
2595 Tripp Rd (61008-7206)
PHONE..................................815 547-0400
**Fax:** 815 625-8745
Mike Hand, *Branch Mgr*
Ravi Talwar, *Manager*
**EMP:** 50 **Privately Held**
**SIC:** 3444 3449 3441 Concrete forms, sheet metal; miscellaneous metalwork; fabricated structural metal
**HQ:** Gerdau Ameristeel Us Inc.
  4221 W Boy Scout Blvd # 600
  Tampa FL 33607
  813 286-8383

### (G-1758)
**GREEN GIANT**
915 E Pleasant St (61008-3396)
PHONE..................................815 544-0438
**Fax:** 815 544-3929
Vince Castle, *Principal*
Ronda Zimmerman, *Human Res Mgr*
Chris Morrison, *Maintence Staff*
Jon Russet, *Maintence Staff*
**EMP:** 2 **EST:** 2007
**SALES (est):** 224.4K **Privately Held**
**SIC:** 3999 Manufacturing industries

### (G-1759)
**GRUPO ANTOLIN ILLINOIS INC**
642 Crystal Pkwy (61008-4065)
PHONE..................................815 544-8020
**Fax:** 815 544-8811
Joseph Maximilan Rogers, *Principal*
Russ Goemaere, *Exec VP*
Roberto Monteros, *Exec VP*
Diego Vizcaino, *Plant Mgr*
Tracey Zimmerman, *QC Mgr*
**EMP:** 180
**SALES (est):** 24MM **Privately Held**
**SIC:** 8741 3714 Management services; motor vehicle parts & accessories
**HQ:** Grupo Antolin-Irausa Sa
  Carretera Madrid-Irun (Burgos) (Km 244,8)
  Burgos 09007
  947 477-700

### (G-1760)
**GYMTEK INCORPORATED**
6853 Indy Dr (61008-8769)
PHONE..................................815 547-0771
**Fax:** 815 547-0552
Mary Yankus, *President*
Richard Yankus, *Opers Mgr*
**EMP:** 19
**SQ FT:** 20,000
**SALES (est):** 3MM **Privately Held**
**WEB:** www.gymtek.net
**SIC:** 3541 Machine tools, metal cutting type

### (G-1761)
**HALLEN BURIAL VAULT INC**
3690 Newburg Rd (61008-8529)
P.O. Box 557 (61008-0557)
PHONE..................................815 544-6138
**Fax:** 815 544-6142
Donald Freund, *President*
**EMP:** 6
**SALES (est):** 808.5K **Privately Held**
**SIC:** 3272 Burial vaults, concrete or precast terrazzo

### (G-1762)
**HOPPERSTAD CUSTOMS**
6860 Imron Dr (61008-8587)
PHONE..................................815 547-7534
Kerry Hopperstad, *Owner*
**EMP:** 2
**SALES (est):** 207.5K **Privately Held**
**WEB:** www.hopperstadcustoms.com
**SIC:** 3711 Motor vehicles & car bodies

### (G-1763)
**INFRASTRUCTURE DEF TECH LLC**
6550 Revlon Dr (61008-8532)
PHONE..................................800 379-1822
Brian Marinielli, *Controller*
Kenneth Carlton,
**EMP:** 2
**SALES (est):** 700K **Privately Held**
**WEB:** www.infrastructure-defense.com
**SIC:** 3499 Barricades, metal

### (G-1764)
**INK ENTERPRISES INC**
Also Called: I E Press & Graphics
1982 Belford North Dr (61008-8565)
PHONE..................................815 547-5515
Donna K Bates, *President*
John W Bates, *Vice Pres*
**EMP:** 5
**SALES (est):** 470K **Privately Held**
**WEB:** www.iepressandgraphics.com
**SIC:** 2752 Commercial printing, lithographic

### (G-1765)
**INTERNATIONAL AUTOMOTIVE**
Also Called: IAC Belvidere
1236 Crosslink Pkwy (61008-6310)
PHONE..................................815 544-2102
Robert S Miller, *President*
**EMP:** 273 **Privately Held**
**SIC:** 3089 Automotive parts, plastic
**HQ:** International Automotive Components Group North America, Inc.
  28333 Telegraph Rd
  Southfield MI 48034
  248 455-7000

### (G-1766)
**JMD SCREW PRODUCTS**
2873 E Fairfield Trl (61008-6455)
PHONE..................................815 505-9113
Jackie Rivera, *Principal*
**EMP:** 3
**SALES (est):** 149.3K **Privately Held**
**SIC:** 3451 Screw machine products

### (G-1767)
**M & M PALTECH INC**
Also Called: Paltech Enterprises Illinois
860 E Jackson St (61008-2332)
PHONE..................................630 350-7890
**Fax:** 815 547-9305
John Swenby, *President*
Ray Rodriguez, *Treasurer*
Alex Ringerst, *Manager*
Larry Johnson, *Admin Sec*
**EMP:** 60
**SQ FT:** 17,000
**SALES (est):** 11.1MM **Privately Held**
**SIC:** 2448 5031 5199 Pallets, wood; lumber, plywood & millwork; baling of wood shavings for mulch

### (G-1768)
**M & R CUSTOM MILLWORK**
Also Called: M&R Custom Mill Work
1979 Belford North Dr (61008-8582)
PHONE..................................815 547-8549
**Fax:** 815 547-6344
Mark B Roden, *Partner*
Renita L Roden, *Partner*
**EMP:** 5
**SALES (est):** 716.1K **Privately Held**
**WEB:** www.mrcustommillwork.com
**SIC:** 2499 2512 2541 2434 Kitchen, bathroom & household ware: wood; upholstered household furniture; wood partitions & fixtures; wood kitchen cabinets; millwork

**Belvidere - Boone County (G-1769)**        **GEOGRAPHIC SECTION**

---

### (G-1769)
**MANITOU AMERICAS INC**
Also Called: Gehl Company
888 Landmark Dr (61008-6715)
PHONE....................................262 334-9461
Kevin Hogan, *President*
Roland Thompson, *Manager*
Alexandra Teleso, *Technology*
**EMP:** 6
**SALES (corp-wide):** 1B **Privately Held**
**SIC:** 3531 3523 Backhoes, tractors, cranes, plows & similar equipment; dozers, tractor mounted: material moving; cranes; excavators: cable, clamshell, crane, derrick, dragline, etc.; farm machinery & equipment; haying machines: mowers, rakes, stackers, etc.; balers; farm: hay, straw, cotton, etc.; harvesters, fruit, vegetable, tobacco, etc.
**HQ:** Manitou Americas, Inc.
    1 Gehl Way
    West Bend WI 53095
    262 334-9461

### (G-1770)
**MCDONNELL COMPONENTS INC**
828 Landmark Dr (61008-6715)
P.O. Box 1678 (61008-1240)
PHONE....................................815 547-9555
**Fax:** 815 547-9556
Tim McDonnell, *President*
Tim Schnoor, *Vice Pres*
Ann Johnson, *Manager*
**EMP:** 52
**SQ FT:** 10,000
**SALES (est):** 5.8MM **Privately Held**
**WEB:** www.mcdonnellcomponents.com
**SIC:** 2452 5031 Panels & sections, prefabricated, wood; lumber, plywood & millwork

### (G-1771)
**MID-WEST FEEDER INC**
Also Called: Midwest Feeder
601 E Pleasant St (61008-3300)
PHONE....................................815 544-2994
**Fax:** 815 544-5440
Cindy Gustafson, *President*
Cynthia Gustafson, *Corp Secy*
Timothy Greenfield, *Vice Pres*
**EMP:** 22
**SQ FT:** 11,000
**SALES (est):** 3.6MM **Privately Held**
**SIC:** 3545 Machine tool attachments & accessories; hopper feed devices

### (G-1772)
**MIDWEST ICE CREAM COMPANY LLC (HQ)**
630 Meadow St (61008-3328)
PHONE....................................815 544-2105
Dale Foltz, *Mng Member*
**EMP:** 13
**SALES (est):** 2.7MM **Publicly Held**
**SIC:** 2026 Fluid milk

### (G-1773)
**NARITA MANUFACTURING INC**
828 Landmark Dr (61008-6715)
PHONE....................................248 345-1777
William Murakami, *Vice Pres*
**EMP:** 10 **EST:** 2012
**SALES (est):** 1.2MM **Privately Held**
**SIC:** 3743 3944 Train cars & equipment, freight or passenger; trains & equipment, toy: electric & mechanical

### (G-1774)
**NASCOTE INDUSTRIES INC**
Magna Exteriors Belvidere
675 Corporate Pkwy (61008-4079)
PHONE....................................419 324-3392
Josh Gasaway, *General Mgr*
Nadine Davis, *Accounting Mgr*
**EMP:** 55
**SALES (corp-wide):** 36.4B **Privately Held**
**SIC:** 3089 Automotive parts, plastic
**HQ:** Nascote Industries, Inc.
    18310 Enterprise Ave
    Nashville IL 62263
    618 327-3286

### (G-1775)
**NORTHERN ILLINOIS WILBERT VLT**
Also Called: Northern Ill Wilbert Vlt Co
845 E Jackson St (61008-2341)
PHONE....................................815 544-3355
**Fax:** 815 544-9601
Michael Banks, *President*
Kathy Banks, *Corp Secy*
**EMP:** 8
**SQ FT:** 15,000
**SALES:** 1MM **Privately Held**
**SIC:** 3272 7261 Burial vaults, concrete or precast terrazzo; funeral service & crematories

### (G-1776)
**NORTHERN PRECISION PLAS INC**
6553 Revlon Dr (61008-7843)
PHONE....................................815 544-8099
**Fax:** 815 544-6313
Robert Milnichuk, *President*
Bob Milnichuk, *Managing Dir*
Jere Eyer, *Admin Sec*
▲ **EMP:** 35
**SQ FT:** 35,000
**SALES (est):** 7.4MM **Privately Held**
**WEB:** www.npp1.com
**SIC:** 3089 Injection molding of plastics; thermoformed finished plastic products

### (G-1777)
**NORTHWEST PALLET SUPPLY CO**
3648 Morreim Dr (61008-6346)
PHONE....................................815 544-6001
**Fax:** 815 544-5299
Walter W Pollack, *President*
Justin Smith, *Opers Mgr*
Mike Meersman, *CFO*
Chris Pollack, *Sales Staff*
Jim Riff, *Director*
▲ **EMP:** 210
**SQ FT:** 156,900
**SALES (est):** 34.4MM **Privately Held**
**WEB:** www.northwestpallet.com
**SIC:** 2448 Wood pallets & skids

### (G-1778)
**PIERCE BOX & PAPER CORPORATION**
4133 Newburg Rd (61008-6700)
PHONE....................................815 547-0117
**Fax:** 815 547-1544
John Menzies, *President*
Donna Perrone, *Treasurer*
C Dennis Juul, *Admin Sec*
**EMP:** 20
**SQ FT:** 42,000
**SALES (est):** 18.1MM **Privately Held**
**WEB:** www.piercebox.com
**SIC:** 5113 2653 Napkins, paper; towels, paper; containers, paper & disposable plastic; corrugated & solid fiber boxes; boxes, corrugated: made from purchased materials

### (G-1779)
**PISTON AUTOMOTIVE LLC**
3458 Morreim Dr (61008-6308)
PHONE....................................313 541-8789
Robert Ajersch, *Finance Dir*
**EMP:** 120
**SALES (corp-wide):** 1B **Privately Held**
**SIC:** 3714 Motor vehicle parts & accessories
**PA:** Piston Automotive, L.L.C.
    12723 Telegraph Rd Ste 1
    Redford MI 48239
    313 541-8674

### (G-1780)
**PREFORMANCE SIGNS**
6940 Imron Dr (61008-8589)
PHONE....................................815 544-5044
Glen Tracy, *Principal*
**EMP:** 5
**SALES (est):** 516.2K **Privately Held**
**SIC:** 3993 Signs & advertising specialties

### (G-1781)
**PRINTWORLD**
319 S State St (61008-3606)
P.O. Box 1106 (61008-1106)
PHONE....................................815 544-1000
Greg Gill, *Principal*
**EMP:** 3
**SALES (est):** 248.6K **Privately Held**
**SIC:** 2759 Commercial printing

### (G-1782)
**RDC LINEAR ENTERPRISES LLC**
6593 Revlon Dr1 (61008-8553)
PHONE....................................815 547-1106
Dennis Schreier,
J Chris Arvidson,
Robert Bauchiero,
▲ **EMP:** 15
**SQ FT:** 21,000
**SALES (est):** 2.2MM **Privately Held**
**SIC:** 3593 Fluid power actuators, hydraulic or pneumatic

### (G-1783)
**ROCKFORD CHEMICAL CO**
915 W Perry St (61008-3498)
PHONE....................................815 544-3476
**Fax:** 815 544-0532
Vann Rossmiller, *President*
**EMP:** 3 **EST:** 1947
**SQ FT:** 20,000
**SALES:** 3MM **Privately Held**
**SIC:** 5074 2899 Boilers, steam; water treating compounds

### (G-1784)
**SPECIAL FASTENER OPERATIONS**
1993 Belford North Dr # 102 (61008-7088)
PHONE....................................815 544-6449
**Fax:** 815 544-6559
William E Truax, *President*
Donna Truax, *Admin Sec*
**EMP:** 4
**SQ FT:** 500
**SALES:** 500K **Privately Held**
**SIC:** 3451 3544 Screw machine products; special dies, tools, jigs & fixtures

### (G-1785)
**STANGER TOOL & MOLD INC**
2713 Winfield Ln (61008-6436)
PHONE....................................847 426-5826
Kevin Stanger, *Owner*
**EMP:** 3
**SQ FT:** 2,400
**SALES:** 350K **Privately Held**
**SIC:** 3089 Injection molded finished plastic products

### (G-1786)
**SUPERIOR COATING CORPORATION**
6860 Indy Dr (61008-8768)
PHONE....................................815 544-3340
**Fax:** 815 544-5205
F Lee Bozeman Jr, *President*
Laurel L Bozeman, *Vice Pres*
**EMP:** 30
**SQ FT:** 25,500
**SALES (est):** 3.7MM **Privately Held**
**WEB:** www.superiorcoating.com
**SIC:** 3479 Coating of metals & formed products

### (G-1787)
**T-REX EXCAVATING INC**
1217 American House Dr (61008-9109)
PHONE....................................815 547-9955
Hermelinda Vargas, *Principal*
**EMP:** 7 **EST:** 2015
**SALES (est):** 458.8K **Privately Held**
**SIC:** 1389 Excavating slush pits & cellars

### (G-1788)
**TAYLOR OFF ROAD RACING**
6925 Imron Dr (61008-8590)
PHONE....................................815 544-4500
**Fax:** 815 547-6882
Scott J Taylor, *President*
**EMP:** 2
**SQ FT:** 8,000
**SALES (est):** 200K **Privately Held**
**WEB:** www.taylorsoffroadracing.com
**SIC:** 3441 3711 7692 Fabricated structural metal; chassis, motor vehicle; welding repair

### (G-1789)
**TLS WINDSLED INC**
507 W 10th St (61008-5639)
PHONE....................................815 262-5791
Terry Soltow, *CEO*
**EMP:** 3
**SALES:** 60K **Privately Held**
**SIC:** 3732 Boat building & repairing

### (G-1790)
**TSM INC**
6859 Belford Indus Dr (61008-8709)
PHONE....................................815 544-5012
Ted Lindstorm, *President*
Linda Lindstorm, *Admin Sec*
**EMP:** 6
**SALES:** 1.2MM **Privately Held**
**SIC:** 3465 Automotive stampings

### (G-1791)
**TWIN TOWERS MARKETING**
Also Called: Twin Towers Embroidery
1231 Logan Ave (61008-4001)
PHONE....................................815 544-5554
Janet Paulsen, *Owner*
**EMP:** 5
**SALES (est):** 320.1K **Privately Held**
**SIC:** 2395 Embroidery products, except schiffli machine

### (G-1792)
**USA MACHINE REBUILDERS**
816 E Pleasant St (61008-3342)
PHONE....................................815 547-6542
Terry Kelly, *Owner*
**EMP:** 5
**SALES (est):** 633.2K **Privately Held**
**WEB:** www.usamachinerebuilders.com
**SIC:** 3541 Machine tools, metal cutting type

### (G-1793)
**VALLEY CUSTOM WOODWORK INC**
1626 Industrial Ct (61008-6345)
PHONE....................................815 544-3939
**Fax:** 815 544-9559
Charles Siracusa, *President*
Greg Dickson, *Project Mgr*
Sharon Siracusa, *Treasurer*
**EMP:** 20
**SQ FT:** 23,000
**SALES (est):** 2.4MM **Privately Held**
**WEB:** www.vcwi.com
**SIC:** 2541 Table or counter tops, plastic laminated

### (G-1794)
**VHD INC**
6833 Irene Rd (61008-8789)
PHONE....................................815 544-2169
**Fax:** 708 544-6130
Michael Vore, *President*
Norland O Bolen, *President*
Kerrill Bolen, *Admin Sec*
▲ **EMP:** 29
**SQ FT:** 10,000
**SALES (est):** 4.9MM **Privately Held**
**WEB:** www.valleyheaderdie.com
**SIC:** 3544 3545 Special dies & tools; reamers, machine tool

### (G-1795)
**WARNER ELECTRIC LLC**
Warner Linear
6593 Revlon Dr Plant 1 1 Plant (61008)
PHONE....................................815 566-4683
Elaine Thomas, *Plant Mgr*
Cheryl Riesselmann, *Design Engr*
**EMP:** 30
**SALES (corp-wide):** 708.9MM **Publicly Held**
**SIC:** 3625 Flow actuated electrical switches
**HQ:** Warner Electric Llc
    449 Gardner St
    South Beloit IL 61080
    815 389-4300

# GEOGRAPHIC SECTION

**(G-1796)**
**WELCH BROS INC**
1000 Town Hall Rd (61008-6300)
PHONE.................................815 547-3000
Britt Lienau, *Sales Staff*
Scott Welch, *Branch Mgr*
**EMP:** 3
**SALES (corp-wide):** 20.3MM **Privately Held**
**SIC: 3272** 5211 Concrete products; lumber & other building materials
**PA:** Welch Bros., Inc.
 1050 Saint Charles St
 Elgin IL 60120
 847 741-6134

**(G-1797)**
**WILLIAM CHARLES CNSTR CO LLC**
Also Called: Irene Quary
4525 Irene Rd (61008-8355)
PHONE.................................815 654-4720
Charles Howard, *Owner*
**EMP:** 6
**SALES (corp-wide):** 172MM **Privately Held**
**SIC: 5032** 1422 Stone, crushed or broken; crushed & broken limestone
**HQ:** William Charles Construction Company, Llc
 5290 Nimtz Rd
 Loves Park IL 61111
 815 654-4700

**(G-1798)**
**YANFENG US AUTOMOTIVE**
775 Logistics Dr (61008-8507)
PHONE.................................779 552-7300
Todd Chase, *Branch Mgr*
**EMP:** 535 **Privately Held**
**SIC: 2531** Seats, automobile
**HQ:** Yanfeng Us Automotive Interior Systems I Llc
 45000 Helm St
 Plymouth MI 48170
 414 524-1200

**(G-1799)**
**YOUNGBERG INDUSTRIES INC**
6863 Indy Dr (61008-8769)
PHONE.................................815 544-2177
**Fax:** 815 544-6440
Thomas Larson, *President*
Denise Larson, *Vice Pres*
Randy Stupka, *Plant Mgr*
Jeff Vincent, *Plant Mgr*
Jeff Kelly, *Purch Dir*
**EMP:** 65
**SQ FT:** 81,075
**SALES:** 13.9MM **Privately Held**
**WEB:** www.youngbergindustries.com
**SIC: 3443** Fabricated plate work (boiler shop)

## Bement
### Piatt County

**(G-1800)**
**CENTRAL ILLINOIS MFG CO**
Also Called: Cim-Tek Filtration
201 N Champaign St (61813-1105)
PHONE.................................217 762-8184
**Fax:** 217 678-2611
James L Ayers, *President*
Eric Brown, *Design Engr*
Linda Masters, *VP Finance*
Vickie Conlin, *Cust Mgr*
Ryan Mulvaney, *Sales Associate*
▲ **EMP:** 95 **EST:** 1956
**SQ FT:** 60,000
**SALES (est):** 25MM **Privately Held**
**WEB:** www.cim-tek.com
**SIC: 3599** Gasoline filters, internal combustion engine, except auto

**(G-1801)**
**PIATT COUNTY SERVICE CO**
Also Called: Platt County Service
878 State Highway 105 (61813-3741)
PHONE.................................217 678-5511
Mark Orr, *Manager*
**EMP:** 8

**SALES (corp-wide):** 29MM **Privately Held**
**WEB:** www.piattfs.com
**SIC: 5999** 2875 5261 Feed & farm supply; fertilizers, mixing only; fertilizer
**PA:** Piatt County Service Co (Inc)
 427 W Marion St Ste 2
 Monticello IL 61856
 217 762-2133

**(G-1802)**
**RHYME OR REASON WOODWORKING**
280 W Moultrie St (61813-1442)
PHONE.................................217 678-8301
Gaila Roberts, *Principal*
**EMP:** 4
**SALES (est):** 295.6K **Privately Held**
**SIC: 2431** Millwork

**(G-1803)**
**WOOD SPECIALTIES INCORPORATED**
964 E 1100 North Rd (61813-3517)
PHONE.................................217 678-8420
**Fax:** 217 678-8052
Jeff Gallivan, *President*
John Gallivan, *Admin Sec*
**EMP:** 12
**SALES (est):** 1MM **Privately Held**
**SIC: 2434** Wood kitchen cabinets

## Benld
### Macoupin County

**(G-1804)**
**3-V INDUSTRIES INC**
110 W Oak St (62009-1550)
PHONE.................................217 835-4453
**Fax:** 217 835-2404
Ed La Roche, *President*
**EMP:** 6
**SQ FT:** 7,500
**SALES:** 800K **Privately Held**
**SIC: 3599** Machine shop, jobbing & repair

**(G-1805)**
**FEMA L & L FOOD SERVICES INC**
Also Called: Fema's
103 N 2nd St (62009-1471)
PHONE.................................217 835-2018
Lonnie J Manalia, *President*
Rhonda L Manalia, *Admin Sec*
**EMP:** 7
**SQ FT:** 2,500
**SALES (est):** 387.3K **Privately Held**
**WEB:** www.femas.com
**SIC: 5812** 2013 2099 2038 Caterers; sausages from purchased meat; food preparations; frozen specialties; meat packing plants

**(G-1806)**
**R & R MACHINING INC**
125 Route 138 (62009-1453)
PHONE.................................217 835-4579
**Fax:** 217 835-4816
Randy Ramseier, *President*
Cindy Rauker, *Vice Pres*
Leo Ramseier, *Treasurer*
**EMP:** 3
**SQ FT:** 2,985
**SALES:** 450K **Privately Held**
**SIC: 3544** 7692 Jigs & fixtures; welding repair

**(G-1807)**
**V-CAM INC**
201 N 7th St (62009-1340)
P.O. Box 102 (62009)
PHONE.................................217 835-4381
**Fax:** 217 835-4401
John Vercoglio, *President*
Lance Vercoglio, *Treasurer*
William Vercoglio, *Admin Sec*
**EMP:** 12
**SQ FT:** 8,000
**SALES (est):** 1MM **Privately Held**
**SIC: 3544** Special dies, tools, jigs & fixtures

## Bensenville
### Dupage County

**(G-1808)**
**3D INDUSTRIES INC**
500 Frontier Way (60106-1191)
PHONE.................................630 616-8702
**Fax:** 847 928-0736
Frank Glavanovits, *President*
Jim Marks, *General Mgr*
Brian Glavanovits, *Manager*
Dave Petrucci, *Manager*
Stephen Odegard, *Info Tech Mgr*
**EMP:** 20
**SQ FT:** 20,000
**SALES (est):** 3.2MM **Privately Held**
**WEB:** www.dietech.net
**SIC: 3544** 3599 Special dies & tools; machine shop, jobbing & repair

**(G-1809)**
**AARON ENGNERED PROCESS EQP INC**
Also Called: Paul O Abbe Division
735 E Green St (60106-2549)
PHONE.................................630 350-2200
Jeffrey Hoffmann, *President*
Allan Cohen, *Vice Pres*
David Bergman, *Engineer*
David Swirley, *Controller*
**EMP:** 9
**SALES:** 3.3MM
**SALES (corp-wide):** 26.7MM **Privately Held**
**WEB:** www.pauloabbe.com
**SIC: 3531** Construction machinery
**PA:** Aaron Equipment Company, Inc.
 735 E Green St
 Bensenville IL 60106
 630 350-2200

**(G-1810)**
**AARON PROCESS EQUIPMENT CO INC**
735 E Green St (60106-2549)
P.O. Box 80 (60106-0080)
PHONE.................................630 350-2200
Alan Cohen, *President*
Michael Cohen, *Vice Pres*
Bob Perna, *Sales Mgr*
Michael Real, *Director*
Leslie S Cohen, *Admin Sec*
▲ **EMP:** 40
**SQ FT:** 250,000
**SALES:** 1.5MM
**SALES (corp-wide):** 26.7MM **Privately Held**
**WEB:** www.aaronprocess.com
**SIC: 3556** Cutting, chopping, grinding, mixing & similar machinery
**PA:** Aaron Equipment Company, Inc.
 735 E Green St
 Bensenville IL 60106
 630 350-2200

**(G-1811)**
**AAXIS ENGRAVERS INC**
230 William St Ste A (60106-3308)
PHONE.................................224 629-4045
**Fax:** 630 543-0835
Elizabeth Alcantar, *President*
**EMP:** 6
**SALES (est):** 630K **Privately Held**
**SIC: 3555** Printing plates

**(G-1812)**
**ABILITY WELDING SERVICE INC**
500 Meyer Rd (60106-1604)
PHONE.................................630 595-3737
**Fax:** 630 595-3738
Walter Kryczka, *President*
Randy Kryczka, *Sales Staff*
Aderine Spirick, *Office Mgr*
**EMP:** 6
**SALES:** 500K **Privately Held**
**SIC: 7692** Welding repair

**(G-1813)**
**ACCURATE PARTS MFG CO**
1100 Industrial Dr (60106-1247)
PHONE.................................630 616-4125
Ozcan Yabukoglu, *President*
▲ **EMP:** 29

**SALES (est):** 4.2MM **Privately Held**
**SIC: 3999** Barber & beauty shop equipment

**(G-1814)**
**ACCUTECH MACHINING INC**
381 Evergreen Ave (60106-2503)
PHONE.................................630 350-2066
**Fax:** 630 350-2068
Jeffrey Szwaya, *President*
Elizabeth Szwaya, *Corp Secy*
Michael James, *Vice Pres*
Natalie Stombock-Szwaya, *Opers Mgr*
Jonathan Tripp, *Manager*
**EMP:** 22 **EST:** 1999
**SQ FT:** 11,000
**SALES (est):** 4.1MM **Privately Held**
**SIC: 3599** Machine shop, jobbing & repair

**(G-1815)**
**ACE METAL CRAFTS COMPANY**
484 Thomas Dr (60106-1619)
PHONE.................................847 455-1010
**Fax:** 847 455-1052
Jean L Pitzo, *President*
Dale Ball, *President*
Kevin Bailey, *Vice Pres*
Keith Stout, *Vice Pres*
Jim Chapman, *VP Mfg*
**EMP:** 105 **EST:** 1960
**SQ FT:** 82,000
**SALES (est):** 42.7MM **Privately Held**
**WEB:** www.acemetal.com
**SIC: 3441** Fabricated structural metal

**(G-1816)**
**ACROFAB**
1100 Entry Dr Unit 1 (60106-3700)
PHONE.................................630 350-7941
Bhupen Patel, *Owner*
**EMP:** 5
**SALES (est):** 746.1K **Privately Held**
**WEB:** www.aerofab.net
**SIC: 3498** Tube fabricating (contract bending & shaping)

**(G-1817)**
**ADVANCE MACHINING**
405 Evergreen Ave (60106-2505)
PHONE.................................630 521-9392
Stefan Szefer, *President*
Stanley Pyrdol, *Vice Pres*
**EMP:** 4
**SQ FT:** 5,000
**SALES (est):** 250K **Privately Held**
**SIC: 3599** Machine shop, jobbing & repair

**(G-1818)**
**ADVANCED DIGITAL & MOLD INC**
833 Eagle Dr (60106-1946)
PHONE.................................630 595-8242
J Alexandersson, *Principal*
**EMP:** 5
**SALES (est):** 549.7K **Privately Held**
**SIC: 3544** Industrial molds

**(G-1819)**
**ADVANCED PRCSION MACHINING LTD**
766 Birginal Dr (60106-1213)
PHONE.................................630 860-2549
Scott R Lamb, *President*
Andrzej Marchwiany, *Admin Sec*
**EMP:** 5
**SQ FT:** 1,200
**SALES (est):** 275K **Privately Held**
**SIC: 3599** Machine shop, jobbing & repair

**(G-1820)**
**ADVANCED THERMAL PROCESSING**
501 Eastern Ave (60106-3811)
PHONE.................................630 595-9000
**Fax:** 630 595-9022
Mark A Bulaw, *President*
Christine Bulaw, *Admin Sec*
**EMP:** 2
**SQ FT:** 18,000
**SALES (est):** 324K **Privately Held**
**SIC: 3398** Metal heat treating

# Bensenville - Dupage County (G-1821)   GEOGRAPHIC SECTION

**(G-1821)**
**AGS MACHINE CO INC**
872 Eagle Dr (60106-1947)
PHONE .................................. 630 766-7777
EMP: 6
SALES (est): 480K  Privately Held
SIC: 3599 Machine Shop

**(G-1822)**
**ALAGOR INDUSTRIES INCORPORATED (PA)**
489 Thomas Dr (60106-1618)
PHONE .................................. 630 766-2910
Fax: 630 766-2912
Richard Rogala, *President*
Lynette Rogala, *Admin Sec*
▼ EMP: 10
SQ FT: 15,000
SALES: 3MM  Privately Held
SIC: 3469 3496 Metal stampings; miscellaneous fabricated wire products

**(G-1823)**
**ALL AMERICAN NUT & CANDY CORP**
930 Fairway Dr (60106-1315)
PHONE .................................. 630 595-6473
Isidor Budina, *CEO*
EMP: 18 EST: 2011
SQ FT: 4,000
SALES: 1.5MM  Privately Held
SIC: 2064 Fruit & fruit peel confections; nuts, candy covered

**(G-1824)**
**ALLIANCE PLASTICS**
830 Fairway Dr Ste 104 (60106-1348)
PHONE .................................. 888 643-1432
Ron Grubbs, *President*
EMP: 4
SALES (est): 327.9K  Privately Held
SIC: 3089 Injection molding of plastics

**(G-1825)**
**ALLMETAL INC**
636 Thomas Dr (60106-1623)
P.O. Box 850 (60106-0850)
PHONE .................................. 630 766-8500
Fax: 630 766-1082
Jeff Andersen, *General Mgr*
Rick Raske, *Safety Mgr*
Dale Klimek, *Human Res Mgr*
Jeffrey Andresen, *Manager*
Corinne Wiegand, *Director*
EMP: 46
SQ FT: 26,000
SALES (corp-wide): 92.9MM  Privately Held
WEB: www.allmetalinc.com
SIC: 3442 Metal doors, sash & trim
PA: Allmetal, Inc.
    1 Pierce Pl Ste 900
    Itasca IL 60143
    630 250-8090

**(G-1826)**
**ALLMETAL INC**
224-230 Foster Ave (60106)
PHONE .................................. 630 766-1407
Fax: 630 766-3180
Vincent Catalano, *General Mgr*
EMP: 15
SALES (corp-wide): 92.9MM  Privately Held
WEB: www.allmetalinc.com
SIC: 3442 3089 Metal doors, sash & trim; injection molding of plastics
PA: Allmetal, Inc.
    1 Pierce Pl Ste 900
    Itasca IL 60143
    630 250-8090

**(G-1827)**
**ALLOYWELD INSPECTION CO INC**
796 Maple Ln (60106-1585)
PHONE .................................. 630 595-2145
Fax: 630 595-2128
Edward J Piecko, *President*
Stanley W Piecko, *Chairman*
Jennifer Anaya, *Vice Pres*
Tamy Piecko, *Info Tech Mgr*
EMP: 22
SQ FT: 7,100
SALES (est): 3.3MM  Privately Held
WEB: www.alloyweldinspection.com
SIC: 1799 7692 8071 8734 Welding on site; welding repair; brazing; testing laboratories; testing laboratories

**(G-1828)**
**ALLSTAR TOOL & MOLDS INC**
799 Eagle Dr Ste A (60106-1995)
PHONE .................................. 630 766-0162
Fred Kovacs, *President*
EMP: 10 EST: 1977
SQ FT: 4,400
SALES: 680K  Privately Held
SIC: 3544 Industrial molds

**(G-1829)**
**ALU-BRA FOUNDRY INC**
630 E Green St (60106-2548)
P.O. Box 68 (60106-0068)
PHONE .................................. 630 766-3112
Fax: 630 766-3307
James E Torkelson, *President*
Joan Torkelson, *Corp Secy*
Amanda Krotz, *Vice Pres*
Tim Fink, *Purch Agent*
Amanda Dimaria, *Manager*
EMP: 80 EST: 1957
SQ FT: 17,000
SALES (est): 17.8MM  Privately Held
WEB: www.alu-bra.com
SIC: 3365 3366 Aluminum foundries

**(G-1830)**
**AM METAL SPINNING CO INC**
756 Larson Ln (60106-1104)
PHONE .................................. 630 616-8634
Larry Fletcher, *President*
EMP: 5
SALES (est): 649K  Privately Held
SIC: 3469 Spinning metal for the trade

**(G-1831)**
**AMCAST INC**
350 Meyer Rd (60106-1615)
PHONE .................................. 630 766-7450
Fax: 630 766-7453
John C Kopp, *President*
Janet Kopp, *Corp Secy*
EMP: 17 EST: 1965
SQ FT: 12,000
SALES (est): 3.3MM  Privately Held
SIC: 3364 3369 3366 3365 Copper & copper alloy die-castings; nonferrous foundries; copper foundries; aluminum foundries

**(G-1832)**
**AMERICAN DENTAL PRODUCTS INC**
603 Country Club Dr Ste B (60106-1329)
PHONE .................................. 630 238-0275
George Nikoli, *President*
Liana Mirea, *Vice Pres*
▲ EMP: 20
SQ FT: 2,000
SALES: 5MM  Privately Held
WEB: www.americandentalproducts.com
SIC: 3843 8072 Dental materials; dental laboratories

**(G-1833)**
**AMERICAN ENGRAVING INC**
151 Wilson Ct (60106-1628)
PHONE .................................. 630 543-2525
Fax: 630 543-2562
Michael Gioia, *President*
Thomas Magarian, *Vice Pres*
▼ EMP: 6
SQ FT: 4,000
SALES (est): 929.5K  Privately Held
WEB: www.americanengraving.net
SIC: 3599 3544 Machine shop, jobbing & repair; special dies, tools, jigs & fixtures

**(G-1834)**
**AMGLO KEMLITE LABORATORIES INC (PA)**
215 Gateway Rd (60106-1952)
PHONE .................................. 630 238-3031
Fax: 630 350-9474
James H Hyland, *Ch of Bd*
Hyland J Grant, *President*
Julie O'Connor, *General Mgr*
Lee Ren, *General Mgr*
Larry A Kerchenfaut, *Managing Dir*
▲ EMP: 100
SQ FT: 20,000
SALES (est): 61.6MM  Privately Held
WEB: www.amglo.com
SIC: 3641 Tubes, electric light

**(G-1835)**
**AMSOIL INC**
485 Thomas Dr (60106-1618)
PHONE .................................. 630 595-8385
Ray Gonzales, *Manager*
EMP: 8
SALES (corp-wide): 120.9MM  Privately Held
WEB: www.amsoil.com
SIC: 2992 3589 2873 3714 Lubricating oils & greases; water filters & softeners, household type; fertilizers: natural (organic), except compost; motor vehicle parts & accessories
PA: Amsoil Inc.
    925 Tower Ave
    Superior WI 54880
    715 392-7101

**(G-1836)**
**ASPEN INDUSTRIES INC**
480 Country Club Dr (60106-1507)
PHONE .................................. 630 238-0611
Ralph Iourio, *President*
John Barry, *President*
Jeff Korpalski, *General Mgr*
▲ EMP: 11 EST: 1999
SQ FT: 12,000
SALES (est): 1MM  Privately Held
WEB: www.aspeninc.com
SIC: 3441 Fabricated structural metal

**(G-1837)**
**AWW 10 INC**
10 Gateway Rd (60106-1949)
PHONE .................................. 630 595-7600
John Baumgardner, *Manager*
EMP: 100
SALES (corp-wide): 7.6B  Publicly Held
SIC: 3452 Screws, metal
HQ: Aww 10, Inc.
    1441 N Wood Dale Rd
    Wood Dale IL 60191
    630 595-0000

**(G-1838)**
**B & M MACHINE INC**
768 Industrial Dr (60106-1305)
PHONE .................................. 630 350-8950
Martin Nicpon, *President*
EMP: 2
SALES (est): 246.8K  Privately Held
SIC: 3578 Adding machines

**(G-1839)**
**B J PLASTIC MOLDING CO**
778 County Line Rd (60106-3277)
PHONE .................................. 630 766-8750
Robert Jacobson, *Manager*
Robert K Jacobsen Jr, *Manager*
EMP: 20
SALES (corp-wide): 10.8MM  Privately Held
WEB: www.bjplastic.com
SIC: 3089 Injection molded finished plastic products
PA: B. J. Plastic Molding Co., Inc
    435 S County Line Rd
    Franklin Park IL 60131
    630 766-3200

**(G-1840)**
**BALA & ANULA FUELS INC**
154 S York Rd (60106-2454)
PHONE .................................. 630 766-1807
EMP: 3
SALES (est): 240.6K  Privately Held
SIC: 2869 Fuels

**(G-1841)**
**BEAN STICH INC**
237 Evergreen Ave (60106-2581)
PHONE .................................. 630 422-1269
Mark Losiak, *President*
Sudhacker G Patel, *Vice Pres*
EMP: 5
SALES: 300K  Privately Held
SIC: 2396 2395 Screen printing on fabric articles; embroidery & art needlework

**(G-1842)**
**BEHABELT USA**
860 Devon Ave (60106-1150)
PHONE .................................. 630 521-9835
Peter Fransemeier, *Exec Dir*
▲ EMP: 6 EST: 2008
SALES (est): 500.3K  Privately Held
SIC: 3052 Rubber & plastics hose & beltings

**(G-1843)**
**BENSENVILLE SCREW PRODUCTS**
796 County Line Rd (60106-3277)
PHONE .................................. 630 860-5222
Fax: 630 860-2709
Mark Tukiendorf, *President*
Tom Tukiendorf, *Plant Mgr*
Bonnie Tukiendorf, *Admin Sec*
EMP: 9
SQ FT: 10,000
SALES: 2MM  Privately Held
WEB: www.bensenvillescrewproducts.com
SIC: 3451 Screw machine products

**(G-1844)**
**BLS ENTERPRISES INC**
Also Called: Tuftads
1120 Thorndale Ave (60106-1144)
PHONE .................................. 630 766-1300
Fax: 630 775-0903
Barry Stoughton, *President*
◆ EMP: 13
SQ FT: 4,800
SALES (est): 1.1MM  Privately Held
WEB: www.tufpads.com
SIC: 3069 Liner strips, rubber

**(G-1845)**
**BOBS BUSINESS INC**
730 Thomas Dr (60106-1625)
PHONE .................................. 630 238-5790
Skip Wolfe, *Sales Mgr*
Judd Smith, *Manager*
EMP: 6
SALES (corp-wide): 7.8MM  Privately Held
SIC: 3949 Bowling equipment & supplies
PA: Bobs' Business, Inc.
    1981 Old West Main St
    Red Wing MN 55066
    651 388-4742

**(G-1846)**
**BRIERGATE TOOL & ENGRG CO**
1007 Industrial Dr (60106-1298)
PHONE .................................. 630 766-7050
Fax: 630 766-3106
Robert L Sbertoli Jr, *President*
Terri Sbertoli, *Corp Secy*
John Sbertoli, *Plant Mgr*
Chris Sbertoli, *Director*
EMP: 10
SQ FT: 20,000
SALES: 1MM  Privately Held
SIC: 3469 3544 Metal stampings; special dies & tools

**(G-1847)**
**BRINKMAN COMPANY INC**
460 Evergreen Ave (60106-2506)
PHONE .................................. 630 595-3640
Howard A Brinkman, *President*
Johnnie Fernandez, *Partner*
EMP: 8 EST: 1944
SQ FT: 4,500
SALES (est): 929.8K  Privately Held
SIC: 2821 Plastics materials & resins

**(G-1848)**
**BSB INTERNATIONAL CORP**
225 James St Ste 4 (60106-3367)
PHONE .................................. 847 791-9272
Bernadette Borek, *President*
EMP: 4
SALES (est): 270K  Privately Held
SIC: 3599 7699 Machine & other job shop work; industrial equipment services

**(G-1849)**
**C N C CENTRAL INC**
177 Il Route 83 (60106-2011)
PHONE .................................. 630 595-1453
Anton L Pondelick, *President*
Lina Pondelick, *Admin Sec*

# GEOGRAPHIC SECTION
## Bensenville - Dupage County (G-1876)

EMP: 8
SQ FT: 6,000
SALES: 2.5MM **Privately Held**
SIC: 3599 3565 Custom machinery; packaging machinery

**(G-1850)**
**CAPABLE CONTROLS INC (PA)**
790 Maple Ln (60106-1513)
PHONE.................................630 860-6514
Ted Singer, *President*
Paul Paluck, *Vice Pres*
EMP: 58
SQ FT: 7,000
SALES (est): 9.9MM **Privately Held**
WEB: www.capablecontrols.com
SIC: 3625 Electric controls & control accessories, industrial

**(G-1851)**
**CAPITAL RUBBER CORPORATION**
1140 Tower Ln (60106-1028)
PHONE.................................630 595-6644
Fax: 630 595-1411
Barbara Feldman, *President*
Bryan Feldman, *Vice Pres*
Kristen Santos, *Manager*
▼ EMP: 11 EST: 1975
SQ FT: 15,000
SALES (est): 4.9MM **Privately Held**
WEB: www.capitalrubbercorp.com
SIC: 5085 3429 Gaskets; clamps & couplings, hose

**(G-1852)**
**CARROLL TOOL & MANUFACTURING**
827 Eagle Dr (60106-1946)
PHONE.................................630 766-3363
Frank Schiffner, *Owner*
EMP: 2
SALES (est): 200K **Privately Held**
SIC: 5085 3544 3442 3363 Industrial tools; special dies, tools, jigs & fixtures; metal doors, sash & trim; aluminum die-castings; plastic containers, except foam

**(G-1853)**
**CAVERO COATINGS COMPANY LLC**
422 County Line Rd (60106-2536)
PHONE.................................630 616-2868
Jose Cavero, *Principal*
EMP: 5
SALES (est): 936.4K **Privately Held**
SIC: 2851 Lacquers, varnishes, enamels & other coatings

**(G-1854)**
**CENTRAL AUTMTC SCREW PDTS INC**
372 Meyer Rd (60106-1615)
PHONE.................................630 766-7966
Fax: 630 766-8016
Daniel Flerlage, *President*
Dennis Flerlage, *Vice Pres*
EMP: 7
SQ FT: 11,000
SALES (est): 1.2MM **Privately Held**
SIC: 3451 Screw machine products

**(G-1855)**
**CENTURY METAL SPINNING CO INC**
430 Meyer Rd (60106-1617)
PHONE.................................630 595-3900
Fax: 630 282-0362
Janet Kaiser, *President*
Andy Rabin, *Opers Mgr*
Danuta Skoczylas, *QC Mgr*
Scott Doebler, *Manager*
EMP: 25 EST: 1933
SQ FT: 25,000
SALES (est): 6.2MM **Privately Held**
WEB: www.centurymetalspinning.com
SIC: 3469 Spinning metal for the trade

**(G-1856)**
**CH MACHINING COMPANY**
1044 Fairway Dr (60106-1317)
PHONE.................................630 595-1050
Fax: 630 595-1050
Andrzej Chomont, *President*
EMP: 3

SALES (est): 446.4K **Privately Held**
SIC: 3541 Machine tools, metal cutting type

**(G-1857)**
**CHEMBLEND OF AMERICA LLC**
240 Foster Ave (60106-1641)
PHONE.................................630 521-1600
John Godina, *President*
Anand Setaram, *Manager*
Tom Hayward, *Director*
▲ EMP: 10
SALES (est): 2.2MM **Privately Held**
SIC: 2833 Medicinals & botanicals

**(G-1858)**
**CHICAGO WHITE METAL CAST INC**
649 N Rte 83 (60106)
PHONE.................................630 595-4424
Fax: 630 595-9160
Eric Treiber, *CEO*
Walter G Treiber, *Chairman*
Michael Dimitroff, *Vice Pres*
Bill Baraglia, *VP Mfg*
William Baraglia, *VP Mfg*
◆ EMP: 200
SQ FT: 136,000
SALES (est): 38.6MM **Privately Held**
WEB: www.cwmtl.com
SIC: 3363 3364 Aluminum die-castings; magnesium & magnesium-base alloy die-castings; zinc & zinc-base alloy die-castings

**(G-1859)**
**CIRCOM INC**
505 W Main St (60106-2137)
PHONE.................................630 595-4460
Fax: 630 595-4615
Lisa Esczuk, *President*
Marlene Rosenberg, *Vice Pres*
Veronica Kayda, *Purchasing*
Phil Moser, *Engineer*
John Hoaglund, *Project Engr*
EMP: 28
SQ FT: 12,000
SALES (est): 6.7MM **Privately Held*
WEB: www.circominc.com
SIC: 3679 3672 3357 8711 Electronic circuits; printed circuit boards; nonferrous wiredrawing & insulating; engineering services; commercial physical research

**(G-1860)**
**CMC TOOL MANUFACTURING**
229 Evergreen Ave (60106-2501)
PHONE.................................630 350-0300
Fax: 630 350-0258
Laurence Chiappe, *President*
Mary Anne Chiappe, *Admin Sec*
EMP: 6 EST: 1978
SQ FT: 5,000
SALES (est): 861.2K **Privately Held**
SIC: 3544 Special dies, tools, jigs & fixtures

**(G-1861)**
**COLLEY ELEVATOR COMPANY**
226 William St (60106-3325)
PHONE.................................630 766-7230
Fax: 630 766-7568
Ray Zomchek, *President*
Pamela Zomchek, *Treasurer*
Mike Rzutto, *Accounts Mgr*
Tj Milici, *Sales Associate*
EMP: 20
SQ FT: 15,000
SALES (est): 3.1MM **Privately Held**
WEB: www.colleyelevator.com
SIC: 7699 1796 3534 Elevators: inspection, service & repair; elevator installation & conversion; elevators & moving stairways

**(G-1862)**
**COLOREX CHEMICAL CO INC**
834 Foster Ave (60106-1510)
PHONE.................................630 238-3124
Yvonne Matsoukas, *President*
EMP: 2 EST: 1962
SQ FT: 5,000
SALES: 1.2MM **Privately Held**
SIC: 2842 5169 Cleaning or polishing preparations; leather dressings & finishes; chemicals & allied products

**(G-1863)**
**COMLINK TECHNOLOGIES INC**
320 Meyer Rd (60106-1615)
P.O. Box 1306, Elmhurst (60126-8306)
PHONE.................................630 279-5445
Robert C Palmer, *President*
Joe Kepinski, *Manager*
EMP: 11
SQ FT: 3,000
SALES (est): 2MM **Privately Held**
WEB: www.comlinktechnologies.com
SIC: 3663 Airborne radio communications equipment

**(G-1864)**
**COMPLETE FLASHINGS INC**
Also Called: C F I
211 Beeline Dr Ste 2 (60106-1640)
PHONE.................................630 595-9725
Mark Rosal, *President*
William Sahagian, *Principal*
Margaret Rosal, *Manager*
EMP: 5
SQ FT: 3,500
SALES (est): 1.3MM **Privately Held**
SIC: 2952 Roofing materials

**(G-1865)**
**CONTRACT PACKAGING PLUS INC**
1239 Spruce Ave (60106-1019)
PHONE.................................708 356-1100
Jeff L Hart, *CEO*
Mery Macgregor, *Manager*
EMP: 7
SALES (est): 670K **Privately Held**
WEB: www.aboutcpp.com
SIC: 7389 2099 Packaging & labeling services; food preparations

**(G-1866)**
**CORE FINISHING INC**
717 Thomas Dr (60106-1624)
PHONE.................................630 521-9635
Fax: 630 521-9659
Corey Coxe, *President*
EMP: 30
SQ FT: 24,000
SALES (est): 2.5MM **Privately Held**
WEB: www.corefinishing.com
SIC: 3479 Coating of metals & formed products

**(G-1867)**
**CORRECT TOOL INC**
869 Fairway Dr (60106-1312)
PHONE.................................630 595-6055
Fax: 630 595-9341
Janusz Szulinski, *President*
Barbara Szulinski, *President*
Mirek Szulinski, *General Mgr*
Marek Kopec, *Engineer*
▲ EMP: 12
SQ FT: 9,000
SALES (est): 2.2MM **Privately Held**
WEB: www.correcttool.com
SIC: 3544 5251 Special dies, tools, jigs & fixtures; tools

**(G-1868)**
**COSMOPOLITAN MACHINE REBUILDER**
346 Evergreen Ave (60106-2504)
PHONE.................................630 595-8141
Fax: 630 595-7429
Wallace Szczekocki, *President*
Leona Szczekocki, *Admin Sec*
EMP: 5
SQ FT: 6,000
SALES (est): 544.4K **Privately Held**
SIC: 3599 Machine shop, jobbing & repair

**(G-1869)**
**COYOTE TRANSPORTATION INC**
600 Thomas Dr (60106-1623)
PHONE.................................630 204-5729
Anthony Varchetto, *President*
Jeff Gosmire, *CFO*
Edgar Arana, *Admin Sec*
EMP: 7
SQ FT: 100,000

SALES: 900K
SALES (corp-wide): 32.6MM **Privately Held**
SIC: 4214 2611 3523 Local trucking with storage; pulp mills, mechanical & recycling processing; balers, farm: hay, straw, cotton, etc.
PA: Pri Group, Llc
600 Thomas Dr
Bensenville IL 60106
630 477-4040

**(G-1870)**
**CP SCREW MACHINE PRODUCTS**
211 Beeline Dr Ste 3 (60106-1640)
PHONE.................................630 766-2313
Fax: 630 766-2609
John M Woodward, *President*
EMP: 15
SQ FT: 9,000
SALES: 975K **Privately Held**
SIC: 3451 Screw machine products

**(G-1871)**
**CREATIVE WERKS LLC (PA)**
222 Sievert Ct (60106-1190)
PHONE.................................630 860-2222
Steve Schroeder, *CEO*
J Rgen Peters, *Principal*
Bob Folkestad, *Vice Pres*
Doug Mauger, *Vice Pres*
Brian Scott, *Opers Mgr*
▲ EMP: 45
SQ FT: 550,000
SALES: 75MM **Privately Held**
WEB: www.creativewerksinc.com
SIC: 3999 Novelties, bric-a-brac & hobby kits

**(G-1872)**
**CROWN TOOL COMPANY INC**
681 Country Club Dr (60106-1324)
PHONE.................................630 766-3050
Fax: 630 766-2648
Walter Wrona, *President*
Ken Wrona, *Finance*
EMP: 4
SQ FT: 6,500
SALES: 500K **Privately Held**
SIC: 3545 3541 3544 Gauges (machine tool accessories); machine tools, metal cutting type; special dies, tools, jigs & fixtures

**(G-1873)**
**CRV INDUSTRIES INC**
Also Called: Crv Lancaster Cams & Indexers
777 Maple Ln (60106-1513)
PHONE.................................630 595-3777
Fax: 630 766-3777
Michael Purner, *President*
Jacquelyn Purner, *Admin Sec*
EMP: 10
SQ FT: 10,000
SALES: 1MM **Privately Held**
WEB: www.crvind.com
SIC: 3599 Machine shop, jobbing & repair

**(G-1874)**
**CSM FASTENER PRODUCTS CO**
1133 Bryn Mawr Ave (60106-1242)
PHONE.................................630 350-8282
Fax: 630 350-8499
Stanley Rosinski, *Principal*
EMP: 7
SALES (est): 655.7K **Privately Held**
SIC: 3452 Bolts, nuts, rivets & washers

**(G-1875)**
**CUSTOM BLADES & TOOLS INC**
1084 Fairway Dr (60106-1317)
PHONE.................................630 860-7650
Henry Wszolek, *President*
EMP: 2
SQ FT: 1,800
SALES (est): 260K **Privately Held**
SIC: 3425 5084 Saw blades & handsaws; industrial machinery & equipment

**(G-1876)**
**CUSTOM MACHINING COMPANY**
401 Evergreen Ave (60106-2590)
PHONE.................................630 766-2600
Fax: 630 766-3062
William Carley, *President*

# Bensenville - Dupage County (G-1877)  GEOGRAPHIC SECTION

Diana Carley, *Corp Secy*
**EMP:** 7
**SQ FT:** 3,000
**SALES (est):** 580K  **Privately Held**
**SIC: 3599** Machine shop, jobbing & repair

### (G-1877)
### CUTTING TOOL INNOVATIONS INC
759 Industrial Dr  (60106-1304)
P.O. Box 50  (60106-0050)
**PHONE** ................................. 630 766-4839
Gohei George Osawa, *CEO*
Denny Denick, *President*
Geoffrey Less, *Vice Pres*
**EMP:** 5
**SALES (est):** 520.7K
**SALES (corp-wide):** 1B  **Privately Held**
**WEB:** www.osgtool.com
**SIC: 3541** Screw & thread machines
**HQ:** Osg Usa, Inc.
  676 E Fullerton Ave
  Glendale Heights IL 60139
  630 790-1400

### (G-1878)
### DELTA SECONDARY INC
1000 Industrial Dr Ste 3d  (60106-1259)
**PHONE** ................................. 630 766-1180
**Fax:** 630 766-1285
Alina Agresto, *President*
Dimitrios Vattis, *Vice Pres*
**EMP:** 40
**SQ FT:** 10,000
**SALES (est):** 3.5MM  **Privately Held**
**SIC: 3471** Finishing, metals or formed products

### (G-1879)
### DESIGNED PLASTICS INC
1133 Bryn Mawr Ave  (60106-1242)
**PHONE** ................................. 630 694-7300
Mark Barnes, *President*
Kathy Barnes, *Corp Secy*
Kim Sullivan, *Project Mgr*
Joe Benka, *Opers Mgr*
Joseph Benka, *Opers Mgr*
**EMP:** 25
**SQ FT:** 20,000
**SALES (est):** 5MM  **Privately Held**
**WEB:** www.designedplastics.com
**SIC: 3089** 3083 Plastic processing; laminated plastics plate & sheet

### (G-1880)
### DISTINCTIVE FOODS LLC
Also Called: Pie Piper
450 Evergreen Ave  (60106-2506)
**PHONE** ................................. 847 459-3600
**Fax:** 630 595-1551
Ron Buck, *Controller*
Josh Harris, *Branch Mgr*
Mike Lopardo, *Manager*
Lori Sproat, *Manager*
Herb Wolfson, *CTO*
**EMP:** 40
**SQ FT:** 20,000
**SALES (corp-wide):** 19.5MM  **Privately Held**
**SIC: 2038** 2051 Frozen specialties; bread, cake & related products
**PA:** Distinctive Foods Llc
  654 Wheeling Rd
  Wheeling IL 60090
  847 459-3600

### (G-1881)
### DOUMAK INC (PA)
1004 Fairway Dr  (60106-1317)
**PHONE** ................................. 800 323-0318
Mark G Schuessler, *President*
Gary G Conway, *Vice Pres*
John A Jeffries, *Shareholder*
◆ **EMP:** 9
**SQ FT:** 225,000
**SALES (est):** 61.3MM  **Privately Held**
**WEB:** www.doumak.com
**SIC: 2064** Marshmallows

### (G-1882)
### DOUMAK INC
1004 Fairway Dr  (60106-1317)
**PHONE** ................................. 630 594-5400
Maria Fernandez, *Manager*
**EMP:** 76

**SALES (corp-wide):** 61.3MM  **Privately Held**
**WEB:** www.doumak.com
**SIC: 2064** Candy & other confectionery products
**PA:** Doumak Inc.
  1004 Fairway Dr
  Bensenville IL 60106
  800 323-0318

### (G-1883)
### DRIVER SERVICES
Also Called: Globe Telecom
120 George St Apt 517  (60106-3177)
**PHONE** ................................. 505 267-8686
Adrian Dorofte, *Principal*
**EMP:** 5
**SALES (est):** 150K  **Privately Held**
**SIC: 4812** 3663 4111 8748 Cellular telephone services; radio & TV communications equipment; airport limousine, scheduled service; telecommunications consultant; domestic freight forwarding

### (G-1884)
### DRUMMOND INDUSTRIES INC
639 Thomas Dr  (60106-1622)
**PHONE** ................................. 773 637-1264
**Fax:** 773 637-1264
Matthew Gieser, *President*
Steve Loerop, *Manager*
**EMP:** 30 **EST:** 1968
**SQ FT:** 28,000
**SALES (est):** 7MM  **Privately Held**
**WEB:** www.drummondindustries.com
**SIC: 3089** Injection molding of plastics

### (G-1885)
### DURABLE MANUFACTURING COMPANY
232 Evergreen Ave Unit B  (60106-2578)
**PHONE** ................................. 630 766-0398
**Fax:** 630 766-0112
Edward Sowin, *Owner*
**EMP:** 12 **EST:** 1953
**SQ FT:** 11,000
**SALES:** 1MM  **Privately Held**
**SIC: 3589** 3585 3564 Water filters & softeners, household type; parts for heating, cooling & refrigerating equipment; blowers & fans

### (G-1886)
### DYNA-TONE LITHO INC
168 Henderson St  (60106-2033)
P.O. Box 871  (60106-0871)
**PHONE** ................................. 630 595-1073
Susan G Martens, *President*
**EMP:** 2
**SALES (est):** 300K  **Privately Held**
**SIC: 2752** Commercial printing, lithographic

### (G-1887)
### E M GLABUS CO INC
420 County Line Rd  (60106-2536)
**PHONE** ................................. 630 766-3027
Dale F Glabus Jr, *President*
Penny Glabus, *Corp Secy*
**EMP:** 10
**SQ FT:** 6,500
**SALES (est):** 1.6MM  **Privately Held**
**SIC: 3599** 3462 Machine shop, jobbing & repair; iron & steel forgings

### (G-1888)
### ECOTURF MIDWEST INC
789 Golf Ln  (60106-1563)
**PHONE** ................................. 630 350-9500
Susan Glatt, *President*
Ed Glatt, *VP Sls/Mktg*
**EMP:** 2
**SQ FT:** 16,000
**SALES:** 300K
**SALES (corp-wide):** 3.1MM  **Privately Held**
**SIC: 3523** Turf & grounds equipment
**PA:** G.A.I.M. Plastics Incorporated.
  789 Golf Ln
  Bensenville IL 60106
  630 350-9500

### (G-1889)
### EDGE MOLD CORPORATION
885 Fairway Dr  (60106-1312)
**PHONE** ................................. 630 616-8108

**Fax:** 630 616-8109
Casey Grzesik, *President*
Irene Grzesik, *Corp Secy*
**EMP:** 6
**SALES:** 300K  **Privately Held**
**WEB:** www.edgemoldco.com
**SIC: 3544** 3364 Industrial molds; nonferrous die-castings except aluminum

### (G-1890)
### ELECTRONIC SYSTEM DESIGN INC
225 Foster Ave  (60106-1631)
**PHONE** ................................. 847 358-8212
**Fax:** 847 358-8214
Harry Rueckel, *President*
Ruth C Rueckel, *Corp Secy*
**EMP:** 3
**SQ FT:** 3,700
**SALES:** 1.6MM  **Privately Held**
**WEB:** www.octamatic.com
**SIC: 3823** 3825 Analyzers, industrial process type; instruments to measure electricity

### (G-1891)
### EMC MACHINING INC
905 Fairway Dr  (60106-1314)
**PHONE** ................................. 630 860-7076
**Fax:** 630 860-2479
Mila Pimentel, *President*
Anna Doma, *Admin Sec*
**EMP:** 10
**SQ FT:** 5,000
**SALES (est):** 1.4MM  **Privately Held**
**SIC: 3599** Machine shop, jobbing & repair

### (G-1892)
### EMLIN COSMETICS INC (PA)
290 Beeline Dr  (60106-1600)
**PHONE** ................................. 630 860-5773
**Fax:** 630 860-6517
Lester Shapiro, *President*
Robert Shapiro, *Vice Pres*
Sandra Geroulis, *Controller*
Norton Shapiro, *Admin Sec*
**EMP:** 25 **EST:** 1964
**SQ FT:** 56,000
**SALES (est):** 4.8MM  **Privately Held**
**WEB:** www.emlin.com
**SIC: 2844** Toilet preparations; hair preparations, including shampoos

### (G-1893)
### ENERSTAR INC
742 Foster Ave  (60106-1509)
**PHONE** ................................. 847 350-3400
Tim Carew, *President*
Ben Pomerantz, *Vice Pres*
Jean Carew, *Treasurer*
**EMP:** 6
**SQ FT:** 2,500
**SALES (est):** 2MM  **Privately Held**
**WEB:** www.enerstar.net
**SIC: 5084** 3823 Industrial machinery & equipment; water quality monitoring & control systems

### (G-1894)
### EXCELLENT BINDERY INC
500 Eastern Ave  (60106-3807)
**PHONE** ................................. 630 766-9050
**Fax:** 630 766-9052
Jozef Borzym, *President*
**EMP:** 20 **EST:** 1998
**SQ FT:** 10,000
**SALES (est):** 1.3MM  **Privately Held**
**SIC: 2789** Binding & repair of books, magazines & pamphlets

### (G-1895)
### FACTORY PLAZA INC
429 Evergreen Ave  (60106-2505)
**PHONE** ................................. 630 616-9999
**Fax:** 630 616-5509
Darek Bosek, *President*
▲ **EMP:** 24
**SALES (est):** 3.2MM  **Privately Held**
**SIC: 3281** Table tops, marble

### (G-1896)
### FEDERAL ENVELOPE COMPANY
608 Country Club Dr  (60106-1303)
**PHONE** ................................. 630 595-2000
**Fax:** 630 595-1212
Howard L Shaw Sr, *Ch of Bd*

Michael Shaw, *President*
Howard Shaw Jr, *Vice Pres*
Kelly Mueller, *CFO*
Raymond Haffertepe, *Treasurer*
▲ **EMP:** 100
**SQ FT:** 106,000
**SALES (est):** 24.6MM  **Privately Held**
**WEB:** www.federalenvelope.com
**SIC: 2677** Envelopes

### (G-1897)
### FINISH LINE HORSE PRODUCTS INC
115 Gateway Rd  (60106-1950)
**PHONE** ................................. 630 694-0000
**Fax:** 630 766-6000
John Howe, *President*
Nick Cinquino, *Opers Staff*
Steve Blanchard, *Sales Mgr*
**EMP:** 22
**SQ FT:** 20,000
**SALES (est):** 5.3MM  **Privately Held**
**WEB:** www.finishlinehorse.com
**SIC: 2834** Veterinary pharmaceutical preparations

### (G-1898)
### FINISHING COMPANY
717 Thomas Dr  (60106-1624)
**PHONE** ................................. 630 521-9635
▲ **EMP:** 90
**SQ FT:** 70,000
**SALES (est):** 8.5MM  **Privately Held**
**WEB:** www.envisionfx.com
**SIC: 3479** 3471 Coating of metals & formed products; plating of metals or formed products

### (G-1899)
### FITPAC CO LTD
14 N Center St 22  (60106-2128)
**PHONE** ................................. 630 428-9077
William Hong, *Principal*
▲ **EMP:** 4
**SALES (est):** 218K  **Privately Held**
**SIC: 3085** 3221 3411 Plastics bottles; glass containers; aluminum cans

### (G-1900)
### FORM-ALL SPRING STAMPING INC
380 Meyer Rd  (60106-1615)
**PHONE** ................................. 630 595-8833
**Fax:** 630 595-9006
Walter Bragiel, *President*
Mary Bragiel, *Vice Pres*
**EMP:** 20 **EST:** 1954
**SQ FT:** 20,000
**SALES:** 2.5MM  **Privately Held**
**SIC: 3469** 3495 Stamping metal for the trade; mechanical springs, precision

### (G-1901)
### FORMCO PLASTICS INC
Also Called: Litestage Lighting Systems
904 Fairway Dr  (60106-1315)
**PHONE** ................................. 630 860-7998
**Fax:** 630 860-9181
Anthony J Tringali III, *CEO*
Joel Tringali, *Admin Sec*
**EMP:** 13
**SQ FT:** 18,000
**SALES (est):** 1.7MM  **Privately Held**
**WEB:** www.litestage.com
**SIC: 3081** Plastic film & sheet

### (G-1902)
### FORSTER TOOL & MFG CO INC
1135 Industrial Dr  (60106-1246)
**PHONE** ................................. 630 616-8177
Maureen Forster, *President*
Nick Bird, *Vice Pres*
Scott Forst, *Vice Pres*
Alonso Chavez, *Manager*
**EMP:** 33
**SQ FT:** 15,000
**SALES (est):** 6MM  **Privately Held**
**WEB:** www.forstertool.com
**SIC: 3544** 3451 3469 Special dies & tools; screw machine products; metal stampings

▲ = Import  ▼ = Export
◆ = Import/Export

## GEOGRAPHIC SECTION
### Bensenville - Dupage County (G-1930)

**(G-1903)**
**G A I M PLASTICS INCORPORATED**
Also Called: G A I M Engineering
789 Golf Ln (60106-1563)
PHONE...................630 350-9500
Edward Glatt, *President*
EMP: 13
SALES (corp-wide): 3.1MM **Privately Held**
WEB: www.gaimway.com
SIC: **3089** Injection molding of plastics
PA: G.A.I.M. Plastics Incorporated.
  789 Golf Ln
  Bensenville IL 60106
  630 350-9500

**(G-1904)**
**GAIM PLASTICS INCORPORATED (PA)**
Also Called: G A I M Engineering
789 Golf Ln (60106-1563)
PHONE...................630 350-9500
Fax: 630 350-9555
Edward W Glatt Jr, *President*
EMP: 16
SQ FT: 13,700
SALES (est): 3.1MM **Privately Held**
WEB: www.gaimway.com
SIC: **3089** Injection molding of plastics

**(G-1905)**
**GATEWAY CABLE INC**
11 Gateway Rd (60106-1948)
PHONE...................630 766-7969
Ronald Flerlage, *Partner*
EMP: 5
SALES (corp-wide): 1.9MM **Privately Held**
SIC: **3679** Harness assemblies for electronic use: wire or cable
PA: Gateway Cable, Inc.
  1998 Ohio St Ste 100
  Lisle IL 60532
  630 766-7969

**(G-1906)**
**GEIB INDUSTRIES INC**
901 E Jefferson St (60106-3232)
PHONE...................847 455-4550
Fax: 847 455-4559
Robert Geib, *President*
Christopher Geib, *President*
Michael A Zalas, *General Mgr*
Thomas Geib, *Vice Pres*
Peter Tinsley, *Sales Mgr*
EMP: 25
SQ FT: 15,000
SALES (est): 36.4MM **Privately Held**
WEB: www.geibind.com
SIC: **5084** 3498 3429 3052 Hydraulic systems equipment & supplies; fabricated pipe & fittings; manufactured hardware (general); rubber & plastics hose & beltings

**(G-1907)**
**GENERAL AIR COMPRESSOR INC**
1078 Fairway Dr (60106-1317)
PHONE...................630 860-1717
George Chicoine, *President*
EMP: 3
SQ FT: 1,400
SALES (est): 444K **Privately Held**
SIC: **3694** Distributors, motor vehicle engine

**(G-1908)**
**GENERAL ELECTRO CORPORATION**
Also Called: Bentronics
1069 Bryn Mawr Ave (60106-1244)
PHONE...................630 595-8989
Fax: 630 595-9071
J Patel, *President*
EMP: 10
SQ FT: 10,500
SALES: 2MM **Privately Held**
WEB: www.generalelectro.com
SIC: **3672** 8711 Printed circuit boards; engineering services

**(G-1909)**
**GIRARD CHEMICAL COMPANY**
605 Country Club Dr Ste F (60106-1330)
PHONE...................630 293-5886
Jeff Girard, *President*
David Girard, *Corp Secy*
EMP: 8
SALES: 1MM **Privately Held**
WEB: www.girardchemical.com
SIC: **2899** Water treating compounds

**(G-1910)**
**GMA INC**
756 Birginal Dr (60106-1213)
PHONE...................630 595-1255
Osvaldo Grano, *President*
Jojo Aquio, *Asst Mgr*
Assumpta Rozal, *Asst Mgr*
EMP: 5
SQ FT: 3,800
SALES (est): 605K **Privately Held**
WEB: www.gmanetwork.com
SIC: **3444** 7692 3441 Sheet metalwork; welding repair; fabricated structural metal

**(G-1911)**
**GOGO LLC**
814 Thorndale Ave (60106-1138)
PHONE...................630 647-1400
EMP: 78
SALES (corp-wide): 596.5MM **Publicly Held**
SIC: **3663** 4812 4813 Radio & TV communications equipment; cellular radio telephone; cellular telephone services; telephone communication, except radio
HQ: Gogo Llc
  111 N Canal St Fl 15
  Chicago IL 60606
  630 647-1400

**(G-1912)**
**GRACELAND CUSTOM PRODUCTS INC**
1017 Graceland Ave (60106)
PHONE...................630 616-4143
Leah Abraham, *President*
Ray Joseph, *Office Mgr*
Ray Tibavido, *Admin Sec*
EMP: 19
SQ FT: 5,000
SALES: 1.8MM **Privately Held**
SIC: **3812** Detection apparatus: electronic/magnetic field, light/heat

**(G-1913)**
**GRAPHIC ENGRAVERS INC**
Also Called: Graphic Photo Engravers
691 Country Club Dr (60106-1324)
PHONE...................630 595-0400
Fax: 630 595-1085
Charles E Zidek, *President*
David Zidek, *Plant Mgr*
Dena Ptak, *Production*
James Zidek, *Treasurer*
Russ Zidek, *Manager*
EMP: 20 EST: 1946
SQ FT: 14,000
SALES (est): 3.2MM **Privately Held**
WEB: www.graphicengravers.com
SIC: **2796** Photoengraving plates, linecuts or halftones

**(G-1914)**
**GROUP 3 ENVELOPE F & S TYPE**
237 Evergreen Ave Ste B (60106-2581)
PHONE...................630 766-1230
Fax: 630 766-1297
Sudhaker Patel, *President*
Phillip Palmer, *Foreman/Supr*
Jyotika Patel, *Admin Sec*
EMP: 3 EST: 1951
SQ FT: 2,200
SALES (est): 300K **Privately Held**
SIC: **3555** Type: lead, steel, brass, copper faced, etc.

**(G-1915)**
**HELENE PRINTING INC**
24 S Addison St Apt 805 (60106-2195)
PHONE...................630 482-3300
Jerry Marchese, *Principal*
EMP: 3 EST: 2007
SALES (est): 269.7K **Privately Held**
SIC: **2759** Commercial printing

**(G-1916)**
**HI PRCISION TL MAKERS MCHY INC**
774 Foster Ave (60106-1509)
PHONE...................630 694-0200
Harold Irving, *President*
EMP: 5
SALES (est): 608.9K **Privately Held**
SIC: **3544** Special dies, tools, jigs & fixtures

**(G-1917)**
**HI-TECH WELDING SERVICES INC**
233 William St (60106-3324)
PHONE...................630 595-8160
Julius Schwarzinger, *President*
Maggy Zols, *Office Mgr*
EMP: 7
SQ FT: 10,000
SALES: 630K **Privately Held**
SIC: **3451** Screw machine products

**(G-1918)**
**I C UNIVERSAL INC**
1040 Fairway Dr (60106-1317)
PHONE...................630 766-1169
Isaac Capistran, *President*
EMP: 2 EST: 1996
SQ FT: 1,200
SALES: 220K **Privately Held**
SIC: **3469** Machine parts, stamped or pressed metal

**(G-1919)**
**INNOVATIVE GRINGING INC**
690 County Line Rd (60106-3260)
PHONE...................630 766-4567
Fax: 630 766-4460
Chris Kik, *President*
EMP: 4
SALES: 300K **Privately Held**
SIC: **3599** Grinding castings for the trade

**(G-1920)**
**INTERMAIL DIRECT MARKETING**
151 Eastern Ave (60106-1159)
PHONE...................630 274-6333
Charles Cerniglia Jr, *President*
EMP: 3
SQ FT: 12,000
SALES: 1MM **Privately Held**
WEB: www.intermaildirect.com
SIC: **3579** Envelope stuffing, sealing & addressing machines

**(G-1921)**
**INTERNATIONAL GOLDEN FOODS INC**
819 Industrial Dr (60106-1306)
PHONE...................630 860-5552
Mansour C Amiran, *President*
Amiran Mansour, *Administration*
▲ EMP: 15
SQ FT: 40,000
SALES (est): 3.5MM **Privately Held**
WEB: www.goldenfood.com
SIC: **2044** 5149 Rice milling; rice, polished

**(G-1922)**
**INTERSOL INDUSTRIES INC**
241 James St (60106-3318)
PHONE...................630 238-0385
Fax: 630 238-9131
Orest Hrynewycz, *President*
Maria Hrynewycz, *Corp Secy*
Roman Hrynewycz, *Vice Pres*
Henry Golde, *Controller*
EMP: 10
SQ FT: 3,000
SALES: 1MM **Privately Held**
WEB: www.intersolind.com
SIC: **3625** 3555 Solenoid switches (industrial controls); printing trades machinery

**(G-1923)**
**IRMKO TOOL WORKS INC**
205 Park St (60106-2556)
PHONE...................630 350-7550
Fax: 630 350-7556
Eric Fox, *President*
Charles Dwyer, *Chairman*
Charlie Dwyer, *Admin Sec*
EMP: 40 EST: 1970
SQ FT: 16,000
SALES (est): 6.4MM **Privately Held**
WEB: www.irmko.com
SIC: **3599** 3471 Machine shop, jobbing & repair; plating & polishing

**(G-1924)**
**ISENBERG BATH CORPORATION**
1325 W Irving Park Rd (60106-1764)
PHONE...................972 510-5916
Abbas Poonawala, *Bd of Directors*
EMP: 6 EST: 2011
SALES (est): 366.5K **Privately Held**
SIC: **3432** Plumbers' brass goods: drain cocks, faucets, spigots, etc.

**(G-1925)**
**J & J INDUSTRIES INC**
107 Gateway Rd (60106-1950)
PHONE...................630 595-8878
Jerry A Haug, *President*
Melanie Haug, *Admin Sec*
EMP: 8
SQ FT: 7,200
SALES: 500K **Privately Held**
SIC: **3053** 2891 3296 Gaskets, packing & sealing devices; adhesives & sealants; mineral wool

**(G-1926)**
**J C EMBROIDERY & SCREEN PRINT**
406 Industrial Dr (60106-1323)
PHONE...................630 595-4670
Fax: 630 595-4675
Jeff Congine, *President*
EMP: 2
SQ FT: 2,800
SALES: 200K **Privately Held**
SIC: **2395** Embroidery products, except schiffli machine

**(G-1927)**
**JEM TOOL & MANUFACTURING CO**
797 Industrial Dr (60106-1304)
PHONE...................630 595-1686
Fax: 630 595-1783
Wesley Cassidy, *President*
Jonathan Cassidy, *Corp Secy*
Sue Cassidy, *Office Mgr*
EMP: 13
SQ FT: 12,000
SALES (est): 1.9MM **Privately Held**
SIC: **3599** Machine shop, jobbing & repair

**(G-1928)**
**JM DIE TOOLING CO**
466 Meyer Rd (60106-1617)
PHONE...................630 616-7776
Fax: 630 616-7778
John Norawa, *President*
EMP: 20
SQ FT: 12,000
SALES (est): 3.6MM **Privately Held**
WEB: www.jmdie.com
SIC: **3544** Special dies, tools, jigs & fixtures

**(G-1929)**
**JM TOOL & DIE LLC**
Also Called: Athena Precision Machining
299 Beeline Dr (60106-1612)
PHONE...................630 595-1274
John Morawa,
EMP: 2 EST: 2010
SALES (est): 293.7K **Privately Held**
SIC: **3544** Mfg Dies/Tools/Jigs/Fixtures

**(G-1930)**
**JOHNSON PRINTING**
729 Il Route 83 Ste 323 (60106-1256)
P.O. Box 1045 (60106-8045)
PHONE...................630 595-8815
Russell Johnson, *Owner*
EMP: 4
SALES (est): 240K **Privately Held**
SIC: **2752** 2759 Commercial printing, lithographic; commercial printing

## Bensenville - Dupage County (G-1931)
### GEOGRAPHIC SECTION

**(G-1931)**
**K & H TOOL CO**
164 Devon Ave (60106-1148)
PHONE...............................630 766-4588
Fax: 630 766-4971
Manuel Cervantes, *President*
EMP: 6
SQ FT: 1,900
SALES: 300K **Privately Held**
SIC: 3544 3599 Jigs & fixtures; machine shop, jobbing & repair

**(G-1932)**
**K B TOOL INC**
211 Beeline Dr Ste 7 (60106-1640)
PHONE...............................630 595-4340
Kenneth Burg, *President*
EMP: 5 EST: 1994
SQ FT: 3,200
SALES (est): 511.4K **Privately Held**
SIC: 3089 3544 Injection molded finished plastic products; dies & die holders for metal cutting, forming, die casting

**(G-1933)**
**K P ENTERPRISES INC**
792 County Line Rd Ste A (60106-3204)
PHONE...............................630 509-2174
Krystyna Pasek, *President*
Jan Pasek, *Admin Sec*
EMP: 3
SALES (est): 410.5K **Privately Held**
SIC: 3599 3544 Machine shop, jobbing & repair; special dies, tools, jigs & fixtures

**(G-1934)**
**KING TOOL AND DIE INC**
210 Gateway Rd (60106-1953)
PHONE...............................630 787-0799
Kevin King, *President*
Shawn King, *Vice Pres*
Jeanne King, *Admin Sec*
EMP: 4
SQ FT: 5,000
SALES: 355K **Privately Held**
SIC: 3544 3469 Special dies, tools, jigs & fixtures; metal stampings

**(G-1935)**
**L D REDMER SCREW PDTS INC**
Also Called: Tanko Screw Products
515 Thomas Dr (60106-1620)
PHONE...............................630 787-0504
Fax: 630 595-0442
Chris Grady, *President*
L D Redmer, *Vice Pres*
Defrancesco Joseph, *Engineer*
Ofelia Berrospe, *Controller*
Bill Landholt, *Sales Mgr*
EMP: 45
SQ FT: 15,000
SALES (est): 11.9MM **Privately Held**
WEB: www.ldredmer.com
SIC: 3451 Screw machine products

**(G-1936)**
**L-V INDUSTRIES INC**
508 Meyer Rd (60106-1604)
PHONE...............................630 595-9251
Fax: 630 595-3801
Jennifer Vinyard, *President*
Jeffrey Vinyard, *Corp Secy*
Jeff Vinyard, *Manager*
EMP: 10
SQ FT: 4,500
SALES (est): 1.5MM **Privately Held**
WEB: www.lvindustries.com
SIC: 3599 3544 Machine shop, jobbing & repair; special dies, tools, jigs & fixtures

**(G-1937)**
**LAKE CABLE LLC**
529 Thomas Dr (60106-1620)
PHONE...............................888 518-8086
Emile Tohme, *President*
John Murakami, *Exec VP*
Dan Borst, *Plant Mgr*
Joel Gonzalez, *Opers Mgr*
Gabriel Lutin, *Prdtn Mgr*
▲ EMP: 194
SQ FT: 65,000
SALES (est): 85.9MM **Privately Held**
WEB: www.lakecable.com
SIC: 3496 Miscellaneous fabricated wire products

**(G-1938)**
**LASER CENTER CORPORATION**
401 Eastern Ave (60106-3810)
PHONE...............................630 422-1975
Yun Chon Kwak, *President*
Donald Shin, *Manager*
EMP: 31
SALES (est): 6.9MM **Privately Held**
SIC: 3444 Sheet metalwork

**(G-1939)**
**LECIP INC**
881 Il Route 83 (60106-1219)
PHONE...............................312 626-2525
Kazuo Ueno, *President*
Koji Isayama, *COO*
Natalie Cornell, *Vice Pres*
Fumitoshi Nakamura, *CFO*
Anne Dowling, *Sr Project Mgr*
▲ EMP: 7
SALES (est): 1.6MM
SALES (corp-wide): 149.4MM **Privately Held**
SIC: 3647 3669 3699 Vehicular lighting equipment; transportation signaling devices; electrical equipment & supplies
PA: Lecip Holdings Corporation
1260-2, Kaminoho
Motosu GIF 501-0
583 243-121

**(G-1940)**
**LESKER COMPANY INC**
528 N York Rd (60106-1607)
P.O. Box 785, Antioch (60002-0785)
PHONE...............................708 343-2277
Fax: 708 343-7369
Robert Lesker, *President*
EMP: 25
SQ FT: 15,000
SALES (est): 3.8MM **Privately Held**
SIC: 3441 Fabricated structural metal

**(G-1941)**
**LEVITON MANUFACTURING CO INC**
700 Golf Ln (60106-1511)
PHONE...............................630 350-2656
Fax: 630 766-6963
Ken Wallace, *Manager*
EMP: 319
SALES (corp-wide): 1.5B **Privately Held**
SIC: 3643 Plugs, electric; caps & plugs, electric: attachment; connectors, electric cord; sockets, electric
PA: Leviton Manufacturing Co., Inc.
201 N Service Rd
Melville NY 11747
631 812-6000

**(G-1942)**
**LRE PRODUCTS INC**
Also Called: Hpfs
733 Maple Ln (60106-1513)
PHONE...............................630 238-8321
Fax: 630 860-7995
Ronald L Yonkee, *President*
Edward P Kasprzycki, *Vice Pres*
Laura Z Stueve, *Treasurer*
▲ EMP: 30
SQ FT: 25,000
SALES (est): 5.2MM **Privately Held**
WEB: www.callhpfs.com
SIC: 3965 3452 Fasteners, buttons, needles & pins; bolts, nuts, rivets & washers

**(G-1943)**
**M COR INC**
227 James St Ste 6 (60106-3374)
P.O. Box 844, Wood Dale (60191-0844)
PHONE...............................630 860-1150
Fax: 630 860-0522
Raymond Mattera, *President*
Larry Mattera, *President*
Richard Mattera, *Vice Pres*
EMP: 13
SQ FT: 2,500
SALES (est): 2MM **Privately Held**
WEB: www.fep-encapsulated-o-rings.com
SIC: 3053 5085 Gaskets, all materials; industrial supplies

**(G-1944)**
**MACHINEX MANUFACTURING CO INC**
225 James St Ste 4 (60106-3367)
PHONE...............................630 766-4210
Stanly Borowiec, *President*
EMP: 4
SALES (est): 276.4K **Privately Held**
SIC: 3599 Machine shop, jobbing & repair

**(G-1945)**
**MARVEL MACHINING CO INC**
231 Evergreen Ave (60106-2501)
PHONE...............................630 350-0075
Fax: 630 350-0869
John Obstalecki, *President*
EMP: 4
SQ FT: 5,000
SALES (est): 650K **Privately Held**
SIC: 3599 Machine shop, jobbing & repair

**(G-1946)**
**MATTHEW WARREN INC**
Also Called: Hi-Perfrmnce Fastening Systems
733 Maple Ln (60106-1513)
PHONE...............................630 860-7766
Jon Emrich, *Sales Mgr*
EMP: 18
SALES (corp-wide): 115.4MM **Privately Held**
HQ: Matthew Warren, Inc.
9501 Tech Blvd Ste 401
Rosemont IL 60018
847 349-5760

**(G-1947)**
**MAVERICK TOOL COMPANY INC**
211 Beeline Dr Ste 5 (60106-1640)
PHONE...............................630 766-2313
John Woodward, *President*
Denise Goorski, *Finance Mgr*
EMP: 20
SQ FT: 3,000
SALES (est): 2.7MM **Privately Held**
SIC: 3545 3544 Cutting tools for machine tools; special dies, tools, jigs & fixtures

**(G-1948)**
**MEDERER GROUP**
745 Birginal Dr Ste B (60106-1220)
PHONE...............................630 860-4587
Herbert Mederer, *Owner*
▲ EMP: 3
SALES (est): 237.8K **Privately Held**
SIC: 2064 Candy & other confectionery products

**(G-1949)**
**MICRO WEST LTD**
326 Evergreen Ave (60106-2504)
P.O. Box 18 (60106-0018)
PHONE...............................630 766-7160
Ivan Kucera, *President*
EMP: 6
SALES (est): 656.5K **Privately Held**
WEB: www.microwestltd.com
SIC: 3643 Current-carrying wiring devices

**(G-1950)**
**MICROTHINCOM INC**
661 Frontier Way (60106-3802)
PHONE...............................630 543-0501
Kenneth Reick, *President*
Daniel O Malley, *Admin Sec*
EMP: 10
SQ FT: 22,000
SALES (est): 1.6MM **Privately Held**
WEB: www.yorktownindustries.com
SIC: 3089 Plastic kitchenware, tableware & houseware

**(G-1951)**
**MIDSTATES CUTTING TOOLS INC**
Also Called: Mid States Tool & Cutter
304 Meyer Rd (60106-1615)
PHONE...............................630 595-0700
James B Surpless Jr, *President*
Lawrence Less, *Mfg Staff*
Matt Gianorio, *VP Sales*
Noreen Lavlle, *Office Mgr*
Joy Macinnis, *Assistant*
EMP: 30 EST: 2005

SALES (est): 6.8MM **Privately Held**
WEB: www.midstates-tool.com
SIC: 3312 Tool & die steel

**(G-1952)**
**MIDWEST GRAPHIC INDUSTRIES**
Also Called: Midwest Graphics
605 Country Club Dr Ste A (60106-1330)
PHONE...............................630 509-2972
Fax: 630 268-0110
James W Panter Jr, *President*
Jefferey Panter, *Treasurer*
Scott W Panter, *Admin Sec*
EMP: 16
SQ FT: 10,000
SALES (est): 1.8MM **Privately Held**
WEB: www.mgimidwest.com
SIC: 2752 2761 Commercial printing, offset; manifold business forms

**(G-1953)**
**MODERN GEAR & MACHINE INC**
406 Evergreen Ave (60106-2506)
PHONE...............................630 350-9173
Fax: 630 350-1607
Kathy Naumowicz, *President*
Darick Naumowicz, *Vice Pres*
EMP: 10
SQ FT: 5,600
SALES (est): 1.6MM **Privately Held**
WEB: www.moderngear.com
SIC: 3541 3462 Gear cutting & finishing machines; iron & steel forgings

**(G-1954)**
**NATIONAL DATA-LABEL CORP**
301 Arthur Ct (60106-3381)
PHONE...............................630 616-9595
Fax: 630 616-0862
William Iovino, *President*
Kent Dahlgren, *Vice Pres*
Dean Maruyama, *Plant Mgr*
Mary Lynn Leland, *Controller*
Bill Iovino, *Sales Executive*
EMP: 20
SQ FT: 25,000
SALES (est): 3.1MM **Privately Held**
WEB: www.nationaldatalabel.com
SIC: 2759 2672 Labels & seals: printing; coated & laminated paper

**(G-1955)**
**NEW WAVE EXPRESS INC**
842 Foster Ave (60106-1510)
PHONE...............................630 238-3129
Fax: 630 238-3140
Takayuki Hanai, *Owner*
▲ EMP: 4
SALES (est): 257.3K **Privately Held**
SIC: 2741 Miscellaneous publishing

**(G-1956)**
**NORTH AMERICA O M C G INC**
Also Called: Omcg North America
857 Industrial Dr Ste 1 (60106-1351)
PHONE...............................630 860-1016
Luigi Magg, *President*
Robert Sears, *Vice Pres*
Kathy Monroe, *Accountant*
EMP: 5
SQ FT: 16,000
SALES (est): 420K **Privately Held**
SIC: 3549 3544 Metalworking machinery; special dies, tools, jigs & fixtures

**(G-1957)**
**NORTHWEST TOOL CO INC**
342 Evergreen Ave (60106-2504)
PHONE...............................630 350-4770
Tomasz Dabkiewicz, *President*
EMP: 4
SQ FT: 1,000
SALES (est): 639K **Privately Held**
SIC: 3599 Machine shop, jobbing & repair

**(G-1958)**
**OMEGA PRINTING INC**
201 William St (60106-3324)
PHONE...............................630 595-6344
Fax: 630 595-0291
Louis J Finger, *President*
Cynthia H Finger, *Vice Pres*
Jeffrey George, *Production*
Patricia Finger, *Finance Dir*
Thomas Isacson, *Info Tech Dir*

# GEOGRAPHIC SECTION
## Bensenville - Dupage County (G-1984)

▲ EMP: 20
SQ FT: 16,000
SALES (est): 4.1MM  Privately Held
WEB: www.omegaprinting.com
SIC: 2752  Commercial printing, offset

### (G-1959)
### OPTI-VUE INC
224 James St (60106-3319)
PHONE..................630 274-6121
Fax: 630 595-1006
Yordan Vulich, *President*
John Vulich, *Vice Pres*
Matthew Vulich, *Vice Pres*
Joseph Vulich, *CFO*
EMP: 4
SQ FT: 13,000
SALES: 500K  Privately Held
WEB: www.aitindustries.com
SIC: 5049  3827  Optical goods; optical instruments & lenses

### (G-1960)
### OSG POWER TOOLS INC
759 Industrial Dr (60106-1304)
PHONE..................630 561-4008
EMP: 200
SALES (est): 12.8MM  Privately Held
SIC: 3541  Mfg Machine Tools-Cutting

### (G-1961)
### OSG USA INC
759 Industrial Dr (60106-1304)
PHONE..................630 274-2100
Gohei Osawa, *Branch Mgr*
EMP: 115
SQ FT: 25,000
SALES (corp-wide): 1B  Privately Held
SIC: 3545  Cutting tools for machine tools
HQ: Osg Usa, Inc.
    676 E Fullerton Ave
    Glendale Heights IL 60139
    630 790-1400

### (G-1962)
### P & A DRIVELINE & MACHINE INC
Also Called: Drivetrain Svc & Components
292 Devon Ave Ste 18 (60106-1145)
PHONE..................630 860-7474
Fax: 630 860-7256
Paresh Patel, *President*
Tim Cobb, *Manager*
Eugene Trojaniak, *Admin Sec*
EMP: 15
SQ FT: 11,200
SALES (est): 6.3MM  Privately Held
SIC: 5013  3599  5531  Truck parts & accessories; machine shop, jobbing & repair; truck equipment & parts

### (G-1963)
### PATKO TOOL & MANUFACTURING
767 Gasoline Aly (60106-1103)
PHONE..................630 616-8802
Chris Pacocha, *President*
EMP: 5
SALES (est): 646.6K  Privately Held
SIC: 3469  Machine parts, stamped or pressed metal

### (G-1964)
### PLASTECH INC
Also Called: Land-O-Tackle
873 Fairway Dr (60106-1312)
PHONE..................630 595-7222
Bob Kenyon, *President*
John Haase, *Vice Pres*
Judy Mussillo, *Admin Sec*
EMP: 12
SQ FT: 12,000
SALES (est): 1.2MM  Privately Held
SIC: 3089  3949  Injection molding of plastics; fishing tackle, general

### (G-1965)
### PONTIAC ENGRAVING
586 Meyer Rd (60106-1604)
PHONE..................630 834-4424
Fax: 630 834-4438
Bruce Solyom, *Owner*
EMP: 3
SQ FT: 2,500
SALES: 120K  Privately Held
SIC: 2796  3545  3544  3452  Engraving on copper, steel, wood or rubber; printing plates; machine tool accessories; special dies, tools, jigs & fixtures; bolts, nuts, rivets & washers; commercial printing

### (G-1966)
### PREMIUM COMPONENTS
1090 Bryn Mawr Ave (60106-1245)
PHONE..................630 521-1700
Lucian Pietreanu, *President*
EMP: 3
SALES (est): 528.7K  Privately Held
SIC: 3714  Motor vehicle transmissions, drive assemblies & parts

### (G-1967)
### PROSPAN MANUFACTURING CO
540 Meyer Rd (60106-1604)
PHONE..................630 860-1930
James Sullivan, *President*
Geralyn Sullivan, *Admin Sec*
EMP: 2
SALES (est): 500K  Privately Held
SIC: 3599  Column clamps & shores

### (G-1968)
### PROSTAT CORPORATION
1072 Tower Ln (60106-1031)
PHONE..................630 238-8883
Fax: 630 238-9717
Stephen Halperin, *President*
Roberta Halperin, *Vice Pres*
Kimberly Becker, *Opers Mgr*
Bobbie Halperin, *Info Tech Mgr*
John Kinnear Jr, *Sr Associate*
EMP: 7
SQ FT: 5,600
SALES (est): 1.4MM  Privately Held
WEB: www.prostatcorp.com
SIC: 3825  3829  3823  Instruments to measure electricity; measuring & controlling devices; industrial instrmnts msrmnt display/control process variable

### (G-1969)
### PROTECTOSEAL COMPANY (PA)
225 Foster Ave (60106-1631)
P.O. Box 95588, Chicago (60694-5588)
PHONE..................630 595-0800
Fax: 630 595-8059
James P Honan, *President*
Clark Huffstutter, *Division Mgr*
Thomas C Piotrowski, *Vice Pres*
Jack Roche, *Mfg Staff*
Jerry Livorsi, *Purchasing*
▲ EMP: 95
SQ FT: 150,000
SALES: 6MM  Privately Held
WEB: www.protectoseal.com
SIC: 3795  5999  Tanks & tank components; safety supplies & equipment

### (G-1970)
### PURELINE TREATMENT SYSTEMS LLC
Also Called: Sterline Bridge
1241 N Ellis St (60106-1118)
PHONE..................847 963-8465
Steve Grassbaugh, *Vice Pres*
John Sokol, *Technical Mgr*
Bradford T Whitmore, *Mng Member*
Lucy Sutton, *Exec Sec*
▲ EMP: 49
SQ FT: 12,000
SALES: 50MM  Privately Held
WEB: www.pureline.net
SIC: 3589  3443  Water treatment equipment, industrial; fumigating chambers, metal plate

### (G-1971)
### QUALITY IRON WORKS INC
449 Evergreen Ave (60106-2505)
PHONE..................630 766-0885
Fax: 630 766-0887
EMP: 17
SQ FT: 5,500
SALES (est): 1.3MM  Privately Held
SIC: 1799  3446  Trade Contractor Mfg Architectural Metalwork

### (G-1972)
### QUALITY PLASTIC PRODUCTS INC
Also Called: Noridge Die & Mold
830 Maple Ln (60106-1546)
PHONE..................630 766-7593
Fax: 630 766-7963
Sten Olsen, *President*
Michael Olsen, *Vice Pres*
EMP: 6
SQ FT: 8,000
SALES (est): 730.6K  Privately Held
SIC: 3089  Injection molding of plastics

### (G-1973)
### QUALITY TECH TOOL INC
759 Industrial Dr (60106-1304)
PHONE..................847 690-9643
Zoran Denic, *President*
Carol Lueth, *General Mgr*
William Rackow, *Vice Pres*
EMP: 42
SQ FT: 11,000
SALES (est): 6.6MM  Privately Held
WEB: www.qualitytechtool.com
SIC: 3545  5251  Drill bits, metalworking; tools

### (G-1974)
### R N I INDUSTRIES INC
Also Called: Advantage Unlimited
236 William St (60106-3325)
PHONE..................630 860-9147
Fax: 630 860-5216
Bradley Jordan, *President*
Scott Gipre, *Manager*
EMP: 22
SQ FT: 22,000
SALES (est): 2MM  Privately Held
WEB: www.adv-unlimited.com
SIC: 3993  Advertising novelties

### (G-1975)
### RACKOW POLYMERS CORPORATION
475 Thomas Dr (60106-1618)
PHONE..................630 766-3982
Fax: 630 766-6742
Mario Rackow, *President*
Ed Matrowski, *Vice Pres*
Ed Modrowski, *Vice Pres*
Bill Swart, *Sales Mgr*
EMP: 30
SQ FT: 60,000
SALES (est): 6.1MM  Privately Held
SIC: 3089  Injection molding of plastics

### (G-1976)
### RASMUSSEN PRESS INC
606 E Green St (60106-2548)
Fax: 630 766-9009
Gregory Rasmussen, *President*
Jerry Rasmussen, *Vice Pres*
EMP: 7
SALES (est): 996.6K  Privately Held
SIC: 2752  2789  7331  2732  Commercial printing, offset; binding only: books, pamphlets, magazines, etc.; direct mail advertising services; book printing; periodicals

### (G-1977)
### REX RADIATOR AND WELDING CO
Also Called: Rex Radiator Sales & Dist
367 Evergreen Ave (60106-2503)
PHONE..................630 595-4664
Fax: 630 595-5057
Bill Rex, *Manager*
EMP: 7
SALES (corp-wide): 3.4MM  Privately Held
SIC: 7539  7692  Radiator repair shop, automotive; automotive welding
PA: Rex Radiator And Welding Co Inc
    1440 W 38th St
    Chicago IL 60609
    312 421-1531

### (G-1978)
### RICH INDUSTRIES INC
489 Thomas Dr (60106-2499)
PHONE..................630 766-9150
Fax: 630 766-6193
Richard Rogala, *President*
Dan Osborn, *General Mgr*
Epifanio Villanueva, *Manager*
▲ EMP: 20
SQ FT: 15,000
SALES (corp-wide): 3MM  Privately Held
WEB: www.richindustries.com
SIC: 3495  Mechanical springs, precision
PA: Alagor Industries, Incorporated
    489 Thomas Dr
    Bensenville IL 60106
    630 766-2910

### (G-1979)
### ROLLYS CONVENIENT FOODS INC
923 Dolores Dr (60106-3427)
PHONE..................630 766-4070
Fax: 630 238-9513
Roland Waller, *President*
Dab Kuffer, *VP Finance*
Judy Graph, *Executive Asst*
EMP: 7
SQ FT: 1,900
SALES (est): 689.6K  Privately Held
WEB: www.capamer.com
SIC: 2038  Pizza, frozen

### (G-1980)
### ROYAL STAIRS CO
300 E Ave (60106)
PHONE..................630 860-2223
Kryspyna Hryszko, *President*
EMP: 5
SALES (est): 470K  Privately Held
SIC: 2431  Staircases & stairs, wood

### (G-1981)
### RPK TECHNOLOGIES INC
272 Judson St (60106-2604)
PHONE..................630 595-0911
Randal Krawiec, *President*
EMP: 3 EST: 2002
SALES (est): 263.7K  Privately Held
SIC: 3563  Spraying & dusting equipment

### (G-1982)
### RPT TONER LLC
475 Supreme Dr (60106-1161)
PHONE..................630 694-0400
Jay Shah,
Induben Patel,
Krishna Patel,
▲ EMP: 50
SQ FT: 50,000
SALES: 9.2MM  Privately Held
SIC: 3955  Print cartridges for laser & other computer printers

### (G-1983)
### RUBICON TECHNOLOGY INC (PA)
900 E Green St (60106-2553)
PHONE..................847 295-7000
Fax: 847 233-0711
Timothy E Brog, *CEO*
Don N Aquilano, *Ch of Bd*
William F Weissman, *President*
Hany Tamim, *COO*
Hal McGee, *Opers Mgr*
▲ EMP: 182
SQ FT: 30,000
SALES: 19.6MM  Publicly Held
WEB: www.rubicon-es2.com
SIC: 3679  Electronic crystals

### (G-1984)
### S & W MANUFACTURING CO INC
216 Evergreen Ave (60106-2502)
PHONE..................630 595-5044
Fax: 630 595-5275
William Burr, *President*
James Langeloh, *General Mgr*
Don E Secor, *Vice Pres*
Pedro Martinez, *Warehouse Mgr*
Milka Ahlstrand, *Controller*
▲ EMP: 45
SQ FT: 35,000
SALES: 11MM  Privately Held
WEB: www.swmanufacturing.com
SIC: 3469  3451  3829  7692  Metal stampings; screw machine products; surveying & drafting equipment; welding repair; machine tool accessories

## Bensenville - Dupage County (G-1985)

**(G-1985)**
**SAN MATEO INC**
1180 Industrial Dr (60106-1247)
P.O. Box 72 (60106-0072)
PHONE ................................. 630 860-6991
Fax: 630 595-4221
Eufracia Orozco, *President*
Hector Martinez, *Vice Pres*
Ray Soto, *Manager*
Lorena Garcia, *Admin Sec*
EMP: 30
SQ FT: 10,000
SALES (est): 5.7MM **Privately Held**
WEB: www.sanmateo.com
SIC: 3444 Sheet metalwork

**(G-1986)**
**SATURN MANUFACTURING COMPANY**
233 Park St (60106-2556)
PHONE ................................. 630 860-8474
Fax: 630 860-8904
William S Beckmeyer III, *President*
Diane Beckmeyer, *Accountant*
Larry Lumb, *Admin Sec*
EMP: 7
SQ FT: 8,870
SALES (est): 1MM **Privately Held**
SIC: 3451 Screw machine products

**(G-1987)**
**SCHLESINGER MACHINERY INC**
820 Maple Ln (60106-1546)
PHONE ................................. 630 766-4074
Fax: 630 766-5008
Michael Schlesinger, *President*
Cathy Schlesinger, *Admin Sec*
EMP: 4
SQ FT: 8,000
SALES: 343.6K **Privately Held**
SIC: 5084 3555 Printing trades machinery, equipment & supplies; printing presses

**(G-1988)**
**SCHOLASTIC TESTING SERVICE**
Also Called: Schools Processing Service
480 Meyer Rd (60106-1617)
PHONE ................................. 630 766-7150
Fax: 630 766-8054
Oliver F Anderhalter, *Principal*
John Kauffman, *Sales Staff*
EMP: 13
SALES (corp-wide): 2.3MM **Privately Held**
WEB: www.ststesting.com
SIC: 8748 2741 Testing service, educational or personnel; miscellaneous publishing
PA: Scholastic Testing Service Inc
4320 Green Ash Dr
Earth City MO 63045
314 739-3650

**(G-1989)**
**SCIENCE SUPPLY SOLUTIONS**
605 Country Club Dr Ste E (60106-1330)
PHONE ................................. 847 981-5500
Robin Webb, *Owner*
▲ EMP: 3 EST: 2009
SALES: 500K **Privately Held**
SIC: 3944 Science kits: microscopes, chemistry sets, etc.

**(G-1990)**
**SERVICE PRO ELECTRIC MTR REPR**
690 Industrial Dr (60106-1319)
PHONE ................................. 630 766-1215
Scott L Gibler, *President*
Ellen Keller, *CFO*
EMP: 5
SQ FT: 3,500
SALES (est): 470K **Privately Held**
SIC: 7694 5571 7999 Electric motor repair; motorcycle parts & accessories; bicycle & motorcycle rental services

**(G-1991)**
**SINGER DATA PRODUCTS INC (PA)**
Also Called: Scribe International Division
790 Maple Ln (60106-1560)
PHONE ................................. 630 860-6500
Fax: 630 860-3672
Theodore Singer, *President*
Robert Brown, *Purch Mgr*
Manny Torres, *Accounting Mgr*
EMP: 8
SQ FT: 9,000
SALES (est): 4.1MM **Privately Held**
SIC: 3577 3581 3579 3578 Printers, computer; automatic vending machines; postage meters; change making machines; audiometers

**(G-1992)**
**SINGER MEDICAL PRODUCTS INC**
790 Maple Ln (60106-1513)
PHONE ................................. 630 860-6500
Theodore Singer, *President*
M Torres, *Director*
EMP: 6
SQ FT: 9,000
SALES: 627.9K
SALES (corp-wide): 4.1MM **Privately Held**
SIC: 3825 Audiometers
PA: Singer Data Products Inc
790 Maple Ln
Bensenville IL 60106
630 860-6500

**(G-1993)**
**SNYDER INDUSTRIES INC**
Also Called: Rmic
736 Birginal Dr (60106-1213)
PHONE ................................. 630 773-9510
Thomas O'Connell, *President*
Bob Moore, *General Mgr*
Mike Blaha, *Engineer*
Sue Hornat, *Sales Mgr*
Michael Morrison, *Sales Executive*
EMP: 90
SALES (corp-wide): 3.7B **Privately Held**
SIC: 3089 1446 2821 Plastic containers, except foam; molding sand mining; molding compounds, plastics
HQ: Snyder Industries, Inc.
6940 O St Ste 100
Lincoln NE 68510
402 465-1206

**(G-1994)**
**SOJUZ ENT**
464 Country Club Dr (60106-1507)
PHONE ................................. 847 215-9400
Karolis Kaminskas, *Owner*
▲ EMP: 1
SALES: 700K **Privately Held**
SIC: 3556 Food products machinery

**(G-1995)**
**SOMIC AMERICA INC**
1080 Tower Ln (60106-1031)
PHONE ................................. 630 274-4423
Peter Fox, *VP Sales*
EMP: 4
SALES (est): 331.7K **Privately Held**
SIC: 3714 Motor vehicle parts & accessories

**(G-1996)**
**SPIRAL-HELIX INC**
500 Industrial Dr (60106-1321)
PHONE ................................. 224 659-7870
Tom Munro, *President*
▲ EMP: 12
SALES (est): 2.5MM
SALES (corp-wide): 869.4MM **Privately Held**
WEB: www.spiral-helix.com
SIC: 3444 Sheet metalwork
HQ: Spiro International Ag
Industriestrasse 173
Boesingen FR
317 403-100

**(G-1997)**
**SPYTEK AEROSPACE CORPORATION**
Also Called: S A
450 Frontier Way Ste D (60106-1170)
PHONE ................................. 847 318-7515
Fax: 630 595-9198
Christopher J Spytek, *President*
Elizabeth Spytek, *Vice Pres*
Michael Spytek, *Engineer*
EMP: 8
SALES: 430K **Privately Held**
SIC: 3599 3769 Machine shop, jobbing & repair; guided missile & space vehicle parts & auxiliary equipment

**(G-1998)**
**STANDARD CAR TRUCK COMPANY**
Also Called: Triangle Engineered Products
701 Maple Ln (60106-1513)
PHONE ................................. 630 860-5511
Fax: 630 860-5607
Joe Lewis, *Principal*
David Watson, *Vice Pres*
EMP: 75
SALES (corp-wide): 2.9B **Publicly Held**
SIC: 3743 3563 Brakes, air & vacuum; railway; air & gas compressors
HQ: Standard Car Truck Company Inc
6400 Shafer Ct Ste 450
Rosemont IL 60018
847 692-6050

**(G-1999)**
**STUDIO COLOR INC**
1140 Industrial Dr (60106-1247)
PHONE ................................. 630 766-3333
Anthony Rallo, *President*
Kurt Seling, *General Mgr*
Roland Stefan, *General Mgr*
Jason Culotta, *Accounts Exec*
Petty Eggert, *Manager*
EMP: 11
SQ FT: 3,600
SALES (est): 1.5MM **Privately Held**
SIC: 2759 Commercial printing

**(G-2000)**
**TAR-B PRECISION MACHINING CORP**
605 Country Club Dr Ste D (60106-1330)
PHONE ................................. 630 521-9771
Maret Wieckowski, *President*
Martha Wieckowska, *Manager*
EMP: 5
SALES (est): 633.4K **Privately Held**
SIC: 3599 Machine shop, jobbing & repair

**(G-2001)**
**THERMO-GRAPHIC LLC**
301 Arthur Ct (60106-3381)
PHONE ................................. 630 350-2226
Fax: 630 250-2227
Alex Lopezalles, *Mng Member*
Rob Feld, *Manager*
EMP: 35
SALES (est): 5.7MM **Privately Held**
SIC: 3993 3089 2759 Displays & cutouts, window & lobby; plastic processing; screen printing

**(G-2002)**
**THREADS UP INC**
1060 Entry Dr (60106-3315)
PHONE ................................. 630 595-2297
Fax: 630 860-1911
Art Barsella, *President*
EMP: 4
SQ FT: 1,690
SALES (est): 446.7K **Privately Held**
WEB: www.threadsupholstery.com
SIC: 3599 Amusement park equipment

**(G-2003)**
**TM AUTOWORKS**
480 Industrial Dr (60106-1323)
PHONE ................................. 630 766-8250
Tossiichi Miyaissi, *Manager*
EMP: 6
SALES (est): 454.1K **Privately Held**
SIC: 7532 3711 Paint shop, automotive; automobile bodies, passenger car, not including engine, etc.

**(G-2004)**
**TMW ENTERPRISES PAVING & MAINT**
179 George St (60106-3105)
PHONE ................................. 630 350-7717
Tyrone Ward, *Owner*
EMP: 20
SALES (est): 2.3MM **Privately Held**
SIC: 2951 Concrete, asphaltic (not from refineries)

**(G-2005)**
**TOTAL CONVEYOR SERVICES INC**
208 Pamela Dr (60106-3282)
PHONE ................................. 630 860-2471
Phillip Puzzo, *President*
EMP: 6
SALES (est): 414.3K **Privately Held**
SIC: 3535 Bulk handling conveyor systems

**(G-2006)**
**TRANSPARENT CONTAINER CO INC**
625 Thomas Dr (60106-1622)
PHONE ................................. 630 860-2666
Keith Smith, *President*
EMP: 50
SALES (corp-wide): 44.3MM **Privately Held**
SIC: 3089 2671 Plastic containers, except foam; trays, plastic; packaging paper & plastics film, coated & laminated
PA: Transparent Container Co., Inc.
325 S Lombard Rd
Addison IL 60101
708 449-8520

**(G-2007)**
**TSA PROCESSING CHICAGO INC**
520 Thomas Dr (60106-1621)
PHONE ................................. 630 860-5900
William Tresten, *President*
Bobby Medus, *Manager*
Monte Sneed, *Admin Sec*
▲ EMP: 8
SALES (est): 1.6MM **Privately Held**
SIC: 3312 Hot-rolled iron & steel products

**(G-2008)**
**ULTRA PACKAGING INC**
534 N York Rd (60106-1607)
PHONE ................................. 630 595-9820
Pamela Stockus, *President*
Pamlea Stockus, *President*
Robert Stockus, *Vice Pres*
Suzanne Waytula, *Office Mgr*
EMP: 9
SALES (est): 1.9MM **Privately Held**
WEB: www.ultrapackaging.com
SIC: 3565 5084 3554 Packaging machinery; industrial machinery & equipment; paper industries machinery

**(G-2009)**
**UNITED LETTER SERVICE INC**
Also Called: United Graphics Mailing Group
1231 N Ellis St (60106-1118)
PHONE ................................. 312 408-2404
Fax: 847 435-1192
Erin Grogan, *President*
John Hayner, *Corp Secy*
Scott Hayner, *Exec VP*
Bob Smetana, *Opers Mgr*
Diane Martin, *Human Res Mgr*
EMP: 19
SQ FT: 52,000
SALES (est): 4.8MM **Privately Held**
WEB: www.unitedletter.com
SIC: 7331 2752 Mailing service; commercial printing, offset

**(G-2010)**
**UPRIGHT NETWORK SERVICES**
101 Eastern Ave (60106-1159)
PHONE ................................. 630 595-5559
Steve Schenk, *President*
Steven A Schenk, *President*
EMP: 4
SALES: 600K **Privately Held**
SIC: 7372 Prepackaged software

**(G-2011)**
**V & A MANUFACTURING**
1054 Fairway Dr (60106-1317)
PHONE ................................. 630 595-1072
Fax: 630 595-8104
Ewa Lesko, *President*
Darek Lesko, *President*
EMP: 5
SQ FT: 1,800
SALES: 1.5MM **Privately Held**
SIC: 3599 Machine shop, jobbing & repair

## GEOGRAPHIC SECTION
## Benton - Franklin County (G-2038)

**(G-2012)**
**VICTOR ENVELOPE MFG CORP**
301 Arthur Ct (60106-3381)
PHONE..................................630 616-2750
Kent Gundlach, *President*
Mary Lynn Leland, *Controller*
Jackie Brooks, *Manager*
Kenneth Seroka, *Admin Sec*
**EMP:** 210
**SQ FT:** 250,000
**SALES (est):** 45.4MM **Privately Held**
**WEB:** www.victorenvelope.com
**SIC:** 2759 Envelopes: printing

**(G-2013)**
**WENLYN SCREW COMPANY INC**
810 Maple Ln (60106-1546)
PHONE..................................630 766-0050
**Fax:** 630 766-1401
Kenneth Hudziak, *President*
Joe Friedmann, *Manager*
**EMP:** 4
**SQ FT:** 7,000
**SALES (est):** 436.9K **Privately Held**
**WEB:** www.wenlyn-screw.com
**SIC:** 3452 3451 Screws, metal; screw machine products

**(G-2014)**
**WEST PRECISION TOOL INC**
447 Evergreen Ave (60106-2592)
PHONE..................................630 766-8304
**Fax:** 630 766-1078
Bill Fielder, *President*
John Schweig, *Vice Pres*
Norma Fielder, *Admin Sec*
**EMP:** 14
**SQ FT:** 5,000
**SALES (est):** 1MM **Privately Held**
**SIC:** 3541 3545 Machine tools, metal cutting type; machine tool accessories

**(G-2015)**
**WINDY ACQUISITION LLC**
Also Called: Gage Food Products
454 Country Club Dr (60106-1507)
PHONE..................................630 595-5744
Francisco Delarosa, *Principal*
Gary Wolf, *CFO*
Dean Calvert,
**EMP:** 44
**SALES (est):** 4.3MM **Privately Held**
**SIC:** 2032 Canned specialties

**(G-2016)**
**WINDY CITY CUTTING DIE INC**
104 Foster Ave (60106-1630)
PHONE..................................630 521-9410
**Fax:** 630 521-9420
John Rzeszot, *President*
William Wiard, *Vice Pres*
John Iwanicki, *Treasurer*
Diana Rutkowski, *Controller*
Annette Russell, *Data Proc Staff*
**EMP:** 29
**SQ FT:** 29,000
**SALES (est):** 5.9MM **Privately Held**
**WEB:** www.windycitycuttingdie.com
**SIC:** 3544 Special dies & tools

**(G-2017)**
**WINDY CITY MUTES**
756 Larson Ln (60106-1104)
PHONE..................................630 616-8634
Larry Fletcher, *President*
Anna Phillips, *Admin Sec*
**EMP:** 6
**SALES:** 50K **Privately Held**
**SIC:** 3931 Musical instruments

**(G-2018)**
**WORLD WIDE ROTARY DIE**
104 Foster Ave (60106-1630)
PHONE..................................630 521-9410
Janusz Iwanicki, *President*
William Wiard, *Vice Pres*
John Kathrein, *Treasurer*
Diana Rutkiwski, *Manager*
Janusz Rzeszot, *Admin Sec*
**EMP:** 7
**SQ FT:** 10,000
**SALES (est):** 808.5K **Privately Held**
**WEB:** www.worldwiderds.com
**SIC:** 3544 Special dies & tools

**(G-2019)**
**XD INDUSTRIES INC**
244 James St (60106-3319)
PHONE..................................630 766-2843
Sebastian Procek, *Owner*
**EMP:** 10
**SALES (est):** 910K **Privately Held**
**SIC:** 3471 7692 Cleaning, polishing & finishing

### Benton
*Franklin County*

**(G-2020)**
**AIRGAS USA LLC**
12238 Petroff Rd (62812-6900)
PHONE..................................618 439-7207
Jewell Sims, *Opers Staff*
Scott Burkitt, *Sales Mgr*
Dan Davis, *Branch Mgr*
**EMP:** 8
**SALES (corp-wide):** 163.9MM **Privately Held**
**SIC:** 5084 5169 2813 Welding machinery & equipment; industrial gases; industrial gases
**HQ:** Airgas Usa, Llc
  259 N Radnor Chester Rd # 100
  Radnor PA 19087
  610 687-5253

**(G-2021)**
**ALL STARS -N- STITCHES INC**
418 E Main St (62812-2154)
P.O. Box 10 (62812-0010)
PHONE..................................618 435-5555
**Fax:** 618 435-5556
Dave Severin, *President*
Penny Severin, *Treasurer*
**EMP:** 7
**SQ FT:** 1,200
**SALES (est):** 590K **Privately Held**
**SIC:** 7389 5999 2759 2395 Cloth cutting, bolting or winding; sign painting & lettering shop; engraving service; banners; screen printing; embroidery products, except schiffli machine

**(G-2022)**
**BENTON EVENING NEWS CO**
111 E Church St (62812-2238)
P.O. Box 877 (62812-0877)
PHONE..................................618 438-5611
**Fax:** 618 435-2413
Danny Malkovich, *President*
Rebecca Malkovich, *Editor*
**EMP:** 3 **EST:** 1921
**SQ FT:** 3,500
**SALES (est):** 140K **Privately Held**
**WEB:** www.bentoneveningnews.com
**SIC:** 2711 2752 Newspapers, publishing & printing; commercial printing, lithographic

**(G-2023)**
**BIO FUELS BY AMERICAN FARMERS**
Also Called: Bfafv
10163 Sugar Creek Rd (62812-4333)
PHONE..................................561 859-6251
Dennis Kinkade, *Mng Member*
John Carlyle,
**EMP:** 12
**SALES (est):** 1.1MM **Privately Held**
**SIC:** 2046 2041 2076 0723 Wet corn milling; flour & other grain mill products; vegetable oil mills; grain milling, custom services

**(G-2024)**
**BRADEN ROCK BIT**
14447 State Highway 34 (62812-6053)
PHONE..................................618 435-4519
**Fax:** 618 435-4520
William Braden, *Owner*
**EMP:** 6
**SALES (est):** 602.2K **Privately Held**
**SIC:** 3532 7699 Bits, except oil & gas field tools, rock; construction equipment repair

**(G-2025)**
**CUSTOM ENTERPRISES**
131 Industrial Park Rd (62812-4541)
PHONE..................................618 439-6626
Deanna Pyszka, *Owner*
Carey Pyszka, *Co-Owner*
**EMP:** 4
**SQ FT:** 3,500
**SALES:** 450K **Privately Held**
**SIC:** 2396 3993 2395 Screen printing on fabric articles; signs & advertising specialties; pleating & stitching

**(G-2026)**
**CUSTOM STAINLESS STEEL INC (PA)**
350 Industrial Park Dr (62812)
P.O. Box 1267 (62812-5267)
PHONE..................................618 435-2605
**Fax:** 618 435-4158
Joe Zsido, *President*
Elizabeth Zsido, *Corp Secy*
Mike Procaccini, *Vice Pres*
**EMP:** 15
**SQ FT:** 13,000
**SALES (est):** 2MM **Privately Held**
**WEB:** www.customstainlesssteel.com
**SIC:** 3429 5091 Marine hardware; boat accessories & parts

**(G-2027)**
**FOUR SEASONS ACE HARDWARE**
11230 State Highway 37 (62812-4400)
PHONE..................................618 439-2101
Marino Presa, *Partner*
Terry Presa, *Partner*
**EMP:** 4
**SQ FT:** 4
**SALES (est):** 532.4K **Privately Held**
**SIC:** 5251 2097 Hardware; manufactured ice

**(G-2028)**
**FRED PIGG DENTAL LAB**
405 E Park St Ste 3 (62812-1971)
P.O. Box 820 (62812-0820)
PHONE..................................618 439-6829
Fred Pigg, *President*
**EMP:** 4
**SQ FT:** 2,000
**SALES (est):** 333K **Privately Held**
**SIC:** 8072 3843 Denture production; dental equipment & supplies

**(G-2029)**
**HUTCHENS-BIT SERVICE INC**
11898 Commerce Ln (62812-6532)
PHONE..................................618 439-9485
**Fax:** 618 439-9487
Kenneth Hutchens, *President*
Betty Hutchens, *Corp Secy*
Tina Hopkins, *Manager*
Danny Robey, *Manager*
▼ **EMP:** 15
**SALES (est):** 2.9MM **Privately Held**
**SIC:** 3533 Bits, oil & gas field tools: rock

**(G-2030)**
**ILLINOIS METER INC**
Also Called: Imco
1500 W Webster St (62812)
P.O. Box 425 (62812-0425)
PHONE..................................618 438-6039
Dennis J Sheley, *President*
**EMP:** 5
**SALES (corp-wide):** 42.7MM **Privately Held**
**SIC:** 3317 5051 Seamless pipes & tubes; pipe & tubing, steel
**PA:** Illinois Meter, Inc.
  4390 Jeffory St
  Springfield IL 62703
  217 529-1672

**(G-2031)**
**INFINITY TOOL MFG LLC**
11648 Skylane Dr (62812-4357)
P.O. Box 488 (62812-0488)
PHONE..................................618 439-4042
Todd Taylor, *COO*
Ryan McCollum, *Sales Staff*
Kenneth D Sentel, *Mng Member*
Bert Beatty, *Manager*
▲ **EMP:** 5 **EST:** 2008
**SALES (est):** 1MM **Privately Held**
**SIC:** 3545 Drills (machine tool accessories)

**(G-2032)**
**JOE ZSIDO SALES & DESIGN INC**
350 Industrial Park Rd (62812)
P.O. Box 1267 (62812-5267)
PHONE..................................618 435-2605
Joe Zsido, *President*
Elizabeth Zsido, *Corp Secy*
Mike Procaccini, *Vice Pres*
**EMP:** 40
**SALES (est):** 4.2MM **Privately Held**
**SIC:** 3312 Stainless steel

**(G-2033)**
**KNIGHT BROS INC**
Also Called: Heritage Custom Trailers
10764 Industrial Park Rd (62812-4537)
PHONE..................................618 439-9626
**Fax:** 618 435-2579
Mark Knight, *President*
Jason Knight, *Vice Pres*
Jill Sanders, *Controller*
**EMP:** 20
**SQ FT:** 35,000
**SALES (est):** 3.4MM **Privately Held**
**WEB:** www.heritagetrailers.com
**SIC:** 3799 5599 Boat trailers; utility trailers

**(G-2034)**
**LAMPLEY OIL INC**
720 W Main St (62812-1367)
PHONE..................................618 439-6288
Steve Lampley, *President*
**EMP:** 5
**SQ FT:** 600
**SALES (est):** 524.4K **Privately Held**
**SIC:** 1311 Crude petroleum production

**(G-2035)**
**MINCON INC**
Also Called: Mincon Rockdrills USA
107 Industrial Park Rd (62812-4541)
P.O. Box 189 (62812-0189)
PHONE..................................618 435-3404
Mike Jones, *President*
Shirley Jones, *Manager*
▲ **EMP:** 20
**SQ FT:** 10,000
**SALES (est):** 3.6MM **Privately Held**
**WEB:** www.percussionbit.com
**SIC:** 3545 Drill bits, metalworking
**HQ:** Mincon Group Public Limited Company
  Smithstown Industrial Estate
  Ballymote

**(G-2036)**
**NATURAL RESOURCES ILL DEPT**
Also Called: Office of Mines & Minerals
503 E Main St (62812-2522)
PHONE..................................618 439-4320
**Fax:** 618 438-8111
Don McBride, *Manager*
**EMP:** 30 **Privately Held**
**WEB:** www.il.gov
**SIC:** 1481 9512 Test boring for nonmetallic minerals; land, mineral & wildlife conservation;
**HQ:** Illinois Department Of Natural Resources
  1 Natural Resources Way # 100
  Springfield IL 62702
  217 782-6302

**(G-2037)**
**NEWMAN WELDING & MACHINE SHOP**
400 W Bond St (62812-1003)
PHONE..................................618 435-5591
**Fax:** 618 435-5591
Lillian Newman, *Owner*
**EMP:** 3 **EST:** 1953
**SQ FT:** 5,440
**SALES (est):** 272K **Privately Held**
**SIC:** 7692 3443 3441 Welding repair; fabricated plate work (boiler shop); fabricated structural metal

**(G-2038)**
**POSITIVE IMPRESSIONS**
14190 State Highway 34 (62812-6041)
PHONE..................................618 438-7030
Allen Lampley, *Owner*
**EMP:** 4 **EST:** 1991

SALES (est): 396.3K **Privately Held**
SIC: 2759 Screen printing

*(G-2039)*
**REND LAKE CARBIDE INC**
11601 Skylane Dr (62812-4364)
P.O. Box 483 (62812-0483)
PHONE..................................618 438-0160
Ken Sentel, *Vice Pres*
▲ EMP: 7
SALES (est): 1.1MM **Privately Held**
SIC: 3532 3533 2819 3545 Drills, bits & similar equipment; bits, oil & gas field tools: rock; carbides; milling cutters

*(G-2040)*
**ROYAL BRASS INC**
1202 Route 14 W (62812-1595)
P.O. Box 594 (62812-0594)
PHONE..................................618 439-6341
Fax: 618 438-0412
Gretchen Leonard, *Opers-Prdtn-Mfg*
EMP: 7
SALES (corp-wide): 54.3MM **Privately Held**
WEB: www.royalbrassandhose.com
SIC: 3492 3533 3429 3052 Hose & tube fittings & assemblies, hydraulic/pneumatic; oil & gas field machinery; manufactured hardware (general); rubber & plastics hose & beltings
PA: Royal Brass, Inc.
1470 Amherst Rd Ste C
Knoxville TN 37909
865 558-0224

*(G-2041)*
**THOMAS PRINTING & STY CO**
301 S Du Quoin St (62812-1460)
PHONE..................................618 435-2801
William F Thomas, *President*
Michael Thomas, *Vice Pres*
EMP: 5 EST: 1956
SQ FT: 2,000
SALES (est): 609.8K **Privately Held**
SIC: 2752 2759 2789 Commercial printing, offset; letterpress printing; bookbinding & related work

*(G-2042)*
**TRI-CITY READY-MIX**
302 E Bond St (62812-2004)
PHONE..................................618 439-2071
Robert Smith, *President*
Norma Smith, *Vice Pres*
Raymond Roberson, *Plant Mgr*
Pamela Smith, *Admin Sec*
EMP: 6
SQ FT: 1,000
SALES: 600K **Privately Held**
SIC: 3273 Ready-mixed concrete

## Berkeley
### Cook County

*(G-2043)*
**AMERICAN DRYER INC**
5700 Mcdermott Dr (60163-1102)
PHONE..................................734 421-2400
Fax: 734 421-5580
Daniel L Rabahy, *President*
Patty Roell, *Office Mgr*
Karen Bennnette, *Manager*
Gail Rabahy, *Admin Sec*
Elisa Vandraiss, *Admin Asst*
▲ EMP: 20
SQ FT: 20,000
SALES (est): 7.2MM **Privately Held**
WEB: www.americandryer.com
SIC: 3634 Dryers, electric: hand & face

*(G-2044)*
**BUHL PRESS**
5656 Mcdermott Dr (60163-1101)
PHONE..................................708 449-8989
Fax: 708 449-8988
Bob Tasch, *VP Opers*
Jim Billsten, *Plant Supt*
Jim Muscarello, *Purch Mgr*
Bruce Plum, *Engineer*
David Berndes, *VP Sales*
EMP: 20
SALES (est): 2.2MM **Privately Held**
SIC: 2741 Miscellaneous publishing

*(G-2045)*
**FUSE LLC**
5656 Mcdermott Dr (60163-1101)
PHONE..................................708 449-8989
Scott Voris, *President*
Ed Gudonis, *CFO*
EMP: 200
SALES (est): 11.3MM **Privately Held**
SIC: 2752 8742 Commercial printing, lithographic; marketing consulting services

*(G-2046)*
**KI INDUSTRIES INC**
5540 Mcdermott Dr (60163-1203)
PHONE..................................708 449-1990
Fax: 708 449-1997
David Goltermann, *President*
Elizabeth Goltermann, *Corp Secy*
Don Mitchell, *Safety Mgr*
Ruth Felske, *Opers Staff*
Gene Emrick, *Purch Mgr*
▲ EMP: 45
SQ FT: 35,000
SALES (est): 12.2MM **Privately Held**
WEB: www.kiindustries.com
SIC: 3089 3643 3446 3432 Plastic processing; current-carrying wiring devices; architectural metalwork; plumbing fixture fittings & trim

*(G-2047)*
**PEBBLEFORK PARTNERS INC**
5656 Mcdermott Dr (60163-1101)
PHONE..................................708 449-8989
Charles P Barkley, *President*
Bruce Plum, *Controller*
Donald Barkley, *Finance*
Karla Scott, *Office Admin*
EMP: 70 EST: 1954
SQ FT: 105,000
SALES (est): 22.2MM **Privately Held**
WEB: www.buhlpress.com
SIC: 2752 Commercial printing, lithographic

*(G-2048)*
**PETERSON ELC PANL MFG CO INC**
5550 Mcdermott Dr (60163-1203)
PHONE..................................708 449-2270
Fax: 708 449-2269
Sue Todd, *CEO*
Richard M Todd Sr, *President*
Richard R Todd Jr, *Vice Pres*
Ron Moretti, *Accountant*
EMP: 18 EST: 1917
SQ FT: 21,000
SALES (est): 7.1MM **Privately Held**
WEB: www.petersonpanel.com
SIC: 3612 3613 Lighting transformers, street & airport; switchboards & parts, power

*(G-2049)*
**PREFERRED PRINTING & GRAPHICS**
5815 Saint Charles Rd (60163-1031)
PHONE..................................708 547-6880
Fax: 708 547-6897
Rosalie Joseph, *Owner*
EMP: 3
SQ FT: 1,500
SALES (est): 240.5K **Privately Held**
SIC: 2752 Commercial printing, offset

*(G-2050)*
**VANEE FOODS COMPANY**
5418 Mcdermott Dr (60163-1299)
PHONE..................................708 449-7300
Fax: 708 449-2558
Aloysius Van Eekeren, *President*
Andrew Van Eekeren, *Vice Pres*
Alex Vaneekeren, *Vice Pres*
Chuck Vaneekeren, *Vice Pres*
Dan Vaneekeren, *Vice Pres*
▲ EMP: 100 EST: 1950
SQ FT: 500,000
SALES (est): 37.4MM **Privately Held**
WEB: www.vaneefoodscompany.com
SIC: 2032 2099 2034 2092 Canned specialties; beef soup: packaged in cans, jars, etc.; seasonings: dry mixes; sauces: gravy, dressing & dip mixes; dried & dehydrated soup mixes; fresh or frozen fish or seafood chowders, soups & stews

*(G-2051)*
**VORIS COMMUNICATION CO INC (PA)**
Also Called: Kelmscott Communications
5656 Mcdermott Dr (60163-1101)
P.O. Box 1090, Aurora (60507-1090)
PHONE..................................630 898-4268
Fax: 630 898-2183
Scott Voris, *President*
Jerry Heitschmidt, *Vice Pres*
Chuck Randazzo, *Vice Pres*
Jason Tews, *Vice Pres*
Rich Tinsley, *Plant Mgr*
EMP: 108
SQ FT: 25,000
SALES (est): 26.3MM **Privately Held**
WEB: www.kelmscottpress.com
SIC: 2752 2791 2789 Commercial printing, lithographic; typesetting; bookbinding & related work

*(G-2052)*
**WESTERLING GROUP**
5311 Saint Charles Rd (60163-1345)
P.O. Box 710, Hillside (60162-0710)
PHONE..................................708 547-8488
Fax: 708 547-8493
Jackie McCulloch, *President*
EMP: 9
SQ FT: 12,500
SALES (est): 1.9MM **Privately Held**
SIC: 2519 5944 Lawn & garden furniture, except wood & metal; silverware

*(G-2053)*
**WORLD DRYER CORPORATION (PA)**
5700 Mcdermott Dr (60163-1196)
PHONE..................................708 449-6950
Fax: 708 449-6958
Dan Storto, *President*
Tom Vic, *President*
Susan Fan, *Vice Pres*
John Potts, *Vice Pres*
Edward Rusick, *CFO*
▲ EMP: 36
SALES (est): 6.6MM **Privately Held**
SIC: 3634 5023 Dryers, electric: hand & face; decorative home furnishings & supplies

## Berwyn
### Cook County

*(G-2054)*
**ABLE PRINTING SERVICE**
6837 Stanley Ave (60402-3041)
PHONE..................................708 788-7115
Fax: 708 788-7164
Herman V Dernaald, *Owner*
Herman Van Dernaald, *Owner*
Ryan Naald, *Manager*
EMP: 7 EST: 1939
SQ FT: 1,800
SALES (est): 1MM **Privately Held**
WEB: www.ableprinting.net
SIC: 2759 Commercial printing

*(G-2055)*
**AD ELECTRIC SIGN INC**
6549 28th St (60402-2787)
PHONE..................................708 222-8000
Orhan Demir, *President*
EMP: 4
SQ FT: 3,600
SALES (est): 431.2K **Privately Held**
SIC: 3993 Neon signs

*(G-2056)*
**ALLIED INSTRUMENT SERVICE INC**
3136 Clarence Ave (60402-3198)
PHONE..................................708 788-1912
Fax: 708 788-2277
Leslie Craggs, *President*
Don Craggs, *Treasurer*
Dave Craggs, *Admin Sec*
EMP: 14
SQ FT: 10,000
SALES: 1.3MM **Privately Held**
WEB: www.alliedinstrument.com
SIC: 7629 7699 3643 Electrical measuring instrument repair & calibration; industrial machinery & equipment repair; power line cable

*(G-2057)*
**BING YEUNG JEWELERS INC**
6916 Cermak Rd (60402-2244)
PHONE..................................708 749-4800
Fax: 708 749-9560
Bing C Yeung, *President*
Acrenonia Yeung, *Corp Secy*
EMP: 4
SQ FT: 1,000
SALES: 320K **Privately Held**
SIC: 3911 5944 Jewelry, precious metal; jewelry stores

*(G-2058)*
**C C P EXPRESS INC**
2630 Highland Ave (60402-2716)
PHONE..................................773 315-0317
Castulo Cortes, *President*
Erica Aguero, *Admin Sec*
EMP: 4
SALES (est): 600.6K **Privately Held**
SIC: 3537 Trucks: freight, baggage, etc.: industrial, except mining

*(G-2059)*
**COMPOSING ROOM INC**
1851 Kenilworth Ave 1 (60402-1614)
PHONE..................................708 795-7523
George Slifka, *President*
Mary Slifka, *Admin Sec*
EMP: 4 EST: 1977
SALES (est): 325.6K **Privately Held**
SIC: 2791 Typesetting

*(G-2060)*
**DIAMOND GRAPHICS OF BERWYN**
6625 26th St Ste 1 (60402-2585)
PHONE..................................708 749-2500
Fax: 708 749-2524
Paul Dimenna, *President*
EMP: 6
SALES (est): 2MM **Privately Held**
SIC: 2752 2791 2789 Commercial printing, offset; typesetting; bookbinding & related work

*(G-2061)*
**EASY TRAC GPS INC**
4234 Ridgeland Ave (60402-4427)
PHONE..................................630 359-5804
Luis R Vera, *President*
EMP: 3
SALES (est): 340.4K **Privately Held**
SIC: 3663 Radio & TV communications equipment

*(G-2062)*
**EDGE COMMUNICATION**
3825 Kenilworth Ave (60402-3911)
PHONE..................................708 749-7818
Christopher Princis, *Owner*
EMP: 9
SALES (est): 540K **Privately Held**
SIC: 7311 2741 Advertising agencies; directories: publishing only, not printed on site

*(G-2063)*
**EL DIA NEWSPAPER**
6331 26th St Apt 1 (60402-5658)
PHONE..................................708 956-7282
Fax: 708 652-6653
George Montesdeoca, *Owner*
EMP: 7
SALES (est): 322.1K **Privately Held**
SIC: 2711 Newspapers

*(G-2064)*
**FATHER & DAUGHTERS PRINTING**
6426 Cermak Rd (60402-2310)
PHONE..................................708 749-8286
Carlos Zepea, *Owner*
EMP: 2
SALES (est): 221K **Privately Held**
SIC: 2759 Commercial printing

# GEOGRAPHIC SECTION

**(G-2065)**
**FEDERAL-MOGUL CORPORATION**
Also Called: Federal Mogul Driveline Pdts
4929 S Mason (60402)
**PHONE** ..................248 354-7700
Allen Gronner, *Manager*
**EMP:** 25
**SALES (corp-wide):** 16.3B **Publicly Held**
**SIC:** 3714  3053  Universal joints, motor vehicle; gaskets & sealing devices
**HQ:** Federal-Mogul Llc
27300 W. 11 Mile Rd
Southfield MI 48034

**(G-2066)**
**FLAMINGOS ICECREAM**
6733 Cermak Rd (60402-2216)
**PHONE** ..................708 749-4287
Gaulupe Lopez, *Owner*
**EMP:** 4
**SALES (est):** 251.5K **Privately Held**
**SIC:** 2024  Ice cream & frozen desserts

**(G-2067)**
**LITTLE VILLAGE PRINTING INC**
3210 Grove Ave Apt 2w (60402-3494)
P.O. Box 243, Riverside (60546-0243)
**PHONE** ..................708 749-4414
Fax: 708 749-4727
William Woznicki, *President*
Virginia Woznicki, *Corp Secy*
**EMP:** 3 **EST:** 1964
**SQ FT:** 900
**SALES (est):** 365K **Privately Held**
**SIC:** 2752  Lithographing on metal

**(G-2068)**
**MASA UNO INC**
6311 Cermak Rd Ste 2 (60402-5466)
**PHONE** ..................708 749-4866
Yolanda Carreon, *President*
**EMP:** 7 **EST:** 2014
**SALES (est):** 714.1K **Privately Held**
**SIC:** 2096  Tortilla chips

**(G-2069)**
**NORTHFIELD BLOCK COMPANY**
Also Called: Chicago Block
5400 W Canal Bank Rd (60402)
**PHONE** ..................708 458-8130
Fax: 708 458-9536
Rick Rasanelli, *Branch Mgr*
**EMP:** 7
**SALES (corp-wide):** 28.6B **Privately Held**
**SIC:** 5032  3271  3272  Masons' materials; blocks, concrete or cinder: standard; concrete products
**HQ:** Northfield Block Company
1 Hunt Ct
Mundelein IL 60060
847 816-9000

**(G-2070)**
**OGDEN TOP & TRIM SHOP INC**
6609 Ogden Ave (60402-3788)
**PHONE** ..................708 484-5422
Carol Nesladek, *Owner*
John Mayer, *Manager*
**EMP:** 7 **EST:** 1947
**SQ FT:** 3,800
**SALES:** 250K **Privately Held**
**SIC:** 7532  3714  2394  2221  Upholstery & trim shop, automotive; motor vehicle parts & accessories; canvas & related products; broadwoven fabric mills, manmade

**(G-2071)**
**ORGANNICA INC**
3437 Maple Ave (60402-3241)
P.O. Box 561 (60402-0561)
**PHONE** ..................312 925-7272
Jennnifer Angone, *Principal*
**EMP:** 4
**SALES:** 3.4K **Privately Held**
**SIC:** 2833  7389  Organic medicinal chemicals: bulk, uncompounded;

**(G-2072)**
**PEREZ HEALTH INCORPORATED**
2215 Oak Park Ave (60402-2220)
**PHONE** ..................708 788-0101
Ricardo Perez, *Owner*
Claudia Villa, *Office Mgr*
**EMP:** 2
**SALES (est):** 321.8K **Privately Held**
**SIC:** 3821  8099  Clinical laboratory instruments, except medical & dental; health & allied services

**(G-2073)**
**PERFECTION SIGNS & GRAPHICS**
6737 Cermak Rd (60402-2216)
**PHONE** ..................708 795-0611
William Langer, *President*
**EMP:** 3
**SALES (est):** 260K **Privately Held**
**SIC:** 5099  3993  Signs, except electric; signs & advertising specialties

**(G-2074)**
**PHYSICIANS RECORD CO INC**
3000 Ridgeland Ave (60402-0724)
**PHONE** ..................800 323-9268
Fax: 708 749-0171
John C Voller, *President*
James Bocek, *Vice Pres*
Christopher Voller, *Vice Pres*
Marcy Voller, *Vice Pres*
Victoria Bocek, *Treasurer*
▼ **EMP:** 56 **EST:** 1907
**SQ FT:** 60,000
**SALES:** 3MM **Privately Held**
**WEB:** www.physiciansrecord.com
**SIC:** 2752  2759  2761  Commercial printing, offset; letterpress printing; manifold business forms

**(G-2075)**
**SWEETENER SUPPLY CORPORATION**
2905 Ridgeland Ave (60402-2781)
**PHONE** ..................708 484-3455
**EMP:** 9
**SALES (corp-wide):** 19.4MM **Privately Held**
**SIC:** 2099  Food preparations
**PA:** Sweetener Supply Corporation
9501 Southview Ave
Brookfield IL 60513
708 588-8400

**(G-2076)**
**TIDD PRINTING CO**
2709 Ridgeland Ave (60402-2730)
**PHONE** ..................708 749-1200
Fax: 708 749-1208
Audrey Zoul, *President*
Eugene Zoul, *Vice Pres*
**EMP:** 5
**SQ FT:** 3,000
**SALES:** 400K **Privately Held**
**SIC:** 2752  2791  2789  2759  Lithographing on metal; typesetting; bookbinding & related work; commercial printing

**(G-2077)**
**VANGARD DISTRIBUTION INC**
2905 Ridgeland Ave (60402-2781)
**PHONE** ..................708 484-9895
**EMP:** 3 **Privately Held**
**SIC:** 2653  3053  Corrugated & solid fiber boxes; packing materials
**PA:** Vangard Distribution, Inc.
9501 Southview Ave
Brookfield IL 60513

**(G-2078)**
**W W BELT INC**
6440 Ogden Ave (60402-3727)
**PHONE** ..................708 788-1855
John Chyna Jr, *President*
Thomas Chyna, *Vice Pres*
**EMP:** 4
**SQ FT:** 5,000
**SALES:** 220K **Privately Held**
**SIC:** 3199  3842  Safety belts, leather; surgical appliances & supplies

**(G-2079)**
**ZEIGLER CHRYSLER DODGE**
Also Called: Zeigler Preowned of Chicago
6539 Ogden Ave (60402-3700)
**PHONE** ..................708 956-7700
Debbie Phillips,
**EMP:** 4
**SALES (est):** 328.5K **Privately Held**
**SIC:** 5013  3714  Automotive supplies & parts; motor vehicle parts & accessories

## Bethalto
### Madison County

**(G-2080)**
**A-Z WELDING**
8373 Militello Ln (62010)
**PHONE** ..................618 259-2515
Brian Zirkelbach, *Owner*
**EMP:** 7
**SALES (est):** 230.5K **Privately Held**
**SIC:** 7692  Welding repair

**(G-2081)**
**EAGLE EXPRESS MAIL LLC**
Also Called: Mail Box Store, The
333 W Bethalto Dr Ste C (62010-1916)
**PHONE** ..................618 377-6245
Eliot L Deters,
**EMP:** 6
**SALES (est):** 852.2K **Privately Held**
**SIC:** 7389  4783  2759  Packaging & labeling services; packing goods for shipping; commercial printing

**(G-2082)**
**PART STOP INC**
5120 State Route 140 (62010-2200)
**PHONE** ..................618 377-5238
Fax: 618 377-5230
Ron Wolkinson, *President*
**EMP:** 9
**SQ FT:** 2,500
**SALES (est):** 1.3MM **Privately Held**
**WEB:** www.partstop.com
**SIC:** 5531  3599  Automotive parts; automotive accessories; machine shop, jobbing & repair

**(G-2083)**
**PERFORMANCE AUTOMOTIVE**
475 S Prairie St (62010-1815)
**PHONE** ..................618 377-0020
Gordon Shifflett, *Owner*
**EMP:** 3
**SALES (est):** 325.5K **Privately Held**
**SIC:** 3599  Machine shop, jobbing & repair

## Bethany
### Moultrie County

**(G-2084)**
**BETHANY PHARMACOL CO INC**
131 Hwy 121 E (61914)
**PHONE** ..................217 665-3395
Jack J Scott, *CEO*
**EMP:** 9
**SALES (est):** 690.1K
**SALES (corp-wide):** 2.6MM **Privately Held**
**SIC:** 2844  Face creams or lotions
**PA:** Bethany Sales Company, Inc.
131 W Main St
Bethany IL 61914
217 665-3395

**(G-2085)**
**MONROE ASSOCIATES INC**
1545 Cr 375e (61914-7048)
P.O. Box 233 (61914-0233)
**PHONE** ..................217 665-3898
Rechele Monroe, *President*
Dennis Monroe, *Vice Pres*
**EMP:** 3
**SALES (est):** 346.6K **Privately Held**
**SIC:** 7379  3571  Computer related consulting services; personal computers (microcomputers)

## Big Rock
### Kane County

**(G-2086)**
**CAM CO INC**
400 Rhodes Ave (60511-2034)
P.O. Box 94 (60511-0094)
**PHONE** ..................630 556-3110
Fax: 630 556-3146
Gregory J Beels, *President*
Ronda Beels, *Admin Sec*
▲ **EMP:** 10
**SQ FT:** 4,000
**SALES (est):** 1.3MM **Privately Held**
**SIC:** 3599  3829  3812  Water leak detectors; measuring & controlling devices; search & navigation equipment

## Blackstone
### Livingston County

**(G-2087)**
**ALLOY SPECIALTIES INC**
32028 N 1500 East Rd (61313-9690)
P.O. Box 212, Ransom (60470-0212)
**PHONE** ..................815 586-4728
Fax: 815 586-4518
James G Coonan, *President*
Richard A Brechlin, *Corp Secy*
Julia K Coonan, *Vice Pres*
Barbara Mikolajzyk, *Manager*
**EMP:** 18 **EST:** 2000
**SQ FT:** 5,000
**SALES (est):** 5.9MM **Privately Held**
**SIC:** 3441  Fabricated structural metal

**(G-2088)**
**PRESTRESS ENGINEERING COMPANY**
Also Called: Prestressed Products Company
15606 E 3200 North Rd (61313-9683)
**PHONE** ..................815 586-4239
Christian Newkirk, *Mfg Staff*
Thomas Dodge, *Branch Mgr*
**EMP:** 20
**SALES (corp-wide):** 2.6MM **Privately Held**
**WEB:** www.pre-stress.com
**SIC:** 3272  Prestressed concrete products
**PA:** Prestress Engineering Company
2220 Il Route 176
Crystal Lake IL 60014
815 459-4545

**(G-2089)**
**VERONA RUBBER WORKS INC**
31577 N 1250 East Rd (61313-9504)
**PHONE** ..................815 673-2929
Benjamin Othon, *Manager*
**EMP:** 12
**SALES (corp-wide):** 1.5MM **Privately Held**
**WEB:** www.veronarubberworks.com
**SIC:** 3069  Molded rubber products
**PA:** Verona Rubber Works, Inc.
31577 N 1250 East Rd
Blackstone IL 61313
815 673-2929

**(G-2090)**
**VERONA RUBBER WORKS INC (PA)**
31577 N 1250 East Rd (61313-9504)
**PHONE** ..................815 673-2929
Mike Othon, *President*
Catherine Othon, *Vice Pres*
Ben Othon, *Safety Mgr*
**EMP:** 13
**SQ FT:** 18,000
**SALES (est):** 1.5MM **Privately Held**
**WEB:** www.veronarubberworks.com
**SIC:** 3069  Custom compounding of rubber materials

## Bloomingdale
### Dupage County

**(G-2091)**
**ABRASIVE-FORM LLC (PA)**
454 Scott Dr (60108-3120)
**PHONE** ..................630 220-3437
John Harig, *President*
Trudy Herrera, *Purch Dir*
Jon Stientjes, *Project Engr*
Chuck Raucci, *CFO*
Greg Zilinsky, *CFO*
**EMP:** 50
**SQ FT:** 73,000
**SALES (est):** 9.6MM **Privately Held**
**SIC:** 3291  Abrasive products

## Bloomingdale - Dupage County (G-2092)

**(G-2092)**
**ALTAK INC**
250 Covington Dr (60108-3106)
PHONE ............................ 630 622-0300
Fax: 630 622-0305
Al Kabeshita, *President*
Miko Kabeshita, *Exec VP*
Minoru Kabeshita, *Vice Pres*
Yutaka Kabeshita, *Vice Pres*
Dawn Berggren, *Purch Mgr*
▲ **EMP:** 85
**SQ FT:** 42,000
**SALES (est):** 23MM **Privately Held**
**WEB:** www.altakinc.com
**SIC: 3496** 5084 Miscellaneous fabricated wire products; industrial machinery & equipment

**(G-2093)**
**AMERILIGHTS INC**
Also Called: A2z Green Lighting
146 Roundtree Ct (60108-3044)
PHONE ............................ 847 219-1476
Manjula Vora, *CEO*
Gordhan Patel, *Admin Sec*
**EMP:** 4
**SALES (est):** 371.7K **Privately Held**
**SIC: 3646** Commercial indusl & institutional electric lighting fixtures

**(G-2094)**
**ARTISTRIES BY TOMMY MUSTO INC**
Also Called: Tommy Rock
159 W Lake St Ste 1 (60108-1052)
PHONE ............................ 630 674-8667
Thomas C Musto, *President*
Donna Musto, *Admin Sec*
**EMP:** 3
**SQ FT:** 3,000
**SALES:** 400K **Privately Held**
**SIC: 3271** 1721 Concrete block & brick; painting & paper hanging

**(G-2095)**
**BEE-JAY INDUSTRIES INC**
148 Paxton Rd (60108-3048)
PHONE ............................ 708 867-4431
Fax: 630 867-5035
Kenneth Fefferman, *President*
Kenneth Fefferman, *President*
Bill Reiner, *Foreman/Supr*
Bette Fefferman, *Finance Dir*
Jan Berschel, *MIS Mgr*
**EMP:** 12
**SQ FT:** 5,000
**SALES (est):** 1MM **Privately Held**
**SIC: 3993** 3961 3911 Advertising novelties; costume jewelry; jewelry, precious metal

**(G-2096)**
**BI-LINK METAL SPECIALTIES INC (PA)**
391 Glen Ellyn Rd (60108-2176)
PHONE ............................ 630 858-5900
Fax: 630 858-5995
David Myers, *President*
Pete Krebs, *General Mgr*
Roy Spangler, *Senior VP*
Ray Ziganto, *Vice Pres*
Nick Dorizas, *Purch Mgr*
▲ **EMP:** 152
**SQ FT:** 90,000
**SALES (est):** 28MM **Privately Held**
**WEB:** www.bi-linkil.com
**SIC: 3469** 3544 Stamping metal for the trade; special dies & tools

**(G-2097)**
**BOBCO ENTERPRISES INC DEL**
212 Garden Way (60108-2919)
PHONE ............................ 773 722-1700
Robert Schultz Sr, *President*
Bonnie Gordon Jones, *Vice Pres*
Robert Schultz Jr, *Vice Pres*
**EMP:** 45
**SQ FT:** 48,000
**SALES (est):** 4.1MM **Privately Held**
**SIC: 3672** 3471 Printed circuit boards; electroplating of metals or formed products

**(G-2098)**
**C & F MACHINE CORP**
176 Covington Dr (60108-3105)
PHONE ............................ 630 924-0300
Fax: 630 924-0312
Julian Kuta, *President*
Theresa Kuta, *Manager*
**EMP:** 12
**SQ FT:** 32,000
**SALES (est):** 1.2MM **Privately Held**
**WEB:** www.cfmach.com
**SIC: 3599** Machine shop, jobbing & repair

**(G-2099)**
**CARE CHILD COMPANIES**
1 Tiffany Pt Ste 115 (60108-2915)
PHONE ............................ 630 295-6770
Dave Funk, *Vice Pres*
**EMP:** 8
**SALES (est):** 442.1K **Privately Held**
**SIC: 2043** Infants' foods, cereal type

**(G-2100)**
**CHICAGO PASTRY INC**
142 N Bloomingdale Rd (60108-1017)
PHONE ............................ 630 529-6161
Fax: 630 529-4824
Egidio Turano, *Purch Dir*
Remo Turano, *Branch Mgr*
**EMP:** 100
**SALES (corp-wide):** 124.2MM **Privately Held**
**SIC: 5149** 5461 2052 2051 Bakery products; bread; cookies & crackers; bread, cake & related products
**PA:** Chicago Pastry, Inc.
6501 Roosevelt Rd
Berwyn IL 60402
708 788-5320

**(G-2101)**
**DAUPHIN ENTERPRISE INC**
Also Called: Cartridge World Bloomingdale
358 W Army Trail Rd # 150 (60108-5605)
PHONE ............................ 630 893-6300
Dominick Dauphin, *Owner*
Christopher Nowak, *Manager*
**EMP:** 3
**SALES (est):** 466.7K **Privately Held**
**SIC: 5112** 3955 Office filing supplies; carbon paper & inked ribbons; print cartridges for laser & other computer printers

**(G-2102)**
**DEL MEDICAL INC**
Also Called: Del Medical Systems Group
241 Covington Dr (60108-3109)
PHONE ............................ 800 800-6006
Walter Schneider, *President*
Marc Lorenzo, *Vice Pres*
Steve Mickelson, *VP Finance*
Eric Sanchez, *Info Tech Mgr*
▲ **EMP:** 17
**SQ FT:** 70,000
**SALES (est):** 23.7MM
**SALES (corp-wide):** 51.1MM **Privately Held**
**WEB:** www.delmedical.com
**SIC: 3844** X-ray apparatus & tubes
**PA:** U.M.G. Inc.
28 Calvert St
Harrison NY 10528
914 835-4600

**(G-2103)**
**DIEQUA CORPORATION (PA)**
180 Covington Dr (60108-3105)
PHONE ............................ 630 980-1133
Fax: 630 980-1232
Meikel Quaas, *President*
Norman Quaas, *Vice Pres*
Tom Culver, *Sales Associate*
Roberto Vasquez, *Sales Associate*
▲ **EMP:** 29
**SQ FT:** 40,000
**SALES:** 10MM **Privately Held**
**WEB:** www.diequa.com
**SIC: 3566** Speed changers (power transmission equipment), except auto

**(G-2104)**
**DIVERSIFIED PRINT GROUP**
358 W Army Trail Rd # 140 (60108-5605)
PHONE ............................ 630 893-8920
Bob Rusty, *Owner*
**EMP:** 4
**SALES (est):** 448.5K **Privately Held**
**SIC: 2752** Commercial printing, lithographic

**(G-2105)**
**ELBA TOOL CO INC**
220 Covington Dr (60108-3105)
PHONE ............................ 847 895-4100
Horst Elendt, *President*
Erich Elendt, *Vice Pres*
Ursula Elendt, *Admin Sec*
**EMP:** 18 **EST:** 1962
**SQ FT:** 20,000
**SALES (est):** 3.2MM **Privately Held**
**WEB:** www.elbatool.com
**SIC: 3544** Industrial molds; dies & die holders for metal cutting, forming, die casting

**(G-2106)**
**ELITE MANUFACTURING TECH INC**
Also Called: Emt
333 Munroe Dr (60108-2639)
PHONE ............................ 630 351-5757
Fax: 630 351-5755
James E Conlon Jr, *CEO*
James O'Keefe, *President*
Ramiro Aranda, *Opers Mgr*
Paul Skrzyniarz, *Opers Staff*
Sarah Anderson, *Purch Dir*
▲ **EMP:** 175
**SQ FT:** 80,000
**SALES:** 32MM **Privately Held**
**WEB:** www.emt333.com
**SIC: 3444** Sheet metalwork

**(G-2107)**
**ENVISION GRAPHICS LLC**
Also Called: Envision 3
225 Madsen Dr (60108-2638)
PHONE ............................ 630 825-1200
Kevin Franz, *CEO*
Tyler Faivre, *Project Mgr*
Chuck Kaiser, *Project Mgr*
Jim Knapp, *Project Mgr*
Tony Vella, *Project Mgr*
**EMP:** 65
**SQ FT:** 50,000
**SALES (est):** 19.1MM **Privately Held**
**WEB:** www.envisiongraphics.com
**SIC: 2759** Commercial printing

**(G-2108)**
**FEDEX OFFICE & PRINT SVCS INC**
369 W Army Trail Rd (60108-2358)
PHONE ............................ 630 894-1800
Nikki Gushes, *Manager*
**EMP:** 13
**SALES (corp-wide):** 50.3B **Publicly Held**
**WEB:** www.kinkos.com
**SIC: 7334** 2791 2789 2752 Photocopying & duplicating services; typesetting; bookbinding & related work; commercial printing, lithographic
**HQ:** Fedex Office And Print Services, Inc.
7900 Legacy Dr
Plano TX 75024
214 550-7000

**(G-2109)**
**GRABER CONCRETE PIPE COMPANY**
24w121 Army Trail Rd (60108-1396)
PHONE ............................ 630 894-5950
Fax: 630 894-6038
Charles R Graber Jr, *President*
Charles S Graber, *Chairman*
Marilyn Graber, *Corp Secy*
Robert Graber, *Manager*
**EMP:** 25 **EST:** 1966
**SQ FT:** 12,500
**SALES (est):** 3.3MM **Privately Held**
**SIC: 3272** Pipe, concrete or lined with concrete

**(G-2110)**
**JOHNSON CONTROLS INC**
153 Stratford Square Mall (60108-2202)
PHONE ............................ 630 351-9407
Fax: 630 351-0337
**EMP:** 5
**SALES (corp-wide):** 36.8B **Privately Held**
**SIC: 2531** Seats, automobile
**PA:** Johnson Controls, Inc.
5757 N Green Bay Ave
Milwaukee WI 53209
414 524-1200

**(G-2111)**
**KORPACK INC**
290 Madsen Dr Bldg 100 (60108-2675)
PHONE ............................ 630 213-3600
Nicholas Novy, *President*
▲ **EMP:** 10
**SQ FT:** 60,000
**SALES:** 7MM **Privately Held**
**SIC: 3565** Packaging machinery

**(G-2112)**
**LAVEZZI PRECISION INC**
250 Madsen Dr (60108-2637)
PHONE ............................ 630 582-1230
Fax: 630 582-1238
Albert J La Vezzi, *President*
Douglas Kremer, *Vice Pres*
George Johnson, *Foreman/Supr*
Gary Ganster, *Purch Dir*
Andy Golak, *Buyer*
**EMP:** 120
**SQ FT:** 90,000
**SALES (est):** 21.7MM **Privately Held**
**WEB:** www.lavezzi.com
**SIC: 3841** Surgical & medical instruments

**(G-2113)**
**LEVITON MANUFACTURING CO INC**
471 Fox Ct (60108-3110)
PHONE ............................ 630 539-0249
Ken Wallace, *Manager*
Everado Rodriguez, *Info Tech Mgr*
**EMP:** 87
**SALES (corp-wide):** 1.5B **Privately Held**
**WEB:** www.leviton.com
**SIC: 3643** Current-carrying wiring devices
**PA:** Leviton Manufacturing Co., Inc.
201 N Service Rd
Melville NY 11747
631 812-6000

**(G-2114)**
**MADDEN COMMUNICATIONS INC**
Also Called: Mbexpress
355 Longview Dr (60108-2640)
PHONE ............................ 630 784-4325
Fax: 630 784-4366
Bill Hendriksen, *Manager*
**EMP:** 46
**SALES (corp-wide):** 173.8MM **Privately Held**
**SIC: 2752** Commercial printing, offset
**PA:** Madden Communications Inc.
901 Mittel Dr
Wood Dale IL 60191
630 787-2200

**(G-2115)**
**MARCUS PRESS**
168 Constitution Dr (60108-1460)
PHONE ............................ 630 351-1857
Janet Marcus, *President*
**EMP:** 4
**SQ FT:** 3,800
**SALES (est):** 380K **Privately Held**
**WEB:** www.marcuspress.com
**SIC: 2752** 2796 2791 2789 Commercial printing, offset; platemaking services; typesetting; bookbinding & related work

**(G-2116)**
**MASTERPIECE FRAMING**
109 S Bloomingdale Rd (60108-1217)
PHONE ............................ 630 893-4390
Matt Puchalski, *President*
**EMP:** 3
**SALES (est):** 280K **Privately Held**
**SIC: 2499** Picture & mirror frames, wood

**(G-2117)**
**MCX PRESS**
355 Longview Dr (60108-2640)
PHONE ............................ 630 784-4325
Bill Hendriksen, *Principal*
▲ **EMP:** 3
**SALES (est):** 191.7K **Privately Held**
**SIC: 2741** Miscellaneous publishing

## GEOGRAPHIC SECTION — Bloomington - Mclean County (G-2145)

**(G-2118)**
**MODERN TUBE LLC (PA)**
193 Rosedale Ct (60108-1477)
PHONE...................................877 848-3300
Michael Anton Jr III, *Mng Member*
Conrad Leupold, *Mng Member*
EMP: 3
SALES (est): 522K **Privately Held**
SIC: 3312  5051  Tubes, steel & iron; tubing, metal

**(G-2119)**
**NATIONAL BOLT & NUT CORP**
144 Covington Dr (60108-3105)
PHONE...................................630 307-8800
Sue P Maggos, *President*
John Kipp, *COO*
Pete Maggos, *Sales Mgr*
Linda Siwe, *Sales Staff*
Kimberly Kipp, *Manager*
▲ EMP: 11 EST: 1996
SQ FT: 116,000
SALES: 3.5MM **Privately Held**
WEB: www.nationalbolt.com
SIC: 3452  Bolts, nuts, rivets & washers

**(G-2120)**
**NEWATER INTERNATIONAL INC**
Also Called: Springsoft International
122 E Lake St (60108-1127)
PHONE...................................630 894-5000
Craig Browart, *President*
Eric Browart, *Vice Pres*
Erick Browark, *Info Tech Dir*
EMP: 10
SQ FT: 1,000
SALES (est): 1.1MM **Privately Held**
SIC: 3589  Water purification equipment, household type

**(G-2121)**
**NOLAN SEALANTS INC**
1 Bloomingdale Pl Apt 104 (60108-1291)
P.O. Box 861 (60108-0861)
PHONE...................................630 774-5713
EMP: 3
SALES (est): 123.2K **Privately Held**
SIC: 2891  Mfg Adhesives/Sealants

**(G-2122)**
**NOW HEALTH GROUP INC (PA)**
Also Called: Now Natural Foods
244 Knollwood Dr Ste 300 (60108-2288)
PHONE...................................630 545-9098
Fax: 630 790-8019
Elwood Richard, *Ch of Bd*
Albert Powers, *President*
Dave Reczek, *General Mgr*
Dan Richard, *General Mgr*
Dan Scoles, *Vice Pres*
▲ EMP: 838
SQ FT: 203,000
SALES (est): 435.8MM **Privately Held**
WEB: www.nowfoods.com
SIC: 2834  Vitamin, nutrient & hematinic preparations for human use

**(G-2123)**
**NOW HEALTH GROUP INC**
Also Called: Now Foods
395 Glen Ellyn Rd (60108-2176)
PHONE...................................888 669-3663
EMP: 838
SALES (corp-wide): 435.8MM **Privately Held**
SIC: 2834  Vitamin, nutrient & hematinic preparations for human use
PA: Now Health Group, Inc.
    244 Knollwood Dr Ste 300
    Bloomingdale IL 60108
    630 545-9098

**(G-2124)**
**PANNON MORD POLISHING**
210 Freeport Dr (60108-1720)
PHONE...................................630 893-9252
EMP: 3
SALES (est): 182.2K **Privately Held**
SIC: 3471  Polishing, metals or formed products

**(G-2125)**
**PARAGON PRINT & MAIL PROD INC**
109 Fairfield Way Ste 202 (60108-1500)
PHONE...................................630 671-2222
Michael Schulkins, *President*
EMP: 2 EST: 2008
SALES (est): 298.7K **Privately Held**
SIC: 2752  Commercial printing, lithographic

**(G-2126)**
**PATRICK CABINETRY INC**
192 Ring Neck Ln (60108-5414)
PHONE...................................630 307-9333
Mike Patrick, *President*
EMP: 3
SALES (est): 295.7K **Privately Held**
SIC: 2512  Upholstered household furniture

**(G-2127)**
**PC-TEL INC (PA)**
471 Brighton Ct (60108-3102)
PHONE...................................630 372-6800
David Neumann, *CEO*
James Giacobazzi, *President*
Rishi Bharadwaj, *Senior VP*
John W Schoen, *CFO*
EMP: 120
SQ FT: 75,517
SALES: 96.7MM **Publicly Held**
WEB: www.pctel.com
SIC: 5731  4812  7372  Antennas; radio telephone communication; prepackaged software

**(G-2128)**
**PEARL DESIGN GROUP LLC**
Also Called: Lakewood Countertop
170 Covington Dr (60108-3105)
PHONE...................................630 295-8401
Fax: 630 295-8545
Jeff Stanley, *Sales Staff*
Bob Carlson,
Ron Brands,
Ken Carlson,
Bob Dirienzo,
EMP: 25
SQ FT: 29,000
SALES (est): 3.8MM **Privately Held**
WEB: www.pearldesigngroup.com
SIC: 2499  Kitchen, bathroom & household ware: wood

**(G-2129)**
**R D S CO**
158 Covington Dr (60108-3105)
PHONE...................................630 893-2990
Scott Perreault, *President*
Dave Wille, *Treasurer*
Stanley Skowron, *Admin Sec*
EMP: 4
SALES (est): 637.6K **Privately Held**
SIC: 3599  Machine shop, jobbing & repair

**(G-2130)**
**RDN MANUFACTURING COMPANY INC**
160 Covington Dr (60108-3105)
PHONE...................................630 893-4500
Fax: 630 893-5010
Robert T Decoursey, *CEO*
Dave Wille, *President*
Scott Fiandalo, *Regl Sales Mgr*
Natalie Folino, *Sales Staff*
EMP: 35
SQ FT: 40,000
SALES (est): 10.2MM **Privately Held**
WEB: www.rdnmfg.com
SIC: 3559  Plastics working machinery

**(G-2131)**
**ROSETTE PRINTING LLC**
517 Widgeon Ln (60108-5416)
PHONE...................................630 295-8500
Tony Amodio, *Manager*
EMP: 2
SALES (est): 200K **Privately Held**
WEB: www.rosetteprinting.com
SIC: 2752  Commercial printing, lithographic

**(G-2132)**
**S & K LABEL CO**
147 Covington Dr (60108-3107)
PHONE...................................630 307-2577
Fax: 630 307-2579
Kenneth J Harvanek, *President*
Diane Erickson, *Office Mgr*
EMP: 4
SALES (est): 420K **Privately Held**
WEB: www.sklabel.com
SIC: 2672  Labels (unprinted), gummed: made from purchased materials

**(G-2133)**
**S & S HINGE COMPANY**
210 Covington Dr (60108-3105)
PHONE...................................630 582-9500
Fax: 630 582-8844
Christopher Stevenson, *President*
Richard St Joseph, *Controller*
Warren Moss, *Accounts Mgr*
Carolyn Kulick, *Manager*
Dan Markel, *Manager*
▼ EMP: 35 EST: 1932
SQ FT: 50,000
SALES (est): 9.1MM **Privately Held**
WEB: www.sandshinge.com
SIC: 3469  Metal stampings

**(G-2134)**
**SAMEL BOTROS**
1 Tiffany Pt Ste G1 (60108-2951)
PHONE...................................847 466-5905
Samuel F Botros, *Principal*
EMP: 5
SALES (est): 445.2K **Privately Held**
SIC: 8099  3845  8011  Blood related health services; laser systems & equipment, medical; gynecologist

**(G-2135)**
**SCHELLERER CORPORATION INC**
Also Called: Signs By Tomorrow
110 Ridge Ave (60108-1209)
PHONE...................................630 980-4567
Fax: 630 980-4899
Gary R Schellerer, *President*
Adam Wagner, *Production*
Carla Schellerer, *Treasurer*
EMP: 65
SQ FT: 24,000
SALES (est): 8.8MM **Privately Held**
WEB: www.bloomingdalesigns.com
SIC: 3993  7532  7319  Signs & advertising specialties; truck painting & lettering; display advertising service

**(G-2136)**
**SEMPER/EXETER PAPER CO LLC**
Also Called: Semper Paper Company
1 Tiffany Pt Ste 300 (60108-2948)
PHONE...................................630 775-9500
Bill Kratohvil, *Branch Mgr*
EMP: 9
SALES (corp-wide): 2.5B **Privately Held**
SIC: 2621  Writing paper
HQ: Semper/Exeter Paper Co Llc
    2617 Legends Way Ste 260
    Crestview Hills KY 41017
    859 341-7100

**(G-2137)**
**SIGN**
Also Called: Sign-A-Rama
369 W Army Trail Rd # 24 (60108-2358)
PHONE...................................630 351-8400
Fax: 630 351-8402
Jacqueline Unger, *President*
EMP: 3
SALES (est): 409.7K **Privately Held**
SIC: 3993  Signs & advertising specialties

**(G-2138)**
**SPECTRON MANUFACTURING**
328 Georgetown Ct Unit C (60108-2055)
PHONE...................................720 879-7605
Greg Askin, *Principal*
Blair Gavan, *Accounts Mgr*
EMP: 7
SALES (est): 370K **Privately Held**
SIC: 1446  3543  3544  Industrial sand; industrial patterns; special dies, tools, jigs & fixtures

**(G-2139)**
**TERCO INC**
459 Camden Dr (60108-3128)
PHONE...................................630 894-8828
Dennis N Ahrens, *CEO*
Dan Ahrens, *President*
Scott Brill, *General Mgr*
David Ahrens, *Corp Secy*
Dennis Brokke, *Vice Pres*
EMP: 22 EST: 1964
SQ FT: 30,000
SALES (est): 6.5MM **Privately Held**
WEB: www.terco.com
SIC: 3565  5084  Packaging machinery; industrial machinery & equipment

**(G-2140)**
**ULTRATECH INC**
251 Covington Dr (60108-3109)
PHONE...................................630 539-3578
Fax: 630 539-4498
Ken Dahm, *President*
Laura Profita, *Manager*
Betty Dahm, *Admin Sec*
EMP: 25
SQ FT: 43,000
SALES: 18.2MM **Privately Held**
WEB: www.ultratechinc.com
SIC: 3444  Sheet metalwork

**(G-2141)**
**WEST SUBURBAN JOURNAL**
229 Esprit Ct (60108-2542)
PHONE...................................708 344-5975
Nicole Trottie, *Owner*
EMP: 3
SALES (est): 157K **Privately Held**
SIC: 2711  Newspapers, publishing & printing

## Bloomington
*Mclean County*

**(G-2142)**
**AKSHAR PLASTIC INC**
1101 Bell St (61701-6979)
PHONE...................................815 635-3536
Bhavana Patel, *President*
Haksmuth Patel, *Vice Pres*
Rita Patel, *Manager*
David Patel, *Asst Mgr*
◆ EMP: 27
SQ FT: 155,000
SALES: 6MM **Privately Held**
SIC: 2821  Molding compounds, plastics

**(G-2143)**
**ALTER TRADING CORPORATION**
501 E Stewart St (61701-6863)
PHONE...................................309 828-6084
William J Bremner, *President*
EMP: 15
SALES (corp-wide): 850.2MM **Privately Held**
SIC: 5093  3312  Metal scrap & waste materials; structural shapes & pilings, steel
HQ: Alter Trading Corporation
    700 Office Pkwy
    Saint Louis MO 63141
    314 872-2400

**(G-2144)**
**AMRIC RESOURCES**
2422 E Washington St # 102 (61704-1611)
PHONE...................................309 664-0391
Patricia Heimerdinger, *President*
EMP: 3
SALES (est): 199.6K **Privately Held**
SIC: 2752  Color lithography

**(G-2145)**
**B AND B AMUSEMENT ILLINOIS LLC**
1404 Mrtin Luther King Dr (61701-1454)
PHONE...................................309 585-2077
Gary R Brewer, *Principal*
EMP: 3 EST: 2012
SALES (est): 381.3K **Privately Held**
SIC: 3999  Coin-operated amusement machines

# Bloomington - Mclean County (G-2146) — GEOGRAPHIC SECTION

### (G-2146)
**B&B AWARDS AND RECOGNITION INC**
Also Called: B & B Awards and Recognition
1210 Towanda Ave Ste 9  (61701-7415)
PHONE ............................ 309 828-9698
Joyce Manard, *Owner*
Dick Manard, *General Mgr*
Tricia Manard, *Graphic Designe*
EMP: 7
SALES (est): 310K  **Privately Held**
WEB: www.b-bawards.com
SIC: 3479  Engraving jewelry silverware, or metal

### (G-2147)
**BEER NUTS  INC**
103 N Robinson St  (61701-5424)
P.O. Box 1327  (61702-1327)
PHONE ............................ 309 827-8580
Fax: 309 827-0914
James A Shirk, *President*
Andrew Shirk, *Admin Sec*
Betty J Shirk, *Admin Sec*
EMP: 80  EST: 1953
SQ FT: 100,000
SALES (est): 20MM  **Privately Held**
WEB: www.beernuts.com
SIC: 2068  Nuts: dried, dehydrated, salted or roasted

### (G-2148)
**BI STATE FURNITURE INC**
Also Called: Bi-State Furniture Rentl & Sls
18 Currency Dr  (61704-9632)
P.O. Box 3587, Davenport IA  (52808-3587)
PHONE ............................ 309 662-6562
Bob Turner, *Manager*
EMP: 6
SALES (corp-wide): 1.5MM  **Privately Held**
WEB: www.astrafurniture.com
SIC: 2519  Household furniture, except wood or metal: upholstered
PA: Bi State Furniture Inc
   513 Fillmore St
   Davenport IA 52802
   319 323-3631

### (G-2149)
**BLOOMINGTON OFFSET PROCESS INC**
1705 S Veterans Pkwy  (61701-7500)
P.O. Box 278  (61702-0278)
PHONE ............................ 309 662-3395
Fax: 309 663-0581
Thomas G Mercier, *President*
Paul L Macfarlane, *Vice Pres*
Kurt Gummerman, *Purch Agent*
Joyce Steinman, *Accounts Exec*
Kristin Milashoski, *Sales Associate*
EMP: 79
SQ FT: 45,000
SALES (est): 15.2MM  **Privately Held**
WEB: www.bopi.com
SIC: 2752  Commercial printing, offset

### (G-2150)
**BLOOMINGTON TENT & AWNING INC**
226 E Market St  (61701-4088)
PHONE ............................ 309 828-3411
Fax: 309 828-2911
Matthew Hagerty, *Owner*
EMP: 6  EST: 1957
SALES (est): 320K  **Privately Held**
SIC: 2394  5999  7359  Canvas & related products; awnings; equipment rental & leasing

### (G-2151)
**CAMTEK  INC**
Also Called: Circuit Assembly & Mfg
2402 E Empire St  (61799-0004)
P.O. Box 5020  (61702-5020)
PHONE ............................ 309 661-0348
Fax: 309 661-1809
Christine Davis, *President*
Angie Stauffer, *Prdtn Mgr*
Jeff Wilson, *Senior Buyer*
Bob Patzer, *QC Mgr*
Marylois Brown, *Controller*
EMP: 70
SQ FT: 60,000
SALES: 13MM  **Privately Held**
WEB: www.camtek-mfg.com
SIC: 3679  Harness assemblies for electronic use: wire or cable

### (G-2152)
**CAPITAL MERCHANT SOLUTIONS INC**
3005 Gill St Ste 2  (61704-3428)
PHONE ............................ 309 452-5990
Fax: 309 452-7035
Christopher Nelson, *CEO*
Russ Link, *President*
Jason Douglass, *Business Mgr*
Cory Nelson, *Vice Pres*
Jeremiah Davis, *Accounts Exec*
EMP: 15
SQ FT: 2,500
SALES (est): 1.9MM  **Privately Held**
WEB: www.cmsprocessing.com
SIC: 4813  7372   ; business oriented computer software

### (G-2153)
**CARGILL  INCORPORATED**
115 S Euclid Ave  (61704-4785)
P.O. Box 1286  (61702-1286)
PHONE ............................ 309 827-7100
Fax: 309 827-7140
Dennis Koss, *Maint Mgr*
Ray Dostal, *Sales/Mktg Mgr*
EMP: 250
SALES (corp-wide): 107.1B  **Privately Held**
WEB: www.cargill.com
SIC: 2075  Soybean oil mills
PA: Cargill, Incorporated
   15407 Mcginty Rd W
   Wayzata MN 55391
   952 742-7575

### (G-2154)
**CENTRAL ILLINOIS DOOR**
1001 Morrissey Dr  (61701-6950)
P.O. Box 5085  (61702-5085)
PHONE ............................ 309 828-0087
Steve Hilliard, *CEO*
Mike Hilliard, *President*
Dale Hilliard, *Vice Pres*
Mike Bradford, *Manager*
EMP: 7
SQ FT: 7,500
SALES (est): 943.8K  **Privately Held**
WEB: www.centralillinoisdoor.com
SIC: 2431  Garage doors, overhead: wood

### (G-2155)
**COPY MAT PRINTING**
1103 Martin Luther King D  (61701-1473)
PHONE ............................ 309 452-1392
Fax: 309 454-3805
Gary Rude, *Owner*
Virginia Rude, *Manager*
EMP: 5  EST: 1978
SQ FT: 3,000
SALES (est): 510K  **Privately Held**
WEB: www.supercopy.com
SIC: 2752  7334  2791  2789  Commercial printing, offset; photocopying & duplicating services; typesetting; bookbinding & related work

### (G-2156)
**CPG PRINTING & GRAPHICS**
1103 Martin Luther King D  (61701-1473)
PHONE ............................ 309 820-1392
Gary Rude, *Executive*
EMP: 3
SALES (est): 284.7K  **Privately Held**
SIC: 2759  Commercial printing

### (G-2157)
**CROWN EQUIPMENT CORPORATION**
Also Called: Crown Lift Trucks
1714 E Hamilton Rd  (61704-9607)
PHONE ............................ 309 663-9200
Scott Furlow, *Branch Mgr*
Steve Bahner, *Manager*
John Jones, *Manager*
Todd Walter, *Manager*
EMP: 17
SALES (corp-wide): 5.5B  **Privately Held**
SIC: 3537  Lift trucks, industrial: fork, platform, straddle, etc.
PA: Crown Equipment Corporation
   44 S Washington St
   New Bremen OH 45869
   419 629-2311

### (G-2158)
**CUSTOM GRAPHICS**
Also Called: C-G Custom Graphics
1212 Towanda Ave Lowr  (61701-7406)
P.O. Box 1667  (61702-1667)
PHONE ............................ 309 828-0717
Fax: 309 828-0122
Daniel Ferguson, *Owner*
EMP: 6  EST: 1962
SQ FT: 1,000
SALES (est): 394.1K  **Privately Held**
SIC: 2791  Typesetting

### (G-2159)
**D J PETERS ORTHOPEDICS LTD**
908 N Hershey Rd Ste 1  (61704-3760)
PHONE ............................ 309 664-6930
Donald S Peters, *President*
Janet L Peters, *Principal*
EMP: 7
SQ FT: 1,500
SALES: 1MM  **Privately Held**
WEB: www.petersorthopedics.com
SIC: 3842  Prosthetic appliances

### (G-2160)
**DANCYN RECOVERY SYSTEMS**
707 N East St  (61701-3059)
PHONE ............................ 309 829-5450
Daniel Kohlenberg, *President*
EMP: 4
SALES (est): 237.3K  **Privately Held**
SIC: 2711  Newspapers

### (G-2161)
**DARNALL PRINTING**
801 W Chestnut St Ste B  (61701-4500)
PHONE ............................ 309 827-7212
Fax: 309 827-7772
Lorrane Darnall, *President*
David Darnall, *Treasurer*
EMP: 3
SALES (est): 320K  **Privately Held**
WEB: www.darnallprinting.com
SIC: 2752  3993  2791  2789  Commercial printing, offset; signs & advertising specialties; typesetting; bookbinding & related work; automotive & apparel trimmings

### (G-2162)
**FAMILY TIME COMPUTING  INC**
Also Called: FTC Family of Companies
4 Yount Dr  (61704-3736)
P.O. Box 1361  (61702-1361)
PHONE ............................ 309 664-1742
Fax: 309 663-5025
Michael Kessler, *President*
Susan Kessler, *Vice Pres*
Zach Lancaster, *Vice Pres*
Nicole Barnett, *Director*
EMP: 11
SALES (est): 1MM  **Privately Held**
WEB: www.ftcpublishing.com
SIC: 7372  Publishers' computer software

### (G-2163)
**FARM WEEK**
Also Called: Illinois Agricultural Assn
1701 Towanda Ave  (61701-2057)
P.O. Box 2901  (61702-2901)
PHONE ............................ 309 557-3140
Fax: 800 998-6090
Philip Nelson, *President*
Ron Warfield, *President*
EMP: 20  EST: 1935
SALES: 2.5MM  **Privately Held**
WEB: www.ilfb.org
SIC: 2711  2741  Newspapers; miscellaneous publishing

### (G-2164)
**FIVE BROTHER INC**
Also Called: Parrott and Assoc Formerly
2905 Gill St Ste B  (61704-8591)
P.O. Box 790  (61702-0790)
PHONE ............................ 309 663-6323
John Parrott, *CEO*
Sandra Parrott, *Corp Secy*
EMP: 4
SALES: 1.3MM  **Privately Held**
SIC: 5651  2253  Family clothing stores; cold weather knit outerwear, including ski wear

### (G-2165)
**FLEXITECH  INC (DH)**
1719 E Hamilton Rd  (61704-9607)
PHONE ............................ 309 664-7828
Fax: 309 665-0679
Randy Ross, *President*
Celso Peirre, *Plant Mgr*
Kevin Jackson, *Chief Engr*
Clint Paul, *Finance*
Jon Dolan, *Manager*
▲ EMP: 180
SALES (est): 35.2MM
SALES (corp-wide): 18.5B  **Privately Held**
SIC: 3492  5013  Fluid power valves & hose fittings; hose & tube fittings & assemblies, hydraulic/pneumatic; automotive supplies & parts

### (G-2166)
**FRANMAR CHEMICAL**
11 Mary Ellen Way  (61701-2014)
P.O. Box 5565  (61702-5565)
PHONE ............................ 309 829-5952
Dan Brown, *Principal*
EMP: 6
SALES (est): 473.8K  **Privately Held**
SIC: 2869  Laboratory chemicals, organic

### (G-2167)
**FREESEN INC**
1523 Cottage Ave  (61701-1503)
P.O. Box 609  (61702-0609)
PHONE ............................ 309 827-4554
Fax: 309 827-5226
Mike Goeken, *Manager*
EMP: 50
SALES (corp-wide): 122.9MM  **Privately Held**
WEB: www.freesen.com
SIC: 2951  1771  Asphalt paving mixtures & blocks; blacktop (asphalt) work
HQ: Freesen Inc.
   3151 Robbins Rd Ste A
   Springfield IL 62704
   217 546-6192

### (G-2168)
**G D S PROFESSIONAL BUS DISPLAY**
Also Called: Gds
1103 Martin Luther King D  (61701-1486)
PHONE ............................ 309 829-3298
Fax: 309 820-8001
Harvey Meister, *Owner*
Brian Glyshaw, *Production*
Brian Leyden, *VP Sales*
Dave Nelson, *Sales Associate*
John Woodall, *Director*
EMP: 25
SQ FT: 120,000
SALES (est): 6.9MM  **Privately Held**
SIC: 5046  3993  Store fixtures & display equipment; signs & advertising specialties

### (G-2169)
**GATEWAY INDUSTRIAL POWER INC**
13958 Roberto Rd Ste 2  (61705-6360)
PHONE ............................ 309 821-1035
Greg Jones, *Manager*
EMP: 5
SALES (corp-wide): 32.9MM  **Privately Held**
SIC: 3585  7538  Refrigeration & heating equipment; diesel engine repair: automotive
PA: Gateway Industrial Power, Inc.
   921 Fournie Ln
   Collinsville IL 62234
   888 865-8675

### (G-2170)
**GENERAL ELECTRIC COMPANY**
1601 General Electric Rd  (61704-2479)
PHONE ............................ 309 664-1513
Fax: 309 664-1444
Ronald Stern, *Vice Pres*
John Brocke, *Plant Mgr*
Tom Jefferson, *Engineer*
Howard Schelt, *Engineer*
Ross Monks, *Human Resources*

▲ = Import  ▼ = Export
◆ = Import/Export

## GEOGRAPHIC SECTION — Bloomington - Mclean County (G-2195)

**EMP:** 250
**SALES (corp-wide):** 123.6B **Publicly Held**
**SIC:** 3625 3613 3643 Starter, electric motor; electric controls & control accessories, industrial; panelboards & distribution boards, electric; current-carrying wiring devices
**PA:** General Electric Company
41 Farnsworth St
Boston MA 02210
617 443-3000

### (G-2171)
### GRANDCENTRAL ENTERPRISES INC
Also Called: AlphaGraphics
716 E Empire St Ste B (61701-8613)
**PHONE** ............................... 309 287-5362
Kunio Ota, *President*
Tomoko Ota, *Admin Sec*
**EMP:** 2
**SQ FT:** 3,300
**SALES (est):** 428.2K **Privately Held**
**SIC:** 2752 Commercial printing, lithographic

### (G-2172)
### GREAT DISPLAY COMPANY LLC
704 S Mclean St (61701-5374)
**PHONE** ............................... 309 821-1037
Jacob Duquenne, *Principal*
Tiffani Hambleton, *Art Dir*
Carina Beaty, *Executive Asst*
Aaron Hambleton,
**EMP:** 10 **EST:** 2010
**SQ FT:** 5,000
**SALES (est):** 860K **Privately Held**
**SIC:** 2759 Decals: printing; posters, including billboards: printing

### (G-2173)
### GRIFOLS SHARED SVCS N AMER INC
511 W Washington St (61701-3809)
**PHONE** ............................... 309 827-3031
Chris Crowell, *Manager*
**EMP:** 3
**SALES (corp-wide):** 548.5MM **Privately Held**
**SIC:** 2836 Plasmas
**HQ:** Grifols Shared Services North America, Inc.
2410 Lillyvale Ave
Los Angeles CA 90032
323 225-2221

### (G-2174)
### GROWMARK ENERGY LLC
1701 Towanda Ave (61701-2057)
**PHONE** ............................... 309 557-6000
**EMP:** 6 **EST:** 2015
**SALES (est):** 341.8K **Privately Held**
**SIC:** 2992 Lubricating oils & greases

### (G-2175)
### GTI SPINDLE TECHNOLOGY INC
Also Called: G T I Spindle
14015 Carole Dr Ste 2 (61705-6202)
**PHONE** ............................... 309 820-7887
**Fax:** 309 820-7897
Tom Hoenig, *Branch Mgr*
**EMP:** 10
**SALES (corp-wide):** 6.6MM **Privately Held**
**WEB:** www.gtispindle.com
**SIC:** 3599 7699 Machine & other job shop work; industrial equipment services
**PA:** Gti Spindle Technology, Inc.
33 Zachary Rd
Manchester NH 03109
603 669-5993

### (G-2176)
### HAJOCA CORPORATION
Also Called: McDonald Supply Div
2047 Ireland Grove Rd B (61704-7109)
P.O. Box 1446 (61702-1446)
**PHONE** ............................... 309 663-7524
**Fax:** 309 663-7545
Kendal Springer, *Manager*
**EMP:** 13
**SALES (corp-wide):** 2.6B **Privately Held**
**WEB:** www.mcdonaldsupply.com
**SIC:** 3431 Plumbing fixtures: enameled iron cast iron or pressed metal
**PA:** Hajoca Corporation
127 Coulter Ave
Ardmore PA 19003
610 649-1430

### (G-2177)
### HEARST COMMUNICATIONS INC
Also Called: The Pantagraph
301 W Washington St (61701-3827)
P.O. Box 2907 (61702-2907)
**PHONE** ............................... 309 829-9000
**Fax:** 309 829-9104
Linda Lindus, *Publisher*
Karen Hansen, *Editor*
Roger Miller, *Editor*
Barry Winterland, *Business Mgr*
Paul Swiech, *COO*
**EMP:** 200
**SALES (corp-wide):** 343.9MM **Privately Held**
**WEB:** www.telegram.com
**SIC:** 2711 Newspapers, publishing & printing
**PA:** Hearst Communications, Inc.
300 W 57th St
New York NY 10019
415 777-7825

### (G-2178)
### HERON BAY INC
Also Called: Fastsigns
1605 General Elc Rd Ste 1 (61704)
**PHONE** ............................... 309 661-1300
**Fax:** 309 661-1305
David Voigts, *President*
**EMP:** 5
**SALES (est):** 420K **Privately Held**
**SIC:** 3993 Signs & advertising specialties

### (G-2179)
### HOLDER PUBLISHING CORPORATION
25 Monarch Dr (61704-9092)
P.O. Box 186 (61702-0186)
**PHONE** ............................... 309 828-7533
Dan Holder, *President*
Judy Holder, *Vice Pres*
**EMP:** 6
**SALES (est):** 530.9K **Privately Held**
**WEB:** www.holderpublishing.com
**SIC:** 2731 2741 Books: publishing only; pamphlets: publishing only, not printed on site; miscellaneous publishing

### (G-2180)
### HOME FOR ALL HEROS NFP
101 Mapehill Dr (61701)
**PHONE** ............................... 309 808-2789
Gary Frazier, *Vice Pres*
**EMP:** 7
**SQ FT:** 7,000
**SALES (est):** 430K **Privately Held**
**SIC:** 2211 Luggage fabrics, cotton

### (G-2181)
### HOWMEDICA OSTEONICS CORP
7 Westport Ct (61704-3732)
**PHONE** ............................... 309 663-6414
**EMP:** 9
**SALES (corp-wide):** 11.3B **Publicly Held**
**SIC:** 3842 Orthopedic appliances
**HQ:** Howmedica Osteonics Corp.
325 Corporate Dr
Mahwah NJ 07430
201 831-5000

### (G-2182)
### ILLINOIS STATE USBC WBA
402 W Hamilton Rd (61704-8610)
**PHONE** ............................... 309 827-6355
Madeline Dotta, *Principal*
**EMP:** 2
**SALES (est):** 291.5K **Privately Held**
**SIC:** 3949 Bowling alleys & accessories

### (G-2183)
### INTEGRATED MEDICAL TECH INC (PA)
2422 E Washington St # 103 (61704-4478)
P.O. Box 5383 (61702-5383)
**PHONE** ............................... 309 662-3614
William Smith, *President*
Norman Hester, *CFO*
**EMP:** 3 **EST:** 2008
**SQ FT:** 4,280
**SALES (est):** 2.1MM **Privately Held**
**SIC:** 3842 3843 3841 Sponges, surgical; sterilizers, hospital & surgical; sterilizers, dental; surgical & medical instruments

### (G-2184)
### J J COLLINS SONS INC
24 Chiswick Cir (61704-7603)
**PHONE** ............................... 309 664-5404
Rick Kuchefski, *Manager*
**EMP:** 20
**SALES (corp-wide):** 32.2MM **Privately Held**
**WEB:** www.jjcollins.com
**SIC:** 2759 Commercial printing
**PA:** J. J. Collins' Sons, Inc.
7125 Janes Ave Ste 200
Woodridge IL 60517
630 960-2525

### (G-2185)
### JACK RUCH QUALITY HOMES INC
Also Called: Jack Ruch Archtctral Mouldings
2908 Gill St Ste 2 (61704-8104)
**PHONE** ............................... 309 663-6595
**Fax:** 309 662-1750
Jack Ruch, *President*
**EMP:** 8
**SALES (est):** 890K **Privately Held**
**SIC:** 1521 3446 6552 2499 New construction, single-family houses; architectural metalwork; subdividers & developers; decorative wood & woodwork

### (G-2186)
### JULY 25TH CORPORATION
Also Called: Starnet Digital Publishing
1708 E Hamilton Rd Ste B (61704-9663)
P.O. Box 1145 (61702-1145)
**PHONE** ............................... 309 664-6444
**Fax:** 309 664-6174
Sandy Adams, *President*
David Mercier, *Chairman*
Karen Crusius, *Vice Pres*
Joann Moore, *Office Mgr*
Scott Martyn, *Manager*
**EMP:** 15
**SQ FT:** 5,000
**SALES (est):** 2MM **Privately Held**
**WEB:** www.starnetdp.com
**SIC:** 2752 2791 Commercial printing, offset; typesetting

### (G-2187)
### K & K TOOL & DIE INC
915 E Oakland Ave (61704-5456)
P.O. Box 1448 (61702-1448)
**PHONE** ............................... 309 829-4479
**Fax:** 309 827-7479
Gene A Kuppersmith, *President*
Frederick H Kuppersmith, *Admin Sec*
**EMP:** 10 **EST:** 1944
**SALES:** 950K **Privately Held**
**SIC:** 3599 7692 3444 Machine shop, jobbing & repair; welding repair; sheet metalwork

### (G-2188)
### KAHUNA LLC
Also Called: Kahuna Atm
807 Arcadia Dr Ste B (61704-6119)
**PHONE** ............................... 888 357-8472
Tammy Cook, *Exec VP*
Josh Hendon, *Vice Pres*
Pamela Philipps, *Vice Pres*
Scott Rathburn, *CFO*
Mark Smith, *VP Finance*
**EMP:** 14
**SALES (est):** 2.4MM **Privately Held**
**SIC:** 3578 Automatic teller machines (ATM)

### (G-2189)
### KELLEY ORNAMENTAL IRON LLC
1206 Towanda Ave Ste 1 (61701-7416)
**PHONE** ............................... 309 820-7540
**Fax:** 309 820-7541
Brian Pinkston, *Manager*
**EMP:** 18
**SALES (corp-wide):** 2.7MM **Privately Held**
**WEB:** www.kelleyiron.com
**SIC:** 3446 Architectural metalwork
**PA:** Kelley Ornamental Iron Llc
4303 N Main St
East Peoria IL 61611
309 697-9870

### (G-2190)
### KIRK WOOD PRODUCTS INC
10424 E 1400 North Rd (61705-6774)
**PHONE** ............................... 309 829-6661
**Fax:** 309 828-6964
Michael Kirk, *President*
**EMP:** 20
**SQ FT:** 60,000
**SALES (est):** 3.9MM **Privately Held**
**SIC:** 2448 Pallets, wood

### (G-2191)
### KRAFT SERVICES
209 S Prospect Rd (61704-4577)
**PHONE** ............................... 309 662-6178
**EMP:** 4
**SALES (est):** 211.6K **Privately Held**
**SIC:** 2022 Processed cheese

### (G-2192)
### L & C IMAGING INC
908 White Oak Rd (61701-2670)
**PHONE** ............................... 309 829-1802
**EMP:** 9
**SALES (est):** 620K **Privately Held**
**SIC:** 3993 Mfg Signs/Advertising Specialties

### (G-2193)
### LEE ENTERPRISES INCORPORATED
301 W Washington St (61701-3827)
**PHONE** ............................... 309 829-9000
Chris Dietiker, *President*
Barry Winterland, *COO*
Diana Cunningham, *Cust Mgr*
Shellie Kelly, *Accounts Exec*
Robin Helenthal, *Manager*
**EMP:** 10
**SALES (corp-wide):** 614.3MM **Publicly Held**
**WEB:** www.lee.net
**SIC:** 2711 Newspapers, publishing & printing
**PA:** Lee Enterprises, Incorporated
201 N Harrison St Ste 600
Davenport IA 52801
563 383-2100

### (G-2194)
### MCLEAN COUNTY ASPHALT CO (PA)
Also Called: Mc Lean County Concrete Co
1100 W Market St (61701-2630)
P.O. Box 3547 (61702-3547)
**PHONE** ............................... 309 827-6115
**Toll Free:** ........................... 877 -
Forrest Kaufman, *President*
Randy Kaufman, *Vice Pres*
Richard Carman, *Controller*
**EMP:** 65
**SQ FT:** 2,000
**SALES (est):** 16.7MM **Privately Held**
**WEB:** www.mc-asphalt.com
**SIC:** 1611 3273 Highway & street paving contractor; ready-mixed concrete

### (G-2195)
### MECHANICAL DEVICES COMPANY
2005 General Electric Rd (61704-1320)
**PHONE** ............................... 309 663-2843
**Fax:** 309 664-0543
Daniel R Sperry, *President*
Robert Waller, *Plant Mgr*
Shane Daniels, *Prdtn Mgr*
Clint Wolfe, *QC Mgr*
Jerry Jones, *Engineer*

## Bloomington - Mclean County (G-2196)

▲ **EMP:** 3 **EST:** 1914
**SALES (est):** 1.4MM **Privately Held**
**SIC:** 3599 Machine shop, jobbing & repair

### (G-2196)
### MERRITT & EDWARDS CORPORATION
302 E Washington St (61701-4041)
**PHONE** .................................. 309 828-4741
Beverly Edwards, *President*
William Edwards, *Vice Pres*
**EMP:** 14
**SQ FT:** 3,500
**SALES (est):** 1.3MM **Privately Held**
**WEB:** www.thecopyshoponline.com
**SIC:** 7334 5943 2789 2752 Blueprinting service; mimeographing; office forms & supplies; bookbinding & related work; commercial printing, lithographic

### (G-2197)
### MICKEY TRUCK BODIES INC
Also Called: Midwest Reconditioning Div
14661 Old Colonial Rd (61705-5947)
**PHONE** .................................. 309 827-8227
Mike Parker, *General Mgr*
**EMP:** 17
**SALES (corp-wide):** 119.3MM **Privately Held**
**WEB:** www.mickeybody.com
**SIC:** 3713 7532 5531 3715 Beverage truck bodies; van bodies; truck bodies (motor vehicles); body shop, trucks; truck equipment & parts; truck trailers; motor vehicles & car bodies; general automotive repair shops
**PA:** Mickey Truck Bodies Inc.
1305 Trinity Ave
High Point NC 27260
336 882-6806

### (G-2198)
### MICROSOFT CORPORATION
2203 E Empire St Ste J (61704-3707)
**PHONE** .................................. 309 665-0113
Dave Youkers, *Branch Mgr*
**EMP:** 100
**SALES (corp-wide):** 85.3B **Publicly Held**
**WEB:** www.microsoft.com
**SIC:** 7372 Application computer software
**PA:** Microsoft Corporation
1 Microsoft Way
Redmond WA 98052
425 882-8080

### (G-2199)
### MIDWEST MARKETING DISTRS INC
Sun Gard Window Fashions
904 S Eldorado Rd (61704-6073)
**PHONE** .................................. 309 663-6972
**EMP:** 4
**SALES (corp-wide):** 1.5MM **Privately Held**
**SIC:** 5719 3081 Ret Misc Homefurnishings Mfg Unsupported Plastic Film/Sheet
**PA:** Midwest Marketing Distributors, Inc.
2000 E War Memorial Dr # 2
Peoria IL 61614
309 688-8858

### (G-2200)
### MIDWEST MOLDING SOLUTIONS
3001 Gill St (61704-8508)
**PHONE** .................................. 309 663-7374
Joseph G Diemer, *President*
▲ **EMP:** 10
**SQ FT:** 3,000
**SALES:** 3MM **Privately Held**
**SIC:** 3089 Plastic processing

### (G-2201)
### MINERVA SPORTSWEAR INC
608 Iaa Dr (61701-2217)
**PHONE** .................................. 309 661-2387
**Fax:** 309 661-8458
Tony Todaro, *President*
Louis Todaro, *Admin Sec*
**EMP:** 12
**SQ FT:** 5,500
**SALES (est):** 1.7MM **Privately Held**
**SIC:** 5611 3993 2396 2395 Clothing, sportswear, men's & boys'; signs & advertising specialties; automotive & apparel trimmings; pleating & stitching; screen printing

### (G-2202)
### MONSANTO COMPANY
14018 Carole Dr (61705-6327)
**PHONE** .................................. 309 829-6640
Barbara Schweigert, *Safety Mgr*
Tom Floyd, *Branch Mgr*
Steven Fenton, *Manager*
**EMP:** 62
**SALES (corp-wide):** 13.5B **Publicly Held**
**SIC:** 2879 Agricultural chemicals
**PA:** Monsanto Company
800 N Lindbergh Blvd
Saint Louis MO 63167
314 694-1000

### (G-2203)
### MORAN AUTO PARTS AND MCH SP
Also Called: Jopac Companies, The
1001 Croxton Ave Bldg 1 (61701-7207)
**PHONE** .................................. 309 663-6449
John Rice, *Owner*
**EMP:** 12 **EST:** 1947
**SQ FT:** 23,000
**SALES (est):** 1.4MM **Privately Held**
**SIC:** 5013 5531 3599 Automotive supplies & parts; automotive parts; machine shop, jobbing & repair

### (G-2204)
### MORRIS PACKAGING LLC (PA)
211 N Williamsburg Dr A (61704-7735)
**PHONE** .................................. 309 663-9100
**Fax:** 309 663-4455
Scott Henderson, *Vice Pres*
Joshua Frantz, *Accountant*
Dawn Gaddis, *Accountant*
Chris Spence, *Cust Mgr*
Amy Adams, *Client Mgr*
**EMP:** 9
**SQ FT:** 2,000
**SALES (est):** 2.2MM **Privately Held**
**WEB:** www.morrispkg.com
**SIC:** 2674 2673 Flour bags: made from purchased materials; shipping bags or sacks, including multiwall & heavy duty; food storage & frozen food bags, plastic

### (G-2205)
### NEON NIGHTS DJ SVC
2902 Essington St (61705-6539)
**PHONE** .................................. 309 820-9000
**EMP:** 3
**SALES (est):** 140K **Privately Held**
**SIC:** 2813 Mfg Industrial Gases

### (G-2206)
### NESTLE USA INC
Also Called: Nestle Confections Factory
2501 Beich Rd (61705-6558)
**PHONE** .................................. 309 829-1031
Howard Baker, *Plant Mgr*
Al Guest, *Financial Exec*
Larry Popp, *Manager*
Charles Sauer, *Director*
**EMP:** 139
**SALES (corp-wide):** 88.4B **Publicly Held**
**WEB:** www.nestleusa.com
**SIC:** 2023 Evaporated milk
**HQ:** Nestle Usa, Inc.
800 N Brand Blvd
Glendale CA 91203
818 549-6000

### (G-2207)
### ORIGINAL SMITH PRINTING INC (DH)
Also Called: O S P
2 Hardman Dr (61701-6934)
**PHONE** .................................. 309 663-0325
**Fax:** 309 662-6566
Rockie Zeigler, *President*
Kirsten Smith, *General Mgr*
Amy Fuller, *Prdtn Mgr*
Marie Albert, *Purchasing*
Gerald Oaks, *Purchasing*
**EMP:** 59 **EST:** 1929
**SQ FT:** 60,000
**SALES (est):** 34.3MM
**SALES (corp-wide):** 4.5B **Privately Held**
**SIC:** 2752 Commercial printing, offset
**HQ:** Commercial Print Group, Inc.
1750 Northway Dr
North Mankato MN 56003
507 625-2828

### (G-2208)
### PANTAGRAPH PRINTING AND STY CO (PA)
217 W Jefferson St (61701-3927)
**PHONE** .................................. 309 829-1071
Michael G Dolan, *President*
Ted Fowler, *Engineer*
Bernard Beoletto, *Sales Mgr*
**EMP:** 17 **EST:** 1860
**SQ FT:** 40,000
**SALES (est):** 9MM **Privately Held**
**SIC:** 2752 2759 2732 Commercial printing, offset; commercial printing; book printing

### (G-2209)
### PANTAGRAPH PUBLISHING CO (PA)
Also Called: Farmercityjournal.com
301 W Washington St (61701-3803)
P.O. Box 2907 (61702-2907)
**PHONE** .................................. 309 829-9000
Linda Lindus, *President*
Henry Bird, *Publisher*
Julie Bechtel, *Publisher*
Tyler Gillette, *Technology*
**EMP:** 13
**SALES (est):** 933.4K **Privately Held**
**SIC:** 2711 Newspapers

### (G-2210)
### PARADIGM BIOAVIATION LLC
2933 E Empire St (61704-5452)
**PHONE** .................................. 309 663-2303
Orval Yarger,
**EMP:** 12
**SALES (est):** 1.2MM **Privately Held**
**SIC:** 2869 Industrial organic chemicals

### (G-2211)
### PELLA CORPORATION
Also Called: Pella Window Door
1407 N Veterans Pkwy B3 (61704-6425)
**PHONE** .................................. 309 663-7132
**Fax:** 309 662-4666
Terry Kieswetter, *Branch Mgr*
**EMP:** 316
**SALES (corp-wide):** 2.1B **Privately Held**
**SIC:** 2431 Windows, wood
**PA:** Pella Corporation
102 Main St
Pella IA 50219
641 621-1000

### (G-2212)
### PELLA CORPORATION
Also Called: Pella Window Door
1407 N Veterans Pkwy B3 (61704-6425)
**PHONE** .................................. 309 663-7132
Terry Kieswetter, *Branch Mgr*
**EMP:** 316
**SALES (corp-wide):** 2.1B **Privately Held**
**SIC:** 2431 Windows, wood
**PA:** Pella Corporation
102 Main St
Pella IA 50219
641 621-1000

### (G-2213)
### PELLA CORPORATION
Also Called: Pella Window Door
1407 N Veterans Pkwy B3 (61704-6425)
**PHONE** .................................. 309 663-7132
Terry Kieswetter, *Branch Mgr*
**EMP:** 316
**SALES (corp-wide):** 2.1B **Privately Held**
**SIC:** 2431 Windows, wood
**PA:** Pella Corporation
102 Main St
Pella IA 50219
641 621-1000

### (G-2214)
### PELLA CORPORATION
Also Called: Pella Window Door
1407 N Veterans Pkwy B3 (61704-6425)
**PHONE** .................................. 309 663-7132
Terry Kieswetter, *Branch Mgr*
**EMP:** 316
**SALES (corp-wide):** 2.1B **Privately Held**
**SIC:** 2431 Windows, wood
**PA:** Pella Corporation
102 Main St
Pella IA 50219
641 621-1000

### (G-2215)
### PRIDE PACKAGING LLC
211 Williamsburg Dr A (61704-7735)
**PHONE** .................................. 309 663-9100
Amy Adams, *Accountant*
Jim Morris,
Orlando Martinez,
Amy Vogel,
**EMP:** 3
**SALES (est):** 210K **Privately Held**
**WEB:** www.pridepkg.com
**SIC:** 2674 2673 Flour bags: made from purchased materials; plastic & pliofilm bags

### (G-2216)
### PROGRSSIVE IMPRSSIONS INTL INC (HQ)
1 Hardman Dr (61701-6934)
**PHONE** .................................. 309 664-0444
Jamie Huff, *President*
Barry Carr, *President*
Ken Orr, *General Mgr*
Kim Armstrong, *Business Mgr*
Art Calamari, *Senior VP*
**EMP:** 119 **EST:** 1991
**SQ FT:** 65,000
**SALES (est):** 29.5MM
**SALES (corp-wide):** 4.5B **Privately Held**
**WEB:** www.whateverittakes.com
**SIC:** 8742 2752 2759 Marketing consulting services; commercial printing, lithographic; commercial printing
**PA:** Taylor Corporation
1725 Roe Crest Dr
North Mankato MN 56003
507 625-2828

### (G-2217)
### R G HANSON COMPANY INC (PA)
211 S Prospect Rd Ste 4 (61704-4907)
P.O. Box 1408 (61702-1408)
**PHONE** .................................. 309 661-9200
**Fax:** 309 663-2659
Thomas R Hanson, *President*
Mary Gerwig, *Finance Dir*
Elaine Mountjoy, *Accounting Mgr*
**EMP:** 10
**SALES (est):** 5MM **Privately Held**
**WEB:** www.rghanson.com
**SIC:** 5084 3599 Industrial machinery & equipment; custom machinery

### (G-2218)
### RETTICK ENTERPRISES INC
Also Called: Right Angle Tool Division
13958 Roberto Rd Ste 1 (61705-6360)
**PHONE** .................................. 309 275-4967
James R Rettick, *President*
**EMP:** 4 **EST:** 1974
**SALES (est):** 281K **Privately Held**
**WEB:** www.ratd.com
**SIC:** 0116 3444 Soybeans; sheet metalwork

### (G-2219)
### ROAD READY SIGNS (PA)
Also Called: Traffic Sign Store, The
1231 N Mason St (61701-1648)
**PHONE** .................................. 309 828-1007
**Fax:** 309 728-2337
Randy Kull, *Partner*
Melvin Kull, *Partner*
**EMP:** 10
**SQ FT:** 1,400
**SALES (est):** 1.5MM **Privately Held**
**SIC:** 3993 Signs & advertising specialties

### (G-2220)
### ROUT A BOUT SHOP INC
Also Called: Rout-A-Bout
619 W Olive St (61701-4967)
**PHONE** .................................. 309 829-0674
William Smith, *President*
**EMP:** 4
**SALES (est):** 250K **Privately Held**
**SIC:** 3993 Signs & advertising specialties

### (G-2221)
### RUFF QUALITY COMPONENTS
1707 E Hamilton Rd (61704-9607)
**PHONE** .................................. 309 662-0425
Mike Ruff, *Owner*
**EMP:** 25 **EST:** 1994

# GEOGRAPHIC SECTION
## Blue Island - Cook County (G-2247)

SALES (est): 101.9K **Privately Held**
SIC: 2439 Structural wood members

**(G-2222)**
**SELECT SCREEN PRINTS & EMB**
112 Southgate Dr (61704-7683)
PHONE...............................309 829-6511
Fax: 309 829-3624
Charles Stevens, *President*
Michael D Moore, *Treasurer*
Marlene M Crone, *Manager*
Amy Legner, *Director*
Molly Smith, *Assistant*
EMP: 12
SQ FT: 6,000
SALES: 1.1MM **Privately Held**
WEB: www.selectscreenprints.com
SIC: 5137 5136 5699 2395 Women's & children's sportswear & swimsuits; men's & boys' sportswear & work clothing; T-shirts, custom printed; embroidery & art needlework; automotive & apparel trimmings; screen printing

**(G-2223)**
**SIEMENS INDUSTRY INC**
14 Currency Dr (61704-9632)
PHONE...............................309 664-2460
Jeremy Hale, *Project Mgr*
Greg Wommac, *Manager*
EMP: 9
SALES (corp-wide): 89.6B **Privately Held**
WEB: www.sibt.com
SIC: 3822 1796 5084 Air conditioning & refrigeration controls; installing building equipment; conveyor systems
HQ: Siemens Industry, Inc.
1000 Deerfield Pkwy
Buffalo Grove IL 60089
847 215-1000

**(G-2224)**
**SIGNSDIRECT INC**
410 E Lafayette St Ste 1 (61701-6518)
PHONE...............................309 820-1070
Tom Dalton, *President*
◆ EMP: 4
SQ FT: 11,000
SALES (est): 570K **Privately Held**
WEB: www.signsdirect.com
SIC: 3993 Signs & advertising specialties

**(G-2225)**
**SOUTHFIELD CORPORATION**
Also Called: Modahl & Scott
917 E Grove St (61701-4201)
PHONE...............................309 829-1087
Fax: 309 829-1270
John Drew, *Manager*
EMP: 22
SALES (corp-wide): 273.9MM **Privately Held**
WEB: www.prairiegroup.com
SIC: 3273 4212 Ready-mixed concrete; local trucking, without storage
PA: Southfield Corporation
8995 W 95th St
Palos Hills IL 60465
708 344-1000

**(G-2226)**
**STUDLEY PRODUCTS INC (PA)**
903 Morrissey Dr (61701-6949)
PHONE...............................309 663-2313
Gary Wilder, *CEO*
Robert Douglas, *Exec VP*
Toni Jo Wilder, *Vice Pres*
Terry Evans, *Purchasing*
Bill Harroui, *Sls & Mktg Exec*
▲ EMP: 105 EST: 1946
SQ FT: 145,000
SALES (est): 6.9MM **Privately Held**
WEB: www.endustfiltration.com
SIC: 2674 Vacuum cleaner bags; made from purchased materials

**(G-2227)**
**SUPER SIGN SERVICE**
621 W Olive St (61701-4967)
P.O. Box 3336 (61702-3336)
PHONE...............................309 829-9241
Fax: 309 828-7611
William R Smith, *Partner*
George E Kletz Jr, *Partner*
EMP: 12 EST: 1973

SALES (est): 1.5MM **Privately Held**
WEB: www.supersignservice.com
SIC: 3993 Signs & advertising specialties

**(G-2228)**
**SWEET TEMPTATIONS CUPCAKE**
2303 E Washington St 5b (61704-1600)
PHONE...............................309 212-2637
Tim Vance, *President*
EMP: 4
SALES (est): 258.9K **Privately Held**
SIC: 2051 Bread, cake & related products

**(G-2229)**
**T G ENTERPRISES INC**
Also Called: Sportland
2045 Ireland Grove Rd (61704-7103)
PHONE...............................309 662-0508
Fax: 309 663-5196
Robin Juhler, *President*
EMP: 11
SQ FT: 9,200
SALES (est): 2.3MM **Privately Held**
WEB: www.sportlandonline.com
SIC: 5571 3751 4489 Motorcycle dealers; all-terrain vehicles; motor scooters & parts; water taxis

**(G-2230)**
**TAURUS CYCLE**
1 Lafayette Ct (61701-6883)
PHONE...............................309 454-1565
John D Earhart, *Owner*
EMP: 3
SALES (est): 227.9K **Privately Held**
SIC: 3751 Motorcycles & related parts

**(G-2231)**
**TIMPTE INDUSTRIES INC**
2312 W Market St (61705-5147)
PHONE...............................309 820-1095
EMP: 78
SALES (corp-wide): 65.9MM **Privately Held**
SIC: 3715 Semitrailers for truck tractors; trailer bodies
PA: Timpte Industries, Inc.
700 N Broadway Ste 800
Denver CO 80203
303 839-1900

**(G-2232)**
**TOYO USA MANUFACTURING INC**
Also Called: Toyo-Precision USA Mfg Inc
818 Avalon Way (61705-6609)
PHONE...............................309 827-8836
Fax: 309 452-8991
Atsushi Makino, *President*
Yuzuru Otsuka, *Admin Sec*
▲ EMP: 12
SALES (est): 2.5MM
SALES (corp-wide): 2.6MM **Privately Held**
SIC: 3714 Motor vehicle parts & accessories
PA: Toyo Seki Seisakusho, K.K.
3-10-6, Kamitsuchidananaka
Ayase KNG 252-1
467 760-238

**(G-2233)**
**TWIN CITY ELECTRIC INC**
1701 Easy St Ste 5 (61701-6878)
PHONE...............................309 827-0636
Fax: 309 828-9403
Cheryl Mulcahey, *President*
Chloe Misch, *Vice Pres*
Larry Mulcahey, *Treasurer*
Harold Misch, *Supervisor*
EMP: 20
SQ FT: 5,000
SALES (est): 2.3MM **Privately Held**
WEB: www.twin-cityelectric.com
SIC: 1731 3643 Electrical work; current-carrying wiring devices

**(G-2234)**
**TWIN CITY WOOD RECYCLING CORP**
1606 W Oakland Ave (61701-4793)
PHONE...............................309 827-9663
John Wollrab, *President*
Phil McCrackin, *Treasurer*

EMP: 5
SALES (est): 622.9K **Privately Held**
SIC: 2421 2448 4953 Sawdust, shavings & wood chips; wood pallets & skids; recycling, waste materials

**(G-2235)**
**WHERRY MACHINE & WELDING INC**
11 Carri Dr (61705-5188)
PHONE...............................309 828-5423
Fax: 309 829-3551
Byron Young, *President*
Steve Young, *Vice Pres*
Connie Young, *Treasurer*
EMP: 9 EST: 1960
SALES (est): 780K **Privately Held**
WEB: www.wherrymachine.com
SIC: 7692 3599 3441 Welding repair; machine shop, jobbing & repair; fabricated structural metal

**(G-2236)**
**WISH BONE RESCUE**
1007 S Madison St (61701-6646)
PHONE...............................309 212-9210
EMP: 3 EST: 2011
SALES (est): 184.1K **Privately Held**
SIC: 3999 Pet supplies

---
**Blue Island**
*Cook County*
---

**(G-2237)**
**ADVANCED VALVE TECH INC**
Also Called: Avt Service Technologies
12601 Homan Ave (60406-1837)
PHONE...............................877 489-4909
Kevin Murphy, *Branch Mgr*
EMP: 40
SALES (corp-wide): 25MM **Privately Held**
SIC: 3491 Industrial valves
PA: Advanced Valve Technologies, Inc.
800 Busse Rd
Elk Grove Village IL 60007
847 364-3700

**(G-2238)**
**BEST KEPT SECRETS**
2119 121st St (60406-1201)
P.O. Box 43135, Chicago (60643-0135)
PHONE...............................773 431-0353
Valerie Kelley, *CEO*
James Hatcher, *Vice Pres*
EMP: 3
SALES: 100K **Privately Held**
SIC: 5621 7389 2335 Ret Women's Clothing Business Services Mfg Women's/Misses' Dresses

**(G-2239)**
**BLUE ISLAND BEER CO**
13357 Olde Western Ave (60406-2969)
PHONE...............................708 954-8085
EMP: 4
SALES (est): 266.4K **Privately Held**
SIC: 2082 Beer (alcoholic beverage)

**(G-2240)**
**BLUE ISLAND SUN**
12607 Artesian Ave (60406-1705)
PHONE...............................708 388-9033
Joe Gatrell, *Owner*
EMP: 5
SALES (est): 193K **Privately Held**
SIC: 2711 Newspapers

**(G-2241)**
**C-V CSTOM CNTRTOPS CBINETS INC**
12525 Irving Ave (60406-1669)
P.O. Box 87 (60406-0087)
PHONE...............................708 388-5066
Fax: 708 388-5084
Roger Christ, *President*
Robert C Volkart, *Vice Pres*
Todd Christ, *Asst Treas*
EMP: 10
SQ FT: 10,000

SALES (est): 1.2MM **Privately Held**
SIC: 2521 2522 2434 2542 Wood office filing cabinets & bookcases; office furniture, except wood; wood kitchen cabinets; partitions & fixtures, except wood; wood partitions & fixtures

**(G-2242)**
**COLOR TONE PRINTING**
Also Called: J N P
2619 Orchard St (60406-1535)
P.O. Box 183 (60406-0183)
PHONE...............................708 385-1442
Fax: 708 385-7329
Robert James, *Partner*
Nelvia Pittman, *Partner*
EMP: 3
SQ FT: 4,000
SALES (est): 277.4K **Privately Held**
SIC: 2759 2752 2396 Letterpress printing; screen printing; commercial printing, offset; automotive & apparel trimmings

**(G-2243)**
**COLVIN PRINTING**
12958 Ashland Ave (60406-2701)
PHONE...............................708 331-4580
Tanya Colvin, *Principal*
EMP: 5
SALES (est): 499.7K **Privately Held**
SIC: 2759 2752 Commercial printing; commercial printing, lithographic

**(G-2244)**
**CRYOGENIC SYSTEMS EQUIPMENT**
2363 136th St (60406-3233)
PHONE...............................708 385-4216
Brian Sink, *President*
Gary Magdziarz, *Marketing Mgr*
Devin Sink, *Admin Asst*
EMP: 27
SQ FT: 26,000
SALES (est): 6.8MM **Privately Held**
WEB: www.cryobrain.com
SIC: 3559 7699 Cryogenic machinery, industrial; industrial equipment services

**(G-2245)**
**DARLING INTERNATIONAL INC**
Darling Intl Grse Trp Pump Div
3000 Wireton Rd (60406-1861)
PHONE...............................708 388-3223
Dan Ross, *Plant Mgr*
Eugene Schneider, *Sales Staff*
Jerome Levy, *Branch Mgr*
EMP: 47
SALES (corp-wide): 3.4B **Publicly Held**
WEB: www.darlingii.com
SIC: 4953 2048 Refuse collection & disposal services; prepared feeds
PA: Darling Ingredients Inc.
251 Oconnor Ridge Blvd
Irving TX 75038
972 717-0300

**(G-2246)**
**DMARV DESIGN SPECIALTY PRTRS**
13010 Western Ave (60406-2407)
PHONE...............................708 389-4420
Fax: 708 389-4439
Marvin Forbish, *President*
Delores Forbish, *CFO*
EMP: 5
SQ FT: 3,500
SALES (est): 550K **Privately Held**
SIC: 2759 2752 2789 2396 Commercial printing; offset & photolithographic printing; bookbinding & related work; automotive & apparel trimmings

**(G-2247)**
**E B BRONSON & CO INC**
Also Called: Bronson Machine Shop
12826 Irving Ave (60406-2122)
P.O. Box 267 (60406-0267)
PHONE...............................708 385-3600
Fax: 708 385-8485
James U Bronson Jr, *President*
Bruce S Bronson, *Vice Pres*
James U Bronson III, *Vice Pres*
Robt Brower, *Plant Mgr*
EMP: 25 EST: 1896
SQ FT: 18,000

# Blue Island - Cook County (G-2248)

SALES (est): 4.6MM **Privately Held**
SIC: 3599 Machine shop, jobbing & repair

### (G-2248)
### EISENHOWER HIGH SCHOOL - BLUE
12700 Sacramento Ave (60406-1899)
PHONE ................................ 708 385-6815
Nicole Hite, *Principal*
EMP: 5
SALES (est): 159.9K **Privately Held**
SIC: 2711 Newspapers

### (G-2249)
### EMBROIDERY CHOICES
2633 New St (60406-2016)
PHONE ................................ 708 597-9093
Jeanne Dolan, *President*
Terry Schuememann, *Vice Pres*
EMP: 2 EST: 2001
SALES (est): 300K **Privately Held**
SIC: 2395 Embroidery & art needlework

### (G-2250)
### ERIN ROPE CORPORATION
2661 139th St (60406-2805)
PHONE ................................ 708 377-1084
James J Doherty, *President*
Fran Doherty, *Vice Pres*
Tom Leyden, *Marketing Staff*
Amy Colomb, *Administration*
▲ EMP: 15
SQ FT: 30,000
SALES (est): 2.9MM **Privately Held**
WEB: www.erinrope.com
SIC: 2298 3357 Cordage & twine; nonferrous wiredrawing & insulating

### (G-2251)
### G & W ELECTRIC COMPANY
Manufacturers Brass Alum Fndry
3450 127th St (60406-1834)
PHONE ................................ 708 389-8307
Fax: 708 388-9926
Jim Acree, *Vice Chairman*
John Berenc, *Vice Pres*
Dennis Cha, *Vice Pres*
Greg Harper, *Vice Pres*
Van Lear, *Vice Pres*
EMP: 35
SALES (corp-wide): 124MM **Privately Held**
SIC: 3364 3363 3369 Brass & bronze diecastings; aluminum die-castings; nonferrous foundries
PA: G & W Electric Company
     305 W Crossroads Pkwy
     Bolingbrook IL 60440
     708 388-5010

### (G-2252)
### GATLING PRINTING INC
Also Called: Gatlin Chapel
2946 Wireton Rd (60406-1869)
PHONE ................................ 708 388-4746
Fax: 708 396-1315
Lafayett Gatlin, *President*
EMP: 4
SALES (est): 231.8K **Privately Held**
WEB: www.gatling-gun.com
SIC: 2752 Commercial printing, lithographic

### (G-2253)
### GOLDEN HYDRAULIC & MACHINE
2966 Wireton Rd (60406-1869)
PHONE ................................ 708 597-4265
John De Makas, *President*
EMP: 4
SALES (est): 527.4K **Privately Held**
SIC: 7692 Welding repair

### (G-2254)
### GREAT NORTHERN LUMBER INC
2200 Burr Oak Ave (60406-2107)
P.O. Box 43144, Chicago (60643-0144)
PHONE ................................ 708 388-1818
Fax: 708 388-9235
Jeffrey B Currier, *President*
Steve Cushman, *Governor*
Kristine Currier, *Treasurer*
Celeste Burke, *Sales Staff*
Nick Nelson, *Sales Associate*
▲ EMP: 65
SQ FT: 12,000
SALES (est): 1MM **Privately Held**
SIC: 2426 5211 2421 5031 Hardwood dimension & flooring mills; lumber products; sawmills & planing mills, general; lumber: rough, dressed & finished; hardwood veneer & plywood; wood preserving

### (G-2255)
### HARVEY PALLETS INC
2200 138th St (60406-3209)
PHONE ................................ 708 293-1831
Manuel Tavarez, *President*
Jose M Tavarez, *Principal*
Julia Tavarez, *Vice Pres*
Johana Lopez, *Accounts Mgr*
Bernard Packo, *Mktg Dir*
EMP: 120
SQ FT: 225,000
SALES (est): 2.4MM **Privately Held**
WEB: www.harveypallets.com
SIC: 2448 Wood pallets & skids

### (G-2256)
### HOLLYWOOD INTERNATIONAL CO
13636 Western Ave (60406-3277)
PHONE ................................ 708 926-9437
Emil Khoury, *President*
Sam Matanyous, *Principal*
Sam Matanious, *Vice Pres*
▼ EMP: 21
SALES (est): 1.1MM **Privately Held**
SIC: 2844 Hair preparations, including shampoos; shampoos, rinses, conditioners: hair; hair coloring preparations; bleaches, hair

### (G-2257)
### J & G FABRICATING INC
Also Called: Par Fabricating Co
12653 Irving Ave (60406-1652)
PHONE ................................ 708 385-9147
Fax: 708 385-5978
Rafal Gliwiak, *Co-Owner*
Piotr Kajpust, *Co-Owner*
Bob Okroi, *VP Sales*
EMP: 8
SQ FT: 8,900
SALES (est): 750K **Privately Held**
WEB: www.parfabricating.com
SIC: 3444 3443 3441 Sheet metalwork; fabricated plate work (boiler shop); fabricated structural metal

### (G-2258)
### J E TOMES & ASSOCIATES INC
2513 140th Pl (60406-3588)
PHONE ................................ 708 653-5100
Joe Tomes, *President*
Kim Erma, *Manager*
Jim Lucas, *Representative*
EMP: 10
SQ FT: 1,000
SALES (est): 2MM **Privately Held**
WEB: www.jetomes.com
SIC: 3272 5211 Concrete products; lumber & other building materials

### (G-2259)
### KDK UPSET FORGING CO
2645 139th St (60406-3599)
P.O. Box 146 (60406-0146)
PHONE ................................ 708 388-8770
Laxminarayan Mahisekar, *President*
Paul Knez, *Vice Pres*
Mark Lesniewicz, *Sales Mgr*
Larry Mahisekar, *Manager*
EMP: 44 EST: 1947
SQ FT: 34,000
SALES (est): 8.4MM **Privately Held**
WEB: www.kdkforging.com
SIC: 3462 3841 3493 3452 Iron & steel forgings; surgical & medical instruments; steel springs, except wire; bolts, nuts, rivets & washers

### (G-2260)
### KOWAL CUSTOM CABINET & FURN
2900 Wireton Rd (60406)
PHONE ................................ 708 597-3367
Fax: 708 597-4585
Jeff Kowalczyk, *President*
Ray Kowalczyk, *Vice Pres*
Judith Kowalczyk, *Admin Sec*
EMP: 6
SALES (est): 716.6K **Privately Held**
SIC: 2434 2511 Wood kitchen cabinets; wood household furniture

### (G-2261)
### M AND M PALLET INC
2810 Vermont St (60406-1870)
PHONE ................................ 708 272-4447
Fax: 708 333-9056
Rodrigo Munoz, *President*
Elizabeth Munoz, *Manager*
Hector Munoz, *Admin Sec*
EMP: 4 EST: 2006
SALES (est): 522.8K **Privately Held**
SIC: 2448 Pallets, wood & wood with metal

### (G-2262)
### MARATHON SPORTSWEAR INC
12757 Homan Ave (60406-1898)
PHONE ................................ 708 389-5390
James P Piko, *President*
Pat Devine, *Vice Pres*
Michele Jantz, *Prdtn Mgr*
Beth O'Rourke, *Sales Staff*
Beth Rourke, *Manager*
EMP: 30
SQ FT: 8,000
SALES (est): 6MM **Privately Held**
WEB: www.marathonsportswear.net
SIC: 2262 Printing: manmade fiber & silk broadwoven fabrics

### (G-2263)
### MONUMENTAL ART WORKS
2152 Vermont St Ste A2 (60406-2581)
PHONE ................................ 708 389-3038
Ogal Bugayon, *President*
Victor Bugayon, *Co-Owner*
EMP: 4
SQ FT: 600
SALES (est): 360K **Privately Held**
SIC: 3272 3281 Monuments & grave markers, except terrazo; granite, cut & shaped

### (G-2264)
### NATIONAL INTERCHEM LLC
13750 Chatham St (60406-3218)
PHONE ................................ 708 597-7777
Paul Killa, *Manager*
EMP: 4
SQ FT: 10,000
SALES: 1MM
SALES (corp-wide): 24.9MM **Privately Held**
SIC: 2819 2869 Industrial inorganic chemicals; industrial organic chemicals
PA: Rna Corporation
     13750 Chatham St
     Blue Island IL 60406
     708 597-7777

### (G-2265)
### PRINTSOURCE PLUS INC
12128 Western Ave (60406-1328)
PHONE ................................ 708 389-6252
EMP: 8
SQ FT: 2,500
SALES: 600K **Privately Held**
SIC: 2752 2791 2789 2759 Lithographic Coml Print Typesetting Services Bookbinding/Related Work Commercial Printing

### (G-2266)
### RIJON MANUFACTURING COMPANY
Also Called: Rijon Awning
13733 Chatham St (60406-3217)
P.O. Box 125 (60406-0125)
PHONE ................................ 708 388-2295
Fax: 708 388-2298
Wayne Roman, *President*
EMP: 7
SALES (est): 917.2K **Privately Held**
WEB: www.rijonmfgco.com
SIC: 3469 3444 3544 Stamping metal for the trade; awnings, sheet metal; dies & die holders for metal cutting, forming, die casting

### (G-2267)
### RNA CORPORATION (PA)
13750 Chatham St (60406-3218)
PHONE ................................ 708 597-7777
Fax: 708 597-8151
Muhammad Akhtar, *President*
Donna Koney, *Purch Mgr*
Muhammad Saeed, *CFO*
Nadia Akhtar, *Manager*
Gaus Ansari, *Manager*
◆ EMP: 85
SQ FT: 250,000
SALES (est): 24.9MM **Privately Held**
WEB: www.rnacorporation.com
SIC: 2844 Cosmetic preparations

### (G-2268)
### SAVINO ENTERPRISES
12453 Gregory St (60406-1600)
PHONE ................................ 708 385-5277
Anthony Savino, *President*
Pam Savino, *Vice Pres*
EMP: 3
SALES (est): 200K **Privately Held**
SIC: 2752 7389 1751 1521 Commercial printing, offset; swimming pool & hot tub service & maintenance; carpentry work; new construction, single-family houses

### (G-2269)
### SCHROEDERS PALLET SERVICE
13601 Western Ave (60406-5057)
PHONE ................................ 708 371-9046
Dewain Schroeder, *President*
EMP: 6
SALES (est): 760.9K **Privately Held**
SIC: 2448 Pallets, wood & wood with metal

### (G-2270)
### SIGNODE INDUSTRIAL GROUP LLC
Also Called: Down River
14153 Western Ave (60406-3421)
P.O. Box 341, Posen (60469-0341)
PHONE ................................ 708 371-9050
Fax: 708 371-9993
Wayne Dziadosz, *Manager*
EMP: 38 **Privately Held**
SIC: 2679 Paper products, converted
HQ: Signode Industrial Group Llc
     3650 W Lake Ave
     Glenview IL 60026
     847 724-7500

### (G-2271)
### SOLVAY USA INC
14000 Seeley Ave (60406-3261)
PHONE ................................ 708 371-2000
Brad Balint, *Plant Mgr*
Jim Click, *Engineer*
Calvin Trock, *Manager*
EMP: 42
SALES (corp-wide): 11.4MM **Privately Held**
WEB: www.food.us.rhodia.com
SIC: 2819 2869 2843 Inorganic acids, except nitric & phosphoric; industrial organic chemicals; surface active agents
HQ: Solvay Usa Inc.
     504 Carnegie Ctr
     Princeton NJ 08540
     609 860-4000

### (G-2272)
### WILL COUNTY WASTE
12807 Homan Ave (60406-3573)
PHONE ................................ 708 489-9718
Bob Wiersema, *Principal*
EMP: 3
SALES (est): 244.7K **Privately Held**
SIC: 3089 Garbage containers, plastic

### (G-2273)
### XCLUSIVE AUTO SALES & SECURITY
2410 Oak St (60406-2033)
PHONE ................................ 708 897-9990
Gordon Hill, *Principal*
EMP: 5
SALES (est): 222.4K **Privately Held**
SIC: 3728 Wing assemblies & parts, aircraft

# GEOGRAPHIC SECTION
## Bolingbrook - Will County (G-2300)

### Blue Mound
*Macon County*

**(G-2274)**
**YODER JOHN**
2580 N 1500 East Rd (62513-8626)
P.O. Box 111 (62513-0111)
PHONE.....................217 676-3430
John Yoder, *Partner*
**EMP:** 3
**SALES (est):** 227.3K  Privately Held
**SIC:** 3523  0291  Driers (farm): grain, hay & seed; livestock farm, general

### Bolingbrook
*Will County*

**(G-2275)**
**7000 INC**
Also Called: Hmg
856 Fieldcrest Dr (60490-5444)
P.O. Box 9413, Naperville (60567-0413)
PHONE.....................312 800-3612
Mary Gjondla, *CEO*
Fred K Gjondla, *CFO*
**EMP:** 10
**SALES:** 10MM  Privately Held
**SIC:** 3829  7319  3845  3841  Thermometers & temperature sensors; media buying service; patient monitoring apparatus; diagnostic apparatus, medical; management consulting services; computer related maintenance services

**(G-2276)**
**ABB INC**
Also Called: Turbine Charging Unit
1 Territorial Ct Ste A (60440-3671)
PHONE.....................630 759-7428
Fax: 630 771-2109
Rich Napul, *Branch Mgr*
**EMP:** 11
**SALES (corp-wide):** 33.8B  Privately Held
**WEB:** www.elsterelectricity.com
**SIC:** 3511  Turbines & turbine generator sets
**HQ:** Abb Inc.
12040 Regency Pkwy # 200
Cary NC 27518
919 856-2360

**(G-2277)**
**ADVANTAGE SEAL INC**
694 Veterans Pkwy Ste A (60440-4618)
PHONE.....................630 226-0200
Kelly Clark, *President*
Michael Compton, *Vice Pres*
Dennis Spears, *Vice Pres*
Nestor Solis, *Admin Sec*
▲ **EMP:** 14
**SQ FT:** 5,000
**SALES:** 1.3MM  Privately Held
**WEB:** www.advantageseal.com
**SIC:** 3053  Oil seals, rubber

**(G-2278)**
**ARTISTIC DENTAL STUDIO INC**
470 Woodcreek Dr (60440-4913)
PHONE.....................630 679-8686
Fax: 630 679-8680
Jerry Ulaszek, *President*
Kathy Deady, *Accountant*
Jim Oneal, *Mktg Coord*
Anthony Calonico, *Department Mgr*
Paul McGrath, *Manager*
**EMP:** 47
**SQ FT:** 9,300
**SALES (est):** 5.5MM  Privately Held
**WEB:** www.artisticdentalstudio.com
**SIC:** 8072  3843  3842  Dental laboratories; dental equipment & supplies; surgical appliances & supplies

**(G-2279)**
**ATHLLETE LLC**
948 W Briarcliff Rd (60440-5216)
PHONE.....................773 829-3752
Qaisar Imran, *President*
**EMP:** 10
**SALES (est):** 331.8K  Privately Held
**SIC:** 2329  2339  5136  Men's & boys' sportswear & athletic clothing; women's & misses' athletic clothing & sportswear; men's & boys' sportswear & work clothing

**(G-2280)**
**ATLANTIS PRODUCTS INC**
586 Territorial Dr Ste H (60440-4885)
PHONE.....................630 971-9680
Marie Murphy, *President*
Gerhard Schiller, *General Mgr*
Linda Zielinski, *Office Mgr*
**EMP:** 5
**SQ FT:** 3,200
**SALES (est):** 520K  Privately Held
**SIC:** 3446  3315  Railings, bannisters, guards, etc.: made from metal pipe; fence gates posts & fittings: steel

**(G-2281)**
**AWARD EMBLEM MFG CO INC**
179 E South Frontage Rd (60440-3512)
PHONE.....................630 739-0800
R Jason Klein, *President*
Jason Klein, *Controller*
**EMP:** 16 EST: 1946
**SQ FT:** 15,000
**SALES (est):** 2.9MM  Privately Held
**WEB:** www.awardemblem.com
**SIC:** 5999  3911  3993  2395  Trophies & plaques; mountings, gold or silver: pens, leather goods, etc.; signs & advertising specialties; pleating & stitching

**(G-2282)**
**BALDOR ELECTRIC COMPANY**
1055 Remington Blvd Ste B (60440-4616)
PHONE.....................630 296-1400
**EMP:** 157
**SALES (corp-wide):** 33.8B  Privately Held
**SIC:** 3621  Motors & generators
**HQ:** Baldor Electric Company
5711 Rs Boreham Jr St
Fort Smith AR 72901
479 646-4711

**(G-2283)**
**CAPTIVISION INC**
263 Heritage Ct (60490-1432)
PHONE.....................630 235-8763
Randall Klotter, *CEO*
**EMP:** 3 EST: 2015
**SALES (est):** 71.1K  Privately Held
**SIC:** 7372  7389  Business oriented computer software;

**(G-2284)**
**CARPENTER TECHNOLOGY CORP**
Also Called: Carpenter Specialty Alloys
902 Carlow Dr (60490-3100)
PHONE.....................630 771-1020
Bill Goodall, *Manager*
**EMP:** 8
**SALES (corp-wide):** 1.8B  Publicly Held
**WEB:** www.cartech.com
**SIC:** 3312  Stainless steel
**PA:** Carpenter Technology Corporation
1735 Market St Fl 15
Philadelphia PA 19103
610 208-2000

**(G-2285)**
**CASCO MANUFACTURING INC**
600 Territorial Dr Ste C (60440-5128)
PHONE.....................630 771-9555
Jackie K James, *President*
Bunny Horner, *Accounts Mgr*
Alf Knudsen, *Mktg Dir*
Minerva Santiago, *Manager*
**EMP:** 30
**SQ FT:** 14,000
**SALES (est):** 7.9MM  Privately Held
**WEB:** www.cascomanufacturing.com
**SIC:** 3679  Harness assemblies for electronic use: wire or cable

**(G-2286)**
**CHICAGO PASTRY INC**
Knead Dough Bakery
556 Saint James Gate (60440-3635)
PHONE.....................630 972-0404
Fax: 630 972-0051
Rod Wetmort, *General Mgr*
John Kogelman, *Manager*
**EMP:** 150
**SALES (corp-wide):** 124.2MM  Privately Held
**SIC:** 2051  Bakery: wholesale or wholesale/retail combined
**PA:** Chicago Pastry, Inc.
6501 Roosevelt Rd
Berwyn IL 60402
708 788-5320

**(G-2287)**
**CONTINENT CORP**
227 Tiger St (60490-2054)
PHONE.....................773 733-1584
Yuriy Makoviychuk, *General Mgr*
**EMP:** 4
**SALES (est):** 192.5K  Privately Held
**SIC:** 2759  5136  5137  Janitorial service, contract basis

**(G-2288)**
**COPE PLASTICS INC**
4 Territorial Ct (60440-3531)
PHONE.....................630 226-1664
Jane Saale, *President*
**EMP:** 13
**SALES (est):** 1.5MM  Privately Held
**SIC:** 3081  Unsupported plastics film & sheet

**(G-2289)**
**CRANE COMPOSITES INC**
594 Territorial Dr Ste D (60440-5143)
PHONE.....................630 378-9580
Jeff Craney, *President*
**EMP:** 81
**SALES (corp-wide):** 2.7B  Publicly Held
**SIC:** 3089  Panels, building: plastic
**HQ:** Crane Composites, Inc.
23525 W Eames St
Channahon IL 60410
815 467-8600

**(G-2290)**
**CRANE NUCLEAR INC**
Also Called: Crane Valve Services
860 Remington Blvd (60440-4910)
PHONE.....................630 226-4900
Fax: 630 226-4646
David Dwyer, *Engineer*
Jerry Kurowski, *Engineer*
Joann Conroy, *Manager*
**EMP:** 50
**SALES (corp-wide):** 2.7B  Publicly Held
**SIC:** 3492  Electrohydraulic servo valves, metal
**HQ:** Crane Nuclear, Inc.
2825 Cobb Intl Blvd Nw
Kennesaw GA 30152
770 424-6343

**(G-2291)**
**CRETA FARMS USA LLC**
654 Cochise Cir (60440-2684)
PHONE.....................630 282-5964
**EMP:** 6
**SALES (est):** 341.6K  Privately Held
**SIC:** 2013  Sausages & other prepared meats

**(G-2292)**
**CTG ADVANCED MATERIALS LLC**
Also Called: Hc Materials
479 Quadrangle Dr Ste E (60440-3652)
PHONE.....................630 226-9080
**EMP:** 21 EST: 2013
**SALES (est):** 1.8MM  Privately Held
**SIC:** 3812  3845  Manufactures Piezoelectric Single Crystals For Acoustic Transduction Devices

**(G-2293)**
**CTS ADVANCED MATERIALS LLC**
479 Quadrangle Dr Ste E (60440-3652)
PHONE.....................630 226-9080
Kieran O'Sullivan, *President*
John Hager, *Controller*
Michael Pavlikowski, *Manager*
▲ **EMP:** 33
**SALES (est):** 7.8MM
**SALES (corp-wide):** 396.6MM  Publicly Held
**SIC:** 3531  Construction machinery
**HQ:** Cts Electronic Components, Inc.
2375 Cabot Dr
Lisle IL 60532
630 577-8800

**(G-2294)**
**CUPCAKEOLOGIST LLC**
751 E Boughton Rd (60440-2281)
PHONE.....................630 656-2272
Mikhail Milad, *Principal*
**EMP:** 4
**SALES (est):** 295.6K  Privately Held
**SIC:** 2051  Bread, cake & related products

**(G-2295)**
**CUSTOM BOXES INC**
681 W Briarcliff Rd (60440-6146)
PHONE.....................630 364-3944
Amir Bashir, *President*
**EMP:** 3
**SALES (est):** 82.1K  Privately Held
**SIC:** 2711  Newspapers

**(G-2296)**
**D & D MANUFACTURING INC**
500 Territorial Dr (60440-4814)
PHONE.....................888 300-6869
Ed Titus, *Engineer*
Michael Komarek, *Accountant*
Eduardo Frias, *Sales Mgr*
Yuri Steventon, *Cust Mgr*
Steve Capo, *Director*
**EMP:** 7
**SALES (est):** 2MM  Privately Held
**SIC:** 3699  Appliance cords for household electrical equipment

**(G-2297)**
**D & D TOOLING AND MFG INC (PA)**
Also Called: D & D Manufacturing Entps
500 Territorial Dr (60440-4814)
PHONE.....................888 300-6869
William Diedrick, *President*
Mike Shaven, *Plant Mgr*
Tim Hager, *Production*
Steve Harris, *QC Dir*
Fernando Valdez, *QC Dir*
**EMP:** 85
**SALES (est):** 25MM  Privately Held
**WEB:** www.ddmfg.com
**SIC:** 3469  Metal stampings

**(G-2298)**
**D & D TOOLING INC**
500 Territorial Dr (60440-4814)
PHONE.....................630 759-0015
William Diedrick, *President*
Lawrence Diedrick, *Vice Pres*
Jodi Sisson, *Plant Mgr*
Krystyna Szewczyk, *Engineer*
**EMP:** 150
**SQ FT:** 10,000
**SALES (est):** 22.6MM  Privately Held
**WEB:** www.portal.net.au
**SIC:** 3544  Special dies & tools

**(G-2299)**
**DANIEL M POWERS & ASSOC LTD**
575 W Crossroads Pkwy B (60440-5096)
PHONE.....................630 685-8400
Fax: 630 685-8401
Theresa Vanek, *CEO*
Pamela Newman, *Chairman*
Kean Irwin, *District Mgr*
Alan Vanichtheeranont, *COO*
Jerry Grigsby, *Mfg Staff*
▲ **EMP:** 60
**SQ FT:** 110,000
**SALES (est):** 24.3MM  Privately Held
**WEB:** www.powersinet.com
**SIC:** 5046  2541  2521  2434  Store fixtures; store fixtures, wood; wood office furniture; wood kitchen cabinets; millwork

**(G-2300)**
**DE BOER & ASSOCIATES**
736 Dorchester Dr (60440-1161)
PHONE.....................630 972-1600
Douglas De Boer, *Owner*
**EMP:** 2
**SALES:** 250K  Privately Held
**SIC:** 2711  Commercial printing & newspaper publishing combined

## Bolingbrook - Will County (G-2301)

**(G-2301)**
**DEJA INVESTMENTS INC (PA)**
279 Marquette Dr (60440-3600)
P.O. Box 270, Hinsdale (60522-6004)
PHONE................................630 408-9222
Edward K Gignac, *President*
John Hartline, *Vice Pres*
Ken Forsberg, *Mfg Staff*
Vanessa Jackson, *Purchasing*
Nicky Oates, *QC Dir*
**EMP:** 60 **EST:** 1922
**SQ FT:** 43,000
**SALES (est):** 7.1MM **Privately Held**
**SIC:** 2023 2099 2026 2024 Ice cream mix, unfrozen: liquid or dry; yogurt mix; milkshake mix; whipped topping, dry mix; food preparations; fluid milk; ice cream & frozen desserts

**(G-2302)**
**DTRS ENTERPRISES INC**
Also Called: Savile Rumtini
1317 Rosemary Dr (60490-4940)
PHONE................................630 296-6890
Didrielle D Tutt, *President*
Richard Smith, *Vice Pres*
**EMP:** 2
**SALES (est):** 220K **Privately Held**
**SIC:** 5182 7389 2085 Wine & distilled beverages; ; distilled & blended liquors

**(G-2303)**
**EFCO CORPORATION**
595 Territorial Dr Ste A (60440-4631)
PHONE................................630 378-4720
Fax: 630 378-4887
Rob Jones, *Branch Mgr*
**EMP:** 27
**SALES (corp-wide):** 2.1B **Privately Held**
**SIC:** 3442 3354 Metal doors, sash & trim; aluminum extruded products
**HQ:** Efco Corporation
1000 County Rd
Monett MO 65708
800 221-4169

**(G-2304)**
**ELAN INDUSTRIES INC**
650 S Schmidt Rd Ard (60440-9403)
PHONE................................630 679-2000
Todd A Thomas, *President*
John Tomaras, *COO*
James M Ralson, *Vice Pres*
Amy Thomas, *Production*
Brian Frank, *Engineer*
▲ **EMP:** 13
**SQ FT:** 10,000
**SALES:** 10.3MM **Privately Held**
**WEB:** www.elanindustries.com
**SIC:** 3679 Electronic circuits

**(G-2305)**
**ELMHURST-CHICAGO STONE COMPANY**
351 Royce Rd (60440-9053)
PHONE................................630 983-6410
Jim Wilson, *Manager*
**EMP:** 30
**SALES (corp-wide):** 122.7MM **Privately Held**
**SIC:** 1422 3273 3272 1442 Cement rock, crushed & broken-quarrying; ready-mixed concrete; concrete products; construction sand & gravel
**PA:** Elmhurst-Chicago Stone Company
400 W 1st St
Elmhurst IL 60126
630 832-4000

**(G-2306)**
**EPIR INC**
590 Territorial Dr Ste B (60440-4634)
PHONE................................630 842-0893
Fax: 630 771-0204
Paul Boieriu, *President*
**EMP:** 3
**SALES (est):** 260K **Privately Held**
**SIC:** 3674 Semiconductors & related devices

**(G-2307)**
**EPIR TECHNOLOGIES INC**
590 Territorial Dr Ste B (60440-4634)
PHONE................................630 771-0203
Sivalingam Sivananthan, *CEO*
Kasivisvananthan Chelvakumar, *President*
Christoph H Grein, *Vice Pres*
Chelva Kumar, *CFO*
Kasi Chelvakumar, *Finance*
**EMP:** 43
**SQ FT:** 52,000
**SALES (est):** 8.7MM **Privately Held**
**WEB:** www.epir.com
**SIC:** 3674 3812 8731 Infrared sensors, solid state; infrared object detection equipment; commercial physical research

**(G-2308)**
**FEDEX OFFICE & PRINT SVCS INC**
251 S Weber Rd (60490-1502)
PHONE................................630 759-5784
Fax: 630 759-6726
Brandy Lucas, *Branch Mgr*
**EMP:** 5
**SALES (corp-wide):** 50.3B **Publicly Held**
**WEB:** www.kinkos.com
**SIC:** 2759 4822 5099 7334 Commercial printing; facsimile transmission services; signs, except electric; photocopying & duplicating services
**HQ:** Fedex Office And Print Services, Inc.
7900 Legacy Dr
Plano TX 75024
214 550-7000

**(G-2309)**
**FERRARA CANDY COMPANY**
901 Carlow Dr (60490-3240)
PHONE................................630 378-4197
**EMP:** 6
**SALES (corp-wide):** 616.5MM **Privately Held**
**SIC:** 2064 Candy & other confectionery products; chewing candy, not chewing gum; chocolate candy, except solid chocolate; jellybeans
**PA:** Ferrara Candy Company
1 Tower Ln Ste 2700
Oakbrook Terrace IL 60181
708 366-0500

**(G-2310)**
**FLOW PRO PRODUCTS INC**
1000 W Crssrds Pkwy 1 (60490)
PHONE................................815 836-1900
John Ruesch, *President*
Bob Holmgren, *Sales Mgr*
Turhan Tilev, *Manager*
Turhan Tiley, *Admin Sec*
▲ **EMP:** 13
**SQ FT:** 9,000
**SALES (est):** 4.2MM **Privately Held**
**WEB:** www.flowproinc.com
**SIC:** 3569 Filters

**(G-2311)**
**FOREST ENVELOPE COMPANY**
309 E Crossroads Pkwy (60440-3539)
PHONE................................630 515-1200
Fax: 708 515-1212
Jack W Wagner, *President*
John F Wagner, *Vice Pres*
Brian Dietrich, *Accounts Mgr*
Phyllis E Wagner, *Admin Sec*
**EMP:** 43 **EST:** 1976
**SQ FT:** 30,000
**SALES (est):** 12MM **Privately Held**
**WEB:** www.forestenvelope.com
**SIC:** 2677 2759 Envelopes; envelopes: printing

**(G-2312)**
**GENERAL CONVERTING INC**
Also Called: GCI
250 W Crossroads Pkwy (60440-3546)
PHONE................................630 378-9800
Robert W Ruebenson, *President*
John Swanstrom, *Purchasing*
Hardy Schuster, *Engineer*
Shirley V Ruebenson, *Admin Sec*
**EMP:** 60
**SQ FT:** 125,000
**SALES (est):** 16.6MM **Privately Held**
**WEB:** www.generalconverting.com
**SIC:** 2657 Folding paperboard boxes

**(G-2313)**
**GENERAL MOTORS LLC**
1355 Remington Blvd (60490-3254)
PHONE................................815 733-0668
Stephanie Malvie, *Manager*
**EMP:** 200 **Publicly Held**
**SIC:** 3714 5013 Motor vehicle parts & accessories; motor vehicle supplies & new parts
**HQ:** General Motors Llc
300 Renaissance Ctr L1
Detroit MI 48243

**(G-2314)**
**GRAPHIC SCIENCES INC**
582 Territorial Dr Ste A (60440-4603)
PHONE................................630 226-0994
Kent Wishart, *President*
Robert Lee, *Warehouse Mgr*
Dorcie Watson, *Accountant*
**EMP:** 9
**SALES (est):** 1.2MM **Privately Held**
**SIC:** 2899 Ink or writing fluids

**(G-2315)**
**HARMON INC**
100 E Crssrds Pkwy Ste B (60440)
PHONE................................630 759-8060
Wally Zabierek, *General Mgr*
Thomas Niepokoj, *Branch Mgr*
Steve Griest, *Manager*
**EMP:** 20
**SALES (corp-wide):** 1.1B **Publicly Held**
**WEB:** www.harmoninc.com
**SIC:** 3449 Curtain wall, metal; curtain walls for buildings, steel
**HQ:** Harmon, Inc.
7900 Xerxes Ave S # 1800
Bloomington MN 55431
952 944-5700

**(G-2316)**
**HOVI INDUSTRIES INCORPORATED (PA)**
Also Called: Perkins Manfacturing
380 Veterans Pkwy Ste 110 (60440-4667)
PHONE................................815 512-7500
Robert Hoppe Sr, *Ch of Bd*
◆ **EMP:** 38
**SALES (est):** 13.2MM **Privately Held**
**SIC:** 5084 3444 7699 6719 Trucks, industrial; metal housings, enclosures, casings & other containers; sewer cleaning & rodding; investment holding companies, except banks

**(G-2317)**
**HUSSAIN SHAHEEN**
Also Called: Need
1900 Danube Way (60490-6500)
PHONE................................630 405-8009
Shaheen Hussain, *Owner*
**EMP:** 3 **EST:** 2014
**SALES (est):** 144.5K **Privately Held**
**SIC:** 2819 Industrial inorganic chemicals

**(G-2318)**
**IFCO**
400 W Crssrds Pkwy Ste A (60440)
PHONE................................630 226-0650
Jim Hillock, *General Mgr*
**EMP:** 6 **EST:** 2009
**SALES (est):** 988.9K **Privately Held**
**SIC:** 2448 Pallets, wood

**(G-2319)**
**IMI MANUFACTURING INC**
694 Veterans Pkwy Ste B (60440-3599)
PHONE................................630 771-0003
Theodore Hofmeister Jr, *President*
Diane Hofmeister, *Admin Sec*
**EMP:** 6
**SQ FT:** 5,000
**SALES (est):** 540K **Privately Held**
**SIC:** 3599 Custom machinery

**(G-2320)**
**IMPRO INDUSTRIES USA INC**
375 Sw Frontage Rd Ste D (60440)
PHONE................................630 759-0280
Letian Qin, *Engineer*
**EMP:** 5 **Privately Held**
**SIC:** 3369 Castings, except die-castings, precision
**HQ:** Impro Industries Usa, Inc.
21660 Copley Dr Ste 100
Diamond Bar CA 91765
909 396-6525

**(G-2321)**
**INSTITUTIONAL EQUIPMENT INC (PA)**
Also Called: Iei
704 Veterans Pkwy Ste B (60440-4612)
PHONE................................630 771-0990
Fax: 630 771-0994
Franklin Fiene, *President*
James Schultz, *Vice Pres*
Kathy Epler, *Personnel Exec*
Susan Enlow, *Admin Sec*
**EMP:** 27
**SQ FT:** 21,000
**SALES (est):** 12.2MM **Privately Held**
**WEB:** www.ieiusa.net
**SIC:** 5046 3556 Commercial cooking & food service equipment; food products machinery

**(G-2322)**
**INTEGRATED LIGHTING TECH INC (PA)**
Also Called: Integrating Green Technologies
1317 Rosemary Dr (60490-4940)
PHONE................................630 750-3786
Carl Tutt, *President*
**EMP:** 1
**SALES (est):** 258K **Privately Held**
**SIC:** 3674 7389 Light emitting diodes;

**(G-2323)**
**INTERSCIENCE TECHNOLOGIES INC**
Also Called: Interscience International
205 Sunshine Dr Bldg 100 (60490-1543)
PHONE................................630 759-4444
Stuart Lagerbauer, *President*
Kirk Kenneth, *Vice Pres*
**EMP:** 7
**SALES:** 100K **Privately Held**
**WEB:** www.mailpower.net
**SIC:** 7372 4813 Prepackaged software; telephone communication, except radio

**(G-2324)**
**INTERSTATE CARGO INC**
380 Internationale Dr A (60440-3638)
PHONE................................630 701-7744
Ilhom Bobohonov, *President*
Nelly Shukur, *Manager*
**EMP:** 24 **EST:** 2013
**SQ FT:** 9,000
**SALES (est):** 4.4MM **Privately Held**
**SIC:** 3537 Truck trailers, used in plants, docks, terminals, etc.

**(G-2325)**
**ISHOT PRODUCTS INC**
558 Payton Ln (60440-3520)
P.O. Box 1668 (60440-7368)
PHONE................................312 497-4190
Christopher R Fliger, *President*
▲ **EMP:** 6
**SQ FT:** 900
**SALES:** 200K **Privately Held**
**SIC:** 3861 Tripods, camera & projector

**(G-2326)**
**J DESIGN WORKS INC**
210 Ironbark Way (60440-3076)
PHONE................................847 812-0891
John Williams, *President*
▲ **EMP:** 2
**SALES:** 1MM **Privately Held**
**SIC:** 2393 Textile bags

**(G-2327)**
**JERNBERG INDUSTRIES LLC**
Also Called: Jernberg of Bolingbrook
455 Gibraltar Dr (60440-3617)
PHONE................................630 972-7000
Larry Wolyniet, *Manager*
**EMP:** 130
**SALES (corp-wide):** 3.9B **Publicly Held**
**SIC:** 3462 Iron & steel forgings
**HQ:** Jernberg Industries, Llc
328 W 40th Pl
Chicago IL 60609
773 268-3004

**(G-2328)**
**JEWEL OSCO INC**
Also Called: Jewel-Osco 3013
1200 W Boughton Rd (60440-6568)
PHONE................................630 226-1892

▲ = Import ▼=Export
◆ =Import/Export

## GEOGRAPHIC SECTION
**Bolingbrook - Will County (G-2354)**

Fax: 630 226-0260
Steven Ranch, *Manager*
**EMP:** 100
**SALES (corp-wide):** 58.8B **Privately Held**
**WEB:** www.jewelosco.com
**SIC:** 5411 5912 5421 2051 Supermarkets, chain; drug stores & proprietary stores; meat & fish markets; bread, cake & related products
**HQ:** Jewel Osco, Inc.
150 E Pierce Rd Ste 200
Itasca IL 60143
630 948-6000

**(G-2329)**
**JOHN MORRELL & CO**
Also Called: Saratoga Food Specialties
771 W Crssroads Pkwy Ste A (60490)
P.O. Box 39604
**PHONE**..................630 993-8763
**Fax:** 630 993-8732
Wade McGeorge, *Branch Mgr*
James Bajna, *Manager*
**EMP:** 225
**SQ FT:** 95,000 **Privately Held**
**WEB:** www.johnmorrell.com
**SIC:** 2099 Seasonings & spices
**HQ:** Morrell John & Co
805 E Kemper Rd
Cincinnati OH 45246
513 782-3800

**(G-2330)**
**KAM GROUP INC**
486 W North Frontage Rd (60440-4904)
**PHONE**..................630 679-9668
MEI Zheng, *Principal*
Dan Liberty, *Accounts Exec*
Daniel Liberty, *Accounts Exec*
Michael LI, *Manager*
▲ **EMP:** 13
**SALES (est):** 1.6MM **Privately Held**
**SIC:** 2673 Bags: plastic, laminated & coated

**(G-2331)**
**KENT PRECISION FOODS GROUP INC**
1000 Dalton Ln Ste A (60490-3258)
**PHONE**..................630 226-0071
Mike Saniat, *Vice Pres*
Josh Cantwell, *Director*
Mimi Pappas, *Admin Asst*
**EMP:** 22
**SALES (corp-wide):** 613.2MM **Privately Held**
**WEB:** www.precisionfoods.com
**SIC:** 2034 2024 Dehydrated fruits, vegetables, soups; ice cream & frozen desserts
**HQ:** Kent Precision Foods Group, Inc.
11457 Olde Cabin Rd # 100
Saint Louis MO 63141
314 567-7400

**(G-2332)**
**KENT PRECISION FOODS GROUP INC**
1000 Dalton Ln Ste A (60490-3258)
**PHONE**..................630 226-0498
Pat Brundige, *Branch Mgr*
**EMP:** 22
**SALES (corp-wide):** 613.2MM **Privately Held**
**SIC:** 2034 Dehydrated fruits, vegetables, soups
**HQ:** Kent Precision Foods Group, Inc.
11457 Olde Cabin Rd # 100
Saint Louis MO 63141
314 567-7400

**(G-2333)**
**KPS CAPITAL PARTNERS LP**
Also Called: MST Div
455 Gibraltar Dr (60440-3617)
**PHONE**..................630 972-7000
M E Wheeler, *CEO*
Larry Wolyniec, *Executive*
**EMP:** 4
**SALES (corp-wide):** 2.3B **Privately Held**
**SIC:** 3559 Automotive related machinery
**PA:** Kps Capital Partners, Lp
485 Lexington Ave Fl 31
New York NY 10017
212 338-5100

**(G-2334)**
**KRACK CORPORATION**
890 Remington Blvd Ste A (60440-4994)
**PHONE**..................630 250-0187
Gordon Shaw, *Principal*
Kathern Chung, *Controller*
Steve Touge, *VP Human Res*
Nichole Nicholson, *Human Res Dir*
Steven Pouge, *Human Res Dir*
◆ **EMP:** 30
**SQ FT:** 225,000
**SALES (est):** 4.9MM
**SALES (corp-wide):** 64.6B **Privately Held**
**WEB:** www.hussmann.com
**SIC:** 3585 Refrigeration equipment, complete
**HQ:** Hussmann Corporation
12999 St Charles Rock Rd
Bridgeton MO 63044
314 291-2000

**(G-2335)**
**LINCOLN ELECTRIC COMPANY**
115 E Crlroads Pkwy Ste A (60440)
**PHONE**..................630 783-3600
Dave Thayer, *Principal*
**EMP:** 11
**SALES (corp-wide):** 2.2B **Publicly Held**
**WEB:** www.subarc-welding.com
**SIC:** 5085 5169 2796 Welding supplies; gases, compressed & liquefied; electrotype plates
**HQ:** Lincoln Electric Company
22801 Saint Clair Ave
Euclid OH 44117
216 481-8100

**(G-2336)**
**LITHOTYPE COMPANY INC**
594 Territorial Dr Ste G (60440-5143)
**PHONE**..................630 771-1920
Bruce Weintraub, *Branch Mgr*
**EMP:** 12
**SALES (corp-wide):** 39MM **Privately Held**
**WEB:** www.lithotype.com
**SIC:** 2752 Wrappers, lithographed
**PA:** Lithotype Company, Inc.
333 Point San Bruno Blvd
South San Francisco CA 94080
650 871-1750

**(G-2337)**
**LOCKER ROOM SCREEN PRINTING**
253 S Schmidt Rd (60440-2746)
**PHONE**..................630 759-2533
**Fax:** 630 759-5532
Tom Pondel, *Owner*
**EMP:** 3
**SQ FT:** 1,700
**SALES:** 350K **Privately Held**
**SIC:** 2759 2396 Screen printing; automotive & apparel trimmings

**(G-2338)**
**LURE GROUP LLC**
5 Privett Ct (60490-2016)
**PHONE**..................630 222-6515
Marc A Eltoft,
**EMP:** 2
**SALES (est):** 215.5K **Privately Held**
**SIC:** 2752 8742 Commercial printing, lithographic; marketing consulting services

**(G-2339)**
**MANDYS KITCHEN & GRILL** ✪
Also Called: A-Z Stepping Stones
431u N Bolingbrook Dr (60440)
**PHONE**..................630 348-2264
Neenah Powell, *President*
Delicia Bowling, *Vice Pres*
**EMP:** 7 **EST:** 2016
**SALES (est):** 95.9K **Privately Held**
**SIC:** 5812 2051 Eating places; family restaurants; restaurant, family: independent; caterers; bakery: wholesale or wholesale/retail combined

**(G-2340)**
**MENASHA PACKAGING COMPANY LLC**
800 S Weber Rd Ste A (60490-5612)
**PHONE**..................815 639-0144
**EMP:** 200

**SALES (corp-wide):** 1.8B **Privately Held**
**SIC:** 2653 Sheets, corrugated: made from purchased materials
**HQ:** Menasha Packaging Company, Llc
1645 Bergstrom Rd
Neenah WI 54956
920 751-1000

**(G-2341)**
**METALS & METALS LLC**
Also Called: Metalsupermarkets LLC
999 Remington Blvd Ste C (60440-4871)
**PHONE**..................630 866-4200
Shirin Lakdawala,
**EMP:** 5
**SQ FT:** 5,000
**SALES:** 500K **Privately Held**
**SIC:** 3441 Fabricated structural metal

**(G-2342)**
**MINNESOTA OFFICE TECHNOLOGY**
4 Territorial Ct Ste S (60440-3531)
**PHONE**..................312 236-0400
**EMP:** 3
**SALES (est):** 270.1K
**SALES (corp-wide):** 10.7B **Publicly Held**
**SIC:** 3823 Programmers, process type
**PA:** Xerox Corporation
201 Merritt 7
Norwalk CT 06851
203 968-3000

**(G-2343)**
**MISS JOANS CUPCAKES**
1899 Marne Rd (60490-4593)
**PHONE**..................630 881-5707
**EMP:** 4
**SALES (est):** 230.7K **Privately Held**
**SIC:** 2051 Bread, cake & related products

**(G-2344)**
**MOHAWK INDUSTRIES INC**
969 Veterans Pkwy Ste B (60490-3520)
**PHONE**..................630 972-8000
**Fax:** 630 972-5715
Gary Bengtson, *Sales & Mktg St*
Natalie Neace, *Marketing Staff*
Joe Zasaitis, *Supervisor*
**EMP:** 70
**SALES (corp-wide):** 8.9B **Publicly Held**
**WEB:** www.mohawkind.com
**SIC:** 2273 Wilton carpets; rugs, tufted
**PA:** Mohawk Industries, Inc.
160 S Industrial Blvd
Calhoun GA 30701
706 629-7721

**(G-2345)**
**MOLEX LLC**
575 Veterans Pkwy Ste A (60440-4622)
**PHONE**..................630 527-4363
Jim Kicher, *Branch Mgr*
**EMP:** 7
**SALES (corp-wide):** 27.4B **Privately Held**
**SIC:** 3679 3643 3357 Antennas, receiving; electronic circuits; connectors & terminals for electrical devices; communication wire; fiber optic cable (insulated)
**HQ:** Molex, Llc
2222 Wellington Ct
Lisle IL 60532
630 969-4550

**(G-2346)**
**MOLEX LLC**
575 Veterans Pkwy Ste A (60440-4622)
**PHONE**..................630 969-4747
Robert Bartos, *Manager*
Jim Kicher, *Executive*
**EMP:** 30
**SALES (corp-wide):** 27.4B **Privately Held**
**WEB:** www.molex.com
**SIC:** 3678 Electronic connectors
**HQ:** Molex, Llc
2222 Wellington Ct
Lisle IL 60532
630 969-4550

**(G-2347)**
**MPS CHICAGO INC**
315 Eisenhower Ln S (60440)
**PHONE**..................630 932-5583
**Fax:** 630 691-2168
Judy Clohessy, *Administration*

**EMP:** 50
**SALES (corp-wide):** 14.1B **Publicly Held**
**WEB:** www.jetlitho.com
**SIC:** 2759 Commercial printing
**HQ:** Mps Chicago, Inc.
1500 Centre Cir
Downers Grove IL 60515
630 932-9000

**(G-2348)**
**MULTI-PLASTICS INC**
606 Territorial Dr Ste C (60440-4936)
**PHONE**..................630 226-0580
Stewart Smolkovich, *Principal*
Mike Budd, *Marketing Mgr*
**EMP:** 40
**SALES (corp-wide):** 208MM **Privately Held**
**WEB:** www.multi-plastics.com
**SIC:** 3089 3081 Plastic processing; unsupported plastics film & sheet
**PA:** Multi-Plastics, Inc.
7770 N Central Dr
Lewis Center OH 43035
740 548-4894

**(G-2349)**
**MUSIC SOLUTIONS**
490 Woodcreek Dr Ste D (60440-1394)
**PHONE**..................630 759-3033
Steve Dollinger, *Partner*
Ronald Lukowski, *Partner*
**EMP:** 10
**SQ FT:** 2,000
**SALES:** 320K **Privately Held**
**WEB:** www.musicsolutionsstore.com
**SIC:** 5735 3931 Record & prerecorded tape stores; guitars & parts, electric & nonelectric; musical instruments, electric & electronic

**(G-2350)**
**NETRANIX ENTERPRISE**
336 Pinto Dr (60440-1724)
Carlos Johnson, *CEO*
Anitra Thomas, *COO*
**EMP:** 10
**SALES (est):** 398.8K **Privately Held**
**SIC:** 1521 2211 General remodeling, single-family houses; apparel & outerwear fabrics, cotton

**(G-2351)**
**NEVERIA MICHOACANA LLC**
132 N Bolingbrook Dr (60440-2350)
**PHONE**..................630 783-3518
**EMP:** 3
**SALES (est):** 162.6K **Privately Held**
**SIC:** 2024 Ice cream, bulk

**(G-2352)**
**NEW YORK & COMPANY INC**
639 E Boughton Rd Ste 135 (60440-3138)
**PHONE**..................630 783-2910
Heidi Velasquez, *Manager*
**EMP:** 17
**SALES (corp-wide):** 929MM **Publicly Held**
**WEB:** www.nyco.com
**SIC:** 5621 2389 5137 Women's specialty clothing stores; men's miscellaneous accessories; women's & children's clothing
**PA:** New York & Company, Inc.
330 W 34th St Fl 9
New York NY 10001
212 884-2000

**(G-2353)**
**NEXUS SUPPLY CONSORTIUM INC**
13g Fernwood Dr (60440-2926)
**PHONE**..................630 649-2868
Lavenia Tyler, *President*
Dorian Yamini, *Principal*
**EMP:** 7
**SALES (est):** 365.8K **Privately Held**
**SIC:** 7359 5045 2731 Office machine rental, except computers; computers, peripherals & software; books: publishing & printing

**(G-2354)**
**NON-METALS INC**
486 W North Frontage Rd (60440-4904)
**PHONE**..................630 378-9866
May Zhao, *President*

# Bolingbrook - Will County (G-2355)

Peter Wu, *Vice Pres*
Charles Zheng, *Manager*
▲ **EMP:** 6
**SQ FT:** 3,600
**SALES (est):** 1MM **Privately Held**
**WEB:** www.nonmetals.com
**SIC: 3053** 5085 Gaskets, packing & sealing devices; gaskets & seals
**PA:** China National Non-Metallic Materials Corporation
No.11, Beishuncheng St., Xizhimen Beijing
106 225-2263

## (G-2355)
### ONE ACCORD UNITY NFP
1886 Marne Rd (60490-4596)
**PHONE**....................630 649-0793
Nathaniel Smith, *CEO*
**EMP:** 4
**SALES (est):** 250.9K **Privately Held**
**SIC: 2721** Periodicals; periodicals: publishing only; statistical reports (periodicals): publishing only

## (G-2356)
### PANCON ILLINOIS LLC
440 Quadrangle Dr Ste A (60440-3455)
**PHONE**....................630 972-6400
**EMP:** 7
**SALES (est):** 330K **Privately Held**
**SIC: 3643** Mfg Conductive Wiring Devices

## (G-2357)
### PERFECTVISION MFG INC
1 Gateway Ct Ste Aa (60440-4669)
**PHONE**....................630 226-9890
Jay Siler, *Manager*
**EMP:** 111
**SALES (corp-wide):** 80.9MM **Privately Held**
**SIC: 3679** Antennas, satellite: household use
**PA:** Perfectvision Manufacturing, Inc.
16101 La Grande Dr
Little Rock AR 72223
501 955-0032

## (G-2358)
### PERKINS MANUFACTURING CO
380 Veterans Pkwy Ste 110 (60440-4667)
**PHONE**....................708 482-9500
Robert Hoppe, *President*
Terry Dilmore, *General Mgr*
Roger Phalert, *Controller*
Cheryl Waite, *Admin Sec*
▲ **EMP:** 28
**SQ FT:** 38,000
**SALES (est):** 4.5MM
**SALES (corp-wide):** 13.2MM **Privately Held**
**WEB:** www.perkinsmfg.com
**SIC: 3423** Jacks: lifting, screw or ratchet (hand tools)
**PA:** Hovi Industries, Incorporated
380 Veterans Pkwy Ste 110
Bolingbrook IL 60440
815 512-7500

## (G-2359)
### PRATER INDUSTRIES INC (HQ)
Also Called: Prater-Sterling
2 Sammons Ct (60440-4995)
**PHONE**....................630 679-3200
**Fax:** 630 759-6099
Robert W Prater, *Ch of Bd*
Robert Scott Prater, *President*
Jerry Olson, *Manager*
▲ **EMP:** 55 **EST:** 1925
**SALES (est):** 23.1MM
**SALES (corp-wide):** 25.1MM **Privately Held**
**SIC: 3556** 3523 3559 3613 Food products machinery; grinders, commercial, food; grading, cleaning, sorting machines, fruit, grain, vegetable; feed grinders, crushers & mixers; chemical machinery & equipment; control panels, electric; machine tools, metal cutting type; manufactured hardware (general)
**PA:** Industrial Magnetics, Inc.
1385 S M 75
Boyne City MI 49712
231 582-3100

## (G-2360)
### PRES-ON CORPORATION
Also Called: Pres-On Tape & Gasket
2600 E 107th St (60440-3196)
**PHONE**....................630 628-2255
**Fax:** 630 628-8025
Henry J Gianatasio, *President*
▲ **EMP:** 50 **EST:** 1949
**SALES (est):** 14.3MM **Privately Held**
**WEB:** www.pres-on.com
**SIC: 3053** 3842 3086 Gasket materials; surgical appliances & supplies; plastics foam products

## (G-2361)
### PROFESSIONAL PRINTERS
349 Marian Ct (60440-2118)
**PHONE**....................630 739-7761
David Prodehl, *Owner*
**EMP:** 3
**SQ FT:** 1,600
**SALES:** 100K **Privately Held**
**SIC: 2752** Commercial printing, lithographic

## (G-2362)
### QUAD/GRAPHICS INC
1000 Remington Blvd # 300 (60440-5114)
**PHONE**....................630 343-4400
Joel Weber, *Sales Staff*
Keith Smith, *Manager*
Jeff Stood, *Manager*
**EMP:** 509
**SALES (corp-wide):** 4.3B **Publicly Held**
**SIC: 2752** Commercial printing, lithographic
**PA:** Quad/Graphics Inc.
N61w23044 Harrys Way
Sussex WI 53089
414 566-6000

## (G-2363)
### QUALITY BLUE & OFFSET PRINTING
7 Sunshine Ct (60490-5578)
**PHONE**....................630 759-8035
**Fax:** 630 759-8036
John Albarracin, *Owner*
**EMP:** 4 **EST:** 1990
**SALES:** 100K **Privately Held**
**SIC: 2752** 7334 2759 Commercial printing, lithographic; photocopying & duplicating services; commercial printing

## (G-2364)
### REGAL JOHNSON CO
229 Christine Way (60440-6138)
**PHONE**....................630 885-0688
Chunyu Tang, *President*
**EMP:** 3
**SALES:** 5MM **Privately Held**
**SIC: 1081** Metal mining services

## (G-2365)
### SALISBURY ELEC SAFETY LLC
Also Called: Salisbury By Honeywell
101 E Crssroads Pkwy Ste A (60440)
**PHONE**....................877 406-4501
Mate Olds, *General Mgr*
Jim Sabo, *Plant Mgr*
WEI MEI, *Accounts Mgr*
Dennis Craig, *Director*
Scott Clary,
▲ **EMP:** 420
**SQ FT:** 115,000
**SALES (est):** 121.7MM
**SALES (corp-wide):** 39.3B **Publicly Held**
**SIC: 3842** Clothing, fire resistant & protective
**PA:** Honeywell International Inc.
115 Tabor Rd
Morris Plains NJ 07950
973 455-2000

## (G-2366)
### SESAME SOLUTIONS LLC
279 Beaudin Blvd (60440-5520)
**PHONE**....................630 427-3400
Tina Smith, *Manager*
Tj Harkins,
▲ **EMP:** 25
**SALES (est):** 3.2MM **Privately Held**
**WEB:** www.sesamesolutions.com
**SIC: 2068** Seeds: dried, dehydrated, salted or roasted

## (G-2367)
### SHAKTHI SOLAR INC
590 Territorial Dr Ste B (60440-4881)
**PHONE**....................630 842-0893
Paul Boieriu, *Admin Sec*
**EMP:** 3
**SALES (est):** 200.9K **Privately Held**
**SIC: 3674** Semiconductors & related devices

## (G-2368)
### SIGN & BANNER EXPRESS
540 E Boughton Rd (60440-2181)
**PHONE**....................630 783-9700
**Fax:** 630 783-8204
Kevin Parker, *Owner*
Rob Pacanti, *Sales Staff*
**EMP:** 3
**SQ FT:** 2,500
**SALES (est):** 240K **Privately Held**
**SIC: 3993** 7336 Signs & advertising specialties; graphic arts & related design

## (G-2369)
### SIGNS BY CUSTOM CUTTING INC
300 Dean Cir (60440-1827)
**PHONE**....................630 759-2734
Victor Drapal, *Principal*
**EMP:** 3
**SALES (est):** 282.8K **Privately Held**
**SIC: 3993** Signs & advertising specialties

## (G-2370)
### SILK 21 SCREEN PRINTING AND EM
505 N Pinecrest Rd (60440-2139)
**PHONE**....................630 972-4250
Willie Smith, *Owner*
**EMP:** 2 **EST:** 2011
**SALES (est):** 201.6K **Privately Held**
**SIC: 2752** Commercial printing, lithographic

## (G-2371)
### SMART PIXEL INC
590 Territorial Dr Ste B (60440-4881)
**PHONE**....................630 771-0206
Sivalingam Sivananthan, *President*
**EMP:** 2
**SALES:** 1.2MM **Privately Held**
**SIC: 3812** Detection apparatus: electronic/magnetic field, light/heat

## (G-2372)
### SMART SYSTEMS INC
554 Territorial Dr (60440-4814)
**PHONE**....................630 343-3333
Fred Halberg, *President*
Vivana Gutierrez, *Accounts Mgr*
▲ **EMP:** 47
**SALES (est):** 6.5MM **Privately Held**
**SIC: 3625** 5531 Relays & industrial controls; automotive & home supply stores

## (G-2373)
### SONOCO DISPLAY & PACKAGING LLC
Also Called: Sonoco Corrflex
101 E Crossroads Pkwy (60440-3690)
**PHONE**....................630 972-1990
Rosa Martinez, *Branch Mgr*
**EMP:** 95
**SALES (corp-wide):** 4.7B **Publicly Held**
**SIC: 3086** Packaging & shipping materials, foamed plastic
**HQ:** Sonoco Display & Packaging, Llc
555 Aureole St
Winston Salem NC 27107
336 784-0445

## (G-2374)
### SONY/ATV MUSIC PUBLISHING LLC
351 Internationale Dr (60440-3628)
**PHONE**....................630 739-8129
**EMP:** 25
**SALES (corp-wide):** 66.9B **Privately Held**
**SIC: 2741** Music book & sheet music publishing
**HQ:** Sony/Atv Music Publishing Llc
25 Madison Ave Fl 24
New York NY 10010
212 833-7730

## (G-2375)
### SPEP ACQUISITION CORP
Also Called: Sierra Pacific Engrg & Pdts
1 Gateway Ct Ste E (60440-4671)
**PHONE**....................310 608-0693
Larry Mirick, *Branch Mgr*
**EMP:** 29
**SALES (corp-wide):** 17.9MM **Privately Held**
**SIC: 3429** 5072 8711 Manufactured hardware (general); hardware; engineering services
**PA:** S.P.E.P. Acquisition Corp.
4041 Via Oro Ave
Long Beach CA 90810
310 608-0693

## (G-2376)
### STEVENSON SALES & SERVICE LLC
410 Stevenson Dr (60440-3094)
**PHONE**....................630 972-0330
Sue Platt, *Finance Mgr*
Daniel Stevenson, *Mng Member*
Julie View, *Manager*
**EMP:** 2
**SALES (est):** 572.2K **Privately Held**
**SIC: 3531** Construction machinery

## (G-2377)
### TECHNICS INC
1000 W Crossroads Pkwy J (60490-3512)
**PHONE**....................630 215-3742
Thomas Edwards, *President*
▲ **EMP:** 2
**SALES (est):** 668.5K **Privately Held**
**WEB:** www.technicsglobal.com
**SIC: 3829** Testing equipment: abrasion, shearing strength, etc.

## (G-2378)
### THYSSENKRUPP MATERIALS NA INC
905 Carlow Dr (60490-5607)
**PHONE**....................630 563-3365
**EMP:** 5
**SALES (corp-wide):** 44.2B **Privately Held**
**SIC: 5051** 5162 3444 Metals service centers & offices; aluminum bars, rods, ingots, sheets, pipes, plates, etc.; plastics sheets & rods; sheet metalwork
**HQ:** Thyssenkrupp Materials Na, Inc.
22355 W 11 Mile Rd
Southfield MI 48033
248 233-5600

## (G-2379)
### TIM WALLACE LDSCP SUP CO INC (PA)
1481 W Boughton Rd (60490-1552)
P.O. Box 277, Plainfield (60544-0277)
**PHONE**....................630 759-6813
**Fax:** 630 759-8153
Tim Wallace, *President*
Doris Wallace, *Manager*
**EMP:** 10
**SQ FT:** 3,200
**SALES (est):** 3.3MM **Privately Held**
**WEB:** www.snowplowsupply.com
**SIC: 5261** 3531 Nurseries & garden centers; snow plow attachments

## (G-2380)
### VISION INTEGRATED GRAPHICS
605 Territorial Dr Ste A (60440-4648)
**PHONE**....................708 570-7900
Tammy German, *Warehouse Mgr*
Greg Burdett, *VP Finance*
Mike Wienke, *Sales Mgr*
Betsy Farmer, *Accounts Exec*
Philip Pitluck, *Accounts Exec*
**EMP:** 150
**SALES (corp-wide):** 66.3MM **Privately Held**
**SIC: 2759** 2752 2732 2741 Commercial printing; commercial printing, lithographic; book printing; miscellaneous publishing
**PA:** Vision Integrated Graphics Group Llc
208 S Jefferson St Fl 3
Chicago IL 60661
312 373-6300

# GEOGRAPHIC SECTION

**Bourbonnais - Kankakee County (G-2407)**

**(G-2381)**
**WEG ELECTRIC MOTORS**
2 Gateway Ct (60440-4879)
PHONE .................................. 630 226-5688
EMP: 3
SALES (est): 335.4K **Privately Held**
SIC: 5521 3699 Automobiles, used cars only; electrical equipment & supplies

**(G-2382)**
**WEST LIBERTY FOODS LLC**
750 S Schmidt Rd (60440-4813)
PHONE .................................. 603 679-2300
EMP: 351 **Privately Held**
SIC: 2015 Turkey processing & slaughtering
PA: West Liberty Foods, L.L.C.
228 W 2nd St
West Liberty IA 52776

**(G-2383)**
**WESTROCK CONVERTING COMPANY**
365 Crossing Rd (60440-3620)
PHONE .................................. 630 783-6700
Fax: 630 783-9675
Kelley Landry, *Project Engr*
Greg Grasso, *Branch Mgr*
EMP: 20
SALES (corp-wide): 14.1B **Publicly Held**
WEB: www.rocktenn.com
SIC: 3086 Packaging & shipping materials, foamed plastic
HQ: Westrock Converting Company
504 Thrasher St
Norcross GA 30071
770 246-9982

**(G-2384)**
**WINDY CITY WIRE AND CONNECTIVI (PA)**
386 Internationale Dr H (60440-3602)
PHONE .................................. 630 633-4500
Richard Galgano, *CEO*
Courtney Usenick, *Vice Pres*
Justin Itzkowitz, *Buyer*
Dan Hughes, *Nat'l Sales Mgr*
Marty Eck, *Sales Mgr*
▼ EMP: 85
SQ FT: 110,000
SALES (est): 40.2MM **Privately Held**
SIC: 3355 Aluminum wire & cable

## Bonfield
### Kankakee County

**(G-2385)**
**NDY MANUFACTURING INC**
4590 N 11000w Rd (60913-7076)
PHONE .................................. 815 426-2330
Kenneth Shoup, *President*
Sheri Shoup, *Office Mgr*
Gary Dumontelle, *Supervisor*
EMP: 8
SALES (est): 1.5MM **Privately Held**
SIC: 3523 Farm machinery & equipment

## Bourbonnais
### Kankakee County

**(G-2386)**
**ALEXANDER SIGNS & DESIGNS INC**
1511 Commerce Dr (60914-4644)
PHONE .................................. 815 933-3100
Fax: 815 933-1121
Anna Alexander, *President*
EMP: 4
SALES (est): 211.1K **Privately Held**
WEB: www.alexanderconstruction.com
SIC: 3993 Signs & advertising specialties

**(G-2387)**
**AMBASSADOR STEEL CORPORATION**
1050 Saint George Rd (60914-9596)
PHONE .................................. 815 929-3770
Fax: 815 258-9715
Rod Fuss, *Manager*
EMP: 13
SALES (corp-wide): 16.2B **Publicly Held**
SIC: 3441 Building components, structural steel
HQ: Ambassador Steel Corporation
1340 S Grandstaff Dr
Auburn IN 46706
260 925-5440

**(G-2388)**
**B & B PUBLISHING CO INC**
Also Called: Herald Country Market, The
500 Brown Blvd (60914-2328)
PHONE .................................. 815 933-1131
Fax: 815 933-3785
Susan Olszewski, *President*
Toby Olszewski, *Publisher*
John Olszewski, *General Mgr*
Bob Glade, *Admin Sec*
Robert Olszewski, *Admin Sec*
EMP: 15 EST: 1975
SQ FT: 3,000
SALES (est): 1MM **Privately Held**
WEB: www.bbherald.com
SIC: 2711 Newspapers

**(G-2389)**
**BELSON STEEL CENTER SCRAP INC**
1685 N State Route 50 (60914-9303)
PHONE .................................. 815 932-7416
Marc Pozan, *President*
Fred Mancuso, *Vice Pres*
Kevin J Kennell, *CFO*
EMP: 25 EST: 2001
SQ FT: 25,000
SALES (est): 18.2MM **Privately Held**
SIC: 5093 3341 Ferrous metal scrap & waste; secondary nonferrous metals

**(G-2390)**
**BRONTE PRESS**
6712 N 4180w Rd (60914-4142)
PHONE .................................. 815 932-5192
Paul Pruchniki, *Partner*
Suzanne Pruchnicki, *Partner*
Suzanne Pruchniki, *Partner*
Elmira Wilkey, *Partner*
EMP: 3
SALES (est): 200K **Privately Held**
SIC: 2732 Book printing

**(G-2391)**
**C & M ENGINEERING**
110 Mooney Dr Ste 8 (60914-2172)
PHONE .................................. 815 932-3388
Fax: 815 932-5506
Jim Mertin, *Partner*
Mike Chamness, *Partner*
Scott Chamness, *Manager*
EMP: 4
SQ FT: 1,800
SALES (est): 340K **Privately Held**
SIC: 3519 3714 Gas engine rebuilding; motor vehicle parts & accessories

**(G-2392)**
**CB&I LLC**
Also Called: CB & I Water
1035 E 5000n Rd (60914-4231)
P.O. Box 681508, Franklin TN (37068-1508)
PHONE .................................. 815 936-5440
Gary Beaty, *Manager*
EMP: 7
SALES (corp-wide): 10.6B **Privately Held**
SIC: 3443 Tanks, standard or custom fabricated: metal plate
HQ: Cb&I Llc
2103 Research Forest Dr
The Woodlands TX 77380
832 513-1000

**(G-2393)**
**DABRICO INC**
1555 Commerce Dr (60914-4600)
PHONE .................................. 815 939-0580
Efrain Davila, *President*
Nohra Davila, *Admin Sec*
▲ EMP: 21
SQ FT: 7,200
SALES (est): 5.8MM **Privately Held**
WEB: www.dabrico.com
SIC: 3559 Pharmaceutical machinery

**(G-2394)**
**DUTCH VALLEY PARTNERS LLC**
4067 E 4000n Rd (60914-4094)
PHONE .................................. 815 937-8812
John Rietveld, *Mng Member*
Kathleen Rosenberg, *Manager*
▲ EMP: 30
SQ FT: 1,500
SALES: 1.5MM **Privately Held**
SIC: 0161 5083 3523 Onion farm; planting machinery & equipment; potato diggers, harvesters & planters

**(G-2395)**
**ENTERPRISE PALLET INC**
1166 E 6000n Rd (60914-4451)
PHONE .................................. 815 928-8546
Fax: 815 839-5400
Thomas Edison, *President*
EMP: 10
SQ FT: 16,000
SALES (est): 760K **Privately Held**
SIC: 2448 5031 2426 Pallets, wood; lumber: rough, dressed & finished; hardwood dimension & flooring mills

**(G-2396)**
**FISHER & LUDLOW INC**
1115 E 5000n Rd (60914-4229)
PHONE .................................. 815 932-1200
Fax: 708 932-4557
Bob Vangeertry, *Branch Mgr*
Robert Van Geertry, *Executive*
EMP: 60
SALES (corp-wide): 103.9K **Privately Held**
WEB: www.amico-online.com
SIC: 3446 Open flooring & grating for construction
PA: Fisher & Ludlow Inc
750 Appleby Line Suite 1
Burlington ON L7L 2
905 632-2121

**(G-2397)**
**GREG LAMBERT CONSTRUCTION**
Also Called: Lambert Bridge & Iron
5485 N 5000e Rd (60914-4136)
P.O. Box 1111 (60914-7111)
PHONE .................................. 815 468-7361
Fax: 815 468-7376
Greg Lambert, *Owner*
Jean Timmermann, *Opers Mgr*
EMP: 27
SQ FT: 1,200
SALES (est): 4.7MM **Privately Held**
SIC: 3441 Fabricated structural metal

**(G-2398)**
**H & H CUSTOM WOODWORKING INC**
Also Called: H & H Custom Countertops
1858 N State Route 50 # 5 (60914-4522)
PHONE .................................. 815 932-6820
Fax: 815 932-1160
Patrick M Haynes, *President*
Laura C Haynes, *Admin Sec*
EMP: 42
SALES (est): 3.2MM **Privately Held**
WEB: www.hhcustomwoodworking.com
SIC: 2431 Millwork

**(G-2399)**
**HOSTMANN STEINBERG INC**
4 Windsor Ct (60914-1639)
PHONE .................................. 815 401-5493
Tom Borbowski, *Opers-Prdtn-Mfg*
EMP: 12
SQ FT: 7,000
SALES (corp-wide): 1.3MM **Privately Held**
WEB: www.hostmann-steinberg.com
SIC: 2893 Printing ink
HQ: Hostmann Steinberg Inc
2850 Festival Dr
Kankakee IL 60901
502 968-5961

**(G-2400)**
**INNOVATIVE MOBILE MARKETING**
1511 Commerce Dr (60914-4644)
PHONE .................................. 815 929-1029
Matt Alexander, *President*
▲ EMP: 17
SALES (est): 1.7MM **Privately Held**
WEB: www.innovativemobile.com
SIC: 2451 Mobile buildings: for commercial use

**(G-2401)**
**JB & S MACHINING**
1675 Enterprise Way (60914)
PHONE .................................. 815 258-4007
Ricky Daniel, *Owner*
EMP: 4
SQ FT: 6,000
SALES (est): 363.4K **Privately Held**
SIC: 3441 Fabricated structural metal

**(G-2402)**
**MEASURED PLASTICS INC**
Also Called: Measured Plastics Gleason
861 E 6000n Rd (60914-4140)
PHONE .................................. 815 939-4408
Shirley Harding, *President*
Steven Duby, *Corp Secy*
Joshua Klein, *Accounts Exec*
EMP: 6
SQ FT: 30,000
SALES: 317.8K **Privately Held**
SIC: 0781 3535 Horticulture services; robotic conveyors

**(G-2403)**
**NUCOR STEEL KANKAKEE INC**
1 Nucor Way (60914-3213)
PHONE .................................. 815 937-3131
John J Fierrola, *CEO*
James Darsey, *President*
Alex Weisselberg, *President*
Johnny Jacobs, *General Mgr*
Matthew Brooks, *Principal*
▲ EMP: 330
SALES (est): 121.8MM
SALES (corp-wide): 16.2B **Publicly Held**
WEB: www.nsknk.com
SIC: 3312 3547 3449 Blast furnaces & steel mills; rolling mill machinery; miscellaneous metalwork
PA: Nucor Corporation
1915 Rexford Rd Ste 400
Charlotte NC 28211
704 366-7000

**(G-2404)**
**O & P KINETIC**
453 S Main St (60914-1918)
PHONE .................................. 815 401-7260
Aaron Hays, *President*
Arron Hays, *President*
EMP: 3
SALES (est): 234.8K **Privately Held**
SIC: 5047 3842 Artificial limbs; braces, orthopedic

**(G-2405)**
**PALO VERDE SUSPENSION INC**
4136 W 6940n Rd (60914-4208)
PHONE .................................. 815 939-2196
Jeremy Wilkey, *CEO*
Richard Sawipskas, *President*
EMP: 5 EST: 2000
SALES (est): 395.5K **Privately Held**
SIC: 3446 Acoustical suspension systems, metal

**(G-2406)**
**SAWMILL CONSTRUCTION INC**
5265 E 4000n Rd (60914-4447)
PHONE .................................. 815 937-0037
Tim Jones, *President*
Donna Jones, *Admin Sec*
EMP: 3
SALES (est): 310K **Privately Held**
SIC: 2421 Sawmills & planing mills, general

**(G-2407)**
**TGRV LLC (HQ)**
Also Called: Allegra Coal City
1032 Margaux (60914-4531)
PHONE .................................. 815 634-2102
Todd Garcia, *Mng Member*
Ryan Voigt,
EMP: 7 EST: 2015

SALES: 1MM **Privately Held**
SIC: **8742** 7331 7389 7374 Marketing consulting services; mailing service; design services; computer graphics service; signs & advertising specialties; family clothing stores

*(G-2408)*
**TMS INTERNATIONAL LLC**
Also Called: IMS
1 Nucor Way (60914-3213)
PHONE..................................815 939-9460
EMP: 8 **Privately Held**
SIC: **3295** 3341 Minerals, Ground Or Treated, Nsk

*(G-2409)*
**WW HENRY COMPANY LP**
150 Mooney Dr (60914-2124)
PHONE..................................815 933-8059
Fax: 815 933-4326
Mark Litton, *Manager*
EMP: 70
SALES (corp-wide): 756.5K **Privately Held**
SIC: **2891** Adhesives
HQ: The W W Henry Company L P
400 Ardex Park Dr
Aliquippa PA 15001
704 203-5000

## Braceville
### Grundy County

*(G-2410)*
**ILLINOIS RECOVERY GROUP I**
2390 S Broadway Rd (60407-9096)
PHONE..................................815 230-7920
Scott Mering, *Owner*
EMP: 3
SALES (est): 478.7K **Privately Held**
SIC: **2611** Pulp manufactured from waste or recycled paper

## Bradford
### Stark County

*(G-2411)*
**GREEN GABLES COUNTRY STORE**
201 Bonita Ave (61421-5305)
PHONE..................................309 897-7160
Robert Rouse, *Principal*
EMP: 60
SALES (est): 2.4MM **Privately Held**
SIC: **2511** Wood household furniture

## Bradley
### Kankakee County

*(G-2412)*
**AIRGAS USA LLC**
184 N Kinzie Ave (60915-1742)
PHONE..................................815 935-7750
Fax: 815 937-4895
David Silva, *Sales Associate*
Lane Heatherwick, *Branch Mgr*
Rob Hernadez, *Manager*
Matt Reiniche, *Manager*
Ken Sutton, *Manager*
EMP: 5
SALES (corp-wide): 163.9MM **Privately Held**
SIC: **3548** Gas welding equipment
HQ: Airgas Usa, Llc
259 N Radnor Chester Rd # 100
Radnor PA 19087
610 687-5253

*(G-2413)*
**BARRINGTON COMPANY**
195 N Euclid Ave (60915-1773)
PHONE..................................815 933-3233
Mike Bysina, *President*
Pam Newbury, *General Mgr*
Jody Polka, *Manager*
EMP: 3

SALES: 300K **Privately Held**
SIC: **2676** Feminine hygiene paper products

*(G-2414)*
**BUNGE OILS INC**
725 N Kinzie Ave (60915-1228)
PHONE..................................815 523-8129
Galhardo Flavio, *Project Mgr*
Scotts Springer, *Branch Mgr*
Lesa Johnson, *Manager*
Reynaldo Cruz, *Project Leader*
Carrie L Abrassart, *Senior Mgr*
EMP: 35 **Privately Held**
WEB: www.bungeoils.com
SIC: **2076** Vegetable oil mills
HQ: Bunge Oils, Inc.
11720 Borman Dr
Saint Louis MO 63146
314 292-2000

*(G-2415)*
**BUNGE OILS INC**
885 N Kinzie Ave (60915-1230)
PHONE..................................815 939-3631
Jeff Wilken, *COO*
Gustavo Karnincic, *Plant Mgr*
Andrey Makarenko, *Opers Mgr*
Patty Mickler, *Purch Agent*
Ricardo Assmann, *Engineer*
EMP: 55 **Privately Held**
WEB: www.bungeoils.com
SIC: **2079** 2077 Edible fats & oils; animal & marine fats & oils
HQ: Bunge Oils, Inc.
11720 Borman Dr
Saint Louis MO 63146
314 292-2000

*(G-2416)*
**BYPAK INC**
195 N Euclid Ave (60915-1773)
PHONE..................................815 933-2870
Michael Bysina, *President*
Raymond A Boldt, *Admin Sec*
Pam Newbury, *Administration*
EMP: 5
SQ FT: 1,000
SALES (est): 1MM **Privately Held**
SIC: **2679** Paper products, converted

*(G-2417)*
**CROWN CORK & SEAL USA INC**
1035 E North St (60915-1299)
PHONE..................................815 933-9351
Fax: 815 933-5925
Ed House, *Plant Mgr*
John Zumpf, *Safety Mgr*
Sharon Britt, *Executive*
EMP: 155
SALES (corp-wide): 8.2B **Publicly Held**
WEB: www.crowncork.com
SIC: **3411** 3354 Metal cans; aluminum extruded products
HQ: Crown Cork & Seal Usa, Inc.
1 Crown Way
Philadelphia PA 19154
215 698-5100

*(G-2418)*
**CSL BEHRING LLC**
1201 N Kinzie Ave (60915-1298)
P.O. Box 511, Kankakee (60901-0511)
PHONE..................................815 932-6773
Fax: 815 802-3333
Carey Miailovich, *COO*
Shailaja Ravola, *Project Mgr*
Sandra Banjamin, *Purch Mgr*
Byron Suprendant, *Purch Agent*
Michael Bartkovsky, *Research*
EMP: 400
SALES (corp-wide): 5.9B **Privately Held**
SIC: **2836** 3841 Blood derivatives; plasmas; surgical & medical instruments
HQ: Csl Behring L.L.C.
1020 1st Ave
King Of Prussia PA 19406

*(G-2419)*
**DAWN FOOD PRODUCTS INC**
785 N Kinzie Ave (60915-1228)
PHONE..................................815 933-0600
Jim Holland, *Marketing Staff*
Bernard Hinke, *Manager*
EMP: 240

SALES (corp-wide): 1.8B **Privately Held**
WEB: www.dawnfoods.com
SIC: **2076** 2013 2087 2079 Vegetable oil mills; sausages & other prepared meats; flavoring extracts & syrups; edible fats & oils; meat packing plants
HQ: Dawn Food Products, Inc.
3333 Sargent Rd
Jackson MI 49201

*(G-2420)*
**DURA PRODUCTS CORPORATION**
Also Called: Durabilt Division
2 E Bradford Dr (60915-1260)
PHONE..................................815 939-1399
Robert Pye, *President*
Nancy N Pye, *Vice Pres*
Randy Wermuth, *Manager*
EMP: 6
SQ FT: 15,000
SALES (est): 918.8K **Privately Held**
SIC: **3519** 5084 3714 Diesel engine rebuilding; industrial machinery & equipment; motor vehicle parts & accessories

*(G-2421)*
**FILTERS TO YOU**
183 E North St (60915-1268)
PHONE..................................815 939-0700
Kathy Landrey, *Principal*
EMP: 2 EST: 2010
SALES (est): 243.5K **Privately Held**
SIC: **3569** Filters

*(G-2422)*
**G & G STUDIOS /BROADWAY PRTG**
Also Called: G & G Printing
345 W Broadway St (60915-2237)
PHONE..................................815 933-8181
Mark Gravlin, *President*
Marian E Gravlin, *Vice Pres*
Karen Cross, *Treasurer*
EMP: 11
SQ FT: 7,500
SALES (est): 970K **Privately Held**
SIC: **2752** 7335 7336 Commercial printing, offset; commercial photography; graphic arts & related design

*(G-2423)*
**GREIF INC**
150 E North St (60915-1264)
PHONE..................................815 935-7575
Jeffrey Lahey, *Plant Mgr*
Mary Bloom, *Purchasing*
Jeff Lahey, *Branch Mgr*
EMP: 30
SALES (corp-wide): 3.3B **Publicly Held**
WEB: www.greif.com
SIC: **3089** 3412 Pallets, plastic; metal barrels, drums & pails
PA: Greif, Inc.
425 Winter Rd
Delaware OH 43015
740 549-6000

*(G-2424)*
**HANSENS MFRS WIN COVERINGS (PA)**
200 N Washington Ave (60915-1676)
PHONE..................................815 935-0010
Fax: 815 935-5393
Jeff F Hansen, *Partner*
F Harry Hansen, *Partner*
Jeff Lambert, *Partner*
EMP: 12
SQ FT: 45,000
SALES (est): 4.7MM **Privately Held**
WEB: www.hansenswindowcoverings.com
SIC: **5714** 2591 Draperies; curtains; blinds vertical; window shades

*(G-2425)*
**KANKAKEE INDUSTRIAL TECH**
359 S Kinzie Ave (60915-2433)
PHONE..................................815 933-6683
Trent Thompson, *President*
Philip Thompson, *Admin Sec*
EMP: 10
SALES (est): 4.2MM **Privately Held**
SIC: **5063** 7694 Motors, electric; electric motor repair

*(G-2426)*
**MILLS MACHINING**
295 Stebbings Ct Ste 4 (60915-1288)
PHONE..................................815 933-9193
Scott Mills, *Owner*
EMP: 5
SALES: 500K **Privately Held**
SIC: **3599** Machine shop, jobbing & repair

*(G-2427)*
**MX TECH INC**
450 S Schuyler Ave (60915-2344)
PHONE..................................815 936-6277
Jeremy Wilkey, *President*
▲ EMP: 3 EST: 1992
SALES: 550K **Privately Held**
WEB: www.mx-tech.com
SIC: **3751** Motorcycles, bicycles & parts

*(G-2428)*
**PEDDINGHAUS CORPORATION (PA)**
300 N Washington Ave (60915-1600)
PHONE..................................815 937-3800
Fax: 815 937-4003
Carl G Peddinghaus, *President*
Kenneth Coulter, *President*
Ted Trybek, *Regional Mgr*
Greg Kubick, *Corp Secy*
Terry Chinn, *Vice Pres*
◆ EMP: 240 EST: 1977
SQ FT: 72,500
SALES (est): 125.7MM **Privately Held**
WEB: www.peddinghaus.com
SIC: **3541** Numerically controlled metal cutting machine tools

*(G-2429)*
**Q SC DESIGN**
230 E Broadway St (60915-2300)
PHONE..................................815 933-6777
Steve Staniszeski, *Owner*
EMP: 4
SALES (est): 290.2K **Privately Held**
SIC: **3993** 5099 Signs & advertising specialties; signs, except electric

*(G-2430)*
**REDD REMEDIES INC**
211 S Quincy Ave (60915-2517)
PHONE..................................815 614-2083
Dan Chapman, *President*
EMP: 10
SALES (est): 1.6MM **Privately Held**
SIC: **2834** Vitamin preparations

*(G-2431)*
**S & S HEATING & SHEET METAL**
222 N Industrial Dr (60915-1279)
PHONE..................................815 933-1993
Fax: 815 938-8045
Winnie Sippel, *President*
EMP: 5
SQ FT: 20,000
SALES (est): 1.1MM **Privately Held**
SIC: **1711** 1761 3444 Warm air heating & air conditioning contractor; sheet metalwork; sheet metalwork

*(G-2432)*
**SECTIONAL SNOW PLOW**
101 N Euclid Ave (60915-1754)
PHONE..................................815 932-7569
Jeff Sexton, *General Mgr*
EMP: 50
SALES (est): 5.2MM **Privately Held**
SIC: **2851** Removers & cleaners

*(G-2433)*
**SECURITY METAL PRODUCTS INC**
101 Lawn St (60915-1631)
PHONE..................................815 933-3307
Edwin A Benson, *President*
EMP: 3
SALES (est): 210.6K **Privately Held**
SIC: **3353** Aluminum sheet & strip

*(G-2434)*
**STRUCTURAL STEEL SYSTEMS LIMI**
Also Called: Peddinghause
300 N Washington Ave (60915-1646)
PHONE..................................815 937-3800
Carl G Peddinghause, *General Mgr*

# GEOGRAPHIC SECTION

**Bridgeview - Cook County (G-2460)**

Peddinghause Corporation, *General Ptnr*
Terry Chinn, *Vice Pres*
Greg Carpenter, *Engineer*
Jim Magnuson, *Engineer*
▲ **EMP:** 18
**SQ FT:** 38,000
**SALES:** 3.6MM **Privately Held**
**SIC: 3317** Steel pipe & tubes

## (G-2435)
### U S FILTERS
404 E Broadway St (60915-1702)
**PHONE** ................................ 815 932-8154
**EMP:** 2 **EST:** 2010
**SALES (est):** 200K **Privately Held**
**SIC: 3569** Mfg General Industrial Machinery

## (G-2436)
### UNIVERSAL PALLET INC
368 S Michigan Ave (60915-2271)
**PHONE** ................................ 815 928-8546
Michael Krueger, *Principal*
**EMP:** 8
**SALES (est):** 671.1K **Privately Held**
**SIC: 2448** Wood pallets & skids

## Breese
### Clinton County

## (G-2437)
### ARROW SHED LLC (HQ)
Also Called: Arrow Group Industries
1101 N 4th St (62230-1755)
**PHONE** ................................ 618 526-4546
**Fax:** 618 526-4617
Robert Silinski, *Mng Member*
Peter Moore, *Info Tech Dir*
◆ **EMP:** 40 **EST:** 1945
**SQ FT:** 12,000
**SALES (est):** 60.7MM
**SALES (corp-wide):** 39.4MM **Privately Held**
**WEB:** www.spacemakersheds.com
**SIC: 3448** Buildings, portable; prefabricated metal; farm & utility buildings
**PA:** Shelterlogic Corp.
  150 Callender Rd
  Watertown CT 06795
  860 945-6442

## (G-2438)
### ARROW SHED LLC
Also Called: Arrow Group Indust
1101 N 4th St (62230-1755)
**PHONE** ................................ 618 526-4546
Larry Goodwin, *Vice Pres*
David Cross, *Vice Pres*
Stephen Weilbacher, *Safety Mgr*
Donna Eversgerd, *Director*
**EMP:** 200
**SALES (corp-wide):** 39.4MM **Privately Held**
**WEB:** www.spacemakersheds.com
**SIC: 3448** Farm & utility buildings
**HQ:** Arrow Shed, Llc
  1101 N 4th St
  Breese IL 62230
  618 526-4546

## (G-2439)
### BEELMAN READY-MIX INC
8200 Old Us Highway 50 (62230-3921)
**PHONE** ................................ 618 526-0260
**Fax:** 618 526-0263
Kurt Becker, *General Mgr*
**EMP:** 10 **Privately Held**
**WEB:** www.beelmanrm.com
**SIC: 5211** 3273 Lumber & other building materials; ready-mixed concrete
**PA:** Beelman Ready-Mix, Inc.
  1 Racehorse Dr
  East Saint Louis IL 62205

## (G-2440)
### BREESE PUBLISHING CO INC (PA)
Also Called: Breese Journal
8060 Old Us Highway 50 (62230-3924)
P.O. Box 405 (62230-0405)
**PHONE** ................................ 618 526-7211
**Fax:** 618 526-2590
Steven H Mahlandt, *President*

Steven Mahlandt, *President*
David Mahlandt, *Vice Pres*
Quentin Glasscock, *Plant Mgr*
Stan Holtmann, *Sales Staff*
▼ **EMP:** 2
**SALES (est):** 15.2MM **Privately Held**
**WEB:** www.breesepub.com
**SIC: 2752** 2711 Commercial printing, offset; newspapers, publishing & printing

## (G-2441)
### CANDLE ENTERPRISES INC
580 N 2nd St (62230-1650)
**PHONE** ................................ 618 526-8070
Martha Ribbings, *Principal*
**EMP:** 3
**SALES (est):** 142.7K **Privately Held**
**SIC: 3999** Candles

## (G-2442)
### COMPOUND BOW RIFLE SIGHT INC
Also Called: Peep Eliminator
1004 S Walnut St (62230-4118)
**PHONE** ................................ 618 526-4427
Melvin Deien, *President*
Janet Deien, *Admin Sec*
**EMP:** 4
**SALES:** 150K **Privately Held**
**SIC: 3949** Archery equipment, general

## (G-2443)
### EXCEL BOTTLING CO
488 S Broadway (62230-1805)
**PHONE** ................................ 618 526-7159
**Fax:** 618 526-7187
Paul Meier, *President*
Joseph Meier, *Vice Pres*
**EMP:** 8 **EST:** 1937
**SQ FT:** 4,000
**SALES (est):** 1.1MM **Privately Held**
**SIC: 2086** 5149 Soft drinks: packaged in cans, bottles, etc.; soft drinks

## (G-2444)
### FOODS & THINGS INC
604 N 1st St (62230-1626)
**PHONE** ................................ 618 526-4478
Lois Garcia, *Partner*
Diane Hummert, *Partner*
**EMP:** 4
**SALES (est):** 281K **Privately Held**
**SIC: 2035** Seasonings & sauces, except tomato & dry

## (G-2445)
### ILLINOIS EMBROIDERY SERVICE
Also Called: Logo's & More
580 N 2nd St (62230-1650)
**PHONE** ................................ 618 526-8006
Martha Ribbing, *Owner*
Daniel Ribbing, *Co-Owner*
**EMP:** 4
**SQ FT:** 2,300
**SALES (est):** 221.6K **Privately Held**
**SIC: 2395** Embroidery & art needlework

## (G-2446)
### QUAD-COUNTY READY MIX CORP
11 S Plum St (62230)
P.O. Box 211 (62230-0211)
**PHONE** ................................ 618 526-7130
**Fax:** 618 526-0530
Phillip Timmerman, *Manager*
**EMP:** 7
**SALES (corp-wide):** 18.9MM **Privately Held**
**SIC: 3273** Ready-mixed concrete
**PA:** Quad-County Ready Mix Corp.
  300 W 12th St
  Okawville IL 62271
  618 243-6430

## (G-2447)
### REHKEMPER & SONS INC (PA)
17817 Saint Rose Rd (62230-2503)
**PHONE** ................................ 618 526-2269
**Fax:** 618 526-2810
Jerome Rehkemper, *President*
Mike Rehkemper, *Vice Pres*
Craig Becker, *Plant Mgr*
**EMP:** 45
**SQ FT:** 20,000

**SALES (est):** 21.6MM **Privately Held**
**SIC: 2439** Trusses, except roof: laminated lumber; trusses, wooden roof

## (G-2448)
### STRAT-O-SPAN BUILDINGS INC (PA)
7980 Old Us Highway 50 (62230-3820)
**PHONE** ................................ 618 526-4566
**Fax:** 618 526-2584
Mark Stratmann, *President*
Tom Stratmann, *Vice Pres*
Mary Moran, *Treasurer*
**EMP:** 4
**SQ FT:** 50,000
**SALES (est):** 1.1MM **Privately Held**
**WEB:** www.strat-o-span.com
**SIC: 2452** 3448 3441 2439 Farm buildings, prefabricated or portable: wood; buildings, portable: prefabricated metal; fabricated structural metal; structural wood members

## Bridgeport
### Lawrence County

## (G-2449)
### BINDERY MAINTENANCE SERVICES
777 E State St (62417-2105)
P.O. Box 63 (62417-0063)
**PHONE** ................................ 618 945-7480
Gary Cornes, *Owner*
**EMP:** 3
**SALES (est):** 100K **Privately Held**
**SIC: 2782** Blankbooks & looseleaf binders

## (G-2450)
### BRIDGEPORT AIR COMPRSR & TL CO
Also Called: B M S Tool & Equipment Co
745 Monroe St (62417-1119)
**PHONE** ................................ 618 945-7163
**Fax:** 618 945-9020
Max R Schauf, *Owner*
**EMP:** 4
**SQ FT:** 10,000
**SALES (est):** 302K **Privately Held**
**SIC: 5075** 3563 5085 Compressors, air conditioning; air & gas compressors including vacuum pumps; tools

## (G-2451)
### DARNELL WELDING
9210 Lanterman Rd (62417-2021)
P.O. Box 1 (62417-0001)
**PHONE** ................................ 618 945-9538
David Darnell, *Owner*
Jeannie Darnell, *Office Mgr*
**EMP:** 4
**SALES:** 250K **Privately Held**
**SIC: 7692** Welding repair

## (G-2452)
### FIVE P DRILLING INC
10585 Cabin Hill Dr (62417-4012)
**PHONE** ................................ 618 943-9771
Carl Price, *President*
Jana Price, *Corp Secy*
Flossie Price, *Vice Pres*
**EMP:** 27
**SALES:** 900K **Privately Held**
**SIC: 1381** Drilling oil & gas wells

## (G-2453)
### JONES BROTHERS MCH & WLDG INC
145 E Olive St (62417)
**PHONE** ................................ 618 945-4609
Bobby Jones, *Principal*
**EMP:** 1 **EST:** 2013
**SALES (est):** 248K **Privately Held**
**SIC: 7692** Automotive welding

## (G-2454)
### REX ENERGY CORPORATION
Rr 1 Box 197 (62417)
**PHONE** ................................ 618 943-8700
**Fax:** 618 943-4501
Brian Clayton, *Principal*
Jack Shawver, *COO*
**EMP:** 25

**SALES (corp-wide):** 139MM **Publicly Held**
**SIC: 1311** Crude petroleum & natural gas production
**PA:** Rex Energy Corporation
  366 Walker Dr
  State College PA 16801
  814 278-7267

## (G-2455)
### RUCKERS MKIN BATCH CANDIES INC
777 Rucker St (62417)
P.O. Box 27 (62417-0027)
**PHONE** ................................ 618 945-7778
Ernest L Hoh, *President*
Richard R Rucker, *President*
Mike Mann, *District Mgr*
Chad Rucker, *Vice Pres*
Robert F Rucker, *Admin Sec*
▲ **EMP:** 25
**SQ FT:** 20,000
**SALES (est):** 3.5MM **Privately Held**
**WEB:** www.makinbatch.com
**SIC: 2064** Candy & other confectionery products

## (G-2456)
### TEAM ENERGY LLC (PA)
Also Called: Swager & Associates
Rr 1 Box 197 (62417)
P.O. Box 3677, Evansville IN (47735-3677)
**PHONE** ................................ 618 943-1010
**Fax:** 618 943-5301
David Britton, *Engineer*
Dennis Swager, *Engineer*
**EMP:** 7
**SQ FT:** 9,200
**SALES (est):** 1.2MM **Privately Held**
**WEB:** www.teamenergyllc.com
**SIC: 1389** 1311 Oil consultants; crude petroleum production

## Bridgeview
### Cook County

## (G-2457)
### A & R SCREENING LLC
8417 Beloit Ave (60455-1717)
**PHONE** ................................ 708 598-2480
**Fax:** 708 598-1422
Jo-Ellen Doranzo, *President*
Joe Doran, *Principal*
John Laroy, *Vice Pres*
**EMP:** 12
**SQ FT:** 3,500
**SALES:** 400K **Privately Held**
**SIC: 2759** 2396 Screen printing; automotive & apparel trimmings

## (G-2458)
### A R TECH & TOOL INC
8620 S Thomas Ave (60455-1880)
**PHONE** ................................ 708 599-5745
Andrew Rytych, *President*
**EMP:** 4
**SQ FT:** 2,400
**SALES:** 250K **Privately Held**
**SIC: 3599** 3545 3544 Machine shop, jobbing & repair; machine tool accessories; special dies, tools, jigs & fixtures

## (G-2459)
### AIR-X REMANUFACTURING CORP
8909 Odell Ave (60455-1913)
**PHONE** ................................ 708 598-0044
James R Dibiase, *President*
**EMP:** 3
**SQ FT:** 24,000
**SALES (est):** 285K **Privately Held**
**SIC: 3714** Air brakes, motor vehicle

## (G-2460)
### ALLEGHENY LUDLUM LLC
Also Called: ATI Allegheny Ludlum
8687 S 77th Ave (60455-1800)
**PHONE** ................................ 708 974-8801
Cory Hextall, *Branch Mgr*
**EMP:** 46 **Publicly Held**
**WEB:** www.alleghenyludlum.com
**SIC: 5051** 3312 Steel; strip, metal; stainless steel

---

(PA)=Parent Co (HQ)=Headquarters (DH)=Div Headquarters
○ = New Business established in last 2 years

HQ: Allegheny Ludlum, Llc
1000 Six Ppg Pl
Pittsburgh PA 15222
412 394-2800

**(G-2461)**
**ALLIANCE DOOR AND HARDWARE LLC**
9015-17 Odell Ave (60455)
PHONE..................630 451-7070
Jimenez Arthur, *CEO*
**EMP:** 4 **EST:** 2013
**SALES (est):** 596.4K **Privately Held**
**SIC:** 5031 2431 3442 Doors; door frames, wood; window & door frames

**(G-2462)**
**ALWAN PRINTING INC**
7825 S Roberts Rd (60455-1405)
PHONE..................708 598-9600
Berj M Khaleel, *CEO*
Yacoub Khaleel, *President*
Frances McLearn, *Manager*
Edward McHugh, *Graphic Designe*
**EMP:** 10
**SQ FT:** 8,000
**SALES (est):** 2MM **Privately Held**
**SIC:** 2752 Commercial printing, lithographic

**(G-2463)**
**AMERICA DISPLAY INC**
10061 S 76th Ave (60455-2430)
PHONE..................708 430-7000
**Fax:** 708 576-4200
Amer Odeh, *President*
Monica Odeh, *CFO*
Renee Zielinska, *Admin Sec*
**EMP:** 11
**SQ FT:** 8,500
**SALES:** 4MM **Privately Held**
**WEB:** www.americadisplay.com
**SIC:** 3999 Advertising display products

**(G-2464)**
**AMERICAN WILBERT VAULT CORP (PA)**
7525 W 99th Pl (60455-2404)
P.O. Box 2309 (60455-6309)
PHONE..................708 366-3210
**Fax:** 708 366-3281
David Reichle, *President*
Eric Urbano, *CFO*
Camille Powell, *Admin Sec*
**EMP:** 15 **EST:** 1924
**SQ FT:** 12,300
**SALES (est):** 5.3MM **Privately Held**
**WEB:** www.americanwilbert.com
**SIC:** 3272 Burial vaults, concrete or precast terrazzo

**(G-2465)**
**AMIS INC**
Also Called: Alexi's One Stop Shop
7506 W 90th St (60455-2123)
PHONE..................708 598-9700
Alex Stevens, *General Mgr*
**EMP:** 3
**SALES (est):** 355.6K **Privately Held**
**SIC:** 3465 5065 7538 Body parts, automobile: stamped metal; radio parts & accessories; general automotive repair shops

**(G-2466)**
**APCO ENTERPRISES INC**
9901 S 76th Ave (60455-2402)
PHONE..................708 430-7333
Greg Hinton, *President*
**EMP:** 9
**SQ FT:** 15,000
**SALES (est):** 710K **Privately Held**
**SIC:** 2842 5169 Cleaning or polishing preparations; specialty cleaning & sanitation preparations

**(G-2467)**
**APCO PACKAGING INC**
9901 S 76th Ave (60455-2402)
PHONE..................708 430-7333
**Fax:** 708 430-8775
Gregory Hinton, *President*
Elbert Hinton, *President*
Al Hinton, *Vice Pres*
Clarence Totleben, *Plant Mgr*
Jeff Krucek, *Project Mgr*
▲ **EMP:** 24
**SQ FT:** 40,000
**SALES (est):** 7.4MM **Privately Held**
**WEB:** www.apcopackaging.com
**SIC:** 2841 Soap & other detergents

**(G-2468)**
**ART CNC MACHINING LLC**
Also Called: Accurate Reliable Technology
9824 Industrial Dr (60455-2327)
PHONE..................708 907-3090
Joseph Lis, *Principal*
Krzysztof Strychacz,
Stanislaw Slota,
**EMP:** 3
**SALES (est):** 157.9K **Privately Held**
**SIC:** 3575 8711 Keyboards, computer, office machine; engineering services

**(G-2469)**
**BAK ELECTRIC**
7951 S Oketo Ave (60455-1533)
PHONE..................708 458-3578
**Fax:** 773 778-7473
Gene Bak, *President*
**EMP:** 3 **EST:** 1979
**SQ FT:** 11,000
**SALES (est):** 210K **Privately Held**
**SIC:** 7694 5999 Electric motor repair; motors, electric

**(G-2470)**
**BIRON STUDIO GENERAL SVCS INC**
Also Called: Seba Signs and Printing
7352 W 79th St (60455-1529)
PHONE..................708 229-2600
Wojciech Chramiec, *President*
**EMP:** 8
**SQ FT:** 1,400
**SALES (est):** 600K **Privately Held**
**SIC:** 3993 Signs & advertising specialties

**(G-2471)**
**BLAZ-MAN GEAR INC**
7461 W 93rd St Ste F (60455-2172)
PHONE..................708 599-9700
**Fax:** 708 599-9802
Ed Blaszynski, *President*
Michelle Blaszynski, *Vice Pres*
**EMP:** 5
**SQ FT:** 2,500
**SALES (est):** 700K **Privately Held**
**SIC:** 3462 Gears, forged steel

**(G-2472)**
**BRIDGEVIEW CUSTOM KIT CABINETS**
8655 Beloit Ave (60455-1776)
PHONE..................708 598-1221
Tino Antonini, *President*
Brenda Sandidge, *Admin Sec*
**EMP:** 10
**SQ FT:** 5,000
**SALES (est):** 1.2MM **Privately Held**
**SIC:** 2434 Wood kitchen cabinets

**(G-2473)**
**BRIDGEVIEW MACHINING INC**
9009 S Thomas Ave (60455-2204)
PHONE..................708 599-4060
Edward Chorzepa, *President*
**EMP:** 5
**SQ FT:** 5,300
**SALES (est):** 530K **Privately Held**
**SIC:** 3599 Machine shop, jobbing & repair

**(G-2474)**
**CAROUSEL CHECKS INC**
8906 S Harlem Ave (60455-1909)
PHONE..................708 599-8576
**Fax:** 708 381-5469
Andrew Crim, *President*
John Scoza, *President*
Jason Ward, *COO*
Heather Blackburn, *Vice Pres*
Dennis Crim, *Vice Pres*
▲ **EMP:** 10
**SQ FT:** 5,000
**SALES (est):** 3.2MM **Privately Held**
**WEB:** www.carouselchecks.com
**SIC:** 2782 Checkbooks

**(G-2475)**
**CAVANAUGH GOVERNMENT GROUP LLC**
8432 Beloit Ave (60455-1774)
PHONE..................630 210-8668
Michael Cavanaugh, *CEO*
**EMP:** 10
**SALES:** 12MM **Privately Held**
**SIC:** 3714 Motor vehicle parts & accessories

**(G-2476)**
**CHICAGO CAN CONVEYOR CORP**
8912 Moore Dr (60455-1920)
P.O. Box 2008 (60455-6008)
PHONE..................708 430-0988
**Fax:** 708 430-1997
Matthew M Bakosh, *President*
Jeanne Bakosh, *Bookkeeper*
**EMP:** 4
**SQ FT:** 800
**SALES (est):** 370K **Privately Held**
**SIC:** 3535 Conveyors & conveying equipment

**(G-2477)**
**CIMENTOS N VOTORANTIM AMER INC**
Also Called: Prairie Material
7601 W 79th St (60455-1115)
PHONE..................708 458-0400
Jim Munro, *President*
Raeann Fracek, *Vice Pres*
**EMP:** 22
**SALES (est):** 3.9MM **Privately Held**
**SIC:** 3255 Cement, clay refractory

**(G-2478)**
**CLOVER CUSTOM COUNTERS INC**
9220 S Octavia Ave (60455-2108)
PHONE..................708 598-8912
**Fax:** 708 598-8912
Pam Baio, *President*
Jerry Baio, *Vice Pres*
**EMP:** 5
**SQ FT:** 2,400
**SALES:** 500K **Privately Held**
**SIC:** 2541 1799 Table or counter tops, plastic laminated; counter top installation

**(G-2479)**
**COMMERCIAL FABRICATORS INC (PA)**
7247 S 78th Ave Ste 1 (60455-1091)
PHONE..................708 594-1199
**Fax:** 708 496-1261
Francesco Scaglia, *President*
Evelyn Scaglia, *Corp Secy*
Frank Chmelir, *Vice Pres*
Greg Chmelir, *Vice Pres*
**EMP:** 9
**SQ FT:** 105,000
**SALES (est):** 10.8MM **Privately Held**
**WEB:** www.commercialfabricators.com
**SIC:** 3441 Expansion joints (structural shapes), iron or steel

**(G-2480)**
**CREATIVE COVERS INC**
7508 W 90th St (60455-2123)
PHONE..................708 233-6880
Brigit Calderon, *President*
**EMP:** 4
**SALES (est):** 270.1K **Privately Held**
**SIC:** 2394 Liners & covers, fabric: made from purchased materials

**(G-2481)**
**D & M WELDING INC**
8314 S 77th Ave (60455-1737)
PHONE..................708 233-6080
**Fax:** 708 233-6760
Dave Bakker, *President*
**EMP:** 5
**SQ FT:** 2,100
**SALES (est):** 572.4K **Privately Held**
**SIC:** 3441 7692 Fabricated structural metal; welding repair

**(G-2482)**
**DEAN PATTERSON**
Also Called: Patterson Printing & Signs
9208 S Oketo Ave Unit B (60455-2100)
PHONE..................708 430-0477
**Fax:** 708 430-0314
Dean Patterson, *Owner*
**EMP:** 4
**SALES (est):** 313.8K **Privately Held**
**SIC:** 2621 3993 2679 5699 Printing paper; letters for signs, metal; tags & labels, paper; T-shirts, custom printed

**(G-2483)**
**DIAMOND WHOLESALE GROUP INC**
7325 W 87th St (60455-1823)
PHONE..................708 529-7495
Rami Zayed, *President*
**EMP:** 2 **EST:** 2011
**SALES (est):** 218.6K **Privately Held**
**SIC:** 2131 Chewing & smoking tobacco

**(G-2484)**
**DK SURFACE HARDENING INC**
7424 W 90th St (60455-2122)
PHONE..................708 233-9095
**EMP:** 3 **EST:** 2015
**SALES (est):** 180.3K **Privately Held**
**SIC:** 3398 Brazing (hardening) of metal

**(G-2485)**
**DUNAJEC BAKERY & DELI**
8339 S Harlem Ave (60455-1718)
PHONE..................773 585-9611
Jan Zych, *Owner*
**EMP:** 14 **EST:** 2000
**SALES (est):** 1.3MM **Privately Held**
**SIC:** 2051 Bread, cake & related products

**(G-2486)**
**ECONOPIN**
8540 S Thomas Ave (60455-1701)
PHONE..................708 599-5002
Gerhard Haigis, *Principal*
**EMP:** 6
**SALES (est):** 789.8K **Privately Held**
**SIC:** 3565 Canning machinery, food

**(G-2487)**
**EDDIE GAPASTIONE**
Also Called: Bella Cabinet
8927 S Octavia Ave (60455-1911)
PHONE..................708 430-3881
Eddie Gapastione, *Owner*
**EMP:** 2
**SQ FT:** 2,350
**SALES:** 200K **Privately Held**
**WEB:** www.bellacabinet.com
**SIC:** 1751 2541 2521 2517 Cabinet building & installation; wood partitions & fixtures; wood office furniture; wood television & radio cabinets; wood household furniture; wood kitchen cabinets

**(G-2488)**
**ELITE MACHINING CO**
8435 S 77th Ct (60455-1744)
PHONE..................708 308-0947
Dariusz Fudala, *President*
**EMP:** 8
**SALES (est):** 590K **Privately Held**
**SIC:** 3444 Sheet metalwork

**(G-2489)**
**FISHER PRINTING INC (PA)**
8640 S Oketo Ave (60455-1827)
PHONE..................708 598-1500
**Fax:** 708 598-7530
Will Fischer, *CEO*
Thomas Fischer, *Chairman*
Tom Scarpati, *COO*
Brad Fischer, *Vice Pres*
John Klabacha, *Sales Dir*
**EMP:** 150 **EST:** 1933
**SQ FT:** 60,000
**SALES (est):** 74.1MM **Privately Held**
**WEB:** www.fisherprinting.com
**SIC:** 2752 Commercial printing, offset

**(G-2490)**
**FISHER PRINTING INC**
8645 S Thomas Ave (60455-1828)
PHONE..................708 598-9266
Tom Fischer, *President*

**GEOGRAPHIC SECTION**          **Bridgeview - Cook County (G-2515)**

**EMP:** 120
**SALES (est):** 8.3MM **Privately Held**
**SIC:** 2711 2752 Commercial printing & newspaper publishing combined; commercial printing, lithographic

### (G-2491)
### FLEETPRIDE INC
7400 W 87th St (60455-1826)
**PHONE** .................................. 708 430-2081
Peter E Pasdach, *Branch Mgr*
**EMP:** 200
**SALES (corp-wide):** 1.3B **Privately Held**
**SIC:** 5013 3715 Truck parts & accessories; truck trailers
**PA:** Fleetpride, Inc.
600 Las Colinas Blvd E # 400
Irving TX 75039
469 249-7500

### (G-2492)
### FORMED FASTENER MFG INC
Also Called: Hardware Representatives
7247 S 78th Ave Ste 1 (60455-1091)
**PHONE** .................................. 708 496-1219
Francesco Scaglia, *President*
Jame Gear, *Purchasing*
**EMP:** 46
**SQ FT:** 20,000
**SALES (est):** 7.5MM
**SALES (corp-wide):** 10.8MM **Privately Held**
**WEB:** www.commercialfabricators.com
**SIC:** 3452 Bolts, metal; nuts, metal; screws, metal
**PA:** Commercial Fabricators, Inc.
7247 S 78th Ave Ste 1
Bridgeview IL 60455
708 594-1199

### (G-2493)
### GEAR PRODUCTS & MFG INC
9007 S Thomas Ave (60455-2204)
**PHONE** .................................. 708 344-0875
Michael Rasmussen, *President*
Paul Michaud, *Corp Secy*
Bill Herbert, *Exec VP*
**EMP:** 6
**SQ FT:** 5,500
**SALES (est):** 1.1MM **Privately Held**
**SIC:** 3462 Gear & chain forgings

### (G-2494)
### GERHARD DESIGNING & MFG INC
8540 S Thomas Ave Ste A (60455-1706)
**PHONE** .................................. 708 599-4664
**Fax:** 708 599-4673
Gerhard A Haigis, *President*
Joseph Giorgetti, *Facilities Mgr*
Nicolette Vlahaikis, *Admin Sec*
**EMP:** 26
**SQ FT:** 32,600
**SALES:** 4.6MM **Privately Held**
**WEB:** www.econopin.com
**SIC:** 3549 3544 Metalworking machinery; special dies & tools

### (G-2495)
### GOLDEN GRAIN COMPANY
7700 W 71st St (60455-1051)
**PHONE** .................................. 708 458-7020
**Fax:** 708 458-7023
Stewart Seaton, *Principal*
Tom Winters, *Plant Mgr*
Dan Arcury, *Controller*
Dave Corazzi, *Manager*
Jesus Vega, *Info Tech Mgr*
**EMP:** 8
**SALES (est):** 4.3MM **Privately Held**
**SIC:** 5149 2098 Pasta & rice; macaroni products (e.g. alphabets, rings & shells), dry

### (G-2496)
### HANSEN PRINTING CO INC
9745 Industrial Dr Ste 10 (60455-2331)
**PHONE** .................................. 708 599-1500
**Fax:** 708 599-1594
Bruce Hansen, *President*
Dorothy Hansen, *Corp Secy*
Russ Hansen, *Vice Pres*
**EMP:** 43
**SQ FT:** 21,000
**SALES (est):** 6.7MM **Privately Held**
**WEB:** www.hansenprintingco.com
**SIC:** 2752 Business forms, lithographed

### (G-2497)
### HAUS SIGN INCORPORATED
8907 Moore Dr (60455-1910)
**PHONE** .................................. 708 598-8740
**EMP:** 2
**SALES (est):** 217.9K **Privately Held**
**SIC:** 3993 Signs & advertising specialties

### (G-2498)
### ILLINOIS TOOL WORKS INC
Also Called: Signode
7201 S 78th St (60455)
**PHONE** .................................. 708 325-2300
Janet Love, *Vice Pres*
Jeff Hochleuter, *Opers-Prdtn-Mfg*
**EMP:** 160
**SALES (corp-wide):** 13.6B **Publicly Held**
**SIC:** 3443 3053 Fabricated plate work (boiler shop); gaskets, packing & sealing devices
**PA:** Illinois Tool Works Inc.
155 Harlem Ave
Glenview IL 60025
847 724-7500

### (G-2499)
### ILLINOIS TOOL WORKS INC
7701 W 71st St (60455-1050)
**PHONE** .................................. 708 458-7320
Dennis Miller, *Vice Pres*
**EMP:** 180
**SALES (corp-wide):** 13.6B **Publicly Held**
**SIC:** 3499 Strapping, metal
**PA:** Illinois Tool Works Inc.
155 Harlem Ave
Glenview IL 60025
847 724-7500

### (G-2500)
### INDUSPAC RTP INC
8100 77th Ave (60455-1566)
P.O. Box 1582, Mebane NC (27302-1582)
**PHONE** .................................. 919 484-9484
Paul Gaulin, *President*
Paul Krebbs, *General Mgr*
Gregory E Clifford, *Principal*
Dennis L Silver, *Principal*
Diane Russel, *Accountant*
**EMP:** 31
**SALES (est):** 3.5MM
**SALES (corp-wide):** 101.7MM **Privately Held**
**SIC:** 2449 Rectangular boxes & crates, wood
**PA:** Groupe Emballage Specialise S.E.C.
1805 50e Av
Lachine QC H8T 3
514 636-7951

### (G-2501)
### J & B TRUCK SERVICES LTD
9012 S Oketo Ave (60455-2156)
**PHONE** .................................. 708 430-8760
Jaroslaw Zalewski, *President*
**EMP:** 7
**SQ FT:** 10,000
**SALES:** 790K **Privately Held**
**SIC:** 3694 Engine electrical equipment

### (G-2502)
### JJ WOOD WORKING
9016 Odell Ave (60455-2128)
**PHONE** .................................. 708 426-6854
**EMP:** 3
**SALES (est):** 205.4K **Privately Held**
**SIC:** 2431 Millwork

### (G-2503)
### JO MO ENTERPRISES INC
Also Called: Vince & Sons Pasta Co
7825 W 87th Pl (60455-1864)
**PHONE** .................................. 708 599-8098
**Fax:** 708 599-8009
Robert Okon, *President*
Michael Okon, *Vice Pres*
**EMP:** 14
**SQ FT:** 10,000
**SALES:** 973.3K **Privately Held**
**SIC:** 2099 2038 2098 5142 Packaged combination products: pasta, rice & potato; spaghetti & meatballs, frozen; macaroni & spaghetti; dinners, frozen

### (G-2504)
### LRM GRINDING CO INC
7333 S 76th Ave (60455-1107)
**PHONE** .................................. 708 458-7878
Lee R Miller, *President*
Jennifer Miller, *Principal*
Michelle Miller, *Principal*
Laurie Ann Vogler, *Admin Sec*
Cathy Hine,
**EMP:** 70
**SQ FT:** 3,500
**SALES:** 1.2MM **Privately Held**
**SIC:** 3493 3599 Flat springs, sheet or strip stock; grinding castings for the trade

### (G-2505)
### MACDERMID ENTHONE INC
9809 Industrial Dr (60455-2313)
**PHONE** .................................. 708 598-3210
**Fax:** 708 598-1719
Barbara Mirowski, *Purchasing*
Ken Crouch, *Engineer*
Bob Fournier, *Manager*
Peter Ruddick, *Manager*
**EMP:** 40
**SQ FT:** 49,000
**SALES (corp-wide):** 3.5B **Publicly Held**
**WEB:** www.enthone.com
**SIC:** 2899 Plating compounds
**HQ:** Macdermid Enthone Inc.
350 Frontage Rd
West Haven CT 06516
203 934-8611

### (G-2506)
### MANITEX INTERNATIONAL INC (PA)
9725 Industrial Dr (60455-2304)
**PHONE** .................................. 708 430-7500
**Fax:** 708 430-1335
David J Langevin, *Ch of Bd*
Lubomir T Litchev, *President*
Andrew M Rooke, *President*
Bruce Steele, *Business Mgr*
Scott Rolston, *Vice Pres*
▲ **EMP:** 141
**SQ FT:** 39,000
**SALES:** 288.9MM **Publicly Held**
**WEB:** www.veri-tek.com
**SIC:** 3537 3536 Industrial trucks & tractors; forklift trucks; lift trucks, industrial: fork, platform, straddle, etc.; hoists, cranes & monorails

### (G-2507)
### MENASHA PACKAGING COMPANY LLC
7770 W 71st St (60455-1051)
**PHONE** .................................. 708 728-0372
**EMP:** 151
**SALES (corp-wide):** 1.8B **Privately Held**
**SIC:** 2653 Sheets, corrugated: made from purchased materials
**HQ:** Menasha Packaging Company, Llc
1645 Bergstrom Rd
Neenah WI 54956
920 751-1000

### (G-2508)
### MICRON METAL FINISHING LLC
8585 S 77th Ave (60455-1779)
**PHONE** .................................. 708 599-0055
Mary Agrusa, *Accounts Mgr*
Ed Warda, *Director*
Watt Bradley,
Rauter Scott,
**EMP:** 42
**SALES (est):** 8.9MM **Privately Held**
**SIC:** 3479 Aluminum coating of metal products

### (G-2509)
### MIDWEST CONTROL CORP
9063 S Octavia Ave (60455-2185)
**PHONE** .................................. 708 599-1331
**Fax:** 708 599-1408
Ed J Tunstall, *President*
Mavis Wasil, *Treasurer*
Deborah Guerra, *Shareholder*
Linda Tunstall, *Shareholder*
Diane Wasil, *Admin Sec*
**EMP:** 15
**SQ FT:** 12,000
**SALES (est):** 3MM **Privately Held**
**WEB:** www.midwestcontrolcorp.com
**SIC:** 3613 8711 Panel & distribution boards & other related apparatus; engineering services

### (G-2510)
### MIDWEST PRESS BRAKE DIES INC
7520 W 100th Pl (60455-2407)
**PHONE** .................................. 708 598-3860
**Fax:** 708 598-3876
Anton Berger, *President*
Karoline Berger, *Corp Secy*
Christine Gunther, *Vice Pres*
**EMP:** 19 EST: 1970
**SQ FT:** 11,000
**SALES (est):** 2.7MM **Privately Held**
**WEB:** www.midwestpressbrake.com
**SIC:** 3544 Special dies, tools, jigs & fixtures

### (G-2511)
### MURRAYS DISC AUTO STORES INC
7100 W 87th St (60455-2051)
**PHONE** .................................. 708 430-8155
Jeff Brown, *Manager*
**EMP:** 3 **Publicly Held**
**WEB:** www.murraysdiscount.com
**SIC:** 7699 7694 5531 Engine repair & replacement, non-automotive; rebuilding motors, except automotive; automotive parts
**HQ:** Murray's Discount Auto Stores, Inc.
8080 Haggerty Rd
Belleville MI 48111
734 957-8080

### (G-2512)
### N CONTOUR CONCEPTS INC
7415 W 90th St (60455-2121)
**PHONE** .................................. 708 599-9571
Luke Klinski, *President*
Mary Ann Klinski, *Vice Pres*
**EMP:** 6 EST: 2008
**SQ FT:** 6,000
**SALES:** 1.5MM **Privately Held**
**SIC:** 3599 Machine shop, jobbing & repair

### (G-2513)
### NABLUS SWEETS INC (PA)
8320 S Harlem Ave (60455-1719)
**PHONE** .................................. 708 529-3911
Mohommad Ahmad, *President*
▲ **EMP:** 8
**SQ FT:** 5,000
**SALES (est):** 2.3MM **Privately Held**
**SIC:** 2051 5461 Cakes, pies & pastries; pastries

### (G-2514)
### NIELSEN & BAINBRIDGE LLC
7830 W 71st St Ste 1 (60455-1093)
**PHONE** .................................. 708 546-2135
Jack Eisenberg, *Principal*
**EMP:** 90 **Privately Held**
**SIC:** 2499 5065 5113 3663 Picture frame molding, finished; electronic parts & equipment; industrial & personal service paper; radio & TV communications equipment
**HQ:** Nielsen & Bainbridge, Llc
12303 Tech Blvd Ste 950
Austin TX 78727
512 506-8844

### (G-2515)
### NORMAN FILTER COMPANY LLC
9850 Industrial Dr (60455-2324)
**PHONE** .................................. 708 233-5521
**Fax:** 708 430-5961
Phillip Netznik, *President*
Gary Uebel, *General Mgr*
Judy Harty, *Vice Pres*
David Ito, *Vice Pres*
Dale Lippold, *Vice Pres*
▼ **EMP:** 71
**SQ FT:** 60,000
**SALES (est):** 16MM **Privately Held**
**SIC:** 3569 Filters

## Bridgeview - Cook County (G-2516)

**(G-2516)**
**P & G KEENE ELEC RBLDRS LLC**
8432 Beloit Ave (60455-1774)
PHONE..................................708 430-5770
Lynette Castiglione, CFO
Sam Castiglione, Mng Member
▲ EMP: 28
SALES: 6.5MM Privately Held
SIC: 3694 Engine electrical equipment

**(G-2517)**
**PACO CORPORATION**
9945 Industrial Dr (60455-2408)
PHONE..................................708 430-2424
Fax: 708 430-0056
Raymond P Paice, President
Greg Paice, General Mgr
Esther Paice, Admin Sec
EMP: 14 EST: 1963
SQ FT: 20,000
SALES (est): 2.7MM Privately Held
WEB: www.pacograting.com
SIC: 3446 3441 Gratings, tread: fabricated metal; fabricated structural metal

**(G-2518)**
**PACTIV LLC**
7701 W 79th St (60455-1411)
PHONE..................................708 924-2402
EMP: 238 Privately Held
SIC: 2673 Food storage & trash bags (plastic)
HQ: Pactiv Llc
1900 W Field Ct
Lake Forest IL 60045
847 482-2000

**(G-2519)**
**PRAIRIE GROUP MANAGEMENT LLC**
7601 W 79th St Ste 1 (60455-1409)
PHONE..................................708 458-0400
Kort Alcorn, Manager
Bobby Oremous,
EMP: 99
SALES (est): 9.9MM Privately Held
SIC: 3273 Ready-mixed concrete

**(G-2520)**
**PRAIRIE PACKAGING INC**
7701 W 79th St (60455-1411)
PHONE..................................708 563-8670
Benjamin Chapiro, Vice Pres
Roger Kovack, Vice Pres
Gary Wayne, Purch Mgr
Russ Geer, Design Engr
Marian Barta, Human Res Mgr
EMP: 3 Privately Held
SIC: 3089 Cups, plastic, except foam
HQ: Prairie Packaging, Inc.
7200 S Mason Ave
Bedford Park IL 60638
708 496-1172

**(G-2521)**
**QUAKER OATS COMPANY**
7700 W 71st St (60455-1051)
PHONE..................................708 458-7090
Samuel De Ocampo, Buyer
Jason Roggenbauer, Branch Mgr
EMP: 185
SALES (corp-wide): 62.8B Publicly Held
WEB: www.quakeroats.com
SIC: 2086 Bottled & canned soft drinks
HQ: The Quaker Oats Company
555 W Monroe St Fl 1
Chicago IL 60661
312 821-1000

**(G-2522)**
**R & L SIGNS INC**
7430 W 90th St (60455-2122)
PHONE..................................708 233-0112
Rodolfo Cobos, President
EMP: 3
SALES (est): 140K Privately Held
SIC: 3993 Signs & advertising specialties

**(G-2523)**
**REBUILDERS ENTERPRISES INC**
9004 S Octavia Ave (60455-2126)
PHONE..................................708 430-0030
Gerald C Roberts, President
EMP: 3
SQ FT: 2,400
SALES (est): 310K Privately Held
WEB: www.rebuildersenterprises.com
SIC: 3714 3563 3511 3491 Motor vehicle brake systems & parts; air & gas compressors; turbines & turbine generator sets; industrial valves

**(G-2524)**
**RITEWAY BRAKE DIES INC**
7440 W 100th Pl (60455-2437)
PHONE..................................708 430-0795
Fax: 708 430-0978
Richard Bernecker, President
David Bernecker, Corp Secy
Bruno Bernecker, Shareholder
EMP: 19
SQ FT: 20,000
SALES (est): 4.2MM Privately Held
WEB: www.ritewaybrakedies.com
SIC: 3542 Press brakes; brakes, metal forming

**(G-2525)**
**ROSE PALLET LLC**
7647 W 100th Pl Ste D (60455-2434)
PHONE..................................708 333-3000
Brian Wesson, Principal
Mia Allen, Vice Pres
EMP: 8
SALES (est): 1.4MM Privately Held
SIC: 2448 Pallets, wood

**(G-2526)**
**RYANS GLASS & METAL INC (PA)**
7549 W 99th Pl (60455-2404)
PHONE..................................708 430-7790
Dave Ryan, President
Michael W Ryan, Vice Pres
Mark Margolis, Admin Sec
EMP: 4
SALES (est): 626.5K Privately Held
SIC: 3442 Metal doors, sash & trim

**(G-2527)**
**SCHAEFF LIFT TRUCK INC**
Also Called: Manitex Material Handling Div
9725 Industrial Dr (60455-2304)
PHONE..................................708 430-5301
Fax: 708 430-6803
Bob Litchev, President
Otto Wiltezk, Director
Paul Jarrell, Admin Sec
▲ EMP: 33
SQ FT: 20,000
SALES: 5.8MM
SALES (corp-wide): 288.9MM Publicly Held
WEB: www.schaeffinc.com
SIC: 3537 Forklift trucks
PA: Manitex International, Inc.
9725 Industrial Dr
Bridgeview IL 60455
708 430-7500

**(G-2528)**
**SIGNODE SUPPLY CORPORATION**
7701 W 71st St (60455-1050)
PHONE..................................708 458-7320
Fax: 708 458-0631
Jeff Hochleutner, Principal
Larry Ruud, Engineer
EMP: 146
SALES (est): 31.6MM Privately Held
SIC: 3499 Strapping, metal
HQ: Signode Industrial Group Llc
3650 W Lake Ave
Glenview IL 60026
847 724-7500

**(G-2529)**
**SOUTHFIELD CORPORATION**
Also Called: Chain O'Lakes Ready-Mixed Co
7601 W 79th St (60455-1115)
PHONE..................................708 362-2520
Steve Locicero, Plant Mgr
Sergio Martinez, Plant Mgr
Paul Blatner, Opers Mgr
Robert F Detten, Controller
Brad Burke, Finance
EMP: 48
SALES (corp-wide): 273.9MM Privately Held
WEB: www.prairiegroup.com
SIC: 3273 Ready-mixed concrete
PA: Southfield Corporation
8995 W 95th St
Palos Hills IL 60465
708 344-1000

**(G-2530)**
**SOUTHFIELD CORPORATION**
Evanston Fuel & Mtl Co Div
7601 W 79th St (60455-1115)
P.O. Box 1123, Oak Lawn (60455-0123)
PHONE..................................708 458-0400
Alan Oremus, President
EMP: 100
SALES (corp-wide): 273.9MM Privately Held
WEB: www.prairiegroup.com
SIC: 3273 Ready-mixed concrete
PA: Southfield Corporation
8995 W 95th St
Palos Hills IL 60465
708 344-1000

**(G-2531)**
**STAMPEDE MEAT INC (PA)**
7351 S 78th Ave (60455-1185)
PHONE..................................773 376-4300
Fax: 708 376-9349
Brock Furlong, CEO
Bill Kulach, President
Mike Asleson, Business Mgr
Alicia Talavera, Business Mgr
Raymond McKiernan, Senior VP
▲ EMP: 1000
SQ FT: 140,000
SALES: 320MM Privately Held
SIC: 2013 Prepared beef products from purchased beef; prepared pork products from purchased pork

**(G-2532)**
**SUPER-DRI CORP**
9707 S 76th Ave (60455-2309)
P.O. Box 267, Coalville UT (84017-0267)
PHONE..................................708 599-8700
William R Battersby, President
Raymond Battersby, Admin Sec
EMP: 3
SALES (est): 330.4K Privately Held
SIC: 2899 Essential oils

**(G-2533)**
**SUPERIOR PILING INC**
7247 S 78th Ave Ste 2 (60455-1091)
PHONE..................................708 496-1196
Francesco Scaglia, President
Frank Chmelir, Vice Pres
Gregg Chmelir, Vice Pres
Michael Bernitt, Manager
Howard Fletcher, MIS Mgr
EMP: 5
SQ FT: 42,000
SALES (est): 1.4MM Privately Held
WEB: www.superiorpiling.com
SIC: 3312 Structural shapes & pilings, steel

**(G-2534)**
**TIBOR MACHINE PRODUCTS INC (PA)**
7400 W 100th Pl (60455-2406)
PHONE..................................708 499-0017
Fax: 708 499-6803
Mark A Lindemulder, CEO
Jerry L Stockton, Exec VP
Mike Costello, Buyer
Adam Bykowski, QC Mgr
Christopher Sulicz, Engineer
EMP: 75
SQ FT: 75,000
SALES (est): 22.6MM Privately Held
SIC: 3599 Machine shop, jobbing & repair

**(G-2535)**
**VCNA PRAIRIE INC (PA)**
7601 W 79th St Ste 1 (60455-1409)
PHONE..................................708 458-0400
Richard Olsen, President
David Plummer, President
Jonna Kolton, Office Mgr
Robert Stineman, Manager
Richard Stoker, Manager
EMP: 58
SALES (est): 294.1MM Privately Held
SIC: 3273 Ready-mixed concrete

**(G-2536)**
**VCNA PRAIRIE ILLINOIS INC**
7601 W 79th St Ste 1 (60455-1409)
PHONE..................................708 458-0400
EMP: 12
SALES (est): 1.9MM Privately Held
SIC: 3273 Ready-mixed concrete

**(G-2537)**
**VCNA PRAIRIE INDIANA INC**
Also Called: Prairie Material
7601 W 79th St Ste 1 (60455-1409)
PHONE..................................708 458-0400
Fax: 708 458-7626
Richard Olson, President
Terri Peuquet, Manager
Mike Pistilli, Manager
G Bridge, Administration
EMP: 25
SALES: 950K Privately Held
SIC: 3272 Concrete products

**(G-2538)**
**WE ARE DONE LLC**
8407 S 77th Ave (60455-1738)
PHONE..................................708 598-7100
Wally Bransen, CEO
Edward S Piszynski, Principal
Sarah Trumbull, Vice Pres
Mike Cohen, Director
▲ EMP: 29
SALES (est): 10.2MM Privately Held
SIC: 2813 Aerosols

**(G-2539)**
**WESTROCK CP LLC**
7601 S 78th Ave (60455-1200)
PHONE..................................708 458-8100
Rick Wrobel, QC Dir
Pat Feeny, Branch Mgr
EMP: 86
SALES (corp-wide): 14.1B Publicly Held
WEB: www.smurfit-stone.com
SIC: 2631 Paperboard mills
HQ: Westrock Cp, Llc
504 Thrasher St
Norcross GA 30071

---

## Brighton
### Macoupin County

**(G-2540)**
**GAIL E STEPHENS**
Also Called: Versatile Machining
110 Ransom St (62012-4403)
P.O. Box 238 (62012-0238)
PHONE..................................618 372-0140
Gail E Stephens, Owner
Mike Stephens, Manager
EMP: 4
SQ FT: 4,400
SALES (est): 500K Privately Held
SIC: 3541 3544 3599 3728 Machine tools, metal cutting type; special dies & tools; custom machinery; aircraft parts & equipment

**(G-2541)**
**H & B HAMS**
202 W Plum St (62012-1242)
P.O. Box 172 (62012-0172)
PHONE..................................618 372-8690
Randy Burns, President
EMP: 9
SQ FT: 2,500
SALES (est): 1.5MM Privately Held
SIC: 5147 2013 Meats, cured or smoked; sausages & other prepared meats

**(G-2542)**
**HISTORIC TIMBER & PLANK INC**
16092 Lageman Ln (62012-3831)
PHONE..................................618 372-4546
Joe Adams, President
EMP: 20
SALES: 2.2MM Privately Held
SIC: 2426 2431 Flooring, hardwood; woodwork, interior & ornamental

# GEOGRAPHIC SECTION

## Broadview - Cook County (G-2567)

**(G-2543)**
**OLIN CORPORATION**
15025 State Highway 111  (62012-1978)
PHONE..................................618 258-2245
Roger Jones, *Branch Mgr*
**EMP:** 8
**SALES (corp-wide):** 5.5B  **Publicly Held**
**WEB:** www.olin.com
**SIC:** 3351  Copper rolling & drawing
**PA:** Olin Corporation
    190 Carondelet Plz # 1530
    Saint Louis MO 63105
    314 480-1400

**(G-2544)**
**PIASA PLASTICS INC**
Also Called: Clear Stand
615 N Main St  (62012-1043)
P.O. Box 27  (62012-0027)
PHONE..................................618 372-7516
Steve Wilken, *President*
Roma Wilken, *Vice Pres*
**EMP:** 8
**SQ FT:** 5,700
**SALES (est):** 400K  **Privately Held**
**WEB:** www.clearstands.com
**SIC:** 3993  Signs & advertising specialties

**(G-2545)**
**TAMMY SMITH**
14 Willow Way  (62012-2403)
PHONE..................................618 372-8410
**EMP:** 3
**SALES (est):** 230.1K  **Privately Held**
**SIC:** 3851  Mfg Ophthalmic Goods

**(G-2546)**
**WILMOUTH MACHINE WORKS INC**
1723 Terpening Rd  (62012-1529)
PHONE..................................618 372-3189
David Wilmouth, *President*
Karen Wilmouth, *Vice Pres*
**EMP:** 5
**SALES (est):** 500K  **Privately Held**
**SIC:** 3599  3441  Machine shop, jobbing & repair; fabricated structural metal

## Brimfield
### Peoria County

**(G-2547)**
**KRESS CORPORATION (PA)**
227 W Illinois St  (61517-8069)
PHONE..................................309 446-3395
Fax: 309 446-9625
Rita S Kress, *President*
Willie Hedgespeth, *COO*
Dawn Maninno, *Opers Staff*
Edward Pryor, *Production*
Rob Mahalic, *Purch Agent*
◆ **EMP:** 100
**SQ FT:** 200,000
**SALES (est):** 28.9MM  **Privately Held**
**WEB:** www.kresscarrier.com
**SIC:** 3531  Trucks, off-highway

**(G-2548)**
**OAK LEAF OUTDOORS INC**
Also Called: Lone Wolf Portable Treestand
10216 W Civil Defense Rd  (61517-9444)
P.O. Box 62, Edwards  (61528-0062)
PHONE..................................309 691-9653
Jared Schlipf, *President*
Mike Walston, *COO*
Jeff Weaver, *Vice Pres*
**EMP:** 12
**SALES (est):** 1.5MM  **Privately Held**
**SIC:** 3949  Hunting equipment

## Bristol
### Kendall County

**(G-2549)**
**PRO GLASS CORPORATION**
9318 Corneils Rd  (60512-9772)
PHONE..................................630 553-3141
Fax: 630 553-3144
Bob Mayerle, *President*
Debra Mayerle, *Vice Pres*
**EMP:** 4
**SQ FT:** 390
**SALES (est):** 478.2K  **Privately Held**
**SIC:** 3231  3083  Windshields, glass: made from purchased glass; laminated plastics plate & sheet

## Broadlands
### Champaign County

**(G-2550)**
**SMITH AND SON MACHINE SHOP**
454 County Road 2400 E  (61816-9734)
PHONE..................................217 260-3257
Steven Smith, *Owner*
**EMP:** 3  **EST:** 2008
**SALES:** 100K  **Privately Held**
**SIC:** 3599  Machine shop, jobbing & repair

## Broadview
### Cook County

**(G-2551)**
**A & H LITHOPRINT  INC**
2540 S 27th Ave  (60155-3851)
PHONE..................................708 345-1196
Fax: 708 345-1225
Patricia Ashley, *CEO*
David Ashley, *President*
Jennifer Ashley, *Vice Pres*
Mike Rubin, *Manager*
Ken Nemes, *Consultant*
**EMP:** 19
**SQ FT:** 16,000
**SALES (est):** 5.6MM  **Privately Held**
**WEB:** www.ahlithoprint.com
**SIC:** 2752  Commercial printing, offset

**(G-2552)**
**AAM-RO CORPORATION**
Also Called: Abrading Machinery Division
3110 S 26th Ave  (60155-4524)
PHONE..................................708 343-5543
Fax: 708 343-5547
Richard J Carey, *President*
Bunny Carey, *Vice Pres*
**EMP:** 18
**SQ FT:** 31,000
**SALES (est):** 3MM  **Privately Held**
**WEB:** www.aamroco.com
**SIC:** 3471  5084  Cleaning & descaling metal products; tumbling (cleaning & polishing) of machine parts; industrial machinery & equipment

**(G-2553)**
**ACME WIRE PRODUCTS  LLC**
2915 S 18th Ave Fl 1  (60155-4735)
PHONE..................................708 345-4430
Fax: 708 345-6051
Mike Kucera, *Engineer*
Maria Echeverria, *CFO*
Ares Vessol, *VP Human Res*
Bernie Echeverria, *Mng Member*
Irene Orquiz, *Office Admin*
▲ **EMP:** 30
**SQ FT:** 30,000
**SALES (est):** 6.4MM  **Privately Held**
**WEB:** www.acmewirepro.com
**SIC:** 3496  Miscellaneous fabricated wire products

**(G-2554)**
**ACTIVE GRINDING & MFG CO**
Also Called: Agmaco
1800 Parkes Dr  (60155-3956)
PHONE..................................708 344-0510
Fax: 708 344-5041
Richard A Pevitts, *CEO*
Carl Santucci, *President*
Virginia Pevitts, *Corp Secy*
Paula Limperis, *Asst Sec*
**EMP:** 15  **EST:** 1945
**SQ FT:** 15,000
**SALES (est):** 750K  **Privately Held**
**WEB:** www.activegrinding.com
**SIC:** 3545  3599  3823  Gauges (machine tool accessories); machine shop, jobbing & repair; industrial instrmnts msrmnt display/control process variable

**(G-2555)**
**ALL PRINTING & GRAPHICS INC (PA)**
2250 S 14th Ave  (60155-4002)
PHONE..................................708 450-1512
Fax: 708 344-3029
Hoyett Owens, *CEO*
Kim Popek, *President*
Betty Owens, *Vice Pres*
Scott Slate, *Finance*
**EMP:** 17
**SQ FT:** 15,000
**SALES (est):** 1.9MM  **Privately Held**
**WEB:** www.allprintinginc.com
**SIC:** 2752  2789  Commercial printing, offset; bookbinding & related work

**(G-2556)**
**ALTON INDUSTRIES INC**
2700 S 21st Ave  (60155-4640)
PHONE..................................708 865-2000
Fax: 708 865-2012
Alfred C Saporito Sr, *President*
**EMP:** 15
**SQ FT:** 12,000
**SALES (est):** 1MM  **Privately Held**
**SIC:** 3471  Coloring & finishing of aluminum or formed products

**(G-2557)**
**ANDREW DISTRIBUTION INC (PA)**
1841 Gardner Rd  (60155-4401)
P.O. Box 1099, Melrose Park  (60161-1099)
PHONE..................................708 410-2400
Charlie Malek, *President*
Charles Murphree, *Business Mgr*
Nahrine Malek, *Admin Sec*
**EMP:** 23
**SALES (est):** 8.2MM  **Privately Held**
**SIC:** 2711  Newspapers

**(G-2558)**
**APH CUSTOM WOOD & METAL PDTS**
2801 S 25th Ave  (60155-4531)
PHONE..................................708 410-1274
Henry Kruski, *Owner*
▲ **EMP:** 5
**SALES (est):** 363.7K  **Privately Held**
**SIC:** 2499  Carved & turned wood

**(G-2559)**
**ARROW PNEUMATICS  INC**
Also Called: AP
2111 W 21st St  (60155-4627)
PHONE..................................708 343-6177
Fax: 708 343-1907
Jerry R Brown, *CEO*
Benny Kawa, *President*
Steve Fligel, *Plant Mgr*
Rikki Thompson, *Purch Agent*
Jim Loughran, *Engineer*
▲ **EMP:** 55  **EST:** 1914
**SQ FT:** 60,000
**SALES (est):** 16.6MM  **Privately Held**
**WEB:** www.arrowpneumatics.com
**SIC:** 3569  Filters

**(G-2560)**
**ARTISTIC ENGRAVING CORPORATION**
2929 S 18th Ave Ste B  (60155-4736)
PHONE..................................708 409-0149
Mary Baldwin, *President*
Kevin Baldwin, *Corp Secy*
**EMP:** 3
**SQ FT:** 1,500
**SALES:** 160K  **Privately Held**
**WEB:** www.artistic-eng.com
**SIC:** 3993  Signs & advertising specialties

**(G-2561)**
**BELDEN MACHINE CORPORATION**
2500 Braga Dr  (60155-3943)
PHONE..................................708 344-4600
Len Sainati, *President*
Dave Carver, *Treasurer*
Diane Parpet, *Manager*
Jeff Wilson, *Technical Staff*
Al Wennerstrom, *Admin Sec*
**EMP:** 15
**SQ FT:** 20,000
**SALES (est):** 2.9MM  **Privately Held**
**WEB:** www.beldenmachine.com
**SIC:** 3541  5084  Machine tools, metal cutting type; industrial machinery & equipment

**(G-2562)**
**BELDEN TOOLS  INC**
2500 Braga Dr  (60155-3989)
PHONE..................................708 344-4600
Fax: 708 344-0245
Perry Sainati, *President*
Oliver Gaess, *President*
Al Wennerstrom, *Mfg Mgr*
Norman Dziedzic, *Engineer*
Rick Kalata, *Engineer*
◆ **EMP:** 30
**SQ FT:** 26,000
**SALES (est):** 7.4MM  **Privately Held**
**WEB:** www.beldenuniversal.com
**SIC:** 3545  Machine tool attachments & accessories

**(G-2563)**
**BMC 1092  INC**
Also Called: Solo Laboratories
2200 Parkes Dr  (60155-3949)
PHONE..................................708 544-2200
Brian Corcoran, *President*
William Kokum, *Vice Pres*
Lisa Patel, *QA Dir*
Helmut Schuster, *Engineer*
Bill Kokum, *Office Mgr*
**EMP:** 20
**SALES (est):** 5.5MM  **Privately Held**
**SIC:** 2844  Hair preparations, including shampoos

**(G-2564)**
**BOMEL TOOL MANUFACTURING CO**
2111 Roberts Dr  (60155-4630)
PHONE..................................708 343-3663
John E Gorman, *President*
Jim Oles, *General Mgr*
Jim Bures, *Controller*
**EMP:** 110
**SQ FT:** 50,000
**SALES (est):** 16.8MM  **Privately Held**
**SIC:** 3544  3469  Special dies, tools, jigs & fixtures; metal stampings

**(G-2565)**
**CENTRAL STEEL FABRICATORS**
2100 Parkes Dr  (60155-3951)
PHONE..................................708 652-2037
Fax: 773 247-3307
Gregory D Johnston, *President*
Miguel J Jaimes, *General Mgr*
Mike Murzanski, *Vice Pres*
Dave Antrim, *Purch Agent*
Greg Lawton, *Sales Executive*
▼ **EMP:** 40  **EST:** 1904
**SQ FT:** 70,000
**SALES (est):** 10.4MM  **Privately Held**
**WEB:** www.centralsteelfab.com
**SIC:** 3449  Miscellaneous metalwork

**(G-2566)**
**CHASE PRODUCTS CO**
2727 Gardner Rd  (60155-4413)
P.O. Box 70, Maywood  (60153-0070)
PHONE..................................708 865-1000
Fax: 708 865-7041
Donald R Virzi, *Vice Ch Bd*
Judith Albazi, *President*
Judy Albazi, *Vice Pres*
Kevin Smith, *Production*
Toni Gurgonne, *Purchasing*
◆ **EMP:** 60  **EST:** 1949
**SQ FT:** 100,000
**SALES (est):** 34.5MM  **Privately Held**
**WEB:** www.chaseltd.com
**SIC:** 2813  3544  2879  2851  Aerosols; special dies, tools, jigs & fixtures; agricultural chemicals; paints & allied products

**(G-2567)**
**CHICAGO CLAMP COMPANY**
2350 S 27th Ave  (60155-3855)
PHONE..................................708 343-8311
Sarah Holmgren, *Principal*
Kevin Barry, *Mng Member*
**EMP:** 5

# Broadview - Cook County (G-2568)

SALES: 179.2K **Privately Held**
SIC: 3462 5251 Construction or mining equipment forgings, ferrous; hardware

### (G-2568)
### CLASSIC COLOR INC
2424 S 25th Ave (60155-3874)
PHONE ..................... 708 484-0000
Fax: 708 344-2233
Raymond E Bell, *President*
Christopher Pirrone, *Business Mgr*
Jeffrey Hernandez, *Vice Pres*
Sara Isiminger, *Production*
Gail Selir, *Production*
EMP: 105
SALES: 25MM **Privately Held**
WEB: www.classiccolor.com
SIC: 2752 Commercial printing, lithographic

### (G-2569)
### CLEMENTS NATIONAL COMPANY (HQ)
Also Called: Cadillac Products
2150 Parkes Dr (60155-3951)
PHONE ..................... 708 594-5890
Reginald W Barrett, *CEO*
Sabit Inan, *Vice Pres*
Sharon Paradowski, *Purch Agent*
Brandon Wall, *Design Engr*
Andrea Nehrbass, *Sales Staff*
▲ EMP: 5
SQ FT: 50,000
SALES (est): 20MM **Privately Held**
WEB: www.cadillacproducts.com
SIC: 3542 3648 3643 3634 Machine tools, metal forming type; lighting equipment; electric connectors; fans, exhaust & ventilating, electric: household

### (G-2570)
### CLEMENTS NATIONAL COMPANY
2150 Parkes Dr (60155-3951)
PHONE ..................... 708 594-5890
Fax: 773 594-2481
Bill Croft, *Branch Mgr*
EMP: 40 **Privately Held**
WEB: www.cadillacproducts.com
SIC: 3589 Commercial cleaning equipment
HQ: Clements National Company
2150 Parkes Dr
Broadview IL 60155
708 594-5890

### (G-2571)
### DE ENTERPRISES INC
Also Called: Interntional Chem Formulations
1945 Gardner Rd (60155-3701)
PHONE ..................... 708 345-8088
Frank A De Santis, *President*
Laura De Santis, *Vice Pres*
Theresa Russo, *Office Mgr*
▼ EMP: 10
SQ FT: 8,000
SALES (est): 1.5MM **Privately Held**
WEB: www.de-enterprises.com
SIC: 2821 2899 Acrylic resins; chemical preparations

### (G-2572)
### DOWNEY INVESTMENTS INC
2125 Gardner Rd (60155-2826)
PHONE ..................... 708 345-8000
David Wasz, *CEO*
Bernard L Downey, *President*
Robert Pokrywka, *Vice Pres*
D Smith, *Vice Pres*
Paul Wiesbach, *Plant Mgr*
▼ EMP: 260 EST: 1958
SQ FT: 320,000
SALES (est): 28.9MM **Privately Held**
WEB: www.bldowney.com
SIC: 3479 Coating of metals & formed products

### (G-2573)
### DURABILT DYVEX INC
Also Called: Durabilt Manufacturing
2545 S 25th Ave (60155-3856)
PHONE ..................... 708 397-4673
Fax: 773 622-7270
Thomas J Durbin, *President*
▲ EMP: 16
SQ FT: 30,000
SALES: 1MM **Privately Held**
WEB: www.durabiltusa.com
SIC: 3317 3423 3496 3429 Steel pipe & tubes; wrenches, hand tools; chain, welded; tackle blocks, metal; stabilizing bars (cargo), metal

### (G-2574)
### ELEVATOR CABLE & SUPPLY CO
Also Called: E C S
2741 S 21st Ave (60155-4639)
PHONE ..................... 708 338-9700
Fax: 708 338-9781
Raymond J Allen, *President*
Reid Goodrich, *CFO*
▲ EMP: 30
SQ FT: 21,000
SALES (est): 8.3MM **Privately Held**
WEB: www.escalatorparts.com
SIC: 3534 2821 Elevators & equipment; plastics materials & resins

### (G-2575)
### ELKAY MANUFACTURING COMPANY
2700 S 17th Ave (60155-4778)
PHONE ..................... 708 681-1880
Fax: 708 681-2961
August R Campeotto, *Materials Mgr*
Brennan Studer, *Opers Staff*
Tim Wilde, *Mfg Staff*
Mark Whittington, *Opers-Prdtn-Mfg*
Gregg Sorrentino, *Purch Mgr*
EMP: 500
SALES (corp-wide): 1.1B **Privately Held**
WEB: www.elkayusa.com
SIC: 3431 3585 3432 3261 Sinks: enameled iron, cast iron or pressed metal; refrigeration & heating equipment; plumbing fixture fittings & trim; vitreous plumbing fixtures
PA: Elkay Manufacturing Company Inc
2222 Camden Ct
Oak Brook IL 60523
630 574-8484

### (G-2576)
### ELKAY MANUFACTURING COMPANY
2700 S 17th Ave (60155-4778)
PHONE ..................... 630 574-8484
Bradford Svensson, *Principal*
Phil Roberto, *Vice Pres*
EMP: 5
SALES (corp-wide): 1.1B **Privately Held**
SIC: 3431 Metal sanitary ware
PA: Elkay Manufacturing Company Inc
2222 Camden Ct
Oak Brook IL 60523
630 574-8484

### (G-2577)
### FFG RESTORATION INC
Also Called: SERVPRO La Grnge Prk/N Rvrside
2737 S 12th Ave (60155-4836)
PHONE ..................... 708 240-4873
James Frangella, *President*
EMP: 15 EST: 2009
SALES (est): 2.9MM **Privately Held**
SIC: 3823 Water quality monitoring & control systems

### (G-2578)
### FIDELITY BINDERY COMPANY
2829 S 18th Ave (60155-4782)
PHONE ..................... 708 343-6833
Fax: 708 343-5061
Earl Williams, *Owner*
Randy Williams, *Accounts Mgr*
EMP: 40 EST: 1964
SQ FT: 20,000
SALES (est): 3.2MM **Privately Held**
WEB: www.fidelityprint.com
SIC: 2789 2752 Bookbinding & related work; commercial printing, lithographic

### (G-2579)
### FIDELITY PRINT CMMNCATIONS LLC
2829 S 18th Ave 33 (60155-4725)
PHONE ..................... 708 343-6833
Earl Williams, *Ch of Bd*
Nichole Williams, *President*
Bernard Williams, *Vice Pres*
Randy Williams, *Manager*
EMP: 42
SQ FT: 20,000
SALES (est): 9.3MM **Privately Held**
WEB: www.fidelityberlin.com
SIC: 2752 Commercial printing, lithographic

### (G-2580)
### FINANCIAL GRAPHIC SERVICES INC (PA)
Also Called: Fgs
2910 S 18th Ave (60155-4727)
PHONE ..................... 708 343-0448
Fax: 630 585-8165
Richard Malacina Sr, *President*
Dennis Sasso, *Exec VP*
Mark Leber, *Senior VP*
Richard Malacina Jr, *Vice Pres*
Gaspar Vincente, *Plant Mgr*
EMP: 100
SQ FT: 25,000
SALES (est): 54.2MM **Privately Held**
SIC: 2759 Financial note & certificate printing & engraving

### (G-2581)
### G MESSMORE COMPANY
2000 S 25th Ave (60155-2817)
P.O. Box 1136, La Grange Park (60526-9236)
PHONE ..................... 708 343-8114
Fax: 708 482-0231
Gary Lynn Messmore, *President*
Linda H Messmore, *Admin Sec*
EMP: 5
SQ FT: 3,000
SALES (est): 683.4K **Privately Held**
SIC: 3451 3599 Screw machine products; machine & other job shop work

### (G-2582)
### GRAYMILLS CORPORATION
2601 S 25th Ave (60155-4535)
PHONE ..................... 773 477-4100
Fax: 773 477-8673
Craig Sheilds, *Ch of Bd*
Linda Shields, *VP Admin*
Peg Esposito, *Purch Mgr*
Mary Allen, *Human Resources*
John Bosselli, *Marketing Staff*
▲ EMP: 72
SQ FT: 94,000
SALES (est): 21.9MM **Privately Held**
SIC: 3561 3559 Pumps & pumping equipment; degreasing machines, automotive & industrial

### (G-2583)
### HEADLY MANUFACTURING CO (PA)
2700 23rd St (60155-4512)
PHONE ..................... 708 338-0800
Fax: 708 338-3322
Albert Giusfredi, *President*
Jim Oles, *General Mgr*
Michael Corrigan, *Controller*
Randy Giusfredi, *Manager*
Bill Reda, *Manager*
EMP: 82 EST: 1921
SQ FT: 22,000
SALES (est): 23.9MM **Privately Held**
WEB: www.headlymfg.com
SIC: 3469 3544 Machine parts, stamped or pressed metal; special dies, tools, jigs & fixtures

### (G-2584)
### HEADLY MANUFACTURING CO
Also Called: Headly Mfg
2111 Roberts Dr (60155-4630)
PHONE ..................... 708 338-0800
EMP: 51
SALES (corp-wide): 23.9MM **Privately Held**
SIC: 3544 3469 Special dies, tools, jigs & fixtures; automobile license tags, stamped metal
PA: Headly Manufacturing Co.
2700 23rd St
Broadview IL 60155
708 338-0800

### (G-2585)
### ILLINOIS TOOL WORKS INC
Also Called: ITW Shakeproof Group
2550 S 27th Ave (60155-3851)
PHONE ..................... 708 681-3891
Jerry De Witz, *General Mgr*
Steve Johnson, *Plant Mgr*
Tom Roberto, *Plant Mgr*
Wilson Hernandez, *Info Tech Mgr*
EMP: 50
SALES (corp-wide): 13.6B **Publicly Held**
SIC: 3429 Metal fasteners
PA: Illinois Tool Works Inc.
155 Harlem Ave
Glenview IL 60025
847 724-7500

### (G-2586)
### ILLINOIS TOOL WORKS INC
ITW Shakeproof Industrial Pdts
2550 S 27th Ave (60155-3851)
PHONE ..................... 708 343-0728
Fax: 708 681-3690
Richard Hensley, *QC Dir*
Roberta Calvert, *Branch Mgr*
EMP: 18
SALES (corp-wide): 13.6B **Publicly Held**
SIC: 3452 3469 Washers; metal stampings
PA: Illinois Tool Works Inc.
155 Harlem Ave
Glenview IL 60025
847 724-7500

### (G-2587)
### INTEL PRINTING INC
1805 Beach St (60155-2862)
PHONE ..................... 708 343-1144
John Gilbert, *President*
Charles Libman, *Admin Sec*
EMP: 6
SQ FT: 8,000
SALES: 1.5MM **Privately Held**
WEB: www.intelprinting.com
SIC: 2752 Commercial printing, offset

### (G-2588)
### JOHNSON POWER LTD (PA)
2530 Braga Dr (60155-3943)
P.O. Box 6399, Maywood (60155-6399)
PHONE ..................... 708 345-4300
Fax: 708 345-4315
Lisa C Johnson Honig, *President*
Robert Honig, *Vice Pres*
Arlene Johnson, *Treasurer*
Pat Callen, *Controller*
▲ EMP: 41
SQ FT: 22,000
SALES: 15MM **Privately Held**
WEB: www.johnsonpower.com
SIC: 3714 Drive shafts, motor vehicle

### (G-2589)
### JOSEPHS FOOD PRODUCTS CO INC
2759 S 25th Ave (60155-4533)
PHONE ..................... 708 338-4090
Fax: 708 338-0191
Reginald Van Eekeren, *President*
Aloysius Van Eekeren, *Admin Sec*
EMP: 240
SQ FT: 170,000
SALES (est): 27.1MM **Privately Held**
SIC: 2099 Spices, including grinding

### (G-2590)
### KARNAK MIDWEST LLC
2601 Gardner Rd (60155-4411)
PHONE ..................... 708 338-3388
Fax: 708 338-0444
John McDermott, *General Mgr*
EMP: 14
SALES (corp-wide): 19.9MM **Privately Held**
SIC: 2952 Roofing materials
HQ: Karnak Midwest, L.L.C.
330 Central Ave
Clark NJ 07066
732 388-0300

### (G-2591)
### KELVYN PRESS INC (HQ)
Also Called: Financial Graphic Service
2910 S 18th Ave (60155-4733)
PHONE ..................... 708 343-0448
Fax: 708 343-0452

# GEOGRAPHIC SECTION
## Broadview - Cook County (G-2614)

Richard J Malacina, *President*
Gary Malacine, *General Mgr*
Richard Malacina Jr, *Vice Pres*
Lynn Suchecki, *Safety Mgr*
Nancy Overholt, *CFO*
**EMP:** 100
**SQ FT:** 100,000
**SALES (est):** 41.9MM **Privately Held**
**SIC:** 2752 Commercial printing, lithographic

**(G-2592)**
### LINDE GAS NORTH AMERICA LLC
2000 S 25th Ave Ste S (60155-2818)
**PHONE**................630 857-6460
Kirk Phelps, *Area Mgr*
**EMP:** 15
**SALES (corp-wide):** 17.9B **Privately Held**
**SIC:** 2813 Oxygen, compressed or liquefied; nitrogen; argon; hydrogen
**HQ:** Linde Gas North America Llc
200 Somerset Corp Blvd # 7000
Bridgewater NJ 08807
800 932-0803

**(G-2593)**
### LINDE GAS NORTH AMERICA LLC
2000 S 25th Ave Ste S (60155-2818)
**PHONE**................708 345-0894
Mark D Weller, *Chairman*
**EMP:** 14
**SALES (corp-wide):** 17.9B **Privately Held**
**SIC:** 3829 Breathalyzers
**HQ:** Linde Gas North America Llc
200 Somerset Corp Blvd # 7000
Bridgewater NJ 08807
800 932-0803

**(G-2594)**
### LITHOGRAPHIC INDUSTRIES INC
2445 Gardner Rd (60155-3798)
**PHONE**................773 921-7955
**Fax:** 708 865-0738
Louis A Ebeqrt, *President*
Cimon Mathews, *Engineer*
Roman A Ebert IV, *CFO*
Paula A Ebert, *Treasurer*
**EMP:** 45
**SQ FT:** 63,000
**SALES (est):** 12MM **Privately Held**
**WEB:** www.lithographic.com
**SIC:** 2752 Commercial printing, offset

**(G-2595)**
### MIDWEST INK CO
2701 S 12th Ave (60155-4836)
**PHONE**................708 345-7177
Frank Hannon, *President*
Joe Hannon, *Exec VP*
Joseph Hannon, *Admin Sec*
▲ **EMP:** 30
**SQ FT:** 20,000
**SALES (est):** 6.2MM **Privately Held**
**WEB:** www.midwestink.com
**SIC:** 2893 Printing ink

**(G-2596)**
### MIDWEST-DESIGN INC
2350 S 27th Ave (60155-3855)
**PHONE**................708 615-1572
**EMP:** 2 **EST:** 1994
**SQ FT:** 6,700
**SALES:** 475K **Privately Held**
**SIC:** 3644 Mfg Nonconductive Wiring Devices

**(G-2597)**
### MODERN PRINTING COLORS INC
1951 W 21st St (60155-4626)
**PHONE**................708 681-5678
Suresh Mahajan, *President*
Neerah Mahajan, *Vice Pres*
John Sergeant, *Sales Staff*
Guy McCormick, *Marketing Staff*
Gumaro Lopez, *Lab Dir*
▲ **EMP:** 15
**SALES (est):** 4.9MM **Privately Held**
**WEB:** www.moderncolors.com
**SIC:** 2899 7389 Ink or writing fluids; demonstration service

**(G-2598)**
### MOREY INDUSTRIES INC
Also Called: Westmont Engineering Company
2000 Beach St (60155-2833)
**PHONE**................708 343-3220
**Fax:** 708 343-1956
Douglas Morey, *President*
Michelle Reynolds, *Controller*
Scott Morey, *Admin Sec*
**EMP:** 110 **EST:** 1958
**SQ FT:** 40,000
**SALES (est):** 26.9MM **Privately Held**
**WEB:** www.westmontengineering.com
**SIC:** 3441 1796 1791 Fabricated structural metal; machinery installation; structural steel erection

**(G-2599)**
### MULLINS FOOD PRODUCTS INC
2200 S 25th Ave (60155-4584)
**PHONE**................708 344-3224
**Fax:** 708 344-3224
Jeanne Gannon, *President*
Ed Mullins, *General Mgr*
Michael Mullins, *COO*
Gary Saatkamp, *Safety Dir*
Rich Vlach, *Safety Dir*
**EMP:** 405
**SQ FT:** 325,000
**SALES (est):** 129.5MM **Privately Held**
**WEB:** www.mullinsfood.com
**SIC:** 2033 2035 Tomato products: packaged in cans, jars, etc.; barbecue sauce: packaged in cans, jars, etc.; catsup: packaged in cans, jars, etc.; dressings, salad: raw & cooked (except dry mixes)

**(G-2600)**
### MULTI SWATCH CORPORATION
Also Called: M.S.i
2600 S 25th Ave Ste Y (60155-4514)
**PHONE**................708 344-9440
**Fax:** 708 344-9461
John M Mozis, *President*
John Holly, *Managing Dir*
▲ **EMP:** 87
**SALES (est):** 12.2MM
**SALES (corp-wide):** 72.5MM **Privately Held**
**WEB:** www.architex-ljh.com
**SIC:** 2782 Sample books
**PA:** Architectural Textiles U.S.A., Inc.
3333 Commercial Ave
Northbrook IL 60062
847 205-1333

**(G-2601)**
### PARKER-HANNIFIN CORPORATION
Refrigeration Specialties
2445 S 25th Ave (60155-3858)
**PHONE**................708 681-6300
**Fax:** 708 681-5311
Darryl Miller, *Branch Mgr*
Mark Chase, *Manager*
Andres Valles, *Executive*
**EMP:** 45
**SALES (corp-wide):** 11.3B **Publicly Held**
**WEB:** www.parker.com
**SIC:** 3491 5078 Industrial valves; refrigeration equipment & supplies
**PA:** Parker-Hannifin Corporation
6035 Parkland Blvd
Cleveland OH 44124
216 896-3000

**(G-2602)**
### PRECISION CNNCTING ROD SVC INC
Also Called: Pcr Machining
2600 W Cermak Rd (60155-4505)
**PHONE**................708 345-3700
**Fax:** 708 345-7727
Richard Farrar, *President*
Edessa Farrar, *Vice Pres*
**EMP:** 12 **EST:** 1927
**SQ FT:** 20,000
**SALES (est):** 2.8MM **Privately Held**
**WEB:** www.connectingrod.com
**SIC:** 3714 Connecting rods, motor vehicle engine

**(G-2603)**
### PRINCIPAL MANUFACTURING CORP
2800 S 19th Ave (60155-4754)
**PHONE**................708 865-7500
**Fax:** 708 865-7632
Paul A Barnett, *President*
Benjamin Barnett, *Vice Pres*
Rick Barnett, *VP Mfg*
Gregory Keating, *Opers Staff*
Edward Farrer, *Purch Dir*
▲ **EMP:** 350 **EST:** 1957
**SQ FT:** 80,000
**SALES (est):** 112.9MM **Privately Held**
**WEB:** www.priman.com
**SIC:** 3469 Stamping metal for the trade

**(G-2604)**
### PRINTING ARTS CMMNICATIONS LLC
2001 W 21st St (60155-4632)
**PHONE**................708 938-1600
**Fax:** 708 938-1717
Ed Kristak, *General Mgr*
James Kosowski, *Vice Pres*
John Myszka, *Vice Pres*
John Earnest, *Project Mgr*
Kathy Pike, *Credit Staff*
**EMP:** 50
**SQ FT:** 60,000
**SALES (est):** 17.8MM **Privately Held**
**WEB:** www.printingartscommunications.com
**SIC:** 2752 Commercial printing, lithographic

**(G-2605)**
### PURES FOOD SPECIALTIES LLC
2929 S 25th Ave (60155-4529)
**PHONE**................708 344-8884
**Fax:** 708 344-8703
Elliott Pure, *President*
Jonathan Pure, *Vice Pres*
Ruth Pure, *Admin Sec*
**EMP:** 50 **EST:** 1989
**SQ FT:** 68,000
**SALES (est):** 10.2MM **Privately Held**
**WEB:** www.puresfood.com
**SIC:** 2052 Cookies

**(G-2606)**
### R A KERLEY INK ENGINEERS INC (PA)
2700 S 12th Ave (60155-4837)
**PHONE**................708 344-1295
**Fax:** 708 865-5759
John J Whalen, *President*
Jim O'Neill, *Controller*
Doug Miller, *Technical Staff*
Jim Oneil, *Director*
Betty K Whalen, *Admin Sec*
▼ **EMP:** 24
**SQ FT:** 12,000
**SALES (est):** 3.8MM **Privately Held**
**SIC:** 2893 Printing ink

**(G-2607)**
### RE-DO-IT CORP
1950 Beach St (60155-2861)
**PHONE**................708 343-7125
**Fax:** 708 343-7101
Virginia Donatell, *President*
Miss V Donatell, *Project Mgr*
John Donatell, *Opers Mgr*
**EMP:** 6 **EST:** 1990
**SQ FT:** 15,000
**SALES:** 700K **Privately Held**
**WEB:** www.redoit.org
**SIC:** 7699 3714 3593 Hydraulic equipment repair; motor vehicle parts & accessories; fluid power cylinders & actuators

**(G-2608)**
### RICTER CORPORATION
Also Called: A & H Bindery, The
2600 Lexington St (60155-2857)
**PHONE**................708 344-3300
**Fax:** 708 344-8712
Richard Bergman, *President*
Terence Murphy, *Vice Pres*
Frank Lempke, *Manager*
**EMP:** 12 **EST:** 1945
**SQ FT:** 12,500
**SALES (est):** 1.5MM **Privately Held**
**WEB:** www.ahbindery.com
**SIC:** 2789 Rebinding books, magazines or pamphlets

**(G-2609)**
### RIPA LLC
Also Called: Printing Arts
2001 W 21st St (60155-4632)
**PHONE**................708 938-1600
James Kosowski, *Mng Member*
John Kosowski,
John Ropski,
**EMP:** 5
**SALES (est):** 1.4MM **Privately Held**
**SIC:** 8741 2759 2621 Management services; commercial printing; wrapping & packaging papers

**(G-2610)**
### ROBERT BOSCH LLC (HQ)
Also Called: Automotive Group
2800 S 25th Ave (60155-4532)
**PHONE**................248 876-1000
**Fax:** 708 786-3544
Tim Frasier, *President*
Mike Mansuetti, *President*
Giles Wallis, *General Mgr*
Scott Winchip, *General Mgr*
Werner Struth, *Chairman*
◆ **EMP:** 500
**SALES:** 10.8B
**SALES (corp-wide):** 236.4MM **Privately Held**
**WEB:** www.boschservice.com
**SIC:** 3714 3694 5013 5064 Motor vehicle parts & accessories; motor vehicle brake systems & parts; motor vehicle electrical equipment; motors, starting: automotive & aircraft; distributors, motor vehicle engine; automotive supplies & parts; automotive engines & engine parts; motor vehicle; packaging machinery; deburring machines
**PA:** R O B E R T B O S C H S T I F T U N G Gesellschaft Mit Beschrankter Haftung
Heidehofstr. 31
Stuttgart 70184
711 460-840

**(G-2611)**
### ROHBI ENTERPRISES INC
3020 S 25th Ave (60155-4503)
**PHONE**................708 343-2004
Ronald Gustafson, *President*
Helen Gustafson, *Corp Secy*
**EMP:** 7 **EST:** 1978
**SQ FT:** 14,500
**SALES (est):** 1.1MM **Privately Held**
**SIC:** 3599 Machine shop, jobbing & repair

**(G-2612)**
### SOURCE TECHNOLOGY
2150 Parkes Dr (60155-3951)
**PHONE**................281 894-6171
**EMP:** 1 **EST:** 2008
**SALES (est):** 280.7K **Privately Held**
**SIC:** 3829 Pressure transducers
**PA:** Winchester Electronics Corporation
55 Water St
Norwalk CT 06854

**(G-2613)**
### STAR THERMOPLASTIC ALLOYS AND (PA)
Also Called: Star Thermoplastics
2121 W 21st St (60155-4634)
**PHONE**................708 343-1100
**Fax:** 708 343-1110
Thomas A Dieschbourg, *President*
Mena Ramiez, *Manager*
**EMP:** 50
**SQ FT:** 30,000
**SALES (est):** 6.7MM **Privately Held**
**WEB:** www.starthermoplastics.com
**SIC:** 2821 Thermoplastic materials

**(G-2614)**
### STAR THERMOPLASTIC ALLOYS AND
Also Called: Star Plastics
2121 W 21st St (60155-4634)
**PHONE**................708 343-1100
Tom Dieschburg, *Manager*
**EMP:** 14

**SALES (corp-wide):** 6.7MM **Privately Held**
**WEB:** www.starthermoplastics.com
**SIC:** 2821 2822 Thermoplastic materials; synthetic rubber
**PA:** Star Thermoplastic Alloys And Rubbers, Inc.
2121 W 21st St
Broadview IL 60155
708 343-1100

*(G-2615)*
### STRIKEFORCE BOWLING LLC
Also Called: Kr Strikeforce Bowling
2001 Parkes Dr (60155-3952)
**PHONE** ................................. 800 297-8555
**Fax:** 708 888-1400
Brian Nendza, *Accountant*
Brad Handelman, *Mng Member*
▲ **EMP:** 20
**SQ FT:** 80,000
**SALES (est):** 4.5MM **Privately Held**
**SIC:** 3949 Sporting & athletic goods

*(G-2616)*
### THUNDER TOOL CORP
2800 S 18th Ave (60155-4753)
**PHONE** ................................. 708 544-4742
**Fax:** 708 544-5625
Ryczard Baczyski, *President*
Joe Nagorzawski, *Vice Pres*
**EMP:** 12
**SQ FT:** 10,000
**SALES (est):** 1.3MM **Privately Held**
**WEB:** www.thundertool.com
**SIC:** 3599 Machine shop, jobbing & repair

*(G-2617)*
### TOTAL CONTROL SPORTS INC
2000 S 25th Ave Ste C (60155-2820)
**PHONE** ................................. 708 486-5800
Peter J Parenti, *President*
Amber Patton, *Manager*
Diane M Parenti, *Admin Sec*
**EMP:** 3 EST: 2009
**SALES (est):** 367.9K **Privately Held**
**SIC:** 3949 Softball equipment & supplies

*(G-2618)*
### TURBO TOOL & MOLD CO
3045 S 26th Ave (60155-4525)
**PHONE** ................................. 708 615-1730
Mike Turbonic, *President*
**EMP:** 4
**SQ FT:** 3,000
**SALES (est):** 533.2K **Privately Held**
**SIC:** 3599 3544 Machine shop, jobbing & repair; special dies, tools, jigs & fixtures

*(G-2619)*
### VIBRO/DYNAMICS CORPORATION
2443 Braga Dr (60155-3941)
**PHONE** ................................. 708 345-2050
**Fax:** 708 345-2225
Hal Reinke, *President*
Keith Leatherwood, *Vice Pres*
Steven Veroeven, *Vice Pres*
Lori Home, *Traffic Mgr*
Mike Jacobs, *Purchasing*
▲ **EMP:** 20
**SQ FT:** 25,000
**SALES (est):** 5.2MM **Privately Held**
**SIC:** 3499 Machine bases, metal

*(G-2620)*
### WESTMONT METAL MFG LLC
2350 S 27th Ave (60155-3855)
**PHONE** ................................. 708 343-0214
**Fax:** 708 343-0215
Philip Solo, *General Mgr*
Roberto Lugar, *Engineer*
James Stephan, *Engineer*
Douglas H Morey, *Mng Member*
**EMP:** 15
**SQ FT:** 26,000
**SALES (est):** 4.1MM **Privately Held**
**WEB:** www.westmontmetal.com
**SIC:** 3441 Fabricated structural metal

---

## Brookfield
### Cook County

*(G-2621)*
### 10 4 IRP INC
8846 47th St (60513-2532)
**PHONE** ................................. 708 485-1040
Mara Lopez, *President*
Marcelino Bacerott, *Vice Pres*
**EMP:** 2
**SALES:** 300K **Privately Held**
**SIC:** 3469 Automobile license tags, stamped metal

*(G-2622)*
### AWNINGS UNLIMITED INC
9445 Ogden Ave (60513-1849)
P.O. Box 25 (60513-0025)
**PHONE** ................................. 708 485-6769
**Fax:** 708 485-4276
Harold Volman Jr, *President*
Jeff Russler, *Vice Pres*
Edna Volman, *Admin Sec*
**EMP:** 4
**SQ FT:** 5,000
**SALES:** 700K **Privately Held**
**SIC:** 3444 Awnings, sheet metal

*(G-2623)*
### BELMONT ELECTRO CO INC
8920 47th St (60513-2417)
**PHONE** ................................. 773 472-4641
**Fax:** 773 472-4925
Dennis Sell, *President*
**EMP:** 6
**SQ FT:** 3,000
**SALES:** 427.5K **Privately Held**
**SIC:** 7694 3621 Electric motor repair; motors & generators

*(G-2624)*
### BLANDO G MFG JEWELERS
9228 Broadway Ave (60513-1252)
**PHONE** ................................. 708 387-0014
Gino A Blando, *President*
Guy Blando Sr, *President*
Gary J Blando, *Corp Secy*
Gino Blando, *Vice Pres*
**EMP:** 7
**SQ FT:** 3,200
**SALES:** 250K **Privately Held**
**SIC:** 7631 3911 5944 Diamond setter; jewelry repair services; jewelry mountings & trimmings; jewelry, precious stones & precious metals

*(G-2625)*
### BOYLESTON 21ST CENTURY LLC
9118 47th St Ste 3 (60513-2768)
**PHONE** ................................. 708 387-2012
Robert Sandstone, *President*
**EMP:** 2
**SALES (est):** 369.7K **Privately Held**
**WEB:** www.boylstonprv.com
**SIC:** 3822 Steam pressure controls, residential or commercial type

*(G-2626)*
### BXB INTL INC
9101 Sahler Ave Apt 1 (60513-2482)
**PHONE** ................................. 312 240-1966
Bob Bassari, *President*
**EMP:** 9
**SALES (est):** 696.6K **Privately Held**
**WEB:** www.bassari.com
**SIC:** 2253 2353 5632 5944 T-shirts & tops, knit; baseball caps; handbags; watches; jewelry, precious stones & precious metals

*(G-2627)*
### CHICAGO DEPORTIVO GROUP INC
3748 Cleveland Ave (60513-1510)
P.O. Box 411 (60513-0411)
**PHONE** ................................. 708 387-7724
Jesus Aguilar, *Principal*
**EMP:** 3
**SALES (est):** 112.3K **Privately Held**
**SIC:** 2711 Newspapers

*(G-2628)*
### COMPRHNSIVE PRSTHTICS ORTHTICS (PA)
Also Called: MD Labs
8400 Brookfield Ave Ste 1 (60513-2091)
**PHONE** ................................. 708 387-9700
Mark Devens, *President*
Corinne Devens, *General Mgr*
Don McComb, *CPA*
Peggy Blake, *Manager*
**EMP:** 13
**SQ FT:** 6,500
**SALES (est):** 2MM **Privately Held**
**WEB:** www.mdoandp.com
**SIC:** 3842 Braces, orthopedic; abdominal supporters, braces & trusses; cervical collars; limbs, artificial

*(G-2629)*
### CULEN TOOL & MANUFACTURING CO
9128 47th St Ste 1 (60513-2496)
**PHONE** ................................. 708 387-1580
Stephen Culen, *President*
Cynthia Culen, *Vice Pres*
**EMP:** 6
**SQ FT:** 12,500
**SALES (est):** 951.3K **Privately Held**
**SIC:** 3469 Metal stampings

*(G-2630)*
### E R WAGNER MANUFACTURING CO
Also Called: Stocker Hinge Mfg Co
8822 47th St (60513-2516)
P.O. Box 149 (60513-0149)
**PHONE** ................................. 708 485-3400
**Fax:** 708 485-0058
Russ Dunlap, *Opers Staff*
Jared Schilling, *Buyer*
Chuck Gambo, *Chief Engr*
Rick Fingar, *Natl Sales Mgr*
William Hayes, *Branch Mgr*
**EMP:** 105
**SALES (corp-wide):** 58.1MM **Privately Held**
**WEB:** www.erwagner.com
**SIC:** 3429 Manufactured hardware (general)
**PA:** E. R. Wagner Manufacturing Company
4611 N 32nd St
Milwaukee WI 53209
414 449-8237

*(G-2631)*
### ENDOFIX LTD
9118 Ogden Ave Ste 1 (60513-1974)
**PHONE** ................................. 708 715-3472
Stephanie R McCollom, *CEO*
John McCollom, *President*
**EMP:** 5
**SQ FT:** 408
**SALES:** 1MM **Privately Held**
**SIC:** 3841 3541 Surgical instruments & apparatus; machine tool replacement & repair parts, metal cutting types

*(G-2632)*
### FLEETWOOD PRESS INC
9321 Ogden Ave (60513-1817)
**PHONE** ................................. 708 485-6811
Bernard A Kowalski, *President*
Carmella Kowalski, *Admin Sec*
**EMP:** 3
**SQ FT:** 1,500
**SALES (est):** 424.9K **Privately Held**
**SIC:** 2752 7372 2791 2789 Commercial printing, offset; prepackaged software; typesetting; bookbinding & related work; commercial printing

*(G-2633)*
### GARCOA INC
8838 Brookfield Ave (60513-2783)
**PHONE** ................................. 708 905-5118
**EMP:** 99
**SALES (corp-wide):** 85.8MM **Privately Held**
**SIC:** 5122 2844 Cosmetics, perfumes & hair products; toilet preparations
**PA:** Garcoa, Inc
26135 Mureau Rd Ste 100
Calabasas CA 91302
818 225-0375

*(G-2634)*
### GEAR & REPAIR
9100 Plainfield Rd Ste 13 (60513-2458)
**PHONE** ................................. 708 387-0144
Gary Vimont, *Owner*
**EMP:** 2
**SALES:** 600K **Privately Held**
**SIC:** 5085 3462 Industrial supplies; iron & steel forgings

*(G-2635)*
### IMPERIAL KITCHENS & BATH INC
8918 Ogden Ave (60513-2006)
**PHONE** ................................. 708 485-0020
**Fax:** 708 485-2880
Larry Rychlowski, *President*
Edward Pudalek, *Treasurer*
**EMP:** 10
**SQ FT:** 6,400
**SALES:** 1.9MM **Privately Held**
**WEB:** www.imperialkitchensandbaths.com
**SIC:** 1751 2511 2541 Cabinet building & installation; wood household furniture; cabinets, except refrigerated: show, display, etc.: wood

*(G-2636)*
### JD PRO PRODUCTIONS INC
4123 Maple Ave (60513-1915)
**PHONE** ................................. 708 485-2126
Jerrold Dobes, *President*
Patricia Dobes, *Admin Sec*
**EMP:** 2
**SALES (est):** 239K **Privately Held**
**WEB:** www.jdprod.com
**SIC:** 2791 Typographic composition, for the printing trade

*(G-2637)*
### MARGES AUNT POTATO SALAD
3938 Arthur Ave (60513-1927)
**PHONE** ................................. 708 612-2300
Bill Schmakel, *Owner*
**EMP:** 1
**SALES:** 200K **Privately Held**
**SIC:** 2099 Potatoes, dried: packaged with other ingredients

*(G-2638)*
### NEWHEALTH SOLUTIONS LLC
3935 Sunnyside Ave (60513-2842)
**PHONE** ................................. 803 627-8378
Tyler Masterson, *CEO*
Chris Legros, *COO*
**EMP:** 3 EST: 2011
**SALES (est):** 215.5K **Privately Held**
**SIC:** 2834 Vitamin preparations

*(G-2639)*
### NICKS METAL FABG & SONS
9132 47th St (60513-2397)
**PHONE** ................................. 708 485-1170
**Fax:** 708 485-1171
Nick Tepavchevich Jr, *President*
Nick Tepavchevich Sr, *President*
Thomas Tepavchevich, *Treasurer*
Gloria Tepavchevich, *Admin Sec*
**EMP:** 18 EST: 1949
**SQ FT:** 11,000
**SALES (est):** 3.8MM **Privately Held**
**SIC:** 3441 3446 Fabricated structural metal; architectural metalwork

*(G-2640)*
### PANEL WINDOW CO INC
9509 Ogden Ave (60513-1841)
**PHONE** ................................. 708 485-0310
**Fax:** 708 485-0310
Keith Wouk, *President*
**EMP:** 6 EST: 1959
**SQ FT:** 7,000
**SALES (est):** 548.7K **Privately Held**
**SIC:** 3231 Products of purchased glass

*(G-2641)*
### PRIORITY PRINT
9433 Ogden Ave (60513-1896)
**PHONE** ................................. 708 485-7080
**Fax:** 708 485-7083
Will Knippenberg, *Owner*
**EMP:** 3
**SQ FT:** 3,500

# GEOGRAPHIC SECTION

SALES (est): 200K  Privately Held
SIC: 2752  2759  2396  Commercial printing, lithographic; offset & photolithographic printing; commercial printing; automotive & apparel trimmings

**(G-2642)**
**SMILE OF BROOKFIELD**
9144 Broadway Ave  (60513-1304)
PHONE............................708 485-7754
Payal Shah, *Principal*
EMP: 2
SALES (est): 225.7K  Privately Held
SIC: 3843  Enamels, dentists'

**(G-2643)**
**TAILORED INC**
9520 47th St Ste 2  (60513-2833)
PHONE............................708 387-9854
Fax: 708 387-9856
Kristine Vrhel, *President*
Marianne Spevacek, *COO*
Arlaina Tibensky, *Vice Pres*
EMP: 9  EST: 1946
SQ FT: 4,200
SALES (est): 270K  Privately Held
WEB: www.tailorbiz.com
SIC: 2391  2392  Draperies, plastic & textile: from purchased materials; bedspreads & bed sets: made from purchased materials

**(G-2644)**
**TENCO HYDRO INC OF ILLINOIS**
4620 Forest Ave  (60513-2594)
PHONE............................708 387-0700
Fax: 708 387-0732
Albert W Lee, *President*
Sandy Monaco, *Accountant*
Kevin Walsh, *Sales Mgr*
EMP: 6  EST: 1980
SQ FT: 10,000
SALES (est): 1MM  Privately Held
WEB: www.tencohydro.com
SIC: 3589  Sewage & water treatment equipment

**(G-2645)**
**THOMAS FINE STAIRS INC**
9110 47th St  (60513-2419)
PHONE............................708 387-9506
William Thomas, *CEO*
EMP: 4
SALES (est): 746.1K  Privately Held
SIC: 2431  Staircases & stairs, wood

**(G-2646)**
**VANGARD DISTRIBUTION INC (PA)**
9501 Southview Ave  (60513-1529)
PHONE............................708 588-8400
Joseph P Gardella, *President*
Thomas Pelafas, *Marketing Staff*
Paul M Julien, *Admin Sec*
▲ EMP: 2
SQ FT: 30,000
SALES (est): 995.9K  Privately Held
SIC: 2653  3053  Corrugated & solid fiber boxes; packing materials

### Buckner
**Franklin County**

**(G-2647)**
**CHRISTOPHER CONCRETE PRODUCTS**
110 N Mine Rd  (62819)
P.O. Box 60  (62819-0060)
PHONE............................618 724-2951
Bert Bonner, *Owner*
Aaron Simion, *Vice Pres*
Shane Bonner, *Sales Staff*
EMP: 6  EST: 1965
SALES: 500K  Privately Held
SIC: 3272  6513  3523  1771  Septic tanks, concrete; apartment building operators; farm machinery & equipment; concrete work

### Buda
**Bureau County**

**(G-2648)**
**VAN-PACKER CO**
302 Mill St  (61314-9539)
P.O. Box 307  (61314-0307)
PHONE............................309 895-2311
Fax: 309 895-3891
Lauren Schulz, *President*
Lauren C Schulz, *President*
Dixey Headley, *Manager*
▲ EMP: 41
SQ FT: 82,000
SALES (est): 8.4MM  Privately Held
SIC: 3272  Concrete products, precast

### Buffalo
**Sangamon County**

**(G-2649)**
**TROTTERS MANUFACTURING CO**
101 S West St  (62515-6228)
P.O. Box 176  (62515-0176)
PHONE............................217 364-4540
Fax: 217 364-4180
Robert Turley, *President*
Dale Turley, *Vice Pres*
Linda Turley, *Admin Sec*
EMP: 8
SQ FT: 10,500
SALES (est): 1MM  Privately Held
WEB: www.trottersmfg.com
SIC: 5531  7699  7692  Automotive tires; farm machinery repair; welding repair

### Buffalo Grove
**Lake County**

**(G-2650)**
**AD SPECIAL TZ INC**
2456 Palazzo Ct  (60089-4677)
PHONE............................847 845-6767
Robyn Gomberg, *President*
Michael Gomberg, *Treasurer*
EMP: 4
SALES (est): 220K  Privately Held
SIC: 3993  Signs & advertising specialties

**(G-2651)**
**AEVERIE INC**
129 Manchester Ct  (60089-6706)
PHONE............................844 238-3743
Rajesh Manghat, *Managing Dir*
EMP: 8
SALES (est): 225.2K  Privately Held
SIC: 7372  7371  Business oriented computer software; computer software development & applications

**(G-2652)**
**AIM GRAPHIC MACHINERY LTD**
Also Called: Aim Business Printers
1374 Abbott Ct  (60089-2378)
PHONE............................847 215-8000
Fax: 847 215-8002
Beverly Sussman, *Partner*
Howard Sussman, *Partner*
Richard Sussman, *Partner*
EMP: 15
SQ FT: 10,000
SALES (est): 1.6MM  Privately Held
WEB: www.aimbusinessprinters.com
SIC: 3955  Print cartridges for laser & other computer printers

**(G-2653)**
**ALL FOAM PRODUCTS CO (PA)**
Also Called: All Foam Pdts Safety Foam Proc
2546 Live Oak Ln  (60089-4609)
PHONE............................847 913-9741
Fax: 847 913-0731
Myrna Steinlauf, *President*
Shelly Silver, *Corp Secy*
Debbie Irlbacker, *Vice Pres*
Marvin Steinlauf, *Vice Pres*
EMP: 6
SQ FT: 3,200
SALES: 795K  Privately Held
WEB: www.allfoam.com
SIC: 3086  Plastics foam products

**(G-2654)**
**ALLIED GRAPHICS INC**
1398 Busch Pkwy  (60089-4505)
PHONE............................847 419-8830
Charles W Schmidt, *President*
Tina Lutz, *Office Mgr*
Rebecca Schmidt, *Admin Sec*
▲ EMP: 2
SQ FT: 3,689
SALES (est): 378.1K  Privately Held
SIC: 5112  7336  2759  2752  Stationery; graphic arts & related design; commercial printing; commercial printing, lithographic

**(G-2655)**
**ALLSTAR EMBROIDERY**
240 Blackthorn Dr  (60089-6341)
PHONE............................847 913-1133
Mike Spector, *Owner*
EMP: 3
SQ FT: 900
SALES (est): 234.8K  Privately Held
SIC: 7389  2395  Textile & apparel services; embroidery products, except schiffli machine

**(G-2656)**
**AMCOR FLEXIBLES LLC (HQ)**
2150 E Lake Cook Rd  (60089-1862)
PHONE............................224 313-7000
Ron Delia, *CEO*
Tom Cochran, *President*
Larry Frevert, *Technical Mgr*
Frederick Patterson, *Engineer*
Carine Faucher, *Manager*
◆ EMP: 250
SQ FT: 200,000
SALES (est): 243.3MM
SALES (corp-wide): 9.4B  Privately Held
SIC: 2671  2621  2821  3081  Plastic film, coated or laminated for packaging; packaging paper; plastics materials & resins; packing materials, plastic sheet; closures, stamped metal
PA: Amcor Ltd
  109 Burwood Rd
  Hawthorn VIC 3122
  392 269-000

**(G-2657)**
**AMERICAN NEEDLE INC (PA)**
Also Called: Amer Needle & Novelty
1275 Busch Pkwy  (60089-4536)
PHONE............................847 215-0011
Fax: 847 215-0013
Robert Kronenberger, *President*
Darla Marabotti, *Finance Dir*
Karen Garcia, *Credit Mgr*
James Stringwell, *VP Sales*
Eric Slagter, *Manager*
◆ EMP: 45  EST: 1918
SQ FT: 45,000
SALES (est): 18MM  Privately Held
WEB: www.americanneedle.com
SIC: 2353  Hats & caps

**(G-2658)**
**AMERISRCBERGEN SOLUTIONS GROUP**
Also Called: Medselect
1400 Busch Pkwy  (60089-4541)
PHONE............................847 808-2600
Bob Rasmussen, *CEO*
Brett Grauss, *Vice Pres*
Michael Sutin, *Engineer*
David Sinyard, *CFO*
David Schott, *Sales Mgr*
▲ EMP: 37  EST: 2001
SQ FT: 4,000
SALES (est): 5.7MM
SALES (corp-wide): 146.8B  Publicly Held
WEB: www.medselectsystems.com
SIC: 3841  Surgical & medical instruments
PA: Amerisourcebergen Corporation
  1300 Morris Dr Ste 100
  Chesterbrook PA 19087
  610 727-7000

**(G-2659)**
**AMIC GLOBAL INC (PA)**
353 Hastings Dr  (60089-6941)
PHONE............................847 600-3590
Baojun Liu, *President*
Robert Leptich, *Vice Pres*
Ashley Liu, *Opers Mgr*
▲ EMP: 7
SALES (est): 1.1MM  Privately Held
WEB: www.amic-inc.com
SIC: 2621  5084  5113  Tissue paper; metal refining machinery & equipment; cups, disposable plastic & paper; dishes, disposable plastic & paper

**(G-2660)**
**ARXIUM INC**
1400 Busch Pkwy  (60089-4541)
PHONE............................847 808-2600
Niels Erik Hansen, *CEO*
Ravee Navaretnam, *COO*
Randy Howorth, *Exec VP*
Keith Goodale, *Opers Mgr*
Dennis Peters, *Safety Mgr*
EMP: 180  EST: 2004
SQ FT: 208,000
SALES (est): 25.8MM
SALES (corp-wide): 36MM  Privately Held
SIC: 3845  7371  Electromedical equipment; custom computer programming services
PA: Arxium Inc
  96 Nature Park Way
  Winnipeg MB R3P 0
  204 943-0066

**(G-2661)**
**BAXTER DIAGNOSTICS INC**
900 Corporate Grove Dr  (60089-4507)
PHONE............................201 337-1212
Fax: 847 777-3333
Tim Anderson, *President*
Phillip Baxter, *General Mgr*
William Mayo, *Principal*
Deb Snider, *Vice Pres*
Jerry Newbrough, *Project Mgr*
▲ EMP: 19
SALES (est): 1.7MM  Privately Held
SIC: 3841  Surgical & medical instruments

**(G-2662)**
**BECHARA SIM**
Also Called: MEI
121 Willow Pkwy  (60089-4635)
PHONE............................847 913-9950
Sim Bechar, *President*
Jeff Bechar, *Vice Pres*
Judith Bechar, *Vice Pres*
Vicki Benrud, *Buyer*
Kevin Guillemette, *Accounts Mgr*
▲ EMP: 14
SALES (est): 1.7MM  Privately Held
SIC: 5065  3699  Electronic parts & equipment; electrical equipment & supplies

**(G-2663)**
**BERRY GLOBAL INC**
800 Corporate Grove Dr  (60089-4512)
PHONE............................847 541-7900
Vin Raby, *President*
Gary Abraham, *Manager*
EMP: 125
SALES (corp-wide): 6.4B  Publicly Held
SIC: 3089  Injection molding of plastics
HQ: Berry Global, Inc.
  101 Oakley St
  Evansville IN 47710
  812 424-2904

**(G-2664)**
**BERTSCHE ENGINEERING CORP**
711 Dartmouth Ln  (60089-6902)
PHONE............................847 537-8757
Fax: 847 537-1113
Richard W Bertsche, *President*
Tristan Bertsche, *Engineer*
Steve E Jacobson, *Engineer*
Linda Bertsche, *Admin Sec*
▲ EMP: 16
SQ FT: 12,000

# Buffalo Grove - Lake County (G-2665) — GEOGRAPHIC SECTION

SALES (est): 3.8MM  Privately Held
WEB: www.bertsche.com
SIC: 3541  3545  Machine tools, metal cutting type; machine tool replacement & repair parts, metal cutting types; machine tool attachments & accessories

### (G-2665)
**BIAS POWER  INC**
975 Deerfield Pkwy  (60089-4511)
PHONE.....................847 419-9180
Fax: 847 215-2914
John Muntean, *President*
Robert T Geras, *President*
Heidi Peddle, *Accounting Mgr*
Viren Modi, *Product Mgr*
▲ EMP: 7
SALES (est): 720K  Privately Held
WEB: www.biaspower.com
SIC: 3679  Static power supply converters for electronic applications

### (G-2666)
**BLACKJACK LIGHTING**
2961 Kingston Dr  (60089-6308)
PHONE.....................847 941-0588
Chad Bell, *Credit Mgr*
EMP: 3  EST: 2014
SALES (est): 451.9K  Privately Held
SIC: 3646  Commercial indusl & institutional electric lighting fixtures

### (G-2667)
**BPREX HEALTHCARE PACKAGING INC (DH)**
Also Called: Rexam
600 Deerfield Pkwy  (60089-7050)
PHONE.....................800 537-0178
Frank C Brown, *CEO*
Scott Brandon, *Manager*
Jerry Allen, *Director*
Gustavo Rodriguez, *Director*
Peggy B Harrington, *Admin Sec*
◆ EMP: 85
SALES (est): 1.9B
SALES (corp-wide): 6.4B  Publicly Held
SIC: 3565  Packaging machinery
HQ: Berry Global, Inc.
   101 Oakley St
   Evansville IN 47710
   812 424-2904

### (G-2668)
**BRAINDOK LLC**
2104 Birchwood Ln  (60089-6683)
PHONE.....................847 877-1586
Bishwajeet Kumar, *Principal*
Dhruv Kumar, *Principal*
Promila Kumar, *Principal*
EMP: 3
SALES (est): 211.7K  Privately Held
SIC: 7373  7372  8243  8748  Systems engineering, computer related; prepackaged software; software training, computer; systems engineering consultant, ex. computer or professional

### (G-2669)
**BRANSON ULTRASONICS CORP**
1585 Barclay Blvd  (60089-4518)
P.O. Box 73174, Chicago  (60673-7174)
PHONE.....................847 229-0800
Fax: 847 229-0861
Joe Belanger, *Sales Mgr*
Joe Bellenger, *Manager*
EMP: 8
SALES (corp-wide): 14.5B  Publicly Held
SIC: 3699  3548  3541  Welding machines & equipment, ultrasonic; welding apparatus; machine tools, metal cutting type
HQ: Branson Ultrasonics Corporation
   41 Eagle Rd Ste 1
   Danbury CT 06810
   203 796-0400

### (G-2670)
**BRIAN PAUL  INC**
Also Called: 3e Graphics & Printing
721 Alsace Ct  (60089-7735)
PHONE.....................847 398-8677
Rick Ebel, *President*
Rick J Ebel, *Admin Sec*
EMP: 49
SQ FT: 35,000
SALES (est): 6.9MM  Privately Held
WEB: www.3elitho.com
SIC: 2752  Commercial printing, lithographic

### (G-2671)
**BURDEENS JEWELRY LTD**
1151 W Lake Cook Rd  (60089-1956)
PHONE.....................847 459-8980
Dennis H Burdeen, *President*
Sandra B Burdeen, *Vice Pres*
EMP: 7
SQ FT: 3,000
SALES (est): 994.6K  Privately Held
SIC: 5944  3911  Jewelry, precious stones & precious metals; jewelry, precious metal

### (G-2672)
**CHICAGO SHOW  INC**
851 Asbury Dr  (60089-4525)
PHONE.....................847 955-0200
Fax: 847 955-9996
James Snediker, *CEO*
Robert R Snediker Jr, *President*
Phil Marco, *Vice Pres*
Ryan Nodorf, *Project Mgr*
Brian Snediker, *Manager*
▲ EMP: 20  EST: 1902
SQ FT: 12,000
SALES (est): 3.5MM  Privately Held
WEB: www.chicagoshow.com
SIC: 3993  Advertising artwork; displays & cutouts, window & lobby

### (G-2673)
**CITA TECHNOLOGIES  LLC**
975 Deerfield Pkwy  (60089-4511)
PHONE.....................847 419-9118
Charles Liang, *Mng Member*
Kevin Hsueh,
▲ EMP: 8
SALES (est): 866.8K  Privately Held
SIC: 3679  Scales, except laboratory

### (G-2674)
**COAST CRANE COMPANY (HQ)**
1110 W Lake Cook Rd # 220  (60089-1944)
PHONE.....................847 215-6500
Nick Matthews, *President*
Mike Heacock, *General Mgr*
Kyle Buchanan, *Area Mgr*
Nick Drake, *Area Mgr*
Robert Magana, *Area Mgr*
▼ EMP: 122
SQ FT: 12,000
SALES (est): 80K  Publicly Held
SIC: 5084  7353  7389  3531  Cranes, industrial; cranes & aerial lift equipment, rental or leasing; crane & aerial lift service; construction machinery; equipment rental & leasing

### (G-2675)
**COFFEE BREWMASTERS USA LLC**
351 Hastings Dr  (60089-6941)
PHONE.....................773 294-9665
Sean Baumgartner,
EMP: 10
SALES (est): 283.4K  Privately Held
SIC: 2095  Coffee extracts

### (G-2676)
**CONCEPTS AND CONTROLS INC**
2530 Apple Hill Ct N  (60089-4650)
PHONE.....................847 478-9296
Anant Venkateswar, *President*
EMP: 10
SQ FT: 4,500
SALES: 250K  Privately Held
WEB: www.conceptsandcontrols.com
SIC: 3599  8742  Custom machinery; automation & robotics consultant

### (G-2677)
**CONOPCO  INC**
491 Arborgate Ln  (60089-1603)
PHONE.....................847 520-8002
David Seiffert, *Branch Mgr*
EMP: 3
SALES (corp-wide): 55.5B  Privately Held
SIC: 2024  Ice cream, packaged: molded, on sticks, etc.
HQ: Conopco, Inc.
   700 Sylvan Ave
   Englewood Cliffs NJ 07632
   201 894-2727

### (G-2678)
**CONSOLIDATED FOAM  INC**
Also Called: Gardien
1670 Barclay Blvd  (60089-4523)
PHONE.....................847 850-5011
Michael Levitt, *CEO*
Daniel Levitt, *President*
Maryjane Permann, *Manager*
▲ EMP: 10
SQ FT: 8,000
SALES (est): 1.9MM  Privately Held
WEB: www.consolidatedfoam.com
SIC: 3089  Planters, plastic

### (G-2679)
**CONTROL WEIGH**
100 Lake Blvd Apt 677  (60089-4367)
PHONE.....................847 540-8260
Howard Schwartz, *Owner*
EMP: 5
SQ FT: 3,000
SALES (est): 334.1K  Privately Held
WEB: www.controlweigh.com
SIC: 3596  5084  Industrial scales; industrial machinery & equipment

### (G-2680)
**CORPAK MEDSYSTEMS  INC (HQ)**
1001 Asbury Dr  (60089-4528)
PHONE.....................847 537-4601
Fax: 847 541-9526
Thomas I Kuhn, *President*
Michael Shaughnessy, *President*
Robert McVey, *Vice Pres*
Stephanie Wasielewski, *Vice Pres*
Germaine Tobias, *Prdtn Mgr*
◆ EMP: 131
SQ FT: 76,000
SALES (est): 30.1MM
SALES (corp-wide): 62.1MM  Privately Held
SIC: 3841  Surgical & medical instruments
PA: Linden, Llc
   111 S Wacker Dr Ste 3350
   Chicago IL 60606
   312 506-5657

### (G-2681)
**COTTAGE COLLAGE**
449 White Pine Rd  (60089-3325)
PHONE.....................847 541-7205
Joann Salyers, *Owner*
EMP: 3
SALES (est): 79.5K  Privately Held
SIC: 2395  Embroidery products, except schiffli machine

### (G-2682)
**DADUM INC**
Also Called: Dadum Die & Design
950 Beechwood Rd  (60089-3240)
PHONE.....................847 541-7851
Gene Johnson, *President*
Diana Johnson, *Vice Pres*
EMP: 5
SALES: 150K  Privately Held
SIC: 3544  7699  3469  Special dies, tools, jigs & fixtures; professional instrument repair services; metal stampings

### (G-2683)
**DEERFIELD BAKERY**
201 N Buffalo Grove Rd  (60089-1748)
PHONE.....................847 520-0068
Henry Schmitt, *Owner*
Joy Faster, *Manager*
EMP: 4  EST: 2015
SALES (est): 157K  Privately Held
SIC: 2052  Bakery products, dry

### (G-2684)
**DELL SOFTWARE  INC**
975 Weiland Rd Unit 200  (60089-7051)
PHONE.....................630 836-0503
Fax: 630 836-8431
EMP: 100
SALES (corp-wide): 45.6B  Privately Held
SIC: 7372  Prepackaged Software Services
HQ: Dell Software, Inc.
   4 Polaris Way
   Aliso Viejo CA 92656
   949 754-8000

### (G-2685)
**DELTA MOLDING LLC**
421 Thompson Blvd  (60089-1032)
PHONE.....................847 414-7773
David B Shelton, *Principal*
David Shelton,
EMP: 4
SALES (est): 180.6K  Privately Held
SIC: 3842  Prosthetic appliances

### (G-2686)
**DES PLAINES PRINTING  LLC**
Also Called: John S Swift of Des Plaines
999 Commerce Ct  (60089-2375)
PHONE.....................847 465-3300
Robert Hagen, *Accounts Mgr*
Michael H Ford,
Deane M Fraser,
Kent T Lyons,
EMP: 15  EST: 1878
SQ FT: 35,000
SALES (est): 1.8MM
SALES (corp-wide): 15.7MM  Privately Held
WEB: www.dppc.com
SIC: 2752  Commercial printing, offset
PA: John S Swift Company Incorporated
   999 Commerce Ct
   Buffalo Grove IL 60089
   847 465-3300

### (G-2687)
**DIECASM  LLC**
540 Hawthorne Rd  (60089-4743)
PHONE.....................877 343-2276
James Cowen, *Mng Member*
EMP: 1
SALES: 400K  Privately Held
SIC: 3944  5511  Automobile & truck models, toy & hobby; new & used car dealers

### (G-2688)
**DISCOUNT COMPUTER SUPPLY INC**
871 Shambliss Ln  (60089-1242)
PHONE.....................847 883-8743
Rick Rodriguez, *President*
EMP: 2
SALES: 400K  Privately Held
WEB: www.ediscountcomputer.com
SIC: 2678  2865  5045  Papeteries & writing paper sets; color lakes or toners; computers, peripherals & software

### (G-2689)
**EAGLE TEST SYSTEMS  INC (HQ)**
2200 Millbrook Dr  (60089-4614)
PHONE.....................847 367-8282
Leonard A Foxman, *President*
Steven Dollens, *President*
Adam B Plummer, *President*
Theodore D Foxman, *COO*
Ken Daub, *Vice Pres*
EMP: 38
SQ FT: 96,000
SALES (est): 54.6MM
SALES (corp-wide): 1.7B  Publicly Held
WEB: www.eagletest.com
SIC: 3825  Test equipment for electronic & electrical circuits
PA: Teradyne, Inc.
   600 Riverpark Dr
   North Reading MA 01864
   978 370-2700

### (G-2690)
**ELECTRONIC ASSEMBLY CORP**
2400 Millbrook Dr  (60089-4698)
PHONE.....................847 793-4400
Peter Strandwitz, *President*
Syed Raza, *Engineer*
Cindy Greenbaum, *Director*
EMP: 100
SALES (corp-wide): 2.5B  Publicly Held
SIC: 3672  Printed circuit boards
HQ: Electronic Assembly Corporation
   55 Jewelers Park Dr
   Neenah WI 54956
   920 722-3451

# GEOGRAPHIC SECTION
## Buffalo Grove - Lake County (G-2716)

**(G-2691)**
**ENGINEERED MATERIALS INC (PA)**
89 Chestnut Ter (60089-6620)
**PHONE**..................847 821-8280
Keith Donaldson, *President*
Robert B Tweed, *Admin Sec*
▲ **EMP:** 2
**SALES (est):** 900.3K **Privately Held**
**WEB:** www.staticintercept.com
**SIC:** 2673 Plastic bags: made from purchased materials

**(G-2692)**
**EPIX INC**
381 Lexington Dr (60089-6934)
**PHONE**..................847 465-1818
**Fax:** 847 465-1919
Howard Dreizen, *President*
Alfred C Petersen, *Vice Pres*
Erik Peterson, *Engineer*
Kirsten Gimm, *Office Mgr*
Kristen Gim, *Manager*
**EMP:** 9
**SQ FT:** 15,000
**SALES:** 2.7MM **Privately Held**
**WEB:** www.eepix.com
**SIC:** 3577 Computer peripheral equipment

**(G-2693)**
**FEDEX OFFICE & PRINT SVCS INC**
76 W Dundee Rd (60089-3758)
**PHONE**..................847 459-8008
Todd Johnson, *Manager*
**EMP:** 9
**SALES (corp-wide):** 50.3B **Publicly Held**
**WEB:** www.kinkos.com
**SIC:** 7334 2791 2789 Photocopying & duplicating services; typesetting; bookbinding & related work
**HQ:** Fedex Office And Print Services, Inc.
   7900 Legacy Dr
   Plano TX 75024
   214 550-7000

**(G-2694)**
**FISHER CONTAINER CORP**
Also Called: Fisher Container Corp
1111 Busch Pkwy (60089-4504)
**PHONE**..................847 541-0000
**Fax:** 847 541-0075
Donald E Fisher, *CEO*
Michael D Fisher, *President*
Marilyn Versten, *Exec VP*
Brad Fisher, *Vice Pres*
Peter Manno, *Vice Pres*
▲ **EMP:** 91
**SQ FT:** 60,000
**SALES (est):** 23.7MM **Privately Held**
**WEB:** www.fishercontainer.com
**SIC:** 2673 5162 2671 3081 Plastic bags: made from purchased materials; plastics products; plastic film, coated or laminated for packaging; unsupported plastics film & sheet

**(G-2695)**
**FISHER CONTAINER HOLDINGS LLC (PA)**
1111 Busch Pkwy (60089-4504)
**PHONE**..................847 541-0000
Kevin Keneally, *CEO*
**EMP:** 0
**SALES (est):** 10MM **Privately Held**
**SIC:** 6719 2673 5162 2671 Holding Company Mfg Plstc/Coat Paper Bag Whol Plastic Mtrl/Shapes Mfg Packaging Paper/Film Mfg Unsupport Plstc Film

**(G-2696)**
**FLEXTRONICS INTL USA INC**
700 Corporate Grove Dr (60089-4554)
**PHONE**..................847 383-1529
Mike Marashli, *Manager*
Dave Vanyek, *Manager*
Rick Williams, *Technician*
**EMP:** 38
**SALES (corp-wide):** 24.4B **Privately Held**
**SIC:** 3089 Injection molding of plastics
**HQ:** Flextronics International Usa, Inc.
   6201 America Center Dr
   San Jose CA 95002

**(G-2697)**
**FLUID LOGIC INC**
1001 Commerce Ct (60089-2362)
**PHONE**..................847 459-2202
Robert Popke, *President*
Andrew Huggins, *Vice Pres*
Myra Antman, *Controller*
**EMP:** 4
**SALES (est):** 457K **Privately Held**
**SIC:** 3492 Control valves, fluid power: hydraulic & pneumatic

**(G-2698)**
**FORD GUM & MACHINE COMPANY INC**
1615 Barclay Blvd (60089-4544)
**PHONE**..................847 955-0003
Greene Steve, *Vice Pres*
Darlene Sheley, *Human Res Mgr*
David Plotnick, *Mktg Dir*
Steve Gold, *Branch Mgr*
Javier Lopez, *Manager*
**EMP:** 18
**SALES (corp-wide):** 57MM **Privately Held**
**SIC:** 2067 5441 Chewing gum; candy
**PA:** Ford Gum & Machine Company, Inc.
   18 Newton Ave
   Akron NY 14001
   716 542-4561

**(G-2699)**
**GLOBAL MATERIAL TECH INC (PA)**
Also Called: Gmt
750 W Lake Cook Rd # 480 (60089-2074)
**PHONE**..................847 495-4700
Norman Soep, *President*
Edwin Jones, *VP Admin*
David Colbert, *Vice Pres*
Alex Krupnik, *Vice Pres*
Robert Krebs, *CFO*
▲ **EMP:** 147 **EST:** 1977
**SQ FT:** 150,000
**SALES (est):** 95.6MM **Privately Held**
**WEB:** www.gmt-inc.com
**SIC:** 3291 Steel wool

**(G-2700)**
**H A GARTENBERG & COMPANY**
260 Blackthorn Dr (60089-6341)
**PHONE**..................847 821-7590
Melvin Gartenberg, *President*
Robert Gartenberg, *Treasurer*
**EMP:** 10
**SQ FT:** 30,000
**SALES (est):** 582K **Privately Held**
**SIC:** 2034 2011 2899 2891 Fruits, dried or dehydrated, except freeze-dried; vegetables, dried or dehydrated (except freeze-dried); dried meats from meat slaughtered on site; chemical preparations; adhesives & sealants; industrial organic chemicals; industrial inorganic chemicals

**(G-2701)**
**HAND TOOL AMERICA**
45 Buckingham Ln (60089-6729)
**PHONE**..................847 947-2866
Pingfeng Zhang, *Principal*
▲ **EMP:** 3
**SALES (est):** 160K **Privately Held**
**SIC:** 3423 Plumbers' hand tools

**(G-2702)**
**HEART & SOUL MEMORIES INC**
1938 Sheridan Rd (60089-8019)
**PHONE**..................847 478-1931
Staci Kamp, *President*
Kim Raphaeli, *Vice Pres*
**EMP:** 2
**SALES (est):** 228.3K **Privately Held**
**SIC:** 2782 Scrapbooks

**(G-2703)**
**HERITAGE PRODUCTS CORPORATION**
1398 Busch Pkwy (60089-4505)
**PHONE**..................847 419-8835
Charles W Schmidt, *President*
**EMP:** 3
**SQ FT:** 2,750

**SALES (est):** 273.5K **Privately Held**
**SIC:** 3089 2741 Plastic processing; miscellaneous publishing

**(G-2704)**
**HEXACOMB CORPORATION (DH)**
1296 Barclay Blvd (60089-4500)
**PHONE**..................847 955-7984
Alexander Toeldte, *President*
Ken Berry, *Opers Staff*
Chuck Soper, *Sales Mgr*
Bill Peterson, *Sales Staff*
Jon Mullica, *Manager*
**EMP:** 2
**SQ FT:** 10,000
**SALES (est):** 65.5MM
**SALES (corp-wide):** 5.7B **Publicly Held**
**SIC:** 2671 2499 Paper coated or laminated for packaging; decorative wood & woodwork
**HQ:** Boise Packaging Holdings Corp
   1955 W Field Ct
   Lake Forest IL 60045
   847 482-3000

**(G-2705)**
**HMC HOLDINGS LLC (PA)**
720 Dartmouth Ln (60089-6902)
**PHONE**..................847 541-5070
John Veleris, *Ch of Bd*
George Garis, *CFO*
▲ **EMP:** 23
**SALES (est):** 20MM **Privately Held**
**WEB:** www.hmcholdings.com
**SIC:** 3469 2542 Boxes: tool, lunch, mail, etc.: stamped metal; cabinets: show, display or storage: except wood

**(G-2706)**
**ILLINOIS TOOL WORKS INC**
Also Called: Signode
180 Hastings Dr (60089-6989)
**PHONE**..................847 215-8925
Dennis Gorman, *Controller*
**EMP:** 24
**SALES (corp-wide):** 13.6B **Publicly Held**
**SIC:** 3565 3499 5051 Packaging machinery; strapping, metal; metals service centers & offices
**PA:** Illinois Tool Works Inc.
   155 Harlem Ave
   Glenview IL 60025
   847 724-7500

**(G-2707)**
**ILLINOIS TOOL WORKS INC**
2550 Millbrook Dr (60089-4694)
P.O. Box 804358, Chicago (60680-4105)
**PHONE**..................847 724-7500
Oguz Arif, *Branch Mgr*
**EMP:** 92
**SALES (corp-wide):** 13.6B **Publicly Held**
**SIC:** 3089 Injection molded finished plastic products
**PA:** Illinois Tool Works Inc.
   155 Harlem Ave
   Glenview IL 60025
   847 724-7500

**(G-2708)**
**INGREDIENTS INC**
1130 W Lake Cook Rd # 320 (60089-1976)
**PHONE**..................847 419-9595
Deborah Stewart, *CEO*
James Stewart, *President*
Samantha Dungey, *Opers Mgr*
▲ **EMP:** 9
**SQ FT:** 3,000
**SALES (est):** 1.6MM **Privately Held**
**WEB:** www.ingredientsinc.com
**SIC:** 2099 Food preparations

**(G-2709)**
**INK STOP INC**
330 Foxford Dr (60089-6302)
**PHONE**..................847 478-0631
Phillip Cole, *President*
**EMP:** 3
**SALES (est):** 250K **Privately Held**
**SIC:** 3955 Print cartridges for laser & other computer printers

**(G-2710)**
**INTERNATIONAL TONER CORP (PA)**
1081 Johnson Dr (60089-6917)
**PHONE**..................847 276-2700
Craig Funk, *President*
Luis Morales, *Warehouse Mgr*
Thomas J Nolan, *Controller*
Daniel Minaghan, *Info Tech Dir*
▲ **EMP:** 8
**SQ FT:** 10,000
**SALES (est):** 1.9MM **Privately Held**
**SIC:** 3861 Toners, prepared photographic (not made in chemical plants)

**(G-2711)**
**ISEWA LLC**
2104 Birchwood Ln (60089-6683)
**PHONE**..................847 877-1586
Vinod Jhajharia,
Bishwajeet Kumar,
Virendra Singh,
**EMP:** 3
**SALES (est):** 190K **Privately Held**
**SIC:** 7373 7372 Computer integrated systems design; application computer software

**(G-2712)**
**J STEWART & CO**
1130 W Lake Cook Rd # 320 (60089-1976)
**PHONE**..................847 419-9595
Deborah Stewart, *CEO*
James Stewart, *President*
**EMP:** 8
**SQ FT:** 4,000
**SALES:** 6.7MM **Privately Held**
**SIC:** 2879 Agricultural chemicals; agricultural disinfectants

**(G-2713)**
**JOHN S SWIFT COMPANY INC (PA)**
999 Commerce Ct (60089-2375)
P.O. Box 5529 (60089-5529)
**PHONE**..................847 465-3300
**Fax:** 847 465-3309
John S Swift III, *Ch of Bd*
Michael Ford, *President*
Deane M Fraser, *Senior VP*
Rick Frydrych, *Vice Pres*
Bill Zimmerman, *Vice Pres*
▲ **EMP:** 50 **EST:** 1912
**SQ FT:** 55,000
**SALES (est):** 15.7MM **Privately Held**
**WEB:** www.jssco.com
**SIC:** 2752 Commercial printing, offset

**(G-2714)**
**K&S INTERNATIONAL INC**
901 Deerfield Pkwy (60089-4511)
**PHONE**..................847 229-0202
**Fax:** 847 229-1001
Kenneth B Glazer, *President*
Scott Glazer, *Vice Pres*
Christy Keller, *VP Sales*
▲ **EMP:** 8
**SQ FT:** 30,000
**SALES (est):** 1.6MM **Privately Held**
**WEB:** www.ksintl.com
**SIC:** 2421 Flooring (dressed lumber), softwood

**(G-2715)**
**K1 SPEED-ILLINOIS INC**
Also Called: K1 Speed Buffalo Grove
301 Hastings Dr (60089-6941)
**PHONE**..................847 941-9400
David Danglard, *President*
Eddie Makowski, *General Mgr*
Susan Graver, *Mktg Dir*
▲ **EMP:** 7 **EST:** 2013
**SALES (est):** 228.1K
**SALES (corp-wide):** 25.3MM **Privately Held**
**SIC:** 3599 Amusement park equipment
**PA:** K1 Speed, Inc.
   17221 Von Karman Ave
   Irvine CA 92614
   949 250-0242

**(G-2716)**
**KOBAC**
1007 Commerce Ct (60089-2362)
**PHONE**..................847 520-6000

# Buffalo Grove - Lake County (G-2717)

EMP: 3
SALES (est): 184.5K **Privately Held**
SIC: 3471 Plating & polishing

**(G-2717)**
**KOBELCO ADVNCED CTING AMER INC**
1007 Commerce Ct (60089-2362)
PHONE..................847 520-6000
Fax: 847 520-6222
Kazuki Takahara, *President*
Yoshinobu Hosokawa, *Admin Sec*
EMP: 900
SALES (est): 49.5MM
SALES (corp-wide): 15.5B **Privately Held**
SIC: 3479 Coating or wrapping steel pipe
HQ: Kobe Steel Usa Holdings Inc.
535 Madison Ave Fl 5
New York NY 10022
212 751-9400

**(G-2718)**
**KOMAX CORPORATION (HQ)**
1100 E Corp Grove Dr (60089)
PHONE..................847 537-6640
Fax: 847 537-5751
Tim Macalpine, *President*
Chris V Ehrenkrook, *General Mgr*
Erich Moeri, *General Mgr*
Peter Everham, *Corp Secy*
Kevin Feil, *Warehouse Mgr*
▲ EMP: 61
SQ FT: 50,000
SALES (est): 18.7MM
SALES (corp-wide): 368.7MM **Privately Held**
WEB: www.komaxusa.com
SIC: 3599 Machine & other job shop work
PA: Komax Holding Ag
Industriestrasse 6
Dierikon LU
414 550-455

**(G-2719)**
**KOP-COAT INC**
Valvtect Petroleum Products
1608 Barclay Blvd (60089-4523)
PHONE..................847 272-2278
Fax: 847 272-4260
Gerald H Nessenson, *Principal*
Paul Craufurd, *Regional Mgr*
Marvin Griffin, *VP Sales*
Jeff Kingsley, *Sales Staff*
Mike Puskar, *Sales Staff*
EMP: 18
SQ FT: 1,200
SALES (corp-wide): 4.8B **Publicly Held**
WEB: www.kop-coat.com
SIC: 2899 Fuel tank or engine cleaning chemicals
HQ: Kop-Coat, Inc.
3040 William Pitt Way
Pittsburgh PA 15238
412 227-2426

**(G-2720)**
**LACERTUS BRANDING LLC**
1569 Barclay Blvd (60089-4518)
PHONE..................224 523-5100
Jerold Isaacson,
Michael Okun,
EMP: 10
SQ FT: 8,000
SALES (est): 25MM **Privately Held**
SIC: 2041 Doughs, frozen or refrigerated

**(G-2721)**
**LASER EXPRESSIONS LTD**
165 N Arlngton Hgts Rd (60089-1783)
PHONE..................847 419-9600
Conni Rydz Karsten, *President*
Bob Karsten, *Admin Sec*
EMP: 5
SQ FT: 1,340
SALES (est): 211.4K **Privately Held**
SIC: 7336 2791 Graphic arts & related design; typesetting

**(G-2722)**
**LAW BULLETIN PUBLISHING CO**
Sullivan Law
1360 Abbott Ct (60089-2378)
PHONE..................847 883-9100
Debra Weatherford, *Manager*
EMP: 15
SQ FT: 1,000
SALES (corp-wide): 69MM **Privately Held**
WEB: www.chicagozoning.com
SIC: 2741 Directories: publishing only, not printed on site
PA: Law Bulletin Publishing Co Inc
415 N State St Ste 1
Chicago IL 60654
312 416-1860

**(G-2723)**
**LED LIGHTING INC**
1555 Barclay Blvd (60089-4518)
PHONE..................847 412-4880
William C Hood, *President*
Julie Smith, *Accountant*
Kristin Burt, *Business Dir*
◆ EMP: 10 EST: 2004
SQ FT: 2,000
SALES (est): 2.3MM **Privately Held**
SIC: 3646 Commercial indusl & institutional electric lighting fixtures

**(G-2724)**
**LEICA MCROSYSTEMS HOLDINGS INC**
1700 Leider Ln (60089-6622)
PHONE..................800 248-0123
Fax: 847 405-0030
Henry Smith, *President*
Deborah Rowells, *President*
Jules Lapin, *Manager*
Armin Hopf, *Director*
Albin Szklany, *Admin Sec*
EMP: 10 EST: 1999
SQ FT: 83,100
SALES (est): 2.9MM
SALES (corp-wide): 6.2B **Publicly Held**
SIC: 5049 3827 Optical goods; optical instruments & lenses; optical instruments & apparatus
HQ: Leica Microsystems Gmbh
Ernst-Leitz-Str. 17-37
Wetzlar 35578
644 129-0

**(G-2725)**
**LEICA MICROSYSTEMS INC**
1700 Leider Ln (60089-6622)
PHONE..................847 405-0123
Sandra Ostrowski, *Branch Mgr*
EMP: 8
SALES (corp-wide): 16.8B **Publicly Held**
WEB: www.leica-microsystems.com
SIC: 3827 3841 Optical instruments & lenses; surgical & medical instruments
HQ: Leica Microsystems Inc.
1700 Leider Ln
Buffalo Grove IL 60089
847 405-0123

**(G-2726)**
**LEICA MICROSYSTEMS INC (HQ)**
1700 Leider Ln (60089-6622)
PHONE..................847 405-0123
Fax: 847 405-0164
Matthias Weber, *President*
Cynthia Manley, *General Mgr*
Claudia Moch, *Editor*
Vanessa Lurquin, *Business Mgr*
Albin Szklany, *Corp Secy*
▲ EMP: 150
SQ FT: 37,000
SALES (est): 113MM
SALES (corp-wide): 16.8B **Publicly Held**
WEB: www.leica-microsystems.com
SIC: 3827 3841 3821 Optical instruments & lenses; optical instruments & apparatus; diagnostic apparatus, medical; laboratory apparatus & furniture
PA: Danaher Corporation
2200 Penn Ave Nw Ste 800w
Washington DC 20037
202 828-0850

**(G-2727)**
**LIVINGSTON INNOVATIONS LLC**
1377 Barclay Blvd (60089-4501)
PHONE..................847 808-0900
Megan Millman, *Manager*
Troy Livingston, *Manager*
EMP: 4
SALES (est): 257.8K **Privately Held**
SIC: 3499 Wheels: wheelbarrow, stroller, etc.: disc, stamped metal; machine bases, metal

# GEOGRAPHIC SECTION

**(G-2728)**
**LONG GROVE CONFECTIONERY CO (PA)**
Also Called: Mangel & Co
333 Lexington Dr (60089-6934)
PHONE..................847 459-3100
Fax: 847 459-4871
John Mangel II, *CEO*
John Mangel III, *Vice Pres*
W David Mangel, *Vice Pres*
Amanda Hughes, *Purch Mgr*
Nick Quartano, *Sales Mgr*
▲ EMP: 50
SQ FT: 65,000
SALES (est): 20.3MM **Privately Held**
SIC: 5441 2064 Confectionery; candy & other confectionery products

**(G-2729)**
**MACLEAN FASTENER SERVICES LLC**
Also Called: Tramac
355 W Dundee Rd Ste 105 (60089-3500)
PHONE..................847 353-8402
Larry Owrutsky, *Accounts Mgr*
Larry Bryk,
▲ EMP: 5
SALES (est): 460K **Privately Held**
SIC: 3743 Railroad equipment

**(G-2730)**
**MANGEL AND CO (PA)**
333 Lexington Dr (60089-6542)
PHONE..................847 459-3100
John Mangel II, *President*
Hilda Mangel, *Vice Pres*
William D Mangel, *Vice Pres*
EMP: 40 EST: 1887
SQ FT: 1,200
SALES (est): 6.3MM **Privately Held**
SIC: 5992 5947 5921 2099 Flowers, fresh; gift shop; wine; cider, nonalcoholic

**(G-2731)**
**MARKING SPECIALISTS/POLY**
Also Called: Marking Specialists Group
1000 Asbury Dr Ste 2 (60089-4551)
PHONE..................847 793-8100
Cliff Modlin, *President*
Larry Lynn, *QA Dir*
Doug Ferguson, *Sales Staff*
Michael Finkelman, *Marketing Staff*
Martin Cibich, *Executive*
EMP: 10
SQ FT: 20,000
SALES (est): 3.3MM **Privately Held**
WEB: www.marking-specialists.com
SIC: 3999 3993 2752 Identification badges & insignia; signs & advertising specialties; commercial printing, lithographic

**(G-2732)**
**MARVEL INDUSTRIES INCORPORATED (PA)**
700 Dartmouth Ln (60089-6902)
PHONE..................847 325-2930
E Kurt Berg, *Ch of Bd*
EMP: 2 EST: 1947
SQ FT: 6,000
SALES (est): 1.3MM **Privately Held**
SIC: 3537 Industrial trucks & tractors

**(G-2733)**
**MBH PROMOTIONS INC**
1108 Gail Dr (60089-1138)
PHONE..................847 634-2411
EMP: 1 EST: 1998
SALES (est): 200K **Privately Held**
SIC: 5199 2759 Whol Nondurable Goods Commercial Printing

**(G-2734)**
**MEDICAL MEMORIES LLC**
2274 Avalon Dr (60089-4682)
PHONE..................847 478-0078
Craig Schnierow,
EMP: 5
SALES (est): 455.2K **Privately Held**
SIC: 2731 Textbooks: publishing & printing

**(G-2735)**
**MERIDIAN LABORATORIES INC**
1130 W Lake Cook Rd # 202 (60089-1994)
PHONE..................847 808-0081

William Zhao, *President*
Jingou Liu, *Vice Pres*
EMP: 4
SALES (est): 247.8K **Privately Held**
SIC: 2834 Powders, pharmaceutical

**(G-2736)**
**MID OAKS INVESTMENTS LLC (PA)**
750 W Lake Cook Rd # 460 (60089-2090)
PHONE..................847 215-3475
Wayne C Kocourek, *CEO*
Michael A Kocourek, *President*
David L Crouch, *Managing Dir*
Christopher Willis, *Vice Pres*
David A Boyle, *CFO*
EMP: 5
SALES (est): 711.5MM **Privately Held**
WEB: www.midoaks.com
SIC: 6726 3089 Investment offices; plastic kitchenware, tableware & houseware

**(G-2737)**
**MIDWEST SEALING PRODUCTS INC**
1001 Commerce Ct (60089-2362)
PHONE..................847 459-2202
Fax: 847 459-2208
Andrew Huggins, *President*
Robert Popke, *Vice Pres*
Myra Antman, *Controller*
EMP: 35
SQ FT: 18,000
SALES (est): 6.9MM **Privately Held**
SIC: 3053 3069 Gaskets, all materials; molded rubber products

**(G-2738)**
**MONNEX INTERNATIONAL INC (PA)**
330 Hastings Dr (60089-6940)
PHONE..................847 850-5263
Moon S Yun, *CEO*
James Wallace, *President*
Andre Wallace, *COO*
Meagan Anderson, *Accounts Mgr*
Tony W Yun, *Director*
▲ EMP: 45
SQ FT: 4,000
SALES (est): 9MM **Privately Held**
SIC: 3363 3451 3679 4225 Aluminum die-castings; screw machine products; electronic circuits; general warehousing & storage

**(G-2739)**
**MORSE AUTOMOTIVE CORPORATION (PA)**
Also Called: Morse Heavy Duty
750 W Lake Cook Rd # 480 (60089-2074)
PHONE..................773 843-9000
Fax: 773 843-9100
Peter Morse, *CEO*
Jay McCrory, *Exec VP*
David Dixon, *Purchasing*
Robert Kurasz, *CFO*
Robert Murasz, *CFO*
▲ EMP: 700
SQ FT: 180,000
SALES (est): 116.2MM **Privately Held**
WEB: www.morseauto.com
SIC: 3714 Motor vehicle brake systems & parts

**(G-2740)**
**MY EYE DOCTOR**
158 Mchenry Rd (60089-1767)
PHONE..................847 325-4440
Fax: 847 325-4443
Adam Keno, *President*
EMP: 4
SALES (corp-wide): 1MM **Privately Held**
SIC: 3851 5995 Lenses, ophthalmic; opticians
PA: My Eye Doctor
29 E Madison St Ste 808
Chicago IL 60602
312 782-4208

**(G-2741)**
**NAGANO INTERNATIONAL CORP**
999 Deerfield Pkwy (60089-4511)
PHONE..................847 537-0011
Yoshitaka Nagano, *President*

▲ = Import ▼ = Export
◆ = Import/Export

# GEOGRAPHIC SECTION

**Buffalo Grove - Lake County (G-2766)**

Hiromi Shiratori, *Vice Pres*
Ray Nakagawa, *Financial Exec*
Yukio Nagano, *Director*
Tadao Inui, *Admin Sec*
▲ **EMP:** 7
**SQ FT:** 34,000
**SALES (est):** 1.4MM **Privately Held**
**WEB:** www.naganoproducts.com
**SIC:** 3492 Hose & tube fittings & assemblies, hydraulic/pneumatic

**(G-2742)**
### NECTA SWEET INC
Also Called: Nsi
1554 Barclay Blvd (60089-4530)
P.O. Box 321, Lincolnshire (60069-0321)
**PHONE** .................................... 847 215-9955
Paul Przybyla, *President*
Nancy Parker, *Sales Executive*
▲ **EMP:** 49
**SQ FT:** 3,000
**SALES (est):** 9.2MM **Privately Held**
**WEB:** www.nectasweet.com
**SIC:** 2869 2062 2099 2087 Sweeteners, synthetic; cane sugar refining; food preparations; flavoring extracts & syrups

**(G-2743)**
### NEMERA BUFFALO GROVE LLC (DH)
600 Deerfield Pkwy (60089-7050)
**PHONE** .................................... 847 541-7900
Heather Strait, *Manager*
Scott Kennedy,
Elizabeth De Longeaux,
◆ **EMP:** 300
**SALES (est):** 92.9MM
**SALES (corp-wide):** 64.5MM **Privately Held**
**SIC:** 3841 Surgical & medical instruments

**(G-2744)**
### NEMERA BUFFALO GROVE LLC
800 Corporate Grove Dr (60089-4512)
**PHONE** .................................... 847 325-3629
**EMP:** 4
**SALES (est):** 537.4K **Privately Held**
**SIC:** 3841 Mfg Surgical/Medical Instruments

**(G-2745)**
### NEMERA BUFFALO GROVE LLC
800 Corporate Grove Dr (60089-4512)
**PHONE** .................................... 847 325-3628
**EMP:** 3
**SALES (corp-wide):** 64.5MM **Privately Held**
**SIC:** 3841 Surgical & medical instruments
**HQ:** Nemera Buffalo Grove Llc
600 Deerfield Pkwy
Buffalo Grove IL 60089
847 541-7900

**(G-2746)**
### NEMERA US HOLDING INC (DH)
600 Deerfield Pkwy (60089-7050)
**PHONE** .................................... 847 325-3620
**EMP:** 18 **EST:** 2015
**SALES (est):** 90.5MM
**SALES (corp-wide):** 61.5MM **Privately Held**
**SIC:** 3841 Mfg Surgical/Medical Instruments
**HQ:** Nemera La Verpilliere
20 Avenue De La Gare
La Verpilliere 38290
474 940-654

**(G-2747)**
### NESTLE USA INC
Also Called: Nestle Clinical Nutrition
2150 E Lake Cook Rd # 800 (60089-1862)
**PHONE** .................................... 847 808-5404
**Fax:** 847 940-6635
Jack Kennedy, *Human Res Dir*
Bill Bartnick, *Branch Mgr*
**EMP:** 100
**SALES (corp-wide):** 88.4B **Publicly Held**
**WEB:** www.nestleusa.com
**SIC:** 5149 5047 2099 2087 Natural & organic foods; medical equipment & supplies; food preparations; flavoring extracts & syrups; canned specialties

**HQ:** Nestle Usa, Inc.
800 N Brand Blvd
Glendale CA 91203
818 549-6000

**(G-2748)**
### NESTLE USA INC
Also Called: Nestles Nutrition
2150 E Lake Cook Rd # 800 (60089-1862)
**PHONE** .................................... 847 808-5300
Roy Reed, *Branch Mgr*
**EMP:** 139
**SALES (corp-wide):** 88.4B **Publicly Held**
**WEB:** www.nestleusa.com
**SIC:** 2023 2033 2064 2047 Evaporated milk; canned milk, whole; cream substitutes; fruits: packaged in cans, jars, etc.; tomato paste: packaged in cans, jars, etc.; tomato sauce: packaged in cans, jars, etc.; candy & other confectionery products; breakfast bars; dog food; cat food; pasta, uncooked: packaged with other ingredients; canned specialties
**HQ:** Nestle Usa, Inc.
800 N Brand Blvd
Glendale CA 91203
818 549-6000

**(G-2749)**
### OUTDOOR ENVIRONMENTS LLC
288 S Buffalo Grove Rd (60089-2148)
**PHONE** .................................... 847 325-5000
Michael Pasternak, *Owner*
**EMP:** 2
**SALES (est):** 260.2K **Privately Held**
**SIC:** 3829 Weather tracking equipment

**(G-2750)**
### PANASONIC CORP NORTH AMERICA
Also Called: Panasonic Fctry Solutions Amer
1000 Asbury Dr (60089-4551)
**PHONE** .................................... 847 637-9700
Alex Shimada, *President*
Fei Ding, *Engineer*
Julian Rebolledo, *Engineer*
Michele Pishko, *Manager*
Jack Sobkowicz, *Manager*
**EMP:** 160
**SALES (corp-wide):** 64.6B **Privately Held**
**WEB:** www.panasonic.com
**SIC:** 3535 Robotic conveyors
**HQ:** Panasonic Corporation Of North America
2 Riverfront Plz Ste 200
Newark NJ 07102
201 348-7000

**(G-2751)**
### PHILOS TECHNOLOGIES INC
1011 Commerce Ct (60089-2362)
**PHONE** .................................... 630 945-2933
Samuel Ko, *CEO*
▲ **EMP:** 6
**SQ FT:** 4,500
**SALES (est):** 1MM **Privately Held**
**SIC:** 2899 Heat treating salts

**(G-2752)**
### PILLOW FACTORY INC (DH)
900 Busch Pkwy (60089-4503)
**PHONE** .................................... 847 680-3388
**Fax:** 847 367-0620
Michael D Green, *President*
Alfred Kaminski, *Mfg Staff*
Thomas Shaw, *Rsch/Dvlpt Mgr*
Terry Voelker, *Manager*
John Chandler II, *Admin Sec*
▲ **EMP:** 12
**SQ FT:** 38,000
**SALES (est):** 15.4MM
**SALES (corp-wide):** 166.9MM **Privately Held**
**SIC:** 2392 Pillows, bed: made from purchased materials
**HQ:** Encompass Group, L.L.C.
615 Macon St
Mcdonough GA 30253
770 957-3981

**(G-2753)**
### PILLSBURY COMPANY LLC
135 N Arlington Heghts (60089-8213)
**PHONE** .................................... 847 541-8888
Ron Krass, *Branch Mgr*
**EMP:** 6

**SALES (corp-wide):** 17.6B **Publicly Held**
**WEB:** www.pillsbury.com
**SIC:** 2041 Flour & other grain mill products
**HQ:** The Pillsbury Company Llc
1 General Mills Blvd
Minneapolis MN 55426

**(G-2754)**
### PLEXUS CORP
Also Called: Plexus Manufacturing Solutions
2400 Millbrook Dr (60089-4698)
**PHONE** .................................... 847 793-4400
**Fax:** 847 793-4481
Steve Ver Keilen, *Opers Staff*
Joanne Straz, *Branch Mgr*
**EMP:** 323
**SALES (corp-wide):** 2.5B **Publicly Held**
**SIC:** 3672 Printed circuit boards
**PA:** Plexus Corp.
1 Plexus Way
Neenah WI 54956
920 969-6000

**(G-2755)**
### POTTER RENDERING CO
Also Called: Potter Sausage
750 W Lake Cook Rd # 485 (60089-2069)
P.O. Box 689, Durant OK (74702-0689)
**PHONE** .................................... 580 924-2414
Billy Campbell, *CEO*
Shannon Kelso, *Human Res Dir*
**EMP:** 7
**SALES (est):** 634.9K **Privately Held**
**SIC:** 2077 Animal & marine fats & oils

**(G-2756)**
### PROFILE PRODUCTS LLC (HQ)
750 W Lake Cook Rd # 440 (60089-2090)
**PHONE** .................................... 847 215-1144
**Fax:** 847 215-1267
John A Schoch Jr, *President*
Jay Molnar, *Vice Pres*
Michael Robeson, *Technical Mgr*
Cal Stuart, *CFO*
Brandon Arnold, *Accountant*
◆ **EMP:** 26
**SQ FT:** 10,000
**SALES (est):** 77.4MM
**SALES (corp-wide):** 86.9MM **Privately Held**
**WEB:** www.conwedfibers.com
**SIC:** 2611 1459 Pulp manufactured from waste or recycled paper; pulp produced from wood base; fuller's earth mining
**PA:** Platte River Equity Iii, L.P.
200 Fillmore St Ste 200
Denver CO 80206
303 292-7300

**(G-2757)**
### PSA EQUITY LLC (PA)
485 E Half Day Rd Ste 500 (60089-8808)
**PHONE** .................................... 847 478-6000
Robert Harris, *Sales Dir*
Cyze James, *Mng Member*
Doherty Thomas B,
Duncan Joe,
Louzan Robert,
**EMP:** 11
**SALES (est):** 15.6MM **Privately Held**
**SIC:** 3089 7331 Identification cards, plastic; direct mail advertising services

**(G-2758)**
### REXAM DEVICES LLC
800 Corporate Grove Dr (60089-4512)
**PHONE** .................................... 847 325-3629
Scott Kennedy,
▲ **EMP:** 12
**SALES (est):** 1.9MM **Privately Held**
**SIC:** 3841 Surgical & medical instruments

**(G-2759)**
### RF TECHNOLOGIES INC (PA)
330 Lexington Dr (60089-6933)
**PHONE** .................................... 618 377-2654
**Fax:** 618 377-1320
Babak Noorian, *President*
Steven Combs, *COO*
Mary Ann Trittschua, *VP Opers*
Fiona Noorian, *Opers Mgr*
Cherie Ingold, *Production*
▲ **EMP:** 44
**SQ FT:** 25,000

**SALES (est):** 5.7MM **Privately Held**
**WEB:** www.rftechno.com
**SIC:** 3669 Burglar alarm apparatus, electric; emergency alarms; intercommunication systems, electric

**(G-2760)**
### ROYAL TOUCH CARWASH
1701 Weiland Rd (60089-6885)
**PHONE** .................................... 847 808-8600
**Fax:** 847 808-9070
John Inreibe, *Branch Mgr*
**EMP:** 9
**SALES (corp-wide):** 1.4MM **Privately Held**
**SIC:** 3089 Injection molding of plastics
**PA:** Royal Touch Carwash
2711 Mannheim Rd
Des Plaines IL 60018
773 447-0403

**(G-2761)**
### SAP ACQUISITION CO LLC
1200 Barclay Blvd (60089-4500)
**PHONE** .................................... 847 229-1600
Jerry Starr,
Michael Lewis,
Gene Wisenwoski,
▲ **EMP:** 27
**SQ FT:** 86,000
**SALES (est):** 2.7MM **Privately Held**
**SIC:** 3089 Floor coverings, plastic

**(G-2762)**
### SBA WIRELESS INC
1287 Barclay Blvd Ste 200 (60089-4514)
**PHONE** .................................... 847 215-8720
Sam Agam, *President*
Mina Agam, *Admin Sec*
▲ **EMP:** 26
**SALES (est):** 3.3MM **Privately Held**
**SIC:** 3651 3579 Speaker systems; time clocks & time recording devices

**(G-2763)**
### SCHULTES PRECISION MFG INC
Also Called: Rex Gauge Division
1250 Busch Pkwy (60089-4538)
**PHONE** .................................... 847 465-0300
**Fax:** 847 998-9340
Otto J Schultes, *President*
Rick Ruppert, *General Mgr*
Joe Climaco, *QC Mgr*
Ricardo Meraz, *QC Mgr*
Phil Maki, *Engineer*
**EMP:** 100 **EST:** 1946
**SQ FT:** 65,000
**SALES (est):** 20.3MM **Privately Held**
**WEB:** www.schultes.com
**SIC:** 3599 3829 Machine shop, jobbing & repair; testing equipment: abrasion, shearing strength, etc.

**(G-2764)**
### SCOTTS COMPANY LLC
700 Eastwood Ln (60089-6905)
**PHONE** .................................... 847 777-0700
Frank Wilson, *Branch Mgr*
**EMP:** 40
**SALES (corp-wide):** 2.8B **Publicly Held**
**WEB:** www.scottscompany.com
**SIC:** 2873 Fertilizers: natural (organic), except compost
**HQ:** The Scotts Company Llc
14111 Scottslawn Rd
Marysville OH 43040
937 644-3729

**(G-2765)**
### SCT ALTERNATIVE INC
1655 Barclay Blvd (60089-4544)
**PHONE** .................................... 847 215-7488
Vadim Katsman, *CEO*
**EMP:** 10
**SALES:** 430K **Privately Held**
**WEB:** www.sctalt.com
**SIC:** 7372 Prepackaged software

**(G-2766)**
### SIEMENS INDUSTRY INC
740 Weidner Rd Apt 203 (60089-3386)
**PHONE** .................................... 847 520-9084
**EMP:** 97

# Buffalo Grove - Lake County (G-2767)

SALES (corp-wide): 89.6B  Privately Held
SIC: 3822  Air conditioning & refrigeration controls; thermostats & other environmental sensors
HQ: Siemens Industry, Inc.
1000 Deerfield Pkwy
Buffalo Grove IL 60089
847 215-1000

### (G-2767)
### SIEMENS INDUSTRY INC (DH)
1000 Deerfield Pkwy  (60089-4547)
PHONE..................................847 215-1000
Judy Marks, CEO
Kevin Lewis, Business Mgr
Kay Meggers, Senior VP
Albrecht Neumann, Vice Pres
Kim Truelsen, Project Mgr
◆ EMP: 1200
SALES (est): 3.7B
SALES (corp-wide): 89.6B  Privately Held
WEB: www.sibt.com
SIC: 3822  5063  3669  1731  Air conditioning & refrigeration controls; thermostats & other environmental sensors; electric alarms & signaling equipment; emergency alarms; safety & security specialization; security systems services; relays & industrial controls
HQ: Siemens Corporation
300 New Jersey Ave Nw # 10
Washington DC 20001
202 434-4800

### (G-2768)
### SIEMENS INDUSTRY INC
887 Deerfield Pkwy  (60089-4511)
PHONE..................................847 215-1000
Kenneth McQuillen, Marketing Mgr
David Matula, Branch Mgr
Gino Fiore, Manager
Swaminathan Arunachalam, Info Tech Mgr
Kim Finke, Technology
EMP: 87
SALES (corp-wide): 89.6B  Privately Held
SIC: 3822  Air conditioning & refrigeration controls; thermostats & other environmental sensors
HQ: Siemens Industry, Inc.
1000 Deerfield Pkwy
Buffalo Grove IL 60089
847 215-1000

### (G-2769)
### SIEMENS MED SOLUTIONS USA INC
Also Called: Ultrasound Div - Buffalo Grove
2500 Millbrook Dr Ste B  (60089-4694)
PHONE..................................847 793-4429
Martin Klein, CFO
EMP: 15
SALES (corp-wide): 89.6B  Privately Held
SIC: 3845  Electromedical equipment
HQ: Siemens Medical Solutions Usa, Inc.
40 Liberty Blvd
Malvern PA 19355
610 219-6300

### (G-2770)
### SIGMA BIO MEDICS INDUSTRIES
Also Called: Sigma Digital Xray
1607 Barclay Blvd  (60089-4544)
P.O. Box 5666  (60089-5666)
PHONE..................................847 419-0669
Kim Antol, President
EMP: 6
SQ FT: 10,000
SALES (est): 570K  Privately Held
SIC: 3861  Photographic processing chemicals

### (G-2771)
### SIGN-A-RAMA OF BUFFALO GROVE
352 Lexington Dr  (60089-6933)
PHONE..................................847 215-1535
Fax: 847 215-1704
Sherri Shodes, President
Chuck Hodes, Human Res Mgr
EMP: 7
SALES (est): 450K  Privately Held
SIC: 3993  5199  Signs & advertising specialties; advertising specialties

### (G-2772)
### SIGNS FOR SUCCESS INC
1538 Madison Dr  (60089-6830)
PHONE..................................847 800-4870
Susan Chesler, President
EMP: 12
SALES (est): 1.2MM  Privately Held
WEB: www.signsforsuccess.net
SIC: 3993  Signs & advertising specialties

### (G-2773)
### SIRIUS AUTOMATION INC
1558 Barclay Blvd  (60089-4530)
PHONE..................................847 607-9378
Justin Lu, President
Tony Cox, President
Kim Smith, General Mgr
EMP: 10
SALES (est): 1.2MM  Privately Held
SIC: 3821  Laboratory apparatus & furniture

### (G-2774)
### SONOMA ORTHOPEDIC PRODUCTS INC
1388 Busch Pkwy  (60089-4505)
PHONE..................................847 807-4378
Charles Nelson, CEO
Rick Epstein, CEO
Carlos Gonzalez, Vice Pres
Kyle Lappin, Vice Pres
David Rardin, Vice Pres
EMP: 13
SQ FT: 5,000
SALES (est): 2.4MM  Privately Held
SIC: 3841  Surgical & medical instruments

### (G-2775)
### SST FORMING ROLL INC
1318 Busch Pkwy  (60089-4505)
PHONE..................................847 215-6812
Aki Washinushi, President
Stan Green, Opers Mgr
Shinsho American Corp, Shareholder
▲ EMP: 6
SQ FT: 2,000
SALES (est): 1.2MM  Privately Held
SIC: 3599  Custom machinery

### (G-2776)
### STATELINE RENEWABLE FUELS LLC
6 Regent Ct W  (60089-1941)
PHONE..................................608 931-4634
Jacob Ramsey, Principal
EMP: 3
SALES (est): 182.5K  Privately Held
SIC: 2869  Fuels

### (G-2777)
### STATIONARY STUDIO LLC (PA)
460 Newtown Dr  (60089-6407)
PHONE..................................847 541-2499
Marc Redman,
Renee Redman,
EMP: 2
SALES (est): 210.7K  Privately Held
WEB: www.thestationerystudio.com
SIC: 2759  Invitation & stationery printing & engraving

### (G-2778)
### SUPERIOR AMERICAN PLASTICS CO
1200 Barclay Blvd  (60089-4500)
PHONE..................................847 229-1600
Fax: 847 229-1909
Richard S Bezark, President
EMP: 32
SALES (est): 6.8MM  Privately Held
WEB: www.superioramerican.com
SIC: 3089  Floor coverings, plastic

### (G-2779)
### SYNAX INC
1374 Abbott Ct  (60089-2378)
PHONE..................................224 352-2927
Yan Svidovsky, President
Natalya Svidovsky, Manager
EMP: 12
SQ FT: 10,000
SALES (est): 1.2MM  Privately Held
SIC: 3541  Machine tools, metal cutting type

### (G-2780)
### TENEX CORPORATION
1282 Barclay Blvd  (60089-4500)
PHONE..................................847 504-0400
Albert B Cheris, President
Kathy Wojcik, Marketing Staff
▲ EMP: 35
SQ FT: 3,000
SALES (est): 9.2MM  Privately Held
SIC: 3089  Plastic kitchenware, tableware & houseware; plastic hardware & building products

### (G-2781)
### THERMOHELP INC
12 River Oaks Cir W  (60089-8805)
P.O. Box 4984  (60089-4984)
PHONE..................................847 821-7130
Alex Shubs, President
Yelena Roginsky, Vice Pres
EMP: 5
SQ FT: 1,500
SALES (est): 430K  Privately Held
SIC: 2299  Insulating felts

### (G-2782)
### TOSHIBA AMERICA ELECTRONIC
2150 E Lake Cook Rd  (60089-1862)
PHONE..................................847 484-2400
Laura Hubbard, Manager
Jessie Wang, Technical Staff
EMP: 9
SALES (corp-wide): 48.4B  Privately Held
SIC: 3674  Semiconductors & related devices
HQ: Toshiba America Electronic Components Inc
9740 Irvine Blvd Ste D700
Irvine CA 92618
949 462-7700

### (G-2783)
### U4G GROUP LLC
1425 Mchenry Rd Ste 209  (60089-1332)
PHONE..................................847 821-6061
Anthony Melikhov, Principal
Patrick Lindemann, CFO
EMP: 5
SALES (est): 224.3K  Privately Held
SIC: 7372  Application computer software

### (G-2784)
### UNICOMP TYPOGRAPHY INC
1137 Lockwood Ct E  (60089-1173)
PHONE..................................847 821-0221
Wilfred Johnson, President
Andrew Johnson, Corp Secy
EMP: 4  EST: 1975
SQ FT: 1,500
SALES (est): 367.5K  Privately Held
SIC: 2791  7336  Typesetting, computer controlled; graphic arts & related design

### (G-2785)
### UNITED ADHESIVES INC
820 Port Clinton Ct E  (60089-6675)
PHONE..................................224 436-0077
Xiarong Peng, President
EMP: 7
SALES (est): 680K  Privately Held
SIC: 2891  Epoxy adhesives

### (G-2786)
### US LBM RIDOUT HOLDINGS LLC (DH)
1000 Corporate Grove Dr  (60089-4550)
PHONE..................................877 787-5267
EMP: 2
SALES (est): 9.5MM
SALES (corp-wide): 2.1B  Privately Held
SIC: 5031  2431  6719  Lumber, plywood & millwork; doors, wood; investment holding companies, except banks

### (G-2787)
### V-TEX INC
Also Called: Uncommon Threads
1027 Busch Pkwy  (60089-4504)
PHONE..................................847 325-4140
Fax: 847 279-1493
Scott H Verson, President
Joy Cameron, Bookkeeper
◆ EMP: 20
SQ FT: 1,500
SALES (est): 2.9MM  Privately Held
SIC: 2326  5131  Service apparel (baker, barber, lab, etc.), washable: men's; textile converters

### (G-2788)
### VAPOR CORPORATION
Also Called: Vapor Bus International
1010 Johnson Dr  (60089-6918)
PHONE..................................847 777-6400
William E Kassling, Ch of Bd
Clement R Arrison, President
Keith Nippes, President
John Condon, Vice Pres
Robert Gallant, Vice Pres
▲ EMP: 408
SQ FT: 330,000
SALES (est): 65MM
SALES (corp-wide): 2.9B  Publicly Held
SIC: 3743  3443  Interurban cars & car equipment; boilers: industrial, power, or marine
PA: Westinghouse Air Brake Technologies Corporation
1001 Airbrake Ave
Wilmerding PA 15148
412 825-1000

### (G-2789)
### VERNON TOWNSHIP OFFICES
3050 N Main St  (60089-2727)
PHONE..................................847 634-4600
Fax: 847 634-1569
Kyle Steininger, Trustee
Michael Theisen, Trustee
Jeffrey Barlow, Sales Executive
Bill Peterson, Manager
Barbara Barnabee, Manager
EMP: 21
SALES (est): 2.9MM  Privately Held
WEB: www.vernontownship.com
SIC: 8111  2711  Taxation law; newspapers

### (G-2790)
### VISIPLEX INC
1287 Barclay Blvd  (60089-4514)
PHONE..................................847 918-0250
Sam Agam, CEO
Karen Rosen, Controller
▲ EMP: 26
SQ FT: 16,500
SALES (est): 4.5MM  Privately Held
SIC: 3663  Radio broadcasting & communications equipment

### (G-2791)
### VISIPLEX INC
1287 Barclay Blvd Ste 100  (60089-4514)
PHONE..................................847 229-0250
Fax: 847 229-0259
Sam Agam, President
▼ EMP: 15
SQ FT: 8,000
SALES (est): 2.6MM  Privately Held
WEB: www.biocommsystems.com
SIC: 3663  5065  Pagers (one-way); paging & signaling equipment

### (G-2792)
### WELLINGTON DRIVE TECH US
1407 Barclay Blvd  (60089-4537)
P.O. Box 4929  (60089-4929)
PHONE..................................847 922-5098
Greg Allen, CEO
Bruce Farquharson, Vice Pres
Steve Hodgson, Sales Staff
Clayton Thomas, Marketing Staff
Susan Tieven, Program Mgr
EMP: 4  EST: 1994
SALES (est): 506.1K
SALES (corp-wide): 1.2MM  Privately Held
SIC: 3621  Motors & generators
PA: Wellington Drive Technologies Limited
21 Arrenway Drive
Auckland,  0632
947 704-15

### (G-2793)
### WES-TECH INC
720 Dartmouth Ln  (60089-6999)
PHONE..................................847 541-5070
Fax: 847 541-0096
John Veleris, President
Keith McGovern, Plant Mgr
Michael Slaga, Materials Mgr

Martin Vavrich, *Warehouse Mgr*
Mike Ferguson, *Engineer*
**EMP:** 8
**SALES (est):** 1.8MM **Privately Held**
**SIC:** 3594 Fluid power pumps & motors

**(G-2794)**
**WES-TECH AUTOMTN SOLUTIONS LLC**
720 Dartmouth Ln (60089-6999)
**PHONE** ................................. 847 541-5070
Dan Voelker, *Vice Pres*
Jason Arends, *Engineer*
Dennis Robb, *Engineer*
George Garifalis, *CFO*
Donald Gross, *Info Tech Mgr*
**EMP:** 65
**SQ FT:** 45,000
**SALES (est):** 22MM **Privately Held**
**SIC:** 3535 3549 Conveyors & conveying equipment; belt conveyor systems, general industrial use; robotic conveyors; assembly machines, including robotic

**(G-2795)**
**WOUNDWEAR INC**
1440 Larchmont Dr (60089-1038)
P.O. Box 6008 (60089-6008)
**PHONE** ................................. 847 634-1700
Dr Joel Spatt, *President*
Marleen Spatt, *Admin Sec*
**EMP:** 3 **EST:** 1999
**SQ FT:** 1,500
**SALES:** 75K **Privately Held**
**SIC:** 3841 Veterinarians' instruments & apparatus

**(G-2796)**
**YANMAR (USA) INC**
901 Corporate Grove Dr (60089-4508)
**PHONE** ................................. 847 541-1900
**Fax:** 847 541-2161
Fumihiro Kano, *President*
Jacqueline Wooster, *Business Mgr*
Julie Pratt-Willey, *Senior Buyer*
Norman Garrett, *Engineer*
Kerry Johnson, *Sls & Mktg Exec*
▼ **EMP:** 3
**SQ FT:** 72,000
**SALES (est):** 430K
**SALES (corp-wide):** 40.9MM **Privately Held**
**SIC:** 3524 5084 Lawn & garden mowers & accessories; engines & parts, diesel
**HQ:** Yanmar Co.,Ltd.
1-32, Chayamachi, Kita-Ku
Osaka OSK 530-0
663 766-211

### Buffalo Prairie
*Rock Island County*

**(G-2797)**
**REASONS INC**
Also Called: Reason's Locker
18510 206th Sw (61237)
**PHONE** ................................. 309 537-3424
**Fax:** 309 537-3424
Steve Reason, *President*
Amy Saddoris, *Business Mgr*
Bonnie Reason, *Treasurer*
Greg Boruff, *Sales Executive*
**EMP:** 2 **EST:** 1964
**SQ FT:** 1,500
**SALES (est):** 249.1K **Privately Held**
**WEB:** www.reasonsprairiepride.com
**SIC:** 5399 5722 5251 2011 Country general stores; electric household appliances; hardware; meat packing plants

### Bull Valley
*Mchenry County*

**(G-2798)**
**DEBOURG CORP**
10004 Bull Valley Rd (60098-8185)
**PHONE** ................................. 815 338-7852
Bjorn Debourg, *President*
Leslie Schermerhorn, *Vice Pres*
**EMP:** 3

**SALES (est):** 260K **Privately Held**
**SIC:** 2899 Fuel treating compounds

### Buncombe
*Johnson County*

**(G-2799)**
**SOUTHERN ILLINOIS POWER COOP**
Also Called: Southern Illinois Material
Rr 37 Box N (62912)
P.O. Box 5 (62912-0005)
**PHONE** ................................. 618 995-2371
**Fax:** 618 995-9537
Brian Cross, *Manager*
**EMP:** 3
**SALES (corp-wide):** 204.7MM **Privately Held**
**SIC:** 2911 Asphalt or asphaltic materials, made in refineries
**PA:** Southern Illinois Power Co-Operative
11543 Lake Of Egypt Rd
Marion IL 62959
618 964-1448

**(G-2800)**
**SOUTHERN ILLINOIS STONE CO (DH)**
4800 State Rt 37 N (62912)
P.O. Box 880, Cape Girardeau MO (63702-0880)
**PHONE** ................................. 573 334-5261
Richard C Neubert, *President*
Jim Weeks, *Chairman*
Del Elfrink, *Treasurer*
Stewart Fuhrmann, *Admin Sec*
**EMP:** 10 **EST:** 1950
**SQ FT:** 300
**SALES (est):** 33.9MM
**SALES (corp-wide):** 77.1MM **Privately Held**
**SIC:** 1611 1422 3272 Highway & street construction; crushed & broken limestone; concrete products used to facilitate drainage

**(G-2801)**
**SOUTHERN ILLINOIS STONE CO**
4800 Hwy 37 N (62912)
**PHONE** ................................. 618 995-2392
Pearl Gibbons, *Manager*
**EMP:** 40
**SALES (corp-wide):** 77.1MM **Privately Held**
**SIC:** 1422 5032 Limestones, ground; stone, crushed or broken
**HQ:** Southern Illinois Stone Co Inc
4800 State Rt 37 N
Buncombe IL 62912
573 334-5261

**(G-2802)**
**WEAVER EQUIPMENT LLC**
Also Called: Weaver Equitment Co
1240 Mount Pleasant Rd (62912-3327)
**PHONE** ................................. 618 833-5521
Ruth Weaver, *President*
**EMP:** 6
**SALES:** 1.4MM **Privately Held**
**SIC:** 3523 Farm machinery & equipment

### Bunker Hill
*Macoupin County*

**(G-2803)**
**ALL TYPE HYDRAULICS CORP**
149 S Washington St (62014-1315)
P.O. Box 11 (62014-0011)
**PHONE** ................................. 618 585-4844
John Chapman, *President*
**EMP:** 4
**SQ FT:** 6,000
**SALES (est):** 548.1K **Privately Held**
**SIC:** 3492 Hose & tube fittings & assemblies, hydraulic/pneumatic

**(G-2804)**
**BUNKER HILL PUBLICATION**
Also Called: Gazette News Office
150 N Washington St (62014)
**PHONE** ................................. 618 585-4411
**Fax:** 618 585-3354
John Galer, *President*
**EMP:** 8
**SALES:** 250K **Privately Held**
**SIC:** 2711 Job printing & newspaper publishing combined

**(G-2805)**
**JETS COMPUTING INC**
200 S Brighton St (62014-1344)
**PHONE** ................................. 618 585-6676
James Dorrington, *President*
Ben Dorrington, *Vice Pres*
**EMP:** 4
**SALES (est):** 346.9K **Privately Held**
**WEB:** www.jetscomputing.com
**SIC:** 3571 Electronic computers

### Burbank
*Cook County*

**(G-2806)**
**ALLPRO FLEET MAINT SYSTEMS**
8614 Lamon Ave (60459-2827)
**PHONE** ................................. 708 430-1400
Ken Michols, *Principal*
**EMP:** 2 **EST:** 2009
**SALES (est):** 218.3K **Privately Held**
**SIC:** 3211 Window glass, clear & colored

**(G-2807)**
**COPAR CORPORATION**
Also Called: Copar International
5744 W 77th St (60459-1305)
**PHONE** ................................. 708 496-1859
**Fax:** 708 496-0079
Stephen R Schmidt, *President*
Gail Schmidt, *Vice Pres*
Jesse Hughes, *Prdtn Mgr*
Michael Venner, *Software Engr*
**EMP:** 45 **EST:** 1953
**SQ FT:** 27,300
**SALES (est):** 10.7MM **Privately Held**
**WEB:** www.copar.com
**SIC:** 3625 3579 Control equipment, electric; paper handling machines

**(G-2808)**
**MARCA INDUSTRIES INC**
5901 W 79th St 400 (60459-1272)
**PHONE** ................................. 773 884-4500
**Fax:** 773 767-8320
Annette Golden, *President*
Leticia Dudek, *Managing Dir*
Rami Ikhreishi, *Managing Dir*
Bruce Golden, *Principal*
John Khamis, *CTO*
**EMP:** 30
**SALES (est):** 2.3MM **Privately Held**
**WEB:** www.marcaindustries.com
**SIC:** 3999 Manufacturing industries

**(G-2809)**
**PAT 24 INC**
7107 W 79th St (60459-1005)
**PHONE** ................................. 708 336-8671
Patrycja Heldak, *Principal*
**EMP:** 4
**SALES (est):** 380.5K **Privately Held**
**SIC:** 3356 Tin

**(G-2810)**
**TIFB MEDIA GROUP INC**
Also Called: Massage Chair Deals
7608 Lockwood Ave (60459-1433)
**PHONE** ................................. 844 862-4391
Feras Ballout, *President*
**EMP:** 5
**SQ FT:** 2,500
**SALES:** 500K **Privately Held**
**SIC:** 3634 Massage machines, electric, except for beauty/barber shops

### Burlington
*Kane County*

**(G-2811)**
**D & M CUSTOM INJECTION M**
Also Called: D & M Plastics
150 French Rd (60109-1112)
P.O. Box 158 (60109-0158)
**PHONE** ................................. 847 683-2054
**Fax:** 847 683-2731
Steve Motisi, *President*
Michael Teofilovich, *Chairman*
Diane Teofilovich, *Corp Secy*
Scott Hagen, *COO*
Robert Flammini, *Vice Pres*
**EMP:** 100
**SQ FT:** 10,000
**SALES (est):** 19.9MM **Privately Held**
**WEB:** www.dmplastics.com
**SIC:** 3089 Injection molding of plastics

**(G-2812)**
**KUNVERJI ENTERPRISE CORP**
Also Called: Veejay Plstic Injction Molding
395 S Main St (60109-1045)
P.O. Box 367 (60109-0367)
**PHONE** ................................. 847 683-2954
**Fax:** 847 683-2590
Shanti Satra, *President*
**EMP:** 15
**SALES (est):** 600K **Privately Held**
**SIC:** 3999 Manufacturing industries

**(G-2813)**
**OWEN PLASTICS LLC**
Also Called: D&M Plastics
150 French Rd (60109-1112)
P.O. Box 158 (60109-0158)
**PHONE** ................................. 847 683-2054
Peyton H Owen Jr, *CEO*
Scott Hagen, *COO*
**EMP:** 45
**SQ FT:** 58,237
**SALES (est):** 5.4MM **Privately Held**
**SIC:** 3089 Injection molding of plastics

**(G-2814)**
**VEEJAY PLASTICS INC**
Also Called: Miniature Injection Molding
395 S Main St (60109-1045)
**PHONE** ................................. 847 683-2954
George Klebansky, *President*
Nadja Fell, *Director*
**EMP:** 15 **EST:** 1965
**SQ FT:** 8,000
**SALES (est):** 900K **Privately Held**
**SIC:** 3089 Injection molding of plastics

### Burnham
*Cook County*

**(G-2815)**
**CALUMET LUBR CO LTD PARTNR**
14000 S Mackinaw Ave (60633-1623)
**PHONE** ................................. 708 832-2463
Henry Banach, *Opers-Prdtn-Mfg*
Joe Lapota, *Sales Staff*
Bart A Banach, *Marketing Staff*
**EMP:** 18
**SQ FT:** 4,000
**SALES (corp-wide):** 3.6B **Publicly Held**
**WEB:** www.calumetspecialty.com
**SIC:** 2992 2842 Oils & greases, blending & compounding; specialty cleaning, polishes & sanitation goods
**HQ:** Calumet Lubricants Co., Limited Partnership
2780 Waterfront Pkwy Ste 200 E
Indianapolis IN 46214
317 328-5660

**(G-2816)**
**DENNCO INC (PA)**
14350 S Saginaw Ave (60633-2008)
**PHONE** ................................. 708 862-0070
**Fax:** 708 862-0097
Dennis I Slomski Jr, *President*
Tricia Yakas, *Vice Pres*
Beverly Slomski, *Treasurer*

EMP: 4
SQ FT: 20,000
SALES (est): 1.5MM  Privately Held
WEB: www.dennco.com
SIC: 2087  2099 Extracts, flavoring; syrups, flavoring (except drink); dessert mixes & fillings

## Burnside
### Hancock County

**(G-2817)**
**SIMMONS LIGHTNING PROTECTION**
2094 E County Road 2115 (62330-4024)
PHONE ............................. 217 746-3971
Raymond Simmons, *Owner*
Judith Smimmons, *Admin Sec*
EMP: 3
SALES (est): 180K  Privately Held
SIC: 3643 Lightning protection equipment

## Burr Ridge
### Dupage County

**(G-2818)**
**A & M WOOD PRODUCTS INC**
9900 S Madison St Unit A (60527-2704)
PHONE ............................. 630 323-2555
Fax: 630 323-3221
Melvin Marwitz, *President*
Sharon Marwitz, *Vice Pres*
Wesley Buege, *Executive*
EMP: 8
SQ FT: 30,000
SALES (est): 700K  Privately Held
SIC: 2449 2431 Boxes, wood: wirebound; moldings & baseboards, ornamental & trim; moldings, wood: unfinished & prefinished; trim, wood

**(G-2819)**
**ACCELERATED PHARMA INC**
15w155 81st St (60527-7903)
PHONE ............................. 773 517-0789
Michael Fonstein, *CEO*
Daniel Perez, *Ch of Bd*
Ekaterina Nikolaevskaya, *COO*
Randy S Saluck, *CFO*
Dmitry Prudnikov, *Chief Mktg Ofcr*
EMP: 7
SALES (est): 304.1K  Privately Held
SIC: 2834 Pharmaceutical preparations

**(G-2820)**
**ADS LLC**
Also Called: Hydra-Stop
144 Tower Dr (60527-6173)
PHONE ............................. 256 430-3366
Brett Hanes, *General Mgr*
J G Wood, *Vice Pres*
Indre Lauraitis, *Senior Buyer*
Sandra Stanley, *Purchasing*
Michael Baich, *Finance*
EMP: 65
SALES (corp-wide): 2.1B  Publicly Held
SIC: 3545 8742 3541 3498 Machine tool accessories; foreign trade consultant; machine tools, metal cutting type; fabricated pipe & fittings; valves & pipe fittings
HQ: Ads Llc
  340 The Bridge St Ste 204
  Huntsville AL 35806
  256 430-3366

**(G-2821)**
**ALBERT VIVO UPHOLSTERY CO INC**
836 Lakeview Ln (60527-5629)
PHONE ............................. 312 226-7779
Fax: 312 226-6125
Albert Vivo, *President*
Anita Knitter, *Manager*
EMP: 8
SALES (est): 440K  Privately Held
SIC: 7641 5712 2519 Reupholstery; furniture repair & maintenance; furniture stores; household furniture, except wood or metal: upholstered

**(G-2822)**
**AMERIGUARD CORPORATION**
Also Called: Colonade Interiors II
7701 S Grant St (60527-5999)
PHONE ............................. 630 986-1900
EMP: 7
SQ FT: 10,000
SALES: 750K  Privately Held
SIC: 2392 2653 3496 3999 Mfg Household Furnishing Mfg Corrugated/Fiber Box Mfg Misc Fab Wire Prdts Mfg Misc Products Whol Appliances/Tv/Radio

**(G-2823)**
**AUGUSTA LABEL CORP**
7938 S Madison St (60527-5806)
PHONE ............................. 630 537-1961
Ryan Orniston, *President*
Kaylee Baumbach, *Graphic Designe*
EMP: 3 EST: 2014
SALES (est): 206.6K  Privately Held
SIC: 2752 Commercial printing, lithographic

**(G-2824)**
**BIOCONCEPTS INC (HQ)**
100 Tower Dr Ste 101 (60527-8916)
PHONE ............................. 630 986-0007
Fax: 630 986-0151
Tom Gavin, *President*
EMP: 6
SALES (est): 909K
SALES (corp-wide): 459.1MM  Publicly Held
WEB: www.orthotic.com
SIC: 3842 Prosthetic appliances; foot appliances, orthopedic
PA: Hanger, Inc.
  10910 Domain Dr Ste 300
  Austin TX 78758
  512 777-3800

**(G-2825)**
**BRONSON & BRATTON INC**
220 Shore Dr (60527-5881)
PHONE ............................. 630 986-1815
Fax: 630 655-3801
Mark Bronson, *President*
Anne McClary, *Vice Pres*
Ginny Collins, *Mfg Mgr*
Mike Noramczyk, *Engineer*
Michael Slaski, *Engineer*
EMP: 106
SQ FT: 33,000
SALES (est): 21MM  Privately Held
SIC: 3544 5085 Special dies & tools; forms (molds), for foundry & plastics working machinery; punches, forming & stamping; abrasives; bort; diamonds, industrial: natural, crude

**(G-2826)**
**C HOFBAUER INC**
11433 Ridgewood Ln (60527-5136)
PHONE ............................. 630 920-1222
Charles Hofbauer, *President*
Stephaine Hofbauer, *Admin Sec*
EMP: 8
SQ FT: 1,500
SALES (est): 17MM  Privately Held
SIC: 3679 Electronic circuits

**(G-2827)**
**CAPERS NORTH AMERICA LLC**
760 Village Ctr Dr Ste 250 (60527)
PHONE ............................. 708 995-7500
Reed Konnerth, *CEO*
EMP: 10
SALES (est): 221.8K  Privately Held
SIC: 7372 Prepackaged software

**(G-2828)**
**CARL STAHL DECORCBLE INNOVTNS**
8080 S Madison St (60527-5808)
PHONE ............................. 312 454-2996
Fax: 312 474-1789
David Barger, *Manager*
Zdenek A Fremund,
Patrick S Kelly,
◆ EMP: 11
SQ FT: 10,000

SALES (est): 2.1MM
SALES (corp-wide): 273.9MM  Privately Held
WEB: www.decorcable.com
SIC: 2542 5039 Partitions & fixtures, except wood; architectural metalwork; metals service centers & offices
HQ: Carl Stahl Sava Industries, Inc.
  4 N Corporate Dr
  Riverdale NJ 07457
  973 835-0882

**(G-2829)**
**CENTRAL DECAL COMPANY INC**
6901 High Grove Blvd (60527-7583)
PHONE ............................. 630 325-9892
Fax: 630 325-9878
Robert Kaplan, *President*
Howard C Kaplan III, *President*
Howard Kaplan Jr, *Vice Pres*
Jennifer Loconte, *Admin Sec*
EMP: 70 EST: 1957
SQ FT: 30,000
SALES (est): 15.6MM  Privately Held
WEB: www.centraldecal.com
SIC: 2759 Decals: printing

**(G-2830)**
**CMB PRINTING INC**
15w700 79th St Unit 4 (60527-7964)
PHONE ............................. 630 323-1110
Thomas Banis, *President*
EMP: 18
SQ FT: 10,000
SALES (est): 2.8MM  Privately Held
SIC: 2752 2791 2789 Commercial printing, lithographic; typesetting; bookbinding & related work

**(G-2831)**
**CNH CAPITAL AMERICA LLC (DH)**
Also Called: Geocap Financial Solutions
6900 Veterans Blvd (60527-5640)
PHONE ............................. 630 887-2233
Derci Alcantara, *Managing Dir*
Brett Davis, *Managing Dir*
Stephen Hatton, *Managing Dir*
Mike Morrone, *Managing Dir*
Vladimir Kovalenko, *Business Mgr*
EMP: 20
SALES (est): 6.2MM
SALES (corp-wide): 26.3B  Privately Held
SIC: 3523 Farm machinery & equipment

**(G-2832)**
**CNH INDUSTRIAL AMERICA LLC**
Also Called: Cnh Case Construction
6900 Veterans Blvd (60527-5640)
PHONE ............................. 706 629-5572
EMP: 50
SALES (corp-wide): 26.3B  Privately Held
SIC: 3531 3523 6159 Construction machinery; tractors, construction; bulldozers (construction machinery); loaders, shovel: self-propelled; farm machinery & equipment; tractors, farm; combines (harvester-threshers); cotton pickers & strippers; agricultural loan companies; machinery & equipment finance leasing
HQ: Cnh Industrial America Llc
  700 St St
  Racine WI 53404
  262 636-6011

**(G-2833)**
**CNH INDUSTRIAL AMERICA LLC**
Also Called: Case New Holl Burr Ridge Opera
6900 Veterans Blvd (60527-5640)
PHONE ............................. 630 887-2233
James Grupka, *Engineer*
Alex Willey, *Engineer*
Leonard Betting, *Project Engr*
Jerry Brinkley, *Project Engr*
George Butkovich, *Project Engr*
EMP: 208
SALES (corp-wide): 26.3B  Privately Held
SIC: 3523 Farm machinery & equipment
HQ: Cnh Industrial America Llc
  700 St St
  Racine WI 53404
  262 636-6011

**(G-2834)**
**DAUBERT INDUSTRIES INC (PA)**
700 S Central Ave (60527)
PHONE ............................. 630 203-6800
Fax: 630 203-6907
Matthew Puz, *President*
Matt Puz, *Principal*
Harry A Fischer, *Vice Chairman*
Galman Roy, *COO*
Peter Miehl, *Vice Pres*
◆ EMP: 10
SQ FT: 6,000
SALES: 73.1MM  Privately Held
SIC: 2899 5169 2891 Rust resisting compounds; rustproofing chemicals; adhesives & sealants

**(G-2835)**
**DAUBERT VCI INC (HQ)**
1333 Burr Ridge Pkwy # 200 (60527-6423)
PHONE ............................. 630 203-6800
Fax: 630 203-6900
M Lawrence Garman, *President*
John R Cosbey, *Corp Secy*
Galman Roy, *COO*
Peter Miehl, *Vice Pres*
Chris Pieroni, *Vice Pres*
EMP: 10
SQ FT: 14,000
SALES (est): 3.6MM
SALES (corp-wide): 73.1MM  Privately Held
WEB: www.daubertvci.com
SIC: 2672 Chemically treated papers: made from purchased materials
PA: Daubert Industries, Inc.
  700 S Central Ave
  Burr Ridge IL 60527
  630 203-6800

**(G-2836)**
**DEARBORN TOOL & MFG INC**
7749 S Grant St (60527-5944)
PHONE ............................. 630 655-1260
Fax: 630 655-1268
Anthony J Hadley Jr, *President*
Penny Koetz, *Opers Mgr*
Cheryl Hadley, *Admin Sec*
EMP: 35
SQ FT: 12,500
SALES (est): 7.4MM  Privately Held
SIC: 3541 3544 Numerically controlled metal cutting machine tools; screw machines, automatic; special dies, tools, jigs & fixtures

**(G-2837)**
**DOUBLE GOOD LLC**
Also Called: Popcorn Palace
16w030 83rd St (60527-5802)
P.O. Box 490, Westmont (60559-0490)
PHONE ............................. 630 568-5544
Pablo Peralta, *Plant Mgr*
Rauf Durosinmi, *Controller*
Mark Biondi, *VP Mktg*
Timothy J Heitmann, *Mng Member*
EMP: 10
SQ FT: 53,000
SALES (est): 2MM  Privately Held
WEB: www.popcornpalace.com
SIC: 2064 Popcorn balls or other treated popcorn products

**(G-2838)**
**ENGINE EFFICIENCY SYSTEMS LLC**
6125 S Madison St (60527-5165)
PHONE ............................. 630 590-5241
Stuart Parry, *Principal*
Geannine Lynch, *Admin Sec*
Brian Aiello,
Joseph Lynch,
EMP: 10
SQ FT: 10,000
SALES (est): 546.1K  Privately Held
SIC: 3519 Internal combustion engines

**(G-2839)**
**ET PRODUCTS LLC**
8128 S Madison St (60527-5854)
PHONE ............................. 800 325-5746
EMP: 3 EST: 2010
SALES (est): 324.1K  Privately Held
SIC: 2911 Fuel additives

**(G-2840)**
**ETCON CORP**
Also Called: Electric Supply Direct
7750 S Grant St  (60527-5945)
PHONE..............................630 325-6100
Fax: 630 325-6838
Joseph Rocci, *President*
Mark Mars, *Controller*
Joseph Mulack, *Sales Staff*
Elizabeth Rocci, *Admin Sec*
▲ **EMP:** 15
**SQ FT:** 35,000
**SALES (est):** 3.2MM **Privately Held**
**SIC: 3825** 3661 Demand meters, electric; volt meters; telephone & telegraph apparatus

**(G-2841)**
**EVONIK CORPORATION**
7420 S County Line Rd  (60527-7947)
PHONE..............................630 230-0176
Zachary Woods, *Sales Staff*
Chien-Chih Chen, *Marketing Staff*
Mark Lee, *Manager*
**EMP:** 3
**SALES (corp-wide):** 2.3B **Privately Held**
**SIC: 2869** Industrial organic chemicals
**HQ:** Evonik Corporation
299 Jefferson Rd
Parsippany NJ 07054
973 929-8000

**(G-2842)**
**FLOWSERVE US INC**
161 Tower Dr Ste D  (60527-7818)
PHONE..............................630 655-5700
Ed Hand, *Technical Mgr*
David Vasil, *Manager*
**EMP:** 30
**SALES (corp-wide):** 3.9B **Publicly Held**
**SIC: 3053** Gaskets, packing & sealing devices
**HQ:** Flowserve Fsd Corporation
2100 Factory St
Kalamazoo MI 49001
269 226-3954

**(G-2843)**
**FUSION SYSTEMS INCORPORATED**
Also Called: Fusion OEM
6951 High Grove Blvd  (60527-7583)
PHONE..............................630 323-4115
Fax: 630 323-3697
Craig Zoberis, *President*
Phil Lullo, *Mfg Dir*
Jacob Miller, *Project Mgr*
James Torres, *Engineer*
Jeff Lacrosse, *Controller*
▲ **EMP:** 45
**SQ FT:** 10,000
**SALES (est):** 11.1MM **Privately Held**
**WEB:** www.fusionems.com
**SIC: 3823** Industrial process measurement equipment; computer interface equipment for industrial process control

**(G-2844)**
**GE HEALTHCARE INC**
161 Tower Dr Ste A  (60527-7818)
PHONE..............................312 243-0787
**EMP:** 19 **Privately Held**
**SIC: 2833** Medicinals & botanicals
**HQ:** Ge Healthcare Inc.
100 Results Way
Marlborough MA 01752
800 292-8514

**(G-2845)**
**GEOTEST INSTRUMENT CORP (PA)**
241 S Frontage Rd Ste 38  (60527-6169)
PHONE..............................847 869-7645
Peter Bach, *President*
Jeffrey Lenz, *Purch Mgr*
Michael Granovsky, *Engineer*
Mary Sylvia, *Manager*
▲ **EMP:** 2
**SQ FT:** 2,000
**SALES (est):** 480K **Privately Held**
**WEB:** www.geotestinst.com
**SIC: 5084** 3829 Measuring & testing equipment, electrical; geophysical or meteorological electronic equipment

**(G-2846)**
**GREAT LAKES WASHER COMPANY**
Also Called: Prestige Threaded Products Co
127 Tower Dr  (60527-5779)
PHONE..............................630 887-7447
Suzanne Jasiak, *President*
Robert H Strawbridge III, *Admin Sec*
▲ **EMP:** 10
**SQ FT:** 7,500
**SALES (est):** 1.2MM **Privately Held**
**SIC: 3452** 5085 Washers, metal; fasteners, industrial: nuts, bolts, screws, etc.

**(G-2847)**
**GSI TECHNOLOGIES LLC**
311 Shore Dr  (60527-5859)
PHONE..............................630 325-8181
Fax: 630 325-2597
David G Austin, *CEO*
Rick Mental, *Business Mgr*
Erik Sventeckis, *Business Mgr*
Dominic Robert Zaccone II, *Vice Pres*
Suzanne M Zaccone, *Vice Pres*
▲ **EMP:** 60
**SQ FT:** 40,650
**SALES (est):** 24.6MM **Privately Held**
**WEB:** www.gsitech.com
**SIC: 2791** 2759 Typesetting: letterpress & screen printing; screen printing; flexographic printing

**(G-2848)**
**H G ACQUISITION CORP (PA)**
7020 High Grove Blvd  (60527-7595)
PHONE..............................630 382-1000
Mark S Holecek, *President*
Michael Hussey, *COO*
Bruce Parkey, *Opers Mgr*
Nan Harrison, *Manager*
Katherine Hajna, *Prgrmr*
**EMP:** 5
**SQ FT:** 6,500
**SALES (est):** 2.8MM **Privately Held**
**SIC: 2731** Books: publishing only

**(G-2849)**
**HANSEN TECHNOLOGIES CORP (HQ)**
681 Commerce St  (60527-7599)
PHONE..............................706 335-5551
Fax: 630 528-0755
Tony Ricci, *President*
Mark Sebben, *Vice Pres*
Christopher Knowles, *VP Opers*
Kay Standridge, *Purchasing*
Bryant Crane, *Engineer*
◆ **EMP:** 94
**SQ FT:** 55,000
**SALES (est):** 16.1MM
**SALES (corp-wide):** 3.7B **Publicly Held**
**WEB:** www.hantech.com
**SIC: 3822** 5078 Air conditioning & refrigeration controls; refrigeration controls (pressure); refrigeration equipment & supplies
**PA:** Roper Technologies, Inc.
6901 Prof Pkwy E Ste 200
Sarasota FL 34240
941 556-2601

**(G-2850)**
**HELIGEAR ACQUISITION CO**
Northstar Aerospace Chicago
1000 Burr Ridge Pkwy  (60527-0849)
PHONE..............................708 728-2055
Bryan Cheek, *Vice Pres*
**EMP:** 7
**SALES (corp-wide):** 267.3MM **Privately Held**
**SIC: 3724** Aircraft engines & engine parts
**PA:** Heligear Acquisition Co.
6006 W 73rd St
Bedford Park IL 60638
708 728-2000

**(G-2851)**
**HOLLAND APPLIED TECHNOLOGIES (HQ)**
7050 High Grove Blvd  (60527-7595)
PHONE..............................630 325-5130
David Chaney, *President*
Robert Soukup, *Vice Pres*
◆ **EMP:** 47
**SQ FT:** 50,000

**SALES (est):** 43.6MM **Privately Held**
**WEB:** www.hollandapt.com
**SIC: 5084** 5169 3537 Industrial machinery & equipment; industrial chemicals; skids, metal
**PA:** Harry Holland & Son, Inc.
7050 High Grove Blvd
Burr Ridge IL 60527
630 325-5130

**(G-2852)**
**HYDRA-STOP LLC**
144 Tower Dr Ste A  (60527-5785)
PHONE..............................708 389-5111
Amy Van Meter, *CFO*
**EMP:** 35
**SALES (est):** 1.2MM **Privately Held**
**SIC: 3491** Mfg Industrial Valves

**(G-2853)**
**INNOVA GLOBAL LLC**
Also Called: Innova Uev
16w235 83rd St Ste A  (60527-5863)
PHONE..............................630 568-5609
Roman Kuropas, *Mng Member*
Clifford Harstad,
**EMP:** 5 **EST:** 2011
**SALES (est):** 543.1K **Privately Held**
**SIC: 3621** Generators for gas-electric or oil-electric vehicles

**(G-2854)**
**INNOVA SYSTEMS INC**
8330 S Madison St Ste 60  (60527-6595)
PHONE..............................630 920-8880
Cheryl Nordstrom, *President*
**EMP:** 5
**SALES (est):** 825.9K **Privately Held**
**SIC: 3851** Ophthalmic goods

**(G-2855)**
**INNOVA UEV LLC**
16w235 83rd St Ste A  (60527-5863)
PHONE..............................630 568-5609
Roman Kuropas, *President*
**EMP:** 11
**SQ FT:** 10,000
**SALES (est):** 710.5K **Privately Held**
**SIC: 3711** Automobile assembly, including specialty automobiles

**(G-2856)**
**INTEGRAL AUTOMATION INC**
Also Called: Premier Tool Works
16 W 171 Shore Ct  (60527)
PHONE..............................630 654-4300
Lucien J Wroblewski, *President*
Bill Wirth, *Opers Mgr*
Colleen Alday, *Manager*
▼ **EMP:** 15
**SQ FT:** 9,000
**SALES (est):** 1.2MM **Privately Held**
**WEB:** www.premiertool.com
**SIC: 3542** 8711 3825 Spring winding & forming machines; engineering services; logic circuit testers

**(G-2857)**
**INTELLIGENT INSTRUMENT SY**
16w251 S Frontage Rd # 23  (60527-6163)
PHONE..............................630 323-3911
Wang Zhao, *Owner*
▲ **EMP:** 2 **EST:** 2009
**SALES (est):** 257.6K **Privately Held**
**SIC: 3931** Musical instruments

**(G-2858)**
**INVEROM CORPORATION**
16w235 83rd St Ste A  (60527-5863)
PHONE..............................630 568-5609
Roman M Kuropas, *CEO*
**EMP:** 6
**SALES (est):** 3MM **Privately Held**
**SIC: 5084** 3571 Industrial machinery & equipment; electronic computers

**(G-2859)**
**JB MFG & SCREW MACHINE**
16w154 Hillside Ln  (60527-6296)
PHONE..............................630 850-6978
Jerzy Roginski, *Principal*
**EMP:** 3
**SALES (est):** 153.4K **Privately Held**
**SIC: 3451** Screw machine products

**(G-2860)**
**JINDILLI BEVERAGES LLC**
8100 S Madison St  (60527-5854)
PHONE..............................630 581-5697
Morgan Roy, *President*
Jim Richards,
▲ **EMP:** 2 **EST:** 2012
**SALES (est):** 295.3K **Privately Held**
**SIC: 2844** Face creams or lotions

**(G-2861)**
**KOHLER CO**
775 Village Center Dr  (60527-4518)
PHONE..............................630 323-7674
Craig Lieffring, *Project Mgr*
Francoise Lewis, *Purch Agent*
Jamie Winstead, *Buyer*
Miriam Huntley, *Branch Mgr*
Melissa Hand, *Manager*
**EMP:** 48
**SALES (corp-wide):** 8B **Privately Held**
**SIC: 3431** Metal sanitary ware
**PA:** Kohler Co.
444 Highland Dr
Kohler WI 53044
920 457-4441

**(G-2862)**
**LABORATORY BUILDERS INC**
166 Shore Dr  (60527-5836)
PHONE..............................630 598-0216
Trudy Chragal, *President*
▲ **EMP:** 4
**SQ FT:** 3,000
**SALES (est):** 965.7K **Privately Held**
**WEB:** www.labbuildersinc.com
**SIC: 3821** Laboratory apparatus & furniture

**(G-2863)**
**M CA CHICAGO**
7065 Veterans Blvd  (60527-5624)
PHONE..............................312 384-1220
Steve Lamb, *Principal*
**EMP:** 3
**SALES (est):** 355.7K **Privately Held**
**SIC: 3494** Valves & pipe fittings

**(G-2864)**
**MARS CHOCOLATE NORTH AMER LLC**
15w660 79th St  (60527-5987)
PHONE..............................630 850-9898
Gil Wright, *Engineer*
Rose Verona, *Branch Mgr*
**EMP:** 220
**SALES (corp-wide):** 35B **Privately Held**
**WEB:** www.kilic-kalkan.com
**SIC: 2066** 2064 Chocolate & cocoa products; candy & other confectionery products
**HQ:** Mars Chocolate North America, Llc
800 High St
Hackettstown NJ 07840
908 852-1000

**(G-2865)**
**MEADEN PRECISION MACHINED PDTS**
Also Called: Meaden Screw Products Company
16w210 83rd St  (60527-5827)
PHONE..............................630 655-0888
John A Meaden Jr, *Ch of Bd*
Thomas F Meaden, *President*
Jerry Paskovich, *General Mgr*
Robert Rackow, *VP Finance*
Maureen Meaden, *Admin Sec*
▲ **EMP:** 75 **EST:** 1939
**SQ FT:** 46,250
**SALES (est):** 17.7MM **Privately Held**
**WEB:** www.meaden.com
**SIC: 3451** Screw machine products

**(G-2866)**
**MEDTEXT INC**
Also Called: H D C
15w560 89th St  (60527-6356)
PHONE..............................630 325-3277
Ona Daugirdas, *President*
John Thomas Daugirdas, *Vice Pres*
**EMP:** 6 **EST:** 1992
**SALES:** 600K **Privately Held**
**WEB:** www.medtext.com
**SIC: 2721** Trade journals: publishing & printing

## Burr Ridge - Dupage County (G-2867)

**(G-2867)**
**MIDWEST OUTDOORS LTD**
Also Called: Fishing Facts
111 Shore Dr (60527-5885)
 PHONE...................................630 887-7722
 Fax: 630 887-1958
 Eugene Laulunen, *President*
 Gail E Laulunen, *President*
 Jeff Scharf, *Sales Mgr*
 Roger Cormier, *Sales Staff*
 Dan Ferris, *Sales Staff*
 **EMP:** 20
 **SALES (est):** 2.9MM **Privately Held**
 **WEB:** www.fishingfacts.com
 **SIC:** 2721 7812 2791 2752 Magazines: publishing & printing; television film production; typesetting; commercial printing, lithographic

**(G-2868)**
**MIDWEST PROMOTIONAL GROUP CO**
16w 211 S Frontage Rd (60527)
 PHONE...................................708 563-0600
 Casey Krajewski, *President*
 David Lewandowski, *President*
 Don Lewandowski, *Chairman*
 Rick Daignault, *Exec VP*
 John Duzansky, *Vice Pres*
 **EMP:** 44
 **SQ FT:** 16,500
 **SALES (est):** 8.8MM **Privately Held**
 **WEB:** www.midwestgrp.com
 **SIC:** 5199 7336 3993 Calendars; advertising specialties; silk screen design; advertising novelties

**(G-2869)**
**MONOGRAMS & MORE**
7926 S Madison St (60527-5806)
P.O. Box 244, Hinsdale (60522-0244)
 PHONE...................................630 789-8424
 Sharon Keogh, *President*
 Diane Kiolbasa, *Vice Pres*
 **EMP:** 5
 **SQ FT:** 540
 **SALES (est):** 390K **Privately Held**
 **SIC:** 5699 5947 7299 7389 Sports apparel; gift shop; stitching services; engraving service; photocopying & duplicating services; pleating & stitching

**(G-2870)**
**NANOPHASE TECHNOLOGIES CORP**
453 Commerce St (60527-7500)
 PHONE...................................630 771-6747
 Fax: 630 323-1221
 Nancy Baldwin, *VP Human Res*
 Bob Roseland, *Branch Mgr*
 Jamee Adkins, *Manager*
 Phil Coatney, *Manager*
 Mohammad Ali, *Director*
 **EMP:** 15
 **SALES (corp-wide):** 10.7MM **Publicly Held**
 **WEB:** www.nanophase.com
 **SIC:** 3299 3399 Ceramic fiber; powder, metal
 **PA:** Nanophase Technologies Corp
  1319 Marquette Dr
  Romeoville IL 60446
  630 771-6708

**(G-2871)**
**NOVA TRONICS INC**
7701 S Grant St Ste C (60527-7253)
 PHONE...................................630 455-1034
 Fax: 630 455-1062
 Matt Novak, *Owner*
 **EMP:** 4
 **SALES (est):** 333.1K **Privately Held**
 **WEB:** www.novatronicsinc.com
 **SIC:** 3629 Static elimination equipment, industrial

**(G-2872)**
**PACKAGING AM INC**
537 87th St (60527-8362)
 PHONE...................................630 568-9506
 **EMP:** 1
 **SALES:** 3MM **Privately Held**
 **SIC:** 3081 Packing materials, plastic sheet

**(G-2873)**
**PACKAGING DESIGN CORPORATION**
101 Shore Dr (60527-5887)
 PHONE...................................630 323-1354
 Fax: 630 323-2802
 Howard Jones, *President*
 Scott H Jones, *President*
 George Budlovsky, *Design Engr*
 Bennie Nelson, *Accounts Mgr*
 David Flaischaker, *Maintence Staff*
 **EMP:** 30
 **SQ FT:** 35,000
 **SALES (est):** 7.1MM **Privately Held**
 **WEB:** www.pack-design.com
 **SIC:** 2653 Corrugated boxes, partitions, display items, sheets & pad

**(G-2874)**
**PANATROL CORPORATION**
161 Tower Dr Ste D (60527-7818)
 PHONE...................................630 655-4700
 Fax: 708 496-0426
 Bruce Krebbers, *President*
 Diane Chrones, *Controller*
 Dean Chrones, *Admin Sec*
 **EMP:** 20
 **SQ FT:** 22,600
 **SALES (est):** 3.5MM **Privately Held**
 **WEB:** www.panatrol.com
 **SIC:** 3625 3629 Relays & industrial controls; electronic generation equipment

**(G-2875)**
**PRECISION GAGE COMPANY**
100 Shore Dr (60527-5819)
 PHONE...................................630 655-2121
 Fax: 630 655-3073
 Barbara L Layland, *President*
 Roger Layland, *Vice Pres*
 H K Layland Jr, *Admin Sec*
 ◆ **EMP:** 10
 **SQ FT:** 10,000
 **SALES (est):** 1.7MM **Privately Held**
 **WEB:** www.precisiongageco.com
 **SIC:** 3545 Measuring tools & machines, machinists' metalworking type

**(G-2876)**
**PYRAMID SCIENCES INC**
9425 S Madison St (60527-6850)
 PHONE...................................630 974-6110
 Folim Halaka, *President*
 **EMP:** 3
 **SALES (est):** 100K **Privately Held**
 **SIC:** 2835 In vitro & in vivo diagnostic substances

**(G-2877)**
**RICK STYFER**
Also Called: Creative Menu's Plus
200 Lakewood Cir (60527-6340)
 PHONE...................................630 734-3244
 Rick Styfer, *Owner*
 Jane Soto, *Manager*
 **EMP:** 3
 **SQ FT:** 5,000
 **SALES (est):** 170K **Privately Held**
 **SIC:** 2752 2759 Menus, lithographed; menus: printing

**(G-2878)**
**ROCKWELL AUTOMATION INC**
180 Harvester Dr Ste 190 (60527-6693)
 PHONE...................................414 382-3662
 Bert Acanfora, *Area Mgr*
 Harry Curnow, *Area Mgr*
 On Emmert, *Area Mgr*
 Robert Kotowski, *Project Mgr*
 Karen Kostrzewa, *Sales Engr*
 **EMP:** 75 **Publicly Held**
 **SIC:** 3625 Relays & industrial controls
 **PA:** Rockwell Automation, Inc.
  1201 S 2nd St
  Milwaukee WI 53204

**(G-2879)**
**SCRIBES INC**
7725 S Grant St Ste 1 (60527-7274)
 PHONE...................................630 654-3800
 Fax: 630 654-3803
 James J Finnegan, *President*
 Joan K Finnegan, *Corp Secy*
 Tom Tompkins, *VP Sls/Mktg*
 Linda Meyer, *Technology*
 Debbie Hartman, *Director*
 **EMP:** 8
 **SALES (est):** 1.2MM **Privately Held**
 **WEB:** www.scribe.com
 **SIC:** 2759 Commercial printing

**(G-2880)**
**SIGN CONTRACTORS**
16w143 Hillside Ln (60527-6269)
 PHONE...................................708 795-1761
 Ken Cichon, *President*
 **EMP:** 2
 **SQ FT:** 1,500
 **SALES (est):** 200K **Privately Held**
 **SIC:** 3993 Signs & advertising specialties

**(G-2881)**
**SPYCO INDUSTRIES INC**
Also Called: Spyco Tool Co
7029 High Grove Blvd (60527-7593)
 PHONE...................................630 655-5900
 Fax: 630 655-5997
 John Spytek, *President*
 Christine Spytek, *Corp Secy*
 Robert Spytek, *Vice Pres*
 Linda Spytek, *Manager*
 **EMP:** 40
 **SQ FT:** 15,000
 **SALES (est):** 7.6MM **Privately Held**
 **WEB:** www.spycoind.com
 **SIC:** 3599 Machine shop, jobbing & repair

**(G-2882)**
**STI HOLDINGS INC**
Also Called: Midwest Utility
15w700 N Frontage Rd # 140 (60527-7544)
 PHONE...................................630 789-2713
 Ray O'Donnell, *President*
 **EMP:** 12
 **SALES (corp-wide):** 266.7MM **Privately Held**
 **WEB:** www.stoughtontrailers.com
 **SIC:** 3715 3537 Semitrailers for truck tractors; industrial trucks & tractors
 **PA:** Sti Holdings, Inc.
  416 S Academy St
  Stoughton WI 53589
  608 873-2500

**(G-2883)**
**TECHNY ADVISORS LLC**
Also Called: Gifts For You
109 Shore Dr (60527-5818)
 PHONE...................................630 771-0095
 Frederick Allen, *Opers Mgr*
 Kristen Metoyer, *Opers Mgr*
 Richard Nichols, *QC Mgr*
 Peter Pesce, *VP Mktg*
 Melissa McVeigh, *Marketing Staff*
 ▲ **EMP:** 18
 **SALES (est):** 5.1MM **Privately Held**
 **SIC:** 3499 Novelties & giftware, including trophies

**(G-2884)**
**TEGRITY INC**
1333 Burr Ridge Pkwy # 250 (60527-6423)
 PHONE...................................800 411-0579
 Isaac Segal, *President*
 Brian Kirby, *President*
 Mona Leung, *CFO*
 Hong Nguyen, *Accountant*
 Curtis Waters, *Sales Dir*
 **EMP:** 30
 **SQ FT:** 1,000
 **SALES:** 1.7MM
 **SALES (corp-wide):** 1.4B **Privately Held**
 **WEB:** www.tegrity.com
 **SIC:** 7372 8732 Educational computer software; educational research
 **HQ:** Mcgraw-Hill Global Education, Llc
  2 Penn Plz Fl 20
  New York NY 10121
  646 766-2000

**(G-2885)**
**TOWER PLASTICS MFG INC**
181 Shore Ct Ste 2 (60527-5850)
 PHONE...................................847 788-1700
 David R Miller, *President*
 **EMP:** 6 **EST:** 1970
 **SQ FT:** 10,000
 **SALES (est):** 763.7K **Privately Held**
 **WEB:** www.towerplastics.com
 **SIC:** 2782 Blankbooks & looseleaf binders; looseleaf binders & devices

**(G-2886)**
**TRC ENVIRONMENTAL CORP**
7521 Brush Hill Dr (60527-7575)
 PHONE...................................630 953-9046
 Scott Miller, *President*
 **EMP:** 6 **EST:** 1996
 **SALES (est):** 1.2MM
 **SALES (corp-wide):** 465.1MM **Publicly Held**
 **SIC:** 3829 Aircraft & motor vehicle measurement equipment
 **PA:** Trc Companies, Inc.
  650 Suffolk St
  Lowell MA 01854
  978 970-5600

**(G-2887)**
**TREND MACHINERY INC**
7475 S Madison St Ste 5 (60527-1635)
 PHONE...................................630 655-0030
 Fax: 630 655-0147
 John J Gordon, *President*
 Robert Gordon, *Vice Pres*
 Thomas Pruyne, *Engineer*
 Donald Strange, *Engineer*
 **EMP:** 6
 **SQ FT:** 5,000
 **SALES (est):** 1.2MM **Privately Held**
 **WEB:** www.trendmachinery.com
 **SIC:** 3625 Control equipment, electric

**(G-2888)**
**TUSCHALL ENGINEERING CO INC**
15w700 79th St Unit 1 (60527-7958)
 PHONE...................................630 655-9100
 Fax: 630 655-9109
 James C Tuschall, *CEO*
 James C Tuschall Sr, *President*
 Hazel Tuschall, *Corp Secy*
 Carolyn Dalby, *Vice Pres*
 Dr John Tuschall Jr, *Vice Pres*
 **EMP:** 25
 **SQ FT:** 12,000
 **SALES (est):** 4.3MM **Privately Held**
 **WEB:** www.tuschalleng.com
 **SIC:** 1791 7389 3446 Structural steel erection; building inspection service; architectural metalwork

**(G-2889)**
**TUTHILL CORPORATION (PA)**
8500 S Madison St (60527-6284)
 PHONE...................................630 382-4900
 Fax: 630 382-4999
 Thomas M Carmazzi, *CEO*
 Mark Hampshire, *President*
 Richard Liebson, *Division Mgr*
 D Ross, *Division Mgr*
 Donald Mateer, *General Mgr*
 ◆ **EMP:** 35 **EST:** 1927
 **SQ FT:** 16,000
 **SALES (est):** 307.6MM **Privately Held**
 **WEB:** www.tuthill.com
 **SIC:** 3561 3586 3524 Pumps & pumping equipment; gasoline pumps, measuring or dispensing; blowers & vacuums, lawn

**(G-2890)**
**UNIMODE INC**
11s104 S Jackson St (60527-6885)
 PHONE...................................773 343-6754
 Arunas Zabielskas, *Principal*
 **EMP:** 2
 **SALES (est):** 205.7K **Privately Held**
 **SIC:** 2431 Millwork

**(G-2891)**
**UNITED FOOD INGREDIENTS INC**
15w700 S Frontage Rd (60527-7930)
 PHONE...................................630 655-9494
 David Jacobson, *President*
 Jim Audet, *Vice Pres*
 ▲ **EMP:** 5
 **SQ FT:** 60,000
 **SALES (est):** 622.6K **Privately Held**
 **SIC:** 2099 Food preparations

**(G-2892)**
**USA DRIVES INC**
7900 S Madison St (60527-5806)
 PHONE...................................630 323-1282
 Fax: 630 323-1390
 Phillip E Reilly, *President*

James Schmidt, *Vice Pres*
Robert Carlson, *Treasurer*
Sherrie Delong, *Director*
Theodore P Woerner, *Admin Sec*
**EMP:** 32
**SQ FT:** 24,000
**SALES (est):** 5.9MM  Privately Held
**WEB:** www.usadrivesinc.com
**SIC:** 3625  Timing devices, electronic

**(G-2893)**
**WESTROCK CP LLC**
8170 S Madison St (60527-5854)
**PHONE**.................................630 655-6951
Charles Timko, *Branch Mgr*
**EMP:** 9
**SALES (corp-wide):** 14.1B  Publicly Held
**WEB:** www.sto.com
**SIC:** 2421  Sawmills & planing mills, general
**HQ:** Westrock Cp, Llc
    504 Thrasher St
    Norcross GA 30071

**(G-2894)**
**WESTROCK RKT COMPANY**
Athena Industries
51 Shore Dr Ste 1 (60527-5888)
**PHONE**.................................630 325-9670
David Linn, *Engineer*
Dale Razee, *Branch Mgr*
Martin Harper, *Branch Mgr*
April Alvarado, *Manager*
**EMP:** 50
**SALES (corp-wide):** 14.1B  Publicly Held
**WEB:** www.rocktenn.com
**SIC:** 2653  Hampers, solid fiber: made from purchased materials
**HQ:** Westrock Rkt Company
    504 Thrasher St
    Norcross GA 30071
    770 448-2193

**(G-2895)**
**WHOLESALE POINT INC**
260 Shore Ct (60527-5815)
**PHONE**.................................630 986-1700
Lisa Haddad, *President*
Kamal J Haddad, *Senior VP*
**EMP:** 12
**SQ FT:** 18,000
**SALES (est):** 5MM  Privately Held
**WEB:** www.wholesalepoint.com
**SIC:** 5047  3841  Medical & hospital equipment; medical equipment & supplies; surgical & medical instruments

**(G-2896)**
**WINLIND SKINCARE LLC**
80 Burr Ridge Pkwy (60527-0832)
**PHONE**.................................630 789-9408
▼ **EMP:** 6
**SALES (est):** 410K  Privately Held
**SIC:** 5999  2834  7389  Ret Misc Merchandise Mfg Pharmaceutical Preparations Business Services At Non-Commercial Site

## Bushnell
### Mcdonough County

**(G-2897)**
**ARCHER-DANIELS-MIDLAND COMPANY**
Also Called: ADM
160 E Main St (61422-1724)
P.O. Box 90 (61422-0090)
**PHONE**.................................309 772-2141
**Fax:** 309 772-2377
Greg Shaw, *Branch Mgr*
G A Andreas Jr, *Manager*
**EMP:** 20
**SALES (corp-wide):** 62.3B  Publicly Held
**WEB:** www.admworld.com
**SIC:** 5153  2099  2032  Grains; food preparations; canned specialties
**PA:** Archer-Daniels-Midland Company
    77 W Wacker Dr Ste 4600
    Chicago IL 60601
    312 634-8100

**(G-2898)**
**BUSHNELL ILLINOIS TANK CO**
Also Called: Schuld-Bushnell
650 W Davis St (61422-1120)
P.O. Box 179 (61422-0179)
**PHONE**.................................309 772-3106
**Fax:** 309 772-2045
Ernest R Schuld, *President*
Deana Nell, *Admin Sec*
▲ **EMP:** 60
**SQ FT:** 50,000
**SALES (est):** 21.5MM  Privately Held
**SIC:** 3523  Farm machinery & equipment; hog feeding, handling & watering equipment; cattle feeding, handling & watering equipment

**(G-2899)**
**BUSHNELL LOCKER SERVICE**
330 Green St (61422-1770)
**PHONE**.................................309 772-2783
**Fax:** 309 772-3140
Larry Mason, *President*
Beth Mason, *Corp Secy*
**EMP:** 8
**SQ FT:** 2,000
**SALES (est):** 337.7K  Privately Held
**SIC:** 0751  2011  4222  1521  Slaughtering: custom livestock services; meat packing plants; warehousing, cold storage or refrigerated; storage, frozen or refrigerated goods; general remodeling, single-family houses

**(G-2900)**
**BUSHNELL WELDING & RADIATOR**
120 Charles St (61422-1740)
P.O. Box 141 (61422-0141)
**PHONE**.................................309 772-9289
Kyle Pico, *Owner*
**EMP:** 3
**SALES (est):** 75K  Privately Held
**SIC:** 7692  7539  Automotive welding; radiator repair shop, automotive

**(G-2901)**
**CORTELYOU EXCAVATING**
494 W Davis St (61422-1116)
P.O. Box 148 (61422-0148)
**PHONE**.................................309 772-2922
David Cortelyou, *Owner*
**EMP:** 2
**SALES (est):** 300K  Privately Held
**SIC:** 1794  3272  1711  Excavation work; concrete products; septic system construction

**(G-2902)**
**DUNTEMAN AND CO**
115 E Twyman St (61422-1320)
**PHONE**.................................309 772-2166
Darrell Dunteman, *Owner*
**EMP:** 3
**SALES (est):** 296.8K  Privately Held
**SIC:** 3599  Amusement park equipment

**(G-2903)**
**KITCHEN COOKED INC**
110 Industrial Park Rd (61422-1185)
**PHONE**.................................309 772-2798
**Fax:** 309 772-3778
Corey Starcevich, *Financial Exec*
**EMP:** 25
**SALES (corp-wide):** 3.5MM  Privately Held
**SIC:** 2096  Potato chips & other potato-based snacks; popcorn, already popped (except candy covered)
**PA:** Kitchen Cooked, Inc
    632 N Main St
    Farmington IL 61531
    309 245-2191

**(G-2904)**
**MACOMB CONCRETE PRODUCTS INC**
11 Hillcrest Dr (61422-9740)
Rural Route 1, Macomb (61455)
**PHONE**.................................309 772-3826
Dave Cadwalader, *President*
Rhonda Calwalader, *Treasurer*
**EMP:** 2  EST: 1949
**SQ FT:** 2,400
**SALES (est):** 253.9K  Privately Held
**SIC:** 5032  3271  3272  Concrete building products; blocks, concrete or cinder: standard; concrete products

**(G-2905)**
**MCDONOUGH DEMOCRAT INC**
358 E Main St (61422-1338)
P.O. Box 269 (61422-0269)
**PHONE**.................................309 772-2129
**Fax:** 309 772-3994
David S Norton, *President*
Phyllis Gould, *Manager*
**EMP:** 16
**SALES (est):** 2.2MM  Privately Held
**SIC:** 2752  Commercial printing, offset

**(G-2906)**
**MID STATE GRAPHICS (PA)**
496 W Harris Ave (61422-1016)
**PHONE**.................................309 772-3843
Dennis King, *Owner*
Linda King, *Co-Owner*
**EMP:** 2
**SALES (est):** 368.7K  Privately Held
**SIC:** 2396  Linings, apparel: made from purchased materials

**(G-2907)**
**NORFORGE AND MACHINING INC**
195 N Dean St (61422-1743)
**PHONE**.................................309 772-3124
Patricia S Hayes, *President*
**EMP:** 70
**SQ FT:** 90,000
**SALES (est):** 18.6MM  Privately Held
**WEB:** www.norforge.com
**SIC:** 3462  3429  Iron & steel forgings; manufactured hardware (general)

**(G-2908)**
**S & P FARMS**
19485 N 1700th Rd (61422-9453)
**PHONE**.................................309 772-3936
Steven C Hess, *Owner*
**EMP:** 1
**SALES:** 750K  Privately Held
**SIC:** 3523  Driers (farm): grain, hay & seed

**(G-2909)**
**VAUGHAN & BUSHNELL MFG CO**
201 W Main St (61422-1350)
**PHONE**.................................309 772-2131
W Parks, *Purchasing*
W H Mourning, *Engineer*
Laverne Parks, *Controller*
Elmer Heikes, *Personnel*
Lavoni Manning, *Sales Staff*
**EMP:** 250
**SQ FT:** 60,000
**SALES (corp-wide):** 40MM  Privately Held
**WEB:** www.vbmfg.com
**SIC:** 3423  Hooks: bush, grass, baling, husking, etc.; axes & hatchets
**PA:** Vaughan & Bushnell Manufacturing Company
    11414 Maple Ave
    Hebron IL 60034
    815 648-2446

## Butler
### Montgomery County

**(G-2910)**
**R MACHINING INC**
705 Elm St (62015-1020)
**PHONE**.................................217 532-2174
**Fax:** 217 532-2174
Ron Reynolds, *President*
Diane Reynolds, *Admin Sec*
**EMP:** 8
**SALES (est):** 878.3K  Privately Held
**SIC:** 3599  7692  Machine & other job shop work; welding repair

## Byron
### Ogle County

**(G-2911)**
**ASPHALT MAINTENANCE**
8579 N River Dr (61010-9432)
**PHONE**.................................815 234-7325
Steve Tilbury, *Principal*
**EMP:** 3
**SALES (est):** 213.3K  Privately Held
**SIC:** 2951  Asphalt paving mixtures & blocks

**(G-2912)**
**AUSTIN-WESTRAN LLC (PA)**
602 E Blackhawk Dr (61010-8940)
P.O. Box 921 (61010-0921)
**PHONE**.................................815 234-2811
Bill Diemel, *President*
Brad Staman, *Purch Mgr*
Amy Rasch, *Purchasing*
Zachary Robinson, *Engineer*
Nadine Dahms, *Controller*
▲ **EMP:** 125  EST: 2001
**SQ FT:** 200,000
**SALES (est):** 37.8MM  Privately Held
**WEB:** www.austinwestran.com
**SIC:** 3567  3444  2514  Industrial furnaces & ovens; sheet metalwork; tables, household: metal

**(G-2913)**
**BYRON BLACKTOP INC**
Also Called: Rabine Paving
3499 E Tower Rd (61010-8824)
**PHONE**.................................815 234-2225
Kevin Herbig, *Branch Mgr*
**EMP:** 3
**SALES (corp-wide):** 665.3K  Privately Held
**SIC:** 2951  Paving mixtures
**PA:** Byron Blacktop Inc
    1291 Kysor Dr
    Byron IL 61010
    815 234-8115

**(G-2914)**
**BYRON BLACKTOP INC (PA)**
1291 Kysor Dr (61010-8828)
P.O. Box 934 (61010-0934)
**PHONE**.................................815 234-8115
Dennis Herbig, *President*
Liv Sorrisso, *Manager*
**EMP:** 2
**SQ FT:** 400
**SALES:** 665.3K  Privately Held
**SIC:** 3531  Asphalt plant, including gravel-mix type

**(G-2915)**
**DANE INDUSTRIES LLC**
Also Called: PQ Ovens
602 E Blackhawk Dr. (61010-8940)
P.O. Box 921 (61010-0921)
**PHONE**.................................815 234-2811
Michael Schrom, *Controller*
Troy Berg,
**EMP:** 99
**SALES (est):** 6.3MM  Privately Held
**SIC:** 3567  Industrial furnaces & ovens

**(G-2916)**
**INFRATROL LLC**
602 E Blackhawk Dr (61010-8940)
**PHONE**.................................779 475-3098
William Diemel, *President*
Steven Onsager, *Vice Pres*
**EMP:** 32
**SQ FT:** 80,000
**SALES (est):** 172K  Privately Held
**SIC:** 3567  Industrial furnaces & ovens

**(G-2917)**
**INTERNTIONAL METAL FINSHG SVCS**
Also Called: Lights On Service
8692 Glacier Dr (61010-9766)
**PHONE**.................................815 234-5254
Alan Titterton, *President*
Pondelea Titterton, *Admin Sec*
**EMP:** 3
**SALES (est):** 224.8K  Privately Held
**SIC:** 3471  Plating & polishing

**(G-2918)**
**QUALITY METAL FINISHING CO**
421 N Walnut St (61010)
P.O. Box 922 (61010-0922)
PHONE.....................................815 234-2711
Fax: 815 234-2243
Mario Bortoli, *Ch of Bd*
Matthew Bortoli, *President*
Rachel Bockman, *Safety Mgr*
Bill Wohrley, *Controller*
Chad Worman, *Manager*
▲ **EMP:** 145 **EST:** 1947
**SQ FT:** 150,000
**SALES (est):** 34.2MM **Privately Held**
**WEB:** www.qmfco.com
**SIC: 3364** Zinc & zinc-base alloy die-castings

**(G-2919)**
**ROCK VALLEY PUBLISHING LLC**
Also Called: Northern Orgle County Temple
418 W Blackhawk Dr (61010-8634)
P.O. Box 982 (61010-0982)
PHONE.....................................815 234-4821
Randy Johnson, *Manager*
**EMP:** 3
**SALES (corp-wide):** 4.5MM **Privately Held**
**WEB:** www.rvpublishing.com
**SIC: 2711** Newspapers: publishing only, not printed on site
**PA:** Rock Valley Publishing Llc
11512 N 2nd St
Machesney Park IL 61115
815 467-6397

**(G-2920)**
**ROGERS READY MIX & MTLS INC (PA)**
8128 N Walnut St (61010)
P.O. Box 250 (61010-0250)
PHONE.....................................815 234-8212
Fax: 815 234-2927
Toby Rogers, *President*
Robert Rogers, *Vice Pres*
Mark Jewell, *Controller*
**EMP:** 80 **EST:** 1965
**SQ FT:** 7,000
**SALES (est):** 14.3MM **Privately Held**
**SIC: 3273** 5032 1442 Ready-mixed concrete; aggregate; construction sand & gravel

**(G-2921)**
**SHERWIN INDUSTRIES INC**
149 S Fox Run Ln (61010-9577)
PHONE.....................................815 234-8007
Steven Schultz, *Partner*
**EMP:** 20
**SALES (est):** 1.5MM **Privately Held**
**SIC: 2951** Asphalt paving mixtures & blocks

**(G-2922)**
**SSN LLC**
Also Called: Supply Solutions Network
4875 E Nordic Woods Dr (61010-9306)
PHONE.....................................815 978-8729
Peter Devries, *CEO*
▲ **EMP:** 6
**SALES:** 100K **Privately Held**
**SIC: 2759** 7389 Commercial printing;

## Cahokia
### St. Clair County

**(G-2923)**
**JET AVIATION ST LOUIS INC (DH)**
6400 Curtiss Steinberg Dr (62206-1458)
PHONE.....................................618 646-8000
Fax: 618 646-8877
Robert Smith, *President*
Kurt Sutterer, *President*
Michael Mueller, *General Mgr*
Heinz Aebi, *Senior VP*
Stephan Bruhin, *Senior VP*
**EMP:** 99 **EST:** 1957
**SQ FT:** 160,000
**SALES (est):** 36MM
**SALES (corp-wide):** 31.3B **Publicly Held**
**WEB:** www.jetaviation.com
**SIC: 4581** 5172 3721 5088 Aircraft servicing & repairing; aircraft storage at airports; airport terminal services; aircraft fueling services; aircraft; aircraft & parts
**HQ:** Jet Aviation International Inc
1515 Perimeter Rd
West Palm Beach FL 33406
561 478-9066

**(G-2924)**
**PRAXAIR DISTRIBUTION INC**
9 Judith Ln (62206-1352)
PHONE.....................................314 664-7900
Jim Loesche, *Plant Mgr*
Ray Chapman, *Manager*
Russ Cooner, *Data Proc Staff*
Ken Marshall, *Director*
**EMP:** 28
**SALES (corp-wide):** 10.5B **Publicly Held**
**SIC: 5084** 5169 7359 2813 Welding machinery & equipment; gases, compressed & liquefied; equipment rental & leasing; industrial gases
**HQ:** Praxair Distribution, Inc.
10 Riverview Dr
Danbury CT 06810
203 837-2000

**(G-2925)**
**RONALD ALLEN**
Also Called: Concept Cleaning Service
1920 Marseilles Dr (62206-2624)
PHONE.....................................314 568-1446
Ronald Allen, *Owner*
**EMP:** 18
**SALES (est):** 691.1K **Privately Held**
**SIC: 3822** 7389 Hardware for environmental regulators;

**(G-2926)**
**STELLAR MANUFACTURING COMPANY**
1647 Sauget Business Blvd (62206-1455)
PHONE.....................................618 823-3761
Fax: 618 337-0003
Thomas V Connelly, *President*
Jerry Lewinski, *Vice Pres*
Matthew Grant, *Plant Engr*
Tiffany Coney, *Human Res Mgr*
Mark Scott, *Manager*
**EMP:** 80
**SQ FT:** 130,000
**SALES (est):** 28.7MM **Privately Held**
**WEB:** www.stellarmfg.com
**SIC: 2819** 3661 Industrial inorganic chemicals; telephone & telegraph apparatus

## Cairo
### Alexander County

**(G-2927)**
**CAIRO DIAGNOSTIC CENTER**
13289 Kessler Rd (62914-3101)
PHONE.....................................618 734-1500
Susie Gies, *Administration*
**EMP:** 10
**SALES (est):** 215.6K **Privately Held**
**SIC: 2835** In vitro & in vivo diagnostic substances

**(G-2928)**
**CAIRO DRY KILNS INC**
14372 State Highway 37 (62914-3180)
P.O. Box 547 (62914-0547)
PHONE.....................................618 734-1039
Fax: 618 734-1053
Dennis Farrow, *President*
Linda Hanes, *General Mgr*
Terry Farrow, *Vice Pres*
**EMP:** 36
**SQ FT:** 12,000
**SALES (est):** 5.7MM **Privately Held**
**SIC: 2421** Kiln drying of lumber

**(G-2929)**
**FARROW LUMBER CO**
Hwy 37 N (62914)
PHONE.....................................618 734-0255
Dennis Farrow, *President*
Linda Farrow, *Corp Secy*
**EMP:** 3
**SQ FT:** 12,000
**SALES (est):** 1.3MM **Privately Held**
**WEB:** www.farrowlumber.com
**SIC: 5031** 2421 Lumber: rough, dressed & finished; custom sawmill

## Caledonia
### Boone County

**(G-2930)**
**BACH TIMBER & PALLET INC**
8858 Grove St (61011-9604)
PHONE.....................................815 885-3774
Robert Bach, *President*
David Bach, *Corp Secy*
Rick Bach, *Vice Pres*
Douglas Bach, *Treasurer*
**EMP:** 5
**SALES (est):** 745.8K **Privately Held**
**SIC: 2448** 2421 Pallets, wood & wood with metal; sawmills & planing mills, general

**(G-2931)**
**CHRISTIANSEN SAWMILL AND LOG**
20080 Grade School Rd (61011-9527)
PHONE.....................................815 315-7520
Dale Christiansen, *Owner*
Matthew Christiansen, *Co-Owner*
**EMP:** 3
**SALES:** 225K **Privately Held**
**SIC: 2421** 2426 2411 Sawmills & planing mills, general; hardwood dimension & flooring mills; logging

**(G-2932)**
**H M C PRODUCTS INC**
7165 Greenlee Dr (61011-9613)
PHONE.....................................815 885-1900
Fax: 815 398-9439
David R Kreissler, *President*
Chris Canfield, *Purch Dir*
Gary Hallberg, *Purchasing*
Jeff Brown, *Engineer*
David Wise, *Design Engr*
**EMP:** 50
**SQ FT:** 10,000
**SALES (est):** 13.4MM **Privately Held**
**WEB:** www.hmcproducts.com
**SIC: 3599** Machine shop, jobbing & repair

**(G-2933)**
**MCCURDY TOOL & MACHINING CO**
1912 Krupke Rd (61011-9567)
PHONE.....................................815 765-2117
Fax: 815 765-3128
F Laverne McCurdy, *President*
Barbara McCurdy, *Finance Other*
**EMP:** 60
**SQ FT:** 15,000
**SALES (est):** 8.1MM **Privately Held**
**SIC: 3544** Special dies & tools

**(G-2934)**
**SERAPH INDUSTRIES LLC**
1175 Krupke Rd (61011-9567)
PHONE.....................................815 222-9686
Vance Hirst Sr, *President*
Vance Hirst Jr, *Vice Pres*
**EMP:** 5
**SQ FT:** 150
**SALES:** 1MM **Privately Held**
**SIC: 3312** Plate, steel; sheet or strip, steel, cold-rolled: own hot-rolled; sheet or strip, steel, hot-rolled

## Calumet City
### Cook County

**(G-2935)**
**ASHLAND CHEMICAL INCORPORATED**
14201 Paxton Ave (60409-3235)
PHONE.....................................708 891-0760
Fax: 708 891-4822
Joe Zemen, *Principal*
**EMP:** 8
**SALES (est):** 1.2MM **Privately Held**
**SIC: 2821** Plastics materials & resins

**(G-2936)**
**CAPLES-EL TRANSPORT INC**
560 Buffalo Ave (60409-3415)
PHONE.....................................708 300-2727
Yahco Caples, *President*
Ruby Caples, *Corp Secy*
**EMP:** 2 **EST:** 2013
**SALES (est):** 221.3K **Privately Held**
**SIC: 3537** 4213 7389 Trucks, tractors, loaders, carriers & similar equipment; contract haulers;

**(G-2937)**
**DOREENS PIZZA INC (PA)**
Also Called: Doreen's Gourmet Frozen Pizza
130 State St (60409-2754)
PHONE.....................................708 862-7499
Fax: 708 862-7498
Robert Wisz, *President*
Lisa Carroll, *Treasurer*
**EMP:** 10
**SQ FT:** 8,000
**SALES:** 2MM **Privately Held**
**SIC: 2038** 5142 5812 Pizza, frozen; packaged frozen goods; eating places

**(G-2938)**
**GELITA USA CHICAGO**
10 Wentworth Ave (60409-2744)
PHONE.....................................708 891-8400
Paulo Reimann, *President*
Shirley Basta, *Opers Mgr*
Thomas Ploog, *Purch Agent*
Bill Simmons, *QC Mgr*
Thiago Antunes, *Engineer*
▲ **EMP:** 16
**SALES (est):** 5.7MM **Privately Held**
**SIC: 2899** Gelatin

**(G-2939)**
**GENERAL MILLS INC**
1600 Huntington Dr (60409-5404)
P.O. Box 368, West Chicago (60186-0368)
PHONE.....................................630 231-1140
Dan Huebner, *Vice Pres*
James Jackson, *Engineer*
Bruce Walker, *Engineer*
Doug Helm, *Project Engr*
Gloria Lorenz, *Personnel*
**EMP:** 500
**SALES (corp-wide):** 16.5B **Publicly Held**
**WEB:** www.generalmills.com
**SIC: 2043** 2099 2098 Cereal breakfast foods; food preparations; macaroni & spaghetti
**PA:** General Mills, Inc.
1 General Mills Blvd
Minneapolis MN 55426
763 764-7600

**(G-2940)**
**GPA MEDIA INC**
228 157th St (60409-4806)
PHONE.....................................773 968-3728
Jacqueline Jackson, *President*
**EMP:** 5 **EST:** 2010
**SALES (est):** 318.3K **Privately Held**
**SIC: 2731** Book publishing

**(G-2941)**
**HARBISONWALKER INTL INC**
1400 Huntington Dr (60409-5464)
PHONE.....................................708 474-5350
Linda Hargis, *Finance*
Guenter Karhut, *Marketing Staff*
Steve Pirtel, *Branch Mgr*
**EMP:** 8
**SALES (corp-wide):** 923MM **Privately Held**
**WEB:** www.hwr.com
**SIC: 3255** Clay refractories
**HQ:** Harbisonwalker International, Inc.
1305 Cherrington Pkwy # 100
Moon Township PA 15108
412 375-6600

**(G-2942)**
**HEAVY HITTERS LLC**
304 153rd Pl (60409-4106)
PHONE.....................................630 258-2991
Thomas Pharris, *Mng Member*
**EMP:** 3

**GEOGRAPHIC SECTION**  **Cambridge - Henry County (G-2967)**

SALES (est): 138.5K  Privately Held
SIC: 3993  Signs & advertising specialties

**(G-2943)**
**HERMANITAS CUPCAKES**
1067 Stewart Ave  (60409-2007)
PHONE..............................708 620-9396
Gabriela Diaz, *Principal*
EMP: 3  EST: 2010
SALES (est): 74K  Privately Held
SIC: 2051  Bread, cake & related products

**(G-2944)**
**JPMORGAN CHASE BANK NAT ASSN**
1783 River Oaks Dr  (60409-5003)
PHONE..............................708 868-1274
Charles Walls, *Branch Mgr*
EMP: 6
SALES (corp-wide): 105.4B  Publicly Held
SIC: 3578  Automatic teller machines (ATM)
HQ: Jpmorgan Chase Bank, National Association
    1111 Polaris Pkwy
    Columbus OH 43240
    614 436-3055

**(G-2945)**
**KAY MANUFACTURING COMPANY**
602 State St  (60409-2041)
PHONE..............................708 862-6800
Fax: 708 862-8122
Brian Pelke, *President*
Steven C Pelke, *COO*
Scott Dekker, *Vice Pres*
Sophie Robertson, *Purchasing*
Dennis Balui, *Manager*
EMP: 150  EST: 1946
SQ FT: 96,000
SALES (est): 27.8MM  Privately Held
WEB: www.kaymfg.com
SIC: 3714  Transmission housings or parts, motor vehicle

**(G-2946)**
**MEATS BY LINZ  INC (PA)**
414 State St  (60409-2618)
P.O. Box 59  (60409-0059)
PHONE..............................708 862-0830
Fax: 708 868-3626
Robert Linz, *President*
Frederick Linz, *Vice Pres*
Becky Robbins, *Vice Pres*
Jose Polanco, *Opers Staff*
Matt Lewman, *Purchasing*
▼ EMP: 44  EST: 1961
SQ FT: 10,000
SALES (est): 22.4MM  Privately Held
WEB: www.meatsbylinz.com
SIC: 5147  5812  2013  2011  Meats, cured or smoked; meats, fresh; eating places; sausages & other prepared meats; meat packing plants

**(G-2947)**
**ONE LOVE**
96 River Oaks Ctr Ste T13  (60409-5547)
PHONE..............................708 832-1740
Robin Henderson, *Owner*
EMP: 2
SALES (est): 210.7K  Privately Held
SIC: 2844  Toilet preparations

**(G-2948)**
**PLASTIC SERVICES AND PRODUCTS**
Also Called: Plastics Color-Chip
14201 Paxton Ave  (60409-3235)
PHONE..............................708 868-3800
Fax: 708 868-3808
Ray Lachapelle, *Division Pres*
EMP: 70
SQ FT: 20,000
SALES (corp-wide): 1.3B  Privately Held
SIC: 2851  Paints & allied products
HQ: Plastic Services And Products
    12243 Branford St
    Sun Valley CA 91352
    818 896-1101

**(G-2949)**
**PLASTICS COLOR & COMPOUNDING**
14201 Paxton Ave  (60409-3235)
PHONE..............................708 868-3800
Jim Christie, *President*
Lori M Johnson, *Exec VP*
Thomas Stackhouse, *Engineer*
David McGowan, *MIS Mgr*
EMP: 100
SQ FT: 4,000
SALES (est): 13.4MM
SALES (corp-wide): 1.3B  Privately Held
WEB: www.plasticscolor.com
SIC: 2821  Plastics materials & resins
HQ: Plastics Color Corporation
    14201 Paxton Ave
    Calumet City IL 60409
    708 868-3800

**(G-2950)**
**PLASTICS COLOR CORP ILLINOIS**
14201 Paxton Ave  (60409-3235)
P.O. Box 1474  (60409-7474)
PHONE..............................708 868-3800
Doug Borgsdorf, *President*
Joe Byrne, *President*
Timothy Workman, *Vice Pres*
Thomas Stackhouse, *Engineer*
John Schwab, *Controller*
▲ EMP: 75
SQ FT: 70,000
SALES (est): 17MM
SALES (corp-wide): 1.3B  Privately Held
SIC: 2816  2851  Inorganic pigments; paints & allied products
HQ: Plastic Services And Products
    12243 Branford St
    Sun Valley CA 91352
    818 896-1101

**(G-2951)**
**PLASTICS COLOR CORPORATION (DH)**
14201 Paxton Ave  (60409-3235)
PHONE..............................708 868-3800
Doug Borgsdorf, *CEO*
Timothy Workman, *Ch of Bd*
Joe Byrne, *President*
T C Cheong, *CFO*
Sal Cuccio, *VP Finance*
EMP: 6
SQ FT: 40,000
SALES (est): 70MM
SALES (corp-wide): 1.3B  Privately Held
WEB: www.plasticscolor.com
SIC: 3559  Plastics working machinery
HQ: Plastic Services And Products
    12243 Branford St
    Sun Valley CA 91352
    818 896-1101

**(G-2952)**
**ROMAN DECORATING PRODUCTS LLC**
824 State St  (60409-2533)
PHONE..............................708 891-0770
John W Penland, *President*
Dennis Skrabak, *Vice Pres*
Jeffrey Hartz, *CFO*
Robin Patrick, *VP Sales*
▲ EMP: 50
SQ FT: 100,000
SALES: 15.3MM  Privately Held
SIC: 2891  Adhesives & sealants

**(G-2953)**
**ROMAN HOLDINGS CORPORATION**
824 State St  (60409-2533)
PHONE..............................708 891-0770
Harry J Bruce, *Ch of Bd*
Richard P Bessette, *President*
Philip G Bessette, *Vice Pres*
Gerald M Russo, *CFO*
Donna Acanfora, *Asst Controller*
EMP: 70
SQ FT: 120,000
SALES: 20MM  Privately Held
WEB: www.romandec.com
SIC: 2891  Adhesives

**(G-2954)**
**SILVER LINE**
1550 Huntington Dr  (60409-5402)
PHONE..............................708 832-9100
Fax: 708 832-9261
Ken Silverman, *President*
EMP: 8
SALES (est): 459K  Privately Held
SIC: 2499  Decorative wood & woodwork

**(G-2955)**
**SMART CHOICE MOBILE  INC**
1856 Sibley Blvd  (60409-2229)
PHONE..............................708 933-6851
EMP: 14
SALES (corp-wide): 5.9MM  Privately Held
SIC: 3661  Telephone sets, all types except cellular radio
PA: Smart Choice Mobile, Inc.
    7667 W 95th St Ste 300
    Hickory Hills IL 60457
    708 581-4904

---
**Calumet Park**
*Cook County*
---

**(G-2956)**
**AMERICAN HOME ALUMINIUM CO**
Also Called: American Home Aluminum Co
12127 S Paulina St  (60827-5319)
PHONE..............................773 925-9442
Robert Roe, *President*
EMP: 1
SALES: 250K  Privately Held
SIC: 3444  Gutters, sheet metal

**(G-2957)**
**CIGAR MIX & DETAIL SHOP**
12408 S Ashland Ave  (60827-5704)
PHONE..............................708 396-1826
Eugene White, *Principal*
EMP: 3
SALES (est): 227.7K  Privately Held
SIC: 3273  Ready-mixed concrete

**(G-2958)**
**CLARK  TASHAUNDA**
Also Called: Ddazzledistributors
12406 S Morgan St  (60827-6225)
PHONE..............................708 247-8274
Tashaunda Clark, *Owner*
EMP: 3
SALES (est): 127.2K  Privately Held
SIC: 3369  3613  Machinery castings, non-ferrous: ex. alum., copper, die, etc.; power circuit breakers; circuit breakers, air; distribution boards, electric; generator control & metering panels

**(G-2959)**
**COLUMBIAN ROPE COMPANY**
12010 S Paulina St  (60827-5318)
PHONE..............................888 593-7999
Stephen G Ludt, *Branch Mgr*
EMP: 105
SALES (corp-wide): 13.4MM  Privately Held
SIC: 2298  Rope, except asbestos & wire
PA: Columbian Rope Company
    145 Towery St
    Guntown MS 38849
    662 348-2241

**(G-2960)**
**CONTINENTAL MIDLAND**
1340 W 127th St  (60827-6129)
PHONE..............................708 441-1000
EMP: 3  EST: 2007
SALES (est): 160K  Privately Held
SIC: 3451  5072  5251  Mfg Screw Machine Products Whol Hardware Ret Hardware

**(G-2961)**
**GOSPEL SYNERGY MAGAZINE INC**
12649 S Ashland Ave  (60827-6015)
PHONE..............................708 272-6640
Andre L Carter, *President*
EMP: 3

SALES (est): 30K  Privately Held
SIC: 2721  7313  Magazines: publishing only, not printed on site; magazine advertising representative

**(G-2962)**
**KAY & CEE**
1204 W 127th St  (60827-6107)
PHONE..............................773 425-9169
Kristine Knowles West, *Owner*
EMP: 6
SALES (est): 246.2K  Privately Held
SIC: 3672  Printed circuit boards

**(G-2963)**
**MOBILE MINI INC**
12658 S Winchester Ave # 2  (60827-5608)
PHONE..............................708 297-2004
Fax: 708 824-2829
Joe Ruffo, *Branch Mgr*
Christpher Thomas, *Manager*
EMP: 30
SALES (corp-wide): 508.6MM  Publicly Held
WEB: www.mobilemini.com
SIC: 3448  3441  3412  7359  Buildings, portable: prefabricated metal; fabricated structural metal; drums, shipping: metal; shipping container leasing
PA: Mobile Mini, Inc.
    4646 E Van Buren St # 400
    Phoenix AZ 85008
    480 894-6311

**(G-2964)**
**UNICORD CORPORATION**
Also Called: Unicord Companies, The
12010 S Paulina St  (60827-5318)
PHONE..............................708 385-7999
Fax: 708 385-8395
Arman Moseni, *President*
Sharon Garry, *Manager*
◆ EMP: 50
SQ FT: 30,000
SALES (est): 8.5MM  Privately Held
WEB: www.unicordcorp.com
SIC: 2298  Twine, cord & cordage

---
**Cambridge**
*Henry County*
---

**(G-2965)**
**CAMBRIDGE CHRONICLE**
119 W Exchange St  (61238-1158)
P.O. Box 5  (61238-0005)
PHONE..............................309 937-3303
Fax: 309 937-3303
Sandy Hull, *Manager*
EMP: 3
SALES (est): 135.7K  Privately Held
SIC: 2711  Newspapers

**(G-2966)**
**CAMBRIDGE PATTERN WORKS**
105 E Railroad St  (61238-1167)
PHONE..............................309 937-5370
Fax: 309 937-5371
David R Anderson, *Owner*
EMP: 4  EST: 1978
SQ FT: 1,600
SALES (est): 338K  Privately Held
SIC: 3312  3543  Blast furnaces & steel mills; industrial patterns

**(G-2967)**
**CSI MANUFACTURING INC**
Hwy 81 E  (61238)
PHONE..............................309 937-2653
Sandra Casteel, *Corp Secy*
Gale Casteel, *Manager*
EMP: 50
SALES (corp-wide): 6.9MM  Privately Held
WEB: www.csihomesonline.com
SIC: 2452  Modular homes, prefabricated, wood
PA: Csi Manufacturing Inc
    419 E Court St
    Cambridge IL
    309 937-5544

**(G-2968)**
**LIBERTY GROUP PUBLISHING**
Also Called: Geneseo Publication
119 W Exchange St (61238-1158)
P.O. Box 132 (61238-0132)
PHONE..................................309 937-3303
Tim Evans, *Principal*
EMP: 3
SALES (corp-wide): 1.6MM **Privately Held**
WEB: www.geneseorepublic.com
SIC: 2759 2711 Commercial printing; newspapers
PA: Liberty Group Publishing
 108 W 1st St
 Geneseo IL 61254
 309 944-1779

**(G-2969)**
**RAILCRAFT NEXIM DESIGN**
12165 N 850th Ave (61238-9293)
PHONE..................................309 937-2360
Fax: 309 937-5525
Richard Nelson, *Owner*
▲ EMP: 3
SALES: 1MM **Privately Held**
SIC: 2599 5712 Factory furniture & fixtures; furniture stores

## Cameron
### Warren County

**(G-2970)**
**MIDWEST AWNINGS INC**
2201 155th St (61423-9543)
P.O. Box 1382, Galesburg (61402-1382)
PHONE..................................309 762-3339
Fax: 309 343-6837
Mike Haun, *President*
EMP: 8
SQ FT: 7,000
SALES (est): 902.6K **Privately Held**
SIC: 2394 3444 5999 5199 Awnings, fabric: made from purchased materials; sheet metalwork; awnings; tarpaulins

## Camp Point
### Adams County

**(G-2971)**
**AUNTIE MMMMS**
105 N Ohio St (62320-1365)
PHONE..................................217 509-6012
Jeffrey Green, *Owner*
EMP: 4 EST: 2009
SALES (est): 201.2K **Privately Held**
SIC: 2051 Cakes, bakery: except frozen

**(G-2972)**
**ELLIOTT PUBLISHING INC**
202 E State St (62320-1114)
P.O. Box 200 (62320-0200)
PHONE..................................217 593-6515
Jim Elliott, *President*
Marcia Elliott, *Vice Pres*
Lisa Newell, *Exec Dir*
EMP: 6
SALES (est): 361.8K **Privately Held**
WEB: www.elliott-publishing.com
SIC: 2711 Newspapers, publishing & printing

**(G-2973)**
**GOLDEN LOCKER INC (PA)**
1880 E 2400th St (62320-2130)
PHONE..................................217 696-4456
Bob Albers, *President*
EMP: 8 EST: 1943
SALES (est): 661.9K **Privately Held**
SIC: 2011 2013 Meat packing plants; sausages & other prepared meats

## Campbell Hill
### Jackson County

**(G-2974)**
**APAC II LLC**
39 Schatte Rd (62916-2509)
PHONE..................................618 426-1338
Abraham J Beachy, *Mng Member*
EMP: 6
SALES (est): 610.8K **Privately Held**
SIC: 3089 Plastics products

**(G-2975)**
**DUSTY LANE WOOD PRODUCTS**
295 Dusty Ln (62916-2421)
PHONE..................................618 426-9045
Ruben Mast, *Owner*
Carolyn Mast, *Owner*
EMP: 2
SALES: 330K **Privately Held**
SIC: 2499 Decorative wood & woodwork

**(G-2976)**
**MAST HARNESS SHOP**
Also Called: Sunny Brook Farm
488 Post Oak Rd (62916-2009)
PHONE..................................217 543-3463
Fax: 217 543-2515
Eli F Schlabach, *General Ptnr*
Kenneth S Schlabach, *Ltd Ptnr*
Merle S Schlabach, *Ltd Ptnr*
Rebecca S Schlabach, *Ltd Ptnr*
Rosemary S Schlabach, *Ltd Ptnr*
EMP: 25
SQ FT: 10,808
SALES (est): 2.2MM **Privately Held**
SIC: 3199 5191 Harness or harness parts; harness wholesale

**(G-2977)**
**MILLCRAFT**
2116 Trico Rd (62916-2111)
PHONE..................................618 426-9819
Gary Miller, *Owner*
Dorothea Miller, *Co-Owner*
EMP: 5
SALES (est): 200K **Privately Held**
SIC: 2434 Wood kitchen cabinets

**(G-2978)**
**MISSELHORN WELDING & MACHINES**
310 S Main St (62916-2525)
PHONE..................................618 426-3714
Fax: 618 426-3832
David Misselhorn, *Owner*
EMP: 3
SALES: 200K **Privately Held**
SIC: 7692 Welding repair

**(G-2979)**
**WK MACHINE**
Also Called: Wk Drainage
98 Catalpa Ln (62916-2257)
PHONE..................................618 426-3423
Edwin Beachy, *Owner*
EMP: 2
SALES (est): 235.6K **Privately Held**
SIC: 3599 Machine shop, jobbing & repair

## Canton
### Fulton County

**(G-2980)**
**ABEL VAULT & MONUMENT CO INC**
1001 E Linn St (61520-9401)
PHONE..................................309 647-0105
Bill Ayers, *Manager*
EMP: 5
SALES (corp-wide): 2.5MM **Privately Held**
SIC: 5999 3272 Monuments, finished to custom order; concrete products
PA: Abel Vault & Monument Co Inc
 1917 N 8th St
 Pekin IL
 309 346-4186

**(G-2981)**
**BASEMENT DEWATERING SYSTEMS**
3100 N Main St (61520-1043)
PHONE..................................309 647-0331
Jerry Jarnagin, *President*
Edward L Ketcham, *Treasurer*
Lori McLouth, *Marketing Staff*
Scott Strode, *Director*
Dennis Dawson, *Admin Sec*
EMP: 16
SQ FT: 6,600
SALES (est): 2.1MM **Privately Held**
WEB: www.basementde-watering.com
SIC: 1521 6531 3564 2851 General remodeling, single-family houses; real estate agents & managers; blowers & fans; paints & allied products

**(G-2982)**
**BLUE BLAZE COAL CPITL RESOURCE**
Also Called: Capitol Resource and Inv Co
420 W Locust St (61520-1646)
P.O. Box 40 (61520-0040)
PHONE..................................309 647-2000
Fax: 309 789-2810
Ron Starnes, *President*
Mark All, *Principal*
EMP: 40
SQ FT: 6,000
SALES (est): 2.7MM **Privately Held**
SIC: 1221 1222 Strip mining, bituminous; bituminous coal-underground mining

**(G-2983)**
**CAMILLES OF CANTON INC**
1400 S Avenue B (61520-3412)
PHONE..................................309 647-7403
Ralph Plunk Jr, *President*
Todd Miller, *Vice Pres*
Camille Plunk, *Treasurer*
Marsha Miller, *Admin Sec*
EMP: 7
SQ FT: 6,000
SALES (est): 150K **Privately Held**
SIC: 5999 5699 2395 Trophies & plaques; T-shirts, custom printed; embroidery & art needlework

**(G-2984)**
**CANTON REDI-MIX INC**
Also Called: Lb Staley Elmwood
22381 N State Highway 78 (61520-8376)
PHONE..................................309 668-2261
Fax: 309 668-2177
James M Curry, *President*
Jon Vrabel, *Vice Pres*
Adam Hoff, *Treasurer*
Jamie Staley, *Bookkeeper*
EMP: 12
SQ FT: 40,000
SALES: 1MM **Privately Held**
SIC: 3273 Ready-mixed concrete

**(G-2985)**
**CANTON REDI-MIX INC**
1130 W Locust St (61520-9681)
PHONE..................................309 647-0019
Lydia E Davis, *President*
Patrick J Davis, *Vice Pres*
EMP: 25
SALES (est): 2.6MM **Privately Held**
SIC: 3273 Ready-mixed concrete

**(G-2986)**
**FOULK ELECTRIC INC**
200 E Alder Rd (61520-9204)
PHONE..................................309 435-7006
Keith W Foulk, *President*
EMP: 4 EST: 2014
SALES (est): 317K **Privately Held**
SIC: 3699 Electrical equipment & supplies

**(G-2987)**
**FULTON COUNTY REHABILITATION (PA)**
500 N Main St (61520-1830)
PHONE..................................309 647-6510
Fax: 309 647-3040
Rex Lewis, *Exec Dir*
EMP: 35
SQ FT: 14,000
SALES: 1.7MM **Privately Held**
SIC: 8361 8331 2448 Rehabilitation center, residential: health care incidental; job training & vocational rehabilitation services; wood pallets & skids

**(G-2988)**
**JARVIS WELDING CO**
124 E Pine St (61520-2799)
PHONE..................................309 647-0033
Fax: 309 647-3808
Brad Jarvis, *Partner*
Randy Jarvis, *Partner*
EMP: 4 EST: 1922
SQ FT: 4,800
SALES (est): 518.2K **Privately Held**
SIC: 7699 7692 3441 Boiler repair shop; aircraft & heavy equipment repair services; welding repair; fabricated structural metal

**(G-2989)**
**MARTIN PUBLISHING CO**
Also Called: Fulton County Democrat
31 S Main St (61520-2605)
PHONE..................................309 647-9501
Fax: 309 547-3055
Robert Martin, *Manager*
EMP: 5
SALES (corp-wide): 2.4MM **Privately Held**
WEB: www.masoncountydemocrat.com
SIC: 2711 Newspapers
PA: Martin Publishing Co.
 217 W Market St
 Havana IL 62644
 309 543-2000

**(G-2990)**
**MARTIN PUBLISHING CO**
Also Called: Martin Publishing Company
31 S Main St (61520-2605)
PHONE..................................309 647-9501
Fax: 309 647-9511
Carole Phillips, *Sales Mgr*
EMP: 15
SALES (corp-wide): 2.4MM **Privately Held**
SIC: 2711 Newspapers
PA: Martin Publishing Co.
 217 W Market St
 Havana IL 62644
 309 543-2000

**(G-2991)**
**MCCLOSKEY EYMAN MLONE MFG SVCS**
37 S 1st Ave (61520-2610)
PHONE..................................309 647-4000
Fax: 309 647-4071
John Eyman, *President*
Becky Eyman, *Treasurer*
EMP: 7
SQ FT: 14,000
SALES: 400K **Privately Held**
SIC: 7699 7692 Industrial machinery & equipment repair; welding repair

**(G-2992)**
**PRO GRAPHICS INK**
322 N 15th Ave (61520-2331)
PHONE..................................309 647-2526
Brenda Promen, *Principal*
EMP: 3
SALES (est): 186.4K **Privately Held**
SIC: 2752 Commercial printing, lithographic

**(G-2993)**
**TRAC EQUIPMENT COMPANY INC**
12 Enterprise Dr (61520-9688)
PHONE..................................309 647-5066
Anthony J Fahrenbruch, *President*
Allen Fahrenbruch, *Vice Pres*
EMP: 2
SQ FT: 800
SALES: 600K **Privately Held**
SIC: 5084 3425 Industrial machinery & equipment; saw blades & handsaws

# GEOGRAPHIC SECTION

Carbondale - Jackson County (G-3017)

## Capron
### Boone County

**(G-2994)**
**CAPRON MFG CO (PA)**
200 Burr Oak Rd (61012-9600)
PHONE....................815 569-2301
Fax: 815 569-2125
John Svabek, *President*
Pat Stanley, *Facilities Mgr*
Dan Lucas, *Opers Staff*
Eric Olsen, *Opers Staff*
Steve McBride, *QC Mgr*
▲ EMP: 60
SQ FT: 75,000
SALES (est): 9.5MM **Privately Held**
WEB: www.capronmfg.com
SIC: **3471** Chromium plating of metals or formed products; plating of metals or formed products

**(G-2995)**
**K K O INC**
100 E Grove St (61012-7710)
P.O. Box 187 (61012-0187)
PHONE....................815 569-2324
Fax: 815 569-2371
Eliza Moravec, *Principal*
EMP: 2 EST: 2010
SALES (est): 206K **Privately Held**
SIC: **2599** Furniture & fixtures

**(G-2996)**
**KEATING OF CHICAGO INC**
100 E Grove St (61012-7710)
P.O. Box 187 (61012-0187)
PHONE....................815 569-2324
Chris Moravec, *VP Opers*
Jack Lee, *Branch Mgr*
Mark Larson, *Manager*
EMP: 25
SALES (corp-wide): 28.6MM **Privately Held**
WEB: www.keatingofchicago.com
SIC: **3589** 3641 3634 3564 Commercial cooking & foodwarming equipment; electric lamps; electric housewares & fans; blowers & fans; food products machinery
PA: Keating Of Chicago, Inc.
8901 W 50th St
Mc Cook IL 60525
708 246-3000

**(G-2997)**
**MELINDA I RHODES (PA)**
15423 Capron Rd (61012-9519)
PHONE....................815 569-2789
Melinda Rhodes, *Owner*
EMP: 2
SALES (est): 210.7K **Privately Held**
SIC: **2051** Bread, cake & related products

**(G-2998)**
**SURFACE MANUFACTURING COMPANY**
135 S 4th St (61012-8702)
P.O. Box 410 (61012-0410)
PHONE....................815 569-2362
Fax: 815 569-2216
Patrick Bryan, *President*
Fred Bryan, *Vice Pres*
EMP: 18
SQ FT: 20,000
SALES (est): 1.6MM **Privately Held**
SIC: **3471** Chromium plating of metals or formed products; plating of metals or formed products

## Carbondale
### Jackson County

**(G-2999)**
**1187 CREATIVE LLC**
201 E Main St Ste 2-I (62901-3027)
PHONE....................618 457-1187
Jon Greenstreet,
Kay Doiser,
Zak Quart,
EMP: 11

SALES (est): 919.7K **Privately Held**
SIC: **3993** Signs & advertising specialties

**(G-3000)**
**ADAMS PRINTING CO**
2350 N Mcroy Dr (62901-5629)
PHONE....................618 529-2396
Francis Ward Adams Jr, *Owner*
EMP: 5
SQ FT: 3,000
SALES: 300K **Privately Held**
WEB: www.adamsprinting.com
SIC: **2752** 2789 Lithographing on metal; bookbinding & related work

**(G-3001)**
**CAPE PROSTHETICS-ORTHOTICS INC**
Also Called: Novacare Prosthetics Orthotics
2355 Sweets Dr Ste G (62902-7294)
PHONE....................618 457-4692
David S Chernow, *President*
Kris Levan, *Marketing Staff*
Richard Thiele, *Branch Mgr*
Maureen Fitzpatrick, *Manager*
Jennifer Priddy, *Supervisor*
EMP: 5
SALES (corp-wide): 203.4MM **Privately Held**
SIC: **5999** 3842 Artificial limbs; orthopedic & prosthesis applications; surgical appliances & supplies
HQ: Cape Prosthetics-Orthotics, Inc.
44 Doctors Park
Cape Girardeau MO 63703
573 334-6401

**(G-3002)**
**CARBONDALE NIGHT LIFE**
Also Called: Carbondale Times
701 W Main St (62901-2643)
PHONE....................618 549-2799
Fax: 618 549-3664
Jason Thomas, *Mng Member*
Jayme Long, *Manager*
Donna Besser, *Director*
EMP: 12
SALES (est): 760.2K **Privately Held**
WEB: www.carbondaletimes.com
SIC: **2711** Commercial printing & newspaper publishing combined

**(G-3003)**
**COLEMAN LAWN EQUIPMENT INC**
210 E Walnut St (62901-3033)
PHONE....................618 529-0181
Fax: 618 529-0182
Marsha Smith, *Branch Mgr*
EMP: 4
SALES (corp-wide): 2.5MM **Privately Held**
WEB: www.colemanlawnequip.com
SIC: **3524** Lawn & garden equipment
PA: Coleman Lawn Equipment Inc
5511 State Route 150
Steeleville IL 62288
618 965-3903

**(G-3004)**
**COM-PAC INTERNATIONAL INC**
800 W Industrial Park Rd (62901-5514)
P.O. Box 2707 (62902-2707)
PHONE....................618 529-2421
Fax: 618 529-2234
Gregory S Sprehe, *CEO*
Donald K Wright, *Exec VP*
Diana Isaacs, *Purch Mgr*
Tina Rhinehart, *Purch Mgr*
Chris Pemberton, *Engineer*
▲ EMP: 180
SQ FT: 60,000
SALES (est): 44.2MM **Privately Held**
WEB: www.com-pac.com
SIC: **3089** Holders: paper towel, grocery bag, etc.: plastic

**(G-3005)**
**DAILY EGYPTIAN SIU NEWSPAPER**
1100 Lincoln Dr Rm 1259 (62901-4306)
PHONE....................618 536-3311
Fax: 618 453-1992
Debbie Clay, *Purch Mgr*
EMP: 75

SALES (est): 2.5MM **Privately Held**
SIC: **2711** 5994 Newspapers, publishing & printing; newsstand

**(G-3006)**
**EMAC INC**
Also Called: Equipment Monitor & Control
2390 Emac Ln (62902-7293)
P.O. Box 2042 (62902-2042)
PHONE....................618 529-4525
Fax: 618 457-0110
Eric Rossi, *President*
◆ EMP: 42
SQ FT: 8,000
SALES: 10MM **Privately Held**
WEB: www.emacinc.com
SIC: **7371** 3571 3823 8711 Computer software systems analysis & design, custom; computers, digital, analog or hybrid; computer interface equipment for industrial process control; engineering services; switchgear & switchboard apparatus; electronic research

**(G-3007)**
**ET SIMONDS MATERIALS COMPANY**
1500 N Oakland Ave (62901-5518)
P.O. Box 3928 (62902-3928)
PHONE....................618 457-8191
Stephen B Simonds, *President*
Kathryn S Stevens, *Admin Sec*
EMP: 40
SALES (est): 1.5MM
SALES (corp-wide): 67MM **Privately Held**
SIC: **2951** Asphalt & asphaltic paving mixtures (not from refineries)
PA: The Simonds Group Ltd
1500 N Oakland Ave
Carbondale IL 62901
618 457-8191

**(G-3008)**
**H & H DRILLING CO**
59 Pineview Rd (62901-5429)
PHONE....................618 529-3697
Lester Holcomb, *President*
Timothy Holcomb, *Vice Pres*
EMP: 3 EST: 1999
SALES (est): 274.3K **Privately Held**
SIC: **3533** Drill rigs

**(G-3009)**
**HAAKES AWNING**
2525 Edgewood Ln (62901-6309)
PHONE....................618 529-4808
Larry C Haake, *Owner*
EMP: 3
SALES: 100K **Privately Held**
SIC: **2211** 2394 2221 5999 Awning stripes, cotton; canvas & related products; broadwoven fabric mills, manmade; awnings

**(G-3010)**
**HENRY PRINTING INC**
975 Charles Rd (62901-6300)
P.O. Box 2706 (62902-2706)
PHONE....................618 529-3040
Fax: 618 549-0686
John M Henry, *President*
EMP: 9
SQ FT: 7,800
SALES (est): 1.6MM **Privately Held**
SIC: **2752** 7334 Commercial printing, offset; photocopying & duplicating services

**(G-3011)**
**ILLINI READY MIX INC (PA)**
801 W Industrial Park Rd (62901-5515)
P.O. Box 2107 (62902-2107)
PHONE....................618 734-0287
Edward Simonds, *President*
Katherine Stevens, *Vice Pres*
Victor Basse, *Opers Mgr*
Michael McClay, *Treasurer*
EMP: 1
SALES (est): 2.8MM **Privately Held**
WEB: www.etsimonds.com
SIC: **3273** Ready-mixed concrete

**(G-3012)**
**ILLINI READY MIX INC**
801 W Industrial Park Rd (62901-5515)
PHONE....................618 529-1626

Doug Harris, *Manager*
EMP: 5
SALES (corp-wide): 2.8MM **Privately Held**
WEB: www.etsimonds.com
SIC: **3273** Ready-mixed concrete
PA: Illini Ready Mix, Inc
801 W Industrial Park Rd
Carbondale IL 62901
618 734-0287

**(G-3013)**
**INTERTAPE POLYMER CORP**
Also Called: Intertape Polymer Group
2200 N Mcroy Dr (62901-5628)
PHONE....................618 549-2131
Curtis Clarke, *Opers Mgr*
Art Farrell, *Accounts Mgr*
Jason Kopinski, *Marketing Staff*
Craig Hoedel, *Manager*
EMP: 70
SALES (corp-wide): 808.8MM **Privately Held**
SIC: **2672** Tape, pressure sensitive: made from purchased materials
HQ: Intertape Polymer Corp.
100 Paramount Dr Ste 300
Sarasota FL 34232
941 727-5788

**(G-3014)**
**LEE ENTERPRISES INCORPORATED**
Also Called: Southern Illinoisan
710 N Illinois Ave (62901-1283)
P.O. Box 2108 (62902-2108)
PHONE....................618 529-5454
Fax: 618 457-2935
Cyndie Sonsteng, *President*
Dennis Derossett, *Publisher*
Cara Recine, *Editor*
Charles Rich, *Controller*
Richard Johnston, *Loan Officer*
EMP: 200
SALES (corp-wide): 614.3MM **Publicly Held**
WEB: www.lee.net
SIC: **2711** 2752 7313 Newspapers: publishing only, not printed on site; commercial printing, lithographic; newspaper advertising representative
PA: Lee Enterprises, Incorporated
201 N Harrison St Ste 600
Davenport IA 52801
563 383-2100

**(G-3015)**
**MAC-WELD INC**
Also Called: Mac-Weld Partnership
612 San Diego Rd (62901-0611)
PHONE....................618 529-1828
Fax: 618 549-1642
Gerald Kaufmann, *President*
Clinton W Taylor, *Vice Pres*
Lynette Taylor, *Treasurer*
Greg Few, *Sales Mgr*
Debra Kaufmann, *Admin Sec*
EMP: 9
SALES (est): 450K **Privately Held**
SIC: **5013** 7539 5084 3599 Automotive engines & engine parts; machine shop, automotive; welding machinery & equipment; machine shop, jobbing & repair

**(G-3016)**
**OTIS ELEVATOR COMPANY**
201 W Kennicott St (62901-1230)
PHONE....................618 529-3411
Charles Johnson, *Branch Mgr*
EMP: 12
SALES (corp-wide): 57.2B **Publicly Held**
WEB: www.otis.com
SIC: **5084** 7699 3534 Elevators; professional instrument repair services; dumbwaiters
HQ: Otis Elevator Company
1 Carrier Pl
Farmington CT 06032
860 674-3000

**(G-3017)**
**OVIS LOADER ATTACHMENTS INC**
1555 S Wall St (62901-3732)
PHONE....................618 203-2757
William Wright, *President*

---

(PA)=Parent Co (HQ)=Headquarters (DH)=Div Headquarters
○ = New Business established in last 2 years

2017 Harris Illinois Industrial Directory

# Carbondale - Jackson County (G-3018) — GEOGRAPHIC SECTION

Nathan Wright, *Vice Pres*
**EMP:** 3
**SALES (est):** 342.3K **Privately Held**
**SIC: 3531** Subsoiler attachments, tractor mounted

### (G-3018)
### PRAIRIE FARMS DAIRY INC
742 N Illinois Ave (62901-1283)
**PHONE** ..................................... 618 457-4167
**Fax:** 618 549-5608
Ron Diuquid, *General Mgr*
**EMP:** 34
**SALES (corp-wide):** 1.8B **Privately Held**
**WEB:** www.prairiefarms.com
**SIC: 2026** 0241 Milk processing (pasteurizing, homogenizing, bottling); milk production
**PA:** Prairie Farms Dairy, Inc.
1100 Broadway
Carlinville IL 62626
217 854-2547

### (G-3019)
### PRINTING PLANT
606 S Illinois Ave Ste 1 (62901-2852)
**PHONE** ..................................... 618 529-3115
**Fax:** 618 529-3116
James Myers, *Partner*
Larry Fehmel, *Partner*
Sharon Fehmel, *Partner*
Cynthia Myers, *Partner*
Alix Bruce, *Manager*
**EMP:** 4
**SQ FT:** 1,200
**SALES (est):** 370K **Privately Held**
**SIC: 2752** Commercial printing, offset

### (G-3020)
### QUICK SIGNS
1260 N Reed Station Rd (62902-7310)
**PHONE** ..................................... 618 549-0747
**Fax:** 618 549-1356
Jeffrey Martin, *Owner*
Lori Martin, *Manager*
**EMP:** 3
**SALES (est):** 181K **Privately Held**
**WEB:** www.quicksigns.org
**SIC: 3993** Signs & advertising specialties

### (G-3021)
### RAINBOW PURE WATER INC
610 Sneed Rd (62902-0488)
**PHONE** ..................................... 618 985-4670
Tary Bishing, *President*
Carol Bisching, *Admin Sec*
**EMP:** 4
**SQ FT:** 15,000
**SALES (est):** 200K **Privately Held**
**SIC: 2086** Pasteurized & mineral waters, bottled & canned

### (G-3022)
### RUDON ENTERPRISES INC
Also Called: Carbondale Trophy Co
118 N Illinois Ave (62901-1450)
**PHONE** ..................................... 618 457-0441
**Fax:** 618 549-0866
Ruth Dalessio, *President*
Dominick Dalessio, *Vice Pres*
Jordan Wren, *Sales Staff*
**EMP:** 4
**SQ FT:** 5,000
**SALES:** 250K **Privately Held**
**WEB:** www.carbondaletrophy.com
**SIC: 3914** 3999 Trophies, plated (all metals); plaques, picture, laminated

### (G-3023)
### SKELCHER CONCRETE PRODUCTS
490 San Diego Rd (62901-0811)
**PHONE** ..................................... 618 457-2930
**Fax:** 618 457-2930
Cliff Skelcher, *Partner*
Paul M Skelcher, *Partner*
**EMP:** 5
**SQ FT:** 5,000
**SALES (est):** 609.3K **Privately Held**
**SIC: 3272** Manhole covers or frames, concrete; septic tanks, concrete; ties, railroad: concrete

### (G-3024)
### SOUTHERN ILLINOIS UNIVERSITY
Also Called: Printing & Duplicating
210 Physical Plant Dr (62901-4308)
**PHONE** ..................................... 618 453-2268
**Fax:** 618 453-1643
Rich Bauer, *Superintendent*
**EMP:** 17
**SALES (corp-wide):** 742.1MM **Privately Held**
**SIC: 2752** Commercial printing, lithographic
**HQ:** Southern Illinois University Inc
1400 Douglas Dr
Carbondale IL 62901
618 536-3475

### (G-3025)
### THOMAS PUBLISHING PRINTING DIV
701 W Main St (62901-2643)
**PHONE** ..................................... 618 351-6655
Dan Sitarz, *Principal*
**EMP:** 2
**SALES (est):** 218.9K **Privately Held**
**SIC: 2759** 2741 Commercial printing; miscellaneous publishing

### (G-3026)
### WE INTERNATIONAL
54 Oakview Rd (62901-8125)
**PHONE** ..................................... 618 549-1784
William W Liao, *Owner*
Elizabeth Liao, *Owner*
▲ **EMP:** 3 **EST:** 1995
**SALES (est):** 283.4K **Privately Held**
**SIC: 3629** Electronic generation equipment

### (G-3027)
### WEATHERFORD SIGNS
219 Weatherford Ln (62902-7780)
P.O. Box 2995 (62902-2995)
**PHONE** ..................................... 618 529-2000
**Fax:** 618 549-7446
Larry Weatherford, *Owner*
**EMP:** 5
**SQ FT:** 1,800
**SALES (est):** 368K **Privately Held**
**SIC: 3993** Signs & advertising specialties

### (G-3028)
### WINN STAR INC
395 S Wolf Creek Rd Fl 1 (62902-0551)
P.O. Box 213, Marion (62959-0213)
**PHONE** ..................................... 618 964-1811
**Fax:** 618 964-1812
Thomas J Throgmorton, *President*
Gwen Kelly, *Corp Secy*
Julia Throgmorton, *Vice Pres*
**EMP:** 5
**SQ FT:** 20,000
**SALES:** 250K **Privately Held**
**SIC: 3812** 2899 Search & navigation equipment; chemical preparations

### (G-3029)
### Z-PATCH INC
800 W Industrial Park Rd (62901-5514)
P.O. Box 2707 (62902-2707)
**PHONE** ..................................... 618 529-2431
Greg Sprehe, *President*
Donald Wright, *Vice Pres*
Amy Galloway, *Controller*
**EMP:** 20
**SQ FT:** 10,000
**SALES (est):** 1.4MM **Privately Held**
**SIC: 3545** Machine tool accessories

---

## Carlinville
*Macoupin County*

### (G-3030)
### AREA DIESEL SERVICE INC (PA)
Also Called: ADC
1300 University St (62626-9620)
P.O. Box 115 (62626-0115)
**PHONE** ..................................... 217 854-2641
**Fax:** 217 854-8972
Val Leefers, *President*
Curtis Owens, *Parts Mgr*
Von Leefers, *Treasurer*
Kathy Ward, *Accountant*
Dave Coonrod, *Mktg Dir*
▲ **EMP:** 38
**SQ FT:** 10,000
**SALES (est):** 10.9MM **Privately Held**
**WEB:** www.areadiesel.com
**SIC: 5531** 5084 3724 3714 Truck equipment & parts; engines & parts, diesel; aircraft engines & engine parts; motor vehicle parts & accessories; turbines & turbine generator sets

### (G-3031)
### CARLINVILLE WASTE WATER PLANTS
1345 Mayo St (62626-1966)
**PHONE** ..................................... 217 854-6506
Pat Bouillon, *Superintendent*
**EMP:** 4
**SALES:** 350K **Privately Held**
**SIC: 3589** Sewage & water treatment equipment

### (G-3032)
### CENTRAL ILLINOIS STEEL COMPANY (PA)
Also Called: Cisco
21050 Route 4 (62626-3525)
P.O. Box 78 (62626-0078)
**PHONE** ..................................... 217 854-3251
**Fax:** 217 854-4771
Daniel M Millard, *President*
Mark Millard, *Vice Pres*
Tim Millard, *Vice Pres*
Ann Girinchik, *Admin Sec*
Chris Millard, *Admin Sec*
**EMP:** 36
**SQ FT:** 80,000
**SALES:** 45MM **Privately Held**
**SIC: 5051** 3441 Steel; fabricated structural metal

### (G-3033)
### CENTRAL MACHINING INC
502 W 1st North St (62626-1683)
**PHONE** ..................................... 217 854-6646
Jon Theivagt, *Vice Pres*
**EMP:** 2
**SALES (est):** 391.5K **Privately Held**
**SIC: 3599** Machine shop, jobbing & repair

### (G-3034)
### CHARLES K EICHEN
Also Called: Eichen's Saw Mill
20002 Claremont Rd (62626-4046)
**PHONE** ..................................... 217 854-9751
Mike K Eichen, *President*
Steve Eichen, *Vice Pres*
**EMP:** 7
**SALES (est):** 376.7K **Privately Held**
**SIC: 5211** 2421 5031 Lumber & other building materials; sawmills & planing mills, general; lumber, plywood & millwork; lumber: rough, dressed & finished

### (G-3035)
### CUBBY HOLE OF CARLINVILLE INC (PA)
Also Called: Cubby Hole, The
12472 Route 108 (62626-3615)
**PHONE** ..................................... 217 854-8511
**Fax:** 217 854-5306
Dale Tosh, *President*
Nancy Tosh, *Admin Sec*
**EMP:** 14
**SQ FT:** 6,000
**SALES (est):** 1MM **Privately Held**
**WEB:** www.cubbyholeonline.com
**SIC: 2396** 2395 3993 Screen printing on fabric articles; embroidery & art needlework; signs & advertising specialties

### (G-3036)
### EAST SIDE JERSEY DAIRY INC (HQ)
1100 Broadway (62626-1183)
**PHONE** ..................................... 217 854-2547
Terry Carter, *Manager*
**EMP:** 30
**SQ FT:** 10,000
**SALES:** 62MM
**SALES (corp-wide):** 1.8B **Privately Held**
**SIC: 2026** Milk processing (pasteurizing, homogenizing, bottling)

**PA:** Prairie Farms Dairy, Inc.
1100 Broadway
Carlinville IL 62626
217 854-2547

### (G-3037)
### EICHEN LUMBER CO INC
20002 Claremont Rd (62626-4046)
**PHONE** ..................................... 217 854-9751
**Fax:** 217 854-3017
Michael Eichen, *President*
Charles K Eichen, *Owner*
Steve Eichen, *Admin Sec*
**EMP:** 7 **EST:** 1962
**SALES:** 500K **Privately Held**
**SIC: 2421** 2426 Sawmills & planing mills, general; hardwood dimension & flooring mills

### (G-3038)
### EXXON MOBIL CORPORATION
Monterey Coal
14491 Brushy Mound Rd (62626)
**PHONE** ..................................... 217 854-3291
**Fax:** 217 854-6807
Joe Barber, *Purchasing*
Ron Yates, *Marketing Mgr*
Howard Schultz, *Manager*
Jim Bailer, *Manager*
**EMP:** 300
**SALES (corp-wide):** 226B **Publicly Held**
**SIC: 1241** 1222 Coal mining services; bituminous coal-underground mining
**PA:** Exxon Mobil Corporation
5959 Las Colinas Blvd
Irving TX 75039
972 444-1000

### (G-3039)
### HUYEAR TRUCKING INC
708 Sumner St (62626-1169)
**PHONE** ..................................... 217 854-3551
Robert H Huyear, *President*
Wilma Huyear, *Corp Secy*
**EMP:** 6
**SALES (est):** 370K **Privately Held**
**SIC: 4212** 1422 5191 6221 Local trucking, without storage; crushed & broken limestone; fertilizer & fertilizer materials; commodity brokers, contracts

### (G-3040)
### INTEGRATED MEDIA INC
Also Called: Illini Tech Services
909 Broadway Ste B (62626-1196)
**PHONE** ..................................... 217 854-6260
**Fax:** 217 854-2206
Kevin Walker, *President*
Matthew Hupp, *Info Tech Mgr*
**EMP:** 10
**SQ FT:** 2,000
**SALES (est):** 620K **Privately Held**
**WEB:** www.int-media.com
**SIC: 7374** 7311 2754 Computer graphics service; advertising consultant; commercial printing, gravure

### (G-3041)
### KUCHAR COMBINE PERFORMANCE
Also Called: Kuchar High Perfomance Parts
300 Route 4 (62626-4111)
**PHONE** ..................................... 217 854-9838
George Kuchar, *President*
**EMP:** 4
**SQ FT:** 3,600
**SALES (est):** 311.3K **Privately Held**
**WEB:** www.kucharcombines.com
**SIC: 3523** 4731 Combines (harvester-threshers); freight transportation arrangement

### (G-3042)
### MACOUPIN COUNTY ENQUIRER INC
125 E Main St (62626-1726)
P.O. Box 200 (62626-0200)
**PHONE** ..................................... 217 854-2534
**Fax:** 217 854-2535
Christopher Schmitt, *President*
Susan Braham, *Vice Pres*
**EMP:** 20 **EST:** 1852
**SQ FT:** 30,000

# GEOGRAPHIC SECTION

Carmi - White County (G-3069)

SALES (est): 1.3MM  Privately Held
SIC: 2711  2752  2791  2789  Newspapers; commercial printing, offset; typesetting; bookbinding & related work; commercial printing

**(G-3043)**
**MACOUPIN ENERGY LLC**
14300 Brushy Mound Rd  (62626-2385)
PHONE.................................217 854-3291
EMP: 14
SALES (est): 1.2MM  Privately Held
SIC: 1241  Coal mining services

**(G-3044)**
**MACOUPIN ENERGY LLC**
Also Called: Shay Mine No. 1
14300 Brushy Mound Rd  (62626-2385)
PHONE.................................217 854-3291
Todd Leverton, *Branch Mgr*
EMP: 115
SALES (corp-wide): 40.8MM  Privately Held
SIC: 1241  Coal mining services
PA: Macoupin Energy Llc
  211 N Broadway Ste 2600
  Saint Louis MO 63102
  314 932-6112

**(G-3045)**
**MADISON FARMS BUTTER COMPANY (PA)**
1100 Broadway  (62626-1183)
PHONE.................................217 854-2547
Paul Benne, *Partner*
EMP: 15
SALES (est): 3.2MM  Privately Held
SIC: 2021  Creamery butter; butter oil

**(G-3046)**
**PM MACHINE SHOP**
706 N Broad St  (62626-1023)
PHONE.................................217 854-3504
Fax: 217 854-3504
Pete Maguire, *Owner*
EMP: 1
SQ FT: 2,000
SALES: 250K  Privately Held
WEB: www.pmmachineshop.com
SIC: 3599  Machine shop, jobbing & repair

**(G-3047)**
**PRAIRIE FARMS DAIRY INC (PA)**
1100 Broadway  (62626-1183)
PHONE.................................217 854-2547
Fax: 217 854-6426
Ed Mullins, *CEO*
Fred Kuenstler, *President*
Ronnie G McMillan, *Vice Pres*
Pat Callahan, *Plant Supt*
Mario Turner, *Plant Supt*
EMP: 135  EST: 1971
SQ FT: 10,000
SALES: 1.8B  Privately Held
WEB: www.prairiefarms.com
SIC: 2026  Milk processing (pasteurizing, homogenizing, bottling)

**(G-3048)**
**WILLS MILLING AND HARDWOOD INC**
9674 Colt Rd  (62626-2240)
PHONE.................................217 854-9056
Fax: 217 854-7895
Bryan Wills, *President*
Charles Wills, *President*
Brian Wills, *General Mgr*
Scott Wills, *Vice Pres*
Amy Wills, *Admin Sec*
EMP: 24
SQ FT: 30,000
SALES (est): 3.9MM  Privately Held
WEB: www.willsmilling.com
SIC: 2431  Millwork

## Carlock
### Mclean County

**(G-3049)**
**COVINGTON SERVICE INSTALLATION**
1907 County Road 275 N  (61725-9014)
PHONE.................................309 376-4921
Wayne Covington, *Owner*
EMP: 3
SALES (est): 526.5K  Privately Held
SIC: 3589  Garbage disposers & compactors, commercial

**(G-3050)**
**DANIEL MFG  INC**
273 County Road 1850 E  (61725-9013)
PHONE.................................309 963-4227
Fax: 309 963-5227
Tim Daniel, *President*
Harley Daniel, *General Mgr*
Luke Daniel, *General Mgr*
Lou Daniel, *Corp Secy*
Ross Walker, *Supervisor*
EMP: 12
SQ FT: 30,000
SALES (est): 2MM  Privately Held
WEB: www.danielmfg.com
SIC: 7692  3444  Welding repair; sheet metalwork

**(G-3051)**
**J AND J PRFMCE POWDR COATING**
410 E Washington St  (61725-9440)
PHONE.................................309 376-4340
James Dolan, *President*
EMP: 2
SALES (est): 291.6K  Privately Held
SIC: 2952  Roofing felts, cements or coatings

## Carlyle
### Clinton County

**(G-3052)**
**ARCHI-CEPTS**
1630 Franklin St  (62231-1727)
PHONE.................................618 594-8810
Roger Rolves, *Owner*
EMP: 3  EST: 2008
SALES (est): 234.2K  Privately Held
SIC: 2499  Decorative wood & woodwork

**(G-3053)**
**CARLYLE SAND & GRAVEL LTD**
11842 State Route 127  (62231-3314)
P.O. Box 106  (62231-0106)
PHONE.................................618 594-8263
Brian Bailey, *Principal*
EMP: 3  EST: 2008
SALES (est): 254.1K  Privately Held
SIC: 1442  Construction sand & gravel

**(G-3054)**
**HUELS OIL COMPANY**
16320 Old Us Highway 50  (62231-2408)
PHONE.................................877 338-6277
Fax: 618 594-2831
Ronald Huels, *President*
Geralyn Huels, *Vice Pres*
EMP: 12
SQ FT: 8,000
SALES (est): 18.3MM  Privately Held
SIC: 5172  2992  Fuel oil; lubricating oils

**(G-3055)**
**JERRY BERRY CONTRACTING CO**
1691 Kane St  (62231-1128)
PHONE.................................618 594-3339
EMP: 4  EST: 1969
SALES (est): 230K  Privately Held
SIC: 1771  1794  3273  Concrete Contractor Excavation Contractor Mfg Ready-Mixed Concrete

**(G-3056)**
**LUEBBERS WELDING & MFG INC**
2420 Old State Rd  (62231-2412)
P.O. Box 248  (62231-0248)
PHONE.................................618 594-2489
Fax: 618 594-2483
Ron Luebbers, *President*
Dana Luebbers, *Corp Secy*
Kevin Luebbers, *Vice Pres*
EMP: 15
SQ FT: 20,000
SALES (est): 1.3MM  Privately Held
SIC: 3599  3444  3443  7692  Machine shop, jobbing & repair; concrete forms, sheet metal; tanks, standard or custom fabricated: metal plate; welding repair

**(G-3057)**
**QUAD-COUNTY READY MIX CORP**
2090 Washington St  (62231-1624)
P.O. Box 24  (62231-0024)
PHONE.................................618 594-2732
Fax: 618 594-2736
Charles Meyer, *Manager*
EMP: 10
SALES (corp-wide): 18.9MM  Privately Held
SIC: 3273  Ready-mixed concrete
PA: Quad-County Ready Mix Corp.
  300 W 12th St
  Okawville IL 62271
  618 243-6430

**(G-3058)**
**SEIFFERTS LOCKER & MEAT PROC**
Also Called: Seifferts Meat Proc & Lckr
1370 Fairfax St  (62231-1705)
PHONE.................................618 594-3921
Michael Seiffert, *Owner*
EMP: 18
SQ FT: 2,400
SALES: 165K  Privately Held
SIC: 2013  5421  5147  Sausages & other prepared meats; meat markets, including freezer provisioners; meats, fresh

**(G-3059)**
**SIMONTON HARDWOOD LUMBER LLC**
16515 Post Oak Rd  (62231-3033)
PHONE.................................618 594-2132
Fax: 618 594-8456
Donna Simonton, *Corp Secy*
William C Simonton, *Mng Member*
EMP: 11  EST: 1961
SALES: 3.8MM  Privately Held
SIC: 2421  2448  2426  Sawmills & planing mills, general; wood pallets & skids; hardwood dimension & flooring mills

**(G-3060)**
**TIMKEN COMPANY**
Also Called: Timken Rail Bearing Service
2210 Franklin St  (62231-1635)
PHONE.................................618 594-4545
Fax: 618 594-8560
Kathy Varel, *Opers Mgr*
Kevin Neal, *Manager*
EMP: 35
SALES (corp-wide): 2.6B  Publicly Held
SIC: 3568  Power transmission equipment
PA: The Timken Company
  4500 Mount Pleasant St Nw
  North Canton OH 44720
  234 262-3000

**(G-3061)**
**WISE CO  INC**
3750 Industrial Dr  (62231-6124)
PHONE.................................618 594-4091
Andy Berry, *Plant Mgr*
John Copper, *Manager*
EMP: 173
SALES (corp-wide): 45.2MM  Privately Held
SIC: 5013  2531  Seat covers; public building & related furniture
PA: The Wise Co Inc
  5828 Shelby Oaks Dr
  Memphis TN 38134
  901 388-0155

## Carmi
### White County

**(G-3062)**
**BROOKSTONE RESOURCES INC**
1615 Oak St  (62821-1371)
PHONE.................................618 382-2893
Rich Kingston, *Partner*
EMP: 4  EST: 2001

SALES (est): 346.8K  Privately Held
SIC: 1311  Crude petroleum & natural gas production

**(G-3063)**
**CAMPBELL ENERGY LLC**
1238 County Road 1500 N  (62821-4630)
PHONE.................................618 382-3939
Matt Campbell,
Jack Campbell,
John Campbell,
EMP: 5
SALES (est): 967.6K  Privately Held
SIC: 1389  Oil field services

**(G-3064)**
**CARMI TIMES**
323 E Main St  (62821-1810)
P.O. Box 190  (62821-0190)
PHONE.................................618 382-4176
Robert Beskow, *Editor*
Barry Cleveland, *Manager*
Cheryl Trout, *Manager*
EMP: 12
SALES (est): 512.9K  Privately Held
SIC: 2711  Newspapers

**(G-3065)**
**CARTER ANNA BROOKS LLC**
1238 County Road 1500 N  (62821-4630)
PHONE.................................618 382-3939
Jakob Campbell, *Principal*
EMP: 3
SALES (est): 165.2K  Privately Held
SIC: 1311  Crude petroleum production

**(G-3066)**
**ELASTEC  INC (PA)**
Also Called: Elastec / American Marine
1309 W Main St  (62821-1389)
PHONE.................................618 382-2525
Fax: 618 382-3610
Donald L Wilson, *CEO*
Peter Cheney, *Regional Mgr*
Jeff Cantrell, *Vice Pres*
Jeff Elliott, *Design Engr*
Jeffry H Bohleber, *CFO*
◆ EMP: 130
SQ FT: 57,000
SALES (est): 20.7MM  Privately Held
WEB: www.in-situburn.com
SIC: 3599  3567  Custom machinery; incinerators, metal: domestic or commercial

**(G-3067)**
**EVERGREEN ENERGY LLC**
645 W Illinois Hwy 14  (62821)
P.O. Box 103  (62821-0103)
PHONE.................................618 384-9295
Abbey Alvin, *Office Mgr*
Edward Bruce,
Gary Evans,
Scott Pugsley,
EMP: 4
SALES (est): 416.5K  Privately Held
SIC: 1381  Drilling oil & gas wells

**(G-3068)**
**GEO N MITCHELL DRLG CO INC**
1239 County Road 1500 N  (62821-4600)
P.O. Box 550  (62821-0550)
PHONE.................................618 382-2343
Fax: 618 384-2435
Chris A Mitchell, *President*
Ryan Mitchell, *Engineer*
Ron Wooten, *VP Finance*
Brad Richards, *Exec Dir*
EMP: 1
SALES (est): 436.1K  Privately Held
WEB: www.mitchell-drilling.com
SIC: 1381  Drilling oil & gas wells

**(G-3069)**
**GHOLSON PUMP & REPAIRS CO**
725 County Road 1450 N  (62821-4814)
PHONE.................................618 382-4730
Tim Gholson, *Owner*
EMP: 3
SALES (est): 190K  Privately Held
SIC: 1389  Oil & gas wells: building, repairing & dismantling

# Carmi - White County (G-3070)

**(G-3070)**
**JIM HALEY OIL PRODUCTION CO**
1415 W Main St (62821-1390)
P.O. Box 547 (62821-0547)
PHONE.................................618 382-7338
Fax: 618 382-2870
Jim Haley, *President*
Rebecca Drone, *Manager*
EMP: 10
SALES (est): 698.9K **Privately Held**
SIC: 1311 Crude petroleum production

**(G-3071)**
**KEROGEN RESOURCES INC**
645 Il Highway 14 (62821-4815)
PHONE.................................618 382-3114
Gary L Evans, *President*
EMP: 2
SALES (est): 250K **Privately Held**
WEB: www.kerogenresources.com
SIC: 1311 Crude petroleum & natural gas

**(G-3072)**
**KOONTZ SERVICES**
1598 County Road 1100 E (62821-4503)
PHONE.................................618 375-7613
Lois Koontz, *Owner*
EMP: 7
SQ FT: 2,520
SALES: 600K **Privately Held**
SIC: 1389 4212 Acidizing wells; liquid haulage, local

**(G-3073)**
**LES WILSON INC**
205 Industrial Ave (62821-2211)
P.O. Box 331 (62821-0331)
PHONE.................................618 382-4667
Fax: 618 382-5313
Robert L Wilson, *President*
Stephanie L Wilson, *Treasurer*
Justin Mugge, *Manager*
Jema Mitchell, *Administration*
EMP: 150 EST: 1942
SQ FT: 10,000
SALES (est): 29.7MM **Privately Held**
WEB: www.leswilson.com
SIC: 1381 Drilling oil & gas wells

**(G-3074)**
**MARSHALL ELECTRIC INC**
1707 Oak St Ste B (62821-2367)
P.O. Box 455 (62821-0455)
PHONE.................................618 382-3932
Fax: 618 382-1115
Wade Richard Marshall Jr, *President*
EMP: 10
SALES (est): 1.8MM **Privately Held**
SIC: 3613 1731 Panel & distribution boards & other related apparatus; control panels, electric; electrical work

**(G-3075)**
**MITCHCO FARMS LLC**
1239 County Road 1500 N (62821-4600)
P.O. Box 254 (62821-0254)
PHONE.................................618 382-5032
George N Mitchell, *Owner*
EMP: 15
SQ FT: 4,000
SALES (est): 1.1MM **Privately Held**
SIC: 1311 1389 Crude petroleum production; servicing oil & gas wells

**(G-3076)**
**ODANIEL TRUCKING CO**
1249 County Road 1500 N (62821-4600)
PHONE.................................618 382-5371
Fax: 618 382-7402
Ed O'Daniel Jr, *President*
William Edwards, *Vice Pres*
John E Mann, *Vice Pres*
EMP: 55
SQ FT: 15,000
SALES (est): 5.6MM **Privately Held**
WEB: www.odanielinc.com
SIC: 4212 3273 1611 1771 Coal haulage, local; ready-mixed concrete; general contractor, highway & street construction; driveway, parking lot & blacktop contractors

**(G-3077)**
**R ENERGY LLC**
1001 E Main St (62821)
P.O. Box 357 (62821-0357)
PHONE.................................618 382-7313
Rebecca R Drone, *Principal*
EMP: 4
SALES (est): 229K **Privately Held**
SIC: 1389 Oil & gas field services

**(G-3078)**
**ROARK OIL FIELD SERVICES INC**
1036 County Road 1575 N (62821-4500)
P.O. Box 88 (62821-0088)
PHONE.................................618 382-4703
Patt Morris, *President*
Herbert Roark, *President*
Judith Morris, *Admin Sec*
EMP: 3
SALES: 100K **Privately Held**
SIC: 1389 Oil field services

**(G-3079)**
**RON ABSHER**
Also Called: Ron Absher Auto Center
1500 Oak St Ste C (62821-1372)
P.O. Box 311 (62821-0311)
PHONE.................................618 382-4646
Ronald Absher, *Owner*
Jane Absher, *Co-Owner*
EMP: 4
SALES (est): 272.6K **Privately Held**
SIC: 1311 Crude petroleum & natural gas production

**(G-3080)**
**SHAWNEE EXPLORATION PARTNERS**
115 Smith St (62821-1426)
PHONE.................................618 382-3223
EMP: 3
SALES (est): 99.1K **Privately Held**
SIC: 1311 Crude petroleum & natural gas production

**(G-3081)**
**VIBRACOUSTIC USA INC**
Also Called: Mixing Division
1500 E Main St (62821-2116)
PHONE.................................618 382-5891
Deanna McInerney, *Asst Controller*
Cindy Harris, *Office Mgr*
Rick Estes, *Manager*
EMP: 50
SALES (corp-wide): 2B **Privately Held**
SIC: 3061 2891 2822 Mechanical rubber goods; adhesives & sealants; synthetic rubber
HQ: Vibracoustic Usa, Inc.
400 Aylworth Ave
South Haven MI 49090
269 637-2116

**(G-3082)**
**VIBRACOUSTIC USA INC**
102 Industrial Ave (62821-2261)
PHONE.................................618 382-2318
Dan Johnston, *Manager*
Dan Johnson, *Manager*
EMP: 115
SALES (corp-wide): 2B **Privately Held**
SIC: 3061 3714 3053 Mechanical rubber goods; motor vehicle parts & accessories; gaskets, packing & sealing devices
HQ: Vibracoustic Usa, Inc.
400 Aylworth Ave
South Haven MI 49090
269 637-2116

**(G-3083)**
**WARREN SERVICE COMPANY**
1714 Oak St (62821-2368)
P.O. Box 372 (62821-0372)
PHONE.................................618 384-2117
Douglas S Warren, *Owner*
EMP: 6
SALES: 1.5MM **Privately Held**
SIC: 1389 Oil field services

**(G-3084)**
**WHITE COUNTY COAL LLC (DH)**
1525 County Rd 1300 N (62821)
P.O. Box 457 (62821-0457)
PHONE.................................618 382-4651
Fax: 618 382-8629
Joseph W Craft III, *President*
Karen Pharr, *Human Res Mgr*
Patty Woodruff, *Manager*
Thomas Pearson,
Gary Rathburn,
▲ EMP: 106 EST: 1979
SQ FT: 1,000
SALES (est): 75.9MM
SALES (corp-wide): 1.9B **Publicly Held**
SIC: 1221 Surface mining, bituminous
HQ: Alliance Coal, Llc
1717 S Boulder Ave # 400
Tulsa OK 74119
918 295-7600

**(G-3085)**
**WILPRO**
205 Industrial Ave (62821-2211)
PHONE.................................618 382-4667
Bob Wilson, *Owner*
Leslie W Wilson, *Co-Owner*
Justin Mugge, *Controller*
EMP: 3
SALES: 500K **Privately Held**
SIC: 1389 Pumping of oil & gas wells

## Carol Stream
*Dupage County*

**(G-3086)**
**360 DIGITAL PRINT INC**
262 Tubeway Dr (60188-2214)
PHONE.................................630 682-3601
Lee Rady, *Principal*
Jim Boaha, *Opers Staff*
EMP: 4
SQ FT: 5,400
SALES: 1.2MM **Privately Held**
SIC: 2752 Commercial printing, lithographic

**(G-3087)**
**A J ANTUNES & CO**
Also Called: Roundup Food Equipment Div
180 Kehoe Blvd (60188-1814)
P.O. Box 87700 (60188-7700)
PHONE.................................630 784-1000
Fax: 630 784-1655
Virginia M Antunes, *Ch of Bd*
Glenn Bullock, *President*
Steve Deppe, *President*
Olga Flores, *Business Mgr*
Daniel Schmidt, *Business Mgr*
▲ EMP: 200 EST: 1955
SQ FT: 115,000
SALES (est): 80.3MM **Privately Held**
WEB: www.antunes.com
SIC: 3589 Commercial cooking & food-warming equipment

**(G-3088)**
**ABERDEEN TECHNOLOGIES INC**
272 Commonwealth Dr (60188-2449)
PHONE.................................630 665-8590
Fax: 630 260-0999
John Michael, *President*
John M Schmitz, *President*
Susan M Vanmeter, *Admin Sec*
EMP: 15
SQ FT: 7,500
SALES (est): 2.3MM **Privately Held**
WEB: www.aberdeentech.com
SIC: 3544 3089 Special dies, tools, jigs & fixtures; molding primary plastic

**(G-3089)**
**ACCURATE WIRE STRIP FRMING INC**
175 Tubeway Dr (60188-2249)
PHONE.................................630 260-1000
Fax: 630 260-0033
Richard Durante, *President*
Jack Domingo, *Vice Pres*
Jeff Durante, *Vice Pres*
Steve Domingo, *VP Opers*
EMP: 10
SQ FT: 11,000
SALES (est): 2MM **Privately Held**
WEB: www.accuratewsf.com
SIC: 3496 3469 3315 Miscellaneous fabricated wire products; metal stampings; wire & fabricated wire products

**(G-3090)**
**ADVANCED AUDIO TECHNOLOGY INC**
Also Called: Aat
200 Easy St Ste E (60188-2399)
PHONE.................................630 665-3344
Fax: 630 665-3347
Robert Atkins, *President*
EMP: 4
SQ FT: 4,000
SALES: 1MM **Privately Held**
WEB: www.advancedaudio.net
SIC: 3652 Magnetic tape (audio): prerecorded

**(G-3091)**
**AEROFAST INC**
360 Gundersen Dr (60188-2422)
PHONE.................................630 668-6575
Fax: 630 668-6597
Nadine Martens, *CEO*
Gary Miller, *President*
EMP: 33 EST: 1958
SQ FT: 10,000
SALES (est): 5.3MM **Privately Held**
WEB: www.aerofastinc.com
SIC: 3965 Straight pins: steel or brass

**(G-3092)**
**AFI INDUSTRIES INC**
Also Called: A F I
475 Kehoe Blvd (60188-1879)
PHONE.................................630 462-0400
Fax: 630 462-1024
Robert Kleckner, *President*
Paul Wood, *Manager*
Patricia Kleckner, *Admin Sec*
▲ EMP: 35
SQ FT: 130,000
SALES (est): 9.2MM **Privately Held**
WEB: www.afiindusties.com
SIC: 3451 3452 3965 Screw machine products; screws, metal; bolts, metal; fasteners

**(G-3093)**
**AGENA MANUFACTURING CO**
360 Gundersen Dr (60188-2422)
PHONE.................................630 668-5086
Fax: 630 668-6597
Jack Martens, *President*
EMP: 30
SQ FT: 5,000
SALES (est): 1.8MM **Privately Held**
SIC: 3496 7699 3444 3429 Miscellaneous fabricated wire products; lock & key services; sheet metalwork; manufactured hardware (general)

**(G-3094)**
**AJ OSTER LLC**
180 Alexandra Way (60188-2048)
PHONE.................................630 260-0950
Fax: 630 260-1102
Randy Otdyke, *Plant Mgr*
Larry Pandocchi, *Materials Mgr*
Robert James, *Manager*
Tom Nelson, *Manager*
EMP: 150
SALES (corp-wide): 1.3B **Publicly Held**
SIC: 3366 Copper foundries; brass foundry
HQ: A.J. Oster, Llc
301 Metro Center Blvd # 204
Warwick RI 02886
401 736-2600

**(G-3095)**
**ALALI ENTERPRISES INC**
Also Called: Coffee News of Dupage County
1228 Narragansett Rd (60188-6054)
P.O. Box 1018, Lombard (60148-8018)
PHONE.................................630 827-9231
Syed H Jaffery, *President*
Zakia Fatima, *Vice Pres*
EMP: 2
SALES (est): 230.1K **Privately Held**
SIC: 2721 Magazines: publishing & printing

## GEOGRAPHIC SECTION
## Carol Stream - Dupage County (G-3118)

**(G-3096)**
**ALLEN ENTERTAINMENT MANAGEMENT**
Also Called: Chicago Lifesttyle, The
471 Essex Pl (60188-9229)
PHONE.................................630 752-0903
Haven Allen, *Owner*
**EMP:** 25
**SQ FT:** 2,000
**SALES:** 150K **Privately Held**
**SIC: 8742** 2721 Business consultant; public utilities consultant; magazines: publishing & printing

**(G-3097)**
**ALLURED PUBLISHING CORPORATION**
Also Called: Global Cosmetics Industry
336 Gundersen Dr Ste A (60188-2403)
PHONE.................................630 653-2155
Janet Ludwig, *President*
Annette Delagrange, *Publisher*
Karen Newman, *Publisher*
Nancy Allured, *Principal*
Stanley Allured, *Chairman*
**EMP:** 50
**SQ FT:** 11,000
**SALES (est):** 7MM **Privately Held**
**WEB:** www.allured.com
**SIC: 2741** 2721 Miscellaneous publishing; trade journals: publishing only, not printed on site

**(G-3098)**
**AMERICAN FLANGE & MFG CO INC (HQ)**
Also Called: Trisure Closures Worldwide
290 Fullerton Ave (60188-1895)
PHONE.................................630 665-7900
Fax: 630 665-7720
David B Fischer, *President*
Michael C Patton, *Principal*
Joachem Van Der Schaaf, *Principal*
Jeff Beeber, *Safety Mgr*
Wayne Avers, *Engineer*
▲ **EMP:** 30 **EST:** 1950
**SQ FT:** 135,000
**SALES (est):** 7MM
**SALES (corp-wide):** 3.3B **Publicly Held**
**WEB:** www.tri-sure.com
**SIC: 3466** Crowns & closures
**PA:** Greif, Inc.
425 Winter Rd
Delaware OH 43015
740 549-6000

**(G-3099)**
**AMERICAN LITHO INCORPORATED**
175 Mercedes Dr (60188-9409)
PHONE.................................630 682-0600
**EMP:** 856
**SALES (corp-wide):** 313.7MM **Privately Held**
**SIC: 2752** 2759 2789 7331 Lithographic Coml Print Commercial Printing Bookbinding/Related Work Direct Mail Ad Svcs
**PA:** American Litho, Incorporated
175 Mercedes Dr
Carol Stream IL 60188
630 462-1700

**(G-3100)**
**AMERICAN LITHO INCORPORATED**
175 Mercedes Dr (60188-9409)
PHONE.................................630 462-1700
Fax: 630 462-3800
Mike Fontana, *President*
Frank Arostegui, *Managing Dir*
Mike Gruper, *Business Mgr*
Joe Bulgarelli, *Vice Pres*
Sam Dentino, *Vice Pres*
▲ **EMP:** 350
**SQ FT:** 300,000
**SALES (est):** 189.8MM **Privately Held**
**WEB:** www.alitho.com
**SIC: 2752** Commercial printing, offset

**(G-3101)**
**AMERICAN PRECISION ELEC INC (PA)**
Also Called: A.P.e
25w624 Saint Charles Rd (60188-2062)
PHONE.................................630 510-8080
Fax: 630 510-8084
Michael Hall, *President*
Jim Kopp, *Vice Pres*
Suresh Patel, *Engineer*
James A Kopp, *Admin Sec*
▲ **EMP:** 65
**SQ FT:** 30,000
**SALES (est):** 16.6MM **Privately Held**
**WEB:** www.ape-inc.net
**SIC: 3679** Electronic circuits

**(G-3102)**
**AMERICAN SLIDE-CHART CO (PA)**
25w 550 Geneva Rd (60188)
P.O. Box 111, Wheaton (60187-0111)
PHONE.................................630 665-3333
Fax: 630 665-3491
David P Johnson, *President*
Don Hoff, *General Mgr*
Leslie Lehman, *Production*
Joe Raguso, *Purch Mgr*
Mary Beth, *Manager*
**EMP:** 80
**SQ FT:** 39,000
**SALES (est):** 11.1MM **Privately Held**
**WEB:** www.americanslidechart.com
**SIC: 2752** Promotional printing, lithographic; calendars, lithographed

**(G-3103)**
**AMERICO CHEMICAL PRODUCTS INC**
551 Kimberly Dr (60188-1835)
PHONE.................................630 588-0830
Fax: 630 588-0930
Christopher Bozin, *President*
Scott Schaff, *Sales Staff*
Lisa Phiel, *Manager*
Kristie Bozin, *Admin Sec*
**EMP:** 20
**SQ FT:** 28,000
**SALES (est):** 10.3MM **Privately Held**
**WEB:** www.americochemical.com
**SIC: 5169** 2819 5199 Chemicals & allied products; industrial inorganic chemicals; packaging materials

**(G-3104)**
**ARCON RING AND SPECIALTY CORP**
123 Easy St (60188-2314)
PHONE.................................630 682-5252
Fax: 630 682-5259
John Barker, *President*
Diane H Barker, *Corp Secy*
Diane Barker, *CFO*
John Debello, *Manager*
**EMP:** 12
**SQ FT:** 10,000
**SALES (est):** 4.4MM **Privately Held**
**WEB:** www.arconring.com
**SIC: 5051** 3496 Metals service centers & offices; miscellaneous fabricated wire products

**(G-3105)**
**ARMADA NUTRITION LLC**
285 Fullerton Ave (60188-1886)
PHONE.................................931 451-7808
Donald K Thorp,
**EMP:** 3
**SALES (corp-wide):** 217.9MM **Privately Held**
**SIC: 2023** Powdered whey
**HQ:** Armada Nutrition Llc
4637 Port Royal Rd
Spring Hill TN 37174
931 451-7808

**(G-3106)**
**ART JEWEL ENTERPRISES LTD**
Also Called: Eagle Grips
460 Randy Rd (60188-2120)
PHONE.................................630 260-0400
Fax: 630 260-0486
Raj Singh, *President*
Indira Singh, *Admin Sec*
**EMP:** 10
**SQ FT:** 5,000
**SALES (est):** 1.3MM **Privately Held**
**WEB:** www.eaglegrips.com
**SIC: 3484** 3421 5941 3161 Guns (firearms) or gun parts, 30 mm. & below; knives: butchers', hunting, pocket, etc.; sporting goods & bicycle shops; luggage; hardwood dimension & flooring mills

**(G-3107)**
**AUTOTECH TECH LTD PARTNR**
363 Saint Paul Blvd (60188-5208)
PHONE.................................563 359-7501
**EMP:** 3 **Privately Held**
**SIC: 3625** Industrial electrical relays & switches
**PA:** Autotech Technologies Limited Partnership
4140 Utica Ridge Rd
Bettendorf IA 52722

**(G-3108)**
**AUTOTECH TECH LTD PARTNR**
Also Called: LTI
343 Saint Paul Blvd (60188-1851)
PHONE.................................630 668-8886
Thomas Allen, *President*
Shankar Krishnamoorthy, *Vice Pres*
Raj Tiwari, *Vice Pres*
Rakesh Kahetarpal, *Engineer*
Shekhar Taneja, *Engineer*
**EMP:** 25 **Privately Held**
**SIC: 3625** 3676 3661 5065 Switches, electronic applications; resistor networks; telephones & telephone apparatus; electronic parts & equipment
**PA:** Autotech Technologies Limited Partnership
4140 Utica Ridge Rd
Bettendorf IA 52722

**(G-3109)**
**AUTUMN WOODS LTD (PA)**
375 Gundersen Dr (60188-2421)
PHONE.................................630 668-2080
Fax: 630 668-2146
Garry Dedick, *President*
Yvonne Dedick, *Treasurer*
**EMP:** 21
**SQ FT:** 10,400
**SALES (est):** 2.5MM **Privately Held**
**WEB:** www.autumnwoodscabinetry.com
**SIC: 2434** Wood kitchen cabinets; vanities, bathroom: wood

**(G-3110)**
**AVG ADVANCED TECHNOLOGIES LP**
Also Called: Uticor Technology
343 Saint Paul Blvd (60188-1851)
PHONE.................................630 668-3900
Fax: 630 668-4676
Shalabh Kumar, *CEO*
Electronic Support Systems Cor, *General Ptnr*
April Peterson, *Purch Mgr*
Dick Glover, *Controller*
**EMP:** 1000
**SQ FT:** 30,000
**SALES (est):** 71.1MM **Privately Held**
**SIC: 3672** 3661 3824 3822 Printed circuit boards; telephones & telephone apparatus; fluid meters & counting devices; auto controls regulating residntl & coml environmt & applncs; relays & industrial controls

**(G-3111)**
**AVG GROUP OF COMPANIES (HQ)**
Also Called: Avg LTI
363 Saint Paul Blvd (60188-5208)
PHONE.................................630 668-8886
Fax: 630 668-0341
Shalli Kuma, *President*
Vikram Kumar, *Vice Pres*
Rakesh Kahetarpal, *Chief Engr*
Linda Wooten, *Human Res Dir*
Melanie Smallwood, *Human Res Mgr*
**EMP:** 19
**SALES (est):** 9MM **Privately Held**
**SIC: 3679** Electronic circuits

**(G-3112)**
**BANNER SERVICE CORPORATION (PA)**
Also Called: Banner Medical
494 E Lies Rd (60188-9425)
PHONE.................................630 653-7500
Fax: 630 653-7555
Mark Redding, *Ch of Bd*
Tom Kehn, *General Mgr*
Justin Mautz, *Plant Mgr*
Bill Norlander, *Opers Staff*
Dave Hallin, *QC Mgr*
▲ **EMP:** 108 **EST:** 1961
**SQ FT:** 75,000
**SALES (est):** 54.2MM **Privately Held**
**WEB:** www.bargrind.com
**SIC: 3599** 5051 Custom machinery; steel; aluminum bars, rods, ingots, sheets, pipes, plates, etc.

**(G-3113)**
**BELCAR PRODUCTS INC**
500 Randy Rd Ste B (60188-2174)
PHONE.................................630 462-1950
Fax: 630 462-1965
James R Bellandi, *President*
Carol A Bellandi, *Corp Secy*
Sharon Newton, *Manager*
Paul Verkinderen, *Manager*
**EMP:** 9
**SQ FT:** 2,000
**SALES (est):** 3.6MM **Privately Held**
**WEB:** www.belcarproducts.com
**SIC: 5085** 5084 3545 3541 Tools; machine tools & metalworking machinery; machine tool accessories; machine tools, metal cutting type

**(G-3114)**
**BENJAMIN MOORE & CO**
320 Fullerton Ave Ste 200 (60188-1866)
PHONE.................................708 343-6000
Fax: 708 343-2359
Jerry Dean, *Manager*
M Kolind, *Administration*
**EMP:** 175
**SALES (corp-wide):** 223.6B **Publicly Held**
**SIC: 2851** 5198 Varnishes; paints, varnishes & supplies
**HQ:** Benjamin Moore & Co.
101 Paragon Dr
Montvale NJ 07645
201 573-9600

**(G-3115)**
**BLACKHAWK CORRUGATED LLC**
700 Kimberly Dr (60188-9406)
PHONE.................................844 270-2296
**EMP:** 48 **EST:** 2015
**SALES (est):** 120.7K **Privately Held**
**SIC: 2653** Corrugated & solid fiber boxes

**(G-3116)**
**BLACKHAWK COURTYARDS LLC**
700 Kimberly Dr (60188-9406)
PHONE.................................416 298-8101
Stephen Yap, *Bookkeeper*
Jim Williamson, *Mng Member*
**EMP:** 6
**SALES (est):** 295.1K **Privately Held**
**SIC: 2653** Corrugated & solid fiber boxes; corrugated boxes, partitions, display items, sheets & pad

**(G-3117)**
**BLACKHAWK INDUSTRIAL DIST INC**
245 E Lies Rd (60188-9421)
PHONE.................................773 736-9600
Frank Bertucci, *General Mgr*
**EMP:** 10 **Privately Held**
**SIC: 3541** 3545 Grinding machines, metalworking; machine tool accessories
**PA:** Blackhawk Industrial Distribution, Inc.
1501 Sw Expressway Dr
Broken Arrow OK 74012

**(G-3118)**
**BLASTLINE USA INC**
Also Called: Blastline USA
226 S Westgate Dr Ste B (60188-2229)
PHONE.................................630 871-0147

---
(PA)=Parent Co (HQ)=Headquarters (DH)=Div Headquarters
✪ = New Business established in last 2 years

2017 Harris Illinois Industrial Directory

## Carol Stream - Dupage County (G-3119)

Charly Lonappan, *Admin Sec*
▼ **EMP**: 6
**SQ FT**: 13,500
**SALES (est)**: 4.3MM **Privately Held**
**SIC**: 5084 5085 3589 Paint spray equipment, industrial; industrial supplies; sandblasting equipment

### (G-3119)
### BOTTLE-FREE WATER
350 S Main Pl (60188-2448)
**PHONE**.................................630 462-6807
**EMP**: 4
**SALES (est)**: 154.7K **Privately Held**
**SIC**: 2086 Pasteurized & mineral waters, bottled & canned

### (G-3120)
### BUCKNER SAND CO (PA)
290 S Main Pl Ste 101 (60188-2476)
**PHONE**.................................630 653-3700
Stephanie Chodera, *Principal*
**EMP**: 4
**SALES (est)**: 1MM **Privately Held**
**SIC**: 1442 Sand mining

### (G-3121)
### CABINETS & GRANITE DIRECT LLC
1175 N Gary Ave (60188-9423)
**PHONE**.................................630 588-8886
Ivan Chen, *Manager*
Jasmine Ni,
▲ **EMP**: 10
**SALES (est)**: 1.6MM **Privately Held**
**SIC**: 5031 2434 5211 Kitchen cabinets; wood kitchen cabinets; cabinets, kitchen

### (G-3122)
### CAC CORPORATION (PA)
Also Called: C A C
307 E Lies Rd (60188-9421)
**PHONE**.................................630 221-5200
**Fax**: 630 221-9567
James J Coduti, *President*
Frances Geier, *Corp Secy*
Barbara Johnson, *Manager*
Stan Stiewak, *Manager*
Mark Wallace, *Manager*
**EMP**: 40
**SQ FT**: 40,000
**SALES (est)**: 4.5MM **Privately Held**
**SIC**: 3469 3544 Metal stampings; special dies, tools, jigs & fixtures

### (G-3123)
### CAMBRDG PRINTING CORP
780 W Army Trail Rd (60188-9297)
**PHONE**.................................630 510-2100
**EMP**: 3 **EST**: 2002
**SALES**: 300K **Privately Held**
**SIC**: 2752 Lithographic Commercial Printing

### (G-3124)
### CAPITAL ADVANCED TECHNOLOGIES
309 Village Dr (60188-1828)
**PHONE**.................................630 690-1696
**Fax**: 630 690-2498
Robert Laschinski, *President*
Anna Laschinski, *Corp Secy*
Dan Blasengane, *Finance Mgr*
**EMP**: 8
**SQ FT**: 6,000
**SALES (est)**: 1.3MM **Privately Held**
**WEB**: www.capitaladvanced.com
**SIC**: 3679 Electronic circuits

### (G-3125)
### CARTPAC INC
Also Called: Frain Group
245 E North Ave (60188-2021)
**PHONE**.................................630 283-8979
**Fax**: 630 510-1101
Richard E Frain Jr, *President*
Robert Palmer, *General Mgr*
Steve Yonk, *CFO*
Chris Hoster, *Controller*
Lynne Fucarino, *Human Res Mgr*
**EMP**: 40
**SALES (est)**: 9.5MM **Privately Held**
**SIC**: 3565 7699 3556 Carton packing machines; industrial machinery & equipment repair; food products machinery

### (G-3126)
### CENTRAL CHEMICAL AND SERVICE
262 Carlton Dr (60188-2406)
**PHONE**.................................630 653-9200
**Fax**: 630 653-9232
Edward L Weller III, *President*
Edward L Weller Jr, *Vice Pres*
Diane M Weller, *Treasurer*
Niwanna M Weller, *Admin Sec*
**EMP**: 15
**SQ FT**: 17,000
**SALES (est)**: 3.7MM **Privately Held**
**SIC**: 2899 2851 Ink or writing fluids; paints & allied products

### (G-3127)
### CHICAGO ENVELOPE INC (PA)
Also Called: C.E. Printed Products
685 Kimberly Dr (60188-9403)
**PHONE**.................................630 668-0400
**Fax**: 630 668-2164
Robert Ohr, *President*
Cheryl Vermillion, *Vice Pres*
Doug Horvath, *Prdtn Mgr*
Scott Hagevold, *Production*
Stef Querry, *Cust Mgr*
**EMP**: 50
**SQ FT**: 21,000
**SALES (est)**: 11.2MM **Privately Held**
**SIC**: 2752 Business form & card printing, lithographic

### (G-3128)
### CHRISTIANITY TODAY INTL
465 Gundersen Dr (60188-2498)
**PHONE**.................................630 260-6200
**Fax**: 630 260-0114
Harold B Smith, *CEO*
Katelyn Beaty, *Managing Dir*
Mark Galli, *Editor*
Samuel Ogles, *Editor*
Ted Olsen, *Editor*
**EMP**: 168 **EST**: 1955
**SQ FT**: 25,000
**SALES (est)**: 11.1MM **Privately Held**
**WEB**: www.cticlassifieds.com
**SIC**: 2721 Magazines: publishing only, not printed on site

### (G-3129)
### CJT KOOLCARB INC (PA)
Also Called: C J T
494 Mission St (60188-9417)
P.O. Box 5941 (60197-5941)
**PHONE**.................................630 690-5933
**Fax**: 630 690-6355
Andrew Piasecki, *President*
Don Egland, *General Mgr*
Wayne Henson, *Business Mgr*
Michael Luedtke, *Vice Pres*
Thomas Trost, *Vice Pres*
▲ **EMP**: 115 **EST**: 2005
**SQ FT**: 68,000
**SALES (est)**: 35.4MM **Privately Held**
**WEB**: www.cjtkoolcarb.com
**SIC**: 3545 Drills (machine tool accessories); drill bits, metalworking; reamers, machine tool

### (G-3130)
### CLARK GEAR WORKS INC
1218 Saratoga Dr (60188-4644)
**PHONE**.................................630 561-2320
Jeffrey L Clark, *President*
Lori A Clark, *Treasurer*
**EMP**: 9
**SALES**: 50K **Privately Held**
**SIC**: 3462 Gears, forged steel

### (G-3131)
### COAL FIELD DEVELOPMENT CO
290 S Main Pl Ste 101 (60188-2476)
**PHONE**.................................630 653-3700
Dj Oppermann, *President*
Stephanie Chodera, *Vice Pres*
**EMP**: 3
**SQ FT**: 500
**SALES (est)**: 323K **Privately Held**
**SIC**: 1241 Coal mining services

### (G-3132)
### COCA COLA
Also Called: Coca-Cola
775 East Dr (60188-9410)
**PHONE**.................................630 588-8786
**EMP**: 4 **EST**: 2013
**SALES (est)**: 354.1K **Privately Held**
**SIC**: 2086 Bottled & canned soft drinks

### (G-3133)
### COLLEENS CONFECTION
190 Easy St Ste I (60188-3515)
**PHONE**.................................630 653-2231
Richard J Hamilton, *Owner*
▼ **EMP**: 4
**SQ FT**: 1,750
**SALES (est)**: 227.1K **Privately Held**
**WEB**: www.colleensconfections.com
**SIC**: 2064 Candy & other confectionery products

### (G-3134)
### COLONIAL BAG CORPORATION
205 Fullerton Ave (60188-1886)
**PHONE**.................................630 690-3999
**Fax**: 630 690-1571
Howard F Anderson, *President*
Ernesto Coria, *Plant Mgr*
Mary Gee, *Marketing Staff*
William Kindorf, *Admin Sec*
▲ **EMP**: 98
**SQ FT**: 70,000
**SALES (est)**: 25.5MM **Privately Held**
**WEB**: www.colonialbag.com
**SIC**: 2673 Trash bags (plastic film): made from purchased materials; plastic bags: made from purchased materials

### (G-3135)
### CONAGRA FODS FD INGRDIENTS INC
Also Called: Spicetec
193 Alexandra Way (60188-2047)
**PHONE**.................................630 682-5600
**Fax**: 630 682-5734
Charles Rudow, *Branch Mgr*
**EMP**: 7
**SALES (corp-wide)**: 11.6B **Publicly Held**
**SIC**: 2087 Flavoring extracts & syrups
**HQ**: Conagra Foods Food Ingredients Company, Inc.
1 Conagra Dr
Omaha NE 68102
402 240-4000

### (G-3136)
### COPIES OVERNIGHT INC (PA)
Also Called: Copresco
262 Commonwealth Dr (60188-2449)
**PHONE**.................................630 690-2000
**Fax**: 630 690-0531
Stephen Johnson, *President*
Chuck Legorreta, *Sr Corp Ofcr*
Charles Legorreta, *Admin Sec*
Monica Hayek, *Admin Asst*
**EMP**: 12
**SQ FT**: 14,000
**SALES (est)**: 3.6MM **Privately Held**
**WEB**: www.copresco.com
**SIC**: 2732 Books: printing & binding

### (G-3137)
### CORE COMPONENTS INC
154 Easy St (60188-2314)
**PHONE**.................................630 690-0520
Amy Adams, *President*
**EMP**: 19
**SQ FT**: 1,000
**SALES (est)**: 1.4MM **Privately Held**
**SIC**: 3625 5063 Relays & industrial controls; electrical apparatus & equipment

### (G-3138)
### CORE PIPE PRODUCTS INC
Also Called: Tube Line Stainless
170 Tubeway Dr (60188-2250)
**PHONE**.................................630 690-7000
**Fax**: 630 690-9701
Joseph Romanelli Sr, *President*
Debbie Tsamoulos, *Human Res Dir*
William Berndt, *Admin Sec*
Steve Romanelli, *Admin Sec*
▲ **EMP**: 120
**SQ FT**: 85,000
**SALES (est)**: 28.7MM **Privately Held**
**WEB**: www.gerlin.com
**SIC**: 3462 Flange, valve & pipe fitting forgings, ferrous

### (G-3139)
### DAINICHI MACHINERY INC
745 Kimberly Dr (60188-9407)
**PHONE**.................................630 681-1572
Yutaka Koyama, *President*
Hidekazu Kawase, *Vice Pres*
▲ **EMP**: 2
**SQ FT**: 12,180
**SALES**: 393.1K
**SALES (corp-wide)**: 32.1MM **Privately Held**
**WEB**: www.dainichi-machinery.com
**SIC**: 7699 3541 Industrial machinery & equipment repair; industrial tool grinding; lathes, metal cutting & polishing
**PA**: Dainichi Kinzoku Kogyo Co.,Ltd.
3-7-31, Chibune, Nishiyodogawa-Ku
Osaka OSK 555-0
648 085-392

### (G-3140)
### DAVES AUTO REPIAR
211 E Saint Charles Rd (60188-2308)
**PHONE**.................................630 682-4411
Dave Deiszke, *Owner*
**EMP**: 4
**SALES (est)**: 188.1K **Privately Held**
**WEB**: www.daves-radiator-auto.com
**SIC**: 3599 Air intake filters, internal combustion engine, except auto

### (G-3141)
### DAVIES MOLDING LLC
350 Kehoe Blvd (60188-1818)
**PHONE**.................................630 510-8188
**Fax**: 630 510-0994
Justin Thomas, *QC Mgr*
Lori Barera, *CFO*
Lois Armstrong, *Sales Dir*
Derran Smith, *Mng Member*
George Huerta, *Manager*
▲ **EMP**: 125 **EST**: 1933
**SQ FT**: 99,000
**SALES (est)**: 31.7MM
**SALES (corp-wide)**: 1.3B **Privately Held**
**WEB**: www.daviesmolding.com
**SIC**: 3089 3825 Extruded finished plastic products; instruments to measure electricity
**HQ**: Pettibone L.L.C.
27501 Bella Vista Pkwy
Warrenville IL 60555
630 353-5000

### (G-3142)
### DECORE TOOL & MFG INC
159 Easy St (60188-2314)
**PHONE**.................................630 681-9760
Scott Decore, *President*
**EMP**: 16
**SALES (est)**: 2.7MM **Privately Held**
**SIC**: 3544 Special dies, tools, jigs & fixtures

### (G-3143)
### DESIGN METALS FABRICATION INC
361 Randy Rd Ste 106 (60188-1869)
**PHONE**.................................630 752-9060
Thang Nguyen, *President*
**EMP**: 8 **EST**: 2008
**SALES (est)**: 1.5MM **Privately Held**
**SIC**: 3441 Fabricated structural metal

### (G-3144)
### DONKEY BRANDS LLC
Also Called: Donkey Chips
281 Carlton Dr (60188-2405)
**PHONE**.................................630 251-2007
Amanda Gallo,
Dominic Gallo,
Lauren Pisljar,
Robert Pisljar,
**EMP**: 13
**SQ FT**: 6,600
**SALES (est)**: 2.2MM **Privately Held**
**SIC**: 2096 Tortilla chips

### (G-3145)
### DYNACUT INDUSTRIES INC
Also Called: Dyna Cut Industries
500 Randy Rd Ste A (60188-2175)
**PHONE**.................................630 462-1900
James R Bellandi, *President*
Carol Bellandi, *Corp Secy*
**EMP**: 20

## GEOGRAPHIC SECTION — Carol Stream - Dupage County (G-3170)

SQ FT: 4,000
SALES (est): 4.1MM Privately Held
SIC: 3545 Machine tool accessories

**(G-3146)**
**EQUI-CHEM INTERNATIONAL INC**
510 Tower Blvd (60188-9426)
P.O. Box 10249, Chicago (60610-0249)
PHONE..................................630 784-0432
Luis C Lovis, President
Louis Lovis Jr, Development
▼ EMP: 10
SQ FT: 20,000
SALES (est): 1.3MM Privately Held
WEB: www.equichem.com
SIC: 2099 2087 Food preparations; flavoring extracts & syrups

**(G-3147)**
**ERGOSEAL INC (PA)**
Also Called: Norman Technology
346 Commerce Dr (60188-1809)
PHONE..................................630 462-9600
Fax: 630 462-3600
Athanasios Hilaris, CEO
John Hilaris, Ch of Bd
Lou Kamvisis, Prdtn Mgr
Nick Lirakos, Engineer
George Waring, Marketing Mgr
▲ EMP: 27
SQ FT: 17,000
SALES: 5.6MM Privately Held
WEB: www.ergoseal.com
SIC: 3561 Pumps & pumping equipment

**(G-3148)**
**EUROPEAN WOOD WORKS INC**
1151 Woodlake Dr (60188-6028)
PHONE..................................773 662-6607
Krzysztof Lukaszek, President
EMP: 4 EST: 2010
SQ FT: 7,000
SALES (est): 31.1K Privately Held
SIC: 2431 Millwork

**(G-3149)**
**EXTRUDED SOLUTIONS INC**
322 Saint Paul Blvd (60188-1852)
PHONE..................................630 871-6450
Treysta Battiato, President
Melissa Battiato, CFO
Victor Battiato, Sales Mgr
Lucien Battiato, Admin Sec
▼ EMP: 6
SQ FT: 6,000
SALES (est): 915.3K Privately Held
SIC: 3089 Automotive parts, plastic

**(G-3150)**
**FERN MANUFACTURING COMPANY**
333 Kimberly Dr (60188-1836)
PHONE..................................630 260-9350
Fax: 630 260-9412
William R Fern, President
Linda Fern, Office Mgr
Laurel Fern, Admin Sec
EMP: 6 EST: 1977
SQ FT: 17,220
SALES (est): 979.6K Privately Held
WEB: www.fernmanco.com
SIC: 3599 Machine shop, jobbing & repair

**(G-3151)**
**FIC AMERICA CORP (HQ)**
485 E Lies Rd (60188-9422)
PHONE..................................630 871-7609
Fax: 630 871-2938
Kenzo Yanase, President
Tsukasa Ishimaru, General Mgr
William T Murakami, Vice Pres
Nolberto Esparza, Opers Staff
Brian Parkes, Production
▲ EMP: 670
SQ FT: 700,000
SALES: 227.1MM
SALES (corp-wide): 3.6B Privately Held
WEB: www.ficamerica.com
SIC: 3469 Metal stampings
PA: Futaba Industrial Co., Ltd.
1, Ochaya, Hashimecho
Okazaki AIC 444-0
564 312-211

**(G-3152)**
**FLEXOGRAFIX INC**
27 W 136 St Charles (60188)
PHONE..................................630 350-0100
Ken Pavett, President
EMP: 10
SQ FT: 5,000
SALES (est): 1.6MM Privately Held
WEB: www.flexografix.com
SIC: 2759 Flexographic printing

**(G-3153)**
**FONA**
525 Randy Rd (60188-2121)
PHONE..................................630 462-1414
Joseph Slawek, Principal
EMP: 3
SALES (est): 197.7K Privately Held
SIC: 2087 Flavoring extracts & syrups

**(G-3154)**
**FORTUNA BAKING COMPANY**
149 Easy St (60188-2314)
PHONE..................................630 681-3000
Pete Fourtounis, President
George Fourtounis, President
EMP: 3
SALES (est): 364.1K Privately Held
SIC: 2051 Bread, cake & related products

**(G-3155)**
**FOX METAL SERVICES INC**
1064 Baybrook Ln (60188-2957)
PHONE..................................847 439-9696
Fax: 847 439-9730
Joseph Cholewa, President
Donna Guasta, Office Mgr
EMP: 12
SALES (est): 940K Privately Held
SIC: 3499 3444 7389 Machine bases, metal; sheet metalwork; metal cutting services

**(G-3156)**
**GALAXY CIRCUITS INC**
383 Randy Rd (60188-1802)
PHONE..................................630 462-1010
Fax: 630 462-1815
Anil Patel, President
Kanti Patel, Vice Pres
Jeff Boyle, Manager
Shankar Patel, Shareholder
Pankaj Patel, Admin Sec
▲ EMP: 20
SQ FT: 15,000
SALES (est): 4MM Privately Held
WEB: www.galaxycircuits.com
SIC: 3672 Printed circuit boards

**(G-3157)**
**GERLIN INC**
Also Called: Core Pipe
170 Tubeway Dr (60188-2250)
PHONE..................................630 653-5232
Steve Romanelli, President
Timothy Warren, Vice Pres
Jim Roder, Purch Agent
Bill Burn, CFO
Bill Berndt, Finance
▲ EMP: 1 EST: 1984
SALES (est): 289.6K Privately Held
SIC: 3498 3317 Fabricated pipe & fittings; pipes, seamless steel

**(G-3158)**
**GIVAUDAN FLAVORS CORPORATION**
Also Called: Spicetec Flavors & Seasonings
195 Alexandra Way (60188-2047)
PHONE..................................630 682-5600
Mauricio Graber, President
Chuck Woods, Chief Mktg Ofcr
EMP: 188
SALES (corp-wide): 1.1B Privately Held
WEB: www.conagra.com
SIC: 2099 2038 2013 Food preparations; dessert mixes & fillings; seasonings & spices; ready-to-eat meals, salads & sandwiches; frozen specialties; dinners, frozen & packaged; lunches, frozen & packaged; sausages & other prepared meats
HQ: Givaudan Flavors Corporation
1199 Edison Dr
Cincinnati OH 45216
513 948-8000

**(G-3159)**
**GLEN LAKE INC**
285 Fullerton Ave (60188-1886)
P.O. Box 2463, Naperville (60567-2463)
PHONE..................................630 668-3492
Fax: 630 668-1434
Deborah Tritt, President
Ricki Matz, Office Mgr
John Tritt, Manager
EMP: 12
SQ FT: 132,000
SALES (est): 1.1MM Privately Held
WEB: www.glenlake.com
SIC: 2045 Prepared flour mixes & doughs

**(G-3160)**
**GLOBE TICKET**
350 Randy Rd Ste 1 (60188-1831)
PHONE..................................847 258-1000
Robert Dawson, Principal
▲ EMP: 3
SALES (est): 319.6K Privately Held
SIC: 2759 Commercial printing

**(G-3161)**
**GRAPHIC PACKAGING HOLDING CO**
Also Called: Altivity Packaging
400 E North Ave (60188-2130)
PHONE..................................630 260-6500
Fax: 630 260-6864
Mike Egan, General Mgr
Bill Lawlor, Purch Mgr
Larry Geller, Persnl Mgr
Tommy Woods, Executive
EMP: 400 Publicly Held
SIC: 2631 2657 2653 Folding boxboard; folding paperboard boxes; corrugated & solid fiber boxes
PA: Graphic Packaging Holding Company
1500 Riveredge Pkwy # 100
Atlanta GA 30328

**(G-3162)**
**GRAPHIC PACKAGING INTL INC**
400 E North Ave (60188-2130)
PHONE..................................630 260-6500
Howard Droege, Branch Mgr
Conrad Kulinowski, Manager
Patricia Vanlandinhem, Manager
Michael Okeefe, Director
EMP: 6 Publicly Held
SIC: 2631 Container board
HQ: Graphic Packaging International, Inc.
1500 Riveredge Pkwy # 100
Atlanta GA 30328
770 240-7200

**(G-3163)**
**GRAPHIC PACKAGING INTL INC**
Also Called: Altivity Packaging
400 E North Ave (60188-2130)
P.O. Box 105, Cantonment FL (32533-0105)
PHONE..................................630 260-6500
Jack Forbes, Principal
Tony F Hancock, Vice Pres
Nancy Glass, Personnel
EMP: 228 Publicly Held
SIC: 2674 2631 Bags: uncoated paper & multiwall; folding boxboard
HQ: Graphic Packaging International, Inc.
1500 Riveredge Pkwy # 100
Atlanta GA 30328
770 240-7200

**(G-3164)**
**GREEN ORGANICS INC**
290 S Main Pl Ste 103 (60188-2476)
PHONE..................................630 871-0108
Fax: 630 588-1107
Joe Mazza, President
David A Gravel, Vice Pres
Magie Cieloski, Controller
EMP: 10
SALES (est): 1.2MM Privately Held
WEB: www.greenorganics.net
SIC: 2875 Compost

**(G-3165)**
**HART & COOLEY INC**
Commercial Products Group
815 Kimberly Dr (60188-1801)
PHONE..................................630 665-5549
Bernard Roy, Principal
EMP: 250
SALES (corp-wide): 36.8B Privately Held
SIC: 3446 Registers (air), metal
HQ: Hart & Cooley, Inc.
5030 Corp Exch Blvd Se
Grand Rapids MI 49512
616 656-8200

**(G-3166)**
**HILL ENGINEERING INC**
373 Randy Rd (60188-1802)
PHONE..................................630 315-5070
Bruce Dewey, President
Tim Schreader, Purch Agent
Terry Reedy, Engineer
James Gafkowski, Design Engr
Elmer Utley, Sales Executive
EMP: 20
SQ FT: 30,000
SALES (est): 4.1MM
SALES (corp-wide): 482.1MM Privately Held
WEB: www.hillengr.com
SIC: 3544 Special dies & tools
HQ: Formtek Inc
711 Ogden Ave
Lisle IL 60532
630 285-1500

**(G-3167)**
**HOPE PUBLISHING COMPANY**
Also Called: Providence Press
380 S Main Pl (60188-2475)
PHONE..................................630 665-3200
Fax: 630 665-2552
John Shorney, President
Jane Holstein, Editor
Scott Shorney, Vice Pres
Steve Shorney, Vice Pres
Janice Geever-Stone, Bookkeeper
EMP: 16 EST: 1892
SQ FT: 10,000
SALES (est): 2.1MM Privately Held
WEB: www.hopepublishing.com
SIC: 2731 2741 Book music: publishing only, not printed on site; miscellaneous publishing

**(G-3168)**
**HOUSE OF GRAPHICS**
370 Randy Rd (60188-1880)
PHONE..................................630 682-0810
Fax: 630 682-0964
Phillis Herbold, President
Jill Lewaniak, Vice Pres
John Leaf, Plant Mgr
Rida Brown, Purch Agent
C Robert Herbold, Manager
EMP: 25 EST: 1969
SQ FT: 34,500
SALES (est): 4.2MM Privately Held
WEB: www.houseofgraphics.com
SIC: 2752 2791 2789 Commercial printing, offset; typesetting; bookbinding & related work

**(G-3169)**
**ILLINOIS TAG CO**
287 Commonwealth Dr (60188-2450)
P.O. Box 4082, Wheaton (60189-4082)
PHONE..................................773 626-0542
Robert A Oliva, President
Nancy Oliva, Business Mgr
Frank Oliva, Purch Mgr
EMP: 20
SQ FT: 1,300
SALES (est): 2.4MM Privately Held
SIC: 2679 2759 2671 Tags & labels, paper; commercial printing; packaging paper & plastics film, coated & laminated

**(G-3170)**
**ILLINOIS TOOL WORKS INC**
Transtech
475 N Gary Ave (60188-1820)
PHONE..................................630 752-4000
Fax: 630 752-4463
Robert Hitchcock, General Mgr
Sheryl Elliott, Accountant
Jud Broome, Manager
Robert McCormack, Director
EMP: 65
SQ FT: 130,000
SALES (corp-wide): 13.6B Publicly Held
SIC: 2754 Commercial printing, gravure

## Carol Stream - Dupage County (G-3171)   GEOGRAPHIC SECTION

PA: Illinois Tool Works Inc.
155 Harlem Ave
Glenview IL 60025
847 724-7500

**(G-3171)**
**ILLINOIS TOOL WORKS INC**
ITW Linx
425 N Gary Ave (60188-1823)
PHONE..............................630 315-2150
Fax: 630 315-2151
E S Santi, *President*
EMP: 104
SALES (corp-wide): 13.6B **Publicly Held**
SIC: 3089 Injection molded finished plastic products
PA: Illinois Tool Works Inc.
155 Harlem Ave
Glenview IL 60025
847 724-7500

**(G-3172)**
**IMTRAN INDUSTRIES INC**
475 N Gary Ave (60188-1820)
PHONE..............................630 752-4000
Joe Olson, *President*
Kenneth Harris, *Vice Pres*
Douglas Parker, *Vice Pres*
Chris Sobaszek, *Opers Mgr*
Ted Beaupre, *Manager*
EMP: 75
SALES (est): 2.4MM **Privately Held**
SIC: 2759 3555 Commercial printing; printing trades machinery

**(G-3173)**
**INTERNATIONAL PAPER COMPANY**
139 Fullerton Ave (60188-1825)
PHONE..............................630 653-3500
Pat Leggett, *Branch Mgr*
EMP: 10
SALES (corp-wide): 21B **Publicly Held**
SIC: 2621 Paper mills
PA: International Paper Company
6400 Poplar Ave
Memphis TN 38197
901 419-9000

**(G-3174)**
**INTERSTATE POWER SYSTEMS INC**
Also Called: Interstate Power Systemd
210 Alexandra Way (60188-2068)
PHONE..............................630 871-1111
Rochelle Protho, *Accounting Mgr*
Myron Birschbach, *Branch Mgr*
EMP: 10
SQ FT: 50,000
SALES (corp-wide): 250MM **Privately Held**
SIC: 3714 5084 Motor vehicle parts & accessories; industrial machinery & equipment
HQ: Interstate Power Systems, Inc.
2501 American Blvd E
Minneapolis MN 55425
952 854-2044

**(G-3175)**
**ISA CHICAGO**
470 Mission St Unit 7 (60188-9424)
PHONE..............................630 317-7169
Mohammed Inayat, *Principal*
EMP: 4
SALES (est): 610.7K **Privately Held**
SIC: 3911 Cigar & cigarette accessories

**(G-3176)**
**JASON OF ILLINOIS INC**
Also Called: Jason Industrial
221 S Westgate Dr Ste N2 (60188-2053)
PHONE..............................630 752-0600
Fax: 630 752-0680
Philip Cohenca, *President*
Kristina Pariso, *General Mgr*
Emmy Cohenca, *Corp Secy*
Tom Tesoro, *VP Sls/Mktg*
Liz Hidalgo, *Assistant*
▲ EMP: 21
SQ FT: 25,000
SALES: 5MM **Privately Held**
SIC: 3052 3492 5085 Rubber & plastics hose & beltings; hose & tube fittings & assemblies, hydraulic/pneumatic; industrial supplies

**(G-3177)**
**JPMORGAN CHASE BANK NAT ASSN**
411 S Schmale Rd (60188-2416)
PHONE..............................630 653-1270
Andrew Keppy, *Financial Exec*
Scott Wurkus, *Manager*
Amy Smith, *Manager*
EMP: 30
SALES (corp-wide): 105.4B **Publicly Held**
WEB: www.chase.com
SIC: 2782 Bank checkbooks & passbooks
HQ: Jpmorgan Chase Bank, National Association
1111 Polaris Pkwy
Columbus OH 43240
614 436-3055

**(G-3178)**
**KIK INTERNATIONAL INC**
780 W Army Trail Rd 209 (60188-9297)
PHONE..............................905 660-0444
Kathleen Lucia, *Principal*
EMP: 18
SALES (est): 2.8MM **Privately Held**
SIC: 2842 Cleaning or polishing preparations

**(G-3179)**
**KLIMP INDUSTRIES INC**
175 Tubeway Dr (60188-2249)
PHONE..............................630 682-0752
Fax: 630 790-0673
James R Bonde, *President*
Katherine Porter, *Principal*
Steve Reinke, *CTO*
EMP: 5
SALES (est): 477.1K **Privately Held**
WEB: www.klimpindustries.com
SIC: 3496 Wire fasteners

**(G-3180)**
**KLIMP INDUSTRIES INC**
175 Tubeway Dr (60188-2249)
P.O. Box 709, Warrenville (60555-0709)
PHONE..............................630 790-0600
James R Bonde, *President*
Richard Durante, *Vice Pres*
Jeff Durante, *Manager*
EMP: 4
SALES: 1MM **Privately Held**
SIC: 3496 Wire fasteners

**(G-3181)**
**KNS COMPANIES INC**
475 Randy Rd (60188-2119)
P.O. Box 88762 (60188-0762)
PHONE..............................630 665-9010
Fax: 630 665-1819
Raymond Bellino, *President*
Edwin F Poland, *President*
Karen Gould, *Office Mgr*
Karen McMahin, *Manager*
Theresa Barton, *Info Tech Mgr*
EMP: 14
SQ FT: 15,000
SALES (est): 4.9MM **Privately Held**
WEB: www.knscompanies.com
SIC: 2821 2851 3081 Epoxy resins; paints & allied products; unsupported plastics film & sheet

**(G-3182)**
**KOWALSKI MEMORIALS INC**
195 Kehoe Blvd Ste 1 (60188-5202)
PHONE..............................630 462-7226
Fax: 630 462-7380
Peter Kowalski, *President*
Holly Klemz, *Manager*
EMP: 5
SQ FT: 3,200
SALES (est): 772.3K **Privately Held**
SIC: 3272 5087 Monuments & grave markers, except terrazo; cemetary supplies & equipment

**(G-3183)**
**LEW ELECTRIC FITTINGS CO**
371 Randy Rd (60188-1802)
P.O. Box 470, Saint Charles (60174-0470)
PHONE..............................630 665-2075
Fax: 708 345-6490
John E Romer, *CEO*
Graham Romer, *President*
Susan Cozzi, *CFO*

▲ EMP: 18 EST: 1901
SQ FT: 17,000
SALES: 6MM **Privately Held**
WEB: www.lewelectric.com
SIC: 3644 Outlet boxes (electric wiring devices)

**(G-3184)**
**LEWIS PROCESS SYSTEMS INC**
294 Commonwealth Dr (60188-2449)
PHONE..............................630 510-8200
Fax: 630 510-8397
Alfred E Gudenkauf, *President*
Bernice Gudenkauf, *Corp Secy*
EMP: 10 EST: 1972
SQ FT: 10,000
SALES (est): 956.7K **Privately Held**
SIC: 3444 5085 7692 3494 Sheet metalwork; valves & fittings; welding repair; valves & pipe fittings; fabricated plate work (boiler shop)

**(G-3185)**
**LINDE LLC**
640 Kimberly Dr (60188-9402)
PHONE..............................630 690-3010
Mike Totteleer, *Manager*
EMP: 10
SALES (corp-wide): 17.9B **Privately Held**
SIC: 5169 2813 Chemicals & allied products; industrial gases
HQ: Linde Llc
200 Somerset Corporate Bl
Bridgewater NJ 08807
908 464-8100

**(G-3186)**
**LOMA INTERNATIONAL INC**
Also Called: Loma Systems
550 Kehoe Blvd (60188-1838)
PHONE..............................630 588-0900
Fax: 630 588-1394
Hugh Zentmyer, *President*
Pradeep Rochliani, *General Mgr*
Mark Lemire, *Business Mgr*
Heather Bradley, *Purch Agent*
Anita Cline, *Purchasing*
▲ EMP: 80
SQ FT: 51,000
SALES (est): 54.7MM
SALES (corp-wide): 13.6B **Publicly Held**
WEB: www.loma.com
SIC: 5065 3535 5084 Electronic parts & equipment; conveyors & conveying equipment; industrial machinery & equipment
PA: Illinois Tool Works Inc.
155 Harlem Ave
Glenview IL 60025
847 724-7500

**(G-3187)**
**MAAC MACHINERY CO INC**
590 Tower Blvd (60188-9426)
PHONE..............................630 665-1700
Fax: 630 665-7795
Paul V Alongi, *Founder*
Mike Assian, *QA Dir*
Paul Ryan, *Marketing Staff*
James Alongi, *Admin Sec*
EMP: 40
SQ FT: 46,000
SALES (est): 11.2MM **Privately Held**
WEB: www.maacsales.com
SIC: 3559 5084 Plastics working machinery; industrial machinery & equipment

**(G-3188)**
**MALLOF ABRUZINO NASH MKTG INC**
Also Called: Man Marketing
765 Kimberly Dr (60188-9407)
PHONE..............................630 929-5200
Fax: 630 752-9288
Edward G Mallof, *President*
Matt Nash, *Vice Pres*
EMP: 26
SQ FT: 10,900
SALES (est): 5.1MM **Privately Held**
WEB: www.manmarketing.com
SIC: 7311 2752 Advertising agencies; commercial printing, offset

**(G-3189)**
**MASTER MARKETING INTL INC**
Also Called: Magnetstreet
280 Gerzevske Ln (60188-2049)
PHONE..............................630 909-1846
Larry Smith, *Plant Mgr*
Neville B Baird, *Manager*
EMP: 15
SALES (corp-wide): 23.8MM **Privately Held**
WEB: www.magnetstreet.com
SIC: 3993 Advertising novelties
PA: Master Marketing International, Inc.
280 Gerzevske Ln
Carol Stream IL 60188
630 653-5525

**(G-3190)**
**MASTER MARKETING INTL INC (PA)**
Also Called: Magnetstreet
280 Gerzevske Ln (60188-2049)
PHONE..............................630 653-5525
Fax: 630 681-1516
Neville B Baird, *Ch of Bd*
Brian Baird, *President*
Jake Witham, *Regional Mgr*
David Baird, *Vice Pres*
Mark Syswerda, *Vice Pres*
▲ EMP: 35
SQ FT: 10,000
SALES (est): 23.8MM **Privately Held**
WEB: www.magnetstreet.com
SIC: 2759 Promotional printing; invitation & stationery printing & engraving

**(G-3191)**
**MASTER-CAST INC**
155 E Saint Charles Rd B (60188-2081)
P.O. Box 387, Batavia (60510-0387)
PHONE..............................630 879-3866
Fax: 630 879-0390
Timothy Guerin, *President*
Brian Guerin, *Vice Pres*
Ben Aguilera, *Executive*
Jill Guerin, *Executive*
EMP: 20
SQ FT: 18,000
SALES (est): 4.5MM **Privately Held**
WEB: www.mastercastfoundry.com
SIC: 3363 Aluminum die-castings

**(G-3192)**
**MEDIA ASSOCIATES INTL INC**
Also Called: M A I
351 S Main Pl Ste 230 (60188-2455)
PHONE..............................630 260-9063
Mark Carpenter, *Ch of Bd*
John D Maust, *President*
Dawn Jewell, *Publications*
Robert Reekie, *Director*
Ramon Rocha, *Director*
EMP: 16
SQ FT: 802
SALES: 706.5K **Privately Held**
SIC: 8742 8331 2731 Business consultant; sheltered workshop; pamphlets: publishing only, not printed on site

**(G-3193)**
**METALS TECHNOLOGY CORPORATION**
120 N Schmale Rd (60188-2151)
PHONE..............................630 221-2500
Fax: 630 221-0120
John B Bell, *President*
Thomas J Bell, *President*
Jerome Bell Jr, *Vice Pres*
Ed Vandyck, *QC Dir*
Darin Meschberger, *Engineer*
EMP: 115
SQ FT: 70,000
SALES (est): 29.3MM **Privately Held**
WEB: www.metalstechnology.com
SIC: 3398 Metal heat treating

**(G-3194)**
**MEYERCORD REVENUE INC**
475 Village Dr (60188-1830)
PHONE..............................630 682-6200
Fax: 630 682-6345
Jim E Bonhivert, *President*
John Sprawka, *General Mgr*
Manuel Garza, *Prdtn Mgr*
Jeff Domelen, *Plant Engr*

# GEOGRAPHIC SECTION

## Carol Stream - Dupage County (G-3220)

**EMP:** 50
**SALES (est):** 9.1MM Privately Held
**SIC:** 2752 Commercial printing, lithographic
**HQ:** Sicpa Securink, Corp.
8000 Research Way
Springfield VA 22153
703 455-8050

### (G-3195)
**MGN TOOL & MFG CO INC**
373 Randy Rd (60188-1802)
**PHONE**.....................630 849-3575
Michael Nawroth, Owner
**EMP:** 3 **EST:** 2011
**SALES (est):** 261.8K Privately Held
**SIC:** 3999 Barber & beauty shop equipment

### (G-3196)
**MICRON MOLD & MFG INC**
1085 Idaho St (60188-1348)
**PHONE**.....................630 871-9531
Josekutty Parackal, President
Benny Parackal, Vice Pres
**EMP:** 4
**SQ FT:** 2,000
**SALES:** 135K Privately Held
**SIC:** 3089 Molding primary plastic

### (G-3197)
**MICROWAVE RES & APPLICATIONS**
190 Easy St Ste A (60188-3500)
**PHONE**.....................630 480-7456
Wayne G Love, President
James C Stratton, Vice Pres
**EMP:** 3
**SQ FT:** 3,200
**SALES (est):** 382K Privately Held
**WEB:** www.microwaveresearch.com
**SIC:** 3631 8733 Microwave ovens, including portable: household; safety research, noncommercial

### (G-3198)
**MIDWEST COACH BUILDERS INC**
Also Called: Mobility Masters
200 Easy St Ste I (60188-2399)
**PHONE**.....................630 690-1420
**Fax:** 630 690-1420
William Karris, President
David Edwards, Vice Pres
**EMP:** 4
**SQ FT:** 2,000
**SALES (est):** 350K Privately Held
**SIC:** 3711 Automobile assembly, including specialty automobiles

### (G-3199)
**MIDWEST WOODCRAFTERS INC**
26w415 Saint Charles Rd (60188-1942)
**PHONE**.....................630 665-0901
**Fax:** 630 665-1091
Michael Allessi, President
Russell Krella, Admin Sec
**EMP:** 6
**SALES (est):** 630K Privately Held
**SIC:** 2431 2517 2434 Millwork; wood television & radio cabinets; wood kitchen cabinets

### (G-3200)
**MJS-CN LLC**
Also Called: Connie's Naturals,
191 S Gary Ave Ste 180 (60188-2058)
**PHONE**.....................630 580-7200
Marc Stolfe,
Ivan Matsunaga,
▲ **EMP:** 15
**SALES (est):** 1.8MM Privately Held
**SIC:** 2038 Frozen specialties

### (G-3201)
**MULTITECH COLD FORMING LLC**
250 Kehoe Blvd (60188-1816)
**PHONE**.....................630 949-8200
Mike Cuhns, Engrg Mgr
Rahul Parikh, Mng Member
▲ **EMP:** 25
**SALES (est):** 3.6MM Privately Held
**SIC:** 3451 3452 3965 Screw machine products; rivets, metal; fasteners

**PA:** Multitech Industries, Inc.
350 Village Dr
Carol Stream IL 60188

### (G-3202)
**MULTITECH INDUSTRIES INC (PA)**
350 Village Dr (60188-1828)
**PHONE**.....................630 784-9200
Rahul Parikh, President
Sandra Rutkas, Controller
Thomas Falcone, Admin Sec
▲ **EMP:** 25
**SQ FT:** 46,000
**SALES (est):** 81.6MM Privately Held
**SIC:** 3559 Automotive related machinery

### (G-3203)
**MULTITECH MCHNED CMPONENTS LLC**
250 Kehoe Blvd (60188-1816)
**PHONE**.....................630 949-8200
Thomas Falcone, Mng Member
Rahul Parikh,
▲ **EMP:** 30
**SALES (est):** 8MM Privately Held
**SIC:** 3559 Automotive related machinery

### (G-3204)
**NATIONAL DATA SVCS CHICAGO INC (HQ)**
Also Called: Diamond Marketing Solutions
900 Kimberly Dr (60188-1859)
**PHONE**.....................630 597-9100
**Fax:** 630 443-7476
Bruce D'Angello, CEO
Paula Kudlinski, President
Michael Nevolo, President
Mark Peterson, President
John Puffer, President
**EMP:** 114
**SALES (est):** 41.5MM
**SALES (corp-wide):** 57.8MM Privately Held
**WEB:** www.dmsolutions.com
**SIC:** 7371 7331 2759 Custom computer programming services; direct mail advertising services; commercial printing
**PA:** Diamond Marketing Solutions Group, Inc.
900 Kimberly Dr
Carol Stream IL 60188
630 597-9100

### (G-3205)
**NEW WORLD PRODUCTS INC**
494 Mission St (60188-9417)
**PHONE**.....................630 690-5625
Chuck Trose, President
Eugene Lurye, Vice Pres
◆ **EMP:** 7
**SALES (est):** 724.7K Privately Held
**SIC:** 3545 Cutting tools for machine tools

### (G-3206)
**NOVA METALS INC**
279 Commonwealth Dr (60188-2450)
**PHONE**.....................630 690-4300
**Fax:** 630 690-9317
Scott Lorenz, President
Steve Maniaci, Treasurer
▼ **EMP:** 12
**SQ FT:** 15,000
**SALES (est):** 1.5MM Privately Held
**SIC:** 3444 Sheet metalwork

### (G-3207)
**NTA PRECISION AXLE CORPORATION**
795 Kimberly Dr (60188-9407)
**PHONE**.....................630 690-6300
Jason Coolidge, Engineer
Jason Cotte, Engineer
Todd Damte, Engineer
Shinji Yamamoto, Engineer
Lindsay Longtin, Accounting Mgr
▲ **EMP:** 260
**SALES:** 120MM
**SALES (corp-wide):** 6B Privately Held
**SIC:** 3714 Bearings, motor vehicle
**PA:** Ntn Corporation
1-3-17, Kyomachibori, Nishi-Ku
Osaka OSK 550-0
664 435-001

### (G-3208)
**OASIS AUDIO LLC**
289 S Main Pl (60188-2425)
**PHONE**.....................630 668-5367
Rick Pritikin, General Mgr
Kyle Zehr, Production
Susanne Anhalt, Sales Mgr
Martha Schuelke, Manager
Tammy Faxel, Director
**EMP:** 8
**SALES (est):** 721.7K Privately Held
**SIC:** 2731 Book publishing

### (G-3209)
**ON TIME ENVELOPES & PRINTING**
615 Kimberly Dr (60188-9403)
**PHONE**.....................630 682-0466
Syed Zaidi, Owner
**EMP:** 5 **EST:** 2008
**SALES (est):** 500K Privately Held
**SIC:** 2759 Commercial printing

### (G-3210)
**PACKAGING PERSONIFIED INC (PA)**
246 Kehoe Blvd (60188-1816)
**PHONE**.....................630 653-1655
**Fax:** 630 653-0344
Dominic Imburgia, President
Dan Imburgia, General Mgr
Joe Imburgia, Plant Mgr
Glenn Rebsch, Plant Mgr
Lynne Ryan, Purchasing
**EMP:** 120
**SQ FT:** 100,000
**SALES (est):** 45.5MM Privately Held
**WEB:** www.packagingpersonified.com
**SIC:** 2673 Plastic bags: made from purchased materials

### (G-3211)
**PARVIN-CLAUSS SIGN CO INC**
165 Tubeway Dr (60188-2249)
**PHONE**.....................866 490-2877
**Fax:** 630 510-2074
Robert A Clauss, President
Cynthia Wiles, Business Mgr
Al Paprocki, Plant Mgr
John Bolger, Purchasing
Brian Davis, Sales Mgr
**EMP:** 42
**SQ FT:** 10,000
**SALES (est):** 7.3MM Privately Held
**WEB:** www.parvinclauss.com
**SIC:** 7389 3993 Sign painting & lettering shop; signs & advertising specialties

### (G-3212)
**PHOTO TECHNIQUES CORP**
399 Gundersen Dr (60188-2421)
**PHONE**.....................630 690-9360
Randy Johnson, Manager
**EMP:** 46
**SALES (corp-wide):** 4.8MM Privately Held
**WEB:** www.nptec.com
**SIC:** 2759 Screen printing
**PA:** Photo Techniques Corp.
387 Gundersen Dr
Carol Stream IL 60188
630 690-9360

### (G-3213)
**PHOTO TECHNIQUES CORP (PA)**
Also Called: Nameplate & Panel Technology
387 Gundersen Dr (60188-2421)
**PHONE**.....................630 690-9360
**Fax:** 630 690-9365
Lisa Savegnago, President
Randy Johnson, Vice Pres
Dave Savegnago, Vice Pres
Jeff Friedman, QC Mgr
Marybeth Racz, Administration
**EMP:** 45
**SQ FT:** 20,000
**SALES (est):** 4.8MM Privately Held
**WEB:** www.nptec.com
**SIC:** 3479 3083 2759 3993 Name plates: engraved, etched, etc.; laminated plastics plate & sheet; screen printing; signs & advertising specialties; packaging paper & plastics film, coated & laminated

### (G-3214)
**PIERCE & STEVENS CHEMICAL**
245 Kehoe Blvd (60188-1815)
**PHONE**.....................630 653-3800
**Fax:** 630 510-0927
**EMP:** 4 **EST:** 2010
**SALES (est):** 320K Privately Held
**SIC:** 2891 Mfg Adhesives/Sealants

### (G-3215)
**PREFERRED FASTENERS INC**
250 S Westgate Dr (60188-2243)
**PHONE**.....................630 510-0200
John Waichulis, President
Tony Waichulis, Plant Mgr
Don Bothwell, Purchasing
George Gora, Sales Staff
**EMP:** 5
**SQ FT:** 5,500
**SALES (est):** 852K Privately Held
**SIC:** 3451 5072 Screw machine products; bolts, nuts & screws

### (G-3216)
**PREMIER HEALTH CONCEPTS LLC**
780 W Army Trail Rd (60188-9297)
**PHONE**.....................630 575-1059
Michelle Bucaro, Marketing Mgr
Michael Gentile Jr,
▲ **EMP:** 5
**SALES (est):** 5MM Privately Held
**SIC:** 2833 Vitamins, natural or synthetic: bulk, uncompounded

### (G-3217)
**PRIME SYSTEMS INC**
Also Called: Prime Uv
416 Mission St (60188-9414)
**PHONE**.....................630 681-2100
Elinor Midlik, President
Elias Baer, Editor
Erich Rassow, Vice Pres
Bruce Foster, Engineer
Juliet Midlik, Regl Sales Mgr
▲ **EMP:** 45
**SQ FT:** 80,000
**SALES (est):** 8.9MM Privately Held
**WEB:** www.primeuv.com
**SIC:** 3826 Ultraviolet analytical instruments

### (G-3218)
**PRINCE CASTLE LLC (DH)**
355 Kehoe Blvd (60188-1833)
**PHONE**.....................630 462-8800
**Fax:** 630 462-9076
Randy Garvin, President
N L Terry, President
Michael Valentino, Principal
Jim Chapman, Vice Pres
Victor Palomino, Vice Pres
◆ **EMP:** 135
**SQ FT:** 187,500
**SALES:** 97.4MM
**SALES (corp-wide):** 223.6B Publicly Held
**WEB:** www.princecastle.com
**SIC:** 3589 Commercial cooking & food-warming equipment
**HQ:** Marmon Industrial Llc
181 W Madison St Fl 26
Chicago IL 60602
312 372-9500

### (G-3219)
**PRINCE FABRICATORS INC**
Also Called: Prince Fabricators Division
745 N Gary Ave (60188-1812)
**PHONE**.....................630 588-0088
Nancy Miller, President
Edward K Miller, Vice Pres
Bob Oriole, Opers Mgr
Bob Granger, Controller
Cara Andrea, Manager
**EMP:** 22
**SALES (est):** 3.5MM Privately Held
**SIC:** 3444 Sheet metal specialties, not stamped

### (G-3220)
**PRINCE INDUSTRIES INC (PA)**
Also Called: Prince Industries Shanghai
745 N Gary Ave (60188-1812)
**PHONE**.....................630 588-0088
Mark S Miller, CEO
Gregory W Roskuszka, President

## Carol Stream - Dupage County (G-3221)

Edward Miller, *Counsel*
Mark Paluch, *Vice Pres*
Kevin Koehler, *VP Opers*
▲ **EMP:** 185 **EST:** 1956
**SQ FT:** 65,000
**SALES (est):** 67.8MM **Privately Held**
**WEB:** www.princeind.com
**SIC:** 3545 Machine tool accessories

**(G-3221)**
**PRINOVA SOLUTIONS LLC**
285 Fullerton Ave (60188-1886)
**PHONE**..................630 868-0359
Donald K Thorp, *President*
Ronald E Juergens, *Vice Pres*
Daniel T Thorp, *Vice Pres*
Donald P Cepican, *CFO*
◆ **EMP:** 25
**SQ FT:** 25,000
**SALES (est):** 7.5MM
**SALES (corp-wide):** 217.9MM **Privately Held**
**SIC:** 2869 2099 Flavors or flavoring materials, synthetic; food preparations
**PA:** Prinova Group Llc
285 Fullerton Ave
Carol Stream IL 60188
630 868-0300

**(G-3222)**
**PROFESSNL MLING PRTG SVCS INC**
269 Commonwealth Dr (60188-2450)
**PHONE**..................630 510-1000
**Fax:** 630 510-1003
Jennifer Rawls, *CEO*
Samuel Bonafede, *President*
Tom Rawls, *General Mgr*
Adam Levine, *Sales Mgr*
**EMP:** 10
**SQ FT:** 12,000
**SALES:** 1MM **Privately Held**
**SIC:** 2752 7331 Commercial printing, lithographic; mailing service

**(G-3223)**
**PUBLISHERS GRAPHICS LLC (PA)**
140 Della Ct (60188-2200)
**PHONE**..................630 221-1850
**Fax:** 630 221-1870
Sheri Herring, *Project Mgr*
Catherine Hoffmann, *CFO*
Lisa Hendrickson, *Marketing Staff*
Nick A Lewis, *Mng Member*
**EMP:** 49
**SQ FT:** 10,000
**SALES (est):** 11.5MM **Privately Held**
**WEB:** www.pubgraphics.com
**SIC:** 2759 Commercial printing

**(G-3224)**
**Q-MATIC TECHNOLOGIES INC**
355 Kehoe Blvd (60188-1817)
**PHONE**..................847 263-7324
**Fax:** 847 263-7367
L Burtea, *General Mgr*
Sanda L Burtea, *Manager*
**EMP:** 9
**SQ FT:** 6,000
**SALES (est):** 1.7MM
**SALES (corp-wide):** 223.6B **Publicly Held**
**WEB:** www.q-maticovens.com
**SIC:** 3556 Food products machinery
**HQ:** Prince Castle Llc
355 Kehoe Blvd
Carol Stream IL 60188
630 462-8800

**(G-3225)**
**R D NIVEN & ASSOCIATES LTD**
955 Kimberly Dr (60188-1806)
**PHONE**..................630 580-6000
**Fax:** 630 580-5690
Don Hubbard, *President*
Bev Sampson, *President*
Jamie Zettlmeier, *President*
Fred Musnicki, *Senior VP*
Ken Vandermeulen, *Vice Pres*
▲ **EMP:** 50
**SQ FT:** 154,000
**SALES (est):** 9.6MM **Privately Held**
**WEB:** www.niven.net
**SIC:** 3993 Signs & advertising specialties

**(G-3226)**
**R T M PRECISION MACHINING INC**
739 Kimberly Dr (60188-9407)
**PHONE**..................630 595-0946
Stanislaw Tokarz, *President*
Henry Kuprinski, *Vice Pres*
Chris Tokarz, *Manager*
**EMP:** 4
**SQ FT:** 3,200
**SALES:** 500K **Privately Held**
**WEB:** www.rtmpm.com
**SIC:** 3541 Cutoff machines (metalworking machinery)

**(G-3227)**
**RAINBOW DUSTERS INTERNATIONAL**
135 E Saint Charles Rd F2 (60188-2078)
**PHONE**..................770 627-3575
Matt Lineberper, *President*
**EMP:** 4
**SALES (est):** 355.4K **Privately Held**
**SIC:** 5074 3991 Plumbing & hydronic heating supplies; brushes for vacuum cleaners, carpet sweepers, etc.

**(G-3228)**
**RICHARD OCHWAT SPECIALTY ENTP**
Also Called: Rose Limited International
385 S Schmale Rd (60188-2756)
**PHONE**..................630 682-0800
Richard Ochwat, *Partner*
Theodore Keyzis, *Partner*
**EMP:** 2
**SQ FT:** 2,500
**SALES (est):** 222.1K **Privately Held**
**SIC:** 5047 3269 Hospital equipment & supplies; medical equipment & supplies; stoneware pottery products

**(G-3229)**
**ROYAL DIE & STAMPING CO INC (HQ)**
125 Mercedes Dr (60188-9409)
**PHONE**..................630 766-2685
**Fax:** 630 766-0401
Henrik Freitag, *CEO*
Erik Freitag, *President*
Andres Vazquez, *Opers Mgr*
Karl Kimmel, *Materials Mgr*
Martha Rojas, *Mfg Staff*
▲ **EMP:** 145
**SQ FT:** 78,000
**SALES (est):** 32.8MM
**SALES (corp-wide):** 161.2MM **Privately Held**
**WEB:** www.royaldie.com
**SIC:** 3544 3469 Dies & die holders for metal cutting, forming, die casting; industrial molds; metal stampings
**PA:** Igp Industries, Llc
101 Mission St Ste 1500
San Francisco CA 94105
415 882-4550

**(G-3230)**
**RYESON CORPORATION (HQ)**
Also Called: Sturtvant Richmont Torque Pdts
555 Kimberly Dr (60188-1835)
**PHONE**..................847 455-8677
Raymond Reynertson, *President*
Edward J Lehner, *Exec VP*
Gene Lezaj, *Vice Pres*
Robert C J Klein, *CFO*
Ron Berg, *Manager*
▲ **EMP:** 55
**SQ FT:** 30,000
**SALES (est):** 9.3MM
**SALES (corp-wide):** 3.4B **Publicly Held**
**WEB:** www.srtorque.com
**SIC:** 3545 3423 3829 Measuring tools & machines, machinists' metalworking type; hand & edge tools; measuring & controlling devices
**PA:** Snap-On Incorporated
2801 80th St
Kenosha WI 53143
262 656-5200

**(G-3231)**
**SAINT-GOBAIN ABRASIVES INC**
Also Called: Superabrasives
200 Fullerton Ave (60188-1826)
**PHONE**..................630 238-3315
**Fax:** 630 238-3300
Bernard Courtmans, *Sales Mgr*
K Jang, *Sales Mgr*
Barbara CHI, *Regl Sales Mgr*
Mike Kornaus, *Manager*
**EMP:** 125
**SALES (corp-wide):** 185.8MM **Privately Held**
**WEB:** www.sgabrasives.com
**SIC:** 3291 Abrasive products
**HQ:** Saint-Gobain Abrasives, Inc.
1 New Bond St
Worcester MA 01606
508 795-5000

**(G-3232)**
**SAINT-GOBAIN ABRASIVES INC**
Also Called: Super-Cut Abrasives
200 Fullerton Ave (60188-1826)
**PHONE**..................630 868-8060
Urban Kurczek, *Marketing Staff*
Samuel H Odeh, *Branch Mgr*
Ted Christle, *Technology*
**EMP:** 169
**SALES (corp-wide):** 185.8MM **Privately Held**
**SIC:** 3291 3559 3545 Wheels, abrasive; coated abrasive products; sandpaper; concrete products machinery; diamond cutting tools for turning, boring, burnishing, etc.; dressers, abrasive wheel: diamond point or other
**HQ:** Saint-Gobain Abrasives, Inc.
1 New Bond St
Worcester MA 01606
508 795-5000

**(G-3233)**
**SAVEX MANUFACTURING COMPANY**
170 Easy St (60188-2314)
**PHONE**..................630 668-7219
**Fax:** 630 668-7289
George Wimpffen, *President*
Max Wimpffen, *General Mgr*
Eva Wimpffen, *Corp Secy*
**EMP:** 5
**SQ FT:** 12,000
**SALES (est):** 953.9K **Privately Held**
**WEB:** www.savex.us
**SIC:** 3841 Surgical & medical instruments

**(G-3234)**
**SCALE RAILROAD EQUIPMENT**
Also Called: All Nation Line Division
23w546 Saint Charles Rd (60188-2868)
**PHONE**..................630 682-9170
William Pope, *President*
Danny Pope, *Vice Pres*
**EMP:** 2
**SQ FT:** 1,900
**SALES (est):** 217K **Privately Held**
**SIC:** 3944 Railroad models: toy & hobby

**(G-3235)**
**SCALE-TRONIX INC**
Also Called: Factory Location
288 Carlton Dr (60188-2406)
P.O. Box 15, Wheaton (60187-0015)
**PHONE**..................630 653-3377
**Fax:** 630 653-3448
Mike Conroy, *Purchasing*
Don Winkleman, *Manager*
**EMP:** 14
**SALES (est):** 4.1MM **Privately Held**
**SIC:** 3545 5046 3842 3596 Scales, measuring (machinists' precision tools); scales, except laboratory; surgical appliances & supplies; scales & balances, except laboratory
**PA:** Scale-Tronix, Inc.
4341 State Street Rd
Skaneateles NY 13152
914 948-8117

**(G-3236)**
**SCHMOLZ BCKENBACH USA HOLDINGS**
365 Village Dr (60188-1828)
**PHONE**..................630 682-3900
**EMP:** 4
**SALES (est):** 249.7K
**SALES (corp-wide):** 26.2MM **Privately Held**
**SIC:** 3449 Miscellaneous metalwork
**HQ:** Ims Group Holding Gmbh
Eupener Str. 70
Dusseldorf 40549
211 509-2315

**(G-3237)**
**SEACO DATA SYSTEMS INC**
1360 Rolling Oaks Dr (60188-4606)
**PHONE**..................630 876-2169
Michael Wade, *President*
**EMP:** 70
**SALES (est):** 4MM **Privately Held**
**SIC:** 3679 Electronic components

**(G-3238)**
**SENSIO AMERICA LLC (PA)**
270 Tubeway Dr (60188-2214)
**PHONE**..................877 501-5337
Jeffrey Condrady, *CEO*
David Zinn, *President*
Terry Delong, *Vice Pres*
Adam Giordano, *Opers Mgr*
Gary Rutherford, *Director*
▲ **EMP:** 12
**SQ FT:** 7,000
**SALES:** 5.2MM **Privately Held**
**SIC:** 3648 Lighting equipment

**(G-3239)**
**SERAC INC (DH)**
160 E Elk Trl (60188-9300)
**PHONE**..................630 510-9343
**Fax:** 630 510-9357
Acyr Borges, *CEO*
Marc Binet, *President*
Andre Jj Graffin, *President*
Rudolph Jamrock, *Project Mgr*
Robert Niklinski, *Project Mgr*
▲ **EMP:** 40 **EST:** 1981
**SQ FT:** 40,000
**SALES (est):** 8.5MM **Privately Held**
**WEB:** www.serac-group.com
**SIC:** 3565 Packaging machinery
**HQ:** Serac Group
12 Route De Mamers
La Ferte Bernard 72400
243 602-828

**(G-3240)**
**SIEBER TOOL ENGINEERING LP**
344 Commerce Dr (60188-1809)
**PHONE**..................630 462-9370
**Fax:** 630 462-0143
Werner Gruse, *Manager*
**EMP:** 10
**SQ FT:** 10,800
**SALES (est):** 1.7MM
**SALES (corp-wide):** 5.6MM **Privately Held**
**WEB:** www.siebertool.com
**SIC:** 3545 5085 3544 3542 Cutting tools for machine tools; tools; special dies, tools, jigs & fixtures; machine tools, metal forming type
**PA:** Ergoseal, Inc.
346 Commerce Dr
Carol Stream IL 60188
630 462-9600

**(G-3241)**
**SOLID IMPRESSIONS INC**
26w455 Saint Charles Rd (60188-1942)
**PHONE**..................630 543-7300
**Fax:** 630 543-7313
John Mantia, *Mng Member*
Beth Gear, *Graphic Designe*
**EMP:** 5
**SQ FT:** 1,500
**SALES (est):** 864.6K **Privately Held**
**WEB:** www.solid-impressions.com
**SIC:** 2752 2791 Commercial printing, offset; typesetting

# GEOGRAPHIC SECTION
## Carol Stream - Dupage County (G-3267)

**(G-3242)**
**SONY ELECTRONICS INC**
1064 Idaho St (60188-1310)
PHONE..................630 773-7500
Catherine Wozney, *Manager*
**EMP:** 227
**SALES (corp-wide):** 66.9B **Privately Held**
**SIC:** 3651 Household audio & video equipment
**HQ:** Sony Electronics Inc.
16535 Via Esprillo Bldg 1
San Diego CA 92127
858 942-2400

**(G-3243)**
**SPECIALTY PUBLISHING COMPANY**
Also Called: Start Magazine
135 E Saint Charles Rd D (60188-2078)
PHONE..................630 933-0844
Fax: 630 933-0845
Peggy Smedley, *President*
Benoit Jouffrey, *Vice Pres*
David Smedley, *Vice Pres*
David Smedoey, *Vice Pres*
Lynne Flakus, *Social Dir*
**EMP:** 25
**SQ FT:** 8,000
**SALES (est):** 3.2MM **Privately Held**
**WEB:** www.specialtypub.com
**SIC:** 2721 Periodicals

**(G-3244)**
**SQUEEGEE BROTHERS INC (PA)**
398 E Saint Charles Rd (60188-2115)
PHONE..................630 510-9152
Jim Fruzyna, *President*
Joe Fruzyna, *Partner*
**EMP:** 10
**SALES (est):** 799.8K **Privately Held**
**SIC:** 2759 Commercial printing

**(G-3245)**
**STABILOC LLC**
Also Called: Swiveloc
545 Kimberly Dr (60188-1805)
PHONE..................586 412-1147
Jill Fata, *Accountant*
Thomas McClanaghan,
Jeff Webber, *Administration*
David Stadler,
**EMP:** 3
**SQ FT:** 2,000
**SALES (est):** 677.6K **Privately Held**
**WEB:** www.stabiloc.com
**SIC:** 3699 Security devices

**(G-3246)**
**STAND FAST GROUP LLC**
Also Called: Ipr Group
710 Kimberly Dr (60188-9406)
PHONE..................630 600-0900
Jim Cunningham, *CFO*
Joe Dimaggio, *Sales Staff*
Jay Carman, *Mng Member*
Keith Carman, *Admin Sec*
Jake Carman, *Training Spec*
**EMP:** 90
**SQ FT:** 17,000
**SALES:** 46MM **Privately Held**
**SIC:** 2653 Corrugated & solid fiber boxes
**PA:** Stand Fast Packaging Products Incorporated
710 Kimberly Dr
Carol Stream IL 60188
630 600-0900

**(G-3247)**
**STAND FAST PACKAGING PDTS INC (PA)**
710 Kimberly Dr (60188-9406)
PHONE..................630 600-0900
Fax: 630 543-6390
Jay Carman, *CEO*
Scott Carman, *President*
John Carman Jr, *Vice Pres*
Blerina Rakipaj, *Accountant*
Cheryl Wheeler, *Human Res Mgr*
**EMP:** 90
**SQ FT:** 100,000
**SALES (est):** 46MM **Privately Held**
**SIC:** 2653 Boxes, corrugated: made from purchased materials

**(G-3248)**
**STANDARD REGISTER INC**
150 E Saint Charles Rd A (60188-2052)
PHONE..................630 784-6810
Fax: 630 784-6934
Mike Reed, *Branch Mgr*
**EMP:** 150
**SALES (corp-wide):** 4.5B **Privately Held**
**WEB:** www.stdreg.com
**SIC:** 2761 Manifold business forms
**HQ:** Standard Register, Inc.
600 Albany St
Dayton OH 45417
937 221-1000

**(G-3249)**
**STANDEX INTERNATIONAL CORP**
Also Called: Mold-Tech Midwest
279 E Lies Rd (60188-9421)
PHONE..................630 588-0400
Matt Crost, *Branch Mgr*
**EMP:** 25
**SALES (corp-wide):** 751.5MM **Publicly Held**
**SIC:** 7389 3544 Engraving service; special dies, tools, jigs & fixtures
**PA:** Standex International Corporation
11 Keewaydin Dr
Salem NH 03079
603 893-9701

**(G-3250)**
**STEWARTS PRVATE BLEND FODS INC (PA)**
301 Carlton Dr (60188-2405)
PHONE..................773 489-2500
Fax: 773 489-2148
Donald Stwewart Jr, *President*
Robert Stewart, *Vice Pres*
Elita Pagan, *Prdtn Mgr*
Tom Waszikowski, *Sales Mgr*
Steve Blair, *Director*
**EMP:** 29 **EST:** 1913
**SQ FT:** 48,000
**SALES (est):** 5.6MM **Privately Held**
**SIC:** 2095 2099 Coffee roasting (except by wholesale grocers); tea blending

**(G-3251)**
**STORAGE BATTERY SYSTEMS LLC**
179 Easy St (60188-2314)
PHONE..................630 221-1700
Fax: 630 221-1701
Joseph Depola, *Principal*
Dennis Morriss, *Manager*
**EMP:** 8
**SALES (corp-wide):** 13.5MM **Privately Held**
**SIC:** 3691 3612 5063 Storage batteries; transformers, except electric; batteries
**PA:** Storage Battery Systems, Llc
N56w16665 Ridgewood Dr
Menomonee Falls WI 53051
262 703-5800

**(G-3252)**
**TEAM CNCEPT PRTG THRMGRPHY INC**
540 Tower Blvd (60188-9426)
PHONE..................630 653-8326
Fax: 630 653-9256
Anthony E Rouse, *President*
Jeff Howicz, *Vice Pres*
Vincent Minini, *Vice Pres*
**EMP:** 50
**SQ FT:** 25,000
**SALES (est):** 11.2MM **Privately Held**
**WEB:** www.teamconceptprinting.com
**SIC:** 2759 2752 Commercial printing; commercial printing, lithographic

**(G-3253)**
**TECHNOLOGY ONE WELDING INC**
210 Easy St Ste D (60188-3544)
PHONE..................630 871-1296
John Kotvan, *President*
▲ **EMP:** 4
**SQ FT:** 2,250
**SALES:** 500K **Privately Held**
**SIC:** 7692 Welding repair

**(G-3254)**
**TEMPO HOLDINGS INC (PA)**
Also Called: Tempo Graphics
455 E North Ave (60188-2123)
PHONE..................630 462-8200
Fax: 630 462-0350
Peter Vouros, *President*
Michael Palucci, *Corp Secy*
John McGough, *Vice Pres*
Kim Harden, *Plant Mgr*
**EMP:** 50
**SQ FT:** 102,000
**SALES (est):** 12.6MM **Privately Held**
**WEB:** www.tempographics.com
**SIC:** 2752 Commercial printing, offset

**(G-3255)**
**TITAN TOOL WORKS LLC**
615 Kimberly Dr (60188-9403)
P.O. Box 1130, Libertyville (60048-4130)
PHONE..................630 221-1080
Eric Chizzo, *Office Mgr*
David Bogetz, *Mng Member*
**EMP:** 11
**SALES (est):** 980.5K **Privately Held**
**SIC:** 7692 3599 Welding repair; machine shop, jobbing & repair

**(G-3256)**
**TODAY GOURMET FOODS ILL LLC**
1087 Country Glen Ln (60188-2931)
PHONE..................847 401-9192
Ronald Kalck, *Principal*
**EMP:** 3
**SALES (est):** 173.6K **Privately Held**
**SIC:** 2099 Food preparations

**(G-3257)**
**TYNDALE HOUSE PUBLISHERS INC (PA)**
351 Executive Dr (60188-2420)
P.O. Box 80, Wheaton (60187-0080)
PHONE..................630 668-8300
Fax: 630 668-9092
Mark D Taylor, *President*
Jeff Johnson, *COO*
Paul Mathews, *Exec VP*
Timothy Bensen, *Buyer*
Lyda Ellis, *Accountant*
◆ **EMP:** 181
**SQ FT:** 415,000
**SALES:** 73.5MM **Privately Held**
**WEB:** www.tyndale.com
**SIC:** 2731 Books: publishing only

**(G-3258)**
**TYNDALE HOUSE PUBLISHERS INC**
370 Executive Dr (60188-2420)
PHONE..................630 668-8300
David Ruba, *Manager*
**EMP:** 78
**SALES (corp-wide):** 73.5MM **Privately Held**
**SIC:** 2731 1541 Books: publishing only; industrial buildings & warehouses
**PA:** Tyndale House Publishers, Inc.
351 Executive Dr
Carol Stream IL 60188
630 668-8300

**(G-3259)**
**UNIFAB MFG INC**
450 Saint Paul Blvd (60188-4917)
PHONE..................630 682-8970
Fax: 630 682-8972
Tam Nguyen, *President*
**EMP:** 25
**SQ FT:** 1,000
**SALES (est):** 5.2MM **Privately Held**
**SIC:** 3444 Sheet metalwork

**(G-3260)**
**VALBRUNA STAINLESS INC**
370 Village Dr (60188-1828)
PHONE..................630 871-5524
Craig Hockings, *Branch Mgr*
**EMP:** 10
**SALES (corp-wide):** 602.2MM **Privately Held**
**WEB:** www.valbrunastainless.com
**SIC:** 3312 Blast furnaces & steel mills
**HQ:** Valbruna Stainless, Inc.
2400 Taylor St
Fort Wayne IN 46802
260 434-2800

**(G-3261)**
**VAXCEL INTERNATIONAL CO LTD**
121 E North Ave (60188-1400)
PHONE..................630 260-0067
C Chen, *President*
Richard Chen, *Exec VP*
Eric Haugh, *Manager*
▲ **EMP:** 50
**SALES (est):** 10.3MM **Privately Held**
**SIC:** 3645 5063 Residential lighting fixtures; lighting fixtures

**(G-3262)**
**VITAMINS INC**
315 Fullerton Ave (60188-1865)
PHONE..................773 483-4640
James F Carozza, *President*
**EMP:** 8
**SQ FT:** 6,900
**SALES (corp-wide):** 7.4MM **Privately Held**
**WEB:** www.vitamins.com
**SIC:** 2834 2833 2087 Vitamin preparations; medicinals & botanicals; flavoring extracts & syrups
**PA:** Vitamins, Inc.
315 Fullerton Ave
Carol Stream IL 60188

**(G-3263)**
**WALEGA PRECISION COMPANY INC**
205 Kehoe Blvd Ste 3 (60188-1897)
PHONE..................630 682-5000
Adam Walega, *President*
Jennifer Walega, *Admin Sec*
**EMP:** 6
**SQ FT:** 5,000
**SALES (est):** 610K **Privately Held**
**SIC:** 3541 Machine tool replacement & repair parts, metal cutting types

**(G-3264)**
**WAVES FLUID SOLUTIONS LLC**
350 S Schmale Rd Ste 17 (60188-2794)
PHONE..................630 765-7533
Sherry Ramzy, *Mng Member*
Bishoy Tanyous,
**EMP:** 5
**SQ FT:** 1,000
**SALES:** 750K **Privately Held**
**SIC:** 5085 3621 3443 3561 Seals, industrial; industrial fittings; electric motor & generator parts; heat exchangers, condensers & components; industrial pumps & parts; filters, general line: industrial; industrial valves

**(G-3265)**
**WEATHERTOP WOODCRAFT**
26w282 Macarthur Ave (60188-2266)
Dick Malacek, *Owner*
**EMP:** 3
**SALES (est):** 260.3K **Privately Held**
**WEB:** www.weathertop.net
**SIC:** 5092 3993 3231 2499 Toys & hobby goods & supplies; signs & advertising specialties; products of purchased glass; wood products

**(G-3266)**
**WESTROCK CP LLC**
450 E North Ave (60188-2130)
PHONE..................630 384-5200
Michael Streny, *Manager*
James Mackowski, *Manager*
Sueann Daniels, *Comp Lab Dir*
**EMP:** 100
**SALES (corp-wide):** 14.1B **Publicly Held**
**SIC:** 2653 Boxes, corrugated: made from purchased materials
**HQ:** Westrock Cp, Llc
504 Thrasher St
Norcross GA 30071

**(G-3267)**
**WESTROCK CP LLC**
450 E North Ave (60188-2130)
PHONE..................630 260-3500
Joe Leblanc, *Manager*

## Carol Stream - Dupage County (G-3268)

**EMP:** 70
**SALES (corp-wide):** 14.1B **Publicly Held**
**WEB:** www.sto.com
**SIC:** 2631 Paperboard mills
**HQ:** Westrock Cp, Llc
504 Thrasher St
Norcross GA 30071

### (G-3268)
### WHEATON RESOURCE CORP
Also Called: Wheaton Brace
380 S Schmale Rd Ste 121 (60188-2790)
**PHONE** ............................... 630 690-5795
**Fax:** 630 690-8448
Catherine Chong, *President*
**EMP:** 5
**SALES (est):** 460K **Privately Held**
**SIC:** 5999 3842 Orthopedic & prosthesis applications; surgical appliances & supplies

### (G-3269)
### WOODWORKING UNLIMITED INC
23w450 Burdette Ave (60188-2144)
**PHONE** ............................... 630 469-7023
Sally Kennard, *President*
Angela Kovich, *Office Mgr*
**EMP:** 12
**SQ FT:** 5,000
**SALES:** 1.2MM **Privately Held**
**SIC:** 2541 1799 Cabinets, lockers & shelving; home/office interiors finishing, furnishing & remodeling; counter top installation

## Carpentersville
### Kane County

### (G-3270)
### A SCHULMAN INC
400 Maple Ave Ste A (60110-1978)
**PHONE** ............................... 847 426-3350
Raza Naseri, *Plant Mgr*
**EMP:** 40
**SALES (corp-wide):** 2.5B **Publicly Held**
**WEB:** www.ferro.com
**SIC:** 2821 Molding compounds, plastics
**PA:** A. Schulman, Inc.
3637 Ridgewood Rd
Fairlawn OH 44333
330 666-3751

### (G-3271)
### ACME INDUSTRIAL COMPANY
441 Maple Ave (60110-1939)
**PHONE** ............................... 847 428-3911
**Fax:** 847 428-1820
John W Evans, *President*
Megan Evans, *General Mgr*
Esther A Schron, *Chairman*
Gary Woytko, *Prdtn Mgr*
Bill Hauschild, *Facilities Mgr*
▼ **EMP:** 110
**SQ FT:** 30,000
**SALES (est):** 23.8MM
**SALES (corp-wide):** 79.8MM **Privately Held**
**WEB:** www.acmeindustrial.com
**SIC:** 3545 Drill bushings (drilling jig); precision measuring tools
**PA:** Jergens, Inc.
15700 S Waterloo Rd
Cleveland OH 44110
216 486-5540

### (G-3272)
### ADVANCED POLYMER ALLOYS LLC
400 Maple Ave Ste A (60110-1978)
**PHONE** ............................... 847 836-8119
E David Santoleri,
**EMP:** 5
**SALES (est):** 813.9K **Privately Held**
**WEB:** www.apainfo.com
**SIC:** 2822 Ethylene-propylene rubbers, EPDM polymers

### (G-3273)
### AMERICAN PRECISION MACHINE
845 Commerce Pkwy (60110-1721)
**PHONE** ............................... 847 428-5950
John Groth, *President*
Carol Johnson, *Office Mgr*
**EMP:** 11
**SQ FT:** 16,000
**SALES (est):** 1.5MM **Privately Held**
**SIC:** 3599 3451 Machine shop, jobbing & repair; screw machine products

### (G-3274)
### AMLING DONUTS INC
Also Called: Country Donuts
98 N Kennedy Dr (60110-1671)
**PHONE** ............................... 847 426-5327
**EMP:** 24
**SALES (corp-wide):** 29MM **Privately Held**
**SIC:** 2051 Bread, Cake, And Related Products
**PA:** Amling Donuts, Inc.
181 Virginia St
Crystal Lake IL 60014
815 455-2028

### (G-3275)
### AUTONETICS INC
425 Maple Ave (60110-1939)
**PHONE** ............................... 847 426-8525
**Fax:** 847 426-6951
Robert Trzaska, *President*
Stanley Trzaska, *Vice Pres*
Walter Cwik, *VP Opers*
Dave Edwards, *Purchasing*
Christine Trzaska, *Treasurer*
**EMP:** 10
**SQ FT:** 10,000
**SALES (est):** 1MM **Privately Held**
**WEB:** www.autoneticsinc.com
**SIC:** 3451 Screw machine products

### (G-3276)
### BLI LEGACY INC (PA)
1013 Tamarac Dr (60110-1967)
**PHONE** ............................... 847 428-6059
**Fax:** 847 428-7180
Brian M Kelly, *President*
David Nattrass, *Vice Pres*
Gary Nattrass, *Vice Pres*
Mike Sanchez, *Vice Pres*
Michael Sanchez, *VP Opers*
**EMP:** 25
**SQ FT:** 20,000
**SALES (est):** 23.5MM **Privately Held**
**WEB:** www.bulklift.com
**SIC:** 7389 3089 Packaging & labeling services; plastic containers, except foam

### (G-3277)
### BULK LIFT INTERNATIONAL LLC
Also Called: Right Bag On Time, The
1013 Tamarac Dr (60110-1967)
**PHONE** ............................... 847 428-6059
Brian M Kelly, *President*
**EMP:** 3 **EST:** 2015
**SALES (est):** 99.8K **Privately Held**
**SIC:** 2674 3443 5999 Shipping bags or sacks, including multiwall & heavy duty; liners/lining; packaging materials: boxes, padding, etc.

### (G-3278)
### CARPENTERSVILLE QUARRY INC
800 Bolz Rd (60110-1179)
**PHONE** ............................... 847 836-1550
Robert Pawelkl, *Manager*
Mike Frenzel, *Manager*
**EMP:** 14 **EST:** 2000
**SALES (est):** 2.4MM **Privately Held**
**SIC:** 1459 Clays (common) quarrying

### (G-3279)
### CASTER WAREHOUSE INC
1011 Tamarac Dr (60110-1967)
**PHONE** ............................... 847 836-5712
**Fax:** 847 836-5754
Bart Thomas, *Sales Associate*
Peter Im, *Branch Mgr*
Steve Angelastro, *Manager*
**EMP:** 15
**SALES (corp-wide):** 9.2MM **Privately Held**
**SIC:** 3562 3312 Casters; wheels
**PA:** Caster Warehouse, Inc.
4405 Business Park Ct Sw
Lilburn GA 30047
800 522-5998

### (G-3280)
### COATING METHODS INCORPORATED
853 Commerce Pkwy (60110-1721)
**PHONE** ............................... 847 428-8800
**Fax:** 847 428-8800
Chuck Rowe, *President*
**EMP:** 13
**SQ FT:** 15,000
**SALES (est):** 1.8MM **Privately Held**
**WEB:** www.coatingmethods.com
**SIC:** 3479 Painting of metal products

### (G-3281)
### CROSS CONTAINER CORPORATION
400 Maple Ave Ste B (60110-1978)
**PHONE** ............................... 847 844-3200
**Fax:** 847 844-3241
Gerald Matlock, *President*
Clark Beckway, *Sales Mgr*
Keith Chambers, *Accounts Mgr*
Ken Lima, *Sales Staff*
**EMP:** 50
**SQ FT:** 260,000
**SALES:** 10.5MM **Privately Held**
**SIC:** 2653 Boxes, corrugated: made from purchased materials

### (G-3282)
### DANA MOLDED
810 Commerce Pkwy (60110-1721)
**PHONE** ............................... 847 783-1800
David Hidding, *President*
**EMP:** 4
**SALES (est):** 460.5K **Privately Held**
**SIC:** 3089 Molding primary plastic

### (G-3283)
### DONALD KRANZ
Also Called: Cabcraft
10 W Main St Fl 1 (60110-1720)
**PHONE** ............................... 847 428-1616
**Fax:** 847 548-5199
Donald Kranz, *Owner*
**EMP:** 4
**SALES (est):** 183.8K **Privately Held**
**WEB:** www.cabcraft.com
**SIC:** 2434 2521 Wood kitchen cabinets; wood office furniture

### (G-3284)
### GARD ROGARD INC
250 Williams St (60110-1848)
**PHONE** ............................... 847 836-7700
Howard Klehm Sr, *President*
Sue Carsello, *Purch Agent*
Nancy Klehm, *Admin Sec*
**EMP:** 69
**SALES (est):** 5.4MM **Privately Held**
**SIC:** 2879 Agricultural chemicals

### (G-3285)
### GRAYHILL INC
459 Maple Ave (60110-1998)
**PHONE** ............................... 847 428-6990
**Fax:** 847 428-6038
Joseph Lamonica, *Plant Mgr*
Adam Tesch, *Production*
Jeff Goodmanson, *Branch Mgr*
Helen Roberts, *Supervisor*
**EMP:** 120
**SALES (corp-wide):** 160.6MM **Privately Held**
**WEB:** www.grayhill.com
**SIC:** 3679 3643 Electronic switches; current-carrying wiring devices
**PA:** Grayhill, Inc
561 W Hillgrove Ave
La Grange IL 60525
708 354-1040

### (G-3286)
### GROTH MANUFACTURING
845 Commerce Pkwy (60110-1721)
**PHONE** ............................... 847 428-5950
John Groth, *President*
Carol Johnson, *Office Mgr*
**EMP:** 31

**SALES (est):** 6.9MM **Privately Held**
**WEB:** www.grothmfg.com
**SIC:** 3451 Screw machine products

### (G-3287)
### I PULLOMA PAINTS
1 Day Ln (60110-1846)
**PHONE** ............................... 847 426-4140
**Fax:** 847 426-7467
Pulloma Kamdar, *President*
**EMP:** 10
**SALES (est):** 2MM **Privately Held**
**SIC:** 2851 Paints & allied products; lacquers, varnishes, enamels & other coatings

### (G-3288)
### ILLINOIS WOOD FIBER PRODUCTS
99 Day Ln (60110-1846)
**PHONE** ............................... 847 836-6176
**Fax:** 847 836-6176
Stephen Johansen, *President*
**EMP:** 4
**SQ FT:** 200
**SALES (est):** 330K **Privately Held**
**SIC:** 2499 Mulch, wood & bark

### (G-3289)
### JACK BEALL VERTICAL SERVICE IN
2085 Orchard Ln (60110-3337)
**PHONE** ............................... 847 426-7958
Jack Beall, *Principal*
**EMP:** 4
**SALES (est):** 308.7K **Privately Held**
**SIC:** 2591 Blinds vertical

### (G-3290)
### KDM ENTERPRISES LLC
820 Commerce Pkwy (60110-1721)
**PHONE** ............................... 877 591-9768
**Fax:** 847 783-0396
Joseph Marzullo, *CFO*
Newman Larry,
▲ **EMP:** 43 **EST:** 2000
**SQ FT:** 52,000
**SALES (est):** 26.3MM **Privately Held**
**SIC:** 2621 4731 Paper mills; freight transportation arrangement

### (G-3291)
### M & M EXPOSED AGGREGATE CO
Also Called: M & M Patio Stone Company
155 S Washington St (60110-2625)
**PHONE** ............................... 847 551-1818
**Fax:** 847 551-1836
Norman Mitchell Sr, *President*
Lester Mitchell, *Treasurer*
Robert Zutoft, *Sales Staff*
**EMP:** 6 **EST:** 1976
**SALES:** 380K **Privately Held**
**SIC:** 3272 3271 Furniture, garden: concrete; concrete products, precast; concrete block & brick; blocks, concrete: landscape or retaining wall

### (G-3292)
### NATION INC
400 Maple Ave Ste B (60110-1978)
**PHONE** ............................... 847 844-7300
Jerry Matlock, *President*
George B Craig, *General Mgr*
▲ **EMP:** 50
**SQ FT:** 60,000
**SALES (est):** 5MM **Privately Held**
**SIC:** 2653 2671 Boxes, corrugated: made from purchased materials; paper coated or laminated for packaging

### (G-3293)
### OXYTECH SYSTEMS INC
852 Commerce Pkwy (60110-1721)
**PHONE** ............................... 847 888-8611
Doug Hammer, *Partner*
John Dziedzic, *Partner*
Jack Karas, *Partner*
Richard Slosarski, *Sales Mgr*
Leo Caproni, *Sales Staff*
**EMP:** 10
**SALES (est):** 200K **Privately Held**
**WEB:** www.oxytechsystems.com
**SIC:** 3567 Infrared ovens, industrial

## GEOGRAPHIC SECTION

### Carthage - Hancock County (G-3317)

**(G-3294)**
**PERFORMANCE INDUSTRIES INC**
Also Called: Metal Substrates
20 Lake Marian Rd  (60110-1929)
PHONE..................972 393-6881
Mike Van Patten, *President*
**EMP:** 40
**SQ FT:** 75,000
**SALES (est):** 6.7MM **Privately Held**
**SIC:** 3441  Fabricated structural metal

**(G-3295)**
**PERFORMANCE STAMPING CO INC**
20 Lake Marian Rd  (60110-1929)
PHONE..................847 426-2233
**Fax:** 708 426-2368
David B Maxwell, *President*
Tim Marth, *COO*
W Jean Spencer, *Vice Pres*
Frank Fleming, *Engineer*
Dave Hallin, *Engineer*
▲ **EMP:** 50 EST: 1971
**SQ FT:** 75,000
**SALES (est):** 17MM **Privately Held**
**WEB:** www.performancestamping.com
**SIC:** 3469  3544  Stamping metal for the trade; special dies & tools

**(G-3296)**
**POLYNT COMPOSITES USA INC (DH)**
99 E Cottage Ave  (60110-1803)
PHONE..................847 428-2657
Rosario Valido, *CEO*
Kevin Brolsma, *General Mgr*
Scott Kaphingst, *General Mgr*
Sergio Conni, *Exec VP*
Chuck Doebler, *Plant Mgr*
▲ **EMP:** 120
**SALES (est):** 316.6MM
**SALES (corp-wide):** 423.9K **Privately Held**
**SIC:** 2821  Polyurethane resins; polyethylene resins

**(G-3297)**
**PRAIRIE STATE INDUSTRIES INC**
1009 Tamarac Dr  (60110-1967)
P.O. Box 1509, Batavia  (60510-6509)
PHONE..................847 428-3641
Alan Leard, *President*
Roxann Leard, *Vice Pres*
Michael Swanson, *Sales Staff*
Joanne Campbell, *Manager*
**EMP:** 10 EST: 1964
**SQ FT:** 26,000
**SALES (est):** 910K **Privately Held**
**SIC:** 3444  3496  3441  Casings, sheet metal; machine guards, sheet metal; miscellaneous fabricated wire products; fabricated structural metal

**(G-3298)**
**PRESS PROOF PRINTING**
180 S Western Ave  (60110-1738)
PHONE..................847 466-7156
Sante Furio, *President*
**EMP:** 2
**SALES (est):** 234.4K **Privately Held**
**SIC:** 2752  Commercial printing, lithographic

**(G-3299)**
**QUARTERS CONCESSIONS INC**
4064 Stratford Ln  (60110-3414)
PHONE..................847 343-4864
Tom Thebault, *Principal*
**EMP:** 3 EST: 2010
**SALES (est):** 296.3K **Privately Held**
**SIC:** 3131  Quarters

**(G-3300)**
**QUILTMASTER INC**
1 S Wisconsin St  (60110-2697)
PHONE..................847 426-6741
**Fax:** 847 426-6977
Raymond A Weishaar, *President*
Robert C Weishaar, *Vice Pres*
**EMP:** 35 EST: 1967
**SQ FT:** 20,000
**SALES (est):** 2.2MM **Privately Held**
**WEB:** www.quiltmaster.com
**SIC:** 2395  2392  Quilting & quilting supplies; quilted fabrics or cloth; quilting, for the trade; comforters & quilts: made from purchased materials; bedspreads & bed sets: made from purchased materials

**(G-3301)**
**REVCOR  INC (PA)**
251 Edwards Ave  (60110-1941)
PHONE..................847 428-4411
**Fax:** 847 426-4630
John Reichwein Jr, *CEO*
Lee Frick, *Vice Pres*
Craig Hall, *Vice Pres*
Paul Vogel, *Vice Pres*
Chuck Omalley, *Plant Mgr*
▲ **EMP:** 300
**SQ FT:** 80,000
**SALES (est):** 81.4MM **Privately Held**
**WEB:** www.revcor.com
**SIC:** 3564  3089  Blowers & fans; blowers & fans; injection molded finished plastic products

**(G-3302)**
**REVCOR INC**
250 Illinois St  (60110)
PHONE..................847 428-4411
John Reichwein, *CEO*
**EMP:** 1 EST: 2015
**SALES (est):** 210K **Privately Held**
**SIC:** 3564  3089  Blowers & fans; blowers & fans; injection molded finished plastic products

**(G-3303)**
**STANLEY MACHINING & TOOL CORP (PA)**
425 Maple Ave  (60110-1939)
PHONE..................847 426-4560
Stanley Trzaska, *CEO*
Krysyna Trzaska, *President*
Tony Beyer, *General Mgr*
Walter Cwik, *General Mgr*
Christopher Mikucki, *Plant Mgr*
▲ **EMP:** 95
**SQ FT:** 110,000
**SALES (est):** 31.9MM **Privately Held**
**WEB:** www.stanleymachining.com
**SIC:** 3599  Machine shop, jobbing & repair

**(G-3304)**
**VIDEO REFURBISHING SVCS INC**
Also Called: Inflight Entertainment Pdts
850 Commerce Pkwy  (60110-1721)
PHONE..................847 844-7366
Robert Hickey, *President*
James Shipley, *COO*
Richard Kuta, *QC Mgr*
Dan Olstinske, *Sales Dir*
Cheffjeff Malek, *Chief Mktg Ofcr*
◆ **EMP:** 20 EST: 2002
**SQ FT:** 7,510
**SALES (est):** 3.4MM **Privately Held**
**WEB:** www.videorefurbishing.com
**SIC:** 3728  Aircraft parts & equipment

### Carrier Mills
*Saline County*

**(G-3305)**
**AMY SCHUTT**
Also Called: Girls In The Garage
420 N Thompson St  (62917-1141)
PHONE..................618 994-7405
Amy Schutt, *Principal*
**EMP:** 3
**SALES (est):** 249.4K **Privately Held**
**SIC:** 7539  2759  Automotive repair shops; screen printing

**(G-3306)**
**CATERPILLAR GLOBL MIN AMER LLC**
Also Called: Caterpilar
9580 Highway 13 W  (62917-2013)
PHONE..................618 982-9000
Pat Higgins, *Manager*
**EMP:** 75
**SALES (corp-wide):** 38.5B **Publicly Held**
**SIC:** 3532  7629  Mining machinery; electrical repair shops
**HQ:** Caterpillar Global Mining America, Llc
2045 W Pike St
Houston PA 15342
724 743-1200

### Carrollton
*Greene County*

**(G-3307)**
**GREENE JERSEY SHOPPERS (PA)**
428 N Main St  (62016-1146)
PHONE..................217 942-3626
Albert Scott III, *Owner*
**EMP:** 9 EST: 1846
**SQ FT:** 2,000
**SALES (est):** 799.8K **Privately Held**
**WEB:** www.greendaily.com
**SIC:** 2711  Newspapers: publishing only, not printed on site

**(G-3308)**
**MARY MCHELLE WINERY VINYRD LLC**
Rr 2 Box 7a  (62016-9601)
PHONE..................217 942-6250
David C Nelson,
▲ **EMP:** 11
**SALES (est):** 1MM **Privately Held**
**WEB:** www.marymichellewinery.com
**SIC:** 2084  Wines

### Carterville
*Williamson County*

**(G-3309)**
**BEST DESIGNS  INC**
11521 Kevin Ln  (62918-3384)
PHONE..................618 985-4445
Mark Shasteen, *CEO*
Rona Shasteen, *President*
Lyndon Forby, *COO*
Joan Shasteen, *Vice Pres*
**EMP:** 18
**SQ FT:** 1,000
**SALES (est):** 2.9MM **Privately Held**
**WEB:** www.amerseal.com
**SIC:** 3011  Tire sundries or tire repair materials, rubber

**(G-3310)**
**CARTERVILLE COURIER**
122 S Division St  (62918-1478)
PHONE..................618 985-6187
Devin Miller, *Principal*
**EMP:** 5
**SALES (est):** 176.7K **Privately Held**
**SIC:** 2711  Newspapers

**(G-3311)**
**CELLAR  LLC (PA)**
Also Called: Walker's Bluff
326 Vermont Rd  (62918-3105)
PHONE..................618 956-9900
**EMP:** 4
**SALES (est):** 585.1K **Privately Held**
**SIC:** 2084  Wines

### Carthage
*Hancock County*

**(G-3312)**
**COKEL WELDING SHOP**
117 S Madison St  (62321-1332)
PHONE..................217 357-3312
Lawrence Cokel, *Owner*
Richard Cokel, *Co-Owner*
**EMP:** 7
**SALES:** 100K **Privately Held**
**SIC:** 7692  1799  Welding repair; welding on site

**(G-3313)**
**DEMOCRAT COMPANY CORP**
Also Called: Hancock County Journal-Pilot
31 N Washington St  (62321-1450)
P.O. Box 478  (62321-0478)
PHONE..................217 357-2149
**Fax:** 217 357-2177
Mark Smidt, *Manager*
**EMP:** 6
**SALES (corp-wide):** 220.6MM **Privately Held**
**WEB:** www.dailydem.com
**SIC:** 2711  Commercial printing & newspaper publishing combined
**HQ:** The Democrat Company Corp
1226 Avenue H
Fort Madison IA 52627
319 372-6421

**(G-3314)**
**GARY GRIMM & ASSOCIATES INC**
1204 Buchanan St  (62321-1510)
P.O. Box 378  (62321-0378)
PHONE..................217 357-3401
**Fax:** 217 357-6763
Gary Grimm, *President*
Phoebe Wear, *Vice Pres*
Donna Hills, *Accountant*
Sandy Kleopfer, *Manager*
▲ **EMP:** 9
**SALES (est):** 600K **Privately Held**
**SIC:** 2731  2721  Book publishing; magazines: publishing only, not printed on site

**(G-3315)**
**MERRITT FARM EQUIPMENT INC**
Also Called: Merritt Rv
1875 E County Road 2000 N  (62321-3023)
PHONE..................217 746-5331
Richard Merritt, *President*
Marlena Siverly, *Corp Secy*
**EMP:** 6
**SQ FT:** 6,100
**SALES (est):** 1.3MM **Privately Held**
**SIC:** 5561  7538  7692  Recreational vehicle dealers; recreational vehicle parts & accessories; recreational vehicle repairs; welding repair

**(G-3316)**
**METHODE ELECTRONICS INC**
Automotive Electronic Controls
111 W Buchanan St  (62321-1250)
P.O. Box 130  (62321-0130)
PHONE..................217 357-3941
**Fax:** 217 357-6200
William Jensen, *Exec VP*
Dave Wessel, *Plant Mgr*
Bill Green, *Mfg Staff*
Doug Scott, *Purchasing*
Doug Dougherty, *Engineer*
**EMP:** 1500
**SQ FT:** 30,000
**SALES (corp-wide):** 809.1MM **Publicly Held**
**WEB:** www.methode.com
**SIC:** 3678  3714  3643  3625  Electronic connectors; motor vehicle parts & accessories; current-carrying wiring devices; relays & industrial controls; switchgear & switchboard apparatus
**PA:** Methode Electronics, Inc
7401 W Wilson Ave
Chicago IL 60706
708 867-6777

**(G-3317)**
**MORTON BUILDINGS  INC**
1825 E Us Highway 136  (62321-3540)
P.O. Box 318  (62321-0318)
PHONE..................217 357-3713
**Fax:** 217 357-2143
Jim Hills, *Manager*
**EMP:** 9
**SALES (corp-wide):** 499.4MM **Privately Held**
**WEB:** www.mortonbuildings.com
**SIC:** 3448  5039  Prefabricated metal buildings; prefabricated structures
**PA:** Morton Buildings, Inc.
252 W Adams St
Morton IL 61550
800 447-7436

## Carthage - Hancock County (G-3318)

**(G-3318)**
**NORTHERN ILLINOIS GAS COMPANY**
Also Called: Nicor Gas
1375 Buchanan St (62321-1574)
PHONE..................217 357-3105
Fax: 217 357-3752
David Schoff, *Branch Mgr*
**EMP:** 12
**SALES (corp-wide):** 19.9B **Publicly Held**
**WEB:** www.nicor.com
**SIC:** 4924 1382 4923 Natural gas distribution; oil & gas exploration services; gas transmission & distribution
**HQ:** Northern Illinois Gas Company
1844 W Ferry Rd
Naperville IL 60563
630 983-8676

**(G-3319)**
**WEBER MEAT INC**
515 Miller St (62321-1126)
PHONE..................217 357-2130
Julie Weber, *Principal*
**EMP:** 3
**SALES (est):** 156.1K **Privately Held**
**SIC:** 5421 2011 Meat markets, including freezer provisioners; meat packing plants

## Cary
### Mchenry County

**(G-3320)**
**A B KELLY INC**
212 W Main St Ste 5 (60013-2769)
PHONE..................847 639-1022
Fax: 847 639-1063
William Braun, *President*
Jamie Garcia, *Vice Pres*
Patrice Beck, *Admin Sec*
**EMP:** 5
**SALES:** 198K **Privately Held**
**SIC:** 2391 3081 7641 2394 Curtains & draperies; vinyl film & sheet; reupholstery & furniture repair; upholstery work; re-upholstery; canvas & related products

**(G-3321)**
**ACCURATE RADIATION SHIELDING**
206 Cleveland St (60013-2971)
PHONE..................847 639-5533
Fax: 847 639-2088
Blake Denker, *President*
Joseph Pesce, *Vice Pres*
Michelle Rivelli, *Office Mgr*
**EMP:** 7
**SQ FT:** 22,000
**SALES (est):** 1MM **Privately Held**
**WEB:** www.accurateshield.com
**SIC:** 3842 5047 Radiation shielding aprons, gloves, sheeting, etc.; hospital equipment & supplies

**(G-3322)**
**ACTION PUMP CO**
170 Chicago St (60013-2948)
PHONE..................847 516-3636
Fax: 847 516-0033
Robert M Barrett, *President*
Marty Barrett, *Vice Pres*
Rick Newtson, *Director*
Mary Ann Barrett, *Admin Sec*
▲ **EMP:** 15
**SQ FT:** 17,000
**SALES (est):** 4.5MM **Privately Held**
**WEB:** www.actionpump.com
**SIC:** 3561 Pumps & pumping equipment

**(G-3323)**
**AEROSTARS INC**
6413 Kingsbridge Dr (60013-1485)
P.O. Box 962 (60013-0962)
PHONE..................847 736-8171
David Monroe, *Corp Secy*
**EMP:** 3
**SALES:** 90K **Privately Held**
**SIC:** 3721 Aircraft

**(G-3324)**
**AIRGUN DESIGNS USA INC**
401 Florine Ct (60013-1501)
PHONE..................847 520-7507
David Zupan, *President*
Marcia Purse, *Office Mgr*
**EMP:** 5
**SQ FT:** 2,000
**SALES (est):** 494.5K **Privately Held**
**WEB:** www.airgun.com
**SIC:** 3944 5941 5091 Air rifles, toy; sporting goods & bicycle shops; firearms, sporting

**(G-3325)**
**AMPAC FLEXICON LLC (DH)**
Also Called: Ampac Flexibles
165 Chicago St (60013-2948)
PHONE..................847 639-3530
Fax: 847 639-6828
Cathy Lebron, *Accounts Mgr*
Ken Seperack, *Marketing Staff*
Renee Flinton, *Manager*
Brian Scampini, *Director*
▲ **EMP:** 72 **EST:** 2004
**SQ FT:** 58,000
**SALES (est):** 13.4MM
**SALES (corp-wide):** 1.3B **Privately Held**
**WEB:** www.flexiconinc.net
**SIC:** 2671 Plastic film, coated or laminated for packaging; paper coated or laminated for packaging
**HQ:** Ampac Holdings, Llc
12025 Tricon Rd
Cincinnati OH 45246
513 671-1777

**(G-3326)**
**AMPAC HOLDINGS LLC**
165 Chicago St (60013-2948)
PHONE..................847 639-3530
**EMP:** 16
**SALES (corp-wide):** 1.3B **Privately Held**
**SIC:** 2673 Plastic bags: made from purchased materials
**HQ:** Ampac Holdings, Llc
12025 Tricon Rd
Cincinnati OH 45246
513 671-1777

**(G-3327)**
**APTARGROUP INC**
Aptar Cary
1160 Silver Lake Rd (60013-1658)
PHONE..................847 639-2124
Joe Heinlein, *Vice Pres*
John Washabaugh, *Plant Mgr*
Jon Werner, *Project Mgr*
Steve Shaffer, *Engineer*
Shyam Kotak, *Accounts Mgr*
**EMP:** 400
**SALES (corp-wide):** 2.3B **Publicly Held**
**SIC:** 3499 3561 3491 Aerosol valves, metal; pumps & pumping equipment; industrial valves
**PA:** Aptargroup, Inc.
475 W Terra Cotta Ave E
Crystal Lake IL 60014
815 477-0424

**(G-3328)**
**BFW COATING**
740 Industrial Dr Ste G (60013-3373)
PHONE..................847 639-2155
Bill Wilson, *Owner*
**EMP:** 2
**SALES (est):** 275.6K **Privately Held**
**SIC:** 3089 Plastics products

**(G-3329)**
**C & B SERVICES**
6305 Lake Shore Dr (60013-1267)
PHONE..................847 462-8484
Cassandra Booker, *Owner*
**EMP:** 4
**SALES (est):** 214K **Privately Held**
**SIC:** 3679 7389 Electronic components;

**(G-3330)**
**CHIRCH GLOBAL MFG LLC**
Also Called: H F K
320 Cary Point Dr (60013-2973)
PHONE..................815 385-5600
Anthony L Chirchcirillo,
**EMP:** 15
**SQ FT:** 72,000
**SALES (est):** 5MM **Privately Held**
**WEB:** www.hfkmfg.com
**SIC:** 3469 3544 Metal stampings; die sets for metal stamping (presses)

**(G-3331)**
**CUSTOM CYLINDER INC**
700 Industrial Dr Ste I (60013-1950)
PHONE..................847 516-6467
Fax: 847 516-6470
Andrew A Durik, *President*
Pauline Vance, *Accounting Mgr*
Svitlana Melnykova, *Accountant*
**EMP:** 20
**SALES (est):** 4.4MM **Privately Held**
**WEB:** www.customcylinders.com
**SIC:** 3593 Fluid power cylinders, hydraulic or pneumatic

**(G-3332)**
**D M C MOLD & TOOL CORP**
740 Industrial Dr Ste H (60013-3373)
PHONE..................847 639-3098
Fax: 847 639-3285
Dustin Carlson, *President*
Virginia Carlson, *Vice Pres*
Steve Lazenby, *Opers Mgr*
Jason Franklin, *Engineer*
Leo Rivas, *Engineer*
**EMP:** 8
**SQ FT:** 4,500
**SALES (est):** 1.3MM **Privately Held**
**WEB:** www.dmcmold.com
**SIC:** 3544 Special dies, tools, jigs & fixtures

**(G-3333)**
**DEBORAH MORRIS GULBRANDSON PT**
Also Called: Cary Physcl Therapy Spt Rehab
2615 3 Oaks Rd Ste 1a (60013-6123)
PHONE..................847 639-4140
Fax: 847 516-8098
Deborah Gulbrandson, *President*
Sharon Stober, *Manager*
**EMP:** 12
**SALES (est):** 1MM **Privately Held**
**SIC:** 8049 3842 Physical therapist; surgical appliances & supplies

**(G-3334)**
**DECORE-ATIVE SPECIALTIES**
387 Oakmont Dr (60013-1179)
PHONE..................630 947-6294
Matthew Landvick, *Principal*
**EMP:** 314
**SALES (corp-wide):** 191MM **Privately Held**
**SIC:** 2431 Doors, wood
**PA:** Decore-Ative Specialties
2772 Peck Rd
Monrovia CA 91016
626 254-9191

**(G-3335)**
**DOD TECHNOLOGIES INC**
675 Industrial Dr (60013-1944)
PHONE..................815 788-5200
Daniel O'Donnell, *President*
Kathy Damato, *Manager*
▲ **EMP:** 8
**SQ FT:** 4,500
**SALES (est):** 3MM **Privately Held**
**WEB:** www.dodtec.com
**SIC:** 3829 Gas detectors

**(G-3336)**
**DURAFLEX INC**
765 Industrial Dr (60013-1918)
PHONE..................847 462-1007
Fax: 847 462-1450
Dean Dellacecca, *President*
Laura Hill, *Accounts Mgr*
Mark Saban, *Manager*
Dave Bernardini, *Technology*
Jenn Jones-Reynolds, *Data Proc Exec*
▲ **EMP:** 50
**SQ FT:** 22,000
**SALES (est):** 11MM **Privately Held**
**WEB:** www.duraflexinc.com
**SIC:** 3498 3599 3769 Pipe fittings, fabricated from purchased pipe; flexible metal hose, tubing & bellows; bellows, industrial: metal; bellows assemblies, missiles: metal

**(G-3337)**
**DUREX INDUSTRIES INC**
305 Cary Point Dr (60013-2974)
PHONE..................847 462-2706
Edward Hinz, *President*
**EMP:** 1
**SALES (est):** 823.1K **Privately Held**
**SIC:** 3567 Electrical furnaces, ovens & heating devices, exc. induction

**(G-3338)**
**DUREX INTERNATIONAL CORP**
Also Called: Durex Industries
190 Detroit St (60013-2979)
PHONE..................847 639-5600
Fax: 847 639-2199
Edward Hinz, *President*
Janet Jackson, *CFO*
Annette Porro, *Credit Mgr*
Terry Smith, *Regl Sales Mgr*
Randy Nelson, *Admin Sec*
▲ **EMP:** 225
**SQ FT:** 120,000
**SALES (est):** 73.3MM **Privately Held**
**WEB:** www.durexindustries.com
**SIC:** 3567 3829 3823 Electrical furnaces, ovens & heating devices, exc. induction; thermometers & temperature sensors; temperature measurement instruments, industrial

**(G-3339)**
**EXPERIMENTAL AIRCRAFT EXAMINER**
69 Mohawk St (60013-1877)
PHONE..................847 226-0777
Edward Finnegan, *Principal*
**EMP:** 3
**SALES (est):** 123.6K **Privately Held**
**SIC:** 2711 Newspapers, publishing & printing

**(G-3340)**
**FAST LANE APPLICATIONS LLC**
219 Fox St (60013-6110)
PHONE..................815 245-2145
Brian Lane, *President*
Kevin Lane, *President*
Danette Lane, *CFO*
**EMP:** 3 **EST:** 2012
**SALES (est):** 177K **Privately Held**
**SIC:** 7372 Business oriented computer software

**(G-3341)**
**FLOCON INC (PA)**
339 Cary Point Dr (60013-2974)
PHONE..................815 444-1500
Fax: 815 444-1501
Richard W Ballot, *CEO*
Patricia Ballot, *Vice Pres*
▲ **EMP:** 43
**SQ FT:** 35,000
**SALES (est):** 4.7MM **Privately Held**
**SIC:** 3491 Industrial valves

**(G-3342)**
**FLOTEK INC**
339 Cary Point Dr (60013-2974)
P.O. Box 609 (60013-0609)
PHONE..................815 943-6816
Ron Kieras, *Managing Dir*
**EMP:** 6
**SALES (est):** 1MM **Privately Held**
**SIC:** 3089 Injection molding of plastics

**(G-3343)**
**FUGIEL RAILROAD SUPPLY CORP**
700 Industrial Dr Ste E (60013-1950)
P.O. Box 158 (60013-0158)
PHONE..................847 516-6862
Fax: 847 516-7099
Kathleen Fugiel, *President*
Robert Fugiel, *Vice Pres*
Jason Hettermann, *VP Opers*
**EMP:** 5
**SALES (est):** 867.1K **Privately Held**
**WEB:** www.fugiel.com
**SIC:** 3743 5088 Railroad equipment; railroad equipment & supplies

**(G-3344)**
**GAGE GRINDING COMPANY INC (PA)**
40 Detroit St Unit D (60013-6605)
PHONE..................847 639-3888
Fax: 847 639-3988
Gary Fischer, *President*
**EMP:** 15 **EST:** 1961

# GEOGRAPHIC SECTION
## Cary - Mchenry County (G-3370)

SQ FT: 9,000
SALES (est): 1.9MM Privately Held
SIC: 3599 Machine shop, jobbing & repair

**(G-3345)**
**GALAXY INDUSTRIES INC**
231 Jandus Rd (60013-2861)
PHONE..........................847 639-8580
Joseph M Lebar, *Ch of Bd*
Kenneth Lebar, *Vice Pres*
Steve J Lebar, *Treasurer*
Martin J Lebar, *Admin Sec*
▲ EMP: 100
SQ FT: 55,000
SALES (est): 9.8MM Privately Held
WEB: www.galaxydrill.com
SIC: 5084 5082 3423 3545 Drilling equipment, excluding bits; drilling bits; tapping attachments; metalworking tools (such as drills, taps, dies, files); masonry equipment & supplies; masons' hand tools; drill bits, metalworking

**(G-3346)**
**GENERAL ASSEMBLY & MFG CORP**
750 Industrial Dr Ste B (60013-1988)
PHONE..........................847 516-6462
Fax: 847 516-7452
Paul A Tomaszek, *President*
Mike Hamby, *Corp Secy*
Rick Bursh, *Vice Pres*
Eva Walker, *Purchasing*
Kelly Brauch, *Manager*
EMP: 45
SQ FT: 30,000
SALES (est): 6.2MM Privately Held
WEB: www.generalassembly.com
SIC: 7389 3491 Packaging & labeling services; industrial valves

**(G-3347)**
**GENERAL LAMINATING COMPANY**
179 Northwest Hwy Ste 3 (60013-6601)
PHONE..........................847 639-8770
Fax: 847 639-8606
Don Cooper, *Owner*
EMP: 3
SQ FT: 5,000
SALES: 250K Privately Held
SIC: 2679 2672 Paperboard products, converted; cardboard: pasted, laminated, lined, or surface coated; coated & laminated paper

**(G-3348)**
**GLAMOX AQUA SIGNAL CORPORATION (DH)**
1125 Alexander Ct (60013-1892)
PHONE..........................847 639-6412
Jan Berner, *Ch of Bd*
Alena Heede, *President*
Jorg Koch-Losekamm, *Principal*
Greg Gibson, *Purch Mgr*
Kathy Jordan, *Accountant*
▲ EMP: 16
SQ FT: 20,300
SALES (est): 2.1MM
SALES (corp-wide): 758.2MM Privately Held
WEB: www.glamox.com
SIC: 3646 3647 Commercial indusl & institutional electric lighting fixtures; boat & ship lighting fixtures
HQ: Glamox Aqua Signal Gmbh
Von-Thunen-Str. 12
Bremen 28307
421 489-30

**(G-3349)**
**GLOBER MANUFACTURING COMPANY**
625 Spruce Tree Dr (60013-3144)
PHONE..........................847 829-4883
Richard P Glowacki, *Ch of Bd*
John M Glowacki, *Vice Pres*
Lori Baisden, *Office Mgr*
EMP: 12 EST: 1946
SQ FT: 3,050

SALES (est): 890K Privately Held
WEB: www.globerinc.com
SIC: 2514 2519 2511 Metal household furniture; furniture, household: glass, fiberglass & plastic; wood household furniture

**(G-3350)**
**HARTLAND CUTTING TOOLS INC**
240 Jandus Rd (60013-2862)
PHONE..........................847 639-9400
Fax: 847 639-7555
Mike Polizzi, *President*
Wendy Kanter, *Opers Mgr*
Rick Luchetti, *Manager*
EMP: 14
SQ FT: 14,000
SALES (est): 2.5MM Privately Held
WEB: www.hartlandtool.com
SIC: 3541 5084 3545 Machine tools, metal cutting type; industrial machinery & equipment; machine tool accessories

**(G-3351)**
**HORIZON STEEL TREATING INC**
Also Called: Trucut
231 Jandus Rd (60013-2861)
PHONE..........................847 639-4030
Joseph R Lebar, *President*
Steven J Lebar, *Admin Sec*
▲ EMP: 100
SQ FT: 10,000
SALES (est): 9.9MM Privately Held
SIC: 3398 Metal Heat Treating

**(G-3352)**
**ILLINOIS BLOWER INC**
Also Called: Ibi
750 Industrial Dr Ste E (60013-1988)
PHONE..........................847 639-5500
Fax: 847 639-9527
Tyler S Barth, *President*
Imtiaz Mohammed, *Business Mgr*
Craig Cummins, *Corp Secy*
Matt Fewell, *Project Mgr*
David Magart, *QC Mgr*
▲ EMP: 85
SQ FT: 75,000
SALES: 25MM Privately Held
WEB: www.illinoisblower.com
SIC: 3564 Blowing fans: industrial or commercial; exhaust fans: industrial or commercial; ventilating fans: industrial or commercial

**(G-3353)**
**ILLINOIS PRO-TURN INC**
309 Cary Point Dr Ste F (60013-2901)
PHONE..........................847 462-1870
Daniel Lamz, *President*
EMP: 8
SALES (est): 1.7MM Privately Held
SIC: 3089 Molding primary plastic

**(G-3354)**
**INSERTECH LLC (PA)**
711 Indl Dr (60013)
PHONE..........................847 516-6184
Fax: 847 516-6486
David Butt, *Mng Member*
Greg Vanicek, *Manager*
Robert Harney,
◆ EMP: 55
SQ FT: 30,000
SALES (est): 30.1MM Privately Held
WEB: www.insertech.net
SIC: 3089 Injection molding of plastics; plastic processing

**(G-3355)**
**INSERTECH INTERNATIONAL INC**
711 Industrial Dr (60013-1962)
PHONE..........................847 416-6184
EMP: 40
SALES (est): 5MM Privately Held
SIC: 3089 Injection molded finished plastic products

**(G-3356)**
**KOFLO CORPORATION**
309 Cary Point Dr Ste A (60013-2901)
PHONE..........................847 516-3700
Fax: 847 516-3724
James Federighi, *President*

Anthony Federighi, *Exec VP*
EMP: 10
SQ FT: 12,000
SALES (est): 2.3MM Privately Held
WEB: www.koflo.com
SIC: 3559 3531 Refinery, chemical processing & similar machinery; construction machinery

**(G-3357)**
**LGB INDUSTRIES**
91 Fairfield Ln (60013-1945)
P.O. Box 99 (60013-0099)
PHONE..........................847 639-1691
Fax: 847 459-8119
Larry G Bachner, *Owner*
EMP: 7
SQ FT: 2,000
SALES (est): 371.2K Privately Held
SIC: 3714 7515 Motor vehicle parts & accessories; passenger car leasing

**(G-3358)**
**LUXURY LIVING INC**
5 Tamarack Ct (60013-2469)
P.O. Box 3622, Barrington (60011-3622)
PHONE..........................847 845-3863
Diane Pawelko, *President*
Edmund Pawelko, *CFO*
▲ EMP: 6
SALES (est): 600K Privately Held
SIC: 3999 Pet supplies

**(G-3359)**
**MASTER CABINETS**
209 Cleveland St Ste D (60013-2978)
PHONE..........................847 639-1323
Johann Merkhofer, *Owner*
EMP: 3
SALES (est): 90K Privately Held
SIC: 2431 2511 2434 Millwork; wood household furniture; wood kitchen cabinets

**(G-3360)**
**MITCHELL ARCFT EXPENDABLES LLC**
1160 Alexander Ct (60013-1892)
PHONE..........................847 516-3773
Craig Cero, *VP Finance*
Terri Wood, *Accounting Mgr*
EMP: 47 EST: 1996
SALES: 10.8MM Privately Held
SIC: 3721 Aircraft

**(G-3361)**
**MULTIMAIL SOLUTIONS**
700 Industrial Dr (60013-1957)
PHONE..........................847 516-9977
Douglas Conte, *Principal*
EMP: 3
SALES (est): 217.1K Privately Held
SIC: 3579 Mailing machines

**(G-3362)**
**NORSKOBOK PRESS**
7001 Owl Way (60013-6029)
PHONE..........................847 516-0085
L Schwartz, *Principal*
EMP: 4
SALES (est): 195.8K Privately Held
SIC: 2741 Miscellaneous publishing

**(G-3363)**
**PFIZER INC**
2323 Grove Ln (60013-2830)
PHONE..........................847 639-3020
Liz Boern, *Branch Mgr*
EMP: 52
SALES (corp-wide): 52.8B Publicly Held
WEB: www.pfizer.com
SIC: 2879 Fungicides, herbicides
PA: Pfizer Inc.
235 E 42nd St
New York NY 10017
212 733-2323

**(G-3364)**
**PLASPROS INC**
511 Cove Dr (60013-6307)
PHONE..........................847 639-6492
Sherry L Hull, *Principal*
EMP: 5
SALES (est): 277.5K Privately Held
SIC: 3089 Plastics products

**(G-3365)**
**RAMCO TOOL & MANUFACTURING**
760 Industrial Dr Ste I (60013-1989)
PHONE..........................847 639-9899
Fax: 847 639-9904
Don M Beene Jr, *President*
Don M Beene Sr, *Treasurer*
Shirley Beene, *Admin Sec*
EMP: 10 EST: 1964
SQ FT: 6,000
SALES (est): 1.6MM Privately Held
WEB: www.ramcomachine.com
SIC: 3599 Machine shop, jobbing & repair

**(G-3366)**
**RENNER & CO**
160 Chicago St (60013-2948)
PHONE..........................847 639-4900
Fax: 847 639-4910
James W Renner, *President*
Robert A Renner, *Corp Secy*
EMP: 10 EST: 1933
SQ FT: 13,500
SALES (est): 1MM Privately Held
SIC: 3499 Novelties & specialties, metal

**(G-3367)**
**RESTORATIONS UNLIMITED II INC**
304 Jandus Rd (60013-3002)
PHONE..........................847 639-5818
Ralph Morey, *President*
EMP: 4
SQ FT: 4,000
SALES: 200K Privately Held
WEB: www.ru2inc.com
SIC: 7532 3711 Antique & classic automobile restoration; automobile assembly, including specialty automobiles

**(G-3368)**
**RIVERSHORE PRESS**
24762 N River Shore Dr (60013-9721)
PHONE..........................847 516-8105
Fax: 847 516-8135
William Wegner, *President*
Melissa Wegner, *Vice Pres*
EMP: 2
SQ FT: 1,800
SALES: 225K Privately Held
SIC: 2752 Commercial printing, lithographic; offset & photolithographic printing

**(G-3369)**
**ROSS AND WHITE COMPANY**
1090 Alexander Ct (60013-1890)
P.O. Box 970 (60013-0970)
PHONE..........................847 516-3900
Fax: 847 516-3989
Jeffrey A Ross, *President*
Roy A Schuetz, *Vice Pres*
Michael J Holzer, *Marketing Staff*
EMP: 15 EST: 1933
SQ FT: 20,000
SALES (est): 3.4MM Privately Held
WEB: www.rossandwhite.com
SIC: 3589 3582 3443 High pressure cleaning equipment; commercial laundry equipment; fabricated plate work (boiler shop)

**(G-3370)**
**SAGE PRODUCTS LLC (HQ)**
3909 3 Oaks Rd (60013-1804)
PHONE..........................815 455-4700
Scott Brown, *President*
Eric Cunningham, *Vice Pres*
Paul H Hanifl, *Vice Pres*
Alan McCandless, *Vice Pres*
Richard Napponelli, *Vice Pres*
◆ EMP: 277
SQ FT: 620,000
SALES (est): 147.5MM
SALES (corp-wide): 11.3B Publicly Held
WEB: www.sageproducts.com
SIC: 3842 5047 Surgical appliances & supplies; medical & hospital equipment
PA: Stryker Corporation
2825 Airview Blvd
Portage MI 49002
269 385-2600

## Cary - Mchenry County (G-3371)

**GEOGRAPHIC SECTION**

**(G-3371)**
**SIGNX CO INC**
508 Cary Algonquin Rd (60013-6712)
PHONE .................... 847 639-7917
Fax: 847 639-5231
Edward D Synek, *President*
EMP: 6
SALES (est): 440K **Privately Held**
WEB: www.signx.com
SIC: 3993 Signs & advertising specialties

**(G-3372)**
**SPEED TECH TECHNOLOGY INC**
314 Cary Point Dr (60013-2975)
PHONE .................... 847 516-2001
John Mykytiuk, *President*
William Mykytiuk, *Vice Pres*
Lilian Mykytiuk, *Admin Sec*
EMP: 9
SQ FT: 8,000
SALES (est): 790K **Privately Held**
SIC: 3519 5013 Gasoline engines; automotive engines & engine parts

**(G-3373)**
**SPOTLIGHT YOUTH THEATER**
755 Industrial Dr (60013-1962)
PHONE .................... 847 516-2298
Darlene Panko, *Managing Dir*
Carolyn Sibley, *Principal*
Miriam Masey, *Mktg Dir*
EMP: 8
SALES (est): 1MM **Privately Held**
SIC: 3648 Spotlights

**(G-3374)**
**T D J GROUP INC**
760 Industrial Dr Ste A (60013-1989)
PHONE .................... 847 639-1113
Fax: 847 639-3867
Redmond R Clark PHD, *President*
Robert Burton, *Vice Pres*
Mary Harvey, *Manager*
EMP: 9
SQ FT: 20,000
SALES (est): 1MM **Privately Held**
WEB: www.blastox.com
SIC: 2899 5169 8732 Chemical supplies for foundries; chemicals, industrial & heavy; research services, except laboratory

**(G-3375)**
**TADD LLC**
Also Called: Light Efficient Design
188 Northwest Hwy Ste 301 (60013-2987)
PHONE .................... 847 380-3540
Tim Taylor, *Owner*
Mary Didier, *Opers Mgr*
Daniel Taylor, *Regl Sales Mgr*
Michael Benz, *VP Mktg*
Jon Fredrikson, *Marketing Staff*
▲ EMP: 12
SALES (est): 8.1MM **Privately Held**
SIC: 3229 Bulbs for electric lights

**(G-3376)**
**TECHNIMOLD TOOL CORPORATION**
500 Cary Algonquin Rd # 1 (60013-2095)
PHONE .................... 847 639-4226
Fax: 847 639-4242
Dennis Crounse, *President*
EMP: 12
SQ FT: 13,000
SALES (est): 1.2MM **Privately Held**
SIC: 3089 Injection molding of plastics

**(G-3377)**
**TRU-CUT INC**
231 Jandus Rd (60013-2861)
PHONE .................... 847 639-2090
Fax: 847 639-1981
Kenneth W Lebar, *President*
Steve J Lebar, *Vice Pres*
Pat Ritschke, *Purch Agent*
Joseph A Lebar, *Treasurer*
Steve Conrad, *Info Tech Mgr*
▲ EMP: 60
SQ FT: 55,000
SALES (est): 9.6MM **Privately Held**
WEB: www.trucutmfg.com
SIC: 3545 3546 Drill bits, metalworking; power-driven handtools

**(G-3378)**
**TRUE VALUE COMPANY**
201 Jandus Rd (60013-2861)
PHONE .................... 847 639-5383
Allen Mangrum, *Safety Mgr*
Robert Marlewski, *Opers Staff*
William Caprel, *Purch Mgr*
Susan Henkel, *Purch Agent*
Aybars Gultekin, *Engineer*
EMP: 5
SALES (corp-wide): 1.5B **Privately Held**
SIC: 5072 2851 3991 Hardware; paints & paint additives; paint & varnish brushes
PA: True Value Company
 8600 W Bryn Mawr Ave 100s
 Chicago IL 60631
 773 695-5000

**(G-3379)**
**XACT WIRE EDM CORP**
720 Industrial Dr Ste 126 (60013-1992)
PHONE .................... 847 516-0903
Fax: 847 516-1287
Noel Rivera, *Project Engr*
Jason Mueller, *Manager*
Jason Mueler, *Manager*
Joe Soyer, *Manager*
EMP: 11
SALES (corp-wide): 7.3MM **Privately Held**
WEB: www.xactedm.com
SIC: 3599 Electrical discharge machining (EDM)
PA: Xact Wire E.D.M., Corp.
 N8w22399 Johnson Dr
 Waukesha WI 53186
 262 549-9005

## Casey
### Clark County

**(G-3380)**
**ASHLEY OIL CO**
508 Deere Run Ln (62420-1936)
P.O. Box 486 (62420-0486)
PHONE .................... 217 932-2112
Wilford Ashley, *President*
EMP: 3
SALES (est): 346.2K **Privately Held**
SIC: 1311 Crude petroleum production

**(G-3381)**
**CHARLES INDUSTRIES LTD**
Charles Marine Products
400 Se 8th St (62420-2054)
PHONE .................... 217 932-2068
Fax: 217 932-2003
Bob Miller, *Maint Spvr*
Larry Budd, *Engineer*
Trent Wallace, *Engineer*
Dave Cazzell, *Controller*
Terri Bishop, *Personnel*
EMP: 55
SALES (corp-wide): 132.1MM **Privately Held**
WEB: www.charlesmarine.com
SIC: 3661 3629 Telephones & telephone apparatus; battery chargers, rectifying or nonrotating
PA: Charles Industries, Ltd.
 5600 Apollo Dr
 Rolling Meadows IL 60008
 847 806-6300

**(G-3382)**
**CHARLES INDUSTRIES LTD**
503 Ne 15th St (62420-2174)
PHONE .................... 217 932-5294
Michael Henderson, *Plant Mgr*
Bob Miller, *Maint Spvr*
Tina Gard, *Purch Agent*
Shelly Garner, *Purch Agent*
Trent Wallace, *Engineer*
EMP: 57
SALES (corp-wide): 132.1MM **Privately Held**
WEB: www.charlesmarine.com
SIC: 3661 5065 3575 Telephones & telephone apparatus; telephone equipment; computer terminals, monitors & components
PA: Charles Industries, Ltd.
 5600 Apollo Dr
 Rolling Meadows IL 60008
 847 806-6300

**(G-3383)**
**GARVER INC**
10234 N 230th St (62420-3249)
PHONE .................... 217 932-2441
Jason Garver, *President*
Patricia Garver, *Treasurer*
EMP: 6
SALES (est): 927K **Privately Held**
WEB: www.garver.com
SIC: 0721 2434 Crop spraying services; wood kitchen cabinets

**(G-3384)**
**GOBLE MANUFACTURING INC**
704 W Main St (62420-1256)
PHONE .................... 217 932-5615
James Goble, *CEO*
EMP: 5
SALES (est): 569.7K **Privately Held**
SIC: 3999 Manufacturing industries

**(G-3385)**
**HORIZONTAL SYSTEMS INC**
14305 N State Highway 49 (62420-3041)
P.O. Box 277 (62420-0277)
PHONE .................... 217 932-6218
Fax: 217 932-6059
Doug Knierim, *President*
Jim Knierim, *President*
Jim Yates, *Vice Pres*
Deb Hawkins, *Manager*
EMP: 6
SQ FT: 7,500
SALES (est): 925.6K **Privately Held**
SIC: 1311 Crude petroleum production

**(G-3386)**
**HUTTON WELDING SERVICE INC**
11995 N 180th St (62420-3100)
PHONE .................... 217 932-5585
Fax: 217 932-5585
David S Hutton, *President*
Debby Hutton, *Admin Sec*
EMP: 2
SQ FT: 5,000
SALES (est): 441.9K **Privately Held**
SIC: 7692 Welding repair

**(G-3387)**
**L & J PRODUCERS INC**
3795 E 700th Rd (62420-3603)
PHONE .................... 217 932-5639
Terry Montgomery, *President*
Denice Whaley, *Admin Sec*
EMP: 2
SALES (est): 211.9K **Privately Held**
SIC: 1311 Crude petroleum & natural gas production

**(G-3388)**
**LEGACY VULCAN LLC**
Midwest Division
9129 N 230th St (62420)
P.O. Box 128 (62420-0128)
PHONE .................... 217 932-2611
Fax: 217 932-5265
Ron Sparks, *Manager*
Brian Hartke, *Manager*
Ron Shields, *Manager*
EMP: 12
SALES (corp-wide): 3.5B **Publicly Held**
WEB: www.vulcanmaterials.com
SIC: 1442 Construction sand & gravel
HQ: Legacy Vulcan, Llc
 1200 Urban Center Dr
 Vestavia AL 35242
 205 298-3000

**(G-3389)**
**MID ILLINOIS QUARRY COMPANY**
9129 N 230th St (62420)
P.O. Box 128 (62420-0128)
PHONE .................... 217 932-2611
Jeff Light, *Principal*
EMP: 3
SALES (est): 317.8K **Privately Held**
SIC: 1429 Slate, crushed & broken-quarrying

PA: Charles Industries, Ltd.
 5600 Apollo Dr
 Rolling Meadows IL 60008
 847 806-6300

**(G-3390)**
**MILLER FERTILIZER INC (PA)**
601 W Main St (62420-1257)
PHONE .................... 217 382-4241
Fax: 217 382-5724
Kim Fritts, *President*
Greg Keller, *Admin Sec*
EMP: 9
SQ FT: 600
SALES (est): 2.5MM **Privately Held**
SIC: 5191 2875 Fertilizer & fertilizer materials; fertilizers, mixing only

**(G-3391)**
**REPORTER INC (PA)**
216 S Central Ave (62420-1726)
P.O. Box 158 (62420-0158)
PHONE .................... 217 932-5211
Rickie Williams, *President*
Ken Wilmering, *President*
EMP: 21
SALES (est): 1.6MM **Privately Held**
SIC: 2711 Newspapers, publishing & printing

**(G-3392)**
**WESCOM PRODUCTS**
503 Ne 15th St (62420-2174)
PHONE .................... 217 932-5292
Mike Henderson, *Plant Mgr*
EMP: 5
SALES (est): 471K **Privately Held**
SIC: 3661 5065 Telephones & telephone apparatus; telephone & telegraphic equipment

## Caseyville
### St. Clair County

**(G-3393)**
**BELZONA GATEWAY INC**
8124 Bunkum Rd (62232-2104)
PHONE .................... 888 774-2984
Brian Portera, *Owner*
EMP: 3
SALES (est): 282.2K **Privately Held**
SIC: 2851 Shellac (protective coating)

**(G-3394)**
**BRECKENRIDGE MATERIAL COMPANY**
10 Tucker Dr (62232-2328)
PHONE .................... 618 398-4141
Jeb Santan, *Principal*
EMP: 28
SALES (corp-wide): 67.4MM **Privately Held**
SIC: 3273 Ready-mixed concrete
PA: Breckenridge Material Company
 2833 Breckenridge Ind Ct
 Saint Louis MO 63144
 314 962-1234

**(G-3395)**
**EAST SIDE TOOL & DIE CO INC**
2762 N 89th St (62232-2315)
PHONE .................... 618 397-1633
Fax: 618 398-1914
James Quinn, *President*
Joan Quinn, *Corp Secy*
Anthony T Quinn, *Vice Pres*
EMP: 10
SQ FT: 15,000
SALES (est): 1.3MM **Privately Held**
SIC: 3544 Special dies & tools

**(G-3396)**
**H & R TOOL & MACHINE CO**
19 W Scates St (62232-1549)
P.O. Box 450 (62232-0450)
PHONE .................... 618 344-7683
Fax: 618 344-7689
Gary Hollowich, *President*
EMP: 4 EST: 1961
SQ FT: 4,800
SALES: 289K **Privately Held**
SIC: 3599 3544 Machine shop, jobbing & repair; special dies, tools, jigs & fixtures

**(G-3397)**
**ILLINI CONCRETE INC**
10 Tucker Dr (62232-2328)
PHONE .................... 618 398-4141

GEOGRAPHIC SECTION
Centralia - Marion County (G-3420)

Jeb Santan, *Manager*
**EMP:** 5
**SALES (corp-wide):** 3.4MM **Privately Held**
**SIC:** 3273 Ready-mixed concrete
**PA:** Illini Concrete, Inc
1300 E A St
Belleville IL 62221
618 235-4141

*(G-3398)*
**JESSIS HIDEOUT**
421 S Main St (62232-1819)
**PHONE**..................................618 343-4346
**EMP:** 7
**SALES (est):** 469.5K **Privately Held**
**SIC:** 2064 5812 Candy bars, including chocolate covered bars; barbecue restaurant

*(G-3399)*
**JOSEPH D SMITHIES**
Also Called: Signs N Such
7409 N Illinois St (62232-2067)
**PHONE**..................................618 632-6141
**Fax:** 618 632-1967
Joseph Smithies, *Owner*
Joseph D Smithies, *Owner*
**EMP:** 3
**SALES:** 165K **Privately Held**
**SIC:** 3993 Signs & advertising specialties

*(G-3400)*
**PURE 111**
923 Far Oaks Dr (62232-2814)
**PHONE**..................................618 558-7888
Amy L Katsikas, *Principal*
**EMP:** 3
**SALES (est):** 161K **Privately Held**
**SIC:** 3231 Medical & laboratory glassware: made from purchased glass

## Catlin
### Vermilion County

*(G-3401)*
**CROP PRODUCTION SERVICES INC**
12895 E Lyons Rd (61817)
P.O. Box 530 (61817-0530)
**PHONE**..................................217 427-2181
Randy Snyder, *Site Mgr*
Clint Hawkins, *Manager*
**EMP:** 9
**SALES (corp-wide):** 13.6B **Privately Held**
**WEB:** www.cropproductionservices.com
**SIC:** 2875 Fertilizers, mixing only
**HQ:** Crop Production Services, Inc.
3005 Rocky Mountain Ave
Loveland CO 80538
970 685-3300

## Cave In Rock
### Hardin County

*(G-3402)*
**HASTIE MINING & TRUCKING (PA)**
Hwy 146 (62919)
Rural Route 1 Box 55 (62919-9711)
**PHONE**..................................618 289-4536
**Fax:** 618 289-4539
Donald Hastie, *Partner*
Robert Hastie, *Partner*
**EMP:** 35
**SQ FT:** 2,240
**SALES:** 19.2MM **Privately Held**
**WEB:** www.hastiemining.com
**SIC:** 1442 1479 4212 1422 Gravel mining; fluorspar mining; local trucking, without storage; crushed & broken limestone

*(G-3403)*
**LAFARGE NORTH AMERICA INC**
Rr 1 (62919-9801)
P.O. Box 267 (62919-0267)
**PHONE**..................................618 289-3404
**EMP:** 27
**SALES (corp-wide):** 26.6B **Privately Held**
**SIC:** 3241 Cement, hydraulic

**HQ:** Lafarge North America Inc.
8700 W Bryn Mawr Ave LI
Chicago IL 60631
703 480-3600

## Centralia
### Marion County

*(G-3404)*
**AMERICAN EQUIPMENT & MCH INC**
2400 S Wabash Ave (62801-6188)
**PHONE**..................................618 533-3857
Robert D Moore, *President*
Michael O McKown, *Admin Sec*
▲ **EMP:** 80
**SQ FT:** 460,000
**SALES (est):** 16.4MM
**SALES (corp-wide):** 4B **Privately Held**
**SIC:** 3532 Stamping mill machinery (mining machinery)
**PA:** Murray Energy Corporation
46226 National Rd W
Saint Clairsville OH 43950
740 338-3100

*(G-3405)*
**BIG 3 PRECISION PRODUCTS INC (PA)**
2923 S Wabash Ave (62801-6284)
P.O. Box A (62801-9199)
**PHONE**..................................618 533-3251
Alan J Scheidt, *President*
Mike Marz, *General Mgr*
Susan Niepoetter, *Corp Secy*
Brooks Alcorn, *Safety Mgr*
Roger Heinzmann, *Opers Staff*
▲ **EMP:** 130
**SQ FT:** 142,205
**SALES (est):** 51.2MM **Privately Held**
**WEB:** www.big3precision.com
**SIC:** 3544 3599 3469 Special dies & tools; custom machinery; metal stampings

*(G-3406)*
**CENTRALIA MACHINE & FAB INC**
306 S Chestnut St (62801-3822)
P.O. Box 1686 (62801-9124)
**PHONE**..................................618 533-9010
Robert P Gilbert, *President*
**EMP:** 1
**SALES (est):** 270K **Privately Held**
**SIC:** 3537 Industrial trucks & tractors

*(G-3407)*
**CENTRALIA MORNING SENTINEL**
232 E Broadway (62801-3251)
**PHONE**..................................618 532-5601
Dan Nickels, *General Mgr*
**EMP:** 100
**SALES (est):** 4.2MM **Privately Held**
**SIC:** 2711 Newspapers

*(G-3408)*
**CENTRALIA PRESS LTD (PA)**
Also Called: Centralia Sentinel
232 E Broadway (62801-3251)
P.O. Box 627 (62801-9110)
**PHONE**..................................618 532-5604
**Fax:** 618 532-1212
John A Perrine, *President*
Dan Nichols, *Business Mgr*
William Perrine, *Admin Sec*
**EMP:** 81
**SQ FT:** 9,000
**SALES (est):** 10.9MM **Privately Held**
**WEB:** www.morningsentinel.com
**SIC:** 2711 Job printing & newspaper publishing combined

*(G-3409)*
**CLINTON COUNTY MATERIALS CORP**
Also Called: Quad-County Rdymx Centralia
100 Rhodes St (62801-2359)
**PHONE**..................................618 533-4252
**Fax:** 618 533-4108
Mike Johnson, *Manager*
**EMP:** 10

**SALES (corp-wide):** 1.8MM **Privately Held**
**SIC:** 3273 Ready-mixed concrete
**PA:** Clinton County Materials Corp
300 W 12th St
Okawville IL 62271
618 243-6430

*(G-3410)*
**CORRUGATED CONVERTING EQP**
306 S Chestnut St (62801-3822)
P.O. Box 1686 (62801-9124)
**PHONE**..................................618 532-2138
**Fax:** 618 532-3447
Steve Gilbert, *President*
Cindy Pitts, *Office Mgr*
**EMP:** 10
**SQ FT:** 20,000
**SALES (est):** 1.2MM **Privately Held**
**WEB:** www.corrugatedindustry.com
**SIC:** 5084 3443 7692 3544 Industrial machinery & equipment; fabricated plate work (boiler shop); welding repair; special dies, tools, jigs & fixtures

*(G-3411)*
**DEMOULIN BROTHERS & COMPANY**
302 Swan Ave (62801-6128)
**PHONE**..................................618 533-3810
**Fax:** 618 533-3810
Bernadette Lowe, *Manager*
**EMP:** 48
**SALES (corp-wide):** 16MM **Privately Held**
**SIC:** 2389 Men's miscellaneous accessories
**PA:** Demoulin Brothers & Company
1025 S 4th St
Greenville IL 62246
618 664-2000

*(G-3412)*
**DURATECH CORPORATION**
2520 S Wabash Ave (62801)
P.O. Box 1720 (62801-9124)
**PHONE**..................................618 533-8891
**Fax:** 618 533-9248
Joe Fulton, *President*
Shelia Kapes, *Corp Secy*
Lisa Graham, *Manager*
**EMP:** 5
**SQ FT:** 18,500
**SALES (est):** 788.9K **Privately Held**
**WEB:** www.duratechcorporation.com
**SIC:** 3089 Plastic & fiberglass tanks

*(G-3413)*
**ENGINEERED FLUID INC (PA)**
Also Called: E F I
1308 N Maple St (62801-2417)
P.O. Box 723 (62801-9111)
**PHONE**..................................618 533-1351
**Fax:** 618 533-1459
Bill Goodspeed, *President*
Patricia Pawlisa, *COO*
Gary Beer, *Vice Pres*
George Wooten, *Vice Pres*
Dustin Diedrich, *Project Mgr*
**EMP:** 107 **EST:** 1962
**SQ FT:** 9,000
**SALES (est):** 26.7MM **Privately Held**
**WEB:** www.engineeredfluid.com
**SIC:** 3561 3613 3491 Pumps & pumping equipment; control panels, electric; industrial valves

*(G-3414)*
**ENGINEERED FLUID INC**
1308 N Maple St (62801-2417)
**PHONE**..................................618 533-1351
Deppto Goodbe, *Manager*
**EMP:** 100
**SALES (corp-wide):** 26.7MM **Privately Held**
**WEB:** www.engineeredfluid.com
**SIC:** 3561 Pumps & pumping equipment
**PA:** Engineered Fluid, Inc.
1308 N Maple St
Centralia IL 62801
618 533-1351

*(G-3415)*
**G-M SERVICES**
309 Country Club Rd (62801-3741)
**PHONE**..................................618 532-2324
Gregory Marcum, *Owner*
**EMP:** 4
**SALES:** 250K **Privately Held**
**WEB:** www.g-mservices.com
**SIC:** 3823 1711 Water quality monitoring & control systems; plumbing, heating, air-conditioning contractors

*(G-3416)*
**GRAPHIC PACKAGING INTL INC**
2333 S Wabash Ave (62801-6187)
P.O. Box 787 (62801-9113)
**PHONE**..................................618 533-2721
Paul Delong, *Prdtn Mgr*
Carol Maxey, *Persnl Dir*
Tammie Taylor, *Persnl Mgr*
Arthur Rideout, *Manager*
Victoria Moore, *Manager*
**EMP:** 97 **Publicly Held**
**SIC:** 2657 Folding paperboard boxes
**HQ:** Graphic Packaging International, Inc.
1500 Riveredge Pkwy # 100
Atlanta GA 30328
770 240-7200

*(G-3417)*
**GREENS MACHINE SHOP**
315 E Kell St (62801-2335)
**PHONE**..................................618 532-4631
**Fax:** 618 532-4631
David Stover, *Owner*
**EMP:** 3 **EST:** 1917
**SQ FT:** 1,600
**SALES (est):** 230K **Privately Held**
**SIC:** 3599 7692 Machine shop, jobbing & repair; welding repair

*(G-3418)*
**ILLINOIS CENTRAL GULF CAR SHOP**
600 Gilmore St (62801-5212)
**PHONE**..................................618 533-8281
**Fax:** 618 533-3332
Reif Palmer, *General Mgr*
Dick Adreon, *Supervisor*
**EMP:** 54
**SALES (est):** 4.9MM **Privately Held**
**SIC:** 3743 7532 Railroad equipment; tops (canvas or plastic), installation or repair: automotive

*(G-3419)*
**INTERMOUNTAIN ELECTRONICS INC**
400 Swan Ave (62801-6220)
**PHONE**..................................618 339-6743
Rick Benedict, *Branch Mgr*
**EMP:** 9
**SALES (corp-wide):** 86MM **Privately Held**
**SIC:** 3699 Household electrical equipment
**PA:** Intermountain Electronics, Inc. Of Price, Utah
1511 S Highway 6
Price UT 84501
435 637-7160

*(G-3420)*
**JAMES RAY MONROE CORPORATION (PA)**
Also Called: Mitchell Printing
308 W Noleman St (62801-3129)
P.O. Box 950 (62801-9115)
**PHONE**..................................618 532-4575
**Fax:** 618 532-0075
David J Mitchell, *President*
Bruce Jones, *Treasurer*
Nancy Spitler, *Office Mgr*
**EMP:** 10 **EST:** 1976
**SQ FT:** 4,000
**SALES:** 1MM **Privately Held**
**SIC:** 2752 5943 5712 3069 Commercial printing, offset; office forms & supplies; office furniture; stationers' rubber sundries; typewriters & business machines; typesetting

# Centralia - Marion County (G-3421)

**(G-3421)**
**LEE GILSTER-MARY CORPORATION**
100 W Calumet St (62801-4130)
PHONE.............................618 533-4808
Fax: 618 533-4818
Nicole Ellis, *QA Dir*
Wayne Malzhon, *Manager*
EMP: 180
SALES (corp-wide): 1.1B **Privately Held**
WEB: www.gilstermarylee.com
SIC: 5149 2074 Groceries & related products; cottonseed oil mills
HQ: Gilster-Mary Lee Corporation
  1037 State St
  Chester IL 62233
  618 826-2361

**(G-3422)**
**MICHAEL REGGIS CLARK**
Also Called: Kaco Signs
1308 N Elm St (62801-2307)
PHONE.............................618 533-3841
Fax: 618 533-0349
Reggis M Clark, *Owner*
Kay Clark, *Owner*
Reggie Clark, *Owner*
EMP: 3
SQ FT: 2,800
SALES: 130K **Privately Held**
SIC: 3993 Signs & advertising specialties

**(G-3423)**
**NATURAL GAS PIPELINE AMER LLC**
7501 Huey Rd (62801-7115)
PHONE.............................618 495-2211
Fax: 618 495-2698
Larry Ullrick, *Branch Mgr*
Raymond Dekamper, *Manager*
EMP: 25
SALES (corp-wide): 13B **Publicly Held**
SIC: 4922 1311 Natural gas transmission; crude petroleum & natural gas
HQ: Natural Gas Pipeline Company Of America Llc
  1001 Louisiana St
  Houston TX 77002
  713 369-9000

**(G-3424)**
**NEW METAL FABRICATION CORP**
931 S Brookside St (62801-5451)
P.O. Box 473 (62801-9107)
PHONE.............................618 532-9000
Jon Bain, *CEO*
Steve Laxton II, *CFO*
EMP: 22
SALES (est): 4.7MM **Privately Held**
SIC: 3441 Fabricated structural metal

**(G-3425)**
**NU-ART PRINTING**
614 W Broadway (62801-5302)
PHONE.............................618 533-9971
Fax: 618 533-6954
Art Borum, *Owner*
EMP: 6
SALES (est): 290K **Privately Held**
SIC: 2752 2759 3993 2791 Commercial printing, offset; commercial printing; signs & advertising specialties; typesetting; bookbinding & related work; automotive & apparel trimmings

**(G-3426)**
**PINNACLE FOODS GROUP LLC**
100 W Calumet St (62801-4130)
PHONE.............................731 343-4995
Michael D French, *Manager*
EMP: 159
SALES (corp-wide): 2.5B **Publicly Held**
SIC: 2038 Frozen specialties
HQ: Pinnacle Foods Group Llc
  399 Jefferson Rd
  Parsippany NJ 07054

**(G-3427)**
**PIONEER CONTAINER MCHY INC**
1674 Woods Ln (62801-6774)
PHONE.............................618 533-7833
James Michael McMillan, *President*
EMP: 2
SQ FT: 13,500
SALES: 350K **Privately Held**
SIC: 3565 Packaging machinery

**(G-3428)**
**QUALITY SPORT NETS INC**
2330 E Calumet St (62801-6578)
P.O. Box 962 (62801-9115)
PHONE.............................618 533-0700
Daniel Koller, *President*
Daniel N Koller, *President*
Mary Lynn Koller, *Admin Sec*
▲ EMP: 7
SQ FT: 8,000
SALES (est): 757K **Privately Held**
SIC: 3949 Nets: badminton, volleyball, tennis, etc.

**(G-3429)**
**ROSE BUSINESS FORMS & PRINTING**
125 N Walnut St (62801-3134)
PHONE.............................618 533-3032
Fax: 618 533-3039
Phillip McDaniel, *President*
EMP: 5
SQ FT: 8,000
SALES (est): 603.6K **Privately Held**
SIC: 2752 5112 2791 2789 Commercial printing, lithographic; business forms; typesetting; bookbinding & related work; commercial printing

**(G-3430)**
**S & M BASEMENTS**
1633 Walnut Hill Rd (62801-6257)
PHONE.............................618 533-1939
Tommy E Miller, *Partner*
Gary Smith, *Partner*
EMP: 6
SALES (est): 729.2K **Privately Held**
SIC: 3272 Areaways, basement window: concrete

**(G-3431)**
**SAY CHEESE CAKE**
421 W Noleman St (62801-3130)
PHONE.............................618 532-6001
Rick Wooters, *Owner*
EMP: 4
SALES (est): 271.5K **Privately Held**
SIC: 2051 Cakes, bakery: except frozen

**(G-3432)**
**SEIP SERVICE & SUPPLY INC**
221 E Broadway Ste 101 (62801-3250)
PHONE.............................618 532-1923
Kris Kourdouvelis, *President*
Elizabeth B Kourdouvelis, *Vice Pres*
Luann Pugh, *Admin Sec*
EMP: 18 EST: 1956
SQ FT: 1,000
SALES (est): 777.5K **Privately Held**
SIC: 1389 5084 Oil field services; oil well machinery, equipment & supplies

**(G-3433)**
**SHOPPERS WEEKLY INC**
Also Called: Shopper Weekly Publishings
301 E Broadway (62801-3252)
P.O. Box 1223 (62801-9118)
PHONE.............................618 533-7283
Fax: 618 533-7284
Cathy Stuehmeier, *President*
John Stuehmeier, *Corp Secy*
EMP: 10
SALES (est): 820K **Privately Held**
SIC: 2741 Shopping news: publishing only, not printed on site

**(G-3434)**
**SOUTHERN GLASS CO**
1005 Beacham Ave (62801-6401)
P.O. Box 482 (62801-9108)
PHONE.............................618 532-4281
Fax: 618 532-5575
Marc Profancik, *Owner*
EMP: 5 EST: 1950
SQ FT: 2,000
SALES: 240K **Privately Held**
SIC: 1793 3231 Glass & glazing work; products of purchased glass

**(G-3435)**
**SWAN SURFACES LLC**
200 Swan Ave (62801-6124)
PHONE.............................618 532-5673
Fax: 618 532-5673
Larry Hayes, *Purch Agent*
Kevin Kuhnke, *Engineer*
Mike Vincent, *Manager*
Connie Buonaura, *Manager*
EMP: 130
SALES (corp-wide): 46.8MM **Privately Held**
SIC: 3088 3431 3261 2541 Shower stalls, fiberglass & plastic; metal sanitary ware; vitreous plumbing fixtures; wood partitions & fixtures
HQ: Swan Surfaces, Llc
  515 Olive St Ste 900
  Saint Louis MO 63101
  800 325-7008

**(G-3436)**
**TONYS WELDING SERVICE INC**
624 N Elm St (62801-2320)
PHONE.............................618 532-9353
Tony Sloat Sr, *President*
Tony R Sloat Jr, *Vice Pres*
Marilyn Sloat, *Admin Sec*
EMP: 7
SQ FT: 6,000
SALES (est): 910.6K **Privately Held**
SIC: 7692 3441 Welding repair; fabricated structural metal

**(G-3437)**
**WB TRAY LLC**
115 Harting Dr (62801-5903)
PHONE.............................618 918-3821
EMP: 2
SALES (est): 241K **Privately Held**
SIC: 3825 Integrating electricity meters

## Centreville
### St. Clair County

**(G-3438)**
**STEEL REBAR MANUFACTURING LLC**
Also Called: Srm
4926 Church Rd (62207-1392)
PHONE.............................618 920-2748
Donald J Johnson, *Mng Member*
EMP: 8
SQ FT: 25,000
SALES (est): 543.3K **Privately Held**
SIC: 1761 3449 5051 Architectural sheet metal work; bars, concrete reinforcing; fabricated steel; steel

## Cerro Gordo
### Piatt County

**(G-3439)**
**CLARKSON SOY PRODUCTS LLC**
320 E South St (61818-4035)
P.O. Box 80 (61818-0080)
PHONE.............................217 763-9511
Curtis Bennett, *President*
Lynn E Clarkson,
◆ EMP: 7
SALES (est): 796K **Privately Held**
SIC: 2075 Soybean oil, deodorized

## Chadwick
### Carroll County

**(G-3440)**
**CHADWICK MANUFACTURING LTD**
Also Called: US Ignition
224 N Main St (61014)
P.O. Box 85 (61014-0085)
PHONE.............................815 684-5152
Fax: 815 684-5160
Allen L Smith, *Partner*
Dwight Smith, *Partner*
Kay Smith, *Partner*
EMP: 6 EST: 1946
SQ FT: 16,600
SALES: 300K **Privately Held**
WEB: www.chadwickmfg.com
SIC: 3599 3631 3499 3443 Machine shop, jobbing & repair; barbecues, grills & braziers (outdoor cooking); furniture parts, metal; fabricated plate work (boiler shop)

**(G-3441)**
**COMPLIANCESIGNS INC**
Also Called: Compliancesigns.com
56 S Main St (61014)
PHONE.............................800 578-1245
Paul Sandefer, *President*
Corrine Sandefer, *Vice Pres*
Paul Skoog, *Vice Pres*
Doug Stang, *Vice Pres*
Tammy Jones, *Manager*
EMP: 70
SALES: 12.4MM **Privately Held**
WEB: www.compliancesigns.com
SIC: 3993 Signs & advertising specialties

**(G-3442)**
**JOHNSONS PROCESSING PLANT**
201 Il Route 40 E (61014-9368)
Rural Route 2 Box 1 (61014)
PHONE.............................815 684-5183
Greg Adolph, *Owner*
EMP: 7 EST: 1960
SALES (est): 576.8K **Privately Held**
SIC: 2011 2013 Meat packing plants; sausages & other prepared meats

## Chambersburg
### Pike County

**(G-3443)**
**CENTRAL STONE COMPANY**
38084 County Highway 21 (62323-2116)
PHONE.............................217 327-4300
Bruce Mowen, *Branch Mgr*
EMP: 3
SALES (corp-wide): 4.3B **Privately Held**
SIC: 1422 Crushed & broken limestone
HQ: Central Stone Company
  1701 5th Ave
  Moline IL 61265
  309 757-8250

## Champaign
### Champaign County

**(G-3444)**
**ADVANCED FILTRATION SYSTEMS INC (PA)**
3206 Farber Dr (61822-1084)
PHONE.............................217 351-3073
Fax: 217 351-1612
Nickolas Priadka, *President*
Tim Walls, *Safety Mgr*
Robin Parent, *Buyer*
Steve Wayman, *Engineer*
Kevin Quinlan, *Human Res Mgr*
▲ EMP: 139
SQ FT: 228,000
SALES (est): 53.9MM **Privately Held**
SIC: 3599 Oil filters, internal combustion engine, except automotive; gasoline filters, internal combustion engine, except auto

**(G-3445)**
**ALLERTON CHARTER COACH**
714 S 6th St (61820-5708)
P.O. Box 4048, Lisle (60532-9048)
PHONE.............................217 344-2600
Dennis Toeppen, *Principal*
EMP: 5
SALES (est): 401.1K **Privately Held**
SIC: 2295 Coated fabrics, not rubberized

**(G-3446)**
**AM KO ORIENTAL FOODS**
Also Called: Am-Ko Oriental Grocery
101 E Springfield Ave (61820-5309)
PHONE.............................217 398-2922
Soon K Chung, *Partner*
Michael Pulliam, *Partner*
▲ EMP: 2

# GEOGRAPHIC SECTION
## Champaign - Champaign County (G-3475)

**SALES (est):** 261.4K  **Privately Held**
**SIC:** 5411  3993  5499  5947  Grocery stores, independent; signs, not made in custom sign painting shops; health & dietetic food stores; gift, novelty & souvenir shop

### (G-3447)
**AM-DON PARTNERSHIP**
Also Called: SBC
1819 S Neil St Ste A  (61820-7271)
**PHONE**.................................217 355-7750
**Fax:** 217 355-7779
Bob Donahoe, *Manager*
**EMP:** 7
**SALES (corp-wide):** 40.3MM  **Privately Held**
**SIC:** 8742  2741  Sales (including sales management) consultant; miscellaneous publishing
**PA:** Am-Don Partnership
    200 E Randolph St # 7000
    Chicago IL 60601
    312 240-6000

### (G-3448)
**AMERICAN BOTTLING COMPANY**
815 Pioneer St  (61820-2512)
**PHONE**.................................217 356-0577
Dale McElhanew, *Manager*
**EMP:** 27
**SALES (corp-wide):** 6.4B  **Publicly Held**
**SIC:** 2086  Bottled & canned soft drinks
**HQ:** The American Bottling Company
    5301 Legacy Dr
    Plano TX 75024

### (G-3449)
**AMERICAN CLASSIFIEDS INC**
505 E University Ave C  (61820-3848)
**PHONE**.................................217 356-4804
Gabriele Cooper, *General Mgr*
**EMP:** 18
**SALES (corp-wide):** 1.5MM  **Privately Held**
**SIC:** 2711  Newspapers, publishing & printing
**PA:** American Classifieds Inc
    1634 N 1st St
    Abilene TX 79601
    325 673-4521

### (G-3450)
**ANDY DALLAS & CO**
Also Called: Dallas & Co Costumes & Magic
101 E University Ave  (61820-4110)
**PHONE**.................................217 351-5974
**Fax:** 217 351-9255
Andrew Dallas, *President*
Barb Dallas, *Treasurer*
Alexis Barnett, *Mktg Dir*
**EMP:** 10
**SQ FT:** 12,000
**SALES (est):** 773.6K  **Privately Held**
**SIC:** 5947  5699  7299  2389  Novelties; party favors; costumes, masquerade or theatrical; costume rental; costumes

### (G-3451)
**APTIMMUNE BIOLOGICS INC**
60 Hazelwood Dr  (61820-7460)
**PHONE**.................................217 377-8866
Federico Zuckermann, *President*
**EMP:** 4
**SALES (est):** 100K  **Privately Held**
**SIC:** 2834  Pharmaceutical preparations

### (G-3452)
**AQUEOUS SOLUTIONS LLC**
301 N Neil St Ste 400  (61820-3169)
**PHONE**.................................217 531-1206
Craig Bethke, *Principal*
Carla Barcus, *Sales Dir*
Brian Farrell, *Info Tech Mgr*
Katelyn Zatwarnicki, *Info Tech Mgr*
**EMP:** 2  **EST:** 2011
**SALES (est):** 256.9K  **Privately Held**
**SIC:** 7372  Application computer software

### (G-3453)
**AT HOME MAGAZINE**
15 E Main St  (61820-3625)
**PHONE**.................................217 351-5282
Deanne Johnson, *Manager*
**EMP:** 3

**SALES (est):** 135.2K  **Privately Held**
**SIC:** 2721  Periodicals: publishing only

### (G-3454)
**ATSP INNOVATIONS LLC**
60 Hazelwood Dr  (61820-7460)
**PHONE**.................................217 239-1703
David Carroll, *Info Tech Mgr*
James Economy,
Andreas Polycarpou,
**EMP:** 4
**SALES (est):** 384.7K  **Privately Held**
**SIC:** 2821  Plastics materials & resins

### (G-3455)
**AUTONOMIC MATERIALS INC**
495 County Road 1300 N  (61822-9746)
**PHONE**.................................217 863-2023
Joe Giuliani, *CEO*
Gerald Wilson, *Office Mgr*
**EMP:** 11
**SALES (est):** 1MM  **Privately Held**
**SIC:** 2851  Paints & allied products

### (G-3456)
**BELL RACING USA LLC**
Also Called: Bell Racing Co
301 Mercury Dr Ste 8  (61822-9654)
**PHONE**.................................217 239-5355
Kyle Kietzmann, *President*
Carole Tempel, *Opers Mgr*
▲ **EMP:** 8  **EST:** 2010
**SALES (est):** 1.1MM  **Privately Held**
**SIC:** 3949  Helmets, athletic

### (G-3457)
**BOW BROTHERS CO INC**
3108 W Springfield Ave  (61822-2865)
**PHONE**.................................217 359-0555
Jeffery Wandell, *President*
**EMP:** 5
**SALES (est):** 213.7K  **Privately Held**
**SIC:** 2396  Automotive & apparel trimmings

### (G-3458)
**BRG SPORTS INC**
301 Mercury Dr Ste 8  (61822-9654)
**PHONE**.................................217 819-5187
Robert Booth, *Principal*
**EMP:** 4  **Privately Held**
**SIC:** 3949  Sporting & athletic goods
**HQ:** Brg Sports, Inc.
    9801 W Higgins Rd
    Rosemont IL 60018
    831 461-7500

### (G-3459)
**BUZARD PIPE ORGAN BUILDERS LLC**
Also Called: Buzard Pipe Organ Craftsmen
112 W Hill St  (61820-8643)
**PHONE**.................................217 352-1955
**Fax:** 217 352-1981
Mark Dirksen, *Business Mgr*
Charles Eames, *Exec VP*
Shane Rhoades, *Production*
John P Buzard, *Mng Member*
Dave Brown, *Manager*
▲ **EMP:** 17
**SQ FT:** 20,000
**SALES:** 1.2MM  **Privately Held**
**WEB:** www.buzardorgans.com
**SIC:** 3931  7699  Pipes, organ; organ tuning & repair

### (G-3460)
**CAMPUS SPORTSWEAR INCORPORATED**
710 S 6th St Ste B  (61820-9200)
P.O. Box 2482  (61825-2482)
**PHONE**.................................217 344-0944
**Fax:** 217 344-6946
Tom Coleman, *President*
Jedd Swisher, *Vice Pres*
**EMP:** 10  **EST:** 1948
**SQ FT:** 2,700
**SALES (est):** 800K  **Privately Held**
**WEB:** www.campussportswearinc.com
**SIC:** 2759  Commercial printing

### (G-3461)
**CARDTHARTIC LLC**
30102 Research Rd  (61822)
**PHONE**.................................217 239-5895
Ed Middleworth, *Manager*

Pam Hills, *Director*
Joanna Steven,
**EMP:** 12
**SQ FT:** 5,000
**SALES (est):** 1.3MM  **Privately Held**
**WEB:** www.cardthartic.com
**SIC:** 2771  Greeting cards

### (G-3462)
**CAST21 INC**
60 Hazelwood Dr  (61820-7460)
**PHONE**.................................847 772-8547
Ashley Moy, *CEO*
Justin Brooks, *COO*
**EMP:** 3
**SALES (est):** 117.4K  **Privately Held**
**SIC:** 3841  8711  Surgical & medical instruments; engineering services

### (G-3463)
**CBANA LABS INC (PA)**
2021 S 1st St Ste 206  (61820-7484)
**PHONE**.................................217 819-5201
Tim Hoerr, *President*
Curtis Ray, *Vice Pres*
Qingmei Chen, *Research*
Junghoon Yeom, *Research*
**EMP:** 7
**SQ FT:** 7,500
**SALES:** 300K  **Privately Held**
**WEB:** www.cbana.com
**SIC:** 3826  5049  Analytical instruments; analytical instruments

### (G-3464)
**CDS OFFICE SYSTEMS INC**
3108 Farber Dr Ofc  (61822-1074)
**PHONE**.................................217 351-5046
Jay Watson, *Owner*
**EMP:** 15
**SALES (corp-wide):** 132.4MM  **Privately Held**
**SIC:** 5044  2759  5999  Office equipment; commercial printing; photocopy machines
**PA:** C.D.S. Office Systems Incorporated
    612 S Dirksen Pkwy
    Springfield IL 62703
    800 367-1508

### (G-3465)
**CENTRAL IL BUSINESS MAGAZINE**
15 E Main St  (61820-3625)
**PHONE**.................................217 351-5281
Greta Hale, *Principal*
**EMP:** 5
**SALES (est):** 232.5K  **Privately Held**
**SIC:** 2759  Magazines: printing

### (G-3466)
**CISCO SYSTEMS INC**
2302 Fox Dr  (61820-2000)
**PHONE**.................................217 363-4500
Carl Helle, *Branch Mgr*
**EMP:** 4
**SALES (corp-wide):** 49.2B  **Publicly Held**
**WEB:** www.cisco.com
**SIC:** 3577  Computer peripheral equipment
**PA:** Cisco Systems, Inc.
    170 W Tasman Dr
    San Jose CA 95134
    408 526-4000

### (G-3467)
**CLARK PRINTING & MARKETING**
501 Mercury Dr  (61822-9649)
**PHONE**.................................217 363-5300
David Clark, *Owner*
**EMP:** 3
**SALES (est):** 240.9K  **Privately Held**
**SIC:** 2759  Commercial printing

### (G-3468)
**COMMON GROUND PUBLISHING LLC**
2001 S 1st St Ste 202  (61820-7478)
**PHONE**.................................217 328-0405
Andrew Jeakins, *Treasurer*
Matthew Robinson, *Manager*
William Cope, *CTO*
**EMP:** 25
**SALES:** 50K  **Privately Held**
**SIC:** 2731  Book publishing

### (G-3469)
**COMPUTING INTEGRITY INC**
3102 Valleybrook Dr  (61822-6112)
**PHONE**.................................217 355-4469
**EMP:** 1
**SQ FT:** 1,200
**SALES:** 400K  **Privately Held**
**SIC:** 7372  Software Development

### (G-3470)
**COUNTY MATERIALS CORP**
702 N Edwin St  (61821-2537)
**PHONE**.................................217 352-4181
Scott Boma, *Branch Mgr*
**EMP:** 33
**SALES (corp-wide):** 422.4MM  **Privately Held**
**WEB:** www.ctymaterials.com
**SIC:** 3271  5211  3273  3272  Blocks, concrete or cinder: standard; lumber & other building materials; masonry materials & supplies; ready-mixed concrete; concrete products; construction sand & gravel
**PA:** County Materials Corp.
    205 North St
    Marathon WI 54448
    715 443-2434

### (G-3471)
**CREATIVE MARBLE INC**
4002 Kearns Dr  (61822-9247)
**PHONE**.................................217 359-7271
**Fax:** 217 359-9862
Richard Atwood, *President*
**EMP:** 6
**SALES (est):** 500K  **Privately Held**
**SIC:** 3281  2821  Marble, building: cut & shaped; plastics materials & resins

### (G-3472)
**DABEL INCORPORATED**
Also Called: A & A Graphx
602 E Green St  (61820-5770)
P.O. Box 373, Savoy  (61874-0373)
**PHONE**.................................217 398-3389
Debbie Able, *President*
Mike Alves, *Vice Pres*
**EMP:** 9
**SQ FT:** 1,800
**SALES (est):** 794.4K  **Privately Held**
**SIC:** 2396  2395  Screen printing on fabric articles; pleating & stitching

### (G-3473)
**DALKEY ARCHIVE PRESS**
Also Called: Dalkey Archive Press, The University Of Illinois 6  (61820)
**PHONE**.................................217 244-5700
**Fax:** 309 438-7422
John Obrien, *Sales Mgr*
Jonathan Dykes, *Marketing Mgr*
Ian Dreiblatt, *Manager*
Lee Rourke, *Manager*
Cailin Neal, *Director*
▲ **EMP:** 8
**SALES:** 1.6MM  **Privately Held**
**WEB:** www.dalkeyarchive.com
**SIC:** 2731  Book publishing

### (G-3474)
**DESERT SOUTHWEST FITNESS INC**
Also Called: Dswfitness
1607 N Market St  (61820-2220)
**PHONE**.................................520 292-0011
Gwen Hyatt, *President*
Pat Ryan, *Vice Pres*
**EMP:** 8
**SQ FT:** 2,000
**SALES (est):** 1.1MM
**SALES (corp-wide):** 31.6MM  **Privately Held**
**WEB:** www.dswfitness.com
**SIC:** 5192  2721  Magazines; magazines: publishing & printing
**PA:** Human Kinetics, Inc.
    1607 N Market St
    Champaign IL 61820
    217 351-5076

### (G-3475)
**DOTS UT INC**
2716 W Clark Rd Ste E  (61822-2842)
**PHONE**.................................217 390-3286
Yuri T Didenko, *President*
**EMP:** 5

# Champaign - Champaign County (G-3476)   GEOGRAPHIC SECTION

SQ FT: 1,800
SALES: 50K **Privately Held**
WEB: www.utdots.com
SIC: **3823** Electrolytic conductivity instruments, industrial process

**(G-3476)**
**EASY PAY & DATA INC**
902 N Country Fair Dr # 6 (61821-2300)
PHONE.................................217 398-9729
Donna Greene, *President*
Lue Patterson, *CFO*
EMP: 6
SALES (est): 801.9K **Privately Held**
SIC: **3571** Electronic computers

**(G-3477)**
**ECOOL LLC**
350 N Walnut St (61820-3619)
PHONE.................................309 966-3701
Dave Smith, *President*
Gerald Schmidt,
EMP: 5 EST: 2014
SQ FT: 100,000
SALES: 43.3K **Privately Held**
SIC: **3585** **2891** Refrigeration & heating equipment; sealants

**(G-3478)**
**EDEN PARK ILLUMINATION INC**
903 N Country Fair Dr (61821-3259)
PHONE.................................217 403-1866
Bill Thalheimer, *CEO*
Sung-Jin Park, *Vice Pres*
EMP: 9
SALES (est): 1.5MM **Privately Held**
SIC: **3641** Electric lamps

**(G-3479)**
**EFFIMAX SOLAR**
60 Hazelwood Dr (61820-7460)
PHONE.................................217 550-2422
Rui Cai, *CEO*
EMP: 4
SALES (est): 316K **Privately Held**
SIC: **3674** Semiconductors & related devices

**(G-3480)**
**EMBEDOR TECHNOLOGIES INC**
60 Hazelwood Dr (61820-7460)
PHONE.................................202 681-0359
Bill Spencer, *President*
Kirill Mechitov, *Treasurer*
Gul Agha, *Admin Sec*
EMP: 3 EST: 2014
SQ FT: 43,000
SALES (est): 190.7K **Privately Held**
SIC: **3823** Data loggers, industrial process type; telemetering instruments, industrial process type

**(G-3481)**
**EP PURIFICATION INC**
2105 W Park Ct (61821-2986)
PHONE.................................217 693-7950
Cy Herring, *CEO*
Sungjin Park, *CTO*
EMP: 14
SQ FT: 7,500
SALES: 300K **Privately Held**
SIC: **3589** Water purification equipment, household type

**(G-3482)**
**EP TECHNOLOGY CORPORATION USA**
Also Called: E P Computer
1401 Interstate Dr (61822-1172)
PHONE.................................217 351-7888
Fax: 217 351-7825
Kevin Wan, *President*
Greg Birckbichler, *Opers Staff*
Andrew Xie, *Research*
Michael Ambrose, *Human Res Dir*
Helena Lin, *Sales Mgr*
▲ EMP: 70
SALES (est): 13.2MM **Privately Held**
WEB: www.eptco.com
SIC: **5734** **8742** **7372** Computer & software stores; protective devices, security; application computer software

**(G-3483)**
**EPIWORKS INC**
1606 Rion Dr (61822-9598)
PHONE.................................217 373-1590
Quesnell J Hartmann, *President*
Ronald L Chez, *Chairman*
David A Ahmari, *Exec VP*
Curt Dickinson, *Materials Mgr*
Brad Roof, *Engineer*
▲ EMP: 55 EST: 1997
SQ FT: 25,000
SALES (est): 18.7MM
SALES (corp-wide): 827.2MM **Publicly Held**
WEB: www.epiworks.com
SIC: **3674** Semiconductors & related devices
PA: Ii-Vi Incorporated
 375 Saxonburg Blvd
 Saxonburg PA 16056
 724 352-4455

**(G-3484)**
**EXCARB INC**
4404 Ironwood Ln (61822-9337)
PHONE.................................217 493-8477
James Eden, *President*
Sung Jin Park, *Vice Pres*
EMP: 3
SQ FT: 800
SALES (est): 164K **Privately Held**
SIC: **3699** Electrical equipment & supplies

**(G-3485)**
**FEDEX OFFICE & PRINT SVCS INC**
505 S Mattis Ave (61821-4276)
PHONE.................................217 355-3400
Jamie Fairbanks, *General Mgr*
EMP: 30
SALES (corp-wide): 50.3B **Publicly Held**
WEB: www.kinkos.com
SIC: **7334** **2789** **2759** **7221** Photocopying & duplicating services; bookbinding & related work; commercial printing; photographic studios, portrait
HQ: Fedex Office And Print Services, Inc.
 7900 Legacy Dr
 Plano TX 75024
 214 550-7000

**(G-3486)**
**FIRST STATE BANK**
101 E Windsor Rd (61820-7754)
P.O. Box 6990 (61826-6990)
PHONE.................................217 239-3000
Fax: 217 239-1164
William Blickhan, *Loan Officer*
Joel Oschwald, *Branch Mgr*
EMP: 7
SALES (corp-wide): 15.2MM **Privately Held**
SIC: **2621** Bank note paper
HQ: First State Bank
 201 W Main St
 Monticello IL 61856
 217 762-9431

**(G-3487)**
**GILL ATHLETICS**
2808 Gemini Ct (61822-9648)
PHONE.................................800 637-3090
Gill Athletics, *CEO*
▼ EMP: 2
SALES (est): 262.8K **Privately Held**
SIC: **3949** Sporting & athletic goods

**(G-3488)**
**GLASS FX**
202 S 1st St (61820)
PHONE.................................217 359-0048
Fax: 217 359-4800
Richard Taylor, *Owner*
EMP: 7
SQ FT: 1,400
SALES (est): 534.8K **Privately Held**
WEB: www.glassfx.com
SIC: **3231** **7699** **3471** Stained glass: made from purchased glass; china & glass repair; plating & polishing

**(G-3489)**
**GLD INDUSTRIES INC**
4411 Southford Trace Dr (61822-8565)
PHONE.................................217 390-9594
Brad Giffel, *President*

Brian Downing, *COO*
EMP: 3
SALES (est): 153.2K **Privately Held**
SIC: **7379** **3825** **3571** **7389** Computer related consulting services; test equipment for electronic & electric measurement; electronic computers;

**(G-3490)**
**GLUCOSENTIENT INC**
60 Hazelwood Dr (61820-7460)
PHONE.................................217 487-4087
Tian Lan, *Principal*
EMP: 5 EST: 2011
SALES (est): 387.1K **Privately Held**
SIC: **2835** In vitro diagnostics

**(G-3491)**
**GRANDE DIVA HAIR SALON**
1711 W John St Apt 6 (61821-3746)
PHONE.................................217 383-0023
Shawna Bass,
EMP: 20
SALES (est): 504.6K **Privately Held**
SIC: **3999** Sterilizers, barber & beauty shop

**(G-3492)**
**HARAN TECHNOLOGIES LLC**
1804 Vale St (61822-3563)
PHONE.................................217 239-1628
Kiruba Haran,
EMP: 3
SALES (est): 121.3K **Privately Held**
SIC: **3621** Mfg Motors/Generators

**(G-3493)**
**HARAN VENTURES LLC**
Also Called: Haran Technologies
1804 Vale St (61822-3563)
PHONE.................................217 239-1628
Kiruba Haran, *CEO*
EMP: 3
SALES (est): 103.7K **Privately Held**
SIC: **8748** **3621** Systems analysis & engineering consulting services

**(G-3494)**
**HERFF JONES LLC**
Herff Jones Cap & Gowns
1000 N Market St (61820-3009)
PHONE.................................217 351-9500
Tom Tanton, *General Mgr*
Ken Langlois, *Vice Pres*
Pam Schrock, *Purch Mgr*
Pam Shrock, *Purchasing*
Mark Taylor, *Sls & Mktg Exec*
EMP: 10
SALES (corp-wide): 1.1B **Privately Held**
WEB: www.herffjones.com
SIC: **3911** Rings, finger: precious metal
HQ: Herff Jones, Llc
 4501 W 62nd St
 Indianapolis IN 46268
 800 419-5462

**(G-3495)**
**HOTTINGER BLDWIN MSREMENTS INC**
Also Called: Hbm Somat
1806 Fox Dr Ste A (61820-7278)
PHONE.................................217 328-5359
James Cirk, *Branch Mgr*
EMP: 20
SALES (corp-wide): 1.6B **Privately Held**
WEB: www.ncode.com
SIC: **3541** Machine tools, metal cutting type
HQ: Hottinger Baldwin Measurements, Inc.
 19 Bartlett St
 Marlborough MA 01752
 508 624-4500

**(G-3496)**
**HUDSON TECHNOLOGIES INC**
3402 N Mattis Ave (61822-1082)
P.O. Box 1541, Pearl River NY (10965)
PHONE.................................217 373-1414
Kevin Zugibe, *Principal*
Brian Coleman, *COO*
Chuck Harkins, *Vice Pres*
Stephen Mandracchia, *Vice Pres*
Robert Stoody, *Vice Pres*
EMP: 30

SALES (corp-wide): 105.4MM **Publicly Held**
SIC: **1711** **2869** Refrigeration contractor; fluorinated hydrocarbon gases
PA: Hudson Technologies, Inc.
 1 Blue Hill Plz Ste 1541
 Pearl River NY 10965
 845 735-6000

**(G-3497)**
**IEP QUALITY INC**
2705 N Salisbury Ct (61821-6900)
PHONE.................................217 840-0570
Gdavid Frye, *Principal*
Susan Carty, *Principal*
James Shriner, *Principal*
Stephen Zahos, *Principal*
EMP: 4
SALES (est): 152.9K **Privately Held**
SIC: **7372** **8299** Educational computer software; educational services

**(G-3498)**
**ILLINI MATTRESS COMPANY INC**
514 S Country Fair Dr (61821-3638)
PHONE.................................217 359-0156
Fax: 217 353-7487
Charles E Stout Jr, *President*
Charles E Spout Jr, *President*
Jan Spout, *Manager*
EMP: 6
SALES (est): 764.5K **Privately Held**
WEB: www.illinimattress.com
SIC: **2515** Mattresses & foundations

**(G-3499)**
**ILLINI MEDIA CO (PA)**
Also Called: Wpgu-FM
512 E Green St Fl 3 (61820-6483)
PHONE.................................217 337-8300
Mary Cory, *Publisher*
Heather Mayer, *Editor*
Amara Enyia, *Vice Pres*
Ross Bessinger, *Mktg Dir*
Mark Jaeger, *Marketing Staff*
EMP: 300 EST: 1911
SQ FT: 10,000
SALES: 1.9MM **Privately Held**
WEB: www.dailyillini.com
SIC: **2711** **4832** **2741** **2721** Newspapers: publishing only, not printed on site; radio broadcasting stations; yearbooks: publishing & printing; periodicals

**(G-3500)**
**ILLINOIS NI CAST LLC**
Also Called: Alloy Engineering & Casting Co
1700 W Washington St (61821-2412)
PHONE.................................217 398-3200
Fax: 217 398-3208
Thomas Wright, *Vice Pres*
Amy Shibibi, *CTO*
Rich Grimm,
EMP: 1
SALES (est): 245.3K
SALES (corp-wide): 42.9MM **Privately Held**
SIC: **3317** **3325** Steel pipe & tubes; steel foundries
PA: Wirco, Inc.
 105 Progress Way
 Avilla IN 46710
 260 897-3768

**(G-3501)**
**INSTY-PRINTS OF CHAMPAIGN INC**
1822 Glenn Park Dr (61821-2400)
PHONE.................................217 356-6166
Fax: 217 356-6297
Richard Bishop, *President*
EMP: 7 EST: 1977
SALES: 370K **Privately Held**
SIC: **2752** **2789** Commercial printing, lithographic; bookbinding & related work

**(G-3502)**
**INTELLIWHEELS INC**
60 Hazelwood Dr (61820-7460)
PHONE.................................630 341-1942
Scott Daigle, *CEO*
EMP: 6
SALES (est): 370K **Privately Held**
SIC: **3842** Surgical appliances & supplies

## Champaign - Champaign County

**(G-3503)**
**ISS MEDICAL INC**
1602 Newton Dr (61822-1061)
PHONE .................................. 217 359-8681
Beniamino Barbieri, *President*
**EMP:** 4
**SQ FT:** 22,000
**SALES (est):** 158.8K **Privately Held**
**SIC:** 3841 Diagnostic apparatus, medical

**(G-3504)**
**JPMORGAN CHASE BANK NAT ASSN**
201 W University Ave # 1 (61820-8802)
PHONE .................................. 217 353-4234
Carol Welch, *Manager*
**EMP:** 6
**SALES (corp-wide):** 105.4B **Publicly Held**
**SIC:** 3578 Automatic teller machines (ATM)
**HQ:** Jpmorgan Chase Bank, National Association
1111 Polaris Pkwy
Columbus OH 43240
614 436-3055

**(G-3505)**
**KAELCO ENTRMT HOLDINGS INC**
3 Henson Pl Ste 1 (61820-7858)
PHONE .................................. 217 600-7815
**EMP:** 3 **EST:** 2013
**SQ FT:** 1,000
**SALES (est):** 80.2K **Privately Held**
**SIC:** 7819 2741 7929 Motion Picture Services Misc Publishing Entertainment

**(G-3506)**
**KELLEY VAULT CO INC**
Also Called: Kelley Crematory
1901 W Springer Dr (61821-2468)
PHONE .................................. 217 355-5551
Bonnie B Kelley, *President*
Roland W Kelley, *Corp Secy*
Richard Herr, *Vice Pres*
**EMP:** 13 **EST:** 1928
**SQ FT:** 1,400
**SALES (est):** 1.9MM **Privately Held**
**SIC:** 3272 Burial vaults, concrete or pre-cast terrazzo

**(G-3507)**
**KRAFT HEINZ FOODS COMPANY**
1701 W Bradley Ave (61821-2201)
PHONE .................................. 217 378-1900
Fax: 217 378-2068
James Grimley, *Plant Mgr*
David Tucker, *Opers Spvr*
Al Rude, *Purch Agent*
Su Collier, *Engineer*
Brad Rauchfuss, *Human Resources*
**EMP:** 75
**SALES (corp-wide):** 26.4B **Publicly Held**
**WEB:** www.kraftfoods.com
**SIC:** 2099 2098 2035 2026 Food preparations; macaroni & spaghetti; pickles, sauces & salad dressings; fluid milk; cheese, natural & processed; local trucking with storage
**HQ:** Kraft Heinz Foods Company
1 Ppg Pl Ste 3200
Pittsburgh PA 15222
412 456-5700

**(G-3508)**
**KWS CEREALS USA LLC**
4101 Colleen Dr (61822-3501)
PHONE .................................. 815 200-2666
Ken Davis, *Mng Member*
Stefan Bruns,
Juergen Leitzke,
Eric Ricard,
**EMP:** 3 **EST:** 2010
**SALES (est):** 79.9K
**SALES (corp-wide):** 1.1B **Privately Held**
**SIC:** 2041 2043 Grain mills (except rice); coffee substitutes, made from grain
**PA:** Kws Saat Se
Grimsehlstr. 31
Einbeck 37574
556 131-10

**(G-3509)**
**LABTHERMICS TECHNOLOGIES**
701 Devonshire Dr Ste B5 (61820-7328)
PHONE .................................. 217 351-7722
Peter Taylor, *CEO*
Eric Landau, *President*
Jeffrey Kouzmanoff, *Engineer*
Ron Johnston, *Director*
**EMP:** 7
**SQ FT:** 4,000
**SALES (est):** 600K **Privately Held**
**WEB:** www.labthermics.com
**SIC:** 3841 Surgical & medical instruments

**(G-3510)**
**LITANIA SPORTS GROUP INC**
Also Called: Gill Athletics
601 Mercury Dr (61822-9675)
P.O. Box 1790 (61824-1790)
PHONE .................................. 217 367-8438
Fax: 217 239-2255
C David Hodge, *President*
Steve Vogelsang, *Vice Pres*
Bridget Schuering, *Purch Agent*
Jerry Jondrecki, *Purchasing*
Judy Woz, *Purchasing*
◆ **EMP:** 135 **EST:** 1918
**SQ FT:** 225,000
**SALES (est):** 26.4MM **Privately Held**
**WEB:** www.gillathletics.com
**SIC:** 3949 Track & field athletic equipment

**(G-3511)**
**LITTELFUSE INC**
2110 S Oak St (61820-0903)
PHONE .................................. 217 531-3100
Mark Cooperman, *Branch Mgr*
**EMP:** 7
**SALES (corp-wide):** 1B **Publicly Held**
**SIC:** 3699 Electrical equipment & supplies
**PA:** Littelfuse, Inc.
8755 W Higgins Rd Ste 500
Chicago IL 60631
773 628-1000

**(G-3512)**
**MBM BUSINESS ASSISTANCE INC**
Also Called: Fastsigns
313 N Mattis Ave Ste 114 (61821-7901)
PHONE .................................. 217 398-6600
Fax: 217 403-0885
James Murphy, *President*
Linda Murphy, *Corp Secy*
**EMP:** 3
**SQ FT:** 3,700
**SALES (est):** 360.3K **Privately Held**
**SIC:** 3993 8243 5999 Signs & advertising specialties; operator training, computer; banners, flags, decals & posters

**(G-3513)**
**MEALPLOT INC**
60 Hazelwood Dr (61820-7460)
PHONE .................................. 217 419-2681
Jeanette Andrade, *CEO*
Manabu Nakamura, *Vice Pres*
**EMP:** 3 **EST:** 2014
**SALES (est):** 105.5K **Privately Held**
**SIC:** 7372 Prepackaged software

**(G-3514)**
**MILLER ROGER WESTON**
Also Called: Miller Enterprises
2611 W Cardinal Rd (61822)
PHONE .................................. 217 352-0476
Fax: 217 352-2266
Roger Weston Miller, *Owner*
**EMP:** 5
**SQ FT:** 36,000
**SALES:** 1MM **Privately Held**
**SIC:** 1794 3599 1711 Excavation & grading, building construction; machine shop, jobbing & repair; mechanical contractor

**(G-3515)**
**MIMOSA ACOUSTICS INC**
335 N Fremont St (61820-3612)
PHONE .................................. 217 359-9740
Patricia Jeng, *President*
Jan Painter, *Vice Pres*
Mike Katzenbach, *Engineer*
Don Wallace, *Engineer*
Jont Allen, *Manager*
**EMP:** 9
**SQ FT:** 1,100
**SALES:** 300K **Privately Held**
**WEB:** www.mimosaacoustics.com
**SIC:** 3842 8099 Hearing aids; hearing testing service

**(G-3516)**
**MMPCU LIMITED**
Also Called: Minuteman Press
905 S Neil St Ste B (61820-6567)
PHONE .................................. 217 355-0500
Fax: 217 355-0081
Paul Conforti, *Principal*
Nani Baker, *Principal*
Dick Carlson, *Principal*
Corrine Conforti, *Principal*
**EMP:** 5 **EST:** 2000
**SQ FT:** 1,250
**SALES (est):** 410K **Privately Held**
**WEB:** www.mmpcu.com
**SIC:** 2752 3555 Commercial printing, lithographic; printing presses

**(G-3517)**
**NEWS GAZETTE INC**
15 E Main St (61820-3641)
P.O. Box 677 (61824-0677)
PHONE .................................. 217 351-5252
Marajen Stevick Chinigo, *Ch of Bd*
John Hirschfeld, *President*
Michael Ovca, *CFO*
**EMP:** 245
**SQ FT:** 10,000
**SALES (est):** 10.4MM
**SALES (corp-wide):** 63.7MM **Privately Held**
**SIC:** 2711 Newspapers, publishing & printing
**PA:** The News-Gazette Inc
15 E Main St
Champaign IL 61820
217 351-5252

**(G-3518)**
**NEWS-GAZETTE INC**
810 Hamilton Dr (61820-6814)
PHONE .................................. 217 351-8128
John Foreman, *Principal*
**EMP:** 3
**SALES (est):** 127.5K **Privately Held**
**SIC:** 2711 Newspapers, publishing & printing

**(G-3519)**
**NEWS-GAZETTE INC (PA)**
Also Called: News Gazette
15 E Main St (61820-3641)
P.O. Box 423, Ballwin MO (63022-0423)
PHONE .................................. 217 351-5252
Fax: 217 351-5374
John Foreman, *President*
Tim Evans, *General Mgr*
Amelia Benner, *Editor*
Will Brumleve, *Editor*
Niko Dugan, *Editor*
**EMP:** 300
**SQ FT:** 15,000
**SALES (est):** 63.7MM **Privately Held**
**SIC:** 2711 Newspapers, publishing & printing

**(G-3520)**
**NITROGEN LABS INC**
618 W Hill St (61820-3323)
PHONE .................................. 312 504-8134
Giraldo Rosales, *President*
**EMP:** 3
**SALES (est):** 260.8K **Privately Held**
**SIC:** 2813 Nitrogen

**(G-3521)**
**OBITER RESEARCH LLC**
2809 Gemini Ct (61822-9647)
PHONE .................................. 217 359-1626
Chad Boulanger, *CEO*
William Boulanger, *General Mgr*
Alexei Pushechnikov, *Research*
Lauri Schultz, *Engineer*
Judy Herbert, *Comptroller*
**EMP:** 12
**SQ FT:** 2,300
**SALES:** 1.2MM **Privately Held**
**WEB:** www.obires.com
**SIC:** 2833 Medicinal chemicals

**(G-3522)**
**OCEANCOMM INCORPORATED**
60 Hazelwood Dr (61820-7460)
PHONE .................................. 800 757-3266
Andrew Singer, *Principal*
**EMP:** 6
**SALES (est):** 261.4K **Privately Held**
**SIC:** 3577 3812 Input/output equipment, computer; search & navigation equipment

**(G-3523)**
**PEPSI-COLA CHMPIGN URBANA BTLR**
Also Called: Pepsico
1306 W Anthony Dr (61821-1199)
PHONE .................................. 217 352-4126
Fax: 217 239-3949
Michael Comet, *President*
John P Trebellas, *Principal*
Bruce Thompson, *Treasurer*
John T Comet, *Admin Sec*
**EMP:** 75
**SQ FT:** 50,000
**SALES (est):** 12.3MM **Privately Held**
**SIC:** 2086 Carbonated soft drinks, bottled & canned

**(G-3524)**
**PETRONICS INC**
60 Hazelwood Dr Rm 216 (61820-7460)
PHONE .................................. 608 630-6527
Michael Friedman, *Principal*
**EMP:** 3
**SQ FT:** 200
**SALES (est):** 120K **Privately Held**
**SIC:** 3944 Electronic toys

**(G-3525)**
**PHOTONICARE INC**
60 Hazelwood Dr (61820-7460)
PHONE .................................. 405 880-7209
Ryan Shelton, *President*
Stephen Boppart, *Director*
**EMP:** 2
**SALES (est):** 251.7K **Privately Held**
**SIC:** 3841 Surgical & medical instruments

**(G-3526)**
**PLASTIPAK PACKAGING INC**
3310 W Springfield Ave (61822-2869)
PHONE .................................. 217 398-1832
Fax: 217 352-8420
Dennis Nuesmeyer, *Plant Mgr*
Mark Trott, *Materials Mgr*
Johnny Smith, *Engineer*
Julia Jamerson, *Controller*
Eric Schumacher, *Controller*
**EMP:** 300
**SALES (corp-wide):** 36.3MM **Privately Held**
**WEB:** www.plastipak.com
**SIC:** 3089 3085 Pallets, plastic; plastics bottles
**HQ:** Plastipak Packaging, Inc.
41605 Ann Arbor Rd E
Plymouth MI 48170
734 455-3600

**(G-3527)**
**POLYVINYL RECORD CO**
717 S Neil St (61820-5203)
PHONE .................................. 217 403-1752
Matt Lunsford, *President*
Darcie Lunsford, *Owner*
Mark Kenny, *Sales Mgr*
Sara Chabot, *Manager*
Andrew Desantis, *Manager*
**EMP:** 4
**SALES (est):** 300K **Privately Held**
**WEB:** www.polyvinylrecords.com
**SIC:** 5735 5961 2782 Records; record &/or tape (music or video) club, mail order; record albums

**(G-3528)**
**PRE PACK MACHINERY INC**
520 S Country Fair Dr (61821-3668)
P.O. Box 3875 (61826-3875)
PHONE .................................. 217 352-1010
Fax: 217 352-1119
Rick Martin, *President*
Steve Bray, *Vice Pres*
**EMP:** 4
**SQ FT:** 5,000

# Champaign - Champaign County (G-3529)

SALES (est): 721.5K  **Privately Held**
WEB: www.prepackmachinery.com
SIC: **3565**  7359  3556  3535  Packaging machinery; rental store, general; food products machinery; conveyors & conveying equipment

### (G-3529)
### PREMIER PRINTING ILLINOIS INC
Also Called: Premier Print Group
3104 Farber Dr  (61822-1074)
PHONE..................217 359-2219
Dan Paulson, *CEO*
Larry Baker, *General Mgr*
Kevin Netherton, *General Mgr*
Bob Spence, *Prdtn Mgr*
Wanda Kanagy, *Sales Executive*
EMP: 96
SALES (est): 15.4MM  **Privately Held**
SIC: **2759**  Commercial printing

### (G-3530)
### PRENOSIS INC
210 Hazelwood Dr Ste 103  (61822-7488)
PHONE..................949 246-3113
Bobby Reddy Jr, *President*
EMP: 6
SALES (est): 515.2K  **Privately Held**
SIC: **2835**  In vitro diagnostics

### (G-3531)
### PSYONIC INC
60 Hazelwood Dr  (61820-7460)
PHONE..................773 888-3252
Aadeel Akhtar, *CEO*
Patrick Slade, *Chief Engr*
EMP: 4
SALES (est): 149.2K  **Privately Held**
SIC: **3842**  Limbs, artificial

### (G-3532)
### RESEARCH PRESS COMPANY
2612 N Mattis Ave  (61822-1053)
P.O. Box 7886  (61826-7886)
PHONE..................217 352-3273
Fax: 217 352-1221
David R Parkinson, *Ch of Bd*
Russell Pence, *President*
Cythia Martin, *Principal*
Ann O Parkinson, *Principal*
Buddy Lane, *Warehouse Mgr*
EMP: 14
SQ FT: 10,500
SALES: 2.5MM  **Privately Held**
WEB: www.researchpress.com
SIC: **2731**  Books: publishing only; pamphlets: publishing only, not printed on site

### (G-3533)
### RICHARDSON IRONWORKS LLC
313 N Mattis Ave Ste 208  (61821-2461)
PHONE..................217 359-3333
EMP: 5
SALES (est): 440K  **Privately Held**
SIC: **2514**  Mfg Metal Household Furniture

### (G-3534)
### ROCKWELL AUTOMATION INC
2802 W Bloomington Rd  (61822-9548)
PHONE..................217 373-0800
Fax: 217 373-0888
Andy Slupecki, *General Mgr*
Jason Semovoski, *Opers Mgr*
Timothy Jennings, *Production*
EMP: 150  **Publicly Held**
SIC: **3625**  Electric controls & control accessories, industrial
PA: Rockwell Automation, Inc.
1201 S 2nd St
Milwaukee WI 53204

### (G-3535)
### SAFELITE GLASS CORP
719 S Neil St  (61820-5203)
PHONE..................877 800-2727
EMP: 3
SALES (corp-wide): 2.9B  **Privately Held**
SIC: **3231**  Windshields, glass: made from purchased glass
HQ: Safelite Glass Corp.
7400 Safelite Way
Columbus OH 43235
614 210-9000

### (G-3536)
### SENFORMATICS LLC
601 W Green St  (61820-5012)
P.O. Box 2790  (61825-2790)
PHONE..................217 419-2571
Joshua Peschel, *President*
EMP: 5
SALES (est): 137.2K  **Privately Held**
SIC: **8742**  3731  Automation & robotics consultant; submersible marine robots, manned or unmanned

### (G-3537)
### SERIONIX
60 Hazelwood Dr  (61820-7460)
PHONE..................651 503-3930
James Langer, *Principal*
EMP: 3
SALES (est): 255.7K  **Privately Held**
SIC: **2821**  Plastics materials & resins

### (G-3538)
### SHUNK CORP
47 E Kenyon Rd  (61820-2216)
PHONE..................217 398-2636
Daniel Shunk, *Principal*
EMP: 6
SALES (est): 967.9K  **Privately Held**
SIC: **2851**  Removers & cleaners

### (G-3539)
### SILGAN WHITE CAP CORPORATION
Also Called: Silgan Holdings Inc
3209 Farber Dr  (61822-1456)
PHONE..................217 398-1600
Fax: 217 398-5970
Kim Howarter, *QC Dir*
Dennis Turman, *Branch Mgr*
Jim Warstler, *Maintence Staff*
EMP: 109
SALES (corp-wide): 3.6B  **Publicly Held**
WEB: www.silganclosures.com
SIC: **3411**  Metal cans
HQ: Silgan White Cap Corporation
4 Landmark Sq Ste 400
Stamford CT 06901

### (G-3540)
### SILVER MACHINE SHOP INC
713 N Market St  (61820-3004)
PHONE..................217 359-5717
Fax: 217 359-9065
Scott Silver, *President*
John Silver, *Principal*
Margaret Silver, *Treasurer*
EMP: 8
SALES (est): 867.3K  **Privately Held**
SIC: **7692**  3599  3444  3441  Welding repair; machine shop, jobbing & repair; sheet metalwork; fabricated structural metal

### (G-3541)
### SOMAT CORPORATION (PA)
2202 Fox Dr Ste A  (61820-7595)
PHONE..................800 578-4260
Fax: 217 328-6576
Jim Kirk, *CEO*
Steve Fleet, *Corp Secy*
Chad Larson, *Production*
Scott Burner, *CFO*
Brad Giffel, *CTO*
EMP: 27
SQ FT: 10,000
SALES (est): 2MM  **Privately Held**
WEB: www.somat.com
SIC: **3577**  Input/output equipment, computer

### (G-3542)
### SONISTIC
60 Hazelwood Dr Ste 230g  (61820-7460)
PHONE..................217 377-9698
Aaron Jones, *Principal*
EMP: 3
SALES (est): 186.9K  **Privately Held**
SIC: **3651**  Household audio & video equipment

### (G-3543)
### SOUTHFIELD CORPORATION
Also Called: Central Hauling
3200 W Springfield Ave  (61822-2867)
PHONE..................217 398-4300
Kevin Tervin, *Branch Mgr*
Carl Bleichner, *Manager*
EMP: 15
SALES (corp-wide): 273.9MM  **Privately Held**
WEB: www.prairiegroup.com
SIC: **3251**  Structural brick & blocks
HQ: Southfield Corporation
8995 W 95th St
Palos Hills IL 60465
708 344-1000

### (G-3544)
### SPECTROCLICK INC
904 Mayfair Rd  (61821-4437)
PHONE..................217 356-4829
Dr Alexander Scheeline, *President*
EMP: 2
SALES (est): 288.5K  **Privately Held**
SIC: **3826**  Analytical instruments

### (G-3545)
### SPORT REDI-MIX LLC (PA)
401 Wilbur Ave  (61822-1319)
P.O. Box 292  (61824-0292)
PHONE..................217 355-4222
Fax: 217 356-5014
Chris Spencer, *Sales Executive*
Christopher Q Knipfer, *Mng Member*
Chris Kinpfer, *Mng Member*
Chad Burned, *Manager*
Kevin Wilhelm, *Manager*
EMP: 25 EST: 2001
SALES (est): 4.3MM  **Privately Held**
WEB: www.sportredimix.com
SIC: **3241**  5251  Cement, hydraulic; tools

### (G-3546)
### STALEY CONCRETE CO
4106 Kearns Dr  (61822-8531)
PHONE..................217 356-9533
Fax: 217 239-0002
Ron Kenny, *President*
Alan Nathan, *Professor*
EMP: 22
SALES (est): 3.6MM  **Privately Held**
WEB: www.staleyconcrete.com
SIC: **3273**  Ready-mixed concrete

### (G-3547)
### STANS SPORTSWORLD INC
47 E Green St  (61820-5311)
PHONE..................217 359-8474
Fax: 217 359-0449
Cameron S Wallace, *President*
Micha Griskell, *Marketing Staff*
EMP: 4
SQ FT: 3,000
SALES: 600K  **Privately Held**
WEB: www.stanssportsworldinc.com
SIC: **5199**  2396  2395  3993  Advertising specialties; screen printing on fabric articles; embroidery & art needlework; signs & advertising specialties

### (G-3548)
### STARFIRE INDUSTRIES LLC
2109 S Oak St Ste 100  (61820-0914)
PHONE..................217 721-4165
Brian E Jurczyk, *President*
Robert A Stubbers,
EMP: 33
SQ FT: 12,000
SALES: 820K  **Privately Held**
WEB: www.starfireindustries.com
SIC: **3764**  3844  3671  8731  Guided missile & space vehicle engines, research & devel.; nuclear irradiation equipment; transmittal, industrial & special purpose electron tubes; commercial physical research; commercial research laboratory

### (G-3549)
### TE SHURT SHOP INC
Also Called: Teshurt
711 S Wright St  (61820-5710)
PHONE..................217 344-1226
Fax: 217 344-0014
Robert Sammons, *President*
Greg Grieme, *Treasurer*
Michele Fassett, *Manager*
Sarah Staker, *Manager*
EMP: 17
SQ FT: 3,500

SALES: 950K  **Privately Held**
WEB: www.teshurt.com
SIC: **5611**  2759  Clothing, sportswear, men's & boys'; letterpress & screen printing

### (G-3550)
### TROPHYTIME INC
223 S Locust St  (61820-4125)
PHONE..................217 351-7958
Fax: 217 351-3109
Keith Bowman, *Owner*
Sharon Aultman, *Executive*
EMP: 7
SQ FT: 3,600
SALES (est): 916.3K  **Privately Held**
SIC: **5999**  3993  Trophies & plaques; signs & advertising specialties

### (G-3551)
### UNDERWOOD DENTAL LABORATORIES
301 N 1st St  (61820-4121)
P.O. Box 1158, Mattoon  (61938-1158)
PHONE..................217 398-0090
Fax: 217 398-8098
Richard Kepp, *President*
Ron Hatfield, *Vice Pres*
Harold Turner, *Treasurer*
James Hone, *Admin Sec*
EMP: 10
SQ FT: 4,000
SALES (est): 810K  **Privately Held**
SIC: **8072**  3843  Dental laboratories; dental equipment & supplies

### (G-3552)
### UNIVERSITY OF ILLINOIS
Also Called: Document Services
54 E Gregory Dr  (61820-6607)
PHONE..................217 333-9350
Barbara Childers, *Director*
EMP: 50
SALES (corp-wide): 3.8B  **Privately Held**
SIC: **2752**  Commercial printing, lithographic
PA: University Of Illinois
506 S Wright St Rm 364
Urbana IL 61801
217 333-1000

### (G-3553)
### VARSITY STRIPING & CNSTR CO
2601 W Cardinal Rd  (61822)
P.O. Box 3055  (61826-3055)
PHONE..................217 352-2203
Fax: 258-8339
Bonnie B Kemper, *President*
Kristen S Kemper, *Corp Secy*
EMP: 30 EST: 1981
SQ FT: 3,000
SALES (est): 2.3MM  **Privately Held**
WEB: www.varsitystriping.com
SIC: **1721**  3993  Pavement marking contractor; signs & advertising specialties

### (G-3554)
### VERTICAL TOWER PARTNER
2626 Midwest Ct  (61822-8929)
PHONE..................217 819-3040
Darrin Peters, *Principal*
EMP: 4
SALES (est): 438.3K  **Privately Held**
SIC: **2591**  Blinds vertical

### (G-3555)
### VESUVIUS CRUCIBLE COMPANY (DH)
1404 Newton Dr  (61822-1069)
P.O. Box 4014  (61824-4014)
PHONE..................217 351-5000
Jerry Taylor, *General Mgr*
Gary Polk, *Business Mgr*
Michael Cunningham, *COO*
Patrick Bikard, *Vice Pres*
Dave Hutzayluk, *Vice Pres*
▲ EMP: 4  EST: 1916
SQ FT: 85,000
SALES (est): 531.5MM
SALES (corp-wide): 1.7B  **Privately Held**
SIC: **3297**  5051  Nonclay refractories; foundry products

# GEOGRAPHIC SECTION

Channahon - Will County (G-3580)

**(G-3556)**
**VESUVIUS U S A CORPORATION (DH)**
Also Called: Foseco
1404 Newton Dr (61822-1069)
P.O. Box 4080 (61824-4080)
PHONE..................217 351-5000
Fax: 217 351-5031
Glenn Cowie, *President*
Chad Beukema, *Asst Treas*
Jeannie Deck, *Sales Staff*
Steven Delcotto, *Admin Sec*
◆ **EMP:** 180 **EST:** 1966
**SALES (est):** 483MM
**SALES (corp-wide):** 1.7B **Privately Held**
**WEB:** www.vesuvius.com
**SIC: 5085** 3297 Refractory material; non-clay refractories; graphite refractories: carbon bond or ceramic bond
**HQ:** Vesuvius Crucible Company
1404 Newton Dr
Champaign IL 61822
217 351-5000

**(G-3557)**
**VISUAL INFORMATION TECH INC**
60 Hazelwood Dr (61820-7460)
PHONE..................217 841-2155
Randall J Sandone, *CEO*
**EMP:** 4
**SALES (est):** 220K **Privately Held**
**SIC: 7372** Prepackaged software

**(G-3558)**
**WANT ADS OF CHAMPAIGN INC (PA)**
Also Called: Thrifty Nckel Amrcn Clssifieds
505 E University Ave C (61820-3847)
PHONE..................217 356-4804
Fax: 217 356-4970
Denny Merrifield, *President*
**EMP:** 10
**SALES (est):** 1.4MM **Privately Held**
**SIC: 2711** 2741 Newspapers: publishing only, not printed on site; miscellaneous publishing

**(G-3559)**
**WARBLER OF ILLINOIS COMPANY**
3127 Village Office Pl (61822-7673)
P.O. Box 5131, Springfield (62705-5131)
PHONE..................301 520-0438
Linda K May, *President*
Mark Cullen, *Counsel*
Windy Cardis, *Vice Pres*
**EMP:** 6
**SALES:** 950K **Privately Held**
**SIC: 3826** Environmental testing equipment

**(G-3560)**
**WEISKAMP SCREEN PRINTING**
312 S Neil St (61820-4914)
PHONE..................217 398-8428
Fax: 217 398-8467
Edward Weiskamp, *Owner*
Todd Duncan, *Executive*
**EMP:** 9
**SALES (est):** 700K **Privately Held**
**SIC: 2759** 3993 2396 Commercial printing; signs & advertising specialties; automotive & apparel trimmings

**(G-3561)**
**WIRCO INC**
1700 W Washington St (61821-2412)
PHONE..................217 398-3200
**EMP:** 85
**SALES (corp-wide):** 42.9MM **Privately Held**
**SIC: 3544** 3496 3322 3599 Industrial molds; woven wire products; malleable iron foundries; machine shop, jobbing & repair
**PA:** Wirco, Inc.
105 Progress Way
Avilla IN 46710
260 897-3768

**(G-3562)**
**WOLFRAM RESEARCH INC (PA)**
100 Trade Centre Dr 6th (61820-6858)
P.O. Box 6059 (61826-6059)
PHONE..................217 398-0700
Fax: 217 398-0747
Stephen Wolfram, *President*
Alex Upellini, *Area Mgr*
Steven Alexander, *COO*
Sarah Duensing, *Project Mgr*
Michael Trott, *Opers Mgr*
**EMP:** 148
**SQ FT:** 60,000
**SALES (est):** 86.6MM **Privately Held**
**WEB:** www.stephenwolfram.com
**SIC: 7372** Prepackaged software

**(G-3563)**
**XEROX CORPORATION**
1211 Hagan St (61820-2508)
PHONE..................217 355-5460
C Armstrong, *Branch Mgr*
**EMP:** 75
**SALES (corp-wide):** 10.7B **Publicly Held**
**WEB:** www.xerox.com
**SIC: 3861** Photographic equipment & supplies
**PA:** Xerox Corporation
201 Merritt 7
Norwalk CT 06851
203 968-3000

## Channahon
### Will County

**(G-3564)**
**AIR PRODUCTS AND CHEMICALS INC**
25915 S Frontage Rd (60410-8723)
PHONE..................815 423-5032
Mark Steinman, *Branch Mgr*
**EMP:** 23
**SALES (corp-wide):** 9.5B **Publicly Held**
**WEB:** www.airproducts.com
**SIC: 2813** Industrial gases
**PA:** Air Products And Chemicals, Inc.
7201 Hamilton Blvd
Allentown PA 18195
610 481-4911

**(G-3565)**
**AMERICAS STYRENICS LLC**
26332 S Frontage Rd (60410-5288)
PHONE..................815 418-6403
Jon Timbers, *Mng Member*
Bonnie J Haydel, *Admin Asst*
**EMP:** 92 **Privately Held**
**SIC: 2821** Plastics materials & resins
**PA:** Americas Styrenics Llc
24 Waterway Ave Ste 1200
The Woodlands TX 77380

**(G-3566)**
**CRANE COMPOSITES INC (DH)**
23525 W Eames St (60410-3220)
PHONE..................815 467-8600
Jeff Craney, *President*
David Reuter, *District Mgr*
Rob Hancock, *Vice Pres*
Mike Miller, *Vice Pres*
Jack Stambaugh, *Vice Pres*
◆ **EMP:** 253 **EST:** 1954
**SQ FT:** 145,000
**SALES (est):** 89.5MM
**SALES (corp-wide):** 2.7B **Publicly Held**
**WEB:** www.kemlite.net
**SIC: 3089** Panels, building: plastic

**(G-3567)**
**CRANE COMPOSITES INC**
Also Called: Kemlite Sequentia Products
23525 W Eames St (60410-3220)
PHONE..................815 467-1437
Fax: 815 467-8666
Robert Barney, *Vice Pres*
Michael Sheron, *Opers-Prdtn-Mfg*
Jack Stambaugh, *VP Sales*
Brayan Esquivel, *Sales Mgr*
Daniel Pedraza, *Sales Mgr*
**EMP:** 173
**SALES (corp-wide):** 2.7B **Publicly Held**
**WEB:** www.kemlite.net
**SIC: 3089** Panels, building: plastic

**HQ:** Crane Composites, Inc.
23525 W Eames St
Channahon IL 60410
815 467-8600

**(G-3568)**
**CROSSLINK COATINGS CORPORATION**
24115 S Municipal Dr (60410-8710)
P.O. Box 777 (60410-0777)
PHONE..................815 467-7970
Fax: 815 467-7997
Dale B Boddeker, *President*
Wilson Stonebraker Sr, *Vice Pres*
Mignon S Boddekker, *Treasurer*
Joann Stonebraker, *Admin Sec*
**EMP:** 5
**SQ FT:** 8,000
**SALES (est):** 1MM **Privately Held**
**SIC: 3479** 2899 Coating of metals & formed products; ink or writing fluids

**(G-3569)**
**DEDICATED TCS LLC**
23330 S Frontage Rd W (60410-8648)
PHONE..................815 467-9560
Jim Coleman, *Manager*
**EMP:** 12
**SALES (corp-wide):** 3.5MM **Privately Held**
**SIC: 3792** Travel trailers & campers
**PA:** Dedicated Tcs, Llc
2700 175th St
Lansing IL 60438
708 474-2580

**(G-3570)**
**DIAMOND QUALITY MANUFACTURING**
24109 S Northern Ill Dr (60410-5358)
PHONE..................815 521-4184
Fax: 815 521-4185
Joseph Majewski, *Owner*
**EMP:** 8
**SALES (est):** 1.2MM **Privately Held**
**SIC: 3999** Manufacturing industries

**(G-3571)**
**DIVERSIFIED CPC INTL INC (DH)**
24338 W Durkee Rd (60410-9719)
PHONE..................815 423-5991
Fax: 815 423-5627
Bill Auriemma, *CEO*
John P Dowd II, *Vice Pres*
William A Frauenheim III, *Vice Pres*
William Frauenheim, *Vice Pres*
Bill Madigan, *Vice Pres*
◆ **EMP:** 25
**SQ FT:** 9,600
**SALES:** 145MM
**SALES (corp-wide):** 35.1B **Privately Held**
**WEB:** www.diversifiedcpc.com
**SIC: 2813** 5169 Industrial gases; aerosols
**HQ:** Sumitomo Corporation Of Americas
300 Madison Ave
New York NY 10017
212 207-0700

**(G-3572)**
**DOW CHEMICAL COMPANY**
26332 S Frontage Rd (60410-5592)
PHONE..................815 423-5921
Michael E Lewis, *Vice Pres*
Dave Schaeffer, *Vice Pres*
John Herod, *Traffic Mgr*
Greg Kuhn, *Manager*
Robert Hawkins, *Manager*
**EMP:** 158
**SALES (corp-wide):** 48.1B **Publicly Held**
**WEB:** www.dow.com
**SIC: 2821** 3086 Plastics materials & resins; plastics foam products
**PA:** The Dow Chemical Company
2030 Dow Ctr
Midland MI 48674
989 636-1000

**(G-3573)**
**EMC**
22824 W Winchester Dr (60410-3308)
PHONE..................480 225-5498
Joseph J Simon, *President*
Ryan Kucera, *Consultant*
**EMP:** 5
**SALES (est):** 432.3K **Privately Held**
**SIC: 3572** Computer storage devices

**(G-3574)**
**EXCEL MACHINE & TOOL**
24050 S Northern Ill Dr (60410-5183)
PHONE..................815 467-1177
Fax: 815 467-1178
Richard Sorg, *President*
**EMP:** 6
**SQ FT:** 5,000
**SALES (est):** 969.2K **Privately Held**
**SIC: 3599** Custom machinery

**(G-3575)**
**EXPRESS CARE**
24361 W Eames St (60410-5594)
PHONE..................815 521-2185
Robert Bond, *President*
**EMP:** 3
**SALES (est):** 231.2K **Privately Held**
**SIC: 2899** Oil treating compounds

**(G-3576)**
**INEOS STYROLUTION AMERICA LLC**
25846 S Frontage Rd (60410-5222)
PHONE..................815 423-5541
**EMP:** 5
**SALES (corp-wide):** 40B **Privately Held**
**SIC: 2869** Industrial organic chemicals
**HQ:** Ineos Styrolution America Llc
4245 Meridian Pkwy # 151
Aurora IL 60504
630 820-9500

**(G-3577)**
**LODERS CROKLAAN BV**
24708 W Durkee Rd (60410-5249)
PHONE..................815 730-5200
Don Grubba, *General Mgr*
Patrick Low, *Pastor*
Ken Cinzio, *VP Opers*
Karen Baldacci, *Production*
Kevin Quick, *Engineer*
**EMP:** 154
**SALES (corp-wide):** 3.7K **Privately Held**
**SIC: 2079** 2045 Edible oil products, except corn oil; doughs, frozen or refrigerated: from purchased flour
**HQ:** Loders Croklaan B.V.
Hogeweg 1
Wormerveer
756 292-911

**(G-3578)**
**LODERS CROKLAAN USA LLC**
24708 W Durkee Rd (60410-5249)
PHONE..................815 730-5200
Fax: 815 730-5202
Mike Molenkamp, *CFO*
Lori King, *Sales Mgr*
David Corp, *Manager*
Jill Papesh, *Director*
Julian Veitch,
▲ **EMP:** 180
**SQ FT:** 100
**SALES:** 440MM
**SALES (corp-wide):** 3.7K **Privately Held**
**SIC: 2079** Edible oil products, except corn oil
**HQ:** Loders Croklaan B.V.
Hogeweg 1
Wormerveer
756 292-911

**(G-3579)**
**MCNDT PIPELINE LTD (PA)**
24154 S Northern Ill Dr (60410-5391)
P.O. Box 545 (60410-0545)
PHONE..................815 467-5200
Fax: 815 467-7868
Cindy McCain, *President*
Jim McCain, *Vice Pres*
**EMP:** 6
**SALES:** 1MM **Privately Held**
**SIC: 1389** 8734 Pipe testing, oil field service; construction, repair & dismantling services; testing laboratories

**(G-3580)**
**MECHANICAL INDUS STL SVCS INC (PA)**
24226 S Northern Ill Dr (60410-5111)
PHONE..................815 521-1725
Fax: 815 521-1732
Michael Hannon, *President*
Robert Filotto, *CFO*

# Channahon - Will County (G-3581)

Kevin Hannon, *Sales Mgr*
Karen Jacobs, *Office Mgr*
Robert Hartley, *Manager*
**EMP:** 30
**SQ FT:** 14,000
**SALES (est):** 7.4MM **Privately Held**
**SIC: 1791** 3446 3441 Structural steel erection; architectural metalwork; fabricated structural metal

**(G-3581)**
**MIDWEST EDM SPECIALTIES INC**
24108 S Northern Ill Dr (60410-5391)
**PHONE**............815 521-2130
Richard Thompson, *President*
Pam Jones, *Bookkeeper*
**EMP:** 6
**SQ FT:** 2,000
**SALES (est):** 675.4K **Privately Held**
**WEB:** www.midwestedm.com
**SIC: 3599** Machine shop, jobbing & repair

**(G-3582)**
**NEKG HOLDINGS INC**
26709 S Kimberly Ln (60410-5408)
**PHONE**............815 383-1379
Erik Harrington, *President*
Neil Harrington, *Principal*
Karen Harrington, *Admin Sec*
**EMP:** 3
**SALES:** 500K **Privately Held**
**SIC: 3452** Bolts, nuts, rivets & washers

**(G-3583)**
**PRICE TECH GROUP ILLINOIS LLC (PA)**
25210-B W Reed St (60410)
P.O. Box 486 (60410-0486)
**PHONE**............815 521-4667
**Fax:** 815 521-4668
Brandon A Hamilton, *Manager*
Daniel A Hamilton,
**EMP:** 3
**SQ FT:** 20,000
**SALES (est):** 890.9K **Privately Held**
**SIC: 2999** Waxes, petroleum: not produced in petroleum refineries

**(G-3584)**
**ROMAR CABINET & TOP CO INC**
23949 S Northern Ill Dr (60410-5181)
**PHONE**............815 467-4452
**Fax:** 815 467-9985
Anthony De Angelis, *President*
Bob Hill, *President*
Robert Hill, *Vice Pres*
Anthony Bellettiere, *Sales Staff*
Brian Parker, *Sales Staff*
**EMP:** 100
**SQ FT:** 40,000
**SALES (est):** 14.6MM **Privately Held**
**WEB:** www.romarcabinet.com
**SIC: 2434** Wood kitchen cabinets

**(G-3585)**
**SCOTTS COMPANY LLC**
23580 W Bluff Rd (60410-8614)
**PHONE**............815 467-1605
Mickey Conner, *Office Mgr*
Anita Wood, *Branch Mgr*
Mike Davitt, *Manager*
**EMP:** 40
**SALES (corp-wide):** 2.8B **Publicly Held**
**WEB:** www.scottscompany.com
**SIC: 2873** Fertilizers: natural (organic), except compost
**HQ:** The Scotts Company Llc
14111 Scottslawn Rd
Marysville OH 43040
937 644-3729

**(G-3586)**
**SMID HEATING & AIR**
23864 W Sussex Dr (60410-3064)
P.O. Box 828, Plainfield (60544-0828)
**PHONE**............815 467-0362
Robert Smid, *President*
**EMP:** 1
**SALES:** 500K **Privately Held**
**SIC: 1711** 3444 Heating systems repair & maintenance; sheet metalwork

**(G-3587)**
**TESTA STEEL CONSTRUCTORS INC**
22449 Thomas Dilon Dr (60410)
P.O. Box 51 (60410-0051)
**PHONE**............815 729-4777
**Fax:** 815 729-4795
Michael J Testa, *President*
**EMP:** 11
**SALES (est):** 2.4MM **Privately Held**
**SIC: 3441** Fabricated structural metal

## Chapin
### Morgan County

**(G-3588)**
**TRAILERS INC**
Also Called: Trailers Machine & Welding
1839 Saint Pauls Ch Rd (62628-4008)
**PHONE**............217 472-6000
Marsha Schoth, *President*
**EMP:** 3
**SQ FT:** 5,000
**SALES (est):** 356.2K **Privately Held**
**SIC: 7692** 7539 3599 Welding repair; machine shop, automotive; machine shop, jobbing & repair

## Charleston
### Coles County

**(G-3589)**
**3RD BASE BAR**
18263 E County Road 400n (61920-6601)
**PHONE**............217 644-2424
Jeanne Oliver, *Owner*
**EMP:** 4
**SALES (est):** 229K **Privately Held**
**SIC: 2599** Bar, restaurant & cafeteria furniture

**(G-3590)**
**BLUESCOPE BUILDINGS N AMER INC**
890 W State St (61920-1086)
**PHONE**............217 348-7676
Darrell Duahoo, *Branch Mgr*
**EMP:** 42 **Privately Held**
**WEB:** www.butlermfg.com
**SIC: 3448** Prefabricated metal buildings
**HQ:** Bluescope Buildings North America, Inc.
1540 Genessee St
Kansas City MO 64102

**(G-3591)**
**CCAR INDUSTRIES**
200 W Locust Ave (61920-1044)
**PHONE**............217 345-3300
Christine Puckle, *Exec Dir*
**EMP:** 30
**SALES (corp-wide):** 7MM **Privately Held**
**SIC: 3999** Barber & beauty shop equipment
**PA:** Ccar Industries
1530 Lincoln Ave
Charleston IL 61920
217 345-7058

**(G-3592)**
**CHARLESTON CONCRETE SUPPLY CO**
Also Called: Charleston Farrier Contruction
2417 18th St (61920-4344)
**PHONE**............217 345-6404
**Fax:** 217 345-6403
Jerry Tarble, *President*
John Tarble, *Vice Pres*
Ronald Murphy, *Treasurer*
**EMP:** 10
**SALES (est):** 1.3MM **Privately Held**
**SIC: 3273** Ready-mixed concrete

**(G-3593)**
**CHARLESTON COUNTY MARKET**
Also Called: Walker's Supersaver Foods
551 W Lincoln Ave (61920-2443)
**PHONE**............217 345-7031
**Fax:** 217 345-5324
Robert L Walker, *President*
Wilbur D Walker, *Corp Secy*
Heather Miller, *Executive*
**EMP:** 80
**SALES (est):** 5.4MM **Privately Held**
**SIC: 5411** 2052 2051 Grocery stores, independent; cookies & crackers; bread, cake & related products

**(G-3594)**
**CHARLESTON GRAPHICS INC**
807a 18th St (61920-2936)
Jeff Browning, *CEO*
Lori D Browning, *President*
Dennis Grant, *President*
William O Browning, *Chairman*
Betty Jo Browning, *Vice Pres*
**EMP:** 3
**SALES (est):** 230K **Privately Held**
**SIC: 7336** 2791 Commercial art & graphic design; typesetting

**(G-3595)**
**COCA-COLA REFRESHMENTS USA INC**
1321 Loxa Rd (61920-7690)
**PHONE**............217 348-1001
Dale Usinger, *Manager*
**EMP:** 11
**SALES (corp-wide):** 41.8B **Publicly Held**
**SIC: 7319** 5499 2086 Distribution of advertising material or sample services; beverage stores; carbonated beverages, nonalcoholic: bottled & canned
**HQ:** Coca-Cola Refreshments Usa, Inc.
2500 Windy Ridge Pkwy Se
Atlanta GA 30339
770 989-3000

**(G-3596)**
**DIETZGEN CORPORATION**
1555 N 5th St (61920-1181)
**PHONE**............217 348-8111
Darren A Letang, *President*
**EMP:** 12
**SALES (corp-wide):** 55.4MM **Privately Held**
**SIC: 2679** Paper products, converted
**PA:** Dietzgen Corporation
121 Kelsey Ln Ste G
Tampa FL 33619
813 286-4767

**(G-3597)**
**GANO WELDING SUPPLIES INC**
320 Railroad Ave (61920-1416)
P.O. Box 295 (61920-0295)
**PHONE**............217 345-3777
**Fax:** 217 345-3783
Patrick Slaughter, *President*
T K Slaughter, *Vice Pres*
**EMP:** 12
**SQ FT:** 2,400
**SALES (est):** 4.6MM **Privately Held**
**WEB:** www.ganowelding.com
**SIC: 5084** 2813 5169 Welding machinery & equipment; acetylene; chemicals & allied products

**(G-3598)**
**GAVINA GRAPHICS**
1920 18th St (61920-3611)
**PHONE**............217 345-9228
Kurby Johnson, *Owner*
**EMP:** 12
**SALES (est):** 699.4K **Privately Held**
**SIC: 2395** Embroidery & art needlework

**(G-3599)**
**ILLINOIS TOOL WORKS INC**
Also Called: Hi-Cone Div
1155 N 5th St (61920-1173)
**PHONE**............217 345-2166
Andrew Albin, *General Mgr*
Keith Waggoner, *Executive*
**EMP:** 50
**SQ FT:** 80,000
**SALES (corp-wide):** 13.6B **Publicly Held**
**SIC: 3086** 3565 5199 Packaging & shipping materials, foamed plastic; packaging machinery; packaging materials
**PA:** Illinois Tool Works Inc.
155 Harlem Ave
Glenview IL 60025
847 724-7500

**(G-3600)**
**INDIGO CIGAR FACTORY**
503 7th St (61920-2027)
**PHONE**............217 348-1514
Marvin Mirick, *Owner*
**EMP:** 3
**SALES (est):** 191.4K **Privately Held**
**SIC: 3999** Cigarette & cigar products & accessories

**(G-3601)**
**J J COLLINS SONS INC**
2351 Madison Ave (61920-9382)
**PHONE**............217 345-7606
**Fax:** 217 348-1852
Robert Heywood, *Plant Mgr*
Jeffrey Phillips, *Plant Mgr*
Mark Lasky, *Project Mgr*
Jim Collins Jr, *Manager*
Michael Wolfe, *Supervisor*
**EMP:** 100
**SALES (corp-wide):** 30MM **Privately Held**
**WEB:** www.jjcollins.com
**SIC: 2752** Business forms, lithographed
**PA:** J. J. Collins' Sons, Inc.
7125 Janes Ave Ste 200
Woodridge IL 60517
630 960-2525

**(G-3602)**
**JOHN KILLOUGH DPM CWS (PA)**
1301 Deerpath (61920-8734)
**PHONE**............217 348-3339
John R Killough, *President*
**EMP:** 4
**SALES (est):** 486K **Privately Held**
**SIC: 3949** Sporting & athletic goods

**(G-3603)**
**LESTER BUILDING SYSTEMS LLC**
890 W State St (61920-1086)
**PHONE**............217 348-7676
**Fax:** 217 345-7159
Ed Janowski, *Branch Mgr*
**EMP:** 35
**SALES (corp-wide):** 78.1MM **Privately Held**
**WEB:** www.lesterbuildings.com
**SIC: 2452** Prefabricated buildings, wood
**PA:** Lester Building Systems, Llc
1111 2nd Ave S
Lester Prairie MN 55354
320 395-5212

**(G-3604)**
**MID-ILLINOIS CONCRETE INC**
Also Called: Charleston Ready Mix
2417 18th St (61920-4344)
**PHONE**............217 345-6404
Robert Kepley, *Manager*
**EMP:** 3
**SALES (corp-wide):** 17.2MM **Privately Held**
**WEB:** www.mid-illinoisconcrete.com
**SIC: 3272** Concrete products
**PA:** Mid-Illinois Concrete, Inc.
1805 S 4th St
Effingham IL
217 342-2115

**(G-3605)**
**NANCYS LETTERING SHOP**
1115 Lincoln Ave (61920-3009)
**PHONE**............217 345-6007
**Fax:** 217 348-6000
Nancy Beabout, *Owner*
**EMP:** 3
**SQ FT:** 1,824
**SALES (est):** 165.8K **Privately Held**
**WEB:** www.nancyslettering.com
**SIC: 5699** 2396 Sports apparel; designers, apparel; automotive & apparel trimmings

**(G-3606)**
**OCE-VAN DER GRINTEN NV**
Also Called: Oce Bruning
815 Reasor Dr (61920-9405)
**PHONE**............217 348-8111
Noreen Connolly, *Branch Mgr*
**EMP:** 47

**SALES (corp-wide):** 30.7B **Privately Held**
**SIC: 2679** Pressed fiber & molded pulp products except food products
**HQ:** Oce Holding B.V.
Sint Urbanusweg 43
Venlo 5914
773 592-222

**(G-3607)**
### PAAP PRINTING
507 Jackson Ave (61920-2031)
**PHONE**.................................217 345-6878
**Fax:** 217 345-6878
Cathy Paap, *Partner*
Terry Paap, *Partner*
**EMP:** 5
**SQ FT:** 1,600
**SALES (est):** 589.5K **Privately Held**
**SIC: 2752** Commercial printing, lithographic

**(G-3608)**
### PRO-TRAN INC
1671 Olive Ave (61920-1207)
**PHONE**.................................217 348-9353
Pierre Chouinard, *President*
Darla Chouinard, *Treasurer*
**EMP:** 3
**SQ FT:** 7,500
**SALES (est):** 453.7K **Privately Held**
**SIC: 3441** 3443 3444 7699 Fabricated structural metal; tanks for tank trucks, metal plate; sheet metalwork; tank repair & cleaning services; welding on site

**(G-3609)**
### RKM ENTERPRISES
Also Called: Sign Appeal
1003 Madison Ave (61920-1667)
**PHONE**.................................217 348-5437
Robert Murphy, *Principal*
**EMP:** 2
**SALES:** 250K **Privately Held**
**WEB:** www.robertmurphy.com
**SIC: 3993** Signs & advertising specialties

**(G-3610)**
### SAFETY STORAGE INC
855 N 5th St (61920-1153)
**PHONE**.................................217 345-4422
**Fax:** 217 298-9716
Lynn R Dufek, *CEO*
Michael Ames, *President*
Dean Alcott, *General Mgr*
Eric Rienbolt, *General Mgr*
Brian Keown, *Opers Mgr*
▼ **EMP:** 70
**SQ FT:** 70,000
**SALES (est):** 18.1MM
**SALES (corp-wide):** 94.4MM **Privately Held**
**WEB:** www.safetystorage.com
**SIC: 3448** Prefabricated metal buildings
**PA:** Lone Star Investment Advisors Llc
4455 L B Johnson Fwy 30
Dallas TX 75244
972 702-7390

**(G-3611)**
### SEWING SALON
718 Jackson Ave (61920-2004)
**PHONE**.................................217 345-3886
**Fax:** 217 345-3886
Mary K Jenkins, *Owner*
Kathy Jenkins, *Co-Owner*
Lowell Jenkins, *Co-Owner*
**EMP:** 4
**SQ FT:** 2,000
**SALES:** 75K **Privately Held**
**SIC: 7219** 2395 Garment making, alteration & repair; embroidery products, except schiffli machine

**(G-3612)**
### SPENCE MONUMENTS CO
525 W State St (61920-1366)
**PHONE**.................................217 348-5992
Daniel Spence, *Owner*
**EMP:** 6
**SQ FT:** 1,900
**SALES:** 500K **Privately Held**
**SIC: 3272** 3281 Grave markers, concrete; monuments, concrete; cut stone & stone products

**(G-3613)**
### STEARNS PRINTING OF CHARLESTON
Also Called: Printco Printing
304 8th St (61920-1504)
**PHONE**.................................217 345-7518
**Fax:** 217 345-7534
Kevin Jenkins, *President*
Colleen Ames, *Manager*
**EMP:** 4
**SQ FT:** 3,300
**SALES (est):** 286.1K **Privately Held**
**SIC: 2789** 2791 Bookbinding & related work; typesetting

**(G-3614)**
### VESUVIUS U S A CORPORATION
955 N 5th St (61920-1160)
P.O. Box 290 (61920-0290)
**PHONE**.................................217 345-7044
**Fax:** 217 345-7124
Carl Corbin, *Project Mgr*
Darren Cloud, *Engineer*
Shawn Coffman, *CPA*
Lorie King, *Personnel*
Steve Slaminko, *Manager*
**EMP:** 150
**SALES (corp-wide):** 1.7B **Privately Held**
**WEB:** www.vesuvius.com
**SIC: 3297** 5085 Graphite refractories: carbon bond or ceramic bond; refractory material
**HQ:** Vesuvius U S A Corporation
1404 Newton Dr
Champaign IL 61822
217 351-5000

**(G-3615)**
### WENDELL ADAMS (PA)
Also Called: Adams Memorials
1286 W State St (61920-8602)
**PHONE**.................................217 345-9587
Wendell Adams, *Owner*
Candy Landon, *Office Mgr*
▲ **EMP:** 30
**SQ FT:** 15,000
**SALES (est):** 10MM **Privately Held**
**WEB:** www.adamsmemorials.com
**SIC: 5999** 3281 1411 Monuments, finished to custom order; cut stone & stone products; dimension stone

**(G-3616)**
### WINNING STITCH
725 Windsor Rd (61920-7474)
**PHONE**.................................217 348-8279
Doris Hill, *Owner*
**EMP:** 6
**SALES (est):** 379.9K **Privately Held**
**WEB:** www.winningstitch.com
**SIC: 2395** 2396 5699 5621 Emblems, embroidered; automotive & apparel trimmings; formal wear; bridal shops

## Chatham
### Sangamon County

**(G-3617)**
### CENTRAL STATES PALLETS
26 Highland Ln (62629-1015)
**PHONE**.................................217 494-2710
Gary Bowsher, *Principal*
**EMP:** 4 **EST:** 2007
**SALES (est):** 346.1K **Privately Held**
**SIC: 2448** Pallets, wood & wood with metal

**(G-3618)**
### CHATHAM PLASTICS INC
7 Kemp Dr (62629-9769)
**PHONE**.................................217 483-1481
Scott Moore, *President*
▲ **EMP:** 4
**SALES (est):** 370K **Privately Held**
**WEB:** www.chathamplastics.com
**SIC: 3089** Molding primary plastic

**(G-3619)**
### EVANS HEATING AND AIR INC
6172 Lick Rd (62629)
P.O. Box 46 (62629-0046)
**PHONE**.................................217 483-8440
**Fax:** 217 483-8441
**EMP:** 7

**SQ FT:** 10,500
**SALES:** 800K **Privately Held**
**SIC: 3444** 7623 Mfg Sheet Metalwork Refrigeration Service/Repair

**(G-3620)**
### FEHRING ORNAMENTAL IRON WORKS
10128 Gilreath Rd (62629-8625)
**PHONE**.................................217 483-6727
Lewis Fehring, *President*
Jim Clanton, *Corp Secy*
William D Nickel, *Vice Pres*
Dave Young, *Vice Pres*
Greg Stephens, *Safety Dir*
**EMP:** 14
**SQ FT:** 30,000
**SALES (est):** 1.5MM **Privately Held**
**SIC: 3448** 1799 7699 7692 Buildings, portable: prefabricated metal; ornamental metal work; blacksmith shop; welding repair; architectural metalwork; fabricated structural metal

**(G-3621)**
### HENRY TECHNOLOGIES INC (HQ)
Also Called: Henry Tech Inc Intl Sls Co
701 S Main St (62629-1655)
**PHONE**.................................217 483-2406
Michael Giordano, *President*
Sandy Macdonald, *General Mgr*
Greg Gutzman, *Maint Spvr*
David Frenk, *Engineer*
Ron Ceminsky, *Sales Mgr*
▲ **EMP:** 4 **EST:** 1914
**SQ FT:** 101,000
**SALES (est):** 86.5MM
**SALES (corp-wide):** 117.2MM **Privately Held**
**WEB:** www.henrytech.com
**SIC: 3491** 3585 3567 3564 Gas valves & parts, industrial; automatic regulating & control valves; regulators (steam fittings); refrigeration equipment, complete; evaporative condensers, heat transfer equipment; industrial furnaces & ovens; blowers & fans; machine tool accessories; valves & pipe fittings
**PA:** Hendricks Holding Company, Inc.
690 3rd St Ste 300
Beloit WI 53511
608 362-8981

**(G-3622)**
### HENRY TECHNOLOGIES INC
701 S Main St (62629-1655)
**PHONE**.................................217 483-2406
Al Paxton, *Sr Corp Ofcr*
Rob Davis, *Purch Mgr*
Tom Maggio, *Purch Mgr*
Charles Mogle, *Engineer*
Dan Rothe, *Engineer*
**EMP:** 78
**SQ FT:** 65,000
**SALES (corp-wide):** 117.2MM **Privately Held**
**WEB:** www.henrytech.com
**SIC: 3585** Refrigeration equipment, complete
**HQ:** Henry Technologies, Inc.
701 S Main St
Chatham IL 62629
217 483-2406

**(G-3623)**
### JOSTENS INC
114 W Walnut St (62629-1068)
**PHONE**.................................217 483-8989
Todd Lawrence, *Branch Mgr*
**EMP:** 39
**SALES (corp-wide):** 13.2B **Publicly Held**
**SIC: 3911** Rings, finger: precious metal
**HQ:** Jostens, Inc.
3601 Minnesota Dr Ste 400
Minneapolis MN 55435
952 830-3300

**(G-3624)**
### KOKES KID ZONE
1033 Jason Pl (62629-2018)
P.O. Box 514 (62629-0514)
**PHONE**.................................217 483-4615
**EMP:** 4 **EST:** 2008

**SALES (est):** 240K **Privately Held**
**SIC: 3663** Mfg Radio/Tv Communication Equipment

**(G-3625)**
### SPRINGFIELD WOODWORKS
6651 Wesley Chapel Rd (62629-8717)
**PHONE**.................................217 483-7234
Moore Springfield, *Owner*
**EMP:** 3
**SALES:** 96K **Privately Held**
**SIC: 2499** Chair cane, rattan or reed

## Chatsworth
### Livingston County

**(G-3626)**
### ACE PLASTICS INC
7942 N 3350 East Rd (60921-8117)
**PHONE**.................................815 635-1368
Sachin Patel, *President*
**EMP:** 10
**SQ FT:** 13,000
**SALES:** 1.6MM **Privately Held**
**SIC: 4953** 4785 3089 Recycling, waste materials; toll operations; plastic processing

**(G-3627)**
### PRINSCO INC
111 E Pine St (60921-9368)
P.O. Box 727 (60921-0727)
**PHONE**.................................815 635-3131
Nick Nissen, *Branch Mgr*
Derrick Nissen, *Manager*
Jeremy Duininck, *Director*
**EMP:** 30
**SALES (corp-wide):** 93.4MM **Privately Held**
**WEB:** www.prinsco.com
**SIC: 3559** Plastics working machinery
**PA:** Prinsco, Inc.
1717 16th St Ne Fl 3
Willmar MN 56201
320 978-4116

**(G-3628)**
### QUANEX HOMESHIELD LLC
32140 E 830 North Rd (60921-8184)
**PHONE**.................................815 635-3171
Steve Simonson, *COO*
**EMP:** 24 **Publicly Held**
**SIC: 3444** Sheet metalwork
**HQ:** Quanex Homeshield, Llc
311 W Coleman St
Rice Lake WI 54868
715 234-9061

**(G-3629)**
### QUANEX HOMESHIELD LLC
32140 E 830 North Rd (60921-8184)
**PHONE**.................................815 635-3171
Kevin Delaney, *Principal*
**EMP:** 12
**SALES (est):** 4MM **Publicly Held**
**SIC: 3353** Aluminum sheet, plate & foil
**PA:** Quanex Building Products Corporation
1800 West Loop S Ste 1500
Houston TX 77027

## Chebanse
### Iroquois County

**(G-3630)**
### CLIFTON CHEMICAL COMPANY (PA)
160 S Locust St (60922-2057)
P.O. Box 25 (60922-0025)
**PHONE**.................................815 697-2343
**Fax:** 815 697-2754
Rick Kuntz, *President*
**EMP:** 4
**SQ FT:** 7,200
**SALES (est):** 1.2MM **Privately Held**
**WEB:** www.cliftonchemical.com
**SIC: 2842** 7389 Specialty cleaning preparations; window cleaning preparations; packaging & labeling services

## Chebanse - Iroquois County (G-3631)

**(G-3631)**
**NORDMEYER GRAPHICS**
100 Dieter Rd (60922-2104)
P.O. Box 238 (60922-0238)
PHONE...............................815 697-2634
Kevin Nordmeyer, *Owner*
**EMP:** 3
**SALES (est):** 245.9K **Privately Held**
**WEB:** www.ngsigns.com
**SIC:** 3993 Signs & advertising specialties

**(G-3632)**
**WOLFE BURIAL VAULT CO INC**
310 N Oak St (60922-2016)
PHONE...............................815 697-2012
**Fax:** 815 697-2015
Rodney Wolfe, *President*
Rod Wolfe, *Principal*
**EMP:** 4
**SQ FT:** 7,800
**SALES (est):** 415.7K **Privately Held**
**SIC:** 3272 Burial vaults, concrete or pre-cast terrazzo

### Chenoa
### Mclean County

**(G-3633)**
**CHENOA LOCKER INC**
8 N Veto St (61726-1006)
P.O. Box 31 (61726-0031)
PHONE...............................815 945-7323
Terry Bittner, *President*
Dana Muir, *Manager*
**EMP:** 8
**SALES (est):** 1.1MM **Privately Held**
**SIC:** 2011 7299 Meat packing plants; butcher service, processing only

**(G-3634)**
**MELTERS AND MORE**
512 N Division St (61726-1052)
PHONE...............................815 419-2043
Raymond Henry Sr, *Partner*
**EMP:** 6 **EST:** 2015
**SALES (est):** 602.7K **Privately Held**
**SIC:** 3443 Water tanks, metal plate; metal parts; chutes & troughs; troughs, industrial: metal plate

**(G-3635)**
**RELIABLE AUTOTECH USA LLC**
600 N Division St (61726-9322)
PHONE...............................815 945-7838
Debasish Chakravarty, *Principal*
Sutapa Chakravarty, *Principal*
Kishor Ashokrao Salunkhe,
**EMP:** 8 **EST:** 1976
**SQ FT:** 16,000 **Privately Held**
**WEB:** www.jgfab.com
**SIC:** 3444 3479 Sheet metalwork; painting of metal products

**(G-3636)**
**WEBER METAL PRODUCTS INC**
10702 E 1400 North Rd (61726-9082)
PHONE...............................815 844-3169
**Fax:** 815 842-2328
Stanley R Weber, *President*
Marsha Weber, *Treasurer*
**EMP:** 12
**SQ FT:** 14,500
**SALES (est):** 1.6MM **Privately Held**
**WEB:** www.webermetalproducts.com
**SIC:** 3599 3451 Machine shop, jobbing & repair; custom machinery; screw machine products

### Cherry Valley
### Winnebago County

**(G-3637)**
**ACME SCREW CO**
125 E State St (61016-7707)
P.O. Box 906, Wheaton (60187-0906)
PHONE...............................815 332-7548
RI Litten, *Manager*
Jeannette Winthers, *Info Tech Dir*
**EMP:** 10
**SQ FT:** 1,500
**SALES (corp-wide):** 20.8MM **Privately Held**
**WEB:** www.acmecompanies.com
**SIC:** 3463 3451 Nonferrous forgings; screw machine products
**PA:** Acme Screw Co.
1201 W Union Ave
Wheaton IL 60187
630 665-2200

**(G-3638)**
**ATLAS COMPONENTS INC**
4055 S Perryville Rd (61016-9729)
P.O. Box 5423, Rockford (61125-0423)
PHONE...............................815 332-4904
**Fax:** 815 332-5311
Michael Karceski, *President*
Tina Fiser, *Manager*
**EMP:** 50
**SQ FT:** 15,500
**SALES (est):** 11.3MM **Privately Held**
**WEB:** www.atlasci.com
**SIC:** 2439 Trusses, wooden roof

**(G-3639)**
**BAR CODE DR INC**
4337 S Perryville Rd (61016-9100)
PHONE...............................815 547-1001
Lynn Godina, *President*
**EMP:** 4
**SALES (est):** 190K **Privately Held**
**SIC:** 2711 Commercial printing & newspaper publishing combined

**(G-3640)**
**CHERRY VALLEY FEED SUPPLIES**
1595 S Bell School Rd (61016-9362)
PHONE...............................815 332-7665
Bob Kramer, *President*
**EMP:** 4
**SALES (est):** 390.7K **Privately Held**
**SIC:** 2048 Dry pet food (except dog & cat)

**(G-3641)**
**ENGINEERED FLUID PWR CON CONS**
Also Called: Fluid Power Concrete Lifting
3637 Cutty Sark Rd (61016-9649)
PHONE...............................815 332-3344
Perry Hockhammer, *Owner*
**EMP:** 3
**SQ FT:** 2,400
**SALES:** 150K **Privately Held**
**SIC:** 1771 3531 Concrete work; cranes

**(G-3642)**
**EVAC NORTH AMERICA INC (DH)**
Also Called: Evac Environmental Solutions
1445 Huntwood Dr (61016-9560)
PHONE...............................815 654-8300
Kenneth Postle, *President*
Sheila Kadet, *General Mgr*
Marjukka Lemmetti, *General Mgr*
Kim Rice, *General Mgr*
Tom Obermann, *Engineer*
◆ **EMP:** 30
**SALES (est):** 7.4MM
**SALES (corp-wide):** 2.2B **Publicly Held**
**WEB:** www.avac.com
**SIC:** 3561 3589 Pumps & pumping equipment; sewage & water treatment equipment

**(G-3643)**
**F P M LLC**
Fpm Ipsen
648 Bypass Us Hwy 20 (61016)
PHONE...............................815 332-4961
**Fax:** 815 332-3022
Dan Neiber, *Plant Mgr*
Bernadette Bennett, *Controller*
Tony Schiame, *Sales Mgr*
Rudolf Vedo, *Marketing Mgr*
Bryan Ames, *Branch Mgr*
**EMP:** 60
**SALES (corp-wide):** 40.8MM **Privately Held**
**WEB:** www.fpmht.com
**SIC:** 3398 Metal heat treating
**PA:** F P M, L.L.C.
1501 Lively Blvd
Elk Grove Village IL 60007
847 228-2525

**(G-3644)**
**FPM HEAT TREATING**
648 Us Highway 20 (61016-9545)
PHONE...............................815 332-4961
**Fax:** 815 332-3022
**EMP:** 14
**SALES (est):** 2.8MM **Privately Held**
**SIC:** 3398 Metal Heat Treating

**(G-3645)**
**IPSEN INC (DH)**
984 Ipsen Rd (61016-3800)
PHONE...............................815 332-4941
**Fax:** 815 332-3074
Geoffrey Somary, *President*
Claude Bertrand, *Exec VP*
Pierre Boulud, *Exec VP*
Etienne De Blois, *Exec VP*
Eric Drape, *Exec VP*
◆ **EMP:** 150
**SQ FT:** 110,000
**SALES:** 90MM
**SALES (corp-wide):** 105.9K **Privately Held**
**WEB:** www.ipsen-intl.com
**SIC:** 3567 Industrial furnaces & ovens
**HQ:** Ipsen International Holding Gmbh
Flutstr. 78
Kleve 47533
282 180-40

**(G-3646)**
**L & S LABEL PRINTING INC**
Also Called: Photo Copy Service
4337 S Perryville Rd # 102 (61016-9100)
PHONE...............................815 964-6753
**Fax:** 815 964-9868
Dave Roliardi, *President*
**EMP:** 4
**SQ FT:** 14,000
**SALES (est):** 848K **Privately Held**
**WEB:** www.photocopyservice.com
**SIC:** 2672 2752 7334 Labels (unprinted), gummed: made from purchased materials; commercial printing, offset; photocopying & duplicating services

**(G-3647)**
**SHELVING AND BATH UNLIMITED**
Also Called: Closet Concpts By Shlvng Unlim
4337 S Perryville Rd # 103 (61016-9100)
PHONE...............................815 378-3328
Joseph Weller, *President*
Wanda Handlin, *Office Mgr*
**EMP:** 3
**SALES:** 500K **Privately Held**
**SIC:** 2541 Cabinets, lockers & shelving

**(G-3648)**
**TOP NOTCH TOOL & SUPPLY INC**
3175 Tuggle Dr (61016-9283)
PHONE...............................815 633-6295
**Fax:** 815 633-6307
Lyle Zellner, *President*
Shana Fuller, *Admin Sec*
**EMP:** 5
**SQ FT:** 3,450
**SALES (est):** 470K **Privately Held**
**WEB:** www.topnotchtool.net
**SIC:** 3599 5085 3545 3544 Machine shop, jobbing & repair; industrial tools; machine tool accessories; special dies, tools, jigs & fixtures

**(G-3649)**
**WEILAND WELDING INC**
4727 Lindbloom Ln (61016-9111)
PHONE...............................815 580-8079
Anita Weiland, *Principal*
**EMP:** 2
**SALES (est):** 298.4K **Privately Held**
**SIC:** 7692 Welding repair

### Chester
### Randolph County

**(G-3650)**
**ARDENT MILLS LLC**
Also Called: Conagra
101 Water St (62233-1843)
P.O. Box 369 (62233-0369)
PHONE...............................618 826-2371
**Fax:** 618 826-4154
Alan Bindel, *Branch Mgr*
**EMP:** 31
**SALES (corp-wide):** 30.3B **Publicly Held**
**WEB:** www.conagra.com
**SIC:** 2041 2048 5149 Flour & other grain mill products; prepared feeds; flour
**HQ:** Ardent Mills Llc
1875 Lawrence St Ste 1400
Denver CO 80202
800 851-9618

**(G-3651)**
**BLAZING COLOR INC**
1007 State St (62233-1657)
PHONE...............................618 826-3001
Kenneth Wagner, *President*
**EMP:** 3
**SQ FT:** 5,000
**SALES:** 950K **Privately Held**
**WEB:** www.blazingfast.com
**SIC:** 2759 2791 Commercial printing; typesetting

**(G-3652)**
**CHESTER BRASS AND ALUMINUM**
Also Called: Chester Foundry
600 Barron St (62233-1548)
P.O. Box 30 (62233-0030)
PHONE...............................618 826-2391
**Fax:** 618 826-3115
Jeffrey Lutz, *President*
**EMP:** 11 **EST:** 1955
**SQ FT:** 6,000
**SALES:** 420K **Privately Held**
**SIC:** 3365 3366 Aluminum & aluminum-based alloy castings; castings (except die): bronze

**(G-3653)**
**CHESTER DAIRY COMPANY INC (PA)**
Also Called: Farm Fresh Str D&M Dar Stores
1915 State St (62233-1115)
P.O. Box 605 (62233-0605)
PHONE...............................618 826-2394
**Fax:** 618 826-2395
Jason Ohlau, *President*
Elizabeth Ohlau, *Admin Sec*
**EMP:** 17 **EST:** 1931
**SQ FT:** 10,000
**SALES (est):** 15.3MM **Privately Held**
**WEB:** www.randesterillinois.com
**SIC:** 2026 Fluid milk; fermented & cultured milk products

**(G-3654)**
**CHESTER DAIRY COMPANY INC**
1912 Swanwick St (62233-1127)
P.O. Box 605 (62233-0605)
PHONE...............................618 826-2395
Barbara Johnson, *Manager*
**EMP:** 4
**SALES (corp-wide):** 15.3MM **Privately Held**
**WEB:** www.chesterillinois.com
**SIC:** 2026 Fluid milk; fermented & cultured milk products
**PA:** Chester Dairy Company, Inc.
1915 State St
Chester IL 62233
618 826-2394

**(G-3655)**
**EBERS DRILLING CO**
4318 State Route 150 (62233-3218)
PHONE...............................618 826-5398
Lonny Ebers, *Owner*
**EMP:** 5
**SALES:** 325K **Privately Held**
**SIC:** 1031 1381 Lead ores mining; drilling oil & gas wells

## GEOGRAPHIC SECTION
## Chicago - Cook County (G-3680)

**(G-3656)**
**GILSTER-MARY LEE CORPORATION**
111 Industrial Dr (62233-2555)
PHONE ..............................618 826-3102
Fax: 618 826-3102
Wayne Stipe, *Traffic Mgr*
Shane Rock, *Manager*
Bob Smith, *Director*
Leanne Kilpatrick, *Executive*
EMP: 6
SALES (corp-wide): 1.1B **Privately Held**
SIC: 3999 Barber & beauty shop equipment
HQ: Gilster-Mary Lee Corporation
1037 State St
Chester IL 62233
618 826-2361

**(G-3657)**
**GILSTER-MARY LEE CORPORATION (HQ)**
1037 State St (62233-1657)
P.O. Box 227 (62233-0227)
PHONE ..............................618 826-2361
Fax: 618 826-2973
Donald E Welge, *President*
Timothy Petzolt, *General Mgr*
Steve Elrod, *Superintendent*
Michael W Welge, *Exec VP*
Delbert Dethrow, *Vice Pres*
▼ EMP: 600
SQ FT: 145,000
SALES (est): 1.1B **Privately Held**
WEB: www.gilstermarylee.com
SIC: 2043 2098 2099 2045 Cereal breakfast foods; macaroni products (e.g. alphabets, rings & shells); dry; popcorn; packaged: except already popped; blended flour: from purchased flour; plastic containers, except foam
PA: Mary Lee Packaging Corporation
1037 State St
Chester IL 62233
618 826-2361

**(G-3658)**
**LEE GILSTER-MARY CORPORATION**
981 State St (62233-1654)
P.O. Box 227 (62233-0227)
PHONE ..............................618 826-2361
Donald Wegle, *President*
Toby Ellner, *Director*
EMP: 5
SALES (corp-wide): 1.1B **Privately Held**
WEB: www.gilstermarylee.com
SIC: 2098 2043 2099 2045 Macaroni products (e.g. alphabets, rings & shells), dry; cereal breakfast foods; popcorn, packaged: except already popped; blended flour: from purchased flour; plastic containers, except foam
HQ: Gilster-Mary Lee Corporation
1037 State St
Chester IL 62233
618 826-2361

**(G-3659)**
**MARY LEE PACKAGING CORPORATION (PA)**
Also Called: Gilster-Mary Lee
1037 State St (62233-1657)
P.O. Box 227 (62233-0227)
PHONE ..............................618 826-2361
Donald E Welge, *President*
Gerry Stolt, *Purchasing*
Michael W Welge, *Treasurer*
Karen Biermann, *Manager*
◆ EMP: 40 EST: 1969
SALES (est): 1.1B **Privately Held**
SIC: 2043 2099 3089 2098 Corn flakes: prepared as cereal breakfast food; syrups; plastic containers, except foam; macaroni & spaghetti

**(G-3660)**
**RANDOLPH COUNTY HERALD TRIBUNE**
1205 Swanwick St (62233-1667)
P.O. Box 269 (62233-0269)
PHONE ..............................618 826-2385
Fax: 618 826-5181
Mike Reed, *President*
Melody Rodgers, *Publisher*
EMP: 11
SQ FT: 3,000
SALES (est): 510K **Privately Held**
WEB: www.gatehousemedia.com
SIC: 2711 Newspapers, publishing & printing

## Chicago
### Cook County

**(G-3661)**
**10TH MAGNITUDE LLC**
20 N Wacker Dr Ste 530 (60606-2803)
PHONE ..............................224 628-9047
Alex Brown, *CEO*
Mike Denton, *Vice Pres*
Kelly McClure, *Vice Pres*
Bibi Petrovits, *Vice Pres*
EMP: 25
SALES (est): 2.9MM **Privately Held**
SIC: 8748 3572 Business consulting; computer storage devices

**(G-3662)**
**2 M TOOL COMPANY INC**
Also Called: Mince Master
6530 W Dakin St (60634-2412)
PHONE ..............................773 282-0722
Fax: 773 282-9744
Milivoje Mihailovic, *President*
Vesna Doyle, *Vice Pres*
Ruzica Mihailovic, *Treasurer*
Vladan Mihailovic, *Admin Sec*
EMP: 12
SQ FT: 12,000
SALES (est): 1.2MM **Privately Held**
WEB: www.mincemaster.com
SIC: 3599 Machine shop, jobbing & repair

**(G-3663)**
**2000PLUS GROUPS INC (PA)**
Also Called: CRESCENT FOODS
4343 W 44th Pl (60632-4303)
PHONE ..............................800 939-6268
Fax: 773 247-6199
Ahmad A Adam, *President*
Fateh Riyal, *Vice Pres*
EMP: 130
SQ FT: 26,300
SALES: 26.1MM **Privately Held**
WEB: www.crescenthalal.com
SIC: 2015 Poultry slaughtering & processing; duck slaughtering & processing; poultry sausage, luncheon meats & other poultry products

**(G-3664)**
**21ST CENTURY US-SINO SERVICES**
Also Called: Sea Horse Blinds
500 W 18th St Ste 2 (60616-1486)
PHONE ..............................312 808-9328
Jimmy Lee, *President*
▲ EMP: 5
SALES: 800K **Privately Held**
SIC: 2591 Window blinds

**(G-3665)**
**233 SKYDECK LLC**
233 S Wacker Dr (60606-7147)
PHONE ..............................312 875-9448
Tom Sakoral,
EMP: 7
SALES (est): 791.5K **Privately Held**
SIC: 3822 Building services monitoring controls, automatic

**(G-3666)**
**2L TECHNOLOGIES LLC**
445 N Franklin St (60654-4901)
PHONE ..............................312 526-3900
Fax: 312 666-8414
Luca Lanzetta, *Principal*
▲ EMP: 5
SALES (est): 525.2K **Privately Held**
SIC: 3545 Tools & accessories for machine tools

**(G-3667)**
**3B MEDIA INC**
401 N Michigan Ave # 1200 (60611-4255)
PHONE ..............................312 563-9363
Ops Dir, *Branch Mgr*
EMP: 14
SALES (corp-wide): 5.9MM **Privately Held**
SIC: 2731 5735 5736 6794 Book music: publishing only, not printed on site; record & prerecorded tape stores; musical instrument stores; patent owners & lessors; advertising agencies
PA: 3b Media, Inc.
401 N Michigan Ave # 1200
Chicago IL 60611
312 563-9363

**(G-3668)**
**3PRIMEDX INC**
191 N Wacker Dr Ste 1500 (60606-1899)
PHONE ..............................312 621-0643
Charles Polsky, *CEO*
Samuel Dudley, *Director*
EMP: 5
SQ FT: 500
SALES (est): 479.3K **Privately Held**
SIC: 2835 In vitro & in vivo diagnostic substances

**(G-3669)**
**5 RABBIT CERVECERIA INC**
Also Called: 5 Rabbit Brewery
6398 W 74th St (60638-6129)
PHONE ..............................312 265-8316
Andres Araya, *CEO*
Isaac Showaki, *Principal*
EMP: 16 EST: 2010
SALES (est): 2.8MM **Privately Held**
SIC: 3556 Brewers' & maltsters' machinery

**(G-3670)**
**555 INTERNATIONAL INC**
Paul D Metal Products
2225 W Pershing Rd (60609-2210)
PHONE ..............................773 847-1400
James Geier, *Manager*
EMP: 25
SALES (corp-wide): 20.7MM **Privately Held**
WEB: www.newstarlighting.com
SIC: 3446 3646 3442 3444 Architectural metalwork; commercial indusl & institutional electric lighting fixtures; metal doors, sash & trim; sheet metalwork
PA: 555 International, Inc.
4501 S Western Blvd
Chicago IL 60609
773 869-0555

**(G-3671)**
**555 INTERNATIONAL INC**
New Star Custom Lighting Co
4000 S Bell Ave (60609-2208)
PHONE ..............................773 869-0555
James Geier, *Manager*
EMP: 25
SALES (corp-wide): 20.7MM **Privately Held**
WEB: www.newstarlighting.com
SIC: 3646 Commercial indusl & institutional electric lighting fixtures
PA: 555 International, Inc.
4501 S Western Blvd
Chicago IL 60609
773 869-0555

**(G-3672)**
**555 INTERNATIONAL INC (PA)**
Also Called: 555 MANUFACTURING DIV OF:
4501 S Western Blvd (60609-3026)
PHONE ..............................773 869-0555
Paul Ohadi, *CEO*
James Geier, *President*
Donald Luken, *CFO*
Donald J Luken, *Admin Sec*
▲ EMP: 60
SQ FT: 60,000
SALES (est): 20.7MM **Privately Held**
WEB: www.newstarlighting.com
SIC: 2542 Fixtures: display, office or store: except wood

**(G-3673)**
**57TH STREET BOOKCASE & CABINET**
1455 E 55th Pl (60637-1875)
PHONE ..............................773 363-3038
Arthur Devenport, *Owner*
Scott Mc Williams, *Manager*
EMP: 14

SALES (est): 1MM **Privately Held**
SIC: 5712 2541 Cabinet work, custom; cabinets, except refrigerated: show, display, etc.: wood

**(G-3674)**
**57TH STREET BOOKCASE & CABINET**
1443 E 56th St (60637-1865)
PHONE ..............................312 867-1669
Scott McWilliams, *Principal*
EMP: 5
SALES (corp-wide): 1.3MM **Privately Held**
SIC: 2434 Wood kitchen cabinets
PA: 57th Street Bookcase & Cabinet
1043 Chicago Ave Ste A
Evanston IL 60202
847 492-8780

**(G-3675)**
**773 LLC**
Also Called: Ch Distillery
564 W Randolph St (60661-2218)
PHONE ..............................312 707-8780
Mark Lucas, *Managing Dir*
Tanya Kregul, *CFO*
Ali Schwartz, *Mktg Dir*
Tremaine Atkinson,
Beth Boyle,
▲ EMP: 4 EST: 2012
SALES (est): 382K **Privately Held**
SIC: 2085 Vodka (alcoholic beverage)

**(G-3676)**
**78 BRAND CO**
Also Called: 78 Red Ketchup
1655 S Blue Island Ave (60608-2133)
PHONE ..............................312 344-1602
Patrick Pilewski, *Managing Prtnr*
Bernard Utrata, *Partner*
▲ EMP: 8
SALES: 300K **Privately Held**
SIC: 2033 Tomato products: packaged in cans, jars, etc.

**(G-3677)**
**A & B MACHINE WORKS INC**
460 N Union Ave (60654-5567)
PHONE ..............................312 733-7888
Fax: 312 733-7614
Dario Chiappini, *President*
Gulia Chiappini, *Vice Pres*
John Chiappini, *Treasurer*
Mickey Sodergren, *Office Mgr*
EMP: 7
SQ FT: 6,400
SALES (est): 1MM **Privately Held**
SIC: 3599 Machine shop, jobbing & repair

**(G-3678)**
**A & B METAL POLISHING INC**
1900 S Washtenaw Ave (60608-2428)
PHONE ..............................773 847-1077
Joseph Norvilas, *President*
Maria Norvilas, *Admin Sec*
EMP: 11
SQ FT: 3,500
SALES (est): 1.3MM **Privately Held**
SIC: 3471 3441 Finishing, metals or formed products; fabricated structural metal

**(G-3679)**
**A & E RUBBER STAMP CORP**
215 N Desplaines St 2n (60661-1243)
PHONE ..............................312 575-1416
Fax: 312 575-8614
Phillip T De Francisco, *President*
William De Francisco, *Vice Pres*
Leona Martinez, *Admin Sec*
EMP: 3 EST: 1950
SQ FT: 2,200
SALES (est): 416.6K **Privately Held**
WEB: www.aerubberstamp.com
SIC: 3953 5943 3993 Marking devices; writing supplies; signs & advertising specialties

**(G-3680)**
**A & F PALLET SERVICE INC**
4333 S Knox Ave (60632-4347)
PHONE ..............................773 767-9500
Fax: 773 767-9504
Jose Muniz, *President*
EMP: 12

Chicago - Cook County (G-3681)

SQ FT: 50,000
SALES: 1MM **Privately Held**
SIC: 2448 Wood pallets & skids

**(G-3681)**
**A - SQUARE MANUFACTURING INC**
3939 S Karlov Ave (60632-3813)
PHONE..................................800 628-6720
EMP: 10 **Privately Held**
SIC: 3499 Fire- or burglary-resistive products
PA: A - Square Manufacturing, Inc.
1100 S Kostner Ave
Chicago IL 60624

**(G-3682)**
**A - SQUARE MANUFACTURING INC (PA)**
1100 S Kostner Ave (60624-3835)
PHONE..................................800 628-6720
Andrez J Komar, *President*
EMP: 30
SALES: 4.1MM **Privately Held**
SIC: 3499 Fire- or burglary-resistive products

**(G-3683)**
**A AND R CUSTOM CHROME**
6528 S Lavergne Ave (60638-5807)
PHONE..................................708 728-1005
James Faxon, *Director*
EMP: 3
SALES (est): 165.5K **Privately Held**
SIC: 3471 Chromium plating of metals or formed products

**(G-3684)**
**A ASHLAND LOCK COMPANY (PA)**
Also Called: Ashland Lock & SEC Solutions
2510 N Ashland Ave (60614-2004)
PHONE..................................773 348-5106
Fax: 773 348-9559
Anne M Gruber, *President*
James E Gruber, *Vice Pres*
Elaine Rivkin, *Office Mgr*
Shaun Ingram, *IT/INT Sup*
Steve Kurek, *IT/INT Sup*
EMP: 12
SQ FT: 3,000
SALES (est): 1.6MM **Privately Held**
WEB: www.ashlandlock.com
SIC: 3429 7699 5251 1751 Locks or lock sets; locksmith shop; builders' hardware; door locks & lock sets; window & door installation & erection

**(G-3685)**
**A CLOSET WHOLESALER**
1155 N Howe St (60610-2473)
PHONE..................................312 654-1400
Allen Brown, *Owner*
Beatriz Anguiano, *Admin Sec*
EMP: 15
SALES (est): 1.3MM **Privately Held**
SIC: 2511 China closets

**(G-3686)**
**A DIVISION OF A&A STUDIOS INC**
350 N Ogden Ave Ste 10 (60607-1117)
PHONE..................................312 278-1144
Anthony Vizzari, *President*
Andrea Vizzari, *Vice Pres*
EMP: 10
SALES: 610K **Privately Held**
SIC: 3861 Photographic equipment & supplies

**(G-3687)**
**A FINKL & SONS CO (HQ)**
Also Called: Finkl Steel - Chicago
1355 E 93rd St (60619-8004)
P.O. Box 92576 (60675-2576)
PHONE..................................773 975-2510
Fax: 773 248-8459
Bruce C Liimatainen, *CEO*
Joseph E Curci, *President*
David Laurenson, *Vice Pres*
Tim Neatl, *Vice Pres*
Tim Neatl, *Vice Pres*
◆ EMP: 351
SQ FT: 462,240

SALES (est): 182.2MM
SALES (corp-wide): 2.4B **Privately Held**
WEB: www.finkl.com
SIC: 3312 Ingots, steel; forgings, iron & steel
PA: Schmolz+Bickenbach Ag
Landenbergstrasse 11
Luzern LU
415 814-000

**(G-3688)**
**A G WELDING**
4711 W Lake St (60644-2710)
PHONE..................................773 261-0575
Fax: 773 261-0577
Adolfo Gaona, *President*
EMP: 6
SQ FT: 10,000
SALES (est): 497.4K **Privately Held**
SIC: 7692 3444 Welding repair; sheet metalwork

**(G-3689)**
**A JULE ENTERPRISE INC**
Also Called: Blasart
2219 W Grand Ave (60612-1511)
PHONE..................................312 243-6950
Julia F Kelly, *President*
EMP: 4
SQ FT: 20,000
SALES (est): 260K **Privately Held**
SIC: 2499 2796 5199 5961 Picture frame molding, finished; etching on copper, steel, wood or rubber; printing plates; gifts & novelties; gift items, mail order

**(G-3690)**
**A NEW DAIRY COMPANY**
Also Called: Randolph Dairy
1234 W Randolph St (60607-1604)
PHONE..................................312 421-1234
George R Schuster, *President*
Steven Schuster, *Vice Pres*
EMP: 38
SQ FT: 19,000
SALES (est): 23.4MM **Privately Held**
WEB: www.anewdairy.com
SIC: 5143 2013 2038 Cheese; milk & cream, fluid; butter; yogurt; smoked meats from purchased meat; frozen specialties; dinners, frozen & packaged

**(G-3691)**
**A P L PLASTICS**
3501 W Fillmore St (60624-4312)
PHONE..................................773 265-1370
Jeff Dennis, *Owner*
EMP: 5
SALES (est): 310K **Privately Held**
SIC: 3089 Plastics products

**(G-3692)**
**A TO Z TYPE & GRAPHIC INC**
Also Called: Digital Publishing Group
1703 N Vine St (60614-5119)
PHONE..................................312 587-1887
Paul Hanover, *President*
Maynard Kabak, *Treasurer*
EMP: 8
SQ FT: 3,200
SALES (est): 580K **Privately Held**
SIC: 7336 2791 Graphic arts & related design; typesetting

**(G-3693)**
**A TRUSTWORTHY SUP SOURCE INC**
6047 N Central Park Ave (60659-3204)
PHONE..................................773 480-0255
Marcella Davis, *Principal*
EMP: 2
SALES (est): 317.6K **Privately Held**
SIC: 2653 2731 5112 3993 Corrugated & solid fiber boxes; textbooks: publishing only, not printed on site; stationery & office supplies; letters for signs, metal; business oriented computer software

**(G-3694)**
**A&J PAVING INC**
1911 N Sayre Ave (60707-3839)
PHONE..................................773 889-9133
Anthony Cocco, *President*
Joseph Cocco Jr, *Admin Sec*
EMP: 2

SALES (est): 280.1K **Privately Held**
SIC: 3272 1611 Concrete products; surfacing & paving

**(G-3695)**
**A-F ACQUISITION LLC** ◯
Also Called: Pullman Innovations
2701 E 100th St (60617-5317)
PHONE..................................773 978-5130
Brandon Boomsma, *Mng Member*
Brian Boomsma,
Steve Deboer,
Matt Dyer,
EMP: 16 EST: 2016
SQ FT: 16,000
SALES (est): 1.9MM **Privately Held**
SIC: 2079 Cooking oils, except corn: vegetable refined

**(G-3696)**
**A-KORN ROLLER INC (PA)**
3545 S Morgan St (60609-1590)
PHONE..................................773 254-5700
Fax: 773 650-7355
Michael E Koren, *President*
Lisa Rodriguez, *Accountant*
Charles Koren, *Sales Mgr*
Michael Rogers, *Cust Mgr*
Mark Akers, *Sales Staff*
▲ EMP: 25
SQ FT: 20,000
SALES (est): 11.4MM **Privately Held**
WEB: www.a-kornroller.com
SIC: 3555 Printing trades machinery

**(G-3697)**
**AA PALLET INC**
900 W 49th Pl (60609-5153)
PHONE..................................773 536-3699
Fax: 773 536-1766
Donald Somerville, *President*
Don Huske, *Principal*
EMP: 20
SQ FT: 33,000
SALES (est): 3.5MM **Privately Held**
WEB: www.aapalletinc.com
SIC: 2448 Wood pallets & skids

**(G-3698)**
**AA SUPERB FOOD CORPORATION**
3823 S Halsted St (60609-1612)
PHONE..................................773 927-3233
Sandy Tsai, *President*
EMP: 44
SALES (est): 5.8MM **Privately Held**
SIC: 2032 Chinese foods: packaged in cans, jars, etc.

**(G-3699)**
**AA-GEM CORPORATION**
4221 N Lawndale Ave (60618-2008)
PHONE..................................773 539-9303
Marilyn Pauga, *President*
EMP: 3
SALES (est): 237.7K **Privately Held**
SIC: 2819 Industrial inorganic chemicals

**(G-3700)**
**AAA MOLD FINISHERS INC**
7208 W Pratt Ave (60631-1159)
PHONE..................................773 775-3977
Brian Miller, *President*
Judith Miler, *Admin Sec*
EMP: 6
SQ FT: 6,000
SALES: 210K **Privately Held**
SIC: 3471 Polishing, metals or formed products

**(G-3701)**
**AABBITT ADHESIVES INC (PA)**
Also Called: Advance Adhesives
2403 N Oakley Ave (60647-2093)
PHONE..................................773 227-2700
Fax: 773 227-2103
Benjamin B Sarmas, *President*
Louise Sarmas, *Corp Secy*
Daniel Sarmas, *Vice Pres*
David Sarmas, *Vice Pres*
Gregory Sarmas, *Vice Pres*
EMP: 60
SQ FT: 67,500

SALES (est): 16.9MM **Privately Held**
WEB: www.aabbitt.com
SIC: 2891 3087 2821 Adhesives; custom compound purchased resins; plastics materials & resins

**(G-3702)**
**AABBITT ADHESIVES INC**
Also Called: Advance Adhesives
601 W 81st (60620)
PHONE..................................773 723-6780
Daniel Sarmas, *Manager*
EMP: 35
SALES (corp-wide): 16.9MM **Privately Held**
WEB: www.aabbitt.com
SIC: 2891 Adhesives
PA: Aabbitt Adhesives, Inc.
2403 N Oakley Ave
Chicago IL 60647
773 227-2700

**(G-3703)**
**AAKASH SPICES & PRODUCE INC**
6404 N Fairfield Ave (60645-5211)
PHONE..................................773 916-4100
Girish Ray, *Agent*
EMP: 10
SALES (est): 706.8K **Privately Held**
SIC: 2099 Seasonings & spices

**(G-3704)**
**ABBEY METAL SERVICES INC**
820 W 120th St (60643-5532)
PHONE..................................773 568-0330
Fax: 773 568-7349
Mark W Okonski, *President*
Alfred G Bialkowski, *Treasurer*
EMP: 12 EST: 1954
SQ FT: 32,000
SALES (est): 2.7MM **Privately Held**
SIC: 3443 Fabricated plate work (boiler shop)

**(G-3705)**
**ABBOTT LABORATORIES**
6235 N Newark Ave (60631-2109)
P.O. Box 319022 (60631-9022)
PHONE..................................847 937-2210
Lynn Pavlis Jenkins, *Principal*
EMP: 764
SALES (corp-wide): 20.8B **Publicly Held**
SIC: 2834 Pharmaceutical preparations
PA: Abbott Laboratories
100 Abbott Park Rd
Abbott Park IL 60064
224 667-6100

**(G-3706)**
**ABBOTT SCOTT MANUFACTURING CO**
4215 W Grand Ave (60651-1857)
PHONE..................................773 342-7200
Fax: 773 342-1610
Joel Michaels, *President*
Lawrence Roseman, *Corp Secy*
Dale Schmoldt, *Vice Pres*
John Mayer, *Controller*
▲ EMP: 40
SQ FT: 40,000
SALES (est): 9.4MM **Privately Held**
WEB: www.scottabbott.com
SIC: 3469 3599 3451 3444 Metal stampings; machine shop, jobbing & repair; screw machine products; sheet metalwork

**(G-3707)**
**ABC INC**
190 N State St Fl 7 (60601-3310)
PHONE..................................312 980-1000
Fax: 312 440-9285
Christine Reller, *Vice Pres*
Kim Pastor, *Manager*
Josefina Leon, *Director*
EMP: 30 **Publicly Held**
WEB: www.abc.com
SIC: 4832 2721 Radio broadcasting stations; periodicals
HQ: Abc, Inc.
77 W 66th St Rm 100
New York NY 10023
212 456-7777

# GEOGRAPHIC SECTION
### Chicago - Cook County (G-3734)

**(G-3708)**
**ABCO METALS CORPORATIONS**
1020 W 94th St (60620-3664)
PHONE...................................773 881-1504
Ray L Ebinger, *President*
Allen Ebinger, *Vice Pres*
**EMP:** 13
**SQ FT:** 20,000
**SALES (est):** 2MM **Privately Held**
**SIC:** 5093 4953 3341 Metal scrap & waste materials; refuse systems; secondary nonferrous metals

**(G-3709)**
**ABLE DIE & MOLD INC**
4239 N Oak Park Ave # 217 (60634-1410)
PHONE...................................773 282-3652
Fax: 773 478-9570
John Krottner, *President*
**EMP:** 2
**SQ FT:** 2,500
**SALES:** 250K **Privately Held**
**SIC:** 3544 Dies, plastics forming; forms (molds), for foundry & plastics working machinery

**(G-3710)**
**ABLE ELECTROPOLISHING CO INC**
2001 S Kilbourn Ave (60623-2390)
PHONE...................................773 277-1600
Fax: 773 277-1655
Don Esser, *President*
James Murnane, *VP Opers*
Doug Johnson, *Controller*
Scott Potter, *Sales Executive*
Adolfo Maldonado, *Supervisor*
**EMP:** 22
**SALES (est):** 6.8MM **Privately Held**
**SIC:** 1081 Metal mining services

**(G-3711)**
**ABUNDANCE HOUSE TREASURE NFP**
1309 S Kedzie Ave (60623-1840)
PHONE...................................312 788-4316
Ernest Jones, *Vice Pres*
Farrah Brown, *Asst Sec*
**EMP:** 3 **EST:** 2015
**SQ FT:** 1,500
**SALES (est):** 132.3K **Privately Held**
**SIC:** 1389 Construction, repair & dismantling services

**(G-3712)**
**ABUNDANT VENTURE INNOVATION AC**
Also Called: Avia, LLC
111 E Wacker Dr Ste 300 (60601-4206)
PHONE...................................312 291-1910
Derek Baird, *Vice Pres*
Peggy E Baxter, *Vice Pres*
Ariana Klitzner, *Vice Pres*
Amanda Schleede, *Opers Mgr*
Mitch Corwin, *Director*
**EMP:** 4
**SALES (est):** 294.2K **Privately Held**
**SIC:** 3825 Network analyzers

**(G-3713)**
**ABYSS SALON INC**
67 E 16th St Ste 5 (60616-1275)
PHONE...................................312 880-0263
Sharon E Miles-Gilty, *President*
David Gilty, *Vice Pres*
Sharon E Miles Gilty, *Purch Dir*
**EMP:** 4
**SQ FT:** 950
**SALES:** 85K **Privately Held**
**WEB:** www.theabysssalon.com
**SIC:** 7241 2844 Barber shops; hair stylist, men; manicure preparations

**(G-3714)**
**ACCESS CASTERS**
10141 S Western Ave (60643-1927)
P.O. Box 43138 (60643-0138)
PHONE...................................773 881-4186
James Russell, *President*
Michael Hyland, *Vice Pres*
**EMP:** 3
**SALES (est):** 665.6K **Privately Held**
**SIC:** 3069 Castings, rubber

**(G-3715)**
**ACCESS INTERNATIONAL INC**
Also Called: A I 2
180 N Stetson Ave (60601-6706)
PHONE...................................312 920-9366
Douglas Katich, *President*
Dave Contreras, *Exec VP*
David Contreras, *Vice Pres*
Derek Morgan, *Vice Pres*
Dorothy Zwierz, *Vice Pres*
**EMP:** 25
**SQ FT:** 6,000
**SALES (est):** 2.6MM **Privately Held**
**WEB:** www.ai2.com
**SIC:** 7371 7372 Computer software development; business oriented computer software

**(G-3716)**
**ACCESS JAPAN LLC**
5130 N Bernard St (60625-4802)
PHONE...................................773 583-7183
John Coomes,
**EMP:** 3
**SALES:** 950K **Privately Held**
**SIC:** 3699 Electrical equipment & supplies

**(G-3717)**
**ACCIONA WINDPOWER N AMER LLC**
333 W Wacker Dr Ste 1500 (60606-1226)
PHONE...................................319 643-9463
Donald Points, *CFO*
**EMP:** 8
**SALES (corp-wide):** 3.5B **Privately Held**
**SIC:** 3511 Turbines & turbine generator sets
**HQ:** Acciona Windpower North America, Llc
155 Fawcett Dr
West Branch IA 52358

**(G-3718)**
**ACCORN GRAN NATURAL STONE INC (PA)**
Also Called: Acorn Granite & Marble
2727 W Madison St (60612-2035)
PHONE...................................312 663-5000
Fax: 773 533-7101
Shankar Vuyyuru, *President*
Tejomai Vuyyuru, *President*
Joanna Buba, *Admin Sec*
▲ **EMP:** 5
**SQ FT:** 8,000
**SALES (est):** 614.3K **Privately Held**
**WEB:** www.acornmarble.com
**SIC:** 3281 Granite, cut & shaped

**(G-3719)**
**ACCURATE ENGINE & MACHINE INC**
5053 W Diversey Ave (60639-1609)
PHONE...................................773 237-4942
Rey Villareal, *President*
**EMP:** 2
**SALES:** 250K **Privately Held**
**SIC:** 7539 3714 Automotive repair shops; motor vehicle parts & accessories

**(G-3720)**
**ACCURATE METAL FABRICATING LLC**
1657 N Kostner Ave (60639-4704)
PHONE...................................773 235-0400
Raymond J Meinsen Jr, *President*
Raymond Scott Meinsen, *Vice Pres*
John H Forchette Jr, *Plant Mgr*
Joan C Meinsen, *Admin Sec*
**EMP:** 70 **EST:** 1939
**SQ FT:** 53,000
**SALES (est):** 11MM **Privately Held**
**SIC:** 3993 3599 3441 Displays & cutouts, window & lobby; machine shop, jobbing & repair; fabricated structural metal

**(G-3721)**
**ACCURATE PERFORATING CO INC**
Also Called: Standard Perforating & Mfg
3636 S Kedzie Ave (60632-2786)
PHONE...................................773 254-3232
Fax: 773 254-9453
Aaron J Kamins, *President*
Larry H Cohen, *Owner*
Phillip Penner, *Vice Pres*
Joe Zumerling, *Purchasing*
Rebecca Stringer, *Controller*
**EMP:** 90
**SQ FT:** 175,000
**SALES (est):** 38MM **Privately Held**
**WEB:** www.accurateperforating.com
**SIC:** 3469 Perforated metal, stamped

**(G-3722)**
**ACCURATE PRODUCTS INCORPORATED**
4645 N Ravenswood Ave (60640-4573)
PHONE...................................773 878-2200
Fax: 773 878-3290
Graham Satherlie, *President*
Tim J Satherlie, *Plant Mgr*
Shawn Satherlie, *QC Mgr*
Raissa Ledesma, *Accounting Mgr*
Ofelia Palabrica, *Finance*
▲ **EMP:** 28
**SQ FT:** 20,000
**SALES (est):** 12MM **Privately Held**
**WEB:** www.accurate-prod.com
**SIC:** 3069 5085 Molded rubber products; rubber goods, mechanical

**(G-3723)**
**ACCURATE TOOL & MFG CORP**
350 N La Salle Dr # 1100 (60654-5131)
PHONE...................................708 652-4266
Fax: 708 652-4443
Charles E Dobes, *President*
Dorothy Dobes, *Vice Pres*
Kathy Restivo, *Office Mgr*
**EMP:** 17 **EST:** 1966
**SQ FT:** 25,000
**SALES (est):** 1.9MM **Privately Held**
**SIC:** 3544 3599 Special dies, tools, jigs & fixtures; machine shop, jobbing & repair

**(G-3724)**
**ACCURO MEDICAL PRODUCTS LLC**
70 W Madison St Ste 3200 (60602-4901)
PHONE...................................800 669-4757
Todd Hubbard, *Mng Member*
Michael Hennessy,
**EMP:** 8
**SALES (est):** 760K **Privately Held**
**SIC:** 3841 Medical instruments & equipment, blood & bone work

**(G-3725)**
**ACE ACTION ELEVATOR SERVICES**
619 N Lotus Ave (60644-1514)
PHONE...................................773 708-1666
George Emmerich, *Principal*
**EMP:** 3
**SALES (est):** 235.8K **Privately Held**
**SIC:** 3534 Elevators & moving stairways

**(G-3726)**
**ACE BAKERIES**
3241 S Halsted St (60608-6605)
PHONE...................................312 225-4973
Fax: 312 225-6849
Lisa Pack, *Owner*
**EMP:** 10
**SALES (est):** 440K **Privately Held**
**WEB:** www.acebakeries.com
**SIC:** 2051 5461 Bread, cake & related products; bakeries

**(G-3727)**
**ACE PLATING COMPANY**
Also Called: Ace Industries
3433 W 48th Pl (60632-3026)
PHONE...................................773 376-1800
Fax: 773 927-4544
Michael Holewinski, *President*
David Flores, *Vice Pres*
**EMP:** 35 **EST:** 1962
**SQ FT:** 40,000
**SALES (est):** 4.4MM **Privately Held**
**WEB:** www.aceindustries.net
**SIC:** 3471 3544 3469 Plating of metals or formed products; special dies, tools, jigs & fixtures; metal stampings

**(G-3728)**
**ACE SANDBLAST COMPANY (DEL)**
Also Called: Ace Sand Blast
4601 W Roscoe St (60641-4484)
PHONE...................................773 777-6654
Fax: 773 777-7562
Robert Largay, *President*
Robert Largary Jr, *Vice Pres*
Julianne Largay, *Vice Pres*
Norma Pesola, *Bookkeeper*
**EMP:** 13 **EST:** 1942
**SQ FT:** 35,000
**SALES (est):** 1.3MM **Privately Held**
**SIC:** 3599 3471 Machine shop, jobbing & repair; plating & polishing

**(G-3729)**
**ACJ PARTNERS LLC**
11552 S Bell Ave (60643-4714)
PHONE...................................630 745-1335
Astor Rogers, *President*
**EMP:** 3 **EST:** 2008
**SQ FT:** 3,000
**SALES (est):** 220K **Privately Held**
**SIC:** 2759 Commercial printing

**(G-3730)**
**ACL INC**
840 W 49th Pl (60609-5151)
PHONE...................................773 285-0295
Frank Ungari, *President*
John Olmstead, *Sr Corp Ofcr*
Tony Banks, *Vice Pres*
Dan Cooke, *Purch Dir*
Diane Potts, *Controller*
▲ **EMP:** 16
**SQ FT:** 18,000
**SALES (est):** 6.2MM **Privately Held**
**WEB:** www.aclstaticide.com
**SIC:** 2819 3825 3812 2842 Industrial inorganic chemicals; instruments to measure electricity; search & navigation equipment; specialty cleaning, polishes & sanitation goods

**(G-3731)**
**ACME BUTTON & BUTTONHOLE CO**
Also Called: Acme Sales
4638 N Ravenswood Ave # 2 (60640-4510)
PHONE...................................773 907-8400
Fax: 773 907-8476
Seymour Ferdman, *President*
Barbara Ferdman, *Vice Pres*
**EMP:** 3 **EST:** 1937
**SALES (est):** 19.9K **Privately Held**
**SIC:** 3965 2395 3961 Buttons & parts; buckles & buckle parts; permanent pleating & pressing, for the trade; costume jewelry

**(G-3732)**
**ACME CONTROL SERVICE INC**
6140 W Higgins Ave (60630-1845)
PHONE...................................773 774-9191
Fax: 773 774-3737
Robert Huening, *President*
Shirley M Huening, *Corp Secy*
Mark Huening, *Vice Pres*
Steven Huening, *Vice Pres*
Chris Molinaro, *Sales Dir*
**EMP:** 25
**SQ FT:** 5,000
**SALES (est):** 4.1MM **Privately Held**
**WEB:** www.acmecontrol.com
**SIC:** 7699 7694 Thermostat repair; armature rewinding shops

**(G-3733)**
**ACME METALLIZING CO INC**
5958 S Central Ave (60638-3711)
PHONE...................................773 767-7000
Fax: 773 767-9759
Edward Lupie, *President*
**EMP:** 10 **EST:** 1955
**SALES (est):** 640K **Privately Held**
**SIC:** 3479 Etching & engraving

**(G-3734)**
**ACME SPINNING COMPANY INC**
Also Called: Ace Industries
3433 W 48th Pl Fl 1 (60632-3026)
PHONE...................................773 927-2711
Michael Holewinski, *President*

Mary Holewinski, *Admin Sec*
▲ **EMP:** 14 **EST:** 1954
**SQ FT:** 24,000
**SALES (est):** 1.7MM **Privately Held**
**WEB:** www.acmespinningcompany.com
**SIC: 3469** Stamping metal for the trade; spinning metal for the trade

### (G-3735)
### ACO INC
Also Called: Aeronautical Electric Company
5656 N Northwest Hwy (60646-6136)
**PHONE** .................................. 773 774-5200
**Fax:** 773 774-7946
William Nordlof, *President*
Michelle Nordlof, *Controller*
Virginia Nordlof, *Admin Sec*
**EMP:** 26
**SQ FT:** 10,500
**SALES:** 1.2MM **Privately Held**
**WEB:** www.aeronauticalelectric.com
**SIC: 3651** 3644 3643 3641 Household audio & video equipment; noncurrent-carrying wiring services; current-carrying wiring devices; electric lamps; manufactured hardware (general)

### (G-3736)
### ACORN WIRE AND IRON WORKS LLC
2035 S Racine Ave (60608-3201)
**PHONE** .................................. 312 243-6414
**Fax:** 312 243-8069
John Stitt, *Manager*
Dean Wynne,
▼ **EMP:** 20 **EST:** 1913
**SQ FT:** 30,000
**SALES (est):** 3.4MM **Privately Held**
**WEB:** www.acornwire.com
**SIC: 3496** Miscellaneous fabricated wire products

### (G-3737)
### ACP TOWER HOLDINGS LLC (PA)
311 S Wacker Dr Ste 4300 (60606-6655)
**PHONE** .................................. 800 835-8527
**EMP:** 7
**SALES (est):** 25.5MM **Privately Held**
**SIC: 3663** 7372 Cellular radio telephone; prepackaged software

### (G-3738)
### ACRYLIC DESIGN WORKS INC
5023 W 66th St (60638-6403)
**PHONE** .................................. 773 843-1300
Mike Palka, *President*
Robert Palka, *Vice Pres*
Eva Kupcek, *Manager*
**EMP:** 10
**SALES (est):** 1.2MM **Privately Held**
**SIC: 2824** Acrylic fibers

### (G-3739)
### ACTA PUBLICATIONS
4848 N Clark St (60640-4711)
**PHONE** .................................. 773 989-3036
**Fax:** 773 271-7399
Gregory Pierce, *President*
**EMP:** 5
**SQ FT:** 5,000
**SALES (est):** 648.2K **Privately Held**
**WEB:** www.actapublications.com
**SIC: 2731** 3652 3695 Books: publishing only; pamphlets: publishing only, not printed on site; magnetic tape (audio): prerecorded; magnetic tape; video recording tape, blank

### (G-3740)
### ACTION ADVERTISING INC
2420 S Michigan Ave (60616-2302)
**PHONE** .................................. 312 791-0660
**Fax:** 312 791-0625
Merilyn Rutsky, *President*
**EMP:** 3
**SQ FT:** 8,000
**SALES:** 240K **Privately Held**
**SIC: 2399** 1799 8742 Banners, made from fabric; flags, fabric; sign installation & maintenance; merchandising consultant

### (G-3741)
### ACTIVE OFFICE SOLUTIONS
Also Called: Active Copier
3839 W Devon Ave (60659-1024)
**PHONE** .................................. 773 539-3333
Charlie Jung, *Principal*
**EMP:** 10
**SALES (est):** 891.9K **Privately Held**
**SIC: 3955** Print cartridges for laser & other computer printers

### (G-3742)
### ADA HOLDING COMPANY INC (HQ)
211 E Chicago Ave B29 (60611-2678)
**PHONE** .................................. 312 440-2897
Wiiliam Zimmerman, *CEO*
Linda Forscello, *Controller*
Andrew Reynolds, *Finance*
Christopher Maag, *Executive*
**EMP:** 15
**SQ FT:** 7,000
**SALES (est):** 9.7MM
**SALES (corp-wide):** 132.8MM **Privately Held**
**SIC: 8748** 2721 2711 Business consulting; magazines: publishing & printing; commercial printing & newspaper publishing combined
**PA:** American Dental Association
211 E Chicago Ave
Chicago IL 60611
312 440-2500

### (G-3743)
### ADAMS ELEVATOR EQUIPMENT CO (DH)
Also Called: Schindler Logistics Center
100 S Wacker Dr Ste 1250 (60606-4004)
**PHONE** .................................. 847 581-2900
**Fax:** 847 965-9114
Robert Schreck, *CEO*
Marie McIntosh, *General Mgr*
Rick Stumpf, *General Mgr*
Gerald Adams, *Marketing Staff*
**EMP:** 38 **EST:** 1930
**SQ FT:** 135,000
**SALES (est):** 10.9MM
**SALES (corp-wide):** 9.5B **Privately Held**
**WEB:** www.adamselevator.com
**SIC: 7389** 3534 3825 3312 Field warehousing; elevators & equipment; signal generators & averagers; locomotive wheels, rolled
**HQ:** Schindler Enterprises Inc.
20 Whippany Rd
Morristown NJ 07960
973 397-6500

### (G-3744)
### ADDISON CENTRAL PATHOLOGY
5645 W Addison St (60634-4403)
**PHONE** .................................. 847 685-9326
Vickie Rezai, *Principal*
**EMP:** 3 **EST:** 2013
**SALES (est):** 270.2K **Privately Held**
**SIC: 3841** Diagnostic apparatus, medical

### (G-3745)
### ADDISON PRECISION TECH LLC
4343 S Oakley Ave (60609-3018)
**PHONE** .................................. 773 626-4747
Ryan Cunningham,
**EMP:** 3
**SALES (est):** 99.9K **Privately Held**
**SIC: 3317** Steel pipe & tubes

### (G-3746)
### ADE INC (PA)
1430 E 130th St (60633-2399)
**PHONE** .................................. 773 646-3400
**Fax:** 773 646-3919
Lewis C Lofgren, *CEO*
Jason C Lofgren, *President*
Nancy Christien Zidek, *Controller*
Jason Lofgren, *Sales Executive*
▲ **EMP:** 20
**SQ FT:** 92,000
**SALES (est):** 5.1MM **Privately Held**
**WEB:** www.ade-usa.com
**SIC: 3086** 2821 2675 Insulation or cushioning material, foamed plastic; plastics materials & resins; die-cut paper & board

### (G-3747)
### ADEL TOOL CO LLP
4640 N Ronald St (60706-4782)
**PHONE** .................................. 708 867-8530
**Fax:** 708 867-7773
Casimir C Sobczak, *Partner*
Dorothy M Sobczak, *Partner*
Donna Barone, *Purchasing*
**EMP:** 3
**SQ FT:** 6,100
**SALES (est):** 377K **Privately Held**
**WEB:** www.adelnibbler.com
**SIC: 3423** Hand & edge tools

### (G-3748)
### ADELLO BIOLOGICS LLC
3440 S Dearborn St # 300 (60616-5074)
**PHONE** .................................. 312 235-3665
**Fax:** 847 760-0610
Thomas Flynn, *Vice Chairman*
Richard Phillips, *Purch Mgr*
Noushin Rahimi, *QA Dir*
Jason LI, *Manager*
Oscar Solis, *Manager*
**EMP:** 3
**SALES (corp-wide):** 5.1MM **Privately Held**
**SIC: 2834** Pharmaceutical preparations
**PA:** Therapeutic Proteins, Inc.
20 New England Ave
Piscataway NJ 08854
312 620-1500

### (G-3749)
### ADFLOW NETWORKS
203 N Lasalle St Ste 2100 (60601)
**PHONE** .................................. 866 423-3569
Sean Donnell, *Manager*
Katelyn Minaker, *Manager*
**EMP:** 3 **Privately Held**
**SIC: 7372** Prepackaged software

### (G-3750)
### ADHEREON CORPORATION
222 Mdse Mart Plz # 1230 (60654-1103)
**PHONE** .................................. 312 997-5002
Kelley Folino, *CEO*
**EMP:** 4
**SALES (est):** 149.2K **Privately Held**
**SIC: 3841** Surgical & medical instruments

### (G-3751)
### ADJUSTABLE CLAMP COMPANY (PA)
Also Called: Pony Tools
404 N Armour St (60642-6323)
P.O. Box 1899, Oak Park (60304-0605)
**PHONE** .................................. 312 666-0640
**Fax:** 312 666-2723
Daniel V Holman, *Ch of Bd*
Joseph Krueger, *President*
Steve Stompanato, *VP Mfg*
Linda Willford, *Treasurer*
Robert Slaveck, *Finance*
▲ **EMP:** 121
**SQ FT:** 10,000
**SALES (est):** 29.7MM **Privately Held**
**WEB:** www.adjustableclamp.com
**SIC: 3429** 3423 3545 Clamps, metal; hand & edge tools; vises, machine (machine tool accessories)

### (G-3752)
### ADM HOLDINGS LLC
191 N Wacker Dr Ste 1500 (60606-1899)
**PHONE** .................................. 312 634-8100
Marc D Bassewitz, *President*
**EMP:** 3
**SALES (corp-wide):** 62.3B **Publicly Held**
**SIC: 2046** Wet corn milling
**HQ:** Adm Holdings, Llc
4666 E Faries Pkwy
Decatur IL 62526
217 424-5200

### (G-3753)
### ADM MILLING CO
1300 W Carroll Ave Fl 2 (60607-1165)
**PHONE** .................................. 312 666-2465
**Fax:** 312 666-4277
Craig A Fischer, *President*
Cecil Garst, *Plant Supt*
Charles Adams, *Opers-Prdtn-Mfg*
**EMP:** 50
**SQ FT:** 187,000
**SALES (corp-wide):** 62.3B **Publicly Held**
**WEB:** www.admmilling.com
**SIC: 2041** Flour mills, cereal (except rice); grain mills (except rice)
**HQ:** Adm Milling Co.
8000 W 110th St Ste 300
Overland Park KS 66210
913 491-9400

### (G-3754)
### ADNAMA INC
1513 S State St (60605-2804)
**PHONE** .................................. 312 922-0509
Aleda Goodwin, *President*
**EMP:** 2
**SALES:** 330K **Privately Held**
**SIC: 3993** Signs & advertising specialties

### (G-3755)
### ADP PALLET INC
7300 S Kostner Ave (60629-5821)
**PHONE** .................................. 773 638-3800
Everardo Saldana, *President*
Edgardo Saldana, *Vice Pres*
**EMP:** 10
**SALES:** 1MM **Privately Held**
**SIC: 2448** Pallets, wood

### (G-3756)
### ADSENSA CORPORATION
404 S Wells St Fl 5 (60607-3964)
**PHONE** .................................. 312 559-2881
Martin Anderson, *President*
Suman Palit, *Info Tech Dir*
Nicole Maaguo, *Director*
**EMP:** 3 **EST:** 2011
**SALES (est):** 210K **Privately Held**
**SIC: 3695** Computer software tape & disks: blank, rigid & floppy

### (G-3757)
### ADVANCE AUTOMATION COMPANY
3526 N Elston Ave (60618-5692)
**PHONE** .................................. 773 539-7633
**Fax:** 773 539-7299
Joseph Hanley Jr, *President*
Annette Stollenwerk, *Treasurer*
Michael Hanley, *Admin Sec*
**EMP:** 12
**SQ FT:** 15,000
**SALES (est):** 2.6MM **Privately Held**
**WEB:** www.advanceautomationco.co
**SIC: 3593** Fluid power cylinders, hydraulic or pneumatic

### (G-3758)
### ADVANCE ENAMELING CO
5849 S Bishop St (60636-1712)
**PHONE** .................................. 773 737-7356
**Fax:** 773 737-7378
Jerry Grunert, *President*
Kurt Grunert, *Vice Pres*
**EMP:** 50
**SQ FT:** 72,000
**SALES (est):** 5.2MM **Privately Held**
**SIC: 3479** Coating of metals & formed products

### (G-3759)
### ADVANCE EQUIPMENT MFG CO
4615 W Chicago Ave (60651-3386)
**PHONE** .................................. 773 287-8220
**Fax:** 773 287-9889
John Wedakind, *President*
Mildred Wedakind, *Vice Pres*
Richard Bodenstab, *Admin Sec*
Deanne Shallcross, *Admin Sec*
▲ **EMP:** 14 **EST:** 1919
**SQ FT:** 20,000
**SALES (est):** 3.1MM **Privately Held**
**SIC: 3423** 5072 Hand & edge tools; hand tools

### (G-3760)
### ADVANCE INSTANT PRINTING CO
5 S Wabash Ave Ste 414 (60603-3507)
**PHONE** .................................. 312 346-0986
**Fax:** 312 346-8541
Dinesh M Patel, *President*
**EMP:** 2
**SQ FT:** 1,200

SALES: 240K **Privately Held**
SIC: 2752 7334 2761 2759 Commercial printing, offset; photocopying & duplicating services; manifold business forms; commercial printing; book printing

**(G-3761)**
**ADVANCE PLASTIC CORP**
4866 W Cortland St (60639-4632)
PHONE.....................................773 637-5922
Fax: 773 637-8237
William Mason III, *President*
Lisa A Mason, *Treasurer*
EMP: 12
SQ FT: 3,500
SALES (est): 1.8MM **Privately Held**
SIC: 3089 Injection molding of plastics

**(G-3762)**
**ADVANCE PRINTERS MACHINE SHOP**
4271 N Elston Ave (60618-1899)
PHONE.....................................773 588-3169
Fax: 773 588-2608
Edwin H Dolatowski, *President*
Cindy Lehmen, *Corp Secy*
EMP: 5 EST: 1919
SQ FT: 6,200
SALES: 500K **Privately Held**
SIC: 3599 Machine shop, jobbing & repair

**(G-3763)**
**ADVANCE SCREW PRODUCTS INC**
5160 W Homer St (60639-4417)
PHONE.....................................773 237-0034
Fax: 773 237-6847
Frank W Tomzik, *President*
Frederick Tomzik, *Corp Secy*
Kenneth Tomzik, *Vice Pres*
Jean Tomzik, *Controller*
EMP: 17
SQ FT: 25,000
SALES (est): 3MM **Privately Held**
SIC: 3451 Screw machine products

**(G-3764)**
**ADVANCE STEEL SERVICES INC**
4722 W Harrison St (60644-5122)
PHONE.....................................773 619-2977
Ninos Oshana, *President*
Patricia Daugherty, *Accounts Mgr*
▼ EMP: 2
SQ FT: 7,500
SALES (est): 256.1K **Privately Held**
SIC: 5051 3312 1791 Steel decking; structural shapes & pilings, steel; bars & bar shapes, steel, cold-finished: own hot-rolled; bars, iron: made in steel mills; structural steel erection

**(G-3765)**
**ADVANCE UNIFORM COMPANY**
33 E 13th St Ste 1 (60605-2381)
PHONE.....................................312 922-1797
Fax: 312 922-8654
Joan Bovit, *President*
Mark Bovit, *Corp Secy*
EMP: 10 EST: 1956
SQ FT: 12,000
SALES: 1.5MM **Privately Held**
SIC: 5699 2326 2337 Uniforms; work uniforms; uniforms, except athletic: women's, misses' & juniors'

**(G-3766)**
**ADVANCE WHEEL CORPORATION**
5335 S Western Blvd Ste H (60609-5450)
PHONE.....................................773 471-5734
Fax: 773 471-5724
William L Dods, *President*
Hector Oliva, *Plant Mgr*
Kevin Rohrbecher, *Sales Staff*
John Korpak, *Admin Sec*
▲ EMP: 70
SQ FT: 100,000
SALES (est): 14.6MM **Privately Held**
WEB: www.advancewheel.com
SIC: 3714 Wheel rims, motor vehicle

**(G-3767)**
**ADVANCE WORLD TRADE INC (PA)**
Also Called: A.W.T. World Trade
4321 N Knox Ave (60641-1906)
PHONE.....................................773 777-0909
Fax: 773 777-0909
Michael Green, *President*
Jorge Fuentes, *Plant Mgr*
Stanley Komrowski, *Engineer*
Sid Cohen, *Controller*
Edward Murphy, *Personnel Exec*
▲ EMP: 60
SQ FT: 85,000
SALES (est): 37.6MM **Privately Held**
WEB: www.awt-gpi.com
SIC: 5084 3555 Printing trades machinery, equipment & supplies; printing trades machinery

**(G-3768)**
**ADVANCED CSTM ENRGY SLTONS INC**
Also Called: Aces
2545 W Diversey Ave (60647-7172)
PHONE.....................................312 428-9540
Lucas Payne, *Ch of Bd*
▲ EMP: 86 EST: 2012
SQ FT: 6,000
SALES: 15MM **Privately Held**
SIC: 3648 7389 Public lighting fixtures;

**(G-3769)**
**ADVANCED FLEXIBLE MTLS LLC**
Also Called: Afm Heatsheets
2 N La Salle St Ste 1200 (60602-4056)
PHONE.....................................770 222-6000
Chris Falk,
Clay Hunter,
EMP: 10
SQ FT: 2,000
SALES (est): 642.5K **Privately Held**
SIC: 2395 Quilted fabrics or cloth

**(G-3770)**
**ADVANCED MACHINE CO INC**
4450 W Belmont Ave (60641-4529)
PHONE.....................................773 545-9790
Fax: 773 545-9760
Beniamin Grama, *President*
EMP: 3
SALES: 200K **Privately Held**
SIC: 3545 Machine tool accessories

**(G-3771)**
**ADVANCED ON-SITE CONCRETE INC**
5308 W Grand Ave (60639-3010)
PHONE.....................................773 622-7836
Fax: 773 622-8660
James Viola, *President*
Natalia Viola, *Admin Sec*
EMP: 20
SALES (est): 5.6MM **Privately Held**
SIC: 5032 3273 Concrete mixtures; ready-mixed concrete

**(G-3772)**
**ADVANCED STROBE PRODUCTS INC**
7227 W Wilson Ave (60706-4705)
PHONE.....................................708 867-3100
Fax: 708 867-1103
Jaro Bijak, *CEO*
Joanna Borkowska, *General Mgr*
Katherine Beres, *Vice Pres*
Greg Koniecko, *Purchasing*
Andrzej Bujnowski, *Engineer*
▲ EMP: 62
SQ FT: 28,000
SALES (est): 18.4MM **Privately Held**
WEB: www.strobelamps.com
SIC: 3641 3679 Electric lamps; electronic loads & power supplies

**(G-3773)**
**ADVANCED WINDOW CORP**
4935 W Le Moyne St (60651-1519)
PHONE.....................................773 379-3500
Fax: 773 379-4060
Robert Gibes, *President*
Jack Gibes, *Vice Pres*
Janucz Gibes, *Vice Pres*
Mario Pydych, *Marketing Staff*
Marek Kowalczyk, *Manager*
EMP: 27
SQ FT: 85,000
SALES: 9.6MM **Privately Held**
WEB: www.advancedwindow.biz
SIC: 3089 5211 Window frames & sash, plastic; lumber & other building materials

**(G-3774)**
**ADVANTAGE MANUFACTURING INC**
1458 N Lamon Ave (60651-1512)
PHONE.....................................773 626-2200
Andrew Radziwonski, *President*
Chris Halat, *Manager*
▲ EMP: 15
SALES (est): 3.2MM **Privately Held**
SIC: 3442 Window & door frames

**(G-3775)**
**ADVANTAGE STRUCTURES LLC**
10554 S Muskegon Ave (60617-5708)
PHONE.....................................773 734-9305
James Purgatorio, *General Mgr*
Joe Vaccaro,
EMP: 1
SALES (est): 285.2K
SALES (corp-wide): 2.2MM **Privately Held**
SIC: 2655 Fiber shipping & mailing containers
PA: J M Vaccaro Trucking Inc
10554 S Muskegon Ave
Chicago IL 60617
773 734-9305

**(G-3776)**
**ADVERTISERS BINDERY INC**
739 S Clark St Fl 3 (60605-1760)
PHONE.....................................312 939-4995
Fax: 312 939-4238
John J Burke Jr, *President*
Diane Burke, *Treasurer*
EMP: 10 EST: 1945
SQ FT: 12,000
SALES (est): 900.7K **Privately Held**
SIC: 2789 7331 Bookbinding & repairing: trade, edition, library, etc.; direct mail advertising services

**(G-3777)**
**AERODYNE INCORPORATED**
Also Called: Aeromotive
2612 W Barry Ave (60618-7145)
PHONE.....................................773 588-2905
Carl Dumele, *Principal*
EMP: 5
SALES: 750K **Privately Held**
SIC: 3694 Engine electrical equipment

**(G-3778)**
**AETNA ENGINEERING WORKS INC**
12001 S Calumet Ave (60628-6798)
PHONE.....................................773 785-0489
Fax: 773 785-7374
Richard J Zajeski, *President*
Richard Messinger, *Vice Pres*
Felicia Harrington, *Manager*
Linda Michaels, *Manager*
EMP: 23
SQ FT: 34,000
SALES (est): 2.5MM **Privately Held**
SIC: 1791 3441 3446 3444 Structural steel erection; fabricated structural metal; ornamental metalwork; sheet metalwork; studs & joists, sheet metal

**(G-3779)**
**AFAM CONCEPT INC**
Also Called: Jf Labs
7401 S Pulaski Rd Ste A (60629-5843)
PHONE.....................................773 838-1336
Fax: 773 838-1379
Akhtar Ali, *President*
Sue Houlihan, *President*
Gene Sims, *CFO*
Faiyaz Ahmed, *Finance*
Carnell Billups, *Human Res Mgr*
◆ EMP: 150
SQ FT: 200,000
SALES (est): 24.5MM **Privately Held**
SIC: 3999 Hair & hair-based products

**(G-3780)**
**AFFINNOVA INC**
233 S Wacker Dr Ste 6225 (60606-6465)
PHONE.....................................781 464-4700
Waleed Al Atraqchi, *Branch Mgr*
EMP: 3
SALES (corp-wide): 41.5MM **Privately Held**
SIC: 7379 7372 Computer related consulting services; business oriented computer software
PA: Affinnova, Inc.
265 Winter St Ste 4
Waltham MA 02451
781 487-2200

**(G-3781)**
**AFSHAR INC**
Also Called: Blazing Beads
3224 W Altgeld St (60647-2506)
PHONE.....................................773 645-8922
Anahit Afshar, *President*
EMP: 3
SALES (est): 210.5K **Privately Held**
SIC: 3911 Jewelry, precious metal

**(G-3782)**
**AGILENT TECHNOLOGIES INC**
4187 Collection Center Dr (60693-0041)
PHONE.....................................800 227-9770
EMP: 34
SALES (corp-wide): 4.2B **Publicly Held**
SIC: 3825 Instruments to measure electricity
PA: Agilent Technologies, Inc.
5301 Stevens Creek Blvd
Santa Clara CA 95051
408 345-8886

**(G-3783)**
**AHEAD LLC (PA)**
401 N Michigan Ave # 3400 (60611-4249)
PHONE.....................................312 924-4492
Fax: 312 924-5076
Daniel Adamany, *CEO*
Aaron Nack, *COO*
Eugene Kagan, *Vice Pres*
Bridget Wesley, *Project Mgr*
Kelly Kennon, *Opers Staff*
EMP: 100
SQ FT: 3,500
SALES (est): 51.9MM **Privately Held**
SIC: 7372 Business oriented computer software

**(G-3784)**
**AI IND**
Also Called: Ai Industries
4015 W Carroll Ave (60624-1802)
PHONE.....................................773 265-6640
Bryan Benson, *CEO*
Arbok Ives, *Principal*
EMP: 30
SALES: 950K **Privately Held**
SIC: 2326 Men's & boys' work clothing

**(G-3785)**
**AIDAR EXPRESS INC**
2814 W Arthur Ave Apt 1 (60645-5292)
PHONE.....................................773 757-3447
Marat Tolonov, *Owner*
EMP: 2
SALES: 250K **Privately Held**
SIC: 3537 Trucks: freight, baggage, etc.: industrial, except mining

**(G-3786)**
**AIRGAS INC**
12722 S Wentworth Ave (60628-7251)
PHONE.....................................773 785-3000
Kevin Spellman, *Branch Mgr*
EMP: 17
SALES (corp-wide): 163.9MM **Privately Held**
WEB: www.airgas.com
SIC: 5169 5084 3548 2911 Industrial gases; industrial machinery & equipment; welding apparatus; petroleum refining; industrial gases
HQ: Airgas, Inc.
259 N Radnor Chester Rd # 100
Radnor PA 19087
610 687-5253

## Chicago - Cook County (G-3787)

**(G-3787)**
**AIRGAS INC**
12745 S Wentworth Ave (60628-7252)
PHONE..................773 785-3000
Fax: 773 264-0391
Jim Cleary, *Branch Mgr*
**EMP:** 6
**SALES (corp-wide):** 163.9MM **Privately Held**
**WEB:** www.airproducts.com
**SIC: 2813** Industrial gases
**HQ:** Airgas, Inc.
259 N Radnor Chester Rd # 100
Radnor PA 19087
610 687-5253

**(G-3788)**
**AIRPORT AVIATION PROFESSIONALS**
5757 S Cicero Ave (60638-3817)
PHONE..................773 948-6631
Jeff Crosby, *Exec Dir*
**EMP:** 4
**SALES (est):** 320K **Privately Held**
**SIC: 3728** Refueling equipment for use in flight, airplane

**(G-3789)**
**AIRWAYS VIDEO INC**
Also Called: Airways Digital Media
4055 W Peterson Ave # 204 (60646-6182)
PHONE..................773 539-8400
Steve Zaransky, *President*
**EMP:** 4
**SQ FT:** 1,300
**SALES (est):** 663.9K **Privately Held**
**SIC: 3823** Digital displays of process variables

**(G-3790)**
**AKERS PACKAGING SERVICE INC**
1037 E 87th St (60619-6398)
PHONE..................773 731-2900
Fax: 773 731-2907
Ralph Bateman, *Safety Mgr*
Rick Atkinson, *Accounting Dir*
Michael Akey Jr, *Branch Mgr*
Jim Hoechst, *Manager*
Harry Kowalski, *Director*
**EMP:** 95
**SALES (corp-wide):** 73.4MM **Privately Held**
**WEB:** www.akers-pkg.com
**SIC: 2653** Boxes, corrugated: made from purchased materials
**PA:** Akers Packaging Service, Inc.
2820 Lefferson Rd
Middletown OH 45044
513 422-6312

**(G-3791)**
**AKZO NOBEL CHEMICALS LLC (DH)**
525 W Van Buren St # 1600 (60607-3845)
PHONE..................312 544-7000
Fax: 312 544-7320
Paul Radlinski, *Managing Dir*
Paul Nolan, *Top Exec*
Graeme Armstrong, *Senior VP*
Blake Holder, *Vice Pres*
John Nowak, *Research*
◆ **EMP:** 250
**SALES (est):** 642.9MM
**SALES (corp-wide):** 15B **Privately Held**
**WEB:** www.akzo-nobel.com
**SIC: 2841** Soap & other detergents
**HQ:** Akzo Nobel Inc.
525 W Van Buren St Fl 16
Chicago IL 60607
312 544-7000

**(G-3792)**
**AKZO NOBEL FUNCTIONAL CHEM LLC (HQ)**
Also Called: Akzonobel
525 W Van Buren St # 1600 (60607-3845)
PHONE..................312 544-7000
Fax: 312 544-7408
Marco Wijnands, *CEO*
John Wolff, *President*
Egbert Henstra, *General Mgr*
Janice Lucchesi, *General Mgr*
Inna Patriki, *General Mgr*
▲ **EMP:** 56

**SALES (est):** 149.7MM
**SALES (corp-wide):** 15B **Privately Held**
**WEB:** www.akzonobel-chemicals.com
**SIC: 2869** Industrial organic chemicals
**PA:** Akzo Nobel N.V.
Christian Neefestraat 2
Amsterdam
889 697-555

**(G-3793)**
**AKZO NOBEL INC (HQ)**
Also Called: Akzonobel
525 W Van Buren St Fl 16 (60607-3835)
PHONE..................312 544-7000
Ton Bchner, *CEO*
Philip E Radtke, *President*
Ruud Joosten, *General Mgr*
Conrad Keijzer, *General Mgr*
Ian Thorn, *General Mgr*
◆ **EMP:** 225
**SALES (est):** 3B
**SALES (corp-wide):** 15B **Privately Held**
**WEB:** www.akzonobelusa.com
**SIC: 2869** 2851 2834 3841 Industrial organic chemicals; paints & paint additives; lacquers, varnishes, enamels & other coatings; pharmaceutical preparations; hemodialysis apparatus; analytical instruments; industrial inorganic chemicals
**PA:** Akzo Nobel N.V.
Christian Neefestraat 2
Amsterdam
889 697-555

**(G-3794)**
**AKZO NOBEL SURFC CHEMISTRY LLC (DH)**
525 W Van Buren St Fl 16 (60607-3835)
PHONE..................312 544-7000
N Stapel, *Managing Dir*
Greg Katzke, *QC Mgr*
Alan Lenderman, *Technical Mgr*
Mary Allen, *Credit Staff*
Terrence M Rauen, *Mng Member*
◆ **EMP:** 10
**SALES (est):** 59.3MM
**SALES (corp-wide):** 15B **Privately Held**
**SIC: 2869** Laboratory chemicals, organic
**HQ:** Akzo Nobel Inc.
525 W Van Buren St Fl 16
Chicago IL 60607
312 544-7000

**(G-3795)**
**ALANSON MANUFACTURING LLC**
4408 W Cermak Rd (60623-2905)
PHONE..................773 762-2530
Fax: 773 762-1477
Tom Marmitt, *General Mgr*
Jerry Tamburrino,
**EMP:** 15
**SQ FT:** 13,000
**SALES (est):** 4.6MM **Privately Held**
**SIC: 3483** Ammunition components

**(G-3796)**
**ALBERTO DAZA**
Also Called: Technoweld
4243 W Arthington St (60624-3507)
PHONE..................773 638-9880
Alberto Daza, *Owner*
**EMP:** 10
**SALES (est):** 432.3K **Privately Held**
**SIC: 7692** Welding repair

**(G-3797)**
**ALCON LABORATORIES INC**
400 W Superior St (60654-3409)
PHONE..................312 751-6200
Kevin Ryan, *CFO*
**EMP:** 50
**SALES (corp-wide):** 48.5B **Privately Held**
**WEB:** www.cibasoft.com
**SIC: 3851** Contact lenses
**HQ:** Alcon Laboratories, Inc.
6201 South Fwy
Fort Worth TX 76134
817 293-0450

**(G-3798)**
**ALCON TOOL & MFG CO INC**
5266 N Elston Ave (60630-1673)
P.O. Box 480421, Niles (60714-0421)
PHONE..................773 545-8742
**EMP:** 10 **EST:** 1946

**SQ FT:** 8,000
**SALES (est):** 93.3K **Privately Held**
**SIC: 3545** 3544 3469 3643 Mfg Machine Tool Access Mfg Dies/Tools/Jigs/Fixt Mfg Metal Stampings Mfg Conductive Wire Dvcs Mfg Crowns/Closures

**(G-3799)**
**ALE SYNDICATE BREWERS LLC**
2601 W Diversey Ave (60647-1817)
PHONE..................773 340-2337
Jesse Evans,
Samuel Evans,
**EMP:** 7
**SALES (est):** 1.1MM **Privately Held**
**SIC: 5181** 2082 Ale; ale (alcoholic beverage)

**(G-3800)**
**ALEGRIA COMPANY**
2952 N Kilbourn Ave (60641-5360)
PHONE..................608 726-2336
Lina Rodriguez, *Partner*
**EMP:** 200
**SALES (est):** 13.5MM **Privately Held**
**SIC: 3571** Electronic computers

**(G-3801)**
**ALESSCO INC (PA)**
Also Called: Flip Flop Puzzle Mats
2237 N Janssen Ave (60614-3017)
PHONE..................773 327-7919
Fax: 773 348-9943
Jeffrey A D'Alessio, *President*
Michael Hallenborg, *Sales Mgr*
Alex Chellberg, *Sales Associate*
Jay Dean, *Marketing Staff*
Gary A D'Alessio, *Admin Sec*
◆ **EMP:** 15
**SQ FT:** 3,500
**SALES (est):** 13MM **Privately Held**
**WEB:** www.alessco.com
**SIC: 3961** 3069 2542 Earrings, except precious metal; necklaces, except precious metal; bracelets, except precious metal; ornaments, costume, except precious metal & gems; floor coverings, rubber; partitions & fixtures, except wood

**(G-3802)**
**ALEX DISPLAYS & CO**
401 N Leavitt St (60612-1617)
PHONE..................312 829-2948
Fax: 312 829-8505
Charles Felder, *CEO*
Steven Felder, *President*
Steve Felder, *President*
Michael Aviles, *Vice Pres*
Neal Marks, *Vice Pres*
**EMP:** 12 **EST:** 1959
**SQ FT:** 38,000
**SALES (est):** 2MM **Privately Held**
**WEB:** www.alexdisplays.com
**SIC: 2541** Display fixtures, wood

**(G-3803)**
**ALEX SMART INC**
1800 W Grace St Apt 322 (60613-6086)
PHONE..................773 244-9275
Jay Blumenfeld, *President*
Peter Merced, *Sales Staff*
Maria Martinez, *Manager*
**EMP:** 4
**SQ FT:** 3,500
**SALES (est):** 450K **Privately Held**
**SIC: 2771** Greeting cards

**(G-3804)**
**ALFRED ROBINSON**
Also Called: Al Jr's Glass
7525 S Evans Ave (60619-1917)
PHONE..................773 487-5777
Alfred Robinson, *Owner*
**EMP:** 3
**SALES (est):** 120K **Privately Held**
**SIC: 3231** Mirrored glass

**(G-3805)**
**ALL CELL TECHNOLOGIES LLC**
Also Called: Allcell
2321 W 41st St (60609-2215)
PHONE..................773 922-1155
Said Al-Hallaj, *Managing Prtnr*
Nazar Al-Khayat, *Vice Pres*
Azeezat Tijjani, *Opers Mgr*

Mario McKinney, *Opers Staff*
Madhushree Ghosh, *Engineer*
▲ **EMP:** 44 **EST:** 2015
**SQ FT:** 10,000
**SALES (est):** 3.9MM **Privately Held**
**WEB:** www.allcelltech.com
**SIC: 3691** Batteries, rechargeable

**(G-3806)**
**ALL ELECTRIC MTR REPR SVC INC (PA)**
6726 S Ashland Ave (60636-3430)
PHONE..................773 925-2404
Fax: 773 925-8816
Patrick Macias, *President*
Mark Stabosz, *Vice Pres*
**EMP:** 12
**SQ FT:** 5,000
**SALES (est):** 2MM **Privately Held**
**SIC: 7699** 7694 5084 5999 Pumps & pumping equipment repair; electric motor repair; pumps & pumping equipment; motors, electric

**(G-3807)**
**ALL PRINTING & GRAPHICS INC**
125 S Clark St Fl 3 (60603-4048)
PHONE..................773 553-3049
Ralph Folks, *Manager*
**EMP:** 5
**SALES (corp-wide):** 1.9MM **Privately Held**
**WEB:** www.allprintinginc.com
**SIC: 2752** Commercial printing, lithographic
**PA:** All Printing & Graphics, Inc.
2250 S 14th Ave
Broadview IL 60155
708 450-1512

**(G-3808)**
**ALL SHE WROTE**
825 W Armitage Ave (60614-4307)
PHONE..................773 529-0100
Fax: 773 529-1265
Wendy Beard, *Owner*
**EMP:** 17
**SALES (est):** 2.7MM **Privately Held**
**SIC: 2759** Invitation & stationery printing & engraving

**(G-3809)**
**ALL WOOD OR METAL RADIATOR COV**
2933 W Greenleaf Ave (60645-2915)
PHONE..................773 973-7328
Fax: 773 973-2123
Martin Rudolph, *Owner*
**EMP:** 3
**SALES (est):** 170K **Privately Held**
**SIC: 3433** Room & wall heaters, including radiators

**(G-3810)**
**ALLEGRO PUBLISHING INC**
2421 N Artesian Ave (60647-1902)
PHONE..................847 565-9083
Robert Mueller, *CEO*
Nathan Wysocki, *Director*
▼ **EMP:** 2
**SQ FT:** 2,000
**SALES (est):** 200K **Privately Held**
**WEB:** www.mwmeetings.com
**SIC: 2731** Book publishing

**(G-3811)**
**ALLEN LARSON**
Also Called: Galactic Clothing
1914 N Washtenaw Ave (60647-4222)
PHONE..................773 454-2210
**EMP:** 3
**SALES (est):** 76K **Privately Held**
**SIC: 2389** Mfg Apparel/Accessories

**(G-3812)**
**ALLEN PAPER COMPANY**
641 W Lake St Ste L101 (60661-1058)
PHONE..................312 454-4500
Fax: 312 454-9934
Charles Walther, *President*
Alice Johnson, *Corp Secy*
Josh Katzman, *Vice Pres*
**EMP:** 7
**SQ FT:** 10,000

## GEOGRAPHIC SECTION
### Chicago - Cook County (G-3839)

SALES: 860K **Privately Held**
WEB: www.allenpapercompany.com
SIC: **3955** 5112 Ribbons, inked: typewriter, adding machine, register, etc.; stationery; computer paper; business forms

**(G-3813)**
### ALLIANCE FOR ILLINOIS MFG
8420 W Bryn Mawr Ave (60631-3479)
PHONE.................................773 594-9292
Fax: 773 594-5916
Chris Multhauf, *Principal*
Ron Thompson,
Pam McDonough,
Dean Stork,
EMP: 1
SALES: 361.6K **Privately Held**
SIC: **3999** Hair curlers, designed for beauty parlors

**(G-3814)**
### ALLIANCE GRAPHICS
1652 W Ogden Ave Apt 4 (60612-3491)
PHONE.................................312 280-8000
Fax: 312 243-1100
Richard Haft, *Owner*
EMP: 3
SQ FT: 1,000
SALES: 250K **Privately Held**
SIC: **2752** 7331 Commercial printing, offset; mailing service

**(G-3815)**
### ALLIED GEAR CO
4901 W Arthington St (60644-5208)
PHONE.................................773 287-8742
Fax: 773 287-4720
Norman Teiber, *President*
Antoinette M Teiber, *Corp Secy*
EMP: 7 EST: 1946
SQ FT: 25,000
SALES (est): 1.2MM **Privately Held**
WEB: www.alliedgear.com
SIC: **3566** 3568 3462 Gears, power transmission, except automotive; sprockets (power transmission equipment); iron & steel forgings

**(G-3816)**
### ALLIED METAL CO (PA)
1300 N Kostner Ave (60651-1605)
PHONE.................................312 225-2800
Fax: 312 225-1161
Joel Fink, *President*
Barry Cohen, *Vice Pres*
Hal Jernigan, *Vice Pres*
Paul Lemkey, *Vice Pres*
Paul Lemke, *VP Prdtn*
▲ EMP: 30 EST: 1955
SQ FT: 60,000
SALES (est): 36.6MM **Privately Held**
WEB: www.alliedmetalcompany.com
SIC: **3341** Aluminum smelting & refining (secondary); zinc smelting & refining (secondary)

**(G-3817)**
### ALLIED PRINTING INC
Also Called: Allied Print & Copy
5640 N Broadway St (60660-4414)
PHONE.................................773 334-5200
Khoushab Alam, *President*
EMP: 3
SALES (est): 310K **Privately Held**
SIC: **2759** Commercial printing

**(G-3818)**
### ALLIED TELESIS INC
Also Called: ATI
123 N Wacker Dr Ste 2130 (60606-1777)
PHONE.................................312 726-1990
Dan Stellop, *Branch Mgr*
EMP: 70
SALES (corp-wide): 264.8MM **Privately Held**
SIC: **3577** 7373 Computer peripheral equipment; local area network (LAN) systems integrator
HQ: Allied Telesis, Inc.
19800 North Creek Pkwy # 100
Bothell WA 98011
408 519-8700

**(G-3819)**
### ALLIGATOR REC & ARTIST MGT INC
Also Called: Eyeball Music
1441 W Devon Ave (60660-1311)
PHONE.................................773 973-7736
Fax: 773 973-2088
Bruce Iglauer, *President*
Joann Auster, *Controller*
Kerry Peace, *Sales Staff*
Cody McGinnes, *Office Mgr*
Mark Steffen, *Manager*
▼ EMP: 15
SQ FT: 8,600
SALES: 2.8MM **Privately Held**
WEB: www.allig.com
SIC: **3652** 8742 Phonograph record blanks; business consultant

**(G-3820)**
### ALLSCRIPTS HEALTHCARE LLC
222 Merchandise Mart Plz (60654-1103)
PHONE.................................312 506-1200
EMP: 3
SALES (corp-wide): 1.5B **Publicly Held**
SIC: **7372** Prepackaged software
HQ: Allscripts Healthcare, Llc
8529 Six Forks Rd
Raleigh NC 27615
919 847-8102

**(G-3821)**
### ALLSCRIPTS HEALTHCARE LLC
222 Merchandise Mart Plz (60654-1103)
PHONE.................................800 334-8534
EMP: 3
SALES (corp-wide): 1.5B **Publicly Held**
SIC: **7372** Prepackaged software
HQ: Allscripts Healthcare, Llc
8529 Six Forks Rd
Raleigh NC 27615
919 847-8102

**(G-3822)**
### ALLSCRPTS HLTHCARE SLTIONS INC (PA)
222 Merchandise Mart Plz (60654-1103)
PHONE.................................312 506-1200
Fax: 312 506-1201
Paul M Black, *CEO*
Michael A Klayko, *Ch of Bd*
Marian Chitu, *President*
Alan Fowles, *President*
Richard Poulton, *President*
EMP: 130
SQ FT: 1,000,000
SALES: 1.5B **Publicly Held**
SIC: **7372** Prepackaged software

**(G-3823)**
### ALLSCRPTS HLTHCARE SLTIONS INC
222 Merchandise Mart Plz # 2024 (60654-1103)
PHONE.................................312 506-1200
Fax: 847 680-3573
Paul Black, *CEO*
Steven Katz, *Exec VP*
Jim Ufheil, *VP Sales*
Greg Boyer, *Manager*
Bonnie Scharado, *Manager*
EMP: 160
SALES (corp-wide): 1.5B **Publicly Held**
SIC: **7372** Prepackaged software
PA: Allscripts Healthcare Solutions, Inc.
222 Merchandise Mart Plz
Chicago IL 60654
312 506-1200

**(G-3824)**
### ALLTECH ASSOCIATES INC (HQ)
Also Called: Grace Dvson Discovery Sciences
415 S Kilpatrick Ave (60644-4923)
PHONE.................................773 261-2252
Fax: 847 948-1078
Lafred E Festa, *President*
Bonnie Przybylski, *Principal*
Sharon McKinley, *Vice Pres*
Thomas W Rendl, *Vice Pres*
Steve Lang, *Purchasing*

EMP: 100 EST: 1970
SQ FT: 60,000
SALES (est): 46.9MM
SALES (corp-wide): 1.6B **Publicly Held**
WEB: www.chromatography.com
SIC: **3826** Chromatographic equipment, laboratory type
PA: W. R. Grace & Co.
7500 Grace Dr
Columbia MD 21044
410 531-4000

**(G-3825)**
### ALLWOOD CABINET
3343 W Columbus Ave (60652-2548)
PHONE.................................773 778-1242
Milan Biljan, *Partner*
Luka Biljan, *Partner*
EMP: 7 EST: 1951
SQ FT: 5,000
SALES: 350K **Privately Held**
SIC: **2434** Wood kitchen cabinets

**(G-3826)**
### ALLY GLOBAL CORPORATION
Also Called: Ally International Trading
6033 N Sheridan Rd 23d (60660-3003)
PHONE.................................773 822-3373
Tony Liu, *President*
EMP: 7
SALES (est): 785.7K **Privately Held**
WEB: www.allyglobalgroup.com
SIC: **3546** 3572 5045 5065 Power-driven handtools; computer storage devices; computers, peripherals & software; electronic parts & equipment

**(G-3827)**
### ALOMAR INC
5 S Wabash Ave Ste 316 (60603-3518)
PHONE.................................312 855-0714
Omar Alvarez, *President*
Onelio Alvarez, *Vice Pres*
Maria G Alvarez, *Treasurer*
▲ EMP: 3
SQ FT: 1,400
SALES: 1.1MM **Privately Held**
WEB: www.alomar.com
SIC: **3911** 5094 Jewelry, precious metal; jewelry

**(G-3828)**
### ALPHA INDUSTRIES MGT INC
Also Called: Isoflex Packaging
1650 E 95th St (60617-4706)
PHONE.................................773 359-8000
EMP: 75
SALES (corp-wide): 1.3B **Privately Held**
SIC: **3081** Plastic film & sheet; polyethylene film
PA: Alpha Industries Management, Inc.
Page And Schuyler Ave
Lyndhurst NJ 07071
201 933-6000

**(G-3829)**
### ALPHA PACKAGING MINNESOTA INC
Also Called: Technigraph
6824 Paysphere Cir (60674-0068)
PHONE.................................507 454-3830
Beth Hoven, *Branch Mgr*
EMP: 3 **Privately Held**
SIC: **3085** Plastics bottles
HQ: Alpha Packaging (Minnesota) Inc.
850 W 3rd St
Winona MN 55987
507 454-3830

**(G-3830)**
### ALPHA PAGES LLC (PA)
107 W Van Buren St # 203 (60605-1054)
PHONE.................................847 733-1740
Jeff Joseph, *CEO*
EMP: 7
SALES: 1.5MM **Privately Held**
SIC: **7313** 3823 Printed media advertising representatives; computer interface equipment for industrial process control

**(G-3831)**
### ALPHA PCB DESIGNS INC
6815 W Higgins Ave (60656-2009)
PHONE.................................773 631-5543
Dean Bassias, *President*
▲ EMP: 4

SQ FT: 3,000
SALES (est): 621.8K **Privately Held**
SIC: **3672** Printed circuit boards

**(G-3832)**
### ALPINA MANUFACTURING LLC
6460 W Cortland St (60707-4011)
PHONE.................................773 202-8887
Fax: 773 202-8826
Darius Augustine, *CEO*
◆ EMP: 35
SQ FT: 100,000
SALES: 9.9MM **Privately Held**
SIC: **3499** Picture frames, metal

**(G-3833)**
### ALPS GROUP INC
55 E Monroe St Ste 3800 (60603-6030)
PHONE.................................815 469-3800
EMP: 3
SALES (corp-wide): 626.5K **Privately Held**
SIC: **3421** Cutlery
PA: Alps Group, Inc.
8779 W Laraway Rd
Frankfort IL 60423
815 469-3800

**(G-3834)**
### ALSTER MACHINING CORP
4243 W Diversey Ave (60639-2002)
PHONE.................................773 384-2370
Fax: 773 384-2374
Adam Widula, *President*
EMP: 10
SQ FT: 16,000
SALES (est): 1.5MM **Privately Held**
SIC: **3599** Machine shop, jobbing & repair

**(G-3835)**
### ALTA VISTA GRAPHIC CORPORATION
3435 N Kimball Ave (60618-5516)
PHONE.................................773 267-2530
Ernesto Pedroza, *President*
Maria Wantuck, *Vice Pres*
Andrea Lebron, *Production*
EMP: 10
SQ FT: 15,000
SALES (est): 1.6MM **Privately Held**
WEB: www.altavistagraphics.com
SIC: **7336** 2752 Graphic arts & related design; commercial printing, lithographic

**(G-3836)**
### ALTA VISTA SOLUTIONS INC
2035 W Grand Ave (60612-1501)
PHONE.................................312 473-3050
Ernesto Pedroza, *President*
EMP: 15
SQ FT: 25,000
SALES (est): 516.5K **Privately Held**
SIC: **2759** Commercial printing

**(G-3837)**
### ALTATHERA PHARMACEUTICALS LLC
200 S Wacker Dr Ste 3100 (60606-5877)
PHONE.................................312 445-8900
Brandon Kashfian, *President*
Merrill Barden, *Vice Pres*
Mahlaqa Patel, *Vice Pres*
Jay Welsh, *Vice Pres*
Patricia Dunnigan, *Manager*
EMP: 9
SALES (est): 1.3MM **Privately Held**
SIC: **2834** Pharmaceutical preparations

**(G-3838)**
### ALTMAN & KOEHLER FOUNDRY
505 W Root St (60609-2733)
PHONE.................................773 373-7737
Fax: 773 373-7737
EMP: 5
SQ FT: 9,300
SALES: 110K **Privately Held**
SIC: **3365** 3369 Aluminum Foundry Non-ferrous Metal Foundry

**(G-3839)**
### ALTMAN PATTERN AND FOUNDRY CO
6820 W 63rd St (60638-4026)
PHONE.................................773 586-9100
Fax: 773 586-9107

# Chicago - Cook County (G-3840)

Ronald Altman, *President*
Virginia Altman, *Vice Pres*
Mary Altman, *Treasurer*
**EMP:** 15
**SQ FT:** 12,000
**SALES:** 800K **Privately Held**
**SIC:** 3365 3366 Aluminum foundries; brass foundry

**(G-3840)**
**ALVAREZ & MARSAL INC**
540 W Madison St Fl 18 (60661-7698)
**PHONE**..................312 601-4220
Corey Martens, *Managing Dir*
Christopher Bryan, *Vice Pres*
Richard Stone, *Vice Pres*
Thomas Downey, *Finance Mgr*
Robert Novak, *Marketing Mgr*
**EMP:** 50
**SALES (corp-wide):** 194.3MM **Privately Held**
**SIC:** 8742 3523 3448 Financial consultant; farm machinery & equipment; prefabricated metal buildings
**HQ:** Alvarez & Marsal, Inc.
600 Madison Ave Fl 8
New York NY 10022
212 759-4433

**(G-3841)**
**AM HARPER PRODUCTS INC**
Also Called: A.M.H. Products
2300 W Jarvis Ave Apt 3 (60645-1777)
**PHONE**..................312 767-8283
Andre Harper, *CEO*
Dejaney Hinds, *President*
Jermaine Moodie, *General Mgr*
Damion Beckford, *Business Mgr*
Melissa Harper, *COO*
**EMP:** 10
**SALES (est):** 335.7K **Privately Held**
**SIC:** 5699 2841 5999 Customized clothing & apparel; designers, apparel; textile soap; toiletries, cosmetics & perfumes

**(G-3842)**
**AM2PAT INC (PA)**
Also Called: Salient Hct
3034 W Devon Ave (60659-1455)
**PHONE**..................847 726-9443
Dushyant Patel, *President*
▲ **EMP:** 7
**SQ FT:** 4,400
**SALES (est):** 2.4MM **Privately Held**
**SIC:** 2834 Pills, pharmaceutical

**(G-3843)**
**AMAG MANUFACTURING INC**
4940 S East End Ave 11c (60615-3159)
**PHONE**..................773 667-5184
Michael Ahasay, *President*
Bruce Strong, *Corp Secy*
Dana Norwick, *Vice Pres*
**EMP:** 6
**SQ FT:** 800
**SALES (est):** 363K **Privately Held**
**SIC:** 3443 3496 Metal parts; miscellaneous fabricated wire products

**(G-3844)**
**AMBERLEAF CABINETRY INC**
1400 W 37th St (60609-2109)
**PHONE**..................773 247-8282
**EMP:** 11
**SALES (est):** 1.2MM **Privately Held**
**SIC:** 2434 Wood kitchen cabinets

**(G-3845)**
**AMENITIES HOME DESIGN**
Also Called: Cynthia Espy
1529 W Glenlake Ave (60660-1825)
**PHONE**..................312 421-2450
Cynthia E Espy, *Owner*
**EMP:** 2
**SQ FT:** 500
**SALES:** 200K **Privately Held**
**WEB:** www.amenitieshome.com
**SIC:** 2353 Hats, caps & millinery

**(G-3846)**
**AMER SPORTS COMPANY (HQ)**
8750 W Bryn Mawr Ave (60631-3655)
**PHONE**..................773 714-6400
Hekey Takala, *Ch of Bd*
Gary Diehl, *President*
Juha Vaisanen, *President*

Sari Homanen, *Human Res Mgr*
Brett Jacobson, *Regl Sales Mgr*
◆ **EMP:** 350
**SQ FT:** 100,000
**SALES:** 691.9MM
**SALES (corp-wide):** 2.7B **Privately Held**
**SIC:** 3949 Sporting & athletic goods; golf equipment; baseball equipment & supplies, general; tennis equipment & supplies
**PA:** Amer Sports Oyj
Konepajankuja 6
Helsinki 00510
207 122-500

**(G-3847)**
**AMERICAN ADVERTISING ASSOC INC**
9101 S Lake Shore Dr (60617)
**PHONE**..................773 312-5110
Noe Rinconeno, *President*
**EMP:** 3
**SALES (est):** 88.3K **Privately Held**
**SIC:** 7319 2759 5131 3993 Display advertising service; letterpress & screen printing; advertising literature: printing; flags & banners; signs & advertising specialties

**(G-3848)**
**AMERICAN AIR FILTER CO INC**
Also Called: AAF International
24828 Network Pl (60673-1248)
P.O. Box 35690 (60654)
**PHONE**..................502 637-0011
Michelle Ecken, *Marketing Staff*
**EMP:** 86
**SALES (corp-wide):** 17.9B **Privately Held**
**SIC:** 3564 Filters, air: furnaces, air conditioning equipment, etc.
**HQ:** American Air Filter Company, Inc.
9920 Corporate Campus Dr # 2200
Louisville KY 40223
502 637-0011

**(G-3849)**
**AMERICAN ASSN ENDODONTISTS**
211 E Chicago Ave # 1100 (60611-2687)
**PHONE**..................312 266-7255
**Fax:** 312 266-9867
Jerry McDonald, *CFO*
Alama Hundik, *Manager*
James M Drinan, *Exec Dir*
M Drinan, *Exec Dir*
Samuel W O Glesby, *Bd of Directors*
**EMP:** 24
**SQ FT:** 7,880
**SALES:** 9.5MM **Privately Held**
**SIC:** 8621 2721 Medical field-related associations; comic books: publishing only, not printed on site

**(G-3850)**
**AMERICAN ASSOCIATION OF INDIVI (PA)**
Also Called: Aaii
625 N Michigan Ave # 401 (60611-3110)
**PHONE**..................312 280-0170
**Fax:** 312 280-1625
James B Cloonan, *Ch of Bd*
John D Markese, *President*
Robert Hormats, *Vice Chairman*
Harry L Madorin, *Corp Secy*
Ted Cfa, *Vice Pres*
**EMP:** 28
**SQ FT:** 8,000
**SALES:** 6MM **Privately Held**
**SIC:** 6282 7331 2731 8621 Investment advisory service; mailing list management; mailing list brokers; books: publishing only; professional membership organizations

**(G-3851)**
**AMERICAN BAR ASSOCIATION (PA)**
321 N Clark St Ste Ll2 (60654-7598)
**PHONE**..................312 988-5000
**Fax:** 312 988-5177
Michael E Burke, *Ch of Bd*
Linda Klein, *President*
John W Anderson, *Managing Prtnr*
Peter Morrill, *General Mgr*
Monica Buckley, *Editor*

**EMP:** 700
**SQ FT:** 160,000
**SALES:** 151.7MM **Privately Held**
**WEB:** www.abanet.org
**SIC:** 8621 2721 2731 Bar association; magazines: publishing only, not printed on site; books: publishing only

**(G-3852)**
**AMERICAN BAR FOUNDATION**
750 N Lk Shr Dr Fl 4th (60611-4557)
**PHONE**..................312 988-6500
**Fax:** 312 988-6579
Lucinda Underwood, *General Mgr*
Mary Aileen, *Editor*
Patricia Brennan, *COO*
Katharine Hannaford, *Development*
Mary Cavallini, *CFO*
**EMP:** 60
**SQ FT:** 15,000
**SALES:** 6.5MM **Privately Held**
**WEB:** www.americanbarfoundation.com
**SIC:** 8733 8111 2741 Research institute; legal services; miscellaneous publishing

**(G-3853)**
**AMERICAN CAMPAIGNS**
5333 W Lake St (60644-2433)
**PHONE**..................773 261-6800
Tom Hendrick, *Principal*
**EMP:** 3
**SALES (est):** 207.3K **Privately Held**
**SIC:** 2759 Commercial printing

**(G-3854)**
**AMERICAN CHAMBER OF**
Also Called: Accr
5 S Wabash Ave Ste 1405a (60603-3104)
**PHONE**..................312 960-9400
Brad Apland, *President*
Scott Apland, *Principal*
Susan Roth, *Manager*
Marvin Schwartz, *Director*
**EMP:** 25
**SALES (est):** 2.5MM **Privately Held**
**SIC:** 2731 Book publishing

**(G-3855)**
**AMERICAN CITY BUS JOURNALS INC**
Also Called: City Business Journals Network
233 N Michigan Ave # 1810 (60601-5802)
**PHONE**..................312 873-2200
**Fax:** 312 337-6931
Megan Omeara, *Branch Mgr*
Joepsh Di Pietro, *Manager*
Filomena Volpe, *Manager*
**EMP:** 3
**SALES (corp-wide):** 1.6B **Privately Held**
**SIC:** 2721 Trade journals: publishing only, not printed on site
**HQ:** American City Business Journals, Inc.
120 W Morehead St Ste 400
Charlotte NC 28202
704 973-1000

**(G-3856)**
**AMERICAN ENLIGHTENMENT LLC**
Also Called: Luckyprints
2023 W Carroll Ave Ste 45 (60612-1693)
**PHONE**..................773 687-8996
Adam Smith,
**EMP:** 5
**SALES (est):** 172.3K **Privately Held**
**SIC:** 2396 5699 Screen printing on fabric articles; customized clothing & apparel

**(G-3857)**
**AMERICAN GRINDING & MACHINE CO (PA)**
2000 N Mango Ave (60639-2899)
**PHONE**..................773 889-4343
**Fax:** 773 889-3781
Greg Leonard, *President*
Todd Proffitt, *Production*
Scott Collins, *VP Sls/Mktg*
John Kehoe, *Manager*
Michael Davenport, *Admin Sec*
**EMP:** 66
**SQ FT:** 11,000
**SALES (est):** 12.1MM **Privately Held**
**SIC:** 3599 5051 7692 Machine shop, jobbing & repair; steel; welding repair

**(G-3858)**
**AMERICAN HOSP ASSN SVCS DEL (HQ)**
155 N Wacker Dr Ste 400 (60606-1719)
**PHONE**..................312 422-2000
**Fax:** 312 422-4700
Jonathan Lord, *COO*
Sidney Jacob, *Treasurer*
Fredric J Entin, *Admin Sec*
James Henderson, *Asst Sec*
**EMP:** 25
**SALES:** 4.5MM
**SALES (corp-wide):** 126.3MM **Privately Held**
**SIC:** 2721 2731 8721 Periodicals; book publishing; billing & bookkeeping service
**PA:** American Hospital Association
155 N Wacker Dr Ste 400
Chicago IL 60606
312 422-3000

**(G-3859)**
**AMERICAN LABELMARK COMPANY (PA)**
Also Called: Labelmaster Division
5724 N Pulaski Rd (60646-6797)
**PHONE**..................773 478-0900
**Fax:** 773 478-6054
Gary S Mostow, *Ch of Bd*
Dwight Curtis, *President*
Tracie Cady, *General Mgr*
Clay Moore, *Principal*
Bob Richard, *Vice Pres*
◆ **EMP:** 120
**SQ FT:** 90,000
**SALES (est):** 61.2MM **Privately Held**
**WEB:** www.alc-net.com
**SIC:** 2752 2731 2754 5192 Commercial printing, offset; advertising posters, lithographed; poster & decal printing, lithographic; book publishing; labels: gravure printing; posters: gravure printing; books, periodicals & newspapers; safety equipment; publishers' computer software

**(G-3860)**
**AMERICAN LIBRARY ASSOCIATION**
Also Called: Booklist
50 E Huron St (60611-2788)
**PHONE**..................312 280-5718
Bill Ott, *CEO*
Linda Cohen, *Sales Staff*
Daniel Kaplan, *Mktg Dir*
William R Gordon, *Branch Mgr*
Julia Smith, *Assoc Editor*
**EMP:** 25
**SALES (corp-wide):** 54.3MM **Privately Held**
**WEB:** www.alawash.org
**SIC:** 2721 Periodicals
**PA:** American Library Association
50 E Huron St
Chicago IL 60611
312 944-6780

**(G-3861)**
**AMERICAN MACHINE TOOLS INC**
5864 N Northwest Hwy (60631-2641)
**PHONE**..................773 775-6285
**Fax:** 773 442-0314
Michael Desjardins, *President*
▼ **EMP:** 7
**SQ FT:** 1,000
**SALES:** 5MM **Privately Held**
**WEB:** www.americanmachinetools.com
**SIC:** 3541 3542 3545 Machine tools, metal cutting type; machine tools, metal forming type; machine tool accessories

**(G-3862)**
**AMERICAN MACHINING & WLDG INC**
6009 S New England Ave (60638-4005)
**PHONE**..................773 586-2585
**Fax:** 773 586-2993
Stanley Sieczka, *President*
Joe Sieczka, *Vice Pres*
Andy Sieczka, *Treasurer*
▲ **EMP:** 25
**SQ FT:** 11,000
**SALES (est):** 6.1MM **Privately Held**
**SIC:** 3599 7692 Machine shop, jobbing & repair; welding repair

## GEOGRAPHIC SECTION
## Chicago - Cook County (G-3887)

**(G-3863)**
**AMERICAN MEDICAL ASSOCIATION (PA)**
Also Called: AMA SUBSCRIPTIONS
330 N Wabash Ave # 39300 (60611-5885)
PHONE...................312 464-5000
Fax: 312 464-5837
James Madera, *CEO*
Andrew W Gurman, *President*
Annette Flanagin, *General Mgr*
Sarah Sanders, *Principal*
Benjamin Schanker, *Principal*
**EMP:** 800 **EST:** 1847
**SQ FT:** 360,000
**SALES:** 284.3MM **Privately Held**
**WEB:** www.amajournals.com
**SIC:** 8621 2721 6321 6282 Medical field-related associations; trade journals: publishing only, not printed on site; reinsurance carriers, accident & health; investment advice

**(G-3864)**
**AMERICAN MEDICAL ASSOCIATION**
American Medical News
515 N State St Fl 9 (60654-9104)
PHONE...................312 464-2555
Fax: 312 464-2580
Bob Cook, *Editor*
David Glendinning, *Editor*
Sher Watts, *Editor*
Robert Hobert, *Vice Pres*
Chris Theodore, *VP Human Res*
**EMP:** 30
**SALES (corp-wide):** 284.3MM **Privately Held**
**WEB:** www.amajournals.com
**SIC:** 2721 Trade journals: publishing & printing
**PA:** American Medical Association Inc
330 N Wabash Ave # 39300
Chicago IL 60611
312 464-5000

**(G-3865)**
**AMERICAN METAL MFG INC**
6323 N Avondale Ave # 125 (60631-1958)
PHONE...................847 651-6097
Tim Blanks, *President*
**EMP:** 2
**SQ FT:** 15,000
**SALES (est):** 220K **Privately Held**
**SIC:** 3499 Aerosol valves, metal

**(G-3866)**
**AMERICAN METAL PERFORATING INC**
3201 W 36th Pl (60632-2741)
PHONE...................773 523-8884
Fax: 773 523-9323
David Y Kamins, *President*
Doris J Kamins, *Admin Sec*
**EMP:** 10
**SQ FT:** 15,000
**SALES (est):** 1.3MM **Privately Held**
**WEB:** www.perforate.net
**SIC:** 3469 Perforated metal, stamped

**(G-3867)**
**AMERICAN NAME PLATE & METAL DE**
4501 S Kildare Ave (60632-4477)
PHONE...................773 376-1400
Fax: 773 376-2236
Michael Stevens, *President*
Mark Hofmeister, *Vice Pres*
Bob Desbles, *Sales Mgr*
**EMP:** 25 **EST:** 1934
**SQ FT:** 45,000
**SALES (est):** 3.6MM **Privately Held**
**WEB:** www.americannameplate.com
**SIC:** 3993 3083 2672 2671 Name plates: except engraved, etched, etc.: metal; plastic finished products, laminated; coated & laminated paper; packaging paper & plastics film, coated & laminated; automotive & apparel trimmings

**(G-3868)**
**AMERICAN NICKEL WORKS INC**
1223 W Lake St (60607-1601)
PHONE...................312 942-0070
Fax: 312 942-0080
Robert Schultz, *President*
Arthur Shultz, *Shareholder*
Florence Shultz, *Shareholder*
**EMP:** 21 **EST:** 1951
**SQ FT:** 20,000
**SALES (est):** 2.1MM **Privately Held**
**SIC:** 3471 Plating of metals or formed products; polishing, metals or formed products

**(G-3869)**
**AMERICAN PLATING & MFG CO**
Also Called: Amplate
3941 S Keeler Ave (60632-3815)
PHONE...................773 890-4907
Fax: 773 843-1207
Karl Urban, *President*
Clara Lyall, *Manager*
**EMP:** 16 **EST:** 1903
**SQ FT:** 14,000
**SALES (est):** 2.1MM **Privately Held**
**WEB:** www.apmchicago.com
**SIC:** 3931 3471 Musical instruments; plating & polishing

**(G-3870)**
**AMERICAN RACK COMPANY**
Also Called: Belke Manufacturing Company
5810 N Northwest Hwy (60631-2641)
PHONE...................773 763-7309
Fax: 773 763-7421
W L Faulman, *President*
Michael R Faulman, *Treasurer*
Dan Close, *Manager*
Phyllis Faulman, *Admin Sec*
**EMP:** 45 **EST:** 1921
**SALES (est):** 4.6MM
**SALES (corp-wide):** 54.2MM **Privately Held**
**WEB:** www.associatedrack.com
**SIC:** 3559 3494 3443 3412 Metal finishing equipment for plating, etc.; valves & pipe fittings; fabricated plate work (boiler shop); metal barrels, drums & pails; paints & allied products; partitions & fixtures, except wood
**PA:** Associated Rack Corporation
70 Athens Dr
Mount Juliet TN 37122
615 288-4204

**(G-3871)**
**AMERICAN SCIENCE & SURPLUS INC**
5316w N Milwaukee Ave (60630)
PHONE...................773 763-0313
Fax: 773 763-1369
Joey Walker, *Manager*
**EMP:** 15
**SALES (corp-wide):** 10.6MM **Privately Held**
**WEB:** www.sciplus.com
**SIC:** 3944 Science kits: microscopes, chemistry sets, etc.; dishes, toy
**PA:** American Science & Surplus, Inc.
7410 N Lehigh Ave
Niles IL 60714
847 647-0011

**(G-3872)**
**AMERICAN SCIENCE AND TECH CORP (PA)**
1367 W Chicago Ave (60642-5661)
PHONE...................312 433-3800
Ali Manesh, *President*
**EMP:** 2
**SALES (est):** 536.2K **Privately Held**
**SIC:** 3728 Aircraft parts & equipment

**(G-3873)**
**AMERICAN SEA AND AIR**
2600 W Peterson Ave (60659-4098)
PHONE...................773 262-5960
Fax: 773 262-5953
Philip Marcus, *Owner*
Phillip Marcus, *Owner*
**EMP:** 10
**SQ FT:** 900
**SALES (est):** 510K **Privately Held**
**SIC:** 3743 Railroad equipment, except locomotives

**(G-3874)**
**AMERICAN SIGN & LIGHTING CO**
350 N La Salle Dr # 1100 (60654-5126)
PHONE...................847 258-8151
Todd Jackson, *CEO*
Jordan Uditsky, *President*
Joe Voyles, *Sales Staff*
Ty King, *Director*
▲ **EMP:** 22
**SQ FT:** 10,000
**SALES (est):** 2.3MM **Privately Held**
**WEB:** www.american-sign.com
**SIC:** 3993 1799 Electric signs; sign installation & maintenance

**(G-3875)**
**AMERICAN SODA FTN EXCH INC**
455 N Oakley Blvd (60612-1452)
PHONE...................312 733-5000
Fax: 312 733-3621
Ray Schy, *President*
Phil Schy, *Vice Pres*
Terry Schy, *Treasurer*
**EMP:** 14
**SQ FT:** 15,000
**SALES (est):** 3.7MM **Privately Held**
**SIC:** 5046 7699 3585 Restaurant equipment & supplies; soda fountain fixtures, except refrigerated; restaurant equipment repair; soda fountains, parts & accessories

**(G-3876)**
**AMERICAN SPECIALTY TOY**
432 N Clark St Ste 305 (60654-4536)
PHONE...................312 222-0984
Kathleen J Mc Hugh, *President*
**EMP:** 3
**SQ FT:** 850
**SALES (est):** 2MM **Privately Held**
**WEB:** www.astratoy.org
**SIC:** 3944 5084 Games, toys & children's vehicles; industrial machinery & equipment

**(G-3877)**
**AMERICAN TAPE MEASURES**
6717 W Foster Ave (60656-2137)
PHONE...................312 208-0282
Fax: 773 327-6318
Kurt Pusczan, *President*
Anne Pusczan, *Admin Sec*
**EMP:** 3 **EST:** 1962
**SQ FT:** 2,000
**SALES (est):** 97K **Privately Held**
**WEB:** www.americantapemeasures.com
**SIC:** 3999 7311 Tape measures; advertising agencies

**(G-3878)**
**AMERICAN TITANIUM WORKS LLC**
30 N La Salle St Ste 2200 (60602-7504)
PHONE...................312 327-3178
Thomas F Sax, *CEO*
Laura Abzal, *Executive Asst*
**EMP:** 2
**SALES (est):** 228.3K **Privately Held**
**SIC:** 3356 Titanium

**(G-3879)**
**AMERICAN TRADE & COML SVC LLC** ✪
Also Called: Atcs LLC
303 S Halsted St Apt 3 (60661-5418)
PHONE...................202 910-8808
Armond Arsalan, *Principal*
**EMP:** 12 **EST:** 2017
**SALES:** 20MM **Privately Held**
**SIC:** 2519 5021 3199 5199 Household furniture, except wood or metal: upholstered; furniture; shoes, leather; leather goods, except footwear, gloves, luggage, belting

**(G-3880)**
**AMERICAN TRADE MAGAZINES LLC**
566 W Lake St Ste 420 (60661-5205)
PHONE...................312 497-7707
Donald Feinstein, *Sales Dir*
Charles R Thompson,
**EMP:** 4
**SALES (est):** 390K **Privately Held**
**SIC:** 2721 Magazines: publishing & printing

**(G-3881)**
**AMERICAN TROPHY & AWARD CO INC**
Also Called: American Dragway Trophy Co
1006 S Michigan Ave # 503 (60605-2216)
PHONE...................312 939-3252
Fax: 312 939-3255
Ben Goldberg, *President*
**EMP:** 3
**SQ FT:** 5,000
**SALES:** 500K **Privately Held**
**SIC:** 3499 Trophies, metal, except silver

**(G-3882)**
**AMERICAN WHEEL CORP**
5939 W 66th St (60638-6205)
PHONE...................708 458-9141
Bill Dods, *President*
**EMP:** 20
**SALES (est):** 4.6MM **Privately Held**
**WEB:** www.american-wheel.com
**SIC:** 3714 Wheels, motor vehicle

**(G-3883)**
**AMERICAN WILBERT VAULT CORP**
11118 S Rockwell St (60655-1900)
PHONE...................773 238-2746
**EMP:** 18
**SALES (corp-wide):** 6.4MM **Privately Held**
**SIC:** 3272 Mfg Concrete Products
**PA:** American Wilbert Vault Corp.
7525 W 99th Pl
Bridgeview IL 60455
708 366-3210

**(G-3884)**
**AMERICAS COMMUNITY BANKERS**
Also Called: P & D Center
363 W Erie St Fl 4 (60654-6903)
PHONE...................312 644-3100
Bob Clifford, *Branch Mgr*
**EMP:** 22
**SQ FT:** 4,500
**SALES (corp-wide):** 7.1MM **Privately Held**
**SIC:** 4225 2759 2782 General warehousing & storage; envelopes: printing; stationery: printing; looseleaf binders & devices
**PA:** Americas Community Bankers
900 19th St Nw Ste 400
Washington DC

**(G-3885)**
**AMERICN FOREIGN LANG NEWSPAPER**
55 E Jackson Blvd Ste 920 (60604-4249)
PHONE...................312 368-4815
Rich Bourjaily, *Owner*
Paul Bourjaily, *Personnel Exec*
**EMP:** 25
**SALES (est):** 698.6K **Privately Held**
**SIC:** 2711 Newspapers

**(G-3886)**
**AMERISCAN DESIGNS INC**
4147 W Ogden Ave (60623-2877)
PHONE...................773 542-1291
Fax: 773 542-1298
William W Mac Williams, *President*
Bill Mac Williams, *President*
Janet Harrell, *Vice Pres*
Nina Lasalle, *Project Mgr*
Aaron Meyer, *Project Mgr*
▲ **EMP:** 55
**SQ FT:** 65,000
**SALES (est):** 16.4MM **Privately Held**
**WEB:** www.ameriscandesigns.com
**SIC:** 5712 2434 2431 3083 Cabinet work, custom; wood kitchen cabinets; millwork; laminated plastics plate & sheet

**(G-3887)**
**AMEROPAN OIL CORP**
3301 S California Ave (60608-5113)
PHONE...................773 847-4400
Fax: 773 847-4882
Jeff Guzman, *Manager*
**EMP:** 10

## Chicago - Cook County (G-3888)

SALES (est): 1.8MM **Privately Held**
SIC: 3443 Fuel tanks (oil, gas, etc.): metal plate

**(G-3888)**
**AMIBERICA INC**
3701 S Ashland Ave (60609-2130)
PHONE..................773 247-3600
William Diaz, *President*
Chris Vargas, *General Mgr*
John Kaminski, *Engineer*
Martin Kosiek, *Sales Executive*
Joseph Sidebotham, *Manager*
▼ EMP: 20
SQ FT: 56,000
SALES (est): 5.3MM **Privately Held**
WEB: www.amiberica.com
SIC: 3559 3567 Metal finishing equipment for plating, etc.; industrial furnaces & ovens

**(G-3889)**
**AMITY PACKING COMPANY INC (PA)**
4220 S Kildare Ave (60632-3930)
PHONE..................312 942-0270
Fax: 312 942-0413
Brian Tyler, *President*
Bruce Degonia, *Vice Pres*
Roger A Pfiel, *Vice Pres*
Joe Pirelli, *Opers Staff*
Sue Flynn, *Credit Mgr*
▼ EMP: 59 EST: 1966
SQ FT: 100,000
SALES: 60MM **Privately Held**
WEB: www.amitypacking.com
SIC: 5147 5812 2011 Meats, fresh; eating places; meat packing plants

**(G-3890)**
**AMK ENTERPRISES CHICAGO INC**
3605 S Calumet Ave (60653-1103)
PHONE..................312 523-7212
Allyson Kennon, *CEO*
EMP: 5
SALES: 350K **Privately Held**
SIC: 3999 5023 7389 Manufacturing industries; home furnishings; interior design services

**(G-3891)**
**AMK KITCHEN BAR**
1954 W Armitage Ave (60622-1024)
PHONE..................773 270-4115
EMP: 5
SALES (est): 320.7K **Privately Held**
SIC: 2599 Bar, restaurant & cafeteria furniture

**(G-3892)**
**AMOCO TECHNOLOGY COMPANY (DEL) (DH)**
200 E Randolph St # 2100 (60601-6432)
PHONE..................312 861-6000
Robert C Carr, *President*
Noreen Froning, *Info Tech Mgr*
F J Sroka, *Admin Sec*
EMP: 200
SALES (est): 52.5MM
SALES (corp-wide): 183B **Privately Held**
SIC: 2835 3821 7374 7372 In vitro & in vivo diagnostic substances; laser beam alignment devices; computer time-sharing; application computer software; solar cells; silicon wafers, chemically doped; laser scientific & engineering instruments
HQ: Bp Corporation North America Inc.
501 Westlake Park Blvd
Houston TX 77079
281 366-2000

**(G-3893)**
**AMP AMERICAS LLC (PA)**
Also Called: AMP CNG
1130 W Monroe St Ste 1 (60607-2500)
PHONE..................312 300-6700
Nate Laurell, *CEO*
Donna Rolf, *President*
Sam Bramfeld, *Senior VP*
Obi Ofoegbu, *Opers Mgr*
Saad Qais, *CFO*
EMP: 17

SALES (est): 3.1MM **Privately Held**
SIC: 2869 5171 Fuels; petroleum bulk stations

**(G-3894)**
**AMPHENOL EEC INC**
Also Called: Electrical Equipment Corp
4050 N Rockwell St (60618-3721)
PHONE..................773 463-8343
Fax: 773 463-8344
R Adam Norwitt, *President*
Darryl Marks, *Engineer*
Antoinette Ryan, *Manager*
▲ EMP: 30
SALES (est): 5MM
SALES (corp-wide): 6.2B **Publicly Held**
SIC: 3643 Electric connectors
PA: Amphenol Corporation
358 Hall Ave
Wallingford CT 06492
203 265-8900

**(G-3895)**
**AMS LLC**
2445 N Seminary Ave (60614-2239)
PHONE..................773 904-7740
Fax: 312 850-3047
Ronald Quick, *President*
EMP: 4
SQ FT: 3,000
SALES: 4MM **Privately Held**
SIC: 3365 Aluminum foundries

**(G-3896)**
**AMSTED INDUSTRIES INCORPORATED (PA)**
180 N Stetson Ave (60601-6808)
PHONE..................312 645-1700
Fax: 312 819-8504
W Robert Reum, *Ch of Bd*
Edward Brosius, *Counsel*
Thomas Petermann, *Counsel*
Marilyn Franson, *Vice Pres*
Steven Obendorf, *Vice Pres*
◆ EMP: 277 EST: 1902
SQ FT: 18,000
SALES (est): 1.9B **Privately Held**
WEB: www.amsted.com
SIC: 3443 3325 3585 3321 Cooling towers, metal plate; railroad car wheels, cast steel; refrigeration & heating equipment; gray & ductile iron foundries; freight cars & equipment

**(G-3897)**
**AMSTED INDUSTRIES INCORPORATED**
2 Prudential Plaza 180 (60601)
PHONE..................312 645-1700
Chris Athas, *Counsel*
EMP: 10
SALES (corp-wide): 1.9B **Privately Held**
SIC: 3443 Cooling towers, metal plate
PA: Amsted Industries Incorporated
180 N Stetson Ave
Chicago IL 60601
312 645-1700

**(G-3898)**
**AMSTED RAIL COMPANY INC**
Asf-Keystone
10 S Riverside Plz Fl 10 (60606-3728)
PHONE..................312 258-8000
Ronald Barker, *President*
Brian Hawkins, *Manager*
EMP: 65
SALES (corp-wide): 1.9B **Privately Held**
WEB: www.asf-keystone.com
SIC: 3743 Railroad equipment
HQ: Amsted Rail Company, Inc.
311 S Wacker Dr Ste 5300
Chicago IL 60606

**(G-3899)**
**AMSTED RAIL COMPANY INC (HQ)**
311 S Wacker Dr Ste 5300 (60606-6630)
PHONE..................312 922-4501
John Wories, *President*
Jay Monaco, *President*
Gary Wagner, *General Mgr*
Jon Schumacher, *COO*
William O'Donnell, *Senior VP*
◆ EMP: 277

SALES (est): 541MM
SALES (corp-wide): 1.9B **Privately Held**
SIC: 3743 Railroad equipment
PA: Amsted Industries Incorporated
180 N Stetson Ave
Chicago IL 60601
312 645-1700

**(G-3900)**
**ANASH EDUCATIONAL INSTITUTE**
2929 W Greenleaf Ave (60645-2915)
PHONE..................773 338-7704
Fax: 773 338-7811
Moshe Miller, *Director*
Yochanan Nathan, *Director*
EMP: 8
SALES (est): 435.9K **Privately Held**
SIC: 2741 Miscellaneous publishing

**(G-3901)**
**ANDERSON CASTING COMPANY INC**
1721 W Carroll Ave (60612)
PHONE..................312 733-1185
Walter Magiera Jr, *President*
Sophie Magiera, *Corp Secy*
EMP: 6 EST: 1946
SQ FT: 10,000
SALES (est): 898.9K **Privately Held**
SIC: 3364 3363 3369 3366 Brass & bronze die-castings; aluminum die-castings; nonferrous foundries; copper foundries; aluminum foundries

**(G-3902)**
**ANDERSON SHUMAKER COMPANY**
824 S Central Ave (60644-5501)
PHONE..................773 287-0874
Fax: 773 287-0031
Richard J Tribble, *President*
Donald Sutrina, *Vice Pres*
Bob Pollmann, *Accounting Mgr*
Ginny Morgan, *Human Res Mgr*
Ron Wolf, *Sales Mgr*
▲ EMP: 40 EST: 1902
SQ FT: 34,300
SALES (est): 14.5MM **Privately Held**
WEB: www.andersonshumaker.com
SIC: 3463 3462 Nonferrous forgings; iron & steel forgings

**(G-3903)**
**ANDREWS AUTOMOTIVE COMPANY**
10055 S Torrence Ave (60617-5337)
PHONE..................773 768-1122
Fax: 773 768-5234
David C Andrews, *President*
EMP: 18
SQ FT: 22,000
SALES (est): 3.5MM **Privately Held**
SIC: 5013 3061 3089 Automotive supplies & parts; automotive rubber goods (mechanical); corrugated panels, plastic

**(G-3904)**
**ANDREWS CARAMEL LLC**
6620 W Dakin St (60634-2413)
PHONE..................773 286-2224
A Lee Stamper, *CEO*
Bradlee F Stamper,
EMP: 15
SQ FT: 10,000
SALES (est): 712.6K **Privately Held**
SIC: 2064 Candy & other confectionery products

**(G-3905)**
**ANDYS DELI AND MIKOLAJCZYK (PA)**
4021 W Kinzie St (60624-1807)
PHONE..................773 722-1000
Fax: 773 722-7928
Andrzej Kolasa, *President*
Jacek Zak, *General Mgr*
Keena Bobrzynski, *Accountant*
Simon Kolasa, *Sales Executive*
Halina Kolasa, *Admin Sec*
▲ EMP: 20 EST: 1918
SQ FT: 1,000

SALES (est): 4.6MM **Privately Held**
WEB: www.andysdeli.com
SIC: 5411 2013 Delicatessens; sausages from purchased meat

**(G-3906)**
**ANEES UPHOLSTERY**
1500 S Western Ave Ste 3 (60608-1828)
PHONE..................312 243-2919
Fax: 312 243-2920
Anees Jaber, *Owner*
Marika Jaber, *Sales Executive*
EMP: 1
SALES (est): 235.1K **Privately Held**
SIC: 7641 2211 Upholstery work; furniture denim

**(G-3907)**
**ANGELS HEAVENLY FUNERAL HOME**
1811 W 103rd St (60643-2816)
PHONE..................773 239-8700
Jimmie Higgins, *Mng Member*
EMP: 5 EST: 2015
SALES (est): 172.3K **Privately Held**
SIC: 2396 5087 Veils & veiling: bridal, funeral, etc.; cemetery & funeral directors' equipment & supplies

**(G-3908)**
**ANIMATED ADVG TECHNIQUES INC**
Also Called: Central Die Cutting
210 S Desplaines St (60661-5500)
PHONE..................312 372-4694
Fax: 312 559-9088
Jim March, *President*
EMP: 5 EST: 1943
SQ FT: 10,000
SALES: 800K **Privately Held**
SIC: 7319 2675 Display advertising service; die-cut paper & board

**(G-3909)**
**ANJEL SCENTS LLC**
6657 S Minerva Ave (60637-4360)
PHONE..................313 729-0719
Parkinson Anjel A, *Principal*
EMP: 3
SALES (est): 209.2K **Privately Held**
SIC: 2844 Toilet preparations

**(G-3910)**
**ANNAKA ENTERPRISES**
8917 S Commercial Ave (60617-3202)
PHONE..................773 768-5490
Alexander Annang, *Owner*
EMP: 4
SALES (est): 130K **Privately Held**
SIC: 5949 2299 Fabric, remnants; textile goods

**(G-3911)**
**ANNAS DRAPERIES & ASSOCIATES**
5908 W Montrose Ave (60634-1625)
PHONE..................773 282-1365
Dodd Otic, *President*
EMP: 3
SALES (est): 271.5K **Privately Held**
SIC: 5714 2211 Curtains; draperies & drapery fabrics, cotton

**(G-3912)**
**ANNS BAKERY INC**
2158 W Chicago Ave (60622-5257)
PHONE..................773 384-5562
Fax: 773 384-5594
Walter Siryj, *President*
EMP: 7
SQ FT: 3,000
SALES: 800K **Privately Held**
SIC: 5461 2051 Bread; cakes; pastries; bread, all types (white, wheat, rye, etc): fresh or frozen; crullers, except frozen; pastries, e.g. danish: except frozen

**(G-3913)**
**ANOTHER CHANCE COMMUNITY DEV**
1641 W 79th St (60620-4212)
PHONE..................773 998-1641
Kenyatta Smith, *CEO*
EMP: 30

SALES (est): 3MM **Privately Held**
SIC: 2013 Sausages & other prepared meats

**(G-3914)**
**ANSONIA COPPER & BRASS INC (PA)**
900 N Michigan Ave # 1600 (60611-6539)
PHONE..................866 607-7066
▲ EMP: 125
SQ FT: 900,000
SALES (est): 21.9MM **Privately Held**
WEB: www.ansoniacb.com
SIC: 3351 3331 3315 Copper rolling & drawing; brass rolling & drawing; primary copper; steel wire & related products

**(G-3915)**
**ANTARES COMPUTER SYSTEMS INC**
Also Called: ACS
8114 S Maryland Ave # 12 (60619-5191)
PHONE..................773 783-8855
Maurice Johnson, *President*
Ida Johnson, *Vice Pres*
EMP: 5
SALES (est): 300K **Privately Held**
SIC: 3571 3577 Personal computers (microcomputers); computer peripheral equipment

**(G-3916)**
**ANTIGUA CASA SHERRY-BRENER (PA)**
3145 W 63rd St (60629-2749)
PHONE..................773 737-1711
James Sherry, *Partner*
Thomas Boodel, *Partner*
Eve Warren, *Partner*
EMP: 2
SQ FT: 10,000
SALES (est): 1MM **Privately Held**
WEB: www.guitarramagazine.com
SIC: 5099 2731 2721 Musical instruments; book music: publishing only, not printed on site; magazines: publishing only, not printed on site

**(G-3917)**
**ANTOLAK MANAGEMENT CO INC**
Also Called: Fastsigns
447 E Ohio St (60611-3626)
PHONE..................312 464-1800
Fax: 312 464-1374
Dan Antolak, *President*
EMP: 6
SALES (est): 900.5K **Privately Held**
SIC: 3993 Signs & advertising specialties

**(G-3918)**
**ANYLOGIC N AMER LTD LBLTY CO**
20 N Wacker Dr Ste 2044 (60606-3002)
PHONE..................312 635-3344
Yulia Levadnaya, *Office Mgr*
John Yedinak,
Timofey Popkov,
Andrei Vorshchez,
EMP: 8 EST: 2009
SQ FT: 850
SALES: 4.2MM **Privately Held**
SIC: 7371 7372 Custom computer programming services; prepackaged software

**(G-3919)**
**ANYTIME WINDOW CLEANING INC**
2517 N Monticello Ave (60647-1113)
PHONE..................773 235-5677
David Bernstein, *Owner*
EMP: 4
SALES (est): 264.5K **Privately Held**
SIC: 2842 Window cleaning preparations

**(G-3920)**
**APAC 90 TEXAS HOLDING INC**
Also Called: Port Arthur News
401 N Wabash Ave Ste 740 (60611-3583)
PHONE..................312 321-2299
Larry J Perrotto, *President*
George R Sample, *Vice Chairman*
Robert Legg, *Treasurer*
Charles Cowan, *Admin Sec*
Ricky Williams, *Admin Sec*
EMP: 4
SQ FT: 15,000
SALES (est): 213K **Privately Held**
SIC: 2711 Newspapers; commercial printing & newspaper publishing combined

**(G-3921)**
**APEX COLORS**
1031 W Bryn Mawr Ave 1a (60660-4657)
P.O. Box 3966, Barrington (60011-3966)
PHONE..................219 764-3301
Paul Bykowski, *President*
Siddhartha Zalani, *President*
EMP: 3
SALES (est): 253.3K **Privately Held**
SIC: 2865 Color pigments, organic

**(G-3922)**
**API PUBLISHING SERVICES LLC**
Also Called: Smith Bucklin & Associates
330 N Wabash Ave Ste 2000 (60611-7621)
PHONE..................312 644-6610
Fax: 312 321-6846
Thomas Morgan, *CEO*
Michelle Miller, *COO*
Gaylen Camera, *Vice Pres*
Danny Dunn, *Project Mgr*
Greg Grosvenor, *Treasurer*
EMP: 20
SQ FT: 12,000
SALES (est): 4MM
SALES (corp-wide): 137.4MM **Privately Held**
SIC: 2721 Periodicals: publishing & printing
PA: Smithbucklin Corporation
    330 N Wabash Ave
    Chicago IL 60611
    312 644-6610

**(G-3923)**
**APOLLO PLASTICS CORPORATION**
5333 N Elston Ave (60630-1610)
PHONE..................773 282-9222
Fax: 773 282-2763
John Lucas, *CEO*
Alberto Silva, *President*
Donald Lucas, *Corp Secy*
David Lucas, *Vice Pres*
Craig Doescher, *Engineer*
▲ EMP: 60 EST: 2000
SALES (est): 9.6MM
SALES (corp-wide): 15.9MM **Privately Held**
SIC: 3089 Casting of plastic
PA: Specialty Manufacturers, Inc.
    2410 Executive Dr Ste 201
    Indianapolis IN
    317 241-1111

**(G-3924)**
**APOSTROPHE BRANDS**
225 W Hubbard St Ste 600 (60654-4916)
PHONE..................312 832-0300
Fax: 312 944-0043
Steve Berg, *Exec VP*
Brad Treysar,
▲ EMP: 15
SALES (est): 2.2MM **Privately Held**
SIC: 2085 Rum (alcoholic beverage)

**(G-3925)**
**APPLIED HYDRAULIC SERVICES**
944 N Spaulding Ave (60651-4135)
PHONE..................773 638-8500
Fax: 773 638-3114
Wayne A Mc Guire, *President*
Gudrun Jocis, *Corp Secy*
▲ EMP: 5 EST: 1981
SQ FT: 5,000
SALES: 1.6MM **Privately Held**
WEB: www.ahscorp.net
SIC: 3594 Fluid power pumps & motors

**(G-3926)**
**APPLIED HYDRAULICS CORPORATION**
944 N Spaulding Ave (60651-4135)
PHONE..................773 638-8500
Michael McGuire, *President*
EMP: 3
SALES: 950K **Privately Held**
SIC: 3594 Fluid power pumps & motors

**(G-3927)**
**APPLUS TECHNOLOGIES INC (PA)**
120 S La Salle St # 1450 (60603-3449)
PHONE..................312 661-1604
Fax: 312 661-1618
Darrin Greene, *CEO*
Brenda Ackarman-Sioson, *Opers Staff*
Celia Forsythe, *CFO*
Anne Hagerty, *Finance Mgr*
Rob Enright, *Accountant*
EMP: 33
SALES: 46.3MM **Privately Held**
SIC: 7373 3577 7379 7371 Computer integrated systems design; optical scanning devices; computer related maintenance services; computer software development & applications

**(G-3928)**
**APRIMO US LLC**
Also Called: Aprimo Marketing Operations Uk
230 W Monroe St Ste 1200 (60606-4704)
PHONE..................877 794-8556
Michael Nelson, *CFO*
EMP: 90
SALES (est): 1.3MM **Privately Held**
SIC: 7372 Application computer software

**(G-3929)**
**APTEAN HOLDINGS INC**
2000 N Racine Ave (60614-4045)
PHONE..................773 975-3100
Gene Climer, *Manager*
EMP: 15
SALES (corp-wide): 714.1MM **Privately Held**
SIC: 7372 Prepackaged software
HQ: Aptean Holdings, Inc.
    450 E 96th St Ste 300
    Indianapolis IN 46240
    317 249-1700

**(G-3930)**
**ARACON DRPERY VNTIAN BLIND LTD**
Also Called: Aracon Venetian Blind-Drapery
3015 N Kedzie Ave (60618-6906)
PHONE..................773 252-1281
Gregory Struhar, *CEO*
EMP: 7
SQ FT: 4,500
SALES (est): 1MM **Privately Held**
SIC: 2591 2391 Venetian blinds; draperies, plastic & textile: from purchased materials

**(G-3931)**
**ARCANUM ALLOY DESIGN INC**
3440 S Dearborn St 206s (60616-5074)
PHONE..................219 508-5531
Daniel Bullard, *CEO*
Joseph McDermott, *COO*
Adam Thomas, *Research*
EMP: 5
SALES (est): 460K **Privately Held**
SIC: 3312 Blast furnaces & steel mills

**(G-3932)**
**ARCELOR MITTAL USA LLC**
1 S Dearborn St Ste 1800 (60603-2308)
PHONE..................312 899-3500
Laurie Elbe, *CEO*
Michael Rippey, *President*
Andrew Reynolds, *Division Mgr*
Ronald Allen, *Human Resources*
Jennifer Austin, *Human Resources*
EMP: 14
SALES (est): 1.7MM **Privately Held**
SIC: 3291 Abrasive metal & steel products
HQ: Arcelormittal Limited
    Avis House
    Manchester M38 9
    161 703-9073

**(G-3933)**
**ARCELORMITTAL SOUTH CHICAGO**
1 S Dearborn St Ste 2100 (60603-2307)
PHONE..................312 899-3300
Fax: 773 768-6407
Michael Rippey, *President*
Marc Jeske, *Admin Sec*
EMP: 2
SALES (est): 224.3K **Privately Held**
SIC: 3315 Steel wire & related products

**(G-3934)**
**ARCELORMITTAL USA LLC**
Also Called: Arcelormittal USA of Chicago
1 S Dearborn St Ste 2100 (60603-2307)
PHONE..................312 899-3400
Ronnie Masliansky, *General Mgr*
David Trachtenberg, *General Mgr*
Vaidya Sethuraman, *Vice Pres*
Keith Nagel, *Engng Exec*
Laurie Elbe, *Manager*
EMP: 225 **Privately Held**
SIC: 3325 Rolling mill rolls, cast steel; alloy steel castings, except investment; railroad car wheels, cast steel
HQ: Arcelormittal Usa Llc
    1 S Dearborn St Ste 1800
    Chicago IL 60603
    312 346-0300

**(G-3935)**
**ARCELORMITTAL USA LLC (HQ)**
1 S Dearborn St Ste 1800 (60603-2308)
PHONE..................312 346-0300
John L Brett, *CEO*
Paul Liebenson, *General Mgr*
Larry Meyer, *General Mgr*
Brad Davey, *Principal*
Daniel G Mull, *Principal*
◆ EMP: 277
SQ FT: 53,484
SALES (est): 4.4B **Privately Held**
SIC: 3312 3325 3356 3316 Blast furnaces & steel mills; rolling mill rolls, cast steel; tin; cold finishing of steel shapes
PA: Arcelormittal Sa
    Boulevard D'avranches 24-26
    Luxembourg
    479 21 -

**(G-3936)**
**ARCHER ENGINEERING COMPANY**
3154 S Archer Ave (60608-6293)
PHONE..................773 247-3501
Fax: 773 247-4840
Ronald Lanie, *President*
Virginia Lanie, *Admin Sec*
EMP: 7 EST: 1951
SQ FT: 24,000
SALES: 1.3MM **Privately Held**
WEB: www.archerengineeringco.com
SIC: 3451 Screw machine products

**(G-3937)**
**ARCHER INDUSTRIES & SUPPLIES**
3452 N Knox Ave (60641-3744)
PHONE..................773 777-2698
Walter Kula, *President*
Krystyna Kula, *Admin Sec*
EMP: 3
SQ FT: 4,000
SALES: 300K **Privately Held**
WEB: www.archerindustries.com
SIC: 3312 3444 Coated or plated products; sheet metalwork

**(G-3938)**
**ARCHER MANUFACTURING CORP**
4439 S Knox Ave (60632-4343)
PHONE..................773 585-7181
Fax: 773 585-3028
Stan Sekula, *President*
EMP: 25 EST: 1948
SQ FT: 28,000
SALES (est): 4.9MM **Privately Held**
WEB: www.archermfg.com
SIC: 3469 3599 Stamping metal for the trade; machine shop, jobbing & repair

**(G-3939)**
**ARCHER METAL & PAPER CO**
Also Called: C & R Scrap Metal
4619 S Knox Ave (60632-4805)
PHONE..................773 585-3030
Fax: 773 585-3031
Ron Nisson, *Owner*
Ronald Nisson, *Principal*
EMP: 10
SQ FT: 10,000

## Chicago - Cook County (G-3940)

SALES (est): 1.9MM **Privately Held**
SIC: **5093** 4953 3341 3312 Scrap & waste materials; refuse systems; secondary nonferrous metals; blast furnaces & steel mills

**(G-3940)**
**ARCHER TINNING & RE-TINNING CO (PA)**
1019 W 47th St (60609-3325)
PHONE..................................773 927-7240
Fax: 773 927-9083
Arjen Byvoets, *President*
Toby Byvoets, *Director*
EMP: 12 EST: 1931
SQ FT: 10,000
SALES (est): 928.8K **Privately Held**
SIC: **3471** Plating of metals or formed products

**(G-3941)**
**ARCHER-DANIELS-MIDLAND COMPANY (PA)**
Also Called: ADM
77 W Wacker Dr Ste 4600 (60601-1667)
P.O. Box 1470, Decatur (62525-1820)
PHONE..................................312 634-8100
Fax: 217 424-4383
Juan R Luciano, *Ch of Bd*
Donald Chen, *President*
Pierre Duprat, *President*
Scott Fredericksen, *President*
Vikram Luthar, *President*
◆ EMP: 600 EST: 1902
SALES: 62.3B **Publicly Held**
WEB: www.admworld.com
SIC: **2046** 2041 2075 2074 Wet corn milling; high fructose corn syrup (HFCS); corn starch; corn oil products; wheat flour; soybean oil mills; cottonseed oil, cake or meal; grain elevators; malt; malt byproducts

**(G-3942)**
**ARCHITECTURAL FAN COIL INC**
3900 W Palmer St (60647-2216)
PHONE..................................312 399-1203
Harvey Dessler, *President*
EMP: 3
SALES (est): 424.9K **Privately Held**
WEB: www.afancoil.com
SIC: **3564** Air purification equipment

**(G-3943)**
**ARDAGH METAL BEVERAGE USA INC**
8770 W Bryn Mawr Ave # 175 (60631-3515)
PHONE..................................773 399-3000
Claude Marbach, *CEO*
Thomas Holz, *CFO*
Curt Rothlisberger, *Credit Staff*
EMP: 75
SALES: 1B **Privately Held**
SIC: **3411** Metal cans

**(G-3944)**
**ARGUS BREWERY**
11314 S Front Ave (60628-5007)
PHONE..................................773 941-4050
Patrick R Jensen, *Owner*
Joseph Mengel, *VP Sales*
Nicholas Lubovich, *Manager*
Mary Bruski, *Admin Asst*
EMP: 7
SALES (est): 476.6K **Privately Held**
SIC: **2082** Beer (alcoholic beverage)

**(G-3945)**
**ARMBRUST PAPER TUBES INC**
6255 S Harlem Ave (60638-3906)
PHONE..................................773 586-3232
Fax: 773 586-8997
Michael Johnstone, *President*
Bernerd Armbrust, *President*
John Armbrust, *Traffic Mgr*
Mark Armbrust, *VP Sales*
EMP: 22
SQ FT: 85,000
SALES (est): 4.1MM **Privately Held**
WEB: www.tubesrus.com
SIC: **2542** 2655 3089 2653 Partitions & fixtures, except wood; tubes, fiber or paper: made from purchased material; cans, fiber: made from purchased material; cores, fiber: made from purchased material; plastic containers, except foam; corrugated & solid fiber boxes; setup paperboard boxes; paperboard mills

**(G-3946)**
**ARMITAGE WELDING**
3212 W Armitage Ave (60647-3716)
PHONE..................................773 772-1442
Manuel Vasquez, *Owner*
EMP: 4
SALES (est): 441.3K **Privately Held**
SIC: **1799** 7692 Athletic & recreation facilities construction; welding repair

**(G-3947)**
**ARRO CORPORATION**
Also Called: Arro Packing
10459 S Muskegon Ave (60617-5727)
PHONE..................................773 978-1251
Patrick Gaughan, *President*
Joseph Litza, *Engineer*
Angie Nowakowski, *Manager*
EMP: 8
SALES (corp-wide): 644MM **Privately Held**
SIC: **5141** 2045 4225 Groceries, general line; pancake mixes, prepared: from purchased flour; general warehousing & storage
PA: Arro Corporation
7440 Santa Fe Dr
Hodgkins IL 60525
708 352-8200

**(G-3948)**
**ARROWEYE SOLUTIONS INC (PA)**
549 W Randolph St Ste 200 (60661-2225)
PHONE..................................312 253-9400
Narinder Dahiya, *CEO*
Mica Moseley, *Senior VP*
Jeff Lipa, *Vice Pres*
Betty Mitchell, *Vice Pres*
Mary Strutynski, *Vice Pres*
EMP: 30
SQ FT: 40,000
SALES (est): 20.4MM **Privately Held**
SIC: **2759** Card printing & engraving, except greeting

**(G-3949)**
**ART BOOKBINDERS OF AMERICA**
451 N Claremont Ave (60612-1440)
PHONE..................................312 226-4100
Fax: 312 226-7560
Mario Poulet, *President*
Greg Poulet, *Vice Pres*
Louis B Poulet, *Vice Pres*
Jackie Lic, *Accounts Mgr*
EMP: 28
SQ FT: 24,000
SALES (est): 4MM **Privately Held**
WEB: www.abofa.com
SIC: **7334** 2789 Photocopying & duplicating services; bookbinding & related work; bookbinding & repairing: trade, edition, library, etc.

**(G-3950)**
**ART IN PRINT REVIEW**
3500 N Lake Shore Dr (60657-1815)
PHONE..................................773 697-9478
Susan Tallman, *President*
EMP: 3
SALES (est): 150.5K **Privately Held**
SIC: **2721** 2741 Periodicals: publishing only; miscellaneous publishing

**(G-3951)**
**ART MEDIA RESOURCES INC**
1965 W Pershing Rd Ste 4 (60609-2319)
PHONE..................................312 663-5350
Fax: 312 663-5177
Shane Suvikapornkul, *President*
Kurt Heintz, *Producer*
▲ EMP: 3

SALES (est): 250K **Privately Held**
WEB: www.paragonbook.com
SIC: **2731** 5192 Books: publishing only; books

**(G-3952)**
**ART OF SHAVING - FL LLC**
520 N Michigan Ave # 122 (60611-6985)
PHONE..................................312 527-1604
Alex Davidson, *Branch Mgr*
EMP: 3
SALES (corp-wide): 65.3B **Publicly Held**
SIC: **2844** Toilet preparations
HQ: The Art Of Shaving - Fl Llc
6100 Blue Lagoon Dr # 150
Miami FL 33126

**(G-3953)**
**ART-FLO SHIRT & LETTERING CO**
Also Called: AF
6939 W 59th St (60638-3205)
PHONE..................................708 656-5422
Michael Dastice, *President*
Joanne Zendol, *President*
James M Dastice, *Vice Pres*
Valerie Dastice, *QC Mgr*
Bill Hanna, *Info Tech Mgr*
EMP: 23 EST: 1959
SQ FT: 13,000
SALES (est): 10.8MM **Privately Held**
WEB: www.artflo.com
SIC: **5136** 5137 2396 2759 Sportswear, men's & boys'; sportswear, women's & children's; screen printing on fabric articles; commercial printing; pleating & stitching

**(G-3954)**
**ARTEMIDE INC**
351 W Hubbard St Ste 602 (60654-4486)
PHONE..................................312 475-0100
Fax: 312 475-0112
Mary Graham, *Principal*
EMP: 5 **Privately Held**
SIC: **3648** Lighting fixtures, except electric: residential
HQ: Artemide Inc.
250 Karin Ln
Hicksville NY 11801
631 694-9292

**(G-3955)**
**ARTHUR COYLE PRESS**
2730 W Coyle Ave (60645-3018)
P.O. Box 59435 (60659-0435)
PHONE..................................773 465-8418
Jerome Yanoff, *Owner*
EMP: 1
SALES: 700K **Privately Held**
WEB: www.arthurcoylepress.com
SIC: **2741** 2731 Business service newsletters: publishing & printing; book publishing

**(G-3956)**
**ARTISAN HANDPRINTS INC**
4234 N Pulaski Rd (60641-2398)
PHONE..................................773 725-1799
Fax: 773 725-0316
Murray Plotkin, *President*
Oszaldo Rodriguez, *Manager*
▼ EMP: 8
SQ FT: 8,500
SALES (est): 908.6K **Privately Held**
SIC: **2759** Screen printing

**(G-3957)**
**ARTISTRY ENGRAVING & EMBOSSING**
6000 N Northwest Hwy (60631-2518)
PHONE..................................773 775-4888
Fax: 773 775-0064
Dorothy K Johnsen, *President*
Michael Gattuso, *Vice Pres*
Tami Gattuso, *Vice Pres*
EMP: 9 EST: 1956
SQ FT: 12,000
SALES: 1MM **Privately Held**
SIC: **2759** 2796 2791 Invitation & stationery printing & engraving; platemaking services; typesetting

**(G-3958)**
**ARTPOL PRINTING INC**
7011 W Higgins Ave (60656-1901)
PHONE..................................773 622-0498
Fax: 773 622-0754
Wojzak Zalog, *President*
Jolata Kowlik, *Vice Pres*
EMP: 3
SQ FT: 1,800
SALES: 480K **Privately Held**
WEB: www.artpolprinting.com
SIC: **2759** Commercial printing

**(G-3959)**
**ARTS & LETTERS MARSHALL SIGNS**
Also Called: Marshall Sign Co
3610 S Albany Ave (60632-2309)
PHONE..................................773 927-4442
Luis Cazares, *President*
EMP: 5
SQ FT: 12,000
SALES (est): 460K **Privately Held**
SIC: **3993** Electric signs

**(G-3960)**
**ASHLAND ABC CHOICE INC**
7903 S Ashland Ave (60620-4336)
PHONE..................................773 488-7800
Samed Yusuf, *President*
EMP: 3
SALES (est): 227.6K **Privately Held**
SIC: **2834** Pills, pharmaceutical

**(G-3961)**
**ASHLAND ALUMINUM COMPANY INC**
1925 N Mendell St (60642-1223)
P.O. Box 190, New Hudson MI (48165-0190)
PHONE..................................773 278-6440
Fax: 773 278-1106
Norman M Yoelin, *President*
Michael L Yoelin, *Vice Pres*
EMP: 10
SQ FT: 50,000
SALES (est): 1.5MM **Privately Held**
SIC: **3355** 3353 Coils, wire aluminum: made in rolling mills; aluminum sheet, plate & foil

**(G-3962)**
**ASHLAND FUEL & QUICK LUBE**
5901 S Ashland Ave (60636-1708)
PHONE..................................773 434-8870
Ali Salem, *Principal*
EMP: 3
SALES (est): 348.5K **Privately Held**
SIC: **2869** Fuels

**(G-3963)**
**ASI SIGN SYSTEMS INC**
2650c W Bradley Pl (60618-4717)
PHONE..................................773 478-5241
Fax: 773 871-0382
Erin Carey, *Partner*
Susan Dutka, *Project Mgr*
Gus Santana, *Project Mgr*
EMP: 6
SALES (corp-wide): 20.4MM **Privately Held**
SIC: **3993** Signs & advertising specialties
PA: Asi Sign Systems, Inc.
8181 Jetstar Dr Ste 110
Irving TX 75063
214 352-9140

**(G-3964)**
**ASPEN FOODS INC**
1115 W Fulton Market (60607-1213)
PHONE..................................312 829-7282
Fax: 312 829-7410
Michael Fields, *President*
Ken Springer, *Opers Staff*
Michael Lazarus, *Plt & Fclts Mgr*
Hank Paasmer, *Engineer*
Denise Coleman, *Human Res Dir*
EMP: 150
SQ FT: 45,000
SALES: 28.1MM
SALES (corp-wide): 1.9B **Privately Held**
SIC: **2015** Chicken, processed: fresh; chicken, processed: frozen; turkey, processed: fresh

HQ: Koch Meat Co., Inc.
1300 Higgins Rd Ste 100
Park Ridge IL 60068
847 384-8018

**(G-3965)**
**ASSEMBLERS INC**
2850 W Columbus Ave (60652-1620)
PHONE.................................773 378-3000
Fax: 773 378-2000
Joel Rosenbacher, *President*
Tim Hansen, *COO*
Gigi Salcedo, *Vice Pres*
Leyvy Diaz, *Project Mgr*
Reece Resendiz, *Opers Mgr*
▲ **EMP:** 250
**SQ FT:** 480,000
**SALES:** 10MM **Privately Held**
**WEB:** www.assemblers.com
**SIC:** 3999 7389 Advertising display products; packaging & labeling services

**(G-3966)**
**ASSET PARTNERS INC**
Also Called: Innovalink
4403 W Lawrence Ave # 200 (60630-2513)
PHONE.................................312 224-8300
David Wadsworth, *CEO*
David Oei, *Info Tech Mgr*
David Patel, *Info Tech Mgr*
**EMP:** 8
**SALES (est):** 631.1K **Privately Held**
**SIC:** 7372 Prepackaged software

**(G-3967)**
**ASSOCIATED ATTRACTIONS ENTPS**
4834 S Halsted St 14 (60609)
PHONE.................................773 376-1900
Fax: 773 579-3694
Steve Johnson, *President*
Chuck Huser, *General Mgr*
**EMP:** 12
**SQ FT:** 50,000
**SALES:** 725K **Privately Held**
**SIC:** 7359 3993 Party supplies rental services; signs & advertising specialties

**(G-3968)**
**ASSOCIATED GROUP HOLDINGS LLC (PA)**
30 S Wacker Dr Ste 1600 (60606-7432)
PHONE.................................312 662-5488
Tim Ritchie, *CEO*
Beth Warloe, *Assistant VP*
Bradley Dame, *Vice Pres*
Jim Hanson, *CFO*
Michael Pokora, *Relations*
**EMP:** 1 **EST:** 2012
**SALES (est):** 137.6MM **Privately Held**
**SIC:** 3448 Prefabricated metal buildings

**(G-3969)**
**ASSOCIATED PUBLICATIONS INC**
Also Called: Complete Woman
875 N Michigan Ave # 3434 (60611-1981)
PHONE.................................312 266-8680
Jim L Spurlock, *President*
Kim Bigelow, *Prdtn Mgr*
Leslie Bryan, *Assoc Editor*
Oostra Lindsey, *Assoc Editor*
Kourtney McKay, *Art Dir*
▲ **EMP:** 13 **EST:** 1978
**SALES (est):** 2MM **Privately Held**
**WEB:** www.associatedpub.com
**SIC:** 2721 Magazines: publishing only, not printed on site

**(G-3970)**
**ASSOCIATED RACK CORPORATION**
Also Called: American Rack
5810 N Northwest Hwy (60631-2641)
PHONE.................................616 554-6004
W Faulkman, *Branch Mgr*
**EMP:** 14
**SALES (corp-wide):** 54.2MM **Privately Held**
**SIC:** 2542 3444 3443 Partitions & fixtures, except wood; sheet metalwork; fabricated plate work (boiler shop)

**PA:** Associated Rack Corporation
70 Athens Dr
Mount Juliet TN 37122
615 288-4204

**(G-3971)**
**ASSOCIATION MANAGEMENT CENTER**
8735 W Higgins Rd Ste 300 (60631-2738)
P.O. Box 3781, Oak Brook (60522-3781)
PHONE.................................847 375-4700
Dagny M Engle, *President*
Jeff Engle, *Principal*
Mark Engle, *Principal*
Barbara Hofmaier, *Editor*
June Pinyo, *Editor*
**EMP:** 100
**SALES (est):** 19.4MM **Privately Held**
**SIC:** 8742 2721 Administrative services consultant; trade journals: publishing & printing

**(G-3972)**
**AT&T CORP**
1 S Wacker Dr Ste 3900 (60606-4635)
PHONE.................................312 602-4108
James Hsu, *Empl Rel Mgr*
Bob Allen, *Branch Mgr*
Keith Raimbault, *Info Tech Mgr*
**EMP:** 12
**SALES (corp-wide):** 163.7B **Publicly Held**
**WEB:** www.att.com
**SIC:** 3661 3677 Autotransformers for telephone switchboards; electronic coils, transformers & other inductors
HQ: At&T Corp.
1 At&T Way
Bedminster NJ 07921
800 403-3302

**(G-3973)**
**AT&T TELEHOLDINGS INC (HQ)**
Also Called: AT&T Midwest
30 S Wacker Dr Fl 34 (60606-7413)
PHONE.................................800 257-0902
Edward Whitacre Jr, *Ch of Bd*
Andrew M Geisse, *President*
William Craft, *CFO*
Ben Reenders, *Marketing Staff*
Jeannie Balsam, *Info Tech Mgr*
**EMP:** 4
**SQ FT:** 146,000
**SALES (est):** 6.1B
**SALES (corp-wide):** 163.7B **Publicly Held**
**WEB:** www.ameritech.com
**SIC:** 4813 4812 2741 5065 Telephone communication, except radio; local telephone communications; long distance telephone communications; cellular telephone services; paging services; directories, telephone: publishing only, not printed on site; telephone equipment; machinery & equipment finance leasing; security systems services
PA: At&T Inc.
208 S Akard St
Dallas TX 75202
210 821-4105

**(G-3974)**
**ATHENA DESIGN GROUP INC**
3500 S Morgan St 1 (60609-1524)
PHONE.................................312 733-2828
Christopher Huang, *President*
▲ **EMP:** 27
**SALES (est):** 4.4MM **Privately Held**
**SIC:** 2752 7311 7336 3993 Commercial printing, lithographic; advertising agencies; advertising consultant; commercial art & graphic design; signs & advertising specialties; direct mail advertising services

**(G-3975)**
**ATHLETIC SEWING MFG CO (PA)**
7449 W Irving Park Rd # 1 (60634-2183)
PHONE.................................773 589-0361
Fax: 773 589-9493
Liz Quilici, *President*
Sylvia Helms, *Corp Secy*
Gwen Gialo, *Manager*
**EMP:** 30
**SQ FT:** 5,000

**SALES (est):** 2.5MM **Privately Held**
**SIC:** 2329 Men's & boys' athletic uniforms; hockey uniforms: men's, youths' & boys'

**(G-3976)**
**ATK FOODS INC (PA)**
Also Called: Sausages By Amy
1143 W Lake St (60607-1618)
PHONE.................................312 829-2250
Richard Kurzawski, *CEO*
Amylu T Kurzawski, *President*
Ed Kleinie, *Vice Pres*
Ed Kleine, *VP Opers*
Mike Rudnicki, *Prdtn Mgr*
**EMP:** 40 **EST:** 1926
**SQ FT:** 27,000
**SALES (est):** 8.2MM **Privately Held**
**WEB:** www.leonssausage.com
**SIC:** 2013 Sausages from purchased meat; luncheon meat from purchased meat

**(G-3977)**
**ATLANTIC PRESS INC**
6721 W 73rd St (60638-6006)
PHONE.................................708 496-2400
Chuck Walloga, *Sales Mgr*
Larry McInerney, *Branch Mgr*
**EMP:** 57
**SALES (corp-wide):** 35.5MM **Privately Held**
**SIC:** 2752 Commercial printing, offset
PA: Atlantic Press, Inc.
6721 W 73rd St
Bedford Park IL 60638
708 496-2400

**(G-3978)**
**ATLAS ABC CORPORATION**
1855 E 122nd St (60633-2401)
PHONE.................................773 646-4500
Barry Zekelman, *CEO*
Jill McCormack, *Manager*
▲ **EMP:** 288
**SALES (est):** 74.1MM **Privately Held**
**WEB:** www.atlastube.com
**SIC:** 3317 Tubes, seamless steel
HQ: Atlas Holding Inc.
1855 E 122nd St
Chicago IL 60633

**(G-3979)**
**ATLAS COPCO COMPRESSORS LLC**
75 Remittance Dr # 3009 (60675-3009)
PHONE.................................281 590-7500
**EMP:** 19
**SALES (corp-wide):** 10.9B **Privately Held**
**SIC:** 3563 3621 Air & gas compressors; motors & generators
HQ: Atlas Copco Compressors Llc
3042 Suthcross Blvd 102
Rock Hill SC 29730
803 817-7000

**(G-3980)**
**ATLAS HOLDING INC (HQ)**
1855 E 122nd St (60633-2401)
PHONE.................................773 646-4500
Barry Zekelman, *CEO*
Dave Seeger, *President*
Andrew Klaus, *Vice Pres*
Michael McNamara, *Vice Pres*
Jeff Cole, *Plant Mgr*
◆ **EMP:** 11
**SALES (est):** 91.4MM **Privately Held**
**WEB:** www.atlastube.com
**SIC:** 3317 Tubes, seamless steel

**(G-3981)**
**ATLAS MAINTENANCE SERVICE INC**
2055 N Kedzie Ave (60647-3703)
PHONE.................................773 486-3386
Piotr Fadrowski, *President*
**EMP:** 3
**SALES (est):** 203.1K **Privately Held**
**SIC:** 3559 Automotive maintenance equipment

**(G-3982)**
**ATLAS MANUFACTURING**
4114 N Ravenswood Ave (60613-1786)
PHONE.................................773 327-3005
Fax: 773 327-5787
John K Lane, *Principal*

▲ **EMP:** 3
**SALES (est):** 233.5K **Privately Held**
**SIC:** 3999 Manufacturing industries

**(G-3983)**
**ATLAS MATERIAL TSTG TECH LLC**
Kaan Engineering
1800 W Belle Plaine Ave F (60613-1827)
PHONE.................................773 327-4520
Fax: 773 248-9027
Joel Goldberg, *President*
James Meindl, *QC Dir*
John Laswell, *Engineer*
Donald Elderts, *VP Finance*
Gwen Collins, *Executive*
**EMP:** 30
**SALES (est):** 3.8B **Publicly Held**
**WEB:** www.atlas-mts.com
**SIC:** 3569 3599 8734 Testing chambers for altitude, temperature, ordnance, power; machine shop, jobbing & repair; product testing laboratory, safety or performance
HQ: Atlas Material Testing Technology Llc
1500 Bishop Ct
Mount Prospect IL 60056
773 327-4520

**(G-3984)**
**ATLAS TUBE (CHICAGO) LLC**
1855 E 122nd St (60633-2401)
PHONE.................................773 646-4500
Barry Zekelman, *CEO*
Tom Muth, *President*
David Seager, *President*
Tony Frabotta, *Vice Pres*
Michael Miles, *Project Engr*
▼ **EMP:** 500
**SALES (est):** 155.9MM **Privately Held**
**SIC:** 3317 3644 Pipes, seamless steel; electric conduits & fittings
PA: Zekelman Industries, Inc.
227 W Monroe St Ste 2600
Chicago IL 60606

**(G-3985)**
**ATLAS UNIFORM COMPANY**
1412 W Wa Blvd Fl 2 (60607-1844)
PHONE.................................312 492-8527
Fax: 773 725-6191
Steve Grys, *President*
**EMP:** 7
**SALES (est):** 513.7K **Privately Held**
**SIC:** 5699 2326 2337 Uniforms; work uniforms; uniforms, except athletic: women's, misses' & juniors'

**(G-3986)**
**ATM AMERICA CORP**
1900 N Austin Ave Ste 69 (60639-5042)
PHONE.................................800 298-0030
Manzar T Zuberi, *President*
MO Akindtu, *Purchasing*
Ron Stansbury, *Sales/Mktg Dir*
Phil Masteangello, *Finance Mgr*
Ted Zuberi, *Sales Staff*
◆ **EMP:** 50 **EST:** 1976
**SQ FT:** 50,000
**SALES (est):** 8MM **Privately Held**
**WEB:** www.atmamericacorp.com
**SIC:** 2842 2992 2844 3545 Specialty cleaning preparations; lubricating oils; shampoos, rinses, conditioners: hair; machine tool accessories; soap & other detergents

**(G-3987)**
**ATOMOWELD CO**
5515 W Montrose Ave (60641-1331)
PHONE.................................773 736-5577
Fax: 773 736-5515
Robert Porada, *President*
**EMP:** 2 **EST:** 1938
**SQ FT:** 2,500
**SALES:** 750K **Privately Held**
**SIC:** 7692 3544 Welding repair; special dies, tools, jigs & fixtures

**(G-3988)**
**ATTUNE MEDICAL**
3440 S Dearborn St 215-S (60616-5074)
PHONE.................................312 994-0174
Erik Kulstad, *CEO*
**EMP:** 25

# Chicago - Cook County (G-3989)     GEOGRAPHIC SECTION

SALES (est): 646.2K **Privately Held**
SIC: 3841 Surgical & medical instruments

### (G-3989)
### AURORA NARINDER
Also Called: Number One
4549 N Clark St (60640-5406)
PHONE.................773 275-2100
EMP: 2
SQ FT: 2,500
SALES (est): 211.8K **Privately Held**
SIC: 2341 5122 5999 Mfg Women's/Youth Underwear Whol Drugs/Sundries Ret Misc Merchandise

### (G-3990)
### AUTO INJURY SOLUTIONS INC
222 Merchandise Mart Plz # 900 (60654-1103)
PHONE.................312 229-2704
Matthew Elges, *President*
Elisa Lazarus, *Vice Pres*
Melissa Loew, *Vice Pres*
Liz Luppino-Heck, *Vice Pres*
Tina Senftle, *Vice Pres*
EMP: 157 EST: 2008
SALES (est): 6.3MM
SALES (corp-wide): 3.7B **Privately Held**
SIC: 7372 Prepackaged software
HQ: Ccc Information Services Inc.
222 Mchds Mart Plz 900
Chicago IL 60654
312 222-4636

### (G-3991)
### AUTOMATIC ANODIZING CORP
3340 W Newport Ave (60618-5594)
PHONE.................773 478-3304
Fax: 773 478-3307
Howard Penner, *President*
Scott Penner, *Vice Pres*
Ted Penner, *Admin Sec*
EMP: 25
SQ FT: 20,000
SALES (est): 3.4MM **Privately Held**
SIC: 3471 2851 Anodizing (plating) of metals or formed products; paints & allied products

### (G-3992)
### AUTOMATIC PRECISION INC
4609 N Ronald St (60706-4718)
PHONE.................708 867-1116
Fax: 630 867-1121
Peter Bulat, *President*
Chris Bulat, *Vice Pres*
Tom Yarka, *Purchasing*
Miguel Ballesteros, *Engineer*
John Bulat, *Treasurer*
▲ EMP: 30
SQ FT: 20,000
SALES (est): 5.5MM **Privately Held**
WEB: www.automaticprecision.com
SIC: 3451 3545 Screw machine products; precision tools, machinists'

### (G-3993)
### AUTONOMY INC
303 E Wacker Dr Ste 2700 (60601-7804)
PHONE.................312 580-9100
Fax: 312 508-9140
Zia Bhatti, *Manager*
Rizwan Khan, *Director*
EMP: 25
SALES (corp-wide): 50.1B **Publicly Held**
WEB: www.iwov.com
SIC: 7372 Business oriented computer software
HQ: Autonomy Inc.
1 Market Plz Fl 19
San Francisco CA 94105

### (G-3994)
### AUTOTECH TECH LTD PARTNR
28617 Network Pl (60673-1286)
PHONE.................563 359-7501
Hyder Han, *General Mgr*
EMP: 25 **Privately Held**
SIC: 3625 Industrial electrical relays & switches
PA: Autotech Technologies Limited Partnership
4140 Utica Ridge Rd
Bettendorf IA 52722

### (G-3995)
### AVAILABLE BUSINESS GROUP INC
Also Called: Source 4-Integrated Business
3944 S Morgan St (60609-2511)
PHONE.................773 247-4141
Fax: 773 247-1313
Patrick Fitzgerald, *President*
Kathy Shine, *Vice Pres*
David Helms, *CFO*
Bill O'Donnell, *Accounts Exec*
Matthew James, *Marketing Mgr*
EMP: 75
SQ FT: 39,000
SALES (est): 10.2MM
SALES (corp-wide): 69.9MM **Privately Held**
SIC: 2752 2759 Commercial printing, lithographic; commercial printing, offset; business forms; printing
PA: Dominion Holdings, Inc.
3473 Brandon Ave Sw
Roanoke VA 24018
540 989-6848

### (G-3996)
### AVAN TOOL & DIE CO INC
4612 W Maypole Ave (60644-2726)
PHONE.................773 287-1670
Fax: 773 287-9732
John J Brownfield, *President*
EMP: 15 EST: 1957
SQ FT: 12,000
SALES: 1MM **Privately Held**
SIC: 3599 3544 3451 3369 Machine shop, jobbing & repair; special dies, tools, jigs & fixtures; screw machine products; nonferrous foundries

### (G-3997)
### AVECTRA INC
10 S Wacker Dr Ste 1120 (60606-7508)
PHONE.................312 425-9094
Fax: 312 924-7301
Kevin Ordonez, *Manager*
EMP: 20
SALES (corp-wide): 51.5MM **Privately Held**
SIC: 7372 Prepackaged software
HQ: Avectra, Inc.
7901 Jones Branch Dr Fl 5
Mc Lean VA 22102

### (G-3998)
### AVENIR PUBLISHING INC
Also Called: Ddc Journal
65 E Wacker Pl Ste 400 (60601-7203)
PHONE.................312 577-7200
Jim Potter, *President*
Natalie Bartolozzi, *Senior VP*
Chris Broadbent, *VP Sales*
Ryan Nolen, *Accounts Exec*
Jack Hamilton, *Sales Staff*
▲ EMP: 25
SALES (est): 2MM **Privately Held**
SIC: 2741 Miscellaneous publishing

### (G-3999)
### AVENUE METAL MANUFACTURING CO
1640 W Ogden Ave (60612-3288)
PHONE.................312 243-3483
Fax: 312 243-0017
James N Brunetti, *President*
Basil N Brunetti, *Treasurer*
EMP: 14 EST: 1953
SQ FT: 14,200
SALES (est): 2MM **Privately Held**
WEB: www.avenuemetal.com
SIC: 3444 1796 Restaurant sheet metalwork; ducts, sheet metal; ventilators, sheet metal; installing building equipment

### (G-4000)
### AVERY DNNSON RET INFO SVCS LLC
15178 Collection Ctr Dr (60693-0151)
PHONE.................626 304-2000
EMP: 3
SALES (corp-wide): 6B **Publicly Held**
SIC: 2671 Packaging paper & plastics film, coated & laminated

HQ: Avery Dennison Retail Information Services, Llc
207 N Goode Ave Fl 6
Glendale CA 91203

### (G-4001)
### AVOCET POLYMER TECH INC
4047 W 40th St (60632-3901)
PHONE.................773 523-2872
Raphael Lee, *President*
Ashley Harris, *Manager*
James Helke, *Administration*
Judy Marrero, *Administration*
EMP: 4
SALES (est): 736.9K **Privately Held**
WEB: www.avocetcorp.com
SIC: 5122 2834 Pharmaceuticals; pharmaceutical preparations

### (G-4002)
### AVTEC (USA) POWERTRAIN CORP
2023 N Halsted St (60614-4371)
PHONE.................773 708-9686
Kelly Cunninghman, *President*
▲ EMP: 1
SALES (est): 1MM **Privately Held**
SIC: 3743 Railroad locomotives & parts, electric or nonelectric

### (G-4003)
### AWARD/VISIONPS INC
208 S Jefferson St (60661-5600)
PHONE.................331 318-7800
Steven Smits, *CEO*
Douglas Powell, *President*
Charles Sherman, *Exec VP*
Darin Johnson, *Vice Pres*
Adrienne Castrovillari, *Accounts Mgr*
EMP: 2
SQ FT: 80,000
SALES (est): 494.2K **Privately Held**
WEB: www.visionps.com
SIC: 2759 2752 2732 2741 Commercial printing; commercial printing, lithographic; book printing; miscellaneous publishing

### (G-4004)
### AWARDS AND MORE INC
8544 S Pulaski Rd (60652-3631)
PHONE.................773 581-7771
Gerald Skizas, *President*
EMP: 5
SQ FT: 1,200
SALES (est): 631K **Privately Held**
SIC: 3499 5999 Trophies, metal, except silver; trophies & plaques

### (G-4005)
### AWNINGS EXPRESS
2415 W 24th Pl (60608-4701)
PHONE.................773 579-1437
Javier Ortega, *Owner*
EMP: 3
SALES (est): 173.5K **Privately Held**
SIC: 3993 Signs & advertising specialties

### (G-4006)
### AXLETECH INTERNATIONAL
Also Called: Heat Treat
1120 W 119th St (60643-5106)
PHONE.................773 264-1234
Fax: 773 264-4321
Mark Garfien, *President*
Jay Litcher, *General Mgr*
Donald Garfield, *Vice Pres*
Chet Lempicki, *Controller*
▲ EMP: 63
SQ FT: 70,000
SALES (est): 18.1MM **Privately Held**
WEB: www.htcoa.com
SIC: 3398 Shot peening (treating steel to reduce fatigue); annealing of metal; brazing (hardening) of metal

### (G-4007)
### AXLETECH INTERNATIONAL LLC
Also Called: US Gear
1020 W 119th St (60643-5216)
PHONE.................877 547-3907
Michael Lobaugh, *Prdtn Mgr*
Paul Blanchard, *Sales Mgr*
Julia Tresh,
EMP: 11

SALES (est): 1.9MM **Privately Held**
SIC: 3714 Motor vehicle parts & accessories

### (G-4008)
### AXODE CORP
35 E Wacker Dr Ste 670 (60601-2114)
PHONE.................312 578-9897
Nicolas Vendryes, *CEO*
Daniel Mangel, *Technical Mgr*
EMP: 2
SALES (est): 211.9K **Privately Held**
WEB: www.axode.com
SIC: 3823 Industrial instrmnts msrmnt display/control process variable

### (G-4009)
### AZCON INC (PA)
Also Called: Azcon Metals
820 W Jackson Blvd # 425 (60607-3396)
P.O. Box 616, Alton (62002-0616)
PHONE.................312 559-3100
Fax: 312 559-1543
Richard A Secrist Jr, *President*
Louis Mantia Jr, *CFO*
Dennis Sullivan, *CFO*
Lance Caldwell, *Sales Staff*
Mark Schofield, *Supervisor*
EMP: 50
SALES (est): 77.9MM **Privately Held**
SIC: 5093 3341 Scrap & waste materials; secondary nonferrous metals

### (G-4010)
### AZTEC MATERIAL SERVICE CORP (PA)
3624 W 26th St Fl 2 (60623-3936)
PHONE.................773 521-0909
Fax: 773 521-0641
Joel Arce, *President*
Jim Acre, *Sales Staff*
Marium Ramirez, *Manager*
EMP: 8
SQ FT: 2,000
SALES (est): 3.3MM **Privately Held**
SIC: 3273 Ready-mixed concrete

### (G-4011)
### AZTEC PLASTIC COMPANY
1747 W Carroll Ave (60612-2503)
PHONE.................312 733-0900
Fax: 773 685-1987
Martin S Wielgus, *President*
EMP: 20
SQ FT: 10,000
SALES (est): 4.6MM **Privately Held**
WEB: www.aztecplastic.com
SIC: 3089 Injection molded finished plastic products

### (G-4012)
### AZTECA FOODS INC (PA)
5005 S Nagle Ave (60638-1318)
P.O. Box 427, Summit Argo (60501-0427)
PHONE.................708 563-6600
Fax: 708 563-0331
Arthur R Velasquez, *CEO*
Renee Velasquez Togher, *President*
Julie Forbes, *Vice Pres*
Nannette Zander, *Vice Pres*
Jim Decloste, *Plant Mgr*
▲ EMP: 140
SQ FT: 120,000
SALES (est): 30.4MM **Privately Held**
SIC: 2096 2099 Tortilla chips; tortillas, fresh or refrigerated

### (G-4013)
### AZTECA JEWELRY (PA)
3334 N Lincoln Ave (60657-1108)
PHONE.................773 929-0796
Juan Romero, *President*
EMP: 3
SQ FT: 2,100
SALES (est): 395.8K **Privately Held**
SIC: 5944 3911 5094 Jewelry stores; jewelry, precious metal; jewelry

### (G-4014)
### B & B FORMICA APPLIERS INC
5617 W Grand Ave (60639-2910)
PHONE.................773 804-1015
Fax: 773 804-1057
Alex Polazkowyj, *President*
Jerry Wereszczak, *Vice Pres*
Carmen Toro, *Admin Asst*

# GEOGRAPHIC SECTION

Chicago - Cook County (G-4042)

**EMP:** 15
**SQ FT:** 18,000
**SALES:** 1.1MM  **Privately Held**
**WEB:** www.b-bformica.com
**SIC:** 3083  2521  5722  5712  Plastic finished products, laminated; wood office furniture; kitchens, complete (sinks, cabinets, etc.); furniture stores; wood partitions & fixtures; wood kitchen cabinets

### (G-4015)
### B & G SHEET METAL
3056 W Walton St  (60622-4348)
**PHONE**...................................773 265-6121
Bill Papageorgiou, *Partner*
George Moutidis, *Partner*
**EMP:** 3
**SQ FT:** 3,500
**SALES (est):** 502.5K  **Privately Held**
**SIC:** 3444  Sheet metalwork

### (G-4016)
### B & J WIRE  INC
1919 S Fairfield Ave # 1  (60608-2498)
**PHONE**...................................877 787-9473
**Fax:** 773 927-9520
Veronica Ronnie Soltysiak, *President*
Xavier Garcia, *Vice Pres*
Veronica Soltysiak, *Manager*
Bernard Linkowski, *Director*
Josephine Soltysiak, *Admin Sec*
**EMP:** 45
**SQ FT:** 80,000
**SALES (est):** 11.2MM  **Privately Held**
**WEB:** www.bjwire.com
**SIC:** 3496  3444  Miscellaneous fabricated wire products; shelving, made from purchased wire; sheet metalwork

### (G-4017)
### B & S AUTO REBUILDERS INC
3513 N Cicero Ave  (60641)
**PHONE**...................................773 283-3763
Ben Zachara, *President*
**EMP:** 3
**SQ FT:** 1,000
**SALES (est):** 292.9K  **Privately Held**
**SIC:** 3519  Gas engine rebuilding

### (G-4018)
### B & T POLISHING CO
2433 W Fulton St  (60612)
**PHONE**...................................847 658-6415
**Fax:** 312 666-3410
Allen Svejcar, *President*
John Svejcar, *Corp Secy*
Ellen Svejcar, *Vice Pres*
**EMP:** 30 EST: 1946
**SQ FT:** 43,000
**SALES:** 2.2MM  **Privately Held**
**SIC:** 3471  Polishing, metals or formed products; plating of metals or formed products

### (G-4019)
### B B M PACKING CO INC
874 N Milwaukee Ave  (60642-4107)
**PHONE**...................................312 243-1061
**Fax:** 312 243-7544
Dimitra Baziotes, *President*
Costa Michalopoulos, *Admin Sec*
**EMP:** 7
**SQ FT:** 1,200
**SALES (est):** 6MM  **Privately Held**
**SIC:** 5147  5142  2013  Meats, fresh; meat, frozen: packaged; poultry, frozen: packaged; sausages & other prepared meats

### (G-4020)
### B P I PRINTING & DUPLICATING (PA)
3223 N Lakewood Ave  (60657)
**PHONE**...................................773 327-7300
Lawrence Berland, *President*
**EMP:** 15
**SALES (est):** 2.3MM  **Privately Held**
**SIC:** 2752  Commercial printing, lithographic

### (G-4021)
### B P I PRINTING & DUPLICATING
Also Called: University Printing
3950 S Morgan St  (60609-2511)
**PHONE**...................................773 822-0111
**Fax:** 773 822-0134
Lawrence Berland, *CEO*

**EMP:** 23
**SALES (corp-wide):** 2.3MM  **Privately Held**
**SIC:** 2752  Commercial printing, lithographic
**PA:** B P I Printing & Duplicating Inc
  3223 N Lakewood Ave
  Chicago IL 60657
  773 327-7300

### (G-4022)
### B-CLEAN LAUNDROMAT INC
5419 S Halsted St  (60609-6168)
**PHONE**...................................678 983-5492
Ronald Martinez II, *President*
Maria S Hernandez, *Vice Pres*
**EMP:** 5 EST: 2015
**SQ FT:** 5,040
**SALES (est):** 289.9K  **Privately Held**
**SIC:** 3582  Washing machines, laundry: commercial, incl. coin-operated; dryers, laundry: commercial, including coin-operated

### (G-4023)
### BA LE MEAT PROCESSING & WHL CO
2405 W Ardmore Ave  (60659-5007)
**PHONE**...................................773 506-2499
**Fax:** 773 506-2405
Son Tran, *President*
Lee Tran, *General Mgr*
Amy Nguyen, *Vice Pres*
Teresa Ortiz, *Manager*
**EMP:** 12
**SQ FT:** 5,000
**SALES:** 795K  **Privately Held**
**SIC:** 2013  5147  Sausages & other prepared meats; meats & meat products

### (G-4024)
### BABAK INC
Also Called: Ambassador Printing
1 N La Salle St  (60602-3902)
**PHONE**...................................312 419-8686
**Fax:** 312 419-8687
Taha Hosseini Tabrizi, *President*
**EMP:** 2
**SQ FT:** 1,200
**SALES (est):** 210K  **Privately Held**
**SIC:** 2752  2791  Commercial printing, offset; typesetting

### (G-4025)
### BAGCRAFTPAPERCON I LLC (DH)
Also Called: Packaging Dynamics
3900 W 43rd St  (60632-3490)
**PHONE**...................................620 856-2800
Phil Harris, *CEO*
Dan Vice, *General Mgr*
Tom Ellsworth, *Exec VP*
Richard Cote, *Vice Pres*
Chuck Hathaway, *Vice Pres*
▲ **EMP:** 215
**SQ FT:** 150,000
**SALES (est):** 237MM
**SALES (corp-wide):** 2.2B  **Publicly Held**
**WEB:** www.packaging-dynamics.com
**SIC:** 2671  2674  2673  3497  Packaging paper & plastics film, coated & laminated; paper bags: made from purchased materials; bags: plastic, laminated & coated; metal foil & leaf; commercial printing

### (G-4026)
### BAHK EYE CENTER INC
Also Called: Bahk Eye Care
5441 N Lincoln Ave  (60625-2222)
**PHONE**...................................773 561-1199
**Fax:** 773 561-2124
Herri C Park Od, *President*
Harold J Park, *Admin Sec*
**EMP:** 2
**SQ FT:** 2,300
**SALES:** 350K  **Privately Held**
**SIC:** 3851  5995  Eyeglasses, lenses & frames; contact lenses; optical goods stores

### (G-4027)
### BAKA VITALIY
Also Called: Interntonal Creative RES Group
2224 W Chicago Ave  (60622-4827)
**PHONE**...................................773 370-5522
Vitaliy Baka, *Owner*

**EMP:** 5
**SALES (est):** 142.9K  **Privately Held**
**SIC:** 7379  2741  7311  ;  miscellaneous publishing; advertising agencies

### (G-4028)
### BAKED
2246 W North Ave  (60647-5443)
**PHONE**...................................773 384-7655
Jennifer Bridget Kane, *Owner*
**EMP:** 4
**SALES (est):** 272.9K  **Privately Held**
**SIC:** 2024  Ice cream & frozen desserts

### (G-4029)
### BAKER & NOSH
1303 W Wilson Ave  (60640-5508)
**PHONE**...................................773 989-7393
Bill Millholland, *Principal*
**EMP:** 4
**SALES (est):** 364.5K  **Privately Held**
**SIC:** 2051  Cakes, bakery: except frozen

### (G-4030)
### BALANSTAR CORPORATION (PA)
Also Called: Balancing Services
5030 W Lake St  (60644-2501)
**PHONE**...................................773 261-5034
**Fax:** 773 261-5030
Erwin Schulz, *President*
John Taylor, *General Mgr*
**EMP:** 10
**SQ FT:** 10,000
**SALES (est):** 1.4MM  **Privately Held**
**SIC:** 3545  Balancing machines (machine tool accessories)

### (G-4031)
### BALDI CANDY CO (PA)
Also Called: Chicago Candy & Nut
3425 N Kimball Ave  (60618-5505)
**PHONE**...................................773 463-7600
Craig Leva, *President*
**EMP:** 50 EST: 1950
**SQ FT:** 80,000
**SALES:** 35MM  **Privately Held**
**WEB:** www.arwayconfections.com
**SIC:** 2064  Chewing candy, not chewing gum

### (G-4032)
### BALDI CANDY CO
Also Called: Arway Confections
3323 W Newport Ave  (60618-5509)
**PHONE**...................................773 267-5770
**Fax:** 773 267-0610
Craig Leva, *President*
**EMP:** 60
**SALES (corp-wide):** 35MM  **Privately Held**
**SIC:** 2066  Chocolate & cocoa products
**PA:** Baldi Candy Co.
  3425 N Kimball Ave
  Chicago IL 60618
  773 463-7600

### (G-4033)
### BALLOTREADY INC
1626 N Honore St  (60622-1308)
**PHONE**...................................301 706-0708
Alexandra Niemczewski, *CEO*
Alexandra C Niemczewski, *President*
Aviva Rosman, *COO*
**EMP:** 3 EST: 2015
**SALES (est):** 111.4K  **Privately Held**
**SIC:** 2741  Miscellaneous publishing

### (G-4034)
### BALON INTERNATIONAL CORP
Also Called: R T Beverage
5410 W Roosevelt Rd 133a  (60644-1478)
**PHONE**...................................773 379-7779
**Fax:** 773 379-7919
Ramon Travieso, *President*
Patrick Travieso, *CFO*
Kim Kanakes, *Admin Sec*
▲ **EMP:** 32
**SQ FT:** 26,000
**SALES (est):** 5.9MM  **Privately Held**
**SIC:** 2086  5499  Carbonated beverages, nonalcoholic: bottled & canned; beverage stores

### (G-4035)
### BAND OF SHOPPERS  INC
Also Called: Whittl
2669 N Greenview Ave F  (60614-1180)
**PHONE**...................................312 857-4250
Michael Zivin, *CEO*
Hemant Kashyap, *COO*
**EMP:** 5
**SQ FT:** 1,000
**SALES (est):** 415K  **Privately Held**
**SIC:** 2741

### (G-4036)
### BANDGRIP INC
311 S Wacker Dr Ste 650  (60606-6728)
**PHONE**...................................844 968-6322
Fred Smith, *CEO*
Keith Hoglund, *COO*
**EMP:** 5
**SALES (est):** 198.4K  **Privately Held**
**SIC:** 3841  Surgical & medical instruments

### (G-4037)
### BANYAN TECHNOLOGIES  INC
1452 E 53rd St Fl 2  (60615-4512)
**PHONE**...................................312 967-9885
Sanchit Mulmuley, *CEO*
Rishi Bhat, *Chief Engr*
**EMP:** 3
**SALES (est):** 71.1K  **Privately Held**
**SIC:** 7372  Prepackaged software

### (G-4038)
### BAR CODE GRAPHICS  INC
65 E Wacker Pl Ste 1800  (60601-7247)
**PHONE**...................................312 664-0700
**Fax:** 312 664-4939
Robert Verb, *CEO*
Andrew Verb, *President*
Jonathan Verb, *COO*
Lois Verb, *Vice Pres*
Lori Williams, *Production*
**EMP:** 19
**SQ FT:** 5,500
**SALES (est):** 1.8MM  **Privately Held**
**WEB:** www.barcode-us.com
**SIC:** 7336  2759  Package design; labels & seals: printing

### (G-4039)
### BAR CODES INC
200 W Monroe St Fl 10  (60606-5009)
**PHONE**...................................800 351-9962
Dan Nettesheim, *CEO*
John Griffin, *Manager*
▲ **EMP:** 19
**SALES (est):** 2.6MM  **Privately Held**
**SIC:** 5112  3577  3663  Office supplies; bar code (magnetic ink) printers; digital encoders

### (G-4040)
### BAR-B-QUE INDUSTRIES INC
Also Called: Henry J'S Famous Foods
4460 W Armitage Ave  (60639-3574)
**PHONE**...................................773 227-5400
**Fax:** 773 227-0414
Forest Krisco, *President*
Cindy Krisco, *Corp Secy*
Diana Smithe, *Office Mgr*
**EMP:** 12
**SQ FT:** 15,000
**SALES (est):** 2.4MM  **Privately Held**
**SIC:** 2013  2011  Corned beef from purchased meat; canned meats (except baby food), meat slaughtered on site

### (G-4041)
### BARDASH & BUKOWSKI INC
Also Called: National Printing Resources
329 W 18th St Ste 908  (60616-1772)
**PHONE**...................................312 829-2080
Michael Bardash, *President*
Allison Fimbianti, *Office Mgr*
James Bukowski, *Admin Sec*
**EMP:** 4
**SQ FT:** 2,000
**SALES (est):** 399.4K  **Privately Held**
**SIC:** 2752  Commercial printing, lithographic

### (G-4042)
### BARKAAT FOODS  LLC
3810 S Halsted St  (60609-1611)
**PHONE**...................................773 376-8723
S I A Khan, *Mng Member*

# Chicago - Cook County (G-4043)

Shafiuddin Irfan A Khan, *Mng Member*
Rizwan Khan, *Manager*
**EMP:** 25
**SALES (est):** 4.1MM **Privately Held**
**SIC:** 2099 Food preparations

### (G-4043)
### BARKER METAL CRAFT INC
2955 N California Ave (60618-7702)
**PHONE**.................................773 588-9300
**Fax:** 773 588-9309
Ronald Kedzorski, *President*
Barbara Kedzorski, *Treasurer*
**EMP:** 8
**SQ FT:** 7,500
**SALES:** 790K **Privately Held**
**WEB:** www.radiatorcover.com
**SIC:** 3444 3446 3443 Sheet metalwork; architectural metalwork; fabricated plate work (boiler shop)

### (G-4044)
### BARKS PUBLICATIONS INC
Also Called: Electrmchnical Bench Reference
500 N Michigan Ave # 901 (60611-3777)
**PHONE**.................................312 321-9440
Horace B Barks, *President*
Elsie Dickson, *Principal*
Kevin Jones, *Senior Editor*
**EMP:** 10 **EST:** 1969
**SQ FT:** 2,500
**SALES (est):** 1.3MM **Privately Held**
**WEB:** www.barks.com
**SIC:** 2721 2731 Magazines: publishing only, not printed on site; books: publishing only

### (G-4045)
### BAROQUE SILVERSMITH INC (PA)
55 E Washington St # 302 (60602-2103)
**PHONE**.................................312 357-2813
**Fax:** 312 357-1999
Hagop Dirilen, *Exec VP*
**EMP:** 2
**SALES (est):** 384.7K **Privately Held**
**WEB:** www.baroquesilversmith.com
**SIC:** 3914 3471 Silversmithing; plating & polishing

### (G-4046)
### BARREL MAKER PRINTING
3065 N Rockwell St Ste 8 (60618-7925)
**PHONE**.................................773 490-3065
Justin Moore, *Principal*
**EMP:** 5
**SALES (est):** 551.2K **Privately Held**
**SIC:** 2752 Commercial printing, lithographic

### (G-4047)
### BARRY CALLEBAUT USA LLC
2144 Paysphere Cir (60674-0021)
**PHONE**.................................312 496-7300
**EMP:** 5
**SALES (corp-wide):** 35MM **Privately Held**
**SIC:** 2066 8741 Chocolate; management services
**HQ:** Barry Callebaut U.S.A. Llc
600 W Chicago Ave Ste 860
Chicago IL 60654

### (G-4048)
### BARRY CALLEBAUT USA LLC (DH)
600 W Chicago Ave Ste 860 (60654-2530)
**PHONE**.................................312 496-7300
David S Johnson, *President*
Willy Geeraerts, *General Mgr*
Jesus Valencia, *General Mgr*
Edgar Garbelotto, *Business Mgr*
James G Hagedorn, *Vice Pres*
◆ **EMP:** 277
**SQ FT:** 10,000
**SALES (est):** 618.4MM
**SALES (corp-wide):** 35MM **Privately Held**
**SIC:** 2066 8741 Chocolate; administrative management
**HQ:** Barry Callebaut Ag
Westpark
ZUrich ZH
432 040-404

### (G-4049)
### BARRY SIGNS INC
6950 W Imlay St (60631-1771)
**PHONE**.................................773 327-1183
Robert Szymanski, *President*
Janice Szymanski, *Corp Secy*
**EMP:** 3
**SQ FT:** 1,200
**SALES:** 200K **Privately Held**
**SIC:** 3993 Signs & advertising specialties; signs, not made in custom sign painting shops

### (G-4050)
### BARSANTI WOODWORK CORPORATION
3838 W 51st St (60632-3614)
**PHONE**.................................773 284-6888
**Fax:** 773 284-1662
Eugene Barsanti, *President*
Constance Barsanti, *Corp Secy*
Gene Monyak, *Plant Mgr*
Bill Bartolucci, *Purchasing*
Art Pollen, *Controller*
**EMP:** 50 **EST:** 1978
**SQ FT:** 58,000
**SALES (est):** 7.3MM **Privately Held**
**WEB:** www.barsantiwoodwork.com
**SIC:** 2431 Millwork

### (G-4051)
### BARTEC ORB INC
4724 S Christiana Ave (60632-3016)
**PHONE**.................................773 927-8600
**Fax:** 773 927-8620
Doug Korslund, *President*
Jason Sewell, *Vice Pres*
**EMP:** 20
**SALES (est):** 5.6MM **Privately Held**
**SIC:** 3444 8711 3672 3533 Sheet metalwork; designing: ship, boat, machine & product; printed circuit boards; oil & gas field machinery

### (G-4052)
### BASS BROTHER INCORPORATED
4441 W Fillmore St (60624-4405)
**PHONE**.................................773 638-7628
Mark N Bass, *President*
**EMP:** 3
**SALES (corp-wide):** 3MM **Privately Held**
**SIC:** 2842 Specialty cleaning, polishes & sanitation goods
**PA:** Bass Brother, Incorporated
2720 S River Rd Ste 146
Des Plaines IL 60018

### (G-4053)
### BASSWOOD ASSOCIATES INC (PA)
Also Called: AlphaGraphics
1017 W Washington Blvd (60607-2119)
**PHONE**.................................312 240-9400
**Fax:** 312 226-6636
Sheila Moran, *President*
Mike Moran, *General Mgr*
Richard Moran, *Vice Pres*
Jeff Magnussen, *Sales Mgr*
**EMP:** 15
**SQ FT:** 4,800
**SALES (est):** 5.8MM **Privately Held**
**SIC:** 2752 2672 Commercial printing, lithographic; coated & laminated paper

### (G-4054)
### BATES ABRASIVE PRODUCTS INC
Also Called: Marvel Abrasive Products
6230 S Oak Park Ave (60638-4016)
**PHONE**.................................773 586-8700
**Fax:** 773 586-0187
Leslie Branch, *President*
Barbara Branch, *Vice Pres*
▲ **EMP:** 35
**SQ FT:** 35,000
**SALES (est):** 3.9MM **Privately Held**
**WEB:** www.marvelabrasives.com
**SIC:** 3291 Abrasive products

### (G-4055)
### BATH SOLUTIONS INC
Also Called: BSI-Bath Solutions
858 W Armitage Ave (60614-4383)
**PHONE**.................................817 429-2318

Thomas H Wolf, *President*
▲ **EMP:** 10
**SQ FT:** 100,000
**SALES:** 40.5MM **Privately Held**
**WEB:** www.globaldecor.com
**SIC:** 3634 Housewares, excluding cooking appliances & utensils

### (G-4056)
### BAXALTA US INC
135 S Lasalle St Ste 3425 (60603)
**PHONE**.................................312 648-2244
**EMP:** 10
**SALES (corp-wide):** 6.4B **Privately Held**
**SIC:** 2835 Blood derivative diagnostic agents
**HQ:** Baxalta Us Inc.
1 Baxter Pkwy
Deerfield IL 60015
224 948-2000

### (G-4057)
### BAY FOODS INC
1026 E Jackson Blvd (60607)
P.O. Box 1455 (60690-1455)
**PHONE**.................................312 346-5757
George A Bay, *President*
James N Bay Jr, *Admin Sec*
**EMP:** 35
**SQ FT:** 5,000
**SALES (est):** 4.2MM **Privately Held**
**SIC:** 2041 Flour mixes

### (G-4058)
### BAY VALLEY FOODS LLC
Also Called: Schwartz Pickle
4401 W 44th Pl (60632-4305)
**PHONE**.................................773 927-7700
**Fax:** 773 927-3750
Gary Newman, *General Mgr*
**EMP:** 100
**SALES (corp-wide):** 6.1B **Publicly Held**
**SIC:** 2033 Canned fruits & specialties
**HQ:** Bay Valley Foods, Llc
3200 Riverside Dr Ste A
Green Bay WI 54301
800 558-4700

### (G-4059)
### BAYS ENGLISH MUFFIN CORP
1026 W Jackson Blvd (60607-2914)
P.O. Box 1455 (60690-1455)
**PHONE**.................................312 829-5253
George A Bay, *President*
Marti Swendson, *Opers Mgr*
Steve Sembler, *Controller*
Steve Semler, *Controller*
Robert Buonauro, *Manager*
**EMP:** 35 **EST:** 1940
**SQ FT:** 30,000
**SALES (est):** 8MM **Privately Held**
**WEB:** www.bays.com
**SIC:** 2051 Breads, rolls & buns

### (G-4060)
### BAYS MICHIGAN CORP
1026 W Jackson Blvd (60607-2914)
P.O. Box 1455 (60690-1455)
**PHONE**.................................312 346-5757
James N Bay Sr, *President*
George A Bay, *Treasurer*
Kerry Clayton, *Manager*
James N Bay Jr, *Admin Sec*
**EMP:** 30
**SQ FT:** 5,000
**SALES (est):** 4.2MM **Privately Held**
**SIC:** 2051 Breads, rolls & buns

### (G-4061)
### BE GROUP INC
Also Called: Contractor Advisors
1507 E 53rd St (60615-4573)
**PHONE**.................................312 436-0301
Suzanne Stantley, *President*
**EMP:** 4
**SALES (est):** 130.4K **Privately Held**
**SIC:** 2721 7374 7389 8611 Magazines: publishing only, not printed on site; service bureau, computer; convention & show services; contractors' association; training & development consultant

### (G-4062)
### BE PRODUCTS INC
180 W Washington St Fl 10 (60602-2315)
**PHONE**.................................312 201-9669

**EMP:** 6
**SALES (est):** 682.1K **Privately Held**
**SIC:** 2844 Mfg Toilet Preparations

### (G-4063)
### BEACON SOLUTIONS INC
111 E Wacker Dr Ste 3000 (60601-4803)
**PHONE**.................................303 513-0469
Gabe Vehosky, *CEO*
**EMP:** 15
**SQ FT:** 2,500
**SALES (est):** 428K **Privately Held**
**SIC:** 2711 Newspapers

### (G-4064)
### BEAN PRODUCTS INC
1500 S Western Ave Ste 40 (60608-1819)
**PHONE**.................................312 666-3600
**Fax:** 312 666-3629
Chuck Blumenthal, *President*
▲ **EMP:** 21
**SQ FT:** 14,000
**SALES (est):** 2.2MM **Privately Held**
**WEB:** www.beanproducts.com
**SIC:** 2392 2833 Cushions & pillows; medicinals & botanicals

### (G-4065)
### BEAR-STEWART CORPORATION (PA)
1025 N Damen Ave (60622-3637)
**PHONE**.................................773 276-0400
**Fax:** 773 276-3512
Clifford Brooks, *President*
Michael Hossman, *Corp Secy*
Gary Posner, *Controller*
**EMP:** 20
**SQ FT:** 45,000
**SALES (est):** 10.4MM **Privately Held**
**WEB:** www.bearstewart.com
**SIC:** 2033 5149 2045 2051 Jams, including imitation: packaged in cans, jars, etc.; jellies, edible, including imitation: in cans, jars, etc.; baking supplies; prepared flour mixes & doughs; bread, cake & related products; food preparations; frozen bakery products, except bread

### (G-4066)
### BEARING SALES CORPORATION (PA)
4153 N Kostner Ave (60641-1928)
**PHONE**.................................773 282-8686
**Fax:** 773 282-3323
John Hilton, *Ch of Bd*
James B White, *President*
Jim White, *President*
John Baldacci, *Vice Pres*
Nancy Johansen, *Credit Mgr*
▲ **EMP:** 23
**SQ FT:** 30,000
**SALES (est):** 11.6MM **Privately Held**
**WEB:** www.bearingsales.com
**SIC:** 5085 3399 3568 3366 Bearings; metal powders, pastes & flakes; power transmission equipment; copper foundries

### (G-4067)
### BEARINGS MANUFACTURING COMPANY
Also Called: BMC
1033 N Kolmar Ave (60651-3337)
**PHONE**.................................773 583-6703
**Fax:** 773 278-6758
Steven Sivo, *President*
Jeffrey Walls, *Vice Pres*
Dennis Driebergen, *Manager*
Jeff Walls, *Manager*
Charles Huddleston, *MIS Mgr*
**EMP:** 12
**SQ FT:** 12,200
**SALES (corp-wide):** 11.7MM **Privately Held**
**WEB:** www.bdsbearing.com
**SIC:** 3568 3562 Bearings, bushings & blocks; ball & roller bearings
**PA:** Bearings Manufacturing Company
15157 Foltz Pkwy
Strongsville OH 44149
440 846-5517

## GEOGRAPHIC SECTION
### Chicago - Cook County (G-4094)

**(G-4068)**
**BEARSE MANUFACTURING CO**
Also Called: Bearse USA
3815 W Cortland St (60647-4691)
PHONE..................................773 235-8710
Fax: 773 235-8716
Thomas F Auer, *President*
Joseph E Auer, *Vice Pres*
▲ EMP: 100 EST: 1921
SQ FT: 50,000
SALES (est): 16.4MM **Privately Held**
WEB: www.bearseusa.com
SIC: 2393 5099 5949 Textile bags; bags & containers, except sleeping bags: textile; cases, carrying; patterns: sewing, knitting & needlework

**(G-4069)**
**BEATRICE COMPANIES INC**
2 N La Salle St (60602-3702)
PHONE..................................602 225-2000
Fax: 312 558-4167
EMP: 20 EST: 1986
SALES (est): 3.3MM **Privately Held**
SIC: 2033 2079 2032 2038 Mfg Canned Fruits/Vegtbl

**(G-4070)**
**BEAUTY VAULT LLC**
3355 N Lincoln Ave Ste 14 (60657-1107)
PHONE..................................773 621-5189
Amanda N Perez, *Principal*
EMP: 3
SALES (est): 202.6K **Privately Held**
SIC: 3272 Burial vaults, concrete or pre-cast terrazzo

**(G-4071)**
**BEECKEN PETTY OKEEFE & CO LLC (PA)**
131 S Dearborn St Ste 122 (60603-5581)
PHONE..................................312 435-0300
Kenneth O'Keefe, *Managing Dir*
Brian F Chambers, *Vice Pres*
Peter Magas, *Vice Pres*
Grant Patrick, *Vice Pres*
Troy Phillips, *Vice Pres*
EMP: 561
SALES (est): 125.9MM **Privately Held**
WEB: www.bpoc.com
SIC: 6799 3841 Venture capital companies; surgical & medical instruments

**(G-4072)**
**BEL BRANDS USA INC (DH)**
30 S Wacker Dr Ste 3000 (60606-7459)
PHONE..................................312 462-1500
Lance Chambers, *President*
Didier Aziza, *Vice Pres*
Pelin Tomay, *Vice Pres*
Vladimir Homola, *Opers Staff*
Francine Moudry, *Opers Staff*
▲ EMP: 40
SQ FT: 130,000
SALES (est): 137.4MM
SALES (corp-wide): 8MM **Privately Held**
WEB: www.kaukauna.com
SIC: 2022 Natural cheese; processed cheese

**(G-4073)**
**BEL MAR WIRE PRODUCTS INC**
2343 N Damen Ave (60647-3352)
PHONE..................................773 342-3800
Anastase Marinos, *President*
George Marinos, *Treasurer*
EMP: 15
SQ FT: 28,000
SALES (est): 2.2MM **Privately Held**
SIC: 3496 2542 Miscellaneous fabricated wire products; partitions & fixtures, except wood

**(G-4074)**
**BEL-AIR MANUFACTURING INC**
3525 W Potomac Ave (60651-2231)
PHONE..................................773 276-7550
Fax: 773 276-1506
Frank Defrank, *President*
Mustafa Macit, *Plant Mgr*
EMP: 16
SQ FT: 40,000
SALES (est): 1.3MM **Privately Held**
WEB: www.belairmfg.com
SIC: 3544 3469 Special dies & tools; stamping metal for the trade

**(G-4075)**
**BELAIR HD STUDIOS LLC**
2233 S Throop St (60608-5002)
PHONE..................................312 254-5188
Clyde Scott, *CEO*
EMP: 30
SQ FT: 35,000
SALES: 180MM **Privately Held**
SIC: 7335 2711 Commercial photography; commercial printing & newspaper publishing combined

**(G-4076)**
**BELLA PHARMACEUTICALS INC** ✪
3101 W Devon Ave (60659-1407)
PHONE..................................773 279-5350
Michael B Younan, *CEO*
EMP: 3 EST: 2016
SALES (est): 123.2K **Privately Held**
SIC: 2834 Pharmaceutical preparations

**(G-4077)**
**BELLAFLORA FOODS LTD**
4334 W Chicago Ave (60651-3422)
PHONE..................................773 252-6113
Fax: 773 252-7085
Roy Pier Dominici, *President*
Rosetta Dominici, *Treasurer*
Gino Riccardi, *Sales Mgr*
Tom Behnke, *Manager*
Maria Ramirez, *Manager*
▲ EMP: 25
SQ FT: 20,000
SALES (est): 8.3MM **Privately Held**
SIC: 2098 5812 Macaroni & spaghetti; noodles (e.g. egg, plain & water), dry; macaroni products (e.g. alphabets, rings & shells), dry; eating places

**(G-4078)**
**BELLWOOD INDUSTRIES INC (PA)**
4351 W Roosevelt Rd (60624-3839)
PHONE..................................773 522-1002
Fax: 773 522-3514
Gerald Cychosz, *Owner*
Joesph Palik, *General Mgr*
EMP: 8 EST: 1970
SQ FT: 2,800
SALES: 900K **Privately Held**
SIC: 3471 Electroplating of metals or formed products

**(G-4079)**
**BELOVED CHARACTERS LTD**
Also Called: My Finished Book
6456 W 64th Pl Apt 3 (60638-5050)
P.O. Box 388931 (60638-8931)
PHONE..................................773 599-0073
Margaret Kairis, *President*
EMP: 4
SALES (est): 234.8K **Privately Held**
WEB: www.belovedcharacters.com
SIC: 2731 7389 Book publishing;

**(G-4080)**
**BELRICH INC**
2341 N Lister Ave (60614-2981)
Fax: 773 342-2341
Elmer Bell, *President*
Jose R Alvarez, *Treasurer*
EMP: 6 EST: 1969
SQ FT: 5,000
SALES (est): 630K **Privately Held**
SIC: 3451 Screw machine products

**(G-4081)**
**BELVIN J & F SHEET METAL CO**
675 N Milwaukee Ave (60642-5920)
PHONE..................................312 666-5222
Fax: 312 666-5223
Javier Tellez, *President*
Ben Belvin, *Chairman*
Fidel Tellez, *Vice Pres*
Carrie Clayton, *Admin Sec*
EMP: 5
SALES (est): 400K **Privately Held**
SIC: 3444 Sheet metal specialties, not stamped

**(G-4082)**
**BENDINGER BRUCE CRTVE COMM IN**
Also Called: Copy Workshop, The
2144 N Hudson Ave Ste 1 (60614-4572)
PHONE..................................773 871-1179
Fax: 773 281-4643
Lorelei Bendinger, *President*
Bruce Bendinger, *Exec VP*
EMP: 6
SALES (est): 629K **Privately Held**
SIC: 2731 8742 2741 Book publishing; marketing consulting services; miscellaneous publishing

**(G-4083)**
**BENEFICIAL REUSE MGT LLC (PA)**
372 W Ontario St Ste 501 (60654-5779)
PHONE..................................312 784-0300
Ann Weis, *Office Mgr*
Andy Gilbert Jr, *CTO*
Robert C Spoerri,
David Schuurman,
EMP: 15
SALES (est): 5.8MM **Privately Held**
SIC: 3822 Auto controls regulating residntl & coml environmt & applncs

**(G-4084)**
**BENTLEYS PET STUFF LLC**
509 N La Salle Dr (60654-7108)
PHONE..................................312 222-1012
Burdette Beckmann, *Owner*
EMP: 3
SALES (corp-wide): 1.4MM **Privately Held**
SIC: 3999 Pet supplies
HQ: Bentley's Pet Stuff, Llc
4192 Ill Rte 83 Ste C
Long Grove IL 60047
224 567-4700

**(G-4085)**
**BERINGER AERO USA INC**
4118 N Nashville Ave (60634-1429)
PHONE..................................708 667-7891
Glibert Beringer, *President*
EMP: 5
SALES (est): 323.5K **Privately Held**
SIC: 3728 Wheels, aircraft

**(G-4086)**
**BERLAND PRINTING INC**
Also Called: Berland Communications
3950 S Morgan St (60609-2511)
PHONE..................................773 702-1999
Fax: 773 327-8666
Lawrence Berland, *President*
Bob Berland, *President*
Theresa Herrera, *Vice Pres*
Jim Ratner, *Info Tech Mgr*
EMP: 25 EST: 1933
SQ FT: 10,000
SALES (est): 4.5MM **Privately Held**
WEB: www.bpi-printing.com
SIC: 2752 Commercial printing, lithographic

**(G-4087)**
**BERT PACKING CO INC**
170 N Green St (60607-2313)
PHONE..................................312 733-0346
Baron Bridgeford, *President*
EMP: 1
SALES (est): 276.2K
SALES (corp-wide): 140MM **Publicly Held**
WEB: www.bridgford.com
SIC: 2013 Snack sticks, including jerky: from purchased meat
HQ: Bridgford Foods Corporation
1308 N Patt St
Anaheim CA 92801
714 526-5533

**(G-4088)**
**BERTEAU-LOWELL PLTG WORKS INC**
2320 W Fullerton Ave (60647-3298)
PHONE..................................773 276-3135
Fax: 773 276-4502
Jim Elies, *President*
James D Elies, *President*
John Kobatch, *Accountant*
Christine Davis, *Manager*
EMP: 33 EST: 1930
SQ FT: 50,000
SALES (est): 4MM **Privately Held**
SIC: 3471 Plating of metals or formed products

**(G-4089)**
**BESLEYS ACCESSORIES INC**
Also Called: Robert Daskal Group
4541 N Ravenswood Ave # 203 (60640-5296)
PHONE..................................773 561-3300
Fax: 773 561-2106
Arlene Bunis, *President*
Lisa Morton, *Controller*
Robert Daskal, *Info Tech Mgr*
Dan Dugas, *Info Tech Mgr*
Peter Hartshorn, *MIS Mgr*
EMP: 8
SQ FT: 11,000
SALES (est): 740K **Privately Held**
WEB: www.robertdaskal.com
SIC: 2323 2339 2331 2392 Neckties, men's & boys': made from purchased materials; neckwear & ties: women's, misses' & juniors'; scarves, hoods, headbands, etc.: women's; blouses, women's & juniors': made from purchased material; household furnishings

**(G-4090)**
**BEST CHICAGO MEAT COMPANY LLC**
Also Called: Glenmark Burgers
4649 W Armitage Ave (60639-3405)
PHONE..................................773 523-8161
Patrick Floyd, *Controller*
EMP: 15
SALES (est): 4.7MM **Privately Held**
SIC: 2011 Meat by-products from meat slaughtered on site

**(G-4091)**
**BEST CROUTONS LLC**
1140 S Washtenaw Ave (60612-4016)
PHONE..................................773 927-8200
Robert Beavers Jr, *CEO*
Stephanie Waldschmidt, *Bookkeeper*
Brandon Beavers,
EMP: 15
SALES (est): 4.2MM **Privately Held**
SIC: 2099 Bread crumbs, not made in bakeries
PA: Beavers Holdings, Llc
3550 Hobson Rd Fl 3
Woodridge IL 60517

**(G-4092)**
**BEST DIAMOND PLASTICS LLC**
1401 E 98th St (60628-1701)
PHONE..................................773 336-3485
Bob Beavers, *Exec VP*
▲ EMP: 10
SALES (est): 3.2MM **Privately Held**
SIC: 2656 Straws, drinking: made from purchased material

**(G-4093)**
**BEST NEON SIGN CO INC**
6025 S New England Ave (60638-4005)
PHONE..................................773 586-2700
Fax: 773 586-7587
Marvin Goldzweig, *President*
Michael Goldzweig, *Treasurer*
Rose Sanders, *Accounts Mgr*
Steve Goldzweig, *Admin Sec*
EMP: 19
SQ FT: 12,000
SALES (est): 2.5MM **Privately Held**
SIC: 3993 1799 Neon signs; signs, not made in custom sign painting shops; sign installation & maintenance

**(G-4094)**
**BEST PALLET COMPANY LLC (PA)**
Also Called: Great Lakes Pallet
166 W Washington St # 300 (60602-2311)
PHONE..................................312 242-4009
Fax: 815 637-1555
Michael Faas, *Plant Mgr*
Bradley Huber, *Treasurer*
Andrew Urnezis, *Sales Dir*
Lori Mackey, *Manager*
Joseph S Messer,

## Chicago - Cook County (G-4095) — GEOGRAPHIC SECTION

EMP: 4
SQ FT: 3,000
SALES (est): 2.8MM  Privately Held
SIC: 2448  Pallets, wood & wood with metal

**(G-4095)**
**BETTER EARTH LLC**
2444 W 16th St Ste 4r  (60608-1731)
PHONE..............................844 243-6333
John Hamilton, Mng Member
EMP: 3
SALES (est): 103.6K  Privately Held
SIC: 3299  Ceramic fiber

**(G-4096)**
**BEVERAGE ART INC**
Also Called: Bev Art HM Brewing Winemaking
10033 S Western Ave  (60643-1925)
PHONE..............................773 881-9463
Fax: 773 233-1445
Greg Fischer, President
EMP: 5
SQ FT: 2,000
SALES (est): 765K  Privately Held
WEB: www.bev-art.com
SIC: 2084  Wines, brandy & brandy spirits

**(G-4097)**
**BEVERAGE FLAVORS INTL LLC**
Also Called: B F I
3150 N Campbell Ave  (60618-7921)
PHONE..............................773 248-3860
Jenna Satterthwaite, Office Mgr
Barbara Martinez, Manager
Daniel T Manoogian,
▼ EMP: 10
SALES (est): 2.1MM  Privately Held
SIC: 2087  Beverage bases

**(G-4098)**
**BEVERLY SHEAR MFG CORPORATION**
3004 W 111th St Ste 1  (60655-2292)
PHONE..............................773 233-2063
Fax: 773 238-0028
Joseph A Nebel, President
Rose Christensen, Vice Pres
Bob Christensen, Purch Mgr
Donna Stork, Sales Staff
EMP: 6  EST: 1931
SQ FT: 2,000
SALES (est): 460K  Privately Held
SIC: 3444  3549  3541  Sheet metalwork; metalworking machinery; machine tools, metal cutting type

**(G-4099)**
**BF FOODS  INC**
Also Called: Bellaflora Foods
4334 W Chicago Ave  (60651-3422)
PHONE..............................773 252-6113
Randall Krebs, President
Greg Raisanen, Principal
Jay L Dolgin, Director
EMP: 25
SALES (est): 3.8MM  Privately Held
SIC: 2043  Cereal breakfast foods

**(G-4100)**
**BF MANUFACTURING LLC**
Also Called: Green Field Operation
3810 S Halsted St  (60609-1611)
PHONE..............................312 446-1163
Ahmed Khan, Mng Member
EMP: 70
SALES (est): 4.2MM  Privately Held
SIC: 2038  Frozen specialties

**(G-4101)**
**BGF PERFORMANCE SYSTEMS LLC**
5454 N Bernard St  (60625-4614)
P.O. Box 256643  (60625-8691)
PHONE..............................773 539-7099
Brad G Frieswyk,
Brad Frieswyk, Graphic Designe
EMP: 1
SALES: 400K  Privately Held
WEB: www.bgfperformance.com
SIC: 8748  2731  Educational consultant; textbooks: publishing & printing

**(G-4102)**
**BHS MEDIA LLC**
Also Called: Bh Sports
123 W Madison St Ste 1600  (60602-4699)
PHONE..............................312 701-0000
Kevin Harrington, Mng Member
EMP: 30  EST: 2012
SALES (est): 2MM  Privately Held
SIC: 2721  Magazines: publishing only, not printed on site

**(G-4103)**
**BIAGIOS GOURMET FOODS INC**
Also Called: Suparossa Pizza
7319 W Lawrence Ave  (60706-3503)
PHONE..............................708 867-4641
Fax: 630 867-3800
Salvatore Cirrincione, President
Lisa Ozians, Finance Other
Rose Cirrincione, Admin Sec
▲ EMP: 20
SQ FT: 30,000
SALES (est): 2.4MM  Privately Held
WEB: www.suparossa.com
SIC: 2038  5812  Frozen specialties; pizza, frozen; caterers

**(G-4104)**
**BIG TEN NETWORK SERVICES LLC**
Also Called: Btn
600 W Chicago Ave Ste 875  (60654-2531)
PHONE..............................312 329-3666
Mark Silverman, President
Elizabeth Conlisk, Vice Pres
Matt Nikkila, Graphic Designe
EMP: 68
SALES (est): 28.1MM  Privately Held
SIC: 3663  Television broadcasting & communications equipment

**(G-4105)**
**BIGHAND INC (DH)**
125 S Wacker Dr Ste 300  (60606-4421)
PHONE..............................312 893-5906
Jon Ardron, CEO
Chuck Pindell, Sales Dir
Earl Konietzko, Accounts Mgr
Megan Euteneuer, Regl Sales Mgr
Jay Philbrick, Regl Sales Mgr
EMP: 13
SALES (est): 3.8MM
SALES (corp-wide): 35.6MM  Privately Held
SIC: 7372  Prepackaged software
HQ: Bighand Limited
    27-29 Union Street
    London SE1 1
    207 940-5900

**(G-4106)**
**BILLS SHADE & BLIND SERVICE (PA)**
765 E 69th Pl  (60637-4158)
PHONE..............................773 493-5000
Leon Jackson, President
R Dardon, Controller
EMP: 6  EST: 1932
SQ FT: 26,250
SALES: 900K  Privately Held
SIC: 2591  Venetian blinds; window shades

**(G-4107)**
**BIMBO BAKERIES USA  INC**
2503 S Blue Island Ave  (60608-4903)
PHONE..............................773 254-3578
EMP: 21
SALES (corp-wide): 13.7B  Privately Held
SIC: 2051  Mfg Bread/Related Products
HQ: Bimbo Bakeries Usa, Inc
    255 Business Center Dr # 200
    Horsham PA 19044
    215 347-5500

**(G-4108)**
**BIO STAR FILMS  LLC**
4848 S Hoyne Ave  (60609-4028)
PHONE..............................773 254-5959
Jerome Starr, Principal
Bill Lavelle, Controller
Mitch Atamian, Executive
Alfred Teo,
Gene Wisniewski,
EMP: 9
SALES (est): 1.3MM  Privately Held
WEB: www.biostarfilms.com
SIC: 2392  7389  Sheets, fabric: made from purchased materials; artists' agents & brokers

**(G-4109)**
**BIOELEMENTS  INC**
4043 N Ravenswood Ave # 216  (60613-5685)
PHONE..............................773 525-3509
Jessica Finlay, Marketing Staff
Callie Lushina, Branch Mgr
Loren Kaminski, Consultant
EMP: 15
SALES (corp-wide): 5.7MM  Privately Held
WEB: www.bioelements.com
SIC: 2844  Beauty shops; cosmetic preparations
PA: Bioelements, Inc.
    3502 E Boulder St
    Colorado Springs CO 80909
    719 260-0297

**(G-4110)**
**BIOFORCE NANOSCIENCES INC**
6248 N Lakewood Ave  (60660-1907)
PHONE..............................515 233-8333
Kerry Frey, COO
Gregory D Brown, CFO
Trisha Newbanks, Controller
Jennifer Albers, Accountant
EMP: 2
SALES (est): 204.8K
SALES (corp-wide): 1.2MM  Publicly Held
WEB: www.bioforcenano.com
SIC: 2836  Biological products, except diagnostic
PA: Bioforce Nanosciences Holdings, Inc.
    1615 Golden Aspen Dr
    Ames IA 50010
    515 233-8333

**(G-4111)**
**BIRD DOG BAY  INC**
2010 W Fulton St  (60612-2359)
PHONE..............................312 631-3108
Steve Mayer, President
Joel Keller, Mktg Dir
Eric Stefenson, Business Dir
EMP: 1
SALES (est): 313.4K  Privately Held
WEB: www.birdogbay.com
SIC: 5136  2253  3961  Men's & boys' clothing; collar & cuff sets, knit; cuff-links & studs, except precious metal & gems

**(G-4112)**
**BIRD-X  INC**
Also Called: Yates Motloid
300 N Oakley Blvd  (60612-2216)
PHONE..............................312 226-2473
Fax: 312 226-2480
Dennis Tilles, President
Jill Galindo, Accountant
Kory Baker, Natl Sales Mgr
Mark Miller, Natl Sales Mgr
Joshua Pierce, Accounts Mgr
▲ EMP: 39
SALES (est): 13.2MM  Privately Held
WEB: www.indus-tool.com
SIC: 5087  5075  5047  2899  Extermination & fumigation equipment & supplies; warm air heating equipment & supplies; dental laboratory equipment; chemical preparations

**(G-4113)**
**BISHOP IMAGE GROUP  INC**
4018 W Irving Park Rd  (60641)
PHONE..............................312 735-8153
Nick Baloun, Marketing Staff
Chris Bishop,
Kristin Swanson,
Chad Taylor,
EMP: 5
SALES (est): 845.5K  Privately Held
WEB: www.bishoptaylorgroup.com
SIC: 3577  Graphic displays, except graphic terminals

**(G-4114)**
**BISHOPS ENGRV & TROPHY SVC INC**
Also Called: Bets
6708 W Belmont Ave  (60634-4848)
PHONE..............................773 777-5014
Linda Bishop, President
Kendal Bishop, General Mgr
Laurence Bishop, Vice Pres
EMP: 7
SQ FT: 8,000
SALES (est): 150K  Privately Held
WEB: www.bets-engraving.com
SIC: 3479  5094  Etching & engraving; trophies

**(G-4115)**
**BITTER END YACHT CLUB INTL**
875 N Michigan Ave # 3707  (60611-1915)
PHONE..............................312 506-6205
Fax: 312 944-2860
Dana Hokin, President
John Glynn, VP Sls/Mktg
Christopher Johnson, Controller
Eva Shillingford, Sales Staff
Robert Gorman, Manager
EMP: 10
SALES (est): 1MM
SALES (corp-wide): 27.8MM  Privately Held
SIC: 7389  2452  Hotel & motel reservation service; purchasing service; marinas, prefabricated, wood
PA: Century America Llc
    1 Thorndal Cir Ste 2
    Darien CT 06820
    203 655-8735

**(G-4116)**
**BIZ 3 PUBLICITY**
1321 N Milwaukee Ave  (60622-9151)
PHONE..............................773 342-3331
Kathryn Frazier, Owner
Chelsi Zollner, Prdtn Mgr
EMP: 6  EST: 2008
SALES (est): 299.4K  Privately Held
SIC: 2741  Miscellaneous publishing

**(G-4117)**
**BIZBASH MEDIA  INC**
5437 N Ashland Ave  (60640-1153)
PHONE..............................312 436-2525
Robert Fitzgerald, Branch Mgr
EMP: 5
SALES (corp-wide): 11MM  Privately Held
SIC: 2759  Advertising literature: printing
PA: Bizbash Media, Inc.
    115 W 27th St Fl 8
    New York NY 10001
    646 638-3600

**(G-4118)**
**BJS WELDING SERVICES ETC CO**
1521 E 83rd St  (60619-4645)
PHONE..............................773 964-5836
Brandon Shearer,
EMP: 7
SALES (est): 372.8K  Privately Held
SIC: 3441  7389  Dam gates, metal plate;

**(G-4119)**
**BLACK BISON WATER SERVICES LLC (PA)**
953 W Fulton St U 2 2 U  (60607)
PHONE..............................630 272-5935
Richard C Kreul, CEO
Matt Kruger, Managing Prtnr
Joe Solari, Managing Prtnr
Justin Haigler, Partner
James Schaffner, Vice Pres
EMP: 4
SALES (est): 7.6MM  Privately Held
SIC: 1381  Drilling oil & gas wells

**(G-4120)**
**BLACK POINT STUDIOS LLC**
1937 N Winchester Ave # 1  (60622-1094)
PHONE..............................773 791-2377
Stan Miskiewicz,
Alejandro Gil,
EMP: 27
SQ FT: 4,000

# GEOGRAPHIC SECTION

Chicago - Cook County (G-4147)

SALES: 1.2MM  Privately Held
SIC: 7819  3861  Visual effects production; film, sensitized motion picture, X-ray, still camera, etc.

**(G-4121)**
**BLACK SWAN MANUFACTURING CO**
4540 W Thomas St  (60651-3387)
PHONE..................773 227-3700
Fax: 773 227-3705
Jeffrey Lichten, *President*
Francine Mills Lichten, *Vice Pres*
Juanita Vargas, *Executive Asst*
Luz Galvan, *Admin Sec*
▲ EMP: 17  EST: 1928
SQ FT: 15,000
SALES (est): 5.4MM  Privately Held
WEB: www.blackswanmfg.com
SIC: 2851  2891  3432  3053  Putty; sealing compounds for pipe threads or joints; cement, except linoleum & tile; plumbing fixture fittings & trim; gaskets, packing & sealing devices; chemical preparations; soap & other detergents

**(G-4122)**
**BLANDINGS LTD**
Also Called: Singer, Ralph Co
2635 W Fletcher St  (60618-7109)
PHONE..................773 478-3542
Fax: 773 478-3437
Stanford Smith, *President*
Carole Smith, *Corp Secy*
EMP: 6  EST: 1921
SQ FT: 6,000
SALES (est): 557.2K  Privately Held
SIC: 3961  3911  2395  Costume jewelry; jewelry apparel, non-precious metals; jewelry, precious metal; pleating & stitching

**(G-4123)**
**BLOMMER CHOCOLATE COMPANY**
600 W Kinzie St  (60654-5585)
PHONE..................800 621-1606
Fax: 312 226-4141
Richard Blommer, *President*
Robert Karr, *General Mgr*
Jeffrey Rasinski, *Assistant VP*
Larry Carroll, *Opers Mgr*
Ch-Owen Silva, *Opers Mgr*
▲ EMP: 100
SALES (est): 10.5MM  Privately Held
SIC: 2066  Chocolate

**(G-4124)**
**BLOMMER MACHINERY COMPANY**
600 W Kinzie St  (60654-5512)
PHONE..................312 226-7700
Joseph W Blommer, *President*
Melissa Tisoncik, *Research*
Henry J Blommer Jr, *Treasurer*
EMP: 5  EST: 1939
SQ FT: 10,000
SALES (est): 620K  Privately Held
SIC: 3556  3443  Chocolate processing machinery; fabricated plate work (boiler shop)

**(G-4125)**
**BLUE COMET TRANSPORT INC**
4919 W Parker Ave  (60639-1713)
PHONE..................773 617-9512
Refugio Noria, *Owner*
EMP: 3
SALES (est): 189.1K  Privately Held
SIC: 2448  4491  4789  Cargo containers, wood; marine cargo handling; cargo loading & unloading services

**(G-4126)**
**BLUE SOFTWARE  LLC**
Also Called: Schwak
8430 W Bryn Mawr Ave # 1100  (60631-3473)
PHONE..................773 957-1669
Scott Strong, *CEO*
Paul Leib, *CFO*
Diana Turgeon, *Human Res Dir*
EMP: 87

SALES (est): 7.4MM  Privately Held
SIC: 7372  7311  Business oriented computer software; advertising agencies

**(G-4127)**
**BLUEAIR  INC**
100 N La Salle St # 1900  (60602-3523)
PHONE..................888 258-3247
Bengt Rittri, *President*
Katie Merchant, *Manager*
Nicholas Nowak, *Associate*
▲ EMP: 13
SALES (est): 2.6MM  Privately Held
WEB: www.blueair.com
SIC: 3634  Air purifiers, portable
HQ: Blueair Ab
    Karlavagen 108
    Stockholm 115 2
    867 945-00

**(G-4128)**
**BLUEBIRD LANES**
3900 W Columbus Ave  (60652-3751)
PHONE..................773 582-2828
Fax: 773 582-1233
William Brennan, *Owner*
EMP: 6
SALES (est): 230K  Privately Held
SIC: 3949  Bowling alleys & accessories

**(G-4129)**
**BLUEMASTIFF GROUP LLC**
903 W 35th St Ste 562  (60609-1539)
PHONE..................708 704-3529
Samuel Winters, *Manager*
EMP: 4
SALES (est): 180K  Privately Held
SIC: 1442  Construction sand & gravel

**(G-4130)**
**BLUETOWN SKATEBOARD CO LLC**
1344 N Oakley Blvd Ste 2  (60622-3048)
PHONE..................312 718-4786
Jeshua Neuhaus, *Principal*
EMP: 3  EST: 2012
SALES (est): 151.4K  Privately Held
SIC: 3949  Skateboards

**(G-4131)**
**BLUSTOR PMC  INC**
401 N Michigan Ave # 1200  (60611-4255)
PHONE..................312 265-3058
Finis Conner, *CEO*
Mark Bennett, *COO*
EMP: 8
SALES (est): 445.9K  Privately Held
SIC: 3699  Security control equipment & systems

**(G-4132)**
**BMT PRNTING CRTGRAPH ESPCLISTS**
12941 S Exchange Ave  (60633-1225)
PHONE..................773 646-4700
Brian Twardosz, *Owner*
EMP: 5
SALES (est): 279.6K  Privately Held
SIC: 2752  Commercial printing, lithographic

**(G-4133)**
**BMW SPORTSWEAR INC**
Also Called: Better Mens Wear
3967 W Madison St  (60624-2337)
PHONE..................773 265-0110
Fax: 773 265-0110
Yousuf Tabani, *President*
EMP: 3
SQ FT: 2,400
SALES: 1.6MM  Privately Held
SIC: 5611  5661  2329  Men's & boys' clothing stores; clothing, sportswear, men's & boys'; men's shoes; men's & boys' sportswear & athletic clothing

**(G-4134)**
**BOBBI SCREEN PRINTING**
4573 S Archer Ave  (60632-2961)
PHONE..................773 847-8200
Fax: 773 247-3062
Bobbi Moore, *President*
EMP: 6
SALES: 250K  Privately Held
SIC: 2396  Screen printing on fabric articles

**(G-4135)**
**BOEING AEROSPACE - TAMS INC (HQ)**
100 N Riverside Plz  (60606-2016)
PHONE..................312 544-2000
Cindy Malawy, *President*
Rae Henderson, *Manager*
EMP: 6
SALES (est): 1.4MM
SALES (corp-wide): 94.5B  Publicly Held
SIC: 3721  Airplanes, fixed or rotary wing; helicopters; research & development on aircraft by the manufacturer
PA: The Boeing Company
    100 N Riverside Plz
    Chicago IL 60606
    312 544-2000

**(G-4136)**
**BOEING COMPANY (PA)**
100 N Riverside Plz  (60606-2016)
P.O. Box 3707, Seattle WA  (98124-2207)
PHONE..................312 544-2000
Fax: 312 544-2082
Dennis A Muilenburg, *Ch of Bd*
Antonio De Palma, *Managing Dir*
J Michael Luttig, *Exec VP*
Theodore Colbert III, *Senior VP*
Gregory L Hyslop, *Senior VP*
EMP: 277  EST: 1916
SALES: 94.5B  Publicly Held
WEB: www.boeing.com
SIC: 3721  3663  3761  3764  Airplanes, fixed or rotary wing; helicopters; research & development on aircraft by the manufacturer; airborne radio communications equipment; guided missiles, complete; guided missiles & space vehicles, research & development; propulsion units for guided missiles & space vehicles; guided missile & space vehicle engines, research & devel.; search & navigation equipment; defense systems & equipment; aircraft control systems, electronic; navigational systems & instruments; aircraft body & wing assemblies & parts

**(G-4137)**
**BOEING IRVING COMPANY**
100 N Riverside Plz Fl 35  (60606-2016)
PHONE..................312 544-2000
James A Bell, *President*
Julia Ho, *Engineer*
Andrew Matthews, *Engineer*
Lisa Dantzler, *Sales Dir*
EMP: 1001
SALES (est): 127MM
SALES (corp-wide): 94.5B  Publicly Held
SIC: 3663  Airborne radio communications equipment
PA: The Boeing Company
    100 N Riverside Plz
    Chicago IL 60606
    312 544-2000

**(G-4138)**
**BOEING LTS INC**
100 N Riverside Plz  (60606-2016)
PHONE..................312 544-2000
Jim McNerney, *President*
EMP: 286
SALES (est): 35.4MM
SALES (corp-wide): 94.5B  Publicly Held
SIC: 3721  Airplanes, fixed or rotary wing
PA: The Boeing Company
    100 N Riverside Plz
    Chicago IL 60606
    312 544-2000

**(G-4139)**
**BOLD DIAGNOSTICS  LLC**
222 Merchandise Mart Plz  (60654-1103)
PHONE..................806 543-5743
Kyle Miller, *Manager*
Sean Connell, *Manager*
Jay Pandit, *Manager*
EMP: 4  EST: 2015
SALES (est): 239K  Privately Held
SIC: 3841  7389  Blood pressure apparatus;

**(G-4140)**
**BOM BON CORP**
3748 W 26th St  (60623-3826)
PHONE..................773 277-8777
Louis Perea, *Principal*

EMP: 8
SALES (est): 615.2K  Privately Held
SIC: 2051  Cakes, bakery: except frozen

**(G-4141)**
**BONANNO VINTNERS  LLC**
2614 N Paulina St  (60614-1018)
P.O. Box 57239  (60657-7347)
PHONE..................773 477-8351
Bonanno Matthew, *Principal*
Matthew Bonanno, *Webmaster*
EMP: 4
SALES (est): 217.1K  Privately Held
SIC: 2084  Wines, brandy & brandy spirits

**(G-4142)**
**BONE & RATTLE  INC**
Also Called: R.ryvette
320 W Ohio St Ste 3w  (60654-7887)
PHONE..................312 813-8830
Sue Chang,
EMP: 7
SALES (est): 436.4K  Privately Held
SIC: 3144  Dress shoes, women's

**(G-4143)**
**BOOKENDS PUBLISHING**
2001 N Halsted St Ste 201  (60614-4365)
PHONE..................312 988-1500
Thomas Kuczmarski, *Partner*
Susan Kuczmarski, *Partner*
Lyn Prandall, *Finance Mgr*
EMP: 3
SALES (est): 188K  Privately Held
SIC: 2731  Books: publishing & printing

**(G-4144)**
**BOOTHS AND UPHOLSTERY BY RAY**
Also Called: Ray's Booths
1400 W 37th St  (60609-2109)
PHONE..................773 523-3355
Fax: 773 523-1018
Ray Irizarry, *Owner*
EMP: 7
SQ FT: 10,000
SALES: 52K  Privately Held
WEB: www.raysbooths.com
SIC: 2599  2541  7641  2531  Bar furniture; counter & sink tops; reupholstery & furniture repair; public building & related furniture; upholstered household furniture

**(G-4145)**
**BORGWARNER TRANSM SYSTEMS INC**
10807 S Fairfield Ave  (60655-1722)
PHONE..................815 469-7819
Michael Oswald, *Manager*
EMP: 438
SALES (corp-wide): 9B  Publicly Held
SIC: 3714  Transmission housings or parts, motor vehicle
HQ: Borgwarner Transmission Systems Inc.
    3800 Automation Way # 500
    Auburn Hills MI 48326
    248 754-9200

**(G-4146)**
**BORNY ENTERPRISE CORP** ✪
625 N Michigan Ave # 1001  (60611-3110)
PHONE..................646 662-1514
Oleg Arepyev, *President*
EMP: 4  EST: 2016
SALES (est): 145.3K  Privately Held
SIC: 3452  Bolts, nuts, rivets & washers

**(G-4147)**
**BOSCH SFTWR INNOVATIONS CORP**
161 N Clark St Ste 3550  (60601-3333)
PHONE..................312 368-2500
David Kim, *CEO*
Kieran Hennessey, *Sales Staff*
Sean Guargena, *Sales Associate*
Christina Gruen, *Marketing Mgr*
Ashley Wenson, *Marketing Staff*
EMP: 40
SQ FT: 4,216
SALES (est): 7.5MM
SALES (corp-wide): 236.4MM  Privately Held
WEB: www.de.bosch.com
SIC: 7372  Prepackaged software

## Chicago - Cook County (G-4148) — GEOGRAPHIC SECTION

HQ: Robert Bosch Gesellschaft Mit
Beschrankter Haftung
Robert-Bosch-Platz 1
Gerlingen  70839
711 811-0

**(G-4148)**
**BOSLEY MEDICAL INSTITUTE**
676 N Michigan Ave # 3850  (60611-2883)
PHONE.................................312 642-5252
EMP: 4
SALES (est): 411.7K  **Privately Held**
SIC: 3841  Surgical & medical instruments

**(G-4149)**
**BOSTIC PUBLISHING COMPANY**
3236 N Sacramento Ave  (60618-5826)
PHONE.................................773 551-7065
James Bostic, President
EMP: 2
SALES (est): 254.9K  **Privately Held**
SIC: 2732  Book printing

**(G-4150)**
**BOWEN  GUERRERO & HOWE LLC**
825 W Chicago Ave  (60642-5408)
PHONE.................................312 447-2370
Sean Conner, Editor
Amie Kesler, Editor
Corey Bowen, Mng Member
EMP: 95
SQ FT: 9,000
SALES (est): 1.2MM  **Privately Held**
SIC: 2721  Magazines: publishing only, not printed on site

**(G-4151)**
**BOX FORM  INC**
1334 W 43rd St  (60609-3308)
PHONE.................................773 927-8808
Fax: 773 927-8891
Amanda Choi, CFO
EMP: 25
SQ FT: 55,000
SALES (est): 4.9MM  **Privately Held**
SIC: 2656  2657  Paper cups, plates, dishes & utensils; folding paperboard boxes

**(G-4152)**
**BOZKI  INC**
205 W Wacker Dr Ste 1320  (60606-1447)
PHONE.................................312 767-2122
EMP: 5
SALES (est): 224.8K  **Privately Held**
SIC: 3679  Headphones, radio

**(G-4153)**
**BP PRODUCTS NORTH AMERICA INC**
BP Oil Supply, Company
30 S Wacker Dr Ste 900  (60606-7403)
PHONE.................................312 594-7689
EMP: 99
SALES (corp-wide): 222.8B  **Privately Held**
SIC: 2911  5172  Petroleum Refiner Whol Petroleum Products
HQ: Bp Products North America Inc.
501 Westlake Park Blvd
Houston TX 77079
281 366-2000

**(G-4154)**
**BPN CHICAGO**
875 N Michigan Ave # 1850  (60611-2975)
PHONE.................................312 799-4100
Mauricio Sabogal, CEO
Elizabeth Ross, President
Donald Morrison, COO
Neil Smith, Senior VP
EMP: 20
SALES (est): 2.7MM  **Privately Held**
SIC: 7311  3695  Advertising consultant; magnetic & optical recording media

**(G-4155)**
**BRAINSTORM USA**
3525 W Peterson Ave # 107  (60659-3324)
PHONE.................................773 509-1227
Fax: 773 509-1443
Victoria Garces, Owner
EMP: 15
SALES (est): 613.6K  **Privately Held**
WEB: www.brainstormusa.com
SIC: 7372  Prepackaged software

**(G-4156)**
**BRAINWARE COMPANY**
4802 N Broadway St 201a  (60640-3622)
P.O. Box 4099037  (60640)
PHONE.................................773 250-6465
Roger Stark, CEO
EMP: 4
SQ FT: 1,700
SALES (est): 299.6K  **Privately Held**
SIC: 7372  Educational computer software

**(G-4157)**
**BRAINWORX STUDIO**
6531 N Albany Ave  (60645-4103)
PHONE.................................773 743-8200
Fax: 773 743-9334
Mercedes Santos, President
Theresa Volpe, Vice Pres
Sandy Petroshius, Director
EMP: 15
SQ FT: 5,000
SALES (est): 1.1MM  **Privately Held**
WEB: www.brainworxstudio.com
SIC: 2731  Book publishing

**(G-4158)**
**BRASS CREATIONS INC**
5610 W Bloomingdale Ave # 4  (60639-4113)
PHONE.................................773 237-7755
Fax: 773 237-7755
Bill Sobanski, President
EMP: 5
SQ FT: 6,000
SALES: 200K  **Privately Held**
SIC: 3312  Structural shapes & pilings, steel

**(G-4159)**
**BREAKER PRESS CO INC**
Also Called: Commercial Printers
2421 S Western Ave  (60608-4704)
PHONE.................................773 927-1666
Fax: 773 927-3676
Richard J Lewandowski, President
Michael J Lewandowsk, Vice Pres
EMP: 6
SQ FT: 2,500
SALES: 1.1MM  **Privately Held**
WEB: www.breakerpress.com
SIC: 2752  2791  Commercial printing, offset; typesetting, computer controlled

**(G-4160)**
**BREAKROOM BREWERY**
2925 W Montrose Ave  (60618-1403)
PHONE.................................773 564-9534
Eric Padilla, Principal
EMP: 9
SALES (est): 962.3K  **Privately Held**
SIC: 2082  Malt beverages

**(G-4161)**
**BRENNER TANK SERVICES LLC**
803 E 120th St  (60628-5743)
PHONE.................................773 468-6390
Robert Agnew, Branch Mgr
EMP: 5
SALES (corp-wide): 1.8B  **Publicly Held**
SIC: 3443  Tanks for tank trucks, metal plate
HQ: Brenner Tank Services Llc
N3760 Hwys 12 & 16 E
Mauston WI 53948
608 847-4131

**(G-4162)**
**BREVITY  LLC**
1750 N Clybourn Ave  (60614-9356)
PHONE.................................312 375-3996
Leonard Wanger,
EMP: 12
SALES (est): 256K  **Privately Held**
SIC: 7372  Prepackaged Software Services

**(G-4163)**
**BREWERS BOTTLERS & BEV CORP**
7233 N Sheridan Rd Ste 5  (60626-5495)
PHONE.................................773 262-9711
EMP: 6
SALES (est): 615.2K  **Privately Held**
SIC: 2086  Bottled & canned soft drinks

**(G-4164)**
**BRICKS INC**
3425 S Kedzie Ave Ste 1  (60623-5181)
PHONE.................................773 523-5718
Fax: 773 523-1458
Kim Schmitt, Owner
EMP: 14
SALES (corp-wide): 6.9MM  **Privately Held**
WEB: www.bricksinc.net
SIC: 3271  Concrete block & brick
PA: Bricks Inc
723 S Lasalle St
Aurora IL 60505
630 897-6926

**(G-4165)**
**BRIDGELINE DIGITAL  INC**
30 N La Salle St Ste 2000  (60602-4346)
PHONE.................................312 784-5720
EMP: 6
SALES (corp-wide): 15.9MM  **Publicly Held**
SIC: 7372  Prepackaged software
PA: Bridgeline Digital, Inc.
80 Blanchard Rd
Burlington MA 01803
781 376-5555

**(G-4166)**
**BRIDGEPORT PHARMACY INC**
3201 S Wallace St  (60616-3501)
PHONE.................................312 326-3200
Fax: 312 791-9650
Snehal Bhavsar, President
EMP: 5
SALES (est): 783.2K  **Privately Held**
SIC: 2834  Adrenal pharmaceutical preparations

**(G-4167)**
**BRIDGEPORT STEEL SALES INC**
2730 S Hillock Ave  (60608-5712)
PHONE.................................312 326-4800
Fax: 312 326-7967
Willie Conrad, President
Bernice Jordan, Admin Sec
EMP: 10
SQ FT: 5,000
SALES (est): 2.2MM  **Privately Held**
SIC: 3441  Fabricated structural metal

**(G-4168)**
**BRIDGFORD FOODS CORPORATION**
Also Called: Bridgford Marketing
170 N Green St  (60607-2313)
PHONE.................................312 733-0300
Fax: 312 733-0320
Allan L Bridgford Sr, CEO
H W Bridgford, Ch of Bd
John V Simmons, President
William L Bridgford, Chairman
Barren Bridgford, COO
▲ EMP: 375
SQ FT: 225,000
SALES (est): 103.6MM
SALES (corp-wide): 140MM  **Publicly Held**
WEB: www.bridgford.com
SIC: 2013  Prepared pork products from purchased pork; prepared beef products from purchased beef; sausages from purchased meat; sausages & related products, from purchased meat
HQ: Bridgford Foods Corporation
1308 N Patt St
Anaheim CA 92801
714 526-5533

**(G-4169)**
**BRIGHT METALS FINISHING CORP**
3905 W Armitage Ave  (60647-3405)
PHONE.................................773 486-2312
Randall Smith, President
Judy Lambros,
EMP: 8
SALES (est): 696.5K  **Privately Held**
SIC: 3471  Anodizing (plating) of metals or formed products

**(G-4170)**
**BRITE DENTAL  PC (PA)**
Also Called: American Brite Dental
5917 S Pulaski Rd  (60629-4515)
PHONE.................................773 735-8353
Fadi Aqeil, President
EMP: 33
SALES (est): 30.9MM  **Privately Held**
SIC: 3843  Enamels, dentists'

**(G-4171)**
**BRITE SITE SUPPLY INC**
4616 W Fullerton Ave  (60639-1816)
PHONE.................................773 772-7300
Fax: 773 772-7631
Andreas Vassilos, President
EMP: 5
SQ FT: 18,000
SALES (est): 600K  **Privately Held**
WEB: www.britesite.net
SIC: 2842  5087  2899  Specialty cleaning preparations; janitors' supplies; chemical preparations

**(G-4172)**
**BRITESEED  LLC**
4660 N Ravenswood Ave  (60640-4510)
PHONE.................................206 384-0311
Hariharan Subramanian, Vice Pres
Mayank Vijayvergia, Marketing Staff
Jonathan Gunn, CTO
Paul Fehrenbacher,
EMP: 5
SALES (est): 489.5K  **Privately Held**
SIC: 3841  Surgical & medical instruments

**(G-4173)**
**BROCKWAY STANDARD INC**
1440 S Kilbourn Ave  (60623-1033)
PHONE.................................773 893-2100
William Eichlin, Principal
EMP: 4
SALES (est): 265.7K  **Privately Held**
SIC: 3411  Metal cans

**(G-4174)**
**BROHMAN INDUSTRIES  INC**
2635 N Kildare Ave  (60639-2051)
PHONE.................................630 761-8160
Fax: 773 489-6584
Herschel Brohman, President
Greg Rau, Managing Dir
Jim Russell, Managing Dir
Rand Thomas, Vice Pres
Thomas Rand, VP Finance
EMP: 18
SQ FT: 30,000
SALES (est): 4.5MM  **Privately Held**
WEB: www.harbro.net
SIC: 2679  2673  Labels, paper: made from purchased material; plastic bags: made from purchased materials

**(G-4175)**
**BRONZE MEMORIAL INC**
Also Called: Wagner Brass Foundry
1842 N Elston Ave  (60642-1216)
PHONE.................................773 276-7972
Richard Wagner, President
EMP: 7
SQ FT: 5,000
SALES (est): 480K  **Privately Held**
SIC: 3499  Tablets, bronze or other metal

**(G-4176)**
**BROS LITHOGRAPHING COMPANY**
1326 W Washington Blvd  (60607-1984)
PHONE.................................312 666-0919
Fax: 312 666-0441
EMP: 9 EST: 1945
SQ FT: 38,000
SALES: 900K  **Privately Held**
SIC: 2752  Lithographic Commercial Printing

**(G-4177)**
**BROWN & MILLER LITERARY ASSOC**
410 S Michigan Ave # 460  (60605-1390)
PHONE.................................312 922-3063
Danielle Egan-Miller, President
Danielle Egan Miller, President
Lawrence Browne, Agent
EMP: 3

SALES (est): 247.2K  Privately Held
WEB: www.mpdinc.net
SIC: 2731  Book publishing

**(G-4178)**
**BROWN LINE METAL WORKS LLC**
4001 N Ravenswood Ave 303a (60613-6126)
PHONE.....................312 884-7644
James Werner,
▲ EMP: 6
SALES (est): 660.4K  Privately Held
SIC: 3621  Torque motors, electric

**(G-4179)**
**BRUSS COMPANY**
Also Called: Golden Trophy Steaks
3548 N Kostner Ave (60641-3898)
PHONE.....................773 282-2900
Fax: 773 282-6966
Donnie Smith, *President*
Anthony Cericola, *General Mgr*
Anthony Cericoa, *Principal*
Dan Bernkopf, *Vice Pres*
Maryellen Mulligan, *Engineer*
▲ EMP: 230 EST: 1937
SQ FT: 52,000
SALES (est): 126.6MM
SALES (corp-wide): 36.8B  Publicly Held
WEB: www.goldentrophysteaks.com
SIC: 5147  5142  2013  2011  Meats, fresh; meat, frozen; packaged; sausages & other prepared meats; meat packing plants
HQ: Tyson Fresh Meats, Inc.
    800 Stevens Port Dr
    Dakota Dunes SD 57049
    605 235-2061

**(G-4180)**
**BSC IMPORTS INCORPORATED**
Also Called: Purple Clay Pottery
213 N Morgan St Unit 2c (60607-1721)
PHONE.....................773 844-4788
▲ EMP: 3
SQ FT: 2,000
SALES (est): 120K  Privately Held
SIC: 3269  Mfg Pottery Products

**(G-4181)**
**BUCKTOWN POLYMERS**
1658 N Milwaukee Ave # 421 (60647-6905)
PHONE.....................312 436-1460
EMP: 2
SALES (est): 277.5K  Privately Held
SIC: 5162  2671  Plastics products; packaging paper & plastics film, coated & laminated

**(G-4182)**
**BUFF & GO INC**
47 W Polk St Ste 100-558 (60605-2000)
P.O. Box 8558 (60680-8558)
PHONE.....................773 719-4436
Leatrice Woody, *President*
EMP: 3
SALES (est): 160K  Privately Held
SIC: 3999  5999  Furniture, barber & beauty shop; business machines & equipment

**(G-4183)**
**BULLEN MIDWEST  INC (PA)**
Also Called: Nuance Solutions
900 E 103rd St Ste D (60628-3091)
PHONE.....................773 785-2300
Fax: 773 785-9969
Jim Flanagan, *President*
Cornelius J Houtsma, *Exec VP*
Matt Ahrens, *Vice Pres*
John J Flanagan Jr, *Vice Pres*
William G Haag, *Vice Pres*
EMP: 20
SQ FT: 64,000
SALES (est): 26.2MM  Privately Held
WEB: www.nuancesol.com
SIC: 2841  2842  2819  2869  Soap: granulated, liquid, cake, flaked or chip; detergents, synthetic organic or inorganic alkaline; scouring compounds; floor waxes; disinfectants, household or industrial plant; industrial inorganic chemicals; industrial organic chemicals

**(G-4184)**
**BUREAU OF NATIONAL AFFAIRS**
6692 N Sioux Ave (60646-2845)
PHONE.....................773 775-8801
Michael Bologna, *President*
EMP: 4
SALES (est): 212.2K  Privately Held
WEB: www.cwit2.org
SIC: 2741  Miscellaneous publishing

**(G-4185)**
**BURGOPAK LIMITED**
213 W Institute Pl # 301 (60610-3121)
PHONE.....................312 255-0827
Fax: 312 255-0972
Jeremy Light, *Branch Mgr*
EMP: 20  Privately Held
SIC: 2671  7336  Packaging paper & plastics film, coated & laminated; commercial art & graphic design
HQ: Burgopak Limited
    Unit A, Flatiron Yard
    London
    207 089-1950

**(G-4186)**
**BURRITO BEACH LLC**
233 N Michigan Ave C023 (60601-5502)
PHONE.....................312 861-1986
Greg Chusble, *Owner*
EMP: 11  Privately Held
SIC: 3421  Table & food cutlery, including butchers'
PA: Burrito Beach L.L.C.
    414 N Orleans St Ste 402
    Chicago IL 60654

**(G-4187)**
**BUSINESS FORMS FINISHING SVC**
5410 S Sayre Ave (60638-2218)
PHONE.....................773 229-0230
Fax: 708 222-6808
Raymond Wojcik, *President*
Joe Martin, *Vice Pres*
Len Hauskey, *Asst Treas*
EMP: 6 EST: 1956
SQ FT: 6,000
SALES (est): 350K  Privately Held
SIC: 2789  2675  Binding only: books, pamphlets, magazines, etc.; die-cut paper & board

**(G-4188)**
**BUSINESS INSURANCE (PA)**
150 N Michigan Ave # 1800 (60601-7553)
PHONE.....................877 812-1587
Fax: 312 280-3174
Keith Crain, *CEO*
Nick White, *Publisher*
Martin J Ross III, *Managing Dir*
Charmain Benton, *Editor*
Stuart Collins, *Editor*
EMP: 20
SALES (est): 1.7MM  Privately Held
WEB: www.businessinsurance.com
SIC: 2721  Periodicals

**(G-4189)**
**BUSINESS SYSTEMS CONSULTANTS**
333 N Michigan Ave # 912 (60601-3965)
PHONE.....................312 553-1253
Fax: 312 553-1256
Jon R Guenther, *President*
Will Steinke, *Accountant*
EMP: 12
SQ FT: 3,000
SALES (est): 1MM  Privately Held
WEB: www.bscichicago.com
SIC: 7372  Prepackaged software

**(G-4190)**
**BUSINESS VALUATION GROUP INC**
400 N La Salle Dr # 3905 (60654-8539)
PHONE.....................312 595-1900
Thomas E Holl, *President*
EMP: 3
SALES (est): 310K  Privately Held
WEB: www.bvgi.net
SIC: 3578  7389  Calculating & accounting equipment; financial services

**(G-4191)**
**BUSTER SERVICES  INC**
Also Called: Fiber Options Div
3301 W 47th Pl (60632-3012)
PHONE.....................773 247-2070
Michael J Finn, *President*
David Levinson, *Vice Pres*
Mary Bochenek, *Accounts Mgr*
EMP: 50
SQ FT: 40,000
SALES (est): 15.1MM  Privately Held
WEB: www.recyclingservices.com
SIC: 5093  2611  Waste paper & cloth materials; pulp mills

**(G-4192)**
**BUSY BEAVER BUTTON COMPANY**
3407 W Armitage Ave (60647-3719)
PHONE.....................773 645-3359
Christen Carter, *President*
Denise Gibson, *Marketing Staff*
Joel Carter, *Manager*
EMP: 6
SALES (est): 675K  Privately Held
SIC: 3999  Buttons: Red Cross, union, identification

**(G-4193)**
**BUTCHER BLOCK FURN BY ONEILL**
Also Called: O'Neill Products
555 W 16th St (60616-1146)
PHONE.....................312 666-9144
Larry Grossmann, *President*
Don Marubio, *General Mgr*
EMP: 6
SALES (est): 518.5K  Privately Held
SIC: 2511  Wood household furniture

**(G-4194)**
**BWAY CORPORATION**
3200 S Kilbourn Ave (60623-4829)
PHONE.....................773 254-8700
Terry Kline, *CEO*
Steve Johnson, *Plant Mgr*
Charles Cleary, *Accountant*
Matt Sawicki, *Manager*
EMP: 117
SALES (corp-wide): 831.7MM  Privately Held
SIC: 3411  3089  Metal cans; plastic containers, except foam
HQ: Bway Corporation
    8607 Roberts Dr Ste 250
    Atlanta GA 30350
    770 645-4800

**(G-4195)**
**BWAY PARENT COMPANY  INC (HQ)**
3200 S Kilbourn Ave (60623-4829)
PHONE.....................773 890-3300
Kenneth M Roessler, *CEO*
Thomas S Souleles, *President*
Tarek Maguid, *COO*
Leslie L Bradshaw, *Exec VP*
Michael A Noel, *Exec VP*
EMP: 14
SALES (est): 629.2MM  Privately Held
SIC: 3411  3089  Metal cans; can lids & ends, metal; oil cans, metal; plastic containers, except foam; tubs, plastic (containers)

**(G-4196)**
**BYCAP  INC**
5505 N Wolcott Ave (60640-1019)
PHONE.....................773 561-4976
Fax: 773 561-5095
Peter C Berry, *President*
Joanne Tecic, *Controller*
Joanne P Tecic, *Admin Sec*
EMP: 20
SALES (est): 3MM  Privately Held
WEB: www.bycap.com
SIC: 3675  3577  Electronic capacitors; computer peripheral equipment

**(G-4197)**
**BYTEBIN LLC**
516 N Ogden Ave 55 (60642-6421)
PHONE.....................312 286-0740
Michael Smith,
Jason Pearl,
Quinn M Stephens,
EMP: 3
SALES (est): 146.1K  Privately Held
SIC: 7371  7372  Computer software development; application computer software

**(G-4198)**
**C & B WELDERS INC**
2645 W Monroe St (60612-2820)
PHONE.....................773 722-0097
Fax: 773 722-8107
Arlan Burton, *President*
Marcy Salinas, *Manager*
Julie Burton, *Admin Sec*
EMP: 8
SQ FT: 10,000
SALES (est): 300K  Privately Held
SIC: 7692  Welding repair

**(G-4199)**
**C & C BAKERY INC**
2655 W Huron St (60612-1142)
PHONE.....................773 276-4233
John M Bottigliero, *President*
Carl Phillips, *Admin Sec*
EMP: 3 EST: 1953
SQ FT: 2,500
SALES (est): 150K  Privately Held
SIC: 2051  Bread, all types (white, wheat, rye, etc): fresh or frozen

**(G-4200)**
**C & C CAN CO INC**
1838 W Grand Ave (60622-6230)
PHONE.....................312 421-2372
William Choporis, *President*
Antonia Choporis, *Admin Sec*
EMP: 3 EST: 1939
SQ FT: 2,500
SALES (est): 124K  Privately Held
SIC: 3469  Stamping metal for the trade

**(G-4201)**
**C & L PRINTING COMPANY**
228 S Wabash Ave Ste 260 (60604-2398)
PHONE.....................312 235-0380
Fax: 312 235-0380
Stephen Chan, *Partner*
Jack Lee, *Partner*
Mike Chan, *Manager*
EMP: 10
SALES (est): 1.4MM  Privately Held
WEB: www.candlprinting.com
SIC: 2752  Commercial printing, lithographic

**(G-4202)**
**C & S STEEL RULE DIE CO INC**
4305 S Homan Ave (60632-3523)
PHONE.....................773 254-4027
Charles Spicuzza, *President*
EMP: 4
SQ FT: 3,500
SALES (est): 250K  Privately Held
SIC: 3544  Dies, steel rule

**(G-4203)**
**C F ANDERSON & CO**
701 S Lasalle St Fl 2 (60605)
PHONE.....................312 341-0850
Fax: 312 341-9255
Frank Lipo, *President*
John Lipo, *Opers-Prdtn-Mfg*
Mary Vrablik, *Personnel*
Thomas Lipo, *Officer*
EMP: 10
SQ FT: 12,000
SALES (est): 500K  Privately Held
WEB: www.clevelandfolder.com
SIC: 3555  3554  2631  Printing trades machinery; folding machines, paper; paperboard mills

**(G-4204)**
**C H MILLERY LLC**
6430 S Ashland Ave (60636-2717)
PHONE.....................773 476-7525
Audrey Wright,
EMP: 15
SQ FT: 8,500
SALES (est): 1.1MM  Privately Held
SIC: 2389  Uniforms & vestments

## Chicago - Cook County (G-4205)

**(G-4205)**
**C STREETER ENTERPRISE**
28 E Jackson Blvd Fl 10 (60604-2263)
PHONE..................................773 858-4388
Cynthia Streeter, *President*
EMP: 4
SALES: 45K **Privately Held**
SIC: 3633 Household laundry equipment

**(G-4206)**
**C2 IMAGING LLC**
600 W Van Buren St # 604 (60607-3760)
PHONE..................................312 238-3800
Glen Hoffmann, *Manager*
EMP: 20 **Privately Held**
SIC: 2754 2759 Commercial printing, gravure; commercial printing
PA: C2 Imaging, Llc
  201 Plaza Two
  Jersey City NJ 07311

**(G-4207)**
**CA INC**
123 N Wacker Dr Ste 2125 (60606-1766)
PHONE..................................312 201-8557
EMP: 7
SALES (corp-wide): 4.2B **Publicly Held**
PA: Ca, Inc.
  520 Madison Ave Fl 22
  New York NY 10022
  800 225-5224

**(G-4208)**
**CABANAS MANUFACTURING JEWELERS**
9 N Wabash Ave Ste 555 (60602-4729)
PHONE..................................312 726-0333
Edward Guini, *President*
EMP: 4
SQ FT: 900
SALES: 500K **Privately Held**
SIC: 3911 Jewelry, precious metal

**(G-4209)**
**CABWORKS LLC**
Also Called: Wsm Enterprises
2701 N Pulaski Rd (60639-2119)
PHONE..................................773 588-1731
Marshall Waksmundzki,
Shaun Summerville,
Richard Waksmunski,
EMP: 20
SQ FT: 35,000
SALES (est): 4.3MM **Privately Held**
WEB: www.cabworks.com
SIC: 3534 Elevators & equipment

**(G-4210)**
**CADE COMMUNICATIONS INC**
3018 N Sheridan Rd Apt 2s (60657-5525)
PHONE..................................773 477-7184
Michel K Cade, *President*
Ann H Cade, *Vice Pres*
EMP: 2
SALES: 220K **Privately Held**
WEB: www.cadecommunications.com
SIC: 2741 8748 Miscellaneous publishing; publishing consultant

**(G-4211)**
**CADUCEUS COMMUNICATIONS INC**
Also Called: Craft Beer Institute
4043 N Ravenswood Ave # 309 (60613-1155)
PHONE..................................773 549-4800
Ray Daniels, *President*
Virginia Thomas, *Manager*
EMP: 6
SQ FT: 1,200
SALES (est): 661.7K **Privately Held**
SIC: 8743 2721 Public relations & publicity; periodicals

**(G-4212)**
**CAFETINE PANIO**
2706 W Division St (60622-2853)
PHONE..................................773 697-8007
Beti Guevara, *Owner*
EMP: 4 EST: 2011
SALES (est): 288.4K **Privately Held**
SIC: 3421 Table & food cutlery, including butchers'

**(G-4213)**
**CAL-ILL GASKET CO**
4716 W Rice St (60651-3329)
PHONE..................................773 287-9605
Brian Burkross, *President*
Joann Gram, *Office Mgr*
EMP: 13
SQ FT: 9,500
SALES (est): 1.7MM **Privately Held**
SIC: 3496 3089 3053 Miscellaneous fabricated wire products; extruded finished plastic products; gaskets, all materials

**(G-4214)**
**CALDWELL LETTER SERVICE INC**
4500 S Kolin Ave Ste 1 (60632-4461)
PHONE..................................773 847-0708
Fax: 312 455-0717
Patricia K Perry, *President*
Will J Perry, *Vice Pres*
EMP: 25
SQ FT: 130,000
SALES (est): 4.2MM **Privately Held**
WEB: www.cls4mail.com
SIC: 7331 2752 Mailing service; commercial printing, offset

**(G-4215)**
**CALIFORNIA MUFFLER AND BRAKES**
5059 S California Ave (60632-2006)
PHONE..................................773 776-8990
Magnolia Zepeda, *Principal*
EMP: 5
SALES (est): 67.2K **Privately Held**
SIC: 3714 7538 Mufflers (exhaust), motor vehicle; general automotive repair shops

**(G-4216)**
**CALLAHAN MINING CORPORATION**
Also Called: Galena Mine Division
104 S Michigan Ave # 900 (60603-5906)
PHONE..................................312 489-5800
James A Sabala, *Treasurer*
Tom Angelos, *Controller*
William Boyd, *Admin Sec*
▼ EMP: 74
SQ FT: 10,000
SALES: 30MM
SALES (corp-wide): 665.7MM **Publicly Held**
SIC: 1044 Silver ores
PA: Coeur Mining, Inc.
  104 S Michigan Ave # 900
  Chicago IL 60603
  312 489-5800

**(G-4217)**
**CALLPOD INC**
850 W Jackson Blvd # 400 (60607-3032)
PHONE..................................312 829-2680
Darren G Guccione, *President*
Lauren Word, *Sales Staff*
Craig Lurey, *CTO*
▲ EMP: 13
SALES (est): 3.4MM **Privately Held**
WEB: www.callpod.com
SIC: 3663 Microwave communication equipment

**(G-4218)**
**CALUMET CONTAINER CORP**
12440 S Stony Island Ave (60633-2404)
PHONE..................................773 646-3653
Dale Fancher, *President*
▲ EMP: 10
SALES (est): 910K **Privately Held**
SIC: 3089 Plastic containers, except foam

**(G-4219)**
**CALUMET RUBBER CORP**
3545 S Normal Ave Ste A (60609-1799)
PHONE..................................773 536-6350
Fax: 773 536-6378
Edward T Woike, *President*
EMP: 5
SQ FT: 18,000
SALES (est): 1MM **Privately Held**
SIC: 3061 Appliance rubber goods (mechanical)

**(G-4220)**
**CAM SYSTEMS**
20 N Wacker Dr Ste 4015 (60606-3111)
PHONE..................................800 208-3244
Robert Nienhouse, *CEO*
EMP: 3
SALES (est): 274.2K **Privately Held**
SIC: 7389 2721 ; periodicals

**(G-4221)**
**CAMBRIDGE BRANDS MFG INC (DH)**
7401 S Cicero Ave (60629-5818)
PHONE..................................773 838-3400
Ellen R Gordon, *President*
G Howard Ember Jr, *Vice Pres*
Barry Bowen, *Treasurer*
Lucille Crocille, *Exec Sec*
EMP: 4
SALES (est): 32.6MM
SALES (corp-wide): 521.1MM **Publicly Held**
SIC: 2064 Candy & other confectionery products

**(G-4222)**
**CAMEO CONTAINER CORPORATION**
1415 W 44th St (60609-3333)
PHONE..................................773 254-1030
Fax: 773 254-5817
Patrick Moore, *President*
Chuck Hynes, *Controller*
Paul Mueller, *Manager*
EMP: 239
SQ FT: 165,000
SALES (est): 34.9MM **Privately Held**
WEB: www.cameocontainer.com
SIC: 2653 2542 Boxes, corrugated: made from purchased materials; partitions & fixtures, except wood

**(G-4223)**
**CAMERON ELECTRIC MOTOR CORP**
551 W Lexington St (60607-4308)
PHONE..................................312 939-5770
John Nomikos, *President*
Soter Nomikos, *Corp Secy*
Mary Nomikos, *Vice Pres*
EMP: 10
SQ FT: 4,500
SALES (est): 1.1MM **Privately Held**
SIC: 7694 Electric motor repair; rebuilding motors, except automotive

**(G-4224)**
**CAMMUN LLC**
345 N Canal St Apt 1408 (60606-1366)
PHONE..................................312 628-1201
Kevin Day, *CTO*
EMP: 5
SALES (est): 130.5K **Privately Held**
SIC: 2741

**(G-4225)**
**CAMS INC**
1960 N Lincoln Park W # 2207 (60614-5487)
PHONE..................................773 929-3656
William S Griffith, *President*
Tim Knudsen, *Finance*
Scott Kolar, *Admin Sec*
EMP: 3
SALES: 500K **Privately Held**
SIC: 3545 3599 Cams (machine tool accessories); machine shop, jobbing & repair

**(G-4226)**
**CANDYALITY (PA)**
3737 N Southport Ave # 1 (60613-6185)
PHONE..................................773 472-7800
Fax: 773 472-7876
Terese Mc Donald, *Owner*
EMP: 7
SALES (est): 720K **Privately Held**
SIC: 2064 Candy & other confectionery products

**(G-4227)**
**CANTARERO PALLETS INC**
1900 N Austin Ave (60639-5010)
PHONE..................................773 413-7017
Anwar Cantarero, *President*
EMP: 8 EST: 2011
SALES (est): 1MM **Privately Held**
SIC: 2448 Pallets, wood & wood with metal

**(G-4228)**
**CANYON FOODS INC**
1150 W 40th St (60609-2505)
PHONE..................................773 890-9888
EMP: 3
SALES (est): 205.7K **Privately Held**
SIC: 2099 Food preparations

**(G-4229)**
**CAPITOL CARTON COMPANY (PA)**
Also Called: Capitol Containers
346 N Justine St Ste 406 (60607-1014)
PHONE..................................312 563-9690
Fax: 312 563-9780
Neil R Gurevitz, *President*
Jeffery Gurebitz, *Corp Secy*
Pat Mazzulo, *Accountant*
Tim Milligan, *Sales Staff*
Catherine Milligan, *Manager*
EMP: 24
SQ FT: 70,000
SALES (est): 3.5MM **Privately Held**
SIC: 2653 2657 2655 2631 Boxes, corrugated: made from purchased materials; folding paperboard boxes; fiber cans, drums & similar products; paperboard mills; partitions & fixtures, except wood; office furniture, except wood

**(G-4230)**
**CAPITOL CARTON COMPANY**
1917 W Walnut St (60612-2405)
PHONE..................................312 491-2220
Fax: 312 491-2221
James Wodarczyk, *Branch Mgr*
EMP: 25
SALES (corp-wide): 3.5MM **Privately Held**
SIC: 2653 Boxes, corrugated: made from purchased materials
PA: Capitol Carton Company
  346 N Justine St Ste 406
  Chicago IL 60607
  312 563-9690

**(G-4231)**
**CAPSIM MGT SIMULATIONS INC**
55 E Monroe St Ste 3210 (60603-5824)
PHONE..................................312 477-7200
Craig Watters, *CEO*
Daniel Smith, *President*
EMP: 36
SQ FT: 2,000
SALES (est): 5.4MM **Privately Held**
WEB: www.capsim.com
SIC: 7372 Educational computer software

**(G-4232)**
**CAPSONIC AUTOMOTIVE INC**
4219 Solutions Ctr (60677-4002)
Drawer Rawer Rawer Rawe (60677-0001)
PHONE..................................915 872-3585
EMP: 400 **Privately Held**
SIC: 3625 Motor controls & accessories; switches, electric power
PA: Capsonic Automotive, Inc.
  460 2nd St
  Elgin IL 60123

**(G-4233)**
**CAPTAIN CURTS FOOD PRODUCTS**
Also Called: Captaincurtfoods.com
8206 S Cottage Grove Ave (60619-5302)
PHONE..................................773 783-8400
Fax: 773 783-8500
Curtis Briggs, *CEO*
Hilda Briggs, *President*
Lamont Meeks, *Principal*
EMP: 27
SQ FT: 12,000
SALES (est): 8MM **Privately Held**
SIC: 2033 5812 Barbecue sauce: packaged in cans, jars, etc.; American restaurant

**(G-4234)**
**CAPTAINS EMPORIUM INC**
1200 W 35th St (60609-1305)
PHONE..................................773 972-7609
Fax: 773 276-2343

# GEOGRAPHIC SECTION
## Chicago - Cook County (G-4259)

Don Glasell, *President*
Nancy Zangerle, *Vice Pres*
**EMP:** 2
**SALES (est):** 202.6K **Privately Held**
**WEB:** www.captainsemporium.com
**SIC:** 3914 8748 Trophies; business consulting

### (G-4235)
### CARAMEL-A BAKERY LTD
Also Called: Caramela Bakery
3945 W Armitage Ave (60647-3450)
**PHONE**....................773 227-2635
Andreas Georgopoulos, *CEO*
**EMP:** 22
**SALES (est):** 1.9MM **Privately Held**
**SIC:** 2053 Frozen bakery products, except bread

### (G-4236)
### CARAUSTAR INDUSTRIES INC
Also Called: Chicago Carton Plant
555 N Tripp Ave (60624-1066)
**PHONE**....................773 308-7622
Shawn Zeck, *General Mgr*
Tim Nebel, *QC Mgr*
Brian Coffe, *Branch Mgr*
**EMP:** 50
**SALES (corp-wide):** 1.5B **Privately Held**
**WEB:** www.caraustar.com
**SIC:** 2657 Folding paperboard boxes
**PA:** Caraustar Industries, Inc.
5000 Astell Pwdr Sprng Rd
Austell GA 30106
770 948-3101

### (G-4237)
### CARBIT CORPORATION (PA)
Also Called: Carbit Paint Co
927 W Blackhawk St (60642-2519)
**PHONE**....................312 280-2300
**Fax:** 312 280-7326
James S Westerman, *President*
David Westerman Sr, *Vice Pres*
Clyde Gebhardt, *Sales Staff*
Chip Bevan, *Consultant*
**EMP:** 42 **EST:** 1925
**SQ FT:** 84,000
**SALES (est):** 7.6MM **Privately Held**
**WEB:** www.carbit.com
**SIC:** 2851 Paints & paint additives; enamels; lacquers, varnishes, enamels & other coatings

### (G-4238)
### CARBON ON CHICAGO LLC
810 N Marshfield Ave (60622-5129)
**PHONE**....................312 225-3200
John Falduto, *Principal*
**EMP:** 8
**SALES (est):** 1MM **Privately Held**
**SIC:** 3421 Table & food cutlery, including butchers'

### (G-4239)
### CARBON SOLUTIONS GROUP LLC
1130 W Monroe St Ste 1 (60607-2500)
**PHONE**....................312 638-9077
Kory Trapp, *Principal*
Matthew Wessels, *Marketing Staff*
Dylan Debiasi, *Manager*
Rory Mahesh Gopaul,
**EMP:** 15
**SALES (est):** 2.6MM **Privately Held**
**SIC:** 3624 Carbon & graphite products

### (G-4240)
### CARDINAL PALLET CO
505 W 43rd St (60609-2718)
**PHONE**....................773 725-5387
**Fax:** 773 285-8495
Thomas J Murrihy Jr, *President*
Brian Murrihy, *Sales Executive*
**EMP:** 25
**SQ FT:** 50,000
**SALES (est):** 5.1MM **Privately Held**
**WEB:** www.cardinalpallet.com
**SIC:** 2448 7699 Pallets, wood; skids, wood; pallet repair

### (G-4241)
### CARDWELL WESTINGHOUSE COMPANY
Also Called: Wabtec
8400 S Stewart Ave (60620-1754)
**PHONE**....................773 483-7575
**Fax:** 773 483-9797
David J Meyer, *Vice Pres*
David Myer, *Opers Mgr*
Scott Natschke, *Engineer*
Michelle Elem, *Controller*
Rosa Miller, *Finance Mgr*
▲ **EMP:** 62
**SALES (est):** 33MM
**SALES (corp-wide):** 2.9B **Publicly Held**
**WEB:** www.wabtecglobalservices.com
**SIC:** 3743 Freight cars & equipment
**HQ:** Wabtec Corporation
1001 Airbrake Ave
Wilmerding PA 15148

### (G-4242)
### CAREMATIX INC
Also Called: Wellness Monitoring
209 W Jackson Blvd # 800 (60606-6907)
**PHONE**....................312 627-9300
**Fax:** 312 627-9309
Sukhwant Khanuja, *CEO*
Sandeep Garg, *Vice Pres*
Preety Singh, *Accounts Mgr*
Deepak Pandey, *Director*
**EMP:** 20
**SQ FT:** 5,500
**SALES (est):** 3.1MM **Privately Held**
**WEB:** www.carematix.com
**SIC:** 3845 Ultrasonic scanning devices, medical

### (G-4243)
### CARGILL INCORPORATED
12200 S Torrence Ave (60617-7200)
**PHONE**....................773 375-7255
**Fax:** 773 978-8357
Jill Bayer, *Manager*
Phil Trylong, *Manager*
**EMP:** 12
**SALES (corp-wide):** 107.1B **Privately Held**
**WEB:** www.cargill.com
**SIC:** 2079 2992 Edible fats & oils; lubricating oils & greases
**PA:** Cargill, Incorporated
15407 Mcginty Rd W
Wayzata MN 55391
952 742-7575

### (G-4244)
### CARIBBEAN AMERICAN BKG CO INC
1539 W Howard St (60626-1707)
**PHONE**....................773 761-0700
**Fax:** 773 761-0764
Michael Humes, *President*
Michael G Humes, *President*
Ken Jarosch, *Bd of Directors*
Melissa Hollingsworth, *Administration*
**EMP:** 5
**SQ FT:** 6,000
**SALES:** 600K **Privately Held**
**WEB:** www.caribbeanamericanbakery.com
**SIC:** 2051 Bread, cake & related products

### (G-4245)
### CARSTENS INCORPORATED
7310 W Wilson Ave (60706-4787)
**PHONE**....................708 669-1500
**Fax:** 708 867-1007
Barbara Vanderkloot, *President*
Barbara Block Vanderkloot, *President*
Daniel C Ingersoll, *Controller*
Christopher Chisom, *Cust Mgr*
Kyle Cieslak, *Mktg Dir*
▲ **EMP:** 100 **EST:** 1886
**SQ FT:** 100,000
**SALES (est):** 15.3MM **Privately Held**
**WEB:** www.carstens.com
**SIC:** 3841 Surgical & medical instruments

### (G-4246)
### CARUS PUBLISHING COMPANY (HQ)
Also Called: Cricket Magazine Group
70 E Lake St Ste 800 (60601-5913)
**PHONE**....................603 924-7209
**Fax:** 312 701-1728

Jason Patenaude, *President*
Edmund Fish, *President*
Aric Holsinger, *Admin Sec*
▲ **EMP:** 1
**SQ FT:** 12,000
**SALES (est):** 2.2MM
**SALES (corp-wide):** 10.4MM **Privately Held**
**WEB:** www.caruspub.com
**SIC:** 2731 Book music: publishing & printing; textbooks: publishing only, not printed on site
**PA:** Epals, Inc
13625 Dulles Tech Dr A
Herndon VA 20171
703 885-3400

### (G-4247)
### CARUS PUBLISHING COMPANY
Also Called: Cricket Publishing
70 E Lake St Ste 800 (60601-5913)
**PHONE**....................312 701-1720
Andre Carus, *President*
**EMP:** 14
**SALES (corp-wide):** 10.4MM **Privately Held**
**WEB:** www.caruspub.com
**SIC:** 2731 Book publishing
**HQ:** Carus Publishing Company
70 E Lake St Ste 800
Chicago IL 60601
603 924-7209

### (G-4248)
### CASE PALUCH & ASSOCIATES INC
Also Called: Orca Graphic House
1806 W Greenleaf Ave (60626-2304)
**PHONE**....................773 465-0098
**Fax:** 773 465-0020
Kathleen Case Paluch, *President*
Dennis A Paluch, *President*
Suzi Barsale, *Vice Pres*
**EMP:** 7
**SQ FT:** 9,000
**SALES (est):** 592.1K **Privately Held**
**WEB:** www.paluchmemorials.com
**SIC:** 2791 2752 7336 2789 Typesetting, computer controlled; commercial printing, offset; commercial art & graphic design; bookbinding & related work

### (G-4249)
### CASPER ERNEST E HAIRGOODS
Also Called: E Casper Hairpieces
6033 N Cicero Ave (60646-4301)
**PHONE**....................773 545-2800
Ernest E Casper, *Owner*
**EMP:** 5
**SQ FT:** 1,000
**SALES (est):** 65.6K **Privately Held**
**SIC:** 7241 3999 5699 Hair stylist, men; wigs, including doll wigs, toupees or wiglets; wigs, toupees & wiglets

### (G-4250)
### CASSETICA SOFTWARE INC
22 W Washington St # 1500 (60602-1607)
**PHONE**....................312 546-3668
**EMP:** 3
**SALES:** 800K **Privately Held**
**SIC:** 7372 Prepackaged Software Services

### (G-4251)
### CAST RITE STEEL CASTING CORP
2135 W Carroll Ave (60612-1689)
**PHONE**....................312 738-2900
Robert Kluk, *President*
Rosa Pena, *Manager*
**EMP:** 17
**SQ FT:** 10,000
**SALES (est):** 1.1MM **Privately Held**
**SIC:** 3325 Alloy steel castings, except investment

### (G-4252)
### CASTING HOUSE INC
5 S Wabash Ave Ste 614 (60603-3291)
**PHONE**....................312 782-7160
**Fax:** 312 782-7153
Jason W Borgstahl, *President*
Lisa Bartasius, *Production*
Jamie Paun, *Production*

Vance West, *Draft/Design*
Justin Shelby, *Treasurer*
**EMP:** 15
**SQ FT:** 2,000
**SALES (est):** 2.4MM **Privately Held**
**SIC:** 3911 Jewelry, precious metal

### (G-4253)
### CASTRO FOODS WHOLESALE INC
1365 W 37th St (60609-2108)
**PHONE**....................773 869-0641
Alejandro Castro, *President*
**EMP:** 28
**SQ FT:** 17,000
**SALES:** 5MM **Privately Held**
**SIC:** 2099 2032 Tortillas, fresh or refrigerated; tamales: packaged in cans, jars, etc.

### (G-4254)
### CASWARD TOOL WORKS INC
1422 N Kilpatrick Ave (60651-1624)
**PHONE**....................773 486-4900
Zdzislaw Szmajlo, *President*
Jessie Szamjlo, *Manager*
**EMP:** 6
**SQ FT:** 5,000
**SALES (est):** 600K **Privately Held**
**SIC:** 3599 7692 Machine shop, jobbing & repair; welding repair

### (G-4255)
### CATALINA GRAPHICS INC
2325 W Farwell Ave Apt 3s (60645-4759)
P.O. Box 598112 (60659-8112)
**PHONE**....................773 973-7780
Richard Bordwell, *President*
**EMP:** 2
**SQ FT:** 1,400
**SALES (est):** 289.8K **Privately Held**
**SIC:** 2752 Lithographing on metal

### (G-4256)
### CATALYST CHICAGO
332 S Michigan Ave Ste 37 (60604-4434)
**PHONE**....................312 427-4830
**Fax:** 312 427-6130
Veronica Anderson, *Principal*
Carlos Azcoitia, *Principal*
Tim King, *Principal*
John Myers, *Research*
James Trapp, *CIO*
**EMP:** 8
**SALES (est):** 510.2K **Privately Held**
**SIC:** 2731 Books: publishing only

### (G-4257)
### CATAPULT MARKETING
233 N Michigan Ave # 810 (60601-5525)
**PHONE**....................312 216-4460
Paul Kramer, *Branch Mgr*
**EMP:** 51
**SALES (corp-wide):** 22.8MM **Privately Held**
**SIC:** 3599 Catapults
**PA:** Catapult Marketing
55 Post Rd W Ste 1
Westport CT 06880
203 682-4000

### (G-4258)
### CATHOLIC PRESS ASSN OF THE US
205 W Monroe St (60606-5013)
**PHONE**....................312 380-6789
Timothy M Walter, *Director*
**EMP:** 3
**SALES:** 662.7K **Privately Held**
**SIC:** 2711 Newspapers, publishing & printing

### (G-4259)
### CAXTON CLUB
Also Called: CAXTON CLUB CHICAGO, THE
60 W Walton St (60610-3305)
**PHONE**....................312 266-8825
Don Chatham, *President*
Jacqueline Vossler, *Admin Sec*
**EMP:** 4
**SQ FT:** 1,000
**SALES:** 129.9K **Privately Held**
**SIC:** 5961 2731 Book club, mail order; book clubs: publishing only, not printed on site

Chicago - Cook County (G-4260)   GEOGRAPHIC SECTION

**(G-4260)**
**CBC RESTAURANT CORP**
Also Called: Corner Bakery Cafe
2711 W George St (60618-7810)
PHONE ....................................773 463-0665
Fax: 773 463-1560
Anthony Machias, Manager
Tony Mathias, Manager
EMP: 80
SALES (corp-wide): 5.6B Privately Held
SIC: 2051 Bakery: wholesale or wholesale/retail combined
HQ: Cbc Restaurant Corp.
  12700 Park Central Dr # 1300
  Dallas TX 75251
  972 619-4100

**(G-4261)**
**CD LLC**
363 W Erie St Ste 400w (60654-6906)
PHONE ....................................312 275-5747
Bryan Villkno, Sales Mgr
Brad Emalfarb, Manager
Scott Emalfarb,
Hal Emalfarb,
EMP: 10
SALES: 500K Privately Held
SIC: 3829 Measuring & controlling devices

**(G-4262)**
**CDC GROUP INC**
Also Called: Chicago Drapery & Carpet
140 S Dearborn St Ste 420 (60603-5233)
PHONE ....................................847 480-8830
Sam Lallas, President
Renee Lallas, Vice Pres
Charles Lipuma, Vice Pres
Jenine M Destefano, Accounts Mgr
Karen Alcantar, Manager
EMP: 25
SQ FT: 2,500
SALES (est): 2.3MM Privately Held
SIC: 2391 5023 Curtains, window: made from purchased materials; draperies, plastic & textile: from purchased materials; curtains; draperies; venetian blinds; vertical blinds

**(G-4263)**
**CDI COMPUTERS (US) CORP**
Also Called: CDI Computer Dealers
500 N Michigan Ave # 600 (60611-3777)
PHONE ....................................888 226-5727
Saar Pikar, CEO
Erez Pikar, President
Naipaul Sheosankar, CFO
Michael McKean, Sales Mgr
EMP: 4 EST: 2010
SALES (est): 1.5MM
SALES (corp-wide): 46.4MM Privately Held
SIC: 7373 3577 5734 Value-added resellers, computer systems; computer peripheral equipment; computer software & accessories
PA: Cdi Computer Dealers Inc
  130 South Town Centre Blvd
  Markham ON L6G 1
  905 946-1119

**(G-4264)**
**CDI CORP**
3440 N Knox Ave (60641-3744)
PHONE ....................................773 205-2960
Fax: 773 394-2965
Robert Tucker, President
Joe Karsznia, Opers Staff
Katie Flynn, Sales Dir
Joe Nardi, Software Dev
▲ EMP: 14
SQ FT: 5,700
SALES: 647K Privately Held
WEB: www.cdi-corp.com
SIC: 2752 Decals, lithographed

**(G-4265)**
**CEDAR CONCEPTS CORPORATION**
4100 S Packers Ave (60609-2425)
PHONE ....................................773 890-5790
Fax: 773 890-1606
Linda McGill Boasmond, President
Ladipo Famodu, Research
▲ EMP: 31
SQ FT: 60,000
SALES (est): 14.3MM Privately Held
WEB: www.cedarconcepts.com
SIC: 2869 5169 2841 2843 Industrial organic chemicals; chemicals & allied products; soap & other detergents; surface active agents; toilet preparations

**(G-4266)**
**CEDILLE CHICAGO NFP**
Also Called: CEDILLE RECORDS
1205 W Balmoral Ave (60640-1308)
PHONE ....................................773 989-2515
Fax: 773 989-2517
James Ginsburg, President
Constance Wilson, Business Mgr
Julie Polanski, Director
EMP: 4 EST: 1989
SQ FT: 1,750
SALES: 387K Privately Held
WEB: www.cedillerecords.org
SIC: 3652 Compact laser discs, prerecorded

**(G-4267)**
**CELLAS CONFECTIONS INC (HQ)**
7401 S Cicero Ave (60629-5818)
PHONE ....................................773 838-3400
Ellen Gordon, President
Melvin J Gordon, Vice Pres
Dan Drechney, Controller
Edgar Llanos, Manager
EMP: 65
SALES (est): 8.3MM
SALES (corp-wide): 521.1MM Publicly Held
WEB: www.tootsie-roll.com
SIC: 2064 Candy & other confectionery products
PA: Tootsie Roll Industries, Inc.
  7401 S Cicero Ave
  Chicago IL 60629
  773 838-3400

**(G-4268)**
**CEMEX CEMENT INC**
12101 S Doty Ave (60633-2322)
PHONE ....................................773 995-5100
Larry Woodward, Branch Mgr
Dave White, Manager
EMP: 5
SALES (corp-wide): 12.2B Privately Held
SIC: 3241 Portland cement
HQ: Cemex Cement, Inc.
  10100 Katy Fwy Ste 300
  Houston TX 77043
  713 650-6200

**(G-4269)**
**CENTER-111 W BURNHAM WASH LLC**
111 W Washington St (60602-2703)
PHONE ....................................312 368-5320
Fax: 312 807-4948
Bonnie Boden, General Mgr
Todd Siegel,
EMP: 22
SQ FT: 600,000
SALES (est): 3.9MM Privately Held
SIC: 2531 Benches for public buildings

**(G-4270)**
**CENTRAL CAN COMPANY INC**
3200 S Kilbourn Ave (60623-4829)
PHONE ....................................773 254-8700
Fax: 773 254-9127
Kenneth Roessler, President
Charles Hushka, Plant Mgr
James Kral, Plant Engr
Tony Such, Controller
Barbara Snyder, Manager
▲ EMP: 180 EST: 1925
SQ FT: 300,000
SALES: 23.4MM
SALES (corp-wide): 831.7MM Privately Held
WEB: www.centralcancompany.com
SIC: 3411 3412 Metal cans; metal barrels, drums & pails
HQ: Bway Corporation
  8607 Roberts Dr Ste 250
  Atlanta GA 30350
  770 645-4800

**(G-4271)**
**CENTRAL MOLDED PRODUCTS LLC**
1978 N Lockwood Ave (60639-3097)
PHONE ....................................773 622-4000
Fax: 773 637-8692
Robert G Garritano,
Thomas Garritano,
EMP: 17 EST: 1934
SQ FT: 15,000
SALES (est): 2.8MM Privately Held
SIC: 3089 Injection molded finished plastic products

**(G-4272)**
**CENTRAL STEEL AND WIRE COMPANY**
3000 W 51st St (60632-2198)
PHONE ....................................773 471-3800
Frank Troike, Chairman
Ray Fiala, Branch Mgr
Frank Budz, Manager
Gene Miller, Prgrmr
Michael Cronin, Bd of Directors
EMP: 100
SQ FT: 1,200
SALES (corp-wide): 599.1MM Publicly Held
WEB: www.centralsteel.com
SIC: 3315 Steel wire & related products
PA: Central Steel And Wire Company
  3000 W 51st St
  Chicago IL 60632
  773 471-3800

**(G-4273)**
**CENTRIC MFG SOLUTIONS INC**
875 N Michigan Ave # 3614 (60611-1803)
PHONE ....................................815 315-9258
Mario Perez, President
Rebecca Perez, Vice Pres
EMP: 7
SALES (est): 810.8K Privately Held
WEB: www.centricms.com
SIC: 3542 Machine tools, metal forming type

**(G-4274)**
**CENTUP INDUSTRIES LLC**
1901 W Chicago Ave Apt 2 (60622-7863)
PHONE ....................................312 291-1687
Leonard Kendall, CEO
EMP: 3 EST: 2013
SQ FT: 2,000
SALES (est): 169.1K Privately Held
SIC: 2741 Miscellaneous publishing

**(G-4275)**
**CENTURY ALUMINUM COMPANY (PA)**
1 S Wacker Dr Ste 1000 (60606-4616)
PHONE ....................................312 696-3101
Fax: 312 696-3102
Michael A Bless, President
Gunnar Gudlaugsson, Managing Dir
Ragnar Gudmundsson, Managing Dir
Lawrence Frost, Exec VP
Jesse E Gary, Exec VP
▲ EMP: 122
SALES (est): 1.3B Publicly Held
WEB: www.centuryca.com
SIC: 3334 Primary aluminum

**(G-4276)**
**CENTURY FILTER PRODUCTS INC**
2939 N Oakley Ave (60618-8029)
PHONE ....................................773 477-1790
Victor La Porta, President
George Koltse, Vice Pres
EMP: 5
SQ FT: 5,000
SALES (est): 853.2K Privately Held
WEB: www.centuryplatingco.com
SIC: 3569 5084 Filters, general line: industrial; industrial machinery & equipment

**(G-4277)**
**CENTURY SPRING CORPORATION**
4045 W Thorndale Ave (60646-6011)
PHONE ....................................800 237-5225
James Frelka, Principal
EMP: 2 EST: 2008
SALES (est): 204.7K Privately Held
SIC: 5051 3495 Metals service centers & offices; wire springs

**(G-4278)**
**CENVEO INC**
3001 N Rockwell St (60618-7917)
PHONE ....................................636 240-5817
Frank Ball, Branch Mgr
EMP: 81 Publicly Held
SIC: 2752 Commercial printing, lithographic
PA: Cenveo, Inc.
  200 First Stamford Pl # 200
  Stamford CT 06902

**(G-4279)**
**CENVEO INC**
Also Called: Mail-Well
3001 N Rockwell St (60618-7917)
PHONE ....................................773 267-1717
Terry Long, General Mgr
Gene Hanyzewski, COO
Michael Delsignore, Vice Pres
James Bolda, Purch Mgr
Nancie Fleurimont, Executive
EMP: 65
SQ FT: 160,000 Publicly Held
WEB: www.mail-well.com
SIC: 2677 Envelopes
PA: Cenveo, Inc.
  200 First Stamford Pl # 200
  Stamford CT 06902

**(G-4280)**
**CENVEO INC**
Also Called: Mail-Well
2950 N Campbell Ave (60618-7904)
P.O. Box 99444 (60693-9444)
PHONE ....................................773 539-0411
Pete Correll, Manager
EMP: 76 Publicly Held
SIC: 2752 Commercial printing, lithographic
PA: Cenveo, Inc.
  200 First Stamford Pl # 200
  Stamford CT 06902

**(G-4281)**
**CENVEO CORPORATION**
Also Called: Mail-Well
5445 N Elston Ave (60630-1456)
PHONE ....................................312 286-6400
Fax: 773 286-6921
EMP: 250 Publicly Held
SIC: 2677 Envelopes
HQ: Cenveo Corporation
  200 First Stamford Pl # 200
  Stamford CT 06902
  303 790-8023

**(G-4282)**
**CERA LTD**
5542 N Lakewood Ave (60640-1313)
PHONE ....................................773 334-1042
Ronald Rhyce, President
EMP: 3
SQ FT: 2,000
SALES (est): 172.6K Privately Held
SIC: 3842 Orthopedic appliances

**(G-4283)**
**CERTIFIED BUSINESS FORMS INC**
5732 W Patterson Ave (60634-2620)
PHONE ....................................773 286-8194
Fax: 773 685-5523
Charles J Schneider, President
Charles J Scheider, Treasurer
EMP: 3
SQ FT: 600
SALES: 300K Privately Held
WEB: www.certifiedbusinessforms.com
SIC: 5112 2761 Business forms; manifold business forms

**(G-4284)**
**CGC CORPORATION**
7401 S Cicero Ave (60629-5818)
PHONE ....................................773 838-3400
EMP: 65 EST: 2014
SALES (est): 165.7K
SALES (corp-wide): 521.1MM Publicly Held
SIC: 2064 Breakfast bars

# GEOGRAPHIC SECTION
## Chicago - Cook County (G-4310)

HQ: Cella's Confections Inc
7401 S Cicero Ave
Chicago IL 60629
773 838-3400

**(G-4285)**
**CHALLENGE PRINTERS**
4354 W Armitage Ave (60639-3507)
**PHONE** ..................... 773 252-0212
**Fax:** 773 252-0059
Taide Villasenor, *Owner*
**EMP:** 5
**SALES:** 300K **Privately Held**
**SIC: 2752** 2791 2789 2759 Commercial printing, lithographic; typesetting; bookbinding & related work; commercial printing

**(G-4286)**
**CHAMBERS GASKET & MFG CO**
4701 W Rice St (60651-3377)
**PHONE** ..................... 773 626-8800
**Fax:** 773 626-1430
Heide Kenny, *President*
Joan Finnegan, *Personnel*
Peter Madler, *Sales Mgr*
Ronald Owens, *Marketing Staff*
Christopher Kenny,
**EMP:** 40 **EST:** 1937
**SQ FT:** 65,000
**SALES (est):** 10.1MM **Privately Held**
**WEB:** www.chambersgasket.com
**SIC: 3053** Gaskets, packing & sealing devices

**(G-4287)**
**CHANNELED RESOURCES INC (PA)**
Also Called: C. R. I.
240 N Ashland Ave (60607-1422)
**PHONE** ..................... 312 733-4200
**Fax:** 312 733-1628
Calvin S Frost Jr, *President*
Richard Barrett, *General Mgr*
David Robinson, *General Mgr*
Steve Atlas, *Business Mgr*
Paula Russell, *Vice Pres*
◆ **EMP:** 20
**SQ FT:** 5,000
**SALES (est):** 16.2MM **Privately Held**
**WEB:** www.channeledresources.com
**SIC: 2672** 5093 Chemically treated papers: made from purchased materials; coated paper, except photographic, carbon or abrasive; waste paper

**(G-4288)**
**CHAR CRUST CO INC**
3017 N Lincoln Ave (60657-4242)
**PHONE** ..................... 773 528-0600
Bernard Silver, *President*
**EMP:** 3
**SQ FT:** 5,000
**SALES (est):** 414.4K **Privately Held**
**WEB:** www.charcrust.com
**SIC: 2099** Seasonings: dry mixes

**(G-4289)**
**CHARLES AUTIN LIMITED**
Also Called: Kwok's Food Service
1801 S Canal St (60616-1522)
**PHONE** ..................... 312 432-0888
**Fax:** 312 432-0886
Charlie Chun, *President*
Chris Lui, *Accounts Mgr*
**EMP:** 80
**SQ FT:** 16,500
**SALES (est):** 38MM **Privately Held**
**SIC: 2013** 5147 2015 Prepared beef products from purchased beef; prepared pork products from purchased pork; meats & meat products; chicken slaughtering & processing

**(G-4290)**
**CHARLES CICERO FINGERHUT (PA)**
Also Called: Charles Fingerhut Bakeries
5537 W Cermak Rd (60804-2218)
**PHONE** ..................... 708 652-3643
**Fax:** 708 652-3665
Herbert Fingerhut Sr, *President*
Francis Fingerhut, *Treasurer*
**EMP:** 14
**SQ FT:** 7,500
**SALES (est):** 1.3MM **Privately Held**
**SIC: 2051** Bread, cake & related products; bread, all types (white, wheat, rye, etc): fresh or frozen; cakes, bakery: except frozen; pastries, e.g. danish: except frozen

**(G-4291)**
**CHARLES H KERR PUBLISHING CO**
1726 W Jarvis Ave (60626-1606)
**PHONE** ..................... 773 262-1329
Carlos Cortez, *President*
Penelope Rosemont, *Corp Secy*
**EMP:** 6
**SQ FT:** 500
**SALES (est):** 526.8K **Privately Held**
**SIC: 2731** 5192 Books: publishing only; books

**(G-4292)**
**CHARLES HORBERG JEWELERS INC**
5 S Wabash Ave Ste 706 (60603-3197)
**PHONE** ..................... 312 263-4924
**Fax:** 312 263-3323
Charles Horberg, *President*
Sandra Horberg, *Treasurer*
**EMP:** 3 **EST:** 1967
**SQ FT:** 800
**SALES (est):** 544.5K **Privately Held**
**SIC: 5094** 5944 3911 Jewelry; jewelry, precious stones & precious metals; jewelry, precious metal

**(G-4293)**
**CHARLES N BENNER INC**
Also Called: Bcs Industries
401 N Western Ave Ste 4 (60612-1418)
**PHONE** ..................... 312 829-4300
**Fax:** 312 829-4341
Brian Benner, *President*
Gail Benner, *Corp Secy*
▲ **EMP:** 25
**SQ FT:** 40,000
**SALES (est):** 2.3MM **Privately Held**
**WEB:** www.buildmykitchen.com
**SIC: 2434** Wood kitchen cabinets

**(G-4294)**
**CHARLOTTE LOUISE TATE**
Also Called: Mickhali Local Distributors
1304 E 87th St (60619-7025)
**PHONE** ..................... 773 849-3236
Charlotte Tate, *Owner*
Michael Harris, *Administration*
**EMP:** 3
**SALES (est):** 114K **Privately Held**
**SIC: 3694** Ignition apparatus & distributors

**(G-4295)**
**CHASE SECURITY SYSTEMS INC**
5947 N Milwaukee Ave (60646-5419)
P.O. Box 30179 (60630-0179)
**PHONE** ..................... 773 594-1919
**Fax:** 773 594-0078
Charles Villanueva, *CEO*
J Springman, *Vice Pres*
**EMP:** 5
**SALES (est):** 550K **Privately Held**
**SIC: 3699** 8742 3446 3357 Security control equipment & systems; marketing consulting services; architectural metalwork; nonferrous wiredrawing & insulating

**(G-4296)**
**CHATEAU FOOD PRODUCTS INC**
6137 W Cermak Rd (60804-2024)
**PHONE** ..................... 708 863-4207
**Fax:** 708 863-5806
Donald L Shotola, *President*
M Anita Shotola, *Corp Secy*
**EMP:** 10 **EST:** 1927
**SQ FT:** 4,000
**SALES (est):** 944.6K **Privately Held**
**WEB:** www.chateaufoods.com
**SIC: 2051** 2099 2038 Bread, cake & related products; food preparations; frozen specialties

**(G-4297)**
**CHERRY MEAT PACKERS INC**
Also Called: Chicago Meat, The
4750 S California Ave (60632-2016)
**PHONE** ..................... 773 927-1200
**Fax:** 773 927-1520
Robert Vicino, *Vice Pres*
Keith Pozulp, *Vice Pres*
**EMP:** 48 **EST:** 1912
**SQ FT:** 47,000
**SALES (est):** 6.9MM **Privately Held**
**SIC: 2013** 2011 Sausages from purchased meat; cured meats from purchased meat; luncheon meat from purchased meat; meat packing plants

**(G-4298)**
**CHEWY SOFTWARE LLC**
507 W Aldine Ave Apt 1b (60657-3758)
**PHONE** ..................... 773 935-2627
Sherri A Wandler, *Principal*
**EMP:** 2
**SALES (est):** 225.1K **Privately Held**
**SIC: 7372** Prepackaged software

**(G-4299)**
**CHI-TOWN PRINTING INC**
6025 N Cicero Ave (60646-4301)
**PHONE** ..................... 773 577-2500
Thomas P Stapka, *Principal*
**EMP:** 3
**SALES (est):** 239.8K **Privately Held**
**SIC: 2752** Commercial printing, lithographic

**(G-4300)**
**CHICAGO AGENT MAGAZINE**
2000 N Racine Ave (60614-4045)
**PHONE** ..................... 773 296-6001
**Fax:** 773 296-6103
Marry Sepulveda, *CEO*
**EMP:** 7
**SALES (est):** 919.8K **Privately Held**
**WEB:** www.chicagoagentmagazine.com
**SIC: 2721** Periodicals

**(G-4301)**
**CHICAGO ALUM CASTINGS CO INC**
205 W Wacker Dr Ste 1818 (60606-1429)
**PHONE** ..................... 773 762-3009
**Fax:** 773 762-3011
Richard A Wagner, *President*
Richard Gurrieri, *Vice Pres*
Derek Horton, *Manager*
**EMP:** 4 **EST:** 1910
**SQ FT:** 14,000
**SALES (est):** 523.4K **Privately Held**
**WEB:** www.chicagoaluminum.com
**SIC: 3365** Aluminum foundries

**(G-4302)**
**CHICAGO AMERICAN MFG LLC**
4500 W 47th St (60632-4450)
**PHONE** ..................... 773 376-0100
Terry Morgan, *Design Engr*
Allen Marshall, *CFO*
Mark A Herman, *Mng Member*
▲ **EMP:** 200
**SQ FT:** 27,500
**SALES (est):** 46.7MM **Privately Held**
**SIC: 2514** 2542 2531 Metal household furniture; partitions & fixtures, except wood; public building & related furniture

**(G-4303)**
**CHICAGO ANODIZING COMPANY**
4112 W Lake St (60624-1792)
**PHONE** ..................... 773 533-3737
**Fax:** 773 533-3740
Norman Americus, *President*
Victor Oraham, *Vice Pres*
John Serritella, *Vice Pres*
Brian Isola, *Admin Sec*
**EMP:** 65 **EST:** 1948
**SQ FT:** 30,000
**SALES (est):** 9.8MM **Privately Held**
**WEB:** www.chicagoanodizing.com
**SIC: 3479** Aluminum coating of metal products

**(G-4304)**
**CHICAGO ART CENTER CO**
6540 N Washtenaw Ave (60645-5308)
**PHONE** ..................... 773 817-2725
Plamen Iordanov, *President*
**EMP:** 4
**SALES (est):** 215.2K **Privately Held**
**SIC: 3999** Manufacturing industries

**(G-4305)**
**CHICAGO BEVERAGE SYSTEMS LLC**
441 N Kilbourn Ave (60624-1098)
**PHONE** ..................... 773 826-4100
**Fax:** 773 826-8023
James Doney, *President*
Stephen Carnes, *Sales Mgr*
Shaun Kravat, *Sales Staff*
Tony Jankowski, *Manager*
▲ **EMP:** 30
**SALES (est):** 4.9MM **Privately Held**
**SIC: 2082** Beer (alcoholic beverage)

**(G-4306)**
**CHICAGO BOATING PUBLICATIONS**
Also Called: Great Lakes Boating Magazine
851 N La Salle Dr (60610-3276)
**PHONE** ..................... 312 266-8400
Ned Dikman, *President*
Ned F Dikimen, *Editor*
Tom Janus, *Treasurer*
Karen Malonis, *Admin Sec*
**EMP:** 9
**SQ FT:** 1,000
**SALES (est):** 1.2MM **Privately Held**
**SIC: 2721** Magazines: publishing only, not printed on site

**(G-4307)**
**CHICAGO BOOTH MFG INC**
5000 W Roosevelt Rd # 202 (60644-1474)
**PHONE** ..................... 773 378-8400
**Fax:** 773 378-8221
David Bochniak, *President*
Ed Salutric, *Engineer*
Joe Wilkinson, *Accounts Mgr*
Megan Millard, *Sales Staff*
Ash Gupta, *Manager*
**EMP:** 10
**SQ FT:** 25,000
**SALES (est):** 1.8MM **Privately Held**
**WEB:** www.chicagobooth.com
**SIC: 2599** 2541 2531 2511 Restaurant furniture, wood or metal; bar furniture; stools, factory; wood partitions & fixtures; public building & related furniture; wood household furniture

**(G-4308)**
**CHICAGO BRIDAL STORE INC**
2146 W 95th St (60643-1019)
**PHONE** ..................... 773 445-4450
Adamma Turner, *Ch of Bd*
**EMP:** 3
**SALES (est):** 50K **Privately Held**
**SIC: 2335** Women's, juniors' & misses' dresses

**(G-4309)**
**CHICAGO CANDLE COMPANY**
Also Called: Holy Hill Gourmet
2701 N Sayre Ave (60707-1712)
**PHONE** ..................... 773 637-5279
Rose Marrie, *Principal*
**EMP:** 3
**SALES (est):** 190.3K **Privately Held**
**SIC: 5199** 3999 Candles; candles

**(G-4310)**
**CHICAGO CAR SEAL COMPANY**
594 Brookside Rd (60612)
**PHONE** ..................... 773 278-9400
**Fax:** 773 278-3839
Dorothea Nyman, *Corp Secy*
▲ **EMP:** 7 **EST:** 1892
**SQ FT:** 12,000
**SALES (est):** 1MM **Privately Held**
**SIC: 3469** 3496 3429 3357 Metal stampings; miscellaneous fabricated wire products; manufactured hardware (general); nonferrous wiredrawing & insulating

### (G-4311)
**CHICAGO CITIZEN NEWSPPR GROUP (PA)**
Also Called: Chicago Weekend
806 E 78th St (60619-2937)
PHONE..................773 783-1251
Fax: 773 783-1301
William Garth, CEO
EMP: 12
SQ FT: 2,000
SALES (est): 3MM **Privately Held**
SIC: 2711  2791  Newspapers, publishing & printing; typesetting

### (G-4312)
**CHICAGO COPPER & IRON WORKS**
Also Called: Air Van Co
3550 N Spaulding Ave (60618-5523)
PHONE..................773 327-2780
Fax: 773 472-5154
John Heinzl, President
Donna Heinzl, Treasurer
Terry Baker, Admin Sec
EMP: 5
SQ FT: 9,000
SALES: 800K **Privately Held**
WEB: www.chicagocopperandiron.com
SIC: 3599  Machine shop, jobbing & repair

### (G-4313)
**CHICAGO CRUSADER NEWS GROUP (PA)**
6429 S King Dr (60637-3116)
PHONE..................773 752-2500
Fax: 773 752-2817
Dorothy R Leavell, President
John Smith, Vice Pres
Dorothy Gonder, Personnel
EMP: 5
SQ FT: 1,500
SALES: 350K **Privately Held**
SIC: 2711  Newspapers: publishing only, not printed on site

### (G-4314)
**CHICAGO DEFENDER PUBLISHING CO**
4445 S King Dr (60653-3310)
PHONE..................312 225-2400
Fax: 312 225-9231
Tom Picou, President
David Milliner, Publisher
Lloyd Huddleston, Editor
Tresa Smith, Financial Exec
Dyanna Lewis, Accounts Exec
EMP: 50
SALES (est): 3MM **Privately Held**
WEB: www.chicagodefender.com
SIC: 2711  Newspapers: publishing only, not printed on site

### (G-4315)
**CHICAGO DOWEL COMPANY INC**
4700 W Grand Ave (60639-4695)
PHONE..................773 622-2000
Fax: 773 622-2047
Paul R Iacono, President
Ralph J Iacono, President
Russell R Iacono, Vice Pres
Paul Iacono, Manager
▲ EMP: 65
SQ FT: 50,000
SALES (est): 9.2MM **Privately Held**
WEB: www.chicagodowel.com
SIC: 2499  Dowels, wood

### (G-4316)
**CHICAGO DROPCLOTH TARPAULIN CO**
3719 W Lawrence Ave (60625-5712)
PHONE..................773 588-3123
Fax: 773 588-3139
Cheryl Warren, President
Karen Mangurten, Vice Pres
EMP: 30  EST: 1948
SQ FT: 12,750
SALES (est): 3.2MM **Privately Held**
SIC: 2394  Cloth, drop (fabric): made from purchased materials; tarpaulins, fabric: made from purchased materials

### (G-4317)
**CHICAGO DRYER COMPANY**
2200 N Pulaski Rd (60639-3737)
PHONE..................773 235-4430
Bruce W Johnson, President
Marilyn Rivera, Traffic Mgr
Jerry Helma, Purch Mgr
Chuck Anderson, Purch Agent
Richard Chioni, Electrical Engi
◆ EMP: 125  EST: 1896
SQ FT: 55,000
SALES (est): 31.7MM **Privately Held**
WEB: www.chidry.com
SIC: 3582  5087  Commercial laundry equipment; laundry equipment & supplies

### (G-4318)
**CHICAGO EXPORT PACKING CO**
1501 W 38th St (60609-2117)
P.O. Box 1349, Deerfield (60015-6005)
PHONE..................773 247-8911
Fax: 773 247-2830
James Nashan, President
Mike Constantini, General Mgr
Mark Vice, VP Sales
EMP: 40
SQ FT: 78,000
SALES (est): 5.4MM **Privately Held**
WEB: www.chicagoexport.com
SIC: 4225  4783  2441  General warehousing; packing goods for shipping; crating goods for shipping; nailed wood boxes & shook

### (G-4319)
**CHICAGO FILM ARCHIVE NFP**
5746 N Drake Ave (60659-4402)
PHONE..................773 478-3799
Nancy Watrous, President
EMP: 3
SALES: 225.6K **Privately Held**
SIC: 3861  Motion picture film

### (G-4320)
**CHICAGO FLYHOUSE INCORPORATED**
2925 W Carroll Ave (60612-1719)
PHONE..................773 533-1590
Fax: 773 533-1351
Mark Witteveen, President
Brent Miller, Project Mgr
Shannon Nickerson, Project Mgr
Benjamin Cohen, Sales Mgr
▲ EMP: 10
SALES (est): 3.6MM **Privately Held**
SIC: 1796  3731  Machine moving & rigging; marine rigging

### (G-4321)
**CHICAGO GROUP ACQUISITION LLC**
350 N Orleans St Fl 10-S (60654-1975)
PHONE..................312 755-0720
EMP: 3
SALES (est): 135.7K **Privately Held**
SIC: 2711  Newspapers-Publishing/Printing

### (G-4322)
**CHICAGO HARLEY DAVIDSON INC**
66 E Ohio St (60611-2702)
PHONE..................312 274-9666
Michael Nilles, Manager
EMP: 6
SALES (corp-wide): 4.2MM **Privately Held**
WEB: www.chicagoharley.com
SIC: 2389  Men's miscellaneous accessories
PA: Chicago Harley Davidson, Inc.
    6868 N Western Ave
    Chicago IL

### (G-4323)
**CHICAGO HONEYMOONERS LLC**
3341 W Sunnyside Ave # 2 (60625-5425)
PHONE..................312 399-5699
Harlan Wayne Fails,
Rebekah Fails,
EMP: 2
SALES: 500K **Privately Held**
SIC: 2511  Wood household furniture

### (G-4324)
**CHICAGO IRON WORKS CORPORATION (PA)**
439 N Western Ave (60612-1419)
PHONE..................312 829-1062
Fax: 312 829-4665
Frank Galasso, President
EMP: 14
SQ FT: 8,000
SALES (est): 770K **Privately Held**
SIC: 3446  3442  Stairs, staircases, stair treads: prefabricated metal; fire escapes, metal; balconies, metal; fences, gates, posts & flagpoles; metal doors, sash & trim

### (G-4325)
**CHICAGO KITE**
5445 N Harlem Ave (60656-1820)
PHONE..................773 467-1428
Robert Zavell, Owner
EMP: 3
SALES (est): 259.6K **Privately Held**
SIC: 3944  Kites

### (G-4326)
**CHICAGO KNITTING MILLS**
3344 W Montrose Ave (60618-1296)
PHONE..................773 463-1464
Fax: 773 463-1465
Robert Soll, Owner
EMP: 3
SQ FT: 3,800
SALES: 160K **Privately Held**
SIC: 2253  2395  5137  5136  Sweaters & sweater coats, knit; jackets, knit; emblems, embroidered; embroidery products, except schiffli machine; uniforms, women's & children's; uniforms, men's & boys'; women's & misses' outerwear; weft knit fabric mills

### (G-4327)
**CHICAGO LAB PRODUCTS**
660 N Union Ave (60654-5526)
PHONE..................312 942-0730
Fax: 312 666-6041
Bob Carjos, Principal
EMP: 4
SALES (est): 327.1K **Privately Held**
SIC: 3821  Laboratory equipment: fume hoods, distillation racks, etc.

### (G-4328)
**CHICAGO LIGHTHOUSE INDUSTRIES**
1850 W Roosevelt Rd Ste 1 (60608-1247)
PHONE..................312 666-1331
Janet Szlyk, CEO
Michael Meehan, Ch of Bd
Marvin Lader, Vice Chairman
Mary Lynne Januszewski, CFO
Ted Mazola, Treasurer
EMP: 65
SALES (est): 2.1MM **Privately Held**
SIC: 3873  Watches, clocks, watchcases & parts

### (G-4329)
**CHICAGO LOCAL FOODS LLC**
1427 W Willow St (60642)
PHONE..................312 432-6575
Andrew Lutsey, CEO
Ryan Kimura, CFO
Murphy Jim, Manager
Lutsey Andrew, Manager
Julie Martin,
EMP: 37
SALES (est): 5.9MM **Privately Held**
SIC: 5141  2013  Food brokers; boneless meat, from purchased meat

### (G-4330)
**CHICAGO MAILING TUBE COMPANY**
400 N Leavitt St (60612-1618)
PHONE..................312 243-6050
Fax: 312 243-6545
Kenneth R Barmore, President
Keith Shimon, President
▲ EMP: 40
SQ FT: 90,000
SALES (est): 11.2MM **Privately Held**
WEB: www.mailing-tube.com
SIC: 2655  Tubes, fiber or paper: made from purchased material; cores, fiber: made from purchased material; fiber cans, drums & containers

### (G-4331)
**CHICAGO MEAT AUTHORITY INC**
1120 W 47th Pl (60609-4302)
PHONE..................773 254-3811
Fax: 773 254-5841
Jordan Dorfman, President
Scott Hardiman, VP Opers
Dan Wang, CFO
Alana Heber, Marketing Mgr
Bartek Woroniecki, Marketing Staff
EMP: 330
SQ FT: 50,000
SALES (est): 118MM **Privately Held**
WEB: www.chicagomeat.com
SIC: 2011  Meat packing plants

### (G-4332)
**CHICAGO METAL FABRICATORS INC**
3724 S Rockwell St (60632-1051)
PHONE..................773 523-5755
Fax: 773 523-8580
Randy Hauser, President
John Nalbach, President
Alice Cook, Vice Pres
Kevin Condon, Opers Mgr
Robert Kmak, Engineer
EMP: 80  EST: 1923
SQ FT: 200,000
SALES (est): 25MM **Privately Held**
WEB: www.chicagometal.com
SIC: 3469  5084  3498  3441  Metal stampings; industrial machinery & equipment; fabricated pipe & fittings; fabricated structural metal; blast furnaces & steel mills

### (G-4333)
**CHICAGO METAL ROLLED PDTS CO (PA)**
3715 S Rockwell St (60632-1030)
PHONE..................773 523-5757
Fax: 773 650-1439
Joseph Wendt, President
George F Wendt, President
Tina Lawrence, General Mgr
Chester Zarebczan, Traffic Mgr
Raymond Reitz, Treasurer
◆ EMP: 66
SQ FT: 100,000
SALES (est): 21.3MM **Privately Held**
WEB: www.cmrp.com
SIC: 3444  3446  3498  3449  Sheet metalwork; architectural metalwork; fabricated pipe & fittings; miscellaneous metalwork; fabricated structural metal

### (G-4334)
**CHICAGO METALLIC COMPANY LLC**
Also Called: Rockfon
4849 S Austin Ave (60638-1400)
PHONE..................708 563-4600
Fax: 708 563-4849
▲ EMP: 190
SALES (est): 258.1MM
SALES (corp-wide): 2.3B **Privately Held**
SIC: 3446  5033  Architectural metalwork; acoustical suspension systems, metal; roofing, asphalt & sheet metal
PA: Rockwool International A/S
    Hovedgaden 584
    Hedehusene 2640
    465 603-00

### (G-4335)
**CHICAGO MOLDING OUTLET**
5858 S Kedzie Ave Ste 1 (60629-3242)
PHONE..................773 471-6870
Nivene Judeh, President
EMP: 4
SALES (est): 431.5K **Privately Held**
SIC: 3089  Molding primary plastic

## Chicago - Cook County (G-4360)

**(G-4336)**
**CHICAGO MTAL SUP FBRCATION INC**
4940 W Grand Ave (60639-4413)
PHONE ............................ 773 227-6200
Bogdan Bosak, *President*
EMP: 14
SALES (est): 3.2MM **Privately Held**
SIC: 3411 Metal cans

**(G-4337)**
**CHICAGO ORIENTAL CNSTR INC**
Also Called: Chicago Oriental Wholesale Mkt
1835 S Canal St 2f (60616-1522)
PHONE ............................ 312 733-9633
Anna Fang, *Principal*
Frank Fang, *Manager*
EMP: 3
SALES (est): 170K **Privately Held**
SIC: 2099 Sandwiches, assembled & packaged; for wholesale market

**(G-4338)**
**CHICAGO ORNAMENTAL IRON INC**
Also Called: Coi Company
1249 W 47th St (60609)
PHONE ............................ 773 321-9635
Jonathan Samek, *President*
Munish Mehta, *COO*
EMP: 46
SQ FT: 30,000
SALES (est): 15.9MM **Privately Held**
SIC: 3449 3446 1791 Miscellaneous metalwork; curtain wall, metal; curtain walls for buildings, steel; architectural metalwork; stairs, fire escapes, balconies, railings & ladders; balconies, metal; bannisters, made from metal pipe; structural steel erection; iron work, structural

**(G-4339)**
**CHICAGO PIPE BENDING & COIL CO**
4535 W Lake St (60624-1685)
PHONE ............................ 773 379-1918
Phillis E Melton, *Ch of Bd*
Michael Melton, *President*
Robert Melton, *Admin Sec*
EMP: 12
SQ FT: 13,000
SALES (est): 5MM **Privately Held**
WEB: www.chicagopipebending.com
SIC: 5051 3498 3494 3312 Pipe & tubing, steel; pipe fittings, fabricated from purchased pipe; valves & pipe fittings; blast furnaces & steel mills

**(G-4340)**
**CHICAGO PIXELS MULITMEDIA NFP**
5016 N Parkside Ave Apt 2 (60630-4633)
PHONE ............................ 312 513-7949
Gregory Tarczynski, *CEO*
EMP: 3
SALES (est): 155.7K **Privately Held**
SIC: 3674 Semiconductors & related devices

**(G-4341)**
**CHICAGO PRECIOUS MTLS EXCH LLC**
30 S Wacker Dr Fl 22 (60606-7452)
PHONE ............................ 312 854-7084
Macon Foscue, *Mng Member*
David Foscue,
EMP: 7
SALES (est): 743.1K **Privately Held**
SIC: 3339 Precious metals

**(G-4342)**
**CHICAGO PRESS CORPORATION**
1112 N Homan Ave (60651-4007)
PHONE ............................ 773 276-1500
Fax: 773 276-4595
Mitchell H Harrison, *President*
Patrica Mallo, *President*
Paul Monsen, *COO*
Ken Roskowski, *Vice Pres*
Peter Gardenier, *Manager*
EMP: 40 EST: 1927
SQ FT: 68,000
SALES (est): 9.8MM **Privately Held**
WEB: www.chicagopress.net
SIC: 2752 Commercial printing, lithographic; commercial printing, offset

**(G-4343)**
**CHICAGO PRVNCE OF THE SOC JSUS**
Loyola University Press
3441 N Ashland Ave (60657-1301)
PHONE ............................ 773 281-1818
Fax: 773 281-0555
Cathy Joyce, *Editor*
Mark Knapke, *Editor*
Maria Mondragon, *Editor*
Janet Czerwinski, *Prdtn Mgr*
Trudy Weisel, *CFO*
EMP: 25
SALES (corp-wide): 6MM **Privately Held**
WEB: www.loyolapress.com
SIC: 2731 Books: publishing only
PA: Chicago Province Of The Society Of Jesus
2050 N Clark St
Chicago IL 60614
773 975-6363

**(G-4344)**
**CHICAGO REVIEW PRESS INC (PA)**
Also Called: Independent Publishers Group
814 N Franklin St Ste 100 (60610-3813)
PHONE ............................ 312 337-0747
Fax: 312 337-5985
Curtis Matthews Jr, *CEO*
Mark Suchomel, *President*
Cynthia Sherry, *Publisher*
Ellen Hornor, *Editor*
Emily Lewis, *Editor*
▲ EMP: 43
SQ FT: 6,000
SALES (est): 76.5MM **Privately Held**
WEB: www.chicagoreviewpress.com
SIC: 5192 2731 Books; books: publishing only

**(G-4345)**
**CHICAGO SCENIC STUDIOS INC**
1315 N North Branch St (60642-2590)
PHONE ............................ 312 274-9900
Fax: 312 274-9901
Robert F Doepel, *President*
Helen A Doepel, *Vice Pres*
Gary Heitz, *Project Dir*
Jean Burch, *Project Mgr*
Alyce Iversen, *Project Mgr*
EMP: 75
SQ FT: 140,000
SALES (est): 11.6MM **Privately Held**
WEB: www.chicagoscenic.com
SIC: 3999 3993 Theatrical scenery; signs & advertising specialties

**(G-4346)**
**CHICAGO SCHOOL WOODWORKING LLC**
5680 N Northwest Hwy (60646-6136)
PHONE ............................ 773 275-1170
Fax: 773 774-2672
Shaun Devine, *Principal*
EMP: 4
SALES (est): 383K **Privately Held**
SIC: 2431 Millwork

**(G-4347)**
**CHICAGO SENSOR INC**
1736 W Pierce Ave (60622-2130)
PHONE ............................ 773 252-9660
Patrick Bowling, *Principal*
EMP: 9 EST: 2009
SALES (est): 1.5MM **Privately Held**
SIC: 3822 Thermostats & other environmental sensors

**(G-4348)**
**CHICAGO SHIRT & LETTERING CO**
1751 N Harlem Ave (60707-4305)
P.O. Box 8106, Romeoville (60446-8106)
PHONE ............................ 773 745-0222
Fax: 773 745-1775
Rocco Elia, *President*
Kathleen Di Gregorio, *Manager*
EMP: 8
SQ FT: 14,000
SALES (est): 926.3K **Privately Held**
SIC: 2396 5136 Screen printing on fabric articles; sportswear, men's & boys'

**(G-4349)**
**CHICAGO SILK SCREEN SUP CO INC**
882 N Milwaukee Ave (60642-4195)
PHONE ............................ 312 666-1494
Fax: 312 666-1213
Frank Zigmond, *President*
Alan Cajka, *Prdtn Mgr*
EMP: 20 EST: 1956
SQ FT: 14,000
SALES (est): 3.1MM **Privately Held**
SIC: 3953 5085 Stencils, painting & marking; textile printers' supplies

**(G-4350)**
**CHICAGO STEEL CONTAINER CORP**
1846 S Kilbourn Ave (60623-2382)
PHONE ............................ 773 277-2244
Fax: 773 277-1585
Louis J Pileggi, *President*
Phillip Klein, *Plant Mgr*
Juan Chapa, *Manager*
Judith Pileggi, *Technology*
Tony Pileggi, *Admin Sec*
EMP: 45 EST: 1978
SQ FT: 70,000
SALES (est): 11.9MM **Privately Held**
WEB: www.chicagosteelcontainer.com
SIC: 3412 Drums, shipping: metal

**(G-4351)**
**CHICAGO SUN-TIMES FEATURES INC (DH)**
350 N Orleans St Ste 1000 (60654-1700)
PHONE ............................ 312 321-3000
Tim Knight, *CEO*
David Radler, *President*
John Cruickshank, *Publisher*
Michael Cooke, *Editor*
Maria Mareno, *Opers Mgr*
EMP: 1300
SQ FT: 500,000
SALES (est): 66.4MM
SALES (corp-wide): 304.8MM **Privately Held**
SIC: 2711 2752 Newspapers, publishing & printing; commercial printing, lithographic
HQ: Cnlc-Stc, Inc.
350 N Orleans St
Chicago IL 60654
312 321-3000

**(G-4352)**
**CHICAGO SUN-TIMES FEATURES INC**
350 N Orleans St Ste 1000 (60654-1700)
PHONE ............................ 312 321-2043
Fax: 773 890-6971
James Shaffer, *Exec VP*
Bill Tatterson, *Manager*
Paul Davia, *Director*
EMP: 14
SALES (corp-wide): 304.8MM **Privately Held**
SIC: 2711 2741 Newspapers, publishing & printing; miscellaneous publishing
HQ: Chicago Sun-Times Features, Inc.
350 N Orleans St Ste 1000
Chicago IL 60654
312 321-3000

**(G-4353)**
**CHICAGO TANK REMOVAL INC**
70 W Madison St Ste 1400a (60602-4252)
PHONE ............................ 312 214-6144
David L Streich, *President*
EMP: 3
SALES (est): 274.1K **Privately Held**
SIC: 3822 Auto controls regulating residntl & coml environmt & applncs

**(G-4354)**
**CHICAGO TEMPERED GLASS INC**
2945 N Mozart St (60618-7701)
PHONE ............................ 773 583-2300
Fax: 773 583-2312
Adam Kaczynski, *President*
Kathy Rizzo, *Vice Pres*
▲ EMP: 13
SALES (est): 1.7MM **Privately Held**
WEB: www.chicagotemperedglass.com
SIC: 3211 Building glass, flat

**(G-4355)**
**CHICAGO TRANSMISSION PARTS**
3016 N Cicero Ave (60641-5106)
PHONE ............................ 773 427-6100
Fax: 773 427-4457
Jose Borjas, *Owner*
Gia Borjas, *Owner*
EMP: 9
SALES (est): 588.1K **Privately Held**
SIC: 3714 Motor vehicle parts & accessories

**(G-4356)**
**CHICAGO TRIBUNE**
665 W Sheridan Rd (60613-3306)
PHONE ............................ 773 910-6462
Ellen Warren, *Principal*
EMP: 3
SALES (est): 115K **Privately Held**
SIC: 2711 Newspapers

**(G-4357)**
**CHICAGO TRIBUNE COMPANY (HQ)**
435 N Michigan Ave # 200 (60611-4024)
PHONE ............................ 312 222-3232
Fax: 312 222-2598
David Hiller, *President*
Jane Hirt, *Editor*
Ray Hochgesang, *Editor*
Rob Karwath, *Editor*
Jim Kirk, *Editor*
▲ EMP: 2700
SQ FT: 943,000
SALES (est): 681.4MM
SALES (corp-wide): 1.6B **Publicly Held**
SIC: 2711 7383 7389 7331 Newspapers, publishing & printing; news feature syndicate; switchboard operation, private branch exchanges; mailing service
PA: Tronc, Inc.
435 N Michigan Ave
Chicago IL 60611
312 222-9100

**(G-4358)**
**CHICAGO TRIBUNE COMPANY**
Also Called: Tribune Freedom Center
777 W Chicago Ave (60654-2850)
PHONE ............................ 312 222-3232
Dick Malone, *General Mgr*
Reed Gregory, *Manager*
Keith Johnson, *Technical Staff*
EMP: 3
SALES (corp-wide): 1.6B **Publicly Held**
SIC: 2711 Newspapers, publishing & printing
HQ: Chicago Tribune Company
435 N Michigan Ave # 200
Chicago IL 60611
312 222-3232

**(G-4359)**
**CHICAGO TRIBUNE COMPANY**
Also Called: Paginatio
435 N Michigan Ave # 200 (60611-4024)
PHONE ............................ 312 222-8611
EMP: 3
SALES (corp-wide): 1.6B **Publicly Held**
SIC: 2711 Newspapers, publishing & printing
HQ: Chicago Tribune Company
435 N Michigan Ave # 200
Chicago IL 60611
312 222-3232

**(G-4360)**
**CHICAGO TURNRITE CO INC**
4459 W Lake St (60624-1636)
PHONE ............................ 773 626-8404
Fax: 773 626-4863
Ray Carlson, *CEO*
Grant Houda, *Plant Mgr*
Marcotulio Juarez, *Draft/Design*
Scott Kolar, *Engineer*
Lori George, *Office Mgr*
▼ EMP: 43 EST: 1948
SQ FT: 80,000
SALES (est): 10.2MM **Privately Held**
WEB: www.turnrite.com
SIC: 3451 Screw machine products

# Chicago - Cook County (G-4361)   GEOGRAPHIC SECTION

**(G-4361)**
**CHICAGO UNIFORMS COMPANY**
550 W Roosevelt Rd (60607-4917)
PHONE.................................312 913-1006
Benjamin Minow, *President*
▲ EMP: 20
SALES (est): 1.1MM **Privately Held**
SIC: 2326 Work uniforms

**(G-4362)**
**CHICAGO WEEKLY**
1131 E 57th St (60637-1503)
PHONE.................................773 702-7718
EMP: 3
SALES (est): 132.4K **Privately Held**
SIC: 2711 Newspapers

**(G-4363)**
**CHICAGO WIRE DESIGN INC**
1750 N Kimball Ave Ste 1 (60647-4884)
PHONE.................................773 342-4220
Fax: 773 342-1474
Frank Lopez, *President*
Peggy Lopez, *Vice Pres*
Margarito Salgado, *Vice Pres*
Larry Wolfe, *Accountant*
Roberto Avalos, *Office Mgr*
EMP: 50
SQ FT: 55,000
SALES (est): 3.8MM **Privately Held**
SIC: 3496 Woven wire products

**(G-4364)**
**CHICAGONE DEVELOPERS INC**
557 E 75th St (60619-2230)
PHONE.................................773 783-2105
Darryl Hicks, *Branch Mgr*
EMP: 3 **Privately Held**
SIC: 3442 Shutters, door or window: metal
PA: Chicagone Developers, Inc.
   2044 W 163rd St Ste 11
   Markham IL

**(G-4365)**
**CHICAGOS FINEST IRON WORKS**
3319 W Washington Blvd (60624)
PHONE.................................773 646-4484
Fax: 708 895-4484
John Macon, *Owner*
EMP: 10
SALES (est): 386.9K **Privately Held**
SIC: 3446 Ornamental metalwork

**(G-4366)**
**CHINA JOURNAL INC**
2146a S Archer Ave (60616-1514)
PHONE.................................312 326-3228
May Zheng, *President*
▲ EMP: 5
SALES (est): 485K **Privately Held**
SIC: 2721 Periodicals

**(G-4367)**
**CHINESE AMERICAN NEWS**
610 W 31st St (60616-3023)
PHONE.................................312 225-5600
Fax: 312 225-8849
James Chang, *President*
EMP: 6
SQ FT: 2,000
SALES (est): 350K **Privately Held**
WEB: www.canews.com
SIC: 2711 Newspapers

**(G-4368)**
**CHOI BRANDS INC**
3401 W Division St (60651-2356)
PHONE.................................773 489-2800
Fax: 773 489-3030
Tony Choi, *President*
Cynthia Choi, *General Mgr*
Unah Choi, *Vice Pres*
Sue Kang, *Vice Pres*
▲ EMP: 120
SQ FT: 90,000
SALES (est): 12.4MM **Privately Held**
WEB: www.choibrothers.com
SIC: 2326 2337 2329 2339 Work uniforms, work garments, except raincoats: waterproof; industrial garments, men's & boys'; uniforms, except athletic: women's, misses' & juniors'; men's & boys' sportswear & athletic clothing; uniforms, athletic: women's, misses' & juniors'; sewing contractor

**(G-4369)**
**CHRIS DJ MIX LLC**
1408 W Fillmore St (60607-4689)
PHONE.................................312 725-3838
Christopher Calip, *Principal*
EMP: 5 EST: 2012
SALES (est): 318.1K **Privately Held**
SIC: 3273 Ready-mixed concrete

**(G-4370)**
**CHRISTIAN CENTURY**
104 S Michigan Ave # 1100 (60603-5919)
PHONE.................................312 263-7510
Fax: 312 263-7540
Rev John M Buchanan, *President*
Safiya Edwards, *Marketing Staff*
Carol Cahill, *Office Mgr*
Masood Akran, *Manager*
Eboo Patel, *Exec Dir*
▲ EMP: 16
SALES (est): 2.4MM **Privately Held**
WEB: www.christiancentury.org
SIC: 2721 Magazines: publishing only, not printed on site

**(G-4371)**
**CHRISTIANA INDUSTRIES INC**
6500 N Clark St (60626-4097)
PHONE.................................773 465-6330
Fax: 773 465-6271
Robert Ferris, *Ch of Bd*
Ron Smith, *President*
Donald Cencula, *Vice Pres*
Peer Pederson, *Admin Sec*
EMP: 170 EST: 1956
SQ FT: 33,500
SALES (est): 18.4MM **Privately Held**
SIC: 3643 Sockets, electric

**(G-4372)**
**CHRISTOPHER GLASS & ALUMINUM**
3014 W Fillmore St (60612-3925)
PHONE.................................312 256-8500
Fax: 312 256-8501
Abraham Asllani, *President*
Paul Rowan, *Exec VP*
John T Metz, *CFO*
Jackie Walker, *Admin Asst*
EMP: 100
SQ FT: 50,000
SALES: 19.9MM **Privately Held**
SIC: 1793 3446 Glass & glazing work; architectural metalwork

**(G-4373)**
**CHROMIUM INDUSTRIES INC (PA)**
4645 W Chicago Ave (60651-3385)
PHONE.................................773 287-3716
Fax: 773 287-5792
Peter J Heidengren, *President*
Scott Patterson, *General Mgr*
Bruno Lemons, *Vice Pres*
Jim Lame, *Opers Mgr*
John Angelos, *Production*
▲ EMP: 39
SQ FT: 47,000
SALES (est): 5.8MM **Privately Held**
WEB: www.chromiumindustries.com
SIC: 3471 3312 2891 2851 Chromium plating of metals or formed products; blast furnaces & steel mills; adhesives & sealants; paints & allied products; inorganic pigments; platemaking services

**(G-4374)**
**CHURCHILL WILMSLOW CORPORATION**
Also Called: Signs Now
162 N Franklin St Ste 200 (60606-1861)
PHONE.................................312 759-8911
Linda George, *President*
EMP: 5
SQ FT: 40,000
SALES (est): 520K **Privately Held**
WEB: www.chicagosignsnow.com
SIC: 3993 2759 Signs & advertising specialties; commercial printing

**(G-4375)**
**CHURNY COMPANY INC**
200 E Randolph St (60601-6436)
PHONE.................................847 646-5500
Fax: 847 480-5591
Georges El-Zoghbi, *President*
Eddy Yee, *Finance Mgr*
Kim K W Rucker, *Admin Sec*
Tina Shritter, *Admin Sec*
▲ EMP: 473 EST: 1941
SQ FT: 7,500
SALES (est): 715.6K
SALES (corp-wide): 26.4B **Publicly Held**
SIC: 2022 Natural cheese; processed cheese
PA: The Kraft Heinz Company
   200 E Randolph St # 7300
   Chicago IL 60601
   412 456-5700

**(G-4376)**
**CHWEY SOFTWARE LLC**
1246 W George St (60657-4220)
PHONE.................................773 525-6445
Pete Hallenberg, *Owner*
EMP: 20 EST: 2000
SALES (est): 1.3MM **Privately Held**
SIC: 7372 Prepackaged software

**(G-4377)**
**CICERONE CERTIFICATION PROGRAM**
4043 N Ravenswood Ave # 306 (60613-5683)
PHONE.................................773 549-4800
Shana Solarte, *Editor*
Virginia Thomas, *Business Mgr*
Nicole Erny, *Manager*
Pat Fahey, *Manager*
Chris Pisney, *Director*
EMP: 5
SALES (est): 258K **Privately Held**
SIC: 2082 Beer (alcoholic beverage)

**(G-4378)**
**CIMINO MACHINE CORP**
5958 S Central Ave (60638-3711)
P.O. Box 354, Saint Charles (60174-0354)
PHONE.................................773 767-7000
Fax: 773 767-9759
Edward J Lupie, *President*
Debbie Lupie, *Admin Sec*
EMP: 10 EST: 1950
SQ FT: 12,000
SALES (est): 1.3MM **Privately Held**
SIC: 3599 7692 Machine shop, jobbing & repair; automotive welding

**(G-4379)**
**CINTAS CORPORATION**
Also Called: Pride Manufacturing
5600 W 73rd St (60638-6212)
PHONE.................................708 563-2626
Donnie Hicks, *General Mgr*
Christine Duffy, *Principal*
William Riesner, *Vice Pres*
John Gulla, *Mfg Dir*
Ejaz Murtaza, *Opers Mgr*
EMP: 70
SALES (corp-wide): 4.9B **Publicly Held**
WEB: www.cintas-corp.com
SIC: 2337 2326 2339 Uniforms, except athletic: women's, misses' & juniors'; medical & hospital uniforms, men's; women's & misses' outerwear
PA: Cintas Corporation
   6800 Cintas Blvd
   Cincinnati OH 45262
   513 459-1200

**(G-4380)**
**CIRCLE STUDIO STAINED GLASS**
3928 N Elston Ave (60618-4228)
PHONE.................................773 588-4848
Joseph Badalpour, *President*
George Badalpour, *Vice Pres*
Susan Wiltshire, *Manager*
EMP: 2
SQ FT: 3,000
SALES: 200K **Privately Held**
WEB: www.circlestudioinc.net
SIC: 8999 3471 3231 Artist; stained glass art; plating & polishing; products of purchased glass

**(G-4381)**
**CISION US INC (PA)**
130 E Randolph St Fl 7 (60601-6164)
PHONE.................................312 922-2400
Kevin Akeroyd, *CEO*
Jason Edelboim, *President*
Jeremy Thompson, *Managing Dir*
Kenneth Davis, *Editor*
Anna Marevska, *Editor*
EMP: 144 EST: 1892
SQ FT: 50,000
SALES (est): 259.7MM **Privately Held**
WEB: www.bacons.com
SIC: 7389 2741 7331 Press clipping service; miscellaneous publishing; mailing service

**(G-4382)**
**CITY FOODS INC**
Also Called: Bea's Best
4230 S Racine Ave (60609-2526)
P.O. Box 9190 (60609-0190)
PHONE.................................773 523-1566
Fax: 773 523-1414
Kenneth Kohn, *President*
Jerry Kohn, *CFO*
Chris Humberg, *Info Tech Mgr*
John Campbell, *Director*
▼ EMP: 110
SQ FT: 30,000
SALES: 48MM **Privately Held**
SIC: 2011 Meat packing plants

**(G-4383)**
**CITY LIVING DESIGN INC**
401 E Ontario St Apt 1302 (60611-7169)
PHONE.................................312 335-0711
Hollis Favin, *President*
EMP: 3
SALES (est): 471K **Privately Held**
SIC: 7299 2211 2511 Banquet hall facilities; furniture denim; wood household furniture

**(G-4384)**
**CITY OF CHICAGO**
Also Called: Department Streets Sanitation
6441 N Ravenswood Ave # 49 (60626-3927)
PHONE.................................312 744-0940
Fax: 312 742-1231
William Nortkett, *Manager*
EMP: 20 **Privately Held**
WEB: www.ci.chi.il.us
SIC: 2842 9111 4953 Sanitation preparations; ; garbage: collecting, destroying & processing
PA: City Of Chicago
   121 N La Salle St
   Chicago IL 60602
   312 744-5000

**(G-4385)**
**CITY OF CHICAGO**
Also Called: Department Aviation Sign Shop
11601 W Touhy Ave (60666-5047)
PHONE.................................773 686-2254
Rich Meehan, *Branch Mgr*
EMP: 3 **Privately Held**
SIC: 3993 Mfg Signs/Advertising Specialties
PA: City Of Chicago
   121 N La Salle St
   Chicago IL 60602
   312 744-5000

**(G-4386)**
**CITY OF CHICAGO**
Also Called: 13th Ward Office
6500 S Pulaski Rd Fl 2 (60629-5136)
PHONE.................................773 581-8000
Frank Olivo, *Director*
EMP: 8 **Privately Held**
WEB: www.ci.chi.il.us
SIC: 9199 2731 General government administration; ; book publishing
PA: City Of Chicago
   121 N La Salle St
   Chicago IL 60602
   312 744-5000

# GEOGRAPHIC SECTION

Chicago - Cook County (G-4412)

### (G-4387)
**CITY OF CHICAGO**
Also Called: Streets and Sanitation, Dept
4830 W Chicago Ave (60651-3223)
**PHONE**..................312 746-6583
**Fax:** 312 746-5347
Excell Brown, *Administration*
**EMP:** 20 **Privately Held**
**WEB:** www.ci.chi.il.us
**SIC:** 2842 Sanitation preparations, disinfectants & deodorants; sanitation preparations
**PA:** City Of Chicago
 121 N La Salle St
 Chicago IL 60602
 312 744-5000

### (G-4388)
**CITY SCREEN INC (PA)**
Also Called: Pengo Products Company
5540 N Kedzie Ave (60625-3924)
**PHONE**..................773 588-5642
**Fax:** 773 588-5742
Gary Langwell, *President*
Diana Langwell, *Corp Secy*
**EMP:** 8 **EST:** 1941
**SQ FT:** 1,800
**SALES (est):** 1.2MM **Privately Held**
**SIC:** 3496 5063 3446 3444 Screening, woven wire: made from purchased wire; electrical apparatus & equipment; architectural metalwork; sheet metalwork; metal doors, sash & trim; millwork

### (G-4389)
**CITY SUBN AUTO SVC GOODYEAR**
5674 N Northwest Hwy (60646-6136)
**PHONE**..................773 355-5550
**Fax:** 773 355-5553
Soneal Asija, *President*
**EMP:** 4
**SQ FT:** 10,000
**SALES:** 360K **Privately Held**
**SIC:** 5531 5511 7549 3714 Automotive tires; automobiles, new & used; towing service, automotive; motor vehicle parts & accessories; truck rental & leasing, no drivers

### (G-4390)
**CITYZENITH LLC**
Also Called: City Zenith
220 N Green St (60607-1702)
**PHONE**..................312 282-2900
Michael Jansen, *Mng Member*
**EMP:** 12 **EST:** 2013
**SQ FT:** 200
**SALES:** 500K **Privately Held**
**SIC:** 7372 Application computer software

### (G-4391)
**CK ACQUISITION HOLDINGS INC**
13535 S Torrence Ave Q (60633-2164)
**PHONE**..................773 646-0115
Bradley Baker, *President*
William Bright, *Admin Sec*
**EMP:** 14
**SALES (est):** 178.2K
**SALES (corp-wide):** 1MM **Privately Held**
**SIC:** 7538 3714 General automotive repair shops; motor vehicle electrical equipment
**PA:** Kerr Holdings Delaware, Inc.
 2140 S Dupont Hwy
 Camden DE 19934
 800 585-1774

### (G-4392)
**CLASSIC EMBROIDERY INC**
6939 W 59th St (60638-3205)
**PHONE**..................708 485-7034
Anna Chraca, *President*
Ralph Cison, *Vice Pres*
**EMP:** 15
**SALES (est):** 1MM **Privately Held**
**SIC:** 2395 Embroidery & art needlework

### (G-4393)
**CLASSIC MIDWEST DIE MOLD INC**
1140 N Kostner Ave (60651-3499)
**PHONE**..................773 227-8000
**Fax:** 773 227-4605
Luigi Scala Sr, *President*
Steve Morris, *Purch Agent*
Jake Morawski, *Office Mgr*
**EMP:** 10
**SQ FT:** 40,000
**SALES (est):** 2MM **Privately Held**
**WEB:** www.classicmdm.com
**SIC:** 3089 3993 Injection molded finished plastic products; signs & advertising specialties

### (G-4394)
**CLASSIC REMIX**
116 W Illinois St Fl 6w-B (60654-2758)
**PHONE**..................312 915-0521
**EMP:** 4
**SALES (est):** 240K **Privately Held**
**SIC:** 2599 Mfg Furniture/Fixtures

### (G-4395)
**CLASSIC VENDING INC**
Also Called: Classic Group, The
2155 S Carpenter St (60608-4502)
**PHONE**..................773 252-7000
Michael Klong, *President*
Jim Carbone, *COO*
Danny Locash, *Director*
**EMP:** 30
**SALES (est):** 12.8MM **Privately Held**
**SIC:** 5046 3581 Coffee brewing equipment & supplies; automatic vending machines

### (G-4396)
**CLAY VOLLMAR PRODUCTS CO (PA)**
5835 W Touhy Ave (60646-1264)
**PHONE**..................773 774-1234
**Fax:** 773 774-1254
Eric W Schulenburg, *President*
H J Schulenberg, *President*
Eric Schulenberg, *Vice Pres*
Mike Gehlbach, *Manager*
Marilyn Schulenberg, *Admin Sec*
**EMP:** 10
**SQ FT:** 2,000
**SALES (est):** 3.1MM **Privately Held**
**WEB:** www.vollmar.com
**SIC:** 3272 5032 Concrete products; sewer pipe, clay

### (G-4397)
**CLEAN MOTION INC**
4444 W Chicago Ave (60651-3424)
**PHONE**..................607 323-1778
Dionysis Alissandrutos, *President*
**EMP:** 10 **EST:** 2014
**SALES (est):** 637.2K **Privately Held**
**SIC:** 2869 Industrial organic chemicals

### (G-4398)
**CLEARTRIAL LLC**
233 S Wacker Dr Ste 4500 (60606-6376)
**PHONE**..................877 206-4846
Michael Soenen, *Managing Prtnr*
Kelly Larrabee, *Director*
Mike Soenen,
**EMP:** 17 **EST:** 2009
**SALES (est):** 1.6MM
**SALES (corp-wide):** 37B **Publicly Held**
**SIC:** 7372 Educational computer software
**PA:** Oracle Corporation
 500 Oracle Pkwy
 Redwood City CA 94065
 650 506-7000

### (G-4399)
**CLEATS MFG INC (PA)**
Also Called: Cleats Manufacturing Company
1855 S Kilbourn Ave (60623-2307)
**PHONE**..................773 521-0300
Stephen Passannante Jr, *President*
Ernest De Lord, *Treasurer*
**EMP:** 18
**SQ FT:** 25,000
**SALES (est):** 4.2MM **Privately Held**
**WEB:** www.cleatsmfg.com
**SIC:** 3444 3429 1761 Ducts, sheet metal; metal fasteners; sheet metalwork

### (G-4400)
**CLEATS MFG INC**
1701 S Kostner Ave (60623-2338)
**PHONE**..................773 542-0453
**Fax:** 773 542-0487
Jim Wagner, *Manager*
**EMP:** 15
**SALES (corp-wide):** 4.2MM **Privately Held**
**WEB:** www.cleatsmfg.com
**SIC:** 3444 Ducts, sheet metal
**PA:** Cleats Mfg., Inc.
 1855 S Kilbourn Ave
 Chicago IL 60623
 773 521-0300

### (G-4401)
**CLEMENTI PRINTING INC**
2832 N Narragansett Ave (60634-4911)
**PHONE**..................773 622-0795
**Fax:** 773 622-5933
Anthony Clementi, *President*
Christine Clementi, *Admin Sec*
**EMP:** 3
**SQ FT:** 600
**SALES (est):** 337.3K **Privately Held**
**SIC:** 2752 2791 Commercial printing, offset; typesetting

### (G-4402)
**CLIENTLOYALTY LLC** ✪
220 N Green St Ste 6015 (60607-1702)
**PHONE**..................312 307-5716
Kent Barnett, *CEO*
Jeb Metric, *Principal*
Jeffrey Berk, *COO*
**EMP:** 3 **EST:** 2016
**SALES (est):** 104.1K **Privately Held**
**SIC:** 7372 Application computer software

### (G-4403)
**CLINTEX LABORATORIES INC**
140 W 62nd St (60621-3809)
**PHONE**..................773 493-9777
**Fax:** 773 493-9829
Stephen G Luster, *President*
Josie Luster, *Vice Pres*
Nancy Rachell, *Purch Mgr*
Brandon Waiters, *Sales Executive*
Helen Hall, *Admin Asst*
**EMP:** 29
**SQ FT:** 50,000
**SALES (est):** 7.1MM **Privately Held**
**WEB:** www.essationsproducts.com
**SIC:** 2844 Cosmetic preparations

### (G-4404)
**CLOROX PRODUCTS MFG CO**
5063 S Merrimac Ave (60638-1305)
**PHONE**..................708 728-4200
**Fax:** 708 458-0433
Dave Santiango, *Branch Mgr*
Sharon Madderom, *Director*
**EMP:** 104
**SALES (corp-wide):** 5.7B **Publicly Held**
**SIC:** 2842 2819 Bleaches, household: dry or liquid; industrial inorganic chemicals
**HQ:** Clorox Products Manufacturing Company
 1221 Broadway
 Oakland CA 94612

### (G-4405)
**CLOROX PRODUCTS MFG CO**
5064 S Merrimac Ave (60638-1306)
**PHONE**..................708 728-4200
Donald Knauss, *CEO*
◆ **EMP:** 29
**SALES (est):** 6.1MM **Privately Held**
**SIC:** 2842 Specialty cleaning, polishes & sanitation goods; bleaches, household: dry or liquid

### (G-4406)
**CLOVER CLUB BOTTLING CO INC**
356 N Kilbourn Ave (60624-1623)
**PHONE**..................773 261-7100
**Fax:** 773 261-7147
Joseph Troy, *President*
Edward Kennelly, *Vice Pres*
▲ **EMP:** 12 **EST:** 1934
**SQ FT:** 65,000
**SALES (est):** 3.2MM **Privately Held**
**SIC:** 5149 2086 Soft drinks; carbonated beverages, nonalcoholic: bottled & canned

### (G-4407)
**CLOVER SIGNS**
2944 W Montrose Ave Apt 1 (60618-1485)
**PHONE**..................773 588-2828
Kwang Yi, *Owner*
Brandon Samuels, *Graphic Designe*
**EMP:** 4
**SQ FT:** 2,000
**SALES (est):** 205.2K **Privately Held**
**SIC:** 3993 Signs & advertising specialties

### (G-4408)
**CLOVERHILL PASTRY-VEND LLC**
Also Called: Cloverhill Bakery
2035 N Narragansett Ave (60639-3842)
**PHONE**..................773 745-9800
**Fax:** 773 745-1647
Robert Gee III, *President*
Tim Hakin, *COO*
Efrain Hernandez, *Purchasing*
Edward Gee, *Treasurer*
William A Gee IV, *Treasurer*
▼ **EMP:** 55 **EST:** 1961
**SQ FT:** 75,000
**SALES (est):** 36.3MM
**SALES (corp-wide):** 4.3B **Privately Held**
**WEB:** www.cloverhill.com
**SIC:** 2053 2051 Frozen bakery products, except bread; cakes, pies & pastries; bakery products, partially cooked (except frozen)
**PA:** Aryzta Ag
 Talacker 41
 ZUrich ZH 8001
 445 834-200

### (G-4409)
**CLYBOURN METAL FINISHING CO**
2240 N Clybourn Ave (60614-3087)
**PHONE**..................773 525-8162
Tim Collins, *President*
William G Romaniuk, *Corp Secy*
Peter Alonzo, *Plant Mgr*
**EMP:** 50 **EST:** 1944
**SQ FT:** 11,250
**SALES:** 2MM **Privately Held**
**WEB:** www.clybournmetal.com
**SIC:** 3471 5084 Polishing, metals or formed products; industrial machinery & equipment

### (G-4410)
**CLYDE PRINTING COMPANY**
3520 S Morgan St Fl 2a (60609-1582)
**PHONE**..................773 847-5900
**Fax:** 773 847-6470
Collen Woulfe, *President*
John V Woulfe Jr, *Vice Pres*
Fran Montoro, *Manager*
Nancy Woulfe, *Admin Sec*
**EMP:** 10
**SQ FT:** 28,000
**SALES (est):** 1.4MM **Privately Held**
**SIC:** 2752 2791 2759 Commercial printing, offset; typesetting; commercial printing

### (G-4411)
**CMV SHARPER FINISH INC**
4500 W Augusta Blvd (60651-3301)
**PHONE**..................773 276-4800
**Fax:** 773 276-4800
Mark J Camelotto, *President*
Craig Roberts, *Vice Pres*
Venkat Tripurenani, *Vice Pres*
▼ **EMP:** 25
**SALES (est):** 5.3MM **Privately Held**
**WEB:** www.cmvsharperfinish.com
**SIC:** 3582 Ironers, commercial laundry & drycleaning

### (G-4412)
**CNLC-STC INC (DH)**
350 N Orleans St (60654-1975)
**PHONE**..................312 321-3000
Jeff Britt, *Editor*
John Cruickshank, *COO*
Frederic R Lebolt, *Vice Pres*
J David Dodd, *CFO*
Madeline Hester, *Accounts Exec*
**EMP:** 1350
**SQ FT:** 500,000
**SALES (est):** 89.3MM
**SALES (corp-wide):** 304.8MM **Privately Held**
**SIC:** 2711 Newspapers, publishing & printing

---

(PA)=Parent Co (HQ)=Headquarters (DH)=Div Headquarters
✪ = New Business established in last 2 years

HQ: Sun-Times Media Group, Inc.
350 N Orleans St Fl 10
Chicago IL 60654
312 321-2299

**(G-4413)**
**COALESSE**
222 Merchds Mrt Plz 1032 (60654)
PHONE .................................. 312 622-6269
Michelle Riley, *Principal*
Ann Fanizzo, *Regional Mgr*
Dean Travia, *Regional Mgr*
Natasha Sides, *Project Mgr*
Shelley Beechie, *Sales Mgr*
**EMP:** 17
**SALES (est):** 1.9MM **Privately Held**
**SIC: 3553** Furniture makers' machinery, woodworking

**(G-4414)**
**COATING & SYSTEMS INTEGRATION**
47 W Division St Pmb 124 (60610-2954)
PHONE .................................. 312 335-1848
Cole Oehler, *President*
**EMP:** 10
**SQ FT:** 40,000
**SALES (est):** 1.1MM **Privately Held**
**SIC: 3567** 3699 Industrial furnaces & ovens; electrical equipment & supplies

**(G-4415)**
**COCA-COLA REFRESHMENTS USA INC**
12200 S Laramie Ave (60803-3194)
PHONE .................................. 708 597-4700
**Fax:** 708 597-9132
Kevin Morris, *VP Corp Comm*
Thomas Pawelczyk, *Manager*
**EMP:** 100
**SALES (corp-wide):** 41.8B **Publicly Held**
**WEB:** www.cokecce.com
**SIC: 2086** 5149 Soft drinks: packaged in cans, bottles, etc.; carbonated beverages, nonalcoholic: bottled & canned; groceries & related products
**HQ:** Coca-Cola Refreshments Usa, Inc.
2500 Windy Ridge Pkwy Se
Atlanta GA 30339
770 989-3000

**(G-4416)**
**CODE SIXFOUR LLC**
111 W Illinois St (60654-4505)
PHONE .................................. 312 429-4802
Eric Rentsch, *CEO*
**EMP:** 5
**SQ FT:** 1,200
**SALES (est):** 222.5K **Privately Held**
**SIC: 7372** Business oriented computer software

**(G-4417)**
**CODY METAL FINISHING INC**
1620 N Throop St (60642-1515)
PHONE .................................. 773 252-2026
Stephen Obert, *President*
David Yaris, *Vice Pres*
Ismael Lopez, *Plant Mgr*
Margret Obert, *Treasurer*
**EMP:** 15
**SQ FT:** 25,000
**SALES (est):** 1.1MM **Privately Held**
**SIC: 3471** Electroplating of metals or formed products

**(G-4418)**
**COEUR CAPITAL INC**
104 S Michigan Ave (60603-5902)
PHONE .................................. 312 489-5800
Mitchell J Krebs, *President*
Casey M Nault, *Vice Pres*
**EMP:** 6
**SALES (est):** 353K
**SALES (corp-wide):** 665.7MM **Publicly Held**
**SIC: 1081** Metal mining services; metal mining exploration & development services
**PA:** Coeur Mining, Inc.
104 S Michigan Ave # 900
Chicago IL 60603
312 489-5800

**(G-4419)**
**COEUR MINING INC (PA)**
104 S Michigan Ave # 900 (60603-5902)
PHONE .................................. 312 489-5800
Robert E Mellor, *Ch of Bd*
Mitchell J Krebs, *President*
Frank L Hanagarne Jr, *COO*
Casey M Nault, *Senior VP*
Hans J Rasmussen, *Senior VP*
**EMP:** 65
**SALES:** 665.7MM **Publicly Held**
**WEB:** www.coeur.com
**SIC: 1041** 1044 Gold ores mining; gold ores processing; silver ores mining; silver ores processing

**(G-4420)**
**COEUR ROCHESTER INC**
104 S Michigan Ave (60603-5902)
PHONE .................................. 312 661-2436
Rochester Green, *Principal*
**EMP:** 7 **EST:** 2013
**SALES (est):** 810.9K **Privately Held**
**SIC: 1044** Silver ores

**(G-4421)**
**COLD HEADERS INC (PA)**
5514 N Elston Ave 14 (60630-1380)
PHONE .................................. 773 775-7900
**Fax:** 773 775-0779
Bruce Duncan, *President*
Richard Duncan, *Vice Pres*
Dave Effert, *Vice Pres*
Lynn Carlson, *Office Mgr*
Michelle Silk, *Office Mgr*
▲ **EMP:** 18 **EST:** 1962
**SQ FT:** 40,000
**SALES (est):** 4.8MM **Privately Held**
**WEB:** www.coldheaders.com
**SIC: 5072** 3599 Screws; machine shop, jobbing & repair

**(G-4422)**
**COLES APPLIANCE & FURN CO**
4026 N Lincoln Ave (60618-3010)
PHONE .................................. 773 525-1797
**Fax:** 773 525-0728
Barry Krasney, *President*
Kevin Krasney, *General Mgr*
Mari Krasney, *Admin Sec*
**EMP:** 5 **EST:** 1957
**SQ FT:** 10,000
**SALES (est):** 2.9MM **Privately Held**
**WEB:** www.shopcoles.com
**SIC: 5722** 5712 5731 2512 Electric household appliances, small; furniture stores; consumer electronic equipment; television sets; high fidelity stereo equipment; video cameras, recorders & accessories; upholstered household furniture

**(G-4423)**
**COLLAGEN USA INC**
3048 N Milwaukee Ave (60618-6624)
PHONE .................................. 708 716-0251
**EMP:** 2
**SALES (est):** 220K **Privately Held**
**SIC: 2844** Mfg Toilet Preparations/Skin Care Products

**(G-4424)**
**COLLEGE BOUND PUBLICATIONS**
7658 N Rogers Ave (60626-1208)
P.O. Box 6526, Evanston (60204-6526)
PHONE .................................. 773 262-5810
R Craig Sautter, *President*
**EMP:** 2
**SALES (est):** 225.9K **Privately Held**
**SIC: 2721** 8748 Periodicals; publishing consultant

**(G-4425)**
**COLNAGO AMERICA INC**
1528 W Adams St Ste 4b (60607-2450)
PHONE .................................. 312 239-6666
Alessandro Colnago, *President*
Soren Krebs Siekierski, *Admin Sec*
▲ **EMP:** 2
**SQ FT:** 2,500
**SALES (est):** 390.7K **Privately Held**
**SIC: 3751** Frames, motorcycle & bicycle

**(G-4426)**
**COLOR COMMUNICATIONS INC (PA)**
4000 W Fillmore St (60624-3905)
PHONE .................................. 773 638-1400
**Fax:** 773 638-0887
Stanley Lerner, *CEO*
Steven Winter, *President*
Harry Lerner, *Vice Pres*
Cynthia Cornell, *Project Dir*
Renee Smentek, *Project Mgr*
▼ **EMP:** 195
**SQ FT:** 300,000
**SALES (est):** 135.6MM **Privately Held**
**SIC: 2752** 3993 Cards, lithographed; advertising artwork

**(G-4427)**
**COLOR WORKS GRAPHICS INC**
451 N Racine Ave (60642-5841)
PHONE .................................. 847 383-5270
**Fax:** 312 666-0473
Al Jay, *President*
Gary Johnson, *Vice Pres*
Pat Lewis, *Sales Associate*
**EMP:** 20
**SQ FT:** 11,000
**SALES (est):** 2.2MM **Privately Held**
**WEB:** www.cardelinc.com
**SIC: 2796** Color separations for printing

**(G-4428)**
**COLORJAR LLC**
435 N La Salle Dr Ste 201 (60654-4588)
PHONE .................................. 312 489-8510
Timm Bloem, *President*
David Gardner, *Mng Member*
Aj Tarachanowicz, *Software Dev*
**EMP:** 10
**SALES (est):** 1.3MM **Privately Held**
**SIC: 3577** Computer peripheral equipment

**(G-4429)**
**COLORS CHICAGO INC**
420 W Huron St Fl 1 (60654-8475)
PHONE .................................. 312 265-1642
Michael Duff, *President*
**EMP:** 9
**SALES (est):** 714.2K **Privately Held**
**SIC: 3861** 7336 Printing frames, photographic; commercial art & graphic design

**(G-4430)**
**COLT TECHNOLOGY SERVICES LLC**
141 W Jackson Blvd # 2808 (60604-2992)
PHONE .................................. 312 465-2484
Derek Sprunk, *Manager*
**EMP:** 6 **EST:** 2015
**SALES (est):** 297.5K
**SALES (corp-wide):** 1.6B **Privately Held**
**SIC: 3663** Radio & TV communications equipment
**HQ:** Colt Technology Services Group Limited
Beaufort House
London
207 390-3900

**(G-4431)**
**COLUMBIA METAL SPINNING CO**
4351 N Normandy Ave (60634-1395)
PHONE .................................. 773 685-2800
Fred Haberkamp, *President*
Dawn Koleman, *Vice Pres*
**EMP:** 55
**SQ FT:** 45,000
**SALES (est):** 10.3MM **Privately Held**
**WEB:** www.cmspinning.com
**SIC: 3469** Spinning metal for the trade

**(G-4432)**
**COLUMBIA SPORTSWEAR COMPANY**
830 N Michigan Ave Ste 3 (60611-2167)
PHONE .................................. 312 649-3758
Timothy Boyle, *President*
**EMP:** 225
**SALES (corp-wide):** 2.3B **Publicly Held**
**SIC: 2329** Men's & boys' sportswear & athletic clothing
**PA:** Columbia Sportswear Company
14375 Nw Science Park Dr
Portland OR 97229
503 985-4000

**(G-4433)**
**COLUMBUS MEATS INC**
906 W Randolph St Fl 1 (60607-2208)
PHONE .................................. 312 829-2480
George Dervenis, *President*
**EMP:** 9
**SQ FT:** 1,900
**SALES (est):** 667.8K **Privately Held**
**SIC: 5421** 5147 2013 Meat markets, including freezer provisioners; meats, fresh; sausages & other prepared meats

**(G-4434)**
**COM-GRAPHICS INC**
329 W 18th St Fl 10 (60616-1120)
PHONE .................................. 312 226-0900
Denise Kretzer, *President*
Lydia Erickson, *CFO*
Lee Dwyer, *Accountant*
Bruce Turyna, *Sales Executive*
Susan Askew, *Manager*
**EMP:** 70 **EST:** 1980
**SQ FT:** 50,000
**SALES (est):** 8.8MM **Privately Held**
**WEB:** www.cgichicago.com
**SIC: 7389** 2759 7331 Microfilm recording & developing service; commercial printing; mailing service

**(G-4435)**
**COMMERCIAL PALLET INC**
2029 W Hubbard St (60612-1609)
PHONE .................................. 312 226-6699
**Fax:** 312 226-6963
Lester Hagan, *President*
Doris Hagan, *Corp Secy*
Tim Hagan, *Vice Pres*
**EMP:** 30 **EST:** 1978
**SQ FT:** 3,500
**SALES (est):** 2.9MM **Privately Held**
**WEB:** www.commercialpallet.com
**SIC: 7699** 2448 Pallet repair; wood pallets & skids

**(G-4436)**
**COMMUNITY GOSPEL CENTER**
Also Called: Community Optical Service
2880 N Milwaukee Ave (60618-7413)
PHONE .................................. 773 486-7661
**Fax:** 773 486-2821
Richard Geeslin, *Director*
**EMP:** 8
**SALES (est):** 120K **Privately Held**
**SIC: 8661** 3827 Churches, temples & shrines; optical instruments & apparatus

**(G-4437)**
**COMMUNITY MAGAZINE GROUP**
1550 S Indiana Ave (60605-2857)
PHONE .................................. 312 880-0370
Jim Distasio, *Principal*
**EMP:** 4
**SALES (est):** 300K **Privately Held**
**SIC: 2721** Periodicals

**(G-4438)**
**COMPASS MINERALS INTL INC**
9200 S Ewing Ave (60617-4638)
PHONE .................................. 773 978-7258
Joe Betustak, *Finance Mgr*
Fred Sanders, *Info Tech Mgr*
Alex Sharpe, *Info Tech Mgr*
Jerrod Young, *Info Tech Mgr*
Wendy Giardina, *Legal Staff*
**EMP:** 13
**SALES (corp-wide):** 1.1B **Publicly Held**
**SIC: 5169** 2899 Salts, industrial; chemical preparations
**PA:** Compass Minerals International, Inc.
9900 W 109th St Ste 100
Overland Park KS 66210
913 344-9200

**(G-4439)**
**COMPLETELY NUTS INC**
600 E Grand Ave (60611-3419)
PHONE .................................. 847 394-4312
Phil Mostaccio, *President*
Chris Mostaccio, *Admin Sec*
**EMP:** 6

SALES (est): 485.5K  Privately Held
SIC: 2068  Nuts: dried, dehydrated, salted or roasted

**(G-4440)**
**COMPUTER BUSINESS FORMS CO**
6525 N Olmsted Ave  (60631-1495)
PHONE..................................773 775-0155
Fax: 773 775-0975
Mark Niederkorn, *President*
Karen Niederkorn, *Corp Secy*
William Niederkon, *Vice Pres*
EMP: 2
SQ FT: 5,500
SALES (est): 280K  Privately Held
WEB: www.cbfdirect.com
SIC: 5112  2761  Computer paper; manifold business forms

**(G-4441)**
**COMPUTER SVCS & CONSULTING INC**
Also Called: CSC Learning
1613 S Michigan Ave  (60616-1209)
P.O. Box 456, Willow Springs  (60480-0456)
PHONE..................................855 827-8328
Fax: 312 360-0324
Caroline Sanchez Crozier, *President*
Babylon Williams, *Vice Pres*
Terry Crozier, *CFO*
Mark Buhl, *Manager*
Ken Robey, *Manager*
EMP: 20
SQ FT: 8,000
SALES (est): 4.2MM  Privately Held
WEB: www.csc-julex.com
SIC: 7372  7378  7373  Operating systems computer software; educational computer software; computer maintenance & repair; value-added resellers, computer systems; local area network (LAN) systems integrator

**(G-4442)**
**CON-TROL-CURE INC**
Also Called: Uv Process Supply
1229 W Cortland St  (60614-4805)
PHONE..................................773 248-0099
Stephen B Siegel, *President*
EMP: 11
SALES (est): 1.7MM  Privately Held
WEB: www.uvprocess.com
SIC: 3625  3621  Control equipment, electric; motors & generators

**(G-4443)**
**CONA LLC**
3827 N Kenneth Ave  (60641-2815)
PHONE..................................773 750-7485
Peter Litton, *Principal*
EMP: 3
SALES (est): 139.4K  Privately Held
SIC: 7371  7372  Computer software development & applications; computer software development; application computer software

**(G-4444)**
**CONAGRA BRANDS INC (PA)**
Also Called: Conagra Foods
222 Merchandise Mart Plz  (60654-1103)
PHONE..................................312 549-5000
Steven F Goldstone, *Ch of Bd*
Sean M Connolly, *President*
Thomas M McGough, *President*
Thomas P Werner, *President*
Colleen R Batcheler, *Exec VP*
◆ EMP: 250  EST: 1919
SALES: 11.6B  Publicly Held
WEB: www.conagra.com
SIC: 2099  2038  2013  Food preparations; dessert mixes & fillings; seasonings & spices; ready-to-eat meals, salads & sandwiches; frozen specialties; dinners, frozen & packaged; lunches, frozen & packaged; sausages & other prepared meats

**(G-4445)**
**CONAGRA DAIRY FOODS COMPANY (HQ)**
222 Merchandise Mart Plz # 1300  (60654-1010)
PHONE..................................630 848-0975

Richard G Scalise, *President*
Tim Harris, *COO*
◆ EMP: 484
SALES (est): 172.4MM
SALES (corp-wide): 11.6B  Publicly Held
SIC: 2022  Natural cheese; processed cheese
PA: Conagra Brands, Inc.
222 Merchandise Mart Plz
Chicago IL 60654
312 549-5000

**(G-4446)**
**CONCEPT LABORATORIES INC**
Also Called: Pure Valley
1400 W Wabansia Ave  (60642-1522)
PHONE..................................773 395-7300
Joel Heifitz, *CEO*
Adam Lustbader, *President*
John M Zomchek, *VP Opers*
John Zomchek, *VP Opers*
Stephen Sands, *CFO*
▲ EMP: 72
SQ FT: 30,000
SALES: 10.5MM  Privately Held
WEB: www.conceptlabs.com
SIC: 2844  2842  Cosmetic preparations; specialty cleaning, polishes & sanitation goods

**(G-4447)**
**CONDOR MACHINE TOOL**
5315 W 63rd St  (60638-5641)
PHONE..................................773 767-5985
Gerry Wozniak, *Owner*
EMP: 4
SALES (est): 331.1K  Privately Held
SIC: 3541  Machine tool replacement & repair parts, metal cutting types

**(G-4448)**
**CONGRESS PRINTING COMPANY**
2136 S Peoria St  (60608-4526)
PHONE..................................312 733-6599
Fax: 312 733-4095
Carl Reisig, *President*
Anne Reisig, *Treasurer*
Dave Jeffers, *Manager*
EMP: 13  EST: 1922
SQ FT: 10,000
SALES (est): 1.3MM  Privately Held
SIC: 2752  Commercial printing, lithographic

**(G-4449)**
**CONNECTERIORS LLC**
3100 N Clybourn Ave  (60618-6425)
PHONE..................................773 549-3333
Brian Miller,
EMP: 9
SQ FT: 3,000
SALES (est): 1MM  Privately Held
SIC: 3651  Household audio equipment

**(G-4450)**
**CONNECTMEDIA VENTURES LLC**
2538 N Marshfield Ave  (60614-1908)
PHONE..................................773 327-3188
John Miller,
EMP: 6
SQ FT: 1,500
SALES: 3MM  Privately Held
SIC: 7372  Prepackaged software

**(G-4451)**
**CONNELLY-GPM INC**
3154 S California Ave  (60608-5176)
PHONE..................................773 247-7231
Fax: 773 247-7239
Stephen M Klein, *President*
Micheal Weiss, *General Mgr*
▼ EMP: 28  EST: 1875
SQ FT: 17,000
SALES (est): 7.5MM  Privately Held
WEB: www.connellygpm.com
SIC: 3399  3272  3312  Iron, powdered; precast terrazo or concrete products; sponge iron

**(G-4452)**
**CONOPCO INC**
Unilever Bestfoods North Amer
2816 S Kilbourn Ave  (60623-4212)
PHONE..................................773 916-4400

Caroline Stankovich, *Purch Mgr*
Nana N Araya, *Engineer*
Renee Plaza, *Manager*
Jorge Guerrero, *Info Tech Dir*
EMP: 126
SQ FT: 12,800
SALES (corp-wide): 55.5B  Privately Held
SIC: 2844  Toilet preparations
HQ: Conopco, Inc.
700 Sylvan Ave
Englewood Cliffs NJ 07632
201 894-2727

**(G-4453)**
**CONSOLIDATED PRINTING CO INC**
5942 N Northwest Hwy  (60631-2664)
PHONE..................................773 631-2800
Fax: 773 631-2822
Marily K Jones, *President*
Marilyn K Jones, *President*
Ashley Anderson, *Opers Staff*
Jennifer Paoletti, *Mktg Dir*
Maralene Jones, *Manager*
EMP: 11
SQ FT: 9,000
SALES (est): 2.2MM  Privately Held
WEB: www.consolidatedprinting.net
SIC: 2752  Commercial printing, offset

**(G-4454)**
**CONSULATE GENERAL LITHUANIA**
455 N Ctyfrnt Plz Dr # 800  (60611-5504)
PHONE..................................312 397-0382
Fax: 312 397-0385
Giedrius Apuokas, *Manager*
EMP: 6
SALES (est): 450K  Privately Held
SIC: 2752  Commercial printing, lithographic

**(G-4455)**
**CONSUMERBASE LLC**
Also Called: Exact Data
33 N Dearborn St Ste 200  (60602-3100)
PHONE..................................312 600-8000
Fax: 847 864-9026
Larry Organ, *CEO*
Colm Ronan, *COO*
Zora Senat, *Vice Pres*
Hillel Lipson, *Sales Dir*
Rick Cali, *Sales Staff*
EMP: 125
SQ FT: 18,269
SALES (est): 8MM  Privately Held
WEB: www.consumerbase.com
SIC: 7331  2741  Mailing service; telephone & other directory publishing

**(G-4456)**
**CONTEMPO MARBLE & GRANITE INC**
411 N Paulina St  (60622-6318)
PHONE..................................312 455-0022
Mike Losurlello, *President*
Gilbert R Truillo, *Treasurer*
EMP: 8
SQ FT: 7,500
SALES: 600K  Privately Held
SIC: 3281  1743  2541  Marble, building: cut & shaped; tile installation, ceramic; wood partitions & fixtures

**(G-4457)**
**CONTINENTAL ASSEMBLY INC**
4317 N Ravenswood Ave  (60613-1111)
PHONE..................................773 472-8004
Fax: 773 472-8009
Mike Hwang, *President*
Kim So, *Manager*
▲ EMP: 11
SQ FT: 10,000
SALES (est): 350K  Privately Held
SIC: 3679  Electronic circuits

**(G-4458)**
**CONTINENTAL MARKETING INC**
Also Called: CMI Display
5696 N Milwaukee Ave  (60646-6222)
PHONE..................................773 467-8300
Marion Fadrowski, *President*
EMP: 12
SQ FT: 1,500

SALES: 1MM  Privately Held
SIC: 2541  Store & office display cases & fixtures

**(G-4459)**
**CONTINENTAL MATERIALS CORP (PA)**
440 S La Salle St # 3100  (60605-5020)
PHONE..................................312 541-7200
Fax: 312 541-8089
James G Gidwitz, *Ch of Bd*
Mark S Nichter, *CFO*
Jeff Lerner, *Manager*
EMP: 15
SALES: 151.5MM  Publicly Held
WEB: www.contmtl.com
SIC: 3585  3273  5031  Refrigeration & heating equipment; ready-mixed concrete; building materials, exterior; doors

**(G-4460)**
**CONTINENTAL STUDIOS INC**
1300 S Kostner Ave  (60623-1152)
PHONE..................................773 542-0309
Fax: 773 782-1955
Joseph Motroni, *President*
Randy Motroni, *Corp Secy*
Lois Motroni, *Vice Pres*
Mary Motroni, *Vice Pres*
EMP: 38  EST: 1986
SQ FT: 18,000
SALES: 4MM  Privately Held
WEB: www.continentalcraft.com
SIC: 3299  3275  Ornamental & architectural plaster work; gypsum products

**(G-4461)**
**CONTINENTAL WINDOW AND GL CORP**
4311 W Belmont Ave  (60641-4525)
PHONE..................................773 794-1600
Greg Sztejkowski, *President*
Donna Sarniak, *Manager*
▼ EMP: 50
SQ FT: 380,000
SALES (est): 9.3MM  Privately Held
WEB: www.continentalwindowandglass.com
SIC: 3089  Windows, plastic; doors, folding: plastic or plastic coated fabric

**(G-4462)**
**CONTINENTAL WINDOW SOUTH INC**
4600 S Kolmar Ave  (60632-4302)
PHONE..................................773 767-1300
Fax: 773 767-1306
Jessie Gorski, *President*
EMP: 16
SALES (est): 2MM  Privately Held
SIC: 3442  Window & door frames

**(G-4463)**
**CONVERGENT ADVISORS**
22 W Washington St # 1500  (60602-1605)
PHONE..................................312 971-2602
Kenneth Labarge, *Principal*
EMP: 3
SALES (est): 199.3K  Privately Held
SIC: 3674  Semiconductors & related devices

**(G-4464)**
**CONVERSION ENERGY SYSTEMS INC**
200 W Monroe St Ste 1700  (60606-5072)
PHONE..................................312 489-8875
Dominic Sergi, *Ch of Bd*
Blaine Gilles, *President*
Matthew J Tummillo, *Vice Pres*
EMP: 5  EST: 2006
SQ FT: 6,000
SALES (est): 380K  Privately Held
SIC: 2299  Wool waste processing

**(G-4465)**
**COORENS COMMUNICATIONS INC**
2134 W Pierce Ave  (60622-1821)
PHONE..................................773 235-8688
Elaine Coorens, *President*
Larry Clary, *Vice Pres*
EMP: 3

# Chicago - Cook County (G-4466)   GEOGRAPHIC SECTION

SALES (est): 247.7K **Privately Held**
WEB: www.ccisite.com
SIC: 7372 Prepackaged software

**(G-4466)**
**COPYLINE**
9026 S Cregier Ave (60617-3533)
PHONE..................................773 375-8127
Fax: 773 252-8269
Juanita Bratcher, *Principal*
EMP: 3
SALES (est): 241.3K **Privately Held**
SIC: 2721 Periodicals

**(G-4467)**
**CORBETT ACCEL HEALTHCARE GRP C**
Also Called: Potentia
225 N Michigan Ave # 1420 (60601-7653)
PHONE..................................312 475-2505
Fax: 312 988-7675
Scott D Cotherman, *CEO*
Vicki Spellman, *Vice Pres*
Pam Magel, *Admin Sec*
EMP: 5
SQ FT: 42,705
SALES (est): 10.6MM
SALES (corp-wide): 15.4B **Publicly Held**
WEB: www.corbett.us
SIC: 7311 2721 Advertising agencies; periodicals
PA: Omnicom Group Inc.
437 Madison Ave
New York NY 10022
212 415-3600

**(G-4468)**
**COREFX INGREDIENTS LLC (HQ)**
4725 W North Ave Ste 240 (60639-4612)
PHONE..................................773 271-2663
Denis Neville, *CEO*
EMP: 6
SQ FT: 1,200
SALES: 15MM **Privately Held**
SIC: 2023 Dry, condensed, evaporated dairy products
PA: Ornua Co-Operative Limited
Grattan House
Dublin
166 195-99

**(G-4469)**
**CORLESS EQUIPMENT CO**
7155 S Fairfield Ave (60629-2009)
PHONE..................................773 776-8383
Fax: 773 776-8967
Diana Nelson, *President*
EMP: 6 EST: 1962
SALES (est): 328.9K **Privately Held**
WEB: www.corlessequipment.com
SIC: 3546 Power-driven handtools

**(G-4470)**
**CORNELL FORGE COMPANY**
6666 W 66th St (60638-4994)
PHONE..................................708 458-1582
Fax: 708 728-9883
Bill Brewer, *CEO*
William H Brewer, *President*
Ken Mathas, *President*
Edward Czerwien, *Maint Spvr*
Robin Adelman, *Opers Staff*
EMP: 60 EST: 1930
SQ FT: 126,000
SALES (est): 32.9MM **Privately Held**
SIC: 3462 Iron & steel forgings

**(G-4471)**
**CORNERSTONE COMMUNICATIONS**
Also Called: Corner Stone
920 W Wilson Ave (60640-6447)
PHONE..................................773 989-2087
Dawn Mortimer, *President*
Janet Cameron, *Treasurer*
Kurt Mortimer, *Accounts Mgr*
Lyda Jackson, *Sales Staff*
Scott Stahnke, *Director*
EMP: 35
SALES: 33.4K **Privately Held**
SIC: 7336 5812 2721 Package design; eating places; periodicals

**(G-4472)**
**CORNERSTONE COMMUNITY OUTREACH**
Also Called: LELAND HOUSE
4615 N Clifton Ave (60640-5013)
PHONE..................................773 506-4904
Fax: 773 271-8245
Curtiss Mortimer, *President*
Andrew Winter, *Principal*
Sandra Ramsey, *Exec Dir*
Neil Taylor, *Admin Sec*
EMP: 12
SALES (est): 3.1MM **Privately Held**
WEB: www.cornerstonecommunity-outreach.org
SIC: 8322 2731 Outreach program; book publishing

**(G-4473)**
**CORONADO CONSERVATION INC**
5807 S Woodlawn Ave (60637-1610)
PHONE..................................301 512-4671
Shane Durkin, *CEO*
EMP: 3
SALES (est): 94.1K **Privately Held**
SIC: 3261 Vitreous plumbing fixtures

**(G-4474)**
**CORPORATE GRAPHICS AMERICA INC**
5312 N Elston Ave (60630-1611)
PHONE..................................773 481-2100
Fax: 773 481-2110
William Goers, *President*
Mary R Goers, *Vice Pres*
John Kawula, *Prdtn Mgr*
EMP: 16
SQ FT: 11,800
SALES (est): 3.6MM **Privately Held**
WEB: www.printcga.com
SIC: 2752 Commercial printing, offset

**(G-4475)**
**CORPORATE IDENTIFICATION SOLUT**
5563 N Elston Ave (60630-1314)
PHONE..................................773 763-9600
Fax: 773 763-9606
Ben Dehayes, *President*
Natalie Connolly, *Business Mgr*
Mike Shelly, *Project Mgr*
Anna Foote, *Manager*
Sara Wadford, *Graphic Designe*
EMP: 27
SQ FT: 21,000
SALES (est): 8.1MM **Privately Held**
WEB: www.corporateidsolutions.com
SIC: 3993 Signs & advertising specialties

**(G-4476)**
**CORPORATION SUPPLY CO INC (PA)**
205 W Randolph St Ste 610 (60606-1814)
PHONE..................................312 726-3375
Fax: 312 726-4411
David Brenner, *President*
EMP: 20
SQ FT: 8,000
SALES (est): 2MM **Privately Held**
SIC: 7389 2759 5199 5943 Design, commercial & industrial; stock certificates: printing; general merchandise, nondurable; office forms & supplies; notary & corporate seals; stationery & office supplies; commercial printing, lithographic

**(G-4477)**
**COSAS INC**
2170 S Canalport Ave (60608-4535)
PHONE..................................312 492-6100
Sean Brodie, *Principal*
EMP: 4
SALES (est): 380.3K **Privately Held**
SIC: 3645 Garden, patio, walkway & yard lighting fixtures: electric

**(G-4478)**
**COSMEDENT INC**
401 N Michigan Ave # 2500 (60611-4243)
PHONE..................................312 644-9388
Fax: 312 644-9752
Michael O'Malley, *President*
Bennett Cochran, *Export Mgr*
Robert Mopper, *VP Sales*
Mary Malley, *Manager*
Mary O'Malley, *Programmer Anys*
EMP: 21
SQ FT: 2,000
SALES (est): 3.2MM **Privately Held**
WEB: www.cosmedent.com
SIC: 3842 Cosmetic restorations

**(G-4479)**
**COSMOPOLITAN FOOT CARE**
1 S Wacker Dr Fl 11 (60606-4614)
PHONE..................................312 984-5111
Fax: 312 984-5171
Alisa French, *Manager*
EMP: 5
SALES (corp-wide): 543.5K **Privately Held**
WEB: www.hearst.comi.com
SIC: 2721 Periodicals
PA: Charles Kaplan Dpm
220 W 98th St Apt 1k
New York NY 10025
212 663-3668

**(G-4480)**
**COSTER COMPANY**
200 S Wacker Dr Ste 4000 (60606-5821)
PHONE..................................312 541-7200
Ronald J Gidwitz, *President*
Alan K Gidwitz, *Vice Pres*
James G Gidwitz, *Vice Pres*
Nancy Gidwitz, *Vice Pres*
Peter E Gidwitz, *Vice Pres*
EMP: 218
SALES (est): 225.4K **Privately Held**
SIC: 3523 Holding Company Through Which Its Subsidiary Manufactures Farm Equipment

**(G-4481)**
**COTTON GOODS MANUFACTURING CO**
259 N California Ave (60612-1903)
PHONE..................................773 265-0088
Fax: 773 265-0096
Edward J Lewis, *President*
Anne Lewis, *Corp Secy*
Michelle Vine, *Manager*
Kevin Higgins, *Director*
▼ EMP: 18 EST: 1923
SQ FT: 11,000
SALES: 900K **Privately Held**
WEB: www.cottongoodsmfg.com
SIC: 2392 Blankets: made from purchased materials; slip covers & pads; shower curtains: made from purchased materials; tablecloths: made from purchased materials

**(G-4482)**
**COUNTER**
666 W Diversey Pkwy (60614-1511)
PHONE..................................312 666-5335
Fax: 773 935-1997
Edward Mark Casey, *Partner*
EMP: 3 EST: 2008
SALES (est): 298.6K **Privately Held**
SIC: 3131 Counters

**(G-4483)**
**COVERIS HOLDING CORP (DH)**
Also Called: Exopack Holding
8600 W Bryn Mawr Ave (60631-3579)
P.O. Box 5687, Spartanburg SC (29304-5687)
PHONE..................................773 877-3300
Gary Masse, *CEO*
Chuck Quinby, *Business Mgr*
Steve Mullins, *COO*
Rod Reeves, *Technical Mgr*
Michael Alger, *CFO*
EMP: 0
SALES (est): 1.1B **Privately Held**
SIC: 6719 2673 2631 Investment holding companies, except banks; bags: plastic, laminated & coated; container, packaging & boxboard

**(G-4484)**
**COVEY MACHINE INC**
3604 S Morgan St (60609-1526)
PHONE..................................773 650-1530
Fax: 773 650-1533
Michael Koren, *President*
Gary Koren, *General Mgr*
EMP: 14
SQ FT: 20,000
SALES (est): 2.6MM **Privately Held**
WEB: www.coveymachine.com
SIC: 3441 3366 3312 Fabricated structural metal; copper foundries; blast furnaces & steel mills

**(G-4485)**
**COWTAN AND TOUT INC**
222 Merchds Mart Plz 638 (60654)
PHONE..................................312 644-0717
Paula Pikowitz, *Manager*
EMP: 10
SALES (corp-wide): 108.8MM **Privately Held**
SIC: 2297 2621 Nonwoven fabrics; wallpaper (hanging paper)
HQ: Cowtan And Tout, Inc.
205 Hudson St Fl 6
New York NY 10013
212 334-5128

**(G-4486)**
**COZZINI LLC**
4300 W Bryn Mawr Ave (60646-5943)
PHONE..................................773 478-9700
Peter J Samson, *President*
Christopher Brown, *Engineer*
Robert Hillman, *Controller*
EMP: 124
SALES (est): 21.6MM
SALES (corp-wide): 2.2B **Publicly Held**
SIC: 3556 Meat processing machinery
PA: The Middleby Corporation
1400 Toastmaster Dr
Elgin IL 60120
847 741-3300

**(G-4487)**
**CPG FINANCE INC**
Also Called: Coveris
8600 W Bryn Mawr Ave (60631-3579)
PHONE..................................773 877-3300
Michael Alger, *Principal*
Lee Marks, *Vice Pres*
EMP: 2900
SALES (est): 40.6K **Privately Held**
SIC: 3086 Packaging & shipping materials, foamed plastic

**(G-4488)**
**CRAFT DIE CASTING CORPORATION**
1831 N Lorel Ave (60639-4390)
PHONE..................................773 237-9710
Fax: 773 237-7872
James Sanabria, *President*
Susan Sanabria, *Vice Pres*
EMP: 20 EST: 1953
SQ FT: 7,200
SALES (est): 3.3MM **Privately Held**
WEB: www.craftdiecasting.com
SIC: 3364 Zinc & zinc-base alloy die-castings

**(G-4489)**
**CRAFT METAL SPINNING CO**
Also Called: Columbia Metal Spinning Co
4351 N Normandy Ave (60634-1395)
PHONE..................................773 685-4700
Fax: 773 685-8053
Fred Haberkamp, *President*
Elenore Haberkamp, *Vice Pres*
EMP: 15 EST: 1947
SQ FT: 75,000
SALES: 850K **Privately Held**
SIC: 3469 Spinning metal for the trade

**(G-4490)**
**CRAFTMASTER MANUFACTURING INC (DH)**
Also Called: CMI
500 W Monroe St Ste 2010 (60661-3762)
P.O. Box 311, Towanda PA (18848-0311)
PHONE..................................800 405-2233
Robert E Merrill, *President*
Terrence McGarrity, *Superintendent*
John Seymour, *Project Mgr*
Peggie Bolan, *VP Sls/Mktg*
Paul Manchester, *CFO*
◆ EMP: 650
SQ FT: 1,000,000

## GEOGRAPHIC SECTION

**Chicago - Cook County (G-4516)**

SALES (est): 74.4MM
SALES (corp-wide): 22.5B Publicly Held
WEB: www.cmicompany.com
SIC: 2493 Hardboard, tempered
HQ: Jeld-Wen, Inc.
440 S Church St Ste 400
Charlotte NC 28202
800 535-3936

### (G-4491)
### CRAFTSMAN PLTG & TINNING CORP (PA)
1250 W Melrose St (60657-3295)
PHONE..................773 477-1040
Fax: 773 477-4996
James B Blacklidge, President
Anthony J Merges, Vice Pres
Ted Kodama, Plant Engr
Cynthia Blacklidge, Controller
Timothy Blacklidge, Asst Sec
EMP: 37 EST: 1945
SQ FT: 31,000
SALES (est): 5.3MM Privately Held
WEB: www.craftsmanplating.com
SIC: 3471 Plating of metals or formed products

### (G-4492)
### CRAIN COMMUNICATIONS INC (PA)
Also Called: Workforce On Line
150 N Michigan Ave # 1800 (60601-7620)
PHONE..................312 649-5200
Fax: 312 649-7937
Rance Crane, CEO
Kieth Crane, CEO
Clark Bell, Publisher
D Mark, General Mgr
Helmut Kluger, Managing Dir
▲ EMP: 22
SALES (est): 4.1MM Privately Held
WEB: www.hrheadquarters.com
SIC: 2721 Magazines: publishing only, not printed on site

### (G-4493)
### CRAIN COMMUNICATIONS INC
Also Called: Crain's Chicago Business
150 N Michigan Ave # 1800 (60601-7620)
PHONE..................312 649-5411
Fax: 312 280-3150
Jan Parr, Editor
Gloria Scoby, Vice Pres
Francis Scott, Human Res Dir
Donna Ricketts, Human Res Mgr
Allison Arden, VP Sales
EMP: 50
SALES (corp-wide): 225MM Privately Held
WEB: www.crainsnewyork.com
SIC: 2721 Magazines: publishing only, not printed on site
PA: Crain Communications, Inc.
1155 Gratiot Ave
Detroit MI 48207
313 446-6000

### (G-4494)
### CRAIN COMMUNICATIONS INC
Also Called: Advertising Age
150 E Michigan Ave (60601)
PHONE..................312 649-5200
Barry Burr, Owner
Gloria Scoby, Principal
Paul Winston, Editor
Clark Bell, Chief
William Morrow, Exec VP
EMP: 190
SALES (corp-wide): 225MM Privately Held
WEB: www.crainsnewyork.com
SIC: 2721 2711 Magazines: publishing only, not printed on site; newspapers, publishing & printing
PA: Crain Communications, Inc.
1155 Gratiot Ave
Detroit MI 48207
313 446-6000

### (G-4495)
### CRAWFORD SAUSAGE CO INC
2310 S Pulaski Rd (60623-3098)
PHONE..................773 277-3095
Fax: 773 277-7749
John Zicha, President
Gregg Zicha, Manager
EMP: 25
SQ FT: 19,500
SALES (est): 3.2MM Privately Held
WEB: www.crawfordsausage.com
SIC: 2013 Luncheon meat from purchased meat; smoked meats from purchased meat; sausages from purchased meat; frankfurters from purchased meat

### (G-4496)
### CREAPAN USA CORP
401 N Michigan Ave # 1200 (60611-4255)
PHONE..................312 836-3704
Walter Kluit, President
Jan F Marien, Vice Pres
▲ EMP: 2
SQ FT: 500
SALES: 500K Privately Held
SIC: 2038 Waffles, frozen; ethnic foods, frozen
HQ: Bioderij Group International B.V.
Baanhoek 186
Sliedrecht
184 444-800

### (G-4497)
### CREATIVE DESIGNS KITC
Also Called: Creative Design Builders
4355 N Ravenswood Ave (60613-1151)
PHONE..................773 327-8400
Ibrahim Shihadeh, President
Yaser Shihadeh, Vice Pres
Natasa Taseva, Financial Analy
Dora Arana, Officer
▲ EMP: 50
SQ FT: 30,000
SALES (est): 6.2MM Privately Held
WEB: www.usacdb.com
SIC: 1799 6552 2434 1542 Kitchen & bathroom remodeling; subdividers & developers; wood kitchen cabinets; nonresidential construction

### (G-4498)
### CREATIVE DIRECTORY INC
Also Called: Chicago Creative Directory
5219 W Belle Plaine Ave (60641-1460)
PHONE..................773 427-7777
Fax: 312 236-6078
Kurt Hanson, President
Patrick Schoorlemmer, Human Res Dir
EMP: 4
SQ FT: 600
SALES (est): 413.5K Privately Held
WEB: www.creativedir.com
SIC: 2741 Directories: publishing only, not printed on site

### (G-4499)
### CREATIVE INDS TERRAZZO PDTS
1753 N Spaulding Ave (60647-4920)
P.O. Box 47649 (60647-7212)
PHONE..................773 235-9088
Carlo Banducci, President
Teri Granato, Bookkeeper
EMP: 8
SQ FT: 11,000
SALES (est): 1MM Privately Held
SIC: 3272 3281 Terrazzo products, precast; cut stone & stone products

### (G-4500)
### CREATIVE METAL PRODUCTS
Also Called: Kagan Industries
1101 S Kilbourn Ave (60624-3822)
PHONE..................773 638-3200
Fax: 773 638-6500
Stuart Kagan, President
Art Kagan, General Mgr
Dale Kagan, Vice Pres
EMP: 15 EST: 1947
SQ FT: 80,000
SALES: 1MM Privately Held
SIC: 2542 3469 2842 3411 Partitions & fixtures, except wood; ash trays, stamped metal; specialty cleaning preparations; metal cans

### (G-4501)
### CREATIVE PRTG & SMART IDEAS
3406 N Cicero Ave (60641-3718)
PHONE..................773 481-6522
Nikolos Parnassos, Owner
May Parnassos, Co-Owner
EMP: 3
SALES (est): 166.5K Privately Held
SIC: 2759 Commercial printing

### (G-4502)
### CREATIVE WOOD CONCEPTS INC
1680 N Ada St (60642-1504)
PHONE..................773 384-9960
Fax: 773 384-9970
Eric Krause, President
Marc Shannon, General Mgr
Michelle Gadeikis, Finance Mgr
EMP: 8
SQ FT: 7,000
SALES (est): 740K Privately Held
WEB: www.creative-wood-concepts.com
SIC: 2511 2517 Wood household furniture; wood television & radio cabinets

### (G-4503)
### CREST GREETINGS INC
444 W 31st St (60616-3136)
PHONE..................708 210-0800
Fax: 312 326-1522
Steven J Colen, President
Bill Dustin,
EMP: 10
SALES (est): 1.1MM Privately Held
SIC: 5961 5112 2771 2759 Cards, mail order; greeting cards; greeting cards; commercial printing

### (G-4504)
### CREST METAL CRAFT INC
2900 E 95th St (60617-5001)
PHONE..................773 978-0950
Fax: 773 978-7354
Nicklais Horvath, President
Dragan Savich, General Mgr
Maria Horvath, Admin Sec
EMP: 6
SQ FT: 18,500
SALES (est): 1.1MM Privately Held
WEB: www.crestcraft.com
SIC: 3441 Fabricated structural metal

### (G-4505)
### CREW BEACON LLC
1635 W Belmont Ave # 703 (60657-3047)
PHONE..................888 966-4455
Jeff Elliott,
Clark Ho,
William Toffel,
Jason Zola,
EMP: 4
SALES (est): 98.3K Privately Held
SIC: 7372 Business oriented computer software

### (G-4506)
### CROSSTECH COMMUNICATIONS INC
111 N Jefferson St (60661-2306)
PHONE..................312 382-0111
Fax: 312 382-0004
Andrew McPherson, President
Jeffrey Larson, Principal
Glenn Gweke, Manager
Bill Hartwig, Associate
EMP: 20
SQ FT: 12,000
SALES (est): 3.5MM Privately Held
WEB: www.crosstechinc.com
SIC: 2791 2796 7336 Typographic composition, for the printing trade; platemaking services; graphic arts & related design

### (G-4507)
### CROSSTREE INC
1906 N Milwaukee Ave (60647-4321)
PHONE..................773 227-1234
Travis Nam, President
EMP: 4
SQ FT: 2,500
SALES (est): 529.2K Privately Held
SIC: 3446 Ornamental metalwork

### (G-4508)
### CROWDMATRIX FX LLC
333 W Hubbard St Apt 901 (60654-4928)
PHONE..................312 329-1170
Gregory Pine, Principal
Jordan Muloy,
Elijah Wood,
EMP: 3
SALES (est): 121.9K Privately Held
SIC: 7372 Application computer software

### (G-4509)
### CROWLEYS YACHT YARD LAKESIDE
3434 E 95th St (60617-5101)
PHONE..................773 221-9990
Fax: 312 225-6354
John Crowley, Principal
EMP: 13
SALES (est): 2.1MM Privately Held
SIC: 3732 Boats, fiberglass: building & repairing

### (G-4510)
### CRYSTAL WIN & DOOR SYSTEMS LTD
1300 W 35th St (60609-1301)
PHONE..................773 376-6688
Fax: 773 376-6868
Ann Liang, Manager
Ann Ganio, Manager
EMP: 50
SALES (est): 2.1MM Privately Held
WEB: www.crystalwindows.com
SIC: 3211 Window glass, clear & colored
HQ: Crystal Window & Door Systems, Ltd.
3110 Whitestone Expy
Flushing NY 11354
718 961-7300

### (G-4511)
### CSI CHICAGO INC
2216 W Winnemac Ave (60625-1816)
PHONE..................773 665-2226
Gary Wing, President
EMP: 6
SALES (est): 425.5K Privately Held
SIC: 2253 T-shirts & tops, knit

### (G-4512)
### CSITEQ LLC
437 W Division St Apt 316 (60610-1720)
PHONE..................312 265-1509
Olatunde Omosebi, President
▼ EMP: 75
SALES: 82K Privately Held
SIC: 4899 8742 7373 1623 Communication signal enhancement network system; management consulting services; local area network (LAN) systems integrator; oil & gas pipeline construction; filters & strainers, pipeline; aircraft/aerospace flight instruments & guidance systems

### (G-4513)
### CUBIC TRNSP SYSTEMS INC
221 N La Salle St Ste 500 (60601-1208)
PHONE..................312 257-3242
Mike Washington, Business Anlyst
EMP: 7
SALES (corp-wide): 1.4B Publicly Held
SIC: 3829 Fare registers for street cars, buses, etc.
HQ: Cubic Transportation Systems, Inc.
5650 Kearny Mesa Rd
San Diego CA 92111
858 268-3100

### (G-4514)
### CUDNER & OCONNOR CO
Also Called: Candoc
4035 W Kinzie St (60624-1895)
PHONE..................773 826-0200
Fax: 773 826-0477
David Knoll, President
Mary Miller, Vice Pres
EMP: 12 EST: 1935
SQ FT: 15,000
SALES (est): 3.1MM Privately Held
SIC: 2893 Lithographic ink

### (G-4515)
### CULTURE STUDIO LLC
1151 W 40th St (60609-2506)
PHONE..................312 243-8304
Rich Santo, Mng Member
EMP: 20 EST: 2009
SALES (est): 2MM Privately Held
SIC: 2759 Commercial printing

### (G-4516)
### CUPCAKE COUNTER LLC
229 W Madison St (60606-3403)
PHONE..................312 422-0800

Chicago - Cook County (G-4517)  GEOGRAPHIC SECTION

Holly Sjo, *Principal*
EMP: 3
SALES (est): 290.4K **Privately Held**
SIC: 3131 Counters

**(G-4517)**
**CURBSIDE SPLENDOR**
2816 N Kedzie Ave (60618-7602)
PHONE..................224 515-6512
Naomi Huffman, *Editor*
Ben Tanzer, *Director*
EMP: 3
SALES (est): 209.9K **Privately Held**
SIC: 2731 Book publishing

**(G-4518)**
**CUSHING AND COMPANY (PA)**
420 W Huron St (60654-8475)
PHONE..................312 266-8228
Fax: 312 266-8059
Cathleen Cushing Duff, *President*
Joseph X Cushing, *Vice Pres*
Jorge Galvan, *Prdtn Mgr*
Theresa Zallis, *Controller*
Katie Schayer, *Human Res Dir*
EMP: 40
SQ FT: 28,000
SALES (est): 15.5MM **Privately Held**
WEB: www.cushingco.com
SIC: 7334 5049 3861 3952 Blueprinting service; scientific & engineering equipment & supplies; drafting supplies; blueprint cloth or paper, sensitized; lead pencils & art goods; coated & laminated paper

**(G-4519)**
**CUSTOM & HARD TO FIND WIGS**
4065 N Milwaukee Ave (60641-1834)
PHONE..................773 777-0222
Fax: 773 777-4228
EMP: 10
SALES (est): 500.8K **Privately Held**
SIC: 2389 5699 Mfg Apparel/Accessories Ret Misc Apparel/Accessories

**(G-4520)**
**CUSTOM BY LAMAR INC**
1332 W Madison St (60607-1969)
PHONE..................312 738-2160
Lamar Gayles, *President*
EMP: 10
SQ FT: 3,000
SALES (est): 694K **Privately Held**
SIC: 2339 2329 5621 5611 Women's & misses' athletic clothing & sportswear; down-filled clothing: men's & boys'; ready-to-wear apparel, women's; clothing, men's & boys': everyday, except suits & sportswear

**(G-4521)**
**CUSTOM CASE CO INC**
6045 S Knox Ave (60629-5421)
PHONE..................773 585-1164
Fax: 708 585-1167
Brian Reid, *President*
Darin Reid, *Vice Pres*
EMP: 20
SQ FT: 12,000
SALES (est): 1.6MM **Privately Held**
WEB: www.customcasecompany.com
SIC: 3161 Cases, carrying

**(G-4522)**
**CUSTOM FIT SHTMETAL ROOFG CORP**
Also Called: Custom Fit Architectural Mtls
222 N Maplewood Ave (60612-2110)
P.O. Box 12289 (60612-0289)
PHONE..................773 227-9019
Chance Johnson, *President*
EMP: 10
SQ FT: 5,000
SALES (est): 1.2MM **Privately Held**
SIC: 3444 Sheet metalwork

**(G-4523)**
**CUSTOM MAGNETICS INC**
Also Called: James Electronics Div
4050 N Rockwell St (60618-3721)
PHONE..................773 463-6500
Fax: 773 463-1504
Raju Shah, *VP Sales*
Tito Chowdhury, *Branch Mgr*
EMP: 20

SALES (corp-wide): 10.7MM **Privately Held**
WEB: www.custommag.com
SIC: 3677 Electronic transformers
PA: Custom Magnetics Inc
801 W Main St
North Manchester IN 46962
773 463-6500

**(G-4524)**
**CUSTOM MENU INSIGHTS LLC**
Also Called: CMI Foods
20 N Wacker Dr Ste 3705 (60606-3103)
PHONE..................312 237-3860
Alan Macus, *Manager*
Carol Pegnato, *Manager*
Thomas M Fitzpatrick,
Rick Garcia,
◆ EMP: 5
SALES (est): 320K **Privately Held**
SIC: 2099 Ready-to-eat meals, salads & sandwiches

**(G-4525)**
**CUSTOM RAILZ & STAIRZ INC**
6740 S Belt Circle Dr (60638-4706)
PHONE..................773 592-7210
EMP: 2
SALES (est): 274.8K **Privately Held**
SIC: 2431 Staircases, stairs & railings

**(G-4526)**
**CUSTOM SIGN CONSULTANTS INC**
1928 W Fulton St (60612-2404)
PHONE..................312 533-2302
Al Frapolli, *President*
Erik Woolsey, *Vice Pres*
EMP: 7
SQ FT: 3,500
SALES (est): 2MM **Privately Held**
SIC: 3993 Signs, not made in custom sign painting shops

**(G-4527)**
**CUSTOMERGAUGE USA LLC**
401 N Michigan Ave # 1200 (60611-4255)
PHONE..................773 669-5915
Adam Dorrell, *President*
EMP: 7
SALES (est): 299K **Privately Held**
SIC: 7372 Prepackaged software

**(G-4528)**
**CWI DISPLAYS CORP**
4041 W Ogden Ave (60623-2857)
PHONE..................773 277-0040
Deidre Harris, *President*
Mike Martinson, *Vice Pres*
Rober Murphy, *Sales Staff*
Demetrius Brown, *Mktg Dir*
Toni Harris, *Executive*
▲ EMP: 10 EST: 1991
SQ FT: 45,000
SALES (est): 1.8MM **Privately Held**
WEB: www.cwidisplays.com
SIC: 3999 Advertising display products

**(G-4529)**
**CYBORG SYSTEMS INC (DH)**
233 S Wacker Dr Ste 3640 (60606-6363)
PHONE..................312 279-7000
Michael D Blair, *CEO*
Sean Blair, *President*
Paul Martin, *President*
Steven J Weinberg, *President*
Paul Irvine, *Vice Pres*
EMP: 220
SQ FT: 72,000
SALES (est): 20.6MM
SALES (corp-wide): 11.6B **Privately Held**
SIC: 7372 7371 Business oriented computer software; custom computer programming services
HQ: Aon Hewitt Llc
200 E Randolph St Ll3
Chicago IL 60601
312 381-1000

**(G-4530)**
**CYGNUS CORPORATION**
Also Called: Cygnus Corp Packaging Div
340 E 138th St (60827-1828)
PHONE..................773 785-2845
Fax: 773 785-3935
Andrew Friedl, *President*

▲ EMP: 85
SQ FT: 74,400
SALES (est): 36.7MM **Privately Held**
SIC: 2841 Detergents, synthetic organic or inorganic alkaline

**(G-4531)**
**CYN INDUSTRIES INC**
Also Called: Boaters World
1661 N Elston Ave (60642-1545)
PHONE..................773 895-4324
Fax: 773 227-3676
David Ritz, *President*
Randy Draftz, *Sales Staff*
EMP: 12
SQ FT: 15,000
SALES (est): 1.4MM **Privately Held**
SIC: 5551 3728 5088 Marine supplies; aircraft assemblies, subassemblies & parts; marine supplies

**(G-4532)**
**D & E PALLET INC**
14358 Martha St (60633)
PHONE..................708 891-4307
Dena Perez, *President*
EMP: 5
SALES (est): 512.9K **Privately Held**
SIC: 2448 Pallets, wood & wood with metal

**(G-4533)**
**D & H GRANITE AND MARBLE SUP**
1520 W Pershing Rd (60609-2408)
PHONE..................773 869-9988
Fax: 773 869-9188
Rendee Du, *Owner*
Johnny Du, *Co-Owner*
EMP: 20
SALES (est): 1.3MM **Privately Held**
SIC: 3281 Granite, cut & shaped

**(G-4534)**
**D & J METALCRAFT COMPANY INC**
4451 N Ravenswood Ave (60640-5802)
PHONE..................773 878-6446
Fax: 773 878-6328
Ivan Panayotov, *President*
Nicola Aglikin, *Treasurer*
Kostadin Pachof, *Treasurer*
Jeffrey Panayotov, *Accounting Mgr*
Lupe Matos, *Bookkeeper*
EMP: 15
SQ FT: 16,000
SALES (est): 2.2MM **Privately Held**
SIC: 3444 Sheet metal specialties, not stamped

**(G-4535)**
**D & P CONSTRUCTION CO INC (PA)**
5521 N Cmderland Ste 1106 (60656)
PHONE..................773 714-9330
Fax: 773 714-9332
Josephine Di Fronzo, *President*
Kathleen S Clementi, *Admin Sec*
EMP: 29 EST: 1974
SQ FT: 1,200
SALES (est): 3.4MM **Privately Held**
SIC: 3443 4953 Dumpsters, garbage; recycling, waste materials

**(G-4536)**
**D & W MFG CO INC**
3237 W Lake St (60624-2004)
PHONE..................773 533-1542
Fax: 773 533-9456
Michael Leavitt, *President*
Shah Prabip, *Vice Pres*
Dave Holian, *Sales Mgr*
Sharon Brown, *Manager*
▲ EMP: 45 EST: 1963
SQ FT: 40,000
SALES (est): 23.5MM **Privately Held**
WEB: www.dwmfg.com
SIC: 5051 3498 Tubing, metal; tube fabricating (contract bending & shaping)

**(G-4537)**
**D L V PRINTING SERVICE INC**
5825 W Corcoran Pl (60644-1854)
PHONE..................773 626-1661
Bonito Johnson, *President*
Vernita Johnson, *Vice Pres*

Kesha Forrest, *Graphic Designe*
EMP: 12
SALES (est): 1.3MM **Privately Held**
WEB: www.dlvprinting.com
SIC: 2759 2791 2789 2752 Commercial printing; typesetting; bookbinding & related work; commercial printing, lithographic

**(G-4538)**
**D-ORUM CORPORATION**
325 W 103rd St (60628-2503)
PHONE..................773 567-2064
Fax: 773 468-3051
Ernest Daurham, *President*
Claudia Daurham, *Vice Pres*
EMP: 10
SQ FT: 8,000
SALES: 2MM **Privately Held**
SIC: 2844 7231 Shampoos, rinses, conditioners: hair; beauty shops

**(G-4539)**
**D5 DESIGN MET FABRICATION LLC**
441 N Campbell Ave (60612-1146)
PHONE..................773 770-4705
Jonathan Becker,
EMP: 8
SALES (est): 1.5MM **Privately Held**
SIC: 3441 7389 3446 Fabricated structural metal; design services; ornamental metalwork

**(G-4540)**
**DABECCA NATURAL FOODS INC**
700 E 107th St (60628-3806)
P.O. Box 15, Clifton TX (76634-0015)
PHONE..................773 291-1428
David A Pederson, *President*
Bill Vree, *CFO*
Gene Finney, *Executive Asst*
EMP: 150 EST: 1997
SQ FT: 5,000
SALES: 40MM **Privately Held**
WEB: www.dabeccanaturalfoods.com
SIC: 2013 Cured meats from purchased meat

**(G-4541)**
**DABIR SURFACES INC (HQ)**
7447 W Wilson Ave (60706-4548)
PHONE..................708 867-6777
Dave Dzioba, *President*
Ben Boyer, *Branch Mgr*
EMP: 13
SALES (est): 2.9MM
SALES (corp-wide): 809.1MM **Publicly Held**
SIC: 3842 Surgical appliances & supplies
PA: Methode Electronics, Inc
7401 W Wilson Ave
Chicago IL 60706
708 867-6777

**(G-4542)**
**DAILY GENERAL LLC**
2757 W Le Moyne St Ste 2 (60622-1619)
PHONE..................217 273-0719
Elizabeth Daily, *Principal*
EMP: 3
SALES (est): 158.9K **Privately Held**
SIC: 2711 Newspapers, publishing & printing

**(G-4543)**
**DAILY NEWS CONDOMINIUM ASSN**
222 S Racine Ave (60607-2894)
PHONE..................312 492-8526
Agata Lipinsky, *President*
Juan Consuegra, *Admin Sec*
EMP: 22 EST: 2001
SALES (est): 1.4MM **Privately Held**
SIC: 2711 Newspapers, publishing & printing

**(G-4544)**
**DAILY WHALE**
222 W Ontario St (60654-3652)
PHONE..................312 787-5204
Tom Butala, *Principal*
EMP: 3

# GEOGRAPHIC SECTION

**Chicago - Cook County (G-4572)**

SALES (est): 124K **Privately Held**
SIC: 2711 Newspapers, publishing & printing

**(G-4545)**
**DAKKOTA INTEGRATED SYSTEMS LLC**
12525 S Carondolet Ave (60633-1157)
PHONE.................................517 694-6500
Don Canada, *Manager*
EMP: 98
SALES (corp-wide): 273.1MM **Privately Held**
SIC: 3711 Automobile assembly, including specialty automobiles
PA: Dakkota Integrated Systems, Llc
   1875 Holloway Dr
   Holt MI 48842
   517 694-6500

**(G-4546)**
**DALLAS SCRUB**
212 W Superior St (60654-3557)
PHONE.................................312 651-6012
Greg Lilien, *Principal*
EMP: 3
SALES (est): 154.1K **Privately Held**
SIC: 2844 Toilet preparations

**(G-4547)**
**DAMATOS BAKERY**
1125 W Grand Ave (60642-5862)
PHONE.................................312 733-5456
Victor D Amato, *Owner*
Debbie Muller, *Manager*
EMP: 12
SQ FT: 2,500
SALES (est): 1.4MM **Privately Held**
SIC: 2051 Bread, cake & related products

**(G-4548)**
**DAMATOS BAKERY INC**
1332 W Grand Ave (60642-6443)
PHONE.................................312 733-6219
Fax: 312 733-3479
Mateo D'Amato, *President*
Nicola D'Amato, *Treasurer*
EMP: 6
SQ FT: 1,400
SALES (est): 350K **Privately Held**
SIC: 2051  2052  5461 Bakery: wholesale or wholesale/retail combined; breads, rolls & buns; cookies & crackers; bakeries

**(G-4549)**
**DAMRON CORPORATION**
Also Called: Damron Tea
4433 W Ohio St (60624-1054)
PHONE.................................773 265-2724
Fax: 773 826-6004
Selena Boyd-Pitman, *Controller*
Selena Pitman, *Controller*
Kimberly Owen, *Manager*
Ricardo Rodriquez, *Manager*
Ronald Damper, *Admin Sec*
▲ EMP: 25
SQ FT: 50,000
SALES (est): 5.8MM **Privately Held**
WEB: www.damrontea.com
SIC: 3089  2099 Food casings, plastic; tea blending

**(G-4550)**
**DANA ANODIZING INC**
Also Called: Bright Metal Finishing Co
3905 W Armitage Ave (60647-3405)
PHONE.................................773 486-2312
Fax: 773 486-2314
Saleh Omar, *President*
Rima Omar, *Corp Secy*
Omar Beshara, *Vice Pres*
Beshara Omar, *Vice Pres*
EMP: 12 EST: 1978
SQ FT: 18,000
SALES (est): 800K **Privately Held**
SIC: 3471 Anodizing (plating) of metals or formed products

**(G-4551)**
**DANCO CONVERTING**
455 E North Ave Ave (60610)
PHONE.................................847 718-0448
Daniel J Mulvey, *President*
Diana Hollerbach, *Cust Mgr*
Kevin Mulvey, *Sales Staff*
Bob Mulvey, *Director*

▲ EMP: 3
SALES (est): 540.6K **Privately Held**
SIC: 2621 Art paper

**(G-4552)**
**DANGIOS**
3050 W Taylor St (60612-3919)
PHONE.................................773 533-3000
Sergio Dangios, *President*
EMP: 2
SALES (est): 228.4K **Privately Held**
SIC: 3544 Industrial molds

**(G-4553)**
**DANIEL J NICKEL & ASSOCS PC**
3052 N Haussen Ct (60618-6519)
PHONE.................................312 345-1850
Daniel Nickel, *Principal*
EMP: 4
SALES (est): 277.8K **Privately Held**
SIC: 3356 Nickel

**(G-4554)**
**DANIELS SHARPSMART INC (DH)**
Also Called: Daniels Health
111 W Jackson Blvd # 720 (60604-4133)
P.O. Box 7697, Carol Stream (60197-7697)
PHONE.................................312 546-8900
Dan Daniels, *President*
Marla Licht, *General Mgr*
Ryan Ferguson, *Business Mgr*
Adrien Hawkins, *Business Mgr*
Ben Martyn, *Business Mgr*
▲ EMP: 42
SALES (est): 254.7MM
SALES (corp-wide): 62MM **Privately Held**
WEB: www.danielsinternational.com
SIC: 4953  2834 Medical waste disposal; pharmaceutical preparations
HQ: Daniels Corporation International Pty Ltd
   34 Cahill St
   Dandenong VIC 3175
   130 066-7787

**(G-4555)**
**DANIELSON FOOD PRODUCTS INC**
215 W Root St (60609-2899)
PHONE.................................773 285-2111
Fax: 773 285-8514
Thomas R Danielson, *President*
Linda J Danielson, *Corp Secy*
James Tormey, *Vice Pres*
EMP: 20 EST: 1939
SQ FT: 23,000
SALES (est): 3.1MM **Privately Held**
SIC: 2013  5147 Sausages & other prepared meats; meats, fresh

**(G-4556)**
**DANISH MAID BUTTER COMPANY**
8512 S Commercial Ave (60617-2533)
PHONE.................................773 731-8787
Fax: 773 731-9812
Susan E Wagner, *President*
Susan Wagner, *Manager*
EMP: 10 EST: 1959
SQ FT: 18,000
SALES (est): 1.3MM **Privately Held**
SIC: 2021 Creamery butter

**(G-4557)**
**DAPRATO RIGALI INC**
6030 N Northwest Hwy (60631-2518)
PHONE.................................773 763-5511
Fax: 773 763-5522
John Rigali, *President*
Elizabeth Rigali-Galvin, *Corp Secy*
Robert J Rigali Jr, *Vice Pres*
EMP: 40 EST: 1893
SALES (est): 270.8K **Privately Held**
SIC: 3299  3281 Statuary: gypsum, clay, papier mache, metal, etc.; art goods: plaster of paris, papier mache & scagliola; plaques: clay, plaster or papier mache; cut stone & stone products

**(G-4558)**
**DARIOS PALLETS CORP**
339 N California Ave (60612)
PHONE.................................312 421-3413

Jorge Aguilar, *President*
Pedro Perez, *Admin Sec*
◆ EMP: 35
SQ FT: 80,000
SALES: 3.2MM **Privately Held**
SIC: 2448 Pallets, wood & wood with metal

**(G-4559)**
**DARLING INGREDIENTS INC**
3443 S Lawndale Ave (60623-5009)
PHONE.................................773 376-5550
Vince Gryb, *CEO*
EMP: 45
SALES (corp-wide): 3.4B **Publicly Held**
SIC: 2077 Grease rendering, inedible
PA: Darling Ingredients Inc.
   251 Oconnor Ridge Blvd
   Irving TX 75038
   972 717-0300

**(G-4560)**
**DART CONTAINER MICHIGAN LLC**
Also Called: Dart Clearview Film Products
1650 E 95th St (60617-4706)
PHONE.................................312 221-1245
Edward Stollenwerk, *Branch Mgr*
EMP: 4
SALES (corp-wide): 2.5B **Privately Held**
SIC: 2671  2673 Plastic film, coated or laminated for packaging; plastic bags: made from purchased materials
HQ: Dart Container Of Michigan Llc
   3120 Sovereign Dr Ste 4b
   Lansing MI 48911
   888 327-8001

**(G-4561)**
**DAS FOODS LLC (PA)**
2041 W Carroll Ave C222 (60612-1630)
PHONE.................................224 715-9289
Katie Das,
Dhruba Das,
▲ EMP: 3
SALES (est): 322K **Privately Held**
SIC: 2064 Candy & other confectionery products

**(G-4562)**
**DATIX (USA) INC**
155 N Wacker Dr Ste 1930 (60606-1719)
PHONE.................................312 724-7776
Philip Taylor, *Opers Staff*
Jonathan Hazan, *Director*
EMP: 2 EST: 2011
SALES (est): 210.7K **Privately Held**
SIC: 7372 Prepackaged software

**(G-4563)**
**DAVID ARCHITECTURAL METALS INC**
3100 S Kilbourn Ave (60623-4894)
PHONE.................................773 376-3200
Fax: 773 376-6862
Richard Schneider, *President*
John Persat, *Superintendent*
Alan Schneider, *Chairman*
Jeffrey N Schnider, *Vice Pres*
Albert Cacini, *Admin Sec*
EMP: 30
SQ FT: 48,000
SALES (est): 7.6MM **Privately Held**
WEB: www.davidarchitecturalmetals.com
SIC: 3446 Architectural metalwork

**(G-4564)**
**DAVID TEPLICA M D**
803 W Hutchinson St (60613-1616)
PHONE.................................773 296-9900
David Teplica, *Principal*
EMP: 5
SALES (est): 556.2K **Privately Held**
WEB: www.davidteplica.com
SIC: 2821 Plastics materials & resins

**(G-4565)**
**DBP COMMUNICATIONS**
Also Called: Design Business Printing
656 W Randolph St Ste 4w (60661-2164)
PHONE.................................312 263-1569
Fax: 312 346-1732
Robert Kenehan, *President*
Denny Harris, *VP Sales*
Thiele Brandon, *Webmaster*
EMP: 10
SQ FT: 5,000

SALES (est): 1.7MM **Privately Held**
WEB: www.dbpchicago.com
SIC: 2752 Commercial printing, offset

**(G-4566)**
**DBP COMMUNICATIONS INC**
4849 N Milwaukee Ave # 502 (60630-5100)
PHONE.................................312 263-1569
Robert Kenehan, *President*
Jennifer Iglesias, *Accountant*
EMP: 8
SALES (est): 637.7K **Privately Held**
SIC: 7389  2752  5199  5699 Advertising, promotional & trade show services; commercial printing, lithographic; business form & card printing, lithographic; badges; calendars; T-shirts, custom printed

**(G-4567)**
**DE VINE DISTRIBUTORS LLC**
3034 W Devon Ave Ste 104 (60659-1400)
PHONE.................................773 248-7005
Alpana Hansoty, *Mng Member*
▲ EMP: 5
SALES (est): 305.6K **Privately Held**
SIC: 2084  5182 Wines; wine

**(G-4568)**
**DE VRIES INTERNATIONAL INC**
3139 N Lincoln Ave (60657-3114)
PHONE.................................773 248-6695
EMP: 25
SALES (corp-wide): 22.8MM **Privately Held**
SIC: 1389 Lease tanks, oil field: erecting, cleaning & repairing
PA: De Vries International, Inc.
   17671 Armstrong Ave
   Irvine CA 92614
   949 252-1212

**(G-4569)**
**DECIBEL AUDIO INC**
1429 N Milwaukee Ave (60622-2015)
PHONE.................................773 862-6700
Fax: 773 772-9072
Jeremy Lewin, *President*
Adam Morgenstern, *Manager*
EMP: 5
SALES (est): 863.3K **Privately Held**
SIC: 3651 Household audio & video equipment

**(G-4570)**
**DECORATIVE INDUSTRIES INC**
6935 W 62nd St (60638-3901)
PHONE.................................773 229-0015
Fax: 312 666-9755
Bartley Bryerton Sr, *President*
Bartley Bryerton Jr, *Vice Pres*
Jerome Bryerton, *Vice Pres*
Eliana Corral, *Manager*
EMP: 25
SQ FT: 60,000
SALES (est): 9.9MM **Privately Held**
WEB: www.decorativecontainer.com
SIC: 5085  2759 Plastic bottles; screen printing

**(G-4571)**
**DECORATORS SUPPLY CORPORATION**
3610 S Morgan St Ste 2 (60609-1587)
PHONE.................................773 847-6300
Fax: 773 847-6357
Steve Grage, *President*
John Meingast, *Treasurer*
Bill Denis, *Executive*
William Denis, *Admin Sec*
EMP: 40
SQ FT: 35,000
SALES (est): 5.4MM **Privately Held**
WEB: www.decoratorssupply.com
SIC: 2431  3299 Millwork; ornamental & architectural plaster work

**(G-4572)**
**DEDUCTLY LLC**
917 W Washington Blvd (60607-2203)
PHONE.................................312 945-8265
Timothy Lewis, *President*
Robert Guyser, *President*
Erik Miles, *President*
EMP: 4 EST: 2013
SQ FT: 2,600

---

(PA)=Parent Co  (HQ)=Headquarters  (DH)=Div Headquarters
✪ = New Business established in last 2 years

2017 Harris Illinois Industrial Directory

# Chicago - Cook County (G-4573)   GEOGRAPHIC SECTION

SALES (est): 162K **Privately Held**
SIC: 7372 Application computer software

**(G-4573)**
**DEEP VALUE INC**
10 S Riverside Plz # 1800 (60606-3728)
PHONE .................................. 312 239-0143
Harish Devarajan, *President*
EMP: 45 EST: 2004
SALES (est): 2.2MM **Privately Held**
SIC: 7372 Word processing computer software

**(G-4574)**
**DEKS NORTH AMERICA INC**
2700 W Roosevelt Rd (60608-1048)
PHONE .................................. 312 219-2110
Jim Sharp, *President*
Anthony R Taglia, *Principal*
Ted Hanusiha, *Cust Svc Mgr*
EMP: 3 EST: 2013
SALES (est): 451K
SALES (corp-wide): 144.5MM **Privately Held**
SIC: 3432 2952 Plumbing fixture fittings & trim; roofing materials
HQ: Deks Industries Pty Ltd
U 5 841 Mountain Hwy
Bayswater VIC 3153
387 278-800

**(G-4575)**
**DELANTE GROUP INC**
35 E Wacker Dr Ste 900 (60601-2120)
PHONE .................................. 312 493-4371
EMP: 3
SALES (est): 190K **Privately Held**
SIC: 7372 Application Software

**(G-4576)**
**DELICIAS BRIANNA**
4911 N Western Ave (60625-1921)
PHONE .................................. 773 409-4394
Hector H Gutierrez, *President*
EMP: 1 EST: 2011
SALES (est): 207.4K **Privately Held**
SIC: 3421 Table & food cutlery, including butchers'

**(G-4577)**
**DELL COVE SPICE CO**
4900 N Hermitage Ave 3 (60640-3404)
PHONE .................................. 312 339-8389
EMP: 3
SALES (est): 229.7K **Privately Held**
SIC: 2099 5149 5499 Seasonings & spices; condiments; spices & herbs

**(G-4578)**
**DELOBIAN FOODS**
7424 N Western Ave (60645-1707)
PHONE .................................. 773 564-0913
Olubambo O Opanuga, *Owner*
EMP: 6
SALES (est): 413.5K **Privately Held**
SIC: 2099 Food preparations

**(G-4579)**
**DELTA METAL PRODUCTS CO**
Also Called: Pinter Sheet Metal Work
1953 N Latrobe Ave (60639-3011)
PHONE .................................. 773 745-9220
Albert E Pinter, *Owner*
EMP: 7
SQ FT: 9,600
SALES (est): 574.7K **Privately Held**
SIC: 3469 Metal stampings

**(G-4580)**
**DELUXE PRINTING**
2816 S Wentworth Ave # 1 (60616-2762)
PHONE .................................. 312 225-0061
Fax: 312 225-8406
Pong Pong Wong, *President*
Michelle Chau, *Admin Sec*
EMP: 3
SALES (est): 289.2K **Privately Held**
SIC: 2759 2752 Commercial printing; commercial printing, lithographic

**(G-4581)**
**DEMETER MILLWORK LLC**
2324 W Fulton St (60612-2208)
PHONE .................................. 312 224-4440
E Gabriel Izsak, *Principal*
EMP: 8 EST: 2010

SALES (est): 1.4MM **Privately Held**
SIC: 2431 Millwork

**(G-4582)**
**DENISE ALLEN ROBINSON INC**
Also Called: Neesh By Dar
4510 N Ravenswood Ave (60640-5202)
PHONE .................................. 773 275-8080
Denise A Robinson, *President*
▲ EMP: 10
SQ FT: 7,000
SALES (est): 1.4MM **Privately Held**
WEB: www.neeshbydar.com
SIC: 2253 Sweaters & sweater coats, knit

**(G-4583)**
**DENTALEZ ALABAMA INC**
Also Called: Nevin Labs
5000 S Halsted St (60609-5130)
PHONE .................................. 773 624-4330
Fax: 773 624-7337
Bob Nevin, *Sales Mgr*
Ed Holland, *Branch Mgr*
Bill Webb, *Manager*
Juan Silva, *Planning*
EMP: 200
SALES (corp-wide): 69.8MM **Privately Held**
WEB: www.dentalez.com
SIC: 3843 Dental equipment & supplies
HQ: Dentalez Alabama, Inc.
2500 S Us Highway 31
Bay Minette AL 36507
251 937-6781

**(G-4584)**
**DEPUTANTE INC**
4113 W Newport Ave (60641-4009)
P.O. Box 412298 (60641-7898)
PHONE .................................. 773 545-9531
EMP: 5 EST: 2004
SALES (est): 360K **Privately Held**
SIC: 2844 Mfg Toilet Preparations

**(G-4585)**
**DESHAMUSIC INC**
Also Called: Sge Group, The
1645 W Ogden Ave Unit 713 (60612-4390)
PHONE .................................. 818 257-2716
Omar D Harris, *CEO*
EMP: 5
SALES (est): 486K **Privately Held**
WEB: www.deshamusic.com
SIC: 8741 7922 7389 2741 Management services; entertainment promotion; music distribution systems; music book & sheet music publishing; popular music groups or artists

**(G-4586)**
**DESITALK CHICAGO LLC**
2652 W Devon Ave Ste B (60659-1811)
PHONE .................................. 773 856-0545
Sudhir Parikh, *Mng Member*
EMP: 25
SALES (est): 1.2MM **Privately Held**
SIC: 2759 Newspapers: printing

**(G-4587)**
**DEVCO CASTING**
5 S Wabash Ave Ste 407 (60603-3503)
PHONE .................................. 312 456-0076
Deveci Sali, *President*
EMP: 3
SALES (est): 232.5K **Privately Held**
SIC: 3325 Alloy steel castings, except investment

**(G-4588)**
**DEVILS DUE PUBLISHING**
3021 W Diversey Ave Apt 2 (60647-0021)
PHONE .................................. 773 412-6427
Josh Blaylock, *President*
Susan Bishop, *Administration*
▲ EMP: 6
SALES (est): 614.4K **Privately Held**
WEB: www.devilsdue.net
SIC: 2741 Miscellaneous publishing

**(G-4589)**
**DEX MEDIA INC**
200 E Randolph St Fl 70 (60601-6915)
PHONE .................................. 312 240-6000
Bruce Diserow, *Principal*
EMP: 15

SALES (corp-wide): 1.8B **Privately Held**
WEB: www.rhdonnelley.com
SIC: 2741 Miscellaneous publishing
PA: Dex Media, Inc.
2200 W Airfield Dr
Dfw Airport TX 75261
972 453-7000

**(G-4590)**
**DEZIGN SEWING INC**
4001 N Rvnswd Ave 505 (60613)
PHONE .................................. 773 549-4336
Fax: 773 549-7085
Barbara Vincent, *President*
Anne Rohner, *Vice Pres*
EMP: 8
SQ FT: 5,000
SALES (est): 924.2K **Privately Held**
WEB: www.dezignsewing.com
SIC: 2591 2391 Drapery hardware & blinds & shades; curtains & draperies

**(G-4591)**
**DGS IMPORT INC**
5513 N Cumberland Ave (60656-1471)
PHONE .................................. 847 595-7016
Peter Stevens, *CEO*
Thomas Vogt, *President*
Joseph Roth, *Admin Sec*
▲ EMP: 30 EST: 2012
SALES (est): 8.8MM
SALES (corp-wide): 43.9MM **Privately Held**
SIC: 3993 Signs & advertising specialties
PA: Dgs Retail, Inc.
60 Maple St Ste 100
Mansfield MA 02048
508 660-1886

**(G-4592)**
**DIAGNOSTIC PHOTONICS INC**
222 Merchandise Mart Plz # 1230 (60654-4342)
PHONE .................................. 312 320-5478
Andrew Cittatine, *President*
Andrew Cittadine, *General Mgr*
Anna Somera, *Manager*
Adam Zysk, *Director*
Stephen Boppart, *Officer*
EMP: 4
SALES (est): 322K **Privately Held**
SIC: 3841 Diagnostic apparatus, medical

**(G-4593)**
**DIAMOND DOGS**
3800 W Montrose Ave (60618-1017)
PHONE .................................. 773 267-0069
EMP: 3
SALES (est): 173.7K **Privately Held**
SIC: 3999 Pet supplies

**(G-4594)**
**DIANAS BANANAS INC**
2733 W Harrison St (60612-3422)
PHONE .................................. 773 638-6800
Robert Carmody, *President*
EMP: 11
SQ FT: 33,000
SALES (est): 1.2MM **Privately Held**
WEB: www.ocd3.com
SIC: 2038 Frozen specialties

**(G-4595)**
**DIAZ PRINTING**
4725 W Grand Ave (60639-4602)
PHONE .................................. 773 887-3366
Ruben Diaz, *CEO*
EMP: 2
SALES (est): 220K **Privately Held**
SIC: 2759 Commercial printing

**(G-4596)**
**DICOM TRANSPORTATION GROUP LP (PA)**
676 N Michigan Ave # 3700 (60611-2883)
PHONE .................................. 312 255-4800
Scott Dobak, *Manager*
EMP: 5 EST: 2014
SALES (est): 15.2MM **Privately Held**
SIC: 3537 Trucks: freight, baggage, etc.: industrial, except mining

**(G-4597)**
**DIEBOLDS CABINET SHOP**
1938 N Springfield Ave (60647-3489)
PHONE .................................. 773 772-3076

Fax: 773 772-8814
Richard A Diebold Jr, *Partner*
John P Diebold, *Partner*
Richard G Diebold III, *Partner*
Anton Habath, *Manager*
EMP: 5 EST: 1937
SQ FT: 6,000
SALES (est): 729.1K **Privately Held**
SIC: 2521 2511 Wood office furniture; wood household furniture

**(G-4598)**
**DIGISTITCH EMBROIDERY & DESIGN**
6535 W Archer Ave (60638-2438)
PHONE .................................. 773 229-8630
Patricia Vainisi, *President*
Gina Viviano, *Owner*
EMP: 4
SALES (est): 275K **Privately Held**
SIC: 2395 Embroidery & art needlework

**(G-4599)**
**DIGITAL FACTORY INC (PA)**
917 E 78th St Apt 203w (60619-3239)
PHONE .................................. 708 320-9879
Lawrence Griffith, *CEO*
EMP: 5
SALES (est): 1.7MM **Privately Held**
SIC: 3993 Signs & advertising specialties

**(G-4600)**
**DIGITAL GREENSIGNS INC**
1606 W Grace St (60613-2710)
PHONE .................................. 312 624-8550
Christopher Bissonnette, *Principal*
EMP: 3
SALES (est): 254.9K **Privately Held**
SIC: 3993 Signs & advertising specialties

**(G-4601)**
**DIGITAL H2O INC**
18 S Michigan Ave Fl 12 (60603-3200)
PHONE .................................. 847 456-8424
Brandon Pearlman, *President*
Michael Chavez, *Manager*
Scott Rothbarth, *Analyst*
EMP: 11
SALES (est): 283.7K **Privately Held**
SIC: 7371 1382 Computer software development & applications; oil & gas exploration services
HQ: Genscape, Inc.
1140 Garvin Pl
Louisville KY 40203
502 583-3435

**(G-4602)**
**DIGITAL HUB LLC**
1040 N Halsted St (60642-4222)
PHONE .................................. 312 943-6161
Fax: 312 943-6207
Tony Mraz, *Manager*
Liz Kossik, *Director*
Charles J Anzilotti,
EMP: 29
SALES (est): 6MM **Privately Held**
WEB: www.digitalhubchicago.com
SIC: 2759 Commercial printing

**(G-4603)**
**DIKE-O-SEAL INCORPORATED**
3965 S Keeler Ave (60632-3879)
PHONE .................................. 773 254-3224
Fax: 773 254-7222
Thomas Slepski, *President*
James P Doyle, *Vice Pres*
John M Palka, *Treasurer*
Catherine M Palka, *Admin Sec*
EMP: 14 EST: 1954
SQ FT: 16,500
SALES (est): 1.1MM **Privately Held**
WEB: www.dike-o-seal.com
SIC: 3089 3053 8711 3544 Plastic hardware & building products; gaskets, packing & sealing devices; consulting engineer; special dies, tools, jigs & fixtures

**(G-4604)**
**DIMEND SCAASI LTD**
5 S Wabash Ave Ste 1734 (60603-3057)
PHONE .................................. 312 857-1700
Isaac Gottesman, *President*
EMP: 5

## GEOGRAPHIC SECTION
### Chicago - Cook County (G-4633)

SALES (est): 641.8K **Privately Held**
SIC: 3915 Jewelers' materials & lapidary work

**(G-4605)**
**DINKELS BAKERY INC**
3329 N Lincoln Ave (60657-1107)
PHONE.....................773 281-7300
Fax: 773 281-6169
Norman Dinkel, *President*
Luke Karl, *Vice Pres*
Holly Dinkel, *Manager*
Jill Glascott, *Manager*
Helen Hanke, *Manager*
EMP: 25
SQ FT: 15,000
SALES (est): 1.4MM **Privately Held**
WEB: www.dinkels.com
SIC: 5461 5961 5149 2052 Bread; cakes; cookies; mail order house; bakery products; cookies & crackers; bread, cake & related products

**(G-4606)**
**DINO DESIGN INCORPORATED**
6538 N Milwaukee Ave (60631-1750)
PHONE.....................773 763-4223
Fax: 773 966-0457
Chris Kowalski, *President*
Christopher Kowarski, *Shareholder*
EMP: 4
SQ FT: 3,200
SALES (est): 356.5K **Privately Held**
SIC: 2361 Girls' & children's dresses, blouses & shirts

**(G-4607)**
**DINO PUBLISHING LLC**
350 W Hubbard St Ste 400 (60654-6900)
PHONE.....................312 822-9266
Amy Wideman, *Editor*
Robyn Bendle, *Prdtn Dir*
Annie Brown, *Accounts Mgr*
Annie Ethridge, *Accounts Exec*
Douglas A Leik, *Manager*
EMP: 4
SALES (est): 240K **Privately Held**
WEB: www.dinopublishing.com
SIC: 2741 Miscellaneous publishing

**(G-4608)**
**DIRECT MARKETING 1 CORPORATION**
Also Called: Aqua Farm
9701 S Lowe Ave (60628-1012)
PHONE.....................773 234-9122
Lori Becton, *President*
Wayne Harris, *Opers Mgr*
EMP: 25 EST: 2012
SALES: 300K **Privately Held**
SIC: 2013 Sausages & related products, from purchased meat

**(G-4609)**
**DIRTT ENVMTL SOLUTIONS INC**
325 N Wells St Ste 1000 (60654-7023)
PHONE.....................312 245-2870
Mogens Smed, *CEO*
Tracy Baker, *COO*
Scott Jenkins, *CFO*
Miles Nixon, *Controller*
Dagmar Spoelgen, *Manager*
▲ EMP: 145
SQ FT: 81,000
SALES (est): 19.1MM **Privately Held**
WEB: www.dirtt.net
SIC: 2522 2521 Office furniture, except wood; wood office furniture

**(G-4610)**
**DISCUSS MUSIC EDUCATION CO**
2720 W Winnemac Ave Apt 1 (60625-2778)
PHONE.....................773 561-2796
Les Dean, *Owner*
EMP: 4
SALES: 34K **Privately Held**
WEB: www.discusmusic.com
SIC: 3999 Education aids, devices & supplies

**(G-4611)**
**DISPLAY GRAPHICS SYSTEMS LLC**
4900 S Rockwell St (60632-1431)
PHONE.....................800 706-9670
Mark D Person, *President*
EMP: 3
SALES (est): 235.7K **Privately Held**
SIC: 3577 Graphic displays, except graphic terminals

**(G-4612)**
**DISPLAY PLAN LPDG**
Also Called: Displayplan US
1901 N Clybourn Ave # 400 (60614-5090)
PHONE.....................773 525-3787
Fax: 773 525-2390
Anne McNeill, *Owner*
Charles Somers, *Manager*
EMP: 21 EST: 2008
SALES (est): 1.5MM **Privately Held**
SIC: 2599 Factory furniture & fixtures

**(G-4613)**
**DIVERSFIED ILL GREEN WORKS LLC**
2419 W Byron St (60618-3709)
PHONE.....................773 544-7777
Tim Roach, *CEO*
Leslie Bowman, *CFO*
EMP: 75
SALES (est): 1.3MM **Privately Held**
SIC: 0111 2045 Wheat; pizza mixes: from purchased flour

**(G-4614)**
**DIXON PALLET SERVICE**
10340 S Lowe Ave (60628-2326)
PHONE.....................773 238-9569
James Earl Dixon, *Principal*
EMP: 8
SALES (est): 520K **Privately Held**
SIC: 2448 Pallets, wood & wood with metal

**(G-4615)**
**DJR INC**
Also Called: Meilahn Manufacturing Company
5900 W 65th St (60638-5406)
PHONE.....................773 581-5204
Fax: 773 581-5404
Gary R Clarin, *President*
Lori Kosch, *Office Mgr*
David Sawyer, *Admin Sec*
EMP: 16 EST: 1870
SQ FT: 23,000
SALES: 1.9MM **Privately Held**
SIC: 2521 5046 Bookcases, office: wood; cabinets, office: wood; shelving, commercial & industrial

**(G-4616)**
**DMI INFORMATION PROCESS CENTER**
5090 W Harrison St (60644-5141)
PHONE.....................773 378-2644
Mary Denson, *Exec Dir*
EMP: 25
SQ FT: 7,000
SALES: 120.8K **Privately Held**
SIC: 8243 2711 Data processing schools; newspapers

**(G-4617)**
**DNEPR TECHOLOGIES INC**
3304 N Broadway St # 163 (60657-3517)
PHONE.....................773 603-3360
Marian Cotor, *President*
▼ EMP: 11
SQ FT: 1,600
SALES: 398.6K **Privately Held**
SIC: 2329 Shirt & slack suits: men's, youths' & boys'

**(G-4618)**
**DO YOU SEE WHAT I SEE ENTERTAI**
Also Called: Do You See Entertainment
2544 W North Ave Apt 3d (60647-5225)
PHONE.....................773 612-1269
Jeff Ramsey, *CEO*
Robert Jones, *President*
Christopher Snyder, *Vice Pres*
Joseph Carver, *CFO*
EMP: 5

SALES (est): 302.7K **Privately Held**
SIC: 2731 Book music: publishing & printing

**(G-4619)**
**DO-RITE DONUTS**
50 W Randolph St (60601-3207)
PHONE.....................312 422-0150
Harris D'Antignac, *Partner*
EMP: 5 EST: 2013
SALES (est): 299.8K **Privately Held**
SIC: 2051 Doughnuts, except frozen

**(G-4620)**
**DOBINSKI MARKETING**
3843 N Fremont St (60613-3001)
PHONE.....................773 248-5880
Richard S Dobinski, *Principal*
EMP: 3
SALES (est): 179.9K **Privately Held**
SIC: 2721 Magazines: publishing & printing

**(G-4621)**
**DOCTORS CHOICE INC**
Also Called: Nuway Distributors
600 W Cermak Rd Ste 1a (60616-4880)
PHONE.....................312 666-1111
Daniel L Gray, *President*
Frank Hunt, *Opers Mgr*
Johnny Lundy, *Opers Mgr*
Allen Lundy, *Consultant*
EMP: 9 EST: 2002
SALES (est): 1.4MM **Privately Held**
SIC: 5722 5047 3841 Electric household appliances; medical equipment & supplies; surgical & medical instruments

**(G-4622)**
**DOLLAR MIX**
3744 W 63rd St (60629-4023)
PHONE.....................773 582-7110
Eduardo Cruc, *Owner*
EMP: 4
SALES (est): 390.3K **Privately Held**
SIC: 3273 Ready-mixed concrete

**(G-4623)**
**DOMINIQUE GRAVES**
Also Called: Nique Soul Catering
6800 S Cornell Ave 1c (60649-1418)
PHONE.....................773 368-5289
Dominique Graves, *Owner*
EMP: 6
SALES (est): 208.3K **Privately Held**
SIC: 2099 Ready-to-eat meals, salads & sandwiches

**(G-4624)**
**DOMINO FOODS INC**
Also Called: Domino Sugar
2905 S Western Ave (60608-5221)
PHONE.....................773 254-8282
Richard Clinton, *QC Mgr*
Ed Furgat, *Branch Mgr*
EMP: 30
SQ FT: 55,000
SALES (corp-wide): 286.8MM **Privately Held**
WEB: www.dominospecialtyingredients.com
SIC: 2062 Cane sugar refining; granulated cane sugar from purchased raw sugar or syrup
HQ: Domino Foods Inc.
99 Wood Ave S Ste 901
Iselin NJ 08830
732 590-1173

**(G-4625)**
**DOMINO FOODS INC**
Also Called: Domino Sugar
2400 E 130th St (60633-1725)
PHONE.....................773 646-2203
Jack Slater, *Mfg Staff*
Lou Delich, *Opers-Prdtn-Mfg*
EMP: 19
SALES (corp-wide): 286.8MM **Privately Held**
WEB: www.dominospecialtyingredients.com
SIC: 2099 Sugar
HQ: Domino Foods Inc.
99 Wood Ave S Ste 901
Iselin NJ 08830
732 590-1173

**(G-4626)**
**DONERMEN LLC**
2849 W Belmont Ave A (60618-5897)
P.O. Box 2219 (60690-2219)
PHONE.....................773 430-2828
Floyd Nicholas G, *Managing Prtnr*
Philip Naumann, *Mng Member*
EMP: 6
SQ FT: 1,800
SALES: 520K **Privately Held**
SIC: 3713 Truck bodies (motor vehicles)

**(G-4627)**
**DONGHIA SHOWROOMS INC**
631 Merchandise Mart 63 (60654)
PHONE.....................312 822-0766
Sam Kahn, *Sales Staff*
Linda Stevens, *Manager*
EMP: 7
SALES (corp-wide): 7.3MM **Privately Held**
SIC: 2395 5231 Quilted fabrics or cloth; paint, glass & wallpaper
PA: Donghia Showrooms Inc
500 Bic Dr Ste 200
Milford CT 06461
203 701-2940

**(G-4628)**
**DONNELLEY AND SONS CO R R**
5858 W 73rd St (60638-6216)
PHONE.....................708 924-6200
Tina Koester, *Principal*
EMP: 2
SALES (est): 239.8K **Privately Held**
SIC: 3555 Printing trades machinery

**(G-4629)**
**DONNELLEY FINANCIAL LLC**
111 S Wacker Dr Ste 3500 (60606-4300)
PHONE.....................312 326-8000
Eric A Eisenstein, *Senior VP*
EMP: 12
SALES (corp-wide): 6.9B **Publicly Held**
SIC: 2752 Commercial printing, lithographic
HQ: Donnelley Financial Llc
55 Water St Lowr L1
New York NY 10041
212 425-0298

**(G-4630)**
**DONR CO**
61 W 15th St Apt 401 (60605-3607)
PHONE.....................773 895-3359
Amadou Lam, *CEO*
EMP: 3
SALES (est): 71.1K **Privately Held**
SIC: 7372 7389 Application computer software;

**(G-4631)**
**DONTRELL PERCY**
11257 S Bishop St (60643-4467)
PHONE.....................773 418-4900
EMP: 14
SALES (est): 378.4K **Privately Held**
SIC: 1389 Construction, repair & dismantling services

**(G-4632)**
**DORENFEST GROUP LTD**
444 N Michigan Ave # 1200 (60611-3959)
PHONE.....................312 464-3000
Sheldon I Dorenfest, *President*
Larry Pawola, *General Mgr*
John Blume, *Vice Pres*
Mitch Work, *Vice Pres*
EMP: 80
SQ FT: 15,000
SALES (est): 4.4MM **Privately Held**
WEB: www.dorenfest.com
SIC: 8742 2721 Hospital & health services consultant; trade journals: publishing only, not printed on site

**(G-4633)**
**DOS BRO CORP**
Also Called: Quicker Printers
6116 N Broadway St (60660-2502)
PHONE.....................773 334-1919
Fax: 773 334-1022
Matthew Gilliana, *President*
Sargon Gilliana, *Treasurer*
EMP: 6

# Chicago - Cook County (G-4634)  GEOGRAPHIC SECTION

SALES (est): 779.5K **Privately Held**
WEB: www.quickerprinters.com
SIC: 2752 Commercial printing, lithographic

### (G-4634)
### DOT BLACK GROUP
329 W 18th St Ste 800 (60616-1103)
PHONE..................312 204-8000
Jim Bossemeyer, *Principal*
Brian Berndt, *Prdtn Mgr*
EMP: 3
SALES (est): 282K **Privately Held**
SIC: 2791 Typesetting

### (G-4635)
### DOT PRESS LLC
1941 W Fulton St (60612-2403)
PHONE..................312 421-0293
Jose Luis Galindo, *Mng Member*
Nilda Esparza,
EMP: 8
SQ FT: 3,400
SALES (est): 1.3MM **Privately Held**
WEB: www.dotpress.us
SIC: 2759 Commercial printing

### (G-4636)
### DOUGHMAN DON & ASSOC
222 Merchandise Mart Plz # 947 (60654-1311)
PHONE..................312 321-1011
Carol Curry, *Owner*
EMP: 3
SALES (est): 183.1K **Privately Held**
SIC: 2339 Women's & misses' accessories

### (G-4637)
### DOVE FOUNDATION
Also Called: Magnify Peace
5056 N Marine Dr Apt C4 (60640-6324)
PHONE..................312 217-3683
Barbara Mc Donald, *CEO*
Wanda Mc Donald, *Treasurer*
EMP: 4 EST: 2007
SALES (est): 349.6K **Privately Held**
SIC: 2678 Writing paper & envelopes: made from purchased materials

### (G-4638)
### DOVER INDUSTRIAL CHROME INC
Also Called: Tvj Electroforming Division
2929 N Campbell Ave (60618-7903)
PHONE..................773 478-2022
Fax: 773 478-0008
EMP: 5
SQ FT: 16,000
SALES: 500K **Privately Held**
SIC: 3471 3479 Electroplating And Electroforming Of Metals Or Formed Products

### (G-4639)
### DOW JONES & COMPANY INC
1 S Wacker Dr Ste 2100 (60606-4677)
PHONE..................312 580-1023
Fax: 312 750-4153
Kevin Helliker, *Editor*
John Prestbo, *Editor*
Gregory Giangrande, *Chairman*
Gayle Gossen, *Business Mgr*
Michael Witt, *Vice Pres*
EMP: 90
SALES (corp-wide): 8.2B **Publicly Held**
WEB: www.dowjones.com/index.asp
SIC: 2711 2721 Newspapers: publishing only, not printed on site; magazines: publishing only, not printed on site; periodicals: publishing only
HQ: Dow Jones & Company, Inc.
 1211 Avenue Of The Americ
 New York NY 10036
 609 627-2999

### (G-4640)
### DPE INCORPORATED
7647 S Kedzie Ave (60652-1507)
PHONE..................773 306-0105
Jose Marquez, *General Mgr*
EMP: 6 EST: 2013
SALES: 900K **Privately Held**
SIC: 2211 2395 2759 Apparel & outerwear fabrics, cotton; embroidery & art needlework; screen printing

### (G-4641)
### DR EARLES LLC
2930 S Michigan Ave # 100 (60616-3270)
PHONE..................312 225-7200
Robert Earles,
Andrea Earles,
Brian Johnson,
EMP: 5
SQ FT: 2,000
SALES: 70K **Privately Held**
WEB: www.dr-earles.com
SIC: 2834 Pharmaceutical preparations

### (G-4642)
### DRAG CITY
2921 N Cicero Ave (60641-5131)
P.O. Box 476867 (60647-0980)
PHONE..................312 455-1015
Fax: 312 455-1057
Daniel Koretzky, *Owner*
Dan Osborn, *Co-Owner*
Rian Murphy, *Sales Staff*
Sara Hays, *Marketing Mgr*
▲ EMP: 8
SALES (est): 770K **Privately Held**
WEB: www.dragcity.com
SIC: 3652 7389 Pre-recorded records & tapes; music recording producer

### (G-4643)
### DREHOBL ART GLASS COMPANY
5108 W Irving Park Rd (60641-2624)
PHONE..................773 286-2566
Chris Drehobl, *Owner*
EMP: 3
SALES (est): 208.8K **Privately Held**
SIC: 3231 Products of purchased glass

### (G-4644)
### DRIG CORPORATION
437 W Division St Apt 316 (60610-1720)
PHONE..................312 265-1509
Olatunde Omosebi, *CEO*
EMP: 7 EST: 2012
SALES (est): 753.2K **Privately Held**
SIC: 2911 7389 5171 5172 Diesel fuels; jet fuels; oils, fuel; ; petroleum bulk stations & terminals; petroleum terminals; gases, liquefied petroleum (propane); aircraft fueling services

### (G-4645)
### DS SERVICES OF AMERICA INC
Also Called: Hinckley Springs
6055 S Harlem Ave (60638-3984)
PHONE..................773 586-8600
Jun Tanaka, *Vice Pres*
Tom Houlihan, *Branch Mgr*
EMP: 250
SQ FT: 76,000
SALES (corp-wide): 3.2B **Privately Held**
WEB: www.suntorywatergroup.com
SIC: 2086 5149 7359 Water, pasteurized: packaged in cans, bottles, etc.; water, distilled; mineral or spring water bottling; equipment rental & leasing
HQ: Ds Services Of America, Inc.
 2300 Windy Ridge Pkwy Se 500n
 Atlanta GA 30339
 770 933-1400

### (G-4646)
### DUBOIS CHEMICALS GROUP INC
7025 W 66th Pl (60638-4703)
PHONE..................708 458-2000
EMP: 4
SALES (est): 194.6K **Privately Held**
SIC: 2869 Industrial organic chemicals
PA: Dubois Chemicals, Inc.
 3630 E Kemper Rd
 Cincinnati OH 45241

### (G-4647)
### DUDE PRODUCTS INC
1744 W Beach Ave U2 (60622-2108)
PHONE..................773 661-1126
Sean Riley, *President*
Ryan Meegan, *Principal*
Brian Wilkin, *Principal*
Jeffrey Klimkowski, *Admin Sec*
EMP: 4

SALES (est): 307.7K **Privately Held**
SIC: 2621 2676 Sanitary tissue paper; sanitary paper products

### (G-4648)
### DUDEK & BOCK SPRING MFG CO (PA)
5100 W Roosevelt Rd (60644-1437)
PHONE..................773 379-4100
Fax: 773 379-0230
John Dudek, *President*
Thomas Berg, *Vice Pres*
John Schneider, *Vice Pres*
Jerzy Siwek, *Plant Mgr*
Thomas Regan, *Opers Staff*
▲ EMP: 185
SQ FT: 250,000
SALES (est): 51MM **Privately Held**
WEB: www.dudek-bock.com
SIC: 3493 3496 3469 Steel springs, except wire; miscellaneous fabricated wire products; metal stampings

### (G-4649)
### DUMORE SUPPLIES INC
Also Called: Do It Best
2525 S Wabash Ave (60616-2308)
P.O. Box 16200 (60616-0200)
PHONE..................312 949-6260
Fax: 312 949-6268
Howard Rosenstein, *President*
Arlene Leshner, *Treasurer*
Joe Richards, *Marketing Staff*
Lindsey Rosenstein, *Director*
Deena Rosenstein, *Admin Sec*
EMP: 14
SQ FT: 17,300
SALES (est): 2.2MM **Privately Held**
WEB: www.dumoresupplies.com
SIC: 5251 3429 5063 5074 Hardware; manufactured hardware (general); electrical apparatus & equipment; light bulbs & related supplies; plumbing & hydronic heating supplies; chemicals & allied products; industrial equipment services

### (G-4650)
### DUN-WEL LITHOGRAPH CO INC
3338 N Ravenswood Ave (60657-2047)
PHONE..................773 327-8811
Fax: 773 327-1317
Guy Grundhoefer, *President*
Julie Grundhoefer, *Admin Sec*
EMP: 4 EST: 1948
SQ FT: 5,600
SALES (est): 634.2K **Privately Held**
SIC: 2752 Lithographing on metal

### (G-4651)
### DUNAMIS INTERNATIONAL
1239 W Madison St (60607-2172)
PHONE..................773 504-5733
EMP: 4 EST: 2009
SALES (est): 300K **Privately Held**
SIC: 2851 Paints And Allied Products, Nec

### (G-4652)
### DUO NORTH AMERICA
329 W 18th St Ste 607 (60616-1120)
PHONE..................312 421-7755
Francois Frezzouls, *President*
Karine Ravetto, *Manager*
EMP: 3 EST: 1998
SALES (est): 900K **Privately Held**
SIC: 7319 2399 Display advertising service; banners, pennants & flags

### (G-4653)
### DUO USA INCORPORATED
Also Called: Duo Display
329 W 18th St Ste 714 (60616-1121)
PHONE..................312 421-7755
Philippe Beille, *President*
Francois Frezouls, *Principal*
Nicolas Crestin, *Mktg Dir*
Richard Kirsch, *Manager*
Michelle Podmohly, *Graphic Designe*
▲ EMP: 4
SALES (est): 330K **Privately Held**
SIC: 2541 5046 Display fixtures, wood; store fixtures & display equipment

### (G-4654)
### DUPLI GROUP INC
3628 N Lincoln Ave (60613-3516)
PHONE..................773 549-5285

Fax: 773 549-4222
Walter E Mc Cormack Jr, *President*
Mike Thomas, *Prdtn Mgr*
Bill Boope, *Sales Mgr*
Robert Dombrowski, *Accounts Mgr*
Rich Roth, *Accounts Exec*
EMP: 10 EST: 1948
SQ FT: 14,000
SALES (est): 1.8MM **Privately Held**
SIC: 2796 2752 2791 Lithographic plates, positives or negatives; commercial printing, lithographic; typesetting

### (G-4655)
### DURACELL COMPANY
181 W Madison St Fl 44 (60602-4510)
PHONE..................203 796-4000
EMP: 7
SALES (corp-wide): 223.6B **Publicly Held**
SIC: 3691 Alkaline cell storage batteries
HQ: The Duracell Company
 14 Research Dr
 Bethel CT 06801
 203 796-4000

### (G-4656)
### DURITE SCREW CORPORATION
1815 N Long Ave 35 (60639-4326)
PHONE..................773 622-3410
Fax: 773 622-3722
Edmund Nowak Jr, *President*
Patricia Nowak, *Treasurer*
EMP: 23
SQ FT: 15,000
SALES (est): 4.6MM **Privately Held**
WEB: www.duritescrewcorp.com
SIC: 3451 Screw machine products

### (G-4657)
### DURO ART INDUSTRIES INC (PA)
Also Called: Duro Decal Co
1832 W Juneway Ter (60626-1016)
PHONE..................773 743-3430
Fax: 773 743-3882
Kurt Rathslag, *President*
Thomas C Rathslag Jr, *General Mgr*
Les Frick, *Sales Mgr*
Thomas Rathlag Jr, *Admin Sec*
▲ EMP: 80
SQ FT: 80,000
SALES (est): 9.2MM **Privately Held**
SIC: 3952 Paints, except gold & bronze: artists'; brushes, air, artists'; canvas board, artists'; lettering instruments, artists'

### (G-4658)
### DUVAS USA LIMITED
676 N Michigan Ave # 2800 (60611-2883)
PHONE..................312 266-1420
Thomas Rissman, *Director*
Paul Clark, *Bd of Directors*
Anthony Kruglinski, *Bd of Directors*
Simon Murad, *Bd of Directors*
EMP: 4
SALES (est): 195K **Privately Held**
SIC: 3699 Security devices

### (G-4659)
### DYNACRON
1017 N Cicero Ave (60651-3202)
PHONE..................773 378-0736
Scott Rempala, *President*
EMP: 2 EST: 2007
SALES (est): 220K **Privately Held**
SIC: 2899 Corrosion preventive lubricant

### (G-4660)
### DYSON INC (DH)
600 W Chicago Ave Ste 275 (60654-2813)
PHONE..................312 469-5950
Ed Culley, *President*
Glen Andrew, *Managing Dir*
James Dyson, *Principal*
Richard Brown, *Business Mgr*
Valerie Hawk, *Business Mgr*
▲ EMP: 100
SQ FT: 10,000
SALES (est): 42MM
SALES (corp-wide): 710.2K **Privately Held**
WEB: www.dyson.com
SIC: 3635 Household vacuum cleaners

# GEOGRAPHIC SECTION

**Chicago - Cook County (G-4687)**

HQ: Dyson Limited
Tetbury Hill
Malmesbury WILTS SN16
166 682-7272

**(G-4661)**
**DYSON B2B INC**
600 W Chicago Ave Ste 275 (60654-2813)
PHONE.................................312 469-5950
Fax: 312 469-5951
James Dyson, *President*
Diane Skinkle, *Controller*
Chris Burnham, *Human Res Mgr*
Jacinta Tan, *Human Res Mgr*
Jamie Ettwein, *Manager*
▲ EMP: 25
SALES (est): 3.5MM
SALES (corp-wide): 710.2K Privately Held
SIC: 3634 Dryers, electric: hand & face
HQ: Dyson, Inc.
600 W Chicago Ave Ste 275
Chicago IL 60654
312 469-5950

**(G-4662)**
**E & H TUBING INC (PA)**
Also Called: Indiana Steel & Tube
4401 W Roosevelt Rd (60624-3841)
PHONE.................................773 522-3100
EMP: 13
SALES (est): 8.2MM Privately Held
SIC: 3317 Mfg Steel Pipe/Tubes

**(G-4663)**
**E & L COMMUNICATION**
2644 W 47th St (60632-1350)
PHONE.................................773 890-1656
Fax: 773 890-2467
EMP: 8
SALES (est): 349.7K Privately Held
SIC: 2711 Newspapers-Publishing/Printing

**(G-4664)**
**E & R POWDER COATINGS INC**
3729 W 49th St (60632-3601)
PHONE.................................773 523-9510
Mark Clausius, *President*
Paulette Clausius, *Vice Pres*
Mandi Prestianni, *Manager*
EMP: 45
SQ FT: 38,000
SALES (est): 6.2MM Privately Held
WEB: www.erpowdercoatings.com
SIC: 3479 Coating of metals & formed products

**(G-4665)**
**E GORNELL & SONS INC**
2241 N Knox Ave (60639-3486)
PHONE.................................773 489-2330
Fax: 773 489-1102
Gus H Treslo, *President*
Ericka Swaim, *General Mgr*
Marjorie Gornell, *Vice Pres*
Daniel Proctor, *Plant Mgr*
Dick Mitchell, *Purch Mgr*
▲ EMP: 36 EST: 1892
SQ FT: 30,000
SALES (est): 5.8MM Privately Held
WEB: www.gornellbrush.com
SIC: 3991 7389 Brushes, household or industrial; design, commercial & industrial

**(G-4666)**
**E J KUPJACK & ASSOCIATES INC**
2233 S Throop St Apt 319 (60608-5011)
PHONE.................................847 823-6661
Fax: 847 823-6664
Henry Kupjack, *President*
Jay Kupjack, *Admin Sec*
EMP: 4 EST: 1938
SQ FT: 3,500
SALES: 275K Privately Held
SIC: 3999 3944 Models, general, except toy; games, toys & children's vehicles

**(G-4667)**
**E N M COMPANY**
Also Called: E N M Digital Counters
5617 N Northwest Hwy (60646-6177)
PHONE.................................773 775-8400
Fax: 773 775-5968
Nicholas G Polydoris, *President*
Fran Klein, *Vice Pres*

Stan Kocol, *Chief Engr*
Gloria Polydoris, *Treasurer*
Lynn George, *Admin Sec*
▲ EMP: 100 EST: 1957
SQ FT: 80,000
SALES (est): 19.9MM Privately Held
SIC: 3824 3625 3568 3699 Counters, revolution; electronic totalizing counters; mechanical counters; timing devices, electronic; sprockets (power transmission equipment); pulleys, power transmission; electrical equipment & supplies; switchgear & switchboard apparatus; computer storage devices

**(G-4668)**
**E SOLUTIONS BUSINESS** ✪
300 N La Salle Dr # 4925 (60654-3406)
PHONE.................................855 324-3339
Sharon Douglas, *CEO*
EMP: 32 EST: 2016
SALES (est): 1.2MM Privately Held
SIC: 3679 Commutators, electronic

**(G-4669)**
**E-J INDUSTRIES INC**
1275 S Campbell Ave (60608-1013)
PHONE.................................312 226-5023
Fax: 312 226-5976
Keith Weitzman, *President*
Karen Soltysiak, *Purchasing*
Peter Nina, *Accountant*
EMP: 55 EST: 1942
SQ FT: 170,000
SALES (est): 10.8MM Privately Held
WEB: www.e-industries.com
SIC: 2599 Restaurant furniture, wood or metal; hotel furniture

**(G-4670)**
**E-Z TREE RECYCLING INC**
7050 S Dorchester Ave (60637-4704)
PHONE.................................773 493-8600
Michael Q Fowler, *President*
Yolanda E Fowler, *Admin Sec*
EMP: 6
SALES (est): 1MM Privately Held
SIC: 5099 2499 5989 5211 Firewood; mulch, wood & bark; wood (fuel); lumber & other building materials; lumber, plywood & millwork; sawmills & planing mills, general

**(G-4671)**
**EAGLE MACHINE COMPANY**
1725 W Walnut St (60612-2523)
PHONE.................................312 243-7407
Fax: 312 243-7431
Sigmund Kamionka, *President*
EMP: 5
SQ FT: 10,000
SALES (est): 613.6K Privately Held
SIC: 3599 7692 Machine shop, jobbing & repair; welding repair

**(G-4672)**
**EAR HUSTLE 411 LLC**
123 W Madison St Ste 806 (60602-4620)
PHONE.................................773 616-3598
Christine Campbell, *Mng Member*
Joanne Miller, *Mng Member*
Lesley Taylor, *Mng Member*
EMP: 3
SALES: 75K Privately Held
SIC: 2711 Newspapers

**(G-4673)**
**EARL AD INC**
2201 S Union Ave Ste 2 (60616-2159)
PHONE.................................312 666-7106
Fax: 312 666-1305
Michael Hoffman, *President*
Roberta Hoffman, *Vice Pres*
EMP: 4
SALES (est): 394.5K Privately Held
SIC: 2759 2396 Screen printing; advertising literature: printing; automotive & apparel trimmings

**(G-4674)**
**EARL G GRAVES LTD**
Also Called: Black Enterprize Magazine
625 N Michigan Ave # 422 (60611-3110)
PHONE.................................312 664-8667
Fax: 312 988-9770
Tracy Randle, *Manager*

EMP: 4
SALES (corp-wide): 18.7MM Privately Held
WEB: www.blackenterprise.com
SIC: 2721 Periodicals
PA: Earl G. Graves, Ltd.
260 Madison Ave Ste 11
New York NY 10016
212 242-8000

**(G-4675)**
**EARL G GRAVES PUBG CO INC**
625 N Michigan Ave # 401 (60611-3110)
PHONE.................................312 274-0682
EMP: 4
SALES (corp-wide): 20.7MM Privately Held
SIC: 2721 Magazine Publisher
HQ: Earl G. Graves Publishing Co., Inc.
260 Madison Ave Ste 11
New York NY 10016
212 242-8000

**(G-4676)**
**EARLY EDITION**
69 W Washington St LI10 (60602-3139)
PHONE.................................312 345-0786
Sadrudi Noorani, *Principal*
EMP: 5
SALES (est): 314K Privately Held
SIC: 2711 Newspapers, publishing & printing

**(G-4677)**
**EARSHOT INC**
560 W Washington Blvd # 240 (60661-2695)
PHONE.................................773 383-1798
David Rush, *CEO*
Joanna Lichter, *Mktg Dir*
EMP: 12
SQ FT: 1,100
SALES (est): 632.9K Privately Held
SIC: 7372 Application computer software

**(G-4678)**
**EARTHS HEALING CAFE LLC**
1942 W Montrose Ave Ste 1 (60613-1187)
PHONE.................................773 728-0598
Aluko Aleksander,
Salmon Samantha,
EMP: 9
SALES (est): 1.1MM Privately Held
SIC: 2834 Vitamin, nutrient & hematinic preparations for human use

**(G-4679)**
**EARTHSAFE SYSTEMS INC (PA)**
2041 W Carroll Ave (60612-1630)
PHONE.................................312 226-7600
Bill Edwards, *President*
EMP: 12
SQ FT: 7,300
SALES (est): 1.6MM Privately Held
WEB: www.earthsafe.com
SIC: 3312 5084 8711 Pipes & tubes; industrial machinery & equipment; professional engineer

**(G-4680)**
**EAST BALT BAKERY OF FLORIDA**
1801 W 31st Pl (60608-6144)
PHONE.................................407 933-2222
Frank Kuchuris, *Ch of Bd*
John Petenes, *President*
EMP: 430
SQ FT: 50,000
SALES (est): 40.1MM
SALES (corp-wide): 1.5B Privately Held
SIC: 2051 Buns, bread type: fresh or frozen
HQ: East Balt Us, Llc
1801 W 31st Pl
Chicago IL 60608

**(G-4681)**
**EAST BALT COMMISSARY LLC**
Also Called: East Balt Bakeries
1801 W 31st Pl (60608-6199)
PHONE.................................773 376-4444
Fax: 773 376-8137
Mark Bendix, *CEO*
David Dvorak, *Exec VP*
Gerry Bilek, *Vice Pres*
Mike Labosky, *Vice Pres*

David Watkins, *CFO*
EMP: 5
SALES (est): 83K Privately Held
SIC: 2051 Bakery: wholesale or wholesale/retail combined

**(G-4682)**
**EAST WEST MARTIAL ARTS SUPS**
5544 N Western Ave (60625-2217)
PHONE.................................773 878-7711
Fax: 773 878-6847
Kyung Sun Shin, *President*
Jay Shin, *Manager*
EMP: 5
SQ FT: 30,000
SALES (est): 787K Privately Held
SIC: 5091 5941 3842 3699 Athletic goods; martial arts equipment & supplies; surgical appliances & supplies; electrical equipment & supplies; special dies, tools, jigs & fixtures; carpets & rugs

**(G-4683)**
**EASTERN ACCENTS INC**
Also Called: Feathersound
4201 W Belmont Ave (60641-4621)
PHONE.................................773 604-7300
Ridvan Tatargil, *President*
Siw Tatargil, *Principal*
Ron Jericho, *CFO*
EMP: 220
SQ FT: 88,000
SALES (est): 17.9MM
SALES (corp-wide): 79.6MM Privately Held
WEB: www.easternaccents.com
SIC: 2392 5719 7389 Cushions & pillows; beddings & linens; interior designer
PA: Ezine Incorporated
4201 W Belmont Ave
Chicago IL 60641
773 866-1212

**(G-4684)**
**EASTERN KITCHEN & BATH**
401 N Western Ave Ste 1 (60612-1418)
PHONE.................................312 492-7248
Fax: 312 492-7258
Kuithen Chen, *Owner*
▲ EMP: 3
SALES (est): 194.2K Privately Held
SIC: 1411 Granite, dimension-quarrying

**(G-4685)**
**EATON INFLATABLE LLC**
Also Called: Pump It Up Chicago
821 W Eastman St (60642-2609)
PHONE.................................312 664-7867
Scott Peterson, *Principal*
EMP: 30
SALES (est): 2MM Privately Held
SIC: 2599 Inflatable beds

**(G-4686)**
**EAZYPOWER CORPORATION**
2321 N Keystone Ave (60639-3709)
PHONE.................................773 278-5000
Burton Kozak, *President*
EMP: 35
SALES (corp-wide): 1MM Privately Held
SIC: 3699 5063 5999 Household electrical equipment; electrical apparatus & equipment; electronic parts & equipment
PA: Eazypower Corporation
60639 W Belden St Ste 10
Chicago IL 60639
773 278-5000

**(G-4687)**
**EAZYPOWER CORPORATION (PA)**
60639 W Belden St Ste 10 (60639)
PHONE.................................773 278-5000
Burton Kozak, *President*
Ira Kozak, *Vice Pres*
Joan Kozak, *Vice Pres*
▲ EMP: 9
SQ FT: 40,000
SALES (est): 1MM Privately Held
WEB: www.eazypower.com
SIC: 3699 5072 Household electrical equipment; power tools & accessories

---

(PA)=Parent Co (HQ)=Headquarters (DH)=Div Headquarters
✪ = New Business established in last 2 years

2017 Harris Illinois
Industrial Directory

# Chicago - Cook County (G-4688)

**(G-4688)**
**EBLING ELECTRIC COMPANY**
2222 W Hubbard St (60612-1614)
PHONE...................312 455-1885
Fax: 312 455-1892
Charles Salemi, *President*
EMP: 12 EST: 1937
SQ FT: 12,000
SALES (est): 840K Privately Held
SIC: 7694 Electric motor repair

**(G-4689)**
**EBONYENERGY PUBLISHING INC NFP**
Also Called: The Gem Group
10960 S Prospect Ave (60643-3442)
PHONE...................773 851-5159
Cheryl Katherine Wash, *President*
EMP: 3
SALES: 10K Privately Held
WEB: www.ebonyenergy.com
SIC: 2731 Book publishing

**(G-4690)**
**EBRO FOODS INC**
Also Called: Ebro Packing Company
1330 W 43rd St (60609-3308)
PHONE...................773 696-0150
Zenaida E Abreu, *President*
Richard Fernandez, *Purchasing*
Silvio Vega Jr, *Treasurer*
Pedro Morales, *Sales Dir*
Carlos Camacho, *Sales Mgr*
▼ EMP: 80
SQ FT: 56,000
SALES (est): 46.1MM Privately Held
WEB: www.ebrofoods.com
SIC: 2032 Mexican foods: packaged in cans, jars, etc.

**(G-4691)**
**ECD-NETWORK LLC**
320 W Ohio St Ste 3w (60654-7887)
PHONE...................917 670-0821
Kyoko Crawford, *CEO*
Jean Christophe Lapiere,
EMP: 5
SQ FT: 500
SALES (est): 160.7K Privately Held
SIC: 7372 Business oriented computer software

**(G-4692)**
**ECO-PUR SOLUTIONS LLC**
694 Veterans Pkwy Ste F (60606)
PHONE...................630 917-8789
David Frank, *Mng Member*
▲ EMP: 4
SALES (est): 250K Privately Held
SIC: 2891 Adhesives & sealants

**(G-4693)**
**ECOCO INC**
1830 N Lamon Ave (60639-4512)
PHONE...................773 745-7700
Aaron Tiram, *President*
Georgi Honigsblum, *Plant Mgr*
Lois Terrell, *Office Mgr*
Dina Piersawl, *Consultant*
Jonathan Tiram, *Senior Mgr*
▲ EMP: 40
SQ FT: 85,000
SALES (est): 11.4MM Privately Held
WEB: www.ecocoinc.com
SIC: 2844 7231 Hair preparations, including shampoos; shampoos, rinses, conditioners: hair; beauty shops

**(G-4694)**
**ED STAN FABRICATING CO**
Also Called: Stan-Ed Metal Mfg Co
4859 W Ogden Ave (60804-3662)
PHONE...................708 863-7668
Fax: 708 863-7672
Edward A Wadas, *President*
Mitch Piznarski, *Manager*
Melanie Wadas, *Admin Sec*
EMP: 6 EST: 1952
SQ FT: 2,475
SALES: 290K Privately Held
SIC: 3469 3446 3444 3443 Stamping metal for the trade; perforated metal, stamped; architectural metalwork; sheet metalwork; fabricated plate work (boiler shop); fabricated structural metal

**(G-4695)**
**EDGAR PALLETS**
4122 W Ogden Ave (60623-2821)
PHONE...................773 454-8919
Edgar J Mendez, *Owner*
EMP: 4 EST: 2009
SALES (est): 313.5K Privately Held
SIC: 2448 Pallets, wood & wood with metal

**(G-4696)**
**EDMARK VISUAL IDENTIFICATION**
4552 N Kilbourn Ave (60630-4120)
PHONE...................800 923-8333
Fax: 773 427-8997
Ed Yerke, *Owner*
EMP: 2
SALES: 250K Privately Held
SIC: 3999 Identification tags, except paper

**(G-4697)**
**EDMUND D SCHMELZIE & SONS**
29 E Madison St Ste 1214 (60602-4472)
PHONE...................312 782-7230
Carl Schmelzie, *President*
Paul Schmelzie, *Vice Pres*
EMP: 3
SQ FT: 1,000
SALES: 500K Privately Held
SIC: 3915 Jewel cutting, drilling, polishing, recutting or setting

**(G-4698)**
**EDQU MEDIA LLC**
9158 S Michigan Ave (60619-6619)
PHONE...................773 803-9793
Gregory Edwards, *CEO*
Sara Edwards, *President*
EMP: 3
SALES (est): 123.9K Privately Held
SIC: 7371 7372 7812 7389 Computer software writers, freelance; computer software development; application computer software; motion picture & video production;

**(G-4699)**
**EDSAL MANUFACTURING CO INC (PA)**
4400 S Packers Ave (60609-3388)
PHONE...................773 475-3020
Fax: 773 254-1303
Bruce Saltzberg, *Principal*
Bruce Murray, *Safety Dir*
James Chruszczyk, *Opers Mgr*
Joseph Zaplatosch, *Materials Mgr*
David Wojtowicz, *Opers Staff*
▲ EMP: 1200 EST: 1952
SQ FT: 700,000
SALES (est): 318.9MM Privately Held
WEB: www.edsal.com
SIC: 2599 2542 2522 Factory furniture & fixtures; shelving, office & store: except wood; cabinets: show, display or storage: except wood; office furniture, except wood

**(G-4700)**
**EDSAL MANUFACTURING CO INC**
1555 W 44th St (60609-3335)
PHONE...................773 475-3013
Denise White, *Principal*
Julie Lonergan, *Admin Asst*
EMP: 68
SALES (corp-wide): 318.9MM Privately Held
SIC: 2599 2542 2522 Factory furniture & fixtures; shelving, office & store: except wood; office furniture, except wood
PA: Edsal Manufacturing Company, Inc.
4400 S Packers Ave
Chicago IL 60609
773 475-3020

**(G-4701)**
**EDUCATION PARTNERS PROJECT LTD**
4800 S Chicago Beach Dr 1901s (60615-7032)
PHONE...................773 675-6643
Vernon McCallum, *Director*
Malika Diamond, *Director*
Gloria McCallum, *Director*
EMP: 4

SALES (est): 241.1K Privately Held
SIC: 8111 8742 8732 3953 Legal services; business consultant; educational research; seal presses, notary & hand

**(G-4702)**
**EDVENTURE PROMOTIONS INC**
770 N La Salle Dr Ste 500 (60654-5267)
PHONE...................312 440-1800
Edward I Levy, *President*
EMP: 2
SQ FT: 1,500
SALES (est): 297.9K Privately Held
SIC: 3993 5199 Signs & advertising specialties; advertising specialties

**(G-4703)**
**EDWARD FIELDS INCORPORATED**
222 Merchandise Mart Plz # 635 (60654-1026)
PHONE...................312 644-0400
Fax: 312 644-0951
Susan Mackenzie, *Manager*
EMP: 4
SALES (corp-wide): 13.4MM Privately Held
WEB: www.edwardfieldsinc.com
SIC: 2273 Carpets & rugs
PA: Edward Fields, Incorporated
150 E 58th St Ste 1101
New York NY 10155
212 310-0400

**(G-4704)**
**EGAN VISUAL/WEST INC**
222 W Merchandise Mart Pl Ste 1079 (60654)
PHONE...................800 266-2387
Jim Egan, *CEO*
Sean Brown, *President*
Kieth Caines, *Director*
Thomas Karras, *Administration*
EMP: 2
SQ FT: 6,500
SALES (est): 345.2K
SALES (corp-wide): 7MM Privately Held
WEB: www.egan.com
SIC: 3952 2531 2521 Chalk: carpenters', blackboard, marking, tailors', etc.; public building & related furniture; blackboards, wood; wood office furniture; panel systems & partitions (free-standing); office: wood
PA: Egan Visual Inc
300 Hanlan Rd
Woodbridge ON L4L 3
905 851-2826

**(G-4705)**
**EIGHTY NINE ROBOTICS LLC**
Also Called: 89robotics
965 W Chicago Ave (60642-5413)
PHONE...................512 573-9091
Yue Wu, *CEO*
EMP: 3
SALES (est): 63.5K Privately Held
SIC: 7371 7372 8711 8731 Computer software development & applications; business oriented computer software; mechanical engineering; computer (hardware) development; automation & robotics consultant

**(G-4706)**
**EKS FIBER OPTICS LP**
150 N Michigan Ave (60601-7553)
PHONE...................312 291-4482
Ross Engel, *President*
EMP: 3
SALES (est): 183.9K Privately Held
SIC: 3661 Fiber optics communications equipment

**(G-4707)**
**EL ENCANTO PRODUCTS INC**
4041 W Ogden Ave Ste 12 (60623-2806)
PHONE...................773 940-1807
Horacio Rodriguez, *President*
EMP: 15
SQ FT: 10,000
SALES (est): 7MM Privately Held
SIC: 2022 Cheese, natural & processed

**(G-4708)**
**EL MORO DE LETRAN CHURROS & BA**
Also Called: Don Churro
1626 S Blue Island Ave (60608-2134)
PHONE...................312 733-3173
Deletran Moro, *Principal*
EMP: 12
SALES (est): 289.8K
SALES (corp-wide): 1.1MM Privately Held
SIC: 2051 5812 Bread, cake & related products; ethnic food restaurants
PA: Molina Enterprises Llc
534 Mary Ave
Collinsville IL

**(G-4709)**
**EL POPOCATAPETL INDUSTRIES INC**
4246 W 47th St (60632-4402)
PHONE...................773 843-0888
Elizabeth A Avina, *President*
EMP: 96
SALES (corp-wide): 10.8MM Privately Held
SIC: 2096 Corn chips & other corn-based snacks
PA: El Popocatapetl Industries, Inc.
1854 W 21st St
Chicago IL 60608
312 421-6143

**(G-4710)**
**EL POPOCATAPETL INDUSTRIES INC (PA)**
Also Called: Tortilleria Industries
1854 W 21st St (60608-2715)
PHONE...................312 421-6143
Ernesto Avina, *President*
Margaret Avina, *Admin Sec*
EMP: 34
SQ FT: 7,200
SALES (est): 10.8MM Privately Held
SIC: 2099 Tortillas, fresh or refrigerated

**(G-4711)**
**EL SOL DECHICAGO NEWSPAPER**
4217 W Fullerton Ave (60639-2069)
PHONE...................773 235-7655
Fernando Moreno, *Principal*
EMP: 5
SALES (est): 243.1K Privately Held
SIC: 2711 Newspapers, publishing & printing

**(G-4712)**
**EL TRADICIONAL**
7647 S Kedzie Ave (60652-1507)
PHONE...................773 925-0335
EMP: 3 EST: 2007
SALES (est): 90K Privately Held
SIC: 2099 Mfg Food Preparations

**(G-4713)**
**EL-MILAGRO INC (PA)**
3050 W 26th St (60623-4130)
PHONE...................773 579-6120
Fax: 773 650-4690
Raphael Lopez, *President*
Jerry Slowik, *VP Finance*
Raulinda Sierra, *Office Mgr*
Jesus Lopez, *Admin Sec*
Linda Lopez, *Admin Sec*
▲ EMP: 300
SQ FT: 3,000
SALES (est): 132.1MM Privately Held
WEB: www.elmilagro.com
SIC: 2099 5812 Tortillas, fresh or refrigerated; Mexican restaurant

**(G-4714)**
**EL-MILAGRO INC**
2919 S Western Ave Fl 1 (60608-5221)
PHONE...................773 650-1614
Fax: 773 579-2407
Phil Crookham, *Plant Mgr*
Bobby Morales, *Plant Mgr*
Monro Lopez, *Branch Mgr*
Hortencia Calderon, *Manager*
Tony Rojas, *Supervisor*
EMP: 200

# GEOGRAPHIC SECTION
## Chicago - Cook County (G-4742)

**SALES (corp-wide):** 132.1MM **Privately Held**
**WEB:** www.elmilagro.com
**SIC: 2099** 5812 Tortillas, fresh or refrigerated; Mexican restaurant
**PA:** El-Milagro, Inc.
3050 W 26th St
Chicago IL 60623
773 579-6120

### (G-4715)
### EL-RANCHERO FOOD PRODUCTS
4457 S Kildare Ave (60632-4316)
**PHONE** .................... 773 843-0430
Salvadore Hernandez, *Owner*
**EMP:** 15
**SALES (corp-wide):** 6.4MM **Privately Held**
**SIC: 2096** Tortilla chips
**PA:** El-Ranchero Food Products
2547 S Kedzie Ave
Chicago IL 60623
773 847-9167

### (G-4716)
### EL-RANCHERO FOOD PRODUCTS (PA)
2547 S Kedzie Ave (60623-4008)
**PHONE** .................... 773 847-9167
Salvador Hernandez, *Owner*
Juan Hernandez, *Manager*
Sandra Valtez, *Administration*
▲ **EMP:** 25
**SQ FT:** 2,500
**SALES (est):** 6.4MM **Privately Held**
**SIC: 2096** 2099 Tortilla chips; food preparations

### (G-4717)
### ELANZA TECHNOLOGIES INC
500 N Michigan Ave # 600 (60611-3754)
**PHONE** .................... 312 396-4187
Tanvir Bukht, *CEO*
David Nancrede, *Chairman*
**EMP:** 40 **EST:** 2001
**SQ FT:** 2,000
**SALES (est):** 3.5MM **Privately Held**
**WEB:** www.elanzatech.com
**SIC: 3661** Telephone & telegraph apparatus

### (G-4718)
### ELDEST DAUGHTER LLC
1305 N Damen Ave (60622-1936)
**PHONE** .................... 949 677-7385
Griffin Caprio, *Chief Engr*
Matt Kowalec, *CFO*
Brett Moody,
**EMP:** 3
**SALES (est):** 183K **Privately Held**
**SIC: 3841** Surgical instruments & apparatus

### (G-4719)
### ELECTRIC MOTOR CORP
3865 N Milwaukee Ave (60641-2883)
**PHONE** .................... 773 725-1050
**Fax:** 773 725-1169
Isabell Siegel, *President*
Charlene Kozlowsky, *Admin Sec*
◆ **EMP:** 25
**SQ FT:** 18,000
**SALES (est):** 4.3MM **Privately Held**
**WEB:** www.electricmotorcorp.com
**SIC: 7694** 3621 Electric motor repair; rebuilding motors, except automotive; motors, electric

### (G-4720)
### ELECTRO-MATIC PRODUCTS CO
2235 N Knox Ave (60639-3487)
**PHONE** .................... 773 235-4010
**Fax:** 773 235-7317
Eric A Littwin, *President*
Daniel Bacchiere, *Vice Pres*
Amy Howe, *Office Mgr*
Robin Clark, *Technology*
Kenneth M Littwin, *Admin Sec*
**EMP:** 10 **EST:** 1946
**SQ FT:** 20,000
**SALES (est):** 3.7MM **Privately Held**
**WEB:** www.em-chicago.com
**SIC: 3625** 3545 3629 3823 Electric controls & control accessories, industrial; chucks: drill, lathe or magnetic (machine tool accessories); rectifiers (electrical apparatus); industrial instrmnts msrmnt display/control process variable

### (G-4721)
### ELECTRO-TECHNIC PRODUCTS INC
4642 N Ravenswood Ave (60640-4592)
**PHONE** .................... 773 561-2349
**Fax:** 773 561-3130
Gerald T Cuzelis, *President*
Greg Vig, *Engineer*
Pam Browder, *Admin Asst*
**EMP:** 17 **EST:** 1942
**SQ FT:** 10,000
**SALES (est):** 1.2MM **Privately Held**
**SIC: 3812** 3699 Search & detection systems & instruments; electrical equipment & supplies

### (G-4722)
### ELECTRONICA AVIATION LLC
150 S Wacker Dr Ste 2403 (60606-4103)
**PHONE** .................... 407 498-1092
Simon Agassian,
**EMP:** 5
**SQ FT:** 500
**SALES (est):** 202.2K **Privately Held**
**SIC: 3728** Research & dev by manuf., aircraft parts & auxiliary equip

### (G-4723)
### ELEMENT BARS INC
Also Called: Elementbars.com
5001 W Belmont Ave (60641-4236)
**PHONE** .................... 888 411-3536
Jonathan Miller, *President*
Jonathan Kelley, *Vice Pres*
**EMP:** 13
**SALES:** 850K **Privately Held**
**WEB:** www.elementbars.com
**SIC: 2064** Candy & other confectionery products

### (G-4724)
### ELEMENT14 INC
Also Called: Newark Element 14
300 S Riverside Plz # 2200 (60606-6765)
P.O. Box 94151, Palatine (60094-4151)
**PHONE** .................... 773 784-5100
Gert Labuschagne, *President*
Jim Seifert, *Senior VP*
Chris Binion, *Vice Pres*
**EMP:** 30
**SALES (est):** 6.7MM **Privately Held**
**SIC: 3678** Electronic connectors

### (G-4725)
### ELEMENTAL ART JEWELRY
5917 N Broadway St (60660-3526)
**PHONE** .................... 773 844-4812
**EMP:** 3 **EST:** 2011
**SALES (est):** 199.6K **Privately Held**
**SIC: 2819** Mfg Industrial Inorganic Chemicals

### (G-4726)
### ELEMENTS GROUP
2033 N Larrabee St (60614-4418)
**PHONE** .................... 312 664-2252
**EMP:** 5
**SALES (est):** 602.5K **Privately Held**
**SIC: 2819** Mfg Industrial Inorganic Chemicals

### (G-4727)
### ELFI LLC
Also Called: Elfi Wall Systems
6001 S Knox Ave (60629)
**PHONE** .................... 815 439-1833
Eric Kocis, *Managing Dir*
George Modrovic, *Mng Member*
▼ **EMP:** 25
**SQ FT:** 50,000
**SALES (est):** 4.8MM **Privately Held**
**WEB:** www.elfiwallsystem.com
**SIC: 3449** 8711 3448 Miscellaneous metalwork; energy conservation engineering; building construction consultant; prefabricated metal buildings

### (G-4728)
### ELG METALS INC
103rd St The Calumet Riv (60617)
**PHONE** .................... 773 374-1500
Rich Jones, *General Mgr*
**EMP:** 42
**SALES (corp-wide):** 3.8B **Privately Held**
**SIC: 3312** 3341 Stainless steel; secondary nonferrous metals
**HQ:** Elg Metals, Inc.
369 River Rd
Mckeesport PA 15132
412 672-9200

### (G-4729)
### ELI MORRIS GROUP LLC
Also Called: MORris&wade
4335 W 21st St (60623-2764)
**PHONE** .................... 773 314-7173
Larry Morris,
**EMP:** 4
**SALES (est):** 244.5K **Privately Held**
**SIC: 2851** 7389 Removers & cleaners;

### (G-4730)
### ELIS CHEESECAKE COMPANY
6701 W Forest Preserve Dr (60634-1470)
**PHONE** .................... 773 205-3800
**Fax:** 773 205-3801
Marc S Schulman, *President*
Jolene Worthington, *Exec VP*
Joseph Nogal, *Vice Pres*
Peter Rainsford, *Vice Pres*
Mary Gale, *Project Mgr*
▼ **EMP:** 220
**SQ FT:** 65,000
**SALES (est):** 47.1MM **Privately Held**
**WEB:** www.ccake.com
**SIC: 2053** 5812 Cakes, bakery: frozen; pies, bakery: frozen; pastries (danish): frozen; eating places

### (G-4731)
### ELITE FABRICATION INC
1524 W Jarvis Ave (60626-2188)
**PHONE** .................... 773 274-4474
Sean Kelley, *President*
**EMP:** 7
**SQ FT:** 15,000
**SALES (est):** 700K **Privately Held**
**SIC: 3443** Fabricated plate work (boiler shop)

### (G-4732)
### ELITE PRECIOUS METALS INC
1440 W Taylor St Ste 315 (60607-4623)
**PHONE** .................... 312 929-3055
Brian Schilling, *President*
**EMP:** 6
**SALES:** 1.5MM **Privately Held**
**SIC: 3339** Precious metals

### (G-4733)
### ELMOS TOMBSTONE SERVICE
6023 S State St (60621-3930)
**PHONE** .................... 773 643-0200
Hosea Knox, *Owner*
Bobbie Knox, *Co-Owner*
**EMP:** 3
**SALES (est):** 257.1K **Privately Held**
**SIC: 3272** Tombstones, precast terrazzo or concrete

### (G-4734)
### ELMOT INC
4923 W Fullerton Ave (60639-2505)
**PHONE** .................... 773 791-7039
Eugene Ballarin, *President*
**EMP:** 4
**SQ FT:** 800
**SALES (est):** 339.1K **Privately Held**
**SIC: 7694** 7699 Electric motor repair; industrial equipment services

### (G-4735)
### ELONA BIOTECHNOLOGIES INC
55 E Monroe St Ste 3800 (60603-6030)
**PHONE** .................... 317 865-4770
Ron Zimmerman, *President*
Donna Zimmerman, *Vice Pres*
Arthur Patterson, *Plant Mgr*
**EMP:** 11
**SQ FT:** 10,000
**SALES:** 2MM
**SALES (corp-wide):** 19.7B **Privately Held**
**WEB:** www.ivax.com
**SIC: 8731** 2869 Commercial physical research; laboratory chemicals, organic
**HQ:** Ivax Corporation
4400 Biscayne Blvd
Miami FL 33137
305 329-3795

### (G-4736)
### ELSTON MATERIALS LLC
1420 N Elston Ave (60642-2418)
**PHONE** .................... 773 235-3100
Alex Puig,
Leonard Puig,
Luis Puig,
**EMP:** 9 **EST:** 2008
**SQ FT:** 43,000
**SALES (est):** 2.6MM **Privately Held**
**SIC: 3271** 5082 5211 Concrete block & brick; general construction machinery & equipment; lumber & other building materials

### (G-4737)
### EMBODIED LABS INC
222 Merchandise Mart Plz (60654-1103)
**PHONE** .................... 336 971-5886
Carrie Shaw, *CEO*
Thomas Leahy, *Co-Owner*
Ryan Lebar, *Co-Owner*
Erin Washington, *Co-Owner*
**EMP:** 4
**SALES (est):** 115.2K **Privately Held**
**SIC: 7372** Educational computer software

### (G-4738)
### EMEELYS SOCKS AND MORE
2415 1/2 W 63rd St (60629-1203)
**PHONE** .................... 847 529-3026
**EMP:** 3
**SALES (est):** 88.8K **Privately Held**
**SIC: 2252** Socks

### (G-4739)
### EMERALD BIOFUELS LLC (PA)
300 N La Salle Dr # 4925 (60654-3406)
**PHONE** .................... 847 420-0898
Howard Jensen,
James Baclawski,
David Drew,
Robert Fleming,
**EMP:** 3
**SALES (est):** 367.6K **Privately Held**
**SIC: 2869** Industrial organic chemicals

### (G-4740)
### EMERALD MACHINE INC
4641 S Halsted St (60609-4415)
P.O. Box 9269 (60609-0269)
**PHONE** .................... 773 924-3659
**Fax:** 773 924-7453
Robert Matz, *President*
Dianne Krawczyk, *Vice Pres*
**EMP:** 6
**SQ FT:** 5,500
**SALES:** 350K **Privately Held**
**SIC: 3599** 7692 3444 Machine shop, jobbing & repair; welding repair; sheet metalwork

### (G-4741)
### EMERALD ONE LLC
300 N La Salle Dr # 4925 (60654-3406)
**PHONE** .................... 601 529-6793
David Drew,
James Baclawski,
Robert Fleming,
Howard Jensen,
**EMP:** 3
**SQ FT:** 10,000
**SALES (est):** 153.6K **Privately Held**
**SIC: 2869** Industrial organic chemicals
**PA:** Emerald Biofuels Llc
300 N La Salle Dr # 4925
Chicago IL 60654

### (G-4742)
### EMERSON ELECTRIC CO
Also Called: Blending and Transfer Systems
222 W Adams St Ste 400 (60606-5308)
**PHONE** .................... 312 803-4321
**EMP:** 29
**SALES (corp-wide):** 14.5B **Publicly Held**
**SIC: 3533** Oil & gas field machinery

# Chicago - Cook County (G-4743)  GEOGRAPHIC SECTION

**PA:** Emerson Electric Co.
8000 West Florissant Ave
Saint Louis MO 63136
314 553-2000

**(G-4743)**
**EMHART TEKNOLOGIES LLC**
12337 Collections Ctr Dr (60693-0123)
P.O. Box 73141 (60673-7141)
**PHONE** ......877 364-2781
**EMP:** 17
**SALES (corp-wide):** 11.4B **Publicly Held**
**WEB:** www.helicoil.com
**SIC: 3541** Machine tools, metal cutting type
**HQ:** Emhart Teknologies Llc
480 Myrtle St
New Britain CT 06053
800 783-6427

**(G-4744)**
**EMMERT JOHN**
Also Called: Coca-Cola
1401 N Cicero Ave (60651-1600)
**PHONE** ......773 292-6580
John Emmert, *Principal*
▼ **EMP:** 13 **EST:** 2007
**SALES (est):** 2.7MM **Privately Held**
**SIC: 2086** Bottled & canned soft drinks

**(G-4745)**
**EMPIRE HARD CHROME INC (PA)**
1615 S Kostner Ave (60623-2336)
**PHONE** ......773 762-3156
William G Horne Jr, *CEO*
Steven J Wallin, *President*
Mark Zetterquist, *General Mgr*
Thomas Boland, *Vice Pres*
Dolores Horne, *Vice Pres*
**EMP:** 108
**SQ FT:** 40,000
**SALES (est):** 22.5MM **Privately Held**
**WEB:** www.empirehardchrome.com
**SIC: 3471 3599** Electroplating of metals or formed products; polishing, metals or formed products; grinding castings for the trade

**(G-4746)**
**EMPIRE HARD CHROME INC**
1537 S Wood St (60608-1919)
**PHONE** ......312 226-7548
**Fax:** 312 226-7549
Thomas Boland, *Vice Pres*
Rich Warunek, *Vice Pres*
Richard Hill, *Plant Mgr*
Steve Walien, *Plant Mgr*
**EMP:** 150
**SALES (corp-wide):** 22.5MM **Privately Held**
**WEB:** www.empirehardchrome.com
**SIC: 3471** Plating & polishing
**PA:** Empire Hard Chrome, Inc.
1615 S Kostner Ave
Chicago IL 60623
773 762-3156

**(G-4747)**
**EMS ACRYLICS & SILK SCREENER (PA)**
4840 W Diversey Ave (60639-1704)
**PHONE** ......773 777-5656
**Fax:** 773 777-8222
Eileen M Macey, *President*
Colette Healy, *Vice Pres*
Robert Somogyi, *Vice Pres*
**EMP:** 10
**SQ FT:** 6,000
**SALES (est):** 1.4MM **Privately Held**
**SIC: 7336 3089 2821** Silk screen design; plastic processing; plastics materials & resins

**(G-4748)**
**ENAMELED STEEL AND SIGN CO**
4568 W Addison St (60641-3886)
**PHONE** ......773 481-2270
**Fax:** 773 777-6393
George Davies, *President*
Ed Arrison, *General Mgr*
Jean Davies, *Vice Pres*
Frank Colabufo, *Chief Engr*
Annette Kriese, *Office Mgr*
**EMP:** 23 **EST:** 1902
**SQ FT:** 56,000
**SALES (est):** 3.3MM **Privately Held**
**WEB:** www.epagecity.com
**SIC: 3479 3471 3231** Coating of metals & formed products; finishing, metals or formed products; industrial glassware: made from purchased glass

**(G-4749)**
**ENCYCLOPAEDIA BRITANNICA INC (HQ)**
325 N Lasalle St Ste 200 (60654)
**PHONE** ......847 777-2241
**Fax:** 312 347-7399
Jorge Cauz, *President*
Erik Gregersen, *Editor*
Kathy Nakamura, *Editor*
Jacob Safra, *Chairman*
Leah Mansoor, *Senior VP*
▲ **EMP:** 113 **EST:** 1768
**SQ FT:** 88,000
**SALES (est):** 118.1MM **Privately Held**
**WEB:** www.eb.com
**SIC: 2731** Book publishing

**(G-4750)**
**ENERGY ABSORPTION SYSTEMS INC (DH)**
70 W Madison St Ste 2350 (60602-4295)
**PHONE** ......312 467-6750
**Fax:** 312 467-9625
Tim Wallace, *CEO*
Gregory B Mitchell, *President*
Bruce Reimer, *Principal*
Mark Fernandez, *Vice Pres*
Diane Sanchez, *Sls & Mktg Exec*
◆ **EMP:** 39
**SQ FT:** 18,000
**SALES (est):** 13.3MM
**SALES (corp-wide):** 4.5B **Publicly Held**
**WEB:** www.energyabsorption.com
**SIC: 3499 3089** Barricades, metal; injection molded finished plastic products
**HQ:** Quixote Corporation
70 W Madison St Ste 2350
Chicago IL 60602
312 705-8400

**(G-4751)**
**ENERGY VAULT LLC**
363 W Erie St (60654-6903)
**PHONE** ......847 722-1128
Scott Emalfarb, *Principal*
**EMP:** 3
**SALES (est):** 209.9K **Privately Held**
**SIC: 3272** Burial vaults, concrete or precast terrazzo

**(G-4752)**
**ENGINEERED GLASS PRODUCTS LLC (HQ)**
2857 S Halsted St (60608-5902)
**PHONE** ......312 326-4710
Mike Hobbs, *CEO*
Chris Hobbs, *Plant Mgr*
Abigail Martinez, *Project Mgr*
Elliott Lewis, *Materials Mgr*
Dave Fraser, *Controller*
**EMP:** 79 **EST:** 1945
**SQ FT:** 30,000
**SALES (est):** 21.2MM **Privately Held**
**WEB:** www.egpglass.com
**SIC: 3211 3231** Sheet glass; products of purchased glass

**(G-4753)**
**ENGINEERED GLASS PRODUCTS LLC**
929 W Exchange Ave (60609-2530)
**PHONE** ......773 843-1964
David Fraser, *Controller*
Juan Rodriquez, *Branch Mgr*
Jeff Hobbs, *Supervisor*
**EMP:** 35 **Privately Held**
**WEB:** www.egpglass.com
**SIC: 3211 3231** Flat glass; products of purchased glass
**HQ:** Engineered Glass Products Llc
2857 S Halsted St
Chicago IL 60608
312 326-4710

**(G-4754)**
**ENGINEERED GLASS PRODUCTS LLC (PA)**
Also Called: Egp
2857 S Halsted St (60608-5902)
**PHONE** ......312 326-4710
Mike Hobbs, *CEO*
**EMP:** 125
**SQ FT:** 20,000
**SALES (est):** 40.1MM **Privately Held**
**WEB:** www.marsco-mfg.com
**SIC: 3231** Products of purchased glass

**(G-4755)**
**ENGLEWOOD CO OP**
900 W 63rd Pkwy (60621-2000)
**PHONE** ......773 873-1201
Laura Dennis, *Manager*
**EMP:** 3
**SALES (est):** 199.5K **Privately Held**
**SIC: 3272** Housing components, prefabricated concrete

**(G-4756)**
**ENJOY LIFE NATURAL BRANDS LLC (HQ)**
Also Called: Enjoy Life Foods
8770 W Bryn Mawr Ave (60631-3515)
**PHONE** ......773 632-2163
**Fax:** 847 260-0306
Scott Mandell, *CEO*
Philip D Gregorcy, *President*
Tom Lipon, *Vice Pres*
Nick Alex, *CFO*
Carrie Ruswick, *Finance*
**EMP:** 50
**SALES (est):** 24.8MM **Publicly Held**
**WEB:** www.enjoylifefoods.com
**SIC: 2046 2051** Wheat gluten; bread, cake & related products

**(G-4757)**
**ENR GENERAL MACHINING CO**
3725 W 49th St (60632-3601)
P.O. Box 32168 (60632-0168)
**PHONE** ......773 523-2944
**Fax:** 773 523-4483
Eugene Szydlo, *President*
Andrea Portilloo, *Manager*
Richard Szydlo, *Admin Sec*
**EMP:** 20 **EST:** 1964
**SQ FT:** 23,000
**SALES (est):** 4.6MM **Privately Held**
**WEB:** www.enrmachine.com
**SIC: 3599** Machine shop, jobbing & repair

**(G-4758)**
**ENSOURCE INC**
2826 S Union Ave (60616-2539)
**PHONE** ......312 912-1048
Rongsong MEI, *President*
**EMP:** 3 **EST:** 2014
**SALES (est):** 155.4K **Privately Held**
**SIC: 1311** Crude petroleum & natural gas

**(G-4759)**
**ENTERPRISE OIL CO**
3200 S Western Ave (60608-6003)
**PHONE** ......312 487-2025
**Fax:** 773 847-7125
Richard H Kruke, *President*
Dawn Mackie, *Admin Sec*
**EMP:** 23
**SALES (est):** 8.2MM **Privately Held**
**WEB:** www.entoilusa.com
**SIC: 2899 2992** Chemical preparations; lubricating oils & greases

**(G-4760)**
**ENTERPRISE SIGNS INC**
10447 S Hale Ave Apt 1 (60643-2878)
**PHONE** ......773 614-8324
**Fax:** 708 388-2585
Leo Milashoski, *Owner*
**EMP:** 4 **EST:** 1951
**SQ FT:** 3,000
**SALES (est):** 210K **Privately Held**
**SIC: 7389 2396 3993 7532** Sign painting & lettering shop; screen printing on fabric articles; signs & advertising specialties; truck painting & lettering

**(G-4761)**
**ENTERPRISES ONE STOP**
48 E Garfield Blvd (60615-4603)
**PHONE** ......773 924-5506
**Fax:** 773 924-5539
Eddy Baker, *Manager*
**EMP:** 4 **EST:** 2009
**SALES (est):** 407.1K **Privately Held**
**SIC: 3589** Car washing machinery

**(G-4762)**
**ENTREPRENEUR MEDIA INC**
205 W Wacker Dr Ste 1820 (60606-1428)
**PHONE** ......312 923-0818
Steve Meisner, *Manager*
**EMP:** 3
**SALES (corp-wide):** 17.4MM **Privately Held**
**SIC: 2721** Magazines: publishing only, not printed on site
**PA:** Entrepreneur Media, Inc.
18061 Fitch
Irvine CA 92614
949 261-2325

**(G-4763)**
**ENVESTNET INC (PA)**
35 E Wacker Dr Ste 2400 (60601-2310)
**PHONE** ......312 827-2800
**Fax:** 312 827-2801
Judson Bergman, *Ch of Bd*
Anil Arora, *Vice Ch Bd*
Bob Auclair, *President*
William Crager, *President*
Josh Mayer, *COO*
**EMP:** 185
**SQ FT:** 43,000
**SALES:** 578.1MM **Publicly Held**
**SIC: 7389 6282 7372** Financial services; investment advice; prepackaged software; business oriented computer software

**(G-4764)**
**ENVESTNET RTRMENT SLUTIONS LLC (HQ)**
35 E Wacker Dr (60601-2314)
**PHONE** ......312 827-7957
Babu Slvadasan, *President*
Kelly Michel, *Officer*
**EMP:** 5
**SALES (est):** 2MM
**SALES (corp-wide):** 578.1MM **Publicly Held**
**SIC: 6411 7372 7389** Pension & retirement plan consultants; business oriented computer software; financial services
**PA:** Envestnet, Inc.
35 E Wacker Dr Ste 2400
Chicago IL 60601
312 827-2800

**(G-4765)**
**ENVIRONMENTAL SYSTEMS RES INST**
Also Called: Esri
221 N La Salle St Ste 863 (60601-1314)
**PHONE** ......312 609-0966
**Fax:** 312 609-0963
Michael Johnson, *Manager*
Crystal Dorn, *Technical Staff*
**EMP:** 3
**SALES (corp-wide):** 1B **Privately Held**
**WEB:** www.esri.com
**SIC: 7372** Prepackaged software
**PA:** Environmental Systems Research Institute, Inc.
380 New York St
Redlands CA 92373
909 793-2853

**(G-4766)**
**ENVISION UNLIMITED**
Also Called: Halas Vocational Center
8562 S Vincennes Ave (60620-1942)
**PHONE** ......773 651-1100
**Fax:** 773 651-8637
Stanley F Watson, *Manager*
**EMP:** 250

## GEOGRAPHIC SECTION

Chicago - Cook County (G-4792)

SALES (corp-wide): 23.2MM **Privately Held**
WEB: www.careinthehome.com
SIC: **8322** 2392 8331 Social services for the handicapped; household furnishings; job training & vocational rehabilitation services
PA: Envision Unlimited
8 S Michigan Ave Ste 1700
Chicago IL 60603
312 346-6230

**(G-4767)**
**EPUBLISHING INC**
720 N Franklin St (60654-7214)
PHONE .................................. 312 768-6800
Connell Trey, *Principal*
Andy Kowl, *Senior VP*
EMP: 5
SALES (est): 480K **Privately Held**
SIC: **7372** Publishers' computer software

**(G-4768)**
**EQUILON ENTERPRISES LLC**
Also Called: Shell Oil Products U S
1001 W Jackson Blvd (60607-2913)
PHONE .................................. 312 733-1849
Bob Stambolic, *Branch Mgr*
EMP: 15
SALES (corp-wide): 233.5B **Privately Held**
WEB: www.shellus.com
SIC: **5541** 2911 Filling stations, gasoline; petroleum refining
HQ: Equilon Enterprises Llc
910 Louisiana St Ste 2
Houston TX 77002
713 241-6161

**(G-4769)**
**EQUINOX GROUP INC**
329 W 18th St Ste 1000 (60616-1122)
PHONE .................................. 312 226-7002
Fax: 312 226-4754
Joe Jeschawitz, *President*
Yolanda Catledge, *Accounting Mgr*
Yolanda Catlegde, *Office Mgr*
EMP: 17
SQ FT: 18,000
SALES: 2MM **Privately Held**
SIC: **3469** Metal stampings

**(G-4770)**
**EQUITRADE GROUP**
225 W Washington St # 2200 (60606-2418)
PHONE .................................. 312 499-9500
Jaime Angulo, *President*
Christopher Chavez, *Manager*
John D Beam, *Admin Sec*
▼ EMP: 2
SQ FT: 300
SALES (est): 1.5MM **Privately Held**
SIC: **2013** Sausages & other prepared meats

**(G-4771)**
**ERASERMITT INCORPORATED**
2001 S Michigan Ave 18q (60616-1735)
PHONE .................................. 312 842-2855
Duane Lewis, *President*
Artis Lewis, *Treasurer*
Diane Lewis, *Admin Sec*
EMP: 3
SALES (est): 240K **Privately Held**
SIC: **3952** 7389 Eraser guides & shields;

**(G-4772)**
**ERIE VEHICLE COMPANY**
60 E 51st St (60615-2192)
PHONE .................................. 773 536-6300
Fax: 773 536-5779
Edward F Kean, *President*
Michael L Kean, *Corp Secy*
Tim Kean, *Controller*
William Kean, *Sales Staff*
EMP: 13
SQ FT: 27,500
SALES (est): 2MM **Privately Held**
SIC: **3713** 5084 Truck bodies (motor vehicles); hydraulic systems equipment & supplies

**(G-4773)**
**ERQ SYSTEMS INC**
10439 S Maplewood Ave (60655-1024)
PHONE .................................. 815 469-1072
James J Broad, *President*
Sal Cerda, *General Mgr*
EMP: 22
SALES (est): 1.5MM **Privately Held**
SIC: **3443** Industrial vessels, tanks & containers

**(G-4774)**
**ERROR FREE SOFTWARE LLC**
Also Called: Aichar
200 S Wacker Dr Ste 2400 (60606-5811)
PHONE .................................. 312 461-0300
Alexei Gitter, *President*
John Koltes, *Corp Secy*
EMP: 35 EST: 1997
SQ FT: 13,000
SALES (est): 4.5MM **Privately Held**
WEB: www.archelon-us.com
SIC: **3695** Computer software tape & disks: blank, rigid & floppy

**(G-4775)**
**ERVA TOOL & DIE COMPANY**
3100 W Grand Ave (60622-4324)
PHONE .................................. 773 533-7806
Fax: 773 533-7826
Erwin J Heyek, *President*
Theresia Heyek, *Corp Secy*
▲ EMP: 4
SQ FT: 17,000
SALES (est): 450K **Privately Held**
WEB: www.erva.com
SIC: **3544** 3469 7692 Die sets for metal stamping (presses); stamping metal for the trade; welding repair

**(G-4776)**
**ESCO LIGHTING INC**
3254 N Kilbourn Ave (60641-4505)
PHONE .................................. 773 427-7000
Fax: 773 427-7007
Donna Franklin, *President*
DK Klotz, *Plant Supt*
Thomas Franklin, *Admin Sec*
◆ EMP: 30 EST: 1975
SQ FT: 25,000
SALES (est): 7.4MM **Privately Held**
WEB: www.escolighting.com
SIC: **3646** Commercial indusl & institutional electric lighting fixtures

**(G-4777)**
**ESQUIFY INC**
805 W Buckingham Pl 2w (60657-2301)
PHONE .................................. 917 553-3741
Drew Stern, *CEO*
Scott Stuart, *Co-Owner*
EMP: 4
SALES (est): 178K **Privately Held**
SIC: **7372** 7389 Business oriented computer software;

**(G-4778)**
**ESSANNAY SHOW IT INC**
451 W Grand Ave (60642)
PHONE .................................. 312 733-5511
Fax: 312 733-0016
Christopher Chambers, *President*
Kevin Chambers, *Office Mgr*
▲ EMP: 5 EST: 1964
SQ FT: 3,000
SALES (est): 770K **Privately Held**
WEB: www.essannay.com
SIC: **3861** 7359 7377 7389 Motion picture apparatus & equipment; equipment rental & leasing; computer rental & leasing;

**(G-4779)**
**ESSENTIAL CREATIONS**
2112 W 95th St (60643-1118)
PHONE .................................. 773 238-1700
Fax: 312 267-0321
Sandtricia Strickland, *Owner*
EMP: 5
SQ FT: 1,600
SALES: 125K **Privately Held**
SIC: **2395** 7336 Embroidery & art needlework; silk screen design

**(G-4780)**
**ESTEE BEDDING COMPANY**
945 E 93rd St (60619-7813)
PHONE .................................. 800 521-7378
Fax: 773 374-4034
Timothy Enright, *President*
Richard Rowan, *General Mgr*
Colleen McGrath, *Manager*
Patricia Enright, *Admin Sec*
▲ EMP: 29 EST: 1924
SQ FT: 150,000
SALES: 8.4MM **Privately Held**
WEB: www.esteebedding.com
SIC: **2515** Mattresses, innerspring or box spring

**(G-4781)**
**ESTRUCTURAS INC**
2232 S Pulaski Rd (60623-3051)
P.O. Box 83, Glenview (60025-0083)
PHONE .................................. 773 522-2200
Fax: 773 522-2294
Valentine Isasi, *Principal*
EMP: 15
SALES (est): 1.1MM **Privately Held**
SIC: **7692** Welding repair

**(G-4782)**
**EUREKA CHEMICAL LABS INC**
4701 S Whipple St (60632-2023)
P.O. Box 576, La Porte IN (46352-0576)
PHONE .................................. 773 847-9672
Fax: 773 722-0965
Aris Tsaras, *President*
EMP: 3
SQ FT: 12,000
SALES (est): 48.8K **Privately Held**
WEB: www.eureka-inc.com
SIC: **2819** Industrial inorganic chemicals

**(G-4783)**
**EUROPEAN CLASSIC BAKERY**
5930 N Elston Ave (60646-5508)
PHONE .................................. 773 774-8755
Milena Kulzic, *Owner*
EMP: 4
SALES (est): 229.4K **Privately Held**
SIC: **2051** Bread, cake & related products

**(G-4784)**
**EVAN LEWIS INC**
3368 N Elston Ave (60618-5831)
PHONE .................................. 773 539-0402
Fax: 773 539-2496
Evan Lewis, *President*
EMP: 2
SALES (est): 257.9K **Privately Held**
WEB: www.evanlewisinc.com
SIC: **2514** Novelty furniture, household: metal

**(G-4785)**
**EVANG LTHN CH DR MRTN LUTH KG**
Also Called: Lutheran Magazine
8765 W Higgins Rd Ste 600 (60631-4100)
PHONE .................................. 773 380-2540
Linda M Delloff, *Editor*
Jeff Favre, *Editor*
Elizabeth Hunter, *Editor*
Bruce Davidson, *Vice Pres*
Victoria Jimenez, *Vice Pres*
EMP: 10
SALES (corp-wide): 991.6K **Privately Held**
SIC: **2721** 8661 Magazines: publishing only, not printed on site; religious organizations
PA: Evangelical Lutheran Church Of Dr Martin Luther
5344 S Francisco Ave
Chicago IL 60632
773 776-8104

**(G-4786)**
**EVANS FOOD GROUP LTD (HQ)**
4118 S Halsted St (60609-2693)
PHONE .................................. 773 254-7400
Jose Luis Prado, *CEO*
Humberto Iniguez, *Vice Pres*
Rick Howard, *Plant Engr Mgr*
Sandra Cebana, *Manager*
EMP: 31
SQ FT: 100,000
SALES (est): 53.2MM
SALES (corp-wide): 1.6B **Privately Held**
SIC: **2096** Pork rinds
PA: Wind Point Partners, L.P.
676 N Michigan Ave # 3700
Chicago IL 60611
312 255-4800

**(G-4787)**
**EVANS FOODS INC (DH)**
Also Called: Mac's Snacks
4118 S Halsted St (60609-2693)
PHONE .................................. 773 254-7400
Fax: 773 254-7791
Alex Silva, *CEO*
Jim Speakes, *President*
Jim Frazier, *Vice Pres*
▼ EMP: 65
SQ FT: 100,000
SALES (est): 20.2MM
SALES (corp-wide): 1.6B **Privately Held**
WEB: www.evansfood.com
SIC: **2096** Pork rinds
HQ: Evans Food Group Ltd.
4118 S Halsted St
Chicago IL 60609
773 254-7400

**(G-4788)**
**EVAPCO INC**
62140 Collection Ctr (60693-0621)
PHONE .................................. 410 756-2600
EMP: 33
SALES (corp-wide): 432.8MM **Privately Held**
SIC: **3443** Cooling towers, metal plate
PA: Evapco, Inc.
5151 Allendale Ln
Taneytown MD 21787
410 756-2600

**(G-4789)**
**EVENTION LLC**
121 W Wacker Dr Ste 3200 (60601-1781)
PHONE .................................. 773 733-4256
Brian Roth, *Mng Member*
Erik Nejman, *Mng Member*
EMP: 25 EST: 2004
SQ FT: 4,500
SALES: 28MM **Privately Held**
SIC: **7372** 7373 Business oriented computer software; systems software development services

**(G-4790)**
**EVERPURSE INC**
212 W Superior St (60654-3557)
PHONE .................................. 650 204-3212
Elizabeth Salcedo, *CEO*
Daniel Salcedo, *Bd of Directors*
EMP: 5 EST: 2012
SALES (est): 748.2K **Privately Held**
SIC: **3677** Transformers power supply, electronic type

**(G-4791)**
**EVOYS CORP**
Also Called: Yoos Imports
4142 W Lawrence Ave (60630-2823)
PHONE .................................. 773 736-4200
SE Lee, *President*
EMP: 2
SQ FT: 3,000
SALES: 8MM **Privately Held**
SIC: **3678** Electronic connectors

**(G-4792)**
**EVRAZ INC NA (DH)**
Also Called: Evraz Oregon Steel
200 E Randolph St # 7800 (60601-6436)
PHONE .................................. 312 533-3621
Fax: 773 533-3611
Conrad Winkler, *President*
Will Baker, *General Mgr*
Robert Franco, *General Mgr*
Tim Oliver, *General Mgr*
Sonya M Pease, *General Mgr*
▲ EMP: 150 EST: 1986
SQ FT: 12,300
SALES (est): 1B
SALES (corp-wide): 7.7B **Privately Held**
WEB: www.evrazincna.com
SIC: **3312** 3317 3325 Plate, steel; bar, rod & wire products; rails, steel or iron; steel pipe & tubes; tubes, seamless steel; railroad car wheels, cast steel

# Chicago - Cook County (G-4793)

**(G-4793)**
**EW BREDEMEIER AND CO**
6625 W Diversey Ave (60707-2218)
PHONE.................................773 237-1600
Fax: 773 276-0198
Roland Leupolt, *President*
Denise Adkins, *Admin Sec*
EMP: 13 EST: 2002
SALES (est): 1.8MM **Privately Held**
SIC: 2231 Upholstery fabrics, wool

**(G-4794)**
**EXCEL MACHINING INC**
5654 W 65th St (60638-5502)
PHONE.................................773 585-6666
Bob Ciszek, *President*
Chris Ciszek, *Vice Pres*
EMP: 7
SQ FT: 6,400
SALES (est): 1MM **Privately Held**
SIC: 3599 Machine & other job shop work; machine shop, jobbing & repair

**(G-4795)**
**EXPANDED METAL PRODUCTS CORP**
Also Called: Empcor
4633 S Knox Ave (60632-4805)
PHONE.................................773 735-4500
Fax: 773 735-9885
Mark J Polan, *President*
Mark Polan, *President*
Ann Polan, *Corp Secy*
Jon Soehren, *Admin Sec*
EMP: 14 EST: 1958
SQ FT: 20,000
SALES (est): 1.2MM **Privately Held**
WEB: www.empcor.com
SIC: 3444 3449 Studs & joists, sheet metal; lath, expanded metal

**(G-4796)**
**EXPERT LOCKSMITH INC**
100 W Randolph St (60601-3218)
PHONE.................................917 751-9267
Ofir Ohana, *Owner*
EMP: 4
SALES (est): 300K **Privately Held**
SIC: 3429 Locks or lock sets

**(G-4797)**
**EXPRESS PUBLISHING INC**
Also Called: Pole Express Publishing
6121 W Belmont Ave (60634-4004)
PHONE.................................773 725-6218
Fax: 773 725-6238
Janusz Wasewicz, *President*
Yanush Wasewicz, *President*
EMP: 8
SALES: 250K **Privately Held**
WEB: www.ex-usa.com
SIC: 2721 Periodicals

**(G-4798)**
**EXPRI PUBLISHING & PRINTING**
2328 W Touhy Ave (60645-3414)
PHONE.................................773 274-5955
Joseph Mihailidis, *President*
Theodora Kyrtsos, *Admin Sec*
EMP: 2
SQ FT: 2,700
SALES (est): 210K **Privately Held**
WEB: www.expriprinting.com
SIC: 2752 Commercial printing, lithographic

**(G-4799)**
**EXTERIOR SERVICES**
327 E 115th St (60628-5016)
PHONE.................................773 660-1457
Fax: 773 928-7174
Ronald Justice, *Partner*
Bob Snell, *Partner*
EMP: 6
SQ FT: 4,800
SALES (est): 813.9K **Privately Held**
WEB: www.exteriorservices.net
SIC: 3496 Miscellaneous fabricated wire products

**(G-4800)**
**EYE CANDY OPTICS CORPORATION**
2121 W Division St Ste 1e (60622-2948)
PHONE.................................773 697-7370
Fax: 773 697-9975
Renee Russo, *Principal*
EMP: 5
SALES (est): 649.6K **Privately Held**
SIC: 3851 Eyeglasses, lenses & frames

**(G-4801)**
**F AND L PALLETS INC**
3018 S Spaulding Ave Fl 1 (60623-4747)
PHONE.................................773 364-0798
Faustino Juarez, *President*
EMP: 5
SALES: 1MM **Privately Held**
SIC: 2448 5031 Pallets, wood & wood with metal; pallets, wood

**(G-4802)**
**F B WILLIAMS CO**
10017 S Claremont Ave (60643-1921)
PHONE.................................773 233-4255
Robert Williams, *President*
EMP: 5
SQ FT: 12,000
SALES (est): 398.7K **Privately Held**
SIC: 3469 3991 3429 Stamping metal for the trade; brooms & brushes; manufactured hardware (general)

**(G-4803)**
**F H LEINWEBER CO INC**
346 W 107th Pl (60628-3336)
PHONE.................................773 568-7722
F H Leinweber, *President*
Nick Foresta, *Manager*
EMP: 20
SALES (corp-wide): 1.7MM **Privately Held**
SIC: 2891 1752 3272 2851 Sealants; floor laying & floor work; concrete products; paints & allied products
PA: F. H. Leinweber Co., Inc.
9812 S Cicero Ave
Oak Lawn IL 60453
708 424-7000

**(G-4804)**
**F HYMAN & CO**
1329 N Clybourn Ave Fl 1 (60610-1797)
PHONE.................................312 664-3810
Fax: 312 664-3811
Ravindra Kobawala, *President*
Pallavi Kobawala, *Vice Pres*
Ashwin Shah, *Admin Sec*
▲ EMP: 7
SQ FT: 5,000
SALES (est): 658.5K **Privately Held**
SIC: 2241 Cotton narrow fabrics

**(G-4805)**
**F KREUTZER & CO**
2646 W Madison St (60612-2064)
PHONE.................................773 826-5767
Fax: 773 826-5769
Stephen J Kreutzer, *President*
Frank M Kreutzer, *Treasurer*
Anna M Kreutzer, *Admin Sec*
EMP: 4
SQ FT: 10,000
SALES (est): 800K **Privately Held**
SIC: 3444 3441 3366 Sheet metalwork; fabricated structural metal; copper foundries

**(G-4806)**
**F M AQUISITION CORP**
Also Called: Content That Works
3750 N Lake Shore Dr 8d (60613-4238)
PHONE.................................773 728-8351
Paul A Camp, *President*
Carley Lintz, *Editor*
Matthew Miller, *Editor*
Jen Champion-Gobel, *Vice Pres*
Kaitlyn Nowicki, *Pub Rel Mgr*
EMP: 9
SQ FT: 1,500
SALES (est): 914.3K **Privately Held**
WEB: www.contentthatworks.com
SIC: 2741 Directories: publishing & printing

**(G-4807)**
**F T I INC**
416 W Erie St (60654-5705)
PHONE.................................312 943-4015
Carl Vespa, *President*
EMP: 20
SALES (est): 1.7MM **Privately Held**
WEB: www.fti.com
SIC: 3825 Instruments for measuring electrical quantities

**(G-4808)**
**FABBRI SAUSAGE MANUFACTURING**
166 N Aberdeen St (60607-1606)
PHONE.................................312 829-6363
Fax: 312 829-0396
Ray Fabbri, *President*
Lawrence Fabbri, *Admin Sec*
EMP: 38
SQ FT: 30,000
SALES (est): 6.2MM **Privately Held**
SIC: 2013 5147 5142 2011 Sausages from purchased meat; roast beef from purchased meat; meats, fresh; meat, frozen: packaged; meat packing plants

**(G-4809)**
**FABRICATING & WELDING CORP**
12246 S Halsted St (60628-6400)
PHONE.................................773 928-2050
Fax: 773 928-4950
Pasquale Del Cotto, *President*
Gregory Del Cotto, *Vice Pres*
Steve Samelak, *Engineer*
Albin F Franks, *Accountant*
Liset Ontiverous, *Admin Sec*
EMP: 21 EST: 1945
SQ FT: 30,000
SALES (est): 6MM **Privately Held**
WEB: www.fabricatingandwelding.com
SIC: 3441 7692 Fabricated structural metal; welding repair

**(G-4810)**
**FAITHS DESIGNS**
Also Called: Faiths Jewelry Designs
7916 S Kingston Ave (60617-1285)
PHONE.................................773 768-5804
Faith Davis, *Owner*
EMP: 5
SALES (est): 180K **Privately Held**
SIC: 3961 Costume jewelry

**(G-4811)**
**FAMOUS LUBRICANTS INC**
124 W 47th St (60609-4696)
PHONE.................................773 268-2555
Fax: 773 268-5815
Vaughn Hapeman II, *President*
James Goodale, *Treasurer*
Mary Thompson, *Admin Sec*
EMP: 8 EST: 1907
SQ FT: 18,000
SALES: 2.5MM **Privately Held**
SIC: 2992 5172 Lubricating oils & greases; lubricating oils & greases

**(G-4812)**
**FANTASTIC LETTERING INC**
5644 W Lawrence Ave (60630-3220)
PHONE.................................773 685-7650
Tony Didlik, *President*
EMP: 6
SALES (est): 500K **Privately Held**
WEB: www.fantasticlettering.com
SIC: 2759 2396 Screen printing; automotive & apparel trimmings

**(G-4813)**
**FAR EAST FOOD INC**
Also Called: Far East Trading Co
1836 S Canal St (60616-1502)
PHONE.................................312 733-1688
Fax: 312 733-7917
Lydia Chen, *President*
▲ EMP: 5
SQ FT: 185,000
SALES: 1MM **Privately Held**
SIC: 5141 2099 Food brokers; food preparations

**(G-4814)**
**FASHAHNN CORPORATION**
8016 S Cottage Grove Ave (60619-4004)
PHONE.................................773 994-3132
Fax: 773 994-0839
EMP: 3
SALES (est): 240K **Privately Held**
SIC: 2337 5621 5611 2339 Mfg Women/Miss Suit/Coat Ret Women's Clothing Ret Men's/Boy's Clothing Mfg Women/Miss Outerwear

**(G-4815)**
**FAST FORWARD ENERGY INC**
Also Called: Bean and Body
2023 W Carroll Ave (60612-1691)
PHONE.................................312 860-0978
Ben Heins, *President*
EMP: 4
SALES (est): 400K **Privately Held**
SIC: 2086 Bottled & canned soft drinks

**(G-4816)**
**FAST SIGNS**
Also Called: Fastsigns
1101 W Belmont Ave (60657-3312)
PHONE.................................773 698-8115
Todd Fisher, *Owner*
EMP: 5 EST: 2014
SALES (est): 121.8K **Privately Held**
SIC: 3993 Signs & advertising specialties

**(G-4817)**
**FAST TRACK PRINTING INC**
2715 W Touhy Ave (60645-3007)
PHONE.................................773 761-9400
Fax: 773 775-7050
John Petergal, *President*
EMP: 4
SQ FT: 3,000
SALES (est): 290K **Privately Held**
SIC: 2759 Commercial printing

**(G-4818)**
**FASTSIGNS**
118 N Halsted St (60661-1042)
PHONE.................................312 344-1765
EMP: 4
SALES (est): 163.2K **Privately Held**
SIC: 3993 Signs & advertising specialties

**(G-4819)**
**FASTSIGNS**
180 N Wacker Dr Ste 100 (60606-1612)
PHONE.................................312 332-7446
Fax: 312 332-3106
Meme Peyovich, *President*
Mimi Graveline, *Sales Mgr*
EMP: 3
SQ FT: 1,100
SALES (est): 834.9K **Privately Held**
SIC: 3993 Signs & advertising specialties

**(G-4820)**
**FATHER MARCELLOS & SON**
645 W North Ave (60610-1011)
PHONE.................................312 654-2565
Fax: 312 654-0373
Bill Bauer, *Owner*
EMP: 130
SALES (est): 2.1MM **Privately Held**
SIC: 5812 5813 2051 Italian restaurant; drinking places; bread, cake & related products

**(G-4821)**
**FBS GROUP INC**
6513 W 64th St (60638-4913)
PHONE.................................773 229-8675
Fax: 773 229-1990
Maryann Hutson, *President*
Mat Hutson Jr, *Admin Sec*
EMP: 10
SQ FT: 10,000
SALES (est): 900K **Privately Held**
SIC: 1791 3496 3446 3444 Structural steel erection; miscellaneous fabricated wire products; architectural metalwork; sheet metalwork; fabricated structural metal

**(G-4822)**
**FBSA LLC**
4545 W Augusta Blvd (60651-3315)
PHONE.................................773 524-2440
Craig Freedman, *Managing Prtnr*
EMP: 188 EST: 2011
SALES (est): 8.3MM
SALES (corp-wide): 142.1MM **Privately Held**
SIC: 2531 Seats, miscellaneous public conveyances

# GEOGRAPHIC SECTION

Chicago - Cook County (G-4847)

PA: Freedman Seating Company
4545 W Augusta Blvd
Chicago IL 60651
773 524-2440

**(G-4823)**
**FEDERAL UNIFORM LLC**
4015 W Carroll Ave (60624-1802)
PHONE .................... 847 658-5470
Arbok Ives,
Steven A Grys,
EMP: 3
SQ FT: 22,000
SALES: 800K **Privately Held**
SIC: 2326 Work uniforms

**(G-4824)**
**FEDERATED PAINT MFG CO (PA)**
5812 S Homan Ave (60629-3637)
PHONE .................... 708 345-4848
John Bauchwitz, *CEO*
Norman Wechter, *President*
Chris Sanek, *General Mgr*
Marshall Wechter, *Corp Secy*
▲ EMP: 17 EST: 1948
SQ FT: 100,000
SALES (est): 1.7MM **Privately Held**
SIC: 2851 Paints & allied products; varnishes; lacquer: bases, dopes, thinner; enamels

**(G-4825)**
**FEDEX OFFICE & PRINT SVCS INC**
1 S Sangamon St (60607-2617)
PHONE .................... 312 492-8355
Fax: 312 492-8538
Chrises Carter, *Branch Mgr*
EMP: 4
SALES (corp-wide): 50.3B **Publicly Held**
SIC: 2752 Commercial printing, lithographic
HQ: Fedex Office And Print Services, Inc.
7900 Legacy Dr
Plano TX 75024
214 550-7000

**(G-4826)**
**FEDEX OFFICE & PRINT SVCS INC**
744 W Fullerton Ave (60614-7583)
PHONE .................... 773 472-3066
Fax: 773 472-3381
Ervin Hughes, *Manager*
EMP: 6
SALES (corp-wide): 50.3B **Publicly Held**
SIC: 2752 Commercial printing, lithographic
HQ: Fedex Office And Print Services, Inc.
7900 Legacy Dr
Plano TX 75024
214 550-7000

**(G-4827)**
**FEDEX OFFICE & PRINT SVCS INC**
71 E Jackson Blvd (60604-4101)
PHONE .................... 312 341-9644
Fax: 312 341-9618
Wanda Crossley, *Manager*
EMP: 11
SALES (corp-wide): 50.3B **Publicly Held**
SIC: 7389 7334 5099 2752 Packaging & labeling services; photocopying & duplicating services; signs, except electric; commercial printing, lithographic
HQ: Fedex Office And Print Services, Inc.
7900 Legacy Dr
Plano TX 75024
214 550-7000

**(G-4828)**
**FEDEX OFFICE & PRINT SVCS INC**
540 N Michigan Ave (60611-3890)
PHONE .................... 312 755-0325
EMP: 10
SALES (corp-wide): 47.4B **Publicly Held**
SIC: 7389 7334 5099 2752 Business Services Photocopying Service Whol Durable Goods Lithographic Coml Print
HQ: Fedex Office And Print Services, Inc.
7900 Legacy Dr
Dallas TX 75024
214 550-7000

**(G-4829)**
**FEDEX OFFICE & PRINT SVCS INC**
505 N Michigan Ave (60611-3827)
PHONE .................... 312 595-0768
Fax: 312 944-0378
Brian Phillips, *Branch Mgr*
EMP: 11
SALES (corp-wide): 50.3B **Publicly Held**
SIC: 7389 7334 5099 2752 Packaging & labeling services; photocopying & duplicating services; signs, except electric; commercial printing, lithographic
HQ: Fedex Office And Print Services, Inc.
7900 Legacy Dr
Plano TX 75024
214 550-7000

**(G-4830)**
**FEDEX OFFICE & PRINT SVCS INC**
720 S Michigan Ave (60605-2116)
PHONE .................... 312 663-1149
Fax: 312 663-1341
Basia Norcheska, *Branch Mgr*
EMP: 11
SALES (corp-wide): 50.3B **Publicly Held**
SIC: 7389 7334 5099 2752 Packaging & labeling services; photocopying & duplicating services; signs, except electric; commercial printing, lithographic
HQ: Fedex Office And Print Services, Inc.
7900 Legacy Dr
Plano TX 75024
214 550-7000

**(G-4831)**
**FEDEX OFFICE & PRINT SVCS INC**
444 N Wells St Fl 1 (60654-4522)
PHONE .................... 312 670-4460
Erick Holmes, *Opers Mgr*
John Hurley, *Manager*
Heath McAdams, *Admin Mgr*
EMP: 18
SALES (corp-wide): 50.3B **Publicly Held**
WEB: www.kinkos.com
SIC: 7334 2791 2789 2759 Photocopying & duplicating services; typesetting; bookbinding & related work; commercial printing
HQ: Fedex Office And Print Services, Inc.
7900 Legacy Dr
Plano TX 75024
214 550-7000

**(G-4832)**
**FELICE HOSIERY CO INC (PA)**
632 W Roosevelt Rd (60607-4912)
PHONE .................... 312 922-3710
Felice Nelson,
Irving Weinberg, *Vice Pres*
EMP: 1
SQ FT: 3,500
SALES (est): 1.1MM **Privately Held**
SIC: 2252 2251 Men's, boys' & girls' hosiery; dyeing & finishing women's full- & knee-length hosiery

**(G-4833)**
**FELICE HOSIERY COMPANY INC**
632 W Roosevelt Rd (60607-4912)
PHONE .................... 312 922-3710
Felice Nelson, *President*
EMP: 23
SQ FT: 9,500
SALES (est): 1.3MM **Privately Held**
SIC: 2252 Anklets & socks

**(G-4834)**
**FELLOWSHIP BLACK LIGHT**
2859 W Wilcox St (60612-3649)
P.O. Box 5369 (60680-5369)
PHONE .................... 773 826-7790
Fax: 773 826-7792
Walter McCray, *Pastor*
EMP: 3
SQ FT: 27,000
SALES (est): 223.9K **Privately Held**
WEB: www.gospelizers.com
SIC: 2721 5699 5942 5621 Periodicals: publishing only; T-shirts, custom printed; book stores; women's clothing stores

**(G-4835)**
**FEMALE HEALTH COMPANY (PA)**
Also Called: VERU HEALTHCARE
150 N Michigan Ave # 1580 (60601-7553)
PHONE .................... 312 595-9123
Fax: 312 595-9122
O B Parrish, *Ch of Bd*
Mitchell Steiner, *President*
Robert H Getzenberg, *Exec VP*
Martin Tayler, *Exec VP*
Michele Greco, *CFO*
EMP: 47
SALES: 22.1MM **Publicly Held**
WEB: www.femalehealth.com
SIC: 3069 Birth control devices, rubber

**(G-4836)**
**FERALLOY CORPORATION (HQ)**
8755 W Higgins Rd Ste 970 (60631-2735)
PHONE .................... 503 286-8869
Fax: 773 380-1535
Carlos Rodriguez Borjas, *President*
John A Hirt, *Vice Pres*
Jack D Love, *Vice Pres*
Sam Meyers, *Opers Mgr*
Mike Borzych, *Credit Staff*
▲ EMP: 20
SQ FT: 10,000
SALES (est): 350.3MM
SALES (corp-wide): 8.6B **Publicly Held**
WEB: www.feralloy.com
SIC: 5051 3471 3444 3312 Iron or steel flat products; plating & polishing; sheet metalwork; blast furnaces & steel mills
PA: Reliance Steel & Aluminum Co.
350 S Grand Ave Ste 5100
Los Angeles CA 90071
213 687-7700

**(G-4837)**
**FERNANDEZ WINDOWS CORP**
2535 S Ridgeway Ave (60623-3831)
PHONE .................... 773 762-2365
Juan Fernandez, *Principal*
EMP: 3
SALES (est): 263.6K **Privately Held**
SIC: 3952 Chalk: carpenters', blackboard, marking, tailors', etc.

**(G-4838)**
**FERTILIZER INC**
Also Called: National Liquid Fertilizer
5820 W 66th St (60638-6204)
PHONE .................... 708 458-8615
Fax: 708 458-8644
Bruce Nutt, *President*
EMP: 6 EST: 1956
SQ FT: 25,000
SALES: 800K **Privately Held**
WEB: www.nationalliquidfertilizer.com
SIC: 2873 Nitrogenous fertilizers

**(G-4839)**
**FGS INC**
815 W Van Buren St # 302 (60607-3566)
PHONE .................... 312 421-3060
Fax: 312 421-3609
Thomas R Schaefer, *President*
Ryan Garth, *Exec VP*
Chuck Libman, *Exec VP*
Kevin Vertone, *Exec VP*
Ryan Doyle, *Vice Pres*
▲ EMP: 10
SALES (est): 2.1MM **Privately Held**
SIC: 2752 2759 Commercial printing, lithographic; commercial printing

**(G-4840)**
**FIBERFORGE CORPORATION**
70 W Madison St Ste 2300 (60602-4250)
PHONE .................... 970 945-9377
Dave Cornelius, *CEO*
David Cramer, *COO*
Jon Fox Rubin PHD, *Exec VP*
Michael Glen, *CFO*
Susan Goldberg, *Marketing Staff*
EMP: 40
SQ FT: 11,000
SALES (est): 4.8MM **Privately Held**
WEB: www.fiberforge.com
SIC: 3728 3999 Aircraft parts & equipment; chairs, hydraulic, barber & beauty shop

**(G-4841)**
**FIBERLINK LLC**
230 E Ohio St Ste 212 (60611-3267)
PHONE .................... 312 951-8500
Kenneth Anderson,
EMP: 4
SALES (est): 402.2K
SALES (corp-wide): 1.7B **Publicly Held**
SIC: 3366 Copper foundries
HQ: Zayo Group, Llc
1805 29th St Unit 2050
Boulder CO 80301
303 381-4683

**(G-4842)**
**FIBRE-TEC PARTITIONS LLC**
5301 S Western Blvd Ste 1 (60609-5425)
PHONE .................... 773 436-4028
Fax: 773 436-4110
Leonard Ingolia, *General Mgr*
Tom Dodson, *Manager*
John Cantalupo,
Tom Dawson,
Terry Jannotta,
EMP: 45
SQ FT: 65,000
SALES (est): 9.1MM **Privately Held**
WEB: www.fibre-tec.com
SIC: 2611 Pulp manufactured from waste or recycled paper

**(G-4843)**
**FINAL CALL INC (PA)**
Also Called: Final Call Newspaper, The
734 W 79th St (60620-2424)
PHONE .................... 773 602-1230
James G Muhammad, *Editor*
Paula Muhammad, *Financial Exec*
Dewayne Muhammad, *Manager*
EMP: 10 EST: 1985
SALES (est): 6MM **Privately Held**
WEB: www.finalcall.com
SIC: 2711 2731 Newspapers, publishing & printing; books: publishing & printing; pamphlets: publishing & printing

**(G-4844)**
**FINCHS BEER COMPANY LLC**
1800 W Walnut St (60612-2526)
PHONE .................... 773 919-8012
Ben Finch, *Mng Member*
Paul Finch,
EMP: 5
SALES: 500K **Privately Held**
SIC: 2082 5181 Beer (alcoholic beverage); beer & other fermented malt liquors

**(G-4845)**
**FINE ARTS ENGRAVING CO**
311 S Wacker Dr Ste 300 (60606-6699)
PHONE .................... 800 688-4400
Joseph L Fontana Sr, *President*
Curt Bennitt, *Vice Pres*
Gil Voltaggio, *Mktg Dir*
EMP: 6
SALES (est): 485.2K **Privately Held**
SIC: 2759 Commercial printing

**(G-4846)**
**FINE LINE PRINTING**
5181 S Archer Ave (60632-4758)
PHONE .................... 773 582-9709
Fax: 773 582-3391
Mark Stone, *Owner*
EMP: 4
SALES (est): 281.3K **Privately Held**
SIC: 2752 2791 2759 Commercial printing, lithographic; typesetting; commercial printing

**(G-4847)**
**FINISHED METALS INCORPORATED**
6146 S New England Ave (60638-4008)
PHONE .................... 773 229-1600
Ronald Fisher, *President*
Mary Francis Johnstone, *Admin Sec*
EMP: 10 EST: 1961
SQ FT: 30,000
SALES (est): 2MM **Privately Held**
WEB: www.finishedmetals.com
SIC: 3471 Polishing, metals or formed products

## Chicago - Cook County (G-4848)

**(G-4848)**
**FINISHING TOUCH INC**
5580 N Northwest Hwy (60630-1116)
PHONE.................................773 774-7349
Fax: 773 774-5403
Mark A Silich, *President*
Suzanne L Silich, *Admin Sec*
EMP: 14
SQ FT: 6,000
SALES (est): 800K  Privately Held
WEB: www.thefinishingtouchinc.com
SIC: 3471  Polishing, metals or formed products

**(G-4849)**
**FIRST IMPRESSION OF CHICAGO**
218 E 79th St (60619-2802)
PHONE.................................773 224-3434
Fax: 773 234-7864
Hayes A Bynum, *Owner*
EMP: 6
SQ FT: 8,000
SALES (est): 546.6K  Privately Held
SIC: 2791 2759 2789 7336  Typesetting; commercial printing; business forms: printing; bookbinding & related work; graphic arts & related design

**(G-4850)**
**FISH KING INC**
5228 W Giddings St (60630-3602)
PHONE.................................773 736-4974
Frank Suerth, *President*
Eileen Bond, *Admin Sec*
EMP: 6
SALES (est): 701.2K  Privately Held
SIC: 2048  Fish food; frozen pet food (except dog & cat); dry pet food (except dog & cat)

**(G-4851)**
**FISHER CONTROLS INTL LLC**
1124 Tower Rd (60673-0001)
P.O. Box 73735 (60673-7735)
PHONE.................................847 956-8020
EMP: 82
SALES (corp-wide): 14.5B  Publicly Held
SIC: 3491  Industrial valves
HQ: Fisher Controls International Llc
   205 S Center St
   Marshalltown IA 50158
   641 754-3011

**(G-4852)**
**FISHEYE SERVICES INCORPORATED**
Also Called: Fisheye Grahphics
5443 N Broadway St (60640-1703)
PHONE.................................773 942-6314
Lee Nagen, *President*
EMP: 2
SQ FT: 1,000
SALES (est): 210K  Privately Held
SIC: 2759 2791 2789 2752  Commercial printing; typesetting; bookbinding & related work; commercial printing, lithographic

**(G-4853)**
**FIVE STAR DESSERTS AND FOODS**
8559 S Constance Ave (60617-2220)
PHONE.................................773 375-5100
Gwendolyn Meeks, *Owner*
EMP: 4
SALES (est): 301.5K  Privately Held
SIC: 2024  Ice cream & frozen desserts

**(G-4854)**
**FIXTURE COMPANY**
8770 W Bryn Mawr Ave (60631-3515)
PHONE.................................847 214-3100
James Buster, *General Mgr*
Mark Menke, *Manager*
EMP: 7
SQ FT: 37,000
SALES (est): 871.6K  Privately Held
WEB: www.thefixtureco.com
SIC: 3534  3613 1796  Elevators & moving stairways; switchgear & switchboard apparatus; installing building equipment

**(G-4855)**
**FIXTURE HARDWARE CO (PA)**
Also Called: Product Emphasis
4711 N Lamon Ave (60630-3896)
PHONE.................................773 777-6100
Fax: 773 685-8316
Roger Wolf, *President*
Todd Carmichael, *Vice Pres*
Robert Anderson, *Project Mgr*
Nate Greaney, *Project Mgr*
Dave Haffey, *Project Mgr*
▲ EMP: 50 EST: 1920
SQ FT: 72,000
SALES (est): 7.8MM  Privately Held
WEB: www.fhcfixture.com
SIC: 2542 2591  Fixtures: display, office or store: except wood; showcases (not refrigerated): except wood; racks, merchandise display or storage: except wood; counters or counter display cases: except wood; shade, curtain & drapery hardware

**(G-4856)**
**FLEISCHMANNS VINEGAR CO INC**
4801 S Oakley Ave (60609-4035)
PHONE.................................773 523-2817
Kurt Avery, *Branch Mgr*
EMP: 15
SALES (corp-wide): 3.4B  Publicly Held
WEB: www.breadworld.com
SIC: 2099  Vinegar
HQ: Fleischmann's Vinegar Company, Inc.
   12604 Hiddencreek Way A
   Cerritos CA 90703
   562 483-4619

**(G-4857)**
**FLEX LIGHTING II LLC**
25 E Washington St # 510 (60602-1732)
PHONE.................................312 929-3488
Mike Casper, *President*
Shawn Pucylowski, *VP Opers*
Eric Blair, *Engineer*
Nicholas Eccles, *Engineer*
Mike Valitchka, *Sales Mgr*
EMP: 5
SALES (est): 670K  Privately Held
SIC: 3648  Lighting equipment

**(G-4858)**
**FLEX-O-GLASS INC (PA)**
Also Called: Warp Bros
4647 W Augusta Blvd Ste 1 (60651-3310)
PHONE.................................773 261-5200
Fax: 773 261-5204
Harold G Warp, *President*
Lawrence Cohen, *Credit Mgr*
Euphelia De Pasquale, *Admin Sec*
EMP: 95 EST: 1924
SQ FT: 300,000
SALES (est): 42.1MM  Privately Held
WEB: www.flexoglass.com
SIC: 3081 3082 2673 2394  Plastic film & sheet; unsupported plastics profile shapes; bags: plastic, laminated & coated; canvas & related products

**(G-4859)**
**FLEX-O-GLASS INC**
Also Called: Industrial Packaging Division
1100 N Cicero Ave Ste 1 (60651-3214)
PHONE.................................773 379-7878
Joine Fabino, *Purch Agent*
Thomas Shultz, *Persnl Dir*
Frank Kostecki, *Human Res Mgr*
Jeff Whittington, *Sales Executive*
Harold Warp, *Branch Mgr*
EMP: 8
SALES (corp-wide): 42.1MM  Privately Held
WEB: www.flexoglass.com
SIC: 3081 3082  Plastic film & sheet; unsupported plastics profile shapes
PA: Flex-O-Glass, Inc.
   4647 W Augusta Blvd Ste 1
   Chicago IL 60651
   773 261-5200

**(G-4860)**
**FLEXAN LLC (PA)**
Also Called: F M I
6626 W Dakin St (60634-2879)
PHONE.................................773 685-6446
Fax: 773 685-6630
Jim Fitzgerald, *CEO*
Bruce Cohan, *President*
Nabil Boufakhreddine, *Vice Pres*
Darren Zhao, *Opers Mgr*
Ken Walton, *QA Dir*
▲ EMP: 131 EST: 1977
SQ FT: 65,000
SALES (est): 37.8MM  Privately Held
WEB: www.flexan.com
SIC: 3069  Molded rubber products

**(G-4861)**
**FLEXICRAFT INDUSTRIES INC (PA)**
2315 W Hubbard St (60612-1403)
PHONE.................................312 738-3588
Fax: 312 421-6327
Paul Berg, *President*
Doug Limberg, *Controller*
Jann Dechristopher, *Accounts Mgr*
Steve Rongione, *Marketing Mgr*
Douglas S Limberg, *Admin Sec*
▲ EMP: 17
SALES (est): 2.7MM  Privately Held
SIC: 3069 3498 5085 5074  Expansion joints, rubber; fabricated pipe & fittings; industrial supplies; plumbing & hydronic heating supplies

**(G-4862)**
**FLIRTY CUPCAKES LLC**
1101 W Lake St Ste 303 (60607-1640)
PHONE.................................312 545-1096
Chris Sewall, *Principal*
EMP: 6
SALES (est): 431.4K  Privately Held
SIC: 2051  Bread, cake & related products

**(G-4863)**
**FLORIDA FRUIT JUICES INC**
Also Called: California Pure Delite Juice & 7001 W 62nd St (60638-3924)
PHONE.................................773 586-6200
Fax: 773 586-6651
Donald Franko Sr, *President*
Don Franko Jr, *Vice Pres*
EMP: 25 EST: 1959
SQ FT: 50,000
SALES (est): 6.5MM  Privately Held
SIC: 2033 2086  Fruit juices: fresh; bottled & canned soft drinks

**(G-4864)**
**FMC SUBSEA SERVICE INC**
200 E Randolph St Fl 66 (60601-6803)
PHONE.................................312 861-6174
William Schumann, *Exec VP*
EMP: 4
SALES (est): 44K
SALES (corp-wide): 790.7K  Privately Held
WEB: www.fmctechnologies.com
SIC: 3533  Oil & gas drilling rigs & equipment
HQ: Technipfmc Us Holdings Inc.
   11740 Katy Fwy
   Houston TX 77079
   281 591-4000

**(G-4865)**
**FMC TECHNOLOGIES INC**
Also Called: Blending and Transfer Systems
222 W Adams St Ste 400 (60606-5308)
PHONE.................................312 803-4321
John T Gremp, *CEO*
Zachary Hockaday, *Design Engr*
EMP: 9 EST: 2000
SALES (est): 611.8K  Privately Held
SIC: 1321  Natural gas liquids

**(G-4866)**
**FOCAL POINT LIGHTING INC**
4201 S Pulaski Rd (60632-3415)
PHONE.................................773 247-9494
Peter Thornton, *President*
Camillo Catuara, *Manager*
EMP: 200
SALES (est): 312.7K  Privately Held
SIC: 3646  Commercial indusl & institutional electric lighting fixtures

**(G-4867)**
**FOCAL POINT LLC (PA)**
Also Called: Focal Point Lighting
4141 S Pulaski Rd (60632-3414)
PHONE.................................773 247-9494
Fax: 773 247-8484
Ken Czech, *President*
Zach Payne, *Project Mgr*
Mark Bendigkeit, *Senior Buyer*
Tasha Ramos, *Senior Buyer*
Alan Bond, *Engineer*
▲ EMP: 110
SQ FT: 102,000
SALES (est): 27.4MM  Privately Held
SIC: 3646  Commercial indusl & institutional electric lighting fixtures

**(G-4868)**
**FOLA COMMUNITY ACTION SERVICES**
8014 S Ashland Ave (60620-4317)
PHONE.................................773 487-4310
Fax: 773 487-4320
Fload Floaoadinde, *Owner*
EMP: 10
SALES (est): 1.5MM  Privately Held
SIC: 2842  Specialty cleaning preparations

**(G-4869)**
**FOODA INC**
363 W Erie St Ste 500e (60654-0500)
PHONE.................................312 752-4352
Julia Dryden, *Principal*
Jason Stulberg, *COO*
Erin Himes, *Accounts Exec*
Orazio Buzza, *Director*
EMP: 34
SALES (est): 1.1MM  Privately Held
SIC: 5812 7372  Eating places; business oriented computer software

**(G-4870)**
**FOODSERVICE DATABASE CO INC**
5724 W Diversey Ave (60639-1203)
PHONE.................................773 745-9400
Fax: 773 745-7432
Ray Mitchell, *President*
Anthony Smith, *Vice Pres*
Mary Manieri, *Office Mgr*
EMP: 10
SALES (est): 670K  Privately Held
WEB: www.fsdbco.com
SIC: 2741  Atlas, map & guide publishing

**(G-4871)**
**FORBIDDEN ROOT A BENEFIT LLC**
444 N Michigan Ave (60611-3903)
PHONE.................................312 464-7910
Robert Finkel, *CEO*
EMP: 4 EST: 2013
SALES (est): 496.5K  Privately Held
SIC: 2082  Beer (alcoholic beverage)

**(G-4872)**
**FOREST LEE LLC**
440 N Wells St Ste 530 (60654-4566)
PHONE.................................312 379-0032
John Cunningham,
Thomas Engel,
EMP: 2
SALES: 5MM  Privately Held
SIC: 3552  Knot tying machines, textile

**(G-4873)**
**FOREVER FLY LLC**
934 N Waller Ave (60651-2649)
PHONE.................................312 981-9161
EMP: 3
SALES (est): 190K  Privately Held
SIC: 2329 2331  Mfg Men's/Boy's Clothing Mfg Women's/Misses' Blouses

**(G-4874)**
**FORMCRAFT TOOL COMPANY**
6453 S Bell Ave (60636-2598)
PHONE.................................773 476-8727
Fax: 773 476-8787
William Matevich, *President*
EMP: 12 EST: 1948
SQ FT: 15,000
SALES (est): 2MM  Privately Held
SIC: 3679  Microwave components

**(G-4875)**
**FORTE PRINT CORPORATION**
3139 W Chicago Ave (60622-4364)
PHONE.................................773 391-0105
Francisco Forte, *President*
Leticia Arce, *Administration*

# GEOGRAPHIC SECTION
## Chicago - Cook County (G-4903)

**EMP:** 3
**SQ FT:** 600
**SALES (est):** 162.2K **Privately Held**
**SIC:** 2759 Commercial printing

### (G-4876)
### FORTELLA COMPANY INC
Also Called: Fortella Forture Cookies
214 W 26th St (60616-2204)
**PHONE**.................................312 567-9000
Herman H Wong, *President*
Brenda Wong, *General Mgr*
Betty Wong, *Vice Pres*
▲ **EMP:** 7
**SQ FT:** 6,250
**SALES:** 1MM **Privately Held**
**SIC:** 2052 Cookies

### (G-4877)
### FOTOFAB LLC
Also Called: Fotofabrication
3758 W Belmont Ave (60618-5246)
**PHONE**.................................773 463-6211
Dan Brumlik, *CEO*
Charles Cohen, *President*
Scott Bekemeyer, *Chairman*
Richard Sobon, *Prdtn Mgr*
Sencer Sofuoglu, *Engineer*
**EMP:** 50
**SALES (est):** 8.5MM **Privately Held**
**SIC:** 3499 Fire- or burglary-resistive products

### (G-4878)
### FOTOFABRICATION CORP
3758 W Belmont Ave (60618-5292)
**PHONE**.................................773 463-6211
**Fax:** 773 463-3387
Jamie K Howton, *President*
Dan Brumlik, *Chairman*
Charles Cohen, *Vice Pres*
Chadwick Torkelson, *Design Engr*
Torrance Cobb, *Manager*
**EMP:** 40 **EST:** 1967
**SQ FT:** 18,500
**SALES (est):** 7.7MM **Privately Held**
**WEB:** www.fotofab.com
**SIC:** 3545 Precision tools, machinists'

### (G-4879)
### FOUR WHITE SOCKS LLC
270 E Pearson St Apt 1502 (60611-2696)
**PHONE**.................................312 257-6456
Kopp Suzanne, *Principal*
**EMP:** 4
**SALES (est):** 312.8K **Privately Held**
**SIC:** 2252 Socks

### (G-4880)
### FOX INTERNATIONAL CORP
Also Called: Bremner-Davis Eductl Systems
7366 N Greenview Ave (60626-1924)
**PHONE**.................................773 465-3634
Kathleen S Fox, *President*
**EMP:** 10
**SALES:** 1MM **Privately Held**
**SIC:** 3532 5049 Sedimentation machinery, mineral; scientific instruments

### (G-4881)
### FRAGRANCE ISLAND
641 E 79th St (60619-3036)
**PHONE**.................................773 488-2700
Mohammad Babul, *Owner*
▲ **EMP:** 4 **EST:** 2007
**SALES (est):** 449.2K **Privately Held**
**SIC:** 2899 5199 Oils & essential oils; gifts & novelties

### (G-4882)
### FRAHTEX INC
2650 W Belden Ave Apt 214 (60647-3087)
**PHONE**.................................773 796-7914
Natalia Garayda, *President*
**EMP:** 4
**SALES (est):** 460K **Privately Held**
**SIC:** 3537 Trucks, tractors, loaders, carriers & similar equipment

### (G-4883)
### FRANK A EDMUNDS & CO INC (PA)
6111 S Sayre Ave (60638-3911)
**PHONE**.................................773 586-2772
Dennis J Clegg, *President*
Jim Mann, *Vice Pres*
Paul Stepuzick, *Vice Pres*
▲ **EMP:** 14
**SQ FT:** 35,000
**SALES (est):** 1.4MM **Privately Held**
**WEB:** www.frankedmunds.com
**SIC:** 2499 Picture & mirror frames, wood

### (G-4884)
### FRANK O CARLSON & CO INC
3622 S Morgan St Ste 2r (60609-1576)
**PHONE**.................................773 847-6900
Rose Carlson, *President*
Matt Pendowski, *President*
David Carlson, *Treasurer*
Chris Carlson, *Manager*
▲ **EMP:** 11
**SQ FT:** 28,000
**SALES:** 1.5MM **Privately Held**
**WEB:** www.focarlson.com
**SIC:** 3993 Signs & advertising specialties

### (G-4885)
### FRANKLIN FUELING SYSTEMS INC
21054 Network Pl (60673-1210)
**PHONE**.................................207 283-0156
Don Kenny, *President*
**EMP:** 6
**SALES (corp-wide):** 949.8MM **Publicly Held**
**SIC:** 3586 Gasoline pumps, measuring or dispensing
**HQ:** Franklin Fueling Systems, Inc.
3760 Marsh Rd
Madison WI 53718
608 838-8786

### (G-4886)
### FREDERICS FRAME STUDIO INC
1230 W Jackson Blvd (60607-2814)
**PHONE**.................................312 243-2950
**Fax:** 312 243-4673
Frederick S Baker, *President*
Scot Campbell, *Director*
Amy Baker, *Admin Sec*
Lisa Baker, *Admin Sec*
**EMP:** 12 **EST:** 1952
**SQ FT:** 30,000
**SALES (est):** 470K **Privately Held**
**WEB:** www.fredericsframestudio.com
**SIC:** 2499 3499 3089 Picture & mirror frames, wood; picture frames, metal; plastic kitchenware, tableware & houseware

### (G-4887)
### FREEDMAN SEATING COMPANY (PA)
4545 W Augusta Blvd (60651-3338)
**PHONE**.................................773 524-2440
**Fax:** 773 252-7450
Gerald Freedman, *CEO*
Craig Freedman, *President*
Christy Nunes, *Managing Dir*
Dan Cohen, *Vice Pres*
Robert Anoff, *Opers Mgr*
▲ **EMP:** 250
**SQ FT:** 233,000
**SALES (est):** 142.1MM **Privately Held**
**WEB:** www.freedmanseating.com
**SIC:** 2531 Seats, miscellaneous public conveyances; vehicle furniture; cabs for off-highway trucks

### (G-4888)
### FREEDOM FUEL & FOOD INC
8950 S Ashland Ave (60620-4952)
**PHONE**.................................773 233-5350
**EMP:** 3
**SALES (est):** 256.7K **Privately Held**
**SIC:** 2869 Fuels

### (G-4889)
### FREIGHTCAR AMERICA INC (PA)
2 N Rverside Plz Ste 1300 (60606)
**PHONE**.................................800 458-2235
**Fax:** 312 928-0890
Joseph E McNeely, *President*
Gus Tosoni, *General Mgr*
Jeffrey Klamar, *Vice Pres*
Mike Macmahon, *Vice Pres*
Joseph Maliekel, *Vice Pres*
◆ **EMP:** 78
**SQ FT:** 15,540
**SALES:** 523.7MM **Publicly Held**
**WEB:** www.freightcaramerica.com
**SIC:** 3743 Railroad equipment; train cars & equipment, freight or passenger

### (G-4890)
### FRESENIUS USA INC
2277 W Howard St (60645-1922)
**PHONE**.................................773 262-7147
Catherine Apuhin, *Principal*
**EMP:** 40
**SALES (corp-wide):** 17.5B **Privately Held**
**SIC:** 2834 Intravenous solutions
**HQ:** Fresenius Usa, Inc.
4040 Nelson Ave
Concord CA 94520
925 288-4218

### (G-4891)
### FRIEDRICH KLATT AND ASSOCIATES
5240 S Hyde Park Blvd (60615-4213)
**PHONE**.................................773 753-1806
**Fax:** 773 288-1376
Dan Friedrich, *Partner*
Marcia Klatt, *Partner*
**EMP:** 5
**SQ FT:** 3,900
**SALES (est):** 672.9K **Privately Held**
**WEB:** www.friedrichklatt.com
**SIC:** 7379 8243 5734 7372 Computer related consulting services; operator training, computer; computer & software stores; business oriented computer software

### (G-4892)
### FRIENDS FUEL
8200 S Kedzie Ave (60652-3329)
**PHONE**.................................773 434-9387
George Dinker, *Manager*
**EMP:** 4
**SALES (est):** 328.7K **Privately Held**
**SIC:** 2869 Fuels

### (G-4893)
### FT MOTORS INC
5929 S Ashland Ave Apt 29 (60636-1708)
**PHONE**.................................773 737-5581
Anthony Jones Taylor, *President*
Fred Bello, *Vice Pres*
**EMP:** 16
**SALES (est):** 1.4MM **Privately Held**
**SIC:** 3714 Motor vehicle engines & parts

### (G-4894)
### FULL COURT PRESS INC
9146 S Pleasant Ave (60643-6011)
**PHONE**.................................773 779-1135
Michael Ryan, *President*
**EMP:** 2
**SALES:** 500K **Privately Held**
**SIC:** 2752 Commercial printing, lithographic

### (G-4895)
### FULL LINE PRINTING INC
361 W Chicago Ave (60654-5125)
**PHONE**.................................312 642-8080
**Fax:** 312 642-9271
Jeff Juhasz, *President*
Stephen Juhasz, *Vice Pres*
Cindy Noga-Juhasz, *Sales Staff*
**EMP:** 9
**SQ FT:** 4,500
**SALES (est):** 890K **Privately Held**
**WEB:** www.fulllineprinting.com
**SIC:** 2752 Commercial printing, offset

### (G-4896)
### FULTON STREET BREWERY LLC
Also Called: Goose Island Beer Company
1800 W Fulton St (60612-2512)
**PHONE**.................................312 915-0071
**Fax:** 312 733-1692
Robert Kenney, *Vice Pres*
Michael Poat, *Production*
Jason Karras, *QC Mgr*
William Carlisle, *Accountant*
Aurora Garcia, *Human Res Mgr*
▲ **EMP:** 30
**SALES (est):** 8.5MM **Privately Held**
**SIC:** 2082 Malt beverages

**HQ:** Anheuser-Busch, Llc
1 Busch Pl
Saint Louis MO 63118
314 632-6777

### (G-4897)
### FUTURES MAGAZINE INC
107 W Van Buren St # 203 (60605-1054)
**PHONE**.................................312 846-4600
Steve Zwick, *Principal*
Yesenia Duran, *Editor*
David Friedman, *CFO*
**EMP:** 3
**SALES (est):** 832.6K
**SALES (corp-wide):** 1.5MM **Privately Held**
**SIC:** 2721 Magazines: publishing & printing
**PA:** The Alpha Pages Llc
107 W Van Buren St # 203
Chicago IL 60605
847 733-1740

### (G-4898)
### FUTURO FOODS INC
3848 N Pioneer Ave (60634-2048)
**PHONE**.................................773 418-2720
Omar Segovia, *Principal*
**EMP:** 3
**SALES (est):** 186.1K **Privately Held**
**SIC:** 2099 Food preparations

### (G-4899)
### G B HOLDINGS INC
600 N Kilbourn Ave (60624-1041)
**PHONE**.................................773 265-3000
Dennis Greenspon, *President*
Steve Greenspon, *Vice Pres*
Lawrence Greenspon, *Treasurer*
David Pollens, *VP Finance*
**EMP:** 117
**SQ FT:** 150,000
**SALES (est):** 13.8MM **Privately Held**
**SIC:** 3432 Plumbing fixture fittings & trim

### (G-4900)
### G E MATHIS COMPANY
6100 S Oak Park Ave (60638-4014)
**PHONE**.................................773 586-3800
**Fax:** 773 586-0070
Lael Mathis, *President*
Craig Mathis, *Vice Pres*
Paul Mathis, *Vice Pres*
James Wright, *Plant Mgr*
Don Umbriaco, *Project Mgr*
▲ **EMP:** 96 **EST:** 1905
**SQ FT:** 125,000
**SALES (est):** 37MM **Privately Held**
**WEB:** www.gemathis.com
**SIC:** 3443 Fabricated plate work (boiler shop)

### (G-4901)
### G I A PUBLICATIONS INC (PA)
7404 S Mason Ave (60638-6230)
**PHONE**.................................708 496-3800
**Fax:** 708 496-2130
Edward J Harris, *CEO*
Alexander Harris, *President*
Gladys Guerrero, *General Mgr*
Clarence Reiels, *Editor*
Rett Richards, *Editor*
▲ **EMP:** 48
**SQ FT:** 50,000
**SALES (est):** 7.2MM **Privately Held**
**WEB:** www.giamusic.com
**SIC:** 2741 Music books: publishing & printing; music, sheet: publishing & printing

### (G-4902)
### G Y INDUSTRIES LLC
70 W Madison St Ste 2300 (60602-4250)
**PHONE**.................................708 210-1300
**Fax:** 708 210-0808
Bill Dustin,
**EMP:** 12 **EST:** 2000
**SQ FT:** 28,000
**SALES (est):** 1.6MM **Privately Held**
**WEB:** www.fsgcrest.com
**SIC:** 2759 Letterpress & screen printing

### (G-4903)
### G&E TRANSPORTATION INC (HQ)
Also Called: GE Transportation
500 W Monroe St (60661-3671)
**PHONE**.................................404 350-6497

# Chicago - Cook County (G-4904)

Fax: 312 621-6504
Gheorghe Ioan Tomsa, *President*
Jonathan Nolfi, *Manager*
Elena Tomsa, *Admin Sec*
**EMP:** 22
**SALES (est):** 6.3MM
**SALES (corp-wide):** 123.6B **Publicly Held**
**SIC: 1381** 3743 8742 Drilling oil & gas wells; locomotives & parts; transportation consultant
**PA:** General Electric Company
41 Farnsworth St
Boston MA 02210
617 443-3000

*(G-4904)*
## G2 CROWD INC
Also Called: G2 Labs
20 N Wacker Dr Ste 1800 (60606-2905)
**PHONE**..................847 748-7559
Godard Abel, *CEO*
Adrienne Weissman, *Chief Mktg Ofcr*
**EMP:** 12
**SQ FT:** 1,600
**SALES (est):** 1.2MM **Privately Held**
**SIC: 7372** 7371 5045 Business oriented computer software; computer software development & applications; computer software

*(G-4905)*
## GABEL & SCHUBERT BRONZE
4500 N Ravenswood Ave (60640-5202)
**PHONE**..................773 878-6800
Thomas A Hillis, *President*
**EMP:** 12 **EST:** 1973
**SQ FT:** 11,000
**SALES:** 1.1MM **Privately Held**
**WEB:** www.gabelandschubert.com
**SIC: 3993** 3999 Name plates: except engraved, etched, etc.: metal; plaques, picture, laminated

*(G-4906)*
## GABRIEL ENTERPRISES
1734 W North Ave (60622-2147)
**PHONE**..................773 342-8705
Poothakalil M Gabriel, *President*
Saramma Gabriel, *Corp Secy*
**EMP:** 4 **EST:** 1974
**SQ FT:** 6,000
**SALES:** 280K **Privately Held**
**SIC: 5136** 5099 2396 Men's & boys' clothing; hats, men's & boys'; cases, carrying; automotive & apparel trimmings

*(G-4907)*
## GADGETWORLD ENTERPRISES INC
10956 S Western Ave (60643-3234)
**PHONE**..................773 703-0796
James Grider, *CEO*
Sheila Edwards, *Vice Pres*
Erica Edwards, *Opers Dir*
**EMP:** 5
**SQ FT:** 10,000
**SALES (est):** 200K **Privately Held**
**SIC: 2051** Bakery: wholesale or wholesale/retail combined

*(G-4908)*
## GALAXY EMBROIDERY INC
1211 S Western Ave (60608-1151)
**PHONE**..................312 243-8991
Gabriel Arcos, *President*
Teresa Galvin, *Vice Pres*
**EMP:** 3 **EST:** 2006
**SALES (est):** 253K **Privately Held**
**SIC: 2395** Embroidery & art needlework

*(G-4909)*
## GALLAS LABEL & DECAL
Also Called: Andrews Decal & Label Company
6559 N Avondale Ave (60631-1521)
**PHONE**..................773 775-1000
Fax: 773 775-1001
Gary Gallas, *President*
**EMP:** 10 **EST:** 1946
**SQ FT:** 16,000

**SALES (est):** 1.9MM **Privately Held**
**WEB:** www.andrewsdecal.com
**SIC: 2752** 2759 2672 Commercial printing, lithographic; transfers, decalcomania or dry: lithographed; letterpress printing; flexographic printing; screen printing; coated & laminated paper

*(G-4910)*
## GALLERIA RETAIL TECH SOLUTIONS
401 N Michigan Ave (60611-4255)
**PHONE**..................312 822-3437
Peter Lee, *Principal*
Steve Richards, *Manager*
**EMP:** 10
**SALES (corp-wide):** 5.4MM **Privately Held**
**WEB:** www.galleria-rts.com
**SIC: 7372** Prepackaged software
**HQ:** Relex Solutions Uk Limited
Brundrett House
Stoke-On-Trent STAFFS ST7 2

*(G-4911)*
## GALLOY AND VAN ETTEN INC (PA)
11756 S Halsted St (60628-5823)
P.O. Box 288145 (60628-8145)
**PHONE**..................773 928-4800
Fax: 773 928-4129
Bernard Vanetten Jr, *President*
John Vanetten, *Corp Secy*
**EMP:** 27 **EST:** 1899
**SQ FT:** 20,000
**SALES (est):** 7.9MM **Privately Held**
**WEB:** www.galloyvanetten.com
**SIC: 5032** 1741 3281 Stone, crushed or broken; marble building stone; marble masonry, exterior construction; cut stone & stone products

*(G-4912)*
## GAMESTOP INC
800 N Kedzie Ave (60651-4100)
**PHONE**..................773 568-0457
Robert Alan Lloyd, *Vice Pres*
**EMP:** 7
**SALES (corp-wide):** 8.6B **Publicly Held**
**SIC: 5945** 5092 3944 Hobby, toy & game shops; video games; video game machines, except coin-operated
**HQ:** Gamestop, Inc.
625 Westport Pkwy
Grapevine TX 76051

*(G-4913)*
## GAMESTOP CORP
3951 N Broadway St (60613-3039)
**PHONE**..................773 545-9602
Julian Paul Raines, *CEO*
**EMP:** 5
**SALES (corp-wide):** 8.6B **Publicly Held**
**SIC: 5945** 5092 3944 Hobby, toy & game shops; video games; video game machines, except coin-operated
**PA:** Gamestop Corp.
625 Westport Pkwy
Grapevine TX 76051
817 424-2000

*(G-4914)*
## GANJI KLAMES
Also Called: Babylon Travel & Tour Service
3418 W Bryn Mawr Ave (60659-3410)
**PHONE**..................773 478-9000
Klames Ganji, *Owner*
**EMP:** 4
**SQ FT:** 1,000
**SALES (est):** 158.5K **Privately Held**
**SIC: 2711** 4724 Newspapers, publishing & printing; tourist agency arranging transport, lodging & car rental

*(G-4915)*
## GANNETT SATELLITE INFO NETWRK
225 N Michigan Ave # 1600 (60601-7757)
**PHONE**..................312 216-1407
Gracia Martore, *CEO*
**EMP:** 5
**SALES (est):** 237.1K **Privately Held**
**SIC: 2711** Newspapers, publishing & printing

*(G-4916)*
## GAST MONUMENTS INC (PA)
1900 W Peterson Ave (60660-3111)
**PHONE**..................773 262-2400
Fax: 773 262-7400
Tom Gast, *Manager*
James Gast, *Director*
John Gast, *Director*
**EMP:** 7
**SQ FT:** 5,000
**SALES (est):** 1MM **Privately Held**
**SIC: 5999** 3281 Monuments, finished to custom order; cut stone & stone products

*(G-4917)*
## GATEWAY CONSTRUCTION COMPANY
Also Called: Gateway Erectors
2723 E Hammond Ave (60633-2053)
**PHONE**..................708 868-2926
Fax: 708 868-1438
Kenneth Crowell, *Branch Mgr*
**EMP:** 50
**SALES (corp-wide):** 20.1MM **Privately Held**
**SIC: 3496** Concrete reinforcing mesh & wire
**PA:** Gateway Construction Company Inc
3150 W Hirsch St
Melrose Park IL
708 344-1444

*(G-4918)*
## GATORADE COMPANY (DH)
555 W Monroe St Fl 1 (60661-3700)
**PHONE**..................312 821-1000
Charles I Maniscalco, *President*
Carla Hassan, *Vice Pres*
Victoria Ingram, *Vice Pres*
Eric Wenner, *Research*
Mary Doherty, *Comms Dir*
▼ **EMP:** 1200
**SQ FT:** 300,000
**SALES (est):** 165.5MM
**SALES (corp-wide):** 62.8B **Publicly Held**
**WEB:** www.gatorade.com
**SIC: 2086** 5149 Bottled & canned soft drinks; beverages, except coffee & tea
**HQ:** The Quaker Oats Company
555 W Monroe St Fl 1
Chicago IL 60661
312 821-1000

*(G-4919)*
## GATTO INDUSTRIAL PLATERS INC
4620 W Roosevelt Rd (60644-1430)
**PHONE**..................773 287-0100
Fax: 773 287-6047
George Gatto, *President*
Juan Arroyo, *COO*
Robert N Swanson, *Vice Pres*
Andy Gruda, *QC Mgr*
Dominick Gatto, *Treasurer*
**EMP:** 185
**SQ FT:** 211,000
**SALES (est):** 26.2MM **Privately Held**
**WEB:** www.gattoplaters.com
**SIC: 3471** Finishing, metals or formed products

*(G-4920)*
## GAW-OHARA ENVELOPE CO (PA)
500 N Sacramento Blvd (60612-1024)
P.O. Box 325, Western Springs (60558-0325)
**PHONE**..................773 638-1200
**EMP:** 40 **EST:** 1913
**SQ FT:** 70,000
**SALES (est):** 28.4MM **Privately Held**
**SIC: 2677** Mfg Envelopes

*(G-4921)*
## GBN NAILS LLC
1822 W 95th St (60643-1104)
**PHONE**..................773 881-8880
Trang Le,
**EMP:** 5
**SALES:** 300K **Privately Held**
**WEB:** www.gbn2000.com
**SIC: 3999** 7231 Fingernails, artificial; beauty shops

*(G-4922)*
## GELSCRUBS
1100 W Cermak Rd Ste B501 (60608-4688)
**PHONE**..................312 243-4612
Dave Hunt, *Manager*
▲ **EMP:** 2
**SALES (est):** 262.1K **Privately Held**
**SIC: 2326** Medical & hospital uniforms, men's

*(G-4923)*
## GEM ACQUISITION COMPANY INC
Also Called: Gem Business Forms
5942 S Central Ave (60638-3711)
**PHONE**..................773 735-3300
Fax: 773 735-4626
Katharine Owens, *President*
Christopher J Owens, *Vice Pres*
**EMP:** 15 **EST:** 1940
**SQ FT:** 13,000
**SALES (est):** 1.4MM **Privately Held**
**SIC: 2761** Manifold business forms

*(G-4924)*
## GEMA INC (PA)
Also Called: Ballert Orthopedic of Chicago
2434 W Peterson Ave (60659-4113)
**PHONE**..................773 508-6690
Fax: 773 878-6603
Gene P Bernardoni, *President*
Mary Evans, *Marketing Staff*
Carlos A Carmona, *Director*
Mark Edelheit, *Admin Sec*
**EMP:** 7
**SALES:** 5MM **Privately Held**
**SIC: 3842** 5047 3841 Surgical appliances & supplies; artificial limbs; surgical & medical instruments

*(G-4925)*
## GENERAL DESIGN JEWELERS INC
5 S Wabash Ave Ste 217 (60603-3522)
**PHONE**..................312 201-9047
Fax: 312 201-0589
Arturo Tobias, *President*
Jose Tobias, *Vice Pres*
**EMP:** 7
**SQ FT:** 3,200
**SALES (est):** 1MM **Privately Held**
**SIC: 3911** Jewelry, precious metal

*(G-4926)*
## GENERAL DYNAMICS ADV INF SYS
50 S La Salle St (60603-1008)
**PHONE**..................703 876-3000
**EMP:** 151
**SALES (corp-wide):** 31.3B **Publicly Held**
**SIC: 3571** Electronic computers
**HQ:** General Dynamics Mission Systems, Inc
12450 Fair Lakes Cir # 800
Fairfax VA 22033
703 263-2800

*(G-4927)*
## GENERAL MACHINE & TL WORKS INC
313 W Chestnut St (60610-3093)
**PHONE**..................312 337-2177
Fax: 312 337-0244
Julius G Howard Jr, *President*
William J Howard, *Vice Pres*
**EMP:** 10
**SQ FT:** 12,500
**SALES:** 2MM **Privately Held**
**SIC: 3599** Machine & other job shop work

*(G-4928)*
## GENERAL MACHINERY & MFG CO
Also Called: Gmmco
2634 N Keeler Ave (60639-2169)
**PHONE**..................773 235-3700
Fax: 773 235-3786
Eric Junkunc, *President*
Noel Junkunc, *Treasurer*
Kiven Curth, *Manager*
Katryzna Gladys, *Manager*
Kevin Curth, *Admin Sec*
**EMP:** 15 **EST:** 1918

# GEOGRAPHIC SECTION

Chicago - Cook County (G-4957)

SQ FT: 20,000
SALES: 12MM  Privately Held
WEB: www.gmmco.com
SIC: 3724  3429  3544  3469  Aircraft engines & engine parts; casket hardware; special dies, tools, jigs & fixtures; metal stampings; sheet metalwork

**(G-4929)**
**GENERAL PACKAGING PRODUCTS INC**
1700 S Canal St  (60616-1108)
PHONE.................................312 226-5611
Fax: 312 226-4027
Bill Troth, *Exec VP*
Jerry Guthrie, *Vice Pres*
Mark Mehring, *Controller*
Debbie Sands, *Cust Mgr*
Dick Bell, *Manager*
▲ EMP: 90  EST: 1932
SQ FT: 51,000
SALES (est): 20MM
SALES (corp-wide): 2.2B  Publicly Held
WEB: www.generalpk.com
SIC: 2754  2671  2759  Rotogravure printing; packaging paper & plastics film, coated & laminated; paper coated or laminated for packaging; flexographic printing
HQ: Packaging Dynamics Corporation
3900 W 43rd St
Chicago IL 60632
773 254-8000

**(G-4930)**
**GENERAL PALLET**
13513 S Calumet Ave  (60827-1834)
PHONE.................................773 660-8550
Hermen Delgado, *Owner*
EMP: 3
SALES (est): 180K  Privately Held
SIC: 2448  Pallets, wood & wood with metal

**(G-4931)**
**GENERAL PRESS COLORS LTD**
53 W Jackson Blvd # 1115  (60604-3566)
PHONE.................................630 543-7878
Fax: 630 543-4657
Casimir J Grabacki, *CEO*
Richard J Kuebel, *President*
Andrew S Grabacki, *Vice Pres*
Gregory C Grabacki, *Vice Pres*
▲ EMP: 50
SQ FT: 40,000
SALES (est): 11.8MM  Privately Held
WEB: www.gpclflush.com
SIC: 2865  Color pigments, organic

**(G-4932)**
**GENERAL PRODUCTS**
Also Called: G P Albums
4045 N Rockwell St  (60618-3797)
PHONE.................................773 463-2424
Fax: 773 463-3028
Raymond Kalwajtys, *General Mgr*
Arlene Newburn, *CFO*
Anne Henning, *Marketing Mgr*
Ronald Kalwajtys, *Mng Member*
Vic Kalwajtis, *Manager*
▲ EMP: 28  EST: 1934
SQ FT: 70,000
SALES (est): 3.9MM  Privately Held
WEB: www.gpalbums.com
SIC: 2782  Scrapbooks, albums & diaries; albums

**(G-4933)**
**GENERAL SURFACE HARDENING (PA)**
2108 W Fulton St  (60612-2314)
PHONE.................................312 226-5472
Fax: 312 226-0243
Stanley Peebles, *President*
Kerrie Padua, *Office Mgr*
EMP: 30
SQ FT: 12,500
SALES (est): 3.8MM  Privately Held
WEB: www.gshinc.net
SIC: 3398  Metal heat treating

**(G-4934)**
**GENESIS COMICS GROUP**
2631 S Ind Ave Apt 1410  (60616)
PHONE.................................312 544-7473
Samuel L Gilbert, *Owner*
EMP: 4

SALES (est): 237.4K  Privately Held
SIC: 2721  Comic books: publishing & printing

**(G-4935)**
**GENESIS PRINT & COPY SVCS INC**
8319 S Stony Island Ave  (60617-1758)
PHONE.................................773 374-1020
Frankie Payne, *CEO*
EMP: 4
SALES (est): 375.3K  Privately Held
SIC: 2759  Commercial printing

**(G-4936)**
**GENEVA WOOD FUELS LLC**
2550 N Lakeview Ave S2206  (60614-8368)
PHONE.................................773 296-0700
Jonathan Kahn,
EMP: 21
SALES (est): 2.2MM  Privately Held
SIC: 2493  Reconstituted wood products

**(G-4937)**
**GENTNER FABRICATION INC**
2847 W 47th Pl  (60632-2030)
PHONE.................................773 523-2505
Fax: 773 523-2515
Christopher Gentner, *President*
EMP: 12
SALES (est): 1.4MM  Privately Held
SIC: 3441  Fabricated structural metal

**(G-4938)**
**GENUINE PARTS COMPANY**
Also Called: NAPA Auto Parts
1225 W Roosevelt Rd  (60608)
PHONE.................................630 293-1300
Cliff Watts, *Manager*
EMP: 13
SALES (corp-wide): 15.3B  Publicly Held
WEB: www.genpt.com
SIC: 5531  3714  5013  Automobile & truck equipment & parts; motor vehicle parts & accessories; automotive supplies & parts
PA: Genuine Parts Company
2999 Wildwood Pkwy
Atlanta GA 30339
770 953-1700

**(G-4939)**
**GENUINE SCOOTERS LLC**
2700 W Grand Ave  (60612-1118)
PHONE.................................773 271-8514
Fax: 773 271-8518
Mary Lindberg, *Opers Mgr*
Massimo Cippoleta, *Parts Mgr*
Carolyn Meyer, *Sales Mgr*
Dean Christofano, *Manager*
Zac Compton, *Manager*
▲ EMP: 8
SALES (est): 5.4MM  Privately Held
WEB: www.genuinescooters.com
SIC: 3751  Motor scooters & parts

**(G-4940)**
**GEOKAT GRANITE**
4460 W Lexington St  (60624-3427)
PHONE.................................773 265-1423
Fax: 773 265-1442
George Pantelic, *Owner*
▲ EMP: 5
SALES (est): 537.7K  Privately Held
WEB: www.geokatgranite.com
SIC: 3281  Granite, cut & shaped

**(G-4941)**
**GEORG JENSEN INC**
959 N Michigan Ave  (60611-1304)
PHONE.................................312 642-9160
Fax: 312 642-4016
David Chu, *CEO*
EMP: 4
SALES (corp-wide): 120.5K  Privately Held
SIC: 5719  5944  3911  China; silverware; jewelry apparel
HQ: Georg Jensen Inc
580 Broadway Rm 506
New York NY 10012
212 850-9830

**(G-4942)**
**GEORGE ERCKMAN JEWELERS**
55 E Washington St # 807  (60602-2680)
PHONE.................................312 263-7380

Linda Erckman, *Owner*
EMP: 6
SQ FT: 600
SALES (est): 520K  Privately Held
SIC: 3911  Jewelry, precious metal

**(G-4943)**
**GEORGE LAUTERER CORPORATION**
Also Called: Geo Lauterer
310 S Racine Ave  (60607-2841)
PHONE.................................312 913-1881
Fax: 312 913-1811
Earl Joyce, *CEO*
John Joyce, *Vice Pres*
Patrick Joyce, *Vice Pres*
EMP: 30  EST: 1881
SQ FT: 10,000
SALES (est): 2.5MM  Privately Held
SIC: 2399  5199  7389  3993  Flags, fabric; banners, made from fabric; pennants; emblems, badges & insignia: from purchased materials; gifts & novelties; engraving service; signs & advertising specialties; automotive & apparel trimmings

**(G-4944)**
**GEORGE NOTTOLI & SONS INC**
Also Called: Original Nottoli & Sons
7652 W Belmont Ave  (60634-3110)
PHONE.................................773 589-1010
George A Nottoli, *President*
Loretta Nottoli, *Treasurer*
EMP: 5
SQ FT: 2,000
SALES (est): 640K  Privately Held
WEB: www.nottoli.com
SIC: 2013  5411  Sausages & other prepared meats; grocery stores, independent

**(G-4945)**
**GEORGE S MUSIC ROOM**
5700 S Cicero Ave Ste 59  (60638-3843)
PHONE.................................773 767-4676
George Daniel, *Owner*
EMP: 5
SALES (est): 376.3K  Privately Held
SIC: 2782  Record albums

**(G-4946)**
**GEORGIES GREEK TASTY FOOD INC**
2527 W Carmen Ave  (60625-2607)
PHONE.................................773 987-1298
Georgia Orr, *Principal*
EMP: 3
SALES (est): 158.6K  Privately Held
SIC: 2099  Food preparations

**(G-4947)**
**GERARDO AND QUINTANA AUTO ELC**
4034 W 63rd St  (60629-4639)
PHONE.................................773 424-0634
Rosa Quintana, *President*
EMP: 4
SALES (est): 232K  Privately Held
SIC: 3699  7538  7539  Electrical equipment & supplies; general automotive repair shops; automotive repair shops

**(G-4948)**
**GERMAN AMERICAN NAT CONGRESS (PA)**
4740 N Western Ave Fl 2  (60625-2013)
PHONE.................................773 561-9181
Fax: 773 561-9207
Beverly Pochatko, *President*
EMP: 2
SQ FT: 500
SALES: 511.6K  Privately Held
SIC: 8641  2711  Social club, membership; newspapers: publishing only, not printed on site

**(G-4949)**
**GF PARENT LLC (PA)**
676 N Michigan Ave  (60611-2883)
PHONE.................................312 255-4800
Eric Beringause, *CEO*
EMP: 2
SQ FT: 30,000
SALES (est): 597.8K  Privately Held
SIC: 2022  5451  Mfg Cheese Ret Dairy Products

**(G-4950)**
**GIANT GLOBES INC**
4433 W Montana St  (60639-1915)
PHONE.................................773 772-2917
Eugene Protas, *Principal*
EMP: 2
SALES (est): 220.4K  Privately Held
SIC: 3542  Bending machines

**(G-4951)**
**GIBA ELECTRIC**
4054 W Warwick Ave  (60641-3142)
PHONE.................................773 685-4420
EMP: 2  EST: 2008
SALES (est): 200K  Privately Held
SIC: 3699  Mfg Electrical Equipment/Supplies

**(G-4952)**
**GILBERT SPRING CORPORATION**
2301 N Knox Ave  (60639-3415)
PHONE.................................773 486-6030
Fax: 773 486-5402
Anthony E Indihar Jr, *President*
Patricia Indihar, *Vice Pres*
▲ EMP: 30
SQ FT: 23,000
SALES (est): 5.5MM  Privately Held
SIC: 3469  3493  Stamping metal for the trade; torsion bar springs

**(G-4953)**
**GL LED LLC** ✪
Also Called: Led Signs Led Lighting
501 W 18th St  (60616-1147)
PHONE.................................312 600-9363
Ate Guo, *Mng Member*
EMP: 5  EST: 2016
SALES (est): 50.6K  Privately Held
SIC: 3993  Signs & advertising specialties

**(G-4954)**
**GLASS CONCEPTS LLC**
1956 W 17th St  (60608-1902)
PHONE.................................773 650-0520
Dominic Hernandez, *Sr Project Mgr*
Sean McEneaney,
EMP: 13
SALES (est): 2MM  Privately Held
SIC: 3231  Doors, glass: made from purchased glass

**(G-4955)**
**GLENMARK INDUSTRIES LTD**
4545 S Racine Ave Ste 1  (60609-3384)
PHONE.................................773 927-4800
Fax: 773 847-2946
Dave Van Kampen, *President*
John Dobias, *Opers Staff*
Dominic Pinto, *Purchasing*
Dominick Pinto, *Purchasing*
Sharon Birkett, *QC Dir*
EMP: 250
SQ FT: 50,000
SALES (est): 65MM  Privately Held
SIC: 2013  Sausages & other prepared meats

**(G-4956)**
**GLENVIEW PHARMA INC**
6404 N Fairfield Ave  (60645-5211)
PHONE.................................773 856-3205
Aakash Ray, *Agent*
EMP: 10
SALES (est): 740K  Privately Held
SIC: 2834  Druggists' preparations (pharmaceuticals)

**(G-4957)**
**GLOBAL CONTRACT MFG INC**
Also Called: Gcm
156 N Jefferson St # 300  (60661-1411)
PHONE.................................312 432-6200
Robert Wolters Jr, *President*
Danielle Wolters, *Corp Secy*
▲ EMP: 2  EST: 1994
SALES (est): 235.9K  Privately Held
WEB: www.gcmusa.com
SIC: 3089  3631  Plastic kitchenware, tableware & houseware; household cooking equipment

# Chicago - Cook County (G-4958)  GEOGRAPHIC SECTION

**(G-4958)**
**GLOBAL MATERIAL TECH INC**
Also Called: Rhodes/American
2825 W 31st St (60623-5102)
PHONE.............................773 247-6000
Fax: 773 247-8343
Alex Krupnik, *Principal*
Steve Bouse, *Business Mgr*
Ed Jones, *Vice Pres*
Yury Grinberg, *Electrical Engi*
Michael Carr, *MIS Mgr*
**EMP:** 120
**SALES (corp-wide):** 95.6MM **Privately Held**
**WEB:** www.gmt-inc.com
**SIC: 3291** 5198 Aluminum oxide (fused) abrasives; paints, varnishes & supplies
**PA:** Global Material Technologies, Incorporated
  750 W Lake Cook Rd # 480
  Buffalo Grove IL 60089
  847 495-4700

**(G-4959)**
**GLOBAL PHARMA DEVICE SOLUTIONS**
6454 W 74th St (60638-6009)
PHONE.............................708 212-5801
Mathew Azuh, *President*
Valerie Hart, *Office Mgr*
Norma Guerrero, *Manager*
**EMP:** 4
**SALES (est):** 223.6K **Privately Held**
**SIC: 2834** Pharmaceutical preparations

**(G-4960)**
**GLOBAL TECHNOLOGIES I LLC (PA)**
Also Called: Strateg Telekom
980 N Michigan Ave # 1400 (60611-7500)
PHONE.............................312 255-8350
Joseph Machulla, *President*
**EMP:** 56
**SQ FT:** 14,000
**SALES (est):** 11.3MM **Privately Held**
**SIC: 1731** 1041 4813 4789 Energy management controls; underground gold mining; telephone communication, except radio; cargo loading & unloading services; underground iron ore mining; electronic media advertising representatives

**(G-4961)**
**GLOBAL TELEPHONY MAGAZINE**
330 N Wabash Ave Ste 2300 (60611-7619)
PHONE.............................312 840-8405
CAM Bishop, *President*
**EMP:** 45
**SALES (est):** 2.1MM
**SALES (corp-wide):** 8.4MM **Privately Held**
**WEB:** www.globalepoint.com
**SIC: 2721** Periodicals
**PA:** Global Epoint, Inc.
  339 Cheryl Ln
  City Of Industry CA 91789
  909 598-6588

**(G-4962)**
**GLUE INC**
5701 N Sheridan Rd Apt 4m (60660-4793)
PHONE.............................312 451-4018
Craig Easly, *Principal*
**EMP:** 3
**SALES (est):** 135.6K **Privately Held**
**SIC: 2891** Adhesives & sealants

**(G-4963)**
**GM CASTING HOUSE INC**
5 S Wabash Ave Ste 614 (60603-3291)
PHONE.............................312 782-7160
Bernie Czerwinski, *President*
Jason Borgstahl, *Principal*
Justin Shelby, *Admin Sec*
**EMP:** 12 **EST:** 2003
**SALES (est):** 1.5MM **Privately Held**
**SIC: 3364** Nonferrous die-castings except aluminum

**(G-4964)**
**GMD MOBILE PRESSURE WSHG SVCS**
539 N Saint Louis Ave (60624-1352)
PHONE.............................773 826-1903
Dwain Williamson, *Principal*
**EMP:** 3
**SALES (est):** 120.3K **Privately Held**
**SIC: 2711** Newspapers, publishing & printing

**(G-4965)**
**GMI PACKAGING CO**
1600 E 122nd St (60633-2359)
PHONE.............................734 972-7389
Joyce Mueller, *President*
**EMP:** 30
**SALES (corp-wide):** 1.5MM **Privately Held**
**SIC: 3535** Bulk handling conveyor systems
**PA:** Gmi Packaging Co.
  1371 Centennial Ln
  Ann Arbor MI 48103
  734 972-7389

**(G-4966)**
**GMM HOLDINGS LLC**
175 E Delaware Pl Unit 6 (60611-1756)
PHONE.............................312 255-9830
Raymond Chung, *General Mgr*
Ravin Gandhi, *Mng Member*
**EMP:** 10 **EST:** 2007
**SQ FT:** 3,500
**SALES (est):** 10MM **Privately Held**
**SIC: 2819** Catalysts, chemical

**(G-4967)**
**GODBEY INDUSTRIES**
4417 N Hermitage Ave (60640-5301)
PHONE.............................773 769-4391
Charles Godbey, *Owner*
**EMP:** 3
**SALES (est):** 105.9K **Privately Held**
**SIC: 3999** Manufacturing industries

**(G-4968)**
**GODIVA CHOCOLATIER INC**
845 N Michigan Ave Fl 4 (60611-2252)
PHONE.............................312 280-1133
Laurie Vaquera, *Manager*
**EMP:** 16 **Privately Held**
**WEB:** www.godiva.com
**SIC: 2066** Chocolate
**HQ:** Godiva Chocolatier, Inc.
  333 W 34th St Fl 6
  New York NY 10001
  212 984-5900

**(G-4969)**
**GOEDUCATION LLC**
Also Called: Conferences I/O
321 N Clark St Ste 2550 (60654-4754)
PHONE.............................312 800-1838
John Pytel, *General Mgr*
Megan Lehrman, *Vice Pres*
Marisa Wolf, *Exec Dir*
Thomas Dickson, *Director*
Brynne Mancuso, *Director*
**EMP:** 5
**SQ FT:** 200
**SALES (est):** 306K **Privately Held**
**SIC: 7372** Educational computer software

**(G-4970)**
**GOGO LLC (DH)**
111 N Canal St Fl 15 (60606-7205)
PHONE.............................630 647-1400
Michael J Small, *President*
Tim Twohig, *Partner*
Margee Elias, *Exec VP*
Anand K Chari, *Exec VP*
Ash A Eldifrawi, *Exec VP*
**EMP:** 448
**SQ FT:** 55,000
**SALES (est):** 259.7MM
**SALES (corp-wide):** 596.5MM **Publicly Held**
**WEB:** www.aircell.com
**SIC: 3663** 4812 4813 4899 Radio & TV communications equipment; cellular radio telephone; cellular telephone services; telephone communication, except radio; data communication services
**HQ:** Gogo Intermediate Holdings Llc
  1250 N Arlington Rd
  Itasca IL 60143
  630 647-1400

**(G-4971)**
**GOLD STANDARD BAKING INC (PA)**
3700 S Kedzie Ave (60632-2768)
PHONE.............................773 523-2333
Fax: 773 523-7381
Yianny Caparos, *President*
Constantin Caparos, *General Mgr*
Connie Holston, *Business Mgr*
Jill Lecroy, *Business Mgr*
Alex Salgado, *Plant Mgr*
**EMP:** 146
**SQ FT:** 150,000
**SALES (est):** 57.2MM **Privately Held**
**WEB:** www.gsbaking.com
**SIC: 2051** Bakery: wholesale or wholesale/retail combined

**(G-4972)**
**GOLDA HOUSE**
3128 W 41st St (60632-2428)
PHONE.............................773 927-0140
**EMP:** 4 **EST:** 2001
**SALES (est):** 160K **Privately Held**
**SIC: 2711** Newspapers-Publishing/Printing

**(G-4973)**
**GOLDEN DRAGON FORTUNE COOKIES**
2323 S Archer Ave (60616-1828)
PHONE.............................312 842-8199
Fax: 312 842-0090
Shing K Tom, *President*
Kean Tom, *Vice Pres*
Michael Tom, *Vice Pres*
Choi Kam Tom, *Treasurer*
Dorothy Lee, *Manager*
**EMP:** 10
**SQ FT:** 25,000
**SALES (est):** 958.4K **Privately Held**
**SIC: 2052** Cookies

**(G-4974)**
**GOLDEN HILL INGREDIENTS LLC**
851 W Grand Ave (60642-6564)
PHONE.............................773 406-3409
▲ **EMP:** 3
**SALES (est):** 5MM **Privately Held**
**SIC: 2099** Rice, uncooked: packaged with other ingredients

**(G-4975)**
**GOLDFISH SWIM SCHOOL LINCOLN**
Also Called: Goldfish Swim Schl Roskow Vlg
2630 W Bradley Pl (60618-4704)
PHONE.............................773 588-7946
Robert Ryan, *Mng Member*
Kathy Ryan, *Mng Member*
**EMP:** 30
**SALES (est):** 2.7MM **Privately Held**
**SIC: 2369** Bathing suits & swimwear: girls', children's & infants'

**(G-4976)**
**GOLFCO INC**
Also Called: Delta Golf
4727 W Montrose Ave (60641-1504)
P.O. Box 21, Golf (60029-0021)
PHONE.............................773 777-7877
Fax: 773 777-6543
Joseph R Morisco, *President*
▲ **EMP:** 20
**SQ FT:** 35,000
**SALES (est):** 2.1MM **Privately Held**
**SIC: 3949** Shafts, golf club

**(G-4977)**
**GOOD WORLD NOODLE INC**
2522 S Halsted St (60608-5931)
PHONE.............................312 326-0441
Miu Ching Lam, *President*
Yuk Lem, *Admin Sec*
**EMP:** 4
**SALES (est):** 300.9K **Privately Held**
**SIC: 2099** Noodles, uncooked: packaged with other ingredients

**(G-4978)**
**GOODMAN DISTRIBUTION INC**
815 W Pershing Rd Ste C (60609-1405)
PHONE.............................773 376-8214
Dott Templeton, *Branch Mgr*
**EMP:** 6
**SALES (corp-wide):** 17.9B **Privately Held**
**SIC: 3567** Heating units & devices, industrial: electric
**HQ:** Goodman Distribution, Inc.
  1426 Ne 8th Ave
  Ocala FL 34470
  352 620-2727

**(G-4979)**
**GOOSE HOLDINGS INC**
Also Called: Goose Island Brewer
1800 W Fulton St (60612-2512)
PHONE.............................312 226-1119
John R Hall, *President*
Claudia Jendron, *Manager*
**EMP:** 45
**SALES (est):** 7.3MM **Privately Held**
**WEB:** www.gooseislandbeer.com
**SIC: 2082** 5813 Malt beverages; drinking places
**HQ:** Anheuser-Busch Companies, Llc
  1 Busch Pl
  Saint Louis MO 63118
  314 632-6777

**(G-4980)**
**GORDON CAPLAN INC**
2040 W North Ave (60647-7496)
PHONE.............................773 489-3300
Gordon M Caplan, *President*
**EMP:** 9 **EST:** 1922
**SQ FT:** 45,000
**SALES (est):** 1.1MM **Privately Held**
**SIC: 5112** 5111 2677 2621 Envelopes; fine paper; envelopes; paper mills

**(G-4981)**
**GOURMET GORILLA INC (PA)**
1200 W Cermak Rd (60608-3221)
PHONE.............................877 219-3663
Jason Weedon, *CEO*
Danielle Hrzic, *President*
Jared Jaggers, *Purch Mgr*
Keelia Murphy, *Asst Office Mgr*
**EMP:** 17 **EST:** 2014
**SQ FT:** 24,000
**SALES:** 4.4MM **Privately Held**
**SIC: 5812** 2099 Caterers; ready-to-eat meals, salads & sandwiches

**(G-4982)**
**GRACE ENTERPRISES INC**
2050 W Devon Ave Ste 2 (60659-2231)
PHONE.............................773 465-5300
**EMP:** 26 **Privately Held**
**SIC: 2759** Commercial printing
**PA:** Grace Enterprises, Inc.
  2050 W Devon Ave Ste 2
  Chicago IL 60659

**(G-4983)**
**GRACE ENTERPRISES INC (PA)**
Also Called: Eco Print Mail Consultants
2050 W Devon Ave Ste 2 (60659-2231)
PHONE.............................773 465-5300
K M Eapen, *President*
Ajith Eapen, *Vice Pres*
Bill Grace, *Plant Mgr*
Titus M Eapen, *Admin Sec*
**EMP:** 4
**SQ FT:** 3,500
**SALES:** 3.8MM **Privately Held**
**WEB:** www.keralax.com
**SIC: 2759** Commercial printing

**(G-4984)**
**GRAND PRINTING & GRAPHICS INC**
105 W Madison St Ste 1100 (60602-4600)
PHONE.............................312 218-6780
James Marshall, *President*
Bruce Frentz, *Vice Pres*
James Kellas, *Treasurer*
**EMP:** 12
**SQ FT:** 7,000
**SALES (est):** 1.8MM **Privately Held**
**SIC: 2752** Commercial printing, lithographic

**(G-4985)**
**GRANITE DESIGNS OF ILINOIS**
945 N California Ave (60622-4478)
PHONE.............................773 772-5300
Bart Bysekiwizz, *President*
**EMP:** 8

## GEOGRAPHIC SECTION
## Chicago - Cook County (G-5012)

SALES (est): 970.6K Privately Held
SIC: 3281 Granite, cut & shaped

**(G-4986)**
**GRANITE GALLERY INC**
3430 W Henderson St (60618-5405)
PHONE.....................773 279-9200
Lester Gizynski, *President*
◆ EMP: 3
SALES (est): 267.9K Privately Held
SIC: 3993 5211 Signs & advertising specialties; lumber & other building materials

**(G-4987)**
**GRANJA & SONS PRINTING**
2707 S Pulaski Rd (60623-4412)
PHONE.....................773 762-3840
Fax: 773 277-1346
Ignacio Granja Sr, *Partner*
Agustin Granja, *Partner*
Ignacio Granja Jr, *Partner*
EMP: 10
SQ FT: 5,000
SALES (est): 550K Privately Held
SIC: 2759 2752 Letterpress printing; commercial printing, lithographic

**(G-4988)**
**GRAPHBURY MACHINES LLC**
5800 N Western Ave (60659-5003)
PHONE.....................754 779-4285
Adrina Gutierrez, *Manager*
EMP: 4
SALES (corp-wide): 4.2MM Privately Held
SIC: 3565 Packaging machinery
PA: Graphbury Machines, Llc
610 Baeten Rd Ste 3
Green Bay WI 54304
754 779-4285

**(G-4989)**
**GRAPHIC IMAGE CORPORATION**
Also Called: G I C
2035 W Grand Ave (60612-1501)
PHONE.....................312 829-7800
Fax: 312 829-7900
John Markasovic, *President*
Frank Markosovic, *Vice Pres*
Paula Mark, *Manager*
Louise M Markasovic, *Admin Sec*
EMP: 12
SQ FT: 10,000
SALES (est): 2.4MM Privately Held
SIC: 2752 2796 2791 Commercial printing, lithographic; platemaking services; typesetting

**(G-4990)**
**GRAPHIC PARTS INTL INC**
4321 N Knox Ave (60641-1906)
PHONE.....................773 725-4900
Michael Green, *President*
EMP: 15
SQ FT: 15,000
SALES (est): 3.4MM Privately Held
SIC: 3469 Machine parts, stamped or pressed metal

**(G-4991)**
**GRAPHIC PRESS**
545 N Dearborn St # 3002 (60654-2658)
PHONE.....................312 909-6100
John Semora, *CEO*
EMP: 3
SALES (est): 170K Privately Held
SIC: 2741 Miscellaneous publishing

**(G-4992)**
**GRAPHICS GROUP LLC**
4600 N Olcott Ave (60706-4604)
PHONE.....................708 867-5500
Bill Stout, *President*
Paul Milewski, *Exec VP*
Roxanne Garlinger, *Project Mgr*
Aaron Warner, *Technology*
EMP: 65
SQ FT: 50,000
SALES (est): 322.7K Privately Held
SIC: 2752 2791 2789 2759 Commercial printing, offset; typesetting; bookbinding & related work; commercial printing

**(G-4993)**
**GRAYMON GRAPHICS INC**
4934 S Rockwell St (60632-1431)
PHONE.....................773 737-0176
Martin Moncaba, *President*
EMP: 4
SALES: 250K Privately Held
SIC: 3993 Signs, not made in custom sign painting shops

**(G-4994)**
**GREAT BOOKS FOUNDATION**
233 N Michigan Ave # 420 (60601-2298)
PHONE.....................312 332-5870
Fax: 312 407-0334
Joseph Coulson, *CEO*
Karlo Flowers, *General Mgr*
Jennifer Kleiman, *Editor*
Mary Williams, *Editor*
Mary Sweeton, *Senior VP*
▲ EMP: 31
SQ FT: 12,500
SALES: 4.9MM Privately Held
SIC: 2731 8299 Books: publishing only; educational services

**(G-4995)**
**GREAT DANE LIMITED PARTNERSHIP (HQ)**
Also Called: Great Dane Trailers
222 N Lasalle St Ste 920 (60601)
PHONE.....................773 254-5533
Fax: 773 254-5533
William H Crown, *President*
Sam Gupta, *Vice Pres*
Jean Vapakin, *Engineer*
Adam Sheridan, *Manager*
Michael Molitor, *Associate*
▼ EMP: 100
SALES (est): 513.4MM
SALES (corp-wide): 1.4B Privately Held
WEB: www.greatdanetrailers.com
SIC: 3715 Truck trailers; demountable cargo containers
PA: Henry Crown And Company
222 N La Salle St # 2000
Chicago IL 60601
312 236-6300

**(G-4996)**
**GREAT LAKES ENVMTL MAR DEL**
39 S La Salle St Ste 308 (60603-1603)
PHONE.....................312 332-3377
Fax: 312 332-3379
Paul A Kakuris, *President*
John Swenson, *Admin Sec*
EMP: 3
SQ FT: 600
SALES (est): 274.8K Privately Held
SIC: 3272 8711 Concrete products; marine engineering

**(G-4997)**
**GREAT LAKES FORGE COMPANY**
Also Called: Lock & Roll Trailer Hitch
2141 S Spaulding Ave (60623-3321)
PHONE.....................773 277-2800
Gregory Russell, *President*
Ralph Russell III, *Admin Sec*
EMP: 7
SQ FT: 20,000
SALES: 500K Privately Held
WEB: www.locknroll.com
SIC: 3462 3799 3714 Iron & steel forgings; ornamental metal forgings, ferrous; trailer hitches; trailer hitches, motor vehicle

**(G-4998)**
**GREAT LAKES PACKING CO INTL**
1535 W 43rd St (60609-3329)
PHONE.....................773 927-6660
Fax: 773 927-8587
Robert Oates, *President*
▼ EMP: 6 EST: 1959
SQ FT: 22,000
SALES (est): 670K Privately Held
SIC: 2011 Meat packing plants

**(G-4999)**
**GREAT SOFTWARE LABORATORY INC**
60 E Monroe St Unit 4301 (60603-2765)
PHONE.....................630 655-8905
Sunil Gaitonde, *Principal*
EMP: 5
SALES (est): 450.4K Privately Held
SIC: 7372 Prepackaged software
PA: Great Software Laboratory Private Limited
No.8 Plot No.74-75
Pune MH

**(G-5000)**
**GREATLAKES ARCHITECTURAL MILLW**
2135 W Fulton St (60612-2313)
PHONE.....................312 829-7110
Odonnell Winchester, *Mng Member*
EMP: 24
SQ FT: 3,000
SALES: 6MM Privately Held
SIC: 2426 2431 Carvings, furniture: wood; interior & ornamental woodwork & trim

**(G-5001)**
**GREG EL- INC**
Also Called: El Greg Pizza
6024 N Keystone Ave (60646-5210)
PHONE.....................773 478-9050
Fax: 773 478-9073
Helen Kayaloglou, *President*
John Kay, *Manager*
Gregory Lereno, *Admin Sec*
EMP: 14
SQ FT: 4,000
SALES (est): 2.4MM Privately Held
WEB: www.elgreg.com
SIC: 2038 Frozen specialties

**(G-5002)**
**GREGORY LAMAR & ASSOC INC**
Also Called: Fingers
345 N La Salle Dr # 2103 (60654-6101)
PHONE.....................312 595-1545
Alfred D Gregory, *President*
Edward Lamar, *Vice Pres*
EMP: 2
SQ FT: 1,800
SALES: 400K Privately Held
WEB: www.fingers.net
SIC: 3842 Splints, pneumatic & wood

**(G-5003)**
**GRIFFIN PLATING CO INC**
1636 W Armitage Ave (60622-1203)
PHONE.....................773 342-5181
Dan Griffin, *President*
Tom Griffin, *Vice Pres*
EMP: 9
SALES (est): 250K Privately Held
SIC: 3471 Plating of metals or formed products; polishing, metals or formed products

**(G-5004)**
**GRIFFITH LABORATORIES USA INC**
Innova Flavors
1437 W 37th St (60609-2110)
PHONE.....................773 523-7509
Judy Ambriz, *Buyer*
Dee Sansone, *Purchasing*
Kelly Akel, *Manager*
Mike Scanlan, *Director*
EMP: 40
SALES (corp-wide): 756.3MM Privately Held
SIC: 2034 Dried & dehydrated vegetables
HQ: Griffith Foods Inc.
12200 S Central Ave
Alsip IL 60803
708 371-0900

**(G-5005)**
**GROUP 329 LLC (PA)**
Also Called: Caps Group, The
329 W 18th St Ste 800 (60616-1103)
PHONE.....................312 828-0200
Fax: 312 828-9888
John Reilly,
James Lederer,
Robin Simon,
EMP: 5

SALES (est): 9.1MM Privately Held
SIC: 7389 7336 2791 Design services; graphic arts & related design; typesetting

**(G-5006)**
**GROUPE LACASSE LLC (PA)**
222 Merchandise Mart Plz (60654-1103)
PHONE.....................312 670-9100
Sylvain Garneau, *President*
Rich Blickley, *General Mgr*
Kevin Glynn, *Exec VP*
Carl Nelson, *Accounts Mgr*
Joshua Benton, *Marketing Staff*
▼ EMP: 20 EST: 1981
SALES: 37.3MM Privately Held
SIC: 2522 2521 2512 Desks, office: except wood; chairs, office: padded or plain, except wood; cabinets, office: except wood; bookcases, office: except wood; desks, office: wood; chairs, office: padded, upholstered or plain: wood; cabinets, office: wood; panel systems & partitions (free-standing), office: wood; upholstered household furniture

**(G-5007)**
**GUARDIAN EQUIPMENT INC**
1140 N North Branch St (60642-4201)
PHONE.....................312 447-8100
Steven Kersten, *President*
Mike Adkins, *General Mgr*
Carsten Birch, *General Mgr*
Donald Schoen, *Vice Pres*
Steven Kinate, *Design Engr*
▲ EMP: 30 EST: 1975
SQ FT: 17,000
SALES (est): 6.3MM Privately Held
WEB: www.gesafety.com
SIC: 3842 5084 3432 Surgical appliances & supplies; safety equipment; plumbing fixture fittings & trim

**(G-5008)**
**GUERO PALLETS**
2525 S Rockwell St (60608-4806)
PHONE.....................312 593-4276
Agustin Razo, *President*
EMP: 8
SALES (est): 1.2MM Privately Held
SIC: 2448 Pallets, wood & wood with metal

**(G-5009)**
**GUESS INC**
605 N Michigan Ave # 200 (60611-3115)
PHONE.....................312 440-9592
Armand Marciano, *Principal*
EMP: 25
SALES (corp-wide): 2.2B Publicly Held
SIC: 2325 Men's & boys' jeans & dungarees
PA: Guess, Inc.
1444 S Alameda St
Los Angeles CA 90021
213 765-3100

**(G-5010)**
**GUESS WHACKIT & HOPE INC**
Also Called: Gard, Ron
1883 N Milwaukee Ave (60647-4464)
PHONE.....................773 342-4273
Fax: 773 342-4277
Ronald J Gard, *President*
EMP: 1
SQ FT: 7,000
SALES: 350K Privately Held
SIC: 7922 2511 Scenery design, theatrical; wood household furniture

**(G-5011)**
**GULF COAST SWITCHING CO LLC**
224 S Michigan Ave # 600 (60604-2505)
PHONE.....................312 324-7353
EMP: 3 EST: 2009
SALES (est): 173.7K Privately Held
SIC: 3679 Electronic switches

**(G-5012)**
**GULF PETROLEUM LLC**
71 W Hubbard St Apt 4701 (60654-4629)
PHONE.....................312 803-0373
Kimberly Starks, *CEO*
EMP: 3
SALES (est): 104.3K Privately Held
SIC: 1311 7389 Crude petroleum & natural gas;

# Chicago - Cook County (G-5013) — GEOGRAPHIC SECTION

**(G-5013)**
**GUS BERTHOLD ELECTRIC COMPANY (PA)**
1900 W Carroll Ave (60612-2402)
PHONE..................312 243-5767
Fax: 312 243-5811
Roderick Berthold, *President*
Charles Berthold, *Chairman*
Joseph H Breskovich, *Vice Pres*
Scott Sremaniak, *Engineer*
F Barlstta, *Admin Asst*
▲ **EMP:** 34 **EST:** 1925
**SQ FT:** 30,000
**SALES (est):** 13MM **Privately Held**
**SIC:** 3613 3822 3643 Switchboards & parts, power; switchboard apparatus, except instruments; auto controls regulating residntl & coml environmt & applncs; current-carrying wiring devices

**(G-5014)**
**GYOOD**
2048 W Belmont Ave (60618-6412)
PHONE..................773 360-8810
Sushil H Narsinghani, *Principal*
**EMP:** 4
**SALES (est):** 212.6K **Privately Held**
**SIC:** 2024 Ice cream, bulk

**(G-5015)**
**GYPSOIL PELLETIZED PDTS LLC**
Also Called: Beneficial Reuse Management
372 W Ontario St Ste 501 (60654-5779)
PHONE..................312 784-0300
Robert Spoerri,
**EMP:** 15
**SALES (est):** 771.1K **Privately Held**
**SIC:** 3822 Auto controls regulating residntl & coml environmt & applncs
**PA:** Beneficial Reuse Management Llc
372 W Ontario St Ste 501
Chicago IL 60654

**(G-5016)**
**GYRO PROCESSING INC**
3338 N Ashland Ave (60657-2109)
PHONE..................800 491-0733
Fax: 708 547-7793
Jose Parra, *President*
Ramon Iniguez, *Vice Pres*
Javier Iniguez, *Plant Mgr*
Adriana Samaniego, *MIS Mgr*
**EMP:** 45
**SQ FT:** 39,000
**SALES (est):** 3.9MM **Privately Held**
**SIC:** 3471 Finishing, metals or formed products

**(G-5017)**
**H & B MACHINE CORPORATION**
1943 W Walnut St (60612-2405)
PHONE..................312 829-4850
Fax: 312 829-8451
Philip J Bracht, *President*
Evelyn Bracht, *Corp Secy*
George Bracht, *Vice Pres*
**EMP:** 4
**SQ FT:** 5,000
**SALES (est):** 489.4K **Privately Held**
**WEB:** www.hbmachine.com
**SIC:** 3599 3537 3536 Machine shop, jobbing & repair; industrial trucks & tractors; hoists, cranes & monorails

**(G-5018)**
**H & H FABRIC CUTTERS**
4431 W Rice St (60651-3457)
PHONE..................773 772-1904
Alexandro Herdia, *Owner*
**EMP:** 4
**SALES:** 190K **Privately Held**
**SIC:** 7389 2329 Sewing contractor; riding clothes:, men's, youths' & boys'

**(G-5019)**
**H B PRODUCTS INCORPORATED**
4625 W 63rd St (60629-5504)
PHONE..................773 735-0936
Fax: 773 735-9866
James Hamann, *President*
George Hamann, *Treasurer*
**EMP:** 3 **EST:** 1978
**SQ FT:** 3,500
**SALES:** 550K **Privately Held**
**SIC:** 3599 3544 Machine shop, jobbing & repair; special dies, tools, jigs & fixtures

**(G-5020)**
**H B TAYLOR CO**
4830 S Christiana Ave (60632-3092)
PHONE..................773 254-4805
Fax: 773 254-4563
Saul Juskaitis, *President*
Martin Ives, *Vice Pres*
Jeralyn Kane, *Office Mgr*
**EMP:** 37
**SQ FT:** 25,000
**SALES (est):** 8MM **Privately Held**
**WEB:** www.hbtaylor.com
**SIC:** 2087 Extracts, flavoring; food colorings

**(G-5021)**
**H HAL KRAMER CO**
4318 N Western Ave (60618-1622)
PHONE..................773 539-9648
Helmut H Kramer, *President*
**EMP:** 4
**SQ FT:** 2,200
**SALES (corp-wide):** 200K **Privately Held**
**SIC:** 2679 Wallboard, decorated: made from purchased material
**PA:** H. Hal Kramer Co.
1865 Old Willow Rd # 231
Northfield IL 60093
847 441-0213

**(G-5022)**
**H KRAMER & CO**
1345 W 21st St (60608-3111)
PHONE..................312 226-6600
Fax: 312 226-4713
Howard K Chapman Jr, *President*
Richard Shovan, *Superintendent*
Adam Chapman, *Exec VP*
William O'Brien, *Exec VP*
Brian Wagner, *Exec VP*
▲ **EMP:** 150 **EST:** 1888
**SQ FT:** 125,000
**SALES (est):** 49.6MM **Privately Held**
**WEB:** www.hkramer.net
**SIC:** 3341 Brass smelting & refining (secondary)

**(G-5023)**
**H R SLATER CO INC**
2050 W 18th St (60608-1816)
PHONE..................312 666-1855
Fax: 312 666-1856
Robert Kurzka, *President*
Daniel Moore, *Sales Mgr*
Steven Sporleder, *Manager*
Bill St Hilaire, *Admin Sec*
**EMP:** 11 **EST:** 1920
**SQ FT:** 10,000
**SALES (est):** 2.1MM **Privately Held**
**SIC:** 3545 3555 3537 3423 Machine tool attachments & accessories; printing trades machinery; industrial trucks & tractors; hand & edge tools

**(G-5024)**
**H WATSON JEWELRY CO**
29 E Madison St Ste 1007 (60602-4407)
PHONE..................312 236-1104
Fax: 312 236-5314
James Watson, *Owner*
**EMP:** 4
**SQ FT:** 1,100
**SALES:** 780K **Privately Held**
**SIC:** 3911 5944 Jewelry, precious metal; jewelry, precious stones & precious metals

**(G-5025)**
**H&R BLOCK INC**
Also Called: H & R Block
8065 S Ccero Ave Unit 30b (60652)
PHONE..................773 582-3444
**EMP:** 10
**SALES (corp-wide):** 3B **Publicly Held**
**WEB:** www.hrblock.com
**SIC:** 7291 6794 7372 4822 Tax return preparation services; franchises, selling or licensing; application computer software; electronic mail
**PA:** H&R Block, Inc.
1 H&R Block Way
Kansas City MO 64105
816 854-3000

**(G-5026)**
**HACH COMPANY**
2207 Collection Center Dr (60693-0022)
PHONE..................800 227-4224
**EMP:** 143
**SALES (corp-wide):** 16.8B **Publicly Held**
**SIC:** 3826 Analytical instruments
**HQ:** Hach Company
5600 Lindbergh Dr
Loveland CO 80538
970 669-3050

**(G-5027)**
**HACKETT PRECISION COMPANY INC**
Also Called: Hpc Automation
70 W Madison St Ste 2300 (60602-4250)
PHONE..................615 227-3136
Joel Pepper, *President*
Eric Hender, *Chairman*
Alton Miles, *Vice Pres*
David Schleicher, *Vice Pres*
Rick Barksdale, *Treasurer*
▲ **EMP:** 42
**SQ FT:** 40,000
**SALES (est):** 5.6MM **Privately Held**
**WEB:** www.aavin.com
**SIC:** 3559 Automotive related machinery
**PA:** Aavin Llc
1245 1st Ave Se
Cedar Rapids IA 52402
319 247-1072

**(G-5028)**
**HADLEY GEAR MANUFACTURING CO**
4444 W Roosevelt Rd (60624-3840)
PHONE..................773 722-1030
Fax: 773 722-6570
John Davey, *President*
Dennis Kempski, *Vice Pres*
Harvey Pestine, *Controller*
**EMP:** 17 **EST:** 1950
**SQ FT:** 24,000
**SALES (est):** 3.6MM **Privately Held**
**WEB:** www.hadleygear.com
**SIC:** 3566 3452 3568 3462 Gears, power transmission, except automotive; screws, metal; sprockets (power transmission equipment); iron & steel forgings; nonferrous rolling & drawing

**(G-5029)**
**HAFNER DUPLICATING COMPANY**
601 S La Salle St (60605-1725)
PHONE..................312 362-0120
Michael Shallberg, *Principal*
**EMP:** 3
**SALES (est):** 279.4K **Privately Held**
**SIC:** 3577 Printers & plotters

**(G-5030)**
**HAFNER PRINTING CO INC**
601 S La Salle St Ste 150 (60605-1726)
PHONE..................312 362-0120
Michael Shallberg, *President*
Jan Simonson, *Purchasing*
**EMP:** 10 **EST:** 1987
**SQ FT:** 6,000
**SALES (est):** 1.3MM **Privately Held**
**SIC:** 2752 7334 2759 Commercial printing, offset; photocopying & duplicating services; commercial printing

**(G-5031)**
**HAGGIN MARKETING INC**
Also Called: Chicago Catalog
343 W Erie St Ste 600 (60654-5789)
PHONE..................312 343-2611
Charlene Gervais, *Branch Mgr*
**EMP:** 15
**SALES (corp-wide):** 15.6MM **Privately Held**
**WEB:** www.hagginmarketing.com
**SIC:** 2741 Catalogs: publishing & printing
**PA:** Haggin Marketing, Inc.
100 Shoreline Hwy A200
Mill Valley CA 94941
415 289-1110

**(G-5032)**
**HAIRLINE CREATIONS INC (PA)**
5850 W Montrose Ave 54 (60634-1748)
PHONE..................773 282-5454
Fax: 773 282-5449
Paul Finamore, *President*
Elizabeth Jaskula, *General Mgr*
**EMP:** 15 **EST:** 1963
**SQ FT:** 5,400
**SALES (est):** 5.5MM **Privately Held**
**WEB:** www.hairlinecreations.com
**SIC:** 3999 5699 7389 Hair & hair-based products; wigs, toupees & wiglets; styling, wigs

**(G-5033)**
**HAKIMIAN GEM CO**
Also Called: Ace of Diamonds
5 S Wabash Ave Ste 1212 (60603-3136)
PHONE..................312 236-6969
Fax: 312 236-4785
Fred Hakimian, *President*
**EMP:** 6
**SQ FT:** 800
**SALES (est):** 1.1MM **Privately Held**
**WEB:** www.hakimiangem.com
**SIC:** 5094 3911 5944 Precious stones (gems); diamonds (gems); jewelry; jewelry, precious metal; jewelry stores

**(G-5034)**
**HALE DEVICES INC (PA)**
Also Called: Aiwa
965 W Chicago Ave (60642-5413)
PHONE..................305 394-4119
Joseph Born, *CEO*
▲ **EMP:** 5 **EST:** 2011
**SQ FT:** 60,000
**SALES:** 1.4MM **Privately Held**
**SIC:** 3678 Electronic connectors

**(G-5035)**
**HALF ACRE BEER COMPANY**
4257 N Lincoln Ave (60618-2953)
PHONE..................773 248-4038
Gabriel Magliaro, *President*
▲ **EMP:** 19
**SALES (est):** 3.8MM **Privately Held**
**SIC:** 2082 Malt beverages

**(G-5036)**
**HALLSTAR COMPANY (PA)**
120 S Riverside Plz # 1620 (60606-3911)
PHONE..................312 554-7400
John J Paro, *CEO*
George A Vincent, *Ch of Bd*
Brad Pentzien, *Business Mgr*
Keith Carlson, *Vice Pres*
Gail A Gerono, *Vice Pres*
▲ **EMP:** 142
**SQ FT:** 20,000
**SALES (est):** 56.9MM **Privately Held**
**WEB:** www.hallstar.com
**SIC:** 2869 5169 Plasticizers, organic: cyclic & acyclic; industrial chemicals

**(G-5037)**
**HALLSTAR SERVICES CORP**
120 S Riverside Plz # 1620 (60606-3911)
PHONE..................312 554-7400
Richard M Trojan, *President*
William J Holbrook, *Admin Sec*
**EMP:** 3 **EST:** 2004
**SALES (est):** 81.8K **Privately Held**
**SIC:** 2869 5169 Plasticizers, organic: cyclic & acyclic; industrial chemicals

**(G-5038)**
**HALSTED PACKING HOUSE CO**
445 N Halsted St (60642-6518)
PHONE..................312 421-5147
William Davos, *Owner*
**EMP:** 6
**SQ FT:** 2,000
**SALES (est):** 400.7K **Privately Held**
**SIC:** 2011 2013 Lamb products from lamb slaughtered on site; sausages & other prepared meats

**(G-5039)**
**HAMPDEN CORPORATION**
1550 W Carroll Ave # 207 (60607-1035)
PHONE..................312 583-3000
Joseph Wein, *Chairman*
Roger Hohl, *Vice Pres*
▲ **EMP:** 26 **EST:** 1922

## GEOGRAPHIC SECTION

**Chicago - Cook County (G-5065)**

SQ FT: 22,000
**SALES (est):** 4.7MM **Privately Held**
**WEB:** www.hampdenwatch.com
**SIC:** 3873 Watches & parts, except crystals & jewels

**(G-5040)**
**HANDCUT FOODS LLC**
1441 W Willow St (60642)
**PHONE**.................................312 239-0381
Melanie Faetz, *Accounts Mgr*
Meghan Provencher, *Executive*
Andrew Osterman,
**EMP:** 85
**SALES (est):** 9.1MM **Privately Held**
**SIC:** 2034 2022 2015 Dried & dehydrated fruits; cheese spreads, dips, pastes & other cheese products; variety meats (fresh edible organs), poultry

**(G-5041)**
**HANJITECH INC**
5750 W Bloomingdale Ave (60639-4138)
**PHONE**.................................847 707-5611
Hyon Kun Byon, *President*
**EMP:** 5
**SALES (est):** 280K **Privately Held**
**SIC:** 3559 5065 5199 Mfg Misc Industry Machinery Whol Electronic Parts/Equipment Whol Nondurable Goods

**(G-5042)**
**HANLON GROUP LTD**
1872 N Clybourn Ave # 504 (60614-4964)
**PHONE**.................................773 525-3666
John T Hanlon, *President*
Catherine Sheridan, *Admin Sec*
**EMP:** 3
**SALES (est):** 4MM **Privately Held**
**SIC:** 2671 5162 2821 Packaging paper & plastics film, coated & laminated; plastics materials & basic shapes; plastics materials & resins

**(G-5043)**
**HARBOR VILLAGE LLC**
2241 W Howard St (60645-1908)
**PHONE**.................................773 338-2222
Don Schein,
**EMP:** 5 **EST:** 2012
**SALES (est):** 264.2K **Privately Held**
**SIC:** 2241 Narrow fabric mills

**(G-5044)**
**HARDT ELECTRIC**
415 E North Water St (60611-5594)
**PHONE**.................................312 822-0869
C Hardt, *Principal*
**EMP:** 2
**SALES (est):** 207.1K **Privately Held**
**SIC:** 3699 1731 Electrical equipment & supplies; electrical work

**(G-5045)**
**HARDWOOD LINE MANUFACTURING CO**
4045 N Elston Ave (60618-2193)
**PHONE**.................................773 463-2600
**Fax:** 773 463-9222
Anton Lazaro Sr, *CEO*
Anton E Lazaro Jr, *President*
Frank Pusateri, *General Mgr*
Bill Matusiak, *Chief Engr*
Debbie Fryer, *Accounting Mgr*
**EMP:** 20 **EST:** 1937
SQ FT: 15,000
**SALES (est):** 5.1MM **Privately Held**
**WEB:** www.hardwoodline.com
**SIC:** 3559 3089 Electroplating machinery & equipment; plastic containers, except foam

**(G-5046)**
**HARMON INC**
4161 S Morgan St (60609-2516)
P.O. Box 74794 (60609)
**PHONE**.................................312 726-5050
Jeff Arsenau, *Branch Mgr*
Tom Pichman, *Branch Mgr*
**EMP:** 72

**SALES (corp-wide):** 1.1B **Publicly Held**
**WEB:** www.harmoninc.com
**SIC:** 1793 7536 5039 3231 Glass & glazing work; automotive glass replacement shops; exterior flat glass: plate or window; interior flat glass: plate or window; products of purchased glass; tempered glass: made from purchased glass; windshields, glass: made from purchased glass; window glass, clear & colored; sash, door or window: metal
**HQ:** Harmon, Inc.
7900 Xerxes Ave S # 1800
Bloomington MN 55431
952 944-5700

**(G-5047)**
**HARRINGTON KING PRFORATING INC**
5655 W Fillmore St (60644-5504)
P.O. Box 22, Berwyn (60402-0022)
**PHONE**.................................773 626-1800
William Jakosz, *Manager*
**EMP:** 110
**SALES (corp-wide):** 42.2MM **Privately Held**
**WEB:** www.hkperf.com
**SIC:** 3469 Metal stampings
**PA:** The Harrington & King Perforating Co Inc
5655 W Fillmore St
Chicago IL 60644
773 626-1800

**(G-5048)**
**HARRIS WILLIAM & COMPANY INC (PA)**
Also Called: William Harris Investors
191 N Wacker Dr Ste 1500 (60606-1899)
**PHONE**.................................312 621-0590
**Fax:** 312 621-0857
Jack R Polsky, *CEO*
Irving B Harris, *Ch of Bd*
Adam Langsam, *COO*
Ann Wolf, *Treasurer*
Carolyn Watson, *Accountant*
**EMP:** 50
**SALES (est):** 134.5MM **Privately Held**
**WEB:** www.whicapital.com
**SIC:** 6799 3317 Investment clubs; steel pipe & tubes

**(G-5049)**
**HARRISON HARMONICAS LLC**
4541 N Ravenswood Ave # 203 (60640-5296)
**PHONE**.................................312 379-9427
Michael Peloquin, *Mng Member*
Bradley Harrison,
John Noel,
**EMP:** 7
SQ FT: 1,100
**SALES (est):** 460K **Privately Held**
**WEB:** www.harrisonharmonicas.com
**SIC:** 3931 Harmonicas

**(G-5050)**
**HARTMAN PUBLISHING GROUP LTD**
Also Called: N'Digo
1006 S Michigan Ave # 200 (60605-2254)
**PHONE**.................................312 822-0202
**Fax:** 312 822-0288
Hermene D Hartman, *President*
Deborah Williams, *CFO*
Reggie Spears, *Manager*
**EMP:** 10
SQ FT: 10,000
**SALES (est):** 982.2K **Privately Held**
**WEB:** www.ndigo.com
**SIC:** 2711 Newspapers: publishing only, not printed on site

**(G-5051)**
**HARTMARX CORPORATION**
101 N Wacker Dr (60606-1784)
**PHONE**.................................312 357-5325
**Fax:** 312 444-2679
Homi Patel, *CEO*
**EMP:** 16
**SALES (est):** 1.4MM **Privately Held**
**SIC:** 2211 Apparel & outerwear fabrics, cotton

**(G-5052)**
**HARVEST FOOD GROUP INC**
Also Called: Chicago Custom Packing
4412 W 44th St (60632-4349)
**PHONE**.................................773 847-3313
**Fax:** 773 847-3343
Cara Hahne, *Opers Mgr*
Julieta Espinosa, *QA Dir*
Brad Gavelek, *CFO*
Howard Schmidt, *Sales Staff*
Bob Healy, *Branch Mgr*
**EMP:** 10
**SALES (corp-wide):** 50.2MM **Privately Held**
**WEB:** www.harvestfoodgroup.com
**SIC:** 2037 Frozen fruits & vegetables
**PA:** Harvest Food Group, Inc.
30w260 Butterfield Rd 201b
Warrenville IL 60555
630 821-4000

**(G-5053)**
**HATCHER ASSOCIATES INC**
1612 N Throop St (60642-1515)
**PHONE**.................................773 252-2171
**Fax:** 773 252-2758
John Cecchini, *President*
Franco Cecchini, *Vice Pres*
Greg Kiesow, *Software Dev*
Larry Cecchini, *Shareholder*
Rob Cecchini, *Shareholder*
**EMP:** 14
SQ FT: 10,000
**SALES (est):** 2.1MM **Privately Held**
**WEB:** www.hatchermodels.com
**SIC:** 3544 Forms (molds), for foundry & plastics working machinery

**(G-5054)**
**HATS FOR YOU**
7509 W Belmont Ave (60634-3317)
**PHONE**.................................773 481-1611
Margaret Foltyn, *Owner*
**EMP:** 4
**SALES (est):** 430.4K **Privately Held**
**SIC:** 2353 Hats & caps

**(G-5055)**
**HAUTE NOIR MEDIA GROUP INC**
Also Called: Haute Noir Magzine
220 N Green St (60607-1702)
**PHONE**.................................312 869-4526
Gina Vaughn, *CEO*
Mark Topps, *Sales Mgr*
Deborah Martin, *Exec Sec*
**EMP:** 3
**SALES (est):** 47.3K **Privately Held**
**SIC:** 2741 7941 7221 7336 ; sports field or stadium operator, promoting sports events; photographer, still or video; commercial art & graphic design; booking agency, theatrical

**(G-5056)**
**HAYMARKET BREWING COMPANY LLC**
Also Called: Haymarket Pub & Brewery
737 W Randolph St (60661-2103)
**PHONE**.................................312 638-0700
Janna Mestan, *General Mgr*
Kris Nielsen, *Human Resources*
Steven Forbes, *Mng Member*
Pete Crowley,
**EMP:** 7 **EST:** 2010
**SALES (est):** 220K **Privately Held**
**SIC:** 5813 2082 Bars & lounges; beer (alcoholic beverage)

**(G-5057)**
**HD HUDSON MANUFACTURING CO (PA)**
500 N Michigan Ave Fl 23 (60611-3766)
**PHONE**.................................312 644-2830
**Fax:** 312 644-7989
Robert C Hudson Jr, *Ch of Bd*
R C Hudson III, *President*
W A Hudson, *President*
Manuel Lluberas, *Editor*
Wayne Beissel, *Plant Mgr*
◆ **EMP:** 45 **EST:** 1929
SQ FT: 13,639

**SALES:** 65MM **Privately Held**
**WEB:** www.hdhudson.com
**SIC:** 3523 Sprayers & spraying machines, agricultural; dusters, mechanical: agricultural

**(G-5058)**
**HEALTH ADMINISTRATION PRESS**
1 N Franklin St Ste 1600 (60606-3421)
**PHONE**.................................312 424-2800
Thomas Dolan, *Owner*
Kaye Humbert, *Marketing Mgr*
**EMP:** 90
**SALES (est):** 4.9MM **Privately Held**
**SIC:** 2741 Miscellaneous publishing

**(G-5059)**
**HEALTH KING ENTERPRISE INC**
Also Called: Balanceuticals Group
238 W 31st St Ste 1 (60616-3600)
**PHONE**.................................312 567-9978
Xingwu Liu, *President*
◆ **EMP:** 4
**SALES (est):** 1.5MM **Privately Held**
**WEB:** www.healthkingenterprise.com
**SIC:** 2023 Dietary supplements, dairy & non-dairy based

**(G-5060)**
**HEALTHCARE RESEARCH LLC**
744 N Wells St Fl 3 (60654-3521)
**PHONE**.................................773 592-3508
Brandi Kurtyka, *CEO*
**EMP:** 10 **EST:** 2013
**SALES (est):** 492.2K **Privately Held**
**SIC:** 7372 Application computer software

**(G-5061)**
**HEALTHENGINE**
875 N Michigan Ave # 3100 (60611-1803)
**PHONE**.................................312 340-8555
**EMP:** 5
**SALES (est):** 429.7K **Privately Held**
**SIC:** 7372 Prepackaged software

**(G-5062)**
**HEALTHLEADERS INC**
1404 N Cleveland Ave (60610-1108)
**PHONE**.................................312 932-0848
Chris Cote, *Manager*
Chris Ahern, *CIO*
Stephen Ham, *Info Tech Mgr*
**EMP:** 40
**SALES (est):** 2.3MM **Privately Held**
**WEB:** www.healthleaders.com
**SIC:** 2721 Magazines: publishing only, not printed on site

**(G-5063)**
**HEALTHY-TXT LLC**
950 W Monroe St Unit 813 (60607-2987)
**PHONE**.................................630 945-1787
Sharon Schreiber, *Partner*
Vishal Mehta, *Partner*
**EMP:** 8 **EST:** 2011
**SALES (est):** 308.2K **Privately Held**
**SIC:** 7372 7389 Application computer software;

**(G-5064)**
**HEARST CORPORATION**
Also Called: Magazine Advertising Dept
333 W Wacker Dr Ste 950 (60606-1250)
**PHONE**.................................312 984-5166
**Fax:** 312 984-5110
Kathy Black, *President*
Robin Billie, *Director*
**EMP:** 50
**SALES (corp-wide):** 6.4B **Privately Held**
**WEB:** www.hearstcorp.com
**SIC:** 2721 Magazines: publishing & printing
**PA:** The Hearst Corporation
300 W 57th St Fl 42
New York NY 10019
212 649-2000

**(G-5065)**
**HEARST CORPORATION**
Also Called: Elle Magazine
333 W Wacker Dr Ste 950 (60606-1250)
**PHONE**.................................312 984-5100
Kelly Mair, *Manager*
**EMP:** 50

# Chicago - Cook County (G-5066)  GEOGRAPHIC SECTION

SALES (corp-wide): 6.4B **Privately Held**
WEB: www.popphoto.com
SIC: 2721 Magazines: publishing only, not printed on site
PA: The Hearst Corporation
    300 W 57th St Fl 42
    New York NY 10019
    212 649-2000

### (G-5066)
### HEAT ARMOR LLC
4400 W 45th St Ste B (60632-4304)
PHONE..................................773 938-1030
Lori Herlihy, *Manager*
Thomas Herlihy Jr,
▼ EMP: 10
SQ FT: 50,000
SALES: 950K **Privately Held**
SIC: 3711 Motor vehicles & car bodies

### (G-5067)
### HEAVY QUIP INCORPORATED
55 W Wacker Dr Ste 1120 (60601-1796)
PHONE..................................312 368-7997
Howard Gossage, *President*
Steve Farkas, *CFO*
Rita Qin, *Accountant*
◆ EMP: 17 EST: 2010
SALES (est): 3.7MM **Privately Held**
SIC: 3519 Engines, diesel & semi-diesel or dual-fuel

### (G-5068)
### HEICO COMPANIES LLC (PA)
70 W Madison St Ste 5600 (60602-4211)
PHONE..................................312 419-8220
E A Roskovensky, *President*
Emily Heisley Stoeckel, *Chairman*
Don Walther, *Exec VP*
Susan Fattore, *Vice Pres*
Kathy Watts, *Vice Pres*
◆ EMP: 15
SQ FT: 40,000
SALES (est): 1.7B **Privately Held**
SIC: 3315 3589 3448 3531 Wire, ferrous/iron; wire products, ferrous/iron: made in wiredrawing plants; sewage & water treatment equipment; sewer cleaning equipment, power; shredders, industrial & commercial; prefabricated metal buildings; prefabricated metal buildings; construction machinery; cranes; logging equipment; cranes, locomotive; electrical work; radio & television switching equipment

### (G-5069)
### HEIM GROUP
7201 S Narragansett Ave (60638-6017)
PHONE..................................708 496-7403
Pat Heim, *CEO*
Rick Bartke, *Exec VP*
George Horcaha, *Purch Mgr*
Ziggy Zajdel, *Electrical Engi*
Zizzy Zajgeo, *Electrical Engi*
▲ EMP: 5
SALES (est): 810.4K **Privately Held**
SIC: 3545 Tools & accessories for machine tools

### (G-5070)
### HENDERSON CO INC
6020 N Keating Ave (60646-4902)
PHONE..................................773 628-7216
Jack Henderson, *President*
John Ryan, *QC Dir*
Erin Boyle-Condon, *Office Mgr*
Kathleen Wilson, *Technical Staff*
EMP: 10
SQ FT: 5,500
SALES (est): 1.3MM **Privately Held**
SIC: 2791 7336 2796 Typographic composition, for the printing trade; commercial art & graphic design; color separations for printing

### (G-5071)
### HENNIG GASKET & SEALS INC
2350 W Cullerton St (60608-2515)
PHONE..................................312 243-8270
Fax: 312 243-7855
James E Hennig, *President*
EMP: 7
SQ FT: 9,000
SALES (est): 2.7MM **Privately Held**
WEB: www.henniggasket.com
SIC: 5085 3053 Gaskets & seals; gaskets; seals, industrial; gaskets & sealing devices

### (G-5072)
### HENRY CROWN AND COMPANY (PA)
Also Called: CC Industries
222 N La Salle St # 2000 (60601-1120)
PHONE..................................312 236-6300
Fax: 312 899-5039
James S Crown, *President*
Richard Goodman, *General Ptnr*
Bill Fleckenstein, *Asst Treas*
John Merritt, *Human Res Dir*
Christopher C Lawrence, *Personnel*
▲ EMP: 180
SQ FT: 35,000
SALES (est): 1.4B **Privately Held**
SIC: 2514 Lawn furniture: metal

### (G-5073)
### HENRY-LEE & COMPANY LLC
549 W Randolph St Ste 500 (60661-2208)
PHONE..................................312 648-1575
Fax: 312 648-4309
John Brooks, *Purch Agent*
Sheldon Mann, *Mng Member*
Robert Mann,
▲ EMP: 15 EST: 1957
SALES (est): 3.1MM **Privately Held**
WEB: www.henry-lee.com
SIC: 2211 Denims

### (G-5074)
### HENSAAL MANAGEMENT GROUP INC
4632 W Monroe St (60644-4605)
PHONE..................................312 624-8133
Fax: 312 624-8130
Kenneth M Hennings, *President*
Rick Humphries, *Vice Pres*
Bonnie Hennings, *Admin Sec*
EMP: 7
SQ FT: 1,100
SALES: 5.5MM **Privately Held**
SIC: 5141 2099 5145 Food brokers; seasonings & spices; snack foods

### (G-5075)
### HEPALINK USA INC (PA)
233 S Wacker Dr Ste 9300 (60606-6319)
PHONE..................................630 206-1788
Shawn Lu, *CFO*
EMP: 7
SALES (est): 25.7MM **Privately Held**
SIC: 2834 Pharmaceutical preparations

### (G-5076)
### HERALD NEWSPAPERS INC
Also Called: Hyde Park Herald
1525 E 53rd St Ste 920 (60615-3096)
PHONE..................................773 643-8533
Fax: 773 643-8542
Bruce Sagan, *President*
Susan Walker, *Vice Pres*
John Kennedy, *Production*
Merna Leslie, *Human Res Dir*
EMP: 20
SQ FT: 5,000
SALES (est): 1.2MM **Privately Held**
WEB: www.hpherald.com
SIC: 2711 Newspapers, publishing & printing

### (G-5077)
### HERBALAND INC (PA)
3127 N Milwaukee Ave (60618-6629)
PHONE..................................773 267-7225
Christopher Diegai, *President*
EMP: 2
SALES (est): 245.9K **Privately Held**
SIC: 2833 Drugs & herbs: grading, grinding & milling

### (G-5078)
### HERCULES IRON WORKS INC
846 W Superior St (60642-5944)
PHONE..................................312 226-2405
Fax: 312 226-2403
Julie Porfiropoulos, *President*
EMP: 10
SQ FT: 12,000
SALES (est): 1.7MM **Privately Held**
SIC: 3441 3446 Building components, structural steel; architectural metalwork

### (G-5079)
### HERFF JONES LLC
Also Called: Nystrom
3333 N Elston Ave (60618-6098)
PHONE..................................773 463-1144
Fax: 773 463-1924
Ron B Ebbole, *VP Opers*
P Ferino, *Controller*
John Boneck, *Personnel*
Patrick McKeon, *Branch Mgr*
James Cerza, *Systems Admin*
EMP: 75
SALES (corp-wide): 1.1B **Privately Held**
WEB: www.herffjones.com
SIC: 3911 Rings, finger: precious metal
HQ: Herff Jones, Llc
    4501 W 62nd St
    Indianapolis IN 46268
    800 419-5462

### (G-5080)
### HERMITAGE GROUP INC
5151 N Ravenswood Ave (60640-2722)
PHONE..................................773 561-3773
Fax: 773 561-4422
Robert A Brenner, *President*
Sara R Brenner, *Corp Secy*
EMP: 25
SQ FT: 10,000
SALES (est): 2.2MM **Privately Held**
WEB: www.hermitageart.com
SIC: 2741 2759 2752 Miscellaneous publishing; commercial printing; commercial printing, lithographic

### (G-5081)
### HERNER-GEISSLER WDWKG CORP
400 N Hermitage Ave (60622-6206)
PHONE..................................312 226-3400
Fax: 312 226-4621
Anthony Herner Sr, *President*
Becky Dittmer, *Treasurer*
Jeffrey J Herner, *Admin Sec*
EMP: 55 EST: 1965
SQ FT: 25,000
SALES (est): 7.7MM **Privately Held**
WEB: www.industrialcouncil.com
SIC: 2521 Wood office furniture

### (G-5082)
### HERTZBERG ERNST & SONS
Also Called: Monastery Hill Bindery
1751 W Belmont Ave (60657-3019)
PHONE..................................773 525-3518
Fax: 773 525-4820
Blair Clark, *President*
Rhoda H Clark, *Chairman*
▲ EMP: 40 EST: 1868
SQ FT: 13,000
SALES (est): 6.7MM **Privately Held**
WEB: www.monasteryhill.com
SIC: 2752 3172 3199 Menus, lithographed; leather cases; embossed leather goods

### (G-5083)
### HEXAGON METROLOGY INC
Also Called: Hexagon Marketing
440 N Wells St (60654-4545)
PHONE..................................312 624-8786
EMP: 3
SALES (corp-wide): 2.9B **Privately Held**
SIC: 3823 Industrial instrmnts msrmnt display/control process variable
HQ: Hexagon Metrology, Inc.
    250 Circuit Dr
    North Kingstown RI 02852
    401 886-2000

### (G-5084)
### HH BACKER ASSOCIATES INC
Also Called: Pet Age Magazine
18 S Michigan Ave # 1100 (60603-3233)
PHONE..................................312 578-1818
Fax: 312 578-1819
Patty Backer, *Ch of Bd*
Mark Mitera, *Vice Pres*
Karen Pedroni, *Admin Sec*
David Harvey, *Relations*
EMP: 17
SALES (est): 2MM **Privately Held**
WEB: www.hhbacker.com
SIC: 2721 7389 Trade journals: publishing only, not printed on site; trade show arrangement

### (G-5085)
### HIG CHEMICALS HOLDINGS
4650 S Racine Ave (60609-3321)
PHONE..................................773 376-9000
Anthony Tamer, *President*
EMP: 240
SALES (est): 15MM **Privately Held**
SIC: 2899 Chemical preparations

### (G-5086)
### HIGGINS BROS INC
1428 W 37th St (60609-2109)
PHONE..................................773 523-0124
Fax: 773 523-1471
Thomas Higgins, *President*
Ron Gentile, *Vice Pres*
EMP: 10
SQ FT: 5,000
SALES: 600K **Privately Held**
WEB: www.midamericasteeldrum.com
SIC: 5085 3412 2823 Drums, new or reconditioned; metal barrels, drums & pails; cellulosic manmade fibers

### (G-5087)
### HIGH PERFORMANCE ENTP INC
Also Called: High Performance Uniforms
3500 N Kostner Ave (60641-3807)
PHONE..................................773 283-1778
Sabrina Gershkovich, *President*
Alex Khakham, *Manager*
▲ EMP: 20
SQ FT: 8,000
SALES (est): 1.3MM **Privately Held**
SIC: 2326 5136 Work uniforms; uniforms, men's & boys'

### (G-5088)
### HILL-ROM HOLDINGS INC (PA)
2 Prudential Plz Ste 4100 (60601)
PHONE..................................312 819-7200
Rolf A Classon, *Ch of Bd*
John J Greisch, *President*
Carlos Alonso, *President*
Alton Shader, *President*
Taylor Smith, *President*
EMP: 300 EST: 1969
SALES: 2.6B **Publicly Held**
WEB: www.hillenbrand.com
SIC: 3841 7352 Surgical & medical instruments; medical equipment rental

### (G-5089)
### HILLSHIRE BRANDS COMPANY (HQ)
Also Called: Sara Lee Food & Beverage
400 S Jefferson St Fl 1 (60607-3812)
PHONE..................................312 614-6000
Fax: 630 726-3712
Sean M Connolly, *President*
Thao Dekool, *Sr Corp Ofcr*
Andrew P Callahan, *Exec VP*
Kent B Magill, *Exec VP*
Judith Sprieser, *Exec VP*
▼ EMP: 277 EST: 1942
SQ FT: 230,000
SALES (est): 3.6B
SALES (corp-wide): 36.8B **Publicly Held**
SIC: 2013 2051 2053 Sausages & other prepared meats; breads, rolls & buns; frozen bakery products, except bread
PA: Tyson Foods, Inc.
    2200 W Don Tyson Pkwy
    Springdale AR 72762
    479 290-4000

### (G-5090)
### HILLSHIRE BRANDS COMPANY
Superior Coffee & Foods
400 S Jefferson St Fl 1 (60607-3812)
PHONE..................................312 614-6000
Jeff Kozak, *Branch Mgr*
EMP: 30
SALES (corp-wide): 36.8B **Publicly Held**
SIC: 2013 2015 Sausages & other prepared meats; poultry slaughtering & processing

▲ = Import ▼ = Export ◆ = Import/Export

HQ: The Hillshire Brands Company
400 S Jefferson St Fl 1
Chicago IL 60607
312 614-6000

**(G-5091)**
**HINCKLEY & SCHMITT INC**
Also Called: Hinckley Springs
6055 S Harlem Ave (60638-3985)
**PHONE**................................773 586-8600
**Fax:** 773 586-8613
David A Krishcok, *President*
▲ **EMP:** 2190
**SQ FT:** 55,000
**SALES (est):** 147.2MM
**SALES (corp-wide):** 72.3MM **Privately Held**
**WEB:** www.suntory.com
**SIC: 2086** 5149 7359 Water, pasteurized: packaged in cans, bottles, etc.; water, distilled; mineral or spring water bottling; equipment rental & leasing
HQ: Suntory International Corp.
600 3rd Ave Fl 21
New York NY 10016
212 891-6600

**(G-5092)**
**HLH ASSOCIATES**
Also Called: PPG Aerospace
1701 E 122nd St (60633-2362)
**PHONE**................................773 646-5900
Duane Utter, *Principal*
**EMP:** 15
**SALES (corp-wide):** 3.2MM **Privately Held**
**SIC: 2851** Coating, air curing
PA: Hlh Associates
3700 S Water St Ste 100
Pittsburgh PA 15203
412 261-6500

**(G-5093)**
**HM WITT & CO**
3313 W Newport Ave (60618-5509)
**PHONE**................................773 250-5000
H Matthew Witt IV, *President*
▼ **EMP:** 20
**SQ FT:** 26,500
**SALES (est):** 2.6MM **Privately Held**
**WEB:** www.hmwitt.com
**SIC: 3993** Signs & advertising specialties

**(G-5094)**
**HMK MATTRESS HOLDINGS LLC**
3216 N Broadway St (60657-3515)
**PHONE**................................773 472-7390
**EMP:** 3
**SALES (corp-wide):** 1.6B **Privately Held**
**SIC: 2515** Mattresses & foundations
HQ: Hmk Mattress Holdings Llc
1000 S Oyster Bay Rd
Hicksville NY 11801
800 934-6848

**(G-5095)**
**HMM PALLETS INC**
3344 S Lawndale Ave (60623-5006)
**PHONE**................................773 927-3448
**Fax:** 773 927-3106
Hector M Munoz, *President*
**EMP:** 2
**SALES (est):** 250K **Privately Held**
**SIC: 2448** Pallets, wood & wood with metal

**(G-5096)**
**HOKU SOLAR POWER I LLC**
125 S Clark St Fl 17 (60603-4035)
**PHONE**................................312 803-4972
Kevin Hirsch, *CFO*
Mike Luo, *Mng Member*
**EMP:** 10
**SALES (est):** 893.8K **Privately Held**
**SIC: 3674** Solar cells

**(G-5097)**
**HOLCIM (US) INC**
3221 E 95th St (60617-5160)
**PHONE**................................773 721-8352
Bob Garza, *Manager*
**EMP:** 4
**SQ FT:** 600
**SALES (corp-wide):** 26.6B **Privately Held**
**WEB:** www.holcim.com/us
**SIC: 3241** Portland cement

HQ: Holcim (Us) Inc.
6211 N Ann Arbor Rd
Dundee MI 48131
734 529-4278

**(G-5098)**
**HOLCIM (US) INC**
Also Called: Skyway Facility
3020 E 103rd St (60617-5809)
**PHONE**................................773 731-1320
John Goetz, *Facilities Mgr*
Tim Noss, *Maint Spvr*
Mark Combs, *Manager*
**EMP:** 27
**SQ FT:** 600
**SALES (corp-wide):** 26.6B **Privately Held**
**WEB:** www.holcim.com/us
**SIC: 3241** 3295 Cement, hydraulic; minerals, ground or treated
HQ: Holcim (Us) Inc.
6211 N Ann Arbor Rd
Dundee MI 48131
734 529-4278

**(G-5099)**
**HOLIDAY BRIGHT LIGHTS INC (PA)**
Also Called: Holidynamics
954 W Wa Blvd Ste 705 (60607-2224)
**PHONE**................................312 226-8281
Rich Martini, *CEO*
Greg Dondelinger, *CFO*
Steve Harrison, *Director*
Dave Daugherty,
Aric Kulm,
▲ **EMP:** 8
**SQ FT:** 8,000
**SALES:** 4MM **Privately Held**
**SIC: 5063** 3646 Lighting fixtures, commercial & industrial; commercial indusl & institutional electric lighting fixtures

**(G-5100)**
**HOMAN BINDERY**
1112 N Homan Ave (60651-4007)
**PHONE**................................773 276-1500
Mitchell Harrison, *Partner*
J S Harrison Trust, *Partner*
Mitchell H Harrison, *Principal*
Jerome Harrison, *Trustee*
**EMP:** 25
**SQ FT:** 20,000
**SALES (est):** 2.6MM **Privately Held**
**SIC: 2789** Binding only: books, pamphlets, magazines, etc.

**(G-5101)**
**HOME CITY ICE (PA)**
Also Called: Jefferson Ice
2248 N Natchez Ave (60707-3424)
**PHONE**................................773 622-9400
**Fax:** 773 622-7955
Robert H Rustman, *President*
**EMP:** 15
**SQ FT:** 31,000
**SALES (est):** 1.5MM **Privately Held**
**WEB:** www.jeffersonice.com
**SIC: 2097** Manufactured ice

**(G-5102)**
**HOME PDTS INTL - N AMER INC (HQ)**
4501 W 47th St (60632-4407)
**PHONE**................................773 890-1010
George Hamilton, *CEO*
Kathy Evans, *Senior VP*
Grant Fagan, *Senior VP*
John Pugh, *Vice Pres*
Dennis Doheny, *CFO*
◆ **EMP:** 300 **EST:** 1952
**SQ FT:** 300,000
**SALES (est):** 207.6MM
**SALES (corp-wide):** 414.3MM **Privately Held**
**SIC: 3089** 3499 Boxes, plastic; organizers for closets, drawers, etc.; plastic; ironing boards, metal
PA: Home Products International, Inc.
4501 W 47th St
Chicago IL 60632
773 890-1010

**(G-5103)**
**HOME SPECIALTY CONNECTION INC**
4955 N Damen Ave Apt 1r (60625-1394)
**PHONE**................................815 363-1934
Janet Michel, *President*
**EMP:** 8
**SALES:** 341K **Privately Held**
**SIC: 3651** Household audio & video equipment

**(G-5104)**
**HOMNAY MAGAZINE**
1114 W Argyle St (60640-3610)
**PHONE**................................773 334-6655
Khanh Tran, *Owner*
**EMP:** 3
**SALES (est):** 160.1K **Privately Held**
**SIC: 2721** Magazines: publishing only, not printed on site

**(G-5105)**
**HONEY BEAR HAM**
1160 W Grand Ave Ste 1 (60642-5837)
**PHONE**................................312 942-1160
**Fax:** 312 942-1951
Julie Connell, *President*
**EMP:** 20
**SALES (est):** 1.7MM **Privately Held**
**SIC: 2013** Ham, roasted: from purchased meat

**(G-5106)**
**HONEYWELL INTERNATIONAL INC**
1 Bank One Plz (60670-0001)
**PHONE**................................480 353-3020
**EMP:** 718
**SALES (corp-wide):** 39.3B **Publicly Held**
**SIC: 3724** Aircraft engines & engine parts; research & development on aircraft engines & parts; turbines, aircraft type
PA: Honeywell International Inc.
115 Tabor Rd
Morris Plains NJ 07950
973 455-2000

**(G-5107)**
**HONEYWELL INTERNATIONAL INC**
24004 Network Pl (60673-1240)
**PHONE**................................973 455-2000
Brad Birdsell, *Branch Mgr*
**EMP:** 657
**SALES (corp-wide):** 39.3B **Publicly Held**
**WEB:** www.honeywell.com
**SIC: 3724** Aircraft engines & engine parts
PA: Honeywell International Inc.
115 Tabor Rd
Morris Plains NJ 07950
973 455-2000

**(G-5108)**
**HONG KONG MARKET CHICAGO INC**
2425 S Wallace St (60616-1855)
**PHONE**................................312 791-9111
Thomas Lamb, *President*
**EMP:** 6
**SALES (est):** 234.7K **Privately Held**
**SIC: 5148** 5141 2032 Banana ripening; food brokers; beans & bean sprouts, canned, jarred, etc.
PA: Hop Kee Incorporated
2425 S Wallace St
Chicago IL 60616

**(G-5109)**
**HOP KEE INCORPORATED (PA)**
Also Called: Hong Kong Market
2425 S Wallace St (60616-1855)
**PHONE**................................312 791-9111
**Fax:** 312 791-1324
Thomas Lam, *President*
Gloria F Lam, *Treasurer*
▲ **EMP:** 33
**SQ FT:** 42,500
**SALES (est):** 18MM **Privately Held**
**WEB:** www.orientaldelicacies.com
**SIC: 5148** 5141 2032 2099 Banana ripening; food brokers; beans & bean sprouts, canned, jarred, etc.; food preparations; cookies & crackers; pickles, sauces & salad dressings

**(G-5110)**
**HOPKINS MACHINE CORPORATION**
4243 W Diversey Ave (60639-2002)
**PHONE**................................773 772-2800
**Fax:** 773 772-5733
Adam Widula, *President*
Alicia Widula, *Vice Pres*
**EMP:** 7
**SQ FT:** 16,000
**SALES:** 1MM **Privately Held**
**WEB:** www.hopkinsmachinery.com
**SIC: 3599** Machine shop, jobbing & repair

**(G-5111)**
**HORAN GLASS BLOCK INC**
6742 W Archer Ave (60638-2333)
**PHONE**................................773 586-4808
**Fax:** 773 586-4730
Kenneth J Schoreder, *President*
Marilyn Schoreder, *Treasurer*
▲ **EMP:** 3
**SALES (est):** 319.3K **Privately Held**
**WEB:** www.horanglassblock.com
**SIC: 3211** 1793 Flat glass; glass & glazing work

**(G-5112)**
**HORIZON FUEL CELL AMERICAS**
18 S Michigan Ave # 1200 (60603-3210)
**PHONE**................................312 316-8050
**EMP:** 5
**SALES (est):** 586.2K **Privately Held**
**SIC: 2869** Fuels

**(G-5113)**
**HORIZON METALS INC**
3925 N Pulaski Rd (60641-2931)
**PHONE**................................773 478-8888
**Fax:** 773 478-8378
Bruce Pinsof, *President*
Karen Pinsof, *Admin Sec*
**EMP:** 19
**SALES (est):** 3.8MM **Privately Held**
**SIC: 3356** 3339 Precious metals; primary nonferrous metals

**(G-5114)**
**HORSEHEAD CORPORATION**
2701 E 114th St (60617-6449)
**PHONE**................................773 933-9260
**Fax:** 773 933-9272
Mike Holezman, *Manager*
**EMP:** 44
**SALES (corp-wide):** 414.9MM **Privately Held**
**SIC: 3339** Zinc smelting (primary), including zinc residue
HQ: American Zinc Recycling Corp.
4955 Steubenville Pike
Pittsburgh PA 15205
724 774-1020

**(G-5115)**
**HORWEEN LEATHER COMPANY**
2015 N Elston Ave Ste 1 (60614-3943)
**PHONE**................................773 772-2026
**Fax:** 773 772-9235
Arnold Horween Jr, *President*
Thomas Culliton, *Corp Secy*
John Culliton, *Vice Pres*
Christopher Koelblinger, *VP Prdtn*
Dan Cordova, *Prdtn Mgr*
▲ **EMP:** 175 **EST:** 1905
**SQ FT:** 260,000
**SALES (est):** 29MM **Privately Held**
**WEB:** www.horween.com
**SIC: 3111** Hides: tanning, currying & finishing

**(G-5116)**
**HOSTFORWEB INCORPORATED**
7061 N Kedzie Ave Ste 302 (60645-2857)
**PHONE**................................312 343-4678
Alex Korneyev, *President*
**EMP:** 2
**SALES (est):** 265.5K **Privately Held**
**SIC: 7372** Operating systems computer software

## Chicago - Cook County (G-5117)

**(G-5117)**
**HOT FOOD BOXES INC**
4109 W Lake St (60624-1719)
P.O. Box 1089, Mooresville IN (46158-5089)
PHONE.................................773 533-5912
EMP: 25 EST: 1948
SQ FT: 32,000
SALES (est): 2.5MM
SALES (corp-wide): 8.9MM Privately Held
SIC: 3556 3444 Mfg Food Products Machinery Mfg Sheet Metalwork
PA: Gm Specialties Inc
4107 W Lake St
Chicago IL
773 533-5912

**(G-5118)**
**HOT MEXICAN PEPPERS INC**
2215 W 47th St (60609-4013)
PHONE.................................773 843-9774
Alejandro L Correa, *President*
◆ EMP: 2
SALES (est): 294.2K Privately Held
SIC: 2034 Dried & dehydrated fruits

**(G-5119)**
**HOTEL AMERIKA**
434 W Briar Pl Apt 4 (60657-4776)
PHONE.................................219 508-9418
David Lazar, *Exec Dir*
EMP: 3
SALES (est): 102.6K Privately Held
SIC: 2721 Magazines: publishing & printing

**(G-5120)**
**HOTVAPES LTD**
7240 N Milwaukee Ave (60647)
PHONE.................................775 468-8273
Tim Roche, *President*
EMP: 15
SALES: 3MM Privately Held
SIC: 5993 3634 Tobacco stores & stands; cigarette lighters, electric

**(G-5121)**
**HOUGHTON INTERNATIONAL INC**
6600 S Nashville Ave (60638-4910)
PHONE.................................610 666-4000
Fax: 773 408-5416
Mike Artson, *Managing Dir*
Robert Jesanis, *Sales Staff*
John V Livaich, *Branch Mgr*
EMP: 18 Privately Held
WEB: www.houghtonintl.com
SIC: 2869 2992 2899 2842 Hydraulic fluids, synthetic base; re-refining lubricating oils & greases; rust arresting compounds, animal or vegetable oil base; cutting oils, blending: made from purchased materials; heat treating salts; cleaning or polishing preparations; processing assistants
HQ: Houghton International Inc.
945 Madison Ave
Norristown PA 19403
610 666-4000

**(G-5122)**
**HOWARD MEDICAL COMPANY**
1690 N Elston Ave (60642-1530)
PHONE.................................773 278-1440
Fax: 773 278-9513
Ross Litton, *President*
Bernie Litton, *Vice Pres*
Bill Chilcutt, *Sls & Mktg Exec*
Mark Litton, *Sales Associate*
Michael Puckett, *Manager*
▲ EMP: 9
SALES (est): 3.4MM Privately Held
WEB: www.howardmedical.com
SIC: 5047 2782 Medical equipment & supplies; ledgers & ledger sheets

**(G-5123)**
**HOWE CORPORATION**
1650 N Elston Ave (60642-1585)
PHONE.................................773 235-0200
Fax: 773 235-1530
Mary C Howe, *President*
Avinash Ahuja, *Exec VP*
Jean Spiegelmuth, *Senior VP*
John Myrda, *Plant Mgr*
A Chaidez, *Purch Mgr*
▲ EMP: 37 EST: 1912
SQ FT: 60,000
SALES (est): 10.5MM Privately Held
WEB: www.howecorp.com
SIC: 3585 3563 3498 3443 Refrigeration equipment, complete; ice making machinery; compressors for refrigeration & air conditioning equipment; air & gas compressors; fabricated pipe & fittings; fabricated plate work (boiler shop)

**(G-5124)**
**HP INTERACTIVE INC**
2461 W Balmoral Ave (60625-2301)
PHONE.................................773 681-4440
Boulos Mikhail, *President*
EMP: 5
SALES (est): 299.4K Privately Held
SIC: 2741

**(G-5125)**
**HQ PRINTERS INC**
200 N La Salle St Lbby 2 (60601-1046)
PHONE.................................312 782-2020
Fax: 312 782-3714
Prakash Patel, *President*
EMP: 2
SQ FT: 2,000
SALES (est): 650K Privately Held
SIC: 7334 2752 2791 2789 Photocopying & duplicating services; business forms, lithographed; typesetting; bookbinding & related work

**(G-5126)**
**HU-FRIEDY MFG CO LLC (PA)**
Also Called: American Dental
3232 N Rockwell St (60618-5935)
PHONE.................................773 975-3975
Fax: 773 975-5168
Ron Saslow, *Ch of Bd*
Ken Serota, *President*
Dick Saslow, *Chairman*
Sam Marin, *Credit Staff*
Patrick Bernardi, *Mktg Dir*
▲ EMP: 277 EST: 1908
SQ FT: 80,000
SALES (est): 125.5MM Privately Held
SIC: 3843 Dental hand instruments

**(G-5127)**
**HUB MANUFACTURING COMPANY INC**
Also Called: Hub Stamping & Mfg Co
1212 N Central Park Ave (60651-2299)
PHONE.................................773 252-1373
Gerald F Benda, *President*
Chris Munoz, *Office Mgr*
EMP: 28
SQ FT: 36,000
SALES (est): 2MM Privately Held
WEB: www.HubManufacturing.com
SIC: 3469 3364 3498 Stamping metal for the trade; zinc & zinc-base alloy die-castings; fabricated pipe & fittings

**(G-5128)**
**HYBRIS (US) CORPORATION (DH)**
20 N Wacker Dr Ste 2900 (60606-3101)
PHONE.................................312 265-5010
Fax: 773 265-5013
Ariel Ludi, *CEO*
Carsten Thoma, *President*
Michael Zips, *COO*
Steven Kramer, *Exec VP*
Katrin Gunter, *Senior VP*
EMP: 30
SQ FT: 14,000
SALES (est): 7.9MM
SALES (corp-wide): 23.3B Privately Held
SIC: 7371 7372 Software programming applications; computer software systems analysis & design, custom; business oriented computer software
HQ: Hybris Ag
Bahnhofplatz
Zug ZG
433 333-939

**(G-5129)**
**HYLAN DESIGN LTD**
329 W 18th St Ste 700 (60616-1122)
PHONE.................................312 243-7341
Fax: 312 243-9955
Theodore H Schultz, *President*
Angelo Mitchello, *Project Mgr*
Elizabeth Schultz, *Admin Sec*
EMP: 4
SQ FT: 7,500
SALES (est): 750K Privately Held
WEB: www.hylandesign.com
SIC: 2599 5712 2541 2511 Cabinets, factory; furniture stores; wood partitions & fixtures; wood household furniture; wood kitchen cabinets; millwork

**(G-5130)**
**HYPERERA INC**
Also Called: (A DEVELOPMENT STAGE ENTERPRISE)
2316 S Wentworth Ave Fl 1 (60616-2014)
PHONE.................................312 842-2288
Zhi Yong LI, *Ch of Bd*
WEI Wu, *President*
Hong Tao Bai, *Vice Pres*
Simon Bai, *CFO*
Nan Su, *CTO*
EMP: 17
SQ FT: 350
SALES: 162.8K Privately Held
SIC: 7372 Prepackaged software

**(G-5131)**
**I M M INC**
Also Called: International Marketing & Mfg
5262 S Kolmar Ave (60632-4711)
PHONE.................................773 767-3700
Fax: 773 767-3750
Anne K Stewart, *President*
Peggy Levato, *Office Mgr*
EMP: 10
SQ FT: 39,000
SALES (est): 1.1MM Privately Held
WEB: www.imm.com
SIC: 2679 4226 2392 2211 Paper products, converted; special warehousing & storage; household furnishings; broadwoven fabric mills, cotton

**(G-5132)**
**I P G WAREHOUSE LTD**
Also Called: Independent Publishers Group
600 N Pulaski Rd (60624-1059)
PHONE.................................773 722-5527
Kurt Matthews, *CEO*
Mark Suchonel, *President*
Berianne Bramman, *Publisher*
Richard Bahena, *Opers Mgr*
Teresa Gamboa, *CFO*
▲ EMP: 24 EST: 2002
SALES (est): 2.2MM Privately Held
WEB: www.ipgbook.com
SIC: 1541 2741 Industrial buildings & warehouses; miscellaneous publishing

**(G-5133)**
**I Q INFINITY LLC**
7624 S Wood St (60620-4448)
PHONE.................................773 651-2556
Fred Sampson, *President*
▲ EMP: 3
SALES (est): 173.5K Privately Held
SIC: 2893 Printing ink

**(G-5134)**
**IB SOURCE INC**
Also Called: Cie Source
516 N Ogden Ave Ste 111 (60642-6421)
PHONE.................................312 698-7062
Andrew T Culley, *President*
John J Cummins, *Admin Sec*
EMP: 7
SALES (est): 770K Privately Held
SIC: 2731 Book publishing

**(G-5135)**
**IBARRA GROUP LLC**
3100 S Homan Ave (60623-5018)
PHONE.................................773 650-0503
Roberts Ibarra, *Mng Member*
Rosa Ibarra,
EMP: 2
SQ FT: 6,000
SALES (est): 200K Privately Held
SIC: 3446 Business consulting

**(G-5136)**
**ICON ACQUISITION HOLDINGS LP (PA)**
680 N Lake Shore Dr (60611-4546)
PHONE.................................312 751-8000
EMP: 3
SALES (est): 56.5MM Privately Held
SIC: 7812 4841 2721 Motion picture production; video production; cable & other pay television services; periodicals

**(G-5137)**
**ICREAM GROUP LLC**
1537 N Milwaukee Ave # 1 (60622-2209)
PHONE.................................773 342-2834
EMP: 2
SALES (est): 210K Privately Held
SIC: 2024 Mfg Ice Cream/Frozen Desert

**(G-5138)**
**IDEA MEDIA SERVICES LLC**
600 W Chicago Ave Ste 1 (60654-2802)
PHONE.................................312 226-2900
Tom Later, *Office Mgr*
Erik Gershfeld, *Manager*
EMP: 12
SQ FT: 3,000
SALES (est): 2.3MM Privately Held
WEB: www.ideareplication.com
SIC: 3652 Compact laser discs, prerecorded

**(G-5139)**
**IDEA TOOL & MANUFACTURING CO**
5615 S Claremont Ave (60636-1011)
P.O. Box 520, La Grange (60525-0520)
PHONE.................................312 476-1080
Fax: 773 476-8259
Lou Hontschel, *Purch Mgr*
Eric Sund, *Director*
EMP: 51
SALES (est): 3.6MM Privately Held
SIC: 3544 Special dies & tools

**(G-5140)**
**IDEAL BOX CO (PA)**
4800 S Austin Ave (60638-1484)
PHONE.................................708 594-3100
Fax: 708 594-3109
Scott Eisen, *President*
Stephen Eisen, *Chairman*
Yale Eisen, *COO*
Jeff Craig, *Vice Pres*
Mike Sebring, *VP Opers*
▲ EMP: 200 EST: 1924
SQ FT: 310,000
SALES: 80MM Privately Held
WEB: www.idealbox.com
SIC: 2653 3993 Boxes, corrugated: made from purchased materials; display items, corrugated: made from purchased materials; signs & advertising specialties

**(G-5141)**
**IDEAL MEDIA LLC (PA)**
200 E Randolph St # 7000 (60601-6436)
P.O. Box 823212, Philadelphia PA (19182-3212)
PHONE.................................312 456-2822
Brian Reshefsky,
Tim Cramer,
◆ EMP: 3
SALES (est): 5MM Privately Held
WEB: www.idealmediallc.com
SIC: 2721 Magazines: publishing only, not printed on site

**(G-5142)**
**IDEVCONCEPTS INC**
100 E 14th St Apt 904 (60605-3666)
PHONE.................................312 351-1615
Mario Mamalis, *President*
Derek Demas, *Director*
EMP: 5
SALES (est): 177.3K Privately Held
SIC: 7371 7372 7389 Computer software development; custom computer programming services; application computer software;

**(G-5143)**
**IDX CORPORATION**
Also Called: Idx Chicago
224-230 W Huron St (60654)
PHONE.................................312 600-9783
Mayur Patadia, *General Mgr*
EMP: 15
SALES (corp-wide): 416.7MM Privately Held
SIC: 2542 Office & store showcases & display fixtures

**PA:** Idx Corporation
1 Rider Trail Plaza Dr
Earth City MO 63045
314 739-4120

### (G-5144)
### IEG LLC
350 N Orleans St Ste 1200  (60654-2105)
PHONE.................................312 944-1727
Laren Ukman, *CEO*
Lesa Ukman, *CEO*
Dan Kowitz, *COO*
Jim Andrews, *Senior VP*
Jeff Bail, *Vice Pres*
**EMP:** 50
**SQ FT:** 27,000
**SALES (est):** 7.3MM
**SALES (corp-wide):** 17.7B  **Privately Held**
**WEB:** www.sponsorship.com
**SIC: 8748**  2721  Business consulting; magazines: publishing only, not printed on site
**HQ:** Group M Worldwide, Llc
498 7th Ave
New York NY 10018
212 297-7000

### (G-5145)
### IEMCO CORPORATION
Also Called: Illinois Engraving & Mfg Co
4530 N Ravenswood Ave  (60640-5202)
PHONE.................................773 728-4400
**Fax:** 773 728-4438
Wayne Tumminello, *President*
Nathan Tumminello, *Engineer*
**EMP:** 6
**SQ FT:** 5,600
**SALES:** 500K  **Privately Held**
**WEB:** www.illinoisengraving.com
**SIC: 3544**  3479  3953  2796  Special dies & tools; etching & engraving; marking devices; platemaking services; commercial printing

### (G-5146)
### IESCO INC
5235 W 65th St Unit B  (60638-5700)
PHONE.................................708 594-1250
**Fax:** 708 594-1256
John M Doody, *President*
Cheryl Mizyed, *Manager*
Barbara Doody, *Admin Sec*
**EMP:** 20 EST: 1943
**SQ FT:** 50,000
**SALES (est):** 5.2MM  **Privately Held**
**SIC: 7694**  Electric motor repair

### (G-5147)
### IGNITE USA LLC
Also Called: Ignite Design
180 N La Salle St Ste 700  (60601-2503)
PHONE.................................312 432-6223
**Fax:** 312 432-6223
Sami El-Saden,
Karen Wolters,
Robert Wolters Sr,
▲ **EMP:** 45
**SQ FT:** 15,000
**SALES (est):** 10.9MM
**SALES (corp-wide):** 13.2B  **Publicly Held**
**WEB:** www.igniteusa.com
**SIC: 3411**  Food & beverage containers
**HQ:** Ignite Holdings, Inc.
954 W Washington Blvd # 735
Chicago IL 60607
312 432-6223

### (G-5148)
### IGUANAMED LLC
363 W Erie St Ste 200e  (60654-7061)
PHONE.................................312 546-4182
Ryan Hertz, *Marketing Staff*
Gregory Lilien, *Mng Member*
Mary Kuknos, *Manager*
Ryan Saunders,
▲ **EMP:** 6
**SALES (est):** 6MM  **Privately Held**
**WEB:** www.walrusbrands.com
**SIC: 2337**  2326  Uniforms, except athletic: women's, misses' & juniors'; medical & hospital uniforms, men's

### (G-5149)
### IHEARTCOMMUNICATIONS INC
Also Called: 1035 Kiss
875 N Michigan Ave # 3100  (60611-1803)
PHONE.................................312 255-5100
**EMP:** 30
**SALES (corp-wide):** 6.2B  **Publicly Held**
**SIC: 3663**  Mfg Radio/Tv Communication Equipment
**HQ:** Iheartcommunications, Inc.
200 E Basse Rd
San Antonio TX 78209
210 822-2828

### (G-5150)
### IKAN CREATIONS LLC ✪
2010 S Wabash Ave Ste H  (60616-1775)
PHONE.................................312 204-7333
Jason Frazier, *President*
**EMP:** 5 EST: 2016
**SQ FT:** 700
**SALES (est):** 156.7K  **Privately Held**
**SIC: 2396**  7812  7819  7929  Screen printing on fabric articles; music video production; sound (effects & music production), motion picture; entertainers & entertainment groups; entertainers

### (G-5151)
### IL INTERNATIONAL LLC (PA)
1720 N Elston Ave  (60642-1532)
PHONE.................................773 276-0070
Marion Cameron, *Principal*
Steve Henrickson, *Vice Pres*
**EMP:** 5
**SALES (est):** 9.2MM  **Privately Held**
**SIC: 3356**  Precious metals

### (G-5152)
### ILIGHT TECHNOLOGIES INC (PA)
Also Called: Optiva Signs
118 S Clinton St Ste 370  (60661-3661)
PHONE.................................312 876-8630
**Fax:** 312 876-8631
Sean Callahan, *CEO*
Mark Cleaver, *President*
Eddy Willette, *Opers Staff*
Sandy Butler, *Purchasing*
Matt Bilbrey, *Engineer*
▲ **EMP:** 12
**SQ FT:** 4,000
**SALES (est):** 3.6MM  **Privately Held**
**SIC: 3648**  Lighting equipment

### (G-5153)
### ILL BATTERY SPXCIALISTS L
4120 W Belmont Ave  (60641-4616)
PHONE.................................773 478-8600
Bill Luncas, *Owner*
**EMP:** 6
**SALES (est):** 766.6K  **Privately Held**
**SIC: 3691**  Storage batteries

### (G-5154)
### ILLINOIS BAKING
10839 S Langley Ave  (60628-3814)
PHONE.................................773 995-7200
**Fax:** 773 995-6982
**EMP:** 4 EST: 2010
**SALES (est):** 170K  **Privately Held**
**SIC: 2051**  Mfg Bread/Related Products

### (G-5155)
### ILLINOIS CASKET COMPANY
6747 S Halsted St  (60621-1813)
PHONE.................................773 483-4500
Willis E Webb, *Owner*
**EMP:** 4
**SQ FT:** 1,100
**SALES (est):** 180K  **Privately Held**
**SIC: 3995**  Burial caskets

### (G-5156)
### ILLINOIS ENGINEERED PDTS INC
2035 S Racine Ave  (60608-3201)
PHONE.................................312 850-3710
**Fax:** 312 850-4736
Dean Wynne, *President*
Michael Patella, *General Mgr*
Laura Marzullo, *Accounting Mgr*
Carina Diaz, *VP Sales*
Brad Chainey, *Sales Mgr*
▲ **EMP:** 20

**SQ FT:** 150,000
**SALES (est):** 5.1MM  **Privately Held**
**WEB:** www.illinoisengineeredproducts.com
**SIC: 3312**  3315  Rails, steel or iron; fence gates posts & fittings: steel

### (G-5157)
### ILLINOIS FIBRE SPECIALTY CO (PA)
Also Called: I F S C O Industries
4301 S Western Blvd  (60609-3089)
PHONE.................................773 376-1122
**Fax:** 773 376-3111
Casimir W Kasper, *President*
Timothy C Kasper, *Exec VP*
Edward Svancara, *Vice Pres*
Kathy Ramski, *Personnel*
Donna Bodell, *Executive*
**EMP:** 25
**SQ FT:** 72,000
**SALES (est):** 3.5MM  **Privately Held**
**SIC: 3429**  5032  5131  Furniture hardware; drywall materials; piece goods & other fabrics

### (G-5158)
### ILLINOIS STEEL SERVICE INC (PA)
1127 S Washtenaw Ave  (60612-4015)
PHONE.................................312 926-7440
**Fax:** 312 929-4338
James Robertson, *President*
E Katz, *Corp Secy*
Charlotte Robertson, *Vice Pres*
**EMP:** 62
**SQ FT:** 60,000
**SALES (est):** 6MM  **Privately Held**
**WEB:** www.iss-steel.com
**SIC: 3449**  5051  3441  3429  Miscellaneous metalwork; iron & steel (ferrous) products; structural shapes, iron or steel; steel; fabricated structural metal; manufactured hardware (general); steel pipe & tubes; blast furnaces & steel mills

### (G-5159)
### ILLINOIS WINDOW SHADE CO
Also Called: Brookline Shade Company
6250 N Broadway St  (60660-1903)
PHONE.................................773 743-6025
**Fax:** 773 743-1749
Joan Lichtfuss, *President*
Jerald Lichtfuss, *Corp Secy*
Bill Lichtfuss, *Sales Mgr*
**EMP:** 9 EST: 1905
**SQ FT:** 12,000
**SALES (est):** 1.1MM  **Privately Held**
**WEB:** www.brooklineshade.com
**SIC: 2591**  Window shades

### (G-5160)
### ILLUMIVATION STUDIOS LLC
2415 W 19th St Unit 3  (60608-3054)
PHONE.................................312 261-5561
Michael Dunbar, *Mng Member*
**EMP:** 4 EST: 2011
**SALES (est):** 315.6K  **Privately Held**
**SIC: 3999**  Theatrical scenery

### (G-5161)
### IMAGINATION PUBLISHING LLC
Also Called: Baumer Financial Publishing
600 W Fulton St Ste 600  (60661-1256)
PHONE.................................312 887-1000
**Fax:** 312 887-1003
Alma Bahman, *Editor*
Jordan Berger, *Editor*
Tessa D'Agosta, *Editor*
Megan Dawson, *Editor*
Roderick Kelly, *Editor*
**EMP:** 50
**SQ FT:** 17,500
**SALES:** 10MM  **Privately Held**
**WEB:** www.imaginepub.com
**SIC: 2721**  2741  Magazines: publishing only, not printed on site; newsletter publishing

### (G-5162)
### IMANAGE LLC (PA)
540 W Madison St Ste 2400  (60661-2562)
PHONE.................................312 667-7000
Neil Araujo, *CEO*
Rafiq Mohammadi, *Vice Pres*
Ray Scheppach, *CFO*
Jessica Martens, *Credit Staff*

Dan Carmel, *Chief Mktg Ofcr*
**EMP:** 160 EST: 2015
**SQ FT:** 26,000
**SALES:** 76MM  **Privately Held**
**SIC: 7372**  Business oriented computer software

### (G-5163)
### IMANIS ORIGINAL BEAN PIES & F
3931 S Leavitt St  (60609-2203)
PHONE.................................773 716-7007
Imani Muhammad, *President*
**EMP:** 4 EST: 2015
**SALES (est):** 116.1K  **Privately Held**
**SIC: 2053**  Mfg Frozen Bakery Products

### (G-5164)
### IMEDIA NETWORK INC
3414 N Milwaukee Ave 2n  (60641-3936)
PHONE.................................847 331-1774
Horatiu Boeriu, *President*
**EMP:** 1 EST: 2009
**SALES:** 300K  **Privately Held**
**SIC: 2741**  Miscellaneous publishing

### (G-5165)
### IMPERIAL GROUP MFG INC
311 W Superior St Ste 510  (60654-3537)
PHONE.................................615 325-9224
**EMP:** 325
**SALES (corp-wide):** 651.7MM  **Privately Held**
**SIC: 3715**  Truck trailers; trailer bodies; truck trailer chassis
**PA:** Imperial Group Manufacturing, Inc.
4545 Airport Rd
Denton TX 76207
940 565-8505

### (G-5166)
### IMPERIAL OIL INC
4346 N Western Ave  (60618-1647)
PHONE.................................773 866-1235
Mahboob Abbas, *President*
**EMP:** 2
**SALES (est):** 237.1K  **Privately Held**
**SIC: 3713**  Automobile wrecker truck bodies

### (G-5167)
### IMPERIAL PLATING COMPANY ILL
7030 W 60th St  (60638-3102)
PHONE.................................773 586-3500
**Fax:** 773 229-0962
Walter Kuziel Jr, *President*
Charles Brass, *Vice Pres*
Anthony Kuziel, *VP Prdtn*
Rebeca Pavon, *QC Mgr*
Rebecc Hernandez, *Office Mgr*
**EMP:** 44
**SQ FT:** 40,000
**SALES:** 3.2MM  **Privately Held**
**WEB:** www.imperialplating.com
**SIC: 3471**  Electroplating of metals or formed products; buffing for the trade; polishing, metals or formed products

### (G-5168)
### IMPERIAL STORE FIXTURES INC
3768 N Clark St  (60613-3810)
PHONE.................................773 348-1137
**Fax:** 773 348-0508
Rose T Stranc, *President*
Edward L Stranc Jr, *Admin Sec*
**EMP:** 8
**SQ FT:** 3,000
**SALES (est):** 1.2MM  **Privately Held**
**SIC: 2542**  2431  Shelving, office & store: except wood; millwork

### (G-5169)
### IMPERIAL ZINC CORP (PA)
Also Called: Imperial Metals Group
1031 E 103rd St  (60628-3007)
PHONE.................................773 264-5900
David Kozin, *President*
Dave Goss, *General Mgr*
Michael Weinger, *Corp Secy*
Marc D Spellman, *Admin Sec*
▲ **EMP:** 80
**SQ FT:** 110,000
**SALES (est):** 29.6MM  **Privately Held**
**WEB:** www.imperialzinc.com
**SIC: 3341**  Secondary nonferrous metals

## Chicago - Cook County (G-5170)

**(G-5170)**
**IMPRESSIVE IMPRESSIONS**
329 W 18th St Ste 306  (60616-1772)
PHONE..................312 432-0501
Fax: 312 432-0503
Carlos Ibarra, *Owner*
Dorothy Ibarra, *Co-Owner*
Dave Ransom, *Personnel Exec*
EMP: 4
SALES: 395K  Privately Held
WEB: www.impressiveimpressions.com
SIC: 2759  Commercial printing

**(G-5171)**
**IN3GREDIENTS INC**
Also Called: Gelnex
30 N Michigan Ave Ste 505  (60602-3836)
PHONE..................312 577-4275
Felipe Chaluppe, *Owner*
Ana Espinosa, *Manager*
▲ EMP: 3
SALES (est): 411.1K  Privately Held
SIC: 2899  Gelatin

**(G-5172)**
**INDEPENDENCE INC**
47 E Oak St Ste 2w  (60611-1867)
PHONE..................312 675-2105
EMP: 4
SALES (est): 81.1K  Privately Held
SIC: 2329  Men's & boys' leather, wool & down-filled outerwear

**(G-5173)**
**INDEPENDENCE TUBE CORPORATION (HQ)**
6226 W 74th St  (60638-6196)
PHONE..................708 496-0380
Fax: 708 563-1950
Dave Grohne, *CEO*
Phillip Alonzo, *Division Mgr*
John Anton, *Division Mgr*
Christopher Ambrosini, *VP Mfg*
Gary Olson, *Foreman/Supr*
◆ EMP: 90
SQ FT: 220,000
SALES (est): 49.6MM
SALES (corp-wide): 16.2B  Publicly Held
WEB: www.independencetube.com
SIC: 3317  Tubes, wrought; welded or lock joint
PA: Nucor Corporation
    1915 Rexford Rd Ste 400
    Charlotte NC 28211
    704 366-7000

**(G-5174)**
**INDIA TRIBUNE LTD (PA)**
3304 W Peterson Ave  (60659-3510)
PHONE..................773 588-5077
Fax: 773 588-7011
Prashant Shah, *President*
Eric Shah, *Publisher*
John Massey, *Manager*
Ravi Ponangi, *Officer*
EMP: 8 EST: 1977
SQ FT: 5,000
SALES: 800K  Privately Held
WEB: www.indiatribune.com
SIC: 2721  2711  Periodicals: publishing only; newspapers

**(G-5175)**
**INDIGO DIGITAL PRINTING LLC**
900 S Wabash Ave Side  (60605-2239)
PHONE..................312 753-3025
Catalin Nedelcu, *Mng Member*
Augustina Nedelcu,
EMP: 3
SQ FT: 1,600
SALES (est): 100K  Privately Held
SIC: 2752  Commercial printing, lithographic

**(G-5176)**
**INDUSTRIAL FENCE INC (PA)**
1300 S Kilbourn Ave  (60623-1045)
PHONE..................773 521-9900
Fax: 773 521-9904
Mike Saltijeral, *CEO*
Miguel A Saltijeral, *President*
Alan Tutje, *CFO*
Maria E Saltijeral, *Admin Sec*
EMP: 42 EST: 1999
SQ FT: 80,000
SALES: 20.6MM  Privately Held
SIC: 3446  1799  1611  Fences or posts, ornamental iron or steel; fence construction; highway signs & guardrails

**(G-5177)**
**INDUSTRIAL INSTRUMENT SVC CORP**
5643 W 63rd Pl  (60638-5515)
PHONE..................773 581-3355
Fax: 773 767-1501
Armon Schmidt, *President*
Majorie Schmidt, *Vice Pres*
EMP: 6 EST: 1959
SQ FT: 1,700
SALES (est): 830K  Privately Held
SIC: 5084  7699  3546  3545  Metalworking machinery; industrial machinery & equipment repair; power-driven handtools; machine tool accessories

**(G-5178)**
**INDUSTRIAL MINT WLDG MACHINING**
1431 W Pershing Rd  (60609-2407)
P.O. Box 385, Kingsbury IN  (46345-0385)
PHONE..................773 376-6526
Fax: 773 376-0631
Katie Hayes, *Human Res Dir*
Gary Steindler, *Sales Staff*
Stephen Sularski, *Manager*
EMP: 85
SQ FT: 69,500
SALES (corp-wide): 25.1MM  Privately Held
SIC: 7699  7692  3441  Industrial equipment services; welding repair; fabricated structural metal
PA: Industrial Maintenance Welding & Machining Co Inc
    2nd & Hupp Rd
    Kingsbury IN 46345
    219 393-5531

**(G-5179)**
**INDUSTRIAL PIPE AND SUPPLY CO**
5100 W 16th St  (60804-1926)
PHONE..................708 652-7511
Fax: 708 652-7529
Stuart J Feinberg, *President*
William J Bero, *Vice Pres*
Dwight Schrimsher, *Plant Mgr*
EMP: 45
SQ FT: 51,000
SALES (est): 16.6MM  Privately Held
SIC: 5085  3569  3498  3312  Valves & fittings; sprinkler systems, fire: automatic; fabricated pipe & fittings; blast furnaces & steel mills

**(G-5180)**
**INDUSTRIAL SERVICE SOLUTIONS (PA)**
875 N Michigan Ave  (60611-1803)
PHONE..................917 609-6979
Jim Rogers, *CEO*
EMP: 10
SALES (est): 22MM  Privately Held
SIC: 7694  3625  5063  6719  Electric motor repair; motor controls, electric; motors, electric; investment holding companies, except banks

**(G-5181)**
**INDUSTRYREADYCOM INC**
2950 W Carroll Ave Ste 3  (60612-1755)
PHONE..................773 575-7001
Vince Marrocco, *President*
Reginald Destin, *Vice Pres*
EMP: 2
SQ FT: 8,400
SALES: 200K  Privately Held
SIC: 3949  Skateboards

**(G-5182)**
**INFINISCENE INC**
25 W Hubbard St Fl 5  (60654-5644)
PHONE..................630 567-0452
Stuart Grubbs, *President*
Aaron Hassell, *COO*
EMP: 7
SALES (est): 246K  Privately Held
SIC: 7372  Prepackaged software

**(G-5183)**
**INFINITY METAL SPINNING INC**
10247 S Avenue O  (60617-5904)
PHONE..................773 731-4467
Moises Tellez, *President*
Joseph Tellez, *Vice Pres*
EMP: 9
SALES: 200K  Privately Held
SIC: 3542  Machine tools, metal forming type

**(G-5184)**
**INFOR (US) INC**
Also Called: Ssa Global
8725 W Higgins Rd  (60631-2716)
PHONE..................312 279-1245
Teshome Kassa, *Branch Mgr*
EMP: 65
SALES (corp-wide): 2.6B  Privately Held
SIC: 7372  Prepackaged software
HQ: Infor (Us), Inc.
    13560 Morris Rd Ste 4100
    Alpharetta GA 30004
    678 319-8000

**(G-5185)**
**INFOR (US) INC**
Also Called: Ssa Global Technologies, Inc
500 W Madison St Fl 22  (60661-2557)
PHONE..................312 258-6000
Mike Brooks, *Vice Pres*
Stan Hill, *Accounts Mgr*
Kevin Fee, *Accounts Exec*
Michael Greenough, *Branch Mgr*
Maureen Carrigan, *Manager*
EMP: 225
SALES (corp-wide): 3.3B  Privately Held
SIC: 7372  Prepackaged software
HQ: Infor (Us), Inc.
    13560 Morris Rd Ste 4100
    Alpharetta GA 30004
    678 319-8000

**(G-5186)**
**INFORMATION RESOURCES INC**
150 N Clinton St  (60661-1402)
PHONE..................312 474-3380
Manish Shah, *Vice Pres*
Allan Russ, *Human Res Mgr*
Susan Cuptavetos, *Manager*
S Zagorski, *Systems Analyst*
EMP: 5
SALES (corp-wide): 610.8MM  Privately Held
WEB: www.infores.com
SIC: 7372  8732  Prepackaged software; business research service
PA: Information Resources, Inc
    150 N Clinton St
    Chicago IL 60661
    312 726-1221

**(G-5187)**
**INFORMATION RESOURCES INC (PA)**
Also Called: Infoscan
150 N Clinton St  (60661-1402)
PHONE..................312 726-1221
Fax: 312 715-2591
Rick Lenny, *Ch of Bd*
Andrew Appel, *President*
Lawrence Benjamin, *President*
Beverly A Grant, *President*
Nigel Howlett, *President*
EMP: 1500
SQ FT: 250,000
SALES (est): 610.8MM  Privately Held
WEB: www.infores.com
SIC: 7372  Prepackaged software

**(G-5188)**
**INFORMATION RESOURCES INC**
550 W Washington Blvd # 6  (60661-2595)
PHONE..................312 474-8900
Steve Frenda, *Exec VP*
Joseph Durret, *Manager*
Rakesh Shah, *Software Engr*
Cheryl Smith, *Database Admin*
Kirsty Harris-Clarke, *Director*
EMP: 900
SALES (corp-wide): 610.8MM  Privately Held
WEB: www.infores.com
SIC: 7372  8732  Prepackaged software; market analysis or research
PA: Information Resources, Inc
    150 N Clinton St
    Chicago IL 60661
    312 726-1221

**(G-5189)**
**INFORMATION USA INC**
Also Called: Hirise Promotions & Marketing
1555 N Dearborn Pkwy Ofc  (60610-7426)
PHONE..................312 943-6288
Fax: 312 943-7064
Kim Mc Coy, *Mktg Dir*
Debbie Samson, *Director*
EMP: 3
SALES (corp-wide): 871.9K  Privately Held
SIC: 2731  Books: publishing only
PA: Information Usa, Inc.
    3909 Prospect St
    Kensington MD 20895
    301 929-8400

**(G-5190)**
**ING BANK FSB**
21 E Chestnut St  (60611-2050)
PHONE..................312 981-1236
James Cummings, *Principal*
EMP: 3  Publicly Held
SIC: 3944  Banks, toy
HQ: Ing Bank Fsb
    802 Delaware Ave
    Wilmington DE 19801

**(G-5191)**
**INGERSOLL-RAND COMPANY**
15768 Collection Ctr Dr  (60693-0157)
PHONE..................704 655-4000
EMP: 26  Privately Held
SIC: 3561  3563  2899  Pumps & pumping equipment; air & gas compressors including vacuum pumps; corrosion preventive lubricant
HQ: Ingersoll-Rand Company
    800 Beaty St Ste B
    Davidson NC 28036
    704 655-4000

**(G-5192)**
**INGLOT ELECTRONICS CORP**
Also Called: Inelco
4878 N Elston Ave  (60630-2578)
PHONE..................773 286-5881
Fax: 773 286-4811
Christopher Inglot, *CEO*
Andrew Platowski, *President*
John Bosch, *Vice Pres*
Kerry Kaczmare, *Purch Dir*
Kerry Kacz, *Manager*
▲ EMP: 58 EST: 1964
SQ FT: 28,000
SALES (est): 9.5MM  Privately Held
WEB: www.inglotelec.com
SIC: 3677  5065  3643  3621  Electronic transformers; coil windings, electronic; inductors, electronic; electronic parts & equipment; current-carrying wiring devices; motors & generators; transformers, except electric

**(G-5193)**
**INGREDION INCORPORATED**
Also Called: Corn Products International
141 W Jackson Blvd # 340  (60604-2992)
PHONE..................708 551-2600
A J Didominicis, *Manager*
EMP: 8
SALES (corp-wide): 5.7B  Publicly Held
WEB: www.cornproducts.com
SIC: 2046  Wet corn milling
PA: Ingredion Incorporated
    5 Westbrook Corporate Ctr # 500
    Westchester IL 60154
    708 551-2600

**(G-5194)**
**INK SPOT PRINTING**
2 N Riverside Plz Ste 365  (60606-2620)
PHONE..................773 528-0288
Fax: 773 528-0239
Stuart Fisher, *Owner*
Sura Fisher, *Co-Owner*

Todd Fisher, *Co-Owner*
EMP: 6
SQ FT: 5,000
SALES (est): 420K  Privately Held
SIC: 2752  2791  Commercial printing, offset; typesetting

**(G-5195)**
**INKDOT LLC**
2032 W Fulton St 263a  (60612-2302)
PHONE..................................630 768-6415
John Larkin, *Mng Member*
EMP: 2
SALES: 300K  Privately Held
SIC: 2752  Photo-offset printing

**(G-5196)**
**INKLING**
6723 N Greenview Ave  (60626-4207)
PHONE..................................312 376-8129
Adam Siegel, *Principal*
EMP: 3
SALES: 250K  Privately Held
SIC: 7372  Business oriented computer software

**(G-5197)**
**INKPARTNERS CORPORATION**
3662 S Hermitage Ave  (60609-1219)
PHONE..................................773 843-1786
Roberto Perez, *President*
EMP: 7
SQ FT: 7,000
SALES (est): 660K  Privately Held
SIC: 2752  Commercial printing, lithographic

**(G-5198)**
**INNERWORKINGS INC (PA)**
600 W Chicago Ave Ste 850  (60654-2529)
PHONE..................................312 642-3700
Fax: 312 642-3704
Jack M Greenberg, *Ch of Bd*
Eric D Belcher, *President*
Oren Azar, *Vice Pres*
Oliver Kimberley, *Vice Pres*
Doug Kraay, *Vice Pres*
▲ EMP: 100
SALES: 1B  Publicly Held
WEB: www.iwprint.com
SIC: 2752  7374  7372  Commercial printing, lithographic; data processing & preparation; publishers' computer software

**(G-5199)**
**INNOPHOS INC**
512 E 138th St  (60803)
PHONE..................................773 468-2300
Rashad Nuruddin, *Plant Engr*
Eric Haaijer, *Branch Mgr*
EMP: 5
SALES (corp-wide): 725.3MM  Publicly Held
WEB: www.innophos.com
SIC: 2874  2819  Phosphates; industrial inorganic chemicals
HQ: Innophos, Inc.
    259 Prospect Plains Rd A
    Cranbury NJ 08512
    609 495-2495

**(G-5200)**
**INNOVATIVE MAG DRIVE LLC**
6911 W 59th St  (60638-3205)
PHONE..................................630 543-4240
Manfred Klein, *Principal*
EMP: 3
SALES (est): 142.6K  Privately Held
SIC: 3568  Mfg Power Transmission Equipment

**(G-5201)**
**INNOVATIVE SPORTS TRAINING INC**
3711 N Ravenswood Ave # 150  (60613-3599)
PHONE..................................773 244-6470
Lee Johnson, *President*
Meredith Evans, *Office Mgr*
Monika Bhuta, *Technical Staff*
EMP: 1
SQ FT: 2,000
SALES (est): 285.8K  Privately Held
WEB: www.innsport.com
SIC: 3825  Measuring instruments & meters, electric

**(G-5202)**
**INOPRINTS**
700 N Green St Ste 503  (60642-5474)
PHONE..................................312 994-2351
Jovim Ventura, *Principal*
EMP: 2
SALES (est): 228.3K  Privately Held
SIC: 2752  Business form & card printing, lithographic

**(G-5203)**
**INRULE TECHNOLOGY INC**
651 W Washington Blvd # 500  (60661-2125)
PHONE..................................312 648-1800
Paul Hessinger, *CEO*
David Labe, *CFO*
Loren Goodman, *CTO*
Rik Chomko, 
EMP: 24
SQ FT: 3,000
SALES (est): 3.9MM  Privately Held
WEB: www.inrule.com
SIC: 7372  Prepackaged software

**(G-5204)**
**INSIDE COUNCIL**
222 S Riverside Plz # 620  (60606-5808)
PHONE..................................312 654-3500
Charles H Carman, *President*
Thomas Dugan, *Publisher*
Thomas Goodman, *Publisher*
Brad Blickstein, *General Mgr*
Nat Flavin, *Principal*
EMP: 14
SQ FT: 6,800
SALES (est): 1.1MM  Privately Held
WEB: www.cltmag.com
SIC: 2721  8111  Trade journals: publishing only, not printed on site; legal services

**(G-5205)**
**INSTANT COLLATING SERVICE INC**
2443 W 16th St  (60608-1780)
PHONE..................................312 243-4703
Fax: 312 243-4559
Cecelia Calandrino, *President*
Cynthia Redwood, *Vice Pres*
Harvey Honig, *Treasurer*
EMP: 12
SQ FT: 25,000
SALES: 750K  Privately Held
SIC: 2789  Trade binding services

**(G-5206)**
**INSTANTWHIP-CHICAGO INC**
1535 N Cicero Ave  (60651-1619)
PHONE..................................773 235-5588
James Ring, *General Mgr*
EMP: 15
SALES (corp-wide): 6.7MM  Privately Held
SIC: 2026  2099  2024  Whipped topping, except frozen or dry mix; food preparations; ice cream & frozen desserts
PA: Instantwhip-Chicago, Inc.
    2200 Cardigan Ave
    Columbus OH 43215
    614 488-2536

**(G-5207)**
**INSTITUTE FOR PUBLIC AFFAIRS**
Also Called: In These Times
2040 N Milwaukee Ave Fl 2  (60647-4002)
PHONE..................................773 772-0100
Fax: 773 772-4180
Jeff Allen, *Publisher*
Jeremy Gantz, *Editor*
Joel Blifus, *Director*
EMP: 12
SQ FT: 8,000
SALES: 3.2MM  Privately Held
WEB: www.inthesetimes.com
SIC: 2721  Magazines: publishing & printing

**(G-5208)**
**INTEGRATED INDUSTRIES INC**
4201 W 36th St Ste 1  (60632-3826)
PHONE..................................773 299-1970
Maureen Godino, *Principal*
EMP: 5
SALES (corp-wide): 5.4MM  Privately Held
SIC: 3999  Atomizers, toiletry
PA: Integrated Industries, Inc.
    1 Penville Rd
    Woodbridge NJ 07095
    732 283-1910

**(G-5209)**
**INTEL CORPORATION**
21003 Network Pl  (60673-1210)
PHONE..................................408 765-8080
Sam Habbal, *Branch Mgr*
EMP: 57
SALES (corp-wide): 59.3B  Publicly Held
SIC: 3674  7372  Semiconductors & related devices; prepackaged software
PA: Intel Corporation
    2200 Mission College Blvd
    Santa Clara CA 95054
    408 765-8080

**(G-5210)**
**INTER SWISS LTD**
5410 W Roosevelt Rd # 242  (60644-1478)
PHONE..................................773 379-0400
Fax: 773 473-7779
Debbie Seidel, *Principal*
Colin Rittgers, *Director*
EMP: 14
SALES (est): 2MM  Privately Held
SIC: 2531  Seats, railroad

**(G-5211)**
**INTERESTING PRODUCTS INC**
Also Called: Design Lab
328 N Albany Ave  (60612-1718)
PHONE..................................773 265-1100
Larry Schoeneman, *President*
EMP: 3
SQ FT: 30,000
SALES (est): 290K  Privately Held
WEB: www.interesting-products.com
SIC: 3999  Theatrical scenery

**(G-5212)**
**INTERFACEFLOR LLC**
600 W Van Buren St # 800  (60607-3708)
PHONE..................................312 775-6307
Fax: 630 281-3567
Andy Knaebel, *COO*
EMP: 36
SALES (corp-wide): 958.6MM  Publicly Held
SIC: 2273  Finishers of tufted carpets & rugs
HQ: Interfaceflor, Llc
    1503 Orchard Hill Rd
    Lagrange GA 30240
    706 882-1891

**(G-5213)**
**INTERFACEFLOR LLC**
440 N Wells St Ste 200  (60654-4550)
PHONE..................................312 836-3389
EMP: 20
SALES (corp-wide): 1B  Publicly Held
SIC: 2273  Mfg Carpets/Rugs
HQ: Interfaceflor, Llc
    1503 Orchard Hill Rd
    Lagrange GA 30240
    706 882-1891

**(G-5214)**
**INTERFACEFLOR LLC**
222 Merchandise Mart Plz # 130  (60654-1103)
PHONE..................................312 822-9640
Fax: 312 822-7240
Greg Colando, *Branch Mgr*
EMP: 16
SALES (corp-wide): 958.6MM  Publicly Held
WEB: www.ca.interfaceinc.com
SIC: 2273  Carpets & rugs
HQ: Interfaceflor, Llc
    1503 Orchard Hill Rd
    Lagrange GA 30240
    706 882-1891

**(G-5215)**
**INTERIOR TECTONICS LLC**
1716 N Cleveland Ave  (60614-5603)
PHONE..................................312 515-7779
Pamela De Varela,
EMP: 5
SQ FT: 1,100
SALES: 700K  Privately Held
WEB: www.interiortectonics.com
SIC: 5712  3699  Furniture stores; security devices

**(G-5216)**
**INTERMEC TECHNOLOGIES CORP**
375 W Erie St Apt 314  (60654-5793)
PHONE..................................312 475-0106
Deepak Mishra, *Branch Mgr*
EMP: 3
SALES (corp-wide): 39.3B  Publicly Held
WEB: www.intermec.net
SIC: 3577  Printers, computer
HQ: Intermec Technologies Corporation
    16201 25th Ave W
    Lynnwood WA 98087
    425 348-2600

**(G-5217)**
**INTERMERICAN CLINICAL SVCS INC**
2651 W Division St  (60622-2851)
PHONE..................................773 252-1147
Ana E Castellanos, *President*
EMP: 9 EST: 1997
SALES (est): 1MM  Privately Held
SIC: 3821  Clinical laboratory instruments, except medical & dental

**(G-5218)**
**INTERMINAL SERVICES**
2040 E 106th St  (60617-6455)
PHONE..................................773 978-8129
Mike Roe, *Manager*
▲ EMP: 20
SALES (est): 954.9K  Privately Held
SIC: 1221  Unit train loading facility, bituminous or lignite

**(G-5219)**
**INTERNATIONAL BUS MCHS CORP**
Also Called: IBM
222 S Riverside Plz # 1  (60606-5808)
PHONE..................................312 423-6640
John Morris, *General Mgr*
Dan Beal, *Vice Pres*
EMP: 200
SALES (corp-wide): 79.9B  Publicly Held
SIC: 3572  Computer storage devices; computer auxiliary storage units
PA: International Business Machines Corporation
    1 New Orchard Rd Ste 1
    Armonk NY 10504
    914 499-1900

**(G-5220)**
**INTERNATIONAL COLLEGE SURGEONS (PA)**
Also Called: Interntnal Mseum Srgcal Scence
1516 N Lake Shore Dr Fl 3  (60610-6652)
PHONE..................................312 642-6502
Fax: 312 787-1624
Fidel Ruiz-Healy, *President*
Mark Golden, *Vice Pres*
Jennifer Tran, *Controller*
Justina Doyle, *Manager*
Lindsey Thieman, *Manager*
EMP: 4
SQ FT: 20,000
SALES: 773K  Privately Held
SIC: 8621  2721  8412  Medical field-related associations; periodicals: publishing only; museum

**(G-5221)**
**INTERNATIONAL NEWS**
4917 N Milwaukee Ave 14  (60630-2105)
PHONE..................................773 283-8323
Alok Patel, *President*
EMP: 4 EST: 2013
SALES (est): 216.3K  Privately Held
SIC: 2711  Newspapers

**(G-5222)**
**INTERNATIONAL PAPER COMPANY**
5300 W 73rd St  (60638-6502)
PHONE..................................708 728-8200

# Chicago - Cook County (G-5223)   GEOGRAPHIC SECTION

Gary Randolph, *Plant Mgr*
Gary Randolph, *Plant Mgr*
Brian Totzke, *Safety Mgr*
Patty Salvi, *Human Res Dir*
Janie Gibson, *Accounts Mgr*
**EMP:** 130
**SQ FT:** 150,000
**SALES (corp-wide):** 21B **Publicly Held**
**WEB:** www.internationalpaper.com
**SIC: 2653** Corrugated boxes, partitions, display items, sheets & pad
**PA:** International Paper Company
6400 Poplar Ave
Memphis TN 38197
901 419-9000

**(G-5223)**
**INTERNATIONAL TACTICAL TRAININ**
915 N Racine Ave Apt 2se (60642-0008)
**PHONE** .............................. 872 221-4886
Bethany Drucker, *President*
**EMP:** 9
**SALES (est):** 430.4K **Privately Held**
**SIC: 3999** 8748 Badges, metal: policemen, firemen, etc.; safety training service

**(G-5224)**
**INTERNATIONAL WOOD DESIGN INC**
941 N California Ave (60622-4478)
**PHONE** .............................. 773 227-9270
Julian Pyjor, *President*
**EMP:** 3
**SALES (est):** 229.8K **Privately Held**
**SIC: 2511** Wood household furniture

**(G-5225)**
**INTERNTIONAL CASINGS GROUP INC (PA)**
Also Called: I C G
4420 S Wolcott Ave (60609-3159)
**PHONE** .............................. 773 376-9200
Alon Nir, *President*
Jay Gotteiner, *General Mgr*
Tom Sanecki, *General Mgr*
John Neavill, *Opers Mgr*
Bryan Schultz, *Controller*
▼ **EMP:** 90
**SQ FT:** 52,000
**SALES (est):** 28MM **Privately Held**
**SIC: 2013** Sausage casings, natural; frozen meats from purchased meat

**(G-5226)**
**INTERSPORTS SCREEN PRINTING**
2407 N Central Park Ave (60647-2326)
**PHONE** .............................. 773 489-7383
Mario Saduirre, *Principal*
**EMP:** 2
**SALES (est):** 210.7K **Privately Held**
**WEB:** www.intersportsmall.com
**SIC: 2752** Commercial printing, lithographic

**(G-5227)**
**INTERSTATE MECHANICAL INC**
1882 S Normal Ave 1 (60616-1013)
**PHONE** .............................. 312 961-9291
Henry Tam, *President*
**EMP:** 1
**SALES (est):** 250K **Privately Held**
**SIC: 3531** Construction machinery

**(G-5228)**
**INTRA-CUT DIE CUTTING INC**
5559 N Northwest Hwy (60630-1130)
**PHONE** .............................. 773 775-6228
**Fax:** 773 775-1530
Angie Wilson, *President*
Joe Bellisario, *Vice Pres*
**EMP:** 10
**SQ FT:** 10,000
**SALES (est):** 1.8MM **Privately Held**
**WEB:** www.intra-cut.net
**SIC: 2675** Paper die-cutting

**(G-5229)**
**INTREPID TOOL INDUSTRIES LLC**
Everede Tool Company Div
5296 N Northwest Hwy (60630-1246)
**PHONE** .............................. 773 467-4200
**Fax:** 773 467-4210

Antonio Gallegos, *Plant Mgr*
Keith Browning, *Mfg Spvr*
John Husar, *Engineer*
Chris Woznicki, *Office Mgr*
Bret Tayne, *Manager*
**EMP:** 35
**SALES (corp-wide):** 9.7MM **Privately Held**
**SIC: 3541** 3545 Machine tools, metal cutting type; cutting tools for machine tools
**PA:** Intrepid Tool Industries, Llc
10895 N Slr Cnyn Way 10 Ste 100
Surprise AZ 85379
623 414-4800

**(G-5230)**
**INVEKTEK LLC**
2039 N Lincoln Ave Unit P (60614-4531)
**PHONE** .............................. 312 343-0600
Rob Loomis, *Managing Dir*
**EMP:** 3 **EST:** 2015
**SALES (est):** 146.7K **Privately Held**
**SIC: 3625** Controls for adjustable speed drives

**(G-5231)**
**INVENERGY WIND FIN CO III LLC**
1 S Wacker Dr Ste 1900 (60606-4644)
**PHONE** .............................. 312 224-1400
Matt Giblin, *Project Mgr*
Michael Polsky, *Mng Member*
Mark Geibel, *Manager*
**EMP:** 3
**SALES (est):** 21.5K **Privately Held**
**SIC: 3612** Power & distribution transformers

**(G-5232)**
**INVESTMENT INFORMATION SVCS**
Also Called: Perritt Capital Mangement
300 S Wacker Dr Ste 2880 (60606-6703)
**PHONE** .............................. 312 669-1650
Jerold Perritt PHD, *Manager*
**EMP:** 3
**SALES (corp-wide):** 3.6MM **Privately Held**
**WEB:** www.perrittcap.com
**SIC: 2721** Statistical reports (periodicals): publishing only
**PA:** Investment Information Services Inc
300 S Wacker Dr Ste 2880
Chicago IL 60606
312 669-1650

**(G-5233)**
**INVISIBLE INSTITUTE**
6100 S Blackstone Ave (60637-2912)
**PHONE** .............................. 415 669-4691
Rajiv Clair, *Treasurer*
Jamie Kalven, *Exec Dir*
**EMP:** 6
**SALES (est):** 423.5K **Privately Held**
**SIC: 7372** Publishers' computer software

**(G-5234)**
**INVISIO COMMUNICATIONS INC**
150 N Michigan Ave # 1950 (60601-7553)
**PHONE** .............................. 412 327-6578
Lars Hojgard Hansen, *CEO*
Thomas Larson, *CFO*
Raymond Clarke, *Director*
**EMP:** 8
**SALES (est):** 319.7K **Privately Held**
**SIC: 3663** 7389 Carrier equipment, radio communications;

**(G-5235)**
**INX INTERNATIONAL INK CO**
5001 S Mason Ave (60638-1416)
**PHONE** .............................. 708 496-3600
**Fax:** 708 562-0370
James Kochanny, *General Mgr*
Dennis Magdziak, *Vice Pres*
Patricia Vukas, *Purchasing*
Jason Graunke, *Manager*
**EMP:** 20
**SQ FT:** 25,000
**SALES (corp-wide):** 1.3B **Privately Held**
**SIC: 2893** Printing ink
**HQ:** Inx International Ink Co
150 N Martingale Rd # 700
Schaumburg IL 60173
630 382-1800

**(G-5236)**
**IPURSE INC**
70 W Madison St (60602-4252)
**PHONE** .............................. 312 344-3449
Robin Trehan, *President*
**EMP:** 15
**SQ FT:** 600
**SALES (est):** 597.7K **Privately Held**
**SIC: 3171** Women's handbags & purses

**(G-5237)**
**IQ7 TECHNOLOGY INC**
161 E Chicago Ave (60611-2601)
**PHONE** .............................. 917 670-1715
Christopher E Olofson, *President*
**EMP:** 9
**SALES (est):** 247K **Privately Held**
**SIC: 7372** Business oriented computer software

**(G-5238)**
**IRON CASTLE INC**
3847 S Kedzie Ave (60632-2730)
**PHONE** .............................. 773 890-0575
**Fax:** 773 890-1492
Hamidreza Alaviharisi, *CEO*
**EMP:** 15
**SALES (est):** 1.3MM **Privately Held**
**SIC: 3446** 2499 Fences or posts, ornamental iron or steel; snow fence, wood

**(G-5239)**
**IRONFORM HOLDINGS CO (PA)**
311 W Superior St Ste 510 (60654-3537)
**PHONE** .............................. 312 374-4810
Terence Wogan, *CEO*
**EMP:** 12
**SALES (est):** 118.7MM **Privately Held**
**SIC: 3469** 3444 Metal stampings; sheet metalwork

**(G-5240)**
**ISACHS SONS INC**
4500 S Kolin Ave Ste 1a (60632-4460)
**PHONE** .............................. 312 733-2815
**Fax:** 312 666-9108
Steve Sachs, *President*
Sach Hyman, *Manager*
▲ **EMP:** 10
**SALES (est):** 1.1MM **Privately Held**
**SIC: 2843** Leather finishing agents

**(G-5241)**
**ISE INC**
222 Merchandise Mart Plz (60654-1103)
**PHONE** .............................. 703 319-0390
Jehad Verjee, *CEO*
Shaffique Verjee, *COO*
**EMP:** 49
**SALES (est):** 2.5MM **Privately Held**
**SIC: 2522** Desks, office: except wood; tables, office: except wood

**(G-5242)**
**ISIS3D LLC**
1210 E 54th St (60615-5202)
**PHONE** .............................. 516 426-5410
Stephanie Avalos-Bock, *Principal*
**EMP:** 4
**SALES (est):** 380.1K **Privately Held**
**SIC: 3559** Robots, molding & forming plastics

**(G-5243)**
**ISKY NORTH AMERICA INC (PA)**
47 W Polk St Ste 208 (60605-2157)
**PHONE** .............................. 937 641-1368
Delin Hu, *President*
Fan LI, *Admin Sec*
**EMP:** 2
**SALES (est):** 229.3K **Privately Held**
**SIC: 2879** Agricultural chemicals

**(G-5244)**
**ISRAEL LEVY DIAMND CUTTERS INC**
29 E Madison St Ste 700 (60602-4543)
**PHONE** .............................. 312 368-8540
Israel Levy, *President*
Kim Penegor, *Controller*
Ken Smith, *Manager*
Albert Levy, *Admin Sec*
Noah Levy, *Admin Sec*
**EMP:** 50
**SQ FT:** 13,000

**SALES (est):** 6.4MM **Privately Held**
**SIC: 3915** Jewelers' materials & lapidary work

**(G-5245)**
**IT TRANSPORTATION COMPANY**
5156 W Winnemac Ave (60630-2330)
**PHONE** .............................. 773 383-5073
Aleksandar Pavicevic, *President*
**EMP:** 17
**SALES (est):** 950K **Privately Held**
**SIC: 3537** Industrial trucks & tractors

**(G-5246)**
**ITERATIVE THERAPEUTICS INC**
2201 W Campbell Park Dr (60612-4092)
**PHONE** .............................. 773 455-7203
Barry Arnason, *President*
David White, *Treasurer*
Cindy Bayley, *Director*
Mark Jensen, *Admin Sec*
**EMP:** 4
**SALES (est):** 360.1K **Privately Held**
**SIC: 2834** Pharmaceutical preparations

**(G-5247)**
**ITERUM THERAPEUTICS US LIMITED**
200 S Monroe St Ste 1575 (60606-5136)
**PHONE** .............................. 312 763-3975
Judith Matthews, *President*
**EMP:** 6
**SALES (est):** 294.2K **Privately Held**
**SIC: 2834** Pharmaceutical preparations

**(G-5248)**
**IVAN CARLSON ASSOCIATES INC**
2224 W Fulton St (60612-2206)
**PHONE** .............................. 312 829-4616
**Fax:** 312 829-1308
Jeff Mueller, *General Mgr*
Tina Marie Carson, *Chairman*
Scott Carlson, *Vice Pres*
Scott T Carson, *Vice Pres*
Earl Huntley, *Controller*
**EMP:** 26
**SALES (est):** 4MM **Privately Held**
**WEB:** www.ivancarlson.com
**SIC: 7922** 3993 2542 Scenery design, theatrical; signs & advertising specialties; partitions & fixtures, except wood

**(G-5249)**
**IXTAPA FOODS**
6135 S Nottingham Ave (60638-3909)
**PHONE** .............................. 773 788-9701
Humberto Cano, *Principal*
Bernard Rose, *Vice Pres*
▲ **EMP:** 3
**SALES (est):** 432.9K **Privately Held**
**SIC: 5141** 2099 5149 Groceries, general line; food preparations; groceries & related products

**(G-5250)**
**J & A SHEET METAL SHOP INC**
1800 N Campbell Ave (60647-4303)
**PHONE** .............................. 773 276-3739
**Fax:** 773 276-5151
Andy Favilla, *President*
Joe Favilla, *Vice Pres*
Silvia Reger, *Office Mgr*
**EMP:** 20
**SQ FT:** 13,000
**SALES (est):** 3.7MM **Privately Held**
**SIC: 3599** 3644 3613 Machine shop, jobbing & repair; electric outlet, switch & fuse boxes; cubicles (electric switchboard equipment)

**(G-5251)**
**J & J MR QUICK PRINT INC**
Also Called: J & J Printing
5729 S Archer Ave (60638-1617)
**PHONE** .............................. 773 767-7776
**Fax:** 773 767-9498
Sally Rodzak, *President*
James Rodzak, *Treasurer*
John Rodzak, *Admin Sec*
**EMP:** 5
**SQ FT:** 3,000
**SALES:** 350K **Privately Held**
**SIC: 2752** 2791 2789 Commercial printing, offset; typesetting; bookbinding & related work

# GEOGRAPHIC SECTION
## Chicago - Cook County (G-5281)

**(G-5252)**
**J & J SILK SCREENING**
5316 S Monitor Ave (60638-2716)
PHONE....................773 838-9000
Monserrate Wright, *Principal*
**EMP:** 3
**SALES (est):** 185.5K **Privately Held**
**SIC:** 2759 Screen printing

**(G-5253)**
**J & J WOODWORK FURNITURE INC**
7001 W 66th Pl (60638-4703)
PHONE....................708 563-9581
Janusz Kas, *President*
Jozef Skwirek, *Vice Pres*
**EMP:** 2
**SALES (est):** 284.3K **Privately Held**
**SIC:** 2511 Wood household furniture

**(G-5254)**
**J & S TOOL INC**
4142 W Lake St (60624-1718)
**Fax:** 773 826-1106
Steven Venci, *President*
**EMP:** 4
**SQ FT:** 3,000
**SALES (est):** 581.4K **Privately Held**
**SIC:** 3544 3599 Special dies & tools; machine shop, jobbing & repair

**(G-5255)**
**J B BURLING GROUP LTD**
540 W Aldine Ave Ste 6 (60657-3889)
PHONE....................773 327-5362
Jerry J Field, *Exec VP*
**EMP:** 3
**SALES (est):** 148.9K **Privately Held**
**SIC:** 3999 Manufacturing industries

**(G-5256)**
**J B WATTS COMPANY INC**
Also Called: Impac Products
6224 S Vernon Ave (60637-2320)
PHONE....................773 643-1855
**Fax:** 773 342-5650
James B Watts Sr, *President*
James B Watts Jr, *Vice Pres*
Barbara Hunt, *Admin Sec*
**EMP:** 4
**SALES (est):** 277.6K **Privately Held**
**SIC:** 2819 5169 5085 Industrial inorganic chemicals; chemicals & allied products; fasteners & fastening equipment

**(G-5257)**
**J C COMMUNICATIONS COMPANY**
318 W Adams St Ste 1406 (60606-5173)
P.O. Box 6563 (60606-0563)
PHONE....................312 236-5122
**Fax:** 312 236-3297
John Stark, *President*
**EMP:** 4
**SALES (est):** 345.7K **Privately Held**
**WEB:** www.starks-news.com
**SIC:** 2741 Miscellaneous publishing

**(G-5258)**
**J C DECAUX NEW YORK INC**
3959 S Morgan St (60609-2512)
PHONE....................312 456-2999
**Fax:** 312 456-2998
Nicholas Clochard-Bossue, *COO*
Raul Arana, *Maint Spvr*
Joseph Kaplan, *Accounts Exec*
**EMP:** 50
**SALES (corp-wide):** 9.2MM **Privately Held**
**SIC:** 2531 Benches for public buildings
**HQ:** J C Decaux New York Inc
3 Park Ave Fl 33
New York NY 10016
646 834-1200

**(G-5259)**
**J G UNIFORMS INC**
Also Called: J G B Uniforms & Career AP
5949 W Irving Park Rd (60634-2618)
PHONE....................773 545-4644
**Fax:** 773 545-3388
Halina Gala, *President*
Gregory Gala, *General Mgr*
Linda Hernandez, *Opers Mgr*
Joseph Gala, *Admin Sec*
**EMP:** 8
**SQ FT:** 1,900
**SALES (est):** 1MM **Privately Held**
**SIC:** 2311 Policemen's uniforms: made from purchased materials; military uniforms, men's & youths': purchased materials; firemen's uniforms: made from purchased materials

**(G-5260)**
**J J MATA INC**
2524 W Devon Ave (60659-1904)
PHONE....................773 750-0643
Zeena Patel, *President*
Anand Patel, *Owner*
**EMP:** 3
**SALES (est):** 213.8K **Privately Held**
**SIC:** 2037 Fruit juices

**(G-5261)**
**J OSHANA & SON PRINTING**
4021 W Irving Park Rd (60641-2926)
PHONE....................773 283-8311
**Fax:** 773 283-2512
Ron Oshana, *Principal*
**EMP:** 3
**SQ FT:** 3,100
**SALES (est):** 308.8K **Privately Held**
**SIC:** 2752 2791 Commercial printing, offset; typesetting

**(G-5262)**
**J P PRINTING INC**
5639 W Division St (60651-1141)
PHONE....................773 626-5222
**Fax:** 773 626-5249
Veronica Polk, *President*
**EMP:** 4
**SQ FT:** 1,200
**SALES (est):** 530K **Privately Held**
**WEB:** www.jpprinting.org
**SIC:** 5111 2791 Printing & writing paper; typesetting

**(G-5263)**
**J R HUSAR INC**
Also Called: Husar Picture Frame
1631 W Carroll Ave (60612-2501)
PHONE....................312 243-7888
**Fax:** 312 243-7999
Jeffery R Husar, *President*
Jeffery R Husar, *President*
Thomas Lynch, *Vice Pres*
**EMP:** 18
**SQ FT:** 25,000
**SALES (est):** 2.8MM **Privately Held**
**SIC:** 2499 Picture & mirror frames, wood

**(G-5264)**
**J T C INC**
Also Called: Ncc
4710 W North Ave (60639-4613)
PHONE....................773 292-9262
**Fax:** 773 292-0723
Al Cantar, *President*
Juan Berez, *Superintendent*
Robert Mann, *Manager*
**EMP:** 17
**SALES (est):** 2.6MM **Privately Held**
**SIC:** 3568 Power transmission equipment

**(G-5265)**
**JAALI BEAN INC**
1941 Wesy Oakdale Ave (60657)
PHONE....................312 730-5095
Brian Junkins, *President*
Monila Junkins, *Principal*
**EMP:** 2 **EST:** 2011
**SALES:** 300K **Privately Held**
**SIC:** 2032 5141 Ethnic foods: canned, jarred, etc.; food brokers

**(G-5266)**
**JABBER LABS INC**
175 N Harbor Dr Apt 2902 (60601-7879)
PHONE....................607 227-6353
Gustavo Bitdinger, *CEO*
**EMP:** 10
**SALES (est):** 281.9K **Privately Held**
**SIC:** 7372 Application computer software

**(G-5267)**
**JAC US INC**
Also Called: Mia Bossi
2444 W 16th St Ste 4 (60608-1731)
PHONE....................312 421-2268
**Fax:** 312 421-2294
Janet Lee, *President*
▲ **EMP:** 20
**SALES (est):** 1.5MM **Privately Held**
**WEB:** www.miabossi.com
**SIC:** 2399 Diapers, except disposable: made from purchased materials

**(G-5268)**
**JACKHAMMER**
6406 N Clark St (60626-4913)
PHONE....................773 743-5772
Rudolph Johnson, *Principal*
**EMP:** 2 **EST:** 2007
**SALES (est):** 261.2K **Privately Held**
**SIC:** 2599 Bar, restaurant & cafeteria furniture

**(G-5269)**
**JACOBS BOILER & MECH INDS INC**
6632 W Diversey Ave (60707-2217)
PHONE....................773 385-9900
**Fax:** 773 622-6632
Matthew D Jacobs, *President*
Victoria Ottenfeld, *Office Mgr*
Thomas G Jacobs, *Shareholder*
Joseph J Jacobs, *Admin Sec*
Joseph Jacobs, *Admin Sec*
**EMP:** 25
**SQ FT:** 15,000
**SALES (est):** 4.1MM **Privately Held**
**WEB:** www.jacobsboiler.com
**SIC:** 7699 7692 7629 3564 Boiler repair shop; welding repair; electrical repair shops; blowers & fans; blast furnaces & steel mills; plumbing & hydronic heating supplies

**(G-5270)**
**JAFFEE INVESTMENT PARTNR LP**
410 N Michigan Ave # 400 (60611-4213)
PHONE....................312 321-1515
Richard M Jaffee, *General Ptnr*
Karen Jaffee Cofsky, *General Ptnr*
Susan Jaffee Hardin, *General Ptnr*
Daniel S Jaffee, *General Ptnr*
Nancy E Jaffee, *General Ptnr*
**EMP:** 125
**SALES (est):** 3.6MM **Privately Held**
**SIC:** 6733 2842 3295 Personal investment trust management; sweeping compounds, oil or water absorbent, clay or sawdust; cat box litter

**(G-5271)**
**JAGOLI**
401 N Western Ave Ste 2 (60612-1418)
PHONE....................312 563-0583
Daniel G Garcia, *Owner*
Linda Didonato, *Sales Staff*
**EMP:** 9
**SALES (est):** 689.6K **Privately Held**
**SIC:** 2519 Household furniture

**(G-5272)**
**JAIL EDUCATION SOLUTIONS INC**
Also Called: Edovo
215 W Superior St Ste 600 (60654-8576)
PHONE....................773 263-0718
Brian Hill, *President*
**EMP:** 23 **EST:** 2013
**SALES (est):** 4.8MM **Privately Held**
**SIC:** 3999 Business consulting

**(G-5273)**
**JAIX LEASING COMPANY**
2 N Riverside Plz (60606-2600)
PHONE....................312 928-0850
Ted Baun, *Principal*
**EMP:** 5
**SALES (est):** 433.8K **Privately Held**
**SIC:** 3743 Railroad car rebuilding

**(G-5274)**
**JAMES PRECIOUS METALS PLATING**
5700 N Northwest Hwy (60646-6138)
PHONE....................773 774-8700
**Fax:** 773 774-3817
Ken Jacobsen, *President*
Tony Martinez, *Plant Mgr*
Luis Carrasco, *Engineer*
Beth Christiensen, *Office Mgr*
Francisco Ocampo, *Manager*
**EMP:** 10 **EST:** 1950
**SQ FT:** 6,000
**SALES:** 750K **Privately Held**
**SIC:** 3471 Electroplating of metals or formed products

**(G-5275)**
**JAMEX JEWELRY INC**
5 S Wabash Ave Ste 404 (60603-3501)
PHONE....................312 726-7867
**Fax:** 312 726-7869
Ronald Daley, *President*
**EMP:** 3
**SALES (est):** 170.7K **Privately Held**
**SIC:** 3911 Jewelry, precious metal

**(G-5276)**
**JANITOR LTD**
218 N Jefferson St # 202 (60661-1121)
PHONE....................773 936-3389
Cory Hohs,
Noah Levens,
**EMP:** 3 **EST:** 2013
**SALES (est):** 187.5K **Privately Held**
**SIC:** 7372 Application computer software

**(G-5277)**
**JANLER CORPORATION**
6545 N Avondale Ave (60631-1583)
PHONE....................773 774-0166
Carol K Ebel, *President*
Carol K Ebell, *President*
Dave Dziak, *Engineer*
John Neton, *Engineer*
Nick Ospina, *Sls & Mktg Exec*
▼ **EMP:** 40
**SQ FT:** 14,500
**SALES (est):** 9.5MM **Privately Held**
**WEB:** www.janler.com
**SIC:** 3544 3089 Forms (molds), for foundry & plastics working machinery; industrial molds; injection molding of plastics

**(G-5278)**
**JANS GRAPHICS INC**
Also Called: Ink Well
2 N Riverside Plz Ste 365 (60606-2620)
PHONE....................312 644-4700
**Fax:** 312 644-4703
Alvin Holtzman, *President*
Judith Holtzman, *Treasurer*
Steve Hirschfeld, *VP Sales*
**EMP:** 12
**SQ FT:** 2,600
**SALES:** 1.6MM **Privately Held**
**WEB:** www.inkwellchicago.com
**SIC:** 2752 7336 Commercial printing, lithographic; graphic arts & related design

**(G-5279)**
**JANSSEN PHARMACEUTICA INC**
20 N Wacker Dr Ste 1442 (60606-2906)
PHONE....................312 750-0507
Paula Costa, *Owner*
**EMP:** 14
**SALES (corp-wide):** 71.8B **Publicly Held**
**WEB:** www.janau.jnj.com
**SIC:** 2833 Anesthetics, in bulk form
**HQ:** Janssen Pharmaceuticals Inc
1125 Trnton Harbourton Rd
Titusville NJ 08560
609 730-2000

**(G-5280)**
**JARRIES SHOE BAGS**
107 S Parkside Ave (60644-3944)
PHONE....................773 379-4044
Jarrie Brown, *Principal*
**EMP:** 3
**SALES (est):** 169.9K **Privately Held**
**SIC:** 2393 Textile bags

**(G-5281)**
**JAS DAHERN SIGNS**
3257 S Harding Ave (60623-4912)
PHONE....................773 254-0717
Patty Bowermaster, *Principal*
**EMP:** 3
**SALES (est):** 170K **Privately Held**
**SIC:** 3993 Signs & advertising specialties

Chicago - Cook County (G-5282)

**(G-5282)**
**JASON LAU JEWELRY**
29 E Madison St Ste 1107 (60602-4492)
PHONE..................312 750-1028
Fax: 312 750-0886
Jason W Lau, *Owner*
EMP: 4
SALES (est): 409.5K **Privately Held**
SIC: 3911 5094 Jewelry, precious metal; jewelry

**(G-5283)**
**JAV MACHINE CRAFT INC**
4624 N Oketo Ave (60706-4601)
PHONE..................708 867-8608
Fax: 708 867-5464
Kenneth Valin, *President*
Casey Holik, *Manager*
EMP: 7 EST: 1950
SQ FT: 9,000
SALES (est): 1.2MM **Privately Held**
SIC: 3599 7692 Machine shop, jobbing & repair; welding repair

**(G-5284)**
**JAY CEE PLASTIC FABRICATORS**
2133 W Mclean Ave (60647-4524)
PHONE..................773 276-1920
Fax: 773 276-0491
Jerome J Boruch, *President*
Mabel M Kuras, *Admin Sec*
EMP: 10
SQ FT: 11,000
SALES (est): 710K **Privately Held**
SIC: 3089 Plastic hardware & building products; washers, plastic; bearings, plastic

**(G-5285)**
**JCDECAUX CHICAGO LLC**
3959 S Morgan St (60609-2512)
PHONE..................312 456-2999
Bernard Parisot, *President*
EMP: 30
SALES (est): 3.9MM
SALES (corp-wide): 9.2MM **Privately Held**
WEB: www.jcdecauxchicago.com
SIC: 2531 Public building & related furniture
HQ: Jcdecaux North America, Inc.
3 Park Ave Fl 33
New York NY 10016
646 834-1200

**(G-5286)**
**JCG INDUSTRIES INC**
Also Called: Aspen Foods
1115 W Fulton Market (60607-1213)
PHONE..................312 829-7282
Micheal Fields, *President*
Hasan Delikaia, *Rsch/Dvlpt Dir*
Judy Scully, *Human Res Dir*
Jeanne Meeder, *Executive*
EMP: 150
SALES (corp-wide): 121.3MM **Privately Held**
SIC: 2015 Chicken, processed: fresh; chicken, processed: frozen; turkey, processed: fresh
PA: Jcg Industries, Inc.
4404 W Berteau Ave
Chicago IL 60641
847 384-5940

**(G-5287)**
**JELD-WEN INC**
500 W Monroe St Ste 2010 (60661-3762)
PHONE..................312 544-5041
EMP: 159
SALES (corp-wide): 22.5B **Publicly Held**
WEB: www.cmicompany.com
SIC: 2493 Reconstituted wood products
HQ: Jeld-Wen, Inc.
440 S Church St Ste 400
Charlotte NC 28202
800 535-3936

**(G-5288)**
**JELLYVISION INC**
848 W Eastman St Ste 104 (60642-2635)
PHONE..................312 266-0606
Amanda Lannert, *President*
Harry N Gottlieb, *Chairman*
Josh Fosburg, *Vice Pres*
Kelli Kaufmann, *Opers Staff*
Elizabeth Baxter, *Production*
EMP: 100
SALES (est): 12.6MM **Privately Held**
WEB: www.jellyvision.com
SIC: 7372 Prepackaged software

**(G-5289)**
**JEM ASSOCIATES LTD (PA)**
5206 N Meade Ave (60630-1041)
PHONE..................847 808-8377
Fax: 773 763-2296
Joseph E Murrow, *Partner*
Geraldine Murrow, *Partner*
EMP: 1
SALES (est): 305.8K **Privately Held**
SIC: 2759 Commercial printing

**(G-5290)**
**JEN-SKO-VEC MACHINING & ENGRG**
5335 S Western Blvd (60609-5450)
PHONE..................773 776-7400
Fax: 773 776-7457
Phil Jenskovec, *Partner*
Paul Jenskovec, *Partner*
Rene Jenskovec, *Accountant*
EMP: 5
SQ FT: 8,000
SALES (est): 350K **Privately Held**
SIC: 3599 Machine shop, jobbing & repair

**(G-5291)**
**JENNY CAPP CO**
6605 S Harvard Ave (60621-3125)
PHONE..................773 217-0057
Jennipher Adkins, *Vice Pres*
EMP: 10
SQ FT: 4,500
SALES (est): 331.8K **Privately Held**
SIC: 2353 7389 2339 Mfg Hats/Caps/Millinery Business Services Mfg Women's/Misses' Outerwear

**(G-5292)**
**JENSEN PLATING WORKS INC (PA)**
183844 N Western Ave (60647)
PHONE..................773 252-7733
Thomas Jensen, *President*
▼ EMP: 20 EST: 1898
SQ FT: 3,000
SALES (est): 3.2MM **Privately Held**
SIC: 3471 Electroplating of metals or formed products

**(G-5293)**
**JENSEN PLATING WORKS INC**
1842 N Western Ave (60647-4382)
PHONE..................773 252-7733
Tom Jensen, *President*
EMP: 15
SALES (corp-wide): 3.2MM **Privately Held**
SIC: 3471 Electroplating of metals or formed products
PA: Jensen Plating Works Inc
183844 N Western Ave
Chicago IL 60647
773 252-7733

**(G-5294)**
**JERNBERG INDUSTRIES LLC (DH)**
328 W 40th Pl (60609-2815)
PHONE..................773 268-3004
George Thanopoulos, *CEO*
Michael Keslar, *General Mgr*
Phil Troha, *Senior Engr*
Robert Koscicki, *Treasurer*
Richard Donnely, *Controller*
EMP: 160
SQ FT: 400,000
SALES (est): 106.1MM
SALES (corp-wide): 3.9B **Publicly Held**
SIC: 3462 3463 Iron & steel forgings; nonferrous forgings
HQ: Hhi Forging, Llc
2727 W 14 Mile Rd
Royal Oak MI 48073
248 284-2900

**(G-5295)**
**JERO MEDICAL EQP & SUPS INC**
4444 W Chicago Ave (60651-3424)
PHONE..................773 305-4193
Obie C Wordlaw, *Ch of Bd*
Dr Julia A Bowen, *President*
Al Payne, *VP Finance*
Shirley Wordlaw, *Admin Sec*
▲ EMP: 27
SQ FT: 17,000
SALES (est): 5.1MM **Privately Held**
WEB: www.jeromedical.com
SIC: 5047 7699 8742 2389 Medical equipment & supplies; professional instrument repair services; hospital & health services consultant; disposable garments & accessories

**(G-5296)**
**JESUS PEOPLE USA FULL GOS**
Also Called: Lakefront Supply
5242 N Elston Ave (60630-1609)
PHONE..................773 989-2083
Fax: 773 282-5701
Terry Gaffron, *Manager*
EMP: 7
SALES (corp-wide): 18MM **Privately Held**
WEB: www.grrrecords.com
SIC: 2952 Roofing materials
PA: Jesus People, U.S.A., Full Gospel Ministries
2950 N Western Ave
Chicago IL 60618
773 252-1812

**(G-5297)**
**JET INDUSTRIES INC**
6025 S Oak Park Ave (60638-4011)
PHONE..................773 586-8900
Fax: 773 586-9636
Elizabeth Twardowski, *President*
John Twardowski, *Vice Pres*
EMP: 35
SQ FT: 18,000
SALES (est): 7.9MM **Privately Held**
SIC: 3441 3599 7692 Fabricated structural metal; machine shop, jobbing & repair; welding repair

**(G-5298)**
**JET RACK CORP**
6200 S New England Ave (60638-4083)
PHONE..................773 586-2150
Fax: 773 586-0114
George Samiotakis, *President*
Andrew Kittridge, *Vice Pres*
Adeline Kasprzyk, *Finance Other*
EMP: 20
SQ FT: 19,600
SALES (est): 2.8MM **Privately Held**
SIC: 2542 7699 3479 3443 Racks, merchandise display or storage: except wood; metal reshaping & replating services; coating of metals with plastic or resins; fabricated plate work (boiler shop); paints & allied products

**(G-5299)**
**JEWEL OSCO INC**
Also Called: Jewel-Osco 3407
5516 N Clark St (60640-1214)
PHONE..................773 728-7730
Dennis Corsco, *Branch Mgr*
EMP: 145
SALES (corp-wide): 58.8B **Privately Held**
WEB: www.jewelosco.com
SIC: 5411 2051 Supermarkets, chain; bread, cake & related products;
HQ: Jewel Osco, Inc.
150 E Pierce Rd Ste 200
Itasca IL 60143
630 948-6000

**(G-5300)**
**JEWEL OSCO INC**
Also Called: Jewel-Osco 3443
5343 N Broadway St (60640-2311)
PHONE..................773 784-1922
Paul Scyscka, *Manager*
Tom Cassidy, *Manager*
EMP: 150

SALES (corp-wide): 58.8B **Privately Held**
WEB: www.jewelosco.com
SIC: 5411 2051 5461 Supermarkets, chain; bread, cake & related products; bakeries
HQ: Jewel Osco, Inc.
150 E Pierce Rd Ste 200
Itasca IL 60143
630 948-6000

**(G-5301)**
**JF INDUSTRIES INC**
7751 W Rosedale Ave (60631-2201)
PHONE..................773 775-8840
Joe Fragola, *President*
EMP: 3
SALES (est): 400K **Privately Held**
SIC: 1731 3629 3999 General electrical contractor; electronic generation equipment; barber & beauty shop equipment

**(G-5302)**
**JHELSA METAL POLSG FABRICATION**
1900 N Austin Ave Ste 71 (60639-5017)
PHONE..................773 385-6628
Fax: 773 385-6632
Jorge Henaine, *President*
EMP: 7
SALES (est): 560K **Privately Held**
WEB: www.jhelsa.com
SIC: 3471 Polishing, metals or formed products

**(G-5303)**
**JIFFY METAL PRODUCTS INC**
5025 W Lake St (60644-2599)
PHONE..................773 626-8090
Fax: 773 626-1529
Jim Mueller, *President*
Teresa Muller, *Vice Pres*
EMP: 8 EST: 1939
SQ FT: 25,000
SALES (est): 1.2MM **Privately Held**
SIC: 3469 3443 Stamping metal for the trade; fabricated plate work (boiler shop)

**(G-5304)**
**JIM NOODLE & RICE**
2819 N Lincoln Ave (60657-4201)
PHONE..................773 935-5923
Woiawit Suwannit, *President*
EMP: 4
SALES (est): 353.1K **Privately Held**
SIC: 2098 Noodles (e.g. egg, plain & water), dry

**(G-5305)**
**JIMMYBARS**
Also Called: Jimmy's Healthy Foods
2558 W 16th St Fl 5th (60608-1751)
PHONE..................888 676-7971
James Simon, *CEO*
Annette Del Prete, *Founder*
EMP: 8
SALES (est): 313K **Privately Held**
SIC: 2099 Food preparations

**(G-5306)**
**JINNY CORP**
3505 N Kimball Ave (60618-5507)
PHONE..................773 588-7200
EMP: 3
SALES (est): 350K **Privately Held**
SIC: 2721 Magazine Publication

**(G-5307)**
**JLO METAL PRODUCTS CO A CORP**
5841 W Dickens Ave (60639-4095)
PHONE..................773 889-6242
Fax: 773 889-2129
John L Oberrieder Jr, *President*
Corey Long, *Plant Mgr*
Scott Harris, *Buyer*
John Roberts, *QC Mgr*
Corinne Vargas, *Human Res Mgr*
EMP: 80
SQ FT: 100,000
SALES (est): 15.8MM **Privately Held**
WEB: www.jlometal.com
SIC: 3469 3411 Stamping metal for the trade; metal cans

## GEOGRAPHIC SECTION

Chicago - Cook County (G-5335)

**(G-5308)**
**JO SNOW INC**
2852 W Lyndale St (60647-2908)
PHONE..................................773 732-3045
Melissa Dawn Yen, *President*
EMP: 3
SALES (est): 226.8K **Privately Held**
SIC: 2087 2063 Cocktail mixes, nonalcoholic; sugar syrup from sugar beets

**(G-5309)**
**JOES PRINTING**
6025 N Cicero Ave (60646-4301)
PHONE..................................773 545-6063
Fax: 773 545-7841
Joe Solaka, *Owner*
EMP: 3
SQ FT: 1,200
SALES: 300K **Privately Held**
SIC: 2752 3953 2789 2759 Commercial printing, offset; marking devices; bookbinding & related work; commercial printing

**(G-5310)**
**JOHN BEAN TECHNOLOGIES CORP (PA)**
Also Called: JBT
70 W Madison St Ste 4400 (60602-4546)
PHONE..................................312 861-5900
Fax: 312 861-5897
Thomas G Giacomini, *Ch of Bd*
David C Burdakin, *Division Pres*
Steven R Smith, *Division Pres*
Jason T Clayton, *Exec VP*
James L Marvin, *Exec VP*
EMP: 40
SQ FT: 24,000
SALES: 1.3B **Publicly Held**
SIC: 3556 3585 3537 Food products machinery; refrigeration & heating equipment; containers (metal), air cargo

**(G-5311)**
**JOHN BEYER RACE CARS**
10718 S Homan Ave (60655-2610)
PHONE..................................773 779-5313
Olive Beyer, *Principal*
EMP: 3
SALES (est): 278.5K **Privately Held**
SIC: 3711 Automobile assembly, including specialty automobiles

**(G-5312)**
**JOHN BUECHNER INC**
8 S Michigan Ave Ste 607 (60603-3467)
PHONE..................................312 263-2226
Fax: 312 263-6127
John Buechner, *President*
Margaret Krizmanic, *Corp Secy*
Clifford Wallace, *Vice Pres*
EMP: 5
SQ FT: 1,700
SALES (est): 2MM **Privately Held**
WEB: www.johnbuechner.com
SIC: 3911 5094 Jewelry, precious metal; precious stones & metals

**(G-5313)**
**JOHN CRANE INC (HQ)**
227 W Monroe St Ste 1800 (60606-5053)
PHONE..................................312 605-7800
Fax: 847 967-3915
Duncan Gillis, *President*
Gustavo Cerruti, *General Mgr*
Dan Clark, *General Mgr*
Gilberto Hernandez, *Counsel*
Paul Roberts, *Sr Corp Ofcr*
▲ EMP: 650 EST: 1917
SQ FT: 450,000
SALES (est): 1.6B
SALES (corp-wide): 4.1B **Privately Held**
WEB: www.johncrane.com
SIC: 3053 Gaskets & sealing devices; packing materials
PA: Smiths Group Plc
    4th Floor
    London SW1Y
    207 004-1600

**(G-5314)**
**JOHN HOFMEISTER & SON INC**
Also Called: Hofhaus
2386 S Blue Island Ave (60608-4228)
PHONE..................................773 847-0700
Fax: 773 847-6707
Matt Hofmeister, *President*
Robert Bukala, *Vice Pres*
Mark J Rataj, *Vice Pres*
Chris Chin, *Production*
Justo Sanchez, *Plant Engr*
▼ EMP: 60
SQ FT: 60,000
SALES (est): 15.9MM **Privately Held**
WEB: www.hofhaus.com
SIC: 2011 Hams & picnics from meat slaughtered on site

**(G-5315)**
**JOHN J MOESLE WHOLESALE MEATS**
Also Called: Moesle Meat Company
4725 S Talman Ave (60632-1406)
PHONE..................................773 847-4900
Fax: 773 847-5200
John J Moesle Jr, *President*
Barbara Moesle, *Corp Secy*
Michael Moesle, *Vice Pres*
EMP: 15 EST: 1945
SQ FT: 26,000
SALES (est): 2.2MM **Privately Held**
SIC: 2013 5147 Prepared pork products from purchased pork; meats & meat products

**(G-5316)**
**JOHN MANEELY COMPANY**
Also Called: Wheatland Tube Company
4435 S Western Blvd (60609-3024)
PHONE..................................773 254-0617
Fax: 773 254-2244
Shawn Londrie, *Principal*
Pete Lira, *Purchasing*
Humberto Hijuelos, *Engrg Dir*
Robert E Stefanak, *Engrg Dir*
Areli Cazares, *Human Res Mgr*
EMP: 150
SQ FT: 115,000 **Privately Held**
SIC: 3317 3498 3312 3083 Pipes, seamless steel; fabricated pipe & fittings; blast furnaces & steel mills; laminated plastics plate & sheet; electric conduits & fittings
HQ: Wheatland Tube, Llc
    227 W Monroe St Ste 2600
    Chicago IL 60606
    312 275-1600

**(G-5317)**
**JOHNNY RCKETS FIREWRKS DISPLAY**
4410 N Hamilton Ave (60625-1789)
PHONE..................................847 501-1270
John G Panchisin, *President*
▲ EMP: 2
SALES (est): 201.9K **Privately Held**
SIC: 2899 Flares, fireworks & similar preparations

**(G-5318)**
**JOHNNY VANS SMOKEHOUSE**
924 W Gordon Ter Apt 3 (60613-2079)
PHONE..................................773 750-1589
Brandi Kay Landreth, *Partner*
EMP: 3
SALES (est): 186.1K **Privately Held**
SIC: 2099 Sauces: dry mixes

**(G-5319)**
**JOHNSON CONTROLS INC**
850 W Jackson Blvd # 420 (60607-3047)
PHONE..................................312 829-5956
Regina Malone, *Training Spec*
EMP: 6
SALES (corp-wide): 36.8B **Privately Held**
SIC: 3714 5063 Motor vehicle parts & accessories; electrical supplies
PA: Johnson Controls, Inc.
    5757 N Green Bay Ave
    Milwaukee WI 53209
    414 524-1200

**(G-5320)**
**JOHNSON PUBLISHING COMPANY LLC (PA)**
Also Called: Fashion Fair Cosmetics Div
200 S Michigan Ave Fl 21 (60604-2473)
PHONE..................................312 322-9200
Fax: 312 322-9375
Clarisa Wilson, *President*
Kathy Chaney, *Editor*
Ericka Goodman, *Editor*
Christian Margena, *Editor*
Linda Johnson Rice, *Chairman*
▼ EMP: 250 EST: 1942
SQ FT: 110,000
SALES (est): 69.2MM **Privately Held**
SIC: 2721 2731 2844 Periodicals: publishing only; books: publishing only; cosmetic preparations; hair preparations, including shampoos

**(G-5321)**
**JOHNSON STEEL RULE DIE CO**
5410 W Roosevelt Rd # 228 (60644-1480)
PHONE..................................773 921-4334
Fax: 773 921-4336
William Drew, *President*
Kevin Barnes, *Vice Pres*
EMP: 12 EST: 1951
SQ FT: 10,000
SALES (est): 1.6MM **Privately Held**
SIC: 3544 Dies, steel rule

**(G-5322)**
**JONES SOFTWARE CORP**
Also Called: J-Soft Tech
531 S Plymouth Ct Ste 104 (60605-1510)
PHONE..................................312 952-0011
Kevin Jones, *CEO*
Kenya Brooks, *President*
EMP: 5
SALES (est): 141.8K **Privately Held**
SIC: 7372 7371 3991 Educational computer software; computer software development & applications; push brooms

**(G-5323)**
**JORDAN PAPER BOX COMPANY**
5045 W Lake St (60644-2596)
PHONE..................................773 287-5362
Fax: 773 287-5362
John M Jordan, *President*
Corinne F Jordan, *Vice Pres*
EMP: 20
SQ FT: 32,000
SALES (est): 1MM **Privately Held**
WEB: www.jordanpaperarts.com
SIC: 2652 2653 2657 2441 Setup paperboard boxes; corrugated & solid fiber boxes; folding paperboard boxes; nailed wood boxes & shook

**(G-5324)**
**JORGE A CRUZ**
240 N Harding Ave (60624-1836)
PHONE..................................773 722-2828
Jorge Cruz, *Principal*
EMP: 4 EST: 2008
SALES (est): 250.3K **Privately Held**
SIC: 7532 3711 Paint shop, automotive; automobile bodies, passenger car, not including engine, etc.

**(G-5325)**
**JORIKI LLC**
1220 W Wrightwood Ave (60614-1224)
PHONE..................................312 848-1136
James Langer,
EMP: 3 EST: 2013
SALES (est): 190.2K **Privately Held**
SIC: 2331 Women's & misses' blouses & shirts

**(G-5326)**
**JOSCO INC**
Also Called: American Speedy Printing
4830 N Harlem Ave (60706-3506)
PHONE..................................708 867-7189
Josephine Harrison, *President*
Joseph Harrison Jr, *Shareholder*
Joseph Harrison Sr, *Admin Sec*
EMP: 5
SQ FT: 1,500
SALES (est): 717.3K **Privately Held**
SIC: 2752 2791 2789 Commercial printing, offset; typesetting; bookbinding & related work

**(G-5327)**
**JOSEPH C WOLF**
5 S Wabash Ave Ste 1018 (60603-3156)
PHONE..................................312 332-3135
Gerald Wolf, *Owner*
EMP: 4
SALES (est): 750K **Privately Held**
SIC: 3911 Jewelry, precious metal

**(G-5328)**
**JOSEPH COPPOLINO**
Also Called: Coppolinos Itln BF Grill & Bar
4455 W 55th St (60632-4736)
PHONE..................................773 735-8647
Joseph Coppolino, *Owner*
EMP: 4
SALES (est): 240.5K **Privately Held**
SIC: 3011 Tires & inner tubes

**(G-5329)**
**JPMORGAN CHASE & CO**
9138 S Commercial Ave (60617-4307)
PHONE..................................773 978-3408
Roman Rodriguez, *Principal*
EMP: 12
SALES (corp-wide): 105.4B **Publicly Held**
SIC: 3644 Insulators & insulation materials, electrical
PA: Jpmorgan Chase & Co.
    270 Park Ave Fl 38
    New York NY 10017
    212 270-6000

**(G-5330)**
**JPMORGAN CHASE BANK NAT ASSN**
353 W 83rd St (60620-1700)
PHONE..................................773 994-2490
Lisa Walker, *Branch Mgr*
EMP: 4
SALES (corp-wide): 105.4B **Publicly Held**
SIC: 3644 Insulators & insulation materials, electrical
HQ: Jpmorgan Chase Bank, National Association
    1111 Polaris Pkwy
    Columbus OH 43240
    614 436-3055

**(G-5331)**
**JR BAKERY**
Also Called: Cheese Cake
2841 W Howard St (60645-1228)
PHONE..................................773 465-6733
Fax: 773 465-8671
Janet Rosing, *President*
Steve Esko, *Manager*
Ruth Sheinhart, *Administration*
EMP: 32
SQ FT: 3,600
SALES (est): 5.2MM **Privately Held**
SIC: 2051 2052 Cakes, bakery: except frozen; cookies & crackers

**(G-5332)**
**JR INDUSTRIES LLC**
4218 N California Ave (60618-1513)
PHONE..................................773 908-5317
Jesse Richardson, *Mng Member*
EMP: 13
SALES (est): 1.7MM **Privately Held**
SIC: 3999 Atomizers, toiletry

**(G-5333)**
**JR PLASTICS LLC**
Also Called: Stylemaster
2850 W Columbus Ave (60652-1620)
PHONE..................................773 523-5454
Fax: 773 523-9975
Martha Williams, *CEO*
EMP: 120
SALES (est): 10.8MM **Privately Held**
SIC: 3089 Plastic kitchenware, tableware & houseware

**(G-5334)**
**JTOOR LLC**
Also Called: J Toor Menswear
900 N Michigan Ave 308a (60611-6530)
PHONE..................................312 291-8249
Jivesh Toor, *President*
EMP: 6
SALES: 500K **Privately Held**
SIC: 2329 Men's & boys' sportswear & athletic clothing

**(G-5335)**
**JUICE TYME INC (PA)**
Also Called: Bevolution Group
4401 S Oakley Ave (60609-3020)
PHONE..................................773 579-1291
Fax: 773 579-1251

# Chicago - Cook County (G-5336)

## GEOGRAPHIC SECTION

Sam Lteif, *CEO*
Philip L Scott, *President*
Matt Martens, *COO*
Jerry Desmond, *Exec VP*
Jay W Erskin, *Senior VP*
◆ **EMP:** 18
**SQ FT:** 30,000
**SALES:** 50MM **Privately Held**
**WEB:** www.juicetyme.com
**SIC: 2033** 2037 Canned fruits & specialties; frozen fruits & vegetables

### (G-5336)
### JURY VERDICT REPORTER
415 N State St Ste 1 (60654-4607)
**PHONE**..................312 644-7800
Sandy Macfarland, *CEO*
**EMP:** 5
**SALES (est):** 257.3K **Privately Held**
**SIC: 2711** Newspapers, publishing & printing

### (G-5337)
### JUST ICE INC
1400 W 46th St (60609-3225)
**PHONE**..................773 301-7323
Rosanna Lloyd, *President*
**EMP:** 5
**SQ FT:** 900
**SALES:** 374K **Privately Held**
**SIC: 2097** Block ice

### (G-5338)
### JUST SASHES
5952 W Addison St (60634-4213)
**PHONE**..................773 205-1429
John R Videckis, *Owner*
**EMP:** 3
**SALES (est):** 254.3K **Privately Held**
**SIC: 2431** Window sashes, wood

### (G-5339)
### JUST TURKEY
4353 S Cottage Grove Ave (60653-3513)
**PHONE**..................708 957-2222
**EMP:** 4 **EST:** 2011
**SALES (est):** 278.6K **Privately Held**
**SIC: 3421** Table & food cutlery, including butchers'

### (G-5340)
### JUVENESSE BY ELAINE GAYLE INC
680 N Lake Shore Dr # 1007 (60611-4546)
**PHONE**..................312 944-1211
**Fax:** 312 944-8822
Elaine B Gayle, *President*
Margaret Grzeszczuk, *MIS Mgr*
Joseph Cochrane, *Admin Sec*
**EMP:** 5
**SQ FT:** 1,000
**SALES (est):** 614K **Privately Held**
**SIC: 2844** 5122 Cosmetic preparations; cosmetics

### (G-5341)
### K & K ABRASIVES & SUPPLIES
5161 S Millard Ave (60632-3797)
**PHONE**..................773 582-9500
**Fax:** 773 582-9532
Carl Kaplan, *President*
Edward Kaplan, *Treasurer*
Phil Marrone, *Controller*
Phyllis Wyman, *Office Mgr*
**EMP:** 20
**SQ FT:** 20,000
**SALES (est):** 5MM **Privately Held**
**SIC: 5085** 3291 Abrasives; abrasive products

### (G-5342)
### K FLEYE DESIGNS
532 N Long Ave (60644-1952)
**PHONE**..................773 531-0716
Kelley D Moseley, *Owner*
**EMP:** 4
**SALES (est):** 212.9K **Privately Held**
**SIC: 3961** Costume jewelry; costume novelties

### (G-5343)
### K H STEUERNAGEL TECHNICAL LTG
4114 N Ravenswood Ave # 1 (60613-1786)
**PHONE**..................773 327-4520

Burkhard Severon, *President*
**EMP:** 3 **EST:** 1979
**SALES (est):** 384.7K
**SALES (corp-wide):** 3.8B **Publicly Held**
**WEB:** www.atlas-mts.com
**SIC: 3821** Laboratory apparatus & furniture
**HQ:** Atlas Material Testing Technology Llc
1500 Bishop Ct
Mount Prospect IL 60056
773 327-4520

### (G-5344)
### K THREE WELDING SERVICE INC
814 W 120th St (60643-5532)
**PHONE**..................708 563-2911
**Fax:** 708 458-7404
Michael T Kuper, *President*
**EMP:** 7
**SQ FT:** 9,800
**SALES (est):** 1.3MM **Privately Held**
**SIC: 3441** 3446 7692 3444 Fabricated structural metal; railings, prefabricated metal; welding repair; sheet metalwork

### (G-5345)
### K&I LIGHT KANDI LED INC
2600 N Cicero Ave (60639-1767)
**PHONE**..................773 745-1533
Ihsan B Paterson, *President*
▲ **EMP:** 4
**SALES (est):** 426.1K **Privately Held**
**SIC: 3645** Residential lighting fixtures

### (G-5346)
### K+S MONTANA HOLDINGS LLC (DH)
123 N Wacker Dr (60606-1743)
**PHONE**..................312 807-2000
**EMP:** 9
**SALES (est):** 1.1B
**SALES (corp-wide):** 3.6B **Privately Held**
**SIC: 2899** Salt
**HQ:** K+S Finance Belgium Bvba
Culliganlaan 2, Internal Postal Box G
Machelen (Bt.)
240 311-80

### (G-5347)
### K+S SALT LLC (DH)
123 N Wacker Dr Fl 6 (60606-1743)
**PHONE**..................844 789-3991
Norbert Steiner, *Chairman*
Michael Resetar, *Facilities Dir*
Fabian Broll, *Marketing Mgr*
Ulrike Cohrs, *Marketing Mgr*
Elisa Euler, *Marketing Mgr*
**EMP:** 1
**SALES (est):** 1.1B
**SALES (corp-wide):** 3.6B **Privately Held**
**SIC: 2899** 5149 5169 Salt; salt, edible; salts, industrial

### (G-5348)
### K-DISPLAY CORP
6150 S Oak Park Ave (60638-4014)
**PHONE**..................773 586-2042
**Fax:** 773 586-2070
Michael Kubacki, *President*
Karen Kubacki, *Vice Pres*
Len Kubacki, *Treasurer*
**EMP:** 14
**SQ FT:** 30,000
**SALES (est):** 2.1MM **Privately Held**
**WEB:** www.k-display.com
**SIC: 3993** Displays & cutouts, window & lobby

### (G-5349)
### K-METAL PRODUCTS INCORPORATED
2310 W 78th St (60620-5801)
**PHONE**..................773 476-2700
Kay Delfosse, *President*
Lisa A Sparks, *Vice Pres*
**EMP:** 6
**SQ FT:** 3,200
**SALES (est):** 500K **Privately Held**
**SIC: 3469** Stamping metal for the trade

### (G-5350)
### KAE DJ PUBLISHING
12003 S Pulaski Rd # 202 (60803-1221)
**PHONE**..................773 233-2609
Kathy Jones, *Principal*

**EMP:** 3 **EST:** 2007
**SALES (est):** 157.8K **Privately Held**
**SIC: 2741** Miscellaneous publishing

### (G-5351)
### KAI LEE COUTURE INC
5612 S King Dr (60637-1266)
**PHONE**..................773 426-1668
Kira Lee, *President*
**EMP:** 4
**SALES:** 30K **Privately Held**
**SIC: 2341** Nightgowns & negligees: women's & children's

### (G-5352)
### KAISER MANUFACTURING CO
1440 N Pulaski Rd (60651-1935)
**PHONE**..................773 235-4705
**Fax:** 773 235-5176
Thomas Kaiser, *President*
Mary Lee Geesbreght, *Corp Secy*
Phillip Kaiser Jr, *Vice Pres*
**EMP:** 134 **EST:** 1945
**SALES (est):** 9.7MM **Privately Held**
**WEB:** www.kaisermfg.com
**SIC: 3444** Sheet metalwork

### (G-5353)
### KALAMAZOO OUTDOOR GOURMET LLC (HQ)
810 W Washington Blvd (60607-2302)
**PHONE**..................312 423-8770
**Fax:** 312 276-4466
Jennifer Timins, *Business Mgr*
Derrick Bregenzer, *Engineer*
Geralyn Aguinaldo, *Regl Sales Mgr*
Melissa York, *VP Mktg*
Spencer Flynn, *Marketing Staff*
▼ **EMP:** 2
**SQ FT:** 7,500
**SALES (est):** 2.7MM
**SALES (corp-wide):** 6.1MM **Privately Held**
**WEB:** www.kalamazoogourmet.com
**SIC: 3631** Barbecues, grills & braziers (outdoor cooking)
**PA:** Synetro Group, Llc
810 W Washington Blvd
Chicago IL 60607
312 372-2600

### (G-5354)
### KALENA LLC
1937 N Mohawk St (60614-5219)
**PHONE**..................773 598-0033
Tarik Tahini,
David Venouziou,
**EMP:** 4
**SALES (est):** 1MM **Privately Held**
**SIC: 2086** Mfg Bottled/Canned Soft Drinks

### (G-5355)
### KALTBAND NORTH AMERICA INC
3750 N Lake Shore Dr 16a (60613-4238)
**PHONE**..................773 248-6684
James C Nedwick, *President*
Micheal Luthi, *Chairman*
Regina Brown, *Regional Mgr*
Hansruedi Gautschi, *Vice Pres*
Daniel Luthi, *Vice Pres*
▲ **EMP:** 17
**SQ FT:** 3,200
**SALES (est):** 3.3MM **Privately Held**
**WEB:** www.kaltbandna.com
**SIC: 3325** 3312 Alloy steel castings, except investment; bars & bar shapes, steel, hot-rolled
**HQ:** Kaltband Ag
Unterwerkstrasse 3
Reinach AG
627 659-999

### (G-5356)
### KAMA ENTERPRISES INC
4925 N Newcastle Ave (60656-3907)
**PHONE**..................773 551-9642
Marian Pobozniak, *President*
**EMP:** 2
**SALES (est):** 216.4K **Privately Held**
**SIC: 3714** Choker rods, motor vehicle

### (G-5357)
### KANA SOFTWARE INC
30 S Wacker Dr Ste 1300 (60606-7466)
**PHONE**..................312 447-5600

Erin Kana, *Branch Mgr*
**EMP:** 3 **Publicly Held**
**SIC: 7372** Prepackaged software
**HQ:** Kana Software, Inc.
2550 Walsh Ave Ste 120
Santa Clara CA 95051
650 614-8300

### (G-5358)
### KANE GRAPHICAL CORPORATION
2255 W Logan Blvd (60647-2114)
**PHONE**..................773 384-1200
Michael N Kane, *President*
Jonathan Kane, *Treasurer*
Elaina Wong, *Cust Svc Mgr*
**EMP:** 30
**SQ FT:** 40,000
**SALES (est):** 4MM **Privately Held**
**WEB:** www.kanegraphical.com
**SIC: 7336** 3993 Silk screen design; signs & advertising specialties

### (G-5359)
### KAPLAN INC
Also Called: Kaplan Educational Center
205 W Randolph St (60606-1867)
**PHONE**..................312 263-4344
Peter Slevin, *Branch Mgr*
**EMP:** 32
**SALES (corp-wide):** 2.4B **Publicly Held**
**SIC: 2711** Newspapers
**HQ:** Kaplan, Inc.
6301 Kaplan Univ Ave
Fort Lauderdale FL 33309
212 492-5800

### (G-5360)
### KAREN YOUNG
Also Called: Loose Petals
10 W Elm St Apt 900 (60610-5015)
**PHONE**..................312 202-0142
Karen Young, *Owner*
**EMP:** 10
**SALES (est):** 774.7K **Privately Held**
**SIC: 2771** 5947 Greeting cards; gift, novelty & souvenir shop

### (G-5361)
### KARL LAMBRECHT CORP
4204 N Lincoln Ave (60618-2902)
**PHONE**..................773 472-5442
**Fax:** 773 472-2724
Alvin Lambrecht, *President*
Frances Lambrecht, *Principal*
Vinod Vats, *Chief Engr*
Raymond Lambrecht, *Treasurer*
Karl Lambrecht, *Human Res Dir*
**EMP:** 22
**SQ FT:** 22,000
**SALES:** 4.1MM **Privately Held**
**SIC: 3827** Lenses, optical: all types except ophthalmic; prisms, optical; polarizers

### (G-5362)
### KARMA YACHT SALES LLC (PA)
3231 S Halsted St Apt 3s (60608-6613)
**PHONE**..................773 254-0200
**Fax:** 773 254-0201
Kristan McClintock, *Mktg Dir*
Sarah Angell, *Marketing Mgr*
Louis Sandoval, *Mng Member*
**EMP:** 6
**SALES (est):** 1.4MM **Privately Held**
**WEB:** www.karmayachtsales.com
**SIC: 5551** 7699 3732 Motor boat dealers; boat repair; boats, fiberglass: building & repairing

### (G-5363)
### KASIAS DELI INC (PA)
440 N Oakley Blvd (60612-1453)
**PHONE**..................312 666-2900
**Fax:** 312 666-2904
Kasmira Bober, *President*
Chris Bober, *Manager*
▲ **EMP:** 12
**SQ FT:** 3,500
**SALES (est):** 2.2MM **Privately Held**
**WEB:** www.kasiaspierogi.com
**SIC: 2038** Ethnic foods, frozen

### (G-5364)
### KASTLE THERAPEUTICS LLC
181 W Madison St Ste 3745 (60602-4640)
**PHONE**..................312 883-5695

Tony Smolcich,
**EMP:** 6
**SALES (est):** 356K  **Privately Held**
**SIC: 2834**  Pharmaceutical preparations

**(G-5365)**
**KAYE LEE & COMPANY INC**
5 S Wabash Ave Ste 200  (60603-3520)
**PHONE**..................................312 236-9686
**Fax:** 312 236-5832
Anthony Liacone, *President*
Mark Engle, *Vice Pres*
**EMP:** 6  **EST:** 1950
**SQ FT:** 1,750
**SALES:** 1.9MM  **Privately Held**
**SIC: 5944**  3911 7631 Jewelry, precious stones & precious metals; jewel settings & mountings, precious metal; jewelry repair services

**(G-5366)**
**KAZMIER TOOLING INC**
6001 S Oak Park Ave  (60638-4011)
**PHONE**..................................773 586-0300
**Fax:** 773 586-6777
Shawn J Ofarrell, *President*
Mike O Farrell, *Office Mgr*
Brian O Farrell, *Admin Sec*
**EMP:** 8
**SQ FT:** 12,500
**SALES (est):** 1.1MM  **Privately Held**
**WEB:** www.kazmiertooling.com
**SIC: 3542**  Brakes, metal forming

**(G-5367)**
**KCP METAL FABRICATIONS INC**
Also Called: Associated Metal Mfg
5475 N Northwest Hwy  (60630-1133)
**PHONE**..................................773 775-0318
**Fax:** 773 775-6409
Conrad Pioli, *President*
Kevin Clarke, *Mktg Dir*
Jeff Chardell, *Marketing Staff*
Karin Pioli, *Admin Sec*
**EMP:** 43  **EST:** 1982
**SQ FT:** 11,187
**SALES (est):** 10.7MM  **Privately Held**
**WEB:** www.kcpmetal.com
**SIC: 3444**  Sheet metalwork

**(G-5368)**
**KCURA LLC (PA)**
231 S Lasalle St Fl 8  (60604)
**PHONE**..................................312 263-1177
Andrew Sieja, *CEO*
Jason Ream, *CFO*
Jessica Davison, *Accountant*
Rob Fischer, *Manager*
Keith M Lieberman,
**EMP:** 500  **EST:** 2015
**SALES (est):** 55.6MM  **Privately Held**
**SIC: 7372**  5045 Business oriented computer software; computer software

**(G-5369)**
**KELLER ORTHOTICS INC (PA)**
2451 N Lincoln Ave  (60614-1509)
**PHONE**..................................773 929-4700
**Fax:** 773 929-4725
H Peter Keller, *President*
Rosa Maria Keller, *Admin Sec*
**EMP:** 11
**SQ FT:** 3,500
**SALES (est):** 1.3MM  **Privately Held**
**WEB:** www.kellerorthotics.com
**SIC: 3842**  Braces, orthopedic

**(G-5370)**
**KELLOGG COMPANY**
2945 W 31st St  (60623-5104)
**PHONE**..................................773 254-0900
**Fax:** 847 254-0795
James Jenness, *CEO*
Dave McMurray, *President*
A Krawetz, *Vice Pres*
Don Laughlin, *Vice Pres*
Debi Weishaar, *Opers Mgr*
**EMP:** 500
**SALES (corp-wide):** 13B  **Publicly Held**
**WEB:** www.kelloggs.com
**SIC: 2043**  Cereal breakfast foods
**PA:** Kellogg Company
   1 Kellogg Sq
   Battle Creek MI 49017
   269 961-2000

**(G-5371)**
**KELLOGG COMPANY**
750 E 110th St  (60628-3826)
**PHONE**..................................773 995-7200
Bob Green, *Manager*
**EMP:** 703
**SALES (corp-wide):** 13B  **Publicly Held**
**WEB:** www.kelloggs.com
**SIC: 2043**  Cereal breakfast foods; corn flakes: prepared as cereal breakfast food; rice: prepared as cereal breakfast food; wheat flakes: prepared as cereal breakfast food
**PA:** Kellogg Company
   1 Kellogg Sq
   Battle Creek MI 49017
   269 961-2000

**(G-5372)**
**KELLY CORNED BEEF CO CHICAGO**
Also Called: Kelly Eisenberg
3531 N Elston Ave  (60618-5631)
**PHONE**..................................773 588-2882
**Fax:** 773 588-0810
Howard Eisenberg, *President*
Carol Ayres, *Controller*
Carol Years, *Controller*
Ed Eisenberg, *Manager*
Calvin Eisenberg, *Admin Sec*
▼ **EMP:** 45
**SQ FT:** 1,200
**SALES (est):** 38.9MM  **Privately Held**
**WEB:** www.kellyeisenberg.com
**SIC: 5147**  2017 Meats, fresh; meats, cured or smoked; meat packing plants

**(G-5373)**
**KELLY FLOUR COMPANY**
260 E Chestnut St # 4406  (60611-2401)
**PHONE**..................................312 933-3104
Marilyn Kelly, *President*
Nancy Lee Savard, *Admin Sec*
**EMP:** 2
**SALES (est):** 230K  **Privately Held**
**SIC: 2023**  2015 Powdered milk; eggs, processed: dehydrated

**(G-5374)**
**KELLY SYSTEMS INC (PA)**
422 N Western Ave  (60612-1491)
**PHONE**..................................312 733-3224
**Fax:** 312 733-6971
Walter M Kelly Jr, *President*
Michael J Kelly, *Vice Pres*
Phil McGeever, *Materials Mgr*
Connie Saliba, *Safety Mgr*
Jim Feirck, *Purchasing*
**EMP:** 28  **EST:** 1904
**SQ FT:** 20,000
**SALES (est):** 7.9MM  **Privately Held**
**WEB:** www.kellytubesystems.com
**SIC: 3535**  1796 7699 Pneumatic tube conveyor systems; installing building equipment; industrial equipment services

**(G-5375)**
**KEMIS KOLLECTIONS**
6007 S Wood St Apt 2  (60636-2253)
**PHONE**..................................773 431-2037
Kemi Ijaola, *Principal*
**EMP:** 3
**SALES (est):** 25K  **Privately Held**
**SIC: 3999**  Candles

**(G-5376)**
**KEMPNER COMPANY INC**
629 W Cermak Rd Ste 201  (60616-2260)
**PHONE**..................................312 733-1606
James Kempner, *President*
◆ **EMP:** 10
**SQ FT:** 15,000
**SALES (est):** 1.4MM  **Privately Held**
**SIC: 2431**  Interior & ornamental woodwork & trim; wood kitchen cabinets

**(G-5377)**
**KERALA EXPRESS NEWSPAPER**
2050 W Devon Ave Apt 1w  (60659-2152)
**PHONE**..................................773 465-5359
**Fax:** 773 465-3800
K M Eathen, *President*
Titus Eapen, *VP Mktg*
**EMP:** 5  **EST:** 1992
**SALES:** 500K  **Privately Held**
**SIC: 2711**  Newspapers, publishing & printing

**(G-5378)**
**KESHER STAM**
2817 W Touhy Ave  (60645-2901)
**PHONE**..................................773 973-7826
Stam Kesher, *Owner*
**EMP:** 4
**SALES (est):** 290K  **Privately Held**
**SIC: 3911**  Rosaries or other small religious articles, precious metal

**(G-5379)**
**KESTLER DIGITAL PRINTING INC**
2845 W 48th Pl  (60632-2012)
**PHONE**..................................773 581-5918
Mario R Kestler, *President*
**EMP:** 17
**SALES (est):** 2.7MM  **Privately Held**
**SIC: 2759**  Commercial printing

**(G-5380)**
**KEYSTONE PRINTING SERVICES**
2451 N Harlem Ave  (60707-2047)
**PHONE**..................................773 622-7210
John Iozzo, *President*
**EMP:** 2
**SQ FT:** 1,500
**SALES (est):** 270K  **Privately Held**
**SIC: 2752**  Commercial printing, offset

**(G-5381)**
**KIDDE FIRE TRINER HOLDINGS LLC (PA)**
155 N Wacker Dr Ste 4150  (60606-1788)
**PHONE**..................................312 219-7900
William R Lane, *President*
**EMP:** 6  **EST:** 2013
**SALES (est):** 10.3MM  **Privately Held**
**SIC: 3699**  Electronic training devices

**(G-5382)**
**KIDSBOOKS LLC (PA)**
3535 W Peterson Ave  (60659-3212)
**PHONE**..................................773 509-0707
**Fax:** 773 509-0404
Dan Blau, *Mng Member*
David Corrente, *Manager*
Jodi Olesek, *Manager*
▲ **EMP:** 5
**SQ FT:** 3,400
**SALES (est):** 5MM  **Privately Held**
**WEB:** www.kidsbooks.com
**SIC: 2731**  Books: publishing only

**(G-5383)**
**KIM & SCTTS GRMET PRETZELS INC**
2107 W Carroll Ave  (60612-1603)
**PHONE**..................................800 578-9478
**Fax:** 312 243-9972
Kimberly Holstein, *President*
Ted Beilman, *Vice Pres*
Scott Holstein, *Vice Pres*
**EMP:** 70
**SQ FT:** 40,000
**SALES (est):** 5.6MM
**SALES (corp-wide):** 992.7MM  **Publicly Held**
**WEB:** www.ksgp.com
**SIC: 2051**  Bread, all types (white, wheat, rye, etc): fresh or frozen
**PA:** J & J Snack Foods Corp.
   6000 Central Hwy
   Pennsauken NJ 08109
   856 665-9533

**(G-5384)**
**KIMBALL OFFICE INC**
325 N Wells St Ste 100  (60654-7023)
**PHONE**..................................800 349-9827
**Fax:** 312 644-8768
Brent Johnson, *Business Mgr*
Michael Donahue, *Vice Pres*
Allen Parker, *Vice Pres*
Monica Canton, *Site Mgr*
Laura Gardner, *Office Mgr*
**EMP:** 10
**SALES (corp-wide):** 635.1MM  **Publicly Held**
**SIC: 2522**  Office desks & tables: except wood
**HQ:** Kimball Office Inc.
   1600 Royal St
   Jasper IN 47549
   812 482-1600

**(G-5385)**
**KIMS MENSWEAR LTD**
326 E 47th St  (60653-4004)
**PHONE**..................................773 373-2237
Sung Kim, *Owner*
**EMP:** 3
**SALES (est):** 116.2K  **Privately Held**
**SIC: 2329**  Men's & boys' clothing

**(G-5386)**
**KIRBY SHEET METAL WORKS INC**
Also Called: Mark Radtke Co Division
4209 S Western Blvd  (60609-2280)
**PHONE**..................................773 247-6477
**Fax:** 773 247-5753
Jack Young, *President*
Phil Kirk, *Vice Pres*
Robert Novick, *Vice Pres*
**EMP:** 20  **EST:** 1924
**SQ FT:** 12,000
**SALES (est):** 3.9MM  **Privately Held**
**SIC: 1761**  3444 Sheet metalwork; sheet metalwork

**(G-5387)**
**KLEIN PRINTING INC**
Also Called: I AM A Print Shoppe
3035 W Fullerton Ave  (60647-2807)
**PHONE**..................................773 235-2121
**Fax:** 773 235-1154
Ralph Klein, *President*
Lillian Klein, *Vice Pres*
Jesus Cruz, *Manager*
**EMP:** 7  **EST:** 1957
**SQ FT:** 6,800
**SALES:** 750K  **Privately Held**
**SIC: 2752**  2759 7334 2791 Commercial printing, offset; thermography; photocopying & duplicating services; typesetting; bookbinding & related work

**(G-5388)**
**KLOECKNER METALS CORPORATION**
Alpha Processing
13535 S Torrence Ave # 10  (60633-2164)
**PHONE**..................................773 646-6363
**Fax:** 773 646-6689
Dan Zekai, *General Mgr*
**EMP:** 10
**SALES (corp-wide):** 6B  **Privately Held**
**WEB:** www.macsteelusa.com
**SIC: 3354**  Coils, rod, extruded, aluminum
**HQ:** Kloeckner Metals Corporation
   500 Colonial Center Pkwy # 500
   Roswell GA 30076
   678 259-8800

**(G-5389)**
**KNIGHT PACKAGING GROUP INC**
4651 W 72nd St  (60629-5809)
**PHONE**..................................773 585-2035
Donald McCann, *CEO*
Thomas Kemp, *President*
Robert Brannigan, *Vice Pres*
Mary Rusin, *Vice Pres*
**EMP:** 6
**SALES (est):** 677.5K  **Privately Held**
**SIC: 3565**  Packing & wrapping machinery

**(G-5390)**
**KNIGHT PAPER BOX COMPANY (PA)**
Also Called: Knight Packaging Group
4651 W 72nd St  (60629-5882)
**PHONE**..................................773 585-2035
**Fax:** 773 585-3824
Anderson Field, *President*
Thomas D Kemp, *Principal*
Robert Killelea, *CFO*
Milan Cannon, *Branch Mgr*
▲ **EMP:** 72  **EST:** 1950
**SQ FT:** 110,000

## Chicago - Cook County (G-5391)

SALES (est): 18.9MM  Privately Held
WEB: www.knightpaperbox.com
SIC: 2657  Folding paperboard boxes

### (G-5391)
### KNIGHTHOUSE MEDIA INC
Also Called: Knighthouse Publishing
150 N Michigan Ave # 900  (60601-7524)
PHONE..................312 676-1100
Christopher Schofield, Principal
EMP: 9
SALES (est): 899.1K  Privately Held
SIC: 2741  Communication services

### (G-5392)
### KNOCK ON METAL INC (PA)
221 N La Salle St # 3315  (60601-1206)
PHONE..................312 372-4569
Van A Schwab, President
EMP: 2
SALES (est): 450.1K  Privately Held
SIC: 3369  Lead castings, except die-castings

### (G-5393)
### KNOX CAPITAL HOLDINGS LLC
212 W Kinzie St  (60654-4747)
PHONE..................312 402-1425
EMP: 4
SALES (est): 382.9K  Privately Held
SIC: 3561  Pumps & pumping equipment

### (G-5394)
### KOCH INDUSTRIES INC
9 E Superior St  (60611-3763)
PHONE..................312 867-1295
EMP: 3
SALES (corp-wide): 27.4B  Privately Held
SIC: 2911  5169  5172  Petroleum refining; chemicals & allied products; petroleum products
PA: Koch Industries, Inc.
  4111 E 37th St N
  Wichita KS 67220
  316 828-5500

### (G-5395)
### KOCH INDUSTRIES INC
3259 E 100th St  (60617-5416)
PHONE..................773 375-3700
Mike Gibson, Branch Mgr
Dave Bever, Manager
Dave Severson, Director
EMP: 37
SALES (corp-wide): 27.4B  Privately Held
WEB: www.kochind.com
SIC: 2999  Coke (not from refineries), petroleum
PA: Koch Industries, Inc.
  4111 E 37th St N
  Wichita KS 67220
  316 828-5500

### (G-5396)
### KOCH MEAT CO INC
Also Called: Aspen Foods
4404 W Berteau Ave  (60641-1907)
PHONE..................847 384-5940
Fax: 773 286-1390
Tyler Davis, Plant Mgr
Manglo Bonilla, Opers Staff
Joe Koch, QC Mgr
Rosann Gra, Human Res Mgr
Larry Smith, Sales Staff
EMP: 375
SALES (corp-wide): 1.9B  Privately Held
SIC: 5142  2015  Packaged frozen goods; poultry slaughtering & processing
HQ: Koch Meat Co., Inc.
  1300 Higgins Rd Ste 100
  Park Ridge IL 60068
  847 384-8018

### (G-5397)
### KOCOUR CO
4800 S Saint Louis Ave  (60632-3091)
PHONE..................773 847-1111
Fax: 773 847-3399
Leslie Kocour Jr, Ch of Bd
Dan Johnson, President
Dennis Masarik, President
Iris A Poltrock, Admin Sec
EMP: 20 EST: 1923
SQ FT: 40,000
SALES (est): 4.8MM  Privately Held
SIC: 3829  5085  2842  Testing equipment: abrasion, shearing strength, etc.; industrial supplies; specialty cleaning, polishes & sanitation goods

### (G-5398)
### KODIAK LLC
4320 S Knox Ave  (60632-4342)
PHONE..................248 545-7520
Laura McQiugg, Manager
Shaeyanne Mooter,
EMP: 20
SALES (est): 2MM  Privately Held
SIC: 2653  Corrugated & solid fiber boxes

### (G-5399)
### KODIAK LLC
Also Called: Packpors
4320 S Knox Ave  (60632-4342)
PHONE..................773 284-9975
Peter Langkamp, General Mgr
Kathy Dunn, Sales Staff
Anthony J Mooter, Mng Member
Leonard Horton, Mng Member
John Madigan, Mng Member
EMP: 20
SQ FT: 85,000
SALES (est): 3.8MM  Privately Held
WEB: www.kodiak.com
SIC: 2653  Display items, corrugated: made from purchased materials

### (G-5400)
### KOEBERS PROSTHETIC ORTHPD LAB (PA)
3834 W Irving Park Rd # 1  (60618-3122)
PHONE..................309 676-2276
Fax: 773 539-5535
Amit Bhanti, CEO
Donald Smerko, President
Todd Nelson, COO
Loretta Smerko, Vice Pres
EMP: 8
SQ FT: 5,000
SALES: 850K  Privately Held
SIC: 3842  Limbs, artificial; braces, orthopedic

### (G-5401)
### KOEHLER BINDERY INC
3802 W Montrose Ave  (60618-1088)
PHONE..................773 539-7979
Ronald Hackl, Vice Pres
Walter J Hackl II, Treasurer
EMP: 5
SALES (est): 626.5K  Privately Held
SIC: 2789  Bookbinding & related work

### (G-5402)
### KOLCRAFT ENTERPRISES INC (PA)
1100 W Monroe St Ste 200  (60607-2528)
PHONE..................312 361-6315
Sanfred Koltun, Ch of Bd
Thomas N Koltun, President
Sharon M Danko, Corp Secy
Edward Bretschger, Senior VP
Andrew Newmark, Senior VP
▲ EMP: 75
SQ FT: 75,000
SALES (est): 63.2MM  Privately Held
SIC: 2515  Mattresses, containing felt, foam rubber, urethane, etc.

### (G-5403)
### KONEKT INC
Also Called: Hologram
111 W Illinois St  (60654-4505)
PHONE..................773 733-0471
Benjamin Forgan, President
Pat Wilbur, CTO
EMP: 2
SALES (est): 281.1K  Privately Held
SIC: 5072  3674  Hardware; integrated circuits, semiconductor networks, etc.

### (G-5404)
### KONVEAU INC
805 E Drexel Sq  (60615-3781)
PHONE..................312 476-9385
Jason Johnson, CEO
Jason Triche, Co-Owner
EMP: 4
SALES (est): 98.3K  Privately Held
SIC: 7372  Application computer software

### (G-5405)
### KOREAN AIR
5600 Mannheim Rd  (60666-1007)
P.O. Box 66259  (60666-0259)
PHONE..................773 686-2730
Fax: 773 686-0735
Joong Lee, Manager
EMP: 7
SALES (corp-wide): 9.7B  Privately Held
SIC: 3812  Flight recorders
HQ: Korean Air
  8133 Leesburg Pike # 630
  Vienna VA 22182
  571 633-9768

### (G-5406)
### KOREX CHICAGO LLC
6200 W 51st St Ste 7  (60638-1349)
PHONE..................708 458-4890
Carol Ellis,
James Barca,
Ofelia Pugeda,
EMP: 26
SALES (est): 8.6MM  Privately Held
SIC: 2812  Alkalies & chlorine

### (G-5407)
### KOREX CORPORATION
6200 W 51st St Ste 6  (60638-1349)
PHONE..................708 458-4890
Chris Kambesis, CEO
EMP: 2
SALES (est): 624.2K  Privately Held
SIC: 2842  Specialty cleaning, polishes & sanitation goods

### (G-5408)
### KOVAL INC
5121 N Ravenswood Ave Grw  (60640-5386)
PHONE..................773 944-0089
Robert Birnecker, CEO
Sonat Birnecker, President
Mariah Veis, Office Mgr
▲ EMP: 12
SALES (est): 1.8MM  Privately Held
SIC: 2085  Distilled & blended liquors

### (G-5409)
### KOZA
13548 S Burley Ave  (60633-1842)
PHONE..................773 646-0958
Jon P Koza, Owner
EMP: 6
SALES (est): 344.6K  Privately Held
SIC: 2731  Book publishing

### (G-5410)
### KRAFT HEINZ COMPANY (PA)
200 E Randolph St # 7300  (60601-7012)
P.O. Box 57, Pittsburgh PA  (15230-0057)
PHONE..................412 456-5700
Bernardo Hees, CEO
Alexandre Behring, Ch of Bd
John T Cahill, Vice Ch Bd
Emin Mammadov, President
Raphael Oliveira, President
EMP: 277
SALES: 26.4B  Publicly Held
SIC: 2033  2038  2032  2098  Tomato sauce: packaged in cans, jars, etc.; frozen specialties; baby foods, including meats: packaged in cans, jars, etc.; bean sprouts: packaged in cans, jars, etc.; soups, except seafood: packaged in cans, jars, etc.; macaroni & spaghetti

### (G-5411)
### KREL LABORATORIES INC
388 N Avers Ave  (60624-1892)
PHONE..................773 826-4487
Fax: 773 826-4562
Michael D Mitchell, President
Michael Ratliff, Vice Pres
Delores Thorns, Office Mgr
Dalaura Throns, Office Mgr
Sansi Mitchell, Shareholder
EMP: 14
SQ FT: 15,000
SALES (est): 1.7MM  Privately Held
SIC: 3471  Plating & polishing; electroplating of metals or formed products; buffing for the trade; polishing, metals or formed products

### (G-5412)
### KROH-WAGNER INC
2331 N Pulaski Rd  (60639-3798)
PHONE..................773 252-2031
Fax: 773 252-4482
Robert C Wagner, President
Margaret Wagner, Vice Pres
Cathy Wagner, Marketing Mgr
EMP: 20
SQ FT: 20,000
SALES (est): 3.7MM  Privately Held
WEB: www.krohwagner.com
SIC: 3317  3442  3449  3444  Tubing, mechanical or hypodermic sizes: cold drawn stainless; moldings & trim, except automobile: metal; miscellaneous metalwork; sheet metalwork; fabricated structural metal; copper rolling & drawing

### (G-5413)
### KRUEGER INTERNATIONAL INC
Also Called: Ki
1181 Merchandise Mart  (60654)
PHONE..................312 467-6850
Dave Fairburn, Manager
EMP: 15
SALES (corp-wide): 616.6MM  Privately Held
WEB: www.ki.com
SIC: 2752  Commercial printing, lithographic
PA: Krueger International, Inc.
  1330 Bellevue St
  Green Bay WI 54302
  920 468-8100

### (G-5414)
### KUNZ GLOVE CO INC
1532 W Fulton St  (60607-1004)
PHONE..................312 733-8780
Fax: 312 733-5474
Kevin G Deady, President
Connie Kreitler, Office Admin
▲ EMP: 39 EST: 1900
SQ FT: 20,000
SALES (est): 6.3MM  Privately Held
WEB: www.kunzglove.com
SIC: 3151  2381  Gloves, leather: work; fabric dress & work gloves

### (G-5415)
### KW PLASTICS
Also Called: Kw Container
270 S State St  (60604)
PHONE..................708 757-5140
Steven Lux, General Mgr
Mick Langford, Supervisor
EMP: 15
SALES (corp-wide): 69.8MM  Privately Held
SIC: 3081  Polypropylene film & sheet
PA: Kw Plastics
  279 Pike County Lake Rd
  Troy AL 36079
  334 566-1563

### (G-5416)
### KYLON MIDWEST
238 E 108th St Apt 2w  (60628-3676)
PHONE..................773 699-3640
Karolyn Wright, Principal
EMP: 4
SALES: 400K  Privately Held
SIC: 3678  Electronic connectors

### (G-5417)
### L & B GLOBAL POWER LLC
5231 W Cullom Ave  (60641-1402)
PHONE..................847 323-0770
Ozhekim Ismail Reha,
Dimitre Doudin,
▲ EMP: 2
SALES (est): 200K  Privately Held
SIC: 3825  7389  Integrating electricity meters;

### (G-5418)
### L & L FLOORING INC
Also Called: Carpet One
3071 N Lincoln Ave  (60657-4207)
PHONE..................773 935-9314
Fax: 773 935-8735
Joel Schreiner, Manager
EMP: 30

# GEOGRAPHIC SECTION

**Chicago - Cook County (G-5443)**

SALES (corp-wide): 18.9MM **Privately Held**
SIC: 5713 2273 Floor covering stores; carpets & rugs
PA: L. & L. Flooring, Inc.
3071 N Lincoln Ave
Chicago IL
773 528-3355

## (G-5419)
### L & M WELDING INC
4619 W Armitage Ave (60639-3405)
PHONE..................................773 237-8500
Fax: 773 889-7774
Luis Salas, *CEO*
Manuel Gomez, *Vice Pres*
▲ EMP: 10
SQ FT: 10,000
SALES: 300K **Privately Held**
SIC: 3449 Bars, concrete reinforcing; fabricated steel

## (G-5420)
### L A BEDDING CORP
3421 W 48th Pl (60632-3026)
PHONE..................................773 715-9641
Luis Martines Sr, *President*
EMP: 6
SALES (est): 640.7K **Privately Held**
SIC: 2515 Mattresses & bedsprings

## (G-5421)
### L A MOTORS INCORPORATED
4034 N Tripp Ave (60641-1942)
PHONE..................................773 736-7305
Art Ambriz, *President*
EMP: 3 EST: 2008
SALES: 57K **Privately Held**
SIC: 7694 7539 7538 5531 Rebuilding motors, except automotive; automotive repair shops; engine repair; automotive parts

## (G-5422)
### L E D TOOL & DIE INC
12625 S Kroll Dr (60803-3221)
PHONE..................................708 597-2505
Edward Data, *President*
Louise Data, *Corp Secy*
Edward F Data, *Vice Pres*
EMP: 4
SQ FT: 1,800
SALES: 180K **Privately Held**
SIC: 3544 7692 Special dies & tools; welding repair

## (G-5423)
### L-DATA CORPORATION
203 N La Salle St # 2169 (60601-1267)
PHONE..................................312 552-7855
Florin Dragomir, *President*
Cesar Quintero, *Consultant*
Ann E Harris, *Officer*
EMP: 32 EST: 1971
SQ FT: 2,200
SALES: 9.2MM **Privately Held**
SIC: 7372 5045 Educational computer software; anti-static equipment & devices; computer software; computers; terminals, computer

## (G-5424)
### LA CRIOLLA INC
907 W Randolph St (60607-2207)
PHONE..................................312 243-8882
Fax: 312 243-8698
Carmen L Maldonado, *President*
Sylvia Maldonado, *Vice Pres*
EMP: 30
SQ FT: 6,000
SALES (est): 7.6MM **Privately Held**
SIC: 5149 2099 Spices & seasonings; natural & organic foods; dried or canned foods; food preparations

## (G-5425)
### LA MEXICANA TORTILLERIA INC
Also Called: Tortilleria La Mexicana
2703 S Kedzie Ave (60623-4735)
PHONE..................................773 247-5443
Fax: 773 247-9004
Rudolph Guerrero, *President*
Rod Yadgarov, *Manager*
EMP: 50
SQ FT: 27,500
SALES (est): 7.1MM **Privately Held**
SIC: 2099 Tortillas, fresh or refrigerated

## (G-5426)
### LA RAZA CHICAGO INC
Also Called: La Raza Newspaper
200 S Michigan Ave # 1600 (60604-2402)
PHONE..................................312 870-7000
Fax: 312 870-7020
Robert Armband, *President*
Carlos Nauzo, *General Mgr*
Alfred Cavazos, *Human Res Mgr*
Hugo Jordan, *Accounts Exec*
Naul Valdez, *Sales Staff*
EMP: 46
SALES (est): 3.2MM **Privately Held**
WEB: www.laraza.com
SIC: 2711 Newspapers

## (G-5427)
### LA RON JEWELERS
5 S Wabash Ave Ste 806 (60603-3184)
PHONE..................................312 263-3898
Larry Shtulman, *Owner*
EMP: 7 EST: 1943
SALES (est): 674.4K **Privately Held**
WEB: www.laronjewelers.com
SIC: 3911 Jewelry, precious metal

## (G-5428)
### LA-Z-BOY INCORPORATED
2647 N Elston Ave (60647-2018)
PHONE..................................773 384-4440
Greg A Brinks, *Treasurer*
Jack Monteleone, *Executive*
EMP: 134
SALES (corp-wide): 1.5B **Publicly Held**
SIC: 2512 Chairs: upholstered on wood frames
PA: La-Z-Boy Incorporated
1 La Z Boy Dr
Monroe MI 48162
734 242-1444

## (G-5429)
### LABAQUETTE KEDZIE INC
5859 S Kedzie Ave (60629-3212)
PHONE..................................773 925-0455
Julie Urebe, *Owner*
EMP: 4
SALES (est): 273K **Privately Held**
SIC: 2051 Bakery: wholesale or wholesale/retail combined

## (G-5430)
### LABELS UNLIMITED INCORPORATED
Also Called: Hospital Labels Co Div
3400 W 48th Pl (60632-3075)
PHONE..................................773 523-7500
Fax: 773 523-7571
Michael Shiel, *President*
Bill Woolf, *Corp Secy*
Joe Okrzesik, *Plant Mgr*
Steve Van Dort, *Graphic Designe*
Jason Wynkoop, *Graphic Designe*
EMP: 45
SQ FT: 60,000
SALES (est): 7.1MM **Privately Held**
WEB: www.labelsunlimited.net
SIC: 2759 2752 2672 2671 Flexographic printing; screen printing; letterpress printing; commercial printing, offset; tape, pressure sensitive: made from purchased materials; packaging paper & plastics film, coated & laminated

## (G-5431)
### LACAVA
1100 W Cermak Rd Ste B403 (60608-0496)
PHONE..................................773 637-9600
Fax: 312 666-4873
Celine Coucaud, *General Mgr*
Carmine Lacava, *Principal*
Andy Muo, *Accounts Mgr*
EMP: 2 EST: 2010
SALES (est): 344.8K **Privately Held**
SIC: 2599 Furniture & fixtures

## (G-5432)
### LACAVA LLC
Also Called: Lacava Design
6630 W Wrightwood Ave (60707-2228)
PHONE..................................773 637-9600
Fax: 773 637-9601
Carmine Lacava, *General Mgr*
Justin Berkowsky, *Accounts Mgr*
Jeremy Sterling, *Accounts Mgr*
Anna Popielarz, *Office Mgr*
Sachin Sharma, *Manager*
▲ EMP: 50
SQ FT: 100,000
SALES: 10.9MM **Privately Held**
WEB: www.lacavadesign.com
SIC: 3432 3261 2434 2521 Plumbing fixture fittings & trim; vitreous plumbing fixtures; bathroom accessories/fittings, vitreous china or earthenware; vanities, bathroom: wood; wood office furniture

## (G-5433)
### LACY ENTERPRISES INC
724 E 104th St (60628-3019)
PHONE..................................773 264-2557
Clemon Lacy, *President*
Gladys Lacy, *Vice Pres*
EMP: 3
SALES: 80K **Privately Held**
SIC: 3713 Dump truck bodies

## (G-5434)
### LAFARGE BUILDING MATERIALS INC (DH)
8700 W Bryn Mawr Ave 300n (60631-3512)
PHONE..................................678 746-2000
Jean M Lechene, *CEO*
Peter L Keeley, *CEO*
Robert Fiolek, *CFO*
Ron Hightower, *Finance Mgr*
Frank Twupack, *Credit Mgr*
▲ EMP: 100
SQ FT: 30,000
SALES (est): 615.8MM
SALES (corp-wide): 26.6B **Privately Held**
SIC: 3241 3274 3273 3271 Masonry cement; natural cement; portland cement; lime; ready-mixed concrete; blocks, concrete or cinder: standard
HQ: Lafarge North America Inc.
8700 W Bryn Mawr Ave Ll
Chicago IL 60631
703 480-3600

## (G-5435)
### LAFARGE NORTH AMERICA INC (DH)
8700 W Bryn Mawr Ave Ll (60631-3535)
PHONE..................................703 480-3600
Bernard L Kasriel, *CEO*
Isaac Preston, *CEO*
John Stull, *President*
Kenneth R Ball, *General Mgr*
Eric Boucher, *General Mgr*
▲ EMP: 120
SALES (est): 3.8B
SALES (corp-wide): 26.6B **Privately Held**
WEB: www.lafargenorthamerica.com
SIC: 3241 3273 3272 3271 Cement, hydraulic; portland cement; ready-mixed concrete; concrete products; precast terrazo or concrete products; prestressed concrete products; cylinder pipe, prestressed or pretensioned concrete; blocks, concrete or cinder: standard; construction sand & gravel; construction sand mining; gravel mining; asphalt paving mixtures & blocks; paving mixtures; asphalt & asphaltic paving mixtures (not from refineries)
HQ: Lafarge
61 Rue Des Belles Feuilles
Paris 75116
144 341-111

## (G-5436)
### LAFARGE NORTH AMERICA INC
8700 W Bryn Mawr Ave Ll (60631-3535)
PHONE..................................773 372-1000
H T Ricie, *Controller*
Steve Lawler, *Manager*
EMP: 27
SALES (corp-wide): 26.6B **Privately Held**
WEB: www.lafargenorthamerica.com
SIC: 3241 Cement, hydraulic
HQ: Lafarge North America Inc.
8700 W Bryn Mawr Ave Ll
Chicago IL 60631
703 480-3600

## (G-5437)
### LAFARGE NORTH AMERICA INC
2150 E 130th St (60633-2300)
PHONE..................................773 646-5228
Fax: 773 646-1813
Angela Brown, *Safety Dir*
Anthony Gianakis, *Plant Mgr*
Maik Strecker, *VP Mktg*
Frank Lavarowicv, *Manager*
Bob Nowicki, *Manager*
EMP: 4
SALES (corp-wide): 26.6B **Privately Held**
WEB: www.lafargenorthamerica.com
SIC: 3241 Cement, hydraulic
HQ: Lafarge North America Inc.
8700 W Bryn Mawr Ave Ll
Chicago IL 60631
703 480-3600

## (G-5438)
### LAGUNITAS BREWING COMPANY
2607 W 17th St (60608-1823)
PHONE..................................773 522-1308
Brandon Greenwood, *Branch Mgr*
EMP: 200 **Privately Held**
SIC: 2082 Malt beverages
HQ: The Lagunitas Brewing Company
1280 N Mcdowell Blvd
Petaluma CA 94954

## (G-5439)
### LAKE MEDIA SERVICES INC
333 N Michigan Ave # 1831 (60601-4108)
PHONE..................................312 739-0423
Larry Cooke, *President*
Corrina Davey, *Med Doctor*
Charles Powell, *Manager*
Will Steinke, *Technical Staff*
Sima Shah, *Gnrl Med Prac*
EMP: 3 EST: 1998
SQ FT: 3,000
SALES: 500K **Privately Held**
WEB: www.lakemedia.com
SIC: 2752 Commercial printing, offset

## (G-5440)
### LAKE PACIFIC PARTNERS LLC
120 S La Salle St # 1510 (60603-3574)
PHONE..................................312 578-1110
Fax: 312 578-1414
William R Voss,
EMP: 500
SALES (est): 34.5MM **Privately Held**
WEB: www.lakepacific.com
SIC: 6211 3089 2013 2011 Investment firm, general brokerage; food casings, plastic; sausages & other prepared meats; meat packing plants

## (G-5441)
### LAKE STREET PALLETS
4600 W Armitage Ave (60639-3406)
PHONE..................................773 889-2266
Florence Rogers, *President*
Patricia Cuevas, *Vice Pres*
Chuck Rogers, *Treasurer*
Carlos Cuevas, *Admin Sec*
EMP: 8
SALES: 100K **Privately Held**
SIC: 7699 2448 Pallet repair; wood pallets & skids

## (G-5442)
### LAKEFRONT ROOFING SUPPLY
977 W Cermak Rd (60608-4518)
PHONE..................................312 275-0270
Fax: 312 275-0266
Tim Bock, *Manager*
EMP: 5
SALES (corp-wide): 18MM **Privately Held**
SIC: 3444 Roof deck, sheet metal
HQ: Lakefront Roofing Supply
2950 N Western Ave
Chicago IL 60618
773 509-0400

## (G-5443)
### LAKEFRONT ROOFING SUPPLY (HQ)
Also Called: Jesus People USA Full Gospel M
2950 N Western Ave (60618-8021)
PHONE..................................773 509-0400
Fax: 773 275-0270

# Chicago - Cook County (G-5444)    GEOGRAPHIC SECTION

Tim Bock, *General Mgr*
Rick J Mills, *CFO*
Sarah Giles, *Financial Exec*
Chris Spicer, *Human Res Mgr*
Kathy Anderson, *Human Resources*
**EMP:** 28
**SALES (est):** 11.9MM
**SALES (corp-wide):** 18MM **Privately Held**
**SIC:** 3444  2952  Sheet metalwork; siding, sheet metal; roofing materials
**PA:** Jesus People, U.S.A., Full Gospel Ministries
2950 N Western Ave
Chicago IL 60618
773 252-1812

## (G-5444)
### LAKEFRONT SCULPTURE EXHIBIT
1807 N Orleans St Ste 1s  (60614-7377)
**PHONE**....................312 719-0207
Vi Jaley, *Owner*
Bob Guthman, *Vice Pres*
**EMP:** 4
**SALES:** 95.2K **Privately Held**
**SIC:** 3299  Architectural sculptures: gypsum, clay, papier mache, etc.

## (G-5445)
### LAKESIDE LITHOGRAPHY LLC
1600 S Laflin St  (60608-2123)
**PHONE**....................312 243-3001
Ed Susralski, *General Mgr*
Louie Vandermeer, *Manager*
Lee Nadler,
▼ **EMP:** 25
**SQ FT:** 60,000
**SALES (est):** 4MM
**SALES (corp-wide):** 30MM **Privately Held**
**SIC:** 2752  Lithographing on metal
**PA:** Lakeside Metals, Inc.
7000 S Adams St Ste 210
Willowbrook IL 60527
630 850-3800

## (G-5446)
### LAKEVIEW ENERGY LLC (PA)
300 W Adams St Ste 830  (60606-5109)
**PHONE**....................312 386-5897
Tim Cowhig, *Chairman*
Earmonn Byrne, *COO*
Charles Stremick, *Vice Pres*
Jim Galvin, *CFO*
Steve Meyer, *CFO*
**EMP:** 22 **EST:** 2010
**SALES (est):** 8.7MM **Privately Held**
**SIC:** 2869  3621  3523  Fuels; windmills, electric generating; windmills for pumping water, agricultural

## (G-5447)
### LAKEVIEW ORAL AND MAXILLOFACIA
1628 W Belmont Ave  (60657-3018)
**PHONE**....................773 327-9500
Kam Patel MD, *Owner*
**EMP:** 3
**SALES (est):** 376.1K **Privately Held**
**SIC:** 2844  Oral preparations

## (G-5448)
### LAMBDA PUBLICATIONS INC
Also Called: Windy City Times
5443 N Broadway St # 101  (60640-1703)
**PHONE**....................773 871-7610
Tracy Baim, *President*
Jean Albright, *Manager*
**EMP:** 10
**SALES (est):** 630K **Privately Held**
**WEB:** www.wctimes.com
**SIC:** 2721  2711  Magazines: publishing only, not printed on site; newspapers

## (G-5449)
### LAMINATION SPECIALTIES CORP (PA)
Also Called: LSI STEEL PROCESSING DIVISION
235 N Artesian Ave  (60612-2148)
**PHONE**....................312 243-2181
**Fax:** 312 243-2873
Robert E Stewart, *CEO*
Albert Delighter, *President*
George Mason, *Safety Mgr*
Sean Hussey, *Regl Sales Mgr*
Joe Hurlburt, *Sales Engr*
▲ **EMP:** 75 **EST:** 1956
**SQ FT:** 56,000
**SALES (est):** 14.8MM **Privately Held**
**WEB:** www.lsisteel.com
**SIC:** 3469  Metal stampings

## (G-5450)
### LAMINATION SPECIALTIES CORP
Also Called: LSI Steel Processing Division
4444 S Kildare Ave  (60632-4345)
**PHONE**....................773 254-7500
**Fax:** 773 927-1246
Len Lococo, *Personnel*
Kenneth H Rober, *Branch Mgr*
**EMP:** 30
**SQ FT:** 108,400
**SALES (corp-wide):** 14.8MM **Privately Held**
**WEB:** www.lsisteel.com
**SIC:** 3469  Metal stampings
**PA:** Lamination Specialties Corp.
235 N Artesian Ave
Chicago IL 60612
312 243-2181

## (G-5451)
### LAMINET COVER COMPANY
Also Called: Lamco Advertising Specialties
4900 W Bloomingdale Ave  (60639-4562)
**PHONE**....................773 622-6700
**Fax:** 773 622-6705
Frank Lieber, *CEO*
Michael Lieber, *President*
Leigh Deyoung, *Sales Mgr*
Michael Briney, *CIO*
Lynne G Lieber, *Admin Sec*
▲ **EMP:** 25
**SQ FT:** 25,000
**SALES (est):** 5.3MM **Privately Held**
**WEB:** www.laminet.com
**SIC:** 2673  Plastic bags: made from purchased materials; garment & wardrobe bags, (plastic film)

## (G-5452)
### LAMONICA ORNAMENTAL IRON WORKS
3311 W Chicago Ave  (60651-4107)
**PHONE**....................773 638-6633
**Fax:** 773 638-7976
Rob Lamonica, *President*
Dominic Lamonaca, *Vice Pres*
**EMP:** 5
**SQ FT:** 1,600
**SALES (est):** 300K **Privately Held**
**SIC:** 3446  1791  Architectural metalwork; iron work, structural

## (G-5453)
### LAMPHOLDERS ASSEMBLIES INC
4106 N Nashville Ave  (60634-1429)
**PHONE**....................773 205-0005
Mae Valentino, *President*
▲ **EMP:** 9
**SQ FT:** 3,500
**SALES (est):** 500K **Privately Held**
**SIC:** 3648  3641  Lighting equipment; electric lamps

## (G-5454)
### LAMPSHADE INC
4041 W Ogden Ave Ste 1  (60623-2857)
P.O. Box 23199  (60623-0199)
**PHONE**....................773 522-2300
**Fax:** 773 522-5589
Michael A Lawlor, *President*
Leonora Figeroa, *Vice Pres*
▲ **EMP:** 17
**SQ FT:** 19,000
**SALES (est):** 2.8MM **Privately Held**
**WEB:** www.lampshade.net
**SIC:** 3645  Lamp shades, metal

## (G-5455)
### LANDAU REAL ESTATE SVCS LLC
Also Called: Landau RES
9936 S Green St  (60643-2202)
**PHONE**....................312 379-9146
Kenneth Gray,
**EMP:** 6
**SALES (est):** 266.3K **Privately Held**
**SIC:** 3842  Cosmetic restorations

## (G-5456)
### LANDMAN DENTAL
625 N Michigan Ave # 1020  (60611-3114)
**PHONE**....................312 266-6480
Tina Kilgore, *Manager*
**EMP:** 2
**SALES (est):** 241.2K **Privately Held**
**SIC:** 3843  Enamels, dentists'

## (G-5457)
### LANE TECHNICAL SALES INC
6465 N Avondale Ave  (60631-1909)
**PHONE**....................773 775-1613
Peter Haak, *President*
Mike Bosco, *VP Sales*
▲ **EMP:** 25
**SALES (est):** 4.6MM **Privately Held**
**WEB:** www.lanetechsales.com
**SIC:** 3679  Electronic circuits

## (G-5458)
### LANG EXTERIOR INC (PA)
Also Called: Lang Exterior Mfg Co
2323 W 59th St  (60636-1518)
**PHONE**....................773 737-4500
**Fax:** 773 737-4144
Darb Lang, *President*
Eugene Lang, *Admin Sec*
**EMP:** 61 **EST:** 1953
**SQ FT:** 180,000
**SALES (est):** 21.2MM **Privately Held**
**WEB:** www.langexterior.com
**SIC:** 3442  3211  3229  Storm doors or windows, metal; insulating glass, sealed units; blocks & bricks, glass

## (G-5459)
### LAPHAM-HICKEY STEEL CORP (PA)
5500 W 73rd St  (60638-6587)
**PHONE**....................708 496-6111
**Fax:** 708 496-8504
William M Hickey Jr, *President*
Rick Oconnell, *Vice Pres*
Larry Chezewski, *Plant Mgr*
Dennis Berger, *Opers Mgr*
Rick Miller, *Opers Mgr*
▲ **EMP:** 150 **EST:** 1926
**SQ FT:** 200,000
**SALES (est):** 305.3MM **Privately Held**
**WEB:** www.lapham-hickey.com
**SIC:** 5051  3398  3355  3317  Bars, metal; strip, metal; tubing, metal; metal heat treating; aluminum rolling & drawing; steel pipe & tubes; cold finishing of steel shapes

## (G-5460)
### LAQUEUS INC
Also Called: Andria Lieu
7435 N Western Ave  (60645-1735)
**PHONE**....................773 508-1993
**Fax:** 773 508-5298
Andria Lieu, *President*
▲ **EMP:** 15
**SQ FT:** 3,500
**SALES (est):** 4.5MM **Privately Held**
**WEB:** www.laqueus.com
**SIC:** 2339  Women's & misses' athletic clothing & sportswear

## (G-5461)
### LAREDO FOODS INC
Also Called: Laredo Spices & Herbs
3401 W Cermak Rd  (60623-3240)
**PHONE**....................773 762-1500
**Fax:** 773 762-1569
Art Jimenez, *President*
Mary B Jimenez, *Treasurer*
Art Jeminus, *Sales Executive*
**EMP:** 20
**SQ FT:** 22,000
**SALES (est):** 2.9MM **Privately Held**
**SIC:** 5149  5145  2099  Spices & seasonings; sauces; snack foods; food preparations

## (G-5462)
### LARENTIA LED LLC
2010 W Fulton St  (60612-2359)
**PHONE**....................312 291-9111
Roxann Smith,
Laura Hagen,
**EMP:** 15
**SALES (est):** 1MM **Privately Held**
**SIC:** 3645  3646  Residential lighting fixtures; commercial indusl & institutional electric lighting fixtures

## (G-5463)
### LASNER BROS INC
Also Called: Lasner Beauty Supply
3649 N Ashland Ave  (60613-3617)
**PHONE**....................773 935-7383
Daniel Lasner, *Vice Pres*
**EMP:** 5 **EST:** 1940
**SQ FT:** 3,000
**SALES:** 600K **Privately Held**
**WEB:** www.lasnerbeautysupply.com
**SIC:** 5087  2844  Beauty parlor equipment & supplies; toilet preparations

## (G-5464)
### LASONS LABEL CO
5666 N Northwest Hwy  (60646-6161)
**PHONE**....................773 775-2606
**Fax:** 773 775-8618
William A Lasiewicz, *President*
Fleming Potter, *Founder*
Bernard M Lasiewicz, *Treasurer*
Geoff Bell, *Producer*
Angie Lau, *Producer*
**EMP:** 2
**SQ FT:** 5,000
**SALES (est):** 279.9K **Privately Held**
**SIC:** 2759  2796  2789  2672  Letterpress printing; labels & seals: printing; platemaking services; bookbinding & related work; coated & laminated paper; packaging paper & plastics film, coated & laminated

## (G-5465)
### LATINO ARTS & COMMUNICATIONS
3514 W Diversey Ave 212  (60647-1233)
**PHONE**....................773 501-0029
Ruben Calderon, *CEO*
**EMP:** 4
**SALES (est):** 316.8K **Privately Held**
**SIC:** 3663  Radio & TV communications equipment

## (G-5466)
### LATTICE ENERGY LLC
175 N Harbor Dr Apt 3205  (60601-7881)
**PHONE**....................312 861-0115
Lewis Larsen, *President*
Helene Berglund, *Treasurer*
**EMP:** 7
**SALES (est):** 710K **Privately Held**
**SIC:** 2819  Nuclear fuel scrap, reprocessing

## (G-5467)
### LAUREL MANUFACTURING LLC
5700 N Lincoln Ave # 203  (60659-4731)
**PHONE**....................773 961-8545
Jennie Rasinski, *Financial Exec*
Roger Weston, *Mng Member*
Neel Shetill,
▲ **EMP:** 9
**SALES (est):** 1.3MM **Privately Held**
**SIC:** 3369  White metal castings (lead, tin, antimony), except die

## (G-5468)
### LAUREN LEIN LTD
208 W Kinzie St Ste 3  (60654-4911)
**PHONE**....................312 527-1714
Lauren Lein-Santos, *Partner*
**EMP:** 25
**SQ FT:** 2,000
**SALES:** 1.2MM **Privately Held**
**SIC:** 2339  2369  Women's & misses' outerwear; girls' & children's outerwear

## (G-5469)
### LAVELL GENERAL HANDYMAN SVCS
8150 S Anthony Ave  (60617-1727)
**PHONE**....................773 691-3101
Lavell Bolden, *Principal*
**EMP:** 5
**SALES (est):** 243.4K **Privately Held**
**SIC:** 3432  Plumbing fixture fittings & trim

## GEOGRAPHIC SECTION

**Chicago - Cook County (G-5493)**

**(G-5470)**
**LAW BULLETIN PUBLISHING CO (PA)**
Also Called: Real Estate Communications
415 N State St Ste 1 (60654-4674)
PHONE..................312 416-1860
Fax: 312 644-1215
L Macfarland Jr, *Ch of Bd*
B Macfarland, *President*
Brewster McFarland, *President*
Bernard Judge, *Editor*
Peter Fazio, *Exec VP*
EMP: 150 EST: 1854
SQ FT: 60,000
SALES (est): 69MM **Privately Held**
WEB: www.chicagozoning.com
SIC: **2741** Guides: publishing & printing; directories: publishing & printing; business service newsletters: publishing & printing

**(G-5471)**
**LAWNDALE FORGING & TOOL WORKS**
2141 S Spaulding Ave (60623-3321)
PHONE..................773 277-2800
Fax: 773 277-9622
Ralph Russell, *President*
Gregory Russell, *General Mgr*
Greg Rusell, *Vice Pres*
EMP: 7 EST: 1916
SQ FT: 12,500
SALES: 575K **Privately Held**
SIC: **3462** 3452 3446 3443 Iron & steel forgings; bolts, nuts, rivets & washers; architectural metalwork; fabricated plate work (boiler shop); hand & edge tools; blast furnaces & steel mills

**(G-5472)**
**LAWRENCE RGAN CMMNICATIONS INC (PA)**
316 N Michigan Ave # 400 (60601-3773)
PHONE..................312 960-4100
Fax: 312 960-4105
Mark Ragan, *CEO*
Marc Thiessen, *President*
Ralph Gaillard, *Publisher*
Rebecca Anderson, *Editor*
Scott Lester, *Editor*
EMP: 43 EST: 1970
SQ FT: 10,000
SALES: 11.7MM **Privately Held**
WEB: www.pinpub.com
SIC: **2721** Periodicals

**(G-5473)**
**LAWTER INC (DH)**
200 N La Salle St # 2600 (60601-1060)
PHONE..................312 662-5700
Ichiro Taninaka, *President*
Yoshihiro Hasegawa, *Chairman*
Corry Manderson, *Business Mgr*
Peter Biesheuvel, *Vice Pres*
Kevin Wu, *Plant Mgr*
▲ EMP: 24
SALES (est): 157.3MM
SALES (corp-wide): 684.2K **Privately Held**
SIC: **2899** 2851 Chemical preparations; paints & allied products
HQ: Lawter Capital B.V.
Ankerkade 81
Maastricht
433 525-354

**(G-5474)**
**LAYSTROM MANUFACTURING CO**
3900 W Palmer St (60647-2216)
PHONE..................773 342-4800
Fax: 773 342-9762
Robert A Laystrom, *President*
Jeff Dec, *Plant Mgr*
Cindy Weglarz, *Opers Staff*
Barbara Hartwig, *Purchasing*
Ed Suerth, *Purchasing*
EMP: 55 EST: 1950
SQ FT: 75,000
SALES: 9MM **Privately Held**
WEB: www.laystrom.com
SIC: **3441** 3444 3469 3465 Fabricated structural metal; sheet metalwork; electronic enclosures, stamped or pressed metal; machine parts, stamped or pressed metal; stamping metal for the trade; automotive stampings; special dies, tools, jigs & fixtures; welding repair

**(G-5475)**
**LAZARE PRINTING CO INC**
709 W Wrightwood Ave # 1 (60614-2599)
PHONE..................773 871-2500
Fax: 773 871-2536
David Bullard, *President*
EMP: 8
SQ FT: 8,000
SALES: 1MM **Privately Held**
WEB: www.lazareprinting.com
SIC: **2752** 2759 Commercial printing, offset; letterpress printing

**(G-5476)**
**LCG SALES INC**
5410 W Roosevelt Rd # 231 (60644-1439)
PHONE..................773 378-7455
Fax: 773 378-3403
Laura Gordon, *President*
Edward Clamage, *Vice Pres*
◆ EMP: 100
SQ FT: 89,000
SALES (est): 11.4MM **Privately Held**
SIC: **3999** Army-Navy goods

**(G-5477)**
**LDR GLOBAL INDUSTRIES LLC**
600 N Kilbourn Ave (60624-1041)
PHONE..................773 265-3000
Hillel Tropper, *CEO*
Moshe Tropper, *President*
David Pollans, *Vice Pres*
Baruch Travitsky, *CFO*
▲ EMP: 80
SALES (est): 14.6MM
SALES (corp-wide): 31.7MM **Privately Held**
SIC: **3432** 5074 Plumbing fixture fittings & trim; plumbing fittings & supplies
PA: Coda Resources Ltd.
960 Alabama Ave
Brooklyn NY 11207
718 649-1666

**(G-5478)**
**LE PETIT PAIN HOLDINGS LLC (PA)**
676 N Michigan Ave (60611-2883)
PHONE..................312 981-3770
Mike Schultz, *Manager*
EMP: 6 EST: 2013
SALES (est): 172.8MM **Privately Held**
SIC: **2051** Bakery: wholesale or wholesale/retail combined

**(G-5479)**
**LEAN PROTEIN TEAM LLC** ✪
235 W Van Buren St (60607-3918)
PHONE..................440 525-1532
Christopher Arlinghaus, *Mng Member*
Dave Gooch,
Alan Knuckman,
EMP: 3 EST: 2017
SQ FT: 5,900
SALES: 20K **Privately Held**
SIC: **2015** Poultry Processing

**(G-5480)**
**LEAPFROG PRODUCT DEV LLC**
159 N Racine Ave Ste 3e (60607-1651)
PHONE..................312 229-0089
Rick Ellison, *President*
Jill Pearson, *VP Sls/Mktg*
Ellison Richard E,
Richard E Ellison,
Sward Kurtis M,
▲ EMP: 10 EST: 2009
SALES (est): 1.6MM **Privately Held**
SIC: **3999** Barber & beauty shop equipment

**(G-5481)**
**LEARNING SEED LLC**
208 S Jefferson St # 402 (60661-5650)
P.O. Box 617880 (60661-7880)
PHONE..................847 540-8855
Fax: 847 540-0854
Joseph Lombardo, *Mng Member*
Christine Schrank,
EMP: 5
SALES (est): 481.6K **Privately Held**
SIC: **3999** 7812 Education aids, devices & supplies; educational motion picture production

**(G-5482)**
**LEE ALLISON COMPANY INC**
1820 W Webster Ave # 301 (60614-2927)
PHONE..................773 276-7172
Leslie Allison, *President*
Jeff Fortier, *Business Mgr*
EMP: 3
SQ FT: 5,000
SALES (est): 414.6K **Privately Held**
WEB: www.leeallison.com
SIC: **2323** Men's & boys' neckwear

**(G-5483)**
**LEE ARMAND & CO LTD**
840 N Milwaukee Ave (60642-4103)
PHONE..................312 455-1200
Fax: 312 455-1210
Norman P Olson, *President*
Kyle Bretland, *Sales Staff*
Alan Vesely, *Office Mgr*
M J Forbes, *Admin Sec*
EMP: 26 EST: 1941
SQ FT: 20,000
SALES (est): 3MM **Privately Held**
WEB: www.armandlee.com
SIC: **2499** 7641 Picture & mirror frames, wood; antique furniture repair & restoration

**(G-5484)**
**LEE QUIGLEY COMPANY**
5301 W 65th St Ste D (60638-5640)
PHONE..................708 563-1600
Anita Kasper, *Branch Mgr*
EMP: 5
SALES (corp-wide): 16.6MM **Privately Held**
SIC: **3471** 5169 Finishing, metals or formed products; chemicals & allied products
PA: The Lee Quigley Company
700 Rockmead Dr Ste 216
Kingwood TX 77339
281 358-9608

**(G-5485)**
**LEE WEITZMAN FURNITURE INC**
1500 S Western Ave Ste 4 (60608-1828)
PHONE..................312 243-3009
Fax: 312 243-8854
Lee Weitzman, *President*
EMP: 8
SQ FT: 5,500
SALES (est): 1.1MM **Privately Held**
SIC: **2511** Novelty furniture: wood

**(G-5486)**
**LEG UP LLC**
639 W Diversey Pkwy # 205 (60614-1535)
PHONE..................312 282-2725
Shelby Mason, *CEO*
EMP: 5 EST: 2010
SALES (est): 526.4K **Privately Held**
SIC: **2339** 4215 Leotards: women's, misses' & juniors'; package delivery, vehicular

**(G-5487)**
**LEGACY VULCAN LLC**
Also Called: Pershing Road Recycle
3910 S Racine Ave (60609-2537)
PHONE..................773 890-2360
Cosme Velasquez, *Manager*
EMP: 6
SALES (corp-wide): 3.5B **Publicly Held**
WEB: www.vulcanmaterials.com
SIC: **3272** Concrete products
HQ: Legacy Vulcan, Llc
1200 Urban Center Dr
Vestavia AL 35242
205 298-3000

**(G-5488)**
**LEGGETT & PLATT INCORPORATED**
13535 S Torrence Ave (60633-2164)
EMP: 92
SALES (corp-wide): 3.7B **Publicly Held**
SIC: **2515** Box springs, assembled
PA: Leggett & Platt, Incorporated
1 Leggett Rd
Carthage MO 64836
417 358-8131

**(G-5489)**
**LEGGETT & PLATT INCORPORATED**
205 W Wacker Dr Ste 922 (60606-1244)
PHONE..................708 458-1800
EMP: 3
SALES (corp-wide): 3.7B **Publicly Held**
SIC: **2515** Box springs, assembled; mattresses, innerspring or box spring; chair & couch springs, assembled; bedsprings, assembled
PA: Leggett & Platt, Incorporated
1 Leggett Rd
Carthage MO 64836
417 358-8131

**(G-5490)**
**LEGGETT & PLATT INCORPORATED**
Also Called: Leggett & Platt 0338
6755 W 65th St (60638-4801)
PHONE..................708 458-1800
Kevin Ehle, *Vice Pres*
Sherwin Wang, *Purch Dir*
John Wainwright, *Branch Mgr*
Wally Crey, *Manager*
EMP: 30
SALES (corp-wide): 3.7B **Publicly Held**
SIC: **2431** Mfg Millwork
PA: Leggett & Platt, Incorporated
1 Leggett Rd
Carthage MO 64836
417 358-8131

**(G-5491)**
**LEGISTEK LLC**
211 W Wacker Dr 201 (60606-1217)
PHONE..................312 399-4891
Peter Moore, *CEO*
EMP: 3 EST: 2014
SALES (est): 234.3K **Privately Held**
SIC: **7372** 7389 Business oriented computer software;

**(G-5492)**
**LEO A BACHRACH JEWELERS INC**
Also Called: Leo Bachrach and Son
55 E Washington St # 801 (60602-2103)
PHONE..................312 263-3111
Fax: 312 263-3112
Leo A Bachrach, *President*
Mark Bachrach, *Treasurer*
Audrey Bachrach, *Admin Sec*
EMP: 4
SQ FT: 1,000
SALES (est): 436.5K **Privately Held**
WEB: www.leobachrachjewelers.com
SIC: **3911** 5944 Jewelry, precious metal; jewelry, precious stones & precious metals

**(G-5493)**
**LEO BURNETT COMPANY INC (HQ)**
Also Called: A R C
35 W Wacker Dr Fl 21 (60601-1755)
PHONE..................312 220-5959
Fax: 312 220-3299
Thomas L Bernardin, *CEO*
Leo Burnett Milan, *CEO*
Bob Raidt, *President*
Richard Stoddart, *President*
Judy John, *Managing Prtnr*
EMP: 148 EST: 1999
SQ FT: 615,000
SALES (est): 244.3MM
SALES (corp-wide): 28.2MM **Privately Held**
WEB: www.leoburnett.com
SIC: **7311** 3993 Advertising agencies; signs & advertising specialties

# Chicago - Cook County (G-5494)    GEOGRAPHIC SECTION

PA: Publicis Groupe S.A.
133 Avenue Des Champs Elysees
Paris 75008
144 437-000

**(G-5494)**
**LEOS SIGN**
1334 N Kostner Ave (60651-1604)
PHONE.................773 227-2460
Leonina Rodriguez, *Owner*
EMP: 3
SALES (est): 165K **Privately Held**
SIC: 3993 Signs & advertising specialties

**(G-5495)**
**LESTER LAMPERT INC**
57 E Oak St (60611)
PHONE.................312 944-6888
Fax: 312 943-9898
Lester Lampert, *CEO*
David Lampert, *President*
Susan Skarren, *Corp Secy*
Maureen Lampert, *Vice Pres*
Pamela Harnett, *Prdtn Mgr*
EMP: 26 **EST**: 1966
SQ FT: 8,000
SALES (est): 5.3MM **Privately Held**
WEB: www.lesterlampert.com
SIC: 3911 5944 Jewelry, precious metal; jewelry, precious stones & precious metals

**(G-5496)**
**LEVI STRAUSS & CO**
1552 N Milwaukee Ave (60622-2284)
PHONE.................773 486-3900
Fax: 773 486-7634
Elaine Deveney, *Manager*
EMP: 15
SALES (corp-wide): 4.5B **Privately Held**
WEB: www.levistrauss.com
SIC: 2325 2339 Jeans: men's, youths' & boys'; jeans: women's, misses & juniors'
PA: Levi Strauss & Co.
1155 Battery St
San Francisco CA 94111
415 501-6000

**(G-5497)**
**LEW-EL TOOL & MANUFACTURING CO**
1935 N Leclaire Ave (60639-4422)
PHONE.................773 804-1133
Fax: 773 804-1412
Richard J Milburn, *President*
Maureen Milburn, *Corp Secy*
Jack Milburn, *Plant Mgr*
Andrea Milburn, *Office Mgr*
EMP: 15
SQ FT: 10,000
SALES (est): 2.9MM **Privately Held**
WEB: www.leweltool.com
SIC: 3493 3544 3496 3469 Cold formed springs; special dies & tools; miscellaneous fabricated wire products; metal stampings; wire springs

**(G-5498)**
**LEXI GROUP INC**
3023 N Clark St Ste 778 (60657-5200)
PHONE.................866 675-1683
Lyndsay Palkon, *President*
EMP: 1
SALES (est): 961.9K **Privately Held**
SIC: 3085 5023 8742 Plastics bottles; home furnishings; management consulting services

**(G-5499)**
**LEXINGTON LEATHER GOODS CO**
5414 W Roosevelt Rd (60644-1467)
PHONE.................773 287-5500
Fax: 630 287-5585
Camerina Torres, *Principal*
▲ EMP: 13
SALES (est): 3MM **Privately Held**
SIC: 2674 Bags: uncoated paper & multi-wall

**(G-5500)**
**LEYBOLD USA INC**
25968 Network Pl (60673-1259)
PHONE.................724 327-5700
Lori Arola, *President*
EMP: 25
SALES (corp-wide): 10.9B **Privately Held**
SIC: 3821 Vacuum pumps, laboratory
HQ: Leybold Usa Inc.
5700 Mellon Rd
Export PA 15632
724 327-5700

**(G-5501)**
**LIBATION CONTAINER INC**
4519 N Mozart St (60625-3816)
P.O. Box 43085 (60643-0085)
PHONE.................312 287-4524
Lawrence Brown, *President*
Cynthia Hing, *Vice Pres*
Cynthia Hing Brown, *Admin Sec*
EMP: 11 **EST**: 2010
SALES (est): 1.2MM **Privately Held**
SIC: 3221 3229 Glass containers; bottles for packing, bottling & canning: glass; glassware, art or decorative

**(G-5502)**
**LIBERTY TIRE RECYCLING LLC**
2044 N Dominick St (60614-3006)
PHONE.................773 871-6360
Ken Lakin, *Principal*
Mario Aguirre, *Info Tech Mgr*
EMP: 8 **Privately Held**
SIC: 3011 5014 4953 Tires & inner tubes; tires & tubes; recycling, waste materials
HQ: Liberty Tire Recycling, Llc
625 Liberty Ave Ste 3100
Pittsburgh PA 15222
412 562-1700

**(G-5503)**
**LIGHT OF MINE LLC**
Also Called: Lom
401 N Michigan Ave # 1200 (60611-4255)
PHONE.................312 840-8570
Suzette E Webb,
EMP: 3
SALES (est): 306.8K **Privately Held**
WEB: www.thelomgroup.com
SIC: 3671 3711 3672 3625 Cathode ray tubes, including rebuilt; ambulances (motor vehicles), assembly of; circuit boards, television & radio printed; industrial electrical relays & switches

**(G-5504)**
**LIGHTITECH LLC**
200 W Superior St Ste 400 (60654-3556)
PHONE.................847 910-4177
Patricia N Harada,
EMP: 1
SALES (est): 225K **Privately Held**
SIC: 1731 3648 Energy management controls; lighting equipment

**(G-5505)**
**LIMITLESS COFFEE LLC**
Also Called: Limitless Coffee & Tea
316 N Elizabeth St (60607-1120)
PHONE.................630 779-3778
Matt Matros,
Craig Alexander,
Chris Fanucchi,
EMP: 40
SQ FT: 2,300
SALES (est): 1.7MM **Privately Held**
SIC: 2095 Coffee extracts

**(G-5506)**
**LINCOLN BARK LLC**
858 W Armitage Ave 240 (60614-4383)
PHONE.................800 428-4027
Bobbye Cochran,
EMP: 3
SALES (est): 218.5K **Privately Held**
SIC: 2047 Dog & cat food

**(G-5507)**
**LINCOLN PARK BREWERY INC**
Also Called: Goose Island Brew Pub
1800 N Clybourn Ave Ste B (60614-4895)
PHONE.................312 915-0071
John Hall, *President*
Reggie Snead, *General Mgr*
EMP: 70
SQ FT: 16,000
SALES (est): 3MM **Privately Held**
SIC: 5812 2082 Eating places; beer (alcoholic beverage)

**(G-5508)**
**LINCOLN SQUARE PRINTING**
4607 N Western Ave Fl 1 (60625-2022)
PHONE.................773 334-9030
Hazem Beia, *Partner*
EMP: 3
SALES (est): 250K **Privately Held**
SIC: 2759 Commercial printing

**(G-5509)**
**LINDA LEVINSON DESIGNS INC**
111 E Oak St 3 (60611-1202)
PHONE.................312 951-6943
Fax: 312 951-8397
Linda Levinson, *President*
EMP: 4
SQ FT: 2,500
SALES (est): 369.4K **Privately Held**
WEB: www.lindalevinsondesigns.com
SIC: 3965 2396 Buckles & buckle parts; automotive & apparel trimmings

**(G-5510)**
**LINE OF ADVANCE NFP**
2126 W Armitage Ave Apt 3 (60647-4594)
PHONE.................312 768-0043
Matt Marcus, *Admin Sec*
EMP: 3
SALES (est): 8.5K **Privately Held**
SIC: 2741 Miscellaneous publishing

**(G-5511)**
**LINEAR DIMENSIONS INC**
445 E Ohio St Ste 350 (60611-3382)
PHONE.................312 321-1810
Fax: 312 321-1830
Ronel W Giedt, *President*
Mike Ward, *Exec VP*
David W Conway, *Technical Staff*
EMP: 10
SQ FT: 1,800
SALES (est): 2MM **Privately Held**
WEB: www.lineardimensions.com
SIC: 3674 Computer logic modules

**(G-5512)**
**LINK TOOLS INTL (USA) INC**
2440 N Lakeview Ave (60614-2872)
PHONE.................773 549-3000
Fax: 773 248-4927
John B Davidson, *President*
Ted Weldon, *VP Mktg*
Tim Bregenzer, *Director*
▲ EMP: 5
SALES (est): 609.9K **Privately Held**
WEB: www.link-tools.com
SIC: 3423 3546 Hand & edge tools; power-driven handtools

**(G-5513)**
**LINKEDHEALTH SOLUTIONS**
700 N Green St (60642-5996)
PHONE.................312 600-6684
Lawrence Miller, *CEO*
EMP: 15
SALES (est): 563.2K **Privately Held**
SIC: 7372 Prepackaged software

**(G-5514)**
**LINN WEST PAPER COMPANY**
4649 N Magnolia Ave (60640-4940)
PHONE.................773 561-3839
Doug Scott, *Chairman*
EMP: 2
SALES (est): 219.1K **Privately Held**
SIC: 2679 Paperboard products, converted

**(G-5515)**
**LINX**
1807 W Sunnyside Ave 2c (60640-5892)
PHONE.................847 910-5303
Alan Rosenfield, *Mng Member*
EMP: 3
SALES (est): 1MM **Privately Held**
SIC: 3999 Barber & beauty shop equipment

**(G-5516)**
**LINX ENTERPRISES LLC**
5051 S Forrestville Ave (60615-2428)
P.O. Box 437404 (60643-7404)
PHONE.................224 409-2206
Asia Taylor,
Paris King,
EMP: 3

SALES (est): 73.4K **Privately Held**
SIC: 7389 7812 7929 7336 Music recording producer; motion picture & video production; music video production; motion picture production & distribution, television; entertainers & entertainment groups; commercial art & graphic design; cakes, bakery: except frozen; music distribution apparatus

**(G-5517)**
**LIQUIDFIRE**
8554 W Rascher Ave Apt 2n (60656-1321)
PHONE.................312 376-7448
Kim Sykes, *Owner*
EMP: 8
SALES (est): 433.5K **Privately Held**
WEB: www.liquidfirehosting.com
SIC: 7372 Prepackaged software

**(G-5518)**
**LITETRONICS TECHNOLOGIES INC**
Also Called: Life Tronics International
6969 W 73rd St (60638-6025)
PHONE.................708 333-6707
Robert C Sorensen, *President*
Thomas Hendrickson, *Vice Pres*
EMP: 6
SQ FT: 30,000
SALES (est): 1MM
SALES (corp-wide): 8.7MM **Privately Held**
WEB: www.litetronics.com
SIC: 3648 Lighting equipment
PA: Litetronics International, Inc.
6969 W 73rd St
Chicago IL 60638
708 389-8000

**(G-5519)**
**LITHUANIAN CATHOLIC PRESS**
Also Called: DRAUGAS PUBLISHING
4545 W 63rd St (60629-5532)
PHONE.................773 585-9500
Fax: 773 585-8284
Marian Remys, *President*
Valentine Krumplis, *Vice Pres*
Silvia Krumplis, *Office Mgr*
EMP: 20
SQ FT: 2,000
SALES (est): 647.1K **Privately Held**
SIC: 2711 2791 2759 2752 Newspapers: publishing only, not printed on site; typesetting; commercial printing; commercial printing, lithographic; periodicals

**(G-5520)**
**LITHUANIAN PRESS INC**
2711 W 71st St (60629-2005)
PHONE.................773 776-3399
Fax: 773 776-7059
Domas Adomaitis, *President*
Edmund Jasiunas, *President*
Vyt Radcius, *Principal*
EMP: 3
SALES (est): 55.3K **Privately Held**
SIC: 2721 Periodicals; periodicals: publishing only

**(G-5521)**
**LITTELFUSE INC (PA)**
8755 W Higgins Rd Ste 500 (60631-2701)
PHONE.................773 628-1000
Fax: 847 391-0146
Gordon Hunter, *Ch of Bd*
David W Heinzmann, *President*
Ryan K Stafford, *Exec VP*
Matthew J Cole, *Senior VP*
Ian Highley, *Senior VP*
EMP: 700 **EST**: 1927
SQ FT: 54,838
SALES: 1B **Publicly Held**
WEB: www.littelfuse.com
SIC: 3613 3679 Fuses & fuse equipment; electronic circuits

**(G-5522)**
**LITTELFUSE INC**
8755 W Higgins Rd Ste 300 (60631-4016)
PHONE.................773 628-1000
Howard B Witt, *President*
EMP: 20
SALES (corp-wide): 1B **Publicly Held**
WEB: www.littelfuse.com
SIC: 3625 Control circuit relays, industrial

# GEOGRAPHIC SECTION

**PA:** Littelfuse, Inc.
8755 W Higgins Rd Ste 500
Chicago IL 60631
773 628-1000

**(G-5523)**
**LIVE DAILY LLC**
2627 W Lunt Ave (60645-3216)
**PHONE**..................................312 286-6706
**EMP:** 4
**SALES (est):** 201.6K **Privately Held**
**SIC:** 2711 Newspapers-Publishing/Printing

**(G-5524)**
**LIVEGIFT INC**
Also Called: Caysh
222 Merchandise Mart Plz (60654-1103)
**PHONE**..................................312 725-4514
David Aronson, *CEO*
**EMP:** 4
**SALES:** 100K **Privately Held**
**SIC:** 2759 Card printing & engraving, except greeting

**(G-5525)**
**LIVEONE INC**
333 N Michigan Ave # 2800 (60601-3901)
**PHONE**..................................312 282-2320
Jimmy Chamberlin, *CEO*
Timothy C Ganschow, *President*
**EMP:** 8
**SALES (est):** 916.8K **Privately Held**
**SIC:** 3823 Digital displays of process variables

**(G-5526)**
**LKQ BROADWAY AUTO PARTS INC**
500 W Madison St Ste 2800 (60661-2506)
**PHONE**..................................312 621-1950
Chad Damron, *President*
**EMP:** 3
**SALES (est):** 181.6K **Privately Held**
**SIC:** 3357 Automotive wire & cable, except ignition sets: nonferrous

**(G-5527)**
**LLOYD M HUGHES ENTERPRISES INC**
Also Called: Laundryworld
6331 S Martin L King Dr (60637-3114)
**PHONE**..................................773 363-6331
Lloyd M Hughes, *President*
**EMP:** 6
**SQ FT:** 6,250
**SALES (est):** 492.2K **Privately Held**
**SIC:** 7215 7389 2329 Laundry, coin-operated; interior decorating; athletic (warmup, sweat & jogging) suits: men's & boys'

**(G-5528)**
**LMS INNOVATIONS INC** ✪
Also Called: Work Song Productions
2734 W Leland Ave Apt 3 (60625-3792)
**PHONE**..................................312 613-2345
Laura St John, *President*
Marlon St John, *Vice Pres*
**EMP:** 3 **EST:** 2016
**SALES (est):** 89.2K **Privately Held**
**SIC:** 2731 2741 8299 8748 Textbooks: publishing only, not printed on site; music books: publishing only, not printed on site; educational services; educational consultant; educational aids & electronic training materials

**(G-5529)**
**LOADSENSE TECHNOLOGIES LLC**
1658 N Milwaukee Ave # 512 (60647-6905)
**PHONE**..................................312 239-0146
Kennard L Wottowa, *Principal*
▲ **EMP:** 3
**SALES (est):** 244.7K **Privately Held**
**SIC:** 3596 Bathroom scales; truck (motor vehicle) scales

**(G-5530)**
**LOGAN SQUARE ALUMINUM SUP INC (PA)**
Also Called: Remodelers Supply Center
2500 N Pulaski Rd (60639-2107)
**PHONE**..................................773 235-2500
**Fax:** 773 235-1860

Louis Silver, *President*
Claire Wilson, *Mktg Dir*
Dave Lambert, *Branch Mgr*
Barry Cohodus, *Manager*
Nathan Silver, *Admin Sec*
▲ **EMP:** 60
**SQ FT:** 250,000
**SALES (est):** 101.1MM **Privately Held**
**WEB:** www.remodelerssupply.com
**SIC:** 5211 3089 Lumber & other building materials; windows, plastic

**(G-5531)**
**LOGAN SQUARE ALUMINUM SUP INC**
Also Called: Studio 41
204 W 83rd St (60620-1703)
**PHONE**..................................773 846-8300
Paul Panitch, *Branch Mgr*
Paul Pantich, *Manager*
**EMP:** 20
**SALES (corp-wide):** 101.1MM **Privately Held**
**WEB:** www.remodelerssupply.com
**SIC:** 3442 Window & door frames
**PA:** Logan Square Aluminum Supply, Inc.
2500 N Pulaski Rd
Chicago IL 60639

**(G-5532)**
**LOGAN SQUARE ALUMINUM SUP INC**
Also Called: Remodeler's Supply Center
2622 N Pulaski Rd (60639-2118)
**PHONE**..................................773 278-3600
**Fax:** 773 235-6712
Chuck Liszka, *Branch Mgr*
**EMP:** 170
**SALES (corp-wide):** 101.1MM **Privately Held**
**WEB:** www.remodelerssupply.com
**SIC:** 3442 Window & door frames; screen & storm doors & windows; metal doors
**PA:** Logan Square Aluminum Supply, Inc.
2500 N Pulaski Rd
Chicago IL 60639

**(G-5533)**
**LOGICGATE INC**
214 W Ohio St Fl 1 (60654-8741)
**PHONE**..................................312 279-2775
Matthew Kunkel, *CEO*
Jonathan Siegler, *COO*
Daniel Campbell, *Officer*
**EMP:** 10
**SALES (est):** 637.9K **Privately Held**
**SIC:** 7371 7372 7379 8748 Computer software development; business oriented computer software; computer related consulting services; business consulting

**(G-5534)**
**LOKMAN ENTERPRISES INC**
7240 N Ridge Blvd Apt 102 (60645-2039)
**PHONE**..................................773 654-0525
Lokman Hossain, *CEO*
R Khan, *Treasurer*
B Khan, *Admin Sec*
**EMP:** 4 **EST:** 2014
**SALES:** 50K **Privately Held**
**SIC:** 2048 7389 Poultry feeds;

**(G-5535)**
**LOMBARD ARCHTCTRAL PRCAST PDTS**
4245 W 123rd St (60803-1805)
**PHONE**..................................708 389-1060
George E Lombard, *President*
Floyd Page, *Exec VP*
John Lombard, *Vice Pres*
**EMP:** 40
**SQ FT:** 50,000
**SALES (est):** 313.9K
**SALES (corp-wide):** 784.8K **Privately Held**
**WEB:** www.lappco.com
**SIC:** 3272 1791 Concrete products, precast; precast concrete structural framing or panels, placing of
**PA:** The Lombard Investment Company
4245 W 123rd St
Alsip IL 60803
708 389-1060

**(G-5536)**
**LONELYBRAND LLC (PA)**
118 W Kinzie St (60654-4508)
**PHONE**..................................312 880-7506
Nicholas Kinports, *Founder*
**EMP:** 4
**SALES (est):** 1.8MM **Privately Held**
**SIC:** 7372 Business oriented computer software

**(G-5537)**
**LONG VIEW PUBLISHING CO INC**
Also Called: People's Weekly World
3339 S Halsted St Ste 4 (60608-6883)
**PHONE**..................................773 446-9920
Terrie Albano, *Publisher*
C Atkins, *Editor*
Mariya Strauss, *Editor*
Barb Russum, *Branch Mgr*
Jenn Delgado, *Executive*
**EMP:** 12
**SALES (corp-wide):** 4.3MM **Privately Held**
**SIC:** 2711 Newspapers, publishing & printing
**PA:** Long View Publishing Co Inc
235 W 23rd St Fl 4
New York NY
212 924-2523

**(G-5538)**
**LOOP ATTACHMENT CO**
1509 N Hudson Ave Apt 3 (60610-5833)
**PHONE**..................................847 922-0642
Evan J Derman, *COO*
Christopher Peterson, *Ch Credit Ofcr*
Daniel Selden, *CTO*
▲ **EMP:** 3
**SALES (est):** 245.9K **Privately Held**
**SIC:** 3069 Molded rubber products

**(G-5539)**
**LOOP AUTOMOTIVE LLC**
303 W Ohio St Apt 2609 (60654-7971)
**PHONE**..................................847 912-9090
Konstantin Selikhov,
**EMP:** 30
**SALES (est):** 1.1MM **Privately Held**
**SIC:** 3089 5013 Automotive parts, plastic; automotive supplies & parts

**(G-5540)**
**LOPEZ PLUMBING SYSTEMS INC**
5816 S Claremont Ave (60636)
**PHONE**..................................773 424-8225
Josue Lopez, *President*
**EMP:** 5 **EST:** 2010
**SALES (est):** 700K **Privately Held**
**SIC:** 3822 Water heater controls

**(G-5541)**
**LOREN GIROVICH**
Also Called: Carline Leathers
5328 N Wayne Ave (60640-2211)
**PHONE**..................................773 334-1444
Loren Girovich, *President*
John Martin, *Vice Pres*
**EMP:** 5
**SALES:** 1MM **Privately Held**
**SIC:** 5136 5137 2387 3172 Leather & sheep lined clothing, men's & boys'; leather & sheep lined clothing, women's & children's; purses; apparel belts; wallets

**(G-5542)**
**LORENZOS DELECTABLE LLC**
4552 S Lamon Ave (60638-1958)
**PHONE**..................................773 791-3327
Lorenzo Crawford, *CEO*
Genesis Crawford, *President*
Aamir Hodari, *General Mgr*
Angela Purdom, *Exec VP*
Rodney Purdom, *CFO*
**EMP:** 5 **EST:** 2013
**SALES (est):** 254.1K **Privately Held**
**SIC:** 2024 5143 Ice cream & frozen desserts; dairy based frozen desserts; frozen dairy desserts

**(G-5543)**
**LOS GAMAS INC**
3333 W Armitage Ave (60647-3717)
**PHONE**..................................872 829-3514

Alejandro Gama, *President*
**EMP:** 6 **EST:** 2012
**SALES:** 580K **Privately Held**
**SIC:** 2099 Tortillas, fresh or refrigerated

**(G-5544)**
**LOS MANGOS**
Also Called: Los Mangos I
3058 S Avers Ave (60623-4542)
**PHONE**..................................773 542-1522
**EMP:** 5
**SALES (est):** 276.5K **Privately Held**
**SIC:** 2024 Ice cream & frozen desserts

**(G-5545)**
**LOS PRIMOS PALLETS INC**
2013 W Ferdinand St (60612-1549)
**PHONE**..................................773 418-3584
Juan Rodriguez, *President*
Jose Martinez, *Manager*
**EMP:** 4 **EST:** 2009
**SALES (est):** 317.8K **Privately Held**
**SIC:** 2448 Pallets, wood & wood with metal

**(G-5546)**
**LOSO TRUCKING INC**
55 E Monroe St Ste 3800 (60603-6030)
**PHONE**..................................312 601-2231
Ronald Harris, *President*
**EMP:** 3
**SALES (est):** 138.9K **Privately Held**
**SIC:** 3537 Trucks, tractors, loaders, carriers & similar equipment

**(G-5547)**
**LOUIS MESKAN BRASS FOUNDRY INC**
Also Called: Meskan Foundry
2007 N Major Ave 13 (60639-2951)
**PHONE**..................................773 237-7662
**Fax:** 773 237-7706
David Meskan, *President*
Allen Meskan, *Exec VP*
Bruce Mell, *Sls & Mktg Exec*
Stephanie Mell, *Marketing Staff*
Lisa Meskan, *Manager*
**EMP:** 102
**SQ FT:** 90,000
**SALES:** 17.7MM **Privately Held**
**WEB:** www.meskan.com
**SIC:** 3366 3365 Castings (except die): brass; aluminum & aluminum-based alloy castings

**(G-5548)**
**LOVE JOURNEY INC** ✪
8121 S Colfax Ave (60617-1203)
**PHONE**..................................773 447-5591
Janine Ingram, *CEO*
**EMP:** 3 **EST:** 2016
**SALES (est):** 83.9K **Privately Held**
**SIC:** 3999 7389 Mfg Misc Products Business Serv Non-Commercial Site

**(G-5549)**
**LOYAL CASKET CO**
134 S California Ave (60612-3671)
P.O. Box 12277 (60612-0277)
**PHONE**..................................773 722-4065
**Fax:** 773 722-7362
Anthony Kolaski, *President*
Dale Malachuk, *Principal*
Jerome Kolaski, *Corp Secy*
**EMP:** 15 **EST:** 1945
**SQ FT:** 50,000
**SALES (est):** 2.4MM **Privately Held**
**SIC:** 3995 Burial caskets

**(G-5550)**
**LPI WORLDWIDE INC**
4821 S Aberdeen St (60609-4312)
**PHONE**..................................773 826-8600
Norman H Wexler, *President*
**EMP:** 5
**SALES (est):** 521.2K **Privately Held**
**SIC:** 3441 Fabricated structural metal

**(G-5551)**
**LPZ INC**
2919 S Western Ave (60608-5221)
**PHONE**..................................773 579-6120
Rafael Lopez, *President*
Jesus Lopez, *Admin Sec*
**EMP:** 3

## Chicago - Cook County (G-5552)

SALES (est): 208.8K **Privately Held**
SIC: **2032** Tortillas: packaged in cans, jars etc.

**(G-5552)**
**LSC COMMUNICATIONS INC (PA)**
191 N Wacker Dr Ste 1400 (60606-1921)
PHONE...................773 272-9200
Thomas J Quinlan III, *Ch of Bd*
Janet Halpin, *Vice Pres*
Andrew B Coxhead, *CFO*
Suzanne S Bettman, *Officer*
Kent A Hansen,
EMP: 100
SALES (est): 13B **Publicly Held**
SIC: **2732 2721 2621** Book printing; magazines: publishing & printing; catalog, magazine & newsprint papers

**(G-5553)**
**LSC COMMUNICATIONS US LLC (HQ)**
191 N Wacker Dr Ste 1400 (60606-1921)
PHONE...................844 572-5720
Thomas J Quinlan III, *CEO*
EMP: 277
SALES (est): 2.8B
SALES (corp-wide): 13B **Publicly Held**
SIC: **2732 2721 2621** Book printing; magazines: publishing & printing; catalog, magazine & newsprint papers
PA: Lsc Communications, Inc.
191 N Wacker Dr Ste 1400
Chicago IL 60606
773 272-9200

**(G-5554)**
**LSK IMPORT**
100 S Wacker Dr Ste 700 (60606-4028)
PHONE...................847 342-8447
Steve Kaplan, *Principal*
▲ EMP: 2
SALES (est): 296.7K **Privately Held**
SIC: **2752** Commercial printing, lithographic

**(G-5555)**
**LSL INDUSTRIES INC**
Also Called: Lsl Health Care
5535 N Wolcott Ave (60640-1019)
P.O. Box 352, Northbrook (60065-0352)
PHONE...................773 878-1100
Fax: 773 878-9100
Ashok Luthra, *President*
Nisar Ahmed, *Opers Mgr*
Tony Huffman, *Safety Mgr*
Artis Carroll, *Finance Mgr*
Jerry Czaja, *Finance*
▲ EMP: 84
SQ FT: 20,000
SALES (est): 31MM **Privately Held**
SIC: **3841 3842** Surgical & medical instruments; surgical appliances & supplies

**(G-5556)**
**LUBY PUBLISHING INC**
Also Called: Billiards Digest
55 E Jackson Blvd Ste 401 (60604-4307)
PHONE...................312 341-1110
Fax: 312 341-1469
Keith Hamilton, *President*
Barb Peltz, *Sales Mgr*
Sally Samaan, *Advt Staff*
Kim Levandowski, *Manager*
Andrew Noteman, *Manager*
EMP: 17 EST: 1913
SQ FT: 8,000
SALES (est): 3MM **Privately Held**
WEB: www.lubypublishing.com
SIC: **2721 2741** Trade journals: publishing only, not printed on site; directories: publishing only, not printed on site

**(G-5557)**
**LUCKSFOOD**
1109 W Argyle St (60640-3609)
PHONE...................773 878-7778
Enpen Chen, *Owner*
EMP: 4
SALES (est): 197.2K **Privately Held**
SIC: **2051** Bread, cake & related products

**(G-5558)**
**LUDIS FOODS ADAMS INC**
23 E Adams St (60603-5603)
PHONE...................312 939-2877
EMP: 3
SALES (est): 81K **Privately Held**
SIC: **2099** Mfg Food Preparations

**(G-5559)**
**LUKE GRAPHICS INC**
6000 N Northwest Hwy (60631-2518)
P.O. Box 31816 (60631-0816)
PHONE...................773 775-6733
Fax: 773 836-7338
Frances Lukasik, *President*
Kim Irving, *Assistant VP*
▲ EMP: 11
SQ FT: 3,000
SALES (est): 1.2MM **Privately Held**
WEB: www.lukegraphicsinc.com
SIC: **2752** Commercial printing, offset

**(G-5560)**
**LULULEMON USA INC**
1627 N Damen Ave (60647-5507)
PHONE...................773 227-1869
EMP: 3
SALES (corp-wide): 2.3B **Privately Held**
SIC: **2339** Sportswear, women's
HQ: Lululemon Usa Inc.
2201 140th Ave E
Sumner WA 98390
604 732-6124

**(G-5561)**
**LULUS**
2401 S Ridgeway Ave (60623-3833)
PHONE...................773 865-8978
Erika Lechuga, *Owner*
EMP: 4
SALES (est): 309.9K **Privately Held**
SIC: **3421** Table & food cutlery, including butchers'

**(G-5562)**
**LUMENART LTD**
3333 W 47th St (60632-2940)
PHONE...................773 254-0744
Derrick Gurski, *President*
▲ EMP: 5
SALES (est): 1.2MM **Privately Held**
SIC: **5063 3645** Lighting fixtures; residential lighting fixtures

**(G-5563)**
**LUMENART LTD**
320 N Damen Ave Ste D300 (60612-2442)
PHONE...................773 254-0744
Darrick Gurski, *Partner*
Christine Mason, *Manager*
▲ EMP: 7
SALES: 2MM **Privately Held**
WEB: www.lumenart.net
SIC: **3645** Residential lighting fixtures

**(G-5564)**
**LUMENERGI INC**
70 W Madison St Ste 2300 (60602-4250)
PHONE...................866 921-4652
Barry Weinbaum, *President*
Bennett Johnston, *President*
William Astary, *Senior VP*
Peter M Schwartz, *Vice Pres*
Andrew Savadelis, *CFO*
▲ EMP: 25
SQ FT: 9,800
SALES (est): 3.8MM **Privately Held**
SIC: **3612** Ballasts for lighting fixtures

**(G-5565)**
**LUMINA INC**
512 N Racine Ave (60642-5842)
P.O. Box 47146 (60647-0003)
PHONE...................312 829-8970
Rocco Saliano, *President*
EMP: 2
SQ FT: 200
SALES (est): 260K **Privately Held**
WEB: www.luminafireworks.com
SIC: **2899** Fireworks

**(G-5566)**
**LUMINESCENCE MEDIA GROUP NFP**
3740 N Lake Shore Dr (60613-4237)
PHONE...................312 602-3302
Mitchell Lieber, *Exec Dir*
EMP: 4
SALES: 120K **Privately Held**
SIC: **3999** Education aids, devices & supplies

**(G-5567)**
**LUNA IT SERVICES**
1658 N Milwaukee Ave # 222 (60647-6905)
PHONE...................213 537-2764
Stephen Richardson, *Principal*
EMP: 8
SALES: 500K **Privately Held**
SIC: **3575** Computer terminals

**(G-5568)**
**LUNA MATTRESS TRANSPORT INC**
3357 W 47th Pl (60632-3041)
PHONE...................773 847-1812
Muhammad Jabara, *President*
EMP: 17
SQ FT: 55,000
SALES: 3.2MM **Privately Held**
SIC: **2515 4731** Mattresses & bedsprings; freight transportation arrangement

**(G-5569)**
**LUSTER PRODUCTS INC (PA)**
1104 W 43rd St (60609-3342)
PHONE...................773 579-1800
Fax: 773 579-1912
Blondell Luster, *Ch of Bd*
Jory Luster, *President*
Fred Luster II, *Vice Pres*
Sonia Luster, *Vice Pres*
Drenda Turner, *Marketing Staff*
◆ EMP: 400 EST: 1955
SQ FT: 200,000
SALES: 82.8K **Privately Held**
WEB: www.lusterproducts.com
SIC: **2844** Hair preparations, including shampoos; shampoos, rinses, conditioners: hair

**(G-5570)**
**LUXURY MBL & GRAN DESIGN INC**
3206 N Kilpatrick Ave (60641-4421)
PHONE...................773 656-2125
Beatriz Trigueros, *President*
EMP: 5
SQ FT: 5,000
SALES (est): 610.3K **Privately Held**
SIC: **3281** Cut stone & stone products

**(G-5571)**
**LV VENTURES INC (PA)**
233 S Wacker Dr Ste 2150 (60606-6370)
PHONE...................312 993-1800
William Farley, *President*
Martin Pajor, *Vice Pres*
Todd Sluzas, *CFO*
EMP: 5 EST: 1982
SALES (est): 37.5MM **Privately Held**
WEB: www.magnus-farley.com
SIC: **3544 3568 3519** Special dies, tools, jigs & fixtures; railroad car journal bearings; diesel, semi-diesel or duel-fuel engines, including marine

**(G-5572)**
**LV VENTURES INC**
Farley Indstries/ Frt Ogf Loom
233 S Wacker Dr Ste 2150 (60606-6370)
PHONE...................312 993-1758
Patty McDonald, *Manager*
EMP: 30
SALES (corp-wide): 37.5MM **Privately Held**
WEB: www.magnus-farley.com
SIC: **3544 6799 3567** Special dies, tools, jigs & fixtures; investors; electrical furnaces, ovens & heating devices, exc. induction
PA: Lv Ventures, Inc.
233 S Wacker Dr Ste 2150
Chicago IL 60606
312 993-1800

**(G-5573)**
**LYKO WOODWORKING & CNSTR**
4157 N Elston Ave (60618-2107)
PHONE...................773 583-4561
Ireneusz Lyko, *President*
EMP: 6
SQ FT: 2,844
SALES (est): 744.7K **Privately Held**
SIC: **2434 1751 2431** Wood kitchen cabinets; carpentry work; millwork

**(G-5574)**
**LYON & HEALY HARPS INC**
168 N Ogden Ave (60607-1465)
PHONE...................312 786-1881
Fax: 312 226-1502
Victor Salvi, *President*
▲ EMP: 3
SALES (est): 552.5K **Privately Held**
SIC: **3931** Harps & parts

**(G-5575)**
**LYON & HEALY HOLDING CORP (HQ)**
168 N Ogden Ave (60607-1412)
PHONE...................312 786-1881
Antonio Forero, *Ch of Bd*
Ronald Koltz, *CFO*
Natalie Bilik, *Sales Staff*
▲ EMP: 25
SQ FT: 65,000
SALES (est): 13.3MM **Privately Held**
WEB: www.lyonhealy.com
SIC: **3931 5736** Harps & parts; string instruments
PA: L.A.M. - Les Arts Mecaniques Sa
Rue De La Sagne 17
Ste-Croix VD
223 204-242

**(G-5576)**
**M & G GRAPHICS INC**
3500 W 38th St (60632-3306)
PHONE...................773 247-1596
Fax: 773 247-1806
Josephine Meyer, *President*
Bob Meyer Jr, *Vice Pres*
John Weiss, *Prdtn Mgr*
Brian Parshall, *Accounts Mgr*
Donna Calandriello, *Manager*
EMP: 22
SQ FT: 40,000
SALES (est): 4.1MM **Privately Held**
WEB: www.m-g-graphics.com
SIC: **2759 2796 2789 2741** Commercial printing; color separations for printing; bookbinding & related work; miscellaneous publishing

**(G-5577)**
**M & I HEATING AND COOLING INC**
6405 N Campbell Ave (60645-5313)
PHONE...................773 743-7073
Musan Imamovic, *Owner*
Bahrija Imamovic, *Office Mgr*
Elzana Imamovic, *Admin Sec*
EMP: 4
SALES (est): 492.7K **Privately Held**
SIC: **3585** Parts for heating, cooling & refrigerating equipment

**(G-5578)**
**M & S INDUSTRIAL CO INC**
4334 W Division St (60651-1713)
PHONE...................773 252-1616
Fax: 773 252-5092
Andrew Metelski, *President*
Stanley Nowak, *Vice Pres*
Andrew Sniezynski, *Vice Pres*
John Biernat, *Treasurer*
Alexandra Spalek, *Admin Sec*
EMP: 25
SQ FT: 16,000
SALES: 1.5MM **Privately Held**
SIC: **3599** Machine shop, jobbing & repair

**(G-5579)**
**M B JEWELERS INC**
Also Called: Royal Casting
29 E Madison St Ste 1835 (60602-4865)
PHONE...................312 853-3490
Fax: 312 853-3492
Yacoub Boyrazian, *President*
Michael Boyrazian, *Corp Secy*

## GEOGRAPHIC SECTION

**EMP:** 2
**SALES:** 275K  **Privately Held**
**SIC:** 3915  3911  Jewelers' castings; jewel cutting, drilling, polishing, recutting or setting; jewelry, precious metal

*(G-5580)*
### M G M DISPLAYS INC
4956 S Monitor Ave  (60638-1544)
**PHONE**.....................................708 594-3699
**Fax:** 708 594-3696
Mark Perrone, *President*
Milt Plude, *Vice Pres*
**EMP:** 3
**SQ FT:** 25,000
**SALES:** 1MM  **Privately Held**
**WEB:** www.mgmdisplays.com
**SIC:** 3993  7319  Advertising artwork; displays & cutouts, window & lobby; display advertising service

*(G-5581)*
### M HANDELSMAN & CO
Also Called: Hanco
6124 N Saint Louis Ave  (60659-2228)
**PHONE**.....................................312 427-0784
**Fax:** 312 427-0787
Bernard Lifchez, *Ch of Bd*
Stuart Berger, *President*
Craig Darlow, *Vice Pres*
Marilyn Berger, *Admin Sec*
**EMP:** 10
**SQ FT:** 20,000
**SALES:** 1.3MM  **Privately Held**
**SIC:** 2329  Men's & boys' sportswear & athletic clothing

*(G-5582)*
### M INC
Also Called: Mattaliano Furniture
205 W Wacker Dr Ste 307  (60606-1487)
**PHONE**.....................................312 853-0512
Darcy Bonner, *President*
**EMP:** 7  **EST:** 1938
**SALES (est):** 941.3K  **Privately Held**
**SIC:** 2511  Wood household furniture

*(G-5583)*
### M K ADVANTAGE INC
1055 W Bryn Mawr Ave F216
(60660-4691)
**PHONE**.....................................773 902-5272
Christopher Schaf, *President*
**EMP:** 12
**SALES (est):** 871.1K  **Privately Held**
**SIC:** 7379  3695  Computer related consulting services; computer software tape & disks: blank, rigid & floppy

*(G-5584)*
### M MAURITZON & COMPANY INC
3939 W Belden Ave  (60647-2207)
**PHONE**.....................................773 235-6000
Steven Karlin, *President*
Charles Karlin, *Principal*
Sean Karlin, *Vice Pres*
John Sokolowski, *Manager*
▲ **EMP:** 50
**SQ FT:** 110,000
**SALES (est):** 9.6MM  **Privately Held**
**WEB:** www.mauritzononline.com
**SIC:** 2394  Tarpaulins, fabric: made from purchased materials

*(G-5585)*
### M PUTTERMAN & CO LLC (HQ)
4834 S Oakley Ave  (60609-4036)
**PHONE**.....................................773 927-4120
**Fax:** 773 650-6046
Sandy Grobarcik, *Controller*
Tom Byrne, *Marketing Staff*
Alan Berman,
Joan Koza,
Edward Reicin,
▲ **EMP:** 63
**SQ FT:** 52,000
**SALES (est):** 12.2MM
**SALES (corp-wide):** 34.2MM  **Privately Held**
**WEB:** www.mputterman.com
**SIC:** 3089  2394  Plastic processing; canvas & related products
**PA:** Mpc Group Llc
4834 S Oakley Ave
Chicago IL 60609
773 927-4120

*(G-5586)*
### M PUTTERMAN & CO LLC
1581 E 98th St  (60628-1731)
P.O. Box 94603  (60690-4603)
**PHONE**.....................................773 734-1000
Ron Young, *Vice Pres*
Adella Savercool, *Sales Staff*
**EMP:** 3
**SALES (corp-wide):** 34.2MM  **Privately Held**
**WEB:** www.mputterman.com
**SIC:** 2394  Canvas & related products
**HQ:** M. Putterman & Co. Llc
4834 S Oakley Ave
Chicago IL 60609
773 927-4120

*(G-5587)*
### M SQUARED INDUSTRIES LLC
828 W Grace St  (60613-5758)
**PHONE**.....................................708 606-2603
Matthew R Stawiarski, *Principal*
**EMP:** 2
**SALES (est):** 106.8K  **Privately Held**
**SIC:** 3999  Manufacturing industries

*(G-5588)*
### M WELLS PRINTING CO
329 W 18th St Ste 502  (60616-1121)
**PHONE**.....................................312 455-0400
**Fax:** 312 455-0800
Michael E Wells, *Owner*
**EMP:** 6
**SQ FT:** 3,500
**SALES (est):** 890K  **Privately Held**
**SIC:** 2759  8742  2761  2752  Promotional printing; marketing consulting services; manifold business forms; commercial printing, lithographic; die-cut paper & board; automotive & apparel trimmings

*(G-5589)*
### M& L NOODLE
1130 W Argyle St  (60640-3610)
**PHONE**.....................................773 878-3333
**EMP:** 4
**SALES (est):** 146.7K  **Privately Held**
**SIC:** 2098  Noodles (e.g. egg, plain & water), dry

*(G-5590)*
### M&J HAULING INC
2048 W Hubbard St  (60612-1610)
**PHONE**.....................................312 342-6596
Marian Flasch, *President*
Micheal Stevens, *Vice Pres*
John Flasch, *Treasurer*
**EMP:** 4
**SALES (est):** 340K  **Privately Held**
**SIC:** 3537  Industrial trucks & tractors

*(G-5591)*
### MAB PHARMACY INC
2643 W Division St Ste 1  (60622-7276)
**PHONE**.....................................773 342-5878
Mahendra T Amin, *President*
**EMP:** 4
**SALES (est):** 440K  **Privately Held**
**SIC:** 2834  Pharmaceutical preparations

*(G-5592)*
### MACHINE TOOL ACC & MFG CO
1915 W Fullerton Ave  (60614-1915)
**PHONE**.....................................773 489-0903
**Fax:** 773 489-4466
Tibor Halasz, *President*
**EMP:** 2  **EST:** 1967
**SQ FT:** 3,000
**SALES (est):** 302.9K  **Privately Held**
**WEB:** www.mtachicago.com
**SIC:** 3545  3599  3498  3462  Boring machine attachments (machine tool accessories); machine shop, jobbing & repair; fabricated pipe & fittings; iron & steel forgings; bolts, nuts, rivets & washers; thread mills

*(G-5593)*
### MACHINEX TECHNOLOGIES INC
8770 W Bryn Mawr Ave # 1300
(60631-3515)
**PHONE**.....................................773 867-8801
Nicolas Belanger, *President*
Nicholas Belanger, *President*
Paul Fortier, *Vice Pres*
Pierre Pare, *Vice Pres*
**EMP:** 100
**SALES (est):** 14.3MM  **Privately Held**
**SIC:** 3535  Conveyor systems; conveyors & conveying equipment

*(G-5594)*
### MACNEAL HOSPITAL
4009 W 59th St  (60629-4511)
**PHONE**.....................................773 581-2199
Edhermila Herrera, *Principal*
**EMP:** 4
**SALES (est):** 307.6K  **Privately Held**
**SIC:** 2835  Pregnancy test kits

*(G-5595)*
### MADE BY HANDS INC
3501 N Southport Ave # 352  (60657-1475)
**PHONE**.....................................773 761-4200
Ava Berry, *Co-President*
Dena Hirschberg, *Co-President*
Paul Nork, *VP Sales*
Nancy Good, *Director*
**EMP:** 2
**SALES (est):** 215.1K  **Privately Held**
**WEB:** www.made-by-hands.com
**SIC:** 3944  5945  Craft & hobby kits & sets; hobby & craft supplies

*(G-5596)*
### MADEMOISELLE INC
4200 W Schubert Ave  (60639-2017)
**PHONE**.....................................773 394-4555
Scott Goldstein, *CEO*
**EMP:** 10  **EST:** 1930
**SQ FT:** 8,000
**SALES:** 1.3MM  **Privately Held**
**SIC:** 2353  2337  2339  Hats, trimmed: women's, misses' & children's; capes, except fur or rubber: women's, misses' & juniors'; collar & cuff sets: women's, misses' & juniors'; scarves, hoods, headbands, etc.: women's

*(G-5597)*
### MADISON CAPITAL PARTNERS CORP (PA)
500 W Madison St Ste 3890  (60661-4593)
**PHONE**.....................................312 277-0323
**Fax:** 312 277-0163
Larry W Gies, *President*
Christopher Domke, *Managing Dir*
Aaron J Vangetson, *Vice Pres*
Brent Campbell, *CFO*
John E Udelhofen, *CFO*
▲ **EMP:** 6
**SQ FT:** 6,000
**SALES (est):** 194.6MM  **Privately Held**
**WEB:** www.madisoncapitalpartners.net
**SIC:** 3542  8741  Machine tools, metal forming type; management services

*(G-5598)*
### MADISON INDS HOLDINGS LLC (PA)
500 W Madison St Ste 3890  (60661-4593)
**PHONE**.....................................312 277-0156
Larry W Gies, *President*
Aaron J Vangetson, *Senior VP*
John E Udelhofen, *Treasurer*
**EMP:** 0
**SALES (est):** 191.6MM  **Privately Held**
**SIC:** 6719  5051  3443  3316  Investment holding companies, except banks; steel; fabricated plate work (boiler shop); cold finishing of steel shapes

*(G-5599)*
### MAGAZINE PLUS
2445 N Clark St  (60614-7777)
**PHONE**.....................................773 281-4106
Mohammed Sultan, *Principal*
**EMP:** 5
**SALES (est):** 401.8K  **Privately Held**
**SIC:** 2721  5993  Magazines: publishing & printing; tobacco stores & stands

*(G-5600)*
### MAGIC SOLUTIONS INC
5455 N Sheridan Rd # 3809  (60640-1958)
**PHONE**.....................................312 647-8688
Maksym Kolodii, *President*
**EMP:** 3
**SALES (est):** 103.6K  **Privately Held**
**SIC:** 3965  Fasteners, buttons, needles & pins

*(G-5601)*
### MAGID GLOVE SAFETY MFG CO LLC
1805 N Hamlin Ave  (60647-4651)
**PHONE**.....................................773 384-2070
**EMP:** 485
**SALES (corp-wide):** 162.5MM  **Privately Held**
**SIC:** 3151  2381  Mfg & Whol Leather & Woven Work Gloves
**PA:** Magid Glove & Safety Manufacturing Co Llc
1300 Naperville Dr
Romeoville IL 60446
773 384-2070

*(G-5602)*
### MAGNETIC SIGNS
4922 S Western Ave  (60609-4742)
**PHONE**.....................................773 476-6551
**Fax:** 773 476-7553
James Sommer, *Owner*
**EMP:** 6  **EST:** 2007
**SALES (est):** 470K  **Privately Held**
**SIC:** 3993  Signs & advertising specialties

*(G-5603)*
### MAGNUS SCREW PRODUCTS CO
1818 N Latrobe Ave  (60639-4351)
**PHONE**.....................................773 889-2344
**Fax:** 773 889-2980
Edward A Magnuski Jr, *President*
Mitchell Magnuski, *Vice Pres*
Eric Sutton, *Manager*
Terrence Magnuski, *Admin Sec*
**EMP:** 20
**SQ FT:** 9,000
**SALES:** 4.3MM  **Privately Held**
**WEB:** www.magnusmachine.com
**SIC:** 3451  Screw machine products

*(G-5604)*
### MAID O MIST LLC
3217 N Pulaski Rd  (60641-4795)
**PHONE**.....................................773 685-7300
**Fax:** 773 685-7332
Warren Alm,
◆ **EMP:** 50
**SALES:** 5MM  **Privately Held**
**SIC:** 3585  Refrigeration & heating equipment

*(G-5605)*
### MAKOWSKIS REAL SAUSAGE CO
2710 S Poplar Ave  (60608-5909)
**PHONE**.....................................312 842-5330
**Fax:** 312 842-5414
Nicole Makowski, *President*
John Kuzel, *Manager*
**EMP:** 40  **EST:** 1919
**SQ FT:** 30,000
**SALES (est):** 6.4MM  **Privately Held**
**SIC:** 2013  Sausages from purchased meat; luncheon meat from purchased meat

*(G-5606)*
### MALCA-AMIT NORTH AMERICA INC
5 S Wabash Ave Ste 1414  (60603-3093)
**PHONE**.....................................312 346-1507
**Fax:** 312 346-1896
Suzanne Clark, *Manager*
Suzanne A Clark, *Manager*
**EMP:** 7
**SALES (corp-wide):** 46.9MM  **Privately Held**
**SIC:** 3462  Armor plate, forged iron or steel
**PA:** Malca-Amit North America, Inc.
580 5th Ave Lbby 1
New York NY 10036
212 840-8330

*(G-5607)*
### MALTHANDLINGCOM LLC
800 N Winthrop Ave S 2  (60660)
**PHONE**.....................................773 888-7718
Marc Marashi, *Sales Staff*
Richard Riley, *Mng Member*
▲ **EMP:** 3
**SQ FT:** 6,000

# Chicago - Cook County (G-5608)

SALES (est): 778.9K **Privately Held**
**SIC: 3523** Cleaning machines for fruits, grains & vegetables

### (G-5608)
### MALVAES SOLUTIONS INCORPORATED
4243 W Ogden Ave (60623-2931)
PHONE..................................773 823-1034
Jesse Malvaes, *Director*
**EMP:** 5
**SALES (est):** 251.7K **Privately Held**
**SIC: 4953** 2448 Recycling, waste materials; pallets, wood

### (G-5609)
### MANUFCTRERS CLARING HSE OF ILL (PA)
4875 N Elston Ave (60630-2551)
PHONE..................................773 545-6300
Fax: 773 545-7356
W Paul Nagel, *President*
William W Nagel, *Corp Secy*
**EMP:** 7
**SQ FT:** 4,000
**SALES (est):** 1.4MM **Privately Held**
**WEB:** www.mchonline.com
**SIC: 7322** 7323 2731 Collection agency, except real estate; credit clearinghouse; books: publishing only

### (G-5610)
### MAPLEHURST BAKERIES LLC
Rubschlager Baking
3220 W Grand Ave (60651-4180)
PHONE..................................773 826-1245
Diana Bell, *Finance Dir*
**EMP:** 24
**SALES (corp-wide):** 35.5B **Privately Held**
**SIC: 2051** Bread, all types (white, wheat, rye, etc): fresh or frozen
**HQ:** Maplehurst Bakeries, Llc
50 Maplehurst Dr
Brownsburg IN 46112
317 858-9000

### (G-5611)
### MARANTHA WRLD RVVAL MINISTRIES (PA)
Also Called: Maranatha Christian Revival Ch
4301 W Diversey Ave (60639-2027)
PHONE..................................773 384-7717
Fax: 773 384-3892
Nahum Rosario, *Pastor*
Cynthia Rosario, *Exec Dir*
Carmen Figueroa, *Admin Sec*
**EMP:** 1
**SQ FT:** 37,000
**SALES (est):** 901.3K **Privately Held**
**WEB:** www.revivalmusic.net
**SIC: 8661** 2731 Christian Reformed Church; textbooks: publishing only, not printed on site

### (G-5612)
### MARCELLS PALLET INC (PA)
4221 W Ferdinand St (60624-1016)
PHONE..................................773 265-1200
**EMP:** 5
**SALES (est):** 829.4K **Privately Held**
**SIC: 3537** Pallets, metal

### (G-5613)
### MARCO LIGHTING COMPONENTS INC (PA)
457 N Leavitt St (60612-1597)
PHONE..................................312 829-6900
Fax: 312 829-6083
Mario Salamone, *President*
Janet Salamone, *Corp Secy*
Vicki Vitez, *Asst Sec*
**EMP:** 14
**SQ FT:** 40,000
**SALES (est):** 1.8MM **Privately Held**
**WEB:** www.marcolighting.com
**SIC: 3441** Fabricated structural metal

### (G-5614)
### MARENA MARENA TWO INC
665 W Sheridan Rd (60613-3306)
PHONE..................................773 327-0619
Marjorie M Noland, *President*
**EMP:** 6
**SQ FT:** 200

SALES (est): 810K **Privately Held**
**SIC: 2339** Women's & misses' outerwear

### (G-5615)
### MARGIES BRANDS INC
6122 S Dorchester Ave (60637-2811)
PHONE..................................773 643-1417
Wilbur Reneau, *President*
Georgia Arnolds, *President*
Margie Reneau, *Chairman*
Dawn Acevado, *Exec VP*
Avery Johnson, *Exec VP*
**EMP:** 27
**SALES (est):** 3.7MM **Privately Held**
**WEB:** www.margiesbrands.com
**SIC: 2033** 2099 Jams, jellies & preserves: packaged in cans, jars, etc.; syrups

### (G-5616)
### MARIAH MEDIA INC
444 N Michigan Ave # 3350 (60611-3903)
PHONE..................................312 222-1100
Fax: 312 222-1189
Lisa Glass, *Manager*
**EMP:** 5
**SALES (corp-wide):** 15.6MM **Privately Held**
**SIC: 2721** Periodicals: publishing only
**PA:** Mariah Media, Inc.
400 Market St
Santa Fe NM 87501
505 989-7100

### (G-5617)
### MARIEGOLD BAKE SHOPPE
5752 N California Ave (60659-4726)
PHONE..................................773 561-1978
Carmelita Bagtus, *Owner*
**EMP:** 5
**SALES (est):** 166.1K **Privately Held**
**SIC: 5812** 2051 Eating places; bakery: wholesale or wholesale/retail combined

### (G-5618)
### MARIES CUSTOM MADE CHOIR ROBES
3838 W Madison St (60624-2334)
PHONE..................................773 826-1214
Fax: 773 826-5229
Marie Pickett, *Owner*
**EMP:** 3
**SQ FT:** 5,000
**SALES (est):** 260.5K **Privately Held**
**SIC: 2384** Robes & dressing gowns

### (G-5619)
### MARIETTA CORPORATION
Also Called: Cygnus D/B/A Marietta Chicago
340 E 138th St (60827-1828)
PHONE..................................773 816-5137
Rey Salvadore, *Manager*
**EMP:** 200
**SALES (corp-wide):** 306MM **Privately Held**
**SIC: 2841** 5122 5131 5139 Soap: granulated, liquid, cake, flaked or chip; toiletries; toilet articles; toilet preparations; perfumes; sewing accessories; hair accessories; shoe accessories; display equipment, except refrigerated; packaging & labeling services
**HQ:** Marietta Corporation
37 Huntington St
Cortland NY 13045
607 753-6746

### (G-5620)
### MARIN SOFTWARE INCORPORATED
140 S Dearborn St 300a (60603-5204)
PHONE..................................312 267-2083
Efrat Aharonovich, *Marketing Mgr*
Sohail Khan, *Technology*
Maulik Shah, *Software Engr*
Diran Hafiz, *Director*
Rupesh Sharma, *Associate Dir*
**EMP:** 3 **Publicly Held**
**SIC: 7372** Prepackaged software
**PA:** Marin Software Incorporated
123 Mission St Fl 27
San Francisco CA 94105

### (G-5621)
### MARIO ESCOBAR
Also Called: Mr Cake
4608 W Diversey Ave Ste 1 (60639-1805)
PHONE..................................773 202-8497
Mario Escobar, *Owner*
**EMP:** 2
**SALES (est):** 206.4K **Privately Held**
**SIC: 3556** Ovens, bakery

### (G-5622)
### MARKETING & TECHNOLOGY GROUP
Also Called: Mmt
1415 N Dayton St Ste 115 (60642-7033)
PHONE..................................312 266-3311
Fax: 312 266-3363
Jim Franklin, *Ch of Bd*
Mark Lefens, *President*
Debbie Weiss, *Controller*
Nathan Greenhalgh, *Assoc Editor*
Lindasey Klingele, *Executive Asst*
▲ **EMP:** 21
**SALES (est):** 2.8MM **Privately Held**
**WEB:** www.plateonline.com
**SIC: 2721** Magazines: publishing only, not printed on site

### (G-5623)
### MARMON ENGINEERED COMPONENTS (DH)
181 W Madison St Fl 26 (60602-4510)
PHONE..................................312 372-9500
Elwood Petchel, *President*
**EMP:** 3
**SALES (est):** 28MM
**SALES (corp-wide):** 223.6B **Publicly Held**
**SIC: 3699** Electrical equipment & supplies
**HQ:** The Marmon Group Llc
181 W Madison St Ste 2600
Chicago IL 60602
312 372-9500

### (G-5624)
### MARMON GROUP LLC (DH)
Also Called: Pan American Screw Div
181 W Madison St Ste 2600 (60602-4504)
PHONE..................................312 372-9500
Frank Ptak, *CEO*
▲ **EMP:** 3 **EST:** 1973
**SQ FT:** 1,000
**SALES (est):** 507.9MM
**SALES (corp-wide):** 223.6B **Publicly Held**
**SIC: 3452** 5072 Bolts, nuts, rivets & washers; bolts, nuts & screws
**HQ:** Union Tank Car Company
175 W Jackson Blvd # 2100
Chicago IL 60604
312 431-3111

### (G-5625)
### MARMON HOLDINGS INC (HQ)
181 W Madison St Ste 2600 (60602-4504)
PHONE..................................312 372-9500
Frank Ptak, *President*
Thomas J Pritzker, *Chairman*
John Nichols, *Vice Chairman*
Robert W Webb, *Senior VP*
Robert C Gluth, *Vice Pres*
◆ **EMP:** 75
**SQ FT:** 33,000
**SALES (est):** 5.8B
**SALES (corp-wide):** 223.6B **Publicly Held**
**SIC: 5051** 3351 3743 4741 Metals service centers & offices; copper pipe; tubing, copper & copper alloy; wire, copper & copper alloy; railway motor cars; rental of railroad cars; caulking tools, hand; can openers, not electric; water treatment equipment, industrial; water purification equipment, household type
**PA:** Berkshire Hathaway Inc.
3555 Farnam St Ste 1440
Omaha NE 68131
402 346-1400

### (G-5626)
### MARMON INDUSTRIAL LLC (DH)
181 W Madison St Fl 26 (60602-4510)
PHONE..................................312 372-9500
John Nichols, *President*
Robert W Webb, *Senior VP*

Lawrence Rist, *Vice Pres*
Bob Lorch, *CFO*
Maria Battaglia, *Analyst*
◆ **EMP:** 6
**SQ FT:** 33,000
**SALES (est):** 798.4MM
**SALES (corp-wide):** 223.6B **Publicly Held**
**SIC: 3743** 4741 3589 6159 Railway motor cars; rental of railroad cars; water treatment equipment, industrial; machinery & equipment finance leasing; fasteners; control valves, fluid power: hydraulic & pneumatic
**HQ:** Marmon Holdings, Inc.
181 W Madison St Ste 2600
Chicago IL 60602
312 372-9500

### (G-5627)
### MARMON INDUSTRIES LLC (DH)
181 W Madison St Ste 2600 (60602-4504)
PHONE..................................312 372-9500
Robert A Pritzker, *President*
Robert C Gluth, *Vice Pres*
Robert W Webb, *Vice Pres*
Doug Wilkinson, *Manager*
◆ **EMP:** 4 **EST:** 1969
**SQ FT:** 33,000
**SALES (est):** 47.6MM **Publicly Held**
**SIC: 3465** 3621 3714 Hub caps, automobile: stamped metal; rotors, for motors; wheels, motor vehicle; brake drums, motor vehicle
**HQ:** Rockwood Holding Company
200 W Madison St Fl 38
Chicago IL
312 750-8400

### (G-5628)
### MARMON RET & END USER TECH INC (DH)
181 W Madison St Fl 26 (60602-4510)
PHONE..................................312 372-9500
Robert B Davidson, *Principal*
Christina Washington, *Administration*
**EMP:** 6
**SALES (est):** 324MM
**SALES (corp-wide):** 223.6B **Publicly Held**
**SIC: 2599** Restaurant furniture, wood or metal
**HQ:** Marmon Holdings, Inc.
181 W Madison St Ste 2600
Chicago IL 60602
312 372-9500

### (G-5629)
### MARMON RETAIL SERVICES INC (DH)
181 W Madison St (60602-4510)
PHONE..................................312 332-0317
Richard Winted,
**EMP:** 8
**SQ FT:** 33,000
**SALES (est):** 407.6MM
**SALES (corp-wide):** 223.6B **Publicly Held**
**SIC: 2541** 2542 Store fixtures, wood; fixtures, store: except wood
**HQ:** Marmon Holdings, Inc.
181 W Madison St Ste 2600
Chicago IL 60602
312 372-9500

### (G-5630)
### MARS CHOCOLATE NORTH AMER LLC
Also Called: M&M Mars
2019 N Oak Park Ave (60707-3360)
PHONE..................................662 335-8000
Cahrles Painter, *Principal*
Micah Bosley, *Production*
Ruben Chacon, *Production*
Russ Basile, *Purchasing*
Garry Barney, *Engineer*
**EMP:** 590
**SALES (corp-wide):** 35B **Privately Held**
**WEB:** www.kilic-kalkan.com
**SIC: 2064** 2066 Candy & other confectionery products; chocolate & cocoa products
**HQ:** Mars Chocolate North America, Llc
800 High St
Hackettstown NJ 07840
908 852-1000

## GEOGRAPHIC SECTION
## Chicago - Cook County (G-5655)

**(G-5631)**
**MARSHALL MANUFACTURING LLC**
2300 N Lincoln Park W  (60614-3456)
PHONE..............................312 914-7288
Derek Marshall,
EMP: 5
SALES (est): 175.6K  Privately Held
SIC: 3999  Novelties, bric-a-brac & hobby kits

**(G-5632)**
**MARTIN PETER ASSOCIATES INC**
2650 W Montrose Ave Ste 1  (60618-1560)
PHONE..............................773 478-2400
Fax: 773 478-4009
Rich Hawkins, *President*
Edward Hamlin, *Founder*
EMP: 16
SQ FT: 4,825
SALES (est): 644K  Publicly Held
SIC: 7372  Prepackaged software
HQ: Lagan Technologies, Inc.
  200 W Jackson Blvd # 1350
  Chicago IL

**(G-5633)**
**MARTINEZ PRINTING LLC**
2714 N Mulligan Ave  (60639-1028)
PHONE..............................773 732-8108
Martinez Ricardo, *Principal*
Hector Martinez,
Ricardo Martinez,
EMP: 2  EST: 2013
SALES (est): 251K  Privately Held
SIC: 2752  Commercial printing, lithographic

**(G-5634)**
**MARUICHI LEAVITT PIPE TUBE LLC**
3655 Solutions Ctr  (60677-3006)
PHONE..............................800 532-8488
David Klima, *Branch Mgr*
EMP: 4
SALES (corp-wide): 1.2B  Privately Held
SIC: 3317  Seamless pipes & tubes
HQ: Maruichi Leavitt Pipe & Tube, Llc
  1717 W 115th St
  Chicago IL 60643
  773 239-7700

**(G-5635)**
**MARUICHI LEAVITT PIPE TUBE LLC (HQ)**
1717 W 115th St  (60643-4398)
PHONE..............................773 239-7700
T Konishi, *President*
Parry D Katsafanas, *COO*
Joe Fattori, *Vice Pres*
S Honda, *Vice Pres*
Bill Goodrich, *Plant Mgr*
▲ EMP: 125
SQ FT: 1,000,000
SALES: 26.1MM
SALES (corp-wide): 1.2B  Privately Held
WEB: www.leavitt-tube.com
SIC: 3317  Seamless pipes & tubes
PA: Maruichi Steel Tube Ltd.
  3-9-10, Kitahorie, Nishi-Ku
  Osaka OSK 550-0
  665 310-101

**(G-5636)**
**MARV-O-LUS MANUFACTURING CO (PA)**
Also Called: Sign Holders Supply
220 N Washtenaw Ave  (60612-2014)
PHONE..............................773 826-1717
Fax: 773 265-1800
Michael Glassenberg, *President*
Mike Brody, *Vice Pres*
◆ EMP: 12
SQ FT: 24,500
SALES: 3MM  Privately Held
WEB: www.marvolus.com
SIC: 2542  2541 Fixtures: display, office or store: except wood; display fixtures, wood

**(G-5637)**
**MARVEL ABRASIVES PRODUCTS LLC**
6230 S Oak Park Ave  (60638-4016)
PHONE..............................800 621-0673
Lelsie J Branch, *President*
Barbara Branch, *Vice Pres*
Craig Pickell,
▲ EMP: 13
SALES (est): 1.7MM  Privately Held
SIC: 3291  Abrasive products

**(G-5638)**
**MARVEL ELECTRIC CORPORATION (PA)**
3425 N Ashland Ave  (60657-1396)
PHONE..............................773 327-2644
Fax: 773 327-0820
William Janisch, *Ch of Bd*
Jeff Janisch, *President*
Arlene L Janisch, *Vice Pres*
Ross E Wollrab, *Engineer*
Audrey Halloran, *Office Mgr*
EMP: 70  EST: 1955
SQ FT: 30,000
SALES (est): 10.5MM  Privately Held
SIC: 3677  3612 3564  Electronic transformers; inductors, electronic; transformers, except electric; blowers & fans

**(G-5639)**
**MARVEL GROUP INC**
3800 W 44th St  (60632-3520)
PHONE..............................773 523-4804
John Dellamore, *President*
EMP: 245
SQ FT: 44,300
SALES (corp-wide): 102MM  Privately Held
WEB: www.marvelgroup.com
SIC: 2522  2521 Office furniture, except wood; wood office furniture
PA: The Marvel Group Inc
  3843 W 43rd St
  Chicago IL 60632
  773 523-4804

**(G-5640)**
**MARVEL GROUP INC (PA)**
3843 W 43rd St  (60632-3409)
PHONE..............................773 523-4804
Fax: 773 237-0358
John J Dellamore, *President*
Chris Bone, *Vice Pres*
Joe Fortin, *Vice Pres*
Michael Glab, *Vice Pres*
Ken Wolfanger, *Vice Pres*
▲ EMP: 180  EST: 1946
SQ FT: 120,000
SALES (est): 102MM  Privately Held
WEB: www.marvelgroup.com
SIC: 2522  Office furniture, except wood

**(G-5641)**
**MARVEL GROUP INC**
4417 S Springfield Ave  (60632)
PHONE..............................773 523-4804
John Dellamore, *Branch Mgr*
EMP: 15
SALES (corp-wide): 102MM  Privately Held
WEB: www.marvelgroup.com
SIC: 2522  Office furniture, except wood
PA: The Marvel Group Inc
  3843 W 43rd St
  Chicago IL 60632
  773 523-4804

**(G-5642)**
**MARZEYA BAKERY INC**
8908 S Commercial Ave  (60617-3201)
PHONE..............................773 374-7855
Jose Luis Padilla, *President*
Irma Padilla, *Corp Secy*
EMP: 5
SQ FT: 1,300
SALES (est): 437.9K  Privately Held
SIC: 2051  5461 Bread, cake & related products; bakeries

**(G-5643)**
**MASTER PAPER BOX COMPANY INC**
3641 S Iron St  (60609-1322)
PHONE..............................773 927-0252
Fax: 773 927-8086
Bill Farago Sr, *President*
John Buber, *Plant Mgr*
Samuel Yozze, *Plant Mgr*
Lauren Farago, *Manager*
EMP: 103
SQ FT: 103,000
SALES (est): 22MM  Privately Held
WEB: www.masterpaperbox.com
SIC: 2657  2652 Folding paperboard boxes; setup paperboard boxes

**(G-5644)**
**MASTER POLISHING & BUFFING**
10247 S Avenue O  (60617-5904)
PHONE..............................773 731-3883
Fax: 773 731-3885
Roberto Ramirez, *Owner*
EMP: 5
SALES (est): 443.6K  Privately Held
SIC: 3471  Buffing for the trade

**(G-5645)**
**MASTER TAPE PRINTERS INC**
4517 N Elston Ave  (60630-4420)
PHONE..............................773 283-8273
Fax: 773 685-1555
Robert Grant, *President*
Caryne Casey, *Corp Secy*
Andy Casey, *Vice Pres*
Terese Grant, *Vice Pres*
Tony Lentini, *Sales Staff*
EMP: 20
SQ FT: 6,200
SALES (est): 2.9MM  Privately Held
WEB: www.mastertapeprinters.com
SIC: 2759  Flexographic printing

**(G-5646)**
**MASTER WELL COMB CO INC**
Also Called: Master Chemical Co
1830 N Lamon Ave  (60639-4512)
PHONE..............................847 540-8300
Fax: 847 540-8385
William J Mealey, *President*
Sunnie Mealey, *Manager*
EMP: 10
SQ FT: 49,000
SALES (est): 2MM  Privately Held
WEB: www.krewcomb.com
SIC: 2844  Shampoos, rinses, conditioners: hair; shaving preparations; toilet preparations

**(G-5647)**
**MASTERCRAFT FURN RFNISHING INC**
3140 W Chicago Ave  (60622-4320)
PHONE..............................773 722-5730
Fax: 773 722-2603
James Antoni, *President*
Marina Antoni, *Admin Sec*
EMP: 19  EST: 1939
SQ FT: 16,000
SALES (est): 1.3MM  Privately Held
WEB: www.mastercraftfurniture.net
SIC: 7641  2511 2521 Furniture refinishing; reupholstery; wood household furniture; wood office furniture

**(G-5648)**
**MASUD JEWELERS INC**
Also Called: Superior Findings
17 N Wabash Ave Ste 430  (60602-4871)
PHONE..............................312 236-0547
Jose Masud, *President*
EMP: 5  EST: 1976
SQ FT: 1,000
SALES (est): 590K  Privately Held
SIC: 5094  3911 7631 Precious stones & metals; jewelry, precious metal; jewelry repair services

**(G-5649)**
**MATCHLESS METAL POLISH COMPANY (PA)**
840 W 49th Pl  (60609-5196)
PHONE..............................773 924-1515
Fax: 773 924-5513
Frank Ungari, *CEO*
John Denman, *VP Opers*
Mike Krapez, *Purchasing*
Bob Lavorgna, *Natl Sales Mgr*
Lyndon Posch, *Marketing Staff*
▲ EMP: 50  EST: 1885
SQ FT: 45,000
SALES (est): 14.5MM  Privately Held
WEB: www.matchlessmetal.com
SIC: 2842  3291 Metal polish; polishing wheels

**(G-5650)**
**MATCHLESS PARISIAN NOVELTY INC (PA)**
840 W 49th Pl  (60609-5151)
PHONE..............................773 924-1515
Frank Ungari, *President*
Rose Sherlock, *Office Mgr*
EMP: 2
SALES (est): 1MM  Privately Held
SIC: 3965  Button backs & parts

**(G-5651)**
**MATERIAL SERVICE RESOURCES (HQ)**
222 N La Salle St # 1200  (60601-1003)
PHONE..............................630 325-7736
Lester Crown, *Ch of Bd*
Michael Stanczak, *President*
Walter Serwa, *VP Finance*
Gerald Ratner, *Admin Sec*
EMP: 100
SQ FT: 80,000
SALES (est): 99.3MM
SALES (corp-wide): 31.3B  Publicly Held
SIC: 1442  1221 Construction sand mining; gravel mining; bituminous coal & lignite-surface mining
PA: General Dynamics Corporation
  2941 Frview Pk Dr Ste 100
  Falls Church VA 22042
  703 876-3000

**(G-5652)**
**MATHEU TOOL WORKS INC**
2426 N Clybourn Ave Fl 1  (60614-1918)
PHONE..............................773 327-9274
Fax: 773 327-5562
Ellis Matheu, *President*
Cornella Matheu, *Admin Sec*
EMP: 3
SQ FT: 4,000
SALES (est): 270K  Privately Held
SIC: 3545  Machine tool attachments & accessories

**(G-5653)**
**MATISS INC**
2101 S Carpenter St Ste 2  (60608-4547)
PHONE..............................773 418-1895
EMP: 19  Privately Held
SIC: 2591  Window shade rollers & fittings
PA: Matiss, Inc.
  51 Harrison St Fl 5
  Hoboken NJ 07030

**(G-5654)**
**MATRIX NORTH AMERCN CNSTR INC (HQ)**
Also Called: Matrix Nac
1 E Wacker Dr Ste 1110  (60601-1474)
PHONE..............................312 754-6605
Jason W Turner, *President*
J Steven Harker, *Senior VP*
Troy Blair, *Vice Pres*
James J Collins Jr, *Vice Pres*
James Faroh, *Vice Pres*
EMP: 1
SALES (est): 1.2MM
SALES (corp-wide): 1.3B  Publicly Held
SIC: 5063  1389 8711 Electrical construction materials; construction, repair & dismantling services; building construction consultant
PA: Matrix Service Company
  5100 E Skelly Dr Ste 700
  Tulsa OK 74135
  918 838-8822

**(G-5655)**
**MATRIX PRECISION CORPORATION**
6154 W Belmont Ave  (60634-4042)
PHONE..............................773 283-1739
Wesley Zoltowski, *President*
EMP: 5
SALES (est): 380.8K  Privately Held
SIC: 3599  Machine shop, jobbing & repair

# Chicago - Cook County (G-5656)

**(G-5656)**
**MATTHEW WARREN INC**
Also Called: Automatic Spring Coiling
4045 W Thorndale Ave (60646-6011)
**PHONE**..................773 539-5600
Fax: 773 539-1109
**EMP:** 100
**SALES (corp-wide):** 115.4MM **Privately Held**
**SIC:** 3493 3495 Steel springs, except wire; wire springs
**HQ:** Matthew Warren, Inc.
9501 Tech Blvd Ste 401
Rosemont IL 60018
847 349-5760

**(G-5657)**
**MAUSER USA LLC**
903 N Kilpatrick Ave (60651-3326)
**PHONE**..................773 261-2332
Mark Zymon, *Branch Mgr*
**EMP:** 8
**SALES (corp-wide):** 6.9B **Privately Held**
**SIC:** 3412 Barrels, shipping: metal
**HQ:** Mauser Usa, Llc
2 Tower Center Blvd 20-1
East Brunswick NJ 08816
732 353-7100

**(G-5658)**
**MAXI-MIX INC**
1416 W Willow St (60642-1524)
**PHONE**..................773 489-6747
Luis Puig Sr, *President*
Alex Puig, *Principal*
Leonard Puig, *Vice Pres*
Luis Puig Jr, *Vice Pres*
Nidia Puig, *Treasurer*
**EMP:** 8
**SQ FT:** 20,000
**SALES (est):** 529.2K **Privately Held**
**WEB:** www.maxi-mix.com
**SIC:** 3255 Mortars, clay refractory

**(G-5659)**
**MAXS SCREEN MACHINE INC (PA)**
Also Called: Msm Promotions
6125 N Nrthwst Hwy Frnt 1 (60631-2175)
**PHONE**..................773 878-4949
Fax: 773 878-4888
Jeff Maksud, *President*
Walter Abraham, *Vice Pres*
Yvonne Valdez, *Sales Mgr*
Steve Maksud, *Manager*
Venessa Martinez, *Admin Sec*
**EMP:** 9
**SQ FT:** 6,000
**SALES (est):** 1.9MM **Privately Held**
**WEB:** www.msmpromotions.com
**SIC:** 2396 3993 Screen printing on fabric articles; signs & advertising specialties

**(G-5660)**
**MAY WOOD INDUSTRIES INC**
12636 S Springfield Ave (60803-1411)
**PHONE**..................708 489-1515
Fax: 708 489-1734
Nancy Gee, *President*
**EMP:** 15 **EST:** 1951
**SQ FT:** 15,000
**SALES:** 2.8MM **Privately Held**
**SIC:** 2431 Millwork

**(G-5661)**
**MAYNARD INC**
2341 N Milwaukee Ave (60647-2984)
**PHONE**..................773 235-5225
Fax: 773 235-5226
Maynard Kier, *President*
Jeffrey Kier, *Vice Pres*
**EMP:** 5
**SQ FT:** 4,000
**SALES:** 200K **Privately Held**
**SIC:** 2844 Cosmetic preparations

**(G-5662)**
**MAZEL & CO INC (PA)**
4300 W Ferdinand St (60624-1095)
**PHONE**..................773 533-1600
Fax: 773 533-9490
Joel Handelman, *President*
Ralph Handelman, *Treasurer*
Erica Strey, *Sales Staff*
▲ **EMP:** 17
**SQ FT:** 80,000
**SALES (est):** 18.5MM **Privately Held**
**WEB:** www.mazelandco.com
**SIC:** 5032 3496 Concrete building products; concrete reinforcing mesh & wire

**(G-5663)**
**MBURGER II (PA)**
5 W Ontario St (60654-7700)
**PHONE**..................312 428-3548
Mike Heberlein, *Principal*
**EMP:** 5
**SALES (est):** 531.8K **Privately Held**
**SIC:** 3421 Table & food cutlery, including butchers'

**(G-5664)**
**MCCLENDON HOLDINGS LLC**
Also Called: McClendon Holdings Affiliates
7200 S Exchange Ave Ste A (60649-2526)
P.O. Box 490050 (60649-0013)
**PHONE**..................773 251-2314
John McClendon, *President*
**EMP:** 4
**SALES (est):** 76.5K **Privately Held**
**SIC:** 8742 5169 5047 2819 Management consulting services; chemicals & allied products; medical & hospital equipment; charcoal (carbon), activated

**(G-5665)**
**MCCONNELL CHASE SOFTWARE WORKS**
360 E Randolph St # 3202 (60601-5069)
**PHONE**..................312 540-1508
Joseph K McConnell, *Owner*
**EMP:** 3
**SQ FT:** 1,600
**SALES (est):** 148.5K **Privately Held**
**SIC:** 7372 Prepackaged software

**(G-5666)**
**MCCRACKEN LABEL CO**
5303 S Keeler Ave (60632-4209)
P.O. Box 32256 (60632-0256)
**PHONE**..................773 581-8860
Fax: 773 581-7916
John F Coaker III, *President*
Michael Polizzi, *General Mgr*
James Coaker, *Treasurer*
Gina Connors, *Art Dir*
Theresa Gutierrez, *Assistant*
◆ **EMP:** 40
**SQ FT:** 69,900
**SALES (est):** 8MM **Privately Held**
**SIC:** 2759 5023 Letterpress printing; flexographic printing; glassware

**(G-5667)**
**MCGILL ASPHALT CONSTRUCTION CO**
4956 S Monitor Ave (60638-1544)
**PHONE**..................708 924-1755
Dwayne McGill, *Owner*
**EMP:** 6
**SALES (est):** 365K **Privately Held**
**SIC:** 3295 Minerals, ground or treated

**(G-5668)**
**MCKLEIN COMPANY LLC**
Also Called: McKlein Company
4447 W Cortland St Ste A (60639-5115)
**PHONE**..................773 235-0600
Fax: 773 378-5800
Chettha Saetia, *Vice Pres*
Joy Diaz, *Accounting Mgr*
Parinda Saetia,
▲ **EMP:** 17
**SQ FT:** 29,042
**SALES:** 7.4MM **Privately Held**
**WEB:** www.mckleinusa.com
**SIC:** 3161 Attache cases

**(G-5669)**
**MEAD FLUID DYNAMICS INC**
4114 N Knox Ave (60641-1999)
**PHONE**..................773 685-6800
Fax: 773 685-7002
Bill Gorski, *President*
Jeff Von Esh, *VP Opers*
Ed Quinto, *QC Mgr*
David Gillhouse, *Info Tech Dir*
▲ **EMP:** 50
**SQ FT:** 38,000
**SALES (est):** 11.1MM
**SALES (corp-wide):** 128.7MM **Privately Held**
**WEB:** www.mead-usa.com
**SIC:** 3492 3593 3494 Control valves, fluid power: hydraulic & pneumatic; fluid power cylinders & actuators; valves & pipe fittings
**PA:** Bimba Manufacturing Company Inc
25150 S Governors Hwy
University Park IL 60484
708 534-8544

**(G-5670)**
**MEAD JOHNSON & COMPANY LLC**
Also Called: Mead Johnson Nutrition
225 N Canal St (60606-1791)
**PHONE**..................847 832-2420
Jane Hall, *Buyer*
Tom Deweerdt, *Controller*
Warren Lee, *Sales Mgr*
Mable Chan, *Marketing Mgr*
Peter Kasper Jakobsen, *Branch Mgr*
**EMP:** 10 **Privately Held**
**SIC:** 2099 2834 2032 Food preparations; pharmaceutical preparations; canned specialties
**HQ:** Mead Johnson & Company, Llc
2400 W Lloyd Expy
Evansville IN 47712
812 429-5000

**(G-5671)**
**MEAD JOHNSON NUTRITION COMPANY (PA)**
225 N Canal St 25 (60606-1791)
**PHONE**..................312 466-5800
Peter Kasper Jakobsen, *President*
**EMP:** 25
**SALES:** 3.7B **Privately Held**
**WEB:** www.bms.com
**SIC:** 2023 2834 Baby formulas; vitamin preparations

**(G-5672)**
**MEADOWBROOK LLC**
Also Called: Land of Nod, The
900 W North Ave (60642-2506)
**PHONE**..................312 475-9903
Fax: 312 255-9904
Jamie Cohen, *Bd of Directors*
**EMP:** 4 **Privately Held**
**SIC:** 2511 Children's wood furniture
**HQ:** Meadowbrook L.L.C.
8135 River Dr
Morton Grove IL 60053
847 656-4700

**(G-5673)**
**MEATBALL VAULT ORIGINAL**
131 N Clinton St Ste 21 (60661-1507)
**PHONE**..................312 285-2090
Leslie Cahill, *Principal*
**EMP:** 3
**SALES (est):** 211K **Privately Held**
**SIC:** 3272 Burial vaults, concrete or precast terrazzo

**(G-5674)**
**MECHANICAL ENGINEERING PDTS**
1319 W Lake St (60607-1511)
**PHONE**..................312 421-3375
Fax: 312 421-3376
Jon Knudsen, *President*
Anne-Judine Knudsen, *Admin Sec*
**EMP:** 3 **EST:** 1922
**SQ FT:** 36,000
**SALES (est):** 396.9K **Privately Held**
**SIC:** 3494 3594 3561 Pipe fittings; fluid power pumps & motors; pumps & pumping equipment

**(G-5675)**
**MEDACTA USA INC**
1556 W Carroll Ave (60607-1030)
**PHONE**..................312 878-2381
Andrew McLeod, *President*
Eric Dremel, *President*
John Thro, *CFO*
Matthew Hamil, *Sales Associate*
**EMP:** 80
**SALES (est):** 9.5MM **Privately Held**
**SIC:** 5047 3172 Orthopedic equipment & supplies; personal leather goods
**PA:** Medacta International Sa
Strada Regina
Castel San Pietro TI
916 966-060

**(G-5676)**
**MEDFORD AERO ARMS LLC**
4541 N Ravenswood Ave (60640-5296)
**PHONE**..................773 961-7686
Stuart Urkov, *Mng Member*
Kurt Wilhelm,
Luke Wojtasik,
**EMP:** 5
**SALES (est):** 242.3K **Privately Held**
**SIC:** 3549 Metalworking machinery

**(G-5677)**
**MEDIAFLY INC**
150 N Michigan Ave # 2000 (60601-7569)
**PHONE**..................312 281-5175
Carson V Conant, *CEO*
Johnathan S Evarts, *COO*
Lou Jacob, *Vice Pres*
Teddy Herman, *Administration*
**EMP:** 5
**SQ FT:** 18,000
**SALES (est):** 1.1MM **Privately Held**
**WEB:** www.mediafly.com
**SIC:** 7372 Prepackaged software

**(G-5678)**
**MEDIATEC PUBLISHING INC (PA)**
111 E Wacker Dr Ste 1200 (60601-4203)
**PHONE**..................312 676-9900
Norman B Kamikow, *President*
Norman B Kamikowq, *Editor*
John R Taggart, *Exec VP*
Gwen Connelly, *Senior VP*
Diane Landsman, *Director*
**EMP:** 22 **EST:** 1999
**SALES:** 10MM **Privately Held**
**WEB:** www.mediatecpub.com
**SIC:** 2721 2741 7389 Magazines: publishing only, not printed on site; catalogs: publishing & printing; decoration service for special events

**(G-5679)**
**MEDIATEC PUBLISHING INC**
111 E Wacker Dr Ste 1200 (60601-4203)
**PHONE**..................510 834-0100
Gwen Connelly, *Opers Dir*
Kendra Chaplin, *Production*
John Taggart, *Branch Mgr*
**EMP:** 11
**SALES (corp-wide):** 10MM **Privately Held**
**SIC:** 2721 Periodicals: publishing only
**PA:** Mediatec Publishing, Inc
111 E Wacker Dr Ste 1200
Chicago IL 60601
312 676-9900

**(G-5680)**
**MEGAMEDIA ENTERPRISES INC**
Also Called: Austin Voice Newspaper
5236 W North Ave (60639-4467)
**PHONE**..................773 889-0880
Isaac Jones, *CEO*
Bradley Cummings, *Treasurer*
Andrew Griffin, *Admin Sec*
**EMP:** 10
**SALES (est):** 651.8K **Privately Held**
**SIC:** 2711 7929 Newspapers; entertainment service

**(G-5681)**
**MEINHARDT DIAMOND TOOL CO**
3800 W Belmont Ave (60618-5206)
**PHONE**..................773 267-3260
Fax: 773 267-7461
Roy F Scholz, *President*
La Scholz, *Corp Secy*
**EMP:** 8 **EST:** 1941
**SQ FT:** 3,500
**SALES (est):** 680K **Privately Held**
**SIC:** 3545 3291 Diamond cutting tools for turning, boring, burnishing, etc.; abrasive products

# GEOGRAPHIC SECTION
## Chicago - Cook County (G-5703)

**(G-5682)**
**MEKANISM INC**
950 W Washington Blvd (60607-2217)
PHONE .................................... 415 908-4000
Jason Harris, *CEO*
EMP: 15
SALES (corp-wide): 10.1MM **Privately Held**
SIC: 3993 Advertising artwork
PA: Mekanism, Inc.
  640 2nd St Fl 3
  San Francisco CA 94107
  415 908-4000

**(G-5683)**
**MELLISH & MURRAY CO (PA)**
Also Called: Aero Flash Signal
1700 W Fulton St (60612-2510)
PHONE .................................... 312 733-3513
Fax: 312 733-0192
Cari A Murray, *President*
Patricia Garnica, *General Mgr*
Debora Panza, *Treasurer*
EMP: 10 EST: 1894
SALES (est): 3.2MM **Privately Held**
WEB: www.mellishmurray.com
SIC: 3444 3647 3564 3441 Sheet metal specialties, not stamped; vehicular lighting equipment; blowing fans: industrial or commercial; fabricated structural metal

**(G-5684)**
**MELLISH & MURRAY CO**
Also Called: Aeroflash Signal
1700 W Fulton St (60612-2510)
PHONE .................................... 312 379-0335
Pat Garnica, *Purchasing*
Cari A Murray, *Finance Other*
EMP: 15
SQ FT: 12,000
SALES (corp-wide): 3.2MM **Privately Held**
WEB: www.mellishmurray.com
SIC: 3567 3444 Induction heating equipment; sheet metalwork
PA: Mellish & Murray Co.
  1700 W Fulton St
  Chicago IL 60612
  312 733-3513

**(G-5685)**
**MENASHA PACKAGING COMPANY LLC**
4545 W Palmer St (60639-3421)
PHONE .................................... 773 227-6000
Emilio Diaz, *Plant Supt*
Kurt Erdmann, *Manager*
EMP: 127
SALES (corp-wide): 1.8B **Privately Held**
SIC: 2653 Display items, corrugated: made from purchased materials
HQ: Menasha Packaging Company, Llc
  1645 Bergstrom Rd
  Neenah WI 54956
  920 751-1000

**(G-5686)**
**MENASHA PACKAGING COMPANY LLC**
350 N Clark St Ste 300 (60654-4980)
PHONE .................................... 312 880-4620
Dana Zubik, *Personnel Assit*
EMP: 500
SALES (corp-wide): 1.8B **Privately Held**
SIC: 2653 Display items, corrugated: made from purchased materials
HQ: Menasha Packaging Company, Llc
  1645 Bergstrom Rd
  Neenah WI 54956
  920 751-1000

**(G-5687)**
**MER-PLA INC**
Also Called: T-G Ad Service
4535 W Fullerton Ave (60639-1933)
PHONE .................................... 847 530-9798
Fax: 773 384-8658
John Goldman, *President*
Andrew Brodell, *Vice Pres*
Joseph Rosey, *Vice Pres*
Richard Schuster, *Vice Pres*
Norm Capitani, *Controller*
EMP: 12 EST: 1961
SQ FT: 16,000
SALES: 800K **Privately Held**
SIC: 3993 2396 Displays & cutouts, window & lobby; automotive & apparel trimmings

**(G-5688)**
**MERCURY PLASTICS INC**
4535 W Fullerton Ave (60639-1933)
PHONE .................................... 888 884-1864
Fax: 773 486-1175
Richard Goldman, *President*
Jim Launer, *General Mgr*
Andrew Brodell, *Vice Pres*
Dave Halley, *Vice Pres*
Robin Harle, *Buyer*
▲ EMP: 40 EST: 1955
SQ FT: 145,000
SALES (est): 10.8MM **Privately Held**
WEB: www.mercuryplastics.net
SIC: 3993 3089 Displays & cutouts, window & lobby; thermoformed finished plastic products

**(G-5689)**
**MEREDITH CORP**
Also Called: Country Home Magazine
333 N Michigan Ave # 1500 (60601-4000)
PHONE .................................... 312 580-1623
Fax: 312 337-1632
Ted Meredith, *Principal*
Brad Wyckoff, *COO*
Mike Lacy, *Director*
EMP: 100
SALES (est): 4.6MM
SALES (corp-wide): 1.6B **Publicly Held**
WEB: www.meredithcorporation.com
SIC: 2721 Periodicals
PA: Meredith Corporation
  1716 Locust St
  Des Moines IA 50309
  515 284-3000

**(G-5690)**
**MERGE HEALTHCARE INCORPORATED (HQ)**
71 S Wacker Dr Ste 2 (60606-4716)
PHONE .................................... 312 565-6868
Fax: 312 565-6870
George Kotlarz, *President*
Gary D Bowers, *President*
Jacques Cornet, *President*
Loris Sartor, *President*
Antonio Wells, *President*
EMP: 148
SQ FT: 22,633
SALES: 212.3MM
SALES (corp-wide): 79.9B **Publicly Held**
WEB: www.merge.com
SIC: 7373 3841 Computer integrated systems design; diagnostic apparatus, medical
PA: International Business Machines Corporation
  1 New Orchard Rd Ste 1
  Armonk NY 10504
  914 499-1900

**(G-5691)**
**MERISANT COMPANY (DH)**
125 S Wacker Dr Ste 3150 (60606-4414)
PHONE .................................... 312 840-6000
Fax: 312 840-5541
Paul Block, *President*
Brian Alsvig, *Vice Pres*
Dan Beck, *Vice Pres*
Jonathan W Cole, *Vice Pres*
Angelo Di Benedetto, *Vice Pres*
▼ EMP: 10
SQ FT: 26,300
SALES (est): 150MM **Privately Held**
SIC: 2869 Industrial organic chemicals
HQ: Flavors Holdings Inc.
  35 E 62nd St
  New York NY 10065
  212 572-8677

**(G-5692)**
**MERISANT FOREIGN HOLDINGS I (DH)**
33 N Dearborn St Ste 200 (60602-3100)
PHONE .................................... 312 840-6000
Paul Block, *Ch of Bd*
Megan Kinsler, *Credit Mgr*
▲ EMP: 15
SALES (est): 8.1MM **Privately Held**
SIC: 2869 Sweeteners, synthetic

HQ: Merisant Us, Inc.
  125 S Wacker Dr Ste 3150
  Chicago IL 60606
  312 840-6000

**(G-5693)**
**MERISANT US INC (DH)**
125 S Wacker Dr Ste 3150 (60606-4414)
PHONE .................................... 312 840-6000
Albert Manzone, *CEO*
Brian Alsvig, *Vice Pres*
Jane Boyce, *Vice Pres*
Trisha Rosado, *CFO*
Megan C Kinsler, *Credit Mgr*
◆ EMP: 287
SQ FT: 10,000
SALES (est): 150MM **Privately Held**
WEB: www.merisant.com
SIC: 2869 Sweeteners, synthetic
HQ: Merisant Company
  125 S Wacker Dr Ste 3150
  Chicago IL 60606
  312 840-6000

**(G-5694)**
**MERIT TOOL ENGINEERING CO INC**
4827 W Wilson Ave (60630-3879)
PHONE .................................... 773 283-1114
Fax: 773 283-0008
Roger W Lewis, *President*
Helen E Lewis, *Corp Secy*
EMP: 5
SQ FT: 5,000
SALES: 400K **Privately Held**
SIC: 3599 3549 3545 3544 Machine shop, jobbing & repair; metalworking machinery; machine tool accessories; special dies, tools, jigs & fixtures

**(G-5695)**
**MERRILL CORPORATION**
311 S Wacker Dr Ste 1800 (60606-6620)
PHONE .................................... 312 263-3524
Fax: 312 786-9900
Robin Clarke, *Safety Mgr*
Jean Goodwin, *VP Sales*
John Berner, *Regl Sales Mgr*
Tony Harvath, *Mktg Dir*
Mark Rossi, *Branch Mgr*
EMP: 200
SALES (corp-wide): 579.3MM **Privately Held**
WEB: www.merrillcorp.com
SIC: 2759 Commercial printing
PA: Merrill Corporation
  1 Merrill Cir
  Saint Paul MN 55108
  651 646-4501

**(G-5696)**
**MERRILL CORPORATION**
200 W Jackson Blvd Fl 11 (60606-6910)
PHONE .................................... 312 386-2200
Fax: 312 930-5985
Frankie Gray, *Opers Staff*
Peter Day, *Branch Mgr*
Ron Smith, *MIS Dir*
EMP: 150
SALES (corp-wide): 579.3MM **Privately Held**
WEB: www.merrillcorp.com
SIC: 2759 7334 Commercial printing; photocopying & duplicating services
PA: Merrill Corporation
  1 Merrill Cir
  Saint Paul MN 55108
  651 646-4501

**(G-5697)**
**MERRILL FINE ARTS ENGRV INC (HQ)**
311 S Wacker Dr Ste 300 (60606-6699)
PHONE .................................... 312 786-6300
Joseph Fontana III, *President*
Greg Jones, *Exec VP*
Daniel Fontana, *Vice Pres*
▲ EMP: 100
SQ FT: 38,000
SALES (est): 12.8MM
SALES (corp-wide): 579.3MM **Privately Held**
WEB: www.faeco.com
SIC: 2759 2752 Stationery: printing; lithographing on metal

PA: Merrill Corporation
  1 Merrill Cir
  Saint Paul MN 55108
  651 646-4501

**(G-5698)**
**MESSAGE MEDIUMS LLC**
Also Called: Signal
222 Merchandise Mart Plz # 1818 (60654-1103)
PHONE .................................... 877 450-0075
Robert Hess, *Senior VP*
Jeffrey Judge, *Mng Member*
Zachary Rivest, *Software Dev*
Chris Watland, 
EMP: 14
SALES (est): 1.1MM **Privately Held**
SIC: 7372 Prepackaged software

**(G-5699)**
**METAL FINISHING RESEARCH CORP**
4025 S Princeton Ave (60609-2825)
PHONE .................................... 773 373-0800
Fax: 773 373-8184
Ernest Walen, *President*
James Casey, *Admin Sec*
EMP: 14
SQ FT: 20,000
SALES (est): 2.8MM **Privately Held**
WEB: www.heatbath.com
SIC: 2819 2899 Industrial inorganic chemicals; chemical preparations
HQ: Heatbath Corporation
  107 Front St
  Indian Orchard MA 01151
  413 452-2000

**(G-5700)**
**METAL MANAGEMENT INC**
9331 S Ewing Ave (60617-4641)
PHONE .................................... 773 721-1100
Miguel Milaro, *Manager*
EMP: 25
SQ FT: 1,200
SALES (corp-wide): 3.4B **Privately Held**
WEB: www.mtlm.com
SIC: 5093 3341 Scrap & waste materials; secondary nonferrous metals
HQ: Metal Management, Inc.
  200 W Madison St Ste 3600
  Chicago IL 60606
  312 645-0700

**(G-5701)**
**METAL MANAGEMENT INC**
1509 W Cortland St (60642-1215)
PHONE .................................... 773 489-1800
Mary Cook, *Manager*
Juan Bargas, *Manager*
EMP: 20
SQ FT: 9,300
SALES (corp-wide): 3.4B **Privately Held**
WEB: www.mtlm.com
SIC: 5093 3341 Scrap & waste materials; secondary nonferrous metals
HQ: Metal Management, Inc.
  200 W Madison St Ste 3600
  Chicago IL 60606
  312 645-0700

**(G-5702)**
**METCO TREATING AND DEV CO**
Also Called: Able Electropolishing
2001 S Kilbourn Ave (60623-2311)
PHONE .................................... 773 277-1600
John Glass, *President*
Dough Johnson, *Accountant*
Scott Potter, *Sales Mgr*
EMP: 100
SQ FT: 40,000
SALES (est): 11.1MM **Privately Held**
WEB: www.ableelectropolishing.com
SIC: 3471 Polishing, metals or formed products

**(G-5703)**
**METHODE DEVELOPMENT CO**
7401 W Wilson Ave (60706-4548)
PHONE .................................... 708 867-6777
Albert C Chiappetta, *Principal*
EMP: 75
SQ FT: 15,000

## Chicago - Cook County (G-5704)

SALES (est): 12.6MM
SALES (corp-wide): 809.1MM **Publicly Held**
WEB: www.methode.com
SIC: 3678 3672 3644 3643 Electronic connectors; printed circuit boards; non-current-carrying wiring services; current-carrying wiring devices; transformers, except electric; nonferrous wiredrawing & insulating
PA: Methode Electronics, Inc
    7401 W Wilson Ave
    Chicago IL 60706
    708 867-6777

### (G-5704)
### METHODE ELECTRONICS INC (PA)
7401 W Wilson Ave (60706-4548)
PHONE ................... 708 867-6777
Fax: 708 867-6999
Walter J Aspatore, *Ch of Bd*
Christopher J Hornung, *Vice Ch Bd*
Donald W Duda, *President*
Marc Dunham, *Vice Pres*
Timothy R Glandon, *Vice Pres*
▲ EMP: 300 EST: 1946
SQ FT: 15,000
SALES: 809.1MM **Publicly Held**
WEB: www.methode.com
SIC: 3678 3674 3676 3672 Electronic connectors; semiconductor circuit networks; microcircuits, integrated (semiconductor); resistor networks; printed circuit boards; wiring boards; test equipment for electronic & electrical circuits; current-carrying wiring devices; bus bars (electrical conductors); connectors & terminals for electrical devices

### (G-5705)
### METOMIC CORPORATION
Also Called: Gearon Company, The
2944 W 26th St (60623-4194)
PHONE ................... 773 247-4716
Fax: 773 247-2563
Sam Palumbo Jr, *President*
Paul Bernstein, *Vice Pres*
Peter Palumbo, *Vice Pres*
▲ EMP: 20
SQ FT: 11,000
SALES (est): 4.2MM **Privately Held**
WEB: www.metomic.com
SIC: 3451 3645 Screw machine products; residential lighting fixtures

### (G-5706)
### METRAFLEX COMPANY
2323 W Hubbard St (60612-1403)
PHONE ................... 312 738-3800
S G Nudel, *CEO*
James Richter, *President*
D R Limberg, *Principal*
Bob Kish, *Prdtn Mgr*
Marty Rogin, *Engineer*
▲ EMP: 60
SQ FT: 59,000
SALES (est): 14.7MM **Privately Held**
WEB: www.metraflex.com
SIC: 3494 3824 3441 3411 Valves & pipe fittings; fluid meters & counting devices; expansion joints (structural shapes), iron or steel; metal cans

### (G-5707)
### METROPOLITAN BREWING LLC
5121 N Ravenswood Ave (60640-5386)
PHONE ................... 773 474-6893
Douglas E Hurst, *CEO*
Tracy Hurst, *Mng Member*
EMP: 7
SALES (est): 607.6K **Privately Held**
SIC: 2082 Near beer

### (G-5708)
### MEXICANDY DISTRIBUTOR INC
2332 S Blue Island Ave (60608-4314)
PHONE ................... 773 847-0024
Erick Hauser, *President*
EMP: 7 EST: 2004
SALES (est): 677.6K **Privately Held**
SIC: 2064 Candy & other confectionery products; candy bars, including chocolate covered bars

### (G-5709)
### MEXICO DISTRIBUTOR INC
2286 S Blue Island Ave (60608-4345)
Jose A Gonzalez, *President*
EMP: 5
SALES: 1MM **Privately Held**
SIC: 2099 Chili pepper or powder

### (G-5710)
### MEXICO ENTERPRISE CORPORATION
6859 W 64th Pl (60638-4898)
PHONE ................... 920 568-8900
Olga Ramirez, *Owner*
EMP: 5
SALES (est): 352.4K **Privately Held**
SIC: 2032 Mexican foods: packaged in cans, jars, etc.

### (G-5711)
### MEXIFEAST FOODS INC
8414 S Brandon Ave 2 (60617-2658)
PHONE ................... 773 356-6386
Nancy Andrade, *President*
Edward Andrade, *Vice Pres*
Jose Andrade, *Treasurer*
EMP: 3
SQ FT: 400
SALES: 60K **Privately Held**
SIC: 2032 5149 Tamales: packaged in cans, jars, etc.; cooking oils & shortenings

### (G-5712)
### MEYER STEEL DRUM INC
2000 S Kilbourn Ave (60623-2310)
PHONE ................... 773 522-3030
Fax: 773 522-7360
Brian T Meyer Jr, *Branch Mgr*
EMP: 25
SALES (corp-wide): 70MM **Privately Held**
SIC: 3412 5085 Drums, shipping: metal; drums, new or reconditioned
PA: Meyer Steel Drum, Inc.
    3201 S Millard Ave
    Chicago IL 60623
    773 376-8376

### (G-5713)
### MEYER STEEL DRUM INC (PA)
Also Called: Ideal Gerit Drum Ring Mfg
3201 S Millard Ave (60623-5078)
PHONE ................... 773 376-8376
Fax: 773 376-7060
William Meyer, *President*
Edward Meyer, *Corp Secy*
John Brazis, *Controller*
Michael Prack, *Sales Mgr*
▲ EMP: 180
SQ FT: 85,000
SALES: 70MM **Privately Held**
WEB: www.meyersteeldrum.com
SIC: 3412 5085 Drums, shipping: metal; drums, new or reconditioned

### (G-5714)
### MFP HOLDING CO (DH)
1414 S Western Ave (60608-1802)
PHONE ................... 312 666-3366
Wyman C Harris, *Ch of Bd*
Doss Samikkannu, *President*
Victor Villalavazo, *Credit Mgr*
Ken Hufsdaver, *VP Mktg*
EMP: 9
SQ FT: 145,000
SALES (est): 10.3MM
SALES (corp-wide): 2.2B **Publicly Held**
SIC: 2531 5021 6512 5064 Public building & related furniture; public building furniture; shopping center, property operation only; electric household appliances
HQ: Sagus International, Inc.
    1302 Industrial Blvd
    Temple TX 76504
    630 413-5540

### (G-5715)
### MFZ VENTURES INC
Also Called: Aluminum Case Co
3333 W 48th Pl (60632-3052)
PHONE ................... 773 247-4611
Fax: 773 247-8376
Ken McDonald, *President*
Linda Jamerson, *COO*
EMP: 5 EST: 1945
SQ FT: 11,050
SALES: 700K **Privately Held**
SIC: 3499 3469 3911 3161 Boxes for packing & shipping, metal; metal stampings; precious metal cases; cases, carrying

### (G-5716)
### MHS LTD
Also Called: Wear-Flex Slings
6616 W Irving Park Rd (60634-2435)
PHONE ................... 773 736-3333
Fax: 773 736-3332
Barry Young, *Branch Mgr*
Roy Norton, *Agent*
EMP: 10
SALES (corp-wide): 2.2MM **Privately Held**
WEB: www.wear-flex.com
SIC: 2298 3537 3496 3429 Nets, seines, slings & insulator pads; industrial trucks & tractors; miscellaneous fabricated wire products; manufactured hardware (general); broadwoven fabric mills, manmade
PA: Mhs Ltd.
    4959 Home Rd
    Winston Salem NC 27106
    336 767-2641

### (G-5717)
### MHUB
Also Called: Catalyze
965 W Chicago Ave (60642-5413)
PHONE ................... 773 580-1485
Haven Allen, *President*
William Fienup, *Vice Pres*
Manas Mehandru, *Admin Sec*
EMP: 3 EST: 2013
SALES (est): 323K **Privately Held**
SIC: 3842 Infant incubators

### (G-5718)
### MI-TE FAST PRINTERS INC (PA)
Also Called: Mi-Te Printing & Graphics
180 W Washington St Fl 2 (60602-4450)
PHONE ................... 312 236-8352
Fax: 312 236-1486
Thomas Sackley, *President*
Taryn Geary, *Sales Staff*
Sandra Sackley, *Admin Sec*
EMP: 27
SALES (est): 4MM **Privately Held**
WEB: www.miteweddinginvitations.com
SIC: 2752 Commercial printing, offset

### (G-5719)
### MIC QUALITY SERVICE INC
3500 S Morgan St (60609-1524)
PHONE ................... 847 778-5676
Genj Genj Guo, *President*
Wenxiu Zhao, *CFO*
◆ EMP: 25
SQ FT: 20,000
SALES (est): 2.1MM **Privately Held**
SIC: 3639 Major kitchen appliances, except refrigerators & stoves

### (G-5720)
### MICHAELANGELO FOODS LLC
1800 N Pulaski Rd (60639-4916)
PHONE ................... 773 425-3498
Michaelangelo Alvarez, *Mng Member*
EMP: 1 EST: 2008
SQ FT: 3,600
SALES: 350K **Privately Held**
SIC: 2032 Italian foods: packaged in cans, jars, etc.

### (G-5721)
### MICHALS ACCESSORY MART INC
Also Called: Michals-Kagan & Associates
55 E Washington St # 601 (60602-2103)
PHONE ................... 312 263-0066
Fax: 312 263-0069
Larry Michals, *President*
Cris Myers, *Admin Sec*
EMP: 3 EST: 1932
SQ FT: 2,000
SALES (est): 290K **Privately Held**
SIC: 5944 3911 Jewelry, precious stones & precious metals; watches; jewelry, precious metal

### (G-5722)
### MICHELANGELO & DONATA BURDI
6411 W Addison St (60634-3809)
PHONE ................... 773 427-1437
Michelangelo Burdi, *Owner*
EMP: 12
SALES (est): 767.4K **Privately Held**
SIC: 3714 Transmissions, motor vehicle

### (G-5723)
### MICRO THREAD CORPORATION
Also Called: Micro Tech Components
6260 N Northwest Hwy (60631-1617)
P.O. Box 31219 (60631-0219)
PHONE ................... 773 775-1200
William Chong, *President*
Patrick T S Wong, *Vice Pres*
Irene Chong, *Manager*
Ngor Wong Chong, *Admin Sec*
EMP: 12
SQ FT: 20,000
SALES (est): 1MM **Privately Held**
WEB: www.microthreadcorp.com
SIC: 3325 Rolling mill rolls, cast steel

### (G-5724)
### MICROLUTION INC
6635 W Irving Park Rd (60634-2410)
PHONE ................... 773 282-6495
Andrew Phillip, *President*
Jeff Perkins, *Mfg Staff*
Brendon Divincenzo, *Engineer*
Edward Ingerman, *Engineer*
Eric Lentz, *Engineer*
EMP: 25
SQ FT: 4,000
SALES (est): 6.4MM
SALES (corp-wide): 3.7B **Privately Held**
WEB: www.microlution-inc.com
SIC: 3599 Bellows, industrial: metal
PA: Georg Fischer Ag
    Amsler-Laffon-Strasse 9
    Schaffhausen SH
    526 311-111

### (G-5725)
### MID CITY PRINTING SERVICE
5566 N Northwest Hwy (60630-1116)
PHONE ................... 773 777-5400
Fax: 773 777-0235
Stanley Jasiuwienas, *President*
Janina Przybylowska, *Treasurer*
EMP: 7
SQ FT: 4,000
SALES (est): 1MM **Privately Held**
SIC: 2752 2791 2789 2759 Commercial printing, offset; typesetting; bookbinding & related work; commercial printing

### (G-5726)
### MID PACK
4610 W West End Ave (60644-2759)
PHONE ................... 773 626-3500
Fax: 773 854-4954
Mark Scott, *Manager*
EMP: 2 EST: 2003
SALES (est): 235.2K **Privately Held**
SIC: 2067 Chewing gum

### (G-5727)
### MID-AMERICAN ELEVATOR CO INC (PA)
Also Called: USA Hoist Company
820 N Wolcott Ave (60622-4937)
PHONE ................... 773 486-6900
Fax: 773 486-1450
Robert R Bailey Jr, *Ch of Bd*
Brian Selke, *President*
Robert R Bailey III, *President*
Cullen Bailey, *Corp Secy*
Greg Selke, *Vice Pres*
▲ EMP: 130
SQ FT: 24,000
SALES (est): 48.3MM **Privately Held**
WEB: www.spacesaverparking.com
SIC: 1796 7699 3823 3535 Elevator installation & conversion; elevators: inspection, service & repair; controllers for process variables, all types; conveyors & conveying equipment; elevators & moving stairways

# GEOGRAPHIC SECTION
## Chicago - Cook County (G-5753)

**(G-5728)**
**MID-AMERICAN ELEVATOR EQP CO**
820 N Wolcott Ave (60622-4937)
PHONE..................................773 486-6900
Robert R Bailey Jr, *Chairman*
Litschewski Jacka, *Vice Pres*
Andreananna Triliegi, *Admin Sec*
**EMP:** 35
**SALES:** 2MM **Privately Held**
**SIC: 3823** Industrial instrmnts msrmnt display/control process variable

**(G-5729)**
**MID-CITY DIE & MOLD CORP**
1743 N Keating Ave (60639-4688)
PHONE..................................773 278-4844
**Fax:** 773 278-5289
Timothy Sterrett, *President*
Robin Sterrett, *Vice Pres*
**EMP:** 2
**SQ FT:** 2,300
**SALES:** 250K **Privately Held**
**SIC: 3544** 8711 Dies, steel rule; forms (molds), for foundry & plastics working machinery; consulting engineer

**(G-5730)**
**MID-STATES WIRE PROC CORP**
4642 W Maypole Ave (60644-2787)
P.O. Box 44550 (60644-0560)
PHONE..................................773 379-3775
**Fax:** 773 379-5053
T W Richer, *President*
Howard Richer, *President*
**EMP:** 10
**SQ FT:** 13,500
**SALES (est):** 988.9K **Privately Held**
**SIC: 3316** Cold-rolled strip or wire

**(G-5731)**
**MID-WEST SCREW PRODUCTS INC (PA)**
3523 N Kenton Ave (60641-3819)
PHONE..................................773 283-6032
**Fax:** 773 284-4496
Walter E Lisowski, *President*
Kenneth Lisowski, *Vice Pres*
Joe Faron, *Plant Mgr*
Jeff Wolford, *Foreman/Supr*
Virginia Lisowski, *Treasurer*
**EMP:** 36 **EST:** 1946
**SQ FT:** 15,000
**SALES (est):** 6.6MM **Privately Held**
**WEB:** www.m-wsp.com
**SIC: 3451** Screw machine products

**(G-5732)**
**MIDAMERICAN PRTG SYSTEMS INC**
1716 W Grand Ave (60622-6084)
PHONE..................................312 663-4720
**Fax:** 312 663-0680
Jerry Freund, *President*
Bruce Miller, *Principal*
Joel Amettis, *Vice Pres*
Art Chiappetta, *Vice Pres*
Leo Douglas, *Vice Pres*
**EMP:** 50
**SQ FT:** 27,000
**SALES (est):** 12.1MM **Privately Held**
**WEB:** www.midamericanprint.com
**SIC: 2752** 2759 Commercial printing, offset; business forms: printing; envelopes: printing

**(G-5733)**
**MIDCO INTERNATIONAL INC**
Also Called: Emberglo Div of Midco Intl
4140 W Victoria St (60646-6790)
PHONE..................................773 604-8700
**Fax:** 773 604-4070
Keith Malek, *CEO*
Teryl A Stanger, *President*
Hal F Beyer III, *Chairman*
John Kopera, *Project Mgr*
John Sobie, *Opers Staff*
▲ **EMP:** 50 **EST:** 1941
**SQ FT:** 82,000
**SALES:** 12.3MM **Privately Held**
**WEB:** www.emberglo.com
**SIC: 3433** 3567 3589 Gas burners, domestic; gas burners, industrial; incinerators, metal: domestic or commercial; cooking equipment, commercial

**(G-5734)**
**MIDLAND INDUSTRIES INC**
1424 N Halsted St (60642-2618)
PHONE..................................312 664-7300
**Fax:** 312 664-7371
Laurence S Spector, *President*
Tim Mohs, *Vice Pres*
Peter Russel, *Vice Pres*
Peter Russell, *Vice Pres*
Chad Spector, *Marketing Mgr*
◆ **EMP:** 42 **EST:** 1955
**SQ FT:** 35,000
**SALES (est):** 16.4MM **Privately Held**
**WEB:** www.zincbig.com
**SIC: 3356** 5093 Zinc & zinc alloy bars, plates, sheets, etc.; nonferrous metals scrap

**(G-5735)**
**MIDLAND METAL PRODUCTS CO**
1200 W 37th St (60609-2187)
PHONE..................................773 927-5700
**Fax:** 773 927-1456
Suzanne Z Mc Donald, *President*
Marcus A Mc Donald, *Principal*
Melissa Smogur, *Project Mgr*
Michael Zyer, *Production*
Aaron Blaisdell, *Purch Dir*
**EMP:** 75
**SQ FT:** 110,000
**SALES (est):** 17.8MM **Privately Held**
**WEB:** www.midlandmetalproducts.com
**SIC: 2542** 3499 Racks, merchandise display or storage: except wood; novelties & specialties, metal

**(G-5736)**
**MIDWAY CAP COMPANY**
1239 W Madison St Ste 3 (60607)
PHONE..................................773 384-0911
**Fax:** 312 243-1555
Merle Spertoli, *President*
Dave Lajb, *Vice Pres*
Monica Galimdo, *Admin Sec*
**EMP:** 20
**SQ FT:** 17,000
**SALES:** 2.5MM **Privately Held**
**SIC: 2353** Police hats & caps

**(G-5737)**
**MIDWAY CAP COMPANY**
4513 W Armitage Ave (60639-3403)
PHONE..................................773 384-0911
**Fax:** 773 384-0949
Merle Stertoli, *President*
**EMP:** 20
**SALES (est):** 980K **Privately Held**
**SIC: 2353** Uniform hats & caps

**(G-5738)**
**MIDWAY FOOD LLC**
3937 S Lowe Ave (60609-2600)
PHONE..................................773 294-0730
Malek Almassad, 
**EMP:** 5
**SALES (est):** 139.9K **Privately Held**
**SIC: 2015** 2092 2037 3411 Poultry, processed: frozen; fresh or frozen packaged fish; vegetables, quick frozen & cold pack, excl. potato products; potato products, quick frozen & cold pack; food & beverage containers

**(G-5739)**
**MIDWAY GAMES INC (HQ)**
2704 W Roscoe St (60618-5910)
PHONE..................................773 961-2222
**Fax:** 773 961-2376
Matthew V Booty, *Ch of Bd*
Deborah K Fulton, *Senior VP*
Miguel Iribarren, *Senior VP*
Ryan G O'Desky, *CFO*
Sara Beck, *Human Res Dir*
**EMP:** 37
**SALES (est):** 27.6MM **Privately Held**
**WEB:** www.midway.com
**SIC: 7372** Home entertainment computer software

**(G-5740)**
**MIDWAY INDUSTRIES INC**
Also Called: Midway Windows and Doors
6750 S Belt Circle Dr (60638-4706)
PHONE..................................708 594-2600
**Fax:** 708 594-1508
Arthur J Strauss Jr, *CEO*
Jerome E Joseph, *President*
Rose Dus, *Controller*
Sharon Burke, *Manager*
Jerry Oksanen, *Manager*
**EMP:** 150
**SQ FT:** 91,000
**SALES (est):** 32.8MM **Privately Held**
**WEB:** www.midwayindustries.com
**SIC: 3442** Metal doors; window & door frames; screen & storm doors & windows

**(G-5741)**
**MIDWEST AIR PRO INC**
2054 N New England Ave (60707-3328)
PHONE..................................773 622-4566
Rosette Viola, *President*
Michael Viola, *Admin Sec*
**EMP:** 4
**SALES (est):** 660.8K **Privately Held**
**SIC: 3564** Air cleaning systems

**(G-5742)**
**MIDWEST CANVAS CORP (PA)**
4635 W Lake St (60644-2798)
PHONE..................................773 287-4400
**Fax:** 773 854-2017
Barry A Handwerker, *President*
Scott Kramer, *Plant Mgr*
Donnie Lytton, *Engineer*
Paul Winn, *Sales Dir*
Steve Rosen, *CIO*
◆ **EMP:** 175 **EST:** 1947
**SQ FT:** 200,000
**SALES (est):** 108.5MM **Privately Held**
**WEB:** www.midwestcanvas.com
**SIC: 3081** 3089 Plastic film & sheet; laminating of plastic

**(G-5743)**
**MIDWEST GALVANIZING INC**
7400 S Damen Ave (60636-3722)
P.O. Box 528140 (60652-8140)
PHONE..................................773 434-2682
**Fax:** 773 434-2912
James Kucia, *President*
Ed Finnegan, *President*
**EMP:** 15
**SQ FT:** 60,000
**SALES (est):** 740K **Privately Held**
**SIC: 3479** 3471 Galvanizing of iron, steel or end-formed products; hot dip coating of metals or formed products; plating & polishing

**(G-5744)**
**MIDWEST GOLD STAMPERS INC**
5707 N Northwest Hwy (60646-6137)
PHONE..................................773 775-5253
**Fax:** 773 775-5267
Terrence Strauch, *President*
Dave Brown, *Controller*
Dave Smith, *Sales Staff*
**EMP:** 15 **EST:** 1977
**SQ FT:** 17,500
**SALES (est):** 121.5K **Privately Held**
**WEB:** www.midwestgoldstampers.com
**SIC: 2789** 3554 2759 Gold stamping on books; die cutting & stamping machinery; paper converting; embossing on paper

**(G-5745)**
**MIDWEST LAW PRINTING CO INC**
Also Called: Photex
226 S Wabash Ave Fl 4 (60604-2332)
PHONE..................................312 431-0185
Manish Shah, *President*
Patrick Kessler, *Vice Pres*
**EMP:** 7 **EST:** 1954
**SQ FT:** 5,000
**SALES (est):** 498.1K **Privately Held**
**SIC: 2721** 7334 2759 2752 Periodicals; photocopying & duplicating services; commercial printing; commercial printing, lithographic

**(G-5746)**
**MIDWEST MANUFACTURING & DISTRG**
6025 N Keystone Ave (60646-5209)
PHONE..................................773 866-1010
Erno Bakondi, *President*
Klara Bakondi, *Admin Sec*

**EMP:** 15
**SQ FT:** 12,500
**SALES (est):** 3.9MM **Privately Held**
**SIC: 3444** Sheet metal specialties, not stamped

**(G-5747)**
**MIDWEST MODEL AIRCRAFT CO**
Also Called: K & S Engineering
6917 W 59th St (60638-3205)
PHONE..................................773 229-0741
**Fax:** 773 586-8556
Wallace M Simmers, *President*
Wally Findysz, *Vice Pres*
Jim Hankowski, *Plant Mgr*
Gerald Hartlaub, *Controller*
Evelyn Simmers, *Admin Sec*
◆ **EMP:** 19
**SQ FT:** 13,000
**SALES (est):** 4.2MM **Privately Held**
**WEB:** www.ksmetals.com
**SIC: 3351** 3354 Tubing, copper & copper alloy; aluminum pipe & tube

**(G-5748)**
**MIDWEST ORTHOTIC SERVICES LLC**
5521 N Cumberland Ave (60656-1572)
PHONE..................................773 930-3770
**EMP:** 26
**SALES (corp-wide):** 18.7MM **Privately Held**
**SIC: 3842** Braces, orthopedic
**PA:** Midwest Orthotic Services, Llc
17530 Dugdale Dr
South Bend IN 46635
574 233-3352

**(G-5749)**
**MIDWEST SOCKS LLC**
4120 N Leamington Ave (60641-1432)
PHONE..................................773 283-3952
Zelek Rosalena, *Principal*
**EMP:** 3 **EST:** 2015
**SALES (est):** 88.8K **Privately Held**
**SIC: 2252** Socks

**(G-5750)**
**MIDWEST SWISS EMBROIDERIES CO**
5590 N Northwest Hwy (60630-1178)
PHONE..................................773 631-7120
**Fax:** 773 631-1178
Marvin Mazzucchelli, *President*
John Mazzucchelli, *Exec VP*
Sue Maher, *Office Mgr*
Dorothy Mazzucchelli, *Admin Sec*
**EMP:** 20 **EST:** 1935
**SQ FT:** 15,000
**SALES (est):** 935K **Privately Held**
**SIC: 2395** 2397 Emblems, embroidered; schiffli machine embroideries

**(G-5751)**
**MIDWEST TOOL INC**
4055 W Peterson Ave # 205 (60646-6183)
PHONE..................................773 588-1313
Mitchell Zamost, *President*
Linda Gorski, *Manager*
**EMP:** 4
**SALES (est):** 448.3K **Privately Held**
**SIC: 3699** Electrical equipment & supplies

**(G-5752)**
**MIDWEST UNCUTS INC**
Also Called: Midwest Labs
5585 N Lynch Ave (60630-1417)
PHONE..................................312 664-3131
Susan Nutgrass, *Opers Mgr*
Robert Pretzie, *Manager*
**EMP:** 11
**SALES (corp-wide):** 2.4B **Privately Held**
**WEB:** www.midwestlabs.com
**SIC: 3851** Eyeglasses, lenses & frames
**HQ:** Midwest Uncuts Inc
1812 N 7th St
Indianola IA 50125
515 961-6593

**(G-5753)**
**MIDWESTERN RUST PROOF INC**
3636 N Kilbourn Ave (60641-3643)
PHONE..................................773 725-6636
Garth Davies, *President*

# Chicago - Cook County (G-5754)   GEOGRAPHIC SECTION

Vicky Ryans, *Accounting Mgr*
Patrick Wiklacz, *Sales Staff*
▲ EMP: 100
SALES (est): 12.8MM **Privately Held**
WEB: www.midwesternrustproof.com
SIC: 3471  Plating & polishing

**(G-5754)**
**MIFAB  INC (PA)**
1321 W 119th St  (60643-5109)
PHONE..................................773 341-3030
Michael J Whiteside, *President*
Mike Bellavance, *COO*
Paul Lacourciere, *Vice Pres*
Courtlen Hagemeyer, *CFO*
Andrew Haines, *Sales Mgr*
▲ EMP: 35
SALES (est): 10.3MM **Privately Held**
SIC: 3432  Plumbing fixture fittings & trim

**(G-5755)**
**MIGALA REPORT**
566 W Adams St Ste 404  (60661-3677)
PHONE..................................312 948-0260
Dan Migala, *Principal*
EMP: 3
SALES (est): 203.8K **Privately Held**
SIC: 2711  Newspapers

**(G-5756)**
**MIGHTY HOOK  INC**
1017 N Cicero Ave  (60651-3202)
PHONE..................................773 378-1909
Fax: 773 378-2803
Scott Rempala, *President*
Sergio Rivera, *General Mgr*
Elaine Kozil, *Office Mgr*
Mike Jones, *Manager*
Edward Rolison, *Admin Sec*
▲ EMP: 30
SQ FT: 51,000
SALES (est): 5MM **Privately Held**
WEB: www.mightyhook.com
SIC: 2298  3452  Wire rope centers; bolts, nuts, rivets & washers

**(G-5757)**
**MIHALIS MARINE**
1224 W 91st St  (60620-3505)
PHONE..................................773 445-6220
Tracy Howard, *Owner*
EMP: 5
SALES (est): 425.3K **Privately Held**
SIC: 7692  Welding repair

**(G-5758)**
**MIKES ANODIZING CO**
859 N Spaulding Ave  (60651-4134)
PHONE..................................773 722-5778
Fax: 773 722-1177
Michael S Balice, *President*
Nick Balice, *General Mgr*
Michelle Balice Jr, *Corp Secy*
EMP: 48 EST: 1946
SQ FT: 50,000
SALES (est): 4.9MM **Privately Held**
SIC: 3471  Anodizing (plating) of metals or formed products

**(G-5759)**
**MILITARY MEDICAL NEWS**
55 E Jackson Blvd # 1820  (60604-4466)
PHONE..................................312 368-4860
Paul Stevens, *President*
EMP: 21
SALES (est): 614K **Privately Held**
SIC: 2711  Newspapers

**(G-5760)**
**MILLERCOORS LLC (HQ)**
250 S Wacker Dr Ste 800  (60606-5888)
P.O. Box 5293, Parsippany NJ  (07054-6293)
PHONE..................................312 496-2700
Gavin Hattersley, *CEO*
Tom Cardella, *Division Pres*
Ed McBrien, *Division Pres*
Alan Clark, *Vice Chairman*
Bradley Bangert, *Area Pres*
◆ EMP: 800
SQ FT: 225,000
SALES: 2B
SALES (corp-wide): 4.8B **Publicly Held**
WEB: www.millercoors.com
SIC: 2082  Beer (alcoholic beverage)

PA: Molson Coors Brewing Company
1801 Calif St Ste 4600
Denver CO 80202
303 927-2337

**(G-5761)**
**MILLERCOORS LLC**
150 S Wacker Dr Ste 2520  (60606-4202)
PHONE..................................312 496-2700
Vivian Ford-Barney, *Branch Mgr*
EMP: 20
SALES (corp-wide): 4.8B **Publicly Held**
SIC: 2082  Malt beverages
HQ: Millercoors Llc
250 S Wacker Dr Ste 800
Chicago IL 60606
312 496-2700

**(G-5762)**
**MILLERS EUREKA  INC**
2121 W Hubbard St  (60612-1611)
PHONE..................................312 666-9383
Fax: 312 666-9209
Carol Miller, *President*
Jim Householder, *Controller*
Betty J Miller, *Admin Sec*
EMP: 10
SQ FT: 16,000
SALES (est): 3.5MM **Privately Held**
SIC: 5051  3446  7692  Steel; railings, bannisters, guards, etc.; made from metal pipe; welding repair

**(G-5763)**
**MILLIKEN & COMPANY**
222 Merchandise Mart Plz # 1149
(60654-1167)
PHONE..................................800 241-4826
Robert Dillon, *Branch Mgr*
EMP: 14
SALES (corp-wide): 3.3B **Privately Held**
WEB: www.milliken.com
SIC: 5023  2273  Carpets; carpets & rugs
PA: Milliken & Company
920 Milliken Rd
Spartanburg SC 29303
864 503-2020

**(G-5764)**
**MILLIKEN & COMPANY**
Also Called: Keystone Aniline
2501 W Fulton St  (60612-2103)
PHONE..................................312 666-2015
J Harold Chandler, *Manager*
EMP: 65
SALES (corp-wide): 3.3B **Privately Held**
SIC: 2819  Industrial inorganic chemicals
PA: Milliken & Company
920 Milliken Rd
Spartanburg SC 29303
864 503-2020

**(G-5765)**
**MILLS PALLET**
4500 W Roosevelt Rd  (60624-3842)
PHONE..................................773 533-6458
Fax: 773 533-9416
Robert Zirves, *President*
Leon Fullett, *Accountant*
Greg Rohde, *Manager*
EMP: 12
SALES (est): 1.2MM **Privately Held**
WEB: www.millspallet.com
SIC: 2448  7699  Pallets, wood; pallet repair

**(G-5766)**
**MILVIA**
222 Merchandise Mart Plz 1427a
(60654-1419)
PHONE..................................312 527-3403
EMP: 3 EST: 2011
SALES (est): 238.3K **Privately Held**
SIC: 3842  Mfg Surgical Appliances/Supplies

**(G-5767)**
**MING TRADING LLC**
2845 W 48th Pl  (60632-2012)
PHONE..................................773 442-2221
Peter Ming,
▲ EMP: 3 EST: 2014
SQ FT: 3,000
SALES: 500K **Privately Held**
SIC: 3999  Pet supplies

**(G-5768)**
**MINIMILL TECHNOLOGIES INC**
505 N Lake Shore Dr # 5407  (60611-6446)
PHONE..................................315 857-7107
Kamala G Rajan, *President*
Srinivasan Balaji, *Vice Pres*
Donnie Parks, *VP Opers*
Erin Procopio, *Office Mgr*
EMP: 2
SALES (est): 212.3K **Privately Held**
SIC: 2431  Millwork

**(G-5769)**
**MIO MED ORTHOPEDICS INC**
2502 N Clark St 212  (60614-1850)
PHONE..................................773 477-8991
Fax: 773 477-4001
Mark Sorensen, *President*
EMP: 3
SALES (est): 399.7K **Privately Held**
SIC: 3842  Surgical appliances & supplies

**(G-5770)**
**MIRACLE PRESS COMPANY**
2951 W Carroll Ave  (60612-1788)
PHONE..................................773 722-6176
Fax: 773 722-1136
John G Novak, *President*
Bruce Novak, *Vice Pres*
Nancy Novak, *Vice Pres*
George Novak, *Treasurer*
EMP: 15 EST: 1933
SQ FT: 24,000
SALES (est): 2.5MM **Privately Held**
WEB: www.miraclepress.com
SIC: 2752  2671  Commercial printing, lithographic; packaging paper & plastics film, coated & laminated

**(G-5771)**
**MISSION OF OUR LADY OF MERCY (PA)**
Also Called: Mercy Home For Boys and Girls
1140 W Jackson Blvd Ste 1  (60607-3884)
PHONE..................................312 738-7568
Fax: 312 738-1598
L Scott Donahue, *CEO*
Jennifer L Kemper, *Sls & Mktg Exec*
Kimberly Majewaski, *Comms Dir*
Dee Atkins, *Exec Dir*
EMP: 9
SQ FT: 76,000
SALES (est): 10.5MM **Privately Held**
WEB: www.mercyhome.org
SIC: 8361  2752  Residential care for children; commercial printing, offset

**(G-5772)**
**MISSION PRESS  INC**
600 W Cermak Rd Ste 1a  (60616-4880)
PHONE..................................312 455-9501
Michael Smith, *President*
Sara Domdey, *Graphic Designe*
EMP: 5
SQ FT: 4,000
SALES (est): 540K **Privately Held**
WEB: www.printingthatrocks.com
SIC: 2752  Commercial printing, lithographic

**(G-5773)**
**MITCHEL HOME**
3652 N Tripp Ave  (60641-3037)
PHONE..................................773 205-9902
Fax: 773 202-1928
John Mitchel, *Partner*
Kathy Mitchel, *Partner*
Denham Lorraine, *Executive*
EMP: 4
SALES (est): 272.1K **Privately Held**
WEB: www.mitchelhome.com
SIC: 2519  Household furniture

**(G-5774)**
**MITEL NETWORKS  INC**
70 W Madison St Ste 1600  (60602-4262)
PHONE..................................312 479-9000
John Uehling, *Vice Pres*
EMP: 13
SALES (corp-wide): 987.6MM **Privately Held**
SIC: 3661  Telephones & telephone apparatus

HQ: Mitel Networks, Inc.
1146 N Alma School Rd
Mesa AZ 85201
480 961-9000

**(G-5775)**
**MITTAL STEEL USA INC**
1 S Dearborn St Ste 1800  (60603-2308)
PHONE..................................312 899-3440
Fax: 312 899-3300
Lance Alberti, *General Mgr*
Vaidya Sethuraman, *CFO*
Jose Cisneros, *Manager*
Eric Drabick, *Supervisor*
Krist Pirovsky, *Supervisor*
▲ EMP: 11
SALES (est): 844.9K **Privately Held**
SIC: 3312  Plate, steel

**(G-5776)**
**MIX KITCHEN**
610 N Fairbanks Ct Ste 3a  (60611-4899)
PHONE..................................312 649-0330
John F Adair, *Principal*
EMP: 7
SALES (est): 600.3K **Privately Held**
SIC: 3273  Ready-mixed concrete

**(G-5777)**
**MK SIGNS INC**
4900 N Elston Ave Ste M  (60630-2573)
PHONE..................................773 545-4444
Fax: 773 545-0042
Ralph Cilia, *President*
Anthony Cilia Jr, *Corp Secy*
April Moran, *Asst Controller*
Tony Cilia Jr, *Admin Sec*
▲ EMP: 46
SQ FT: 18,000
SALES (est): 5.5MM **Privately Held**
WEB: www.mksigns.net
SIC: 3993  1799  7336  Neon signs; signs, not made in custom sign painting shops; sign installation & maintenance; art design services

**(G-5778)**
**MK TILE INK**
5851 S Neenah Ave  (60638-3314)
PHONE..................................773 964-8905
Marcin Krol, *Principal*
EMP: 1
SALES: 522K **Privately Held**
SIC: 1743  5211  5032  3272  Tile installation, ceramic; tile, ceramic; ceramic wall & floor tile; tile, precast terrazzo or concrete; floor tile

**(G-5779)**
**MLEVEL INC**
205 W Wacker Dr Ste 820  (60606-1460)
PHONE..................................888 564-5395
Jordan Fladell, *CEO*
David G Cutler, *President*
Holly Bonelli, *Business Anlyst*
Josh Felix, *Director*
Ashley Kiebach, *Business Dir*
EMP: 32 EST: 2014
SALES (est): 1.3MM **Privately Held**
SIC: 7372  Educational computer software

**(G-5780)**
**MOBILEHOP TECHNOLOGY LLC**
838 W 31st St Unit 3g  (60608-5874)
PHONE..................................312 504-3773
EMP: 3 EST: 2011
SALES (est): 180K **Privately Held**
SIC: 7372  Prepackaged Software Services

**(G-5781)**
**MODERN GRAPHIC SYSTEMS INC**
4922 S Western Ave  (60609-4742)
PHONE..................................773 476-6898
James Sommer, *CEO*
Lucille G Sommer, *Vice Pres*
EMP: 6
SQ FT: 6,250
SALES: 600K **Privately Held**
WEB: www.amagneticsign.com
SIC: 3552  Silk screens for textile industry

# GEOGRAPHIC SECTION
## Chicago - Cook County (G-5807)

**(G-5782)**
**MODERN LIGHTING TECH LLC**
1751 W Grand Ave (60622-6050)
PHONE.................................312 624-9267
EMP: 5 EST: 2012
SQ FT: 8,500
SALES (est): 380K Privately Held
SIC: 3641 Mfg Electric Lamps

**(G-5783)**
**MODERN LUXURY MEDIA LLC**
Also Called: Cs Magazine Front Desk Chicago
33 W Monroe St Ste 2100 (60603-5410)
PHONE.................................312 274-2500
Fax: 312 274-2501
Allison Mitchell, Editor
Ralph Gago, Business Mgr
Chloe Doherty, Accounts Exec
Logan Walsh, Mktg Coord
Starr Scuderi, Branch Mgr
EMP: 30
SALES (corp-wide): 1.1B Publicly Held
SIC: 2721 Periodicals
HQ: Modern Luxury Media, Llc
243 Vallejo St
San Francisco CA 94111
404 443-0004

**(G-5784)**
**MODERN PROCESS EQUIPMENT INC**
3125 S Kolin Ave (60623-4890)
PHONE.................................773 254-3929
Fax: 773 254-3935
D Ephraim, President
Hector Cotto, Plant Mgr
Chris Spatz, Engineer
Stephen Chu, Design Engr
Lizzie Ephraim, Sls & Mktg Exec
EMP: 50 EST: 1957
SQ FT: 50,000
SALES (est): 14.1MM Privately Held
WEB: www.mpechicago.com
SIC: 8711 3556 Engineering services; grinders, commercial, food

**(G-5785)**
**MODERN SPECIALTIES COMPANY**
Also Called: Progress Dusters Division
661 W Lake St (60661-1034)
PHONE.................................312 648-5800
Fax: 312 648-1333
Gerissa French, President
Bob Rosenberg, General Mgr
Robert Dean French, Shareholder
▲ EMP: 7 EST: 1929
SQ FT: 6,000
SALES (est): 1.1MM Privately Held
WEB: www.themodernspecialtiescompany.com
SIC: 3421 3999 3541 3423 Knives: butchers', hunting, pocket, etc.; knife blades & blanks; dusters, feather; machine tools, metal cutting type; hand & edge tools; broadwoven fabric mills, wool

**(G-5786)**
**MODERN SPROUT LLC**
1451 N Ashland Ave (60622-8087)
PHONE.................................312 342-2114
Nicholas J Behr, Mng Member
Sarah D Burrows, Mng Member
EMP: 2 EST: 2013
SALES (est): 228.3K Privately Held
SIC: 3999 Hydroponic equipment

**(G-5787)**
**MOES RIVER NORTH LLC**
155 W Kinzie St (60654-4514)
PHONE.................................312 245-2000
EMP: 3
SALES (est): 137.3K Privately Held
SIC: 3421 Table & food cutlery, including butchers'

**(G-5788)**
**MOHICAN PETROLEUM INC**
21 S Clark St Ste 3980 (60603-2017)
PHONE.................................312 782-6385
F M Bransfield, President
Charles Bransfield, Vice Pres
Dorothy Huntoon, Treasurer
Erika Schroederus, Manager
James Murphy, Admin Sec
EMP: 4
SALES (est): 1MM Privately Held
WEB: www.mohicanpetroleum.com
SIC: 1382 Oil & gas exploration services

**(G-5789)**
**MOLD EXPRESS INC**
8142 W Frest Preserve Ave (60634-2908)
PHONE.................................773 766-0874
EMP: 2 EST: 2013
SALES (est): 214.8K Privately Held
SIC: 3544 Industrial molds

**(G-5790)**
**MOLD-RITE PLASTICS LLC (HQ)**
30 N La Salle St Ste 2425 (60602-3361)
P.O. Box 160, Plattsburgh NY (12901-0160)
PHONE.................................518 561-1812
Rick Gardner, Facilities Mgr
Tom Recny, CFO
Jeff Titherington, VP Sales
Brian Bauerbach,
Christina Benard, Analyst
◆ EMP: 179
SQ FT: 335,000
SALES (est): 131.3MM Privately Held
WEB: www.mrpcap.com
SIC: 3089 Closures, plastic

**(G-5791)**
**MOM DAD & ME (PA)**
7601 S Cicero Ave Ste 1970 (60652)
PHONE.................................773 735-9606
James Ching, Owner
▲ EMP: 2
SALES (est): 257.7K Privately Held
SIC: 2335 Wedding gowns & dresses

**(G-5792)**
**MONDA WINDOW & DOOR CORP**
4101 W 42nd Pl (60632-3938)
PHONE.................................773 254-8888
Elias Abubeker, President
Mindy Ouyang, Manager
Min Ouyang, Admin Sec
▲ EMP: 25
SQ FT: 50,000
SALES (est): 7.5MM Privately Held
WEB: www.mondawindow.com
SIC: 3354 2431 3089 3353 Aluminum extruded products; windows, wood; washers, plastic; aluminum sheet, plate & foil

**(G-5793)**
**MONDELEZ GLOBAL LLC**
Also Called: Nabisco
7300 S Kedzie Ave (60629-3595)
PHONE.................................773 925-4300
Fax: 773 476-6269
Dave Lamy, General Mgr
Tom Barnas, Maint Spvr
Gary Trider, Mfg Staff
William Lundgren, Engineer
George Dappert, Finance Mgr
EMP: 21 Publicly Held
WEB: www.kraftfoods.com
SIC: 2052 2099 Cookies; food preparations
HQ: Mondelez Global Llc
3 Parkway N Ste 300
Deerfield IL 60015
847 943-4000

**(G-5794)**
**MONETT METALS INC**
Also Called: Horizon Metals
3925 N Pulaski Rd (60641-2931)
PHONE.................................773 478-8888
Steve Lamm, Manager
EMP: 5
SALES (corp-wide): 566.9MM Privately Held
WEB: www.monettsteel.com
SIC: 3325 Steel foundries
HQ: Monett Metals Inc.
101 Industrial Dr
Monett MO 65708
417 235-6053

**(G-5795)**
**MONITOR PUBLISHING INC**
6304 N Nagle Ave Ste B (60646-3614)
PHONE.................................773 205-0303
Fax: 773 205-5252
Jack Zaworski, President
EMP: 6
SALES (est): 381.2K Privately Held
WEB: www.infopl.com
SIC: 2731 2721 Book publishing; periodicals

**(G-5796)**
**MONOGEN INC**
140 S Dearborn St Ste 420 (60603-5233)
PHONE.................................847 573-6700
Norman J Pressman, President
EMP: 40 EST: 1996
SALES (est): 5.1MM Privately Held
SIC: 3841 Medical instruments & equipment, blood & bone work; diagnostic apparatus, medical

**(G-5797)**
**MONTAUK CHICAGO INC**
401 N Wells St Ste 108a (60654-7026)
PHONE.................................312 951-5688
Tim Zyto, President
EMP: 3
SALES (est): 218.2K Privately Held
WEB: www.montauksofa.com
SIC: 5712 2599 Furniture stores; furniture & fixtures

**(G-5798)**
**MONTROSE GLASS & MIRROR CORP**
3916 W Montrose Ave Fl 1 (60618-1019)
PHONE.................................773 478-6433
Fax: 773 478-8880
Paul Sikar, President
Galina Sikar, Vice Pres
EMP: 3
SQ FT: 3,500
SALES (est): 371.9K Privately Held
SIC: 5231 5719 3231 3211 Glass; mirrors; products of purchased glass; flat glass

**(G-5799)**
**MOODY BIBLE INST OF CHICAGO (PA)**
820 N La Salle Dr (60610-3263)
PHONE.................................312 329-4000
Fax: 312 329-2099
Jerry Jenkins, Ch of Bd
Paul Nyquist, President
William Thrasher, Division Mgr
Michael Kane, Dean
Erwin Lutzer, Pastor
◆ EMP: 575 EST: 1886
SQ FT: 100,000
SALES: 111.9MM Privately Held
WEB: www.moody.edu
SIC: 8661 8299 8221 4832 Religious organizations; bible school; professional schools; radio broadcasting stations; books: publishing only

**(G-5800)**
**MOODY BIBLE INST OF CHICAGO**
Also Called: Moody Press A Division of MBI
210 W Chestnut St (60610-3112)
PHONE.................................312 329-2102
Cessandra Dillon, Publisher
Gregory Thornton, Branch Mgr
Duane Koenig, Manager
EMP: 50
SALES (corp-wide): 111.9MM Privately Held
WEB: www.moody.edu
SIC: 8741 2721 2731 Administrative management; periodicals; book publishing
PA: The Moody Bible Institute Of Chicago
820 N La Salle Dr
Chicago IL 60610
312 329-4000

**(G-5801)**
**MOON GUY HONG FOOD INC**
3823 S Halsted St (60609-1612)
PHONE.................................773 927-3233
Fax: 773 927-4529
Chiu Kit Leung, President
EMP: 12
SQ FT: 17,500
SALES (est): 500K Privately Held
SIC: 2038 2099 Ethnic foods, frozen; food preparations

**(G-5802)**
**MOORE NORTH AMERICA FIN INC**
111 S Wacker Dr Ste 3600 (60606-4300)
PHONE.................................847 607-6000
Ed Tyler, Principal
EMP: 4
SALES (est): 273.3K
SALES (corp-wide): 6.9B Publicly Held
SIC: 2761 Manifold business forms
PA: R. R. Donnelley & Sons Company
35 W Wacker Dr Ste 3650
Chicago IL 60601
312 326-8000

**(G-5803)**
**MORAN GRAPHICS INC**
Also Called: AlphaGraphics
1017 W Wa Blvd Unit 101 (60607-2108)
PHONE.................................312 226-3900
Sheila D Moran, President
Richard F Moran, Vice Pres
Judy Serrano, Manager
EMP: 26
SQ FT: 1,500
SALES (est): 4.1MM Privately Held
SIC: 2752 Commercial printing, lithographic

**(G-5804)**
**MORAN PROPERTIES INC**
1407 N Dearborn St (60610-1505)
PHONE.................................312 440-1962
Susan J Moran, President
John McDonough, Treasurer
EMP: 2
SALES (est): 264.6K Privately Held
SIC: 1382 Oil & gas exploration services

**(G-5805)**
**MORGEN TRANSPORTATION INC**
Also Called: Black Hstory Educatonal Netwrk
8 S Michigan Ave Ste 1600 (60603-3576)
PHONE.................................773 405-1250
Marcus Alston, CEO
Tracey Alston, President
EMP: 7
SQ FT: 3,000
SALES (est): 800K Privately Held
SIC: 2732 Books: printing only

**(G-5806)**
**MORRIS KURTZON INCORPORATED**
Also Called: Kurtzon Lighting
1420 S Talman Ave (60608-1693)
PHONE.................................773 277-2121
Fax: 773 277-9164
Daniel Koch, CEO
Victor Morales, General Mgr
Andrew Koch, Purchasing
Kamla Koch, Human Res Mgr
Henry Bradford, Marketing Staff
EMP: 22 EST: 1946
SQ FT: 75,000
SALES (est): 8.4MM Privately Held
WEB: www.kurtzon.com
SIC: 3646 Fluorescent lighting fixtures, commercial

**(G-5807)**
**MORTON INTERNATIONAL LLC (HQ)**
Also Called: Morton Salt
123 N Wacker Dr Ste 2400 (60606-1760)
PHONE.................................312 807-2696
Fax: 312 807-3286
Mark L Roberts, President
James Swanson, COO
Elizabeth Nohe, Vice Pres
Carol Panozzo, Vice Pres
Ed Fasulo, Plant Mgr
▲ EMP: 250
SALES (est): 639.6MM
SALES (corp-wide): 3.6B Privately Held
WEB: www.mortonintl.com
SIC: 2891 2851 2822 1479 Adhesives; lacquers, varnishes, enamels & other coatings; polysulfides (thiokol); salt & sulfur mining; salt

## Chicago - Cook County (G-5808)

PA: K+S Ag
Bertha-Von-Suttner-Str. 7
Kassel 34131
561 930-10

**(G-5808)**
**MORTON INTERNATIONAL LLC**
Mortan Salt
1357 N Elston Ave (60642-2417)
PHONE..............................773 235-2341
Fax: 773 235-1015
Frank L Castelluccio, *Branch Mgr*
**EMP:** 16
**SALES (corp-wide):** 3.6B **Privately Held**
**SIC: 1479** Salt & sulfur mining
HQ: Morton International, Llc
123 N Wacker Dr Ste 2400
Chicago IL 60606
312 807-2696

**(G-5809)**
**MORTON SALT INC (DH)**
Also Called: Chicago Salt Service
444 W Lake St Ste 3000 (60606-0090)
PHONE..............................312 807-2000
Fax: 312 807-2152
Christian Herrmann, *CEO*
Robert Alberico, *Vice Pres*
Matt Beliveau, *Vice Pres*
Guy Leblanc, *Vice Pres*
Elizabeth Nohe, *Vice Pres*
◆ **EMP:** 250
**SQ FT:** 95,838
**SALES (est):** 1.1B
**SALES (corp-wide):** 3.6B **Privately Held**
**SIC: 2891** 2851 2822 1479 Adhesives & sealants; paints & allied products; synthetic rubber; salt & sulfur mining; chemical preparations

**(G-5810)**
**MORTON YOKOHAMA INC**
123 N Wacker Dr Fl 27 (60606-1763)
PHONE..............................312 807-2000
James J Fuerholzer, *President*
**EMP:** 13
**SALES (est):** 1.6MM **Privately Held**
**SIC: 2891** Sealants; adhesives

**(G-5811)**
**MOSAICOS INC**
4948 N Pulaski Rd (60630-2813)
PHONE..............................773 777-8453
Lisa M Bannelos, *President*
George A Bannelos, *Admin Sec*
**EMP:** 5
**SALES (est):** 643.9K **Privately Held**
**WEB:** www.mosaicostile.com
**SIC: 3253** Ceramic wall & floor tile

**(G-5812)**
**MOTAMED MEDICAL PUBLISHING CO**
7141 N Kedzie Ave # 1504 (60645-2847)
PHONE..............................773 761-6667
Dr Hosein A Motamed, *President*
**EMP:** 3
**SALES (est):** 206.9K **Privately Held**
**SIC: 2731** Textbooks: publishing only, not printed on site

**(G-5813)**
**MOTOR ROW DEVELOPMENT CORP**
2303 S Mich Ave Ste Assoc (60616)
PHONE..............................773 525-3311
Fax: 773 665-7914
Paul Zucker, *President*
**EMP:** 1
**SALES (est):** 281.1K **Privately Held**
**SIC: 3714** Motor vehicle parts & accessories

**(G-5814)**
**MOTORMAKERS DE KALB CREDIT UN**
Also Called: GE Motors
3726 N Wayne Ave (60613-3723)
PHONE..............................815 756-6381
Gerald Miller, *Vice Ch Bd*
Walter Kaster, *President*
Marion H Giesecke, *Treasurer*
Floyd Schroeder, *Technology*
Reg Lemoine, *Executive*
**EMP:** 5

**SQ FT:** 450
**SALES (est):** 500K **Privately Held**
**SIC: 6062** 3621 State credit unions, not federally chartered; motors & generators

**(G-5815)**
**MOTOROLA MOBILITY HOLDINGS LLC (HQ)**
222 Merchandise Mart Plz # 1600 (60654-1103)
PHONE..............................847 523-5000
Dennis Woodside, *CEO*
Rick Osterloh, *President*
Daniel M Moloney, *President*
Harvey Zou, *Managing Dir*
Charlie Gross, *Business Mgr*
▲ **EMP:** 8
**SALES:** 3.5B
**SALES (corp-wide):** 38.7B **Privately Held**
**SIC: 3663** Radio & TV communications equipment; mobile communication equipment
PA: Lenovo Group Limited
23/F Taikoo Place Lincoln Hse
Quarry Bay HK
251 638-38

**(G-5816)**
**MOTOROLA MOBILITY LLC**
222 Merchandise Mart Plz (60654-1103)
PHONE..............................847 523-5000
**EMP:** 4
**SALES (corp-wide):** 38.7B **Privately Held**
**SIC: 3669** Intercommunication systems, electric
HQ: Motorola Mobility Llc
222 Merchandise Mart Plz
Chicago IL 60654

**(G-5817)**
**MOTOROLA MOBILITY LLC (DH)**
222 Merchandise Mart Plz (60654-1103)
P.O. Box 391597, Mountain View CA (94039-1597)
PHONE..............................800 668-6765
Fax: 847 523-6441
Rick Osterloh, *President*
Aymar De Lencquesaing, *President*
Sanjay Jha, *President*
Iqbal Arshad, *Senior VP*
Kouji Kodera, *Senior VP*
▲ **EMP:** 346
**SALES (est):** 761.1MM
**SALES (corp-wide):** 38.7B **Privately Held**
**SIC: 3663** 4812 Mobile communication equipment; cellular telephone services

**(G-5818)**
**MOTOROLA SOLUTIONS INC (PA)**
500 W Monroe St Ste 4400 (60661-3781)
PHONE..............................847 576-5000
Fax: 847 538-2250
Gregory Q Brown, *Ch of Bd*
Mark S Hacker, *Exec VP*
John P Molloy, *Exec VP*
John K Wozniak, *Vice Pres*
Gino A Bonanotte, *CFO*
**EMP:** 225 **EST:** 1928
**SALES:** 6B **Publicly Held**
**WEB:** www.motorola.com
**SIC: 3663** 3661 Radio & TV communications equipment; mobile communication equipment; pagers (one-way); cellular radio telephone; modems; multiplex equipment, telephone & telegraph

**(G-5819)**
**MOXIE APPAREL LLC**
222 S Morgan St Ste 3c (60607-3728)
PHONE..............................312 243-9040
**EMP:** 3
**SALES (corp-wide):** 1.6MM **Privately Held**
**SIC: 2329** Mfg Men's/Boy's Clothing
PA: Moxie Apparel Llc
145 E 27th St Apt 11g
New York NY 10016
212 779-0195

**(G-5820)**
**MP STEEL CHICAGO LLC**
5757 W Ogden Ave Ste 4 (60804-3881)
PHONE..............................773 242-0853
Jack Desai, *General Mgr*
Jim Perkne, *Manager*

**EMP:** 50
**SALES (est):** 5.6MM **Privately Held**
**SIC: 3398** Metal heat treating

**(G-5821)**
**MPC CONTAINMENT INTL LLC**
4834 S Oakley Ave (60609-4036)
PHONE..............................773 927-4120
John Belknap, *General Mgr*
Morgan Widder, *Project Mgr*
Ben Beiler,
▲ **EMP:** 99
**SALES (est):** 6.2MM **Privately Held**
**SIC: 3999** Manufacturing industries

**(G-5822)**
**MPC CONTAINMENT SYSTEMS LLC (HQ)**
4834 S Oakley Ave (60609-4036)
PHONE..............................773 927-4121
Benjamin Beiler, *Mng Member*
Edward Reicin, *Bd of Directors*
Alan Berman,
Edward E Reicin,
**EMP:** 65
**SQ FT:** 52,000
**SALES (est):** 21.8MM
**SALES (corp-wide):** 34.2MM **Privately Held**
**SIC: 2394** Canvas & related products
PA: Mpc Group Llc
4834 S Oakley Ave
Chicago IL 60609
773 927-4120

**(G-5823)**
**MPC CONTAINMENT SYSTEMS LLC**
4834 S Oakley Ave (60609-4036)
PHONE..............................773 734-1000
Julio Oceuguera, *Branch Mgr*
**EMP:** 35
**SALES (corp-wide):** 34.2MM **Privately Held**
**SIC: 2394** Canvas & related products
HQ: Mpc Containment Systems Llc
4834 S Oakley Ave
Chicago IL 60609
773 927-4121

**(G-5824)**
**MPC GROUP LLC (PA)**
4834 S Oakley Ave (60609-4036)
PHONE..............................773 927-4120
Benjamin Beiler, *CEO*
Alan Berman,
Edward Reicin,
**EMP:** 2
**SALES (est):** 34.2MM **Privately Held**
**WEB:** www.mpcgroup.net
**SIC: 2394** 3089 Canvas & related products; plastic processing

**(G-5825)**
**MRC POLYMERS INC (PA)**
3307 S Lawndale Ave (60623-5007)
PHONE..............................773 890-9000
Fax: 773 890-9007
Paul Binks, *President*
Brett Miller, *General Mgr*
Sergio Cabrales, *Plant Mgr*
Buddy Self, *Opers Mgr*
Jayme Dood, *Purch Dir*
▲ **EMP:** 100
**SQ FT:** 75,000
**SALES (est):** 19MM **Privately Held**
**WEB:** www.mrcpolymers.com
**SIC: 2821** Polycarbonate resins; polypropylene resins; polyesters

**(G-5826)**
**MSI GREEN INC**
1958 W Grand Ave (60622-6232)
PHONE..............................312 421-6550
Irene Weiss, *President*
Marc Weiss, *Vice Pres*
**EMP:** 4 **EST:** 2012
**SALES (est):** 563.6K **Privately Held**
**SIC: 2023** 2033 2064 Dry, condensed, evaporated dairy products; fruits & fruit products in cans, jars, etc.; candy & other confectionery products

**(G-5827)**
**MT GREENWOOD EMBROIDERY**
3136 W 111th St (60655-2206)
PHONE..............................773 779-5798
Fax: 773 779-4760
Sam Costas, *President*
**EMP:** 1
**SQ FT:** 2,400
**SALES (est):** 200K **Privately Held**
**SIC: 7336** 2395 Silk screen design; embroidery & art needlework

**(G-5828)**
**MU DAI LLC**
35 E Wacker Dr Fl 14 (60601-2314)
PHONE..............................312 982-0040
Shanon Marks, *CEO*
Patrick J Bickett, *COO*
Deborah Davis, *Accounts Mgr*
Steven Spieczny, *Officer*
Russ Burns,
**EMP:** 14
**SQ FT:** 10,000
**SALES:** 1.5MM **Privately Held**
**SIC: 7372** 7336 7373 7371 Prepackaged software; commercial art & graphic design; art design services; computer integrated systems design; custom computer programming services

**(G-5829)**
**MULLEN FOODS LLC**
6740 N Edgebrook Ter (60646-2703)
PHONE..............................773 716-9001
James Mullen,
**EMP:** 6
**SALES (est):** 424.2K **Privately Held**
**SIC: 2033** Canned fruits & specialties

**(G-5830)**
**MULLER QUAKER DAIRY LLC**
555 W Monroe St Fl 7 (60661-3706)
P.O. Box 049003 (60604)
PHONE..............................312 821-1000
Stefan Muller,
Ted Herrod,
Hainer Kamps,
Natalie Reed,
Manfred Weiss,
▲ **EMP:** 201 **EST:** 2010
**SALES (est):** 670.8K
**SALES (corp-wide):** 13.5B **Privately Held**
**SIC: 2023** Yogurt mix
PA: Dairy Farmers Of America, Inc.
1405 N 98th St
Kansas City KS 66111
816 801-6455

**(G-5831)**
**MULTI ART PRESS**
7560 N Milwaukee Ave (60631-4444)
PHONE..............................773 775-0515
Fax: 847 647-7305
Sam Kuraishi, *President*
Sal Falhan, *Vice Pres*
Alham Kuraishi, *Vice Pres*
**EMP:** 4
**SQ FT:** 2,600
**SALES (est):** 220K **Privately Held**
**SIC: 2752** 7334 2789 2759 Commercial printing, offset; photocopying & duplicating services; bookbinding & related work; commercial printing

**(G-5832)**
**MULTI PACKAGING SOLUTIONS INC**
Also Called: Chicago Paper Tub & Can
4221 N Normandy Ave (60634-1402)
PHONE..............................773 283-9500
Marc Shore, *CEO*
**EMP:** 5
**SALES (corp-wide):** 14.1B **Publicly Held**
**SIC: 2759** 2731 2761 3089 Commercial printing; screen printing; letterpress printing; tags: printing; books: publishing & printing; continuous forms, office & business; identification cards, plastic; arts & crafts equipment & supplies; packaging paper & plastics film, coated & laminated
HQ: Multi Packaging Solutions, Inc.
150 E 52nd St Ste 2800
New York NY 10022
646 885-0005

## GEOGRAPHIC SECTION

**Chicago - Cook County (G-5858)**

**(G-5833)**
**MUNOZ FLOUR TORTILLERIA INC**
1707 W 47th St (60609-3823)
**PHONE**..................773 523-1837
**Fax:** 773 843-8348
Oscar Munoz, *President*
Mario Garza, *Manager*
**EMP:** 10
**SALES (est)** 679.6K **Privately Held**
**SIC: 2099** Tortillas, fresh or refrigerated

**(G-5834)**
**MURFF ENTERPRISES LLC**
9331 S Clyde Ave (60617-3745)
**PHONE**..................203 685-5556
Daniel Murff,
**EMP:** 4
**SALES (est)** 125.1K **Privately Held**
**SIC: 3999** Manufacturing industries

**(G-5835)**
**MURO PALLETS CORP**
5208 S Mozart St (60632-2248)
**PHONE**..................773 640-8606
Javier Muro, *Principal*
**EMP:** 3
**SALES (est)** 153.9K **Privately Held**
**SIC: 2448** Pallets, wood & wood with metal

**(G-5836)**
**MURPHY BROTHERS ENTERPRISES**
Also Called: Andee Boiler & Welding Co
7649 S State St (60619-2316)
**PHONE**..................773 874-9020
**Fax:** 773 874-1136
Jeffrey Murphy, *President*
Timothy R Murphy, *Vice Pres*
William J Murphy, *Admin Sec*
**EMP:** 15
**SQ FT:** 8,000
**SALES (est)** 1.4MM **Privately Held**
**SIC: 7699** 7692 Boiler repair shop; welding repair

**(G-5837)**
**MURRIHY PALLET CO**
1919 W 74th St (60636-3747)
P.O. Box 9054 (60609-0054)
**PHONE**..................615 370-7000
**Fax:** 773 471-4200
John Murrihy Sr, *President*
John Murrihy Jr, *Vice Pres*
**EMP:** 20
**SALES (est)** 3.2MM **Privately Held**
**WEB:** www.murrihypallet.com
**SIC: 2448** 7699 Pallets, wood; skids, wood; pallet repair

**(G-5838)**
**MWW FOOD PROCESSING USA LLC**
Also Called: Thurne USA
4300 W Bryn Mawr Ave (60646-5943)
**PHONE**..................800 582-1574
Selim A Bassoul, *President*
Selim Bassoul, *President*
Stephen Numm, *General Mgr*
Bob Hillman, *Controller*
**EMP:** 5 **EST:** 2015
**SALES (est):** 586.6K
**SALES (corp-wide):** 2.2B **Publicly Held**
**SIC: 3556** Food products machinery; cutting, chopping, grinding, mixing & similar machinery; grinders, commercial, food; mixers, commercial, food
**PA:** The Middleby Corporation
 1400 Toastmaster Dr
 Elgin IL 60120
 847 741-3300

**(G-5839)**
**MY EYE DOCTOR (PA)**
29 E Madison St Ste 808 (60602-3298)
**PHONE**..................312 782-4208
**Fax:** 312 782-4635
Ralph Keno, *President*
Blanche Keno, *Admin Sec*
▲ **EMP:** 6
**SQ FT:** 750
**SALES (est)** 1MM **Privately Held**
**SIC: 3851** 5995 Lenses, ophthalmic; contact lenses, prescription

**(G-5840)**
**MY LOCAL BEACON LLC**
73 W Monroe St Ste 323 (60603-4910)
**PHONE**..................888 482-6691
Shijo Mathew, *Vice Pres*
**EMP:** 5
**SALES (est)** 270K **Privately Held**
**SIC: 7372** Prepackaged software

**(G-5841)**
**MY OWN MEALS INC**
Also Called: J&M Food Products Company
5410 W Roosevelt Rd # 301 (60644-1490)
**PHONE**..................773 378-6505
**Fax:** 773 378-6416
Mary Anne Jackson, *President*
Maria Duarte, *Branch Mgr*
**EMP:** 5
**SALES (corp-wide):** 15.2MM **Privately Held**
**WEB:** www.myownmeals.com
**SIC: 2099** Food preparations
**PA:** My Own Meals, Inc.
 400 Lake Cook Rd Ste 107
 Deerfield IL 60015
 847 948-1118

**(G-5842)**
**MY-SIGNGUYCOM INC**
5570 N Lynch Ave (60630-1453)
**PHONE**..................888 223-9703
Dmitry Kuzmenko, *President*
**EMP:** 3
**SALES (est)** 284.8K **Privately Held**
**SIC: 3993** Signs & advertising specialties

**(G-5843)**
**MYBREAD LLC**
Also Called: Gluten Free Bakery
2000 W Fulton St (60612-2364)
**PHONE**..................312 600-9633
Daniel Gallagher, *President*
**EMP:** 4
**SALES (est)** 231K **Privately Held**
**SIC: 5461** 2052 2051 Bread; bakery products, dry; bread, cake & related products

**(G-5844)**
**MYERSON LLC (PA)**
Also Called: Pinnacle
5106 N Ravenswood Ave (60640-2713)
**PHONE**..................312 432-8200
**Fax:** 312 563-9535
Jim Swartout, *COO*
Joe Heery, *CFO*
Janine Pierre, *Human Res Mgr*
Phil Gorski, *Sales Mgr*
Melissa Salem, *Manager*
**EMP:** 2
**SALES (est)** 527.2K **Privately Held**
**WEB:** www.myersontooth.com
**SIC: 3843** Teeth, artificial (not made in dental laboratories)

**(G-5845)**
**MYHOMEEQ LLC**
1741 N Western Ave (60647-6513)
**PHONE**..................773 328-7034
John Blaser, *Manager*
Robert Weissbourd,
**EMP:** 3
**SALES (est)** 113K **Privately Held**
**SIC: 7372** Prepackaged software

**(G-5846)**
**N E S TRAFFIC SAFETY**
8770 W Bryn Mawr Ave (60631-3515)
**PHONE**..................312 603-7444
Garry Culver, *Principal*
**EMP:** 10
**SALES (est)** 1MM **Privately Held**
**SIC: 3669** Traffic signals, electric

**(G-5847)**
**NABLUS SWEETS INC**
4800 N Kedzie Ave (60625)
**PHONE**..................708 205-6534
**EMP:** 30
**SALES (corp-wide):** 1.7MM **Privately Held**
**SIC: 2061** 5461 Mfg Raw Cane Sugar Retail Bakery
**PA:** Nablus Sweets Inc.
 8320 S Harlem Ave
 Bridgeview IL 60455
 708 529-3911

**(G-5848)**
**NACME STEEL PROCESSING LLC**
Also Called: National Processing Co-Plant 1
429 W 127th St (60628-7109)
**PHONE**..................773 468-3309
**Fax:** 773 468-2868
John Dubrock, *General Mgr*
Jim J Parker, *Manager*
Bill Shukitis, *Manager*
**EMP:** 60
**SALES (est)** 13.3MM **Privately Held**
**SIC: 3312** Blast furnaces & steel mills

**(G-5849)**
**NADIG NEWSPAPERS INC**
Also Called: Northwest Side Press
4937 N Milwaukee Ave (60630-2114)
**PHONE**..................773 286-6100
Glenn Nadig, *President*
Randy Erickson, *Advt Staff*
**EMP:** 16
**SQ FT:** 5,500
**SALES (est)** 1.1MM **Privately Held**
**WEB:** www.nadignewspapers.com
**SIC: 2711** Newspapers, publishing & printing

**(G-5850)**
**NAK WON KOREAN BAKERY**
3746 W Lawrence Ave (60625-5726)
**PHONE**..................773 588-8769
To Mon Cha, *Owner*
**EMP:** 3
**SALES (est)** 126.3K **Privately Held**
**SIC: 2051** 5963 Cakes, bakery: except frozen; direct selling establishments

**(G-5851)**
**NAMASTE LABORATORIES LLC (HQ)**
310 S Racine Ave Fl 8 (60607-2841)
**PHONE**..................708 824-1393
**Fax:** 708 388-4656
Clarisa Wilson, *CEO*
Clyde Burks, *COO*
Jaspreet Singh, *Controller*
Linga Kanugula, *Finance*
Vikram Bali, *Sales Dir*
◆ **EMP:** 80
**SQ FT:** 100,000
**SALES (est):** 88.2MM
**SALES (corp-wide):** 846MM **Privately Held**
**SIC: 2844** Hair preparations, including shampoos
**PA:** Dabur India Limited
 Dabur Corporate Office,
 Ghaziabad UP 20101
 120 418-2100

**(G-5852)**
**NANOFAST INC**
416 N Erie St (60654-5771)
**PHONE**..................312 943-4223
**Fax:** 312 337-7718
Carl Vespa, *President*
S Nakagi, *Treasurer*
J Ireland, *Admin Sec*
**EMP:** 25 **EST:** 1963
**SQ FT:** 60,000
**SALES (est)** 2.9MM **Privately Held**
**SIC: 3825** Digital test equipment, electronic & electrical circuits; analog-digital converters, electronic instrumentation type

**(G-5853)**
**NARDA INC**
Also Called: North Amercn Ret Dealers Assn
222 S Riverside Plz (60606-5808)
**PHONE**..................312 648-2300
Tom Drake, *Exec Dir*
Deal - Robert Goldberg, *General Counsel*
**EMP:** 11
**SQ FT:** 6,500
**SALES (est)** 149.9K **Privately Held**
**WEB:** www.narda.com
**SIC: 8611** 2721 5961 Merchants' association; trade journals: publishing & printing; catalog & mail-order houses

**(G-5854)**
**NARRATIVE HEALTH NETWORK INC**
1201 S Prrie Ave Apt 4103 (60605)
**PHONE**..................312 600-9154
Paul Abraham, *CEO*
Lakshmi Halasyamani, *Sr Exec VP*
Stefan Abraham, *Treasurer*
Tarun Abraham, *Admin Sec*
**EMP:** 7 **EST:** 2015
**SALES (est)** 275.6K **Privately Held**
**SIC: 7372** Application computer software

**(G-5855)**
**NAS MEDIA GROUP INC**
6324 S Kimbark Ave # 400 (60637-3967)
**PHONE**..................773 824-0242
Michael Gardner, *CEO*
**EMP:** 13
**SALES (corp-wide):** 1.3MM **Privately Held**
**SIC: 2741** 8748 Business service newsletters: publishing & printing; business consulting
**PA:** Nas Media Group Inc
 424 Brookwood Ter 2
 Olympia Fields IL 60461
 312 371-7499

**(G-5856)**
**NATAZ SPECIALTY COATINGS INC**
3300 W 31st St (60623-5016)
**PHONE**..................773 247-7030
John J Francis, *President*
Michael K Francis, *Vice Pres*
Nia Gardner, *Manager*
▼ **EMP:** 12 **EST:** 1927
**SQ FT:** 25,000
**SALES (est)** 1.5MM **Privately Held**
**WEB:** www.pureasphalt.com
**SIC: 2952** 2899 2891 2851 Asphalt felts & coatings; chemical preparations; adhesives & sealants; paints & allied products; soap & other detergents

**(G-5857)**
**NATIONAL ASSOCIATION REALTORS (PA)**
Also Called: REALTOR MAGAZINE
430 N Michigan Ave Lowr 2 (60611-4088)
**PHONE**..................800 874-6500
**Fax:** 312 329-8873
Dale Stinton, *CEO*
Steve Brown, *President*
Maurice Veissi, *President*
John Pierpoint, *Principal*
Terrence M McDermott, *Exec VP*
**EMP:** 250
**SQ FT:** 180,000
**SALES:** 214.1MM **Privately Held**
**WEB:** www.realtor.org
**SIC: 8611** 2721 8299 Trade associations; periodicals: publishing & printing; educational service, nondegree granting: continuing educ.

**(G-5858)**
**NATIONAL ASSOCIATION REALTORS**
430 N Michigan Ave Lowr 2 (60611-4088)
P.O. Box 92497 (60675-2497)
**PHONE**..................800 874-6500
Robert Goldberg, *Vice Pres*
Douglas Hinderer, *Vice Pres*
John Pierpoint, *VP Finance*
Dale Stinton, *Manager*
Marian Leon, *Manager*
**EMP:** 250
**SALES (corp-wide):** 214.1MM **Privately Held**
**WEB:** www.realtor.org
**SIC: 8611** 2721 8299 Trade associations; periodicals: publishing & printing; educational service, nondegree granting: continuing educ.
**PA:** National Association Of Realtors
 430 N Michigan Ave Lowr 2
 Chicago IL 60611
 800 874-6500

# Chicago - Cook County (G-5859)

**GEOGRAPHIC SECTION**

**(G-5859)**
**NATIONAL BEEF PACKING CO LLC**
Also Called: National Beef Packing Intl
30 N Michigan Ave # 1702 (60602-3643)
PHONE..............................312 332-6166
Mark Domanski, *President*
EMP: 3
SALES (corp-wide): 10.8B **Publicly Held**
WEB: www.nationalbeef.com
SIC: 2011 Meat packing plants
HQ: National Beef Packing Company, L.L.C.
  12200 N Ambassador Dr # 101
  Kansas City MO 64163
  800 449-2333

**(G-5860)**
**NATIONAL BISCUIT COMPANY**
7300 S Kedzie Ave (60629-3595)
PHONE..............................773 925-0654
Dave Lamy, *Principal*
EMP: 4
SALES (est): 258.4K **Privately Held**
SIC: 2051 Cakes, bakery: except frozen

**(G-5861)**
**NATIONAL CASEIN COMPANY (PA)**
601 W 80th St (60620-2502)
PHONE..............................773 846-7300
Fax: 773 487-5709
Hope T Cook, *President*
Ervin Kitzmiller, *General Mgr*
Charles Cook, *Vice Pres*
Nigel Martin, *VP Mfg*
David Lowery, *Plant Mgr*
▲ EMP: 30 EST: 1921
SQ FT: 50,000
SALES (est): 10.5MM **Privately Held**
SIC: 2891 Glue; adhesives

**(G-5862)**
**NATIONAL CASEIN NEW JERSEY INC (PA)**
601 W 80th St (60620-2502)
PHONE..............................773 846-7300
Charles L Cook, *President*
Hope T Cook, *Vice Pres*
Roger Quackenbush, *Manager*
Daniel Ferrarrio, *Admin Sec*
▲ EMP: 5 EST: 1951
SQ FT: 50,000
SALES (est): 2.6MM **Privately Held**
SIC: 2891 Adhesives

**(G-5863)**
**NATIONAL CASEIN OF CALIFORNIA (PA)**
601 W 80th St (60620-2502)
PHONE..............................773 846-7300
Richard A Cook, *President*
Charles L Cook, *Vice Pres*
David Lowery, *Plant Mgr*
Tom Schillaci, *Plant Mgr*
Norman Evans, *Treasurer*
▼ EMP: 55
SQ FT: 75,000
SALES: 6MM **Privately Held**
SIC: 2891 2821 Glue; plastics materials & resins

**(G-5864)**
**NATIONAL MATERIAL LP**
Also Called: Cox Metal Processing
12100 S Stony Island Ave (60633-2430)
PHONE..............................773 646-6300
Fax: 773 646-0973
Quentin Morlier, *Sales Engr*
Eddie Mendoza, *Manager*
EMP: 28
SALES (corp-wide): 649.5MM **Privately Held**
WEB: www.nmlp.com
SIC: 3312 Sheet or strip, steel, hot-rolled
PA: National Material L.P.
  1965 Pratt Blvd
  Elk Grove Village IL 60007
  847 806-7200

**(G-5865)**
**NATIONAL MICRO SYSTEMS INC**
2 E 8th St Ste 100 (60605-2122)
PHONE..............................312 566-0414
Terry R Peters, *President*
Bernard Linzmeier, *Vice Pres*
Richard Peters, *Treasurer*
Barbara Peters, *Admin Sec*
EMP: 5
SALES (est): 75K **Privately Held**
SIC: 3571 7378 3823 Electronic computers; computer maintenance & repair; industrial instrmnts msrmnt display/control process variable

**(G-5866)**
**NATIONAL PORGES RADIATOR CORP**
320 W 83rd St (60620-1704)
PHONE..............................773 224-3000
Fax: 773 224-3020
James Porges, *President*
EMP: 18
SQ FT: 23,000
SALES (est): 3.3MM **Privately Held**
WEB: www.radiatorcores.com
SIC: 3714 Radiators & radiator shells & cores, motor vehicle

**(G-5867)**
**NATIONAL POWER CORP**
4330 W Belmont Ave (60641-4524)
PHONE..............................773 685-2662
Ira Alport, *President*
Thomas Vrablik, *President*
Joel Alport, *Vice Pres*
Juan Manzo, *Opers Mgr*
Zaira Estrada, *Buyer*
▲ EMP: 50
SQ FT: 23,000
SALES (est): 14.5MM **Privately Held**
SIC: 3691 Batteries, rechargeable

**(G-5868)**
**NATIONAL RUBBER STAMP CO INC**
5320 N Lowell Ave Apt 311 (60630-1780)
PHONE..............................773 281-6522
Fax: 773 281-6953
Donna Heintz, *President*
Wayne Heintz, *Vice Pres*
EMP: 2 EST: 1933
SQ FT: 3,000
SALES: 280K **Privately Held**
SIC: 3953 3479 7389 Marking devices; cancelling stamps, hand: rubber or metal; date stamps, hand: rubber or metal; name plates: engraved, etched, etc.; engraving service

**(G-5869)**
**NATIONWIDE FOODS INC**
Also Called: Brookfield Farms
700 E 107th St (60628-3806)
PHONE..............................773 787-4900
Fax: 773 264-1270
Frank Swan, *Ch of Bd*
Dennis Gleason, *President*
Tom Fitzgibbons, *Human Res Dir*
Patrick Keable, *MIS Mgr*
David Peterson, *Executive*
EMP: 500 EST: 1969
SQ FT: 115,000
SALES: 125MM **Privately Held**
WEB: www.brookfieldfarm.org
SIC: 2013 5142 5147 Corned beef from purchased meat; meat, frozen: packaged; meats, fresh

**(G-5870)**
**NATURES AMERICAN CO**
3105 N Ashland Ave (60657-3013)
PHONE..............................630 246-4274
Kevin Hannan, *CEO*
Tyler Page, *Finance Dir*
Jay Sebben, *Admin Sec*
EMP: 8
SALES: 700K **Privately Held**
WEB: www.natureshand.com
SIC: 2041 Grain cereals, cracked

**(G-5871)**
**NATURES HEALING REMEDIES INC**
7742 W Addison St (60634-3018)
PHONE..............................773 589-9996
Leon Kolodziej, *President*
June Demma, *Manager*
EMP: 12
SALES (est): 1.4MM **Privately Held**
WEB: www.natureshealingremedies.com
SIC: 2833 Drugs & herbs: grading, grinding & milling

**(G-5872)**
**NAUTIC GLOBAL GROUP LLC**
333 W Wacker Dr Ste 600 (60606-1284)
PHONE..............................574 457-5731
Ernie Shimall, *Info Tech Dir*
Mitch Carr, *Director*
Steven L Smilay,
▼ EMP: 4
SALES (est): 838.8K **Privately Held**
SIC: 3732 Boat building & repairing

**(G-5873)**
**NAVIGON INC**
200 W Madison St Ste 650 (60606-3412)
PHONE..............................312 268-1500
Johannes Angenvoort, *President*
Michael Roach, *President*
Andreas Hecht, *Senior VP*
Iris Korzilius, *Project Mgr*
Sonja Brennecke, *Human Resources*
▲ EMP: 65
SALES (est): 7.2MM **Privately Held**
WEB: www.navigon.com
SIC: 3812 Search & navigation equipment

**(G-5874)**
**NAVILLUS WOODWORKS LLC**
2100 N Major Ave (60639-2901)
PHONE..............................312 375-2680
Daniel F Sullivan, *Mng Member*
EMP: 6
SALES: 1MM **Privately Held**
SIC: 2431 3549 Millwork; cutting & slitting machinery

**(G-5875)**
**NAYLOR AUTOMOTIVE ENGRG CO INC**
4645 S Knox Ave (60632-4805)
PHONE..............................773 582-6900
Fax: 773 582-6985
Paul Januska, *President*
Kimberly Natalino, *Sales Mgr*
Nancy Huemmer, *Manager*
EMP: 18 EST: 1950
SQ FT: 17,000
SALES (est): 3MM **Privately Held**
SIC: 7539 3714 3568 Automotive repair shops; motor vehicle parts & accessories; power transmission equipment

**(G-5876)**
**NAYLOR PIPE COMPANY (PA)**
1230 E 92nd St (60619-7997)
PHONE..............................773 721-9400
Fax: 773 721-9494
William B Skeates, *Ch of Bd*
John J Czulno, *President*
Michael T O'Rourke, *Exec VP*
Russell A Blais, *Vice Pres*
Kevin Joyce, *Vice Pres*
EMP: 180 EST: 1925
SQ FT: 150,000
SALES (est): 26.8MM **Privately Held**
WEB: www.naylorpipe.com
SIC: 3317 Pipes, seamless steel; tubes, seamless steel

**(G-5877)**
**NDUJA ARTISANS CO**
2817 N Harlem Ave (60707-1638)
PHONE..............................312 550-6991
Agostino Fiasche, *President*
Tony Fiasche, *President*
EMP: 2
SALES: 500K **Privately Held**
SIC: 2015 Poultry sausage, luncheon meats & other poultry products

**(G-5878)**
**NEA AGORA PACKING CO**
1056 W Taylor St (60607-4223)
PHONE..............................312 421-5130
Rose Musollami, *Owner*
EMP: 3
SQ FT: 2,500
SALES (est): 342.3K **Privately Held**
SIC: 5147 5421 2013 2011 Meats, fresh; meat markets, including freezer provisioners; sausages & other prepared meats; meat packing plants

**(G-5879)**
**NEAL-SCHUMAN PUBLISHERS INC**
50 E Huron St (60611-2729)
PHONE..............................312 944-6780
Patricia G Schuman, *President*
EMP: 10
SQ FT: 2,600
SALES (est): 680K **Privately Held**
WEB: www.neal-schuman.com
SIC: 2731 Books: publishing only

**(G-5880)**
**NEFAB INC**
3105 N Ashland Ave 394 (60657-3013)
PHONE..............................705 748-4888
Eric Howe, *President*
Atul Swarup, *Controller*
▲ EMP: 7
SQ FT: 1,000
SALES (est): 1.5MM
SALES (corp-wide): 380.8MM **Privately Held**
SIC: 2631 Container, packaging & boxboard
HQ: Nefab Ab
  Slottsgatan 14
  Jonkoping 553 2
  771 590-000

**(G-5881)**
**NEGS & LITHO INC**
Also Called: Business Express R & A Prtg
6501 N Avondale Ave (60631-1521)
PHONE..............................847 647-7770
Fax: 847 355-5766
Arthur Milbrandt, *President*
Allen Milbrandt, *Vice Pres*
Aida Rodriguez, *Office Mgr*
EMP: 4
SQ FT: 3,500
SALES: 300K **Privately Held**
SIC: 2752 7331 7374 7338 Commercial printing, offset; mailing service; data processing service; word processing service; typesetting

**(G-5882)**
**NEIMAN BROS CO INC**
Also Called: Neiman Brothers Co
3322 W Newport Ave (60618-5595)
PHONE..............................773 463-3000
Fax: 773 463-3181
Laura Neiman, *President*
Joe Ruzakovich, *Warehouse Mgr*
Patrick Cass, *Executive*
Phyllis Neiman, *Admin Sec*
▲ EMP: 26 EST: 1920
SQ FT: 35,000
SALES (est): 14.3MM **Privately Held**
WEB: www.neimanbrothers.com
SIC: 5149 2099 2087 Flour; honey; baking supplies; food preparations; flavoring extracts & syrups

**(G-5883)**
**NELSON & LAVOLD MANUFACTURING**
1530 N Halsted St 34 (60642-2528)
PHONE..............................312 943-6300
Fax: 312 664-0879
Thor Sveinsvoll, *President*
EMP: 6 EST: 1946
SQ FT: 9,700
SALES (est): 831.7K **Privately Held**
SIC: 3451 Screw machine products

**(G-5884)**
**NELSON - HARKINS INDS INC**
5301 N Kedzie Ave (60625-4799)
PHONE..............................773 478-6243
Fax: 773 478-8227
Thomas Harkins, *President*
Donald P Harkins Jr, *Vice Pres*
Randal P Harkins, *Treasurer*
EMP: 27
SQ FT: 21,000
SALES (est): 3.9MM **Privately Held**
SIC: 3993 3953 3446 3365 Signs, not made in custom sign painting shops; letters for signs, metal; marking devices; architectural metalwork; aluminum foundries; wood partitions & fixtures

# GEOGRAPHIC SECTION
## Chicago - Cook County (G-5914)

**(G-5885)**
**NEON ART**
4752 N Avers Ave (60625-6201)
PHONE...................773 588-5883
Hochul Shin, *Owner*
**EMP:** 3
**SALES (est):** 140K **Privately Held**
**SIC:** 3993 Electric signs; neon signs

**(G-5886)**
**NEON DESIGN INC**
3722 N Ashland Ave (60613-3602)
PHONE...................773 880-5020
Fax: 773 880-5107
Peter Schwaba, *President*
Joan Schwaba, *Admin Sec*
**EMP:** 3
**SQ FT:** 2,500
**SALES:** 375K **Privately Held**
**WEB:** www.neondesign.com
**SIC:** 5046 3993 Neon signs; signs & advertising specialties

**(G-5887)**
**NEON EXPRESS SIGNS**
5026 N Broadway St (60640-3006)
PHONE...................773 463-7335
**EMP:** 4
**SALES (est):** 334.4K **Privately Held**
**SIC:** 3993 Mfg Signs/Advertising Specialties

**(G-5888)**
**NEON SHOP INC**
2247 N Western Ave (60647-3142)
PHONE...................773 227-0303
Fax: 773 227-3334
Tom Brickler, *President*
**EMP:** 4
**SQ FT:** 1,000
**SALES (est):** 433.8K **Privately Held**
**SIC:** 3993 Neon signs

**(G-5889)**
**NEUROTHERAPEUTICS PHARMA INC**
8750 W Bryn Mawr Ave # 440 (60631-3545)
PHONE...................773 444-4180
Fax: 773 444-4188
Stephen D Collins, *President*
Brian Williams, *Vice Pres*
**EMP:** 7
**SALES (est):** 700K **Privately Held**
**SIC:** 2834 Pharmaceutical preparations

**(G-5890)**
**NEW C F & I INC**
Also Called: Rockey Mountain Steel Mills
200 E Randolph St # 7800 (60601-6436)
PHONE...................312 533-3555
William Swindels, *Chairman*
Rob Simon, *Vice Pres*
Jennifer Murray, *Vice Pres*
Steven Rowan, *Vice Pres*
David Cranston, *VP Opers*
▲ **EMP:** 750
**SQ FT:** 10,000
**SALES (est):** 66.9MM
**SALES (corp-wide):** 7.7B **Privately Held**
**SIC:** 3312 Blast furnaces & steel mills
**HQ:** Evraz Inc. Na
  200 E Randolph St # 7800
  Chicago IL 60601
  312 533-3621

**(G-5891)**
**NEW CITY COMMUNICATIONS**
Also Called: New City News
770 N Halsted St Ste 183 (60642-7889)
PHONE...................312 243-8786
Fax: 312 243-8802
Brian Hieggelke, *President*
Toni Nealie, *Editor*
Elliot Reichart, *Editor*
Ben Schulman, *Editor*
Don Vandermyer, *Business Mgr*
**EMP:** 29
**SQ FT:** 6,638
**SALES (est):** 3.5MM **Privately Held**
**WEB:** www.newcity.com
**SIC:** 2752 2791 2711 Newspapers, lithographed only; typesetting; newspapers

**(G-5892)**
**NEW PACKING COMPANY**
1249 W Lake St (60607-1519)
P.O. Box 7726 (60680-7726)
PHONE...................312 666-1314
Fax: 312 666-8698
Kurt Kreiger, *President*
John Gray, *General Mgr*
**EMP:** 15 **EST:** 1949
**SALES (est):** 1.9MM **Privately Held**
**SIC:** 2013 Sausages from purchased meat; bacon, side & sliced: from purchased meat; prepared pork products from purchased pork

**(G-5893)**
**NEW SBL INC**
1001 W 45th St Ste B (60609-3347)
PHONE...................773 376-8280
Yuk C Chan, *President*
Crystal Xu, *Accountant*
Yu HEI Tung, *Manager*
**EMP:** 34
**SQ FT:** 12,000
**SALES (est):** 5.7MM **Privately Held**
**SIC:** 2499 Food handling & processing products, wood

**(G-5894)**
**NEW SPECIALTY PRODUCTS INC**
Also Called: Barbeque Select
1421 W 47th St (60609-3233)
P.O. Box 9273 (60609-0273)
PHONE...................773 847-0230
Paul H Buehler, *President*
**EMP:** 23
**SALES (est):** 3.9MM **Privately Held**
**SIC:** 2035 2013 2015 Pickles, sauces & salad dressings; prepared beef products from purchased beef; prepared pork products from purchased pork; chicken, processed: fresh

**(G-5895)**
**NEW SPIN CYCLE**
1400 E 47th St Ste A (60653-4520)
PHONE...................773 952-7490
Kirk Bargle, *Owner*
**EMP:** 7 **EST:** 2012
**SALES (est):** 443.8K **Privately Held**
**SIC:** 3582 Commercial laundry equipment

**(G-5896)**
**NEW STAR CUSTOM LIGHTING CO**
4000 S Bell Ave (60609-2208)
PHONE...................773 254-7827
Fax: 773 254-6811
Ronald Stone, *President*
James Geier, *Principal*
Lloyd Vermeland, *Vice Pres*
Ricardo Lopez, *Plant Mgr*
John Persky, *Regl Sales Mgr*
▲ **EMP:** 25
**SQ FT:** 15,000
**SALES (est):** 6.1MM **Privately Held**
**SIC:** 3646 Commercial indusl & institutional electric lighting fixtures

**(G-5897)**
**NEW TASTE GOOD NOODLE INC**
2559 S Archer Ave (60608-5915)
PHONE...................312 842-8980
Fax: 312 842-8648
WEI Min Xu, *Admin Sec*
**EMP:** 5
**SALES (est):** 501.1K **Privately Held**
**SIC:** 2099 Noodles, uncooked: packaged with other ingredients

**(G-5898)**
**NEW WORLD TRNSP SYSTEMS**
5895 N Rogers Ave (60646-5953)
PHONE...................773 509-5931
Edward Marx Jr, *Principal*
**EMP:** 2
**SALES (est):** 263.8K **Privately Held**
**SIC:** 3799 Transportation equipment

**(G-5899)**
**NEWLY WEDS FOODS INC (PA)**
4140 W Fullerton Ave (60639-2198)
PHONE...................773 489-7000
Fax: 773 292-7636
Charles T Angell, *President*
Jack Conway, *General Mgr*
John Norton, *General Mgr*
Kent Bergene, *Senior VP*
John J Seely, *Senior VP*
◆ **EMP:** 600 **EST:** 1932
**SQ FT:** 375,000
**SALES (est):** 2MM **Privately Held**
**WEB:** www.newlywedsfoods.com
**SIC:** 2099 Bread crumbs, not made in bakeries; sugar powdered from purchased ingredients; seasonings & spices

**(G-5900)**
**NEWLY WEDS FOODS INC**
4849 N Milwaukee Ave # 700 (60630-2394)
PHONE...................773 628-6900
Brian Johnson, *Branch Mgr*
**EMP:** 67
**SALES (corp-wide):** 2MM **Privately Held**
**SIC:** 3691 Alkaline cell storage batteries
**PA:** Newly Weds Foods, Inc.
  4140 W Fullerton Ave
  Chicago IL 60639
  773 489-7000

**(G-5901)**
**NEWS & LETTERS**
59 E Van Buren St (60605-1230)
PHONE...................312 663-0839
Fax: 773 663-9069
Al Walchirk, *Principal*
**EMP:** 3
**SALES (est):** 120.9K **Privately Held**
**SIC:** 2711 Newspapers

**(G-5902)**
**NEWSPAPER NATIONAL NETWORK**
500 N Michigan Ave # 2210 (60611-3776)
PHONE...................312 644-1142
**EMP:** 4
**SALES (est):** 190.9K **Privately Held**
**SIC:** 2711 Newspapers-Publishing/Printing

**(G-5903)**
**NEWSPAPER SOLUTIONS INC**
4968 N Milwaukee Ave 1n (60630-2385)
PHONE...................773 930-3404
Daniel Harris, *Principal*
**EMP:** 9
**SALES (est):** 551.9K **Privately Held**
**SIC:** 2711 Newspapers

**(G-5904)**
**NEWSWEB CORPORATION (PA)**
1645 W Fullerton Ave (60614-1919)
PHONE...................773 975-5727
Fax: 773 975-6975
Fred J Eychaner, *President*
Charles Gross, *President*
Andy Sanchez, *Manager*
Jon Barry, *Admin Sec*
**EMP:** 46
**SALES (est):** 9.7MM **Privately Held**
**WEB:** www.newswebcorporation.com
**SIC:** 2752 Newspapers, lithographed only

**(G-5905)**
**NEWTEC WINDOW & DOOR INC**
3159 W 36th St (60632-2303)
PHONE...................773 869-9888
Fax: 773 869-0888
Zhengming Lei, *President*
Magda Bernat, *Manager*
Shanle Chen, *Admin Sec*
**EMP:** 25
**SALES (est):** 4.5MM **Privately Held**
**SIC:** 2521 Wood office furniture

**(G-5906)**
**NEXHAND INC**
2500 N Lakeview Ave (60614-1846)
PHONE...................619 820-2988
Micah Mackison, *CEO*
**EMP:** 3 **EST:** 2011
**SALES (est):** 215K **Privately Held**
**SIC:** 3841 Surgical & medical instruments

**(G-5907)**
**NEXTPOINT INC**
4043 N Ravenswood Ave (60613-1155)
PHONE...................773 929-4000
Rakesh Madhava, *CEO*
Tricia Boguslawski, *Vice Pres*
Dakota Dux, *Senior Engr*
Jodi Hrbek, *Bus Dvlpt Dir*
Lauren Chingo, *Finance Mgr*
**EMP:** 20
**SALES (est):** 2.3MM **Privately Held**
**SIC:** 7372 Application computer software

**(G-5908)**
**NFC COMPANY INC**
Also Called: NFC Suburban
2944 N Leavitt St (60618-8115)
PHONE...................773 472-6468
Fax: 773 472-2022
Norbert Francis, *President*
**EMP:** 5
**SQ FT:** 3,000
**SALES (est):** 1.1MM **Privately Held**
**SIC:** 5046 8742 2087 Restaurant equipment & supplies; soda fountain fixtures, except refrigerated; management consulting services; flavoring extracts & syrups

**(G-5909)**
**NGUYEN CHAU**
Also Called: Chicago Apparel Company
2311 W Howard St (60645-1503)
PHONE...................773 506-1066
Chau Nguyen, *Principal*
**EMP:** 5
**SALES (est):** 350K **Privately Held**
**SIC:** 2339 Sportswear, women's

**(G-5910)**
**NICKEL COMPOSITE COATINGS INC**
6454 W 74th St (60638-6009)
PHONE...................708 563-2780
Fax: 708 563-2788
Philip Fabiyi, *President*
Tristan Fabiyi, *Plant Mgr*
Norma Guerrero, *QC Mgr*
Valerie Hart, *Manager*
**EMP:** 20
**SALES (est):** 1.6MM **Privately Held**
**WEB:** www.ncccoat.com
**SIC:** 3479 Varnishing of metal products

**(G-5911)**
**NICKEL PUTTER**
1229 N North Branch St (60642-2473)
PHONE...................312 337-7888
**EMP:** 5
**SALES (est):** 22.4K **Privately Held**
**SIC:** 3356 Nickel

**(G-5912)**
**NICKELODEON MAGAZINES INC**
Also Called: Nickelodeon Jr Mag Chicago
401 N Michigan Ave # 2200 (60611-4255)
PHONE...................312 836-0668
Scott Sherman, *Branch Mgr*
Karen Moses, *Info Tech Mgr*
Rob Glaser, *Technical Staff*
Katelyn Kroneman, *Director*
**EMP:** 3
**SALES (corp-wide):** 12.4B **Publicly Held**
**SIC:** 2721 Magazines: publishing only, not printed on site
**HQ:** Nickelodeon Magazines Inc
  1633 Broadway Fl 7
  New York NY 10019
  212 541-1949

**(G-5913)**
**NIEDERMAIER INC (PA)**
Also Called: Niedermaier Furniture
1700 N Throop St (60642-1517)
PHONE...................312 492-9400
Judith Niedermaier, *President*
Jeffrey Niedermaier, *Vice Pres*
Rio Hamilton, *Manager*
**EMP:** 20 **EST:** 1965
**SQ FT:** 110,000
**SALES (est):** 5MM **Privately Held**
**WEB:** www.niedermaier.com
**SIC:** 2522 5021 Office furniture, except wood; office & public building furniture

**(G-5914)**
**NIEMAN & CONSIDINE INC**
Also Called: Uk Sailmakers
2323 S Michigan Ave (60616-2104)
PHONE...................312 326-1053
James Considine, *President*
Patrick Considine, *Vice Pres*
Mike Considine, *Sales Mgr*
Kate Swanson, *Manager*

# Chicago - Cook County (G-5915)     GEOGRAPHIC SECTION

EMP: 10
SQ FT: 10,000
SALES: 1.5MM **Privately Held**
SIC: 2394 5551 Sails: made from purchased materials; boat dealers

**(G-5915)**
**NIESE WALTER MACHINE MFG CO**
6551 N Olmsted Ave (60631-1414)
PHONE..................773 774-7337
Fax: 773 774-6587
Walter Niese Jr, *President*
Karen Niese, *Corp Secy*
Steve Niese, *Vice Pres*
EMP: 7 EST: 1960
SQ FT: 6,500
SALES: 1MM **Privately Held**
SIC: 3599 7629 Machine shop, jobbing & repair; electrical repair shops

**(G-5916)**
**NIGHTINGALE CORP**
222 Merchandise Mart Plz # 1078 (60654-1197)
PHONE..................800 363-8954
Wr Breen, *President*
Ed Breen, *Vice Pres*
Gerry Adam, *Vice Pres*
Jose Paiva, *Vice Pres*
Yuyan Liu, *Controller*
EMP: 90
SQ FT: 795
SALES: 34MM **Privately Held**
SIC: 2522 2521 Mfg Nonwood Office Furn Mfg Wood Office Furn

**(G-5917)**
**NIJHUIS WATER TECHNOLOGY INC**
560 W Washington Blvd # 320 (60661-2693)
PHONE..................312 466-9900
Ronald Ruijtenberg, *President*
Thomas Thorelli, *Admin Sec*
EMP: 5
SALES (est): 708.9K **Privately Held**
SIC: 3589 Water treatment equipment, industrial

**(G-5918)**
**NIKE INC**
8510 S Cottage Grove Ave (60619-6116)
PHONE..................773 846-5460
Fax: 773 994-8880
Henderson Foster, *Manager*
Vanessa Wallace, *Manager*
EMP: 50
SALES (corp-wide): 32.3B **Publicly Held**
WEB: www.nike.com
SIC: 3021 Rubber & plastics footwear
PA: Nike, Inc.
   1 Sw Bowerman Dr
   Beaverton OR 97005
   503 671-6453

**(G-5919)**
**NIKKEI AMERICA HOLDINGS INC**
Also Called: Japan Economic Journal
125 S Wacker Dr Ste 1080 (60606-4432)
PHONE..................312 263-8877
Shinichi Yamashita, *Branch Mgr*
EMP: 3
SALES (corp-wide): 1.7B **Privately Held**
WEB: www.nikkei.com
SIC: 2711 Newspapers
HQ: Nikkei America Holdings, Inc
   1325 Avenue Of The Americ
   New York NY

**(G-5920)**
**NO SURRENDER INC (PA)**
Also Called: Something Old, Something New
1056 W Belmont Ave (60657-3326)
PHONE..................773 929-7920
Jack Mages, *President*
EMP: 8
SQ FT: 13,000
SALES (est): 1.3MM **Privately Held**
WEB: www.nosurrender.com
SIC: 5065 5651 2671 Security control equipment & systems; unisex clothing stores; packaging paper & plastics film, coated & laminated

**(G-5921)**
**NOBERT PLATING CO**
340 N Ashland Ave (60607-1015)
PHONE..................312 421-4040
Fax: 312 421-5120
Diann Sickles, *President*
Rob Sickles, *Vice Pres*
Danny Rangel, *Safety Mgr*
Yolanda Amaro, *Purch Mgr*
Jamie Sickles, *QC Mgr*
EMP: 5 EST: 1903
SQ FT: 45,000
SALES (est): 996.5K **Privately Held**
WEB: www.nobertplating.com
SIC: 3471 Electroplating of metals or formed products

**(G-5922)**
**NOGI BRANDS LLC**
2106 W Erie St (60612-1320)
PHONE..................312 371-7974
Paul Rashid, *Principal*
EMP: 3
SALES (est): 170K **Privately Held**
SIC: 2032 Canned specialties

**(G-5923)**
**NOODLE PARTY**
4205 W Lawrence Ave (60630-2728)
PHONE..................773 205-0505
Nisanart Konkrasung, *President*
EMP: 8 EST: 2008
SALES (est): 525.6K **Privately Held**
SIC: 2098 Noodles (e.g. egg, plain & water), dry

**(G-5924)**
**NOON HOUR FOOD PRODUCTS INC (PA)**
Also Called: Swedish Food Products
215 N Desplaines St Fl 1 (60661-1072)
PHONE..................312 382-1177
Fax: 312 382-9420
Paul A Buhl, *President*
Peter S Buhl, *Exec VP*
Larry Buhl, *Vice Pres*
William L Buhl, *Vice Pres*
Pat Freeman, *Controller*
EMP: 35 EST: 1876
SALES (est): 13.6MM **Privately Held**
WEB: www.noonhourfoods.com
SIC: 5149 2034 Groceries & related products; potato products, dried & dehydrated

**(G-5925)**
**NORDEX USA INC (DH)**
300 S Wacker Dr Ste 1500 (60606-6762)
PHONE..................208 383-6500
Jrgen Zeschky, *CEO*
Ralf Sigrist, *President*
William Lutz, *Vice Pres*
Bernard Scherbarthold, *CFO*
Billy Chapman, *Manager*
◆ EMP: 85
SQ FT: 15,000
SALES (est): 76.5MM
SALES (corp-wide): 3.5B **Privately Held**
SIC: 3511 7389 Turbines & turbine generator sets; industrial & commercial equipment inspection service
HQ: Nordex Energy Gmbh
   Langenhorner Chaussee 600
   Hamburg 22419
   403 003-0100

**(G-5926)**
**NORDSON ASYMTEK INC**
25033 Network Pl (60673-1250)
PHONE..................760 431-1919
EMP: 101
SALES (corp-wide): 1.8B **Publicly Held**
SIC: 3823 Industrial flow & liquid measuring instruments
HQ: Nordson Asymtek, Inc.
   2747 Loker Ave W
   Carlsbad CA 92010
   760 431-1919

**(G-5927)**
**NORFOLK SOUTHERN CORPORATION**
2543 W Columbus Ave (60629-2058)
PHONE..................773 933-5698
Fax: 773 933-5640
George Marx, *Opers Staff*
Brad Carper, *Branch Mgr*
EMP: 5
SALES (corp-wide): 9.8B **Publicly Held**
SIC: 2531 Seats, railroad
PA: Norfolk Southern Corporation
   3 Commercial Pl Ste 1a
   Norfolk VA 23510
   757 629-2680

**(G-5928)**
**NORKIN JEWELRY CO INC**
55 E Washington St # 203 (60602-2103)
PHONE..................312 782-7311
Fax: 312 782-5369
Galina Norkin, *President*
EMP: 20
SQ FT: 1,900
SALES (est): 1.9MM **Privately Held**
SIC: 3911 7631 5094 Jewelry, precious metal; jewelry repair services; diamonds (gems); precious stones (gems)

**(G-5929)**
**NORRIDGE JEWELRY**
29 E Madison St Ste 1202 (60602-4485)
PHONE..................312 984-1036
Richard J Kohler, *Owner*
David Kohler, *Co-Owner*
EMP: 4
SALES (est): 277.9K **Privately Held**
SIC: 2452 Modular homes, prefabricated, wood

**(G-5930)**
**NORTH AMERICAN BEAR CO INC (PA)**
1200 W 35th St (60609-1305)
PHONE..................773 376-3457
Fax: 773 247-9861
Paul Levy, *CEO*
Raymond Miller, *COO*
Melissa Bullock, *Vice Pres*
Steven Isenberg, *Vice Pres*
Michelle Sterling, *Opers Mgr*
▲ EMP: 28
SQ FT: 2,000
SALES (est): 3.9MM **Privately Held**
WEB: www.nabear.com
SIC: 3942 Stuffed toys, including animals

**(G-5931)**
**NORTH AMERICAN DIE CASTNG ASSN**
5439 W Lawrence Ave (60630-3451)
PHONE..................773 202-1000
Dennis A Parker CPA, *President*
EMP: 3
SALES: 36.2K **Privately Held**
SIC: 3544 Special dies & tools

**(G-5932)**
**NORTH AMERICAN FUND III LP (PA)**
135 S La Salle St # 3225 (60603-4177)
PHONE..................312 332-4950
Charles L Palmer, *Managing Prtnr*
▲ EMP: 3
SQ FT: 3,000
SALES (est): 61.4MM **Privately Held**
SIC: 3089 5162 Injection molding of plastics; plastics resins

**(G-5933)**
**NORTH AMERICAN JEWELERS INC**
5 S Wabash Ave Ste 1512 (60603-3087)
P.O. Box 11408 (60611-0408)
PHONE..................312 425-9000
Kurt Steckbeck, *President*
Ryan Degood, *Sr Corp Ofcr*
Dan Coghlan, *Vice Pres*
Martin Weinberger, *CFO*
EMP: 70
SQ FT: 7,500
SALES (est): 17.5MM **Privately Held**
SIC: 5094 3915 Diamonds (gems); jewelers' findings & materials

**(G-5934)**
**NORTH HALSTED DENTAL SPA**
3710 N Halsted St (60613-3910)
PHONE..................773 296-0325
Michael Griffin, *Owner*
EMP: 2
SALES (est): 200.6K **Privately Held**
SIC: 3843 Enamels, dentists'

**(G-5935)**
**NORTH POINT INVESTMENTS INC (PA)**
70 W Madison St Ste 3500 (60602-4224)
PHONE..................312 977-4386
William A Bryant, *President*
Dale G Marcus, *Treasurer*
Ken Gallagher, *Controller*
Barry J Shkolnik, *Agent*
EMP: 2
SALES (est): 10.5MM **Privately Held**
SIC: 3531 5063 3677 3621 Construction machinery; electrical apparatus & equipment; electronic coils, transformers & other inductors; motors & generators

**(G-5936)**
**NORTH SAILS GROUP LLC**
1665 N Elston Ave (60642-1545)
PHONE..................773 489-1308
Fax: 773 489-9820
Perry Lewis, *Manager*
EMP: 4 **Privately Held**
WEB: www.northsails.com
SIC: 2394 7641 Sails: made from purchased materials; reupholstery & furniture repair
HQ: North Sails Group, Llc
   125 Old Gate Ln Ste 7
   Milford CT 06460
   203 874-7548

**(G-5937)**
**NORTH-WEST DRAPERY SERVICE**
4507 N Milwaukee Ave (60630-3711)
PHONE..................773 282-7117
Fax: 773 282-6882
Brian C Lydon, *President*
EMP: 8
SQ FT: 2,380
SALES (est): 923.1K **Privately Held**
SIC: 2391 Curtains & draperies

**(G-5938)**
**NORTHWEST DENTAL PROSTHETICS**
6124 N Milwaukee Ave # 16 (60646-3820)
PHONE..................773 505-9191
Thomas Abele, *President*
Brian Abele, *Vice Pres*
EMP: 4
SQ FT: 1,400
SALES (est): 250K **Privately Held**
SIC: 3843 Dental equipment & supplies

**(G-5939)**
**NORTHWEST PIPE COMPANY**
1050 N State St Fl Mezz7 (60610)
PHONE..................312 587-8702
Tom Baas, *Branch Mgr*
EMP: 158
SALES (corp-wide): 156.2MM **Publicly Held**
SIC: 3317 Steel pipe & tubes
PA: Northwest Pipe Company
   5721 Se Columbia Way # 200
   Vancouver WA 98661
   360 397-6250

**(G-5940)**
**NORTHWEST PREMIER PRINTING**
5421 W Addison St (60641-3203)
PHONE..................773 736-1882
Fax: 773 736-1730
Lee Stroh, *President*
James Henaghan, *Vice Pres*
Jeanne Henaghan, *Treasurer*
EMP: 5
SQ FT: 8,000
SALES: 850K **Privately Held**
SIC: 2752 2791 2789 2759 Commercial printing, lithographic; typesetting; bookbinding & related work; commercial printing

**(G-5941)**
**NORTHWEST PUBLISHING LLC**
Also Called: Chicago Collection Magazine
500 N Dearborn St # 1014 (60654-3363)
PHONE..................312 329-0600

Fax: 312 329-0610
Louis Weiss, *Mng Member*
Elizabeth Goodchild, *Director*
EMP: 5
SALES (est): 1MM **Privately Held**
WEB: www.chicagocollection.com
SIC: 2721 Magazines: publishing only, not printed on site

**(G-5942)**
**NORTHWESTERN CUP & LOGO INC**
41 W 84th St Fl 1 (60620-1251)
PHONE..................773 874-8000
Timothy Rand, *President*
EMP: 8
SQ FT: 500
SALES (est): 920.7K **Privately Held**
SIC: 3089 Cups, plastic, except foam

**(G-5943)**
**NORTHWSTERN GLOBL HLTH FNDTION**
2707 N Lincoln Ave Apt B (60614-1363)
P.O. Box 1969, Evanston (60204-1969)
PHONE..................214 207-9485
Kara Palamountain, *President*
EMP: 3
SALES: 1.4MM **Privately Held**
SIC: 3999 Manufacturing industries

**(G-5944)**
**NORWAY PRESS INC**
400 W 76th St Ste 1105 (60620-1641)
PHONE..................773 846-9422
Samuel Hill, *President*
EMP: 5
SALES (est): 350K **Privately Held**
WEB: www.norwaypressinc.com
SIC: 2759 Commercial printing

**(G-5945)**
**NORWOOD HOUSE PRESS INC**
6150 N Milwaukee Ave # 2 (60646-3821)
P.O. Box 316598 (60631-6598)
PHONE..................866 565-2900
Patti Hall, *President*
Frank Radell, *Sales Dir*
▲ EMP: 2
SALES (est): 295.8K **Privately Held**
SIC: 2741 Miscellaneous publishing

**(G-5946)**
**NORWOOD INDUSTRIES INC**
Also Called: Norwood Paper
7001 W 60th St (60638-3101)
PHONE..................773 788-1508
Fax: 773 788-1528
Kathleen A Zeman, *CEO*
Laura Z Martin, *President*
Robert I Zeman III, *Vice Pres*
Tracy Alvarez, *Natl Sales Mgr*
Amy Hogue, *Natl Sales Mgr*
EMP: 13
SQ FT: 130,000
SALES (est): 4MM **Privately Held**
SIC: 2679 Paper products, converted

**(G-5947)**
**NOVALEX THERAPEUTICS INC**
2242 W Harrison St # 201 (60612-3719)
PHONE..................630 750-9334
Michael Johnson, *Principal*
Shahila Christie, *Principal*
Elizabeth Woods, *Vice Pres*
EMP: 4
SALES (est): 397.1K **Privately Held**
SIC: 2834 Druggists' preparations (pharmaceuticals)

**(G-5948)**
**NOVIAN HEALTH INC**
Also Called: Novilase Chicago
430 W Erie St Ste 500 (60654-5732)
PHONE..................312 266-7200
Henry R Appelbaum, *President*
Eugene Bajorinas, *Vice Pres*
Jessica Topolosky, *Office Mgr*
Marti Delay, *Office Admin*
Kambiz Dowlatshahi, *Medical Dir*
EMP: 6 EST: 1991
SALES (est): 710K **Privately Held**
WEB: www.novianhealth.com
SIC: 3841 Surgical lasers

**(G-5949)**
**NOVO CARD PUBLISHERS INC**
5410 W Roosevelt Rd # 302 (60644-1875)
P.O. Box 486, Techny (60082-0486)
PHONE..................847 947-8090
K Chae, *Principal*
EMP: 4
SALES (est): 739.2K **Privately Held**
SIC: 2721 Periodicals

**(G-5950)**
**NOVUM PHARMA LLC**
640 N La Salle Dr Ste 670 (60654-3763)
PHONE..................877 404-4724
Gavin Toepke, *Business Mgr*
Elizabeth Coggins, *Sales Mgr*
Michael Cutler, *Sales Mgr*
Brandon Parks, *Sales Mgr*
Anne Powell, *Sales Mgr*
EMP: 10 EST: 2015
SQ FT: 3,372
SALES (est): 997K **Privately Held**
SIC: 2834 Pharmaceutical preparations

**(G-5951)**
**NRTX LLC**
1454 W Melrose St Ste 2 (60657-2116)
PHONE..................224 717-0465
Matthieu Chardon,
EMP: 3
SALES (est): 217.9K **Privately Held**
SIC: 3841 Diagnostic apparatus, medical

**(G-5952)**
**NU VISION MEDIA INC**
1327 W Wa Blvd Ste 102b (60607-2193)
PHONE..................773 495-5254
Roland S Martin, *President*
EMP: 2
SALES (est): 204.7K **Privately Held**
SIC: 3825 Multimeters

**(G-5953)**
**NU-DELL MANUFACTURING CO INC (PA)**
Also Called: Nu-Dell Plastics
400 E Randolph St (60601-7329)
PHONE..................847 803-4500
Fax: 847 803-4584
David M Block, *CEO*
Michael Miller, *Mfg Mgr*
Beverly Berg, *Treasurer*
Bill Howard, *Manager*
James Luety, *Manager*
▲ EMP: 10 EST: 1926
SQ FT: 3,200
SALES (est): 10.6MM **Privately Held**
SIC: 3993 3089 2499 3281 Signs & advertising specialties; plastic hardware & building products; picture frame molding, finished; cut stone & stone products; public building & related furniture

**(G-5954)**
**NUCURRENT INC**
641 W Lake St Ste 304 (60661-1308)
PHONE..................312 575-0388
Jacob Babcock, *CEO*
Bob Giometti, *Vice Pres*
Michael Gotlieb, *Vice Pres*
Megha Maripuri, *Treasurer*
Vinit Singh, *Senior Mgr*
EMP: 8
SALES (est): 500.9K **Privately Held**
SIC: 3663 Antennas, transmitting & communications

**(G-5955)**
**NUESTRO MUNDO NEWSPAPER (PA)**
3339 S Halsted St (60608-6882)
PHONE..................773 446-9920
EMP: 3
SALES (est): 915K **Privately Held**
SIC: 2711 Newspapers, publishing & printing

**(G-5956)**
**NUTRASWEET COMPANY (DH)**
222 Merchandise Mart Plz # 936 (60654-1103)
PHONE..................312 873-5000
Fax: 312 873-5053
Craig Petray, *CEO*
Larry Benjamin, *President*

William Schumacher, *CFO*
▲ EMP: 9
SALES (est): 2MM **Privately Held**
SIC: 2869 Industrial organic chemicals
HQ: Nutrasweet Property Holdings, Inc.
222 Merchandise Mart Plz
Chicago IL 60654
312 873-5000

**(G-5957)**
**O & K AMERICAN CORP (HQ)**
4630 W 55th St (60632-4908)
PHONE..................773 767-2500
Kazuta Oku, *President*
Takao Oku, *Chairman*
Michal Pasek, *Mfg Mgr*
Gerard Blake, *Maint Spvr*
Pam Storcz, *Manager*
▲ EMP: 90
SQ FT: 150,000
SALES (est): 34.7MM
SALES (corp-wide): 294.4MM **Privately Held**
WEB: www.oandkamerican.com
SIC: 3312 Blast furnace & related products
PA: O&K Company Limited
2-8-81, Nakajima, Nishiyodogawa-Ku
Osaka OSK 555-0
664 710-110

**(G-5958)**
**O & W WIRE CO INC**
7816 S Oakley Ave (60620-5814)
PHONE..................773 776-5919
Fax: 773 776-5829
Wenceslao Ramirez, *President*
EMP: 10
SQ FT: 13,900
SALES (est): 1.3MM **Privately Held**
SIC: 3312 Wire products, steel or iron

**(G-5959)**
**O SIGNS INC**
325 N Hoyne Ave (60612-1636)
PHONE..................312 888-3386
Patrick M Oleary, *President*
EMP: 3
SALES (est): 250.3K **Privately Held**
SIC: 3993 Signs & advertising specialties

**(G-5960)**
**O2COOL LLC**
168 N Clinton St Ste 500 (60661-1423)
PHONE..................312 951-6700
Fax: 312 951-6707
Linda Usher, *CEO*
Eric Junkel, *Engineer*
Debbie Weiss, *Controller*
Jason Yau, *Controller*
Carl Go, *Accounting Mgr*
▲ EMP: 20
SQ FT: 7,500
SALES (est): 5.6MM **Privately Held**
SIC: 3634 Fans, electric: desk

**(G-5961)**
**O2M TECHNOLOGIES LLC**
2242 W Harrison St Ste 20 (60612-3719)
PHONE..................773 910-8533
Mrignayani Kotecha,
Boris Epel,
Howard Halpern,
EMP: 3
SALES (est): 128K **Privately Held**
SIC: 3826 Magnetic resonance imaging apparatus

**(G-5962)**
**OAKLEY INC**
835 N Michigan Ave # 7000 (60611-2228)
PHONE..................312 787-2545
Colin Baden, *CEO*
EMP: 2
SALES (est): 286.8K **Privately Held**
SIC: 3827 Optical alignment & display instruments

**(G-5963)**
**OBAN COMPOSITES LLC**
1300 W Belmont Ave # 311 (60657-3200)
PHONE..................866 607-0284
Ralph Reichert,
EMP: 7 EST: 2009
SQ FT: 2,000

SALES (est): 481.7K **Privately Held**
SIC: 5941 3949 Sporting goods & bicycle shops; sporting & athletic goods

**(G-5964)**
**OBRIEN ARCHITECTURAL MTLS INC**
858 W Armitage Ave # 205 (60614-4383)
PHONE..................773 868-1065
John O'Brien, *President*
EMP: 10 EST: 2007
SALES (est): 2MM **Privately Held**
SIC: 3441 Fabricated structural metal

**(G-5965)**
**OCCIDENTAL CHEMICAL CORP**
4201 W 69th St (60629-5718)
PHONE..................773 284-0079
Fax: 773 284-7809
Donna Fiscus,
EMP: 19
SQ FT: 2,700
SALES (corp-wide): 10.4B **Publicly Held**
WEB: www.oxychem.com
SIC: 2874 Phosphatic fertilizers
HQ: Occidental Chemical Corporation
5005 Lyndon B Johnson Fwy # 2200
Dallas TX 75244
972 404-3800

**(G-5966)**
**OCCLY LLC**
2835 N Sheffield Ave (60657-5081)
PHONE..................773 969-5080
Marc Harris, *Mng Member*
EMP: 3
SQ FT: 2,000
SALES (est): 133.4K **Privately Held**
SIC: 3699 Electrical equipment & supplies

**(G-5967)**
**OCHEM INC**
2201 W Campbell Park Dr (60612-4160)
PHONE..................847 403-7044
EMP: 18
SALES (corp-wide): 2MM **Privately Held**
SIC: 2899 Chemical preparations
PA: Ochem, Inc.
9044 Buckingham Park Dr
Des Plaines IL 60016
847 403-7044

**(G-5968)**
**ODWALLA INC**
2837 N Cambridge Ave (60657-6018)
PHONE..................773 687-8667
EMP: 39
SALES (corp-wide): 41.8B **Publicly Held**
SIC: 2033 Fruit juices: packaged in cans, jars, etc.
HQ: Odwalla, Inc.
1 Coca Cola Plz Nw
Atlanta GA 30313
479 721-6260

**(G-5969)**
**OFFSPRINGS INC**
Also Called: Vertical Blinds Factory
1451 W Webster Ave (60614-3049)
PHONE..................773 525-1800
Jay Pinsky, *President*
EMP: 6
SALES (est): 480K **Privately Held**
SIC: 2591 5719 Drapery hardware & blinds & shades; window furnishings

**(G-5970)**
**OGDEN FOODS LLC (PA)**
4320 W Ogden Ave (60623-2924)
PHONE..................773 277-8207
Barsh Janusz,
Janusz Barsh,
Eva Jakubowski,
EMP: 22
SQ FT: 27,000
SALES: 1MM **Privately Held**
SIC: 2013 Boneless meat, from purchased meat

**(G-5971)**
**OGDEN FOODS LLC**
4325 W Ogden Ave (60623-2925)
PHONE..................773 801-0125
Dorota Mietus, *Branch Mgr*
EMP: 8

# Chicago - Cook County (G-5972)  GEOGRAPHIC SECTION

SALES (corp-wide): 1MM  Privately Held
SIC: 2013  Boneless meat, from purchased meat
PA: Ogden Foods Llc
4320 W Ogden Ave
Chicago IL 60623
773 277-8207

### (G-5972)
### OGDEN MINUTEMAN INC
3939 W Ogden Ave  (60623-2486)
PHONE.................................773 542-6917
Musa Tadros, Owner
EMP: 4
SALES (est): 326.5K  Privately Held
SIC: 2752  Commercial printing, offset

### (G-5973)
### OGDEN OFFSET PRINTERS INC
6150 S Archer Ave  (60638-2641)
PHONE.................................773 284-7797
Fax: 773 284-7798
Sandra H William, President
John Williams, Vice Pres
EMP: 4
SQ FT: 4,800
SALES: 500K  Privately Held
SIC: 2752  3993  2789  Commercial printing, offset; signs & advertising specialties; bookbinding & related work

### (G-5974)
### OHIO PULP MILLS INC (PA)
737 N Michigan Ave # 1450  (60611-2615)
PHONE.................................312 337-7822
Robert Mendelson, President
Thomas Imming, President
David Mendelson, Exec VP
David Berkenstein, Treasurer
EMP: 13
SQ FT: 5,088
SALES (est): 3.3MM  Privately Held
SIC: 2611  Pulp manufactured from waste or recycled paper

### (G-5975)
### OIL-DRI CORPORATION AMERICA (PA)
410 N Michigan Ave # 400  (60611-4293)
PHONE.................................312 321-1515
Fax: 312 321-9525
Richard M Jaffee, Ch of Bd
Joseph C Miller, Vice Ch Bd
Daniel S Jaffee, President
Mark E Lewry, COO
Karen Cofsky, Vice Pres
EMP: 90
SALES: 262.3MM  Publicly Held
WEB: www.oildri.com
SIC: 2842  3295  Sweeping compounds, oil or water absorbent, clay or sawdust; earths, ground or otherwise treated; cat box litter; filtering clays, treated

### (G-5976)
### OIL-DRI CORPORATION AMERICA
410 N Michigan Aveste 400  (60611)
PHONE.................................312 321-1516
Carol Groom, Manager
EMP: 500
SALES (corp-wide): 262.3MM  Publicly Held
WEB: www.oildri.com
SIC: 1459  3295  Clays (common) quarrying; cat box litter
PA: Oil-Dri Corporation Of America
410 N Michigan Ave # 400
Chicago IL 60611
312 321-1515

### (G-5977)
### OKAMURA CORP
222 Merchandise Mart Plz 11-124  (60654-4333)
PHONE.................................312 645-0115
Lorna Walters, Principal
Akiko Soma, Manager
▲ EMP: 8
SALES (est): 1.3MM  Privately Held
SIC: 3571  Electronic computers

### (G-5978)
### OLD FASHIONED MEAT CO INC
920 W Fulton Market  (60607-1309)
PHONE.................................312 421-4555
Fax: 312 421-8037
Roberto Casmilo, President
Thomas G Stapleton, President
Veronica Castillo, Controller
EMP: 4
SQ FT: 2,000
SALES (est): 1.1MM  Privately Held
SIC: 5147  2013  Meats & meat products; sausages & other prepared meats

### (G-5979)
### OLD GARY INC (DH)
Also Called: Post-Tribune
350 N Orleans St Fl 10  (60654-1975)
PHONE.................................219 648-3000
Fax: 219 648-3235
Boni L Fine, Publisher
Eileen Brown, Editor
Joe Puchek, Editor
John Feczko, Director
Michele Hunkele, Director
EMP: 15  EST: 1909
SQ FT: 30,000
SALES (est): 19.1MM
SALES (corp-wide): 304.8MM  Privately Held
SIC: 2711  Newspapers, publishing & printing
HQ: Sun-Times Media Group, Inc.
350 N Orleans St Fl 10
Chicago IL 60654
312 321-2299

### (G-5980)
### OLD STYLE IRON WORKS INC
7843 S Claremont Ave  (60620-5812)
PHONE.................................773 265-5787
Fax: 773 476-4431
EMP: 7
SQ FT: 10,000
SALES (est): 840K  Privately Held
SIC: 3441  1791  3446  Structural Metal Fabrication Structural Steel Erection Mfg Architectural Metalwork

### (G-5981)
### OLDCASTLE BUILDINGENVELOPE INC
4161 S Morgan St  (60609-2516)
PHONE.................................773 523-8400
John Janik, Sales Mgr
Philip F Albrecht, Manager
EMP: 6
SALES (corp-wide): 28.6B  Privately Held
WEB: www.oldcastleglass.com
SIC: 3231  5231  Tempered glass: made from purchased glass; insulating glass: made from purchased glass; glass
HQ: Oldcastle Buildingenvelope, Inc.
5005 Lndn B Jnsn Fwy 10 Ste 1050
Dallas TX 75244
214 273-3400

### (G-5982)
### OLIVE MOUNT MART
3536 W 63rd St  (60629-3712)
PHONE.................................773 476-4964
Nick Salem, Principal
EMP: 2
SALES (est): 200K  Privately Held
SIC: 3561  Cylinders, pump

### (G-5983)
### OLIVE SPARTATHLON OIL & GRE
6301 N Tripp Ave  (60646-4524)
PHONE.................................312 782-9855
Barbara Koutsogergas, President
Maria K Alexakis, Admin Sec
▲ EMP: 3
SALES (est): 130.4K  Privately Held
SIC: 2079  Olive oil

### (G-5984)
### OLIVIA R AGUILAR-CAMACHO
Also Called: Ibbysscrubs
5757 N Sheridan Rd  (60660-4746)
PHONE.................................773 600-6864
Olivia R Aguilar, Owner
EMP: 1
SALES: 600K  Privately Held
SIC: 2211  Scrub cloths

### (G-5985)
### OLSHAWS INTERIOR SERVICES
407 S Peoria St  (60607-3511)
PHONE.................................312 421-3131
Bright Jeon, President
Sue Jeon, Treasurer
EMP: 3  EST: 1948
SQ FT: 3,500
SALES (est): 295.4K  Privately Held
SIC: 2391  7349  5719  2591  Draperies, plastic & textile: from purchased materials; window blind cleaning; venetian blinds; drapery hardware & blinds & shades

### (G-5986)
### OLYMPIA MEAT PACKERS  INC
Also Called: Olympic Meat Packing
810 W Randolph St  (60607-2308)
PHONE.................................312 666-2222
George Tsoukas, President
EMP: 3
SQ FT: 1,200
SALES (est): 965.9K  Privately Held
SIC: 5147  5421  2011  Meats, fresh; meat markets, including freezer provisioners; meat packing plants

### (G-5987)
### OLYMPIC TROPHY AND AWARDS CO
5860 N Northwest Hwy  (60631-2641)
PHONE.................................773 631-9500
Fax: 773 631-7780
Susan McMahon, President
Lawrence McCann, CTO
EMP: 13
SALES (est): 1.5MM  Privately Held
SIC: 3499  2759  3993  2396  Novelties & giftware, including trophies; trophies, metal, except silver; novelties & specialties, metal; screen printing; signs & advertising specialties; automotive & apparel trimmings

### (G-5988)
### OMAR MEDICAL SUPPLIES  INC (PA)
Also Called: OMAR SUPPLIES
345 E Wacker Dr Unit 4601  (60601-5275)
PHONE.................................708 922-4377
Fax: 708 283-8106
Willie Wilson, President
Roxanne Jackson, Vice Pres
Jaime Contreas, Accounts Mgr
Dale Wilson, Manager
◆ EMP: 40  EST: 1997
SQ FT: 75,000
SALES: 53.7MM  Privately Held
WEB: www.omarinc.com
SIC: 5085  5047  2259  Industrial supplies; dental equipment & supplies; dyeing & finishing knit gloves & mittens

### (G-5989)
### OMG HANDBAGS LLC
2045 W Grand Ave Ste 202  (60612-1577)
PHONE.................................847 337-9499
Ann Narter,
▲ EMP: 4
SALES (est): 340K  Privately Held
SIC: 2393  Textile bags

### (G-5990)
### ONE SHOT LLC
1701 E 122nd St  (60633-2362)
PHONE.................................773 646-5900
Tom Klaypatch, Finance
Jack Cuadra,
EMP: 20
SALES (est): 2MM
SALES (corp-wide): 33.6MM  Privately Held
WEB: www.spraylat.com
SIC: 2851  Paints & allied products
PA: Talyarps Corporation
143 Sparks Ave
Pelham NY 10803
914 699-3030

### (G-5991)
### ONEILL PRODUCTS INC
Also Called: Midwest Marine Div
555 W 16th St  (60616-1146)
PHONE.................................312 243-3413

Fax: 312 243-3415
Larry Grossman, President
Mary Grossman, Corp Secy
EMP: 2
SQ FT: 2,500
SALES: 500K  Privately Held
SIC: 5085  2511  Rubber goods, mechanical; wood household furniture

### (G-5992)
### ONION INC
730 N Franklin St Ste 701  (60654-7203)
PHONE.................................312 751-0503
Peter Haise, Manager
EMP: 10
SALES (corp-wide): 15.4MM  Privately Held
WEB: www.onionavclub.com
SIC: 2721  Magazines: publishing & printing
PA: Onion Inc.
730 N Franklin St Ste 701
Chicago IL 60654
312 751-0503

### (G-5993)
### ONION INC (PA)
Also Called: Onion Company, The
730 N Franklin St Ste 701  (60654-7203)
PHONE.................................312 751-0503
Steve Hannah, CEO
Mike McAvoy, President
Kristine Desrochers, Partner
Adam Albright-Hanna, Editor
Alexander Blechman, Editor
EMP: 10
SALES (est): 15.4MM  Privately Held
WEB: www.onionavclub.com
SIC: 2721  Magazines: publishing & printing

### (G-5994)
### OPEN KITCHENS  INC (PA)
1161 W 21st St  (60608-3397)
PHONE.................................312 666-5334
Fax: 312 666-9242
Terese M Fiore, President
Tim Lacey, General Mgr
Anthony Fiore, VP Opers
Ketan Baman, CPA
Linda Padilla, Human Res Mgr
EMP: 120
SQ FT: 65,000
SALES: 27.9MM  Privately Held
SIC: 2099  Food preparations

### (G-5995)
### OPEN KITCHENS  INC
2141 S Racine Ave  (60608-3222)
PHONE.................................312 666-5334
Terese Fiore, Branch Mgr
Linda Padilla, Admin Asst
EMP: 25
SALES (corp-wide): 27.9MM  Privately Held
SIC: 5812  2099  2038  4215  Eating places; food preparations; frozen specialties; courier services, except by air
PA: Open Kitchens, Inc.
1161 W 21st St
Chicago IL 60608
312 666-5334

### (G-5996)
### OPSDIRT  LLC
948 N Winchester Ave # 3  (60622-4963)
PHONE.................................773 412-1179
Jeffrey Waugh,
Brian Garriotte,
Jason Garriotte,
Mike Kostorowski,
Jay Walley,
EMP: 6
SALES (est): 542.4K  Privately Held
SIC: 2899  7389  Fusees: highway, marine or railroad.

### (G-5997)
### OPTIMUS ADVANTAGE LLC
10 S Lasalle  (60606)
PHONE.................................847 905-1000
Michael Harris, Principal
EMP: 3
SQ FT: 2,000
SALES (est): 63.5K  Privately Held
SIC: 7371  7372  Computer software systems analysis & design, custom; application computer software

## GEOGRAPHIC SECTION
## Chicago - Cook County (G-6023)

**(G-5998)**
**ORACLE CORPORATION**
980 N Michigan Ave # 1400 (60611-7500)
PHONE.................................773 404-9300
Fax: 312 335-0735
Diane Cleary, *Branch Mgr*
**EMP:** 310
**SALES (corp-wide):** 37B **Publicly Held**
**SIC:** 7372 Prepackaged software
**PA:** Oracle Corporation
500 Oracle Pkwy
Redwood City CA 94065
650 506-7000

**(G-5999)**
**ORACLE CORPORATION**
330 N Wabash Ave Ste 2400 (60611-7618)
PHONE.................................312 692-5270
Greg Hilbrich, *Vice Pres*
John Womeldorff, *Project Mgr*
Manu Parikh, *Consultant*
Alex Kallend, *Systs Prg Mgr*
James Schoessling, *Director*
**EMP:** 191
**SALES (corp-wide):** 37B **Publicly Held**
**SIC:** 7372 Prepackaged software
**PA:** Oracle Corporation
500 Oracle Pkwy
Redwood City CA 94065
650 506-7000

**(G-6000)**
**ORACLE CORPORATION**
233 S Wacker Dr Ste 4500 (60606-6406)
PHONE.................................262 957-3000
Sriram Kalyanaraman, *Vice Pres*
Narayan Nayar, *Vice Pres*
Mary Martyak, *Project Mgr*
Roger Lewis, *Engineer*
James Torzewski, *Sales Dir*
**EMP:** 302
**SALES (corp-wide):** 37B **Publicly Held**
**SIC:** 7372 Business oriented computer software
**PA:** Oracle Corporation
500 Oracle Pkwy
Redwood City CA 94065
650 506-7000

**(G-6001)**
**ORACLE HCM USER GROUP INC**
330 N Wabash Ave Ste 2000 (60611-7621)
PHONE.................................312 222-9350
**EMP:** 2
**SALES:** 1.1MM **Privately Held**
**SIC:** 7372 Prepackaged Software Services

**(G-6002)**
**ORACLE SYSTEMS CORPORATION**
401 N Michigan Ave # 2200 (60611-4255)
P.O. Box 3140 (60654-0140)
PHONE.................................312 245-1580
Amy Carlton, *Editor*
Theresa Wojtalewicz, *Editor*
Frank Stefano, *Sr Corp Ofcr*
Stacy Dalton, *Vice Pres*
Kim Wiatr, *Opers Mgr*
**EMP:** 30
**SALES (corp-wide):** 37B **Publicly Held**
**WEB:** www.forcecapital.com
**SIC:** 7372 7371 Prepackaged software; custom computer programming services
**HQ:** Oracle Systems Corporation
500 Oracle Pkwy
Redwood City CA 94065
650 506-7000

**(G-6003)**
**ORBIS RPM LLC**
4400 W 45th St (60632-4304)
PHONE.................................773 376-9775
Angel Barreto, *Branch Mgr*
**EMP:** 6
**SALES (corp-wide):** 1.8B **Privately Held**
**WEB:** www.cartonplast.com
**SIC:** 3081 Polypropylene film & sheet
**HQ:** Orbis Rpm, Llc
1055 Corporate Center Dr
Oconomowoc WI 53066
262 560-5000

**(G-6004)**
**ORBIT ROOM**
2959 N California Ave (60618-7702)
PHONE.................................773 588-8540
Dirk Nebbeling, *Principal*
**EMP:** 7
**SALES (est):** 560.8K **Privately Held**
**SIC:** 2064 Candy bars, including chocolate covered bars

**(G-6005)**
**ORCHARD HILL CABINETRY INC (PA)**
Also Called: Builders Cabinet Supply
401 N Western Ave Ste 3 (60612-1418)
PHONE.................................312 829-4300
Brian Benner, *President*
Derek Poloski, *VP Opers*
Gail Benner, *Treasurer*
**EMP:** 26
**SALES (est):** 6.8MM **Privately Held**
**SIC:** 2434 Wood kitchen cabinets

**(G-6006)**
**ORECX**
1 N La Salle St Ste 1375 (60602-4351)
PHONE.................................312 895-5292
Fax: 312 895-5220
Bruce Kaskey, *CEO*
Ralph Atallah, *President*
Steve Kaiser, *Co-Founder*
Bruce D Kaskey, *CFO*
Craig McCue, *VP Sales*
**EMP:** 15
**SALES (est):** 1MM **Privately Held**
**SIC:** 7372 Prepackaged software

**(G-6007)**
**ORIENTAL KITCHEN CORPORATION (PA)**
Also Called: R R Sausage Factory
223 N Justine St (60607-1403)
PHONE.................................312 738-2850
Fax: 312 666-4442
Roman P Badiola, *President*
Rosario Manio, *Vice Pres*
Cleo S Badiola, *Admin Sec*
**EMP:** 7
**SALES (est):** 605K **Privately Held**
**SIC:** 2013 2011 Sausages from purchased meat; pork, cured: from purchased meat; meat packing plants

**(G-6008)**
**ORIENTAL KITCHEN CORPORATION**
223 N Justine St (60607-1403)
PHONE.................................312 738-2850
Rose Manio, *Manager*
**EMP:** 7
**SALES (corp-wide):** 605K **Privately Held**
**SIC:** 2013 Sausages from purchased meat
**PA:** Oriental Kitchen Corporation
223 N Justine St
Chicago IL 60607
312 738-2850

**(G-6009)**
**ORIENTAL NOODLE**
3808 W Lawrence Ave (60625-7856)
PHONE.................................773 279-1595
Nancy Truong, *Principal*
**EMP:** 4
**SALES (est):** 276.8K **Privately Held**
**SIC:** 2098 Macaroni & spaghetti

**(G-6010)**
**ORIGAMI RISK LLC (PA)**
222 Merchandise Mart Plz # 2300 (60654-1172)
PHONE.................................312 546-6515
Earne Bentley, *Vice Pres*
Wesley P Foster, *Vice Pres*
Kathy Buesch, *Finance*
Chris Bennett, *Sales Dir*
Jason Franks, *Sales Dir*
**EMP:** 1
**SALES (est):** 535.5K **Privately Held**
**SIC:** 7372 Business oriented computer software

**(G-6011)**
**ORIGINAL FERRARA INC**
Also Called: Original Ferrara Bakery
2210 W Taylor St (60612-4234)
PHONE.................................312 666-2200
Fax: 312 666-2008
Nello V Ferrara, *Ch of Bd*
William J Davy, *President*
Nella Davy, *Vice Pres*
**EMP:** 16 **EST:** 1908
**SQ FT:** 14,000
**SALES:** 750K **Privately Held**
**WEB:** www.ferrarabakery.com
**SIC:** 5149 5461 2051 Bakery products; bakeries; bread; cakes; cookies; bread, cake & related products

**(G-6012)**
**ORIGINAL GREEK SPECIALTIES**
Also Called: Olympia Gyros Co
5757 W 59th St (60638-3721)
PHONE.................................773 735-2250
Fax: 773 735-9108
Andre Papantoniou, *President*
Joanne Barera, *Office Mgr*
Kosta Papantoniou, *Admin Sec*
**EMP:** 20
**SQ FT:** 28,000
**SALES (est):** 4.5MM **Privately Held**
**SIC:** 2013 Frozen meats from purchased meat

**(G-6013)**
**ORIGINAL SHUTTER MAN**
1231 W 74th Pl (60636-4143)
PHONE.................................773 966-7160
James Johnson, *Founder*
**EMP:** 4
**SALES (est):** 407K **Privately Held**
**SIC:** 2431 Door shutters, wood

**(G-6014)**
**ORLAND SPORTS LTD**
Also Called: Club House Designs
5610 W Bloomingdale Ave # 1 (60639-4113)
PHONE.................................773 685-3711
Jon Sollberger, *Principal*
**EMP:** 5
**SALES (est):** 378.3K **Privately Held**
**SIC:** 2395 Embroidery & art needlework

**(G-6015)**
**ORLANDI STATUARY COMPANY**
1801 N Central Park Ave (60647-4703)
PHONE.................................773 489-0303
Fax: 773 489-2159
Fabio Orlandi, *President*
Dani Orlandi, *Vice Pres*
Bianca Orlandi, *Sales Dir*
▲ **EMP:** 54
**SQ FT:** 70,000
**SALES (est):** 6MM **Privately Held**
**WEB:** www.orlandicustom.com
**SIC:** 3999 3299 3272 Mannequins; art goods: plaster of paris, papier mache & scagliola; concrete products

**(G-6016)**
**ORSOLINIS WELDING & FABG**
3040 W Carroll Ave (60612-1722)
PHONE.................................773 722-9855
Fax: 773 722-9860
Theresa Orsolini, *President*
Joseph Orsolini, *Vice Pres*
Robert Orsolini, *Vice Pres*
Debbie Auggello, *Admin Sec*
▲ **EMP:** 15 **EST:** 1965
**SQ FT:** 30,000
**SALES:** 1.4MM **Privately Held**
**SIC:** 7692 3446 3441 Welding repair; architectural metalwork; fabricated structural metal

**(G-6017)**
**ORTHO SEATING LLC**
4444 W Ohio St (60624-1053)
PHONE.................................773 276-3539
Fax: 773 265-5610
Mark Levit, *General Mgr*
Mark Beguzman, *General Mgr*
Iakovos Platis, *General Mgr*
T Platis, *General Mgr*
Mirna Miranda, *Controller*
▲ **EMP:** 12
**SQ FT:** 28,000
**SALES (est):** 1.7MM **Privately Held**
**SIC:** 2522 5021 Chairs, office: padded or plain, except wood; chairs

**(G-6018)**
**ORTMAN-MCCAIN CO**
2303 W 18th St (60608-1808)
PHONE.................................312 666-2244
Nancy Newberger, *President*
David Allison, *Vice Pres*
Brian Sparks, *Plant Mgr*
**EMP:** 8 **EST:** 1947
**SQ FT:** 18,000
**SALES (est):** 915.5K **Privately Held**
**WEB:** www.ortman-mccain.com
**SIC:** 3555 3563 Printing trades machinery; air & gas compressors

**(G-6019)**
**ORVIS COMPANY INC**
142 E Ontario St Ste 1 (60611-5424)
PHONE.................................312 440-0662
Fax: 312 587-8713
Tj Roy, *General Mgr*
Nate Jenkins, *Office Mgr*
**EMP:** 10
**SALES (corp-wide):** 197MM **Privately Held**
**WEB:** www.orvis.com
**SIC:** 5961 5941 3949 Catalog sales; fitness & sporting goods, mail order; sporting goods & bicycle shops; fishing tackle, general
**PA:** The Orvis Company Inc
178 Conservation Way
Sunderland VT 05250
802 362-3622

**(G-6020)**
**OSCARS FOODS INC (PA)**
6125 W Belmont Ave (60634-4004)
PHONE.................................773 622-6822
Fax: 773 622-8344
Oscar Gramata, *President*
Lolita Gramata, *Admin Sec*
**EMP:** 8
**SQ FT:** 4,000
**SALES:** 750K **Privately Held**
**WEB:** www.oscarsfoods.com
**SIC:** 2013 Sausages from purchased meat; smoked meats from purchased meat; bacon, side & sliced: from purchased meat

**(G-6021)**
**OSI INDUSTRIES LLC**
Auto & Sons Stockyards
4545 S Racine Ave (60609-3371)
PHONE.................................773 847-2000
Fax: 773 847-0136
Ken Hertenstein, *Transptn Dir*
Eric Smith, *Plant Mgr*
John Dobias, *Opers-Prdtn-Mfg*
George Krzesinski, *Treasurer*
Joseph Sendelbach, *Treasurer*
**EMP:** 340
**SQ FT:** 20,000
**SALES (corp-wide):** 2.9B **Privately Held**
**SIC:** 5147 2013 Meats & meat products; sausages & other prepared meats
**HQ:** Osi Industries, Llc
1225 Corp Blvd Ste 105
Aurora IL 60505
630 851-6600

**(G-6022)**
**OSORIO IRON WORKS**
4515 W Thomas St (60651-3319)
PHONE.................................773 772-4060
Fax: 773 772-4184
Rueben Osorio, *President*
Martino Osorio, *Admin Sec*
**EMP:** 13
**SQ FT:** 750
**SALES (est):** 1.3MM **Privately Held**
**SIC:** 3446 Fences or posts, ornamental iron or steel

**(G-6023)**
**OTIS ELEVATOR COMPANY**
651 W Washington Blvd 1n (60661-2140)
PHONE.................................312 454-1616
Fax: 312 454-0217
Quanstrom Lillian, *Warehouse Mgr*
Alan Lindroth, *Marketing Staff*
Kun Peng, *Sr Project Mgr*
Kyle Franzen, *Manager*
**EMP:** 60
**SALES (corp-wide):** 57.2B **Publicly Held**
**WEB:** www.otis.com
**SIC:** 3446 3534 Elevator guide rails; elevators & equipment

# Chicago - Cook County (G-6024) — GEOGRAPHIC SECTION

HQ: Otis Elevator Company
1 Carrier Pl
Farmington CT 06032
860 674-3000

**(G-6024)**
**OTTOS DRAPERY SERVICE INC**
5219 W Cullom Ave (60641-1402)
PHONE .................... 773 777-7755
Otto Perez, *President*
**EMP:** 5
**SALES:** 200K **Privately Held**
**SIC: 2591** Drapery hardware & blinds & shades

**(G-6025)**
**OTUS LLC**
900 N Michigan Ave # 1600 (60611-1542)
PHONE .................... 312 229-7648
Andrew Bluhm,
Ally Erskine, *Executive Asst*
**EMP:** 32
**SALES (est):** 101.8K **Privately Held**
**SIC: 7372** Educational computer software

**(G-6026)**
**OUTDOOR SPACE LLC**
Also Called: Synlawn of Chicago
3120 N Sheffield Ave # 1 (60657-9314)
PHONE .................... 773 857-5296
**Fax:** 773 857-5297
**EMP:** 30
**SQ FT:** 10,000
**SALES (est):** 2.7MM **Privately Held**
**SIC: 3523** Mfg Turf

**(G-6027)**
**OUTPUT MEDICAL INC**
4660 N Ravenswood Ave (60640-4510)
PHONE .................... 630 430-8024
Jay Joshi, *CEO*
**EMP:** 3
**SQ FT:** 100
**SALES (est):** 108.2K **Privately Held**
**SIC: 3845** Automated blood & body fluid analyzers, except laboratory

**(G-6028)**
**OVERGRAD INC**
2545 W Diversey Ave # 215 (60647-7408)
PHONE .................... 312 324-4952
Ryan Hoch, *CEO*
Kevin Hoffman, *Co-Owner*
**EMP:** 4
**SQ FT:** 373
**SALES (est):** 98.3K **Privately Held**
**SIC: 7372** Educational computer software

**(G-6029)**
**OVERT PRESS INC**
4625 W 53rd St (60632-4903)
PHONE .................... 773 284-0909
**Fax:** 773 284-8833
Eileen Turcich, *President*
David Roach, *Business Mgr*
George W Turcich, *Corp Secy*
**EMP:** 35
**SQ FT:** 15,000
**SALES (est):** 4.2MM **Privately Held**
**WEB:** www.overtpress.com
**SIC: 2759** 7374 2752 2677 Letterpress printing; data processing service; commercial printing, lithographic; envelopes

**(G-6030)**
**OVERTON CHICAGO GEAR CORP**
2823 W Fulton St (60612-1705)
PHONE .................... 773 638-0508
**Fax:** 773 638-7161
Donald Brown, *CEO*
Chris Boudreau, *Production*
Adam Arters, *Finance*
Ramze Dahleh, *Human Resources*
▲ **EMP:** 62 **EST:** 1913
**SQ FT:** 46,000
**SALES (est):** 18.9MM **Privately Held**
**WEB:** www.cgdoj.com
**SIC: 3566** Reduction gears & gear units for turbines, except automotive; drives, high speed industrial, except hydrostatic; gears, power transmission, except automotive

**(G-6031)**
**OWANZA CORPORATION**
300 N La Salle Dr # 4295 (60654-3406)
PHONE .................... 312 281-2900
Emily Harrison, *Director*
**EMP:** 6
**SALES (est):** 185.9K **Privately Held**
**SIC: 7372** Prepackaged software

**(G-6032)**
**OWENS WELDING & FABRICATING**
548 N Sacramento Blvd (60612-1022)
PHONE .................... 773 265-9900
Steve Ben Dov, *President*
**EMP:** 10
**SALES (est):** 740K **Privately Held**
**SIC: 3441** Fabricated structural metal

**(G-6033)**
**OWN THE NIGHT APP**
1735 N Paulina St Apt 305 (60622-1461)
PHONE .................... 773 216-0245
Kevin Yu, *Principal*
John Sun, *Principal*
Paul Zhang, *Principal*
**EMP:** 3
**SALES (est):** 122.1K **Privately Held**
**SIC: 7372** Application computer software

**(G-6034)**
**OXXFORD CLOTHES XX INC (HQ)**
1220 W Van Buren St Fl 7 (60607-2842)
PHONE .................... 312 829-3600
**Fax:** 312 666-1751
Spencer Hayes, *Ch of Bd*
Sergio Casalena, *President*
David Brignoni, *Store Mgr*
Matthew Svejcar, *Prdtn Mgr*
Terrelle Hall, *Accountant*
**EMP:** 223
**SQ FT:** 105,000
**SALES (est):** 25.9MM
**SALES (corp-wide):** 317.5MM **Privately Held**
**WEB:** www.oxxfordclothes.com
**SIC: 2325** 2311 Men's & boys' trousers & slacks; suits, men's & boys': made from purchased materials; jackets, tailored suit-type: men's & boys'; tailored dress & sport coats: men's & boys'
**PA:** Tom James Company
263 Seaboard Ln
Franklin TN 37067
615 771-1122

**(G-6035)**
**OZINGA CHICAGO READY MIX CON**
1818 E 103rd St (60617-5641)
PHONE .................... 312 432-5700
**EMP:** 43
**SALES (corp-wide):** 221.8MM **Privately Held**
**SIC: 3273** Ready-mixed concrete
HQ: Ozinga Chicago Ready Mix Concrete, Inc
2255 S Lumber St
Chicago IL 60616

**(G-6036)**
**OZINGA CHICAGO READY MIX CON**
2001 N Mendell St (60614-3033)
PHONE .................... 773 862-2817
Rick Schicitano, *Manager*
**EMP:** 40
**SQ FT:** 53,700
**SALES (corp-wide):** 221.8MM **Privately Held**
**SIC: 3273** Ready-mixed concrete
HQ: Ozinga Chicago Ready Mix Concrete, Inc
2255 S Lumber St
Chicago IL 60616

**(G-6037)**
**OZINGA CHICAGO READY MIX CON (HQ)**
2255 S Lumber St (60616-2198)
PHONE .................... 847 447-0353
Justin Ozinga, *President*
Mattew Huisman, *Treasurer*
Barry N Voorn, *Admin Sec*
**EMP:** 40
**SQ FT:** 17,000
**SALES (est):** 27.7MM
**SALES (corp-wide):** 221.8MM **Privately Held**
**SIC: 3273** Ready-mixed concrete
**PA:** Ozinga Bros., Inc.
19001 Old Lagrange Rd # 30
Mokena IL 60448
708 326-4200

**(G-6038)**
**OZINGA CHICAGO READY MIX CON**
2255 S Lumber St (60616-2198)
PHONE .................... 312 432-5700
Tom Van Etten, *Manager*
**EMP:** 60
**SQ FT:** 3,800
**SALES (corp-wide):** 221.8MM **Privately Held**
**SIC: 3273** Ready-mixed concrete
HQ: Ozinga Chicago Ready Mix Concrete, Inc
2255 S Lumber St
Chicago IL 60616

**(G-6039)**
**P B A CORP**
522 N Western Ave (60612)
PHONE .................... 312 666-7370
**EMP:** 13 **EST:** 1963
**SQ FT:** 12,000
**SALES (est):** 97.2K **Privately Held**
**SIC: 3471** 3312 Plating/Polishing Service Blast Furnace-Steel Works

**(G-6040)**
**P S GREETINGS INC (PA)**
Also Called: Fantus Paper Products
5730 N Tripp Ave (60646-6741)
PHONE .................... 708 831-5340
**Fax:** 773 267-6055
Mark McCracken, *President*
Don Wilkin, *Sales Mgr*
Rose Bargas, *Accounts Mgr*
Ryan Cozzo, *Info Tech Mgr*
Patricia Lobosco, *Admin Sec*
▲ **EMP:** 150
**SQ FT:** 125,000
**SALES (est):** 44.7MM **Privately Held**
**WEB:** www.psgreetings.com
**SIC: 2771** Greeting cards

**(G-6041)**
**P&L GROUP LTD**
24 E 107th St (60628-3502)
PHONE .................... 773 660-1930
Pamela McElvane, *Principal*
Daisy Chan, *Director*
**EMP:** 12
**SALES (est):** 1.3MM **Privately Held**
**SIC: 2721** Magazines: publishing & printing

**(G-6042)**
**P-AMERICAS LLC**
Also Called: Pepsico
1400 W 35th St (60609-1311)
PHONE .................... 773 893-2300
**Fax:** 773 893-2306
Lucy Hanik, *Accountant*
Cathy Okrzesik, *Marketing Mgr*
Tom Beyak, *Marketing Staff*
George Augustin, *Branch Mgr*
Megan Carlson, *Manager*
**EMP:** 500
**SALES (corp-wide):** 62.8B **Publicly Held**
**SIC: 2086** Carbonated soft drinks, bottled & canned
HQ: P-Americas Llc
1 Pepsi Way
Somers NY

**(G-6043)**
**P-AMERICAS LLC**
Also Called: Pepsico
4931 S Union Ave (60609)
PHONE .................... 773 451-4499
**Fax:** 773 451-4423
**EMP:** 123
**SALES (corp-wide):** 62.8B **Publicly Held**
**SIC: 2086** Carbonated soft drinks, bottled & canned
HQ: P-Americas Llc
1 Pepsi Way
Somers NY

**(G-6044)**
**P-AMERICAS LLC**
Also Called: Pepsico
555 W Monroe St Ste 1 (60661-3605)
PHONE .................... 312 821-2266
Robert Scharringhausen, *Principal*
Rich Beck, *Sr Corp Ofcr*
Jair Cole, *Plant Mgr*
Ruth Potes, *Project Mgr*
Yolanda Cannella, *Buyer*
**EMP:** 75
**SALES (corp-wide):** 62.8B **Publicly Held**
**SIC: 2086** 5149 Bottled & canned soft drinks; soft drinks
HQ: P-Americas Llc
1 Pepsi Way
Somers NY

**(G-6045)**
**P-AMERICAS LLC**
Also Called: Pepsico
650 W 51st St (60609-5221)
PHONE .................... 773 624-8013
**Fax:** 773 451-4420
Rich Schutzenhofer, *President*
Alex Quintero, *Project Mgr*
Mike Booker, *Engineer*
John Schutt, *Human Res Dir*
Andy Ramirez, *Branch Mgr*
**EMP:** 150
**SALES (corp-wide):** 62.8B **Publicly Held**
**SIC: 2086** Carbonated soft drinks, bottled & canned
HQ: P-Americas Llc
1 Pepsi Way
Somers NY

**(G-6046)**
**P-K TOOL & MFG CO (PA)**
4700 W Le Moyne St (60651-1682)
PHONE .................... 773 235-4700
Philip P Kaiser Jr, *President*
Thomas P Kaiser, *President*
Roger Behrens, *Senior VP*
Bill Collatz, *Plant Mgr*
Darrin Nunley, *Plant Mgr*
**EMP:** 100
**SQ FT:** 40,000
**SALES (est):** 24.9MM **Privately Held**
**WEB:** www.pktool.com
**SIC: 3469** 3545 3549 Stamping metal for the trade; precision tools, machinists'; machine tool attachments & accessories; assembly machines, including robotic

**(G-6047)**
**PAANI FOODS INC**
6167 N Broadway St # 300 (60660-2501)
PHONE .................... 312 420-4624
◆ **EMP:** 10
**SALES:** 500K **Privately Held**
**SIC: 2038** 5142 Mfg & Whol Frozen Foods

**(G-6048)**
**PAASCHE AIRBRUSH CO**
4311 N Normandy Ave (60634-1395)
PHONE .................... 773 867-9191
**Fax:** 773 867-9198
John Pettersen, *President*
Vallie Pettersen, *President*
Ruth Cogan, *Vice Pres*
Brian Pettersen, *Vice Pres*
Steve Pettersen, *Vice Pres*
▲ **EMP:** 68 **EST:** 1904
**SQ FT:** 60,000
**SALES (est):** 12.6MM **Privately Held**
**WEB:** www.paascheairbrush.com
**SIC: 3952** 3563 3444 3443 Brushes, air, artists'; robots for industrial spraying, painting, etc.; spraying outfits: metals, paints & chemicals (compressor); air & gas compressors including vacuum pumps; sheet metalwork; fabricated plate work (boiler shop)

**(G-6049)**
**PAC TEAM US PRODUCTIONS LLC**
4447 W Armitage Ave (60639-3573)
PHONE .................... 773 360-8960
John Gedeon, *Project Mgr*
**EMP:** 7 **EST:** 2015

**SALES (est):** 643.3K  **Privately Held**
**SIC: 2541** 2434  Display fixtures, wood; wood kitchen cabinets

**(G-6050)**
### PACAP LLC
4753 N Broadway St # 1034  (60640-4990)
**PHONE** .................................. 773 754-7089
Deyuan Pan,
**EMP:** 5  **EST:** 2012
**SALES (est):** 302.1K  **Privately Held**
**SIC: 3575**  Computer terminals
**PA:** Fujian Guoguang Electronic Science And Technology Co., Ltd.
No.160, Jiangbin Blvd., Mawei, Economic And Technology Developme
Fuzhou
591 839-8961

**(G-6051)**
### PACE INDUSTRIES INC (PA)
2545 W Polk St  (60612-4127)
**PHONE** .................................. 312 226-5500
**Fax:** 312 226-0164
James Palka, *President*
Jack Dullaghan, *COO*
Richard Bontkowski, *Vice Pres*
Bob Rekart, *Chief Engr*
Mike Prasch, *CFO*
◆ **EMP:** 100
**SQ FT:** 100,000
**SALES (est):** 58.8MM  **Privately Held**
**SIC: 2434** 2514 3645  Vanities, bathroom: wood; medicine cabinets & vanities: metal; residential lighting fixtures

**(G-6052)**
### PACIFIC GRANITES INC
5 S Wabash Ave Ste 511  (60603-3485)
**PHONE** .................................. 312 835-7777
Mihir Karia, *Principal*
**EMP:** 8
**SALES (est):** 644.3K  **Privately Held**
**SIC: 1423**  Crushed & broken granite

**(G-6053)**
### PACKAGING CORPORATION AMERICA
Also Called: PCA Chicago Container
5445 W 73rd St  (60638-6500)
**PHONE** .................................. 708 821-1600
Ron Danczyk, *Vice Pres*
Steven Possler, *Branch Mgr*
**EMP:** 86
**SALES (corp-wide):** 5.7B  **Publicly Held**
**SIC: 2653**  Corrugated boxes, partitions, display items, sheets & pad
**PA:** Packaging Corporation Of America
1955 W Field Ct
Lake Forest IL 60045
847 482-3000

**(G-6054)**
### PACKAGING CORPORATION AMERICA
Also Called: PCA
5230 W Roosevelt Rd  (60644-1438)
**PHONE** .................................. 773 378-8700
Prafulla D'Souza, *Sales Dir*
Nate McFadyen, *Representative*
**EMP:** 3
**SALES (corp-wide):** 5.7B  **Publicly Held**
**SIC: 2653**  Corrugated & solid fiber boxes
**PA:** Packaging Corporation Of America
1955 W Field Ct
Lake Forest IL 60045
847 482-3000

**(G-6055)**
### PACKAGING DYNAMICS CORPORATION (DH)
Also Called: Bagcraft
3900 W 43rd St  (60632-3421)
**PHONE** .................................. 773 254-8000
**Fax:** 773 254-8204
Richard Goulet, *General Mgr*
Patrick T Chamblis, *Exec VP*
Suzette Martyka, *Vice Pres*
Dan Vice, *Vice Pres*
Russ Wanke, *Vice Pres*
▲ **EMP:** 282
**SALES (est):** 487.7MM
**SALES (corp-wide):** 2.2B  **Publicly Held**
**SIC: 2671**  Packaging paper & plastics film, coated & laminated
**HQ:** Hilex Poly Co. Llc
101 E Carolina Ave
Hartsville SC 29550
843 857-4800

**(G-6056)**
### PACKAGING DYNAMICS OPER CO
3900 W 43rd St  (60632-3421)
**PHONE** .................................. 773 843-8000
Phillip D Harris, *Principal*
**EMP:** 4
**SALES (est):** 266.1K
**SALES (corp-wide):** 2.2B  **Publicly Held**
**SIC: 2671**  Paper coated or laminated for packaging
**HQ:** Packaging Dynamics Corporation
3900 W 43rd St
Chicago IL 60632
773 254-8000

**(G-6057)**
### PAKET CORPORATION
Also Called: Packet
9165 S Lake Shore Dr  (60617-4407)
**PHONE** .................................. 773 221-7300
**Fax:** 773 221-7316
Mark O'Malley, *President*
David Alvarez, *Vice Pres*
Stella Diaz, *Vice Pres*
Matt Zoeller, *Vice Pres*
Selina Grankowski, *Human Res Mgr*
**EMP:** 50
**SQ FT:** 105,000
**SALES (est):** 7.3MM  **Privately Held**
**WEB:** www.paketcorp.com
**SIC: 7389** 2844  Packaging & labeling services; face creams or lotions

**(G-6058)**
### PAKISTAN NEWS
6033 N Sheridan Rd  (60660-3003)
**PHONE** .................................. 773 271-6400
Ifti Nasim, *Manager*
**EMP:** 4
**SALES (est):** 163.7K  **Privately Held**
**SIC: 2711**  Newspapers

**(G-6059)**
### PALEO PRIME LLC
1106 W Newport Ave Apt 3  (60657-1513)
**PHONE** .................................. 312 659-6596
Casey M McMillin, *Mng Member*
**EMP:** 1
**SALES:** 200K  **Privately Held**
**SIC: 2052**  Cookies

**(G-6060)**
### PALETERIA AZTECA INC
Also Called: Paleteria Azteca 2
3119 W Cermak Rd  (60623-3451)
**PHONE** .................................. 773 277-1423
Sabas Guzman, *President*
▲ **EMP:** 4
**SALES (est):** 368.7K  **Privately Held**
**SIC: 2024**  Ice cream, bulk

**(G-6061)**
### PALETERIA EL SABOR
1639 W 18th St  (60608-2835)
**PHONE** .................................. 312 243-2308
Jose C Fierro, *President*
**EMP:** 4  **EST:** 2011
**SALES (est):** 300.2K  **Privately Held**
**SIC: 2024**  Ice cream & frozen desserts

**(G-6062)**
### PALETERIA EL SABOR DE MICHOACN
2456 W 47th St  (60632-1336)
**PHONE** .................................. 773 376-3880
Angelica Barajas, *President*
**EMP:** 3
**SALES (est):** 251.2K  **Privately Held**
**SIC: 2024**  Ice cream, bulk

**(G-6063)**
### PALLET BASE LLC
1000 W Wa Blvd Unit 229  (60607-2115)
**PHONE** .................................. 312 316-6137
Brian J McCarthy, *Principal*
**EMP:** 3
**SALES (est):** 173.8K  **Privately Held**
**SIC: 2448**  Pallets, wood & wood with metal

**(G-6064)**
### PALM LABS ADHESIVES LLC ○
2550 N Lakeview Ave  (60614-2045)
**PHONE** .................................. 773 799-8470
**EMP:** 3  **EST:** 2017
**SALES (est):** 123.2K  **Privately Held**
**SIC: 2891**  Adhesives

**(G-6065)**
### PALMER PRINTING INC
739 S Clark St Fl 1  (60605-1760)
**PHONE** .................................. 312 427-7150
**Fax:** 312 427-5387
Ciro A Rossini, *Ch of Bd*
Edmund Rossini, *President*
Gene Modloff, *General Mgr*
Douglas Doolittle, *Sales Mgr*
**EMP:** 38  **EST:** 1935
**SQ FT:** 15,000
**SALES (est):** 8MM  **Privately Held**
**WEB:** www.palmer-printing.com
**SIC: 2752** 2732  Commercial printing, offset; book printing

**(G-6066)**
### PALMGREN STEEL PRODUCTS INC
4444 W Ohio St  (60624-1053)
**PHONE** .................................. 773 265-5700
**Fax:** 773 265-5740
Mark Lebit, *President*
Suriya Ramachandra, *General Mgr*
Ernie Torkilsen, *VP Sales*
**EMP:** 10
**SQ FT:** 60,000
**SALES (est):** 888.5K
**SALES (corp-wide):** 25.1MM  **Privately Held**
**WEB:** www.palmgren.com
**SIC: 3545**  Vises, machine (machine tool accessories); rotary tables
**PA:** The C H Hanson Company
2000 N Aurora Rd
Naperville IL 60563
630 848-2000

**(G-6067)**
### PANCHOS ICE CREAM
4055 W 31st St  (60623-4904)
**PHONE** .................................. 773 254-3141
Hilda Magallon, *Owner*
Jeffe Perez, *Manager*
**EMP:** 6
**SQ FT:** 180
**SALES (est):** 250K  **Privately Held**
**SIC: 2024**  Ice cream & ice milk

**(G-6068)**
### PANDA GRAPHICS INC
451 N Racine Ave Fl 1  (60642-5841)
**PHONE** .................................. 312 666-7642
Aljay Juozaitis, *President*
Mary E Borowczyk, *Office Mgr*
**EMP:** 3
**SALES (est):** 250K  **Privately Held**
**SIC: 2752** 2759  Lithographing on metal; commercial printing, offset; letterpress printing

**(G-6069)**
### PANDADERIA EL ACAMBARO
1720 W 18th St  (60608-1914)
**PHONE** .................................. 312 666-6316
**EMP:** 6
**SALES (est):** 447.6K  **Privately Held**
**SIC: 3565**  Bread wrapping machinery

**(G-6070)**
### PAOLI INC
222 Merchandise Mart Plz # 380  (60654-1245)
**PHONE** .................................. 312 644-5509
▲ **EMP:** 4
**SALES (est):** 440K  **Privately Held**
**SIC: 2521**  Mfg Office Furniture-Nonwood

**(G-6071)**
### PAPA CHARLIES INC
1800 S Kostner Ave  (60623-2339)
**PHONE** .................................. 773 522-7900
**Fax:** 773 522-7864
Joe Hall, *President*
Chris Hall, *Vice Pres*
George Rackos, *Vice Pres*
Mellisa Elmore, *Office Mgr*
**EMP:** 25
**SQ FT:** 20,000
**SALES (est):** 11.4MM  **Privately Held**
**WEB:** www.papacharlies.com
**SIC: 2013**  Sausages & other prepared meats

**(G-6072)**
### PAPIROS GRAPHICS
4557 W 59th St  (60629-5437)
**PHONE** .................................. 773 581-3000
Rodolfo A Alvarado, *Partner*
**EMP:** 4
**SALES (est):** 388.2K  **Privately Held**
**SIC: 2752**  Commercial printing, lithographic

**(G-6073)**
### PAPPONE INC
Also Called: Pasta Pappone
2041 W Carroll Ave C214  (60612-1692)
**PHONE** .................................. 630 234-4738
Jonathan P Mulholland, *CEO*
**EMP:** 5  **EST:** 2013
**SQ FT:** 1,200
**SALES (est):** 350.5K  **Privately Held**
**SIC: 5499** 2033  Gourmet food stores; spaghetti & other pasta sauce: packaged in cans, jars, etc.

**(G-6074)**
### PAPYRUS PRESS INC
3441 W Grand Ave  (60651-4001)
**PHONE** .................................. 773 342-0700
**Fax:** 773 342-3063
Gus Lymperopoulos, *President*
Constantine Lymperopoulos, *President*
Nick Lymperopoulos, *Vice Pres*
Angelos Sidereas, *Treasurer*
**EMP:** 10
**SQ FT:** 25,000
**SALES (est):** 1.1MM  **Privately Held**
**SIC: 2759** 2752 2791 2396  Screen printing; commercial printing, offset; typesetting; automotive & apparel trimmings

**(G-6075)**
### PARADE PUBLICATIONS INC
500 N Michigan Ave # 910  (60611-3741)
**PHONE** .................................. 312 661-1620
**Fax:** 312 661-0776
Heather Faust, *Sales/Mktg Mgr*
Beverly Vacval, *Manager*
**EMP:** 12
**SQ FT:** 3,000
**SALES (corp-wide):** 354MM  **Privately Held**
**SIC: 2721**  Magazines: publishing only, not printed on site
**HQ:** Parade Publications, Inc.
711 3rd Ave
New York NY 10017
212 450-7000

**(G-6076)**
### PARAGON SPRING COMPANY
4435 W Rice St Ste 45  (60651-3457)
**PHONE** .................................. 773 489-6300
**Fax:** 773 489-6356
Marilyn L Whittle, *CEO*
Amy L Whittle, *President*
**EMP:** 20  **EST:** 1945
**SQ FT:** 32,000
**SALES (est):** 4.4MM  **Privately Held**
**SIC: 3493** 3312 3469 3496  Flat springs, sheet or strip stock; wire products, steel or iron; stamping metal for the trade; miscellaneous fabricated wire products; wire springs

**(G-6077)**
### PARAMOUNT PLASTICS INC
140 S Dearborn St Ste 420  (60603-5233)
**PHONE** .................................. 815 834-4100
**Fax:** 815 834-1410
Doug Mulay, *President*
Larry Scales, *Principal*
Peggy Scales, *Corp Secy*
Carolyn Mills, *QC Mgr*
Nancy Powers, *Finance Dir*
**EMP:** 80
**SQ FT:** 120,000
**SALES (est):** 17.4MM  **Privately Held**
**SIC: 3089**  Injection molding of plastics

## Chicago - Cook County (G-6078)

**(G-6078)**
**PARAMOUNT PLASTICS LLC**
140 S Dearborn St Ste 420 (60603-5233)
PHONE.................................815 834-4100
Fax: 815 834-1920
Doug Mulay,
Matt Simpson,
Ken Swanick,
**EMP:** 100
**SQ FT:** 140,000
**SALES (est):** 14.4MM **Privately Held**
**WEB:** www.paramountplastics.net
**SIC:** 2131 Chewing tobacco

**(G-6079)**
**PARAMOUNT TRUCK BODY CO INC**
2107 W Fulton St (60612-2313)
PHONE.................................312 666-6441
Fax: 312 666-4215
Joseph Smolucha, *President*
Greg Smolucha, *Corp Secy*
Stephanie Smolucha, *Vice Pres*
Ronald Havrianek, *CPA*
**EMP:** 20
**SQ FT:** 15,000
**SALES (est):** 4MM **Privately Held**
**SIC:** 3713 3715 Truck bodies (motor vehicles); trailer bodies

**(G-6080)**
**PARAMOUNT WIRE SPECIALTIES**
4106 W Chicago Ave 10 (60651-3622)
PHONE.................................773 252-5636
Fax: 773 252-5636
James E Macy, *President*
Mary Macy, *Admin Sec*
**EMP:** 18 **EST:** 1949
**SQ FT:** 12,000
**SALES (est):** 2.2MM **Privately Held**
**SIC:** 3496 7692 3993 3645 Lamp frames, wire; welding repair; signs & advertising specialties; residential lighting fixtures

**(G-6081)**
**PARENTEAU STUDIOS**
3401 N Knox Ave (60641-3728)
PHONE.................................312 337-8015
Fax: 312 337-7139
Paul Parenteau, *Owner*
Helen Waserztrum, *Controller*
**EMP:** 20
**SQ FT:** 58,500
**SALES (est):** 1.4MM **Privately Held**
**WEB:** www.parenteaustudios.com
**SIC:** 2391 7641 2514 2512 Draperies, plastic & textile: from purchased materials; reupholstery; household furniture: upholstered on metal frames; upholstered household furniture; mattresses & bedsprings

**(G-6082)**
**PARISO INC**
Also Called: V P Plating
1836 N Lockwood Ave (60639-4353)
PHONE.................................773 889-4383
Victor V Pariso, *President*
John P Pariso, *Vice Pres*
Sandra J Pariso, *Director*
**EMP:** 10 **EST:** 1919
**SQ FT:** 10,000
**SALES (est):** 1.8MM **Privately Held**
**WEB:** www.vpmetalcoat.com
**SIC:** 3471 Electroplating of metals or formed products; polishing, metals or formed products

**(G-6083)**
**PARK PACKING COMPANY INC**
4107 S Ashland Ave (60609-2331)
PHONE.................................773 254-0100
Fax: 773 254-9414
Athanasios Bairaktaris, *President*
Thomas A Birkrktirs, *Sales Mgr*
Emily Bairaktaris, *Admin Sec*
**EMP:** 28
**SQ FT:** 10,000
**SALES (est):** 11.8MM **Privately Held**
**SIC:** 5147 2011 5421 2013 Meats, fresh; meat packing plants; meat & fish markets; sausages & other prepared meats; slaughtering: custom livestock services

**(G-6084)**
**PARK-HIO FRGED MCHNED PDTS LLC**
Also Called: Kropp Forge
5301 W Roosevelt Rd (60804-1224)
PHONE.................................708 652-6691
Fax: 708 652-6696
Thomas Pollard, *President*
Les Havlik, *Controller*
▲ **EMP:** 85
**SQ FT:** 450,000
**SALES (est):** 37.3MM
**SALES (corp-wide):** 1.2B **Publicly Held**
**WEB:** www.kroppforge.com
**SIC:** 3462 Iron & steel forgings
**HQ:** Park-Ohio Industries, Inc.
6065 Parkland Blvd Ste 1
Cleveland OH 44124
440 947-2000

**(G-6085)**
**PARK-OHIO INDUSTRIES INC**
Park Ohio Forged Machined Pdts
5301 W Roosevelt Rd (60804-1224)
PHONE.................................708 652-6691
John Chrzanowski, *Senior VP*
Vickey Weber, *QC Mgr*
Rochelle Kosmos, *Branch Mgr*
David Hill,
**EMP:** 85
**SALES (corp-wide):** 1.2B **Publicly Held**
**WEB:** www.pkoh.com.cn
**SIC:** 3911 Medals, precious or semi-precious metal
**HQ:** Park-Ohio Industries, Inc.
6065 Parkland Blvd Ste 1
Cleveland OH 44124
440 947-2000

**(G-6086)**
**PARKER HOUSE SAUSAGE COMPANY (PA)**
4605 S State St (60609-4699)
PHONE.................................773 538-1112
Fax: 773 285-0903
Michael Parker, *CEO*
Robin McFolling, *President*
Azieb Parker, *Admin Sec*
▲ **EMP:** 33 **EST:** 1920
**SQ FT:** 37,000
**SALES (est):** 4.7MM **Privately Held**
**SIC:** 2013 Sausages from purchased meat

**(G-6087)**
**PARROT PRESS**
4484 S Archer Ave (60632-2846)
PHONE.................................773 376-6333
Fax: 773 376-6333
David Hines, *Owner*
**EMP:** 3
**SQ FT:** 1,800
**SALES (est):** 170K **Privately Held**
**SIC:** 2752 2789 Commercial printing, offset; bookbinding & related work

**(G-6088)**
**PASTAFRESH CO**
Also Called: Pastafresh Homemade Pasta
3418 N Harlem Ave (60634-3605)
PHONE.................................773 745-5888
Anthony Bartucci, *President*
Gino Bartucci, *Admin Sec*
▲ **EMP:** 4
**SQ FT:** 1,200
**SALES (est):** 359.6K **Privately Held**
**SIC:** 2099 2098 2035 Packaged combination products: pasta, rice & potato; pasta, uncooked: packaged with other ingredients; macaroni & spaghetti; pickles, sauces & salad dressings

**(G-6089)**
**PASTORELLI FOOD PRODUCTS INC**
901 W Lake St (60607)
PHONE.................................312 455-1006
Noe Lara, *Manager*
Linda Fraid, *Administration*
**EMP:** 3
**SQ FT:** 61,000
**SALES (corp-wide):** 2.2MM **Privately Held**
**WEB:** www.pastorelli.com
**SIC:** 2032 2033 2099 2079 Italian foods: packaged in cans, jars, etc.; spaghetti: packaged in cans, jars, etc.; pizza sauce: packaged in cans, jars, etc.; vinegar; cooking oils, except corn: vegetable refined; vegetable shortenings (except corn oil)
**PA:** Pastorelli Food Products, Inc.
162 N Sangamon St
Chicago IL 60607
312 666-2041

**(G-6090)**
**PAUL D METAL PRODUCTS INC**
2225 W Pershing Rd (60609-2210)
PHONE.................................773 847-1400
Fax: 773 847-1451
Farshid Paul Ohadi, *President*
David Nohava, *Vice Pres*
Marina Guzeman, *Manager*
**EMP:** 55
**SQ FT:** 180,000
**SALES (est):** 7.6MM **Privately Held**
**SIC:** 3646 3446 Commercial indusl & institutional electric lighting fixtures; architectural metalwork

**(G-6091)**
**PAUL SISTI**
Also Called: Paul Sisti Studio
3520 N Lake Shore Dr (60657-1860)
PHONE.................................773 472-5615
Fax: 773 472-5615
Paul Sisti, *Owner*
**EMP:** 3
**SALES:** 60K **Privately Held**
**SIC:** 7219 2339 Dressmaking service, material owned by customer; women's & misses' outerwear

**(G-6092)**
**PAYMENT PATHWAYS INC**
8745 W Higgins Rd Ste 240 (60631-4020)
PHONE.................................312 346-9400
Richard Obrien, *President*
**EMP:** 3
**SALES (est):** 153.2K **Privately Held**
**SIC:** 2741 Telephone & other directory publishing

**(G-6093)**
**PEAK HEALTHCARE ADVISORS LLC**
Also Called: Battle Balls Bubble Soccer
4043 N Ravenswood Ave # 225 (60613-5682)
PHONE.................................646 479-0005
Randy Carlson, *CEO*
**EMP:** 4
**SALES (est):** 138.6K **Privately Held**
**SIC:** 3949 Team sports equipment

**(G-6094)**
**PECHINEY CAST PLATE**
8770 W Bryn Mawr Ave Fl 9 (60631-3515)
P.O. Box 58447, Los Angeles CA (90058-0447)
PHONE.................................847 299-0220
Tom Reynolds, *General Mgr*
Charles Sheperd, *Controller*
**EMP:** 120 **EST:** 1940
**SQ FT:** 611,000
**SALES (est):** 14.7MM **Privately Held**
**SIC:** 3353 Mfg Aluminum Sheet/Foil

**(G-6095)**
**PEER FOODS INC (HQ)**
1200 W 35th St Fl 3 (60609-1305)
PHONE.................................773 927-1440
Larry O' Connell, *President*
David Henson, *Opers Mgr*
Tom Grantner, *Research*
Donna Recupido, *Treasurer*
Tom Sutton, *Accounting Dir*
**EMP:** 2
**SQ FT:** 10,000
**SALES (est):** 1.4MM
**SALES (corp-wide):** 81MM **Privately Held**
**SIC:** 2011 Meat packing plants

**PA:** Peer Foods Group, Inc.
1200 W 35th St Fl 3
Chicago IL 60609
773 927-1440

**(G-6096)**
**PEERLESS**
4855 S Racine Ave (60609-4320)
PHONE.................................773 294-2667
Bill A Dowell, *Principal*
**EMP:** 3
**SALES (est):** 398.9K **Privately Held**
**SIC:** 3552 Embroidery machines

**(G-6097)**
**PEGAS WINDOW INC**
4100 W Grand Ave Ste 1 (60651-1882)
PHONE.................................773 394-6466
Fax: 773 394-6470
Krzysztof Nowak, *President*
Mirso Dragavic, *Corp Secy*
Roman Yactkowskyy, *Vice Pres*
**EMP:** 5
**SALES (est):** 2MM **Privately Held**
**SIC:** 3442 Screen & storm doors & windows

**(G-6098)**
**PEKAY MACHINE & ENGRG CO INC**
2520 W Lake St (60612-2108)
PHONE.................................312 829-5530
Fax: 312 829-3388
Jules T Parisi Jr, *President*
Charles J Parisi, *Vice Pres*
Jean Parisi, *Asst Sec*
**EMP:** 13 **EST:** 1945
**SQ FT:** 25,000
**SALES (est):** 2.4MM **Privately Held**
**WEB:** www.pekay.com
**SIC:** 3559 3498 Foundry machinery & equipment; tube fabricating (contract bending & shaping)

**(G-6099)**
**PENDRAGON SOFTWARE CORPORATION**
118 S Clinton St Ste 570 (60661-5771)
PHONE.................................847 816-9660
Daniel Phillips, *President*
Blake Dalzin, *Sales Mgr*
John Lee, *Software Dev*
Samantha Attaguile, *Executive Asst*
**EMP:** 5
**SQ FT:** 1,800
**SALES (est):** 470K **Privately Held**
**WEB:** www.pendragonsoftware.com
**SIC:** 7372 7371 Computer software development & applications

**(G-6100)**
**PENTON MEDIA INC**
Also Called: Penton Media - Aviation Week
24652 Network Pl (60673-1246)
PHONE.................................212 204-4200
**EMP:** 3
**SALES (corp-wide):** 1.4B **Privately Held**
**SIC:** 2721 7389 7313 7375 Periodicals; advertising, promotional & trade show services; printed media advertising representatives; on-line data base information retrieval
**HQ:** Penton Media, Inc.
1166 Avenue Of The Americ
New York NY 10036
212 204-4200

**(G-6101)**
**PEOPLE AGAINST DIRTY MFG PBC**
720 E 111th St (60628-4669)
PHONE.................................415 568-4600
Drew Fraser, *COO*
**EMP:** 66
**SALES (est):** 12.1MM **Privately Held**
**SIC:** 2841 Soap & other detergents
**HQ:** Ecover Co-Ordination Center Nv
Steenovenstraat 1, Internal Postal Box A
Malle
323 309-2500

## GEOGRAPHIC SECTION
## Chicago - Cook County (G-6126)

### (G-6102)
**PEOPLEADMIN INC**
4611 N Ravenswood Ave # 201 (60640-7564)
**PHONE**..................877 637-5800
**EMP:** 50
**SALES (corp-wide):** 21.4MM **Privately Held**
**SIC: 7372** 8299 Educational computer software; educational services
**PA:** Peopleadmin, Inc.
  805 Las Cimas Pkwy # 400
  Austin TX 78746
  877 637-5800

### (G-6103)
**PEOPLES TRIBUNE**
2421 W Pratt Blvd (60645-4603)
**PHONE**..................773 486-3551
Laura Garcia, *Principal*
**EMP:** 30
**SALES (est):** 1.1MM **Privately Held**
**SIC: 2711** Newspapers, publishing & printing

### (G-6104)
**PEORIA PACKING LTD (PA)**
1307 W Lake St (60607-1511)
**PHONE**..................312 226-2600
**Fax:** 312 226-8752
Harry Katsiavelos, *President*
Louis Manis, *Vice Pres*
Georgia Katsiavelos, *Admin Sec*
**EMP:** 15
**SQ FT:** 18,000
**SALES (est):** 11MM **Privately Held**
**SIC: 2011** 5147 5421 Meat packing plants; meats & meat products; meat markets, including freezer provisioners

### (G-6105)
**PEPSICO INC**
555 W Monroe St Fl 1 (60661-3700)
**PHONE**..................312 821-1000
Deb Hertler, *Vice Pres*
Jim Lynch, *Vice Pres*
Jim Freeman, *Project Mgr*
Jill Struzik, *Project Mgr*
Eric Wenner, *Research*
**EMP:** 3
**SALES (corp-wide):** 62.8B **Publicly Held**
**SIC: 2086** 2087 2096 Bottled & canned soft drinks; flavoring extracts & syrups; potato chips & similar snacks
**PA:** Pepsico, Inc.
  700 Anderson Hill Rd
  Purchase NY 10577
  914 253-2000

### (G-6106)
**PERADATA TECHNOLOGY CORP**
4324 N Damen Ave (60618-1706)
**PHONE**..................631 588-2216
Kevin Kanakos, *President*
**EMP:** 40
**SALES:** 3MM **Privately Held**
**WEB:** www.peradata.com
**SIC: 3577** Computer peripheral equipment

### (G-6107)
**PERVASIVE HEALTH INC**
1 N La Salle St Ste 1825 (60602-3933)
**PHONE**..................312 257-2967
Paul Magelli, *CEO*
Geoff Phillips, *CFO*
Leigh Sauceda, *Accountant*
**EMP:** 5
**SALES (est):** 481.1K **Privately Held**
**SIC: 7372** 7373 Business oriented computer software; computer integrated systems design

### (G-6108)
**PETEGO EGR LLC**
8 S Michigan Ave Ste 1601 (60603-3314)
**PHONE**..................312 726-1341
Emanuele Bianchi,
▲ **EMP:** 8
**SQ FT:** 14,000
**SALES (est):** 990.2K **Privately Held**
**WEB:** www.petego.com
**SIC: 3999** 5199 Pet supplies; pet supplies

### (G-6109)
**PETER TROOST MONUMENT CO**
6605 S Pulaski Rd (60629-5137)
**PHONE**..................773 585-0242
Frank Troost, *Manager*
**EMP:** 5
**SQ FT:** 2,300
**SALES (corp-wide):** 14MM **Privately Held**
**WEB:** www.troost.com
**SIC: 3281** 5999 Cut stone & stone products; monuments, finished to custom order
**PA:** Peter Troost Monument Co.
  4300 Roosevelt Rd
  Hillside IL
  708 544-0916

### (G-6110)
**PETERS CONSTRUCTION**
3441 W Grand Ave (60651-4001)
**PHONE**..................773 489-5555
Aracela Perez, *Owner*
**EMP:** 9
**SALES (est):** 1.1MM **Privately Held**
**SIC: 2431** 1751 1521 Millwork; carpentry work; new construction, single-family houses

### (G-6111)
**PETERSON BROTHERS PLASTICS**
2929 N Pulaski Rd (60641-5421)
**PHONE**..................773 286-5666
**Fax:** 773 286-5888
Kenneth Peterson, *President*
Keith Peterson, *Vice Pres*
Kevin Peterson, *Admin Sec*
**EMP:** 12 **EST:** 1943
**SQ FT:** 16,000
**SALES (est):** 2MM **Privately Held**
**WEB:** www.petersenplastics.com
**SIC: 5162** 3993 Plastics materials; signs, not made in custom sign painting shops

### (G-6112)
**PETOTE LLC**
2444 W 16th St Ste 4 (60608-1731)
**PHONE**..................312 455-0873
**Fax:** 312 455-1368
Janet Lee,
▲ **EMP:** 7
**SALES (est):** 821.9K **Privately Held**
**WEB:** www.petote.com
**SIC: 3999** Pet supplies

### (G-6113)
**PETRA MANUFACTURING CO**
Also Called: Screenprint Products
6600 W Armitage Ave (60707-3908)
**PHONE**..................773 622-1475
**Fax:** 773 622-9448
Norman C Hoffberg, *President*
Cheryl Visockis, *Vice Pres*
Tom Cordina, *Controller*
Pat Walczewski, *Sales Staff*
▲ **EMP:** 70 **EST:** 1933
**SQ FT:** 68,000
**SALES (est):** 9.7MM **Privately Held**
**WEB:** www.petramanufacturing.com
**SIC: 2396** 2385 2671 Printing & embossing on plastics fabric articles; screen printing on fabric articles; aprons, waterproof: made from purchased materials; gowns, plastic: made from purchased materials; plastic film, coated or laminated for packaging

### (G-6114)
**PETRO CHEM ECHER ERHARDT LLC**
Also Called: Petro-Chem Industries Div
2628 S Sacramento Ave (60623-5118)
**PHONE**..................773 847-7535
**Fax:** 773 847-7595
Charles Schroeder, *Manager*
**EMP:** 8
**SQ FT:** 15,000
**SALES (est):** 1.4MM **Privately Held**
**WEB:** www.petrochemind.com
**SIC: 7699** 3443 Boiler & heating repair services; fabricated plate work (boiler shop)

### (G-6115)
**PFINGSTEN PARTNERS LLC (PA)**
300 N Lasalle St 5400 (60654)
**PHONE**..................312 222-8707
Phillip D Bronsteatter, *Finance*
Jeffrey A Channey, *Finance*
Thomas J Gaul, *Finance*
Nick R Johansson, *Finance*
Ryan T Lavelle, *Finance*
◆ **EMP:** 13
**SQ FT:** 6,800
**SALES (est):** 152.1MM **Privately Held**
**WEB:** www.pfingstenpartners.com
**SIC: 5065** 6211 3679 3578 Video equipment, electronic; investment firm, general brokerage; electronic switches; coin counters

### (G-6116)
**PFINGSTEN PARTNERS FUND IV LP**
300 N La Salle Dr (60654-3406)
**PHONE**..................312 222-8707
Phillip D Bronsteatter, *Vice Pres*
Matthew P Schloop, *Vice Pres*
Jeffrey A Cote, *CFO*
Andrew W Petri, *Controller*
Thomas S Bagley,
**EMP:** 276
**SALES:** 168K
**SALES (corp-wide):** 152.1MM **Privately Held**
**SIC: 2511** Porch furniture & swings: wood
**PA:** Pfingsten Partners, L.L.C.
  300 N LaSalle St 5400
  Chicago IL 60654
  312 222-8707

### (G-6117)
**PHILS AUTO BODY**
833 W 35th St (60609-1511)
**PHONE**..................773 847-7156
Phil Winstead, *Principal*
**EMP:** 7
**SALES (est):** 342.1K **Privately Held**
**SIC: 7532** 3713 3711 Body shop, automotive; truck & bus bodies; automobile bodies, passenger car, not including engine, etc.

### (G-6118)
**PHOENIX ELECTRIC MFG CO**
3625 N Halsted St (60613-4394)
**PHONE**..................773 477-8855
**Fax:** 773 477-0867
Sanford Bank, *Ch of Bd*
Norberto Anselmi, *President*
Saul Perez, *Vice Pres*
Douglas Bank, *Sales Mgr*
Claudio Orellana, *Manager*
▲ **EMP:** 44 **EST:** 1936
**SQ FT:** 15,000
**SALES (est):** 7.4MM **Privately Held**
**WEB:** www.phoenixelectric.com
**SIC: 3089** Handles, brush or tool: plastic

### (G-6119)
**PHOENIX INTL PUBLICATIONS INC**
Also Called: Pikids
8501 W Higgins Rd Ste 300 (60631-2812)
**PHONE**..................312 739-4400
Vincent Douglas, *CEO*
Liam Qian, *Senior VP*
Liang Qian, *Senior VP*
Alen Qin, *CFO*
▲ **EMP:** 300
**SALES:** 100MM
**SALES (corp-wide):** 59.9MM **Privately Held**
**SIC: 5942** 2731 Children's books; books: publishing & printing
**HQ:** Jiangsu Phoenix Publishing And Media Corporation Limited
  27/F, Block B, Phoenix Plaza, No.1 Hunan Road
  Nanjing 21000
  258 365-7811

### (G-6120)
**PHOENIX TREE PUBLISHING INC**
5660 N Jersey Ave (60659-3626)
**PHONE**..................773 251-0309
▲ **EMP:** 3
**SALES (est):** 301.9K **Privately Held**
**SIC: 2741** Miscellaneous publishing

### (G-6121)
**PICKLES SORREL INC**
Also Called: Puckered Pickle
5610 W Taylor St (60644-5507)
**PHONE**..................773 379-4748
**Fax:** 773 379-4738
Steven Nathan, *President*
Wayne Newman, *Vice Pres*
**EMP:** 15
**SQ FT:** 12,000
**SALES (est):** 3.1MM **Privately Held**
**WEB:** www.puckeredpickle.com
**SIC: 2035** Pickles, vinegar

### (G-6122)
**PILLA EXEC INC**
2447 W 80th St (60652-2863)
**PHONE**..................312 882-8263
James Perkins, *CEO*
**EMP:** 3
**SQ FT:** 700
**SALES (est):** 180K **Privately Held**
**SIC: 6798** 3253 5511 Real estate investment trusts; ceramic wall & floor tile; automobiles, new & used

### (G-6123)
**PILZ AUTOMTN SAFETY LTD PARTNR**
7021 Solutions Ctr (60677-7000)
**PHONE**..................734 354-0272
**EMP:** 3
**SALES (corp-wide):** 358.9MM **Privately Held**
**SIC: 3625** Relays & industrial controls
**HQ:** Pilz Automation Safety, Limited Partnership
  7150 Commerce Blvd
  Canton MI 48187

### (G-6124)
**PINNACLE PUBLISHING INC**
316 N Michigan Ave Cl20 (60601-3773)
**PHONE**..................218 444-2180
**EMP:** 10
**SALES:** 4.5MM **Privately Held**
**WEB:** www.edgequest.com
**SIC: 2721** 2731 Trade journals: publishing & printing; book publishing

### (G-6125)
**PIONEER FORMS INC**
3921 N Elston Ave (60618-4227)
**PHONE**..................773 539-8587
**Fax:** 773 539-5057
Kwang Lim Rah, *President*
Yunhee Rah, *Vice Pres*
**EMP:** 5
**SQ FT:** 10,000
**SALES (est):** 420K **Privately Held**
**SIC: 2759** Business forms: printing

### (G-6126)
**PIONEER NEWSPAPERS INC (DH)**
Also Called: Pioneer Press
350 N Orleans St Fl 10 (60654-1975)
**PHONE**..................847 486-0600
**Fax:** 847 486-7416
Nancy Riles, *Business Mgr*
Mark Cohen, *COO*
Greg Powell, *Vice Pres*
Michael Sperling, *Vice Pres*
Louis Skonieczny, *Credit Mgr*
**EMP:** 230
**SQ FT:** 38,500
**SALES (est):** 34.3MM
**SALES (corp-wide):** 304.8MM **Privately Held**
**WEB:** www.pioneerlocal.com
**SIC: 2711** Newspapers, publishing & printing
**HQ:** Sun-Times Media Group, Inc.
  350 N Orleans St Fl 10
  Chicago IL 60654
  312 321-2299

## Chicago - Cook County (G-6127)   GEOGRAPHIC SECTION

**(G-6127)**
**PIONEER PRINTING SERVICE INC**
1340 N Astor St  (60610-2171)
PHONE .................................. 312 337-4283
Fax: 312 943-6387
Deborah Schnitzius, *President*
Frances Schnitzius, *Treasurer*
EMP: 3
SQ FT: 5,000
SALES (est): 306.3K **Privately Held**
SIC: 2752 2759 Commercial printing, offset; commercial printing

**(G-6128)**
**PIPELINE TRADING SYSTEMS LLC**
1 S Dearborn St Ste 2100  (60603-2307)
PHONE .................................. 312 212-4288
Fax: 312 212-4286
Marilou Giustini, *Director*
EMP: 3
SALES (corp-wide): 12.6MM **Privately Held**
SIC: 3699 Electronic training devices
HQ: Pipeline Trading Systems Llc
  60 E 42nd St Ste 624
  New York NY 10165
  212 370-8354

**(G-6129)**
**PIPESTONE PASSAGES**
5407 S Avers Ave  (60632-3724)
PHONE .................................. 773 735-2488
Larry Podwika, *Partner*
Nancy Jenkober, *Partner*
EMP: 4
SALES: 40K **Privately Held**
SIC: 2731 Book publishing

**(G-6130)**
**PITCHFORK MEDIA INC**
3317 W Fullerton Ave  (60647-2513)
PHONE .................................. 773 395-5937
Fax: 773 395-5992
EMP: 40
SALES (est): 5.5MM **Privately Held**
SIC: 2721 Periodicals-Publishing/Printing

**(G-6131)**
**PITNEY BOWES INC**
3640 N Bosworth Ave 3s  (60613-5371)
PHONE .................................. 773 755-5808
Alan Montague, *Principal*
EMP: 35
SALES (corp-wide): 3.4B **Publicly Held**
SIC: 3579 Mailing machines
PA: Pitney Bowes Inc.
  3001 Summer St Ste 3
  Stamford CT 06905
  203 356-5000

**(G-6132)**
**PITNEY BOWES INC**
230 W Monroe St Ste 1150  (60606-4805)
PHONE .................................. 312 419-7114
Fax: 312 782-6447
John Trotta, *Vice Pres*
Joe Dvoinik, *Manager*
Crystal Weidel, *Manager*
Paulette Westnuy, *Manager*
Mal Byrne, *Director*
EMP: 12
SALES (corp-wide): 3.4B **Publicly Held**
SIC: 3579 7359 Postage meters; business machine & electronic equipment rental services
PA: Pitney Bowes Inc.
  3001 Summer St Ste 3
  Stamford CT 06905
  203 356-5000

**(G-6133)**
**PIVOT POINT USA INC (PA)**
Also Called: Pivot Point Beauty School
8725 W Higgins Rd Ste 700  (60631-2700)
PHONE .................................. 800 886-4247
Karen Wilkin-Donachie, *CEO*
Sharon Retson, *General Mgr*
Ron Beible, *Principal*
Ken Angermeier, *Vice Pres*
Kevin Cameron, *Vice Pres*
▲ EMP: 75
SQ FT: 42,000
SALES (est): 26.8MM **Privately Held**
SIC: 2731 5087 Books: publishing only; beauty parlor equipment & supplies

**(G-6134)**
**PIVOTAL PRODUCTION LLC**
356 E Sutherland St  (60619)
P.O. Box 198545  (60619-8545)
PHONE .................................. 773 726-7706
Letitia Jenkins, *CEO*
EMP: 3 EST: 2008
SQ FT: 1,000
SALES: 2K **Privately Held**
SIC: 2844 Toilet preparations

**(G-6135)**
**PLANTER INC**
Also Called: Victory Division of Planter
1820 N Major Ave  (60639-4118)
PHONE .................................. 773 637-7777
Fax: 773 637-7799
Steven Kite, *President*
Eric Priceman, *Vice Pres*
Stan Rosenberg, *Vice Pres*
Alan Starks, *Vice Pres*
Karen Marino, *Manager*
▲ EMP: 75 EST: 1948
SQ FT: 45,000
SALES (est): 13.4MM **Privately Held**
WEB: www.buyvictory.com
SIC: 3499 3599 Trophies, metal, except silver; machine shop, jobbing & repair

**(G-6136)**
**PLASTICREST PRODUCTS INC**
4519 W Harrison St  (60624-3099)
PHONE .................................. 773 826-2163
Fax: 773 826-4227
Robert W Pauley, *President*
▲ EMP: 10 EST: 1942
SQ FT: 17,000
SALES (est): 1.5MM **Privately Held**
WEB: www.spgppi.com
SIC: 3469 3089 3172 2657 Boxes, stamped metal; boxes, plastic; personal leather goods; folding paperboard boxes

**(G-6137)**
**PLASTICS D-E-F**
3065 W Armitage Ave  (60647-5911)
PHONE .................................. 312 226-4337
Fax: 312 674-5152
Jack H Beck, *Partner*
Robert Klovstad, *Partner*
EMP: 4
SQ FT: 2,500
SALES: 200K **Privately Held**
SIC: 2673 Bags: plastic, laminated & coated

**(G-6138)**
**PLASTICS PRINTING GROUP INC**
5414 W Roosevelt Rd  (60644-1467)
PHONE .................................. 312 421-7980
Lee Masover, *President*
Alfred Johnson, *Project Mgr*
Dave Jones, *Project Mgr*
Brian Drucker, *Accounts Mgr*
Chris Gangy, *Admin Sec*
EMP: 11
SQ FT: 13,500
SALES (est): 2.1MM **Privately Held**
SIC: 2759 2675 2396 Screen printing; die-cut paper & board; automotive & apparel trimmings

**(G-6139)**
**PLATT LUGGAGE INC**
Also Called: Platt Cases
4051 W 51st St  (60632-4294)
PHONE .................................. 773 838-2000
Fax: 773 838-2010
Marc Platt, *President*
Alan Evavold, *VP Sales*
Kathleen Anweiler, *Sales Mgr*
Regina Nash, *Manager*
Walley Smreczak, *Manager*
▲ EMP: 75 EST: 1921
SQ FT: 70,000
SALES (est): 14.6MM **Privately Held**
SIC: 3161 3089 Attache cases; cases, plastic

**(G-6140)**
**PLAYER SPORTS LTD**
2956 W Peterson Ave  (60659-3810)
PHONE .................................. 773 764-4111
Anthony Chronis, *Partner*
James Chronis, *Partner*
EMP: 3
SQ FT: 4,600
SALES (est): 513.8K **Privately Held**
SIC: 5091 2261 Sporting & recreation goods; screen printing of cotton broadwoven fabrics

**(G-6141)**
**PLYMOUTH TUBE COMPANY**
4555 W Armitage Ave  (60639-3403)
PHONE .................................. 773 489-0226
Tony Campbell, *General Mgr*
CAM Valle, *General Mgr*
Ed Reid, *Opers Mgr*
Dewey Green, *QC Mgr*
Craig Pidcock, *Engineer*
EMP: 98
SALES (corp-wide): 278.9MM **Privately Held**
WEB: www.plymouth.com
SIC: 3317 3354 Tubes, seamless steel; tubes, wrought: welded or lock joint; shapes, extruded aluminum; tube, extruded or drawn, aluminum
PA: Plymouth Tube Company
  29w 150 Warrenville Rd
  Warrenville IL 60555
  630 393-3550

**(G-6142)**
**PMC CONVERTING CORP**
5080 N Kimberly Ave # 107  (60630-1770)
PHONE .................................. 773 481-2269
Fax: 773 481-2311
Rocio Medina, *President*
Lorena Medina, *Vice Pres*
EMP: 7
SALES (est): 714K **Privately Held**
SIC: 2675 Paper die-cutting

**(G-6143)**
**PNE WIND USA INC**
150 N Michigan Ave # 1500  (60601-7570)
PHONE .................................. 773 329-3705
Roland Stanze, *President*
EMP: 3
SALES (est): 456.7K **Privately Held**
SIC: 3511 Turbines & turbine generator sets

**(G-6144)**
**PNG TRANSPORT LLC**
3543 S Parnell Ave Apt B  (60609-1796)
P.O. Box 166787  (60616-6787)
PHONE .................................. 312 218-8116
Peter Ng, *President*
EMP: 2
SALES: 230K **Privately Held**
SIC: 2421 Building & structural materials, wood

**(G-6145)**
**POERSCH METAL MANUFACTURING CO**
4027 W Kinzie St  (60624-1807)
PHONE .................................. 773 722-0890
Fax: 773 722-4122
Robert C Kruse Sr, *President*
EMP: 14
SQ FT: 6,000
SALES (est): 2.5MM **Privately Held**
WEB: www.poerschmetal.com
SIC: 3844 3861 X-ray apparatus & tubes; photographic equipment & supplies

**(G-6146)**
**POETRY FOUNDATION**
Also Called: Poetry Magazine
61 W Superior St  (60654-5457)
PHONE .................................. 312 787-7070
Fax: 312 787-6650
John Kenney, *Ch of Bd*
Robert Polito, *President*
Fred Sasaki, *Publisher*
Sarah Dodson, *Editor*
Don Share, *Editor*
EMP: 25
SQ FT: 22,000
SALES: 12.4MM **Privately Held**
WEB: www.poetrymagazine.org
SIC: 2721 Magazines: publishing only, not printed on site

**(G-6147)**
**POETS STUDY INC**
4366 N Elston Ave  (60641-2146)
PHONE .................................. 773 286-1355
Fax: 773 286-1210
Alfred Schuch, *President*
EMP: 7 EST: 1939
SQ FT: 2,700
SALES: 700K **Privately Held**
SIC: 2759 2791 2752 Card printing & engraving, except greeting; typesetting; commercial printing, lithographic

**(G-6148)**
**POLAMER INC**
Also Called: Polamer & Parcel Travel Svc
6401 N Milwaukee Ave  (60646)
PHONE .................................. 773 774-3600
Ledia Janowski, *Manager*
EMP: 5
SALES (corp-wide): 20.7MM **Privately Held**
WEB: www.polamerusa.com
SIC: 2449 Shipping cases & drums, wood: wirebound & plywood
PA: Polamer, Inc
  3094 N Milwaukee Ave
  Chicago IL 60618
  773 685-8222

**(G-6149)**
**POLLACK SERVICE**
3701 N Ravenswood Ave  (60613-3553)
PHONE .................................. 773 528-8096
Gerald Pollack, *Principal*
Lynn L Pollack, *Agent*
EMP: 65
SALES (est): 1.9MM **Privately Held**
WEB: www.pollackservices.com
SIC: 2389 Regalia

**(G-6150)**
**POLLARD BROS MFG CO**
5504 N Northwest Hwy  (60630-1188)
PHONE .................................. 773 763-6868
Fax: 773 763-4466
Jason Hein, *President*
Steve F Hein, *Admin Sec*
EMP: 11 EST: 1921
SQ FT: 20,000
SALES (est): 1.5MM **Privately Held**
WEB: www.pollardbros.com
SIC: 2599 Factory furniture & fixtures

**(G-6151)**
**POLONIA BOOK STORE INC**
4738 N Milwaukee Ave  (60630-3614)
PHONE .................................. 773 481-6968
Mira Puacz, *President*
EMP: 3
SQ FT: 8,200
SALES (est): 189.7K **Privately Held**
WEB: www.polonia.com
SIC: 5942 2731 Book stores; books: publishing only

**(G-6152)**
**POLPRESS INC**
Also Called: Polpress Priniting
5566 N Northwest Hwy  (60630-1116)
PHONE .................................. 773 792-1200
Fax: 773 792-1209
Roman Majewski, *President*
Gile Montanez, *Administration*
EMP: 6
SQ FT: 2,000
SALES: 1MM **Privately Held**
SIC: 2752 Commercial printing, offset

**(G-6153)**
**POLYAIR INTER PACK INC**
808 E 113th St  (60628-5150)
PHONE .................................. 773 995-1818
Joe Miller, *Branch Mgr*
EMP: 70 **Privately Held**

# GEOGRAPHIC SECTION

Chicago - Cook County (G-6178)

SIC: 3433 2394 3949 3086 Solar heaters & collectors; liners & covers, fabric: made from purchased materials; water sports equipment; packaging & shipping materials, foamed plastic; plastic film, coated or laminated for packaging; unsupported plastics film & sheet

### (G-6154)
**POLYCORP ILLINOIS INC (PA)**
3620 W 38th St (60632-3308)
PHONE..................................773 847-7575
Michael Chorpash, *CEO*
Elliott Pearlman, *Ch of Bd*
Diana Oboijvitz, *Manager*
John Smith, *Manager*
▲ EMP: 73
SQ FT: 75,000
SALES (est): 6.8MM **Privately Held**
SIC: 7699 3999 5085 4953 Plastics products repair; custom pulverizing & grinding of plastic materials; drums, new or reconditioned; refuse collection & disposal services

### (G-6155)
**POLYSYSTEMS INC (PA)**
30 N La Salle St Ste 3600 (60602-2586)
PHONE..................................312 332-2114
Fax: 312 332-2391
Roger W Smith, *President*
Robert Arendt, *COO*
R Thomas Herget, *Exec VP*
John Adduci, *Vice Pres*
Matt Covalle, *Vice Pres*
EMP: 80
SQ FT: 30,000
SALES (est): 11.5MM **Privately Held**
WEB: www.polysystems.com
SIC: 7374 7372 7373 Computer timesharing; application computer software; computer systems analysis & design

### (G-6156)
**POP BOX LLC**
1700 W Irving Park Rd # 302 (60613-2559)
PHONE..................................630 509-2281
Joy Kitt, *Mng Member*
Catherine Berthault,
Francois Berthault,
EMP: 10
SQ FT: 7,000
SALES (est): 362.2K **Privately Held**
SIC: 2099 Food preparations

### (G-6157)
**PORCELAIN ENAMEL FINISHERS**
1530 S State St Apt 1018 (60605-2987)
PHONE..................................312 808-1560
EMP: 6 EST: 1945
SQ FT: 3,600
SALES (est): 300K **Privately Held**
SIC: 3469 3479 3545 3264 Mfg Metal Stampings Coating/Engraving Svcs Mfg Machine Tool Access Mfg Porcelain Elc Supply Mfg Adhesives/Sealants

### (G-6158)
**POWER PARTNERS LLC**
Also Called: Devon Discount Pharmacy
1542 W Devon Ave (60660-1344)
PHONE..................................773 465-8688
Karen Wheet, *Regl Sales Mgr*
Andreas Iskos, *Mng Member*
Jiten Patel,
Andy Politis,
EMP: 6
SQ FT: 400
SALES (est): 1.4MM **Privately Held**
SIC: 2834 Pharmaceutical preparations

### (G-6159)
**POWERCOCO LLC**
1658 N Milwaukee Ave # 546 (60647-6905)
PHONE..................................614 323-5890
Christopher Henneforth,
Tyler Beuerlein,
Jaisen Freeman,
Christopher Hunter,
Steve Vasquez,
EMP: 6
SALES (est): 627.5K **Privately Held**
SIC: 2086 7389 Bottled & canned soft drinks;

### (G-6160)
**POWERSCHOOL GROUP LLC**
Also Called: Sungard
2290 Collection Center Dr (60693-0022)
PHONE..................................610 867-9200
EMP: 15
SALES (corp-wide): 1.9B **Privately Held**
SIC: 7372 Prepackaged Software Services
HQ: Powerschool Group Llc
150 Parkshore Dr
Folsom CA 95630
916 288-1636

### (G-6161)
**PPG ARCHITECTURAL FINISHES INC**
Also Called: Glidden Professional Paint Ctr
3641 S Washtenaw Ave (60632-1645)
PHONE..................................773 523-6333
EMP: 100
SALES (corp-wide): 14.7B **Publicly Held**
WEB: www.gliddenpaint.com
SIC: 2891 2046 2821 2869 Adhesives & sealants; adhesives; industrial starch; edible starch; plastics materials & resins; industrial organic chemicals; flavors or flavoring materials, synthetic; perfume materials, synthetic; vanillin, synthetic
HQ: Ppg Architectural Finishes, Inc.
1 Ppg Pl
Pittsburgh PA 15272
412 434-3131

### (G-6162)
**PPG INDUSTRIES INC**
1701 E 122nd St (60633-2362)
PHONE..................................773 646-5900
Brodgon Kelly, *Director*
EMP: 23
SALES (corp-wide): 14.7B **Publicly Held**
SIC: 2851 Paints & allied products
PA: Ppg Industries, Inc.
1 Ppg Pl
Pittsburgh PA 15272
412 434-3131

### (G-6163)
**PPG INDUSTRIES INC**
1701 E 122nd St (60633-2362)
PHONE..................................773 646-5900
Fax: 773 646-3743
Thomas McLaughlin, *Branch Mgr*
EMP: 50
SALES (corp-wide): 14.7B **Publicly Held**
WEB: www.spraylat.com
SIC: 2851 2891 Paints, waterproof; paints: oil or alkyd vehicle or water thinned; plastics base paints & varnishes; adhesives & sealants
PA: Ppg Industries, Inc.
1 Ppg Pl
Pittsburgh PA 15272
412 434-3131

### (G-6164)
**PPG INDUSTRIES INC**
Also Called: PPG 5527
345 N Morgan St (60607-1322)
PHONE..................................312 666-2277
Dave Bartozi, *Manager*
EMP: 24
SALES (corp-wide): 14.7B **Publicly Held**
WEB: www.ppg.com
SIC: 2851 Paints & allied products
PA: Ppg Industries, Inc.
1 Ppg Pl
Pittsburgh PA 15272
412 434-3131

### (G-6165)
**PRACTICE LAW MANAGEMENT MAG**
321 N Clark St (60654-4714)
PHONE..................................312 988-6114
Doug Simpson, *COO*
John O Hearn, *Director*
EMP: 10
SALES (est): 675.9K **Privately Held**
SIC: 2721 Periodicals

### (G-6166)
**PRAIRIE PACKAGING INC**
7200 S Mason Ave (60638-6226)
PHONE..................................708 496-2900
Joseph Krippel, *Vice Pres*
Mike Bledsoe, *Purch Agent*
Mark Pearce, *Engineer*
Phil Gingras, *Manager*
Joseph Pollaro, *Manager*
EMP: 11 **Privately Held**
SIC: 3089 3421 Kitchenware, plastic; plates, plastic; table & food cutlery, including butchers'
HQ: Prairie Packaging, Inc.
7200 S Mason Ave
Bedford Park IL 60638
708 496-1172

### (G-6167)
**PRAIRIE WI-FI SYSTEMS**
935 W Chestnut St Ste 530 (60642-5491)
P.O. Box 12994 (60612-5076)
PHONE..................................515 988-3260
Andrew Tomka, *Principal*
EMP: 3
SALES (est): 176.8K **Privately Held**
SIC: 8748 7372 7371 7359 Systems engineering consultant, ex. computer or professional; educational computer software; business oriented computer software; computer software development; electronic equipment rental, except computers

### (G-6168)
**PRECISION DIALOGUE DIRECT INC (PA)**
5501 W Grand Ave (60639-2909)
PHONE..................................773 237-2264
Fax: 773 237-3577
Thomas Rogers, *President*
David Joss, *President*
Jenna Hunger, *Business Mgr*
Jim Jung, *Business Mgr*
Ross Priester, *Business Mgr*
EMP: 100
SQ FT: 86,000
SALES (est): 36.1MM **Privately Held**
WEB: www.nwmail.com
SIC: 7331 2752 Mailing service; commercial printing, offset

### (G-6169)
**PRECISION DIE CUTTING & FINISH**
4027 W Le Moyne St (60651-1930)
PHONE..................................773 252-5625
Fax: 773 252-7092
William Bardeleben, *President*
EMP: 8 EST: 1974
SQ FT: 7,000
SALES (est): 950K **Privately Held**
WEB: www.precisiondiecutting.com
SIC: 2653 2796 2789 2675 Display items, corrugated: made from purchased materials; display items, solid fiber: made from purchased materials; platemaking services; bookbinding & related work; die-cut paper & board

### (G-6170)
**PRECISION FORMING STAMPING CO**
2419 W George St (60618-7930)
PHONE..................................773 489-6868
Fax: 773 278-3153
Kathy Hill, *President*
Stanley Sulikowski, *Plant Mgr*
Richard Hansen, *Purchasing*
Kay Josetti, *Manager*
EMP: 30
SQ FT: 16,000
SALES (est): 4.1MM **Privately Held**
SIC: 3469 3496 Metal stampings; miscellaneous fabricated wire products

### (G-6171)
**PRECISION REMANUFACTURING INC**
4520 W Fullerton Ave (60639-1934)
PHONE..................................773 489-7225
Fax: 773 489-7463
John Kaufman Beidler Jr, *President*
Tom McDonald, *Engineer*
Jerald Joseph Mudryj, *Admin Sec*
EMP: 12
SQ FT: 10,000
SALES (est): 1.7MM **Privately Held**
SIC: 3714 Steering mechanisms, motor vehicle

### (G-6172)
**PRECISION SCREW MACHINING CO**
3511 N Kenton Ave (60641-3819)
PHONE..................................773 205-4280
Sandra Greene, *President*
Hilliard Franklin Greene, *President*
Hilliard Greene, *Vice Pres*
EMP: 10 EST: 1946
SALES (est): 975.2K **Privately Held**
SIC: 3743 3451 Railroad locomotives & parts, electric or nonelectric; screw machine products

### (G-6173)
**PREFERRED FOODS PRODUCTS INC**
1421 W 47th St (60609-3233)
P.O. Box 9273 (60609-0273)
PHONE..................................773 847-0230
Fax: 773 847-1201
Paul Buehler, *President*
Nathan Anderson, *Vice Pres*
EMP: 15
SQ FT: 20,000
SALES (est): 1.3MM **Privately Held**
SIC: 2013 Sausages & other prepared meats

### (G-6174)
**PREFERRED FREEZER SERVICES OF**
4500 W 42nd Pl (60632-0001)
PHONE..................................773 254-9500
Kosta Anezirjs, *Sales Mgr*
▲ EMP: 10 EST: 2012
SALES (est): 1.3MM **Privately Held**
SIC: 3821 Freezers, laboratory

### (G-6175)
**PREFERRED PRINTING SERVICE**
2343 W Roosevelt Rd (60608-1193)
PHONE..................................312 421-2343
Fax: 312 421-0222
J Robert Jayko, *President*
Gregory Jayko, *Vice Pres*
Maureen Kunak, *Financial Exec*
Blythe Mathews, *Financial Exec*
John Sims, *Branch Mgr*
EMP: 3
SALES: 100K **Privately Held**
SIC: 2759 2752 2791 2789 Letterpress printing; commercial printing, offset; typesetting; bookbinding & related work; coated & laminated paper; packaging paper & plastics film, coated & laminated

### (G-6176)
**PREFLIGHT LLC**
200 N Lasalle Ste 1400 (60601)
PHONE..................................312 935-2804
EMP: 4
SALES (est): 355.3K **Privately Held**
SIC: 3537 Industrial trucks & tractors

### (G-6177)
**PREMIER INTERNATIONAL ENTPS**
221 N La Salle St Ste 900 (60601-1300)
PHONE..................................312 857-2200
Jim Hempleman, *President*
Valerie Hollaender, *Office Mgr*
Brian Cacioppo, *Consultant*
Steve Novak, *Sr Consultant*
EMP: 20
SALES: 50.5K **Privately Held**
WEB: www.premier-international.com
SIC: 7371 7379 7372 Computer software development & applications; computer related consulting services; prepackaged software

### (G-6178)
**PREMIER METAL WORKS INC**
1616 S Clinton St (60616-1110)
PHONE..................................312 226-7414
Fax: 312 226-2539
Andrew Michyeta III, *President*
Andrew Michyeta IV, *Vice Pres*
EMP: 8
SQ FT: 18,000
SALES (est): 690K **Privately Held**
SIC: 3469 Stamping metal for the trade

## Chicago - Cook County (G-6179)

**(G-6179)**
**PREMIERE AUTO SERVICE**
727 S Jefferson St (60607-3608)
P.O. Box 6973 (60680-6973)
PHONE..................................773 275-8785
Benjamin Dam, *President*
Ming Ng, *Vice Pres*
**EMP:** 7
**SQ FT:** 6,000
**SALES:** 500K **Privately Held**
**SIC:** 3714 5013 Motor vehicle parts & accessories; automotive engines & engine parts; automotive supplies & parts

**(G-6180)**
**PRESENTATION STUDIOS INTL LLC**
Also Called: Laser Art Studio
1435 W Fulton St (60607-1109)
PHONE..................................312 733-8160
**Fax:** 312 432-4366
John Andrew Metelnick, *Mng Member*
Jason Tooms, *Manager*
Dave Wegter, *Manager*
William Bauman, *Director*
Andy Metelnick, *Director*
**EMP:** 11 **EST:** 1998
**SALES (est):** 1.4MM **Privately Held**
**SIC:** 3699 Laser welding, drilling & cutting equipment

**(G-6181)**
**PRESS SYNDICATION GROUP LLC**
2850 N Pulaski Rd Unit 9 (60641-5456)
PHONE..................................646 325-3221
Niels Warren Winter, *Mng Member*
**EMP:** 5 **EST:** 2015
**SQ FT:** 55,000
**SALES (est):** 218.2K **Privately Held**
**SIC:** 2731 Book publishing

**(G-6182)**
**PRESSURE VESSEL SERVICE INC**
12260 S Carondolet Ave (60633-1197)
PHONE..................................773 913-7700
Paul Winkley, *Principal*
Timothy Nicholson, *Vice Pres*
Al McAlpine, *Opers Mgr*
Karen Handloser, *Controller*
Dale Price, *Manager*
**EMP:** 18
**SALES (corp-wide):** 497MM **Privately Held**
**SIC:** 2899 Chemical preparations
**PA:** Pressure Vessel Service, Inc.
10900 Harper Ave
Detroit MI 48213
313 921-1200

**(G-6183)**
**PREVUE PET PRODUCTS INC (PA)**
Also Called: Prevue Hendyrx
224 N Maplewood Ave (60612-2110)
PHONE..................................773 722-1052
**Fax:** 312 243-4224
Richard C Savitt, *CEO*
Jason Savitt, *President*
Mike Fradimiko, *Vice Pres*
Felipe Mendoza, *Warehouse Mgr*
Michael Fratamico, *CFO*
▲ **EMP:** 15
**SQ FT:** 50,000
**SALES (est):** 4.4MM **Privately Held**
**WEB:** www.prevuepet.com
**SIC:** 3999 5199 Pet supplies; pet supplies

**(G-6184)**
**PRIDE IN GRAPHICS INC**
739 S Clark St Fl 2 (60605-1760)
PHONE..................................312 427-2000
**Fax:** 312 939-0993
John Ekizian, *Ch of Bd*
Mike Ekizian, *President*
Todd Minuth, *Plant Mgr*
**EMP:** 12 **EST:** 1953
**SQ FT:** 10,000
**SALES:** 1.9MM **Privately Held**
**SIC:** 2752 Commercial printing, offset; lithographing on metal

**(G-6185)**
**PRIME DENTAL MANUFACTURING**
4555 W Addison St (60641-3816)
PHONE..................................773 283-2914
Pedro Segura, *President*
Adres Segura, *Chairman*
Javier Alvarez, *QA Dir*
Gabriel Anaya, *Research*
▲ **EMP:** 30
**SQ FT:** 6,000
**SALES (est):** 4.8MM **Privately Held**
**WEB:** www.primedentalmfg.com
**SIC:** 3843 Denture materials

**(G-6186)**
**PRIME GROUP INC**
Also Called: Prime Group Realty Trust
122 S Michigan Ave # 2040 (60603-6194)
PHONE..................................312 922-3883
Donald H Faloon, *Exec VP*
Jeffrey A Patterson, *Exec VP*
Murray J Aschler, *Senior VP*
Philip A Hoffer, *Senior VP*
James Hoffman, *Senior VP*
**EMP:** 7
**SALES (corp-wide):** 17.3MM **Privately Held**
**SIC:** 3531 Marine related equipment
**PA:** The Prime Group Inc
120 N Lasalle St Fl 32
Chicago IL 60602
312 917-1500

**(G-6187)**
**PRIMO GRANITO LLC**
4527 N Mobile Ave (60630-3021)
PHONE..................................773 282-6391
Joseph Litza,
Linda Kuczma,
**EMP:** 10
**SQ FT:** 11,000
**SALES:** 800K **Privately Held**
**SIC:** 3281 Building stone products; household articles, except furniture: cut stone

**(G-6188)**
**PRIMROSE CANDY CO**
4111 W Parker Ave (60639-2176)
PHONE..................................800 268-9522
**Fax:** 773 276-7411
Mark Puch, *President*
Jeff Puch, *Vice Pres*
Rachel Deahl, *Production*
Jackie Gredell, *Production*
Jessica Peretti, *Production*
▲ **EMP:** 103 **EST:** 1928
**SQ FT:** 130,000
**SALES (est):** 38.4MM **Privately Held**
**WEB:** www.primrosecandy.com
**SIC:** 2064 Lollipops & other hard candy

**(G-6189)**
**PRINT RITE INC**
Also Called: Trade Print
7748 W Addison St (60634-3018)
PHONE..................................773 625-0792
John Pratola, *President*
Tony Salkeld, *Opers Mgr*
Mary Salkeld, *Office Mgr*
**EMP:** 1
**SQ FT:** 3,000
**SALES:** 600K **Privately Held**
**SIC:** 2731 2752 Book publishing; commercial printing, lithographic

**(G-6190)**
**PRINT SERVICE & DIST ASSN PSDA**
401 N Michigan Ave (60611-4255)
PHONE..................................312 321-5120
Tressa McLaughlin, *President*
Emily Marxer, *Sales Dir*
**EMP:** 2
**SALES (est):** 234.8K **Privately Held**
**SIC:** 2752 Commercial printing, lithographic

**(G-6191)**
**PRINTED BLOG INC**
216 S Jefferson St Ll1 (60661-5608)
PHONE..................................312 924-1040
**EMP:** 4

**SALES (est):** 166.5K **Privately Held**
**SIC:** 2711 Newspapers, publishing & printing

**(G-6192)**
**PRINTERS ROW LLC**
500 S Dearborn St (60605-1502)
PHONE..................................312 435-0411
**Fax:** 312 362-0814
Gregory A Page, *Office Mgr*
**EMP:** 2
**SALES (est):** 210K **Privately Held**
**SIC:** 2752 Commercial printing, lithographic

**(G-6193)**
**PRINTERS ROW LOFT**
732 S Fincl Pl Ste Mgmt (60605)
PHONE..................................312 431-1019
**EMP:** 2 **EST:** 2010
**SALES (est):** 209.2K **Privately Held**
**SIC:** 2752 Commercial printing, lithographic

**(G-6194)**
**PRINTERS SQUARE CONDO ASSN**
680 S Federal St (60605-1844)
PHONE..................................312 765-8794
Michael Pfammatter, *Principal*
**EMP:** 2 **EST:** 2012
**SALES (est):** 244.4K **Privately Held**
**SIC:** 2752 Commercial printing, lithographic

**(G-6195)**
**PRINTING IN REMEBRANCE INC**
8248 S Cottage Grove Ave (60619-5302)
PHONE..................................773 874-8700
Tiffany Hall, *President*
Anthony Hall, *Vice Pres*
**EMP:** 12 **EST:** 2012
**SALES (est):** 1.3MM **Privately Held**
**SIC:** 2759 Commercial printing

**(G-6196)**
**PRINTING ON ASHLAND INC**
8227 S Ashland Ave Ste 1 (60620-4682)
PHONE..................................773 488-4707
Onesa Aton, *President*
Rodney Payton, *Senior VP*
**EMP:** 4
**SQ FT:** 1,750
**SALES (est):** 350K **Privately Held**
**SIC:** 2752 Commercial printing, lithographic

**(G-6197)**
**PRINTS CHICAGO INC**
1230 W Jackson Blvd (60607-2814)
PHONE..................................312 243-6481
Fred Baker, *Principal*
**EMP:** 4
**SALES (est):** 231.6K **Privately Held**
**SIC:** 2711 Commercial printing & newspaper publishing combined

**(G-6198)**
**PRIORITY PRINTING**
6942 W Diversey Ave (60707-1725)
PHONE..................................773 889-6021
Fred Edwards, *Owner*
**EMP:** 4
**SQ FT:** 5,000
**SALES (est):** 360.7K **Privately Held**
**SIC:** 2752 2796 Commercial printing, offset; platemaking services

**(G-6199)**
**PRISM COMMERCIAL PRINTING CTRS (PA)**
6957 W Archer Ave (60638-2330)
PHONE..................................630 834-4443
Cynthia Bieniek, *President*
Brian Bieniek, *Admin Sec*
Lewis Guza, *Administration*
**EMP:** 9
**SQ FT:** 1,500
**SALES (est):** 2.1MM **Privately Held**
**SIC:** 2752 2796 2791 2789 Commercial printing, offset; platemaking services; typesetting; bookbinding & related work

**(G-6200)**
**PRISM COMMERCIAL PRINTING CTRS**
6901 W 59th St (60638-3205)
PHONE..................................773 229-2620
**Fax:** 773 229-2628
Cynthia Bieniek, *Branch Mgr*
**EMP:** 3
**SQ FT:** 4,000
**SALES (corp-wide):** 2.1MM **Privately Held**
**SIC:** 2752 Commercial printing, offset
**PA:** Prism Corp Commercial Printing Centers
6957 W Archer Ave
Chicago IL 60638
630 834-4443

**(G-6201)**
**PRISM COMMERCIAL PRINTING CTRS**
6130 S Pulaski Rd (60629-4628)
PHONE..................................773 735-5400
Frank Lazarz, *Branch Mgr*
**EMP:** 5
**SALES (corp-wide):** 2.1MM **Privately Held**
**SIC:** 2752 Commercial printing, lithographic
**PA:** Prism Corp Commercial Printing Centers
6957 W Archer Ave
Chicago IL 60638
630 834-4443

**(G-6202)**
**PRO IMAGE PROMOTIONS INC**
2006 W Chicago Ave (60622-5559)
PHONE..................................773 292-1111
Roberto A Vergara, *President*
Maribel Vergara, *Accounts Mgr*
Issable Cantra, *Manager*
**EMP:** 2
**SALES (est):** 212.6K **Privately Held**
**SIC:** 2759 Screen printing

**(G-6203)**
**PRO TEC METAL FINISHING CORP**
1428 N Kilpatrick Ave (60651-1624)
PHONE..................................773 384-7853
**Fax:** 773 384-4449
Dale Weincouff, *President*
**EMP:** 8
**SQ FT:** 10,000
**SALES:** 750K **Privately Held**
**SIC:** 2899 3471 Chemical preparations; plating & polishing

**(G-6204)**
**PRODICO TECHNOLOGIES LLC**
6508 S Dorchester Ave (60637-4409)
PHONE..................................312 498-5152
Douglass Bevel,
**EMP:** 2
**SALES (est):** 200K **Privately Held**
**SIC:** 3841 Surgical & medical instruments

**(G-6205)**
**PRODUCTIGEAR INC**
1900 W 34th St (60608-6894)
PHONE..................................773 847-4505
**Fax:** 773 847-6348
Richard Wieker, *President*
Dorothy Stevens, *Vice Pres*
**EMP:** 35 **EST:** 1946
**SQ FT:** 9,000
**SALES (est):** 8.5MM **Privately Held**
**WEB:** www.productigear.com
**SIC:** 3566 3568 3462 Speed changers (power transmission equipment), except auto; power transmission equipment; iron & steel forgings

**(G-6206)**
**PRODUCTION TOOL COMPANIES LLC (PA)**
1229 E 74th St (60619-2098)
PHONE..................................773 288-4400
**Fax:** 773 288-4569
Joe Dangelo, *Vice Pres*
Michael Madigan, *Data Proc Dir*
Stanley Malec, *Director*
▲ **EMP:** 45
**SQ FT:** 125,000

# GEOGRAPHIC SECTION
## Chicago - Cook County (G-6233)

**SALES (est):** 6.4MM  *Privately Held*
**WEB:** www.productiontoolcompanies.com
**SIC:** 3599  Machine & other job shop work

**(G-6207)**
### PRODUCTIVE EDGE LLC (PA)
Also Called: Open Point Solutions
11 E Illinois St Fl 2  (60611-5654)
**PHONE**..................312 561-9000
Bill McCall, *Senior VP*
Senthil Bellukutty, *Vice Pres*
Dave Pellissier, *Vice Pres*
Tom Dicicco, *Project Mgr*
Jon Maher, *Project Mgr*
**EMP:** 60
**SQ FT:** 500
**SALES (est):** 11.2MM  *Privately Held*
**SIC:** 7371 7372 Computer software development & applications; prepackaged software

**(G-6208)**
### PROFESSIONAL FREEZING SVCS LLC
7035 W 65th St  (60638-4603)
**PHONE**..................773 847-7500
Karen Grzywacz, *CEO*
Edward Grzywacz, *President*
Jennifer Ramirez, *Manager*
**EMP:** 6
**SALES (est):** 1.6MM  *Privately Held*
**SIC:** 5064 5421 3822 Refrigerators & freezers; freezer provisioners, meat; temperature controls, automatic

**(G-6209)**
### PROFESSIONAL GEM SCIENCES INC
5 S Wabash Ave Ste 315  (60603-3517)
**PHONE**..................312 920-1541
**Fax:** 312 920-1554
Myriam Tashtey, *President*
**EMP:** 7
**SALES (est):** 618.9K  *Privately Held*
**WEB:** www.progem.com
**SIC:** 1499 8734 Gem stones (natural) mining; testing laboratories

**(G-6210)**
### PROGRESS PRINTING CORPORATION
3324 S Halsted St Ste 1  (60608-6799)
**PHONE**..................773 927-0123
**Fax:** 773 927-5804
Martin Gapshis, *President*
Marilyn Gapshis, *Corp Secy*
**EMP:** 23 EST: 1933
**SQ FT:** 20,000
**SALES (est):** 3.2MM  *Privately Held*
**SIC:** 2759 2752 2791 2789 Letterpress printing; commercial printing, offset; typesetting; bookbinding & related work

**(G-6211)**
### PROGRESSIVE BRONZE WORKS INC
3550 N Spaulding Ave  (60618-5523)
**PHONE**..................773 463-5500
**Fax:** 773 463-0589
Joseph E Rossi, *President*
Bobbi Rossi, *Admin Sec*
**EMP:** 25 EST: 1935
**SQ FT:** 33,000
**SALES (est):** 3.1MM  *Privately Held*
**SIC:** 3499  Novelties & specialties, metal

**(G-6212)**
### PROGRESSIVE COATING CORP
900 S Cicero Ave  (60644-5213)
**PHONE**..................773 261-8900
**Fax:** 773 261-8902
Joseph Tompa, *President*
Diana Tompa, *Treasurer*
**EMP:** 15
**SQ FT:** 30,000
**SALES (est):** 1.1MM  *Privately Held*
**SIC:** 3479 Coating of metals & formed products

**(G-6213)**
### PROGRESSIVE SHEET METAL INC
2850 S Tripp Ave  (60623-4336)
**PHONE**..................773 376-1155
**Fax:** 773 376-9556

Juan Gallegos, *President*
Julio Gallegos, *Vice Pres*
Isidro Luque, *Controller*
**EMP:** 9 EST: 1960
**SQ FT:** 2,200
**SALES (est):** 1.1MM  *Privately Held*
**SIC:** 3444  Sheet metalwork

**(G-6214)**
### PROGRESSIVE SYSTEMS NETWRK INC
329 W 18th St Ste 605  (60616-1103)
**PHONE**..................312 382-8383
**Fax:** 312 382-8819
Jeff Stangel, *President*
Jerry Piaskowy, *Vice Pres*
Scott Veitch, *Info Tech Mgr*
**EMP:** 4
**SQ FT:** 5,000
**SALES (est):** 780K  *Privately Held*
**WEB:** www.progressivesys.net
**SIC:** 5111 2752 7373 8743 Printing & writing paper; commercial printing, offset; office computer automation systems integration; promotion service

**(G-6215)**
### PROMOTIONAL TS
1211 S Western Ave  (60608-1151)
**PHONE**..................312 243-8991
Gabriel Arcos, *Owner*
**EMP:** 3
**SALES (est):** 100K  *Privately Held*
**SIC:** 2395 Embroidery products, except schiffli machine

**(G-6216)**
### PROMUS EQUITY PARTNERS LLC (PA)
30 S Wacker Dr Ste 1600  (60606-7432)
**PHONE**..................312 784-3990
Zach Musso, *Mng Member*
Steven Brown, *Mng Member*
Charlie Adair, *Business Dir*
Meredith Mays, *Shareholder*
Anders Rosenquist, *Associate*
**EMP:** 11
**SALES (est):** 34MM  *Privately Held*
**SIC:** 3499 5999 Doors, safe & vault: metal; vaults & safes

**(G-6217)**
### PROSHIP INC
29 N Wacker Dr Ste 700  (60606-3228)
**PHONE**..................312 332-7447
**EMP:** 3
**SALES (corp-wide):** 23.6MM  *Privately Held*
**SIC:** 7371 7372 5734 Custom Computer Programing Prepackaged Software Services
**HQ:** Proship, Inc.
400 N Executive Dr # 210
Brookfield WI 53005
414 302-2929

**(G-6218)**
### PROTUS CONSTRUCTION
1429 N Oakley Blvd  (60622-1848)
**PHONE**..................773 405-9999
Stanislaw Swierczyk, *Owner*
**EMP:** 5
**SALES (est):** 303.4K  *Privately Held*
**SIC:** 1389 Construction, repair & dismantling services

**(G-6219)**
### PROVISUR TECHNOLOGIES
222 N La Salle St  (60601-1003)
**PHONE**..................312 284-4698
Brian Perkins, *Exec VP*
Paul Heskens, *Vice Pres*
William Wight, *Vice Pres*
Imad Hamdan, *Plant Mgr*
Melissa Casiano, *Opers Mgr*
**EMP:** 3
**SALES (est):** 390.2K  *Privately Held*
**SIC:** 8731 3621 Commercial physical research; motors & generators

**(G-6220)**
### PSYCHIATRIC ASSESSMENTS INC
Also Called: Adaptive Testing Technologies
217 N Jefferson St # 601  (60661-1103)
**PHONE**..................312 878-6490
Yehuda Cohen, *Principal*
**EMP:** 2
**SALES (est):** 291.6K  *Privately Held*
**SIC:** 7372 8748 Business oriented computer software; testing services

**(G-6221)**
### PTM BIOLABS INC
2201 W Campbell Park Dr  (60612-4092)
**PHONE**..................312 802-6843
Zhongyi Cheng, *President*
Ying Ming Zhao, *Treasurer*
Peter Lee, *Accounts Mgr*
Lexi Lai, *Consultant*
Hsiao Lai, *Associate*
**EMP:** 4
**SALES:** 300K  *Privately Held*
**SIC:** 2836 Biological products, except diagnostic

**(G-6222)**
### PUBLIC GOOD SOFTWARE INC
20 N Wacker Dr Ste 3405  (60606-3102)
**PHONE**..................877 941-2747
Jason Kunesh, *CEO*
Chris Gansen, *CTO*
Brian Bonenberger, *Software Engr*
**EMP:** 12
**SQ FT:** 900
**SALES (est):** 503.3K  *Privately Held*
**SIC:** 7372 Business oriented computer software

**(G-6223)**
### PUBLISHING PROPERTIES LLC (DH)
350 N Orleans St Fl 10  (60654-1975)
**PHONE**..................312 321-2299
Michael Mackey, *Principal*
**EMP:** 2
**SALES (est):** 712.8K
**SALES (corp-wide):** 304.8MM  *Privately Held*
**SIC:** 2711 7313 Newspapers; electronic media advertising representatives; printed media advertising representatives

**(G-6224)**
### PUBLISHING TASK FORCE
Also Called: Italian Trade Agency
401 N Michigan Ave # 1720  (60611-4255)
**PHONE**..................312 670-4360
Mateo Picarillo, *Director*
**EMP:** 10
**SALES (est):** 565K  *Privately Held*
**SIC:** 2741 Miscellaneous publishing

**(G-6225)**
### PULLMAN SUGAR LLC
700 E 107th St  (60628-3806)
**PHONE**..................773 260-9180
Brian Boomsma, *President*
Brandon Boomsma, *Vice Pres*
Steve Deboer, *CFO*
Kenneth Pawlowski, *Manager*
Jay Earnshaw, *IT/INT Sup*
▲ **EMP:** 42
**SQ FT:** 100,000
**SALES (est):** 20.7MM
**SALES (corp-wide):** 195.1MM  *Privately Held*
**SIC:** 2062 Cane sugar refining
**PA:** Dutch Farms, Inc.
700 E 107th St
Chicago IL 60628
773 660-0900

**(G-6226)**
### PUNCH PRODUCTS MANUFACTURING
Also Called: A-Punch Products Mfg Co
500 S Kolmar Ave  (60624-3095)
**PHONE**..................773 533-2800
**Fax:** 773 533-2800
Moin Shaikh, *President*
Paul Seligman, *Sales Staff*
Shaukat Kazi, *Admin Sec*
**EMP:** 35
**SQ FT:** 24,000

**SALES (est):** 1.5MM  *Privately Held*
**SIC:** 3053 3086 2672 3842 Gaskets & sealing devices; insulation or cushioning material, foamed plastic; adhesive papers, labels or tapes: from purchased material; surgical appliances & supplies; machine tools, metal forming type; pressed & blown glass

**(G-6227)**
### PUNCH SKIN CARE INC
2155 W Belmont Ave Ste 34  (60618-6471)
**PHONE**..................702 333-2510
Michael Crown, *President*
**EMP:** 22 EST: 2014
**SQ FT:** 6,000
**SALES (est):** 1.2MM  *Privately Held*
**SIC:** 2844  Toilet preparations

**(G-6228)**
### PURE ASPHALT COMPANY
Also Called: Pure Alphalt
3455 W 31st Pl  (60623-5082)
**PHONE**..................773 247-7030
**Fax:** 773 247-7066
Karl Brinkmann, *Division Mgr*
Hector Covarrubias, *Accounts Mgr*
Alan Brooker, *Info Tech Mgr*
Michael K Francis, *Admin Sec*
**EMP:** 15
**SALES (est):** 4.8MM  *Privately Held*
**SIC:** 2952  Asphalt felts & coatings

**(G-6229)**
### PURE LIGHTING LLC
1718 W Fullerton Ave  (60614-1922)
**PHONE**..................773 770-1130
John Kay, *Engineer*
Michael Shulan, *Project Engr*
Bill Nichols, *Controller*
Mike Donovan, *VP Sales*
Gina Gasbarre, *Marketing Mgr*
▲ **EMP:** 13
**SALES (est):** 1.5MM  *Privately Held*
**SIC:** 3646 Commercial indusl & institutional electric lighting fixtures

**(G-6230)**
### PUZZLES BUS OFF SOLUTIONS INC
47 W Polk St  (60605-2000)
**PHONE**..................773 891-7688
John Sullen, *President*
Michele Sullen, *Admin Sec*
**EMP:** 2 EST: 2012
**SALES (est):** 235.7K  *Privately Held*
**SIC:** 3944  Puzzles

**(G-6231)**
### PVS CHEMICAL SOLUTIONS INC
12260 S Carondolet Ave  (60633-1197)
**PHONE**..................773 933-8800
D A Price, *Technical Mgr*
Scott Ribo, *Manager*
Dale Price, *Manager*
**EMP:** 36
**SALES (corp-wide):** 497MM  *Privately Held*
**SIC:** 2819 2899 2869 Sulfur chloride; chemical preparations; industrial organic chemicals
**HQ:** Pvs Chemical Solutions, Inc.
10900 Harper Ave
Detroit MI 48213
313 921-1200

**(G-6232)**
### PYAR & COMPANY LLC
1749 N Cleveland Ave  (60614-5602)
P.O. Box 14814 (60614-8532)
**PHONE**..................312 451-5073
Paula Queen,
Shalini Gupta,
**EMP:** 4 EST: 2011
**SALES (est):** 279.7K  *Privately Held*
**SIC:** 2392 3651 5023 Cushions & pillows; pillows, stereo; linens, table

**(G-6233)**
### PYROPHASE INC
5000 S Cornell Ave 18c  (60615-3041)
**PHONE**..................773 324-8645
Jeff Presley, *President*
Iman Safari, *Engineer*
Rosemarie Snow, *Associate*

# Chicago - Cook County (G-6234)  GEOGRAPHIC SECTION

**EMP:** 4
**SALES:** 950K  **Privately Held**
**SIC:** 1389  Oil & gas field services

**(G-6234)**
**Q LOTUS HOLDINGS INC**
520 N Kingsbury St # 1810  (60654-8772)
**PHONE**...................312 379-1800
Gary A Rosenberg, *Ch of Bd*
Jorge Gonzalez, *CFO*
Ingrid Diaz, *Admin Sec*
**EMP:** 3
**SALES (est):** 376.6K  **Privately Held**
**SIC:** 1011  7389  Iron ores; financial services

**(G-6235)**
**QABOSS PARTNERS**
27 N Wacker Dr Ste 155  (60606-2800)
**PHONE**...................312 203-4290
Kvi El, *Partner*
**EMP:** 300
**SALES (est):** 13.6MM  **Privately Held**
**SIC:** 3663  Radio & TV communications equipment; mobile communication equipment;

**(G-6236)**
**QAPRINTSCOM**
Also Called: Q and A Media Service
2721 S Halsted St  (60608-5906)
**PHONE**...................312 404-2130
Ada Yang, *Principal*
**EMP:** 5
**SALES (est):** 614.9K  **Privately Held**
**SIC:** 2752  Business form & card printing, lithographic

**(G-6237)**
**QST INDUSTRIES INC (PA)**
Also Called: Q S T
550 W Adams St Ste 200  (60661-3665)
**PHONE**...................312 930-9400
**Fax:** 312 930-0118
Lacramioara Curcan, *General Mgr*
Alex Danch, *Vice Pres*
Michael Danch, *Vice Pres*
Sal Paterna, *Vice Pres*
Dick Shanhouse, *Vice Pres*
◆ **EMP:** 50
**SQ FT:** 20,000
**SALES (est):** 180.4MM  **Privately Held**
**WEB:** www.johnsolomon.com
**SIC:** 2396  2392  2754  Automotive & apparel trimmings; household furnishings; commercial printing, lithographic

**(G-6238)**
**QST INDUSTRIES INC**
Samuel Haber Son Division
550 W Adams St Ste 200  (60661-3665)
**PHONE**...................312 930-9400
**Fax:** 312 648-0312
Charee Sontep, *Human Res Mgr*
Jeff Carlevato, *Manager*
**EMP:** 55
**SALES (corp-wide):** 180.4MM  **Privately Held**
**WEB:** www.johnsolomon.com
**SIC:** 2396  Automotive & apparel trimmings
**PA:** Qst Industries, Inc.
550 W Adams St Ste 200
Chicago IL 60661
312 930-9400

**(G-6239)**
**QT INFO SYSTEMS INC**
141 W Jackson Blvd 1255a  (60604-3192)
**PHONE**...................800 240-8761
Terrence Linn, *Principal*
Terry Linn, *Vice Pres*
**EMP:** 15
**SQ FT:** 500
**SALES (est):** 1MM  **Privately Held**
**SIC:** 2741

**(G-6240)**
**QUADRAMED CORPORATION**
440 N Wells St Ste 505  (60654-4584)
**PHONE**...................312 396-0700
Margaret Jones, *Finance Mgr*
Joanne August, *Branch Mgr*
Joanne Agust, *Technical Staff*
Jill Marcotte, *Technical Staff*
**EMP:** 23

**SALES (corp-wide):** 2.1B  **Privately Held**
**WEB:** www.quadramed.com
**SIC:** 8742  7322  7373  7372  Hospital & health services consultant; collection agency, except real estate; computer integrated systems design; prepackaged software; custom computer programming services
**HQ:** Quadramed Corporation
12110 Sunset Hills Rd # 600
Reston VA 20190
703 709-2300

**(G-6241)**
**QUAKER MANUFACTURING LLC**
321 N Clark St  (60654-4714)
**PHONE**...................312 222-7111
Pamela S Hewitt, *Senior VP*
Sarah E Bergman, *Mng Member*
Stuart Kurtz, *Analyst*
**EMP:** 10
**SALES (est):** 729.7K
**SALES (corp-wide):** 62.8B  **Publicly Held**
**WEB:** www.quakeroats.com
**SIC:** 2043  Cereal breakfast foods
**HQ:** The Quaker Oats Company
555 W Monroe St Fl 1
Chicago IL 60661
312 821-1000

**(G-6242)**
**QUAKER OATS COMPANY (HQ)**
555 W Monroe St Fl 1  (60661-3716)
**PHONE**...................312 821-1000
Jose Luis Prado, *President*
Rich Schutzenhofer, *President*
Thomas Ryan, *General Mgr*
John B Kavanagh, *Counsel*
Natalie Browne, *Vice Pres*
◆ **EMP:** 1000 **EST:** 1901
**SQ FT:** 300,000
**SALES (est):** 3.5B
**SALES (corp-wide):** 62.8B  **Publicly Held**
**WEB:** www.quakeroats.com
**SIC:** 2086  2043  2045  2052  Bottled & canned soft drinks; cereal breakfast foods; flours & flour mixes, from purchased flour; rice cakes; granola & muesli, bars & clusters; rice, uncooked: packaged with other ingredients; pasta, uncooked: packaged with other ingredients; maple syrup
**PA:** Pepsico, Inc.
700 Anderson Hill Rd
Purchase NY 10577
914 253-2000

**(G-6243)**
**QUAKER OATS EUROPE INC (HQ)**
555 W Monroe St Fl 1  (60661-3716)
**PHONE**...................312 821-1000
Gary Rodkin, *President*
**EMP:** 5
**SALES (est):** 543.4K
**SALES (corp-wide):** 62.8B  **Publicly Held**
**SIC:** 2043  2045  Cereal breakfast foods; flours & flour mixes, from purchased flour
**PA:** Pepsico, Inc.
700 Anderson Hill Rd
Purchase NY 10577
914 253-2000

**(G-6244)**
**QUALITEX COMPANY**
4248 N Elston Ave  (60618-1894)
**PHONE**...................773 506-8112
**Fax:** 773 463-5731
Harry Campagna, *President*
Freddi Campagna, *Treasurer*
Morry Freidlander, *Sales Staff*
Ava B Campagna, *Admin Sec*
▼ **EMP:** 16 **EST:** 1943
**SALES (est):** 3.2MM  **Privately Held**
**SIC:** 2842  3582  Drycleaning preparations; commercial laundry equipment

**(G-6245)**
**QUALITY ARMATURE INC**
5259 W Grand Ave  (60639-3043)
**PHONE**...................773 622-3951
Michele Rubino, *President*
Michele Filomeno, *President*
Filomena Rubino, *Corp Secy*
**EMP:** 7
**SQ FT:** 6,000

**SALES (est):** 1.1MM  **Privately Held**
**WEB:** www.qualityarmature.com
**SIC:** 7694  Armature rewinding shops; electric motor repair

**(G-6246)**
**QUALITY CROUTONS INC**
1155 W 40th St  (60609-2506)
**PHONE**...................773 927-8200
**Fax:** 773 927-8228
David M Moore, *President*
Dan Harding, *Engineer*
**EMP:** 40
**SQ FT:** 40,000
**SALES (est):** 6.9MM  **Privately Held**
**WEB:** www.qualitycroutons.com
**SIC:** 2051  2052  7389  Bread, cake & related products; cookies & crackers; packaging & labeling services

**(G-6247)**
**QUALITY OPTICAL INC**
4610 N Lincoln Ave  (60625-2008)
**PHONE**...................773 561-0870
**Fax:** 773 561-4185
Ted Carillo, *Owner*
**EMP:** 3
**SQ FT:** 3,200
**SALES (est):** 213.2K  **Privately Held**
**SIC:** 5995  3851  3827  Eyeglasses, prescription; ophthalmic goods; optical instruments & lenses

**(G-6248)**
**QUALITY TOOL & MACHINE INC**
8050 S Constance Ave  (60617-1027)
**PHONE**...................773 721-8655
**Fax:** 773 768-1289
Anthony Martincic Jr, *President*
Anton Martincic Jr, *President*
**EMP:** 6 **EST:** 1940
**SQ FT:** 7,000
**SALES (est):** 500K  **Privately Held**
**SIC:** 3544  7692  Special dies, tools, jigs & fixtures; welding repair

**(G-6249)**
**QUAM-NICHOLS COMPANY**
234 E Marquette Rd Ste 1  (60637-4090)
**PHONE**...................773 488-5800
**Fax:** 773 488-6944
Randy Moore, *Vice Pres*
Denise Toliver, *Purchasing*
Bruce Arndt, *CFO*
David Formet, *Accounts Mgr*
Joda Boykin, *Sales Staff*
▲ **EMP:** 108 **EST:** 1930
**SQ FT:** 120,000
**SALES (est):** 21.3MM  **Privately Held**
**WEB:** www.quamspeakers.com
**SIC:** 3651  Loudspeakers, electrodynamic or magnetic

**(G-6250)**
**QUANTUM CORPORATION**
1 S Wacker Dr  (60606-4614)
**PHONE**...................312 372-2857
Kevin Marston, *Manager*
**EMP:** 90
**SALES (corp-wide):** 505.3MM  **Publicly Held**
**WEB:** www.quantum.com
**SIC:** 3572  Computer storage devices
**PA:** Quantum Corporation
224 Airport Pkwy Ste 550
San Jose CA 95110
408 944-4000

**(G-6251)**
**QUANTUM NOVA TECHNOLOGIES**
2207 E 70th Pl  (60649-2271)
**PHONE**...................773 386-6816
James Render, *Principal*
**EMP:** 3
**SALES (est):** 235.9K  **Privately Held**
**SIC:** 3572  Computer storage devices

**(G-6252)**
**QUANTUM PARTNERS LLC**
2035 W Evergreen Ave  (60622-1908)
**PHONE**...................312 725-4668
Ling Liu, *Principal*
**EMP:** 6
**SALES (est):** 591.8K  **Privately Held**
**SIC:** 3572  Computer storage devices

**(G-6253)**
**QUANTUM9 INC**
303 W Erie St Ste L101  (60654-3968)
**PHONE**...................888 716-0404
**EMP:** 3
**SALES (est):** 94.5K  **Privately Held**
**SIC:** 3572  Computer storage devices

**(G-6254)**
**QUARASAN GROUP INC**
1 E Wacker Dr Ste 1900  (60601-1902)
**PHONE**...................312 981-2540
**Fax:** 312 981-2507
Randi Brill, *President*
Dennis Light, *Editor*
Robert S Taylor, *Vice Pres*
Maribel Irizarry, *Accountant*
Bob Taylor, *Financial Exec*
**EMP:** 75
**SQ FT:** 50,400
**SALES (est):** 6.9MM  **Privately Held**
**WEB:** www.quarasan.com
**SIC:** 2741  7389  8748  Miscellaneous publishing; artists' agents & brokers; business consulting

**(G-6255)**
**QUARTIX INC**
500 N Michigan Ave # 1607  (60611-5066)
**PHONE**...................855 913-6663
Andrew Walters, *President*
David Bridge, *CFO*
Russell Green, *CPA*
Andrew Kirk, *Director*
**EMP:** 14
**SALES (est):** 164.2K  **Privately Held**
**SIC:** 3812  Search & navigation equipment; navigational systems & instruments

**(G-6256)**
**QUESTILY LLC (PA)**
3619 N Claremont Ave  (60618-4817)
**PHONE**...................312 636-6657
John Miniati, *CEO*
**EMP:** 3
**SALES (est):** 15K  **Privately Held**
**SIC:** 7372  7389  Educational computer software

**(G-6257)**
**QUESTILY LLC**
2 N La Salle St Fl 14  (60602-3702)
**PHONE**...................312 636-6657
John Miniati, *CEO*
**EMP:** 4
**SALES (corp-wide):** 15K  **Privately Held**
**SIC:** 7372  Educational computer software
**PA:** Questily Llc
3619 N Claremont Ave
Chicago IL 60618
312 636-6657

**(G-6258)**
**QUINCY LAB INC**
1928 N Leamington Ave  (60639-4421)
**PHONE**...................773 622-2428
**Fax:** 773 622-2282
Anthony Guanci Jr, *President*
Cheri McKown, *Principal*
Peggy Riley, *Office Mgr*
**EMP:** 35
**SQ FT:** 38,000
**SALES:** 2MM  **Privately Held**
**WEB:** www.quincylab.com
**SIC:** 3821  3842  3567  Ovens, laboratory; incubators, laboratory; surgical appliances & supplies; industrial furnaces & ovens

**(G-6259)**
**QUIXOTE CORPORATION (HQ)**
70 W Madison St Ste 2350  (60602-4295)
**PHONE**...................312 705-8400
**Fax:** 312 467-1356
Bruce Reimer, *President*
Jeffery S Held, *Vice Pres*
George Reed, *Vice Pres*
Joan R Riley, *Vice Pres*
Kenneth Clark, *Opers Mgr*
◆ **EMP:** 33 **EST:** 1969
**SQ FT:** 21,000

# GEOGRAPHIC SECTION

Chicago - Cook County (G-6284)

**SALES (est):** 33.1MM
**SALES (corp-wide):** 4.5B **Publicly Held**
**WEB:** www.quixotecorp.com
**SIC:** 3089 4899 Plastic hardware & building products; communication signal enhancement network system; radar station operation
**PA:** Trinity Industries, Inc.
2525 N Stemmons Fwy
Dallas TX 75207
214 631-4420

**(G-6260)**
## QUIXOTE TRANSPORTATION SAFETY
70 W Madison St Ste 2350 (60602-4295)
**PHONE** .................................. 312 467-6750
Leslie Jezuit, *President*
James E Connell, *General Mgr*
Daniel Gorey, *CFO*
James D Crowley, *VP Sales*
Joan Riley, *Admin Sec*
**EMP:** 90
**SQ FT:** 19,000
**SALES (est):** 8.7MM
**SALES (corp-wide):** 4.5B **Publicly Held**
**SIC:** 3499 3089 Barricades, metal; injection molded finished plastic products
**HQ:** Quixote Corporation
70 W Madison St Ste 2350
Chicago IL 60602
312 705-8400

**(G-6261)**
## R & B POWDER COATINGS INC
4000 S Bell Ave (60609-2208)
**PHONE** .................................. 773 247-8300
**Fax:** 773 247-6131
Tony Cash, *President*
Lois Thompson, *Vice Pres*
Kathy De Pino, *Sales Executive*
Kathy Depino, *Manager*
**EMP:** 30
**SQ FT:** 40,000
**SALES (est):** 4.3MM **Privately Held**
**WEB:** www.rbpowder.com
**SIC:** 3479 Painting, coating & hot dipping

**(G-6262)**
## R & E QUALITY MFG CO
7005 W School St (60634-3647)
**PHONE** .................................. 773 286-6846
Edward Gray, *Owner*
**EMP:** 3
**SALES:** 200K **Privately Held**
**SIC:** 3312 Tool & die steel

**(G-6263)**
## R & J TRUCKING AND RECYCL INC
6650 S Oak Park Ave (60638-4812)
**PHONE** .................................. 708 563-2600
Balbina Alvear, *President*
Julian Cadalan, *General Mgr*
**EMP:** 12
**SALES:** 3.4MM **Privately Held**
**SIC:** 2611 4212 Pulp manufactured from waste or recycled paper; local trucking, without storage

**(G-6264)**
## R A R MACHINE & MANUFACTURING
5750 N Melvina Ave (60646-6122)
**PHONE** .................................. 630 260-9591
Ronald Carlson, *President*
Mary Katherine Carlson, *Corp Secy*
**EMP:** 25
**SQ FT:** 12,500
**SALES:** 1.2MM **Privately Held**
**SIC:** 3599 7692 Machine shop, jobbing & repair; welding repair

**(G-6265)**
## R C INDUSTRIES INC
1420 N Lamon Ave (60651-1512)
**PHONE** .................................. 773 378-1118
**Fax:** 773 378-5063
Robert A Calabrese, *President*
Mildred J Calabrese, *Corp Secy*
Stuart Schwartz, *Exec VP*
Schwartz Stuart, *Manager*
**EMP:** 12
**SQ FT:** 16,500

**SALES (est):** 1.1MM **Privately Held**
**SIC:** 3471 2851 Finishing, metals or formed products; paints & allied products

**(G-6266)**
## R E Z PACKAGING INC
3735 S Racine Ave (60609-2137)
**PHONE** .................................. 773 247-0800
Debra Zarazee, *President*
Richard Zarazee, *Treasurer*
**EMP:** 4
**SQ FT:** 20,000
**SALES:** 500K **Privately Held**
**SIC:** 2842 Specialty cleaning preparations; deodorants, nonpersonal

**(G-6267)**
## R L D COMMUNICATIONS INC (PA)
Also Called: Box Office Magazine
725 S Wells St Fl 4 (60607-4521)
**PHONE** .................................. 312 338-7007
**Fax:** 773 338-1884
Robert L Dietmeier, *Principal*
Dan Johnson, *Principal*
Lois Dietmeier, *Admin Sec*
**EMP:** 4
**SALES (est):** 654K **Privately Held**
**SIC:** 2721 Trade journals: publishing only, not printed on site

**(G-6268)**
## R MADERITE INC
1616 N Washtenaw Ave (60647-5231)
**PHONE** .................................. 773 235-1515
**Fax:** 773 235-1527
**EMP:** 2 EST: 2006
**SALES (est):** 230K **Privately Held**
**SIC:** 5211 2499 Ret Lumber/Building Materials Mfg Wood Products

**(G-6269)**
## R POPERNIK CO INC
2313 W 59th St (60636-1518)
**PHONE** .................................. 773 434-4300
**Fax:** 773 434-4345
Ronald J Popernik, *CEO*
Marielena White, *President*
Michelle Kibler, *Corp Secy*
**EMP:** 15
**SQ FT:** 22,800
**SALES (est):** 2.5MM **Privately Held**
**SIC:** 2759 2673 Flexographic printing; food storage & frozen food bags, plastic

**(G-6270)**
## R R DONNELLEY & SONS COMPANY (PA)
Also Called: RR Donnelley
35 W Wacker Dr Ste 3650 (60601-1840)
**PHONE** .................................. 312 326-8000
**Fax:** 312 326-8543
John C Pope, *Ch of Bd*
Daniel L Knotts, *President*
John Pecaric, *Exec VP*
Jeffrey G Gorski, *Senior VP*
Terry D Peterson, *CFO*
**EMP:** 277 EST: 1864
**SALES:** 6.9B **Publicly Held**
**WEB:** www.rrdonnelley.com
**SIC:** 2754 2759 2752 2732 Commercial printing, gravure; catalogs: gravure printing, not published on site; magazines: gravure printing, not published on site; directories: gravure printing, not published on site; commercial printing, letterpress printing; commercial printing, offset; books: printing & binding; direct mail advertising services; graphic arts & related design

**(G-6271)**
## R R STREET & CO INC
4600 S Tripp Ave (60632-4419)
**PHONE** .................................. 773 247-1190
L Ross Beard, *President*
**EMP:** 50
**SQ FT:** 19,500
**SALES (corp-wide):** 42.2MM **Privately Held**
**WEB:** www.4streets.com
**SIC:** 2842 Cleaning or polishing preparations

**PA:** R. R. Street & Co., Inc.
215 Shuman Blvd Ste 403
Naperville IL 60563
630 416-4244

**(G-6272)**
## R R STREET & CO INC
2353 S Blue Island Ave (60608-4227)
**PHONE** .................................. 773 254-1277
Ross Beard, *Vice Pres*
Clarence Overby, *Manager*
**EMP:** 13
**SALES (corp-wide):** 42.2MM **Privately Held**
**WEB:** www.4streets.com
**SIC:** 2842 Drycleaning preparations
**PA:** R. R. Street & Co., Inc.
215 Shuman Blvd Ste 403
Naperville IL 60563
630 416-4244

**(G-6273)**
## R S OWENS & CO INC
Also Called: Elegance In Awards & Gifts
5535 N Lynch Ave (60630-1417)
**PHONE** .................................. 773 282-6000
**Fax:** 773 545-4501
Scott Siegel, *President*
Leslie Neumann, *Division Mgr*
Shirlie L Siegel, *Corp Secy*
Mark Avenson, *Vice Pres*
Mark Psaros, *Vice Pres*
▲ **EMP:** 251
**SQ FT:** 82,000
**SALES (est):** 47.6MM **Privately Held**
**WEB:** www.rsowens.com
**SIC:** 3499 3999 3911 3961 Trophies, metal, except silver; plaques, picture, laminated; medals, precious or semi-precious metal; pins (jewelry), precious metal; pins (jewelry), except precious metal

**(G-6274)**
## R T P INC
Also Called: Minuteman Press
1249 N Clybourn Ave (60610-6655)
**PHONE** .................................. 312 664-6150
Gary Allison, *President*
Sarah Allison, *Treasurer*
Joe Hernandez, *Marketing Mgr*
**EMP:** 4
**SALES (est):** 460K **Privately Held**
**SIC:** 2752 Commercial printing, lithographic

**(G-6275)**
## R-K PRESS BRAKE DIES INC
12512 S Springfield Ave (60803-1409)
**PHONE** .................................. 708 371-1756
**Fax:** 708 371-8068
Tom Bosinski, *President*
Dan Orseske, *Sales Staff*
Russ McDaniel, *Office Mgr*
Russ McDanniel, *Manager*
**EMP:** 18
**SQ FT:** 20,000
**SALES (est):** 3.2MM **Privately Held**
**WEB:** www.rkbrakedies.com
**SIC:** 3542 3544 Press brakes; special dies, tools, jigs & fixtures

**(G-6276)**
## RA-UJAMAA INC
622 E 47th St (60653-4210)
**PHONE** .................................. 773 373-8585
Ronney McCarthy, *President*
**EMP:** 2
**SQ FT:** 800
**SALES:** 250K **Privately Held**
**SIC:** 3993 Signs & advertising specialties

**(G-6277)**
## RACHEL SWITALL MAG GROUP NFP
1441b W Wrightwood Ave (60614-1121)
**PHONE** .................................. 773 344-7123
Rachel Switall, *CEO*
**EMP:** 4
**SALES (est):** 164.9K **Privately Held**
**SIC:** 2711 Newspapers: publishing only, not printed on site

**(G-6278)**
## RACINE PAPER BOX MANUFACTURING
3522 W Potomac Ave (60651-2230)
**PHONE** .................................. 773 227-3900
**Fax:** 773 227-3983
Navnit Patel, *President*
Atul Patel, *Vice Pres*
Robert Patel, *Purchasing*
Savita Patel, *Admin Sec*
**EMP:** 20
**SQ FT:** 29,000
**SALES:** 450K **Privately Held**
**SIC:** 2652 3944 2675 2657 Setup paperboard boxes; games, toys & children's vehicles; die-cut paper & board; folding paperboard boxes

**(G-6279)**
## RADIO FLYER INC
6515 W Grand Ave (60707-3436)
**PHONE** .................................. 773 637-7100
**Fax:** 773 637-8874
Robert Pasin, *President*
Paul Pasin, *Exec VP*
Kim Lefko, *Senior VP*
Miteshkumar Shah, *QA Dir*
Lucux Law, *Engineer*
▲ **EMP:** 50 EST: 1930
**SALES (est):** 14.3MM **Privately Held**
**WEB:** www.radioflyer.com
**SIC:** 3944 Wagons: coaster, express & play; children's

**(G-6280)**
## RADIOFX INC ✪
1953 N Clybourn Ave (60614-4945)
**PHONE** .................................. 773 255-8069
John Wanzung, *CEO*
**EMP:** 3 EST: 2016
**SALES (est):** 78.2K **Privately Held**
**SIC:** 7372 Application computer software

**(G-6281)**
## RADIONIC HI-TECH INC
6625 W Diversey Ave (60707-2218)
**PHONE** .................................. 773 804-0100
Jeffrey Winton, *President*
**EMP:** 52
**SQ FT:** 85,000
**SALES (est):** 7MM **Privately Held**
**SIC:** 3629 3641 3648 3643 Battery chargers, rectifying or nonrotating; lamps, incandescent filament, electric; lamps, fluorescent, electric; lighting equipment; starting switches, fluorescent

**(G-6282)**
## RADIONIC INDUSTRIES INC
6625 W Diversey Ave (60707-2218)
**PHONE** .................................. 773 804-0100
**Fax:** 773 804-0180
Jeff Winton, *President*
Jim Eckl, *Manager*
Joyce Elliott, *Manager*
Daniel Winton, *Admin Sec*
Marla Fine, *Administration*
▲ **EMP:** 110
**SQ FT:** 85,000
**SALES (est):** 19.8MM **Privately Held**
**WEB:** www.radionic.net
**SIC:** 3612 Fluorescent ballasts; lighting transformers, fluorescent

**(G-6283)**
## RADIUS SOLUTIONS INCORPORATED
150 N Michigan Ave # 300 (60601-7524)
**PHONE** .................................. 312 648-0800
David Taylor, *President*
Kevin Blakey, *Opers Staff*
**EMP:** 11
**SALES (est):** 1MM **Privately Held**
**SIC:** 7372 Business oriented computer software

**(G-6284)**
## RAHMANIMS IMPORTS INC (PA)
Also Called: RI Diamonds
5 S Wabash Ave Ste 1211 (60603-3135)
**PHONE** .................................. 312 236-2200
Naser Rahmanim, *President*
Vahideh Rahmanim, *Vice Pres*
Afsaneh Rahmanim, *Admin Sec*
**EMP:** 8

## Chicago - Cook County (G-6285)

SQ FT: 2,100
SALES (est): 656.9K **Privately Held**
WEB: www.ridiamonds.com
SIC: 3911 5094 Jewelry, precious metal; jewelry

**(G-6285)**
**RAIL FORGE**
2001 W Wabansia Ave # 101 (60647-5566)
PHONE...............................630 561-4989
Keith Ishaug, *Principal*
EMP: 4
SALES (est): 308.7K **Privately Held**
SIC: 3452 Screws, metal

**(G-6286)**
**RAILWAY PROGRAM SERVICES INC**
Also Called: Rpsi
6235 S Oak Park Ave (60638-4015)
PHONE...............................708 552-4000
Gregory R Winsor, *President*
Scott Ward, *Opers Mgr*
James Schmidt, *Opers Staff*
EMP: 9 EST: 1993
SQ FT: 2,000
SALES (est): 977.3K
SALES (corp-wide): 11.7MM **Privately Held**
WEB: www.ramptechinc.com
SIC: 3743 Railroad car rebuilding
PA: Steelhead Corporation
    6235 S Oak Park Ave
    Chicago IL 60638
    708 552-4000

**(G-6287)**
**RAIN PUBLICATION INC**
65 E Wacker Pl Ste 930 (60601-7251)
PHONE...............................312 284-2444
Kurt Hanson, *President*
Linda Spitz, *General Mgr*
EMP: 6
SQ FT: 400
SALES (est): 250K **Privately Held**
WEB: www.kurthanson.com
SIC: 2741 Newsletter publishing

**(G-6288)**
**RAINBOW ART INC**
2224 W Grand Ave (60612-1512)
PHONE...............................312 421-5600
Fax: 312 421-1451
Norman Korenthal, *President*
Jack Korenthal, *President*
Susan Korenthal, *Vice Pres*
Kathy Duncan, *Office Mgr*
EMP: 15 EST: 1941
SQ FT: 9,600
SALES (est): 1.8MM **Privately Held**
WEB: www.rainbowartinc.com
SIC: 3479 2759 3471 2396 Coating of metals & formed products; imprinting; plating & polishing; automotive & apparel trimmings

**(G-6289)**
**RAINBOW FABRICS INC**
620 W Roosevelt Rd (60607-4912)
PHONE...............................312 356-9979
Jagan Dhamisha, *President*
EMP: 2
SALES (est): 260K **Privately Held**
SIC: 2299 Fabrics: linen, jute, hemp, ramie

**(G-6290)**
**RAPID CIRCULAR PRESS INC**
526 N Western Ave (60612-1422)
PHONE...............................312 421-5611
Fax: 312 421-5610
George Korecky, *President*
Barry Korecky, *Vice Pres*
Audry Korecky, *Treasurer*
Sherry Gabrilators, *Office Mgr*
Sherry Gabrielatos, *Manager*
EMP: 15 EST: 1955
SQ FT: 12,500
SALES: 1.2MM **Privately Held**
WEB: www.rapidcircularpress.com
SIC: 2752 2791 2759 2741 Commercial printing, lithographic; circulars, lithographed; typesetting; commercial printing; miscellaneous publishing

**(G-6291)**
**RAPID DISPLAYS INC (PA)**
Also Called: Cadaco Division
4300 W 47th St (60632-4404)
PHONE...............................773 927-5000
Fax: 773 927-9281
David P Abramson, *CEO*
Earl Abramson, *Chairman*
Cadaco John, *Sr Corp Ofcr*
Alan Foshay, *Vice Pres*
Brian McCormick, *Vice Pres*
▲ EMP: 250 EST: 1938
SQ FT: 350,000
SALES (est): 158.3MM **Privately Held**
WEB: www.rapiddisplays.com
SIC: 2675 3944 Die-cut paper & board; board games, children's & adults'

**(G-6292)**
**RAPID DISPLAYS INC**
4300 W 47th St (60632-4404)
PHONE...............................773 927-1500
Mark Abramson, *General Mgr*
EMP: 100
SALES (corp-wide): 156.5MM **Privately Held**
WEB: www.rapiddisplays.com
SIC: 2084 Wines
PA: Rapid Displays, Inc.
    4300 W 47th St
    Chicago IL 60632
    773 927-5000

**(G-6293)**
**RAPID EXECUTION SERVICES LLC**
141 W Jackson Blvd 300a (60604-2992)
PHONE...............................312 789-4358
EMP: 3 EST: 2014
SALES (est): 281K **Privately Held**
SIC: 6231 7373 7372 Security & commodity exchanges; systems integration services; computer-aided system services; business oriented computer software

**(G-6294)**
**RAPID WIRE FORMS INC**
6932 W 62nd St (60638-3934)
PHONE...............................773 586-6600
Mary Iuliano, *President*
Anthony Iuliano, *Vice Pres*
EMP: 5
SALES (est): 586.7K **Privately Held**
SIC: 3496 Miscellaneous fabricated wire products

**(G-6295)**
**RAVENS WOOD PHARMACY**
4211 N Cicero Ave (60641-1651)
PHONE...............................708 667-0525
EMP: 4
SALES (est): 187K **Privately Held**
SIC: 5912 5122 2834 Ret Drugs/Sundries Whol Drugs/Sundries Mfg Pharmaceutical Preparations

**(G-6296)**
**RAWNATURE5 LLC**
3026 W Carroll Ave (60612-1722)
PHONE...............................312 800-3239
Dustin Baker, *President*
Chris Fanucchi, *Vice Pres*
EMP: 13
SALES (est): 1.1MM **Privately Held**
SIC: 2099 5141 Food preparations; food brokers

**(G-6297)**
**RAYTRANS DISTRIBUTION SVCS INC (HQ)**
600 W Chicago Ave Ste 725 (60654-2522)
P.O. Box 1719, Matteson (60443-4719)
PHONE...............................708 503-9940
Douglas R Waggonerr, *President*
Douglas R Waggoner, *President*
Tyler Ellison, *Exec VP*
David B Menzel, *CFO*
James Ray, *Treasurer*
EMP: 10
SQ FT: 3,300

SALES (est): 5.2MM
SALES (corp-wide): 1.7B **Publicly Held**
SIC: 8742 4731 7372 Distribution channels consultant; transportation agents & brokers; prepackaged software
PA: Echo Global Logistics, Inc.
    600 W Chicago Ave Ste 725
    Chicago IL 60654
    800 354-7993

**(G-6298)**
**RAZE VAPOR**
329 W Evergreen Ave (60610-1814)
PHONE...............................415 596-2697
EMP: 5 EST: 2009
SALES (est): 426.6K **Privately Held**
SIC: 2131 Smoking tobacco

**(G-6299)**
**RCP PUBLICATIONS INC**
3449 N Sheffield Ave (60657-1613)
P.O. Box 3486 (60654-0486)
PHONE...............................773 227-4066
Robert Avakian, *President*
William Klingel, *Vice Pres*
Christopher Menchine, *Treasurer*
EMP: 8
SQ FT: 2,500
SALES (est): 340K **Privately Held**
SIC: 2711 2721 Newspapers; periodicals

**(G-6300)**
**RE MET CORP**
Also Called: United American Metals
2246 W Hubbard St (60612-1614)
PHONE...............................312 733-6700
Fax: 312 733-6710
William Renotti, *President*
Alan Renotti, *Vice Pres*
EMP: 6
SQ FT: 20,000
SALES: 1.3MM **Privately Held**
SIC: 3339 Tin refining (primary); lead smelting & refining (primary); zinc refining (primary), including slabs & dust

**(G-6301)**
**REACH CHICAGO LLC**
350 N Orleans St Fl 10-S (60654-1975)
PHONE...............................312 923-1028
EMP: 3
SALES (est): 117K **Privately Held**
SIC: 2711 Newspapers, publishing & printing

**(G-6302)**
**REAL ESTATE NEWS CORP**
Also Called: Chicago Going Out Guide
3525 W Peterson Ave T10 (60659-3312)
PHONE...............................773 866-9900
Fax: 773 866-1626
Steven N Polydoris, *President*
EMP: 7
SQ FT: 2,900
SALES (est): 912.9K **Privately Held**
WEB: www.chicagobridemagazine.com
SIC: 2721 Periodicals

**(G-6303)**
**REAL TASTE NOODLES MFG INC**
1838 S Canal St (60616-1502)
PHONE...............................312 738-1893
Charlie Len, *President*
EMP: 3 EST: 2000
SQ FT: 5,000
SALES (est): 200K **Privately Held**
SIC: 2099 Noodles, fried (Chinese)

**(G-6304)**
**REAL TIMES INC OF ILLINOIS**
200 S Michigan Ave # 1700 (60604-2402)
PHONE...............................312 225-2400
Clarence Nixon, *President*
Tom Picou, *Chairman*
Frank McGee, *Accounts Mgr*
EMP: 14
SQ FT: 19,000
SALES (est): 485.9K
SALES (corp-wide): 8.9MM **Privately Held**
SIC: 2711 Newspapers: publishing only, not printed on site

PA: Real Times Ii Llc
    4445 S Dr Mrtn Lther King Martin Luther King
    Chicago IL 60653
    312 225-2400

**(G-6305)**
**REAL TIMES II LLC (PA)**
Also Called: Chicago Defender Newspaper
4445 S Dr Mrtn Lther King Martin Luther King (60653)
PHONE...............................312 225-2400
Michael House, *President*
Kurt Cherry, *CFO*
EMP: 2
SALES (est): 8.9MM **Privately Held**
SIC: 2711 Newspapers: publishing only, not printed on site

**(G-6306)**
**REALCLEARPOLITICS (PA)**
6160 N Cicero Ave Ste 410 (60646-4337)
PHONE...............................773 255-5846
David Desrosiers, *Principal*
Emmeline Zhao, *Editor*
Melissa Farnum, *Business Mgr*
Kori Kemble, *Sales Dir*
EMP: 8
SALES (est): 1MM **Privately Held**
SIC: 2711 Newspapers

**(G-6307)**
**REALIZE INC**
Also Called: Realize.ai
1803 W 95th St 509 (60643-1103)
PHONE...............................312 566-8759
Alexander Risman, *CEO*
Robert Russell, *CFO*
Sea Chen, *Officer*
EMP: 3
SALES (est): 76.9K **Privately Held**
SIC: 7372 Business oriented computer software

**(G-6308)**
**REALTOR MAGAZINE**
Also Called: National Associates Realtors
430 N Michigan Ave Fl 9 (60611-4011)
PHONE...............................312 329-1928
Fax: 312 329-5960
Stacy Moncrieff, *Principal*
Mary Glick, *Info Tech Mgr*
Jan Hope, *Info Tech Mgr*
EMP: 12
SALES (est): 1.1MM **Privately Held**
WEB: www.realtormag.com
SIC: 2721 Magazines: publishing & printing

**(G-6309)**
**REB STEEL EQUIPMENT CORP (PA)**
Also Called: REB Storage Systems Intl
4556 W Grand Ave (60639-4734)
PHONE...............................773 252-0400
Fax: 773 252-0303
Thomas E Lesko, *CEO*
Lori Palmer, *Exec VP*
William Welton, *Senior VP*
Mike Baily, *Vice Pres*
Joseph Budz, *Vice Pres*
▼ EMP: 50
SQ FT: 100,000
SALES (est): 41.5MM **Privately Held**
WEB: www.rebsteel.com
SIC: 5046 5084 5021 2542 Commercial equipment; shelving, commercial & industrial; materials handling machinery; lockers; shelving, office & store: except wood; racks, merchandise display or storage: except wood; lockers (not refrigerated): except wood

**(G-6310)**
**REBEL SCREENERS INC**
820 W Jackson Blvd # 400 (60607-3026)
PHONE...............................312 525-2670
Fax: 312 525-2712
Edward Wormser, *President*
Scott Stephens, *President*
Erna Rokosz, *Human Res Mgr*
▲ EMP: 70
SQ FT: 10,000
SALES (est): 4.4MM **Privately Held**
SIC: 2396 Screen printing on fabric articles

# GEOGRAPHIC SECTION
## Chicago - Cook County (G-6336)

**(G-6311)**
**RECLAMATION LLC**
1720 N Elston Ave (60642-1532)
PHONE..................510 441-2305
Nancy Hoeffer, *Vice Pres*
Edward Watkins, *Mng Member*
Sipi Metals Corporation,
**EMP:** 4
**SQ FT:** 9,000
**SALES:** 2MM **Privately Held**
**WEB:** www.reclamation.net
**SIC:** 3341 Secondary precious metals

**(G-6312)**
**RECORD INC**
207 E Ohio St Ste 164 (60611-4092)
PHONE..................312 985-7270
Brian Timpone, *Publisher*
**EMP:** 9 **EST:** 2013
**SQ FT:** 727
**SALES (est):** 268.9K **Privately Held**
**SIC:** 2711 Newspapers: publishing only, not printed on site

**(G-6313)**
**RECSOLU INC**
Also Called: Yello
55 E Monroe St Ste 3600 (60603-6032)
P.O. Box 1235 (60690-1235)
PHONE..................312 517-3200
Jason Weingarden, *CEO*
Dan Bartfield, *President*
David Stiefel, *Senior VP*
Kelley Clark, *Vice Pres*
Brian Burke, *CFO*
**EMP:** 32
**SQ FT:** 3,700
**SALES (est):** 6.3MM **Privately Held**
**SIC:** 7371 7372 7373 Computer software writing services; computer software development; business oriented computer software; application computer software; systems software development services

**(G-6314)**
**RECYCLED PAPER GREETINGS INC**
111 N Canal St Ste 700 (60606-7210)
PHONE..................773 348-6410
**Fax:** 773 929-7123
Leonard Levine, *COO*
Philip Friedmann, *Vice Pres*
Dale Shearer, *Purchasing*
Michael Keiser, *Treasurer*
Kathy Harty, *VP Sales*
▲ **EMP:** 25 **EST:** 1972
**SQ FT:** 75,000
**SALES:** 4.7MM
**SALES (corp-wide):** 2.3B **Privately Held**
**WEB:** www.recycledpapergreetings.com
**SIC:** 2771 5199 Greeting cards; gifts & novelties
**HQ:** American Greetings Corporation
1 American Blvd
Cleveland OH 44145
216 252-7300

**(G-6315)**
**RED STREAK HOLDINGS COMPANY**
350 N Orleans St Fl 10-S (60654-1975)
PHONE..................312 321-3000
Cyrus F Friedheim Jr, *President*
**EMP:** 3
**SALES (est):** 104.3K **Privately Held**
**SIC:** 2711 Newspapers, publishing & printing

**(G-6316)**
**REDBOX WORKSHOP LTD**
3121 N Rockwell St (60618-7919)
PHONE..................773 478-7077
**Fax:** 773 478-7177
Pamela L Parker, *President*
Pamela Parker, *President*
Tony Labrosse, *Partner*
Anthony Labrosse, *Vice Pres*
Emily Kneer, *Project Mgr*
**EMP:** 22
**SQ FT:** 17,000
**SALES (est):** 4.4MM **Privately Held**
**WEB:** www.labrosseltd.com
**SIC:** 2541 2531 2426 Showcases, except refrigerated: wood; public building & related furniture; frames for upholstered furniture, wood

**(G-6317)**
**REDSHELF INC**
Also Called: Redshelf/Virdocs
500 N Dearborn St # 1200 (60654-3347)
PHONE..................312 878-8586
Tim Haitaian, *CFO*
Shannon Godfrey, *Sales Staff*
Katie Callaghan, *Marketing Mgr*
**EMP:** 6
**SALES (est):** 101.6K **Privately Held**
**SIC:** 2741 Miscellaneous publishing

**(G-6318)**
**REED-UNION CORPORATION (PA)**
875 N Michigan Ave # 3718 (60611-1946)
PHONE..................312 644-3200
**Fax:** 312 644-3577
Peter D Goldman, *President*
Carol Burns, *Manager*
Carol Goldman, *Admin Sec*
**EMP:** 10 **EST:** 1929
**SQ FT:** 3,500
**SALES:** 2.2MM **Privately Held**
**WEB:** www.nufinish.com
**SIC:** 2842 Automobile polish

**(G-6319)**
**REFINED HAYSTACK LLC**
230 W Superior St 2f (60654-3595)
PHONE..................773 627-3534
Sabrina Vodnik,
**EMP:** 3
**SQ FT:** 200
**SALES (est):** 146.3K **Privately Held**
**SIC:** 2711 Newspapers: publishing only, not printed on site

**(G-6320)**
**REGAL CUT STONE LLC**
4213 W Chicago Ave (60651-3518)
PHONE..................773 826-8796
Melisa Anderson, *Manager*
Gary Gofron,
**EMP:** 13
**SALES (est):** 1.2MM **Privately Held**
**SIC:** 3281 Cut stone & stone products

**(G-6321)**
**REGAL HEALTH FOODS INTL INC**
3705 W Grand Ave (60651-2236)
PHONE..................773 252-1044
**Fax:** 773 252-0817
Gregory Piatigorsky, *President*
◆ **EMP:** 50
**SQ FT:** 25,000
**SALES (est):** 9.9MM **Privately Held**
**WEB:** regalsnacks.com
**SIC:** 2068 Salted & roasted nuts & seeds

**(G-6322)**
**REGENCY HAND LAUNDRY**
2739 N Racine Ave (60614-1205)
PHONE..................773 871-3950
Michael Park, *Owner*
**EMP:** 6
**SALES (est):** 243K **Privately Held**
**SIC:** 7216 3589 Drycleaning plants, except rugs; servicing machines, except dry cleaning, laundry: coin-oper.

**(G-6323)**
**REGENT AUTOMOTIVE ENGINEERING**
2107 N Cicero Ave (60639-3309)
PHONE..................773 889-5744
Peter Roumbos, *Partner*
Don Roumbos, *Partner*
**EMP:** 3 **EST:** 1954
**SQ FT:** 2,000
**SALES (est):** 274K **Privately Held**
**SIC:** 3593 3599 Fluid power cylinders, hydraulic or pneumatic; crankshafts & camshafts, machining; machine shop, jobbing & repair

**(G-6324)**
**REGENT WINDOW FASHIONS LLC**
Also Called: JP O'Callaghan
917 W Irving Park Rd (60613-4585)
PHONE..................773 871-6400
**Fax:** 773 871-6534
John Ellis, *Owner*
**EMP:** 3 **EST:** 1946
**SQ FT:** 2,400
**SALES (est):** 220K **Privately Held**
**SIC:** 2591 5719 1799 Blinds vertical; window furnishings; venetian blinds; vertical blinds; window shades; window treatment installation

**(G-6325)**
**REGGIOS PIZZA INC (PA)**
340 W 83rd St (60620-1704)
PHONE..................773 488-1411
**Fax:** 773 783-7333
John Clark Jr, *President*
Pearl Clark, *Corp Secy*
Sydney Ward, *CFO*
Shelly Horner, *Sales Staff*
Darryl Pennington, *MIS Mgr*
**EMP:** 70
**SQ FT:** 36,000
**SALES (est):** 8MM **Privately Held**
**SIC:** 5812 2038 Pizzeria, independent; pizza, frozen

**(G-6326)**
**REINO TOOL & MANUFACTURING CO**
Also Called: Chicago Wire
3668 N Elston Ave (60618-4316)
PHONE..................773 588-5800
Donald R Michonski, *President*
Martin Michonski, *Vice Pres*
Dennis Kane, *Engineer*
Caryn Chemers, *Manager*
**EMP:** 16 **EST:** 1962
**SQ FT:** 5,000
**SALES:** 810K **Privately Held**
**WEB:** www.chicagowire.com
**SIC:** 3545 3443 3496 3452 Precision tools, machinists'; cylinders, pressure: metal plate; miscellaneous fabricated wire products; bolts, nuts, rivets & washers; screw machine products; steel wire & related products

**(G-6327)**
**RELAY SERVICES MFG CORP**
1300 N Pulaski Rd Ste 12 (60651-1932)
PHONE..................773 252-2700
**Fax:** 773 252-0300
Hugo Francisco, *President*
Joann Kas, *Office Mgr*
**EMP:** 11 **EST:** 1943
**SQ FT:** 8,200
**SALES (est):** 1.2MM **Privately Held**
**WEB:** www.relayserviceco.com
**SIC:** 3625 3679 3612 Relays, for electronic use; electronic switches; specialty transformers

**(G-6328)**
**RELIABLE ASPHALT CORPORATION (PA)**
3741 S Pulaski Rd (60623-4927)
PHONE..................773 254-1121
**Fax:** 773 254-7489
Michael Vondra, *President*
Donna Elischer, *Corp Secy*
Sam Aprile, *Vice Pres*
Bill Howorth, *Vice Pres*
Mike Murphy, *Opers Mgr*
**EMP:** 17
**SQ FT:** 3,000
**SALES (est):** 2.2MM **Privately Held**
**SIC:** 2951 Asphalt & asphaltic paving mixtures (not from refineries)

**(G-6329)**
**RELIABLE GALVANIZING COMPANY (PA)**
819 W 88th St (60620-2668)
PHONE..................773 651-2500
**Toll Free:**..................888  -
**Fax:** 773 488-7100
Daniel D Sugarman, *Ch of Bd*
Michael Eisner, *President*
Dale Wolak, *Manager*
Dale Wolek, *Admin Sec*
**EMP:** 42
**SQ FT:** 55,000
**SALES (est):** 4.7MM **Privately Held**
**WEB:** www.reliablegalvanizing.com
**SIC:** 3479 Galvanizing of iron, steel or end-formed products; hot dip coating of metals or formed products

**(G-6330)**
**RELIABLE PLATING CORPORATION**
1538 W Lake St (60607-1468)
PHONE..................312 421-4747
**Fax:** 312 421-4599
James R Greenwell, *President*
Judy Welsh, *Controller*
Coult Greenwell, *VP Sales*
Ann Ortiz, *Manager*
Maria Zermeno, *Manager*
**EMP:** 75
**SQ FT:** 50,000
**SALES (est):** 11MM **Privately Held**
**WEB:** www.reliableplating.com
**SIC:** 3471 Finishing, metals or formed products; chromium plating of metals or formed products

**(G-6331)**
**RELIEFWATCH INC**
1425 E 53rd St Fl 2 (60615)
PHONE..................646 678-2336
Daniel Yu, *CEO*
**EMP:** 7
**SALES (est):** 390K **Privately Held**
**SIC:** 7372 7371 8243 Application computer software; business oriented computer software; custom computer programming services; software training, computer

**(G-6332)**
**RENEGADE STEEL**
1458 S Canal St (60607-5201)
PHONE..................716 903-2506
Stephen Salgot, *General Ptnr*
Albert Shinners, *General Ptnr*
**EMP:** 5
**SALES (est):** 279.6K **Privately Held**
**SIC:** 3448 Prefabricated metal buildings

**(G-6333)**
**RENEW PACKAGING LLC**
2444 W 16th St Ste 4r (60608-1731)
PHONE..................312 421-6699
John Hamilton,
◆ **EMP:** 7
**SQ FT:** 18,000
**SALES (est):** 1.1MM **Privately Held**
**SIC:** 5113 2673 Bags, paper & disposable plastic; bags: plastic, laminated & coated

**(G-6334)**
**RENSEL-CHICAGO INC (PA)**
2300 N Kilbourn Ave (60639-3402)
PHONE..................773 235-2100
Brian H Johnson, *President*
**EMP:** 14
**SQ FT:** 35,000
**SALES (est):** 6.4MM **Privately Held**
**SIC:** 3861 3625 3089 Screens, projection; noise control equipment; injection molding of plastics

**(G-6335)**
**RENT-A-CENTER INC**
3145 S Ashland Ave # 103 (60608-6248)
PHONE..................773 376-8883
**Fax:** 773 376-1777
Claud Echoles, *Manager*
**EMP:** 6
**SALES (corp-wide):** 2.9B **Publicly Held**
**WEB:** www.rentcenter.com
**SIC:** 3699 Appliance cords for household electrical equipment
**PA:** Rent-A-Center, Inc.
5501 Headquarters Dr
Plano TX 75024
972 801-1100

**(G-6336)**
**RESCO 8 LLC**
Also Called: Piece
1927 W North Ave (60622-1316)
PHONE..................773 772-4422
**Fax:** 773 772-3747

# Chicago - Cook County (G-6337)

Brent Holten, *General Mgr*
William Jacobs, *Mng Member*
▲ **EMP:** 70
**SALES (est):** 2.1MM **Privately Held**
**SIC:** 5812 2082 Pizza restaurants; beer (alcoholic beverage)

### (G-6337)
### RESONANCE MEDICAL LLC
222 Merchandise Mart Plz (60654-1103)
**PHONE**.................................229 292-2094
Christopher Heddon, *CEO*
**EMP:** 5
**SALES (est):** 461.1K **Privately Held**
**SIC:** 3841 Surgical & medical instruments

### (G-6338)
### RESTORING PATH
Also Called: CRUSHERS CLUB
1406 W 64th St (60636-2816)
**PHONE**.................................773 424-7023
Sally Hazelgrove, *President*
**EMP:** 19 **EST:** 2013
**SALES (est):** 146.4K **Privately Held**
**SIC:** 3949 Gloves, sport & athletic: boxing, handball, etc.

### (G-6339)
### RETAILOUT INC
719 S State St (60605-2541)
**PHONE**.................................312 786-4312
Tom Lourmas, *Director*
◆ **EMP:** 20
**SALES (est):** 1.3MM **Privately Held**
**SIC:** 3571 Electronic computers

### (G-6340)
### REUM CORPORATION
140 S Dearborn St Ste 420 (60603-5233)
**PHONE**.................................847 625-7386
▲ **EMP:** 120
**SALES (est):** 13MM
**SALES (corp-wide):** 57MM **Privately Held**
**SIC:** 3089 Mfg Plastic Products
**PA:** Rm Trust Gmbh
  Heidelberger Str. 64
  Hopfingen 74746
  628 357-0

### (G-6341)
### REVOLUTION COMPANIES INC
Also Called: Mission Popcorn
332 S Michigan Ave # 1032 (60604-4434)
**PHONE**.................................800 826-4083
Malik Thomas, *CEO*
**EMP:** 30 **EST:** 2011
**SQ FT:** 3,500
**SALES (est):** 2.1MM **Privately Held**
**SIC:** 2096 Potato chips & other potato-based snacks

### (G-6342)
### REX CARTON COMPANY INC
4528 W 51st St (60632-4597)
**PHONE**.................................773 581-4115
**Fax:** 773 581-4120
Gildo Mazzolin, *Ch of Bd*
Ronald Lemar, *President*
Sal Arena, *General Mgr*
Amy Mazzolin, *Vice Pres*
Greg Fleck, *Purchasing*
**EMP:** 30
**SQ FT:** 125,000
**SALES (est):** 11.6MM **Privately Held**
**WEB:** www.rexcarton.com
**SIC:** 2653 2657 Boxes, corrugated: made from purchased materials; folding paperboard boxes

### (G-6343)
### REX RADIATOR AND WELDING CO (PA)
1440 W 38th St (60609-2114)
**PHONE**.................................312 421-1531
William H Rex, *President*
Stephen C Rex, *Treasurer*
Robert A Rex, *Admin Sec*
**EMP:** 7
**SQ FT:** 4,000
**SALES (est):** 3.4MM **Privately Held**
**SIC:** 7539 7692 Radiator repair shop, automotive; welding repair; automotive welding

### (G-6344)
### REXAM BEVERAGE CAN COMPANY (DH)
8770 W Bryn Mawr Ave Fl 8 (60631-3515)
**PHONE**.................................773 399-3000
**Fax:** 773 399-3354
William R Barker, *CEO*
Rich Grimley, *President*
John Niemryk, *Vice Pres*
Gene Pawula, *Vice Pres*
Mark Stafford, *VP Opers*
◆ **EMP:** 125 **EST:** 1929
**SQ FT:** 275,000
**SALES (est):** 1B
**SALES (corp-wide):** 9B **Publicly Held**
**SIC:** 3411 Food & beverage containers; aluminum cans
**HQ:** Ball Inc.
  4201 Congress St Ste 340
  Charlotte NC 28209
  704 551-1500

### (G-6345)
### REXAM BEVERAGE CAN COMPANY
1101 W 43rd St (60609-3340)
**PHONE**.................................773 247-4646
Glenn Barnett, *Plant Mgr*
Don Black, *QC Dir*
Catalin Neacsu, *Plant Engr*
Kevin Farrell, *Human Res Dir*
**EMP:** 105
**SALES (corp-wide):** 9B **Publicly Held**
**SIC:** 3411 Aluminum cans
**HQ:** Rexam Beverage Can Company
  8770 W Bryn Mawr Ave Fl 8
  Chicago IL 60631
  773 399-3000

### (G-6346)
### RGB LIGHTS INC
6045 N Keystone Ave (60646-5209)
**PHONE**.................................312 421-6080
Brett Gardner, *CEO*
Jameson Green, *President*
Julie Green, *COO*
Glenn West, *Accounts Exec*
Peter Carroll, *Marketing Staff*
▲ **EMP:** 12
**SQ FT:** 10,000
**SALES (est):** 3MM **Privately Held**
**SIC:** 3646 5063 3645 Commercial indusl & institutional electric lighting fixtures; lighting fittings & accessories; residential lighting fixtures

### (G-6347)
### RH DEVELOPMENT
9431 S Claremont Ave (60643-6746)
**PHONE**.................................773 331-3772
Renard J Harvey Jr, *Owner*
**EMP:** 12
**SALES (est):** 291.9K **Privately Held**
**SIC:** 2395 Pleating & stitching

### (G-6348)
### RH PREYDA COMPANY (PA)
Also Called: Hall Shrpning Stnes A Rh Pryda
333 N Michigan Ave # 3000 (60601-4048)
**PHONE**.................................212 880-1477
Oscar Cozzini, *President*
Monika Cozzini, *Vice Pres*
**EMP:** 13 **EST:** 2013
**SQ FT:** 2,000
**SALES (est):** 1.4MM **Privately Held**
**SIC:** 3291 Abrasive products

### (G-6349)
### RI-DEL MFG INC (PA)
Also Called: Power Parts Sign Co
1754 W Walnut St (60612-2524)
**PHONE**.................................312 829-8720
**Fax:** 312 829-8770
Stephen Hrajnoha, *President*
James Hrajnoha, *Admin Sec*
▲ **EMP:** 56
**SQ FT:** 40,000
**SALES (est):** 13.1MM **Privately Held**
**WEB:** www.ridelmfg.com
**SIC:** 3599 7692 3441 3469 Machine shop, jobbing & repair; welding repair; fabricated structural metal; stamping metal for the trade

### (G-6350)
### RIBBON SUPPLY COMP
5448 W Fullerton Ave (60639-1452)
**PHONE**.................................773 237-7979
G John Wilson, *President*
**EMP:** 10 **EST:** 1925
**SQ FT:** 2,000
**SALES (est):** 939.3K **Privately Held**
**SIC:** 2396 3961 Ribbons & bows, cut & sewed; pins (jewelry), except precious metal

### (G-6351)
### RIBBON WEBBING CORPORATION
4711 W Division St (60651-1638)
**PHONE**.................................773 287-1221
**Fax:** 773 287-1222
Jae C Chang, *President*
Luke Chang, *General Mgr*
Timothy E Johnson, *Vice Pres*
Anna Kim, *Manager*
Soon Jin Chang, *Admin Sec*
◆ **EMP:** 145 **EST:** 1981
**SALES (est):** 1MM **Privately Held**
**WEB:** www.ribbonwebbing.com
**SIC:** 2241 Webbing, woven

### (G-6352)
### RICHARDSON SEATING CORPORATION
2545 W Arthington St (60612-4107)
**PHONE**.................................312 829-4040
**Fax:** 312 829-8337
Earl Lichtenstein, *President*
Ron Maslovsky, *Sales Staff*
Sharon Lichtenstien, *Admin Sec*
Ira Lichtenstein, *Relations*
▲ **EMP:** 40 **EST:** 1975
**SQ FT:** 75,000
**SALES (est):** 7.5MM **Privately Held**
**WEB:** www.richardsonseating.com
**SIC:** 2522 Office chairs, benches & stools, except wood

### (G-6353)
### RICKARD CIRCULAR FOLDING CO
Also Called: Rickard Bindery
325 N Ashland Ave (60607-1077)
**PHONE**.................................312 243-6300
**Fax:** 312 243-6323
Jack Rickard, *Ch of Bd*
Kevin Rickard, *President*
Pete Noteman, *Manager*
Bonnie Rickard, *Admin Sec*
**EMP:** 85 **EST:** 1900
**SQ FT:** 80,000
**SALES (est):** 4MM **Privately Held**
**WEB:** www.rickardbindery.com
**SIC:** 2789 Bookbinding & related work; pamphlets, binding

### (G-6354)
### RICO COMPUTERS ENTERPRISES INC
7022 W 73rd Pl (60638-5921)
**PHONE**.................................708 594-7426
**Fax:** 708 594-7478
John Rico, *President*
Guadalupe Rico, *Corp Secy*
Antonio Rico, *Vice Pres*
**EMP:** 13
**SQ FT:** 500
**SALES (est):** 1MM **Privately Held**
**WEB:** www.ricoenterprises.com
**SIC:** 7378 3571 7371 Computer maintenance & repair; electronic computers; computer software development & applications

### (G-6355)
### RIDDLE MCINTYRE INC
175 N Franklin St Frnt 1 (60606-1835)
**PHONE**.................................312 782-3317
**Fax:** 312 782-3319
Hee Kang, *President*
Frank Kang, *Manager*
Wha Kang, *Admin Sec*
**EMP:** 6 **EST:** 1916
**SQ FT:** 2,300
**SALES (est):** 440K **Privately Held**
**SIC:** 5699 2321 Custom tailor; men's & boys' furnishings

### (G-6356)
### RIGHTHAND TECHNOLOGIES INC
7450 W Wilson Ave (60706-4549)
**PHONE**.................................773 774-7600
Steve Valentor, *President*
Jeff Slawicki, *COO*
Nicole Stafford, *Purch Mgr*
Naomi Marnell, *QC Mgr*
Steven Davis, *Engineer*
▲ **EMP:** 50
**SQ FT:** 25,000
**SALES (est):** 13.6MM **Privately Held**
**WEB:** www.righthandtech.com
**SIC:** 3672 Printed circuit boards

### (G-6357)
### RIGHTSOURCE DIGITAL SVCS INC
Also Called: RDS Digital
2242 W Harrison St # 201 (60612-3719)
**PHONE**.................................888 774-2201
Nuha Nazy, *President*
Claudette Halwagy, *Business Mgr*
Emilia Rogowska, *Vice Pres*
**EMP:** 12 **EST:** 2015
**SQ FT:** 25,000
**SALES (est):** 107.6K **Privately Held**
**SIC:** 7389 7374 2752 Presorted mail service; ; optical scanning data service; commercial printing, lithographic

### (G-6358)
### RINDA TECHNOLOGIES INC
4563 N Elston Ave Fl 1 (60630-4214)
**PHONE**.................................773 736-6633
Edward Rinda, *President*
▲ **EMP:** 10
**SQ FT:** 2,600
**SALES (est):** 1.4MM **Privately Held**
**WEB:** www.rinda.com
**SIC:** 3695 Computer software tape & disks: blank, rigid & floppy

### (G-6359)
### RINKER BOAT COMPANY
333 W Wacker Dr Ste 600 (60606-1284)
**PHONE**.................................574 457-5731
Robert Moran, *CEO*
**EMP:** 29
**SALES (est):** 6.5MM **Privately Held**
**SIC:** 3731 Offshore supply boats, building & repairing

### (G-6360)
### RISK NEVER DIE INC
1001 W 15th St Unit 222 (60608-2765)
**PHONE**.................................708 240-4194
**EMP:** 5
**SALES (est):** 310K **Privately Held**
**SIC:** 3544 Mfg Dies/Tools/Jigs/Fixtures

### (G-6361)
### RIVALFLY NATIONAL NETWORK LLC
320 W Ohio St (60654-6566)
**PHONE**.................................847 867-8660
Allen Marrinson, *Mng Member*
Rich Babich,
Albert Goodman,
**EMP:** 6
**SQ FT:** 1,500
**SALES (est):** 227.1K **Privately Held**
**SIC:** 7372 Business oriented computer software

### (G-6362)
### RIVER NORTH HAND
356 W Superior St (60654-3416)
**PHONE**.................................312 335-9669
Michael D Demaio,
**EMP:** 2
**SALES (est):** 210K **Privately Held**
**SIC:** 3589 Car washing machinery

### (G-6363)
### RIVERSIDE GRAPHICS CORPORATION
2 N Riverside Plz Ste 365 (60606-2620)
**PHONE**.................................312 372-3766
**Fax:** 312 372-7233
Patrick Monahan, *President*
John Denoyer, *President*
Paul Sato, *Sales Staff*
Terry Vigor, *Sales Staff*

# GEOGRAPHIC SECTION
## Chicago - Cook County (G-6390)

Carol Denoyer, *Admin Sec*
**EMP:** 9
**SQ FT:** 3,000
**SALES (est):** 1.6MM **Privately Held**
**WEB:** www.riversidegx.com
**SIC: 2752** Commercial printing, offset

### (G-6364)
### RKF ENTERPRISES
7331 S Michigan Ave Ste 1 (60619-1618)
**PHONE** .................................. 773 723-7038
Khan Franklin, *Owner*
Robert Franklin, *Owner*
**EMP:** 3 **EST:** 1988
**SALES (est):** 165.3K **Privately Held**
**SIC: 2789** Bookbinding & repairing: trade, edition, library, etc.

### (G-6365)
### RM LUCAS CO
3211 S Wood St (60608-6118)
**PHONE** .................................. 773 523-4300
**EMP:** 35
**SALES (corp-wide):** 15.6MM **Privately Held**
**SIC: 2891** 1761 Adhesives & sealants; roofing contractor
**PA:** R.M. Lucas Co.
 12400 S Laramie Ave
 Alsip IL 60803
 773 523-4300

### (G-6366)
### RNFL ACQUISITION LLC
Also Called: Michigan Renewable Carbon
70 W Madison St Ste 2300 (60602-4250)
**PHONE** .................................. 651 442-6011
Jim Mennell, *CEO*
Rico Biasetti, *President*
Todd Smreker, *Vice Pres*
Sean Pearson, *Controller*
**EMP:** 50
**SALES (est):** 7.8MM
**SALES (corp-wide):** 10.8MM **Privately Held**
**SIC: 3624** Carbon specialties for electrical use
**PA:** Biogenic Reagents, Llc
 133 1st Ave N
 Minneapolis MN 55401
 651 442-6011

### (G-6367)
### ROBERT B SCOTT OCULARISTS LTD (PA)
111 N Wabash Ave Ste 1620 (60602-3453)
**PHONE** .................................. 312 782-3558
**Fax:** 312 372-4449
Roland B Scott, *President*
Bonny Scott, *Treasurer*
Vivian Scott, *Admin Sec*
**EMP:** 1
**SQ FT:** 1,600
**SALES (est):** 6.9MM **Privately Held**
**SIC: 5169** 3851 3842 Chemicals & allied products; eyes, glass & plastic; surgical appliances & supplies

### (G-6368)
### ROBERT KOESTER (PA)
Also Called: Delmark Records
4121 N Rockwell St (60618-2822)
**PHONE** .................................. 773 539-5001
**Fax:** 773 539-5004
Robert Koester, *Owner*
Steve Wagner, *Producer*
Susan Koester, *Admin Asst*
**EMP:** 5
**SQ FT:** 6,500
**SALES (est):** 1.6MM **Privately Held**
**WEB:** www.delmark.com
**SIC: 5735** 3652 Compact discs; records; audio tapes, prerecorded; compact laser discs, prerecorded; phonograph records, prerecorded; magnetic tape (audio): prerecorded

### (G-6369)
### ROBERT-LESLIE PUBLISHING LLC
4147 N Ravenswood Ave # 301 (60613-2472)
P.O. Box 1514, Jonesboro AR (72403-1514)
**PHONE** .................................. 773 935-8358
Judith Coffey, *CEO*
Beth Wise, *Editor*
Marilyn Overby, *Manager*
Kristey Rothgery, *Manager*
Daniel Wasp, *Manager*
**EMP:** 3
**SALES (est):** 226.6K **Privately Held**
**SIC: 2741** Miscellaneous publishing

### (G-6370)
### ROBERTS SHEET METAL WORKS INC
4447 W Kinzie St (60624-1601)
**PHONE** .................................. 773 626-3811
Frank Czarkowski, *Owner*
**EMP:** 20
**SALES (corp-wide):** 2.7MM **Privately Held**
**SIC: 2542** Showcases (not refrigerated): except wood
**PA:** Robert's Sheet Metal Works, Inc.
 4347 W Kinzie St
 Chicago IL
 773 626-3811

### (G-6371)
### ROBIN HOOD MAT & QUILTING CORP (PA)
4800 S Richmond St (60632-2007)
**PHONE** .................................. 312 953-2960
Robin Hood, *Principal*
**EMP:** 5
**SALES (est):** 474.5K **Privately Held**
**SIC: 2515** Mattresses & bedsprings

### (G-6372)
### ROBIT INC (HQ)
639 W Diversey Pkwy # 217 (60614-1535)
**PHONE** .................................. 708 667-7892
Jussi Rautiainen, *President*
David Delorne, *Vice Pres*
**EMP:** 1
**SQ FT:** 200,000
**SALES:** 2MM
**SALES (corp-wide):** 48.9MM **Privately Held**
**SIC: 3533** Drilling tools for gas, oil or water wells
**PA:** Robit Oyj
 Vikkiniitynite 9
 Lempaala 33880
 331 403-400

### (G-6373)
### ROCK BOTTOM MINNEAPOLIS INC
Also Called: Rock Bottom Chicago
1 W Grand Ave (60654-4806)
**PHONE** .................................. 312 755-9339
**Fax:** 312 755-0164
Jennifer Thompson, *Manager*
**EMP:** 75 **Privately Held**
**SIC: 5812** 2082 5813 American restaurant; caterers; beer (alcoholic beverage); drinking places
**HQ:** Rock Bottom Of Minneapolis, Inc.
 8001 Arista Pl Unit 500
 Broomfield CO 80021
 763 537-5080

### (G-6374)
### ROCKET FUEL INC
205 N Michigan Ave # 2900 (60601-6901)
**PHONE** .................................. 207 520-9075
Richard Frankel, *President*
Abhinav Gupta, *Admin Sec*
**EMP:** 10
**SALES (est):** 1.5MM **Privately Held**
**SIC: 2869** Fuels

### (G-6375)
### ROCKING HORSE
2535 N Milwaukee Ave (60647-2629)
**PHONE** .................................. 773 486-0011
Alex Psolakides, *Principal*
**EMP:** 3
**SALES (est):** 284.2K **Privately Held**
**SIC: 3944** Rocking horses

### (G-6376)
### ROCKTENN
1415 W 44th St (60609-3333)
**PHONE** .................................. 773 254-1030
Diane Anderson, *General Mgr*
Christine Catrambone, *General Mgr*
Paul Mimura, *Engineer*
Mark Cooper, *Info Tech Mgr*
**EMP:** 14
**SALES (est):** 2.8MM **Privately Held**
**SIC: 2631** Linerboard; container, packaging & boxboard

### (G-6377)
### ROCKWELL METAL PRODUCTS INC
3232 W Cermak Rd (60623-3312)
**PHONE** .................................. 773 762-7030
**Fax:** 773 762-7031
Rudy Lung, *President*
Jane Taccola, *Admin Sec*
▲ **EMP:** 8 **EST:** 1949
**SQ FT:** 12,000
**SALES (est):** 660K **Privately Held**
**SIC: 3469** Machine parts, stamped or pressed metal

### (G-6378)
### RODALE INC
65 E Wacker Pl Ste 1101 (60601-7216)
**PHONE** .................................. 312 726-0365
Randt Holloway, *Manager*
**EMP:** 13
**SALES (corp-wide):** 435.6MM **Privately Held**
**WEB:** www.rodale.com
**SIC: 2721** Periodicals
**PA:** Rodale Inc.
 400 S 10th St
 Emmaus PA 18049
 800 848-4735

### (G-6379)
### ROESERS BAKERY
3216 W North Ave (60647-4985)
**PHONE** .................................. 773 489-6900
**Fax:** 773 489-6933
John Roeser III, *Owner*
**EMP:** 25
**SQ FT:** 7,500
**SALES (est):** 2.7MM **Privately Held**
**WEB:** www.roeserscakes.com
**SIC: 2051** 2024 Bakery: wholesale or wholesale/retail combined; ice cream & ice milk

### (G-6380)
### ROGERS CUSTOM TRIMS INC
2101 N Monitor Ave (60639-2820)
**PHONE** .................................. 773 745-6577
**Fax:** 773 745-7765
Steven Klein, *President*
Carol Klein, *Treasurer*
Majorie Klein, *Admin Sec*
**EMP:** 9
**SQ FT:** 5,000
**SALES:** 500K **Privately Held**
**WEB:** www.rogerstrims.com
**SIC: 2241** 5713 2391 Trimmings, textile; floor covering stores; curtains & draperies

### (G-6381)
### ROGERS LOOSE LEAF CO
1555 W Fulton St (60607-1011)
**PHONE** .................................. 312 226-1947
**Fax:** 312 226-3005
James Stuercke, *President*
**EMP:** 18 **EST:** 1930
**SQ FT:** 15,000
**SALES (est):** 1.7MM **Privately Held**
**WEB:** www.rogerslooseleafco.com
**SIC: 2754** Music sheet: gravure printing, not published on site

### (G-6382)
### ROHNER ENGRAVING INC
1112 N Homan Ave (60651-4007)
**PHONE** .................................. 773 244-8343
David Rohner, *President*
**EMP:** 2
**SQ FT:** 3,000
**SALES (est):** 249.5K **Privately Held**
**WEB:** www.rohnerdigital.com
**SIC: 2759** Stationery: printing

### (G-6383)
### ROHNER LETTERPRESS INC
Also Called: Rohner Press
1112 N Homan Ave (60651-4007)
**PHONE** .................................. 773 248-0800
**Fax:** 773 248-8655
Bruno Rohner, *President*
**EMP:** 11
**SQ FT:** 5,000
**SALES (est):** 1.5MM **Privately Held**
**WEB:** www.rohner1.com
**SIC: 2759** Letterpress printing

### (G-6384)
### ROLL ROLL MET FABRICATORS INC
2310 W 58th St (60636-1516)
**PHONE** .................................. 773 434-1315
Antonio Alvarez, *President*
Marina Alvarez, *Admin Sec*
**EMP:** 24
**SQ FT:** 87,000
**SALES (est):** 2.5MM **Privately Held**
**SIC: 3499** Machine bases, metal

### (G-6385)
### ROLLED EDGE INC
Also Called: Chicago Paper Tube & Can Co.
4221 N Normandy Ave (60634-1402)
**PHONE** .................................. 773 283-9500
**Fax:** 773 283-9501
John Dudlak, *President*
Jonathan Dudlak, *General Mgr*
Molly Dudlak, *Exec VP*
Chrissy Cabay, *Sls & Mktg Exec*
Margo Damolaris, *Marketing Staff*
▲ **EMP:** 25
**SQ FT:** 65,000
**SALES (est):** 7.3MM **Privately Held**
**WEB:** www.chicagopapertube.com
**SIC: 2655** Tubes, fiber or paper: made from purchased material

### (G-6386)
### ROMA PACKING CO
2354 S Leavitt St (60608-4030)
**PHONE** .................................. 773 927-7371
**Fax:** 773 927-7370
Steve Lombardi, *President*
Marsha Caputo, *Corp Secy*
Marcia Caputo, *Vice Pres*
**EMP:** 7
**SQ FT:** 3,125
**SALES (est):** 750K **Privately Held**
**SIC: 5147** 2013 Meats, fresh; sausages from purchased meat

### (G-6387)
### ROMAINE EMPIRE LLC
Also Called: Farmer's Fridge
155 N Wacker Dr Ste 4250 (60606-1750)
**PHONE** .................................. 312 229-0099
Dave Kuipers, *CFO*
Luke Saunders,
**EMP:** 20 **EST:** 2013
**SALES (est):** 484K **Privately Held**
**SIC: 5962** 2099 Food vending machines; ready-to-eat meals, salads & sandwiches

### (G-6388)
### ROMAN ELECTRIC
6054 W Giddings St (60630-3109)
**PHONE** .................................. 773 777-9246
Cesar Roman, *Principal*
**EMP:** 4
**SALES (est):** 439.2K **Privately Held**
**SIC: 3699** Electrical equipment & supplies

### (G-6389)
### ROME METAL MFG INC
4612 W Ohio St (60644-1794)
**PHONE** .................................. 773 287-1755
**Fax:** 773 287-7155
**EMP:** 6 **EST:** 1904
**SQ FT:** 12,000
**SALES:** 400K **Privately Held**
**SIC: 3444** 3443 2542 2522 Sheet metal specialties, not stamped; fabricated plate work (boiler shop); partitions & fixtures, except wood; office furniture, except wood; household furnishings

### (G-6390)
### ROOMS REDUX CHICAGO INC
6033 N Sheridan Rd 25d (60660-3003)
**PHONE** .................................. 312 835-1192
Philip George Popowici, *Principal*
**EMP:** 10
**SALES (est):** 832.6K **Privately Held**
**WEB:** www.roomsreduxchicago.com
**SIC: 2511** Bed frames, except water bed frames: wood

## Chicago - Cook County (G-6391) — GEOGRAPHIC SECTION

**(G-6391)**
**ROOSEVELT TORCH**
18 S Michigan Ave Rm 515  (60603-3200)
PHONE ..................... 312 281-3242
Kristen Strobde, *Principal*
EMP: 10
SALES (est): 446K  Privately Held
SIC: 2711  Newspapers, publishing & printing

**(G-6392)**
**ROQ INNOVATION  LLC**
3201 S Talumet Ave  (60616)
PHONE ..................... 917 770-2403
Raquel Graham, *President*
EMP: 4
SALES: 80K  Privately Held
SIC: 2389  7389  Apparel for handicapped;

**(G-6393)**
**RORKE & RILEY SPECIALTY B**
3712 N Broadway St # 252  (60613-4235)
PHONE ..................... 773 929-2522
Peter Page, *President*
EMP: 4
SALES (est): 224K  Privately Held
WEB: www.rorkeriley.com
SIC: 2086  Carbonated soft drinks, bottled & canned

**(G-6394)**
**ROSCOR CORPORATION (PA)**
Also Called: Discount Video Warehouse
140 S Dearborn St Ste 420  (60603-5233)
PHONE ..................... 847 299-8080
Fax: 847 299-4206
Paul Roston, *President*
James Skupien, *Division Mgr*
Bennett N Grossman, *Vice Pres*
Mitch Roston, *Vice Pres*
Robert Strutzel, *Vice Pres*
EMP: 95  EST: 1917
SQ FT: 33,000
SALES (est): 12.9MM  Privately Held
WEB: www.roscor.com
SIC: 3663  Radio & TV communications equipment; mobile communication equipment; studio equipment, radio & television broadcasting; satellites, communications

**(G-6395)**
**ROSE PACKING COMPANY  INC**
4900 S Major Ave  (60638-1589)
PHONE ..................... 708 458-9300
Victor Jacobellis, *Div Sub Head*
Jim Vandenbergh, *Vice Pres*
Peter Rose, *Branch Mgr*
Charmaine Jeske, *Data Proc Mgr*
Paul Michalak, *Director*
EMP: 530
SQ FT: 135,000
SALES (corp-wide): 256.8MM  Privately Held
SIC: 2011  2013  Pork products from pork slaughtered on site; sausages & other prepared meats
PA: Rose Packing Company, Inc.
   65 S Barrington Rd
   South Barrington IL 60010
   847 381-5700

**(G-6396)**
**ROSENGARD SUE JWLY DESIGN LTD**
2210 S Halsted St  (60608-4522)
PHONE ..................... 312 733-1133
Fax: 312 733-1236
Sue Rosengard, *President*
EMP: 2
SQ FT: 800
SALES (est): 211.1K  Privately Held
SIC: 3911  Jewelry, precious metal

**(G-6397)**
**ROSHAN AG  INC**
Also Called: Rosen Printing Services
3525 W Peterson Ave # 120  (60659-3313)
PHONE ..................... 773 267-1635
Asnan Ghaziani, *CEO*
Roshan A Ghaziani, *President*
EMP: 4  EST: 2008
SALES (est): 284.3K  Privately Held
SIC: 2759  Commercial printing

**(G-6398)**
**ROTATION DYNAMICS CORPORATION**
Also Called: Rotadyne Precision Mch Roller
6120 S New England Ave  (60638-4008)
PHONE ..................... 630 769-9700
Fax: 773 229-9092
Ed Narakas, *Mfg Dir*
Timu Gallies, *Manager*
Mark Dejvoda, *Manager*
Mark Vejvoda, *Manager*
Michael Rekau, *Director*
EMP: 20
SQ FT: 18,400
SALES (corp-wide): 128.8MM  Privately Held
SIC: 3861  3354  2796  Graphic arts plates, sensitized; aluminum extruded products; platemaking services
PA: Rotation Dynamics Corporation
   8140 Cass Ave
   Darien IL 60561
   630 769-9255

**(G-6399)**
**ROTATION DYNAMICS CORPORATION**
Also Called: Ideal Roller
2512 W 24th St  (60608-3709)
PHONE ..................... 773 247-5600
Fax: 773 247-0876
J Kaminski, *Sales Staff*
Len Kruizenga, *Manager*
Sonia Llamas, *Manager*
Kevin Wesolowski, *Manager*
EMP: 77
SALES (corp-wide): 128.8MM  Privately Held
SIC: 3555  3061  2796  Printing trades machinery; mechanical rubber goods; platemaking services
PA: Rotation Dynamics Corporation
   8140 Cass Ave
   Darien IL 60561
   630 769-9255

**(G-6400)**
**ROWBOAT CREATIVE  LLC**
2649 N Kildare Dock 1 On  (60639)
PHONE ..................... 773 675-2628
Lucas Guariglia,
Joseph Zangrilli,
EMP: 14  EST: 2010
SALES (est): 1.7MM  Privately Held
SIC: 2759  Commercial printing

**(G-6401)**
**ROYAL ENVELOPE CORPORATION**
4114 S Peoria St  (60609-2521)
PHONE ..................... 773 376-1212
Fax: 773 376-0011
Mike Pusatera, *President*
Anthony Pusatera, *President*
Matt Pusatera, *General Mgr*
Eileen Pusatera, *Vice Pres*
Roman Heredia, *Plant Mgr*
EMP: 60
SQ FT: 55,000
SALES (est): 22.8MM  Privately Held
WEB: www.royalenv.com
SIC: 2677  Envelopes

**(G-6402)**
**RR DONNELLEY & SONS COMPANY**
230 W Monroe St Ste 2500  (60606-4902)
PHONE ..................... 312 332-4345
Greg Sutter, *Manager*
EMP: 22
SALES (corp-wide): 6.9B  Publicly Held
WEB: www.moore.com
SIC: 5112  2752  Business forms; office supplies; commercial printing, lithographic
PA: R. R. Donnelley & Sons Company
   35 W Wacker Dr Ste 3650
   Chicago IL 60601
   312 326-8000

**(G-6403)**
**RR DONNELLEY & SONS COMPANY**
35 W Wacker Dr Ste 3650  (60601-1840)
PHONE ..................... 312 326-8000
Michael Manzella, *Manager*
EMP: 56
SALES (corp-wide): 6.9B  Publicly Held
WEB: www.moore.com
SIC: 2761  Manifold business forms
PA: R. R. Donnelley & Sons Company
   35 W Wacker Dr Ste 3650
   Chicago IL 60601
   312 326-8000

**(G-6404)**
**RR DONNELLEY & SONS COMPANY**
111 S Wacker Dr Fl 36  (60606-4300)
PHONE ..................... 312 236-8000
EMP: 109
SALES (corp-wide): 11.2B  Publicly Held
SIC: 2754  2759  0752  2732  Gravure Commercial Printing
PA: R.R. Donnelley & Sons Company
   35 W Wacker Dr Ste 3650
   Chicago IL 60601
   312 326-8000

**(G-6405)**
**RR DONNELLEY PRINTING CO LP (HQ)**
Also Called: R R Donnelley
111 S Wacker Dr Ste 3500  (60606-4304)
PHONE ..................... 312 326-8000
Fax: 312 681-6200
Ronald Daly, *President*
Monica Forhmann, *Vice Pres*
Thomas Quinlan, *CFO*
Kevin Smith, *CFO*
Anthony Malandro, *Human Res Dir*
▲ EMP: 3
SQ FT: 220,000
SALES (est): 689.6MM
SALES (corp-wide): 6.9B  Publicly Held
SIC: 2754  2752  5085  Rotogravure printing; commercial printing, offset; industrial supplies
PA: R. R. Donnelley & Sons Company
   35 W Wacker Dr Ste 3650
   Chicago IL 60601
   312 326-8000

**(G-6406)**
**RRD NETHERLANDS LLC**
111 S Wacker Dr  (60606-4302)
PHONE ..................... 312 326-8000
Thomas J Quinlan III, *President*
EMP: 10
SALES (est): 819.1K
SALES (corp-wide): 6.9B  Publicly Held
SIC: 2754  Commercial printing, gravure
PA: R. R. Donnelley & Sons Company
   35 W Wacker Dr Ste 3650
   Chicago IL 60601
   312 326-8000

**(G-6407)**
**RS OWENS DIV ST REGIS LLC**
5535 N Lynch Ave  (60630-1417)
PHONE ..................... 773 282-6000
Richard Sirkser, *President*
Mark Psaros, *Manager*
▲ EMP: 80  EST: 2012
SALES (est): 8.5MM  Privately Held
SIC: 3914  Trophies, plated (all metals)

**(G-6408)**
**RSM INTERNATIONAL**
1 S Wacker Dr  (60606-4614)
PHONE ..................... 312 634-4762
Donna Sciarappa, *Regional Mgr*
Danny Sutantyo, *Manager*
David Fiszer, *Consultant*
Brian Becker, *Bd of Directors*
Hussain Hasan, *Bd of Directors*
EMP: 3  EST: 2015
SALES (est): 108.7K  Privately Held
SIC: 2721  Periodicals

**(G-6409)**
**RTC INDUSTRIES  INC**
3101 S Kedzie Ave Apt S  (60623-5111)
PHONE ..................... 847 640-2400
Fax: 773 376-5216
Fernando Deguzman, *Project Mgr*
John Lopotko, *Indstl Engineer*
Jenny Tanquary, *Accounting Mgr*
Iqbal Khan, *Manager*
Ralph Shirley, *Supervisor*
EMP: 100
SALES (corp-wide): 257.9MM  Privately Held
WEB: www.rtc.com
SIC: 3993  2671  2542  Displays & cutouts, window & lobby; packaging paper & plastics film, coated & laminated; partitions & fixtures, except wood
PA: Rtc Industries, Inc
   2800 Golf Rd
   Rolling Meadows IL 60008
   847 640-2400

**(G-6410)**
**RTENERGY LLC**
2100 N Southport Ave  (60614-4090)
PHONE ..................... 773 975-2598
EMP: 10
SALES (est): 910K  Privately Held
WEB: www.rtenergy.com
SIC: 3699  1731  High-energy particle physics equipment; energy management controls

**(G-6411)**
**RUBIN BROTHERS  INC**
2241 S Halsted St  (60608-4521)
PHONE ..................... 312 942-1111
Fax: 312 942-1871
David A Rubin, *President*
Miguel Garcia, *Vice Pres*
Terry Rubin, *Marketing Staff*
EMP: 140
SQ FT: 85,000
SALES (est): 24.3MM  Privately Held
SIC: 2326  Industrial garments, men's & boys'

**(G-6412)**
**RUBIN MANUFACTURING  INC**
2241 S Halsted St  (60608-4521)
PHONE ..................... 312 942-1111
David Rubin, *President*
▲ EMP: 285
SQ FT: 85,000
SALES (est): 35.9MM  Privately Held
SIC: 2211  Apparel & outerwear fabrics, cotton

**(G-6413)**
**RUBSCHLAGER BAKING CORPORATION**
3220 W Grand Ave Ste 1  (60651-4194)
PHONE ..................... 773 826-1245
Fax: 773 826-6619
Paul A Rubschlager, *President*
Joan Rubschlager, *Treasurer*
EMP: 2
SQ FT: 43,000
SALES (est): 586.2K
SALES (corp-wide): 35.5B  Privately Held
WEB: www.rubschlagerbaking.com
SIC: 2051  Bread, all types (white, wheat, rye, etc): fresh or frozen
HQ: Weston Foods Us, Inc.
   50 Maplehurst Dr
   Brownsburg IN 46112
   317 858-9000

**(G-6414)**
**RUDD CONTAINER CORPORATION**
4600 S Kolin Ave  (60632-4497)
PHONE ..................... 773 847-7600
Fax: 773 847-7930
Darrell Rudd, *Ch of Bd*
Ted Bihun, *Vice Pres*
Kyle O'Bradovich, *Plant Mgr*
Errol Dolin, *Sales Mgr*
Zachary Rudd, *Sales Associate*
EMP: 60  EST: 1920
SQ FT: 93,000
SALES (est): 14.7MM  Privately Held
SIC: 2653  5113  Boxes, corrugated: made from purchased materials; corrugated & solid fiber boxes

**(G-6415)**
**RUSSELL DOOT INC**
11 E Hubbard St Ste 301  (60611-5636)
PHONE ..................... 312 527-1437
Fax: 312 527-3959
Stewart Russell, *Partner*
Peter Doot, *Partner*
EMP: 6
SQ FT: 2,000

SALES (est): 852.4K  Privately Held
SIC: 3993 2759 2396 2399 Signs & advertising specialties; commercial printing; automotive trimmings, fabric; banners, pennants & flags

**(G-6416)**
**RYAN MEAT COMPANY**
6719 S State St  (60637-3997)
PHONE...................773 783-3840
Fax: 773 783-4718
Corneilios Ryan, *President*
Gerald Ryan, *Corp Secy*
Jerry Crofton, *Vice Pres*
EMP: 7
SQ FT: 4,700
SALES (est): 1.6MM  Privately Held
SIC: 5147 2013 2011 Meats, fresh; sausages & other prepared meats; meat packing plants

**(G-6417)**
**RYCOLINE PRODUCTS  LLC**
5540 N Northwest Hwy  (60630-1134)
P.O. Box 97043  (60690-7043)
PHONE...................773 775-6755
Connie Gill, *Human Resources*
Charles L Palmer,
Gary Anderson,
Norman J Nichol,
◆ EMP: 143 EST: 1957
SQ FT: 40,000
SALES (est): 26.8MM
SALES (corp-wide): 6.7B  Privately Held
WEB: www.rycoline.com
SIC: 2842 3555 2899 Cleaning or polishing preparations; printing trades machinery; chemical preparations
HQ: Sun Chemical Corporation
  35 Waterview Blvd Ste 100
  Parsippany NJ 07054
  973 404-6000

**(G-6418)**
**S & B FINISHING CO  INC**
3005 W Franklin Blvd  (60612-1007)
PHONE...................773 533-0033
Fax: 773 533-8400
Kenneth Spielman, *President*
Marcy Roth, *Admin Sec*
EMP: 55 EST: 1977
SQ FT: 35,000
SALES (est): 8.7MM  Privately Held
SIC: 3479 Painting, coating & hot dipping

**(G-6419)**
**S & C ELECTRIC COMPANY (PA)**
6601 N Ridge Blvd  (60626-3997)
PHONE...................773 338-1000
Fax: 773 338-3657
Kyle Seymour, *President*
Andrew Jones, *Managing Dir*
Anna Miranda, *COO*
Witold Bik, *Vice Pres*
John Crain, *Vice Pres*
◆ EMP: 1900 EST: 1911
SQ FT: 1,200,000
SALES (est): 870.1MM  Privately Held
WEB: www.sandc.com
SIC: 3613 3643 3625 8711 Fuses, electric; switches, electric power except snap, push button, etc.; switchgear & switchgear accessories; current-carrying wiring devices; relays & industrial controls; engineering services

**(G-6420)**
**S & G STEP TOOL INC**
5203 N Rose St  (60656-1014)
PHONE...................773 992-0808
Fax: 773 992-0811
Sabin Torlo, *President*
Gregory Matiasek, *Vice Pres*
EMP: 5
SQ FT: 4,000
SALES (est): 470.4K  Privately Held
SIC: 3423 Hand & edge tools

**(G-6421)**
**S & S KEYTAX INC**
4608 W 20th St  (60804-2511)
PHONE...................708 656-9221
Fax: 708 656-9451
James Stoner III, *President*
Alex Barbosa, *Manager*
EMP: 13
SQ FT: 6,000
SALES (est): 1.1MM  Privately Held
SIC: 3469 3961 Automobile license tags, stamped metal; keychains, except precious metal

**(G-6422)**
**S V C PRINTING CO**
3008 N Laramie Ave  (60641-5010)
PHONE...................773 286-2219
Frank Canino, *Owner*
Dominica Canino, *Co-Owner*
Barbara Canino, *Vice Pres*
EMP: 3 EST: 1939
SQ FT: 3,000
SALES (est): 60K  Privately Held
SIC: 2759 Letterpress printing

**(G-6423)**
**SABINAS FOOD PRODUCTS INC**
1509 W 18th St  (60608-2803)
PHONE...................312 738-2412
Antonio Avina, *President*
Alex Reynoso, *Vice Pres*
EMP: 25
SQ FT: 9,000
SALES (est): 1MM  Privately Held
SIC: 2099 Tortillas, fresh or refrigerated

**(G-6424)**
**SAFE FAIR FOOD COMPANY LLC**
318 W Adams St Ste 700c  (60606-5131)
PHONE...................904 930-4277
Will Holsworth, *CEO*
Javier Retamar, *CFO*
Tati Rezende, *CFO*
Ashley Maynard, *Finance Dir*
EMP: 10
SQ FT: 1,500
SALES (est): 2.5MM  Privately Held
SIC: 2096 Potato chips & similar snacks

**(G-6425)**
**SAFE-T-QUIP CORPORATION**
2300 N Kilbourn Ave  (60639-3402)
PHONE...................773 235-2100
Brian Johnson, *President*
Marianne Degroot, *Vice Pres*
EMP: 12
SALES (est): 1.1MM
SALES (corp-wide): 6.4MM  Privately Held
SIC: 3089 3296 Injection molding of plastics; mineral wool
PA: Rensel-Chicago, Inc.
  2300 N Kilbourn Ave
  Chicago IL 60639
  773 235-2100

**(G-6426)**
**SAFECHARGE LLC**
2506 N Clark St Ste 176  (60614-1848)
PHONE...................248 866-9428
Douglas R Charron,
David Adams,
EMP: 3
SALES (est): 255K  Privately Held
SIC: 3629 5021 Battery chargers, rectifying or nonrotating; lockers

**(G-6427)**
**SAFEGUARD SCIENTIFICS  INC**
3400 N Kildare Ave Apt 1r  (60641-3849)
PHONE...................312 234-9828
Bob Portogallo, *Principal*
EMP: 3
SALES (corp-wide): 18.5MM  Publicly Held
SIC: 2761 Manifold business forms
PA: Safeguard Scientifics, Inc.
  170 N Radnor Chstr Rd # 200
  Wayne PA 19087
  610 293-0500

**(G-6428)**
**SAGE VERTICAL GRDN SYSTEMS LLC**
730 W Randolph St Ste 300  (60661-2147)
PHONE...................312 234-9655
Richard Gasaway, *CEO*
Richard V Gasaway, *President*
EMP: 11 EST: 2014
SALES (est): 1.1MM  Privately Held
SIC: 2591 Blinds vertical

**(G-6429)**
**SAINT MARY FUEL COMPANY**
6700 S Ashland Ave  (60636-3414)
PHONE...................773 918-1681
Simon Abraham, *Owner*
EMP: 4
SALES (est): 605.9K  Privately Held
SIC: 2869 Fuels

**(G-6430)**
**SAINTS VOLO & OLHA UK CATH PAR**
2245 W Superior St  (60612-1327)
PHONE...................312 829-5209
Fax: 312 829-4113
Izan Krotec, *Pastor*
EMP: 4 EST: 1968
SALES (est): 212.2K  Privately Held
SIC: 8661 2752 Catholic Church; lithographing on metal

**(G-6431)**
**SALAMANDER STUDIOS CHICAGO INC**
Also Called: Stockwell Greetings
5410 W Roosevelt Rd # 306  (60644-1875)
PHONE...................773 379-2211
Judith R Gillman, *President*
John Fenwick, *Vice Pres*
▲ EMP: 15
SQ FT: 30,000
SALES (est): 1.3MM  Privately Held
WEB: www.asalamandercard.com
SIC: 2771 Greeting cards

**(G-6432)**
**SALESFORCECOM  INC**
205 W Wacker Dr Fl 22  (60606-1216)
PHONE...................312 361-3555
EMP: 4
SALES (corp-wide): 8.3B  Publicly Held
SIC: 7372 Business oriented computer software
PA: Salesforce.Com, Inc.
  1 Market Ste 300
  San Francisco CA 94105
  415 901-7000

**(G-6433)**
**SALESFORCECOM  INC**
111 W Illinois St  (60654-4505)
PHONE...................312 288-3600
EMP: 9
SALES (corp-wide): 8.3B  Publicly Held
SIC: 7372 Business oriented computer software
PA: Salesforce.Com, Inc.
  1 Market Ste 300
  San Francisco CA 94105
  415 901-7000

**(G-6434)**
**SALMONS AND BROWN**
44 E Superior St 1  (60611-2506)
PHONE...................312 929-6756
EMP: 8 EST: 2010
SALES (est): 320K  Privately Held
SIC: 2321 2335 Mfg Men's/Boy's Furnishings Mfg Women's/Misses' Dresses

**(G-6435)**
**SALSEDO PRESS INC**
3139 W Chicago Ave  (60622-4364)
PHONE...................773 533-9900
Fax: 773 533-9304
Victor Cortes, *President*
Pat Gleason, *Corp Secy*
Maria Arroyo, *Shareholder*
Chris Burke, *Shareholder*
Juan Carlos Martinez, *Shareholder*
EMP: 12
SQ FT: 12,500
SALES (est): 1.2MM  Privately Held
WEB: www.salsedopress.com
SIC: 2752 Commercial printing, offset

**(G-6436)**
**SANCHEM INC**
1600 S Canal St  (60616-1199)
PHONE...................312 733-6100
Fax: 312 733-7432
Estelle Flicher, *President*
John Fletcher, *Manager*
Jonathan J Flicher, *Admin Sec*
▼ EMP: 22

SALES (est): 5.6MM  Privately Held
WEB: www.sanchem.com
SIC: 2899 Rust resisting compounds; corrosion preventive lubricant

**(G-6437)**
**SANDERSON AND ASSOCIATES**
400 N Racine Ave Apt 211  (60642-6096)
PHONE...................312 829-4350
Fax: 312 829-4360
Rhonda Sanderson, *Owner*
Samantha Amato, *Vice Pres*
Remy Vaudelle, *Art Dir*
EMP: 10
SALES (est): 810K  Privately Held
SIC: 8743 2721 Public relations services; periodicals

**(G-6438)**
**SANDOVAL FENCES CORP**
Also Called: Sandoval Fences Company
855 N Cicero Ave  (60651-3229)
PHONE...................773 287-0279
Fax: 773 237-7972
Jesus Rodriguez, *President*
Leticia Rodriguez, *Manager*
Regina Rodriguez, *Admin Sec*
EMP: 5 EST: 2000
SQ FT: 24,900
SALES (est): 832.6K  Privately Held
WEB: www.sandovalfences.com
SIC: 3446 1799 1791 Fences or posts, ornamental iron or steel; fence construction; ornamental metal work; structural steel erection; building front installation metal; iron work, structural

**(G-6439)**
**SANGO EMBROIDERY**
5220 S Pulaski Rd  (60632-4222)
PHONE...................773 582-4354
Julio Santiagio, *Owner*
EMP: 6 EST: 1998
SALES (est): 232.1K  Privately Held
SIC: 2395 Embroidery products, except schiffli machine

**(G-6440)**
**SANSABELT**
101 N Wacker Dr  (60606-1784)
PHONE...................312 357-5119
Warwick Jones, *Principal*
John Hermann, *Technology*
EMP: 3
SALES (est): 172.6K  Privately Held
SIC: 2329 Men's & boys' clothing

**(G-6441)**
**SANTANA & DAUGHTER INC**
5959 W Dickens Ave  (60639-4032)
PHONE...................773 237-1818
Jose Santana, *President*
EMP: 3
SALES (est): 91.1K  Privately Held
SIC: 2396 2261 Screen printing on fabric articles; plisse printing of cotton broadwoven fabrics

**(G-6442)**
**SANTUCCI ENTERPRISES**
6345 W Warwick Ave  (60634-2432)
PHONE...................773 286-5629
Carmen Santucci, *Owner*
EMP: 4
SALES (est): 333.5K  Privately Held
SIC: 3677 3621 Electronic coils, transformers & other inductors; motors & generators

**(G-6443)**
**SAPORITO FINISHING CO**
Also Called: Accurate Anodizing Division
3130 S Austin Blvd  (60804-3729)
PHONE...................708 222-5300
Frank Voltarel, *Branch Mgr*
EMP: 50
SALES (corp-wide): 22.8MM  Privately Held
WEB: www.saporitofinishing.com
SIC: 3471 Anodizing (plating) of metals or formed products
PA: Saporito Finishing Co.
  3119 S Austin Blvd
  Cicero IL 60804
  708 222-5300

## Chicago - Cook County (G-6444)

**(G-6444)**
**SARCO PUTTY COMPANY**
5959 S Knox Ave  (60629-5498)
PHONE .................................. 773 735-5577
Fax: 773 735-9819
Myrtle Sarsfield, *President*
James Sarsfield, *Vice Pres*
Denise Sarsfield, *Treasurer*
Edward Sarsfield III, *Admin Sec*
EMP: 4
SQ FT: 16,000
SALES (est): 800K  **Privately Held**
SIC: 2851  2891  Putty; caulking compounds; sealing compounds for pipe threads or joints; sealing compounds, synthetic rubber or plastic

**(G-6445)**
**SARCOL**
3050 W Taylor St  (60612-3998)
PHONE .................................. 773 533-3000
Fax: 773 533-3003
Sergio Rodriguez, *President*
EMP: 4  EST: 2010
SALES (est): 333.1K  **Privately Held**
SIC: 3369  Nonferrous foundries

**(G-6446)**
**SARJ KALIDAS  LLC**
Also Called: Jays Import and Wholesale
1344 N Western Ave  (60622-2923)
Rural Route 1000, Maywood  (60153)
PHONE .................................. 708 865-9134
Jatin Patel, *Mng Member*
Riten Patel, *Manager*
▲ EMP: 52
SALES: 13MM  **Privately Held**
SIC: 5199  5162  3999  Lighters, cigarette & cigar; plastics products; cigarette lighters, except precious metal

**(G-6447)**
**SAVO GROUP  LTD**
Also Called: Savo Headquarters
155 N Wacker Dr Ste 1000  (60606-1731)
PHONE .................................. 312 276-7700
Fax: 312 506-1701
Mark O'Connell, *CEO*
Carleton A Larsen, *President*
Mark F O'Connel, *President*
Kurt Andersen, *Exec VP*
Suzanne Martin, *Exec VP*
EMP: 123
SQ FT: 42,000
SALES (est): 27.1MM  **Privately Held**
WEB: www.savogroup.com
SIC: 7372  5734  Prepackaged software; software, business & non-game

**(G-6448)**
**SAZERAC NORTH AMERICA  INC (HQ)**
75 Remittance Dr # 3312  (60675-3312)
PHONE .................................. 502 423-5225
Mark Brown, *President*
John Barron, *Accounts Mgr*
▲ EMP: 25
SALES (est): 61.2MM
SALES (corp-wide): 314.4MM  **Privately Held**
SIC: 2085  Distilled & blended liquors
PA: Sazerac Company, Inc.
3850 N Causeway Blvd # 1695
Metairie LA 70002
504 831-9450

**(G-6449)**
**SC INDUSTRIES  INC (PA)**
Also Called: Mdhearingaid
917 W Wa Blvd Ste 202  (60607-2203)
PHONE .................................. 312 366-3899
Sreekant Cherukuri, *President*
Sreenivas Cherukuri, *COO*
EMP: 8
SALES (est): 3.2MM  **Privately Held**
SIC: 3842  Hearing aids

**(G-6450)**
**SCHAUMBURG REVIEW**
Also Called: Pioneer Press
350 N Orleans St Fl 10  (60654-1700)
PHONE .................................. 847 998-3400
Fax: 847 486-7450
EMP: 14

SALES (est): 1MM  **Privately Held**
SIC: 2711  7313  Newspapers-Publishing/Printing Advertising Representative

**(G-6451)**
**SCHELLHORN PHOTO TECHNIQUES**
3916 N Elston Ave Ste 1  (60618-4287)
PHONE .................................. 773 267-5141
Fax: 773 267-0933
John Prince, *President*
Mike Post, *Vice Pres*
Jose Maisonet, *Admin Sec*
EMP: 10  EST: 1963
SQ FT: 6,500
SALES (est): 1MM  **Privately Held**
WEB: www.schellhorn.biz
SIC: 7336  7335  3555  2791  Silk screen design; photographic studio, commercial; printing trades machinery; typesetting; commercial printing

**(G-6452)**
**SCHNEIDER ELECTRIC USA  INC**
311 S Wacker Dr Ste 4550  (60606-6622)
PHONE .................................. 312 697-4770
Ken Bruno, *Vice Pres*
Matthew Lesniewski, *Info Tech Mgr*
Rachel M Shedd, *Director*
EMP: 5
SALES (corp-wide): 241K  **Privately Held**
SIC: 3613  Circuit breakers, air
HQ: Schneider Electric Usa, Inc.
800 Federal St
Andover MA 01810
978 975-9600

**(G-6453)**
**SCHOLARSHIP SOLUTIONS LLC**
Also Called: Stars Online
318 W Adams St Ste 1600  (60606-5100)
PHONE .................................. 847 859-5629
Kurt H Reilly, *CEO*
Dennis Leise, *QA Dir*
Chris Jerles, *Business Anlyst*
Shpendi Jashari, *Software Engr*
EMP: 14  EST: 2012
SQ FT: 13,868
SALES (est): 866.7K  **Privately Held**
SIC: 7372  Application computer software

**(G-6454)**
**SCHOLD MACHINE CORPORATION**
7201 W 64th Pl  (60638-4692)
PHONE .................................. 708 458-3788
Fax: 708 458-3866
Jerome P Tippett, *Ch of Bd*
Karen Varnes, *Admin Sec*
EMP: 20  EST: 1949
SQ FT: 35,000
SALES (est): 5.6MM  **Privately Held**
SIC: 3559  Chemical machinery & equipment

**(G-6455)**
**SCHULZE AND BURCH BISCUIT CO (PA)**
1133 W 35th St  (60609-1485)
PHONE .................................. 773 927-6622
Fax: 773 376-4528
Kevin M Boyle, *President*
Sorrell John, *General Mgr*
David Hensler, *Vice Pres*
Joseph Lynch, *Vice Pres*
James McBride, *Vice Pres*
▲ EMP: 277  EST: 1976
SQ FT: 400,000
SALES (est): 93.6MM  **Privately Held**
WEB: www.toastem.com
SIC: 2051  2052  2099  Bread, cake & related products; cookies & crackers; food preparations

**(G-6456)**
**SCIAKY  INC**
4915 W 67th St  (60638-6408)
PHONE .................................. 708 594-3841
Fax: 708 594-9831
Scott Phillips, *CEO*
William S Phillips, *President*
Robert Salo, *General Mgr*
Nicholas Slobidsky, *Engineer*

Ralph Thompson, *Engineer*
EMP: 50
SQ FT: 155,000
SALES (est): 13MM
SALES (corp-wide): 105.7MM  **Privately Held**
WEB: www.sciaky.com
SIC: 3699  Electron beam metal cutting, forming or welding machines; laser welding, drilling & cutting equipment
PA: Phillips Service Industries, Inc.
14492 N Sheldon Rd # 374
Plymouth MI 48170
734 853-5000

**(G-6457)**
**SCIBOR UPHOLSTERING & GALLERY**
12210 S Harlem Ave  (60643)
PHONE .................................. 708 671-9700
Yvonne Scibor, *President*
EMP: 3
SQ FT: 3,700
SALES (est): 309.5K  **Privately Held**
SIC: 5712  7641  2512  Custom made furniture, except cabinets; reupholstery; upholstered household furniture

**(G-6458)**
**SCIENCE SOLUTIONS  LLC (PA)**
5000 W Roosevelt Rd Dock29  (60644-1789)
PHONE .................................. 773 261-1197
Greg Rubin, *Mng Member*
Dean Gangbar,
Manjit Singh,
EMP: 4
SQ FT: 20,000
SALES (est): 932.5K  **Privately Held**
SIC: 2842  Cleaning or polishing preparations

**(G-6459)**
**SCORPION GRAPHICS  INC**
3221 W 36th St  (60632-2701)
PHONE .................................. 773 927-3203
Fax: 773 927-3402
Maria Collins, *President*
Richard Collins, *Vice Pres*
EMP: 14  EST: 1995
SQ FT: 4,000
SALES (est): 1.8MM  **Privately Held**
SIC: 2396  Screen printing on fabric articles

**(G-6460)**
**SCOTT JANCZAK**
Also Called: Blaz Cartage
6285 N Knox Ave  (60646-5032)
PHONE .................................. 773 545-7233
Scott Janczak, *Owner*
EMP: 8
SALES (est): 667.6K  **Privately Held**
SIC: 3537  Trucks, tractors, loaders, carriers & similar equipment

**(G-6461)**
**SCREW MACHINE ENGRG CO INC**
6425 N Avondale Ave  (60631-1998)
PHONE .................................. 773 631-7600
Fax: 773 631-1838
Richard C Baumgart, *President*
Bob Baumgar, *Vice Pres*
EMP: 45  EST: 1937
SQ FT: 22,000
SALES (est): 9MM  **Privately Held**
WEB: www.screwmacheng.com
SIC: 3451  Screw machine products

**(G-6462)**
**SCRN LLC**
1132 W Fulton Market  (60607-1219)
PHONE .................................. 847 513-4082
Sean Daw, *Mng Member*
Samuel Landers,
◆ EMP: 2
SQ FT: 900
SALES: 550K  **Privately Held**
SIC: 3663  Cellular radio telephone

**(G-6463)**
**SDR CORP**
Also Called: Stuart Hale Company
4350 W Ohio St  (60624-1051)
PHONE .................................. 773 638-1800
Dave Schulman, *President*

Stuart Schulman, *Treasurer*
Dean Erickson, *Sales Dir*
Rochelle Schulman, *Admin Sec*
▲ EMP: 4  EST: 1942
SQ FT: 9,375
SALES: 798.5K  **Privately Held**
WEB: www.stuarthale.com
SIC: 2099  2077  Food preparations; animal & marine fats & oils

**(G-6464)**
**SEA-RICH CORP**
Also Called: American Cotton Products Div
5000 W Roosevelt Rd # 104  (60644-1474)
PHONE .................................. 773 261-6633
Fax: 773 533-0226
EMP: 8
SQ FT: 17,000
SALES: 750K  **Privately Held**
SIC: 5199  2211  5113  2221  Whol Nondurable Goods Cotton Brdwv Fabric Mill Whol Indstl/Svc Paper Manmad Brdwv Fabric Mill

**(G-6465)**
**SEADOG**
1500 W Division St  (60642-3344)
PHONE .................................. 773 235-8100
Sompol Chaosaowapa, *President*
EMP: 4  EST: 2010
SALES (est): 343.9K  **Privately Held**
SIC: 3421  Table & food cutlery, including butchers'

**(G-6466)**
**SEAMCRAFT INTERNATIONAL LLC**
5610 W Bloomingdale Ave # 4  (60639-4113)
PHONE .................................. 773 417-4002
Edward Kuhr, *Mng Member*
Linda Steward, *Manager*
Richard Lefauve Jr,
Darek Mecinski,
▼ EMP: 22
SALES: 1.2MM  **Privately Held**
SIC: 2399  3161  2394  Emblems, badges & insignia; sample cases; liners & covers, fabric: made from purchased materials

**(G-6467)**
**SEATS & STOOLS INC**
2711 N Bosworth Ave  (60614-1109)
P.O. Box 577706  (60657-7338)
PHONE .................................. 773 348-7900
Allen Hilder, *President*
▲ EMP: 1
SALES (est): 208.2K  **Privately Held**
SIC: 2599  Stools, factory

**(G-6468)**
**SECOND CHILD**
954 W Armitage Ave Fl 1  (60614-4222)
PHONE .................................. 773 883-0880
Amy Helgren, *Owner*
EMP: 4
SALES (est): 359.8K  **Privately Held**
WEB: www.2ndchild.com
SIC: 2339  Maternity clothing

**(G-6469)**
**SECRETARY OF STATE ILLINOIS**
Also Called: Jessie White Drvers Svcs Fclty
9901 S King Dr  (60628-1523)
PHONE .................................. 773 660-4963
EMP: 12  **Privately Held**
SIC: 3469  Automobile license tags, stamped metal
HQ: Secretary Of State, Illinois
213 State House
Springfield IL 62706
217 782-2201

**(G-6470)**
**SECURESLICE INC**
6300 N Rockwell St  (60659-1838)
PHONE .................................. 800 984-0494
Ismail Mohammed, *Exec Dir*
EMP: 50  EST: 2012
SALES (est): 1.6MM  **Privately Held**
SIC: 7379  7372  Computer data escrow service; ; business oriented computer software

## GEOGRAPHIC SECTION
## Chicago - Cook County (G-6498)

**(G-6471)**
**SEDIA SYSTEMS INC (PA)**
1820 W Hubbard St Ste 300 (60622-6290)
PHONE................................312 212-8010
Wilson Troup III, *President*
Fran Fritzman, *Controller*
▲ **EMP:** 9
**SQ FT:** 3,500
**SALES (est):** 3.7MM **Privately Held**
**WEB:** www.sediasystems.com
**SIC:** 2531 Public building & related furniture

**(G-6472)**
**SEE ALL INDUSTRIES INC (PA)**
3623 S Laflin Pl (60609-1397)
PHONE................................773 927-3232
**Fax:** 773 927-7742
Carmela Celenza, *President*
Joseph C Celenza, *Vice Pres*
Gerald Celenza, *Treasurer*
Joseph Celenza Jr, *Admin Sec*
▲ **EMP:** 16
**SQ FT:** 30,000
**SALES:** 4MM **Privately Held**
**WEB:** www.seeall.com
**SIC:** 3231 Mirrored glass

**(G-6473)**
**SEE WHAT YOU SEND INC**
2300 N Lincoln Park W (60614-3456)
PHONE................................781 780-1483
Chris Stacey, *President*
Salvatore Migliaccio, *Treasurer*
**EMP:** 3
**SALES (est):** 145.5K **Privately Held**
**SIC:** 7372 7389 Application computer software;

**(G-6474)**
**SEEC TRASPORTATION CORP**
190 S Lasalle Ste 2100 (60603)
PHONE................................800 215-4003
Sabrina Chambers, *President*
**EMP:** 4
**SQ FT:** 965
**SALES (est):** 149.8K **Privately Held**
**SIC:** 3743 Train cars & equipment, freight or passenger

**(G-6475)**
**SELECT SNACKS COMPANY INC**
825 E 99th St (60628-1526)
PHONE................................773 933-2167
Joseph Shankland, *President*
Chuck Leifheid, *Credit Mgr*
**EMP:** 75
**SALES (est):** 4MM **Privately Held**
**SIC:** 2096 5145 Potato chips & similar snacks; confectionery

**(G-6476)**
**SENSAPHONICS INC**
660 N Milwaukee Ave Ste 1 (60642-8674)
PHONE................................312 432-1714
**Fax:** 312 432-1738
Michael Santucci, *President*
Doris Bell, *Administration*
**EMP:** 5
**SQ FT:** 800
**SALES (est):** 500K **Privately Held**
**WEB:** www.sensaphonics.com
**SIC:** 3842 Surgical appliances & supplies

**(G-6477)**
**SENSIBLE PRODUCTS INC**
7290 W Devon Ave (60631-1620)
P.O. Box 31695 (60631-0695)
PHONE................................773 774-7400
**Fax:** 773 774-6100
Michael G Rubino, *President*
▲ **EMP:** 5
**SQ FT:** 2,000
**SALES:** 600K **Privately Held**
**SIC:** 3545 Machine tool accessories

**(G-6478)**
**SERIOUS ENERGY INC**
1333 N Hickory Ave (60642-2433)
PHONE................................312 515-4606
**EMP:** 48
**SALES (corp-wide):** 11.4MM **Privately Held**
**SIC:** 2531 Public building & related furniture
**PA:** Serious Energy, Inc.
1250 Elko Dr
Sunnyvale CA 94089
408 541-8000

**(G-6479)**
**SERLIN IRON & METAL CO INC**
1810 N Kilbourn Ave (60639-5107)
PHONE................................773 227-3826
**Fax:** 773 252-1075
Mark Kalter, *President*
Mitch Kalter, *Vice Pres*
Evelyn Kalter, *Admin Sec*
**EMP:** 15
**SQ FT:** 32,500
**SALES (est):** 3.1MM **Privately Held**
**SIC:** 5093 3341 Ferrous metal scrap & waste; secondary nonferrous metals

**(G-6480)**
**SERVI-SURE CORPORATION**
2020 W Rascher Ave (60625-1004)
PHONE................................773 271-5900
**Fax:** 773 271-3777
Jon Rosner, *President*
Ronald Mann, *Vice Pres*
Mike Wolfer, *Engineer*
Lissetta Velazquez, *Manager*
**EMP:** 24 **EST:** 1959
**SALES (est):** 3.4MM **Privately Held**
**WEB:** www.servisure.com
**SIC:** 2796 Platemaking services

**(G-6481)**
**SERVICE & MANUFACTURING CORP**
5414c W Roosevelt Rd C (60644-1467)
PHONE................................773 287-5500
Camerina Torres, *President*
Clarence Eisenman, *Vice Pres*
**EMP:** 26
**SALES (est):** 1,000K **Privately Held**
**SIC:** 3161 Sample cases

**(G-6482)**
**SERVICE CUTTING & WELDING**
2911 N Moody Ave (60634-5027)
PHONE................................773 622-8366
Peter Harris, *Owner*
**EMP:** 3
**SALES:** 60K **Privately Held**
**SIC:** 7692 7699 Welding repair; industrial machinery & equipment repair

**(G-6483)**
**SERVICE SHEET METAL WORKS INC**
5000 W 73rd St (60638-6612)
PHONE................................773 229-0031
**Fax:** 773 229-0032
Todd Carmichael, *President*
Roger Wolf, *Vice Pres*
**EMP:** 14 **EST:** 1945
**SQ FT:** 15,000
**SALES (est):** 2MM **Privately Held**
**SIC:** 3444 3312 7692 3993 Sheet metalwork; pipes & tubes; welding repair; signs & advertising specialties; fabricated pipe & fittings; metal stampings

**(G-6484)**
**SEWARD SCREW ACQUISITION LLC**
1835 W Warner Ave (60613-1822)
PHONE................................312 498-9933
Timothy Derry, *President*
**EMP:** 3
**SALES (est):** 142.8K **Privately Held**
**SIC:** 3542 Presses: forming, stamping, punching, sizing (machine tools)

**(G-6485)**
**SEWARD SCREW OPERATING LLC**
1835 W Warner Ave (60613-1822)
PHONE................................312 498-9933
Timothy Derry, *President*
**EMP:** 120
**SALES (est):** 5MM **Privately Held**
**SIC:** 3542 Presses: forming, stamping, punching, sizing (machine tools)

**(G-6486)**
**SFC CHEMICALS LTD**
1031 W Bryn Mawr Ave 1a (60660-4657)
P.O. Box 3966, Barrington (60011-3966)
PHONE................................847 221-2152
Shyam R Zalani,
**EMP:** 3
**SALES (est):** 15MM **Privately Held**
**WEB:** www.sfcltd.com
**SIC:** 2834 Druggists' preparations (pharmaceuticals)

**(G-6487)**
**SHADE BROOKLINE CO**
Also Called: Aberdeen Window Shade Service
6246 N Broadway St (60660-1903)
PHONE................................773 274-5513
**Fax:** 773 274-5599
John Lichtfess, *President*
Ronald J Silverman, *Vice Pres*
Jerry Lichtfuss, *Treasurer*
**EMP:** 13 **EST:** 1924
**SQ FT:** 2,000
**SALES (est):** 1MM **Privately Held**
**SIC:** 2591 2391 7699 Window shades; venetian blinds; draperies, plastic & textile: from purchased materials; window blind repair services

**(G-6488)**
**SHADEMAKER PRODUCTS CORP**
7300 S Kimbark Ave (60619-1430)
P.O. Box 5271, Buffalo Grove (60089-5271)
PHONE................................773 955-0998
Sidney M Levin, *CEO*
**EMP:** 7
**SQ FT:** 25,000
**SALES:** 100K **Privately Held**
**WEB:** www.shademakerproducts.com
**SIC:** 3444 Awnings, sheet metal

**(G-6489)**
**SHARLEN ELECTRIC CO (PA)**
9101 S Baltimore Ave (60617-4417)
P.O. Box 17597 (60617-0597)
PHONE................................773 721-0700
**Fax:** 773 721-9208
William Cullen, *President*
Jim Cullen, *Vice Pres*
Joe Kibbon, *CFO*
Sarah Aguayo, *Human Resources*
Tom Denton, *Telecomm Mgr*
**EMP:** 50
**SQ FT:** 75,000
**SALES (est):** 17.5MM **Privately Held**
**WEB:** www.sharlen.com
**SIC:** 1731 3498 General electrical contractor; tube fabricating (contract bending & shaping)

**(G-6490)**
**SHARPRINT SLKSCRN & GRPHCS**
Also Called: Sharprint Promotional Apparel
4200 W Wrightwood Ave (60639-2023)
PHONE................................877 649-2554
**Fax:** 773 243-5005
George Kilian, *President*
Calvin Hodge, *Safety Mgr*
Maureen Alfonso, *CFO*
Nancy Oiszweski, *Sales Staff*
Wendy Roman, *Sales Staff*
**EMP:** 65
**SQ FT:** 40,000
**SALES (est):** 9.7MM **Privately Held**
**WEB:** www.sharprint.com
**SIC:** 2396 Screen printing on fabric articles

**(G-6491)**
**SHAW INDUSTRIES GROUP INC**
Also Called: Shaw Contract Group
222 Merchandise Mart Plz # 10 (60654-1103)
PHONE................................312 467-1331
**Fax:** 312 467-1339
Greg Klaus, *Principal*
**EMP:** 7
**SALES (corp-wide):** 223.6B **Publicly Held**
**SIC:** 2273 Carpets & rugs
**HQ:** Shaw Industries Group, Inc.
616 E Walnut Ave
Dalton GA 30721
800 441-7429

**(G-6492)**
**SHAWNIMALS LLC**
2023 W Carroll Ave C301 (60612-1691)
PHONE................................312 235-2625
Jen Brody, *Prdtn Mgr*
Shawn Smith, *Manager*
**EMP:** 4
**SQ FT:** 1,400
**SALES (est):** 200K **Privately Held**
**SIC:** 3942 Dolls & stuffed toys; stuffed toys, including animals

**(G-6493)**
**SHAZAK PRODUCTIONS**
6415 N Sacramento Ave (60645-4214)
PHONE................................773 406-9880
Rabbi Moshe Moscowitz, *Principal*
**EMP:** 4
**SALES (est):** 145.3K **Privately Held**
**SIC:** 2711 Newspapers, publishing & printing

**(G-6494)**
**SHEETS & CYLINDER WELDING INC**
4147 W Ogden Ave (60623-2877)
PHONE................................800 442-2200
**Fax:** 773 762-0086
Louis White, *President*
Helen White, *Principal*
**EMP:** 7
**SALES (est):** 610K **Privately Held**
**SIC:** 3441 7692 3444 Fabricated structural metal; welding repair; sheet metalwork

**(G-6495)**
**SHELTER SYSTEMS**
3729 N Ravenswood Ave (60613-3590)
PHONE................................773 281-9270
**Fax:** 773 281-9217
John Jameson, *Owner*
**EMP:** 3
**SQ FT:** 1,500
**SALES:** 225K **Privately Held**
**SIC:** 2394 Canopies, fabric: made from purchased materials

**(G-6496)**
**SHIFTGIG INC**
225 W Hubbard St Ste 302 (60654-4916)
PHONE................................312 763-3003
Edward Lou, *CEO*
Jeff Pieta, *President*
Marc Bronsweig, *Managing Dir*
Mindy Gulledge, *Managing Dir*
Sean Casey, *Chief Engr*
**EMP:** 50 **EST:** 2012
**SQ FT:** 864
**SALES (est):** 5.1MM **Privately Held**
**SIC:** 2741

**(G-6497)**
**SHIIR RUGS LLC**
208 W Kinzie St Ste 5 (60654-4911)
PHONE................................312 828-0400
**EMP:** 3
**SALES (est):** 62K **Privately Held**
**SIC:** 2273 2392 Carpets & rugs; linings, carpet: textile, except felt

**(G-6498)**
**SHOPPERTRAK RCT CORPORATION (DH)**
233 S Wacker Dr Fl 41 (60606-6323)
PHONE................................312 529-5300
Christopher Ainsley, *President*
Bill Martin, *Exec VP*
Todd Starcevich, *Vice Pres*
Beth Bialkowski, *Project Mgr*
Greg Porlier, *Project Mgr*
**EMP:** 10
**SQ FT:** 40,000
**SALES (est):** 40.6MM
**SALES (corp-wide):** 36.8B **Privately Held**
**WEB:** www.shoppertrak.com
**SIC:** 7371 3824 Computer software development & applications; mechanical & electromechanical counters & devices

# Chicago - Cook County (G-6499)

HQ: Sensormatic Electronics, Llc
6600 Congress Ave
Boca Raton FL 33487
561 912-6000

**(G-6499)**
**SHORE CAPITAL PARTNERS LLC (PA)**
1 E Wacker Dr Ste 400 (60601-1815)
PHONE.................312 348-7580
Fax: 312 348-7669
Justin Ishbia, *Partner*
Michael Cooper, *Partner*
John Hennegan, *Partner*
Ryan Kelley, *Partner*
Don Pierce, *Partner*
EMP: 14
SALES (est): 14.7MM **Privately Held**
SIC: 6799 3069 Investors; medical & laboratory rubber sundries & related products

**(G-6500)**
**SHOWCASE CORPORATION (PA)**
233 S Wacker Dr Ste 5150 (60606-6371)
PHONE.................312 651-3000
Jack Noonan, *President*
EMP: 160
SQ FT: 9,000
SALES (est): 20.4MM **Privately Held**
SIC: 7372 7371 Business oriented computer software; custom computer programming services

**(G-6501)**
**SHREE MAHAVIR INC**
Also Called: Print Express
311 S Wacker Dr Ste 4550 (60606-6622)
PHONE.................312 408-1080
Kishore Kuvadia, *President*
Tina Kuvadia, *Admin Sec*
▼ EMP: 5
SQ FT: 1,500
SALES (est): 508.8K **Privately Held**
WEB: www.shreemahavir.com
SIC: 2752 2791 2789 2759 Commercial printing, offset; typesetting; bookbinding & related work; commercial printing; automotive & apparel trimmings

**(G-6502)**
**SHREE PRINTING CORP**
3011 W Irving Park Rd (60618-3513)
PHONE.................773 267-9500
Fax: 773 267-9576
Jagdish Suthar, *President*
Manju J Suthar, *Vice Pres*
Manish Suthar, *Manager*
Himan Suther, *Manager*
EMP: 2
SQ FT: 4,000
SALES (est): 210K **Privately Held**
SIC: 2752 7334 7336 2791 Commercial printing, lithographic; photocopying & duplicating services; commercial art & graphic design; typesetting; bookbinding & related work

**(G-6503)**
**SHUFFLE TECH INTERNATIONAL LLC**
1440 N Kingsbury St # 218 (60642-2651)
PHONE.................312 787-7780
Richard J Schultz, *Mng Member*
Richard Schultz, *Manager*
EMP: 3
SQ FT: 2,000
SALES: 1MM **Privately Held**
SIC: 3949 Shuffleboards & shuffleboard equipment

**(G-6504)**
**SHURE PRODUCTS INC**
Also Called: T.S. Shure
954 W Wa Blvd Ste 515 (60607-2206)
PHONE.................773 227-1001
Thomas S Shure, *President*
Doug Sissom, *Vice Pres*
Doug Sisson, *Vice Pres*
Jerome Foster, *Manager*
▲ EMP: 13
SQ FT: 5,000
SALES (est): 2.8MM **Privately Held**
WEB: www.shureproducts.com
SIC: 3944 2731 Games, toys & children's vehicles; book publishing

**(G-6505)**
**SIEDEN STICKER USA LTD**
1506 W Grand Ave Apt 3e (60642-7525)
PHONE.................312 280-7711
Alice Heredia, *Vice Pres*
EMP: 5
SALES (est): 310K **Privately Held**
SIC: 2389 Men's miscellaneous accessories

**(G-6506)**
**SIGENICS INC (PA)**
3440 S Dearborn St 126s (60616-5074)
PHONE.................312 448-8000
Philip R Troyk, *President*
Douglas A Kerns, *Principal*
David Anderson, *Manager*
Glenn A Demichele, *Admin Sec*
EMP: 11
SQ FT: 3,441
SALES (est): 2.3MM **Privately Held**
WEB: www.sigenics.com
SIC: 8711 8731 8734 3672 Engineering services; biotechnical research, commercial; testing laboratories; printed circuit boards; wafers (semiconductor devices); measuring & controlling devices

**(G-6507)**
**SIGN AMERICA**
Also Called: America International Dist
2748 W Devon Ave (60659-1711)
PHONE.................773 262-7800
Fax: 773 262-7898
Salim Shariff, *Owner*
Loretta Miller, *Sales Staff*
EMP: 4
SALES (est): 210K **Privately Held**
SIC: 3993 Signs & advertising specialties

**(G-6508)**
**SIGN-A-RAMA**
1513 S State St (60605-2804)
PHONE.................312 922-0509
Fax: 312 922-0517
Aleda Goodwin, *President*
Cornelius Goodwin, *Admin Sec*
EMP: 3
SALES (est): 325K **Privately Held**
SIC: 3993 Signs & advertising specialties

**(G-6509)**
**SIGNAL DIGITAL INC (PA)**
111 N Canal St Ste 455 (60606-7202)
PHONE.................312 685-1911
Michael Sands, *President*
Patrick Venetucci, *COO*
Todd Chu, *Senior VP*
Kathy Menis, *Senior VP*
Ana Milicevic, *Senior VP*
EMP: 45
SALES (est): 37.3MM **Privately Held**
SIC: 7372 Application computer software

**(G-6510)**
**SIGNATURE DESIGN & TAILORING**
8027 S Stony Island Ave (60617-1747)
PHONE.................773 375-4915
Valencio Hinton, *Owner*
EMP: 15 EST: 1997
SALES (est): 420K **Privately Held**
SIC: 2311 5611 5621 Jackets, tailored suit-type: men's & boys'; men's & boys' clothing stores; women's clothing stores

**(G-6511)**
**SIGNS NOW**
2525 W Hutchinson St (60618-1503)
PHONE.................800 356-3373
Michele Kunze, *Owner*
EMP: 4
SQ FT: 1,200
SALES (est): 230K **Privately Held**
WEB: www.signsnowchicago.com
SIC: 3993 Signs & advertising specialties

**(G-6512)**
**SIM PARTNERS INC (PA)**
30 N La Salle St Ste 3400 (60602-3337)
PHONE.................800 260-3380
Jonathan Schepke, *President*
Adam Borfman, *Vice Pres*
Saul Delage, *Vice Pres*
Jai Hawkinson, *Vice Pres*
Ellen Allerton, *Human Res Mgr*
EMP: 35
SQ FT: 5,000
SALES: 5MM **Privately Held**
WEB: simpartners.com/
SIC: 2741

**(G-6513)**
**SIMON GLOBAL SERVICES LLC**
5655 N Clark St Ste 5 (60660-4038)
PHONE.................773 334-7794
Gabriel Bedoya, *Principal*
EMP: 4
SALES (est): 290K **Privately Held**
SIC: 2741 Miscellaneous publishing

**(G-6514)**
**SIMPLE MILLS LLC**
444 N Wells St Ste 203 (60654-4522)
PHONE.................312 600-6196
Katlin Smith, *CEO*
EMP: 7
SALES: 2.2MM **Privately Held**
SIC: 2045 Prepared flour mixes & doughs

**(G-6515)**
**SING S NOODLE**
2171 S China Pl (60616-1536)
PHONE.................312 225-2882
Xiu Liu, *Principal*
EMP: 5
SALES (est): 303.9K **Privately Held**
SIC: 2098 Noodles (e.g. egg, plain & water), dry

**(G-6516)**
**SINGER SAFETY COMPANY**
Also Called: UNI-Glide
2300 N Kilbourn Ave (60639-3402)
PHONE.................773 235-2100
Fax: 773 235-0363
Brian Johnson, *President*
Anna Marie Johnson, *Vice Pres*
Gregory Pranski, *Prdtn Mgr*
Tom Kiolbassa, *Controller*
EMP: 17 EST: 1950
SQ FT: 36,000
SALES (est): 5MM
SALES (corp-wide): 6.4MM **Privately Held**
WEB: www.singersafety.com
SIC: 3448 Screen enclosures
PA: Rensel-Chicago, Inc.
2300 N Kilbourn Ave
Chicago IL 60639
773 235-2100

**(G-6517)**
**SIPI METALS CORP (PA)**
1720 N Elston Ave (60642-1532)
PHONE.................773 276-0070
Fax: 773 276-7014
Marion A Cameron, *President*
Robert S Glidden, *Senior VP*
Dennis R Arakelian, *Vice Pres*
Robert Berny, *Vice Pres*
Joris Coopmans, *Vice Pres*
▲ EMP: 120 EST: 1905
SQ FT: 200,000
SALES (est): 28.7MM **Privately Held**
WEB: www.sipimetals.com
SIC: 3339 3341 Gold refining (primary); platinum group metal refining (primary); silver refining (primary); brass smelting & refining (secondary); copper smelting & refining (secondary); zinc smelting & refining (secondary)

**(G-6518)**
**SIR SPEEDY PRINTING**
1711 N Clybourn Ave (60614-5519)
PHONE.................312 337-0774
Fax: 312 337-1792
George Lesniak, *President*
Orlando Rosado, *General Mgr*
Marial Poll, *Vice Pres*
EMP: 4
SALES (est): 620.1K **Privately Held**
SIC: 2752 2791 2789 Commercial printing, lithographic; typesetting; bookbinding & related work

**(G-6519)**
**SIX OAKS COMPANY**
2033 W 108th Pl (60643-3304)
PHONE.................312 343-4037
Michael P Walsh, *President*
EMP: 3
SALES: 500K **Privately Held**
SIC: 3559 Special industry machinery

**(G-6520)**
**SKILLED PLATING CORP**
151618 N Kilpatrick Ave (60651)
PHONE.................773 227-0262
Fax: 773 227-7465
Gary Weincouff, *President*
Dawna Maggard, *Vice Pres*
EMP: 6
SQ FT: 8,300
SALES: 500K **Privately Held**
SIC: 3471 Electroplating of metals or formed products; finishing, metals or formed products

**(G-6521)**
**SKIN CARE SYSTEMS**
119 W Hubbard St Lowr (60654-7579)
PHONE.................312 644-9067
Fax: 312 644-9069
Barbara Leonardi, *President*
Michael Sanders, *Technology*
EMP: 3
SALES (est): 169.2K **Privately Held**
SIC: 7231 3999 Beauty shops; barber & beauty shop equipment

**(G-6522)**
**SKOL MFG CO**
4444 N Ravenswood Ave (60640-5803)
PHONE.................773 878-5959
Fax: 773 878-0320
Raymond Skolorzynski, *President*
Junanita Skolorzynski, *CFO*
Walter Skolorzynski, *Treasurer*
EMP: 20 EST: 1943
SQ FT: 20,000
SALES (est): 4.9MM **Privately Held**
WEB: www.skolmfg.com
SIC: 3499 Machine bases, metal

**(G-6523)**
**SKW INDUSTRIES LLC**
Also Called: Progressive Coating
900 S Cicero Ave (60644-5213)
PHONE.................773 261-8900
Stephen K Walters,
EMP: 15
SALES: 1.2MM **Privately Held**
SIC: 3999 Manufacturing industries

**(G-6524)**
**SKYLINE DESIGN INC**
1240 N Homan Ave Ste 1 (60651-4202)
PHONE.................773 278-4660
Charles Rizzo, *President*
Nick Corriero, *Vice Pres*
◆ EMP: 85 EST: 1982
SQ FT: 120,000
SALES (est): 15.7MM **Privately Held**
WEB: www.skydesign.com
SIC: 3231 Novelties, glass: fruit, foliage, flowers, animals, etc.; furniture tops, glass: cut, beveled or polished; art glass: made from purchased glass

**(G-6525)**
**SKYWAY CEMENT COMPANY LLC**
3020 E 103rd St (60617-5809)
PHONE.................800 643-1808
Wayne Emmer, *Principal*
EMP: 10
SALES (est): 2.2MM **Privately Held**
SIC: 3241 Masonry cement

**(G-6526)**
**SLAYMAKER FINE ART LTD**
Also Called: Slaymaker Galleries
833 W Aldine Ave (60657-2305)
PHONE.................773 348-1450
Woody Slaymaker, *President*
EMP: 9 EST: 1979
SALES (est): 790K **Privately Held**
WEB: www.slaymakerfineartltd.com
SIC: 1522 2741 Residential construction; miscellaneous publishing

## GEOGRAPHIC SECTION

Chicago - Cook County (G-6554)

**(G-6527)**
**SLEE CORPORATION**
Also Called: Crystal Edge
4125 N Kostner Ave  (60641-1928)
**PHONE**.................................773 777-2444
Barry Slee, *President*
Lesley Slee, *Vice Pres*
Cathy Uliasz, *Sales Staff*
◆ **EMP:** 28
**SQ FT:** 42,000
**SALES (est):** 4.7MM **Privately Held**
**WEB:** www.slee.com
**SIC: 3231** Ornamental glass: cut, engraved or otherwise decorated; mirrored glass

**(G-6528)**
**SLEEP6  LLC**
1332 N Halsted St  (60642-2624)
**PHONE**.................................844 375-3376
Robert Taglianetti,
**EMP:** 4
**SALES (est):** 115.8K **Privately Held**
**SIC: 2394** Air cushions & mattresses, canvas

**(G-6529)**
**SLEEPECK PRINTING COMPANY**
70 W Madison St Ste 2300  (60602-4250)
**PHONE**.................................708 544-8900
Michael W Sleepeck, *Ch of Bd*
**EMP:** 200 **EST:** 1904
**SQ FT:** 100,000
**SALES (est):** 26MM **Privately Held**
**SIC: 2752** Commercial printing, offset; lithographing on metal

**(G-6530)**
**SLIDEMATIC PRODUCTS CO**
4520 W Addison St  (60641-3814)
**PHONE**.................................773 545-4213
Mark Magnuson, *President*
Charlie Ripka, *Buyer*
Tina Fields, *Office Mgr*
David L Magnuson, *Admin Sec*
**EMP:** 27
**SALES (est):** 7.5MM **Privately Held**
**SIC: 3469** Metal stampings

**(G-6531)**
**SLIPCHIP CORPORATION**
118 N Clinton St Ste 205  (60661-2332)
**PHONE**.................................312 550-5600
Brian Coe, *CEO*
Rustem Ismagilov, *Principal*
**EMP:** 10
**SALES (est):** 870K **Privately Held**
**SIC: 3826** Spectroscopic & other optical properties measuring equipment

**(G-6532)**
**SMART OFFICE SERVICES INC**
3720 W Chicago Ave  (60651-3820)
P.O. Box 97  (60690-0097)
**PHONE**.................................773 227-1121
Deborah A Smart, *President*
Edrick Smart, *Corp Secy*
**EMP:** 5
**SALES (est):** 490K **Privately Held**
**SIC: 2752** 7334 Commercial printing, lithographic; photocopying & duplicating services

**(G-6533)**
**SMH2 MANUFACTURING LLC**
2041 W Carroll Ave  (60612-1630)
**PHONE**.................................773 793-6643
Stephen A Martin, *Principal*
**EMP:** 3 **EST:** 2015
**SALES (est):** 56.4K **Privately Held**
**SIC: 3999** Manufacturing industries

**(G-6534)**
**SMILE LEE FACES**
4197 S Archer Ave  (60632-1849)
**PHONE**.................................773 376-9999
Andrea Lacayo, *Principal*
**EMP:** 4
**SALES (est):** 399.5K **Privately Held**
**SIC: 3843** Enamels, dentists'

**(G-6535)**
**SMITH POWER TRANSMISSION CO**
5335 S Western Blvd Ste C  (60609-5450)
**PHONE**.................................773 526-5512
**Fax:** 773 526-5515
Robert Smith, *President*
**EMP:** 3
**SQ FT:** 2,000
**SALES (est):** 652.2K **Privately Held**
**SIC: 3569** 5085 Filters; gears

**(G-6536)**
**SMITHFIELD FOODS  INC**
303 E Wacker Dr Ste 1100  (60601-5204)
**PHONE**.................................312 577-5650
Stephanie Martin, *Branch Mgr*
Ron Wells, *Director*
**EMP:** 12 **Privately Held**
**SIC: 2011** Meat packing plants
**HQ:** Smithfield Foods, Inc.
200 Commerce St
Smithfield VA 23430
757 365-3000

**(G-6537)**
**SMOOCHES ICE CREAM**
3559 W Arlington St  (60624)
**PHONE**.................................708 370-0282
Felice Matthews, *Owner*
**EMP:** 3
**SALES (est):** 101.3K **Privately Held**
**SIC: 2024** Ice cream, bulk

**(G-6538)**
**SNAIDERO USA**
222 Mrchnds Mrt Pl 140  (60654)
**PHONE**.................................312 644-6662
**Fax:** 312 644-6665
Brandy Cohen, *Design Engr*
Erika Klimenko, *Branch Mgr*
**EMP:** 3
**SALES (corp-wide):** 7MM **Privately Held**
**WEB:** www.snaidero-la.com
**SIC: 2434** Wood kitchen cabinets
**PA:** Snaidero U.S.A.
20300 S Vt Ave Ste 125
Torrance CA 90502
310 516-8499

**(G-6539)**
**SNOW & GRAHAM LLC**
4021 N Ravenswood Ave  (60613-2409)
**PHONE**.................................773 665-9000
Ebony Chafey,
**EMP:** 8
**SALES (est):** 1.2MM **Privately Held**
**WEB:** www.snowandgraham.com
**SIC: 2621** Stationery, envelope & tablet papers

**(G-6540)**
**SNOWBALL INDUSTRIES**
3404 N Harding Ave  (60618-5136)
**PHONE**.................................773 316-0051
Christopher Cianciola, *Principal*
**EMP:** 3
**SALES (est):** 97.7K **Privately Held**
**SIC: 3999** Manufacturing industries

**(G-6541)**
**SOLO CUP OPERATING CORPORATION**
7575 S Kostner Ave Ste 3  (60652-1151)
**PHONE**.................................847 444-5000
Jean Roberts, *Plant Mgr*
Richard Ignash, *Foreman/Supr*
George Jarke, *Foreman/Supr*
Patricia Marschke, *Purch Agent*
Robert Dusich, *QA Dir*
**EMP:** 150
**SALES (corp-wide):** 1.3B **Privately Held**
**SIC: 3089** 3421 Cups, plastic, except foam; cutlery
**HQ:** Solo Cup Operating Corporation
300 Tr State Intl Ste 200
Lincolnshire IL 60069
847 444-5000

**(G-6542)**
**SOLUTION 3 GRAPHICS  INC**
10547 S Western Ave  (60643-2592)
**PHONE**.................................773 233-3600
George Herzog, *President*
Charles Bennett, *Foreman/Supr*
Charlene Herzog, *Admin Sec*
**EMP:** 14 **EST:** 1966
**SQ FT:** 10,000
**SALES (est):** 1.5MM **Privately Held**
**WEB:** www.regal-print.com
**SIC: 2752** Commercial printing, offset

**(G-6543)**
**SOMMERS & FAHRENBACH INC**
3301 W Belmont Ave  (60618-5578)
**PHONE**.................................773 478-3033
**Fax:** 773 478-2303
Thomas M Sommers, *President*
Daniel Lee, *Opers Spvr*
Robert Walsh, *Treasurer*
Joseph Prieboy, *Office Mgr*
**EMP:** 11 **EST:** 1919
**SQ FT:** 8,000
**SALES (est):** 2MM **Privately Held**
**WEB:** www.sfprinting.net
**SIC: 2752** 2791 2789 Commercial printing, offset; typesetting; bookbinding & related work

**(G-6544)**
**SORINI MANUFACTURING CORP**
Also Called: Soring Ring
2524 S Blue Island Ave  (60608-4934)
**PHONE**.................................773 247-5858
**Fax:** 773 247-7186
Peter M May, *President*
Peter May Jr, *Vice Pres*
Pauline May, *Admin Sec*
▲ **EMP:** 27 **EST:** 1963
**SQ FT:** 40,000
**SALES (est):** 8.8MM **Privately Held**
**WEB:** www.sorini.com
**SIC: 3466** Closures, stamped metal

**(G-6545)**
**SOUDAN METALS COMPANY INC (PA)**
Also Called: Steel Fab & Finish
319 W 40th Pl  (60609-2816)
P.O. Box 9044  (60609-0044)
**PHONE**.................................773 548-7600
**Fax:** 773 548-4803
Thomas A Soudan Sr, *CEO*
Thomas L Soudan Jr, *President*
Peter Soudan, *Sales Mgr*
Derek Wasilewski, *Info Tech Dir*
Tom Connelly, *Info Tech Mgr*
**EMP:** 115
**SQ FT:** 105,000
**SALES (est):** 33.7MM **Privately Held**
**WEB:** www.slitcoils.com
**SIC: 5051** 3316 Steel; cold finishing of steel shapes

**(G-6546)**
**SOUTH CHICAGO PACKING LLC**
945 W 38th St  (60609-1410)
**PHONE**.................................708 589-2400
**Fax:** 708 589-2525
David J Miniat, *President*
John Molton, *CFO*
**EMP:** 100
**SALES (corp-wide):** 101.5MM **Privately Held**
**SIC: 2079** 2077 Compound shortenings; rendering
**PA:** South Chicago Packing Llc
16250 Vincennes Ave
South Holland IL 60473
708 589-2400

**(G-6547)**
**SOUTH SHORE IRON WORKS INC**
407 W 109th St  (60628-3216)
**PHONE**.................................773 264-2267
**Fax:** 773 264-9458
Judith Hartmann, *President*
Fred Hartmann, *Corp Secy*
**EMP:** 28 **EST:** 1924
**SQ FT:** 10,000
**SALES (est):** 6.7MM **Privately Held**
**WEB:** www.ssiw.com
**SIC: 3312** Structural shapes & pilings, steel

**(G-6548)**
**SPACE ORGANIZATION  LTD**
4720 W Walton St  (60651-3331)
**PHONE**.................................312 654-1400
**Fax:** 312 654-1405
Gary Nemoy, *President*
Alan Brownstone, *President*
Keith Perry, *Manager*
**EMP:** 10
**SALES (est):** 826.4K **Privately Held**
**WEB:** www.spaceorganization.net
**SIC: 1751** 2434 Cabinet & finish carpentry; cabinet building & installation; wood kitchen cabinets

**(G-6549)**
**SPACESAVER PARKING COMPANY**
Also Called: Mid American Elevator
820 N Wolcott Ave  (60622-4937)
**PHONE**.................................773 486-6900
**Fax:** 773 486-2438
Robert R Bailey Jr, *Ch of Bd*
Greg Selke, *Vice Pres*
Mark Selke, *Vice Pres*
Tim Moran, *Opers Mgr*
Jacqueline Smith, *Director*
▲ **EMP:** 3
**SALES (est):** 977.1K **Privately Held**
**SIC: 3559** Parking facility equipment & supplies

**(G-6550)**
**SPANISH AMERCN LANGUAG NEWSPAP**
55 E Jackson Blvd # 1820  (60604-4466)
**PHONE**.................................312 368-4840
Paul Steven, *Owner*
**EMP:** 20
**SALES (est):** 556.4K **Privately Held**
**SIC: 2711** Newspapers

**(G-6551)**
**SPARRER SAUSAGE COMPANY INC**
Also Called: El Campeon Food Products
4325 W Ogden Ave  (60623-2925)
**PHONE**.................................773 762-3334
**Fax:** 773 521-9368
Brian Graves, *President*
Robert Rodgers, *Controller*
**EMP:** 120
**SQ FT:** 49,800
**SALES (est):** 16.9MM **Privately Held**
**WEB:** www.sparrers.com
**SIC: 2013** Smoked meats from purchased meat; sausages from purchased meat

**(G-6552)**
**SPARROW SOUND DESIGN**
Also Called: Southport Records
3501 N Southport Ave  (60657-1475)
**PHONE**.................................773 281-8510
**Fax:** 773 472-4330
Bradley Parker, *Partner*
Joanie Pallatto, *Partner*
**EMP:** 5
**SQ FT:** 2,300
**SALES:** 7.8K **Privately Held**
**WEB:** www.chicagosound.com
**SIC: 3652** Pre-recorded records & tapes

**(G-6553)**
**SPARTAN SHEET METAL  INC**
3006 W Bryn Mawr Ave  (60659-3725)
**PHONE**.................................773 895-7266
George Sinodinos, *President*
**EMP:** 2
**SALES (est):** 279.3K **Privately Held**
**SIC: 3444** Sheet metalwork

**(G-6554)**
**SPECIAL TOOL ENGINEERING CO**
4539 S Knox Ave  (60632-4892)
**PHONE**.................................773 767-6690
**Fax:** 773 767-0829
John Kristmann, *President*
Liz Krafthefer, *Purchasing*
Dick Hennessey, *Engineer*
Judi Orsi, *Admin Sec*
**EMP:** 10 **EST:** 1945
**SQ FT:** 14,000
**SALES:** 1MM **Privately Held**
**SIC: 3555** 7692 3535 Printing trades machinery; welding repair; conveyors & conveying equipment

# Chicago - Cook County (G-6555) — GEOGRAPHIC SECTION

### (G-6555)
**SPECIFIED PLATING CO**
320 N Harding Ave (60624-1838)
PHONE.................................773 826-4501
Fax: 773 826-3076
John C Kopecky, *President*
Debra Meyers, *Treasurer*
Helen Lazzarotto, *Admin Sec*
**EMP:** 35 **EST:** 1945
**SQ FT:** 70,000
**SALES (est):** 4.2MM **Privately Held**
**SIC:** 3471 3479 Electroplating of metals or formed products; painting, coating & hot dipping

### (G-6556)
**SPEED INK PRINTING**
3547 W Peterson Ave (60659-3212)
PHONE.................................773 539-9700
Roberto Alvarado, *Supervisor*
**EMP:** 4
**SALES (est):** 429.9K **Privately Held**
**SIC:** 2752 Commercial printing, lithographic

### (G-6557)
**SPEEDY REDI MIX LLC**
6445 S State St (60637-3000)
PHONE.................................773 487-2000
Cordia Forte,
**EMP:** 50
**SALES (est):** 3.3MM **Privately Held**
**SIC:** 3273 Ready-mixed concrete

### (G-6558)
**SPEND RADAR LLC**
311 S Wacker Dr Ste 2270 (60606-6675)
PHONE.................................312 265-0764
Cindy Barlow, *Vice Pres*
Mary Kraft, *VP Finance*
Jim Greenough, *Sales Staff*
Bill Ryan, *Marketing Staff*
Rodney True, *Mng Member*
**EMP:** 30
**SQ FT:** 6,000
**SALES (est):** 2.2MM **Privately Held**
**SIC:** 7372 7379 Application computer software; business oriented computer software; computer related consulting services

### (G-6559)
**SPICY MIX ASIAN AND AMERICAN**
5952 W Roosevelt Rd (60644-1471)
PHONE.................................773 295-5765
Rachadakorn S Arunrung, *President*
**EMP:** 4 **EST:** 2012
**SALES (est):** 279.6K **Privately Held**
**SIC:** 3273 Ready-mixed concrete

### (G-6560)
**SPINNER MEDICAL PRODUCTS INC**
900 N Lake Shore Dr Ste 1 (60611-1544)
PHONE.................................312 944-8700
Gerald R Spinner, *Ch of Bd*
Raymond Spinner, *President*
Millicent Lea, *Corp Secy*
Neal Spinner, *Vice Pres*
Farooq Attawala, *Manager*
**EMP:** 326
**SQ FT:** 375,000
**SALES (est):** 18.5MM **Privately Held**
**SIC:** 3089 Molding primary plastic

### (G-6561)
**SPIRALTECH SUPERIOR DENTAL IMP**
875 N Michigan Ave # 3106 (60611-1803)
PHONE.................................312 440-7777
Jonathan Yahav, *CEO*
Daniel Rosenphal, *Marketing Staff*
**EMP:** 10
**SQ FT:** 2,000
**SALES:** 1MM **Privately Held**
**SIC:** 3843 Orthodontic appliances

### (G-6562)
**SPL-USA LLC**
123 N Wacker Dr (60606-1743)
PHONE.................................312 807-2000
Daniel Nott, *Principal*
**EMP:** 5
**SALES (est):** 378.7K
**SALES (corp-wide):** 3.6B **Privately Held**
**SIC:** 2891 Adhesives & sealants
**HQ:** Morton Salt, Inc.
444 W Lake St Ste 3000
Chicago IL 60606

### (G-6563)
**SPOOKY COOL LABS LLC**
5515 N Cumberland Ave # 810 (60656-4745)
PHONE.................................773 577-5555
Joe Kaminkow,
**EMP:** 40
**SALES (est):** 2.6MM
**SALES (corp-wide):** 741.4MM **Publicly Held**
**SIC:** 7372 Prepackaged software; application computer software
**PA:** Zynga Inc.
699 8th St
San Francisco CA 94103
855 449-9642

### (G-6564)
**SPUDNIK PRESS COOPERATIVE**
1821 W Hubbard St Ste 302 (60622-6273)
PHONE.................................312 563-0302
Angela Lennard, *Principal*
Alison Kleiman, *Vice Pres*
Tom Wilder, *Treasurer*
Megan Klawitter, *Admin Sec*
**EMP:** 11
**SALES:** 192.9K **Privately Held**
**SIC:** 2741 8699 Miscellaneous publishing; charitable organization

### (G-6565)
**SRAM LLC (PA)**
1000 W Fulton Market # 400 (60607-1299)
PHONE.................................312 664-8800
Stanley R Day Jr, *President*
Fk Day, *Exec VP*
Michael D Mercuri, *Vice Pres*
John Nedeau, *Vice Pres*
Edward Herrington, *QC Mgr*
▲ **EMP:** 80
**SQ FT:** 30,000
**SALES (est):** 655.3MM **Privately Held**
**WEB:** www.sram.com
**SIC:** 3751 Gears, motorcycle & bicycle

### (G-6566)
**SSH ENVIRONMENTAL INDS INC (PA)**
875 N Michigan Ave # 4020 (60611-1803)
PHONE.................................312 573-6413
Todd Hamilton, *President*
James Gordon, *Vice Pres*
Boulder Capital, *Shareholder*
**EMP:** 2
**SALES (est):** 7MM **Privately Held**
**SIC:** 3829 Measuring & controlling devices

### (G-6567)
**ST MARYS CEMENT**
12101 S Doty Ave (60633-2322)
PHONE.................................773 995-5100
Dave White, *Principal*
**EMP:** 8
**SALES (est):** 584.3K **Privately Held**
**SIC:** 1422 Cement rock, crushed & broken-quarrying

### (G-6568)
**STAGES CONSTRUCTION INC**
4722 W Harrison St (60644-5122)
PHONE.................................773 619-2977
Nenus Oshana, *President*
**EMP:** 5
**SQ FT:** 7,000
**SALES (est):** 200.5K **Privately Held**
**SIC:** 1799 8711 8741 1389 Construction site cleanup; fence construction; building construction consultant; construction management; construction, repair & dismantling services

### (G-6569)
**STANDARD HEAT TREATING CO INC**
5757 W Ogden Ave (60804-3877)
PHONE.................................708 447-7504
Wendell Matthews, *President*
James Matthews, *Vice Pres*
Wayne Matthews Jr, *Vice Pres*
Walter Santoyl, *Plant Mgr*
**EMP:** 55 **EST:** 1953
**SQ FT:** 35,000
**SALES (est):** 6.5MM **Privately Held**
**SIC:** 3398 Brazing (hardening) of metal; tempering of metal

### (G-6570)
**STANDARD MARBLE & GRANITE**
4551 W 5th Ave (60624-3410)
PHONE.................................773 533-0450
Fax: 773 533-5849
Jeanjacques Porret, *President*
Jean Porret, *President*
Vija Reinfelds, *Corp Secy*
▲ **EMP:** 10
**SQ FT:** 12,000
**SALES (est):** 1MM **Privately Held**
**SIC:** 1743 1741 3281 Terrazzo, tile, marble, mosaic work; marble installation, interior; marble masonry, exterior construction; marble, building: cut & shaped; granite, cut & shaped

### (G-6571)
**STANDARD REGISTER INC**
20 N Wacker Dr Ste 1475 (60606-2915)
PHONE.................................630 784-6833
Charles Grund, *Principal*
David J Caquatto, *Sales & Mktg St*
**EMP:** 13
**SALES (corp-wide):** 4.5B **Privately Held**
**WEB:** www.stdreg.com
**SIC:** 2761 Manifold business forms
**HQ:** Standard Register, Inc.
600 Albany St
Dayton OH 45417
937 221-1000

### (G-6572)
**STANLEY SPRING & STAMPING CORP**
5050 W Foster Ave (60630-1614)
PHONE.................................773 777-2600
Fax: 773 777-3894
Ronald J Banas, *CEO*
Felix Cantu, *Purchasing*
Micheal Godzik, *Controller*
▲ **EMP:** 80 **EST:** 1944
**SQ FT:** 85,000
**SALES (est):** 25.4MM **Privately Held**
**WEB:** www.stanleyspring.com
**SIC:** 3469 3495 3493 Stamping metal for the trade; wire springs; steel springs, except wire

### (G-6573)
**STANRON CORPORATION (PA)**
Also Called: Stanron Steel Specialties Div
5050 W Foster Ave (60630-1614)
PHONE.................................773 777-2600
Ronald J Banas, *President*
Judy Jansen, *Office Mgr*
Frank Petro, *Admin Sec*
**EMP:** 60
**SQ FT:** 2,500
**SALES:** 18MM **Privately Held**
**WEB:** www.stanron.com
**SIC:** 3469 Stamping metal for the trade

### (G-6574)
**STANTON WIND ENERGY LLC**
1 S Wacker Dr Ste 1900 (60606-4644)
PHONE.................................312 224-1400
Invenergy Wind North America L, *Mng Member*
Michael Polsky,
**EMP:** 10
**SALES (est):** 830K **Privately Held**
**SIC:** 3621 Windmills, electric generating

### (G-6575)
**STAR CABINETRY**
4440 W Belmont Ave (60641-4529)
PHONE.................................773 725-4651
Francisco Launas, *President*
**EMP:** 2
**SALES (est):** 202.3K **Privately Held**
**SIC:** 2499 Decorative wood & woodwork

### (G-6576)
**STARFRUIT LLC**
222 Merchandise Mart Plz # 238 (60654-1008)
PHONE.................................312 527-3674
Missy Seffner, *Principal*
**EMP:** 3
**SALES (est):** 179.4K **Privately Held**
**SIC:** 2026 Yogurt

### (G-6577)
**STARLINE DESIGNS**
750 E 43rd St (60653-2947)
PHONE.................................773 683-7506
**EMP:** 4 **EST:** 2010
**SALES:** 100K **Privately Held**
**SIC:** 2262 Manmade Fiber & Silk Finishing Plant

### (G-6578)
**STATE OF ILLINOIS**
Also Called: Office of Spcial Dputy Rceiver
222 Merchandise Mart Plz # 1450 (60654-1103)
PHONE.................................312 836-9500
Fax: 312 836-1944
Asha Puri, *President*
Donna Alt, *Technology*
**EMP:** 137 **Privately Held**
**WEB:** www.idfpr.com
**SIC:** 3663 9651 8742 8111 Radio receiver networks; insurance commission, government; management consulting services; legal services; real estate agents & managers
**HQ:** State Of Illinois
320 W Washington St Fl 3
Springfield IL 62701
217 785-0820

### (G-6579)
**STAY STRAIGHT MANUFACTURING**
4145 W Kinzie St (60624-1715)
PHONE.................................312 226-2137
Louis Brandt, *President*
**EMP:** 4 **EST:** 1999
**SQ FT:** 5,000
**SALES (est):** 495K **Privately Held**
**WEB:** www.staystraight.com
**SIC:** 2521 Wood office furniture

### (G-6580)
**STEEL GUARD INC**
4707 W North Ave (60639-4612)
PHONE.................................773 342-6265
Gonzalo Briseno, *President*
Esther Grau, *Vice Pres*
**EMP:** 10
**SQ FT:** 6,000
**SALES (est):** 1.4MM **Privately Held**
**SIC:** 3089 3496 3446 Fences, gates & accessories: plastic; miscellaneous fabricated wire products; architectural metalwork

### (G-6581)
**STEELCASE INC**
222 Merchandise Mart Plz # 1032 (60654-1175)
P.O. Box 99315 (60693-9315)
PHONE.................................312 321-3720
Fax: 312 321-3860
Carly Johnston, *Consultant*
**EMP:** 12
**SALES (corp-wide):** 3B **Publicly Held**
**WEB:** www.steelcase.com
**SIC:** 2522 2521 Office furniture, except wood; wood office furniture
**PA:** Steelcase Inc.
901 44th St Se
Grand Rapids MI 49508
616 247-2710

### (G-6582)
**STEELWERKS OF CHICAGO LLC**
4257 W Drummond Pl Unit E (60639-2004)
PHONE.................................312 792-9593
Gregory Frost, *Principal*
**EMP:** 5
**SALES (est):** 202K **Privately Held**
**SIC:** 3449 3441 3446 3548 Miscellaneous metalwork; fabricated structural metal; architectural metalwork; stairs, fire escapes, balconies, railings & ladders; welding apparatus

# GEOGRAPHIC SECTION

Chicago - Cook County (G-6609)

**(G-6583)**
**STEINBACH PROVISION COMPANY**
741 W 47th St (60609-4409)
PHONE..................773 538-1511
Fax: 773 538-3131
Tom Steinbach, *President*
Jean Ellitch, *Office Mgr*
**EMP:** 7 **EST:** 1945
**SQ FT:** 7,000
**SALES:** 5MM **Privately Held**
**SIC:** 2011 2013 Meat packing plants; sausages & other prepared meats

**(G-6584)**
**STEINER ELECTRIC COMPANY**
Steiner/Excell Motor Repair
2225 W Hubbard St (60612-1613)
PHONE..................312 421-7220
Ted Mussatti, *Human Res Dir*
Michael Wojtulewicz, *Accounts Mgr*
Pete Reitsch, *Sales Engr*
John Anderson, *Sales Staff*
Jim Gattone, *Sales Staff*
**EMP:** 50
**SALES (corp-wide):** 222MM **Privately Held**
**WEB:** www.stnr.com
**SIC:** 5063 7694 Electrical apparatus & equipment; electrical supplies; electric motor repair
**PA:** Steiner Electric Company
1250 Touhy Ave
Elk Grove Village IL 60007
847 228-0400

**(G-6585)**
**STEINER INDUSTRIES INC**
5801 N Tripp Ave (60646-6013)
PHONE..................773 588-3444
Fax: 773 588-3450
Robert J Steiner, *President*
Rafael Kramer, *General Mgr*
Robert H Gerstein, *Corp Secy*
Kim Maryniarczyk, *Purchasing*
Debbie McHugh, *Sls & Mktg Exec*
▲ **EMP:** 60
**SQ FT:** 45,000 **Privately Held**
**WEB:** www.steinerindustries.com
**SIC:** 3842 Personal safety equipment

**(G-6586)**
**STEINMETZ R (US) LTD**
Also Called: Orli Diamonds
67 E Madison St Ste 1606 (60603-3062)
PHONE..................312 332-0990
Isaac De Kalo, *President*
Eytan De Kalo, *Vice Pres*
**EMP:** 4
**SALES (est):** 676.4K **Privately Held**
**WEB:** www.orlidiamonds.com
**SIC:** 5094 3915 Diamonds (gems); jewelry; diamond cutting & polishing; jewel cutting, drilling, polishing, recutting or setting

**(G-6587)**
**STELLAR PERFORMANCE MFG LLC (PA)**
640 N La Salle Dr Ste 540 (60654-3749)
PHONE..................312 951-2311
▲ **EMP:** 11
**SALES (est):** 2.8MM **Privately Held**
**SIC:** 2821 Plastics materials & resins

**(G-6588)**
**STELLAR RECOGNITION INC**
Also Called: Sports Awards
5544 W Armstrong Ave (60646-6514)
PHONE..................773 282-8060
Fax: 773 282-3019
Roy T Newton, *President*
Vien Tom, *Accountant*
Eileen M Newton, *Admin Sec*
▲ **EMP:** 80
**SQ FT:** 23,000
**SALES (est):** 13.5MM **Privately Held**
**WEB:** www.sportsawardsonline.com
**SIC:** 3914 3999 2396 3993 Trophies, plated (all metals); plaques, picture, laminated; ribbons & bows, cut & sewed; advertising novelties; commercial printing

**(G-6589)**
**STEREO OPTICAL COMPANY INC**
8600 W Catalpa Ave (60656-1116)
PHONE..................773 867-0380
Christophe Condat, *President*
Fouad Amghar, *Project Mgr*
Teri Zelasko, *Opers Mgr*
Lisa Tolson, *Mktg Coord*
Terri Zblasko, *Manager*
**EMP:** 15
**SQ FT:** 10,000
**SALES (est):** 4.2MM
**SALES (corp-wide):** 938.9MM **Privately Held**
**WEB:** www.nationaloptronics.com
**SIC:** 3841 Ophthalmic instruments & apparatus; retinoscopes
**HQ:** Essilor Of America, Inc.
13555 N Stemmons Fwy
Dallas TX 75234
214 496-4000

**(G-6590)**
**STERLING PLATING INC**
4629 N Ronald St (60706-4718)
PHONE..................708 867-6587
Herbert Degrenier, *CEO*
Colette Sherwin, *President*
Marcia Jerzyk, *Admin Sec*
**EMP:** 20
**SQ FT:** 16,000
**SALES:** 2MM **Privately Held**
**WEB:** www.sterling-labs.com
**SIC:** 3471 Electroplating of metals or formed products

**(G-6591)**
**STERLING SPRING LLC (PA)**
Also Called: Wesco
5432 W 54th St (60638-2998)
PHONE..................773 582-6464
Fax: 773 582-0657
Mike Malesky, *General Mgr*
Stanley Graczyk, *Plant Mgr*
Anthony Massaro, *Treasurer*
Eric Dickinson, *Accounts Mgr*
Robert D Dickinson, *Mng Member*
**EMP:** 60
**SQ FT:** 50,000
**SALES:** 19.2MM **Privately Held**
**SIC:** 3495 Wire springs

**(G-6592)**
**STERLING SPRING LLC**
Also Called: Wesco
7171 W 65th St (60638-4605)
PHONE..................773 772-9331
Melissa Trudgen, *Human Resources*
**EMP:** 43
**SALES (corp-wide):** 19.2MM **Privately Held**
**SIC:** 3495 Wire springs
**PA:** Sterling Spring, L.L.C.
5432 W 54th St
Chicago IL 60638
773 582-6464

**(G-6593)**
**STEROIDS LTD**
1255 N State Pkwy (60610-8206)
PHONE..................312 996-2364
**EMP:** 5
**SALES:** 500K **Privately Held**
**SIC:** 2899 Chemical preparations

**(G-6594)**
**STEVEN MADDEN LTD**
1553 N Milwaukee Ave (60622-2009)
PHONE..................773 276-5486
Steve Madden, *Principal*
**EMP:** 75
**SALES (corp-wide):** 1.4B **Publicly Held**
**SIC:** 3143 Men's footwear, except athletic
**PA:** Steven Madden, Ltd.
5216 Barnett Ave
Long Island City NY 11104
718 446-1800

**(G-6595)**
**STEVENS EXHIBITS & DISPLAYS**
3900 S Union Ave (60609-2623)
PHONE..................773 523-3900
Thomas Mc Kernin, *President*
Charles Mc Kernin, *Treasurer*
Edie Fogarty, *Accountant*
Sharon Mc Kernin, *Admin Sec*
**EMP:** 35 **EST:** 1966
**SQ FT:** 94,000
**SALES:** 2MM **Privately Held**
**WEB:** www.stevensexhibits.com
**SIC:** 7389 3993 Trade show arrangement; displays & cutouts, window & lobby

**(G-6596)**
**STEWART INGRDIENTS SYSTEMS INC**
1843 W Fulton St (60612-2511)
PHONE..................312 254-3539
Fax: 312 666-1541
Keith F Stewart, *President*
Bill Braun, *Vice Pres*
Constantine Nicholas, *Treasurer*
Celine Stewart, *Treasurer*
Ross Stewart, *Sales Staff*
**EMP:** 18
**SQ FT:** 15,000
**SALES (est):** 3.7MM **Privately Held**
**WEB:** www.ksfpro.com
**SIC:** 2033 Jellies, edible, including imitation: in cans, jars, etc.; fruits: packaged in cans, jars, etc.

**(G-6597)**
**STOCK MANUFACTURING CO LLC**
316 N Michigan Ave Frnt 2 (60601-3774)
PHONE..................773 265-6640
Ives Areill, *Principal*
**EMP:** 3
**SALES (est):** 231.8K **Privately Held**
**SIC:** 3999 Manufacturing industries

**(G-6598)**
**STONE USA INC**
1234 S Michigan Ave Ste D (60605-2596)
PHONE..................312 356-0988
Thomas Gilkos, *President*
▲ **EMP:** 7
**SALES (est):** 548.4K **Privately Held**
**SIC:** 1411 Dimension stone

**(G-6599)**
**STONEPEAK CERAMICS INC (DH)**
Also Called: Euro West Decorative Surfaces
314 W Superior St Ste 201 (60654-3538)
PHONE..................312 335-0321
Fax: 312 335-0533
Romano Minozzi, *President*
Milko Camellini, *Plant Mgr*
Jordan Wallace, *Purch Mgr*
Jamie Bostaph, *Purchasing*
Andrea Bertelli, *QC Mgr*
▲ **EMP:** 25
**SQ FT:** 15,000
**SALES (est):** 57.3MM **Privately Held**
**WEB:** www.stonepeakceramics.com
**SIC:** 3253 Mosaic tile, glazed & unglazed: ceramic
**HQ:** Granitifiandre Spa
Via Radici Nord 112
Castellarano RE 42014
053 681-9611

**(G-6600)**
**STORIANT INC**
70 W Madison St Ste 2300 (60602-4250)
P.O. Box 182, Marblehead MA (01945-0182)
PHONE..................617 431-8000
Jeffry Flowers, *President*
John Hogan, *Vice Pres*
Rick Ruskin, *VP Sales*
Amy Berenson, *Director*
Susan Pravda, *Admin Sec*
**EMP:** 34
**SQ FT:** 6,500
**SALES (est):** 2.2MM **Privately Held**
**SIC:** 7372 Prepackaged software; business oriented computer software

**(G-6601)**
**STORMS INDUSTRIES INC**
1500 S Western Ave Ste 5 (60608-1828)
PHONE..................312 243-7480
Fax: 312 243-6879
William A Ross, *President*
Dave Murphy, *Principal*
David Gilliam, *Manager*
▲ **EMP:** 35
**SQ FT:** 16,000
**SALES:** 9MM **Privately Held**
**WEB:** www.stormsindustries.com
**SIC:** 5087 3564 Laundry equipment & supplies; filters, air: furnaces, air conditioning equipment, etc.

**(G-6602)**
**STRATEGIC MATERIALS INC**
10330 S Woodlawn Ave (60628-3050)
PHONE..................773 523-2200
Dan Jania, *Manager*
**EMP:** 3
**SQ FT:** 5,000 **Privately Held**
**SIC:** 4953 3231 Recycling, waste materials; products of purchased glass
**HQ:** Strategic Materials, Inc.
16365 Park Ten Pl Ste 200
Houston TX 77084
281 647-2700

**(G-6603)**
**STREAMLINED BAKING CO**
3945 W Armitage Ave (60647-3450)
PHONE..................773 227-2635
Konstantina Georgopoulos, *President*
**EMP:** 14
**SALES:** 500K **Privately Held**
**SIC:** 2051 Cakes, pies & pastries

**(G-6604)**
**STREETWISE**
4554 N Broadway St # 350 (60640-7962)
PHONE..................773 334-6600
James Lobianco, *Exec Dir*
**EMP:** 16
**SQ FT:** 3,500
**SALES:** 796.3K **Privately Held**
**SIC:** 2711 Newspapers, publishing & printing

**(G-6605)**
**STRESS FREE COOKIES INC**
605 N Ridgeway Ave (60624-1274)
PHONE..................312 856-7686
Tony Jarrett, *President*
**EMP:** 6
**SALES:** 25K **Privately Held**
**SIC:** 2052 Cookies & crackers

**(G-6606)**
**STRETCH CHI**
4765 N Lincoln Ave # 207 (60625-2077)
PHONE..................773 420-9355
Carrie L Collins, *Owner*
**EMP:** 2 **EST:** 2011
**SALES (est):** 217.8K **Privately Held**
**SIC:** 3841 Muscle exercise apparatus, ophthalmic

**(G-6607)**
**STRIVE CONVERTING CORPORATION**
4545 W Palmer St (60639-3421)
PHONE..................773 227-6000
Fax: 773 227-2645
Michael K Waite, *President*
Paul Kracun, *Purchasing*
Scott Weldon, *Controller*
Mike Harper, *VP Sales*
Larry Maravilla, *Sales Staff*
▲ **EMP:** 160 **EST:** 1982
**SQ FT:** 235,000
**SALES (est):** 20.2MM **Privately Held**
**SIC:** 2653 Boxes, corrugated: made from purchased materials; display items, corrugated: made from purchased materials

**(G-6608)**
**STRYKER CORPORATION**
Stryker Performance Solutions
350 N Orleans St (60654-1975)
PHONE..................312 386-9780
**EMP:** 412
**SALES (corp-wide):** 11.3B **Publicly Held**
**SIC:** 3841 Surgical instruments & apparatus
**PA:** Stryker Corporation
2825 Airview Blvd
Portage MI 49002
269 385-2600

**(G-6609)**
**STUMPFOLL TOOL & MFG**
1713 W Hubbard St (60622-6213)
PHONE..................312 733-2632

# Chicago - Cook County (G-6610) — GEOGRAPHIC SECTION

**Fax:** 312 733-2632
Joseph Stumpfoll, *Owner*
**EMP:** 7
**SQ FT:** 7,500
**SALES (est):** 300K Privately Held
**SIC:** 3469 3544 Stamping metal for the trade; special dies, tools, jigs & fixtures

### (G-6610)
### STUTZ COMPANY
4450 W Carroll Ave (60624-1696)
**PHONE**................................773 287-1068
**Fax:** 773 287-4303
Gerald L Stutz, *President*
Paul David Stutz, *Corp Secy*
James Stutz, *Vice Pres*
Joette Ojeda, *Purchasing*
▲ **EMP:** 16 EST: 1921
**SQ FT:** 30,000
**SALES (est):** 8.5MM Privately Held
**WEB:** www.stutzcompany.com
**SIC:** 5084 5169 3559 2899 Industrial machinery & equipment; industrial chemicals; metal finishing equipment for plating, etc.; plating compounds

### (G-6611)
### SUCCESS PUBLISHING GROUP INC
Also Called: Comptons Encyclopedia
310 S Michigan Ave Fl 9 (60604-4207)
**PHONE**................................708 565-2681
Fred Bruno, *CEO*
Mike Capetanakis, *President*
**EMP:** 14
**SALES:** 3MM Privately Held
**SIC:** 2731 Textbooks: publishing & printing

### (G-6612)
### SUCCESS VENDING MFG CO LLC
Also Called: International Services
5128 W Irving Park Rd (60641-2624)
**PHONE**................................773 262-1685
Chris Pentell, *Partner*
Steve Zatz, *Partner*
**EMP:** 22
**SQ FT:** 22,000
**SALES:** 14.2MM Privately Held
**SIC:** 3581 Automatic vending machines

### (G-6613)
### SUKIE GROUP INC
4115 W Ogden Ave Ste 1 (60623-2805)
**PHONE**................................773 521-1800
Suk Y Rapavi, *President*
Michael Tinoco, *Manager*
▲ **EMP:** 19
**SQ FT:** 4,000
**SALES (est):** 2.2MM Privately Held
**WEB:** www.globalcases.com
**SIC:** 3111 3161 5099 Case leather; cases, carrying; luggage

### (G-6614)
### SULLIVAN CGLIANO TRAINING CTRS (PA)
Also Called: Advanced Careers Learning Ctrs
203 N La Salle St Fl M18 (60601-1253)
**PHONE**................................312 422-0009
**Fax:** 312 782-3789
Herb Cogluiano, *President*
Larry Pratcher, *Principal*
Shibu Thomas, *Principal*
Sheila Chapman, *Vice Pres*
Mark Gallagher, *Vice Pres*
**EMP:** 4
**SALES (est):** 1MM Privately Held
**SIC:** 7372 Business oriented computer software

### (G-6615)
### SULTRY SATCHELS
8111 S Morgan St (60620-3020)
**PHONE**................................773 873-5718
Cynthia Simmons, *Owner*
Charessa McNeil, *Co-Owner*
**EMP:** 3
**SALES (est):** 100K Privately Held
**SIC:** 2211 Bags & bagging, cotton

### (G-6616)
### SULTRY SATCHELS INC
8159 S Troy St (60652-2616)
**PHONE**................................312 810-1081
Charessa Maiden-Mcneal, *Principal*
**EMP:** 3
**SALES (est):** 175.6K Privately Held
**SIC:** 3161 Satchels

### (G-6617)
### SUMMITT MEDIA GROUP INC
330 N Wabash Ave Ste 2401 (60611-7618)
**PHONE**................................312 222-1010
**Fax:** 312 222-1310
Lloyd Ferguson, *President*
Todd Mathes, *General Mgr*
Iris Zavala, *General Mgr*
Steve Schlegel, *Managing Dir*
Steve Sterling, *Editor*
▲ **EMP:** 30
**SQ FT:** 3,500
**SALES (est):** 4.5MM
**SALES (corp-wide):** 45.4MM Privately Held
**WEB:** www.packworld.com
**SIC:** 2721 Magazines: publishing only, not printed on site
**PA:** Packaging Machinery Manufacturers Institute, Incorporated
11911 Freedom Dr Ste 600
Reston VA 20190
703 243-8555

### (G-6618)
### SUN DOME INC
3641 S Washtenaw Ave (60632-1645)
**PHONE**................................773 890-5350
Ashley Ross, *President*
**EMP:** 12
**SALES (est):** 1.8MM Privately Held
**SIC:** 3089 Closures, plastic

### (G-6619)
### SUN GRAPHIC INC (DH)
5540 N Northwest Hwy (60630-1116)
**PHONE**................................773 775-6755
Charles L Palmer, *Ch of Bd*
Mark Monahan, *Mfg Staff*
Ralph Zarada, *QC Mgr*
James Nowaczyk, *Info Tech Mgr*
David Hill, *Admin Sec*
▼ **EMP:** 35
**SQ FT:** 25,000
**SALES (est):** 5.7MM
**SALES (corp-wide):** 6.7B Privately Held
**WEB:** www.sungraphic.com
**SIC:** 3555 Printing trade parts & attachments
**HQ:** Sun Chemical Corporation
35 Waterview Blvd Ste 100
Parsippany NJ 07054
973 404-6000

### (G-6620)
### SUN-TMES MDIA PRODUCTIONS LLC
350 N Orleans St Ste 10s (60654-1975)
**PHONE**................................312 321-2299
**EMP:** 1
**SALES (est):** 263.6K
**SALES (corp-wide):** 304.8MM Privately Held
**SIC:** 2711 7313 Newspapers; electronic media advertising representatives; printed media advertising representatives
**HQ:** Sun-Times Media Holdings, Llc
350 N Orleans St Ste 1000
Chicago IL 60654

### (G-6621)
### SUN-TIMES MEDIA LLC
350 N Orleans St Ste 1000 (60654-1700)
**PHONE**................................312 321-3000
**Fax:** 312 321-2288
Richard Babcock, *Editor*
Jim Emerson, *Editor*
Julie Parker, *Manager*
Tim Knight,
**EMP:** 68
**SALES (est):** 6.2MM Privately Held
**SIC:** 2711 Newspapers; publishing & printing

### (G-6622)
### SUN-TIMES MEDIA LLC
350 N Orleans St Ste 1000 (60654-1700)
**PHONE**................................312 321-2299
Jeremy Halbreich, *Executive*
Jeremy L Halbreich,
**EMP:** 10
**SALES (est):** 749.6K
**SALES (corp-wide):** 304.8MM Privately Held
**SIC:** 2711 7313 Newspapers; electronic media advertising representatives; printed media advertising representatives
**HQ:** Sun-Times Media Holdings, Llc
350 N Orleans St Ste 1000
Chicago IL 60654

### (G-6623)
### SUN-TIMES MEDIA GROUP INC (DH)
350 N Orleans St Fl 10 (60654-1975)
**PHONE**................................312 321-2299
**Fax:** 312 321-0629
Tim Knight, *CEO*
Jeremy Deedes, *CEO*
Jerry J Strader, *President*
Blair Richard Surkamer, *President*
David C Martin, *Senior VP*
**EMP:** 64
**SQ FT:** 320,000
**SALES (est):** 302.9MM
**SALES (corp-wide):** 304.8MM Privately Held
**WEB:** www.hollinger.com
**SIC:** 2711 Newspapers, publishing & printing

### (G-6624)
### SUN-TIMES MEDIA HOLDINGS LLC (HQ)
350 N Orleans St Ste 1000 (60654-1700)
**PHONE**................................312 321-2299
Timothy P Knight, *CEO*
Rodney O'Neal, *CEO*
Bradley Phillip Bell, *President*
John A Canning, *Chairman*
Michael W Ferro, *Chairman*
**EMP:** 24
**SALES (est):** 304.8MM Privately Held
**SIC:** 2711 Newspapers; publishing & printing
**PA:** Wrapports, Llc
350 N Orleans St 10thf
Chicago IL 60654
312 321-3000

### (G-6625)
### SUN-TIMES MEDIA OPERATIONS LLC
350 N Orleans St Fl 10 (60654-1975)
**PHONE**................................312 321-2299
Jeremy L Halbreich,
**EMP:** 3
**SALES (est):** 115.1K Privately Held
**SIC:** 2711 7313 Newspapers; electronic media advertising representatives; printed media advertising representatives

### (G-6626)
### SUNDSTROM PRESSED STEEL CO
8030 S South Chicago Ave (60617-1029)
**PHONE**................................773 721-2237
**Fax:** 773 721-9534
Richard F Sundstrom, *President*
Herbert D Rentschler, *Vice Pres*
Calvin Thomas, *Manager*
Robert J Barnes, *Admin Sec*
▲ **EMP:** 25
**SQ FT:** 53,000
**SALES (est):** 5.4MM Privately Held
**WEB:** www.cisatlantic.com
**SIC:** 3469 Stamping metal for the trade

### (G-6627)
### SUNNY ENTERPRISES INC
Also Called: Subway 25858
2811 S Kedzie Ave (60623-4712)
**PHONE**................................847 219-1045
Pratik Patel, *President*
Shakuben D Patel, *Vice Pres*
Dilip Patel, *Admin Sec*
**EMP:** 10
**SQ FT:** 2,500
**SALES:** 750K Privately Held
**SIC:** 2099 Ready-to-eat meals, salads & sandwiches

### (G-6628)
### SUNRISE FUTURES LLC
30 S Wacker Dr Ste 1706 (60606-7414)
**PHONE**................................312 612-1041
Allan San, *Principal*
**EMP:** 5
**SALES (est):** 772K Privately Held
**SIC:** 7372 Prepackaged software

### (G-6629)
### SUNRISE HITEK GROUP LLC
5915 N Northwest Hwy (60631-2644)
**PHONE**................................773 792-8880
Jimmy Sun, *President*
▲ **EMP:** 25
**SALES (est):** 1.7MM Privately Held
**SIC:** 2732 5734 Books: printing & binding; computer software & accessories

### (G-6630)
### SUNRISE HITEK SERVICE INC
Also Called: Sunrise Digital
5915 N Northwest Hwy (60631-2644)
**PHONE**................................773 792-8880
**Fax:** 773 792-8881
Libo Sun, *President*
Jimmy Sun, *President*
Steven Miller, *General Mgr*
Fran Sun, *Finance Mgr*
Katie Kelly, *Accounts Mgr*
▲ **EMP:** 20
**SQ FT:** 14,000
**SALES (est):** 3.6MM Privately Held
**WEB:** www.sunrisehitek.com
**SIC:** 2759 7389 2796 2752 Commercial printing; design services; platemaking services; commercial printing, lithographic; miscellaneous publishing

### (G-6631)
### SUNSET HALTHCARE SOLUTIONS INC
180 N Michigan Ave # 2000 (60601-7401)
**PHONE**................................877 578-6738
Christopher Slosar, *President*
Greg Wood, *Vice Pres*
Paul Ruflin, *Sales Dir*
Mike Chorney, *Manager*
Phil Cosens, *Manager*
▲ **EMP:** 40
**SALES (est):** 7.9MM Privately Held
**SIC:** 3841 Cannulae

### (G-6632)
### SUPERIOR GRAPHITE CO (PA)
10 S Riverside Plz # 1470 (60606-3838)
**PHONE**................................312 559-2999
**Fax:** 312 559-9064
Edward O Carney, *President*
Mark Wanta, *General Mgr*
Peter R Carney, *Chairman*
Jorge Ayala, *Business Mgr*
Ron G Pawelko, *Senior VP*
◆ **EMP:** 35
**SALES (est):** 79.8MM Privately Held
**SIC:** 3295 Graphite, natural: ground, pulverized, refined or blended

### (G-6633)
### SUPERIOR GRAPHITE CO
6540 S Laramie Ave (60638-6499)
**PHONE**................................708 458-0006
**Fax:** 708 594-1474
Roberto Diaz, *Opers Mgr*
Denis Murphy, *Branch Mgr*
Gerardo Mora, *Manager*
Sonia Vargas, *Manager*
James Bruley, *Director*
**EMP:** 50
**SQ FT:** 30,000
**SALES (corp-wide):** 79.8MM Privately Held
**SIC:** 3295 3823 3624 2992 Graphite, natural: ground, pulverized, refined or blended; industrial instrmnts msrmnt display/control process variable; carbon & graphite products; lubricating oils & greases
**PA:** Superior Graphite Co.
10 S Riverside Plz # 1470
Chicago IL 60606
312 559-2999

### (G-6634)
### SUPERIOR GRAPHITE CO
4201 W 36th St Bldg Rear (60632-3825)
**PHONE**................................773 890-4100
**Fax:** 773 890-4102
Laura Kroschel, *Traffic Mgr*
Francois Henry, *Research*

▲ = Import ▼ = Export
◆ = Import/Export

Charles Noorman, *Sales Mgr*
Alla Miroshnychenko, *Marketing Staff*
Denis Murphy, *Manager*
**EMP:** 20
**SALES (corp-wide):** 79.8MM **Privately Held**
**SIC:** 3295 Graphite, natural: ground, pulverized, refined or blended
**PA:** Superior Graphite Co.
10 S Riverside Plz # 1470
Chicago IL 60606
312 559-2999

**(G-6635)**
**SUPERIOR MFG GROUP - EUROPE (PA)**
5655 W 73rd St Bestle Par (60638)
**PHONE** .................................. 708 458-4600
John V Wood, *CEO*
Vincent De Phillips, *President*
Charles F Wood, *Vice Pres*
Michael P Wood, *Treasurer*
Robin Brink, *Accounting Mgr*
▲ **EMP:** 10
**SALES (est):** 1.7MM **Privately Held**
**SIC:** 3069 5085 Door mats, rubber; industrial supplies

**(G-6636)**
**SUPERIOR TABLE PAD CO**
3010 N Oakley Ave (60618-8000)
**PHONE** .................................. 773 248-7232
**Fax:** 773 935-7192
Steven Antler, *President*
Geoffrey Garland, *Vice Pres*
**EMP:** 9 **EST:** 1937
**SQ FT:** 10,000
**SALES (est):** 1.2MM **Privately Held**
**WEB:** www.superiortablepad.com
**SIC:** 2392 3949 Pads & padding, table: except asbestos, felt or rattan; sporting & athletic goods

**(G-6637)**
**SUPPLY VISION INC**
220 N Green St (60607-1702)
**PHONE** .................................. 847 388-0064
Mike Powell, *CEO*
Cris Arens, *Principal*
**EMP:** 2
**SALES (est):** 219.8K **Privately Held**
**SIC:** 7372 Business oriented computer software

**(G-6638)**
**SUPREME FRAME & MOULDING CO**
652 W Randolph St (60661-2114)
**PHONE** .................................. 312 930-9056
**Fax:** 312 930-9268
Barry Fript, *President*
Leonard Fript, *Corp Secy*
**EMP:** 10 **EST:** 1935
**SQ FT:** 25,000
**SALES:** 1MM **Privately Held**
**SIC:** 2499 7699 5719 3499 Picture frame molding, finished; picture framing, custom; pictures, wall; picture frames, metal; metal doors, sash & trim

**(G-6639)**
**SUPREME JUICE CO**
1307 S Pulaski Rd (60623-1236)
**PHONE** .................................. 773 277-5800
**Fax:** 773 277-5801
Shabir Kassam, *President*
**EMP:** 13 **EST:** 1989
**SQ FT:** 20,000
**SALES (est):** 2.2MM **Privately Held**
**WEB:** www.beverageonline.com
**SIC:** 2087 Beverage bases

**(G-6640)**
**SURCOM INDUSTRIES INC**
1017 N Cicero Ave (60651-3202)
**PHONE** .................................. 773 378-0736
**Fax:** 773 378-2083
Scott Rempala, *President*
Scott Rampala, *CFO*
Natalie Rempala, *Manager*
**EMP:** 6
**SALES (est):** 451.1K **Privately Held**
**SIC:** 3471 Plating & polishing

**(G-6641)**
**SURFACE SOLUTIONS GROUP LLC**
5492 N Northwest Hwy (60630-1114)
**PHONE** .................................. 773 427-2084
Mike Osterhout, *Plant Mgr*
David Garza, *Office Mgr*
Bruce Nesbitt,
Jackie Mals, *Admin Asst*
George Osterhout,
**EMP:** 60 **EST:** 2011
**SQ FT:** 6,800
**SALES (est):** 5.2MM
**SALES (corp-wide):** 24.4MM **Privately Held**
**SIC:** 3479 Painting, coating & hot dipping
**PA:** Orion Industries, Ltd.
5492 N Northwest Hwy
Chicago IL 60630
773 282-9100

**(G-6642)**
**SURPLUS RECORD LLC**
20 N Wacker Dr Ste 2400 (60606-3004)
**PHONE** .................................. 312 372-9077
Thomas C Scanlan, *President*
**EMP:** 12 **EST:** 1924
**SQ FT:** 3,000
**SALES (est):** 24.8K **Privately Held**
**SIC:** 2721 Periodicals

**(G-6643)**
**SUSTAINABLE HOLDING INC**
7122 S Oglesby Ave (60649-2516)
**PHONE** .................................. 773 324-0407
Brian Smith, *CEO*
Ronald McMillon, *President*
Gerald Christensen, *CTO*
**EMP:** 4
**SALES (est):** 200K **Privately Held**
**SIC:** 3999 5531 7389 Manufacturing industries; automotive accessories;

**(G-6644)**
**SUSTANBLE SLTIONS AMER LED LLC**
Also Called: Sustainable Solutions Amer Led
910 W Van Buren St Ste 6a (60607-7900)
**PHONE** .................................. 866 323-3494
William Ryan, *CEO*
Dale Bianco, *CFO*
**EMP:** 15
**SQ FT:** 30,000
**SALES (est):** 2.8MM **Privately Held**
**SIC:** 3646 Commercial indusl & institutional electric lighting fixtures

**(G-6645)**
**SUZLON WIND ENERGY CORPORATION (HQ)**
8750 W Bryn Mawr Ave # 300 (60631-3521)
**PHONE** .................................. 773 328-5077
**Fax:** 773 444-0588
Duncan Koerbel, *CEO*
Terri Denning, *General Mgr*
Jitendra Deshpande, *General Mgr*
Jaya Prakash, *General Mgr*
Rahul Limje, *COO*
▲ **EMP:** 237
**SALES (est):** 97.5MM **Privately Held**
**WEB:** www.suzlon.com
**SIC:** 3511 Turbines & turbine generator sets

**(G-6646)**
**SWABY MANUFACTURING COMPANY (PA)**
5420 W Roosevelt Rd 300b (60644-1439)
**PHONE** .................................. 773 626-1400
**Fax:** 773 626-3646
Mohammad Khalil, *President*
Kay Khalil, *Office Mgr*
Kuzida Khalil, *Admin Sec*
▲ **EMP:** 8 **EST:** 1893
**SQ FT:** 2,500
**SALES (est):** 4.3MM **Privately Held**
**SIC:** 3561 Pumps, domestic: water or sump; industrial pumps & parts

**(G-6647)**
**SWEET BEGINNINGS LLC**
3726 W Flournoy St (60624-3612)
**PHONE** .................................. 773 638-7058
Brenda Palms Barber, *CEO*
**EMP:** 8
**SALES (est):** 574.8K **Privately Held**
**SIC:** 2099 3999 Honey, strained & bottled; beekeepers' supplies

**(G-6648)**
**SWEET MANUFACTURING CORP**
111 E Chestnut St Apt 36k (60611-6013)
**PHONE** .................................. 847 546-5575
**Fax:** 847 546-9675
Richard K Sweet, *President*
Helen R Sweet, *Admin Sec*
▲ **EMP:** 30
**SQ FT:** 5,000
**SALES (est):** 256.3K **Privately Held**
**WEB:** www.sweetlok.com
**SIC:** 3429 3469 Cabinet hardware; metal stampings

**(G-6649)**
**SWIFT EDUCATION SYSTEMS INC**
332 S Michigan Ave # 1032 (60604-4434)
**PHONE** .................................. 312 257-3751
Louie Huang, *CEO*
Zachary Schneirov, *President*
William Nelson, *Admin Sec*
**EMP:** 3
**SALES (est):** 163.6K **Privately Held**
**SIC:** 7372 Educational computer software

**(G-6650)**
**SWIFT IMPRESSIONS INC**
Also Called: Cut Rate Printers
70 E Lake St Ste 1000 (60601-7627)
**PHONE** .................................. 312 263-3800
**Fax:** 312 372-0005
Tony Musto, *President*
Carolyn Musto, *Vice Pres*
Andrew McNally, *Manager*
**EMP:** 4
**SQ FT:** 940
**SALES (est):** 410K **Privately Held**
**SIC:** 2752 Commercial printing, offset

**(G-6651)**
**SWISS PRODUCTS LP**
4333 W Division St (60651-1792)
**PHONE** .................................. 773 394-6480
**Fax:** 773 394-6475
Senya R Kalpake, *Partner*
Paul Kalpake, *General Ptnr*
**EMP:** 39 **EST:** 1941
**SQ FT:** 50,000
**SALES (est):** 7.4MM **Privately Held**
**WEB:** www.swissfoodproducts.com
**SIC:** 2034 2099 Dehydrated fruits, vegetables, soups; gravy mixes, dry; seasonings: dry mixes; spices, including grinding

**(G-6652)**
**SWISSPORT FUELING INCORPO**
5000 W 63rd St (60638-5719)
**PHONE** .................................. 773 203-5419
**EMP:** 5
**SALES (est):** 695K **Privately Held**
**SIC:** 2869 Fuels

**(G-6653)**
**SWITCHCRAFT INC (HQ)**
5555 N Elston Ave (60630-1386)
**PHONE** .................................. 773 792-2700
**Fax:** 773 792-2129
Keith A Bandolik, *President*
Cheryl Book, *President*
Pantaleon Koulogeorge, *Engineer*
Nicholas Wahoff, *Engineer*
Diane Lazaar, *Regl Sales Mgr*
▲ **EMP:** 365 **EST:** 1946
**SQ FT:** 220,000
**SALES (est):** 74.8MM
**SALES (corp-wide):** 1.3B **Publicly Held**
**WEB:** www.switchcraft.com
**SIC:** 3613 3679 3663 3661 Switchgear & switchboard apparatus; electronic switches; radio & TV communications equipment; telephone cords, jacks, adapters, etc.; electronic connectors; current-carrying wiring devices
**PA:** Heico Corporation
3000 Taft St
Hollywood FL 33021
954 987-4000

**(G-6654)**
**SWITCHCRAFT HOLDCO INC (HQ)**
5555 N Elston Ave (60630-1386)
**PHONE** .................................. 773 792-2700
Keith A Bandolik, *President*
▲ **EMP:** 7
**SALES (est):** 29.1MM
**SALES (corp-wide):** 1.3B **Publicly Held**
**SIC:** 3613 3679 3663 3661 Switchgear & switchboard apparatus; electronic switches; radio & TV communications equipment; telephone cords, jacks, adapters, etc.; electronic connectors; current-carrying wiring devices
**PA:** Heico Corporation
3000 Taft St
Hollywood FL 33021
954 987-4000

**(G-6655)**
**SWITCHED SOURCE LLC**
18 S Michigan Ave Fl 12 (60603-3200)
**PHONE** .................................. 708 207-1479
Charles Murray, *President*
**EMP:** 3
**SALES (est):** 133K **Privately Held**
**SIC:** 3621 Rotary converters (electrical equipment)

**(G-6656)**
**SYMFACT INC**
55 W Monroe St Ste 2900 (60603-5058)
Rural Route 1121 Prk W, Mount Pleasant SC (29466)
**PHONE** .................................. 847 380-4174
Andreas Kyriakakis, *President*
Chris Kraddock, *COO*
Harry Angel, *Vice Pres*
Roland Javet, *CTO*
**EMP:** 35
**SALES (est):** 2.2MM
**SALES (corp-wide):** 2.4MM **Privately Held**
**SIC:** 7372 Prepackaged software
**PA:** Symfact Ag
Bankstrasse 4
Uster ZH 8610
449 051-919

**(G-6657)**
**SYNERGY TECHNOLOGY GROUP INC**
Also Called: Shartega Systems
1250 W Augusta Blvd # 201 (60642-4131)
**PHONE** .................................. 773 305-3500
Jake Kunda, *President*
Nic Connor, *Vice Pres*
**EMP:** 15 **EST:** 2003
**SALES (est):** 1MM **Privately Held**
**SIC:** 7371 7372 7379 Computer software development & applications; prepackaged software; business oriented computer software; computer related consulting services

**(G-6658)**
**SYSTAT SOFTWARE INC (HQ)**
225 N Wash St Ste 425 (60606)
**PHONE** .................................. 408 876-4508
Tanveer Khader, *CEO*
Richard Gall, *President*
Kirti Batavia, *Principal*
Varadha Rajan, *Vice Pres*
Parveen Gill, *Accountant*
**EMP:** 24
**SQ FT:** 4,797
**SALES (est):** 4.1MM **Privately Held**
**SIC:** 7372 Application computer software

**(G-6659)**
**SYSTEM SCIENCE CORPORATION**
1408 W Taylor St Apt 301 (60607-4687)
**PHONE** .................................. 708 214-2264
Andreas Linninger, *President*
**EMP:** 5
**SALES (est):** 508.4K **Privately Held**
**SIC:** 3845 Electromedical equipment

## Chicago - Cook County (G-6660)

**(G-6660)**
**SYSTEM SOFTWARE ASSOCIATES DEL (PA)**
Also Called: Ssa
500 W Madison St Ste 1600 (60661-4555)
PHONE..................................312 258-6000
**Fax:** 312 474-7500
Robert R Carpenter, *Ch of Bd*
Lynn Karbin, *Accounting Mgr*
Walter Pecile, *Info Tech Dir*
Kathleen Galvan, *Analyst*
**EMP:** 22
**SALES (est):** 40.8MM **Privately Held**
**SIC:** 7372 7373 Application computer software; business oriented computer software; computer-aided engineering (CAE) systems service

**(G-6661)**
**SYSTEMS AL SNOW**
801 S Wells St (60607-4520)
PHONE..................................312 846-6026
Karla Figueroa, *Owner*
**EMP:** 3
**SALES (est):** 218K **Privately Held**
**SIC:** 2851 Removers & cleaners

**(G-6662)**
**T 26 INC**
Also Called: 5inch
1110 N Milwaukee Ave (60642-4017)
PHONE..................................773 862-1201
**EMP:** 5
**SALES (est):** 540K **Privately Held**
**SIC:** 3575 Mfg Computer Terminals

**(G-6663)**
**T R COMMUNICATIONS INC**
Also Called: Beverly Review
10546 S Western Ave (60643-2528)
PHONE..................................773 238-3366
**Fax:** 773 238-1492
Robert Olzewski Jr, *President*
Toby Olszewski, *Vice Pres*
Susan Olszewski, *Office Mgr*
Ericka Swanson, *Graphic Designe*
**EMP:** 12
**SQ FT:** 2,000
**SALES (est):** 969.5K **Privately Held**
**WEB:** www.trcom.net
**SIC:** 2741 2791 2711 Business service newsletters; publishing & printing; typesetting; newspapers

**(G-6664)**
**T2 CABINETS INC**
1400 W 37th St (60609-2109)
PHONE..................................312 593-1507
Mao MEI, *Principal*
▲ **EMP:** 13 **EST:** 2008
**SALES (est):** 1.8MM **Privately Held**
**SIC:** 2434 Wood kitchen cabinets

**(G-6665)**
**TAICO DESIGN PRODUCTS INC**
333 N Canal St Apt 3701 (60606-1545)
PHONE..................................773 871-9086
Leon Levy, *President*
Catherine Levy, *Vice Pres*
**EMP:** 3
**SQ FT:** 2,000
**SALES (est):** 502.2K **Privately Held**
**WEB:** www.taicodesign.com
**SIC:** 3089 7389 Injection molding of plastics; design services

**(G-6666)**
**TAILS INC**
Also Called: Chicagoland Tails
4410 N Ravenswood Ave # 1 (60640-5999)
PHONE..................................773 564-9300
Janice Brown, *President*
L Brown, *Publisher*
Dana Cetrola, *Opers Mgr*
Charlene Underly, *Accounts Exec*
**EMP:** 12
**SALES (est):** 1.3MM **Privately Held**
**SIC:** 2721 Magazines: publishing & printing

**(G-6667)**
**TAITT BURIAL GARMENTS**
6649 S Wabash Ave (60637-3034)
PHONE..................................773 483-7424
Ernestine Taitt, *Owner*
**EMP:** 15
**SALES (est):** 530K **Privately Held**
**SIC:** 2389 Disposable garments & accessories

**(G-6668)**
**TALCOTT COMMUNICATIONS CORP (PA)**
Also Called: Giftware News
704 N Wells St Fl 2 (60654-3569)
PHONE..................................312 849-2220
Daniel Von Rabenau, *President*
Cathryn Piccirillo, *Editor*
Ruth Tang, *Manager*
Dayna Fields, *Assoc Editor*
▲ **EMP:** 28
**SQ FT:** 2,700
**SALES (est):** 4.2MM **Privately Held**
**WEB:** www.giftwarenews.com
**SIC:** 2721 Magazines: publishing only, not printed on site

**(G-6669)**
**TAM TAV BAKERY INC**
Also Called: Tel Aviv Kosher Bakery
2944 W Devon Ave (60659-1556)
PHONE..................................773 764-8877
**Fax:** 773 764-8854
David Ackerman, *President*
Esther Sabo, *Vice Pres*
Naftula Basman, *Shareholder*
Diane Ackerman, *Admin Sec*
Judy Glock, *Admin Sec*
**EMP:** 20
**SQ FT:** 3,900
**SALES (est):** 1.2MM **Privately Held**
**SIC:** 5461 5149 2051 Bakeries; bakery products; bread, cake & related products

**(G-6670)**
**TAMPICO BEVERAGES INC**
2425 W Barry Ave (60618-7913)
PHONE..................................773 296-0190
**EMP:** 13
**SALES (corp-wide):** 2.9B **Privately Held**
**SIC:** 2087 Flavoring extracts & syrups
**HQ:** Tampico Beverages Inc.
3106 N Campbell Ave
Chicago IL 60618
773 296-0190

**(G-6671)**
**TAMPICO BEVERAGES INC (DH)**
3106 N Campbell Ave (60618-7921)
PHONE..................................773 296-0190
Scott Miller, *CEO*
Terry Boden, *President*
Mark Kent, *Exec VP*
Pedro Dejesus Jr, *Senior VP*
Dawn Stanislaw, *CFO*
◆ **EMP:** 50
**SQ FT:** 70,000
**SALES (est):** 24.2MM
**SALES (corp-wide):** 2.9B **Privately Held**
**SIC:** 2087 Concentrates, drink; fruit juices: concentrated for fountain use
**HQ:** Houchens Food Group, Inc.
700 Church St
Bowling Green KY 42101
270 843-3252

**(G-6672)**
**TAMPICO PRESS**
1919 S Blue Island Ave (60608-3014)
PHONE..................................312 243-5448
Marcos Urbano, *Owner*
Marcos Urbana, *Partner*
**EMP:** 3
**SQ FT:** 2,500
**SALES (est):** 262.3K **Privately Held**
**SIC:** 2759 2752 Letterpress printing; commercial printing, offset

**(G-6673)**
**TANKLINK CORPORATION**
200 S Wacker Dr Ste 1800 (60606-5911)
PHONE..................................312 379-8397
**Fax:** 847 882-0066
John Crump, *President*
Robert Beering,
**EMP:** 20
**SQ FT:** 7,017
**SALES (est):** 2.8MM
**SALES (corp-wide):** 25.5MM **Privately Held**
**WEB:** www.wdomain.com
**SIC:** 3663 Cellular radio telephone
**HQ:** Telular Corporation
200 S Wacker Dr Ste 1800
Chicago IL 60606
800 835-8527

**(G-6674)**
**TANVAS INC**
Also Called: Kinea Touch
600 W Van Buren St # 710 (60607-3758)
PHONE..................................773 295-6220
Greg Topel, *CEO*
Ed Colgate, *President*
Michael Olley, *Engineer*
Michael Peshkin, *CTO*
**EMP:** 6
**SALES (est):** 1MM **Privately Held**
**SIC:** 3679 Electronic circuits

**(G-6675)**
**TAO TRADING CORPORATION**
1420 W Howard St Apt 201 (60626-1433)
PHONE..................................773 764-6542
Mona K Buechler, *President*
▲ **EMP:** 7
**SALES (est):** 971.3K **Privately Held**
**SIC:** 2531 Chairs, table & arm

**(G-6676)**
**TARGET MARKET NEWS INC**
228 S Wabash Ave Ste 210 (60604-2383)
PHONE..................................312 408-1881
Kenneth Smikle, *President*
**EMP:** 3
**SQ FT:** 400
**SALES (est):** 211.1K **Privately Held**
**WEB:** www.targetmarketnews.com
**SIC:** 8732 2721 Market analysis or research; periodicals

**(G-6677)**
**TARNEY INC**
4520 W North Ave (60639-4723)
PHONE..................................773 235-0331
**Fax:** 773 235-2729
Raymond Peterson, *President*
**EMP:** 20 **EST:** 1970
**SALES (est):** 600K **Privately Held**
**WEB:** www.tarney.com
**SIC:** 3599 3469 Machine shop, jobbing & repair; metal stampings

**(G-6678)**
**TATINE**
4200 W Diversey Ave (60639-2003)
PHONE..................................312 733-0173
Kaytlin Costus, *Manager*
**EMP:** 5 **EST:** 2015
**SALES (est):** 342.9K **Privately Held**
**SIC:** 3999 Candles

**(G-6679)**
**TAUBER BROTHERS TOOL & DIE CO**
4701 N Olcott Ave (60706-4692)
PHONE..................................708 867-9100
**Fax:** 708 867-9323
Joseph P Tauber Jr, *President*
Cynthia Tauber, *Vice Pres*
Adam Cholewa, *Plant Mgr*
Sally Igartua, *Office Mgr*
Louis Velez, *Manager*
**EMP:** 20
**SQ FT:** 30,000
**SALES (est):** 3.5MM **Privately Held**
**SIC:** 3469 3544 3541 Stamping metal for the trade; die sets for metal stamping (presses); machine tools, metal cutting: exotic (explosive, etc.)

**(G-6680)**
**TAYLOR FARMS ILLINOIS INC**
Also Called: Last Minute Gourmet
200 N Artesian Ave (60612-2149)
PHONE..................................312 226-3328
Bruce Taylor, *CEO*
David Monk, *Marketing Staff*
Peter Duda, *Manager*
**EMP:** 300
**SALES (est):** 46.5MM **Privately Held**
**SIC:** 2099 Vegetables, peeled for the trade
**PA:** Taylor Fresh Foods, Inc
150 Main St Ste 400
Salinas CA 93901

**(G-6681)**
**TDR EXPRESS INC**
5231 N Oakview St Apt 3e (60656-3077)
P.O. Box 302, Des Plaines (60016-0005)
PHONE..................................224 805-0070
Dan Balbaie, *President*
Tony S Ardelean, *Admin Sec*
**EMP:** 4
**SALES (est):** 503.5K **Privately Held**
**SIC:** 3537 Trucks: freight, baggage, etc.: industrial, except mining

**(G-6682)**
**TEAM CAST INC**
111 W Washington St # 1865 (60602-2703)
PHONE..................................312 263-0033
Eric Stampinato, *COO*
Olivier Tregarot, *Opers Staff*
Mark Polovick, *VP Sales*
Christophe Trolet, *Sales Mgr*
Sandrine Konnecke, *Marketing Staff*
**EMP:** 3
**SALES (est):** 500K **Privately Held**
**SIC:** 3663 Mobile communication equipment

**(G-6683)**
**TEC FOODS INC**
4300 W Ohio St (60624-1051)
PHONE..................................800 315-8002
**Fax:** 773 638-9170
Anastasios E Costianis, *President*
Elliot Costianis, *General Mgr*
TAS Cospianis, *Financial Exec*
Moscha Costianis, *Admin Sec*
**EMP:** 42
**SQ FT:** 37,000
**SALES (est):** 474.5K **Privately Held**
**WEB:** www.tecfoods.com
**SIC:** 2034 2041 5149 Soup mixes; flour; fruits, dried

**(G-6684)**
**TECHDRIVE INC**
3255 S Dearborn St # 320 (60616-3089)
PHONE..................................312 567-3910
Robert Filler, *CEO*
**EMP:** 7
**SALES (est):** 589.4K **Privately Held**
**WEB:** www.techdrive.com
**SIC:** 2899 Fuel tank or engine cleaning chemicals

**(G-6685)**
**TECHNOX MACHINE & MFG INC**
2619 N Normandy Ave (60707-2225)
PHONE..................................773 745-6800
**Fax:** 773 745-8502
Shamkant S Shirsat, *President*
Myra Pienkos, *Accountant*
Amit Shirsat, *Admin Sec*
**EMP:** 25
**SQ FT:** 35,000
**SALES (est):** 6.1MM **Privately Held**
**WEB:** www.technoxmachine.com
**SIC:** 3541 Machine tool replacement & repair parts, metal cutting types

**(G-6686)**
**TED MULLER**
Also Called: Muller Roofing & Construction
910 S Michigan Ave # 1612 (60605-2356)
PHONE..................................312 435-0978
Ted Muller, *Owner*
**EMP:** 9 **EST:** 1981
**SALES (est):** 519.2K **Privately Held**
**SIC:** 2952 2899 1799 2621 Mastic roofing composition; waterproofing compounds; waterproofing; building & roofing paper, felts & insulation siding

**(G-6687)**
**TEDS CUSTOM CABINETS INC**
5946 S Pulaski Rd (60629-4516)
PHONE..................................773 581-4455
Ted Wisz, *President*
Ted Lech, *Vice Pres*
**EMP:** 6
**SQ FT:** 4,200
**SALES (est):** 725.3K **Privately Held**
**SIC:** 2434 5211 Vanities, bathroom: wood; cabinets, kitchen; bathroom fixtures, equipment & supplies

# GEOGRAPHIC SECTION
Chicago - Cook County (G-6714)

**(G-6688)**
**TEEATUDE INC**
1016 W Jackson Blvd (60607-2914)
PHONE .................................. 312 324-3554
Tamira Russo, *CEO*
**EMP:** 4
**SQ FT:** 1,000
**SALES (est):** 372K  **Privately Held**
**SIC: 2759**  Letterpress & screen printing

**(G-6689)**
**TELCO MACHINE & MANUFACTURING (PA)**
3957 N Normandy Ave (60634-2422)
PHONE .................................. 773 725-4441
Fax: 773 725-4497
Neil David, *President*
Gene Kustra, *Manager*
**EMP:** 25 **EST:** 1980
**SQ FT:** 7,000
**SALES (est):** 3.7MM  **Privately Held**
**SIC: 3599**  Machine shop, jobbing & repair

**(G-6690)**
**TELCO MACHINE & MANUFACTURING**
6610 W Dakin St (60634-2413)
PHONE .................................. 773 725-4441
Anil David, *Branch Mgr*
**EMP:** 6
**SALES (corp-wide):** 3.7MM  **Privately Held**
**SIC: 3599**  Machine shop, jobbing & repair
**PA:** Telco Machine & Manufacturing Inc
3957 N Normandy Ave
Chicago IL 60634
773 725-4441

**(G-6691)**
**TELEDYNE MONITOR LABS INC**
12497 Collection Ctr Dr (60693-0124)
PHONE .................................. 303 792-3300
**EMP:** 7
**SALES (corp-wide):** 2.1B  **Publicly Held**
**SIC: 3671**  Traveling wave tubes
**HQ:** Teledyne Monitor Labs, Inc.
35 Inverness Dr E
Englewood CO 80112
303 792-3300

**(G-6692)**
**TELULAR CORPORATION (HQ)**
Also Called: Telguard
200 S Wacker Dr Ste 1800 (60606-5911)
P.O. Box 7246, Philadelphia PA (19101-7246)
PHONE .................................. 800 835-8527
Fax: 312 379-8310
Doug Milner, *CEO*
Allen Yurko, *President*
Robert Deering, *General Mgr*
Sherry Swehla, *General Mgr*
Brian J Clucas, *Principal*
▲ **EMP:** 99
**SQ FT:** 11,700
**SALES (est):** 25.2MM
**SALES (corp-wide):** 25.5MM  **Privately Held**
**WEB:** www.wdomain.com
**SIC: 3663** 7372  Cellular radio telephone; prepackaged software
**PA:** Acp Tower Holdings, Llc
311 S Wacker Dr Ste 4300
Chicago IL 60606
800 835-8527

**(G-6693)**
**TELZA WELDING INC**
Also Called: Telza Welding Co
1624 N Kilbourn Ave (60639-4716)
PHONE .................................. 773 777-4467
Jesse Kolekosky, *President*
**EMP:** 5
**SQ FT:** 3,000
**SALES (est):** 497.3K  **Privately Held**
**SIC: 7692**  Welding repair

**(G-6694)**
**TEMP-TECH INDUSTRIES INC**
6166 S Sayre Ave (60638-3987)
PHONE .................................. 773 586-2800
Fax: 773 586-2850
Frank Lakis Jr, *President*
Guy Dekker, *Vice Pres*
Roger Mentzer, *Vice Pres*
**EMP:** 33
**SQ FT:** 26,800
**SALES (est):** 4.5MM  **Privately Held**
**SIC: 3231** 3442 2431  Products of purchased glass; metal doors, sash & trim; millwork

**(G-6695)**
**TEMPEL HOLDINGS INC**
5500 N Wolcott Ave (60640-1020)
PHONE .................................. 773 250-8000
Timothy N Taylor, *President*
**EMP:** 8
**SALES (est):** 1MM  **Privately Held**
**SIC: 3469**  Stamping metal for the trade

**(G-6696)**
**TEMPEL STEEL COMPANY (PA)**
5500 N Wolcott Ave (60640-1020)
PHONE .................................. 773 250-8000
Fax: 773 250-8910
Gary Wagner, *CEO*
Richard Buff, *General Mgr*
Christopher Stephan, *Chairman*
Robert Potter, *COO*
David Silvestri, *COO*
▲ **EMP:** 554 **EST:** 1945
**SQ FT:** 5,000
**SALES (est):** 714.1MM  **Privately Held**
**SIC: 3469** 3313 3316 3398  Stamping metal for the trade; electrometallurgical products; cold finishing of steel shapes; metal heat treating; metals service centers & offices

**(G-6697)**
**TEMPEL STEEL COMPANY**
5454 N Wolcott Ave (60640-1018)
PHONE .................................. 773 250-8000
Irfan Khan, *QC Mgr*
Jerry Huffer, *Engineer*
Robert Romain, *Marketing Staff*
Mark Buckner, *Manager*
Rhonda Pencak, *Manager*
**EMP:** 800
**SQ FT:** 46,100
**SALES (corp-wide):** 714.1MM  **Privately Held**
**SIC: 3313**  Electrometallurgical products
**PA:** Tempel Steel Company
5500 N Wolcott Ave
Chicago IL 60640
773 250-8000

**(G-6698)**
**TEMPEL STEEL COMPANY**
5500 N Wolcott Ave (60640-1020)
PHONE .................................. 773 250-8000
Mark Baker, *Branch Mgr*
**EMP:** 650
**SALES (corp-wide):** 714.1MM  **Privately Held**
**SIC: 3399** 3083 2891 3313  Laminating steel; laminated plastics plate & sheet; adhesives & sealants; electrometallurgical products
**PA:** Tempel Steel Company
5500 N Wolcott Ave
Chicago IL 60640
773 250-8000

**(G-6699)**
**TEMPUS HEALTH INC**
600 W Chicago Ave Ste 775 (60654-2526)
PHONE .................................. 312 784-4400
Ryan Fukushima, *COO*
Erik Phelps, *Exec VP*
**EMP:** 25
**SALES (est):** 121.4K  **Privately Held**
**SIC: 7374** 7371 7372  Data processing & preparation; computer software systems analysis & design, custom; business oriented computer software

**(G-6700)**
**TENGGREN-MEHL CO INC**
7019 W Higgins Ave (60656-1901)
PHONE .................................. 773 763-3290
James C Weilandt, *President*
Susan Weilandt, *Vice Pres*
**EMP:** 7 **EST:** 1927
**SQ FT:** 1,400
**SALES (est):** 800K  **Privately Held**
**SIC: 2391**  Curtains & draperies

**(G-6701)**
**TENNANT COMPANY**
Also Called: Florock
1120 W Exchange Ave (60609-2510)
PHONE .................................. 773 376-7132
Byron Beamer, *Business Mgr*
Sharon Payne, *Marketing Staff*
**EMP:** 38
**SALES (corp-wide):** 808.5MM  **Publicly Held**
**SIC: 2851**  Paints & allied products
**PA:** Tennant Company
701 Lilac Dr N
Minneapolis MN 55422
763 540-1200

**(G-6702)**
**TENTH AND BLAKE BEER COMPANY (DH)**
250 S Wacker Dr Ste 800 (60606-5888)
PHONE .................................. 312 496-2759
Tom Cardella, *President*
Gavin Hattersley, *CFO*
**EMP:** 11
**SALES (est):** 10.9MM
**SALES (corp-wide):** 4.8B  **Publicly Held**
**SIC: 2082**  Beer (alcoholic beverage)
**HQ:** Millercoors Llc
250 S Wacker Dr Ste 800
Chicago IL 60606
312 496-2700

**(G-6703)**
**TEPROMARK INTERNATIONAL INC**
140 S Dearborn St Ste 420 (60603-5233)
PHONE .................................. 847 329-7881
Robert J Morris, *President*
Harold Klein, *Vice Pres*
Philip Collins, *Sales Mgr*
**EMP:** 8
**SQ FT:** 15,000
**SALES (est):** 700K  **Privately Held**
**SIC: 2499**  Decorative wood & woodwork

**(G-6704)**
**TESLA MOTORS INC**
1053 W Grand Ave (60642-6556)
PHONE .................................. 312 733-9780
Elon Musk, *President*
**EMP:** 12
**SALES (corp-wide):** 7B  **Publicly Held**
**SIC: 3711** 3714  Motor vehicles & car bodies; cars, electric, assembly of; motor vehicle parts & accessories
**PA:** Tesla, Inc.
3500 Deer Creek Rd
Palo Alto CA 94304
650 681-5000

**(G-6705)**
**TEX TANA INC (PA)**
2243 W Belmont Ave Ste 1 (60618-7289)
PHONE .................................. 773 561-9270
Hans J Weil, *Ch of Bd*
Anat Unruh, *President*
Michael Cook, *Vice Pres*
Cathy Calderon, *Controller*
Clara Marin, *Finance Mgr*
◆ **EMP:** 5 **EST:** 1949
**SQ FT:** 8,000
**SALES (est):** 10MM  **Privately Held**
**WEB:** www.tana-tex.com
**SIC: 2299**  Jute & flax textile products

**(G-6706)**
**TEXTILE INDUSTRIES INC**
2414 W Cullerton St Fl 3 (60608-2401)
PHONE .................................. 312 829-3112
Richard Cogan, *CEO*
Nancy Cogan, *President*
Rita Damitz, *Sales Staff*
Leida Cruz, *Office Mgr*
**EMP:** 7
**SQ FT:** 11,375
**SALES (est):** 650K  **Privately Held**
**WEB:** www.textileind.com
**SIC: 3569**  Filters, general line: industrial

**(G-6707)**
**TEYS (USA) INC**
770 N Halsted St Ste 202 (60642-6930)
PHONE .................................. 312 492-7163
Brad Teys, *CEO*
Allan Teys, *Ch of Bd*
Michael Forrest, *President*
Thomas James Gallagher, *Admin Sec*
Jessica Monge, *Admin Sec*
◆ **EMP:** 9 **EST:** 2000
**SQ FT:** 2,300
**SALES:** 350.3MM  **Privately Held**
**SIC: 2011**  Beef products from beef slaughtered on site

**(G-6708)**
**TFA SIGNS**
5500 N Kedzie Ave (60625-3924)
PHONE .................................. 773 267-6007
**EMP:** 2
**SALES (est):** 248.1K  **Privately Held**
**SIC: 3993**  Signs & advertising specialties

**(G-6709)**
**TFO GROUP LLC**
Also Called: Field Outfitting Co., The
2140 W Fulton St Ste F (60612-2338)
P.O. Box 671, Skokie (60076-0671)
PHONE .................................. 608 469-7519
Ross Paladin, *Owner*
Dan Winders, *COO*
**EMP:** 6
**SQ FT:** 3,000
**SALES:** 8MM  **Privately Held**
**SIC: 2329** 2337  Men's & boys' sportswear & athletic clothing; women's & misses' suits & coats

**(G-6710)**
**THE SYNTEK GROUP INC**
3415 N Pulaski Rd 23 (60641-4025)
PHONE .................................. 773 279-0131
Wan S Shin, *President*
Joon Shin, *Vice Pres*
Michael Shin, *Shareholder*
▲ **EMP:** 5
**SQ FT:** 7,000
**SALES (est):** 916K  **Privately Held**
**SIC: 3679**  Electronic circuits

**(G-6711)**
**THERESE CROWE DESIGN LTD**
Also Called: Crowe, Therese Design
29 E Madison St Ste 1401 (60602-4445)
PHONE .................................. 312 269-0039
Therese Crowe, *President*
**EMP:** 1
**SALES:** 200K  **Privately Held**
**SIC: 3911**  Jewelry, precious metal

**(G-6712)**
**THERMATOME CORPORATION**
2242 W Harrison St # 201 (60612-3719)
PHONE .................................. 312 772-2201
Tom Ryan, *CEO*
Kambiz Dowlatshahi, *President*
Christopher Valadez, *COO*
Fay Stanley, *Admin Sec*
**EMP:** 4
**SALES (est):** 260K  **Privately Held**
**SIC: 3841** 3845  Surgical & medical instruments; electromedical equipment

**(G-6713)**
**THERMOELECTRIC COOLG AMER CORP**
Also Called: T E C A
4048 W Schubert Ave (60639-2122)
PHONE .................................. 773 342-4900
Fax: 773 342-0191
Mike Mikalauskis, *President*
Emily Hutensky, *General Mgr*
Manuel Martinez, *Prdtn Mgr*
Afshin Asadnejad, *Engineer*
Ayesha Grayson, *Manager*
**EMP:** 2
**SALES (est):** 547.2K  **Privately Held**
**WEB:** www.thermoelectric.com
**SIC: 3674**  Solid state electronic devices

**(G-6714)**
**THINKCERCACOM INC**
Also Called: Ithaca Education
440 N Wells St Ste 720 (60654-4548)
PHONE .................................. 224 412-3722
Eileen M Buckley, *CEO*
Abby Ross, *COO*
Josh Tolman, *COO*
Brian Bar, *Vice Pres*
Elizabeth Riley, *Mktg Dir*
**EMP:** 13

# Chicago - Cook County (G-6715) — GEOGRAPHIC SECTION

SALES (est): 891.7K **Privately Held**
SIC: 8299 7372 Educational services; application computer software

**(G-6715)**
**THIRD WRLD PRESS FUNDATION INC**
7822 S Dobson Ave (60619-3204)
P.O. Box 19730 (60619-0730)
PHONE..................................773 651-0700
Fax: 773 651-7286
Donald L Lee, *President*
Bennett Johnson, *Vice Pres*
EMP: 10
SQ FT: 7,100
SALES (est): 48.4K **Privately Held**
SIC: 2731 Books: publishing only

**(G-6716)**
**THIS WEEK IN CHICAGO INC**
Also Called: Key Magazine
226 E Ontario St Fl 3 (60611-7220)
PHONE..................................312 943-0838
Fax: 312 664-6113
Walter L West III, *President*
Jean Lieber, *Advt Staff*
Nancy Vargas, *Office Mgr*
EMP: 12
SQ FT: 3,000
SALES (est): 1.3MM **Privately Held**
SIC: 2721 Magazines: publishing only, not printed on site

**(G-6717)**
**THOMSON QUANTITATIVE ANALYTICS**
230 S La Salle St Ste 688 (60604-1433)
PHONE..................................847 610-0574
Fax: 312 915-6349
William Aronin, *President*
Chris Hanson, *Director*
EMP: 20
SALES (est): 3.8MM
SALES (corp-wide): 3.7B **Publicly Held**
SIC: 5045 7372 7371 Computer software; prepackaged software; custom computer programming services
HQ: Thomson Reuters Corporation
3 Times Sq
New York NY 10036
646 223-4000

**(G-6718)**
**THOMSON REUTERS (LEGAL) INC**
Also Called: Hubbard One
1 N Dearborn St Fl 5 (60602-4349)
PHONE..................................312 873-6800
Anthony E Davis, *Partner*
Preston McKenzie, *Vice Pres*
Chris Lambrecht, *Finance*
Colin Gordon, *Accounts Exec*
Christoph Harttung, *Accounts Exec*
EMP: 9
SALES (corp-wide): 3.7B **Publicly Held**
WEB: www.personnet.com
SIC: 2721 Periodicals: publishing & printing
HQ: Thomson Reuters (Legal) Inc.
610 Opperman Dr
Eagan MN 55123
651 687-7000

**(G-6719)**
**THOMSON REUTERS CORPORATION**
1 N Dearborn St Ste 1400 (60602-4336)
PHONE..................................312 288-4654
Fax: 312 873-6801
Robert D Daleo, *Exec VP*
David Baker, *Site Mgr*
Jane Moran, *CIO*
Rich Carlson, *Info Tech Mgr*
EMP: 89
SALES (corp-wide): 3.7B **Publicly Held**
SIC: 2731 Books: publishing only
HQ: Thomson Reuters Corporation
3 Times Sq
New York NY 10036
646 223-4000

**(G-6720)**
**THOMSON STEEL POLISHING CORP**
6150 S New England Ave (60638-4008)
PHONE..................................773 586-2345
Fax: 773 229-1603
Ronald Fisher, *President*
EMP: 7 EST: 1955
SQ FT: 30,000
SALES (est): 490K **Privately Held**
WEB: www.thomsonsteel.com
SIC: 3471 3479 Polishing, metals or formed products; coating of metals & formed products

**(G-6721)**
**THOUGHTLY CORP**
750 N Rush St Apt 1906 (60611-2581)
PHONE..................................772 559-2008
Chase Perkins, *CEO*
EMP: 3
SALES (est): 150.9K **Privately Held**
SIC: 7372 Application computer software

**(G-6722)**
**THRALL ENTERPRISES INC (PA)**
180 N Stetson Ave (60601-6794)
PHONE..................................312 621-8200
Fax: 312 621-4549
Jeffrey J Thrall, *Ch of Bd*
James R Thrall, *Vice Pres*
Marilynn Thrall, *Vice Pres*
Nancy G Haller, *Treasurer*
Maria Calderon, *Accountant*
◆ EMP: 11
SQ FT: 5,000
SALES (est): 154.6MM **Privately Held**
WEB: www.thrallenterprises.com
SIC: 2893 Printing ink

**(G-6723)**
**THRILLED LLC**
Also Called: Pulpulp
555 W Jackson Blvd # 400 (60661-5700)
PHONE..................................312 404-1929
Jacob Dehart, *Principal*
EMP: 4 EST: 2015
SALES (est): 90.8K **Privately Held**
SIC: 5651 3999 Family clothing stores; framed artwork

**(G-6724)**
**THYSSENKRUPP ELEVATOR CORP**
940 W Adams St (60607-3031)
PHONE..................................312 733-8025
Mike Corson, *Manager*
EMP: 58
SALES (corp-wide): 44.2B **Privately Held**
WEB: www.tyssenkrupp.com
SIC: 3534 Elevators & moving stairways
HQ: Thyssenkrupp Elevator Corporation
11605 Haynes Bridge Rd # 650
Alpharetta GA 30009
678 319-3240

**(G-6725)**
**THYSSENKRUPP NORTH AMERICA INC (HQ)**
111 W Jackson Blvd # 2400 (60604-4154)
PHONE..................................312 525-2800
Torsten Gessner, *CEO*
Derrick Richter, *Principal*
Heinrich Hiesinger, *Chairman*
Amy Gulinson, *Counsel*
Tom Bradsley, *Vice Pres*
EMP: 35
SQ FT: 90,000
SALES (est): 12.6B
SALES (corp-wide): 44.2B **Privately Held**
SIC: 6719 3714 Investment holding companies, except banks; axles, motor vehicle
PA: Thyssenkrupp Ag
Thyssenkrupp Allee 1
Essen 45143
201 844-5641

**(G-6726)**
**TIGHE PUBLISHING SERVICES INC**
1700 W Irving Park Rd # 210 (60613-2599)
PHONE..................................773 281-9100
Fax: 773 281-9110
Suzanne H Tighe, *President*
Kim Sindelar, *Vice Pres*
Austin Tighe, *Vice Pres*
Tracey Randinelli, *Project Mgr*
Cathy Vanpatten, *Project Mgr*
EMP: 19
SALES (est): 2.1MM **Privately Held**
WEB: www.tighepub.com
SIC: 2741 8748 Miscellaneous publishing; business consulting

**(G-6727)**
**TIME OUT CHICAGO PARTNERS LLLP**
247 S State St Ste 1700 (60604-1965)
PHONE..................................312 924-9555
Fax: 312 924-9560
Alison Tocci, *President*
Scott Smith, *Editor*
Kim Russell, *Technology*
Nadine Nakanishi, *Director*
Stephanie Gladney, *Art Dir*
EMP: 23
SALES (est): 3.2MM
SALES (corp-wide): 42.9MM **Privately Held**
SIC: 2759 Magazines: printing
HQ: Time Out Digital Limited
Fourth Floor
London W1T 7
207 813-3000

**(G-6728)**
**TIMKEN DRIVES LLC**
875 N Michigan Ave (60611-1803)
P.O. Box 71523 (60694-1523)
PHONE..................................312 274-9710
Fax: 312 274-1304
Mark Millmore, *Branch Mgr*
EMP: 3
SALES (corp-wide): 2.6B **Publicly Held**
WEB: www.drivesinc.com
SIC: 3462 Chains, forged steel
HQ: Timken Drives, Llc
901 19th Ave
Fulton IL 61252
815 589-2211

**(G-6729)**
**TINI MARTINI**
2169 N Milwaukee Ave (60647-4058)
PHONE..................................773 269-2900
EMP: 3 EST: 2005
SALES (est): 150K **Privately Held**
SIC: 2711 5813 Newspapers-Publishing/Printing Drinking Place

**(G-6730)**
**TITANIUM VENTURES GROUP LLC**
329 W Evergreen Ave (60610-1814)
PHONE..................................312 375-3526
Piunno Matthew, *Principal*
EMP: 3
SALES (est): 191.9K **Privately Held**
SIC: 3356 Titanium

**(G-6731)**
**TJMJ INC**
Also Called: Arvey Paper
1 S Dearborn St Ste 2100 (60603-2307)
PHONE..................................312 315-7780
Mohammed Imran Khan, *President*
D Robert Smusz, *President*
EMP: 14
SALES (est): 5.5MM **Privately Held**
SIC: 2678 Stationery products

**(G-6732)**
**TMB INDUSTRIES INC (PA)**
Also Called: Begel Industries
980 N Michigan Ave # 11400 (60611-4501)
PHONE..................................312 280-2565
Timothy Masek, *Managing Dir*
Joseph Ponteri, *Managing Dir*
Tom Begel, *Chairman*
Courtney Suvada, *Manager*
Tim Masek, *Director*
EMP: 10
SQ FT: 3,000
SALES (est): 69.6MM **Privately Held**
SIC: 6799 3321 Investors; gray & ductile iron foundries

**(G-6733)**
**TODAYS TEMPTATIONS INC**
1900 N Austin Ave Ste 72 (60639-5078)
PHONE..................................773 385-5355
Fax: 773 329-8912
Al Filin, *President*
▲ EMP: 14
SALES (est): 1.2MM **Privately Held**
SIC: 2051 Bakery: wholesale or wholesale/retail combined

**(G-6734)**
**TOGGLE INC (PA)**
2004 Wattles Dr (60614)
PHONE..................................323 882-6339
Adam Johnson, *CEO*
John Cho, *COO*
EMP: 9
SALES (est): 1MM **Privately Held**
SIC: 3571 Computers, digital, analog or hybrid

**(G-6735)**
**TOHO TECHNOLOGY INC**
4809 N Ravenswood Ave (60640-4495)
PHONE..................................773 583-7183
John B Coomes, *President*
Bijan Arianlou, *Sales Mgr*
EMP: 9
SALES (est): 1.4MM **Privately Held**
SIC: 3699 Electrical equipment & supplies

**(G-6736)**
**TOM TOM TAMALES MFG CO INC**
Also Called: Tom Tom Tamales & Baking Co
4750 S Washtenaw Ave (60632-2096)
PHONE..................................773 523-5675
Nick C Petros, *President*
George Devos, *Manager*
George Davelis, *Consultant*
George Anos, *Director*
Chris Lito, *Director*
EMP: 10
SQ FT: 16,000
SALES (est): 995.5K **Privately Held**
SIC: 2032 5149 Tamales: packaged in cans, jars, etc.; bakery products

**(G-6737)**
**TOMCYNDI INC**
Also Called: Chicago Steaks
822 W Exchange Ave (60609-2507)
P.O. Box 9083 (60609-0083)
PHONE..................................773 847-5400
Thomas Summers, *President*
Joe Halper, *Senior VP*
Pablo Sanchez, *Safety Mgr*
Gail Glowacki, *Human Res Mgr*
Curt Strong, *Manager*
EMP: 25
SQ FT: 26,500
SALES (est): 4.4MM **Privately Held**
WEB: www.chicagosteaks.com
SIC: 5147 2013 2011 Meats & meat products; sausages & other prepared meats; meat packing plants

**(G-6738)**
**TOMEK IRON ORIGINALS**
6059 S Oak Park Ave (60638-4011)
PHONE..................................773 788-1750
Tom Gadawski, *President*
EMP: 8
SALES (est): 807.7K **Privately Held**
SIC: 3462 Iron & steel forgings

**(G-6739)**
**TOMMY HO JEWELERS**
5 S Wabash Ave Ste 1503 (60603-3088)
PHONE..................................312 368-8593
Fax: 312 368-1216
Tommy Ho, *Owner*
EMP: 3
SALES (est): 253.1K **Privately Held**
SIC: 5944 3911 Jewelry stores; jewelry, precious metal

**(G-6740)**
**TONY PATTERSON**
Also Called: Street Comedy Records
623 E 89th St (60619-6829)
PHONE..................................773 487-4000
Tony Patterson, *Principal*
EMP: 3 EST: 2000

# GEOGRAPHIC SECTION

## Chicago - Cook County (G-6763)

SALES (est): 130K **Privately Held**
WEB: www.streetcomedyrecords.com
SIC: 3652 Compact laser discs, prerecorded

### (G-6741)
### TOOTSIE ROLL COMPANY INC
7401 S Cicero Ave (60629-5885)
PHONE.....................773 838-3400
Ellen R Gordon, *President*
Barry Bowen, *Treasurer*
G Howard Ember Jr, *VP Finance*
Lucille Crocilla, *Exec Sec*
EMP: 1000
SQ FT: 1,500,000
SALES (est): 132.2MM
SALES (corp-wide): 521.1MM **Publicly Held**
WEB: www.tootsie-roll.com
SIC: 2064 Candy & other confectionery products
HQ: Tootsie Roll Industries, Llc
7401 S Cicero Ave
Chicago IL 60629

### (G-6742)
### TOOTSIE ROLL INDUSTRIES INC (PA)
7401 S Cicero Ave (60629-5885)
PHONE.....................773 838-3400
Fax: 773 838-3534
Ellen R Gordon, *Ch of Bd*
John P Majors, *Vice Pres*
John W Newlin Jr, *VP Mfg*
Barry P Bowen, *Treasurer*
G Howard Ember Jr, *VP Finance*
◆ EMP: 850
SQ FT: 2,354,000
SALES: 521.1MM **Publicly Held**
WEB: www.tootsie-roll.com
SIC: 2064 Candy & other confectionery products

### (G-6743)
### TOOTSIE ROLL INDUSTRIES LLC (HQ)
7401 S Cicero Ave (60629-5885)
PHONE.....................773 245-4202
Ellen Gordon, *President*
G Howard Ember, *CFO*
Barry Bowen, *Treasurer*
EMP: 4
SALES (est): 182.4MM
SALES (corp-wide): 521.1MM **Publicly Held**
SIC: 2064 Candy & other confectionery products
PA: Tootsie Roll Industries, Inc.
7401 S Cicero Ave
Chicago IL 60629
773 838-3400

### (G-6744)
### TOP NOTCH SILK SCREENING
3382 S Archer Ave (60608-6810)
PHONE.....................773 847-6335
Fax: 773 847-6635
Sam Vainisi, *President*
Tony Slezak, *Treasurer*
Thomas Liberti, *Manager*
Pat Vainisi, *Admin Sec*
EMP: 7
SQ FT: 7,500
SALES (est): 590K **Privately Held**
WEB: www.topnotch-tees.com
SIC: 2261 2396 Screen printing of cotton broadwoven fabrics; automotive & apparel trimmings

### (G-6745)
### TOPIARIUS
2950 W Carroll Ave Ste 2 (60612-1755)
PHONE.....................773 475-7784
Craig Jenkins-Sutton, *President*
EMP: 7
SALES (est): 1.4MM **Privately Held**
SIC: 2851 Removers & cleaners

### (G-6746)
### TOPWEB LLC
5450 N Northwest Hwy (60630-1114)
PHONE.....................773 975-0400
Charles Gross, *President*
Patrick O'Toole, *Controller*
EMP: 41
SQ FT: 55,000
SALES (est): 4.8MM
SALES (corp-wide): 9.7MM **Privately Held**
SIC: 2752 Commercial printing, offset
PA: Newsweb Corporation
1645 W Fullerton Ave
Chicago IL 60614
773 975-5727

### (G-6747)
### TORA PRINT SVCS
1500 N Greenview Ave (60642-2669)
PHONE.....................773 252-1000
Thomas Geiser, *Owner*
EMP: 4
SALES (est): 315.6K **Privately Held**
SIC: 2752 Commercial printing, lithographic

### (G-6748)
### TORSTENSON GLASS CO (PA)
3233 N Sheffield Ave (60657-2210)
PHONE.....................773 525-0435
Fax: 773 525-0009
Douglas Studt, *President*
Brad Studt, *Vice Pres*
Steve Deyoung, *Marketing Staff*
Kevin Byczek, *Information Mgr*
▲ EMP: 20 EST: 1889
SQ FT: 50,000
SALES (est): 2.6MM **Privately Held**
WEB: www.tglass.com
SIC: 3231 5039 Products of purchased glass; exterior flat glass: plate or window; interior flat glass: plate or window

### (G-6749)
### TORTILLERIA ATOTONILCO INC
1850 W 47th St (60609-3845)
PHONE.....................773 523-0800
Oscar Munoz, *President*
EMP: 20
SQ FT: 25,200
SALES (corp-wide): 14.2MM **Privately Held**
WEB: www.atotonilcoinc.com
SIC: 5149 5461 2051 Crackers, cookies & bakery products; bakeries; bread, cake & related products
PA: Tortilleria Atotonilco, Inc.
1707 W 47th St
Chicago IL 60609
773 523-0800

### (G-6750)
### TOTALWORKS INC
2240 N Elston Ave (60614-2906)
PHONE.....................773 489-4313
Gail Ludewig, *President*
Bruce Jensen, *Corp Secy*
Carol Gronlund, *CFO*
EMP: 35
SQ FT: 15,000
SALES (est): 3.3MM **Privately Held**
WEB: www.totalworks.net
SIC: 2741 Catalogs: publishing only, not printed on site

### (G-6751)
### TOWER AUTOMOTIVE OPERATIONS I
12350 S Avenue O (60633-1459)
PHONE.....................773 646-6550
Fax: 773 646-6557
Matt Pollick, *Branch Mgr*
EMP: 358
SALES (corp-wide): 1.9B **Publicly Held**
SIC: 3465 Automotive stampings
HQ: Tower Automotive Operations Usa I Llc
17672 N Laurel Park Dr 400e
Livonia MI 48152
248 675-6000

### (G-6752)
### TOWER OIL & TECHNOLOGY CO
Also Called: Industrial Technology
4300 S Tripp Ave (60632-4319)
PHONE.....................773 927-6161
Fax: 773 927-3105
Ron Bielech, *Branch Mgr*
EMP: 35

SALES (corp-wide): 5.2MM **Privately Held**
WEB: www.toweroil.com
SIC: 5172 2992 2899 Petroleum products; lubricating oils & greases; chemical preparations
PA: Tower Oil & Technology Co.
4300 S Tripp Ave
Chicago IL 60632
773 927-6161

### (G-6753)
### TRADINGSCREEN INC
566 W Adams St Ste 350 (60661-3659)
PHONE.....................312 447-0100
Aicha Boti, *Manager*
EMP: 3
SALES (corp-wide): 14.8MM **Privately Held**
SIC: 7372 Prepackaged software
PA: Tradingscreen Inc.
215 Park Ave S Ste 1300
New York NY 10003
212 359-4100

### (G-6754)
### TRAFFCO PRODUCTS LLC
7731 S South Chicago Ave (60619-2721)
PHONE.....................773 374-6645
Alex Degutis, *Vice Pres*
Paul Leitelt, *Mng Member*
Andrew Leitelt,
EMP: 9
SQ FT: 25,000
SALES (est): 500K **Privately Held**
SIC: 3669 Traffic signals, electric

### (G-6755)
### TRAFFICCOM (HQ)
425 W Randolph St (60606-1530)
PHONE.....................773 997-8351
Judson Green, *President*
David Mullen, *CFO*
Eduardo Pletsch, *Finance*
Lawrence M Kaplan, *Admin Sec*
EMP: 7
SALES (est): 969.7K
SALES (corp-wide): 673.3MM **Privately Held**
SIC: 2752 Maps, lithographed
PA: Here Holding Corporation
425 W Randolph St
Chicago IL 60606
312 894-7000

### (G-6756)
### TRAMCO PUMP CO
1500 W Adams St (60607-2485)
PHONE.....................312 243-5800
Fax: 312 243-0702
John P Obermaier, *President*
Tayat Rashid, *Purch Mgr*
EMP: 26
SQ FT: 20,000
SALES (est): 11.1MM **Privately Held**
WEB: www.tramcopump.com
SIC: 3561 5084 3594 Pumps & pumping equipment; processing & packaging equipment; fluid power pumps & motors

### (G-6757)
### TRANSAGRA INTERNATIONAL INC (PA)
155 N Michigan Ave # 720 (60601-7707)
PHONE.....................312 856-1010
Henry A Sakai, *President*
Lisa Sakai, *Vice Pres*
EMP: 2
SQ FT: 450
SALES (est): 1.1MM **Privately Held**
WEB: www.culbac.com
SIC: 2048 Feed supplements

### (G-6758)
### TRANSCO PRODUCTS INC (HQ)
200 N La Salle St # 1550 (60601-1034)
PHONE.....................312 427-2818
Fax: 312 427-4975
Edward Wolbert, *President*
Bruce Alpha, *Vice Pres*
Kevin Hawks, *Project Mgr*
Nathan Miller, *Project Mgr*
Phil Vazquez, *Project Mgr*
▲ EMP: 80
SQ FT: 19,000

SALES: 14.8MM
SALES (corp-wide): 109.8MM **Privately Held**
WEB: www.transcoinc.com
SIC: 3479 3296 Coating of metals & formed products; insulation: rock wool, slag & silica minerals
PA: Transco Inc.
200 N La Salle St # 1550
Chicago IL 60601
312 896-8527

### (G-6759)
### TRANSCO RAILWAY PRODUCTS INC (HQ)
200 N La Salle St # 1550 (60601-1034)
PHONE.....................312 427-2818
Edward Wolbert, *CEO*
J Robert Nelson, *President*
Paul Armstrong, *Division Mgr*
Randy Stinnett, *Business Mgr*
Bruce Alpha, *Vice Pres*
▲ EMP: 6
SQ FT: 19,000
SALES: 76.7MM
SALES (corp-wide): 109.8MM **Privately Held**
SIC: 3743 4789 Railroad equipment; railroad car repair
PA: Transco Inc.
200 N La Salle St # 1550
Chicago IL 60601
312 896-8527

### (G-6760)
### TRANSCO RAILWAY PRODUCTS INC
200 N La Salle St # 1550 (60601-1034)
PHONE.....................419 562-1031
Gary Baren, *Manager*
Paul Beran, *Manager*
Avid Rhoades, *Manager*
Lonny Thompson, *Manager*
EMP: 80
SALES (corp-wide): 109.8MM **Privately Held**
SIC: 3537 3743 Industrial trucks & tractors; railroad equipment
HQ: Transco Railway Products Inc.
200 N La Salle St # 1550
Chicago IL 60601
312 427-2818

### (G-6761)
### TRANSFER LOGISTICS INC
11600 S Burley Ave (60617-7201)
PHONE.....................773 646-0529
Steven C Joseph, *President*
Hal Tolin, *Admin Sec*
Amy Atteberry, *Admin Asst*
EMP: 2
SALES (est): 290K **Privately Held**
SIC: 3537 Loading docks: portable, adjustable & hydraulic

### (G-6762)
### TRANSLUCENT PUBLISHING CORP
222 W Ontario St Ste 410 (60654-3654)
PHONE.....................312 447-5450
Richard Rueckheim, *Director*
EMP: 15 EST: 2013
SALES (est): 1.2MM **Privately Held**
SIC: 2741 Miscellaneous publishing

### (G-6763)
### TREASURE ISLAND FOODS INC
75 W Elm St (60610-2789)
PHONE.....................312 440-1144
Fax: 312 440-9821
Richard Roph, *Manager*
EMP: 75
SALES (corp-wide): 95MM **Privately Held**
WEB: www.dazzlederm.com
SIC: 5411 5992 5421 2051 Grocery stores, independent; florists; meat & fish markets; bread, cake & related products
PA: Treasure Island Foods, Inc.
3460 N Broadway St
Chicago IL 60657
773 327-3880

# Chicago - Cook County (G-6764)

**(G-6764)**
**TREASURE ISLAND FOODS INC**
2121 N Clybourn Ave # 9  (60614-4031)
PHONE.................................773 880-8880
Fax: 773 880-0206
Babe Magnus, *Branch Mgr*
EMP: 150
SALES (corp-wide): 95MM **Privately Held**
WEB: www.dazzlederm.com
SIC: 5411  5992  2051  Grocery stores; florists; bread, cake & related products
PA: Treasure Island Foods, Inc.
3460 N Broadway St
Chicago IL 60657
773 327-3880

**(G-6765)**
**TREASURE ISLAND FOODS INC**
1639 N Wells St  (60614-6001)
PHONE.................................312 642-1105
Fax: 312 642-8736
Richard Roth, *Manager*
Alan Arima, *Manager*
Jerry Riordan, *Manager*
EMP: 75
SALES (corp-wide): 95MM **Privately Held**
WEB: www.dazzlederm.com
SIC: 5411  2051  Grocery stores, chain; bread, cake & related products
PA: Treasure Island Foods, Inc.
3460 N Broadway St
Chicago IL 60657
773 327-3880

**(G-6766)**
**TREATMENT PRODUCTS LTD**
4701 W Augusta Blvd  (60651-3307)
PHONE.................................773 626-8888
Fax: 773 626-6200
Jeff Victor, *President*
Ken Victor, *Vice Pres*
Luis Vasquez, *Representative*
◆ EMP: 40
SQ FT: 60,000
SALES (est): 11MM **Privately Held**
WEB: www.tiregold.com
SIC: 2842  7389  Automobile polish; waxes for wood, leather & other materials; packaging & labeling services

**(G-6767)**
**TREND PUBLISHING INC**
Also Called: Modern Metal Products
625 N Michigan Ave # 1100  (60611-3110)
PHONE.................................312 654-2300
William J D'Alexander, *President*
Neiland Pennington, *Editor*
Traci Fonville, *Business Mgr*
Carlotta Lacy, *Prdtn Mgr*
Wayne Krusen, *Finance Mgr*
EMP: 24
SQ FT: 8,000
SALES (est): 4.1MM **Privately Held**
WEB: www.modernmetals.com
SIC: 2721  Magazines: publishing only, not printed on site

**(G-6768)**
**TRENDLER INC**
4540 W 51st St  (60632-4554)
PHONE.................................773 284-6600
Fax: 773 581-6250
Andreas R Gfesser, *President*
Martin F Gfesser, *President*
Anton Gfesser, *Chairman*
Steven A Gfesser, *Corp Secy*
Mike Kohlstedt, *Manager*
▲ EMP: 45 EST: 1933
SQ FT: 120,000
SALES (est): 12.1MM **Privately Held**
WEB: www.trendler.com
SIC: 3499  2511  Furniture parts, metal; unassembled or unfinished furniture, household: wood; rockers, except upholstered: wood

**(G-6769)**
**TRI INTERNATIONAL CO**
Also Called: Tootsie Roll Industries
7401 S Cicero Ave  (60629-5818)
PHONE.................................773 838-3400
Howard Denver, *CEO*
Ellen R Gordon, *President*
Thomas Corr, *Vice Pres*
John Major, *Vice Pres*
Howard Ember, *CFO*
EMP: 650
SALES (est): 36.5MM
SALES (corp-wide): 521.1MM **Publicly Held**
WEB: www.tootsie-roll.com
SIC: 2064  Chocolate candy, except solid chocolate
PA: Tootsie Roll Industries, Inc.
7401 S Cicero Ave
Chicago IL 60629
773 838-3400

**(G-6770)**
**TRI-LITE INC**
1642 N Besly Ct  (60642-1526)
PHONE.................................773 384-7765
Fax: 773 384-5115
Robert Hearling, *President*
Ricardo Diaz, *General Mgr*
Barry Seid, *Chairman*
Rick Mincher, *Buyer*
Rick Overholtzer, *Buyer*
▲ EMP: 22
SQ FT: 20,000
SALES (est): 5.2MM **Privately Held**
WEB: www.triliteinc.com
SIC: 3647  3648  3646  3669  Automotive lighting fixtures; lighting fixtures, except electric: residential; stage lighting equipment; commercial indusl & institutional electric lighting fixtures, emergency alarms; sirens, electric: vehicle, marine, industrial & air raid; intercommunication systems, electric; electric household fans, heaters & humidifiers

**(G-6771)**
**TRIANGLE PACKAGE MACHINERY CO (PA)**
6655 W Diversey Ave  (60707-2239)
PHONE.................................773 889-0200
Fax: 773 889-4221
Bryan L Muskat, *President*
Mike Summers, *CFO*
Michael Summer, *Finance Dir*
EMP: 170 EST: 1923
SQ FT: 98,000
SALES (est): 26.3MM **Privately Held**
SIC: 3565  Packaging machinery; bag opening, filling & closing machines

**(G-6772)**
**TRIBUNE FINANCE SERVICE CENTER**
435 N Michigan Ave Fl 2  (60611-4024)
PHONE.................................312 595-0783
Fax: 312 329-0420
Bruce A Karsh, *Chairman*
EMP: 1
SALES (est): 221.9K
SALES (corp-wide): 1.6B **Publicly Held**
WEB: www.tribune.com
SIC: 2711  Newspapers, publishing & printing
PA: Tronc, Inc.
435 N Michigan Ave
Chicago IL 60611
312 222-9100

**(G-6773)**
**TRIBUNE PUBLISHING COMPANY LLC (HQ)**
435 N Michigan Ave Fl 2  (60611-4024)
PHONE.................................312 222-9100
Eddy Hartenstein, *Ch of Bd*
Jack Fuller, *President*
John Schram, *Managing Dir*
Kathy Thomson, *COO*
Laverne Horton, *Counsel*
EMP: 20
SALES (est): 1.5B
SALES (corp-wide): 1.6B **Publicly Held**
SIC: 2711  Newspapers
PA: Tronc, Inc.
435 N Michigan Ave
Chicago IL 60611
312 222-9100

**(G-6774)**
**TRIBUNE PUBLISHING COMPANY LLC**
Also Called: Chicago Magazine
435 N Michigan Ave Fl 2  (60611-4024)
PHONE.................................312 832-6711
Fax: 312 222-0287
Susanna Homan, *Publisher*
Jeff Kobbeman, *Controller*
Tom Hanks, *Finance Mgr*
Elizabeth V Goodchild, *Finance*
Kristin Shea, *Adv Dir*
EMP: 55
SALES (corp-wide): 1.6B **Publicly Held**
SIC: 2711  2721  Newspapers; periodicals
HQ: Tribune Publishing Company, Llc
435 N Michigan Ave Fl 2
Chicago IL 60611
312 222-9100

**(G-6775)**
**TRIBUNE TOWER**
435 N Michigan Ave Fl 2  (60611-4024)
PHONE.................................312 981-7200
Kenney Crane, *Principal*
EMP: 11
SALES (est): 1MM **Privately Held**
SIC: 2711  Newspapers, publishing & printing

**(G-6776)**
**TRICO BELTING & SUPPLY COMPANY**
5450 W Roosevelt Rd  (60644-1467)
PHONE.................................773 261-0988
Fax: 773 261-0978
Mike Lader, *Owner*
Lance Watterson, *Manager*
EMP: 15
SALES (corp-wide): 94.7MM **Privately Held**
WEB: www.tricobelt.com
SIC: 3496  Conveyor belts
HQ: Trico Belting & Supply Company
9965 Farr Ct
West Chester OH 45246
513 860-8400

**(G-6777)**
**TRIPNARY LLC**
233 E Wacker Dr  (60601-5104)
PHONE.................................512 554-1911
Abhishek Ghuwalewala,
EMP: 3
SALES (est): 167.1K **Privately Held**
SIC: 7372  7389  Application computer software;

**(G-6778)**
**TRIPPE MANUFACTURING COMPANY**
Also Called: Tripp Lite
1111 W 35th St Fl 12  (60609-1404)
PHONE.................................773 869-1111
Fax: 773 644-6505
Elbert Howell, *CEO*
Glen Haeflinger, *President*
Jeff Novak, *Regional Mgr*
Caroline Perigny, *Business Mgr*
Daniel Sanchez, *Sr Corp Ofcr*
◆ EMP: 500
SQ FT: 950,000
SALES: 380K **Privately Held**
WEB: www.tripplite.com
SIC: 3577  Computer peripheral equipment

**(G-6779)**
**TRITON INDUSTRIES INC (PA)**
1020 N Kolmar Ave  (60651-3343)
PHONE.................................773 384-3700
Fax: 773 384-8748
Marvin R Wortell, *Ch of Bd*
Brenton R Wortell, *President*
Louis Shapiro, *Counsel*
Cindy Churak, *Sls & Mktg Exec*
Thomas Fuss, *CFO*
EMP: 149 EST: 1961
SQ FT: 100,000
SALES (est): 24.2MM **Privately Held**
WEB: www.tritonindustries.com
SIC: 3469  3441  Stamping metal for the trade; electronic enclosures, stamped or pressed metal; kitchen fixtures & equipment: metal, except cast aluminum; fabricated structural metal

**(G-6780)**
**TRIUMPH BOOKS CORP**
814 N Franklin St Fl 3  (60610-3813)
PHONE.................................312 337-0747
Fax: 312 663-3557
Mitchell Rogatz, *President*
Noah Amstadter, *Editor*
Jeff Fedotin, *Editor*
Adam Motin, *Editor*
Bill Ames, *Opers Mgr*
◆ EMP: 22
SQ FT: 4,100
SALES (est): 4.4MM **Privately Held**
SIC: 2731  Books: publishing only

**(G-6781)**
**TRONC INC (PA)**
435 N Michigan Ave  (60611-4066)
PHONE.................................312 222-9100
Justin C Dearborn, *CEO*
Michael W Ferro Jr, *Ch of Bd*
Tony W Hunter, *President*
Timothy E Ryan, *President*
Julie K Xanders, *Exec VP*
EMP: 114
SQ FT: 318,000
SALES (est): 1.6B **Publicly Held**
SIC: 2711  Newspapers; newspapers, publishing & printing

**(G-6782)**
**TROY DESIGN & MANUFACTURING CO**
12359 S Burley Ave  (60633-1296)
PHONE.................................773 646-0804
EMP: 9
SALES (corp-wide): 151.8B **Publicly Held**
SIC: 3999  Barber & beauty shop equipment
HQ: Troy Design & Manufacturing Co
14425 N Sheldon Rd
Plymouth MI 48170
313 592-2300

**(G-6783)**
**TRU SERV CORP**
8600 W Bryn Mawr Ave  (60631-3579)
P.O. Box 31850  (60631-0850)
PHONE.................................773 695-5674
Fax: 773 695-6566
EMP: 18 EST: 2008
SALES (est): 2.4MM **Privately Held**
SIC: 2851  Mfg Paints/Allied Products

**(G-6784)**
**TRU-GUARD MANUFACTURING CO**
10733 S Michigan Ave  (60628-3509)
PHONE.................................773 568-5264
Fax: 773 568-4002
John Brooks, *President*
EMP: 3
SQ FT: 4,000
SALES (est): 210K **Privately Held**
SIC: 3446  1791  3496  3442  Ornamental metalwork; structural steel erection; miscellaneous fabricated wire products; metal doors, sash & trim; millwork

**(G-6785)**
**TRUCKERS OIL PROS INC**
2756 W 35th St  (60632-1604)
PHONE.................................773 523-8990
Fax: 773 523-2464
Michael Marden, *President*
Ponch Acosta, *Admin Sec*
EMP: 11
SQ FT: 20,000
SALES (est): 1.4MM **Privately Held**
SIC: 2992  7542  Oils & greases, blending & compounding; carwashes

**(G-6786)**
**TRUE VALUE COMPANY (PA)**
8600 W Bryn Mawr Ave 100s  (60631-3505)
P.O. Box 31850  (60631-0850)
PHONE.................................773 695-5000
Fax: 773 695-7259
Brent Burger, *Ch of Bd*
John Hartmann, *President*
Richard Grubbs, *Regional Mgr*
Lisa Fortuna, *Business Mgr*
Paul Mezzatesta, *Business Mgr*
▼ EMP: 500 EST: 1953

## GEOGRAPHIC SECTION

Chicago - Cook County (G-6814)

SQ FT: 175,000
SALES: 1.5B  Privately Held
WEB: www.TrueValue.com
SIC: 5072  2851  3991  Hardware; paints & paint additives; paint & varnish brushes

### (G-6787)
### TRUEPAD LLC
180 N Wabash Ave Ste 730  (60601-3600)
PHONE .................................. 847 274-6898
Paul Lazarre,
Scott Hammack,
EMP: 18
SALES (est): 937.6K  Privately Held
SIC: 7372  7389  Business oriented computer software;

### (G-6788)
### TRUEQUEST COMMUNICATIONS LLC
Also Called: Vision Vocation Guide
53 W Jackson Blvd # 1140  (60604-3619)
PHONE .................................. 312 356-9900
Fax: 312 829-7400
Patrice Tuohy, President
Dianne Potter, Prdtn Mgr
Diane Walde, Manager
Curtis Long, Director
Jennifer Tomshack, Director
EMP: 6
SQ FT: 1,800
SALES: 1.2MM  Privately Held
WEB: www.truequest.biz
SIC: 2741  4899  Miscellaneous publishing; data communication services

### (G-6789)
### TRUSTWAVE HOLDINGS INC (DH)
70 W Madison St Ste 600  (60602-4210)
PHONE .................................. 312 750-0950
Robert J McCullen, CEO
Jarrett Benavidez, Managing Dir
Andrew Bokor, Exec VP
Steven Mallia, Vice Pres
Marc Shinbrood, Vice Pres
EMP: 1
SALES (est): 76.9MM  Privately Held
WEB: www.trustwave.com
SIC: 7373  7372  Systems integration services; prepackaged software
HQ: Trustwave Corporation
    70 W Madison St Ste 600
    Chicago IL 60602
    312 873-7500

### (G-6790)
### TRUTH LABS LLC
212 W Superior St Ste 505  (60654-2608)
PHONE .................................. 312 291-9035
EMP: 10
SQ FT: 3,000
SALES: 900K
SALES (corp-wide): 17.4MM  Privately Held
SIC: 7371  7372  Software programming applications; application computer software
PA: Clarity Consulting Inc.
    20 N Wacker Dr Ste 1450
    Chicago IL 60606
    312 863-3100

### (G-6791)
### TUNNEL VISION CONSULTING GROUP
Also Called: Mary A. Metcalf
8844 S Jeffery Blvd  (60617-2909)
P.O. Box 496762  (60649-0084)
PHONE .................................. 773 367-7292
Mary A Metcalf, Principal
Mary Vann, Co-Owner
EMP: 3  EST: 2011
SALES (est): 178.8K  Privately Held
SIC: 3571  3575  3829  7373  Electronic computers; keyboards, computer, office machine; instrument board gauges, automotive: computerized; computer-aided manufacturing (CAM) systems service; operator training, computer

### (G-6792)
### TURFMAPP INC
3550 N Lake Shore Dr  (60657-1944)
PHONE .................................. 703 473-5678
Triratana Sanguanbun, President
Trisikh Sanguanbun, Vice Pres
EMP: 6
SALES (est): 217.2K  Privately Held
SIC: 7372  7389  Prepackaged software;

### (G-6793)
### TURK ELECTRIC SIGN CO
Also Called: Flashtric
3434 N Cicero Ave 3436  (60641-3720)
PHONE .................................. 773 736-9300
Fax: 773 282-5477
Alexander Demir, President
Helen Demir, Corp Secy
Bedia Moallem, Shareholder
EMP: 1
SQ FT: 3,000
SALES: 400K  Privately Held
WEB: www.flashtric.com
SIC: 3993  Electric signs

### (G-6794)
### TURNER AGWARD
Also Called: Intelliginix Consulting Svcs
5642 W Div St Ste 212  (60651)
PHONE .................................. 773 669-8559
Agward Turner, Owner
EMP: 5
SALES (est): 240K  Privately Held
SIC: 1731  7372  7373  8748  Voice, data & video wiring contractor; operating systems computer software; systems engineering, computer related; systems engineering consultant, ex. computer or professional;

### (G-6795)
### TWEETEN FIBRE CO
Also Called: Masters Billiard Chalk
1756 W Hubbard St  (60622-6214)
PHONE .................................. 312 733-7878
Fax: 312 733-0767
Robert R Knight, President
Irvin Nemecek, Vice Pres
Jim Knight, Controller
▲ EMP: 20
SQ FT: 18,000
SALES (est): 2.3MM  Privately Held
WEB: www.tweeten.us
SIC: 3949  Billiard & pool equipment & supplies, general

### (G-6796)
### TWO J S SHEET METAL WORKS INC
5828 S Oakley Ave  (60636-1525)
PHONE .................................. 773 436-9424
Juan Macias, President
Jesus Macias, Vice Pres
EMP: 4
SQ FT: 5,600
SALES (est): 619.1K  Privately Held
SIC: 3444  Sheet metalwork

### (G-6797)
### TWO JS COPIES NOW INC
Also Called: Sir Speedy
6725 N Northwest Hwy  (60631-1319)
PHONE .................................. 847 292-2679
Fax: 847 292-2681
John Crocello, President
Jeanne Crocello, Vice Pres
EMP: 6
SQ FT: 1,200
SALES (est): 832K  Privately Held
WEB: www.sirspeedyrosemont.com
SIC: 2752  Commercial printing, lithographic

### (G-6798)
### TWO TOWER FRAMES INC
Also Called: Safigel
1300 W Belmont Ave # 111  (60657-3240)
PHONE .................................. 773 697-6856
Eric P Sharvelle, President
EMP: 4
SALES (est): 431.4K  Privately Held
SIC: 3827  5048  Optical instruments & lenses; ophthalmic goods; contact lenses; frames, ophthalmic

### (G-6799)
### TWT MARKETING INC
Also Called: Wecaretoo
2719 W Lunt Ave  (60645-3005)
PHONE .................................. 773 274-4470
Shelby Miller, President
Richard Scheafer, Vice Pres
EMP: 2  EST: 1992
SALES (est): 200K  Privately Held
WEB: www.wecaretoo.com
SIC: 4813  2741  ; telephone & other directory publishing

### (G-6800)
### TXTICON LLC
4027 N Kedvale Ave  (60641-2386)
PHONE .................................. 312 860-3378
Fredrick Fugiel,
EMP: 7
SALES (est): 331.2K  Privately Held
SIC: 7372  Application computer software

### (G-6801)
### TYLKA PRINTING INC
4915 W 63rd St  (60638-5810)
PHONE .................................. 773 767-3775
Fax: 773 767-9447
David Tylka, President
Linda Hlado, Vice Pres
EMP: 4
SQ FT: 4,000
SALES: 800K  Privately Held
SIC: 2752  Commercial printing, lithographic; commercial printing, offset

### (G-6802)
### TYLU WIRELESS TECHNOLOGY LLC
3424 S State St  (60616-5374)
PHONE .................................. 312 260-7934
Michael E Aldridge, CEO
Tom Freeburg, Vice Pres
Paul Schaafsma, Vice Pres
EMP: 8
SQ FT: 2,000
SALES (est): 695K  Privately Held
WEB: www.tylu.com
SIC: 3699  7373  4812  Security control equipment & systems; systems software development services; cellular telephone services

### (G-6803)
### U-TRACKING INTERNATIONAL INC
500 N Michigan Ave # 300  (60611-3777)
PHONE .................................. 312 242-6003
EMP: 32
SQ FT: 5,000
SALES: 2.5MM  Privately Held
SIC: 3663  Satellites, communications

### (G-6804)
### UHLIR MANUFACTURING CORP
2642 W Cullerton St  (60608-2422)
PHONE .................................. 773 376-5289
Jim Uhlir, President
Jana Uhlir, Corp Secy
EMP: 6
SQ FT: 5,000
SALES (est): 420.1K  Privately Held
WEB: www.unityusa.com
SIC: 3599  Machine shop, jobbing & repair

### (G-6805)
### UIC
1747 W Roosevelt Rd 145  (60608-1264)
PHONE .................................. 312 413-7697
Octavia Kincaid, Principal
Melissa Zimmerman, Human Resources
EMP: 17
SALES (est): 1.8MM  Privately Held
SIC: 3999  Stage hardware & equipment, except lighting

### (G-6806)
### ULLA OF FINLAND
6221 N Leona Ave  (60646-4829)
PHONE .................................. 773 763-0700
Ulla Marzolf, Managing Prtnr
Serge Marzolf, Partner
EMP: 2
SALES: 200K  Privately Held
SIC: 3961  Costume jewelry

### (G-6807)
### ULTIMATE SIGN CO
5511 W Pensacola Ave  (60641-1335)
PHONE .................................. 773 282-4595
Jack Fraizer, President
Josh Cooper, Bd of Directors
EMP: 6
SALES: 200K  Privately Held
SIC: 3993  Signs & advertising specialties

### (G-6808)
### ULTRA-METRIC TOOL CO
2952 N Leavitt St  (60618-8197)
PHONE .................................. 773 281-4200
Fax: 773 281-6185
Steven Huy, President
Frank Gieger, Vice Pres
EMP: 17
SQ FT: 17,000
SALES (est): 1.7MM  Privately Held
WEB: www.umthermoform.com
SIC: 3599  3544  Machine shop, jobbing & repair; special dies, tools, jigs & fixtures

### (G-6809)
### UMPHREYS MCGEE INC
1530 W Oakdale Ave  (60657-4011)
PHONE .................................. 773 880-0024
Vince Iwinski, Manager
EMP: 3
SALES (est): 263.8K  Privately Held
SIC: 3931  Musical instruments

### (G-6810)
### UNCOMMON RADIANT
2826 W Fitch Ave  (60645-2906)
PHONE .................................. 773 640-1674
Hildi Dvora, President
Yakov Dvora, Vice Pres
▲ EMP: 3
SALES (est): 352.3K  Privately Held
SIC: 3645  Residential lighting fixtures

### (G-6811)
### UNI-GLIDE CORP
2300 N Kilbourn Ave  (60639-3402)
PHONE .................................. 773 235-2100
Brian H Johnson, President
Charlotte Cooper, Personnel
Anna Johnson, Manager
EMP: 7
SALES (est): 296.3K
SALES (corp-wide): 6.4MM  Privately Held
SIC: 2591  5072  Curtain & drapery rods, poles & fixtures; hardware
PA: Rensel-Chicago, Inc.
    2300 N Kilbourn Ave
    Chicago IL 60639
    773 235-2100

### (G-6812)
### UNICHEM CORPORATION
1201 W 37th St  (60609-2122)
PHONE .................................. 773 376-8872
Eugene O Korey, President
Nowell Korey, President
Irv O Korey, Vice Pres
EMP: 12
SQ FT: 25,000
SALES (est): 2.2MM  Privately Held
WEB: www.unichemco.com
SIC: 2841  Soap: granulated, liquid, cake, flaked or chip; detergents, synthetic organic or inorganic alkaline

### (G-6813)
### UNICUT CORPORATION
Also Called: Super Life
1770 W Berteau Ave # 505  (60613-1872)
PHONE .................................. 773 525-4210
Fax: 773 525-7966
Marcel Bolchis, President
EMP: 6
SQ FT: 10,000
SALES (est): 560K  Privately Held
WEB: www.unicut.com
SIC: 3425  3546  Saw blades, chain type; saw blades for hand or power saws; power-driven handtools

### (G-6814)
### UNION FOODS INC
Also Called: Dunkin' Donuts
233 N Michigan Ave  (60601-5519)
PHONE .................................. 201 327-2828
Sirajuddin Virani, President
EMP: 3  EST: 1990
SALES (est): 96.1K  Privately Held
SIC: 5461  2024  5812  Doughnuts; ice cream & frozen desserts; eating places

# Chicago - Cook County (G-6815)   GEOGRAPHIC SECTION

**(G-6815)**
**UNION TANK CAR COMPANY (DH)**
175 W Jackson Blvd # 2100  (60604-2683)
PHONE .................................. 312 431-3111
Fax: 312 347-5707
Kenneth P Fischl, *President*
Robert K Lorch, *Vice Pres*
Mark J Garrette, *CFO*
Robert W Webb, *Admin Sec*
Chuck Weiher, *Administration*
◆ **EMP:** 200
**SQ FT:** 16,000
**SALES (est):** 1.9B
**SALES (corp-wide):** 223.6B **Publicly Held**
**WEB:** www.utlx.com
**SIC:** 3743 4741 4789 5051  Train cars & equipment, freight or passenger; railroad car rebuilding; rental of railroad cars; railroad car repair; metals service centers & offices
**HQ:** Marmon Holdings, Inc.
    181 W Madison St Ste 2600
    Chicago IL 60602
    312 372-9500

**(G-6816)**
**UNION TANK CAR COMPANY**
175 W Jackson Blvd # 2100  (60604-2683)
PHONE .................................. 312 431-3111
Cynthia Rein, *Principal*
Mark J Garrette, *CFO*
Frank S Ptak, *Director*
**EMP:** 136
**SALES (corp-wide):** 223.6B **Publicly Held**
**WEB:** www.utlx.com
**SIC:** 3743  Train cars & equipment, freight or passenger
**HQ:** Union Tank Car Company
    175 W Jackson Blvd # 2100
    Chicago IL 60604
    312 431-3111

**(G-6817)**
**UNIPAQ INC**
2426 W Lyndale St  (60647-3111)
PHONE .................................. 773 252-3000
Fax: 773 252-3001
Dan Christin, *President*
**EMP:** 4
**SQ FT:** 2,500
**SALES:** 1MM **Privately Held**
**WEB:** www.unipaq.com
**SIC:** 3053  Packing materials

**(G-6818)**
**UNIQEMA AMERICAS**
4650 S Racine Ave  (60609-3321)
PHONE .................................. 773 376-9000
Fax: 773 376-0095
Woodson Demeris, *Manager*
**EMP:** 20
**SALES (est):** 3.9MM **Privately Held**
**SIC:** 2899  Chemical preparations

**(G-6819)**
**UNIQUE ENVELOPE CORPORATION**
5958 S Oak Park Ave  (60638-3202)
PHONE .................................. 773 586-0330
Melvin Kozbiel, *President*
Darrell Kozbiel, *Vice Pres*
Colette Kozbiel, *Admin Sec*
**EMP:** 25
**SQ FT:** 40,000
**SALES (est):** 3.9MM **Privately Held**
**SIC:** 2754 2759 2677  Envelopes: gravure printing; commercial printing; envelopes

**(G-6820)**
**UNITED AMERCN HEALTHCARE CORP (PA)**
303 E Wacker Dr Ste 1040  (60601-5216)
PHONE .................................. 313 393-4571
John M Fife, *Ch of Bd*
Joanne Shuey, *Vice Pres*
Jill Tobin, *Vice Pres*
Jagu Vanaharam, *Vice Pres*
Jeaneen Morris, *Opers Staff*
▲ **EMP:** 16
**SQ FT:** 1,000
**SALES:** 8.4MM **Publicly Held**
**WEB:** www.uahc.com
**SIC:** 3841 3699  Surgical & medical instruments; laser welding, drilling & cutting equipment; laser systems & equipment

**(G-6821)**
**UNITED BINDERY SERVICE**
1845 W Carroll Ave  (60612-2589)
PHONE .................................. 312 243-0240
Fax: 312 243-3080
Bruce Kosaka, *Owner*
Jim Yoshimoto, *Vice Pres*
▲ **EMP:** 45
**SQ FT:** 70,000
**SALES (est):** 5.4MM **Privately Held**
**SIC:** 2789  Bookbinding & repairing: trade, edition, library, etc.

**(G-6822)**
**UNITED CONTAINER CORPORATION**
1350 N Elston Ave  (60642-2440)
PHONE .................................. 773 342-2200
Fax: 773 342-4231
Bill Heymann, *President*
Michael Heymann, *Corp Secy*
Florian Seidel, *Manager*
Cindy Heymann, *Shareholder*
Karen Heymann, *Shareholder*
**EMP:** 27
**SQ FT:** 30,000
**SALES (est):** 6.3MM **Privately Held**
**SIC:** 2653  Boxes, corrugated: made from purchased materials; display items, solid fiber: made from purchased materials

**(G-6823)**
**UNITED FENCE CO INC**
722 W 49th Pl  (60609-5199)
PHONE .................................. 773 924-0773
Fax: 773 924-3103
Robert H Hill, *President*
Mildred Hill, *Admin Sec*
**EMP:** 5
**SQ FT:** 15,000
**SALES (est):** 615.8K **Privately Held**
**WEB:** www.unitedfenceco.com
**SIC:** 1799 5039 3446  Fence construction; wire fence, gates & accessories; architectural metalwork

**(G-6824)**
**UNITED FUEL SAVERS LLC**
516 N Ogden Ave  (60642-6421)
PHONE .................................. 312 725-4993
**EMP:** 3
**SALES (est):** 193.8K **Privately Held**
**SIC:** 2869  Fuels

**(G-6825)**
**UNITED PRINTERS INC**
1540 W 44th St  (60609-3334)
PHONE .................................. 773 376-1955
Christina Hernandez, *President*
**EMP:** 3
**SALES (est):** 222.2K **Privately Held**
**SIC:** 2759  Commercial printing

**(G-6826)**
**UNITED SPRING & MANUFACTURING**
830 N Pulaski Rd  (60651-3608)
PHONE .................................. 773 384-8464
Fax: 773 384-8260
Mitchell Celarek, *CEO*
Renee Gonyer, *Vice Pres*
Richard Weisgerber, *Purchasing*
Helen Gonyer, *Treasurer*
Cliff Gonyer, *Sales Mgr*
**EMP:** 20
**SQ FT:** 35,000
**SALES (est):** 3.1MM **Privately Held**
**WEB:** www.unitedspring.net
**SIC:** 3493 3495  Steel springs, except wire; wire springs

**(G-6827)**
**UNITED STATES AUDIO CORP**
Also Called: Kowalik Brothers
1658 W 35th St  (60609-1310)
PHONE .................................. 312 316-2929
Johm Kowalik, *President*
**EMP:** 4 **Privately Held**
**SIC:** 3651  Household audio & video equipment
**PA:** United States Audio Corporation
    411 Crabtree Ln
    Glenview IL 60025

**(G-6828)**
**UNITED STATES GEAR CORPORATION**
Also Called: North American Gear and Axel
1020 W 119th St  (60643-5216)
PHONE .................................. 773 821-5450
Fax: 773 821-0345
Sue Crabtree, *Project Mgr*
Juan Guerra, *Agent*
Pete Hamby, *Director*
**EMP:** 7
**SALES (corp-wide):** 2.2B **Publicly Held**
**WEB:** www.heattreatcorp.com
**SIC:** 3714  Gears, motor vehicle
**HQ:** United States Gear Corporation
    9420 S Stony Island Ave
    Chicago IL
    773 375-4900

**(G-6829)**
**UNITED STATES GYPSUM COMPANY (HQ)**
550 W Adams St Ste 1300  (60661-3692)
PHONE .................................. 312 606-4000
James S Metcalf, *President*
Timothy V Bixler, *Senior VP*
Dominic A Danessa, *Senior VP*
Robert B Waterhouse, *Senior VP*
Joseph M Carson, *Vice Pres*
◆ **EMP:** 385 **EST:** 1901
**SALES (est):** 1.2B
**SALES (corp-wide):** 3B **Publicly Held**
**WEB:** www.usg.com
**SIC:** 3275  Gypsum products; gypsum board; gypsum plaster
**PA:** Usg Corporation
    550 W Adams St
    Chicago IL 60661
    312 436-4000

**(G-6830)**
**UNITY HARDWOODS LLC**
5950 W 66th St Unit C  (60638-6206)
PHONE .................................. 708 701-2943
Michael Dittmer,
Rick Berryman,
Gina Guare,
**EMP:** 14
**SQ FT:** 38,000
**SALES:** 1.6MM **Privately Held**
**SIC:** 2426  Flooring, hardwood

**(G-6831)**
**UNIVERSAL ELECTRIC FOUNDRY INC**
1523 W Hubbard St  (60642-6387)
PHONE .................................. 312 421-7233
Fax: 312 421-0538
Rodney Norwell, *President*
James H Hartman, *Vice Pres*
Michael Rowley, *Manager*
Bonnie Yankura, *Manager*
**EMP:** 33 **EST:** 1912
**SQ FT:** 22,000
**SALES (est):** 8MM **Privately Held**
**WEB:** www.universalfoundry.com
**SIC:** 3325 3351 3365 3369  Alloy steel castings, except investment; bronze rolling & drawing; brass rolling & drawing; aluminum & aluminum-based alloy castings; nonferrous foundries; copper foundries

**(G-6832)**
**UNIVERSAL HOLDINGS I LLC**
Also Called: Smith Brothers Company
70 W Madison St Ste 2300  (60602-4250)
PHONE .................................. 773 847-1005
Steven Silk, *CEO*
Carol Hennessy, *CFO*
▲ **EMP:** 100
**SALES (est):** 20.7MM **Privately Held**
**SIC:** 2064  Cough drops, except pharmaceutical preparations

**(G-6833)**
**UNIVERSAL LIGHTING CORPORATION**
Also Called: Universal Lighting & Clg Sup
3084 S Lock St  (60608-5517)
PHONE .................................. 773 927-2000
Joseph Difazio, *President*
**EMP:** 6
**SALES (est):** 733.8K **Privately Held**
**SIC:** 3641  Electric lamps

**(G-6834)**
**UNIVERSAL OVERALL COMPANY**
1060 W Van Buren St  (60607-2988)
PHONE .................................. 312 226-3336
Fax: 312 226-1986
Sara Eckerling Greenberg, *President*
Jason Greenburg, *General Mgr*
Heather Eckerling, *Vice Pres*
Amy Dunadanc, *Human Res Mgr*
Amy Dunada, *Executive*
◆ **EMP:** 50 **EST:** 1924
**SQ FT:** 112,000
**SALES (est):** 7.6MM **Privately Held**
**WEB:** www.universaloverall.com
**SIC:** 2326  Men's & boys' work clothing

**(G-6835)**
**UNIVERSAL TRNSPT SYSTEMS LLC**
474 N Lake Shore Dr # 5805  (60611-3400)
PHONE .................................. 312 994-2349
David L Summers,
**EMP:** 10
**SALES (est):** 650K **Privately Held**
**SIC:** 3724 7389  Aircraft engines & engine parts;

**(G-6836)**
**UNIVERSITY OF CHICAGO**
University of Chicago Press
1427 E 60th St  (60637-2902)
PHONE .................................. 773 702-1722
Mark Aldenderfer, *Editor*
Susan Allan, *Editor*
Alison Compton, *Editor*
Holly Bland, *Ch Admin Ofcr*
John Kessler, *Sales Dir*
**EMP:** 300
**SALES (corp-wide):** 2.9B **Privately Held**
**WEB:** www.uchicago.edu
**SIC:** 2721 2731  Periodicals: publishing only; books: publishing only
**PA:** The University Of Chicago
    5801 S Ellis Ave Ste 1
    Chicago IL 60637
    773 702-1234

**(G-6837)**
**UNIVERSITY OF CHICAGO**
Also Called: University of Chicago Press
11030 S Langley Ave  (60628-3830)
PHONE .................................. 773 702-7000
Fax: 773 660-2235
Paula Duffy, *President*
T Brent, *Editor*
Andrea Canfield, *Editor*
Karen M Darling, *Editor*
Caterina Maclean, *Editor*
**EMP:** 6
**SALES (corp-wide):** 2.9B **Privately Held**
**WEB:** www.uchicago.edu
**SIC:** 2732 8221  Book printing; university
**PA:** The University Of Chicago
    5801 S Ellis Ave Ste 1
    Chicago IL 60637
    773 702-1234

**(G-6838)**
**UNIVERSITY OF CHICAGO**
Also Called: Steam Plant
6101 S Blackstone Ave  (60637-2911)
PHONE .................................. 773 702-9780
Adam Lucido, *Foreman/Supr*
Dan Carey, *Manager*
**EMP:** 19
**SALES (corp-wide):** 2.9B **Privately Held**
**WEB:** www.uchicago.edu
**SIC:** 3511 8221  Steam turbines; university
**PA:** The University Of Chicago
    5801 S Ellis Ave Ste 1
    Chicago IL 60637
    773 702-1234

**(G-6839)**
**UNIVERSITY PRINTING CO INC**
4001 N Ravenswood Ave # 304  (60613-1154)
PHONE .................................. 773 525-2400
Fax: 773 251-2378
Laura C Mather, *President*

EMP: 3
SQ FT: 3,000
SALES (est): 327.7K Privately Held
SIC: 2752 Commercial printing, lithographic

**(G-6840)**
**UOP LLC**
2820 N Southport Ave (60657-4111)
PHONE.................708 442-3681
Alice Driscoll, Principal
EMP: 133
SALES (corp-wide): 39.3B Publicly Held
SIC: 2819 Catalysts, chemical
HQ: Uop Llc
25 E Algonquin Rd
Des Plaines IL 60016
847 391-2000

**(G-6841)**
**UPPER URBAN GREEN PRPRTY MAINT**
3135 S Throop St (60608-6344)
PHONE.................312 218-5903
Marianne Marrero, President
EMP: 3
SALES (est): 215.7K Privately Held
SIC: 6512 3131 Nonresidential building operators; uppers

**(G-6842)**
**UPS POWER MANAGEMENT INC**
4940 S Kilbourn Ave (60632-4523)
PHONE.................844 877-2288
Jin Zheng, Director
EMP: 10
SQ FT: 20,000
SALES (est): 507K Privately Held
SIC: 3621 Storage battery chargers, motor & engine generator type

**(G-6843)**
**UPWARD BOUND**
3501 W Fillmore St (60624-4312)
PHONE.................773 265-1370
Val Jordan, President
EMP: 3
SALES (est): 177.1K Privately Held
SIC: 3089 Plastics products

**(G-6844)**
**URANTIA CORP**
533 W Diversey Pkwy (60614-1643)
PHONE.................773 248-6616
Richard Keeler, President
Sheila Schneider, Asst Sec
EMP: 10
SALES (est): 483.5K
SALES (corp-wide): 1.2MM Privately Held
SIC: 2731 8661 Book publishing; religious organizations
PA: Urantia Foundation
533 W Diversey Pkwy
Chicago IL 60614
773 525-3319

**(G-6845)**
**URANTIA FOUNDATION (PA)**
533 W Diversey Pkwy (60614-1698)
PHONE.................773 525-3319
Fax: 773 525-7739
Paula Thompson, Managing Dir
MO Siegel, Trustee
J Peregrine, Exec Dir
Catherine Jones, Exec Dir
Jay Peregrine, Exec Dir
EMP: 10 EST: 1950
SQ FT: 4,500
SALES: 1.2MM Privately Held
SIC: 2731 8661 Books: publishing only; religious organizations

**(G-6846)**
**URBAN APPLE LLC**
7027 N Ridge Blvd (60645-3521)
PHONE.................312 912-1377
Palmer Machelle L, Principal
EMP: 2
SALES (est): 210.8K Privately Held
SIC: 3571 Personal computers (microcomputers)

**(G-6847)**
**URBAN IMAGING GROUP INC**
3246 N Elston Ave (60618-5828)
PHONE.................773 961-7500
Richard Chavez Jr, President
Alvaro Patino, Prdtn Mgr
Steve Ballard, Sales Mgr
Gloria Roxas, Office Mgr
EMP: 8
SALES (est): 1MM Privately Held
SIC: 2752 Advertising posters, lithographed

**(G-6848)**
**URBAN OUTFITTERS INC**
Bhldn
8 E Walton St (60611-1413)
PHONE.................312 573-2573
EMP: 4
SALES (corp-wide): 3.5B Publicly Held
SIC: 2335 Wedding gowns & dresses
PA: Urban Outfitters, Inc.
5000 S Broad St
Philadelphia PA 19112
215 454-5500

**(G-6849)**
**URBAN RE MIX LLC**
2361 S State St (60616-2009)
PHONE.................312 360-0011
Mari Ann L Cater, Principal
EMP: 5 EST: 2011
SALES (est): 465.5K Privately Held
SIC: 3273 Ready-mixed concrete

**(G-6850)**
**URBAN RESEARCH PRESS INC**
840 E 87th St Ste 1 (60619-6257)
PHONE.................773 994-7200
Dempsey J Travis, President
EMP: 12
SQ FT: 2,500
SALES (est): 565.4K Privately Held
SIC: 2731 Books: publishing only

**(G-6851)**
**URDU TIMES**
7061 N Kedzie Ave # 1102 (60645-2867)
PHONE.................773 274-3100
Tariq Hawaja, Owner
Nasim Farooqa, Owner
EMP: 4
SALES (est): 190K Privately Held
SIC: 2711 Newspapers

**(G-6852)**
**US ADHESIVES**
1735 W Carroll Ave (60612-2590)
PHONE.................312 829-7438
Fax: 312 829-9733
Brian Creevy, President
Pamela Creevy, Corp Secy
EMP: 7
SALES: 994.5K Privately Held
SIC: 2891 Adhesives & sealants

**(G-6853)**
**US CATHOLIC MAGAZINE**
205 W Monroe St Fl 9 (60606-5060)
PHONE.................312 236-7782
Meinrad Scherer-Emunds, Publisher
John Molyneux, Principal
Barbara Mastrolia, Analyst
EMP: 3 EST: 2008
SALES (est): 169.4K Privately Held
SIC: 2721 Magazines: publishing & printing

**(G-6854)**
**US INTERNATIONAL INC**
Also Called: US International Supply
1950 W Armitage Ave # 1 (60622-1024)
PHONE.................312 671-9207
Urvashi Bhushan, President
▼ EMP: 3
SALES: 50K Privately Held
SIC: 3999 Manufacturing industries

**(G-6855)**
**US PLATING CO INC**
2136 S Sawyer Ave (60623-3337)
PHONE.................773 522-7300
Robert Alley, President
EMP: 11 EST: 1959
SQ FT: 26,000
SALES (est): 1.3MM Privately Held
SIC: 3471 Plating of metals or formed products; finishing, metals or formed products

**(G-6856)**
**US SILICA**
200 S La Salle St # 2100 (60601-1026)
PHONE.................312 589-7539
Bryan Shinn, President
Veronica Lill, Transptn Dir
Michael Ditzler, Facilities Mgr
Keith Parris, Cust Mgr
Wendy Samp, Director
EMP: 14
SALES (est): 6.8MM Privately Held
SIC: 2819 Silica compounds

**(G-6857)**
**USA STAR GROUP OF COMPANY**
4403 N Broadway St (60640-5682)
PHONE.................773 456-6677
Mohammad Faisal, Vice Pres
EMP: 3
SALES (est): 168.1K Privately Held
SIC: 3531 Bucket or scarifier teeth

**(G-6858)**
**USG CORPORATION (PA)**
550 W Adams St (60661-3665)
PHONE.................312 436-4000
Fax: 312 672-4093
Steven F Leer, Ch of Bd
Jennifer F Scanlon, President
Gregory D Salah, President
Dominic A Dannessa, COO
Chris A Rosenthal, Senior VP
EMP: 277
SALES: 3B Publicly Held
WEB: www.gypsumsolutions.com
SIC: 3275 3296 Gypsum products; gypsum board; gypsum plaster; insulating plaster, gypsum; mineral wool insulation products; acoustical board & tile, mineral wool

**(G-6859)**
**USSPICE MILL INC**
4537 W Fulton St (60624-1609)
PHONE.................773 378-6800
Fax: 773 378-0077
Naren M Patel, President
Hansa N Patel, Admin Sec
▲ EMP: 10
SQ FT: 40,000
SALES (est): 1.5MM Privately Held
WEB: www.usspice.com
SIC: 2099 5149 Spices, including grinding; spices & seasonings

**(G-6860)**
**USWAY CORPORATION (PA)**
150 W Maple St Apt 1003 (60610-2893)
P.O. Box 10080 (60610-0080)
PHONE.................773 338-9688
Victor Korzen, CEO
Michael Weide, Chief Engr
▲ EMP: 5
SQ FT: 5,000
SALES: 500K Privately Held
SIC: 3511 5063 Turbines & turbine generator sets; lighting fittings & accessories

**(G-6861)**
**UTC RAILCAR REPAIR SVCS LLC**
161 N Clark St (60601-3206)
PHONE.................312 431-5053
Fax: 312 853-5518
Kenneth P Fischl, President
Jan Makela, General Mgr
Jim McMahon, Senior VP
Robert K Lorch, Vice Pres
Mark J Garrette, CFO
EMP: 937
SQ FT: 56,000
SALES (est): 79MM
SALES (corp-wide): 223.6B Publicly Held
SIC: 4789 3743 5088 4741 Railroad car repair; railroad car rebuilding; transportation equipment & supplies; rental of railroad cars
HQ: Union Tank Car Company
175 W Jackson Blvd # 2100
Chicago IL 60604
312 431-3111

**(G-6862)**
**UTLX MANUFACTURING INC**
175 W Jackson Blvd (60604-2615)
PHONE.................419 698-3820
Gregory Cieslak, Manager
EMP: 8 EST: 2010
SALES (est): 1MM Privately Held
SIC: 3999 Manufacturing industries

**(G-6863)**
**V & N METAL PRODUCTS INC**
2320 W 78th St (60620-5801)
PHONE.................773 436-1855
Fax: 773 436-9774
Vince Egresits, President
Anastasia Egresits, Vice Pres
Linda Huculak, Admin Sec
EMP: 4
SQ FT: 6,000
SALES: 400K Privately Held
SIC: 3499 3446 3444 3443 Stabilizing bars (cargo), metal; architectural metalwork; sheet metalwork; fabricated plate work (boiler shop); fabricated structural metal; manufactured hardware (general)

**(G-6864)**
**V & V SUPREMO FOODS INC (PA)**
2141 S Throop St (60608-4410)
PHONE.................312 733-5652
Fax: 312 421-2855
Gilberto Villasenor, President
Philip Villasenor, General Mgr
Aitza Dulce, Purch Mgr
Guillermo Guitierrez, CFO
Lupe Martinez, Credit Mgr
EMP: 145
SQ FT: 75,000
SALES (est): 57.7MM Privately Held
WEB: www.vvsupremo.com
SIC: 2022 5149 Natural cheese; specialty food items

**(G-6865)**
**V A M D INC**
7035 W Higgins Ave (60656-1976)
PHONE.................773 631-8400
Vidan Lazic, President
Aleks Lazic, Senior VP
Dusica Lazic, Admin Sec
EMP: 6
SQ FT: 4,800
SALES: 1MM Privately Held
SIC: 5147 5421 2013 Meats & meat products; meat & fish markets; sausages & other prepared meats

**(G-6866)**
**V A ROBINSON LTD**
2850 N Pulaski Rd Ste 4r (60641-5456)
PHONE.................773 205-4364
Virgil Robinson III, President
EMP: 5
SALES (est): 440K Privately Held
SIC: 3441 Fabricated structural metal

**(G-6867)**
**V J DOLAN & COMPANY INC**
1830 N Laramie Ave (60639-4486)
PHONE.................773 237-0100
Fax: 773 237-2855
David D Dolan, President
Robbie Mizera, Purch Mgr
Diane Romcoe, Manager
Stephen J Dolan, Admin Sec
EMP: 25
SQ FT: 35,000
SALES (est): 6.2MM Privately Held
WEB: www.vjdolan.com
SIC: 2851 Lacquer: bases, dopes, thinner; stains: varnish, oil or wax

**(G-6868)**
**V P ANODIZING INC**
1819 N Lorel Ave (60639-4330)
PHONE.................773 622-9100
Victor V Pariso, President
EMP: 6
SQ FT: 10,000

# Chicago - Cook County (G-6869)  GEOGRAPHIC SECTION

SALES: 750K  Privately Held
SIC: 3471  Plating & polishing

**(G-6869)**
**V W BROACHING SERVICE INC**
3250 W Lake St  (60624-2003)
PHONE..................................773 533-9000
Fax: 773 533-0763
Russell W Roschman, *President*
D J West Sr, *General Mgr*
Georgiann Dytrych, *Vice Pres*
Brian Gillund, *Plant Mgr*
EMP: 19
SQ FT: 54,000
SALES (est): 3.8MM  Privately Held
WEB: www.vwbroaching.com
SIC: 3599  Machine shop, jobbing & repair; electrical discharge machining (EDM)

**(G-6870)**
**VAN L SPEAKERWORKS INC**
5704 N Western Ave  (60659-5114)
PHONE..................................773 769-0773
Fax: 773 769-0859
John R Van Leishout, *President*
Rosemarie Shelton, *Treasurer*
EMP: 2
SQ FT: 1,500
SALES: 200K  Privately Held
SIC: 7622  5731  3651  Home entertainment repair services; high fidelity stereo equipment; speaker systems

**(G-6871)**
**VANGUARD CHEMICAL CORPORATION**
429 W Ohio St  (60654-4506)
PHONE..................................312 751-0717
Fax: 312 751-2717
Mark Rotblatt, *President*
Maureen Rotblatt, *Vice Pres*
EMP: 15
SALES (est): 1MM  Privately Held
WEB: www.vanguardchemical.com
SIC: 2842  5169  Specialty cleaning, polishes & sanitation goods; chemicals & allied products

**(G-6872)**
**VANTAGE OLEOCHEMICALS INC**
4650 S Racine Ave  (60609-3321)
PHONE..................................773 376-9000
Peter Havens, *Ch of Bd*
Julian Steinberg, *President*
William A Micsky, *President*
Jim Collins, *Controller*
Morgan R Jones, *Admin Sec*
◆ EMP: 29
SQ FT: 3,500
SALES (est): 8MM
SALES (corp-wide): 277.7MM  Privately Held
SIC: 2899  Chemical preparations
PA: Vantage Specialties, Inc.
3938 Porett Dr
Gurnee IL 60031
847 244-3410

**(G-6873)**
**VANTAGE OLEOCHEMICALS INC (DH)**
4650 S Racine Ave  (60609-3321)
PHONE..................................773 376-9000
Fax: 773 376-7428
Julian Steinberg, *CEO*
Robert Drennan, *Ch of Bd*
Anthony Tamer, *President*
Noel Beavis, *COO*
Don Ciancio, *Exec VP*
▲ EMP: 103
SALES (est): 164MM
SALES (corp-wide): 627.1MM  Privately Held
SIC: 2869  2841  5169  Fatty acid esters, aminos, etc.; glycerin, crude or refined: from fats; industrial chemicals
HQ: Vantage Specialty Chemicals, Inc.
4650 S Racine Ave
Chicago IL 60609
800 833-2864

**(G-6874)**
**VANTAGE OLEOCHEMICALS INC**
4650 S Racine Ave  (60609-3321)
PHONE..................................773 376-9000
Don Cancio, *Vice Pres*
Jim Collins, *Controller*
Noel Beavis, *Manager*
Jeff Rubin, *Manager*
EMP: 5
SALES (corp-wide): 627.1MM  Privately Held
SIC: 2899  Chemical preparations
HQ: Vantage Oleochemicals, Inc
4650 S Racine Ave
Chicago IL 60609
773 376-9000

**(G-6875)**
**VANTAGE SPECIALTIES INC**
4650 S Racine Ave  (60609-3321)
PHONE..................................847 244-3410
EMP: 11
SALES (corp-wide): 277.7MM  Privately Held
SIC: 2843  5199  5169  Surface active agents; oils, animal or vegetable; industrial chemicals
PA: Vantage Specialties, Inc.
3938 Porett Dr
Gurnee IL 60031
847 244-3410

**(G-6876)**
**VAS DESIGN INC**
3356 N Milwaukee Ave  (60641-4004)
PHONE..................................773 794-1368
Vas Gabrov, *President*
EMP: 3
SQ FT: 2,900
SALES (est): 243.7K  Privately Held
WEB: www.bestfireplace.com
SIC: 2499  Decorative wood & woodwork

**(G-6877)**
**VCNA PRAIRIE INC**
865 N Peoria St  (60642-5429)
PHONE..................................312 733-0094
Brad Huiner, *Marketing Mgr*
EMP: 1942  Privately Held
SIC: 3272  Building materials, except block or brick: concrete
PA: Vcna Prairie, Inc.
7601 W 79th St Ste 1
Bridgeview IL 60455

**(G-6878)**
**VECTOR CUSTOM FABRICATING INC**
2128 W Fulton St  (60612-2314)
PHONE..................................312 421-5161
Fax: 312 421-2983
Stephen Mueller, *President*
Michael Wilkie, *Treasurer*
Nethen Overley, *Manager*
Barry Hehemann, *Admin Sec*
▲ EMP: 10
SQ FT: 6,000
SALES: 2.3MM  Privately Held
WEB: www.vectorfabricating.com
SIC: 3446  Architectural metalwork

**(G-6879)**
**VELTEX CORPORATION (PA)**
123 W Madison St Ste 1500  (60602-4612)
PHONE..................................312 235-4014
R Preston Roberts, *Ch of Bd*
Wayne Hanson, *President*
Stephen Macklem, *Corp Secy*
Michael Pearl, *COO*
Robert St-Amant, *COO*
EMP: 35
SQ FT: 25,000
SALES: 70MM  Privately Held
WEB: www.veltexcorporation.com
SIC: 2211  5199  Broadwoven fabric mills, cotton; advertising specialties

**(G-6880)**
**VENETIAN MONUMENT COMPANY**
Also Called: Mary Hill Memorials
527 N Western Ave  (60612-1421)
PHONE..................................312 829-9622
Frank P Troost, *President*
Robert F Troost, *Corp Secy*
EMP: 11  EST: 1912
SQ FT: 5,600
SALES: 3MM
SALES (corp-wide): 14MM  Privately Held
WEB: www.troost.com
SIC: 5999  3281  Tombstones; cut stone & stone products
PA: Peter Troost Monument Co.
4300 Roosevelt Rd
Hillside IL
708 544-0916

**(G-6881)**
**VENT PRODUCTS CO INC**
1901 S Kilbourn Ave  (60623-2309)
PHONE..................................773 521-1900
Diana Ehrenfried, *President*
Marsha Passannante, *Vice Pres*
Felix Cantu, *Purch Agent*
Robert Colon, *Natl Sales Mgr*
Tori Gora, *Sales Staff*
EMP: 45  EST: 1962
SQ FT: 60,000
SALES (est): 10.5MM  Privately Held
WEB: www.ventprod.com
SIC: 3444  3564  3442  3441  Sheet metal specialties, not stamped; blowers & fans; metal doors, sash & trim; fabricated structural metal

**(G-6882)**
**VENT URE AIR**
1855 S 54th Ave  (60804-1815)
PHONE..................................708 652-7200
Michael Friedman, *Owner*
EMP: 2
SALES (est): 261.2K  Privately Held
SIC: 3822  Auto controls regulating residntl & coml environmt & applncs

**(G-6883)**
**VENTFABRICS INC**
Also Called: Vent Fabrics
5520 N Lynch Ave  (60630-1418)
PHONE..................................773 775-4477
Fax: 773 775-5065
David Mac Arthur, *President*
Richard Ustrak, *Plant Mgr*
Peg Weinlein, *Office Mgr*
Jim O'Brien, *Manager*
EMP: 17
SQ FT: 13,000
SALES (est): 4MM  Privately Held
WEB: www.ventfabrics.com
SIC: 3585  Refrigeration & heating equipment; air conditioning units, complete: domestic or industrial; heating equipment, complete

**(G-6884)**
**VENTUREDYNE LTD**
Also Called: Chisholm, Boyd & White Company
4101 W 126th St  (60803-1901)
PHONE..................................708 597-7550
Fax: 708 597-0313
Michael T Gerardi, *General Mgr*
Nikolas Wurinaris, *Opers Staff*
Mark Cwiertniak, *Purchasing*
Robert Smith, *Treasurer*
Dale Purdy, *Marketing Staff*
EMP: 26
SALES (corp-wide): 121MM  Privately Held
SIC: 3542  3613  3452  3429  Pressing machines; switchgear & switchboard apparatus; bolts, nuts, rivets & washers; manufactured hardware (general)
PA: Venturedyne, Ltd.
600 College Ave
Pewaukee WI 53072
262 691-9900

**(G-6885)**
**VERENA SOLUTIONS LLC**
650 W Lake St Ste 110  (60661-1028)
PHONE..................................314 651-1908
Michael M Infanger, *Principal*
EMP: 3
SALES (est): 142K  Privately Held
SIC: 3845  Ultrasonic scanning devices, medical

**(G-6886)**
**VERONE PUBLISHING INC**
Also Called: Via Times News Organization
5421 Ne Rver Rd Apt 1605  (60656)
PHONE..................................773 866-0811
Veronica Leighton, *President*
Joe Maurizio, *Vice Pres*
EMP: 7
SALES: 250K  Privately Held
SIC: 2721  Magazines: publishing only, not printed on site

**(G-6887)**
**VERSATILE MATERIALS INC**
600 W 52nd St  (60609-5203)
PHONE..................................773 924-3700
EMP: 5
SALES (est): 550K  Privately Held
SIC: 2891  2816  Mfg Adhesives/Sealants Mfg Inorganic Pigments

**(G-6888)**
**VERTICAL WEB MEDIA LLC**
Also Called: Internet Retailer
125 S Wacker Dr Ste 1900  (60606-4419)
PHONE..................................312 362-0076
Fax: 312 362-9532
Jack Love, *Ch of Bd*
Molly Rogers, *President*
Paul Demery, *Editor*
Allison Enright, *Editor*
Tracy Maple, *Editor*
EMP: 21
SQ FT: 3,400
SALES (est): 4.1MM  Privately Held
WEB: www.internetretailer.com
SIC: 2721  Trade journals: publishing only, not printed on site

**(G-6889)**
**VERTIDRAPES MANUFACTURING INC**
3910 N Central Park Ave  (60618-4105)
P.O. Box 46243  (60646-0243)
PHONE..................................773 478-9272
Ben Lazo, *President*
Emma Lazo, *General Mgr*
EMP: 25
SALES (est): 3.8MM  Privately Held
SIC: 5023  2591  Window covering parts & accessories; window blinds; window shades; shade, curtain & drapery hardware

**(G-6890)**
**VESTITRAK INTL INC**
70 W Madison St Ste 1400  (60602-4267)
PHONE..................................312 236-7100
Nidhir Sreedevan, *CEO*
Celine Kapila, *President*
EMP: 35
SQ FT: 1,000
SALES (est): 1.8MM  Privately Held
WEB: www.vestitrak.com
SIC: 3069  Medical & laboratory rubber sundries & related products

**(G-6891)**
**VETERAN GREENS LLC**
7552 S Union Ave  (60620-2401)
PHONE..................................773 599-9689
Melvin Ward,
William Jones,
Dominique Tatum,
Lawrence Van Meter,
EMP: 4
SALES (est): 210.1K  Privately Held
SIC: 5431  2875  5148  0182  Fruit & vegetable markets; compost; fresh fruits & vegetables; food crops grown under cover;

**(G-6892)**
**VICLARITY INC**
300 N Lasalle St  (60654)
PHONE..................................201 214-5405
Richard Butti, *Vice Pres*
EMP: 9
SQ FT: 2,400
SALES (est): 204.2K  Privately Held
SIC: 7372  Application computer software

# GEOGRAPHIC SECTION
## Chicago - Cook County (G-6920)

**(G-6893)**
**VICTOR FOOD PRODUCTS**
Also Called: Victor's Food
4194 N Elston Ave (60618-1829)
**PHONE**.................773 478-9529
Zenida Brosas, *President*
**EMP:** 4
**SALES:** 270K **Privately Held**
**SIC: 2011** Meat packing plants

**(G-6894)**
**VICTOR LEVY JEWELRY CO INC**
Also Called: National Jewelers Co.
29 E Madison St Ste 1640 (60602-4427)
**PHONE**.................312 782-5297
Victor Levy, *President*
**EMP:** 3
**SQ FT:** 350
**SALES (est):** 290K **Privately Held**
**WEB:** www.worldiamonds.com
**SIC: 3911** 7631 Jewelry, precious metal; rings, finger: precious metal; earrings, precious metal; bracelets, precious metal; jewelry repair services; diamond setter

**(G-6895)**
**VIDA ENTERPRISES INC**
Also Called: Vidas Angels
3000 S Throop St (60608-5813)
**PHONE**.................312 808-0088
Elvira Jimenez-Schreck, *Principal*
**EMP:** 4 **EST:** 2010
**SALES (est):** 241.6K **Privately Held**
**SIC: 2392** 2673 2611 7389 Bags, garment storage: except paper or plastic film; food storage & trash bags (plastic); pulp mills, mechanical & recycling processing;

**(G-6896)**
**VIENNA BEEF LTD (PA)**
2501 N Damen Ave (60647-2101)
**PHONE**.................773 278-7800
John P Bodman, *President*
Howard Eirinberg, *President*
James Bodman, *Chairman*
Jack P Bodman, *Senior VP*
Jack Bodman, *Senior VP*
▼ **EMP:** 39 **EST:** 1893
**SQ FT:** 100,000
**SALES (est):** 90.8MM **Privately Held**
**SIC: 2013** 2035 2053 5411 Prepared beef products from purchased beef; prepared pork products from purchased pork; sausages & related products, from purchased meat; cucumbers, pickles & pickle salting; relishes, fruit & vegetable; cakes, bakery: frozen; delicatessens; groceries & related products; meats & meat products

**(G-6897)**
**VIES NAILS**
3511 N Lincoln Ave Fl 1 (60657-1137)
**PHONE**.................773 281-6485
Jimmy Tran, *Owner*
**EMP:** 4
**SALES (est):** 300.1K **Privately Held**
**SIC: 2844** Manicure preparations

**(G-6898)**
**VIGIL PRINTING INC**
4415 W Lawrence Ave (60630-2510)
**PHONE**.................773 794-8808
**Fax:** 773 794-8922
Michael Pearson, *President*
Rose Pearson, *Admin Sec*
**EMP:** 9
**SQ FT:** 5,000
**SALES:** 800K **Privately Held**
**WEB:** www.vigilprinting.com
**SIC: 2752** 7331 Commercial printing, lithographic; direct mail advertising services

**(G-6899)**
**VIKING PRINTING & COPYING INC**
53 W Jackson Blvd Lbby (60604-3606)
**PHONE**.................312 341-0985
Bill Anderson, *President*
David Anderson, *Vice Pres*
**EMP:** 3
**SQ FT:** 1,200
**SALES (est):** 300K **Privately Held**
**SIC: 2752** 7334 2791 2789 Commercial printing, offset; photocopying & duplicating services; typesetting; bookbinding & related work

**(G-6900)**
**VIRTU**
2034 N Damen Ave (60647-4547)
**PHONE**.................773 235-3790
Julie Horowitz, *Principal*
**EMP:** 4
**SALES (est):** 182.4K **Privately Held**
**SIC: 5947** 5092 3944 Gift shop; arts & crafts equipment & supplies; craft & hobby kits & sets

**(G-6901)**
**VISIBILLITY INC**
225 N Michigan Ave Fl 16 (60601-7668)
**PHONE**.................312 616-5900
Faiz Ahmed, *CEO*
Asif Ahmed, *CTO*
**EMP:** 24 **EST:** 2000
**SALES (est):** 1.3MM
**SALES (corp-wide):** 343.2MM **Publicly Held**
**WEB:** www.bottomline.com
**SIC: 7372** Prepackaged software
**PA:** Bottomline Technologies (De), Inc.
325 Corporate Dr Ste 300
Portsmouth NH 03801
603 436-0700

**(G-6902)**
**VISION I SYSTEMS**
2416 S Canal St (60616-2224)
**PHONE**.................312 326-9188
John Lee, *Owner*
**EMP:** 5
**SALES (est):** 588.5K **Privately Held**
**SIC: 7372** 4813 Prepackaged software;

**(G-6903)**
**VISION INTEGRATED GRAPHICS (PA)**
208 S Jefferson St Fl 3 (60661-5758)
**PHONE**.................312 373-6300
Doug Powell, *CEO*
Steve Smits, *President*
Dan Rose, *General Mgr*
Don Ward, *General Mgr*
Charles Sherman, *Exec VP*
**EMP:** 30
**SQ FT:** 125,000
**SALES (est):** 66.3MM **Privately Held**
**WEB:** www.alphabetapress.com
**SIC: 2752** Commercial printing, lithographic

**(G-6904)**
**VISION SALES & MARKETING INC**
5620 W 51st Forest Vw St (60638)
**PHONE**.................708 496-6016
Mohammad Ali, *President*
▲ **EMP:** 8
**SQ FT:** 35,000
**SALES (est):** 2.3MM **Privately Held**
**SIC: 5169** 5145 2086 3089 Detergents & soaps, except specialty cleaning; candy; carbonated beverages, nonalcoholic: bottled & canned; holders: paper towel, grocery bag, etc.: plastic

**(G-6905)**
**VISUAL MARKETING INC**
154 W Erie St (60654-3987)
**PHONE**.................312 664-9177
**Fax:** 312 664-9473
Lawrence J Zock, *CEO*
Jack Michaelis, *President*
Keith Rojc, *President*
James Spear, *Prdtn Mgr*
Phil Divenere, *Engineer*
▲ **EMP:** 20
**SQ FT:** 16,000
**SALES (est):** 3.5MM **Privately Held**
**WEB:** www.vmichicago.com
**SIC: 3993** Displays & cutouts, window & lobby

**(G-6906)**
**VITA FOOD PRODUCTS INC (PA)**
2222 W Lake St (60612-2281)
**PHONE**.................312 738-4500
Clifford K Bolen, *President*
Howard E Bedford, *Chairman*
R Anthony Nelson, *CFO*
Marty Allen, *Credit Staff*
▲ **EMP:** 100 **EST:** 1898
**SQ FT:** 82,200
**SALES:** 53.6MM **Privately Held**
**WEB:** www.vitafoodproducts.com
**SIC: 2091** 5149 Fish, canned & cured; spices & seasonings

**(G-6907)**
**VITAL PROTEINS LLC**
1564 N Damen Ave Ste 208 (60622-2102)
**PHONE**.................224 544-9110
Kurt Seidensticker, *CEO*
**EMP:** 25
**SALES (corp-wide):** 19MM **Privately Held**
**SIC: 2023** 5499 Dietary supplements, dairy & non-dairy based; vitamin food stores
**PA:** Vital Proteins Llc
545 Busse Rd
Elk Grove Village IL 60007
224 544-9110

**(G-6908)**
**VIVOR LLC**
222 Merchandise Mart Plz (60654-1103)
**PHONE**.................312 967-6379
Ian Manners, *CEO*
**EMP:** 3
**SALES (est):** 146.7K **Privately Held**
**SIC: 7372** Business oriented computer software

**(G-6909)**
**VIZR TECH LLC**
400 N Mcclurg Ct Apt 2906 (60611-4346)
**PHONE**.................312 420-4466
Richard Buchler, *CEO*
**EMP:** 5
**SALES (est):** 128.9K **Privately Held**
**SIC: 7372** Application computer software

**(G-6910)**
**VM ELECTRONICS LLC**
5080 N Kimberly Ave # 110 (60630-1770)
**PHONE**.................847 663-9310
Wayne Pavlovic,
**EMP:** 4
**SALES (est):** 786.8K **Privately Held**
**SIC: 3555** Electrotyping machines

**(G-6911)**
**VMR CHICAGO LLC**
34 E Oak St Fl 7 (60611-1231)
**PHONE**.................312 649-6673
Mark O Gill,
Tina Kourasis,
Elena Salvi,
**EMP:** 10
**SALES (est):** 1.2MM **Privately Held**
**SIC: 2329** Men's & boys' leather, wool & down-filled outerwear

**(G-6912)**
**VOGEL/HILL CORPORATION**
Also Called: Decardy Diecasting
3935 W Shakespeare Ave (60647-3430)
**PHONE**.................773 235-6916
**Fax:** 773 235-7238
William Vogel, *President*
Victoria Vogel, *Vice Pres*
**EMP:** 24 **EST:** 1907
**SQ FT:** 17,000
**SALES (est):** 4.7MM **Privately Held**
**WEB:** www.decardy.com
**SIC: 3364** Zinc & zinc-base alloy die-castings; lead die-castings

**(G-6913)**
**VOLTRONICS INC**
7746 W Addison St (60634-3095)
**PHONE**.................773 625-1779
Edwin E Hedeen, *President*
Claudia Panos, *Vice Pres*
**EMP:** 14
**SQ FT:** 3,500
**SALES (est):** 1.9MM **Privately Held**
**SIC: 3676** Electronic resistors

**(G-6914)**
**VOODOO RIDE LLC**
1341 W Fullerton Ave # 255 (60614-2362)
**PHONE**.................312 944-0465
Christopher Ferraro, *President*
**EMP:** 3
**SQ FT:** 2,000
**SALES:** 4MM
**SALES (corp-wide):** 1.3MM **Privately Held**
**WEB:** www.voodooride.com
**SIC: 2842** Automobile polish
**PA:** Pilot Inc.
13000 Temple Ave
City Of Industry CA 91746
626 937-6988

**(G-6915)**
**VOSGES LTD (PA)**
Also Called: Vosges Haut Chocolate
2950 N Oakley Ave (60618-8010)
**PHONE**.................773 388-5560
**Fax:** 773 772-7917
Katrina Markoff, *President*
Nancy Scher, *Principal*
Caroline Lubbers, *Vice Pres*
Celia Cheng, *Sales Staff*
▲ **EMP:** 82 **EST:** 1997
**SALES (est):** 49.4MM **Privately Held**
**SIC: 5441** 2066 Candy, nut & confectionery stores; chocolate candy, solid

**(G-6916)**
**VOYANT DIAGNOSTICS INC**
1600 S Ind Ave Apt 1101 (60616)
**PHONE**.................630 456-6340
Michael Tu, *President*
Burhan Adhami, *Vice Pres*
**EMP:** 5
**SALES (est):** 229.7K **Privately Held**
**SIC: 2835** In vitro diagnostics

**(G-6917)**
**W & W MUSICAL INSTRUMENT CO**
Also Called: W & W Harp Co
3868 W Grand Ave (60651-2005)
**PHONE**.................773 278-4210
**Fax:** 773 818-0868
Walter Krasicki Jr, *President*
Denise Krasicki, *Vice Pres*
**EMP:** 20
**SALES:** 1MM **Privately Held**
**WEB:** www.venusharps.com
**SIC: 3931** 7699 5736 Harps & parts; musical instrument repair services; musical instrument stores

**(G-6918)**
**W G N FLAG & DECORATING CO**
798488 S Chicago Ave (60617)
**PHONE**.................773 768-8076
**Fax:** 773 768-3138
Carl Porter Jr, *President*
Carl Porter III, *Vice Pres*
Gus Porter, *Vice Pres*
Pamela S Porter, *Admin Sec*
**EMP:** 15 **EST:** 1915
**SALES (est):** 1.4MM **Privately Held**
**WEB:** www.wgnflag.com
**SIC: 2399** 5999 3993 3446 Flags, fabric; pennants; flags; signs & advertising specialties; architectural metalwork

**(G-6919)**
**W KOST MANUFACTURING CO INC**
70 W Madison St Ste 2300 (60602-4250)
**PHONE**.................847 428-0600
Bradley Kost, *President*
Richard Walen, *General Mgr*
Walter Kost, *Chairman*
Anna Hunt, *Human Res Dir*
Patti Lebeau, *Office Mgr*
**EMP:** 200
**SALES (est):** 19.8MM **Privately Held**
**SIC: 2439** 2452 Trusses, wooden roof; trusses, except roof: laminated lumber; prefabricated wood buildings

**(G-6920)**
**W R GRACE & CO**
Also Called: W R Grace Davison Chemical Div
4099 W 71st St (60629-5839)
**PHONE**.................773 838-3200
Pat Murphy, *Plant Mgr*
Troy Miedona, *Opers Staff*
Alan Goeppinger, *Purchasing*
Andrew Farley, *Research*
Colleen Miedona, *Engineer*
**EMP:** 125

# Chicago - Cook County (G-6921)     GEOGRAPHIC SECTION

**SALES (corp-wide):** 1.6B **Publicly Held**
**WEB:** www.grace.com
**SIC:** 3081 2819 Film base, cellulose acetate or nitrocellulose plastic; catalysts, chemical
**PA:** W. R. Grace & Co.
7500 Grace Dr
Columbia MD 21044
410 531-4000

### (G-6921)
### W R GRACE & CO
Also Called: Grace Davison
4001 W 71st St (60629-5801)
**PHONE**..................................708 458-0340
James Hansen, *Mfg Mgr*
Andy Aberdale, *Branch Mgr*
**EMP:** 164
**SALES (corp-wide):** 1.6B **Publicly Held**
**SIC:** 2819 Catalysts, chemical
**PA:** W. R. Grace & Co.
7500 Grace Dr
Columbia MD 21044
410 531-4000

### (G-6922)
### W R GRACE & CO
W R Grace Construction Pdts
6051 W 65th St (60638-5396)
**PHONE**..................................414 354-4400
**Fax:** 708 458-6165
Lorin Lewis, *Mfg Staff*
Neal Jablonski, *Technical Engr*
Russ Victoria, *Project Engr*
**EMP:** 11
**SALES (corp-wide):** 1.6B **Publicly Held**
**WEB:** www.grace.com
**SIC:** 2899 Concrete curing & hardening compounds
**PA:** W. R. Grace & Co.
7500 Grace Dr
Columbia MD 21044
410 531-4000

### (G-6923)
### W R GRACE & CO - CONN
6050 W 51st St (60638-1485)
**PHONE**..................................708 458-0340
Mark Simmis, *Principal*
Sue Dietz, *QC Dir*
Stan Slusser, *Human Res Dir*
**EMP:** 135
**SALES (corp-wide):** 1.6B **Publicly Held**
**WEB:** www.grace.com
**SIC:** 2899 Concrete curing & hardening compounds
**HQ:** W. R. Grace & Co.-Conn.
7500 Grace Dr
Columbia MD 21044
410 531-4000

### (G-6924)
### W R GRACE & CO- CONN
Also Called: W R Grace Construction Pdts
6051 W 65th St (60638-5396)
**PHONE**..................................708 458-9700
James Hansen, *General Mgr*
John Shaw, *Manager*
**EMP:** 16
**SALES (corp-wide):** 1.6B **Publicly Held**
**WEB:** www.grace.com
**SIC:** 3086 2891 2819 3531 Plastics foam products; adhesives & sealants; industrial inorganic chemicals; construction machinery; chemical preparations
**HQ:** W. R. Grace & Co.-Conn.
7500 Grace Dr
Columbia MD 21044
410 531-4000

### (G-6925)
### W R PABICH MANUFACTURING CO
Also Called: Ideal Stitcher & Manufacturing
2323 N Knox Ave (60639-3484)
**PHONE**..................................773 486-4141
**Fax:** 773 486-4812
James F Sullivan, *Vice Pres*
Renee Tracy, *Vice Pres*
**EMP:** 14 **EST:** 1933
**SQ FT:** 14,500
**SALES (est):** 2.4MM **Privately Held**
**SIC:** 3315 Steel wire & related products

### (G-6926)
### W S C INC
70 W Madison St Ste 2300 (60602-4250)
**PHONE**..................................312 372-1121
**EMP:** 3
**SALES (corp-wide):** 82.1MM **Privately Held**
**SIC:** 3571 5045 Electronic computers; computers, peripherals & software
**HQ:** W S C Inc
8938 Ridgeland Ave
Oak Lawn IL

### (G-6927)
### W WHORTON & CO
Also Called: Nasaba Magazine
9029 S Western Ave (60643-6433)
**PHONE**..................................773 445-2400
**Fax:** 773 445-9740
Will Whorton, *Owner*
**EMP:** 4 **EST:** 2000
**SALES (est):** 213.7K **Privately Held**
**WEB:** www.nau.edu
**SIC:** 2721 Magazines: publishing only, not printed on site

### (G-6928)
### W-D TOOL ENGINEERING COMPANY
3128 W Grand Ave (60622-4387)
**PHONE**..................................773 638-2688
**Fax:** 773 638-2690
Walter Dychie, *President*
John Zwarycz, *Vice Pres*
**EMP:** 10
**SQ FT:** 5,000
**SALES (est):** 720K **Privately Held**
**WEB:** www.wdtooleng.com
**SIC:** 3599 Machine & other job shop work

### (G-6929)
### W-R INDUSTRIES INC
2303 W 18th St (60608-1808)
**PHONE**..................................312 733-5200
Nancy Newberger, *President*
David Allison, *Vice Pres*
Anne Arnet, *Office Mgr*
Anne Arndt, *Manager*
▲ **EMP:** 7
**SALES (est):** 1.5MM **Privately Held**
**WEB:** www.w-rindustries.com
**SIC:** 2836 2844 Biological products, except diagnostic; toilet preparations

### (G-6930)
### WABASH PUBLISHING CO INC (PA)
Also Called: Illinois Sports News
906 S Wabash Ave (60605-2205)
**PHONE**..................................312 939-5900
**Fax:** 312 427-0426
Thomas F Kelly III, *President*
John Daly, *Admin Sec*
**EMP:** 6 **EST:** 1927
**SQ FT:** 10,000
**SALES (est):** 1.4MM **Privately Held**
**SIC:** 2741 Miscellaneous publishing; racing forms & programs: publishing & printing

### (G-6931)
### WACO MANUFACTURING CO INC
2233 W Ferdinand St (60612-1584)
**PHONE**..................................312 733-0054
**Fax:** 312 733-3934
Mike Troccoli, *President*
Melinda Williams, *Office Mgr*
Ron Sarno, *Admin Sec*
◆ **EMP:** 15
**SQ FT:** 25,000
**SALES (est):** 2MM **Privately Held**
**SIC:** 2599 7641 2531 2522 Stools with casters (not household or office), metal; reupholstery; public building & related furniture; office furniture, except wood; wood household furniture

### (G-6932)
### WAGNER BRASS FOUNDRY INC
1838 N Elston Ave (60642-1284)
**PHONE**..................................773 276-7907
**Fax:** 773 276-9656
Richard A Wagner, *President*
**EMP:** 9
**SQ FT:** 10,000
**SALES (est):** 1.3MM **Privately Held**
**WEB:** www.wagnerfoundry.com
**SIC:** 3365 3369 3366 Aluminum & aluminum-based alloy castings; nonferrous foundries; copper foundries

### (G-6933)
### WAH KING NOODLE CO INC
5770 S Perry Ave (60621-4057)
**PHONE**..................................773 684-8000
John Tan, *President*
Lawrence Tan, *Exec VP*
John Fong, *Manager*
Rhea Tan, *Admin Sec*
**EMP:** 8
**SQ FT:** 10,000
**SALES (est):** 330K **Privately Held**
**SIC:** 2098 2099 Noodles (e.g. egg, plain & water), dry; food preparations

### (G-6934)
### WAH KING NOODLE CO INC (PA)
5770 S Perry Ave (60621-4057)
**PHONE**..................................323 268-0222
Diana Ling, *General Mgr*
Lawrence Tan, *Vice Pres*
▲ **EMP:** 10
**SQ FT:** 5,000
**SALES (est):** 1.9MM **Privately Held**
**WEB:** www.wahkingnoodle.com
**SIC:** 2099 5149 Pasta, uncooked: packaged with other ingredients; pasta & rice

### (G-6935)
### WALACH MANUFACTURING CO INC
5049 W Diversey Ave (60639-1609)
**PHONE**..................................773 836-2060
**Fax:** 773 836-2161
David Walach, *President*
**EMP:** 10
**SQ FT:** 10,000
**SALES (est):** 3.1MM **Privately Held**
**WEB:** www.walach.com
**SIC:** 3569 3599 3593 Jacks, hydraulic; machine shop, jobbing & repair; fluid power cylinders & actuators

### (G-6936)
### WALT LTD
Also Called: Specialty Precision Tool
433 W Armitage Ave (60614-4547)
**PHONE**..................................312 337-2756
Michael A Walt, *President*
Louisa McCharthy, *CFO*
Sam Walt, *Manager*
**EMP:** 25 **EST:** 1996
**SQ FT:** 30,000
**SALES:** 3MM **Privately Held**
**WEB:** www.waltltd.com
**SIC:** 3441 3544 7692 Fabricated structural metal; special dies & tools; welding repair

### (G-6937)
### WAM VENTURES INC
Also Called: WV Sharp
70 W Madison St Ste 1403 (60602-4252)
**PHONE**..................................312 214-6136
William Minor, *President*
**EMP:** 4
**SALES (est):** 280K **Privately Held**
**SIC:** 3577 5112 Computer peripheral equipment; stationery & office supplies

### (G-6938)
### WAPRO INC
150 N Michigan Ave (60601-7553)
**PHONE**..................................888 927-8677
Magnus Munkahusagan, *President*
Magnus Larsson Munkahusagan, *President*
**EMP:** 2 **EST:** 2010
**SALES (est):** 227.1K **Privately Held**
**SIC:** 3544 Industrial molds

### (G-6939)
### WARBLER DIGITAL INC
20 N Wacker Dr Ste 1200 (60606-2901)
**PHONE**..................................312 924-1056
Mark Dunlap, *President*
Bryan Serkin, *Sales Mgr*
**EMP:** 30
**SALES (est):** 1.4MM **Privately Held**
**SIC:** 7372 7812 Application computer software; video production

### (G-6940)
### WARGAMING (USA) INC (PA)
Also Called: Wargaming West
651 W Washington Blvd # 600 (60661-2122)
**PHONE**..................................312 258-0500
Jeremy Monroe, *President*
**EMP:** 18 **EST:** 2013
**SALES (est):** 27.9MM **Privately Held**
**SIC:** 7372 Application computer software

### (G-6941)
### WATER SAVER FAUCET CO (PA)
701 W Erie St (60654-5503)
**PHONE**..................................312 666-5500
**Fax:** 312 666-8597
Steven A Kersten, *President*
Priscilla Kersten, *Corp Secy*
Jason Cantu, *Opers Mgr*
Geoff Aronson, *Sales Staff*
Ben Anderson, *Sales Associate*
▲ **EMP:** 125 **EST:** 1934
**SQ FT:** 80,000
**SALES (est):** 18.6MM **Privately Held**
**WEB:** www.wsflab.com
**SIC:** 3432 Faucets & spigots, metal & plastic; plumbers' brass goods: drain cocks, faucets, spigots, etc.

### (G-6942)
### WATERS TECHNOLOGIES CORP
4559 Paysphere Cir (60674-0045)
**PHONE**..................................508 482-8365
**EMP:** 10 **Publicly Held**
**SIC:** 3826 Chromatographic equipment, laboratory type
**HQ:** Waters Technologies Corporation,
34 Maple St
Milford MA 01757
508 478-2000

### (G-6943)
### WATERWAY RV LLC MFG HOME
2 N Riverside Plz Ste 800 (60606-2682)
**PHONE**..................................312 207-1835
**Fax:** 312 474-0205
**EMP:** 2
**SALES (est):** 226.2K **Privately Held**
**SIC:** 3999 Manufacturing industries

### (G-6944)
### WAVE MECHANICS NEON
450 N Leavitt St (60612-1544)
**PHONE**..................................312 829-9283
**EMP:** 3
**SALES (est):** 180K **Privately Held**
**SIC:** 3993 Mfg Signs/Advertising Specialties

### (G-6945)
### WAXMAN CANDLES INC
3044 N Lincoln Ave (60657-4208)
**PHONE**..................................773 929-3000
Anne Olson, *Branch Mgr*
**EMP:** 4
**SALES (corp-wide):** 1.2MM **Privately Held**
**SIC:** 3999 5961 5999 Candles; mail order house; candle shops
**PA:** Waxman Candles Inc
609 Massachusetts St
Lawrence KS 66044
785 843-8593

### (G-6946)
### WEALTH PARTNERS PUBLISHING INC
1136 S Delano Ct W B201 (60605-3740)
**PHONE**..................................312 854-2522
Candice Cunningham, *Principal*
**EMP:** 7
**SALES (est):** 258.1K **Privately Held**
**SIC:** 2741 Miscellaneous publishing

### (G-6947)
### WEARY & BAITY INC
Also Called: UPS Stores 2872, The
333 W North Ave Ste F (60610-2587)
**PHONE**..................................312 943-6197
Barbara Weary, *President*
Ray Vaity, *Admin Sec*
**EMP:** 4
**SQ FT:** 1,208

## GEOGRAPHIC SECTION
## Chicago - Cook County (G-6972)

**SALES:** 500K **Privately Held**
**SIC: 5999** 5084 5113 2752 Packaging materials: boxes, padding, etc.; razors, electric; packaging machinery & equipment; processing & packaging equipment; shipping supplies; commercial printing, lithographic

### (G-6948)
### WEB PRODUCTION & FABG INC
448 N Artesian Ave (60612-1446)
**PHONE**.................................312 733-6800
Fax: 312 666-0995
Maureen Kendziera, *President*
**EMP:** 14 **EST:** 1993
**SQ FT:** 10,000
**SALES (est):** 1.9MM **Privately Held**
**SIC: 7692** 3446 1791 3441 Welding repair; gratings, open steel flooring; lintels light gauge steel; structural steel erection; building components, structural steel; joists, open web steel: long-span series

### (G-6949)
### WEBER PRESS INC
5746 N Western Ave (60659-5114)
**PHONE**.................................773 561-9815
Harry Weber, *President*
Peter Weber, *Vice Pres*
**EMP:** 5
**SQ FT:** 5,000
**SALES:** 600K **Privately Held**
**SIC: 2752** 2759 2791 Commercial printing, offset; letterpress printing; typesetting

### (G-6950)
### WEILAND METAL PRODUCTS COMPANY
6437 N Avondale Ave (60631-1909)
**PHONE**.................................773 631-4210
Fax: 773 631-3472
Ken Weiland, *President*
Carmella Beasley, *Office Mgr*
▲ **EMP:** 5 **EST:** 1940
**SQ FT:** 22,500
**SALES (est):** 2MM **Privately Held**
**SIC: 3429** 3452 Manufactured hardware (general); bolts, nuts, rivets & washers

### (G-6951)
### WEILER RUBBER TECHNOLOGIES LLC
4223 W Lake St (60624-1723)
**PHONE**.................................773 826-8900
Sean Duffy, *Mng Member*
▲ **EMP:** 2
**SQ FT:** 1,000
**SALES:** 300K **Privately Held**
**SIC: 2822** Synthetic rubber

### (G-6952)
### WELDING SHOP
Also Called: Andersen Welding
109 W 103rd St (60628-2607)
**PHONE**.................................773 785-1305
Dave Andersen, *Owner*
**EMP:** 2 **EST:** 1917
**SQ FT:** 1,800
**SALES (est):** 221.6K **Privately Held**
**SIC: 7692** Welding repair

### (G-6953)
### WELLS JANITORIAL SERVICE INC
11006 S Michigan Ave # 5 (60628-4352)
**PHONE**.................................872 226-9983
Jamaine J Wells, *President*
**EMP:** 3
**SQ FT:** 850
**SALES (est):** 94.7K **Privately Held**
**WEB:** www.mywjs.com
**SIC: 7349** 7389 2676 Janitorial service, contract basis; ; sanitary paper products; towels, napkins & tissue paper products

### (G-6954)
### WELLS SINKWARE CORP
916 W 21st St (60608-4542)
P.O. Box 166137 (60616-6137)
**PHONE**.................................312 850-3466
Honghai Wang, *President*
Mike Song, *General Mgr*
Patricia Hight, *Accountant*
Eric Chang, *Director*
▲ **EMP:** 2

**SQ FT:** 35,000
**SALES (est):** 2MM **Privately Held**
**SIC: 3261** Sinks, vitreous china

### (G-6955)
### WELLSPRING INVESTMENTS LLC
Also Called: All Seasons Screen Prtg & EMB
5470 N Elston Ave (60630-1454)
**PHONE**.................................773 736-1213
Fax: 773 736-0659
John Marino, *General Mgr*
Judy Reneau,
Randy Reneau,
**EMP:** 5
**SQ FT:** 5,500
**SALES (est):** 750K **Privately Held**
**SIC: 2395** 2396 Embroidery & art needlework; screen printing on fabric articles

### (G-6956)
### WENESCO INC
4700 W Montrose Ave (60641-1503)
P.O. Box 59303 (60659-0303)
**PHONE**.................................773 283-3004
Fax: 773 463-1400
Brian Lowenthal, *President*
Joe Hernandez, *Opers Mgr*
Manny Khan, *Controller*
Wendi Ewalt, *Marketing Mgr*
**EMP:** 12
**SQ FT:** 6,000
**SALES (est):** 2.8MM **Privately Held**
**WEB:** www.wenesco.com
**SIC: 3548** 2899 Soldering equipment, except hand soldering irons; chemical preparations

### (G-6957)
### WENNER MEDIA LLC
Also Called: Rolling Stone Magazine
333 N Michigan Ave # 1105 (60601-4008)
**PHONE**.................................312 660-3040
Maureen Harrison, *Sales/Mktg Mgr*
**EMP:** 7
**SALES (corp-wide):** 108.6MM **Privately Held**
**SIC: 2721** Magazines: publishing & printing
**PA:** Wenner Media Llc
1290 Ave Of The Amer Fl 2
New York NY 10104
212 484-1616

### (G-6958)
### WESCO SPRING COMPANY
4501 S Knox Ave (60632-4899)
**PHONE**.................................773 838-3350
Fax: 773 838-0018
Martha Quezada, *President*
Richard Chudzik, *President*
Tony Carini, *Manager*
Loretta Chudzik, *Admin Sec*
**EMP:** 50 **EST:** 1945
**SQ FT:** 50,000
**SALES (est):** 9.8MM **Privately Held**
**WEB:** www.wescospring.com
**SIC: 3496** 3495 3469 3493 Miscellaneous fabricated wire products; mechanical springs, precision; metal stampings; steel springs, except wire

### (G-6959)
### WESLING PRODUCTS INC
2912 W Lake St (60612-1924)
**PHONE**.................................773 533-2850
Fax: 773 533-2851
S Scott Spirakes, *President*
**EMP:** 6 **EST:** 1923
**SQ FT:** 10,000
**SALES (est):** 500K **Privately Held**
**SIC: 2441** 2449 3861 Cases, wood; wood containers; photographic equipment & supplies

### (G-6960)
### WEST LAKE CONCRETE & RMDLG LLC
2029 N Lavergne Ave (60639-3234)
**PHONE**.................................847 477-8667
Eric Rohde,
Victor Botello,
Noe Gomez,
**EMP:** 3

**SALES (est):** 138.8K **Privately Held**
**SIC: 1771** 1799 3272 3531 Patio construction, concrete; erection & dismantling of forms for poured concrete; floor slabs & tiles, precast concrete; finishers, concrete & bituminous: powered

### (G-6961)
### WEST PUBLISHING CORPORATION
Also Called: Bar/Bri Group
111 W Jackson Blvd # 1700 (60604-3597)
**PHONE**.................................312 894-1690
Fax: 312 873-1674
Patrick Kraska, *Branch Mgr*
**EMP:** 61
**SALES (corp-wide):** 3.7B **Publicly Held**
**WEB:** www.ruttergroup.com
**SIC: 2731** Book publishing
**HQ:** West Publishing Corporation
610 Opperman Dr
Eagan MN 55123
651 687-7000

### (G-6962)
### WEST WATER INC
463 W 24th St Ste 1 (60616-4947)
**PHONE**.................................312 326-7480
Chaolian Chen, *President*
▲ **EMP:** 3
**SALES (est):** 299.9K **Privately Held**
**SIC: 2086** Pasteurized & mineral waters, bottled & canned; mineral water, carbonated: packaged in cans, bottles, etc.

### (G-6963)
### WESTERN DIGITAL TECH INC
15535 Collection Ctr Dr (60693-0155)
**PHONE**.................................949 672-7000
Stephen D Milligan, *Branch Mgr*
**EMP:** 3
**SALES (corp-wide):** 12.9B **Publicly Held**
**SIC: 3572** Computer storage devices
**HQ:** Western Digital Technologies, Inc.
3355 Michelson Dr Ste 100
Irvine CA 92612

### (G-6964)
### WESTERN-CULLEN-HAYES INC (PA)
2700 W 36th Pl (60632-1617)
**PHONE**.................................773 254-9600
Fax: 773 254-1110
Ronald L Mc Daniel, *President*
Barbara Gulick, *Vice Pres*
Jeff Hein, *Foreman/Supr*
Donna Adamus, *Purch Agent*
Tom Burke, *Manager*
**EMP:** 70
**SQ FT:** 81,000
**SALES (est):** 16.8MM **Privately Held**
**SIC: 3643** 3743 3669 Current-carrying wiring devices; railroad equipment; railroad signaling devices, electric

### (G-6965)
### WESTINGHOUSE A BRAKE TECH CORP
Also Called: Wabtec Global Services
8401 S Stewart Ave (60620-1755)
**PHONE**.................................708 596-6730
Fax: 708 596-7858
Ronald Chaney, *Manager*
**EMP:** 35
**SALES (corp-wide):** 2.9B **Publicly Held**
**WEB:** www.wabtecglobalservices.com
**SIC: 3743** Railroad equipment
**PA:** Westinghouse Air Brake Technologies Corporation
1001 Airbrake Ave
Wilmerding PA 15148
412 825-1000

### (G-6966)
### WESTROCK CP LLC
626 E 111th St (60628-4632)
**PHONE**.................................773 264-3516
Mike Tinsdale, *Manager*
**EMP:** 9
**SALES (corp-wide):** 14.1B **Publicly Held**
**WEB:** www.smurfit-stone.com
**SIC: 2631** Paperboard mills
**HQ:** Westrock Cp, Llc
504 Thrasher St
Norcross GA 30071

### (G-6967)
### WESTROCK CP LLC
Stone Southwest
150 N Michigan Ave (60601-7553)
**PHONE**.................................312 346-6600
Fax: 312 580-3377
Roger W Stone, *Ch of Bd*
Joseph McCurley, *Asst Supt*
James Davis, *Senior VP*
John Crimmin, *Vice Pres*
Mark Polivka, *Vice Pres*
**EMP:** 86
**SALES (corp-wide):** 14.1B **Publicly Held**
**SIC: 2631** 2611 2621 2435 Linerboard; container, packaging & boxboard; pulp produced from wood base; newsprint paper; plywood, hardwood or hardwood faced; panels, softwood plywood; veneer stock, softwood; lumber: rough, sawed or planed
**HQ:** Westrock Cp, Llc
504 Thrasher St
Norcross GA 30071

### (G-6968)
### WESTROCK MWV LLC
9540 S Dorchester Ave (60628-1721)
**PHONE**.................................773 221-9015
Judy Steward, *Personnel*
Brian Porrett, *Branch Mgr*
Brian Souza, *Manager*
Virgil Bocian, *Director*
**EMP:** 200
**SQ FT:** 100,000
**SALES (corp-wide):** 14.1B **Publicly Held**
**WEB:** www.meadwestvaco.com
**SIC: 2631** Linerboard
**HQ:** Westrock Mwv, Llc
501 S 5th St
Richmond VA 23219
804 444-1000

### (G-6969)
### WESTROCK RKT COMPANY
Also Called: Undetermined
222 N La Salle St (60601-1003)
**PHONE**.................................312 346-6600
Cooper Gordon, *Vice Pres*
Mark Polivka, *Vice Pres*
Steve Reavis, *Controller*
Sandy Kaehn, *Personnel Exec*
Bruce Smith, *Sales Mgr*
**EMP:** 10000
**SALES (corp-wide):** 14.1B **Publicly Held**
**SIC: 2631** 2653 2621 2674 Container board; corrugated boxes, partitions, display items, sheets & pad; kraft paper; shipping & shopping bags or sacks
**HQ:** Westrock Rkt Company
504 Thrasher St
Norcross GA 30071
770 448-2193

### (G-6970)
### WHI CAPITAL PARTNERS (HQ)
191 N Wacker Dr Ste 1500 (60606-1899)
**PHONE**.................................312 621-0590
Adam Schecter, *Partner*
Eric Cohen, *Partner*
Michael Resnick, *Exec VP*
Joe Caballero, *Manager*
**EMP:** 6
**SALES (est):** 134.5MM **Privately Held**
**SIC: 6799** 3317 Investment clubs; steel pipe & tubes
**PA:** Harris William & Company Inc
191 N Wacker Dr Ste 1500
Chicago IL 60606
312 621-0590

### (G-6971)
### WHITE EAGLE BRANDS INC
Also Called: Paint Glider
7257 W Touhy Ave Ste 102 (60631-4390)
**PHONE**.................................773 631-1764
Thomas Pasinski, *President*
Anthony Yelch, *COO*
**EMP:** 4
**SALES (est):** 389.7K **Privately Held**
**SIC: 3089** Plastic hardware & building products

### (G-6972)
### WHITE EAGLE SPRING &
1637 N Lowell Ave (60639-4888)
**PHONE**.................................773 384-4455

## Chicago - Cook County (G-6973)

Fax: 773 384-5627
Robert Ambroziak, *President*
John Ambroziak, *Treasurer*
Bob L Ambroziak, *Technology*
**EMP:** 12
**SQ FT:** 22,500
**SALES (est):** 2.2MM **Privately Held**
**WEB:** www.whiteeaglespring.com
**SIC:** 3495 3496 Mechanical springs, precision; miscellaneous fabricated wire products

*(G-6973)*
### WHITE PICKET MEDIA INC
Also Called: Kitchens.com
4611 N Ravenswood Ave # 101 (60640-7564)
**PHONE**.................................773 769-8400
Steven Krengel, *President*
Jenna Mattison, *Design Engr*
**EMP:** 13
**SALES (est):** 1.1MM **Privately Held**
**SIC:** 2741 Miscellaneous publishing

*(G-6974)*
### WHITE WAY SIGN & MAINT CO
2722 N Racine Ave (60614-1206)
**PHONE**.................................847 391-0200
Fax: 847 391-0099
Robert B Flannery Jr, *President*
James G Flannery, *Chairman*
Robert B Flannery Sr, *Vice Pres*
Kevin Hofert, *Engineer*
Willard Martens, *CFO*
**EMP:** 200
**SQ FT:** 36,000
**SALES (est):** 28.2MM **Privately Held**
**WEB:** www.whiteway.com
**SIC:** 3993 7629 Electric signs; scoreboards, electric; electrical repair shops

*(G-6975)*
### WHITLEY PRODUCTS INC (HQ)
2 N Rverside Plz Ste 1025 (60606)
**PHONE**.................................574 267-7114
James Cirar, *Vice Pres*
Charles E Jones, *CFO*
Joe Anios, *Info Tech Dir*
▲ **EMP:** 12 **EST:** 1942
**SQ FT:** 120,000
**SALES (est):** 24.6MM
**SALES (corp-wide):** 69.6MM **Privately Held**
**WEB:** www.whitleyproducts.com
**SIC:** 3498 3492 Tube fabricating (contract bending & shaping); hose & tube fittings & assemblies, hydraulic/pneumatic
**PA:** Tmb Industries Inc.
  980 N Michigan Ave # 11400
  Chicago IL 60611
  312 280-2565

*(G-6976)*
### WHITNEY FOODS INC
2541 S Damen Ave (60608-5206)
**PHONE**.................................773 842-8511
Whitney Blake Fitzgerald, *President*
**EMP:** 12
**SALES (est):** 1.8MM **Privately Held**
**SIC:** 2099 Food preparations

*(G-6977)*
### WIELGUS PRODUCT MODELS INC
1435 W Fulton St (60607-1109)
**PHONE**.................................312 432-1950
Fax: 312 432-9366
J Andrew Metelnick, *President*
Andrew Metelnick, *Draft/Design*
Gertrude Metelnick, *Treasurer*
Dennis Cullen, *Sales Staff*
Kurt Komanowski, *Program Mgr*
**EMP:** 25 **EST:** 1950
**SQ FT:** 12,000
**SALES (est):** 3.4MM **Privately Held**
**WEB:** www.wielgus.com
**SIC:** 3999 Models, except toy

*(G-6978)*
### WILIAMS INTERACTIVE LLC
2718 W Roscoe St (60618)
**PHONE**.................................773 961-1920
Orrin Edidin, *CEO*
Jordan Levin, *COO*
Kent Hansen, *CFO*
Tami Samek, *Credit Mgr*

Steve Macaluso, *Admin Sec*
**EMP:** 200
**SALES (est):** 13.5MM
**SALES (corp-wide):** 2.8B **Publicly Held**
**SIC:** 3944 Video game machines, except coin-operated
**HQ:** Wms Industries Inc
  3401 N California Ave
  Chicago IL 60618
  847 785-3000

*(G-6979)*
### WILKENS-ANDERSON COMPANY (PA)
Also Called: Waco
4525 W Division St (60651-1674)
**PHONE**.................................773 384-4433
Fax: 773 384-6260
Bruce Wilkens, *President*
Don Hartman, *General Mgr*
Eric Jensen, *Vice Pres*
Matthew Wilkens, *Research*
Tad Rock, *CFO*
**EMP:** 23
**SQ FT:** 55,000
**SALES (est):** 14.3MM **Privately Held**
**WEB:** www.waco-lab-supply.com
**SIC:** 5049 3829 Scientific instruments; analytical instruments; measuring & controlling devices

*(G-6980)*
### WILL DON CORP
Also Called: O & G Spring & Wire
7171 W 65th St (60638-4605)
**PHONE**.................................773 276-7081
Fax: 773 772-6578
Richard Greg, *President*
**EMP:** 85 **EST:** 1965
**SALES (est):** 12.2MM **Privately Held**
**SIC:** 3496 Miscellaneous fabricated wire products

*(G-6981)*
### WILLDON CORP
Also Called: Oandg Spring and Wire
7171 W 65th St (60638-4605)
**PHONE**.................................773 276-7080
Gregg Pet, *President*
**EMP:** 50
**SALES (est):** 4.7MM **Privately Held**
**WEB:** www.ogspring.com
**SIC:** 3495 3993 3496 Wire springs; signs & advertising specialties; miscellaneous fabricated wire products

*(G-6982)*
### WILLE BROS CO
12600 S Hamlin Ct (60803-1525)
**PHONE**.................................708 388-9000
Wayne Pasquarella, *Opers Staff*
Kevin Jarco, *Manager*
**EMP:** 55
**SALES (corp-wide):** 16.5MM **Privately Held**
**WEB:** www.willebrothers.com
**SIC:** 5211 3273 Cement; ready-mixed concrete
**PA:** Wille Bros., Co.
  11303 Manhattan Monee Rd
  Monee IL 60449
  708 535-4101

*(G-6983)*
### WILLIAM DUDEK MANUFACTURING CO
4901 W Armitage Ave (60639-3214)
**PHONE**.................................773 622-2727
Fax: 773 622-6295
William Dudek, *President*
Victoria Macy, *Treasurer*
Gwen Meyer, *Accountant*
Ingred Peavy, *Human Res Mgr*
Theresa Barcal, *Admin Sec*
◆ **EMP:** 28
**SQ FT:** 23,000
**SALES (est):** 5.3MM **Privately Held**
**WEB:** www.dudekmfg.com
**SIC:** 3496 3469 3493 3444 Miscellaneous fabricated wire products; metal stampings; steel springs, except wire; sheet metalwork; manufactured hardware (general)

*(G-6984)*
### WILLIAM HARRIS LEE & CO INC (PA)
410 S Michigan Ave # 560 (60605-1456)
**PHONE**.................................312 786-0459
William H Lee III, *President*
Bruce Morrow, *General Mgr*
Mark Braunstein, *Marketing Staff*
Maria Macreen, *Assistant*
▲ **EMP:** 20
**SQ FT:** 6,000
**SALES (est):** 1.9MM **Privately Held**
**WEB:** www.whlee.net
**SIC:** 3931 Strings, musical instrument

*(G-6985)*
### WILLIAMS ELECTRONIC GAMES DE (DH)
3401 N California Ave (60618-5809)
**PHONE**.................................773 961-1000
Fax: 773 961-1099
Orrin Edidin, *CEO*
K Fedesna, *Vice Pres*
D Hassler, *Vice Pres*
W Smolucha, *Vice Pres*
Paul Morton, *VP Mfg*
**EMP:** 420
**SQ FT:** 130,000
**SALES (est):** 27.6MM
**SALES (corp-wide):** 2.8B **Publicly Held**
**SIC:** 3999 Coin-operated amusement machines
**HQ:** Wms Games Inc
  3401 N California Ave
  Chicago IL 60618
  773 728-2300

*(G-6986)*
### WILLIAMS ELECTRONIC GAMES DE
Also Called: WMS Gaming
3401 N California Ave (60618-5809)
**PHONE**.................................773 961-1000
Christian Castro, *Electrical Engi*
Kevin Davis, *Human Res Mgr*
Tom Byczek, *Manager*
Michael Rubin, *Sr Software Eng*
Debbi Larocco, *Admin Asst*
**EMP:** 18
**SALES (corp-wide):** 2.8B **Publicly Held**
**SIC:** 3999 Coin-operated amusement machines
**HQ:** Williams Electronic Games, Inc De
  3401 N California Ave
  Chicago IL 60618
  773 961-1000

*(G-6987)*
### WILLOW CREEK ENERGY LLC (PA)
1 S Wacker Dr Ste 1900 (60606-4644)
**PHONE**.................................312 224-1400
Michael Polsky, *President*
Mark Geibel, *Accounts Mgr*
**EMP:** 1
**SQ FT:** 5,000
**SALES (est):** 792.6K **Privately Held**
**SIC:** 3621 Windmills, electric generating

*(G-6988)*
### WILLOW GROUP INC
Also Called: Twg Rsarch Div of Willow Group
1 E Wacker Dr Ste 2700 (60601-1976)
**PHONE**.................................847 277-9400
Fax: 847 277-9401
William G Fergus, *President*
**EMP:** 6
**SQ FT:** 2,500
**SALES (est):** 668.5K **Privately Held**
**WEB:** www.willowgroup.com
**SIC:** 2721 8732 Periodicals: publishing & printing; market analysis or research

*(G-6989)*
### WILMETTE SCREW PRODUCTS
4432 N Elston Ave (60630-4475)
**PHONE**.................................773 725-2626
Fax: 773 725-9405
Charles Raia, *President*
Louis Raia, *President*
**EMP:** 2 **EST:** 1955
**SALES (est):** 350K **Privately Held**
**SIC:** 3451 Screw machine products

*(G-6990)*
### WILSON SPORTING GOODS CO (DH)
8750 W Bryn Mawr Ave Fl 2 (60631-3721)
**PHONE**.................................773 714-6400
Fax: 773 714-4550
Mike Dowse, *President*
Jim Hackett, *General Mgr*
Gretchen Waterman, *General Mgr*
Chris Considine, *Principal*
Craig Kopkash, *Business Mgr*
▲ **EMP:** 280
**SQ FT:** 100,000
**SALES (est):** 689.1MM
**SALES (corp-wide):** 2.7B **Privately Held**
**WEB:** www.wilsonsports.net
**SIC:** 5091 3949 Sporting & recreation goods; sporting & athletic goods; golf equipment; baseball equipment & supplies, general; tennis equipment & supplies
**HQ:** Amer Sports Company
  8750 W Bryn Mawr Ave
  Chicago IL 60631
  773 714-6400

*(G-6991)*
### WILSON SPORTING GOODS CO
Also Called: Wilson Racket Division
8700 W Bryn Mawr Ave (60631-3512)
**PHONE**.................................773 714-6500
Fax: 773 714-6852
Tim Greene, *Opers Staff*
Jim Haneklau, *Natl Sales Mgr*
Bill Hartmann, *Natl Sales Mgr*
Andy Hawley, *Natl Sales Mgr*
Steve Weisbrodt, *Regl Sales Mgr*
**EMP:** 200
**SALES (corp-wide):** 2.7B **Privately Held**
**WEB:** www.wilsonsports.com
**SIC:** 3949 Sporting & athletic goods
**HQ:** Wilson Sporting Goods Co.
  8750 W Bryn Mawr Ave Fl 2
  Chicago IL 60631
  773 714-6400

*(G-6992)*
### WIND POINT PARTNERS LP (PA)
676 N Michigan Ave # 3700 (60611-2838)
**PHONE**.................................312 255-4800
Fax: 312 255-4820
Nathan Brown, *Partner*
Jim Tenbroek, *Partner*
Alex Washington, *Partner*
Bob Cummings, *Managing Dir*
Rebecca Asfour, *Vice Pres*
◆ **EMP:** 11
**SQ FT:** 4,909
**SALES (est):** 1.6B **Privately Held**
**SIC:** 6799 7363 3089 Venture capital companies; help supply services; blister or bubble formed packaging, plastic

*(G-6993)*
### WIND POINT PARTNERS VI LP (HQ)
676 N Michigan Ave # 3700 (60611-2838)
**PHONE**.................................312 255-4800
Bob Cummings, *Partner*
James E Forrest, *Partner*
Michael Mahoney, *Partner*
Michael Solot, *Partner*
James Tenbroek, *Partner*
**EMP:** 5
**SALES (est):** 237.6MM
**SALES (corp-wide):** 1.6B **Privately Held**
**SIC:** 6799 2542 2541 3429 Investors; partitions & fixtures, except wood; wood partitions & fixtures; manufactured hardware (general)
**PA:** Wind Point Partners, L.P.
  676 N Michigan Ave # 3700
  Chicago IL 60611
  312 255-4800

*(G-6994)*
### WINDY CITY DETECTORS SALES
Also Called: Windy City Metal Detector Sls
6435 N Newark Ave (60631-1742)
**PHONE**.................................773 774-5445
Ron Shore, *Owner*
**EMP:** 2
**SALES (est):** 221.1K **Privately Held**
**SIC:** 3669 Metal detectors

## GEOGRAPHIC SECTION
## Chicago - Cook County (G-7018)

**(G-6995)**
**WINDY CITY ENGINEERING INC**
3244 W 30th St (60623-4794)
PHONE.................................773 254-8113
Fax: 773 254-1591
Darryl Wagner, *President*
Diane Wagner, *Corp Secy*
Dale Wagner, *Vice Pres*
**EMP:** 11
**SQ FT:** 10,000
**SALES (est):** 1.9MM **Privately Held**
**SIC:** 3714 Rebuilding engines & transmissions, factory basis

**(G-6996)**
**WINDY CITY LASER SERVICE INC**
820 W 120th St (60643-5532)
PHONE.................................773 995-0188
Jose G Briones, *President*
Jose Briones, *President*
**EMP:** 3
**SALES (est):** 583.3K **Privately Held**
**SIC:** 3699 7699 Laser systems & equipment; industrial equipment services

**(G-6997)**
**WINDY CITY MEDIA GROUP**
5315 N Clark St Ste 3 (60640-2291)
PHONE.................................773 871-7610
Tracy Baim, *Principal*
Kirk Williamson, *Editor*
**EMP:** 5
**SALES (est):** 270K **Privately Held**
**SIC:** 2721 Magazines: publishing only, not printed on site

**(G-6998)**
**WINDY CITY PARROT INC**
2618 W Walton St (60622-4579)
PHONE.................................312 492-9673
Fax: 312 492-9674
Catherine Tobsing, *President*
Mitch Rezman, *Admin Sec*
**EMP:** 5
**SALES (est):** 706.6K **Privately Held**
**WEB:** www.windycityparrot.com
**SIC:** 3942 Stuffed toys, including animals

**(G-6999)**
**WINDY CITY PLASTICS INC**
263 N California Ave (60612-1903)
PHONE.................................773 533-1099
Fax: 773 533-1130
Matthias Wanezek, *President*
Keith Bosker, *Admin Sec*
**EMP:** 5
**SQ FT:** 7,000
**SALES (est):** 665.6K **Privately Held**
**SIC:** 3993 Signs & advertising specialties

**(G-7000)**
**WINDY CITY SILKSCREENING INC**
2715 S Archer Ave (60608-5926)
PHONE.................................312 842-0030
Fax: 312 842-8574
Ronald Szczesniak, *President*
Marybeth Szczesniak, *Vice Pres*
Paul Macchione, *Marketing Staff*
James Szczesniak, *Manager*
**EMP:** 40
**SQ FT:** 15,000
**SALES (est):** 4.2MM **Privately Held**
**WEB:** www.windycitysilkscreening.com
**SIC:** 2396 5699 Screen printing on fabric articles; sports apparel

**(G-7001)**
**WINDY CITY WORD**
5090 W Harrison St (60644-5141)
PHONE.................................773 378-0261
Mary Denson, *Principal*
**EMP:** 2
**SALES (est):** 212.2K **Privately Held**
**SIC:** 2621 Newsprint paper

**(G-7002)**
**WINSCRIBE USA INC (DH)**
8700 W Bryn Mawr Ave 720s (60631-3512)
PHONE.................................773 399-1608
Matthew Weavers, *President*
Natalie Fairbairn, *Opers Mgr*
Jamey Story, *Manager*
Greg Allen, *CTO*
**EMP:** 11
**SQ FT:** 5,000
**SALES (est):** 2.7MM **Privately Held**
**WEB:** www.winscribe.com
**SIC:** 7372 Prepackaged software
**HQ:** Winscribe Inc. Limited
Level 2 95 Hurstmere Rd
Auckland
948 690-10

**(G-7003)**
**WINSIGHT LLC (HQ)**
300 S Riverside Plz # 1600 (60606-6756)
PHONE.................................312 876-0004
Mike Wood Jr, *President*
Joe Carroll, *CFO*
Emily Chmura, *Marketing Staff*
**EMP:** 25
**SALES (est):** 15.9MM **Privately Held**
**SIC:** 2721 Periodicals
**PA:** Redwood Acquisitions, Llc
1101 30th St Nw
Washington DC 20007
202 625-8340

**(G-7004)**
**WINTERS WELDING INC**
7122 S Seeley Ave (60636-3728)
P.O. Box 201026 (60620-7026)
PHONE.................................773 860-7735
Deborah D Miller, *President*
**EMP:** 3
**SALES (est):** 149.8K **Privately Held**
**SIC:** 1799 3446 Fence construction; ornamental metal work; fences or posts, ornamental iron or steel

**(G-7005)**
**WIREMASTERS INCORPORATED**
Also Called: W/M Display Group
1040 W 40th St 1050 (60609-2503)
PHONE.................................773 254-3700
Fax: 773 254-3188
Paul Scriba, *President*
Drew Heinemann, *Vice Pres*
Steve Zimmermann, *Accounts Exec*
Jeff Carroll, *Sales Staff*
Brent Roberts, *Sales Staff*
▲ **EMP:** 50 EST: 1947
**SQ FT:** 76,300
**SALES (est):** 11.1MM **Privately Held**
**WEB:** www.wmdisplay.com
**SIC:** 2542 3499 3993 Office & store showcases & display fixtures; novelties & specialties, metal; miscellaneous fabricated wire products; signs & advertising specialties

**(G-7006)**
**WISEPAK FOODS LLC**
Also Called: Mr. Pak's
4225 N Pulaski Rd (60641-2331)
PHONE.................................773 772-0072
Greg Wiseman,
Jung Pak,
**EMP:** 35
**SQ FT:** 6,000
**SALES:** 2MM **Privately Held**
**SIC:** 2092 Fresh or frozen packaged fish

**(G-7007)**
**WISH COLLECTION**
350 N Ogden Ave Ste 100 (60607-1103)
PHONE.................................205 324-0209
Tal Moise, *Principal*
**EMP:** 6
**SALES (est):** 4.9MM **Privately Held**
**SIC:** 2389 Apparel & accessories
**PA:** Vfish Inc.
2719 N Ashland Ave
Chicago IL 60614
312 423-7839

**(G-7008)**
**WISNIWSKI RCHARD STL RULE DIES**
4422 N Elston Ave (60630-4419)
PHONE.................................773 282-1144
Richard A Wisniewski, *President*
Linda Groselak, *Treasurer*
Steve Groselak, *Manager*
**EMP:** 4
**SQ FT:** 3,000
**SALES (est):** 574.2K **Privately Held**
**SIC:** 3544 Dies & die holders for metal cutting, forming, die casting; dies, steel rule

**(G-7009)**
**WITHOUT A TRACE WEAVER INC (PA)**
3344 W Bryn Mawr Ave (60659-4511)
PHONE.................................773 588-4922
Michael Ehrlich, *President*
Linda Lee Mrkvicka, *Admin Sec*
**EMP:** 12
**SALES:** 980K **Privately Held**
**WEB:** www.withoutatrace.com
**SIC:** 2231 Weaving mill, broadwoven fabrics: wool or similar fabric

**(G-7010)**
**WM F MEYER CO (PA)**
2211 N Elston Ave Ste 103 (60614-2921)
P.O. Box 37, Aurora (60507-0037)
PHONE.................................773 772-7272
Fax: 630 851-4043
William J Meyer, *President*
Eric James, *Manager*
Joe Walz, *Manager*
Tiffany Kraber, *Administration*
**EMP:** 30
**SQ FT:** 40,000
**SALES (est):** 51.8MM **Privately Held**
**WEB:** www.wmfmeyer.com
**SIC:** 5198 5074 5231 5211 Paints; plumbing & hydronic heating supplies; pipes & fittings, plastic; paint & painting supplies; lumber & other building materials; fixtures: display, office or store: except wood

**(G-7011)**
**WM HUBER CABINET WORKS**
2400 N Campbell Ave (60647-1913)
PHONE.................................773 235-7660
Fax: 773 235-0059
Michael Huber, *President*
Daniel Huber, *Corp Secy*
Ervin E Huber, *Vice Pres*
Gary Huber, *Vice Pres*
**EMP:** 50 EST: 1941
**SQ FT:** 34,000
**SALES (est):** 8MM **Privately Held**
**WEB:** www.hubercabinet.com
**SIC:** 2431 2521 Interior & ornamental woodwork & trim; wood office furniture

**(G-7012)**
**WM WRIGLEY JR COMPANY (HQ)**
930 W Evergreen Ave (60642-2437)
PHONE.................................312 280-4710
Fax: 312 644-0353
Martin Radvan, *President*
Tad Moskwa, *Business Mgr*
Peter Hempstead, *Senior VP*
Howard Malovany, *Senior VP*
Gary R Bebee, *Vice Pres*
▼ **EMP:** 345 EST: 1891
**SQ FT:** 453,400
**SALES (est):** 173.1MM
**SALES (corp-wide):** 35B **Privately Held**
**WEB:** www.wrigley.com
**SIC:** 2067 2064 2087 2899 Chewing gum; chewing gum base; candy & other confectionery products; chewing candy, not chewing gum; lollipops & other hard candy; flavoring extracts & syrups; peppermint oil; spearmint oil
**PA:** Mars, Incorporated
6885 Elm St
Mc Lean VA 22101
703 821-4900

**(G-7013)**
**WM WRIGLEY JR COMPANY**
Also Called: Wrigley's
1300 N North Branch St (60642-2731)
PHONE.................................312 205-2300
Sunny Ishikawa, *Manager*
**EMP:** 35
**SALES (corp-wide):** 35B **Privately Held**
**SIC:** 2067 Chewing gum
**HQ:** Wm. Wrigley Jr. Company
930 W Evergreen Ave
Chicago IL 60642
312 280-4710

**(G-7014)**
**WM WRIGLEY JR COMPANY**
600 W Chicago Ave Ste 500 (60654-2282)
PHONE.................................312 644-2121
Howard Malovany, *Vice Pres*
Debbie Doerr, *Sales Staff*
**EMP:** 800
**SALES (corp-wide):** 35B **Privately Held**
**WEB:** www.wrigley.com
**SIC:** 2067 2064 2087 2899 Chewing gum; chewing gum base; candy & other confectionery products; extracts, flavoring; peppermint oil; spearmint oil
**HQ:** Wm. Wrigley Jr. Company
930 W Evergreen Ave
Chicago IL 60642
312 280-4710

**(G-7015)**
**WMS GAMES INC (DH)**
3401 N California Ave (60618-5899)
PHONE.................................773 728-2300
Brian R Gamache, *CEO*
Louis Nicastro, *Ch of Bd*
**EMP:** 15
**SQ FT:** 129,000
**SALES (est):** 61.4MM
**SALES (corp-wide):** 2.8B **Publicly Held**
**WEB:** www.jcir.com
**SIC:** 3999 Coin-operated amusement machines
**HQ:** Wms Industries Inc
3401 N California Ave
Chicago IL 60618
847 785-3000

**(G-7016)**
**WMS GAMING INC**
3401 N California Ave (60618-5899)
PHONE.................................773 961-1747
Rick Martine, *Project Mgr*
Brian Pierce, *Branch Mgr*
**EMP:** 125
**SQ FT:** 29,400
**SALES (corp-wide):** 2.8B **Publicly Held**
**SIC:** 3999 Slot machines
**HQ:** Wms Gaming Inc.
3401 N California Ave
Chicago IL 60618
773 961-1000

**(G-7017)**
**WMS GAMING INC (DH)**
3401 N California Ave (60618-5899)
PHONE.................................773 961-1000
Fax: 773 961-1025
Brian R Gamache, *CEO*
Sebastian Salat, *President*
Rory Block, *Vice Pres*
Sean Hayes, *Project Mgr*
Tim Seckel, *Opers Staff*
◆ **EMP:** 621
**SQ FT:** 130,000
**SALES (est):** 180.1MM
**SALES (corp-wide):** 2.8B **Publicly Held**
**SIC:** 3999 Slot machines
**HQ:** Wms Industries Inc
3401 N California Ave
Chicago IL 60618
847 785-3000

**(G-7018)**
**WMS INDUSTRIES INC (HQ)**
3401 N California Ave (60618-5899)
PHONE.................................847 785-3000
Fax: 773 961-1040
Brian R Gamache, *Ch of Bd*
Orrin J Edidin, *President*
Robert J Bahash, *Principal*
Patricia M Nazemetz, *Principal*
Kenneth Lochiatto, *COO*
**EMP:** 69
**SQ FT:** 350,000
**SALES:** 697.3MM
**SALES (corp-wide):** 2.8B **Publicly Held**
**WEB:** www.wmsgaming.com
**SIC:** 3999 7999 Coin-operated amusement machines; lottery operation
**PA:** Scientific Games Corporation
6650 El Camino Rd
Las Vegas NV 89118
702 897-7150

## Chicago - Cook County (G-7019)

**(G-7019)**
**WODACK ELECTRIC TOOL CORP**
4627 W Huron St (60644-1309)
**PHONE**....................773 287-9866
**EMP:** 10
**SQ FT:** 6,000
**SALES:** 200K **Privately Held**
**SIC: 3546** 3621 3635 Mfg Motors/Generators Mfg Power-Driven Handtools Mfg Home Vacuum Cleaners

**(G-7020)**
**WOLFAM HOLDINGS CORPORATION**
Also Called: Kwik Kopy Printing
120 W Madison St Ste 510 (60602-4418)
**PHONE**....................312 407-0100
**Fax:** 312 407-0383
Darryl Wolf, *President*
Michael Paulson, *Exec Dir*
**EMP:** 8
**SQ FT:** 2,500
**SALES:** 500K **Privately Held**
**SIC: 2759** Thermography

**(G-7021)**
**WOLFSWORD PRESS**
7144 N Harlem Ave 325 (60631-1005)
**PHONE**....................773 403-1144
Valya Lupescu, *President*
Mark P Lupescu, *Admin Sec*
**EMP:** 3
**SALES (est):** 172.2K **Privately Held**
**SIC: 2741** Miscellaneous publishing

**(G-7022)**
**WOOD CREATIONS INCORPORATED (PA)**
Also Called: WCI
3918 W Shakespeare Ave (60647-3431)
**PHONE**....................773 772-1375
**Fax:** 773 772-5712
George Malishewsky, *President*
Ted Pyciak, *Vice Pres*
▲ **EMP:** 5
**SQ FT:** 25,000
**SALES (est):** 1.3MM **Privately Held**
**SIC: 2431** Millwork

**(G-7023)**
**WOOD CREATIONS INCORPORATED**
4627 W Fullerton Ave (60639-1876)
**PHONE**....................773 772-1375
John Ocnei, *Manager*
**EMP:** 8
**SQ FT:** 14,000
**SALES (corp-wide):** 1.3MM **Privately Held**
**SIC: 2431** Millwork
**PA:** Wood Creations Incorporated
3918 W Shakespeare Ave
Chicago IL 60647
773 772-1375

**(G-7024)**
**WOOD SHOP**
Also Called: Woodshop, The
441 E 75th St (60619-2228)
**PHONE**....................773 994-6666
**Fax:** 773 994-6667
Lawrance Dantignac, *Owner*
Marbita Dantignac, *Co-Owner*
**EMP:** 9
**SQ FT:** 3,000
**SALES:** 300K **Privately Held**
**SIC: 2499** 2434 5999 Picture & mirror frames, wood; wood kitchen cabinets; art dealers

**(G-7025)**
**WOODARDS LLC DBA CUSTOM WROUG**
4464 N Elston Ave (60630-4419)
**PHONE**....................773 283-8113
Sanchez Gloria, *Principal*
**EMP:** 4 **EST:** 2014
**SALES (est):** 500.6K **Privately Held**
**SIC: 3312** Rails, steel or iron

**(G-7026)**
**WOODWAYS INDUSTRIES LLC**
850 S Wabash Ave Ste 300 (60605-3642)
**PHONE**....................616 956-3070
**EMP:** 44 **Privately Held**
**SIC: 2434** Wood kitchen cabinets
**PA:** Woodways Industries, Llc
4265 28th St Se Ste A
Grand Rapids MI 49512

**(G-7027)**
**WORDSPACE PRESS LIMITED**
2259 N Kedzie Blvd (60647-2561)
**PHONE**....................773 292-0292
Dave Glowacz, *President*
Jim Nanczek, *Editor*
**EMP:** 3
**SALES:** 100K **Privately Held**
**SIC: 2741** Miscellaneous publishing

**(G-7028)**
**WORLD BOOK INC (DH)**
Also Called: World Book Direct Marketing
180 N La Salle St Ste 900 (60601-2500)
**PHONE**....................312 729-5800
**Fax:** 312 729-5600
Robert D McBride, *President*
Mellonee Carrigan, *Editor*
Lyndsie Manusos, *Editor*
S Richardson, *Editor*
Daniel Zeff, *Editor*
▲ **EMP:** 50 **EST:** 1957
**SALES (est):** 50.3MM
**SALES (corp-wide):** 223.6B **Publicly Held**
**WEB:** www.worldbook.com
**SIC: 2731** 2741 5961 Textbooks: publishing only, not printed on site; atlases: publishing only, not printed on site; books, mail order (except book clubs)
**HQ:** The Scott Fetzer Company
28800 Clemens Rd
Westlake OH 44145
440 892-3000

**(G-7029)**
**WORLD CLASS TECHNOLOGIES INC**
Also Called: Lmsys
70 E Lake St Ste 600 (60601-7642)
**PHONE**....................312 758-3114
Steve Williams, *President*
Marion Williams, *Vice Pres*
**EMP:** 6
**SQ FT:** 5,000
**SALES (est):** 450K **Privately Held**
**SIC: 3842** 3949 Orthopedic appliances; braces, orthopedic; sporting & athletic goods

**(G-7030)**
**WORLD JOURNAL LLC**
2116 S Archer Ave (60616-1514)
**PHONE**....................312 842-8005
**Fax:** 312 842-3749
Tom Lai, *Manager*
Katie Chang, *Manager*
**EMP:** 10
**SQ FT:** 19,000
**SALES (corp-wide):** 54.9MM **Privately Held**
**WEB:** www.wjnews.net
**SIC: 2711** 2791 Newspapers: publishing only, not printed on site; typesetting
**HQ:** World Journal Llc
14107 20th Ave Fl 2
Whitestone NY 11357
718 746-8889

**(G-7031)**
**WORLD JOURNAL LLC**
Also Called: World Journal Chinese Daily
2471 S Archer Ave (60616-1853)
**PHONE**....................312 842-8080
W J Hwang, *Owner*
Jie Cole, *Accounts Exec*
Huey Tzy Chang, *Manager*
**EMP:** 12
**SALES (corp-wide):** 54.9MM **Privately Held**
**WEB:** www.wjnews.net
**SIC: 2711** Newspapers, publishing & printing
**HQ:** World Journal Llc
14107 20th Ave Fl 2
Whitestone NY 11357
718 746-8889

**(G-7032)**
**WORLD OF SOUL INC**
9131 S La Salle St (60620-1410)
P.O. Box 288656 (60628-8656)
**PHONE**....................773 840-4839
Terry Hardy, *President*
**EMP:** 3 **EST:** 2013
**SALES (est):** 174.5K **Privately Held**
**SIC: 3751** 7389 Motorcycles & related parts;

**(G-7033)**
**WORLDS FINEST CHOCOLATE INC (PA)**
Also Called: Cook Chocolate Company
4801 S Lawndale Ave (60632-3065)
**PHONE**....................773 847-4600
**Fax:** 773 847-0996
Edmond F Opler, *Ch of Bd*
Howard Zodikoff, *President*
Rich Mazur, *Vice Pres*
Bill Erickson, *Purch Mgr*
Jim Hammond, *Engineer*
▲ **EMP:** 350
**SQ FT:** 500,000
**SALES (est):** 206.5MM **Privately Held**
**SIC: 2066** 5947 Chocolate & cocoa products; gift, novelty & souvenir shop

**(G-7034)**
**WRAPPING INC**
3600 N Lake Shore Dr (60613-4684)
**PHONE**....................773 871-2898
Leszek Mirecki, *President*
John Badie, *Vice Pres*
**EMP:** 1
**SALES:** 1MM **Privately Held**
**SIC: 3086** Packaging & shipping materials, foamed plastic

**(G-7035)**
**WRAPPORTS LLC (PA)**
350 N Orleans St 10thf (60654-1975)
**PHONE**....................312 321-3000
Timothy P Knight, *CEO*
Bradley Phillip Bell, *President*
Michael W Ferro Jr, *Chairman*
Rich Hummel, *Sales Mgr*
David Wilson, *Accounts Exec*
**EMP:** 23
**SALES (est):** 304.8MM **Privately Held**
**SIC: 7379** 2711 ; newspapers, publishing & printing

**(G-7036)**
**WRENCH**
Also Called: Food Bikes
1208 W Hubbard St (60642)
**PHONE**....................773 609-1698
George Olec,
Oliver Kavanaugh,
**EMP:** 6
**SALES (est):** 320K **Privately Held**
**SIC: 5941** 3751 3568 Bicycle & bicycle parts; motorcycles, bicycles & parts; handle bars, motorcycle & bicycle; drive chains, bicycle or motorcycle

**(G-7037)**
**WRIGHTWOOD TECHNOLOGIES INC**
Also Called: Cherry Instruments
3440 S Dearborn St Ste 39 (60616-5148)
**PHONE**....................312 238-9512
Samuel M Pro, *President*
John Maltby, *Electrical Engi*
Warren R Freidl III, *Bd of Directors*
Warren Friedl, *Admin Sec*
▲ **EMP:** 3
**SQ FT:** 500
**SALES:** 1.3MM **Privately Held**
**WEB:** www.wrightwoodtech.com
**SIC: 3821** Laboratory apparatus & furniture

**(G-7038)**
**WRIGLEY MANUFACTURING CO LLC (DH)**
Also Called: Wrigley's
410 N Michigan Ave (60611-4213)
P.O. Box 3900, Peoria (61612-3900)
**PHONE**....................312 644-2121
Martin Radvan, *President*
Andy Pharoah, *Vice Pres*
Anthony Gedeller, *Treasurer*
Steffy Cetron, *Exec Sec*
▲ **EMP:** 600
**SALES (est):** 116.1MM
**SALES (corp-wide):** 35B **Privately Held**
**WEB:** www.wrigleys.com
**SIC: 2067** Chewing gum
**HQ:** Wm. Wrigley Jr. Company
930 W Evergreen Ave
Chicago IL 60642
312 280-4710

**(G-7039)**
**WRIGLEY MANUFACTURING CO LLC**
Also Called: Wrigley's
1452 N Cherry Ave (60642-7559)
**PHONE**....................312 644-2121
Megan McKellen, *Manager*
**EMP:** 567
**SALES (corp-wide):** 35B **Privately Held**
**SIC: 2067** Chewing gum
**HQ:** Wrigley Manufacturing Company Llc
410 N Michigan Ave
Chicago IL 60611
312 644-2121

**(G-7040)**
**WRIGLEY SALES COMPANY LLC**
410 N Michigan Ave # 1600 (60611-4213)
**PHONE**....................312 644-2121
Ralph P Scozzafoua, *Principal*
Phil Johnson, *Vice Pres*
Greg Ryan, *Finance Mgr*
Shirley Ll, *Human Res Mgr*
Hand Michael, *Human Res Mgr*
▼ **EMP:** 15
**SALES (est):** 3MM
**SALES (corp-wide):** 35B **Privately Held**
**WEB:** www.wrigley.com
**SIC: 2067** Chewing gum
**HQ:** Wm. Wrigley Jr. Company
930 W Evergreen Ave
Chicago IL 60642
312 280-4710

**(G-7041)**
**WSW INDUSTRIAL MAINTENANCE**
2701 E 105th St (60617-5713)
**PHONE**....................773 721-0675
**Fax:** 773 721-1393
Walter S Stuczynski, *President*
Donna Stuczynski, *Admin Sec*
Lorina Stuczynski, *Admin Sec*
**EMP:** 15
**SQ FT:** 20,000
**SALES (est):** 3.1MM **Privately Held**
**SIC: 3441** Fabricated structural metal

**(G-7042)**
**WW ENGINEERING COMPANY LLC**
4321 W 32nd St (60623-4814)
**PHONE**....................773 376-9494
**Fax:** 773 376-0831
Al Giudice,
Thomas F Baldacci,
Claude Giudice,
**EMP:** 15
**SQ FT:** 20,000
**SALES (est):** 4MM **Privately Held**
**SIC: 3443** 3536 7699 Tanks, standard or custom fabricated: metal plate; hoppers, metal plate; hoists, cranes & monorails; industrial machinery & equipment repair

**(G-7043)**
**XAPTUM INC**
222 Merchandise Mart Pl S Ste 1212 (60654)
**PHONE**....................847 404-6205
Rohit Pasam, *CEO*
Brian Gratch, *Exec VP*
Helena Stelnicki, *CFO*

## GEOGRAPHIC SECTION

**Chicago - Cook County (G-7071)**

EMP: 7
SQ FT: 500
SALES (est): 152.8K **Privately Held**
SIC: 7372 Application computer software

**(G-7044)**
**XFORM POWER AND EQP SUPS LLC**
2741 N Pine Grove Ave (60614-6109)
PHONE..................773 260-0209
Nelda Connors, *CEO*
EMP: 4 EST: 2014
SQ FT: 2,000
SALES (est): 297.7K **Privately Held**
SIC: 5063 3621 Generators; motors & generators

**(G-7045)**
**XL MANUFACTURE**
2717 W Lawrence Ave (60625-3490)
PHONE..................773 271-8900
Hristos Lalopoulos, *Principal*
EMP: 3
SALES (est): 246.4K **Privately Held**
SIC: 3999 Manufacturing industries

**(G-7046)**
**XMT SOLUTIONS LLC**
Also Called: Mobell Muscle
1749 N Wells St Apt 2010 (60614-5829)
PHONE..................703 338-9422
Michael Humenansky, *Mng Member*
EMP: 4
SALES: 180K **Privately Held**
SIC: 3949 Exercise equipment

**(G-7047)**
**YANA HOUSE**
7120 S Normal Blvd (60621-3025)
PHONE..................773 874-7120
Fax: 773 874-7120
Charlie Powell, *Exec Dir*
EMP: 3
SALES: 57.1K **Privately Held**
SIC: 3545 Machine tool accessories

**(G-7048)**
**YEARY & ASSOCIATES INC**
Also Called: Yeary Controls
1050 N State St Ste Mez3 (60610)
PHONE..................312 335-1012
Arthur R Yeary, *President*
John Roper, *Sr Associate*
▲ EMP: 5
SALES (est): 175.1K **Privately Held**
SIC: 3592 Carburetors; pistons, rings, valves

**(G-7049)**
**YES PRINT MANAGEMENT INC**
Also Called: Yes Packaging
415 N Aberdeen St Ste 2 (60642-8265)
PHONE..................312 226-4444
Gerald A Cox Jr, *President*
Jerry Cox, *Human Resources*
EMP: 7 EST: 1999
SQ FT: 1,000
SALES (est): 1MM **Privately Held**
WEB: www.yesprintmgt.com
SIC: 2759 Commercial printing

**(G-7050)**
**YFY JUPITER INC**
445 N Wells St Ste 401 (60654-4534)
PHONE..................312 419-8565
Dickie Chan, *General Mgr*
Joe Lin, *General Mgr*
Sean Murphy, *Principal*
Eddie Ho, *Project Dir*
Michelle P Tai, *CFO*
EMP: 47
SALES (corp-wide): 50MM **Privately Held**
SIC: 3577 Printers & plotters
PA: Yfy Jupiter, Inc.
121 S 8th St Ste 800
Minneapolis MN 55402
515 778-3624

**(G-7051)**
**YIELD MANAGEMENT SYSTEMS LLC**
2626 N Lakeview Ave # 2501 (60614-1821)
PHONE..................312 665-1595
Fax: 773 665-1596

Steven Gelb, *Manager*
EMP: 5
SALES (est): 510K **Privately Held**
SIC: 7372 Prepackaged software

**(G-7052)**
**YMC CORP**
Also Called: Canton Noodle Company
481 W 26th St (60616-2235)
PHONE..................312 842-4900
Fax: 312 225-2262
Harry Moy, *President*
Tom Moy, *Treasurer*
James Moy, *Admin Sec*
▲ EMP: 17
SQ FT: 5,000
SALES: 1.5MM **Privately Held**
WEB: www.ymc-europe.com
SIC: 2099 Noodles, fried (Chinese)

**(G-7053)**
**YOLANDA LORENTE LTD (PA)**
4424 N Ravenswood Ave 1 (60640-5803)
PHONE..................773 334-4536
Fax: 773 528-4316
Yolanda Lorente, *President*
Arthur Szefer, *Vice Pres*
▲ EMP: 20
SQ FT: 25,000
SALES (est): 1.2MM **Privately Held**
WEB: www.yolandalorente.com
SIC: 2331 2335 2337 2339 Women's & misses' blouses & shirts; women's, juniors' & misses' dresses; women's & misses' suits & coats; women's & misses' outerwear

**(G-7054)**
**YOUNG INNOVATIONS HOLDINGS LLC (PA)**
111 S Wacker Dr Ste 3350 (60606-4306)
PHONE..................312 506-5600
Anthony Davis, *President*
William Drehkoff, 
EMP: 6
SALES (est): 124.6MM **Privately Held**
SIC: 3843 Dental equipment & supplies

**(G-7055)**
**YOUTOPIA INC**
222 Merchandise Mart Plz # 1212 (60654-4342)
PHONE..................312 593-0859
Simeon Schnapper, *CEO*
EMP: 3
SQ FT: 75,000
SALES (est): 114.8K **Privately Held**
SIC: 7372 Publishers' computer software

**(G-7056)**
**Z A W COLLECTIONS**
11145 S Michigan Ave (60628-4322)
PHONE..................773 568-2031
Fax: 773 264-9445
Mike Smith, *Manager*
EMP: 4 EST: 2001
SALES (est): 205.2K **Privately Held**
SIC: 5651 2299 Unisex clothing stores; textile goods

**(G-7057)**
**Z PRINT INC**
5257 N Central Ave (60630-4656)
PHONE..................773 685-4878
Dariusz Gorecki, *President*
EMP: 6
SALES (est): 430K **Privately Held**
SIC: 2759 Commercial printing

**(G-7058)**
**ZAIBAK BROS (PA)**
35 E Wacker Dr Fl 9 (60601-2314)
PHONE..................312 564-5800
Khaled Elzeibak, *President*
Kevin Zaibak, *Bookkeeper*
Manuel Perez, *Admin Sec*
▲ EMP: 10
SQ FT: 22,000
SALES (est): 2MM **Privately Held**
SIC: 2099 5141 Food preparations; food brokers

**(G-7059)**
**ZEBRA OUTLET**
5750 W Bloomingdale Ave (60639-4138)
PHONE..................312 416-1518

Arman Yavuz, *President*
EMP: 12
SQ FT: 20,000
SALES: 1MM **Privately Held**
SIC: 3555 Copy holders, printers'

**(G-7060)**
**ZEBRA TECHNOLOGIES CORPORATION**
6048 Eagle Way (60678-1060)
PHONE..................847 634-6700
EMP: 400
SALES (corp-wide): 3.5B **Publicly Held**
SIC: 3577 Bar code (magnetic ink) printers
PA: Zebra Technologies Corporation
3 Overlook Pt
Lincolnshire IL 60069
847 634-6700

**(G-7061)**
**ZEKELMAN INDUSTRIES INC (PA)**
Also Called: Energex Tube
227 W Monroe St Ste 2600 (60606-5082)
PHONE..................312 275-1600
Fax: 312 357-1197
Barry Zekelman, *CEO*
Jim Hays, *President*
David Devine, *General Mgr*
Tim Feeney, *General Mgr*
Nicholas Shubat, *General Mgr*
EMP: 50
SQ FT: 10,000
SALES (est): 656.5MM **Privately Held**
WEB: www.jmcsteel.com
SIC: 3317 Pipes, seamless steel

**(G-7062)**
**ZELL CO**
329 W 18th St Ste 507 (60616-1121)
PHONE..................312 226-9191
Fax: 312 226-9093
Eugene Zell, *President*
Meredith Zell, *Admin Sec*
EMP: 6 EST: 1982
SQ FT: 12,000
SALES (est): 829.1K **Privately Held**
WEB: www.zellcompany.com
SIC: 7331 2759 Mailing service; commercial printing

**(G-7063)**
**ZENDER ENTERPRISES LTD**
Also Called: Zender Molding Solutions
3692 N Milwaukee Ave (60641-3032)
PHONE..................773 282-2293
Joyce Zender, *President*
Joe Zender, *Vice Pres*
George Avila, *Dir Ops-Prd-Mfg*
EMP: 8
SQ FT: 10,000
SALES (est): 511.9K **Privately Held**
WEB: www.zemolding.com
SIC: 3544 3089 Industrial molds; injection molding of plastics

**(G-7064)**
**ZENITH FABRICATING COMPANY**
Also Called: Zenfab
1928 N Leamington Ave (60639-4490)
PHONE..................773 622-2601
Cheri McKown, *President*
Cherri McKown, *Controller*
Peggy Riley, *Manager*
Patti Kalal, *Admin Sec*
EMP: 37 EST: 1965
SQ FT: 33,000
SALES (est): 7.7MM **Privately Held**
SIC: 3499 Boxes for packing & shipping, metal

**(G-7065)**
**ZF CHASSIS COMPONENTS LLC**
Also Called: ZF Chassis Systems Tuscaloosa
3400 E 126th St (60633-1293)
PHONE..................773 371-4550
Brad Neuman, *Plant Mgr*
Mark Meyer, *Opers Mgr*
Jane Boudreau, *Safety Mgr*
Phil Danner, *Purch Agent*
Krishna Srireddy, *Engineer*
EMP: 330 **Privately Held**

SIC: 3714 5013 Motor vehicle parts & accessories; automotive supplies & parts
HQ: Zf Chassis Components, Llc
3300 John Conley Dr
Lapeer MI 48446
810 245-2000

**(G-7066)**
**ZF CHASSIS SYSTEMS CHICAGO LLC**
Also Called: Division C
3400 E 126th St (60633-1293)
PHONE..................773 371-4550
Stefan Sommer, *CEO*
Nick Scheele, *COO*
James Curry, *Plant Mgr*
Howard Broadfoot, *Plant Mgr*
Rocco Imbesi, *Facilities Mgr*
▲ EMP: 249
SQ FT: 150,000
SALES (est): 36.7MM **Privately Held**
WEB: www.zf-group.com
SIC: 3714 5013 Motor vehicle parts & accessories; automotive supplies & parts
HQ: Zf Chassis Components, Llc
3300 John Conley Dr
Lapeer MI 48446
810 245-2000

**(G-7067)**
**ZIM MANUFACTURING CO**
6100 W Grand Ave (60639-2752)
PHONE..................773 622-2500
Fax: 773 622-0269
Kenneth Kukla, *President*
Jean Kukla, *Manager*
EMP: 50
SQ FT: 34,000
SALES (est): 7.9MM **Privately Held**
SIC: 3423 Mechanics' hand tools

**(G-7068)**
**ZIMMERMAN BRUSH CO**
Also Called: Zimco
6320 N Whipple St (60659-1420)
PHONE..................773 761-6331
Fax: 773 973-4378
Yale Zimmerman, *President*
EMP: 100
SALES (est): 6.9MM **Privately Held**
SIC: 3991 Brushes, household or industrial

**(G-7069)**
**ZIRLIN INTERIORS INC**
5540 N Broadway St (60640-1406)
PHONE..................773 334-5530
Fax: 773 334-6024
Irving Zirlin, *President*
Paul Zirlin, *Vice Pres*
Shelly Bland, *Treasurer*
Shelly Zirlin, *Manager*
Glenn Zirlin, *Admin Sec*
EMP: 24
SQ FT: 9,000
SALES (est): 3.1MM **Privately Held**
WEB: www.zirlininteriorsinc.com
SIC: 2391 7641 3429 2591 Curtains & draperies; reupholstery; manufactured hardware (general); drapery hardware & blinds & shades

**(G-7070)**
**ZIRMED INC**
111 N Canal St Ste 400 (60606-7203)
PHONE..................312 207-0889
EMP: 16
SALES (corp-wide): 66.4MM **Privately Held**
SIC: 7372 Utility computer software
PA: Zirmed Inc.
888 W Market St Ste 400
Louisville KY 40202
502 473-7709

**(G-7071)**
**ZOES MFGCO LLC**
168 N Sangamon St (60607-2210)
PHONE..................312 666-4018
Phillip Colias Jr, *President*
EMP: 13
SALES (corp-wide): 2.1MM **Privately Held**
SIC: 2842 3131 3111 Polishing preparations & related products; shoe polish or cleaner; footwear cut stock; leather tanning & finishing

# Chicago - Cook County (G-7072)

PA: Zoes Mfgco Llc
166 N Sangamon St 172
Chicago IL
312 666-4018

**(G-7072)**
**ZORCH INTERNATIONAL INC**
223 W Erie St Ste 5nw (60654-3995)
PHONE ................................. 312 751-8010
Mike Wolfe, *CEO*
Julie Trost, *President*
Catherine Kingery, *Vice Pres*
Lauren Senter, *Vice Pres*
Chris Hosler, *Controller*
**EMP:** 43
**SQ FT:** 10,000
**SALES (est):** 13.8MM **Privately Held**
**WEB:** www.zorchit.com
**SIC:** 2759 Promotional printing

**(G-7073)**
**ZORIN MATERIAL HANDLING CO (PA)**
1937 W Wolfram St (60657-4031)
PHONE ................................. 773 342-3818
Jeffrey Farlander, *President*
▼ **EMP:** 1
**SALES (est):** 208.1K **Privately Held**
**WEB:** www.zorinmaterial.com
**SIC:** 5984 3412 Liquefied petroleum gas dealers; drums, shipping: metal

**(G-7074)**
**ZSI-FOSTER INC**
6571 Solutions Ctr (60677-6005)
PHONE ................................. 800 323-7053
**EMP:** 4
**SALES (corp-wide):** 152.1MM **Privately Held**
**SIC:** 3429 Clamps, metal
**HQ:** Zsi-Foster, Inc.
45065 Michigan Ave
Canton MI 48188
734 844-0055

**(G-7075)**
**ZUCHEM INC**
2225 W Harrison St Ste F (60612-4671)
PHONE ................................. 312 997-2150
David Demirjian PHD, *President*
Rajni Aneja, *Vice Pres*
Gina Berdesko, *Project Mgr*
**EMP:** 7
**SALES (est):** 600K **Privately Held**
**WEB:** www.zuchem.com
**SIC:** 2099 Sugar

**(G-7076)**
**ZWEIBEL WORLDWIDE PRODUCTIONS**
212 W Superior St Ste 200 (60654-3562)
PHONE ................................. 312 751-0503
Steve Hannah, *CEO*
Mike McAvoy, *COO*
**EMP:** 14
**SALES (est):** 111K
**SALES (corp-wide):** 15.4MM **Privately Held**
**SIC:** 2711 Newspapers, publishing & printing
**PA:** Onion Inc.
730 N Franklin St Ste 701
Chicago IL 60654
312 751-0503

## Chicago Heights
### Cook County

**(G-7077)**
**AEN INDUSTRIES INC**
Also Called: Clean Shop Division
1522 Union Ave (60411-3511)
PHONE ................................. 708 758-3000
Mike Schreiber, *President*
**EMP:** 15
**SALES (est):** 3.5MM **Privately Held**
**SIC:** 3564 5075 Air purification equipment; air conditioning & ventilation equipment & supplies

**(G-7078)**
**ALCO SPRING INDUSTRIES INC**
2300 Euclid Ave (60411-4085)
PHONE ................................. 708 755-0438
Fax: 708 755-0056
William Kiefer, *President*
Ramiro Aguila, *General Mgr*
Karen Thoma, *Senior VP*
Clayton Baker, *Vice Pres*
Paul Jelinek, *QC Mgr*
▲ **EMP:** 70
**SQ FT:** 150,000
**SALES (est):** 17.7MM **Privately Held**
**WEB:** www.alcospring.com
**SIC:** 3493 Hot wound springs, except wire

**(G-7079)**
**ARSCO**
1001 Washington St (60411-2846)
PHONE ................................. 708 755-1733
Howard Gossage, *Principal*
**EMP:** 10
**SALES:** 950K **Privately Held**
**SIC:** 3714 Motor vehicle engines & parts

**(G-7080)**
**ASHLAND SCREENING CORPORATION**
475 E Joe Orr Rd (60411-1286)
PHONE ................................. 708 758-8800
Fax: 708 758-4436
Robert K Starmann, *President*
**EMP:** 30
**SQ FT:** 50,000
**SALES (est):** 2.5MM **Privately Held**
**WEB:** www.ashlandcontainer.com
**SIC:** 2759 2396 Screen printing; automotive & apparel trimmings

**(G-7081)**
**BAR PROCESSING CORPORATION**
1601 Wentworth Ave Ste 33 (60411-3711)
PHONE ................................. 708 757-4570
Fax: 708 757-6155
Howard Wojtczak, *QC Dir*
Nick Vaandrager, *Engineer*
Jeff Kolbus, *Manager*
**EMP:** 40
**SALES (corp-wide):** 36.3MM **Privately Held**
**SIC:** 3471 3312 Finishing, metals or formed products; polishing, metals or formed products; blast furnaces & steel mills
**HQ:** Bar Processing Corporation
26601 W Huron River Dr
Flat Rock MI 48134
734 782-4454

**(G-7082)**
**BEHR PROCESS CORPORATION**
21701 Mark Collins Dr # 200 (60411-5197)
PHONE ................................. 708 753-0136
Jimmy Taylor, *Branch Mgr*
**EMP:** 59
**SALES (corp-wide):** 7.3B **Publicly Held**
**SIC:** 2851 Paints & paint additives; stains: varnish, oil or wax; varnishes
**HQ:** Behr Process Corporation
3400 W Segerstrom Ave
Santa Ana CA 92704

**(G-7083)**
**BEHR PROCESS CORPORATION**
270 State St Ste 1 (60411-1287)
PHONE ................................. 708 757-6350
Mike Dean, *Plant Mgr*
Jeffrey D Filley, *Branch Mgr*
Pauric McPartlan, *Manager*
**EMP:** 104
**SALES (corp-wide):** 7.3B **Publicly Held**
**WEB:** www.behr.com
**SIC:** 2851 Paints & paint additives; varnish, oil or wax; varnishes
**HQ:** Behr Process Corporation
3400 W Segerstrom Ave
Santa Ana CA 92704

**(G-7084)**
**BULL MOOSE TUBE COMPANY**
555 E 16th St (60411-3731)
PHONE ................................. 708 757-7700
Fax: 708 757-7720
Rick Thyem, *Manager*
Jack Keslin, *Manager*
**EMP:** 100
**SQ FT:** 95,000 **Privately Held**
**WEB:** www.bullmoosetube.com
**SIC:** 3317 Steel pipe & tubes
**HQ:** Bull Moose Tube Company
1819 Clarkson Rd Ste 100
Chesterfield MO 63017
636 537-1249

**(G-7085)**
**C F C INTERNATIONAL**
385 E Joe Orr Rd (60411-1237)
PHONE ................................. 708 753-0679
Greg Jehlik, *President*
Jeff Cosman, *Manager*
**EMP:** 2 **EST:** 1891
**SQ FT:** 28,000
**SALES (est):** 246.4K **Privately Held**
**WEB:** www.cfcintl.com
**SIC:** 7389 2752 2796 2759 Engraving service; commercial printing, offset; platemaking services; commercial printing

**(G-7086)**
**CFC INTERNATIONAL INC**
500 State St (60411-1293)
PHONE ................................. 708 891-3456
Philip M Gresh, *President*
Mike Freeman, *Opers Staff*
**EMP:** 4
**SALES (est):** 93.7K **Privately Held**
**SIC:** 3083 3081 Laminated plastics plate & sheet; unsupported plastics film & sheet

**(G-7087)**
**CFC INTERNATIONAL CORPORATION (HQ)**
Also Called: CFC Applied Holographics
500 State St (60411-1293)
PHONE ................................. 708 323-4131
Nicolas Martino, *President*
Mark Mitravich, *Business Mgr*
William A Herring, *Senior VP*
Ronald Kropp, *Senior VP*
John Schneider, *Vice Pres*
▲ **EMP:** 240
**SQ FT:** 150,000
**SALES:** 69.6MM
**SALES (corp-wide):** 13.6B **Publicly Held**
**WEB:** www.cfcintl.com
**SIC:** 3053 3081 Packing materials; unsupported plastics film & sheet
**PA:** Illinois Tool Works Inc.
155 Harlem Ave
Glenview IL 60025
847 724-7500

**(G-7088)**
**CHICAGO HEIGHTS PALLETS CO**
1200 State St (60411-2968)
P.O. Box 506 (60412-0506)
PHONE ................................. 708 757-7641
Roy Serrano, *President*
**EMP:** 10
**SALES (est):** 910K **Privately Held**
**SIC:** 2448 Pallets, wood & wood with metal

**(G-7089)**
**CHICAGO HEIGHTS STAR TOOL AND**
640 217th St (60411-4327)
PHONE ................................. 708 758-2525
Fax: 708 758-5336
John Montella, *President*
Don Krause, *Engineer*
Thomas Montella, *Treasurer*
Eric Almquist, *Sales Engr*
Pat Bric, *Director*
▲ **EMP:** 13
**SQ FT:** 8,500
**SALES (est):** 2.8MM **Privately Held**
**WEB:** www.startoolanddie.com
**SIC:** 3544 5084 Dies & die holders for metal cutting, forming, die casting; dies, plastics forming; extrusion dies; jigs & fixtures; industrial machinery & equipment

**(G-7090)**
**CHS ACQUISITION CORP**
Also Called: Chicago Heights Steel
211 E Main St (60411-4270)
P.O. Box 1249, Calumet City (60409-1249)
PHONE ................................. 708 756-5648
Fax: 708 756-5628
Bradley R Corral, *President*
Richard R Gollner, *Corp Secy*
▼ **EMP:** 250
**SQ FT:** 250,000
**SALES (est):** 87.4MM **Privately Held**
**WEB:** www.chs.com
**SIC:** 3312 Fence posts, iron & steel; structural shapes & pilings, steel

**(G-7091)**
**CIPRIANIS SPAGHETTI & SAUCE CO**
1025 W End Ave (60411-2742)
PHONE ................................. 708 755-6212
Fax: 708 755-6272
Annette Johnson, *President*
**EMP:** 21
**SQ FT:** 15,000
**SALES:** 2MM **Privately Held**
**SIC:** 2099 Sauces: gravy, dressing & dip mixes

**(G-7092)**
**CITIZENS BANK NATIONAL ASSN**
101 Dixie Hwy (60411-1766)
PHONE ................................. 708 755-0741
Thomas Orcini, *Principal*
Stephen Sheridan, *Human Res Mgr*
**EMP:** 6
**SALES (corp-wide):** 5.7B **Publicly Held**
**SIC:** 3944 Banks, toy
**HQ:** Citizens Bank, National Association
1 Citizens Plz Ste 1
Providence RI 02903
401 282-7000

**(G-7093)**
**COLUMBIA ALUMINUM RECYCL LTD**
400 E Lincoln Hwy (60411-2973)
P.O. Box 751 (60412-0751)
PHONE ................................. 708 758-8888
Fax: 708 758-0029
Jonathan C Markle, *President*
Laura Peterson, *Controller*
Louis H Washauer, *Admin Sec*
**EMP:** 45
**SQ FT:** 150,000
**SALES (est):** 20MM
**SALES (corp-wide):** 1.2B **Publicly Held**
**SIC:** 3341 Secondary nonferrous metals
**HQ:** Real Alloy Recycling, Inc.
3700 Park East Dr Ste 300
Beachwood OH 44122
216 755-8900

**(G-7094)**
**CROSSMARK PRINTING INC**
Olympic Printing
410 Ashland Ave Ste 300 (60411-1679)
PHONE ................................. 708 754-4000
Fax: 708 754-0123
Robert Carstensen, *Branch Mgr*
**EMP:** 6
**SALES (corp-wide):** 1.9MM **Privately Held**
**WEB:** www.ecrossmark.com
**SIC:** 2759 Letterpress printing; screen printing
**PA:** Crossmark Printing, Inc.
18400 76th Ave Ste A
Tinley Park IL 60477
708 532-8263

**(G-7095)**
**DI CICCO CONCRETE PRODUCTS**
128 E 14th St (60411-2779)
P.O. Box 728 (60412-0728)
PHONE ................................. 708 754-5691
Fax: 708 754-5132
Carlo Di Cicco Jr, *CEO*
Luis Galvan, *President*
Larry Sims, *General Mgr*
Corazon Calara, *Treasurer*
Carletta Galvan, *Admin Sec*
**EMP:** 15
**SQ FT:** 16,000
**SALES (est):** 3.3MM **Privately Held**
**SIC:** 3272 Manhole covers or frames, concrete

## Chicago Heights - Cook County (G-7119)

**(G-7096)**
**EVENT CATERING GROUP**
325 W Glengate Ave (60411-1652)
PHONE..................................708 534-3100
Erin Buchmeier, *Principal*
**EMP:** 5
**SALES:** 100K **Privately Held**
**SIC:** 2099 Food preparations

**(G-7097)**
**FH AYER MANUFACTURING CO**
2015 S Halsted St (60411-4283)
P.O. Box 247 (60412-0247)
PHONE..................................708 755-0550
Fax: 708 755-7435
Robert C Debolt, *President*
Frank Smith, *Purch Mgr*
David Kristoff, *Sales Staff*
Bonnie Gonzales, *Office Mgr*
Rick Piunti, *Supervisor*
**EMP:** 45
**SQ FT:** 30,000
**SALES (est):** 8.9MM **Privately Held**
**WEB:** www.fhayer.com
**SIC:** 3599 3561 8734 7629 Machine shop, jobbing & repair; pumps & pumping equipment; testing laboratories; electrical repair shops

**(G-7098)**
**GERRESHEIMER GLASS INC**
1131 Arnold St (60411-2904)
PHONE..................................708 757-6853
Tom Lucas, *Plant Supt*
John Weritz, *Opers Staff*
Mike McCartney, *Plt & Fclts Mgr*
Patrick Gabel, *Purch Agent*
Fred Powers, *Purch Agent*
**EMP:** 200
**SALES (corp-wide):** 1.5B **Privately Held**
**WEB:** www.kimblescience.com
**SIC:** 3231 3221 Products of purchased glass; glass containers
**HQ:** Gerresheimer Glass Inc.
537 Crystal Ave
Vineland NJ 08360
856 692-3600

**(G-7099)**
**GLITECH INC**
330 E Joe Orr Rd Unit 1 (60411-1296)
PHONE..................................708 753-1220
Gary Loyd, *President*
Candace Boyd, *Admin Sec*
**EMP:** 10
**SQ FT:** 37,700
**SALES (est):** 1.1MM **Privately Held**
**SIC:** 3446 Railings, bannisters, guards, etc.: made from metal pipe

**(G-7100)**
**GOODER-HENRICHSEN COMPANY INC (PA)**
2900 State St (60411-4843)
PHONE..................................708 757-5030
Fax: 708 757-3157
Tom Ryan, *President*
Gregg Baldwin, *Vice Pres*
Paul Oconnor, *Vice Pres*
Eric Siew, *Vice Pres*
Diane Wojtanowicz, *Production*
**EMP:** 53 **EST:** 1927
**SQ FT:** 115,000
**SALES (est):** 10.3MM **Privately Held**
**SIC:** 3441 Joists, open web steel: long-span series

**(G-7101)**
**GUNDERSON RAIL SERVICES LLC**
1545 State St (60411-3707)
PHONE..................................866 858-3919
Theodore Quick, *Principal*
**EMP:** 35
**SALES (corp-wide):** 2.6B **Publicly Held**
**SIC:** 3743 Railroad equipment
**HQ:** Gunderson Rail Services Llc
1 Centerpointe Dr Ste 200
Lake Oswego OR 97265
503 684-7000

**(G-7102)**
**HALLMARK CABINET COMPANY**
Also Called: Hallmark Surfaces
3225 Rennie Smith Dr (60411-5565)
PHONE..................................708 757-7807
Fax: 708 757-7822
Anthony S Pappas, *President*
Penny Pappas, *Manager*
Joe Sendra, *Info Tech Mgr*
Judith K Pappas, *Admin Sec*
**EMP:** 70 **EST:** 1980
**SALES (est):** 9.2MM **Privately Held**
**WEB:** www.hallmarktops.com
**SIC:** 2541 7389 Counters or counter display cases, wood;

**(G-7103)**
**INNOPHOS INC**
1101 Arnold St (60411-2904)
PHONE..................................708 757-6111
Susan Turner, *Plant Mgr*
Jerry Norvil, *Buyer*
Robert Petrella, *Engineer*
Don Strohacker, *Engineer*
Joseph Sprouse, *Electrical Engi*
**EMP:** 168
**SALES (corp-wide):** 725.3MM **Publicly Held**
**WEB:** www.innophos.com
**SIC:** 2819 2874 Phosphates, except fertilizers: defluorinated & ammoniated; phosphates
**HQ:** Innophos, Inc.
259 Prospect Plains Rd A
Cranbury NJ 08512
609 495-2495

**(G-7104)**
**J&A PALLETS SERVICE INC**
1225 Arnold St (60411-2905)
PHONE..................................708 333-6601
Antonio Munice, *President*
**EMP:** 10
**SALES (est):** 1.5MM **Privately Held**
**SIC:** 2448 Pallets, wood & wood with metal

**(G-7105)**
**JN PUMP HOLDINGS INC (PA)**
Also Called: Nagle Pumps
1249 Center Ave (60411-2805)
PHONE..................................708 754-2940
Fax: 708 754-2944
James Nagle, *President*
William Hein, *General Mgr*
Kay Sue Nagle, *Vice Pres*
Richard Swanson, *Purch Mgr*
Paul Mell, *Controller*
**EMP:** 19 **EST:** 1946
**SQ FT:** 30,000
**SALES (est):** 2.8MM **Privately Held**
**SIC:** 3561 5084 Pumps & pumping equipment; industrial machinery & equipment

**(G-7106)**
**JOHNSTON & JENNINGS INC**
1200 State St Ste 1 (60411-2968)
PHONE..................................708 757-5375
Fax: 708 757-7787
Craig Yort, *President*
Julie Yort, *Admin Sec*
**EMP:** 7
**SQ FT:** 65,000
**SALES (est):** 1.1MM **Privately Held**
**SIC:** 3321 Gray & ductile iron foundries

**(G-7107)**
**K & A BREAD LLC**
Also Called: Pita Pan Old World Bakery
401 E Joe Orr Rd (60411-1202)
PHONE..................................708 757-7750
Andre Papantoniou,
**EMP:** 100
**SALES (est):** 16MM **Privately Held**
**SIC:** 2051 2053 Breads, rolls & buns; cakes, bakery: except cakes, bakery: frozen

**(G-7108)**
**KEMPCO WINDOW TREATMENTS INC**
74 E 23rd St (60411-4285)
PHONE..................................708 754-4484
Fax: 708 755-9603
Thomas Kemp, *President*
Serge Sokol, *Corp Secy*
Frank Casto, *Vice Pres*
Leo Ankney, *Director*
James Kemp, *Shareholder*
**EMP:** 30
**SQ FT:** 13,000
**SALES (est):** 4.5MM **Privately Held**
**WEB:** www.kempcoworkroom.com
**SIC:** 5023 2211 5131 Draperies; draperies & drapery fabrics, cotton; drapery material, woven

**(G-7109)**
**KEYSTONE CONSOLIDATED INDS INC**
Keystone Calumetals
317 E 11th St (60411-2852)
PHONE..................................708 753-1200
Karen Handley, *Finance Mgr*
Michael Goich, *Branch Mgr*
**EMP:** 33
**SALES (corp-wide):** 1.8B **Publicly Held**
**WEB:** www.keystonesteel.com
**SIC:** 3312 Bar, rod & wire products
**HQ:** Keystone Consolidated Industries, Inc.
5430 Lyndon B Johnson Fwy # 1740
Dallas TX 75240
800 441-0308

**(G-7110)**
**KEYSTONE-CALUMET INC**
317 E 11th St (60411-2852)
PHONE..................................708 753-1200
C Vic Stirnaman, *President*
Leo Alexander, *Human Res Mgr*
Norma Romero, *Human Res Mgr*
Dave Jillson, *Manager*
Sandra K Myers, *Admin Sec*
**EMP:** 21
**SALES (est):** 4.3MM **Privately Held**
**SIC:** 3312 Axles, rolled or forged: made in steel mills

**(G-7111)**
**MARCONI BAKERY COMPANY**
212 E 16th St (60411-3648)
PHONE..................................708 757-6315
Joe Marconi, *President*
William Marconi, *Vice Pres*
**EMP:** 10
**SQ FT:** 2,400
**SALES (est):** 740K **Privately Held**
**SIC:** 2051 Bread, all types (white, wheat, rye, etc): fresh or frozen

**(G-7112)**
**MERCEDES FABRICATION**
57 E 24th St (60411-4177)
PHONE..................................708 709-9240
Fax: 708 709-9280
Tim Mercede, *President*
**EMP:** 18
**SALES (est):** 1.6MM **Privately Held**
**WEB:** www.mercedesfabrication.com
**SIC:** 3449 Bars, concrete reinforcing: fabricated steel

**(G-7113)**
**MINORITY AUTO HDLG SPECIALISTS (HQ)**
22401 Sauk Pointe Dr (60411-4833)
PHONE..................................708 757-8758
Fax: 708 757-8767
Theodore Vance, *President*
Dave Howard, *Manager*
George Klien, *Admin Sec*
**EMP:** 16
**SALES (est):** 13.8MM
**SALES (corp-wide):** 52.5MM **Privately Held**
**SIC:** 4731 3448 Freight forwarding; prefabricated metal buildings
**PA:** T.V. Minority Company, Inc.
9400 Pelham Rd
Taylor MI 48180
313 386-1048

**(G-7114)**
**MORGAN LI LLC**
383 E 16th St (60411-3701)
PHONE..................................708 758-5300
Andrew Rosenband, *CEO*
Jonathan Rosenband, *President*
Phil Rosenband, *Exec VP*
Joseph Downes, *Vice Pres*
Antonio Lopez, *Opers Mgr*
▲ **EMP:** 40
**SQ FT:** 350,000
**SALES:** 20.3MM **Privately Held**
**SIC:** 2541 Store & office display cases & fixtures

**(G-7115)**
**NUFARM AMERICAS INC**
220 E 17th St Fl 2 (60411-3602)
PHONE..................................708 756-2010
Conrad Harwell, *Plant Mgr*
Melissa Keil, *Purch Mgr*
Londra Taylor, *Research*
Gregory Jones, *Engineer*
Kim Schulz, *Cust Mgr*
**EMP:** 60
**SQ FT:** 75,000
**SALES (corp-wide):** 2B **Privately Held**
**WEB:** www.nufarm.com
**SIC:** 2879 Insecticides, agricultural or household
**HQ:** Nufarm Americas Inc.
11901 S Austin Ave Ste A
Alsip IL 60803
708 377-1330

**(G-7116)**
**OZINGA BROS INC**
1750 State St (60411-3710)
PHONE..................................708 326-4200
Bill Clark, *President*
Phil Tempelman, *Opers Mgr*
**EMP:** 80
**SQ FT:** 6,400
**SALES (corp-wide):** 221.8MM **Privately Held**
**SIC:** 3273 Ready-mixed concrete
**PA:** Ozinga Bros., Inc.
19001 Old Lagrange Rd # 30
Mokena IL 60448
708 326-4200

**(G-7117)**
**POLL ENTERPRISES INC**
Also Called: Core Integrated Marketing
209 Glenwood Rd (60411-8217)
PHONE..................................708 756-1120
Howard L Budrow, *President*
Judith L Budrow, *Admin Sec*
Greg Budrow, *Administration*
**EMP:** 18 **EST:** 1983
**SQ FT:** 6,500
**SALES (est):** 3MM **Privately Held**
**WEB:** www.printcrazy.com
**SIC:** 7334 2752 Photocopying & duplicating services; commercial printing, offset

**(G-7118)**
**PTC GROUP HOLDINGS CORP**
Also Called: Dixmor Division
475 E 16th St (60411-3702)
PHONE..................................708 757-4747
Thomas Sprehe, *Plant Mgr*
George Bednar, *Opers Mgr*
Marty Strutz, *Branch Mgr*
**EMP:** 51 **Privately Held**
**SIC:** 3312 3317 3316 Well casings, iron & steel: made in steel mills; steel pipe & tubes; cold finishing of steel shapes
**PA:** Ptc Group Holdings Corp.
6051 Wallace Road Ext # 2
Wexford PA 15090

**(G-7119)**
**RAIL EXCHANGE INC**
1150 State St (60411-3700)
P.O. Box 340 (60412-0340)
PHONE..................................708 757-3317
Fax: 708 757-6828
Dean M Bartolini, *CEO*
Michael Bartolini, *President*
Mike Bartolini, *General Mgr*
Tom Wisinski, *Senior VP*
Cheryl Pohrte, *CFO*
**EMP:** 50
**SQ FT:** 36,000
**SALES (est):** 13.3MM **Privately Held**
**WEB:** www.railexchangeinc.com
**SIC:** 3469 3743 3462 3441 Machine parts, stamped or pressed metal; railroad locomotives & parts, electric or nonelectric; iron & steel forgings; fabricated structural metal

## Chicago Heights - Cook County (G-7120)

**(G-7120)**
**REAL ALLOY RECYCLING INC**
400 E Lincoln Hwy (60411-2973)
P.O. Box 751 (60412-0751)
PHONE..................................708 758-8888
Larry Lipa, *Plant Mgr*
**EMP:** 60
**SALES (corp-wide):** 1.2B **Publicly Held**
**WEB:** www.imcorecycling.com
**SIC:** 3341 Secondary nonferrous metals
**HQ:** Real Alloy Recycling, Inc.
 3700 Park East Dr Ste 300
 Beachwood OH 44122
 216 755-8900

**(G-7121)**
**RHONE-POULENC BASIC CHEM CO**
1101 Arnold St (60411-2995)
PHONE..................................708 757-6111
**Fax:** 708 709-2861
Paul Pruett, *Principal*
**EMP:** 3
**SALES (est):** 283.8K **Privately Held**
**SIC:** 2819 Industrial inorganic chemicals

**(G-7122)**
**RMI INC**
211 E Main St (60411-4270)
PHONE..................................708 756-5640
Brad Corral, *President*
Richard Gollner, *CFO*
Dave Fuss, *Manager*
Nancy Corral, *Admin Sec*
**EMP:** 10
**SALES (est):** 3.6MM **Privately Held**
**SIC:** 3312 Structural & rail mill products

**(G-7123)**
**ROBEY PACKAGING EQP & SVC**
3236 Rennie Smith Dr (60411-5564)
PHONE..................................708 758-8250
Rich Robey, *President*
Patricia Robey, *Corp Secy*
Heather Henle, *Admin Sec*
**EMP:** 4
**SALES (est):** 440K **Privately Held**
**SIC:** 3565 7699 Bag opening, filling & closing machines; industrial machinery & equipment repair

**(G-7124)**
**RUTHMAN PUMP AND ENGINEERING**
Also Called: Nagle Pumps
1249 Center Ave (60411-2805)
PHONE..................................708 754-2940
William Hein, *Manager*
**EMP:** 5
**SALES (corp-wide):** 41.6MM **Privately Held**
**WEB:** www.ruthmannpumpen.de
**SIC:** 3561 Pumps & pumping equipment
**PA:** Ruthman Pump And Engineering, Inc
 1212 Streng St
 Cincinnati OH 45223
 513 559-1901

**(G-7125)**
**S M C GRAPHICS**
1024 Lowe Ave (60411-2731)
PHONE..................................708 754-8973
Manfredo Ciccotelli, *Partner*
Sandra Ciccotelli, *Partner*
▲ **EMP:** 2
**SALES (est):** 280.3K **Privately Held**
**SIC:** 2752 2791 7336 Commercial printing, offset; typesetting; commercial art & graphic design

**(G-7126)**
**SOLVAY USA INC**
1020 State St (60411-2908)
PHONE..................................708 441-6041
**Fax:** 708 441-6086
Dave Harrison, *Systs Engr*
Sam Agle, *Branch Mgr*
**EMP:** 31
**SALES (corp-wide):** 11.4MM **Privately Held**
**WEB:** www.food.us.rhodia.com
**SIC:** 2819 Industrial inorganic chemicals
**HQ:** Solvay Usa Inc.
 504 Carnegie Ctr
 Princeton NJ 08540
 609 860-4000

**(G-7127)**
**STARMONT MANUFACTURING INC**
640 217th St (60411-4327)
PHONE..................................708 758-2525
John Montella, *President*
Thomas Montella, *Admin Sec*
**EMP:** 10
**SQ FT:** 5,000
**SALES (est):** 800K **Privately Held**
**SIC:** 3469 Metal stampings

**(G-7128)**
**SURE PLUS MANUFACTURING CO**
185 E 12th St (60411-2780)
PHONE..................................708 756-3100
Gordon P Henschel, *President*
Paul Henschel, *Vice Pres*
Patti Rivera, *Director*
**EMP:** 64 **EST:** 1965
**SQ FT:** 200,000
**SALES (est):** 8.4MM **Privately Held**
**WEB:** www.sureplus.com
**SIC:** 3231 3714 Mirrors, truck & automobile: made from purchased glass; motor vehicle parts & accessories

**(G-7129)**
**T & J MEATPACKING INC**
635 Glenwood Dyer Rd (60411-8625)
P.O. Box 215, Glenwood (60425-0215)
PHONE..................................708 757-6930
**Fax:** 708 758-8688
Tony Lilovich, *President*
John Lilovich, *Vice Pres*
Rick Havlin, *Manager*
**EMP:** 55 **EST:** 1935
**SQ FT:** 1,100
**SALES (est):** 8MM **Privately Held**
**SIC:** 2011 5147 5421 0751 Meat byproducts from meat slaughtered on site; meats & meat products; meat & fish markets; slaughtering: custom livestock services; sausages & other prepared meats

**(G-7130)**
**TANKO SCRW PRD CORP**
19830 Stoney Island Ave (60411-8671)
PHONE..................................708 418-0300
**Fax:** 708 418-0370
William Landholt, *Principal*
**EMP:** 3
**SALES (est):** 170K **Privately Held**
**SIC:** 3451 Screw machine products

**(G-7131)**
**TGM FABRICATING INC**
57 E 24th St (60411-4177)
PHONE..................................708 533-0857
Rosaoia Turner, *President*
**EMP:** 2 **EST:** 2010
**SALES (est):** 345.9K **Privately Held**
**SIC:** 3441 Fabricated structural metal

**(G-7132)**
**TRIALCO INC (PA)**
900 E Lincoln Hwy Ste 1 (60411-2992)
PHONE..................................708 757-4200
**Fax:** 708 757-3933
Jay Armstrong, *President*
Mike Carroll, *Controller*
Linda Hackel, *Personnel Exec*
Charles Pardo, *Director*
Bruce Kronick, *Admin Sec*
**EMP:** 50
**SQ FT:** 175,000
**SALES (est):** 9.2MM **Privately Held**
**WEB:** www.trialco.net
**SIC:** 3341 Aluminum smelting & refining (secondary)

**(G-7133)**
**TURNCO INC**
Also Called: Turnco Products
2200 S Halsted St (60411-4284)
PHONE..................................708 756-6565
Jerry Hindel Jr, *President*
Michael Langlinais, *Marketing Staff*
**EMP:** 5 **EST:** 1961
**SQ FT:** 7,200
**SALES (est):** 884.4K **Privately Held**
**SIC:** 3451 Screw machine products

**(G-7134)**
**VACUDYNE INCORPORATED (DH)**
375 E Joe Orr Rd (60411-1292)
PHONE..................................708 757-5200
**Fax:** 708 757-7180
Gary Tracy, *President*
George Collins, *Vice Pres*
Ron Tedford, *Plant Mgr*
Mike Strawn, *Purchasing*
John Cook, *Project Engr*
**EMP:** 40 **EST:** 1957
**SQ FT:** 34,000
**SALES (est):** 9.5MM
**SALES (corp-wide):** 62.6MM **Privately Held**
**SIC:** 3559 Tobacco products machinery
**HQ:** Altair Corporation (Del)
 350 Barclay Blvd
 Lincolnshire IL 60069
 847 634-9540

**(G-7135)**
**VESUVIUS U S A CORPORATION**
333 State St (60411-1203)
PHONE..................................708 757-7880
Jack Lee, *Production*
Woody Rothrock, *Purch Mgr*
Cahalan Gibson, *Engineer*
F L Jurotich, *Enginr/R&D Mgr*
Troy Devault, *Manager*
**EMP:** 75
**SALES (corp-wide):** 1.7B **Privately Held**
**WEB:** www.vesuvius.com
**SIC:** 3297 Graphite refractories: carbon bond or ceramic bond
**HQ:** Vesuvius U S A Corporation
 1404 Newton Dr
 Champaign IL 61822
 217 351-5000

**(G-7136)**
**VITELLI CONCRETE PRODUCTS INC**
2410 S Halsted St (60411-4131)
PHONE..................................708 754-5846
Jason Hering, *President*
**EMP:** 4 **EST:** 1900
**SQ FT:** 3,000
**SALES (est):** 520K **Privately Held**
**SIC:** 3272 Concrete products

**(G-7137)**
**ZOETIS LLC**
Also Called: Animal Health Div
400 State St (60411-1242)
PHONE..................................708 757-2592
Bryan Hunt, *Opers-Prdtn-Mfg*
H Pocius, *Engr R&D*
John Baker, *Asst Director*
**EMP:** 70
**SALES (corp-wide):** 4.8B **Publicly Held**
**WEB:** www.alpharma.com
**SIC:** 2833 2834 2048 4225 Antibiotics; pharmaceutical preparations; prepared feeds; general warehousing
**HQ:** Zoetis Llc
 10 Sylvan Way Ste 105
 Parsippany NJ 07054
 800 601-1357

## Chicago Ridge
### Cook County

**(G-7138)**
**ACCURATE INDUSTRIAL SUPPLY CO**
6647 99th St (60415-1294)
PHONE..................................708 422-7050
**Fax:** 708 422-7442
Michael J Saracini, *President*
Rose Saracini, *Vice Pres*
Mary Katherine Saracini, *Admin Sec*
**EMP:** 7
**SQ FT:** 15,000
**SALES (est):** 1.2MM **Privately Held**
**SIC:** 3965 Fasteners, buttons, needles & pins

**(G-7139)**
**AVIATION SERVICES GROUP INC**
Also Called: Aviation Services Group of IL
10524 Major Ave (60415-2033)
PHONE..................................708 425-4700
John Cisla, *Branch Mgr*
**EMP:** 4
**SALES (corp-wide):** 1.4MM **Privately Held**
**SIC:** 3721 Aircraft
**PA:** Aviation Services Group Inc
 4243 E Lake Blvd
 Birmingham AL 35217
 205 849-3848

**(G-7140)**
**CELTIC ENVIRONMENTAL**
6640 99th Pl (60415-1211)
PHONE..................................708 442-5823
Joseph Smrz, *Owner*
**EMP:** 6
**SALES (est):** 918K **Privately Held**
**SIC:** 3292 Asbestos products

**(G-7141)**
**CHICAGO FLORAL PLANTERS INC**
10139 S Harlem Ave (60415-1366)
PHONE..................................708 423-2754
James Wrobel, *President*
Janet Wrobel, *Admin Sec*
**EMP:** 3
**SALES (est):** 230K **Privately Held**
**SIC:** 2449 Containers, plywood & veneer wood

**(G-7142)**
**CHICAGO PARK DISTRICT**
10736 Lombard Ave (60415-2109)
PHONE..................................708 857-2653
**Fax:** 708 636-5758
Kevin King, *Branch Mgr*
**EMP:** 75
**SALES (corp-wide):** 185.1MM **Privately Held**
**SIC:** 3599 Amusement park equipment
**PA:** Chicago Park District
 541 N Fairbanks Ct # 400
 Chicago IL 60611
 312 742-7529

**(G-7143)**
**CLOPAY BUILDING PDTS CO INC**
10047 Virginia Ave Ste A (60415-3716)
PHONE..................................708 346-0901
John Elgin, *Manager*
**EMP:** 5
**SALES (corp-wide):** 1.9B **Publicly Held**
**SIC:** 2431 Garage doors, overhead: wood
**HQ:** Clopay Building Products Company, Inc.
 8585 Duke Blvd
 Mason OH 45040

**(G-7144)**
**CMD CONVEYOR INC**
10008 Anderson Ave (60415-1257)
PHONE..................................708 237-0996
Casey Czochara, *President*
**EMP:** 34
**SQ FT:** 13,000
**SALES (est):** 8.9MM **Privately Held**
**SIC:** 3535 Conveyors & conveying equipment

**(G-7145)**
**CROWLEY-SHEPPARD ASPHALT INC**
6525 99th Pl (60415-1233)
P.O. Box 157 (60415-0157)
PHONE..................................708 499-2900
**Fax:** 708 499-3106
Richard A Sheppard, *President*
Michael J Sheppard, *Vice Pres*
**EMP:** 10 **EST:** 1943
**SQ FT:** 3,000
**SALES (est):** 10MM **Privately Held**
**SIC:** 2951 1771 Asphalt & asphaltic paving mixtures (not from refineries); blacktop (asphalt) work

# GEOGRAPHIC SECTION

**Chillicothe - Peoria County (G-7172)**

**(G-7146)**
**ELITE MCHNING OF CHICAGO RIDGE**
6655 99th St (60415-1208)
PHONE..........................708 423-0767
Fax: 708 423-2614
Matt Osinski, *President*
Raphael O'Sinski, *General Mgr*
Thor Swanson, *Sales Staff*
Beata Drwal, *Manager*
EMP: 7
SALES (est): 1MM **Privately Held**
SIC: **3599** Machine shop, jobbing & repair

**(G-7147)**
**ENTERPRISE AC & HTG CO**
6112 111th St (60415-2105)
PHONE..........................708 430-2212
John Coleman, *Manager*
EMP: 6
SALES (corp-wide): 813.9K **Privately Held**
SIC: **3444** 1711 Sheet metalwork; plumbing, heating, air-conditioning contractors
PA: Enterprise Air Conditioning & Heating Co
6100 W 82nd Pl
Oak Lawn IL 60459
708 430-2212

**(G-7148)**
**GREAT LAKES STAIR & STEEL INC**
10130 Virginia Ave (60415-1378)
PHONE..........................708 430-2323
Don Ziblis, *President*
Tony Ziblis, *Prdtn Mgr*
Sue Ziblis, *Office Mgr*
Michael Mara, *Manager*
EMP: 9
SQ FT: 3,000
SALES (est): 2.4MM **Privately Held**
WEB: www.glstair.com
SIC: **3449** Bars, concrete reinforcing: fabricated steel

**(G-7149)**
**HARRIS PRECISION TOOLS INC**
10081 Anderson Ave (60415-1200)
PHONE..........................708 422-5808
Fax: 708 422-4202
Robert Harris, *President*
Donna Harris, *Admin Sec*
EMP: 6
SQ FT: 6,000
SALES: 300K **Privately Held**
SIC: **3541** 3625 3546 3545 Cutoff machines (metalworking machinery); relays & industrial controls; power-driven handtools; machine tool accessories; cutlery

**(G-7150)**
**HOHMANN & BARNARD ILLINOIS LLC**
9999 Virginia Ave (60415-1368)
P.O. Box 5270, Hauppauge NY (11788-0270)
PHONE..........................773 586-6700
Jack Nappi, *Controller*
Jan Crusing, *Manager*
Ronald Hohmann,
Christopher Hohmann,
Robert Hohmann,
EMP: 34
SQ FT: 34,000
SALES (est): 6MM **Privately Held**
SIC: **3496** 3315 Concrete reinforcing mesh & wire; steel wire & related products

**(G-7151)**
**MIDWEST MIXING INC**
5630 Pleasant Blvd (60415-2306)
PHONE..........................708 422-8140
Fax: 708 422-8100
Robert R Smith, *President*
Gary Grenier, *Corp Secy*
Louis Fandrey, *Manager*
EMP: 6
SQ FT: 7,000
SALES: 800K **Privately Held**
WEB: www.midwestmixing.com
SIC: **3559** 3531 Refinery, chemical processing & similar machinery; chemical machinery & equipment; construction machinery

**(G-7152)**
**MOORE MEMORIALS**
5960 111th St (60415-2275)
PHONE..........................708 636-6532
Fax: 708 636-1054
Maurice Moore Jr, *President*
Patricia Moore, *Vice Pres*
Maurice Moore Sr, *Admin Sec*
EMP: 11
SQ FT: 4,200
SALES (est): 1.4MM **Privately Held**
SIC: **5999** 5039 3281 Gravestones, finished; glass construction materials; cut stone & stone products

**(G-7153)**
**PETRO ENTERPRISES INC**
10242 Ridgeland Ave (60415-1328)
PHONE..........................708 425-1551
Ken Petropolus, *President*
EMP: 5
SALES (est): 510K **Privately Held**
SIC: **2519** 5021 5712 Household furniture, except wood or metal: upholstered; furniture; furniture stores

**(G-7154)**
**PRECISION PRISMATIC INC**
10247 Ridgeland Ave Ste 1 (60415-2807)
PHONE..........................708 424-0905
Joseph Pristo, *President*
EMP: 6
SQ FT: 5,000
SALES: 500K **Privately Held**
SIC: **3545** Precision tools, machinists'

**(G-7155)**
**PRO IMAGE**
670 Chicago Ridge Mall (60415-2606)
PHONE..........................708 422-7471
EMP: 6
SALES (est): 311.2K **Privately Held**
SIC: **7335** 2339 2329 Photographic studio, commercial; athletic clothing: women's, misses & juniors'; men's & boys' sportswear & athletic clothing

**(G-7156)**
**PRODUCT FEEDING SOLUTIONS INC**
5632 Pleasant Blvd (60415-2306)
PHONE..........................630 709-9546
Noel Parlour, *CEO*
Barbara Parlour, *President*
EMP: 5
SQ FT: 2,000
SALES (est): 634.8K **Privately Held**
SIC: **3829** Measuring & controlling devices

**(G-7157)**
**R&R EQUIPMENT PLUS1 INC**
9923 Ridgeland Ave (60415-1262)
PHONE..........................708 529-3931
Rachel Ettawa, *President*
Wayne Ettawa, *Vice Pres*
EMP: 10
SQ FT: 1,500
SALES (est): 412.7K **Privately Held**
SIC: **5084** 3621 5088 Lift trucks & parts; electric motor & generator parts; space propulsion units & parts

**(G-7158)**
**SELCO INDUSTRIES**
6655 Kitty Ave (60415-1286)
PHONE..........................708 499-1060
Fax: 708 499-2080
Joseph Heneghan, *President*
Robert Scellato, *Opers Mgr*
EMP: 8
SQ FT: 18,000
SALES (est): 1.6MM **Privately Held**
SIC: **3446** 5039 Railings, bannisters, guards, etc.: made from metal pipe; stairs, staircases, stair treads: prefabricated metal; joists; structural assemblies, prefabricated: non-wood

**(G-7159)**
**WW TIMBERS INC (PA)**
10150 Virginia Ave Ste K (60415-3715)
PHONE..........................708 423-9112
Fax: 708 423-8855
Philip Weibel, *President*
Debbie Cummings, *Office Mgr*
Leonard Schultz III, *Admin Sec*
EMP: 6
SQ FT: 20,000
SALES (est): 768.2K **Privately Held**
SIC: **2439** Timbers, structural: laminated lumber

## Chillicothe
### Peoria County

**(G-7160)**
**A C GENTROL INC**
100 S 4th St (61523-2245)
P.O. Box 452 (61523-0452)
PHONE..........................309 274-5486
Fax: 309 274-3962
Angelito M Capati, *President*
EMP: 35
SQ FT: 14,000
SALES (est): 7MM **Privately Held**
WEB: www.acgentrol.com
SIC: **3613** Generator control & metering panels; control panels, electric

**(G-7161)**
**ALLIED WELDING INC**
1820 N Santa Fe Ave (61523-1042)
P.O. Box 410 (61523-0410)
PHONE..........................309 274-6227
Fax: 309 274-5448
Terry Nelson, *President*
Scott Crank, *General Mgr*
David Roahrig, *Purch Agent*
Steve Wylie, *Engineer*
Patsy Morrow, *Controller*
EMP: 50
SQ FT: 35,700
SALES (est): 8MM **Privately Held**
WEB: www.alliedwelding.net
SIC: **3599** Machine & other job shop work

**(G-7162)**
**BLUE RIDGE FORGE INC**
316 W Cedar St (61523-1642)
P.O. Box 43 (61523-0043)
PHONE..........................309 274-5377
John Morris, *Vice Pres*
EMP: 6
SALES (est): 872.2K **Privately Held**
SIC: **3315** Welded steel wire fabric

**(G-7163)**
**C J HOLDINGS INC**
Also Called: J & J Manufacturing
110 W Walnut St (61523-1833)
PHONE..........................309 274-3141
Fax: 309 274-2354
Caryn Knop, *President*
Carl A Gross, *Shareholder*
Jackie Gross, *Admin Sec*
EMP: 6 EST: 2004
SQ FT: 15,000
SALES (est): 1.1MM **Privately Held**
SIC: **3469** 7692 3444 3443 Metal stampings; welding repair; sheet metalwork; fabricated plate work (boiler shop)

**(G-7164)**
**EAGLE COMPANIES INC**
4214 E Rome Rd (61523-9384)
PHONE..........................309 686-9054
Fax: 309 686-9359
Timothy J Tobin, *President*
EMP: 10
SQ FT: 24,000
SALES (est): 1.7MM **Privately Held**
WEB: www.eaglemodular.com
SIC: **3448** Prefabricated metal buildings

**(G-7165)**
**FRONTIER SIGNS & LIGHTING**
15419 N 7th St (61523-9241)
PHONE..........................309 694-7300
Fax: 309 694-7377
EMP: 2
SALES (est): 203K **Privately Held**
SIC: **3993** Signs & advertising specialties

**(G-7166)**
**GALENA ROAD GRAVEL INC**
5129 E Truitt Rd (61523-9340)
P.O. Box 50 (61523-0050)
PHONE..........................309 274-6388
Fax: 309 274-5125
Rich Lucas, *President*
Peter Powell, *Vice Pres*
Judy Samayao, *Treasurer*
EMP: 35
SQ FT: 500
SALES (est): 7.3MM
SALES (corp-wide): 9.9MM **Privately Held**
SIC: **1442** Construction sand & gravel
HQ: B.S.C. Holding, Inc.
10955 Lowell Ave Ste 500
Overland Park KS 66210
913 262-7263

**(G-7167)**
**IMAGINATION PRODUCTS CORP**
Also Called: Flexisnake
227 W Cedar St (61523-1638)
PHONE..........................309 274-6223
Scott Turner, *President*
Stephen Turner, *Vice Pres*
EMP: 7
SQ FT: 8,000
SALES: 100K **Privately Held**
SIC: **2842** 3999 5087 Drain pipe solvents or cleaners; pipe cleaners; cleaning & maintenance equipment & supplies

**(G-7168)**
**J T FENNELL CO INC (PA)**
1104 N Front St (61523-1650)
P.O. Box 337 (61523-0337)
PHONE..........................309 274-2145
Fax: 309 274-2147
James T Fennell, *President*
Jerry P Fennell, *Vice Pres*
Scott Meints, *Manager*
John Merdian, *Admin Sec*
EMP: 100 EST: 1946
SQ FT: 90,000
SALES (est): 19.1MM **Privately Held**
SIC: **3599** Machine shop, jobbing & repair

**(G-7169)**
**NOVEL ELECTRONIC DESIGNS INC**
143 N 3rd St (61523-2156)
PHONE..........................309 224-9945
Durwin D Nigus, *President*
Pamela Nigus, *President*
Pamela Niguss, *General Mgr*
EMP: 4
SALES (est): 385K **Privately Held**
SIC: **3679** Electronic circuits

**(G-7170)**
**POWER ENCLOSURES INC (PA)**
100 S 4th St (61523-2245)
P.O. Box 452 (61523-0452)
PHONE..........................309 274-9000
Angelito Capati, *President*
Teresita Capati, *Treasurer*
EMP: 13
SQ FT: 14,000
SALES (est): 1.8MM **Privately Held**
WEB: www.powerenclosures.com
SIC: **3621** Motor housings

**(G-7171)**
**TER-SON CORPORATION**
Also Called: Allied Welding
1801 N Logan St (61523-1102)
P.O. Box 410 (61523-0410)
PHONE..........................309 274-6227
Terry Nelson, *President*
Susan Nelson, *Vice Pres*
Ernest Hostetler Jr, *Treasurer*
Craig Hodge, *Manager*
EMP: 75
SALES (est): 6.7MM **Privately Held**
SIC: **3599** Machine & other job shop work

**(G-7172)**
**WESTERN YEAST COMPANY INC**
305 W Ash St (61523-1603)
PHONE..........................309 274-3160

Fax: 309 274-5107
Keith Turner, *President*
Robert Leiner, *General Mgr*
La Von Turner, *Corp Secy*
Michael Turner Dvm, *Vice Pres*
J W Ones, *Sales Staff*
**EMP:** 20
**SQ FT:** 20,000
**SALES (est):** 2.8MM  Privately Held
**WEB:** www.westernyeast.com
**SIC:** 2048  Prepared feeds

## Chrisman
### Edgar County

**(G-7173)**
**CHRISMAN LEADER**
140 W Madison Ave  (61924-1118)
**PHONE**..................................217 269-2811
Lou Valbert, *Owner*
Joann Travioli, *Manager*
**EMP:** 5
**SQ FT:** 4,000
**SALES (est):** 224.5K  Privately Held
**SIC:** 2711  5994  Newspapers, publishing & printing; news dealers & newsstands

## Christopher
### Franklin County

**(G-7174)**
**SIMION FABRICATION  INC**
901 W Egyptian Ave  (62822)
P.O. Box 33  (62822-0033)
**PHONE**..................................618 724-7331
Fax: 618 724-2120
Darrell Simion, *President*
Rosalee Simion, *Corp Secy*
**EMP:** 8
**SQ FT:** 8,400
**SALES (est):** 900K  Privately Held
**SIC:** 3441  Fabricated structural metal

## Cicero
### Cook County

**(G-7175)**
**ABSOLUTE STONEWORKS INC**
5738 W 26th St  (60804-3223)
**PHONE**..................................708 652-7600
Dean Grozdic, *President*
**EMP:** 4
**SALES (est):** 350K  Privately Held
**SIC:** 3281  Marble, building: cut & shaped; granite, cut & shaped

**(G-7176)**
**ACTIVE GRAPHICS  INC**
5500 W 31st St  (60804-3957)
**PHONE**..................................708 656-8900
George Hayes, *President*
James Radermacher, *CFO*
John Collins, *Director*
Jeremy Hayes, *Admin Sec*
**EMP:** 45
**SQ FT:** 23,000
**SALES (est):** 12.1MM  Privately Held
**WEB:** www.activegraphics.net
**SIC:** 2752  7336  2759  Commercial printing, offset; commercial art & graphic design; commercial printing

**(G-7177)**
**ALANG PATTERN INC**
3635 S 61st Ave  (60804-4147)
**PHONE**..................................773 722-9481
**EMP:** 4
**SALES (est):** 363.9K  Privately Held
**SIC:** 3543  Industrial patterns

**(G-7178)**
**AMD INDUSTRIES  INC (PA)**
4620 W 19th St  (60804-2597)
**PHONE**..................................708 863-8900
Fax: 708 863-2065
David E Allen, *Chairman*
Teresita Rivera, *Controller*
Lydia Allen, *Admin Sec*

◆ **EMP:** 55
**SQ FT:** 130,000
**SALES (est):** 14MM  Privately Held
**SIC:** 3993  Displays & cutouts, window & lobby

**(G-7179)**
**B & B SPECIALTY COMPANY INC**
5133 W 25th Pl  (60804-2908)
**PHONE**..................................708 652-9234
Fax: 708 652-3817
William Harrison, *President*
W H Pickard, *Accountant*
**EMP:** 4  **EST:** 1943
**SQ FT:** 6,250
**SALES (est):** 300K  Privately Held
**SIC:** 3599  Machine shop, jobbing & repair

**(G-7180)**
**BERKSHIRE INVESTMENTS LLC**
Also Called: Chicago Extruded Metals Co
1601 S 54th Ave  (60804-1892)
**PHONE**..................................708 656-7900
Fax: 708 780-3479
Dan Smolen, *Purch Mgr*
Herb Vahldick, *Technical Mgr*
Leon Fridberg, *Engineer*
Dave Cobb, *Manager*
Scott Johnson, *Manager*
**EMP:** 100
**SQ FT:** 204,000
**SALES (est):** 25.8MM  Privately Held
**WEB:** www.berkshireinvestments.com
**SIC:** 3499  Giftware, brass goods

**(G-7181)**
**BROADWIND ENERGY  INC (PA)**
3240 S Central Ave  (60804-3939)
**PHONE**..................................708 780-4800
Fax: 630 637-8472
David P Reiland, *Ch of Bd*
Stephanie K Kushner, *President*
David W Fell, *Vice Pres*
Erik W Jensen, *Vice Pres*
Robert R Rogowski, *Vice Pres*
**EMP:** 106
**SQ FT:** 301,000
**SALES (est):** 180.8MM  Publicly Held
**SIC:** 3511  Turbines & turbine generator sets; turbines & turbine generator sets & parts; turbines & turbine generator set units, complete

**(G-7182)**
**CHURCHILL CABINET COMPANY**
4616 W 19th St  (60804-2502)
**PHONE**..................................708 780-0070
Roger E Duba, *President*
Douglas Duba, *Vice Pres*
Marion Loboz, *Admin Sec*
▲ **EMP:** 50  **EST:** 1904
**SQ FT:** 94,000
**SALES (est):** 9.1MM  Privately Held
**SIC:** 2541  2511  Cabinets, except refrigerated: show, display, etc.: wood; unassembled or unfinished furniture, household: wood

**(G-7183)**
**CICERO IRON METAL & PAPER INC**
5901 W Ogden Ave Ste 7  (60804-3811)
**PHONE**..................................708 863-8601
Fax: 708 863-1364
Bob Hernandez, *President*
**EMP:** 6
**SQ FT:** 10,000
**SALES (est):** 750.8K  Privately Held
**SIC:** 5093  3341  2611  Metal scrap & waste materials; secondary nonferrous metals; pulp mills

**(G-7184)**
**CIRCLE GEAR & MACHINE CO INC**
1501 S 55th Ct  (60804-1842)
**PHONE**..................................708 652-1000
Fax: 708 652-1100
Albert J Knez, *CEO*
Edward Kaske, *President*
Michael McKernin, *President*
Scott Reid, *Vice Pres*
Charlotte Schmidt, *Vice Pres*
▲ **EMP:** 49
**SQ FT:** 125,000

**SALES (est):** 13.6MM  Privately Held
**WEB:** www.circlegear.com
**SIC:** 3566  Gears, power transmission, except automotive

**(G-7185)**
**COREY STEEL COMPANY**
2800 S 61st Ct  (60804-3091)
P.O. Box 5137, Chicago  (60680-5137)
**PHONE**..................................800 323-2750
Fax: 708 735-8100
Mordechai Korf, *CEO*
Paul J Darling II, *President*
John M Decker, *Vice Pres*
John W Kenefick, *Vice Pres*
Kevin A Lavery, *Vice Pres*
▲ **EMP:** 200  **EST:** 1924
**SQ FT:** 600,000
**SALES (est):** 136.1MM
**SALES (corp-wide):** 584.6MM  Privately Held
**WEB:** www.coreysteel.com
**SIC:** 3316  5051  Bars, steel, cold finished, from purchased hot-rolled; aluminum bars, rods, ingots, sheets, pipes, plates, etc.
**PA:** Optima Specialty Steel, Inc.
    200 S Biscayne Blvd # 5500
    Miami FL 33131
    305 375-7560

**(G-7186)**
**CR LAURENCE CO  INC**
Also Called: Crl Glass Machinery
5501 W Ogden Ave  (60804-3507)
**PHONE**..................................773 242-2871
R Carroll, *President*
John Czopek, *General Mgr*
**EMP:** 7
**SALES (corp-wide):** 28.6B  Privately Held
**SIC:** 5072  3559  Hardware; glass making machinery: blowing, molding, forming, etc.
**HQ:** C.R. Laurence Co., Inc.
    2503 E Vernon Ave
    Vernon CA 90058
    323 588-1281

**(G-7187)**
**CYRUS SHANK COMPANY (HQ)**
Also Called: Shank Precision Machine Co
4645 W Roosevelt Rd  (60804-1522)
**PHONE**..................................708 652-2700
Fax: 708 652-2766
Frank Kruppe Jr, *President*
Robert T Kruppe Jr, *Vice Pres*
Tom Hitt, *Financial Exec*
Janice Brandner, *Office Mgr*
**EMP:** 29
**SQ FT:** 14,000
**SALES (est):** 3.7MM
**SALES (corp-wide):** 4.3MM  Privately Held
**WEB:** www.cyrusshank.com
**SIC:** 3491  Industrial valves
**PA:** Shank Manufacturing
    575 Exchange Ct
    Aurora IL
    331 212-5488

**(G-7188)**
**DEFENDER STEEL DOOR & WINDOW (PA)**
6119 W 35th St  (60804-4108)
**PHONE**..................................708 780-7320
Fax: 708 780-7347
Robert Bianco, *President*
Robert Smith, *Corp Secy*
Dawn McKinney, *Purch Agent*
**EMP:** 23
**SQ FT:** 500
**SALES (est):** 2.8MM  Privately Held
**WEB:** www.steel-door.com
**SIC:** 5211  3442  Doors, storm: wood or metal; metal doors, sash & trim

**(G-7189)**
**DI-CARR PRINTING COMPANY**
1630 S Cicero Ave  (60804-1519)
**PHONE**..................................708 863-0069
Fax: 708 863-1331
Larry Jaskunas, *Owner*
Cindy Jaskunas, *Owner*
**EMP:** 3  **EST:** 1946
**SQ FT:** 1,500

**SALES:** 250K  Privately Held
**SIC:** 2752  Commercial printing, offset

**(G-7190)**
**DIECRAFTERS  INC**
1349 S 55th Ct  (60804-1211)
**PHONE**..................................708 656-3336
Fax: 708 656-3386
Robert J Windler, *President*
David Windler, *Vice Pres*
Carmen Falibene, *Controller*
Erik Windler, *Accounts Exec*
Dan Hecker, *Manager*
**EMP:** 30
**SALES (est):** 7.5MM  Privately Held
**WEB:** www.diecrafters.com
**SIC:** 2675  Paperboard die-cutting; cards: die-cut & unprinted: made from purchased materials

**(G-7191)**
**DORBIN METAL STRIP MFG CO INC**
2404 S Cicero Ave  (60804-3442)
**PHONE**..................................708 656-2333
Fax: 708 656-1333
John Dorosz, *President*
Carol Dorosz, *Treasurer*
Dan Kuecker, *Manager*
**EMP:** 12  **EST:** 1938
**SQ FT:** 12,000
**SALES (est):** 2.1MM  Privately Held
**SIC:** 3442  Weather strip, metal

**(G-7192)**
**DUNDICK CORPORATION**
4616 W 20th St  (60804-2593)
**PHONE**..................................708 656-6363
Fax: 708 656-2359
Len Pernecky, *President*
Mike Bran, *Vice Pres*
**EMP:** 40  **EST:** 1944
**SQ FT:** 20,000
**SALES (est):** 6.1MM  Privately Held
**SIC:** 3545  3599  Gauges (machine tool accessories); machine shop, jobbing & repair

**(G-7193)**
**ELECTRONIC PLATING CO**
1821 S 54th Ave  (60804-1815)
**PHONE**..................................708 652-8100
Fax: 708 652-8174
Robert Porcelli, *President*
Carl Porcelli, *Vice Pres*
Belinda Marquez, *Office Mgr*
**EMP:** 30
**SQ FT:** 8,000
**SALES (est):** 4.4MM  Privately Held
**SIC:** 3471  Electroplating of metals or formed products; finishing, metals or formed products

**(G-7194)**
**ELEGANT ACQUISITION LLC**
Also Called: Elegant Packaging
5253 W Roosevelt Rd  (60804-1222)
**PHONE**..................................708 652-3400
Fax: 708 652-6444
Robert Waltz, *COO*
Sheldon Gottlieb, *Vice Pres*
Frank Ambrose, *VP Opers*
Doug Gauert, *VP Sales*
Paul Nelson, *Accounts Mgr*
▲ **EMP:** 80
**SQ FT:** 96,000
**SALES (est):** 23.6MM  Privately Held
**WEB:** www.elegantpackaging.com
**SIC:** 2652  3172  Setup paperboard boxes; sewing cases

**(G-7195)**
**EMCO METALWORKS CO**
1505 S Laramie Ave  (60804-1939)
**PHONE**..................................708 222-1011
Robert Pancoe, *President*
Nate Enriquez, *Manager*
**EMP:** 25
**SQ FT:** 18,000
**SALES (est):** 6.5MM  Privately Held
**SIC:** 3441  Fabricated structural metal

**(G-7196)**
**EXPO ENGINEERED  INC**
1824 S Cicero Ave  (60804-2543)
**PHONE**..................................708 780-7155

Fax: 708 780-7125
Ruben Rivera, President
**EMP:** 1
**SQ FT:** 5,000
**SALES (est):** 203K **Privately Held**
**WEB:** www.expoengineered.com
**SIC:** 3634 Immersion heaters, electric: household; wall heaters, electric: household

**(G-7197)**
### GENERAL ELECTRIC COMPANY
1543 S 54th Ave (60804-1813)
**PHONE**...............................708 780-2600
Fax: 708 780-2642
Eva Garza, QC Dir
Stephanie Bonner, Finance
Laura Whieeis, Manager
Sean Gaughan, Manager
**EMP:** 12
**SALES (corp-wide):** 123.6B **Publicly Held**
**SIC:** 3634 Heating units, for electric appliances
**PA:** General Electric Company
41 Farnsworth St
Boston MA 02210
617 443-3000

**(G-7198)**
### GIANNI INCORPORATED
4615 W Roosevelt Rd (60804-1522)
**PHONE**...............................708 863-6696
Fax: 708 863-4071
Marcello Gianni, President
Gianni Angelo, Treasurer
**EMP:** 58
**SQ FT:** 56,000
**SALES (est):** 10MM **Privately Held**
**WEB:** www.gianniinc.com
**SIC:** 2521 Wood office furniture

**(G-7199)**
### H & H MOTOR SERVICE INC
5130 W 16th St (60804-1927)
**PHONE**...............................708 652-6100
Fax: 708 652-7180
Thomas W Green, President
Larry Fulgenzi, Admin Sec
**EMP:** 7
**SQ FT:** 10,000
**SALES (est):** 1.4MM **Privately Held**
**SIC:** 7694 Electric motor repair

**(G-7200)**
### HARRIS STEEL COMPANY (PA)
1223 S 55th Ct (60804-1297)
**PHONE**...............................708 656-5500
Fax: 708 656-0151
Thomas Eliasek, President
Jack Harris Jr, Chairman
Scott Decker, Plant Mgr
Terry Wilczak, Facilities Mgr
John Medina, Purch Dir
**EMP:** 69 **EST:** 1950
**SQ FT:** 150,000
**SALES (est):** 31.1MM **Privately Held**
**WEB:** www.harrissteelco.com
**SIC:** 5051 3316 Metals service centers & offices; cold finishing of steel shapes

**(G-7201)**
### HAWTHORNE PRESS
5615 W Roosevelt Rd (60804-1229)
**PHONE**...............................708 652-9000
Fax: 708 652-9493
Anthony Sarno, President
**EMP:** 2
**SQ FT:** 1,800
**SALES (est):** 204.7K **Privately Held**
**SIC:** 2759 2789 2752 Commercial printing; bookbinding & related work; commercial printing, lithographic

**(G-7202)**
### HICKMAN WILLIAMS & COMPANY
Also Called: Hickman Williams & Co
1410 S 55th Ct (60804-1840)
**PHONE**...............................708 656-8818
Fax: 708 442-3793
V Valaenziano, Division Mgr
Scott McClain, Vice Pres
Dan Baran, Engineer
John Kalinowski, Manager
Lawrence Gebhardt, Manager
**EMP:** 17
**SQ FT:** 132,000
**SALES (corp-wide):** 195.8MM **Privately Held**
**WEB:** www.hicwilco.com
**SIC:** 1221 4225 3624 Coal preparation plant, bituminous or lignite; general warehousing; carbon & graphite products
**PA:** Hickman, Williams & Company
250 E 5th St Ste 300
Cincinnati OH 45202
513 621-1946

**(G-7203)**
### ICC INTRNTONAL CELSIUS CONCEPT
2385 S 59th Ct (60804)
**PHONE**...............................773 993-4405
Luis Saquimux, Vice Pres
**EMP:** 7
**SALES (est):** 331.4K **Privately Held**
**SIC:** 3569 3585 3571 Robots, assembly line: industrial & commercial; refrigeration & heating equipment; electronic computers

**(G-7204)**
### ILF TECHNOLOGIES LLC
1215 S Laramie Ave (60804-1354)
**PHONE**...............................630 759-1776
Fax: 630 759-1748
Alicia Heimann, Office Mgr
Robert Allison,
Milan Pecharich,
**EMP:** 16
**SALES (est):** 3.1MM **Privately Held**
**WEB:** www.ilftech.com
**SIC:** 3555 Printing trades machinery

**(G-7205)**
### INDUSTRIAL FILTER PUMP MFG CO
5900 W Ogden Ave (60804-3873)
**PHONE**...............................708 656-7800
Fax: 708 656-7806
Paul Eggerstedt, Principal
Tom Anderson, Manager
Brian Carlson, Analyst
**EMP:** 2 **EST:** 2009
**SALES (est):** 356.3K **Privately Held**
**SIC:** 3569 Filters

**(G-7206)**
### INTEGRATED DISPLAY SYSTEMS (PA)
Also Called: IDS Lift-Net
5130 W 16th St (60804-1927)
P.O. Box 170, Evanston (60204)
**PHONE**...............................708 298-9661
Winslow D Soule, President
Parsifal Gomez, Engineer
Larry Fulgenzi, VP Sales
Dominic Beni, Manager
**EMP:** 11
**SQ FT:** 4,000
**SALES (est):** 1.1MM **Privately Held**
**SIC:** 3534 Elevators & equipment

**(G-7207)**
### ITRON CORPORATION DEL (PA)
3131 S Austin Blvd (60804-3730)
**PHONE**...............................708 222-5320
Charles J Saporito Jr, President
John Saporito III, President
Terry Mitchell, Div Sub Head
James Mirabile, Vice Pres
**EMP:** 13 **EST:** 1982
**SQ FT:** 17,000
**SALES (est):** 1.5MM **Privately Held**
**SIC:** 3643 Connectors & terminals for electrical devices

**(G-7208)**
### KAMAN TOOL CORPORATION
3147 S Austin Blvd (60804-3730)
**PHONE**...............................708 652-9023
Fax: 708 652-0940
Ronald W Roderweiss, President
Joan Borek, Office Mgr
**EMP:** 5 **EST:** 1974
**SQ FT:** 8,000
**SALES:** 900K **Privately Held**
**SIC:** 3599 3469 Machine shop, jobbing & repair; stamping metal for the trade

**(G-7209)**
### KOPPERS INDUSTRIES INC
Koppers Carbon Mtls & Chem Div
3900 S Laramie Ave (60804-4523)
**PHONE**...............................708 656-5900
Fax: 708 656-6079
S D Lowe, Plant Mgr
Gregg Bambule, Safety Mgr
Lim Land, Chief Engr
Alan Babjak, Engineer
Ron Smith, Human Res Mgr
**EMP:** 45
**SALES (corp-wide):** 18.8MM **Privately Held**
**WEB:** www.koppers.com
**SIC:** 2865 2911 2869 Cyclic crudes, coal tar; petroleum refining; industrial organic chemicals
**PA:** Koppers Industries, Inc
436 7th Ave Ste 2026
Pittsburgh PA 15219
412 227-2001

**(G-7210)**
### KORINEK & CO INC
4828 W 25th St (60804-3489)
**PHONE**...............................708 652-2870
Fax: 708 242-1917
George F Korinek, President
Scott Korineck, Vice Pres
**EMP:** 7
**SQ FT:** 6,000
**SALES (est):** 1MM **Privately Held**
**WEB:** www.korinek.com
**SIC:** 5149 2033 2051 Bakery products; preserves, including imitation: in cans, jars, etc.; jams, including imitation: packaged in cans, jars, etc.; jellies, edible, including imitation: in cans, jars, etc.; bread, cake & related products

**(G-7211)**
### KRALY TIRE REPAIR MATERIALS
5936 W 35th St (60804-4167)
**PHONE**...............................708 863-5981
Kenneth Kraly, Owner
**EMP:** 3
**SQ FT:** 2,100
**SALES (est):** 250K **Privately Held**
**SIC:** 3011 Tire sundries or tire repair materials, rubber

**(G-7212)**
### LA CASA DEL TEQUILA CORP
6144 W 26th St (60804-3004)
**PHONE**...............................708 652-3640
Eduardo Gutierez, Owner
**EMP:** 6
**SALES (est):** 431K **Privately Held**
**SIC:** 2082 Malt liquors

**(G-7213)**
### LA HISPAMEX FOOD PRODUCTS INC
1859 S 55th Ave (60804-1819)
**PHONE**...............................708 780-1808
Jose A Galvez, President
Jose Aispuro, Manager
**EMP:** 5
**SQ FT:** 10,000
**SALES (est):** 773.8K **Privately Held**
**SIC:** 2022 Processed cheese

**(G-7214)**
### LAWNDALE PRESS INC (PA)
Also Called: Lawndale News
5533 W 25th St (60804-3319)
**PHONE**...............................708 656-6900
Fax: 708 656-2433
Linda Nardini, CEO
Robert Nardini, President
Ashmar Mandou, Editor
James Nardini, Senior VP
Doris Ramirez, Sales Staff
**EMP:** 8
**SQ FT:** 6,000
**SALES (est):** 1.1MM **Privately Held**
**WEB:** www.lawndalenews.com
**SIC:** 2711 Newspapers

**(G-7215)**
### LBP MANUFACTURING LLC (PA)
1325 S Cicero Ave (60804-1404)
**PHONE**...............................800 545-6200

Matt Cook, CEO
Ken Eme, Senior VP
Don Wolski, Vice Pres
David Youngberg, Plant Mgr
Janine Putnam, Production
▲ **EMP:** 92
**SALES (est):** 25.8MM **Privately Held**
**SIC:** 2671 Paper coated or laminated for packaging

**(G-7216)**
### LODOLCE MEAT CO INC
5238 W 24th Pl (60804-2824)
P.O. Box 50718 (60804-0718)
**PHONE**...............................708 863-4655
Phillip Lo Dolce, President
Maria Pawlak, Officer
**EMP:** 5
**SALES:** 1.5MM **Privately Held**
**SIC:** 2013 Corned beef from purchased meat; sausages from purchased meat; cooked meats from purchased meat

**(G-7217)**
### MAH MACHINE COMPANY
3301 S Central Ave (60804-3986)
**PHONE**...............................708 656-1826
Fax: 708 656-4152
Martin Hozjan, CEO
Robert Hozjan, President
Anna Hozjan, Principal
Christopher Hozjan, Vice Pres
Martina Hozjan Ruda, Vice Pres
▲ **EMP:** 105
**SQ FT:** 100,000
**SALES (est):** 35.3MM **Privately Held**
**WEB:** www.mahmachine.com
**SIC:** 3599 7699 Machine shop, jobbing & repair; printing trades machinery & equipment repair

**(G-7218)**
### MARES SERVICE INC
4611 W 34th St (60804-4590)
**PHONE**...............................708 656-1660
Fax: 708 656-9837
Frank Mares Sr, President
Marylou Mares, Vice Pres
**EMP:** 8 **EST:** 1956
**SALES (est):** 1.1MM **Privately Held**
**SIC:** 3711 Wreckers (tow truck), assembly of

**(G-7219)**
### MECANICA EN GENERAL SANTOYO
5222 W 26th St (60804-3331)
**PHONE**...............................708 652-2217
Francisco Santoyo, Owner
**EMP:** 2
**SALES (est):** 219K **Privately Held**
**SIC:** 3011 Automobile tires, pneumatic

**(G-7220)**
### MENARD INC
2333 S Cicero Ave (60804-2451)
**PHONE**...............................708 780-0260
Jim Rowley, Branch Mgr
**EMP:** 50
**SALES (corp-wide):** 15.2B **Privately Held**
**WEB:** www.menards.com
**SIC:** 2431 Millwork
**PA:** Menard, Inc.
5101 Menard Dr
Eau Claire WI 54703
715 876-5911

**(G-7221)**
### METAL-RITE INC
3140 S 61st Ave (60804-3793)
**PHONE**...............................708 656-3832
Fax: 708 656-3834
Mark W Kuchan, President
Kurt Kuchan, Treasurer
Nancy Kuchan, Admin Sec
**EMP:** 15 **EST:** 1965
**SQ FT:** 11,600
**SALES (est):** 3.2MM **Privately Held**
**SIC:** 3444 Sheet metal specialties, not stamped

**(G-7222)**
### MILANS MACHINING & MFG CO INC
1301 S Laramie Ave (60804-1355)
**PHONE**...............................708 780-6600

Fax: 708 780-1314
Milan Pecharich, President
Martha Pecharich, Corp Secy
Marrko Pecharich, Vice Pres
Chuck Scholz, Opers-Prdtn-Mfg
Maria Martinez, Manager
**EMP:** 55
**SQ FT:** 65,000
**SALES (est):** 11.1MM  **Privately Held**
**WEB:** www.milansmachining.com
**SIC:** 3599  7692  3555  3544  Machine shop, jobbing & repair; welding repair; printing trades machinery; special dies, tools, jigs & fixtures; metal stampings

### (G-7223)
### OLYMPIC PETROLEUM CORPORATION (PA)
5000 W 41st St  (60804-4524)
**PHONE** .................................. 708 876-7900
**Fax:** 708 594-9354
Yasar Samarah, President
Amit Shukla, CFO
Dean Mettler, Lab Dir
◆ **EMP:** 75
**SQ FT:** 120,000
**SALES (est):** 38.6MM  **Privately Held**
**SIC:** 2992  Lubricating oils & greases; lubricating oils

### (G-7224)
### ON TIME DECORATIONS INC
1411 S Laramie Ave  (60804-1328)
**PHONE** .................................. 708 357-6072
Victor Loggins, Owner
**EMP:** 14
**SALES:** 500K  **Privately Held**
**SIC:** 3552  Silk screens for textile industry

### (G-7225)
### ROYAL BOX GROUP  LLC (HQ)
Also Called: Royal Continental Box Company
1301 S 47th Ave  (60804-1598)
**PHONE** .................................. 708 656-2020
**Fax:** 708 222-3447
Robert L Mc Ilvaine, President
Angie Bragg, General Mgr
Jay King, General Mgr
J Jordan Nerenberg, Chairman
Tim Benecke, Vice Pres
**EMP:** 277
**SQ FT:** 350,000
**SALES (est):** 215.3MM
**SALES (corp-wide):** 248.1MM  **Privately Held**
**WEB:** www.royalbox.com
**SIC:** 2653  Boxes, corrugated: made from purchased materials
**PA:** Schwarz Partners, L.P.
  3600 Woodview Trce # 300
  Indianapolis IN 46268
  317 290-1140

### (G-7226)
### ROYAL BOX GROUP  LLC
Also Called: Continental Concepts
4600 W 12th Pl  (60804-1501)
**PHONE** .................................. 708 222-4650
Johnny Jones, Plant Mgr
Diane Mucha, CFO
Wayne Provus, Manager
Rose Kulak, Manager
Donald Malzahn, Admin Sec
**EMP:** 10
**SALES (corp-wide):** 248.1MM  **Privately Held**
**WEB:** www.royalbox.com
**SIC:** 2653  Boxes, corrugated: made from purchased materials
**HQ:** Royal Box Group, Llc
  1301 S 47th Ave
  Cicero IL 60804
  708 656-2020

### (G-7227)
### SAFE-AIR OF ILLINOIS  INC
1855 S 54th Ave  (60804-1896)
**PHONE** .................................. 708 652-9100
**Fax:** 708 652-9158
Frank Ruiz, CEO
Michael Friedman, President
Robert Colon, Cust Mgr
Judith Magnus, Office Mgr
**EMP:** 45 EST: 1955
**SQ FT:** 67,000
**SALES (est):** 11.4MM  **Privately Held**
**WEB:** www.safeair-dowco.com
**SIC:** 3444  Ducts, sheet metal

### (G-7228)
### SAPORITO FINISHING CO (PA)
Also Called: Accurate Anodizing Div
3119 S Austin Blvd  (60804-3730)
**PHONE** .................................. 708 222-5300
**Fax:** 708 222-0129
Charles Saporito Jr, President
Gerald Rice, General Mgr
Jerry Rice, General Mgr
Charles Saporito Sr, Chairman
Josephine Saporito, Corp Secy
**EMP:** 92
**SQ FT:** 94,000
**SALES (est):** 22.8MM  **Privately Held**
**WEB:** www.saporitofinishing.com
**SIC:** 3471  Anodizing (plating) of metals or formed products; electroplating of metals or formed products; finishing, metals or formed products

### (G-7229)
### STANDARD HEAT TREATING LLC
5757 W Ogden Ave  (60804-3877)
**PHONE** .................................. 773 242-0853
**Fax:** 708 780-5106
Jack Christ, Mng Member
Greg Loredo, Manager
Greg L Sancho, Manager
**EMP:** 41
**SALES (est):** 8.9MM  **Privately Held**
**WEB:** www.standardht.com
**SIC:** 3398  Metal heat treating

### (G-7230)
### STEEL FABRICATION AND WELDING
3200 S 61st Ave  (60804-3718)
**PHONE** .................................. 773 343-0731
Ignacio Servin, Owner
**EMP:** 6
**SALES:** 170K  **Privately Held**
**SIC:** 3312  1791  Wire products, steel or iron; concrete reinforcement, placing of

### (G-7231)
### STERLING METAL CRAFT  INC
1817 S 55th Ave Ste 3  (60804-1861)
**PHONE** .................................. 708 652-4590
**Fax:** 708 652-4590
Joseph Karam, President
▲ **EMP:** 10
**SALES (est):** 1.6MM  **Privately Held**
**WEB:** www.sterlingmetalcraft.com
**SIC:** 3469  Spinning metal for the trade

### (G-7232)
### SUNTIMEZ ENTERTAINMENT
5811 W Roosevelt Rd  (60804-1136)
**PHONE** .................................. 630 747-0712
**EMP:** 3 EST: 2008
**SALES (est):** 120K  **Privately Held**
**SIC:** 3931  Mfg Musical Instruments

### (G-7233)
### SUPERIOR PIPE STANDARDS INC
3128 S 61st Ave  (60804-3714)
**PHONE** .................................. 708 656-0208
Witold Sulik, President
**EMP:** 8
**SQ FT:** 10,500
**SALES:** 400K  **Privately Held**
**WEB:** www.superiorpipe.com
**SIC:** 3498  Fabricated pipe & fittings

### (G-7234)
### SUPREME FELT & ABRASIVES INC
1633 S 55th Ave  (60804-1817)
**PHONE** .................................. 708 344-0134
**Fax:** 708 344-0285
David McNeilly, President
David Neiman, Vice Pres
**EMP:** 25
**SQ FT:** 20,000
**SALES (est):** 4.5MM  **Privately Held**
**WEB:** www.supremefelt.com
**SIC:** 3053  5199  Gasket materials; felt

### (G-7235)
### TELE GUIA SPANISH TV GUIDE
Also Called: CHI Montes
3116 S Austin Blvd  (60804-3729)
**PHONE** .................................. 708 656-9800
**Fax:** 708 222-6822
Patricia Scolera, Treasurer
Rose Montes, Manager
**EMP:** 22
**SALES (est):** 1.6MM  **Privately Held**
**SIC:** 2741  Miscellaneous publishing

### (G-7236)
### TELE-GUIA INC
Also Called: Tele Guia De Chicago
3116 S Austin Blvd  (60804-3729)
**PHONE** .................................. 708 656-9800
Ezequiel Montes, President
Rose Montes, Vice Pres
Eduardo Fernandez, Director
**EMP:** 12
**SALES:** 1,000K  **Privately Held**
**WEB:** www.teleguia.net
**SIC:** 2741  2791  2721  Guides: publishing & printing; typesetting; periodicals

### (G-7237)
### TELEGUIA INC
Also Called: Elimparcial Newspaper
3116 S Austin Blvd  (60804-3729)
**PHONE** .................................. 708 656-6675
Ezequiel Montes, President
Rose Montes, Vice Pres
**EMP:** 20
**SALES:** 700K  **Privately Held**
**SIC:** 2711  Newspapers, publishing & printing

### (G-7238)
### TERRACE HOLDING COMPANY
1325 S Cicero Ave  (60804-1404)
**PHONE** .................................. 708 652-5600
Barry Silver, President
**EMP:** 930
**SQ FT:** 150,000
**SALES (est):** 72.9MM  **Privately Held**
**SIC:** 3556  Food products machinery

### (G-7239)
### TVO ACQUISITION CORPORATION (PA)
Also Called: John Gillen Company
2540 S 50th Ave  (60804-3416)
**PHONE** .................................. 708 656-4240
**Fax:** 708 656-3203
Thomas V O'Neill, President
Veronica S O'Neill, Vice Pres
Kevin O'Neill, Engineer
**EMP:** 37 EST: 1918
**SQ FT:** 55,000
**SALES (est):** 14.3MM  **Privately Held**
**SIC:** 3541  Machine tools, metal cutting type; screw & thread machines; chucking machines, automatic; milling machines

### (G-7240)
### UNIQUE PRTRS LITHOGRAPHERS INC
5500 W 31st St  (60804-3957)
**PHONE** .................................. 708 656-8900
**Fax:** 708 656-2176
John Collins, President
Charles Deets, Chairman
Steve Deets, Vice Pres
Jane Griffin, Manager
Jim Molineux, Info Tech Dir
**EMP:** 65
**SQ FT:** 26,000
**SALES (est):** 13.8MM  **Privately Held**
**WEB:** www.uniqueprinters.com
**SIC:** 2752  Commercial printing, lithographic

### (G-7241)
### UNIQUE/ACTIVE LLC
5500 W 31st St  (60804-3957)
**PHONE** .................................. 708 656-8900
Steve Deets, COO
Brian Hoban, Plant Mgr
Mike Egan, Production
Tom Howard, Production
Tammy Roberts, Human Res Mgr
**EMP:** 30
**SALES (est):** 6.9MM  **Privately Held**
**SIC:** 2752  Commercial printing, lithographic

### (G-7242)
### UNITED GASKET CORPORATION
1633 S 55th Ave  (60804-1889)
**PHONE** .................................. 708 656-3700
**Fax:** 708 656-6292
Mark Pahios, President
Failon Cindy, CFO
Scott Januszyk, Manager
Cindy Phelan, Executive
▲ **EMP:** 70 EST: 1940
**SQ FT:** 35,000
**SALES (est):** 27.6MM  **Privately Held**
**WEB:** www.unitedgasket.com
**SIC:** 3554  3714  5013  3053  Die cutting & stamping machinery, paper converting; motor vehicle parts & accessories; motor vehicle supplies & new parts; gaskets, packing & sealing devices

### (G-7243)
### V BROTHERS MACHINE CO
4900 W 16th St  (60804-1531)
**PHONE** .................................. 708 652-0062
**Fax:** 708 652-0036
Damjan Vujanovic, President
Dragen Vujanovic, Vice Pres
**EMP:** 20 EST: 1981
**SQ FT:** 23,000
**SALES (est):** 3.3MM  **Privately Held**
**SIC:** 3599  7692  Machine shop, jobbing & repair; welding repair

### (G-7244)
### VEOLIA ES INDUSTRIAL SVCS INC
6001 W Pershing Rd  (60804-4112)
**PHONE** .................................. 708 652-0575
Richard Jania, Project Mgr
Steve Waters, Branch Mgr
**EMP:** 16
**SALES (corp-wide):** 452.1MM  **Privately Held**
**SIC:** 2873  Nitrogenous fertilizers
**HQ:** Veolia Es Industrial Services, Inc.
  4760 World Houston Pkwy # 100
  Houston TX 77032
  713 672-8004

### (G-7245)
### WEST TOWN PLATING INC
5243 W 25th Pl  (60804-3391)
**PHONE** .................................. 708 652-1600
**Fax:** 708 652-0564
Gerald Glab, Ch of Bd
Keith Glab, Vice Pres
Russell Glab, Vice Pres
Emil Kumiega, Plant Mgr
**EMP:** 20 EST: 1953
**SQ FT:** 10,000
**SALES (est):** 2.5MM  **Privately Held**
**SIC:** 3471  Chromium plating of metals or formed products

### (G-7246)
### WIRTZ BEVERAGE ILLINOIS LLC (PA)
Also Called: Wirtz Bev Ill Metro-Chicago
3333 S Laramie Ave  (60804-4520)
**PHONE** .................................. 847 228-9000
Ed Callison, Exec VP
David Lockie, Senior VP
James English, CFO
Alex Gonzalez, Human Resources
Scott Barnett, Sales Mgr
▲ **EMP:** 133
**SALES (est):** 46.7MM  **Privately Held**
**SIC:** 2082  5169  Ale (alcoholic beverage); alcohols

### (G-7247)
### WRIGHT QUICK SIGNS INC
Also Called: Wright Advertising
1347 S Laramie Ave  (60804-1355)
**PHONE** .................................. 708 652-6020
**Fax:** 708 652-6034
Ralph Pontrelli, President
**EMP:** 7 EST: 1967
**SQ FT:** 2,500

SALES (est): 849.1K **Privately Held**
WEB: www.wrightadvertising.com
SIC: **7312** 7311 3993 Outdoor advertising services; advertising agencies; signs & advertising specialties

**(G-7248)**
**ZB IMPORTING INC**
Also Called: Ziyad Brothers Importing
5400 W 35th St (60804-4431)
PHONE..................................708 222-8330
Fax: 708 222-1442
Ibrahim Ziad, *President*
Nassem Ziyad, *General Mgr*
Nezar Ziad, *Admin Sec*
◆ EMP: 85
SQ FT: 150,000
SALES (est): 44.4MM **Privately Held**
WEB: www.ziyad.com
SIC: **5149** 2064 2051 Specialty food items; candy & other confectionery products; bread, all types (white, wheat, rye, etc) fresh or frozen

## Cisco
### Piatt County

**(G-7249)**
**BOYD SPOTTING INC**
1310 N 300 East Rd (61830-6534)
PHONE..................................217 669-2418
Jacquelyn Boyd, *President*
EMP: 5
SALES (est): 719.9K **Privately Held**
SIC: **3792** Travel trailers & campers

## Cisne
### Wayne County

**(G-7250)**
**CISNE IRON WORKS INC**
701 S Jones St (62823)
P.O. Box 511 (62823-0511)
PHONE..................................618 673-2188
Fax: 618 673-2199
Stan Zdan Jr, *President*
EMP: 11
SQ FT: 6,000
SALES (est): 870K **Privately Held**
SIC: **3312** 7692 3441 Stainless steel; welding repair; fabricated structural metal

**(G-7251)**
**DAVE WHITE**
1269 Conty Rod 970 E (62823)
PHONE..................................618 898-1130
Dave White, *Owner*
EMP: 5
SALES (est): 320.5K **Privately Held**
WEB: www.davewhite.me.uk
SIC: **2452** Farm & agricultural buildings, prefabricated wood

**(G-7252)**
**HAROLD L RAY TRUCK & TRCTR SVC**
Hwy 45 N (62823)
P.O. Box 130 (62823-0130)
PHONE..................................618 673-2701
Harold L Ray, *President*
Billye Ray, *Admin Sec*
EMP: 12
SALES (est): 800.2K **Privately Held**
SIC: **4212** 1389 Heavy machinery transport, local; gas field services

## Cissna Park
### Iroquois County

**(G-7253)**
**BAIER HOME CENTER**
120 S 2nd St (60924-6131)
P.O. Box 120 (60924-0120)
PHONE..................................815 457-2300
David L Baier, *Owner*
EMP: 5

SALES (est): 477.1K **Privately Held**
SIC: **3634** Housewares, excluding cooking appliances & utensils

**(G-7254)**
**BAIER PUBLISHING COMPANY**
Also Called: Cissna Park News
119 W Garfield Ave (60924-6125)
P.O. Box 8 (60924-0008)
PHONE..................................815 457-2245
Fax: 815 457-3245
Rick Baier, *President*
Barb Scheiwe, *Manager*
EMP: 5
SQ FT: 8,000
SALES (est): 100K **Privately Held**
SIC: **2711** Newspapers

**(G-7255)**
**KSI CONVEYOR INC**
454 N State Route 49 (60924-8876)
P.O. Box 69 (60924-0069)
PHONE..................................815 457-2403
Adam Renyer, *Prdtn Mgr*
Ronnie Edelman, *Mfg Mgr*
Jaclyn Rokey, *Purch Agent*
Amy Walder, *Purch Agent*
Doug Teske, *QA Dir*
EMP: 63
SALES (corp-wide): 34MM **Privately Held**
SIC: **3523** Farm machinery & equipment
PA: Ksi Conveyor, Inc.
2345 U Rd
Sabetha KS 66534
785 284-0600

## Claremont
### Richland County

**(G-7256)**
**HERSHEYS METAL MEISTER LLC**
Also Called: Hersheys Metal Meister
7405 E Mount Pleasant Ln (62421-2727)
PHONE..................................217 234-4700
Atlee Hershberger, *Sales Mgr*
Nelson Hershberger, *Mng Member*
Jacob Hershberger, *Manager*
Miriam Hershberger,
▲ EMP: 20
SQ FT: 50,000
SALES (est): 2.2MM **Privately Held**
SIC: **3542** 5072 5033 Machine tools, metal forming type; presses: forming, stamping, punching, sizing (machine tools); builders' hardware; insulation materials

## Clarendon Hills
### Dupage County

**(G-7257)**
**J2SYS LLC**
Also Called: J2sys Robot
102 Naperville Rd (60514-1023)
PHONE..................................630 542-1342
Jueli Lin,
Hong Ding,
EMP: 18
SALES: 250K **Privately Held**
SIC: **6531** 7371 3569 5999 Real estate leasing & rentals; computer software development & applications; robots, assembly line: industrial & commercial; electronic parts & equipment

**(G-7258)**
**MEDTEX HEALTH SERVICES INC**
554 Willowcreek Ct (60514-3602)
PHONE..................................630 789-0330
John Maras, *President*
EMP: 2
SALES: 250K **Privately Held**
SIC: **3845** 3841 5047 Electromedical equipment; surgical & medical instruments; medical & hospital equipment

**(G-7259)**
**NALI INC**
Also Called: Simco Formalwear
266 S Prospect Ave (60514-1442)
PHONE..................................708 442-8710
Sonali Sheth, *President*
Prashant Sheth, *Treasurer*
Michaella Hood, *Manager*
▲ EMP: 22
SQ FT: 21,000
SALES: 2.5MM **Privately Held**
SIC: **2389** 5632 5944 Uniforms & vestments; apparel accessories; jewelry stores

**(G-7260)**
**THOLEO DESIGN INC**
418 Ridge Ave (60514-2706)
PHONE..................................630 325-3792
Blake Thoele, *President*
Karin Thoele, *Vice Pres*
EMP: 3 EST: 2000
SALES (est): 253.5K **Privately Held**
SIC: **3069** Rubber floor coverings, mats & wallcoverings

## Clay City
### Clay County

**(G-7261)**
**ABNER TRUCKING CO INC**
207 S 1st St Se (62824-1055)
P.O. Box 375 (62824-0375)
PHONE..................................618 676-1301
Arthur Thomas Abner, *President*
EMP: 9 EST: 1958
SQ FT: 1,800
SALES (est): 753.1K **Privately Held**
SIC: **4212** 1389 Local trucking, without storage; servicing oil & gas wells

**(G-7262)**
**BANGERT CASING PULLING CORP**
1 Industrial Dr (62824)
P.O. Box 441 (62824-0441)
PHONE..................................618 676-1411
Fax: 618 676-1089
Ronald G Bangert, *President*
Andrew Bangert, *Vice Pres*
Naomi Bangert, *Treasurer*
Ronald Bangert II, *Admin Sec*
EMP: 9 EST: 1940
SQ FT: 4,800
SALES (est): 840K **Privately Held**
SIC: **1389** 5084 Oil field services; oil well machinery, equipment & supplies

**(G-7263)**
**DARRELL FICKAS SAWMILL**
940 S 1st St Se (62824-1224)
PHONE..................................618 676-1200
Darrell Sawmill, *Principal*
EMP: 5 EST: 2013
SALES (est): 374.8K **Privately Held**
SIC: **2421** Sawmills & planing mills, general

**(G-7264)**
**FRANCIS L MORRIS**
1377 Angling Rd (62824-2353)
PHONE..................................618 676-1724
Francis L Morris, *Owner*
EMP: 3
SALES (est): 120K **Privately Held**
SIC: **2421** Sawmills & planing mills, general

**(G-7265)**
**J W RUDY CO INC**
506 S 1st St Se (62824-1208)
P.O. Box 485 (62824-0485)
PHONE..................................618 676-1616
Fax: 618 676-1617
Kay Rudy, *President*
Steve Rudy, *Manager*
Crystal Rudy, *Admin Sec*
EMP: 18 EST: 1948
SQ FT: 1,500
SALES (est): 1.1MM **Privately Held**
SIC: **1311** 4212 Crude petroleum production; local trucking, without storage

**(G-7266)**
**M & I ACID COMPANY INC**
1107 S Main St (62824-1165)
P.O. Box 443 (62824-0443)
PHONE..................................618 676-1638
Ivan Brikker, *Vice Pres*
Mick Mason, *Administration*
EMP: 4 EST: 1993
SALES (est): 342.3K **Privately Held**
SIC: **1389** Acidizing wells

**(G-7267)**
**ORDNER WELL SERVICE INC**
946 Sunset Rd Sw (62824-1112)
P.O. Box 402 (62824-0402)
PHONE..................................618 676-1950
Jim Ordner, *President*
EMP: 4
SALES (est): 276.2K **Privately Held**
SIC: **1389** Well logging

**(G-7268)**
**TRI STATE ACID CO INC**
110 Industrial Park (62824)
P.O. Box 343 (62824-0343)
PHONE..................................618 676-1111
Ivan Bricker, *Owner*
EMP: 5
SALES (est): 200.8K **Privately Held**
SIC: **1389** Acidizing wells

## Clayton
### Adams County

**(G-7269)**
**CONCORD CABINETS INC (PA)**
1276 E 2575th St (62324-2716)
PHONE..................................217 894-6507
Fax: 217 894-7064
Gene Daggett, *CEO*
Greg Daggett, *President*
Steven Spilker, *Vice Pres*
Sharron Daggett, *Admin Sec*
EMP: 10
SQ FT: 25,000
SALES: 1MM **Privately Held**
SIC: **2599** 1751 Cabinets, factory; cabinet & finish carpentry

**(G-7270)**
**WEATHERGUARD BUILDINGS**
1654 E 2950th St (62324-2622)
PHONE..................................217 894-6213
Melvin Schrock, *Owner*
EMP: 3
SALES (est): 230.9K **Privately Held**
SIC: **2421** Building & structural materials, wood

## Cleveland
### Henry County

**(G-7271)**
**RIVERSTONE GROUP INC**
Also Called: Cleveland Quarry
1001 N Broadway St (61241-8547)
PHONE..................................309 933-1123
Fax: 309 792-4551
John Swan, *Branch Mgr*
EMP: 18
SALES (corp-wide): 4.3B **Privately Held**
WEB: www.riverstonegrp.com
SIC: **1422** 5032 Crushed & broken limestone; limestone
PA: Riverstone Group, Inc.
1701 5th Ave
Moline IL 61265
309 757-8250

## Clifton
### Iroquois County

**(G-7272)**
**ADVOCATE**
Also Called: Advocate Printing
330 N 4th St (60927-7232)
P.O. Box 548 (60927-0548)
PHONE..................................815 694-2122

Fax: 815 694-2649
Theresa M Simoneau, Owner
Crystal Murray, Creative Dir
**EMP:** 4
**SALES:** 100K  **Privately Held**
**SIC:** 2711  2752  Newspapers, publishing & printing; commercial printing, lithographic

**(G-7273)**
### CHARLES CRANE
Also Called: Crane Equipment
188 E 3100 North Rd  (60927-7205)
PHONE..................................815 258-5375
Charles E Crane, Owner
Mike Brooks, Administration
**EMP:** 3
**SQ FT:** 10,000
**SALES (est):** 442.9K  **Privately Held**
**SIC:** 3523  0191  Farm machinery & equipment; general farms, primarily crop

**(G-7274)**
### JDL GRAPHICS INC
3043 N 1600 East Rd  (60927-7044)
PHONE..................................815 694-2979
Joanne Lachappell, President
**EMP:** 3  **EST:** 1987
**SALES:** 100K  **Privately Held**
**SIC:** 2262  Screen printing: manmade fiber & silk broadwoven fabrics

**(G-7275)**
### SYSTEMS BY LAR INC
841 E 3000 North Rd  (60927-7188)
PHONE..................................815 694-3141
Lynn A Rosenbaum, President
Sally Rosenbaum, Vice Pres
**EMP:** 5  **EST:** 2002
**SALES (est):** 875.3K  **Privately Held**
**SIC:** 3061  Mechanical rubber goods

## Clinton
### De Witt County

**(G-7276)**
### AAK MECHANICAL INC
10962 Riddle Rd  (61727-9373)
PHONE..................................217 935-8501
Steven R Coppenbarger, President
Jodi Karr, Manager
Jennifer Coppenbarger, Admin Sec
**EMP:** 52
**SALES:** 13.3MM  **Privately Held**
**SIC:** 1796  3441  Machinery installation; fabricated structural metal

**(G-7277)**
### ARCHER-DANIELS-MIDLAND COMPANY
Also Called: ADM
714 N Grant St  (61727-1011)
PHONE..................................217 935-3620
Chantel Thompson, QA Dir
**EMP:** 135
**SALES (corp-wide):** 62.3B  **Publicly Held**
**SIC:** 2046  Wet corn milling
**PA:** Archer-Daniels-Midland Company
   77 W Wacker Dr Ste 4600
   Chicago IL 60601
   312 634-8100

**(G-7278)**
### AREA DISPOSAL SERVICE INC
9550 Heritage Rd  (61727-2819)
PHONE..................................217 935-1300
Ken Heuerman, Branch Mgr
**EMP:** 10
**SALES (corp-wide):** 733.6MM  **Privately Held**
**SIC:** 3589  Garbage disposers & compactors, commercial
**HQ:** Area Disposal Service, Inc.
   4700 N Sterling Ave
   Peoria IL 61615
   309 686-8033

**(G-7279)**
### CENTRAL ILLINOIS NEWSPAPERS
Also Called: Clinton Daily Journal
111 S Monroe St  (61727-2057)
P.O. Box 615  (61727-0615)
PHONE..................................217 935-3171

Fax: 217 935-6086
John Tompkins, President
Mike Tompkins, Vice Pres
Susan Munoz, Marketing Staff
Diane Robertson, Receptionist
**EMP:** 4
**SQ FT:** 7,000
**SALES (est):** 457.1K  **Privately Held**
**WEB:** www.rochellenewsleader.com
**SIC:** 2711  2752  Newspapers: publishing only, not printed on site; commercial printing, lithographic
**HQ:** Rochelle Newspapers Inc
   211 E Il Route 38
   Rochelle IL 61068
   815 562-2061

**(G-7280)**
### CYRULIK INC
1100 E Johnson St  (61727)
PHONE..................................217 935-6969
Fax: 217 935-3093
Shelby Cyrulik, President
**EMP:** 4
**SQ FT:** 20,000
**SALES:** 410K  **Privately Held**
**SIC:** 3273  Ready-mixed concrete

**(G-7281)**
### H N C PRODUCTS INC
8631 Sunset Rd  (61727-8987)
PHONE..................................217 935-9100
Fax: 217 935-8938
Chimpiramma Potini, President
Josh McGee, QA Dir
Jerry Wright, Director
Srilatha Potini, Admin Sec
**EMP:** 40
**SQ FT:** 70,000
**SALES (est):** 8.3MM  **Privately Held**
**WEB:** www.hncproducts.com
**SIC:** 3579  2844  Mailing, letter handling & addressing machines; toilet preparations

**(G-7282)**
### HARBACH GILLAN & NIXON INC (PA)
Also Called: H G & N Fertilizer
618 W Van Buren St  (61727-2183)
P.O. Box 457  (61727-0457)
PHONE..................................217 935-8378
Curtis Harbach, President
Bob Anderson, Corp Secy
Gene Kaufman, Controller
Kent Patterson, Accounts Mgr
Robert C Anderson, Admin Sec
**EMP:** 10
**SQ FT:** 2,000
**SALES (est):** 16.7MM  **Privately Held**
**SIC:** 2873  5191  2875  Nitrogenous fertilizers; fertilizer & fertilizer materials; fertilizers, mixing only

**(G-7283)**
### HARBACH NIXON & WILLSON INC (HQ)
618 W Van Buren St  (61727-2183)
P.O. Box 457  (61727-0457)
PHONE..................................217 935-8378
Virgil T Harbach, President
John Buerk, Treasurer
Gene Kaufman, Controller
Richard Graves, Admin Sec
**EMP:** 3
**SALES (est):** 343.2K
**SALES (corp-wide):** 16.7MM  **Privately Held**
**SIC:** 2879  Agricultural chemicals
**PA:** Harbach, Gillan & Nixon, Inc.
   618 W Van Buren St
   Clinton IL 61727
   217 935-8378

**(G-7284)**
### ILLINOIS OIL MARKETING EQP INC
601 E Leander St  (61727-2511)
PHONE..................................217 935-5107
Dan Ballenger, Manager
**EMP:** 15
**SALES (corp-wide):** 22.5MM  **Privately Held**
**WEB:** www.iome.com
**SIC:** 3443  Tanks, standard or custom fabricated: metal plate

**PA:** Illinois Oil Marketing Equipment, Inc.
   850 Brenkman Dr
   Pekin IL 61554
   309 347-1819

**(G-7285)**
### LIBERTY DIVERSIFIED INTL INC
10670 State Highway 10  (61727-9277)
P.O. Box 443  (61727-0443)
PHONE..................................217 935-8361
Fax: 217 935-8364
Thomas Sivil, Manager
**EMP:** 50
**SALES (corp-wide):** 607.8MM  **Privately Held**
**WEB:** www.millercontainer.com
**SIC:** 2653  3412  Boxes, corrugated: made from purchased materials; metal barrels, drums & pails
**PA:** Liberty Diversified International, Inc.
   5600 Highway 169 N
   New Hope MN 55428
   763 536-6600

**(G-7286)**
### M & M PUMP CO
404 S Portland Pl Apt 2  (61727-2388)
PHONE..................................217 935-2517
Fax: 217 935-2622
Carol McClur, President
Rod Wortz, Vice Pres
**EMP:** 4
**SALES (est):** 310K  **Privately Held**
**SIC:** 3589  5084  High pressure cleaning equipment; cleaning equipment, high pressure, sand or steam

**(G-7287)**
### MCELROY METAL MILL INC
10940 State Hwy 10  (61727)
PHONE..................................217 935-9421
Fax: 217 935-6615
Steve Hunter, Purch Agent
Scott Krejci, Sales Staff
John Hinthorne, Branch Mgr
**EMP:** 48
**SQ FT:** 70,000
**SALES (corp-wide):** 381.9MM  **Privately Held**
**WEB:** www.mcelroymetal.com
**SIC:** 3448  Prefabricated metal buildings
**PA:** Mcelroy Metal Mill, Inc.
   1500 Hamilton Rd
   Bossier City LA 71111
   318 747-8000

**(G-7288)**
### RR DONNELLEY & SONS COMPANY
Also Called: Colorforms
900 S Cain St  (61727-2537)
P.O. Box 379  (61727-0379)
PHONE..................................217 935-2113
Fax: 217 935-4813
Jeff Massey, Engineer
Gayle Waddle, Personnel
Keith Gonnerman, Prgrmr
Marty Morris, Director
Kirk Fornella, Executive
**EMP:** 230
**SQ FT:** 160,000
**SALES (corp-wide):** 6.9B  **Publicly Held**
**WEB:** www.moore.com
**SIC:** 2752  2761  Commercial printing, lithographic; manifold business forms
**PA:** R. R. Donnelley & Sons Company
   35 W Wacker Dr Ste 3650
   Chicago IL 60601
   312 326-8000

**(G-7289)**
### TEKNI-PLEX INC
Action Technology
10610 State Highway 10  (61727-9277)
P.O. Box 111  (61727-0111)
PHONE..................................217 935-8311
Fax: 217 935-9132
Bryan Foster, Plant Mgr
Julie Tedrick, Controller
Gary Seitzer, Maintence Staff
**EMP:** 30
**SALES (corp-wide):** 1.1B  **Privately Held**
**SIC:** 3429  Manufactured hardware (general)

**PA:** Tekni-Plex, Inc.
   460 E Swedesford Rd # 3000
   Wayne PA 19087
   484 690-1520

**(G-7290)**
### TRINITY STRUCTURAL TOWERS INC
10000 Tabor Rd  (61727-9645)
PHONE..................................217 935-7900
Ed Pittman, Principal
Thomas Marstein, Facilities Mgr
Mike Calhoun, QC Dir
**EMP:** 15
**SALES (corp-wide):** 4.5B  **Publicly Held**
**SIC:** 3441  3621  Fabricated structural metal; windmills, electric generating
**HQ:** Trinity Structural Towers, Inc.
   2525 N Stemmons Fwy
   Dallas TX 75207
   214 631-4420

## Coal City
### Grundy County

**(G-7291)**
### COAL CITY COURANT
Also Called: Free Press Newspapers
271 S Broadway St  (60416-1534)
P.O. Box 215  (60416-0215)
PHONE..................................815 634-0315
Eric Fisher, President
**EMP:** 3
**SALES (est):** 132.2K  **Privately Held**
**SIC:** 2711  Newspapers

**(G-7292)**
### COAL CITY REDI-MIX CO INC
640 S Mazon St  (60416)
P.O. Box 116  (60416-0116)
PHONE..................................815 634-4455
Fax: 815 634-4470
Steven W Dearth, President
Michael Dearth, Vice Pres
**EMP:** 13
**SQ FT:** 2,000
**SALES (est):** 1.6MM  **Privately Held**
**SIC:** 3273  3241  Ready-mixed concrete; cement, hydraulic

**(G-7293)**
### HESTER CABINETS & MILLWORK
655 S Marguerite St  (60416-1486)
PHONE..................................815 634-4555
Steven R Hester, President
**EMP:** 6  **EST:** 1933
**SQ FT:** 5,000
**SALES (est):** 850.2K  **Privately Held**
**WEB:** www.cabinetmaking.com
**SIC:** 2434  Wood kitchen cabinets

## Coal Valley
### Rock Island County

**(G-7294)**
### COMPLETE CUSTOM WOODWORKS
3 Crestview Dr  (61240-9409)
PHONE..................................309 644-1911
James Jermigan, Owner
**EMP:** 1
**SQ FT:** 1,000
**SALES:** 750K  **Privately Held**
**SIC:** 2521  Cabinets, office: wood

**(G-7295)**
### DEER PROCESSING
11928 Niabi Zoo Rd  (61240-9530)
PHONE..................................309 799-5994
Fax: 309 799-5980
Teri Dean, Owner
**EMP:** 12
**SALES (est):** 596.3K  **Privately Held**
**SIC:** 2011  Meat packing plants

**(G-7296)**
### FCA LLC
2212 Us Highway 6  (61240-9602)
PHONE..................................309 949-3999

Jim Eddy, *Branch Mgr*
**EMP: 43 Privately Held**
**WEB:** www.fcamfg.com
**SIC: 5085** 2653 2441 Industrial supplies; corrugated & solid fiber boxes; nailed wood boxes & shook
**PA:** Fca, Llc
  7601 John Deere Pkwy
  Moline IL 61265

*(G-7297)*
**KONE INC**
Also Called: Kone Escalator Div
2266 Us Highway 6 (61240-9602)
**PHONE**.................................309 945-4961
Godfrey Allen, *Vice Pres*
Tom Nurnberg, *Vice Pres*
Gregg Schipper, *Purch Mgr*
Scott Holbrook, *Buyer*
Rod Mintle, *Buyer*
**EMP: 200**
**SALES (corp-wide): 650.6MM Privately Held**
**WEB:** www.us.kone.com
**SIC: 7699** 3534 Elevators: inspection, service & repair; elevators & moving stairways
**HQ:** Kone Inc.
  4225 Naperville Rd # 400
  Lisle IL 60532
  630 577-1650

*(G-7298)*
**PRAIRIE AREA LIBRARY SYSTEM (PA)**
220 W 23rd Ave (61240-9624)
**PHONE**.................................309 799-3155
Barry Levine, *President*
Penny O'Rouke, *Vice Pres*
Mary Stewrt, *Sales/Mktg Mgr*
Crystal Talbot, *Finance*
Robert McKay, *Exec Dir*
**EMP: 20**
**SALES: 3.1MM Privately Held**
**WEB:** www.quadlinc.com
**SIC: 7372** 8741 8231 Operating systems computer software; management services; libraries

*(G-7299)*
**VALLEY MEATS LLC**
2302 1st St Sr (61240-9408)
P.O. Box 69 (61240-0069)
**PHONE**.................................309 799-7341
Jeff Joeb, *President*
Randy Ehrlich, *Vice Pres*
Richard Koehler, *Vice Pres*
Bonnie L Smolenski, *Admin Sec*
**EMP: 49**
**SALES (est): 6.8MM Privately Held**
**SIC: 8741** 2011 Business management; boxed beef from meat slaughtered on site

## Coatsburg
### Adams County

*(G-7300)*
**AREA FABRICATORS**
1735 Highway 24 (62325-2202)
**PHONE**.................................217 455-3426
**Fax:** 217 455-3427
Ronald Conover, *Partner*
Jeffery A Conover, *Partner*
Steve M Conover, *Partner*
**EMP: 3**
**SALES (est): 441.2K Privately Held**
**SIC: 3441** Fabricated structural metal

## Cobden
### Union County

*(G-7301)*
**COOK SALES INC (PA)**
Also Called: Cook Portable Warehouses
3455 Old Highway 51 N (62920-3666)
P.O. Box 687, Anna (62906-0687)
**PHONE**.................................618 893-2114
Greg Cook, *President*
Mike Miller, *Vice Pres*
Tim Yearack, *Engineer*
Festus Lot, *Sales Staff*

Tedra L Miller, *Admin Sec*
**EMP: 50**
**SQ FT:** 46,500
**SALES (est):** 18.4MM **Privately Held**
**WEB:** www.cookstuff.com
**SIC: 2452** Prefabricated wood buildings

*(G-7302)*
**LINCOLN HERITAGE WINERY LLC**
772 Kaolin Rd (62920-3783)
**PHONE**.................................618 833-3783
Homer L Cissell,
Bonnie Cissell,
**EMP: 2**
**SALES (est): 239.1K Privately Held**
**SIC: 5182** 2084 Wine; wines

*(G-7303)*
**RUSTLE HILL WINERY LLC**
8595 Us Highway 51 N (62920-3145)
**PHONE**.................................618 893-2700
**Fax:** 618 893-2733
Lenore Russell,
**EMP: 2**
**SALES (est): 200.4K Privately Held**
**SIC: 2084** Wines

*(G-7304)*
**SHAWNEE GRAPEVINES LLC**
Also Called: Starview Vineyard
5100 Wing Hill Rd (62920-3211)
**PHONE**.................................618 893-9463
Ron Dalius,
**EMP: 4**
**SALES (est): 263.2K Privately Held**
**SIC: 0762** 2084 Vineyard management & maintenance services; wines

*(G-7305)*
**SPHINX PANEL AND DOOR INC**
317 Locust St (62920-2104)
**PHONE**.................................618 351-9266
Terry A Bovee, *President*
Paul Sutton, *Plant Mgr*
**EMP: 8 EST: 1997**
**SQ FT:** 3,200
**SALES: 1MM Privately Held**
**WEB:** www.sphinxpanel.com
**SIC: 3632** Refrigerators, mechanical & absorption: household

## Coffeen
### Montgomery County

*(G-7306)*
**US MINERALS INC**
796 Cips Trl (62017-2137)
**PHONE**.................................217 534-2370
**Fax:** 217 534-6206
Eric White, *Plant Mgr*
Jean McMullin, *Admin Asst*
**EMP: 15**
**SALES (corp-wide): 34.6MM Privately Held**
**SIC: 3291** Abrasive products
**PA:** U.S. Minerals, Inc.
  18635 West Creek Dr Ste 2
  Tinley Park IL 60477
  219 864-0909

## Colchester
### Mcdonough County

*(G-7307)*
**CENTRAL STONE COMPANY**
5533 E 400th St (62326-1887)
**PHONE**.................................309 776-3900
**Fax:** 309 776-3261
Harvey Fueling, *Manager*
**EMP: 12**
**SALES (corp-wide): 4.3B Privately Held**
**SIC: 1422** 5032 Agricultural limestone, ground; stone, crushed or broken
**HQ:** Central Stone Company
  1701 5th Ave
  Moline IL 61265
  309 757-8250

*(G-7308)*
**YETTER M CO INC EMP B TR**
109 S Mcdonough St (62326-1303)
P.O. Box 358 (62326-0358)
**PHONE**.................................309 776-4111
Bernard Lelan, *President*
**EMP: 1**
**SALES: 2.6MM Privately Held**
**SIC: 3999** Manufacturing industries

*(G-7309)*
**YETTER MANUFACTURING COMPANY (PA)**
Also Called: Yetter Farm Equipment
109 S Mcdonough St (62326-1303)
P.O. Box 358 (62326-0358)
**PHONE**.................................309 776-3222
**Fax:** 309 776-3222
Bernard F Whalen, *President*
Patrick T Whalen, *Vice Pres*
Kristoffer Griffith, *Purch Mgr*
Ron Arteaga, *Purchasing*
Theodore Stull, *Research*
▲ **EMP: 80**
**SQ FT:** 46,500
**SALES (est): 30.7MM Privately Held**
**SIC: 3523** 2542 Farm machinery & equipment; cutters & blowers, ensilage; soil preparation machinery, except turf & grounds; racks, merchandise display or storage: except wood

## Coleta
### Whiteside County

*(G-7310)*
**GIBBS MACHINE CORP**
411 S Main (61081-5117)
**PHONE**.................................815 336-9000
Jerry A Gibbs, *President*
Pam Beyer, *Purchasing*
Susan Hector, *Manager*
Bobbie L Gibbs, *Admin Sec*
**EMP: 20**
**SALES (est): 3.4MM Privately Held**
**SIC: 3599** Machine shop, jobbing & repair

## Colfax
### Mclean County

*(G-7311)*
**TFT INC**
31784 E 1400 North Rd (61728-7523)
**PHONE**.................................309 531-2012
Gerald Thompson, *President*
**EMP: 1**
**SALES: 1MM Privately Held**
**SIC: 3523** Driers (farm): grain, hay & seed

## Collinsville
### Madison County

*(G-7312)*
**ADVANCED PATTERN WORKS LLC**
305 Railroad Ave (62234-2831)
**PHONE**.................................618 346-9039
James Pennebaker, *Corp Counsel*
John Harris, *Mng Member*
Larry Hubbman, *Data Proc Staff*
Susan White, *Admin Asst*
**EMP: 5**
**SALES: 900K Privately Held**
**SIC: 3322** 3543 Malleable iron foundries; industrial patterns

*(G-7313)*
**ALAO TEMITOPE**
Also Called: Topilonio
29 Brookhill Ct (62234-6044)
**PHONE**.................................331 454-3333
Temitope Ajayi, *Owner*
**EMP: 15**
**SALES (est): 550K Privately Held**
**SIC: 2082** 7389 Malt syrups;

*(G-7314)*
**ALEXANDER BREWSTER LLC**
1401 N Bluff Rd (62234-7303)
**PHONE**.................................618 346-8580
John W Thomas Jr,
Zachary A Kaesberg,
Jerod B Thomas,
Jerod Thomas,
Nancy L Thomas,
**EMP: 7**
**SQ FT:** 4,800
**SALES (est): 1.2MM Privately Held**
**WEB:** www.brewsteralexander.com
**SIC: 3651** Video camera-audio recorders, household use

*(G-7315)*
**COLLINSVILLE ICE & FUEL CO**
800 N Bluff Rd (62234-5818)
**PHONE**.................................618 344-3272
**Fax:** 618 344-8213
John J O'Donnell, *President*
Maureen O'Donnell, *Vice Pres*
Martin Odonnell, *Vice Pres*
Sheri O'Donnell, *Admin Sec*
**EMP: 15**
**SQ FT:** 5,000
**SALES (est): 1.6MM Privately Held**
**WEB:** www.collinsviceandfuel.com
**SIC: 1741** 2097 Stone masonry; block ice

*(G-7316)*
**COLLINSVILLE SPORTS STORE**
2211 Vandalia St (62234-4855)
**PHONE**.................................618 345-5588
**Fax:** 618 345-5612
Donna Jesse, *President*
Jerry Jesse, *Vice Pres*
**EMP: 6**
**SQ FT:** 4,000
**SALES (est): 512.9K Privately Held**
**SIC: 3949** Sporting & athletic goods

*(G-7317)*
**CONCRETE UNIT STEP CO INC**
8915 Collinsville Rd (62234-1711)
**PHONE**.................................618 344-7256
William R Poneleit, *President*
**EMP: 3**
**SQ FT:** 1,000
**SALES (est): 356.9K Privately Held**
**SIC: 3272** 3446 Concrete products, pre-cast; steps, prefabricated concrete; architectural metalwork

*(G-7318)*
**CUSTOM WOOD CREATIONS**
776 Timberlane Dr (62234-4132)
**PHONE**.................................618 346-2208
Martin E Plute Jr, *Principal*
**EMP: 2**
**SALES (est): 226.6K Privately Held**
**SIC: 2431** Millwork

*(G-7319)*
**D L AUSTIN STEEL SUPPLY CORP (PA)**
500 Camelot Dr (62234-4717)
P.O. Box 166 (62234-0166)
**PHONE**.................................618 345-7200
**Fax:** 618 345-7203
David Austin Sr, *President*
David L Austin II, *President*
Kathleen Austin, *Corp Secy*
G S Austin, *Manager*
**EMP: 2**
**SQ FT:** 4,200
**SALES (est): 1.1MM Privately Held**
**SIC: 3441** 5051 Fabricated structural metal; metals service centers & offices

*(G-7320)*
**E W ENTERPRISES INC**
1 Meadow Heights Prof Par (62234-4486)
**PHONE**.................................618 345-2244
**Fax:** 618 345-2211
Ronald S Weber, *CEO*
Evelyn M Weber, *President*
◆ **EMP: 4**
**SALES: 2.2K Privately Held**
**SIC: 3952** Pencil holders

## Collinsville - Madison County (G-7321)

**(G-7321)**
**EAGLE PUBLICATIONS INC**
Also Called: Hometown Phone Book
2 Eastport Plaza Dr # 100 (62234-6109)
PHONE.................................618 345-5400
Fax: 618 345-5474
Martin L Norton, *President*
Tammy Norton, *Vice Pres*
EMP: 45
SQ FT: 65,775
SALES (est): 4.5MM **Privately Held**
WEB: www.hometownphonebook.com
SIC: 2711 2741 Newspapers: publishing only, not printed on site; miscellaneous publishing

**(G-7322)**
**EAST BANK NEON INC**
8146 Gass Ln (62234-7009)
PHONE.................................618 345-9517
Dennis Wick, *President*
Sam Glasser, *Manager*
EMP: 8
SALES (corp-wide): 1.1MM **Privately Held**
SIC: 3993 Signs & advertising specialties
PA: East Bank Neon Inc
1511 Washington Ave
Saint Louis MO

**(G-7323)**
**ES INVESTMENTS INC**
1997 Lemontree Ln (62234-5252)
PHONE.................................618 345-6151
Fax: 618 344-2028
Richard Eilering, *President*
Valerie Durley, *Vice Pres*
EMP: 8
SQ FT: 1,000
SALES (est): 701K **Privately Held**
WEB: www.e-smasonry.com
SIC: 1311 Crude petroleum production; natural gas production

**(G-7324)**
**ESI FUEL & ENERGY GROUP LLC**
1997 Lemontree Ln (62234-5252)
PHONE.................................716 465-4289
Valerie Durley, *Partner*
Richard Eilering, *Partner*
Brad Frank, *Partner*
Montie Miner, *Partner*
Kelly Planzo, *Partner*
EMP: 4
SALES (est): 171.1K **Privately Held**
SIC: 2911 4911 Jet fuels; diesel fuels; gases & liquefied petroleum gases; ;

**(G-7325)**
**FOURNIE FARMS INC**
925 Mcdonough Lake Rd (62234-7401)
PHONE.................................618 344-8527
Fax: 618 344-8815
Robert L Fournie, *President*
Dorothy Fournie, *Corp Secy*
EMP: 26
SALES (est): 190K **Privately Held**
SIC: 0161 2035 Vegetables & melons; horseradish, prepared

**(G-7326)**
**G & M INDUSTRIES INC**
208 Yorktown Dr (62234-4352)
P.O. Box 561 (62234-0561)
PHONE.................................618 344-6655
William Graebe, *President*
Annette Graebe, *Vice Pres*
EMP: 4
SQ FT: 2,000
SALES (est): 304.3K **Privately Held**
SIC: 3842 3999 Wheelchairs; desk pads, except paper

**(G-7327)**
**GATEWAY INDUSTRIAL POWER INC (PA)**
Also Called: Gateway Truck and Rfrgn
921 Fournie Ln (62234-7430)
PHONE.................................888 865-8675
Fax: 618 345-2955
John Wagner, *Ch of Bd*
David M Keach, *President*
Zach Wagner, *President*
Kevin Kennedy, *Controller*
EMP: 117
SQ FT: 3,000
SALES (est): 32.9MM **Privately Held**
WEB: www.gipower.com
SIC: 3585 7538 Refrigeration & heating equipment; diesel engine repair: automotive

**(G-7328)**
**J D REFRIGERATION**
Also Called: Darlington Climate Control
6849 Fedder Ln (62234-6507)
PHONE.................................618 345-0041
Dan Darlington, *President*
Jim Kerner, *Corp Secy*
Greg Darlington, *Admin Sec*
EMP: 2
SQ FT: 1,000
SALES (est): 241.2K **Privately Held**
SIC: 1711 3585 Warm air heating & air conditioning contractor; refrigeration & heating equipment

**(G-7329)**
**JDS LABS INC**
909 N Bluff Rd (62234-5803)
PHONE.................................618 366-0475
John Seaber, *President*
EMP: 5
SALES (est): 713.1K **Privately Held**
SIC: 3679 7389 Headphones, radio;

**(G-7330)**
**LONDON SHOE SHOP & WESTERN WR**
125 W Main St (62234-3001)
PHONE.................................618 345-9570
Fax: 618 343-3647
Mark Allard, *Owner*
EMP: 4
SQ FT: 3,000
SALES (est): 323.5K **Privately Held**
SIC: 5661 3143 Custom & orthopedic shoes; shoes, orthopedic; men's footwear, except athletic

**(G-7331)**
**M O W PRINTING INC**
526 Vandalia St (62234-4041)
PHONE.................................618 345-5525
Fax: 618 345-9254
John Meehan Jr, *President*
Kelly Jean Ossola, *Vice Pres*
Darrell Walling, *Vice Pres*
EMP: 11
SQ FT: 8,000
SALES (est): 1.3MM **Privately Held**
SIC: 2752 2791 2789 Commercial printing, lithographic; typesetting; bookbinding & related work

**(G-7332)**
**MADISON COUNTY PUBLICATIONS**
Also Called: Granite City Journals
2 Executive Dr (62234-6120)
PHONE.................................618 344-0265
Lee Bachlet, *Manager*
EMP: 30
SALES (corp-wide): 614.3MM **Publicly Held**
SIC: 2711 Newspapers: publishing only, not printed on site
HQ: Madison County Publications Inc
113 E Clay St
Collinsville IL 62234
618 344-0264

**(G-7333)**
**MADISON COUNTY PUBLICATIONS (DH)**
Also Called: Collinsville Herald Journal
113 E Clay St (62234-3202)
PHONE.................................618 344-0264
Fax: 618 344-3611
Tom Rice, *President*
Carole Fredeking, *General Mgr*
Marcia Dahm, *General Mgr*
EMP: 15
SALES (est): 3.1MM
SALES (corp-wide): 614.3MM **Publicly Held**
SIC: 2711 Newspapers: publishing only, not printed on site

## GEOGRAPHIC SECTION

HQ: Suburban Newspapers Of Greater St. Louis, Inc.
14522 South Outer 40 Rd
Chesterfield MO
314 821-1110

**(G-7334)**
**MANDIS DENTAL LABORATORY**
607 Vandalia St Ste 300 (62234-4081)
PHONE.................................618 345-3777
Nicholas C Mandis, *President*
EMP: 4
SQ FT: 1,500
SALES (est): 403.5K **Privately Held**
SIC: 8072 3843 3842 Crown & bridge production; dental equipment & supplies; surgical appliances & supplies

**(G-7335)**
**MARSH SHIPPING SUPPLY CO LLC (PA)**
Also Called: Mssc
926 Mcdonough Lake Rd E (62234-7437)
PHONE.................................618 343-1006
Craig Eversmann, *President*
John Burnett, *General Mgr*
Shiela Cahill, *QA Dir*
Rita Swettenham, *VP Sls/Mktg*
▼ EMP: 12 EST: 2000
SQ FT: 15,000
SALES (est): 9.5MM **Privately Held**
WEB: www.marshship.com
SIC: 3565 3542 Packaging machinery; marking machines

**(G-7336)**
**MSSC LLC**
926 Mcdonough Lake Rd E (62234-7437)
PHONE.................................618 343-1006
EMP: 4 EST: 2014
SALES (est): 244.8K **Privately Held**
SIC: 3565 Packaging machinery

**(G-7337)**
**PRECISION SERVICE**
Also Called: Herbs License Service
407 W Main St (62234-3004)
PHONE.................................618 345-2047
Fax: 618 346-1057
Larry Hrabusicky, *Owner*
Joe Hrabusicky, *Manager*
EMP: 5
SQ FT: 4,000
SALES (est): 670.3K **Privately Held**
WEB: www.precisionservice.com
SIC: 3556 7699 2599 Bakery machinery; restaurant equipment repair; carts, restaurant equipment

**(G-7338)**
**PROST HEATING & COOLING LLC**
6964 Lebanon Rd (62234-7506)
P.O. Box 95 (62234-0095)
PHONE.................................618 344-3749
Sandra Prost,
EMP: 7
SALES (est): 1MM **Privately Held**
SIC: 3585 Refrigeration & heating equipment

**(G-7339)**
**QUALITY SAND COMPANY INC**
1327 N Bluff Rd (62234-7301)
PHONE.................................618 346-1070
Fax: 618 346-1365
Tony O'Donnell, *President*
Tony O Donnell, *President*
Bob Zoelizer, *Treasurer*
EMP: 7
SQ FT: 500
SALES (est): 589.4K
SALES (corp-wide): 304.8MM **Privately Held**
SIC: 1442 Construction sand mining; gravel mining
PA: Fred Weber, Inc.
2320 Creve Coeur Mill Rd
Maryland Heights MO 63043
314 344-0070

**(G-7340)**
**SASI CORPORATION**
Also Called: Bridal Originals
1700 Saint Louis Rd (62234-1802)
PHONE.................................314 922-7432

Daniel P Shea, *President*
Ronald Sundermeyer, *Exec VP*
Arlene Kirk, *Mfg Staff*
Irene Callahan, *Purch Mgr*
Brenda Page, *Credit Staff*
◆ EMP: 30 EST: 1947
SQ FT: 100,000
SALES (est): 2.6MM **Privately Held**
WEB: www.nadineprom.com
SIC: 2335 Wedding gowns & dresses; gowns, formal

**(G-7341)**
**SEV-REND CORPORATION**
5301 Horseshoe Lake Rd (62234-7423)
PHONE.................................618 301-4130
Robert E Williams Jr, *President*
▲ EMP: 15
SQ FT: 25,685
SALES (est): 4.6MM **Privately Held**
WEB: www.sev-rend.com
SIC: 2679 Tags & labels, paper

**(G-7342)**
**SUBURBAN NEWSPAPERS OF GREATER**
Also Called: Monroe County Clarion
2 Executive Dr (62234-6120)
PHONE.................................618 281-7691
Steve Holt, *Sales/Mktg Mgr*
EMP: 25
SALES (corp-wide): 614.3MM **Publicly Held**
SIC: 2711 Newspapers: publishing only, not printed on site
HQ: Suburban Newspapers Of Greater St. Louis, Inc.
14522 South Outer 40 Rd
Chesterfield MO
314 821-1110

### Colona
*Henry County*

**(G-7343)**
**I80 EQUIPMENT LLC**
20490 E 550th St (61241-8628)
P.O. Box 132 (61241-0132)
PHONE.................................309 949-3701
Mitch Melega, *Accountant*
Jordan Jones, *Sales Staff*
Eric Jones, *Manager*
Jones Erik R,
▼ EMP: 65
SALES (est): 18.8MM **Privately Held**
SIC: 3537 Industrial trucks & tractors

**(G-7344)**
**LAVENDER CREST WINERY**
5401 Us Highway 6 (61241-8617)
PHONE.................................309 949-2565
Martha Rittmueller, *President*
Ron Belshause, *General Mgr*
Greg Backes, *Vice Pres*
Wilbert Rittemuller, *Treasurer*
Gina Backes, *Admin Sec*
EMP: 20
SALES (est): 500K **Privately Held**
WEB: www.lavendercrestwinery.com
SIC: 2084 Wines

**(G-7345)**
**LEONARDS UNIT STEP OF MOLINE**
Also Called: Unit Step Company
24415 Ridge Rd (61241-9064)
PHONE.................................309 792-9641
Glenn J Bear, *President*
EMP: 2
SQ FT: 17,000
SALES (est): 210K **Privately Held**
SIC: 3272 3446 Concrete products, precast; architectural metalwork

**(G-7346)**
**QUAD CITIES DIRECTIONAL BORING**
24190 N High St (61241-8706)
P.O. Box 371 (61241-0371)
PHONE.................................309 792-3070
Tj Timmerman, *President*
EMP: 5

SALES (est): 520K  Privately Held
SIC: 1381  Directional drilling oil & gas wells

**(G-7347)**
**ROCK RIVER ARMS  INC**
1042 Cleveland Rd  (61241-8974)
PHONE....................309 792-5780
Fax: 309 792-5781
Lester C Larson Jr, *President*
Chuck Larson, *Vice Pres*
Sarah Larson, *Purch Mgr*
Gay Larson, *Treasurer*
Tom Carbone, *Sales Staff*
▼ EMP: 60
SQ FT: 15,000
SALES (est): 13.9MM  Privately Held
WEB: www.rockriverarms.com
SIC: 3484  5941  Guns (firearms) or gun parts, 30 mm. & below; sporting goods & bicycle shops

**(G-7348)**
**SOUTHWICK MACHINE & DESIGN CO**
21300 Briar Bluff Rd  (61241)
P.O. Box 578  (61241-0578)
PHONE....................309 949-2868
Robert Southwick, *President*
Peggy Southwick, *Admin Sec*
EMP: 3
SQ FT: 2,500
SALES: 270K  Privately Held
SIC: 3444  3599  7692  1799  Sheet metalwork; machine & other job shop work; welding repair; welding on site

**(G-7349)**
**T&J TURNING INC**
4 Goembel Dr  (61241-9081)
PHONE....................309 738-8762
Anthony Lieving, *President*
Joanne Lieving, *Vice Pres*
EMP: 3
SALES (est): 258.2K  Privately Held
SIC: 3541  Lathes

## Columbia
### Monroe County

**(G-7350)**
**ACTION GRAPHICS AND SIGNS INC**
8802 Summer Rd  (62236-3502)
PHONE....................618 939-5755
Fax: 618 939-5551
Jane Kolmer, *President*
EMP: 4
SQ FT: 3,000
SALES: 500K  Privately Held
SIC: 3993  Signs & advertising specialties

**(G-7351)**
**B&H MACHINE  INC**
251 Southwoods Ctr Ste 1  (62236-2493)
P.O. Box 626  (62236-0626)
PHONE....................618 281-3737
Fax: 618 281-3740
Robert D Wooters, *President*
Len Shields, *General Mgr*
Eric Wooters, *Vice Pres*
Christine Wooters, *Treasurer*
EMP: 10
SQ FT: 3,600
SALES (est): 1.4MM  Privately Held
SIC: 3953  3544  Printing dies, rubber or plastic, for marking machines; special dies, tools, jigs & fixtures

**(G-7352)**
**BESTWORDS ORG CORP**
8934 Trolley Rd  (62236-3422)
P.O. Box 202  (62236-0202)
PHONE....................618 939-4324
EMP: 2 EST: 2000
SALES: 200K  Privately Held
SIC: 2731  Books-Publishing/Printing

**(G-7353)**
**BUDNICK CONVERTING  INC**
200 Admiral Weinel Blvd  (62236-1994)
P.O. Box 197  (62236-0197)
PHONE....................618 281-8090
Fax: 618 281-6308
Ann Wegmann, *President*
Brad Albrech, *Finance*
Michelle Brewer, *Cust Mgr*
Christy Hornacek, *Comms Mgr*
Brad Albrecht, *Info Tech Mgr*
▲ EMP: 110
SQ FT: 48,000
SALES (est): 54.9MM  Privately Held
WEB: www.budnickconverting.com
SIC: 2672  Masking tape: made from purchased materials

**(G-7354)**
**COLUMBIA QUARRY COMPANY (PA)**
210 State Route 158  (62236-3241)
PHONE....................618 281-7631
Fax: 618 281-6120
Charles H Krause Jr, *Ch of Bd*
Klyde Trexler, *President*
R L Trexler, *President*
Donna Eckrich, *Vice Pres*
John Schmidt, *Treasurer*
EMP: 20
SQ FT: 7,000
SALES (est): 14.7MM  Privately Held
WEB: www.columbiaquarry.com
SIC: 1422  Crushed & broken limestone

**(G-7355)**
**COMPUTER PWR SOLUTIONS ILL LTD**
Also Called: Cpsi
235 Southwoods Ctr  (62236-2466)
P.O. Box 108  (62236-0108)
PHONE....................618 281-8898
Michelle Elia, *President*
Joe Dobronski, *Vice Pres*
Gay Sherman, *Sales Dir*
John Bauer, *Sales Associate*
Aziz Elia, *Technology*
EMP: 26
SQ FT: 10,000
SALES (est): 2.4MM  Privately Held
WEB: www.vcasel.com
SIC: 7371  7379  7372  7373  Computer software development; computer related consulting services; prepackaged software; publishers' computer software; application computer software; systems software development services

**(G-7356)**
**CONRAD PRESS LTD**
120 N Main St Stop 1  (62236-1761)
P.O. Box 407  (62236-0407)
PHONE....................618 281-7969
Michael G Conrad, *Partner*
John Conrad, *Partner*
EMP: 3 EST: 1955
SQ FT: 1,500
SALES: 200K  Privately Held
SIC: 2752  2791  Commercial printing, offset; typesetting

**(G-7357)**
**CONTEMPORARY MARBLE INC**
Also Called: McCarty's Contemporary Marble
8533 Hanover Indus Dr  (62236-4635)
PHONE....................618 281-6200
Fax: 618 281-5662
Harold McCarty, *President*
Donna McCarty, *President*
EMP: 4
SQ FT: 12,000
SALES (est): 528.1K  Privately Held
SIC: 3281  Cut stone & stone products; bathroom fixtures, cut stone

**(G-7358)**
**HOYA CORPORATION**
Also Called: Hoya Vision Care
301 Vision Dr  (62236-2474)
PHONE....................618 281-3344
Cindy Bradley, *Controller*
Eric Mueller, *Branch Mgr*
EMP: 175
SALES (corp-wide): 4.3B  Privately Held
SIC: 3851  Ophthalmic goods
HQ: Hoya Corporation
    651 E Corporate Dr
    Lewisville TX 75057
    972 221-4141

**(G-7359)**
**KELLYJO MAKES SCENTS**
3050 Steppig Rd  (62236-4106)
PHONE....................618 281-4241
Kelly Eason, *Principal*
EMP: 3 EST: 2015
SALES (est): 150.1K  Privately Held
SIC: 2844  Toilet preparations

**(G-7360)**
**KNOTT SO SHABBY**
117 W Locust St  (62236-1709)
PHONE....................618 281-6002
EMP: 3
SALES (est): 273.1K  Privately Held
SIC: 2851  Paints & allied products

**(G-7361)**
**ORNAMENTAL IRON SHOP**
148 Hill Castle Dr  (62236-4542)
PHONE....................618 281-6072
Chris Shaw, *Owner*
EMP: 3 EST: 2008
SALES (est): 202.6K  Privately Held
SIC: 7299  5211  3446  1799  Home improvement & renovation contractor agency; fencing; railings, bannisters, guards, etc.: made from metal pipe; ornamental metal work

**(G-7362)**
**ORTHO-CLINICAL DIAGNOSTICS INC**
8 Briarhill Ln  (62236-1004)
PHONE....................618 281-3882
Kathy Bursak, *President*
EMP: 200
SALES (corp-wide): 979.3MM  Privately Held
WEB: www.orthoclinical.com
SIC: 2835  Blood derivative diagnostic agents
PA: Ortho-Clinical Diagnostics, Inc.
    1001 Us Highway 202
    Raritan NJ 08869
    908 218-8000

**(G-7363)**
**THERMO-CRAFT INC**
Also Called: Thermocraft
528 S Main St  (62236-2479)
PHONE....................618 281-7055
Catherine Pirtle, *President*
Charlie Craft, *Principal*
Mary Craft, *Corp Secy*
EMP: 5
SQ FT: 7,500
SALES: 499K  Privately Held
SIC: 2752  2759  Commercial printing, lithographic; commercial printing

**(G-7364)**
**TOWER ROCK STONE COMPANY (PA)**
250 W Sand Bank Rd  (62236-1044)
P.O. Box 50  (62236-0050)
PHONE....................618 281-4106
Jay Luhr, *President*
Sheryl Metzger, *Corp Secy*
Rodney Linker, *Vice Pres*
Michael Luhr, *Vice Pres*
William Shaw, *Vice Pres*
EMP: 10
SQ FT: 25,000
SALES: 41MM  Privately Held
SIC: 1422  Crushed & broken limestone

**(G-7365)**
**TRUSS COMPONENTS INC (PA)**
607 N Main St Ste 100  (62236-1405)
PHONE....................800 678-7877
Mary P Keller, *President*
Wanda Zentay, *Human Res Mgr*
EMP: 12
SQ FT: 26,000
SALES (est): 2.8MM  Privately Held
WEB: www.trusscomponents.com
SIC: 2439  Trusses, wooden roof

## Compton
### Lee County

**(G-7366)**
**JAMES HOWARD CO**
623 W Chestnut St  (61318-9504)
P.O. Box 200  (61318-0200)
PHONE....................815 497-2831
Fax: 815 497-4601
James Mc Innis, *Owner*
Howard Mc Innis, *Co-Owner*
Karen Hamilton, *Sales Staff*
EMP: 5
SQ FT: 6,000
SALES (est): 573.2K  Privately Held
WEB: www.jameshowardco.com
SIC: 5199  2531  3952  Artists' materials; school furniture; lead pencils & art goods

**(G-7367)**
**LOTUS CREATIVE INNOVATIONS LLC**
970 Meluigins Grove Rd  (61318-9727)
PHONE....................815 440-8999
Ashish Gavali, *President*
Delsie Gavili, *President*
EMP: 4
SALES (est): 250K  Privately Held
SIC: 3542  Machine tools, metal forming type

## Concord
### Morgan County

**(G-7368)**
**M & F FABRICATION & WELDING**
2243 Mud Creek Rd  (62631-5026)
PHONE....................217 457-2221
EMP: 3
SALES (est): 140K  Privately Held
SIC: 7692  Welding Repair

## Congerville
### Woodford County

**(G-7369)**
**PREMIER FABRICATION  LLC**
303 County Highway 8  (61729-9511)
P.O. Box 36  (61729-0036)
PHONE....................309 448-2338
Scott Aberle, *President*
Dale Eastman, *Opers Staff*
Steve Grimes, *Director*
▲ EMP: 120
SQ FT: 75,000
SALES: 19MM  Privately Held
SIC: 3599  Machine shop, jobbing & repair

**(G-7370)**
**R & S STEEL CORPORATION**
301 W Washington St  (61729-9745)
P.O. Box 828  (61729)
PHONE....................309 448-2645
Fax: 309 448-2646
Randy Phelps, *President*
Susan Phelps, *Treasurer*
EMP: 2
SQ FT: 9,000
SALES: 350K  Privately Held
SIC: 3599  Machine shop, jobbing & repair

**(G-7371)**
**RIVER VIEW MOTOR SPORTS INC**
1792 Hillside Rd  (61729-9552)
PHONE....................309 467-4569
James Ely, *Owner*
EMP: 3 EST: 2001
SALES (est): 332.1K  Privately Held
SIC: 3647  7011  Motorcycle lamps; motor inn

# Cooksville
## Mclean County

**(G-7372)**
**CRUTCHER MFG**
202 N Jeffrey St (61730-7516)
PHONE..................309 725-3545
EMP: 2
SALES (est): 211.6K Privately Held
SIC: 3999 Manufacturing industries

**(G-7373)**
**WISSMILLER & EVANS ROAD EQP**
Also Called: Wissmiller Welding
102 S Jeffrey St (61730-7534)
P.O. Box 87 (61730-0087)
PHONE..................309 725-3598
Fax: 309 725-3346
Joseph Wissmiller, *President*
Lori Wissmiller, *Admin Sec*
EMP: 3
SALES: 600K Privately Held
SIC: 5251 7692 5082 1799 Snowblowers; welding repair; road construction equipment; welding on site

# Cordova
## Rock Island County

**(G-7374)**
**3M COMPANY**
22614 Route 84 N (61242-9799)
PHONE..................309 654-2291
Fax: 309 654-1364
Jean Sweeney, *Vice Pres*
Tony Harris, *Research*
James Rutenbeck, *Plant Engr Mgr*
Jeff Brinkman, *Engineer*
Greg Carpenter, *Engineer*
EMP: 332
SALES (corp-wide): 30.1B Publicly Held
SIC: 3841 Surgical instruments & apparatus
PA: 3m Company
 3m Center Bldg 22011w02
 Saint Paul MN 55144
 651 733-1110

**(G-7375)**
**FRYER TO FUEL INC**
26700 171st Ave N (61242-9666)
PHONE..................309 654-2875
Harold A Coers, *President*
▲ EMP: 5
SALES (est): 741.5K Privately Held
SIC: 2869 Fuels

**(G-7376)**
**GOLDEN VALLEY HARDSCAPES LLC**
18715 Route 84 N (61242-9757)
PHONE..................309 654-2261
Thomas Messer, *Principal*
EMP: 2
SALES (est): 218.3K Privately Held
SIC: 2499 5154 Mulch or sawdust products, wood; livestock

**(G-7377)**
**MATCON MANUFACTURING INC**
15509 Route 84 N (61242-9002)
P.O. Box 437, Port Byron (61275-0437)
PHONE..................309 755-1020
Donn Larson, *President*
EMP: 40
SALES (est): 3MM Privately Held
SIC: 3312 Structural shapes & pilings, steel

**(G-7378)**
**MATERIAL CONTROL SYSTEMS INC**
Also Called: Matcon 2
15509 Route 84 N (61242-9002)
PHONE..................309 654-9031
Judy Scott, *Branch Mgr*
David McClanahan, *Comp Spec*
EMP: 7
SALES (corp-wide): 26.8MM Privately Held
WEB: www.matconusa.com
SIC: 5099 2542 Containers: glass, metal or plastic; racks, merchandise display or storage: except wood
PA: Material Control Systems, Inc.
 201 N Main St
 Port Byron IL 61275
 309 523-3774

**(G-7379)**
**MELYX INC (PA)**
Also Called: Xylem
18715 Route 84 N (61242-9757)
PHONE..................309 654-2551
Fax: 309 654-2045
Charles Dornfeld, *President*
Marda Kornhaber, *Director*
▲ EMP: 10
SQ FT: 1,200
SALES (est): 4.8MM Privately Held
SIC: 2499 Mulch, wood & bark

**(G-7380)**
**WESTWAY FEED PRODUCTS LLC**
Also Called: Westway Trading
22220 Route 84 N (61242-9664)
PHONE..................309 654-2211
Fax: 309 654-2422
Steve Pohlmaier, *Manager*
EMP: 15
SALES (corp-wide): 8.2B Privately Held
WEB: www.westway.com
SIC: 2048 2061 Feed supplements; raw cane sugar
HQ: Westway Feed Products Llc
 365 Canal St Ste 2929
 New Orleans LA 70130
 504 934-1850

# Cornell
## Livingston County

**(G-7381)**
**DICKS CUSTOM CABINET SHOP**
202 W Main St (61319)
P.O. Box 148 (61319-0148)
PHONE..................815 358-2663
Fax: 815 358-2797
Richard Leonard, *Owner*
EMP: 5
SQ FT: 5,600
SALES (est): 540.2K Privately Held
SIC: 5712 2511 2434 Cabinet work, custom; wood household furniture; wood kitchen cabinets

**(G-7382)**
**VALLEY VIEW INDUSTRIES INC (PA)**
7551e 2500 N Rd (61319)
PHONE..................815 358-2236
Richard Hatzer, *President*
Joan Mullen, *Vice Pres*
William Kenney, *Treasurer*
EMP: 30 EST: 1951
SALES (est): 7.4MM Privately Held
WEB: www.valleyviewind.com
SIC: 1422 4213 4212 Crushed & broken limestone; lime rock, ground; trucking, except local; local trucking, without storage

# Cortland
## Dekalb County

**(G-7383)**
**ALEXANDER LUMBER CO**
Also Called: Coutland Components
164 S Loves Rd (60112-4038)
PHONE..................815 754-1000
Robert Fitz Gerarld, *Manager*
Mike Henninason, *Manager*
EMP: 5
SALES (corp-wide): 474.7K Privately Held
SIC: 2439 5211 Trusses, except roof: laminated lumber; lumber products
HQ: Alexander Lumber Co.
 515 Redwood Dr
 Aurora IL 60506
 630 844-5123

**(G-7384)**
**ALFREDOS IRON WORKS INC**
280 W Lincoln Hwy (60112-8420)
PHONE..................815 748-1177
Luis A De La Cruz, *President*
EMP: 23
SQ FT: 4,037
SALES: 325K Privately Held
WEB: www.alfredoironworks.com
SIC: 3446 1791 1799 3441 Architectural metalwork; structural steel erection; iron work, structural; fence construction; ornamental metal work; fabricated structural metal

**(G-7385)**
**CORTES ENTERPRISE INC**
Also Called: Quality Transport & Recycling
255 W Lincoln Hwy (60112-4079)
P.O. Box 405, Dekalb (60115-0405)
PHONE..................779 777-1061
Luis Cortes, *President*
EMP: 6
SQ FT: 2,000
SALES (est): 1.7MM Privately Held
SIC: 3559 Recycling machinery

**(G-7386)**
**CUSTOM STONE WRKS ACQSTION INC**
165 W Stephenie Dr (60112-4081)
PHONE..................630 669-1119
Jamie Bastone, *Principal*
EMP: 5
SALES (est): 570.4K Privately Held
SIC: 3281 Cut stone & stone products

**(G-7387)**
**D M O INC**
Also Called: Tailwind Furniture
195 W Stephenie Dr (60112-4081)
P.O. Box 129, Maple Park (60151-0129)
PHONE..................815 756-3638
John Oksas, *President*
EMP: 6
SALES: 100K Privately Held
WEB: www.tailwindfurniture.com
SIC: 3553 Furniture makers' machinery, woodworking

**(G-7388)**
**DUN-RITE TOOL & MACHINE CO**
Also Called: Dun-Rite Tooling
55 W Lincoln Hwy (60112-4078)
PHONE..................815 758-5464
Jack Cress, *CEO*
John Connor, *President*
Dick Cress, *Project Engr*
Deirdre Mihm, *Controller*
Kristine Coffine, *Human Res Dir*
EMP: 30
SQ FT: 30,000
SALES (est): 10MM Privately Held
SIC: 3531 3589 5072 Crushers, grinders & similar equipment; shredders, industrial & commercial; power tools & accessories

**(G-7389)**
**JOHNSON SEAT & CANVAS SHOP**
25 S Somonauk Rd (60112-4147)
P.O. Box 548 (60112-0548)
PHONE..................815 756-2037
Fred Johnson, *President*
Fred F Johnson, *Vice Pres*
EMP: 8 EST: 1947
SQ FT: 5,000
SALES: 490K Privately Held
WEB: www.johnsoncanvas.com
SIC: 2394 Canvas & related products

**(G-7390)**
**JUST PARTS INC (PA)**
121 W Elm Ave (60112-4023)
PHONE..................815 756-2184
David N Waters, *President*
▲ EMP: 7
SQ FT: 15,000
SALES (est): 3.6MM Privately Held
WEB: www.justpartsinc.com
SIC: 3714 5013 Motor vehicle electrical equipment; automotive supplies & parts

**(G-7391)**
**KISHWAUKEE FORGE COMPANY**
520 E N Ave (60112)
P.O. Box 369, Dekalb (60115-0369)
PHONE..................815 758-4451
Fax: 815 758-2975
Donald G Jones, *President*
Jeffrey T Jones, *Admin Sec*
EMP: 20
SQ FT: 50,000
SALES (est): 2.9MM
SALES (corp-wide): 18.4MM Privately Held
SIC: 3462 3423 Automotive & internal combustion engine forgings; hand & edge tools
PA: Dekalb Forge Company
 1832 Pleasant St
 Dekalb IL 60115
 815 756-3538

**(G-7392)**
**KRIESE MFG**
231 N Juniper St (60112-4132)
PHONE..................815 748-2683
Patrick Kriese, *President*
Wendy Kriese, *Vice Pres*
EMP: 2
SALES (est): 272.7K Privately Held
SIC: 3548 3999 Welding & cutting apparatus & accessories; manufacturing industries

**(G-7393)**
**MICHAEL BURZA**
Also Called: AM PM Printers
122 E Meadow Dr (60112-4136)
P.O. Box 267 (60112-0267)
PHONE..................815 909-0233
Michael Burza, *Principal*
EMP: 2
SALES (est): 215.6K Privately Held
SIC: 2752 Commercial printing, lithographic

**(G-7394)**
**POWER EQUIPMENT COMPANY**
211 W Stephenie Dr (60112-4082)
PHONE..................815 754-4090
Fax: 815 754-4280
David E Olson, *President*
David H Olson, *President*
Richard Olson, *Vice Pres*
Eric Olson, *Manager*
EMP: 22
SQ FT: 28,000
SALES (est): 21.8MM Privately Held
WEB: www.peco1948.com
SIC: 5083 3679 Lawn & garden machinery & equipment; electronic loads & power supplies

**(G-7395)**
**SUNNY DAY DISTRIBUTING INC**
76 E Meadow Dr (60112-4137)
PHONE..................630 779-8466
Jim Cunningham, *President*
EMP: 1 EST: 2015
SALES: 500K Privately Held
SIC: 2099 Tortillas, fresh or refrigerated

**(G-7396)**
**WALT MACHINE AND TOOL INC**
302 W Lincoln Hwy Ste 6 (60112-7916)
PHONE..................815 754-6484
Fax: 815 754-9078
Dan Walt, *President*
Karla Walt, *Admin Sec*
EMP: 4
SQ FT: 2,400
SALES (est): 481.1K Privately Held
SIC: 3599 Machine shop, jobbing & repair

# GEOGRAPHIC SECTION

Countryside - Cook County (G-7421)

## Cottage Hills
### Madison County

**(G-7397)**
**GM SCRAP METALS**
220 Franklin Ave (62018-1273)
PHONE..................................618 259-8570
Margaret Ivanuck, *Owner*
Paul Ivanuck, *Manager*
EMP: 5
SALES (est): 439.2K  **Privately Held**
SIC: 5093  4953  3341  Ferrous metal scrap & waste; recycling, waste materials; secondary nonferrous metals

## Coulterville
### Randolph County

**(G-7398)**
**BRIAN HOBBS**
Also Called: Handy Helper Fencing
207 E Mill St (62237-1741)
PHONE..................................618 758-1303
Brian Hobbs, *Owner*
EMP: 1
SALES: 230K  **Privately Held**
SIC: 3446  Fences, gates, posts & flagpoles

**(G-7399)**
**CORRPAK  INC**
Also Called: Fabcorr
1231 State Route 13 (62237-3326)
PHONE..................................618 758-2755
Tom Talbert, *Manager*
EMP: 3
SALES (corp-wide): 3.4MM  **Privately Held**
WEB: www.corrpak.com
SIC: 3444  Sheet metalwork
PA: Corrpak, Inc.
    719 Spirit 40 Park Dr
    Chesterfield MO 63005
    636 537-2885

**(G-7400)**
**HNRC DISSOLUTION CO**
12626 Sarah Rd (62237-1916)
PHONE..................................618 758-4501
EMP: 250
SALES (corp-wide): 405.9MM  **Privately Held**
SIC: 1221  Bituminous Coal/Lignite Surface Mining
PA: Hnrc Dissolution Co
    201 E Main St 100
    Lexington KY 40507
    606 327-5450

**(G-7401)**
**LARRYS BETTER BUILT BATTERY**
9321 Deer Run Ln (62237-1943)
PHONE..................................618 758-2011
Gina Burns, *President*
EMP: 2
SQ FT: 100
SALES (est): 210K  **Privately Held**
SIC: 3692  5531  Primary batteries, dry & wet; batteries, automotive & truck

**(G-7402)**
**PEABODY COAL COMPANY**
Also Called: Gateway Mine
13101 Zeigler 11 Rd (62237-2046)
PHONE..................................618 758-2395
Greg Boyce, *Branch Mgr*
EMP: 197
SALES (corp-wide): 4.7B  **Publicly Held**
SIC: 1222  Bituminous coal-underground mining
HQ: Peabody Coal Company
    701 Market St
    Saint Louis MO 63101
    314 342-3400

## Country Club Hills
### Cook County

**(G-7403)**
**AMITY HOSPITAL SERVICES INC**
4921 173rd St Ste 2 (60478-2026)
PHONE..................................708 206-3970
Fax: 708 206-3972
Edward Button, *President*
EMP: 4
SQ FT: 2,500
SALES: 400K  **Privately Held**
SIC: 3821  7699  5999  Sterilizers; hospital equipment repair services; hospital equipment & supplies

**(G-7404)**
**ANHEUSER-BUSCH  LLC**
17751 Hillcrest Dr (60478-4930)
PHONE..................................708 206-2881
W Baker, *Manager*
EMP: 156  **Privately Held**
WEB: www.hispanicbud.com
SIC: 2082  Beer (alcoholic beverage)
HQ: Anheuser-Busch, Llc
    1 Busch Pl
    Saint Louis MO 63118
    314 632-6777

**(G-7405)**
**COOK JV PRINTING**
4061 183rd St (60478-5306)
PHONE..................................708 799-0007
J Cook, *Principal*
EMP: 11
SALES (est): 1.4MM  **Privately Held**
SIC: 2752  Commercial printing, lithographic

**(G-7406)**
**DA CLOSET**
4139 167th St (60478-2035)
PHONE..................................708 206-1414
EMP: 5 EST: 2009
SALES (est): 606K  **Privately Held**
SIC: 2329  Knickers, dress (separate): men's & boys'

**(G-7407)**
**GREAT LAKES LIFTING**
4910 Wilshire Blvd (60478-3153)
PHONE..................................815 931-4825
Don Brooks, *Owner*
Steven Brooks, *Sales Mgr*
EMP: 5
SALES (est): 674.6K  **Privately Held**
SIC: 3272  Building materials, except block or brick: concrete

**(G-7408)**
**HARTS TOP AND CABINET SHOP**
Also Called: Harts Top Shop
4941 173rd St Ste 1 (60478-2030)
PHONE..................................708 957-4666
Fax: 708 957-4941
Kenneth Hartsfield, *Owner*
EMP: 5 EST: 1979
SQ FT: 8,000
SALES (est): 750K  **Privately Held**
SIC: 2541  5211  Table or counter tops, plastic laminated; cabinets, kitchen

**(G-7409)**
**IODON INC**
18610 John Ave (60478-5298)
P.O. Box 21, Dolton (60419-0021)
PHONE..................................708 799-4062
Iona J Boersma, *President*
EMP: 3
SALES (est): 348.8K  **Privately Held**
SIC: 3432  Plumbing fixture fittings & trim

**(G-7410)**
**MIDWEST SIGN & LIGHTING INC**
4910 Wilshire Blvd (60478-3153)
PHONE..................................708 365-5555
Billy Don Brooks, *President*
Frank Nielson, *Vice Pres*
EMP: 7
SQ FT: 3,000
SALES (est): 987.5K  **Privately Held**
SIC: 3993  3648  2752  Signs & advertising specialties; lighting equipment; commercial printing, lithographic

## Countryside
### Cook County

**(G-7411)**
**ADVANCE WELDING & EQUIPMENT**
6688 Joliet Rd (60525-4575)
PHONE..................................630 759-3334
Heather Meyers, *President*
EMP: 16
SALES (est): 1.4MM  **Privately Held**
SIC: 3449  Bars, concrete reinforcing: fabricated steel

**(G-7412)**
**AIRGAS USA LLC**
5235 9th Ave (60525-3629)
PHONE..................................708 354-0813
Veronica Cajkusic, *Plant Mgr*
Veronica Caljkusic, *Branch Mgr*
EMP: 23
SALES (corp-wide): 163.9MM  **Privately Held**
WEB: www.airgas.com
SIC: 5169  5047  2813  Industrial gases; medical & hospital equipment; industrial gases
HQ: Airgas Usa, Llc
    259 N Radnor Chester Rd # 100
    Radnor PA 19087
    610 687-5253

**(G-7413)**
**AIRGAS USA LLC**
5220 East Ave (60525-3133)
PHONE..................................708 482-8400
Fax: 708 579-6602
Patrick Verschelde, *COO*
Rick Udischas, *Research*
David Johns, *Manager*
Christine E Boisrobert, *Info Tech Mgr*
Carlos Helou, *Technology*
EMP: 120
SALES (corp-wide): 163.9MM  **Privately Held**
WEB: www.airliquide.com
SIC: 2813  Industrial gases
HQ: Airgas Usa, Llc
    259 N Radnor Chester Rd # 100
    Radnor PA 19087
    610 687-5253

**(G-7414)**
**AMERICAN GAMING & ELEC INC (HQ)**
Also Called: Wells-Gardner
9500 W 55th St Ste A (60525-7125)
P.O. Box 689, La Grange  (60525-0689)
PHONE..................................708 290-2100
Fax: 708 290-2200
Anthony Spier, *President*
Mike Rudowicz, *Exec VP*
Mike Mazzaroli, *Vice Pres*
Brad Paul, *Engineer*
James F Brace, *CFO*
▲ EMP: 3
SALES (est): 899.2K
SALES (corp-wide): 6.1MM  **Publicly Held**
SIC: 3575  Computer terminals, monitors & components
PA: Ag&E Holdings Inc.
    223 Pratt St
    Hammonton NJ 08037
    609 704-3000

**(G-7415)**
**BARE DEVELOPMENT  INC**
Also Called: Golf Trucks
5425 9th Ave (60525-3604)
PHONE..................................708 352-2273
William Moldenhauer, *President*
Theresa Demetry, *Vice Pres*
Jeff Mielke, *Vice Pres*
Jefferey Mielkey, *Treasurer*
EMP: 10
SALES: 3MM  **Privately Held**
SIC: 3674  Light emitting diodes

**(G-7416)**
**CASA DE MONTE CRISTO**
1332 W 55th St (60525-6541)
PHONE..................................708 352-6668
Sam Julio, *Principal*
EMP: 2
SALES (est): 248.8K  **Privately Held**
SIC: 2121  Cigars

**(G-7417)**
**CHICAGO CHAIN AND TRANSM CO (PA)**
650 E Plainfield Rd (60525-6914)
P.O. Box 705, La Grange  (60525-0705)
PHONE..................................630 482-9000
Fax: 708 482-3021
James D Schwarz, *President*
Ron Triska, *Vice Pres*
Carrie Guinta, *Controller*
Eileen Stratton, *Accountant*
Paul Fletcher, *Sales Mgr*
EMP: 20
SQ FT: 17,500
SALES (est): 11.6MM  **Privately Held**
SIC: 5085  5084  5063  3535  Power transmission equipment & apparatus; bearings, bushings, wheels & gears; industrial machinery & equipment; electrical apparatus & equipment; conveyors & conveying equipment

**(G-7418)**
**CONTAINER HDLG SYSTEMS CORP**
621 E Plainfield Rd (60525-6913)
PHONE..................................708 482-9900
Fax: 708 482-8960
John C Nalbach, *President*
Jerry E Norbut, *Vice Pres*
Jerry Glikis, *Purch Agent*
Ming Huang, *Engineer*
Frank Berndt, *Design Engr*
EMP: 46
SQ FT: 22,000
SALES (est): 13.7MM  **Privately Held**
WEB: www.containerhandlingsystems.com
SIC: 3535  Conveyors & conveying equipment

**(G-7419)**
**COOPERS HAWK PRODUCTION LLC**
430 E Plainfield Rd (60525-6910)
PHONE..................................708 839-2920
Dee Sortino, *CFO*
▲ EMP: 6
SALES (est): 760.2K
SALES (corp-wide): 305.8MM  **Privately Held**
WEB: www.chwinery.com
SIC: 2084  Wines
PA: Cooper's Hawk Intermediate Holding, Llc
    5325 9th Ave
    Countryside IL 60525
    708 839-2920

**(G-7420)**
**COOPERS HWK INTERMEDTE HOLDNG (PA)**
Also Called: Coopers Hawk Winery & Rest
5325 9th Ave (60525-3602)
PHONE..................................708 839-2920
Emily Dock, *General Mgr*
Matthew Foody, *General Mgr*
Ryan Quisenberry, *General Mgr*
Ben Hummer, *Vice Pres*
Tara Snyder, *Vice Pres*
EMP: 136
SALES (est): 305.8MM  **Privately Held**
SIC: 8741  2084  5182  5812  Restaurant management; wines; wine; eating places

**(G-7421)**
**COOPERS HWK INTERMEDTE HOLDNG**
430 E Plainfield Rd (60525-6910)
PHONE..................................708 215-5674
EMP: 14
SALES (corp-wide): 305.8MM  **Privately Held**
SIC: 8741  2084  5182  5812  Restaurant management; wines; wine; eating places

# Countryside - Cook County (G-7422)

PA: Cooper's Hawk Intermediate Holding, Llc
5325 9th Ave
Countryside IL 60525
708 839-2920

**(G-7422)**
**E FORMELLA & SONS INC**
Also Called: Enrico Formella
411 E Plainfield Rd (60525-6909)
PHONE ................................ 708 598-0909
Randy Formella, *President*
Kathy Moore, *Manager*
Kathy Formella, *Admin Sec*
▲ EMP: 20
SQ FT: 33,000
SALES (est): 4.6MM Privately Held
WEB: www.iwanthotpeppers.com
SIC: 2035 Pickled fruits & vegetables

**(G-7423)**
**EAGLE SCREEN PRINT INDS INC**
5326 East Ave (60525-3134)
PHONE ................................ 708 579-1739
Fax: 708 579-1739
Mahendra Patel, *President*
Jeff Weeden, *Sales Staff*
EMP: 15
SQ FT: 9,300
SALES (est): 1.5MM Privately Held
WEB: www.eaglescreenprinting.com
SIC: 2759 Screen printing

**(G-7424)**
**FGFI LLC**
411 E Plainfield Rd (60525-6909)
PHONE ................................ 708 598-0909
Kathy Formella, *Mng Member*
EMP: 38
SALES (est): 2MM Privately Held
SIC: 2079 2035 Cooking oils, except corn: vegetable refined; seasonings & sauces, except tomato & dry

**(G-7425)**
**G BLANDO JEWELERS INC**
Also Called: Blando's Marry ME Jewelry
3 Countryside Plz (60525-3980)
PHONE ................................ 630 627-7963
Gino Blando, *President*
EMP: 4
SQ FT: 3,000
SALES: 865K Privately Held
SIC: 5944 3911 Jewelry stores; jewelry, precious metal

**(G-7426)**
**GALL MACHINE CO**
9640 Joliet Rd (60525-4138)
PHONE ................................ 708 352-2800
Fax: 708 352-2802
John G Harper, *President*
John A Harper, *Vice Pres*
John Zoiss, *Purchasing*
Tiffeney K Harper, *Treasurer*
Mary C Harper, *Admin Sec*
EMP: 10
SQ FT: 15,000
SALES (est): 1.9MM Privately Held
WEB: www.gallmachine.com
SIC: 3496 Miscellaneous fabricated wire products

**(G-7427)**
**GARY W BERGER**
25 Birch St (60525-4170)
P.O. Box 727, La Grange (60525-0727)
PHONE ................................ 708 588-0200
Fax: 708 588-0223
Gary W Berger, *Owner*
EMP: 3
SQ FT: 1,500
SALES: 950K Privately Held
WEB: www.garysbergermd.com
SIC: 8742 3364 Manufacturing management consultant; lead & zinc die-castings

**(G-7428)**
**GOODCO PRODUCTS LLC**
6688 Joliet Rd Ste 185 (60525-4575)
PHONE ................................ 630 258-6384
Jon Bradley,
EMP: 4
SQ FT: 1,000
SALES (est): 547.9K Privately Held
SIC: 3421 3089 5199 Table cutlery, except with handles of metal; clothespins, plastic; matches

**(G-7429)**
**HOGAN WOODWORK INC**
5328 East Ave (60525-3134)
PHONE ................................ 708 354-4525
Fax: 708 354-4543
Martin Hogan, *President*
Joyce Hogan, *Admin Sec*
EMP: 6
SQ FT: 6,200
SALES: 800K Privately Held
SIC: 2431 Millwork; doors & door parts & trim, wood; moldings & baseboards, ornamental & trim; interior & ornamental woodwork & trim

**(G-7430)**
**HOLLYMATIC CORPORATION**
600 E Plainfield Rd (60525-6900)
PHONE ................................ 708 579-3700
Fax: 708 579-1057
James D Azzar, *President*
Marilyn Krische, *General Mgr*
J Wacaser, *Mfg Mgr*
Robert Grebic, *Purch Agent*
Marilyn Kirsche, *Human Res Mgr*
▲ EMP: 55 EST: 1937
SQ FT: 55,000
SALES (est): 35.8MM Privately Held
WEB: www.hollymatic.com
SIC: 5113 3556 2672 Industrial & personal service paper; meat processing machinery; mixers, commercial, food; grinders, commercial, food; sausage stuffers; coated & laminated paper

**(G-7431)**
**HONEY FLUFF DOUGHNUTS**
6566 Joliet Rd (60525-4649)
PHONE ................................ 708 579-1826
Vimala Gupta, *President*
EMP: 3
SQ FT: 1,000
SALES (est): 150K Privately Held
SIC: 5461 2051 Doughnuts; doughnuts, except frozen

**(G-7432)**
**HOUSE OF COLOR**
9912 W 55th St (60525-3612)
PHONE ................................ 708 352-3222
Fax: 708 352-2072
Donald Musillami, *Owner*
EMP: 10
SALES (est): 841K Privately Held
SIC: 2499 5039 Picture & mirror frames, wood; glass construction materials

**(G-7433)**
**HUNT ENTERPRISES INC**
Also Called: Hunt Printing & Graphics
5542 S La Grange Rd (60525-3668)
PHONE ................................ 708 354-8464
Doug May, *President*
William Hunt, *Director*
EMP: 6
SQ FT: 2,000
SALES: 500K Privately Held
WEB: www.huntprinting.com
SIC: 2752 Commercial printing, offset

**(G-7434)**
**INFINITY CMMNCATIONS GROUP LTD**
Also Called: Infinity Signs
5350 East Ave (60525-3134)
PHONE ................................ 708 352-1086
Brian Lappin, *President*
Russell Nicoletti, *Vice Pres*
EMP: 10
SQ FT: 10,000
SALES: 1.4MM Privately Held
SIC: 3993 Signs & advertising specialties

**(G-7435)**
**JEWEL OSCO INC**
Also Called: Jewel-Osco 3154
5545 S Brainard Ave (60525-3542)
PHONE ................................ 708 352-0120
Fax: 708 354-2733
Mary Pruzs, *President*
EMP: 225
SALES (corp-wide): 58.8B Privately Held
WEB: www.jewelosco.com
SIC: 5411 2051 Supermarkets, chain; bread, cake & related products
HQ: Jewel Osco, Inc.
150 E Pierce Rd Ste 200
Itasca IL 60143
630 948-6000

**(G-7436)**
**JOHN R NALBACH ENGINEERING CO**
621 E Plainfield Rd (60525-6913)
PHONE ................................ 708 579-9100
Fax: 708 579-0122
John C Nalbach, *President*
Phil Testa, *VP Mfg*
Tony Anton, *Purchasing*
Thad Przybylowski, *Engineer*
Kevin Loeb, *Project Engr*
EMP: 23 EST: 1945
SQ FT: 74,000
SALES (est): 7.5MM Privately Held
WEB: www.nalbach.com
SIC: 3565 Packing & wrapping machinery

**(G-7437)**
**MINUTEMAN PRESS**
6670 S Brainard Ave # 203 (60525-4621)
PHONE ................................ 630 541-9122
Fax: 630 655-2575
Greg Siedlecki, *Owner*
EMP: 6
SQ FT: 1,800
SALES: 500K Privately Held
SIC: 2752 2791 2789 2759 Commercial printing, lithographic; typesetting; bookbinding & related work; commercial printing

**(G-7438)**
**MINUTEMAN PRESS OF COUNTRYSIDE**
6566 Joliet Rd (60525-4649)
PHONE ................................ 708 354-2190
Fax: 708 354-0454
Christopher Zurowski, *President*
Julie Zurowski, *Vice Pres*
Veronica Zurowski, *Treasurer*
George Zurowski, *Shareholder*
EMP: 4
SQ FT: 1,000
SALES: 480K Privately Held
SIC: 2752 Commercial printing, lithographic

**(G-7439)**
**MITSUBISHI ELECTRIC US INC**
Also Called: Mitsubshi Elevators Escalators
5218 Dansher Rd (60525-3122)
PHONE ................................ 708 354-2900
Fax: 708 354-4261
Bill Zornow, *Opers Mgr*
Kirk R Maier, *Sales Staff*
Jared Elfvin, *Manager*
EMP: 30
SALES (corp-wide): 37.3B Privately Held
WEB: www.diamond-vision.com
SIC: 3534 Elevators & equipment; escalators, passenger & freight
HQ: Mitsubishi Electric Us, Inc.
5900 Katella Ave Ste A
Cypress CA 90630
714 220-2500

**(G-7440)**
**PELSTAR LLC**
Also Called: Health O Meter Professional
9500 W 55th St Ste C (60525-7110)
PHONE ................................ 708 377-0600
Fax: 708 377-0601
Rawley Cashen, *Controller*
Rolly Cashen, *Controller*
Janet Chambers, *Human Resources*
Chris Manning, *Marketing Staff*
Dan J Maeir,
◆ EMP: 20
SQ FT: 160,000
SALES (est): 5.6MM Privately Held
WEB: www.pelouze.com
SIC: 3596 Scales & balances, except laboratory

**(G-7441)**
**ROLLSTOCK INC**
600 E Plainfield Rd (60525-6914)
PHONE ................................ 708 579-3700
James D Azzar, *President*
Donna Enochs, *Credit Mgr*
Sue Briones, *Office Mgr*
Sue Allen, *Administration*
EMP: 6
SALES (est): 830.7K Privately Held
SIC: 3565 Packaging machinery

**(G-7442)**
**SKI SEAL COATING INC**
7100 Pleasantdale Dr (60525-5071)
PHONE ................................ 708 246-5656
Richard Zwolinski, *President*
EMP: 6
SALES (est): 1MM Privately Held
SIC: 2891 Adhesives & sealants

**(G-7443)**
**SOKOL AND COMPANY**
5315 Dansher Rd (60525-3192)
PHONE ................................ 708 482-8250
Fax: 708 482-9750
John S Novak Jr, *President*
Michael Novak, *Production*
Myra Loughrie, *Research*
Ken Crane, *Engineer*
Mathew McNulty, *CFO*
◆ EMP: 100 EST: 1907
SQ FT: 110,000
SALES (est): 44.5MM Privately Held
WEB: www.solofoods.com
SIC: 2099 2033 5149 2091 Cake fillings, except fruit; peanut butter; spaghetti & other pasta sauce: packaged in cans, jars, etc.; jams, jellies & preserves: packaged in cans, jars, etc.; sauces; canned & cured fish & seafoods

**(G-7444)**
**SOLO FOODS**
5315 Dansher Rd (60525-3101)
PHONE ................................ 800 328-7656
EMP: 3 EST: 2012
SALES (est): 220.4K Privately Held
SIC: 2099 Desserts, ready-to-mix

**(G-7445)**
**SUPREME SCREW PRODUCTS**
5227 Dansher Rd (60525-3123)
PHONE ................................ 708 579-3500
Fax: 708 579-3560
EMP: 3 EST: 2013
SALES (est): 192.4K Privately Held
SIC: 3451 Screw machine products

**(G-7446)**
**T & H LEMONT INC**
5118 Dansher Rd (60525-6906)
PHONE ................................ 708 482-1800
Fax: 708 482-1801
John Hillis, *President*
Glenn Hoffmann, *President*
Walter Heller, *Vice Pres*
Thomas Nandory, *Project Mgr*
Mike Poidomani, *Purch Mgr*
▲ EMP: 80
SQ FT: 68,000
SALES (est): 18.5MM
SALES (corp-wide): 907.7MM Privately Held
WEB: www.thlemont.com
SIC: 3544 3325 Special dies, tools, jigs & fixtures; steel foundries
PA: Rowan Technologies, Inc.
10 Indel Ave
Rancocas NJ 08073

**(G-7447)**
**TRINITY BRAND INDUSTRIES INC**
5342 East Ave (60525-3134)
P.O. Box 560, La Grange (60525-0560)
PHONE ................................ 708 482-4980
Ron Supeter, *President*
EMP: 10
SQ FT: 6,000
SALES (est): 890K Privately Held
WEB: www.trinitybrand.com
SIC: 3829 Gauging instruments, thickness ultrasonic

## GEOGRAPHIC SECTION

**(G-7448)**
**TRU VUE INC (HQ)**
9400 W 55th St  (60525-3636)
PHONE .................................. 708 485-5080
Fax: 708 485-5980
Jane Boyce, *President*
Thomas Graham, *Vice Pres*
Jim Hayes, *Vice Pres*
Joe Maxwell, *Vice Pres*
Bob Kozak, *Safety Dir*
◆ EMP: 110
SQ FT: 300,000
SALES (est): 74.8MM
SALES (corp-wide): 1.1B **Publicly Held**
WEB: www.tru-vue.com
SIC: 3211  3496  Picture glass; mats & matting
PA: Apogee Enterprises, Inc.
     4400 W 78th St Ste 520
     Minneapolis MN 55435
     952 835-1874

**(G-7449)**
**VEE PAK LLC**
5321 Dansher Rd  (60525-3125)
PHONE .................................. 708 482-8881
Fax: 708 482-3343
Scott Almquist, *CEO*
Jennifer Lord, *Research*
Brandon Bayston, *Treasurer*
Paul Morrison, *Mktg Dir*
Beverly Pleasant, *Director*
EMP: 150
SALES (corp-wide): 250MM **Privately Held**
WEB: www.veepak.com
SIC: 2844  Cosmetic preparations
PA: Vee Pak, Llc
     6710 River Rd
     Hodgkins IL 60525
     708 482-8881

**(G-7450)**
**VINYL GRAPHICS INC**
Also Called: Sign-A-Rama
35 E Plainfield Rd Ste 2  (60525-3086)
PHONE .................................. 708 579-1234
Shibu Kurian, *President*
EMP: 3
SQ FT: 1,100
SALES (est): 240K **Privately Held**
SIC: 3993  Signs & advertising specialties

**(G-7451)**
**WELCH PACKAGING LLC**
5300 Dansher Rd  (60525-3124)
PHONE .................................. 708 813-1520
Fax: 708 813-1539
Doug Poulston, *Branch Mgr*
EMP: 100
SALES (corp-wide): 160.2MM **Privately Held**
SIC: 2653  Corrugated boxes, partitions, display items, sheets & pad
HQ: Welch Packaging, Llc
     1020 Herman St
     Elkhart IN 46516
     574 295-2460

### Cowden
*Shelby County*

**(G-7452)**
**MILLERS FERTILIZER & FEED**
300 E Cedar St  (62422-1000)
Rr # 1 Box 91  (62422-4085)
PHONE .................................. 217 783-6321
Steve Miller, *Owner*
EMP: 14
SQ FT: 750
SALES (est): 1.7MM **Privately Held**
SIC: 5191  2875  Fertilizer & fertilizer materials; feed; limestone, agricultural; fertilizers, mixing only

### Creal Springs
*Williamson County*

**(G-7453)**
**BELLA TERRA WINERY LLC**
Also Called: Bella T Winery
755 Parker City Rd  (62922-1013)
PHONE .................................. 618 658-8882
Edward Russell,
EMP: 12
SQ FT: 150
SALES (est): 720K **Privately Held**
SIC: 2084  0172  5921  5182  Wines; grapes; wine; wine; recreational vehicle rental

**(G-7454)**
**RIX ENTERPRISE INC**
5891 Saraville Rd  (62922-2204)
PHONE .................................. 618 996-8237
Fax: 618 996-8238
Jason Rix, *President*
Kristi Rix, *Admin Sec*
EMP: 6  EST: 1997
SALES: 300K **Privately Held**
SIC: 3599  Machine & other job shop work

### Crescent City
*Iroquois County*

**(G-7455)**
**AILEYS 3 WELDING**
Rr 24 Box West  (60928)
PHONE .................................. 815 683-2181
Norman Ailey, *Managing Prtnr*
Randy Strom, *Partner*
Bill Weakley, *Partner*
EMP: 3
SALES (est): 216.2K **Privately Held**
SIC: 7692  Welding repair

**(G-7456)**
**SCHEIWES PRINT SHOP**
Also Called: Scheiwes Print and Christn Sup
407 Main St  (60928-8082)
P.O. Box 57  (60928-0057)
PHONE .................................. 815 683-2398
Glenn Scheiwe, *Partner*
Irma Scheiwe, *Partner*
EMP: 3  EST: 1972
SQ FT: 1,875
SALES (est): 394.3K **Privately Held**
SIC: 2752  2759  5999  2789  Commercial printing, offset; screen printing; letterpress printing; religious goods; bookbinding & related work; automotive & apparel trimmings

### Crest Hill
*Will County*

**(G-7457)**
**AMERICAN MARBLE & GRANITE INC**
1930 Donmaur Dr  (60403-1905)
PHONE .................................. 815 741-1710
Fax: 815 741-1712
Phillip Varsek, *President*
EMP: 2
SALES (est): 564.6K **Privately Held**
SIC: 5032  3281  Marble building stone; cut stone & stone products

**(G-7458)**
**FAB WERKS INC**
911 Brian Dr  (60403-2484)
PHONE .................................. 815 724-0317
Fax: 815 724-0318
Kenneth Charles Krier, *President*
Joeseph Krier, *Manager*
Rebecca Lyn Krier, *Admin Sec*
EMP: 25  EST: 1998
SQ FT: 3,000
SALES (est): 5.4MM **Privately Held**
WEB: www.fabwerksinc.com
SIC: 3444  Sheet metalwork

**(G-7459)**
**J M PRINTERS INC (PA)**
Also Called: J M Office Products
510 Pasadena Ave  (60403-2406)
PHONE .................................. 815 727-1579
Fax: 815 727-2605
Glen Conklin, *President*
Mark Conklin, *Treasurer*
EMP: 12  EST: 1965
SQ FT: 7,500
SALES (est): 1.5MM **Privately Held**
SIC: 2752  5112  Commercial printing, lithographic; office supplies

**(G-7460)**
**JOLIET PATTERN WORKS INC**
508 Pasadena Ave  (60403-2406)
PHONE .................................. 815 726-5373
Andrew D Wood, *President*
Robert Benbow, *Vice Pres*
Amy Willingston, *Manager*
EMP: 53  EST: 1946
SQ FT: 67,000
SALES (est): 14MM **Privately Held**
WEB: www.jolietpattern.com
SIC: 2759  3993  Screen printing; displays & cutouts, window & lobby

**(G-7461)**
**JOLIET TECHNOLOGIES LLC**
1724 Tomich Ct  (60403-0940)
PHONE .................................. 815 725-9696
Fax: 815 725-9393
Greg Thornton, *Prdtn Mgr*
John Gierich, *QA Dir*
Clay Johnson,
Gregory Hill,
EMP: 8
SQ FT: 3,000
SALES (est): 1.6MM **Privately Held**
WEB: www.joliettech.com
SIC: 3625  Control equipment, electric

**(G-7462)**
**LEGACY 3D LLC**
2020 N Raynor Ave  (60403-2700)
PHONE .................................. 815 727-5454
Jessica Flengg, *Manager*
Paul Ciesiun,
Walter Lee Mauney,
Richard K Rudie,
EMP: 10
SALES (est): 1MM **Privately Held**
SIC: 3993  7389  Signs & advertising specialties; design services

**(G-7463)**
**METALOCK CORPORATION (PA)**
2021 N Raynor Ave  (60403-2487)
PHONE .................................. 815 666-1560
Fax: 708 839-1603
Tom Breaux, *President*
Frederick W Lewis, *Corp Secy*
EMP: 12
SQ FT: 10,000
SALES (est): 1.3MM **Privately Held**
WEB: www.casting-repairs.com
SIC: 7692  Cracked casting repair

**(G-7464)**
**MORENO AND SONS INC**
2366 Plainfield Rd  (60403-1847)
PHONE .................................. 815 725-8600
Mario Moreno, *President*
EMP: 8
SALES (est): 938K **Privately Held**
SIC: 3949  Gymnasium equipment

**(G-7465)**
**RAILWAY & INDUSTRIAL SVCS INC**
Also Called: Railway & Industrial Spc
2201 N Center St  (60403-2521)
PHONE .................................. 815 726-4224
Fax: 815 726-4265
Richard Vetter, *President*
Daniel T Schwarz, *Vice Pres*
Greg Camacho, *Purch Dir*
Richard E Vetter Jr, *Admin Sec*
EMP: 125
SQ FT: 10,000
SALES (est): 23.4MM **Privately Held**
WEB: www.risinc.com
SIC: 3743  5088  Railroad equipment; railroad car rebuilding; tank freight cars & car equipment; railroad equipment & supplies

**(G-7466)**
**RICH PRODUCTS CORPORATION**
21511 Division St  (60403-2020)
PHONE .................................. 815 729-4509
EMP: 750
SALES (corp-wide): 3.2B **Privately Held**
SIC: 2053  Frozen bakery products, except bread
PA: Rich Products Corporation
     1 Robert Rich Way
     Buffalo NY 14213
     716 878-8000

**(G-7467)**
**SAFELITE GLASS CORP**
Also Called: Safelite Autoglass
2406 Plainfield Rd  (60403-1454)
PHONE .................................. 815 436-6333
Mike Litwiller, *Manager*
EMP: 3
SALES (corp-wide): 2.9B **Privately Held**
SIC: 3231  Windshields, glass: made from purchased glass
HQ: Safelite Glass Corp.
     7400 Safelite Way
     Columbus OH 43235
     614 210-9000

**(G-7468)**
**STELLATO PRINTING INC (PA)**
1801 Jared Dr  (60403-0922)
PHONE .................................. 815 725-1057
Anthony Stellato, *President*
Ericka Zacek, *Production*
EMP: 2
SALES (est): 345.5K **Privately Held**
WEB: www.stellatoprinting.com
SIC: 2752  Commercial printing, lithographic

**(G-7469)**
**TEMPER ENTERPRISES INC**
Also Called: Precision Printing
2218 Plainfield Rd Ste B  (60403-1880)
PHONE .................................. 815 553-0374
Tony Temper, *President*
EMP: 1
SQ FT: 2,800
SALES: 200K **Privately Held**
SIC: 2752  2759  Commercial printing, offset; commercial printing

**(G-7470)**
**USA HOIST COMPANY INC (HQ)**
1000 Sak Dr Unit A  (60403-2562)
PHONE .................................. 815 740-1890
Fax: 815 740-1810
Robert Bailey III, *President*
Robert Bailey IV, *Vice Pres*
Justin Messer, *CFO*
M Cullen Bailey, *Admin Sec*
▲ EMP: 35
SQ FT: 20,000
SALES (est): 23.3MM
SALES (corp-wide): 48.3MM **Privately Held**
WEB: www.usahoist.com
SIC: 5082  7353  3531  Construction & mining machinery; general construction machinery & equipment; heavy construction equipment rental; aerial work platforms: hydraulic/elec. truck/carrier mounted
PA: Mid-American Elevator Company, Inc.
     820 N Wolcott Ave
     Chicago IL 60622
     773 486-6900

### Creston
*Ogle County*

**(G-7471)**
**DAVIDSON GRAIN INCORPORATED**
Also Called: Davidson Farms of Creston
5960 S Woodlawn Rd  (60113)
PHONE .................................. 815 384-3208
Fax: 815 384-4600
Ronald W Davidson, *President*
John Davidson, *Vice Pres*
Hadley Forbes, *Treasurer*
Carol Davidson, *Admin Sec*
EMP: 45

**Creston - Ogle County (G-7472)**      GEOGRAPHIC SECTION

SQ FT: 800
SALES (est): 2.3MM **Privately Held**
SIC: **4212** 3523 Local trucking, without storage; elevators, farm

**(G-7472)**
**HUEBER LLC (PA)**
110 S Main St (60113)
P.O. Box 85 (60113-0085)
PHONE.................................815 393-4879
Fax: 815 384-3751
Jon Hueber, *President*
Joe Male, *Business Mgr*
Jan Hueber, *Vice Pres*
EMP: 12
SQ FT: 4,800
SALES (est): 11.4MM **Privately Held**
WEB: www.hueber.com
SIC: **5191** 5153 2048 Farm supplies; feed; seeds: field, garden & flower; grain elevators; prepared feeds

## Crestwood
### Cook County

**(G-7473)**
**ACCURATE PRINTING INC**
4749 136th St (60445-1968)
PHONE.................................708 824-0058
Fax: 708 824-0212
Thomas J Doyle, *President*
▲ EMP: 3 EST: 1996
SALES (est): 588.4K **Privately Held**
SIC: **2759** Commercial printing

**(G-7474)**
**ALL AMERICAN TROPHY KING INC**
13811 Cicero Ave (60445-1826)
PHONE.................................708 597-2121
Fax: 708 582-3399
James Seidel,
Geraldine Seidel, *Corp Secy*
Chuck Tate, *CTO*
EMP: 10
SQ FT: 14,000
SALES: 1.2MM **Privately Held**
WEB: www.allamericantrophy.com
SIC: **3914** 5094 5999 Trophies; trophies; trophies & plaques

**(G-7475)**
**ALLIED MACHINE TOOL & DYE**
13430 Kolmar Ave (60445-1443)
PHONE.................................708 388-7676
Christopher Galik, *President*
Frances Galik, *Vice Pres*
EMP: 3
SALES (est): 344.9K **Privately Held**
SIC: **3599** Machine & other job shop work

**(G-7476)**
**ALTEC PRINTING LLC**
4931 141st St (60445-2103)
PHONE.................................708 489-2484
John J Nieszel, *Mng Member*
Joseph J Urback,
EMP: 3
SALES (est): 210K **Privately Held**
WEB: www.altecprinting.com
SIC: **2759** Commercial printing

**(G-7477)**
**BEST BRAKE DIE INC**
13434 Kolmar Ave (60445-1443)
PHONE.................................708 388-1896
Fax: 708 388-2658
Dennis Malloy, *President*
John Hughes, *Treasurer*
Tina Malloy, *Office Mgr*
EMP: 7
SQ FT: 10,000
SALES: 750K **Privately Held**
SIC: **3544** Special dies & tools

**(G-7478)**
**CAMCO MANUFACTURING INC**
Also Called: Camco Screw Machine Products
13933 Kildare Ave (60445-2356)
PHONE.................................708 597-4288
Fax: 708 597-4298
Jack Rochon, *President*
Karen Jeziorny, *Bookkeeper*

Karen Jezidrney, *Executive*
EMP: 10
SQ FT: 7,500
SALES: 1MM **Privately Held**
SIC: **3599** 3451 Machine shop, jobbing & repair; screw machine products

**(G-7479)**
**CAMSHOP INDUSTRIAL LLC**
Also Called: Camco Manufacturing
13933 Kildare Ave (60445-2356)
PHONE.................................708 597-4288
Emmanuel Arevalo-Nowell, *Vice Pres*
Mario Arevalo, *Mng Member*
EMP: 8
SALES (est): 634.4K **Privately Held**
SIC: **3451** Screw machine products

**(G-7480)**
**CC DISTRIBUTING SERVICES INC**
Also Called: Smith Brothers Converters
13655 Kenton Ave (60445-1938)
P.O. Box 221047, Chicago (60622-0008)
PHONE.................................800 931-2668
Daniel Eitel, *President*
EMP: 3
SQ FT: 4,000
SALES (est): 1MM **Privately Held**
SIC: **5013** 5531 3714 Exhaust systems (mufflers, tail pipes, etc.); automotive parts; exhaust systems & parts, motor vehicle

**(G-7481)**
**CERTIWELD INC**
13953 Kostner Ave (60445-2205)
PHONE.................................708 389-0148
John Flynn, *President*
EMP: 3
SQ FT: 1,800
SALES (est): 201.5K **Privately Held**
SIC: **7692** Welding repair

**(G-7482)**
**CLASSIC AUTOMATION & TOOL**
4329 136th Ct (60445-1904)
PHONE.................................708 388-6311
Ron Hadar, *President*
EMP: 4
SQ FT: 6,000
SALES (est): 100K **Privately Held**
SIC: **3599** Machine shop, jobbing & repair

**(G-7483)**
**CONTEMPO AUTOGRAPHIC & SIGNS**
Also Called: Signs By Design
13866 Cicero Ave (60445-1883)
PHONE.................................708 371-5499
Fax: 708 371-0969
Chris Gorecki, *Partner*
John Gorecki, *Partner*
Dan Gorecki, *General Mgr*
EMP: 3
SQ FT: 1,400
SALES (est): 309.9K **Privately Held**
SIC: **3993** Signs & advertising specialties

**(G-7484)**
**COUNTY PACKAGING INC**
Also Called: Doosan
13600 Kildare Ave (60445-2326)
PHONE.................................708 597-1100
Fax: 708 597-1105
Jack Kent, *President*
Michael Cerva, *Vice Pres*
Holly Kent, *Treasurer*
Kandice Banker, *Admin Asst*
Joe Pisterzi, *Admin Asst*
▲ EMP: 70
SQ FT: 60,000
SALES (est): 6.9MM **Privately Held**
SIC: **7389** 3694 Packaging & labeling services; automotive electrical equipment

**(G-7485)**
**CRESTWOOD CUSTOM CABINETS**
13960 Kildare Ave (60445-2357)
PHONE.................................708 385-3167
Fax: 708 385-3178
Dennis Kersten, *Partner*
Frank Kersten, *Partner*
EMP: 4 EST: 1961

SQ FT: 4,000
SALES: 250K **Privately Held**
WEB: www.crestwoodcustomcabinets.com
SIC: **2434** 2521 2517 Vanities, bathroom: wood; wood office furniture; wood television & radio cabinets

**(G-7486)**
**CUSTOM WOOD DESIGNS INC**
14237 Kilbourne Ave (60445-2674)
PHONE.................................708 799-3439
Fax: 708 957-9663
Louis Mascitti Jr, *President*
EMP: 3
SQ FT: 4,800
SALES (est): 159.8K **Privately Held**
SIC: **7641** 2511 2434 Reupholstery & furniture repair; wood household furniture; wood kitchen cabinets

**(G-7487)**
**FAMAR FLAVOR LLC**
4711 137th St (60445-1928)
PHONE.................................708 926-2951
Justine Kos,
Martin Pawlus,
EMP: 5
SALES (est): 426.3K **Privately Held**
SIC: **2099** Seasonings & spices; spices, including grinding

**(G-7488)**
**FANNING COMMUNICATIONS INC**
Also Called: Advertising Designs
4701 Midlothian Tpke # 4 (60445-1976)
PHONE.................................708 293-1430
John J Fanning, *President*
Karl Paloucek, *Editor*
Catherine Fanning, *Vice Pres*
John Seno, *Admin Sec*
EMP: 8 EST: 2001
SALES (est): 1.5MM **Privately Held**
WEB: www.chiefengineer.org
SIC: **7311** 8999 2721 7374 Advertising agencies; technical writing; magazines: publishing & printing; computer graphics service; administrative management

**(G-7489)**
**INSCERCO MFG INC**
Also Called: Mailcrafters
4621 138th St (60445-1969)
PHONE.................................708 597-8777
Fax: 708 597-2176
Robert R Kruk, *President*
Anna M Kruk, *Corp Secy*
Robert R Kruk Jr, *Vice Pres*
Larry Solomon, *Purchasing*
Herman Havinga, *Engineer*
EMP: 20 EST: 1968
SQ FT: 20,000
SALES (est): 4.8MM **Privately Held**
WEB: www.inscerco.com
SIC: **3579** Mailing, letter handling & addressing machines

**(G-7490)**
**INTEGRA GRAPHICS AND FORMS INC**
4749 136th St (60445-1968)
PHONE.................................708 385-0950
Fax: 708 385-1717
Rick Richter, *President*
Gene Egan, *Vice Pres*
Eugene Egan, *Admin Sec*
EMP: 10
SQ FT: 5,500
SALES (est): 1.6MM **Privately Held**
WEB: www.integragraphics.com
SIC: **2759** 7389 2789 2752 Commercial printing; brokers' services; bookbinding & related work; commercial printing, lithographic

**(G-7491)**
**KEY WEST METAL INDUSTRIES INC**
13831 Kostner Ave (60445-1912)
PHONE.................................708 371-1470
William A Slabich Jr, *President*
Lou Osika, *Vice Pres*
Brian Carrier, *Plant Mgr*
Brett Dornack, *QC Mgr*
Pat Kafka, *Accounts Mgr*

EMP: 120
SQ FT: 13,000
SALES: 19MM **Privately Held**
SIC: **1711** 3444 3499 Plumbing contractors; sheet metal specialties, not stamped; fire- or burglary-resistive products

**(G-7492)**
**LANDCRAFT AUTO & MARINE INC**
Also Called: Landcraft Marine
13626 Cicero Ave (60445-1937)
PHONE.................................708 385-0717
Keith Lekberg, *President*
Christine Lekberg, *Marketing Staff*
EMP: 10
SQ FT: 3,000
SALES: 500K **Privately Held**
WEB: www.land-craft.com
SIC: **3732** Boats, fiberglass: building & repairing

**(G-7493)**
**MACHINING SYSTEMS CORPORATION**
14003 Kostner Ave (60445-2207)
PHONE.................................708 385-7903
Fax: 708 385-7904
Lucy Fudala, *President*
Stanley Fudala, *Vice Pres*
EMP: 6
SQ FT: 3,600
SALES (est): 630K **Privately Held**
SIC: **3599** Machine & other job shop work

**(G-7494)**
**METRO PAINT SUPPLIES**
14032 Kostner Ave Unit G (60445-2287)
PHONE.................................708 385-7701
Melissa Rizzo, *Manager*
EMP: 3 EST: 2007
SALES (est): 280.8K **Privately Held**
SIC: **2851** 5198 Paints & allied products; paints

**(G-7495)**
**MID-OAK DISTILLERY INC**
4330 Midlothian Tpke # 2 (60445-1975)
PHONE.................................708 925-9318
David Grotto, *Principal*
EMP: 8
SALES (est): 1MM **Privately Held**
SIC: **2085** Distillers' dried grains & solubles & alcohol

**(G-7496)**
**OMEGA PLATING INC**
4704 137th St (60445-1929)
PHONE.................................708 389-5410
Fax: 708 389-3119
Mithabhai Patel, *President*
Jayanpibhai K Patel, *Treasurer*
Shirish Shah, *Admin Sec*
EMP: 15
SQ FT: 15,000
SALES: 2.5MM **Privately Held**
SIC: **3471** 3479 Plating of metals or formed products; coating of metals & formed products

**(G-7497)**
**PALLETMAXX INC**
4818 137th St Ste 1 (60445-1977)
PHONE.................................708 385-9595
Kenneth Conway, *President*
Larry Hackett, *COO*
Todd Conway, *Vice Pres*
Ken Otto, *Sales Staff*
Claudia Hurst, *Director*
EMP: 7
SALES (est): 740K **Privately Held**
WEB: www.palletmaxx.com
SIC: **2448** Wood pallets & skids

**(G-7498)**
**PRECISION IBC INC**
13612 Lawler Ave (60445-1714)
PHONE.................................708 396-0750
Anthony Beard, *Branch Mgr*
EMP: 10 **Privately Held**
SIC: **3443** Water tanks, metal plate
PA: Precision Ibc, Inc.
8054 Mcgowin Dr
Fairhope AL 36532

# GEOGRAPHIC SECTION

## Crystal Lake - Mchenry County (G-7524)

**(G-7499)**
**RIVERCREST SEWING CENTER**
13310 Cicero Ave (60445-1428)
PHONE...................708 385-2516
Wallace Kirby, *Owner*
EMP: 3
SALES (est): 188.2K **Privately Held**
SIC: 3639 Sewing equipment

**(G-7500)**
**ROBERTSON TRANSFORMER CO**
Also Called: Robertson Worldwide
4700 137th St Ste A (60445-4307)
PHONE...................708 388-2315
William Bryant, *CEO*
Dale Marcus, *CFO*
Kenneth Gallagher, *Finance*
Christopher Page, *Administration*
▲ EMP: 40
SQ FT: 70,000
SALES (est): 10.5MM **Privately Held**
WEB: www.robertsontransformer.com
SIC: 3612 3621 5063 Fluorescent lighting transformers; motors & generators; electrical apparatus & equipment
PA: North Point Investments, Inc
70 W Madison St Ste 3500
Chicago IL 60602
312 977-4386

**(G-7501)**
**SCS COMPANY**
13633 Crestview Ct (60445-1830)
PHONE...................708 203-4955
Jeff Nemeh, *President*
Diala Nemeh, *Corp Secy*
EMP: 22
SQ FT: 14,000
SALES: 950K **Privately Held**
SIC: 2842 4959 Specialty cleaning preparations; sweeping service: road, airport, parking lot, etc.

**(G-7502)**
**SENECA PETROLEUM CO INC (PA)**
13301 Cicero Ave (60445-1427)
PHONE...................708 396-1100
Owen E Hulse Jr, *CEO*
Owen E Hulse III, *President*
Robert Schafer, *Vice Pres*
Jim Sellhorn, *Vice Pres*
Catherine Grcevic, *Admin Sec*
EMP: 20 EST: 1921
SQ FT: 8,000
SALES (est): 22.1MM **Privately Held**
SIC: 2911 1611 Asphalt or asphaltic materials, made in refineries; highway & street construction

**(G-7503)**
**SPIRIT CONCEPTS INC**
4365 136th Ct (60445-1904)
PHONE...................708 388-4500
Fax: 708 388-8700
Michael Kupchek III, *President*
Karen Kupchek, *Admin Sec*
EMP: 9
SQ FT: 3,500
SALES (est): 750K **Privately Held**
WEB: www.spiritconcepts.com
SIC: 2511 2517 Wood household furniture; wood television & radio cabinets

**(G-7504)**
**STRICTLY NEON INC**
Also Called: Strictly Signs
4608 137th St Ste D (60445-4305)
PHONE...................708 597-1616
Wally Wysocki, *President*
Walter Wysocki, *President*
Jim Givens, *Vice Pres*
EMP: 8
SQ FT: 1,400
SALES: 950K **Privately Held**
WEB: www.strictlyneon.com
SIC: 3993 1799 Electric signs; neon signs; sign installation & maintenance

**(G-7505)**
**TAL MAR CUSTOM MET FABRICATORS**
4632 138th St (60445-1931)
PHONE...................708 371-0333
Fax: 708 371-4111
James A Cesak, *President*
Bill Babcock, *Engineer*
Ronald Dibasilio, *Treasurer*
Judy Stiegal, *Office Mgr*
Robert Talerico, *Director*
EMP: 72
SQ FT: 25,000
SALES: 15MM **Privately Held**
SIC: 3599 Machine shop, jobbing & repair

**(G-7506)**
**TRIEZENBERG MILLWORK CO**
4737 138th St Ste 202 (60445-4301)
PHONE...................708 489-9062
Clarence Triezenberg, *President*
David Noort, *Admin Sec*
EMP: 4
SQ FT: 10,000
SALES: 590K **Privately Held**
SIC: 5031 5211 2431 2421 Millwork; millwork & lumber; millwork; sawmills & planing mills, general

**(G-7507)**
**VALLEY VIEW INDUSTRIES HC INC**
Also Called: Valley View Specialties
13834 Kostner Ave (60445-1913)
PHONE...................800 323-9369
Fax: 708 597-9959
Howard J Rynberk, *President*
Bonnie Oneill, *Exec VP*
Nancy Schoeneman, *Accounting Mgr*
Dominick Bertucci, *Nat'l Sales Mgr*
Dominic Vertucci, *Sales Executive*
EMP: 50
SQ FT: 75,000
SALES (est): 10.4MM **Privately Held**
SIC: 3271 3524 Blocks, concrete: landscape or retaining wall; lawn & garden equipment

## Crete
### Will County

**(G-7508)**
**BAJA SALES INC**
15 Charles Ct (60417-1508)
PHONE...................708 672-9245
Bob Armbruster, *President*
EMP: 6
SALES: 10MM **Privately Held**
SIC: 2099 Packaged combination products: pasta, rice & potato

**(G-7509)**
**BUILDERS IRONWORKS INC**
399 Greenbriar Dr (60417-1110)
PHONE...................708 672-1047
Rick Wories, *President*
Richard Wories, *President*
Joel Wories, *Vice Pres*
Julie Wories, *Admin Sec*
EMP: 9
SALES (est): 1.2MM **Privately Held**
SIC: 3446 Architectural metalwork

**(G-7510)**
**COMPONENT TOOL & MFG CO**
25416 S Dixie Hwy Ste 1 (60417-3952)
P.O. Box 373 (60417-0373)
PHONE...................708 672-5505
Fax: 708 672-3838
Timothy G Piepenbrink, *President*
Mike Tamez, *Foreman/Supr*
Chrissy Santana, *Admin Sec*
EMP: 13
SQ FT: 7,000
SALES (est): 2.2MM **Privately Held**
SIC: 3544 3599 8711 7692 Special dies, tools, jigs & fixtures; machine shop, jobbing & repair; consulting engineer; welding repair; metal stampings

**(G-7511)**
**COOPER EQUIPMENT COMPANY INC**
763 W Old Monee Rd (60417-3947)
PHONE...................708 367-1291
Fax: 708 367-1294
Scott Cooper, *President*
EMP: 2
SALES (est): 240.8K **Privately Held**
SIC: 2835 7629 In vitro & in vivo diagnostic substances; electrical repair shops

**(G-7512)**
**CRETE TWP**
26730 S Stoney Island Ave (60417-4746)
PHONE...................708 672-3111
Mark Rosandich, *Trustee*
EMP: 3 EST: 2012
SALES (est): 483.5K **Privately Held**
SIC: 3711 Fire department vehicles (motor vehicles), assembly of

**(G-7513)**
**FUEL FITNESS**
1379 Main St (60417-2927)
PHONE...................708 367-0707
David Spoolstra, *Principal*
EMP: 5
SALES (est): 352.2K **Privately Held**
SIC: 2869 Fuels

**(G-7514)**
**GREEN ENERGY SOLUTIONS INC**
30 Cornwall Dr (60417-1004)
PHONE...................708 672-1900
Jeffrey Patchett, *President*
EMP: 11
SALES (est): 950K **Privately Held**
SIC: 2392 Household furnishings

**(G-7515)**
**HOLLAND LP (HQ)**
Also Called: Holland Specialty Vehicles
1000 Holland Dr (60417-2120)
PHONE...................708 672-2300
Fax: 708 672-0119
Philip C Moeller, *President*
Robert Norby, *General Mgr*
Andrew Smith, *General Mgr*
Kevin Flaherty, *Vice Pres*
Miguel Celdran, *Plant Mgr*
▲ EMP: 150
SQ FT: 60,000
SALES: 276.7MM
SALES (corp-wide): 574.2MM **Privately Held**
SIC: 2899 3743 Fluxes: brazing, soldering, galvanizing & welding; railroad equipment
PA: Curran Group, Inc.
286 Memorial Ct
Crystal Lake IL 60014
815 455-5100

**(G-7516)**
**LOTTON ART GLASS CO**
24760 S Country Ln (60417-2658)
PHONE...................708 672-1400
Fax: 708 672-1401
Charles Lotton, *Owner*
Sharon Heinz, *Office Mgr*
EMP: 4
SALES (est): 371.9K **Privately Held**
WEB: www.lottonglass.com
SIC: 3231 3229 Art glass: made from purchased glass; pressed & blown glass

**(G-7517)**
**NATIONAL MACHINE REPAIR INC**
115 W Burville Rd (60417-3324)
PHONE...................708 672-7711
Fax: 708 672-3214
Lou Novelli, *President*
Angelo Novelli, *Vice Pres*
EMP: 18
SQ FT: 33,000
SALES (est): 2.5MM **Privately Held**
WEB: www.nationalmachinerepair.com
SIC: 3599 7629 3441 Machine shop, jobbing & repair; custom machinery; electrical repair shops; fabricated structural metal

**(G-7518)**
**ROCK TOPS INC**
295 W Burville Rd (60417-3340)
P.O. Box 397 (60417-0397)
PHONE...................708 672-1450
Robert Kasper, *President*
EMP: 5
SALES (est): 402.2K **Privately Held**
SIC: 2395 2399 Quilted fabrics or cloth; aprons, breast (harness)

**(G-7519)**
**SOUTHLAND VOICE**
1712 S Dixie Hwy Trlr 133 (60417-3948)
PHONE...................708 214-8582
Barbara Dorman, *Owner*
EMP: 25
SALES (est): 1MM **Privately Held**
SIC: 2711 7389 Newspapers, publishing & printing;

**(G-7520)**
**SUPERIOR MOBILE HOME SERVICE**
3421 E Reichert Dr (60417-4875)
PHONE...................708 672-7799
Kevin Clomp, *President*
Henriette Clomp, *Corp Secy*
EMP: 4
SALES (est): 340K **Privately Held**
SIC: 2451 Mobile homes

## Crossville
### White County

**(G-7521)**
**CITATION OIL & GAS CORP**
Hwy 14 E (62827)
P.O. Box 310 (62827-0310)
PHONE...................618 966-2101
Jim Schreifels, *Manager*
Bryan Dicus, *Manager*
EMP: 28
SALES (corp-wide): 179.7MM **Privately Held**
SIC: 1311 2911 Crude petroleum production; petroleum refining
PA: Citation Oil & Gas Corp.
14077 Cutten Rd
Houston TX 77069
281 891-1000

**(G-7522)**
**COY OIL INC**
503 S State St (62827-1121)
P.O. Box 575, Mount Vernon IN (47620-0575)
PHONE...................618 966-2126
Danny Stewart, *Manager*
EMP: 3
SALES (corp-wide): 825.2K **Privately Held**
SIC: 1381 Directional drilling oil & gas wells
PA: Coy Oil, Inc
7451 Sauerkraut Ln N
Mount Vernon IN 47620
812 838-3146

**(G-7523)**
**ROYAL DRILLING & PRODUCING**
Also Called: Royal Drilling & Production
Hwy 14 (62827)
P.O. Box 329 (62827-0329)
PHONE...................618 966-2221
James Cantrell, *President*
Chris Cantrell, *Vice Pres*
EMP: 3 EST: 1973
SALES (est): 1.4MM **Privately Held**
WEB: www.royaldrilling.com
SIC: 1381 Drilling oil & gas wells

## Crystal Lake
### Mchenry County

**(G-7524)**
**20 20 MEDICAL SYSTEMS INC**
Also Called: K2 Tables
111 Erick St Ste 125 (60014-1314)
PHONE...................815 455-7161
Gary Chianakas, *President*
Karen Chianakas, *Treasurer*
▲ EMP: 7
SALES (est): 530K **Privately Held**
SIC: 3842 Surgical appliances & supplies

## Crystal Lake - Mchenry County (G-7525)

**(G-7525)**
**ABA CUSTOM WOODWORKING**
765 Duffy Dr Ste B (60014-1716)
PHONE .................. 815 356-9663
Roger Schultz, *Principal*
Geri Rosner, *Office Mgr*
EMP: 3
SQ FT: 6,000
SALES: 350K **Privately Held**
SIC: 2499 1751 2521 2511 Decorative wood & woodwork; cabinet & finish carpentry; wood office furniture; wood household furniture; wood kitchen cabinets

**(G-7526)**
**ACCUMATION INC**
6211 Factory Rd (60014-7914)
P.O. Box 387 (60039-0387)
PHONE .................. 815 455-6250
Fax: 815 455-6087
Roland Gigon, *President*
Barbara Pearson, *Office Mgr*
EMP: 17
SQ FT: 10,000
SALES (est): 3MM **Privately Held**
WEB: www.accumation.com
SIC: 3451 Screw machine products

**(G-7527)**
**ALBERT J WAGNER & SON LLC**
2510 Il Route 176 Ste B (60014-2217)
PHONE .................. 815 459-1287
George Rudder, *CEO*
Albert J Wagner III, *Admin Sec*
EMP: 10
SALES (est): 744.2K **Privately Held**
SIC: 3444 Sheet metalwork

**(G-7528)**
**ALL AMERICAN WOOD REGISTER CO**
7103 Sands Rd (60014-6526)
PHONE .................. 815 356-1000
Patti Stasiak, *President*
Tom Stasiak, *Vice Pres*
Kim Reimer, *Human Resources*
Sara Luken, *Marketing Mgr*
EMP: 12
SALES (est): 1MM **Privately Held**
WEB: www.allamericanwood.com
SIC: 2499 3433 2431 Decorative wood & woodwork; heating equipment, except electric; millwork

**(G-7529)**
**ALPHA STAR TOOL AND MOLD INC**
11 Burdent Dr (60014-4233)
PHONE .................. 815 455-2802
Fax: 815 455-2577
John Thurow, *President*
Audrey Thurow, *Corp Secy*
Matthew Thurow, *Manager*
EMP: 18
SQ FT: 12,000
SALES (est): 2.9MM **Privately Held**
SIC: 3544 3089 Dies & die holders for metal cutting, forming, die casting; injection molding of plastics

**(G-7530)**
**ALPHA SWISS INDUSTRIES INC**
Also Called: Asi
700 Tek Dr (60014-8100)
PHONE .................. 815 455-3031
Jeff Koepke, *President*
Joe Rusciano, *Vice Pres*
EMP: 8
SQ FT: 4,500
SALES (est): 1.3MM **Privately Held**
WEB: www.alpha-swiss.com
SIC: 3545 3451 Measuring tools & machines, machinists' metalworking type; precision tools, machinists'; screw machine products

**(G-7531)**
**ALTRAN CORP**
365 E Terra Cotta Ave (60014-3608)
PHONE .................. 815 455-5650
Fax: 815 455-3171
David Peterson, *President*
Peggy J Peterson, *Corp Secy*
Cyril Roger, *Exec VP*
Ludovic Bruillot, *Purch Dir*
Frederic Fougerat, *Comms Dir*
▲ EMP: 28
SQ FT: 9,000
SALES (est): 5.3MM **Privately Held**
WEB: www.altrancorp.com
SIC: 3677 Coil windings, electronic

**(G-7532)**
**AMBROTOS INC**
4219 Belson Ln (60014-6589)
PHONE .................. 815 355-8217
James Kondrat, *President*
EMP: 3
SALES: 75K **Privately Held**
SIC: 3479 Metal coating & allied service

**(G-7533)**
**AMERICAN CALIBRATION INC**
4410 Il Route 176 Ste 11 (60014-3710)
PHONE .................. 815 356-5839
Todd Gibson, *President*
Jean Schoch, *Finance*
Rachel Kempf, *Manager*
Linda Roberts, *Admin Sec*
EMP: 15
SALES: 2.6MM **Privately Held**
SIC: 3599 Machine shop, jobbing & repair

**(G-7534)**
**APTARGROUP INC**
265 Exchange Dr (60014-6230)
PHONE .................. 779 220-4430
EMP: 50
SALES (corp-wide): 2.3B **Publicly Held**
SIC: 3089 Closures, plastic
PA: Aptargroup, Inc.
475 W Terra Cotta Ave E
Crystal Lake IL 60014
815 477-0424

**(G-7535)**
**APTARGROUP INC (PA)**
475 W Terra Cotta Ave E (60014-3407)
PHONE .................. 815 477-0424
Fax: 815 477-0481
King W Harris, *Ch of Bd*
Stephan B Tanda, *President*
Salim Haffar, *President*
Eldon Schaffer, *President*
Gael Touya, *President*
◆ EMP: 277
SALES: 2.3B **Publicly Held**
WEB: www.aptargroup.com
SIC: 3089 3499 Closures, plastic; aerosol valves, metal

**(G-7536)**
**APTARGROUP INTERNATIONAL LLC (HQ)**
475 W Terra Cotta Ave E (60014-3407)
PHONE .................. 815 477-0424
Stephen J Hagge, *CEO*
James Meyer, *Vice Pres*
Robert Kuhn, *Admin Sec*
EMP: 4
SALES (est): 830.6K
SALES (corp-wide): 2.3B **Publicly Held**
SIC: 3089 Boxes, plastic
PA: Aptargroup, Inc.
475 W Terra Cotta Ave E
Crystal Lake IL 60014
815 477-0424

**(G-7537)**
**ARQUILLA INC**
Also Called: X-Cel X-Ray
4220 Waller St Ste 1 (60012-2816)
P.O. Box 1857 (60039-1857)
PHONE .................. 815 455-2470
Fax: 815 455-4732
Guido Arquilla, *President*
Dolores Morris, *Admin Sec*
EMP: 14
SQ FT: 16,000
SALES: 1.8MM **Privately Held**
WEB: www.xcelxray.com
SIC: 3844 5047 X-ray apparatus & tubes; X-ray machines & tubes

**(G-7538)**
**ARROW SHEET METAL COMPANY**
1032 Ascot Dr (60014-8831)
PHONE .................. 815 455-2019
EMP: 35 EST: 1937
SQ FT: 2,000
SALES (est): 3MM **Privately Held**
SIC: 1761 3444 Roofing/Siding Contractor Mfg Sheet Metalwork

**(G-7539)**
**AUTOMATED MFG SOLUTIONS INC**
6126 Factory Rd (60014-7954)
P.O. Box 1616 (60039-1616)
PHONE .................. 815 477-2428
Steven A Gauger, *President*
EMP: 10
SALES: 2MM **Privately Held**
SIC: 3599 Custom machinery

**(G-7540)**
**BBC INNOVATION CORPORATION**
7900 S Illinois Rt 31 (60014)
PHONE .................. 847 458-2334
Dong Sok Han, *President*
▲ EMP: 7
SALES (est): 2MM **Privately Held**
SIC: 3261 Bidets, vitreous china

**(G-7541)**
**BIG BEAM EMERGENCY SYSTEMS INC**
290 E Prairie St (60014-4415)
P.O. Box 518 (60039-0518)
PHONE .................. 815 459-6100
Fax: 815 459-6173
Nikunj H Shah, *President*
Steven J Loria, *Corp Secy*
Thomas Smonskey, *Vice Pres*
Vijay Shah, *Manager*
▲ EMP: 25
SQ FT: 44,000
SALES: 10MM **Privately Held**
WEB: www.bigbeam.com
SIC: 3648 Lighting equipment; lanterns: electric, gas, carbide, kerosene or gasoline

**(G-7542)**
**BOLTSWITCH INC**
6208 Commercial Rd (60014-7991)
PHONE .................. 815 459-6900
Fax: 815 455-7788
John Erickson Sr, *Ch of Bd*
James Erickson, *President*
Douglas Nickels, *Purch Agent*
Eric Maier, *QC Mgr*
John W Erickson Jr, *Treasurer*
◆ EMP: 45
SQ FT: 53,000
SALES: 9.9MM **Privately Held**
WEB: www.boltswitch.com
SIC: 3613 Power circuit breakers

**(G-7543)**
**BRENCO MACHINE AND TOOL INC**
6117 Factory Rd (60014-7953)
PHONE .................. 815 356-5100
Fax: 815 356-5112
Dietrich Bronst, *President*
Birgit Bronst, *Corp Secy*
Mike Schroeter, *Site Mgr*
Debbie Golladay, *Manager*
EMP: 12
SQ FT: 8,700
SALES: 1.5MM **Privately Held**
WEB: www.brencomachine.com
SIC: 3599 Machine shop, jobbing & repair

**(G-7544)**
**BROWN WOODWORKING**
1804 Blue Island Dr (60014-2204)
PHONE .................. 815 477-8333
David Brown, *Owner*
EMP: 3
SALES (est): 227.8K **Privately Held**
SIC: 2499 2434 2431 Decorative wood & woodwork; wood kitchen cabinets; millwork

**(G-7545)**
**BUBBLE BUBBLE INC**
35 Berkshire Dr Ste 3 (60014-7700)
PHONE .................. 815 455-2366
Judy Delaware, *Owner*
EMP: 4
SALES (est): 428.6K **Privately Held**
SIC: 3421 Table & food cutlery, including butchers'

**(G-7546)**
**BUZZ SALES COMPANY INC**
6110 Official Rd (60014-7921)
P.O. Box 463 (60039-0463)
PHONE .................. 815 459-1170
Fax: 815 459-1192
Peter N Anderson, *President*
Roger G Angelkorte, *Vice Pres*
Jeffrey Kohnke, *Vice Pres*
Jerrie Wiltberger, *Office Mgr*
Margaret R Anderson, *Admin Sec*
EMP: 8
SALES (est): 1.6MM **Privately Held**
WEB: www.buzzsales.com
SIC: 2893 2899 Gravure ink; chemical preparations

**(G-7547)**
**C L GRAPHICS INC**
134 Virginia Rd Ste A (60014-3113)
PHONE .................. 815 455-0900
Fax: 815 455-4255
Richard Schildgen, *President*
Nancy Strauss, *Finance Mgr*
Dave Heiden, *Manager*
Mary Knapp, *Manager*
Mike Mack, *Manager*
EMP: 20
SQ FT: 11,000
SALES (est): 3.5MM **Privately Held**
WEB: www.clgraphics.com
SIC: 2759 Promotional printing

**(G-7548)**
**CALCO CONTROLS INC**
Also Called: Calco Cutaways
439 S Dartmoor Dr (60014-8726)
PHONE .................. 847 639-3858
Fax: 847 639-3860
Neil Sivertson, *President*
Owen Schnaper, *General Mgr*
Daniel Fierla, *Prdtn Mgr*
Tom West, *Manager*
EMP: 10
SQ FT: 5,000
SALES: 1MM **Privately Held**
WEB: www.calcocutaways.com
SIC: 3599 3567 Machine shop, jobbing & repair; heating units & devices, industrial: electric

**(G-7549)**
**CAMFIL USA INC**
Also Called: Os Farr
500 S Main St (60014-6205)
PHONE .................. 815 459-6600
Fax: 815 459-5390
Christine Sanders, *Purchasing*
Russ Demayo, *Engineer*
Debbie Clark, *Human Res Dir*
Patricia Lambert, *Branch Mgr*
EMP: 95
SQ FT: 128,000
SALES (corp-wide): 725.6MM **Privately Held**
SIC: 3569 3564 Filters; blowers & fans
HQ: Camfil Usa Inc
1 N Corporate Dr
Riverdale NJ 07457
973 616-7300

**(G-7550)**
**CARE SOLUTIONS INCORPORATED**
365 Millennium Dr Ste D (60012-3747)
PHONE .................. 815 301-4034
Lanie P Lagman, *President*
Lullete Tu-Camara, *Admin Sec*
EMP: 16
SALES (est): 2.4MM **Privately Held**
SIC: 2834 Solutions, pharmaceutical

**(G-7551)**
**CHEMTOOL INCORPORATED**
8200 Ridgefield Rd (60012-2912)
PHONE .................. 815 459-1250
Dean Athens, *General Mgr*
EMP: 75

# GEOGRAPHIC SECTION
## Crystal Lake - Mchenry County (G-7578)

**SALES (corp-wide):** 223.6B  **Publicly Held**
**SIC: 2992** 2899 3471 2842  Lubricating oils & greases; cutting oils, blending; made from purchased materials; rust arresting compounds, animal or vegetable oil base; rust resisting compounds; water treating compounds; plating & polishing; specialty cleaning, polishes & sanitation goods; soap & other detergents
**HQ:** Chemtool Incorporated
  801 W Rockton Rd
  Rockton IL 61072
  815 957-4140

### (G-7552)
### CHICAGO LATEX PRODUCTS INC
345 E Terra Cotta Ave (60014-3608)
P.O. Box 395 (60039-0395)
**PHONE** .................................. 815 459-9680
James Athans, *President*
Susan Bemis, *President*
John Kuetemeyer, *President*
Lyle Bemis, *Vice Pres*
Sue Delisle, *Office Mgr*
**EMP:** 10
**SALES (est):** 816.8K  **Privately Held**
**WEB:** www.chicagolatexproducts.com
**SIC: 2821** 3087 2891 2851  Molding compounds, plastics; custom compound purchased resins; adhesives & sealants; paints & allied products

### (G-7553)
### CHICAGO PLASTIC SYSTEMS INC
440 S Dartmoor Dr (60014-8713)
P.O. Box 304 (60039-0304)
**PHONE** .................................. 815 455-4599
**Fax:** 815 455-6499
Leif R Heggem, *President*
Donna Howell, *Office Mgr*
Dirk F Howell, *Admin Sec*
**EMP:** 28
**SQ FT:** 20,000
**SALES (est):** 8.1MM  **Privately Held**
**WEB:** www.cpsfab.com
**SIC: 3564** 3089  Air purification equipment; plastic & fiberglass tanks

### (G-7554)
### CJCWOOD PRODUCTS INC
Also Called: Millfab
95 Grant St (60014-4394)
**PHONE** .................................. 815 479-5190
John Zirkel, *President*
**EMP:** 45
**SQ FT:** 400
**SALES (est):** 2.6MM  **Privately Held**
**SIC: 3544**  Special dies, tools, jigs & fixtures

### (G-7555)
### CLINTON OIL CORP
250 N Il Route 31 176 (60014-4517)
**PHONE** .................................. 815 356-1124
Dipdi Kapadia, *Business Mgr*
**EMP:** 5
**SALES (est):** 402.7K  **Privately Held**
**SIC: 1389**  Oil & gas field services

### (G-7556)
### COMPONENT PARTS COMPANY
7301 Foxfire Dr (60012-1603)
**PHONE** .................................. 815 477-2323
John Vlk, *President*
▲ **EMP:** 7
**SALES (est):** 705.2K  **Privately Held**
**SIC: 3443**  Metal parts

### (G-7557)
### COVIDIEN LP
815 Tek Dr (60014-8172)
**PHONE** .................................. 815 444-2500
Rui Santos, *Plant Mgr*
Julie Witte, *Senior Buyer*
Lyna Chhor, *Engineer*
Ricardo Guzman, *Engineer*
Jeremy Roberts, *Engineer*
**EMP:** 574  **Privately Held**
**SIC: 3842**  Surgical appliances & supplies
**HQ:** Covidien Lp
  15 Hampshire St
  Mansfield MA 02048
  508 261-8000

### (G-7558)
### CREATIVE BEDDING TECHNOLOGIES
300 Exchange Dr (60014-6290)
**PHONE** .................................. 815 444-9088
**Fax:** 815 444-8810
Anthony Dean, *Principal*
Ted Lazakis, *Plant Mgr*
**EMP:** 2
**SALES (est):** 206.8K  **Privately Held**
**SIC: 3841**  Surgical & medical instruments

### (G-7559)
### CRYSTAL LAKE BEER COMPANY
Also Called: Crystal Lake Brewing
150 N Main St (60014-4433)
**PHONE** .................................. 779 220-9288
John O'Fallon, *President*
Charles Ross, *Admin Sec*
**EMP:** 10 **EST:** 2013
**SQ FT:** 13,200
**SALES:** 250K  **Privately Held**
**SIC: 2082**  Beer (alcoholic beverage)

### (G-7560)
### CSM PRODUCTS INC (DH)
545 Dakota St Ste A (60012-3743)
**PHONE** .................................. 815 444-1671
Greg Sheahen, *President*
**EMP:** 8
**SALES (est):** 1.2MM
**SALES (corp-wide):** 775.7K  **Privately Held**
**SIC: 3825**  Instruments to measure electricity
**HQ:** Csm Computer-Systeme-Messtechnik Gmbh
  Raiffeisenstr. 36
  Filderstadt 70794
  711 779-640

### (G-7561)
### CUMMINS FILTRATION INC
3011 Illinois Rte 176 (60014)
**PHONE** .................................. 931 526-9551
Tom Linebarge, *Branch Mgr*
**EMP:** 5
**SALES (corp-wide):** 17.5B  **Publicly Held**
**SIC: 3714**  Motor vehicle parts & accessories
**HQ:** Cummins Filtration Inc
  26 Century Blvd Ste 500
  Nashville TN 37214
  615 367-0040

### (G-7562)
### CURRAN CONTRACTING COMPANY (HQ)
286 Memorial Ct (60014-6277)
**PHONE** .................................. 815 455-5100
**Fax:** 815 455-7894
Rick Noe, *President*
Bill Curran, *General Mgr*
Tim Curran, *Exec VP*
Dan Curran, *Vice Pres*
Mike Curran, *Vice Pres*
**EMP:** 25
**SQ FT:** 4,000
**SALES:** 8.9MM
**SALES (corp-wide):** 574.2MM  **Privately Held**
**WEB:** www.currancontracting.com
**SIC: 2951** 1611  Asphalt & asphaltic paving mixtures (not from refineries); highway & street construction
**PA:** Curran Group, Inc.
  286 Memorial Ct
  Crystal Lake IL 60014
  815 455-5100

### (G-7563)
### CURRAN GROUP INC (PA)
286 Memorial Ct (60014-6277)
**PHONE** .................................. 815 455-5100
Timothy Curran, *President*
Mike Curran, *President*
Jairus Camarena, *Project Mgr*
Todd Gierke, *CFO*
Jordan Wolf, *Treasurer*
◆ **EMP:** 23
**SQ FT:** 4,000
**SALES (est):** 574.2MM  **Privately Held**
**WEB:** www.currangroup.net
**SIC: 1799** 3253 1611  Welding on site; wall tile, ceramic; highway & street paving contractor

### (G-7564)
### CUTTING EDGE COMMUNICATIONS
764 Grandview Dr (60014-7319)
**PHONE** .................................. 815 788-9419
Myron Hillers, *President*
**EMP:** 2
**SALES (est):** 217.8K  **Privately Held**
**SIC: 4813** 3661  Telephone communication, except radio; fiber optics communications equipment

### (G-7565)
### DALZELL & COMPANY
41 N Williams St (60014-4403)
**PHONE** .................................. 815 477-8816
**Fax:** 815 477-9097
Steve Dalzell, *President*
Jennifer Dalzell, *Vice Pres*
**EMP:** 8
**SALES (est):** 1.5MM  **Privately Held**
**WEB:** www.dalzellandco.com
**SIC: 3911**  Jewelry, precious metal

### (G-7566)
### DELTA-THERM CORPORATION
6711 Sands Rd Ste A (60014-6594)
**PHONE** .................................. 847 526-2407
**Fax:** 312 526-4456
Tom Slagis, *President*
Penelope Lums, *Controller*
Dorothy Rosario, *Accounting Mgr*
Pat Stearns, *Natl Sales Mgr*
Bill Keyes, *Manager*
**EMP:** 18 **EST:** 1968
**SQ FT:** 10,000
**SALES:** 3.6MM  **Privately Held**
**WEB:** www.delta-therm.com
**SIC: 3699** 3567  Heat emission operating apparatus; heating units & devices, industrial; electric

### (G-7567)
### DEMARCO INDUSTRIAL VACUUM CORP
1030 Lutter Dr (60014-8189)
P.O. Box 1138 (60039-1138)
**PHONE** .................................. 815 344-2222
Thomas Demarco, *President*
Christine Demarco, *Vice Pres*
Louis Demarco, *Sales Mgr*
**EMP:** 3
**SALES (est):** 983.3K  **Privately Held**
**SIC: 3563**  Vacuum (air extraction) systems, industrial

### (G-7568)
### DYNA COMP INC
6215 Factory Rd Ste C (60014-7925)
**PHONE** .................................. 815 455-5570
**Fax:** 815 455-5748
Stephen Rasmussen, *President*
**EMP:** 2
**SALES (est):** 307.3K  **Privately Held**
**SIC: 3993** 2331 2321  Signs & advertising specialties; women's & misses' blouses & shirts; men's & boys' furnishings

### (G-7569)
### EAGLE TOOL US LLC
Also Called: Eagle Tool Ram Shop
4014 Northwest Hwy Ste 1a (60014-8211)
**PHONE** .................................. 815 459-4177
Colleen York, *President*
Edward Dedina,
**EMP:** 6
**SQ FT:** 2,000
**SALES (est):** 825.1K  **Privately Held**
**WEB:** www.eagle-tool.us
**SIC: 3544**  Special dies, tools, jigs & fixtures

### (G-7570)
### EAST WEST INTERGRATED THERAPYS
2719 Red Barn Rd (60012-1015)
**PHONE** .................................. 815 788-0574
Christine Rogers, *President*
Nancy Smetters, *Manager*
**EMP:** 4
**SALES (est):** 130K  **Privately Held**
**SIC: 2834**  Medicines, capsuled or ampuled

### (G-7571)
### ELEC EASEL
2600 Behan Rd (60014-2224)
**PHONE** .................................. 815 444-9700
Charles Pettrone, *Principal*
Amber Wheet, *Web Dvlpr*
**EMP:** 2 **EST:** 2007
**SALES (est):** 203K  **Privately Held**
**SIC: 3699**  Electrical equipment & supplies

### (G-7572)
### ELITE KIDS
825 Munshaw Ln (60014-1731)
**PHONE** .................................. 815 451-9600
Lynn Ledford, *Principal*
**EMP:** 3
**SALES (est):** 170K  **Privately Held**
**SIC: 5137** 2369  Children's goods; girls' & children's outerwear

### (G-7573)
### ELM STREET DESIGN INC
3916 Overland Rd (60012-2241)
**PHONE** .................................. 815 455-3622
Merrill Millman, *President*
**EMP:** 4
**SALES:** 200K  **Privately Held**
**SIC: 3993**  Signs & advertising specialties

### (G-7574)
### EVERBLAST INC
820 Mcardle Dr Ste C (60014-8164)
**PHONE** .................................. 815 788-8660
Christopher Hindley, *President*
▲ **EMP:** 4
**SQ FT:** 2,500
**SALES (est):** 621K  **Privately Held**
**WEB:** www.everblast.com
**SIC: 3589**  Sandblasting equipment

### (G-7575)
### FALCON PRESS INC
341 E Crystal Lake Ave (60014-6211)
**PHONE** .................................. 815 455-9099
Rod Russell, *President*
**EMP:** 4
**SQ FT:** 4,000
**SALES (est):** 481.4K  **Privately Held**
**SIC: 2752** 2759  Commercial printing, offset; letterpress printing

### (G-7576)
### FANFEST CORPORATION
Also Called: Fantasy Festival Costume Magic
3604 Oak Knoll Rd (60012-2039)
**PHONE** .................................. 847 658-2000
**EMP:** 5
**SQ FT:** 7,650
**SALES (est):** 537K  **Privately Held**
**WEB:** www.fantasyfestival.com
**SIC: 5699** 7299 2389 5945  Costumes, masquerade or theatrical; costume rental; masquerade costumes; theatrical costumes; hobbies; balloon shops

### (G-7577)
### FAYE JEWELLERY CHEZ
6314 Tilgee Rd (60012)
**PHONE** .................................. 815 477-1818
Jeff Faye, *Owner*
**EMP:** 3
**SQ FT:** 2,000
**SALES (est):** 239K  **Privately Held**
**WEB:** www.jewellerychezfaye.com
**SIC: 5944** 5094 3911  Jewelry, precious stones & precious metals; jewelry; jewelry, precious metal

### (G-7578)
### FIELD MANUFACTURING CORP
1661 Brompton Ln Ste B (60014-2046)
**PHONE** .................................. 815 455-5596
Karla Moreland, *Branch Mgr*
**EMP:** 60
**SALES (corp-wide):** 14.7MM  **Privately Held**
**SIC: 3089**  Injection molding of plastics
**PA:** Field Manufacturing Corp
  2750 Oregon Ct Ste M8
  Torrance CA 90503
  310 781-9292

# Crystal Lake - Mchenry County (G-7579)

## (G-7579)
**FISHSTONE STUDIO INC**
Also Called: Concrete Countertop Supply
110 East St (60014-4407)
**PHONE**.....................815 276-0299
Thomas Fischer, *Principal*
Carrie Fischer, *Principal*
Janice Raczynski, *Principal*
**EMP:** 3
**SALES (est):** 323.3K **Privately Held**
**SIC: 3273** Ready-mixed concrete

## (G-7580)
**G & M MANUFACTURING CORP**
111 S Main St (60014-6249)
**PHONE**.....................815 455-1900
**Fax:** 815 455-1901
Marcia Goerner, *President*
John Goerner, *Vice Pres*
**EMP:** 43
**SQ FT:** 52,000
**SALES (est):** 10.5MM **Privately Held**
**WEB:** www.usgravitics.com
**SIC: 3469** 3465 Electronic enclosures, stamped or pressed metal; automotive stampings

## (G-7581)
**GESKE AND SONS INC (PA)**
400 E Terra Cotta Ave (60014-3611)
**PHONE**.....................815 459-2407
**Fax:** 815 459-2465
Leroy Geske, *President*
Larry G Geske, *Vice Pres*
Adam Geske, *QC Mgr*
**EMP:** 11 **EST:** 1951
**SQ FT:** 8,600
**SALES (est):** 3.6MM **Privately Held**
**SIC: 1611** 2951 4212 4959 Highway & street construction; asphalt & asphaltic paving mixtures (not from refineries); local trucking, without storage; snowplowing

## (G-7582)
**GESKE AND SONS INC**
Also Called: Geske & Sons
400 E Terra Cotta Ave (60014-3611)
**PHONE**.....................815 459-2407
Lori Geske, *Manager*
**EMP:** 3
**SALES (corp-wide):** 3.6MM **Privately Held**
**SIC: 2951** Asphalt & asphaltic paving mixtures (not from refineries)
**PA:** Geske And Sons Inc
400 E Terra Cotta Ave
Crystal Lake IL 60014
815 459-2407

## (G-7583)
**GIL INSTRUMENTS CO**
500 Oxford Ln (60014-5526)
**PHONE**.....................815 459-8764
Richard F Mc Gill, *President*
Sarah F Mc Gill, *Admin Sec*
**EMP:** 4 **EST:** 1970
**SALES (est):** 310K **Privately Held**
**SIC: 7389** 3679 Design, commercial & industrial; harness assemblies for electronic use: wire or cable

## (G-7584)
**GRAY WOLF GRAPHICS INC**
457 S Dartmoor Dr (60014-8712)
**PHONE**.....................815 356-0895
**Fax:** 815 356-0896
Brian Semple, *President*
Ken Kottra, *Vice Pres*
Pete Semple, *Vice Pres*
**EMP:** 14
**SQ FT:** 2,500
**SALES (est):** 2MM **Privately Held**
**SIC: 2752** Commercial printing, lithographic

## (G-7585)
**GROVE DESIGN & ADVERTISING INC**
Also Called: Grove Communications
3918 Valley View Rd (60012-2104)
**PHONE**.....................815 459-4552
Robert A Grzelewski, *President*
Robert W Grzelewski, *President*
Carolyn Grzelewski, *Admin Sec*
**EMP:** 4
**SQ FT:** 12,000
**SALES (est):** 260K **Privately Held**
**WEB:** www.grovecommunications.com
**SIC: 2752** 7311 Commercial printing, offset; advertising agencies

## (G-7586)
**H R LARKE CORP**
999 Saddle Creek Ln (60014-1934)
**PHONE**.....................847 204-2776
Harold Larke,
**EMP:** 5
**SALES (est):** 407.7K **Privately Held**
**SIC: 3694** Motor generator sets, automotive

## (G-7587)
**HARRISON MARTHA PRINT STUDIO**
3222 Carrington Dr (60014-4760)
**PHONE**.....................949 290-8630
Martha Harrison, *Principal*
**EMP:** 4
**SALES (est):** 377.4K **Privately Held**
**SIC: 2752** Commercial printing, lithographic

## (G-7588)
**HOOSIER PRECAST LLC**
2220 Il Route 176 (60014-2218)
**PHONE**.....................815 459-4545
**EMP:** 3 **EST:** 2008
**SALES (est):** 170K **Privately Held**
**SIC: 3272** Precast terrazo or concrete products

## (G-7589)
**HUGHES & SON INC**
Also Called: Hughes Sign Co
652 W Terra Cotta Ave (60014-3462)
P.O. Box 367 (60039-0367)
**PHONE**.....................815 459-1887
**Fax:** 815 459-8872
Dennis Hughes, *President*
Kathryn Hughes, *Corp Secy*
Howard Hughes, *Vice Pres*
Penny Hughes, *Sales Staff*
**EMP:** 6
**SQ FT:** 4,800
**SALES (est):** 609.9K **Privately Held**
**SIC: 1799** 7389 3993 Sign installation & maintenance; sign painting & lettering shop; signs & advertising specialties

## (G-7590)
**HUYGEN CORPORATION (PA)**
1025 Lutter Dr (60014-8190)
P.O. Box 2424 (60039-2424)
**PHONE**.....................815 455-2200
Garrett Wade, *President*
Richard A Wade, *CFO*
Sharon Wade, *Admin Sec*
**EMP:** 6
**SQ FT:** 10,000
**SALES (est):** 901.6K **Privately Held**
**WEB:** www.huygen.com
**SIC: 3825** 5065 7629 3826 Test equipment for electronic & electrical circuits; measuring instruments & meters, electric; electronic parts; electrical equipment repair services; analytical instruments

## (G-7591)
**IDENTATRONICS INC**
2510 Il Route 176 Ste E (60014-2217)
**PHONE**.....................847 437-2654
**Fax:** 847 437-2660
William L Bangston, *President*
Lee Rowland, *Engineer*
Mike Grzegorek, *Sales Mgr*
Carol Hoellen, *Mktg Dir*
Brandy Phelan, *Marketing Staff*
**EMP:** 30
**SQ FT:** 17,000
**SALES (est):** 3.3MM
**SALES (corp-wide):** 12.6MM **Privately Held**
**WEB:** www.identatronics.com
**SIC: 7389** 3089 5084 3651 Laminating service; identification cards, plastic; printing trades machinery, equipment & supplies; household audio & video equipment
**PA:** Prr, Inc.
100 S 5th St Ste 300
Minneapolis MN
612 215-7460

## (G-7592)
**INDUCTION HEAT TREATING CORP**
Also Called: Iht
775 Tek Dr (60014-8172)
**PHONE**.....................815 477-7788
**Fax:** 815 477-7784
David Haimbaugh, *President*
Richard Haimbaugh, *Vice Pres*
Gary Tudor, *Vice Pres*
Thomas Iftner, *QC Mgr*
Roger Sass, *QC Mgr*
**EMP:** 50
**SQ FT:** 35,000
**SALES (est):** 13.3MM **Privately Held**
**WEB:** www.ihtcorp.com
**SIC: 3398** Metal heat treating

## (G-7593)
**JAMETHER INCORPORATED**
Also Called: AlphaGraphics US 590
6294 Northwest Hwy (60014-7933)
**PHONE**.....................815 444-9971
James Davis, *President*
Therese Davis, *Vice Pres*
**EMP:** 5
**SQ FT:** 4,000
**SALES (est):** 600K **Privately Held**
**SIC: 2752** Commercial printing, lithographic

## (G-7594)
**JEMISON ELC BOX SWTCHBOARD INC**
371 E Prairie St Unit H (60014-4412)
P.O. Box 426 (60039-0426)
**PHONE**.....................815 459-4060
Ralph Weger, *President*
Dominick A Scolaro, *Corp Secy*
Mike Weger, *Manager*
Michael C Weger, *Admin Sec*
**EMP:** 8 **EST:** 1957
**SQ FT:** 13,000
**SALES (est):** 1.4MM **Privately Held**
**WEB:** www.jemison.com
**SIC: 3625** 3613 Control equipment, electric; switchboards & parts, power

## (G-7595)
**JME TECHNOLOGIES INC**
2520 Route 176 Bldg 3 (60014)
**PHONE**.....................815 477-8800
Jerald Ewert, *CEO*
Karen Ewert, *Business Mgr*
Charmaine Geffert, *Opers Mgr*
Shawn Lee, *Sales Associate*
**EMP:** 4
**SALES (est):** 1.1MM **Privately Held**
**WEB:** www.jmetechnologies.com
**SIC: 5065** 4581 3827 Electronic parts & equipment; aircraft maintenance & repair services; optical test & inspection equipment

## (G-7596)
**JOHN CRANE INC**
Also Called: Smith, John Crane
29-31 Burdent Dr (60014)
**PHONE**.....................815 459-0420
**Fax:** 815 587-5692
Dan Schoenveck, *General Mgr*
**EMP:** 23
**SALES (corp-wide):** 4.1B **Privately Held**
**WEB:** www.johncrane.com
**SIC: 3295** 3541 Minerals, ground or treated; lapping machines
**HQ:** John Crane Inc.
227 W Monroe St Ste 1800
Chicago IL 60606
312 605-7800

## (G-7597)
**KARLY IRON WORKS INC**
4014 Northwest Hwy Ste 4c (60014-8211)
**PHONE**.....................815 477-3430
Daryl Kendrick, *President*
**EMP:** 5
**SALES (est):** 293.5K **Privately Held**
**SIC: 7692** Welding repair

## (G-7598)
**KELLY & SON FORESTRY & LOG LLC**
1783 Ashford Ln (60014-2013)
**PHONE**.....................815 275-6877
Kelly David C, *Principal*
**EMP:** 3
**SALES (est):** 272.7K **Privately Held**
**SIC: 2411** Logging

## (G-7599)
**KLIMKO INK INC**
Also Called: Kwik Kopy Printing
125 S Virginia St (60014-5845)
**PHONE**.....................815 459-5066
**Fax:** 815 459-2970
Charlie Klimkowski, *President*
Barb Colin, *Manager*
**EMP:** 8
**SQ FT:** 3,200
**SALES (est):** 1.2MM **Privately Held**
**SIC: 2759** Thermography

## (G-7600)
**KNAACK LLC**
Also Called: Knaack Manufacturing
420 E Terra Cotta Ave (60014-3611)
**PHONE**.....................815 459-6020
**Fax:** 815 459-9097
Chad Severson, *President*
Robert Pradelski, *Vice Pres*
William Zbylut, *Chief Mktg Ofcr*
Steve Seibert, *CTO*
Brian Conn,
◆ **EMP:** 100 **EST:** 1960
**SQ FT:** 450,000
**SALES (est):** 61.4MM **Privately Held**
**WEB:** www.knaack.com
**SIC: 3499** Chests, fire or burglary resistive: metal
**HQ:** Werner Co
93 Werner Rd
Greenville PA 16125
724 588-2000

## (G-7601)
**LAC ENTERPRISES INC**
Also Called: Eagle Press
2530 Il Route 176 Ste 9 (60014-2226)
**PHONE**.....................815 455-5044
**Fax:** 815 455-1446
Michael Lacomb, *President*
Debra Lacomb, *Corp Secy*
Susan Kramer, *COO*
**EMP:** 5
**SQ FT:** 2,500
**SALES (est):** 510K **Privately Held**
**SIC: 2752** 2791 2789 Commercial printing, lithographic; typesetting; bookbinding & related work

## (G-7602)
**LEE JENSEN SALES CO INC (PA)**
101 W Terra Cotta Ave (60014-3507)
**PHONE**.....................815 459-0929
**Fax:** 815 459-6458
James Jensen, *President*
Rick Metropulos, *Vice Pres*
Randall Keegan, *Purch Agent*
Karen Balke, *Office Mgr*
**EMP:** 30
**SQ FT:** 5,000
**SALES (est):** 15.1MM **Privately Held**
**WEB:** www.leejensensales.com
**SIC: 5082** 7353 3496 General construction machinery & equipment; heavy construction equipment rental; slings, lifting: made from purchased wire

## (G-7603)
**M M MARKETING**
4501 Il Route 176 Ste B (60014-3711)
**PHONE**.....................815 459-7968
**Fax:** 815 459-4468
Jim Mc Neil, *Owner*
**EMP:** 4
**SALES (est):** 240K **Privately Held**
**SIC: 2791** 2741 7336 2752 Typesetting; miscellaneous publishing; commercial art & graphic design; commercial printing, lithographic

## (G-7604)
**MACHINE TECHNOLOGY INC**
221 Erick St (60014-4594)
**PHONE**.....................815 444-4837
Kurt W Schraut, *President*
James Schraut, *Principal*
Jacob Shaffer, *Manager*
▲ **EMP:** 4

# GEOGRAPHIC SECTION

## Crystal Lake - Mchenry County (G-7631)

SQ FT: 6,000
SALES (est): 310K **Privately Held**
SIC: 3545 Machine tool accessories

**(G-7605)**
**MAGNETIC DEVICES INC**
150 Virginia Rd Ste 5 (60014-7940)
PHONE.................................815 459-0077
EMP: 6
SQ FT: 4,400
SALES: 500K **Privately Held**
SIC: 3677 3621 3612 Mfg Electronic Coils/Transformers Mfg Motors/Generators Mfg Transformers

**(G-7606)**
**MATHEWS COMPANY**
Also Called: Mathew Equipment Company
500 Industrial Rd (60012-3684)
P.O. Box 70 (60039-0070)
PHONE.................................815 459-2210
Fax: 815 459-5889
David L Mathews, *Ch of Bd*
Joseph Shulfer, *President*
Lynn Hummer, *General Mgr*
Jeff Sedlack, *Vice Pres*
Dean Hysen, *Purch Agent*
EMP: 85
SQ FT: 25,000
SALES (est): 25.9MM **Privately Held**
WEB: www.mathewscompany.com
SIC: 3523 Haying machines: mowers, rakes, stackers, etc.; cutters & blowers, ensilage; driers (farm): grain, hay & seed; grounds mowing equipment

**(G-7607)**
**MCGRATH PRESS INC**
Also Called: McGrath Printing Custom Ap Inc.
740 Duffy Dr (60014-8199)
PHONE.................................815 356-5246
Fax: 815 356-5247
Kevin McGrath, *President*
Kevin Mc Grath, *President*
Brian Mueller, *Production*
Bob Benson, *Purchasing*
Dixie Church, *Manager*
EMP: 20
SQ FT: 11,700
SALES (est): 4.2MM **Privately Held**
SIC: 2752 7336 2789 2791 Commercial printing, offset; commercial art & graphic design; bookbinding & related work; typesetting; die-cut paper & board; letterpress & screen printing

**(G-7608)**
**MEDTRONIC INC**
815 Tek Dr (60014-8172)
PHONE.................................815 444-2500
EMP: 8 **Privately Held**
SIC: 3841 Surgical & medical instruments
HQ: Medtronic, Inc.
710 Medtronic Pkwy
Minneapolis MN 55432
763 514-4000

**(G-7609)**
**METO-GRAFICS INC**
111 Erick St Ste 116 (60014-1312)
PHONE.................................847 639-0044
Michael V Emrich, *President*
Julie Tomaso, *Purch Agent*
Chris Craig, *Manager*
EMP: 14
SQ FT: 30,000
SALES (est): 3.6MM **Privately Held**
WEB: www.meto-grafics.com
SIC: 2759 3471 3479 3625 Screen printing; anodizing (plating) of metals or formed products; etching & engraving; etching on metals; relays & industrial controls; switchgear & switchboard apparatus; scales & balances, except laboratory

**(G-7610)**
**METROM RAIL LLC**
1125 Mitchell Ct (60014-1723)
PHONE.................................847 874-7233
Anthony Scala, *Principal*
Rick Carlson, *Manager*
EMP: 10
SALES (est): 1.8MM **Privately Held**
SIC: 3999 Manufacturing industries

**(G-7611)**
**MICRON ENGINEERING CO**
2125 E Dean Woodstock (60039)
P.O. Box 2412 (60039-2412)
PHONE.................................815 455-2888
Fax: 815 455-2855
John Karr, *Owner*
EMP: 3
SALES: 375K **Privately Held**
SIC: 3544 3612 Special dies & tools; transformers, except electric

**(G-7612)**
**MIDWEST MOBILE CANNING LLC**
1228 Westport Rdg (60014-8989)
PHONE.................................815 861-4515
Terry McGinnis, *Mng Member*
EMP: 2 EST: 2013
SALES: 700K **Privately Held**
SIC: 3565 7389 Bottling & canning machinery;

**(G-7613)**
**MILLENNIUM ELECTRONICS INC**
300 Millennium Dr (60012-3740)
PHONE.................................815 479-9755
Fax: 815 479-1153
Duane R Benn, *President*
Marc Damman, *Vice Pres*
Andrew K Miraldi, *Vice Pres*
▲ EMP: 97
SQ FT: 60,000
SALES (est): 12.6MM
SALES (corp-wide): 31MM **Privately Held**
WEB: www.mei2000.net
SIC: 3679 Harness assemblies for electronic use: wire or cable
PA: Adco Circuits, Inc.
2868 Bond St
Rochester Hills MI 48309
248 853-6620

**(G-7614)**
**MODERN FLUID TECHNOLOGY INC**
93 Berkshire Dr Ste F (60014-2809)
PHONE.................................815 356-0001
Louis Licastro Jr, *President*
EMP: 5
SQ FT: 2,300
SALES (est): 1.1MM **Privately Held**
SIC: 7699 3823 8742 Industrial machinery & equipment repair; industrial process control instruments; industry specialist consultants

**(G-7615)**
**MOLD REPAIR AND MANUFACTURING**
2520 Il Route 176 Ste 5 (60014-2227)
PHONE.................................815 477-1332
John Demmikus, *Owner*
EMP: 3 EST: 2008
SALES (est): 75.4K **Privately Held**
SIC: 7699 3999 Repair services; manufacturing industries

**(G-7616)**
**MPD MEDICAL SYSTEMS INC**
2530 Il Route 176 Ste 3 (60014-2226)
PHONE.................................815 477-0707
Thomas Parr, *President*
George Mede, *Vice Pres*
Roger Dittrich, *Treasurer*
▼ EMP: 4
SQ FT: 10,000
SALES (est): 599.1K **Privately Held**
WEB: www.mpdmedical.com
SIC: 2599 Hospital furniture, except beds

**(G-7617)**
**NATIONAL GIFT CARD CORP**
300 Millennium Dr (60012-3740)
PHONE.................................815 477-4288
Fax: 815 477-1290
Adam Van Witzenburg, *CEO*
Douglas Wheeler, *President*
Steve Van Witzenburg, *General Mgr*
Bill St Clair, *Senior VP*
Eric Thiegs, *Senior VP*
EMP: 45
SALES (est): 8.2MM **Privately Held**
SIC: 2771 7334 Greeting cards; photocopying & duplicating services

**(G-7618)**
**NELSON-WHITTAKER LTD**
Also Called: Central Specialties
220 Exchange Dr Ste D (60014-6282)
PHONE.................................815 459-6000
Fax: 815 459-6105
Jay A Maher, *President*
Susan Maher, *Vice Pres*
Joe Mancuso, *Plant Mgr*
Sharri Kapaldo, *Purch Mgr*
Russ Budde, *Sales Mgr*
▲ EMP: 26 EST: 1992
SQ FT: 27,300
SALES (est): 5.6MM **Privately Held**
WEB: www.csltd.com
SIC: 3914 3944 3484 Stainless steel ware; strollers, baby (vehicle); guns (firearms) or gun parts, 30 mm. & below

**(G-7619)**
**NIMCO CORPORATION**
1000 Nimco Dr (60014-1704)
P.O. Box 320 (60039-0320)
PHONE.................................815 459-4200
Fax: 815 459-8119
Larry G Bachner, *CEO*
Jerry G Bachner, *President*
Laverne E Bachner, *Vice Pres*
Kristie Cox, *Manager*
▲ EMP: 55 EST: 1972
SQ FT: 40,000
SALES (est): 14.2MM **Privately Held**
SIC: 3556 Packing house machinery

**(G-7620)**
**NORTHERN ILLINOIS GAS COMPANY**
Also Called: Nicor Gas
300 W Terra Cotta Ave (60014-3512)
PHONE.................................630 983-8676
Fax: 815 455-4688
Cathy Chivari, *Branch Mgr*
Dave Ruffalo, *Real Est Agnt*
EMP: 129
SALES (corp-wide): 19.9B **Publicly Held**
WEB: www.nicor.com
SIC: 4924 1382 4923 Natural gas distribution; oil & gas exploration services; gas transmission & distribution
HQ: Northern Illinois Gas Company
1844 W Ferry Rd
Naperville IL 60563
630 983-8676

**(G-7621)**
**NTPWIND POWER INC**
Also Called: Northtech Power
4702 Rte 176 (60014)
PHONE.................................815 345-1931
Charles Spoto, *President*
EMP: 3
SALES (est): 130.5K **Privately Held**
SIC: 3511 Turbines & turbine generator sets & parts

**(G-7622)**
**NU-METAL PRODUCTS INC**
260 E Prairie St (60014-4413)
PHONE.................................815 459-2075
Fax: 815 459-0435
Francene Weyland, *President*
William H Weyland, *General Mgr*
Cyntheea White, *Corp Secy*
EMP: 18 EST: 1946
SQ FT: 15,000
SALES (est): 3MM **Privately Held**
WEB: www.numetalproducts.com
SIC: 3451 Screw machine products

**(G-7623)**
**OPEN ADVANCED MRI CRYSTL**
820 E Terra Cotta Ave # 102 (60014-3649)
PHONE.................................815 444-1330
Jeff Moore, *Director*
EMP: 5
SALES (est): 574.2K **Privately Held**
SIC: 2835 In vitro & in vivo diagnostic substances

**(G-7624)**
**P F PETTIBONE & CO**
Also Called: P.F.
2220 Il Route 176 A (60014-2218)
P.O. Box 364, Hebron (60034-0364)
PHONE.................................815 344-7811
William J Poggensee III, *President*
Deborah Cherney, *Vice Pres*
Stella M Poggensee, *Admin Sec*
EMP: 5 EST: 1895
SQ FT: 2,000
SALES (est): 870.4K **Privately Held**
WEB: www.pfpettibone.com
SIC: 5199 2752 5192 Badges; commercial printing, offset; books

**(G-7625)**
**PIN UP TATTOO**
424 W Virginia St (60014-5936)
PHONE.................................815 477-7515
EMP: 3
SALES (est): 203.1K **Privately Held**
SIC: 3452 Pins

**(G-7626)**
**POLLACK MANUFACTURING CO LLC**
9418 Butternut Dr (60014-3913)
PHONE.................................815 520-8415
Nicole Pollack, *Principal*
EMP: 3
SALES (est): 100.1K **Privately Held**
SIC: 3999 Manufacturing industries

**(G-7627)**
**PRECISION NEON GLASSWORK**
1324 Knollwood Cir (60014-1829)
PHONE.................................847 428-1200
Curtis Muller, *Owner*
EMP: 2
SQ FT: 2,000
SALES: 200K **Privately Held**
SIC: 3993 5046 Neon signs; neon signs

**(G-7628)**
**PRECISION PLUS PRODUCTS INC**
990 Lutter Dr Ste B (60014-1719)
PHONE.................................815 459-1351
Fax: 815 459-1506
Alexander E Donald, *President*
James C Markel, *Vice Pres*
EMP: 4
SQ FT: 13,000
SALES (est): 494.2K **Privately Held**
SIC: 3599 Machine shop, jobbing & repair

**(G-7629)**
**PRESSURE SPECIALIST INC**
186 Virginia Rd (60014-7904)
PHONE.................................815 477-0007
Fax: 815 477-7395
John R Ripkey, *President*
Nancy Ripkey, *Manager*
▲ EMP: 40
SQ FT: 20,000
SALES (est): 8.8MM **Privately Held**
WEB: www.hoseshop.com
SIC: 3491 Regulators (steam fittings)

**(G-7630)**
**PRESTRESS ENGINEERING COMPANY (PA)**
Also Called: Prestressed Products Company
2220 Il Route 176 (60014-2218)
P.O. Box 100, Marathon WI (54448-0100)
PHONE.................................815 459-4545
Fax: 815 459-6855
Tim Sonnentag, *President*
Robert Stoehr, *CFO*
EMP: 8 EST: 1997
SALES (est): 2.6MM **Privately Held**
WEB: www.pre-stress.com
SIC: 3272 Prestressed concrete products

**(G-7631)**
**PRINTECH OF ILLINOIS INC**
975 Nimco Dr Ste E (60014-1734)
PHONE.................................815 356-1195
Ron Pekovitch, *President*
EMP: 4
SQ FT: 20,000

# Crystal Lake - Mchenry County (G-7632)   GEOGRAPHIC SECTION

**SALES (est):** 280K **Privately Held**
**WEB:** www.printechofil.com
**SIC:** 2752 Commercial printing, lithographic

**(G-7632)**
**PRO TECHMATION INC**
370 E Prairie St Ste 5 (60014-4475)
P.O. Box 1769 (60039-1769)
**PHONE** ........................... 815 459-5909
**Fax:** 815 459-6378
Don Meyer, *President*
Mary Meyer, *Exec VP*
Scott Kokuska, *Plant Mgr*
Vickie Gray, *Office Mgr*
**EMP:** 5
**SALES:** 600K **Privately Held**
**WEB:** www.protechmation.com
**SIC:** 3569 Assembly machines, non-metalworking

**(G-7633)**
**PRO TUFF DECAL INC**
7505 Eastgate Aly (60014-7945)
P.O. Box 1800 (60039-1800)
**PHONE** ........................... 815 356-9160
**Fax:** 815 356-9161
Ross J Teresi, *President*
▲ **EMP:** 40
**SQ FT:** 10,000
**SALES (est):** 6.9MM **Privately Held**
**WEB:** www.protuffdecals.com
**SIC:** 2759 Screen printing

**(G-7634)**
**PROCESS ENGINEERING CORP (PA)**
7426 Virginia Rd (60014-7906)
P.O. Box 279 (60039-0279)
**PHONE** ........................... 815 459-1734
**Fax:** 815 459-3676
Maridelle McKesson, *President*
James M McKesson, *Vice Pres*
Ted McKesson, *Vice Pres*
Tim Boyd, *Engineer*
**EMP:** 17
**SQ FT:** 18,000
**SALES (est):** 2.7MM **Privately Held**
**WEB:** www.proengcorp.com
**SIC:** 3624 Carbon & graphite products

**(G-7635)**
**PROCESSED STEEL COMPANY**
3703 S Il Route 31 (60012-1412)
**PHONE** ........................... 815 459-2400
George A Berry IV, *President*
Kathleen M Martinez, *Admin Sec*
▲ **EMP:** 309
**SALES (est):** 1.8MM
**SALES (corp-wide):** 179.8MM **Privately Held**
**SIC:** 3312 Tool & die steel & alloys
**HQ:** Tc Industries, Inc.
3703 S Il Route 31
Crystal Lake IL 60012
815 459-2401

**(G-7636)**
**RAMCO GROUP LLC**
Also Called: Ramco Tool
764 Tek Dr (60014-8100)
**PHONE** ........................... 847 639-9899
Curtis Kenney, *President*
Sarah Kenney, *Admin Asst*
**EMP:** 12
**SALES (est):** 1.2MM **Privately Held**
**SIC:** 3541 8711 Machine tools, metal cutting type; machine tool design

**(G-7637)**
**RAVEN TREE PRESS LLC**
6213 Factory Rd Ste B (60014-7908)
**PHONE** ........................... 800 323-8270
Dawn Jeffers,
Steve Stiles,
Rob Straebel,
**EMP:** 5
**SALES (est):** 313.7K **Privately Held**
**SIC:** 2731 Book publishing

**(G-7638)**
**REPROGRAPHICS (PA)**
26 Crystal Lake Plz (60014-7929)
**PHONE** ........................... 815 477-1018
**Fax:** 815 477-3839
Herman C Braun, *Owner*
Karl Brown, *Vice Pres*
**EMP:** 4
**SQ FT:** 5,600
**SALES (est):** 783.8K **Privately Held**
**WEB:** www.reprographics.org
**SIC:** 7334 7374 2791 2789 Photocopying & duplicating services; blueprinting service; data processing & preparation; typesetting; bookbinding & related work

**(G-7639)**
**RESEARCH IN MOTION RF INC**
500 Coventry Ln Ste 260 (60014-7592)
**PHONE** ........................... 815 444-1095
Keith Manssen, *Vice Pres*
Anthon Thomas, *Branch Mgr*
**EMP:** 8
**SALES (corp-wide):** 1.3B **Privately Held**
**WEB:** www.phasedarray.com
**SIC:** 3812 3663 Search & navigation equipment; antennas, transmitting & communications
**HQ:** Research In Motion Rf, Inc.
22 Technology Way Fl 5
Nashua NH 03060
603 598-8880

**(G-7640)**
**RFQ LLC**
Also Called: Promoversity
6213 Factory Rd Ste A (60014-7908)
**PHONE** ........................... 815 893-6656
Doug Murphy,
Roberta Ward,
**EMP:** 4 **EST:** 2010
**SALES (est):** 1.3MM
**SALES (corp-wide):** 1.8B **Publicly Held**
**SIC:** 8743 2253 Sales promotion; T-shirts & tops, knit
**PA:** Barnes & Noble Education, Inc.
120 Mountainview Blvd A
Basking Ridge NJ 07920
908 991-2665

**(G-7641)**
**RIDGEFIELD INDUSTRIES CO LLC**
Also Called: Tall Trees Farm
8420 Railroad St (60012-2806)
**PHONE** ........................... 800 569-0316
**Fax:** 815 356-9492
Michael V Mitchell, *Principal*
Tom Bossier, *Manager*
Dan Hamley, *Manager*
▲ **EMP:** 39
**SQ FT:** 25,000
**SALES (est):** 15.1MM **Privately Held**
**WEB:** www.ridgefieldindustries.com
**SIC:** 5023 2426 5713 Wood flooring; flooring, hardwood; floor covering stores

**(G-7642)**
**RITA CORPORATION (PA)**
850 S Route 31 (60014)
P.O. Box 457 (60039-0457)
**PHONE** ........................... 815 337-2500
**Fax:** 312 337-2522
Stephen T Goode Jr, *Ch of Bd*
Brian J Goode, *President*
Jim Cook, *Vice Pres*
Ron Corbick, *Vice Pres*
Jaime McLeer, *Project Mgr*
▲ **EMP:** 50
**SQ FT:** 120,000
**SALES (est):** 36.1MM **Privately Held**
**WEB:** www.ritacorp.com
**SIC:** 2833 2844 2824 5169 Animal oils, medicinal grade: refined or concentrated; face creams or lotions; protein fibers; chemicals & allied products

**(G-7643)**
**RITE-TEC COMMUNICATIONS**
5812 Marietta Dr (60014-4508)
**PHONE** ........................... 815 459-7712
**Fax:** 815 459-7833
John Riska, *Owner*
**EMP:** 6
**SALES (est):** 129.1K **Privately Held**
**SIC:** 8999 7336 2791 2731 Writing for publication; commercial art & graphic design; typesetting; book publishing

**(G-7644)**
**RW TECHNOLOGIES US LLC**
387 E Congress Pkwy A1 (60014-6287)
**PHONE** ........................... 815 444-6887
Troy Richert, *Managing Prtnr*
Micheal Walker,
**EMP:** 10
**SQ FT:** 10,000
**SALES (est):** 1.2MM **Privately Held**
**SIC:** 3672 Printed circuit boards

**(G-7645)**
**SAGE PRODUCTS LLC**
815 Tek Dr (60014-8172)
**PHONE** ........................... 815 455-4700
**Fax:** 815 455-5599
Pam Allen, *Branch Mgr*
**EMP:** 7
**SALES (corp-wide):** 11.3B **Publicly Held**
**SIC:** 3061 Mechanical rubber goods
**HQ:** Sage Products, Llc
3909 3 Oaks Rd
Cary IL 60013
815 455-4700

**(G-7646)**
**SEAN MATTHEW INNOVATIONS INC**
314 Lorraine Dr (60012-3611)
**PHONE** ........................... 815 455-4525
Michael Lohmeyer, *President*
**EMP:** 4
**SALES (est):** 249.8K **Privately Held**
**SIC:** 3999 Manufacturing industries

**(G-7647)**
**SERV-ALL DIE & TOOL COMPANY**
110 Erick St (60014-4534)
**PHONE** ........................... 815 459-2900
**Fax:** 847 459-8456
Dan Johnson, *President*
Bill Meier, *Prdtn Mgr*
Richard Sample, *Treasurer*
Kathy Payne, *CTO*
Dan Schultz, *Info Tech Dir*
**EMP:** 45 **EST:** 1944
**SQ FT:** 60,000
**SALES (est):** 12.2MM **Privately Held**
**WEB:** www.serv-all.com
**SIC:** 3364 3544 Zinc & zinc-base alloy die-castings; special dies & tools

**(G-7648)**
**SEVEN MFG INC**
3513 Deep Wood Dr (60012-1004)
**PHONE** ........................... 815 356-8102
Tanya Lynn Mari, *Principal*
▲ **EMP:** 8
**SALES (est):** 677K **Privately Held**
**SIC:** 3999 Manufacturing industries

**(G-7649)**
**SHAW SUBURBAN MEDIA GROUP INC**
Also Called: Kane County Chronicle
7717 S Il Route 31 (60014-8132)
P.O. Box 250 (60039-0250)
**PHONE** ........................... 815 459-4040
Thomas Shaw, *President*
Sarah Dickey, *Vice Pres*
Sarah Schwarzkopf, *Opers Mgr*
**EMP:** 225
**SALES (est):** 12.9MM
**SALES (corp-wide):** 83.1MM **Privately Held**
**SIC:** 2711 Newspapers, publishing & printing
**PA:** The B F Shaw Printing Company
444 Pine Hill Dr
Dixon IL
815 284-4000

**(G-7650)**
**SHOELACE INC (PA)**
Also Called: Ms. Bossy Boots
23 N Williams St (60014-4403)
P.O. Box 1696, Palatine (60078-1696)
**PHONE** ........................... 847 854-2500
Robert J Guss, *President*
Amber Mullins, *Manager*
**EMP:** 5
**SALES (est):** 388.5K **Privately Held**
**SIC:** 2241 Shoe laces, except leather

**(G-7651)**
**SIGGS RIGS**
3810 S Oak Knoll Rd (60012-2043)
**PHONE** ........................... 847 456-4012
Karen Siggeman, *Principal*
**EMP:** 4
**SALES (est):** 256.7K **Privately Held**
**SIC:** 3949 Hooks, fishing

**(G-7652)**
**SPARTAN ADHESIVES COATINGS CO**
345 E Terra Cotta Ave (60014-3608)
**PHONE** ........................... 815 459-8500
John Kuetemeyer, *President*
John Meyer, *Principal*
Cathy Washburn, *Vice Pres*
Kathy S Washburn, *Admin Sec*
James G Militello,
▲ **EMP:** 11 **EST:** 1969
**SQ FT:** 25,000
**SALES (est):** 2.9MM **Privately Held**
**WEB:** www.spartancompany.com
**SIC:** 2891 Adhesives

**(G-7653)**
**SPARTAN FLAME RETARDANTS INC**
345 E Terra Cotta Ave (60014-3608)
**PHONE** ........................... 815 459-8500
**Fax:** 815 459-8560
John Kuetemeyer, *President*
**EMP:** 10
**SALES (est):** 950K **Privately Held**
**SIC:** 2819 Industrial inorganic chemicals

**(G-7654)**
**STOP & GO INTERNATIONAL INC**
3610 Thunderbird Ln (60012-2089)
**PHONE** ........................... 815 455-9080
William G Merriman, *CEO*
Bonnie F Merriman, *Vice Pres*
▲ **EMP:** 6
**SQ FT:** 3,500
**SALES (est):** 484K **Privately Held**
**WEB:** www.stopngo.com
**SIC:** 3011 5531 Tires & inner tubes; automotive & home supply stores

**(G-7655)**
**SUB-SEM INC**
473 S Dartmoor Dr (60014-8700)
P.O. Box 161 (60039-0161)
**PHONE** ........................... 815 459-4139
**Fax:** 815 459-3369
Ronald Miller, *President*
Mike Lyons, *Vice Pres*
Thomas Mull, *Engineer*
Leslie Miller, *Human Res Mgr*
Rolf P Diehl, *Personnel Exec*
▲ **EMP:** 37
**SQ FT:** 18,600
**SALES (est):** 10.9MM **Privately Held**
**WEB:** www.subsem.com
**SIC:** 3679 Harness assemblies for electronic use: wire or cable

**(G-7656)**
**SUR-FIT CORPORATION**
110 Erick St (60014-4534)
**PHONE** ........................... 815 301-5815
Kevin Belousek, *President*
▲ **EMP:** 20
**SQ FT:** 20,000
**SALES (est):** 4MM **Privately Held**
**SIC:** 3511 Hydraulic turbines

**(G-7657)**
**SYSTEMS LIVE LTD**
6917 Red Barn Rd (60012-1053)
**PHONE** ........................... 815 455-3383
**Fax:** 815 455-3406
J Kennedy Nicholson, *President*
Ken Nicholson, *President*
**EMP:** 4
**SQ FT:** 2,000
**SALES (est):** 231.8K **Privately Held**
**SIC:** 7372 7371 Application computer software; custom computer programming services

## GEOGRAPHIC SECTION

**Cullom - Livingston County (G-7681)**

**(G-7658)**
**T & C METAL CO**
378 E Prairie St (60014-4415)
**PHONE**.................................815 459-4445
Thomas E Lindley Jr, *President*
Cynthia Lindley, *Corp Secy*
**EMP:** 4
**SQ FT:** 5,000
**SALES (est):** 694.3K **Privately Held**
**SIC:** 5093 4953 3341 Nonferrous metals scrap; refuse systems; secondary nonferrous metals

**(G-7659)**
**TAKASAGO INTL CORP USA**
300 Memorial Dr Ste 100 (60014-6273)
**PHONE**.................................815 479-5030
Fax: 815 479-1911
Charles Manley, *Vice Pres*
Takashi Miura, *Vice Pres*
Shi RHO, *Vice Pres*
Kazuhiko Tokoro, *Vice Pres*
Russel Buchanan, *Prdtn Mgr*
**EMP:** 6
**SALES (corp-wide):** 1.2B **Privately Held**
**SIC:** 2844 Perfumes & colognes
**HQ:** Takasago International Corporation (U.S.A)
4 Volvo Dr
Rockleigh NJ 07647
201 767-9001

**(G-7660)**
**TC INDUSTRIES INC (HQ)**
Also Called: Mill Products Division
3703 S Il Route 31 (60012-1412)
**PHONE**.................................815 459-2401
Thomas Z Hayward Jr, *Ch of Bd*
George A Berry IV, *President*
Fred Ballstaedt, *Vice Pres*
Wayne Gritzmacher, *Vice Pres*
Richard Albright, *Plant Mgr*
▼ **EMP:** 205 EST: 1881
**SQ FT:** 500,000
**SALES:** 179.7MM
**SALES (corp-wide):** 179.8MM **Privately Held**
**WEB:** www.tcindustries.com
**SIC:** 3499 3398 Machine bases, metal; metal heat treating
**PA:** Terra Cotta Holdings Co.
3703 S Il Route 31
Crystal Lake IL 60012
815 459-2400

**(G-7661)**
**TECHNIPAQ INC**
975 Lutter Dr (60014-8190)
**PHONE**.................................815 477-1800
Fax: 815 477-0777
Philip Rosenburg, *President*
Janice Rosenburg, *Vice Pres*
Kory Beckman, *Opers Mgr*
Brian Rosenburg, *VP Sales*
Ron Reiner, *Manager*
◆ **EMP:** 160
**SQ FT:** 60,000
**SALES (est):** 25.3MM **Privately Held**
**WEB:** www.technipaq.com
**SIC:** 3089 Laminating of plastic

**(G-7662)**
**TECHNOLOGIES DVLPMNT**
3517 Braberry Ln (60012-2079)
**PHONE**.................................815 943-9922
David Levitan, *Owner*
**EMP:** 5
**SALES (est):** 2MM **Privately Held**
**SIC:** 3083 Laminated plastic sheets

**(G-7663)**
**TELLENAR INC**
727 Tek Dr (60014-8172)
**PHONE**.................................815 356-8044
Fax: 815 356-8140
Richard J Schmidt, *President*
Lawrence Nelson, *Opers Staff*
Lawrence Schmidt, *Admin Sec*
**EMP:** 15
**SQ FT:** 35,000
**SALES (est):** 3.3MM **Privately Held**
**WEB:** www.tellenar.com
**SIC:** 3469 3549 Electronic enclosures, stamped or pressed metal; assembly machines, including robotic

**(G-7664)**
**TERRA COTTA HOLDINGS CO (PA)**
3703 S Il Route 31 (60012-1412)
**PHONE**.................................815 459-2400
Thomas Hayward Jr, *Ch of Bd*
George Berry III, *Vice Ch Bd*
Robert Berry, *President*
George Berry IV, *Exec VP*
Frank Celmer, *CFO*
**EMP:** 25
**SQ FT:** 20,000
**SALES (est):** 179.8MM **Privately Held**
**SIC:** 3499 3398 6531 Machine bases, metal; metal heat treating; real estate agents & managers

**(G-7665)**
**THINK INK INC**
890 Cog Cir (60014-7311)
**PHONE**.................................815 459-4565
Fred Kaiser Sr, *CEO*
Fred Kaiser Jr, *President*
Klara Kaiser, *Treasurer*
Tom Art, *Director*
**EMP:** 8
**SQ FT:** 5,100
**SALES (est):** 1.1MM **Privately Held**
**WEB:** www.think-ink.com
**SIC:** 2759 2396 Screen printing; automotive & apparel trimmings

**(G-7666)**
**TMJ ARCHITECTURAL LLC**
Also Called: T M J
430 Everett Ave (60014-7129)
**PHONE**.................................815 388-7820
Terry Mercer Jr, *President*
**EMP:** 1 EST: 2014
**SALES (est):** 282.5K **Privately Held**
**SIC:** 5033 2952 Roofing & siding materials; roofing materials

**(G-7667)**
**TORQEEDO INC**
171 Erick St Ste A1 (60014-4539)
**PHONE**.................................815 444-8806
Steve Trkla, *President*
Ralf Plieninger, *COO*
Tess Smallridge, *Corp Comm Staff*
Maurice Bajohr, *Manager*
Martin Schwarz, *Manager*
▲ **EMP:** 5
**SALES (est):** 1MM
**SALES (corp-wide):** 14.5MM **Privately Held**
**SIC:** 3621 Electric motor & generator auxillary parts
**PA:** Torqeedo Gmbh
Friedrichshafener Str. 4a
Gilching 82205
815 392-1510

**(G-7668)**
**TRADEVOLVE INC**
4211 Alex Ln (60014-3884)
**PHONE**.................................847 987-9411
Jason Mast, *President*
Daniel Goldstein, *COO*
**EMP:** 4 EST: 2013
**SALES (est):** 165.4K **Privately Held**
**SIC:** 7372 7389 Application computer software;

**(G-7669)**
**TRICAST/PRESFORE CORPORATION**
169 Virginia Rd (60014-7903)
**PHONE**.................................815 459-1820
Truman E Moore, *President*
Jeannie Rapier, *Office Mgr*
**EMP:** 6
**SQ FT:** 9,000
**SALES (est):** 864.5K **Privately Held**
**SIC:** 3365 3369 3366 Aluminum foundries; nonferrous foundries; brass foundry

**(G-7670)**
**TRIUMPH TWIST DRILL CO INC**
Also Called: Northern Division
301 Industrial Rd (60012-3602)
**PHONE**.................................815 459-6250
Fax: 815 459-9291
James H Beck, *Ch of Bd*
Arthur R Beck, *President*
Robert Maxey, *Vice Pres*
Mark M Harwell, *VP Opers*
Norman E Margolin, *CFO*
**EMP:** 500
**SQ FT:** 57,000
**SALES:** 59.5MM
**SALES (corp-wide):** 8.8B **Privately Held**
**WEB:** www.precisiontwistdrill.com
**SIC:** 3545 5084 3546 3544 Cutting tools for machine tools; drill bits, metalworking; industrial machinery & equipment; power-driven handtools; special dies, tools, jigs & fixtures
**HQ:** Precision Twist Drill Co.
301 Industrial Rd
Crystal Lake IL 60012
815 459-2040

**(G-7671)**
**UTILITY BUSINESS MEDIA INC**
Also Called: UTILITY SAFETY & OPS LEADERSHI
360 Memorial Dr Ste 10 (60014-6291)
**PHONE**.................................815 459-1796
Carla Housh, *President*
Kurt Moreland, *Publisher*
Kate Wade, *Business Mgr*
Catherine Cox, *Marketing Staff*
Greg Rokus, *Marketing Staff*
**EMP:** 4
**SALES (est):** 452.3K **Privately Held**
**SIC:** 2721 Periodicals: publishing only

**(G-7672)**
**VARIABLE OPERATIONS TECH INC**
Also Called: Vo-Tech
1145 Paltronics Ct (60014-1729)
**PHONE**.................................815 479-8528
Wojciech Furman, *President*
**EMP:** 21
**SQ FT:** 14,000
**SALES (est):** 6.4MM **Privately Held**
**WEB:** www.vo-tech.net
**SIC:** 3549 3541 3499 3599 Metalworking machinery; machine tools, metal cutting type; linings, safe & vault: metal; machine shop, jobbing & repair

**(G-7673)**
**VERLO MATTRESS OF LAKE GENEVA**
5150 Northwest Hwy Ste 1 (60014-8058)
**PHONE**.................................815 455-2570
Fax: 815 455-1767
Tom Wisniewski, *Manager*
**EMP:** 3
**SALES (corp-wide):** 1.2MM **Privately Held**
**SIC:** 5712 2515 2511 Mattresses; mattresses & bedsprings; wood household furniture
**PA:** Verlo Mattress Of Lake Geneva, Inc
2462 State Road 120
Lake Geneva WI
262 249-0420

**(G-7674)**
**VINYLWORKS INC**
8550 Ridgefield Rd Ste E (60012-2800)
**PHONE**.................................815 477-9680
Joel Berkland, *President*
Bob Turley, *General Mgr*
Kevin McCarthy, *Purch Mgr*
Grant Stahl, *Manager*
Craig Steagall, *Admin Sec*
**EMP:** 5
**SALES (est):** 599.7K **Privately Held**
**SIC:** 2824 Vinyl fibers

**(G-7675)**
**WEEKLY JOURNALS**
7717 S Il Route 31 (60014-8132)
P.O. Box 250 (60039-0250)
**PHONE**.................................815 459-4040
John Rung, *Publisher*
**EMP:** 4 EST: 1984
**SALES (est):** 230.7K **Privately Held**
**SIC:** 2711 Newspapers

**(G-7676)**
**WERNER CO**
420 E Terra Cotta Ave (60014-3611)
**PHONE**.................................815 459-6020
Nilesh Bedarkar, *Engineer*
Frank Carbajal, *Engineer*
Amit Chourey, *Engineer*
Radhika Dhande, *Engineer*
Lokesh Firkey, *Engineer*
**EMP:** 23 **Privately Held**
**SIC:** 3499 3355 3089 3446 Manufacturing industries
**HQ:** Werner Co
93 Werner Rd
Greenville PA 16125
724 588-2000

**(G-7677)**
**WEVAULTCOM LLC**
190 Liberty Rd Unit 3 (60014-8067)
**PHONE**.................................877 938-2858
Eric Peterson,
**EMP:** 20
**SALES (est):** 1.2MM
**SALES (corp-wide):** 5.6MM **Privately Held**
**SIC:** 3572 Computer storage devices
**PA:** Converged Technology Professionals, Inc.
190 Liberty Rd Unit 3
Crystal Lake IL 60014
312 447-7000

**(G-7678)**
**X-RAY CASSETTE REPAIR CO INC**
Also Called: Reina Imaging
6107 Lou St (60014-7916)
**PHONE**.................................815 356-8181
Fax: 815 356-8270
Leo J Reina, *President*
Dawm Farrar, *CFO*
Ronny Bachrach, *Marketing Staff*
Anthony Reina, *Info Tech Mgr*
▲ **EMP:** 25
**SQ FT:** 25,000
**SALES (est):** 4.7MM **Privately Held**
**WEB:** www.xraycassette.com
**SIC:** 3844 7699 X-ray apparatus & tubes; X-ray equipment repair

### Cuba
*Fulton County*

**(G-7679)**
**BANNER PUBLICATIONS**
Also Called: Banner Sale Management Service
350 N 1st St (61427-5117)
P.O. Box 500 (61427-0500)
**PHONE**.................................309 338-3294
Fax: 309 785-5050
Greg Deakin, *Owner*
Stacey Wise, *Human Res Mgr*
**EMP:** 5 EST: 1978
**SALES:** 750K **Privately Held**
**WEB:** www.bannersheepmagazine.com
**SIC:** 2721 5154 2791 Trade journals: publishing only, not printed on site; auctioning livestock; typesetting

**(G-7680)**
**FINISHING TOUCH**
Also Called: Menne's Finishing Touch
15383 E Cheyenne Dr (61427-9431)
**PHONE**.................................309 789-6444
James Menne, *President*
Sandy Menne, *Principal*
**EMP:** 3
**SALES (est):** 230.5K **Privately Held**
**SIC:** 2599 5712 Factory furniture & fixtures; unfinished furniture

### Cullom
*Livingston County*

**(G-7681)**
**EVERGREEN FS INC**
19484 N 3000 East Rd (60929-7093)
**PHONE**.................................815 934-5422
Paul Sutter, *Manager*
**EMP:** 3
**SALES (corp-wide):** 71.3MM **Privately Held**
**WEB:** www.evergreen-fs.com
**SIC:** 2875 Fertilizers, mixing only

**Cullom - Livingston County (G-7682)**       **GEOGRAPHIC SECTION**

PA: Evergreen Fs, Inc
402 N Hershey Rd
Bloomington IL 61704
877 963-2392

**(G-7682)**
**HAHN INDUSTRIES**
300 S Walnut St (60929-7201)
P.O. Box 355 (60929-0355)
PHONE.................................815 689-2133
Fax: 815 689-2855
Marjorie Hahn, *Owner*
Robert Hahn, *Owner*
**EMP:** 5 **EST:** 1960
**SQ FT:** 600
**SALES (est):** 404.1K **Privately Held**
**SIC: 3272** Concrete products

**(G-7683)**
**REGENCY CUSTOM WOODWORKING**
215 E Van Alstyne St (60929-7157)
P.O. Box 337 (60929-0337)
PHONE.................................815 689-2117
Fax: 815 689-2153
James Alling, *President*
Richard Alling, *Vice Pres*
Joan Alling, *Admin Sec*
**EMP:** 15
**SQ FT:** 25,000
**SALES:** 1MM **Privately Held**
**SIC: 2434** 2541 2521 5211 Wood kitchen cabinets; vanities, bathroom: wood; wood partitions & fixtures; wood office furniture; cabinets, kitchen

**(G-7684)**
**REMMERS WELDING AND MACHINE**
17809 N 3500 East Rd (60929-9757)
PHONE.................................815 689-2765
Jim Remmers, *Owner*
**EMP:** 2
**SALES:** 400K **Privately Held**
**SIC: 3599** Machine shop, jobbing & repair

**(G-7685)**
**TECHNIKS LLC**
Also Called: Rko Saw
424 E Jackson St (60929-7100)
PHONE.................................815 689-2748
Carey Wiesner, *General Mgr*
Carey Saw, *Financial Exec*
**EMP:** 24
**SALES (corp-wide):** 1.6B **Privately Held**
**SIC: 7699** 5084 3545 3425 Knife, saw & tool sharpening & repair; machine tools & accessories; machine tool accessories; saw blades & handsaws
HQ: Techniks, Llc
9930 E 56th St
Indianapolis IN 46236

## Custer Park
### Will County

**(G-7686)**
**ALLEN POPOVICH**
23215 Cooper Rd (60481-8450)
PHONE.................................815 712-7404
Allen Popovich, *Owner*
**EMP:** 6
**SALES (est):** 240.7K **Privately Held**
**SIC: 3441** 3544 3599 7692 Fabricated structural metal; special dies, tools, jigs & fixtures; crankshafts & camshafts, machining; welding repair; industrial machinery & equipment repair; agricultural equipment repair services

## Cutler
### Perry County

**(G-7687)**
**KNIGHT HAWK COAL LLC**
7290 County Line Rd (62238)
PHONE.................................618 497-2768
Steve Carter, *Branch Mgr*
**EMP:** 203

**SALES (corp-wide):** 544.3MM **Privately Held**
**SIC: 1241** Coal mining services
PA: Knight Hawk Coal, L.L.C.
500 Cutler Trico Rd
Percy IL 62272
618 426-3662

## Dahinda
### Knox County

**(G-7688)**
**KING SYSTEMS INC (PA)**
1130 Lakeview Rd S (61428-9790)
PHONE.................................309 879-2668
Brent King, *President*
**EMP:** 3
**SQ FT:** 800
**SALES (est):** 397.5K **Privately Held**
**SIC: 3523** Barn, silo, poultry, dairy & livestock machinery; hog feeding, handling & watering equipment; incubators & brooders, farm

## Dahlgren
### Hamilton County

**(G-7689)**
**COUNTERTOP CREATIONS**
6th St And Hwy 142 (62828)
P.O. Box 8 (62828-0008)
PHONE.................................618 736-2700
Fax: 618 736-2500
Steven Dodson, *Owner*
Alberta Dodson, *Co-Owner*
**EMP:** 13
**SALES (est):** 1.2MM **Privately Held**
**SIC: 2541** Counter & sink tops

**(G-7690)**
**HAMILTON COUNTY COAL LLC**
Also Called: Alliance Wor Processing LLC
18033 County Road 500 E (62828-4294)
PHONE.................................618 648-2603
Joseph W Craft III, *CEO*
Brandon Higgs, *Manager*
**EMP:** 310
**SALES:** 123.7MM
**SALES (corp-wide):** 1.9B **Publicly Held**
**SIC: 1241** Coal mining services
HQ: Alliance Coal, Llc
1717 S Boulder Ave # 400
Tulsa OK 74119
918 295-7600

**(G-7691)**
**JACOB CHAMBLISS**
Also Called: Chambliss Welding
127 County Road 600 E (62828-9003)
PHONE.................................618 731-6632
Jacob Chambliss, *Owner*
**EMP:** 3
**SQ FT:** 4,500
**SALES (est):** 114K **Privately Held**
**SIC: 7692** Welding repair

**(G-7692)**
**RAPP CABINETS & WOODWORKS INC**
501 E Illinois Hwy 142 (62828)
P.O. Box 88 (62828-0088)
PHONE.................................618 736-2955
Jim Rapp, *President*
James Rapp, *Owner*
Cletus Rapp, *Vice Pres*
**EMP:** 12
**SALES (est):** 1.4MM **Privately Held**
**SIC: 2541** 2434 Cabinets, lockers & shelving; wood kitchen cabinets

**(G-7693)**
**WHITE OAK RESOURCES LLC**
18033 County Road 500 E (62828-4294)
PHONE.................................618 643-5500
B Scott Spears, *Mng Member*
Ronda Barnard, *Manager*
Jeffery D Brock,
Shyla Hendrickson,
Chris James,
▲ **EMP:** 2008

**SALES (est):** 57.6MM
**SALES (corp-wide):** 1.9B **Publicly Held**
**SIC: 1241** Coal mining services
PA: Alliance Resource Partners Lp
1717 S Boulder Ave # 400
Tulsa OK 74119
918 295-7600

## Dakota
### Stephenson County

**(G-7694)**
**BERNER FOOD & BEVERAGE LLC (PA)**
Also Called: Berner Foods
2034 E Factory Rd (61018-9736)
PHONE.................................815 563-4222
Fax: 815 563-4017
Stephen A Kneubuehl, *CEO*
Bill Marchido, *President*
Edward Kneubuehl, *COO*
Todd Mullane, *Vice Pres*
Zachary Kneubuehl, *Prdtn Mgr*
**EMP:** 290
**SQ FT:** 34,000
**SALES (est):** 121.9MM **Privately Held**
WEB: www.bernerfoods.com
**SIC: 2022** 2026 2095 2086 Cheese spreads, dips, pastes & other cheese products; dips, cheese-based; dips, sour cream based; instant coffee; soft drinks: packaged in cans, bottles, etc.; spaghetti & other pasta sauce: packaged in cans, jars, etc.

## Dallas City
### Hancock County

**(G-7695)**
**D & D CONSTRUCTION CO LLC**
220 Cherry St (62330)
P.O. Box 508 (62330-0508)
PHONE.................................217 852-6631
David Greenig, *Mng Member*
**EMP:** 3
**SALES (est):** 1MM **Privately Held**
**SIC: 3448** Prefabricated metal buildings

**(G-7696)**
**DADANT & SONS INC**
Hwy 9 S (62330)
P.O. Box 237 (62330-0237)
PHONE.................................217 852-3324
Fax: 217 852-3806
Kent Robertson, *Manager*
**EMP:** 10
**SALES (corp-wide):** 32.5MM **Privately Held**
WEB: www.dadant.com
**SIC: 3823** 3444 Industrial process measurement equipment; sheet metalwork
PA: Dadant & Sons, Inc.
51 S 2nd St Ste 2
Hamilton IL 62341
217 847-3324

**(G-7697)**
**JACK BARTLETT**
Also Called: Bartlett Farms
2745 N County Road 2150 (62330-2300)
PHONE.................................217 659-3575
Jack Bartlett, *Owner*
**EMP:** 2
**SALES (est):** 220K **Privately Held**
**SIC: 2452** Farm & agricultural buildings, prefabricated wood

**(G-7698)**
**KINAST INC**
Also Called: Moulder's Friend, The
549 Oak St (62330-1217)
P.O. Box 120 (62330-0120)
PHONE.................................217 852-3525
Fax: 217 852-3256
Steven Kirkenslager, *President*
**EMP:** 3
**SQ FT:** 5,000
**SALES (est):** 332.1K **Privately Held**
**SIC: 3559** 3523 5084 Stone working machinery; farm machinery & equipment; machine tools & metalworking machinery

## Dalton City
### Moultrie County

**(G-7699)**
**WISHZING**
320 S East St (61925-1031)
P.O. Box 191 (61925-0191)
PHONE.................................217 413-8469
Tonya Walker, *Owner*
**EMP:** 20
**SALES:** 20K **Privately Held**
**SIC: 3369** Nonferrous foundries

## Damiansville
### Clinton County

**(G-7700)**
**WIEGMANN WOODWORKING**
105 Sugar Creek Ln (62215-1353)
PHONE.................................618 248-1300
Fax: 618 248-1301
Bobby Wiegmann, *Principal*
**EMP:** 9
**SALES (est):** 1.1MM **Privately Held**
**SIC: 2431** Millwork

## Danvers
### Mclean County

**(G-7701)**
**PROGRESS RAIL SERVICES CORP**
5704 E 1700 North Rd (61732-9251)
PHONE.................................309 963-4425
Rich Harris, *Branch Mgr*
**EMP:** 46
**SALES (corp-wide):** 38.5B **Publicly Held**
**SIC: 4789** 7389 3312 Railroad maintenance & repair services; railroad car repair; metal cutting services; structural & rail mill products
HQ: Progress Rail Services Corporation
1600 Progress Dr
Albertville AL 35950
256 593-1260

## Danville
### Vermilion County

**(G-7702)**
**APF US INC**
2204 Kickapoo Dr (61832-5379)
PHONE.................................217 304-0027
Martin Schwarzenberger, *CEO*
**EMP:** 1
**SALES:** 200K **Privately Held**
**SIC: 3569** General industrial machinery

**(G-7703)**
**ARCONIC INC**
1 Customer Pl (61834-9481)
PHONE.................................217 431-3800
Lee Leathers, *Manager*
Matthew Garth, *Executive*
**EMP:** 53
**SALES (corp-wide):** 12.3B **Publicly Held**
**SIC: 3353** Aluminum sheet & strip; coils, sheet aluminum; plates, aluminum; foil, aluminum
PA: Arconic Inc.
390 Park Ave
New York NY 10022
212 836-2758

**(G-7704)**
**AUTOMATION INTERNATIONAL INC**
Also Called: A I I
1020 Bahls St (61832-3367)
PHONE.................................217 446-9500
Larry E Moss, *President*
Maurice M Taylor Jr, *President*
Brenda Mitchell, *Purchasing*
Amy Waddell, *Purchasing*

Gary Ingold, *Engineer*
▼ **EMP:** 55 **EST:** 1955
**SQ FT:** 80,000
**SALES (est):** 21.1MM **Privately Held**
**WEB:** www.automation-intl.com
**SIC:** 3548 Resistance welders, electric; arc welders, transformer-rectifier

**(G-7705)**
**BES DESIGNS & ASSOCIATES INC (PA)**
2412 Georgetown Rd (61832-8425)
**PHONE**....................217 443-4619
Robert Jackson, *President*
Ted Hollen, *Corp Secy*
**EMP:** 4
**SQ FT:** 4,000
**SALES:** 742.6K **Privately Held**
**SIC:** 2759 Screen printing

**(G-7706)**
**BOBS MARKET & GREENHOUSE**
1118 E Voorhees St (61832-2130)
**PHONE**....................217 442-8155
Robert Wiese, *Owner*
Sharon Wiese, *Partner*
**EMP:** 1
**SQ FT:** 3,000
**SALES:** 300K **Privately Held**
**SIC:** 5431 3272 Fruit stands or markets; vegetable stands or markets; monuments, concrete

**(G-7707)**
**BRAINERD CHEMICAL MIDWEST LLC**
209 Brewer Rd (61834-6707)
P.O. Box 521150, Tulsa OK (74152-1150)
**PHONE**....................918 622-1214
Bruce Schofield, *Manager*
**EMP:** 3
**SALES (corp-wide):** 20.8MM **Privately Held**
**SIC:** 2819 Hydrochloric acid
**HQ:** Brainerd Chemical Midwest Llc
  427 S Boston Ave
  Tulsa OK 74103
  918 622-1214

**(G-7708)**
**BUNGE MILLING INC**
321 E North St (61832-5888)
**PHONE**....................217 442-1801
**EMP:** 139 **Privately Held**
**SIC:** 2041 Mfg Flour/Grain Mill Prooducts
**HQ:** Bunge Milling, Inc.
  11720 Borman Dr
  Saint Louis MO 63146
  314 292-2000

**(G-7709)**
**CHEM-CAST LTD**
1009 Lynch Rd (61834-5804)
**PHONE**....................217 443-5532
**Fax:** 217 443-5533
Kenneth A Craig, *Partner*
Jeffery A Craig, *Vice Pres*
Jeff Craig, *Plant Mgr*
Sal Marino, *Purchasing*
Mark Ottarski, *Director*
**EMP:** 138
**SQ FT:** 140,000
**SALES (est):** 30.2MM **Privately Held**
**WEB:** www.chem-cast.com
**SIC:** 3544 3543 Special dies, tools, jigs & fixtures; industrial patterns

**(G-7710)**
**CREATIVE CABINETS COUNTERTOPS**
3817 N Vermilion St (61832-1159)
**PHONE**....................217 446-6406
**Fax:** 217 446-6400
Chris White, *President*
Allen Norris, *General Mgr*
Linda White, *Vice Pres*
**EMP:** 14
**SQ FT:** 17,000
**SALES:** 1.3MM **Privately Held**
**SIC:** 2434 5031 Wood kitchen cabinets; vanities, bathroom: wood; kitchen cabinets

**(G-7711)**
**CRONKHITE INDUSTRIES INC**
2212 Kickapoo Dr (61832-5379)
**PHONE**....................217 443-3700
**Fax:** 217 443-3778
Cynthia S Cronkhite, *President*
David Mc Dowell, *Vice Pres*
Wade Meade, *Vice Pres*
**EMP:** 14 **EST:** 1972
**SQ FT:** 32,000
**SALES (est):** 3.1MM **Privately Held**
**WEB:** www.cronkhitetrailers.com
**SIC:** 3523 Trailers & wagons, farm

**(G-7712)**
**DANVILLE METAL STAMPING CO INC (PA)**
20 Oakwood Ave (61832-5452)
**PHONE**....................217 446-0647
Judd Peck, *President*
Judd C Peck, *Principal*
Tom Neal, *VP Mfg*
Sue Beck, *Admin Sec*
**EMP:** 12 **EST:** 1946
**SQ FT:** 175,000
**SALES (est):** 74.5MM **Privately Held**
**WEB:** www.danvillemetal.com
**SIC:** 3724 Engine mount parts, aircraft

**(G-7713)**
**DANVILLE METAL STAMPING CO INC**
17 Oakwood Ave (61832-5598)
**PHONE**....................217 446-0647
**Fax:** 217 446-3751
Judd Peck, *President*
**EMP:** 12
**SALES (corp-wide):** 74.5MM **Privately Held**
**WEB:** www.danvillemetal.com
**SIC:** 3724 Engine mount parts, aircraft
**PA:** Danville Metal Stamping Co., Inc.
  20 Oakwood Ave
  Danville IL 61832
  217 446-0647

**(G-7714)**
**DANVILLE METAL STAMPING CO INC**
1100 Martin St (61832-3217)
**PHONE**....................217 446-0647
**EMP:** 8
**SALES (corp-wide):** 74.5MM **Privately Held**
**SIC:** 3724 Engine mount parts, aircraft
**PA:** Danville Metal Stamping Co., Inc.
  20 Oakwood Ave
  Danville IL 61832
  217 446-0647

**(G-7715)**
**DEL STORM PRODUCTS INC**
2003 E Voorhees St (61834-6242)
**PHONE**....................217 446-3377
**Fax:** 217 446-1461
John Ives, *President*
**EMP:** 12 **EST:** 1955
**SQ FT:** 30,000
**SALES (est):** 1.8MM **Privately Held**
**SIC:** 3442 3429 Metal doors, sash & trim; screen & storm doors & windows; manufactured hardware (general)

**(G-7716)**
**ENVIROX LLC**
1938 E Fairchild St (61832-3501)
P.O. Box 2327 (61834-2327)
**PHONE**....................217 442-8596
**Fax:** 217 442-2568
Derek Webber, *Technology*
Patrick Stewart,
Tarylor Stewart,
**EMP:** 45 **EST:** 1999
**SQ FT:** 33,000
**SALES:** 11MM **Privately Held**
**WEB:** www.h2orange2.com
**SIC:** 2869 Industrial organic chemicals

**(G-7717)**
**ESTAD STAMPING & MFG CO**
Also Called: Brennan Engineering
1005 Griggs St (61834-4116)
P.O. Box 825 (61834-0825)
**PHONE**....................217 442-4600
Robert B Rew, *President*

Bill Barglaw, *Vice Pres*
Greg Rew, *Vice Pres*
Eva Cotton, *Treasurer*
**EMP:** 24
**SQ FT:** 35,000
**SALES (est):** 5.3MM **Privately Held**
**WEB:** www.estadstamping.com
**SIC:** 3315 3429 3469 3695 Nails, steel: wire or cut; casket hardware; stamping metal for the trade; drums, magnetic
**PA:** Gemco
  1019 Griggs St
  Danville IL 61832
  217 446-7900

**(G-7718)**
**FAULSTICH PRINTING COMPANY INC**
2001 E Voorhees St (61834-6242)
P.O. Box 732 (61834-0732)
**PHONE**....................217 442-4994
**Fax:** 217 442-4992
Fred J Faulstich, *President*
Con Bateman, *Corp Secy*
William Faulstich, *Vice Pres*
**EMP:** 9 **EST:** 1932
**SQ FT:** 11,000
**SALES:** 782.6K **Privately Held**
**SIC:** 2752 2759 Commercial printing, offset; letterpress printing

**(G-7719)**
**FIBERTEQ LLC**
3650 Southgate Dr (61834-9400)
**PHONE**....................217 431-2111
**Fax:** 217 443-3783
John Johanningsmeier, *Admin Mgr*
▲ **EMP:** 80
**SQ FT:** 150,000
**SALES (est):** 17.2MM **Privately Held**
**WEB:** www.fiberteq.com
**SIC:** 2221 Glass & fiberglass broadwoven fabrics

**(G-7720)**
**FLEX-N-GATE CORPORATION**
Also Called: Bumper Works
3403 Lynch Creek Dr (61834-9388)
**PHONE**....................217 442-4018
**Fax:** 217 442-8541
Karen McGinnis, *Purch Mgr*
Justin Legacy, *Buyer*
Joshua Clouse, *QC Mgr*
Bill Lang, *Manager*
**EMP:** 100
**SALES (corp-wide):** 3.3B **Privately Held**
**WEB:** www.flex-n-gate.com
**SIC:** 3714 Bumpers & bumperettes, motor vehicle
**PA:** Flex-N-Gate Corporation
  1306 E University Ave
  Urbana IL 61802
  217 384-6600

**(G-7721)**
**FLEX-N-GATE CORPORATION**
Also Called: Flex N Gate Plastics
3403 Lynch Creek Dr (61834-9388)
**PHONE**....................217 442-4018
Kevin Lee, *Branch Mgr*
**EMP:** 4
**SALES (corp-wide):** 3.3B **Privately Held**
**WEB:** www.flex-n-gate.com
**SIC:** 3089 Injection molding of plastics
**PA:** Flex-N-Gate Corporation
  1306 E University Ave
  Urbana IL 61802
  217 384-6600

**(G-7722)**
**FREIGHT CAR SERVICES INC**
2313 Cannon St Ste 2 (61832-4200)
**PHONE**....................217 443-4106
**Fax:** 217 443-0750
John E Carroll Jr, *President*
Donna Little, *Business Mgr*
Glenn Caren, *Vice Pres*
Ken Bridges, *VP Opers*
Jean Bates, *Purchasing*
**EMP:** 480

**SALES (est):** 31.4MM
**SALES (corp-wide):** 523.7MM **Publicly Held**
**WEB:** www.freightcaramerica.com
**SIC:** 4789 3743 3537 Railroad car repair; railroad car rebuilding; train cars & equipment, freight or passenger; industrial trucks & tractors
**PA:** Freightcar America, Inc.
  2 N Rverside Plz Ste 1300
  Chicago IL 60606
  800 458-2235

**(G-7723)**
**FREIGHTCAR AMERICA INC**
2313 Cannon St (61832-4200)
**PHONE**....................217 443-4106
Les Wood, *Managing Dir*
Terrence G Heidkamp, *Senior VP*
Michael List, *QC Mgr*
James Melton, *QC Mgr*
Mike Jordan, *Branch Mgr*
**EMP:** 150
**SALES (corp-wide):** 523.7MM **Publicly Held**
**SIC:** 3743 Train cars & equipment, freight or passenger
**PA:** Freightcar America, Inc.
  2 N Rverside Plz Ste 1300
  Chicago IL 60606
  800 458-2235

**(G-7724)**
**FURRY INC**
2005 E Voorhees St (61834-6242)
P.O. Box 453 (61834-0453)
**PHONE**....................217 446-0084
**Fax:** 217 446-0085
Dann E Furry, *President*
**EMP:** 13 **EST:** 1962
**SQ FT:** 20,000
**SALES (est):** 2.8MM **Privately Held**
**WEB:** www.furry.com
**SIC:** 3599 Machine shop, jobbing & repair

**(G-7725)**
**G P COLE INC**
Also Called: Dines Machine & Manufacturing
1120 Industrial St (61832-3351)
**PHONE**....................217 431-3029
**Fax:** 217 431-1946
Gary C Parks, *President*
**EMP:** 15
**SQ FT:** 9,545
**SALES:** 1.5MM **Privately Held**
**SIC:** 3599 Machine shop, jobbing & repair

**(G-7726)**
**GEMCO (PA)**
1019 Griggs St (61832-4116)
P.O. Box 846 (61834-0846)
**PHONE**....................217 446-7900
**Fax:** 217 442-2582
Robert B Rew, *CEO*
Greg Rew, *President*
**EMP:** 38 **EST:** 1941
**SQ FT:** 27,350
**SALES (est):** 5.3MM **Privately Held**
**WEB:** www.gemcoinsulation.com
**SIC:** 3399 Metal fasteners

**(G-7727)**
**GRACE & TRUTH INC**
210 Chestnut St (61832-2633)
**PHONE**....................217 442-1120
**Fax:** 217 442-1163
Sam O Hadley, *President*
Mary K Hassler, *Corp Secy*
Paul Van Ryn, *Vice Pres*
◆ **EMP:** 6 **EST:** 1931
**SQ FT:** 7,200
**SALES:** 313.5K **Privately Held**
**WEB:** www.gtpress.org
**SIC:** 2731 Books: publishing & printing

**(G-7728)**
**GREENWOOD INC (PA)**
Also Called: Greenwood Plastics
1126 N Kimball St (61832-3124)
**PHONE**....................800 798-4900
**Fax:** 217 442-9182
Donna Darby-Walthall, *President*
Dave Rumple, *Purchasing*
Richard Darby, *Treasurer*
Linda Sempsrott, *Admin Sec*
▲ **EMP:** 15

# Danville - Vermilion County (G-7729)

SQ FT: 2,000
SALES (est): 18MM  Privately Held
WEB: www.caminodelsol.com
SIC: 3995  3089  7261  Burial vaults, fiberglass; thermoformed finished plastic products; funeral home

### (G-7729)
### GREENWOOD INC
Also Called: Greenwood Plastics Industries
1126 N Kimball St  (61832-3124)
PHONE..................217 431-6034
Fax: 217 431-8411
Jim Darby, *President*
Tom Edwards, *Branch Mgr*
EMP: 25
SALES (corp-wide): 18MM  Privately Held
WEB: www.caminodelsol.com
SIC: 3089  Thermoformed finished plastic products
PA: Greenwood, Inc.
    1126 N Kimball St
    Danville IL 61832
    800 798-4900

### (G-7730)
### HEARING AID WAREHOUSE INC
1005 N Gilbert St  (61832-3848)
PHONE..................217 431-4700
Jeff Elkin, *President*
EMP: 3
SALES (est): 201.8K  Privately Held
SIC: 3842  5999  Hearing aids; miscellaneous retail stores

### (G-7731)
### HEATCRAFT RFRGN PDTS LLC
Also Called: Heatcraft Refrigeration Pdts
1001 E Voorhees St Ste B  (61832-2145)
PHONE..................217 446-2434
Fax: 217 446-3710
Larry Golen, *President*
Jeff Hummel, *Vice Pres*
Ernie Rumple, *QC Mgr*
Carol Miller, *Human Res Dir*
Richard Hawkins, *Personnel*
EMP: 325
SALES (corp-wide): 3.6B  Publicly Held
WEB: www.heatcraftrpd.com
SIC: 3585  Parts for heating, cooling & refrigerating equipment; condensers, refrigeration
HQ: Heatcraft Refrigeration Products Llc
    2175 W Park Place Blvd
    Stone Mountain GA 30087
    770 465-5600

### (G-7732)
### HOLMES BROS INC
510 Junction St  (61832-4800)
PHONE..................217 442-1430
Fax: 217 442-8936
Robert Muirhead, *President*
Barbara Muirhead, *Vice Pres*
Matthew Muirhead, *Vice Pres*
Jane Towne, *Purch Mgr*
Carrie Buchanan, *Office Mgr*
EMP: 30  EST: 1872
SQ FT: 100,000
SALES (est): 3.3MM  Privately Held
SIC: 3829  3599  Physical property testing equipment; machine shop, jobbing & repair

### (G-7733)
### HONEYWELL INTERNATIONAL INC
209 Brewer Rd  (61834-6707)
Peter Bray, *Purch Dir*
Tim Zimmer, *Manager*
EMP: 28
SALES (corp-wide): 39.3B  Publicly Held
WEB: www.honeywell.com
SIC: 2824  Fluorocarbon fibers
PA: Honeywell International Inc.
    115 Tabor Rd
    Morris Plains NJ 07950
    973 455-2000

### (G-7734)
### HONEYWELL INTERNATIONAL INC
3401 Lynch Creek Dr  (61834-9388)
PHONE..................217 431-3710
Joe Mollica, *Director*

EMP: 3
SALES (corp-wide): 39.3B  Publicly Held
SIC: 3724  Aircraft engines & engine parts
PA: Honeywell International Inc.
    115 Tabor Rd
    Morris Plains NJ 07950
    973 455-2000

### (G-7735)
### HYSTER CO
1010 E Fairchild St  (61832-3393)
PHONE..................217 443-7000
Fax: 217 443-7396
John Bartho, *Vice Pres*
EMP: 9
SALES (est): 1.5MM  Privately Held
SIC: 3536  Hoists, cranes & monorails

### (G-7736)
### HYSTER-YALE GROUP INC
1010 E Fairchild St  (61832-3393)
PHONE..................217 443-7416
Suzanne Adkins, *Sales Mgr*
Brian Barr, *Manager*
Jeff Kline, *Manager*
Tom O'Connell, *Manager*
Tricia Richardson, *Manager*
EMP: 30
SALES (corp-wide): 2.5B  Publicly Held
SIC: 4225  5084  3537  General warehousing & storage; industrial machinery & equipment; industrial trucks & tractors
HQ: Hyster-Yale Group, Inc.
    1400 Sullivan Dr
    Greenville NC 27834
    252 931-5100

### (G-7737)
### ILLINI CASTINGS LLC
1940 E Fairchild St  (61832-3515)
P.O. Box 827  (61834-0827)
PHONE..................217 446-6365
John Widmer, *President*
Rebecca York, *Office Mgr*
▲ EMP: 16  EST: 2009
SALES (est): 4MM
SALES (corp-wide): 140.2MM  Privately Held
SIC: 5093  3743  Metal scrap & waste materials; plastics scrap; waste paper; railroad equipment
PA: Mervis Industries, Inc.
    3295 E Main St Ste C
    Danville IL 61834
    217 442-5300

### (G-7738)
### INDEPENDENT NEWS
Also Called: Independent News, The
2202 Kickapoo Dr  (61832-5379)
PHONE..................217 662-6001
Fax: 217 662-2484
Doyne Lenhart, *Owner*
EMP: 5
SQ FT: 1,000
SALES (est): 140K  Privately Held
WEB: www.lenhartauction.com
SIC: 2711  Newspapers: publishing only, not printed on site

### (G-7739)
### INDIANA PRECISION INC
130 N Jackson St  (61832-4728)
PHONE..................765 361-0247
Chuck Holmes, *Personnel Exec*
Kim Bell, *Manager*
Jim Denman, *Supervisor*
EMP: 15
SALES (est): 2.2MM
SALES (corp-wide): 546.3MM  Privately Held
WEB: www.kaydon.com
SIC: 3089  3599  3544  Injection molding of plastics; machine & other job shop work; special dies, tools, jigs & fixtures
HQ: Kaydon Corporation
    2723 S State St Ste 300
    Ann Arbor MI 48104
    734 747-7025

### (G-7740)
### KAYDON ACQUISITION XII INC
Also Called: Tridan International
130 N Jackson St  (61832-4728)
PHONE..................217 443-3592
Michael Purchase, *CEO*

Bill Benner, *Plant Mgr*
Gary Dobbins, *Opers Mgr*
Bob Cromwell, *Safety Mgr*
Pat Smith, *Opers Staff*
EMP: 30
SALES (est): 6.8MM
SALES (corp-wide): 546.3MM  Privately Held
SIC: 3545  Machine tool accessories
HQ: Kaydon Corporation
    2723 S State St Ste 300
    Ann Arbor MI 48104
    734 747-7025

### (G-7741)
### KELLY PRINTING CO INC
205 Oregon Ave  (61832-4237)
PHONE..................217 443-1792
Fax: 217 443-0869
Thomas Kelly, *President*
Tom Kelly, *Office Mgr*
EMP: 20
SQ FT: 5,000
SALES: 900K  Privately Held
SIC: 2752  2791  2789  2759  Commercial printing, offset; typesetting; bookbinding & related work; commercial printing

### (G-7742)
### KELLYS SIGN SHOP
1004 N Vermilion St  (61832-3057)
PHONE..................217 477-0167
Art Tabels, *Principal*
EMP: 3
SALES (est): 249.7K  Privately Held
SIC: 3993  Signs & advertising specialties

### (G-7743)
### KIK CUSTOM PRODUCTS INC (HQ)
Also Called: Kik Danville
1 W Hegeler Ln  (61832-8341)
PHONE..................217 442-1400
William Smith, *President*
Bill Smith, *Principal*
Valdemar Guerra, *Controller*
Kurt Augustson, *Manager*
Bharet Bhavsar, *Manager*
▲ EMP: 450
SQ FT: 315,000
SALES: 716.3MM
SALES (corp-wide): 496.1K  Privately Held
SIC: 2841  2842  2843  2844  Soap & other detergents; specialty cleaning, polishes & sanitation goods; surface active agents; toilet preparations
PA: Kik Custom Products Inc
    101 Macintosh Blvd
    Concord ON L4K 4
    905 660-0444

### (G-7744)
### KILE MACHINE & TOOL INC
3231 Illini Rd  (61834-6278)
PHONE..................217 446-8616
Fax: 217 446-1496
Albert J Kile, *President*
Anna C Kile, *Corp Secy*
Albet L Kile, *Vice Pres*
Russell W Kile, *Vice Pres*
Stanley J Kile, *Vice Pres*
EMP: 5  EST: 1967
SQ FT: 8,500
SALES: 400K  Privately Held
WEB: www.kilemachinetool.com
SIC: 3466  3545  3452  Crowns & closures; machine tool accessories; bolts, nuts, rivets & washers

### (G-7745)
### LEATHERNECK HARDWARE INC
1017 Bahls St  (61832-3323)
P.O. Box 1142  (61834-1142)
PHONE..................217 431-3096
Fax: 217 442-3613
Dale Carlton, *President*
Connie Carlton, *Corp Secy*
Tom Hanrahan, *Opers Mgr*
Henry Hunt, *Controller*
Bob Brown, *Sales Staff*
▲ EMP: 24
SQ FT: 6,000

SALES (est): 4.9MM  Privately Held
WEB: www.doorhdwe.com
SIC: 3429  Door opening & closing devices, except electrical

### (G-7746)
### LEBANON SEABOARD CORPORATION
Also Called: Lebanon Chemical
508 W Ross Ln  (61834-5137)
P.O. Box 686  (61834-0686)
PHONE..................217 446-0983
Fax: 217 443-6121
Vernon Bishop, *President*
Katherine Bishop, *Vice Pres*
George Hinkle, *Plant Mgr*
Wyatt White, *Safety Mgr*
Bill Kelso, *VP Sls/Mktg*
EMP: 40
SALES (corp-wide): 147.6MM  Privately Held
WEB: www.lebturf.com
SIC: 2875  5191  2048  Fertilizers, mixing only; pesticides; insecticides; chemicals, agricultural; prepared feeds; bird food, prepared
PA: Lebanon Seaboard Corporation
    1600 E Cumberland St
    Lebanon PA 17042
    717 273-1685

### (G-7747)
### LINNE MACHINE COMPANY INC
209 Avenue C  (61832-5498)
PHONE..................217 446-5746
Fax: 217 446-5579
Kim Linne, *President*
Pam Linne, *Vice Pres*
EMP: 3
SQ FT: 3,200
SALES (est): 389.6K  Privately Held
SIC: 3599  7692  Machine shop, jobbing & repair; welding repair

### (G-7748)
### LINWOOD LLC
917 N Walnut St Ste 101  (61832-3911)
PHONE..................217 446-1110
Nathan Byram, *Principal*
EMP: 3  EST: 2007
SALES (est): 270.3K  Privately Held
SIC: 2499  Wood products

### (G-7749)
### LONG CONSTRUCTION SERVICES
617 1/2 E Voorhees St  (61832-2150)
PHONE..................217 443-2876
Fax: 217 443-2887
John N Long, *President*
Jackie Long, *Vice Pres*
EMP: 5
SALES (est): 270K  Privately Held
SIC: 3479  Painting, coating & hot dipping

### (G-7750)
### LUMBER SPECIALISTS INC
137 N Walnut St  (61832-4712)
PHONE..................217 443-8484
Fax: 217 443-8490
John Foreman, *Branch Mgr*
Janet Pettice, *Manager*
Kathy Robinson, *Manager*
EMP: 10
SALES (corp-wide): 63.7MM  Privately Held
SIC: 2711  Newspapers
PA: The News-Gazette Inc
    15 E Main St
    Champaign IL 61820
    217 351-5252

### (G-7751)
### MARBLE MACHINE INC (PA)
21204 Rileysburg Rd  (61834-5892)
PHONE..................217 431-3014
Fax: 217 431-3034
Jeff Marble, *President*
EMP: 23
SQ FT: 25,000
SALES (est): 4MM  Privately Held
SIC: 3599  Machine shop, jobbing & repair

# GEOGRAPHIC SECTION

Danville - Vermilion County (G-7775)

**(G-7752)**
**MARBLE MACHINE INC**
Also Called: Danville Brass and Aluminum
205 Oakwood Ave (61832-5426)
PHONE .................... 217 442-0746
Ken Dale, *Sales/Mktg Mgr*
Mike Hoskins, *Manager*
**EMP:** 3
**SALES (corp-wide):** 4MM **Privately Held**
**SIC:** 3365 3369 Aluminum foundries; nonferrous foundries
**PA:** Marble Machine Inc
21204 Rileysburg Rd
Danville IL 61834
217 431-3014

**(G-7753)**
**MCENGLEVAN INDUS FRNC MFG INC**
Also Called: Mifco
708 Griggs St (61832-4011)
P.O. Box 31 (61834-0031)
PHONE .................... 217 446-0941
Fax: 217 446-0943
William Walter, *President*
William Walter Jr, *Vice Pres*
Nancy Harmon, *Admin Sec*
▼ **EMP:** 3 **EST:** 1938
**SQ FT:** 31,000
**SALES:** 997K **Privately Held**
**WEB:** www.mifco.com
**SIC:** 3567 Industrial furnaces & ovens

**(G-7754)**
**MEL PRICE COMPANY INC (PA)**
Also Called: Mel Price Containers
16395 Lewis Rd (61834)
P.O. Box 1637 (61834-1637)
PHONE .................... 217 442-9092
Fax: 217 443-0914
Melvin L Price, *President*
Jill Price, *Vice Pres*
**EMP:** 10 **EST:** 1976
**SALES:** 289K **Privately Held**
**SIC:** 4212 1794 1442 Local trucking, without storage; excavation & grading, building construction; sand mining; gravel & pebble mining

**(G-7755)**
**MH EQUIPMENT COMPANY**
1010 E Fairchild St (61832-3393)
P.O. Box 847 (61834-0847)
PHONE .................... 217 443-7210
Fax: 217 443-7658
Dan House, *Production*
Ray Seguin, *Branch Mgr*
Dave Greazer, *Manager*
Mike Hidgon, *Manager*
Butch Schnink, *Director*
**EMP:** 100
**SALES (corp-wide):** 237.2MM **Privately Held**
**SIC:** 3537 3634 Forklift trucks; electric household cooking appliances; toasters, electric: household; irons, electric: household; coffee makers, electric: household
**HQ:** Mh Equipment Company
2001 Hartman
Chillicothe IL 61523
309 579-8020

**(G-7756)**
**MIDWEST ELC MTR INC DANVILLE**
819 N Bowman Ave (61832-4031)
P.O. Box 1516 (61834-1516)
PHONE .................... 217 442-5656
Walter Burress, *President*
Zeke Yoho, *Vice Pres*
**EMP:** 4
**SQ FT:** 30,000
**SALES (est):** 579.7K **Privately Held**
**SIC:** 7694 5999 5063 Electric motor repair; motors, electric; motor controls, starters & relays: electric; motors, electric

**(G-7757)**
**MURPHY OIL USA INC**
Also Called: Murphy USA 6511
4105 N Vermilion St (61834-5983)
PHONE .................... 217 442-7882
Fax: 217 442-7882
Beverly Mitchell, *Manager*
Lynn Moore, *Manager*
**EMP:** 5 **Publicly Held**
**WEB:** www.murphyoilusa.com
**SIC:** 2911 Gasoline
**HQ:** Murphy Oil Usa, Inc.
200 E Peach St
El Dorado AR 71730
870 862-6411

**(G-7758)**
**NEWSPAPER HOLDING INC**
17 W North St (61832-5765)
P.O. Box 787 (61834-0787)
PHONE .................... 217 446-1000
Amy Winter, *Branch Mgr*
Carolyn Van Pelt, *Manager*
Tanny Ellis, *Director*
**EMP:** 38 **Privately Held**
**WEB:** www.clintonnc.com
**SIC:** 2711 Newspapers
**HQ:** Newspaper Holding, Inc.
425 Locust St
Johnstown PA 15901
814 532-5102

**(G-7759)**
**PARK ELECTRIC MOTOR SERVICE**
1204 N Collett St (61832-3111)
PHONE .................... 217 442-1977
Laura Park, *President*
Gerald Park, *Corp Secy*
**EMP:** 4 **EST:** 1978
**SQ FT:** 4,000
**SALES (est):** 509.5K **Privately Held**
**SIC:** 7694 5063 Electric motor repair; motors, electric

**(G-7760)**
**PIX NORTH AMERICA INC**
1222 E Voorhees St (61834-6249)
PHONE .................... 217 516-8348
**EMP:** 22
**SALES (corp-wide):** 2.9MM **Privately Held**
**SIC:** 3052 Rubber & plastics hose & beltings
**PA:** Pix North America, Inc.
1901 S Sertoma Ave Unit 1
Sioux Falls SD 57106
855 800-0720

**(G-7761)**
**QUAKER OATS COMPANY**
1703 E Voorhees St (61834-6262)
PHONE .................... 217 443-4995
Fax: 217 443-8641
Jeff Newlin, *QC Mgr*
Steve Risley, *QC Mgr*
Sam Serpico, *QC Mgr*
Tammy Cook, *Engineer*
Deb Kennedy, *Engineer*
**EMP:** 600
**SALES (corp-wide):** 62.8B **Publicly Held**
**WEB:** www.quakeroats.com
**SIC:** 2099 2043 2041 Food preparations; cereal breakfast foods; flour & other grain mill products
**HQ:** The Quaker Oats Company
555 W Monroe St Fl 1
Chicago IL 60661
312 821-1000

**(G-7762)**
**RAHN EQUIPMENT COMPANY**
2400 Georgetown Rd (61832-8425)
PHONE .................... 217 431-1232
Fax: 217 431-1237
Chris Rahn, *President*
Joyce Rahn, *Corp Secy*
**EMP:** 9
**SQ FT:** 10,000
**SALES (est):** 3.7MM **Privately Held**
**SIC:** 5082 5083 3711 General construction machinery & equipment; mowers, power; truck & tractor truck assembly; snow plows (motor vehicles), assembly of

**(G-7763)**
**RATHJE ENTERPRISES INC**
Also Called: Bodine Electric of Decatur
19 Withner St (61832-5326)
P.O. Box 701 (61834-0701)
PHONE .................... 217 443-0022
Fax: 217 443-0027
Mike Dell, *Principal*
**EMP:** 12

**SALES (corp-wide):** 81.7MM **Privately Held**
**WEB:** www.bodineelectricofdecatur.com
**SIC:** 1731 3621 General electrical contractor; motors & generators
**PA:** Rathje Enterprises, Inc.
1845 N 22nd St
Decatur IL 62526
217 423-2593

**(G-7764)**
**ROWDY STAR CUSTOM CREATIONS**
1936 Delong St (61832-2622)
PHONE .................... 217 497-1789
Kathy A Pichon, *Owner*
Kathy Pichon, *Owner*
**EMP:** 3
**SALES (est):** 75K **Privately Held**
**SIC:** 3993 Signs & advertising specialties

**(G-7765)**
**SAND VALLEY SAND & GRAVEL INC**
16395 Lewis Rd (61834)
PHONE .................... 217 446-4210
Melvin Price, *Principal*
**EMP:** 15
**SALES (est):** 783.5K **Privately Held**
**SIC:** 1442 Construction sand & gravel

**(G-7766)**
**SPEEDYS QUICK PRINT**
44 N Vermilion St (61832-5802)
PHONE .................... 217 431-0510
Fax: 217 446-2808
Ivan Solgard, *Owner*
Lynda Solgard, *Co-Owner*
Philip Henschen, *Manager*
**EMP:** 4
**SQ FT:** 3,600
**SALES (est):** 507.2K **Privately Held**
**WEB:** www.speedysquickprint.com
**SIC:** 7334 2752 2791 2789 Photocopying & duplicating services; commercial printing, offset; typesetting; bookbinding & related work

**(G-7767)**
**TEEPAK USA LLC**
915 N Michigan Ave (61834-3500)
PHONE .................... 217 446-6460
Fax: 217 446-4097
Cliff Harper, *Principal*
**EMP:** 2
**SALES (est):** 371K **Privately Held**
**SIC:** 3089 Food casings, plastic

**(G-7768)**
**THERMO TECHNIQUES LLC**
20 Oakwood Ave (61832-5452)
PHONE .................... 217 446-1407
Fax: 217 446-2755
Randy Allison, *General Mgr*
**EMP:** 26
**SALES (est):** 5.3MM
**SALES (est):** 74.5MM **Privately Held**
**WEB:** www.thermotechniques.com
**SIC:** 3398 Metal heat treating; brazing (hardening) of metal
**PA:** Danville Metal Stamping Co., Inc.
20 Oakwood Ave
Danville IL 61832
217 446-0647

**(G-7769)**
**THREADS OF TIME**
207 S Buchanan St (61832-6838)
PHONE .................... 217 431-9202
Fax: 217 431-9234
Melissa Gouty, *Owner*
William R Gouty II, *Co-Owner*
**EMP:** 9
**SALES (est):** 918.5K **Privately Held**
**SIC:** 3639 Sewing machines & attachments, domestic

**(G-7770)**
**THYSSENKRUPP CRANKSHAFT CO LLC (DH)**
Also Called: Thyssenkrupp Automtve Sales &
1000 Lynch Rd (61834-5811)
PHONE .................... 217 431-0060

Brandon Hamilton, *Buyer*
Isaac Tshiofwe, *Electrical Engi*
Kim Dalton, *Accountant*
Steve Wakolbinger, *Manager*
Bernd Huelsebusch, *Info Tech Dir*
◆ **EMP:** 200
**SQ FT:** 175,000
**SALES (est):** 122.6MM
**SALES (corp-wide):** 44.2B **Privately Held**
**SIC:** 3714 3462 Universal joints, motor vehicle; automotive & internal combustion engine forgings

**(G-7771)**
**THYSSENKRUPP CRANKSHAFT CO LLC**
1000 Lynch Rd (61834-5811)
PHONE .................... 217 444-5230
Sandro Escarabelin, *Engineer*
Richard Clark, *Manager*
**EMP:** 25
**SALES (corp-wide):** 44.2B **Privately Held**
**SIC:** 3714 Motor vehicle parts & accessories
**HQ:** Thyssenkrupp Crankshaft Company Llc
1000 Lynch Rd
Danville IL 61834
217 431-0060

**(G-7772)**
**THYSSENKRUPP CRANKSHAFT CO LLC**
1200 International Pl (61834-6291)
PHONE .................... 217 444-5400
Joseph Pycz III, *President*
Rubens Casarin, *Manager*
Bob Shutt, *Manager*
**EMP:** 130
**SALES (corp-wide):** 44.2B **Privately Held**
**SIC:** 3462 Iron & steel forgings
**HQ:** Thyssenkrupp Crankshaft Company Llc
1000 Lynch Rd
Danville IL 61834
217 431-0060

**(G-7773)**
**THYSSENKRUPP CRANKSHAFT CO LLC**
75 Walz Crk (61834-9373)
P.O. Box 1997 (61834-1997)
PHONE .................... 217 444-5500
Adolf Pfeiffer, *Branch Mgr*
**EMP:** 210
**SALES (corp-wide):** 44.2B **Privately Held**
**SIC:** 3714 3462 Universal joints, motor vehicle; iron & steel forgings
**HQ:** Thyssenkrupp Crankshaft Company Llc
1000 Lynch Rd
Danville IL 61834
217 431-0060

**(G-7774)**
**THYSSENKRUPP PRESTA COLD FORGI**
Also Called: Thyssenkrupp Auto Sales Techno
69 Walz Crk (61834-9373)
PHONE .................... 217 431-4212
Richard Clark, *Vice Pres*
Peter Allaart, *Mng Member*
Mike Day, *Manager*
Dennis Stull, *Manager*
Joel Cmillin, *CTO*
**EMP:** 40
**SALES (est):** 5.6MM
**SALES (corp-wide):** 44.2B **Privately Held**
**WEB:** www.thyssenkrupp.com
**SIC:** 3694 Engine electrical equipment
**HQ:** Thyssenkrupp Automotive Sales & Technical Center, Inc.
3155 W Big Beaver Rd # 125
Troy MI 48084

**(G-7775)**
**THYSSNKRUPP PRSTA DANVILLE LLC**
75 Walz Crk (61834-9373)
PHONE .................... 217 444-5500
Carlos Dias, *President*
Ryan Garrison, *Engineer*
Guy Todd, *Credit Staff*
Felicitas Eberl, *Human Res Mgr*

## Danville - Vermilion County (G-7776)

Theresa Hermann, *Human Res Mgr*
◆ **EMP:** 300
**SALES (est):** 105MM
**SALES (corp-wide):** 44.2B **Privately Held**
**SIC:** 3714 Camshafts, motor vehicle
**PA:** Thyssenkrupp Ag
Thyssenkrupp Allee 1
Essen 45143
201 844-5641

**(G-7776)**
**TILTON PATTERN WORKS INC**
21204 Rileysburg Rd (61834-5892)
**PHONE**.................................217 442-1502
Jeff Marble, *President*
**EMP:** 12 **EST:** 1947
**SQ FT:** 4,000
**SALES (est):** 1.4MM **Privately Held**
**SIC:** 3543 3366 Industrial patterns; castings (except die): brass; castings (except die): bronze

**(G-7777)**
**TOWNE MACHINE TOOL COMPANY**
407 S College St (61832-6722)
P.O. Box 685 (61834-0685)
**PHONE**.................................217 442-4910
**Fax:** 217 442-4969
Clinton S Towne, *CEO*
Scott Towne, *Vice Pres*
Randy Williamson, *Manager*
Charlett Towne, *Shareholder*
Curt Towne, *Shareholder*
**EMP:** 17 **EST:** 1950
**SQ FT:** 15,000
**SALES (est):** 4.3MM **Privately Held**
**WEB:** www.townmachine.com
**SIC:** 3556 Food products machinery

**(G-7778)**
**VERMILION STEEL FABRICATION**
Also Called: Electronic Equipment Exchange
3295 E Main St Ste A (61834-9302)
**PHONE**.................................217 442-5300
Adam Mervis, *President*
Micheal Smith, *CFO*
Jennifer Klein, *Treasurer*
▲ **EMP:** 8
**SALES (est):** 868.9K **Privately Held**
**SIC:** 3449 5399 Bars, concrete reinforcing; fabricated steel; warehouse club stores

**(G-7779)**
**VISCOFAN USA INC**
915 Michigan St (61834)
**PHONE**.................................217 444-8000
Phil Hathaway, *Human Res Dir*
Doug Dunningham, *Branch Mgr*
Mike Voorhees, *Senior Mgr*
Troy Pearson, *CIO*
**EMP:** 70
**SALES (corp-wide):** 185MM **Privately Held**
**SIC:** 3089 2013 Food casings, plastic; sausage casings, natural
**HQ:** Viscofan Usa, Inc.
50 County Ct
Montgomery AL 36105
334 396-0092

**(G-7780)**
**WATCHFIRE ENTERPRISES INC (DH)**
1015 Maple St (61832-3200)
**PHONE**.................................217 442-0611
Steve Harriott, *CEO*
Frank Dwyer, *CFO*
Adam Grimes, *CFO*
▲ **EMP:** 23
**SALES:** 130.6MM **Privately Held**
**SIC:** 3993 Electric signs
**HQ:** Watchfire Technologies Holdings Ii, Inc.
1015 Maple St
Danville IL 61832
217 442-0611

**(G-7781)**
**WATCHFIRE SIGNS LLC (DH)**
1015 Maple St (61832-3200)
P.O. Box 850 (61834-0850)
**PHONE**.................................217 442-0611

**Fax:** 217 442-1020
Steve Harriott, *President*
Dave Warns, *Vice Pres*
Frank Dwyer, *CFO*
Steve Davis, *Sales Engr*
◆ **EMP:** 277 **EST:** 1932
**SQ FT:** 195,000
**SALES (est):** 97.5MM
**SALES (corp-wide):** 130.6MM **Privately Held**
**WEB:** www.watchfiresigns.com
**SIC:** 3993 Electric signs
**HQ:** Watchfire Enterprises, Inc.
1015 Maple St
Danville IL 61832
217 442-0611

**(G-7782)**
**WATCHFIRE TECH HOLDINGS I INC (PA)**
1015 Maple St (61832-3200)
**PHONE**.................................217 442-6971
Steve Harriott, *CEO*
**EMP:** 7
**SALES (est):** 130.6MM **Privately Held**
**SIC:** 3993 Electric signs

**(G-7783)**
**WATCHFIRE TECH HOLDINGS II INC (HQ)**
1015 Maple St (61832-3200)
**PHONE**.................................217 442-0611
Steve Harriott, *CEO*
**EMP:** 7
**SALES (est):** 130.6MM **Privately Held**
**SIC:** 3993 Electric signs
**PA:** Watchfire Technologies Holdings I, Inc.
1015 Maple St
Danville IL 61832
217 442-6971

**(G-7784)**
**WESTROCK MWV LLC**
Also Called: Envelope Division
202 Eastgate Dr (61834-9472)
**PHONE**.................................217 442-2247
**Fax:** 217 442-1007
Richard Miller, *Plant Mgr*
Linda Cribes, *Manager*
**EMP:** 25
**SALES (corp-wide):** 14.1B **Publicly Held**
**WEB:** www.meadwestvaco.com
**SIC:** 2631 2791 2752 Linerboard; typesetting; commercial printing, lithographic
**HQ:** Westrock Mwv, Llc
501 S 5th St
Richmond VA 23219
804 444-1000

**(G-7785)**
**WILLIAM INGRAM**
Also Called: Quick Lube
216 S Gilbert St (61832-6232)
**PHONE**.................................217 442-5075
Kevin Davis, *Owner*
**EMP:** 4
**SALES (corp-wide):** 424.6K **Privately Held**
**SIC:** 2992 7549 Lubricating oils; automotive maintenance services
**PA:** William Ingram
Danville IL 61832
217 446-6887

## Darien
### Dupage County

**(G-7786)**
**ACME MARBLE CO INC**
1103 Belair Dr (60561-4013)
**PHONE**.................................630 964-7162
George Binder, *President*
Thomas Satler, *Vice Pres*
Delores Satler, *Admin Sec*
**EMP:** 6
**SQ FT:** 4,000
**SALES:** 300K **Privately Held**
**SIC:** 1743 3281 Marble installation, interior; cut stone & stone products

**(G-7787)**
**ADVANCED GRAPHICS TECH INC**
Also Called: Rotadyne-Decorative Tech GP
8140 Cass Ave (60561-5013)
**PHONE**.................................817 481-8561
Thomas Gilson, *CEO*
Shelby Jones, *Manager*
**EMP:** 200
**SQ FT:** 30,000
**SALES (est):** 16.9MM
**SALES (corp-wide):** 128.8MM **Privately Held**
**SIC:** 3471 3479 Plating of metals or formed products; coating of metals & formed products
**PA:** Rotation Dynamics Corporation
8140 Cass Ave
Darien IL 60561
630 769-9255

**(G-7788)**
**ALL CUT INC**
8195 S Lemont Rd (60561-1755)
**PHONE**.................................630 910-6505
Andrew Widlacki, *President*
Stan Widlacki, *Vice Pres*
**EMP:** 3
**SALES:** 400K **Privately Held**
**WEB:** www.all-cut.com
**SIC:** 3599 Custom machinery

**(G-7789)**
**ANDY WURST**
Also Called: A & W Auto Truck & Trailer
17w411 N Frontage Rd (60561-5407)
**PHONE**.................................630 964-4410
**Fax:** 630 964-4644
Andy Wurst, *Owner*
**EMP:** 4
**SALES (est):** 190K **Privately Held**
**WEB:** www.awtrailer.com
**SIC:** 3799 Trailers & trailer equipment

**(G-7790)**
**ANGELA YANG CHINGJUI**
Also Called: Bridge Wave Electronics
1026 Sean Cir (60561-3877)
**PHONE**.................................630 724-0596
Angela C Yang, *Owner*
**EMP:** 3
**SALES (est):** 235.7K **Privately Held**
**SIC:** 3674 Semiconductors & related devices

**(G-7791)**
**CHEM FREE SOLUTIONS (PA)**
Also Called: Naturally Clean
8420 Evergreen Ln (60561-8400)
**PHONE**.................................630 541-7931
Michael Wallrich, *President*
Dennis Voss, *Principal*
**EMP:** 2
**SQ FT:** 6,500
**SALES (est):** 478K **Privately Held**
**SIC:** 2869 Enzymes

**(G-7792)**
**DAVES WELDING SERVICE INC**
7201 Leonard Dr (60561-4147)
**PHONE**.................................630 655-3224
Dave Norlag, *President*
**EMP:** 4
**SALES (est):** 450K **Privately Held**
**SIC:** 1799 7692 3446 3444 Welding on site; welding repair; architectural metalwork; sheet metalwork;

**(G-7793)**
**EDK CONSTRUCTION INC**
1325 Chapman Dr (60561-5388)
**PHONE**.................................630 853-3484
Elaine Kindt, *CEO*
**EMP:** 2
**SALES (est):** 209.8K **Privately Held**
**WEB:** www.edkconstruction.com
**SIC:** 1442 Gravel mining

**(G-7794)**
**EDMPARTSCOM INC**
8197 S Lemont Rd (60561-1755)
**PHONE**.................................630 427-1603
Iyad Aweidah, *President*
**EMP:** 2
**SQ FT:** 6,000

**SALES:** 500K **Privately Held**
**WEB:** www.riverport-edm.com
**SIC:** 3541 Electrical discharge erosion machines

**(G-7795)**
**GISCO INC**
8193 S Lemont Rd (60561-1755)
**PHONE**.................................630 910-3000
**Fax:** 630 910-3500
Jerry Gisco, *President*
Tania Cogdill, *COO*
Sonia Jewgieniew, *Admin Sec*
**EMP:** 5
**SQ FT:** 6,300
**SALES (est):** 420K **Privately Held**
**SIC:** 3559 Concrete products machinery; stone tumblers

**(G-7796)**
**HONEYWELL INTERNATIONAL INC**
7714 Baker Ct (60561-4549)
**PHONE**.................................630 960-5282
Joe Youthison, *Branch Mgr*
**EMP:** 699
**SALES (corp-wide):** 39.3B **Publicly Held**
**SIC:** 3724 Aircraft engines & engine parts
**PA:** Honeywell International Inc.
115 Tabor Rd
Morris Plains NJ 07950
973 455-2000

**(G-7797)**
**IMPERIAL RIVETS & FASTENERS CO**
7201 Walden Ln (60561-3734)
**PHONE**.................................630 964-0208
**Fax:** 630 963-0289
Samuel Chou, *President*
▲ **EMP:** 3
**SQ FT:** 7,000
**SALES (est):** 290.8K **Privately Held**
**WEB:** www.imperialrivet.com
**SIC:** 3452 Bolts, nuts, rivets & washers; rivets, metal
**PA:** Top Screw Metal Corp.
78, Lane 415, Taiho Rd., Sec. 2,
Changhwa City CHA
472 371-59

**(G-7798)**
**KERINS INDUSTRIES INC**
8408 Wilmette Ave Ste A (60561-6446)
**PHONE**.................................630 515-9111
**Fax:** 630 515-9149
James Kerins, *President*
Sue Kerins, *Corp Secy*
G Kerins, *Vice Pres*
Dave Van Vreede Sales, *Manager*
▲ **EMP:** 2
**SQ FT:** 6,000
**SALES (est):** 315.2K **Privately Held**
**WEB:** www.multihitch.com
**SIC:** 3799 Trailer hitches

**(G-7799)**
**MARKETING CARD TECHNOLOGY LLC**
8245 Lemont Rd (60561-1761)
**PHONE**.................................630 985-7900
**Fax:** 630 985-7300
Pushparaj Venkitsamy, *President*
SRI Lala, *Vice Pres*
Jim Horstman, *Accountant*
**EMP:** 90
**SQ FT:** 5,000
**SALES (est):** 21.9MM **Privately Held**
**SIC:** 7331 2771 Direct mail advertising services; greeting cards

**(G-7800)**
**MIDWEST ULTRASONICS INC**
2000 Harper Rd (60561-6701)
**PHONE**.................................630 434-9458
Stephen B Highland, *Principal*
**EMP:** 4
**SALES (est):** 469.5K **Privately Held**
**SIC:** 3829 Ultrasonic testing equipment

**(G-7801)**
**PRINCE MEAT CO**
8418 Gleneyre Rd (60561-5322)
**PHONE**.................................815 729-2333
Gwen Pasiewicz, *President*

Glenn Pasiewicz, *Vice Pres*
Jean Weck, *Treasurer*
Pauline Pasiewicz, *Admin Sec*
**EMP:** 12
**SQ FT:** 12,000
**SALES (est):** 1.3MM **Privately Held**
**SIC: 5961** 5147 2013 2011 Food, mail order; meats, fresh; sausages & other prepared meats; meat packing plants

**(G-7802)**
**SMART MEDICAL TECHNOLOGY INC**
8404 Wilmette Ave Ste B (60561-6425)
**PHONE**..................................630 964-1689
James Patrick, *CEO*
Matt Hincks, *Vice Pres*
Kenneth King, *Vice Pres*
▲ **EMP:** 12
**SALES (est):** 1.5MM **Privately Held**
**SIC: 3841** Medical instruments & equipment, blood & bone work

**(G-7803)**
**TDS MACHINING INC**
8402 Wilmette Ave Ste B (60561-5433)
**PHONE**..................................630 964-0004
Ted Jablonski, *President*
**EMP:** 10
**SQ FT:** 3,000
**SALES (est):** 1.3MM **Privately Held**
**WEB:** www.tdsmachining.com
**SIC: 3599** Machine shop, jobbing & repair

**(G-7804)**
**WILLOW FARM PRODUCT INC**
Also Called: Wf Machining Product
8193 S Lemont Rd (60561-1755)
**PHONE**..................................630 395-9246
Richard Polivka, *Owner*
**EMP:** 6 **EST:** 2014
**SALES (est):** 545.9K **Privately Held**
**SIC: 3411** Metal cans

### Davis
#### Stephenson County

**(G-7805)**
**EFFECTIVE ENERGY ASSOC LLC**
1979 Sunline Dr (61019-9455)
P.O. Box 57 (61019-0057)
**PHONE**..................................815 248-9280
Bob Abele, *Mng Member*
Jacob Scheid, *Manager*
▼ **EMP:** 5
**SALES:** 250K **Privately Held**
**SIC: 3559** 7389 Refinery, chemical processing & similar machinery;

**(G-7806)**
**HAZEN DISPLAY CORPORATION (PA)**
537 Baintree Rd (61019-9440)
**PHONE**..................................815 248-2925
Gerald E Osowski, *President*
Marvin O Conrad, *Vice Pres*
Bill Gibson, *Office Mgr*
**EMP:** 20 **EST:** 1946
**SQ FT:** 33,000
**SALES (est):** 1.5MM **Privately Held**
**SIC: 3993** 2759 3089 2396 Displays & cutouts, window & lobby; screen printing; plastic processing; automotive & apparel trimmings

**(G-7807)**
**SUMMIT MOLD INC**
Also Called: Summit Precision Machining
10400 E Stanton Rd (61019-9785)
P.O. Box 98 (61019-0098)
**PHONE**..................................815 865-5809
**Fax:** 815 865-5350
Rick Jones, *President*
Lisa Jones, *Vice Pres*
**EMP:** 6
**SQ FT:** 8,000
**SALES (est):** 825K **Privately Held**
**WEB:** www.summitprecisionmachining.com
**SIC: 3599** Machine & other job shop work

**(G-7808)**
**T R MACHINE INC**
103 Il Route 75 E Ste 100 (61019-9584)
**PHONE**..................................815 865-5711
**Fax:** 815 865-5721
Jana Olsen, *President*
Thomas R Olsen, *Vice Pres*
Janet Klever, *Controller*
**EMP:** 36
**SQ FT:** 20,000
**SALES (est):** 8.9MM **Privately Held**
**WEB:** www.trmachine.com
**SIC: 3599** Machine shop, jobbing & repair

**(G-7809)**
**WENGERS SPRINGBROOK CHEESE INC**
12805 N Spring Brook Rd (61019-9719)
**PHONE**..................................815 865-5855
Fred Winger, *President*
John H Wenger, *Vice Pres*
Kelley Olsen, *Office Mgr*
**EMP:** 15
**SALES (est):** 2.6MM **Privately Held**
**SIC: 2022** Cheese, natural & processed

### Davis Junction
#### Ogle County

**(G-7810)**
**DJ LIQUORS INC**
5657 N Junction Way (61020-9433)
**PHONE**..................................815 645-1145
Mark Fritzen, *President*
**EMP:** 4
**SQ FT:** 500
**SALES:** 150K **Privately Held**
**SIC: 2082** Malt liquors

**(G-7811)**
**FOREST CITY SATELLITE**
432 Heartland Dr (61020-9741)
**PHONE**..................................815 639-0500
**EMP:** 4
**SALES (est):** 250.8K **Privately Held**
**SIC: 3663** Cameras, television

**(G-7812)**
**FORM RELIEF TOOL CO INC**
14499 E Il Route 72 (61020-9775)
**PHONE**..................................815 393-4263
**Fax:** 815 393-3143
James Marx, *President*
Judy Marx, *Admin Sec*
**EMP:** 16
**SQ FT:** 5,600
**SALES (est):** 3MM **Privately Held**
**WEB:** www.formrelief.com
**SIC: 3541** 4225 5251 Machine tools, metal cutting type; miniwarehouse, warehousing; tools

**(G-7813)**
**GENSLER GARDENS INC (PA)**
8631 11th St (61020-9604)
**PHONE**..................................815 874-9634
**Fax:** 815 874-9113
William Gensler, *President*
Scott Gensler, *Vice Pres*
Eleanor Gensler, *Admin Sec*
**EMP:** 6
**SALES (est):** 1.7MM **Privately Held**
**WEB:** www.genslergardens.com
**SIC: 2519** 0161 0171 Garden furniture, except wood, metal, stone or concrete; vegetables & melons; berry crops

**(G-7814)**
**ROLL RITE INC**
6549 N Junction Rd (61020-9780)
P.O. Box 153 (61020-0153)
**PHONE**..................................815 645-8600
**Fax:** 815 645-8300
Jerry Hanna, *President*
Patricia Hanna, *Vice Pres*
**EMP:** 4
**SQ FT:** 7,800
**SALES (est):** 1.1MM **Privately Held**
**WEB:** www.rollriteinc.com
**SIC: 3542** 3599 3545 3541 Knurling machines; grinding castings for the trade; machine tool accessories; machine tools, metal cutting type

**(G-7815)**
**SKANDIA INC**
5000 N Il Route 251 (61020-9532)
**PHONE**..................................815 393-4600
**Fax:** 815 393-4522
Tim Theden, *CEO*
Gary Palmer, *President*
Jarrod Triplett, *Vice Pres*
Jeff Vardell, *QC Mgr*
Chris Theden, *Treasurer*
**EMP:** 70
**SQ FT:** 80,000
**SALES (est):** 18.3MM
**SALES (corp-wide):** 32.5MM **Privately Held**
**WEB:** www.skandiaupholsterysupplies.com
**SIC: 4581** 8734 2273 3728 Aircraft maintenance & repair services; aircraft upholstery repair; product testing laboratories; aircraft floor coverings, except rubber or plastic; aircraft parts & equipment
**PA:** Graycliff Partners, Lp
500 5th Ave Fl 47
New York NY 10110
212 300-2900

### Dawson
#### Sangamon County

**(G-7816)**
**ALL WEATHER COURTS INC**
Rr Box 276 (62520)
**PHONE**..................................217 364-4546
**Fax:** 217 364-4436
**EMP:** 4 **EST:** 1962
**SQ FT:** 5,200
**SALES:** 400K **Privately Held**
**SIC: 1629** 1611 2891 Tennis Courts Resurfacing Contractor & Mfg Sealer

### De Kalb
#### Dekalb County

**(G-7817)**
**E B INC**
Also Called: Hiatt Brothers
116 E State St (60115)
P.O. Box 607, Dekalb (60115-0607)
**PHONE**..................................815 758-6646
**Fax:** 815 758-6861
Edward J Bosic, *President*
Eileen S Bosic, *Corp Secy*
Bill Gibbons, *Vice Pres*
Ann Bosic, *Office Mgr*
◆ **EMP:** 10
**SQ FT:** 12,000
**SALES (est):** 1.6MM **Privately Held**
**SIC: 3441** Fabricated structural metal

### De Soto
#### Jackson County

**(G-7818)**
**ANDREW MCDONALD**
Also Called: Flatland Forge & Design
100 N Ash St (62924-1115)
**PHONE**..................................618 867-2323
Andrew McDonald, *Owner*
**EMP:** 3
**SALES:** 50K **Privately Held**
**SIC: 3462** Iron & steel forgings

### Decatur
#### Macon County

**(G-7819)**
**300 BELOW INC**
2999 E Parkway Dr (62526-5296)
**PHONE**..................................217 423-3070
Pete Paulin, *President*
John Koucky, *Vice Pres*
Keith Jewsbury, *Foreman/Supr*
Susan Brown, *Manager*
Dick Mayberry, *Manager*
▲ **EMP:** 6
**SQ FT:** 10,000
**SALES:** 1.7MM **Privately Held**
**WEB:** www.300below.com
**SIC: 3398** 8731 2899 2842 Metal heat treating; energy research; electronic research; rifle bore cleaning compounds; specialty cleaning preparations

**(G-7820)**
**ADM GRAIN COMPANY**
4666 E Faries Pkwy (62526-5678)
**PHONE**..................................217 424-5200
Wendall Carroll, *Opers Staff*
Doug Gooden, *Manager*
**EMP:** 35
**SALES (est):** 24.7MM
**SALES (corp-wide):** 62.3B **Publicly Held**
**SIC: 5153** 2041 Grain elevators; flour & other grain mill products
**PA:** Archer-Daniels-Midland Company
77 W Wacker Dr Ste 4600
Chicago IL 60601
312 634-8100

**(G-7821)**
**ADM HOLDINGS LLC**
350 N Water St (62523-1106)
**PHONE**..................................217 422-7281
**EMP:** 4
**SALES (corp-wide):** 62.3B **Publicly Held**
**SIC: 2046** Wet corn milling
**HQ:** Adm Holdings, Llc
4666 E Faries Pkwy
Decatur IL 62526
217 424-5200

**(G-7822)**
**ADM HOLDINGS LLC (HQ)**
4666 E Faries Pkwy (62526-5678)
P.O. Box 1470 (62525-1820)
**PHONE**..................................217 424-5200
Patricia A Woertz, *CEO*
▼ **EMP:** 1
**SALES (est):** 803.3K
**SALES (corp-wide):** 62.3B **Publicly Held**
**SIC: 2046** Wet corn milling; high fructose corn syrup (HFCS); corn starch; corn oil products
**PA:** Archer-Daniels-Midland Company
77 W Wacker Dr Ste 4600
Chicago IL 60601
312 634-8100

**(G-7823)**
**ADM TRUCKING INC**
2100 N Jasper St (62526-4848)
**PHONE**..................................217 451-4288
**EMP:** 8
**SALES (corp-wide):** 62.3B **Publicly Held**
**SIC: 2046** Wet corn milling
**HQ:** Adm Trucking, Inc.
2501 N Brush College Rd
Decatur IL 62526
217 424-5200

**(G-7824)**
**AIR CASTER LLC** ✪
2887 N Woodford St (62526-4713)
**PHONE**..................................217 877-1237
Filip Van Der Borght,
Mike Skaff,
**EMP:** 25 **EST:** 2016
**SQ FT:** 25,000
**SALES (est):** 1.6MM **Privately Held**
**SIC: 3599** Custom machinery

**(G-7825)**
**AIR INTERNATIONAL C W T US**
675 W South Side Dr (62521-4020)
**PHONE**..................................217 422-1896
Norman Golm, *President*
**EMP:** 3
**SALES (est):** 214.3K **Privately Held**
**SIC: 3724** Research & development on aircraft engines & parts

**(G-7826)**
**AKORN INC**
Also Called: Akorn Pharmaceuticals
1222 W Grand Ave (62522-1412)
**PHONE**..................................217 423-9715
**Fax:** 217 428-8514
Sheila Doolan, *Vice Pres*
Glenn Wickes, *Vice Pres*
Steve Coventry, *Mfg Dir*
Justin Kent, *Opers Spvr*
Jeff Noel, *Purch Dir*

Decatur - Macon County (G-7827)                                    GEOGRAPHIC SECTION

EMP: 125
SALES (corp-wide): 1.1B **Publicly Held**
SIC: 2834 Pharmaceutical preparations
PA: Akorn, Inc.
   1925 W Field Ct Ste 300
   Lake Forest IL 60045
   847 279-6100

**(G-7827)**
**ALEXANDER LUMBER CO**
Also Called: Decatur Counter Top
2729 N 22nd St (62526-2101)
PHONE..................................217 429-2729
Fax: 217 429-3430
Rick Highcock, *Branch Mgr*
EMP: 8
SALES (corp-wide): 474.7K **Privately Held**
WEB: www.hundmanlumber.com
SIC: 2541 Counter & sink tops
HQ: Alexander Lumber Co.
   515 Redwood Dr
   Aurora IL 60506
   630 844-5123

**(G-7828)**
**ALGEN ENTERPRISES LTD**
Also Called: Decatur Machine & Tool Co
2020 E Locust St (62521-1536)
PHONE..................................217 428-4888
Fax: 217 428-9881
Pam Wogoman, *President*
Cindy Kosinski, *Vice Pres*
Alice Stelzriede, *Shareholder*
Kenneth Eugene Stelzriede, *Shareholder*
Tamara Fortner, *Administration*
EMP: 12
SQ FT: 11,000
SALES: 1.5MM **Privately Held**
SIC: 3599 3544 Machine shop, jobbing & repair; special dies, tools, jigs & fixtures

**(G-7829)**
**ALHENCAM SEAL COAT INC**
1887 Sangamon Rd (62521)
P.O. Box 1730 (62525-1730)
PHONE..................................217 422-4605
Fax: 217 422-7109
Bill Camfield, *President*
EMP: 5
SALES (est): 540.3K **Privately Held**
SIC: 2891 Sealants

**(G-7830)**
**ALIGN PRODUCTION SYSTEMS LLC**
2230 N Brush College Rd (62526-5522)
PHONE..................................217 423-6001
Jason Stoecker, *CEO*
Shane Metzger, *COO*
Zhang Jingwei, *Marketing Staff*
EMP: 41
SALES (est): 13.7MM **Privately Held**
SIC: 3537 3535 Industrial trucks & tractors; bulk handling conveyor systems

**(G-7831)**
**ALL SEASONS HEATING & AC**
Also Called: All Seasons Co
167 Excelsior School Rd (62521-8763)
PHONE..................................217 429-2022
Clarence Pickering, *Owner*
EMP: 6
SALES (est): 352.6K **Privately Held**
SIC: 1711 7699 3444 1799 Ventilation & duct work contractor; refrigeration contractor; filter cleaning; hoods, range: sheet metal; steam cleaning of building exteriors

**(G-7832)**
**AMERICAN FIXTURE**
3040 N Norwood Ave (62526-1523)
PHONE..................................217 429-1300
Fax: 217 429-1303
David Lichtenberger, *President*
Jim Lichtenberger, *Vice Pres*
James Lichtenburger, *Vice Pres*
EMP: 6
SALES: 550K **Privately Held**
SIC: 2434 3448 2541 Wood kitchen cabinets; prefabricated metal buildings; wood partitions & fixtures

**(G-7833)**
**ARCHER-DANIELS-MIDLAND COMPANY**
Also Called: ADM
3665 E Division (62525)
PHONE..................................217 424-5882
Rob Jacobson, *Branch Mgr*
EMP: 100
SALES (corp-wide): 62.3B **Publicly Held**
WEB: www.admworld.com
SIC: 2075 Soybean oil mills
PA: Archer-Daniels-Midland Company
   77 W Wacker Dr Ste 4600
   Chicago IL 60601
   312 634-8100

**(G-7834)**
**ARCHER-DANIELS-MIDLAND COMPANY**
Also Called: ADM
466 Ferrys Pkwy (62525)
P.O. Box 1470 (62525-1820)
PHONE..................................217 424-5236
Jerome Pala, *Principal*
EMP: 4
SALES (corp-wide): 62.3B **Publicly Held**
WEB: www.admworld.com
SIC: 2041 Wheat flour
PA: Archer-Daniels-Midland Company
   77 W Wacker Dr Ste 4600
   Chicago IL 60601
   312 634-8100

**(G-7835)**
**ARCHER-DANIELS-MIDLAND COMPANY**
Also Called: Shared Services Center
350 N Water St (62523-1106)
P.O. Box 2576 (62525-2576)
PHONE..................................217 424-5413
Juan R Luciano, *CEO*
EMP: 41
SALES (corp-wide): 62.3B **Publicly Held**
SIC: 2046 2041 2075 2074 Wet corn milling; high fructose corn syrup (HFCS); corn starch; corn oil products; wheat flour; soybean oil mills; cottonseed oil, cake or meal; grain elevators; malt; malt byproducts
PA: Archer-Daniels-Midland Company
   77 W Wacker Dr Ste 4600
   Chicago IL 60601
   312 634-8100

**(G-7836)**
**ARCHER-DANIELS-MIDLAND COMPANY**
Also Called: ADM
2235 N Brush College Rd (62526-5521)
PHONE..................................217 424-5200
Bill Manley, *Manager*
EMP: 58
SALES (corp-wide): 62.3B **Publicly Held**
WEB: www.admworld.com
SIC: 2075 2083 Soybean oil mills; malt
PA: Archer-Daniels-Midland Company
   77 W Wacker Dr Ste 4600
   Chicago IL 60601
   312 634-8100

**(G-7837)**
**ARCHER-DANIELS-MIDLAND COMPANY**
ADM
3883 E Faries Pkwy (62526-5656)
P.O. Box 1470 (62525-1820)
PHONE..................................217 424-5858
Steve McTaggart, *Merchandise Mgr*
Brad Birkholtz, *Manager*
EMP: 49
SALES (corp-wide): 62.3B **Publicly Held**
WEB: www.admworld.com
SIC: 2048 2075 Prepared feeds; soybean oil mills
PA: Archer-Daniels-Midland Company
   77 W Wacker Dr Ste 4600
   Chicago IL 60601
   312 634-8100

**(G-7838)**
**ARCHER-DANIELS-MIDLAND COMPANY**
ADM
4666 E Faries Pkwy Ste 1 (62526-5632)
P.O. Box 1470 (62525-1820)
PHONE..................................217 424-5200
Scott Harmeier, *Superintendent*
John Felton, *COO*
Jim Dubblede, *Vice Pres*
Charles Jenkins, *Vice Pres*
Gary Muruz, *Vice Pres*
EMP: 33
SALES (corp-wide): 62.3B **Publicly Held**
WEB: www.admworld.com
SIC: 2041 Flour & other grain mill products
PA: Archer-Daniels-Midland Company
   77 W Wacker Dr Ste 4600
   Chicago IL 60601
   312 634-8100

**(G-7839)**
**ARCHER-DANIELS-MIDLAND COMPANY**
ADM
3615 E Faries Pkwy (62526-5658)
P.O. Box 1470 (62525-1820)
PHONE..................................217 424-5785
Fax: 217 424-5996
Gary Bingham, *Manager*
EMP: 75
SALES (corp-wide): 62.3B **Publicly Held**
WEB: www.admworld.com
SIC: 2048 Prepared feeds
PA: Archer-Daniels-Midland Company
   77 W Wacker Dr Ste 4600
   Chicago IL 60601
   312 634-8100

**(G-7840)**
**ARCHER-DANIELS-MIDLAND COMPANY**
Also Called: ADM
3700 E Division St (62526-5669)
PHONE..................................217 424-5200
Steve Obrien, *General Mgr*
Gregory Barger, *Manager*
Dick Maloney, *Maintence Staff*
EMP: 58
SALES (corp-wide): 62.3B **Publicly Held**
WEB: www.admworld.com
SIC: 2833 2834 Vitamins, natural or synthetic: bulk, uncompounded; pharmaceutical preparations
PA: Archer-Daniels-Midland Company
   77 W Wacker Dr Ste 4600
   Chicago IL 60601
   312 634-8100

**(G-7841)**
**ARCHER-DANIELS-MIDLAND COMPANY**
4666 E Faries Pkwy Ste 1 (62526-5632)
PHONE..................................217 424-5200
Fax: 217 362-3941
Crocifissa Mandracchia, *General Mgr*
Terry Barnhardt, *Opers Mgr*
Cliff Bruce, *Branch Mgr*
Brad Riley, *Admin Sec*
EMP: 112
SALES (corp-wide): 62.3B **Publicly Held**
SIC: 2046 Wet corn milling
PA: Archer-Daniels-Midland Company
   77 W Wacker Dr Ste 4600
   Chicago IL 60601
   312 634-8100

**(G-7842)**
**AURA SYSTEMS INC**
2345 E Garfield Ave (62526-5125)
PHONE..................................217 423-4100
Fax: 217 423-4001
Mark L Sadorus, *President*
Joyce Sadorus, *Corp Secy*
Lowell Sadorus, *Vice Pres*
EMP: 22
SQ FT: 11,500
SALES: 2.4MM **Privately Held**
SIC: 3599 Custom machinery

**(G-7843)**
**BARTON MANUFACTURING LLC (HQ)**
1395 S Taylorville Rd (62521-4034)
PHONE..................................217 428-0711

Greg Mason, *President*
Sherie Osborne, *Opers Mgr*
Phillip Vanderbordht, *Controller*
▲ EMP: 46
SQ FT: 65,000
SALES (est): 12.2MM **Privately Held**
WEB: www.bartonmfg.com
SIC: 3599 Machine & other job shop work; machine shop, jobbing & repair
PA: Tag-Barton Llc
   1395 S Taylorville Rd
   Decatur IL 62521
   217 428-0711

**(G-7844)**
**BARTON MANUFACTURING LLC**
600 E Wabash Ave (62523-1012)
PHONE..................................217 428-0726
Tony Leffler, *Manager*
EMP: 10
SALES (corp-wide): 12.2MM **Privately Held**
WEB: www.bartonmfg.com
SIC: 7699 7692 Welding equipment repair; tank & boiler cleaning service; welding repair
HQ: Barton Manufacturing Llc
   1395 S Taylorville Rd
   Decatur IL 62521
   217 428-0711

**(G-7845)**
**BENDSEN SIGNS & GRAPHICS INC**
1506 E Mcbride Ave (62526-5082)
PHONE..................................217 877-2345
Fax: 217 877-2347
Tom Pistorius, *President*
Jason Thompson, *Director*
EMP: 10 EST: 1943
SQ FT: 5,000
SALES (est): 1.8MM **Privately Held**
WEB: www.bendsensigns.com
SIC: 1799 7353 3993 3953 Sign installation & maintenance; cranes & aerial lift equipment, rental or leasing; signs & advertising specialties; marking devices

**(G-7846)**
**BODINES BAKING COMPANY**
2136 N Dennis Ave (62526-3523)
PHONE..................................217 853-7707
Amanda Bodine, *Principal*
EMP: 3
SALES (est): 68.6K **Privately Held**
SIC: 2051 Bread, cake & related products

**(G-7847)**
**BOLD MACHINE WORKS INC**
1677 S Taylorville Rd (62521-3950)
PHONE..................................217 428-6644
Fax: 217 428-8071
Donald Williams, *President*
Jennifer Latshaw, *Vice Pres*
Nancy Williams, *Vice Pres*
EMP: 10 EST: 1880
SQ FT: 6,000
SALES (est): 1.5MM **Privately Held**
SIC: 3599 Machine shop, jobbing & repair

**(G-7848)**
**BONE A FIDE PET GROOMING**
1220 E Pershing Rd Ste 1 (62526-4795)
PHONE..................................217 872-0907
James Woodrum, *Partner*
EMP: 3
SALES (est): 79K **Privately Held**
SIC: 0752 3999 Grooming services, pet & animal specialties; pet supplies

**(G-7849)**
**CACHERA AND KLEMM INC**
Also Called: C & K Custom Signs
2271 E Hubbard Ave (62526-2149)
PHONE..................................217 876-7446
Fax: 217 876-7447
Marie Klemm, *President*
Otto Klemm, *Vice Pres*
EMP: 4
SQ FT: 1,900
SALES (est): 433.4K **Privately Held**
WEB: www.cksigns.com
SIC: 3993 Electric signs

# GEOGRAPHIC SECTION

## Decatur - Macon County (G-7875)

**(G-7850)**
**CARDINAL PROFESSIONAL PRODUCTS**
3150 N Woodford St (62526-2834)
PHONE.................714 761-3292
John Sansone, *President*
**EMP:** 8 **EST:** 2010
**SALES (est):** 1.3MM **Privately Held**
**SIC: 2879** 7342 Insecticides & pesticides; pest control services

**(G-7851)**
**CARGILL INCORPORATED**
765 E Pythian Ave (62526-2412)
PHONE.................217 872-7653
Jim Miller, *Branch Mgr*
**EMP:** 12
**SALES (corp-wide):** 107.1B **Privately Held**
**SIC: 3552** Yarn texturizing machines
**PA:** Cargill, Incorporated
 15407 Mcginty Rd W
 Wayzata MN 55391
 952 742-7575

**(G-7852)**
**CARTRIDGE WORLD DECATUR**
215 E Ash Ave Ste D (62526-6159)
PHONE.................217 875-0465
**EMP:** 5
**SALES (est):** 462K **Privately Held**
**SIC: 3955** Carbon Paper And Inked Ribbons

**(G-7853)**
**CATERPILLAR INC**
3000 N 27th St (62525)
P.O. Box 1430 (62525-1809)
PHONE.................217 475-4000
**Fax:** 217 475-4665
Mike Lervaag, *Purch Mgr*
Dan Hanback, *Purchasing*
Keyur Shah, *Senior Engr*
Cathy Mock, *Human Res Mgr*
Rob Bussell, *Branch Mgr*
**EMP:** 650
**SQ FT:** 3,000,000
**SALES (corp-wide):** 38.5B **Publicly Held**
**WEB:** www.cat.com
**SIC: 3713** 3531 Truck & bus bodies; tractors, construction
**PA:** Caterpillar Inc.
 100 Ne Adams St
 Peoria IL 61629
 309 675-1000

**(G-7854)**
**CATERPILLAR INC**
2701 Pershing Rd (62526)
PHONE.................217 424-1809
James Owens, *Branch Mgr*
**EMP:** 355
**SALES (corp-wide):** 38.5B **Publicly Held**
**SIC: 3531** Tractors, construction
**PA:** Caterpillar Inc.
 100 Ne Adams St
 Peoria IL 61629
 309 675-1000

**(G-7855)**
**CENTRAL MACHINING SERVICE**
2057 E Olive St (62526-5136)
PHONE.................217 422-7472
**Fax:** 217 422-7483
Mike Jeffers, *Owner*
**EMP:** 5
**SALES (est):** 524.4K **Privately Held**
**SIC: 3599** 3444 Machine shop, jobbing & repair; sheet metalwork

**(G-7856)**
**CENTRAL SERVICE CENTER**
715 N Bright St (62522-1601)
P.O. Box 979, Kincaid (62540-0979)
PHONE.................217 423-3900
Rodney Stanfill, *Partner*
Marcus Matthews, *Partner*
**EMP:** 5
**SQ FT:** 25,000
**SALES (est):** 330K **Privately Held**
**SIC: 3999** Badges, metal: policemen, firemen, etc.

**(G-7857)**
**CLASSIC PRINTING CO INC**
529 N Martin Luther King (62523-1114)
P.O. Box 497 (62525-0497)
PHONE.................217 428-1733
**Fax:** 217 428-0596
Melvin D Mills, *President*
Debra J Mills, *Admin Sec*
**EMP:** 6 **EST:** 1954
**SALES (est):** 800.9K **Privately Held**
**SIC: 2752** Commercial printing, offset

**(G-7858)**
**CONTINENTAL CARBONIC PDTS INC**
2550 N Brush College Rd (62526-5556)
PHONE.................217 428-2080
**Fax:** 217 424-2325
Robert Wiesemann, *Branch Mgr*
**EMP:** 6
**SALES (corp-wide):** 32.6B **Privately Held**
**SIC: 2813** Dry ice, carbon dioxide (solid)
**HQ:** Continental Carbonic Products, Inc.
 3985 E Harrison Ave
 Decatur IL 62526
 217 428-2068

**(G-7859)**
**CONTINENTAL CARBONIC PDTS INC (DH)**
3985 E Harrison Ave (62526-5534)
PHONE.................217 428-2068
John W Funk, *President*
Steve Barfoot, *Area Mgr*
Nathan Carl, *Area Mgr*
Kyle Smith, *Area Mgr*
Mark D Hatton, *Vice Pres*
**EMP:** 50
**SQ FT:** 12,000
**SALES (est):** 301.2MM
**SALES (corp-wide):** 32.6B **Privately Held**
**WEB:** www.ccpidryice.com
**SIC: 2813** Carbon dioxide; dry ice, carbon dioxide (solid)
**HQ:** Matheson Tri-Gas, Inc.
 150 Allen Rd Ste 302
 Basking Ridge NJ 07920
 908 991-9200

**(G-7860)**
**COUNTRY JOURNAL PUBLISHING CO**
Also Called: Grain Journal
3065 Pershing Ct (62526-1564)
PHONE.................217 877-9660
**Fax:** 217 877-6647
Mark Avery, *President*
Deb Coontz, *Publisher*
Joe Funk, *Editor*
Kendall Trump, *Editor*
Jerry Welter, *Vice Pres*
**EMP:** 16
**SQ FT:** 5,000
**SALES (est):** 2.3MM **Privately Held**
**WEB:** www.millingequipment.com
**SIC: 2721** Magazines: publishing only, not printed on site

**(G-7861)**
**CROWN CORK & SEAL USA INC**
255 W Pershing Rd (62526-3200)
PHONE.................217 872-6100
Cecil Tuyl, *Vice Pres*
**EMP:** 118
**SALES (corp-wide):** 8.2B **Publicly Held**
**WEB:** www.crowncork.com
**SIC: 3411** Metal cans
**HQ:** Crown Cork & Seal Usa, Inc.
 1 Crown Way
 Philadelphia PA 19154
 215 698-5100

**(G-7862)**
**CURRY READY-MIX OF DECATUR**
Also Called: The Curry Companies
2200 N Woodford St (62526-5095)
PHONE.................217 428-7177
**Fax:** 217 428-7178
Lou Marcy, *President*
Larry Laycock, *Manager*
Allen Violette, *CIO*
**EMP:** 15
**SQ FT:** 625

**SALES (est):** 1.6MM
**SALES (corp-wide):** 5.2MM **Privately Held**
**SIC: 3273** Ready-mixed concrete
**PA:** Capitol Ready-Mix, Inc
 1900 E Mason St
 Springfield IL 62702
 217 528-1100

**(G-7863)**
**CUSTOM TROPHIES**
947 N Water St (62523-1020)
PHONE.................217 422-3353
Diane Doty, *Owner*
**EMP:** 3
**SQ FT:** 1,600
**SALES (est):** 200K **Privately Held**
**SIC: 5999** 7336 3993 2396 Trophies & plaques; silk screen design; signs & advertising specialties; automotive & apparel trimmings

**(G-7864)**
**D & M PATTERN CO**
987 Montgomery Ct (62526-1240)
PHONE.................217 877-0064
Donald Kuenzel, *President*
Merrilee Kuenzel, *Corp Secy*
**EMP:** 3
**SQ FT:** 2,500
**SALES (est):** 200K **Privately Held**
**SIC: 3543** Foundry patternmaking

**(G-7865)**
**D C T/PRECISION LLC**
Also Called: Dct
1260 E North St (62521-2001)
P.O. Box 500 (62520-0500)
PHONE.................217 475-0141
**Fax:** 217 475-0246
Judy Burch, *Asst Mgr*
John D Lambrick,
James Gahwiler,
Julia Leurck,
**EMP:** 12
**SQ FT:** 4,800
**SALES (est):** 1.2MM **Privately Held**
**SIC: 3544** Special dies, tools, jigs & fixtures

**(G-7866)**
**DARK MATTER PRINTING**
7 Ridge Dr (62521-5421)
PHONE.................217 791-4059
Chris Morrison, *Principal*
**EMP:** 3
**SALES (est):** 171K **Privately Held**
**SIC: 2752** Commercial printing, lithographic

**(G-7867)**
**DEAN FOODS COMPANY**
965 S Wyckles Rd (62522-1082)
PHONE.................217 428-6726
Carl Johnson, *Manager*
**EMP:** 87 **Publicly Held**
**WEB:** www.deanfoods.com
**SIC: 2026** Fluid milk
**PA:** Dean Foods Company
 2711 N Haskell Ave
 Dallas TX 75204

**(G-7868)**
**DECATUR AERATION INC**
101 Main St (62523)
P.O. Box 1757 (62525-1757)
PHONE.................217 422-6828
Mike Straighter, *President*
**EMP:** 12
**SALES (est):** 960K **Privately Held**
**SIC: 3441** Fabricated structural metal

**(G-7869)**
**DECATUR BLUE PRINT COMPANY**
230 W Wood St (62523-1277)
PHONE.................217 423-7589
**Fax:** 217 423-7580
Dann W Nelson, *President*
Margaret Hickman, *CFO*
Matthew Swarthout, *CTO*
**EMP:** 9
**SQ FT:** 6,000

**SALES (est):** 1.2MM **Privately Held**
**WEB:** www.decaturblue.com
**SIC: 7334** 2752 5049 Blueprinting service; offset & photolithographic printing; engineers' equipment & supplies; drafting supplies

**(G-7870)**
**DECATUR BOTTLING CO**
Also Called: Pepsico
2112 N Brush College Rd (62526-5555)
PHONE.................217 429-5415
**Fax:** 217 429-3039
Michael L Vitale, *President*
G Louis Vitale, *Corp Secy*
Guy L Vitale Jr, *Vice Pres*
Jenny Farmer, *Manager*
**EMP:** 73 **EST:** 1914
**SQ FT:** 45,000
**SALES (est):** 6.3MM **Privately Held**
**SIC: 2086** Carbonated soft drinks, bottled & canned

**(G-7871)**
**DECATUR FOUNDRY INC**
1745 N Illinois St (62526-4932)
PHONE.................217 429-5261
**Fax:** 217 425-2834
Terry R Young, *President*
Tommy L Young, *Vice Pres*
Rex Ragsdale, *Opers Staff*
John E Johnson, *Admin Sec*
**EMP:** 80 **EST:** 1918
**SQ FT:** 205,000
**SALES (est):** 22MM **Privately Held**
**WEB:** www.decaturfoundry.com
**SIC: 3321** Gray iron castings; ductile iron castings

**(G-7872)**
**DECATUR INDUSTRIAL ELC INC (PA)**
Also Called: Kankakee Industrial Technology
1650 E Garfield Ave (62526-5108)
P.O. Box 1188 (62525-1188)
PHONE.................217 428-6621
**Fax:** 217 428-6189
Philip Thompson Sr, *Ch of Bd*
Trent Thompson, *President*
Dean Ortianu, *Controller*
Fred Roth, *Sales Dir*
Vinny Thomas, *Accounts Mgr*
**EMP:** 35 **EST:** 1971
**SQ FT:** 20,000
**SALES (est):** 47.8MM **Privately Held**
**WEB:** www.decaturindustrialelectric.com
**SIC: 5063** 7694 Electrical supplies; electric motor repair

**(G-7873)**
**DECATUR PLATING & MFG CO**
1147 E Garfield Ave (62526-4825)
PHONE.................217 422-8514
**Fax:** 217 422-8515
William J Stuckey, *President*
Lona Stuckey, *Vice Pres*
David Stuckey, *Manager*
**EMP:** 10 **EST:** 1948
**SQ FT:** 12,000
**SALES:** 1.4MM **Privately Held**
**SIC: 3471** Electroplating of metals or formed products

**(G-7874)**
**DECATUR WOOD PRODUCTS LLC**
800 E Garfield Ave (62526-4500)
PHONE.................217 424-2602
**Fax:** 217 424-2608
Steve Richards, *Owner*
Amy Richards,
**EMP:** 2
**SQ FT:** 40,000
**SALES:** 900K **Privately Held**
**SIC: 2448** Pallets, wood

**(G-7875)**
**DECO MANUFACTURING COMPANY**
5054 Cundiff Ct (62526-9649)
PHONE.................217 872-6450
**Fax:** 217 872-6455
Phillip N Jones, *President*
Corey Dauhthery, *General Mgr*
Cary Mundwiler, *Facilities Mgr*

**Decatur - Macon County (G-7876)**  GEOGRAPHIC SECTION

Tracey Waite, *Mfg Staff*
Cory Daugherty, *Manager*
**EMP:** 23 **EST:** 1980
**SQ FT:** 10,000
**SALES (est)** 5.5MM **Privately Held**
**WEB:** www.decomfg.com
**SIC:** 3452 Bolts, metal

**(G-7876)**
**DIXIE CARBONIC INC**
3985 E Harrison Ave (62526-5534)
**PHONE**.................................217 428-2068
Robert Wiesemann II, *President*
John Nemac, *Vice Pres*
Randy Spitz, *CFO*
**EMP:** 61
**SALES:** 12MM
**SALES (corp-wide):** 32.6B **Privately Held**
**SIC:** 2813 Dry ice, carbon dioxide (solid)
**HQ:** Continental Carbonic Products, Inc.
 3985 E Harrison Ave
 Decatur IL 62526
 217 428-2068

**(G-7877)**
**DONNELLY AUTOMOTIVE MACHINE**
Also Called: Carquest Auto Parts
1298 E Eldorado St (62521-2032)
**PHONE**.................................217 428-7414
**Fax:** 217 428-9367
Patrick E Donnelly, *President*
Cecilia M Donnelly, *Corp Secy*
Robert H Donnelly, *Vice Pres*
**EMP:** 14 **EST:** 1950
**SQ FT:** 5,000
**SALES (est):** 2.4MM **Privately Held**
**SIC:** 5531 3599 Automotive parts; machine shop, jobbing & repair

**(G-7878)**
**DYNAGRAPHICS INCORPORATED**
Also Called: Fast Impressions
3220 N Woodford St (62526-2836)
P.O. Box 2730 (62524-2730)
**PHONE**.................................217 876-9950
**Fax:** 217 876-9951
David Bowers, *President*
Dan Niebrugge, *Plant Mgr*
Cindy Staudenmaier, *Controller*
Richard S Bowers, *Admin Sec*
Sheri Martin, *Graphic Designe*
**EMP:** 34
**SQ FT:** 22,000
**SALES (est):** 7.5MM **Privately Held**
**WEB:** www.dynafast.com
**SIC:** 2759 Advertising specialties

**(G-7879)**
**ENSIGN EMBLEM LTD**
2435 E Federal Dr (62526-2160)
**PHONE**.................................217 877-8224
**Fax:** 217 872-9649
Thomas Chambers, *Principal*
Kristine Shreve, *Mktg Dir*
**EMP:** 65
**SALES (corp-wide):** 14.8MM **Privately Held**
**SIC:** 2395 Embroidery products, except schiffli machine
**PA:** Ensign Emblem Ltd.
 1746 Keane Dr
 Traverse City MI 49696
 231 946-7703

**(G-7880)**
**FERGUSON ENTERPRISES INC**
Also Called: Wolseley Indus Group 3194
1226 E Garfield Ave (62526-4923)
**PHONE**.................................217 425-7262
Tim Watring, *Branch Mgr*
**EMP:** 6
**SALES (corp-wide):** 20.8B **Privately Held**
**SIC:** 3399 Iron ore recovery from open hearth slag
**HQ:** Ferguson Enterprises, Inc.
 12500 Jefferson Ave
 Newport News VA 23602
 757 874-7795

**(G-7881)**
**FERGUSON ENTERPRISES INC**
Also Called: Wolseley Industrial Group
500 W Eldorado St (62522-2165)
**PHONE**.................................217 425-7262
Tim Watring, *Branch Mgr*
**EMP:** 6
**SALES (corp-wide):** 20.8B **Privately Held**
**SIC:** 3443 Metal parts
**HQ:** Ferguson Enterprises, Inc.
 12500 Jefferson Ave
 Newport News VA 23602
 757 874-7795

**(G-7882)**
**FISHERMANS QUARTERS**
2886 S Mount Zion Rd (62521-9721)
**PHONE**.................................217 791-5104
Monte Prasun, *Principal*
**EMP:** 3
**SALES (est):** 358.4K **Privately Held**
**SIC:** 3131 Quarters

**(G-7883)**
**FUYAO GLASS ILLINOIS INC**
Also Called: PPG Industries
2768 E Elwin Rd (62521-7848)
**PHONE**.................................217 864-2392
**Fax:** 217 864-6260
Gauthier John, *President*
David Burkett, *Principal*
Shushe Ng WA Ng, *Principal*
**EMP:** 175
**SALES (est):** 37.9MM
**SALES (corp-wide):** 609.8MM **Privately Held**
**SIC:** 3211 5231 3999 Flat glass; glass; atomizers, toiletry
**HQ:** Fuyao Glass America Inc.
 2801 W Stroop Rd
 Dayton OH 45439
 937 496-5777

**(G-7884)**
**GARVER FEEDS (PA)**
222 E Wabash Ave (62523-1092)
**PHONE**.................................217 422-2201
**Fax:** 217 422-0715
Edward Larry Garver Jr, *Partner*
Gene Garver, *Partner*
Shane Garver, *Manager*
**EMP:** 20
**SQ FT:** 5,400
**SALES (est):** 6.9MM **Privately Held**
**SIC:** 5999 5149 2048 Pet food; feed & farm supply; pet foods; prepared feeds

**(G-7885)**
**GRAHAM WELDING INC**
813 E North St (62521-1932)
**PHONE**.................................217 422-1423
**Fax:** 217 422-5779
Charles Graham, *President*
**EMP:** 8
**SQ FT:** 50,000
**SALES (est):** 926.6K **Privately Held**
**SIC:** 7692 Welding repair

**(G-7886)**
**GROHNE CONCRETE PRODUCTS CO**
2594 N Water St (62526-4229)
P.O. Box 828 (62525-0828)
**PHONE**.................................217 877-4197
**Fax:** 217 877-8367
Hal Shintzler, *President*
Tom Grohne, *Vice Pres*
**EMP:** 7
**SALES:** 400.8K
**SALES (corp-wide):** 35.3MM **Privately Held**
**WEB:** www.christy-foltz.com
**SIC:** 3273 Ready-mixed concrete
**PA:** Christy-Foltz, Inc.
 740 S Main St
 Decatur IL 62521
 217 428-8601

**(G-7887)**
**HANGER PROSTHETICS &**
Also Called: Hanger Clinic
1910 S Mount Zion Rd D (62521-8419)
**PHONE**.................................217 429-6656
Sam Liang, *President*
Gunther Konigsmann, *Branch Mgr*
Sheryl Price, *Director*
**EMP:** 7
**SALES (corp-wide):** 459.1MM **Publicly Held**
**SIC:** 3842 Limbs, artificial

**HQ:** Hanger Prosthetics & Orthotics East, Inc.
 33 North Ave Ste 101
 Tallmadge OH 44278
 330 633-9807

**(G-7888)**
**HEINKELS PACKING COMPANY INC**
2005 N 22nd St (62526-4734)
P.O. Box 2134 (62524-2134)
**PHONE**.................................217 428-4401
**Fax:** 217 428-4403
Miles Wright, *President*
Robert Neal Wright, *Corp Secy*
Dennis Heinkel, *Vice Pres*
**EMP:** 22 **EST:** 1912
**SALES:** 3.1MM **Privately Held**
**SIC:** 2011 Sausages from meat slaughtered on site; luncheon meat from meat slaughtered on site; beef products from beef slaughtered on site; pork products from pork slaughtered on site

**(G-7889)**
**HOME CITY ICE COMPANY**
Also Called: Home Ice
2304 N Martn Lthr Kng Jr (62526-4585)
**PHONE**.................................217 877-7733
Lee Ungrund, *Manager*
Lee Unrum, *Manager*
**EMP:** 15
**SALES (corp-wide):** 305.4MM **Privately Held**
**WEB:** www.homecityice.com
**SIC:** 2097 Manufactured ice
**PA:** The Home City Ice Company
 6045 Bridgetown Rd Ste 1
 Cincinnati OH 45248
 513 574-1800

**(G-7890)**
**HUSTON-PATTERSON CORPORATION (PA)**
Also Called: Huston Patterson Printers
123 W North St Fl 4 (62523-3396)
P.O. Box 260 (62525-0260)
**PHONE**.................................217 429-5161
**Fax:** 217 429-9807
Thomas W Kowa, *President*
Stephen E Frantz, *COO*
Donald Ellis, *Vice Pres*
Tonya Kowa Morelli, *Vice Pres*
Zachary Kowa, *Opers Staff*
**EMP:** 65 **EST:** 1895
**SQ FT:** 133,000
**SALES (est):** 25.6MM **Privately Held**
**WEB:** www.hustonpatterson.com
**SIC:** 2752 2791 Commercial printing, offset; typesetting

**(G-7891)**
**ILLINI AEROFAB INC**
4455 W Main St (62522-1055)
**PHONE**.................................217 425-2971
Robert Babb, *President*
**EMP:** 4
**SALES (est):** 322K **Privately Held**
**SIC:** 3721 Aircraft

**(G-7892)**
**ILLINI PRECISION MACHINING INC**
750 E Prairie Ave (62523-1149)
**PHONE**.................................217 425-5780
**Fax:** 217 425-5781
Robert Hauskins, *President*
Rose Hauskins, *Vice Pres*
**EMP:** 9
**SQ FT:** 8,000
**SALES (est):** 740K **Privately Held**
**SIC:** 3599 Machine shop, jobbing & repair

**(G-7893)**
**ILLMO R/X SERVICE**
Also Called: Illmo R/X Services
3373 N Woodford St (62526-2837)
P.O. Box 2138 (62524-2138)
**PHONE**.................................217 877-1192
**Fax:** 217 875-7333
**EMP:** 15
**SALES (corp-wide):** 2.2MM **Privately Held**
**SIC:** 5048 3851 Whol Ophthalmic Goods Mfg Ophthalmic Goods

**PA:** Illmo R/X Service
 52 Progress Pkwy
 Maryland Heights MO
 314 434-6858

**(G-7894)**
**INDUSTRIAL CSTM PWDR CTING INC**
Also Called: Industrial Cstm Powdr Coating
661 E Wood St (62523-1152)
**PHONE**.................................217 423-4272
Nancy Platzbecker, *President*
Bill Platzbecker, *Vice Pres*
**EMP:** 10
**SQ FT:** 3,500
**SALES (est):** 1.1MM **Privately Held**
**SIC:** 3479 Painting, coating & hot dipping

**(G-7895)**
**INDUSTRIAL RUBBER & SUP ENTP**
2670 E Garfield Ave (62526-5325)
**PHONE**.................................217 429-3747
William H Veteto, *President*
Clarence D Golden, *Admin Sec*
**EMP:** 4
**SQ FT:** 2,500
**SALES (est):** 620K **Privately Held**
**SIC:** 5085 3429 3052 Rubber goods, mechanical; manufactured hardware (general); rubber & plastics hose & beltings

**(G-7896)**
**INTERNATIONAL CONTROL SVCS INC**
Also Called: I C S
606 W Imboden Dr (62526-9067)
**PHONE**.................................217 422-6700
**Fax:** 217 422-3205
Dennis M Espinoza, *President*
Daryl Peeks, *Engineer*
Christopher Expinoza, *CFO*
Robert Johnston, *CFO*
William Ginos, *Controller*
▲ **EMP:** 110
**SQ FT:** 50,000
**SALES (est):** 48.2MM **Privately Held**
**SIC:** 3672 Printed circuit boards

**(G-7897)**
**J A K ENTERPRISES INC**
Also Called: Bard Optical
288 N Park St (62523-1306)
**PHONE**.................................217 422-3881
**Fax:** 217 422-3883
Angie Oyer, *Manager*
**EMP:** 6
**SALES (corp-wide):** 9.7MM **Privately Held**
**WEB:** www.bardoptical.com
**SIC:** 5995 3499 3827 Optical goods stores; industrial machinery & equipment; optical instruments & lenses
**PA:** J A K Enterprises, Inc
 8309 N Knoxville Ave # 1
 Peoria IL 61615
 309 693-9540

**(G-7898)**
**JAMIEL INC**
Also Called: A-1 Food & Liquor
151 N Jasper St (62521-2801)
**PHONE**.................................217 423-1000
Amanda Asad, *President*
**EMP:** 3 **EST:** 2010
**SALES (est):** 547.2K **Privately Held**
**SIC:** 5182 3411 Liquor; food & beverage containers

**(G-7899)**
**JARVIS BROS & MARCELL INC (PA)**
1210 S Jasper St (62521-3531)
P.O. Box 1631 (62525-1631)
**PHONE**.................................217 422-3120
Sam Jarvis, *President*
T Stephen Ballance, *Vice Pres*
**EMP:** 2
**SQ FT:** 1,200
**SALES:** 400K **Privately Held**
**SIC:** 1311 Crude petroleum production

# GEOGRAPHIC SECTION
## Decatur - Macon County (G-7925)

**(G-7900)**
**JARVIS DRILLING CO (PA)**
132 S Water St Ste 331 (62523-2376)
P.O. Box 1631 (62525-1631)
PHONE.................................217 422-3120
T Stephen Ballance, *President*
EMP: 2
SALES: 1.2MM **Privately Held**
SIC: 1311 Crude petroleum production

**(G-7901)**
**KATCO ENTERPRISES LLC**
2243 Highland Rd (62521-5905)
PHONE.................................217 429-5855
George Thomas Harris, *Principal*
EMP: 3 EST: 2008
SALES (est): 224.6K **Privately Held**
SIC: 3089 Fences, gates & accessories: plastic

**(G-7902)**
**KELLEY CONSTRUCTION INC**
2454 N 27th St (62526-5262)
P.O. Box 2440 (62524-2440)
PHONE.................................217 422-1800
Fax: 217 422-9635
I Dean Benson, *President*
Gary Cooper, *Vice Pres*
Virginia A Foster, *Treasurer*
Dave W Rathje Jr, *Admin Sec*
EMP: 300
SQ FT: 4,000
SALES (est): 38.8MM **Privately Held**
SIC: 1541 3444 Industrial buildings, new construction; sheet metalwork

**(G-7903)**
**KLAMAN HARDWOOD**
4351 N Macarthur Rd (62526-9332)
PHONE.................................217 972-7888
Timothy Klaman, *Principal*
EMP: 3
SALES (est): 226.2K **Privately Held**
SIC: 2435 Panels, hardwood plywood

**(G-7904)**
**L T PROPERTIES INC (PA)**
1395 S Taylorville Rd (62521-4034)
PHONE.................................217 423-8772
Lawrence Rogers, *President*
Bryan Maple, *Office Mgr*
Thomas J Vaughan, *Admin Sec*
EMP: 3
SQ FT: 12,000
SALES (est): 3.9MM **Privately Held**
SIC: 3599 3531 Machine & other job shop work; construction machinery

**(G-7905)**
**LEE ENTERPRISES INCORPORATED**
Also Called: William Street Press
1605 N Brant Ct (62521-1599)
PHONE.................................217 421-8955
Fax: 217 421-8954
Sue Watts, *Manager*
EMP: 6
SALES (corp-wide): 614.3MM **Publicly Held**
WEB: www.lee.net
SIC: 2711 Newspapers
PA: Lee Enterprises, Incorporated
201 N Harrison St Ste 600
Davenport IA 52801
563 383-2100

**(G-7906)**
**LEE ENTERPRISES INCORPORATED**
Also Called: Herald & Review
601 E William St (62523-1142)
P.O. Box 311 (62525-0311)
PHONE.................................217 421-6920
Fax: 217 421-6913
Michael R Gulledge, *Publisher*
Mike Albright, *Editor*
Jeana Matherly, *Editor*
Scott Perry, *Editor*
John Reidy, *Editor*
EMP: 140
SALES (corp-wide): 614.3MM **Publicly Held**
WEB: www.lee.net
SIC: 2711 Newspapers: publishing only, not printed on site
PA: Lee Enterprises, Incorporated
201 N Harrison St Ste 600
Davenport IA 52801
563 383-2100

**(G-7907)**
**LEE ENTERPRISES INCORPORATED**
Also Called: Prairie Shopper/Business Jurnl
604 E William St (62523-1143)
P.O. Box 311 (62525-0311)
PHONE.................................217 421-8940
Linda Lusk, *Manager*
Nick Meier, *Manager*
EMP: 5
SALES (corp-wide): 614.3MM **Publicly Held**
WEB: www.lee.net
SIC: 2711 2741 Newspapers; miscellaneous publishing
PA: Lee Enterprises, Incorporated
201 N Harrison St Ste 600
Davenport IA 52801
563 383-2100

**(G-7908)**
**LEGACY VULCAN LLC**
Also Called: Macon Sand & Gravel
2855 S Lincoln Memorial P (62522-8812)
PHONE.................................217 963-2196
Fax: 217 963-2494
Tom Heft, *Superintendent*
EMP: 8
SALES (corp-wide): 3.5B **Publicly Held**
WEB: www.vulcanmaterials.com
SIC: 3272 Concrete products
HQ: Legacy Vulcan, Llc
1200 Urban Center Dr
Vestavia AL 35242
205 298-3000

**(G-7909)**
**M E BARBER CO INC**
1660 S Taylorville Rd (62521-3951)
PHONE.................................217 428-4591
Fax: 217 428-4591
D J Hynds, *President*
EMP: 6
SQ FT: 2,000
SALES: 600K **Privately Held**
WEB: www.mebarberco.com
SIC: 3423 3643 Wrenches, hand tools; current-carrying wiring devices

**(G-7910)**
**MACHINE WORKS OF DECATUR INC**
2035 E Garfield Ave (62526-5094)
PHONE.................................217 428-3896
Fax: 217 428-4029
Jeff Conour, *President*
Jemremy Conour, *Principal*
Lynette Conour, *Admin Sec*
EMP: 4
SALES: 390K **Privately Held**
SIC: 3599 Machine & other job shop work

**(G-7911)**
**MCLEAN SUBSURFACE UTILITY**
237 E Stuart Ave (62526-4660)
PHONE.................................336 988-2520
Stacey E Slaw, *Principal*
EMP: 4
SALES (est): 191.3K **Privately Held**
SIC: 1623 8711 1389 8713 Underground utilities contractor; engineering services; testing, measuring, surveying & analysis services; surveying services

**(G-7912)**
**MEDA PHARMACEUTICALS INC**
705 E Eldorado St (62523-1118)
PHONE.................................217 424-8400
Robert Sheridan, *Area Mgr*
Mark Kostreba, *Senior VP*
Gary Evans, *Vice Pres*
Jeffrey Hostler, *Vice Pres*
Sean Adamson, *Warehouse Mgr*
EMP: 100
SQ FT: 32,200
SALES (corp-wide): 2.2B **Privately Held**
SIC: 2834 Druggists' preparations (pharmaceuticals)
HQ: Meda Pharmaceuticals Inc.
265 Davidson Ave Ste 400
Somerset NJ 08873
732 564-2200

**(G-7913)**
**MICROTEK PATTERN INC**
2035 N Jasper St (62526-4847)
PHONE.................................217 428-0433
Nelson Mosley, *President*
Robin Shively, *Treasurer*
EMP: 7 EST: 1996
SQ FT: 3,500
SALES (est): 1MM **Privately Held**
SIC: 3543 Industrial patterns

**(G-7914)**
**MIDSTATE CORE CO**
777 E William St (62521-1950)
P.O. Box 25318 (62525-5318)
PHONE.................................217 429-2673
Fax: 217 429-2679
John R Phillips, *President*
Barbara Phillips, *Corp Secy*
EMP: 25
SQ FT: 14,000
SALES: 1.2MM **Privately Held**
SIC: 3543 Foundry cores

**(G-7915)**
**MIDWEST FIBER INC DECATUR**
1902 N Water St (62526-4353)
PHONE.................................217 424-9460
Ron Shumaker, *President*
Mike Shumaker, *General Mgr*
Jacob Welker, *Opers Staff*
Joy Hangartner, *Sales Staff*
Ron Schumaker, *Manager*
▼ EMP: 40
SQ FT: 27,000
SALES (est): 12.8MM **Privately Held**
WEB: www.decaturrecycle.com
SIC: 5093 4953 3341 Waste paper; refuse systems; secondary nonferrous metals

**(G-7916)**
**MIDWEST PROCESSING COMPANY**
4666 E Faries Pkwy (62526-5630)
PHONE.................................217 424-5200
James Balloun, *General Mgr*
Charles Bayless, *Vice Pres*
Graig Fischer, *Vice Pres*
EMP: 60
SALES (est): 6.2MM
SALES (corp-wide): 62.3B **Publicly Held**
WEB: www.admworld.com
SIC: 2079 Edible fats & oils
PA: Archer-Daniels-Midland Company
77 W Wacker Dr Ste 4600
Chicago IL 60601
312 634-8100

**(G-7917)**
**MILLIKEN VALVE CO INC**
500 W Eldorado St (62522-2165)
PHONE.................................217 425-7410
EMP: 2
SALES (est): 231.7K **Privately Held**
SIC: 3592 Valves

**(G-7918)**
**MUELLER CO LLC**
Gas Products Division
500 W Eldorado St (62522-2165)
P.O. Box 671 (62525-1808)
PHONE.................................217 423-4471
Fax: 217 425-7382
Connor Deering, *Vice Pres*
Jayy Ruffner, *Buyer*
Steve Crawford, *Engineer*
Timothy Hipp, *Engineer*
Jeff Huffman, *Engineer*
EMP: 20
SALES (corp-wide): 1.1B **Publicly Held**
WEB: www.muellerflo.com
SIC: 3533 3592 Gas field machinery & equipment; valves
HQ: Mueller Co. Llc
633 Chestnut St Ste 1200
Chattanooga TN 37450
423 209-4800

**(G-7919)**
**MUELLER COMPANY PLANT 4**
1226 E Garfield Ave (62526-4923)
PHONE.................................217 425-7424
EMP: 3
SALES (est): 258.3K **Privately Held**
SIC: 3399 Iron ore recovery from open hearth slag

**(G-7920)**
**MUNICIPAL ELECTRONICS INC**
2267 E Hubbard Ave (62526-2149)
PHONE.................................217 877-8601
James Gulley, *President*
Robert Gulley, *Vice Pres*
Gary Gulley, *Admin Sec*
EMP: 8
SQ FT: 2,400
SALES: 460K **Privately Held**
WEB: www.municipalelectronics.com
SIC: 7629 3812 Electronic equipment repair; radar systems & equipment

**(G-7921)**
**NEBRASKA PLASTICS INCORPORATED**
354 S Glencoe Ave (62522-2518)
PHONE.................................217 423-9007
EMP: 3 EST: 2010
SALES (est): 166.8K **Privately Held**
SIC: 3089 Plastics products

**(G-7922)**
**ORBIS RPM LLC**
1781 Hubbard Ave (62526-2819)
PHONE.................................217 876-8655
EMP: 16
SALES (corp-wide): 1.8B **Privately Held**
SIC: 3081 Polypropylene film & sheet
HQ: Orbis Rpm, Llc
1055 Corporate Center Dr
Oconomowoc WI 53066
262 560-5000

**(G-7923)**
**ORNAMENTAL METALWORKS INC**
Also Called: Ormco
2136 N Woodford St # 100 (62526-5015)
P.O. Box 977 (62525-0977)
PHONE.................................217 424-2326
Fax: 217 424-2326
Jerry Kieffer, *President*
Phil Wallace, *Vice Pres*
Del Beimfohr, *Treasurer*
EMP: 7 EST: 1934
SQ FT: 48,000
SALES (est): 1.4MM **Privately Held**
SIC: 3441 Building components, structural steel

**(G-7924)**
**OSBORNE PUBLICATIONS INC**
Also Called: Decatur Tribune
132 S Water St Ste 424 (62523-2306)
P.O. Box 1490 (62525-1490)
PHONE.................................217 422-9702
Fax: 217 422-7320
Paul V Osborne, *President*
Janet Osborne, *Vice Pres*
EMP: 4 EST: 1964
SQ FT: 3,500
SALES (est): 349.1K **Privately Held**
SIC: 2711 2791 2759 Newspapers, publishing & printing; typesetting; newspapers: printing

**(G-7925)**
**PARKE & SON INC**
Parke Toll Processing
3523 Rupp Pkwy (62526-2170)
PHONE.................................217 875-0572
Paul Doolen, *Manager*
EMP: 3
SALES (corp-wide): 9.5MM **Privately Held**
WEB: www.parkewarehouses.com
SIC: 2045 Prepared flour mixes & doughs
PA: Parke & Son, Inc.
1800 E Garfield Ave
Decatur IL 62526
217 429-5255

### (G-7926)
**PETERS MACHINE INC**
3765 N Westlawn Ave (62526-9322)
PHONE..................217 875-2578
Fax: 217 875-2772
Jerald L Nelson, *President*
Lacy Berry, *Admin Mgr*
EMP: 18
SQ FT: 20,000
SALES (est): 4MM  Privately Held
WEB: www.petersmachine.com
SIC: 7692  3599  Welding repair; machine shop, jobbing & repair

### (G-7927)
**PIONEER PUMP AND PACKING INC**
1501 N 22nd St (62526-5107)
PHONE..................217 791-5293
EMP: 3
SALES (corp-wide): 30MM  Privately Held
SIC: 3491  Industrial valves
PA: Pioneer Pump And Packing, Inc.
   400 Russell Blvd
   Saint Louis MO 63104
   314 771-0700

### (G-7928)
**PRAIRIE CENTRAL READY MIX**
800 E Mckinley Ave (62526-2409)
PHONE..................217 877-5210
Fax: 217 877-0760
Richard Goken, *Manager*
EMP: 4
SALES (est): 318.3K  Privately Held
SIC: 3273  Ready-mixed concrete

### (G-7929)
**PRAIRIE FARMS DAIRY  INC**
Prarie Frms Dry Dcatr Ice Crm
757 N Morgan St (62521-1241)
P.O. Box 650 (62525-0650)
PHONE..................217 423-3459
Fax: 217 422-5233
Craig Radke, *Safety Mgr*
Michael Vernon, *Sales/Mktg Mgr*
EMP: 62
SALES (corp-wide): 1.8B  Privately Held
WEB: www.prairiefarms.com
SIC: 2026  2024  Milk processing (pasteurizing, homogenizing, bottling); ice cream & frozen desserts
PA: Prairie Farms Dairy, Inc.
   1100 Broadway
   Carlinville IL 62626
   217 854-2547

### (G-7930)
**R & R SERVICES ILLINOIS  INC**
800 E Garfield Ave (62526-4500)
P.O. Box 319, Argenta (62501-0319)
PHONE..................217 424-2602
Jeffery S Rose, *President*
Steve Richards, *Vice Pres*
EMP: 8
SALES (est): 923.1K  Privately Held
SIC: 2448  Wood pallets & skids

### (G-7931)
**RANDYS EXPER-CLEAN**
4925 W Main St (62522-1062)
PHONE..................217 423-1975
Randy Goodrich, *Owner*
EMP: 4
SALES (est): 185.7K  Privately Held
SIC: 7217  3524  Carpet & upholstery cleaning; snowblowers & throwers, residential

### (G-7932)
**RATHJE ENTERPRISES  INC (PA)**
Also Called: BODINE ELECTRIC OF DECATUR
1845 N 22nd St (62526-5113)
P.O. Box 976 (62525-1810)
PHONE..................217 423-2593
Fax: 217 420-4283
David W Rathje, *President*
Harry B Rakers, *President*
Jeanne Jones, *Exec VP*
Warren Elder, *Manager*
Phade Myers, *Manager*
EMP: 265
SQ FT: 57,000
SALES (est): 81.7MM  Privately Held
WEB: www.bodineelectricofdecatur.com
SIC: 1731  7694  5063  Electrical work; armature rewinding shops; electrical supplies

### (G-7933)
**REFRESHMENT SERVICES  INC**
Also Called: Pepsico
2112 N Brush College Rd (62526-5555)
PHONE..................217 429-5415
Al Hudgins, *General Mgr*
Chris Kirn, *General Mgr*
Amy Simoneson, *General Mgr*
Jeff Sutherland, *General Mgr*
Brad Lipcaman, *Sales Mgr*
EMP: 40
SALES (corp-wide): 95.5MM  Privately Held
SIC: 2086  Carbonated soft drinks, bottled & canned
PA: Refreshment Services, Inc.
   1121 Locust St
   Quincy IL 62301
   217 223-8600

### (G-7934)
**RING CONTAINER TECH LLC**
Also Called: Ringwood
2454 E Hubbard Ave (62526-2148)
PHONE..................217 875-5084
Fax: 217 875-7327
Bryan Harris, *Mfg Staff*
Ken Landreth, *Manager*
EMP: 50
SALES (corp-wide): 291.7MM  Privately Held
WEB: www.ringcontainer.com
SIC: 3085  3089  Plastics bottles; blow molded finished plastic products
PA: Ring Container Technologies, Llc.
   1 Industrial Park
   Oakland TN 38060
   800 280-7464

### (G-7935)
**ROSEMOUNT INC**
2241 E Hubbard Ave (62526-2149)
PHONE..................217 877-5278
Teresa Edwards, *Manager*
EMP: 4
SALES (corp-wide): 14.5B  Publicly Held
WEB: www.rosemount.com
SIC: 3823  Industrial instrmnts msrmnt display/control process variable
HQ: Rosemount Inc.
   8200 Market Blvd
   Chanhassen MN 55317
   952 906-8888

### (G-7936)
**ROTARY DRYER PARTS INC**
2590 E Federal Dr Ste 508 (62526-2181)
PHONE..................217 877-2787
Fax: 217 877-2710
Charles Brown, *President*
EMP: 2
SALES (est): 334.9K  Privately Held
SIC: 3621  Motors & generators

### (G-7937)
**S L FIXTURES INC**
2222 E Logan St (62526-5133)
PHONE..................217 423-9907
Fax: 217 423-8810
Matthew Long, *President*
EMP: 5
SQ FT: 3,000
SALES (est): 716.2K  Privately Held
SIC: 2599  3429  Cabinets, factory; cabinet hardware

### (G-7938)
**SAFELITE GLASS CORP**
Also Called: Safelite Group
1303 N Main St (62526-4416)
PHONE..................877 800-2727
EMP: 3
SALES (corp-wide): 2.9B  Privately Held
SIC: 3231  Products of purchased glass
HQ: Safelite Glass Corp.
   7400 Safelite Way
   Columbus OH 43235
   614 210-9000

### (G-7939)
**SEBENS CONCRETE PRODUCTS INC**
7000 E Us Route 36 (62521-9693)
PHONE..................217 864-2824
Fax: 217 864-2824
Kevin Greenfield, *President*
EMP: 6  EST: 1950
SQ FT: 15,000
SALES (est): 807.2K  Privately Held
SIC: 3272  Drain tile, concrete; septic tanks, concrete; tile, precast terrazzo or concrete

### (G-7940)
**SHUR CO OF ILLINOIS**
4350 E Boyd Rd (62521-8535)
PHONE..................217 877-8277
Bill Shorna, *Owner*
EMP: 9
SALES (est): 599.3K  Privately Held
SIC: 2451  5199  Mobile home frames; tarpaulins

### (G-7941)
**SOUTHFIELD CORPORATION**
Also Called: Prairie Central
705 E Mckinley Ave (62526-2407)
PHONE..................217 875-5455
Sally Obrien, *Plant Mgr*
Sally O'Brien, *Manager*
Sally Brien, *Manager*
EMP: 15
SALES (corp-wide): 273.9MM  Privately Held
WEB: www.prairiegroup.com
SIC: 5211  3272  3271  Brick; concrete products; concrete block & brick
PA: Southfield Corporation
   8995 W 95th St
   Palos Hills IL 60465
   708 344-1000

### (G-7942)
**SOUTHFIELD CORPORATION**
800 E Mckinley Ave (62526-2409)
PHONE..................217 877-5210
Dean Bush, *Manager*
EMP: 15
SALES (corp-wide): 273.9MM  Privately Held
WEB: www.prairiegroup.com
SIC: 3273  Ready-mixed concrete
PA: Southfield Corporation
   8995 W 95th St
   Palos Hills IL 60465
   708 344-1000

### (G-7943)
**STAR SILKSCREEN DESIGN INC**
2281 E Hubbard Ave (62526-2149)
PHONE..................217 877-0804
Fax: 217 877-0843
Jon Kozeliski, *President*
Karen Ragee, *Vice Pres*
EMP: 5
SQ FT: 2,700
SALES (est): 600K  Privately Held
SIC: 2396  2395  Screen printing on fabric articles; embroidery & art needlework

### (G-7944)
**STEWART BROTHERS PACKING CO**
1004 N Country Club Rd (62521-1812)
PHONE..................217 422-7741
Jeffrey J Stewart, *Partner*
John J Stewart, *Partner*
EMP: 8  EST: 1935
SQ FT: 1,200
SALES (est): 1.1MM  Privately Held
SIC: 2011  Meat by-products from meat slaughtered on site

### (G-7945)
**STRATAS FOODS LLC**
3601 E Division St (62526-5638)
PHONE..................217 424-5660
Rod Logan, *Branch Mgr*
Eric Kearns, *Supervisor*
EMP: 32  Privately Held
SIC: 2079  Edible fats & oils
PA: Stratas Foods Llc
   7130 Goodlett Frm Pkwy # 200
   Cordova TN 38016

### (G-7946)
**SURE SHINE POLISHING**
1455 N Main St (62526-4418)
PHONE..................217 853-4888
Jason Eddinger, *Principal*
EMP: 3
SALES (est): 145.1K  Privately Held
SIC: 3471  Polishing, metals or formed products

### (G-7947)
**T/CCI MANUFACTURING  LLC (PA)**
2120 N 22nd St (62526-4737)
PHONE..................217 423-0066
Richard J Demirjian, *Mfg Staff*
Marilyn Dillon, *Purchasing*
Eric Droit, *Controller*
Dennis Flaherty, *Controller*
Julie Ward, *Persnl Mgr*
▲ EMP: 111
SALES (est): 55MM  Privately Held
WEB: www.tccimanufacturing.com
SIC: 3714  Air conditioner parts, motor vehicle

### (G-7948)
**TAG-BARTON LLC (PA)**
1395 S Taylorville Rd (62521-4034)
PHONE..................217 428-0711
EMP: 2
SALES (est): 12.2MM  Privately Held
SIC: 3599  6719  Machine & other job shop work; machine shop, jobbing & repair; investment holding companies, except banks

### (G-7949)
**TATE & LYLE AMERICAS LLC (HQ)**
2200 E Eldorado St (62521-1578)
PHONE..................217 421-2964
John Schnake, *CEO*
Richard Delbridge, *Human Res Dir*
Perry Marchisello, *Manager*
Guy Brown, *Director*
◆ EMP: 140
SQ FT: 5,000
SALES (est): 31.2MM
SALES (corp-wide): 3.4B  Privately Held
SIC: 2046  Corn & other vegetable starches
PA: Tate & Lyle Public Limited Company
   1 Kingsway
   London WC2B
   207 257-2100

### (G-7950)
**TATE LYLE INGRDNTS AMRICAS LLC (HQ)**
Also Called: Tate & Lyle Citric Acid
2200 E Eldorado St (62521-1578)
P.O. Box 151 (62525-1801)
PHONE..................217 423-4411
John Schnake, *CEO*
Javed Ahmed, *CEO*
Andrew Bailey, *Business Mgr*
Rob Gibber, *Exec VP*
Robert Gibber, *Exec VP*
◆ EMP: 1145
SQ FT: 500,000
SALES (est): 937.5MM
SALES (corp-wide): 3.4B  Privately Held
WEB: www.aestaley.com
SIC: 2046  Wet corn milling
PA: Tate & Lyle Public Limited Company
   1 Kingsway
   London WC2B
   207 257-2100

### (G-7951)
**TCR SYSTEMS  LLC**
4900 N Brush College Rd (62526-9766)
P.O. Box 3398 (62524-3398)
PHONE..................217 877-5622
Fax: 217 877-5625
Terry Randles, *President*
Gary Davis, *Accountant*
Larry Bonnett, *Supervisor*
Jim Byrge,
John Ellis,
EMP: 100
SQ FT: 280,000
SALES (est): 24.8MM  Privately Held
WEB: www.tcrsystems.com
SIC: 3444  Sheet metalwork

## GEOGRAPHIC SECTION

**Deerfield - Lake County (G-7976)**

**(G-7952)**
**THORNTON WELDING SERVICE INC**
4350 N Route 48 (62526-9654)
P.O. Box 3155 (62524-3155)
**PHONE**..................217 877-0610
Fax: 217 877-0612
Mark Thornton, *President*
Marilyn Thornton, *Vice Pres*
**EMP:** 25
**SQ FT:** 8,040
**SALES (est):** 1.7MM **Privately Held**
**SIC:** 1721 1799 7692 7629 Commercial painting; sandblasting of building exteriors; welding repair; electrical repair shops; plating & polishing

**(G-7953)**
**TIN MAUNG**
1770 E Lake Shore Dr (62521-3832)
**PHONE**..................217 233-1405
Maung Tin, *Principal*
**EMP:** 3
**SALES (est):** 202.5K **Privately Held**
**SIC:** 3356 Tin

**(G-7954)**
**TRUMP PRINTING INC**
Also Called: Trump Direct
1591 N Water St (62526-4441)
P.O. Box 17 (62525-0017)
**PHONE**..................217 429-9001
Fax: 217 429-4305
Dennis Trump, *CEO*
Brad Simpson, *Vice Pres*
**EMP:** 12
**SQ FT:** 9,000
**SALES (est):** 2.1MM **Privately Held**
**WEB:** www.trump-com.com
**SIC:** 2752 2791 2789 Commercial printing, offset; typesetting; bookbinding & related work

**(G-7955)**
**UNION IRON INC (HQ)**
3550 E Mound Rd (62521-8514)
P.O. Box 1038 (62525-1038)
**PHONE**..................217 429-5148
Gary Anderson, *President*
Loren Dresbeck, *Production*
Judith Curry, *Treasurer*
Cauline Greenwelt, *Manager*
Steve Sommerfield, *Admin Sec*
▼ **EMP:** 27
**SQ FT:** 20,000
**SALES (est):** 8.7MM
**SALES (corp-wide):** 393.2MM **Privately Held**
**WEB:** www.unionironworks.com
**SIC:** 3523 3511 Elevators, farm; steam engines
**PA:** Ag Growth International Inc
198 Commerce Dr
Winnipeg MB R3P 0
204 489-1855

**(G-7956)**
**VICTORY PHARMACY DECATUR INC**
Also Called: Victory Medical Equipment
163 N Water St (62523-1309)
**PHONE**..................217 429-8650
Fax: 217 429-8651
Wole Adeoye, *President*
Abiola Adeoye, *Admin Sec*
**EMP:** 34
**SQ FT:** 2,500
**SALES:** 2.9MM **Privately Held**
**SIC:** 3845 5047 Ultrasonic medical equipment, except cleaning; medical equipment & supplies; electro-medical equipment

**(G-7957)**
**VOESTALPINE NORTRAK INC**
690 E Kenwood Ave (62526-4584)
**PHONE**..................217 876-9160
Sean Betty, *Manager*
**EMP:** 100
**SALES (corp-wide):** 12.3B **Privately Held**
**SIC:** 3743 Railroad equipment
**HQ:** Voestalpine Nortrak Inc.
1740 Pacific Ave
Cheyenne WY 82007
307 778-8700

**(G-7958)**
**WABEL TOOL COMPANY**
1020 E Eldorado St (62521-1916)
**PHONE**..................217 429-3656
Fax: 217 429-3099
Virginia M Hornback, *President*
Jenny Hornback, *Principal*
Rudy Hubner, *Vice Pres*
William R Friend, *Treasurer*
Marla Burge, *Office Mgr*
**EMP:** 30
**SQ FT:** 22,000
**SALES (est):** 6.1MM **Privately Held**
**WEB:** www.wabeltool.com
**SIC:** 3599 Machine shop, jobbing & repair

**(G-7959)**
**WHEELS & DEALS**
170 N Oakdale Blvd (62522-1918)
**PHONE**..................217 423-6333
Rick Reynolds, *Owner*
**EMP:** 7
**SALES (est):** 365.3K **Privately Held**
**SIC:** 2711 Newspapers

**(G-7960)**
**WOODWIND SPECIALISTS**
890 W William St (62522-2330)
P.O. Box 1024 (62525-1024)
**PHONE**..................217 423-4122
Sande Hackel, *Owner*
**EMP:** 3 **EST:** 1973
**SQ FT:** 6,000
**SALES:** 24K **Privately Held**
**SIC:** 2499 Decorative wood & woodwork

### Deer Creek
*Tazewell County*

**(G-7961)**
**CENTRAL ILLINOIS TRUSS (PA)**
105 Prospect Dr (61733-1001)
**PHONE**..................309 447-6644
Fax: 309 447-6655
Todd Erwin, *Principal*
**EMP:** 10
**SALES (est):** 273.5K **Privately Held**
**SIC:** 2439 Structural wood members

**(G-7962)**
**COOK FABRICATION SIGNS GRAPHIC**
325 N Deer Crk (61733)
**PHONE**..................309 360-3805
Gary Cook, *Owner*
**EMP:** 3
**SALES (est):** 219.8K **Privately Held**
**SIC:** 3993 Signs & advertising specialties

**(G-7963)**
**DEER CREEK FLANGE PIPE CO INC**
300 N Logan St (61733-9314)
P.O. Box 50 (61733-0050)
**PHONE**..................309 447-6981
Gerald A Rich Jr, *President*
Tammy Rich, *Corp Secy*
Brian Rich, *Vice Pres*
**EMP:** 3
**SQ FT:** 5,000
**SALES (est):** 353.9K **Privately Held**
**SIC:** 3462 Flange, valve & pipe fitting forgings, ferrous

**(G-7964)**
**HOMEWAY HOMES INC**
100 Homeway Ct (61733-9018)
**PHONE**..................309 965-2312
Brian R Schieler, *President*
Rich Schieler, *Plant Mgr*
Tim Gardner, *Project Mgr*
John Rassi, *CFO*
Craig Steffen, *CFO*
**EMP:** 60
**SALES (est):** 11.8MM **Privately Held**
**WEB:** www.homewayhomes.com
**SIC:** 2452 Modular homes, prefabricated, wood

**(G-7965)**
**MARIANNE STRAWN**
Also Called: Aunt Em's Gourmet Popcorn
405 E 1st Ave (61733-9539)
**PHONE**..................309 447-6612
Marianne Strawn, *Owner*
**EMP:** 6
**SALES (est):** 680K **Privately Held**
**SIC:** 2096 Popcorn, already popped (except candy covered)

**(G-7966)**
**TITAN INDUSTRIES INC**
100 Prspect Dr Deer Crk Deer Creek (61733)
P.O. Box 226 (61733-0226)
**PHONE**..................309 440-1010
Angela Rich, *President*
Suzanne M McQueary, *Admin Sec*
**EMP:** 6
**SALES (est):** 1.2MM **Privately Held**
**SIC:** 3441 Fabricated structural metal

### Deer Grove
*Whiteside County*

**(G-7967)**
**H W HOSTETLER & SONS**
Also Called: Prairie View Farms
27445 Hurd Rd (61243-9722)
**PHONE**..................815 438-7816
H W Hostetler, *Owner*
**EMP:** 3 **EST:** 1944
**SALES (est):** 140K **Privately Held**
**SIC:** 0191 3523 General farms, primarily crop; farm machinery & equipment

**(G-7968)**
**STERLING GEAR INC**
Also Called: Stainless Steel Prod
1582 Hoover Rd (61243-9739)
P.O. Box 68 (61243-0068)
**PHONE**..................815 438-4327
Robert Elfline, *President*
▲ **EMP:** 10
**SALES (est):** 544.5K **Privately Held**
**WEB:** www.sterlinggear.com
**SIC:** 3541 Gear cutting & finishing machines

### Deer Park
*Lake County*

**(G-7969)**
**CONTINENTAL AUTO SYSTEMS INC**
21440 W Lake Cook Rd (60010-3609)
**PHONE**..................847 862-5000
Samir Salman, *CEO*
Scott Beutler, *President*
Frank Harazim, *Facilities Mgr*
Thorsten Behrens, *Engineer*
Jim Freimuth, *Engineer*
**EMP:** 1 **EST:** 1998
**SALES (est):** 1.8MM **Privately Held**
**SIC:** 7549 3625 High performance auto repair & service; motor controls, electric

**(G-7970)**
**CONTINENTAL AUTOMOTIVE INC**
Continental Auto Systems Div
21440 W Lake Cook Rd (60010-3609)
**PHONE**..................847 862-6300
John Garner, *Counsel*
Ned Reckamp, *Vice Pres*
Ritu Goel, *Project Mgr*
Teri Walker, *Project Mgr*
Dick Wendelken, *Purchasing*
**EMP:** 24
**SALES (corp-wide):** 42.8B **Privately Held**
**SIC:** 3694 Engine electrical equipment
**HQ:** Continental Automotive, Inc.
1830 Macmillan Park Dr
Fort Mill SC 29707
704 583-8878

**(G-7971)**
**HEALTHWISE GOURMET COFFEES (PA)**
76 Woodberry Rd (60010-3641)
**PHONE**..................847 382-3230
James Couch, *Mng Member*
Michael Reines,
**EMP:** 3
**SQ FT:** 4,000
**SALES:** 1MM **Privately Held**
**SIC:** 2095 Roasted coffee

**(G-7972)**
**LUCKY BRAND DUNGAREES LLC**
20530 N Rand Rd Ste 418 (60010-7237)
**PHONE**..................847 550-1647
Joyce Hughes, *Branch Mgr*
**EMP:** 38
**SALES (corp-wide):** 397.8MM **Privately Held**
**SIC:** 2325 Men's & boys' jeans & dungarees
**PA:** Lucky Brand Dungarees, Llc
540 S Santa Fe Ave
Los Angeles CA 90013
213 443-5700

**(G-7973)**
**NEOVISION USA INC**
21720 W Long Grove Rd C33 (60010-3732)
**PHONE**..................847 533-0541
Howard Leventhal, *President*
**EMP:** 10
**SALES:** 950K **Privately Held**
**SIC:** 3669 Communications equipment

### Deerfield
*Lake County*

**(G-7974)**
**ALPHA INDUSTRIES INC**
1720 Christopher Dr (60015-3912)
**PHONE**..................847 945-1740
Jerry Becker, *Principal*
**EMP:** 4
**SALES (corp-wide):** 73.6MM **Privately Held**
**SIC:** 3999 Barber & beauty shop equipment
**PA:** Alpha Industries, Inc.
14200 Pk Madow Dr Ste 110
Chantilly VA 20151
703 378-1420

**(G-7975)**
**AMERICAN CHEMET CORPORATION (PA)**
Also Called: American Chemet Export
740 Waukegan Rd Ste 202 (60015-4400)
P.O. Box 437 (60015-0437)
**PHONE**..................847 948-0800
Fax: 847 948-0811
W H Shropshire, *President*
Daniel B Brimhall, *Vice Pres*
Kim A Klatt, *Vice Pres*
Brad Smith, *Treasurer*
PC Best, *Admin Sec*
◆ **EMP:** 11
**SQ FT:** 3,300
**SALES:** 218.2MM **Privately Held**
**WEB:** www.chemet.com
**SIC:** 2819 2816 Copper compounds or salts, inorganic; zinc pigments: zinc oxide, zinc sulfide

**(G-7976)**
**AMERICAN IMAGING MGT INC**
540 Lake Cook Rd Ste 300 (60015-5602)
**PHONE**..................847 564-8500
Brandon Cady, *Senior VP*
Neepa Patel, *Senior VP*
Paul Danao, *VP Bus Dvlpt*
James Chow, *CFO*
Joel Cesario, *Marketing Staff*
**EMP:** 20
**SALES (corp-wide):** 84.8B **Publicly Held**
**SIC:** 3841 Diagnostic apparatus, medical
**HQ:** American Imaging Management, Inc.
8600 W Bryn Mawr Ave 800s
Chicago IL 60631
773 864-4600

---

(PA)=Parent Co (HQ)=Headquarters (DH)=Div Headquarters
✪ = New Business established in last 2 years

# Deerfield - Lake County (G-7977) — GEOGRAPHIC SECTION

### (G-7977)
**AMT CORP**
717 Juneway Ave (60015-3526)
PHONE..................847 459-6177
Robert Franks, *President*
EMP: 3
SALES (est): 184.3K **Privately Held**
SIC: 3999 Advertising display products

### (G-7978)
**ARLA GRAPHICS INC**
875 Mountain Dr (60015-1801)
P.O. Box 1204 (60015-6003)
PHONE..................847 470-0005
Fax: 847 470-0605
Lee Bendersky, *President*
EMP: 4
SQ FT: 2,000
SALES (est): 580.9K **Privately Held**
WEB: www.arlagraphics.com
SIC: 2752 Commercial printing, lithographic

### (G-7979)
**ASTELLAS US LLC**
3 Parkway N (60015-2537)
PHONE..................800 888-7704
Yoshihiko Hatanaka, *Principal*
Steve Knowles, *Treasurer*
Bryan Bradford, *Finance*
Mark Niemaszek, *Sales Dir*
Chad Roberts, *Regl Sales Mgr*
EMP: 163
SQ FT: 140,000
SALES: 858.8K
SALES (corp-wide): 11.7B **Privately Held**
SIC: 2834 Pharmaceutical preparations
HQ: Astellas Us Holding, Inc.
1 Astellas Way
Northbrook IL 60062
224 205-8800

### (G-7980)
**ASTELLAS US TECHNOLOGIES INC**
3 Parkway N Ste 300 (60015-2565)
PHONE..................847 317-8800
Makoto Nishimura, *CEO*
Hadir Sesi, *Director*
EMP: 400
SALES (est): 41.6MM
SALES (corp-wide): 11.7B **Privately Held**
SIC: 2834 Mfg Pharmaceutical Preparations
HQ: Astellas Pharma Us, Inc.
1 Astellas Way
Northbrook IL 60062
800 888-7704

### (G-7981)
**BAXALTA EXPORT CORPORATION**
1 Baxter Pkwy (60015-4625)
PHONE..................224 948-2000
Dr Ludwig N Hanton, *CEO*
▼ EMP: 5 EST: 2015
SALES (est): 297.1K
SALES (corp-wide): 6.4B **Privately Held**
SIC: 2834 3841 2835 3842 Pharmaceutical preparations; intravenous solutions; solutions, pharmaceutical; surgical & medical instruments; catheters; medical instruments & equipment, blood & bone work; surgical instruments & apparatus; blood derivative diagnostic agents; surgical appliances & supplies
HQ: Baxalta Incorporated
1200 Lakeside Dr
Bannockburn IL 60015
224 940-2000

### (G-7982)
**BAXALTA WORLD TRADE LLC (DH)**
1 Baxter Pkwy (60015-4625)
PHONE..................224 948-2000
Dr Ludwig N Hanton, *CEO*
EMP: 5
SALES (est): 15MM
SALES (corp-wide): 6.4B **Privately Held**
SIC: 2834 3841 2835 3842 Pharmaceutical preparations; intravenous solutions; solutions, pharmaceutical; surgical & medical instruments; catheters; medical instruments & equipment, blood & bone work; surgical instruments & apparatus; blood derivative diagnostic agents; surgical appliances & supplies
HQ: Baxalta Incorporated
1200 Lakeside Dr
Bannockburn IL 60015
224 940-2000

### (G-7983)
**BAXALTA WORLDWIDE LLC**
1 Baxter Pkwy (60015-4625)
PHONE..................224 948-2000
EMP: 4
SALES (est): 239K
SALES (corp-wide): 6.4B **Privately Held**
SIC: 2834 3841 2835 3842 Pharmaceutical preparations; surgical & medical instruments; blood derivative diagnostic agents; surgical appliances & supplies
HQ: Baxalta Incorporated
1200 Lakeside Dr
Bannockburn IL 60015
224 940-2000

### (G-7984)
**BAXTER GLOBAL HOLDINGS II INC (HQ)**
1 Baxter Pkwy (60015-4625)
PHONE..................847 948-2000
Robert L Parkinson Jr, *CEO*
Jean-Luc Butel, *President*
Selene Mojica, *Principal*
Kathy Azuara, *Vice Pres*
Salvatore Dadouche, *Vice Pres*
▼ EMP: 40
SALES (est): 30.9MM
SALES (corp-wide): 10.1B **Publicly Held**
SIC: 3841 2834 Surgical & medical instruments; pharmaceutical preparations
PA: Baxter International Inc.
1 Baxter Pkwy
Deerfield IL 60015
224 948-2000

### (G-7985)
**BAXTER HEALTHCARE CORPORATION**
1 Baxter Pkwy (60015-4625)
PHONE..................800 422-9837
Peter S Hellman, *Branch Mgr*
EMP: 200
SALES (corp-wide): 10.1B **Publicly Held**
SIC: 2836 Plasmas
HQ: Baxter Healthcare Corporation
1 Baxter Pkwy
Deerfield IL 60015
224 948-2000

### (G-7986)
**BAXTER HEALTHCARE CORPORATION**
1435 Lake Cook Rd (60015-5213)
PHONE..................847 948-2000
Jim Hauert, *Vice Pres*
Wesley Ward, *Project Mgr*
Jennifer McCallister, *Opers Mgr*
Jim Stoner, *Branch Mgr*
Sandy Eden, *Analyst*
EMP: 300
SALES (corp-wide): 10.1B **Publicly Held**
SIC: 3841 Surgical & medical instruments
HQ: Baxter Healthcare Corporation
1 Baxter Pkwy
Deerfield IL 60015
224 948-2000

### (G-7987)
**BAXTER HEALTHCARE CORPORATION**
Baxter Pharmaceutical Solution
1 Baxter Pkwy (60015-4625)
PHONE..................847 948-2000
Joel Titus, *Engineer*
Thomas F Chen, *Branch Mgr*
James Pacella, *Info Tech Dir*
Tom McGrady, *Director*
EMP: 401
SALES (corp-wide): 10.1B **Publicly Held**
SIC: 3841 Surgical & medical instruments
HQ: Baxter Healthcare Corporation
1 Baxter Pkwy
Deerfield IL 60015
224 948-2000

### (G-7988)
**BAXTER INTERNATIONAL INC (PA)**
1 Baxter Pkwy (60015-4634)
PHONE..................224 948-2000
Fax: 847 948-3080
Jose E Almeida, *Ch of Bd*
Giuseppe Accogli, *President*
Brik V Eyre, *President*
Paul Vibert, *President*
Sean Martin, *Vice Pres*
EMP: 1500
SALES: 10.1B **Publicly Held**
SIC: 2834 3841 2835 3842 Pharmaceutical preparations; intravenous solutions; solutions, pharmaceutical; surgical & medical instruments; catheters; medical instruments & equipment, blood & bone work; surgical instruments & apparatus; blood derivative diagnostic agents; surgical appliances & supplies

### (G-7989)
**BAXTER WORLD TRADE CORPORATION (HQ)**
1 Baxter Pkwy (60015-4625)
PHONE..................224 948-2000
Robert Parkinson, *President*
Angelique Lewis, *Opers Mgr*
Line Skoufos, *Opers Mgr*
Steven Wayne, *Facilities Mgr*
Amy Nguyen, *Supervisor*
EMP: 10
SQ FT: 17,915
SALES (est): 142.8MM
SALES (corp-wide): 10.1B **Publicly Held**
SIC: 2834 3841 Intravenous solutions; blood transfusion equipment; hemodialysis apparatus; diagnostic apparatus, medical; needles, suture
PA: Baxter International Inc.
1 Baxter Pkwy
Deerfield IL 60015
224 948-2000

### (G-7990)
**BEAM GLOBAL SPIRITS & WINE LLC (DH)**
Also Called: Beam Suntory
510 Lake Cook Rd (60015-4971)
PHONE..................847 948-8888
Matthew Shattock, *President*
Alonzo Johnson, *President*
Torsten Helbig, *Managing Dir*
Harish Moolchandani, *Managing Dir*
Tom V Wilen, *COO*
◆ EMP: 140
SQ FT: 50,000
SALES (est): 396.1MM
SALES (corp-wide): 72.3MM **Privately Held**
SIC: 2085 Distilled & blended liquors; bourbon whiskey; gin (alcoholic beverage); vodka (alcoholic beverage)
HQ: Beam Suntory Inc.
510 Lake Cook Rd
Deerfield IL 60015
847 948-8888

### (G-7991)
**BEAM SUNTORY INC (DH)**
510 Lake Cook Rd (60015-4971)
PHONE..................847 948-8888
Yasuhiro Fukuyama, *CEO*
Matthew J Shattock, *President*
Albert Baladi, *President*
Nicholas Fink, *President*
Atsushi Koizumi, *President*
◆ EMP: 130
SALES (est): 1.4B
SALES (corp-wide): 72.3MM **Privately Held**
WEB: www.fortunebrands.com
SIC: 2085 Distilled & blended liquors; bourbon whiskey; gin (alcoholic beverage); vodka (alcoholic beverage)
HQ: Suntory Holdings Limited
2-1-40, Dojimahama, Kita-Ku
Osaka OSK 530-0
663 461-682

### (G-7992)
**BNP MEDIA INC**
155 N Pfingsten Rd # 205 (60015-5293)
PHONE..................630 690-4200
Fax: 630 227-0204
Anne Armel, *Publisher*
Thomas Williams, *Publisher*
Scott Hilling, *Marketing Staff*
Linda Johnson, *Branch Mgr*
EMP: 70
SALES (corp-wide): 164.8MM **Privately Held**
SIC: 2721 Trade journals: publishing only, not printed on site
PA: Bnp Media, Inc.
2401 W Big Beaver Rd # 700
Troy MI 48084
248 362-3700

### (G-7993)
**CAPOL LLC**
707 Lake Cook Rd Ste 320 (60015-5276)
PHONE..................224 545-5095
Fax: 224 235-4691
Dr Matthias Seemann, *CEO*
Cahterine Clark, *President*
Bernd Strack, *CFO*
▲ EMP: 8
SALES (est): 912K
SALES (corp-wide): 6.9B **Privately Held**
SIC: 2064 2087 Candy & other confectionery products; glace, for glazing food
HQ: Capol Gmbh
Otto-Hahn-Str. 10
Elmshorn 25337
412 147-740

### (G-7994)
**CF INDUSTRIES INC (HQ)**
4 Parkway N Ste 400 (60015-2590)
PHONE..................847 405-2400
Tony Will, *CEO*
Steve Wilson, *President*
Bert Frost, *Senior VP*
Dennis Kelleher, *Senior VP*
Doug Barnard, *Vice Pres*
◆ EMP: 277
SQ FT: 88,000
SALES (est): 4.3B
SALES (corp-wide): 3.6B **Publicly Held**
WEB: www.cfindustries.com
SIC: 2873 2874 Anhydrous ammonia; urea; phosphoric acid; superphosphates, ammoniated or not ammoniated; diammonium phosphate; calcium meta-phosphate
PA: Cf Industries Holdings, Inc.
4 Parkway N Ste 400
Deerfield IL 60015
847 405-2400

### (G-7995)
**CF INDUSTRIES ENTERPRISES INC**
4 Parkway N Ste 400 (60015-2590)
PHONE..................847 405-2400
Dennis Kelleher, *Principal*
EMP: 3
SALES (est): 449.2K **Privately Held**
SIC: 2873 Nitrogenous fertilizers

### (G-7996)
**CF INDUSTRIES HOLDINGS INC (PA)**
4 Parkway N Ste 400 (60015-2590)
PHONE..................847 405-2400
Fax: 847 405-2730
Stephen A Furbacher, *Ch of Bd*
W Anthony Will, *President*
Douglas C Barnard, *Senior VP*
Christopher D Bohn, *Senior VP*
Bert A Frost, *Senior VP*
EMP: 266
SALES: 3.6B **Publicly Held**
SIC: 2873 2874 Nitrogenous fertilizers; fertilizers: natural (organic), except compost; phosphatic fertilizers

# GEOGRAPHIC SECTION
## Deerfield - Lake County (G-8021)

**(G-7997)**
**CF INDUSTRIES NITROGEN LLC (DH)**
4 Parkway N Ste 400 (60015-2590)
PHONE..................847 405-2400
Burton M Joyce, *Vice Ch Bd*
Lee Wyatt, *Vice Pres*
Jeanie Peterson, *Technical Mgr*
Jake Daigle, *Plant Engr*
Jeff Bald, *Sales Dir*
**EMP:** 115
**SQ FT:** 175,000
**SALES (est):** 222.3MM
**SALES (corp-wide):** 3.6B **Publicly Held**
**WEB:** www.terramed.net
**SIC:** 2875 2873 Fertilizers, mixing only; nitrogenous fertilizers

**(G-7998)**
**CF INDUSTRIES NITROGEN LLC (HQ)**
4 Parkway N Ste 400 (60015-2590)
PHONE..................847 405-2400
W Anthony Will, *CEO*
**EMP:** 15
**SALES (est):** 616.6MM
**SALES (corp-wide):** 3.6B **Publicly Held**
**SIC:** 2873 2874 Nitrogenous fertilizers; phosphatic fertilizers
**PA:** Cf Industries Holdings, Inc.
4 Parkway N Ste 400
Deerfield IL 60015
847 405-2400

**(G-7999)**
**CF INDUSTRIES SALES LLC**
4 Parkway N Ste 400 (60015-2590)
PHONE..................847 405-2400
Tony Will, *CEO*
**EMP:** 360
**SALES (est):** 442.2MM
**SALES (corp-wide):** 3.6B **Publicly Held**
**SIC:** 2873 Nitrogenous fertilizers
**PA:** Cf Industries Holdings, Inc.
4 Parkway N Ste 400
Deerfield IL 60015
847 405-2400

**(G-8000)**
**CONSUMERS DGEST CMMNCTIONS LLC**
520 Lake Cook Rd Ste 500 (60015-5633)
PHONE..................847 607-3000
Arthur Weber, *Partner*
Randy Weber, *Publisher*
Laurie Foster, *Vice Pres*
Stephen Purtell, *Treasurer*
Caren Ettleman, *Manager*
**EMP:** 17
**SALES (est):** 2MM **Privately Held**
**WEB:** www.consumersdigest.com
**SIC:** 2721 Magazines: publishing only, not printed on site

**(G-8001)**
**CONVERGENT GROUP LLC**
521 Deerpath Ct (60015-4104)
PHONE..................847 274-6336
David Ransburg, *Principal*
**EMP:** 3
**SALES (est):** 371.7K **Privately Held**
**SIC:** 3674 Semiconductors & related devices

**(G-8002)**
**CRL INDUSTRIES INC (HQ)**
500 Lake Cook Rd Ste 430 (60015-5268)
PHONE..................847 940-3550
D H Carroll, *Ch of Bd*
Gary J Minta, *Vice Pres*
Gregory Hamilton, *CFO*
David Danielski, *Treasurer*
Kathryn V Heller, *Manager*
▲ **EMP:** 1
**SALES (est):** 17.5MM **Privately Held**
**SIC:** 3553 3549 Sanding machines, except portable floor sanders: woodworking; metalworking machinery
**PA:** Lc Holdings Of Delaware, Inc
500 Lake Cook Rd Ste 430
Deerfield IL 60015
847 940-3550

**(G-8003)**
**DASHIRE INC**
Also Called: Superon Drug
150 Doral Ct (60015-5072)
PHONE..................847 236-0776
Donald Oppenheim, *President*
Shirley Oppenheim, *Admin Sec*
**EMP:** 10
**SQ FT:** 4,500
**SALES (est):** 1.3MM **Privately Held**
**SIC:** 5122 2833 Drugs & drug proprietaries; medicinals & botanicals

**(G-8004)**
**EASTWOOD ENTERPRISES INC**
1020 Chapel Ct (60015-2211)
P.O. Box 219, Highland Park (60035-0219)
PHONE..................847 940-4008
**Fax:** 847 940-4090
Paul D Levi, *President*
Sue E Clements, *Admin Sec*
**EMP:** 51
**SQ FT:** 16,000
**SALES (est):** 6.5MM **Privately Held**
**SIC:** 3599 Machine & other job shop work

**(G-8005)**
**ECO GREEN ANALYTICS LLC**
735 Castlewood Ln (60015-3972)
PHONE..................847 691-1148
Diego Klabjan, *Principal*
**EMP:** 6
**SALES (est):** 558.1K **Privately Held**
**SIC:** 3621 Generators for gas-electric or oil-electric vehicles

**(G-8006)**
**ELEXA CONSUMER PRODUCTS INC**
Also Called: Elexa Commercial Products
2275 Half Day Rd Ste 333 (60015-1277)
PHONE..................773 794-1300
Lawrence Beger, *President*
Randy Estlund, *CFO*
Seth Pychewicz, *Manager*
▲ **EMP:** 350
**SQ FT:** 40,000
**SALES (est):** 37.5MM **Privately Held**
**WEB:** www.bradley-steel.com
**SIC:** 3651 3661 Household audio & video equipment; telephones & telephone apparatus

**(G-8007)**
**FORTUNE BRANDS HOME & SEC INC (PA)**
520 Lake Cook Rd (60015-5611)
PHONE..................847 484-4400
**Fax:** 847 419-4110
Christopher J Klein, *CEO*
David M Thomas, *Ch of Bd*
Michael P Bauer, *President*
Brett E Finley, *President*
David M Randich, *President*
▲ **EMP:** 150
**SALES (est):** 4.9B **Publicly Held**
**SIC:** 2531 2599 3429 3469 Public building & related furniture; cabinets, factory; keys, locks & related hardware; boxes: tool, lunch, mail, etc.: stamped metal

**(G-8008)**
**FUJI IMPULSE AMERICAN CORP**
1735 Lisa Marie Ct (60015-3921)
PHONE..................847 236-9190
Jun Sota, *Principal*
▲ **EMP:** 7 **EST:** 2007
**SALES (est):** 871.9K **Privately Held**
**SIC:** 3565 Packaging machinery

**(G-8009)**
**GLOBEPHARM INC**
313 Pine St (60015-4828)
PHONE..................847 914-0922
Michael Anisfeld, *President*
Daryl Stone, *Vice Pres*
▼ **EMP:** 8
**SALES:** 500K **Privately Held**
**WEB:** www.globepharm.org
**SIC:** 2834 8742 Pharmaceutical preparations; hospital & health services consultant

**(G-8010)**
**HEALTHY LIFE NUTRACEUTICS INC**
500 Lake Cook Rd Ste 350 (60015-5268)
PHONE..................201 253-9053
Ravi Patel, *President*
Swapnil Shah, *Vice Pres*
**EMP:** 5
**SALES (est):** 528.2K **Privately Held**
**SIC:** 5122 2834 Vitamins & minerals; vitamin, nutrient & hematinic preparations for human use

**(G-8011)**
**HERSHEY COMPANY**
1751 Lake Cook Rd (60015-5615)
PHONE..................800 468-1714
**EMP:** 3
**SALES (corp-wide):** 7.4B **Publicly Held**
**SIC:** 2066 Chocolate & cocoa products
**PA:** Hershey Company
100 Crystal A Dr
Hershey PA 17033
717 534-4200

**(G-8012)**
**HIGH TECH RESEARCH INC (PA)**
Also Called: Expert Manufacturing Systems
1020 Milwaukee Ave # 330 (60015-3562)
PHONE..................847 215-9797
**Fax:** 847 215-9796
Steven Birman, *President*
Alex Liberov, *Vice Pres*
Michael Ofrikhter, *Engineer*
**EMP:** 10
**SALES (est):** 2MM **Privately Held**
**WEB:** www.htrmicronite.com
**SIC:** 7371 7372 Computer software development; software programming applications; prepackaged software

**(G-8013)**
**HOLDEN INDUSTRIES INC (PA)**
500 Lake Cook Rd Ste 400 (60015-5269)
PHONE..................847 940-1500
**Fax:** 847 940-1583
Joseph S Haas, *Ch of Bd*
Arthur R Miller, *Exec VP*
Daryl Hively, *Purch Mgr*
Gregory R Hamilton, *CFO*
Donald Hotz, *CFO*
◆ **EMP:** 17
**SALES (est):** 286.1MM **Privately Held**
**SIC:** 2752 2672 3545 3589 Commercial printing, lithographic; adhesive papers, labels or tapes: from purchased material; machine tool accessories; sewage & water treatment equipment; sewer cleaning equipment, power; machine tools, metal cutting type; fabricated structural metal

**(G-8014)**
**ICNET SYSTEMS INC**
1 Baxter Pkwy (60015-4625)
PHONE..................630 836-8073
Brik V Eyre, *President*
Robert J Hombach, *CFO*
Jay Saccaro, *CFO*
David P Scharf, *Admin Sec*
**EMP:** 30 **EST:** 2006
**SALES (est):** 287.3K
**SALES (corp-wide):** 10.1B **Publicly Held**
**SIC:** 7372 Business oriented computer software
**HQ:** Baxter Healthcare Corporation
1 Baxter Pkwy
Deerfield IL 60015
224 948-2000

**(G-8015)**
**J M SIGNS**
1664 Garand Dr (60015-2649)
P.O. Box 132 (60015-0132)
PHONE..................847 945-7446
James Golding, *Owner*
**EMP:** 3
**SALES (est):** 238.5K **Privately Held**
**SIC:** 3993 Signs & advertising specialties

**(G-8016)**
**JAM INTERNATIONAL CO LTD**
Also Called: American Hao Feng Co
500 Lake Cook Rd Ste 350 (60015-5268)
PHONE..................847 827-6391
Ann Shen, *President*
Mary Bullock, *Vice Pres*
Jose Yu, *Manager*
▲ **EMP:** 5
**SQ FT:** 1,800
**SALES (est):** 48.3K **Privately Held**
**SIC:** 2511 Wood household furniture

**(G-8017)**
**JAMES R WILBAT GLASS STUDIO**
924 Woodward Ave (60015-2867)
PHONE..................847 940-0015
James R Wilbat, *President*
Cara Wilbat, *Treasurer*
**EMP:** 3
**SQ FT:** 500
**SALES (est):** 20K **Privately Held**
**SIC:** 3229 Pressed & blown glass

**(G-8018)**
**JII HOLDINGS LLC**
1751 Lake Cook Rd Ste 550 (60015-5624)
PHONE..................847 945-5591
**EMP:** 4
**SALES (est):** 194.8K **Privately Held**
**SIC:** 1231 Anthracite mining

**(G-8019)**
**JIM BEAM BRANDS CO (DH)**
Also Called: James B Beam Import
510 Lake Cook Rd Ste 200 (60015-4964)
PHONE..................847 948-8903
**Fax:** 847 948-0393
Matthew J Shattock, *CEO*
Richard B Reese, *President*
Craig M Smith, *Exec VP*
Joseph J Winkler, *Exec VP*
Beth Bronner, *Senior VP*
◆ **EMP:** 325 **EST:** 1923
**SQ FT:** 50,000
**SALES (est):** 297.3MM
**SALES (corp-wide):** 72.3MM **Privately Held**
**WEB:** www.jbbworldwide.com
**SIC:** 2085 Distilled & blended liquors; bourbon whiskey; gin (alcoholic beverage); vodka (alcoholic beverage)
**HQ:** Beam Suntory Inc.
510 Lake Cook Rd
Deerfield IL 60015
847 948-8888

**(G-8020)**
**JORDAN INDUSTRIES INC (PA)**
1751 Lake Cook Rd Ste 550 (60015-5658)
PHONE..................847 945-5591
**Fax:** 847 945-5698
John W Jordan II, *Ch of Bd*
Thomas H Quinn, *President*
Joseph C Linen, *Senior VP*
Edward F Lilly, *Vice Pres*
Pam Ross, *Vice Pres*
◆ **EMP:** 15
**SQ FT:** 13,411
**SALES (est):** 592.6MM **Privately Held**
**WEB:** www.jordanind.com
**SIC:** 3621 3625 3714 3089 Motors, electric; electric motor & generator auxillary parts; motor starters & controllers, electric; motor vehicle engines & parts; rebuilding engines & transmissions, factory basis; gears, motor vehicle; thermoformed finished plastic products; labels & seals: printing; art, picture frames & decorations; picture frames, ready made

**(G-8021)**
**JORDAN SPECIALTY PLASTICS INC (HQ)**
1751 Lake Cook Rd Ste 550 (60015-5624)
PHONE..................847 945-5591
Lisa Ondrula, *Principal*
Brooke Overgard, *Admin Asst*
**EMP:** 7
**SALES (est):** 167.5MM
**SALES (corp-wide):** 592.6MM **Privately Held**
**SIC:** 3089 3081 Plastic containers, except foam; unsupported plastics film & sheet
**PA:** Jordan Industries, Inc.
1751 Lake Cook Rd Ste 550
Deerfield IL 60015
847 945-5591

# Deerfield - Lake County (G-8022)
## GEOGRAPHIC SECTION

**(G-8022)**
**JP LEATHERWORKS INC**
1038 Somerset Ave (60015-2942)
PHONE.....................847 317-9804
P Grace Blumenthal, *President*
Pamela Grace Blumenthal, *President*
**EMP:** 6
**SALES:** 1MM  **Privately Held**
**WEB:** www.jpleatherworks.com
**SIC: 3961**  Watchbands, base metal

**(G-8023)**
**JSOLO CORP**
Also Called: Minuteman Press
607 Carriage Way (60015-4536)
PHONE.....................847 964-9188
**Fax:** 847 298-1312
James S Solotke, *President*
**EMP:** 4
**SALES (est):** 290K  **Privately Held**
**SIC: 2752**  Commercial printing, lithographic

**(G-8024)**
**KEYSTONE BAKERY HOLDINGS LLC (DH)**
520 Lake Cook Rd (60015-5611)
PHONE.....................603 792-3113
Kevin McDonough, *President*
John Brennan, *Vice Pres*
Phil Streeter, *Vice Pres*
Ed Cassidy, *VP Sales*
Dave Ivey, *Administration*
▲ **EMP:** 1
**SALES (est):** 81.1MM
**SALES (corp-wide):** 35.5B  **Privately Held**
**SIC: 2053**  2051  Doughnuts, frozen; bread, cake & related products
**HQ:** Maplehurst Bakeries, Llc
50 Maplehurst Dr
Brownsburg IN 46112
317 858-9000

**(G-8025)**
**KIMBERLY-CLARK CORPORATION**
2275 Half Day Rd Ste 350 (60015-1277)
PHONE.....................312 371-5166
Wayne R Sanders, *Chairman*
**EMP:** 66
**SALES (corp-wide):** 18.2B  **Publicly Held**
**WEB:** www.kimberly-clark.com
**SIC: 2621**  Paper mills
**PA:** Kimberly-Clark Corporation
351 Phelps Dr
Irving TX 75038
972 281-1200

**(G-8026)**
**KRAFT FOODS ASIA PCF SVCS LLC (HQ)**
3 Parkway N Ste 300 (60015-2565)
PHONE.....................847 943-4000
Irene B Rosenfeld, *CEO*
**EMP:** 3
**SALES (est):** 739.9K  **Publicly Held**
**SIC: 2022**  2013  2095  2043  Processed cheese; natural cheese; spreads, cheese; dips, cheese-based; sausages & other prepared meats; bacon, side & sliced: from purchased meat; frankfurters from purchased meat; luncheon meat from purchased meat; coffee roasting (except by wholesale grocers); freeze-dried coffee; instant coffee; cereal breakfast foods; dressings, salad: raw & cooked (except dry mixes); powders, drink

**(G-8027)**
**LADDER INDUSTRIES INC (DH)**
500 Lake Cook Rd Ste 400 (60015-5269)
PHONE.....................800 360-6789
Gregory Larson, *President*
Tim Gonzalez, *General Mgr*
Joseph S Haas, *Vice Pres*
Arthur R Miller, *Vice Pres*
Gary Chenault, *Plant Mgr*
▲ **EMP:** 26
**SQ FT:** 45,000
**SALES (est):** 5.1MM
**SALES (corp-wide):** 286.1MM  **Privately Held**
**WEB:** www.ladderindustries.com
**SIC: 3449**  Miscellaneous metalwork

**HQ:** Wildeck, Inc.
405 Commerce St
Waukesha WI 53186
262 549-4000

**(G-8028)**
**LC HOLDINGS OF DELAWARE INC (PA)**
500 Lake Cook Rd Ste 430 (60015-5268)
PHONE.....................847 940-3550
D H Carroll, *President*
Gary J Minta, *Vice Pres*
Thomas Z Hayward Jr, *Admin Sec*
▲ **EMP:** 1
**SALES (est):** 14.2MM  **Privately Held**
**SIC: 3553**  3549  5084  3541  Sanding machines, except portable floor sanders: woodworking; metalworking machinery; industrial machinery & equipment; grinding, polishing, buffing, lapping & honing machines; grinding machines, metalworking

**(G-8029)**
**LEWA ACQUISITION CORP**
500 Lake Cook Rd Ste 430 (60015-5268)
PHONE.....................847 940-3535
D H Carroll, *President*
Gary J Minta, *Treasurer*
Thomas Z Hayward Jr, *Admin Sec*
**EMP:** 480
**SALES (est):** 2.9MM  **Privately Held**
**SIC: 0272**  2353  Horses & other equines; hats: cloth, straw & felt

**(G-8030)**
**LUNA AZUL COMMUNICATIONS INC**
1340 Hackberry Rd (60015-4020)
PHONE.....................773 616-0007
Stefan Nikolov, *President*
**EMP:** 20
**SALES (est):** 1.4MM  **Privately Held**
**SIC: 2741**  Miscellaneous publishing

**(G-8031)**
**LUNDBECK LLC (DH)**
6 Parkway N Ste 400 (60015-2522)
PHONE.....................847 282-1000
Sean Nolan, *CEO*
Nancy Shalowitz, *Counsel*
Charles R Krikorian, *Vice Pres*
Michael Burke, *VP Sls/Mktg*
Curtis Rhine, *CFO*
▲ **EMP:** 105  **EST:** 2000
**SQ FT:** 34,000
**SALES (est):** 163.4MM
**SALES (corp-wide):** 4.9B  **Privately Held**
**WEB:** www.ovationpharma.com
**SIC: 2834**  5122  Pharmaceutical preparations; pharmaceuticals
**HQ:** H. Lundbeck A/S
Ottiliavej 9
Valby  2500
363 013-11

**(G-8032)**
**LUNDBECK PHARMACEUTICALS LLC**
6 Parkway N Ste 400 (60015-2522)
PHONE.....................847 282-1000
Peter Anastasiou, *President*
**EMP:** 1000
**SALES (est):** 60.4MM
**SALES (corp-wide):** 4.9B  **Privately Held**
**SIC: 2834**  Pharmaceutical preparations
**HQ:** Lundbeck Llc
6 Parkway N Ste 400
Deerfield IL 60015
847 282-1000

**(G-8033)**
**M L S PRINTING CO INC**
537 Hermitage Dr (60015-4444)
PHONE.....................847 948-8902
John Mc Loughlin, *President*
Elizabeth Mc Loughlin, *Corp Secy*
**EMP:** 3  **EST:** 1957
**SQ FT:** 6,000
**SALES (est):** 240K  **Privately Held**
**SIC: 2752**  2796  2761  2759  Commercial printing, offset; platemaking services; manifold business forms; commercial printing

**(G-8034)**
**MALCOLITE CORPORATION (PA)**
1161 Lake Cook Rd Ste I (60015-5277)
PHONE.....................847 562-1350
**Fax:** 847 736-3774
Jason B Howard, *President*
Anthony Maas, *Sls & Mktg Exec*
Cecile Win, *Marketing Mgr*
**EMP:** 70
**SQ FT:** 36,000
**SALES (est):** 10.4MM  **Privately Held**
**WEB:** www.malcolite.com
**SIC: 3641**  Electric lamps & parts for generalized applications

**(G-8035)**
**MEDICAL ID FASHIONS COMPANY**
Also Called: Webzonepro.com
408 Swan Blvd (60015-3673)
PHONE.....................847 404-6789
Olaf Moetus, *President*
**EMP:** 4  **EST:** 2014
**SALES (est):** 237.3K  **Privately Held**
**SIC: 3961**  Bracelets, except precious metal

**(G-8036)**
**MICHAEL SCOTT INC**
111 Deer Lake Rd Ste 130 (60015-4978)
PHONE.....................847 965-8700
Douglas Cohen, *President*
Michael Cohen, *Vice Pres*
Scott Cohen, *Vice Pres*
Reth Archer, *Office Mgr*
▲ **EMP:** 15
**SQ FT:** 4,400
**SALES (est):** 1.5MM  **Privately Held**
**WEB:** www.scottmichael.com
**SIC: 2511**  Wood household furniture

**(G-8037)**
**MONDELEZ GLOBAL LLC (HQ)**
3 Parkway N Ste 300 (60015-2565)
PHONE.....................847 943-4000
David A Brearton,
Pluehs W Gerhard,
May J Karen,
Irene B Rosenfeld,
▲ **EMP:** 132
**SALES (est):** 5.5B  **Publicly Held**
**SIC: 2052**  2066  3999  2067  Crackers, dry; biscuits, dry; chocolate; candles; chewing gum; cheese, natural & processed; beverage bases

**(G-8038)**
**MONDELEZ INTERNATIONAL INC (PA)**
3 Parkway N Ste 300 (60015-2565)
PHONE.....................847 943-4000
**Fax:** 847 646-7759
Irene B Rosenfeld, *Ch of Bd*
Maurizio Brusadelli, *President*
Timothy P Cofer, *President*
Alejandro R Lorenzo, *President*
Hubert Weber, *President*
♦ **EMP:** 2000
**SALES (est):** 25.9B  **Publicly Held**
**WEB:** www.kraft.com
**SIC: 2022**  2013  2095  2043  Processed cheese; natural cheese; spreads, cheese; dips, cheese-based; sausages & other prepared meats; bacon, side & sliced: from purchased meat; frankfurters from purchased meat; luncheon meat from purchased meat; coffee roasting (except by wholesale grocers); freeze-dried coffee; instant coffee; cereal breakfast foods; dressings, salad: raw & cooked (except dry mixes); powders, drink

**(G-8039)**
**MONDELEZ INTL HOLDINGS LLC (HQ)**
3 Parkway N Ste 300 (60015-2565)
PHONE.....................800 572-3847
**Fax:** 847 317-7296
Carol J Ward,
Jonas Bruzas,
Philip Gregorcy,
**EMP:** 7
**SALES (est):** 11.8MM  **Publicly Held**
**SIC: 2038**  Snacks, including onion rings, cheese sticks, etc.

**(G-8040)**
**MORRIS CODY & ASSOC**
400 Lake Cook Rd Ste 207 (60015-4930)
PHONE.....................847 945-8050
**Fax:** 847 945-5037
Cody Morris, *President*
**EMP:** 4  **EST:** 1973
**SALES (est):** 147.1K  **Privately Held**
**SIC: 2741**  Newsletter publishing

**(G-8041)**
**MULCH CENTER LLC**
21457 Milwaukee Ave (60015-5322)
PHONE.....................847 459-7200
**Fax:** 847 229-0219
James Seckelmann, *Owner*
**EMP:** 28
**SALES (est):** 5.6MM  **Privately Held**
**SIC: 2499**  Mulch, wood & bark

**(G-8042)**
**MY OWN MEALS INC (PA)**
400 Lake Cook Rd Ste 107 (60015-4929)
P.O. Box 334 (60015-0334)
PHONE.....................847 948-1118
Mary A Jackson, *President*
Elizabeth M Doyle, *Vice Pres*
Joseph D Onofrio, *Vice Pres*
Joseph D'Onofrio, *CFO*
▼ **EMP:** 4
**SQ FT:** 1,500
**SALES (est):** 15.2MM  **Privately Held**
**WEB:** www.myownmeals.com
**SIC: 2099**  Food preparations

**(G-8043)**
**NANO GAS TECHNOLOGIES INC**
506 Cambridge Cir (60015-4209)
PHONE.....................586 229-2656
Leonard Bland, *CEO*
Scott Fiedler, *COO*
**EMP:** 5
**SALES (est):** 640.8K  **Privately Held**
**SIC: 3589**  Water treatment equipment, industrial

**(G-8044)**
**NURI CORP**
Also Called: Newport Coffee House
1121 Half Day Rd (60015-1207)
PHONE.....................847 940-7134
**Fax:** 847 940-7501
Danny Chung, *President*
**EMP:** 12
**SQ FT:** 1,809
**SALES (est):** 1.1MM  **Privately Held**
**SIC: 2095**  Coffee roasting (except by wholesale grocers)

**(G-8045)**
**OUTOKUMPU STAINLESS USA LLC**
2275 Half Day Rd Ste 300 (60015-1232)
PHONE.....................847 405-6604
**Fax:** 847 317-1440
Debbie Bradford, *Manager*
**EMP:** 75
**SALES (corp-wide):** 593.1MM  **Privately Held**
**SIC: 3312**  Stainless steel
**HQ:** Outokumpu Stainless Usa, Llc
1 Steel Dr
Calvert AL 36513
847 317-1400

**(G-8046)**
**PREGIS HOLDING I CORPORATION (PA)**
1650 Lake Cook Rd Ste 400 (60015-4747)
PHONE.....................847 597-2200
Glenn M Fischer, *President*
Michael T McDonnell, *President*
**EMP:** 10
**SALES (est):** 207.9MM  **Privately Held**
**SIC: 2671**  5199  7336  Packaging paper & plastics film, coated & laminated; packaging materials; package design

**(G-8047)**
**PREGIS INNOVATIVE PACKG LLC**
1650 Lake Cook Rd Ste 400 (60015-4747)
PHONE.....................847 597-2200
Kevin Baudhuin, *President*
Keith Lavanway, *CFO*

# GEOGRAPHIC SECTION

## Deerfield - Lake County (G-8070)

Sean Condon, *Sales Executive*
Wayne Schobel, *Manager*
**EMP:** 46
**SALES (est):** 15.1MM
**SALES (corp-wide):** 5.6B Privately Held
**SIC:** 2671 5199 Packaging paper & plastics film, coated & laminated; packaging materials
**HQ:** Pregis Llc
  1650 Lake Cook Rd Ste 400
  Deerfield IL 60015
  847 597-9330

### (G-8048)
### PREGIS LLC (HQ)
1650 Lake Cook Rd Ste 400 (60015-4747)
**PHONE** ............................ 847 597-9330
**Fax:** 847 597-9752
Kevin Baudhuin, *President*
Tom Pienkowski, *President*
Tom Wetsch, *President*
Ivan Brewington, *Regional Mgr*
Dan Donofrio, *VP Opers*
◆ **EMP:** 70
**SALES (est):** 324.9MM
**SALES (corp-wide):** 5.6B Privately Held
**SIC:** 3086 Packaging & shipping materials, foamed plastic
**PA:** Olympus Partners, L.P.
  1 Station Pl Ste 4
  Stamford CT 06902
  203 353-5900

### (G-8049)
### PREGIS LLC
1650 Lake Cook Rd Ste 400 (60015-4747)
**PHONE** ............................ 847 597-2200
Kevin J Baudhuin, *President*
D Keith Lavanway, *CFO*
**EMP:** 4000
**SALES (est):** 207.9MM Privately Held
**SIC:** 2671 2673 3086 Packaging paper & plastics film, coated & laminated; bags: plastic, laminated & coated; insulation or cushioning material, foamed plastic; packaging & shipping materials, foamed plastic
**PA:** Pregis Holding I Corporation
  1650 Lake Cook Rd Ste 400
  Deerfield IL 60015

### (G-8050)
### PRINTING YOU CAN TRUST
707 Mallard Ln (60015-3680)
**PHONE** ............................ 224 676-0482
Aaron Marsh, *Owner*
**EMP:** 3 **EST:** 2009
**SALES (est):** 266.5K Privately Held
**SIC:** 2759 Commercial printing

### (G-8051)
### SCHOLL COMMUNICATIONS INC
56 Birchwood Ave (60015-4709)
P.O. Box 560 (60015-0560)
**PHONE** ............................ 847 945-1891
**Fax:** 847 945-1897
Marilyn D Scholl, *President*
David E Scholl, *Exec VP*
**EMP:** 4
**SALES (est):** 291.9K Privately Held
**SIC:** 2759 8742 Directories (except telephone): printing; business consultant; marketing consulting services

### (G-8052)
### SIEMENS HLTHCARE DGNOSTICS INC
1717 Deerfield Rd (60015-3900)
**PHONE** ............................ 847 267-5300
Greg Sorsenson, *CEO*
Erin Camp, *Counsel*
Helen Heifets, *Counsel*
Jessica East, *Project Mgr*
Adam Maniscalco, *Project Mgr*
▲ **EMP:** 49 **EST:** 2005
**SALES (est):** 10.9MM
**SALES (corp-wide):** 89.6B Privately Held
**SIC:** 3841 Surgical & medical instruments
**HQ:** Siemens Healthcare Diagnostics Inc.
  511 Benedict Ave
  Tarrytown NY 10591
  914 631-8000

### (G-8053)
### SIGNATURE BUSINESS SYSTEMS INC
500 Lake Cook Rd Fl 3 (60015-5609)
**PHONE** ............................ 847 459-8500
Michael Silver, *Manager*
**EMP:** 10
**SALES (corp-wide):** 35MM Privately Held
**SIC:** 7371 7372 Custom computer programming services; computer software development; prepackaged software
**PA:** Signature Business Consulting Systems Inc
  105 Feldcrest Ave Ste 404
  Edison NJ 08837
  888 725-2555

### (G-8054)
### SILICON CONTROL INC (PA)
155 N Pfingsten Rd # 360 (60015-5293)
**PHONE** ............................ 847 215-7947
**Fax:** 847 808-9090
Paul Schur, *President*
Pam Topper, *Manager*
**EMP:** 4
**SQ FT:** 2,000
**SALES (est):** 952K Privately Held
**WEB:** www.silicon-control.com
**SIC:** 8711 8731 3825 3823 Consulting engineer; commercial physical research; instruments to measure electricity; industrial instrmnts msrmnt display/control process variable

### (G-8055)
### SIMONTON HOLDINGS INC (DH)
Also Called: Specialty Building Resources
520 Lake Cook Rd (60015-5611)
P.O. Box 1646, Parkersburg WV (26102-1646)
**PHONE** ............................ 304 428-8261
Samuel B Ross II, *Ch of Bd*
Mike Peterson, *Manager*
◆ **EMP:** 15
**SALES (est):** 178.6MM
**SALES (corp-wide):** 72.3MM Privately Held
**SIC:** 3089 5961 3086 5963 Window frames & sash, plastic; mail order house; plastics foam products; direct selling establishments
**HQ:** Beam Suntory Inc.
  510 Lake Cook Rd
  Deerfield IL 60015
  847 948-8888

### (G-8056)
### STAGNITO PARTNERS LLC (HQ)
Also Called: Stagnito Media
570 Lake Cook Rd Ste 310 (60015-4952)
**PHONE** ............................ 224 632-8200
Kollin Stagnito, *CEO*
Jackie Batson, *Prdtn Mgr*
Kyle Stagnito, *CFO*
Katrina Lopez, *Accounts Exec*
Bette J Boyers, *Adv Mgr*
**EMP:** 62
**SALES (est):** 19.9MM
**SALES (corp-wide):** 20.1MM Privately Held
**SIC:** 2721 8742 7389 Magazines: publishing only, not printed on site; marketing consulting services; convention & show services
**PA:** Ensembleiq, Inc.
  4 Middlebury Blvd
  Randolph NJ 07869
  973 607-1300

### (G-8057)
### SYSTEMS PIPING
1625 Half Day Rd (60015-1233)
**PHONE** ............................ 847 948-1373
Karen Vanderbilt, *Owner*
**EMP:** 7
**SALES (est):** 410K Privately Held
**SIC:** 3569 Sprinkler systems, fire: automatic

### (G-8058)
### TAKEDA DEV CTR AMERICAS INC
1 Takeda Pkwy (60015-5713)
**PHONE** ............................ 224 554-6500

Stuart Dollow, *President*
Gita Shipkowitz, *Editor*
Nancy Joseph-Ridge, *Chairman*
Qais Mekki, *Vice Pres*
Greg Murawski, *Project Mgr*
**EMP:** 549
**SALES (est):** 75.9MM
**SALES (corp-wide):** 15.2B Privately Held
**SIC:** 2834 Pharmaceutical preparations
**HQ:** Takeda Pharmaceuticals U.S.A., Inc.
  1 Takeda Pkwy
  Deerfield IL 60015
  224 554-6500

### (G-8059)
### TAKEDA PHARMACEUTICALS NA
1 Takeda Pkwy (60015-5713)
**PHONE** ............................ 972 819-5353
**EMP:** 9 **EST:** 2009
**SALES (est):** 968.1K Privately Held
**SIC:** 2834 Pharmaceutical preparations

### (G-8060)
### TAKEDA PHARMACEUTICALS USA INC (HQ)
1 Takeda Pkwy (60015-5713)
**PHONE** ............................ 224 554-6500
**Fax:** 847 383-3080
Helen Pring, *President*
Mary-Jo Dempson, *President*
Ramona Sequeira, *President*
Hiroaki Ogata, *General Mgr*
Steve Higgins, *District Mgr*
▲ **EMP:** 558
**SALES (est):** 1.7B
**SALES (corp-wide):** 15.2B Privately Held
**SIC:** 2834 Pharmaceutical preparations
**PA:** Takeda Pharmaceutical Company Limited
  4-1-1, Doshomachi, Chuo-Ku
  Osaka OSK 541-0
  662 042-111

### (G-8061)
### TAKEDA PHRMACEUTICALS AMER INC
1 Takeda Pkwy (60015-5713)
**PHONE** ............................ 224 554-6500
Douglas Cole, *President*
Helen Pring, *Treasurer*
Patrick Butler, *Asst Treas*
Guido Giazzon, *Director*
Kenneth D Greisman, *Admin Sec*
**EMP:** 2137
**SALES (est):** 203MM
**SALES (corp-wide):** 15.2B Privately Held
**SIC:** 2834 Pharmaceutical preparations
**HQ:** Takeda Pharmaceuticals U.S.A., Inc.
  1 Takeda Pkwy
  Deerfield IL 60015
  224 554-6500

### (G-8062)
### TERRA NITROGEN COMPANY LP (PA)
4 Parkway N Ste 400 (60015-2542)
**PHONE** ............................ 847 405-2400
W Anthony Will, *President*
Dennis P Kelleher, *CFO*
▲ **EMP:** 2
**SALES:** 418.3MM Publicly Held
**WEB:** www.terranitrogen.com
**SIC:** 2873 Nitrogen solutions (fertilizer)

### (G-8063)
### TEXTURA CORPORATION (HQ)
1405 Lake Cook Rd (60015-5213)
**PHONE** ............................ 866 839-8872
**Fax:** 847 582-1037
Patrick Allin, *President*
Heidi Gluck, *Counsel*
Michael Antis, *Exec VP*
Linda Debruin, *Exec VP*
David Kelly, *Exec VP*
**EMP:** 250
**SQ FT:** 63,000
**SALES:** 86.7MM
**SALES (corp-wide):** 37B Publicly Held
**WEB:** www.texturallc.com
**SIC:** 7372 Prepackaged software
**PA:** Oracle Corporation
  500 Oracle Pkwy
  Redwood City CA 94065
  650 506-7000

### (G-8064)
### VAN STOCKUM KRISTINE
Also Called: Kristine Van Stockum's Hand PA
827 Woodward Ave (60015-2864)
**PHONE** ............................ 847 914-0015
Kristine Van Stockum, *Owner*
**EMP:** 4
**SALES:** 50K Privately Held
**SIC:** 2392 Tablecloths & table settings

### (G-8065)
### VARSITY LOGISTICS INC
1 Parkway N Ste 400s (60015-2551)
**PHONE** ............................ 650 392-7979
Madeline Bottari, *President*
Julian Thomas, *Production*
Igor Kashtan, *Manager*
Stephanie Roundtree, *Programmer Anys*
Mark B Abelson, *Director*
**EMP:** 30
**SQ FT:** 6,000
**SALES (est):** 3.8MM Privately Held
**WEB:** www.varsitylogistics.com
**SIC:** 7372 Prepackaged software; application computer software

### (G-8066)
### VICRON OPTICAL INC
1020 Milwaukee Ave # 235 (60015-3555)
**PHONE** ............................ 847 412-5530
**EMP:** 10
**SQ FT:** 2,000
**SALES:** 1MM Privately Held
**SIC:** 3851 5047 Manufactures And Wholsales Opthalmic Supplies

### (G-8067)
### W-F PROFESSIONAL ASSOC INC
400 Lake Cook Rd Ste 207 (60015-5258)
**PHONE** ............................ 847 945-8050
William Feinberg, *President*
**EMP:** 3
**SALES (est):** 227.8K Privately Held
**WEB:** www.wfprofessional.com
**SIC:** 2741 8748 Miscellaneous publishing; business consulting

### (G-8068)
### WORTH-PFAFF INNOVATIONS INC (PA)
Also Called: Flashcut Cnc
444 Lake Cook Rd Ste 17 (60015-4931)
**PHONE** ............................ 847 940-9305
Ronald K Worth, *President*
Anne Neal, *Opers Mgr*
Eric Pfaff, *Admin Sec*
▲ **EMP:** 6
**SQ FT:** 5,000
**SALES (est):** 3.9MM Privately Held
**WEB:** www.flashcutcnc.com
**SIC:** 5084 3829 Instruments & control equipment; measuring & controlling devices

### (G-8069)
### WOW SIGNS INC
150 Augusta Dr (60015-5069)
**PHONE** ............................ 847 910-4405
Larry Feld, *President*
**EMP:** 6
**SALES (est):** 413.8K Privately Held
**WEB:** www.wowzone.com
**SIC:** 3993 Signs & advertising specialties

### (G-8070)
### ZOOKBINDERS INC
151 S Pfingsten Rd Ste K (60015-4934)
**PHONE** ............................ 847 272-5745
**Fax:** 847 272-5978
Mark Zucker, *President*
Leslie Zucker, *Vice Pres*
Al Kawano, *Plant Mgr*
Greg Martinez, *Opers Mgr*
Jean Stein, *Materials Mgr*
**EMP:** 70
**SALES (est):** 11.7MM Privately Held
**WEB:** www.zookbinders.com
**SIC:** 2782 Albums

## Dekalb
### Dekalb County

**(G-8071)**
**3M DEKALB DISTRIBUTION**
12101 Barber Greene Rd (60115-7901)
PHONE..................815 756-5087
Robert Hughes, *Principal*
◆ EMP: 23
SALES (est): 2.6MM **Privately Held**
SIC: **5199** 3999 Anatomical specimens & research material; atomizers, toiletry

**(G-8072)**
**ACE MACHINE & TOOL**
314 Wood St (60115-4163)
PHONE..................815 793-5077
Elissa Jarke, *Owner*
Ronald Jarke, *Co-Owner*
EMP: 5
SALES: 175K **Privately Held**
SIC: **3559** 7389 Automotive related machinery;

**(G-8073)**
**ALGUS PACKAGING INC**
1212 E Taylor St (60115-4507)
P.O. Box 488 (60115-0488)
PHONE..................815 756-1881
Fax: 815 758-2281
Arthur Gustafson, *President*
Larry Aska, *Vice Pres*
Pat Stoner, *Vice Pres*
Karen Gustafson, *Admin Sec*
Dave Holderness, *Maintence Staff*
EMP: 100
SQ FT: 200,000
SALES (est): 37.6MM **Privately Held**
WEB: www.algus.com
SIC: **3089** 3565 Blister or bubble formed packaging, plastic; packaging machinery

**(G-8074)**
**AMERICAN MARKETING & PUBG LLC**
Also Called: Home Pages
915 E Lincoln Hwy (60115-3941)
P.O. Box 801 (60115-0801)
PHONE..................815 756-2840
Joline Staeheli, *COO*
Chad Campbell, *Exec VP*
Karen Bourdage, *Finance*
Matt Chenoweth, *HR Admin*
Brian Franczak, *VP Sales*
EMP: 35
SQ FT: 1,500
SALES (est): 5.3MM **Privately Held**
WEB: www.homepagesdirectories.com
SIC: **2741** Telephone & other directory publishing

**(G-8075)**
**ARMOLOY OF ILLINOIS INC**
Also Called: Bi Protec
114 Simonds Ave (60115-3969)
PHONE..................815 758-6657
Michael Bejbl, *President*
Pat Bradford, *Plant Mgr*
Larry Lighthall, *Controller*
EMP: 45
SQ FT: 22,750
SALES (est): 3.9MM
SALES (corp-wide): 8.4MM **Privately Held**
WEB: www.armoloy.com
SIC: **3479** Coating of metals & formed products
PA: Investment Holdings Inc
114 Simons Ave
De Kalb IL
815 758-6657

**(G-8076)**
**CASTLE-PRINTECH INC**
121 Industrial Dr (60115-3931)
PHONE..................815 758-5484
Fax: 815 758-0712
John M Gavelda, *President*
EMP: 1 EST: 1990
SALES (est): 200.5K **Privately Held**
SIC: **2759** Commercial printing

**(G-8077)**
**COLE PALLET SERVICES CORP**
1300 Oak St (60115-3559)
P.O. Box 964 (60115-0964)
PHONE..................815 758-3226
Fax: 815 758-2687
Brett Cole, *President*
John Cole, *Vice Pres*
EMP: 35
SQ FT: 37,000
SALES (est): 4.3MM **Privately Held**
SIC: **2448** 2449 Pallets, wood; skids, wood; wood containers

**(G-8078)**
**CONEX CABLE LLC**
1007 E Locust St (60115-3967)
P.O. Box 822 (60115-0822)
PHONE..................800 877-8089
Brian Starr, *Prdtn Mgr*
Raymond Charles Hott,
Renee Kozin,
Melissa Spellman,
▲ EMP: 35
SQ FT: 64,000
SALES (est): 10.5MM **Privately Held**
SIC: **3355** Aluminum wire & cable

**(G-8079)**
**COPY SERVICE INC**
1005 W Lincoln Hwy (60115-3019)
PHONE..................815 758-1151
Fax: 815 758-1152
David Baker, *President*
Nancy Baker, *Manager*
EMP: 5
SQ FT: 7,000
SALES (est): 631.4K **Privately Held**
SIC: **7334** 5943 2791 2789 Photocopying & duplicating services; office forms & supplies; typesetting; bookbinding & related work

**(G-8080)**
**CST INDUSTRIES INC**
Engineered Storage Products Co
345 Harvestore Dr (60115-9646)
PHONE..................815 756-1551
Ron Brotz, *Opers Staff*
Aaron George, *Buyer*
Donna Dulany, *Human Res Mgr*
Chris Forbes, *Sales Dir*
Al Lang, *Mktg Dir*
EMP: 175
SALES (corp-wide): 279.8MM **Privately Held**
WEB: www.tanks.com
SIC: **3448** 3523 3443 Farm & utility buildings; farm machinery & equipment; fabricated plate work (boiler shop)
PA: Cst Industries, Inc.
903 E 104th St Ste 900
Kansas City MO 64131
913 621-3700

**(G-8081)**
**CURRAN CONTRACTING COMPANY**
2220 County Farm Rd (60115-9429)
PHONE..................815 758-8113
Rick Noe, *Principal*
EMP: 8
SALES (corp-wide): 574.2MM **Privately Held**
WEB: www.currancontracting.com
SIC: **1611** 2951 5032 Highway & street construction; asphalt paving mixtures & blocks; paving materials
HQ: Curran Contracting Company
286 Memorial Ct
Crystal Lake IL 60014
815 455-5100

**(G-8082)**
**CURT HERRMANN CONSTRUCTION INC**
512 Maplewood Ave (60115-4214)
PHONE..................815 748-0531
Curt Herrmann, *President*
EMP: 4
SALES: 375K **Privately Held**
SIC: **3131** Counters

**(G-8083)**
**CUSHIONEER INC**
1651 Pleasant St (60115-2604)
PHONE..................815 748-5505
Fax: 815 748-5504
Andrew Swift, *President*
Warren B Swift, *Shareholder*
EMP: 53
SQ FT: 80,000
SALES (est): 9.2MM **Privately Held**
WEB: www.cushioneer.com
SIC: **3086** Packaging & shipping materials, foamed plastic

**(G-8084)**
**CY-TEC INC**
221 Industrial Dr (60115-3933)
P.O. Box 46 (60115-0046)
PHONE..................815 756-8416
Fax: 815 756-8418
Dan Pritchard, *President*
Patrice Pritchard, *Shareholder*
EMP: 5
SQ FT: 14,000
SALES: 600K **Privately Held**
SIC: **3555** Printing trades machinery; presses, gravure; printing trade parts & attachments

**(G-8085)**
**DE KALB PLATING CO INC**
221 Grove St (60115-3701)
PHONE..................815 756-6112
Fax: 815 756-3927
Bruce Miller, *President*
EMP: 7
SQ FT: 7,700
SALES (est): 1MM **Privately Held**
SIC: **3471** Electroplating of metals or formed products

**(G-8086)**
**DEKALB CONFECTIONARY INC (PA)**
149 N 2nd St (60115-3203)
PHONE..................815 758-5990
Fax: 815 758-1182
Thomas Smith, *President*
Sharon Smith, *Vice Pres*
EMP: 16
SQ FT: 3,300
SALES (est): 1.9MM **Privately Held**
SIC: **5441** 2066 Candy, nut & confectionery stores; chocolate & cocoa products

**(G-8087)**
**DEKALB FORGE COMPANY (PA)**
Also Called: Forge Resources Group
1832 Pleasant St (60115-2609)
P.O. Box 369 (60115-0369)
PHONE..................815 756-3538
Fax: 815 756-6958
Donald G Jones, *President*
Jeffrey Jones, *Vice Pres*
Brian Urfer, *Project Mgr*
Scott Holdiman, *Purchasing*
Lance Robinson, *QC Dir*
EMP: 75 EST: 1946
SQ FT: 102,000
SALES (est): 18.4MM **Privately Held**
WEB: www.dekalbforge.com
SIC: **3462** Iron & steel forgings

**(G-8088)**
**DIDDY DOGS INC**
1180 W Lincoln Hwy (60115-2902)
PHONE..................815 517-0451
Jess Parker, *Owner*
Keith L Foster, *Principal*
EMP: 2
SALES (est): 226.2K **Privately Held**
SIC: **5199** 2047 Pets & pet supplies; dogs; dog food

**(G-8089)**
**ELECTROLIZING INC (HQ)**
114 Simonds Ave (60115-3969)
PHONE..................815 758-6657
Jerome Bejbl, *President*
EMP: 2
SQ FT: 1,625
SALES (est): 8.1MM
SALES (corp-wide): 8.4MM **Privately Held**
SIC: **3471** Electroplating & plating
PA: Investment Holdings Inc
114 Simons Ave
De Kalb IL
815 758-6657

**(G-8090)**
**FASTRACK STAIRS & RAILS LTD**
303 N 11th St (60115-3503)
PHONE..................847 531-6252
Bruce Woodbridge, *President*
EMP: 6
SALES (est): 347.5K **Privately Held**
SIC: **3446** Stairs, fire escapes, balconies, railings & ladders

**(G-8091)**
**FORGE RESOURCES GROUP LLC**
1832 Pleasant St (60115-2609)
P.O. Box 369 (60115-0369)
PHONE..................815 758-6400
EMP: 200
SALES (est): 6.9MM **Privately Held**
SIC: **3399** Mfg Primary Metal Products

**(G-8092)**
**FORGE RESOURCES GROUP LLC**
1801 Pleasant St (60115-2608)
PHONE..................815 758-6400
EMP: 191
SALES (corp-wide): 16.2MM **Privately Held**
SIC: **3399** Iron ore recovery from open hearth slag
PA: Forge Resources Group Llc
1832 Pleasant St
Dekalb IL 60115
815 758-6400

**(G-8093)**
**FORGE RESOURCES GROUP LLC (PA)**
1832 Pleasant St (60115-2609)
P.O. Box 369 (60115-0369)
PHONE..................815 758-6400
Donald G Jones, *President*
Jeffrey Jones, *Vice Pres*
Tim Pfeifer, *Engineer*
Kent Paul, *CFO*
Kate Marach, *Accounts Mgr*
EMP: 9
SALES (est): 16.2MM **Privately Held**
SIC: **3462** 3399 Iron & steel forgings; iron ore recovery from open hearth slag

**(G-8094)**
**GEM ELECTRIC MOTOR REPAIR**
1400 E Lincoln Hwy (60115-3971)
PHONE..................815 756-5317
Fax: 815 756-8553
Hirlande Erker, *President*
John Erker, *Corp Secy*
Paul Erker, *Vice Pres*
EMP: 2
SQ FT: 2,500
SALES: 250K **Privately Held**
SIC: **5063** 7694 Motors, electric; electric motor repair

**(G-8095)**
**H A PHILLIPS & CO (PA)**
770 Enterprise Ave (60115-7904)
PHONE..................630 377-0050
Michael Ryan, *CEO*
Steve L Yagla, *Vice Pres*
Brian J Youssi, *Vice Pres*
John Terdina, *Production*
Dave Williams, *Production*
▼ EMP: 30 EST: 1928
SQ FT: 22,000
SALES (est): 8.7MM **Privately Held**
WEB: www.haphillips.com
SIC: **3585** 3491 3443 3822 Refrigeration & heating equipment; industrial valves; fabricated plate work (boiler shop); refrigeration controls (pressure); household refrigerators & freezers

**(G-8096)**
**HERFF JONES LLC**
901 N 1st St Ste 7 (60115-2395)
PHONE..................815 756-4743
Fax: 815 756-4150

## GEOGRAPHIC SECTION
### Dekalb - Dekalb County (G-8121)

Bernard W Elsner, *Manager*
**EMP:** 12
**SALES (corp-wide):** 1.1B **Privately Held**
**WEB:** www.herffjones.com
**SIC:** 3911  Rings, finger: precious metal
**HQ:** Herff Jones, Llc
4501 W 62nd St
Indianapolis IN 46268
800 419-5462

**(G-8097)**
### HORIZON DOWNING LLC
Also Called: Horizon Displays, LLC
1115 E Locust St  (60115-3964)
P.O. Box 827  (60115-0827)
**PHONE** .................................... 815 758-6867
**Fax:** 815 758-6891
Larry Denny, *Systems Staff*
Brian Johnson, *Executive*
Michael J Scherer,
**EMP:** 27
**SQ FT:** 52,500
**SALES (est):** 3.6MM
**SALES (corp-wide):** 18.8MM **Privately Held**
**WEB:** www.horizondisplays.com
**SIC:** 3993  7389  4225  Signs & advertising specialties; advertising artwork; displays & cutouts, window & lobby; promoters of shows & exhibitions; advertising, promotional & trade show services; general warehousing
**PA:** Downing Displays, Inc.
550 Techne Center Dr
Milford OH 45150
513 248-9800

**(G-8098)**
### IDEAL INDUSTRIES INC
1330 E Lincoln Hwy  (60115-3973)
**PHONE** .................................... 815 758-2656
**Fax:** 815 758-4547
Kristen Winnicki, *Area Mgr*
Bill Wildman, *Mfg Dir*
Bill Schleper, *Plant Mgr*
Jake Young, *Opers Mgr*
George Hand, *Opers Staff*
**EMP:** 100
**SALES (corp-wide):** 366.2MM **Privately Held**
**WEB:** www.idealindustries.com
**SIC:** 3315  3643  Wire carts: grocery, household & industrial; current-carrying wiring devices
**PA:** Ideal Industries, Inc.
1375 Park Ave
Sycamore IL 60178
815 895-5181

**(G-8099)**
### J6 POLYMERS LLC
633 Enterprise Ave Ste 3  (60115-7913)
**PHONE** .................................... 815 517-1179
Robert J Wood, *General Mgr*
Sandra Wood, *Mng Member*
Jonathon Wood, *Manager*
James Wood, *Admin Mgr*
**EMP:** 4
**SQ FT:** 6,500
**SALES (est):** 437.3K **Privately Held**
**SIC:** 2822  Ethylene-propylene rubbers, EPDM polymers

**(G-8100)**
### JANELLE PUBLICATIONS INC
116 Twombly Rd  (60115)
P.O. Box 811  (60115-0811)
**PHONE** .................................... 815 756-2300
**Fax:** 815 756-4799
Janet Dawson, *President*
Sten Kresatck, *Vice Pres*
**EMP:** 2
**SQ FT:** 1,350
**SALES:** 350K **Privately Held**
**WEB:** www.janellepublications.com
**SIC:** 2741  8049  Miscellaneous publishing; speech therapist

**(G-8101)**
### L M C INC
Also Called: APM Process Center
1142 Glidden Ave  (60115-4377)
**PHONE** .................................... 815 758-3514
**Fax:** 815 758-3802
Lennart Lindeli, *Ch of Bd*
Gordon D Goranson, *President*

▲ **EMP:** 1
**SQ FT:** 40,000
**SALES (est):** 202.3K **Privately Held**
**WEB:** www.lmcpress.com
**SIC:** 3542  3535  Pressing machines; conveyors & conveying equipment

**(G-8102)**
### LOTHSON GUITARS
10580 Keslinger Rd  (60115-8829)
**PHONE** .................................... 815 756-2031
**Fax:** 815 756-2031
Larry Lothson, *Owner*
**EMP:** 3
**SALES:** 150K **Privately Held**
**SIC:** 5736  3931  String instruments; musical instruments

**(G-8103)**
### LOU PLUCINSKI
Also Called: Sign Shop The
110 Industrial Dr  (60115-3932)
**PHONE** .................................... 815 758-7888
Lou Plucinski, *Owner*
**EMP:** 4
**SQ FT:** 3,200
**SALES:** 300K **Privately Held**
**SIC:** 3993  7532  1799  Signs & advertising specialties; top & body repair & paint shops; glass tinting, architectural or automotive

**(G-8104)**
### LUXIS INTERNATIONAL INC
1292 S 7th St  (60115-4746)
**PHONE** .................................... 800 240-1473
Laura Steubbing, *Principal*
**EMP:** 2
**SALES (est):** 206K **Privately Held**
**SIC:** 2844  Toilet preparations

**(G-8105)**
### MANITOWOC LIFTS AND MFG LLC
155 Harvestore Dr  (60115-8675)
**PHONE** .................................... 815 748-9500
Shirley Cahill, *Accounts Mgr*
Doug Climenhaga,
**EMP:** 6 **EST:** 2010
**SQ FT:** 75,000
**SALES (est):** 847.1K **Privately Held**
**SIC:** 5084  3593  Lift trucks & parts; fluid power cylinders, hydraulic or pneumatic

**(G-8106)**
### MPE BUSINESS FORMS INC
1120 Oak St  (60115-3557)
**PHONE** .................................... 815 748-3676
Twyla S Edwards, *President*
Tom Edwards, *Corp Secy*
**EMP:** 20
**SQ FT:** 65,000
**SALES (est):** 3.8MM **Privately Held**
**SIC:** 2752  Business form & card printing, lithographic

**(G-8107)**
### NANCY J PERKINS
Also Called: Le Print Express
1950 Dekalb Ave Ste D  (60115)
**PHONE** .................................... 815 748-7121
**Fax:** 815 748-8068
Nancy J Perkins, *Owner*
Jim Perkins, *Co-Owner*
David Perkins, *Technical Staff*
Tina Vavra, *Director*
**EMP:** 5
**SQ FT:** 2,500
**SALES:** 550K **Privately Held**
**WEB:** www.leprintdekalb.com
**SIC:** 2759  Invitation & stationery printing & engraving

**(G-8108)**
### NARA DIPS INC
122 E Lincoln Hwy  (60115-3228)
**PHONE** .................................... 773 837-0601
Albert Agha, *Vice Pres*
**EMP:** 5
**SALES (est):** 365.1K **Privately Held**
**SIC:** 2032  Canned specialties

**(G-8109)**
### NATHAN WINSTON SERVICE INC
132 N 3rd St  (60115-3302)
**PHONE** .................................... 815 758-4545

**Fax:** 815 758-6191
Barry Nathan Haber, *CEO*
Carolyn Haber, *President*
**EMP:** 4
**SQ FT:** 1,700
**SALES (est):** 240K **Privately Held**
**WEB:** www.nathanwinston.com
**SIC:** 7389  3993  3953  Engraving service; signs & advertising specialties; marking devices

**(G-8110)**
### NEHRING ELECTRICAL WORKS CO
1005 E Locust St  (60115-3967)
P.O. Box 965  (60115-0965)
**PHONE** .................................... 815 756-2741
**Fax:** 815 756-7048
Raymond C Hott, *President*
David Kozin, *Principal*
Debbie Edmonds, *Credit Mgr*
Nick Johnson, *Sales Mgr*
Fred Weiss, *Admin Sec*
▲ **EMP:** 130 **EST:** 1912
**SQ FT:** 200,000
**SALES (est):** 54.9MM **Privately Held**
**WEB:** www.nehringwire.com
**SIC:** 3351  3355  7692  Wire, copper & copper alloy; aluminum wire & cable; welding repair

**(G-8111)**
### OFFICEMAX NORTH AMERICA INC
2350 Sycamore Rd Ste E  (60115-2000)
**PHONE** .................................... 815 748-3007
**Fax:** 815 748-4072
Dave Schwaller, *Manager*
**EMP:** 25
**SALES (corp-wide):** 11B **Publicly Held**
**WEB:** www.copymax.net
**SIC:** 5712  5943  2759  Office furniture
**HQ:** Officemax North America, Inc.
263 Shuman Blvd
Naperville IL 60563
630 717-0791

**(G-8112)**
### ON PAINT IT COMPANY
140 Tygert Ln  (60115-8259)
P.O. Box 439, Crown Point IN  (46308-0439)
**PHONE** .................................... 219 765-5639
Steven Becker, *Owner*
**EMP:** 3 **EST:** 1980
**SALES (est):** 154.5K **Privately Held**
**SIC:** 3952  Lettering instruments, artists'

**(G-8113)**
### PREMIUM WOOD PRODUCTS INC
436 E Locust St  (60115-3327)
**PHONE** .................................... 815 787-3669
**Fax:** 815 787-9688
Michael A Wood, *President*
Sue Wood, *Accountant*
**EMP:** 30
**SQ FT:** 40,000
**SALES:** 3MM **Privately Held**
**WEB:** www.premiumwoodproducts.com
**SIC:** 2499  Decorative wood & woodwork

**(G-8114)**
### PSYTEC INC
520 Linden Pl  (60115-3130)
P.O. Box 564  (60115-0564)
**PHONE** .................................... 815 758-1415
Renanne Brock, *Manager*
**EMP:** 3
**SALES (est):** 215K **Privately Held**
**SIC:** 2731  5192  Books: publishing only; books

**(G-8115)**
### RIGHT/POINTE COMPANY
234 Harvestore Dr  (60115-8769)
P.O. Box 467  (60115-0467)
**PHONE** .................................... 815 754-5700
**Fax:** 815 754-5702
Patrick Giersch, *President*
S Patrick Giersch, *President*
Spencer Myers, *General Mgr*
George Flannigan, *Manager*
Stephanie Park, *Manager*
**EMP:** 55

**SQ FT:** 16,200
**SALES (est):** 31.7MM **Privately Held**
**SIC:** 2899  2891  Concrete curing & hardening compounds; adhesives & sealants

**(G-8116)**
### ROCK-TENN COMPANY
Also Called: Alliance Display
800 Nestle Ct  (60115-8676)
**PHONE** .................................... 815 756-8913
David Rose, *Manager*
**EMP:** 37
**SALES (corp-wide):** 14.1B **Publicly Held**
**WEB:** www.rocktenn.com
**SIC:** 3086  Packaging & shipping materials, foamed plastic
**HQ:** Westrock Rkt Company
504 Thrasher St
Norcross GA 30071
770 448-2193

**(G-8117)**
### SISLERS ICE INC
274 Harvestore Dr  (60115-8769)
**PHONE** .................................... 815 756-6903
**Fax:** 815 748-4613
Scott Sisler, *President*
**EMP:** 20
**SQ FT:** 7,000
**SALES (est):** 2.7MM **Privately Held**
**SIC:** 2097  5999  5078  Manufactured ice; ice; ice making machines

**(G-8118)**
### SK EXPRESS INC
310 Dietz Ave  (60115-2671)
P.O. Box 1139  (60115-7139)
**PHONE** .................................... 815 748-4388
Saeed Saffaei, *President*
David Petersen, *Engineer*
Salem Parsons, *Manager*
**EMP:** 190
**SQ FT:** 22,000
**SALES (est):** 41.6MM **Privately Held**
**WEB:** www.skexpressinc.com
**SIC:** 3694  Battery cable wiring sets for internal combustion engines

**(G-8119)**
### SONOCO PRTECTIVE SOLUTIONS INC
1401 Pleasant St  (60115-2663)
**PHONE** .................................... 815 787-5244
Dean Kalmerton, *Mfg Staff*
Ron Leach, *Director*
**EMP:** 40
**SQ FT:** 50,000
**SALES (corp-wide):** 4.7B **Publicly Held**
**WEB:** www.tuscarora.com
**SIC:** 3365  3544  Machinery castings, aluminum; special dies, tools, jigs & fixtures
**HQ:** Sonoco Protective Solutions, Inc.
1 N 2nd St
Hartsville SC 29550
843 383-7000

**(G-8120)**
### SOTA SERVICE CTR BY BODINETS
Also Called: Sota Turntable
436 E Locust St  (60115-3327)
**PHONE** .................................... 608 538-3500
**Fax:** 708 361-2970
Mona Lisa Hook, *President*
Kirk Bodinet, *President*
**EMP:** 5
**SQ FT:** 1,200
**SALES (est):** 240.8K **Privately Held**
**WEB:** www.sotaturntables.com
**SIC:** 7622  3679  Home entertainment repair services; recording & playback apparatus, including phonograph

**(G-8121)**
### SOUTHMOOR ESTATES INC
Also Called: Mikari
1032 S 7th St  (60115-4526)
**PHONE** .................................... 815 756-1299
**Fax:** 815 756-1390
Patrick C Lasco, *President*
Kari Lasco, *Corp Secy*
**EMP:** 7
**SALES (est):** 763.6K **Privately Held**
**WEB:** www.southmoorestates.com
**SIC:** 5271  6515  2451  Mobile homes; mobile home site operators; mobile homes

# Dekalb - Dekalb County (G-8122)

### (G-8122)
**SPORTS ALL SORTS AP & DESIGN**
147 N 2nd St Ste 2 (60115-3276)
PHONE..................................815 756-9910
Fax: 815 756-1245
John Launer, *Owner*
EMP: 6
SQ FT: 6,000
SALES (est): 350K **Privately Held**
SIC: 2759 Screen printing

### (G-8123)
**SUPERIOR BUSINESS SOLUTIONS**
308 Laurel Ln (60115-1714)
PHONE..................................815 787-1333
Robert English, *Owner*
EMP: 2
SALES (est): 212.7K **Privately Held**
SIC: 2752 Commercial printing, lithographic

### (G-8124)
**TEGRANT ALLOYD BRANDS INC (DH)**
Also Called: Sonoco Alloyd
1401 Pleasant St (60115-2663)
P.O. Box 627 (60115-0627)
PHONE..................................815 756-8451
Ron Leach, *President*
James L Price, *Senior VP*
Vince Manalio, *Plant Mgr*
Brian Lothson, *Engineer*
Dennis Beck, *Design Engr*
EMP: 325 EST: 1961
SQ FT: 300,000
SALES (est): 101.6MM
SALES (corp-wide): 4.7B **Publicly Held**
SIC: 3089 3565 Blister or bubble formed packaging, plastic; trays, plastic; packaging machinery
HQ: Tegrant Corporation
1401 Pleasant St
Dekalb IL 60115
815 756-8451

### (G-8125)
**TEGRANT CORPORATION (HQ)**
Also Called: Sonoco Protective Solution
1401 Pleasant St (60115-2663)
PHONE..................................815 756-8451
Fax: 815 756-5187
Ron Leach, *President*
Vicki Arthur, *Principal*
Jim Ingallino, *Safety Mgr*
Jerry Knitter, *Engineer*
Tom Marks, *Project Engr*
▼ EMP: 325
SQ FT: 300,000
SALES (est): 688.2MM
SALES (corp-wide): 4.7B **Publicly Held**
WEB: www.alloyd.com
SIC: 2671 Plastic film, coated or laminated for packaging
PA: Sonoco Products Company
1 N 2nd St
Hartsville SC 29550
843 383-7000

### (G-8126)
**TEGRANT HOLDING CORP**
1401 Pleasant St (60115-2663)
P.O. Box 627 (60115-0627)
PHONE..................................815 756-8451
Ronald G Leach, *President*
Jay Hereford, *Corp Secy*
EMP: 3370
SALES (est): 140.1MM
SALES (corp-wide): 4.7B **Publicly Held**
SIC: 3089 3565 Blister or bubble formed packaging, plastic; packing & wrapping machinery
PA: Sonoco Products Company
1 N 2nd St
Hartsville SC 29550
843 383-7000

### (G-8127)
**TIM DETWILER ENTERPRISES INC**
Also Called: Wholesale Gate Co
1140 S 7th St (60115-4528)
PHONE..................................815 758-9950
Fax: 815 748-0510
Tim Detwiler, *President*
Jared Johnsen, *General Mgr*
Rae Detwiler, *Vice Pres*
Abrahams Gage, *Manager*
Thom Battisto, *Info Tech Dir*
▲ EMP: 8 EST: 1967
SQ FT: 9,000
SALES: 500K **Privately Held**
WEB: www.wholesalegate.com
SIC: 3446 Gates, ornamental metal; ornamental metalwork

### (G-8128)
**UNIFIED WIRE AND CABLE COMPANY**
338 Wurlitzer Dr (60115-2675)
P.O. Box 452 (60115-0452)
PHONE..................................815 748-4876
Fax: 815 748-4336
Brian Foley, *President*
Rick Waters, *Purchasing*
Judith Sid, *Admin Sec*
EMP: 20
SQ FT: 25,000
SALES (est): 10.2MM **Privately Held**
WEB: www.unifiedwireandcable.com
SIC: 3357 Nonferrous wiredrawing & insulating

### (G-8129)
**UPPER DECK SPORTS BAR**
241 E Lincoln Hwy (60115-3206)
PHONE..................................815 517-0682
Phyllis Witmer, *Principal*
EMP: 3
SALES (est): 240.2K **Privately Held**
SIC: 3131 Uppers

### (G-8130)
**VIDICON LLC**
300 Harvestore Dr (60115-8680)
PHONE..................................815 756-9600
Ronald J Proesel, *Mng Member*
Daniel Wolf, *Manager*
Robert J Brigham Jr,
EMP: 3
SQ FT: 34,000
SALES (est): 280K **Privately Held**
SIC: 3651 Household video equipment

### (G-8131)
**WELSH INDUSTRIES LTD**
6 Evergreen Cir (60115-2214)
P.O. Box 783 (60115-0783)
PHONE..................................815 756-1111
Fax: 815 756-1224
Michael Welsh, *CEO*
Rosemarie Welsh, *President*
EMP: 50
SQ FT: 14,000
SALES (est): 5.1MM **Privately Held**
WEB: www.welshind.com
SIC: 2395 Emblems, embroidered

### (G-8132)
**WHISKEY ACRES DISTILLING CO**
11504 Keslinger Rd (60115-8810)
PHONE..................................815 739-8711
James Walter, *President*
EMP: 10
SALES: 200K **Privately Held**
SIC: 2085 Distilled & blended liquors

## Delavan
### *Tazewell County*

### (G-8133)
**DELAVAN TIMES**
314 S Locust St (61734-7528)
P.O. Box 199 (61734-0199)
PHONE..................................309 244-7111
Sandra Larimore Denman, *Owner*
EMP: 3
SALES (est): 145.4K **Privately Held**
SIC: 2711 Newspapers

## Depue
### *Bureau County*

### (G-8134)
**DEPUE MECHANICAL INC (PA)**
216 W 4th S (61322)
P.O. Box 80 (61322-0080)
PHONE..................................815 447-2267
Jim Jacobsen Sr, *CEO*
James Jacobsen Jr, *President*
Tom Herrigan, *Treasurer*
Jazmin Velazguez, *Administration*
EMP: 25
SQ FT: 3,000
SALES (est): 13MM **Privately Held**
SIC: 1711 3444 Boiler maintenance contractor; sheet metalwork

## Des Plaines
### *Cook County*

### (G-8135)
**2 FIGS BAKING CO INC**
229 Leahy Cir S (60016-6026)
PHONE..................................847 778-2936
EMP: 4
SALES (est): 208.3K **Privately Held**
SIC: 2051 Bread, cake & related products

### (G-8136)
**3 D CONCRETE DESIGN INC**
1000 Lee St (60016-6515)
PHONE..................................847 297-7968
Nick Desario, *President*
Jim Iatropoulos, *Director*
EMP: 2
SALES (est): 302.5K **Privately Held**
SIC: 3444 Concrete forms, sheet metal

### (G-8137)
**312 AQUAPONICS LLC**
711 S River Rd Apt 812 (60016-4772)
PHONE..................................312 469-0239
Mario Spatafora, *Mng Member*
EMP: 4
SALES: 10K **Privately Held**
SIC: 3999 Manufacturing industries

### (G-8138)
**A HARDY/U S A LTD**
1400 E Touhy Ave Ste 120 (60018-3338)
PHONE..................................847 298-2358
Mark Klevin, *President*
Ken Driscoll, *Exec VP*
Anna Naklarice, *Office Mgr*
EMP: 7
SALES (est): 600K **Privately Held**
SIC: 2084 Wines, brandy & brandy spirits

### (G-8139)
**A WHEELS INC**
666 Garland Pl (60016-4788)
PHONE..................................847 699-7000
EMP: 3 EST: 2015
SALES (est): 68.8K **Privately Held**
SIC: 3291 Wheels, grinding: artificial

### (G-8140)
**ABBOTT LABORATORIES**
215 E Washington St (60016-2925)
P.O. Box 64, North Chicago (60064-0064)
PHONE..................................847 937-6100
Stafford O'Kelly, *Division Pres*
Laura Pfantz, *Business Mgr*
Robert Koska, *Vice Pres*
Scott McKenzie, *Opers Mgr*
Agustin Reyes, *QA Dir*
EMP: 1000
SALES (corp-wide): 20.8B **Publicly Held**
WEB: www.abbott.com
SIC: 2834 Pharmaceutical preparations
PA: Abbott Laboratories
100 Abbott Park Rd
Abbott Park IL 60064
224 667-6100

### (G-8141)
**ABBOTT MOLECULAR INC**
1300 E Touhy Ave (60018-3315)
PHONE..................................224 361-7800
EMP: 3
SALES (corp-wide): 20.8B **Publicly Held**
SIC: 2835 3826 In vitro & in vivo diagnostic substances; analytical instruments
HQ: Abbott Molecular Inc.
1300 E Touhy Ave
Des Plaines IL 60018

### (G-8142)
**ABBOTT MOLECULAR INC (HQ)**
1300 E Touhy Ave (60018-3315)
PHONE..................................224 361-7800
Fax: 224 361-7008
Edward L Michael, *President*
Lisa D Koenig, *Accounts Exec*
▲ EMP: 100
SQ FT: 56,551
SALES (est): 78.8MM
SALES (corp-wide): 20.8B **Publicly Held**
WEB: www.abbottmolecular.com
SIC: 2835 3826 In vitro & in vivo diagnostic substances; analytical instruments
PA: Abbott Laboratories
100 Abbott Park Rd
Abbott Park IL 60064
224 667-6100

### (G-8143)
**ABKI TECH SERVICE INC ◆**
Also Called: Abkitech
764 Meadow Dr (60016-1146)
P.O. Box 1362 (60017-1362)
PHONE..................................847 818-8403
Kitty Thomas, *President*
EMP: 10 EST: 2016
SALES (est): 239.3K **Privately Held**
SIC: 7371 7372 7373 7374 Custom computer programming services; custom computer programming services; application computer software; systems engineering, computer related; service bureau, computer;

### (G-8144)
**ADVANCED FIBER PRODUCTS LLC**
200 Howard Ave Ste 244 (60018-5909)
PHONE..................................847 768-9001
Mark Benton, *General Mgr*
Dennis Gudgel, *Product Mgr*
Richard Durrant, *Senior Mgr*
Julie Durrant,
EMP: 6
SQ FT: 2,000
SALES (est): 1MM
SALES (corp-wide): 9.4MM **Privately Held**
SIC: 3229 Fiber optics strands
PA: Advanced Fiber Products Limited
Hollands Road Industrial Estate
Haverhill CB9 8
144 070-6441

### (G-8145)
**ALL SAINTS MONUMENT CO INC**
20 S River Rd (60016-3457)
PHONE..................................847 824-1248
Fax: 847 297-5462
Frank Troost, *President*
EMP: 2
SALES: 546.6K
SALES (corp-wide): 14MM **Privately Held**
WEB: www.troost.com
SIC: 3281 5999 Monument or burial stone, cut & shaped; monuments & tombstones
PA: Peter Troost Monument Co.
4300 Roosevelt Rd
Hillside IL
708 544-0916

### (G-8146)
**AMCOR PHRM PACKG USA LLC**
1731 S Mount Prospect Rd (60018-1803)
PHONE..................................847 298-5626
Amy Murray, *Buyer*
Lewis Motisi, *QC Dir*
Robert Fisher, *Sales Staff*
Jeff Burke, *Manager*
Richard Beckwith, *Executive*
EMP: 110
SQ FT: 80,000
SALES (corp-wide): 9.4B **Privately Held**
WEB: www.alcanpackaging.com
SIC: 3089 3221 Plastic containers, except foam; glass containers

# GEOGRAPHIC SECTION

**Des Plaines - Cook County (G-8171)**

HQ: Amcor Pharmaceutical Packaging Usa, Llc
625 Sharp St N
Millville NJ 08332
856 327-1540

### (G-8147)
### AMERICAN SOC HM INSPECTORS INC (PA)
Also Called: ASHI
932 Lee St Ste 101 (60016-6594)
PHONE..................847 759-2820
**Fax:** 847 759-1620
Randy Sipe, *President*
Frank Lesh, *Exec Dir*
Mark Lester,
Bill Mason,
**EMP:** 12
**SALES:** 2.8MM **Privately Held**
**WEB:** www.ashi.org
**SIC:** 2721  8621  Trade journals: publishing only, not printed on site; professional membership organizations

### (G-8148)
### AMERICAN WILBERT VAULT CORP
165 S River Rd (60016-3415)
PHONE..................847 824-4415
Brian Doyle, *Branch Mgr*
**EMP:** 9
**SALES (corp-wide):** 5.3MM **Privately Held**
**SIC:** 3272 Concrete products
**PA:** American Wilbert Vault Corp
7525 W 99th Pl
Bridgeview IL 60455
708 366-3210

### (G-8149)
### AMNETIC LLC
1645 S River Rd Ste 8 (60018-2206)
PHONE..................877 877-3678
Fred Kortmann,
**EMP:** 6
**SALES (est):** 267.4K **Privately Held**
**SIC:** 2819 Alkali metals: lithium, cesium, francium, rubidium

### (G-8150)
### ANDERSON SAFFORD MKG GRAPHICS
Also Called: Rubber Stamp Man
570 E Northwest Hwy Ste 7 (60016-2269)
PHONE..................847 827-8968
**Fax:** 847 297-0105
Ralph Kipnis, *President*
Gayle Kipnis, *President*
Madeline Scrima, *Exec VP*
**EMP:** 14
**SQ FT:** 17,000
**SALES (est):** 1.9MM **Privately Held**
**WEB:** www.midweststampman.com
**SIC:** 3953  7336  Marking devices; graphic arts & related design; silk screen design

### (G-8151)
### ARGYLE CUT STONE CO
1046 Woodlawn Ave (60016-3337)
PHONE..................847 456-6210
**Fax:** 847 966-9778
Daniel Peterson, *President*
Alfred Peterson, *President*
B James Larson, *Corp Secy*
**EMP:** 30 EST: 1929
**SQ FT:** 8,125
**SALES:** 900K **Privately Held**
**WEB:** www.argylecutstone.com
**SIC:** 3281  1422  Limestone, cut & shaped; crushed & broken limestone

### (G-8152)
### ASPEN API INC (DH)
Also Called: Organon API
2136 S Wolf Rd (60018-1932)
PHONE..................847 635-0985
Andrea Keith Vasel, *President*
Gene Godawa, *Corp Secy*
▲ **EMP:** 10
**SQ FT:** 6,600

**SALES (est):** 4MM **Privately Held**
**WEB:** www.diosynth.com
**SIC:** 2836  2869  2834  2812 Coagulation products; industrial organic chemicals; pharmaceutical preparations; alkalies & chlorine
**HQ:** Aspen Oss B.V.
Kloosterstraat 6
Oss
412 661-000

### (G-8153)
### ASTEROID GRINDING & MFG INC
2190 S Wolf Rd (60018-1903)
PHONE..................847 298-8109
**Fax:** 847 298-8120
Michael Vigue, *Partner*
James Vigue, *Vice Pres*
Sheryl Lynn Decoteau, *Office Mgr*
Wayne Pope, *Admin Sec*
**EMP:** 43
**SQ FT:** 22,000
**SALES (est):** 8.6MM **Privately Held**
**WEB:** www.asteroidgrinding.com
**SIC:** 3599 Grinding castings for the trade

### (G-8154)
### AXIS INTERNATIONAL MARKETING
1800 S Wolf Rd Ste 2 (60018-1905)
PHONE..................847 297-0744
Linda Chen-Berger, *President*
Andy Berger, *Vice Pres*
Heidi Bassie, *Sales Staff*
▲ **EMP:** 170 EST: 1998
**SQ FT:** 3,000
**SALES (est):** 16.7MM **Privately Held**
**SIC:** 5023  3631 Aluminumware; household cooking equipment

### (G-8155)
### BAS SUCCESS EXPRESS INC
9001 Golf Rd Apt 7h (60016-1966)
PHONE..................847 258-5550
Ionut Blaga, *Principal*
**EMP:** 3
**SALES (est):** 76.2K **Privately Held**
**SIC:** 2711 Newspapers

### (G-8156)
### BAY PLASTICS
1245 E Forest Ave Ste 8 (60018-1564)
PHONE..................847 299-2045
Norman Knurek, *Principal*
▲ **EMP:** 10
**SALES (est):** 1.7MM **Privately Held**
**SIC:** 3089 Plastic processing

### (G-8157)
### BEASTGRIP CO
1269 Rand Rd (60016-3402)
PHONE..................312 283-5283
Vadym Chalenko, *CEO*
**EMP:** 2
**SQ FT:** 4,000
**SALES (est):** 317.3K **Privately Held**
**SIC:** 5043  3827 Photographic equipment & supplies; lenses, optical: all types except ophthalmic

### (G-8158)
### BIO-RAD LABORATORIES INC
1400 E Touhy Ave (60018-3305)
PHONE..................847 699-2217
Dave Reilly, *Vice Pres*
Jeff Larson, *Mfg Dir*
Traci Foster, *Human Res Mgr*
Matthew Nill, *Manager*
**EMP:** 473
**SALES (corp-wide):** 2B **Publicly Held**
**SIC:** 3826 Analytical instruments
**PA:** Bio-Rad Laboratories, Inc.
1000 Alfred Nobel Dr
Hercules CA 94547
510 724-7000

### (G-8159)
### BION ENTERPRISES LTD
Also Called: MBL Bion
455 State St Ste 100 (60016-2280)
PHONE..................847 544-5044
**Fax:** 847 544-5051
Jun Sasaki, *CEO*
Melinda Ascher, *COO*
Judy Rasmussen, *Safety Mgr*

Mike Carroll, *VP Finance*
Svetlana Revina, *Accounting Mgr*
**EMP:** 30 EST: 1978
**SQ FT:** 17,000
**SALES:** 4MM
**SALES (corp-wide):** 3.4B **Privately Held**
**WEB:** www.bionenterprises.com
**SIC:** 2835 In vitro & in vivo diagnostic substances
**HQ:** Mbl International Corporation
15a Constitution Way
Woburn MA 01801
781 939-6964

### (G-8160)
### BODACIOUS BEADS INC
1942 S River Rd (60018-3206)
PHONE..................847 699-7959
Judith Schwab, *President*
**EMP:** 4
**SALES:** 500K **Privately Held**
**WEB:** www.bodaciousbeads.net
**SIC:** 3999 Stringing beads

### (G-8161)
### C M I NOVACAST INC
500 E Touhy Ave Ste B (60018-2644)
PHONE..................847 699-9020
**Fax:** 847 699-9023
Lee Gouwens, *President*
Mary Weaver Gouwens, *Vice Pres*
▲ **EMP:** 15
**SQ FT:** 12,000
**SALES (est):** 4MM **Privately Held**
**WEB:** www.cminovacast.com
**SIC:** 3441 Joists, open web steel: long-span series

### (G-8162)
### CF GEAR HOLDINGS LLC (PA)
Also Called: Process Gear
2064 Mannheim Rd (60018-2909)
PHONE..................847 376-8322
**Fax:** 847 671-6840
Cathy Lancaster, *Controller*
Rishi Chandra,
Salisha Chandra,
**EMP:** 12
**SALES (est):** 3.1MM **Privately Held**
**SIC:** 3599 Machine shop, jobbing & repair

### (G-8163)
### CFC INC
Also Called: Columbus Foods Company
30 E Oakton St (60018-1945)
PHONE..................847 257-8920
Paulette Gagliardo, *President*
Kathryn Miller, *Opers Mgr*
Joe Feely, *Prdtn Mgr*
Rick Cummisford, *QC Dir*
Terence G Matern, *Controller*
▼ **EMP:** 100 EST: 1937
**SQ FT:** 330,000
**SALES (est):** 57.7MM **Privately Held**
**WEB:** www.columbusfoods.com
**SIC:** 2079 Edible fats & oils

### (G-8164)
### CHICAGO DIAL INDICATOR COMPANY
1372 Redeker Rd (60016-3421)
PHONE..................847 827-7186
**Fax:** 847 827-0478
Jerry R Iverson, *CEO*
Erick Iverson, *President*
Wilford Tucker, *COO*
Chuck Fleming, *Buyer*
Kathy Adamiec, *Director*
▲ **EMP:** 35
**SQ FT:** 14,700
**SALES (est):** 7.3MM **Privately Held**
**WEB:** www.dialindicator.com
**SIC:** 3829 Measuring & controlling devices

### (G-8165)
### CHICAGO FAUCET COMPANY (HQ)
2100 Clearwater Dr (60018-5904)
PHONE..................847 803-5000
**Fax:** 847 298-3101
Andreas Nowak, *CEO*
Eric Franklin, *Vice Pres*
Charles Lynch, *Vice Pres*
Manfred Wolpert, *Vice Pres*
Tonya Haltom, *Manager*
▲ **EMP:** 100

**SQ FT:** 135,000
**SALES (est):** 105.3MM
**SALES (corp-wide):** 2.7B **Privately Held**
**WEB:** www.chicagofaucets.com
**SIC:** 3432 Plumbers' brass goods: drain cocks, faucets, spigots, etc.
**PA:** Geberit Ag
Schachenstrasse 77
Jona SG 8645
552 216-111

### (G-8166)
### CHICAGO FAUCET FEDERAL CR UN
2100 Clearwater Dr (60018-1918)
PHONE..................847 803-5000
**EMP:** 10 EST: 2015
**SALES (est):** 594.5K **Privately Held**
**SIC:** 3432 Plumbing fixture fittings & trim

### (G-8167)
### CHICAGO QUADRILL CO
1840 Busse Hwy (60016-6727)
PHONE..................847 824-4196
**Fax:** 847 824-4197
Carl Grunschel Sr, *President*
Gladys Grunschel, *Corp Secy*
Carl Grunschel Jr, *Exec VP*
Karen Grunschel, *Office Mgr*
**EMP:** 9
**SQ FT:** 13,000
**SALES:** 1MM **Privately Held**
**SIC:** 3545  3544  3546 Drilling machine attachments & accessories; dies & die holders for metal cutting, forming, die casting; drill attachments, portable

### (G-8168)
### CHROMATECH PRINTING INC
16 Mary St (60016-3407)
PHONE..................847 699-0333
**Fax:** 847 699-2872
Barbara Vanslambrouck, *President*
Michael Vanslambrouck, *Corp Secy*
**EMP:** 10
**SQ FT:** 18,000
**SALES (est):** 1.8MM **Privately Held**
**WEB:** www.chromatech.com
**SIC:** 2752 Commercial printing, offset

### (G-8169)
### CIBA VISION INC
333 Howard Ave (60018-1907)
PHONE..................847 294-3000
Bernie Bartlette, *General Mgr*
Roman Baginski, *Accountant*
Tom Steiner, *VP Sales*
**EMP:** 2820
**SQ FT:** 340,000
**SALES (est):** 228.8MM
**SALES (corp-wide):** 48.5B **Privately Held**
**WEB:** www.w-j.com
**SIC:** 3851 Contact lenses
**HQ:** Alcon Laboratories, Inc.
6201 South Fwy
Fort Worth TX 76134
817 293-0450

### (G-8170)
### CISCO SYSTEMS INC
9501 Tech Blvd Ste 100 (60018)
PHONE..................847 678-6600
Peter Puczko, *Engineer*
Jeff Schweisthal, *Engineer*
Gordon St Claire, *Engineer*
Brian Marille, *Manager*
Bader Hamdan, *Manager*
**EMP:** 350
**SALES (corp-wide):** 49.2B **Publicly Held**
**WEB:** www.cisco.com
**SIC:** 3577  5065 Data conversion equipment, media-to-media: computer; electronic parts & equipment
**PA:** Cisco Systems, Inc.
170 W Tasman Dr
San Jose CA 95134
408 526-4000

### (G-8171)
### CLOVERDALE CORPORATION
Also Called: AlphaGraphics
1583 Lee St (60018-1518)
PHONE..................847 296-9225
**Fax:** 847 296-9227
Roger Hull, *President*
Mc Evoy Galbreath, *Vice Pres*

# Des Plaines - Cook County (G-8172)

C D Hodges Hull, *Vice Pres*
Janie Dushane Hull, *Admin Sec*
**EMP:** 6
**SQ FT:** 2,000
**SALES:** 870K **Privately Held**
**SIC:** 2752 2789 Commercial printing, lithographic; bookbinding & related work

### (G-8172)
### COLORMETRIC LABORATORIES INC
Also Called: C L I Laboratories
1261 Rand Rd Ste A (60016-3402)
**PHONE** .................................... 847 803-3737
**Fax:** 847 803-3739
Thomas Klingner, *President*
Kristine Klingner, *Admin Sec*
**EMP:** 2 **EST:** 1971
**SQ FT:** 2,400
**SALES:** 275K **Privately Held**
**WEB:** www.clilabs.com
**SIC:** 3821 8071 Laboratory apparatus & furniture; urinalysis laboratory

### (G-8173)
### COMMUNITY ADVANTAGE NETWORK (PA)
1163 Lee St (60016-6516)
**PHONE** .................................... 847 376-8943
**EMP:** 4
**SALES (est):** 507.8K **Privately Held**
**SIC:** 3663 Cellular radio telephone

### (G-8174)
### CONTOUR SAWS INC
900 Graceland Ave (60016)
**PHONE** .................................... 800 259-6834
**Fax:** 847 803-9467
Michael L Wilkie, *Ch of Bd*
Jon Henricks, *Vice Ch Bd*
Chuck B Davis, *Senior VP*
James Tutor, *Vice Pres*
John Whalen, *Vice Pres*
◆ **EMP:** 120
**SQ FT:** 125,000
**SALES (est):** 26.8MM **Privately Held**
**SIC:** 3425 Saw blades for hand or power saws

### (G-8175)
### COPYCO PRINTING INC
95 Bradrock Dr (60018-1937)
**PHONE** .................................... 847 824-4400
**Fax:** 847 824-3770
Leonard F Thomas, *CEO*
Andrew Thomas, *President*
Alan Czarnik, *Exec VP*
David Piper, *Vice Pres*
Steve Schafer, *Technical Staff*
▲ **EMP:** 48 **EST:** 1968
**SQ FT:** 18,000
**SALES (est):** 7.2MM **Privately Held**
**SIC:** 2752 Commercial printing, offset

### (G-8176)
### COPYSET SHOP INC
1801 E Oakton St (60018-2111)
**PHONE** .................................... 847 768-2679
**Fax:** 847 768-2685
Daniel Davidson, *President*
Ed Davidson, *Vice Pres*
**EMP:** 6
**SQ FT:** 7,000
**SALES (est):** 1.2MM **Privately Held**
**WEB:** www.copyset.com
**SIC:** 7334 2791 Photocopying & duplicating services; typesetting

### (G-8177)
### CREATIVE STEEL FABRICATORS
1024 North Ave (60016-3331)
**PHONE** .................................... 847 803-2090
**Fax:** 847 803-2119
William Poreda, *President*
James Cogar, *Corp Secy*
**EMP:** 8
**SQ FT:** 9,550
**SALES:** 1MM **Privately Held**
**SIC:** 3444 3469 3441 3429 Sheet metalwork; metal stampings; fabricated structural metal; manufactured hardware (general)

### (G-8178)
### CRYSTATECH INC
1700 S Mount Prospect Rd (60018-1804)
**PHONE** .................................... 847 768-0500
Eric Klasson, *President*
David Seeger, *Vice Pres*
Kayla Royer, *Controller*
Bryan Petrinec, *Admin Sec*
▲ **EMP:** 10 **EST:** 2000
**SQ FT:** 10,000
**SALES (est):** 590K **Privately Held**
**WEB:** www.crystatech.com
**SIC:** 1389 Construction, repair & dismantling services

### (G-8179)
### DELAVAL MANUFACTURING
1855 S Mount Prospect Rd (60018-1805)
**PHONE** .................................... 847 298-5505
Larry Mitch, *Principal*
Paul Lofgren, *VP Sales*
Parimal Mehta, *Manager*
Brett Olinger, *Manager*
AIA Prashaw, *Manager*
▼ **EMP:** 8
**SALES (est):** 819.2K **Privately Held**
**SIC:** 3999 Coin-operated amusement machines

### (G-8180)
### DELPHI AUTOMOTIVE SYSTEMS LLC
25 E Algonquin Rd (60016-6101)
**PHONE** .................................... 847 391-2000
David Holdenman, *Branch Mgr*
**EMP:** 30 **Privately Held**
**WEB:** www.delphiauto.com
**SIC:** 3714 Exhaust systems & parts, motor vehicle
**HQ:** Delphi Automotive Systems, Llc
5725 Delphi Dr
Troy MI 48098

### (G-8181)
### DELUXE CORPORATION
Also Called: Deluxe Check Printers
1600 E Touhy Ave (60018-3607)
**PHONE** .................................... 847 635-7200
**Fax:** 847 635-4122
Craig Lederman, *Manager*
Len Chlopek, *Manager*
Sonny Marano, *Comp Spec*
**EMP:** 246
**SALES (corp-wide):** 1.8B **Publicly Held**
**WEB:** www.dlx.com
**SIC:** 2782 2759 Checkbooks; commercial printing
**PA:** Deluxe Corporation
3680 Victoria St N
Shoreview MN 55126
651 483-7111

### (G-8182)
### DELUXE JOHNSON (HQ)
Also Called: Johnson Group
1600 E Touhy Ave (60018-3607)
**PHONE** .................................... 847 635-7200
Dennis W Johnson, *Principal*
Dale H Johnson, *Principal*
Jeff Kopelman, *CFO*
▲ **EMP:** 15 **EST:** 1957
**SQ FT:** 20,000
**SALES (est):** 12.5MM
**SALES (corp-wide):** 1.8B **Publicly Held**
**SIC:** 2752 2782 2789 Commercial printing, lithographic; typesetting; bookbinding & related work
**PA:** Deluxe Corporation
3680 Victoria St N
Shoreview MN 55126
651 483-7111

### (G-8183)
### DENTSPLY SIRONA INC
Midwest Dental
901 W Oakton St (60018-1843)
**PHONE** .................................... 847 640-4800
**Fax:** 847 640-4806
Michael Hirsh, *Engineer*
Devon Howe, *Mktg Dir*
Linda Trevenen, *Mktg Dir*
Steve Snyder, *Marketing Mgr*
Steve Cornelius, *Branch Mgr*
**EMP:** 175
**SALES (corp-wide):** 3.7B **Publicly Held**
**WEB:** www.dentsply.com
**SIC:** 3843 Dental equipment & supplies
**PA:** Dentsply Sirona Inc.
221 W Philadelphia St
York PA 17401
717 845-7511

### (G-8184)
### DES PLAINES JOURNAL INC
Also Called: Journal & Topics Newspapers
622 Graceland Ave (60016-4519)
**PHONE** .................................... 847 299-5511
**Fax:** 847 298-8549
Todd C Wessell, *President*
Kelvin Fee, *Vice Pres*
Melody Walker, *VP Sls/Mktg*
Richard Wessell Jr, *Adv Dir*
**EMP:** 70 **EST:** 1931
**SQ FT:** 12,500
**SALES:** 3MM **Privately Held**
**WEB:** www.journal-topics.com
**SIC:** 2711 7331 2791 2752 Newspapers: publishing only, not printed on site; mailing service; typesetting; commercial printing, lithographic

### (G-8185)
### DESIGN GROUP SIGNAGE CORP
2135 Frontage Rd (60018-3009)
**PHONE** .................................... 847 390-0350
**Fax:** 847 390-9231
Bridget Gilmore, *President*
Bridgit Gilmore, *President*
James Gilmore, *Admin Sec*
**EMP:** 12
**SQ FT:** 30,000
**SALES (est):** 1.9MM **Privately Held**
**WEB:** www.designgroupsignage.com
**SIC:** 3993 Signs & advertising specialties

### (G-8186)
### DREAMWORLD GOLF
353 N River Rd (60016-1210)
**PHONE** .................................... 847 803-4757
Bob Okita, *Principal*
**EMP:** 4
**SALES (est):** 404.3K **Privately Held**
**SIC:** 3949 Golf equipment

### (G-8187)
### DURABLE OFFICE PRODUCTS CORP
2475 S Wolf Rd (60018-2603)
**PHONE** .................................... 847 787-0100
**Fax:** 847 787-0311
Wolsens Berger, *General Mgr*
▲ **EMP:** 6
**SALES (est):** 815.1K
**SALES (corp-wide):** 109.9MM **Privately Held**
**SIC:** 2541 Store & office display cases & fixtures
**PA:** Durable Hunke & Jochheim Gmbh & Co. Kg
Westfalenstr. 77-79
Iserlohn 58636
237 166-20

### (G-8188)
### ENTERPRISE SERVICE CORPORATION
5400 Milton Pkwy (60018)
**PHONE** .................................... 773 589-2727
John Schwab, *Branch Mgr*
**EMP:** 3
**SALES (corp-wide):** 638.1K **Privately Held**
**SIC:** 1731 3711 Electric power systems contractors; snow plows (motor vehicles), assembly of
**PA:** Enterprise Service Corporation
2648 Paula Ln
Des Plaines IL 60018
847 299-2727

### (G-8189)
### EPIC METALS CORPORATION
2400 E Devon Ave Ste 205 (60018-4617)
**PHONE** .................................... 847 803-6411
**Fax:** 847 470-5408
Don Landis, *Branch Mgr*
**EMP:** 9
**SALES (corp-wide):** 21.2MM **Privately Held**
**SIC:** 3444 Roof deck, sheet metal
**PA:** Epic Metals Corporation
11 Talbot Ave
Rankin PA 15104
412 351-3913

### (G-8190)
### ERMAK USA INC
2860 S River Rd Ste 145 (60018-6008)
**PHONE** .................................... 847 640-7765
Emre Varisli, *Principal*
▲ **EMP:** 18
**SALES:** 3.7MM
**SALES (corp-wide):** 77.3MM **Privately Held**
**SIC:** 3441 Fabricated structural metal
**PA:** Ermaksan Makina Sanayi Ve Ticaret Anonim Sirketi
Organize Sanayi Bolgesi, No:6
Lacivert Caddesi
Bursa 16120
224 267-1900

### (G-8191)
### EVERGREEN SCALE MODELS INC
65 Bradrock Dr (60018-1937)
**PHONE** .................................... 224 567-8099
Brian Ellerby, *President*
Mary Ellerby, *Vice Pres*
**EMP:** 12 **EST:** 1976
**SALES (est):** 980K **Privately Held**
**SIC:** 3999 2821 Models, general, except toy; plastics materials & resins

### (G-8192)
### EXTON CORP
Also Called: Exton Corporation
1 Innovation Dr (60016-3161)
**PHONE** .................................... 847 391-8100
Mark Simanton, *President*
Kevin Groom, *Chief*
Jim Kreutz, *Plant Mgr*
**EMP:** 107
**SQ FT:** 90,000
**SALES (est):** 12.5MM
**SALES (corp-wide):** 675MM **Privately Held**
**WEB:** www.innovmfg.com
**SIC:** 3444 3469 Sheet metal specialties, not stamped; stamping metal for the trade
**PA:** Ims Companies, Llc
1 Innovation Dr
Des Plaines IL 60016
847 391-8100

### (G-8193)
### FAB-RITE SHEET METAL
74 Bradrock Dr (60018-1938)
**PHONE** .................................... 847 228-0300
Patrick Ryan, *President*
Viggy Lebherz, *Controller*
**EMP:** 15
**SQ FT:** 40,000
**SALES:** 2.5MM **Privately Held**
**SIC:** 3444 Sheet metalwork

### (G-8194)
### FASTENERS FOR RETAIL INC
Also Called: Ffr Merchandising
1600 Birchwood Ave (60018-3004)
**PHONE** .................................... 847 296-5511
Scott Luedke, *Plant Mgr*
**EMP:** 153
**SALES (corp-wide):** 5.6B **Privately Held**
**SIC:** 3089 Extruded finished plastic products
**HQ:** Fasteners For Retail, Inc.
8181 Darrow Rd
Twinsburg OH 44087
330 998-7800

### (G-8195)
### FILTER FRIEND Z INC
2280 Magnolia St (60018-3127)
**PHONE** .................................... 847 824-4049
Mildred Phillips, *President*
**EMP:** 4
**SALES (est):** 276.8K **Privately Held**
**SIC:** 3564 Blower filter units (furnace blowers)

## GEOGRAPHIC SECTION
### Des Plaines - Cook County (G-8219)

**(G-8196)**
**FILTRAN HOLDINGS LLC (PA)**
875 Seegers Rd (60016-3045)
PHONE..................847 635-6670
Larry W Gies Jr, *President*
John E Udelhofen, *Vice Pres*
Brett Wall, *Vice Pres*
Dennis Baran, *CFO*
David J Ball, *Treasurer*
**EMP:** 1
**SALES (est):** 157.6MM **Privately Held**
**SIC: 3433** Heating equipment, except electric

**(G-8197)**
**FILTRAN LLC (HQ)**
875 Seegers Rd (60016-3045)
PHONE..................847 635-6670
**Fax:** 847 635-7724
Brett Wall, *President*
Chris Heidemann, *General Mgr*
Dennis Barn, *Vice Pres*
John Eleftherakis, *Vice Pres*
John E Udelhofen, *Vice Pres*
◆ **EMP:** 240
**SALES (est):** 155.2MM **Privately Held**
**SIC: 3433** Heating equipment, except electric

**(G-8198)**
**FINZER HOLDING LLC (PA)**
Also Called: Finzer Roller Pennsylvania
129 Rawls Rd (60018-1328)
PHONE..................847 390-6200
Grace Devito, *Accounts Mgr*
Bob Dolan, *Manager*
John O Finzer III,
David M Finzer,
**EMP:** 2
**SQ FT:** 36,000
**SALES (est):** 13.2MM **Privately Held**
**SIC: 3069** Rubber hardware

**(G-8199)**
**FINZER ROLLER INC (PA)**
129 Rawls Rd (60018-1328)
PHONE..................847 390-6200
**Fax:** 847 390-6201
John Finzer, *CEO*
David M Finzer, *President*
Ron Bradley, *Plant Mgr*
Patricia Sachs, *Purch Agent*
Mike Hefner, *CFO*
◆ **EMP:** 35
**SQ FT:** 28,000
**SALES (est):** 29.8MM **Privately Held**
**WEB:** www.finzerroller.com
**SIC: 3069** Rubber rolls & roll coverings; roll coverings, rubber

**(G-8200)**
**FOOD SERVICE PUBLISHING CO**
Also Called: Food Industry News
3166 S River Rd Ste 40 (60018)
PHONE..................847 699-3300
**Fax:** 847 699-3307
James S Contis, *President*
Mark Braun, *Publisher*
Terry Minich, *Editor*
Terry Minnich, *Editor*
Cary Miller, *Vice Pres*
**EMP:** 10
**SQ FT:** 2,200
**SALES (est):** 550K **Privately Held**
**SIC: 2711** 2741 2721 Newspapers: publishing only, not printed on site; directories: publishing only, not printed on site; periodicals

**(G-8201)**
**GEPCO INTERNATIONAL INC (HQ)**
1770 Birchwood Ave (60018-3006)
PHONE..................847 795-9555
**Fax:** 847 795-8770
Gary Geppert, *Ch of Bd*
Greg Hansen, *Sales Mgr*
Todd Harrington, *Executive*
▲ **EMP:** 45
**SQ FT:** 60,000
**SALES (est):** 4MM **Publicly Held**
**SIC: 3357** 5065 Communication wire; electronic parts & equipment

**(G-8202)**
**GILCO REAL ESTATE COMPANY**
515 Jarvis Ave (60018-1957)
PHONE..................847 298-1717
Hunter J Gilbertson, *President*
Moises Sanabria, *Superintendent*
Gus Gilbertson, *Vice Pres*
Ted Robinson, *Sales Staff*
Sharron Messina, *Manager*
**EMP:** 50 **EST:** 1938
**SQ FT:** 50,000
**SALES (est):** 2.8MM **Privately Held**
**WEB:** www.gilcoscaffolding.com
**SIC: 1799** 7359 5082 3446 Scaffolding construction; equipment rental & leasing; scaffolding; architectural metalwork

**(G-8203)**
**GTX INC**
300 E Touhy Ave (60018-2611)
PHONE..................847 699-7421
Bom Lee Hee, *Principal*
**EMP:** 3
**SALES (est):** 387.8K **Privately Held**
**SIC: 2992** Lubricating oils

**(G-8204)**
**HIGGINS QUICK PRINT**
Also Called: Higgins Forms & Systems
2410 S River Rd (60018-3201)
PHONE..................847 635-7700
**Fax:** 847 635-7744
Murray Burns, *Owner*
**EMP:** 4
**SALES (est):** 397.5K **Privately Held**
**SIC: 2752** Commercial printing, offset

**(G-8205)**
**HONEYWELL INTERNATIONAL INC**
25 E Algonquin Rd (60016-6101)
P.O. Box 5017 (60017-5017)
PHONE..................847 391-2000
Carlos A Cabrera, *CEO*
Daniel Key, *Vice Pres*
David Kalafut, *Engineer*
Stephen T Wilson, *Engineer*
Mary Oleksiuk, *Human Res Mgr*
**EMP:** 3000
**SQ FT:** 800
**SALES (corp-wide):** 39.3B **Publicly Held**
**WEB:** www.honeywell.com
**SIC: 5013** 3519 Automotive supplies & parts; diesel engine rebuilding
**PA:** Honeywell International Inc.
115 Tabor Rd
Morris Plains NJ 07950
973 455-2000

**(G-8206)**
**HU-FRIEDY MFG CO LLC**
1666 E Touhy Ave (60018-3607)
PHONE..................847 257-4500
Ron Saslow, *Branch Mgr*
**EMP:** 11
**SALES (corp-wide):** 125.5MM **Privately Held**
**SIC: 3999** Barber & beauty shop equipment
**PA:** Hu-Friedy Mfg. Co., Llc
3232 N Rockwell St
Chicago IL 60618
773 975-3975

**(G-8207)**
**ICEBERG ENTERPRISES LLC (PA)**
2700 S River Rd Ste 303 (60018-4107)
PHONE..................847 685-9500
**Fax:** 847 588-8226
Howard Green, *CEO*
Richard Gilbert, *President*
Douglas Nash, *General Mgr*
Richard Fox, *Vice Pres*
David Parzynski Sr, *Vice Pres*
▲ **EMP:** 11
**SQ FT:** 3,700
**SALES (est):** 41.4MM **Privately Held**
**SIC: 3089** Blow molded finished plastic products

**(G-8208)**
**ILLINOIS TOOL WORKS INC**
Also Called: ITW Switches
195 E Algonquin Rd (60016-6197)
PHONE..................847 876-9400
**Fax:** 847 876-9440
Lynn Wesley, *Human Res Mgr*
Brian Truesdale, *Manager*
**EMP:** 180
**SALES (corp-wide):** 13.6B **Publicly Held**
**SIC: 3679** 3643 3621 3613 Electronic switches; current-carrying wiring devices; motors & generators; switchgear & switchboard apparatus; computer peripheral equipment
**PA:** Illinois Tool Works Inc.
155 Harlem Ave
Glenview IL 60025
847 724-7500

**(G-8209)**
**ILLINOIS TOOL WORKS INC**
ITW Nexus
195 E Algonquin Rd (60016-6197)
P.O. Box 2444 (60017-2444)
PHONE..................847 299-2222
**Fax:** 630 390-6183
Mark Udelhofen, *General Mgr*
Rob Proksa, *Mfg Mgr*
Bill Kaempfe, *Purchasing*
David Nadrowski, *Manager*
Don Bennett, *Supervisor*
**EMP:** 170
**SALES (corp-wide):** 13.6B **Publicly Held**
**SIC: 3089** 5085 3469 3965 Injection molding of plastics; industrial supplies; metal stampings; fasteners, buttons, needles & pins
**PA:** Illinois Tool Works Inc.
155 Harlem Ave
Glenview IL 60025
847 724-7500

**(G-8210)**
**IMS COMPANIES LLC (PA)**
1 Innovation Dr (60016-3161)
PHONE..................847 391-8100
**Fax:** 847 391-8354
Mark Simanton, *CEO*
James Talarek, *COO*
Steve Szczech, *Vice Pres*
Kevin Groom, *Chief Mktg Ofcr*
Bert A Getz Jr, *Director*
▼ **EMP:** 58
**SQ FT:** 245,000
**SALES (est):** 607.5MM **Privately Held**
**SIC: 3469** 8711 3679 3714 Metal stampings; engineering services; harness assemblies for electronic use: wire or cable; gears, motor vehicle; sheet metal specialties, not stamped

**(G-8211)**
**IMS ENGINEERED PRODUCTS LLC**
Also Called: Amco Engineering Co
1 Innovation Dr (60016-3161)
PHONE..................847 391-8100
Jesse Flores, *Engineer*
Edward V Anderson, *Treasurer*
Margaret M Amoroso, *Controller*
Kathleen Krol, *Accountant*
Angela Oliver, *Human Res Dir*
▲ **EMP:** 163 **EST:** 2005
**SALES (est):** 44.2MM
**SALES (corp-wide):** 607.5MM **Privately Held**
**SIC: 3444** 2522 3699 3469 Housings for business machines, sheet metal; office cabinets & filing drawers: except wood; filing boxes, cabinets & cases: except wood; office desks & tables: except wood; electrical equipment & supplies; metal stampings; partitions & fixtures, except wood
**PA:** Ims Companies, Llc
1 Innovation Dr
Des Plaines IL 60016
847 391-8100

**(G-8212)**
**INTERMOLDING TECHNOLOGY LLC**
85 Bradrock Dr (60018-1937)
PHONE..................847 376-8517
Helmut Mueller, *President*
Daniel Warmuth, *General Mgr*
**EMP:** 14
**SALES (est):** 2.3MM **Privately Held**
**SIC: 3089** Injection molding of plastics

**(G-8213)**
**INTERNATIONAL PAPER COMPANY**
100 E Oakton St (60018-1956)
PHONE..................847 390-1300
Roger Knapp, *Plant Engr*
Todd Douglas, *Manager*
**EMP:** 23
**SALES (corp-wide):** 21B **Publicly Held**
**SIC: 2621** Paper mills
**PA:** International Paper Company
6400 Poplar Ave
Memphis TN 38197
901 419-9000

**(G-8214)**
**INTRAVATION INC (PA)**
1113 Hewitt Dr (60016-6040)
PHONE..................847 299-6423
Anthony Salah, *President*
Michael Ruddick, *Treasurer*
**EMP:** 1
**SALES (est):** 800K **Privately Held**
**WEB:** www.intravation.com
**SIC: 7372** Application computer software

**(G-8215)**
**J B METAL WORKS INC**
1325 Lee St (60018-1514)
PHONE..................847 824-4253
**Fax:** 847 824-7958
Steven Burval, *President*
Carole Burval, *Corp Secy*
**EMP:** 5 **EST:** 1938
**SQ FT:** 11,000
**SALES (est):** 801.3K **Privately Held**
**WEB:** www.jbmetalworks.com
**SIC: 3446** 3444 3443 3441 Architectural metalwork; sheet metalwork; fabricated plate work (boiler shop); fabricated structural metal

**(G-8216)**
**JEWEL-OSCO INC**
Also Called: Jewel-Osco 3425
1500 Lee St (60018-1544)
PHONE..................847 296-7786
**Fax:** 847 299-3209
Tom Hong, *Manager*
**EMP:** 200
**SALES (corp-wide):** 58.8B **Privately Held**
**WEB:** www.jewelosco.com
**SIC: 5411** 5912 5421 2051 Supermarkets, chain; drug stores & proprietary stores; meat & fish markets; bread, cake & related products
**HQ:** Jewel Osco, Inc.
150 E Pierce Rd Ste 200
Itasca IL 60143
630 948-6000

**(G-8217)**
**JPH ENTERPRISES INC**
Also Called: Citywide Printing
420 Lee St (60016-4610)
PHONE..................847 390-0900
**Fax:** 847 390-6254
James Hess, *President*
**EMP:** 7
**SQ FT:** 5,000
**SALES (est):** 88.2K **Privately Held**
**SIC: 2752** 7334 2796 2791 Commercial printing, offset; photocopying & duplicating services; platemaking services; typesetting; bookbinding & related work; commercial printing

**(G-8218)**
**KING OF SOFTWARE INC**
1232 Willow Ave (60016-4234)
PHONE..................847 354-8745
**EMP:** 3
**SALES (est):** 182.2K **Privately Held**
**SIC: 7372** Prepackaged software

**(G-8219)**
**KRAUS & NAIMER INC**
200 Howard Ave Ste 270 (60018-5910)
PHONE..................847 298-2450
Ray Ploski, *Manager*
Brian Myers, *Technology*

## Des Plaines - Cook County (G-8220)

EMP: 7
SALES (corp-wide): 17MM **Privately Held**
WEB: www.krausnaimer.com
SIC: 3679 Electronic switches
PA: Kraus & Naimer, Inc.
760 New Brunswick Rd
Somerset NJ 08873
732 560-1240

**(G-8220)**
**LA MARCHE MFG CO (PA)**
106 Bradrock Dr (60018-1967)
PHONE.................847 299-1188
Fax: 847 299-3061
Raulf La Marche, *Ch of Bd*
Richard Rutkowski, *President*
Judith La Marche, *Chairman*
Raj Dhiman, *Exec VP*
Rajesh Dhiman, *Exec VP*
▲ EMP: 135
SQ FT: 66,000
SALES: 11.5MM **Privately Held**
WEB: www.lamarchemfg.com
SIC: 3629 Battery chargers, rectifying or nonrotating; inverters, nonrotating: electrical

**(G-8221)**
**LEA & SACHS INC (PA)**
1267 Rand Rd (60016-3402)
P.O. Box 1667 (60017-1667)
PHONE.................847 296-8000
George B Martin, *President*
Robert Martin, *Vice Pres*
EMP: 13 EST: 1937
SQ FT: 4,000
SALES (est): 1.5MM **Privately Held**
WEB: www.leasachs.com
SIC: 2241 Elastic narrow fabrics, woven or braided; elastic webbing

**(G-8222)**
**LEARJET INC**
Also Called: Bombardier Learjet
251 Wille Rd Ste A (60018-1861)
PHONE.................847 553-0172
Dave Hanna, *Branch Mgr*
Susana Andino, *Manager*
Tom Frohlich, *Manager*
Kris Paquin, *Manager*
EMP: 450
SALES (corp-wide): 16.3B **Privately Held**
SIC: 3721 Aircraft
HQ: Learjet Inc.
1 Learjet Way
Wichita KS 67209
316 946-2000

**(G-8223)**
**LEGGETT & PLATT INCORPORATED**
Also Called: Vertex Fasteners
1798 Sherwin Ave (60018-3015)
PHONE.................847 768-6139
Fax: 847 768-7192
Julio Vizuete, *QC Mgr*
Scott Bridges, *Branch Mgr*
EMP: 53
SALES (corp-wide): 3.7B **Publicly Held**
WEB: www.leggett.com
SIC: 3549 3965 Metalworking machinery; fasteners, buttons, needles & pins
PA: Leggett & Platt, Incorporated
1 Leggett Rd
Carthage MO 64836
417 358-8131

**(G-8224)**
**M T M ASSN FOR STANDARDS & RES**
Also Called: MTM ASSOCIATION
1111 E Touhy Ave Ste 280 (60018-5811)
PHONE.................847 299-1111
Fax: 847 299-3509
Knuth Jasker, *Managing Dir*
Alfredo Link, *Managing Dir*
Michael Mitchell, *Vice Pres*
Dirk Rauglas, *Exec Dir*
Lillian Burns, *Meeting Planner*
EMP: 5
SQ FT: 2,700

SALES: 451.8K **Privately Held**
WEB: www.mtm.org
SIC: 7372 8299 Educational computer software; educational service, nondegree granting: continuing educ.

**(G-8225)**
**MAK-SYSTEM CORP**
2720 S River Rd Ste 225 (60018-4111)
PHONE.................847 803-4863
Simon Kiskovski, *President*
Poline Matti, *Sales Staff*
EMP: 16
SALES (est): 2.4MM
SALES (corp-wide): 1.8MM **Privately Held**
SIC: 3695 Computer software tape & disks: blank, rigid & floppy
PA: Mak-System France
10 Avenue De La Grande Armee
Paris 75017
144 090-650

**(G-8226)**
**MANUFACTURING / WOODWORKING**
1054 S River Rd (60016-6745)
PHONE.................847 730-4823
Arthur Szelag, *President*
EMP: 5
SQ FT: 6,000
SALES (est): 189.7K **Privately Held**
SIC: 2434 2517 2521 5712 Wood kitchen cabinets; home entertainment unit cabinets, wood; wood office filing cabinets & bookcases; customized furniture & cabinets; planing mill, millwork

**(G-8227)**
**MARTIN SPROCKET & GEAR INC**
1505 Birchwood Ave (60018-3001)
PHONE.................847 298-8844
Fax: 847 298-2967
Mylan Tyrrell, *Manager*
Tim Dalton, *Manager*
EMP: 13
SALES (corp-wide): 403.8MM **Privately Held**
SIC: 3566 3568 Gears, power transmission, except automotive; power transmission equipment
PA: Martin Sprocket & Gear, Inc.
3100 Sprocket Dr
Arlington TX 76015
817 258-3000

**(G-8228)**
**MAXON SHOOTERS SUPPLIES INC**
Also Called: Maxon Shters Sups Indoor Range
75 Bradrock Dr (60018-1937)
PHONE.................847 298-4867
Fax: 847 298-4885
Thomas Kral, *President*
Barry Levin, *President*
Claudia Levin, *Vice Pres*
William Levin, *Treasurer*
EMP: 4
SQ FT: 1,000
SALES (est): 776.3K **Privately Held**
SIC: 5941 7699 3483 Firearms; gunsmith shop; ammunition components

**(G-8229)**
**MAYATECH CORPORATION**
1000 Graceland Ave (60016-6512)
PHONE.................847 297-0930
Fax: 847 699-7545
Raymond Tibavido, *President*
Richard Brian, *President*
Raymond P Tibavido III, *Corp Secy*
Buddha Mayani, *Vice Pres*
EMP: 32
SQ FT: 28,000
SALES (est): 3.4MM **Privately Held**
SIC: 3554 Paper industries machinery

**(G-8230)**
**MCI SERVICE PARTS INC**
200 E Oakton St (60018-1948)
PHONE.................419 994-4141
Carl Roth, *Principal*
EMP: 60

SALES (corp-wide): 1.5B **Privately Held**
SIC: 5013 7538 3714 3713 Motor vehicle supplies & new parts; general automotive repair shops; motor vehicle parts & accessories; truck & bus bodies
HQ: Mci Service Parts, Inc.
200 E Oakton St
Des Plaines IL 60018
847 285-2000

**(G-8231)**
**MEDCO INC**
55 Bradrock Dr (60018-1937)
P.O. Box 72145 (60018)
PHONE.................847 296-3021
Ronald Zarach, *President*
Andy Nastrazewski, *Vice Pres*
Tom Budys, *Treasurer*
Diane Fitzgerald, *Manager*
EMP: 18 EST: 1962
SQ FT: 22,300
SALES (est): 2.6MM **Privately Held**
SIC: 3599 8711 Mfg Industrial Machinery Engineering Services

**(G-8232)**
**MEITHEAL PHARMACEUTICALS INC**
2340 S River Rd Ste 208 (60018-3223)
PHONE.................773 951-6542
Thomas Shea, *CEO*
Victoria Wohlfeil, *General Counsel*
EMP: 6
SALES (est): 267.4K **Privately Held**
SIC: 2834 Powders, pharmaceutical

**(G-8233)**
**MIGHTY MITES AWARDS AND SONS**
1297 Rand Rd (60016-3402)
PHONE.................847 297-0035
Fax: 847 803-1039
Sam A Donatucci, *President*
Jim Winski, *Opers Mgr*
Mike Donatucci, *Manager*
Virginia Donatucci, *Admin Sec*
EMP: 9
SQ FT: 7,800
SALES (est): 1.4MM **Privately Held**
WEB: www.mightymitesawards.com
SIC: 3499 2396 2326 Trophies, metal, except silver; automotive & apparel trimmings; men's & boys' work clothing

**(G-8234)**
**MONTANA METAL PRODUCTS LLC (HQ)**
Also Called: Mmp
25 Howard Ave (60018-1901)
PHONE.................847 803-6600
Fax: 847 803-6601
Michael Faten, *CFO*
Joe Stephen, *VP Finance*
Pamela Brooks, *Bookkeeper*
Michael Kedryna, *Manager*
Anthony Sobel,
EMP: 115 EST: 1957
SQ FT: 98,500
SALES (est): 23.2MM
SALES (corp-wide): 25.1MM **Privately Held**
SIC: 3444 Sheet metalwork
PA: The Mifsud Group Llc
140 Blaze Industrial Pkwy
Berea OH 44017
216 325-7280

**(G-8235)**
**MOTOR COACH INDS INTL INC (HQ)**
Also Called: Mcli
200 E Oakton St (60018-1948)
PHONE.................847 285-2000
Fax: 847 285-2013
Paul Soubry, *President*
Stephen Kratzer, *Business Mgr*
Louis Quaglia, *Business Mgr*
Mario Gonzalez, *Exec VP*
Timothy J Nalepka, *Vice Pres*
EMP: 125
SALES (est): 414.2MM
SALES (corp-wide): 1.5B **Privately Held**
SIC: 3713 3711 3714 Bus bodies (motor vehicles); buses, all types, assembly of; motor vehicle parts & accessories

PA: New Flyer Industries Inc
711 Kernaghan Ave
Winnipeg MB R2C 3
204 224-1251

**(G-8236)**
**MOTOR COACH INDUSTRIES**
200 E Oakton St (60018-1948)
PHONE.................847 285-2000
EMP: 5
SALES (est): 610.6K **Privately Held**
SIC: 5063 5012 3711 Whol Electrical Equipment Whol Autos/Motor Vehicles Mfg Motor Vehicle/Car Bodies

**(G-8237)**
**MOTUS DIGITAL LLC**
131 Cornell Ave (60016-2128)
PHONE.................972 943-0008
Kieth Brock,
Howard Blietz,
EMP: 25
SALES (est): 2.5MM **Privately Held**
SIC: 3861 Motion picture film

**(G-8238)**
**MOVIE FACTS INC (PA)**
1870 Busse Hwy Ste 200 (60016-6773)
PHONE.................847 299-9700
Fax: 847 299-9732
Glen F Wilmes, *President*
Lawrence Fils, *Treasurer*
Jill Wilmes Ovnik, *Admin Sec*
Jill Wilmes, *Admin Sec*
EMP: 40
SQ FT: 9,000
SALES (est): 8MM **Privately Held**
WEB: www.moviefactsinc.com
SIC: 2731 7313 Pamphlets: publishing only, not printed on site; radio, television, publisher representatives

**(G-8239)**
**MSF GRAPHICS INC**
959 Lee St (60016-6545)
P.O. Box 8164, Northfield (60093-8164)
PHONE.................847 446-6900
Fax: 847 967-0555
Michael S French, *President*
EMP: 6
SALES (est): 480K **Privately Held**
WEB: www.msfgraphics.com
SIC: 2752 2759 2789 Commercial printing, offset; screen printing; bookbinding & related work

**(G-8240)**
**MYECCHO LLC**
550 Graceland Ave Apt 11 (60016-4451)
PHONE.................224 639-3068
Srujesh Shah, *Principal*
Suj Shah,
EMP: 5
SALES (est): 159.8K **Privately Held**
SIC: 8249 7372 Business training services; business oriented computer software

**(G-8241)**
**NIDEC MOTOR CORPORATION**
Merkle-Korff
1905 S Mount Prospect Rd (60018-1856)
PHONE.................847 439-3760
John Brown, *General Mgr*
Teri Anderson, *Vice Chairman*
Chuck Hayward, *Buyer*
Mika S Smith, *Buyer*
Keith Dwyer, *Sales Staff*
EMP: 100
SALES (corp-wide): 10B **Privately Held**
SIC: 3694 Ignition apparatus & distributors
HQ: Nidec Motor Corporation
8050 West Florissant Ave
Saint Louis MO 63136

**(G-8242)**
**NIMLOK COMPANY (PA)**
111 Rawls Rd (60018-1328)
PHONE.................847 647-1012
Fax: 847 647-2044
Gerald Perutz, *Ch of Bd*
Simon Perutz, *President*
Aurelia Sirbu, *Accounts Mgr*
Emma Swales, *Marketing Mgr*
Marc Miziarco, *Manager*
▲ EMP: 64

**SQ FT:** 136,000
**SALES (est):** 14MM  **Privately Held**
**WEB:** www.nimlok.com
**SIC: 3993**  Displays & cutouts, window & lobby

**(G-8243)**
**NIPPON YAKIN AMERICA INC**
2800 S River Rd  (60018-6001)
**PHONE** .................................. 847 685-6644
Masashi Kobayashi, *Principal*
Perry Ohlson, *Sales Mgr*
**EMP:** 5
**SALES (est):** 385.9K
**SALES (corp-wide):** 993.9MM  **Privately Held**
**SIC: 3356**  Tin & tin alloy bars, pipe, sheets, etc.
**PA:** Nippon Yakin Kogyo Co., Ltd.
 1-5-8, Kyobashi
 Chuo-Ku TKY 104-0
 332 721-511

**(G-8244)**
**NU-WAY INDUSTRIES INC**
555 Howard Ave  (60018-1981)
**PHONE** .................................. 847 298-7710
**Fax:** 847 635-8650
Steven Southwell, *President*
Joe Fijak, *Exec VP*
Mary Howard, *Exec VP*
Tracy Corso, *Vice Pres*
Susan Passero, *Materials Mgr*
▲ **EMP:** 250
**SQ FT:** 293,000
**SALES:** 32MM  **Privately Held**
**WEB:** www.nuwayindustries.com
**SIC: 3444**  3469 3599 Sheet metalwork; sheet metal specialties, not stamped; metal housings, enclosures, casings & other containers; stamping metal for the trade; machine shop, jobbing & repair

**(G-8245)**
**OAKLEY SIGNS & GRAPHICS INC**
471 N 3rd Ave  (60016-1160)
**PHONE** .................................. 224 612-5045
Jennifer Elliott, *Human Res Mgr*
Kenneth D Levitt, *Branch Mgr*
**EMP:** 15
**SALES (corp-wide):** 7.7MM  **Privately Held**
**SIC: 3993**  Signs & advertising specialties
**PA:** Oakley Signs & Graphics, Inc.
 650 Northlake Blvd # 520
 Altamonte Springs FL 32701
 407 262-8200

**(G-8246)**
**OCHEM INC (PA)**
9044 Buckingham Park Dr  (60016-5102)
**PHONE** .................................. 847 403-7044
Weizhong Liu, *President*
**EMP:** 2
**SQ FT:** 10,000
**SALES:** 2MM  **Privately Held**
**SIC: 2899**  Chemical preparations

**(G-8247)**
**ORBUS LLC**
Also Called: Nimlok
111 Rawls Rd  (60018-1328)
**PHONE** .................................. 847 647-1012
Simon Perutz, *Branch Mgr*
**EMP:** 135
**SALES (corp-wide):** 76.5MM  **Privately Held**
**SIC: 3999**  Advertising display products
**PA:** Orbus Llc
 9033 Murphy Rd
 Woodridge IL 60517
 630 226-1155

**(G-8248)**
**PACIFIC COAST FEATHER COMPANY**
414 E Golf Rd  (60016-2234)
**PHONE** .................................. 847 827-1210
**EMP:** 9
**SALES (corp-wide):** 410.7MM  **Privately Held**
**SIC: 2392**  Cushions & pillows; comforters & quilts: made from purchased materials
**PA:** Pacific Coast Feather Company
 1964 4th Ave S
 Seattle WA 98134
 206 624-1057

**(G-8249)**
**PAMCO PRINTED TAPE LABEL INC (HQ)**
2200 S Wolf Rd  (60018-1934)
**PHONE** .................................. 847 803-2200
**Fax:** 847 803-2209
Robert Simko, *CEO*
William E Burch, *President*
Jonathan Boucher, *Vice Pres*
Thomas Spielberger, *Vice Pres*
Treina Blair, *CFO*
**EMP:** 150  **EST:** 1990
**SQ FT:** 54,000
**SALES (est):** 29.4MM
**SALES (corp-wide):** 144.5MM  **Privately Held**
**SIC: 2759**  2752 Commercial printing; commercial printing, lithographic
**PA:** Resource Label Group, Llc
 147 Seaboard Ln
 Franklin TN 37067
 615 661-5900

**(G-8250)**
**PARKER-HANNIFIN CORPORATION**
500 S Wolf Rd  (60016-3187)
**PHONE** .................................. 847 298-2400
**EMP:** 115
**SALES (corp-wide):** 11.3B  **Publicly Held**
**SIC: 3593**  Fluid power cylinders, hydraulic or pneumatic
**PA:** Parker-Hannifin Corporation
 6035 Parkland Blvd
 Cleveland OH 44124
 216 896-3000

**(G-8251)**
**PARKWAY METAL PRODUCTS INC**
130 Rawls Rd  (60018-1329)
**PHONE** .................................. 847 789-4000
Ted Martin, *President*
Daniel Brown, *Senior VP*
Tom Raczka, *Office Mgr*
Daniel Winters, *Manager*
**EMP:** 90
**SQ FT:** 71,000
**SALES (est):** 23.6MM  **Privately Held**
**WEB:** www.parkwaymetal.com
**SIC: 3441**  3469 Fabricated structural metal; stamping metal for the trade

**(G-8252)**
**PETNET SOLUTIONS INC**
200 Howard Ave Ste 240  (60018-5909)
**PHONE** .................................. 847 297-3721
Tim Huston, *Manager*
Danny Bingham, *Manager*
John Beyer, *Shareholder*
**EMP:** 4
**SALES (corp-wide):** 89.6B  **Privately Held**
**SIC: 2835**  Radioactive diagnostic substances
**HQ:** Petnet Solutions, Inc.
 810 Innovation Dr
 Knoxville TN 37932
 865 218-2000

**(G-8253)**
**PEXCO LLC (DH)**
1600 Birchwood Ave  (60018-3004)
**PHONE** .................................. 847 296-5511
Brad Thompson, *COO*
Himanshu Patel, *Plant Mgr*
Lisa Navarro, *Purch Mgr*
Lee Hackett, *Engineer*
Glenn Hampton, *Engineer*
▲ **EMP:** 160
**SQ FT:** 96,600
**SALES (est):** 26MM
**SALES (corp-wide):** 1.2B  **Privately Held**
**WEB:** www.porthplastic.com
**SIC: 3089**  Plastic hardware & building products
**HQ:** Porex Technologies Corporation
 1625 Ashton Park Dr Ste A
 South Chesterfield VA 23834
 804 524-4983

**(G-8254)**
**PH TOOL MANUFACTURING**
1200 Andrea Ln  (60018-5501)
**PHONE** .................................. 847 952-9441
Halil Tuskar, *Owner*
**EMP:** 4
**SALES (est):** 244.8K  **Privately Held**
**SIC: 3599**  Machine shop, jobbing & repair

**(G-8255)**
**PHOENIX GRAPHICS INC**
2375 Magnolia St  (60018-3128)
**PHONE** .................................. 847 699-9520
Bruce H Holmberg, *President*
**EMP:** 3  **EST:** 1920
**SQ FT:** 2,000
**SALES (est):** 342.6K  **Privately Held**
**SIC: 2759**  7311 Screen printing; advertising consultant

**(G-8256)**
**PLATINUM TOUCH INDUSTRIES LLC**
471 N 3rd Ave  (60016-1160)
**PHONE** .................................. 773 775-9988
Vincent Gendusa, *Principal*
**EMP:** 8
**SALES (est):** 1.3MM  **Privately Held**
**SIC: 3999**  Manufacturing industries

**(G-8257)**
**PLITEK**
69 Rawls Rd  (60018-1326)
**PHONE** .................................. 847 827-6680
**Fax:** 847 827-6733
Karl K Hoffman, *President*
Joseph Weber, *General Mgr*
Judi Terranova, *Purch Agent*
Roger Engel, *Engineer*
Justin Tivers, *Project Engr*
▲ **EMP:** 62
**SQ FT:** 54,000
**SALES (est):** 21.2MM  **Privately Held**
**WEB:** www.plitek.com
**SIC: 2672**  3089 3053 Coated & laminated paper; plastic processing; gaskets, packing & sealing devices

**(G-8258)**
**POWERPATH MICROPRODUCTS INC**
200 Howard Ave Ste 238  (60018-5909)
**PHONE** .................................. 847 827-6330
**Fax:** 847 827-6433
Kerry Dulin, *President*
Joe L Lekostaj, *Admin Sec*
**EMP:** 3
**SQ FT:** 4,500
**SALES:** 375K  **Privately Held**
**WEB:** www.rosslaresecurity.com
**SIC: 3089**  Injection molding of plastics

**(G-8259)**
**PPG ARCHITECTURAL FINISHES INC**
Also Called: Glidden Professional Paint Ctr
2200 E Devon Ave 111  (60018-4503)
**PHONE** .................................. 847 699-8400
Jim Greer, *General Mgr*
**EMP:** 16
**SALES (corp-wide):** 14.7B  **Publicly Held**
**WEB:** www.gliddenpaint.com
**SIC: 2899**  Concrete curing & hardening compounds
**HQ:** Ppg Architectural Finishes, Inc.
 1 Ppg Pl
 Pittsburgh PA 15272
 412 434-3131

**(G-8260)**
**PRAIRIE GLEN IMAGING CTR LLC**
9680 Golf Rd  (60016-1522)
**PHONE** .................................. 847 296-5366
P Shirazi,
**EMP:** 4
**SALES (est):** 480K  **Privately Held**
**SIC: 3826**  Magnetic resonance imaging apparatus

**(G-8261)**
**PRECISION INSTRUMENTS INC**
1846 Miner St  (60016-4712)
P.O. Box 1306  (60017-1306)
**PHONE** .................................. 847 824-4194
John K Larson, *President*
Andrew Larson, *Vice Pres*
John A Larson, *Vice Pres*
R Glenn Meier, *Vice Pres*
Ron Lundgren, *Plant Mgr*
**EMP:** 56  **EST:** 1938
**SQ FT:** 48,000
**SALES (est):** 5.5MM  **Privately Held**
**WEB:** www.torqwrench.com
**SIC: 3423**  Wrenches, hand tools

**(G-8262)**
**PRECISION PRODUCTS MFG INTL**
1400 E Touhy Ave Ste 402  (60018-3341)
**PHONE** .................................. 847 299-8500
Sam Shadman, *President*
Balu Balaguru, *Vice Pres*
**EMP:** 23
**SQ FT:** 3,000
**SALES (est):** 1.6MM  **Privately Held**
**WEB:** www.ppmiinc.com
**SIC: 3841**  8742 Suction therapy apparatus; manufacturing management consultant

**(G-8263)**
**PRESS TECH INC**
959 Lee St  (60016-6545)
**PHONE** .................................. 847 824-4485
**Fax:** 847 824-4775
Robert Soske, *President*
Edward Soske, *Vice Pres*
Joan Soske, *CFO*
**EMP:** 14
**SQ FT:** 4,400
**SALES (est):** 3.6MM  **Privately Held**
**WEB:** www.inkpaperpride.com
**SIC: 2752**  Commercial printing, offset

**(G-8264)**
**PRIME PRINTING INC**
967 Graceland Ave Ste 5  (60016-6591)
**PHONE** .................................. 847 299-9960
**Fax:** 847 299-9767
Michael Robbins, *President*
Elda Robbins, *Admin Sec*
Biju Jacob, *Analyst*
**EMP:** 3
**SALES:** 200K  **Privately Held**
**SIC: 2752**  Commercial printing, lithographic

**(G-8265)**
**PRINT MANAGEMENT PARTNERS INC (PA)**
Also Called: Go2 Partners
701 Lee St Ste 1050  (60016-4572)
**PHONE** .................................. 847 699-2999
James O'Brien, *President*
Mike Ryan, *Vice Pres*
Jim Grandos, *CFO*
Kelly Koons, *Accounts Mgr*
Debra Piotrowski, *Accounts Mgr*
**EMP:** 22
**SQ FT:** 5,500
**SALES (est):** 38.5MM  **Privately Held**
**WEB:** www.ourpartners.com
**SIC: 8742**  2759 7379 Marketing consulting services; commercial printing; computer related consulting services

**(G-8266)**
**QUALITY NEON SERVICE**
1350 Oakwood Ave Ste A  (60016-6577)
**PHONE** .................................. 847 299-2969
**EMP:** 3  **EST:** 2014
**SALES (est):** 248.7K  **Privately Held**
**SIC: 2813**  Neon

**(G-8267)**
**RAHCO RUBBER INC**
1633 Birchwood Ave  (60018-3003)
**PHONE** .................................. 847 298-4200
**Fax:** 847 298-4201
William R Anton, *President*
Mark Bradham, *Business Mgr*
John M Anton, *Vice Pres*
Stephen Anton, *Vice Pres*
Kevin Magner, *Plt & Fclts Mgr*
**EMP:** 90
**SQ FT:** 57,000

# Des Plaines - Cook County (G-8268)

SALES (est): 18.1MM **Privately Held**
WEB: www.rahcorubber.com
SIC: 3069 Grommets, rubber; washers, rubber; hard rubber products; molded rubber products

**(G-8268)**
**ROGUS TOOL INC**
354 N East River Rd (60016-1224)
PHONE..................847 824-5939
Fax: 847 297-6562
Dennis Rogus, *President*
Bera Rogus, *Admin Sec*
EMP: 3
SALES (est): 160K **Privately Held**
SIC: 3599 3544 Machine shop, jobbing & repair; special dies, tools, jigs & fixtures

**(G-8269)**
**SA INDUSTRIES INC**
1054 S River Rd (60016-6745)
PHONE..................847 730-4823
Arthur Szelag, *President*
EMP: 5
SALES (est): 250K **Privately Held**
SIC: 3553 Woodworking machinery

**(G-8270)**
**SEAVIVOR BOATS**
576 Arlington Ave (60016-3363)
PHONE..................847 297-5953
Logan Kleckles, *President*
EMP: 9 EST: 1977
SALES (est): 558.4K **Privately Held**
SIC: 3732 5551 Boat building & repairing; boat dealers

**(G-8271)**
**SEEDBURO EQUIPMENT COMPANY INC**
2293 S Mount Prospect Rd (60018-1810)
PHONE..................312 738-3700
Thomas E Runyon, *President*
Katherine Reading, *Vice Pres*
Don Schreiber, *Buyer*
Reuben Shaffer, *Buyer*
Cary Hall, *CFO*
▼ EMP: 19 EST: 1912
SQ FT: 13,000
SALES (est): 8.1MM **Privately Held**
WEB: www.seedburo.com
SIC: 3523 5083 0723 Farm machinery & equipment; agricultural machinery; cash grain crops market preparation services

**(G-8272)**
**SEOCLARITY**
2800 S River Rd Ste 290 (60018-6091)
PHONE..................773 831-4500
Mitul Gandhi, *Owner*
Christina West, *Vice Pres*
Chris Sachs, *Human Res Mgr*
Ejaz Arain, *Accounts Mgr*
Rick Behrman, *Accounts Exec*
EMP: 10
SALES (est): 724K **Privately Held**
SIC: 7372 Prepackaged software

**(G-8273)**
**SHERMAR INDUSTRIES LLC**
1245 S Leslie Ln (60018-5563)
PHONE..................847 378-8073
Ronald B Cooper, *Principal*
EMP: 3 EST: 2012
SALES (est): 197.9K **Privately Held**
SIC: 3999 Manufacturing industries

**(G-8274)**
**SHINETOO LIGHTING AMERICA LLC**
1311 Rand Rd (60016-3404)
PHONE..................877 957-7317
Kathryn Ocampo, *Opers Mgr*
Servando Ocampo, *Mng Member*
Jun Qian, *Manager*
EMP: 5 EST: 2013
SALES (est): 488.7K **Privately Held**
SIC: 3648 5063 Lighting equipment; lighting fixtures, commercial & industrial

**(G-8275)**
**SIGNS PLUS**
Also Called: Bill's Auto & Truck Repair
1216 Rand Rd (60016-3403)
PHONE..................847 489-9009
Rob Zimmerman, *Owner*
EMP: 4
SALES (est): 260K **Privately Held**
WEB: www.signsplus1.com
SIC: 3993 Signs & advertising specialties

**(G-8276)**
**SILK SCREENING BY SELEP**
767 W Millers Rd (60016-2563)
PHONE..................847 593-7050
William Selep, *President*
Shirley Selep, *Corp Secy*
EMP: 4 EST: 1958
SQ FT: 150
SALES (est): 270K **Privately Held**
SIC: 2261 2262 Screen printing of cotton broadwoven fabrics; screen printing: man-made fiber & silk broadwoven fabrics

**(G-8277)**
**SMILE AROMATICS INC**
2454 E Dempster St # 422 (60016-5320)
PHONE..................847 759-0350
Elliott Weller, *President*
Daniel Goolsby, *Vice Pres*
EMP: 20
SQ FT: 2,000
SALES (est): 3MM **Privately Held**
SIC: 2844 Perfumes & colognes

**(G-8278)**
**SPECTACLE ZOOM LLC**
8671 Josephine St Apt A (60016-1876)
PHONE..................504 352-7237
Joshua Seib, *Principal*
EMP: 3
SALES (est): 190K **Privately Held**
SIC: 3851 Spectacles

**(G-8279)**
**SPLASH DOG THERAPY INC**
42 N Broadway St (60016-2348)
PHONE..................847 296-4007
Traci Szwed, *Principal*
EMP: 3 EST: 2008
SALES (est): 335K **Privately Held**
SIC: 2836 Veterinary biological products

**(G-8280)**
**SPOUTS OF WATER INC (PA)**
9416 Margail Ave (60016-3811)
PHONE..................303 570-5104
John Kye, *Principal*
Seul Ku, *Principal*
William Raseman, *Director*
EMP: 5 EST: 2013
SALES (est): 134.7K **Privately Held**
SIC: 3269 Filtering media, pottery

**(G-8281)**
**STEPHEN FOSSLER COMPANY**
1600 E Touhy Ave (60018-3607)
PHONE..................847 635-7200
Fax: 815 424-9292
Robert Murray, *CEO*
Steven Fosler, *Principal*
EMP: 60
SQ FT: 16,000
SALES (est): 8.4MM
SALES (corp-wide): 1.8B **Publicly Held**
WEB: www.fossler.com
SIC: 2759 2672 2671 Labels & seals: printing; coated & laminated paper; packaging paper & plastics film, coated & laminated
HQ: New England Business Service, Inc.
500 Main St
Groton MA 01471
978 448-6111

**(G-8282)**
**SUKGYUNG AT INC**
2400 E Devon Ave Ste 283 (60018-4631)
PHONE..................847 298-6570
Hyung Sup Lim, *President*
Eun Hee Ahn, *Director*
◆ EMP: 8
SALES (est): 3MM **Privately Held**
WEB: www.sukgyung.com
SIC: 2834 Powders, pharmaceutical

**(G-8283)**
**SUPREME MANUFACTURING COMPANY**
Also Called: C & L Supreme Mfg Co
1755 Birchwood Ave (60018-3005)
PHONE..................847 297-8212
Louis Spizziri, *President*
Phillip E Spizziri, *Corp Secy*
Peter Spizziri, *Vice Pres*
Chris Spizziri, *Plant Mgr*
Gary O'Gradney, *Manager*
EMP: 35 EST: 1956
SQ FT: 21,000
SALES (est): 8MM **Privately Held**
WEB: www.suprememfg.net
SIC: 3599 3451 Machine shop, jobbing & repair; screw machine products

**(G-8284)**
**SVANACO INC (PA)**
Also Called: Americaneagle.com
2600 S River Rd (60018-3203)
PHONE..................847 699-0300
Fax: 847 699-4207
Norbert Svanascini, *President*
Michael Svanascini, *COO*
Bob Ferguson, *Vice Pres*
Tony Svanascini, *Vice Pres*
Doug Dillon, *Technical Mgr*
EMP: 90
SQ FT: 30,000
SALES (est): 43.4MM **Privately Held**
WEB: www.americaneagle.com
SIC: 7372 Educational computer software

**(G-8285)**
**TECHPOL AUTOMATION INC**
2083 Maple St (60018-3018)
PHONE..................847 347-4765
Janusz M Piotrowski, *Principal*
EMP: 4
SQ FT: 2,200
SALES (est): 400K **Privately Held**
SIC: 3651 Household audio & video equipment

**(G-8286)**
**TIMOTHY DARREY**
Also Called: Universal Display Products
1153 Lee St Bldg 223 (60016-6516)
PHONE..................847 231-2277
Timothy Darrey, *Owner*
EMP: 2
SALES (est): 250K **Privately Held**
SIC: 3993 Signs & advertising specialties

**(G-8287)**
**TOUHY DIAGNOSTIC AT HOME LLC**
1293 Rand Rd (60016-3402)
PHONE..................847 803-1111
Noreen Khan, *President*
Mohammad Akbar Zahid, *Principal*
EMP: 15
SQ FT: 1,000
SALES (est): 1.2MM **Privately Held**
SIC: 3829 Medical diagnostic systems, nuclear

**(G-8288)**
**U O P EQUITEC SERVICES INC**
25 E Algonquin Rd (60016-6100)
PHONE..................847 391-2000
Carlos Guimaraes, *President*
Graeme Donald, *President*
George Davidson, *Treasurer*
Shouvik Dutta, *Info Tech Mgr*
Steven Philoon, *Info Tech Mgr*
EMP: 2000
SALES (est): 148.7MM
SALES (corp-wide): 39.3B **Publicly Held**
SIC: 3533 Oil & gas field machinery
HQ: Universal Oil Products Company
2466 E 22nd St
Tulsa OK

**(G-8289)**
**U OP**
25 E Algonquin Rd (60016-6100)
PHONE..................847 391-2000
Graeme Donald, *President*
▲ EMP: 8

SALES (est): 1.3MM
SALES (corp-wide): 39.3B **Publicly Held**
WEB: www.uop.com
SIC: 2819 8711 Catalysts, chemical; engineering services; chemical engineering
HQ: Uop Llc
25 E Algonquin Rd
Des Plaines IL 60016
847 391-2000

**(G-8290)**
**UNITED LITHOGRAPH INC**
1670 S River Rd (60018-2290)
PHONE..................847 803-1700
Michael Adams, *President*
EMP: 4
SALES (est): 440.3K **Privately Held**
SIC: 2752 7334 2791 2789 Commercial printing, lithographic; photocopying & duplicating services; typesetting; bookbinding & related work

**(G-8291)**
**UNITED WIRE CRAFT INC**
Also Called: United Displaycraft
333 E Touhy Ave (60018-2605)
PHONE..................847 375-3800
Fax: 847 375-3801
Rich Carrigan, *President*
Tony Feudner, *COO*
James Black, *Vice Pres*
Jeffrey Ginger, *Vice Pres*
Gloria Robles, *Project Mgr*
◆ EMP: 225 EST: 1953
SQ FT: 214,000
SALES (est): 57.8MM **Privately Held**
WEB: www.uniteddisplaycraft.com
SIC: 3993 2542 Signs & advertising specialties; partitions & fixtures, except wood

**(G-8292)**
**UOP LLC**
Also Called: Honeywell UOP
50 E Algonquin Rd (60016-6102)
PHONE..................303 791-0311
Fax: 847 391-3330
Gary Lundeen, *Manager*
EMP: 75 EST: 1997
SALES (est): 12.2MM **Privately Held**
SIC: 3724 Aircraft engines & engine parts

**(G-8293)**
**UOP LLC**
175 W Oakton St (60018-1834)
PHONE..................847 391-2000
William J Blasko, *Engineer*
Michael Lunda, *Director*
E Wozniak, *Director*
Megan Everett, *Administration*
EMP: 6
SALES (corp-wide): 39.3B **Publicly Held**
WEB: www.uop.com
SIC: 3826 3823 3621 Analytical instruments; industrial instrmnts msrmnt display/control process variable; motors & generators
HQ: Uop Llc
25 E Algonquin Rd
Des Plaines IL 60016
847 391-2000

**(G-8294)**
**UOP LLC**
201 W Oakton St Ste 2 (60018-1855)
PHONE..................847 391-2540
EMP: 164
SALES (corp-wide): 39.3B **Publicly Held**
SIC: 2819 Catalysts, chemical
HQ: Uop Llc
25 E Algonquin Rd
Des Plaines IL 60016
847 391-2000

**(G-8295)**
**USP HOLDINGS INC**
6250 N Rver Rd Ste 10100 (60018)
PHONE..................847 604-6100
John A Hatherly, *Managing Prtnr*
Frank G Hayes, *Partner*
Terry M Theodore, *Partner*
Ted Cwynar, *Credit Staff*
EMP: 1101 EST: 2012
SALES (est): 75.1MM **Privately Held**
SIC: 3321 3491 Cast iron pipe & fittings; industrial valves

# GEOGRAPHIC SECTION

**(G-8296)**
**V FORMUSA CO**
Also Called: Marconi
2150 Oxford Rd (60018-1920)
**PHONE**..................224 938-9360
**Fax:** 312 421-1286
Robert Johnson, *President*
Pasquale Giampietro, *Mktg Dir*
Suzanne Johnson, *Admin Sec*
▲ **EMP:** 10 **EST:** 1898
**SQ FT:** 25,000
**SALES (est):** 1.1MM **Privately Held**
**WEB:** www.marconi-foods.com
**SIC:** 0723 5141 2079 2035 Vegetable packing services; groceries, general line; edible fats & oils; pickles, sauces & salad dressings; canned fruits & specialties; cheese, natural & processed

**(G-8297)**
**VECTOR MOLD & TOOL INC**
412 Norman Ct (60016-2443)
**PHONE**..................847 437-0110
Frank Mezzano, *President*
**EMP:** 6
**SQ FT:** 3,500
**SALES (est):** 772.3K **Privately Held**
**SIC:** 3089 3544 Injection molding of plastics; special dies, tools, jigs & fixtures

**(G-8298)**
**VERITIV OPERATING COMPANY**
Also Called: Bulkley Dunton Publishing
100 E Oakton St (60018-1956)
**PHONE**..................800 347-9279
**EMP:** 5
**SALES (corp-wide):** 8.3B **Publicly Held**
**SIC:** 2741 Misc Publishing
**HQ:** Veritiv Operating Company
1000 Abernathy Rd
Atlanta GA 30328
770 391-8200

**(G-8299)**
**VISIONARY SOLUTIONS INC**
129 Rawls Rd (60018-1328)
**PHONE**..................847 296-9615
**Fax:** 847 296-9620
Marty Finzer, *Mng Member*
**EMP:** 1
**SALES (est):** 250K **Privately Held**
**SIC:** 5084 3999 Conveyor systems; manufacturing industries

**(G-8300)**
**VITEL INDUSTRIES INC**
1026 North Ave Ste A (60016-3331)
**PHONE**..................847 299-9750
**Fax:** 847 299-7689
John Adams, *President*
Robert Adams, *Vice Pres*
▲ **EMP:** 8
**SALES (est):** 550K **Privately Held**
**SIC:** 2211 5131 Apparel & outerwear fabrics, cotton; upholstery fabrics, woven

**(G-8301)**
**W DIAMOND GROUP CORPORATION (PA)**
Also Called: Hart Schaffner & Marx
1680 E Touhy Ave (60018-3607)
**PHONE**..................646 647-2791
Doug Williams, *CEO*
Kenneth Ragland, *COO*
Loretta Osowski, *Human Res Mgr*
▲ **EMP:** 590
**SQ FT:** 240,000
**SALES (est):** 179.2MM **Privately Held**
**SIC:** 2326 5611 Men's & boys' work clothing; men's & boys' clothing stores

**(G-8302)**
**WESLEY-JESSEN CORPORATION DEL**
333 Howard Ave (60018-1907)
**PHONE**..................847 294-3000
**Fax:** 847 294-3052
Glen Bradley, *President*
Lawrence L Chapoy, *Vice Pres*
Jim McAloon, *Technical Mgr*
Edward Kelly, *CFO*
Kevin Ryan, *Manager*
**EMP:** 1000 **EST:** 1995
**SQ FT:** 340,000
**SALES (est):** 90.1MM
**SALES (corp-wide):** 48.5B **Privately Held**
**WEB:** www.w-j.com
**SIC:** 3851 Contact lenses
**HQ:** Alcon Laboratories, Inc.
6201 South Fwy
Fort Worth TX 76134
817 293-0450

**(G-8303)**
**WEST AGRO INC**
1855 S Mount Prospect Rd (60018-1805)
**PHONE**..................847 298-5505
Terry Mitchell, *Vice Pres*
Larry Mitsch, *Mfg Staff*
Larry Mitseh, *Manager*
Laura Bercovitz, *Manager*
Else Hamayan, *Exec Dir*
**EMP:** 43
**SQ FT:** 100,000
**SALES (corp-wide):** 6.4B **Privately Held**
**WEB:** www.westagro.com
**SIC:** 2879 2842 Agricultural chemicals; specialty cleaning, polishes & sanitation goods
**HQ:** West Agro, Inc.
11100 N Congress Ave
Kansas City MO 64153
816 891-1600

**(G-8304)**
**WHEATON PLASTIC PRODUCTS**
1731 S Mount Prospect Rd (60018-1803)
**PHONE**..................847 298-5626
**Fax:** 847 827-0773
Tom Clark, *Vice Pres*
**EMP:** 4 **EST:** 2002
**SALES (est):** 363.6K **Privately Held**
**SIC:** 3085 Plastics bottles

**(G-8305)**
**WHOLESOME HARVEST BAKING LLC (DH)**
1011 E Touhy Ave Ste 500 (60018-5829)
**PHONE**..................800 550-6810
Dan Curtin, *President*
Orzse Hodi, *VP Mktg*
Emily Liang, *Mktg Dir*
Marsha Brant, *Training Dir*
▼ **EMP:** 50 **EST:** 1961
**SALES (est):** 1.5B
**SALES (corp-wide):** 12.3B **Privately Held**
**WEB:** www.mapleleaffoodsusa.com
**SIC:** 2051 Bagels, fresh or frozen
**HQ:** Canada Bread Company, Limited
10 Four Seasons Pl Suite 1200
Etobicoke ON M9B 6
416 622-2040

**(G-8306)**
**WYKA LLC**
Also Called: Edison Graphics
1515 S Mount Prospect Rd (60018-1324)
**PHONE**..................847 298-0740
**Fax:** 847 298-9507
Steve Breitenstein, *Mng Member*
Nicole Chic, *Manager*
Larae J Breitenstein,
Kenneth Wyka,
Richard J Wyka,
**EMP:** 15 **EST:** 1951
**SQ FT:** 22,000
**SALES (est):** 2.9MM **Privately Held**
**SIC:** 2752 2759 Commercial printing, offset; calendars: printing

**(G-8307)**
**YASKAWA AMERICA INC**
1297 E Walnut Ave (60016-6506)
**PHONE**..................847 887-7909
Terry Willett, *Principal*
Doug D Schenher, *Vice Pres*
**EMP:** 250
**SALES (corp-wide):** 3.4B **Privately Held**
**WEB:** www.methodsmachine.com
**SIC:** 3621 5063 Motors, electric; motors, electric
**HQ:** Yaskawa America, Inc.
2121 Norman Dr
Waukegan IL 60085
847 887-7000

**(G-8308)**
**ZIMMERMAN ENTERPRISES INC (PA)**
Also Called: Best Bus Sales
1216 Rand Rd (60016-3403)
**PHONE**..................847 297-3177
Robert L Zimmerman, *President*
Karen Cameron, *Info Tech Mgr*
**EMP:** 12
**SQ FT:** 43,000
**SALES (est):** 2.2MM **Privately Held**
**WEB:** www.bestbussales.com
**SIC:** 3993 4111 7538 Signs & advertising specialties; bus transportation; general automotive repair shops

## Detroit
### Pike County

**(G-8309)**
**DYNO NOBEL INC**
1353 W Washington St (62363-9549)
P.O. Box 349, Pittsfield (62363-0349)
**PHONE**..................217 285-5531
Brian Jockisch, *Branch Mgr*
**EMP:** 28
**SALES (corp-wide):** 2.5B **Privately Held**
**SIC:** 2892 Explosives
**HQ:** Dyno Nobel Inc.
2795 E Cottonwood Pkwy # 500
Salt Lake City UT 84121
801 364-4800

## Dewey
### Champaign County

**(G-8310)**
**DATA COMM FOR BUSINESS INC (PA)**
2949 County Road 1000 E (61840-9639)
P.O. Box 6329, Champaign (61826-6329)
**PHONE**..................217 897-1741
**Fax:** 217 897-1331
Russell Straayer, *President*
Michael Gadel, *Vice Pres*
John McCain, *Sales Mgr*
Dan Smith, *Manager*
Mark Schank, *Software Dev*
**EMP:** 18
**SQ FT:** 80,000
**SALES (est):** 4.2MM **Privately Held**
**WEB:** www.dcbnet.com
**SIC:** 3669 5065 Intercommunication systems, electric; communication equipment

**(G-8311)**
**PRICE MACHINE INC**
1021 County Road 2850 N (61840-9637)
**PHONE**..................217 892-8958
Kenny Price, *President*
**EMP:** 3
**SQ FT:** 2,400
**SALES (est):** 434.4K **Privately Held**
**SIC:** 3599 Machine & other job shop work

## Dieterich
### Effingham County

**(G-8312)**
**C S C INC**
100 Zumbahlen Ave Ste C (62424-1044)
**PHONE**..................217 925-5908
Rick Seifert, *Principal*
▲ **EMP:** 30
**SALES (est):** 2.1MM **Privately Held**
**SIC:** 1751 2434 Cabinet & finish carpentry; wood kitchen cabinets

**(G-8313)**
**HIGGS WELDING LLC**
101 Zumbahlen Ave (62424-1053)
**PHONE**..................217 925-5999
**Fax:** 217 925-5997
Troy Higgs, *Partner*
Brett Higgs, *Partner*
Jodi Nuxoll, *Office Mgr*
**EMP:** 8
**SALES (est):** 1MM **Privately Held**
**SIC:** 7692 Welding repair

**(G-8314)**
**SEPTIC SOLUTIONS INC**
314 W Center St (62424-1048)
**PHONE**..................217 925-5992
Jesse James, *President*
Casey James, *Sales Staff*
Jodi Mulvey, *Marketing Staff*
Jodi James, *Manager*
◆ **EMP:** 9
**SALES (est):** 4.2MM **Privately Held**
**WEB:** www.septicsolutions.net
**SIC:** 5091 5039 3949 Exercise equipment; septic tanks; exercise equipment

**(G-8315)**
**SRMD SOLUTIONS LLC**
202 W Center St (62424-1012)
**PHONE**..................217 925-5773
Paul Romack, *CEO*
Brad Schumacher, *COO*
**EMP:** 7
**SQ FT:** 4,000
**SALES (est):** 367K **Privately Held**
**SIC:** 3559 7373 Electronic component making machinery; office computer automation systems integration

## Divernon
### Sangamon County

**(G-8316)**
**LEONARD EMERSON**
Also Called: Emerson Press
103 W Dodds St (62530-2301)
P.O. Box 437 (62530-0437)
**PHONE**..................217 628-3441
**Fax:** 217 628-3606
Leonard Emerson, *Owner*
**EMP:** 6
**SQ FT:** 3,000
**SALES (est):** 636.5K **Privately Held**
**WEB:** www.emersonpress.com
**SIC:** 2752 2791 2789 Commercial printing, offset; typesetting; bookbinding & related work

## Dix
### Jefferson County

**(G-8317)**
**BOYD SAWMILL**
Also Called: Garren Sawmill & Farm
19775 N Boyd Ln (62830-3406)
**PHONE**..................618 735-2056
Wendall Klockenga, *President*
**EMP:** 6
**SALES:** 150K **Privately Held**
**SIC:** 0191 2421 2426 General farms, primarily crop; sawmills & planing mills, general; hardwood dimension & flooring mills

**(G-8318)**
**ROYAL FIBERGLASS POOLS INC**
Also Called: The Pool Center
312 Duncan Ln (62830-1467)
**PHONE**..................618 266-7089
**Fax:** 618 266-7658
Clifford Hebert, *President*
Rebecca Hebert, *Vice Pres*
**EMP:** 60
**SQ FT:** 5,000
**SALES (est):** 3.5MM **Privately Held**
**WEB:** www.royalfiberglasspools.com
**SIC:** 3949 1799 Swimming pools, except plastic; swimming pool construction

## Dixmoor
### Cook County

**(G-8319)**
**CHICAGO MAGNESIUM**
14050 Wood St (60426-1157)
**PHONE**..................708 926-9531
**EMP:** 3

**Dixmoor - Cook County (G-8320)**

SALES (est): 197.6K **Privately Held**
SIC: 3356 Magnesium

**(G-8320)**
**ORIENT MACHINING & WELDING INC**
14501 Wood St Ste A (60426-1617)
PHONE...............................708 371-3500
Fax: 708 371-0100
Andrzej Plewa, *President*
Walter Koszarek, *Vice Pres*
EMP: 22
SQ FT: 100,000
SALES (est): 9.6MM **Privately Held**
WEB: www.orientmachine.com
SIC: 3599 3499 7692 Machine shop, jobbing & repair; welding tips, heat resistant: metal; welding repair

## Dixon
### Lee County

**(G-8321)**
**AAA GALVANIZING - JOLIET INC**
Also Called: AAA Galvanizing of Dixon
310 E Progress Dr (61021-9607)
PHONE...............................815 284-5001
Fax: 815 284-5002
Mike Echebarria, *Senior VP*
Mike Echebarria, *Branch Mgr*
EMP: 45
SALES (corp-wide): 858.9MM **Publicly Held**
SIC: 3479 3441 Hot dip coating of metals or formed products; fabricated structural metal
HQ: Aaa Galvanizing - Joliet, Inc.
625 Mills Rd
Joliet IL 60433
815 723-5000

**(G-8322)**
**ALLIED-LOCKE INDUSTRIES INC**
1020 Subic Rd (61021-8358)
PHONE...............................800 435-7752
William Crowson, *Branch Mgr*
EMP: 50
SALES (corp-wide): 73.8MM **Privately Held**
SIC: 3568 Power transmission equipment
PA: Allied-Locke Industries, Incorporated
1088 Corregidor Rd
Dixon IL 61021
815 288-1471

**(G-8323)**
**BONNELL INDUSTRIES INC**
1385 Franklin Grove Rd (61021-9150)
PHONE...............................815 284-3819
Fax: 815 284-8815
Joseph W Bonnell, *President*
Cindy Bonnell, *Corp Secy*
Phillip Megli, *Assistant VP*
Paul Anderson, *Plant Mgr*
Marilyn Foster, *Office Mgr*
EMP: 87
SQ FT: 37,000
SALES: 13MM **Privately Held**
WEB: www.bonnellindustries.com
SIC: 3531 5013 5012 Road construction & maintenance machinery; truck parts & accessories; truck bodies

**(G-8324)**
**BORGWARNER INC**
Also Called: Borg-Warner Emissions Systems
1350 Franklin Grove Rd (61021-9174)
PHONE...............................815 288-1462
Dan Paturra, *Plant Mgr*
Ray L Jones, *Materials Mgr*
Jamie Elliott, *Purch Agent*
Jeff Regllin, *Purchasing*
Joe Struhs, *Sales/Mktg Mgr*
EMP: 250
SQ FT: 100,000
SALES (corp-wide): 9B **Publicly Held**
SIC: 3465 3592 3714 Automotive stampings; carburetors; fuel systems & parts, motor vehicle
PA: Borgwarner Inc.
3850 Hamlin Rd
Auburn Hills MI 48326
248 754-9200

**(G-8325)**
**BORGWARNER INC**
Also Called: Borgwarner Emissions Systems
1350 Franklin Grove Rd (61021-9174)
PHONE...............................815 288-1462
Fax: 815 288-6940
James R Verrier, *CEO*
Phyllis Bonanno, *President*
Ray Jones, *Materials Mgr*
Jennifer Adcock, *Purch Mgr*
Matthew Guthrie, *QC Mgr*
▲ EMP: 2 EST: 2000
SALES (est): 326K **Privately Held**
SIC: 3714 Motor vehicle parts & accessories; transmission housings or parts, motor vehicle

**(G-8326)**
**COILCRAFT INCORPORATED**
924 Jaybee Ave (61021)
P.O. Box 525 (61021-0525)
PHONE...............................815 288-7051
Scott Helfrich, *Branch Mgr*
EMP: 100
SALES (corp-wide): 476.5K **Privately Held**
SIC: 3677 Coil windings, electronic; electronic transformers; filtration devices, electronic
PA: Coilcraft, Incorporated
1102 Silver Lake Rd
Cary IL 60013
847 639-2361

**(G-8327)**
**CUSTOM MACHINE INC**
895 Shop Rd (61021-3281)
PHONE...............................815 284-3820
Fax: 815 284-9164
Gary Haenitsch, *President*
William Haenitsch, *Vice Pres*
EMP: 8 EST: 1976
SQ FT: 8,500
SALES: 680K **Privately Held**
SIC: 3599 Machine shop, jobbing & repair

**(G-8328)**
**DIXON DIRECT LLC**
1226 W 7th St (61021-3412)
PHONE...............................815 284-2211
Peter Lennox, *CEO*
Richard Boysen, *General Mgr*
EMP: 200
SALES (est): 79.8MM
SALES (corp-wide): 771.2K **Privately Held**
WEB: www.dixondirect.com
SIC: 2752 Commercial printing, offset
HQ: Ileos Beauty Usa Corp.
276 5th Ave Rm 1104
New York NY 10001
212 319-6130

**(G-8329)**
**DONALDSON COMPANY INC**
815 W Progress Dr (61021-9655)
PHONE...............................815 288-3374
Fax: 815 288-5079
Marty Kelnhofer, *QC Dir*
Jeff Carson, *Branch Mgr*
EMP: 50
SALES (corp-wide): 2.2B **Publicly Held**
WEB: www.donaldson.com
SIC: 3564 3599 Purification & dust collection equipment; air intake filters, internal combustion engine, except auto
PA: Donaldson Company, Inc.
1400 W 94th St
Minneapolis MN 55431
952 887-3131

**(G-8330)**
**DOWNTOWN SPORTS**
1202 S Galena Ave (61021-3844)
PHONE...............................815 284-2255
Fax: 815 285-1009
Merlin Clausen, *Owner*
EMP: 3
SQ FT: 3,400
SALES: 327K **Privately Held**
SIC: 2395 Embroidery products, except schiffli machine

**(G-8331)**
**FLEX-O-GLASS INC**
1200 Warp Rd (61021-9166)
PHONE...............................815 288-1424
Fax: 815 288-1427
Garry Ofarrell, *Plant Mgr*
Harold G Warp, *Branch Mgr*
G Warp, *Manager*
EMP: 50
SALES (corp-wide): 42.1MM **Privately Held**
WEB: www.flexoglass.com
SIC: 3081 3082 2821 2671 Plastic film & sheet; unsupported plastics profile shapes; plastics materials & resins; packaging paper & plastics film, coated & laminated
PA: Flex-O-Glass, Inc.
4647 W Augusta Blvd Ste 1
Chicago IL 60651
773 261-5200

**(G-8332)**
**FRANKLIN MAINTENANCE**
1597 Nachusa Rd (61021-8804)
PHONE...............................815 284-6806
Larry Crawford, *Owner*
Maggie Crawford, *Co-Owner*
EMP: 3
SALES (est): 118.9K **Privately Held**
SIC: 7692 Cracked casting repair

**(G-8333)**
**GRANITEWORKS**
1220 S Galena Ave (61021-3844)
PHONE...............................815 288-3350
Fax: 815 288-3479
Dan Johns, *Principal*
EMP: 2
SALES (est): 224.4K **Privately Held**
SIC: 2541 Counter & sink tops

**(G-8334)**
**JOHN THOMAS INC**
Also Called: John Thomas Company
1560 Lovett Dr (61021-9623)
PHONE...............................815 288-2343
John Dvorak, *President*
Kole Weaver, *CFO*
EMP: 30
SQ FT: 18,000
SALES: 6.5MM **Privately Held**
WEB: www.crashcushions.com
SIC: 5084 3669 7359 3499 Safety equipment; traffic signals, electric; work zone traffic equipment (flags, cones, barrels, etc.); automobile seat frames, metal; automotive parts, plastic

**(G-8335)**
**JOHNSON CONTROLS INC**
629 N Galena Ave Ste 210 (61021-1664)
PHONE...............................815 288-3859
Karen Stencel, *Purchasing*
William Perry, *Manager*
Ralph Moore, *Director*
Al Schmidt, *Director*
Mark Stencel, *Director*
EMP: 200
SALES (corp-wide): 36.8B **Privately Held**
SIC: 2531 Seats, automobile
PA: Johnson Controls, Inc.
5757 N Green Bay Ave
Milwaukee WI 53209
414 524-1200

**(G-8336)**
**KREIDER SERVICES INCORPORATED (PA)**
Also Called: Hilltop Group Home
500 Anchor Rd (61021-8854)
P.O. Box 366 (61021-0366)
PHONE...............................815 288-6691
Fax: 815 288-1636
Arlan L McClain, *CEO*
Michelle Hamilton, *Facilities Dir*
Paul Roe, *Prdtn Mgr*
Edward Roller, *CFO*
Tom Bowen, *Human Res Mgr*
EMP: 70 EST: 1952
SQ FT: 60,000
SALES (est): 17.8MM **Privately Held**
SIC: 8331 8361 2875 4953 Sheltered workshop; residential care; fertilizers, mixing only; recycling, waste materials

**(G-8337)**
**NEISEWANDER ENTERPRISES INC (PA)**
Also Called: Raynor Garage Door
1101 E River Rd (61021-3252)
P.O. Box 448 (61021-0448)
PHONE...............................815 288-1431
Ray H Neisewander III, *President*
Patrick Kennedy, *Director*
EMP: 1000
SQ FT: 600,000
SALES (est): 269.9MM **Privately Held**
WEB: www.raynorgaragedoor.com
SIC: 3442 2431 3429 Garage doors, overhead: metal; garage doors, overhead: wood; manufactured hardware (general)

**(G-8338)**
**OSMER WOODWORKING INC**
406 E Bradshaw St (61021-1637)
PHONE...............................815 973-5809
Adam Osmer, *President*
EMP: 2
SALES (est): 219.5K **Privately Held**
SIC: 2431 8711 1799 1521 Millwork; building construction consultant; home/office interiors finishing, furnishing & remodeling; kitchen & bathroom remodeling; single-family home remodeling, additions & repairs; general remodeling, single-family houses;

**(G-8339)**
**PLEWS INC (PA)**
Also Called: Plews Edelmann
1550 Franklin Grove Rd (61021-9110)
PHONE...............................815 288-3344
Brett Mueller, *President*
Stephen Venghaus, *President*
Bob Sawyer, *Engineer*
David Babics, *Sls & Mktg Exec*
Tami Borum, *CFO*
◆ EMP: 175
SQ FT: 350,000
SALES (est): 47.5MM **Privately Held**
SIC: 3714 3429 3492 Motor vehicle parts & accessories; manufactured hardware (general); fluid power valves & hose fittings

**(G-8340)**
**QUALITY READY MIX CONCRETE CO**
1569 Franklin Grove Rd (61021-9110)
P.O. Box 321 (61021-0321)
PHONE...............................815 288-6416
Jason Dykema, *Manager*
EMP: 6
SALES (corp-wide): 2.9MM **Privately Held**
SIC: 3273 Ready-mixed concrete
PA: Quality Ready Mix Concrete Co.
14849 Lyndon Rd
Morrison IL 61270
815 772-7181

**(G-8341)**
**RAYNOR MFG CO (HQ)**
Also Called: Raynor Garage Doors
1101 E River Rd (61021-3277)
P.O. Box 448 (61021-0448)
PHONE...............................815 288-1431
Fax: 800 323-7896
Ray N Heisewander III, *President*
Marianna Raynor, *COO*
Dave Babics, *Engineer*
Bob Spratt, *Engineer*
Joe Theby, *VP Human Res*
◆ EMP: 800
SQ FT: 900,000
SALES (est): 269.9MM **Privately Held**
WEB: www.raynor.com
SIC: 3442 7011 3699 2431 Garage doors, overhead: metal; hotels; electrical equipment & supplies; millwork
PA: Neisewander Enterprises Inc.
1101 E River Rd
Dixon IL 61021
815 288-1431

**(G-8342)**
**RAYNOR MFG CO**
Also Called: Raynor Garage Doors
1101 E River Rd (61021-3277)
PHONE...............................815 288-1431

# GEOGRAPHIC SECTION

Dolton - Cook County (G-8368)

Steve Langford, *Manager*
**EMP:** 62
**SALES (corp-wide):** 269.9MM **Privately Held**
**WEB:** www.raynor.com
**SIC:** 3442 Garage doors, overhead: metal
**HQ:** Raynor Mfg. Co.
1101 E River Rd
Dixon IL 61021
815 288-1431

*(G-8343)*
### RENNER QUARRIES LTD (PA)
1700 S Galena Ave Ste 116 (61021-9695)
**PHONE**.................................815 288-6699
Robert Egert, *President*
Gary Egert, *Corp Secy*
Bob Egert, *VP Sales*
Marty Egert, *Office Mgr*
**EMP:** 2
**SQ FT:** 500
**SALES:** 1MM **Privately Held**
**SIC:** 1422 Limestones, ground

*(G-8344)*
### ROCK RIVER READY MIX INC (PA)
2320 S Galena Ave (61021-9608)
P.O. Box 384 (61021-0384)
**PHONE**.................................815 288-2260
Adel A Mobarak, *President*
Mary Frances Mobarak, *Corp Secy*
George Mobarak, *Vice Pres*
Donna Tobey, *Plant Mgr*
Scott Mills, *Admin Sec*
**EMP:** 7
**SQ FT:** 800
**SALES (est):** 6.7MM **Privately Held**
**SIC:** 1442 5032 Construction sand mining; gravel mining; concrete mixtures

*(G-8345)*
### ROCK RIVER READY MIX INC
1905 Mound Hill Rd (61021-9735)
P.O. Box 384 (61021-0384)
**PHONE**.................................815 625-1139
**Fax:** 815 625-8117
Donna Rodriguez, *Manager*
**EMP:** 9
**SALES (corp-wide):** 6.7MM **Privately Held**
**SIC:** 3273 Ready-mixed concrete
**PA:** Rock River Ready Mix, Inc.
2320 S Galena Ave
Dixon IL 61021
815 288-2260

*(G-8346)*
### ROCK RIVER READY-MIX
2320 S Galena Ave (61021-9608)
P.O. Box 384 (61021-0384)
**PHONE**.................................815 288-2269
Adel A Mobarak, *President*
Mary F Mobarak, *Corp Secy*
George Mobarak, *Vice Pres*
J Scott Mills, *Asst Sec*
**EMP:** 30
**SQ FT:** 800
**SALES (est):** 2.1MM
**SALES (corp-wide):** 6.7MM **Privately Held**
**SIC:** 3273 5032 Ready-mixed concrete; gravel; sand, construction
**PA:** Rock River Ready Mix, Inc.
2320 S Galena Ave
Dixon IL 61021
815 288-2260

*(G-8347)*
### SAUK VALLEY PRINTING
113 S Peoria Ave Ste 1 (61021-2905)
**PHONE**.................................815 284-2222
Bob Clardie, *Owner*
**EMP:** 5
**SALES (est):** 252.6K **Privately Held**
**SIC:** 2759 Commercial printing

*(G-8348)*
### SCHEFFLER CUSTOM WOODWORKING
Also Called: Freight House Kit & Bath Str
925 Depot Ave (61021-3548)
**PHONE**.................................815 284-6564
Jerry Scheffler, *President*
Matthew J Scheffler, *Vice Pres*
**EMP:** 4

**SALES (est):** 540K **Privately Held**
**SIC:** 1521 5712 2431 Single-family housing construction; cabinet work, custom; millwork

*(G-8349)*
### SCHRADER-BRIDGEPORT INTL INC
Also Called: Syracuse Guage
1550 Franklin Grove Rd (61021-9110)
**PHONE**.................................815 288-3344
Kelly Mosher, *Principal*
Dave Berg, *Vice Pres*
Vicki Hinson, *Purch Agent*
Benjamin Rieley, *Engineer*
Thomas Nelson, *Manager*
**EMP:** 4
**SALES (corp-wide):** 2.9B **Privately Held**
**WEB:** www.syracusegauge.com
**SIC:** 3491 3823 Industrial valves; industrial instrmnts msrmnt display/control process variable
**HQ:** Schrader-Bridgeport International Inc.
205 Frazier Rd
Altavista VA 24517
434 369-4741

*(G-8350)*
### SEWER EQUIPMENT CO AMERICA
Also Called: Sewer Equipment of Canada
1590 Dutch Rd (61021-8624)
**PHONE**.................................815 835-5566
**Fax:** 847 729-3547
Daniel J O'Brien, *President*
Nathan Berk, *General Mgr*
John Wichmann, *Exec VP*
Joe Gennaro, *Prdtn Mgr*
Stanley Stuart, *Engineer*
**EMP:** 120
**SQ FT:** 6,000
**SALES (est):** 44MM **Privately Held**
**WEB:** www.sewerequip.com
**SIC:** 3589 Sewer cleaning equipment, power

*(G-8351)*
### SGS REFRIGERATION INC
827 W Progress Dr (61021-9609)
**PHONE**.................................815 284-2700
Peter Spellar, *President*
Ray Schmidt, *VP Opers*
Scott Rozanas, *CFO*
Don Chason, *Sales Staff*
Edward Schinner, *Admin Sec*
**EMP:** 22 **EST:** 2011
**SQ FT:** 35,000
**SALES (est):** 6.9MM **Privately Held**
**SIC:** 3585 Refrigeration & heating equipment

*(G-8352)*
### SOUTHFIELD CORPORATION
Also Called: Dixon-Marquette Cement
1914 White Oak Ln (61021-9089)
P.O. Box 468 (61021-0468)
**PHONE**.................................815 284-3357
**Fax:** 815 284-3314
Mark Hill, *Plant Mgr*
Matt Clarage, *Prdtn Mgr*
Larry Setchell, *Opers-Prdtn-Mfg*
Tom Powers, *Purch Mgr*
Jim Clark, *QC Dir*
**EMP:** 150
**SALES (corp-wide):** 273.9MM **Privately Held**
**WEB:** www.prairiegroup.com
**SIC:** 3273 3241 Ready-mixed concrete; cement, hydraulic
**PA:** Southfield Corporation
8995 W 95th St
Palos Hills IL 60465
708 344-1000

*(G-8353)*
### SPECTRUM BRANDS INC
200 E Corporate Dr (61021-9301)
**PHONE**.................................815 285-6500
Steve Randorfer, *Branch Mgr*
**EMP:** 8
**SALES (corp-wide):** 5.2B **Publicly Held**
**SIC:** 3691 Alkaline cell storage batteries
**HQ:** Spectrum Brands, Inc.
3001 Deming Way
Middleton WI 53562
608 275-3340

*(G-8354)*
### ST MARYS CEMENT INC (US)
1914 White Oak Ln (61021-9089)
P.O. Box 468 (61021-0468)
**PHONE**.................................313 842-4600
Bob Unterweger, *Plant Mgr*
Mike Kivlin, *Controller*
Mark Hill, *Manager*
**EMP:** 50 **Privately Held**
**SIC:** 3241 Cement, hydraulic
**HQ:** St. Marys Cement Inc. (U.S.)
9333 Dearborn St
Detroit MI 48209
313 842-4600

*(G-8355)*
### STERLING-ROCK FALLS READY MIX
1905 Mound Hill Rd (61021-9735)
P.O. Box 384 (61021-0384)
**PHONE**.................................815 288-3135
**Fax:** 815 652-8117
Adel Mobarak, *President*
Mary Francis Mobarak, *Corp Secy*
George Mobarak, *Vice Pres*
**EMP:** 12
**SQ FT:** 3,600
**SALES:** 1.2MM **Privately Held**
**SIC:** 3273 Ready-mixed concrete

*(G-8356)*
### TLM ENTERPRISES INC
Also Called: Creative Printing
213 W 1st St (61021-3027)
**PHONE**.................................815 284-5040
Tracey L Montgomery, *President*
Toni L Montgomery, *Vice Pres*
**EMP:** 2
**SQ FT:** 2,000
**SALES (est):** 281K **Privately Held**
**SIC:** 2752 7699 2791 Commercial printing, offset; printing trades machinery & equipment repair; typesetting

*(G-8357)*
### UPM RAFLATAC INC
101 E Corporate Dr (61021-9306)
**PHONE**.................................815 285-6100
Jan-Erik Forsstrom, *Branch Mgr*
**EMP:** 118
**SALES (corp-wide):** 10.3B **Privately Held**
**SIC:** 2672 3083 Coated & laminated paper; laminated plastics plate & sheet
**HQ:** Upm Raflatac, Inc.
400 Broadpointe Dr
Mills River NC 28759
828 651-4800

*(G-8358)*
### UZHAVOOR FUELS INC
707 N Galena Ave (61021-1509)
**PHONE**.................................630 401-6173
Joy Ashish, *Principal*
**EMP:** 4
**SALES (est):** 215.3K **Privately Held**
**SIC:** 2869 Fuels

*(G-8359)*
### WORLD GRANITE INC
1220 S Galena Ave (61021-3844)
**PHONE**.................................815 288-3350
Dan Johns, *President*
**EMP:** 2
**SALES:** 400K **Privately Held**
**SIC:** 3281 Cut stone & stone products

*(G-8360)*
### ZIGLERS MCH & MET WORKS INC
Also Called: Ziglers Machine and Met Works
972 Mile Rd (61021-9016)
**PHONE**.................................815 652-7518
John Zigler, *President*
Kathy Zigler, *Vice Pres*
**EMP:** 2
**SALES (est):** 500K **Privately Held**
**SIC:** 3449 7692 Miscellaneous metalwork; welding repair

*(G-8361)*
### ZUMA CORPORATION
Also Called: M L Products
1335 Chicago Ave (61021-3905)
**PHONE**.................................815 288-7269
Mitch Atkinson, *President*

**EMP:** 2
**SALES (est):** 465.3K **Privately Held**
**SIC:** 5082 3524 Road construction equipment; road construction & maintenance machinery; lawn & garden equipment

## Dolton
*Cook County*

*(G-8362)*
### ABUNDANT LIVING CHRISTIAN CTR
14540 Lincoln Ave (60419-1810)
**PHONE**.................................708 896-6181
**EMP:** 8
**SALES (est):** 583K **Privately Held**
**SIC:** 2531 Mfg Public Building Furniture

*(G-8363)*
### ARDAGH GLASS INC
13850 Cottage Grove Ave (60419-1052)
**PHONE**.................................708 849-4010
Jeremy Holiness, *Maint Spvr*
Vicky Mowers, *Financial Exec*
Rich Krooswyk, *Personnel*
Vrian Houger, *Manager*
**EMP:** 100 **Privately Held**
**WEB:** www.sgcontainers.com
**SIC:** 3221 Glass containers
**HQ:** Ardagh Glass Inc.
10194 Crosspoint Blvd
Indianapolis IN 46256

*(G-8364)*
### B A P ENTERPRISES INC
14235 Cottage Grove Ave (60419-1354)
P.O. Box 610 (60419-0610)
**PHONE**.................................708 849-0900
**Fax:** 708 849-0974
Bruce A Prokop, *President*
Debbie Prokop, *Corp Secy*
Louis A Prokop, *Vice Pres*
**EMP:** 4
**SQ FT:** 3,100
**SALES:** 1MM **Privately Held**
**SIC:** 1711 3599 Heating & air conditioning contractors; machine & other job shop work; machine shop, jobbing & repair

*(G-8365)*
### BALL FOSTER GLASS CONTAINER
13850 Cottage Grove Ave (60419-1052)
**PHONE**.................................708 849-1500
Milt Penenger, *Principal*
**EMP:** 4 **EST:** 1980
**SALES (est):** 233.9K **Privately Held**
**SIC:** 3221 Glass containers

*(G-8366)*
### BELBOZ CORP
742 Evans Ct (60419-2115)
**PHONE**.................................708 856-6099
Kiana Belcher, *President*
**EMP:** 6
**SQ FT:** 200
**SALES:** 62K **Privately Held**
**SIC:** 6531 2759 Real estate managers; promotional printing

*(G-8367)*
### CALUMET BRASS FOUNDRY INC
14610 Lakeside Ave (60419-2023)
P.O. Box 158 (60419-0158)
**PHONE**.................................708 849-3040
**Fax:** 708 849-6343
Catherine Dolan, *President*
Lisa Calumet, *Sales Staff*
**EMP:** 12
**SQ FT:** 25,000
**SALES (est):** 1.3MM **Privately Held**
**SIC:** 3366 Brass foundry

*(G-8368)*
### CARAVAN INGREDIENTS INC
14622 Lakeside Ave (60419-2023)
**PHONE**.................................708 849-8590
John Polley, *Engineer*
Richard Hulfeld, *Manager*
Jerry Jocius, *Manager*
Danielle Gaczkowski, *Technology*
**EMP:** 60

**Dolton - Cook County (G-8369)**

SQ FT: 40,000
**SALES (corp-wide):** 963.3MM **Privately Held**
**WEB:** www.caravaningredients.com
**SIC:** 2099 2087 Food preparations; flavoring extracts & syrups
**HQ:** Caravan Ingredients Inc.
7905 Quivira Rd
Lenexa KS 66215
913 890-5500

**(G-8369)**
**DALMATIAN FIRE EQUIPMENT LTD**
531 Monroe St (60419-1134)
**PHONE**..................708 201-1730
John Rydzewski, *President*
Jennifer Rydzewski, *Treasurer*
Alex Rydzewski, *Admin Sec*
**EMP:** 4
**SALES (est):** 544.4K **Privately Held**
**SIC:** 3699 Fire control or bombing equipment, electronic

**(G-8370)**
**HARRIS LUBRICANTS**
14335 Dorchester Ave (60419-1328)
**PHONE**..................708 849-1935
Carl Harris, *President*
**EMP:** 2
**SQ FT:** 6,000
**SALES:** 875K **Privately Held**
**SIC:** 2992 Oils & greases, blending & compounding

**(G-8371)**
**HOLLAND MANUFACTURING CORP**
13901 Indiana Ave (60419-1169)
P.O. Box 261, South Holland (60473-0261)
**PHONE**..................708 849-1000
**Fax:** 708 849-1199
Kenneth Hoekstra, *President*
David Myroup, *Corp Secy*
John Nelson, *Vice Pres*
Kenya Dower, *Office Admin*
▲ **EMP:** 42
**SQ FT:** 60,000
**SALES (est):** 7.1MM **Privately Held**
**SIC:** 3255 Clay refractories

**(G-8372)**
**IDENTCORP INDUSTRIES**
14209 Maryland Ave (60419-1372)
**PHONE**..................708 896-6407
Daniel Jones, *Owner*
**EMP:** 32
**SALES (est):** 1.3MM **Privately Held**
**WEB:** www.Identicorp.com
**SIC:** 3825 7389 Transducers for volts, amperes, watts, vars, frequency, etc.;

**(G-8373)**
**MIX MATCH LLC**
14725 Drexel Ave (60419-2219)
**PHONE**..................708 201-0009
Lavonne Sanders, *Mng Member*
Burma Kennedy, *Manager*
Britney Sanders,
Ora Sanders,
Micah K Swansey,
**EMP:** 16
**SALES (est):** 1.7MM **Privately Held**
**SIC:** 2064 5145 Popcorn balls or other treated popcorn products; snack foods

**(G-8374)**
**PDQ TOOL & STAMPING CO**
14901 Greenwood Rd (60419-2238)
**PHONE**..................708 841-3000
**Fax:** 708 841-7936
Thomas Miller Jr, *President*
Mark Webb, *General Mgr*
Tim Morris, *QC Dir*
Joann Labarge, *Finance Mgr*
Jan Ehrlich, *Office Mgr*
**EMP:** 30 **EST:** 1975
**SQ FT:** 23,000
**SALES (est):** 4.8MM **Privately Held**
**WEB:** www.pdqtoolandstamping.com
**SIC:** 3544 3469 Die sets for metal stamping (presses); metal stampings

**(G-8375)**
**PROAM SPORTS PRODUCTS**
435 Adams St (60419-1120)
**PHONE**..................708 841-4200
Raymond McClinton Jr, *Principal*
**EMP:** 4
**SALES (est):** 197.3K **Privately Held**
**SIC:** 3949 Sporting & athletic goods

**(G-8376)**
**QSIMAGINATIONSTATION**
14641 Dante Ave (60419-2410)
**PHONE**..................708 928-9622
Taquila Allen, *President*
**EMP:** 5 **EST:** 2013
**SALES (est):** 290.4K **Privately Held**
**SIC:** 3944 Paint sets, children's

**(G-8377)**
**T A U INC**
Also Called: Die Cut Plates
14075 Lincoln Ave (60419-1021)
**PHONE**..................708 841-5757
**Fax:** 708 841-2535
Curt Voss, *President*
Bill Hinton, *Vice Pres*
**EMP:** 3
**SALES (est):** 383.5K **Privately Held**
**SIC:** 3469 3354 Ornamental metal stampings; aluminum extruded products

**(G-8378)**
**YUSRAA INC**
14828 Cottage Grove Ave (60419-2108)
**PHONE**..................312 608-1916
Tajmah Y Al-Faruqi, *Principal*
**EMP:** 2
**SALES (est):** 205K **Privately Held**
**SIC:** 3537 Trucks: freight, baggage, etc.: industrial, except mining

**Dongola**
*Union County*

**(G-8379)**
**CHEERS FOOD FUEL**
510 Ne Front St (62926-2349)
**PHONE**..................618 827-4836
David Godfrey, *Manager*
**EMP:** 3
**SALES (est):** 184.6K **Privately Held**
**SIC:** 2869 Fuels

**Dorsey**
*Madison County*

**(G-8380)**
**AXON TELECOM LLC**
Also Called: Csd
177 Snake Rd (62021-3007)
**PHONE**..................618 278-4606
William Ludwig,
**EMP:** 1
**SALES:** 5MM **Privately Held**
**SIC:** 3661 Fiber optics communications equipment

**(G-8381)**
**MCCANN CONCRETE PRODUCTS INC**
8709 N State Route 159 (62021-1217)
**PHONE**..................618 377-3888
**Fax:** 618 377-7746
Patrick McCann, *President*
Jack McCann, *Vice Pres*
Mark Melvin, *Vice Pres*
Chris McCann, *Sales Engr*
Debbie Christopher, *Sales Staff*
**EMP:** 20
**SQ FT:** 5,000
**SALES (est):** 4.4MM **Privately Held**
**WEB:** www.mccannconcreteproducts.com
**SIC:** 3272 Concrete products

**Dow**
*Jersey County*

**(G-8382)**
**MORRIS PALLET SKIDS INC**
15133 Newbern Rd (62022-3192)
**PHONE**..................618 786-2241
John Abbott, *Exec Dir*
**EMP:** 4 **EST:** 2010
**SALES (est):** 422.1K **Privately Held**
**SIC:** 2448 Pallets, wood & wood with metal

**(G-8383)**
**STINE WOODWORKING LLC**
16376 Bartlett Rd (62022-3030)
**PHONE**..................618 885-2229
David Stine, *Mng Member*
Stephanie Abbajay, *Manager*
**EMP:** 2
**SALES:** 250K **Privately Held**
**SIC:** 2431 Millwork

**Downers Grove**
*Dupage County*

**(G-8384)**
**A LEN RADIATOR SHOPPE INC**
Also Called: A Len Complete Auto Svc Ctr
333 Ogden Ave (60515-3142)
**PHONE**..................630 852-5445
**Fax:** 630 852-5456
Leonard H Senicka, *President*
Cynthia Senicka, *Corp Secy*
Len Senieka, *Opers Staff*
**EMP:** 5
**SQ FT:** 10,000
**SALES:** 1MM **Privately Held**
**SIC:** 5531 5013 7539 7538 Automotive parts; automotive supplies & parts; radiator repair shop, automotive; general automotive repair shops; hose & tube fittings & assemblies, hydraulic/pneumatic

**(G-8385)**
**ADVANCED OZONE TECH INC**
Also Called: Cec, The Ozone Co
2743 Curtiss St (60515-4002)
**PHONE**..................630 964-1300
**Fax:** 630 964-1282
Kathryn V Johnston, *President*
William R Johnston, *Vice Pres*
Hank Bourassa, *Engineer*
Mike Costello, *Engineer*
Kathy Dusso, *Exec Dir*
**EMP:** 10
**SQ FT:** 3,500
**SALES (est):** 1.8MM **Privately Held**
**WEB:** www.aquaxox.com
**SIC:** 3621 Motors & generators

**(G-8386)**
**ALWAYS THERE EXPRESS CORP**
20w538 Elizabeth Dr (60516-7117)
**PHONE**..................773 931-3744
Tadas Jurgaitis, *President*
**EMP:** 20
**SALES (est):** 3.9MM **Privately Held**
**SIC:** 3537 Trucks: freight, baggage, etc.: industrial, except mining

**(G-8387)**
**AMKUS INC**
Also Called: Amkus Rescue Systems
2700 Wisconsin Ave (60515-4226)
P.O. Box 408, Bolingbrook (60440-1097)
**PHONE**..................630 515-1800
Margaret Weigand, *President*
Judy Weigand, *Exec VP*
Michael Kiefer, *Vice Pres*
Alan Painter, *Opers Staff*
Twine Martin, *Purch Agent*
▲ **EMP:** 26
**SQ FT:** 40,000
**SALES (est):** 5.7MM **Privately Held**
**WEB:** www.amkus.com
**SIC:** 3569 Firefighting apparatus

**(G-8388)**
**APOLLO COMPUTER SOLUTIONS INC (PA)**
914 55th St 2 (60515-4954)
**PHONE**..................312 671-3575
Mitchell Fromberg, *President*
**EMP:** 2
**SALES (est):** 294.7K **Privately Held**
**WEB:** www.apollocomputersolutions.com
**SIC:** 3571 Electronic computers

**(G-8389)**
**ARROW GEAR COMPANY (PA)**
2301 Curtiss St (60515-4036)
**PHONE**..................630 969-7640
**Fax:** 630 969-0253
David Goodfellow, *CEO*
James Pielsticer, *Exec VP*
Brett Bodoh, *Mfg Spvr*
Cris Nadela, *Engineer*
Andrew Mazzarella, *CFO*
▲ **EMP:** 250 **EST:** 1947
**SQ FT:** 140,000
**SALES (est):** 45.5MM **Privately Held**
**WEB:** www.arrowgear.com
**SIC:** 3724 3566 3714 3568 Aircraft engines & engine parts; drives, high speed industrial, except hydrostatic; motor vehicle parts & accessories; power transmission equipment; iron & steel forgings; metal heat treating

**(G-8390)**
**ARROW GEAR COMPANY**
5240 Belmont Rd (60515-4340)
**PHONE**..................630 969-7640
**Fax:** 630 241-9022
Joe Arzin, *President*
**EMP:** 25
**SQ FT:** 10,625
**SALES (corp-wide):** 45.5MM **Privately Held**
**WEB:** www.arrowgear.com
**SIC:** 3451 Screw machine products
**PA:** Arrow Gear Company
2301 Curtiss St
Downers Grove IL 60515
630 969-7640

**(G-8391)**
**AZTEC CORPORATION**
Also Called: Rediscover Music
2800 Maple Ave Apt 34a (60515-4150)
**Fax:** 630 305-0782
Allan Shaw, *President*
Genevieve Shaw, *Admin Sec*
**EMP:** 7
**SQ FT:** 1,000
**SALES (est):** 780K **Privately Held**
**WEB:** www.folkera.com
**SIC:** 3652 5099 5961 Compact laser discs, prerecorded; compact discs; tapes & cassettes, prerecorded; record &/or tape (music or video) club, mail order

**(G-8392)**
**BABCOCK & WILCOX POWR GENERATN**
1431 Opus Pl Ste 600 (60515-1170)
**PHONE**..................630 719-5120
Robert Gay, *Vice Pres*
Vernon Wear, *Vice Pres*
Bruce Evenson, *Opers Mgr*
J Shildmer, *Branch Mgr*
Jay Weiss, *CTO*
**EMP:** 10
**SALES (corp-wide):** 1.5B **Publicly Held**
**SIC:** 3511 Steam turbines
**HQ:** The Babcock & Wilcox Company
20 S Van Buren Ave
Barberton OH 44203
330 753-4511

**(G-8393)**
**BAKED APPLE PANCAKE HOUSE**
1224 Ogden Ave (60515-2740)
**PHONE**..................630 515-9000
**EMP:** 5
**SALES (est):** 614.6K **Privately Held**
**SIC:** 3571 Personal computers (microcomputers)

# GEOGRAPHIC SECTION

Downers Grove - Dupage County (G-8418)

### (G-8394)
**BALES MOLD SERVICE INC**
2824 Hitchcock Ave Ste A (60515-4030)
PHONE .................................. 630 852-4665
Fax: 630 852-4687
Stacey Bales, *President*
John Bailey, *General Mgr*
Eric Witte, *QC Mgr*
Harry Raimondi, *Technical Mgr*
Rich Wozniak, *Technical Mgr*
EMP: 40
SQ FT: 28,000
SALES (est): 6MM **Privately Held**
WEB: www.balesmold.com
SIC: **3471** 7692 Polishing, metals or formed products; chromium plating of metals or formed products; electroplating of metals or formed products; welding repair

### (G-8395)
**BASELINE GRAPHICS INC**
5424 Webster St (60515-4916)
PHONE .................................. 630 964-9566
Fax: 630 964-9596
Marry Joe Hobbs, *President*
Marijo Hobbs, *President*
EMP: 3
SQ FT: 10,000
SALES (est): 223.1K **Privately Held**
SIC: **2791** 7336 Typesetting; graphic arts & related design

### (G-8396)
**BECTON DICKINSON AND COMPANY**
Also Called: B D
1400 Opus Pl Ste 805 (60515-5754)
PHONE .................................. 630 743-2006
Jim Meurer, *Manager*
EMP: 8
SALES (corp-wide): 12.4B **Publicly Held**
SIC: **3841** Surgical & medical instruments
PA: Becton, Dickinson And Company
1 Becton Dr
Franklin Lakes NJ 07417
201 847-6800

### (G-8397)
**BLUE DIAMOND ATHLETIC DISP INC**
1933 Loomes Ave (60516-2432)
PHONE .................................. 847 414-9971
Nilmini Posmer, *President*
Kenneth Posmer, *Vice Pres*
EMP: 5
SALES: 54K **Privately Held**
SIC: **3993** Signs & advertising specialties

### (G-8398)
**BMC SOFTWARE INC**
1901 Butterfield Rd # 420 (60515-7915)
PHONE .................................. 331 777-8700
Mark Graham, *President*
John Rotta, *Opers Staff*
Tom Lonergan, *Accounts Exec*
Jim Boland, *VP Mktg*
Chandra Rathore, *Business Anlyst*
EMP: 40
SQ FT: 2,000
SALES (corp-wide): 1.8B **Privately Held**
WEB: www.bmc.com
SIC: **7372** Utility computer software
HQ: Bmc Software, Inc.
2103 Citywest Blvd # 2100
Houston TX 77042
713 918-8800

### (G-8399)
**BUFFALO ARMS**
112 Tower Rd (60515-2312)
PHONE .................................. 630 969-1796
Brice Fawcett, *Owner*
EMP: 3
SALES (est): 217.1K **Privately Held**
SIC: **3949** Sporting & athletic goods

### (G-8400)
**BUHRKE INDUSTRIES LLC**
Also Called: IMS Buhrke-Olson
2500 Curtiss St (60515-4058)
PHONE .................................. 847 981-7550
EMP: 47
SALES (corp-wide): 675MM **Privately Held**
WEB: www.buhrke.com
SIC: **3999** Barber & beauty shop equipment
HQ: Buhrke Industries, Llc
511 W Algonquin Rd
Arlington Heights IL 60005
847 981-7550

### (G-8401)
**C & C PRINTING CONTROLS INC**
5015 Chase Ave (60515-4014)
PHONE .................................. 630 810-0484
Brian Chapas, *President*
EMP: 3
SQ FT: 2,400
SALES (est): 402.4K **Privately Held**
SIC: **3555** Printing trade parts & attachments; printing presses

### (G-8402)
**C AND C MACHINE TOOL SERVICE**
5015 Chase Ave (60515-4014)
PHONE .................................. 630 810-0484
Fax: 630 810-0491
Kathleen Chapas, *President*
Richard Chapas, *Admin Sec*
EMP: 9
SQ FT: 5,400
SALES: 900K **Privately Held**
SIC: **7694** 5084 Rebuilding motors, except automotive; printing trades machinery, equipment & supplies

### (G-8403)
**CAMPBELL CAMIE INC**
2651 Warrenville Rd # 300 (60515-5772)
PHONE .................................. 314 968-3222
Vincent J Doder, *President*
Jim McLarty, *Vice Pres*
David Graebner, *Finance*
EMP: 21 EST: 1946
SQ FT: 18,000
SALES (est): 3.3MM
SALES (corp-wide): 254.8MM **Privately Held**
WEB: www.camie.com
SIC: **2819** 2891 2992 2899 Industrial inorganic chemicals; adhesives; lubricating oils & greases; chemical preparations; industrial organic chemicals
HQ: Plaze, Inc.
2651 Warrenville Rd # 300
Downers Grove IL 60515
630 628-4240

### (G-8404)
**CANADA ORGANIZATION & DEV LLC (HQ)**
3005 Highland Pkwy (60515-5682)
PHONE .................................. 630 743-2563
Robert A Livingston, *President*
EMP: 3 EST: 2002
SALES (est): 64.2MM
SALES (corp-wide): 6.7B **Publicly Held**
SIC: **3561** Pumps & pumping equipment
PA: Dover Corporation
3005 Highland Pkwy # 200
Downers Grove IL 60515
630 541-1540

### (G-8405)
**CEMEC INC (PA)**
1516 Centre Cir (60515-1019)
PHONE .................................. 630 495-9696
Fax: 630 495-9785
James C Klouda, *President*
Marilyn Klouda, *Corp Secy*
Thomas Klouda, *Vice Pres*
John Ray, *Engineer*
Rob Fredres, *Info Tech Dir*
EMP: 3
SQ FT: 3,500
SALES (est): 2.5MM **Privately Held**
SIC: **3677** 8734 3621 Filtration devices, electronic; testing laboratories; motors & generators

### (G-8406)
**CENGAGE LEARNING INC**
Netg Division
2651 Warrenville Rd # 550 (60515-5544)
PHONE .................................. 630 554-0821
Craig Boyd, *Vice Pres*
Wendy Colby, *Vice Pres*
Bill Keen, *Branch Mgr*
Robb Beard, *Manager*
Jim Greenhill, *CTO*
EMP: 4 **Privately Held**
WEB: www.thomsonlearning.com
SIC: **8299** 8742 7372 Educational service, nondegree granting: continuing educ.; training & development consultant; educational computer software
PA: Cengage Learning, Inc.
20 Channel Ctr St
Boston MA 02210

### (G-8407)
**CENTRIC CO INC**
4153 W End Rd (60515-2307)
PHONE .................................. 708 728-9061
Ray Bliss, *President*
EMP: 8
SALES (est): 661.6K **Privately Held**
SIC: **3411** Can lids & ends, metal

### (G-8408)
**CHEMRING ENERGETIC DEVICES INC**
2525 Curtiss St (60515-4060)
PHONE .................................. 630 969-0620
William Currer, *President*
Jonathan Bailey, *Vice Pres*
Robert Glembin, *VP Opers*
Robert Glendin, *VP Opers*
Dave Eisenschmied, *Plant Mgr*
EMP: 111
SQ FT: 55,000
SALES (est): 27.9MM
SALES (corp-wide): 632.5MM **Privately Held**
WEB: www.scotinc.com
SIC: **3812** 3724 Missile guidance systems & equipment; aircraft engines & engine parts
PA: Chemring Group Plc
Roke Manor
Romsey HANTS SO51

### (G-8409)
**CHICAGO CRATE INC**
440 Roe Ct (60516-3904)
PHONE .................................. 708 380-4716
Mark Harrington, *President*
EMP: 5
SALES (est): 471.5K **Privately Held**
SIC: **2449** Rectangular boxes & crates, wood

### (G-8410)
**CHICAGOLAND RACEWAY**
2255 Maple Ave (60515-4404)
PHONE .................................. 708 203-8003
EMP: 3
SALES (est): 101.9K **Privately Held**
SIC: **3644** Raceways

### (G-8411)
**CITGO PETROLEUM CORPORATION**
1201 Ogden Ave (60515-2741)
PHONE .................................. 847 818-1800
Chuck Mavus, *Branch Mgr*
EMP: 5 **Privately Held**
WEB: www.citgo.com
SIC: **2911** Petroleum refining
HQ: Citgo Petroleum Corporation
1293 Eldridge Pkwy
Houston TX 77077
832 486-4000

### (G-8412)
**CLAIRE-SPRAYWAY INC (DH)**
Also Called: Claire Manufacturing
2651 Warrenville Rd # 300 (60515-5772)
PHONE .................................. 630 628-3000
Fax: 630 543-4310
Michael Rohl, *CEO*
Edward Byczynski, *President*
Bob Potvin, *Vice Pres*
Bob Potzin, *VP Sls/Mktg*
Michelle Stella, *Adv Mgr*
▼ EMP: 50
SQ FT: 100,000
SALES (est): 36.5MM
SALES (corp-wide): 254.8MM **Privately Held**
WEB: www.clairemfg.com
SIC: **2842** Cleaning or polishing preparations; deodorants, nonpersonal; disinfectants, household or industrial plant
HQ: Plaze, Inc.
2651 Warrenville Rd # 300
Downers Grove IL 60515
630 628-4240

### (G-8413)
**CLAIRE-SPRAYWAY INC**
2651 Warrenville Rd # 300 (60515-5772)
PHONE .................................. 630 628-3000
Steve Parbs, *Plant Mgr*
Theresa Lavine, *Manager*
EMP: 80
SALES (corp-wide): 254.8MM **Privately Held**
WEB: www.clairemfg.com
SIC: **2813** 2992 2899 2879 Aerosols; lubricating oils & greases; chemical preparations; agricultural chemicals; specialty cleaning, polishes & sanitation goods
HQ: Claire-Sprayway, Inc.
2651 Warrenville Rd # 300
Downers Grove IL 60515
630 628-3000

### (G-8414)
**CLAYMOUNT AMERICAS CORPORATION**
2545 Curtiss St (60515-4059)
PHONE .................................. 630 271-9729
Jan-Willem Overman, *General Mgr*
Walter Jurek, *Engineer*
▲ EMP: 36 EST: 2013
SALES: 4.5MM
SALES (corp-wide): 3.2B **Publicly Held**
SIC: **3844** X-ray apparatus & tubes; hospital equipment & furniture
HQ: Varex Imaging Corporation
1678 S Pioneer Rd
Salt Lake City UT 84104
801 972-5000

### (G-8415)
**COMPTIA LEARNING LLC**
3500 Lacey Rd Ste 100 (60515-5439)
PHONE .................................. 630 678-8490
EMP: 12
SQ FT: 35,000
SALES (est): 760K **Privately Held**
SIC: **7372** 8611 Prepackaged Software Services Business Association

### (G-8416)
**COMPUSYSTEMS INC (PA)**
Also Called: C S I
2651 Warrenville Rd # 400 (60515-5753)
PHONE .................................. 708 344-9070
Fax: 708 786-5568
Clark K Williams, *Ch of Bd*
Chris Williams, *President*
Pat Fallon, *President*
Jen Mitchell, *President*
Paul McCaffray, *Exec VP*
EMP: 133
SQ FT: 27,000
SALES (est): 56MM **Privately Held**
WEB: www.compusystems.com
SIC: **7372** Prepackaged software; business oriented computer software

### (G-8417)
**CONAGRA BRANDS INC**
3250 Lacey Rd Ste 600 (60515-7918)
PHONE .................................. 630 455-5200
EMP: 100
SALES (corp-wide): 11.6B **Publicly Held**
SIC: **2053** Frozen bakery products, except bread
PA: Conagra Brands, Inc.
222 Merchandise Mart Plz
Chicago IL 60654
312 549-5000

### (G-8418)
**CONSCISYS CORP**
1125 Mistwood Pl (60515-1205)
PHONE .................................. 630 810-4444
Scott Carr, *President*

# Downers Grove - Dupage County (G-8419)

**EMP:** 25
**SALES (est):** 1.5MM **Privately Held**
**SIC: 7372** Prepackaged software

### (G-8419)
### CONTEMPORARY CTRL SYSTEMS INC (PA)
2431 Curtiss St (60515-4006)
**PHONE** .................................. 630 963-1993
**Fax:** 630 963-0109
George M Thomas, *President*
Richard Mager, *Finance*
Maria Martinez, *Manager*
Judith L Thomas, *Admin Sec*
Carol Mackey, *Administration*
◆ **EMP:** 25
**SQ FT:** 14,000
**SALES (est):** 8.7MM **Privately Held**
**WEB:** www.ctrlink.com
**SIC: 3577** Computer peripheral equipment

### (G-8420)
### CONTROL MASTERS INC
5235 Katrine Ave (60515-4034)
**PHONE** .................................. 630 968-2390
**Fax:** 630 968-3260
Carl F Horn, *President*
Sherry Duffins, *Manager*
**EMP:** 1
**SQ FT:** 20,000
**SALES (est):** 1.5MM **Privately Held**
**SIC: 8711 3625** Engineering services; relays & industrial controls

### (G-8421)
### CPC AEROSCIENCE INC (PA)
Also Called: Terand Industries
2651 Warrenville Rd # 300 (60515-5772)
**PHONE** .................................. 954 974-5440
Terry Colker, *President*
John Kessler, *Safety Mgr*
Brian Parliment, *CFO*
Brenda Slusher, *Human Res Dir*
Karen Dosher, *VP Mktg*
▲ **EMP:** 2 **EST:** 1961
**SQ FT:** 43,000
**SALES (est):** 5.4MM **Privately Held**
**SIC: 2842** Specialty cleaning, polishes & sanitation goods

### (G-8422)
### CVP SYSTEMS INC
2518 Wisconsin Ave (60515-4230)
**PHONE** .................................. 630 852-1190
**Fax:** 630 852-1386
Wesley Bork, *President*
Laurie Mykleby, *Vice Pres*
Chris V Wandelen, *Vice Pres*
Pat Duranty, *Production*
Ron Stevens, *Production*
◆ **EMP:** 52
**SQ FT:** 30,000
**SALES (est):** 16.1MM **Privately Held**
**WEB:** www.cvpsystems.com
**SIC: 3556 3565 3563** Food products machinery; packaging machinery; air & gas compressors

### (G-8423)
### D S PRECISION TOOL COMPANY
1420 Brook Dr (60515-1025)
**PHONE** .................................. 630 627-0696
**Fax:** 630 627-0698
David Steininger II, *President*
Nancy Lott, *Admin Sec*
**EMP:** 5
**SQ FT:** 3,500
**SALES:** 500K **Privately Held**
**WEB:** www.dscrimp.com
**SIC: 3544** Special dies, tools, jigs & fixtures

### (G-8424)
### DALLAS CORPORATION
4340 Cross St (60515-1715)
**PHONE** .................................. 630 322-8000
**Fax:** 630 322-8008
Lance Haack, *President*
Mary Esposito, *Vice Pres*
**EMP:** 18
**SQ FT:** 10,000
**SALES (est):** 3.5MM **Privately Held**
**WEB:** www.dallascorp.com
**SIC: 5112 4225 2752** Manifold business forms; general warehousing; commercial printing, offset

### (G-8425)
### DEAN B SCOTT
1319 Butterfield Rd # 524 (60515-5621)
P.O. Box 1509, Fort Myers FL (33902-1509)
**PHONE** .................................. 630 960-4455
Dean B Scott, *Owner*
**EMP:** 3
**SALES (est):** 311.7K **Privately Held**
**SIC: 3851** Eyes, glass & plastic

### (G-8426)
### DEE ERECTORS INC
8314 Old Fence Ct (60517-4104)
**PHONE** .................................. 630 327-1185
**EMP:** 3
**SALES (est):** 238.9K **Privately Held**
**SIC: 3325** Steel Foundry

### (G-8427)
### DFK AMERICA INC
2215 Curtiss St (60515-4010)
**PHONE** .................................. 630 324-6793
Dalibor Kanovsky, *President*
▲ **EMP:** 7
**SALES (est):** 1MM **Privately Held**
**SIC: 3537** Cabs, for industrial trucks & tractors

### (G-8428)
### DIAMOND WEB PRINTING LLC
2820 Hitchcock Ave (60515-4041)
**PHONE** .................................. 630 663-0350
**Fax:** 630 663-0353
Gregg Herlin, *Principal*
Charles J Gardella,
Mark Kramer,
George Scharf,
**EMP:** 18
**SQ FT:** 26,000
**SALES (est):** 1.5MM **Privately Held**
**WEB:** www.diamondkmarketing.com
**SIC: 2752 2759** Commercial printing, offset; commercial printing

### (G-8429)
### DICKE TOOL COMPANY (PA)
Also Called: Dicke Safety Products
1201 Warren Ave (60515-3548)
**PHONE** .................................. 630 969-0050
**Fax:** 630 969-3973
Vera D Dicke, *President*
Todd Belobraydich, *Sales Executive*
Lisa Inches, *Manager*
Marilyn Willits, *Manager*
Bill Ribolzi, *Info Tech Dir*
▲ **EMP:** 30 **EST:** 1880
**SQ FT:** 25,000
**SALES (est):** 12.3MM **Privately Held**
**WEB:** www.dicketool.com
**SIC: 3441 3993** Fabricated structural metal; signs & advertising specialties

### (G-8430)
### DOVER ARTIFICIAL LIFT INTL LLC (HQ)
Also Called: Norris Production Solutions
3005 Highland Pkwy (60515-5682)
**PHONE** .................................. 630 743-2563
Robert A Livingston, *CEO*
William C Johnson, *President*
Kevin P Buchanan, *Vice Pres*
Brad M Cerepak, *CFO*
Gary Larson, *CFO*
▲ **EMP:** 15
**SALES (est):** 1.3B
**SALES (corp-wide):** 6.7B **Publicly Held**
**SIC: 3559 3535 3533 3561** Automotive related machinery; bulk handling conveyor systems; oil field machinery & equipment; industrial pumps & parts
**PA:** Dover Corporation
3005 Highland Pkwy # 200
Downers Grove IL 60515
630 541-1540

### (G-8431)
### DOVER CORPORATION (PA)
3005 Highland Pkwy # 200 (60515-5655)
**PHONE** .................................. 630 541-1540
**Fax:** 630 743-2671
Michael F Johnston, *Ch of Bd*
Robert A Livingston, *President*
Patrick M Burns, *Senior VP*
Ivonne M Cabrera, *Senior VP*
Stephen Gary Kennon, *Senior VP*
◆ **EMP:** 150 **EST:** 1947
**SALES:** 6.7B **Publicly Held**
**WEB:** www.dovercorporation.com
**SIC: 3632 3586 3533 3577** Household refrigerators & freezers; measuring & dispensing pumps; oil & gas drilling rigs & equipment; computer peripheral equipment; bar code (magnetic ink) printers; semiconductors & related devices

### (G-8432)
### DOVER ENERGY AUTOMATION LLC (PA)
Also Called: Timberline Manufacturing
3005 Highland Pkwy (60515-5682)
**PHONE** .................................. 630 541-1540
Mike Martindale, *Vice Pres*
Justin Green, *Sales Staff*
**EMP:** 35 **EST:** 2002
**SQ FT:** 11,000
**SALES (est):** 9MM **Privately Held**
**SIC: 3561 3545** Pumps & pumping equipment; machine tool accessories

### (G-8433)
### DOVER EUROPE INC (HQ)
3005 Highland Pkwy # 200 (60515-5682)
**PHONE** .................................. 630 541-1540
Robert A Livingston, *President*
John F Hartner, *President*
Jeffrey S Niew, *President*
William W Spurgeon, *President*
Michael Y Zhang, *President*
**EMP:** 5
**SALES (est):** 18.9MM
**SALES (corp-wide):** 6.7B **Publicly Held**
**SIC: 3531 3542 3565 3534** Construction machinery; machine tools, metal forming type; packaging machinery; elevators & moving stairways
**PA:** Dover Corporation
3005 Highland Pkwy # 200
Downers Grove IL 60515
630 541-1540

### (G-8434)
### DOVER PRTG IDENTIFICATION INC (HQ)
3005 Highland Pkwy # 200 (60515-5682)
**PHONE** .................................. 630 541-1540
Lewis Burns, *CEO*
John F Hartner, *President*
Peter Downe, *Vice Pres*
Daniel McCourt, *Vice Pres*
Bob Schewer, *Vice Pres*
◆ **EMP:** 90
**SQ FT:** 2,600
**SALES (est):** 1.9B
**SALES (corp-wide):** 6.7B **Publicly Held**
**WEB:** www.doverindustries.com
**SIC: 3556 3565 3593 7699** Food products machinery; packaging machinery; fluid power cylinders, hydraulic or pneumatic; industrial equipment services
**PA:** Dover Corporation
3005 Highland Pkwy # 200
Downers Grove IL 60515
630 541-1540

### (G-8435)
### DUPAGE PRODUCTS GROUP
2250 Curtiss St (60515-4054)
**PHONE** .................................. 630 969-7200
**Fax:** 630 969-0310
Jerry Piper, *CEO*
Larry Masters, *Purchasing*
Bruce Sichak, *Director*
**EMP:** 60
**SALES (est):** 4.7MM **Privately Held**
**SIC: 3356** Nonferrous rolling & drawing

### (G-8436)
### DURAVANT (PA)
3500 Lacey Rd Ste 290 (60515-5443)
**PHONE** .................................. 630 635-3910
**EMP:** 9
**SALES (est):** 4.5MM **Privately Held**
**SIC: 3565 3535** Manufacturing Packaging Machinery Conveyors/Equipment

### (G-8437)
### DURAVANT LLC (HQ)
Also Called: Fischbein LLC
3500 Lacey Rd Ste 290 (60515-5443)
**PHONE** .................................. 630 635-3910
Michael J Kachmer, *President*
W L Inglett, *General Mgr*
Vivek Joshi, *Vice Pres*
David Parker, *Vice Pres*
Eleni Yianas, *Vice Pres*
◆ **EMP:** 10
**SALES (est):** 70.1MM
**SALES (corp-wide):** 1.3B **Privately Held**
**SIC: 3559 3565 3535** Bag seaming & closing machines (sewing machinery); packaging machinery; belt conveyor systems, general industrial use
**PA:** Odyssey Investment Partners Llc
590 Madison Ave Fl 39
New York NY 10022
212 351-7900

### (G-8438)
### EARTHGRAINS REFRIGERTD DOUGH P
Also Called: Refrigerated Dough Division
3250 Lacey Rd Ste 600 (60515-7918)
**PHONE** .................................. 630 455-5200
**Fax:** 630 455-5202
Kevin Hunt, *CEO*
▼ **EMP:** 700 **EST:** 1957
**SALES (est):** 150.6MM
**SALES (corp-wide):** 6.1B **Publicly Held**
**WEB:** www.egr.com
**SIC: 2051 2053 2041 2035** Breads, rolls & buns; cakes, pies & pastries; frozen bakery products, except bread; doughs, frozen or refrigerated; dressings, salad: raw & cooked (except dry mixes); mayonnaise; frozen food & ice cream containers; food containers (liquid tight), including milk cartons
**PA:** Treehouse Foods, Inc.
2021 Spring Rd Ste 600
Oak Brook IL 60523
708 483-1300

### (G-8439)
### ELGIN EQUIPMENT GROUP LLC (HQ)
2001 Bttrfield Rd Ste 1020 (60515)
**PHONE** .................................. 630 434-7200
David Hall, *President*
Kerry Koch, *Vice Pres*
Tim Lilly, *VP Opers*
Keith Wilkerson, *Opers Mgr*
Randy Finney, *Prdtn Mgr*
**EMP:** 7
**SALES (est):** 147.3MM
**SALES (corp-wide):** 1.6B **Privately Held**
**SIC: 3532** Mining machinery
**PA:** Audax Group, L.P.
101 Huntington Ave # 2450
Boston MA 02199
617 859-1500

### (G-8440)
### ELGIN NATIONAL INDUSTRIES INC (PA)
2001 Bttrfield Rd Ste 1020 (60515)
**PHONE** .................................. 630 434-7200
**Fax:** 630 434-7246
Fred C Schulte, *Ch of Bd*
David Hall, *President*
Charles D Hall, *President*
Umberto Vergine, *Sr Exec VP*
Lynn C Batory, *Vice Pres*
◆ **EMP:** 13
**SQ FT:** 6,470
**SALES (est):** 92.8MM **Privately Held**
**WEB:** www.ohiorod.com
**SIC: 3532 8711** Mining machinery; crushing, pulverizing & screening equipment; engineering services

### (G-8441)
### EMMETTS TAVERN & BREWING CO
5200 Main St (60515-4688)
**PHONE** .................................. 630 434-8500
Kirsten Swanson, *Principal*
**EMP:** 7
**SALES (corp-wide):** 3MM **Privately Held**
**SIC: 5812 2082 5182** Chicken restaurant; beer (alcoholic beverage); wine & distilled beverages
**PA:** Emmett's Tavern & Brewing Co.
128 W Main St
West Dundee IL 60118
847 428-4500

▲ = Import ▼ = Export
◆ = Import/Export

### (G-8442)
**FEMINA SPORT INC**
5100 Walnut Ave (60515-4066)
PHONE..................................630 271-1876
Roberta Weimer, *President*
EMP: 6
SALES: 245K **Privately Held**
SIC: 2395 Embroidery products, except schiffli machine

### (G-8443)
**FLAVORCHEM CORPORATION (PA)**
Also Called: Orchid Labs
1525 Brook Dr (60515-1024)
PHONE..................................630 932-8100
Fax: 630 932-4626
Ken R Malinowski, *Principal*
Jacqueline Sprovieri, *Corp Secy*
Phillip Sprovieri, *Vice Pres*
David Russo, *Plant Mgr*
Antonio Decristofaro, *Opers Mgr*
◆ EMP: 90
SQ FT: 70,000
SALES (est): 34MM **Privately Held**
WEB: www.flavorchem.com
SIC: 2087 Extracts, flavoring; syrups, flavoring (except drink)

### (G-8444)
**FLORISTS TRANSWORLD DLVRY INC**
3113 Woodcreek Dr (60515-5412)
PHONE..................................630 719-7800
Fax: 630 719-6966
Joe Ernst, *VP Opers*
Becky Sheehan, *CFO*
Becky A Sheehan, *CFO*
Jandy Tomy, *Controller*
Carrie Mininni, *Sales Dir*
▲ EMP: 725
SQ FT: 120,000
SALES (est): 213.3MM
SALES (corp-wide): 1.1B **Publicly Held**
WEB: www.ftdimarketplace.com
SIC: 5193 7389 2771 Florists' supplies; florist telegraph service; greeting cards
PA: Ftd Companies, Inc.
3113 Woodcreek Dr
Downers Grove IL 60515
630 719-7800

### (G-8445)
**FOUNDATION LITHUANIAN MINOR**
908 Rob Roy Pl (60516-3824)
PHONE..................................630 969-1316
Ramunas Buntinas, *Principal*
EMP: 5
SALES: 28.7K **Privately Held**
SIC: 2731 Book publishing

### (G-8446)
**FUSIBOND PIPING SYSTEMS INC**
2615 Curtiss St (60515-4003)
PHONE..................................630 969-4488
Fax: 630 969-2355
Richard H Krause, *President*
Patricia Ann Krause, *Vice Pres*
Craig J Krause, *Treasurer*
Kyle Jo Manowsky, *Admin Sec*
EMP: 18
SQ FT: 32,000
SALES (est): 3.5MM **Privately Held**
WEB: www.fusibond.com
SIC: 3084 5084 Plastics pipe; industrial machinery & equipment

### (G-8447)
**GEOMENTUM INC (HQ)**
Also Called: Geomentum Solutions
3025 Highland Pkwy (60515-5506)
P.O. Box 7063 (60515-7063)
PHONE..................................630 729-7500
Fax: 630 241-9432
Sean Finnegan, *CEO*
Judi Crisileo, *Vice Pres*
Larry Fuchs, *Vice Pres*
Robin Zeldin, *Vice Pres*
Judi Berman, *Buyer*
▲ EMP: 291
SQ FT: 73,500
SALES (est): 63.5MM
SALES (corp-wide): 7.8B **Publicly Held**
WEB: www.nsamedia.com
SIC: 2711 7311 Newspapers; advertising agencies
PA: The Interpublic Group Of Companies Inc
909 3rd Ave Fl 7
New York NY 10022
212 704-1200

### (G-8448)
**GEOMENTUM INC**
Magnet Media
3025 Highland Pkwy (60515-5506)
PHONE..................................630 729-7500
Randy Novak, *Branch Mgr*
EMP: 3
SALES (corp-wide): 7.8B **Publicly Held**
SIC: 2711 7311 Newspapers; advertising agencies
HQ: Geomentum Inc.
3025 Highland Pkwy # 700
Downers Grove IL 60515
630 729-7500

### (G-8449)
**GH PRINTING CO INC (PA)**
5207 Walnut Ave (60515-4025)
PHONE..................................630 960-4115
Fax: 630 960-5313
Gail Herlin, *President*
Gregg Herlin, *Vice Pres*
Todd Herlin, *Marketing Mgr*
EMP: 22
SQ FT: 12,500
SALES (est): 3.3MM **Privately Held**
WEB: www.ghprinting.com
SIC: 2752 7336 Commercial printing, lithographic; graphic arts & related design

### (G-8450)
**GIFT CHECK PROGRAM 2013 INC**
Also Called: Holiday Gift Check Program
1400 Opus Pl Ste 810 (60515-5708)
PHONE..................................630 986-5081
EMP: 3
SALES (est): 172.4K **Privately Held**
SIC: 2015 Turkey, processed

### (G-8451)
**GLANBIA PERFORMANCE NTRTN INC (DH)**
Also Called: Optimum Nutrition
3500 Lacey Rd (60515-5422)
PHONE..................................630 236-0097
Fax: 630 236-8517
Thomas Tench, *CEO*
Paul Freeborn, *Counsel*
Ken Strick, *Senior VP*
Adalberto Luna, *QA Dir*
Chris Mendes, *QA Dir*
◆ EMP: 120
SQ FT: 140,000
SALES (est): 134.2MM **Privately Held**
WEB: www.optimumnutrition.com
SIC: 2833 5149 5122 Vitamins, natural or synthetic: bulk, uncompounded; health foods; vitamins & minerals
HQ: Glanbia, Inc
121 4th Ave S
Twin Falls ID 83301
208 733-7555

### (G-8452)
**GLOBAL GEAR & MACHINING LLC**
2500 Curtiss St (60515-4058)
PHONE..................................630 969-9400
Mark Simington, *President*
David Wilbanks, *Engineer*
Donna Bertolini, *Manager*
Tom Gust, *Manager*
Cori Ooyen, *Manager*
▲ EMP: 127
SQ FT: 130,000
SALES (est): 43.5MM
SALES (corp-wide): 675MM **Privately Held**
WEB: www.globalgearllc.com
SIC: 3714 Gears, motor vehicle
PA: Ims Companies, Llc
1 Innovation Dr
Des Plaines IL 60016
847 391-8100

### (G-8453)
**HAPPY DOG BARKERY**
5118 Main St Ste A (60515-1696)
PHONE..................................630 512-0822
Beth Staley, *Owner*
EMP: 10
SALES (est): 1.2MM **Privately Held**
SIC: 2051 Bakery: wholesale or wholesale/retail combined

### (G-8454)
**HARRIS BOOKBINDING LLC**
5375 Walnut Ave (60515-4108)
PHONE..................................773 287-9414
Greg Goodman, *Mng Member*
EMP: 20
SALES (est): 1.2MM **Privately Held**
SIC: 2789 Bookbinding & related work

### (G-8455)
**HARRY J TRAINOR**
2113 Oxnard Dr (60516-2512)
PHONE..................................630 493-1163
Harry Trainor, *Principal*
EMP: 4
SALES (est): 386.9K **Privately Held**
SIC: 3823 Humidity instruments, industrial process type

### (G-8456)
**HEARTHSIDE FOOD SOLUTIONS LLC (PA)**
3250 Lacey Rd Ste 200 (60515-8384)
PHONE..................................630 967-3600
Richard Sealise, *CEO*
Bob Scalia, *Vice Pres*
John Weller, *Vice Pres*
Tod Bower, *Purch Mgr*
Fred Jasse, *CFO*
▼ EMP: 50
SALES (est): 2.3B **Privately Held**
SIC: 2043 2038 Cereal breakfast foods; snacks, including onion rings, cheese sticks, etc.

### (G-8457)
**HEUFT USA INC**
2820 Thatcher Rd (60515-4051)
PHONE..................................630 395-9521
Fax: 630 968-8767
Carl Bonnan, *General Mgr*
Daniel McKee, *Engineer*
Hans Kolovitsch, *Sales Dir*
John Martinez, *Sales Staff*
Laura Quid, *Mktg Coord*
▲ EMP: 11
SQ FT: 7,500
SALES (est): 6.1MM
SALES (corp-wide): 105.1MM **Privately Held**
SIC: 5065 3699 Electronic parts & equipment; electrical equipment & supplies
HQ: Heuft Systemtechnik Gmbh
Am Wind 1
Burgbrohl 56659
263 656-0

### (G-8458)
**HILLSHIRE BRANDS COMPANY**
3131 Woodcreek Dr (60515-5400)
PHONE..................................630 991-5100
EMP: 11
SALES (corp-wide): 36.8B **Publicly Held**
SIC: 2051 Pies, bakery: except frozen
HQ: The Hillshire Brands Company
400 S Jefferson St Fl 1
Chicago IL 60607
312 614-6000

### (G-8459)
**HIROSE ELECTRIC (USA) INC (HQ)**
2300 Warrenville Rd # 150 (60515-1755)
PHONE..................................630 282-6700
Yasushi Nakamura, *President*
Nick Shuikuia, *General Mgr*
Mitsugu Sugino, *Chairman*
Naoki Shukuya, *Exec VP*
Rick Van Weezel, *VP Sales*
EMP: 55
SQ FT: 40,000
SALES (est): 28.7MM
SALES (corp-wide): 1B **Privately Held**
WEB: www.hirose.com
SIC: 5065 3678 Electronic parts & equipment; electronic connectors
PA: Hirose Electric Co., Ltd.
5-5-23, Osaki
Shinagawa-Ku TKY 141-0
334 915-300

### (G-8460)
**HOLY COW SPORTS INCORPORATED**
5004 Chase Ave (60515-4013)
PHONE..................................630 852-9001
Margaret Buhtanic, *President*
Michael Buhtanic, *Vice Pres*
Mike Butanic, *Project Mgr*
EMP: 10
SALES (est): 1.2MM **Privately Held**
WEB: www.holycowsports.com
SIC: 2261 Screen printing of cotton broadwoven fabrics

### (G-8461)
**HOME MOBILITY SOLUTIONS INC**
Also Called: HMS Elevators
5239 Thatcher Rd (60515-4027)
PHONE..................................630 800-7800
Mike Cleary, *Principal*
EMP: 3
SALES (est): 1.1MM **Privately Held**
SIC: 5084 3534 Elevators; elevators & moving stairways

### (G-8462)
**IFASTGROUPE USA LLC**
2626 Warrenville Rd # 400 (60515-1775)
PHONE..................................450 658-7148
E A Roskovensky, *Principal*
▲ EMP: 5
SALES (est): 460.5K **Privately Held**
SIC: 3315 Steel wire & related products

### (G-8463)
**IMAGE PLUS INC**
4248 Belle Aire Ln Ste 1 (60515-1914)
PHONE..................................630 852-4920
Fax: 630 852-6088
Ronald A Burzynski, *Manager*
EMP: 6
SALES (est): 782.2K **Privately Held**
SIC: 2262 5199 2759 2395 Screen printing: manmade fiber & silk broadwoven fabrics; advertising specialties; screen printing; embroidery products, except schiffli machine; automotive & apparel trimmings

### (G-8464)
**IMS OLSON LLC**
2500 Curtiss St (60515-4058)
PHONE..................................630 969-9400
Norman Sachs, *Mng Member*
EMP: 75
SALES (est): 6.2MM **Privately Held**
SIC: 3544 3469 Special dies, tools, jigs & fixtures; metal stampings

### (G-8465)
**INDEPENDENT OUTDOOR LTD**
5009 Chase Ave (60515-4014)
P.O. Box 273 (60515-0273)
PHONE..................................630 960-2460
Richard D Wood, *President*
Barbara L Wood, *Vice Pres*
EMP: 3
SQ FT: 3,000
SALES (est): 341.1K **Privately Held**
SIC: 3993 7389 Signs & advertising specialties; sign painting & lettering shop

### (G-8466)
**INDUSTRIAL KINETICS INC (PA)**
2535 Curtiss St (60515-4059)
PHONE..................................630 655-0300
George Huber III, *President*
Dwight Pentzien, *Vice Pres*
Richard Robinson, *Project Mgr*
Rich Moldovan, *Mfg Mgr*
Jim Sevening, *Materials Mgr*
▼ EMP: 35
SQ FT: 90,000

## Downers Grove - Dupage County (G-8467)

SALES (est): 10.7MM **Privately Held**
WEB: www.iki.com
SIC: 3535 Unit handling conveying systems

**(G-8467)**
**J WALLACE & ASSOCIATES INC**
1409 Centre Cir (60515-1022)
PHONE..................................630 960-4221
John Wallace, *President*
Annamaire Enger, *Purchasing*
Anna Marie Orseno, *Admin Asst*
EMP: 2
SQ FT: 4,000
SALES (est): 1.2MM **Privately Held**
WEB: www.jwallaceinc.com
SIC: 7319 2653 Display advertising service; corrugated boxes, partitions, display items, sheets & pad

**(G-8468)**
**JUSKIE PRINTING CORP**
2820 Hitchcock Ave Ste E (60515-4062)
PHONE..................................630 663-8833
Mark Spash, *President*
Wendy Bauman, *Office Mgr*
EMP: 3
SQ FT: 2,500
SALES (est): 569.5K **Privately Held**
SIC: 2752 2789 Commercial printing, offset; bookbinding & related work

**(G-8469)**
**K-G SPRAY-PAK INC**
2651 Warrenville Rd # 300 (60515-5772)
PHONE..................................630 543-7600
Mike Magner, *Vice Pres*
EMP: 4
SALES (est): 149.1K **Privately Held**
SIC: 2813 Aerosols

**(G-8470)**
**KRICK ENTERPRISES INC**
Also Called: Signs Now
1548 Ogden Ave (60515-2771)
PHONE..................................630 515-1085
Marlene Krick, *President*
James Krick, *Vice Pres*
EMP: 5
SQ FT: 1,800
SALES: 500K **Privately Held**
SIC: 7389 3993 Sign painting & lettering shop; electric signs

**(G-8471)**
**L & M HARDWARE LTD**
2600 Warrenville Rd # 202 (60515-1761)
PHONE..................................312 805-2752
Willis L Collins, *President*
EMP: 2
SALES (est): 250K **Privately Held**
SIC: 3999 3429 Atomizers, toiletry; animal traps, iron or steel

**(G-8472)**
**LANSA INC**
2001 Butterfield Rd # 102 (60515-5491)
PHONE..................................630 874-7042
Pete Draney, *CEO*
Steven Gapp, *President*
Mark Fredericks, *Vice Pres*
Daniel Trower, *Technology*
Mike Palma, *IT/INT Sup*
EMP: 225
SQ FT: 11,000
SALES: 30MM **Privately Held**
WEB: www.lansa.com
SIC: 7371 7372 Computer software development; educational computer software
PA: Lansa Holdings, Inc.
  2001 Butterfield Rd # 102
  Downers Grove IL 60515
  630 874-7000

**(G-8473)**
**LAUNDRY SERVICES COMPANY**
4805 Pershing Ave (60515-3346)
PHONE..................................630 327-9363
Karl Keefer, *President*
EMP: 4
SALES (est): 554.8K **Privately Held**
SIC: 3452 Washers

**(G-8474)**
**LED BUSINESS SOLUTIONS LLC**
433 Maple Ave (60515-3806)
PHONE..................................844 464-5337
EMP: 10
SALES (est): 670K **Privately Held**
SIC: 3646 Mfg Commercial Lighting Fixtures

**(G-8475)**
**LEXRAY LLC**
3041 Woodcreek Dr Ste 102 (60515-5418)
PHONE..................................630 664-6740
Alex Bratton,
EMP: 10
SQ FT: 3,000
SALES (est): 1.1MM **Privately Held**
SIC: 7372 Prepackaged software

**(G-8476)**
**LINDY MANUFACTURING COMPANY**
5200 Katrine Ave (60515-4033)
PHONE..................................630 963-4126
Fax: 630 963-5308
David A Collins, *President*
Cathy G Collins, *Corp Secy*
Pat Kasva, *Human Res Mgr*
EMP: 30 EST: 1953
SQ FT: 40,000
SALES (est): 6.1MM **Privately Held**
SIC: 3469 Stamping metal for the trade

**(G-8477)**
**LIXI INC**
1438 Brook Dr (60515-1025)
PHONE..................................630 620-4646
Fax: 630 620-7776
EMP: 3 EST: 2008
SALES (est): 170K **Privately Held**
SIC: 3844 Mfg X-Ray Apparatus/Tubes

**(G-8478)**
**LODAAT LLC**
410 40th St (60515-2258)
PHONE..................................630 852-7544
Reggie Patel, *General Mgr*
EMP: 66
SALES (corp-wide): 50MM **Privately Held**
SIC: 2834 Pharmaceutical preparations
PA: Lodaat, Llc
  2 Mid America Plz Ste 800
  Oakbrook Terrace IL 60181
  630 248-2380

**(G-8479)**
**LOFTHOUSE BAKERY PRODUCTS INC**
3250 Lacey Rd Ste 600 (60515-7918)
PHONE..................................630 455-5229
EMP: 6
SALES (corp-wide): 6.1B **Publicly Held**
SIC: 2052 Crackers, dry
HQ: Lofthouse Bakery Products, Inc.
  215 N 700 W Ste A10
  Ogden UT 84404

**(G-8480)**
**LOVEJOY INC (HQ)**
2655 Wisconsin Ave (60515-4299)
PHONE..................................630 852-0500
Fax: 630 852-2120
Mike Hennessey, *Ch of Bd*
Sandy Swaim, *Vice Pres*
Mark Goodrich, *Plant Mgr*
Yongmei LI, *Buyer*
Arif Syed, *Controller*
▲ EMP: 219 EST: 1900
SQ FT: 75,000
SALES: 79.8MM
SALES (corp-wide): 2.6B **Publicly Held**
WEB: www.lovejoy-inc.com
SIC: 3568 Couplings, shaft: rigid, flexible, universal joint, etc.; pulleys, power transmission
PA: The Timken Company
  4500 Mount Pleasant St Nw
  North Canton OH 44720
  234 262-3000

**(G-8481)**
**MACHINE SOLUTION PROVIDERS INC**
Also Called: MSP
2659 Wisconsin Ave (60515-4244)
PHONE..................................630 717-7040
Fax: 630 717-7163
William A Novak, *President*
Michael P O'Brien, *Vice Pres*
Al Davenport, *Purch Mgr*
Audra Kerr, *Buyer*
Frank Baker, *Engineer*
▲ EMP: 55
SQ FT: 45,000
SALES (est): 27.6MM **Privately Held**
WEB: www.msp-inc.net
SIC: 3531 Roofing equipment

**(G-8482)**
**MANSCORE LLC**
1239 Gilbert Ave (60515-4516)
PHONE..................................630 297-7502
James Stocki, *CEO*
EMP: 3
SALES (est): 150K **Privately Held**
SIC: 7372 Application computer software

**(G-8483)**
**MAR COR PURIFICATION INC**
Also Called: Marcor
2850 Hitchcock Ave (60515-4016)
PHONE..................................630 435-1017
Fax: 630 435-1018
Kevin Peers, *Manager*
Kevin Pierce, *Manager*
EMP: 8
SALES (corp-wide): 664.7MM **Publicly Held**
WEB: www.marcorservices.com
SIC: 5999 2834 Water purification equipment; chlorination tablets & kits (water purification)
HQ: Mar Cor Purification, Inc.
  4450 Township Line Rd
  Skippack PA 19474
  800 633-3080

**(G-8484)**
**MAXIMUM PRTG & GRAPHICS INC**
911 Burlington Ave (60515-4716)
PHONE..................................630 737-0270
David Dipple, *President*
EMP: 10
SALES (est): 1.4MM **Privately Held**
SIC: 2752 Commercial printing, lithographic

**(G-8485)**
**MICROGUIDE INC**
1635 Plum Ct (60515-1325)
PHONE..................................630 964-3335
Glenn Krol, *President*
EMP: 3 EST: 1981
SALES (est): 302.8K **Privately Held**
SIC: 3842 Surgical appliances & supplies

**(G-8486)**
**MICROSOFT CORPORATION**
3025 Highland Pkwy # 300 (60515-5533)
PHONE..................................630 725-4000
Alan Silberman, *Managing Prtnr*
Steve Delaney, *Accounts Exec*
Jim Gourley, *Accounts Exec*
Jeff Nyheim, *Manager*
Missy Mazur, *Manager*
EMP: 60
SALES (corp-wide): 85.3B **Publicly Held**
WEB: www.microsoft.com
SIC: 7372 Prepackaged software
PA: Microsoft Corporation
  1 Microsoft Way
  Redmond WA 98052
  425 882-8080

**(G-8487)**
**MIDPOINT PACKAGING LLC**
5157 Thatcher Rd (60515-4029)
P.O. Box 947 (60515-0947)
PHONE..................................630 613-9922
Cory Lee, *Mng Member*
Michael Flanagan,
EMP: 7
SQ FT: 5,000
SALES: 2.5MM **Privately Held**
SIC: 3086 5199 Packaging & shipping materials, foamed plastic; packaging materials

**(G-8488)**
**MOLDTRONICS INC**
703 Rogers St (60515-3735)
PHONE..................................630 968-7000
Fax: 630 968-5068
Henry J Schmidt, *President*
Patrick Bishop, *QC Mgr*
Eileen Schmidt, *Admin Sec*
EMP: 43 EST: 1940
SQ FT: 23,000
SALES (est): 9.7MM **Privately Held**
WEB: www.moldtronics.com
SIC: 3089 3545 3442 Molding primary plastic; machine tool accessories; metal doors, sash & trim

**(G-8489)**
**MOLEX LLC**
Molex Fiber Optics
5224 Katrine Ave (60515-4070)
PHONE..................................630 512-8787
Fax: 630 810-8981
Frederick A Krehbiel, *CEO*
Brett Lane, *Engineer*
Dan McGawan, *Engineer*
Malcolm Phifer, *Engineer*
Tom Stanczyk, *Engineer*
EMP: 14
SALES (corp-wide): 27.4B **Privately Held**
WEB: www.molex.com
SIC: 3678 3679 3643 3357 Electronic connectors; electronic switches; electronic circuits; connectors & terminals for electrical devices; communication wire; fiber optic cable (insulated)
HQ: Molex, Llc
  2222 Wellington Ct
  Lisle IL 60532
  630 969-4550

**(G-8490)**
**MOTEC INC**
555 Rogers St Ste 5 (60515-3776)
PHONE..................................630 241-9595
Fax: 630 241-9597
Joanne Cleaves, *President*
Thomas E Cleaves, *Vice Pres*
▲ EMP: 5
SALES (est): 759.2K **Privately Held**
SIC: 3679 3714 3613 Electronic switches; motor vehicle parts & accessories; switchgear & switchboard apparatus

**(G-8491)**
**MOTOROLA SOLUTIONS INC**
1411 Opus Pl Ste 350 (60515-5717)
PHONE..................................630 353-8000
EMP: 5
SALES (corp-wide): 6B **Publicly Held**
WEB: www.motorola.com
SIC: 3663 Radio & TV communications equipment
PA: Motorola Solutions, Inc.
  500 W Monroe St Ste 4400
  Chicago IL 60661
  847 576-5000

**(G-8492)**
**MPS CHICAGO INC (DH)**
Also Called: Fulfillment Center, The
1500 Centre Cir (60515-1019)
PHONE..................................630 932-9000
Fax: 630 932-1079
George Bogdanovic, *President*
Bee Ruguone, *Prdtn Mgr*
Jeanne Beard, *VP Sales*
Julie Georgas, *Accounts Mgr*
Ronald Emmel, *Marketing Staff*
▲ EMP: 190 EST: 1962
SQ FT: 160,000
SALES: 59.7MM
SALES (corp-wide): 14.1B **Publicly Held**
WEB: www.jetlitho.com
SIC: 2752 3499 Color lithography; novelties & giftware, including trophies
HQ: Multi Packaging Solutions, Inc.
  150 E 42nd St Ste 2800
  New York NY 10022
  646 885-0005

## GEOGRAPHIC SECTION

**Downers Grove - Dupage County (G-8518)**

**(G-8493)**
**NATURES BEST INC (PA)**
3500 Lacey Rd Ste 1200 (60515-5450)
PHONE .................................. 631 232-3355
Hal Katz, *President*
Barbara Blind, *Bookkeeper*
▼ EMP: 20
SQ FT: 18,000
SALES (est): 18.4MM **Privately Held**
WEB: www.naturesbest.com
SIC: 5122 2833 8049 Vitamins & minerals; vitamins, natural or synthetic: bulk, uncompounded; nutrition specialist

**(G-8494)**
**NAVISTAR INC**
3333 Finley Rd (60515-1227)
PHONE .................................. 630 963-0769
Jim Guziak, *Director*
EMP: 66
SALES (corp-wide): 8.1B **Publicly Held**
SIC: 3711 Truck & tractor truck assembly
HQ: Navistar, Inc.
2701 Navistar Dr
Lisle IL 60532
331 332-5000

**(G-8495)**
**NICKELS QUARTERS LLC**
1651 Bolson Dr (60516-2637)
PHONE .................................. 630 514-5779
John Nickels, *Principal*
EMP: 4
SALES (est): 369.2K **Privately Held**
SIC: 3356 Nickel

**(G-8496)**
**NITE OWL PRINTS LLC**
1323 Butterfield Rd # 102 (60515-5620)
PHONE .................................. 630 541-6273
Sandip B Mehta, *Principal*
Sandip Mehta, *Marketing Mgr*
Sejal M Shah,
EMP: 2
SALES (est): 473.9K **Privately Held**
SIC: 2752 Commercial printing, lithographic

**(G-8497)**
**NUTHEME SIGN COMPANY**
2659 Wisconsin Ave (60515-4244)
PHONE .................................. 847 230-0067
Fax: 847 364-5932
Mary Ann Giovenco, *President*
Len Giovenco, *Principal*
James Borys, *VP Opers*
John Miller, *Plant Mgr*
EMP: 6
SQ FT: 3,750
SALES: 150K **Privately Held**
WEB: www.nutheme.com
SIC: 3993 Signs, not made in custom sign painting shops

**(G-8498)**
**OMEGA PUBLISHING SERVICES INC**
1137 Mistwood Pl (60515-1205)
PHONE .................................. 630 968-0440
Richard Wright, *President*
EMP: 2
SALES: 250K **Privately Held**
SIC: 2731 Books: publishing only

**(G-8499)**
**PAPERWORKS**
904 62nd St (60516-1901)
PHONE .................................. 630 969-3218
Fax: 630 969-4319
Ellen Arnold, *Owner*
EMP: 3
SALES (est): 150K **Privately Held**
SIC: 2741 Business service newsletters: publishing & printing

**(G-8500)**
**PAUL D STARK & ASSOCIATES (PA)**
Also Called: Stark Aire Fluid Bed Dryers
509 Blackburn Ct (60516-3919)
PHONE .................................. 630 964-7111
Fax: 630 964-7135
Paul D Stark, *President*
Andy Stark, *Corp Secy*
EMP: 3
SALES: 2.1MM **Privately Held**
SIC: 3567 3564 3443 Driers & redriers, industrial process; air purification equipment; cyclones, industrial: metal plate

**(G-8501)**
**PERRYCO INC (PA)**
Also Called: Enterprise Printing
6920 Webster St (60516-3509)
PHONE .................................. 303 652-8282
Wayne Perry, *President*
Lee Crispe, *CPA*
Donald A Perry, *CPA*
Dayna E Roane, *CPA*
Beverly Perry, *Admin Sec*
EMP: 24
SALES (est): 3MM **Privately Held**
WEB: www.rushvilletimes.com
SIC: 2711 Newspapers, publishing & printing

**(G-8502)**
**PETRO PROP INC**
7948 Highland Ave (60516-4328)
PHONE .................................. 630 910-4738
EMP: 7
SALES (est): 550K **Privately Held**
SIC: 3366 Copper Foundry

**(G-8503)**
**PLAZE INC (HQ)**
Also Called: Plz Aeroscience
2651 Warrenville Rd # 300 (60515-5772)
PHONE .................................. 630 628-4240
John Ferring IV, *Ch of Bd*
Ben Lacroffe, *CFO*
▲ EMP: 150 EST: 1940
SALES (est): 252.3MM
SALES (corp-wide): 254.8MM **Privately Held**
WEB: www.plaze.com
SIC: 5169 2819 Aerosols; charcoal (carbon), activated
PA: Plz Aeroscience Corporation
2651 Warrenville Rd # 300
Downers Grove IL 60515
630 628-3000

**(G-8504)**
**PLUMROSE USA INC (DH)**
1901 Butterfield Rd # 305 (60515-7915)
PHONE .................................. 732 257-6600
Dave Schanzer, *CEO*
Freddy Mortsenen, *Senior VP*
Freddy Mortensen, *Vice Pres*
Debbie Echols, *Safety Mgr*
Keith Strawn, *Purch Dir*
▲ EMP: 50
SALES: 580MM **Privately Held**
SIC: 2011 5147 2013 5149 Hams & picnics from meat slaughtered on site; bacon, slab & sliced from meat slaughtered on site; meats & meat products; sausages & other prepared meats; specialty food items
HQ: Jbs Usa Food Company
1770 Promontory Cir
Greeley CO 80634
970 506-8000

**(G-8505)**
**PLZ AEROSCIENCE CORPORATION (PA)**
2651 Warrenville Rd # 300 (60515-5772)
PHONE .................................. 630 628-3000
Ed Byczynski, *President*
Michael Magner, *Vice Pres*
Ben Lacrosse, *CFO*
EMP: 37
SQ FT: 250,000
SALES (est): 254.8MM **Privately Held**
SIC: 2813 Aerosols

**(G-8506)**
**PORTOLA PACKAGING LLC**
1140 31st St (60515-1212)
PHONE .................................. 630 515-8383
Anthony J Allot,
Joseph A Heaney,
Frank W III Hogan,
EMP: 26
SALES: 11.7MM
SALES (corp-wide): 3.6B **Publicly Held**
SIC: 3089 Closures, plastic
PA: Silgan Holdings Inc.
4 Landmark Sq Ste 400
Stamford CT 06901
203 975-7110

**(G-8507)**
**POWDERED METAL TECH LLC**
Also Called: Love Joy Technology
2655 Wisconsin Ave (60515-4243)
PHONE .................................. 630 852-0500
Michael Hennessy, *Manager*
EMP: 4
SALES (est): 430.1K **Privately Held**
SIC: 3444 Sheet metalwork

**(G-8508)**
**PRACTICE MANAGEMENT INFO CORP**
2001 Butterfield Rd # 310 (60515-1513)
PHONE .................................. 800 633-7467
Fax: 630 964-8873
Meta Rias, *Branch Mgr*
EMP: 30
SALES (corp-wide): 3MM **Privately Held**
WEB: www.medicalbookstore.com
SIC: 2731 Book publishing
PA: Practice Management Information Corporation
4727 Wilshire Blvd # 302
Los Angeles CA 90010
323 954-0224

**(G-8509)**
**PRECISION BRAND PRODUCTS INC**
2250 Curtiss St (60515-4038)
PHONE .................................. 630 969-7200
Terry Piper, *President*
Larry Franczyk, *Vice Pres*
Philip Wernick, *Controller*
Bruce Sichak, *Sales Mgr*
Lorraine Wood, *Sales Associate*
◆ EMP: 44
SQ FT: 50,000
SALES (est): 9.4MM
SALES (corp-wide): 223.6B **Publicly Held**
WEB: www.psteel.com
SIC: 3499 3429 3545 Shims, metal; manufactured hardware (general); machine tool accessories; bits for use on lathes, planers, shapers, etc.; drills (machine tool accessories); gauges (machine tool accessories)
HQ: Precision Steel Warehouse, Incorporated
3500 Wolf Rd
Franklin Park IL 60131
800 323-0740

**(G-8510)**
**PRECISION CIRCUITS INC**
2538 Wisconsin Ave (60515-4230)
PHONE .................................. 630 515-9100
George Cepynsky, *President*
EMP: 19
SQ FT: 3,400
SALES (est): 4.6MM **Privately Held**
SIC: 3679 Electronic circuits

**(G-8511)**
**PRODUCT SERVICE CRAFT INC**
5407 Walnut Ave (60515-4106)
PHONE .................................. 630 964-5160
Fax: 630 964-5161
George Beaton, *President*
Tim Putlak, *Office Mgr*
EMP: 10
SQ FT: 15,000
SALES: 900K **Privately Held**
SIC: 3499 3613 3466 Boxes for packing & shipping, metal; switchgear & switchboard apparatus; crowns & closures

**(G-8512)**
**RAILDECKS INTERMODAL**
1311 Palmer St (60516-2732)
PHONE .................................. 630 442-7676
EMP: 3 EST: 2012
SALES (est): 206.8K **Privately Held**
SIC: 2448 Cargo containers, wood & metal combination

**(G-8513)**
**RESCAR INDUSTRIES INC (PA)**
Also Called: Rescar Co
1101 31st St Ste 250 (60515-5532)
PHONE .................................. 630 963-1114
Joseph F Schieszler, *President*
Marvin Miller, *Project Mgr*
Barry Anstandig, *Treasurer*
Carol Brown, *Accounting Mgr*
Barbara Thomas, *Human Res Dir*
EMP: 45
SQ FT: 13,000
SALES (est): 313.9MM **Privately Held**
WEB: www.rescar.com
SIC: 3743 Railroad car rebuilding

**(G-8514)**
**REXNORD INDUSTRIES LLC**
2400 Curtiss St (60515-4037)
PHONE .................................. 847 520-1428
Fax: 847 537-0788
Marlene Maslovitz, *General Mgr*
Ron Krantz, *Purch Mgr*
Edward Mellinger, *QC Mgr*
Rod Oconnor, *Financial Exec*
Patrice Fassier, *Sales Mgr*
EMP: 98 **Publicly Held**
SIC: 3568 Power transmission equipment
HQ: Rexnord Industries, Llc
247 W Freshwater Way # 200
Milwaukee WI 53204
414 643-3000

**(G-8515)**
**REXNORD INDUSTRIES LLC**
2400 Curtiss St (60515-4037)
P.O. Box Caller # 1482 (60516)
PHONE .................................. 630 969-1770
Mark Cogdon, *General Mgr*
Cathy Palia, *Senior VP*
Gib Ende, *Project Dir*
Herman Ruiz, *Plant Mgr*
Dorothy Matiya, *Purch Mgr*
EMP: 100
SQ FT: 500,000 **Publicly Held**
SIC: 3568 Couplings, shaft: rigid, flexible, universal joint, etc.
HQ: Rexnord Industries, Llc
247 W Freshwater Way # 200
Milwaukee WI 53204
414 643-3000

**(G-8516)**
**REXNORD INDUSTRIES LLC**
2324 Curtiss St (60515-4017)
PHONE .................................. 630 719-2345
Fax: 630 969-8752
EMP: 209
SALES (est): 78K **Publicly Held**
SIC: 3999 Manufacturing industries
PA: Rexnord Corporation
247 W Freshwater Way # 300
Milwaukee WI 53204

**(G-8517)**
**S G S INC**
Also Called: Logic Printing
900 Ogden Ave Ste 190 (60515-2829)
PHONE .................................. 708 544-6061
Hema Gajiwala, *President*
EMP: 2
SQ FT: 500
SALES: 200K **Privately Held**
SIC: 2752 7336 7334 Commercial printing, offset; commercial art & graphic design; photocopying & duplicating services

**(G-8518)**
**SANFORD LP (HQ)**
Also Called: Sanford Brands
3500 Lacey Rd (60515-5422)
PHONE .................................. 770 418-7000
Fax: 630 547-6719
Michael Colk, *President*
Debra Svennizik, *General Mgr*
Rusty Snow, *Vice Pres*
Anthony De Pietro, *Engineer*
Maureen Wolthuis, *VP Sales*
◆ EMP: 600
SQ FT: 205,000
SALES (est): 210MM
SALES (corp-wide): 13.2B **Publicly Held**
SIC: 2891 3951 3952 Adhesives; pens & mechanical pencils; lead pencils & art goods

## Downers Grove - Dupage County (G-8519)

**PA:** Newell Brands Inc.
221 River St
Hoboken NJ 07030
201 610-6600

**(G-8519)**
**SAWIER**
7517 Florence Ave (60516-4482)
**PHONE** ................................. 630 297-8588
Justin Sawier, *President*
**EMP:** 46
**SALES:** 13.9MM **Privately Held**
**SIC: 5999** 3524 Tents; lawn & garden equipment

**(G-8520)**
**SCHNEIDER ELECTRIC USA INC**
3050 Finley Rd Ste 301 (60515-1196)
**PHONE** ................................. 847 925-7773
Bob Stalinger, *Manager*
**EMP:** 7
**SALES (corp-wide):** 241K **Privately Held**
**WEB:** www.squared.com
**SIC: 3613** Switchgear & switchboard apparatus
**HQ:** Schneider Electric Usa, Inc.
800 Federal St
Andover MA 01810
978 975-9600

**(G-8521)**
**SERVICENOW INC**
2001 Butterfield Rd # 240 (60515-1050)
**PHONE** ................................. 630 963-4608
**EMP:** 4
**SALES (corp-wide):** 1.3B **Publicly Held**
**SIC: 7372** Prepackaged software
**PA:** Servicenow, Inc.
2225 Lawson Ln
Santa Clara CA 95054
408 501-8500

**(G-8522)**
**SIEMENS PRODUCT LIFE MGMT SFTW**
Also Called: Siemens PLM Software
2001 Butterfield Rd # 630 (60515-1050)
**PHONE** ................................. 630 437-6700
**Fax:** 630 437-6766
Geoff Halliday, *Principal*
Frank Buchholz, *Senior VP*
Karin Tier, *VP Finance*
Amanda Goodman, *Finance Mgr*
David Bartlett, *Finance*
**EMP:** 34
**SALES (corp-wide):** 89.6B **Privately Held**
**SIC: 7372** Prepackaged software
**HQ:** Siemens Product Lifecycle Management Software Inc.
5800 Granite Pkwy Ste 600
Plano TX 75024
972 987-3000

**(G-8523)**
**SIGNATURE OF CHICAGO INC**
8428 Brookridge Rd (60516-4823)
**PHONE** ................................. 630 271-1876
Roberta Weimer, *President*
**EMP:** 3
**SALES:** 250K **Privately Held**
**SIC: 2395** Embroidery products, except schiffli machine

**(G-8524)**
**SILGAN WHITE CAP AMERICAS LLC**
Also Called: White Cap Illinois
1140 31st St (60515-1212)
**PHONE** ................................. 630 515-8383
**Fax:** 630 515-5326
Ray Torres, *President*
William Callard, *Purchasing*
Christopher Roth, *CFO*
**EMP:** 13 **EST:** 2001
**SALES (est):** 1.8MM
**SALES (corp-wide):** 3.6B **Publicly Held**
**SIC: 3411** 3444 Food & beverage containers; metal housings, enclosures, casings & other containers
**PA:** Silgan Holdings Inc.
4 Landmark Sq Ste 400
Stamford CT 06901
203 975-7110

**(G-8525)**
**SKYLINE INTERNATIONAL INC**
1400 Centre Cir (60515-1013)
**PHONE** ................................. 847 357-9077
Zain Subhani, *President*
▲ **EMP:** 20
**SQ FT:** 8,605
**SALES (est):** 2.5MM **Privately Held**
**SIC: 3679** Electronic circuits

**(G-8526)**
**SPANNAGEL TOOL & DIE**
2732 Wisconsin Ave (60515-4226)
**PHONE** ................................. 630 969-0650
**Fax:** 630 969-0650
Brian Spannagel, *President*
Margaret Spannagel, *Admin Sec*
**EMP:** 20 **EST:** 1920
**SQ FT:** 15,000
**SALES:** 1MM **Privately Held**
**SIC: 3544** 3469 Special dies & tools; metal stampings

**(G-8527)**
**STAGING BY TISH**
345 2nd St (60515-5228)
**PHONE** ................................. 630 852-9595
Patricia Wolf, *Principal*
**EMP:** 3
**SALES (est):** 90.5K **Privately Held**
**SIC: 1099** Metal ores

**(G-8528)**
**SUBURBAN LIFE PUBLICATION**
Also Called: Liberty Subn Chcago Newspapers
1101 31st St Ste 260 (60515-5585)
**PHONE** ................................. 630 368-1100
Caroll Stacklin, *President*
Michelle Herick, *Sr Corp Ofcr*
Nicole Ross, *Vice Pres*
Laura Pass, *Adv Dir*
John Amspaugh, *Manager*
**EMP:** 64
**SQ FT:** 30,000
**SALES (est):** 2.8MM
**SALES (corp-wide):** 83.1MM **Privately Held**
**SIC: 2711** Newspapers
**PA:** The B F Shaw Printing Company
444 Pine Hill Dr
Dixon IL
815 284-4000

**(G-8529)**
**TAGITSOLD INC**
Also Called: Fire Place By Ignite
740 Ogden Ave (60515-2916)
**PHONE** ................................. 630 724-1800
Randall Schorle, *President*
**EMP:** 2
**SALES:** 400K **Privately Held**
**SIC: 3272** Fireplace & chimney material: concrete

**(G-8530)**
**TEASE**
4717 Seeley Ave (60515-3413)
**PHONE** ................................. 630 960-4950
Allan Harris, *Partner*
**EMP:** 4
**SALES (est):** 240K **Privately Held**
**SIC: 2759** Screen printing

**(G-8531)**
**TECHNICAL ORDNANCE INC**
2525 Curtiss St (60515-4060)
**PHONE** ................................. 630 969-0620
Ebby Bryce, *Branch Mgr*
Gregg Eichwedel, *Manager*
Dennis Gulbranson, *Manager*
**EMP:** 201
**SALES (corp-wide):** 42.5MM **Privately Held**
**SIC: 2899** Pyrotechnic ammunition: flares, signals, rockets, etc.
**PA:** Technical Ordnance, Inc.
47600 180th St
Clear Lake SD 57226

**(G-8532)**
**THOR DEFENSE INC**
6121 Plymouth St (60516-1783)
P.O. Box 280 (60515-0280)
**PHONE** ................................. 630 541-5106
Diana Swenson, *CEO*
Severt Swenson III, *President*
**EMP:** 2
**SQ FT:** 2,500
**SALES:** 2MM **Privately Held**
**WEB:** www.thordefense.com
**SIC: 3842** Surgical appliances & supplies

**(G-8533)**
**TMK IPSCO**
2650 Warrenville Rd # 700 (60515-2074)
**PHONE** ................................. 630 874-0078
**Fax:** 630 874-6431
Vicki Avril, *CEO*
Dhiren Panda, *General Mgr*
Peter Smith, *Vice Pres*
Kirsten Augsback, *Production*
Christopher Corwell, *Sales Mgr*
▲ **EMP:** 28
**SALES (est):** 5.2MM **Privately Held**
**SIC: 3317** Seamless pipes & tubes

**(G-8534)**
**TREEHOUSE PRIVATE BRANDS INC**
3250 Lacey Rd Ste 600 (60515-7918)
**PHONE** ................................. 630 455-5265
Charles G Huber Jr, *Branch Mgr*
Richard Dissinger, *Manager*
**EMP:** 10
**SALES (corp-wide):** 6.1B **Publicly Held**
**SIC: 2043** 2052 2068 2035 Cereal breakfast foods; crackers, dry; cookies; nuts: dried, dehydrated, salted or roasted; dressings, salad: raw & cooked (except dry mixes); seasonings & sauces, except tomato & dry
**HQ:** Treehouse Private Brands, Inc.
800 Market St Ste 2600
Saint Louis MO 63101

**(G-8535)**
**UNIQUE ASSEMBLY & DECORATING**
2550 Wisconsin Ave (60515-4242)
**PHONE** ................................. 630 241-4300
**Fax:** 630 241-4306
James Gerberich, *President*
George Brown, *Shareholder*
Lynn Gerberich, *Admin Sec*
▲ **EMP:** 36
**SQ FT:** 20,500
**SALES:** 3MM **Privately Held**
**WEB:** www.uniquepadprinting.com
**SIC: 3089** 2759 Coloring & finishing of plastic products; commercial printing

**(G-8536)**
**VERSATILE CARD TECHNOLOGY INC (PA)**
Also Called: V C T
5200 Thatcher Rd (60515-4053)
**PHONE** ................................. 630 852-5600
**Fax:** 630 852-5817
Pethinaidu Veluchamy, *CEO*
Nicholas Cooney, *President*
Anu Veluchamy, *President*
Push Venktaswamy, *Vice Pres*
Tom Verkler, *Accounting Mgr*
▲ **EMP:** 200
**SQ FT:** 50,000
**SALES (est):** 59.8MM **Privately Held**
**WEB:** www.vct.com
**SIC: 3089** Identification cards, plastic

**(G-8537)**
**VERTEC BIOSOLVENTS INC**
1441 Branding Ave Ste 100 (60515-5624)
**PHONE** ................................. 630 960-0600
**Fax:** 630 960-0660
James Opre, *President*
Skip Laubach, *President*
Gerald Vasek, *Vice Pres*
**EMP:** 8 **EST:** 1997
**SQ FT:** 4,000
**SALES (est):** 1.8MM **Privately Held**
**WEB:** www.vertecbiosolvents.com
**SIC: 2911** Solvents

**(G-8538)**
**VRMC LLC**
3000 Woodcreek Dr Ste 300 (60515-5408)
**PHONE** ................................. 612 210-1868
Robert E Luby Jr,
**EMP:** 6

**SALES:** 950K **Privately Held**
**SIC: 3999** Manufacturing industries

**(G-8539)**
**WAIPUNA USA INC**
Also Called: Waipuna Systems
5126 Walnut Ave (60515-4045)
**PHONE** ................................. 630 514-0364
Jeff Wingren, *CEO*
**EMP:** 3
**SALES:** 190K **Privately Held**
**SIC: 3523** Weeding machines, agricultural

**(G-8540)**
**WALLACE/HASKIN CORP**
900 Ogden Ave 181 (60515-2829)
**PHONE** ................................. 630 789-2882
Kenneth Eng, *President*
Ashley C Eng, *Chairman*
▲ **EMP:** 5 **EST:** 1896
**SQ FT:** 10,000
**SALES (est):** 496.9K **Privately Held**
**SIC: 3556** 3546 3646 5085 Grinders, commercial, food; fish & shellfish processing machinery; power-driven handtools; fluorescent lighting fixtures, commercial; industrial supplies; abrasives & adhesives; saw blades & handsaws; cutlery

**(G-8541)**
**WALNECKS INC**
Also Called: Walneck's Cycle Trader
7923 Janes Ave (60517-3800)
**PHONE** ................................. 630 985-2097
Buzz Walneck, *President*
**EMP:** 2 **EST:** 1981
**SALES (est):** 251.7K **Privately Held**
**WEB:** www.walnecks.com
**SIC: 2721** Magazines: publishing only, not printed on site

**(G-8542)**
**WATERS WIRE EDM SERVICE**
2719 Curtiss St (60515-4002)
**PHONE** ................................. 630 640-3534
Ron Vondrasek, *Owner*
**EMP:** 5
**SQ FT:** 35,000
**SALES:** 400K **Privately Held**
**SIC: 3312** Tool & die steel

**(G-8543)**
**WELKINS LLC**
3000 Woodcreek Dr Ste 300 (60515-5408)
**PHONE** ................................. 877 319-3504
Christopher Blodgett,
**EMP:** 5
**SALES (est):** 455.1K **Privately Held**
**SIC: 3949** 3841 Sporting & athletic goods; surgical & medical instruments; surgical appliances & supplies

**(G-8544)**
**WHITE GRAPHICS INC**
1411 Centre Cir (60515-1022)
**PHONE** ................................. 630 791-0232
Richard T White Jr, *CEO*
Andrew White, *President*
Thomas White, *Vice Pres*
Pamela Kovsky, *Office Mgr*
Joyce R White, *Admin Sec*
**EMP:** 10
**SALES (est):** 1.6MM **Privately Held**
**SIC: 2759** Commercial printing

**(G-8545)**
**WHITE GRAPHICS PRINTING SVCS**
1411 Centre Cir (60515-1022)
**PHONE** ................................. 630 629-9300
Richard T White Jr, *President*
Dee Zaremba, *Plant Mgr*
Pam Bukovsk, *Manager*
Andrew White, *Manager*
Joyce White, *Admin Sec*
**EMP:** 5
**SQ FT:** 15,000
**SALES (est):** 720.1K **Privately Held**
**WEB:** www.whitegraphicschicago.com
**SIC: 2754** 2759 Commercial printing, gravure; commercial printing

## GEOGRAPHIC SECTION

**(G-8546)**
**WINNER CUTTING & STAMPING CO**
1245 Warren Ave  (60515-3548)
PHONE.................................630 963-1800
John Berwanger, *President*
Robert A Simpson, *President*
Ernest Dix, *Vice Pres*
Kevin Phillips, *Vice Pres*
Thomas Slott, *Vice Pres*
**EMP:** 11
**SQ FT:** 10,000
**SALES (est):** 1.9MM  **Privately Held**
**SIC:** 3053  Gaskets, all materials

### Downs
*Mclean County*

**(G-8547)**
**PRAIRIE WOODWORKS INC**
311 S Lincoln St  (61736-7567)
P.O. Box 21  (61736-0021)
PHONE.................................309 378-2418
Fax: 309 378-2418
Ronald Skidmore, *President*
Stephen Stenger, *Treasurer*
**EMP:** 7  **EST:** 1976
**SQ FT:** 10,000
**SALES:** 350K  **Privately Held**
**WEB:** www.prairiewoodworks.com
**SIC:** 2511  2434  2431  Wood household furniture; wood kitchen cabinets; millwork

**(G-8548)**
**TRUELINE INC**
7095 Shaffer Dr  (61736-7547)
PHONE.................................309 378-2571
Kenneth Mysvka, *President*
Matt Lucas, *Natl Sales Mgr*
**EMP:** 20
**SALES (est):** 2.3MM  **Privately Held**
**SIC:** 3569  Assembly machines, non-metalworking

**(G-8549)**
**UNITED OIL CO**
405 S Seminary St  (61736-7583)
P.O. Box 1263, Bloomington  (61702-1263)
PHONE.................................309 378-3049
Bill Chaney, *Owner*
**EMP:** 5
**SALES (est):** 396.5K  **Privately Held**
**SIC:** 1389  Oil & gas field services

### Du Quoin
*Perry County*

**(G-8550)**
**AMERICAN FUR ENTERPRISES**
413 S Greenwood Ave  (62832-2564)
PHONE.................................618 542-2018
Tyrone Lindner, *Owner*
Tyrone Lindner, *Owner*
**EMP:** 3
**SALES:** 38K  **Privately Held**
**SIC:** 3999  Furs, dressed: bleached, curried, scraped, tanned or dyed

**(G-8551)**
**BURKE TOOL & MANUFACTURING INC**
339 E Olive St  (62832-2316)
PHONE.................................618 542-6441
Fax: 618 542-4265
John Burke, *President*
Jeannie Burke, *Vice Pres*
**EMP:** 8
**SQ FT:** 13,000
**SALES (est):** 1MM  **Privately Held**
**WEB:** www.burketool.com
**SIC:** 3599  7692  3625  Machine shop, jobbing & repair; welding repair; relays & industrial controls

**(G-8552)**
**COCA-COLA REFRESHMENTS USA INC**
Hwy 51 S  (62832)
P.O. Box 187  (62832-0187)
PHONE.................................618 542-2101
Fax: 618 542-4561
Jim Walter, *Branch Mgr*
**EMP:** 116
**SALES (corp-wide):** 41.8B  **Publicly Held**
**SIC:** 2086  2087  Carbonated beverages, nonalcoholic: bottled & canned; soft drinks: packaged in cans, bottles, etc.; fruit drinks (less than 100% juice): packaged in cans, etc.; syrups, drink; concentrates, drink
**HQ:** Coca-Cola Refreshments Usa, Inc.
2500 Windy Ridge Pkwy Se
Atlanta GA 30339
770 989-3000

**(G-8553)**
**DUQUOIN DENTAL ASSOCIATES**
1266 S Washington St  (62832-3853)
PHONE.................................618 542-8832
Isaac E Davison, *President*
**EMP:** 4
**SALES (est):** 220K  **Privately Held**
**SIC:** 3843  Dental equipment & supplies

**(G-8554)**
**FIVE STAR INDUSTRIES  INC (PA)**
1308 Wells Street Rd  (62832-4171)
P.O. Box 60  (62832-0060)
PHONE.................................618 542-4880
Fax: 618 542-5556
Byford Reidelberger, *President*
Helen Mayer, *Vice Pres*
Greg Herrin, *Opers Staff*
Tom Emling, *Treasurer*
John Childs, *Controller*
**EMP:** 40
**SQ FT:** 40,000
**SALES:** 3.4MM  **Privately Held**
**WEB:** www.5starind.com
**SIC:** 2511  8361  8331  Wood lawn & garden furniture; rehabilitation center, residential: health care incidental; sheltered workshop

**(G-8555)**
**GE FAIRCHILD MINING EQUIPMENT**
707 N Hickory St  (62832-1238)
Rural Route 51  (62832)
PHONE.................................618 559-3216
Russell T Stokes, *Branch Mgr*
**EMP:** 86
**SALES (corp-wide):** 64.1MM  **Privately Held**
**SIC:** 3532  3535  Mining machinery; conveyors & conveying equipment
**PA:** Ge Fairchild Mining Equipment
200 Fairchild Ln
Glen Lyn VA 24093
540 921-8000

**(G-8556)**
**GENERAL CABLE INDUSTRIES INC**
Also Called: Du Quoin, IL Plant
1453 S Washington St  (62832-3803)
PHONE.................................618 542-4761
Jerry McKinzie, *Plant Mgr*
Andy Small, *Plant Mgr*
Mark Tindle, *Mfg Staff*
Don Schmidt, *Engineer*
Douglas Taylor, *Engineer*
**EMP:** 80  **Publicly Held**
**WEB:** www.generalcable.com
**SIC:** 3351  Wire, copper & copper alloy
**HQ:** General Cable Industries, Inc.
4 Tesseneer Dr
Highland Heights KY 41076
859 572-8000

**(G-8557)**
**PERRY ADULT LIVING INC**
1308 Wells Street Rd  (62832-4171)
PHONE.................................618 542-5421
John Childs, *Manager*
**EMP:** 6
**SALES (est):** 210K  **Privately Held**
**SIC:** 8322  3949  Social services for the handicapped; baskets (creels), fish & bait

**(G-8558)**
**ST NICHOLAS BREWING CO**
12 S Oak St  (62832-1515)
P.O. Box 863  (62832-0863)
PHONE.................................618 318-3556
Theodore Wichmann, *President*
Gary Sullivan, *Partner*
Karen Hand, *Vice Pres*
Sarah Andrew, *Treasurer*
Abby Ancell, *Director*
**EMP:** 5
**SALES (est):** 425.3K  **Privately Held**
**SIC:** 2082  Beer (alcoholic beverage)

### Dundee
*Kane County*

**(G-8559)**
**BRIGHT DESIGNS INC**
14n690 Sleepy Hollow Rd  (60118-9165)
PHONE.................................847 428-6012
Kimberly Bright, *Owner*
**EMP:** 3
**SALES (est):** 50K  **Privately Held**
**SIC:** 2511  5712  Wood household furniture; furniture stores

**(G-8560)**
**CJ DRILLING  INC**
19n041 Galligan Rd  (60118-9536)
PHONE.................................847 854-3888
Tammie A Johnson, *President*
Ryan Allen, *Project Mgr*
Kevin Okeefe, *Materials Mgr*
Kevin Breen, *CFO*
Sheila Lane, *Office Mgr*
**EMP:** 36
**SALES (est):** 15.3MM  **Privately Held**
**SIC:** 1629  3441  4213  7389  Caisson drilling; fabricated structural metal; trucking, except local;

**(G-8561)**
**ENERGY GROUP  INC (PA)**
14 N 679 Isle Rr 25  (60118)
PHONE.................................847 836-2000
Fax: 847 836-9448
Lawrence R Buettner, *President*
Ronald Walblay, *Corp Secy*
**EMP:** 25
**SQ FT:** 3,500
**SALES (est):** 4MM  **Privately Held**
**SIC:** 1382  Oil & gas exploration services

**(G-8562)**
**GROOMSMART INC**
4672 W Main St  (60118-9414)
P.O. Box 447, Belvidere  (61008-0447)
PHONE.................................847 836-6007
Tracy Huey, *Principal*
**EMP:** 6
**SALES (est):** 515.9K  **Privately Held**
**SIC:** 3999  Pet supplies

**(G-8563)**
**LARON OIL CORPORATION**
14 N 679 Rr 25  (60118)
PHONE.................................847 836-2000
Lawrence Buettner, *President*
Ronald Walblay, *Corp Secy*
**EMP:** 8
**SALES (est):** 770K  **Privately Held**
**SIC:** 1382  Oil & gas exploration services

**(G-8564)**
**MAYTEC  INC**
901 Wesemann Dr  (60118-9407)
PHONE.................................847 429-0321
Harold Ley, *President*
Erik Sanke, *Sales Dir*
Thomas Paskiewicz, *Manager*
Dieter Ley, *Admin Sec*
Daisy Ruiz, *Administration*
▲ **EMP:** 9
**SALES (est):** 2.1MM  **Privately Held**
**WEB:** www.maytecinc.com
**SIC:** 3354  Aluminum extruded products

**(G-8565)**
**NORTHERN ILLINOIS MOLD CORP**
17n520 Adams Dr  (60118-9526)
PHONE.................................847 669-2100
Fax: 847 669-2154
Bruce Niggemann, *President*
Steve Pierce, *Purchasing*
**EMP:** 15
**SQ FT:** 20,000
**SALES (est):** 2.1MM  **Privately Held**
**WEB:** www.nimold.com
**SIC:** 3544  Forms (molds), for foundry & plastics working machinery

### Dunlap
*Peoria County*

**(G-8566)**
**BLITZ LURES  LLC**
11919 N Windcrest Ct  (61525-9509)
PHONE.................................309 256-1574
Vance Terry J, *Mng Member*
**EMP:** 4
**SALES (est):** 1.1K  **Privately Held**
**SIC:** 3949  Bait, artificial: fishing; lures, fishing: artificial

**(G-8567)**
**HIDDEN HOLLOW STABLES INC**
9222 Brimfield Jubilee Rd  (61525-9149)
PHONE.................................309 243-7979
Kathy Simpson, *President*
**EMP:** 4
**SALES (est):** 290K  **Privately Held**
**WEB:** www.hiddenhollowstables.com
**SIC:** 7999  5812  1711  3599  Riding stable; eating places; boiler & furnace contractors; machine shop, jobbing & repair

**(G-8568)**
**JANES LETTERING SERVICE INC**
12200 N Brentfield Dr # 13  (61525-9002)
PHONE.................................309 243-7669
Fax: 309 243-7032
Joy Pautler, *President*
Kevin Pautler, *Vice Pres*
**EMP:** 5
**SALES (est):** 423K  **Privately Held**
**SIC:** 2395  Embroidery & art needlework

### Dupo
*St. Clair County*

**(G-8569)**
**CUSTOM BLENDING & PCKAGING OF**
108 Coulter Rd  (62239)
PHONE.................................618 286-1140
Dale Horne, *Mng Member*
Theresa Keith, *Manager*
Carol Schieler, *Director*
Judy Hamilton,
Seelman Craig A,
▲ **EMP:** 11
**SALES (est):** 2.9MM  **Privately Held**
**SIC:** 2841  2813  2843  Soap: granulated, liquid, cake, flaked or chip; aerosols; surface active agents

**(G-8570)**
**EARTHWISE RECYCLED PALLET**
336 Mcbride Ave  (62239-1640)
P.O. Box 162  (62239-0162)
PHONE.................................618 286-6015
Daryll G Mallin, *Owner*
**EMP:** 3
**SALES (est):** 261.8K  **Privately Held**
**SIC:** 2448  Pallets, wood & wood with metal

**(G-8571)**
**HUCKS FOOD FUEL**
110 S Main St  (62239-1348)
PHONE.................................618 286-5111
Fax: 618 286-9515
Amanda Feiser, *Principal*
**EMP:** 15
**SALES (est):** 1MM  **Privately Held**
**SIC:** 2869  Fuels

## Dupo - St. Clair County (G-8572)

**(G-8572)**
**INTERSTATE INDUSTRIAL TECH**
Also Called: Industec
510 N Main St (62239-1126)
PHONE.................................618 286-4900
Merrill W Dawson, *President*
Scott Dawson, *Manager*
Phyllis M Dawson, *Admin Sec*
**EMP:** 6
**SQ FT:** 4,000
**SALES (est):** 510K  **Privately Held**
**WEB:** www.industech.com
**SIC: 3625**  Control equipment, electric

**(G-8573)**
**MILLER MANUFACTURING CO INC**
Miller Group
1610 Design Way (62239-1826)
PHONE.................................636 343-5700
Randy Castle, *President*
**EMP:** 80
**SQ FT:** 100,000
**SALES (corp-wide):** 11MM  **Privately Held**
**SIC: 2541**  Wood partitions & fixtures
**PA:** Miller Manufacturing Co Inc
3301 Castlewood Rd
Richmond VA 23234
804 232-4551

**(G-8574)**
**MULTIPLEX DISPLAY FIXTURE CO**
Also Called: Miller Group Multiplex Div
1610 Design Way (62239-1826)
PHONE.................................800 325-3350
Randy Castle, *President*
Kathy Webster, *Managing Dir*
Elmer Brannaker, *Plant Mgr*
Dick Vogt, *Plant Mgr*
Mike Ebert, *Purch Mgr*
**EMP:** 50
**SQ FT:** 97,000
**SALES:** 9.7MM
**SALES (corp-wide):** 11MM  **Privately Held**
**SIC: 2541**  2542  2434  Display fixtures, wood; partitions & fixtures, except wood; wood kitchen cabinets
**PA:** Miller Manufacturing Co Inc
3301 Castlewood Rd
Richmond VA 23234
804 232-4551

**(G-8575)**
**PROGRESSIVE RECOVERY INC**
700 Industrial Dr (62239-1827)
PHONE.................................618 286-5000
Fax: 618 286-5009
Daniel B Marks, *President*
Jim Laarman, *COO*
Donald Fluchel, *Vice Pres*
Jerry Trunko, *Project Mgr*
Rich Meyer, *Opers Mgr*
**EMP:** 60
**SQ FT:** 60,000
**SALES (est):** 27.4MM  **Privately Held**
**WEB:** www.progressive-recovery.com
**SIC: 3569**  Liquid automation machinery & equipment

**(G-8576)**
**R T P COMPANY**
1610 Design Way Ste B (62239-1826)
PHONE.................................618 286-6100
**EMP:** 3
**SALES (est):** 173.3K  **Privately Held**
**SIC: 3089**  Plastics products

**(G-8577)**
**STELLAR BLENDING & PACKAGING**
1556 Decoma Dr (62239-1824)
P.O. Box 130 (62239-0130)
PHONE.................................314 520-7318
Theresa Pakovich, *Manager*
Daniel G Connelly,
Jerry Lewinski,
Jeffrey C Walker,
**EMP:** 19
**SALES (est):** 2.7MM  **Privately Held**
**SIC: 7389**  2842  Packaging & labeling services; cleaning or polishing preparations

**(G-8578)**
**STERLING PHRM SVCS LLC (PA)**
109 S 2nd St (62239-1351)
PHONE.................................618 286-6060
Tiffany Flynn, *Project Mgr*
Robert G Flynn, *Mng Member*
Robert T Flynn,
**EMP:** 7
**SQ FT:** 3,600
**SALES:** 4MM  **Privately Held**
**SIC: 2834**  Pharmaceutical preparations

**(G-8579)**
**STOLLE CASPER QUAR & CONTG CO**
Also Called: Falling Springs Quarry
2901 Stolle Rd (62239-1635)
PHONE.................................618 337-5212
Sharon Dell, *Manager*
**EMP:** 25
**SALES (corp-wide):** 62.1MM  **Privately Held**
**SIC: 1422**  1411  Crushed & broken limestone; dimension stone
**PA:** Stolle, Casper Quarry & Contracting Co Inc
3003 Stolle Rd
Dupo IL
618 337-3343

**(G-8580)**
**STREBOR SPECIALTIES LLC**
108 Coulter Rd (62239)
P.O. Box 62 (62239-0062)
PHONE.................................618 286-1140
Otto Roberts,
**EMP:** 26
**SQ FT:** 26,000
**SALES (est):** 1.1MM  **Privately Held**
**SIC: 2869**  2992  3499  Industrial organic chemicals; oils & greases, blending & compounding; nozzles, spray: aerosol, paint or insecticide

**(G-8581)**
**TRAUBE CANVAS PRODUCTS INC**
1727 Bluffview Dr (62239-1488)
PHONE.................................618 281-0696
Todd Traube, *President*
Don Traube, *Vice Pres*
**EMP:** 12
**SQ FT:** 2,400
**SALES (est):** 1.2MM  **Privately Held**
**WEB:** www.traubeawning.com
**SIC: 2394**  Awnings, fabric: made from purchased materials; tents: made from purchased materials

**(G-8582)**
**UPCHURCH READY MIX CONCRETE**
200 N 2nd St (62239-1231)
PHONE.................................618 286-4808
Jim Upchurch, *Executive*
**EMP:** 3
**SALES (est):** 189.5K  **Privately Held**
**SIC: 3273**  Ready-mixed concrete

**(G-8583)**
**VERTEX CHEMICAL CORPORATION**
3101 Carondelet Ave (62239-1176)
P.O. Box 277 (62239-0277)
PHONE.................................618 286-5207
Fax: 314 894-2671
Lee Moisio, *Vice Pres*
John Helebusch, *Manager*
John Helebusch, *Manager*
**EMP:** 14
**SALES (corp-wide):** 483.5MM  **Publicly Held**
**WEB:** www.vertexchemical.com
**SIC: 2819**  Bleaching powder, lime bleaching compounds
**HQ:** Vertex Chemical Corporation
11685 Manchester Rd
Saint Louis MO 63131
314 471-0500

**(G-8584)**
**WINNING STREAK INC**
1580 Decoma Dr (62239-1824)
PHONE.................................618 277-8191
Chris Braun, *President*
**EMP:** 20
**SQ FT:** 10,000
**SALES (est):** 3.3MM  **Privately Held**
**WEB:** www.winning-streak.com
**SIC: 2759**  5941  2395  Screen printing; sporting goods & bicycle shops; embroidery & art needlework

## Durand
### Winnebago County

**(G-8585)**
**FOLK RACE CARS**
9027 Freeport Rd (61024-9721)
PHONE.................................815 629-2418
Ron Folk, *Owner*
Brian Folk, *Manager*
**EMP:** 3
**SQ FT:** 2,700
**SALES (est):** 309.2K  **Privately Held**
**WEB:** www.folkracecars.com
**SIC: 3711**  5531  7692  3599  Chassis, motor vehicle; automotive accessories; welding repair; custom machinery; top & body repair & paint shops

**(G-8586)**
**KR MACHINE**
15322 Eicks Rd (61024-9641)
PHONE.................................815 248-2250
Karen Judd, *President*
Laurence Judd Jr, *Vice Pres*
**EMP:** 5
**SALES (est):** 250K  **Privately Held**
**SIC: 3469**  Machine parts, stamped or pressed metal

**(G-8587)**
**MULVAIN WOODWORKS**
14578 Center Rd (61024-9525)
PHONE.................................815 248-2305
Fax: 815 248-3253
Patricia Mulvain, *President*
**EMP:** 5
**SALES (est):** 618.1K  **Privately Held**
**WEB:** www.mulvainwoodworks.com
**SIC: 2421**  2431  Sawmills & planing mills, general; millwork

## Dwight
### Livingston County

**(G-8588)**
**CATERPILLAR INC**
1200 E Mazon Ave (60420-8202)
PHONE.................................815 584-4887
**EMP:** 360
**SALES (corp-wide):** 38.5B  **Publicly Held**
**SIC: 3531**  Construction machinery
**PA:** Caterpillar Inc.
100 Ne Adams St
Peoria IL 61629
309 675-1000

**(G-8589)**
**NEW LENOX MACHINE CO INC**
1200 E Mazon Ave Ste B (60420-8218)
P.O. Box 188 (60420-0188)
PHONE.................................815 584-4866
Fax: 815 584-4877
Alan G Seniw, *President*
Carol Seniw, *Corp Secy*
**EMP:** 10
**SQ FT:** 22,000
**SALES (est):** 1.2MM  **Privately Held**
**WEB:** www.newlenoxmc.com
**SIC: 3599**  8742  3542  Machine & other job shop work; maintenance management consultant; rebuilt machine tools, metal forming types

**(G-8590)**
**PAPER**
204 E Chippewa St (60420-1408)
P.O. Box 245 (60420-0245)
PHONE.................................815 584-1901
Fax: 815 584-2196
Mary Boma, *Owner*
**EMP:** 22  **EST:** 2000
**SALES (est):** 910.6K  **Privately Held**
**WEB:** www.thepaper.com
**SIC: 2711**  Newspapers

**(G-8591)**
**R R DONNELLEY & SONS COMPANY**
R R Donnelley
801 N Union St (60420-7032)
PHONE.................................815 584-2770
Fax: 815 584-4353
Dennis Wall, *Division Mgr*
Clay Webb, *Enginr/R&D Mgr*
Sharron Doyle, *Controller*
Denise Seeman, *Manager*
**EMP:** 900
**SQ FT:** 357,000
**SALES (corp-wide):** 6.9B  **Publicly Held**
**WEB:** www.rrdonnelley.com
**SIC: 2752**  2789  2759  2732  Commercial printing, lithographic; bookbinding & related work; commercial printing; book printing; miscellaneous publishing
**PA:** R. R. Donnelley & Sons Company
35 W Wacker Dr Ste 3650
Chicago IL 60601
312 326-8000

**(G-8592)**
**RIBER CONSTRUCTION INC**
405 S Old Route 66 (60420-1290)
PHONE.................................815 584-3337
Fax: 815 584-3340
Paul Riber, *President*
Patsy Riber, *Corp Secy*
Mark Riber, *Director*
**EMP:** 12  **EST:** 1931
**SQ FT:** 2,400
**SALES:** 3.1MM  **Privately Held**
**SIC: 1622**  3273  Bridge construction; ready-mixed concrete

## Earlville
### Lasalle County

**(G-8593)**
**EARLVILLE COLD STOR LCKR LLC**
101 N East St (60518-8094)
PHONE.................................815 246-9469
Gene Coppes, *Owner*
Margie Coppes, *Co-Owner*
**EMP:** 5  **EST:** 1937
**SQ FT:** 1,000
**SALES (est):** 388.4K  **Privately Held**
**SIC: 2011**  2013  Meat packing plants; sausages & other prepared meats

**(G-8594)**
**FREEDOM SAUSAGE INC**
4155 E 1650th Rd (60518-6192)
PHONE.................................815 792-8276
Fax: 815 792-8283
Mark Wiley, *President*
Paul Wiley, *Vice Pres*
Jim Pfau, *Treasurer*
Dave Gast, *Admin Sec*
**EMP:** 10  **EST:** 1980
**SQ FT:** 6,000
**SALES (est):** 630K  **Privately Held**
**SIC: 7299**  2013  Butcher service, processing only; sausages & other prepared meats

**(G-8595)**
**HOMETOWN NEWS GROUP LP**
107 W Railroad St (60518-3101)
P.O. Box 487 (60518-0487)
PHONE.................................815 246-4600
Andrea Bloom, *Partner*
**EMP:** 9
**SALES (est):** 350K  **Privately Held**
**SIC: 2711**  Newspapers: publishing only, not printed on site

**(G-8596)**
**R&R FLIGHT SERVICE**
Rr 2 (60518)
PHONE.................................815 538-2599
Don Younglove, *Owner*
**EMP:** 5
**SALES (est):** 274.4K  **Privately Held**
**SIC: 3523**  Fertilizing machinery, farm

# GEOGRAPHIC SECTION

East Dubuque - Jo Daviess County (G-8620)

**(G-8597)**
**TSF NET INC**
Also Called: Software Farm, The
402 S Ottawa St (60518-8164)
P.O. Box 477 (60518-0477)
**PHONE** .......... 815 246-7295
John O Foster, *Principal*
**EMP:** 10
**SALES:** 500K **Privately Held**
**SIC:** 7372 4813 Prepackaged software;

## East Alton
### Madison County

**(G-8598)**
**ACE PRINTING CO**
615 E Airline Dr (62024-1913)
**PHONE** .......... 618 259-2711
**Fax:** 618 259-2745
Donald J Mitchell, *Owner*
Carolyn Mitchell, *Owner*
Carolyn Mitchelle, *Co-Owner*
**EMP:** 3
**SQ FT:** 2,700
**SALES:** 145K **Privately Held**
**SIC:** 2759 Commercial printing; visiting cards (including business); printing

**(G-8599)**
**BEALL MANUFACTURING INC (PA)**
Also Called: Supertuf
421 N Shamrock St (62024-1174)
P.O. Box 70 (62024-0070)
**PHONE** .......... 618 259-8154
**Fax:** 618 259-7953
Mark Speciale, *President*
Larry Allen, *General Mgr*
Jim Speciale, *Controller*
Travis Hogan, *Sales Staff*
Art Fultz, *Marketing Mgr*
**EMP:** 50
**SQ FT:** 75,000
**SALES (est):** 14.9MM **Privately Held**
**WEB:** www.supertuf.com
**SIC:** 3523 3495 3524 Farm machinery & equipment; wire springs; lawn & garden equipment

**(G-8600)**
**CSI CUTTING SPECIALIST INC**
421 N Shamrock St (62024-1174)
P.O. Box 70 (62024-0070)
**PHONE** .......... 731 352-5351
Mark Speciale, *President*
John Pieper, *Mfg Dir*
Jim Speciale, *Controller*
**EMP:** 75
**SALES (est):** 10MM
**SALES (corp-wide):** 14.9MM **Privately Held**
**SIC:** 3469 Machine parts, stamped or pressed metal
**PA:** Beall Manufacturing, Inc.
421 N Shamrock St
East Alton IL 62024
618 259-8154

**(G-8601)**
**FLOWERS DISTRIBUTING INC**
Also Called: 7 Up
4605 Hedge Rd (62024)
**PHONE** .......... 618 255-1021
**Fax:** 618 255-1024
Harry Flowers Jr, *President*
**EMP:** 20
**SQ FT:** 5,000
**SALES (est):** 3.2MM **Privately Held**
**SIC:** 2086 Bottled & canned soft drinks

**(G-8602)**
**GBC METALS LLC**
305 Lewis And Clark Blvd (62024-1177)
**PHONE** .......... 618 258-2350
John Wasz, *CEO*
Ken Hale, *Director*
**EMP:** 17
**SALES (corp-wide):** 1.3B **Publicly Held**
**SIC:** 3351 Brass rolling & drawing
**HQ:** Gbc Metals, Llc
427 N Shamrock St
East Alton IL 62024
618 258-2350

**(G-8603)**
**GBC METALS LLC (DH)**
Also Called: Olin Brass
427 N Shamrock St (62024-1174)
**PHONE** .......... 618 258-2350
**Fax:** 618 258-2719
John Walker, *CEO*
Bill Toler, *President*
John J Wasz, *COO*
John Moritz, *Vice Pres*
Tom Werner, *Vice Pres*
◆ **EMP:** 2
**SALES:** 241.9MM
**SALES (corp-wide):** 1.3B **Publicly Held**
**SIC:** 3351 3341 3469 Brass rolling & drawing; copper smelting & refining (secondary); metal stampings
**HQ:** Global Brass And Copper, Inc.
305 Lewis And Clark Blvd
East Alton IL 62024
502 873-3000

**(G-8604)**
**GLOBAL BRASS AND COPPER INC (HQ)**
305 Lewis And Clark Blvd (62024-1177)
**PHONE** .......... 502 873-3000
Michael Psaros, *Ch of Bd*
John Wasz, *President*
Greg Keown, *Vice Pres*
Kelly Funke, *Engineer*
Ed McGillis, *Engineer*
**EMP:** 2
**SALES (est):** 1.2B
**SALES (corp-wide):** 1.3B **Publicly Held**
**SIC:** 3351 3341 3469 1542 Brass rolling & drawing; copper smelting & refining (secondary); metal stampings; commercial & office building, new construction
**PA:** Global Brass And Copper Holdings, Inc.
475 N Marti Rd
Schaumburg IL 60173
847 240-4700

**(G-8605)**
**GLOBAL BRASS AND COPPER INC**
1901 N Roselle Rd (62024)
**PHONE** .......... 618 258-5330
John J Wasz, *CEO*
**EMP:** 1
**SALES (est):** 317.6K
**SALES (corp-wide):** 1.3B **Publicly Held**
**SIC:** 3555 Type: lead, steel, brass, copper faced, etc.
**HQ:** Global Brass And Copper, Inc.
305 Lewis And Clark Blvd
East Alton IL 62024
502 873-3000

**(G-8606)**
**NEWSSOR MANUFACTURING INC**
302 Dry St (62024-1010)
**PHONE** .......... 618 259-1174
Wendell Ross, *President*
**EMP:** 9
**SQ FT:** 7,300
**SALES (est):** 1MM **Privately Held**
**SIC:** 3599 5084 Machine shop, jobbing & repair; industrial machinery & equipment

**(G-8607)**
**OLIN CORPORATION**
Also Called: Olin Fabricated Products
250 Olin Industrial Dr (62024-4400)
**PHONE** .......... 618 258-5668
**Fax:** 618 258-2696
**EMP:** 12
**SALES (corp-wide):** 5.5B **Publicly Held**
**SIC:** 2812 Alkalies & chlorine; caustic soda, sodium hydroxide; chlorine, compressed or liquefied
**PA:** Olin Corporation
190 Carondelet Plz # 1530
Saint Louis MO 63105
314 480-1400

**(G-8608)**
**OLIN CORPORATION**
Also Called: Winchester Ammunition
600 Powder Mill Rd (62024-1273)
**PHONE** .......... 618 258-2000
**Fax:** 618 258-3178
Steven D Goodman, *Superintendent*
Donald Gilkison, *VP Admin*
Brett Flaugher, *Vice Pres*
Larry Stewart, *VP Mfg*
Matt Brueckner, *Plant Mgr*
**EMP:** 150
**SALES (corp-wide):** 5.5B **Publicly Held**
**WEB:** www.olin.com
**SIC:** 3484 Small arms
**PA:** Olin Corporation
190 Carondelet Plz # 1530
Saint Louis MO 63105
314 480-1400

**(G-8609)**
**OLIN ENGINEERED SYSTEMS INC**
427 N Shamrock St (62024-1174)
**PHONE** .......... 618 258-2874
Jeff Haferkamp, *Principal*
**EMP:** 3
**SALES (est):** 244.5K
**SALES (corp-wide):** 5.5B **Publicly Held**
**WEB:** www.olin.com
**SIC:** 3449 Miscellaneous metalwork
**PA:** Olin Corporation
190 Carondelet Plz # 1530
Saint Louis MO 63105
314 480-1400

**(G-8610)**
**RONALD S LEFORS BS CPO**
214 W Saint Louis Ave (62024-1122)
**PHONE** .......... 618 259-1969
Ronald S Lefors, *Owner*
**EMP:** 4
**SQ FT:** 3,500
**SALES (est):** 220K **Privately Held**
**SIC:** 3842 5999 Limbs, artificial; orthopedic & prosthesis applications

**(G-8611)**
**STAAR BALES LESTARGE INC**
Also Called: Neon Works of St Louis
450 W Saint Louis Ave (62024-1123)
**PHONE** .......... 618 259-6366
Christopher Staar, *President*
Dave Kapper, *Principal*
**EMP:** 4
**SQ FT:** 3,200
**SALES (est):** 220K **Privately Held**
**SIC:** 3993 1799 5046 Neon signs; sign installation & maintenance; neon signs

**(G-8612)**
**WEST STAR AVIATION LLC**
2 Airline Ct (62024-2284)
**PHONE** .......... 618 259-3230
Greg Beebee, *Manager*
**EMP:** 5
**SALES (corp-wide):** 82.9MM **Privately Held**
**SIC:** 3663 Satellites, communications
**HQ:** West Star Aviation, Llc
796 Heritage Way
Grand Junction CO 81506
970 243-7500

## East Carondelet
### St. Clair County

**(G-8613)**
**ERIC HARR**
7508 Triple Lakes Rd (62240-1712)
**PHONE** .......... 618 538-7889
Eric Harr, *Owner*
**EMP:** 30
**SALES (est):** 2.3MM **Privately Held**
**WEB:** www.ericharr.com
**SIC:** 3442 Metal doors

**(G-8614)**
**GATEWAY PROPANE LLC**
237 Coulter Rd (62240-1338)
P.O. Box 306, Dupo (62239-0306)
**PHONE** .......... 618 286-3005
Janice Gail Rhine, *Principal*
**EMP:** 3
**SALES (est):** 197.4K **Privately Held**
**SIC:** 2911 Liquefied petroleum gases, LPG

**(G-8615)**
**STERLING PHRM SVCS LLC**
102 Coulter Rd (62240-1346)
**PHONE** .......... 618 286-4116
Jaime Kennedy, *Branch Mgr*
**EMP:** 12
**SALES (corp-wide):** 4MM **Privately Held**
**SIC:** 2834 Pharmaceutical preparations
**PA:** Sterling Pharmaceutical Services, Llc
109 S 2nd St
Dupo IL 62239
618 286-6060

## East Dubuque
### Jo Daviess County

**(G-8616)**
**AGGREGATE MATERIALS COMPANY**
18525 Us Highway 20 W (61025-8505)
**PHONE** .......... 815 747-2430
Harvey Seiler, *Superintendent*
**EMP:** 7
**SALES (corp-wide):** 739.3K **Privately Held**
**SIC:** 1442 Construction sand & gravel
**PA:** Aggregate Materials Company Inc
5 Jones St Ste 1
Dubuque IA 52001
563 583-6642

**(G-8617)**
**EAST DBQUE NTRGN FRTLIZERS LLC**
16675 Us Highway 20 W (61025-8605)
**PHONE** .......... 815 747-3101
Mark A Pytosh, *President*
Bill White, *Exec VP*
John R Walter, *Senior VP*
Neal Barkley, *Vice Pres*
Dan Poster, *Vice Pres*
▲ **EMP:** 145
**SALES (est):** 15.1MM
**SALES (corp-wide):** 4.7B **Publicly Held**
**WEB:** www.rtkmidwest.com
**SIC:** 2873 Ammonium nitrate, ammonium sulfate
**HQ:** Cvr Partners, Lp
2277 Plaza Dr Ste 500
Sugar Land TX 77479
281 207-3200

**(G-8618)**
**KATS MEOW**
288 Sinsinawa Ave (61025-1221)
**PHONE** .......... 815 747-2113
Kathy Runde, *Owner*
**EMP:** 3
**SALES (est):** 144.7K **Privately Held**
**SIC:** 2085 Cocktails, alcoholic

**(G-8619)**
**LANGE SIGN GROUP**
1780 Il Route 35 N (61025-9681)
**PHONE** .......... 815 747-2448
Dan Lange, *Owner*
Sue Lange, *Office Mgr*
**EMP:** 5
**SALES (est):** 437.2K **Privately Held**
**SIC:** 3993 Signs & advertising specialties

**(G-8620)**
**RENTECH DEVELOPMENT CORP**
16675 Us Highway 20 W (61025-8605)
P.O. Box 229 (61025-0229)
**PHONE** .......... 815 747-3101
John Diesch, *Branch Mgr*
Sheri Henschel, *Manager*
Lynn A Stewart, *Admin Sec*
**EMP:** 115
**SALES (corp-wide):** 150.7MM **Publicly Held**
**SIC:** 2873 Nitrogen solutions (fertilizer)
**HQ:** Rentech Development Corporation
4949 S Syracuse St # 320
Denver CO 80237
303 298-8008

# East Dubuque - Jo Daviess County (G-8621)

**(G-8621)**
**S AND K PACKAGING INCORPORATED**
120 N Frentress Lake Rd (61025-9529)
P.O. Box 1681, Dubuque IA (52004-1681)
PHONE.................................563 582-8895
Shawn Stackis, *President*
▲ **EMP:** 5
**SALES (est):** 590K **Privately Held**
**SIC:** 5199 2621 Packaging materials; wrapping & packaging papers

**(G-8622)**
**SCHMALZ PRECAST CONCRETE MFG**
18363 Us Highway 20 W (61025-8514)
PHONE.................................815 747-3939
Michael Schmalz, *CEO*
Marlene Schmalz, *Vice Pres*
**EMP:** 7
**SALES:** 350K **Privately Held**
**SIC:** 3272 Burial vaults, concrete or precast terrazzo; septic tanks, concrete

**(G-8623)**
**SMITHFIELD FARMLAND CORP**
Also Called: Smithfield Food
18531 Us Highway 20 W (61025-8505)
PHONE.................................815 747-8809
Marlene Wand, *Branch Mgr*
**EMP:** 6 **Privately Held**
**SIC:** 2011 Meat packing plants
**HQ:** Smithfield Farmland Corp.
111 Commerce St
Smithfield VA 23430
757 357-3131

**(G-8624)**
**SOCIALCLOAK INC**
399 Sinsinawa Ave (61025-1222)
PHONE.................................650 549-4412
Heath Hutchinson, *CEO*
**EMP:** 5
**SQ FT:** 1,500
**SALES (est):** 155K **Privately Held**
**SIC:** 7372 Publishers' computer software

**(G-8625)**
**TERRY TERRI MULGREW**
521 Montgomery Ave (61025-1034)
PHONE.................................815 747-6248
Terry Mulgree, *Owner*
**EMP:** 4 **EST:** 2000
**SALES (est):** 356.4K **Privately Held**
**SIC:** 2951 Asphalt paving mixtures & blocks

**(G-8626)**
**TOP BLOCK & BRICK INC**
84 N Frentress Lake Rd (61025-9529)
PHONE.................................815 747-3159
Fax: 815 747-3109
Daniel E Petitgout, *President*
Mark Hess, *Manager*
**EMP:** 19
**SQ FT:** 20,000
**SALES (est):** 3.6MM **Privately Held**
**WEB:** www.topblockandbrick.com
**SIC:** 3271 Blocks, concrete or cinder: standard

## East Dundee
### Kane County

**(G-8627)**
**A AND T CIGARETTES IMPORTS**
105 Prairie Lake Rd (60118-9133)
PHONE.................................847 836-9134
Deepti Shah, *President*
Keyur Khambhati, *Accounting Mgr*
◆ **EMP:** 3
**SALES (est):** 193.5K **Privately Held**
**SIC:** 3999 Cigarette & cigar products & accessories

**(G-8628)**
**ADDVALUE2PRINT LLC**
555 Plate Dr Ste 6 (60118-2465)
PHONE.................................847 551-1570
Ivan Verheye, *Partner*
**EMP:** 4
**SALES (est):** 434.3K **Privately Held**
**SIC:** 2752 Commercial printing, lithographic

**(G-8629)**
**CARSON PRINTING INC**
Also Called: Cpiprint
1110 Heinz Dr Ste C (60118-2451)
P.O. Box 1017, West Dundee (60118-7017)
PHONE.................................847 836-0900
Fax: 847 836-0940
Terrence P Carson, *President*
Joie Carson, *Admin Sec*
**EMP:** 2
**SQ FT:** 4,000
**SALES (est):** 200K **Privately Held**
**SIC:** 2752 2796 2791 2759 Lithographing on metal; commercial printing, offset; platemaking services; typesetting; commercial printing; die-cut paper & board

**(G-8630)**
**CUTSHAW INSTLS INC**
216 Dundee Ave (60118-1627)
PHONE.................................847 426-9208
Leo Cutshaw, *Principal*
**EMP:** 3 **EST:** 2007
**SALES (est):** 178.9K **Privately Held**
**SIC:** 3643 Lightning protection equipment

**(G-8631)**
**DAVITZ MOLD CO INC**
570 Rock Road Dr Ste D (60118-2448)
PHONE.................................847 426-4848
Fax: 847 426-4960
David Davitz, *President*
Marlis Davitz, *Vice Pres*
**EMP:** 6
**SQ FT:** 1,500
**SALES:** 900K **Privately Held**
**SIC:** 3544 Special dies, tools, jigs & fixtures; industrial molds; special dies & tools

**(G-8632)**
**DPS DIGITAL PRINT SVC**
555 Plate Dr Ste 4 (60118-2465)
PHONE.................................847 836-7734
David Cohn, *Owner*
**EMP:** 5
**SALES (est):** 483K **Privately Held**
**SIC:** 2752 Commercial printing, lithographic

**(G-8633)**
**DTS AMERICA INC**
427 E 4th St (60118-1308)
PHONE.................................847 783-0401
Fax: 847 695-2601
Terry Aschenbrenner, *President*
Bob Schmidt, *Engineer*
Rob Herrmann, *Project Engr*
**EMP:** 4
**SQ FT:** 3,500
**SALES (est):** 859.2K **Privately Held**
**WEB:** www.dtsamerica.com
**SIC:** 3569 5084 Liquid automation machinery & equipment; industrial machinery & equipment

**(G-8634)**
**DUNDEE DESIGN LLC**
570 Rock Road Dr Ste P (60118-2448)
PHONE.................................847 494-2360
Steve Swanson,
Linda Swanson,
**EMP:** 3
**SQ FT:** 2,750
**SALES (est):** 359.6K **Privately Held**
**SIC:** 3822 Building services monitoring controls, automatic

**(G-8635)**
**DUNDEE TRUCK & TRLR WORKS LLC ◐**
Also Called: Dundee Truck Repair & Wash
407 Christina Dr (60118-3541)
PHONE.................................224 484-8182
Tj Bhathal, *President*
MB Bhathal, *Opers Mgr*
**EMP:** 7 **EST:** 2016
**SQ FT:** 11,000
**SALES (est):** 422.5K **Privately Held**
**SIC:** 7538 7542 3715 General truck repair; truck wash; truck trailers

**(G-8636)**
**FRIGEL NORTH AMERICA INC**
150 Prairie Lake Rd Ste A (60118-9131)
PHONE.................................847 540-0160
Fax: 847 540-0161
Duccio Doris, *CEO*
Stephen Petrakis, *President*
Randy Burgardt, *Opers Mgr*
Lawrence Bowman, *Opers Staff*
Chris Skowronski, *Engineer*
▲ **EMP:** 14
**SALES (est):** 3.4MM **Privately Held**
**SIC:** 3585 5075 Heating equipment, complete; warm air heating & air conditioning

**(G-8637)**
**GENERAL FOAM PLASTICS CORP**
1051 E Main St (60118-2454)
PHONE.................................847 851-9995
Lewis Cheng, *CEO*
**EMP:** 3
**SALES (est):** 220K **Privately Held**
**SIC:** 3086 Plastics foam products

**(G-8638)**
**GMC TECHNOLOGIES INC**
215 Prairie Lake Rd Ste A (60118-9125)
PHONE.................................847 426-8618
Gabriela Alvarez, *President*
Maritza Jagusch, *Treasurer*
M Carolina Vargas, *Admin Sec*
**EMP:** 8
**SALES:** 300K **Privately Held**
**SIC:** 3549 Metalworking machinery

**(G-8639)**
**GOLDEN BAG COMPANY INC**
Also Called: Plastic Bag Manufacturer
290 Illinois St (60118-1112)
PHONE.................................847 836-7766
Fax: 847 836-9988
John CHI, *President*
Juanita Soong, *Exec Dir*
Susan Wu, *Admin Sec*
▲ **EMP:** 12
**SQ FT:** 40,000
**SALES (est):** 3MM **Privately Held**
**SIC:** 2673 Plastic bags: made from purchased materials

**(G-8640)**
**GOLDEN PLASTICS LLC**
Also Called: Golden Bag
290 Illinois St (60118-1112)
P.O. Box 334, Dundee (60118-0334)
PHONE.................................847 836-7766
**EMP:** 12
**SALES (est):** 627.8K **Privately Held**
**SIC:** 2759 3089 Bags, plastic: printing; extruded finished plastic products

**(G-8641)**
**GRADS INC**
Also Called: Custom Flooring Insets
205 Prairie Lake Rd Ste C (60118-9112)
PHONE.................................847 426-3904
Alan Stensrud, *President*
Gordon Smith, *Principal*
Ron Diskin, *Vice Pres*
Sandy Stensrud, *Admin Sec*
**EMP:** 6 **EST:** 1946
**SQ FT:** 5,000
**SALES:** 393.7K **Privately Held**
**SIC:** 2426 1752 Flooring, hardwood; floor laying & floor work

**(G-8642)**
**GREAT SPIRIT HARDWOODS LLC**
7 Jackson St (60118-1318)
PHONE.................................224 801-1969
Don Gleichman Jr, *Manager*
Skip Gleichman, *Manager*
**EMP:** 9
**SALES (est):** 354.5K **Privately Held**
**SIC:** 5211 2511 Millwork & lumber; wood household furniture

**(G-8643)**
**HORIZON DIE COMPANY INC**
160 Windsor Dr (60118-9169)
PHONE.................................847 426-8558
Daniel Badovinac, *President*
Peter Badovinac, *Vice Pres*
Issa Handal, *Engineer*
Stephanie Woods, *Marketing Staff*
Teresa Strach, *Office Admin*
**EMP:** 34
**SQ FT:** 15,000
**SALES (est):** 9.3MM **Privately Held**
**SIC:** 3469 3544 Machine parts, stamped or pressed metal; special dies & tools

**(G-8644)**
**HUMIDITY 2 OPTIMIZATION LLC**
Also Called: H2o
105 Prairie Lake Rd Ste D (60118-9133)
PHONE.................................847 991-7488
Jeff Bossong, *Mng Member*
Anthony Graffia,
Christopher Rosman,
**EMP:** 11
**SALES (est):** 934.1K **Privately Held**
**SIC:** 3823 1731 Humidity instruments, industrial process type; electronic controls installation

**(G-8645)**
**HYDROSIL INTERNATIONAL LTD**
125 Prairie Lake Rd (60118-9126)
PHONE.................................847 741-1600
Fax: 847 741-1616
William Waldschmidt, *President*
▲ **EMP:** 8
**SQ FT:** 5,000
**SALES (est):** 1.4MM **Privately Held**
**WEB:** www.hydrosilintl.com
**SIC:** 3564 Air purification equipment

**(G-8646)**
**ILLINI HI-REACH INC**
15n320 Route 25 Unit A (60118)
PHONE.................................847 428-3311
Mike Gerrard, *Manager*
**EMP:** 12
**SALES (corp-wide):** 11MM **Privately Held**
**SIC:** 3569 Lubrication equipment, industrial
**PA:** Illini Hi-Reach, Inc.
13633 Main St
Lemont IL 60439
630 243-1515

**(G-8647)**
**INTELEX USA LLC**
105 Prairie Lake Rd (60118-9133)
PHONE.................................847 496-1727
Anthony R Graffia, *Principal*
**EMP:** 2
**SALES (est):** 219.3K **Privately Held**
**SIC:** 2259 Towels, knit

**(G-8648)**
**J N MACHINERY CORP**
1081 Rock Road Ln (60118-2444)
PHONE.................................224 699-9161
Daniel F Pierre III, *President*
▲ **EMP:** 5
**SQ FT:** 3,700
**SALES (est):** 896.9K **Privately Held**
**WEB:** www.jnmachinery.com
**SIC:** 3567 Industrial furnaces & ovens

**(G-8649)**
**MAXI-VAC INC**
120 Prairie Lake Rd Ste C (60118-9128)
P.O. Box 668, Dundee (60118-0668)
PHONE.................................630 620-6669
Jeff Lichthardt, *President*
**EMP:** 4
**SALES (est):** 229K **Privately Held**
**SIC:** 3699 Cleaning equipment, ultrasonic, except medical & dental

**(G-8650)**
**ORANGE CRUSH LLC**
507 Rock Road Dr (60118-2446)
PHONE.................................847 428-6176
Phil Doherty, *Plant Supt*
Tim Daniell, *Branch Mgr*
**EMP:** 7
**SALES (corp-wide):** 47.3MM **Privately Held**
**SIC:** 2951 1795 Asphalt paving mixtures & blocks; concrete breaking for streets & highways
**PA:** Orange Crush, L.L.C.
321 Center St
Hillside IL 60162
708 544-9440

# GEOGRAPHIC SECTION

**East Moline - Rock Island County (G-8675)**

**(G-8651)**
**PATRIOT FUELS LLC**
10219 Vine St (60118)
PHONE................................847 551-5946
Fred Huckstorf, *Principal*
EMP: 7
SALES (est): 1MM **Privately Held**
SIC: 2869 Fuels

**(G-8652)**
**PETER FOX**
Also Called: Hqf Manufacturing
578 Rock Road Dr Ste 4 (60118-2450)
P.O. Box 6581, Aurora (60598-0581)
PHONE................................847 428-2249
Peter Fox, *Owner*
EMP: 5
SQ FT: 6,500
SALES: 300K **Privately Held**
SIC: 3965 Fasteners, buttons, needles & pins

**(G-8653)**
**POLYGROUP SERVICES NA INC (PA)**
Also Called: Polygroup Limited
1051 E Main St Ste 218 (60118-2455)
PHONE................................847 851-9995
Lewis Cheng, *CEO*
Antonio Zuany, *Opers Mgr*
▲ EMP: 5
SQ FT: 1,500
SALES (est): 2MM **Privately Held**
SIC: 2599 3999 3699 Inflatable beds; Christmas tree ornaments, except electrical & glass; lawn ornaments; Christmas tree ornaments, electric

**(G-8654)**
**POWER ELECTRONICS INTL INC**
561 Plate Dr Ste 8 (60118-2467)
PHONE................................847 836-2071
Fax: 847 428-7744
Michael Habisohn, *Vice Pres*
Chris Whitcome, *Vice Pres*
William Zaehler, *Safety Mgr*
Lawrence Librare, *Engineer*
Beng Mien, *Engineer*
▲ EMP: 50 EST: 1970
SALES (est): 13.5MM **Privately Held**
WEB: www.peinfo.com
SIC: 3674 Solid state electronic devices

**(G-8655)**
**REX RADIATOR AND WELDING CO**
578 Rock Road Dr Ste 5 (60118-2450)
PHONE................................847 428-1112
Joseph Garboyan, *Manager*
EMP: 5
SALES (corp-wide): 3.4MM **Privately Held**
SIC: 7692 7539 7538 Welding repair; radiator repair shop, automotive; general truck repair
PA: Rex Radiator And Welding Co Inc
1440 W 38th St
Chicago IL 60609
312 421-1531

**(G-8656)**
**S4 INDUSTRIES INC**
140 Prairie Lake Rd (60118-9134)
PHONE................................224 699-9674
James Del RE, *President*
Mike Howlett, *Director*
Michael P Howlett, *Admin Sec*
▲ EMP: 15
SQ FT: 21,000
SALES (est): 4MM **Privately Held**
SIC: 3089 Blow molded finished plastic products

**(G-8657)**
**SUMMIT DESIGN SOLUTIONS INC**
402 Fallbrook Dr (60118-3022)
PHONE................................847 836-8183
Fax: 847 843-0303
Thomas Smigelski, *President*
Dennis Cotner, *Admin Sec*
EMP: 3
SALES (est): 330K **Privately Held**
WEB: www.summitds.com
SIC: 5063 3672 Electrical apparatus & equipment; printed circuit boards

**(G-8658)**
**TERRY TOOL & MACHINING CORP**
563 Commonwealth Dr # 1300 (60118-2487)
PHONE................................847 289-1054
Fax: 847 289-1054
Terrance T Witczak, *President*
Jo Anne Witczak, *Bookkeeper*
EMP: 4
SQ FT: 11,000
SALES: 200K **Privately Held**
WEB: www.terrytool.com
SIC: 3542 7692 3544 Metal deposit forming machines; welding repair; special dies, tools, jigs & fixtures

**(G-8659)**
**TLK INDUSTRIES INC**
130 Prairie Lake Rd Ste A (60118-9130)
PHONE................................847 359-3200
Douglas Sarrazine Jr, *President*
Doug Sarrazine, *Sales Staff*
Beverly Sarrazine, *Admin Sec*
EMP: 60 EST: 1971
SALES (est): 6.1MM **Privately Held**
WEB: www.tlkind.com
SIC: 7389 3444 Design services; sheet metalwork

**(G-8660)**
**TLK TOOL & STAMPING INC**
130 Prairie Lake Rd Ste C (60118-9130)
P.O. Box 340, Carpentersville (60110-0340)
PHONE................................224 293-6941
Kevin Sarrazine, *President*
▲ EMP: 8
SALES (est): 1MM **Privately Held**
SIC: 3469 Metal stampings

**(G-8661)**
**UPLAND CONCRETE**
563 Commonwealth Dr # 1000 (60118-2486)
PHONE................................224 699-9909
EMP: 6
SALES (est): 925K **Privately Held**
SIC: 5211 5032 3273 Cement; concrete & cinder building products; ready-mixed concrete

**(G-8662)**
**XCO INTERNATIONAL INCORPORATED**
1082 Rock Road Ln Ste A (60118-2481)
PHONE................................847 428-2400
Deborah D Kious, *President*
Christopher Kious, *Project Mgr*
Patrick D Ertel, *Admin Sec*
EMP: 10
SQ FT: 2,000
SALES (est): 895.9K **Privately Held**
WEB: www.xco.com
SIC: 3823 Thermocouples, industrial process type

## East Hazel Crest
### Cook County

**(G-8663)**
**ADVANCE IRON WORKS INC**
1325 171st St (60429-1906)
P.O. Box 4169, Saint Charles (60174-9079)
PHONE................................708 798-3540
Robert J Sutphen, *President*
Robert Sutphen, *Vice Pres*
EMP: 16
SQ FT: 10,000
SALES (est): 2.6MM **Privately Held**
SIC: 3441 1791 Fabricated structural metal; structural steel erection

**(G-8664)**
**ALLOY SLING CHAINS INC (PA)**
1406 175th St (60429-1820)
PHONE................................708 647-4900
Fax: 773 647-4913

Duane Kaminski, *President*
John D Murphy, *Vice Pres*
Jason Billows, *Plant Mgr*
Tony Zomparelli, *Sales Mgr*
Michelle S Billows, *Admin Sec*
▲ EMP: 85 EST: 1970
SQ FT: 40,000
SALES (est): 22.8MM **Privately Held**
WEB: www.ascindustries.com
SIC: 3496 Slings, lifting: made from purchased wire

**(G-8665)**
**BROCHEM INDUSTRIES INC**
1229 171st St (60429-1904)
PHONE................................708 206-2874
Charles Mihalov, *President*
EMP: 3
SALES (est): 330K **Privately Held**
SIC: 3589 Water treatment equipment, industrial

**(G-8666)**
**TOOL AUTOMATION ENTERPRISES**
Also Called: T A E Signals Division
1516 175th St Ste A (60429-1892)
PHONE................................708 799-6847
Fax: 708 799-9949
John Kut, *President*
Patrick Kut, *Vice Pres*
Bruce Moorhouse, *Vice Pres*
Patricia McCarthy, *Admin Sec*
EMP: 6 EST: 1961
SQ FT: 27,000
SALES (est): 490K **Privately Held**
SIC: 3669 3469 3647 Railroad signaling devices, electric; metal stampings; flasher lights, automotive

**(G-8667)**
**WELDING SPECIALTIES**
17300 Laflin Ave (60429-1844)
PHONE................................708 798-5388
EMP: 4
SALES: 200K **Privately Held**
SIC: 7692 3444 Welding Repair Mfg Sheet Metalwork

## East Lynn
### Vermilion County

**(G-8668)**
**GREENE WELDING & HARDWARE INC**
Also Called: Galvanized Stairs
41774 N Main St (60932)
P.O. Box 191 (60932-0191)
PHONE................................217 375-4244
Paul S Greene, *Ch of Bd*
Rex A Greene, *President*
Andrew Greene, *Vice Pres*
Rhoda Greene, *Treasurer*
Mike Adams, *Sales Staff*
EMP: 25
SQ FT: 45,000
SALES (est): 3.6MM **Privately Held**
WEB: www.greenebinstairs.com
SIC: 7699 1542 3446 5251 Farm machinery repair; farm building construction; stairs, staircases, stair treads: prefabricated metal; builders' hardware

## East Moline
### Rock Island County

**(G-8669)**
**A1 SKILLED STAFFING**
915 15th Ave (61244-2137)
P.O. Box 364 (61244-0364)
PHONE................................309 281-1400
Shawn Garcia, *Owner*
EMP: 26
SALES (est): 4.1MM **Privately Held**
SIC: 3537 Lift trucks, industrial: fork, platform, straddle, etc.

**(G-8670)**
**ATLAS ROOFING CORPORATION**
Also Called: Atlas Energy Products
3110 Morton Dr (61244-1964)
PHONE................................309 752-7121
Fax: 309 752-7127
Crystal Kitterman, *Accounts Mgr*
Jennifer Sansone, *Accounts Mgr*
Randell Shaffer, *Manager*
EMP: 20
SQ FT: 120,000 **Privately Held**
WEB: www.atlasroofing.com
SIC: 3296 3086 2952 Fiberglass insulation; plastics foam products; asphalt felts & coatings
HQ: Atlas Roofing Corporation
802 Highway 19 N Ste 190
Meridian MS 39307
601 484-8900

**(G-8671)**
**BI STATE STEEL CO**
503 7th St (61244-1459)
PHONE................................309 755-0668
Fax: 309 755-9690
Paul Thomas, *President*
Dennis Ahrens, *Vice Pres*
EMP: 5
SQ FT: 12,000
SALES (est): 934.1K **Privately Held**
SIC: 3441 7692 Fabricated structural metal; welding repair

**(G-8672)**
**CENTRO INC**
1001 13th St (61244-1734)
PHONE................................309 751-9700
Kevin McMichael, *General Mgr*
EMP: 3
SALES (corp-wide): 200MM **Privately Held**
SIC: 3086 Plastics foam products
PA: Centro, Inc.
950 N Bend Dr
North Liberty IA 52317
319 626-3200

**(G-8673)**
**DEERE & COMPANY**
Also Called: John Deere Harvester
1100 13th Ave (61244-1455)
PHONE................................309 765-8000
Coston Anthony, *Area Mgr*
R Kleine, *Div Sub Head*
Randal Sergesketter, *Senior VP*
Victoria Graves, *Vice Pres*
Lanny Johnson, *Safety Dir*
EMP: 24
SALES (corp-wide): 26.6B **Publicly Held**
WEB: www.deere.com
SIC: 3523 Combines (harvester-threshers)
PA: Deere & Company
1 John Deere Pl
Moline IL 61265
309 765-8000

**(G-8674)**
**DEERE & COMPANY**
John Deere Harvester Works
1100 13th Ave (61244-1455)
P.O. Box 1001 (61244)
PHONE................................800 765-9588
Fax: 309 765-6035
Pat Pinkston, *Vice Pres*
Pushpa Manukonda, *Engineer*
Jacob Salowitz, *Engineer*
Bill Lewis, *Business Anylst*
Erin Theusch, *Manager*
EMP: 1500
SALES (corp-wide): 26.6B **Publicly Held**
SIC: 3523 Farm machinery & equipment; tractors, farm; harrows: disc, spring, tine, etc.; plows, agricultural: disc, moldboard, chisel, listers, etc.
PA: Deere & Company
1 John Deere Pl
Moline IL 61265
309 765-8000

**(G-8675)**
**DEERE & COMPANY**
John Deere Harvester Works
1515 5th St (61244-1359)
PHONE................................309 765-8000
Tom Phan, *President*

# East Moline - Rock Island County (G-8676)

Patrick Weber, *Vice Pres*
Pankaj Bhugra, *Engineer*
Vernon Gambleton, *Engineer*
James O'Bryon, *Engineer*
**EMP:** 4
**SALES (corp-wide):** 26.6B  **Publicly Held**
**SIC: 3523**  Farm machinery & equipment; tractors, farm; harrows: disc, spring, tine, etc.; plows, agricultural: disc, moldboard, chisel, listers, etc.
**PA:** Deere & Company
1 John Deere Pl
Moline IL 61265
309 765-8000

### (G-8676)
### DERBYTECH INC
700 16th Ave  (61244-2122)
P.O. Box 576  (61244-0576)
**PHONE**..................................309 755-2662
**Fax:** 309 755-7299
Alan Derbyshire, *President*
Jean Derby, *Office Mgr*
Jean Kapua, *Office Mgr*
Dave Hinkle, *Programmer Anys*
David Serven, *Executive*
**EMP:** 26
**SALES (est):** 4.3MM  **Privately Held**
**WEB:** www.racingteam.com
**SIC: 3571**  5045  5734  7378  Computers, digital, analog or hybrid; computers; computer & software stores; computer maintenance & repair

### (G-8677)
### DS POLISHING & METAL FINSHG
1201 7th St  (61244-1465)
**PHONE**..................................309 755-0544
Melinda Boyd, *President*
Thomas Zinanni, *Vice Pres*
**EMP:** 4
**SQ FT:** 5,000
**SALES (est):** 446.1K  **Privately Held**
**SIC: 3471**  Finishing, metals or formed products

### (G-8678)
### EAST MOLINE HERALD PRINT INC
Also Called: Herald Printing
824 15th Ave  (61244-2136)
**PHONE**..................................309 755-5224
**Fax:** 309 755-5225
John Jondy, *President*
Patrick J Danley, *Vice Pres*
**EMP:** 4
**SQ FT:** 1,200
**SALES (est):** 340K  **Privately Held**
**SIC: 2759**  5943  2791  2752  Letterpress printing; office forms & supplies; typesetting; commercial printing, lithographic

### (G-8679)
### FUN INDUSTRIES INC
627 15th Ave  (61244-1323)
P.O. Box 458  (61244-0458)
**PHONE**..................................309 755-5021
**Fax:** 309 755-1684
Roy Johnston III, *President*
Judy Bowser, *Manager*
**EMP:** 10
**SQ FT:** 17,000
**SALES:** 1MM  **Privately Held**
**WEB:** www.funindustries.com
**SIC: 3999**  Coin-operated amusement machines

### (G-8680)
### GLOBAL FIRE CONTROL INC
1201 7th St Ste 103  (61244-1465)
**PHONE**..................................309 314-0919
**Fax:** 309 755-8310
Jeffrey G Oppenheimer, *CEO*
Terry Johnson, *Info Tech Mgr*
**EMP:** 4
**SALES (est):** 609.5K  **Privately Held**
**WEB:** www.globalfirecontrol.com
**SIC: 3669**  Fire alarm apparatus, electric

### (G-8681)
### HC DUKE & SON LLC
Also Called: Electro Freeze
2116 8th Ave  (61244-1800)
**PHONE**..................................309 755-4553
**Fax:** 309 755-9858

Mark Holden, *Division Mgr*
Dorothy Ball, *General Mgr*
Jim Duke, *Vice Pres*
Dick Bryant, *Purch Dir*
Sue Christensen, *Purchasing*
▲ **EMP:** 150
**SQ FT:** 110,000
**SALES (est):** 48.7MM  **Privately Held**
**WEB:** www.electrofreeze.com
**SIC: 3556**  Ice cream manufacturing machinery
**HQ:** Ali Spa
Via Piero Gobetti 2/A
Cernusco Sul Naviglio MI 20063
029 219-91

### (G-8682)
### I-N-I MACHINING INC
17128 Route 2 & 92  (61244)
P.O. Box 101  (61244-0101)
**PHONE**..................................309 496-1002
Nikki Young, *President*
**EMP:** 6
**SALES (est):** 1MM  **Privately Held**
**SIC: 3541**  Milling machines

### (G-8683)
### KVF-QUAD CORPORATION
808 13th St  (61244-1628)
P.O. Box 795  (61244-0795)
**PHONE**..................................563 529-1916
**Fax:** 309 755-1121
Michael Crotty, *President*
Tim Cain, *General Mgr*
Eric Davis, *Opers Mgr*
Melody Watters, *Human Res Mgr*
Jim Wells, *Sales Engr*
**EMP:** 45 EST: 1976
**SQ FT:** 60,000
**SALES (est):** 7MM  **Privately Held**
**WEB:** www.kvfquad.com
**SIC: 3479**  Coating of metals & formed products

### (G-8684)
### L & M STEEL SERVICES INC
3660 Morton Dr  (61244-1918)
P.O. Box 427  (61244-0427)
**PHONE**..................................309 755-3713
**Fax:** 309 755-0922
Tony Lyttles, *President*
Gerry Meade, *Vice Pres*
Sandra Meade, *Treasurer*
Roxanne Lyttles, *Admin Sec*
**EMP:** 10
**SALES (est):** 1.7MM  **Privately Held**
**SIC: 3441**  Building components, structural steel

### (G-8685)
### LCV COMPANY
919 15th Ave  (61244-2137)
**PHONE**..................................309 738-6452
Lambros C Mihalopoulos, *President*
**EMP:** 6 EST: 1999
**SALES (est):** 48.6K  **Privately Held**
**SIC: 2099**  Food preparations

### (G-8686)
### LIFT SYSTEMS INC (PA)
1505 7th St  (61244-2112)
P.O. Box 906, Moline  (61266-0906)
**PHONE**..................................309 764-9842
Bruce Forster, *President*
Ray Shuman, *Vice Pres*
Brian Wagner, *Vice Pres*
Tim Faccio, *Prdtn Mgr*
Heather Orozco, *Sales Staff*
▼ **EMP:** 72
**SALES (est):** 19.1MM  **Privately Held**
**WEB:** www.liftsystems.com
**SIC: 3536**  Hoists, cranes & monorails

### (G-8687)
### MCLAUGHLIN BODY CO
1400 5th St  (61244)
**PHONE**..................................309 736-6105
T Beinke, *Branch Mgr*
**EMP:** 120
**SALES (corp-wide):** 14.8MM  **Privately Held**
**WEB:** www.mclbody.com
**SIC: 3441**  Fabricated structural metal

**PA:** Mclaughlin Body Co.
2430 River Dr
Moline IL 61265
309 762-7755

### (G-8688)
### MOLINE SEMICON LLC
605 17th Ave  (61244-2045)
**PHONE**..................................309 755-0433
Arvind Sodhani, *Accountant*
Manoj Baheti, *Mng Member*
William Race, *Manager*
**EMP:** 1
**SQ FT:** 800
**SALES:** 250K  **Privately Held**
**SIC: 3674**  Semiconductors & related devices

### (G-8689)
### NIXALITE OF AMERICA INC (PA)
Also Called: Advanced Bird Control
1025 16th Ave  (61244-1424)
P.O. Box 727  (61244-0727)
**PHONE**..................................309 755-8771
**Fax:** 309 755-1865
Marie Gellerstedt, *Ch of Bd*
Cory A Gellerstedt, *President*
John Gellerstedt, *President*
Keith Gellerstedt, *Exec VP*
Jon Gellerstedt, *Admin Sec*
▼ **EMP:** 15
**SQ FT:** 25,000
**SALES (est):** 3.5MM  **Privately Held**
**WEB:** www.nixalite.com
**SIC: 3496**  Miscellaneous fabricated wire products

### (G-8690)
### POWER-SONIC CORPORATION
1300 19th St Ste 200  (61244-2338)
**PHONE**..................................309 752-7750
Roger Lyll, *Principal*
**EMP:** 4
**SALES (corp-wide):** 82.7MM  **Privately Held**
**SIC: 3442**  Rolling doors for industrial buildings or warehouses, metal
**PA:** The Power-Sonic Corporation
7550 Panasonic Way
San Diego CA 92154
619 661-2020

### (G-8691)
### QC SERVICE ASSOCIATES INC
1300 90th St Ste 110  (61244)
P.O. Box 525  (61244-0525)
**PHONE**..................................309 755-6785
Carl McNair, *President*
**EMP:** 30
**SALES (est):** 2.1MM  **Privately Held**
**SIC: 3549**  Assembly machines, including robotic

### (G-8692)
### QUAD CITY ENGINEERING COMPANY
3650 Morton Dr  (61244-1918)
P.O. Box 377  (61244-0377)
**PHONE**..................................309 755-9762
Roger Dolleslager, *President*
William Bessee, *Purchasing*
John Lasley, *Office Mgr*
Tony Rokis, *Supervisor*
**EMP:** 22 EST: 1944
**SQ FT:** 28,000
**SALES (est):** 3.2MM  **Privately Held**
**WEB:** www.quadcityeng.com
**SIC: 3544**  Dies & die holders for metal cutting, forming, die casting; jigs & fixtures

### (G-8693)
### R K PRODUCTS INC
3802 Jean St  (61244-9648)
**PHONE**..................................309 792-1927
Philip Kester, *President*
Marilyn Kaster, *Vice Pres*
**EMP:** 4
**SALES (est):** 300K  **Privately Held**
**SIC: 3523**  Farm machinery & equipment

### (G-8694)
### SIGN TEAM INC
5417 180th St N  (61244-9423)
**PHONE**..................................309 302-0017
Alison Rodriguez, *President*
**EMP:** 2

**SALES (est):** 222K  **Privately Held**
**SIC: 3993**  Signs & advertising specialties

### (G-8695)
### TIMBERLINE PALLET & SKID INC
2500 8th Ave  (61244-1831)
P.O. Box 631  (61244-0631)
**PHONE**..................................309 752-1770
**Fax:** 309 752-1775
Joseph Tindall, *President*
Joseph R Tindall, *President*
Karen Tindall, *Treasurer*
**EMP:** 13
**SQ FT:** 40,000
**SALES:** 1.7MM  **Privately Held**
**SIC: 2448**  5031  Pallets, wood & wood with metal; skids, wood & wood with metal; lumber, plywood & millwork

### (G-8696)
### VALSPAR
3560 5th Ave  (61244-9548)
**PHONE**..................................309 743-7133
**EMP:** 3
**SALES (est):** 281.1K  **Privately Held**
**SIC: 2851**  Paints & allied products

### (G-8697)
### VAN PELT CORPORATION
Also Called: Service Steel Division
2930 Morton Dr  (61244-1959)
**PHONE**..................................313 365-3600
**Fax:** 309 755-3069
Tim Pratt, *QC Mgr*
Roger Vanpelt, *Persnl Mgr*
Robert Schwarm, *Branch Mgr*
**EMP:** 22
**SQ FT:** 87,350
**SALES (corp-wide):** 33.2MM  **Privately Held**
**WEB:** www.servicesteel.com
**SIC: 5051**  3441  3449  Structural shapes, iron or steel; fabricated structural metal; miscellaneous metalwork
**PA:** Van Pelt Corporation
13700 Sherwood St Ste 2
Detroit MI 48212
313 365-3600

### (G-8698)
### WALLACE ENTERPRISES INC
3121 187th Street Ct N  (61244-9501)
**PHONE**..................................309 496-1230
Kevin R Wallace, *President*
**EMP:** 4 EST: 2000
**SALES (est):** 439.8K  **Privately Held**
**SIC: 3844**  Radiographic X-ray apparatus & tubes

## East Peoria
### Peoria County

### (G-8699)
### CATERPILLAR INC
100 Tractor Dr  (61630-1200)
**PHONE**..................................309 494-0138
Rick Auch, *Engineer*
Sarita Kuppili, *Design Engr*
Craig Gardner, *Branch Mgr*
Jason Hussey, *Technical Staff*
**EMP:** 342
**SALES (corp-wide):** 38.5B  **Publicly Held**
**SIC: 3531**  Construction machinery
**PA:** Caterpillar Inc.
100 Ne Adams St
Peoria IL 61629
309 675-1000

## East Peoria
### Tazewell County

### (G-8700)
### AMERIGREEN PALLETS
280 Fondulac Dr  (61611-2602)
**PHONE**..................................309 698-3463
**EMP:** 3 EST: 2009
**SALES (est):** 130K  **Privately Held**
**SIC: 2448**  Mfg Wood Pallets/Skids

# GEOGRAPHIC SECTION

**East Peoria - Tazewell County (G-8730)**

### (G-8701)
**BESSLER WELDING INC**
5313 N Main St (61611-1398)
PHONE..................................309 699-6224
Fax: 309 699-0626
Albert Durst, *President*
David Crumley, *Vice Pres*
**EMP:** 13
**SQ FT:** 2,500
**SALES:** 1MM **Privately Held**
**SIC: 7692** Welding repair

### (G-8702)
**BLIND WILLIAMSON & DRAPERY**
230 Cracklewood Ln (61611-4447)
PHONE..................................309 694-7339
Twila Williamson, *CEO*
Steve Williamson, *Admin Sec*
**EMP:** 2
**SALES (est):** 346.1K **Privately Held**
**SIC: 2591** Drapery hardware & blinds & shades

### (G-8703)
**BOLEY TOOL & MACHINE WORKS INC**
1044 Spring Bay Rd (61611-1395)
PHONE..................................309 694-2722
Fax: 309 694-7879
Warren M Boley, *President*
Dan Weston, *Plant Mgr*
Jill Jacobs, *QC Mgr*
Anne Boley, *CFO*
Frank Boley, *Finance*
**EMP:** 125
**SQ FT:** 99,000
**SALES (est):** 29.1MM **Privately Held**
**WEB:** www.boleytool.com
**SIC: 3519** 5013 3599 3569 Parts & accessories, internal combustion engines; automotive supplies & parts; machine shop, jobbing & repair; assembly machines, non-metalworking

### (G-8704)
**CATERPILLAR INC**
600 W Washington St (61611-2054)
PHONE..................................309 675-1000
Fax: 309 633-8695
**EMP:** 355
**SALES (corp-wide):** 47B **Publicly Held**
**SIC: 3531** Mfg Construction Machinery
**PA:** Caterpillar Inc.
100 Ne Adams St
Peoria IL 61629
309 675-1000

### (G-8705)
**CENTRAL MANUFACTURING COMPANY**
4258 Springfield Rd (61611-9217)
P.O. Box 420, Groveland, (61535-0420)
PHONE..................................309 387-6591
Fax: 309 387-6941
Michael D Mc Lemore, *President*
Diane Zook, *Office Mgr*
**EMP:** 8
**SALES (est):** 2MM **Privately Held**
**WEB:** www.flameball.com
**SIC: 3535** 4213 3443 Conveyors & conveying equipment; trucking, except local; fabricated plate work (boiler shop)

### (G-8706)
**CHIPS ALEECES PITA**
Also Called: Anthony's
308 Illini Dr (61611-1825)
PHONE..................................309 699-8859
Fax: 309 699-6852
Alice Anthony, *Owner*
Steven Anthony, *Opers Mgr*
**EMP:** 5
**SQ FT:** 1,500
**SALES (est):** 406.3K **Privately Held**
**SIC: 2096** Potato chips & similar snacks

### (G-8707)
**CROWN TROPHY**
235 E Washington St Ste C (61611-7004)
PHONE..................................309 699-1766
Fax: 309 699-2066
Shari Prather, *Owner*
**EMP:** 3
**SALES (est):** 130K **Privately Held**
**SIC: 5999** 3479 3993 Trophies & plaques; etching & engraving; signs & advertising specialties

### (G-8708)
**ENERCON ENGINEERING INC (PA)**
201 Altorfer Ln (61611-2038)
PHONE..................................800 218-8831
Fax: 309 694-3703
Lawrence Tangel, *CEO*
Edward J Tangel, *President*
Nicholas Keever, *COO*
Carl Tawney, *Engineer*
Steve Evans, *Electrical Engi*
◆ **EMP:** 185
**SQ FT:** 160,000
**SALES:** 54MM **Privately Held**
**WEB:** www.enercon-eng.com
**SIC: 3613** 3625 Switchgear & switchboard apparatus; control equipment, electric

### (G-8709)
**ENERCON ENGINEERING INC**
301 Altorfer Ln (61611-2039)
PHONE..................................309 694-1418
Sara Jones, *Manager*
**EMP:** 70
**SALES (est):** 2.1MM **Privately Held**
**SIC: 3625** 3613 Relays & industrial controls; switchgear & switchboard apparatus

### (G-8710)
**FOUR SEASONS GUTTER PROTE**
1815 Meadow Ave (61611-3605)
PHONE..................................309 694-4565
Jeff Harper, *Owner*
**EMP:** 4
**SALES (est):** 417.2K **Privately Held**
**SIC: 1761** 3089 Siding contractor; gutters (glass fiber reinforced), fiberglass or plastic

### (G-8711)
**GMH METAL FABRICATION INC**
136 Fleur De Lis Dr (61611-2155)
PHONE..................................309 253-6429
Terry Leong, *President*
Gary M Hagel, *Admin Sec*
**EMP:** 2
**SALES (est):** 213.4K **Privately Held**
**SIC: 3449** Miscellaneous metalwork

### (G-8712)
**HORIZON GRAPHICS**
222 Meadow Ave (61611-6804)
PHONE..................................309 699-4287
Fax: 309 699-2361
Jeff Hickerson, *Partner*
**EMP:** 11
**SALES (est):** 1MM **Privately Held**
**SIC: 2752** Offset & photolithographic printing

### (G-8713)
**ILLINOIS VALLEY GUTTERS INC**
157 Thunderbird Ln (61611-1486)
PHONE..................................309 698-8140
Cristine Rainey, *President*
**EMP:** 5
**SALES (est):** 589.6K **Privately Held**
**SIC: 3444** Gutters, sheet metal

### (G-8714)
**INSULATION SOLUTIONS INC**
401 Truck Haven Rd (61611-1356)
PHONE..................................309 698-0062
Donald L Meyer, *President*
Dario J Lamberti, *Manager*
Ryan McCoy, *Manager*
Cara Paul, *Manager*
Chad Whittington, *Manager*
▲ **EMP:** 17
**SALES (est):** 5MM **Privately Held**
**SIC: 3357** Building wire & cable, nonferrous

### (G-8715)
**J H BENEDICT CO INC**
3211 N Main St (61611-1790)
PHONE..................................309 694-3111
Fax: 309 694-1363
Robert M Jones, *President*
David Gilbert, *Vice Pres*
Chad Miars, *Vice Pres*
Robert Everts, *VP Opers*
Austin Jones, *Foreman/Supr*
**EMP:** 53 **EST:** 1946
**SQ FT:** 26,500
**SALES (est):** 11.8MM **Privately Held**
**WEB:** www.jhbenedict.com
**SIC: 3544** 3545 Special dies, tools, jigs & fixtures; special dies & tools; forms (molds), for foundry & plastics working machinery; machine tool accessories

### (G-8716)
**J&J READY MIX INC**
100 Cass St (61611-2408)
PHONE..................................309 676-0579
Dave Minor, *Principal*
**EMP:** 3
**SALES (est):** 233.9K **Privately Held**
**SIC: 3273** Ready-mixed concrete

### (G-8717)
**JK WILLIAMS DISTILLING LLC**
526 High Point Ln (61611-9327)
PHONE..................................309 839-0591
Jonathan A Williams,
**EMP:** 6
**SALES (est):** 460.8K **Privately Held**
**SIC: 2085** Scotch whiskey; bourbon whiskey; rye whiskey

### (G-8718)
**JOHN KING USA INC**
200 Catherine St Unit 7b (61611-3128)
PHONE..................................309 698-9250
Cristopher Robinson, *President*
Mike Robinson, *General Mgr*
Mary Garber, *Manager*
Barry Ashton, *Admin Sec*
Priscilla Cooper, *Admin Sec*
▲ **EMP:** 8
**SALES (est):** 1.8MM **Privately Held**
**WEB:** www.johnkingchains.com
**SIC: 3568** Belting, chain

### (G-8719)
**JOHNSON CONTROLS INC**
3850 N Main St (61611-5512)
PHONE..................................309 427-2800
Claudius Anderson, *Branch Mgr*
**EMP:** 28
**SALES (corp-wide):** 36.8B **Privately Held**
**SIC: 2531** 5063 Seats, automobile; electrical supplies
**PA:** Johnson Controls, Inc.
5757 N Green Bay Ave
Milwaukee WI 53209
414 524-1200

### (G-8720)
**JTEC INDUSTRIES INC**
201 Carver Ln (61611-3016)
PHONE..................................309 698-9301
Jonathan S Peterson, *President*
Nate Gillespie, *Controller*
Ty Overcash, *Sales Executive*
Lorie Lundeen, *Office Mgr*
Alex Garrison, *Office Admin*
**EMP:** 50
**SQ FT:** 13,500
**SALES (est):** 15.8MM **Privately Held**
**WEB:** www.jtecindustries.com
**SIC: 3089** 4213 Plastic containers, except foam; trailer or container on flat car (TOFC/COFC)

### (G-8721)
**KELLEY ORNAMENTAL IRON LLC (PA)**
Also Called: Kelley Iron Works
4303 N Main St (61611-1455)
PHONE..................................309 697-9870
Fax: 309 697-9871
Sandy Nelson, *Office Mgr*
Joel Hoerr, *Mng Member*
**EMP:** 25 **EST:** 1948
**SALES (est):** 2.7MM **Privately Held**
**WEB:** www.kelleyiron.com
**SIC: 3446** Architectural metalwork

### (G-8722)
**KROGER CO**
201 S Main St (61611-2458)
PHONE..................................309 694-6298
Fax: 309 694-0939
April Smith, *Branch Mgr*
Kelly Ward,
**EMP:** 130
**SALES (corp-wide):** 115.3B **Publicly Held**
**WEB:** www.kroger.com
**SIC: 5411** 5992 5912 2051 Supermarkets, chain; florists; drug stores & proprietary stores; bread, cake & related products
**PA:** The Kroger Co
1014 Vine St Ste 1000
Cincinnati OH 45202
513 762-4000

### (G-8723)
**LAHOOD CONSTRUCTION INC**
3305 N Main St (61611-1566)
PHONE..................................309 699-5080
Fax: 309 699-5087
Joe Lahood, *President*
**EMP:** 35 **EST:** 1991
**SALES (est):** 6MM **Privately Held**
**SIC: 3273** Ready-mixed concrete

### (G-8724)
**METROPOLITAN PRINTERS**
109 E Washington St (61611-2566)
P.O. Box 2416 (61611-0416)
PHONE..................................309 694-1114
Fax: 309 694-2871
**EMP:** 4
**SQ FT:** 1,500
**SALES (est):** 250K **Privately Held**
**SIC: 2752** Lithographic Commercial Printing

### (G-8725)
**MEYER ENTERPRISES LLC (PA)**
401 Truck Haven Rd (61611-1356)
PHONE..................................309 698-0062
Donald L Meyer, *Mng Member*
Thomas Fahey,
Connie Klinkdradt,
James Klinkdradt,
Charles Meyer,
**EMP:** 3 **EST:** 1997
**SQ FT:** 40,000
**SALES (est):** 9.9MM **Privately Held**
**SIC: 5033** 2621 Insulation materials; insulation siding, paper

### (G-8726)
**NEO ORTHOTICS INC**
100 Park Pl (61611-1493)
PHONE..................................309 699-0354
Timothy W Potendyk, *President*
**EMP:** 2
**SALES (est):** 230K **Privately Held**
**SIC: 3842** Orthopedic appliances

### (G-8727)
**OLYMPIA MANUFACTURING INC**
101 Annie Ln (61611-9568)
PHONE..................................309 387-2633
Richard Gedhardt, *President*
**EMP:** 8
**SALES (est):** 475.9K **Privately Held**
**SIC: 3444** Sheet metalwork

### (G-8728)
**PREMIER BEVERAGE SOLUTIONS LLC**
805 Oakwood Rd (61611-1652)
PHONE..................................309 369-7117
Pete Bennett, *Vice Pres*
**EMP:** 2
**SALES:** 200K **Privately Held**
**SIC: 2037** Frozen fruits & vegetables

### (G-8729)
**QUICK PRINT SHOPPE**
500 Fondulac Dr (61611-2161)
PHONE..................................309 694-1204
David R Blair, *Owner*
**EMP:** 3 **EST:** 2001
**SALES:** 200K **Privately Held**
**WEB:** www.quickprintshop.com
**SIC: 2752** Commercial printing, offset

### (G-8730)
**RAYS MACHINE & MFG CO INC**
419 Truck Haven Rd (61611-1356)
PHONE..................................309 699-2121
Fax: 309 699-4825
Hylee Matthew Kemp, *President*

# East Peoria - Tazewell County (G-8731)

EMP: 10 EST: 1971
SALES: 2.1MM
SALES (corp-wide): 8.1MM **Privately Held**
WEB: www.kempmfg.com
SIC: 3599 Machine shop, jobbing & repair
PA: Kemp Manufacturing Company
4310 N Voss St
Peoria IL 61616
309 682-7292

### (G-8731)
**RJ DISTRIBUTING CO**
410 High Point Ln (61611-9479)
PHONE..............................309 685-2794
Fax: 309 688-9489
Robert A Jockisch, *President*
Gordon R Jockisch, *Vice Pres*
Brian Jockisch, *Manager*
▲ EMP: 35 EST: 1945
SQ FT: 20,000
SALES (est): 14.4MM **Privately Held**
WEB: www.rjdistributing.net
SIC: 5181 5182 2869 Beer & other fermented malt liquors; wine; alcohols, non-beverage

### (G-8732)
**ROANOKE CONCRETE PRODUCTS CO**
1275 Spring Bay Rd (61611-9779)
PHONE..............................309 698-7882
Gerald W Hodel Roanoke, *President*
EMP: 15
SALES (corp-wide): 8.6MM **Privately Held**
SIC: 3273 Ready-mixed concrete
PA: Roanoke Concrete Products Co.
1275 Springbay Rd E
Peoria IL 61611
309 698-7882

### (G-8733)
**SELNAR INC (PA)**
Also Called: American Speedy Printing
2460 E Washington St (61611-1859)
PHONE..............................309 699-3977
Fax: 309 699-1196
Randy Hopkins, *President*
Leslie A Hopkins, *Corp Secy*
EMP: 2 EST: 1979
SALES (est): 450K **Privately Held**
SIC: 2759 5943 2752 Commercial printing; office forms & supplies; commercial printing, lithographic

### (G-8734)
**SIMPLEXGRINNELL LP**
686 High Point Ln (61611-9329)
PHONE..............................309 694-8000
Cheryl Bouchez, *Opers Mgr*
Amy Knoll, *Safety Mgr*
Tim Roth, *Manager*
EMP: 60
SALES (corp-wide): 36.8B **Privately Held**
WEB: www.simplexgrinnell.com
SIC: 3669 Emergency alarms
HQ: Simplexgrinnell Lp
4700 Exchange Ct
Boca Raton FL 33431
561 988-7200

### (G-8735)
**SOPHER DESIGN & MANUFACTURING**
3312 Meadow Ave (61611-4639)
PHONE..............................309 699-6419
Terry Sopher, *President*
Jennifer Stout, *Corp Secy*
EMP: 7
SQ FT: 4,500
SALES: 400K **Privately Held**
WEB: www.sopher.net
SIC: 3544 3523 3555 Special dies & tools; farm machinery & equipment; printing trades machinery

### (G-8736)
**TAG TOOL SERVICES INCORPORATED**
Also Called: County Line Tool
3303 N Main St Ste A (61611-6010)
PHONE..............................309 694-2400
Fax: 309 248-7230
Vonda Jones, *President*

Steve Schatsiek, *VP Opers*
Austin L Jones, *Admin Sec*
EMP: 25
SALES (est): 4.3MM **Privately Held**
SIC: 3545 Machine tool accessories

### (G-8737)
**UNITED SEATING & MOBILITY LLC**
125 Thunderbird Ln Ste 1 (61611-5536)
PHONE..............................309 699-0509
Tamas Feitel, *CFO*
EMP: 4
SALES (corp-wide): 123.6MM **Privately Held**
SIC: 3842 Wheelchairs
PA: United Seating & Mobility Llc
975 Hornet Dr
Hazelwood MO 63042
314 731-7867

### (G-8738)
**VERSA PRESS INC**
1465 Spring Bay Rd (61611-9788)
PHONE..............................309 822-0260
Fax: 309 822-8141
Steven J Kennell, *President*
Kristine Losby, *Vice Pres*
Mike Butler, *Foreman/Supr*
Pam Larson, *Production*
Kris Perkins, *Buyer*
EMP: 185
SQ FT: 145,000
SALES (est): 46.7MM **Privately Held**
WEB: www.versapress.com
SIC: 2732 Books: printing & binding

## East Saint Louis
### St. Clair County

### (G-8739)
**ACCU-WRIGHT FIBERGLASS INC**
2393 Carol St (62206-2722)
PHONE..............................618 337-3318
Steve Wright, *President*
EMP: 5
SALES (est): 512.7K **Privately Held**
SIC: 1799 7699 2221 Fiberglass work; boat repair; fiberglass fabrics

### (G-8740)
**AFTON CHEMICAL CORPORATION**
501 Monsanto Ave (62206-1138)
PHONE..............................618 583-1000
James Horvath, *General Mgr*
Damian Barnes, *Vice Pres*
Christopher Conley, *Vice Pres*
Mike Lewis, *Vice Pres*
Carolyn Garrett, *Plant Mgr*
EMP: 292
SALES (corp-wide): 2B **Publicly Held**
SIC: 2869 3566 2899 2841 Industrial organic chemicals; speed changers, drives & gears; chemical preparations; soap & other detergents
HQ: Afton Chemical Corporation
500 Spring St
Richmond VA 23219
804 788-5086

### (G-8741)
**ATLAS READY MIX INC**
2901 Missouri Ave (62205-1122)
PHONE..............................618 271-0774
Greg Upchurch, *President*
EMP: 5 EST: 1951
SALES (est): 209.7K **Privately Held**
SIC: 3273 Ready-mixed concrete

### (G-8742)
**AVTEC INC**
6 Industrial Park (62206-1077)
PHONE..............................618 337-7800
Fax: 618 337-7976
Bouchaib Ziadi, *President*
Joseph Ziadi, *Vice Pres*
Martabeth L Ziadi, *Vice Pres*
Chris Gresick, *VP Sales*
William J Ziadi, *Manager*
EMP: 15
SQ FT: 4,000

SALES (est): 2.8MM **Privately Held**
WEB: www.avteclighting.com
SIC: 3646 Commercial indusl & institutional electric lighting fixtures

### (G-8743)
**BAD GIRLZ ENTERPRISES INC**
414 S 39th St (62207-2614)
PHONE..............................618 215-1428
Daphane Simora, *CEO*
Kisha McCoy, *CFO*
EMP: 162 EST: 2009
SALES (est): 8.3MM **Privately Held**
SIC: 2844 Cosmetic preparations

### (G-8744)
**BEELMAN READY-MIX INC (PA)**
1 Racehorse Dr (62205-1001)
PHONE..............................618 646-5300
Frank Beelman III, *President*
Sam Beelman, *President*
Kiah McCance, *Sales Mgr*
EMP: 36
SALES (est): 12.7MM **Privately Held**
WEB: www.beelmanrm.com
SIC: 3273 Ready-mixed concrete

### (G-8745)
**BLUE NILE TRUCKING LLC**
404 N 27th St (62205-1708)
PHONE..............................618 215-1077
Jai Lavington, *President*
EMP: 3
SALES (est): 214.5K **Privately Held**
SIC: 3537 Straddle carriers, mobile

### (G-8746)
**CHEMTRADE CHEMICALS US LLC**
2500 Kingshighway (62201-2446)
PHONE..............................618 274-4363
Fax: 618 271-5530
Don Brown, *Opers-Prdtn-Mfg*
Scott Lange, *Purchasing*
Brian Wiese, *Manager*
Tricia Phillips, *Administration*
EMP: 25
SALES (corp-wide): 789.3MM **Privately Held**
SIC: 2819 Aluminum sulfate
HQ: Chemtrade Chemicals Us Llc
90 E Halsey Rd
Parsippany NJ 07054
973 515-0900

### (G-8747)
**CONCRETE SUPPLY LLC**
Also Called: Concrete Supply of Illinois
1 Racehorse Dr (62205-1001)
PHONE..............................618 646-5300
Fax: 618 646-5400
Kurt Becker, *General Mgr*
Gary Jansen, *CFO*
Marianne Pelate, *Manager*
EMP: 1
SALES: 1,000K **Privately Held**
SIC: 3273 Ready-mixed concrete

### (G-8748)
**DOUGHERTY E J OIL & STONE SUP**
1501 Lincoln Ave (62204-1041)
PHONE..............................618 271-4414
Fax: 618 874-6773
E J Dougherty Jr, *President*
Deborah L Dougherty, *Admin Sec*
EMP: 7 EST: 1957
SQ FT: 5,000
SALES (est): 1.5MM **Privately Held**
SIC: 5172 2951 Petroleum products; asphalt paving mixtures & blocks

### (G-8749)
**EAST ST LOUIS TRML & STOR CO**
1501 Lincoln Ave (62204-1041)
PHONE..............................618 271-2185
James A Dougherty, *President*
Edward J Dougherty Jr, *Vice Pres*
Mike Oconnel, *Vice Pres*
Debbie Zukowski, *Vice Pres*
Dan Rheaume, *Manager*
EMP: 25
SQ FT: 5,000

SALES (est): 2MM **Privately Held**
SIC: 4231 1389 4226 Trucking terminal facilities; processing service, gas; petroleum & chemical bulk stations & terminals for hire

### (G-8750)
**ELITE IMAGING**
317 Salem Pl Ste 130 (62208-1347)
PHONE..............................618 632-2900
Cathy Fara, *CFO*
Cecil Gray, *Mng Member*
Mary Greteman, *Administration*
EMP: 15
SALES (est): 2.2MM **Privately Held**
SIC: 3841 Diagnostic apparatus, medical

### (G-8751)
**ETHYL CORP**
501 Monsanto Ave (62206-1138)
PHONE..............................618 583-1292
EMP: 3
SALES (est): 189.2K **Privately Held**
SIC: 2869 Industrial organic chemicals

### (G-8752)
**GASKET & SEAL FABRICATORS INC**
1640 Sauget Indl Pkwy (62206-1449)
PHONE..............................314 241-3673
Fax: 618 332-0450
Gerald Johnson, *President*
James S Boos, *President*
Randy Hamilton, *Prdtn Mgr*
Paul Miles, *Marketing Staff*
Donna McArthur, *Manager*
▲ EMP: 20
SQ FT: 40,000
SALES (est): 5MM **Privately Held**
WEB: www.gasketandseal.com
SIC: 3053 Gaskets, all materials

### (G-8753)
**GATEWAY CRUSHING & SCREENING**
3936 Mississippi Ave (62206-1060)
PHONE..............................618 337-1954
Fax: 618 337-8785
Johnny R Baur, *President*
EMP: 20
SALES (est): 1.7MM **Privately Held**
SIC: 1429 Igneous rock, crushed & broken-quarrying

### (G-8754)
**GATEWAY FABRICATORS INC**
633 Collinsville Ave (62201-1309)
P.O. Box 2193 (62202-2193)
PHONE..............................618 271-5700
Kevin J Mocabee, *President*
EMP: 7
SQ FT: 18,000
SALES (est): 600K **Privately Held**
SIC: 3443 Fabricated plate work (boiler shop)

### (G-8755)
**HUNTSMAN P&A AMERICAS LLC**
2051 Lynch Ave (62204-1717)
PHONE..............................618 646-2119
Onika Young, *Human Res Mgr*
Tom Sweeney, *Info Tech Dir*
Mark Olson, *Director*
EMP: 25
SALES (corp-wide): 9.6B **Publicly Held**
WEB: www.rockwoodpigments.com
SIC: 2816 2865 Iron oxide pigments (ochers, siennas, umbers); color pigments, organic
HQ: Huntsman P&A Americas Llc
7011 Muirkirk Rd
Beltsville MD 20705
301 210-3400

### (G-8756)
**ILLINI DIGITAL PRINTING CO**
680 N 20th St (62205-1812)
PHONE..............................618 271-6622
John Eichelberger, *Principal*
EMP: 4
SALES (est): 393.8K **Privately Held**
SIC: 2752 Commercial printing, lithographic

## GEOGRAPHIC SECTION
### Edelstein - Peoria County (G-8780)

**(G-8757)**
**INDUSTRIAL GAS PRODUCTS INC**
2350 Falling Springs Rd (62206-1102)
**PHONE**..................618 337-1030
Robert Clarkson, *President*
Rick Clarkson, *Treasurer*
Steve Laux, *Accountant*
Rhonda Wheeler, *Bookkeeper*
**EMP:** 6
**SQ FT:** 6,500
**SALES (est):** 1.2MM **Privately Held**
**SIC:** 2813 Hydrogen

**(G-8758)**
**K & K METAL WORKS INC**
2034 Saint Clair Ave (62205-1817)
**PHONE**..................618 271-4680
Dana Kincade, *President*
Dennis Kincade, *Vice Pres*
**EMP:** 10
**SALES (est):** 1.7MM **Privately Held**
**SIC:** 3498 7692 Fabricated pipe & fittings; welding repair

**(G-8759)**
**LAUX GRAFIX INC**
3709 Mississippi Ave (62206-1036)
**PHONE**..................618 337-4558
Rich Laux, *Owner*
Adam Sanchez, *Sales Staff*
Dave Berube, *Sales Associate*
Charity Wright, *Marketing Staff*
**EMP:** 4
**SQ FT:** 1,800
**SALES (est):** 250K **Privately Held**
**WEB:** www.newsignsfast.com
**SIC:** 3993 7389 Signs & advertising specialties; printed circuitry graphic layout

**(G-8760)**
**MASTER GUARD SECURITY CO**
6125 State St (62203-1406)
**PHONE**..................618 398-7749
**Fax:** 618 398-7857
Michael Harris, *Partner*
Kevin Harris, *Partner*
Bobby Smith, *Partner*
**EMP:** 3
**SALES:** 80K **Privately Held**
**SIC:** 3462 7381 Iron & steel forgings; security guard service

**(G-8761)**
**MONITOR NEWSPAPER INC**
Also Called: East St Louis Monitor Pubg Co
1501 State St (62205-2011)
P.O. Box 2137 (62202-2137)
**PHONE**..................618 271-0468
**Fax:** 618 271-8443
Anne Jordan, *President*
Clyde Jordan Jr, *Principal*
Anthony Sanders, *Principal*
Ahmad Seea, *Manager*
**EMP:** 6
**SALES:** 400K **Privately Held**
**SIC:** 2711 Newspapers: publishing only, not printed on site

**(G-8762)**
**NATIONAL TOOL & MACHINE CO**
1235 Piggott Ave (62201)
**PHONE**..................618 271-6445
**Fax:** 618 874-3135
**EMP:** 10 **EST:** 1928
**SQ FT:** 6,500
**SALES (est):** 730K **Privately Held**
**SIC:** 3599 7692 Mfg Industrial Machinery Welding Repair

**(G-8763)**
**OLDCASTLE LAWN & GARDEN INC**
Also Called: Oldcastle Lawn & Grdn Midwest
1130 Queeny Ave (62206-1150)
**PHONE**..................618 274-1222
Tim Thomas, *Owner*
Rich Mullen, *Sales Mgr*
**EMP:** 17
**SALES (corp-wide):** 28.6B **Privately Held**
**SIC:** 3524 Lawn & garden equipment
**HQ:** Oldcastle Lawn & Garden, Inc.
900 Ashwood Pkwy Ste 600
Atlanta GA 30338

**(G-8764)**
**PETER BUILT**
2350 Sauget Indus Pkwy (62206-2937)
**PHONE**..................618 337-4000
Claire Larson, *President*
Beckie Collins, *Marketing Staff*
**EMP:** 30
**SALES (est):** 5.6MM **Privately Held**
**SIC:** 3715 Trailer bodies

**(G-8765)**
**PETRA INDUSTRIES INC**
Also Called: Petra Companies The
6400 Collinsville Rd (62201-2526)
P.O. Box 121, Collinsville (62234-0121)
**PHONE**..................618 271-0022
**Fax:** 618 271-0688
A C Musgrave Jr, *President*
Dana Musgrove, *Vice Pres*
Jayce Ralph, *Natl Sales Mgr*
Tyler Scherner, *Merchandise Mgr*
Bobby Witt, *Merchandise Mgr*
◆ **EMP:** 18
**SALES (est):** 6.3MM **Privately Held**
**SIC:** 2812 Alkalies & chlorine

**(G-8766)**
**REAGENT CHEMICAL & RES INC**
1700 S 20th St (62207-1916)
**PHONE**..................618 271-8140
Robert Merseman, *Branch Mgr*
**EMP:** 3
**SALES (corp-wide):** 280MM **Privately Held**
**WEB:** www.biotarget.com
**SIC:** 2819 3949 Sulfur, recovered or refined, incl. from sour natural gas; targets, archery & rifle shooting
**PA:** Reagent Chemical & Research, Inc.
115 Rte 202
Ringoes NJ 08551
908 284-2800

**(G-8767)**
**RESCAR INDUSTRIES INC**
501 Monsanto Ave (62206-1138)
**PHONE**..................618 875-3234
Jeremy Speelman, *Manager*
**EMP:** 4
**SALES (corp-wide):** 313.9MM **Privately Held**
**WEB:** www.rescar.com
**SIC:** 3743 Railroad car rebuilding
**PA:** Rescar Industries, Inc.
1101 31st St Ste 250
Downers Grove IL 60515
630 963-1114

**(G-8768)**
**SAFETY-KLEEN SYSTEMS INC**
3000 Missouri Ave (62205-1125)
**PHONE**..................618 875-8050
Steve Ogdenwald, *President*
**EMP:** 9
**SALES (corp-wide):** 2.7B **Publicly Held**
**SIC:** 2992 4953 Re-refining lubricating oils & greases; refuse systems
**HQ:** Safety-Kleen Systems, Inc.
2600 N Central Expy # 400
Richardson TX 75080
972 265-2000

**(G-8769)**
**SOLVAY CHEMICALS INC**
3500 Missouri Ave (62205-3104)
**PHONE**..................618 274-0755
Homero Villarreal, *Plant Mgr*
Jack Kettler, *Plant Engr*
Jan Pashia, *Financial Exec*
Milton Highhouse, *Branch Mgr*
Cindy Shirley, *Manager*
**EMP:** 41
**SALES (corp-wide):** 11.4MM **Privately Held**
**SIC:** 2819 2869 2899 Fluorine, elemental; industrial organic chemicals; chemical preparations
**HQ:** Solvay Chemicals, Inc.
3737 Buffalo Speedway
Houston TX 77098
713 525-6800

**(G-8770)**
**ST LOUIS FLEXICORE INC**
Also Called: Flexicore Slab
6351 Collinsville Rd (62201-2523)
**PHONE**..................618 531-8691
**Fax:** 618 274-0130
Marvin P Siegele, *President*
Denise Lyons, *Corp Secy*
Kim Moore, *Vice Pres*
Ken Moore, *Vice Pres*
**EMP:** 10 **EST:** 1956
**SQ FT:** 9,000
**SALES (est):** 2.5MM **Privately Held**
**SIC:** 3272 2952 Floor slabs & tiles, precast concrete; roofing tile & slabs, concrete; asphalt felts & coatings

**(G-8771)**
**STONETREE FABRICATION INC**
9 Production Pkwy (62206-1081)
**PHONE**..................618 332-1700
**Fax:** 618 332-1717
Thomas Smugala, *President*
Shari Smugala, *Controller*
**EMP:** 20
**SALES:** 2MM **Privately Held**
**WEB:** www.stonetreefabrications.com
**SIC:** 2434 5712 Vanities, bathroom: wood; customized furniture & cabinets

**(G-8772)**
**SWANSEA BUILDING PRODUCTS INC**
494 N 33rd St (62205-1422)
**PHONE**..................618 874-6282
Cletus Mueth, *President*
David Fournie, *Vice Pres*
**EMP:** 18
**SALES (est):** 2.5MM **Privately Held**
**WEB:** www.buildingproductscorp.com
**SIC:** 3271 Concrete block & brick
**PA:** Building Products Corp.
950 Freeburg Ave
Belleville IL 62220
618 233-4427

**(G-8773)**
**TOP METAL BUYERS INC (PA)**
Also Called: Top Metal Recycling
808 Walnut Ave (62201-2940)
**PHONE**..................314 421-2721
**Fax:** 618 271-7908
Norman Schultz, *President*
Brett Nickel, *Admin Sec*
**EMP:** 16
**SQ FT:** 60,000
**SALES (est):** 6.6MM **Privately Held**
**WEB:** www.topmetal.net
**SIC:** 5093 4953 3341 Junk & scrap; ferrous metal scrap & waste; refuse systems; secondary nonferrous metals

**(G-8774)**
**UNIVERSAL AIR FILTER COMPANY (HQ)**
1624 Sauget Indus Pkwy (62206-1451)
**PHONE**..................618 271-7300
**Fax:** 618 271-8808
Todd C Deibel, *President*
Dan Krupp, *President*
Thomas Olandt, *Business Mgr*
Robert Haas, *Purch Mgr*
Jeffrey Bloese, *Engineer*
**EMP:** 49
**SQ FT:** 45,000
**SALES:** 18MM
**SALES (corp-wide):** 44.6MM **Privately Held**
**WEB:** www.uaf.com
**SIC:** 3564 Filters, air: furnaces, air conditioning equipment, etc.
**PA:** Thompson Street Capital Manager Llc
120 S Central Ave Ste 600
Saint Louis MO 63105
314 727-2112

**(G-8775)**
**WASTEQUIP LLC**
Wastequip Saint Louis
2701 Converse Ave (62207-1728)
**PHONE**..................618 271-6250
Kevin Lolling, *General Mgr*
**EMP:** 20

**SALES (corp-wide):** 556.4MM **Privately Held**
**SIC:** 3443 Dumpsters, garbage
**PA:** Wastequip, Llc
6525 Morrison Blvd # 300
Charlotte NC 28211
704 366-7140

**(G-8776)**
**WASTEQUIP SAINT LOUIS**
2701 Converse Ave (62207-1728)
**PHONE**..................216 292-0625
**Fax:** 618 271-1329
Greg Podell, *President*
Joanna Thompson, *Controller*
John Hentze, *Office Mgr*
**EMP:** 28
**SALES (est):** 3.2MM **Privately Held**
**SIC:** 3537 Trucks, tractors, loaders, carriers & similar equipment

### Easton
*Mason County*

**(G-8777)**
**MAHANS FIBERGLASS**
106 E Main St (62633-9324)
P.O. Box 112 (62633-0112)
**PHONE**..................309 562-7349
**Fax:** 309 562-7341
Jim Mahan, *Owner*
**EMP:** 3
**SALES (est):** 212.9K **Privately Held**
**SIC:** 2221 Fiberglass fabrics

**(G-8778)**
**ONKENS INCORPORATED**
320 E Main St (62633-9325)
P.O. Box 72 (62633-0072)
**PHONE**..................309 562-7477
James H Onken, *President*
Joseph D Onken, *Admin Sec*
▲ **EMP:** 15
**SALES (est):** 2.1MM **Privately Held**
**SIC:** 3441 Fabricated structural metal

### Edelstein
*Peoria County*

**(G-8779)**
**CUSTOM POWER PRODUCTS INC**
Also Called: Cpp
19727 N State Route 40 (61526-9507)
P.O. Box 106 (61526-0106)
**PHONE**..................309 249-2704
**Fax:** 309 249-3003
Lowell Langeland, *President*
Dave Malott, *Engineer*
**EMP:** 6
**SQ FT:** 25,000
**SALES (est):** 1.6MM **Privately Held**
**WEB:** www.custompowerproducts.com
**SIC:** 3613 Switchgear & switchgear accessories

**(G-8780)**
**INTERNATIONAL SUPPLY CO**
2717 W North St (61526-9530)
P.O. Box 17 (61526-0017)
**PHONE**..................309 249-6211
**Fax:** 309 249-2404
E Lee Hofmann, *President*
Becky Hofmann, *Corp Secy*
Duane Dean, *Vice Pres*
Rick Durie, *Vice Pres*
Chad Jenkins, *Engineer*
**EMP:** 90
**SQ FT:** 100,000
**SALES (est):** 31.8MM
**SALES (corp-wide):** 150MM **Privately Held**
**WEB:** www.elhisco.com
**SIC:** 3621 Control equipment for electric buses & locomotives
**PA:** Fibrebond Corporation
1300 Davenport Dr
Minden LA 71055
318 377-1030

## Edwards
*Peoria County*

**(G-8781)**
**AMERICAN BOTTLING COMPANY**
7215 N Kckapoo Edwards Rd (61528-9705)
PHONE................309 693-2777
Fax: 309 693-2810
Paul Beressel, *Office Mgr*
Paul Bersell, *Manager*
EMP: 40
SALES (corp-wide): 6.4B **Publicly Held**
WEB: www.cs-americas.com
SIC: 2086 Soft drinks: packaged in cans, bottles, etc.
HQ: The American Bottling Company
 5301 Legacy Dr
 Plano TX 75024

**(G-8782)**
**KICKAPOO CREEK WINERY**
6605 N Smith Rd (61528-9631)
PHONE................309 495-9463
David Conner, *Owner*
EMP: 7
SALES (est): 853.8K **Privately Held**
SIC: 2084 5921 5947 Wines; wine; gift shop

**(G-8783)**
**MIDWEST PERMA-COLUMN INC**
7407 N Kckapoo Edwards Rd (61528-9705)
PHONE................309 589-7949
Doug Streitmatter, *President*
Phil Ehnle, *Vice Pres*
Ray Blunier, *Treasurer*
David Ehnle, *Manager*
EMP: 4
SALES (est): 668.8K **Privately Held**
SIC: 3272 Concrete products, precast

**(G-8784)**
**R/A HOERR INC**
Also Called: Hoerr Racing Products
9804 W Primrose (61528-9306)
PHONE................309 691-8789
Fax: 309 691-8796
Irv Hoerr, *CEO*
Jason Mitchell, *President*
Derek Woolf, *Purch Mgr*
Bryan Long, *Manager*
◆ EMP: 23
SQ FT: 10,000
SALES (est): 5.1MM **Privately Held**
WEB: www.hrpworld.com
SIC: 3711 7948 Motor vehicles & car bodies; race car owners

**(G-8785)**
**WAYNE PRINTING COMPANY (PA)**
7917 N Kckapoo Edwards Rd (61528-9579)
PHONE................309 691-2496
Fax: 309 691-9379
Kenneth E Hoerr, *President*
Linda Shroff, *Controller*
Bill Jones, *Manager*
Ken Notaro, *Supervisor*
Cindy McCarley, *Director*
EMP: 38 EST: 1990
SQ FT: 34,120
SALES (est): 8.9MM **Privately Held**
WEB: www.waynewag.com
SIC: 2752 Commercial printing, offset

**(G-8786)**
**WAYNE PRINTING COMPANY**
Also Called: Wayne Wagoner Printing
7917 N Kckapoo Edwards Rd (61528-9579)
PHONE................309 691-2496
Scott Hoerr, *President*
Ken Notaro, *General Mgr*
Vicky Nauman, *Plant Mgr*
Bill Britt, *Sales Mgr*
Eric Timm, *Branch Mgr*
EMP: 50
SALES (corp-wide): 8.9MM **Privately Held**
WEB: www.waynewag.com
SIC: 2752 Offset & photolithographic printing
PA: Wayne Printing Company
 7917 N Kckapoo Edwards Rd
 Edwards IL 61528
 309 691-2496

## Edwardsville
*Madison County*

**(G-8787)**
**ANNIES FROZEN CUSTARD**
245 S Buchanan St (62025-2108)
PHONE................618 656-0289
Fax: 618 656-8425
Kay Geiszelman, *Owner*
EMP: 20
SALES (est): 1.1MM **Privately Held**
WEB: www.anniesfrozencustard.com
SIC: 2024 Ice cream & frozen desserts

**(G-8788)**
**ANNS PRINTING & COPYING CO**
Also Called: Ann Printing
219 2nd Ave Ste E (62025-2598)
PHONE................618 656-6878
Kathy Moore, *Owner*
EMP: 3
SQ FT: 1,600
SALES (est): 276.6K **Privately Held**
SIC: 2759 6514 Commercial printing; dwelling operators, except apartments

**(G-8789)**
**B JS PRINTABLES**
1415 Troy Rd (62025-2532)
PHONE................618 656-8625
Fax: 618 656-8625
Brenda Schrage, *Owner*
EMP: 4
SALES: 160K **Privately Held**
WEB: www.bjsprintables.com
SIC: 2396 5136 5611 5137 Fabric printing & stamping; sportswear, men's & boys'; clothing, sportswear, men's & boys'; sportswear, women's & children's; women's sportswear; pleating & stitching

**(G-8790)**
**B QUAD OIL INC**
1405 Troy Rd Ste B (62025-2532)
PHONE................618 656-4419
Bill Blythe, *President*
Robert Rohrkaste, *Corp Secy*
EMP: 3
SALES (est): 319.2K **Privately Held**
SIC: 1311 Crude petroleum production

**(G-8791)**
**BC ENTERPRISES**
99 Shore Dr Sw (62025-5338)
PHONE................618 655-0784
Bret Seavers, *Partner*
Christopher McMiller, *Partner*
EMP: 2
SALES (est): 218.8K **Privately Held**
SIC: 3824 Water meters

**(G-8792)**
**BECK SHOE PRODUCTS COMPANY**
203 W High St (62025-1529)
PHONE................618 656-5819
Fax: 618 656-5897
Gregory Evans, *President*
Edward Page, *VP Opers*
EMP: 1
SQ FT: 1,700
SALES (est): 206.6K **Privately Held**
WEB: www.beckshoepolishers.com
SIC: 3634 Shoe polishers, electric

**(G-8793)**
**BUDGET PRINTING CENTER**
3709 Edwardsville Rd # 1 (62025-7249)
PHONE................618 655-1636
John Sharp, *President*
Jane Stahlhut, *Corp Secy*
EMP: 4
SALES: 150K **Privately Held**
SIC: 2752 2791 Commercial printing, offset; typesetting

**(G-8794)**
**DAVID YATES**
Also Called: Yates Complete Concrete
6407 Sworm Ln (62025-4921)
PHONE................618 656-7879
David Yates, *Owner*
EMP: 4
SALES (est): 150K **Privately Held**
WEB: www.davidyates.com
SIC: 3273 Ready-mixed concrete

**(G-8795)**
**DONUT PALACE**
443 S Buchanan St (62025-2064)
PHONE................618 692-0532
Pete Patel, *Owner*
EMP: 6
SQ FT: 1,500
SALES (est): 180K **Privately Held**
SIC: 5461 2051 Doughnuts; doughnuts, except frozen

**(G-8796)**
**DYNAMI SOLUTIONS LLC**
2 Loggers Trl (62025-5743)
PHONE................618 363-2771
Joe Stoddard, *Opers Staff*
Kevin Ogle, *Mng Member*
Bill Jagoe IV,
J Scott Jagoe,
William R Jagoe IV,
EMP: 6
SALES (est): 426.1K **Privately Held**
WEB: www.dynamisolutions.com
SIC: 7372 Prepackaged software

**(G-8797)**
**EBERHART SIGN & LIGHTING CO (PA)**
104 1st Ave (62025-2574)
PHONE................618 656-7256
Fax: 618 656-7257
Ronald P Eberhart, *President*
Jim Pitts, *Manager*
EMP: 8
SQ FT: 2,200
SALES (est): 1.2MM **Privately Held**
SIC: 3993 1731 Signs & advertising specialties; electrical work

**(G-8798)**
**EDWARDSVILLE MCH & WLDG CO INC**
1509 Troy Rd (62025-2534)
PHONE................618 656-5145
Fax: 618 656-7647
Richard L Hartnagel, *President*
George Hartnagel, *Vice Pres*
Tina Hartnageo, *Admin Sec*
EMP: 4 EST: 1947
SQ FT: 6,500
SALES (est): 350K **Privately Held**
SIC: 3599 7692 Machine shop, jobbing & repair; welding repair

**(G-8799)**
**EDWARDSVILLE PUBLISHING CO**
Also Called: Edwardsville Intelligencer
117 N 2nd St (62025-1938)
PHONE................618 656-4700
Fax: 618 656-7618
Bill Tucker, *Editor*
Bruce E Coury, *Vice Pres*
Pam Roth, *Controller*
Denise Vonderhaar, *Controller*
Amy Schaake, *Adv Dir*
EMP: 73
SALES (est): 5.1MM
SALES (corp-wide): 6.4B **Privately Held**
WEB: www.goedwardsville.com
SIC: 2711 2791 2752 Newspapers, publishing & printing; typesetting; commercial printing, lithographic
PA: The Hearst Corporation
 300 W 57th St Fl 42
 New York NY 10019
 212 649-2000

**(G-8800)**
**EDWARDSVILLE WATER TREATMENT**
3735 Wanda Rd (62025-7401)
PHONE................618 692-7053
Fax: 618 692-7054
Billy Sietz, *Principal*
John Shaw, *Manager*
EMP: 5 EST: 2008
SALES (est): 330.8K **Privately Held**
SIC: 3589 Water treatment equipment, industrial

**(G-8801)**
**FOSTER LEARNING LLC**
900 Timberlake Dr (62025-4107)
PHONE................618 656-6836
Ann Robertson, *Principal*
Edwards Ackad, *Chief Engr*
Thomas Foster, *Treasurer*
EMP: 3
SALES (est): 74.9K **Privately Held**
SIC: 7372 Application computer software; educational computer software

**(G-8802)**
**FRAMERY**
216 E Park St (62025-1711)
PHONE................618 656-5749
EMP: 3 EST: 1979
SALES (est): 160K **Privately Held**
SIC: 3499 Mfg Misc Fabricated Metal Products

**(G-8803)**
**HUBBELL POWER SYSTEMS INC**
131 Enterprise Dr (62025-7436)
PHONE................618 797-5000
EMP: 15
SALES (corp-wide): 3.5B **Publicly Held**
SIC: 3612 3679 3699 3691 Power transformers, electric; power supplies, all types: static; electrical equipment & supplies; nickel cadmium storage batteries
HQ: Hubbell Power Systems, Inc.
 200 Center Point Cir # 200
 Columbia SC 29210
 803 216-2600

**(G-8804)**
**HUBBELL POWER SYSTEMS INC**
Turner Electric
131 Enterprise Dr (62025-7436)
PHONE................618 797-5000
EMP: 23
SALES (corp-wide): 3.3B **Publicly Held**
SIC: 3613 Mfg Switchgear/Switchboards
HQ: Hubbell Power Systems, Inc.
 200 Center Point Cir # 200
 Columbia SC 29210
 803 216-2600

**(G-8805)**
**KSEM INC**
6471 Miller Dr (62025-4927)
PHONE................618 656-5388
Fax: 618 656-5388
Joan Ketcham, *President*
EMP: 3
SQ FT: 4,800
SALES (est): 346.6K **Privately Held**
SIC: 3523 3993 7692 3441 Farm machinery & equipment; signs, not made in custom sign painting shops; welding repair; fabricated structural metal

**(G-8806)**
**LIZOTTE SHEET METAL INC**
632 W Schwarz St (62025-1564)
PHONE................618 656-3066
Paul Lizotte, *President*
Aileen Lizotte, *Corp Secy*
Kent Lizotte, *Vice Pres*
EMP: 4
SQ FT: 3,000
SALES (est): 494.2K **Privately Held**
SIC: 1711 3446 3444 3443 Warm air heating & air conditioning contractor; ventilation & duct work contractor; architectural metalwork; sheet metalwork; fabricated plate work (boiler shop); fabricated structural metal

## GEOGRAPHIC SECTION

### Effingham - Effingham County (G-8834)

**(G-8807)**
**MENASHA PACKAGING COMPANY LLC**
21 W Gtwy Commerce Ctr Dr (62025-2814)
**PHONE**.................................618 931-7805
Elsa Montanez, *General Mgr*
Deborah Vaught, *Financial Analy*
Richard McFarland, *Manager*
**EMP:** 13
**SALES (corp-wide):** 1.8B **Privately Held**
**SIC:** 2653 Sheets, corrugated: made from purchased materials
**HQ:** Menasha Packaging Company, Llc
1645 Bergstrom Rd
Neenah WI 54956
920 751-1000

**(G-8808)**
**MENASHA PACKAGING COMPANY LLC**
9 Gatway Cmmerce Ctr Dr E (62025-2810)
**PHONE**.................................618 501-6040
**EMP:** 140
**SALES (corp-wide):** 1.8B **Privately Held**
**SIC:** 2653 Sheets, corrugated: made from purchased materials
**HQ:** Menasha Packaging Company, Llc
1645 Bergstrom Rd
Neenah WI 54956
920 751-1000

**(G-8809)**
**MIKE SIMON TRUCKING LLC**
3114 Sand Rd (62025-7514)
**PHONE**.................................618 659-8755
Michael Simon, *Mng Member*
**EMP:** 2
**SALES (est):** 270K **Privately Held**
**SIC:** 3537 Industrial trucks & tractors

**(G-8810)**
**NIKKIN FLUX CORP**
512 Phillipena St (62025-1007)
P.O. Box 402 (62025-0402)
**PHONE**.................................618 656-2125
Steven Schoeffler, *President*
Jill Miller, *Purch Mgr*
▲ **EMP:** 5
**SALES (est):** 792.5K **Privately Held**
**WEB:** www.nikkinflux.com
**SIC:** 2819 Industrial inorganic chemicals

**(G-8811)**
**OLIVE OILS & MORE LLC**
1990 Troy Rd Ste A (62025-2596)
**PHONE**.................................618 656-4645
Mary Burke, *Principal*
**EMP:** 3
**SALES (est):** 248.7K **Privately Held**
**SIC:** 2079 Olive oil

**(G-8812)**
**RICHARDS BRICK COMPANY (PA)**
234 Springer Ave (62025-1806)
**PHONE**.................................618 656-0230
John R Motley, *President*
Nick Douglas, *Plant Mgr*
Robert Richards, *CFO*
Chris Tvetene, *Sales Staff*
James Richards, *Admin Sec*
**EMP:** 85
**SQ FT:** 5,000
**SALES (est):** 31.8MM **Privately Held**
**WEB:** www.richardsbrick.com
**SIC:** 5032 3251 Brick, except refractory; brick clay: common face, glazed, vitrified or hollow

**(G-8813)**
**SANITARY STAINLESS SERVICES**
703 Vassar Dr (62025-3169)
**PHONE**.................................618 659-8567
Jonah Cope, *Owner*
**EMP:** 3
**SALES (est):** 113.7K **Privately Held**
**WEB:** www.sanitarystainless.net
**SIC:** 7692 Welding repair

**(G-8814)**
**SJD DIRECT MIDWEST LLC (PA)**
Also Called: Rand Diversified Midwest
21 Gtewy Cmrc Ctr Dr W (62025-2814)
**PHONE**.................................618 931-2151
Mike Waite, *President*
Vera McCarty, *Manager*
David Kauffman,
Stuart Sklovsky,
John P Wuensch,
▲ **EMP:** 6
**SALES (est):** 28.6MM **Privately Held**
**WEB:** www.rand-div.com
**SIC:** 3565 Packing & wrapping machinery

**(G-8815)**
**ST LOUIS SCRAP TRADING LLC**
5 Sunset Hills Blvd N (62025-3732)
**PHONE**.................................618 307-9002
Charles Fred Francis, *Mng Member*
**EMP:** 3
**SALES (est):** 302.7K **Privately Held**
**SIC:** 3312 8748 1795 Blast furnaces & steel mills; business consulting; wrecking & demolition work

**(G-8816)**
**T J S EQUIPMENT INC**
1514 Weber Dr (62025-4104)
**PHONE**.................................618 656-8046
Terrence J Scheibal, *President*
**EMP:** 3
**SALES (est):** 410K **Privately Held**
**SIC:** 5046 3531 Commercial equipment; plows: construction, excavating & grading

**(G-8817)**
**TINSLEY STEEL INC**
2 Oasis Dr (62025-5939)
**PHONE**.................................618 656-5231
**Fax:** 618 656-9040
Greg Tinsley, *President*
Cathy Tinsley, *Corp Secy*
Bob Smith, *Manager*
**EMP:** 8
**SQ FT:** 12,000
**SALES (est):** 2MM **Privately Held**
**SIC:** 3316 3446 3444 3443 Bars, steel, cold finished, from purchased hot-rolled; architectural metalwork; sheet metalwork; fabricated plate work (boiler shop); fabricated structural metal; nonferrous rolling & drawing

**(G-8818)**
**WILSEYS HANDMADE SWEETS LLC**
316 W Park St (62025-1942)
**PHONE**.................................314 504-0851
Lindsey Wulfing, *Principal*
**EMP:** 6
**SALES (est):** 427.7K **Privately Held**
**SIC:** 2053 Cakes, bakery: frozen

**(G-8819)**
**WINKLER PRODUCTS INC**
9029 Pin Oak Rd (62025-6829)
**PHONE**.................................314 421-1926
Edwin Winkler, *President*
Marie Hultz, *Corp Secy*
**EMP:** 5
**SQ FT:** 20,000
**SALES (est):** 380K **Privately Held**
**SIC:** 2657 Folding paperboard boxes

### Effingham
*Effingham County*

**(G-8820)**
**4X4 HEADQUARTERS LLC**
18086 N Highway 45 (62401)
**PHONE**.................................217 540-5337
James McHuge,
**EMP:** 6 **EST:** 2010
**SALES (est):** 702.9K **Privately Held**
**SIC:** 3711 Motor vehicles & car bodies

**(G-8821)**
**AD WORKS INC**
17866 N Us Highway 45 (62401-6708)
**PHONE**.................................217 342-9688
**Fax:** 217 342-5939
David Campbell, *President*
**EMP:** 4
**SQ FT:** 4,000
**SALES (est):** 275K **Privately Held**
**SIC:** 2759 2752 Commercial printing; commercial printing, lithographic

**(G-8822)**
**ADERMANNS WELDING & MCH & CO**
1310 Pike Ave (62401-4270)
P.O. Box 221 (62401-0221)
**PHONE**.................................217 342-3234
**Fax:** 217 342-0230
Steve Bloemer, *President*
Kelly Lidy, *Corp Secy*
Paul Bloemer, *Vice Pres*
**EMP:** 5 **EST:** 1942
**SALES (est):** 330K **Privately Held**
**SIC:** 3599 7692 3441 Machine shop, jobbing & repair; automotive welding; fabricated structural metal

**(G-8823)**
**AIR STAMPING INC**
3 Legend Park (62401-9442)
P.O. Box 568 (62401-0568)
**PHONE**.................................217 342-1283
**Fax:** 217 342-1286
Gene Williams, *President*
Larry Hines, *Vice Pres*
▲ **EMP:** 12
**SQ FT:** 18,800
**SALES (est):** 3.9MM **Privately Held**
**SIC:** 5072 3599 Screws; machine shop, jobbing & repair

**(G-8824)**
**ARCHER-DANIELS-MIDLAND COMPANY**
Also Called: ADM Animal Nutrition
1 Goodlife Dr (62401-3716)
P.O. Box 687 (62401-0687)
**PHONE**.................................217 342-3986
**Fax:** 217 342-3110
Jim Niendiek, *Purch Mgr*
Kent Lockridge, *Purchasing*
Tracy Mintert, *Purchasing*
Richard Worman, *Sales Mgr*
Kyle Taylor, *Branch Mgr*
**EMP:** 44
**SQ FT:** 18,000
**SALES (corp-wide):** 62.3B **Publicly Held**
**WEB:** www.admworld.com
**SIC:** 2048 Prepared feeds
**PA:** Archer-Daniels-Midland Company
77 W Wacker Dr Ste 4600
Chicago IL 60601
312 634-8100

**(G-8825)**
**ATHLETIC IMAGE**
510 W Jaycee Ave Ste 3 (62401-2912)
**PHONE**.................................217 347-7377
**Fax:** 217 347-7376
Jim Smothers, *Owner*
**EMP:** 5
**SALES (est):** 180K **Privately Held**
**SIC:** 2759 Screen printing

**(G-8826)**
**AXIOSONIC LLC**
2600 S Raney St (62401-4219)
**PHONE**.................................217 342-3412
Peter Bonutti, *Principal*
Justin Beyers, *Vice Pres*
**EMP:** 10
**SQ FT:** 5,000
**SALES (est):** 408.2K **Privately Held**
**SIC:** 3845 Ultrasonic medical equipment, except cleaning

**(G-8827)**
**BIERMAN WELDING INC**
1103 S Willow St (62401-4044)
P.O. Box 25 (62401-0025)
**PHONE**.................................217 342-2050
**Fax:** 217 342-2075
James Bierman, *President*
Phillip Bierman, *Vice Pres*
Mark Bierman, *Treasurer*
Barbara Key, *Manager*
Jerry Bierman, *Admin Sec*
**EMP:** 14
**SQ FT:** 4,000
**SALES (est):** 1.6MM **Privately Held**
**SIC:** 7692 7539 Welding repair; trailer repair

**(G-8828)**
**BUCKEYE TERMINALS LLC**
18264 N Highway 45 (62401-6958)
**PHONE**.................................217 342-2336
Chet Greene, *Principal*
Clark Smith, *Mng Member*
**EMP:** 5
**SALES (est):** 306.4K **Privately Held**
**SIC:** 1389 5085 Pipe testing, oil field service; pipeline wrappings, anti-corrosive

**(G-8829)**
**CCI REDI MIX**
2604 N Haarmann St (62401-4272)
**PHONE**.................................217 342-2299
Gary Bartels, *President*
**EMP:** 35
**SALES (est):** 4.6MM **Privately Held**
**SIC:** 3273 Ready-mixed concrete

**(G-8830)**
**CONTINENTAL MILLS INC**
1200 Stevens Ave (62401-4264)
**PHONE**.................................217 540-4000
Julie Klein, *QA Dir*
**EMP:** 140
**SALES (corp-wide):** 261.4MM **Privately Held**
**SIC:** 2045 Flours & flour mixes, from purchased flour
**PA:** Continental Mills, Inc.
18100 Andover Park W
Tukwila WA 98188
253 872-8400

**(G-8831)**
**CONTRACT TRANSPORTATION SYS CO**
711 W Wabash Ave (62401-2605)
**PHONE**.................................217 342-5757
**Fax:** 217 347-2811
Shawn Mohundro, *Manager*
**EMP:** 110
**SALES (corp-wide):** 11.8B **Publicly Held**
**WEB:** www.ctsoh.net
**SIC:** 2851 Paints & allied products
**HQ:** Contract Transportation System Co.
101 W Prospect Ave
Cleveland OH 44115
216 566-2000

**(G-8832)**
**DINGO INC**
14480 N 1025th St (62401-6257)
**PHONE**.................................217 868-5615
Kathy Witkowski, *President*
Kathleen A Witkowski, *President*
Gerald Crisman, *Admin Sec*
**EMP:** 4
**SALES (est):** 276.8K **Privately Held**
**WEB:** www.pappyledeaux.com
**SIC:** 2033 Barbecue sauce: packaged in cans, jars, etc.

**(G-8833)**
**DRAVES INVESTMENT INC**
Also Called: Draves Archery
1707w Ave Of Mid America (62401)
**PHONE**.................................888 678-0251
Jessy Draves, *President*
Toby Draves, *Vice Pres*
Jarrad Phillips, *Manager*
Vicky Draves, *Admin Sec*
**EMP:** 4
**SALES (est):** 462.4K **Privately Held**
**WEB:** www.dravesarchery.com
**SIC:** 3949 Hunting equipment

**(G-8834)**
**DUST LOGGING LLC**
16666 E 2050th Ave (62401-6992)
**PHONE**.................................217 844-2305
Ryan Dust, *Principal*
**EMP:** 3
**SALES (est):** 311.8K **Privately Held**
**SIC:** 2411 Logging

## Effingham - Effingham County (G-8835)

**(G-8835)**
**EFFINGHAM MONUMENT CO INC**
Rr 33 Box E (62401)
P.O. Box 899 (62401-0899)
PHONE .......................... 217 857-6085
Fax: 217 857-1416
Bart Willenborg, *President*
Allen Koester, *Vice Pres*
EMP: 3
SQ FT: 2,400
SALES: 300K **Privately Held**
SIC: 5999 3281 Gravestones, finished; monuments, finished to custom order; cut stone & stone products

**(G-8836)**
**EFFINGHAM SIGNS & GRAPHICS**
1009 S Oak St (62401-1969)
PHONE .......................... 217 347-8711
Fax: 217 347-8711
Alice Hahn, *Owner*
EMP: 7
SQ FT: 6,000
SALES: 700K **Privately Held**
SIC: 7389 3993 Lettering service; signs & advertising specialties

**(G-8837)**
**GOT 2B SCRAPPIN**
1901 S 4th St Ste 11 (62401-4188)
PHONE .......................... 217 347-3600
Bev Esgar, *Manager*
EMP: 3
SALES: (est) 284.1K **Privately Held**
SIC: 2782 Scrapbooks

**(G-8838)**
**HEARTLAND HARDWOODS INC**
20871 N 1600th St (62401-7506)
P.O. Box 84 (62401-0084)
PHONE .......................... 217 844-3312
Fax: 217 844-3326
Mark J Willenborg, *President*
Craig C Willenborg, *Vice Pres*
EMP: 20
SQ FT: 25,000
SALES: 2MM **Privately Held**
WEB: www.heartlandhardwoods.com
SIC: 2426 2431 2421 2411 Furniture stock & parts, hardwood; millwork; sawmills & planing mills, general; logging

**(G-8839)**
**HODGSON MILL INC**
1100 Stevens Ave (62401-4265)
P.O. Box 1048 (62401-1048)
PHONE .......................... 217 347-0105
Fax: 217 347-0198
Robert J Goldstein, *President*
Cathy Goldstein, *Chairman*
Regina Shafer, *Treasurer*
Jeffrey Masters, *Controller*
▲ EMP: 142
SQ FT: 124,256
SALES: (est) 37.6MM **Privately Held**
WEB: www.hodgsonmill.com
SIC: 2041 2045 5141 Flour & other grain mill products; pancake mixes, prepared: from purchased flour; groceries, general line

**(G-8840)**
**J M LUSTIG CUSTOM CABINETS CO**
921 E Fayette Ave (62401-3657)
P.O. Box 26 (62401-0026)
PHONE .......................... 217 342-6661
Fax: 217 342-6661
Isabel Lustig, *President*
EMP: 11 EST: 1925
SQ FT: 16,435
SALES: (est) 990K **Privately Held**
SIC: 2434 2511 2521 2421 Wood kitchen cabinets; wood household furniture; wood office furniture; sawmills & planing mills, general

**(G-8841)**
**JBC HOLDING CO (PA)**
3601 S Banker St (62401-2899)
PHONE .......................... 217 347-7701
Louis Kenter, *Chairman*
James Gibbons, *Vice Pres*
Michael Hamann, *Purch Mgr*
Jane Knicely, *Controller*
Jane Knicely, *Controller*
▼ EMP: 4
SALES: (est) 64.8MM **Privately Held**
SIC: 2541 2542 2511 2099 Wood partitions & fixtures; counters or counter display cases: except wood; wood household furniture; bread crumbs, not made in bakeries

**(G-8842)**
**KINGERY PRINTING COMPANY (PA)**
Also Called: M & D Printing Div
3012 S Banker St (62401-2900)
P.O. Box 727 (62401-0727)
PHONE .......................... 217 347-5151
Fax: 217 536-6992
John Kingery, *Ch of Bd*
Michael C Kingery, *President*
Jeff Hoene, *Business Mgr*
Terry Probst, *Treasurer*
Berta Peugh, *Human Res Mgr*
EMP: 160
SQ FT: 100,000
SALES: 31MM **Privately Held**
WEB: www.kingeryprinting.com
SIC: 2752 Commercial printing, offset

**(G-8843)**
**LANGE ELECTRIC INC**
912 E Fayette Ave (62401-3605)
P.O. Box 912 (62401-0912)
PHONE .......................... 217 347-7626
Fax: 217 347-7629
James H Lange, *President*
Linda Lange, *Corp Secy*
EMP: 3
SQ FT: 3,500
SALES: 350K **Privately Held**
SIC: 7694 5063 Electric motor repair; motors, electric

**(G-8844)**
**LUDWIG MEDICAL INC**
1010 N Parkview St (62401-3152)
PHONE .......................... 217 342-6570
Gerald E Ludwig, *President*
Diana Ludwig, *Corp Secy*
EMP: 3
SALES: (est) 396.5K **Privately Held**
SIC: 3841 3821 Surgical & medical instruments; laboratory apparatus & furniture

**(G-8845)**
**MERZ AIR CONDITIONING AND HTG**
509 S Willow St (62401-3756)
P.O. Box 1305 (62401-1305)
PHONE .......................... 217 342-2323
Glen Freeman, *President*
William Saulle, *Vice Pres*
Brenda Warner, *Sales Staff*
Judie Barnes, *Admin Sec*
EMP: 30
SALES: 5MM **Privately Held**
WEB: www.merzac.com
SIC: 1711 3444 Heating & air conditioning contractors; sheet metalwork

**(G-8846)**
**MIDTOWN FUELS**
503 W Jefferson Ave (62401-2338)
PHONE .......................... 217 347-7191
Sandy Lewis, *Manager*
EMP: 3
SALES: (est) 160.3K **Privately Held**
SIC: 2869 Fuels

**(G-8847)**
**MIDWEST FINISHERS PWDRCTNG**
10235 N 800th St (62401-6507)
PHONE .......................... 217 536-9098
Richard Murphy, *Owner*
EMP: 3
SALES: (est) 217.2K **Privately Held**
SIC: 3399 Powder, metal

**(G-8848)**
**MORROW SHOE AND BOOT INC**
320 W Jefferson Ave (62401-2352)
PHONE .......................... 217 342-6833
William A Morrow, *President*
EMP: 1
SQ FT: 7,500
SALES: 348.2K **Privately Held**
SIC: 3069 5661 Boot or shoe products, rubber; women's boots

**(G-8849)**
**NEW YORK BLOWER COMPANY**
Also Called: Mechanovent
1304 W Jaycee Ave (62401-4226)
PHONE .......................... 217 347-3233
Fax: 217 347-3240
Robert Korfmann, *VP Mfg*
Greg Pelletier, *Manager*
EMP: 60
SALES: (corp-wide): 91.6MM **Privately Held**
WEB: www.nyb.com
SIC: 3564 Ventilating fans: industrial or commercial
PA: The New York Blower Company
7660 S Quincy St
Willowbrook IL 60527
630 794-5700

**(G-8850)**
**NEWSPAPER HOLDING INC**
Also Called: Effingham Daily News
201 N Banker St (62401-2304)
P.O. Box 370 (62401-0370)
PHONE .......................... 217 347-7151
Fax: 217 342-9315
Steve Raymond, *Principal*
Mary Holle, *Editor*
Donna Riley-Gordon, *Editor*
George Weaver, *Vice Pres*
EMP: 65 **Privately Held**
WEB: www.clintonnc.com
SIC: 2711 Newspapers, publishing & printing
HQ: Newspaper Holding, Inc.
425 Locust St
Johnstown PA 15901
814 532-5102

**(G-8851)**
**NOVA SOLUTIONS INC (PA)**
Also Called: Nova The Right Solution
421 Industrial Ave (62401-2835)
P.O. Box 725 (62401-0725)
PHONE .......................... 217 342-7070
John Lechman, *President*
Suzanne Lechman, *Corp Secy*
Teresa Miller, *CFO*
Cindy Fulk, *Manager*
Nicholas Lechman, *Manager*
▲ EMP: 30
SQ FT: 101,000
SALES: (est) 4.2MM **Privately Held**
WEB: www.novadesk.com
SIC: 2521 5021 Wood office furniture; office furniture

**(G-8852)**
**PATTON PRINTING AND GRAPHICS**
902 W Wabash Ave B (62401-1908)
PHONE .......................... 217 347-0220
Fax: 217 342-5617
Dan Patton, *Owner*
Madonna Patton, *Co-Owner*
EMP: 8
SQ FT: 1,800
SALES: 500K **Privately Held**
WEB: www.pattonprinting.com
SIC: 2752 2791 2789 Commercial printing, offset; typesetting; bookbinding & related work

**(G-8853)**
**PEERLESS AMERICA INCORPORATED**
1201 W Wabash Ave (62401-1967)
PHONE .......................... 217 342-0400
Fax: 217 342-0412
Mike Warkins, *President*
Roger Paulman, *President*
Frederick Paulman, *Chairman*
Bruce Brown, *Vice Pres*
John Lohman, *Project Mgr*
▼ EMP: 150 EST: 1912
SALES: (est) 42.8MM **Privately Held**
WEB: www.peerlessofamerica.com
SIC: 3354 3585 3498 3443 Coils, rod, extruded, aluminum; condensers, refrigeration; fabricated pipe & fittings; fabricated plate work (boiler shop)

**(G-8854)**
**QG LLC**
420 Industrial Ave (62401-2834)
PHONE .......................... 217 347-7721
Brian Mulroney, *Branch Mgr*
EMP: 340
SALES: (corp-wide): 4.3B **Publicly Held**
SIC: 2752 Color lithography
HQ: Qg, Llc
N61w23044 Harrys Way
Sussex WI 53089

**(G-8855)**
**QG LLC**
Also Called: Worldcolor Effingham
1200 W Niccum Ave (62401-4217)
PHONE .......................... 217 347-7721
Ken Kobus, *Production*
David Reyes, *Sales Staff*
Dwaine Kinderkhecht, *Branch Mgr*
EMP: 60
SALES: (corp-wide): 4.3B **Publicly Held**
WEB: www.qwdys.com
SIC: 2754 2759 Commercial printing, gravure; commercial printing
HQ: Qg, Llc
N61w23044 Harrys Way
Sussex WI 53089

**(G-8856)**
**R & G MACHINE SHOP INC**
1303 Parker Ave (62401-4233)
PHONE .......................... 217 342-6622
Fax: 217 342-6622
Mike Rieman, *President*
Curt Goeckner, *Admin Sec*
EMP: 10
SQ FT: 2,500
SALES: 1MM **Privately Held**
SIC: 3559 Semiconductor manufacturing machinery

**(G-8857)**
**RUSTY & ANGELA BUZZARD**
Also Called: Effingham Printing Company
205 N 4th St (62401-3461)
P.O. Box 71 (62401-0071)
PHONE .......................... 217 342-9841
Rusty Buzzard, *Owner*
Angela Buzzard, *Co-Owner*
EMP: 3
SQ FT: 1,200
SALES: 110K **Privately Held**
SIC: 2752 2791 2789 2759 Commercial printing, lithographic; typesetting; bookbinding & related work; commercial printing

**(G-8858)**
**SOUTHEASTERN CONTAINER INC**
1200 Mcgrath Ave (62401-4231)
P.O. Box 909, Enka NC (28728-0909)
PHONE .......................... 217 342-9600
Fax: 217 342-9660
Heidi Eichner, *General Mgr*
Heidi Good, *General Mgr*
Ralph Henderson, *Manager*
Matt Childs, *Manager*
Tim Atkinson, *Maintence Staff*
EMP: 50
SALES: (corp-wide): 500K **Privately Held**
SIC: 3085 Plastics bottles
PA: Southeastern Container, Inc.
1250 Sand Hill Rd
Enka NC 28728
828 350-7200

**(G-8859)**
**SPORTS DESIGNS & GRAPHICS**
807 S Maple St (62401-2641)
PHONE .......................... 217 342-2777
Robert Smothers, *President*
EMP: 25
SALES: (est): 1.5MM **Privately Held**
SIC: 2395 Embroidery & art needlework

## GEOGRAPHIC SECTION

**(G-8860)**
**VERSATECH LLC**
1609 W Wernsing Ave Ste D (62401-4274)
PHONE .................................. 217 342-3500
Matthew Repking, *Plant Mgr*
Mitch Stevens, *Project Mgr*
Jon Holland, *Prdtn Mgr*
Paul Pugsley, *Purchasing*
Jeff Dasenbrock, *Research*
**EMP:** 130
**SQ FT:** 75,000
**SALES (est):** 27.9MM **Privately Held**
**SIC:** 8711 3542 Structural engineering; machine tools, metal forming type

**(G-8861)**
**VOGEL MANUFACTURING CO INC**
10862 N 1000th Rd (62401-6568)
PHONE .................................. 217 536-6946
Charles Vogel, *President*
Virginia Vogel, *Corp Secy*
Kevin Vogel, *Vice Pres*
**EMP:** 3
**SALES:** 414K **Privately Held**
**WEB:** www.vogelmanufacturing.com
**SIC:** 3714 Motor vehicle engines & parts

**(G-8862)**
**WAUPACA FOUNDRY INC**
1500 Heartland Blvd (62401-4234)
PHONE .................................. 217 347-0600
**Fax:** 217 342-6933
Bob Harter, *Plant Mgr*
Michael Nikolai, *CFO*
Pamela Mattone, *Controller*
Heather Hartke, *Finance*
Brian Nowak, *Human Res Mgr*
**EMP:** 128
**SALES (corp-wide):** 80.6B **Privately Held**
**SIC:** 3559 3321 3465 Automotive related machinery; ductile iron castings; body parts, automobile: stamped metal
**HQ:** Waupaca Foundry, Inc.
1955 Brunner Dr
Waupaca WI 54981
715 258-6611

**(G-8863)**
**WILLENBORG HARDWOOD INDS INC**
15485 E 1900th Ave (62401-6972)
P.O. Box 632 (62401-0632)
PHONE .................................. 217 844-2082
Dennis Willenborg, *CEO*
Russell Willenborg, *Vice Pres*
Kim Parker, *Treasurer*
**EMP:** 18 **EST:** 1960
**SQ FT:** 20,000
**SALES (est):** 2.8MM **Privately Held**
**SIC:** 2421 Sawmills & planing mills, general

**(G-8864)**
**WORTMAN PRINTING COMPANY INC**
1713 S Banker St (62401-2748)
P.O. Box 38 (62401-0038)
PHONE .................................. 217 347-3775
**Fax:** 217 347-1082
Del Wortman, *President*
Diane Wortman, *Vice Pres*
**EMP:** 8
**SQ FT:** 7,000
**SALES (est):** 847.1K **Privately Held**
**WEB:** www.wortmanprinting.com
**SIC:** 2759 2791 2789 2752 Commercial printing; typesetting; bookbinding & related work; commercial printing, lithographic

### El Paso
*Woodford County*

**(G-8865)**
**AMERICAN BUILDINGS COMPANY**
2101 E Main St (61738-1348)
PHONE .................................. 309 527-5420
**Fax:** 309 527-1522
Adam Scott, *District Mgr*
Dennis Ludwig, *QC Mgr*
Jenni Johnson, *Engineer*
Ken Barnhart, *Sales Executive*
Terry Kuper, *Branch Mgr*
**EMP:** 105
**SQ FT:** 133,000
**SALES (corp-wide):** 16.2B **Publicly Held**
**WEB:** www.americanbuildings.com
**SIC:** 3448 Buildings, portable: prefabricated metal
**HQ:** American Buildings Company
1150 State Docks Rd
Eufaula AL 36027
888 307-4338

**(G-8866)**
**CENTRAL HYDRAULICS INC**
513 State Route 251 (61738-1791)
PHONE .................................. 309 527-5238
**Fax:** 309 527-5240
Chris Porzelius, *President*
**EMP:** 3
**SALES (est):** 300K **Privately Held**
**SIC:** 3569 3714 3594 7699 Jacks, hydraulic; motor vehicle parts & accessories; fluid power pumps & motors; hydraulic equipment repair

**(G-8867)**
**CUSTOM CRAFTED DOOR INC**
2810 County Road 520 N (61738-1793)
PHONE .................................. 309 527-5075
**Fax:** 309 527-3500
Jimmy D Young, *President*
Bonnie Young, *Corp Secy*
Dennis Ortinac, *Vice Pres*
**EMP:** 15
**SQ FT:** 50,000
**SALES (est):** 2.1MM **Privately Held**
**WEB:** www.customcrafteddoor.com
**SIC:** 2431 5211 Doors, wood; millwork & lumber

**(G-8868)**
**E I DU PONT DE NEMOURS & CO**
Also Called: Dupont
2830 Us Highway 24 (61738-1734)
PHONE .................................. 309 527-5115
**Fax:** 309 527-1218
Chuck Hollowell, *Purchasing*
Andy Cich, *Project Engr*
Jean Bates, *Human Res Dir*
Kenneth Cook, *Manager*
Hank Brill, *Manager*
**EMP:** 50
**SALES (corp-wide):** 24.5B **Publicly Held**
**WEB:** www.dupont.com
**SIC:** 2879 Fungicides, herbicides
**PA:** E. I. Du Pont De Nemours And Company
974 Centre Rd
Wilmington DE 19805
302 774-1000

**(G-8869)**
**EL PASO JOURNAL**
51 W Front St (61738-1553)
PHONE .................................. 309 527-8595
**Fax:** 309 527-8850
Kim Kearney, *President*
**EMP:** 3
**SALES (est):** 214.1K **Privately Held**
**SIC:** 2711 Newspapers

**(G-8870)**
**INNOVATIVE INDUSTRIAL SVCS LLC**
700 S Fayette St (61738-1442)
PHONE .................................. 309 527-2035
John Miller, *Vice Pres*
Anas Alrawi, *CTO*
Jack Widmer,
Mary Widmer,
**EMP:** 17
**SQ FT:** 9,000
**SALES (est):** 4.8MM **Privately Held**
**SIC:** 3569 Robots, assembly line: industrial & commercial

**(G-8871)**
**NCI GROUP INC**
21 E Front St (61738-1168)
PHONE .................................. 309 527-3095
**Fax:** 309 527-3094
Kimberly Lauraitis, *Manager*
**EMP:** 79
**SALES (corp-wide):** 1.6B **Publicly Held**
**SIC:** 3448 3446 Prefabricated metal buildings; prefabricated metal components; architectural metalwork
**HQ:** Nci Group, Inc.
10943 N Sam Huston Pkwy W
Houston TX 77064
281 897-7500

### Elburn
*Kane County*

**(G-8872)**
**A E FRASZ INC**
1n545 Brundige Rd (60119-9412)
PHONE .................................. 630 232-6223
Andrew E Frasz, *President*
Gail Frasz, *Admin Sec*
**EMP:** 12
**SQ FT:** 5,400
**SALES (est):** 2.3MM **Privately Held**
**SIC:** 1794 1442 Excavation work; gravel mining

**(G-8873)**
**ACCURAIL INC**
400 W Nebraska St (60119-8300)
P.O. Box 278 (60119-0278)
PHONE .................................. 630 365-6400
**Fax:** 630 365-6499
Dennis Storzek, *President*
Robert B Walker Jr, *Vice Pres*
▲ **EMP:** 12
**SQ FT:** 5,000
**SALES (est):** 750K **Privately Held**
**WEB:** www.accurail.com
**SIC:** 3944 5092 Railroad models: toy & hobby; model kits

**(G-8874)**
**ADVANCED MICRO LITES INC**
205 Dempsey St Ste A (60119-7028)
PHONE .................................. 630 365-5450
Shirley Jaeger, *President*
Dawn Kuefler, *Corp Secy*
Bob Jaeger, *Vice Pres*
▲ **EMP:** 6
**SQ FT:** 4,000
**SALES:** 2MM **Privately Held**
**WEB:** www.advmicrolites.com
**SIC:** 3645 3641 5063 Residential lighting fixtures; electric lamps; light bulbs & related supplies

**(G-8875)**
**AQUATROL INC**
600 E North St (60119-9048)
P.O. Box 8012 (60119-8012)
PHONE .................................. 630 365-2363
**Fax:** 630 365-5434
Bert Lowden, *President*
Eric Lambert, *General Mgr*
▲ **EMP:** 14
**SQ FT:** 20,000
**SALES (est):** 3.3MM **Privately Held**
**WEB:** www.aquatrol.com
**SIC:** 3494 3491 Valves & pipe fittings; industrial valves

**(G-8876)**
**ARCH CHEMICALS INC**
Marine Bio Chemist
809 Hicks Dr Ste A (60119-9062)
PHONE .................................. 630 365-1720
**Fax:** 630 365-1721
Doug Walls, *Opers Mgr*
John Cortell, *Manager*
**EMP:** 3
**SALES (corp-wide):** 4B **Privately Held**
**SIC:** 2899 Water treating compounds
**HQ:** Arch Chemicals, Inc.
1200 Bluegrass Lakes Pkwy
Alpharetta GA 30004
678 624-5800

**(G-8877)**
**BARCAR MANUFACTURING INC**
1 N 081 Thryselius Dr (60119)
P.O. Box 8042 (60119-8042)
PHONE .................................. 630 365-5200
**Fax:** 630 365-5202
Dan Carson Sr, *President*
Dan D Carson Sr, *President*
Dan Carson Jr, *Corp Secy*
▲ **EMP:** 7
**SQ FT:** 6,000
**SALES:** 854.4K **Privately Held**
**SIC:** 3694 Harness wiring sets, internal combustion engines

**(G-8878)**
**BOGART INDUSTRIES LLC**
315 E Reader St (60119-8936)
PHONE .................................. 224 242-4578
Michael Henry Van Bogaert, *Principal*
**EMP:** 3
**SALES (est):** 102.2K **Privately Held**
**SIC:** 3999 Manufacturing industries

**(G-8879)**
**CHEM SPEC CORPORATION**
2n900 Bowgren Dr (60119-8523)
PHONE .................................. 847 891-2133
Ed Reynaert, *President*
**EMP:** 3
**SALES (est):** 295.6K **Privately Held**
**SIC:** 2891 Adhesives & sealants

**(G-8880)**
**CIDER GOULD & APPLE**
2s230 Green Rd (60119-9686)
PHONE .................................. 630 365-2233
Tom Gould, *Owner*
**EMP:** 3
**SALES (est):** 73K **Privately Held**
**SIC:** 2033 Canned fruits & specialties

**(G-8881)**
**CROWN COATINGS COMPANY**
215 W Nebraska St (60119-8309)
PHONE .................................. 630 365-9925
**Fax:** 630 365-9928
Carolyn Popp, *President*
**EMP:** 12
**SQ FT:** 10,000
**SALES (est):** 250K **Privately Held**
**WEB:** www.crowncoatings.com
**SIC:** 5033 2952 Roofing, asphalt & sheet metal; asphalt felts & coatings
**PA:** Drafting & Construction Services, Inc
55 Winthrop New Rd
Sugar Grove IL

**(G-8882)**
**D N M SEALCOATING INC**
300 Railroad St (60119-8358)
PHONE .................................. 630 365-1816
Doug Romando, *President*
Melanie Romando, *Owner*
**EMP:** 5
**SALES (est):** 780K **Privately Held**
**SIC:** 2952 Asphalt felts & coatings

**(G-8883)**
**DRUMBEATERS OF AMERICA INC**
215 W Nebraska St (60119-8309)
PHONE .................................. 630 365-5527
Carolyn Popp, *President*
Mary Brown, *Office Mgr*
▼ **EMP:** 16
**SQ FT:** 10,000
**SALES (est):** 5.4MM **Privately Held**
**WEB:** www.drumbeaters.com
**SIC:** 3532 4953 Crushers, stationary; cleaning machinery, mineral; hazardous waste collection & disposal

**(G-8884)**
**ELBURN MARKET INC**
Also Called: Ream's Meat Market
250 S Main St (60119-9426)
PHONE .................................. 630 365-6461
Randall D Ream, *President*
Phyllis Ream, *Corp Secy*
Janelle Ream, *Vice Pres*
**EMP:** 25 **EST:** 1953
**SQ FT:** 1,800
**SALES (est):** 2MM **Privately Held**
**WEB:** www.elburnmarket.com
**SIC:** 5421 5411 2013 Meat markets, including freezer provisioners; fish markets; grocery stores; sausages from purchased meat

**(G-8885)**
**ELBURN METAL STAMPING INC**
44w210 Keslinger Rd (60119-9702)
P.O. Box 947 (60119-0947)
PHONE .................................. 630 365-2500

## Elburn - Kane County (G-8886)

Fax: 630 365-2506
Steven P Porter, *President*
Lana Porter, *Corp Secy*
Chad Porter, *Manager*
Kathy Porter, *Manager*
▲ **EMP:** 30
**SQ FT:** 50,000
**SALES (est):** 5.2MM  **Privately Held**
**WEB:** www.elburnstamping.com
**SIC:** 3599  3469  Custom machinery; stamping metal for the trade

### (G-8886)
### ELECTRIC CONDUIT CNSTR CO
816 Hicks Dr  (60119-9060)
**PHONE** .................................. 630 293-4474
J E Pfleeger, *President*
Mark Schiavi, *Vice Pres*
Bill Foster, *Project Mgr*
Kristopher Tyler, *Project Mgr*
James Carson, *Foreman/Supr*
**EMP:** 250
**SALES (est):** 57.7MM  **Privately Held**
**SIC:** 1521  3644  1623  3272  Single-family housing construction; electric conduits & fittings; oil & gas pipeline construction; conduits, concrete

### (G-8887)
### ELECTRIC CONDUIT CONSTRUCTION
Also Called: Midwestern Contractors
601 E North St  (60119-9048)
**PHONE** .................................. 630 859-9310
Mark Schiavi, *Vice Pres*
Mike Purpura, *Sales Mgr*
Ryan Dowling, *Info Tech Dir*
**EMP:** 19 **EST:** 2008
**SALES (est):** 3.6MM  **Privately Held**
**SIC:** 3644  Electric conduits & fittings

### (G-8888)
### EMBROIDERY EXPRESS INC
217 Dempsey St Ste C  (60119-9183)
**PHONE** .................................. 630 365-9393
Fax: 630 365-2255
Randy Norris, *President*
Rick Westerlin, *Vice Pres*
**EMP:** 10
**SALES (est):** 761.2K
**SALES (corp-wide):** 5.5MM  **Privately Held**
**WEB:** www.tryadspecialties.com
**SIC:** 2395  Embroidery products, except schiffli machine; emblems, embroidered
**PA:** Tryad Specialties Inc
2015 Dean St Ste 6
Saint Charles IL 60174
630 549-0079

### (G-8889)
### HARRY OTTO PRINTING COMPANY
Also Called: Exclusive Boarding
707 E North St Ste A  (60119-9010)
**PHONE** .................................. 630 365-6111
Fax: 630 365-6124
Thomas Otto, *President*
Cindy Otto, *Vice Pres*
**EMP:** 10 **EST:** 1954
**SQ FT:** 5,000
**SALES (est):** 1.3MM  **Privately Held**
**WEB:** www.ottoprinting.com
**SIC:** 2759  2752  2789  2771  Letterpress printing; commercial printing, offset; edging books, cards or paper; greeting cards

### (G-8890)
### JAHNS STRUCTURE JACKING SYSTEM
Also Called: Jsjs
15 S 1st St  (60119)
P.O. Box 8110  (60119-7200)
**PHONE** .................................. 630 365-2455
Fax: 630 365-2467
William Jahns, *President*
Carol Jahns, *Vice Pres*
**EMP:** 4
**SQ FT:** 4,500
**SALES (est):** 799.6K  **Privately Held**
**WEB:** www.jsjs.com
**SIC:** 3569  Jacks, hydraulic

### (G-8891)
### MEYER MATERIAL CO MERGER CORP
1s194 Il Route 47  (60119-9678)
**PHONE** .................................. 847 658-7811
Fax: 847 658-4514
Steven Warnke, *Principal*
Gary Floit, *Manager*
**EMP:** 15
**SALES (corp-wide):** 26.6B  **Privately Held**
**SIC:** 1442  Construction sand & gravel
**HQ:** Meyer Material Co Merger Corp.
580 S Wolf Rd
Des Plaines IL 60016
815 331-7200

### (G-8892)
### MEYER MATERIAL CO MERGER CORP
1s194 Il Route 47  (60119-9678)
**PHONE** .................................. 847 824-4111
Fax: 847 824-7382
Michael Downey, *Plant Mgr*
Allen Miller, *Plant Mgr*
Dave Young, *Manager*
**EMP:** 50
**SALES (corp-wide):** 26.6B  **Privately Held**
**SIC:** 3273  Ready-mixed concrete
**HQ:** Meyer Material Co Merger Corp.
580 S Wolf Rd
Des Plaines IL 60016
815 331-7200

### (G-8893)
### MEYER MATERIAL CO MERGER CORP
1s194 Il Route 47  (60119-9678)
**PHONE** .................................. 815 568-6119
Fax: 630 357-0482
Steve Warnke, *General Mgr*
Michael Coursey, *Plant Mgr*
**EMP:** 30
**SALES (corp-wide):** 26.6B  **Privately Held**
**SIC:** 3273  1442  Ready-mixed concrete; construction sand & gravel
**HQ:** Meyer Material Co Merger Corp.
580 S Wolf Rd
Des Plaines IL 60016
815 331-7200

### (G-8894)
### MEYER MATERIAL CO MERGER CORP
1s194 Il Route 47  (60119-9678)
**PHONE** .................................. 815 385-4920
Fax: 630 653-3369
Rob Butera, *Manager*
Tony Grosso, *Manager*
Bill Myers, *Manager*
**EMP:** 28
**SALES (corp-wide):** 26.6B  **Privately Held**
**SIC:** 3273  5211  Ready-mixed concrete; lumber & other building materials
**HQ:** Meyer Material Co Merger Corp.
580 S Wolf Rd
Des Plaines IL 60016
815 331-7200

### (G-8895)
### MEYER MATERIAL CO MERGER CORP
1s194 Il Route 47  (60119-9678)
**PHONE** .................................. 815 568-7205
Pat Phyffer, *Manager*
**EMP:** 6
**SALES (corp-wide):** 26.6B  **Privately Held**
**SIC:** 3273  Ready-mixed concrete
**HQ:** Meyer Material Co Merger Corp.
580 S Wolf Rd
Des Plaines IL 60016
815 331-7200

### (G-8896)
### MEYER MATERIAL HANDLING
1s194 Il Route 47  (60119-9678)
**PHONE** .................................. 414 768-1631
Rich Dembinsky, *Plant Mgr*
**EMP:** 5
**SALES (est):** 810.7K  **Privately Held**
**SIC:** 3273  Ready-mixed concrete

### (G-8897)
### MIDWEST TOOL TECHNOLOGY
44w720 Main Street Rd  (60119-8470)
**PHONE** .................................. 630 207-6076
James Erwin, *Owner*
**EMP:** 3
**SQ FT:** 1,200
**SALES (est):** 230K  **Privately Held**
**SIC:** 3544  Industrial molds

### (G-8898)
### MITY INC (PA)
Also Called: Self-Cleaning Strainer Co
700 E North St Ste B  (60119-7009)
P.O. Box 818  (60119-0818)
**PHONE** .................................. 630 365-5030
Fax: 630 365-5033
Melvin J Thryselius, *President*
Gerald Runge, *Vice Pres*
Judy Thryselius, *Office Mgr*
Jerry R Rundee, *Admin Sec*
Jerry R Undee, *Admin Sec*
**EMP:** 4
**SQ FT:** 600
**SALES:** 600K  **Privately Held**
**WEB:** www.scsci.com
**SIC:** 3569  5084  3564  3494  Filters & strainers, pipeline; industrial machinery & equipment; blowers & fans; valves & pipe fittings; metal stampings

### (G-8899)
### MONITOR TECHNOLOGIES LLC
44w320 Keslinger Rd  (60119-9702)
**PHONE** .................................. 630 365-9403
Craig Arussell, *President*
Joe Lewis, *Vice Pres*
Rob Vance, *Vice Pres*
Jeff Cole, *Engineer*
Chris Otte, *Marketing Staff*
▲ **EMP:** 40
**SQ FT:** 30,000
**SALES (est):** 13.9MM  **Privately Held**
**WEB:** www.monitortech.com
**SIC:** 3823  Liquid level instruments, industrial process type; level & bulk measuring instruments, industrial process

### (G-8900)
### NEXPUMP INC
820 Stover Dr Unit B  (60119-8424)
**PHONE** .................................. 630 365-4639
Dan Gierke, *CEO*
Chris Gierke, *Vice Pres*
▲ **EMP:** 5
**SALES (est):** 886.9K  **Privately Held**
**WEB:** www.gierke.com
**SIC:** 3561  Pumps, domestic: water or sump

### (G-8901)
### ODIN INDUSTRIES INC
740 Hicks Dr  (60119-9059)
**PHONE** .................................. 630 365-2475
Fax: 630 365-2150
David Anderson, *President*
Linda Anderson, *Corp Secy*
**EMP:** 15
**SQ FT:** 13,000
**SALES (est):** 2.5MM  **Privately Held**
**WEB:** www.odinindustries.com
**SIC:** 3444  Sheet metalwork; forming machine work, sheet metal

### (G-8902)
### OPTIMAL CONSTRUCTION SVCS INC
843 Shepherd Ln  (60119-7125)
P.O. Box 488  (60119-0488)
**PHONE** .................................. 630 365-5050
Jerald Meister, *President*
**EMP:** 1 **EST:** 2011
**SALES:** 380K  **Privately Held**
**SIC:** 3448  1761  Prefabricated metal buildings; roofing, siding & sheet metal work; gutter & downspout contractor; siding contractor

### (G-8903)
### PERIMETER ACCESS SYS SVCS INC
Also Called: Pass
116 Paul St  (60119-7027)
**PHONE** .................................. 630 556-4283
Michael Wroblewski, *President*

**EMP:** 10
**SALES (est):** 1.5MM  **Privately Held**
**SIC:** 3699  Door opening & closing devices, electrical

### (G-8904)
### PRECISION COMPUTER METHODS
801 Drover St  (60119-8955)
**PHONE** .................................. 630 208-8000
Peter Hart Heinicke, *President*
Karen Heinicke, *Vice Pres*
**EMP:** 4
**SQ FT:** 750
**SALES (est):** 540.3K  **Privately Held**
**SIC:** 7373  3577  5734  Computer systems analysis & design; data conversion equipment, media-to-media: computer; software, business & non-game

### (G-8905)
### PRO ACCESS SYSTEMS INC (PA)
116 Paul St  (60119-7027)
**PHONE** .................................. 630 426-0022
Fax: 630 620-0063
Andrew M Faville, *CEO*
Leslie R Heerdt, *Ch of Bd*
Donald R Parrin, *President*
Ervin E Schlepp, *Exec VP*
Jacob Wilson, *Opers Mgr*
▲ **EMP:** 10
**SQ FT:** 6,000
**SALES (est):** 3.3MM  **Privately Held**
**WEB:** www.edko.com
**SIC:** 3699  Door opening & closing devices, electrical

### (G-8906)
### QUIKRETE CHICAGO
Also Called: PCI
1s950 Lorang Rd  (60119-7719)
**PHONE** .................................. 630 557-8252
Fax: 630 557-8270
John D Petty, *President*
Brian Petty, *Corp Secy*
Nettie Petty, *Vice Pres*
**EMP:** 55
**SQ FT:** 24,000
**SALES (est):** 10.4MM  **Privately Held**
**WEB:** www.pci-il.com
**SIC:** 3272  2899  Concrete products; chemical preparations

### (G-8907)
### R B EVANS CO
808 Hicks Dr  (60119-9060)
**PHONE** .................................. 630 365-3554
Margaret Spelman, *President*
David G Evans, *Vice Pres*
Kenneth Evans, *Vice Pres*
Marsha Fazio, *Admin Sec*
**EMP:** 6
**SQ FT:** 10,000
**SALES:** 600K  **Privately Held**
**WEB:** www.rbevans.com
**SIC:** 3541  3451  Numerically controlled metal cutting machine tools; screw machine products

### (G-8908)
### RADCO INDUSTRIES INC
39w 930 Midan Dr  (60119)
**PHONE** .................................. 630 232-7966
Benjie Smith, *Branch Mgr*
**EMP:** 3
**SALES (corp-wide):** 1.7MM  **Privately Held**
**WEB:** www.radcoind.com
**SIC:** 2819  Industrial inorganic chemicals
**PA:** Radco Industries, Inc.
700 Kingsland Dr
Batavia IL 60510
630 232-7966

### (G-8909)
### RUNGE ENTERPRISES INC
1 N 020 Thryselius Dr  (60119)
P.O. Box 157  (60119-0157)
**PHONE** .................................. 630 365-2000
Fax: 630 365-2362
Gerald Runge, *President*
Barbara Liljehorn, *Admin Sec*
**EMP:** 8
**SQ FT:** 20,000

# GEOGRAPHIC SECTION

Elgin - Kane County (G-8935)

SALES (est): 971.4K  Privately Held
WEB: www.rungeinc.com
SIC: 3599  3469  Machine shop, jobbing & repair; metal stampings

**(G-8910)**
**SIMULATION TECHNOLOGY LLC**
747 Herra St Unit B  (60119-8437)
PHONE..............................630 365-3400
Leland George, *Mng Member*
EMP: 8
SALES (est): 970.4K  Privately Held
SIC: 3699  Automotive driving simulators (training aids), electronic

**(G-8911)**
**SUN OVENS INTERNATIONAL INC**
39w835 Midan Dr Unit F  (60119-7908)
PHONE..............................630 208-7273
Paul M Munsen, *President*
Jessica Anderson, *Office Mgr*
EMP: 15
SQ FT: 10,000
SALES: 1.4MM  Privately Held
WEB: www.sunoven.com
SIC: 3634  3631  Ovens, portable: household; household cooking equipment

**(G-8912)**
**TABLES INC**
835 Drover St  (60119-8955)
PHONE..............................630 365-0741
Thomas Mocchi, *President*
EMP: 3  EST: 1954
SALES (est): 290K  Privately Held
SIC: 2522  3429  2512  2511  Tables, office: except wood; wallcases, office: except wood; manufactured hardware (general); upholstered household furniture; wood household furniture

**(G-8913)**
**TECH-WELD INC**
801 E North St  (60119-9084)
PHONE..............................630 365-3000
Fax: 630 365-0506
Gregory J Lesage, *President*
Linda Lesage, *Office Mgr*
EMP: 15
SQ FT: 10,000
SALES (est): 4.5MM  Privately Held
WEB: www.techweld.net
SIC: 3443  3498  Tanks, standard or custom fabricated: metal plate; tube fabricating (contract bending & shaping)

**(G-8914)**
**TERRAMAC LLC**
724 Hicks Dr  (60119-9059)
PHONE..............................630 365-4800
Monica Coenen, *Marketing Staff*
Lisa A Crimaldi, *Mng Member*
Michael A Crimaldi, *Mng Member*
EMP: 5
SQ FT: 10,000
SALES (est): 1.2MM  Privately Held
SIC: 3531  Construction machinery

**(G-8915)**
**THRYSELIUS MACHINING INC**
44w480 Keslinger Rd  (60119)
P.O. Box 248  (60119-0248)
PHONE..............................630 365-9191
Fax: 630 365-9195
James Thryselius, *President*
Judy Thryselius, *Vice Pres*
EMP: 15
SQ FT: 21,000
SALES (est): 1.7MM  Privately Held
SIC: 3599  Machine shop, jobbing & repair

**(G-8916)**
**TIN MANS GARAGE INC**
39w869 Midan Dr Unit B  (60119-9472)
PHONE..............................630 262-0752
EMP: 4
SALES (est): 437.9K  Privately Held
SIC: 3444  Sheet metalwork

## Eldorado
### Saline County

**(G-8917)**
**BECKS MEDICAL & INDUS GASES**
1411 Locust St  (62930-1629)
PHONE..............................618 273-9019
Carl V Kasiar, *President*
EMP: 15
SALES: 145K  Privately Held
SIC: 3842  Surgical appliances & supplies

**(G-8918)**
**C & D REBUILDERS**
1219 Us Highway 45 N  (62930-3769)
PHONE..............................618 273-9862
Daniel Cummins, *Partner*
David Naas, *Partner*
EMP: 3  EST: 1978
SQ FT: 2,400
SALES (est): 190K  Privately Held
SIC: 3621  3694  7533  Starters, for motors; generators, automotive & aircraft; alternators, automotive; auto exhaust system repair shops; muffler shop, sale or repair & installation

**(G-8919)**
**CAP FACTORY**
816 State St  (62930-1220)
PHONE..............................618 273-9662
Susan Stevens, *Manager*
EMP: 15
SALES (est): 690.1K  Privately Held
WEB: www.capfactory.net
SIC: 2353  Hats, caps & millinery

**(G-8920)**
**FAB CON INDUSTRIES INC**
101 E Deyoung  (62930)
PHONE..............................618 969-9040
Michael K Dover, *Principal*
EMP: 9
SALES (est): 955.7K  Privately Held
SIC: 3999  Manufacturing industries

**(G-8921)**
**QUORUM LABS  LLC**
895 Grayson Rd  (62930-3913)
P.O. Box 29  (62930-0029)
PHONE..............................618 525-5600
David Bartok,
EMP: 3  EST: 2015
SQ FT: 3,200
SALES (est): 120.2K  Privately Held
SIC: 2836  Biological products, except diagnostic

**(G-8922)**
**RDF INC**
2909 Richardson St  (62930-3559)
PHONE..............................618 273-4141
Fax: 618 273-4341
Dale Kjensrud, *President*
Mary Gothard, *Office Mgr*
Janet Melissen, *Admin Sec*
▲ EMP: 18
SQ FT: 16,000
SALES (est): 3.2MM  Privately Held
WEB: www.rdfrubber.com
SIC: 3069  4953  Reclaimed rubber (reworked by manufacturing processes); recycling, waste materials

**(G-8923)**
**SUN-TIMES MEDIA GROUP  INC**
Also Called: Eldorado Daily Journal
1200 Locust St  (62930-1723)
P.O. Box 248, Harrisburg  (62946-0248)
PHONE..............................618 273-3379
Fax: 618 273-3738
Terry Geese, *Editor*
George Wilson, *Manager*
Carol Rann, *Manager*
EMP: 4
SALES (corp-wide): 304.8MM  Privately Held
WEB: www.hollinger.com
SIC: 2711  Newspapers, publishing & printing
HQ: Sun-Times Media Group, Inc.
   350 N Orleans St Fl 10
   Chicago IL 60654
   312 321-2299

**(G-8924)**
**TOWNLEY ENGRG & MFG CO INC**
607 Sutton Rd  (62930)
P.O. Box 531  (62930-0531)
PHONE..............................618 273-8271
Fax: 618 273-3418
Virgil Sanders, *Manager*
Beth Bowers, *Admin Asst*
EMP: 15
SALES (corp-wide): 81.6MM  Privately Held
WEB: www.townley.net
SIC: 3561  3532  3356  Pump jacks & other pumping equipment; mining machinery; nonferrous rolling & drawing
PA: Townley Engineering And Manufacturing Company, Inc.
   10551 Se 110th St Rd
   Candler FL 32111
   352 687-3001

**(G-8925)**
**TRI-COUNTY CHEMICAL  INC (PA)**
2441 Public Rd  (62930-1148)
PHONE..............................618 273-2071
Fax: 618 273-2091
H E Melton, *President*
Jeremy Maloney, *Sales Executive*
EMP: 14  EST: 1956
SQ FT: 8,000
SALES (est): 9.4MM  Privately Held
SIC: 2873  Fertilizers: natural (organic), except compost

**(G-8926)**
**WILDCAT HILLS**
115 Grayson Ln  (62930-3947)
PHONE..............................618 273-8600
EMP: 5
SALES (est): 300.8K  Privately Held
SIC: 1241  Coal mining services

## Eldred
### Greene County

**(G-8927)**
**ASSOCIATED AGRI-BUSINESS INC (PA)**
Also Called: Simfax Agri-Services
229 Elm St  (62027-1002)
P.O. Box 82  (62027-0082)
PHONE..............................618 498-2977
G John Roundcount, *President*
Connie Blackorby, *Office Mgr*
Whitney McIver, *Admin Sec*
EMP: 1
SALES (est): 468.9K  Privately Held
SIC: 6331  7372  Federal crop insurance corporation; prepackaged software

## Elgin
### Kane County

**(G-8928)**
**2ND CINE  INC**
637 Frazier St  (60123-2105)
PHONE..............................773 455-5808
Thomas S Ciciura, *Principal*
EMP: 3
SQ FT: 6,000
SALES (est): 518.5K  Privately Held
SIC: 7819  5043  3861  Consultants, motion picture; equipment rental, motion picture; motion picture cameras, equipment & supplies; motion picture apparatus & equipment

**(G-8929)**
**A J FUNK & CO**
Also Called: Glass Cleaner
1471 Timber Dr  (60123-1898)
PHONE..............................847 741-6760
Fax: 847 741-6767
Patrick Funk, *President*
Lou Carlotti, *Sales Dir*
Barbara Drufke, *Manager*
Barbara Devfkf, *Admin Sec*
EMP: 1  EST: 1941
SQ FT: 24,000
SALES: 2.5MM  Privately Held
WEB: www.glasscleaner.com
SIC: 2842  5169  Window cleaning preparations; chemicals & allied products

**(G-8930)**
**A123 SYSTEMS LLC**
88 Airport Rd  (60123-9324)
PHONE..............................617 778-5700
Edward Kopkowski, *CEO*
EMP: 5  EST: 2013
SALES (est): 502.3K
SALES (corp-wide): 2.9B  Privately Held
SIC: 3691  Batteries, rechargeable
HQ: Wanxiang America Corporation
   88 Airport Rd
   Elgin IL 60123

**(G-8931)**
**ABRASIVE TECHNOLOGY INC**
1175 Bowes Rd  (60123-5541)
PHONE..............................847 888-7100
Yefim Vernik, *Research*
Shahla Amiri, *Branch Mgr*
Kim Bailey, *Manager*
EMP: 50
SALES (corp-wide): 98MM  Privately Held
WEB: www.abrasive-tech.com
SIC: 3291  Abrasive wheels & grindstones, not artificial
PA: Abrasive Technology, Inc.
   8400 Green Meadows Dr N
   Lewis Center OH 43035
   740 548-4100

**(G-8932)**
**ACME DESIGN INC**
37 N Union St  (60123-5334)
PHONE..............................847 841-7400
Clinton Borucki, *President*
Elizabeth Haney, *Marketing Staff*
EMP: 5
SALES (est): 910K  Privately Held
SIC: 3999  Models, except toy

**(G-8933)**
**ACOMTECH MOLD INC**
39w433 Highland Ave Ste 1  (60124-4208)
P.O. Box 5153  (60121-5153)
PHONE..............................847 741-3537
Dave Malo, *President*
Judy Malo, *Vice Pres*
Gary Bolliger, *VP Opers*
EMP: 9
SQ FT: 8,400
SALES (est): 1.4MM  Privately Held
SIC: 2821  3544  Molding compounds, plastics; special dies, tools, jigs & fixtures

**(G-8934)**
**ACSYS LASERTECHNIK US INC (HQ)**
2541 Tech Dr Ste 404  (60124)
PHONE..............................224 699-9572
Gerhard Kimmel, *Ch of Bd*
Andreas Plauschin, *COO*
EMP: 2
SQ FT: 2,300
SALES: 677.1K
SALES (corp-wide): 14.8MM  Privately Held
SIC: 3541  7699  Machine tools, metal cutting type; industrial machinery & equipment repair
PA: Acsys Lasertechnik Gmbh
   Leibnizstr 9
   Kornwestheim  70806
   715 480-8750

**(G-8935)**
**ACTION CABINET SALES INC**
1150 Davis Rd Ste K  (60123-1345)
PHONE..............................847 717-0011
Mary Weine, *President*
Edward J Weine, *President*
EMP: 7

# Elgin - Kane County (G-8936)

SALES (est): 520K **Privately Held**
SIC: **2434** 1751 2541 Wood kitchen cabinets; cabinet building & installation; wood partitions & fixtures

### (G-8936)
### ADMO
2550 Decade Ct Ste A  (60124-7861)
PHONE..................847 741-5777
Fax: 847 741-5540
Deborah Krieps, *Corp Secy*
Curtis Olsen, *Vice Pres*
Vicki Wilder, *Purch Mgr*
Debroah McKines, *Controller*
James McBride, *Finance Dir*
▲ **EMP**: 100
**SQ FT**: 40,000
**SALES (est)**: 39.8MM **Privately Held**
WEB: www.admo.com
SIC: **3089** 3544 Injection molding of plastics; industrial molds

### (G-8937)
### ADVANCE ENGINEERING CORP
Also Called: AEC
440 S Mclean Blvd  (60123-7102)
PHONE..................847 760-9421
Thomas Brown, *President*
Mike Legittino, *Vice Pres*
Brian Paszkiewicz, *Vice Pres*
Kelli Tidmore, *Mktg Dir*
Tahira Pasneem, *Info Tech Mgr*
▲ **EMP**: 40 **EST**: 1950
**SQ FT**: 75,000
**SALES (est)**: 9.6MM **Privately Held**
WEB: www.advengcorp.net
SIC: **3824** Integrating & totalizing meters for gas & liquids

### (G-8938)
### AE SEWER & SEPTICS INC
241 Adams St  (60123-7527)
PHONE..................847 289-9084
Antonio Vialegas, *CEO*
**EMP**: 2
**SALES (est)**: 220K **Privately Held**
SIC: **3321** Sewer pipe, cast iron

### (G-8939)
### AEROMOTIVE SERVICES INC
345 Willard Ave  (60120-6810)
PHONE..................224 535-9220
Carl Dumele, *President*
Tom Carroll, *CFO*
**EMP**: 10
**SALES (est)**: 2MM **Privately Held**
SIC: **3694** Harness wiring sets, internal combustion engines

### (G-8940)
### AGNES & CHRIS GULIK
Also Called: Cds Engineering
408 W Amberside Dr  (60124-7860)
PHONE..................847 931-9641
Chris Gulik, *Principal*
**EMP**: 3
**SALES (est)**: 427.4K **Privately Held**
SIC: **3613** Panel & distribution boards & other related apparatus

### (G-8941)
### AIR GAGE COMPANY
516 Slade Ave  (60120-3028)
PHONE..................847 695-0911
Thomas Fernandez, *President*
Mike Smith, *General Mgr*
Dave Joslyn, *Exec VP*
▲ **EMP**: 104 **EST**: 1965
**SQ FT**: 60,000
**SALES (est)**: 13.6MM **Privately Held**
WEB: www.airgage.com
SIC: **3545** 3823 3825 Gauges (machine tool accessories); industrial instrmnts msrmnt display/control process variable; instruments to measure electricity

### (G-8942)
### ALLEGRA PRINT & IMAGING INC
Also Called: Alegra Printing
909 Davis Rd  (60123-1311)
PHONE..................847 697-1434
Robert S Hanson, *President*
Jack Ottinger, *Manager*
Virginia Hanson, *Admin Sec*
**EMP**: 5
**SQ FT**: 5,500
**SALES (est)**: 600K **Privately Held**
WEB: www.allegramarietta.com
SIC: **2752** 2791 2789 2671 Commercial printing, offset; typesetting; bookbinding & related work; packaging paper & plastics film, coated & laminated; mailing service

### (G-8943)
### ALLIED ASPHALT PAVING CO INC (PA)
1100 Brandt Dr  (60120)
PHONE..................630 289-6080
Fax: 847 695-9262
Dan Plote, *President*
Raymond Plote, *Chairman*
Daniel R Plote, *Vice Pres*
Kim Hulke, *Personnel*
Jerry McAuley, *Manager*
**EMP**: 30 **EST**: 1949
**SQ FT**: 2,000
**SALES (est)**: 5.8MM **Privately Held**
SIC: **1611** 2951 2952 Highway & street paving contractor; asphalt & asphaltic paving mixtures (not from refineries); asphalt felts & coatings

### (G-8944)
### ALPHA ASSEMBLY SOLUTIONS INC
2541 Technology Dr  (60124-7845)
PHONE..................847 426-4241
**EMP**: 134
**SALES (corp-wide)**: 3.5B **Publicly Held**
SIC: **3356** Solder: wire, bar, acid core, & rosin core
HQ: Alpha Assembly Solutions Inc.
300 Atrium Dr Fl 3
Somerset NJ 08873
908 791-3000

### (G-8945)
### ALPHA TOOL & DIE INC
74 Lockman Cir  (60123-1250)
PHONE..................847 622-8849
Matthew Durovey, *President*
**EMP**: 4
**SQ FT**: 5,000
**SALES (est)**: 418.7K **Privately Held**
SIC: **3544** Special dies, tools, jigs & fixtures

### (G-8946)
### ALPHABET SHOP INC
300 Elgin Ave  (60120-8412)
PHONE..................847 888-3150
Fax: 847 888-5588
Sheldon Bernstein, *President*
Paul Tylman, *Vice Pres*
Barbara Trager, *Treasurer*
Robert Smith, *Admin Sec*
**EMP**: 25 **EST**: 1963
**SQ FT**: 26,000
**SALES (est)**: 4.1MM **Privately Held**
WEB: www.alphabetshop.com
SIC: **3993** 2759 Signs & advertising specialties; displays & cutouts, window & lobby; letters for signs, metal; commercial printing

### (G-8947)
### AMERICAN COLLOID COMPANY
Metallurgical Alloy Division
3422 Cameron Dr  (60124-8070)
PHONE..................304 882-2123
**EMP**: 11
**SALES (corp-wide)**: 1.7B **Publicly Held**
SIC: **1459** 2899 Clay/Related Mineral Mining Mfg Chemical Preparations
HQ: American Colloid Company
2870 Forbs Ave
Hoffman Estates IL 60192

### (G-8948)
### AMERICAN INDUSTRIAL DIRECT LLC (PA)
Also Called: Auto Body Tool Mart
2545 Millennium Dr  (60124-7815)
PHONE..................800 382-1200
Gary Ramey, *Controller*
Rosa Lazaro, *Sales Mgr*
Noah Dorfman, *Marketing Staff*
Matthew Dorfman, *Mng Member*
Brian Henke,
▼ **EMP**: 31
**SQ FT**: 30,000
**SALES**: 16MM **Privately Held**
WEB: www.autobodytoolmart.com
SIC: **5013** 5085 3559 Motor vehicle supplies & new parts; industrial supplies; frame straighteners, automobile (garage equipment)

### (G-8949)
### AMERICAN LED LTG SOLUTIONS LLC
1645 Todd Farm Dr  (60123-1146)
PHONE..................847 931-1900
Kevin O'Malley,
Mike Stathkis,
**EMP**: 2
**SALES (est)**: 200K **Privately Held**
WEB: www.americanledsolutions.com
SIC: **3674** Light emitting diodes

### (G-8950)
### AMERICAN NTN BEARING MFG CORP (DH)
Also Called: Anbm
1525 Holmes Rd  (60123-1205)
PHONE..................847 741-4545
Andy Kitajima, *President*
Katsu Miyake, *President*
Mike Bilyk, *General Mgr*
John Welch, *General Mgr*
Bill Murray, *Foreman/Supr*
▲ **EMP**: 380
**SQ FT**: 400,000
**SALES (est)**: 84.7MM
**SALES (corp-wide)**: 6B **Privately Held**
SIC: **3562** Ball bearings & parts; roller bearings & parts
HQ: Ntn Usa Corporation
1600 Bishop Ct
Mount Prospect IL 60056
847 298-4652

### (G-8951)
### AMERICAN WILBERT VAULT CORP
954 Bluff City Blvd  (60120-7594)
PHONE..................847 741-3089
Marc Hejnosz, *Manager*
**EMP**: 3
**SALES (corp-wide)**: 5.3MM **Privately Held**
WEB: www.americanwilbert.com
SIC: **3272** Concrete products
PA: American Wilbert Vault Corp
7525 W 99th Pl
Bridgeview IL 60455
708 366-3210

### (G-8952)
### AMTEC MOLDED PRODUCTS INC
1355 Holmes Rd Ste A  (60123-1244)
PHONE..................815 226-0187
Fax: 815 226-0276
Ganesh Subramanian, *President*
Jayakar Krishnamurphy, *Chairman*
Krushna C Pati, *Admin Sec*
**EMP**: 33
**SQ FT**: 49,000
**SALES**: 4MM
**SALES (corp-wide)**: 39.6MM **Privately Held**
WEB: www.amtecmolded.com
SIC: **3089** Molding primary plastic
HQ: North American Acquisition Corporation
1875 Holmes Rd
Elgin IL 60123

### (G-8953)
### AMTEC PRECISION PRODUCTS INC (PA)
1875 Holmes Rd  (60123-1298)
PHONE..................847 695-8030
Jay Krishnamurphy, *CEO*
Ganesh Subramanian, *President*
Kem Formanski, *Vice Pres*
Krushna Pati, *Controller*
▲ **EMP**: 69
SALES (est): 39.6MM **Privately Held**
SIC: **3714** 3089 3469 Transmission housings or parts, motor vehicle; fuel systems & parts, motor vehicle; motor vehicle transmissions, drive assemblies & parts; injection molding of plastics; machine parts, stamped or pressed metal

### (G-8954)
### ANJAY TRADERS INC
450 Shepard Dr Ste 17h  (60123-7033)
PHONE..................847 888-8562
Fax: 847 888-8142
Jamil Uddin, *President*
▲ **EMP**: 1
**SQ FT**: 50,000
**SALES (est)**: 200K **Privately Held**
WEB: www.anjaytraders.com
SIC: **5091** 3421 Hunting equipment & supplies; cutlery

### (G-8955)
### AQUA COAT INC
1061 Davis Rd  (60123-1313)
PHONE..................815 209-0808
Sven Carstensen, *Principal*
Geogre Cash, *Prdtn Mgr*
**EMP**: 2
**SALES (est)**: 202.8K **Privately Held**
SIC: **3479** Coating, rust preventive

### (G-8956)
### AQUA-TECH CO
1875 Big Timber Rd Ste C  (60123-1150)
PHONE..................847 383-7075
Mark Vera, *President*
Katherine Devine, *Admin Sec*
**EMP**: 9 **EST**: 2009
**SALES (est)**: 737.4K **Privately Held**
SIC: **2048** Fish food

### (G-8957)
### AQUARIUS FLUID PRODUCTS INC
Also Called: Nolan Fire Pump System Testing
2585 Millennium Dr Ste B  (60124-7822)
PHONE..................847 289-9090
J Brian Nolan, *President*
Jennifer N Molner, *VP Opers*
Jennifer Nolan, *Admin Sec*
Rob Nolan, *Admin Sec*
**EMP**: 6
**SQ FT**: 2,000
**SALES (est)**: 1.6MM **Privately Held**
SIC: **3569** Firefighting apparatus & related equipment

### (G-8958)
### ARTISTIC CARTON COMPANY (PA)
Also Called: White Pigeon Paper Co Div
1975 Big Timber Rd  (60123-1139)
PHONE..................847 741-0247
Fax: 847 741-8529
Peter A Traeger, *CEO*
Jeff Zeedyk, *COO*
Mark R Hopkinson, *CFO*
Jerry Hartje, *Natl Sales Mgr*
Shawn Lunt, *Manager*
**EMP**: 50 **EST**: 1935
**SQ FT**: 60,000
**SALES (est)**: 69MM **Privately Held**
WEB: www.artisticcarton.com
SIC: **2631** 2675 2657 Folding boxboard; die-cut paper & board; folding paperboard boxes

### (G-8959)
### ASSOCIATED PROFESSIONALS
665 Tollgate Rd Ste F  (60123-9353)
PHONE..................847 931-0095
Fax: 847 931-0132
**EMP**: 3
**SALES (est)**: 240K **Privately Held**
SIC: **3531** Mfg Construction Machinery

### (G-8960)
### ATLAS BOILER & WELDING COMPANY
424 N Grove Ave  (60120-3612)
P.O. Box 202  (60121-0202)
PHONE..................815 963-3360
Fax: 847 741-4420
Justine Ackmann, *President*
**EMP**: 4

SQ FT: 4,800
SALES (est): 553.8K **Privately Held**
SIC: **7699** 7692 3443 Boiler repair shop; welding repair; fabricated plate work (boiler shop)

### (G-8961)
### AVERUS USA INC (PA)
2410 Vantage Dr (60124-7867)
PHONE...................................800 913-7034
Daryl Mirza, *President*
John Collins, *Vice Pres*
Christie Kaye, *Admin Sec*
EMP: 85
SQ FT: 26,000
SALES (est): 67.2MM **Privately Held**
SIC: **3569** 7349 Filters, general line: industrial; building component cleaning service

### (G-8962)
### B D C INC
1185 Jansen Farm Ct (60123-2595)
PHONE...................................847 741-2233
Fax: 847 741-2290
Thom Carpenter, *President*
Carol Carpenter, *Corp Secy*
D Lee Carpenter, *Vice Pres*
Jerry Traxler, *Plant Mgr*
Adriana Casarrubias, *Purch Dir*
◆ EMP: 30
SQ FT: 20,000
SALES (est): 5.5MM **Privately Held**
WEB: www.cbdinc.net
SIC: **3652** 3679 Pre-recorded records & tapes; electronic circuits

### (G-8963)
### BALL CORPORATION
1717 Gifford Rd (60120-7534)
Fax: 847 888-5680
Jack McGowan, *CFO*
Julia Bearstler, *Human Res Dir*
Scott Hamlin, *Manager*
Jim Denison, *Supervisor*
Craig Autry, *Director*
EMP: 151
SALES (corp-wide): 9B **Publicly Held**
SIC: **3411** Metal cans
PA: Ball Corporation
10 Longs Peak Dr
Broomfield CO 80021
303 469-3131

### (G-8964)
### BELLEN CONTAINER CORPORATION
Also Called: Packaging By Design
1460 Bowes Rd (60123-5539)
P.O. Box 5125 (60121-5125)
PHONE...................................847 741-5600
Fax: 847 741-5666
Joseph Graziano Sr, *President*
Charles J Graziano, *President*
Joseph Graziano Jr, *Vice Pres*
Larry Pierce, *Controller*
Micheal Graziano, *Sales Mgr*
EMP: 35
SQ FT: 34,970
SALES (est): 5.4MM **Privately Held**
WEB: www.packaging-by-design.com
SIC: **7389** 2759 Laminating service; flexographic printing

### (G-8965)
### BFI WASTE SYSTEMS N AMER INC
Also Called: Site 933
1330 Gasket Dr (60120-7543)
PHONE...................................847 429-7370
Fax: 630 429-7383
Kim Davis, *Principal*
Rich Shield, *Purch Dir*
Beverly Perez, *Human Res Mgr*
John Larson, *Manager*
Frank McCoy, *Manager*
EMP: 29
SALES (corp-wide): 9.3B **Publicly Held**
WEB: www.mjes.com
SIC: **4953** 4212 3341 2611 Rubbish collection & disposal; local trucking, without storage; secondary nonferrous metals; pulp mills

HQ: Bfi Waste Systems Of North America, Inc.
2394 E Camelback Rd
Phoenix AZ 85016
480 627-2700

### (G-8966)
### BIRD DOG DIVERSIFIED
1670 Cambridge Dr (60123-1143)
PHONE...................................847 741-0700
Jason Brown,
EMP: 28
SQ FT: 38,400
SALES (est): 340K **Privately Held**
SIC: **3089** Injection molding of plastics

### (G-8967)
### BIZ PINS INC
2111 Big Timber Rd (60123-1123)
PHONE...................................847 695-6212
Fax: 847 695-6247
Daniel McCarty, *President*
▲ EMP: 6
SALES (est): 590.2K **Privately Held**
WEB: www.bizpins.com
SIC: **2299** Felts & felt products

### (G-8968)
### BN DELFI USA INC
530 Cumberland Trl (60123-2670)
PHONE...................................847 280-0447
Nikolas Bismpikis, *President*
EMP: 3 EST: 2011
SALES (est): 145.6K **Privately Held**
SIC: **2022** 2099 Cheese, natural & processed; sugar

### (G-8969)
### BOHLER
2505 Millennium Dr (60123-7815)
PHONE...................................630 883-3000
John Kelly, *Principal*
EMP: 2
SALES (est): 290K **Privately Held**
SIC: **3449** Bars, concrete reinforcing: fabricated steel

### (G-8970)
### BOWL-TRONICS ENTERPRISES INC
1115 Sherwood Ave (60120-2444)
PHONE...................................847 741-4500
Fax: 847 741-0914
Richard Mc Gehee, *President*
EMP: 8
SQ FT: 3,200
SALES (est): 764.8K **Privately Held**
WEB: www.bowl-tronics.com
SIC: **3949** 7629 Bowling equipment & supplies; electronic equipment repair

### (G-8971)
### BRIGITFLEX INC
1725 Fleetwood Dr (60123-7130)
PHONE...................................847 741-1452
Brigit Lawrence, *President*
EMP: 10
SQ FT: 15,000
SALES (est): 1.2MM **Privately Held**
SIC: **3629** Blasting machines, electrical

### (G-8972)
### BTR CONTROLS INC
1570 Todd Farm Dr (60123-1287)
PHONE...................................847 608-9500
Ron Seyk, *President*
Richard Groth, *Vice Pres*
Rik Bruns, *Engineer*
Sandra Seyk, *Admin Sec*
EMP: 9
SQ FT: 15,000
SALES (est): 1.9MM **Privately Held**
WEB: www.btrcontrols.com
SIC: **3625** Control equipment, electric; industrial controls: push button, selector switches, pilot

### (G-8973)
### BUCHER HYDRAULICS INC
2545 Northwest Pkwy (60124-7870)
PHONE...................................847 429-0700
Fax: 847 429-0777
Dan Vaughan, *CEO*
Joel Fornell, *Project Mgr*
Carlos Vidinha, *Materials Mgr*
Kelley Widerstrom, *Buyer*

Jainil Chikani, *Engineer*
EMP: 7
SALES (corp-wide): 2.3B **Privately Held**
WEB: www.bucherhydraulics.com
SIC: **3594** Pumps, hydraulic power transfer
HQ: Bucher Hydraulics, Inc.
1363 Michigan St Ne
Grand Rapids MI 49503
616 458-1306

### (G-8974)
### BYSTRONIC INC (DH)
200 Airport Rd (60123-9325)
PHONE...................................847 214-0300
Robert St Aubin, *President*
Michael Zakrzewski, *President*
Sergey Levitzky, *Managing Dir*
Igor Pinto, *Managing Dir*
Ulrich Troesch, *Chairman*
▲ EMP: 110
SQ FT: 48,300
SALES (est): 36.7MM
SALES (corp-wide): 1.2B **Privately Held**
WEB: www.bystronicusa.com
SIC: **3559** 3541 3699 Glass making machinery: blowing, molding, forming, etc.; machine tools, metal cutting type; laser welding, drilling & cutting equipment
HQ: Bystronic Maschinen Ag
Industriestrasse 5
BUtzberg BE 4922
629 587-777

### (G-8975)
### C&C SEALANTS
576 Covered Bridge Dr (60124-5613)
PHONE...................................708 717-0686
Kevin Carey, *Principal*
EMP: 13
SALES (est): 950K **Privately Held**
SIC: **3011** Tires & inner tubes

### (G-8976)
### CAP & SEAL CO
1591 Fleetwood Dr (60123-7194)
PHONE...................................847 741-3101
Thomas J Brown, *President*
Andrew Nodics, *Controller*
Jeannine Pack, *Manager*
EMP: 27 EST: 1957
SQ FT: 34,000
SALES (est): 3.5MM
SALES (corp-wide): 3.8MM **Privately Held**
WEB: www.capseal.com
SIC: **3469** Metal stampings
PA: Sealco Industries, Inc
1591 Fleetwood Dr
Elgin IL 60123
847 741-3101

### (G-8977)
### CAPSONIC AUTOMOTIVE INC
Also Called: Capsonic Automotive & Arospc
1595 Highpoint Dr (60123-9303)
PHONE...................................847 888-0930
EMP: 4 **Privately Held**
SIC: **3674** Radiation sensors
PA: Capsonic Automotive, Inc.
460 2nd St
Elgin IL 60123

### (G-8978)
### CAPSONIC AUTOMOTIVE INC
Also Called: Capsonic Group
495 Renner Dr (60123-6903)
PHONE...................................847 888-7300
Fax: 847 888-7514
George Albrecht, *Branch Mgr*
EMP: 10 **Privately Held**
SIC: **3625** Motor controls & accessories; switches, electric power
PA: Capsonic Automotive, Inc.
460 2nd St
Elgin IL 60123

### (G-8979)
### CAPSONIC AUTOMOTIVE INC (PA)
460 2nd St (60123-7008)
PHONE...................................847 888-7300
Gregory G Liautaud, *President*
Seth Gutkowski, *Vice Pres*
Tom Schmidtbauer, *Senior Buyer*
Raul Ramirez, *Controller*
Thomas J Gillespie, *Admin Sec*

▲ EMP: 10
SQ FT: 70,000
SALES (est): 122.9MM **Privately Held**
SIC: **3625** 3679 3674 Motor controls & accessories; switches, electric power; harness assemblies for electronic use: wire or cable; radiation sensors

### (G-8980)
### CAPSONIC GROUP LLC (PA)
460 2nd St (60123-7008)
PHONE...................................847 888-7264
Fax: 847 888-7261
Greg G Liautaud, *CEO*
George Albrecht, *Vice Pres*
Magdeline White, *Buyer*
Thomas Gillespie, *CFO*
Kotaro Furuichi, *Manager*
▲ EMP: 441
SQ FT: 72,000
SALES (est): 48.4MM **Privately Held**
WEB: www.capsonic.com
SIC: **3089** Injection molded finished plastic products; injection molding of plastics

### (G-8981)
### CAR - MON PRODUCTS INC
1225 Davis Rd (60123-1365)
PHONE...................................847 695-9000
Fax: 847 695-9078
Fred L Imming, *President*
Sandra K Imming, *Admin Sec*
EMP: 40
SQ FT: 46,000
SALES (est): 10MM **Privately Held**
WEB: www.car-mon.com
SIC: **3564** Exhaust fans: industrial or commercial; air cleaning systems; air purification equipment

### (G-8982)
### CARLSON STI INC
1875 Big Timber Rd Ste A (60123-1149)
PHONE...................................630 232-2460
JC Carlson, *Principal*
EMP: 8 EST: 2009
SALES (est): 1MM **Privately Held**
SIC: **3559** Bag seaming & closing machines (sewing machinery)

### (G-8983)
### CARLSON TOOL & MACHINE COMPANY
Also Called: Carlson STI
1875 Big Timber Rd (60123-1148)
PHONE...................................630 232-2460
Fax: 630 232-2016
John M Carlson, *President*
John Wilson, *Opers Staff*
Alex Tover, *Sales Associate*
Cindy Doede, *Office Mgr*
Dorothy Carlson, *Admin Sec*
▲ EMP: 10 EST: 1937
SQ FT: 45,000
SALES (est): 2.2MM **Privately Held**
WEB: www.carlson-tool.com
SIC: **3559** Broom making machinery

### (G-8984)
### CARMEN MATTHEW LLC
Also Called: Norlux
1225 Bowes Rd (60123-5542)
PHONE...................................630 784-7500
Fax: 630 871-8506
Kevin Ogaard, *Mfg Mgr*
Julianne Baker, *Buyer*
Mahesh Patel, *QC Mgr*
Dave Shuemaker, *QC Mgr*
Greg Bobeczko, *Engineer*
▲ EMP: 56
SQ FT: 12,000
SALES (est): 16.3MM **Privately Held**
WEB: www.norluxcorp.com
SIC: **3648** Lighting equipment

### (G-8985)
### CGK ENTERPRISES INC
Also Called: Tri-State Asphalt Emulsions
695 Church Rd (60123-9308)
PHONE...................................847 888-1362
Fax: 847 214-9078
Todd Weist, *CEO*
Charles Kline, *President*
EMP: 4

# Elgin - Kane County (G-8986)

SALES (est): 956.3K  Privately Held
WEB: www.il-asphalt.org
SIC: 2951  Asphalt & asphaltic paving mixtures (not from refineries)

### (G-8986)
### CHEMTECH PLASTICS INC
765 Church Rd  (60123-9308)
PHONE..............................630 503-6000
Fax: 847 742-6884
Ragnar Korthase, *CEO*
Derek N Popp, *President*
Jeff Nesslar, *Vice Pres*
Enrique Alvarez, *Engineer*
Tom Macdonald, *Engineer*
▲ EMP: 100
SQ FT: 60,000
SALES (est): 33.9MM  Privately Held
WEB: www.chemtechplastics.com
SIC: 3089  Injection molding of plastics

### (G-8987)
### CHICAGO DYE WORKS
18 N State St  (60123-5484)
P.O. Box 703  (60121-0703)
PHONE..............................847 931-7968
Tom Hodge, *Owner*
EMP: 6
SALES: 250K  Privately Held
SIC: 2269  Linen fabrics: dyeing, finishing & printing

### (G-8988)
### CHICAGO STOOL AND CHAIR INC
1230 Saint Charles St  (60120-8445)
PHONE..............................847 289-9955
Heshou Ling, *President*
▲ EMP: 4
SQ FT: 15,000
SALES: 700K  Privately Held
SIC: 2521  Wood office chairs, benches & stools

### (G-8989)
### CHOOCHS
64 S Grove Ave  (60120-6404)
PHONE..............................847 888-0211
Mike Dutirro, *President*
EMP: 2  EST: 2011
SALES (est): 294.5K  Privately Held
SIC: 3421  Table & food cutlery, including butchers'

### (G-8990)
### CHURCH OF BRETHREN INC (PA)
Also Called: Denoninational Headquarters
1451 Dundee Ave  (60120-1694)
P.O. Box 1451  (60121-1451)
PHONE..............................847 742-5100
Fax: 847 742-1618
Donal R Fitzkee, *Ch of Bd*
Connie Burk Davis, *Ch of Bd*
Donald R Fitzkee, *Ch of Bd*
Nevin Dulabaum, *Pastor*
Judy E Keyser, *CFO*
EMP: 80
SQ FT: 70,000
SALES: 9.7MM  Privately Held
WEB: www.brethren.org
SIC: 8661  2721  Brethren Church; magazines: publishing only, not printed on site

### (G-8991)
### CITY ORNAMENTAL IRON WORKS
Also Called: City Iron Works
1140 Morningside Dr  (60123-1437)
PHONE..............................847 888-8898
Fax: 847 888-8898
Tom Walton, *Owner*
EMP: 5
SQ FT: 3,000
SALES (est): 387.4K  Privately Held
SIC: 3315  3446  Ornamental metalwork; sheet metalwork; fabricated plate work (boiler shop); metal doors, sash & trim; fabricated structural metal

### (G-8992)
### CLARIDGE PRODUCTS AND EQP INC
923 N State St  (60123-2146)
PHONE..............................847 991-8822
Fax: 847 991-9057
Mike Denker, *Division Mgr*
Chuck Rhodes, *Project Engr*
EMP: 6
SALES (corp-wide): 102.6MM  Privately Held
WEB: www.claridgeproducts.com
SIC: 2493  2531  Reconstituted wood products; blackboards; wood
PA: Claridge Products And Equipment, Incorporated
601 Highway 62 65 S
Harrison AR 72601
870 743-2200

### (G-8993)
### COBRA METAL WORKS INC
1140 Jansen Farm Dr  (60123-2550)
PHONE..............................847 214-8400
Fax: 847 214-8428
Anton Hirsch, *President*
Carmen Mancini, *Opers Staff*
Cobra Deleon, *Engineer*
Helen Guagliardo, *Controller*
Marcel Oros, *Manager*
▲ EMP: 180  EST: 1997
SALES (est): 76.7MM  Privately Held
WEB: www.cobrametalworks.com
SIC: 3444  Sheet metalwork

### (G-8994)
### COLONY INC (PA)
Also Called: Colony Display
2531 Tech Dr Ste 314  (60124)
PHONE..............................847 426-5300
Jerrold Zich, *President*
Kent West, *Vice Pres*
Jorge De Leon, *Project Mgr*
Bob Button, *Opers Mgr*
Jared Koverman, *Project Engr*
▲ EMP: 25
SQ FT: 250,000
SALES: 50MM  Privately Held
WEB: www.colonydisplay.com
SIC: 2542  2541  Partitions & fixtures, except wood; wood partitions & fixtures

### (G-8995)
### COMPONENT PLASTICS INC
700 Tollgate Rd  (60123-9338)
PHONE..............................847 695-9200
Fax: 847 695-7117
Joseph Valente, *President*
Justin Newlin, *VP Mfg*
Darrick Schlossmann, *Project Mgr*
Prashant Patel, *Project Engr*
Ellen Israel, *Human Res Dir*
▲ EMP: 100
SQ FT: 40,000
SALES (est): 23.3MM  Privately Held
WEB: www.cpielgin.com
SIC: 3089  Injection molding of plastics

### (G-8996)
### COMPONENT SPECIALTY INC (HQ)
412 N State St  (60123-2877)
PHONE..............................847 742-4400
Bruce J Carter, *President*
Nand Kumar, *Vice Pres*
Andy Nuggehalli, *CFO*
▲ EMP: 20
SQ FT: 52,000
SALES (est): 8.8MM
SALES (corp-wide): 32.6MM  Privately Held
SIC: 3599  Machine shop, jobbing & repair
PA: Uca Group, Inc
412 N State St
Elgin IL 60123
847 742-8870

### (G-8997)
### COMPUTERPROX
163 E Chicago St Fl 2  (60120-5523)
PHONE..............................847 516-8560
Greg Gliniecki, *CEO*
Mark Elliot, *Partner*
EMP: 10
SALES (est): 817.3K  Privately Held
WEB: www.computerprox.com
SIC: 3577  Computer peripheral equipment

### (G-8998)
### CONCRETE SPECIALITIES CO INC
1375 Gifford Rd  (60120-7306)
PHONE..............................847 608-1200
Jim Nondorf, *President*
Julie Smith, *Controller*
EMP: 40
SQ FT: 50,000
SALES (est): 2.6MM
SALES (corp-wide): 15.9MM  Privately Held
SIC: 3272  Concrete products
PA: Concrete Specialties Co.
1375 Gifford Rd
Elgin IL 60120
847 608-1200

### (G-8999)
### CONCRETE SPECIALTIES CO (PA)
1375 Gifford Rd  (60120-7306)
PHONE..............................847 608-1200
Fax: 630 608-1205
James Nondorf, *President*
▼ EMP: 44  EST: 1946
SALES (est): 15.9MM  Privately Held
SIC: 3272  Concrete products, precast

### (G-9000)
### CONDOR GRANITES INTL INC
1605 Dundee Ave Ste H  (60120-1678)
PHONE..............................847 635-7214
Jayanti K Patel, *President*
Vishal Patel, *Manager*
Bharat K Thakkar, *Admin Sec*
▲ EMP: 3
SALES (est): 289.2K  Privately Held
SIC: 3281  Granite, cut & shaped

### (G-9001)
### CONTINENTAL DATALABEL INC (PA)
1855 Fox Ln  (60123-7815)
PHONE..............................847 742-1600
Timothy J Flynn, *CEO*
Michael P Nicholas, *President*
Meghan Flynn, *Vice Pres*
Steve Solberg, *Plant Mgr*
Kathy Maegdlin, *Credit Mgr*
▲ EMP: 110
SQ FT: 120,000
SALES (est): 20.5MM  Privately Held
WEB: www.compulabel.com
SIC: 2672  Tape, pressure sensitive: made from purchased materials

### (G-9002)
### CONTROLLINK INCORPORATED
1650 Cambridge Dr  (60123-1143)
PHONE..............................847 622-1100
Fax: 847 622-8600
Gary Dembski, *President*
Boris Bednyak, *Corp Secy*
Tj Gone, *Engineer*
Don Kirchner, *Engineer*
EMP: 30
SQ FT: 20,000
SALES (est): 6.2MM  Privately Held
WEB: www.controllink.com
SIC: 7373  3625  Computer integrated systems design; relays & industrial controls

### (G-9003)
### COOK COMMUNICATIONS MINIS
Chariot Family Publishing
850 N Grove Ave  (60120-2807)
PHONE..............................847 741-5168
David Orriss, *Manager*
EMP: 100
SALES (corp-wide): 22.6MM  Privately Held
WEB: www.cookministries.com
SIC: 2721  2731  2754  Periodicals; book publishing; magazines: gravure printing, not published on site
PA: Cook Communications Ministries International, Inc.
4050 Lee Vance Vw
Colorado Springs CO 80918
719 536-0100

### (G-9004)
### COOK COMMUNICATIONS MINISTRIES
Also Called: Cook, David C
850 N Grove Ave  (60120-2807)
PHONE..............................847 741-0800
Fax: 847 741-2444
Cris Doornbos, *CEO*
EMP: 150
SALES (corp-wide): 22.6MM  Privately Held
WEB: www.cookministries.com
SIC: 8661  2721  2771  2731  Religious organizations; periodicals: publishing & printing; greeting cards; books: publishing & printing; book printing
PA: Cook Communications Ministries International, Inc.
4050 Lee Vance Vw
Colorado Springs CO 80918
719 536-0100

### (G-9005)
### COURT & SLOPE INC
780 Church Rd  (60123-9345)
PHONE..............................847 697-3600
Fax: 847 742-0738
Dean Armentrout, *President*
Dave Hoffman, *Vice Pres*
Malinda Aichholz, *Office Mgr*
EMP: 4  EST: 1967
SQ FT: 6,000
SALES (est): 230K  Privately Held
SIC: 3949  7699  5941  5091  Strings, tennis racket; racquet restringing & equipment repair; tennis goods & equipment; sporting & recreation goods; metalworking machinery

### (G-9006)
### CUSTOM CABINET REFACERS INC
2482 Technology Dr  (60124-7925)
PHONE..............................847 695-8800
David Solari, *President*
EMP: 9
SQ FT: 7,000
SALES (est): 850K  Privately Held
SIC: 2434  Wood kitchen cabinets

### (G-9007)
### CUSTOM FABRICATIONS INC
1625 Weld Rd Ste B  (60123-5800)
PHONE..............................847 531-5912
Fax: 847 531-5934
Scott McConaughay, *President*
EMP: 5
SALES (est): 860.6K  Privately Held
SIC: 3365  Machinery castings, aluminum

### (G-9008)
### D & S COMMUNICATIONS INC (PA)
Also Called: Mako Networks
1355 N Mclean Blvd  (60120-1245)
PHONE..............................847 468-8082
Fax: 815 544-2480
Jason Kaubasak, *President*
Grace Gardner, *General Mgr*
Mike Bryniarski, *Vice Pres*
Brenda Dodd, *Vice Pres*
Anna Ramza, *Project Mgr*
▲ EMP: 60
SQ FT: 54,000
SALES (est): 19.6MM  Privately Held
WEB: www.dscomm.com
SIC: 3661  4812  4813  Telephone & telegraph apparatus; radio telephone communication; telephone communication, except radio

### (G-9009)
### DAVID H POOL
Also Called: Print Loop
1405 Timber Dr Ste B  (60123-1809)
PHONE..............................847 695-5007
David H Pool, *Owner*
EMP: 4
SALES: 170K  Privately Held
SIC: 3552  2262  8743  Silk screens for textile industry; screen printing: manmade fiber & silk broadwoven fabrics; promotion service

# GEOGRAPHIC SECTION
## Elgin - Kane County (G-9034)

**(G-9010)**
**DINAMICA GENERALE US INC**
2300 Galvin Dr (60124-7793)
PHONE...........................815 751-9916
Andrea Ghiraldi, *President*
EMP: 4
SQ FT: 6,114
SALES (est): 202.1K **Privately Held**
SIC: 3823 Industrial instrmnts msrmnt display/control process variable

**(G-9011)**
**DOCUMENT PUBLISHING GROUP**
Also Called: Healthware Systems
2511 Tech Dr Ste 102 (60124)
PHONE...........................847 783-0670
Stephen Gruner, *President*
Kelly Green, *Executive*
EMP: 24
SQ FT: 7,100
SALES (est): 2MM **Privately Held**
SIC: 7371 2759 Computer software development; laser printing

**(G-9012)**
**DOVEE MANUFACTURING INC**
640 Church Rd (60123-9340)
PHONE...........................847 437-8122
Fax: 847 437-8131
John Malina, *Principal*
Amy Malina, *Principal*
EMP: 15 EST: 1944
SQ FT: 10,000
SALES: 3.3MM **Privately Held**
WEB: www.dovee.com
SIC: 3544 3469 Special dies & tools; die sets for metal stamping (presses); metal stampings

**(G-9013)**
**DSM DESOTECH INC (DH)**
Also Called: DSM Functional Materials
1122 Saint Charles St (60120-8498)
PHONE...........................847 697-0400
Fax: 847 695-1748
Steve Hartig, *President*
Rob Crowell, *Vice Pres*
Les Nack, *Vice Pres*
Wanda Baron, *Accountant*
Christine Woollard, *Sales Mgr*
▲ EMP: 200
SQ FT: 80,000
SALES (est): 66.7MM
SALES (corp-wide): 8.3B **Privately Held**
WEB: www.dsmdesotech.com
SIC: 2821 2819 8731 2851 Plastics materials & resins; industrial inorganic chemicals; commercial physical research; paints & allied products
HQ: Dsm Finance Usa Inc.
1408 Columbia Nitrogen Dr
Augusta GA 30901
706 849-6515

**(G-9014)**
**DTV INNOVATIONS LLC (PA)**
2402 Millennium Dr (60124-7827)
PHONE...........................847 919-3550
Scott Lopresto, *Engineer*
Benitius Handjojo,
EMP: 12
SQ FT: 7,000
SALES: 4MM **Privately Held**
SIC: 3663 Television broadcasting & communications equipment

**(G-9015)**
**DYNACAST INC**
195 Corporate Dr (60123-9355)
PHONE...........................847 608-2200
Fax: 847 608-2201
Frank Anaya, *Plant Mgr*
Chuck Dykstra, *QC Mgr*
Jeremy Magee, *QC Mgr*
Nevel Crook, *Engineer*
Jeff Gary, *Engineer*
EMP: 105
SALES (corp-wide): 598.9MM **Privately Held**
SIC: 3364 3369 3365 3363 Zinc & zinc-base alloy die-castings; nonferrous foundries; aluminum foundries; aluminum die-castings
HQ: Dynacast Inc
14045 Ballantyne Ste
Charlotte NC 28277
704 927-2790

**(G-9016)**
**DYNAMIC DOOR SERVICE INC**
1165 Deep Woods Dr (60120-5046)
PHONE...........................847 885-4751
Fax: 847 741-6912
Adam Jaworski, *President*
Christine Jaworski, *Admin Sec*
EMP: 4
SALES (est): 603.9K **Privately Held**
WEB: www.dynamicdoor.com
SIC: 3484 Revolvers or revolver parts, 30 mm. & below

**(G-9017)**
**E A M & J INC**
Also Called: A&E Plastics
1620 Cambridge Dr (60123-1143)
PHONE...........................847 622-9200
Fax: 847 622-9022
Maynard Ostrowski, *President*
Andy Ostrowski, *Foreman/Supr*
Andrew Sarkady, *Sales Mgr*
Alnaz Ali, *Manager*
Ali Alnaz, *Manager*
▲ EMP: 25
SQ FT: 40,000
SALES (est): 5.8MM **Privately Held**
WEB: www.ae-tci.com
SIC: 3089 Molding primary plastic

**(G-9018)**
**EAGLE CABINET INC**
1625 Dundee Ave (60120-1679)
PHONE...........................847 289-9992
Tom Miesoer, *President*
▲ EMP: 2
SALES (est): 231.7K **Privately Held**
SIC: 2434 Wood kitchen cabinets

**(G-9019)**
**EASTVIEW MANUFACTURING INC**
970 Elizabeth St (60120-8455)
PHONE...........................847 741-2514
Fax: 847 741-1777
James McNurney, *President*
EMP: 3
SQ FT: 7,500
SALES (est): 402.5K **Privately Held**
SIC: 3621 3568 3451 Motors, electric; power transmission equipment; screw machine products

**(G-9020)**
**EDM SCORPIO INC**
Also Called: Scorpio Elec Dschrge Machining
84 Joslyn Dr (60120-4578)
PHONE...........................847 931-5164
James M Hickey, *President*
EMP: 3
SQ FT: 5,000
SALES (est): 210K **Privately Held**
SIC: 3599 Electrical discharge machining (EDM)

**(G-9021)**
**ELGIN CAM CO**
425 Shepard Dr (60123-7011)
P.O. Box 334 (60121-0334)
PHONE...........................847 741-1757
Fax: 847 741-1767
Mark Anderson, *President*
Kimberly Christensen, *Corp Secy*
Greg Anderson, *Vice Pres*
EMP: 6 EST: 1962
SALES: 320K **Privately Held**
SIC: 3545 Cams (machine tool accessories)

**(G-9022)**
**ELGIN CENTER PHARMACY INC**
1554 Todd Farm Dr (60123-1287)
PHONE...........................847 697-1600
Arvind B Surti, *President*
Linda Bautisa, *Office Mgr*
EMP: 16
SALES (est): 2.7MM **Privately Held**
SIC: 2834 Pharmaceutical preparations

**(G-9023)**
**ELGIN INDUSTRIES INC (PA)**
1100 Jansen Farm Dr (60123-2555)
PHONE...........................847 742-1720
Fax: 847 742-2220
Martin J Skok Jr, *Ch of Bd*
Chris Anderson, *Exec VP*
Bill Skok, *Vice Pres*
Tom Skok, *Vice Pres*
Melinda Willis, *Opers Mgr*
▲ EMP: 150 EST: 1919
SQ FT: 150,000
SALES (est): 47.9MM **Privately Held**
WEB: www.elginind.com
SIC: 3714 5013 Motor vehicle engines & parts; motor vehicle supplies & new parts

**(G-9024)**
**ELGIN INSTANT PRINT**
293 S Aldine St (60123-7249)
PHONE...........................847 931-9006
Fax: 847 931-9013
Bonnie Pacetti, *President*
Brian Pacetti, *President*
Kathy Brockner, *Vice Pres*
EMP: 5
SQ FT: 2,400
SALES: 350K **Privately Held**
SIC: 2752 7334 2791 2789 Commercial printing, lithographic; photocopying & duplicating services; typesetting; bookbinding & related work

**(G-9025)**
**ELGIN MOLDED PLASTICS INC (PA)**
Also Called: EMPCO-LITE DIV
909 Grace St (60120-8419)
PHONE...........................847 931-2455
Fax: 847 931-2454
Clarence Labar, *President*
Henry Lindner, *Vice Pres*
Jeff Wheeland, *Plant Mgr*
Chris Farwell, *Prdtn Mgr*
Leroy Goff, *Research*
▲ EMP: 100
SQ FT: 80,000
SALES: 11.6MM **Privately Held**
WEB: www.empco-lite.com
SIC: 3089 Injection molded finished plastic products

**(G-9026)**
**ELGIN SWEEPER COMPANY**
1300 W Bartlett Rd (60120-7529)
PHONE...........................847 741-5370
Fax: 847 742-3035
Robert Welding, *CEO*
Mark Weber, *President*
Gary Gembala, *General Mgr*
Sean Lemcke, *Regional Mgr*
Tom Sybilrud, *Regional Mgr*
▼ EMP: 425 EST: 1903
SQ FT: 240,000
SALES (est): 194MM
SALES (corp-wide): 707.9MM **Publicly Held**
WEB: www.elginsweeper.com
SIC: 3711 Street sprinklers & sweepers (motor vehicles), assembly of
PA: Federal Signal Corporation
1415 W 22nd St Ste 1100
Oak Brook IL 60523
630 954-2000

**(G-9027)**
**EMERSON ELECTRIC CO**
1901 South St (60123-6939)
PHONE...........................847 585-8300
Fax: 847 608-0134
Sharon Adams, *President*
Edgar M Purvis Jr, *Exec VP*
Perry Rothenbanm, *Engineer*
Bob Vandusen, *Sales Staff*
James Hamilton, *Product Mgr*
EMP: 100
SQ FT: 25,000
SALES (corp-wide): 14.5B **Publicly Held**
WEB: www.gotoemerson.com
SIC: 3822 Appliance regulators
PA: Emerson Electric Co.
8000 West Florissant Ave
Saint Louis MO 63136
314 553-2000

**(G-9028)**
**ENGINEERED COMPONENTS CO (PA)**
1100 Davis Rd Ste A (60123-1316)
PHONE...........................847 985-8000
Fax: 847 841-7007
Arne A Henriksen, *President*
Jeffrey Henriksen, *Vice Pres*
Jeff Hendrickson, *Safety Mgr*
Diane E Coursey, *Admin Sec*
▲ EMP: 32
SALES: 20MM **Privately Held**
WEB: www.engcomponents.com
SIC: 3965 5085 Fasteners; fasteners, industrial: nuts, bolts, screws, etc.

**(G-9029)**
**ENGINEERED PLASTIC SYSTEMS LLC**
885 Church Rd (60123-9309)
PHONE...........................800 480-2327
Fax: 847 289-8382
John Joyce,
Timothy Andrews,
David Cook,
▲ EMP: 16
SQ FT: 30,000
SALES (est): 4.7MM **Privately Held**
WEB: www.epsplasticlumber.com
SIC: 3082 5211 Unsupported plastics profile shapes; lumber products

**(G-9030)**
**ETON MACHINE CO LTD**
1485 Davis Rd Ste B (60123-1351)
PHONE...........................847 426-3380
Fax: 847 426-3388
Bob Adamek, *President*
Narandera Dhawan, *Vice Pres*
Richard Madla, *Vice Pres*
Brenda Holland, *Manager*
EMP: 10
SQ FT: 14,000
SALES: 1MM **Privately Held**
WEB: www.etonmachine.net
SIC: 3599 7692 Machine shop, jobbing & repair; welding repair

**(G-9031)**
**EZ COMFORT HEATING & AC**
1290 Evergreen Ln (60123-4101)
PHONE...........................630 289-2020
Steven J Marks, *Principal*
EMP: 3
SALES (est): 250K **Privately Held**
SIC: 3585 Heating & air conditioning combination units

**(G-9032)**
**FABRIC IMAGES INC**
325 Corporate Dr (60123-9373)
PHONE...........................847 488-9877
Fax: 847 488-1772
Marco Alvarez, *President*
Patrick W Hayes, *President*
Brittney Schmidt, *Project Mgr*
Vince Graal, *Opers Mgr*
Amy Toneys, *Engineer*
▲ EMP: 80
SQ FT: 55,000
SALES (est): 14.5MM **Privately Held**
SIC: 2399 Banners, made from fabric

**(G-9033)**
**FABRICATORS & MFRS ASSN INTL (PA)**
Also Called: Fma
2135 Point Blvd (60123-7956)
PHONE...........................815 399-8700
Gerald Shankel, *President*
Patricia Lee, *Pub Rel Dir*
Jim Warren, *Education*
EMP: 20 EST: 1970
SQ FT: 38,220
SALES: 14.2MM **Privately Held**
WEB: www.fmanet.org
SIC: 8611 2721 Trade associations; trade journals; publishing only, not printed on site

**(G-9034)**
**FAC ENTERPRISES INC**
2755 Spectrum Dr (60124-7841)
PHONE...........................847 844-4000
Frederick A Campbell, *President*

# Elgin - Kane County (G-9035)  GEOGRAPHIC SECTION

Jane E Campbell, *Admin Sec*
▲ **EMP:** 55
**SQ FT:** 50,000
**SALES (est):** 12MM **Privately Held**
**WEB:** www.geminimoulding.com
**SIC:** 2499 Picture & mirror frames, wood

**(G-9035)**
## FINISH LINE USA INC
1750 Todd Farm Dr Ste A (60123-1137)
**PHONE** ................................... 847 608-7800
Grace Vargas, *President*
William Diaz, *Co-Owner*
Patricio Izquierdo, *Co-Owner*
**EMP:** 15
**SALES (est):** 2.2MM **Privately Held**
**SIC:** 3399 Powder, metal

**(G-9036)**
## FIRST AYD CORPORATION
1325 Gateway Dr (60124-7866)
**PHONE** ................................... 847 622-0001
Thomas R Schreiner, *President*
James K Evans, *Admin Sec*
**EMP:** 100
**SQ FT:** 100,000
**SALES (est):** 29.6MM **Privately Held**
**WEB:** www.1stayd.com
**SIC:** 2842 2841 Sanitation preparations; soap & other detergents

**(G-9037)**
## FIRST PRIORITY INC (PA)
Also Called: Priority Care
1590 Todd Farm Dr (60123-1287)
**PHONE** ................................... 847 531-1215
**Fax:** 847 289-1223
Lawrence F Schneider, *President*
Paul Gutierrez, *Opers Staff*
Ray Letak, *Opers Staff*
Felicia Kemp, *QC Dir*
Michael Barnes, *QC Mgr*
▲ **EMP:** 75
**SQ FT:** 99,000
**SALES (est):** 15.3MM **Privately Held**
**SIC:** 2834 5122 Veterinary pharmaceutical preparations; animal medicines

**(G-9038)**
## FMA COMMUNICATONS INC
2135 Point Blvd (60123-7956)
**PHONE** ................................... 815 227-8284
**Fax:** 815 381-1370
Ed Youdell, *President*
Bob Young, *VP Finance*
Mary Bohnsack, *Admin Sec*
Joe Hamblock, *Maintence Staff*
Alison Chebuhar,
**EMP:** 82
**SQ FT:** 15,000
**SALES (est):** 10.1MM
**SALES (corp-wide):** 14.2MM **Privately Held**
**WEB:** www.thefabricator.com
**SIC:** 2721 Trade journals: publishing only, not printed on site
**PA:** Fabricators & Manufacturers Association, International
2135 Point Blvd
Elgin IL 60123
815 399-8700

**(G-9039)**
## FOUNTAIN PRODUCTS INC
2769 Cascade Falls Cir (60124-3116)
**PHONE** ................................... 630 991-7267
**Fax:** 630 443-1344
Paul J Lamb Jr, *President*
Janette Lamb, *Treasurer*
**EMP:** 2 **EST:** 1930
**SALES (est):** 256.2K **Privately Held**
**SIC:** 3469 Kitchen fixtures & equipment, porcelain enameled

**(G-9040)**
## FOX CONTROLS INC
11n26 Rippburger Rd (60123)
**PHONE** ................................... 847 464-5096
**Fax:** 312 464-5104
Sam G Boytor, *President*
Robert Sore, *Sales Mgr*
Nina Walker, *Office Mgr*
Carol A Boytor, *Admin Sec*
**EMP:** 30
**SQ FT:** 14,000

**SALES (est):** 4.8MM **Privately Held**
**WEB:** www.foxcontrols.com
**SIC:** 3613 5084 Control panels, electric; safety inspection service

**(G-9041)**
## GAMENAMICS INC
2541 Tech Dr Ste 406 (60124)
**PHONE** ................................... 847 844-7688
Catherine Burton, *President*
▲ **EMP:** 15
**SQ FT:** 9,500
**SALES (est):** 1.6MM **Privately Held**
**WEB:** www.gamenamics.com
**SIC:** 3944 Games, toys & children's vehicles

**(G-9042)**
## GEISMAR
1415 Davis Rd (60123-1321)
**PHONE** ................................... 847 697-7510
**EMP:** 3
**SALES (est):** 212.3K **Privately Held**
**SIC:** 3743 Railway maintenance cars

**(G-9043)**
## GEKA MANUFACTURING CORPORATION
1690 Cambridge Dr (60123-1143)
**PHONE** ................................... 224 238-5080
Brad Thompson, *President*
Luis Aguinaga, *Engineer*
Franco Luca Waizendorf, *Admin Sec*
◆ **EMP:** 41
**SALES (est):** 12.9MM **Privately Held**
**SIC:** 2844 Cosmetic preparations
**HQ:** Geka Gmbh
Waizendorf 3
Bechhofen 91572
982 287-01

**(G-9044)**
## GERALI CUSTOM DESIGN INC
1482 Sheldon Dr (60120-8131)
**PHONE** ................................... 847 760-0500
David Gerali, *President*
Ruth Gerali, *Corp Secy*
**EMP:** 65
**SQ FT:** 10,500
**SALES (est):** 10.1MM **Privately Held**
**WEB:** www.geralidesign.com
**SIC:** 2542 2541 1799 Counters or counter display cases: except wood; wood partitions & fixtures; counter top installation

**(G-9045)**
## GIBBON AMERICA INC
801 N State St Ste A (60123-2101)
P.O. Box 7, Dundee (60118-0007)
**PHONE** ................................... 847 931-1255
**Fax:** 847 931-1289
Michael Gibbons, *President*
Robert Olech, *Admin Sec*
**EMP:** 10
**SQ FT:** 20,000
**SALES (est):** 1.3MM **Privately Held**
**SIC:** 5085 2893 Ink, printers'; printing ink

**(G-9046)**
## GIBBON AMERICA II CORP
Also Called: Gibbon Printing Inks
801 N State St Ste A (60123-2101)
P.O. Box 7, Dundee (60118-0007)
**PHONE** ................................... 847 931-1255
Robert Olech, *President*
▲ **EMP:** 15
**SQ FT:** 20,000
**SALES (est):** 2MM **Privately Held**
**WEB:** www.gibbonink.com
**SIC:** 2893 Printing ink

**(G-9047)**
## GIVAUDAN FLAVORS CORPORATION
580 Tollgate Rd Ste A (60123-9320)
**PHONE** ................................... 847 608-6200
**Fax:** 847 608-6201
Dan McCafferty, *Manager*
**EMP:** 133
**SALES (corp-wide):** 1.1B **Privately Held**
**SIC:** 2869 Flavors or flavoring materials, synthetic
**HQ:** Givaudan Flavors Corporation
1199 Edison Dr
Cincinnati OH 45216
513 948-8000

**(G-9048)**
## GLOBAL FIELD SERVICES INTL INC
1875 Fox Ln (60123-7813)
**PHONE** ................................... 847 931-8930
Siegfried Schulz, *President*
**EMP:** 3
**SALES (est):** 299K **Privately Held**
**SIC:** 1799 7692 Welding on site; welding repair

**(G-9049)**
## GMT INC
180 S Melrose Ave (60123-6140)
**PHONE** ................................... 847 697-8161
**Fax:** 847 697-8176
Glenn Bolt, *President*
Jermiah Seah, *President*
Scott Clair, *Prdtn Mgr*
Michelle Dubanowski, *Development*
Margaret Kessel, *Finance Mgr*
**EMP:** 42
**SQ FT:** 30,000
**SALES (est):** 10.8MM **Privately Held**
**WEB:** www.gmtplastics.com
**SIC:** 3089 Thermoformed finished plastic products

**(G-9050)**
## GOOD LITE CO (PA)
1155 Jansen Farm Dr (60123-2596)
**PHONE** ................................... 847 841-1145
**Fax:** 630 841-1149
Robert Rodgers, *President*
Kay Chaplin, *General Mgr*
Chris Greening, *General Mgr*
Tim Collins, *Mktg Dir*
Joe Villari, *Marketing Staff*
▲ **EMP:** 6 **EST:** 1931
**SQ FT:** 10,000
**SALES:** 1MM **Privately Held**
**WEB:** www.good-lite.com
**SIC:** 5047 3841 Medical equipment & supplies; surgical & medical instruments

**(G-9051)**
## GREAT LAKES CLAY & SUPPLY INC
927 N State St (60123-2146)
**PHONE** ................................... 224 535-8127
Timothy Pfiffner, *President*
Alado Marchetti, *Treasurer*
Stephanie Meyer, *Manager*
**EMP:** 5
**SQ FT:** 10,500
**SALES:** 1.4MM **Privately Held**
**WEB:** www.greatclay.com
**SIC:** 5032 5719 3255 Tile & clay products; pottery; clay refractories

**(G-9052)**
## H E WISDOM & SONS INC (HQ)
Also Called: Wisdom Adhesives
1575 Executive Dr (60123-9363)
**PHONE** ................................... 847 841-7002
**Fax:** 847 841-7009
Ed Marzano, *President*
Andrea Steiger, *President*
Tom Rolando, *COO*
Kevin Callahan, *Vice Pres*
Jack Chambers, *Vice Pres*
▲ **EMP:** 20
**SQ FT:** 12,000
**SALES (est):** 21.1MM
**SALES (corp-wide):** 2B **Publicly Held**
**WEB:** www.wisdomadhesives.com
**SIC:** 2295 2891 Resin or plastic coated fabrics; adhesives; glue
**PA:** H.B. Fuller Company
1200 Willow Lake Blvd
Saint Paul MN 55110
651 236-5900

**(G-9053)**
## H E WISDOM & SONS INC
1500 Scottsdale Ct (60123-9365)
**PHONE** ................................... 847 841-7002
**EMP:** 4
**SALES (corp-wide):** 2B **Publicly Held**
**SIC:** 2891 Adhesives & sealants
**HQ:** H. E. Wisdom & Sons, Inc.
1575 Executive Dr
Elgin IL 60123
847 841-7002

**(G-9054)**
## H H INTERANTIONAL INC
1010 Douglas Rd (60120-7507)
**PHONE** ................................... 847 697-7805
Hormoz Homozi, *President*
**EMP:** 3
**SALES:** 250K **Privately Held**
**SIC:** 3081 Unsupported plastics film & sheet

**(G-9055)**
## HANSEN PLASTICS CORP
2758 Alft Ln (60124-7899)
**PHONE** ................................... 847 741-4510
**Fax:** 847 741-0253
David Watermann, *CEO*
Roy D Lilly, *President*
Taylor Reed, *Project Mgr*
Laura Johnson, *QA Dir*
Bob Acerrano, *QC Mgr*
▲ **EMP:** 65
**SQ FT:** 60,000
**SALES (est):** 29.4MM **Privately Held**
**WEB:** www.hansenplastics.com
**SIC:** 3089 Injection molding of plastics

**(G-9056)**
## HANSEN PLASTICS CORP
1300 Abbott Dr (60123-1821)
**PHONE** ................................... 847 741-4510
**EMP:** 3
**SALES (est):** 170.2K **Privately Held**
**SIC:** 3089 Mfg Plastic Products

**(G-9057)**
## HARIG PRODUCTS INC
1875 Big Timber Rd (60123-1148)
P.O. Box 46965, Mount Clemens MI (48046-6965)
**PHONE** ................................... 847 695-1000
Paul Koster, *Vice Pres*
Denny Zummer, *Controller*
**EMP:** 17
**SQ FT:** 40,000
**SALES (est):** 3.6MM
**SALES (corp-wide):** 17MM **Privately Held**
**WEB:** www.harigproducts.com
**SIC:** 3531 Crushers, grinders & similar equipment
**PA:** Tru Tech Systems, Inc.
24550 N River Rd
Mount Clemens MI 48043
586 469-2700

**(G-9058)**
## HARTING INC OF NORTH AMERICA
Also Called: Harting Elektronik
1375 Crispin Dr (60123)
**PHONE** ................................... 847 741-2700
Allan Dickson, *President*
Bryan Kolak, *Director*
**EMP:** 25
**SALES (corp-wide):** 626.6MM **Privately Held**
**SIC:** 3678 Electronic connectors
**HQ:** Harting Inc. Of North America
1370 Bowes Rd
Elgin IL 60123
847 741-1500

**(G-9059)**
## HARTING INC OF NORTH AMERICA (HQ)
1370 Bowes Rd (60123-5556)
**PHONE** ................................... 847 741-1500
**Fax:** 847 741-8257
Dietmar Harting, *Ch of Bd*
Achim Meyer, *General Mgr*
Rolf Baumann, *Managing Dir*
Ellen McMillan, *Managing Dir*
Peter Addison, *Regional Mgr*
▲ **EMP:** 35
**SQ FT:** 50,000
**SALES (est):** 49.9MM
**SALES (corp-wide):** 626.6MM **Privately Held**
**WEB:** www.harting.com
**SIC:** 5065 3678 Connectors, electronic; electronic connectors
**PA:** Harting Ag & Co. Kg
Marienwerder Str. 3
Espelkamp 32339
577 247-0

## GEOGRAPHIC SECTION
### Elgin - Kane County (G-9084)

**(G-9060)**
**HAUMILLER ENGINEERING COMPANY**
445 Renner Dr (60123-6991)
PHONE..................847 695-9111
Fax: 847 695-2092
Russ Holmer, *President*
Art Parsons, *Project Mgr*
Russ Miller, *Engineer*
Pat Phillips, *Engineer*
Dan Speranza, *Engineer*
◆ **EMP:** 105 **EST:** 1953
**SQ FT:** 35,000
**SALES (est):** 24.9MM **Privately Held**
**WEB:** www.haumiller.com
**SIC:** 3599 Custom machinery

**(G-9061)**
**HEALTHWARE SYSTEMS INC**
2511 Tech Dr Ste 102 (60124)
PHONE..................847 783-0670
Steve Gruner, *President*
Dennis Porto, *President*
Jay Kunwar, *Vice Pres*
Patrick Murray, *Vice Pres*
Joe Blazen, *Project Mgr*
**EMP:** 30
**SALES (est):** 3.3MM **Privately Held**
**SIC:** 7372 Prepackaged software

**(G-9062)**
**HENDRICK METAL PRODUCTS LLC**
1320 Gateway Dr (60124-7825)
PHONE..................847 742-7002
Fax: 847 742-7448
Manny Barsoumian, *General Mgr*
Bruce Caldwell, *General Mgr*
Mike Drake, *Principal*
Tracy Wickerheim, *Electrical Engi*
Alicia McHale, *Controller*
**EMP:** 55
**SQ FT:** 76,000
**SALES (est):** 11.8MM **Privately Held**
**SIC:** 3444 Sheet metalwork

**(G-9063)**
**HENKEL CONSUMER GOODS INC**
2175 Point Blvd Ste 180 (60123-9217)
PHONE..................847 426-4552
Rachel Blakeney, *Branch Mgr*
**EMP:** 100
**SALES (corp-wide):** 19.7B **Privately Held**
**SIC:** 2841 Soap & other detergents
**HQ:** Henkel Consumer Goods Inc.
7201 E Henkel Way
Scottsdale AZ 85255
860 571-5100

**(G-9064)**
**HENKEL CORPORATION**
1345 Gasket Dr (60120-7544)
PHONE..................847 468-9200
Michele Johnson, *Project Mgr*
Robert Ludicky, *Research*
Michael Pierce, *Research*
Ron Leonhardt, *Engr R&D*
Steve Roseti, *Sales/Mktg Mgr*
**EMP:** 100
**SALES (corp-wide):** 19.7B **Privately Held**
**SIC:** 2891 5169 Adhesives; chemicals & allied products
**HQ:** Henkel Corporation
1 Henkel Way
Rocky Hill CT 06067
860 571-5100

**(G-9065)**
**HERBS BAKERY INC**
1020 Larkin Ave (60123-5240)
PHONE..................847 741-0249
Fax: 847 742-6883
Lynn Schwartz, *President*
Wendy Wessel, *Vice Pres*
Erick Schwartz, *Admin Sec*
**EMP:** 19
**SQ FT:** 3,400
**SALES (est):** 865.9K **Privately Held**
**WEB:** www.herbsbakery.com
**SIC:** 5461 2051 Bakeries; bread, cake & related products

**(G-9066)**
**HONOR MED MASKINER CORP**
Also Called: Starro Precision P&E
600 Church Rd (60123-9340)
PHONE..................847 741-9400
Patricia Hirsch, *CEO*
Janusz Buz, *Technology*
Hubert Bieniewski, *Admin Sec*
**EMP:** 4
**SALES:** 450K **Privately Held**
**SIC:** 3541 Vertical turning & boring machines (metalworking)

**(G-9067)**
**HOWARD SPORTSWEAR GRAPHICS**
1421 Holmes Rd 1433 (60123-1203)
PHONE..................847 695-8195
Jeff Howard, *President*
Quintin Howard, *Admin Sec*
**EMP:** 30
**SALES (est):** 4.3MM **Privately Held**
**SIC:** 2752 Transfers, decalcomania or dry: lithographed

**(G-9068)**
**HUMBOLDT MFG CO (PA)**
875 Tollgate Rd (60123-9351)
PHONE..................708 456-6300
Fax: 708 456-6355
Dennis E Burgess, *President*
Joseph Bryk, *Corp Secy*
Joe Bryk, *CFO*
June Janyia, *Credit Mgr*
Phyllis Shanoff, *Manager*
◆ **EMP:** 38 **EST:** 1925
**SQ FT:** 45,000
**SALES:** 30MM **Privately Held**
**WEB:** www.humboldtmfg.com
**SIC:** 3829 3821 Surveying & drafting equipment; bunsen burners; laboratory equipment: fume hoods, distillation racks, etc.

**(G-9069)**
**HYDROX CHEMICAL COMPANY INC**
Also Called: Hydrox Laboratories
825 Tollgate Rd Ste B (60123-9326)
PHONE..................847 468-9400
Fax: 847 468-9407
Kappana Ramanandan, *President*
Chris Karrassy, *Production*
Keith Robertson, *QC Mgr*
Brian Gaare, *CFO*
Barrett Peterson, *VP Finance*
▲ **EMP:** 65 **EST:** 1913
**SQ FT:** 85,000
**SALES (est):** 38.8MM **Privately Held**
**SIC:** 2844 2819 2834 2869 Shampoos, rinses, conditioners: hair; peroxides, hydrogen peroxide; veterinary pharmaceutical preparations; industrial organic chemicals

**(G-9070)**
**I W M CORPORATION**
Also Called: Industrial Water Management
399 Hammond Ave (60120-8423)
PHONE..................847 695-0700
Fax: 847 695-0710
Leonard Sneed, *President*
**EMP:** 9
**SQ FT:** 24,000
**SALES (est):** 937.1K **Privately Held**
**WEB:** www.iwmcorporation.com
**SIC:** 8748 5084 2899 Business consulting; industrial machinery & equipment; chemical preparations

**(G-9071)**
**ILLINOIS TOOL WORKS INC**
ITW Shakeproof Auto Div
1201 Saint Charles St (60120-8494)
PHONE..................847 741-7900
Fax: 847 741-8489
Dave Hauner, *Branch Mgr*
Wellard McGuire, *Manager*
**EMP:** 35
**SALES (corp-wide):** 13.6B **Publicly Held**
**SIC:** 3452 3451 Bolts, nuts, rivets & washers; screw machine products

**PA:** Illinois Tool Works Inc.
155 Harlem Ave
Glenview IL 60025
847 724-7500

**(G-9072)**
**ILLINOIS TOOL WORKS INC**
Also Called: ITW Paslode
2501 Galvin Dr (60124-8093)
PHONE..................847 783-5500
David Adame, *Marketing Staff*
**EMP:** 104
**SALES (corp-wide):** 13.6B **Publicly Held**
**SIC:** 3089 3965 3499 2891 Injection molded finished plastic products; closures, plastic; synthetic resin finished products; fasteners; strapping, metal; adhesives & sealants; refrigeration & heating equipment
**PA:** Illinois Tool Works Inc.
155 Harlem Ave
Glenview IL 60025
847 724-7500

**(G-9073)**
**IMAC MOTION CONTROL CORP**
1301 Bowes Rd Ste A (60123-5510)
PHONE..................847 741-4622
John Krezski, *President*
Marc Bennett, *Engineer*
Janelle Carrera, *Marketing Staff*
Terri Legan, *Manager*
**EMP:** 5
**SQ FT:** 10,000
**SALES (est):** 540K **Privately Held**
**WEB:** www.imac-mcc.com
**SIC:** 3861 Motion picture apparatus & equipment

**(G-9074)**
**IMAGE TECHNOLOGY INC**
937 Davis Rd (60123-1311)
PHONE..................847 622-3300
Fax: 847 622-2700
Maganbhai Vekaria, *President*
Bharat Akoliya, *Treasurer*
**EMP:** 12
**SQ FT:** 10,000
**SALES (est):** 1.7MM **Privately Held**
**SIC:** 3672 Printed circuit boards

**(G-9075)**
**IN COLOR GRAPHICS COML PRTG**
1855 Fox Ln (60123-7813)
PHONE..................847 697-0003
Rich Philip, *Owner*
**EMP:** 10 **EST:** 1998
**SALES (est):** 981.6K **Privately Held**
**SIC:** 2759 2752 Commercial printing; commercial printing, lithographic

**(G-9076)**
**INDUCTION INNOVATIONS INC**
1175 Jansen Farm Ct (60123-2595)
PHONE..................847 836-6933
Thomas M Gough, *President*
Steven Gough, *Vice Pres*
Dave Pacholok, *Vice Pres*
▲ **EMP:** 5
**SALES (est):** 1MM **Privately Held**
**WEB:** www.inductioninnovations.com
**SIC:** 3677 Inductors, electronic

**(G-9077)**
**INLAND BROACHING AND TL CO LLC**
1441 Timber Dr (60123-1827)
PHONE..................847 233-0033
Fax: 773 237-0525
Amarnath Nuggehalli,
Nandkumar Nuggehalli,
Vijay Raichura,
**EMP:** 2
**SALES (est):** 240K **Privately Held**
**SIC:** 3541 Broaching machines

**(G-9078)**
**INTEGRITY TECHNOLOGIES LLC**
Also Called: Integratech
1140 Peachtree Ln Unit B (60120-4803)
PHONE..................850 240-6089
John Jinkins,
**EMP:** 3

**SALES (est):** 224.2K **Privately Held**
**SIC:** 3571 5734 Electronic computers; modems, monitors, terminals & disk drives: computers

**(G-9079)**
**INTERNATIONAL PAPER COMPANY**
1300 Bowes Rd (60123-5538)
**EMP:** 172
**SALES (corp-wide):** 21B **Publicly Held**
**SIC:** 2621 Paper mills
**PA:** International Paper Company
6400 Poplar Ave
Memphis TN 38197
901 419-9000

**(G-9080)**
**J M RESOURCES INC**
Also Called: Inland Broaching & Tool Co
1441 Timber Dr (60123-1827)
PHONE..................630 690-7337
Fax: 847 233-9933
Mike Shah, *President*
Mike A Shah, *President*
Jyoti M Shah, *Corp Secy*
Georgia Perez, *Controller*
Michael Cielak, *Webmaster*
**EMP:** 12 **EST:** 1946
**SQ FT:** 17,000
**SALES (est):** 1.2MM **Privately Held**
**SIC:** 3545 7699 3544 Broaches (machine tool accessories); knife, saw & tool sharpening & repair; special dies, tools, jigs & fixtures

**(G-9081)**
**J SCHNEERBERGER CORP**
1380 Gateway Dr Ste 8 (60124-7891)
PHONE..................847 888-3498
Jurg Schneerberger, *President*
Hans Peter Maurer, *Treasurer*
▲ **EMP:** 7
**SQ FT:** 2,500
**SALES (est):** 1.9MM **Privately Held**
**WEB:** www.schneeberger-us.com
**SIC:** 5084 3541 Machine tools & metalworking machinery; grinding machines, metalworking
**PA:** J. Schneeberger Maschinen Holding Ag
Geissbergstrasse 2
Roggwil BE
629 184-111

**(G-9082)**
**JALOR COMPANY**
545 Tollgate Rd Ste E (60123-9305)
PHONE..................847 202-1172
John Goorsky, *Owner*
**EMP:** 3
**SALES (est):** 257.9K **Privately Held**
**WEB:** www.jalorcompany.com
**SIC:** 3441 Fabricated structural metal

**(G-9083)**
**JOHN B SANFILIPPO & SON INC (PA)**
Also Called: FISCHER NUT COMPANY
1703 N Randall Rd (60123-7820)
PHONE..................847 289-1800
Fax: 847 289-1843
Jeffrey T Sanfilippo, *Ch of Bd*
Jasper B Sanfilippo Jr, *President*
Michael J Valentine, *President*
Jeffrey Hunter, *Business Mgr*
Frank S Pellegrino, *Senior VP*
◆ **EMP:** 160 **EST:** 1979
**SQ FT:** 400,000
**SALES:** 952MM **Publicly Held**
**WEB:** www.jbssinc.com
**SIC:** 2068 2064 2099 2096 Nuts: dried, dehydrated, salted or roasted; candy & other confectionery products; peanut butter; dessert mixes & fillings; potato chips & similar snacks; chocolate & cocoa products

**(G-9084)**
**JOHN B SANFILIPPO & SON INC**
Fisher Division
2350 Fox Ln (60123)
PHONE..................847 690-8432
Jasper Sanfilippo, *Treasurer*
Francisco Almazan, *Manager*
**EMP:** 150

Elgin - Kane County (G-9085)    GEOGRAPHIC SECTION

**SALES (corp-wide):** 952MM **Publicly Held**
**WEB:** www.jbssinc.com
**SIC: 2068** 2099 Nuts: dried, dehydrated, salted or roasted; food preparations
**PA:** John B. Sanfilippo & Son, Inc.
1703 N Randall Rd
Elgin IL 60123
847 289-1800

**(G-9085)**
## JR ROYALS ATHLETICS
1073 Compass Pt (60123-8591)
**PHONE**..................224 659-2906
David Zabran, *President*
**EMP:** 20
**SALES (est):** 817.9K **Privately Held**
**SIC: 2257** 7999 8699 Jersey cloth; sports instruction, schools & camps; athletic organizations

**(G-9086)**
## JR TECH INC
1600 Todd Farm Dr Ste A (60123-1141)
**PHONE**..................847 214-8860
Dan Scully, *President*
Joseph Rick, *Vice Pres*
Loraine Scully, *Manager*
**EMP:** 8
**SALES (est):** 1.3MM **Privately Held**
**SIC: 3599** Machine shop, jobbing & repair

**(G-9087)**
## KANEBRIDGE CORPORATION
1125 Gateway Dr (60124-7831)
Joseph McGrath, *President*
**EMP:** 30
**SALES (corp-wide):** 20.7MM **Privately Held**
**SIC: 3452** Bolts, nuts, rivets & washers
**PA:** Kanebridge Corporation
250 Pehle Ave Ste 303
Saddle Brook NJ 07663
201 337-3200

**(G-9088)**
## KIEL MACHINE PRODUCTS
877 Arthur Dr (60120-3115)
Walter D Kiel, *President*
Ruth Kiel, *Vice Pres*
**EMP:** 5 **EST:** 1979
**SQ FT:** 1,200
**SALES (est):** 528.2K **Privately Held**
**SIC: 3451** Screw machine products

**(G-9089)**
## KIM GILMORE
Also Called: Gilmore Marketing Concepts
2250 Point Blvd Ste 321 (60123-7837)
**PHONE**..................847 931-1511
Kim Gilmore, *Owner*
**EMP:** 6
**SALES (est):** 400K **Privately Held**
**SIC: 3993** Signs & advertising specialties

**(G-9090)**
## KINNEY ELECTRICAL MFG CO
678 Buckeye St (60123-2827)
**PHONE**..................847 742-9600
**Fax:** 847 742-3326
Lowell D Naber, *President*
Tim Shelton, *General Mgr*
Greg Bird, *Design Engr*
Richard Markovich, *Design Engr*
Dennis Meyer, *Design Engr*
**EMP:** 80
**SQ FT:** 99,000
**SALES (est):** 38.1MM **Privately Held**
**WEB:** www.kinneyelectric.com
**SIC: 3613** Panelboards & distribution boards, electric; switchboard apparatus, except instruments

**(G-9091)**
## KNIGHT TOOL WORKS INC
1200 Abbott Dr Ste C (60123-1825)
**PHONE**..................847 678-1237
Richard Peterson II, *President*
Elizabeth Peterson, *Corp Secy*
▲ **EMP:** 17 **EST:** 1964
**SQ FT:** 250,000
**SALES:** 1.4MM **Privately Held**
**WEB:** www.knight-toolworks.com
**SIC: 3544** Dies & die holders for metal cutting, forming, die casting

**(G-9092)**
## KREIS TOOL & MFG CO INC
1615 Cambridge Dr (60123-1144)
**PHONE**..................847 289-3700
**Fax:** 847 289-3701
E Stephen Kreis, *President*
Valerie Kreis, *Corp Secy*
Siegfried Kreis, *Vice Pres*
Karl Guenther, *Plant Mgr*
Bob Keller, *Prdtn Mgr*
**EMP:** 30
**SQ FT:** 35,000
**SALES (est):** 8.7MM **Privately Held**
**WEB:** www.kreis.com
**SIC: 3544** 3599 Special dies, tools, jigs & fixtures; machine shop, jobbing & repair

**(G-9093)**
## LASER PRO
978 N Mclean Blvd (60123-2039)
**PHONE**..................847 742-1055
William Grocke, *President*
William A Grocke, *Owner*
Pierce Shannon, *Accounts Mgr*
James Kouris, *Sales Staff*
Jerry Bomer, *Manager*
**EMP:** 5
**SALES (est):** 722.2K **Privately Held**
**SIC: 3861** 5734 Toners, prepared photographic (not made in chemical plants); computer peripheral equipment

**(G-9094)**
## LEHMAN FAST TECH
37w468 Elmer Ct (60124-4810)
P.O. Box 301, South Elgin (60177-0301)
**PHONE**..................847 742-5202
James Lehman, *Owner*
**EMP:** 3
**SQ FT:** 300
**SALES (est):** 245.8K **Privately Held**
**SIC: 3599** 3544 Machine shop, jobbing & repair; special dies, tools, jigs & fixtures

**(G-9095)**
## LINEAR INDUSTRIES INC
2531 Tech Dr Ste 310 (60124)
**PHONE**..................847 428-5793
Gustavo Figueiredo, *President*
Alan Gray, *CFO*
Perry Priestley, *VP Sales*
Claudia Curtis, *Accounts Mgr*
Carl Clouse, *Marketing Staff*
**EMP:** 12
**SALES (est):** 1.3MM **Privately Held**
**SIC: 3663** Radio broadcasting & communications equipment
**PA:** Hitachi Kokusai Linear Equipamentos Eletronicos S/A.
Rod. Br 459 121 A
Santa Rita Do Sapucai MG 37540

**(G-9096)**
## LUBEQ CORPORATION
1380 Gateway Dr Ste 6 (60124-7891)
**PHONE**..................847 931-1020
**Fax:** 847 931-0944
Klaus Pressl, *President*
Tim Hickey, *Vice Pres*
Tiffany Meyer, *Credit Mgr*
Stephanie Pressl, *Analyst*
▲ **EMP:** 10
**SQ FT:** 17,500
**SALES (est):** 6.8MM **Privately Held**
**SIC: 5172** 3561 Lubricating oils & greases; pumps & pumping equipment

**(G-9097)**
## M2M ENTERPRISES LLC
930 Ascot Dr (60123-6759)
P.O. Box 6430 (60121-6430)
**PHONE**..................847 899-7565
Debra Sauder, *Mng Member*
**EMP:** 5
**SALES (est):** 467.8K **Privately Held**
**SIC: 3842** Surgical appliances & supplies

**(G-9098)**
## MACCARB INC
2430 Millennium Dr (60124-7827)
**PHONE**..................877 427-2499
Adam McCarthy, *President*
Orland McCarthy, *Director*
**EMP:** 2
**SQ FT:** 1,500

**SALES:** 1MM **Privately Held**
**WEB:** www.maccarb.com
**SIC: 5169** 2813 3443 Industrial gases; carbon dioxide; cylinders, pressure: metal plate

**(G-9099)**
## MACHINED CONCEPTS LLC
1760 Britannia Dr Ste 8 (60124-7814)
**PHONE**..................847 708-4923
Cindy Kay, *Manager*
Albert Raczynski,
**EMP:** 3
**SALES (est):** 450.4K **Privately Held**
**SIC: 3599** Machine shop, jobbing & repair

**(G-9100)**
## MARSHALL MIDDLEBY INC (HQ)
Also Called: Middleby Cooking Systems Group
1400 Toastmaster Dr (60120-9274)
**PHONE**..................847 289-0204
**Fax:** 847 741-2710
William F Whitman Jr, *Ch of Bd*
Selim A Bassoul, *President*
David B Baker, *CFO*
Martin Lindsay, *Treasurer*
Timothy J Fitzgerald, *Admin Sec*
◆ **EMP:** 200
**SQ FT:** 210,000
**SALES:** 332.8MM
**SALES (corp-wide):** 2.2B **Publicly Held**
**SIC: 3556** 3585 3631 Ovens, bakery; mixers, feed, except agricultural; refrigeration equipment, complete; household cooking equipment
**PA:** The Middleby Corporation
1400 Toastmaster Dr
Elgin IL 60120
847 741-3300

**(G-9101)**
## MASTER MACHINE GROUP
1515 Commerce Dr (60123-9304)
**PHONE**..................847 472-9940
Amy Berchett, *Admin Sec*
**EMP:** 5
**SALES (est):** 560K **Privately Held**
**SIC: 3541** Machine tools, metal cutting type

**(G-9102)**
## MASTER MOLDED PRODUCTS LLC
1000 Davis Rd (60123-1314)
**PHONE**..................847 695-9700
**Fax:** 847 695-9707
John Weinhart, *Exec VP*
Ken Mraz, *Vice Pres*
Art Schueneman, *VP Opers*
Eduardo Rodriguez, *Warehouse Mgr*
Liz Roush, *QC Mgr*
▲ **EMP:** 125 **EST:** 1945
**SQ FT:** 85,000
**SALES (est):** 43MM
**SALES (corp-wide):** 198.4MM **Privately Held**
**WEB:** www.mastermolded.com
**SIC: 3089** Injection molding of plastics
**PA:** Quantum Plastics, Llc
1000 Davis Rd
Elgin IL 60123
847 695-9700

**(G-9103)**
## MATE TECHNOLOGIES INC
1695 Todd Farm Dr (60123-1146)
**PHONE**..................847 289-1010
Steven Matecki, *CEO*
Mark Matecki, *Principal*
Randy Matecki, *Vice Pres*
**EMP:** 10
**SQ FT:** 10,000
**SALES (est):** 1.1MM **Privately Held**
**SIC: 5162** 3089 2851 Plastics products; injection molding of plastics; paints & allied products

**(G-9104)**
## MAVEA LLC
1707 N Randall Rd Ste 200 (60123-9414)
**PHONE**..................905 712-2045
Kevin Chamberlain, *Vice Pres*
Thomas Hose, *Vice Pres*
Stephen Kaplan, *Vice Pres*
Cws Fralix, *Sales Dir*

Elizabeth Cahill, *Marketing Mgr*
▲ **EMP:** 7
**SQ FT:** 2,500
**SALES (est):** 1.7MM **Privately Held**
**SIC: 3569** Filters
**HQ:** Brita Gmbh
Heinrich-Hertz-Str. 4
Taunusstein 65232
612 874-60

**(G-9105)**
## MEF CONSTRUCTION INC
707 Mariner Ct (60120-7606)
**PHONE**..................847 741-8601
Dianna Magana, *President*
**EMP:** 3 **EST:** 2014
**SALES (est):** 218.6K **Privately Held**
**SIC: 1623** 1794 1799 3271 Water & sewer line construction; excavation & grading, building construction; athletic & recreation facilities construction; playground construction & equipment installation; blocks, concrete: landscape or retaining wall;

**(G-9106)**
## META-MEG TOOL CORPORATION
1434 Davis Rd (60123-1322)
**PHONE**..................847 742-3600
**Fax:** 847 742-3626
Robert Schuld, *President*
Barbara Schuld, *Corp Secy*
**EMP:** 5 **EST:** 1975
**SQ FT:** 3,500
**SALES (est):** 500K **Privately Held**
**SIC: 7699** 3544 Plastics products repair; special dies, tools, jigs & fixtures

**(G-9107)**
## METAL FINISHING PROS CORP
41 N Union St (60123-5334)
**PHONE**..................630 883-8339
**EMP:** 3
**SALES (est):** 282.2K **Privately Held**
**SIC: 3471** Cleaning, polishing & finishing

**(G-9108)**
## METAL IMAGES INC
325 Corporate Dr (60123-9373)
**PHONE**..................847 488-9877
Marco Alvarez, *President*
Patrick Hayes, *President*
**EMP:** 6
**SALES (est):** 530K **Privately Held**
**SIC: 3471** Buffing for the trade

**(G-9109)**
## MEYER METAL SYSTEMS INC
1111 Davis Rd (60123-1315)
**PHONE**..................847 468-0500
Craig Meyer, *President*
Kenn Gardio, *Manager*
**EMP:** 12
**SQ FT:** 39,000
**SALES (est):** 2.4MM **Privately Held**
**SIC: 3355** Aluminum rail & structural shapes

**(G-9110)**
## MIDDLEBY CORPORATION (PA)
1400 Toastmaster Dr (60120-9274)
**PHONE**..................847 741-3300
**Fax:** 847 741-9476
Selim A Bassoul, *Ch of Bd*
David Brewer, *COO*
Abhishek Azad, *Exec VP*
Timothy J Fitzgerald, *CFO*
Martin M Lindsay, *Treasurer*
**EMP:** 30
**SQ FT:** 207,000
**SALES:** 2.2B **Publicly Held**
**WEB:** www.middleby.com
**SIC: 3556** 3589 Food products machinery; ovens, bakery; mixers, commercial, food; commercial cooking & foodwarming equipment; cooking equipment, commercial; food warming equipment, commercial

**(G-9111)**
## MIDDLEBY CORPORATION
Also Called: Toastmaster
1400 Toastmaster Dr (60120-9274)
**PHONE**..................847 741-3300
**Fax:** 847 741-0015

# GEOGRAPHIC SECTION

Elgin - Kane County (G-9135)

**EMP:** 20
**SALES (corp-wide):** 2.2B **Publicly Held**
**WEB:** www.middleby.com
**SIC: 3556** 3589 Food products machinery; ovens, bakery; mixers, commercial, food; cooking equipment, commercial; food warming equipment, commercial
**PA:** The Middleby Corporation
1400 Toastmaster Dr
Elgin IL 60120
847 741-3300

**(G-9112)**
**MIDDLEBY WORLDWIDE INC (HQ)**
1400 Toastmaster Dr (60120-9274)
**PHONE**..................847 741-3300
Selim A Bassoul, *CEO*
Tim Fitzgerald, *CFO*
Martin M Lindsay, *Treasurer*
◆ **EMP:** 3
**SALES (est):** 640.2K
**SALES (corp-wide):** 2.2B **Publicly Held**
**SIC: 3556** Food products machinery
**PA:** The Middleby Corporation
1400 Toastmaster Dr
Elgin IL 60120
847 741-3300

**(G-9113)**
**MOTION INDUSTRIES INC**
Also Called: Braas Company
440 Airport Rd Ste J (60123-9301)
**PHONE**..................847 760-6630
Max Rockafellow, *Branch Mgr*
**EMP:** 7
**SALES (corp-wide):** 15.3B **Publicly Held**
**SIC: 3694** Distributors, motor vehicle engine
**HQ:** Motion Industries, Inc.
1605 Alton Rd
Birmingham AL 35210
205 956-1122

**(G-9114)**
**MOTOROLA SOLUTIONS INC**
2520 Galvin Dr (60124-7928)
**PHONE**..................847 576-5000
Matthew West, *General Mgr*
Bob Sanders, *Senior VP*
Greg Billings, *Vice Pres*
Scott Schoepel, *Vice Pres*
Keith Edmonds, *Project Mgr*
**EMP:** 142
**SALES (corp-wide):** 6B **Publicly Held**
**SIC: 3663** Radio & TV communications equipment
**PA:** Motorola Solutions, Inc.
500 W Monroe St Ste 4400
Chicago IL 60661
847 576-5000

**(G-9115)**
**MPR PLASTICS INC**
1551 Scottsdale Ct # 100 (60123-9336)
**PHONE**..................847 468-9950
Paul D Doran, *President*
Kashmir Singh, *Plant Mgr*
Kelly George, *Human Resources*
Jeff Gathman, *Manager*
Adam Tyminski, *Assistant*
▲ **EMP:** 30
**SQ FT:** 25,000
**SALES (est):** 7.9MM **Privately Held**
**WEB:** www.mprplastics.com
**SIC: 3089** Injection molded finished plastic products

**(G-9116)**
**MULTIFILM PACKAGING CORP**
Also Called: Multifoil Packaging
1040 N Mclean Blvd (60123-1709)
**PHONE**..................847 695-7600
**Fax:** 847 695-7645
Olle Mannertorp, *CEO*
Christopher Rogers, *President*
Robert Tate, *Vice Pres*
Chuck Dipietro, *Opers Mgr*
Dave Rohrschneider, *Opers Mgr*
▲ **EMP:** 55
**SQ FT:** 82,200
**SALES:** 24.7MM **Privately Held**
**WEB:** www.multifilm.com
**SIC: 3081** Packing materials, plastic sheet

**(G-9117)**
**NAVIS INDUSTRIES INC**
2500 Tech Dr Ste 100 (60123)
**PHONE**..................224 293-2000
Scott D Griffith, *President*
Pam Marian, *Manager*
▲ **EMP:** 4
**SALES (est):** 956.3K **Privately Held**
**WEB:** www.navisfilms.com
**SIC: 2671** Plastic film, coated or laminated for packaging

**(G-9118)**
**NEWHAVEN DISPLAY INTL INC**
2661 Galvin Ct (60124-8092)
**PHONE**..................847 844-8795
Gary Murrell, *President*
Atif Khan, *Engineer*
Curt Lagerstam, *Engineer*
Sharon Kateshiro, *Accountant*
Annie Nawrocki, *Cust Mgr*
▲ **EMP:** 29
**SALES (est):** 5.8MM **Privately Held**
**SIC: 3612** 3634 3651 3699 Transformers, except electric; electric housewares & fans; household audio & video equipment; electrical equipment & supplies

**(G-9119)**
**NEWOVO PLASTICS LLC**
345 Willard Ave (60120-6810)
**PHONE**..................224 535-8183
Carl Dumele, *CEO*
**EMP:** 6
**SALES (est):** 441.8K **Privately Held**
**SIC: 3089** Injection molding of plastics

**(G-9120)**
**NEXT GEN MANUFACTURING INC**
1330 Crispin Dr Ste 205 (60123-5504)
**PHONE**..................847 289-8444
Carl Bonta, *President*
Kim Ponta, *Admin Sec*
**EMP:** 7 **EST:** 2012
**SQ FT:** 3,600
**SALES:** 560K **Privately Held**
**SIC: 2221** Textile warping, on a contract basis

**(G-9121)**
**NEXUS OFFICE SYSTEMS INC**
2250 Point Blvd Ste 125 (60123-7869)
**PHONE**..................847 836-1095
**Fax:** 847 836-1945
**EMP:** 12
**SALES (corp-wide):** 9.6MM **Privately Held**
**SIC: 3861** Mfg Photographic Equipment/Supplies
**PA:** Nexus Office Systems, Inc.
898 Featherstone Rd
Rockford IL 61107
815 227-0170

**(G-9122)**
**NGS PRINTING INC**
1400 Crispin Dr (60123-5533)
**PHONE**..................847 741-4411
**Fax:** 847 741-2728
Gerhard Landrowski, *President*
Mark Landrowski, *COO*
Kay Ramsey, *Office Mgr*
Erik Landrowski, *Admin Sec*
▲ **EMP:** 45 **EST:** 1957
**SQ FT:** 40,000
**SALES (est):** 9.9MM **Privately Held**
**WEB:** www.ngsprint.com
**SIC: 2759** Screen printing

**(G-9123)**
**NIDEC MOTOR CORPORATION**
Also Called: Elgin Engineering Center
1901 South St (60123-6939)
**PHONE**..................847 585-8430
Mark Fischer, *Research*
**EMP:** 415
**SALES (corp-wide):** 10B **Publicly Held**
**SIC: 3621** Rotors, for motors
**HQ:** Nidec Motor Corporation
8050 West Florissant Ave
Saint Louis MO 63136

**(G-9124)**
**NORTH AMERCN ACQUISITION CORP**
Also Called: Amtec Precision Products
1355 Holmes Rd (60123-1254)
**PHONE**..................847 695-8030
**Fax:** 847 622-4289
Church Russel, *CEO*
Vince Piunti, *Sales Staff*
**EMP:** 100
**SALES (corp-wide):** 39.6MM **Privately Held**
**SIC: 3451** Screw machine products
**HQ:** North American Acquisition Corporation
1875 Holmes Rd
Elgin IL 60123

**(G-9125)**
**NORTH AMERCN ACQUISITION CORP (HQ)**
Also Called: Amtec Precision Products
1875 Holmes Rd (60123-1298)
**PHONE**..................847 695-8030
Jaykar Krishnamurthy, *Ch of Bd*
Ganesh Subramanian, *President*
Kenneth Formanski, *Vice Pres*
Shawn Mock, *Opers Mgr*
Krishana Pati, *Controller*
▲ **EMP:** 126
**SQ FT:** 214,000
**SALES (est):** 39.6MM **Privately Held**
**SIC: 3714** 3089 3469 Transmission housings or parts, motor vehicle; fuel systems & parts, motor vehicle; motor vehicle transmissions, drive assemblies & parts; injection molding of plastics; machine parts, stamped or pressed metal
**PA:** Amtec Precision Products, Inc.
1875 Holmes Rd
Elgin IL 60123
847 695-8030

**(G-9126)**
**NORTHGATE TECHNOLOGIES INC**
1591 Scottsdale Ct (60123-9361)
**PHONE**..................847 608-8900
**Fax:** 847 608-9405
Robert Mantell, *President*
Patrick Treacy, *Materials Mgr*
Barbara Meissner, *Production*
Eric Andersen, *Engineer*
Daniel Washburn, *CFO*
**EMP:** 40
**SQ FT:** 19,000
**SALES (est):** 9.1MM
**SALES (corp-wide):** 3.4MM **Privately Held**
**WEB:** www.northgate-tech.com
**SIC: 3841** 5047 3845 Surgical & medical instruments; medical equipment & supplies; electromedical equipment
**PA:** Trudell Medical Limited
725 Third St
London ON N5V 5
519 455-7060

**(G-9127)**
**OERLIKON BLZERS CATING USA INC**
1181 Jansen Farm Ct (60123-2595)
**PHONE**..................847 695-5200
Jim Williams, *QC Dir*
Darin Swiger, *Manager*
**EMP:** 32
**SALES (corp-wide):** 2.3B **Privately Held**
**WEB:** www.balzers.com
**SIC: 3479** Coating of metals & formed products
**HQ:** Oerlikon Balzers Coating Usa Inc.
1475 E Wdfield Rd Ste 201
Schaumburg IL 60173
847 619-5541

**(G-9128)**
**OLYMPIC CONTROLS CORP**
Also Called: Amperite Co.
1250 Crispin Dr (60123-5531)
**PHONE**..................847 742-3566
Albano Andreini, *President*
David Armon, *Vice Pres*
Donald Dumper, *Vice Pres*
John Scandora, *Vice Pres*
Bill Perkis, *Plant Mgr*

▲ **EMP:** 30
**SQ FT:** 18,000
**SALES (est):** 6.1MM **Privately Held**
**WEB:** www.occorp.com
**SIC: 3625** 3677 Relays & industrial controls; control equipment, electric; coil windings, electronic

**(G-9129)**
**OMNI CONTAINMENT SYSTEMS LLC**
1501 Commerce Drive Elgin (60123)
P.O. Box 12, Algonquin (60102-0012)
**PHONE**..................847 468-1772
Skip Lewis, *Opers Staff*
Gary Weldon, *Manager*
Kevin Chwala,
Brian Chwala,
Christina Chwala,
▼ **EMP:** 6
**SQ FT:** 4,000
**SALES (est):** 615K **Privately Held**
**SIC: 3589** Commercial cooking & food-warming equipment

**(G-9130)**
**ORR MARKETING CORP**
Also Called: Great Holloween Stores
784 Scott Dr (60123-2640)
**PHONE**..................847 401-5171
Orrion Ferguson, *President*
**EMP:** 10
**SALES:** 400K **Privately Held**
**SIC: 8742** 2389 Marketing consulting services; costumes

**(G-9131)**
**ORSTROM WOODWORKING LTD**
1502 Sawgrass Ct (60123-6804)
**PHONE**..................847 697-1163
**EMP:** 3 **EST:** 1999
**SALES (est):** 170K **Privately Held**
**SIC: 2431** Mfg Millwork

**(G-9132)**
**OZINGA CONCRETE PRODUCTS INC**
2521 Tech Dr Ste 212 (60124)
**PHONE**..................847 426-0920
Marty Ozinga, *President*
Dave Lapoint, *Treasurer*
**EMP:** 50
**SQ FT:** 4,000
**SALES (est):** 5MM **Privately Held**
**SIC: 3272** Concrete products

**(G-9133)**
**PADDOCK PUBLICATIONS INC**
385 Airport Rd Ste A (60123-9341)
**PHONE**..................847 608-2700
**EMP:** 243
**SALES (corp-wide):** 122.6MM **Privately Held**
**SIC: 2711** Newspapers
**PA:** Paddock Publications, Inc.
155 E Algonquin Rd
Arlington Heights IL 60005
847 427-4300

**(G-9134)**
**PALAPA COATINGS INC**
325 Corporate Dr (60123-9373)
**PHONE**..................847 628-6360
**Fax:** 847 628-6354
Marco Alvarez, *President*
Kyle Hayes, *Admin Sec*
**EMP:** 8
**SALES (est):** 790K **Privately Held**
**SIC: 3999** Sprays, artificial & preserved

**(G-9135)**
**PARKER-HANNIFIN CORPORATION**
Also Called: Engineered Polymer Systems Div
2565 Northwest Pkwy (60124-7870)
**PHONE**..................847 836-6859
**Fax:** 847 783-4301
Harold McHenry, *Engineer*
Jennifer Battaglia, *Controller*
Dale Burnett, *Branch Mgr*
David Bills, *Manager*
**EMP:** 100

# Elgin - Kane County (G-9136)　　GEOGRAPHIC SECTION

**SALES (corp-wide):** 11.3B  **Publicly Held**
**WEB:** www.parker.com
**SIC:** 3087  Custom compound purchased resins
**PA:** Parker-Hannifin Corporation
　6035 Parkland Blvd
　Cleveland OH 44124
　216 896-3000

## (G-9136)
### PATRICK MANUFACTURING INC
667 N State St  (60123-2801)
**PHONE**...............................847 697-5920
**Fax:** 847 697-5987
Susan Mc Grail, *President*
Jeanette Mc Grail, *Corp Secy*
Patricia Lane, *Vice Pres*
Patty Lane, *Manager*
**EMP:** 20
**SQ FT:** 45,000
**SALES (est):** 5.6MM  **Privately Held**
**WEB:** www.patrickmfg.com
**SIC:** 3493  Steel springs, except wire

## (G-9137)
### PERFECT PIPE & SUPPLY CORP
440 S Mclean Blvd  (60123-7102)
**PHONE**...............................630 628-6728
Thomas Brown, *President*
Thomas Paszkiewicz, *President*
Gene Pogreba, *Project Mgr*
Michael Legittino, *Admin Sec*
▲ **EMP:** 5
**SQ FT:** 8,000
**SALES (est):** 885.3K  **Privately Held**
**SIC:** 3321  5074  Cast iron pipe & fittings; pipes & fittings, plastic

## (G-9138)
### PLASMATREAT USA INC (PA)
Also Called: Plasma Technology Systems
2541 Tech Dr Ste 407  (60124)
**PHONE**...............................847 783-0622
Andreas Stecher, *President*
Nick Rollick, *Vice Pres*
Jeff Leighty, *Sales Staff*
Gita Patel, *Administration*
**EMP:** 19 EST: 2006
**SALES:** 3.5MM  **Privately Held**
**SIC:** 3694  Automotive electrical equipment

## (G-9139)
### PLASTIC POWERDRIVE PDTS LLC
1589 Highpoint Dr  (60123-9303)
**PHONE**...............................847 637-5233
Billmeyer Bruce, *Manager*
**EMP:** 10
**SALES (est):** 1.8MM  **Privately Held**
**SIC:** 3089  Injection molding of plastics

## (G-9140)
### PLASTIC TECHNOLOGIES INC
1200 Abbott Dr  (60123-1825)
**PHONE**...............................847 841-8610
Arthur P Schueler Jr, *President*
Gary Kinberg, *Vice Pres*
Artie Schuler, *Office Mgr*
▲ **EMP:** 20
**SQ FT:** 13,600
**SALES (est):** 4MM  **Privately Held**
**WEB:** www.astrooptics.com
**SIC:** 3648  3465  Reflectors for lighting equipment: metal; automotive stampings

## (G-9141)
### PLASTICS
39w446 Capulet Cir  (60124)
**PHONE**...............................847 931-9391
Jennifer Schwab, *Principal*
**EMP:** 3
**SALES (est):** 218.5K  **Privately Held**
**SIC:** 3089  Molding primary plastic

## (G-9142)
### PLASTIVAL INC
Also Called: Re-Source Building Products
1685 Holmes Rd  (60123-5709)
**PHONE**...............................847 931-4771
Guy David, *President*
Lisa Webster, *Manager*
Jim Quinn, *Admin Sec*
**EMP:** 500

**SALES (est):** 2.8MM  **Privately Held**
**WEB:** www.plastival.com
**SIC:** 3089  Fences, gates & accessories: plastic
**PA:** Cyprium Investment Partners Llc
　200 Public Sq Ste 2020
　Cleveland OH 44114

## (G-9143)
### POLY COMPOUNDING LLC
1390 Gateway Dr Ste 6  (60124-7842)
**PHONE**...............................847 488-0683
**Fax:** 847 488-0687
Scott Crosby, *Mng Member*
John Wolfe,
▲ **EMP:** 9
**SQ FT:** 16,000
**SALES (est):** 1MM  **Privately Held**
**SIC:** 3087  Custom compound purchased resins

## (G-9144)
### POTHOLE PROS
3074 Chalkstone Ave  (60124-8939)
**PHONE**...............................847 815-5789
Andy Carter, *Principal*
**EMP:** 5
**SALES (est):** 435.1K  **Privately Held**
**SIC:** 2951  Asphalt & asphaltic paving mixtures (not from refineries)

## (G-9145)
### PPG INDUSTRIES INC
Also Called: PPG 5534
266 Kimball St  (60120-4202)
**PHONE**...............................847 742-3340
Jeff Molicm, *Branch Mgr*
**EMP:** 24
**SALES (corp-wide):** 14.7B  **Publicly Held**
**WEB:** www.ppg.com
**SIC:** 2851  Paints & allied products
**PA:** Ppg Industries, Inc.
　1 Ppg Pl
　Pittsburgh PA 15272
　412 434-3131

## (G-9146)
### PRECISION DORMER LLC
2511 Tech Dr Ste 113  (60124)
**PHONE**...............................800 877-3745
Frank Tao, *Managing Dir*
Franco Boeche, *Area Mgr*
Marco Schiavi, *Area Mgr*
Robert Carroll, *Purchasing*
Leonardo F Kuriyama, *Research*
◆ **EMP:** 173
**SALES (est):** 56.7MM
**SALES (corp-wide):** 8.8B  **Privately Held**
**SIC:** 3545  Drills (machine tool accessories); cutting tools for machine tools
**HQ:** Sandvik, Inc.
　17-02 Nevins Rd
　Fair Lawn NJ 07410
　201 794-5000

## (G-9147)
### PRICE CIRCUITS LLC
1300 Holmes Rd  (60123-1202)
**PHONE**...............................847 742-4700
Sheeba Job, *Finance Mgr*
Wayne Price,
Sibi Varghese,
**EMP:** 40
**SQ FT:** 22,000
**SALES (est):** 8.8MM  **Privately Held**
**SIC:** 3672  Printed circuit boards

## (G-9148)
### PRINTPACK INC
Flexible Packaging
1400 Abbott Dr  (60123-1882)
**PHONE**...............................847 888-7150
**Fax:** 847 888-5993
Karen O'Connor, *Purch Agent*
Keith Smith, *Engineer*
Thomas Maher, *Personnel*
John Rosauer, *Branch Mgr*
**EMP:** 160
**SALES (corp-wide):** 1.3B  **Privately Held**
**WEB:** www.printpack.com
**SIC:** 2673  3081  2671  Bags: plastic, laminated & coated; plastic film & sheet; packaging paper & plastics film, coated & laminated

**HQ:** Printpack, Inc.
　2800 Overlook Pkwy Ne
　Atlanta GA 30339
　404 460-7000

## (G-9149)
### PROFORMA-PPG INC
158 Dawson Dr  (60120-6409)
**PHONE**...............................847 429-9349
Katherine Labbe, *President*
**EMP:** 4
**SALES (est):** 360K  **Privately Held**
**SIC:** 2754  Business form & card printing, gravure

## (G-9150)
### PROGRESSIVE PUBLICATIONS INC
Also Called: Coupon Magazine
85 Market St Ste 105  (60123-5083)
**PHONE**...............................847 697-9181
David W Schmidt, *President*
Kimberly E Schmidt, *Treasurer*
**EMP:** 4
**SQ FT:** 800
**SALES (est):** 418.2K  **Privately Held**
**SIC:** 2721  Magazines: publishing only, not printed on site

## (G-9151)
### PROQUIS INC
423 Walnut Ave  (60123-7513)
**PHONE**...............................847 278-3230
David Best, *CEO*
William P Best, *President*
Gil Hersh, *Vice Pres*
**EMP:** 11
**SQ FT:** 3,200
**SALES:** 1.8MM  **Privately Held**
**WEB:** www.proquis.com
**SIC:** 7372  7371  7373  8243  Prepackaged software; computer software development & applications; systems software development services; software training, computer; general management consultant

## (G-9152)
### PROTON MULTIMEDIA INC
Also Called: Kult of Athena
1485 Davis Rd Ste A  (60123-1351)
**PHONE**...............................847 531-8664
Ryan Whittlinger, *President*
▲ **EMP:** 3
**SQ FT:** 23,000
**SALES (est):** 700K  **Privately Held**
**SIC:** 3423  Hammers (hand tools)

## (G-9153)
### PULL X MACHINES INC 933
782 Church Rd  (60123-9306)
**PHONE**...............................847 952-9977
Debra Kimberlin, *Vice Pres*
Linda Serino, *Office Mgr*
**EMP:** 3
**SALES (est):** 266.7K  **Privately Held**
**SIC:** 3599  Industrial machinery

## (G-9154)
### PUSKAR PRECISION MACHINING CO
1610 Cambridge Dr  (60123-1143)
**PHONE**...............................847 888-2929
**Fax:** 847 888-2969
Asim Puskar, *President*
Fuad Puskar, *Vice Pres*
Evan Browne, *Director*
**EMP:** 15  EST: 1973
**SQ FT:** 24,000
**SALES (est):** 3MM  **Privately Held**
**SIC:** 3599  Machine shop, jobbing & repair

## (G-9155)
### QUAD-ILLINOIS INC (PA)
Also Called: Shamrock Specialty Packaging
2760 Spectrum Dr  (60124-7841)
**PHONE**...............................847 836-1115
**Fax:** 847 836-5511
James M Owens, *President*
Judi Childress, *Controller*
Fred Sturgeon, *Manager*
**EMP:** 15
**SALES (est):** 21.4MM  **Privately Held**
**SIC:** 5113  3999  5084  4789  Shipping supplies; barber & beauty shop equipment; packaging machinery & equipment; cargo loading & unloading services

## (G-9156)
### QUALITY DIE CASTING CO
1760 Britannia Dr Ste 5  (60124-7814)
**PHONE**...............................847 214-8840
Pamela Cavka, *Owner*
Mirsa Talic, *Vice Pres*
**EMP:** 14
**SQ FT:** 12,100
**SALES (est):** 2.2MM  **Privately Held**
**SIC:** 3364  Zinc & zinc-base alloy die-castings

## (G-9157)
### QUALITY FASTENER PRODUCTS INC
1430 Davis Rd  (60123-1322)
**PHONE**...............................224 330-3162
**EMP:** 2  EST: 2011
**SALES (est):** 242.5K  **Privately Held**
**SIC:** 3559  Special industry machinery

## (G-9158)
### QUALITY TECHNOLOGY INTL INC
Also Called: Qti
1707 N Randall Rd Ste 300  (60123-9412)
**PHONE**...............................847 649-9300
**Fax:** 847 649-9309
Dan Hammes, *President*
Troy Lohrmann, *Vice Pres*
David Gilligan, *Opers Staff*
Steve Joloy, *CFO*
Lawrence Hong, *Treasurer*
◆ **EMP:** 20
**SQ FT:** 4,000
**SALES (est):** 3MM
**SALES (corp-wide):** 42.5B  **Privately Held**
**WEB:** www.qtitech.com
**SIC:** 3999  Seeds, coated or treated, from purchased seeds
**HQ:** Itochu International Inc.
　1251 Avenue Of The Americ
　New York NY 10020
　212 818-8000

## (G-9159)
### QUESTEK MANUFACTURING CORP
2570 Technology Dr  (60124-7884)
**PHONE**...............................847 428-0300
**Fax:** 847 428-7530
Dale R Krueger, *President*
Rick Anderson, *Plant Mgr*
▲ **EMP:** 70
**SQ FT:** 60,000
**SALES (est):** 12.8MM  **Privately Held**
**WEB:** www.questekmex.com
**SIC:** 3625  3644  Electric controls & control accessories, industrial; noncurrent-carrying wiring services

## (G-9160)
### R M TOOL & MANUFACTURING CO
368 Bluff City Blvd Ste 6  (60120-8398)
**PHONE**...............................847 888-0433
**Fax:** 847 888-3229
Russell Mueller, *President*
Fred Mueller, *Corp Secy*
Paul Mueller, *Vice Pres*
**EMP:** 6
**SQ FT:** 3,600
**SALES (est):** 300K  **Privately Held**
**WEB:** www.millanyangle.com
**SIC:** 3599  3312  3544  Machine shop, jobbing & repair; tool & die steel & alloys; special dies, tools, jigs & fixtures

## (G-9161)
### RAYS ELECTRICAL SERVICE LLC
37w904 Us Highway 20  (60124-8125)
**PHONE**...............................847 214-2944
Lisa Sakolari, *Office Mgr*
Ray Sakolari,
**EMP:** 15
**SALES (est):** 1.5MM  **Privately Held**
**SIC:** 1731  1381  7389  Electrical work; directional drilling oil & gas wells;

## (G-9162)
### REGAL STEEL ERECTORS LLC
850 Tollgate Rd  (60123-9300)
**PHONE**...............................847 888-3500

# GEOGRAPHIC SECTION

Michael Bates, *Mng Member*
Brian Bates,
**EMP:** 40
**SALES:** 7MM **Privately Held**
**SIC:** 1791 7692 Structural steel erection; welding repair

**(G-9163)**
### REID COMMUNICATIONS INC
Also Called: Green Book Lenders Guide, The
450 Shepard Dr Ste 11 (60123-7033)
P.O. Box 5000 (60121-5000)
**PHONE** ............................ 847 741-9700
**Fax:** 847 741-9792
David Sears, *President*
Paul Sears, *CFO*
**EMP:** 24
**SALES (est):** 3.4MM **Privately Held**
**WEB:** www.reidcomm.com
**SIC:** 2759 2741 Publication printing; miscellaneous publishing

**(G-9164)**
### RELIANCE TOOL & MFG CO (PA)
Also Called: Rtm Trend
900 N State St Ste 101 (60123-2106)
**PHONE** ............................ 847 695-1235
**Fax:** 847 695-0931
Paul Knowlton, *President*
Ray Salazar, *Purch Agent*
Eric Fritz, *Engineer*
Richard A Roberts, *Director*
**EMP:** 45 **EST:** 1947
**SQ FT:** 27,000
**SALES (est):** 24.1MM **Privately Held**
**WEB:** www.reliancetool.com
**SIC:** 3541 3469 Machine tools, metal cutting type; stamping metal for the trade

**(G-9165)**
### RIEKE OFFICE INTERIORS INC (PA)
Also Called: R O I
2000 Fox Ln (60123-7814)
**PHONE** ............................ 847 622-9711
**Fax:** 847 622-9750
Todd L Rieke, *CEO*
Christopher Matus, *President*
Carol Nelson, *Vice Pres*
Libby Rieke, *Vice Pres*
Lauren Colwell, *Project Mgr*
**EMP:** 51
**SQ FT:** 80,000
**SALES (est):** 13.1MM **Privately Held**
**WEB:** www.rieke.com
**SIC:** 2521 5932 Wood office furniture; office furniture, secondhand; store fixtures & equipment, secondhand

**(G-9166)**
### ROHM AND HAAS COMPANY
2531 Tech Dr Ste 301 (60124)
**PHONE** ............................ 847 426-3245
Firdosi Ansar, *Manager*
**EMP:** 110
**SALES (corp-wide):** 48.1B **Publicly Held**
**SIC:** 2821 Plastics materials & resins
**HQ:** Rohm And Haas Company
100 N Independence Mall W
Philadelphia PA 19106
215 592-3000

**(G-9167)**
### ROSELYNN FASHIONS
900 Elizabeth St (60120-8418)
**PHONE** ............................ 847 741-6000
**Fax:** 847 741-6000
Roselynn Spak, *Owner*
Sam Mancini, *Co-Owner*
**EMP:** 6
**SALES:** 300K **Privately Held**
**WEB:** www.roselynnfashions.com
**SIC:** 2396 5941 5091 2395 Screen printing on fabric articles; sporting goods & bicycle shops; sporting & recreation goods; pleating & stitching

**(G-9168)**
### RPS ENGINEERING INC
1300 Crispin Dr (60123-5532)
P.O. Box 5186 (60121-5186)
**PHONE** ............................ 847 931-1950
**Fax:** 847 931-4274
Richard Stanis, *President*
Tom Clough, *Controller*
Steven Kelly, *Manager*
▲ **EMP:** 18
**SQ FT:** 40,000
**SALES (est):** 6.4MM **Privately Held**
**SIC:** 3444 3535 Siding, sheet metal; conveyors & conveying equipment

**(G-9169)**
### RR DONNELLEY & SONS COMPANY
Also Called: R R Donnelley
168 E Highland Ave Ste 2 (60120-5564)
**PHONE** ............................ 847 622-1026
**Fax:** 847 931-5409
Reganald Farmer, *Purchasing*
Tony Myrie, *Manager*
John Smith, *IT Specialist*
**EMP:** 45
**SALES (corp-wide):** 6.9B **Publicly Held**
**WEB:** www.rrdonnelley.com
**SIC:** 2754 2759 Commercial printing, gravure; commercial printing
**PA:** R. R. Donnelley & Sons Company
35 W Wacker Dr Ste 3650
Chicago IL 60601
312 326-8000

**(G-9170)**
### S & S WELDING & FABRICATION
31w377 Spaulding Rd (60120-7577)
**PHONE** ............................ 847 742-7344
**Fax:** 847 742-0102
Henry Eolz, *President*
Karl Schoder, *General Mgr*
**EMP:** 4
**SQ FT:** 12,000
**SALES (est):** 235K **Privately Held**
**WEB:** www.slswelding.com
**SIC:** 7692 3441 3444 Welding repair; fabricated structural metal; sheet metalwork

**(G-9171)**
### SAFE WATER TECHNOLOGIES INC
996 Bluff City Blvd (60120-7594)
**PHONE** ............................ 847 888-6900
Brett Oleskow, *President*
▲ **EMP:** 8
**SQ FT:** 10,000
**SALES (est):** 1.6MM **Privately Held**
**WEB:** www.swtwater.com
**SIC:** 3589 Water treatment equipment, industrial

**(G-9172)**
### SCHWANOG LLC
1630 Todd Farm Dr (60123-1145)
**PHONE** ............................ 847 289-1055
Richard Bishop, *Sales Engr*
Holger Johannsen, *Manager*
Clemens Guentert,
**EMP:** 1
**SALES (est):** 226.6K **Privately Held**
**SIC:** 2819 Carbides

**(G-9173)**
### SEALCO INDUSTRIES INC (PA)
Also Called: Cap & Seal Company
1591 Fleetwood Dr (60123-7126)
**PHONE** ............................ 847 741-3101
**Fax:** 847 741-0254
Thomas J Brown, *President*
Gary Mayberry, *VP Mfg*
Paul Kurpier, *Controller*
Wendy Schnegelsberg, *Human Resources*
Andrew Knox, *Office Mgr*
▲ **EMP:** 27
**SQ FT:** 34,000
**SALES (est):** 3.8MM **Privately Held**
**SIC:** 3469 Metal stampings

**(G-9174)**
### SEIGLES CABINET CENTER LLC (PA)
1331 Davis Rd (60123-1319)
**PHONE** ............................ 224 535-7034
**Fax:** 847 697-6521
Sally Gange, *Marketing Staff*
Mark S Seigle,
**EMP:** 4 **EST:** 2011
**SALES (est):** 682.5K **Privately Held**
**SIC:** 2434 Wood kitchen cabinets; vanities, bathroom: wood

**(G-9175)**
### SELLSTROM MANUFACTURING CO (DH)
Also Called: Sellstrom Safeguards
300 Coporate Dr (60123)
P.O. Box 355, Palatine (60078-0355)
**PHONE** ............................ 800 323-7402
**Fax:** 847 358-8564
Barbara M Sellstrom, *Ch of Bd*
Chris Baby, *President*
David Peters, *President*
Rusty Franklin, *Vice Pres*
Lawrence P Schmidt, *Treasurer*
▲ **EMP:** 80 **EST:** 1923
**SQ FT:** 96,000
**SALES:** 14.1MM
**SALES (corp-wide):** 3.2MM **Privately Held**
**WEB:** www.sellstrom.com
**SIC:** 3842 Personal safety equipment
**HQ:** Jet Equipment & Tools Ltd
49 Schooner St
Coquitlam BC V3K 0
604 523-8665

**(G-9176)**
### SET SCREW & MFG CO
1210 Saint Charles St (60120-8445)
**PHONE** ............................ 847 717-3700
**Fax:** 847 717-3710
James A Brown, *President*
Dale Engelking, *VP Opers*
Frank Duffy, *Sales Staff*
Michelle Leonard, *Sales Staff*
Marge Brown, *Manager*
▲ **EMP:** 23
**SQ FT:** 25,000
**SALES (est):** 4.8MM **Privately Held**
**WEB:** www.setfast.net
**SIC:** 3452 5085 Bolts, nuts, rivets & washers; fasteners, industrial: nuts, bolts, screws, etc.
**PA:** Mabjab Holdings Inc
1210 Saint Charles St
Elgin IL

**(G-9177)**
### SIEMENS INDUSTRY INC
Also Called: Flender
1401 Madeline Ln (60124-7949)
**PHONE** ............................ 847 931-1990
**Fax:** 847 931-0711
Leen Dijk, *Business Mgr*
Reggie Reid, *Mfg Mgr*
Mark Taylor, *Purchasing*
Dana Webb, *QC Mgr*
Michael Gagliano, *Engineer*
**EMP:** 65
**SALES (corp-wide):** 89.6B **Privately Held**
**WEB:** www.sea.siemens.com
**SIC:** 3566 Speed changers, drives & gears
**HQ:** Siemens Industry, Inc.
1000 Deerfield Pkwy
Buffalo Grove IL 60089
847 215-1000

**(G-9178)**
### SIGMATRON INTERNATIONAL INC
Also Called: Spitfire Controls
1901 South St (60123-6939)
**PHONE** ............................ 847 586-5200
**EMP:** 6 **Publicly Held**
**SIC:** 3672 3677 3679 3549 Printed circuit boards; electronic coils, transformers & other inductors; electronic circuits; assembly machines, including robotic; engine electrical test equipment
**PA:** Sigmatron International, Inc.
2201 Landmeier Rd
Elk Grove Village IL 60007

**(G-9179)**
### SIGNS IN DUNDEE INC
Also Called: Signs By Tomorrow
1028 Dundee Ave (60120-2447)
**PHONE** ............................ 847 742-9530
**Fax:** 847 742-9579
John Pendexter, *President*
**EMP:** 4
**SALES (est):** 270K **Privately Held**
**SIC:** 3993 2396 2752 2759 Signs & advertising specialties; fabric printing & stamping; poster & decal printing, lithographic; poster & decal printing & engraving

**(G-9180)**
### SIKORA PRECISION INC
140 Will Scarlett Ln (60120-9524)
**PHONE** ............................ 847 468-0900
Kurt Sikora, *President*
Margaret Sikora, *Admin Sec*
**EMP:** 4
**SQ FT:** 1,200
**SALES (est):** 175K **Privately Held**
**SIC:** 3089 3599 Injection molding of plastics; machine shop, jobbing & repair

**(G-9181)**
### SIMPLOMATIC MANUFACTURING CO
1616 Berkley St Ste 100 (60123-7083)
**PHONE** ............................ 773 342-7757
**Fax:** 773 342-8329
David Hahn, *President*
Valerie Crazybear, *Accountant*
Tom Voller, *Manager*
Joanne Cipolla, *Shareholder*
Patricia Voller, *Admin Sec*
**EMP:** 30
**SQ FT:** 25,000
**SALES (est):** 6.9MM **Privately Held**
**WEB:** www.simplomatic.com
**SIC:** 3469 3089 Metal stampings; plastic processing

**(G-9182)**
### SIMPSON ELECTRIC COMPANY
853 Dundee Ave (60123-3036)
P.O. Box 99, Lac Du Flambeau WI (54538-0099)
**PHONE** ............................ 847 697-2260
**Fax:** 847 697-1389
Robert Study, *Research*
Cyndy Towalski, *Marketing Mgr*
Art Leppi, *Manager*
**EMP:** 25
**SALES (corp-wide):** 154.9MM **Privately Held**
**SIC:** 3663 3829 3825 Radio & TV communications equipment; measuring & controlling devices; instruments to measure electricity
**HQ:** Simpson Electric Company
520 Simpson Ave
Lac Du Flambeau WI 54538
715 588-3947

**(G-9183)**
### SIMS FAMILY HOLDINGS LLC (PA)
Also Called: PPG
1111 Bowes Rd (60123-5541)
**PHONE** ............................ 847 488-1230
Kevin K Sims,
Charles W Mory,
Richard M Sims,
**EMP:** 84
**SQ FT:** 150,000
**SALES (est):** 60.7MM **Privately Held**
**WEB:** www.provenpartnersgroup.com
**SIC:** 2099 Food preparations

**(G-9184)**
### SKF USA INC
Also Called: SKF Arspace Sling Slutions Div
900 N State St (60123-2104)
**PHONE** ............................ 847 742-0700
Sunil Chrungu, *General Mgr*
Bert Nyenhuis, *General Mgr*
Darin Samuel, *General Mgr*
Carl Orstadius, *Managing Dir*
Bryan Uncapher, *Business Mgr*
**EMP:** 88
**SALES (corp-wide):** 546.3MM **Privately Held**
**WEB:** www.skfusa.com
**SIC:** 3053 Gaskets, packing & sealing devices
**HQ:** Skf Usa Inc.
890 Forty Foot Rd
Lansdale PA 19446
267 436-6000

**(G-9185)**
### SKF USA INC
Also Called: SKF Automotive Division
890 N State St Ste 200 (60123-2177)
**PHONE** ............................ 847 742-0700
Krister Peil, *Vice Pres*
Chuck Thomas, *Buyer*

## Elgin - Kane County (G-9186)

Mike Macgrath, *Manager*
**EMP:** 61
**SALES (corp-wide):** 546.3MM **Privately Held**
**WEB:** www.skfusa.com
**SIC:** 3562 3053 Ball & roller bearings; gaskets, packing & sealing devices
**HQ:** Skf Usa Inc.
890 Forty Foot Rd
Lansdale PA 19446
267 436-6000

### (G-9186)
### SKF USA INC
SKF Sealing Solutions Division
900 N State St (60123-2104)
**PHONE** ................................ 847 742-0700
Linas Maskaliunas, *Engineer*
Matthew Milani, *Engineer*
Rob Pecak, *Engineer*
Udell So, *Electrical Engi*
Andrew Yarrow, *Controller*
**EMP:** 61
**SALES (corp-wide):** 546.3MM **Privately Held**
**WEB:** www.skfusa.com
**SIC:** 3562 3053 3829 3714 Ball & roller bearings; ball bearings & parts; roller bearings & parts; gaskets & sealing devices; oil seals, rubber; vibration meters, analyzers & calibrators; motor vehicle parts & accessories; power transmission equipment
**HQ:** Skf Usa Inc.
890 Forty Foot Rd
Lansdale PA 19446
267 436-6000

### (G-9187)
### SKIMAN SALES INC
850 Villa St (60120-8073)
**PHONE** ................................ 847 888-8200
Dee Pizer, *CEO*
**EMP:** 2
**SALES (est):** 750K **Privately Held**
**SIC:** 2451 Mobile homes, personal or private use

### (G-9188)
### SLIPMATE CO
1693 Todd Farm Dr (60123-1146)
**PHONE** ................................ 847 289-9200
**Fax:** 847 289-1818
Steve Matecki, *CEO*
John S Matecki, *Ch of Bd*
Randy Matecki, *President*
Mark Matecki, *Vice Pres*
Katrina Jones, *Manager*
**EMP:** 30
**SQ FT:** 32,000
**SALES (est):** 4.3MM **Privately Held**
**WEB:** www.slipmate.com
**SIC:** 3479 Coating of metals & formed products

### (G-9189)
### SOUTHERN GRAPHIC SYSTEMS LLC
150 Corporate Dr (60123-9354)
**PHONE** ................................ 847 695-9515
**Fax:** 847 695-9872
Joe O'Connor, *President*
Pat Ryan, *General Mgr*
Dan Kyle, *Plant Mgr*
Raymond Lebrun, *Plant Mgr*
Travis Tolzien, *Project Mgr*
**EMP:** 30
**SALES (corp-wide):** 303.8MM **Privately Held**
**SIC:** 2796 Platemaking services
**HQ:** Southern Graphic Systems, Llc
626 W Main St Ste 500
Louisville KY 40202
502 637-5443

### (G-9190)
### SPINTEX INC
1331 Gateway Dr (60124-7866)
**PHONE** ................................ 847 608-5411
**Fax:** 847 608-5417
Ken Katayama, *President*
Marie Katayama, *Corp Secy*
▲ **EMP:** 9
**SQ FT:** 23,000
**SALES (est):** 1.8MM **Privately Held**
**WEB:** www.spintex.com
**SIC:** 3089 Injection molding of plastics

### (G-9191)
### STANDARD REGISTER INC
2768 Spectrum Dr (60124-7841)
**PHONE** ................................ 847 783-1040
Jim Stewart, *Branch Mgr*
Mike Jackson, *Branch Mgr*
**EMP:** 27
**SALES (corp-wide):** 4.5B **Privately Held**
**SIC:** 2759 Commercial printing
**HQ:** Standard Register, Inc.
600 Albany St
Dayton OH 45417
937 221-1000

### (G-9192)
### STARRO PRECISION PRODUCTS INC
1730 Todd Farm Dr (60123-1142)
**PHONE** ................................ 847 741-9400
Bruce Stark Jr, *President*
Mircea Diaconescu, *Electrical Engi*
**EMP:** 50
**SQ FT:** 37,000
**SALES (est):** 7.1MM **Privately Held**
**SIC:** 3451 Screw machine products

### (G-9193)
### STELFAST INC
2780 Spectrum Dr (60124-7841)
**PHONE** ................................ 847 783-0161
David Gawlik, *Branch Mgr*
**EMP:** 17
**SALES (corp-wide):** 22.1MM **Privately Held**
**SIC:** 3452 Bolts, nuts, rivets & washers
**PA:** Stelfast Inc
22979 Stelfast Pkwy
Strongsville OH 44149
440 879-0077

### (G-9194)
### SUBURBAN PLASTICS CO (PA)
340 Renner Dr (60123-6999)
**PHONE** ................................ 847 741-4900
**Fax:** 847 741-0094
Stuart Baxter, *President*
Jeremy Baxter, *Vice Pres*
Keith Kazmer, *Plant Mgr*
N Olofson, *Plant Mgr*
Steven Akiyama, *Draft/Design*
▲ **EMP:** 325 **EST:** 1946
**SQ FT:** 125,000
**SALES (est):** 95MM **Privately Held**
**WEB:** www.suburbanplastics.com
**SIC:** 3089 Injection molding of plastics

### (G-9195)
### SULLIVAN TOOL AND REPAIR INC
370 Brook St Unit 3 (60120-4153)
**PHONE** ................................ 224 856-5867
John P Sullivan, *President*
**EMP:** 1
**SALES (est):** 294.3K **Privately Held**
**SIC:** 3089 Injection molding of plastics

### (G-9196)
### SUNBURST SHUTTERS ILLINOIS
700 Church Rd (60123-9306)
**PHONE** ................................ 847 697-4000
**Fax:** 847 697-4178
Mathew Thelander, *President*
Matthew Thelander, *President*
Dix Jarman, *Admin Sec*
**EMP:** 15
**SQ FT:** 6,000
**SALES (est):** 1.7MM **Privately Held**
**SIC:** 2431 Window shutters, wood

### (G-9197)
### SUNBURST TECHNOLOGY CORP (HQ)
1550 Executive Dr (60123-9311)
**PHONE** ................................ 800 321-7511
Conall Ryan, *President*
Mark Sotir, *Chairman*
Jenna Bogard, *Engineer*
Steve Klein, *Controller*
Sharry Bekielewski, *Accounting Mgr*
**EMP:** 9

**SALES (est):** 2.9MM **Privately Held**
**SIC:** 7372 7822 3944 Educational computer software; video tapes, recorded: wholesale; games, toys & children's vehicles

### (G-9198)
### SUNSTAR PHARMACEUTICAL INC
1300 Abbott Dr (60123-1821)
**PHONE** ................................ 773 777-4000
Richard McMan, *Ch of Bd*
Tom Studeny, *Controller*
Akane Takemura, *Senior Mgr*
Janet Simpson, *Retailers*
▲ **EMP:** 90
**SALES (est):** 15.1MM
**SALES (corp-wide):** 557MM **Privately Held**
**SIC:** 2834 2844 7389 Tablets, pharmaceutical; vitamin preparations; toothpastes or powders, dentifrices; packaging & labeling services
**HQ:** Sunstar Americas, Inc.
301 E Central Rd
Schaumburg IL 60195
773 777-4000

### (G-9199)
### SUZLON WIND ENERGY CORPORATION
Suzlon Wind Trbine Trining Ctr
2583 Technology Dr (60124-7832)
**PHONE** ................................ 773 328-5077
Charles Clayton, *President*
**EMP:** 9 **Privately Held**
**SIC:** 3511 Turbines & turbine generator sets
**HQ:** Suzlon Wind Energy Corporation
8750 W Bryn Mawr Ave # 300
Chicago IL 60631
773 328-5077

### (G-9200)
### T C I VACUUM FORMING COMPANY
1620 Cambridge Dr (60123-1143)
**PHONE** ................................ 847 622-9100
**Fax:** 847 922-9022
John Vinka, *President*
Don Swiat, *General Mgr*
Maynard Ostrowski, *Vice Pres*
Bob Neuzil, *Plant Mgr*
Joann Spellman, *Office Mgr*
**EMP:** 50 **EST:** 1989
**SQ FT:** 40,000
**SALES (est):** 8.1MM **Privately Held**
**SIC:** 3089 Plastic processing

### (G-9201)
### T P I INC
1172 Price Dr (60120-4656)
**PHONE** ................................ 847 888-0232
Lana Seyller, *President*
Dennis Seyller, *Corp Secy*
**EMP:** 6
**SQ FT:** 14,000
**SALES (est):** 550K **Privately Held**
**SIC:** 2491 Wood preserving

### (G-9202)
### TAYKIT INC
Also Called: Creekside Printing
1175 Davis Rd (60123-1315)
**PHONE** ................................ 847 888-1150
**Fax:** 847 888-1190
Steven Kittay, *President*
Don Anderson, *Accounts Exec*
**EMP:** 35
**SQ FT:** 22,000
**SALES (est):** 6MM **Privately Held**
**WEB:** www.creeksideprinting.com
**SIC:** 2752 Commercial printing, offset

### (G-9203)
### TECH GLOBAL INC
2759 Pinnacle Dr (60124-7943)
**PHONE** ................................ 847 532-4882
James Rocheford, *President*
Gina Wojcik, *Project Mgr*
Diane Lewis, *Purch Mgr*
Kristin Cuellar, *Manager*
▲ **EMP:** 16
**SQ FT:** 11,000

**SALES (est):** 3.9MM **Privately Held**
**WEB:** techglobal.com
**SIC:** 3577 Computer peripheral equipment

### (G-9204)
### TECH GLOBAL INC
2521 Tech Dr Ste 206 (60124)
**PHONE** ................................ 224 623-2000
James Rocheford, *CEO*
**EMP:** 1
**SALES:** 1,000K **Privately Held**
**SIC:** 3571 Electronic computers

### (G-9205)
### TEK-CAST INC
195 Corporate Dr (60123-9355)
**PHONE** ................................ 630 422-1458
John Cahill, *President*
Aiden Walsh, *President*
Simon Newman, *Principal*
Maureen Cahill, *Admin Sec*
▲ **EMP:** 60
**SQ FT:** 10,000
**SALES (est):** 12.1MM **Privately Held**
**SIC:** 3363 Aluminum die-castings

### (G-9206)
### TELEDYNE LECROY INC
2111 Big Timber Rd Ste A (60123-1123)
**PHONE** ................................ 847 888-0450
Jim Kimnetz, *CFO*
**EMP:** 27
**SALES (corp-wide):** 2.1B **Publicly Held**
**SIC:** 3825 3829 3621 3577 Test equipment for electronic & electrical circuits; measuring & controlling devices; motors & generators; computer peripheral equipment; computer terminals
**HQ:** Teledyne Lecroy, Inc.
700 Chestnut Ridge Rd
Chestnut Ridge NY 10977
845 425-2000

### (G-9207)
### TEMP EXCEL PROPERTIES LLC
2520 Vantage Dr (60124-7881)
**PHONE** ................................ 847 844-3845
Rick Powell, *Manager*
**EMP:** 5
**SALES (corp-wide):** 102.6MM **Privately Held**
**WEB:** www.excelsior-hvac.com
**SIC:** 5075 3444 Warm air heating equipment & supplies; air conditioning & ventilation equipment & supplies; furnace casings, sheet metal
**HQ:** Temp Excel Properties, Llc
17725 Volbrecht Rd Ste 1
Lansing IL 60438

### (G-9208)
### TEMP-AIR INC
Temp Heat Division
39 W 107 Highland Ave (60123)
**PHONE** ................................ 847 931-7700
**Fax:** 847 931-7704
Beth Shelby, *Manager*
**EMP:** 10
**SQ FT:** 12,000
**SALES (corp-wide):** 44.9MM **Privately Held**
**SIC:** 3585 Refrigeration & heating equipment
**PA:** Temp-Air, Inc.
3700 W Preserve Blvd
Burnsville MN 55337
800 836-7432

### (G-9209)
### TEMPERATURE EQUIPMENT CORP
Also Called: A Division of TEC
1313 Timber Dr (60123-1826)
**PHONE** ................................ 847 429-0818
**EMP:** 8
**SALES (corp-wide):** 116.5MM **Privately Held**
**SIC:** 3822 Mfg Environmental Controls
**HQ:** Temperature Equipment Corporation
17725 Volbrecht Rd Ste 1
Lansing IL 60438
708 418-0900

# GEOGRAPHIC SECTION
Elgin - Kane County (G-9230)

**(G-9210)**
**TERRI LYNN INC (PA)**
1450 Bowes Rd (60123-5539)
P.O. Box 5118 (60121-5118)
PHONE.....................847 741-1900
Fax: 847 741-1912
Terri L Schuck, *President*
Mark E Graziano, *Corp Secy*
Charles J Graziano, *Vice Pres*
Joseph Graziano, *Purch Agent*
Randy Grazzannio, *Executive*
▼ EMP: 130
SQ FT: 108,000
SALES (est): 44.1MM **Privately Held**
WEB: www.terrilynn.com
SIC: **2068** 2064 2034 Salted & roasted nuts & seeds; candy & other confectionery products; dried & dehydrated fruits

**(G-9211)**
**THOMAS RESEARCH PRODUCTS LLC**
Also Called: Trp
1215 Bowes Rd Ste 1225 (60123-5542)
PHONE......................224 654-8626
Glenn Garbowicz, *CEO*
Warren Hecht, *President*
John Lacorte, *Natl Sales Mgr*
Brian Johnson, *Regl Sales Mgr*
Michael Wypasek, *Corp Comm Staff*
▲ EMP: 15
SQ FT: 4,000
SALES (est): 1.5MM
SALES (corp-wide): 3.5B **Publicly Held**
SIC: **3612** Power & distribution transformers
HQ: Varon Lighting Group, Llc
765 S Il Route 83
Elmhurst IL 60126
630 279-9800

**(G-9212)**
**TOOLING SOLUTIONS INC**
1515 Commerce Dr (60123-9304)
PHONE......................847 472-9940
Fax: 847 472-9941
Glenn Burchette, *President*
Amy Burchette, *Vice Pres*
Greg Lesiak, *Technology*
EMP: 5
SQ FT: 3,000
SALES (est): 670K **Privately Held**
WEB: www.toolingsolutions.com
SIC: **3541** Machine tools, metal cutting type

**(G-9213)**
**TRI-DIM FILTER CORPORATION**
Also Called: I D T
999 Raymond St (60120-8364)
PHONE......................847 695-5822
Margertt Bingman, *Plant Mgr*
Adam Adams, *Purchasing*
Margaret Bingman, *Branch Mgr*
Eli Miles, *Supervisor*
EMP: 35
SALES (corp-wide): 137.7MM **Privately Held**
WEB: www.tridim.com
SIC: **3569** 3564 Filters, general line: industrial; blowers & fans
PA: Tri-Dim Filter Corporation
93 Industrial Dr
Louisa VA 23093
540 967-2600

**(G-9214)**
**TRICOR SYSTEMS INC**
1650 Todd Farm Dr (60123-1145)
PHONE......................847 742-5542
Fax: 847 742-5574
Tim Allen, *President*
Keith Jereb, *Vice Pres*
Phillip Mustes, *Controller*
Tom Allen, *VP Mktg*
EMP: 35
SQ FT: 24,000
SALES: 12.4MM **Privately Held**
WEB: www.tricor-systems.com
SIC: **3829** 3823 3699 8731 Measuring & controlling devices; industrial instrmnts msrmnt display/control process variable; electronic training devices; flight simulators (training aids), electronic; commercial research laboratory

**(G-9215)**
**TRITECH INTERNATIONAL LLC**
1710 Todd Farm Dr (60123-1142)
PHONE......................847 888-0333
Fax: 847 888-3015
Tom Hibsch, *Mfg Mgr*
Kazuyuki Toriyama,
▲ EMP: 8
SQ FT: 10,000
SALES (est): 1.4MM **Privately Held**
WEB: www.tritechinternational.com
SIC: **3312** 5084 Tool & die steel & alloys; tool & die makers' equipment

**(G-9216)**
**TRIUMPH TRUSS & STEEL COMPANY**
1250 Larkin Ave Ste 200 (60123-6078)
PHONE......................815 522-6000
David Watts, *Mng Member*
EMP: 10
SALES (corp-wide): 6.5MM **Privately Held**
SIC: **2439** Trusses, wooden roof
PA: Triumph Truss & Steel Company
11804 S Il Route 47
Huntley IL 60142
847 669-8200

**(G-9217)**
**TUBE & PIPE ASSOCIATION INTL**
Also Called: Fabricators and Mfrs Assn
2135 Point Blvd (60123-7956)
PHONE......................815 399-8700
Fax: 815 399-7279
Jerry Shankel, *President*
Jim Rura, *Plant Mgr*
Rick Strapple, *VP Sales*
Jim Gorzek, *Sales Executive*
Scott Stevens, *Mktg Dir*
EMP: 75
SALES (est): 3.9MM **Privately Held**
SIC: **8611** 2721 Business associations; periodicals

**(G-9218)**
**TYSON FRESH MEATS INC**
2170 Point Blvd Ste 300 (60123-7875)
PHONE......................847 836-5550
Brad Bodine, *Manager*
EMP: 17
SALES (corp-wide): 36.8B **Publicly Held**
SIC: **2011** 2013 3111 4213 Meat packing plants; boxed beef from meat slaughtered on site; pork products from pork slaughtered on site; meat by-products from meat slaughtered on site; sausages & other prepared meats; prepared beef products from purchased beef; prepared pork products from purchased pork; ham, roasted: from purchased meat; leather tanning & finishing; trucking, except local; meat processing machinery
HQ: Tyson Fresh Meats, Inc.
800 Stevens Port Dr
Dakota Dunes SD 57049
605 235-2061

**(G-9219)**
**UNIVERSAL CHEM & COATINGS INC (PA)**
Also Called: Unichem
1975 Fox Ln (60123-7839)
PHONE......................847 931-1700
Daniel Chin, *President*
Frederick V Chin, *Vice Pres*
Andy Marck, *Accounts Mgr*
Daniel Birr, *Lab Dir*
Susan Ernsting, *Admin Sec*
▼ EMP: 25
SQ FT: 50,000
SALES (est): 9.7MM **Privately Held**
WEB: www.unicheminc.com
SIC: **2851** 2891 Coating, air curing; adhesives & sealants

**(G-9220)**
**UNIVERSAL-SPC INC**
412 N State St (60123-2877)
PHONE......................847 742-4400
Nand Kumar, *President*
Bruce J Carter, *Vice Pres*
Amarnath Nuggehalli, *CFO*
EMP: 3
SALES (est): 456.4K
SALES (corp-wide): 32.6MM **Privately Held**
SIC: **3599** 3471 Machine shop, jobbing & repair; plating & polishing
PA: Uca Group, Inc
412 N State St
Elgin IL 60123
847 742-8870

**(G-9221)**
**US SPECIALTY PACKAGING INC**
2760 Spectrum Dr (60124-7841)
PHONE......................847 836-1115
Steven Myers, *President*
Daniel Purcell, *Vice Pres*
EMP: 14
SQ FT: 40,000
SALES (est): 4.8MM **Privately Held**
SIC: **2676** 2515 Sanitary paper products; box springs, assembled

**(G-9222)**
**USACH TECHNOLOGIES INC (HQ)**
1524 Davis Rd (60123-1359)
PHONE......................847 888-0148
Fax: 847 888-0144
Giacomo Antonini, *President*
Richard L Simons, *President*
Diana Szymonik, *General Mgr*
Mike Beckford, *Mfg Staff*
Nancy Cox, *Purch Mgr*
▲ EMP: 42
SQ FT: 34,000
SALES (est): 5.6MM
SALES (corp-wide): 292MM **Publicly Held**
WEB: www.usach.com
SIC: **3541** 5084 7699 Grinding machines, metalworking; metalworking machinery; industrial machinery & equipment repair
PA: Hardinge Inc.
1 Hardinge Dr
Elmira NY 14902
607 734-2281

**(G-9223)**
**VALUE ADDED SERVICES & TECH**
Also Called: Vast
164 Division St Ste 315 (60120-5528)
PHONE......................847 888-8232
James Hanson, *President*
EMP: 5
SQ FT: 1,200
SALES (est): 544.5K **Privately Held**
WEB: www.vastproducts.net
SIC: **3625** Electric controls & control accessories, industrial

**(G-9224)**
**VECCHIO MANUFACTURING OF ILL (PA)**
Also Called: V M I
801d N State St Unit D (60123-2145)
PHONE......................847 742-8429
Sandra Vecchio, *President*
▲ EMP: 10
SQ FT: 21,000
SALES: 950K **Privately Held**
WEB: www.vecchiomfg.com
SIC: **3083** 2493 3281 2531 Plastic finished products, laminated; bulletin boards, wood; blackboards, slate; public building & related furniture

**(G-9225)**
**W J DENNIS & COMPANY**
1111 Davis Rd Ste B (60123-1388)
PHONE......................847 697-4800
Fax: 847 697-4821
Andre Daigle, *President*
Chris Brand, *General Mgr*
Jim Greenlee, *Manager*
Paul Signor, *Info Tech Dir*
▲ EMP: 16 EST: 1900
SQ FT: 37,000
SALES (est): 3.6MM
SALES (corp-wide): 72.2K **Privately Held**
WEB: www.wjdennis-rcr.com
SIC: **3052** 3069 2273 3089 Rubber hose; air line or air brake hose, rubber or rubberized fabric; garden hose, rubber; spray bulbs, rubber; rugs, tufted; plastic hardware & building products; window squeegees; manufactured hardware (general)
HQ: Rcr International Inc
180 Rue De Normandie
Boucherville QC J4B 5
450 670-8100

**(G-9226)**
**WAGNER SYSTEMS INC**
Also Called: Industrial Solutions
300 Airport Rd Unit 1 (60123-1600)
PHONE......................630 503-2400
Fax: 630 503-2377
Hubert Riek, *CEO*
Jerry Trostle, *President*
Matthias Koehler, *General Mgr*
Jeff Porters, *Opers Mgr*
Frank Battista, *Project Engr*
▲ EMP: 21
SQ FT: 1,000
SALES (est): 6.4MM **Privately Held**
WEB: www.wagnersystemsinc.com
SIC: **3559** Paint making machinery

**(G-9227)**
**WALTER TOOL & MFG INC**
1535 Commerce Dr (60123-9304)
PHONE......................847 697-7230
Fax: 847 697-7251
John Walter, *President*
Tony Walter, *Vice Pres*
EMP: 15
SQ FT: 15,000
SALES (est): 3MM **Privately Held**
WEB: www.wtool.com
SIC: **3541** 3599 Numerically controlled metal cutting machine tools; machine shop, jobbing & repair

**(G-9228)**
**WALTERS DISTRIBUTING COMPANY**
1625 Dundee Ave Ste D (60120-1679)
PHONE......................847 468-0941
Neil J Fischer, *President*
Bruce L Fischer, *Vice Pres*
EMP: 7 EST: 1947
SQ FT: 5,500
SALES (est): 1MM **Privately Held**
SIC: **3714** Transmissions, motor vehicle

**(G-9229)**
**WANXIANG USA HOLDINGS CORP (HQ)**
88 Airport Rd Ste 100 (60123-9324)
PHONE......................847 622-8838
Weiding Lu, *CEO*
Gary Wetzel, *COO*
Pin Ni, *Vice Pres*
▲ EMP: 12
SQ FT: 1,000
SALES (est): 62.8MM
SALES (corp-wide): 2.9B **Privately Held**
SIC: **3714** 6211 Motor vehicle parts & accessories; investment firm, general brokerage
PA: Wanxiang Group Corporation
Wanxiang Road,Xiaoshan Economic And Technological Development Zo
Hangzhou
571 828-3299

**(G-9230)**
**WATER SERVICES COMPANY OF ILL**
390 Sadler Ave (60120-8038)
PHONE......................847 697-6623
Fax: 847 742-3700
Michael J Pedone, *President*
Julie Termini, *Manager*
Margarette Pedone, *Admin Sec*
EMP: 8
SQ FT: 50,000
SALES (est): 1.2MM **Privately Held**
WEB: www.water-resources.com
SIC: **3829** 7699 Gauges, motor vehicle: oil pressure, water temperature; professional instrument repair services

# Elgin - Kane County (G-9231)

**(G-9231)**
**WAUCONDA TOOL & ENGINEERING CO**
Also Called: Pep Wauconda
690 Church Rd (60123-9340)
PHONE..................847 608-0602
Fax: 847 608-0662
Corinne Leiner, *Vice Pres*
EMP: 25
SALES (corp-wide): 833.4MM **Publicly Held**
WEB: www.wauconda.com
SIC: 3469 3544 Stamping metal for the trade; special dies, tools, jigs & fixtures
HQ: Wauconda Tool & Engineering Llc
    821 W Algonquin Rd
    Algonquin IL 60102
    847 658-4588

**(G-9232)**
**WEILER ENGINEERING INC**
1395 Gateway Dr (60124-7866)
PHONE..................847 697-4900
Fax: 847 697-4915
Gerhard H Weiler, *President*
Carol Zolp, *President*
Sig Obermann, *Vice Pres*
Mark Danley, *VP Opers*
Mark Danly, *Plant Mgr*
▲ EMP: 100
SQ FT: 120,000
SALES (est): 39.1MM **Privately Held**
WEB: www.weiler-bfs.com
SIC: 3559 Pharmaceutical machinery

**(G-9233)**
**WELCH BROS INC (PA)**
1050 Saint Charles St (60120-8441)
P.O. Box 749 (60121-0749)
PHONE..................847 741-6134
Fax: 847 741-6195
David D Welch, *President*
Mark Welch, *Vice Pres*
Rocky Brandl, *Research*
Michael J Nawrocki, *Controller*
Les Arnold, *Sales Staff*
▲ EMP: 118
SQ FT: 7,200
SALES (est): 20.1MM **Privately Held**
WEB: www.welchbrothers.com
SIC: 3272 5211 Concrete products, pre-cast; septic tanks, concrete; manhole covers or frames, concrete; lumber & other building materials

**(G-9234)**
**WELCH STEEL PRODUCTS INC**
333 Hammond Ave (60120-8421)
P.O. Box 749 (60121-0749)
PHONE..................847 741-2623
Fax: 847 741-5603
David Welch, *President*
EMP: 12
SALES (est): 1.1MM **Privately Held**
SIC: 3462 Iron & steel forgings

**(G-9235)**
**WENCO MANUFACTURING CO INC**
11n261 Muirhead Rd (60124-8225)
PHONE..................630 377-7474
Fax: 630 513-6599
Bonnie Little, *President*
James Little, *Vice Pres*
EMP: 20
SALES (est): 2MM **Privately Held**
SIC: 3452 3469 3545 3423 Bolts, metal; metal stampings; cutting tools for machine tools; hand & edge tools

**(G-9236)**
**WET & FORGET USA A NEW ZEALND**
2521 Tech Dr Ste 209 (60124)
P.O. Box 5805 (60121-5805)
PHONE..................847 428-3894
Brett Perry, *General Ptnr*
Adam Smith, *Natl Sales Mgr*
▲ EMP: 7
SQ FT: 3,000
SALES (est): 1.3MM **Privately Held**
SIC: 3589 Commercial cleaning equipment

**(G-9237)**
**WILLIAMS HALTHCARE SYSTEMS LLC**
158 N Edison Ave (60123-5215)
PHONE..................847 741-3650
Vicki Bradas, *Controller*
Thomas Kenny, *Info Tech Mgr*
Thomas J Kenny, *Administration*
▲ EMP: 60
SQ FT: 10,000
SALES (est): 8.8MM **Privately Held**
WEB: www.williamshealthcare.com
SIC: 3842 Surgical appliances & supplies

**(G-9238)**
**WISDOM ADHESIVES**
350 River Ridge Dr (60123-9370)
PHONE..................847 841-7002
EMP: 3
SALES (est): 155.1K **Privately Held**
SIC: 2891 Adhesives

**(G-9239)**
**WORLD RICHMAN MFG CORP**
2505 Bath Rd (60124-7894)
PHONE..................847 468-8898
Fax: 847 468-8899
David D Huang, *President*
Agnes Meng, *Prdtn Mgr*
Colleen Hadson, *Accountant*
▲ EMP: 11
SQ FT: 40,000
SALES (est): 1.8MM **Privately Held**
WEB: www.worldrichman.com
SIC: 3172 Personal leather goods

**(G-9240)**
**ZENTER CUSTOM CABINETS INC**
363 Bluff City Blvd (60120-8374)
PHONE..................847 488-0744
Juan Zenteno, *President*
EMP: 13
SALES (est): 1.6MM **Privately Held**
SIC: 2434 Wood kitchen cabinets

## Elizabeth
### Jo Daviess County

**(G-9241)**
**CIVIL CONSTRUCTORS INC**
Also Called: Civil Constrs Inc Illinois
1307 W Longhollow Rd (61028-9487)
P.O. Box 750, Freeport (61032-0750)
PHONE..................815 858-2691
Georgia Bussan, *Office Mgr*
Dave Hermsen, *Manager*
EMP: 7
SALES (corp-wide): 153.7MM **Privately Held**
SIC: 1629 1422 Rock removal; crushed & broken limestone
HQ: Civil Constructors, Inc.
    2283 Us Highway 20 E
    Freeport IL 61032
    815 235-2200

**(G-9242)**
**JEANBLANC INTERNATIONAL INC**
Also Called: Ds2 Tech
6686 S Derinda Rd (61028-9512)
PHONE..................815 598-3400
James Jeanblanc, *President*
Denise K Graves, *Executive Asst*
EMP: 2 EST: 1983
SQ FT: 8,000
SALES (est): 750K **Privately Held**
WEB: www.jeanblanc.com
SIC: 2899 5045 Oils & essential oils; computers

**(G-9243)**
**M & W FEED SERVICE**
201 S Ash St (61028-9104)
P.O. Box 294 (61028-0294)
PHONE..................815 858-2412
Fax: 815 858-2413
Marvin J Wurster, *President*
Laurie Wuster, *Vice Pres*
EMP: 4
SQ FT: 3,600
SALES (est): 1.2MM **Privately Held**
SIC: 5191 2048 Farm supplies; feed; prepared feeds

**(G-9244)**
**MD TECHNOLOGIES INC**
6965 S Pleasant Hill Rd (61028-9315)
P.O. Box 60, Galena (61036-0060)
PHONE..................815 598-3143
Fax: 815 598-3110
Bill Merkle, *President*
Melissa Merkle, *Manager*
EMP: 10
SALES (est): 1.4MM **Privately Held**
WEB: www.mdtechnologiesinc.com
SIC: 3841 Diagnostic apparatus, medical; ophthalmic instruments & apparatus

## Elizabethtown
### Hardin County

**(G-9245)**
**FRICKER MACHINE SHOP & SALVAGE**
Rr 1 (62931-9801)
Rural Route Box 16 (62931-9703)
PHONE..................618 285-3271
Jerry Fricker, *Owner*
EMP: 4
SQ FT: 6,000
SALES (est): 247.1K **Privately Held**
SIC: 7692 5093 5052 3713 Welding repair; ferrous metal scrap & waste; coal; truck & bus bodies

**(G-9246)**
**HARDIN COUNTY INDEPENDENT**
2527 W 1st St (62931)
PHONE..................618 287-2361
Julie Smith, *Owner*
EMP: 3
SALES (est): 165.1K **Privately Held**
SIC: 2711 5943 Newspapers, publishing & printing; office forms & supplies

## Elk Grove Village
### Cook County

**(G-9247)**
**24LAND EXPRESS INC**
1460 Mark St (60007-6714)
PHONE..................630 766-2424
Kevin Cho, *President*
Paul Cho, *Principal*
◆ EMP: 4
SALES (est): 303.3K **Privately Held**
SIC: 2741 Miscellaneous publishing

**(G-9248)**
**A & A MACHINE CO INC**
1530 Jarvis Ave (60007-2459)
PHONE..................847 985-4619
Fax: 847 437-6227
Richard A Kehr, *President*
Daniel Kehr, *Vice Pres*
Eleanor Kehr, *Treasurer*
Michelle Kehr, *Office Mgr*
EMP: 2
SQ FT: 5,000
SALES (est): 203.8K **Privately Held**
SIC: 3599 Machine shop, jobbing & repair

**(G-9249)**
**A & J PRINTERS INC**
Also Called: A & J Graphics
809 Dierking Ter (60007-2406)
PHONE..................847 909-9609
David F Compitello, *Principal*
EMP: 2
SALES (est): 201.9K **Privately Held**
SIC: 2752 Commercial printing, lithographic

**(G-9250)**
**A J R INDUSTRIES INC**
117 Gordon St (60007-1182)
PHONE..................847 439-0380
Fax: 847 439-0230
Alan Wojtowicz, *President*
Richard Simantz, *Vice Pres*
Gary Wojtowicz, *Vice Pres*
Pamela Simantz, *Treasurer*
Bob Zurek, *Human Res Mgr*
EMP: 40 EST: 1965
SQ FT: 22,000
SALES (est): 12MM **Privately Held**
SIC: 3728 Gears, aircraft power transmission

**(G-9251)**
**A M P SOFTWARE INC**
455 Vermont Dr (60007-2750)
PHONE..................630 240-5922
Adam M Pajerski, *Owner*
EMP: 1
SALES: 250K **Privately Held**
SIC: 7372 Prepackaged software

**(G-9252)**
**AAP METALS LLC (HQ)**
2200 Pratt Blvd (60007-5917)
PHONE..................847 916-1220
Tom Modrowski, *CEO*
Tom Heneghan, *Exec VP*
Paul Patek, *CFO*
EMP: 64
SALES (est): 33.6MM
SALES (corp-wide): 166.2MM **Privately Held**
SIC: 3312 Stainless steel
PA: Main Steel, Llc
    2200 Pratt Blvd
    Elk Grove Village IL 60007
    847 916-1220

**(G-9253)**
**ABBCO INC**
2401 American Ln (60007-6203)
PHONE..................630 595-7115
Joseph Abbate Jr, *President*
Phillip Cypcar, *Sales Engr*
EMP: 25 EST: 1960
SQ FT: 25,000
SALES (est): 4.5MM **Privately Held**
WEB: www.abbcoinc.net
SIC: 3545 3541 3451 Cutting tools for machine tools; machine tools, metal cutting type; screw machine products

**(G-9254)**
**ABBOTT LABORATORIES**
Abbott Molecular
1800 Brummel Ave (60007-2121)
PHONE..................224 361-7129
EMP: 4
SALES (corp-wide): 20.8B **Publicly Held**
SIC: 2835 In vitro & in vivo diagnostic substances
PA: Abbott Laboratories
    100 Abbott Park Rd
    Abbott Park IL 60064
    224 667-6100

**(G-9255)**
**ABERDON ENTERPRISES**
225 Bond St (60007-1220)
PHONE..................847 228-1300
Kim Komacki, *Principal*
EMP: 12
SALES (est): 1.8MM **Privately Held**
SIC: 3569 7389 General industrial machinery; business services

**(G-9256)**
**ABILITY FASTENERS INC**
685 Fargo Ave (60007-4742)
PHONE..................847 593-4230
Fax: 847 593-5826
John Larsen, *President*
Mary Ann Larsen, *Corp Secy*
Kathy Podulka, *Manager*
Barbara Sutherland, *Manager*
▲ EMP: 10 EST: 1983
SQ FT: 11,000
SALES (est): 2.4MM **Privately Held**
SIC: 5072 3452 3451 3444 Nuts (hardware); bolts; screws; rivets; bolts, nuts, rivets & washers; screw machine products; sheet metalwork

**(G-9257)**
**ABILITY METAL COMPANY**
1355 Greenleaf Ave (60007-5520)
PHONE..................847 437-7040
Fax: 847 437-1089
Tim Selleck, *President*

Steve Mucci, *President*
Beverly Kral, *Purchasing*
Jim Kovacs, *QC Mgr*
Shannon Podgorski, *Engineer*
▲ **EMP:** 42
**SQ FT:** 40,000
**SALES (est):** 7.8MM **Privately Held**
**WEB:** www.abilitymetal.com
**SIC: 3812** Search & navigation equipment; cabin environment indicators; electronic detection systems (aeronautical); radar systems & equipment

*(G-9258)*
## ABRAXIS BIOSCIENCE LLC
1300 Chase Ave (60007-4813)
**PHONE**.................................310 437-7715
**EMP:** 4
**SALES (corp-wide):** 11.2B **Publicly Held**
**SIC: 2834** Pharmaceutical preparations
**HQ:** Abraxis Bioscience, Llc
11755 Wilshire Blvd Fl 20
Los Angeles CA 90025

*(G-9259)*
## ACCELERATED ASSEMBLIES INC
725 Nicholas Blvd (60007-2508)
**PHONE**.................................630 616-6680
Brian Steelglove, *President*
Michelle Hinca, *Shareholder*
Lisette Garcia, *Administration*
**EMP:** 20
**SQ FT:** 13,500
**SALES (est):** 7.4MM **Privately Held**
**SIC: 3679** 3674 3571 3672 Electronic circuits; semiconductors & related devices; electronic computers; printed circuit boards

*(G-9260)*
## ACCULIGHT LLC
2570 United Ln (60007-6819)
**PHONE**.................................630 847-1000
Febin Mootheril, *President*
**EMP:** 3
**SALES (est):** 230.4K **Privately Held**
**SIC: 3641** 5719 Tubes, electric light; lighting fixtures

*(G-9261)*
## ACCURATE DIE CUTTING INC
120 Joey Dr (60007-1304)
**PHONE**.................................847 437-7215
Laura Wolff, *President*
Christopher Ciesiel, *Prdtn Mgr*
**EMP:** 4
**SQ FT:** 2,200
**SALES (est):** 503.4K **Privately Held**
**WEB:** www.accuratedie.com
**SIC: 2789** Trade binding services

*(G-9262)*
## ACCUTRACE INC
2425 Touhy Ave (60007-5331)
**PHONE**.................................847 290-9900
Ramzan Dhanji, *President*
**EMP:** 15
**SALES (est):** 990K **Privately Held**
**WEB:** www.pcb4u.com
**SIC: 3672** Printed circuit boards

*(G-9263)*
## ACE PRECISION TOOL & MFG CO
1612 Landmeier Rd (60007-2478)
**PHONE**.................................847 690-0111
**Fax:** 847 690-0112
James A Glorioso Jr, *President*
**EMP:** 8
**SALES (est):** 1.2MM **Privately Held**
**SIC: 3599** Machine shop, jobbing & repair

*(G-9264)*
## ACME FINISHING COMPANY LLC
1595 Oakton St (60007-2149)
**PHONE**.................................847 640-7890
William Walters, *Principal*
**EMP:** 17
**SALES (est):** 1MM
**SALES (corp-wide):** 4.2MM **Privately Held**
**SIC: 5199** 3999 Packaging materials; atomizers, toiletry

**PA:** Acuity Capital Partners Llc
180 N Stetson Ave
Chicago IL 60601
312 268-5749

*(G-9265)*
## ACME FINISHING COMPANY INC
1595 Oakton St (60007-2149)
**PHONE**.................................847 640-7890
**Fax:** 847 640-0298
Dennis Walters, *President*
Steve Jayhan, *General Mgr*
Wendy Brandt, *Business Mgr*
Jack Walters, *Vice Pres*
Lisa Keener, *Controller*
**EMP:** 80 **EST:** 1933
**SQ FT:** 110,000
**SALES (est):** 12.6MM **Privately Held**
**WEB:** www.acmefinishing.com
**SIC: 3479** Enameling, including porcelain, of metal products; japanning of metal

*(G-9266)*
## ACME INDUSTRIES INC
1325 Pratt Blvd (60007-5710)
**PHONE**.................................847 296-3346
Warren Young, *Ch of Bd*
Fred Young, *President*
Bob Clifford, *Vice Pres*
Larry Wetendorf, *Materials Mgr*
Jack Korenkiewicz, *Opers Staff*
▲ **EMP:** 115 **EST:** 1948
**SQ FT:** 270,000
**SALES (est):** 45.6MM **Privately Held**
**WEB:** www.acmeind.com
**SIC: 3599** Custom machinery

*(G-9267)*
## ACTEGA NORTH AMERICA INC
1550 Carmen Dr Bldg 7 (60007-6502)
**PHONE**.................................847 690-9310
**EMP:** 4 **Privately Held**
**SIC: 2893** Printing ink
**HQ:** Actega North America Inc.
950 S Chester Ave Ste B2
Delran NJ 08075
856 829-6300

*(G-9268)*
## ACTIVE AUTOMATION INC
530 Bennett Rd (60007-1122)
**PHONE**.................................847 427-8100
**Fax:** 847 806-6396
Sam V Marinkovich, *President*
Biba M Marinkovich, *Admin Sec*
**EMP:** 10
**SQ FT:** 11,000
**SALES:** 500K **Privately Held**
**WEB:** www.activeautomation.com
**SIC: 3549** 5084 7389 8742 Assembly machines, including robotic; industrial machinery & equipment; design, commercial & industrial; automation & robotics consultant

*(G-9269)*
## AD IMAGES
2258 Landmeier Rd Ste F (60007-2637)
**PHONE**.................................847 956-1887
**Fax:** 847 956-7071
Kenneth R Haycock, *President*
Donna Delinger, *Admin Sec*
**EMP:** 5
**SQ FT:** 1,000
**SALES:** 300K **Privately Held**
**WEB:** www.adimages.net
**SIC: 2759** 7311 7389 Screen printing; advertising agencies; embroidering of advertising on shirts, etc.

*(G-9270)*
## ADAIR ENTERPRISES INC
1499 Tonne Rd (60007-5003)
**PHONE**.................................847 640-7789
Kenneth Adair, *President*
Chuck Adair, *Admin Sec*
**EMP:** 12
**SQ FT:** 4,000
**SALES (est):** 3.1MM **Privately Held**
**WEB:** www.adairenterprises.com
**SIC: 3492** Hose & tube fittings & assemblies, hydraulic/pneumatic

*(G-9271)*
## ADC DIECASTING LLC
901 Chase Ave (60007-4807)
**PHONE**.................................847 541-3030
**EMP:** 197
**SQ FT:** 120,000
**SALES (corp-wide):** 32MM **Privately Held**
**SIC: 3363** Aluminum die-castings
**PA:** Adc Diecasting, Llc
901 Chase Ave
Elk Grove Village IL 60007
847 541-3030

*(G-9272)*
## ADC DIECASTING LLC (PA)
Also Called: Anderson Die Castings
901 Chase Ave (60007-4807)
**PHONE**.................................847 541-3030
**Fax:** 847 541-4017
Patrick Tang, *President*
Steve Domlaick, *Opers Mgr*
Dave Ohman, *Opers Mgr*
Andy Tang, *Production*
Nancy Bahrs, *QC Mgr*
**EMP:** 3
**SQ FT:** 64,000
**SALES:** 32MM **Privately Held**
**SIC: 3363** Aluminum die-castings

*(G-9273)*
## ADK ARMS INC
2301 Estes Ave (60007-5428)
**PHONE**.................................847 981-9800
Christopher Kozlowski, *President*
Roy Finch, *Vice Pres*
Tadeusz Kozlowski, *Vice Pres*
**EMP:** 3
**SALES (est):** 134.8K **Privately Held**
**SIC: 3541** Machine tools, metal cutting type

*(G-9274)*
## ADK PRODUCTS INC
2821 Old Higgins Rd (60007-6416)
**PHONE**.................................847 710-0021
Bogumila Kozlowski, *President*
**EMP:** 3
**SALES:** 100K **Privately Held**
**SIC: 3499** Fabricated metal products

*(G-9275)*
## ADVANCED EXTRUDER TECH INC
2281 E Devon Ave (60007-6805)
**PHONE**.................................847 238-9651
**Fax:** 847 238-9654
Fred Jalili, *President*
Alan Farkas, *Sales Staff*
**EMP:** 24
**SQ FT:** 40,000
**SALES (est):** 5.3MM **Privately Held**
**WEB:** www.aetextruder.com
**SIC: 2891** Sealing compounds, synthetic rubber or plastic

*(G-9276)*
## ADVANCED PRECISION MFG INC (PA)
Also Called: Apmi
2301 Estes Ave (60007-5428)
**PHONE**.................................847 981-9800
**Fax:** 847 981-9801
Tadeusz Kozlowski, *President*
Chris Kozlowski, *Senior VP*
Becky Kozlowski, *Vice Pres*
**EMP:** 42
**SQ FT:** 25,000
**SALES:** 4MM **Privately Held**
**WEB:** www.apmi.us
**SIC: 3728** 3812 5088 Aircraft body assemblies & parts; search & navigation equipment; transportation equipment & supplies

*(G-9277)*
## ADVANCED STEEL FABRICATION
181 Randall St (60007-1014)
**PHONE**.................................847 956-6565
Alex Varga, *President*
**EMP:** 5
**SQ FT:** 5,000
**SALES (est):** 640K **Privately Held**
**SIC: 3441** Fabricated structural metal

*(G-9278)*
## ADVANCED VALVE TECH INC (PA)
800 Busse Rd (60007-2429)
**PHONE**.................................847 364-3700
Kevin Murphy, *CEO*
Arlene Soverino, *Human Resources*
Fred Bloom, *Director*
Mike Murphy, *Director*
Tony Renton, *Director*
▲ **EMP:** 27
**SQ FT:** 25,000
**SALES:** 25MM **Privately Held**
**SIC: 5074** 3317 Pipes & fittings, plastic; steel pipe & tubes

*(G-9279)*
## ADVANTAGE DIRECT INC
1822 Elmhurst Rd (60007-5911)
P.O. Box 492, Bensenville (60106-0492)
**PHONE**.................................847 427-1185
Amir Mirza, *President*
Huma Mirza, *Manager*
**EMP:** 11
**SQ FT:** 8,900
**SALES (est):** 3.2MM **Privately Held**
**WEB:** www.americancordsets.com
**SIC: 3643** 5063 Plugs, electric; building wire & cable; electronic wire & cable; power wire & cable

*(G-9280)*
## ADVANTAGE TOOL AND MOLD INC
1501 Kathleen Way (60007-3128)
**PHONE**.................................847 301-9020
Bill Stack, *President*
**EMP:** 3
**SQ FT:** 3,600
**SALES:** 700K **Privately Held**
**SIC: 3312** Forgings, iron & steel

*(G-9281)*
## ADVERTISING PRODUCTS INC
Also Called: API
680 Fargo Ave (60007-4701)
**PHONE**.................................847 758-0415
Glenn Rebechini, *CEO*
Doug McDonald, *Administration*
**EMP:** 3
**SQ FT:** 10,000
**SALES (est):** 290K **Privately Held**
**SIC: 3993** Signs & advertising specialties

*(G-9282)*
## AEROTRONIC CONTROLS CO (PA)
2101 Arthur Ave (60007-6089)
**PHONE**.................................847 228-6504
Chris L Seth, *President*
Barry Seth, *Vice Pres*
Larry Jagiello, *Purchasing*
Irene Seth, *Treasurer*
Steve Handing, *Mktg Dir*
▲ **EMP:** 11 **EST:** 1958
**SQ FT:** 82,000
**SALES (est):** 2.2MM **Privately Held**
**SIC: 3672** 3679 Printed circuit boards; power supplies, all types: static

*(G-9283)*
## ALBEA
1500 Midway Ct Ste W9 (60007-6606)
**PHONE**.................................847 439-8220
**Fax:** 847 439-8230
Warren Hendricks, *Manager*
**EMP:** 3
**SALES (est):** 237.2K **Privately Held**
**SIC: 3089** Plastics products

*(G-9284)*
## ALCONIX USA INC
25 Northwest Point Blvd # 800 (60007-1099)
**PHONE**.................................847 717-7407
Kenji Ito, *President*
Frank W Jamieson, *Exec VP*
Yoshihiko Suzuki, *Treasurer*
Kazuo Nezaki, *Admin Sec*
▲ **EMP:** 7
**SALES:** 2.6MM
**SALES (corp-wide):** 1.7B **Privately Held**
**SIC: 5051** 3498 Copper sheets, plates, bars, rods, pipes, etc.; tube fabricating (contract bending & shaping)

**PA:** Alconix Corporation
2-11-1, Nagatacho
Chiyoda-Ku TKY 100-0
335 967-400

### (G-9285)
### ALL WEATHER PRODUCTS CO LLC
1500 Greenleaf Ave (60007-5525)
PHONE..................847 981-0386
John Kruppa, *Accountant*
William S Rossi, *Mng Member*
Bill Rossi,
**EMP:** 13
**SQ FT:** 30,000
**SALES (est):** 3.7MM **Privately Held**
**WEB:** www.awsubstrates.com
**SIC:** 2679 Paper products, converted; paperboard products, converted

### (G-9286)
### ALL-STATE INDUSTRIES INC
Also Called: Alert Manufacturing
2651 Carl Blvd (60007-6718)
PHONE..................847 350-0460
**Fax:** 847 350-0468
Greg Sage, *Branch Mgr*
**EMP:** 70
**SALES (corp-wide):** 60.9MM **Privately Held**
**WEB:** www.all-stateind.com
**SIC:** 5085 3061 3053 Hose, belting & packing; rubber goods, mechanical; mechanical rubber goods; gaskets, packing & sealing devices
**PA:** All-State Industries, Inc.
500 S 18th St
West Des Moines IA 50265
515 223-5843

### (G-9287)
### ALLSTAR FASTENERS INC
1550 Arthur Ave (60007-5733)
PHONE..................847 640-7827
**Fax:** 847 640-0086
Roger Pendroy, *President*
Richard Shacht, *Treasurer*
Allan Vodicka, *Admin Sec*
▲ **EMP:** 50
**SQ FT:** 50,000
**SALES (est):** 8.9MM **Privately Held**
**WEB:** www.allstarfasteners.com
**SIC:** 3452 Screws, metal

### (G-9288)
### ALLSTATE PRINTING INC
620 Bennett Rd (60007-1103)
PHONE..................847 640-4401
Gary Lowmiller, *President*
Kevin Lowmiller, *Vice Pres*
**EMP:** 5
**SQ FT:** 63,000
**SALES (est):** 969.2K **Privately Held**
**SIC:** 2752 Commercial printing, offset

### (G-9289)
### ALPHA OMEGA PLASTICS COMPANY
1099 Touhy Ave (60007-4921)
PHONE..................847 956-8777
**Fax:** 847 956-7171
Lambros Kalamaris, *President*
Lambros Brown, *Plant Mgr*
Maria Theodosis, *Treasurer*
Christina Calamiras, *Office Mgr*
Angeline Beladakis, *Admin Sec*
▼ **EMP:** 55
**SQ FT:** 64,000
**SALES (est):** 12.2MM **Privately Held**
**SIC:** 3089 5162 Plastic processing; plastics materials

### (G-9290)
### ALPHA OMEGA PROFILE EXTRUSION
1099 Touhy Ave (60007-4921)
PHONE..................847 956-8777
Angeline Beladakis, *CEO*
Lambros Kalamaris, *President*
Joanne Limber, *Office Mgr*
▼ **EMP:** 16
**SALES (est):** 1.5MM **Privately Held**
**SIC:** 3524 Edgers, lawn

### (G-9291)
### AM PRECISION MACHINE INC
Also Called: Millusions
170 Lively Blvd (60007-1621)
PHONE..................847 439-9955
**Fax:** 847 439-0483
Margaret Kozlowski, *CEO*
Stanley Kozlowski, *President*
Andy G Kozlowski, *Senior VP*
Krystina Kozlowski, *Vice Pres*
Dave Bullock, *Engineer*
▲ **EMP:** 25
**SQ FT:** 33,500
**SALES (est):** 4MM **Privately Held**
**WEB:** www.amprecision.com
**SIC:** 3599 Machine shop, jobbing & repair

### (G-9292)
### AMAZING CABINETS & DESIGN CORP
2400 Delta Ln (60007-6303)
PHONE..................773 405-0174
Roseli De Paula Marques, *President*
**EMP:** 6
**SQ FT:** 500
**SALES:** 500K **Privately Held**
**SIC:** 7389 3429 Design services; cabinet hardware

### (G-9293)
### AMBER ENGINEERING AND MFG CO
2400 Brickvale Dr (60007-6809)
PHONE..................847 595-6966
**Fax:** 847 595-2114
Sigismund Paul, *President*
Bernard Paul, *Vice Pres*
George Dewey, *Engineer*
**EMP:** 70 **EST:** 1960
**SQ FT:** 50,000
**SALES (est):** 11.5MM **Privately Held**
**SIC:** 8711 3549 3452 Designing: ship, boat, machine & product; assembly machines, including robotic; bolts, nuts, rivets & washers

### (G-9294)
### AMCRAFT MANUFACTURING INC
Also Called: Fabracraft Manufacturing
580 Lively Blvd (60007-2014)
PHONE..................847 439-4565
**Fax:** 847 439-2194
Mark Deutsch, *President*
Bob Dejidow, *Manager*
▼ **EMP:** 14
**SQ FT:** 7,200
**SALES (est):** 2.6MM **Privately Held**
**SIC:** 2393 Textile bags; bags & containers, except sleeping bags: textile

### (G-9295)
### AMERICAN COLOR ALTICOR
1800 Landmeier Rd Ste A (60007-2438)
PHONE..................847 472-7500
Fred Riley, *Principal*
Jim Bonaventura, *VP Sales*
**EMP:** 2
**SALES (est):** 220.3K **Privately Held**
**SIC:** 2759 Commercial printing

### (G-9296)
### AMERICAN DIGITAL CORPORATION
25 Northwest Point Blvd # 200 (60007-1035)
PHONE..................847 637-4300
**Fax:** 847 919-8468
Norbert Wojcik, *President*
Paul J Gute, *Senior VP*
Robert Panos, *Senior VP*
Michael Scoby, *Vice Pres*
Ann Oneill, *VP Human Res*
**EMP:** 38
**SQ FT:** 8,000
**SALES (est):** 16.3MM **Privately Held**
**WEB:** www.americandigital.com
**SIC:** 3577 Computer peripheral equipment

### (G-9297)
### AMERICAN MOLDING TECH INC
Also Called: A M T
2350 Lunt Ave (60007-5610)
PHONE..................847 437-6900
Dimitri Poulos, *President*
Jessica Deas, *Manager*
**EMP:** 25
**SALES (est):** 5.6MM **Privately Held**
**SIC:** 3089 Injection molding of plastics

### (G-9298)
### AMERICAN SPEEDY PRINTING CTRS
859 Oakton St (60007-1904)
PHONE..................847 806-0135
**Fax:** 847 437-3211
Joe Smith, *Owner*
Jim Smith, *Co-Owner*
**EMP:** 25 **EST:** 1988
**SALES (est):** 1.4MM **Privately Held**
**SIC:** 2752 Commercial printing, offset

### (G-9299)
### AMERICAN VULKO TREAD CORP
690 Chase Ave (60007-4802)
PHONE..................847 956-1300
**Fax:** 847 956-1339
Andrew C Bryniczka, *President*
Wayne Johnson, *Treasurer*
Carol Dalton, *Admin Sec*
▲ **EMP:** 12
**SQ FT:** 5,500
**SALES (est):** 2.3MM **Privately Held**
**WEB:** www.avt.us
**SIC:** 3714 Wheels, motor vehicle

### (G-9300)
### AMERICOR ELECTRONICS LTD
675 Lively Blvd (60007-2015)
PHONE..................847 956-6200
**Fax:** 847 956-0300
Thomas Pross, *President*
Marie Logan, *Vice Pres*
▲ **EMP:** 11
**SQ FT:** 5,000
**SALES (est):** 2MM **Privately Held**
**WEB:** www.americor-usa.com
**SIC:** 3643 Current-carrying wiring devices

### (G-9301)
### AMG INTERNATIONAL INC
Also Called: Freeman Products Worldwide
1480 E Devon Ave (60007-5801)
PHONE..................847 439-1001
Dave Shultz, *Manager*
**EMP:** 4
**SALES (corp-wide):** 13.1MM **Privately Held**
**SIC:** 3914 Trophies
**PA:** Amg International Inc
71 Walsh Dr Ste 101
Parsippany NJ 07054
201 475-4800

### (G-9302)
### AMITRON INC
Also Called: Amitron Crop
2001 Landmeier Rd (60007-2422)
PHONE..................847 290-9800
**Fax:** 847 290-9823
Bhagvan Patel, *President*
Milan Mortimer, *Corp Secy*
Akshay Patel, *Plant Mgr*
Chandrika Patel, *Purch Mgr*
Rajani Patel, *Engrg Dir*
▲ **EMP:** 137
**SQ FT:** 73,000
**SALES (est):** 28.2MM **Privately Held**
**WEB:** www.amitroncorp.com
**SIC:** 3672 Printed circuit boards

### (G-9303)
### AMPEL INCORPORATED
925 Estes Ave (60007-4905)
PHONE..................847 952-1900
**Fax:** 847 952-0064
Jay Gopani, *CEO*
**EMP:** 38
**SQ FT:** 34,000
**SALES:** 4MM **Privately Held**
**WEB:** www.ampelinc.com
**SIC:** 3672 Printed circuit boards

### (G-9304)
### AMT (ADDITIVE MFG TECH INC)
1201 Oakton St Ste 1 (60007-2018)
PHONE..................847 258-4475
Francois Reymondet, *President*
Sheila Jackson, *Manager*
**EMP:** 5
**SALES (est):** 374.3K **Publicly Held**
**SIC:** 3699 3544 Laser systems & equipment; industrial molds
**HQ:** Phenix Systems
Par Europeen D Entreprises
Riom 63200
473 334-585

### (G-9305)
### ANAH MACHINE MFG CO
801 Pratt Blvd (60007-5116)
PHONE..................847 228-6450
**Fax:** 847 228-6467
Andrew Kolosa, *President*
**EMP:** 10
**SQ FT:** 17,500
**SALES:** 1MM **Privately Held**
**SIC:** 3599 Machine shop, jobbing & repair

### (G-9306)
### ANGLE METAL MANUFACTURING CO
Also Called: Angle Sheet Metal
1497 Tonne Rd (60007-5003)
PHONE..................847 437-8666
**Fax:** 847 437-8736
Jeff Nowak, *President*
Wayne Wittmeyer, *Vice Pres*
Brian Nowak, *Treasurer*
**EMP:** 4
**SQ FT:** 4,600
**SALES (est):** 577.2K **Privately Held**
**SIC:** 3444 Sheet metalwork

### (G-9307)
### ANGLE TOOL COMPANY
425 Crossen Ave (60007-2003)
PHONE..................847 593-7572
**Fax:** 847 593-7582
**EMP:** 5 **EST:** 1970
**SQ FT:** 8,000
**SALES:** 500K **Privately Held**
**SIC:** 3544 3469 Mfg Dies/Tools/Jigs/Fixtures Mfg Metal Stampings

### (G-9308)
### ANODIZING SPECIALISTS LTD
210 Crossen Ave (60007-1612)
PHONE..................847 437-9495
**Fax:** 847 437-0969
Mike Panoplos, *President*
**EMP:** 9
**SQ FT:** 6,200
**SALES (est):** 100K **Privately Held**
**SIC:** 3471 Anodizing (plating) of metals or formed products; chromium plating of metals or formed products

### (G-9309)
### ANRITSU INFIVIS INC
Also Called: Anritsu Indus Slutions USA Inc
1001 Cambridge Dr (60007-2453)
PHONE..................847 419-9729
Eric Braner, *CEO*
Douglas Dobben, *General Mgr*
Stanley Wilkerson, *Engineer*
Doug Dobben, *CFO*
Erik Brainard, *Sales Mgr*
▲ **EMP:** 33
**SQ FT:** 20,000
**SALES (est):** 9MM
**SALES (corp-wide):** 771.1MM **Privately Held**
**WEB:** www.detectionperfection.com
**SIC:** 2834 Intravenous solutions
**HQ:** Anritsu Infivis Co., Ltd.
5-1-1, Onna
Atsugi KNG 243-0
462 966-700

### (G-9310)
### APHELION PRECISION TECH CORP
1800 Greenleaf Ave (60007-5502)
PHONE..................847 215-7285
Jane Black, *President*
William Black, *Exec VP*
Michael Black, *Vice Pres*
Blake Taubman, *QC Mgr*
Ryan Timm, *QC Mgr*
**EMP:** 45
**SQ FT:** 25,000
**SALES (est):** 10.4MM **Privately Held**
**WEB:** www.aphelions.net
**SIC:** 3599 Machine shop, jobbing & repair

## GEOGRAPHIC SECTION

**Elk Grove Village - Cook County (G-9336)**

**(G-9311)**
**AQUION PARTNERS LTD PARTNR**
2080 Lunt Ave (60007-5606)
PHONE...................847 437-9400
Fax: 847 437-5539
David Cole, *CEO*
Eddie Garmon, *Exec VP*
Jelle Lambrechts, *Accounts Mgr*
David Zindell, *Applctn Conslt*
Samuel Metallo, *Technical Staff*
EMP: 5
SALES (est): 418.6K **Privately Held**
SIC: 2819 Industrial inorganic chemicals

**(G-9312)**
**ARC-TRONICS INC**
1150 Pagni Dr (60007-6686)
PHONE...................847 437-0211
Fax: 847 437-0181
Conrad Goeringer, *CEO*
Michael Goeringer, *President*
Matthew Goeringer, *VP Mfg*
Becky Hauser, *Buyer*
Marla Goerlnge, *CFO*
▲ EMP: 210
SQ FT: 30,000
SALES (est): 66.2MM **Privately Held**
WEB: www.arc-tronics.com
SIC: 3672 3824 3679 Printed circuit boards; mechanical & electromechanical counters & devices; electronic circuits; harness assemblies for electronic use: wire or cable

**(G-9313)**
**ARLINGTON SPECIALTIES INC**
Also Called: Georgetown Spice Company
1515 Carmen Dr (60007-6501)
P.O. Box 1353, Arlington Heights (60006-1353)
PHONE...................847 545-9500
Georgiat Kaplan, *President*
Barry Kaplan, *Vice Pres*
Georgette Kaplan, *Treasurer*
▲ EMP: 4
SQ FT: 1,000
SALES (est): 240K **Privately Held**
SIC: 2099 5499 2045 2051 Spices, including grinding; spices & herbs; cake mixes, prepared: from purchased flour; cakes, bakery: except frozen

**(G-9314)**
**ASCENT MFG CO**
123 Scott St (60007-1210)
PHONE...................847 806-6600
Fax: 847 806-0009
George Daniel, *President*
Marie Daniel, *Corp Secy*
Andy Daniel, *Vice Pres*
Chet Daniel, *Vice Pres*
EMP: 20
SQ FT: 40,000
SALES (est): 4.8MM **Privately Held**
WEB: www.ascentmfgco.com
SIC: 3495 3496 7692 3469 Precision springs; miscellaneous fabricated wire products; welding repair; metal stampings; springs

**(G-9315)**
**ASHLAND DOOR SOLUTIONS LLC**
185 Martin Ln (60007-1309)
PHONE...................773 348-5106
Anne Gruber,
EMP: 3
SALES (est): 151.3K **Privately Held**
SIC: 3429 7699 5251 1751 Manufactured hardware (general); repair services; hardware; carpentry work

**(G-9316)**
**ASSA ABLOY ENTRANCE SYSTEMS US**
Also Called: Besam Entrance Solutions
1630 Jarvis Ave (60007-2404)
PHONE...................847 228-5600
Fax: 847 228-5622
Mike Sumrall, *Manager*
Danny Degott, *Manager*
EMP: 10
SALES (corp-wide): 7.7B **Privately Held**
SIC: 3699 1796 3442 Door opening & closing devices, electrical; installing building equipment; metal doors
HQ: Assa Abloy Entrance Systems Us Inc.
1900 Airport Rd
Monroe NC 28110
704 290-5520

**(G-9317)**
**ASSEMBLY INTERNATIONAL INC**
775 Touhy Ave (60007-4915)
PHONE...................847 437-3120
Fax: 847 437-9668
Indra Patel, *President*
Harshad Patel, *Vice Pres*
Adrian Botezatu, *Opers Mgr*
EMP: 17
SQ FT: 15,000
SALES (est): 2MM **Privately Held**
WEB: www.assemblyint.com
SIC: 3672 Printed circuit boards

**(G-9318)**
**ASTRO MACHINE CORPORATION**
630 Lively Blvd (60007-2016)
PHONE...................847 364-6363
Fax: 847 364-9898
George Selak, *President*
Martin Selak, *Chairman*
Martin M Selak, *Chairman*
Nancy Dedic, *Corp Secy*
Miryana Schubert, *Vice Pres*
▲ EMP: 42
SQ FT: 35,000
SALES: 12MM **Privately Held**
WEB: www.astromachine.com
SIC: 3579 Mailing, letter handling & addressing machines; address labeling machines

**(G-9319)**
**ATLAS COPCO COMPRESSORS LLC**
2501 Landmeier Rd Ste 109 (60007-2622)
P.O. Box 91730, Chicago (60693-1730)
PHONE...................847 640-6067
Fax: 847 981-8958
Erik Arfalk, *Vice Pres*
Tom Borer, *Vice Pres*
Debby Shiflett, *Senior Buyer*
Allen Kuhlman, *Accounts Mgr*
Jack Maly, *Sales Staff*
EMP: 10
SALES (corp-wide): 10.9B **Privately Held**
WEB: www.atlascopco.com
SIC: 3563 Air & gas compressors
HQ: Atlas Copco Compressors Llc
3042 Suthcross Blvd 102
Rock Hill SC 29730
803 817-7000

**(G-9320)**
**ATOMIC ENGINEERING CO**
365 Kent Ave (60007-1901)
PHONE...................847 228-1387
Fax: 847 593-7433
Jacqueline Redmond, *President*
Shirley Borek, *Vice Pres*
EMP: 13 EST: 1952
SALES (est): 1.3MM **Privately Held**
SIC: 3599 3544 Machine shop, jobbing & repair; die sets for metal stamping (presses); jigs & fixtures

**(G-9321)**
**AUTOMATIC PRODUCTION EQUIPMENT**
815 Touhy Ave (60007-4917)
PHONE...................847 439-1448
Donald Schmucker, *President*
Helen Schmucker, *Treasurer*
John Eckler, *Sales Mgr*
EMP: 8
SQ FT: 15,000
SALES (est): 1.9MM **Privately Held**
WEB: www.apeinc.com
SIC: 5084 3541 Industrial machinery & equipment; machine tools, metal cutting type

**(G-9322)**
**AUTOMOTIVE ENGINE SPECIALTIES**
173 Randall St (60007-1014)
PHONE...................847 956-1244
Anthony Schroeder, *Owner*
EMP: 3
SQ FT: 3,700
SALES (est): 220K **Privately Held**
SIC: 3599 Machine shop, jobbing & repair

**(G-9323)**
**AVANA ELECTRIC MOTORS INC**
Also Called: Avana Electrotek
1445 Brummel Ave (60007-2110)
P.O. Box 644 (60009-0644)
PHONE...................847 439-3950
Fax: 847 439-3950
Tom Hannay, *President*
Vivian Woodville, *Accounting Mgr*
Jim Holtzer, *Sales Executive*
EMP: 17 EST: 1943
SQ FT: 15,600
SALES (est): 6.8MM **Privately Held**
SIC: 5063 7694 Motors, electric; motor controls, starters & relays: electric; generators; electric motor repair

**(G-9324)**
**AVISTA GROUP CORPORATION**
Also Called: Avista USA
955 Pratt Blvd (60007-5118)
PHONE...................877 772-8826
Christopher Lee, *President*
Min Moon, *Manager*
▲ EMP: 12
SQ FT: 50,000
SALES: 7MM **Privately Held**
SIC: 2519 Television cabinets, plastic

**(G-9325)**
**AVOCO INTERNATIONAL LLC (PA)**
720 Bonnie Ln (60007-2201)
PHONE...................847 795-0200
Jerome Remien, *Principal*
Edward Lipski, *CFO*
EMP: 6
SQ FT: 3,000
SALES (est): 11.6MM **Privately Held**
SIC: 2032 Ethnic foods: canned, jarred, etc.

**(G-9326)**
**AWNINGS BY ZIP DEE INC**
96 Crossen Ave (60007-1608)
PHONE...................847 640-0460
James G Webb, *President*
Ron Mullins, *Plant Mgr*
▲ EMP: 28
SALES (est): 4.6MM **Privately Held**
SIC: 2394 Canvas & related products

**(G-9327)**
**AXIS MANUFACTURING INC**
2436 Delta Ln (60007-6303)
PHONE...................847 350-0200
Fax: 847 350-0202
Will Pavon, *President*
Alberto Del Gadillo, *Vice Pres*
Amparo Mendoza, *Treasurer*
Jonathan Sirotek, *Director*
Carmen Mendoza, *Admin Sec*
EMP: 14 EST: 1966
SALES (est): 2.5MM **Privately Held**
WEB: www.axismfg.com
SIC: 3599 Custom machinery

**(G-9328)**
**B & M PLASTIC INC**
2001 Arthur Ave (60007-6006)
PHONE...................847 258-4437
Miroslaw Grabowski, *Principal*
EMP: 11
SALES (est): 2.3MM **Privately Held**
SIC: 3089 Air mattresses, plastic

**(G-9329)**
**B & W MACHINE COMPANY INC**
71 Gordon St (60007-1117)
PHONE...................847 364-4500
Fax: 847 364-4505
P Bockstahler, *President*
Peter Bockstahler, *President*
Bernadette Bockstahler, *Admin Sec*
EMP: 5
SQ FT: 5,000
SALES: 300K **Privately Held**
SIC: 3599 7692 Machine shop, jobbing & repair; welding repair

**(G-9330)**
**B AND K MUELLER INDUSTRIES**
2021 Lunt Ave (60007-5605)
PHONE...................847 290-1108
Fax: 847 773-0330
Peter Bricman, *President*
◆ EMP: 9
SALES (est): 815.5K **Privately Held**
SIC: 3999 Manufacturing industries

**(G-9331)**
**B M W INC**
415 Bennett Rd (60007-1006)
PHONE...................847 439-0095
Fax: 847 439-0118
Boris Raslin, *President*
Gary Iklov, *Vice Pres*
Ella Khajan, *Accounts Mgr*
EMP: 25
SQ FT: 17,000
SALES (est): 5.5MM **Privately Held**
WEB: www.wbm-inc.com
SIC: 3599 Machine shop, jobbing & repair

**(G-9332)**
**B S GRINDING INC**
2535 United Ln (60007-6820)
PHONE...................847 787-0770
Fax: 847 956-1798
Ted Boska, *President*
EMP: 5
SQ FT: 4,600
SALES (est): 530K **Privately Held**
SIC: 7389 3599 Grinding, precision: commercial or industrial; machine shop, jobbing & repair

**(G-9333)**
**BALLY FOIL GRAPHICS INC**
1701 Elmhurst Rd (60007-6407)
PHONE...................847 427-1509
Fax: 847 427-1537
Allan L Bally, *President*
EMP: 4
SALES: 200K **Privately Held**
SIC: 2752 2791 2759 Commercial printing, offset; typesetting; commercial printing; publication printing

**(G-9334)**
**BAMS MANUFACTURING CO INC**
421 Bennett Rd (60007-1006)
PHONE...................800 206-0613
Fax: 847 647-6968
David Sverdlik, *President*
EMP: 7
SQ FT: 3,500
SALES (est): 620K **Privately Held**
SIC: 8711 3599 3549 Designing: ship, boat, machine & product; custom machinery; metalworking machinery

**(G-9335)**
**BAYER CORPORATION**
25 Northwest Point Blvd (60007-1056)
PHONE...................847 725-6320
Sang Lyu, *Manager*
EMP: 4
SALES (corp-wide): 49.4B **Privately Held**
SIC: 2821 Polypropylene resins
HQ: Bayer Corporation
100 Bayer Rd
Pittsburgh PA 15205
412 777-2000

**(G-9336)**
**BECKER SPECIALTY CORPORATION (DH)**
2526 Delta Ln (60007-6305)
PHONE...................847 766-3555
Jack McGrew, *Principal*
Mary Hanley, *Controller*
Steven B Chameides, *Admin Sec*
▲ EMP: 17
SALES (est): 35.3MM
SALES (corp-wide): 837.5MM **Privately Held**
WEB: www.beckers-bic.com
SIC: 3677 Electronic coils, transformers & other inductors

# Elk Grove Village - Cook County (G-9337)

HQ: Becker Industrial Coatings Holding Ab
Bruksgarden
Hoganas  263 3
423 385-00

**(G-9337)**
**BECKS LIGHT GAUGE ALUMINUM CO**
1425 Tonne Rd  (60007-5003)
PHONE ................................. 847 290-9990
Greg Beck, *President*
Matt Swanson, *Manager*
EMP: 10
SALES (est): 3.7MM  **Privately Held**
SIC: 5051  3365  Miscellaneous nonferrous products; aluminum foundries

**(G-9338)**
**BELL LITHO INC (PA)**
Also Called: Glo Document Solutions
370 Crossen Ave  (60007-2089)
PHONE ................................. 847 952-3300
Fax: 847 952-8010
Felix Ricci, *President*
Herman A Bellagamba, *Chairman*
Maureen Bellagamba, *Corp Secy*
Martin Bellagamba, *Vice Pres*
Mike Marsek, *Vice Pres*
EMP: 82 EST: 1965
SQ FT: 30,000
SALES (est): 16.8MM  **Privately Held**
WEB: www.bell-litho.com
SIC: 2752  2789  Commercial printing, offset; bookbinding & related work

**(G-9339)**
**BELL LITHO INC**
Also Called: Sun America
1820 Lunt Ave  (60007-5602)
PHONE ................................. 847 290-9300
Nelson McAllister, *Purchasing*
Gary Miller, *Manager*
EMP: 6
SALES (corp-wide): 16.8MM  **Privately Held**
WEB: www.bell-litho.com
SIC: 2752  Commercial printing, offset
PA: Bell Litho, Inc.
370 Crossen Ave
Elk Grove Village IL 60007
847 952-3300

**(G-9340)**
**BELMONT SAUSAGE COMPANY**
2201 Estes Ave  (60007-5426)
PHONE ................................. 847 357-1515
Fax: 847 472-9858
Walter Milica, *President*
Mario Tkacz, *Opers Staff*
Elwira Blicharz, *QC Mgr*
Michael Mulica, *Info Tech Mgr*
▲ EMP: 25 EST: 1963
SALES (est): 5.7MM  **Privately Held**
WEB: www.belmontsausage.com
SIC: 2013  2011  Sausages & other prepared meats; meat packing plants

**(G-9341)**
**BEST METAL EXTRUSIONS INC**
1900 E Devon Ave  (60007-6022)
PHONE ................................. 847 981-0797
Fax: 630 595-4103
Terry Slade, *President*
Juan Gonzalez, *Plant Mgr*
Parker Slade, *Opers Mgr*
Mary Akhavan, *Manager*
EMP: 20
SQ FT: 7,000
SALES (est): 5MM  **Privately Held**
WEB: www.bestmetal.net
SIC: 3544  Extrusion dies

**(G-9342)**
**BIOSYNERGY INC (PA)**
1940 E Devon Ave  (60007-6022)
PHONE ................................. 847 956-0471
Fax: 847 956-6050
Fred K Suzuki, *Ch of Bd*
Laurence Mead, *COO*
Mary K Friske, *Vice Pres*
Jennifer A Rieck, *Vice Pres*
Lauane C Addis, *Admin Sec*
EMP: 5
SQ FT: 10,400
SALES (est): 1.3MM  **Privately Held**
WEB: www.biosynergyinc.com
SIC: 3829  3841  3822  3821  Thermometers & temperature sensors; temperature sensors, except industrial process & aircraft; surgical & medical instruments; auto controls regulating residntl & coml environmt & applncs; laboratory apparatus & furniture

**(G-9343)**
**BLAIR COMPANY**
225 N Arlington Heights R  (60007-1017)
PHONE ................................. 847 439-3980
Fax: 847 439-3983
Michael Lebov, *Owner*
EMP: 5
SALES (est): 1MM  **Privately Held**
SIC: 5049  5047  3821  Laboratory equipment, except medical or dental; hospital furniture; hospital equipment & supplies; laboratory apparatus & furniture

**(G-9344)**
**BLEY LLC**
700 Chase Ave  (60007-4804)
PHONE ................................. 847 290-0117
Keren Nelson, *Accountant*
Regina Heine, *Office Mgr*
David Eggert, *Mng Member*
Krishna Rajagopal,
▲ EMP: 53
SQ FT: 68,000
SALES (est): 10.8MM  **Privately Held**
SIC: 3541  Machine tools, metal cutting type

**(G-9345)**
**BLOCKMASTER ELECTRONICS INC**
1400 Howard St  (60007-2221)
PHONE ................................. 847 956-1680
Fax: 847 956-1690
Joe Sieracki, *President*
Joseph Horak, *Office Mgr*
▲ EMP: 8
SQ FT: 20,000
SALES (est): 640K  **Privately Held**
WEB: www.blockmaster.com
SIC: 3679  Electronic circuits

**(G-9346)**
**BROOKE GRAPHICS LLC**
1331 Greenleaf Ave  (60007-5520)
PHONE ................................. 847 593-1300
Fax: 847 985-9507
Amy Polich, *Manager*
Reed Larson, *CTO*
Thomas James B Bednarke,
Sheila L Bednarke,
EMP: 22
SQ FT: 35,000
SALES (est): 4.3MM  **Privately Held**
SIC: 2759  Commercial printing

**(G-9347)**
**BUCTHEL METAL FINISHING CORP**
1945 Touhy Ave  (60007-5315)
PHONE ................................. 847 427-8704
Fax: 847 427-8706
Abe Yousif, *President*
Lorraine Geruis, *MIS Mgr*
EMP: 12
SQ FT: 10,000
SALES (est): 1.5MM  **Privately Held**
SIC: 3471  Buffing for the trade; polishing, metals or formed products; finishing, metals or formed products

**(G-9348)**
**BUILDEX ELECTRONICS INC**
1734 Elmhurst Rd  (60007-5909)
P.O. Box 130, Wheeling  (60090-0130)
PHONE ................................. 847 437-2299
Fax: 847 437-0885
Bhagvanji J Parecha, *President*
Shobhna Parecha, *Vice Pres*
EMP: 15
SQ FT: 5,000
SALES (est): 2MM  **Privately Held**
WEB: www.buildexelectronics.com
SIC: 3672  Printed circuit boards

**(G-9349)**
**BURSTAN INC**
2530 United Ln  (60007-6819)
PHONE ................................. 847 787-0380
Santon Katka, *President*
EMP: 4
SALES (est): 377.4K  **Privately Held**
SIC: 2752  Commercial printing, lithographic

**(G-9350)**
**BV USA ENTERPRISES**
1680-1682 Carmen Dr  (60007)
PHONE ................................. 224 619-7888
Lan Yin Tsdai, *Officer*
EMP: 3
SALES (est): 159.4K  **Privately Held**
SIC: 5091  3751  Bicycle equipment & supplies; motorcycles, bicycles & parts

**(G-9351)**
**BWAY CORPORATION**
1350 Arthur Ave  (60007-5707)
PHONE ................................. 847 956-0750
Marcelo Osorio, *Manager*
Trevor Maclaughlin, *Manager*
EMP: 146
SALES (corp-wide): 831.7MM  **Privately Held**
SIC: 3411  3089  Metal cans; can lids & ends, metal; oil cans, metal; plastic containers, except foam; tubs, plastic (containers)
HQ: Bway Corporation
8607 Roberts Dr Ste 250
Atlanta GA 30350
770 645-4800

**(G-9352)**
**C U SERVICES  LLC**
725 Parkview Cir  (60007-3330)
PHONE ................................. 847 439-2303
Fax: 847 439-2303
Ramsey Cronfel, *Mng Member*
▲ EMP: 5
SALES (est): 900K  **Privately Held**
WEB: www.cuservices.net
SIC: 5084  3494  Industrial machinery & equipment; valves & pipe fittings

**(G-9353)**
**C2 IMAGING  LLC**
Elk Grove Graphics
1200 Chase Ave  (60007-4826)
PHONE ................................. 847 439-7834
EMP: 45  **Privately Held**
SIC: 2752  Commercial printing, lithographic
PA: C2 Imaging, Llc
201 Plaza Two
Jersey City NJ 07311

**(G-9354)**
**CABINET BROKER LTD**
1061 Rohlwing Rd  (60007-3217)
PHONE ................................. 847 352-1898
Fax: 847 352-2066
Jerry Sitter, *President*
EMP: 1
SALES (est): 350K  **Privately Held**
SIC: 2434  7389  Wood kitchen cabinets; design services

**(G-9355)**
**CABLE COMPANY (PA)**
498 Bonnie Ln  (60007-1908)
PHONE ................................. 847 437-5267
John S Lloyd, *President*
▲ EMP: 23
SQ FT: 12,000
SALES (est): 4.5MM  **Privately Held**
WEB: www.cablecotech.com
SIC: 3663  5063  Television broadcasting & communications equipment; wire & cable

**(G-9356)**
**CARGOIS INC**
2700 Coyle Ave  (60007-6406)
PHONE ................................. 847 357-1901
Jong Han Kwon, *President*
Kisun Park, *Principal*
Tim Lee, *Manager*
▼ EMP: 13
SALES (est): 2.2MM  **Privately Held**
SIC: 2448  Cargo containers, wood

**(G-9357)**
**CARR MACHINE & TOOL INC**
1301 Jarvis Ave  (60007-2387)
PHONE ................................. 847 593-8003
Fax: 847 593-8007
Richard Carr, *President*
Serge Shelepov, *Mfg Mgr*
James R Carr, *Treasurer*
EMP: 8
SQ FT: 7,500
SALES (est): 1.4MM  **Privately Held**
WEB: www.carrmachine.com
SIC: 3599  Machine shop, jobbing & repair

**(G-9358)**
**CATALINA COATING & PLAS INC**
Also Called: Catalina Graphic Films
870 Greenleaf Ave  (60007-5026)
PHONE ................................. 847 806-1340
Fax: 847 806-0296
David Robbins, *Accounts Mgr*
Jim Pluskota, *Office Mgr*
David J Petrow, *Administration*
Mike Petrow, *Administration*
EMP: 11
SALES (corp-wide): 29.5MM  **Privately Held**
WEB: www.catalinagraphicfilms.com
SIC: 3083  5162  3081  Laminated plastics plate & sheet; plastics materials & basic shapes; unsupported plastics film & sheet
PA: Catalina Coating & Plastics, Inc.
27001 Agoura Rd Ste 100
Calabasas CA 91301
818 880-8060

**(G-9359)**
**CATALOG DESIGNERS INC**
106 Buckingham Ct  (60007-3856)
PHONE ................................. 847 228-0025
Robert N Holzheimer, *CEO*
Kathleen Holzheimer, *Vice Pres*
EMP: 4
SALES (est): 444.3K  **Privately Held**
WEB: www.catalogdesigners.com
SIC: 2741  7311  2759  Catalogs: publishing only, not printed on site; advertising agencies; commercial printing

**(G-9360)**
**CATAPULT GLOBAL  LLC**
1000 Lee St  (60007-1208)
PHONE ................................. 847 364-8149
Long S Shouchou,
Frederick Kesselman,
▲ EMP: 10
SQ FT: 25,000
SALES (est): 1.9MM  **Privately Held**
WEB: www.catapultglobal.com
SIC: 3441  Fabricated structural metal

**(G-9361)**
**CENTECH PLASTICS  INC**
Also Called: Cmt
855 Touhy Ave  (60007-4917)
PHONE ................................. 847 364-4433
Fax: 847 364-1144
Mark Hendee, *CEO*
Gyongyi Varhegyi, *President*
Peter Varhegyi, *Vice Pres*
Margaret Cally, *Manager*
▲ EMP: 126
SQ FT: 31,500
SALES (est): 12MM  **Privately Held**
SIC: 3089  Injection molding of plastics

**(G-9362)**
**CENTURY MOLD & TOOL CO**
855 Touhy Ave  (60007-4917)
PHONE ................................. 847 364-5858
Fax: 847 364-6699
Peter Varhegyi, *President*
Gyongyi Varhegyi, *Corp Secy*
EMP: 28
SQ FT: 12,500
SALES (est): 3.3MM  **Privately Held**
WEB: www.centurycentech.com
SIC: 7389  3089  3544  Grinding, precision: commercial or industrial; injection molding of plastics; special dies, tools, jigs & fixtures

**(G-9363)**
**CHALLENGE TOOL CO**
60 Joey Dr  (60007-1302)
PHONE ................................. 847 640-8085

## GEOGRAPHIC SECTION
### Elk Grove Village - Cook County (G-9389)

**Fax:** 847 640-8126
Russell K Stoltz, *Owner*
Kim Fitzgerald, *Finance Other*
Ken Stoltz, *Sales Staff*
**EMP:** 4
**SQ FT:** 6,000
**SALES (est):** 220K **Privately Held**
**WEB:** www.chaltool.com
**SIC:** 3544 Industrial molds; dies, plastics forming; dies & die holders for metal cutting, forming, die casting

### (G-9364)
### CHAMBERS MARKETING OPTIONS
Also Called: Wedding Pages of Chicago, The
1008 Bonaventure Dr (60007-3277)
**PHONE** ............................. 847 584-2626
**Fax:** 847 854-2660
Joe Chambers, *President*
Suzan Chambers, *Admin Sec*
**EMP:** 6
**SQ FT:** 1,200
**SALES (est):** 580.4K **Privately Held**
**SIC:** 5621 7389 2721 Bridal shops; trade show arrangement; periodicals

### (G-9365)
### CHARLESTON INDUSTRIES INC
Also Called: Peterson Alumminum
1005 Tonne Rd (60007-4817)
**PHONE** ............................. 847 228-7150
**Fax:** 847 956-7968
Michael S Peterson, *President*
Michael S Palesny, *Manager*
Mariam Demichael, *Administration*
**EMP:** 3
**SALES (corp-wide):** 66.2MM **Privately Held**
**WEB:** www.cisigns.com
**SIC:** 5046 3993 Commercial equipment; signs & advertising specialties
**HQ:** Charleston Industries, Inc.
101 Industrial Dr
Charleston MS 38921
662 647-5525

### (G-9366)
### CHEM-PLATE INDUSTRIES INC (PA)
1800 Touhy Ave (60007-5314)
**PHONE** ............................. 847 640-1600
**Fax:** 847 640-1699
Martin Straus, *President*
Pedro Gomez, *General Mgr*
Jaclyn Paull, *Purch Agent*
Linette Neal, *QC Dir*
Lisa McKinstry, *Controller*
**EMP:** 80
**SQ FT:** 59,000
**SALES (est):** 56.1MM **Privately Held**
**WEB:** www.chemplateindustries.com
**SIC:** 3398 3471 Metal heat treating; plating & polishing

### (G-9367)
### CHICAGO CIRCUITS CORPORATION
2685 United Ln (60007-6822)
**PHONE** ............................. 847 238-1623
**Fax:** 847 238-9160
Hari Kher, *President*
Mahendra Patel, *Exec VP*
Mike Patel, *Vice Pres*
Rakesh Patel, *Vice Pres*
**EMP:** 16
**SQ FT:** 15,000
**SALES:** 2.2MM **Privately Held**
**WEB:** www.chicagocircuits.com
**SIC:** 3672 5063 Printed circuit boards; circuit breakers

### (G-9368)
### CHICAGO PALLET SERVICE INC (HQ)
1875 Greenleaf Ave (60007-5501)
**PHONE** ............................. 847 439-8754
**Fax:** 312 343-4567
Leo Rodriguez, *President*
Araceli Rodriguez, *Vice Pres*
**EMP:** 32
**SALES (est):** 5.8MM
**SALES (corp-wide):** 8.4MM **Privately Held**
**SIC:** 2448 Wood pallets & skids

**PA:** Chicago Pallet Service Ii, Inc.
1875 Greenleaf Ave
Elk Grove Village IL 60007
847 439-8330

### (G-9369)
### CHICAGO PALLET SERVICE II INC (PA)
1875 Greenleaf Ave (60007-5501)
**PHONE** ............................. 847 439-8330
Amparo Rodriguez, *President*
Sally Rodriguez, *Vice Pres*
**EMP:** 31
**SALES (est):** 8.4MM **Privately Held**
**SIC:** 2448 Pallets, wood & wood with metal

### (G-9370)
### CHICAGO WATERJET INC
42 Martin Ln (60007-1308)
**PHONE** ............................. 847 350-1898
Patrick Hill, *President*
**EMP:** 2 **EST:** 2000
**SQ FT:** 2,500
**SALES (est):** 356.9K **Privately Held**
**WEB:** www.chicagowaterjet.com
**SIC:** 3599 4941 Machine shop, jobbing & repair; water supply

### (G-9371)
### CHICAGOSTYLE WEDDINGS
1008 Bonaventure Dr (60007-3277)
**PHONE** ............................. 847 584-2626
**Fax:** 847 584-2660
Joe Chambers, *Principal*
**EMP:** 5
**SALES (est):** 301.3K **Privately Held**
**SIC:** 2335 Wedding gowns & dresses

### (G-9372)
### CHRISTOPHER R CLINE PRTG LTD
931 Oakton St (60007-1905)
**PHONE** ............................. 847 981-0500
**Fax:** 847 981-0580
Christopher R Cline, *President*
**EMP:** 12
**SQ FT:** 5,000
**SALES (est):** 1.1MM **Privately Held**
**SIC:** 2752 2791 2789 Commercial printing, offset; typesetting; bookbinding & related work

### (G-9373)
### CIM-TECH PLASTICS INC
2670 United Ln (60007-6821)
**PHONE** ............................. 847 350-0900
**Fax:** 847 350-0903
Charles Pertile, *President*
Anthony D'Angelo, *Admin Sec*
Laurie Miller, *Administration*
**EMP:** 16
**SQ FT:** 6,000
**SALES (est):** 2.5MM **Privately Held**
**SIC:** 3089 Plastic processing

### (G-9374)
### CIRCUIT ENGINEERING LLC
1390 Lunt Ave (60007-5620)
**PHONE** ............................. 847 806-7777
Felix Simon, *General Mgr*
Bruce Parker, *Controller*
Tony Serpe, *VP Sales*
Bhavesh Mehta, *Manager*
Roy Elamaaa,
▲ **EMP:** 40
**SQ FT:** 40,000
**SALES (est):** 7.7MM **Privately Held**
**WEB:** www.circuiteng.com
**SIC:** 3672 Printed circuit boards

### (G-9375)
### CLASSIFIED VENTURES
1905 Lunt Ave (60007-5603)
**PHONE** ............................. 847 472-2718
**EMP:** 4
**SALES (est):** 17.2K **Privately Held**
**SIC:** 2711 Newspapers, publishing & printing

### (G-9376)
### CLEAR LAM PACKAGING INC (PA)
1950 Pratt Blvd (60007-5993)
**PHONE** ............................. 847 439-8570
James Sanfilippo, *President*

Louis Belmont, *Vice Pres*
Thomas Caulfield, *CFO*
Kathy Pepsnik, *Human Res Dir*
John Mahr, *Sales Mgr*
▲ **EMP:** 277
**SQ FT:** 155,000
**SALES (est):** 167.9MM **Privately Held**
**SIC:** 2671 Packaging paper & plastics film, coated & laminated

### (G-9377)
### CLEAR LAM PACKAGING INC
Also Called: Map Systems
1900 Pratt Blvd (60007-5906)
**PHONE** ............................. 847 378-1200
Hermes Bidawid, *Vice Pres*
Elaine Chaney, *Vice Pres*
Donald Page, *Engineer*
Bob Keamsen, *Sales Staff*
Tom Wedoff, *Manager*
**EMP:** 60
**SALES (corp-wide):** 167.9MM **Privately Held**
**SIC:** 2821 Molding compounds, plastics
**PA:** Clear Lam Packaging, Inc.
1950 Pratt Blvd
Elk Grove Village IL 60007
847 439-8570

### (G-9378)
### CLINGAN STEEL INC
2525 Arthur Ave (60007-6019)
**PHONE** ............................. 847 228-6200
Robert S Clingan, *President*
Tom Bulwan, *General Mgr*
Tom Buowan, *General Mgr*
Ron Licko, *COO*
Cristina Vargas, *Opers Mgr*
◆ **EMP:** 85
**SALES:** 31.3MM **Privately Held**
**WEB:** www.clingansteel.com
**SIC:** 3316 Cold finishing of steel shapes

### (G-9379)
### CMP ASSOCIATES INC
Also Called: Cmp Anodizing
1340 Howard St (60007-2214)
**PHONE** ............................. 847 956-1313
Werner Langenstrass, *President*
Carol Langenstrass, *Admin Sec*
**EMP:** 12
**SALES (est):** 1.9MM **Privately Held**
**WEB:** www.cmpanodizing.com
**SIC:** 3471 Polishing, metals or formed products

### (G-9380)
### COATINGS APPLICATIONS INC
2671 United Ln (60007-6822)
**PHONE** ............................. 847 238-9408
**Fax:** 847 595-0884
Donato Clemente, *President*
Guy Mele, *Executive*
**EMP:** 40
**SQ FT:** 15,000
**SALES (est):** 5.2MM **Privately Held**
**WEB:** www.coatingsapp.com
**SIC:** 3479 3353 Painting of metal products; aluminum sheet, plate & foil

### (G-9381)
### COLORS FOR PLASTICS INC
2239 Pratt Blvd (60007-5916)
**PHONE** ............................. 847 437-0033
John Dalleska, *Manager*
**EMP:** 5
**SALES (corp-wide):** 21.4MM **Privately Held**
**WEB:** www.colorsforplastics.com
**SIC:** 2816 2865 Inorganic pigments; cyclic crudes & intermediates
**PA:** Colors For Plastics, Inc.
2245 Pratt Blvd
Elk Grove Village IL 60007
847 437-0033

### (G-9382)
### COLORS FOR PLASTICS INC (PA)
2245 Pratt Blvd (60007-5916)
**PHONE** ............................. 847 437-0033
**Fax:** 847 806-0787
John Dalleska, *President*
Robert Dalleska, *Vice Pres*
Gayle Paredes, *Manager*
**EMP:** 75

**SQ FT:** 45,000
**SALES (est):** 21.4MM **Privately Held**
**WEB:** www.colorsforplastics.com
**SIC:** 2816 2865 Inorganic pigments; cyclic crudes & intermediates

### (G-9383)
### COMET TOOL INC
880 Nicholas Blvd (60007-2511)
**PHONE** ............................. 847 956-0126
Hans Wiesmayer, *President*
James W Ray, *President*
Griff Noon, *Vice Pres*
Edward A Zemola, *Vice Pres*
Monika Wiesmayer, *Treasurer*
▲ **EMP:** 50 **EST:** 1968
**SQ FT:** 34,000
**SALES (est):** 798.4K **Privately Held**
**WEB:** www.comettool.com
**SIC:** 3545 3625 Mfg Machine Tool Accessories Mfg Relays/Industrial Controls

### (G-9384)
### COMMERCIAL COPY PRINTING CTR
520 Bennett Rd (60007-1122)
**PHONE** ............................. 847 981-8590
**EMP:** 15 **EST:** 1979
**SQ FT:** 4,000
**SALES:** 1MM **Privately Held**
**SIC:** 2752 2796 2791 2789 Lithographic Coml Print Platemaking Services Typesetting Services Bookbinding/Related Work

### (G-9385)
### COMMERCIAL FINISHES CO LTD
540 Lively Blvd (60007-2014)
**PHONE** ............................. 847 981-9222
**Fax:** 847 981-0698
Sam Legittino, *President*
John Klodnicki, *Vice Pres*
John Koodinicki, *Vice Pres*
Judith Legittino, *Admin Sec*
**EMP:** 23
**SQ FT:** 16,000
**SALES (est):** 1.1MM **Privately Held**
**WEB:** www.cfcpaint.com
**SIC:** 3479 Painting, coating & hot dipping

### (G-9386)
### COMMERCIAL MACHINE SERVICES
1099 Touhy Ave (60007-4921)
P.O. Box 835 (60009-0835)
**PHONE** ............................. 847 806-1901
**Fax:** 847 806-1975
Herbert R Gottelt, *President*
Robert Walser, *Vice Pres*
**EMP:** 10
**SQ FT:** 4,000
**SALES (est):** 1.4MM **Privately Held**
**WEB:** www.callcommercial.com
**SIC:** 7699 7692 3599 Industrial machinery & equipment repair; welding repair; machine shop, jobbing & repair

### (G-9387)
### COMMERCIAL STAINLESS SERVICES
1201 Busse Rd (60007-4820)
**PHONE** ............................. 847 349-1560
Daniel Hansen, *President*
**EMP:** 19
**SALES (est):** 4MM **Privately Held**
**SIC:** 3312 Stainless steel

### (G-9388)
### CONCEPT INDUSTRIES INC
199 Gaylord St (60007-1106)
**PHONE** ............................. 847 258-3545
Robert Renner, *President*
Jack Krafcisin, *Admin Sec*
**EMP:** 4
**SQ FT:** 7,000
**SALES (est):** 895.7K **Privately Held**
**SIC:** 7692 Welding repair

### (G-9389)
### CONNOR SPORTS FLOORING LLC (DH)
1830 Howard St Ste F (60007-2481)
**PHONE** ............................. 847 290-9020
Ronald Cerny, *CEO*

# Elk Grove Village - Cook County (G-9390)

Jon Isaacs, *Vice Pres*
Kenneth Bayne, *CFO*
▼ **EMP:** 87
**SQ FT:** 164,000
**SALES (est):** 25.5MM
**SALES (corp-wide):** 62.5MM **Privately Held**
**WEB:** www.connorfloor.com
**SIC:** 2426 5031 2439 Flooring, hardwood; lumber: rough, dressed & finished; structural wood members
**HQ:** Connor Sport Court International, Llc
5445 W Harold Gatty Dr
Salt Lake City UT 84116
801 972-0260

### (G-9390)
**CONTINENTAL BINDERY CORP**
700 Fargo Ave (60007-4703)
**PHONE** ..............................847 439-6811
**Fax:** 847 439-6847
Tim Hoffman, *President*
Tim Brown, *Opers Mgr*
Sandra Kiefer, *Office Mgr*
Florene Bongi, *Manager*
**EMP:** 100
**SQ FT:** 21,000
**SALES (est):** 11.5MM **Privately Held**
**SIC:** 2789 Binding only: books, pamphlets, magazines, etc.

### (G-9391)
**CONTOUR MACHINING INC**
640 Fargo Ave (60007-4701)
**PHONE** ..............................847 364-0111
**Fax:** 847 364-0117
Gertrude Schneider, *CEO*
Werner Schneider, *President*
**EMP:** 7
**SQ FT:** 5,000
**SALES:** 1MM **Privately Held**
**WEB:** www.contourmachining.net
**SIC:** 3599 Machine shop, jobbing & repair

### (G-9392)
**CONVERTING TECHNOLOGY INC**
Also Called: CTI
1557 Carmen Dr (60007-6501)
**PHONE** ..............................847 290-0590
**Fax:** 847 290-0596
John Norgard, *President*
William Crutchfield, *Treasurer*
Steve Katsenios, *Manager*
Dan McGhee, *Manager*
Rich Belmonte, *Director*
▲ **EMP:** 57
**SQ FT:** 27,600
**SALES (est):** 10.9MM **Privately Held**
**WEB:** www.converting-technology.com
**SIC:** 3544 Dies, steel rule

### (G-9393)
**COOPER LIGHTING LLC**
2550 United Ln (60007-6819)
**PHONE** ..............................312 595-2770
Tony Tarello, *Branch Mgr*
**EMP:** 4 **Privately Held**
**WEB:** www.corelite.com
**SIC:** 3645 Residential lighting fixtures
**HQ:** Cooper Lighting, Llc
1121 Highway 74 S
Peachtree City GA 30269
770 486-4800

### (G-9394)
**COOPER LIGHTING LLC**
400 Busse Rd (60007-2195)
**PHONE** ..............................847 956-8400
**Fax:** 847 806-3894
Dave Arnold, *Branch Mgr*
Russell Burns, *Agent*
**EMP:** 100 **Privately Held**
**WEB:** www.corelite.com
**SIC:** 3645 3646 Residential lighting fixtures; commercial indusl & institutional electric lighting fixtures
**HQ:** Cooper Lighting, Llc
1121 Highway 74 S
Peachtree City GA 30269
770 486-4800

### (G-9395)
**COOPER SMITH INTERNATIONAL INC**
Also Called: SCI
2701 Busse Rd (60007-6102)
**PHONE** ..............................847 595-7572
**Fax:** 708 568-0290
Rich Digiuseppe, *Regional Mgr*
Gary Skeber, *Regional Mgr*
Tom Seaks, *Regl Sales Mgr*
Chuck Neely, *Branch Mgr*
**EMP:** 80
**SALES (corp-wide):** 100.7MM **Privately Held**
**SIC:** 3494 Valves & pipe fittings
**PA:** Smith Cooper International, Inc
2867 Vail Ave
Commerce CA 90040
323 890-4455

### (G-9396)
**CORE-MARK INTERNATIONAL INC**
405 Lively Blvd (60007-2011)
**PHONE** ..............................847 593-1800
Joseph Martin, *Owner*
**EMP:** 4
**SALES (corp-wide):** 14.5B **Publicly Held**
**WEB:** www.core-mark.com
**SIC:** 3089 Plastic containers, except foam
**HQ:** Core-Mark International, Inc.
395 Oyster Point Blvd # 415
South San Francisco CA 94080
650 589-9445

### (G-9397)
**CORRO-SHIELD INTERNATIONAL INC**
2575 United Ln (60007-6820)
**PHONE** ..............................847 298-7770
**Fax:** 847 298-7784
M Grant Brown, *President*
Bret Sneider, *COO*
Hugh Mc Veigh, *Vice Pres*
William Demetros, *Accountant*
Bret Snider, *Manager*
**EMP:** 12
**SQ FT:** 11,000
**SALES:** 1.5MM **Privately Held*
**WEB:** www.corroshield.com
**SIC:** 2821 Epoxy resins

### (G-9398)
**CRAFTSTECH INC**
Also Called: Crafts Technology
91 Joey Dr (60007-1321)
**PHONE** ..............................847 758-3100
**Fax:** 847 758-0162
Thomas Kuhl, *President*
David Le Maistre, *Vice Pres*
Jeffrey Roberts, *Engineer*
Dave Lemaistre, *VP Sales*
Jeffrey Taylor, *Business Dir*
**EMP:** 37 **EST:** 1996
**SQ FT:** 20,000
**SALES:** 7.1MM **Privately Held**
**WEB:** www.craftstech.net
**SIC:** 3545 Machine tool accessories

### (G-9399)
**CREATIVE LABEL INC (PA)**
2450 Estes Ave (60007-5490)
**PHONE** ..............................847 981-3800
Jerry Koril, *CEO*
Gary Koril, *President*
Terri Koril, *Admin Sec*
**EMP:** 75
**SQ FT:** 50,000
**SALES (est):** 11.5MM **Privately Held**
**WEB:** www.labels-decals.com
**SIC:** 2796 2789 2675 Platemaking services; gold stamping on books; die-cut paper & board

### (G-9400)
**CRISTAUX INC**
Also Called: Cristaux International
1343 Brummel Ave (60007-2108)
**PHONE** ..............................773 775-6020
Andre Janus, *President*
▲ **EMP:** 2
**SALES (est):** 227.9K **Privately Held**
**SIC:** 3231 Products of purchased glass

### (G-9401)
**CROSS EXPRESS COMPANY**
153 Crest Ave (60007-1731)
**PHONE** ..............................847 439-7457
**Fax:** 847 879-1142
Tihomir Mintchev, *President*
**EMP:** 2
**SALES (est):** 275.8K **Privately Held**
**SIC:** 2741 Miscellaneous publishing

### (G-9402)
**CURATEK PHARMACEUTICALS LTD**
1965 Pratt Blvd (60007-5905)
**PHONE** ..............................847 806-7674
**Fax:** 847 806-7612
Robert J Borgman, *President*
**EMP:** 3
**SALES (corp-wide):** 916.5K **Privately Held**
**WEB:** www.curatek.com
**SIC:** 2834 Pharmaceutical preparations
**PA:** Curatek Pharmaceuticals Ltd
3773 Howard Hughes Pkwy
Las Vegas NV
702 734-3700

### (G-9403)
**CUSTOM MACHINING & DESIGN LLC**
1510 Midway Ct Ste E5 (60007-6691)
**PHONE** ..............................847 364-2601
**Fax:** 847 364-2603
Edmund Kuzniarowicz, *Principal*
**EMP:** 4
**SALES (est):** 464.6K **Privately Held**
**SIC:** 8742 7539 3545 3544 Marketing consulting services; machine shop, automotive; machine tool accessories; special dies, tools, jigs & fixtures

### (G-9404)
**CUSTOM PLASTICS INC**
Also Called: Custom Accents
1940 Lunt Ave (60007-5634)
**PHONE** ..............................847 439-6770
**Fax:** 847 572-0674
Peter Tisbo, *President*
William Morelock, *General Mgr*
Richard Kneisel, *Vice Pres*
Ray Mendlik, *Vice Pres*
David Phillips, *Vice Pres*
▲ **EMP:** 220
**SQ FT:** 150,000
**SALES (est):** 62.2MM **Privately Held**
**WEB:** www.customaccents.com
**SIC:** 3089 Extruded finished plastic products; injection molded finished plastic products

### (G-9405)
**CUSTOM PLASTICS INC**
1890 Lunt Ave (60007-5602)
**PHONE** ..............................847 640-4723
Steve Berg, *Manager*
**EMP:** 14
**SALES (est):** 2MM **Privately Held**
**SIC:** 3089 Extruded finished plastic products; injection molded finished plastic products

### (G-9406)
**CUTTING EDGE MACHINING INC**
105 Randall St Ste B (60007-1010)
**PHONE** ..............................847 427-1392
**Fax:** 847 427-1469
Steven Campos, *President*
Ron Gokan, *Vice Pres*
**EMP:** 4
**SQ FT:** 5,000
**SALES (est):** 562.3K **Privately Held**
**WEB:** www.cuttingedgemachining.com
**SIC:** 3599 Machine & other job shop work

### (G-9407)
**CWS CABINETS**
225 Stanley St (60007-1558)
**PHONE** ..............................847 258-4468
Mariusz Jerominski, *Principal*
**EMP:** 4
**SALES (est):** 352.7K **Privately Held**
**SIC:** 2434 Wood kitchen cabinets

### (G-9408)
**D & K CUSTOM MACHINE DESIGN**
1795 Commerce Dr (60007-2119)
P.O. Box 1146 (60009-1146)
**PHONE** ..............................847 956-4757
**Fax:** 847 956-0225
Karl Singer, *President*
Lisa Defrancesco, *Purchasing*
Christina Znorski, *Sls & Mktg Exec*
James Kelly, *Sales Mgr*
Marge Hayes, *Sales Executive*
▲ **EMP:** 30
**SQ FT:** 50,000
**SALES (est):** 5.6MM
**SALES (corp-wide):** 38.7MM **Privately Held**
**WEB:** www.dkgroup.net
**SIC:** 3555 Printing trades machinery
**PA:** D & K Group, Inc.
1795 Commerce Dr
Elk Grove Village IL 60007
847 956-0160

### (G-9409)
**D & K GROUP INC (PA)**
1795 Commerce Dr (60007-2119)
P.O. Box 1146 (60009-1146)
**PHONE** ..............................847 956-0160
**Fax:** 847 956-0105
Karl Singer, *President*
Jorn Winkler, *Managing Dir*
Rick Crimmins, *Area Mgr*
Scott Diamond, *Area Mgr*
Mike Owen, *Area Mgr*
▲ **EMP:** 40
**SQ FT:** 135,000
**SALES (est):** 38.7MM **Privately Held**
**WEB:** www.dkgroup.com
**SIC:** 2891 3555 Laminating compounds; printing trades machinery

### (G-9410)
**D & K INTERNATIONAL INC (HQ)**
1795 Commerce Dr (60007-2119)
P.O. Box 1146 (60009-1146)
**PHONE** ..............................847 439-3423
Karl Singer, *President*
Marge Heyes, *Vice Pres*
James Broz, *CFO*
Steve Patton, *Director*
Sally Singer, *Admin Sec*
**EMP:** 47
**SQ FT:** 85,000
**SALES (est):** 20.8MM
**SALES (corp-wide):** 38.7MM **Privately Held**
**WEB:** www.dkgroup.com
**SIC:** 2891 Laminating compounds
**PA:** D & K Group, Inc.
1795 Commerce Dr
Elk Grove Village IL 60007
847 956-0160

### (G-9411)
**D & K MACHINE AND TOOL INC**
1080 Howard St (60007-2208)
**PHONE** ..............................847 439-8691
**Fax:** 847 439-8692
Artur Drewno, *President*
Andrew Kurzynski, *Admin Sec*
**EMP:** 2 **EST:** 1997
**SALES (est):** 326K **Privately Held**
**SIC:** 3599 Machine shop, jobbing & repair

### (G-9412)
**D & S WIRE INC**
2531 E Devon Ave (60007-6313)
**PHONE** ..............................847 766-5520
**Fax:** 847 766-5683
Perry Kospe, *President*
Tom Alexander, *Treasurer*
Perry D Koste, *Treasurer*
Jennie Kropfel, *Office Mgr*
Kristin Kospe, *Admin Sec*
**EMP:** 17 **EST:** 1963
**SQ FT:** 18,000
**SALES (est):** 4.8MM **Privately Held**
**WEB:** www.dswire.com
**SIC:** 3357 Nonferrous wiredrawing & insulating

## GEOGRAPHIC SECTION
### Elk Grove Village - Cook County (G-9436)

**(G-9413)**
**D&W FINE PACK HOLDINGS LLC (HQ)**
1900 Pratt Blvd (60007-5906)
PHONE ..................................... 847 378-1200
David H Randall, *President*
**EMP:** 1 **EST:** 2009
**SALES (est):** 679MM
**SALES (corp-wide):** 711.5MM **Privately Held**
**SIC: 3089** Plastic kitchenware, tableware & houseware
**PA:** Mid Oaks Investments Llc
750 W Lake Cook Rd # 460
Buffalo Grove IL 60089
847 215-3475

**(G-9414)**
**D&W FINE PACK LLC (DH)**
Also Called: D W Packaging Solutions
1900 Pratt Blvd (60007-5906)
PHONE ..................................... 847 378-1200
Dave Randall, *CEO*
Kevin Andrews, *CEO*
Clay Davis, *Senior VP*
Jay Dubois, *Senior VP*
Michael Casula, *Vice Pres*
▲ **EMP:** 550
**SQ FT:** 530,000
**SALES (est):** 679MM
**SALES (corp-wide):** 711.5MM **Privately Held**
**SIC: 3089** Plastic kitchenware, tableware & houseware
**HQ:** D&W Fine Pack Holdings Llc
1900 Pratt Blvd
Elk Grove Village IL 60007
847 378-1200

**(G-9415)**
**D/C EXPORT & DOMESTIC PKG INC (PA)**
Also Called: D/C Group The
1300 E Devon Ave (60007-5831)
PHONE ..................................... 847 593-4200
Fax: 847 593-4209
Carol Cocciemiglio, *President*
Dominick Cocciemiglio Jr, *Corp Secy*
John Cocciemiglio, *Vice Pres*
Paul Michalak, *Vice Pres*
**EMP:** 34
**SQ FT:** 55,000
**SALES (est):** 11.6MM **Privately Held**
**WEB:** www.dcexport.com
**SIC: 4783** 2449 2653 2441 Packing & crating; rectangular boxes & crates, wood; corrugated boxes, partitions, display items, sheets & pad; boxes, wood

**(G-9416)**
**DAIRY DYNAMICS LLC**
17820 Washington St (60007)
P.O. Box 283, Union (60180-0283)
PHONE ..................................... 847 758-7300
Jill Hilgenberg, *Officer*
Herbert J Sewell,
Herbert Sewell,
**EMP:** 12
**SALES (est):** 3.5MM **Privately Held**
**SIC: 2841** Soap & other detergents

**(G-9417)**
**DATASIS CORPORATION**
1687 Elmhurst Rd (60007-6413)
PHONE ..................................... 847 427-0909
Joseph Hassen, *President*
David Bertz, *Exec VP*
Bruce Campbell, *Sales Mgr*
Christina Hassen, *Marketing Mgr*
**EMP:** 16
**SQ FT:** 12,000
**SALES (est):** 2.5MM **Privately Held**
**WEB:** www.datasis.com
**SIC: 7377** 7373 3652 Computer hardware rental or leasing, except finance leasing; computer peripheral equipment rental & leasing; systems software development services; compact laser discs, prerecorded

**(G-9418)**
**DAYTON SUPERIOR CORPORATION**
Also Called: Metal Acesories
2400 Arthur Ave (60007-6017)
PHONE ..................................... 847 391-4700
John Cicearelli, *President*
Jim Eenka, *Vice Pres*
Steven Huston, *Vice Pres*
Edward Rahe, *Engineer*
Jim Benka, *CFO*
▼ **EMP:** 864 **EST:** 1901
**SQ FT:** 25,000
**SALES (est):** 132.4MM **Publicly Held**
**WEB:** www.symons.com
**SIC: 3444** Concrete forms, sheet metal
**HQ:** Dayton Superior Corporation
1125 Byers Rd
Miamisburg OH 45342
937 866-0711

**(G-9419)**
**DEADLINE PRTG CLOR COPYING LLC**
2289 E Devon Ave (60007-6805)
PHONE ..................................... 847 437-9000
George Samp, *Mng Member*
Alan Hugar,
**EMP:** 6
**SQ FT:** 7,200
**SALES:** 1.2MM **Privately Held**
**SIC: 2752** 2789 Commercial printing, offset; bookbinding & related work

**(G-9420)**
**DECO ADHESIVE PDTS 1985 LTD**
Also Called: Deco Labels & Tags
500 Thorndale Ave Ste H (60007)
PHONE ..................................... 847 472-2100
Fax: 847 472-2106
Douglas B Ford, *President*
Kathy De Marco, *Opers Mgr*
Michael Schaid, *Sales Mgr*
**EMP:** 25
**SALES (corp-wide):** 3.6MM **Privately Held**
**SIC: 2679** 2675 2671 Tags & labels, paper; die-cut paper & board; packaging paper & plastics film, coated & laminated
**PA:** Deco Adhesive Products (1985) Limited
28 Greensboro Dr
Etobicoke ON M9W 1
416 247-7878

**(G-9421)**
**DELTA LABORATORIES INC**
2690 Delta Ln (60007-6307)
PHONE ..................................... 630 351-1798
Dennis Fath, *President*
▲ **EMP:** 7 **EST:** 1999
**SALES (est):** 1.4MM **Privately Held**
**SIC: 2844** Cosmetic preparations

**(G-9422)**
**DELTA PRECISION CIRCUITS INC**
1370 Lively Blvd (60007-4926)
PHONE ..................................... 847 758-8000
Fax: 847 758-8010
Mukesh Patel, *President*
Peter Dawravoo, *General Mgr*
Ashok Patel, *Vice Pres*
Janice Rosario, *Sales Staff*
Adesh Patel, *Admin Sec*
▲ **EMP:** 33 **EST:** 1971
**SQ FT:** 35,000
**SALES (est):** 5.2MM **Privately Held**
**WEB:** www.deltacircuits.com
**SIC: 3672** Printed circuit boards

**(G-9423)**
**DENOR GRAPHICS INC**
665 Lunt Ave (60007-5014)
PHONE ..................................... 847 364-1130
Fax: 847 364-4716
Edward W De Luga, *President*
Arleen E De Luga, *Corp Secy*
**EMP:** 10
**SQ FT:** 8,000
**SALES (est):** 1.6MM **Privately Held**
**SIC: 2752** 2791 2789 Commercial printing, offset; typesetting; bookbinding & related work

**(G-9424)**
**DESCO INC**
Also Called: Desco Dryers
1240 Howard St (60007-2267)
PHONE ..................................... 847 439-2130
Fax: 847 439-0029
George J Gambini III, *President*
Lisa M Defily, *CFO*
**EMP:** 6
**SQ FT:** 6,700
**SALES:** 730K **Privately Held**
**WEB:** www.descodryers.com
**SIC: 3559** Metal finishing equipment for plating, etc.

**(G-9425)**
**DESIGN LOFT IMAGING INC**
393 Bianco Dr (60007-4401)
PHONE ..................................... 847 439-2486
Jeffrey Hastings, *President*
Cindy Hastings, *Vice Pres*
**EMP:** 2
**SALES:** 200K **Privately Held**
**WEB:** www.toshiba-machine.com
**SIC: 2395** Embroidery products, except schiffli machine

**(G-9426)**
**DIAMOND SCREEN PROCESS INC**
321 Bond St (60007-1222)
PHONE ..................................... 847 439-6200
Fax: 847 439-6362
Roddy Zukowski, *President*
**EMP:** 8 **EST:** 1956
**SQ FT:** 10,000
**SALES (est):** 1MM **Privately Held**
**WEB:** www.diamondscreen.net
**SIC: 2759** Screen printing

**(G-9427)**
**DIE CRAFT METAL PRODUCTS**
1001 Nicholas Blvd Ste H (60007-2523)
P.O. Box 1104, Plainfield (60544-1104)
PHONE ..................................... 847 593-1433
Fax: 847 593-1970
Arthur Briesch, *CEO*
Pete Norton, *Sales Executive*
**EMP:** 7
**SALES (est):** 1MM **Privately Held**
**SIC: 3544** Special dies & tools

**(G-9428)**
**DIE MOLD JIG GRINDING & MFG**
1485 Landmeier Rd Ste M (60007-2464)
PHONE ..................................... 847 228-1444
Fax: 847 228-7765
Dean Erickson, *President*
**EMP:** 3 **EST:** 1982
**SQ FT:** 1,000
**SALES (est):** 250K **Privately Held**
**SIC: 3544** Industrial molds; jigs & fixtures

**(G-9429)**
**DIEMASTERS MANUFACTURING INC**
2100 Touhy Ave (60007-5325)
PHONE ..................................... 847 640-9900
Fax: 847 640-6292
Virgil Dela, *President*
Charles Brewer, *Vice Pres*
Tom Haring, *Materials Dir*
Bill Curtis, *Plant Mgr*
Jit Mistry, *Project Mgr*
▲ **EMP:** 125
**SALES (est):** 20.7MM **Privately Held**
**WEB:** www.diemasters.net
**SIC: 2396** 3544 3469 3444 Fabric printing & stamping; special dies, tools, jigs & fixtures; metal stampings; sheet metalwork

**(G-9430)**
**DLP COATINGS INC**
2301 Eastern Ave (60007-6814)
PHONE ..................................... 847 350-0113
Richard Murphy, *President*
Jacqueline Murphy, *Corp Secy*
Rachel Garcia, *Manager*
**EMP:** 40
**SQ FT:** 20,000
**SALES (est):** 5.7MM **Privately Held**
**WEB:** www.dlpcoatings.com
**SIC: 3479** Enameling, including porcelain, of metal products; japanning of metal

**(G-9431)**
**DLS CUSTOM EMBROIDERY INC**
Also Called: DLS Printing & Promotions
1665 Tonne Rd (60007-5123)
PHONE ..................................... 847 593-5957
Fax: 847 593-5958
Edward K Schaefer, *President*
Melisa Hoberg, *Vice Pres*
Frank Deneusbourg, *Executive*
**EMP:** 20
**SQ FT:** 5,000
**SALES:** 2.2MM **Privately Held**
**WEB:** www.dlsprint.com
**SIC: 2211** Print cloths, cotton

**(G-9432)**
**DOOSAN INFRACORE AMERICA CORP**
Also Called: Doosan Infrcre Amrca Midw Tech
1701 Howard St Ste F (60007-2479)
PHONE ..................................... 847 437-1010
Jim Shiner, *Manager*
**EMP:** 6
**SALES (corp-wide):** 3.1B **Privately Held**
**WEB:** www.doosanlift.com
**SIC: 3531** Construction machinery
**HQ:** Doosan Machine Tools America Corporation
19a Chapin Rd
Pine Brook NJ 07058
973 618-2500

**(G-9433)**
**DOUMAK INC**
2491 Estes Ave (60007-5422)
PHONE ..................................... 847 981-2180
Fax: 708 640-0013
John Casey, *Controller*
Tim Samson, *Branch Mgr*
Gary Conway, *Director*
**EMP:** 76
**SALES (corp-wide):** 61.3MM **Privately Held**
**WEB:** www.doumak.com
**SIC: 2064** Marshmallows
**PA:** Doumak Inc.
1004 Fairway Dr
Bensenville IL 60106
800 323-0318

**(G-9434)**
**DOW CHEMICAL COMPANY**
2401 Pratt Blvd (60007-5920)
PHONE ..................................... 847 439-2240
Fax: 847 569-3361
David Sizka, *Branch Mgr*
**EMP:** 45
**SALES (corp-wide):** 48.1B **Publicly Held**
**SIC: 2819** 2821 Industrial inorganic chemicals; plastics materials & resins
**HQ:** The Dow Chemical Company
25500 Whitesell St
Hayward CA 94545
510 786-0100

**(G-9435)**
**DRESSER INC**
Becker Precision Equipment
1550 Greenleaf Ave (60007-5525)
PHONE ..................................... 847 437-5940
Fax: 847 437-2549
Narendra Desai, *General Mgr*
Vova Rimboym, *Engineer*
Steven Bowles, *Senior Mgr*
**EMP:** 55
**SALES (corp-wide):** 123.6B **Publicly Held**
**WEB:** www.dresser.com
**SIC: 3491** 3625 3612 3593 Regulators (steam fittings); control equipment, electric; industrial controls: push button, selector switches, pilot; transformers, except electric; fluid power cylinders & actuators; valves & pipe fittings
**HQ:** Dresser, Llc
601 Shiloh Rd
Plano TX 75074
262 549-2626

**(G-9436)**
**DUO GRAPHICS**
1612 Landmeier Rd Ste C (60007-2463)
PHONE ..................................... 847 228-7080
Erin Boomer, *President*

## Elk Grove Village - Cook County (G-9437)

EMP: 4
SQ FT: 3,500
SALES: 170K **Privately Held**
SIC: **2759** 2752 Letterpress printing; commercial printing, offset

**(G-9437)**
**DURABUILT DIE CORP**
619 Woodview Ave (60007-4340)
PHONE..................847 437-2086
Dan Urbina, *President*
Raul Urbina, *Principal*
Evelyn Urbina, *Admin Sec*
EMP: 4
SQ FT: 2,460
SALES (est): 280K **Privately Held**
SIC: **3544** Dies, steel rule

**(G-9438)**
**DURACREST FABRICS**
2474 Delta Ln (60007-6303)
PHONE..................847 350-0030
Ralph Fortino, *President*
EMP: 5
SALES (est): 93.4K **Privately Held**
SIC: **5949** 2399 Fabric stores piece goods; fabricated textile products

**(G-9439)**
**DURATRACK INC**
950 Morse Ave (60007-5108)
PHONE..................847 806-0202
Fax: 847 806-1999
Russell Scott, *President*
Amidee Barnes, *Prdtn Mgr*
Geri Leatherman, *Facilities Mgr*
Julie Scott, *Admin Sec*
Dawn Sheeman, *Administration*
EMP: 25
SQ FT: 30,000
SALES (est): 1.2MM **Privately Held**
WEB: www.duratrak.com
SIC: **3429** Manufactured hardware (general)

**(G-9440)**
**DVA METAL FABRICATION INC**
1427 Tonne Rd (60007-5003)
PHONE..................224 577-8217
Dimitar Atanassov, *Principal*
EMP: 4
SALES (est): 415.7K **Privately Held**
SIC: **3399** Powder, metal

**(G-9441)**
**E B G B INC**
Also Called: Chicago Sign Designs
220 Lively Blvd (60007-1623)
PHONE..................847 228-9333
Fax: 847 228-9335
Gary Becker, *President*
Eric Becker, *Vice Pres*
EMP: 2
SQ FT: 2,500
SALES (est): 290.4K **Privately Held**
WEB: www.chicagosigndesigns.com
SIC: **3993** Signs & advertising specialties

**(G-9442)**
**E C SCHULTZ & CO INC**
333 Crossen Ave (60007-2050)
PHONE..................847 640-1190
Fax: 847 640-1198
Michael Pautz, *President*
James Pautz, *Vice Pres*
Paul Murphy, *Manager*
EMP: 16 EST: 1895
SQ FT: 8,000
SALES: 1.9MM **Privately Held**
SIC: **2796** 3544 Engraving on copper, steel, wood or rubber: printing plates; special dies, tools, jigs & fixtures

**(G-9443)**
**E J WELCH CO INC**
2601 Lively Blvd (60007-6730)
PHONE..................847 238-0100
Mike Gee, *Manager*
EMP: 24
SALES (corp-wide): 61MM **Privately Held**
SIC: **3423** Hand & edge tools
PA: E. J. Welch Co., Inc.
13735 Lakefront Dr
Earth City MO 63045
314 739-2273

**(G-9444)**
**E-M METAL FABRICATOR**
145 Joey Dr (60007-1303)
PHONE..................847 593-9970
Fax: 847 593-7925
Milton R Moscoso, *Principal*
Elva Moscoso, *Post Master*
EMP: 3
SALES (est): 668.6K **Privately Held**
SIC: **3444** Sheet metalwork; metal housings, enclosures, casings & other containers; casings, sheet metal; stove boards, sheet metal

**(G-9445)**
**E-Z ROTATIONAL MOLDER INC**
1001 Nicholas Blvd Ste F (60007-2523)
PHONE..................847 806-1327
Fax: 847 806-1330
Edmund Zalewski, *President*
John Zalewski, *Vice Pres*
Greg Zalewski, *Plant Mgr*
Theresa Zalewski, *Admin Sec*
Peter Zalewski, *Representative*
EMP: 6
SQ FT: 5,000
SALES (est): 758.4K **Privately Held**
SIC: **3089** Molding primary plastic

**(G-9446)**
**EAGLE CONNECTOR CORPORATION**
401 Crossen Ave (60007-2003)
PHONE..................847 593-8737
Fax: 847 956-8190
Henry E Bauerle, *President*
John Bauer, *Vice Pres*
Freida Bauerle, *Treasurer*
Elizabeth Bauer, *Admin Sec*
EMP: 18
SQ FT: 5,000
SALES (est): 1.5MM **Privately Held**
WEB: www.eagleconnector.com
SIC: **3643** Current-carrying wiring devices

**(G-9447)**
**EAST COAST SIGNS ADVERTISING**
1418 Elmhurst Rd (60007-6417)
PHONE..................215 458-9042
Kurt Ripkey, *President*
Melanie Jech, *Vice Pres*
EMP: 95
SALES (est): 5.7MM **Privately Held**
SIC: **3993** Signs & advertising specialties

**(G-9448)**
**ECOLAB INC**
Also Called: Johnson Contrls Authorized Dlr
1060 Thorndale Ave (60007-6747)
PHONE..................847 350-2229
Fax: 847 350-2657
Greg Powers, *Principal*
Iisha Griffin, *QC Mgr*
Abrar Ahmed, *Engineer*
Mark Swisher, *Manager*
EMP: 35
SALES (corp-wide): 13.1B **Publicly Held**
WEB: www.ecolab.com
SIC: **2842** 5075 Specialty cleaning, polishes & sanitation goods; warm air heating & air conditioning
PA: Ecolab Inc.
1 Ecolab Pl
Saint Paul MN 55102
800 232-6522

**(G-9449)**
**EDLONG CORPORATION (PA)**
Also Called: Edlong Flavors
225 Scott St (60007-1212)
PHONE..................847 439-9230
Fax: 847 439-0053
Laurette Rondenet-Smith, *President*
Rick Schultz, *Vice Pres*
Anne Druschitz, *Research*
Dawn Leduc, *Controller*
Dawn J Leduke, *Controller*
▼ EMP: 75 EST: 1914
SQ FT: 120,000
SALES (est): 16MM **Privately Held**
WEB: www.edlong.com
SIC: **2087** Extracts, flavoring

**(G-9450)**
**ELECTRONIC INTERCONNECT CORP**
2375 Estes Ave (60007-5428)
PHONE..................847 364-4848
Fax: 847 364-4892
Pratish Patel, *President*
Dr Bharad Barai, *Chairman*
Melody Mietzke, *Regional Mgr*
Vikas Shaw, *CFO*
Angela Kariwiec, *Manager*
EMP: 99
SQ FT: 25,000
SALES (est): 20.3MM **Privately Held**
WEB: www.eiconnect.com
SIC: **3672** Printed circuit boards

**(G-9451)**
**ELK GROVE CUSTOM SHEET METAL**
106 N Lively Blvd (60007-1329)
PHONE..................847 352-2845
Thomas J Dahm, *President*
Kathleen Dahm, *Admin Sec*
EMP: 10
SQ FT: 3,500
SALES (est): 1.2MM **Privately Held**
SIC: **1796** 1761 3444 1711 Pollution control equipment installation; sheet metalwork; sheet metalwork; heating & air conditioning contractors

**(G-9452)**
**ELK GROVE SIGNS INC**
Also Called: Signs Now
1670 Greenleaf Ave (60007-5527)
PHONE..................847 427-0005
Joe Danco, *President*
▲ EMP: 3
SQ FT: 1,350
SALES (est): 403.6K **Privately Held**
SIC: **3993** Signs & advertising specialties

**(G-9453)**
**ELLA ENGINEERING INCORPORATED**
800 Morse Ave (60007-5106)
PHONE..................847 354-4767
Randy Zitella, *President*
Charles Wulf, *Vice Pres*
EMP: 5 EST: 2014
SQ FT: 15,000
SALES (est): 736.4K **Privately Held**
SIC: **3451** Screw machine products

**(G-9454)**
**EMCO GEARS INC (PA)**
160 King St (60007-1111)
PHONE..................847 220-4327
Fax: 773 539-8792
Richard R Wolfe Sr, *President*
Anthony Scinto, *Engineer*
Jeremy Weinberg, *Engineer*
Michael Chang, *Accountant*
EMP: 30 EST: 1933
SQ FT: 20,000
SALES (est): 5.5MM **Privately Held**
WEB: www.emco-gears.com
SIC: **3462** Gear & chain forgings

**(G-9455)**
**EMPIRE CRANKSHAFTS**
742 Lively Blvd (60007-2203)
PHONE..................847 640-8101
Marc Ortiz, *Office Mgr*
EMP: 3
SALES: 130K **Privately Held**
SIC: **3599** Machine shop, jobbing & repair

**(G-9456)**
**EMSUR USA LLC (HQ)**
2800 Carl Blvd (60007-6721)
PHONE..................847 274-9450
Cynthia Parcher, *CFO*
Clemente Gonazales, *CFO*
▲ EMP: 20
SALES (est): 4.7MM **Privately Held**
SIC: **2023** 5199 2759 Dry, condensed, evaporated dairy products; packaging materials; commercial printing
PA: Laninver Usa Inc
2800 Carl Bulevard
Elk Grove Village IL 60007
847 367-8787

**(G-9457)**
**EN POINTE CABINETRY**
950 Thorndale Ave (60007-6759)
PHONE..................847 787-0777
EMP: 3
SALES (est): 231K **Privately Held**
SIC: **2434** Wood kitchen cabinets

**(G-9458)**
**ENGELHARDT GEAR CO**
2526 American Ln (60007-6265)
PHONE..................847 766-7070
Fax: 847 766-6937
Armin Engelhardt, *President*
Rose Boile, *Manager*
Kathleen Rice, *Manager*
EMP: 20
SQ FT: 10,000
SALES (est): 4.4MM **Privately Held**
WEB: www.gearmaker.com
SIC: **3566** Gears, power transmission, except automotive

**(G-9459)**
**ENGELHARDT-LINK INC**
185 King St (60007-1110)
PHONE..................847 593-5850
Fax: 847 593-5894
Tom Link, *President*
Dorothy Engelhardt, *Corp Secy*
▲ EMP: 9
SQ FT: 10,000
SALES: 1MM **Privately Held**
WEB: www.engelhardtlink.com
SIC: **3931** 5099 Strings, musical instrument; cellos & parts; musical instruments

**(G-9460)**
**ENGINEERED PLASTIC PDTS CORP**
2542 Pratt Blvd (60007-5923)
PHONE..................847 952-8400
Fax: 847 952-9066
Alexander M Curtiss, *President*
Pam Lechner, *Purch Agent*
Donna Fugate, *Manager*
Charles L Michod Jr, *Admin Sec*
EMP: 20 EST: 1976
SQ FT: 6,500
SALES (est): 4.6MM **Privately Held**
WEB: www.eppcorp.com
SIC: **3451** 5162 3089 Screw machine products; plastics sheets & rods; plastic processing

**(G-9461)**
**EPCOR INDUSTRIAL INC**
1325 Louis Ave (60007-2309)
PHONE..................847 545-9212
Jolanta Lis, *CEO*
Jaroslaw Lis, *President*
Daniel Zagulski, *Prdtn Mgr*
EMP: 7
SQ FT: 5,000
SALES: 550K **Privately Held**
SIC: **3542** Machine tools, metal forming type

**(G-9462)**
**EPE INDUSTRIES USA INC**
Also Called: Epe Industries USA Chicago
1109 Kirk St (60007-6738)
PHONE..................800 315-0336
Jose Telles, *Branch Mgr*
EMP: 10
SALES (corp-wide): 37.4MM **Privately Held**
SIC: **3086** Packaging & shipping materials, foamed plastic
HQ: Epe Industries Usa, Inc.
17654 Newhope St Ste A
Fountain Valley CA 92708

**(G-9463)**
**ERA INDUSTRIES INC**
1800 Greenleaf Ave (60007-5502)
PHONE..................847 357-1320
Fax: 847 678-7829
Paul Podedworny, *President*
Jacek Slowinski, *Purchasing*
Daniel Skwierczynsk, *Engineer*
Juana Zelaya, *Manager*
Tracie Glatchak, *Officer*
▲ EMP: 130 EST: 1977
SQ FT: 39,000

# GEOGRAPHIC SECTION
## Elk Grove Village - Cook County (G-9490)

SALES (est): 45.5MM  Privately Held
WEB: www.eraind.com
SIC: 3599  Machine shop, jobbing & repair

**(G-9464)**
**ERELL MANUFACTURING COMPANY**
2678 Coyle Ave  (60007-6404)
PHONE ............................. 847 427-3000
Fax: 847 663-9970
Randy Silton, *President*
Dori Schnieder, *Vice Pres*
EMP: 13
SQ FT: 1,000
SALES (est): 1.4MM  Privately Held
WEB: www.erell.com
SIC: 3999  Advertising curtains

**(G-9465)**
**ETYMOTIC RESEARCH INC**
61 Martin Ln  (60007-1307)
PHONE ............................. 847 228-0006
Fax: 847 228-6836
Mark Piepenbrink, *CEO*
Mead C Killion PHD, *President*
Charles Aldous, *Engineer*
Devan Dauber, *Engineer*
Dave Friesema, *Engineer*
EMP: 44
SQ FT: 25,000
SALES (est): 9.3MM  Privately Held
WEB: www.etymotic.com
SIC: 8732  3842  Research services, except laboratory; hearing aids

**(G-9466)**
**EVERWILL INC**
1400 E Devon Ave  (60007-5801)
PHONE ............................. 847 357-0446
Rob Williams, *Owner*
▲ EMP: 6
SALES (est): 574K  Privately Held
SIC: 2759  Screen printing

**(G-9467)**
**EXCEL COLOR CORPORATION**
110 Martin Ln  (60007-1310)
PHONE ............................. 847 734-1270
Fax: 847 734-1370
William G Osborne, *President*
Vijay Shah, *Manager*
EMP: 4
SQ FT: 16,000
SALES (est): 636K  Privately Held
SIC: 2796  Color separations for printing

**(G-9468)**
**EXCEL ELECTRO ASSEMBLY INC**
1595 Brummel Ave  (60007-2112)
PHONE ............................. 847 621-2500
Hiten Bhanderi, *President*
Rasik Bhanderi, *Vice Pres*
Trushar Patel, *Engineer*
EMP: 12
SQ FT: 10,000
SALES (est): 1MM  Privately Held
WEB: www.excele.com
SIC: 3672  Printed circuit boards

**(G-9469)**
**EXCELL ELECTRONICS CORPORATION**
2425 American Ln  (60007-6203)
PHONE ............................. 847 766-7455
Fax: 847 766-1843
Ushma Patel, *President*
Chandra Dave, *Vice Pres*
Sav Patel, *Vice Pres*
Harry Patel, *Treasurer*
Jon Vukovich, *Sales Mgr*
▲ EMP: 28
SQ FT: 20,000
SALES (est): 5.1MM  Privately Held
WEB: www.excellpcb.com
SIC: 3672  Printed circuit boards

**(G-9470)**
**EXCLUSIVE STONE**
1361 Jarvis Ave  (60007-2303)
PHONE ............................. 847 593-6963
Jeff Mueller, *Principal*
EMP: 3  EST: 2007

SALES (est): 322.1K  Privately Held
SIC: 3469  5211  Kitchen fixtures & equipment, porcelain enameled; masonry materials & supplies

**(G-9471)**
**EXECUTIVE PERFORMANCE FUEL LLC**
1060 Talbots Ln  (60007-7106)
PHONE ............................. 847 364-1933
Ann E Potts, *Principal*
EMP: 3
SALES (est): 224K  Privately Held
SIC: 2869  Fuels

**(G-9472)**
**EXPRESS GRINDING INC**
119 Joey Dr  (60007-1303)
PHONE ............................. 847 434-5827
Fax: 847 434-5822
Bill Rosinski, *Principal*
EMP: 2
SALES (est): 363.5K  Privately Held
SIC: 3599  Grinding castings for the trade

**(G-9473)**
**F P M LLC (PA)**
Also Called: F P M Heat Treating
1501 Lively Blvd  (60007-5029)
PHONE ............................. 847 228-2525
Fax: 847 228-9887
William Koziel, *President*
George Manseau, *General Mgr*
Steve Kinloch, *COO*
Robert Ferry, *Vice Pres*
Robin Nichols, *Plant Mgr*
EMP: 130
SQ FT: 88,000
SALES (est): 40.8MM  Privately Held
WEB: www.fpmht.com
SIC: 3398  Metal heat treating

**(G-9474)**
**FABRICATED METALS CO**
Also Called: Machined Products
2121 Landmeier Rd  (60007-2506)
PHONE ............................. 847 718-1300
Fax: 847 718-1307
David Pingel, *CEO*
Sirinivas Ghejji, *President*
Mohammed Qureshi, *President*
Srinivas Ghejji, *Vice Pres*
▲ EMP: 108
SQ FT: 98,500
SALES (est): 19.5MM  Privately Held
WEB: www.machinedproducts.com
SIC: 3599  Machine shop, jobbing & repair

**(G-9475)**
**FANMAR INC**
901 Greenleaf Ave  (60007-5010)
PHONE ............................. 708 563-0505
Fax: 708 563-0222
Dill Grobes, *President*
John C Nalbach, *Corp Secy*
Sue Gutierrez, *Manager*
EMP: 25  EST: 1965
SQ FT: 28,000
SALES (est): 6.1MM  Privately Held
WEB: www.fanmar.com
SIC: 3599  3444  3645  3469  Machine shop, jobbing & repair; sheet metalwork; residential lighting fixtures; metal stampings; fabricated structural metal; office furniture, except wood

**(G-9476)**
**FASPRO TECHNOLOGIES INC**
165 King St  (60007-1110)
PHONE ............................. 847 364-9999
EMP: 13
SALES (corp-wide): 20.3MM  Privately Held
SIC: 3479  Etching, photochemical
PA: Faspro Technologies, Inc.
500 W Campus Dr
Arlington Heights IL 60004
847 392-9500

**(G-9477)**
**FASTSIGNS**
1701 Howard St Ste C  (60007-2479)
PHONE ............................. 847 981-1965
Fax: 847 981-1964
Bob Rogers, *President*
Bob Rodgers, *Human Res Mgr*

EMP: 3
SALES (est): 282.5K  Privately Held
SIC: 3993  Signs & advertising specialties

**(G-9478)**
**FISA NORTH AMERICA INC**
260 Stanley St  (60007-1557)
PHONE ............................. 847 593-2080
Phil Vaudeleau, *CEO*
John Moczalla, *Regl Sales Mgr*
David Royo, *Manager*
▲ EMP: 5
SALES (est): 600K  Privately Held
WEB: www.fisa.com
SIC: 3699  Cleaning equipment, ultrasonic, except medical & dental

**(G-9479)**
**FL 1**
Also Called: Chicago Offset
128 N Lively Blvd Fl 1  (60007-1330)
PHONE ............................. 847 956-9400
EMP: 11
SQ FT: 8,400
SALES: 2.3MM  Privately Held
SIC: 2752  Lithographic Commercial Printing

**(G-9480)**
**FLUID PUMP SERVICE INC**
Also Called: Fluid Pump Systems
435 Bennett Rd  (60007-1006)
PHONE ............................. 847 228-0750
Fax: 847 228-6541
Thomas Krzak, *President*
Laura Krzak, *Administration*
EMP: 7
SQ FT: 10,000
SALES: 1.7MM  Privately Held
WEB: www.fluidpump.com
SIC: 7699  5084  7694  Pumps & pumping equipment repair; pumps & pumping equipment; motor repair services

**(G-9481)**
**FMI INC**
2382 United Ln  (60007-6815)
PHONE ............................. 847 350-1535
Fax: 847 350-1109
Scott A Severson, *President*
▲ EMP: 60
SQ FT: 10,000
SALES (est): 19.4MM
SALES (corp-wide): 37.8MM  Privately Held
WEB: www.fmimed.com
SIC: 3061  Mechanical rubber goods
PA: Flexan, Llc
6626 W Dakin St
Chicago IL 60634
773 685-6446

**(G-9482)**
**FNA IP HOLDINGS INC**
1825 Greenleaf Ave  (60007-5501)
PHONE ............................. 847 348-1500
Gus Alexander, *President*
Daphne Alexander, *Corp Secy*
William Alexander, *Vice Pres*
Sonja Bell, *Finance*
EMP: 80
SALES (est): 13.6MM  Privately Held
WEB: www.faippowerwasher.com
SIC: 5084  3589  3563  3561  Industrial machinery & equipment; high pressure cleaning equipment; vacuum (air extraction) systems, industrial; pumps & pumping equipment; electric household appliances, major; builders' hardware

**(G-9483)**
**FOCUS POLY**
801 Chase Ave  (60007-4840)
PHONE ............................. 847 981-6890
S Michael, *Manager*
▲ EMP: 4
SALES (est): 573.1K  Privately Held
SIC: 3086  Packaging & shipping materials, foamed plastic

**(G-9484)**
**FOODHANDLER INC**
2301 Lunt Ave  (60007-5625)
PHONE ............................. 866 931-3613
Michael Mattos, *CEO*
Sherri Hager, *Vice Pres*

Katie Farrell, *Manager*
Brian Polk, *Technology*
Barbara Amato, *Administration*
◆ EMP: 70
SQ FT: 30,000
SALES (est): 23.8MM
SALES (corp-wide): 9.1B  Privately Held
WEB: www.foodhandler.com
SIC: 5162  2673  Plastics products; bags: plastic, laminated & coated
PA: Bunzl Public Limited Company
York House, 45 Seymour Street
London  W1H 7
207 725-5000

**(G-9485)**
**FOREST PACKAGING CORPORATION**
1955 Estes Ave  (60007-5415)
PHONE ............................. 847 981-7000
Fax: 847 981-7233
Gregory R Kula, *President*
Kurt Arbeen, *VP Sls/Mktg*
EMP: 40  EST: 1965
SQ FT: 47,000
SALES (est): 16.2MM  Privately Held
WEB: www.forestpkg.com
SIC: 2653  7336  Boxes, corrugated: made from purchased materials; package design

**(G-9486)**
**FORMULA SYSTEMS NORTH AMERICA**
2300 Eastern Ave  (60007-6813)
PHONE ............................. 847 350-0655
Fax: 847 350-0670
John Curzon, *President*
Cornelius Walls, *Vice Pres*
Graham Davies, *Admin Sec*
▲ EMP: 2
SALES (est): 360.4K  Privately Held
SIC: 3534  Elevators & equipment

**(G-9487)**
**FORT DEARBORN COMPANY**
1530 Morse Ave  (60007-5724)
PHONE ............................. 847 357-2300
Bill Samuels, *Director*
EMP: 100  Privately Held
SIC: 2752  Commercial printing, lithographic
HQ: Fort Dearborn Company
1530 Morse Ave
Elk Grove Village IL 60007
847 357-9500

**(G-9488)**
**FORTMAN & ASSOCIATES LTD**
Also Called: Newmax
472 Potomac Ln  (60007-2764)
PHONE ............................. 847 524-0741
Angelika K Fortman, *President*
Stephen A Fortman, *Admin Sec*
EMP: 10
SALES (est): 970K  Privately Held
WEB: www.newmax.com
SIC: 7336  2752  Art design services; offset & photolithographic printing

**(G-9489)**
**FOX MACHINE & TOOL INC**
985 Lively Blvd  (60007-2206)
PHONE ............................. 847 357-1845
Jozef Lisiecki, *President*
EMP: 9
SALES (est): 1MM  Privately Held
SIC: 3599  3545  Custom machinery; machine tool accessories

**(G-9490)**
**FREEMAN PRODUCTS INC**
1225 Arthur Ave  (60007-5705)
PHONE ............................. 847 439-1000
Fax: 847 439-1024
Dan Campion, *Manager*
EMP: 5
SALES (corp-wide): 21.3MM  Privately Held
SIC: 3714  3429  5999  Thermostats, motor vehicle; clamps & couplings, hose; trophies & plaques
PA: Freeman Products, Inc.
71 Walsh Dr Ste 101
Parsippany NJ 07054
201 475-4800

# Elk Grove Village - Cook County (G-9491)

**(G-9491)**
**G T MOTORING INC**
860 Greenleaf Ave (60007-5026)
PHONE.................................847 466-7463
Gregory P Haye, *President*
◆ **EMP:** 1
**SALES:** 350K **Privately Held**
**SIC:** 5015 3465 Automotive parts & supplies, used; body parts, automobile: stamped metal

**(G-9492)**
**G&M METAL**
1970 Estes Ave (60007-5416)
PHONE.................................630 616-1126
Mitch Dejlitko, *Principal*
**EMP:** 6
**SALES (est):** 643.8K **Privately Held**
**SIC:** 3443 Metal parts

**(G-9493)**
**GAGE MANUFACTURING INC**
820 Touhy Ave (60007-4918)
PHONE.................................847 228-7300
Jacqueline Gajewski, *President*
Ed Gajewski, *Sales Staff*
Greg Gajewski, *Director*
**EMP:** 15
**SALES (est):** 3MM **Privately Held**
**SIC:** 3451 Screw machine products

**(G-9494)**
**GAGE TOOL & MANUFACTURING INC**
1025 Pauly Dr (60007-1314)
PHONE.................................847 640-1069
Fax: 847 640-1072
Paul Oroni, *President*
Daniel Oroni, *Manager*
**EMP:** 2
**SQ FT:** 1,200
**SALES (est):** 320.1K **Privately Held**
**SIC:** 3544 Special dies, tools, jigs & fixtures

**(G-9495)**
**GALAXY PRECISION MFG INC**
2636 United Ln (60007-6821)
PHONE.................................847 238-9066
Ellias Kademoglou, *President*
Eva Solis, *Assistant VP*
**EMP:** 15
**SQ FT:** 20,000
**SALES (est):** 2.8MM **Privately Held**
**WEB:** www.galaxyprecision.com
**SIC:** 3599 3544 Machine shop, jobbing & repair; special dies, tools, jigs & fixtures

**(G-9496)**
**GAMMA ALPHA VISUAL**
Also Called: AlphaGraphics
86 Biesterfield Rd (60007-3668)
PHONE.................................847 956-0633
Fax: 847 956-0634
Gregory J Poulos, *Mng Member*
**EMP:** 7
**SALES (est):** 521.4K **Privately Held**
**WEB:** www.pengraphics.com
**SIC:** 7389 2791 2789 2752 Printers' services: folding, collating; typesetting; bookbinding & related work; commercial printing, lithographic

**(G-9497)**
**GENERAL PRECISION MFG LLC**
2670 Greenleaf Ave (60007-5513)
PHONE.................................847 624-4969
Nancy Reuhi,
**EMP:** 6
**SALES (est):** 200.3K **Privately Held**
**SIC:** 3999 Atomizers, toiletry

**(G-9498)**
**GENESIS ELECTRIC & TECH INC**
356 Lively Blvd (60007-2010)
PHONE.................................847 258-5218
Sean Gannon, *President*
**EMP:** 5
**SALES (est):** 207.8K **Privately Held**
**SIC:** 8731 3699 Commercial physical research; electrical equipment & supplies

**(G-9499)**
**GERARD PRINTING COMPANY**
710 Bonnie Ln (60007-2201)
PHONE.................................847 437-6442
Fax: 847 437-5038
Bob Denbroeder, *President*
Robert Denbroeder, *President*
John Denbroeder, *Vice Pres*
**EMP:** 9
**SQ FT:** 4,200
**SALES (est):** 860K **Privately Held**
**WEB:** www.gerardprinting.com
**SIC:** 2752 Commercial printing, offset

**(G-9500)**
**GLOBAL DECOR INC**
1501 Nicholas Blvd (60007-5515)
PHONE.................................847 437-9600
Tom Wolf, *President*
Paul Croisdale, *Vice Pres*
▲ **EMP:** 25
**SQ FT:** 100,000
**SALES (est):** 3.9MM **Privately Held**
**WEB:** www.globaldecorinc.com
**SIC:** 2499 Mfg Wood Products

**(G-9501)**
**GLOBAL ENDOSCOPY INC**
878 Cass Ln (60007-3049)
PHONE.................................847 910-5836
Fax: 630 773-3640
Nick Mircea, *President*
Mary Ann Mircea, *Vice Pres*
**EMP:** 3
**SQ FT:** 2,500
**SALES (est):** 320K **Privately Held**
**SIC:** 3841 Surgical & medical instruments

**(G-9502)**
**GLOBAL STONE INC**
51 Joey Dr (60007-1301)
PHONE.................................847 718-1418
Grzegorz Zamarski, *President*
**EMP:** 5
**SQ FT:** 3,800
**SALES (est):** 576K **Privately Held**
**SIC:** 3281 Granite, cut & shaped

**(G-9503)**
**GLOBAL TOOL & DIE INC**
1355 Tonne Rd (60007-5002)
PHONE.................................847 956-1200
Frank Fudala, *President*
Genene Fudala, *Treasurer*
**EMP:** 5
**SALES (est):** 500K **Privately Held**
**SIC:** 3544 Special dies, tools, jigs & fixtures

**(G-9504)**
**GLOBAL WEB SYSTEMS INC**
742 Cutter Ln (60007-6903)
PHONE.................................630 782-9690
Fax: 630 782-9693
C Doyle Sutherland, *President*
Daniel Kosrow, *Vice Pres*
▲ **EMP:** 15
**SQ FT:** 10,000
**SALES (est):** 2.5MM **Privately Held**
**SIC:** 3555 Printing presses

**(G-9505)**
**GLOBUS FOOD PRODUCTS LLC**
Also Called: Mystic Pizza Food Company
2258 Landmeier Rd Ste A (60007-2637)
PHONE.................................847 378-8221
Patrick Pawlis, *President*
**EMP:** 3
**SALES (est):** 340.5K **Privately Held**
**SIC:** 2038 Frozen specialties

**(G-9506)**
**GRAND PRODUCTS INC (PA)**
1718 Hampshire Dr (60007-2760)
PHONE.................................800 621-6101
Fax: 847 795-0444
David Marofske Jr, *President*
Nicholas Kallas, *President*
David Marofske Sr, *Chairman*
Bill Tweedell, *Finance Dir*
◆ **EMP:** 124
**SQ FT:** 92,608
**SALES (est):** 25.1MM **Privately Held**
**SIC:** 3999 3679 Coin-operated amusement machines; harness assemblies for electronic use: wire or cable

**(G-9507)**
**GRANTE FOODS INTERNATIONAL LLC**
780 Arthur Ave (60007-5233)
PHONE.................................773 751-9551
Anna Kudrytskaya, *Manager*
Dzianis Bahatyrov,
▲ **EMP:** 10
**SQ FT:** 22,000
**SALES (est):** 270.1K **Privately Held**
**SIC:** 5149 2079 2013 Groceries & related products; juices; edible oil products, except corn oil; sausages & other prepared meats

**(G-9508)**
**GRAPHIC INNOVATORS INC**
855 Morse Ave (60007-5105)
PHONE.................................847 718-1516
Fax: 847 875-0030
Michael J Kiley, *CEO*
Scott J Kiley, *President*
Paul Minasian, *Vice Pres*
Irena Rybka, *VP Opers*
Brian Blackmore, *Plant Mgr*
◆ **EMP:** 50
**SQ FT:** 91,000
**SALES (est):** 21.6MM **Privately Held**
**WEB:** www.graphicinnovators.com
**SIC:** 3555 5084 Printing trades machinery; printing presses; printing trades machinery, equipment & supplies

**(G-9509)**
**GRAPHIC PACKAGING INTL INC**
1500 Nicholas Blvd (60007-5516)
PHONE.................................847 437-1700
Fax: 847 956-9291
Jim Sinovich, *General Mgr*
Larry Seaborg, *Opers Mgr*
Diana Diaz, *Personnel Exec*
John Colandrea, *Sales Mgr*
Gary Lapnow, *Sales Mgr*
**EMP:** 409 **Publicly Held**
**SIC:** 2631 Container board
**HQ:** Graphic Packaging International, Inc.
1500 Riveredge Pkwy # 100
Atlanta GA 30328
770 240-7200

**(G-9510)**
**GRAPHIC PACKAGING INTL INC**
1500 Nicholas Blvd (60007-5516)
PHONE.................................847 354-3554
Phil Dimaso, *Opers Staff*
Timothy Jacob, *Accounts Mgr*
David Scheivle, *Branch Mgr*
Rizwan Ali, *IT/INT Sup*
Marlen Ortega, *Director*
**EMP:** 8300 **Publicly Held**
**SIC:** 2631 Folding boxboard; container board
**HQ:** Graphic Packaging International, Inc.
1500 Riveredge Pkwy # 100
Atlanta GA 30328
770 240-7200

**(G-9511)**
**GRECIAN DELIGHT FOODS INC (PA)**
Also Called: Grecian Delight Foods, Inc Del
1201 Tonne Rd (60007-4925)
PHONE.................................847 364-1010
Fax: 847 364-1077
Peter Parthenis Jr, *President*
David Kiel, *President*
Michael Loukis, *Business Mgr*
Greg Graber, *Vice Pres*
Bill Poulos, *Vice Pres*
◆ **EMP:** 180
**SALES (est):** 48.5MM **Privately Held**
**WEB:** www.greciandelight.com
**SIC:** 2051 2011 2099 2013 Bread, all types (white, wheat, rye, etc): fresh or frozen; lamb products from lamb slaughtered on site; food preparations; sausages & other prepared meats

**(G-9512)**
**GREENLEE DIAMOND TOOL CO**
2375 Touhy Ave (60007-5330)
PHONE.................................866 451-3316
Fax: 847 593-3165
Jim Long, *General Mgr*
Vince Pecis, *General Mgr*
Michael L Wilkie, *Principal*
Keith Baxley, *Prdtn Mgr*
Joe Sanders, *Sales Executive*
**EMP:** 25
**SALES (est):** 4.7MM **Privately Held**
**WEB:** www.greenleediamond.com
**SIC:** 3545 Machine tool accessories

**(G-9513)**
**GREENRIDGE FARM INC**
2355 Greenleaf Ave (60007-5508)
PHONE.................................847 434-1803
Michael Madej, *President*
Sebastian Madej, *Vice Pres*
▲ **EMP:** 26 **EST:** 2008
**SALES (est):** 5.5MM **Privately Held**
**SIC:** 2013 Boneless meat, from purchased meat

**(G-9514)**
**H D A FANS INC**
1455 Brummel Ave 300 (60007-2110)
PHONE.................................630 627-2087
Fax: 847 290-0159
Thomas Kubik, *President*
Martin Keller, *President*
Mike Murphy, *Vice Pres*
**EMP:** 6
**SALES:** 500K **Privately Held**
**WEB:** www.hdafan.com
**SIC:** 3564 Aircurtains (blower)

**(G-9515)**
**H S I FIRE AND SAFETY GROUP (PA)**
107 Garlisch Dr (60007-1322)
PHONE.................................847 427-8340
Tom Berricad, *President*
Margeret Fetier, *Manager*
▲ **EMP:** 4 **EST:** 1977
**SQ FT:** 10,000
**SALES (est):** 702.2K **Privately Held**
**SIC:** 3829 Fire detector systems, non-electric

**(G-9516)**
**HANOVER DISPLAYS INC**
1601 Tonne Rd (60007-5123)
PHONE.................................773 334-9934
Gavin Williams, *President*
Brent Anderson, *Opers Mgr*
Thomas Thorelli, *Admin Sec*
▲ **EMP:** 15
**SALES (est):** 2.3MM **Privately Held**
**SIC:** 3993 Signs & advertising specialties

**(G-9517)**
**HASKRIS CO**
100 Kelly St (60007-1012)
PHONE.................................847 956-6420
Daniel M Falotico, *President*
Lorina Pop, *General Mgr*
Steven Szot, *General Mgr*
Ed Rowe, *Prdtn Mgr*
Rob Baer, *Buyer*
**EMP:** 51 **EST:** 1944
**SQ FT:** 24,000
**SALES (est):** 14.4MM **Privately Held**
**WEB:** www.haskris.com
**SIC:** 3585 Coolers, milk & water: electric

**(G-9518)**
**HAUSNER HARD - CHROME INC (PA)**
670 Greenleaf Ave (60007-5084)
PHONE.................................847 439-6010
Fax: 847 439-6027
David J Hausner, *CEO*
Jeffrey Hausner, *President*
John David, *CFO*
John Wiley, *Sales Staff*
Robert Hallstrom, *Sales Executive*
**EMP:** 47
**SQ FT:** 11,500
**SALES:** 15.5MM **Privately Held**
**WEB:** www.hausnerhardchrome.com
**SIC:** 3471 Chromium plating of metals or formed products

**(G-9519)**
**HEADCO INDUSTRIES INC**
Also Called: Bearing Headquarters Co
109 N Lively Blvd (60007-1324)
PHONE.................................847 640-6490
Fax: 847 640-6943
Jim Scardina, *Exec VP*

▲ = Import ▼ = Export
◆ = Import/Export

Ron Brousseau, *Branch Mgr*
**EMP:** 10
**SALES (corp-wide):** 145.7MM **Privately Held**
**WEB:** www.his-tech.com
**SIC:** 5085  5084  3599  Bearings, bushings, wheels & gears; bearings; sprockets; hydraulic systems equipment & supplies; machine shop, jobbing & repair
**PA:** Headco Industries, Inc.
2601 Parkes Dr
Broadview IL 60155
708 681-4400

**(G-9520)**
### HEIDOLPH NA LLC
Also Called: Heidolph North America
1241 Jarvis Ave  (60007-2301)
**PHONE**.................................224 265-9600
James Dawson, *Mng Member*
Deborah Zinsser-Krys,
**EMP:** 18
**SALES (est):** 5.8MM **Privately Held**
**SIC:** 3564  3821  3561  Air cleaning systems; shakers & stirrers; pumps & pumping equipment

**(G-9521)**
### HELIX INTERNATIONAL INC (PA)
Also Called: Helix International Mch Div
2150 Lively Blvd  (60007-5208)
**PHONE**.................................847 709-0666
Jan Jorfald, *President*
Drew Naismith, *Vice Pres*
Aleksandr Antonyuk, *Sales Mgr*
◆ **EMP:** 2
**SALES (est):** 881.3K **Privately Held**
**WEB:** www.helixinternational.com
**SIC:** 3569  Filters

**(G-9522)**
### HELM TOOL COMPANY INCORPORATED
1290 Brummel Ave  (60007-2168)
**PHONE**.................................847 952-9528
**Fax:** 847 364-0863
Helmut Mueller, *President*
Ralf Mueller, *Vice Pres*
Manfred Heumann, *Plant Mgr*
Piotr Niedoba, *Plant Mgr*
Michael Smith, *Purchasing*
**EMP:** 20
**SQ FT:** 22,000
**SALES (est):** 3.9MM **Privately Held**
**WEB:** www.helmtool.com
**SIC:** 3544  Industrial molds

**(G-9523)**
### HFO CHICAGO LLC
555 Busse Rd  (60007-2116)
**PHONE**.................................847 258-2850
Dan Lamberty, *Controller*
Nick Schuchardt,
**EMP:** 17
**SQ FT:** 35,000
**SALES (est):** 3.1MM
**SALES (corp-wide):** 51.8MM **Privately Held**
**SIC:** 3599  5084  Machine & other job shop work; industrial machinery & equipment
**HQ:** Midwest Manufacturing Resources, Inc.
1993 Case Pkwy
Twinsburg OH 44087
330 405-4227

**(G-9524)**
### HILLSHIRE BRANDS COMPANY
Superior Coffee & Foods
1325 Chase Ave  (60007-4812)
**PHONE**.................................847 956-7575
**Fax:** 847 956-9771
Bob Budlow, *Branch Mgr*
Lauren Schumacher, *Manager*
Valerie Brown, *MIS Dir*
Araceli Arzeta, *Administration*
**EMP:** 120
**SALES (corp-wide):** 36.8B **Publicly Held**
**SIC:** 2095  5149  Roasted coffee; groceries & related products
**HQ:** The Hillshire Brands Company
400 S Jefferson St Fl 1
Chicago IL 60607
312 614-6000

**(G-9525)**
### HONTECH INTERNATIONAL CORP
1000 Lee St  (60007-1208)
**PHONE**.................................847 364-9800
Chou Long Shou, *President*
Fred Kesselman, *Opers Mgr*
▲ **EMP:** 10
**SQ FT:** 25,000
**SALES (est):** 3.4MM **Privately Held**
**SIC:** 3444  Sheet metalwork

**(G-9526)**
### HP INC
25 Northwest Point Blvd  (60007-1056)
**PHONE**.................................847 342-2000
Joe Parzech, *Principal*
Robert Mack, *Technical Staff*
**EMP:** 100
**SALES (corp-wide):** 48.2B **Publicly Held**
**SIC:** 3571  5045  Electronic computers; computers
**PA:** Hp Inc.
1501 Page Mill Rd
Palo Alto CA 94304
650 857-1501

**(G-9527)**
### HST MATERIALS INC
1631 Brummel Ave  (60007-2125)
**PHONE**.................................847 640-1803
Kathryn E Miller, *President*
Larry Barch, *QC Dir*
Luca Lanzetta, *Nat'l Sales Mgr*
Wioleta Kielbasinska, *Sales Staff*
Denale Harpling, *Administration*
**EMP:** 12
**SALES (est):** 2.2MM **Privately Held**
**SIC:** 3069  Sponge rubber & sponge rubber products

**(G-9528)**
### HUETONE IMPRINTS INC
90 N Lively Blvd  (60007-1317)
**PHONE**.................................630 694-9610
Bimal Thakkar, *CEO*
**EMP:** 6
**SQ FT:** 6,500
**SALES (est):** 950.9K **Privately Held**
**WEB:** www.huetoneimprints.com
**SIC:** 2759  Screen printing

**(G-9529)**
### I T W DELTAR/DIAMED CORP
830 Lee St  (60007-1205)
**PHONE**.................................847 593-8811
**Fax:** 847 593-5545
Robert L Hamilton Jr, *Vice Pres*
**EMP:** 3
**SALES (est):** 253.3K **Privately Held**
**SIC:** 3089  Plastics products

**(G-9530)**
### I TW DELTAR INSERT MOLDED PDTS
830 Lee St  (60007-1205)
**PHONE**.................................847 593-8811
Robert L Hamilton Jr, *Principal*
**EMP:** 3
**SALES (est):** 237.2K **Privately Held**
**SIC:** 3089  Molding primary plastic

**(G-9531)**
### ICON IDENTITY SOLUTIONS INC (PA)
1418 Elmhurst Rd  (60007-6417)
**PHONE**.................................847 364-2250
Kurt Ripkey, *President*
Tom Hunt, *Exec VP*
Melanee Jech, *Exec VP*
Douglas Long, *Exec VP*
Matt Czyl, *Vice Pres*
**EMP:** 197 **EST:** 1925
**SQ FT:** 21,000
**SALES:** 119MM **Privately Held**
**WEB:** www.iconid.com
**SIC:** 3993  Signs & advertising specialties; neon signs

**(G-9532)**
### ICON IDENTITY SOLUTIONS INC
Imagecare Maintenance
1418 Elmhurst Rd  (60007-6417)
**PHONE**.................................847 364-2250
John P Callan, *Branch Mgr*
**EMP:** 46
**SALES (corp-wide):** 119MM **Privately Held**
**SIC:** 3993  Signs & advertising specialties
**PA:** Icon Identity Solutions, Inc.
1418 Elmhurst Rd
Elk Grove Village IL 60007
847 364-2250

**(G-9533)**
### ILLINOIS BOTTLE MFG CO
701 E Devon Ave  (60007-6702)
**PHONE**.................................847 595-9000
Robert Klekauskas, *President*
Cathy Boldenow, *QC Mgr*
Bruce Ronner, *VP Finance*
John Coursey, *VP Mktg*
Colleen Hughes, *Manager*
▲ **EMP:** 80 **EST:** 1979
**SQ FT:** 225,000
**SALES (est):** 13.8MM **Privately Held**
**WEB:** www.arrowplastic.com
**SIC:** 3089  3085  3999  Plastic containers, except foam; plastics bottles; atomizers, toiletry

**(G-9534)**
### ILLINOIS TOOL WORKS INC
950 Pratt Blvd  (60007-5119)
**PHONE**.................................630 787-3298
**EMP:** 91
**SALES (corp-wide):** 13.6B **Publicly Held**
**SIC:** 3089  Injection molded finished plastic products
**PA:** Illinois Tool Works Inc.
155 Harlem Ave
Glenview IL 60025
847 724-7500

**(G-9535)**
### ILLINOIS TOOL WORKS INC
Also Called: ITW Filtration
830 Lee St  (60007-1205)
**PHONE**.................................847 593-8811
Chris Fredricks, *Manager*
**EMP:** 28
**SALES (corp-wide):** 13.6B **Publicly Held**
**SIC:** 2834  5122  Pharmaceutical preparations; drugs, proprietaries & sundries
**PA:** Illinois Tool Works Inc.
155 Harlem Ave
Glenview IL 60025
847 724-7500

**(G-9536)**
### ILLINOIS TOOL WORKS INC
Also Called: ITW Ramset Red Head
2471 Brickvale Dr  (60007-6810)
**PHONE**.................................847 350-0193
Jim Surjan, *Manager*
**EMP:** 25
**SALES (corp-wide):** 13.6B **Publicly Held**
**SIC:** 2899  Chemical preparations
**PA:** Illinois Tool Works Inc.
155 Harlem Ave
Glenview IL 60025
847 724-7500

**(G-9537)**
### ILLINOIS TOOL WORKS INC
Also Called: ITW Shakeproof-Elk Grove
2700 York Rd  (60007-6315)
**PHONE**.................................847 766-9000
Earl Dineen, *General Mgr*
Jim Nelson, *Engineer*
Debbie Wieker, *Payroll Mgr*
Roy Mathieson, *Manager*
Trini Nunez, *Manager*
**EMP:** 185
**SALES (corp-wide):** 13.6B **Publicly Held**
**SIC:** 3452  Bolts, nuts, rivets & washers
**PA:** Illinois Tool Works Inc.
155 Harlem Ave
Glenview IL 60025
847 724-7500

**(G-9538)**
### IMAGE CIRCUIT INC
925 Estes Ave  (60007-4905)
**PHONE**.................................847 622-3300
Mohan Dungarani, *President*
**EMP:** 9
**SALES:** 850K **Privately Held**
**SIC:** 3672  Printed circuit boards

**(G-9539)**
### IMAGE SYSTEMS BUS SLUTIONS LLC
Also Called: Isbs
1776 Commerce Dr  (60007-2120)
**PHONE**.................................847 378-8249
**Fax:** 847 882-7544
Donna Diekneit, *Sales Mgr*
Claude Avvisati, *Manager*
Sandy Foret, *Manager*
David Boelter,
**EMP:** 30
**SQ FT:** 50,000
**SALES (est):** 6.8MM **Privately Held**
**SIC:** 3299  Images, small: gypsum, clay or papier mache

**(G-9540)**
### IMAGECARE MAINTENANCE SVCS LLC
1418 Elmhurst Rd  (60007-6417)
**PHONE**.................................847 631-3306
Kurt W Ripkey, *President*
**EMP:** 5
**SALES (est):** 3.1MM
**SALES (corp-wide):** 119MM **Privately Held**
**SIC:** 3993  Signs & advertising specialties
**PA:** Icon Identity Solutions, Inc.
1418 Elmhurst Rd
Elk Grove Village IL 60007
847 364-2250

**(G-9541)**
### IMAGINEERING INC
2425 Touhy Ave  (60007-5331)
**PHONE**.................................847 806-0003
**Fax:** 847 806-0004
Khurrum Dhanji, *CEO*
Parvin Dhanji, *President*
Sulaiman Roy, *COO*
Hina Valiani, *Accountant*
Hasnain Patel, *Accounts Exec*
▲ **EMP:** 48
**SQ FT:** 38,000
**SALES (est):** 6.9MM **Privately Held**
**WEB:** www.pcbnet.com
**SIC:** 8711  3672  8731  Electrical or electronic engineering; printed circuit boards; circuit boards, television & radio printed; wiring boards; electronic research

**(G-9542)**
### IMPACT PRTRS & LITHOGRAPHERS
1370 E Higgins Rd  (60007-1603)
**PHONE**.................................847 981-9676
Robert Serna, *President*
Vito Griseta, *Vice Pres*
Bob Serna, *Adv Dir*
Charlene Jurgenson, *Manager*
**EMP:** 37
**SQ FT:** 20,000
**SALES (est):** 4MM **Privately Held**
**WEB:** www.impactprinters.com
**SIC:** 2752  Commercial printing, offset; lithographing on metal

**(G-9543)**
### IMPERIAL STONE COLLECTION
460 Lively Blvd Ste 1  (60007-2022)
**PHONE**.................................847 640-8817
Monika Glowacka, *Principal*
**EMP:** 7 **EST:** 2009
**SALES (est):** 1MM **Privately Held**
**SIC:** 3446  Ornamental metalwork

**(G-9544)**
### INDIUM CORPORATION OF AMERICA
80 Scott St  (60007-1228)
**PHONE**.................................847 439-9134
Joann Warren, *Human Res Mgr*
Paul Gassensmith, *Manager*
**EMP:** 6
**SALES (corp-wide):** 193.5MM **Privately Held**
**SIC:** 7692  Welding repair
**PA:** Indium Corporation Of America
34 Robinson Rd
Clinton NY 13323
800 446-3486

## Elk Grove Village - Cook County (G-9545)

**(G-9545)**
**INFINITYBOX LLC**
1410 Brummel Ave (60007-2111)
PHONE..................847 232-1991
Edwin Harris,
EMP: 4
SALES (est): 246.3K  Privately Held
SIC: 3714  Automotive wiring harness sets

**(G-9546)**
**INK SOLUTIONS LLC (PA)**
800 Estes Ave (60007-4904)
PHONE..................847 593-5200
John Jilek, COO
John P Jilek Sr, Mng Member
Martin Morrissey, Manager
Alan Berna, Supervisor
Carl Hirsch,
▲ EMP: 15
SQ FT: 19,700
SALES (est): 18MM  Privately Held
WEB: www.INKSOLUTIONS.us
SIC: 2851  Lithographic varnishes

**(G-9547)**
**INK SYSTEMS INC**
800 Estes Ave (60007-4904)
PHONE..................847 427-2200
Fax: 847 427-1500
John Jilek, President
EMP: 9
SALES (corp-wide): 42.9MM  Privately Held
WEB: www.inksystemsinc.com
SIC: 2893  Printing ink
PA: Ink Systems, Inc.
    2311 S Eastern Ave
    Commerce CA 90040
    323 720-4000

**(G-9548)**
**INNOVO CORP**
2385 United Ln (60007-6816)
PHONE..................847 616-0063
Bob Kinsley, President
Jan Jakimiec, Vice Pres
Anna Turek, Manager
Ron Bochat, Technology
Adam Szczepaniec, Admin Sec
EMP: 12
SQ FT: 10,000
SALES (est): 2.6MM  Privately Held
WEB: www.innovo.us
SIC: 3552  Dyeing machinery, textile

**(G-9549)**
**INTEGRATED MEASUREMENT SYSTEMS**
600 Bonnie Ln (60007-1912)
P.O. Box 1568 (60009-1568)
PHONE..................847 956-1940
Kenneth S Norman, President
EMP: 5
SQ FT: 2,500
SALES (est): 906.6K  Privately Held
WEB: www.intmeasys.com
SIC: 3596  Industrial scales

**(G-9550)**
**INTEGRATED PACKG & FASTENER**
1678 Carmen Dr (60007-6504)
PHONE..................847 439-5730
Fax: 847 640-8894
Mark Ryan, President
Jill Rozehon, Corp Secy
Jill Louise, Opers Mgr
Jill Rozhon, Sales Staff
◆ EMP: 78
SALES (est): 10.4MM  Privately Held
WEB: www.integratedpack.com
SIC: 3565  Packaging machinery

**(G-9551)**
**INTERFLO INDUSTRIES INC**
695 Lunt Ave (60007-5014)
PHONE..................847 228-0606
Fax: 847 228-0687
Leonard Gluck, President
▼ EMP: 5
SQ FT: 3,000
SALES (est): 480K  Privately Held
SIC: 2842  2841  Industrial plant disinfectants or deodorants; soap & other detergents

**(G-9552)**
**INTERNATIONAL PAPER COMPANY**
25 Northwest Point Blvd # 300 (60007-1033)
PHONE..................847 228-7227
Paul Baylog, Accounts Exec
Tom Dupuis, Manager
EMP: 139
SALES (corp-wide): 21B  Publicly Held
WEB: www.internationalpaper.com
SIC: 2621  Paper mills
PA: International Paper Company
    6400 Poplar Ave
    Memphis TN 38197
    901 419-9000

**(G-9553)**
**INTERNATIONAL PROC CO AMER**
Also Called: Iosso Products Co
1485 Lively Blvd (60007-5094)
PHONE..................847 437-8400
Richard C Iosso, President
Marianne Iosso, Vice Pres
Grace Iosso, Admin Sec
▲ EMP: 30
SQ FT: 26,000
SALES (est): 7MM  Privately Held
WEB: www.iosso.com
SIC: 3398  3341  3471  Brazing (hardening) of metal; secondary nonferrous metals; plating & polishing

**(G-9554)**
**INTRATEK INC**
54 N Lively Blvd (60007-1317)
PHONE..................847 640-0007
Fax: 847 640-0009
Ken Patel, President
Jignesh Patel, Vice Pres
EMP: 4
SQ FT: 4,000
SALES (est): 425.5K  Privately Held
WEB: www.intratekpcb.com
SIC: 8711  3672  Professional engineer; printed circuit boards

**(G-9555)**
**IRVING PRESS INC**
2530 United Ln (60007-6180)
PHONE..................847 595-6650
Fax: 708 595-6610
Gerald W Gaul, President
Thomas Maheu, Opers Mgr
EMP: 26
SQ FT: 20,000
SALES (est): 4.8MM  Privately Held
WEB: www.irvingpress.com
SIC: 2752  Commercial printing, offset

**(G-9556)**
**J & E SEATING LLC**
Also Called: Mlp Seating
950 Pratt Blvd (60007-5119)
PHONE..................847 956-1700
Ralph Samuel, Mng Member
EMP: 21 EST: 2013
SQ FT: 32,000
SALES (est): 1.9MM  Privately Held
SIC: 2522  Office chairs, benches & stools, except wood

**(G-9557)**
**J D GRAPHIC CO INC**
1101 Arthur Ave (60007-5289)
PHONE..................847 364-4000
James De Blasio Jr, President
Connie Santoro, Opers Mgr
Jimmy Deblasio, Purch Mgr
Nick Deblasio, Marketing Staff
Crista Deblasio, Admin Asst
EMP: 40
SQ FT: 40,000
SALES (est): 8.6MM  Privately Held
WEB: www.jdgraphic.com
SIC: 2752  2796  2789  Commercial printing, offset; platemaking services; bookbinding & related work

**(G-9558)**
**J R FRIDRICH INC**
1830 Lunt Ave (60007-5602)
P.O. Box 621, Wood Dale (60191-0621)
PHONE..................847 439-1554
Fax: 847 439-3765
George Fridrich, President
Barbara Fridrich, Corp Secy
EMP: 14
SALES (est): 1.7MM  Privately Held
SIC: 3993  Displays & cutouts, window & lobby

**(G-9559)**
**JACKSON SPRING & MFG CO**
299 Bond St (60007-1220)
PHONE..................847 952-8850
Fax: 847 952-8909
Robert Kupczak, President
Robert Kunkle, Vice Pres
Ron Meyers, Opers Mgr
Al Matusiak, Safety Mgr
Fred Martinez, Opers Staff
EMP: 58  EST: 1961
SQ FT: 55,000
SALES (est): 12.7MM  Privately Held
WEB: www.jacksonspring.com
SIC: 3495  Mechanical springs, precision

**(G-9560)**
**JARVIS CORP**
Also Called: Jarvis Lighting
1950 Estes Ave (60007-5416)
PHONE..................800 363-1075
Kirby Corkill, CEO
EMP: 27 EST: 2002
SALES (est): 7.2MM  Privately Held
SIC: 3646  Commercial indusl & institutional electric lighting fixtures

**(G-9561)**
**JEROME REMIEN CORPORATION**
409 Busse Rd (60007-2114)
P.O. Box 1067, Northbrook (60065-1067)
PHONE..................847 806-0888
Jerome Remien, President
Susan Winters, Marketing Staff
EMP: 11
SQ FT: 3,000
SALES (est): 500K  Privately Held
WEB: www.honorgardsystems.com
SIC: 3499  3429  Locks, safe & vault: metal; manufactured hardware (general)

**(G-9562)**
**JESCORP INC**
1900 Pratt Blvd (60007-5906)
PHONE..................847 378-1200
Fax: 847 290-1282
John E Sanfilippo, President
James J Sanfilippo, Vice Pres
EMP: 85
SQ FT: 60,000
SALES (est): 15.7MM
SALES (corp-wide): 167.9MM  Privately Held
WEB: www.clearlam.com
SIC: 3565  3699  Packing & wrapping machinery; electrical equipment & supplies
PA: Clear Lam Packaging, Inc.
    1950 Pratt Blvd
    Elk Grove Village IL 60007
    847 439-8570

**(G-9563)**
**JOHNSON & JOHNSON**
1350 Estes Ave (60007-5404)
PHONE..................847 640-5400
Fax: 847 640-4618
EMP: 3
SALES (corp-wide): 67.2B  Publicly Held
SIC: 2676  Mfg Consumer Products
PA: Johnson & Johnson
    1 Johnson And Johnson Plz
    New Brunswick NJ 08933
    732 524-0400

**(G-9564)**
**JOONG-ANG DAILY NEWS**
Also Called: The Korea Centl Daily Chicago
790 Busse Rd (60007-2118)
PHONE..................847 228-7200
Fax: 847 427-9627
Gwang Jang, President
Daniel Um, Vice Pres
▲ EMP: 35
SQ FT: 3,400
SALES (est): 2MM  Privately Held
SIC: 2711  2741  Commercial printing & newspaper publishing combined; miscellaneous publishing

**(G-9565)**
**JRD LABS LLC**
2613 Greenleaf Ave (60007-5512)
PHONE..................847 818-1076
Mark Weinberg, President
◆ EMP: 5
SQ FT: 1,000
SALES (est): 756K  Privately Held
WEB: www.jrdlabsupply.com
SIC: 3826  Analytical instruments

**(G-9566)**
**JSC PRODUCTS INC**
2270 Elmhurst Rd (60007-6309)
PHONE..................847 290-9520
John M Carrol, President
EMP: 5
SALES (est): 747.8K  Privately Held
SIC: 2631  Paperboard mills; cardboard

**(G-9567)**
**JW EXPRESS**
440 Lively Blvd (60007-2012)
PHONE..................630 697-1037
Jerry Niewiara, Principal
EMP: 9
SALES (est): 474.9K  Privately Held
SIC: 2741  Miscellaneous publishing

**(G-9568)**
**K & L LOOSELEAF PRODUCTS INC**
425 Bonnie Ln (60007-1907)
PHONE..................847 357-9733
Fax: 847 439-3389
Ken Fairbanks Jr, President
Ben Bodkins, Opers Mgr
Jim Boeing, Safety Mgr
EMP: 60
SQ FT: 16,000
SALES (est): 8.1MM  Privately Held
WEB: www.kllooseleaf.com
SIC: 2782  5199  Looseleaf binders & devices; advertising specialties

**(G-9569)**
**K V F COMPANY (PA)**
950 Lively Blvd (60007-2254)
PHONE..................847 437-5100
Fax: 847 437-5103
Luis A Luna, President
Mathew Harman, Mfg Staff
Toni Quigley, Financial Exec
Madison Carrasco, Director
EMP: 48
SQ FT: 26,400
SALES (est): 4.6MM  Privately Held
WEB: www.kvfcompany.com
SIC: 3471  3398  Finishing, metals or formed products; sand blasting of metal parts; metal heat treating

**(G-9570)**
**K V F COMPANY**
1325 Landmeier Rd (60007-2411)
PHONE..................847 437-5019
Manuel Luna, Manager
EMP: 14
SALES (corp-wide): 4.6MM  Privately Held
WEB: www.kvfcompany.com
SIC: 3471  3398  Finishing, metals or formed products; sand blasting of metal parts; metal heat treating
PA: K V F Company
    950 Lively Blvd
    Elk Grove Village IL 60007
    847 437-5100

**(G-9571)**
**KAVALIERGLASS NORTH AMER INC**
1301 Brummel Ave (60007-2108)
PHONE..................847 364-7303
Greg Bittner, President
EMP: 10
SALES (est): 644K  Privately Held
SIC: 3221  Glass containers

# GEOGRAPHIC SECTION

Elk Grove Village - Cook County (G-9597)

**(G-9572)**
**KERRY INC**
Also Called: Kerry Ingredients and Flavours
1301 Mark St  (60007-6711)
PHONE..................847 595-1003
**EMP:** 8  **Privately Held**
**SIC: 2051**  Bread, cake & related products
**HQ:** Kerry Inc.
3330 Millington Rd
Beloit WI 53511
608 363-1200

**(G-9573)**
**KERRY INGREDIENTS & FLAVOURS**
1301 Mark St  (60007-6711)
PHONE..................847 595-1003
Bill Day, *Principal*
Stuart McCarroll, *Vice Pres*
Michael Kolbuk, *Controller*
Michael Reda, *VP Finance*
**EMP:** 14
**SALES (est):** 2.5MM  **Privately Held**
**SIC: 2051**  Bakery: wholesale or wholesale/retail combined

**(G-9574)**
**KITCHEN TRANSFORMATION INC**
Also Called: Payless For Granite
1410 Jarvis Ave  (60007-2306)
PHONE..................847 758-1905
Paul Batashev, *President*
▲ **EMP:** 12 **EST:** 2011
**SQ FT:** 10,000
**SALES:** 3.5MM  **Privately Held**
**SIC: 3281**  Granite, cut & shaped

**(G-9575)**
**KKT CHILLERS  INC**
1280 Landmeier Rd  (60007-2410)
PHONE..................847 734-1600
Erica Alvi, *Vice Pres*
Wolfgang Corpus, *Vice Pres*
Christopher Barnes, *Treasurer*
Andrea Lmelunann, *Asst Treas*
Dina Shamoon, *Admin Mgr*
▲ **EMP:** 10
**SALES (est):** 2.2MM
**SALES (corp-wide):** 1.6B  **Privately Held**
**SIC: 3432**  8741  Plumbing fixture fittings & trim; management services
**HQ:** Ait-Deutschland Gmbh
Industriestr. 3
Kasendorf  95359
922 899-060

**(G-9576)**
**KLASS ELECTRIC COMPANY INC**
101 Kelly St Ste C  (60007-1029)
PHONE..................847 437-5555
Bettie Sevcik, *Principal*
**EMP:** 19 **EST:** 2009
**SALES (est):** 3.8MM  **Privately Held**
**SIC: 3699**  Electrical equipment & supplies

**(G-9577)**
**KLEIN TOOLS  INC**
Also Called: Turn Key Forging
2300 E Devon Ave  (60007-6120)
PHONE..................847 228-6999
Brian Bykowski, *Engineer*
Mike S Klein, *Office Mgr*
Ernest Pawelczyk, *Branch Mgr*
**EMP:** 78
**SALES (corp-wide):** 344.9MM  **Privately Held**
**WEB:** www.kleintools.com
**SIC: 3423**  3199 3469 2899  Hand & edge tools; belting for machinery: solid, twisted, flat, etc.: leather; safety belts, leather; metal stampings; chemical preparations; partitions & fixtures, except wood; fabric dress & work gloves
**PA:** Klein Tools, Inc.
450 Bond St
Lincolnshire IL 60069
847 821-5500

**(G-9578)**
**KOPP WELDING INC**
991 Oakton St  (60007-1905)
PHONE..................847 593-2070
**Fax:** 847 593-2086

Adam Kopp, *President*
Kathy Kopp, *Vice Pres*
**EMP:** 7
**SALES (est):** 1MM  **Privately Held**
**SIC: 3548**  Electric welding equipment

**(G-9579)**
**KOREA DAILY NEWS**
790 Busse Rd  (60007-2118)
PHONE..................847 545-1767
Gwangho Jang, *CEO*
**EMP:** 50
**SALES:** 5MM  **Privately Held**
**SIC: 2711**  Newspapers, publishing & printing

**(G-9580)**
**KURZ TRANSFER PRODUCTS LP**
220 Martin Ln  (60007-1311)
PHONE..................847 228-0001
**Fax:** 847 228-0230
Tony Flaim, *Branch Mgr*
**EMP:** 4
**SALES (corp-wide):** 77.8MM  **Privately Held**
**WEB:** www.kurzusa.com
**SIC: 4225**  3497  General warehousing & storage; gold foil or leaf
**PA:** Kurz Transfer Products, Lp
3200 Woodpark Blvd
Charlotte NC 28206
704 927-3700

**(G-9581)**
**L & M TOOL & DIE CO INC**
1570 Louis Ave  (60007-2314)
PHONE..................847 364-9760
**Fax:** 847 364-9771
Lars Gosell, *President*
Christopher Gosell, *Engineer*
Erik Gosell, *Engineer*
Marilyn Gosell, *Admin Sec*
**EMP:** 5 **EST:** 1979
**SQ FT:** 12,000
**SALES:** 1.3MM  **Privately Held**
**SIC: 3544**  Special dies, tools, jigs & fixtures

**(G-9582)**
**LA-CO INDUSTRIES  INC (PA)**
Also Called: Markal Company
1201 Pratt Blvd  (60007-5746)
PHONE..................847 427-3220
**Fax:** 847 826-7130
Daniel Kleiman, *CEO*
George Bowman, *President*
Michael Goluszka, *VP Mfg*
Eric Person, *Mfg Mgr*
Julie Gann, *Safety Mgr*
◆ **EMP:** 145 **EST:** 1935
**SQ FT:** 80,000
**SALES (est):** 28.5MM  **Privately Held**
**WEB:** www.laco.com
**SIC: 2891**  2899  Sealants; fluxes: brazing, soldering, galvanizing & welding

**(G-9583)**
**LANINVER USA INC (PA)**
2800 Carl Bulevard  (60007)
PHONE..................847 367-8787
Clemente Gonzales, *President*
**EMP:** 2 **EST:** 2013
**SALES (est):** 4.7MM  **Privately Held**
**SIC: 2759**  Commercial printing

**(G-9584)**
**LARSEN ENVELOPE CO  INC**
165 Gaylord St  (60007-1106)
PHONE..................847 952-9020
**Fax:** 847 952-9045
Leonard R Larsen Jr, *President*
Helen Larsen, *Corp Secy*
Jack Story, *Vice Pres*
Paul Kowal, *Manager*
Helen M Larsen, *Admin Sec*
**EMP:** 22
**SQ FT:** 7,500
**SALES (est):** 3.6MM  **Privately Held**
**WEB:** www.larsenenvelope.com
**SIC: 2754**  Envelopes: gravure printing

**(G-9585)**
**LASER PLUS TECHNOLOGIES LLC**
2450 American Ln  (60007-6204)
PHONE..................847 787-9017
**Fax:** 847 787-9019
Julian Kuta, *Vice Pres*
Karen Schwartz, *Engineer*
Jason Schawrtz, *Mng Member*
**EMP:** 4
**SQ FT:** 10,000
**SALES (est):** 568.5K  **Privately Held**
**WEB:** www.laserpls.com
**SIC: 7389**  3441  Metal cutting services; fabricated structural metal

**(G-9586)**
**LASER TECHNOLOGY GROUP INC**
1029 Charlela Ln Apt 407  (60007-3225)
PHONE..................847 524-4088
Don McNeil, *President*
**EMP:** 3
**SALES:** 11K  **Privately Held**
**SIC: 2893**  Printing ink

**(G-9587)**
**LAUBER TOOL CO INC**
Also Called: Tool & Die
170 Seegers Ave  (60007-1615)
PHONE..................847 228-5969
**Fax:** 847 228-5982
Anton Lauber, *President*
**EMP:** 4
**SQ FT:** 5,000
**SALES (est):** 350K  **Privately Held**
**WEB:** www.laubertool.com
**SIC: 3544**  Special dies, tools, jigs & fixtures

**(G-9588)**
**LAWRENCE FOODS INC**
2200 Lunt Ave  (60007-5685)
PHONE..................847 437-2400
**Fax:** 847 437-2567
Lester Lawrence, *CEO*
Andy Balafas, *General Mgr*
Keith Appling, *Exec VP*
Sravani Chancharem, *QC Mgr*
Varun Bhakta, *Engineer*
▼ **EMP:** 250
**SQ FT:** 200,000
**SALES (est):** 107.3MM  **Privately Held**
**WEB:** www.lawrencefoods.com
**SIC: 2033**  2099  Canned fruits & specialties; food preparations

**(G-9589)**
**LC INDUSTRIES  INC**
Also Called: Lewis N Clark Travel ACC
2781 Katherine Way  (60007-6746)
PHONE..................312 455-0500
**Fax:** 312 455-0005
Michael Smerling, *President*
Brian Luczak, *Controller*
Cherie Corbisiero, *Marketing Staff*
Rae L Smerling, *Admin Sec*
▲ **EMP:** 27
**SQ FT:** 30,000
**SALES (est):** 5.6MM  **Privately Held**
**WEB:** www.lewisnclark.com
**SIC: 3161**  Luggage

**(G-9590)**
**LEE INDUSTRIES  INC**
Also Called: Groen Process Equipment Div
1900 Pratt Blvd  (60007-5906)
P.O. Box 688, Philipsburg PA  (16866-0688)
PHONE..................847 462-1865
Hermes Bidawid, *Vice Pres*
Elaine Chaney, *Vice Pres*
Donald Page, *Engineer*
Anthony Dalman, *Sales Staff*
Ron Rosati, *Branch Mgr*
**EMP:** 120
**SALES (corp-wide):** 89.7MM  **Privately Held**
**WEB:** www.unifiedbrands.net
**SIC: 3589**  3556 3531 3511  Cooking equipment, commercial; food products machinery; construction machinery; turbines & turbine generator sets; fabricated plate work (boiler shop); commercial cooking & food service equipment

**PA:** Lee Industries, Inc.
210 4th St Sw
Conover NC 28613
828 464-8318

**(G-9591)**
**LEGACY FOODS MFG LLC**
498 Franklin Ln  (60007-2702)
PHONE..................224 639-5297
Phillip M Graff, *Mng Member*
John Barajan, *Manager*
**EMP:** 3
**SALES (est):** 220K  **Privately Held**
**SIC: 2099**  Sauces: gravy, dressing & dip mixes

**(G-9592)**
**LEGACY FOODS MFG LLC**
2775 Katherine Way  (60007-6746)
PHONE..................847 595-9106
John Barajas, *Principal*
Steve Sallenback, *Principal*
Phil Graff,
**EMP:** 14
**SALES (est):** 3.6MM  **Privately Held**
**SIC: 2035**  2033  Pickles, sauces & salad dressings; barbecue sauce: packaged in cans, jars, etc.

**(G-9593)**
**LEGACY VULCAN  LLC**
Also Called: Elk Grove Recycle
1520 Midway Ct  (60007-6605)
PHONE..................847 437-4181
Dave Kwoznewski, *Principal*
Sue Stasch, *Opers Staff*
James Lillwitz, *Project Engr*
John Vanick, *Manager*
**EMP:** 22
**SALES (corp-wide):** 3.5B  **Publicly Held**
**WEB:** www.vulcanmaterials.com
**SIC: 1442**  Construction sand & gravel
**HQ:** Legacy Vulcan, Llc
1200 Urban Center Dr
Vestavia AL 35242
205 298-3000

**(G-9594)**
**LEMOY INTERNATIONAL INC (PA)**
Also Called: Ideas
95 King St  (60007-1108)
PHONE..................847 427-0840
**Fax:** 847 427-1367
William Lee, *President*
**EMP:** 3
**SALES (est):** 1.3MM  **Privately Held**
**SIC: 5047**  3843 3841  Dental equipment & supplies; dental equipment; surgical & medical instruments

**(G-9595)**
**LIFESPAN BRANDS LLC**
1200 Thorndale Ave  (60007-6749)
PHONE..................630 315-3300
Clay Farnsworth, *President*
Michael Kehrmann, *Senior VP*
Tom Spain, *Opers Staff*
Joe Kostelc, *CFO*
▲ **EMP:** 18
**SQ FT:** 70,000
**SALES:** 19.4MM  **Privately Held**
**WEB:** www.lavaworld.com
**SIC: 3645**  3596  Residential lighting fixtures; bathroom scales

**(G-9596)**
**LIGHTOLIER GENLYTE INC**
951 Busse Rd  (60007-2400)
PHONE..................847 364-8250
**Fax:** 847 364-4117
Gary Basista, *President*
Jeff Ridgell, *Vice Pres*
Vince Lanius, *Director*
**EMP:** 56
**SALES (est):** 3.4MM  **Privately Held**
**SIC: 3645**  Residential lighting fixtures

**(G-9597)**
**LITTLE LADY FOODS INC (PA)**
Also Called: Primerro Frozen Foods
2323 Pratt Blvd  (60007-5918)
PHONE..................847 806-1440
**Fax:** 847 806-0026
Rick Anderson, *CEO*
John Geocaris, *Principal*

# Elk Grove Village - Cook County (G-9598)

Mark Pickett, *Vice Pres*
Steven Kunkle, *VP Opers*
Edward Mulloy, *Plant Mgr*
**EMP:** 230 **EST:** 1960
**SQ FT:** 200,000
**SALES (est):** 142.6MM **Privately Held**
**WEB:** www.littleladyfoods.com
**SIC:** 2038 2099 Pizza, frozen; food preparations

### (G-9598)
**LOYOLA PAPER COMPANY**
951 Lunt Ave (60007-5091)
**PHONE** ............................ 847 956-7770
**Fax:** 847 956-6897
Joan Lavezzorio, *President*
Nicholas Lavezzorio, *President*
Nancy Cygen, *Office Mgr*
**EMP:** 40 **EST:** 1969
**SQ FT:** 75,000
**SALES (est):** 12.9MM **Privately Held**
**WEB:** www.loyolapaper.com
**SIC:** 2679 7389 Paperboard products, converted; interior designer

### (G-9599)
**LUDWIG DAIRY PRODUCTS INC (PA)**
1270 Mark St (60007-6708)
**PHONE** ............................ 847 860-8646
Miroslaw Gebka, *President*
Sebastian Gebka, *General Mgr*
Henes Dobrzycki, *Manager*
▲ **EMP:** 7
**SQ FT:** 5,000
**SALES (est):** 2.8MM **Privately Held**
**SIC:** 2022 Cheese, natural & processed

### (G-9600)
**LUMISOURCE LLC**
2950 Old Higgins Rd (60007-6500)
**PHONE** ............................ 847 699-8988
Shui-Yu Lee, *President*
Irene Lee, *Vice Pres*
Steve Lee, *Vice Pres*
Lashuundra Charief, *Manager*
◆ **EMP:** 20
**SQ FT:** 37,500
**SALES (est):** 6.4MM **Privately Held**
**WEB:** www.lumisource.com
**SIC:** 3643 Lamp sockets & receptacles (electric wiring devices)

### (G-9601)
**M & J MANUFACTURING CO INC**
1450 Jarvis Ave (60007-2380)
**PHONE** ............................ 847 364-6066
**Fax:** 847 364-6134
Joseph Soehn, *President*
Michael Howard, *Vice Pres*
Joe Soehn Jr, *Vice Pres*
Matt Soehn, *Vice Pres*
**EMP:** 10 **EST:** 1967
**SQ FT:** 8,000
**SALES:** 1MM **Privately Held**
**SIC:** 3599 7692 Machine shop, jobbing & repair; welding repair

### (G-9602)
**M & R PRECISION MACHINING INC**
680 Lively Blvd (60007-2016)
**PHONE** ............................ 847 364-1050
**Fax:** 847 364-1055
Richard G Beunhauer, *Principal*
Irma Beinhauer, *Treasurer*
Gerhard Beinhauer, *Human Res Dir*
▲ **EMP:** 30
**SQ FT:** 19,000
**SALES (est):** 6.7MM **Privately Held**
**WEB:** www.mrprecision.com
**SIC:** 3599 Machine shop, jobbing & repair

### (G-9603)
**M I E AMERICA INC**
420 Bennett Rd (60007-1007)
**PHONE** ............................ 847 981-6100
**Fax:** 847 981-3232
Gunther Kuel, *President*
Norman Von Hollen, *Vice Pres*
Linda Andel, *Accountant*
▲ **EMP:** 11
**SQ FT:** 10,000
**SALES (est):** 2.5MM
**SALES (corp-wide):** 11MM **Privately Held**
**WEB:** www.mieamerica.com
**SIC:** 3829 Nuclear instrument modules
**PA:** Mie Medical Imaging Electronics Gmbh
Hauptstr. 112
Seth 23845
419 499-770

### (G-9604)
**M S A PRINTING CO**
850 Touhy Ave (60007-4918)
**PHONE** ............................ 847 593-5699
**Fax:** 847 593-1054
Ross Diederich, *President*
Peggy Diederich, *Admin Sec*
**EMP:** 3
**SQ FT:** 5,000
**SALES (est):** 270K **Privately Held**
**SIC:** 2759 2752 2796 2675 Letterpress printing; commercial printing, offset; platemaking services; die-cut paper & board

### (G-9605)
**MACHINED METALS MANUFACTURING**
1450 Jarvis Ave (60007-2306)
**PHONE** ............................ 847 364-6116
Matthias Soehn, *President*
Joseph Soehn, *Admin Sec*
**EMP:** 30
**SQ FT:** 8,000
**SALES (est):** 1.6MM **Privately Held**
**WEB:** www.machined-metals.com
**SIC:** 3599 Machine shop, jobbing & repair

### (G-9606)
**MAGNETIC INSPECTION LAB INC**
Also Called: M I L
1401 Greenleaf Ave (60007-5536)
**PHONE** ............................ 847 437-4488
**Fax:** 847 437-4538
Robert L Schiewe, *President*
Annie Gandhi, *Vice Pres*
Jay Gandhi, *Vice Pres*
Tim Schiewe, *Vice Pres*
Adam Schrader, *Opers Mgr*
**EMP:** 85
**SQ FT:** 35,000
**SALES (est):** 20MM **Privately Held**
**WEB:** www.milinc.com
**SIC:** 8734 7692 3471 2899 Metallurgical testing laboratory; welding repair; plating & polishing; chemical preparations

### (G-9607)
**MAIN STEEL LLC (PA)**
2200 Pratt Blvd (60007-5917)
**PHONE** ............................ 847 916-1220
Tom Modrowski, *CEO*
Paul Patek, *CFO*
▲ **EMP:** 35 **EST:** 2014
**SALES (est):** 166.2MM **Privately Held**
**SIC:** 3312 Stainless steel

### (G-9608)
**MAIN STEEL POLISHING CO INC (PA)**
Also Called: Main Steel - Corporate 6001
2200 Pratt Blvd (60007-5917)
**PHONE** ............................ 847 916-1220
Keith Medick, *CEO*
Michael Folley, *General Mgr*
Bob Haas, *General Mgr*
George Bogan, *Exec VP*
Mark McCool, *Vice Pres*
▲ **EMP:** 35 **EST:** 1980
**SQ FT:** 15,000
**SALES (est):** 29.2MM **Privately Held**
**SIC:** 3471 Finishing, metals or formed products; buffing for the trade

### (G-9609)
**MAJESTIC SPRING INC**
Also Called: Coil lt
1390 Jarvis Ave (60007-2304)
**PHONE** ............................ 847 593-8887
**Fax:** 847 593-8954
John Giourdas, *President*
**EMP:** 10
**SQ FT:** 5,000
**SALES:** 875K **Privately Held**
**WEB:** www.majesticspring.com
**SIC:** 3495 Wire springs

### (G-9610)
**MAPES & SPROWL STEEL LLC**
1100 E Devon Ave (60007-5274)
**PHONE** ............................ 800 777-1025
**Fax:** 847 364-0137
Christopher Hutter, *Principal*
Paul D Douglass, *Principal*
**EMP:** 2
**SALES (est):** 1MM
**SALES (corp-wide):** 128.5MM **Privately Held**
**SIC:** 3315 Steel wire & related products
**PA:** Union Partners 1 Llc
1400 16th St Ste 250
Oak Brook IL 60523
630 822-7000

### (G-9611)
**MARATHON TECHNOLOGIES INC**
Also Called: MTI
800 Nicholas Blvd (60007-2511)
**PHONE** ............................ 847 378-8572
**Fax:** 847 228-1770
Jerry Kozlowski, *President*
Jerzy Kozlowski, *President*
Mark Kozlowski, *General Mgr*
Anne Starck, *Office Mgr*
**EMP:** 40
**SQ FT:** 15,000
**SALES (est):** 7.3MM **Privately Held**
**WEB:** www.marathontechnologies.com
**SIC:** 3599 Machine shop, jobbing & repair

### (G-9612)
**MARVCO TOOL & MANUFACTURING**
775 Lively Blvd (60007-2202)
P.O. Box 524 (60009-0524)
**PHONE** ............................ 847 437-4900
**Fax:** 847 437-4925
Marvin Harrigan, *President*
Michael Harrigan, *Vice Pres*
**EMP:** 5
**SQ FT:** 11,000
**SALES (est):** 833K **Privately Held**
**WEB:** www.marvcotool.com
**SIC:** 3553 3549 3546 3535 Saws, power: bench & table, except portable: woodworking; metalworking machinery; power-driven handtools; conveyors & conveying equipment

### (G-9613)
**MATERIAL SCIENCES CORPORATION**
2250 Pratt Blvd (60007-5917)
**PHONE** ............................ 847 439-2210
Daniel Fondriest, *Manager*
**EMP:** 25
**SALES (corp-wide):** 110.1MM **Privately Held**
**SIC:** 3479 Painting of metal products
**PA:** Material Sciences Corporation
6855 Commerce Blvd
Canton MI 48187
734 207-4444

### (G-9614)
**MATTHEW WARREN INC**
Also Called: Rumco
989 Pauly Dr (60007-1312)
**PHONE** ............................ 847 364-5000
**Fax:** 847 364-4104
Sebastian Janas, *Sales Staff*
Dan Bishop, *Branch Mgr*
**EMP:** 20
**SALES (corp-wide):** 115.4MM **Privately Held**
**SIC:** 3452 Bolts, nuts, rivets & washers; screws, metal; spring pins, metal
**HQ:** Matthew Warren, Inc.
9501 Tech Blvd Ste 401
Rosemont IL 60018
847 349-5760

### (G-9615)
**MAYEKAWA USA INC (DH)**
1850 Jarvis Ave (60007-2440)
**PHONE** ............................ 773 516-5070
Tadashi Maekawa, *President*
Takeo Kanazawa, *COO*
Linda Ford, *Human Res Mgr*
Irene Hurtado, *Accounts Mgr*
Saeiji Daito, *Administration*
▲ **EMP:** 12
**SQ FT:** 35,000
**SALES (est):** 35.9MM **Privately Held**
**SIC:** 3585 5078 3563 Refrigeration equipment, complete; refrigeration equipment & supplies; air & gas compressors
**HQ:** Mayekawa Mfg. Co., Ltd.
3-14-15, Botan
Koto-Ku TKY 135-0
336 428-181

### (G-9616)
**MEA INC**
2600 American Ln (60007-6270)
**PHONE** ............................ 847 766-9040
**Fax:** 630 350-1951
Townes Comer, *President*
Marge Dombrowski, *General Mgr*
William T Comer, *Vice Pres*
**EMP:** 23 **EST:** 1963
**SQ FT:** 13,000
**SALES (est):** 8.5MM **Privately Held**
**WEB:** www.meaincorporated.com
**SIC:** 3593 8711 3492 Fluid power actuators, hydraulic or pneumatic; mechanical engineering; electrohydraulic servo valves, metal

### (G-9617)
**MEDALIST INDUSTRIES INC**
Also Called: C-Tech Systems Division
2700 Elmhurst Rd (60007-6315)
**PHONE** ............................ 847 766-9000
**Fax:** 847 766-3645
James S Dahlke, *President*
Michael Gregg, *Vice Pres*
James G Gumm, *Vice Pres*
William C O'Loughlin, *Vice Pres*
James A Lathrop, *Treasurer*
**EMP:** 9 **EST:** 1954
**SALES:** 126MM
**SALES (corp-wide):** 13.6B **Publicly Held**
**SIC:** 3452 Screws, metal; bolts, metal; nuts, metal; washers, metal
**PA:** Illinois Tool Works Inc.
155 Harlem Ave
Glenview IL 60025
847 724-7500

### (G-9618)
**MET PLASTICS**
333 King St (60007-1114)
**PHONE** ............................ 847 228-5070
**Fax:** 847 228-5673
**EMP:** 3
**SALES (est):** 144.2K **Privately Held**
**SIC:** 3089 3544 Plastics products; special dies, tools, jigs & fixtures

### (G-9619)
**MET2PLASTIC LLC**
Also Called: Met Plastics
701 Lee St (60007-1121)
**PHONE** ............................ 847 228-5070
Michael P Walter, *President*
Jim Van Dahm, *General Mgr*
Jeff Freebus, *Purch Agent*
Wayne Maurer, *QC Mgr*
**EMP:** 40
**SQ FT:** 30,000
**SALES (est):** 8.8MM
**SALES (corp-wide):** 99.7K **Privately Held**
**WEB:** www.metplastics.com
**SIC:** 3089 Injection molding of plastics
**HQ:** Dedienne Multiplasturgy
Zac Des Champs Chouette 2
Saint Aubin Sur Gaillon 27600

### (G-9620)
**METAL IMPACT LLC**
1501 Oakton St (60007-2101)
**PHONE** ............................ 847 718-0192
**Fax:** 847 718-9360
Kevin Prunsky, *Ch of Bd*
Barbara Ostron, *Human Res Dir*
Newell John, *Mng Member*
Prunsky Kevin, *Mng Member*
Tom Lowkitz, *Maintence Staff*
**EMP:** 100
**SQ FT:** 175,000

# GEOGRAPHIC SECTION
## Elk Grove Village - Cook County (G-9644)

SALES (est): 21.4MM
SALES (corp-wide): 80.6MM **Privately Held**
SIC: 3544 Extrusion dies
PA: Thunderbird Llc
  1501 Oakton St
  Elk Grove Village IL 60007
  847 718-9300

### (G-9621)
### METAL IMPACT SOUTH LLC
1501 Oakton St (60007-2101)
PHONE.................847 718-9300
EMP: 11
SALES (corp-wide): 80.6MM **Privately Held**
SIC: 3354 Aluminum extruded products
HQ: Metal Impact South Llc
  795 Sam T Barkley Dr
  New Albany MS 38652
  662 538-6500

### (G-9622)
### METAL RESOURCES INTL LLC
1965 Pratt Blvd (60007-5905)
PHONE.................847 806-7200
Fax: 847 806-7237
Cyrus Tang, *President*
National Material,
▲ EMP: 14
SALES (est): 4.6MM **Privately Held**
SIC: 3325 Rolling mill rolls, cast steel

### (G-9623)
### METRIC MACHINE SHOP INC
101 Kelly St Ste D (60007-1029)
PHONE.................847 439-9891
Edward Rybecki, *President*
EMP: 4
SALES: 350K **Privately Held**
SIC: 3599 Machine & other job shop work

### (G-9624)
### MGB ENGINEERING COMPANY (PA)
1099 Touhy Ave (60007-4921)
PHONE.................847 956-7444
Michael Beladakis, *President*
Lambros Kalamaris, *Plant Mgr*
Maria Theodosis, *Treasurer*
Angie Beladakis, *Admin Sec*
EMP: 20
SQ FT: 64,000
SALES (est): 7MM **Privately Held**
SIC: 3559 3542 Plastics working machinery; machine tools, metal forming type

### (G-9625)
### MICHAEL A GREENBERG MD LTD
Also Called: Illinois Dermatological Center
800 Biesterfield Rd # 3002 (60007-3364)
PHONE.................847 364-4717
Michael Greenberg, *Owner*
Trevor Powell, *Office Mgr*
EMP: 10
SQ FT: 1,100
SALES (est): 1.4MM **Privately Held**
WEB: www.anovelvision.com
SIC: 8011 2731 Dermatologist; physicians' office, including specialists; book publishing

### (G-9626)
### MIDACO CORPORATION
2000 Touhy Ave (60007-5368)
PHONE.................847 593-8420
Fax: 847 593-8451
Michael P Cayley, *President*
Malcolm Keith, *Vice Pres*
Vincent Storelli, *Design Engr*
Mary T Baran, *Treasurer*
Robert Dunbar, *VP Sales*
EMP: 40
SQ FT: 40,000
SALES (est): 10MM **Privately Held**
WEB: www.midaco-corp.com
SIC: 3599 3537 Custom machinery; machine shop, jobbing & repair; pallets, metal

### (G-9627)
### MIDWAY GRINDING INC
1451 Lunt Ave (60007-5621)
PHONE.................847 439-7424
Fax: 847 439-7459
Jerry Malachowski, *President*
Dorothy Malachowski, *Corp Secy*
Peter Gudek, *Manager*
Michael Malachowsky, *Manager*
Tony Szafranski, *Manager*
EMP: 45 EST: 1978
SQ FT: 30,000
SALES (est): 7.9MM **Privately Held**
WEB: www.midwaygrinding.com
SIC: 3599 Machine & other job shop work; grinding castings for the trade

### (G-9628)
### MIDWAY MACHINE PRODUCTS & SVCS
2690 American Ln (60007-6208)
PHONE.................847 860-8180
Juan D Guemez, *President*
EMP: 5
SALES (est): 612.5K **Privately Held**
WEB: www.midwaymachineproducts.com
SIC: 3451 Screw machine products

### (G-9629)
### MILLENNIUM MARKING COMPANY (DH)
2600 Greenleaf Ave (60007-5513)
PHONE.................847 806-1750
Fax: 847 806-1751
Paul Demartini, *President*
Dan Cork, *Vice Pres*
Robert Sterrett, *Vice Pres*
Diane Rogers, *Purch Mgr*
Mark Klage, *Regl Sales Mgr*
◆ EMP: 38
SQ FT: 20,000
SALES (est): 8.5MM
SALES (corp-wide): 4.1MM **Privately Held**
WEB: www.millmarking.com
SIC: 3953 5112 Marking devices; marking devices
HQ: Trodat Usa Llc
  48 Heller Park Ln
  Somerset NJ 08873
  732 562-9500

### (G-9630)
### MISSION CONTROL SYSTEMS INC
700 Oakton St (60007-1903)
PHONE.................847 956-7650
Fax: 847 956-7660
Scott Medford, *President*
Gary Chapman, *Principal*
Brad Kodi, *Principal*
Jillynn Degrenier, *Manager*
EMP: 16
SQ FT: 10,300
SALES (est): 4.6MM **Privately Held**
WEB: www.missioncontrolsystems.com
SIC: 3625 Electric controls & control accessories, industrial

### (G-9631)
### MIYANO MACHINERY USA INC (DH)
2316 Touhy Ave (60007-5329)
PHONE.................630 766-4141
Tsugio Sasaki, *President*
Jinho Park, *Engineer*
Sasaki Tsugio, *Treasurer*
Imad Tsay, *Manager*
Henry Marchionne, *Director*
▲ EMP: 20
SQ FT: 182,450
SALES (est): 4.3MM
SALES (corp-wide): 2.7B **Privately Held**
WEB: www.miyano-usa.com
SIC: 5084 3541 Metalworking machinery; numerically controlled metal cutting machine tools
HQ: Citizen Machinery Co.,Ltd.
  4107-6, Miyota, Miyotamachi
  Kita Saku-Gun NAG 389-0
  267 325-900

### (G-9632)
### MK SYSTEMS INCORPORATED (PA)
1455 Brummel Ave (60007-2110)
PHONE.................847 709-6180
Brien Buelow, *President*
Curtis Benson, *Sales Engr*
Frank Nevsimal, *Sales Associate*
Andrew Kirkel, *Marketing Staff*
Jacqueline Hovey, *Manager*
EMP: 14
SALES (est): 3.2MM **Privately Held**
SIC: 3599 Machine & other job shop work

### (G-9633)
### MLP SEATING CORP
950 Pratt Blvd (60007-5119)
PHONE.................847 956-1700
Fax: 847 956-1776
Ralph D Samuel, *President*
Goerge Stembridge, *QC Dir*
Jennie Betti, *Manager*
Judy Laux, *Technology*
Michelle C Samuel, *Admin Sec*
▼ EMP: 25 EST: 1946
SQ FT: 43,000
SALES (est): 5.2MM **Privately Held**
WEB: www.mlpseating.com
SIC: 2522 2521 Chairs, office: padded or plain, except wood; stools, office: except wood; wood office furniture

### (G-9634)
### MODERN AIDS INC
201 Bond St (60007-1220)
PHONE.................847 437-8600
Fax: 847 437-8602
Douglas E Croft, *President*
Larry A Lewis, *Admin Sec*
EMP: 20
SQ FT: 11,000
SALES (est): 5.1MM **Privately Held**
SIC: 3842 Gauze, surgical

### (G-9635)
### MONOTYPE IMAGING INC
985 Busse Rd (60007-2400)
PHONE.................847 718-0400
Frank Mercuri, *Production*
Benjamin Richard, *Accounts Mgr*
David Harned, *Manager*
Satoshi Asari, *Manager*
Dieter Jancart, *Manager*
EMP: 11
SALES (corp-wide): 203.4MM **Publicly Held**
SIC: 7371 7372 Custom computer programming services; prepackaged software
HQ: Monotype Imaging Inc.
  600 Unicorn Park Dr
  Woburn MA 01801

### (G-9636)
### MOSS HOLDING COMPANY (HQ)
2600 Elmhurst Rd (60007-6312)
P.O. Box 36547 Treasury, Chicago (60694-0001)
PHONE.................847 238-4200
Dan Patterson, *President*
Mark Ollinger, *CFO*
Yvonne Illenberg, *Accountant*
▲ EMP: 160
SALES (est): 68.4MM
SALES (corp-wide): 78.8MM **Privately Held**
SIC: 2399 2541 2211 Banners, pennants & flags; store & office display cases & fixtures; stretch fabrics, cotton
PA: Century Park Capital Partners, Llc
  2101 Rosecrans Ave # 4275
  El Segundo CA 90245
  310 867-2210

### (G-9637)
### MOSS INC
2600 Elmhurst Rd (60007-6312)
P.O. Box 248, Belfast ME (04915-0248)
PHONE.................800 341-1557
Fax: 207 930-6002
Dan Patterson, *President*
Bob Frey, *Exec VP*
Dan Scandiff, *Exec VP*
Sarah Browning, *Senior VP*
Vijay Hingorani, *Senior VP*
EMP: 5
SALES (est): 263K **Privately Held**
SIC: 2759 Commercial printing

### (G-9638)
### MOTION ACCESS LLC
775 Nicholas Blvd (60007-2508)
PHONE.................847 357-8832
Fax: 847 357-8834
Michael Valencia, *Marketing Staff*
Robert Oakley, *Mng Member*
▲ EMP: 30
SALES (est): 3.7MM **Privately Held**
SIC: 2431 Doors & door parts & trim, wood

### (G-9639)
### MOTOR OIL INC
2250 Arthur Ave (60007-6011)
PHONE.................847 956-7550
Fax: 847 956-0399
Thomas G Sullivan, *President*
EMP: 10
SQ FT: 5,000
SALES: 1.1MM **Privately Held**
WEB: www.motoroilinc.com
SIC: 2992 5172 Oils & greases, blending & compounding; lubricating oils & greases

### (G-9640)
### MSC PRE FINISH METALS EGV INC (HQ)
2250 Pratt Blvd (60007-5917)
PHONE.................847 439-2210
Gerald G Nadig, *Ch of Bd*
Douglas M Rose, *President*
James Waclawik Sr, *CFO*
EMP: 230
SQ FT: 233,000
SALES (est): 55.4MM
SALES (corp-wide): 110.1MM **Privately Held**
SIC: 3479 3471 3399 Coating of metals & formed products; electroplating of metals or formed products; laminating steel
PA: Material Sciences Corporation
  6855 Commerce Blvd
  Canton MI 48187
  734 207-4444

### (G-9641)
### MUELLER INDUSTRIES INC
2021 Lunt Ave (60007-5605)
PHONE.................847 290-1108
Peter Berkman, *Manager*
EMP: 150
SALES (corp-wide): 2B **Publicly Held**
SIC: 3351 Copper & copper alloy pipe & tube
PA: Mueller Industries, Inc.
  8285 Tournament Dr # 150
  Memphis TN 38125
  901 753-3200

### (G-9642)
### MUELLER MFG CORP (PA)
Also Called: Mueller Metal Products
300 Lively Blvd (60007-2010)
P.O. Box 129 (60009-0129)
PHONE.................847 640-1666
Fax: 847 640-1675
Anton Mueller, *President*
Anne Mueller, *Treasurer*
Eric Hauser, *Sales Mgr*
Kathleen Anderson, *Director*
Ronald Mueller, *Admin Sec*
EMP: 30
SQ FT: 90,000
SALES (est): 2.2MM **Privately Held**
WEB: www.muellermfg.com
SIC: 3469 5084 Stamping metal for the trade; industrial machinery & equipment

### (G-9643)
### MUELLER ORNA IR WORKS INC
655 Lively Blvd (60007-2015)
PHONE.................847 758-9941
Fax: 847 758-9945
Robert C Mueller, *President*
Lynn Parquette, *Treasurer*
Marilyn Mueller, *Admin Sec*
EMP: 10 EST: 1933
SALES (est): 1.9MM **Privately Held**
WEB: www.ornamentaliron.net
SIC: 3446 Fences or posts, ornamental iron or steel; railings, prefabricated metal; gates, ornamental metal

### (G-9644)
### NACME STEEL PROCESSING LLC
1965 Pratt Blvd (60007-5905)
PHONE.................847 806-7226
Grant Kottemeyer, *Principal*
Diana Palido, *Manager*
Diana Puldo, *Manager*

# Elk Grove Village - Cook County (G-9645)

**EMP**: 7
**SALES (est)**: 510K **Privately Held**
**SIC**: 3312 Blast furnaces & steel mills

**(G-9645)**
### NAMCO AMERICA INC
951 Cambridge Dr (60007-2434)
**PHONE**.................................847 264-5610
Kenji Hisatsune, *CEO*
Frank Cosentino, *Vice Pres*
Mehdi Eghbal, *Vice Pres*
Patrick O'Brien, *Opers Mgr*
James Roycroft, *Purch Mgr*
▲ **EMP**: 25
**SALES (est)**: 3.3MM
**SALES (corp-wide)**: 5.4B **Privately Held**
**WEB**: www.namcobandai.com
**SIC**: 3999 Coin-operated amusement machines
**HQ**: Bandai Namco Holdings Usa Inc.
   2120 Park Pl Ste 120
   El Segundo CA 90245

**(G-9646)**
### NATIONAL MATERIAL COMPANY LLC (PA)
1965 Pratt Blvd (60007-5905)
**PHONE**.................................847 806-7200
Dan Howell, *Controller*
**EMP**: 50
**SALES (est)**: 53.1MM **Privately Held**
**SIC**: 3341 3399 3315 Aluminum smelting & refining (secondary); aluminum atomized powder; wire, ferrous/iron

**(G-9647)**
### NATIONAL METAL FABRICATORS LLC
2395 Greenleaf Ave (60007-5508)
**PHONE**.................................847 439-5321
**Fax**: 847 439-4774
William T Bonine Jr, *President*
Steve Kint, *Owner*
Mike Bollero, *Vice Pres*
Jon Miller, *Vice Pres*
Jim Slater, *Webmaster*
◆ **EMP**: 34
**SQ FT**: 56,000
**SALES (est)**: 8.6MM **Privately Held**
**SIC**: 3441 Fabricated structural metal

**(G-9648)**
### NBS CORPORATION
1501 Tonne Rd (60007-5004)
**PHONE**.................................847 860-8856
Jim Straus, *Manager*
**EMP**: 3
**SALES (corp-wide)**: 6.9MM **Privately Held**
**SIC**: 3965 Fasteners
**PA**: Nbs Corporation
   3100 E Slauson Ave
   Vernon CA 90058
   323 923-1627

**(G-9649)**
### NEFAB PACKAGING N CENTL LLC
850 Mark St (60007-6704)
**Fax**: 847 595-7230
Mike Pectorelli, *Manager*
**EMP**: 143
**SALES (est)**: 17.5MM
**SALES (corp-wide)**: 380.8MM **Privately Held**
**SIC**: 2448 2449 2441 Pallets, wood & wood with metal; skids, wood & wood with metal; rectangular boxes & crates, wood; nailed wood boxes & shook
**HQ**: Nefab Packaging, Inc.
   204 Airline Dr Ste 100
   Coppell TX 75019
   469 444-5264

**(G-9650)**
### NEW CHICAGO WHOLESALE BKY INC
Also Called: Chicago Gourmet Wholesale Bky
795 Touhy Ave (60007-4915)
Rural Route 795 Touhy (60007)
**PHONE**.................................847 981-1600
Juliana Achimas, *President*
Mario Achimas, *Marketing Staff*
Andrea Achimas, *Office Mgr*
**EMP**: 42
**SQ FT**: 20,000
**SALES (est)**: 887K **Privately Held**
**WEB**: www.cgwbakery.com
**SIC**: 5149 2053 2051 Bakery products; cakes, bakery: frozen; cakes, bakery: except frozen

**(G-9651)**
### NIDEC MOTOR CORPORATION
Merkle-Korff Industries
25 Northwest Point Blvd # 900 (60007-1056)
**PHONE**.................................847 439-3760
Kevin Machalek, *Vice Pres*
**EMP**: 75
**SALES (corp-wide)**: 10B **Privately Held**
**SIC**: 3621 Motors, electric
**HQ**: Nidec Motor Corporation
   8050 West Florissant Ave
   Saint Louis MO 63136

**(G-9652)**
### NISSEI AMERICA INC
721 Landmeier Rd (60007-4757)
**PHONE**.................................847 228-5000
**Fax**: 847 228-6700
Peter Pollack, *Manager*
**EMP**: 8
**SALES (corp-wide)**: 323.1MM **Privately Held**
**WEB**: www.nisseiamerica.com
**SIC**: 5084 3089 Industrial machinery & equipment; extruded finished plastic products
**HQ**: Nissei America, Inc.
   1480 N Hancock St
   Anaheim CA 92807
   714 693-3000

**(G-9653)**
### NORDENT MANUFACTURING INC
610 Bonnie Ln (60007-2379)
**PHONE**.................................847 437-4780
**Fax**: 847 437-4786
Richard Martin, *President*
Peter Martin, *Principal*
Joe Martin, *Vice Pres*
Robert Tatum, *Vice Pres*
Dave Schero, *Opers Staff*
**EMP**: 20 **EST**: 1969
**SQ FT**: 5,000
**SALES**: 5.5MM **Privately Held**
**WEB**: www.nordent.com
**SIC**: 3843 7699 3841 Dental equipment; dental instrument repair; surgical & medical instruments

**(G-9654)**
### NORTH AMERICAN EN INC
776 Lunt Ave (60007-5025)
**PHONE**.................................847 952-3680
**Fax**: 847 690-0171
Louis Brosio, *CEO*
Michael Brosio, *President*
Silvano Boswell, *General Mgr*
Jaime Santiago, *Plant Mgr*
David Brosio, *Treasurer*
**EMP**: 17 **EST**: 1998
**SQ FT**: 5,000
**SALES (est)**: 2.3MM **Privately Held**
**WEB**: www.northamericanen.com
**SIC**: 3471 Plating of metals or formed products

**(G-9655)**
### NORTH SHORE CONSULTANTS INC
Also Called: En Es Cee Technology
613 Thorndale Ave (60007-4334)
**PHONE**.................................847 290-1599
**Fax**: 773 286-1974
Audrey Wojtecki, *President*
Dennis Wojtecki, *Treasurer*
**EMP**: 5
**SALES (est)**: 460K **Privately Held**
**WEB**: www.enescee.com
**SIC**: 2891 8748 5169 Adhesives; business consulting; chemicals & allied products

**(G-9656)**
### NORTHWEST MOLD & MACHINE CORP
131 Martin Ln (60007-1309)
**PHONE**.................................847 690-1501
Stanouy Kaczor, *President*
**EMP**: 5
**SQ FT**: 2,000
**SALES (est)**: 600K **Privately Held**
**SIC**: 3599 Machine shop, jobbing & repair

**(G-9657)**
### NU-WAY ELECTRONICS INC
Also Called: Nuway Electronics
165 Martin Ln (60007-1309)
**PHONE**.................................847 437-7120
William N Aldeen, *President*
Alina Rymsza, *Controller*
**EMP**: 36
**SQ FT**: 15,000
**SALES (est)**: 6.7MM **Privately Held**
**WEB**: www.nuway.net
**SIC**: 3679 5065 Harness assemblies for electronic use: wire or cable; electronic parts

**(G-9658)**
### NUMALLIANCE - NORTH AMER INC
1361 Howard St (60007-2213)
P.O. Box 576, Durant IA (52747-0576)
**PHONE**.................................847 439-4500
Joel Etienne, *President*
Ludovic Vallet, *COO*
Frank Arena, *Sales Mgr*
▲ **EMP**: 7 **EST**: 1978
**SQ FT**: 2,500
**SALES (est)**: 6.3MM **Privately Held**
**WEB**: www.properzi.com
**SIC**: 3599 Machine & other job shop work
**PA**: Numalliance
   Parc D Activites
   Saint Michel Sur Meurthe
   329 583-615

**(G-9659)**
### O R LASERTECHNOLOGY INC
1420 Howard St (60007-2221)
**PHONE**.................................847 593-5711
Yhushua Resnik, *President*
Uri Resnik, *Vice Pres*
Howard Davis, *Manager*
**EMP**: 7
**SQ FT**: 8,900
**SALES (est)**: 1.2MM
**SALES (corp-wide)**: 9.6MM **Privately Held**
**WEB**: www.orlaserwelding.com
**SIC**: 3699 Laser welding, drilling & cutting equipment
**PA**: O. R. Lasertechnologie Gmbh
   Dieselstr. 15
   Dieburg 64807
   607 120-9890

**(G-9660)**
### OAKLEY INDUSTRIAL MCHY INC
1601 Lunt Ave (60007-5616)
**PHONE**.................................847 966-0052
Carl T Kamys, *CEO*
**EMP**: 24 **EST**: 2010
**SALES (est)**: 6.1MM **Privately Held**
**SIC**: 3567 Heating units & devices, industrial: electric

**(G-9661)**
### OCTAVIA TOOL & GAGE COMPANY
135 Kelly St (60007-1011)
**PHONE**.................................847 913-9233
**Fax**: 847 297-3379
Larry Rust, *President*
**EMP**: 4 **EST**: 1957
**SQ FT**: 1,500
**SALES**: 500K **Privately Held**
**SIC**: 3544 3469 Special dies, tools, jigs & fixtures; metal stampings

**(G-9662)**
### OHARE SPRING COMPANY INC
930 Lee St (60007-1207)
**PHONE**.................................847 298-1360
John Schneider, *President*
Jim Vyleta, *General Mgr*
Kathy Schneider, *Human Res Mgr*
**EMP**: 20 **EST**: 1964
**SQ FT**: 28,000
**SALES (est)**: 4.4MM **Privately Held**
**WEB**: www.oharespring.com
**SIC**: 3495 3469 3496 Mechanical springs, precision; stamping metal for the trade; wire winding

**(G-9663)**
### OLDCASTLE BUILDINGENVELOPE INC
2901 Lively Blvd (60007-6735)
**PHONE**.................................630 250-7270
Fred Stella, *Manager*
**EMP**: 20
**SALES (corp-wide)**: 28.6B **Privately Held**
**WEB**: www.oldcastleglass.com
**SIC**: 3231 Tempered glass: made from purchased glass; insulating glass: made from purchased glass
**HQ**: Oldcastle Buildingenvelope, Inc.
   5005 Lndn B Jnsn Fwy 10 Ste 1050
   Dallas TX 75244
   214 273-3400

**(G-9664)**
### OMEGA MOULDING NORTH AMER INC
1420 Thorndale Ave (60007-6751)
**PHONE**.................................630 509-2397
Jose Avita, *Branch Mgr*
**EMP**: 4 **Privately Held**
**SIC**: 2431 Moldings, wood: unfinished & prefinished
**PA**: Omega Moulding North America, Inc.
   1 Sawgrass Dr
   Bellport NY 11713

**(G-9665)**
### OMEGA ROYAL GRAPHICS INC
1621 Brummel Ave (60007-2125)
**PHONE**.................................847 952-8000
**Fax**: 847 952-8071
Kenneth Grimshaw, *President*
Kenneth David, *Vice Pres*
Ann Grimshaw, *Treasurer*
**EMP**: 10
**SQ FT**: 15,000
**SALES**: 1.3MM **Privately Held**
**SIC**: 2752 Commercial printing, offset

**(G-9666)**
### ONLINE ELECTRONICS INC
Also Called: Overnite Protos
1261 Jarvis Ave (60007-2301)
**PHONE**.................................847 871-1700
**Fax**: 847 290-8691
Aziz Ajani, *CEO*
Dilkhush Bhayani, *President*
**EMP**: 35
**SALES (est)**: 4.1MM **Privately Held**
**WEB**: www.pcborder.com
**SIC**: 3672 8711 Printed circuit boards; electrical or electronic engineering

**(G-9667)**
### OPTIMAL AUTOMATICS CO
120 Stanley St (60007-1554)
**PHONE**.................................847 439-9110
John Georgis, *President*
Majel Coza, *Data Proc Dir*
▼ **EMP**: 7 **EST**: 1972
**SQ FT**: 8,000
**SALES (est)**: 1.1MM **Privately Held**
**SIC**: 3589 3556 Commercial cooking & foodwarming equipment; food products machinery

**(G-9668)**
### P M S CONSOLIDATED
2400 E Devon Ave (60007-6034)
**PHONE**.................................847 364-0011
**Fax**: 847 364-0015
Kurt Walker, *Plant Mgr*
**EMP**: 5
**SALES (est)**: 468.2K **Privately Held**
**SIC**: 2816 Inorganic pigments

**(G-9669)**
### PARAGON AUTOMATION INC
1410 Brummel Ave (60007-2111)
**PHONE**.................................847 593-0434
**Fax**: 847 593-2014
Donald Schreiner, *President*
Robert Jaeger, *Corp Secy*
Nathan A Baraglia, *Vice Pres*

Jacky Schreiner, *Office Mgr*
Jaclyn Schreiner-Vanko, *Office Mgr*
**EMP:** 14 **EST:** 1977
**SQ FT:** 17,500
**SALES:** 1.5MM **Privately Held**
**WEB:** www.paragonautomation.com
**SIC:** 3599 Custom machinery

### (G-9670)
### PARKER-HANNIFIN CORPORATION
Also Called: Mobile Systems
850 Arthur Ave (60007-5215)
**PHONE**..................847 258-6200
Jason Coolick, *Engineer*
Donald E Washkewicz, *Manager*
**EMP:** 120
**SALES (corp-wide):** 11.3B **Publicly Held**
**WEB:** www.parker.com
**SIC:** 3492 Fluid power valves & hose fittings
**PA:** Parker-Hannifin Corporation
6035 Parkland Blvd
Cleveland OH 44124
216 896-3000

### (G-9671)
### PAULSON PRESS INC
Also Called: Paulson's Litho
904 Cambridge Dr (60007-2435)
**PHONE**..................847 290-0080
**Fax:** 847 290-0140
Ben Letto, *President*
Paul Letto, *Vice Pres*
Anthony Letto, *Treasurer*
Vince Letto, *Admin Sec*
**EMP:** 28
**SQ FT:** 20,000
**SALES (est):** 5.8MM **Privately Held**
**SIC:** 2752 Commercial printing, offset; lithographing on metal

### (G-9672)
### PCB EXPRESS INC
600 E Higgins Rd Ste 2c (60007-1500)
**PHONE**..................847 952-8896
Pragna Patel, *President*
Bobbie Goldberg, *Sales Executive*
**EMP:** 3
**SALES:** 1.5MM **Privately Held**
**WEB:** www.pcbontime.com
**SIC:** 3672 Printed circuit boards

### (G-9673)
### PERFECTION PLATING INC
775 Morse Ave (60007-5184)
**PHONE**..................847 593-6506
**Fax:** 847 593-5239
Randy G Zitella, *Principal*
Chuck Wulf, *Vice Pres*
Alex Tomanovich, *Mktg Dir*
Douglas A Hanson, *Admin Sec*
**EMP:** 120
**SQ FT:** 65,000
**SALES (est):** 18.3MM **Privately Held**
**WEB:** www.perfectionplate.com
**SIC:** 3471 Electroplating & plating

### (G-9674)
### PERMATRON CORPORATION
2020 Touhy Ave (60007-5318)
**PHONE**..................847 434-1421
Leslye Sandberg, *President*
Kevin Mehaffey, *General Mgr*
Tod Oberg, *Sales Mgr*
JP Calubaquib, *Accounts Mgr*
John Rappaport, *Accounts Mgr*
▲ **EMP:** 20
**SQ FT:** 13,000
**SALES (est):** 4.5MM **Privately Held**
**WEB:** www.permatron.com
**SIC:** 1711 3564 Plumbing, heating, air-conditioning contractors; filters, air: furnaces, air conditioning equipment, etc.

### (G-9675)
### PETE FRCANO SONS CSTM HM BLDRS
1225 Howard St (60007-2219)
**PHONE**..................847 258-4626
Pete Fricano, *President*
**EMP:** 11
**SALES (est):** 158.8K **Privately Held**
**SIC:** 1521 1542 2842 New construction, single-family houses; commercial & office buildings, renovation & repair; specialty cleaning preparations

### (G-9676)
### PETERSEN ALUMINUM CORPORATION (PA)
Also Called: Pac-Clad Metal Roofing
1005 Tonne Rd (60007-4817)
**PHONE**..................847 228-7150
**Fax:** 800 722-7150
Michael L Petersen, *Ch of Bd*
John Palesny, *President*
Greg Beane, *Regional Mgr*
Thomas Creigh, *Vice Pres*
Jonathon Snyder, *Vice Pres*
▲ **EMP:** 52
**SQ FT:** 80,000
**SALES (est):** 66.2MM **Privately Held**
**WEB:** www.pac-clad.com
**SIC:** 3353 3316 3354 3448 Flat rolled shapes, aluminum; sheet, steel, cold-rolled: from purchased hot-rolled; aluminum extruded products; panels for prefabricated metal buildings; metals service centers & offices; aluminum bars, rods, ingots, sheets, pipes, plates, etc.; steel; signs & advertising specialties

### (G-9677)
### PETERSEN FINISHING CORPORATION (PA)
1005 Tonne Rd (60007-4817)
**PHONE**..................847 228-7150
John P Paleczny, *President*
Michael Petersen, *Vice Pres*
William Kurth, *Shareholder*
Ann Petersen, *Shareholder*
Kathryn Petersen, *Shareholder*
**EMP:** 3
**SQ FT:** 80,000
**SALES (est):** 1MM **Privately Held**
**SIC:** 3471 Anodizing (plating) of metals or formed products

### (G-9678)
### PHOENIX BINDING CORP
Also Called: American Binding
1100 Pratt Blvd (60007-5122)
**PHONE**..................847 981-1111
Hanry Isbell, *President*
Christine Kelstrom, *Office Mgr*
**EMP:** 70
**SQ FT:** 35,000
**SALES:** 2.3MM **Privately Held**
**WEB:** www.americanbinding.com
**SIC:** 2789 Binding only: books, pamphlets, magazines, etc.

### (G-9679)
### PHOENIX TOOL CORP
700 Lunt Ave (60007-5025)
**PHONE**..................847 956-1886
Henry E Bauerle, *President*
Frieda Bauerle, *Admin Sec*
▲ **EMP:** 14
**SQ FT:** 12,800
**SALES (est):** 2.4MM **Privately Held**
**WEB:** www.phoenixtool.com
**SIC:** 3544 3599 Industrial molds; machine shop, jobbing & repair

### (G-9680)
### PILLARHOUSE USA INC
201 Lively Blvd (60007-1622)
**PHONE**..................847 593-9080
**Fax:** 847 593-9084
Jonathan Wol, *President*
Adrian De'ath, *Vice Pres*
Theresa Tellez, *Manager*
Jacqueline Wray, *Admin Sec*
**EMP:** 10
**SQ FT:** 15,000
**SALES:** 9MM **Privately Held**
**WEB:** www.pillarhouseusa.com
**SIC:** 5084 7699 7694 Machine tools & metalworking machinery; industrial machinery & equipment repair; coil winding service

### (G-9681)
### PINE ENVIRONMENTAL SVCS LLC
1450 Elmhurst Rd (60007-6417)
**PHONE**..................847 718-1246
**Fax:** 847 718-1423
Brigitt Hinde, *Branch Mgr*
**EMP:** 4
**SALES (corp-wide):** 371.7MM **Privately Held**
**SIC:** 3826 Environmental testing equipment
**HQ:** Pine Environmental Services Llc
92 N Main St Bldg 20
Windsor NJ 08561

### (G-9682)
### PITTCO ARCHITECTURAL MTLS INC
1530 Landmeier Rd (60007-2416)
**PHONE**..................800 992-7488
**Fax:** 847 593-9946
Alfred Shapiro, *CEO*
Elly Hansen, *Corp Secy*
Todd Tewksbury, *Project Mgr*
Richard Massei, *Sales Executive*
Steve Knudson, *Manager*
**EMP:** 7
**SQ FT:** 100,000
**SALES (est):** 2.1MM **Privately Held**
**WEB:** www.pittcometals.com
**SIC:** 3442 Casements, aluminum; store fronts, prefabricated, metal

### (G-9683)
### PK CORPORATION
527 Newberry Dr (60007-2740)
**PHONE**..................847 879-1070
Petre Kazakov, *President*
**EMP:** 7
**SALES (est):** 856.8K **Privately Held**
**SIC:** 3715 Truck trailers

### (G-9684)
### PMI CARTONING INC
850 Pratt Blvd (60007-5117)
**PHONE**..................847 437-1427
**Fax:** 847 437-1627
Branko Tisma, *President*
Branko Vukotic, *Managing Dir*
John Bamas, *Vice Pres*
Lilly Tisma, *Vice Pres*
Zheetkah Moarjanovic, *Plant Mgr*
**EMP:** 100
**SQ FT:** 110,000
**SALES (est):** 19.3MM **Privately Held**
**WEB:** www.pmicartoning.com
**SIC:** 3565 Packaging machinery

### (G-9685)
### POLYFORM PRODUCTS COMPANY
1901 Estes Ave (60007-5415)
**PHONE**..................847 427-0020
**Fax:** 847 427-0426
Denice Steinmann, *President*
Wayne Marsh, *Vice Pres*
Ray Simmons, *VP Opers*
Kimberly Rausch, *Engineer*
Michael Baumer, *VP Finance*
◆ **EMP:** 40
**SQ FT:** 58,000
**SALES (est):** 8.4MM **Privately Held**
**WEB:** www.sculpey.com
**SIC:** 3952 5945 3295 2821 Modeling clay; hobby, toy & game shops; minerals, ground or treated; plastics materials & resins

### (G-9686)
### POLYONE CORPORATION
2400 E Devon Ave (60007-6034)
**PHONE**..................847 364-0011
Therese Staron, *Purch Agent*
Kurt Walker, *Branch Mgr*
Bohdan Pihaniuk, *Systems Staff*
**EMP:** 89 **Publicly Held**
**WEB:** www.polyone.com
**SIC:** 2865 2851 2816 Dyes & pigments; paints & allied products; inorganic pigments
**PA:** Polyone Corporation
33587 Walker Rd
Avon Lake OH 44012

### (G-9687)
### POSSEHL CONNECTOR SVCS SC INC
1521 Morse Ave (60007-5781)
**PHONE**..................803 366-8316
Darrell Shaw, *Branch Mgr*
**EMP:** 40 **Privately Held**
**WEB:** www.possehlconnector.com
**SIC:** 3643 3471 Electric connectors; plating & polishing
**HQ:** Possehl Connector Services S.C., Inc.
445 Bryant Blvd
Rock Hill SC 29732
803 366-8316

### (G-9688)
### POST PRESS PRODUCTION INC (PA)
Also Called: Pp3
2601 Lively Blvd (60007-6730)
**PHONE**..................630 860-9833
Steven Olandese, *President*
John J Mascari, *Vice Pres*
**EMP:** 16
**SQ FT:** 68,000
**SALES (est):** 2.9MM **Privately Held**
**SIC:** 2782 Blankbooks & looseleaf binders

### (G-9689)
### POWELL TREE CARE INC
212 E Devon Ave (60007-4037)
P.O. Box 1514 (60009-1514)
**PHONE**..................847 364-1181
David Powell, *President*
**EMP:** 4
**SALES (est):** 260K **Privately Held**
**SIC:** 0783 1629 2411 4959 Tree trimming services for public utility lines; removal services, bush & tree; land clearing contractor; wood chips, produced in the field; snowplowing; wood (fuel)

### (G-9690)
### POWER LUBE LLC
1461 Busse Rd (60007-5323)
**PHONE**..................847 806-7022
Jeno Han, *Manager*
**EMP:** 5
**SALES (est):** 640.5K **Privately Held**
**SIC:** 2911 Oils, lubricating

### (G-9691)
### PRE FNISH MTALS MRRISVILLE INC
2250 Pratt Blvd (60007-5917)
**PHONE**..................847 439-2211
**Fax:** 847 806-6486
Gerald Nadig, *Ch of Bd*
Jim Powlak, *Controller*
Martin A Scott, *Sales Mgr*
▲ **EMP:** 75
**SQ FT:** 116,000
**SALES (est):** 7.5MM
**SALES (corp-wide):** 110.1MM **Privately Held**
**SIC:** 3479 3621 Painting, coating & hot dipping; coating of metals & formed products; coating of metals with plastic or resins; painting of metal products; motors & generators
**HQ:** Msc Pre Finish Metals (Egv) Inc.
2250 Pratt Blvd
Elk Grove Village IL 60007
847 439-2210

### (G-9692)
### PRECISION GRINDING INC
2375 American Ln (60007-6201)
**PHONE**..................847 238-1000
**Fax:** 847 238-1014
Shamkant Shirsat, *President*
Walter Malek, *Vice Pres*
**EMP:** 8
**SQ FT:** 8,500
**SALES:** 850K **Privately Held**
**SIC:** 3599 Machine shop, jobbing & repair

### (G-9693)
### PRECISION INC
2210 Elmhurst Rd (60007-6309)
**PHONE**..................847 593-2947
**Fax:** 847 228-6838
James De Roche, *President*
**EMP:** 3

## Elk Grove Village - Cook County (G-9694)

SALES (est): 265.8K  **Privately Held**
SIC: 3599  Machine shop, jobbing & repair

### (G-9694)
### PRECISION INK CORPORATION
151 Stanley St  (60007-1555)
PHONE.................................847 952-1500
Rod Cartwright, *President*
EMP: 10
SQ FT: 6,000
SALES (est): 2MM  **Privately Held**
SIC: 2893  Printing ink

### (G-9695)
### PRECISION PROCESS CORP
1401 Brummel Ave  (60007-2110)
PHONE.................................847 640-9820
Fax: 847 952-8121
Vladimir A Moskin, *President*
Mikhail Lyakhovetskiy, *General Mgr*
Kris Parzatka, *Engineer*
EMP: 26
SQ FT: 14,000
SALES (est): 5.2MM  **Privately Held**
WEB: www.pp-corp.com
SIC: 3544  Special dies & tools

### (G-9696)
### PRESS AMERICA INC
661 Fargo Ave  (60007-4742)
PHONE.................................847 228-0333
Fax: 847 228-7333
Martin D'Amico, *President*
Pete Catino, *Prdtn Mgr*
Mike Grimm, *Consultant*
Debra D'Amico, *Admin Sec*
▲ EMP: 30
SQ FT: 12,500
SALES (est): 5.6MM  **Privately Held**
SIC: 2752  Commercial printing, offset

### (G-9697)
### PRIMEDGE INC (PA)
1281 Arthur Ave  (60007-5705)
PHONE.................................224 265-6600
Fax: 773 478-8689
Ivo Cozzini, *President*
Tom Mazuchowski, *President*
Randy Rhude, *Exec VP*
Peter Samson, *Exec VP*
Marcelo Zocchi, *Exec VP*
◆ EMP: 160
SQ FT: 70,000
SALES (est): 37.6MM  **Privately Held**
SIC: 3556  5072  Meat processing machinery; cutlery

### (G-9698)
### PRINTING WORKS INC
2485 E Devon Ave  (60007-6212)
PHONE.................................847 860-1920
Fax: 847 860-0038
Patricia Whelan, *President*
Charles Spittler, *Corp Secy*
William Whelan, *Vice Pres*
Bill Whalen, *Manager*
Nick Tornabene, *CTO*
EMP: 4
SQ FT: 4,000
SALES: 350K  **Privately Held**
WEB: www.theprintingworks.com
SIC: 2752  2791  2789  2759  Commercial printing, offset; typesetting; bookbinding & related work; commercial printing; automotive & apparel trimmings; truck rental & leasing, no drivers

### (G-9699)
### PROTEPO LTD (PA)
906 Mayfair Ct  (60007-3478)
PHONE.................................847 466-1023
Lynette Sowler, *President*
Lynette Fowler, *President*
Vasilis Katsoulis, *CTO*
EMP: 5
SQ FT: 500
SALES: 1MM  **Privately Held**
SIC: 7372  Prepackaged software

### (G-9700)
### PULSARLUBE USA INC
1480 Howard St  (60007-2221)
PHONE.................................847 593-5300
Yun J Yang, *President*
▲ EMP: 5

SALES (est): 400K  **Privately Held**
WEB: www.pulsarlubeusa.com
SIC: 3569  Lubrication equipment, industrial

### (G-9701)
### PULVER INC
Also Called: Mailers Company
575 Bennett Rd  (60007-1101)
PHONE.................................847 734-9000
Patrick Pulver, *President*
Dawn Pulver, *Admin Sec*
EMP: 20
SQ FT: 50,000
SALES (est): 4.8MM  **Privately Held**
WEB: www.mailersco.com
SIC: 2631  Container, packaging & boxboard

### (G-9702)
### QUALITY PAPER INC
1855 Greenleaf Ave  (60007-5501)
PHONE.................................847 258-3999
Marty Riley, *President*
EMP: 15 EST: 2012
SALES (est): 1.5MM  **Privately Held**
SIC: 2679  Paperboard products, converted

### (G-9703)
### QUANTUM ENGINEERING INC
801 Chase Ave Ste G  (60007-4836)
P.O. Box 784  (60009-0784)
PHONE.................................847 640-1340
Diane Hubball, *President*
David Wano, *General Mgr*
EMP: 7 EST: 1999
SQ FT: 12,000
SALES (est): 1MM  **Privately Held**
SIC: 3544  Special dies & tools

### (G-9704)
### QUANTUM STORAGE SYSTEMS
2600 United Ln  (60007-6821)
PHONE.................................630 274-6610
EMP: 2
SALES (est): 237.4K  **Privately Held**
SIC: 2541  Shelving, office & store, wood

### (G-9705)
### QWIK-TIP INC
2415 E Higgins Rd  (60007-2605)
PHONE.................................847 640-7387
Warren Osborn, *President*
EMP: 3
SALES (est): 284.5K  **Privately Held**
WEB: www.qwiktip.com
SIC: 3714  Motor vehicle body components & frame

### (G-9706)
### R & G SPRING CO INC
1451 Landmeier Rd Ste L  (60007-2462)
PHONE.................................847 228-5640
Fax: 847 228-5643
Roman Hudec, *Owner*
Elizabeth Hudec, *Vice Pres*
EMP: 4
SQ FT: 120,000
SALES (est): 280K  **Privately Held**
SIC: 3493  3495  5085  Steel springs, except wire; wire springs; springs

### (G-9707)
### RAINBOW COLORS INC
935 Lee St  (60007-1206)
PHONE.................................847 640-7700
Pankaj Patel, *President*
Leah Asselin, *General Mgr*
EMP: 12 EST: 2008
SALES (est): 2.2MM  **Privately Held**
SIC: 3083  Plastic finished products, laminated

### (G-9708)
### RANDALL PUBLICATIONS (PA)
1840 Jarvis Ave  (60007-2440)
PHONE.................................847 437-6604
Michael Goldstein, *Editor*
Luann Harrold, *Accountant*
EMP: 20
SALES (est): 1.8MM  **Privately Held**
SIC: 2721  Periodicals

### (G-9709)
### RANDALL PUBLISHING INC
Also Called: Gear Technology
1425 Lunt Ave  (60007-5621)
P.O. Box 1426  (60009-1426)
PHONE.................................847 437-6604
Michael Goldstein, *President*
William Stott, *Editor*
Richard Goldstein, *Vice Pres*
Dave Friedman, *Sales Mgr*
David Ropinski, *Director*
EMP: 12
SALES (est): 1.2MM  **Privately Held**
WEB: www.geartechnology.com
SIC: 2721  5084  Magazines: publishing only, not printed on site; industrial machinery & equipment

### (G-9710)
### REALLY USEFUL BOXES INC
2791 Katherine Way  (60007-6746)
PHONE.................................847 238-0444
Michael Pickles, *President*
Barry Silverman, *Sales Mgr*
EMP: 13
SALES (est): 1.7MM
SALES (corp-wide): 61.3MM  **Privately Held**
SIC: 3089  Boxes, plastic
HQ: Really Useful Products Ltd
    Unit 2
    Normanton  WF6 1
    192 489-8477

### (G-9711)
### REBECHINI STUDIO INC (PA)
Also Called: 680 Design
680 Fargo Ave  (60007-4701)
PHONE.................................847 364-8600
Fax: 847 470-0324
Glenn Rebechini, *Owner*
Larry Goone, *General Mgr*
Vince Papp, *Foreman/Supr*
EMP: 12
SQ FT: 11,200
SALES (est): 2.6MM  **Privately Held**
WEB: www.rsi-design.com
SIC: 3993  3479  3999  8999  Signs, not made in custom sign painting shops; letters for signs, metal; displays & cutouts, window & lobby; etching on metals; plaques, picture, laminated; sculptor's studio; marking devices

### (G-9712)
### REDEEN ENGRAVING INC
670 Chase Ave  (60007-4802)
PHONE.................................847 593-6500
Fax: 847 593-6512
Floyd Redeen, *President*
Adele Adams, *Sales Mgr*
EMP: 8 EST: 1960
SQ FT: 6,000
SALES (est): 741.9K  **Privately Held**
SIC: 2759  3544  Embossing on paper; special dies, tools, jigs & fixtures

### (G-9713)
### RELIANCE SPECIALTY PDTS INC
855 Morse Ave  (60007-5105)
PHONE.................................847 640-8923
Mark Skiersch, *President*
Laurie Lamantia, *Sales Staff*
Marisa Luna, *Manager*
Cynthia Marciniak, *Info Tech Mgr*
▲ EMP: 10
SQ FT: 30,000
SALES (est): 2.3MM  **Privately Held**
WEB: www.relspec.com
SIC: 2869  Industrial organic chemicals

### (G-9714)
### REPRO-GRAPHICS INC
1900 Arthur Ave  (60007-6005)
PHONE.................................847 439-1775
Fax: 847 439-1883
John Schiele, *President*
Steve Funk, *CFO*
Barb Hedman, *Controller*
Joe Madonia, *Accounts Exec*
Andy Olcott, *Director*
EMP: 70
SQ FT: 50,000
SALES (est): 22.1MM  **Privately Held**
WEB: www.schielegroup.com
SIC: 2752  Commercial printing, offset

### (G-9715)
### REXAM BEVERAGE CAN COMPANY
2520 Lively Blvd  (60007-6727)
PHONE.................................847 238-3200
Mike Gogola, *Project Mgr*
Bob Walsh, *Opers Mgr*
Ray Arriola, *Purchasing*
Robert Diaz, *Purchasing*
Mark Scales, *Manager*
EMP: 110
SALES (corp-wide): 9B  **Publicly Held**
SIC: 3411  Metal cans
HQ: Rexam Beverage Can Company
    8770 W Bryn Mawr Ave Fl 8
    Chicago IL 60631
    773 399-3000

### (G-9716)
### RJ STUCKEL CO INC
94 Garlisch Dr  (60007-1316)
PHONE.................................800 789-7220
Fax: 847 593-6027
Robert W Stuckel, *President*
Diane Denn, *Controller*
▲ EMP: 20
SQ FT: 35,000
SALES (est): 4.1MM  **Privately Held**
WEB: www.rjstuckel.com
SIC: 3469  3544  Stamping metal for the trade; die sets for metal stamping (presses)

### (G-9717)
### ROLLEX CORPORATION (PA)
800 Chase Ave  (60007-4806)
PHONE.................................847 437-3000
Fax: 847 437-5671
Bruce Stevens, *Ch of Bd*
James L Brittingham, *President*
Bill Smith, *Vice Pres*
Mike Shield, *Mfg Dir*
Elizabeth Meza, *Opers Staff*
EMP: 125 EST: 1950
SQ FT: 120,000
SALES (est): 95.2MM  **Privately Held**
WEB: www.rollex.com
SIC: 3444  Gutters, sheet metal; siding, sheet metal

### (G-9718)
### ROPAK CENTRAL INC
Also Called: Linpac Ropak Packaging Central
1350 Arthur Ave  (60007-5741)
PHONE.................................847 956-0750
Fax: 847 956-0756
Kenneth Roessler, *President*
Ralph Nelson, *General Mgr*
Ronald W Cameron, *Vice Pres*
Terry Drainer, *Plant Mgr*
Greg Toft, *Controller*
▲ EMP: 85 EST: 1979
SQ FT: 161,000
SALES (est): 20.7MM
SALES (corp-wide): 831.7MM  **Privately Held**
WEB: www.ropakcorp.com
SIC: 3089  Blow molded finished plastic products; injection molded finished plastic products; plastic containers, except foam
HQ: Ropak Corporation
    10540 Talbert Ave 200w
    Fountain Valley CA 92708
    714 845-2845

### (G-9719)
### ROTARY PAPER MANIFOLD
2300 Arthur Ave  (60007-6015)
PHONE.................................847 758-7800
Yarka Sena, *Principal*
EMP: 5
SALES (est): 817.8K  **Privately Held**
SIC: 2679  Paper products, converted

### (G-9720)
### ROYAL FOODS & FLAVORS INC
2456 American Ln  (60007-6204)
PHONE.................................847 595-9166
Fax: 847 595-9690
Harish Gadhvi, *President*
Dan Bhagat, *Manager*
▲ EMP: 10
SQ FT: 10,000
SALES (est): 1.4MM  **Privately Held**
SIC: 2099  2087  Seasonings: dry mixes; flavoring extracts & syrups

# GEOGRAPHIC SECTION
## Elk Grove Village - Cook County (G-9747)

**(G-9721)**
**RR DEFENSE SYSTEMS INC**
341 Lively Blvd (60007-2009)
PHONE..........................312 446-9167
Merriellyn Kett, *CEO*
**EMP:** 9
**SQ FT:** 5,000
**SALES (est):** 88.8K **Privately Held**
**SIC:** 3482 3484 Small arms ammunition; small arms

**(G-9722)**
**S AND S ASSOCIATES INC**
Also Called: Trademark Products
1016 Bonaventure Dr (60007-3277)
PHONE..........................847 584-0033
**Fax:** 847 584-0287
Larry Scanlon, *President*
**EMP:** 6
**SQ FT:** 2,500
**SALES (est):** 559.2K **Privately Held**
**SIC:** 3993 3953 5999 Signs & advertising specialties; embossing seals & hand stamps; rubber stamps

**(G-9723)**
**S B LIQUIDATING COMPANY**
Also Called: Spiral Binding of Illinois
1100 Touhy Ave (60007-4924)
PHONE..........................847 758-9500
**Fax:** 847 758-9572
Bruce L Kappele, *President*
Robert Frankiewicz, *Corp Secy*
Olivia Macias, *Office Mgr*
**EMP:** 65
**SQ FT:** 60,000
**SALES (est):** 4.5MM **Privately Held**
**SIC:** 2789 Bookbinding & related work

**(G-9724)**
**S P INDUSTRIES INC**
Also Called: Sp Industries
1455 Elmhurst Rd (60007-6400)
PHONE..........................847 228-2851
Ron Dimaria, *President*
Michael Sniegowski, *Technology*
**EMP:** 45
**SALES (corp-wide):** 1.5B **Privately Held**
**WEB:** www.relianceglass.com
**SIC:** 3231 Products of purchased glass
**HQ:** S P Industries, Inc.
935 Mearns Rd
Warminster PA 18974
215 672-7800

**(G-9725)**
**S-P PRODUCTS INC**
730 Pratt Blvd (60007-5115)
P.O. Box 128, Glenview (60025-0128)
PHONE..........................847 593-8595
**Fax:** 847 593-8629
Peter A Vrame, *President*
Suresh Patel, *VP Prdtn*
Marcos Garcia, *Sales Mgr*
Peggy Klotz, *Accounts Mgr*
**EMP:** 16
**SQ FT:** 15,000
**SALES (est):** 3.7MM **Privately Held**
**SIC:** 3646 3643 Commercial indusl & institutional electric lighting fixtures; current-carrying wiring devices

**(G-9726)**
**SAMMY USA CORP**
800 Arthur Ave (60007-5215)
PHONE..........................847 364-9787
**Fax:** 847 364-9787
Yoshiharu Suzuki, *President*
James Miskell, *Vice Pres*
David Kane, *Manager*
**EMP:** 45
**SQ FT:** 70,000
**SALES (est):** 4.4MM
**SALES (corp-wide):** 11.2MM **Privately Held**
**WEB:** www.sammyusa.com
**SIC:** 3695 Computer software tape & disks: blank, rigid & floppy
**PA:** Sammy Corp.
4-1-1, Kandasurugadai
Chiyoda-Ku TKY
332 946-811

**(G-9727)**
**SANFORD CHEMICAL CO INC**
1945 Touhy Ave (60007-5369)
PHONE..........................847 437-3530
**Fax:** 773 437-0905
Sanford Arenberg, *President*
Sylve Schwartz, *Corp Secy*
Barbara Arenberg, *Vice Pres*
Joy Doherty, *Credit Mgr*
John Arenberg, *Sales Mgr*
**EMP:** 10 **EST:** 1956
**SALES (est):** 1.5MM **Privately Held**
**SIC:** 2891 2841 2879 2843 Adhesives; detergents, synthetic organic or inorganic alkaline; fungicides, herbicides; leather finishing agents; chemical preparations; industrial inorganic chemicals

**(G-9728)**
**SAVAGE BROS COMPANY**
1825 Greenleaf Ave (60007-5501)
PHONE..........................847 981-3000
**Fax:** 847 981-3010
Robert Parmley, *President*
Charles Kirelawich, *Vice Pres*
Jorge Aguirre, *Opers Staff*
William Bauer, *Engineer*
Daniel Sampey, *Manager*
▼ **EMP:** 65 **EST:** 1855
**SQ FT:** 25,000
**SALES:** 10MM **Privately Held**
**WEB:** www.savagebros.com
**SIC:** 3556 Confectionery machinery; smokers, food processing equipment

**(G-9729)**
**SAVE ON PRINTING INC**
1451 Landmeier Rd (60007-2454)
PHONE..........................847 922-7855
Luis Trevino, *Owner*
**EMP:** 5
**SALES (est):** 250K **Privately Held**
**SIC:** 2752 Commercial printing, lithographic

**(G-9730)**
**SAWS UNLIMITED INC**
494 Bonnie Ln (60007-1908)
PHONE..........................847 640-7450
Horst Stange, *President*
Barbara Moore, *Administration*
**EMP:** 4
**SQ FT:** 5,000
**SALES (est):** 599.1K **Privately Held**
**SIC:** 3425 3546 Saw blades for hand or power saws; saws & sawing equipment

**(G-9731)**
**SCHIELE GRAPHICS INC**
Also Called: Schiele Group
1880 Busse Rd (60007-5718)
PHONE..........................847 434-5455
**Fax:** 847 434-5465
John Schiele, *President*
Frank Grana, *COO*
Brian Conlin, *Prdtn Mgr*
John Kontek, *Production*
Larry Plecki, *Production*
**EMP:** 60 **EST:** 1948
**SQ FT:** 40,000
**SALES (est):** 23.8MM **Privately Held**
**WEB:** www.schielegroup.com/
**SIC:** 2752 2791 Commercial printing, offset; typesetting

**(G-9732)**
**SCREEN MACHINE INCORPORATED**
1025 Criss Cir (60007-1203)
PHONE..........................847 439-2233
**Fax:** 847 439-2247
Dave Rhyan, *President*
Norman Lysiak, *Vice Pres*
**EMP:** 9
**SQ FT:** 4,000
**SALES:** 582.8K **Privately Held**
**WEB:** www.thescreenmachineco.net
**SIC:** 2752 5137 5136 2396 Offset & photolithographic printing; sportswear, women's & children's; shirts, men's & boys'; automotive & apparel trimmings

**(G-9733)**
**SELAH USA INC**
1501 Jarvis Ave (60007-2401)
PHONE..........................847 758-0702
Jun Kim, *Owner*
▲ **EMP:** 6
**SALES (est):** 637.6K **Privately Held**
**SIC:** 2759 Screen printing

**(G-9734)**
**SENTRY SPRING & MFG CO**
184 Inverness Ct (60007-7077)
PHONE..........................847 584-9391
Joseph Janus, *Owner*
**EMP:** 3
**SALES (est):** 210K **Privately Held**
**SIC:** 3999 Manufacturing industries

**(G-9735)**
**SHARP METAL PRODUCTS**
140 Joey Dr (60007-1304)
PHONE..........................847 439-5393
**Fax:** 847 439-1717
George W Prisching, *President*
Craig Prisching, *Vice Pres*
Cecilia A Prisching, *Admin Sec*
**EMP:** 8
**SALES (est):** 1.1MM **Privately Held**
**SIC:** 3544 Special dies & tools

**(G-9736)**
**SHOPPE DE LEE INC**
2625 American Ln Ste A (60007-6214)
PHONE..........................847 350-0580
Thomas Lee, *President*
Dorothy Lee, *Corp Secy*
Gerald Lee, *Vice Pres*
**EMP:** 3
**SQ FT:** 4,000
**SALES:** 200K **Privately Held**
**SIC:** 2512 Upholstered household furniture

**(G-9737)**
**SIGMATRON INTERNATIONAL INC (PA)**
2201 Landmeier Rd (60007-2616)
PHONE..........................847 956-8000
**Fax:** 847 640-4528
Gary R Fairhead, *Ch of Bd*
Greg Fairhead, *Exec VP*
Gregory A Fairhead, *Exec VP*
Rajesh B Upadhyaya, *Exec VP*
Daniel P Camp, *Vice Pres*
▲ **EMP:** 7
**SQ FT:** 124,300
**SALES:** 253.9MM **Publicly Held**
**WEB:** www.sigmatronintl.com
**SIC:** 3672 3677 3679 3549 Printed circuit boards; electronic coils, transformers & other inductors; electronic circuits; assembly machines, including robotic; engine electrical test equipment

**(G-9738)**
**SIGN PALACE INC**
68 N Lively Blvd (60007-1317)
PHONE..........................847 228-7446
**Fax:** 847 640-1343
Joseph Holik, *President*
Darlene Holik, *Admin Sec*
**EMP:** 6
**SQ FT:** 7,000
**SALES (est):** 500K **Privately Held**
**WEB:** www.signpalace.com
**SIC:** 7389 3993 Sign painting & lettering shop; signs & advertising specialties

**(G-9739)**
**SIGNATURE INNOVATIONS LLC**
1171 Landmeier Rd (60007-2408)
P.O. Box 464, Wood Dale (60191-0464)
PHONE..........................847 758-9600
Tom Koczur, *General Mgr*
Patrick Ryan, *Office Mgr*
Thomas Koczur, *Mng Member*
▲ **EMP:** 5
**SALES (est):** 934.1K **Privately Held**
**WEB:** www.signatureinnovations.com
**SIC:** 5023 1752 2426 2511 Wood flooring; wood floor installation & refinishing; carvings, furniture: wood; flooring, hardwood; parquet flooring, hardwood; coffee tables: wood

**(G-9740)**
**SIGNS NOW**
1670 Greenleaf Ave (60007-5527)
PHONE..........................847 427-0005
Bonnie McCulla, *President*
James McCulla, *Vice Pres*
**EMP:** 4
**SALES:** 200K **Privately Held**
**SIC:** 3993 Signs & advertising specialties

**(G-9741)**
**SKILD MANUFACTURING INC**
160 Bond St Fl 1 (60007-1297)
PHONE..........................847 437-1717
**Fax:** 847 437-0760
Alison Graunke, *President*
Jim Graunke, *Vice Pres*
Wendy Maniscalco, *Vice Pres*
Greg Malloy, *Engineer*
**EMP:** 24 **EST:** 1953
**SQ FT:** 20,000
**SALES:** 3.5MM **Privately Held**
**WEB:** www.skildmfg.com
**SIC:** 3599 Machine shop, jobbing & repair

**(G-9742)**
**SOLAR SPRING COMPANY**
Also Called: Solar Spring & Wire Forms
345 Criss Cir (60007-1224)
PHONE..........................847 437-7838
**Fax:** 847 437-6468
Oscar Diaz, *President*
Yarissa Diaz, *Supervisor*
▲ **EMP:** 103 **EST:** 1979
**SQ FT:** 80,000
**SALES (est):** 23.9MM **Privately Held**
**WEB:** www.solarspring.com
**SIC:** 3495 3496 Mechanical springs, precision; miscellaneous fabricated wire products

**(G-9743)**
**SONIC MANUFACTURING CORP**
Also Called: Sonic Tool Mfg
950 Lee St (60007-1207)
PHONE..........................847 228-0015
Frank Sommer, *President*
George Sommer, *President*
John Sommer, *Vice Pres*
Mark Sommer, *Vice Pres*
Irene Sommer, *Treasurer*
**EMP:** 15 **EST:** 1965
**SQ FT:** 18,000
**SALES (est):** 3.1MM **Privately Held**
**WEB:** www.sonicmfgcorp.com
**SIC:** 3599 Machine shop, jobbing & repair

**(G-9744)**
**SONOSCAN INC (PA)**
2149 Pratt Blvd (60007-5914)
PHONE..........................847 437-6400
**Fax:** 847 437-1550
Lawrence W Kessler, *President*
Tom Kleinschmidt, *VP Opers*
Sandy Brand, *Facilities Mgr*
Tom Kleinshmidt, *Opers Staff*
Gary Vinzant, *Production*
▼ **EMP:** 67
**SQ FT:** 40,000
**SALES (est):** 20.3MM **Privately Held**
**SIC:** 3829 8734 8731 Ultrasonic testing equipment; testing laboratories; commercial research laboratory

**(G-9745)**
**SOURCE UNITED LLC**
Also Called: C N Tool
689 Chase Ave (60007-4801)
PHONE..........................847 956-1459
Kris Malorny,
Radosav Trninich,
**EMP:** 5
**SQ FT:** 1,300
**SALES (est):** 679.6K **Privately Held**
**SIC:** 3599 Machine shop, jobbing & repair

**(G-9746)**
**SPF SUPPLIES INC**
300 Scott St (60007-1215)
PHONE..........................847 454-9081
Richard Spiess, *President*
Mike Goodman, *Sales Staff*
**EMP:** 4
**SQ FT:** 2,500
**SALES:** 200K **Privately Held**
**SIC:** 3559 Chemical machinery & equipment

**(G-9747)**
**SPG USA INC**
501 Lively Blvd (60007-2013)
PHONE..........................847 439-4949

# Elk Grove Village - Cook County (G-9748)

Daniel Kim, *CEO*
Chang Ho Kim, *President*
▲ EMP: 5
SQ FT: 9,000
SALES (est): 16MM **Privately Held**
SIC: 3621 5063 Motors, electric; motors, electric

**(G-9748)**
**SPORT INCENTIVES INC**
1050 Pauly Dr (60007-1315)
PHONE..................847 427-8650
Fax: 847 427-8670
Susan Jesselson, *President*
Mark Jesselson, *Vice Pres*
Sheri Willis, *Marketing Staff*
EMP: 12
SQ FT: 10,000
SALES (est): 1.1MM **Privately Held**
WEB: www.smartincentives.com
SIC: 2599 Stools, factory

**(G-9749)**
**SPX CORPORATION**
Genfare, A Division of Spx.
800 Arthur Ave (60007-5215)
PHONE..................847 593-8855
Peter Datka, *Human Res Mgr*
Datka Peter, *Personnel Exec*
Dan Reichard, *Sales Executive*
Roy Purnell, *Marketing Mgr*
Kim Green, *Branch Mgr*
EMP: 108
SQ FT: 53,000
SALES (corp-wide): 1.4B **Publicly Held**
WEB: www.spx.com
SIC: 3443 Cooling towers, metal plate
PA: Spx Corporation
   13320a Balntyn Corp Pl
   Charlotte NC 28277
   980 474-3700

**(G-9750)**
**SRC ELECTRIC LLC**
360 Bennett Rd (60007-1005)
PHONE..................224 404-6103
EMP: 4
SALES (est): 141.4K **Privately Held**
SIC: 3699 Electrical equipment & supplies

**(G-9751)**
**STANDARD RUBBER PRODUCTS CO**
Also Called: S R P
120 Seegers Ave (60007-1650)
P.O. Box 797 (60009-0797)
PHONE..................847 593-5630
Fax: 847 593-5634
Larry Gualano, *President*
Rita Schmidt, *Corp Secy*
Al Gualano, *Vice Pres*
John Schmidt, *Vice Pres*
Terri Welch, *Buyer*
EMP: 48 EST: 1946
SQ FT: 14,500
SALES (est): 10.3MM **Privately Held**
WEB: www.srpco.com
SIC: 3069 3053 3087 3061 Sponge rubber & sponge rubber products; washers, rubber; gaskets, all materials; custom compound purchased resins; mechanical rubber goods; industrial organic chemicals; plastics materials & resins

**(G-9752)**
**STANGE INDUSTRIAL GROUP**
494 Bonnie Ln (60007-1908)
PHONE..................847 640-8470
Horst Stange, *President*
Arif Jasarevic, *Sales Staff*
EMP: 8
SALES (est): 1.2MM **Privately Held**
SIC: 3546 Drill attachments, portable

**(G-9753)**
**STAR ACQUISITION INC**
825 Pratt Blvd (60007-5116)
PHONE..................847 439-0605
EMP: 5
SALES (est): 236.2K **Privately Held**
SIC: 3672 Printed circuit boards

**(G-9754)**
**STAR DIE MOLDING INC**
2741 Katherine Way (60007-6746)
PHONE..................847 766-7952
Fax: 630 766-8029
Johan Peterse, *President*
Betty Petersen, *President*
Johan Petersen, *Vice Pres*
Tim Malak, *Controller*
Gail Seyller, *Human Res Mgr*
▲ EMP: 69 EST: 1957
SQ FT: 21,000
SALES (est): 23.3MM **Privately Held**
SIC: 3089 3544 Plastic processing; industrial molds

**(G-9755)**
**STAR ELECTRONICS CORP**
825 Pratt Blvd (60007-5116)
P.O. Box 104, Itasca (60143-0104)
PHONE..................847 439-0605
Fax: 847 439-0872
Subash Patel, *President*
Ramanlal Patel, *Treasurer*
Vinod Patel, *Treasurer*
EMP: 36
SQ FT: 22,000
SALES (est): 6.1MM **Privately Held**
WEB: www.starelectronicsinc.com
SIC: 3672 Circuit boards, television & radio printed

**(G-9756)**
**STARK TOOLS AND SUPPLY INC**
1001 Fargo Ave Ste 105 (60007-4706)
P.O. Box 7454, Libertyville (60048-7454)
PHONE..................847 772-8974
Daniel Pahng, *President*
EMP: 5
SALES: 100K **Privately Held**
SIC: 3423 Hand & edge tools

**(G-9757)**
**STERN PINBALL INC**
2001 Lunt Ave (60007-5605)
PHONE..................708 345-7700
Gary Stern, *President*
Arnie Mahler, *COO*
George Gomez, *Vice Pres*
Kevin Schechtel, *Vice Pres*
Michael Odonnell, *VP Opers*
▼ EMP: 59
SQ FT: 40,000
SALES (est): 12.7MM **Privately Held**
WEB: www.sternpinball.com
SIC: 3999 Coin-operated amusement machines

**(G-9758)**
**STOCK GEARS INC**
1801 Vermont Dr (60007-2752)
PHONE..................224 653-9489
Fax: 847 827-6103
Bruce Billmeyer, *President*
EMP: 15
SQ FT: 11,000
SALES (est): 1.6MM **Privately Held**
WEB: www.stockgearsinc.com
SIC: 3089 3568 3545 3462 Injection molding of plastics; power transmission equipment; machine tool accessories; iron & steel forgings; manufactured hardware (general)

**(G-9759)**
**STYLENQUAZA LLC**
750 Pratt Blvd (60007-5115)
PHONE..................847 981-0191
EMP: 4 **Privately Held**
SIC: 3281 Building stone products
HQ: Stylenquaza, Llc
   11620 Goodnight Ln # 100
   Dallas TX 75229

**(G-9760)**
**SUNG JI USA**
Also Called: Chicago Off Set
128 N Lively Blvd (60007-1330)
PHONE..................847 956-9400
Fax: 847 956-4811
Daniel Kim, *General Mgr*
EMP: 10
SALES (est): 939.3K **Privately Held**
SIC: 2752 Commercial printing, lithographic

**(G-9761)**
**SUNRISE DISTRIBUTORS INC (PA)**
Also Called: Sunrise Foods
2411 United Ln (60007-6818)
PHONE..................630 400-8786
Yousuf Karim, *President*
Farhan Karim, *Vice Pres*
Muhammad Ahmad, *Manager*
▲ EMP: 6
SQ FT: 28,000
SALES (est): 6MM **Privately Held**
SIC: 5149 3321 5499 2041 Rice, polished

**(G-9762)**
**SUNRISE ELECTRONICS INC**
130 Martin Ln (60007-1310)
PHONE..................847 357-0500
Ashok Patel, *President*
Jigar Patel, *Vice Pres*
▲ EMP: 28
SQ FT: 18,000
SALES (est): 4.9MM **Privately Held**
WEB: www.sunrisepcb.com
SIC: 3672 Printed circuit boards

**(G-9763)**
**SUPREME TAMALE CO**
1495 Brummel Ave (60007-2110)
PHONE..................773 622-3777
Fax: 773 622-3350
John Paklaian, *President*
Don Griffin, *Manager*
EMP: 6
SQ FT: 6,250
SALES (est): 600K **Privately Held**
WEB: www.supremetamale.com
SIC: 2032 2038 Tamales: packaged in cans, jars, etc.; frozen specialties

**(G-9764)**
**SYNCHEM INC**
1400 Chase Ave (60007-4825)
PHONE..................847 298-2436
Wuping MA, *President*
Zhiqiang Fang, *Vice Pres*
Min Yang, *Research*
Larry Heuing, *Bookkeeper*
Jeffrey Heilbrunn, *Manager*
EMP: 12
SQ FT: 4,000
SALES (est): 1.2MM **Privately Held**
WEB: www.synchem.com
SIC: 2833 Medicinal chemicals

**(G-9765)**
**SYNERGY MECH SOLUTIONS INC**
55 N Lively Blvd (60007-1323)
P.O. Box 1485 (60009-1485)
PHONE..................847 437-4500
Thomas R Sullivan, *President*
Pete Psaras, *Sales Engr*
EMP: 6
SQ FT: 2,000
SALES: 6MM **Privately Held**
SIC: 3585 Heating & air conditioning combination units

**(G-9766)**
**SYSTEMS & ELECTRONICS INC**
190 Gordon St (60007-1120)
PHONE..................847 228-0985
Fax: 847 228-1164
Andy Lobato, *President*
Paul Howrihane, *Engineer*
George Grove, *Marketing Staff*
James Putman, *Manager*
Douglas Shoemaker, *Administration*
EMP: 20
SQ FT: 14,500
SALES (est): 2.3MM **Privately Held**
WEB: www.sei-sdrs.com
SIC: 8731 3728 Commercial physical research; electronic research; aircraft parts & equipment

**(G-9767)**
**TAISEI LAMICK USA INC**
1801 Howard St (60007-2484)
PHONE..................847 258-3283
Yoshinari Kimura, *President*
▲ EMP: 10
SALES (est): 1.9MM **Privately Held**
SIC: 3565 Packaging machinery

**(G-9768)**
**TAPE CASE LTD**
150 Gaylord St (60007-1107)
PHONE..................847 299-7880
Martin Lahart, *President*
Mary Grace Castillo, *Manager*
◆ EMP: 21
SALES (est): 18.5MM **Privately Held**
SIC: 5085 2891 7389 Adhesives, tape & plasters; adhesives & sealants;

**(G-9769)**
**TEAM IMPRESSIONS INC**
Also Called: T E A M
360 Scott St (60007-1215)
PHONE..................847 357-9270
Fax: 847 357-9280
Ronald C Felici, *President*
Mary Drogos, *Manager*
EMP: 22
SQ FT: 12,000
SALES (est): 3.3MM **Privately Held**
WEB: www.teamimpressions.net
SIC: 2759 Commercial printing; flexographic printing

**(G-9770)**
**TEAM PLAY INC**
201 Crossen Ave (60007-1611)
PHONE..................847 952-7533
Fax: 847 952-7534
Frank Pellegrini, *President*
Ken Fedesna, *COO*
Ad Pellegrini, *Vice Pres*
Geno Giuntoli, *VP Sales*
Jeff Bykowski, *Accounts Mgr*
▲ EMP: 15
SQ FT: 15,000
SALES (est): 4.1MM **Privately Held**
WEB: www.teamplayinc.com
SIC: 3861 Printing equipment, photographic

**(G-9771)**
**TECH STAR DESIGN AND MFG**
116 N Lively Blvd (60007-1318)
PHONE..................847 290-8676
Fax: 847 290-8309
Frank Sedlasek, *President*
Lois Sedlasek, *Corp Secy*
EMP: 10
SALES (est): 1.1MM **Privately Held**
WEB: www.techstardesign.com
SIC: 3679 8731 Electronic circuits; electronic research

**(G-9772)**
**TECH-MATE INC**
1671 Virginia Dr (60007-2961)
PHONE..................847 352-9690
Anita Marie Pucci, *President*
Mark Stephen Pucci, *Admin Sec*
EMP: 3
SALES (est): 270K **Privately Held**
SIC: 2821 Plastics materials & resins

**(G-9773)**
**TECHPACK INC**
1500 Midway Ct Ste W9 (60007-6606)
PHONE..................847 439-8220
Robert Epley, *President*
Warren Henricks, *Manager*
EMP: 32
SALES (est): 3.4MM **Privately Held**
SIC: 2844 Cosmetic preparations

**(G-9774)**
**TECHPRINT INC**
2330 Eastern Ave (60007-6813)
PHONE..................847 616-0109
Fax: 847 616-0323
Michael Roth, *President*
Ralph Hlavin, *General Mgr*
Ronald Roth, *Vice Pres*
John Roth, *Engineer*
Cathy Roth, *Manager*
EMP: 17
SALES: 800K **Privately Held**
WEB: www.e-techprint.com
SIC: 2759 2752 2789 Commercial printing; commercial printing, lithographic; bookbinding & related work

## GEOGRAPHIC SECTION
## Elk Grove Village - Cook County (G-9800)

**(G-9775)**
**TEMPIL INC (HQ)**
1201 Pratt Blvd (60007-5708)
PHONE..........................908 757-8300
Daniel Kleiman, *CEO*
Roger Hornburger, *General Mgr*
Leroy Frank, *Manager*
Maria Henson, *Manager*
Alfred Fleury, *Director*
**EMP:** 8
**SQ FT:** 30,000
**SALES (est):** 1MM
**SALES (corp-wide):** 28.5MM  **Privately Held**
**WEB:** www.tempil.com
**SIC:** 2869  Laboratory chemicals, organic
**PA:** La-Co Industries, Inc.
  1201 Pratt Blvd
  Elk Grove Village IL 60007
  847 427-3220

**(G-9776)**
**TERNKIRST TL & DIE & MCH WORKS**
355 Lively Blvd (60007-2009)
PHONE..........................847 437-8360
Fax: 847 437-5993
Franz Kirchgatterer, *President*
Otto Ternes, *Vice Pres*
Christina Finnestad, *Manager*
**EMP:** 18
**SQ FT:** 10,000
**SALES (est):** 2.9MM  **Privately Held**
**SIC:** 3599  3544  Machine shop, jobbing & repair; special dies & tools

**(G-9777)**
**THREE JS INDUSTRIES INC**
701 Landmeier Rd (60007-4757)
PHONE..........................847 640-6080
Fax: 847 640-6081
Joanne Marozza, *President*
Judy Garnmeister, *Vice Pres*
Jennifer Herz, *Vice Pres*
**EMP:** 19
**SQ FT:** 15,000
**SALES (est):** 2.3MM  **Privately Held**
**WEB:** www.threejsindustries.com
**SIC:** 3471  Plating of metals or formed products

**(G-9778)**
**THUNDERBIRD LLC (PA)**
1501 Oakton St (60007-2101)
PHONE..........................847 718-9300
John Newell,
Kevin Prunsky,
**EMP:** 8
**SALES (est):** 80.6MM  **Privately Held**
**SIC:** 3599  Machine & other job shop work

**(G-9779)**
**TIGERFLEX CORPORATION**
801 Estes Ave (60007-4903)
PHONE..........................847 439-1766
Fax: 847 640-8372
Hitoya Kodama, *President*
Yuki Okubo, *Accounts Mgr*
Fred Bobzien, *Admin Sec*
▲ **EMP:** 1120  **EST:** 1978
**SQ FT:** 50,000
**SALES (est):** 188MM
**SALES (corp-wide):** 356.5MM  **Privately Held**
**SIC:** 3052  Plastic hose
**PA:** Tigers Polymer Corporation
  1-4-1, Higashimachi, Shinsenri
  Toyonaka OSK 560-0
  668 341-551

**(G-9780)**
**TIME EMBROIDERY**
2201 Lively Blvd (60007-5209)
PHONE..........................847 364-4371
Christina Clifton, *Principal*
**EMP:** 4
**SALES (est):** 373.4K  **Privately Held**
**SIC:** 2395  Embroidery products, except schiffli machine

**(G-9781)**
**TISHMA ENGINEERING LLC**
850 Pratt Blvd (60007-5117)
PHONE..........................847 755-1200
**EMP:** 4
**SALES:** 300K  **Privately Held**
**SIC:** 3999  Mfg Misc Products

**(G-9782)**
**TOMEN AMERICA INC**
25 Nw Point Boulev Ste 490 (60007)
PHONE..........................847 439-8500
Glenn Gawlik, *Branch Mgr*
**EMP:** 56
**SALES (corp-wide):** 69.6B  **Privately Held**
**SIC:** 5153  5169  5031  5131  Grains; chemicals & allied products; lumber: rough, dressed & finished; plywood; textiles, woven; finishing plants, cotton
**HQ:** Tomen America Inc.
  805 3rd Ave Fl 16
  New York NY 10022
  212 355-3600

**(G-9783)**
**TOP GALLANT INC**
648 Dauphine Ct Unit E (60007-3574)
PHONE..........................847 981-5521
Lee Prager, *Owner*
John Beggs, *Director*
**EMP:** 15
**SALES (est):** 1.6MM  **Privately Held**
**SIC:** 3429  Marine hardware

**(G-9784)**
**TOPY PRECISION MFG INC (DH)**
1375 Lunt Ave (60007-5619)
PHONE..........................847 228-5902
Fax: 847 228-1599
Koichi Kevin Maruyama, *President*
Toshi Oguchi, *President*
Hiromitsu Oshida, *Principal*
Nick Sasaki, *Vice Pres*
Mike Knowlton, *Plant Mgr*
▲ **EMP:** 51
**SQ FT:** 52,000
**SALES (est):** 23.3MM
**SALES (corp-wide):** 1.8B  **Privately Held**
**SIC:** 3465  3399  Automotive stampings; metal fasteners
**HQ:** Topy Fasteners,Ltd.
  5652-36, Sasaga
  Matsumoto NAG 399-0
  263 256-219

**(G-9785)**
**TOTAL PLASTICS INC**
505 Busse Rd (60007-2116)
PHONE..........................847 593-5000
Fax: 847 593-5333
Jeff Zonsius, *General Mgr*
**EMP:** 10
**SALES (corp-wide):** 923.9MM  **Privately Held**
**SIC:** 2821  5162  Plastics materials & resins; plastics materials & basic shapes
**HQ:** Total Plastics Resources Llc
  2810 N Burdick St Ste A
  Kalamazoo MI 49004
  269 344-0009

**(G-9786)**
**TOTAL TOOLING TECHNOLOGY INC**
1475 Elmhurst Rd (60007-6400)
PHONE..........................847 437-5135
Fax: 847 437-5329
Paul Majerus, *President*
James Majerus, *Vice Pres*
Patty Majerus, *Bookkeeper*
**EMP:** 10
**SQ FT:** 5,000
**SALES (est):** 1MM  **Privately Held**
**WEB:** www.totaltoolingtechnology.com
**SIC:** 3541  7699  3553  3546  Machine tools, metal cutting type; industrial machinery & equipment repair; woodworking machinery; power-driven handtools

**(G-9787)**
**TOWER METAL PRODUCTS LP (PA)**
1965 Pratt Blvd (60007-5905)
PHONE..........................847 806-7200
Fax: 847 806-7222
Audie Tang, *Partner*
Cyrus Tang,
**EMP:** 2
**SQ FT:** 100,000
**SALES (est):** 5.1MM  **Privately Held**
**SIC:** 3341  Aluminum smelting & refining (secondary)

**(G-9788)**
**TRAVEL CADDY INC**
Also Called: Travelon
700 Touhy Ave (60007-4916)
PHONE..........................847 621-7000
Fax: 847 621-7001
Donald E Godshaw, *President*
Roberto M Mustacchi, *CFO*
Kathy Curtin, *VP Mktg*
Tanya Krivtsov, *Manager*
Joy Lancaster, *Manager*
▲ **EMP:** 50  **EST:** 1978
**SQ FT:** 39,000
**SALES (est):** 10.2MM  **Privately Held**
**WEB:** www.travelon.com
**SIC:** 3161  3792  Traveling bags; travel trailers & campers

**(G-9789)**
**TREND TECHNOLOGIES LLC**
737 Fargo Ave (60007-4702)
PHONE..........................847 640-2382
Michal Cabaj, *Engineer*
Katie Kasprzycki, *Human Res Mgr*
Mark Boratto, *Sales Mgr*
Dan Precour, *Branch Mgr*
**EMP:** 200
**SALES (corp-wide):** 159MM  **Privately Held**
**SIC:** 3089  3544  Molding primary plastic; special dies, tools, jigs & fixtures
**HQ:** Trend Technologies, Llc
  4626 Eucalyptus Ave
  Chino CA 91710
  909 597-7861

**(G-9790)**
**TRI GUARDS INC**
80 N Lively Blvd (60007-1317)
PHONE..........................847 537-8444
Fax: 847 537-8507
George Triunfol, *President*
Anne Triunfol, *Vice Pres*
Mary Lou Hazell, *Accounting Mgr*
**EMP:** 15  **EST:** 1970
**SQ FT:** 10,000
**SALES (est):** 1.3MM  **Privately Held**
**WEB:** www.tri-guards.com
**SIC:** 3089  Plastic hardware & building products

**(G-9791)**
**TRI-STAR ENGINEERING INC**
2455 Pan Am Blvd (60007-6209)
PHONE..........................847 595-3377
Fax: 847 766-3377
Robert Lindstrom, *President*
Alan Wicker, *Treasurer*
Rita Nardi, *Manager*
Judy Lindstrom, *Admin Sec*
**EMP:** 33
**SQ FT:** 2,500
**SALES (est):** 4.9MM  **Privately Held**
**WEB:** www.tristareng.com
**SIC:** 3544  3545  Special dies, tools, jigs & fixtures; machine tool accessories

**(G-9792)**
**TRIAD TRUCKING LLC**
836 S Arlington Hts Rd (60007-3667)
PHONE..........................847 833-9276
Brooke Hudson,
**EMP:** 5
**SALES (est):** 751.8K  **Privately Held**
**SIC:** 3537  Trucks: freight, baggage, etc.: industrial, except mining

**(G-9793)**
**TRIMACO LLC**
1215 Landmeier Rd (60007-2433)
P.O. Box 2300, Morrisville NC (27560)
PHONE..........................919 674-3476
Vito Ancona, *Manager*
**EMP:** 21
**SALES (corp-wide):** 99MM  **Privately Held**
**SIC:** 2679  Paper products, converted
**PA:** Trimaco, Llc
  2300 Gateway Centre Blvd # 200
  Morrisville NC 27560
  919 674-3476

**(G-9794)**
**TSD MANUFACTURING CO INC**
825 Chase Ave (60007-4805)
PHONE..........................630 238-8750
Fax: 630 238-8752
Semyon Trakhtenburg, *President*
**EMP:** 12
**SQ FT:** 6,000
**SALES (est):** 1.7MM  **Privately Held**
**SIC:** 3599  Custom machinery

**(G-9795)**
**ULRICH KAEPPLER**
Also Called: Kaeppler Machining
1693 Elmhurst Rd (60007-6413)
PHONE..........................847 290-0220
Ulrich Kaeppler, *Owner*
▲ **EMP:** 5
**SALES (est):** 543.5K  **Privately Held**
**SIC:** 3599  Machine shop, jobbing & repair

**(G-9796)**
**ULTRA SPECIALTY HOLDINGS INC**
1360 Howard St (60007-2214)
PHONE..........................847 437-8110
Fax: 847 437-0748
Hans Scheel, *President*
Victor Zarecky, *Corp Secy*
Thaddeus Haderspeck, *Vice Pres*
Tony Phipps, *Mfg Staff*
**EMP:** 24  **EST:** 1964
**SQ FT:** 22,400
**SALES (est):** 4.6MM  **Privately Held**
**WEB:** www.ultraspecialties.com
**SIC:** 3599  3544  Machine shop, jobbing & repair; special dies, tools, jigs & fixtures

**(G-9797)**
**UNI-LABEL AND TAG CORPORATION**
Also Called: Varimed Division
1121 Pagni Dr (60007-6602)
PHONE..........................847 956-8900
Fax: 847 981-9577
Donna J Zgonina, *CEO*
Dan Mallek, *Sales Staff*
Mike Laziewicz, *Sales Associate*
**EMP:** 35  **EST:** 1975
**SQ FT:** 20,000
**SALES (est):** 5.4MM  **Privately Held**
**WEB:** www.arpeco.com
**SIC:** 2759  2671  2241  Labels & seals: printing; packaging paper & plastics film, coated & laminated; narrow fabric mills

**(G-9798)**
**UNITECH INDUSTRIES INC**
1461 Elmhurst Rd (60007-6400)
PHONE..........................847 357-8800
Fax: 847 357-8804
Atamjit Singh, *President*
Yash Sutariya, *Vice Pres*
Holanda Singh, *Admin Sec*
**EMP:** 18
**SQ FT:** 7,000
**SALES (est):** 2.6MM  **Privately Held**
**WEB:** www.unitechindustriesinc.com
**SIC:** 3471  Electroplating & plating

**(G-9799)**
**UNITED CMRA BINOCULAR REPR LLC**
2525 Busse Rd (60007-6118)
PHONE..........................630 595-2525
Fax: 630 595-2526
Steve Schuldt, *President*
Frank Soukup, *General Mgr*
Maribeth Wlodarczyk, *General Mgr*
Antoinette Sciacca, *Principal*
Renee Miastkowski, *Vice Pres*
**EMP:** 20
**SQ FT:** 7,500
**SALES (est):** 4.2MM  **Privately Held**
**WEB:** www.unitedcamera.com
**SIC:** 7699  7819  3652  Photographic equipment repair; video tape or disk reproduction; pre-recorded records & tapes

**(G-9800)**
**UNIVERSAL BROACHING INC**
1203 Pagni Dr (60007-6604)
PHONE..........................847 228-1440
Fax: 847 228-5115
Frances Hehn, *President*

# Elk Grove Village - Cook County (G-9801)

**GEOGRAPHIC SECTION**

Frances A Hehn, *President*
Ronald Hehn, *President*
Ronald P Hehn Jr, *Vice Pres*
**EMP:** 12
**SQ FT:** 10,000
**SALES:** 1MM **Privately Held**
**SIC:** 3541 3545 7692 5085 Broaching machines; broaches (machine tool accessories); welding repair; industrial tools

### (G-9801)
**UNIVERSAL CHEM & COATINGS INC**
1124 Elmhurst Rd (60007-2615)
**PHONE** ............................... 847 297-2001
**Fax:** 847 297-5752
Frederick Chun, *Vice Pres*
Fredrick Chin, *Vice Pres*
**EMP:** 25
**SALES (corp-wide):** 9.7MM **Privately Held**
**WEB:** www.unicheminc.com
**SIC:** 2819 2891 2851 Industrial inorganic chemicals; adhesives & sealants; paints & allied products
**PA:** Universal Chemicals And Coatings, Inc.
1975 Fox Ln
Elgin IL 60123
847 931-1700

### (G-9802)
**UNIVERSAL SCIENTIFIC ILL INC**
Also Called: Universal Scientific III Inc
2101 Arthur Ave (60007-6089)
**PHONE** ............................... 847 228-6464
Chris L Seth, *President*
Barry Seth, *Vice Pres*
Joan Northrup, *Manager*
**EMP:** 24
**SQ FT:** 82,000
**SALES (est):** 2.2MM **Privately Held**
**WEB:** www.usipcb.com
**SIC:** 3672 Printed circuit boards
**PA:** Aerotronic Controls Co.
2101 Arthur Ave
Elk Grove Village IL 60007
847 228-6504

### (G-9803)
**VAL CUSTOM CABINETS & FLRG INC**
2656 American Ln (60007)
**PHONE** ............................... 708 790-8373
Valeriy Yenakiy, *President*
**EMP:** 4
**SALES (est):** 31.9K **Privately Held**
**SIC:** 2434 Wood kitchen cabinets

### (G-9804)
**VALEE INC (PA)**
Also Called: Insty-Prints
859 Oakton St (60007-1904)
**PHONE** ............................... 847 364-6464
**Fax:** 847 364-6571
Valerie Roesti, *President*
Lee Roesti, *Vice Pres*
**EMP:** 6
**SQ FT:** 6,000
**SALES (est):** 1.1MM **Privately Held**
**WEB:** www.elkgroveinsty.com
**SIC:** 2752 7334 2791 2759 Commercial printing, offset; photocopying & duplicating services; typesetting; commercial printing

### (G-9805)
**VENTEC USA LLC**
720 Lee St (60007-1116)
**PHONE** ............................... 847 621-2261
Jack Pattie, *Mng Member*
▲ **EMP:** 8
**SALES:** 8MM **Privately Held**
**SIC:** 1021 Copper ore milling & preparation

### (G-9806)
**VERSON ENTERPRISES INC**
870 Cambridge Dr (60007-2437)
**PHONE** ............................... 847 364-2600
**Fax:** 847 364-2899
James Glover, *President*
Roger Anderson, *Corp Secy*
Esther Reilly, *Manager*
**EMP:** 19
**SQ FT:** 5,000
**SALES (est):** 1.9MM **Privately Held**
**WEB:** www.graftel.com
**SIC:** 8734 3826 Testing laboratories; analytical instruments

### (G-9807)
**VERTEX DISTRIBUTION**
1680 Elmhurst Rd (60007-6418)
**PHONE** ............................... 847 437-0400
Fred Hacket, *Manager*
▲ **EMP:** 2
**SALES (est):** 629.9K **Privately Held**
**SIC:** 3965 Fasteners

### (G-9808)
**VIDEOJET TECHNOLOGIES INC**
1855 Estes Ave (60007-5413)
**PHONE** ............................... 630 238-3900
Jonathan Hinkemeyer, *Vice Pres*
Robert Weaver, *Technical Mgr*
Daniel Bottens, *Manager*
Peter Ryan, *Technology*
Peter Papantos, *Director*
**EMP:** 55
**SALES (corp-wide):** 16.8B **Publicly Held**
**WEB:** www.videojet.com
**SIC:** 3579 Addressing machines, plates & plate embossers
**HQ:** Videojet Technologies Inc.
1500 N Mittel Blvd
Wood Dale IL 60191
630 860-7300

### (G-9809)
**VITAL PROTEINS LLC (PA)**
545 Busse Rd (60007-2116)
**PHONE** ............................... 224 544-9110
Kurt Seidensticker, *Mng Member*
Laura Seidensticker,
**EMP:** 27
**SALES:** 19MM **Privately Held**
**SIC:** 5499 2023 Vitamin food stores; dietary supplements, dairy & non-dairy based

### (G-9810)
**VOESTLPINE PRECISION STRIP LLC**
901 Morse Ave (60007-5107)
**PHONE** ............................... 847 227-5272
**Fax:** 847 437-6033
Darryl Christman, *Engineer*
Tom Kiolbassa, *VP Finance*
Wayne Kralka, *Mktg Dir*
Udeo Coehler, *Mng Member*
Darryl Christmas, *Manager*
▲ **EMP:** 65
**SALES (est):** 21.2MM **Privately Held**
**SIC:** 3325 Steel foundries

### (G-9811)
**WEYERHAEUSER COMPANY**
Also Called: Elk Grove Corrugated Plant
1800 Nicholas Blvd (60007-5903)
**PHONE** ............................... 847 439-1111
Paul Bosley, *Branch Mgr*
**EMP:** 147
**SALES (corp-wide):** 6.3B **Publicly Held**
**SIC:** 2653 Corrugated boxes, partitions, display items, sheets & pad
**PA:** Weyerhaeuser Company
220 Occidental Ave S
Seattle WA 98104
206 539-3000

### (G-9812)
**WHITE RACKER CO INC**
420 Lively Blvd (60007-2012)
**PHONE** ............................... 847 758-1640
**Fax:** 847 758-1741
Kenneth F Rogalski, *President*
▲ **EMP:** 5 **EST:** 1895
**SALES (est):** 713.2K **Privately Held**
**WEB:** www.whiteracker.com
**SIC:** 3599 3471 3432 Machine shop, jobbing & repair; plating & polishing; plumbing fixture fittings & trim

### (G-9813)
**WILCOR SOLID SURFACE INC**
55 Randall St (60007-1013)
**PHONE** ............................... 630 350-7703
J Bradford Reamer, *President*
**EMP:** 15
**SQ FT:** 5,000
**SALES (est):** 1.1MM **Privately Held**
**WEB:** www.wilcorusa.com
**SIC:** 1799 2541 2434 2821 Counter top installation; counters or counter display cases, wood; wood kitchen cabinets; plastics materials & resins

### (G-9814)
**WILLIE WASHER MFG CO**
2101 Greenleaf Ave (60007-5507)
**PHONE** ............................... 847 956-1344
**Fax:** 847 956-7943
William Neumann, *President*
Jamie Brabeck, *General Mgr*
Bill Fortney, *COO*
Diane Newmann, *Treasurer*
Bob Urlakis, *Sales Mgr*
**EMP:** 115 **EST:** 1973
**SQ FT:** 140,000
**SALES (est):** 23MM **Privately Held**
**WEB:** www.williewasher.com
**SIC:** 3469 3452 Stamping metal for the trade; washers, metal

### (G-9815)
**WOODLOGIC CUSTOM MILLWORK INC**
505 Bonnie Ln (60007-1909)
**PHONE** ............................... 847 640-4500
Richard Theis, *President*
**EMP:** 20
**SALES (est):** 3.3MM **Privately Held**
**SIC:** 2499 Decorative wood & woodwork

### (G-9816)
**WOOGL CORPORATION**
Also Called: Allegra Marketing Print & Mail
859 Oakton St (60007-1904)
**PHONE** ............................... 847 806-1160
Joseph W Smith, *President*
Christine Accardo, *General Mgr*
James Smith, *Vice Pres*
Doug Zirkel, *Sales Mgr*
Doug Rebok, *Marketing Staff*
**EMP:** 23
**SQ FT:** 7,000
**SALES (est):** 3.2MM **Privately Held**
**WEB:** www.allegradigital.com
**SIC:** 2752 2796 2791 2789 Commercial printing, offset; platemaking services; typesetting; bookbinding & related work

### (G-9817)
**WRIGHT TECHNOLOGIES INC**
1380 Howard St (60007-2214)
**PHONE** ............................... 847 439-4150
Kazimierz Aleszczyk, *President*
**EMP:** 9
**SQ FT:** 8,400
**SALES (est):** 950K **Privately Held**
**SIC:** 3599 Machine shop, jobbing & repair

### (G-9818)
**WUNDERLICH DIAMOND TOOL CORP**
1330 Howard St (60007-2200)
**PHONE** ............................... 847 437-9904
**Fax:** 847 439-4856
Jakub Wunderlich, *President*
Mark Wunderlich, *Vice Pres*
**EMP:** 13
**SQ FT:** 10,000
**SALES (est):** 2.3MM **Privately Held**
**WEB:** www.wunderlichdiamond.com
**SIC:** 3545 Diamond cutting tools for turning, boring, burnishing, etc.

### (G-9819)
**WYNRIGHT CORPORATION (DH)**
2500 York Rd (60007-6319)
**PHONE** ............................... 847 595-9400
Kevin Ambrose, *CEO*
John Chapman, *General Mgr*
Clint Lasher, *Division Pres*
Robert Liebe, *Division Pres*
Kenneth Dickerson, *COO*
▲ **EMP:** 100
**SQ FT:** 50,000
**SALES (est):** 397.4MM
**SALES (corp-wide):** 2.8B **Privately Held**
**WEB:** www.wynright.com
**SIC:** 5084 3535 8711 Industrial machinery & equipment; materials handling machinery; lift trucks & parts; conveyors & conveying equipment; engineering services
**HQ:** Daifuku Webb Holding Company
34375 W 12 Mile Rd
Farmington Hills MI 48331
248 553-1000

### (G-9820)
**X-L-ENGINEERING CORP**
Also Called: Cnc Induistries
330 Crossen Ave (60007-2002)
**PHONE** ............................... 847 364-4750
Kurt Wenhack, *Plant Mgr*
Kurt Wendhack, *Manager*
**EMP:** 20
**SALES (corp-wide):** 15.6MM **Privately Held**
**WEB:** www.xleng.com
**SIC:** 3451 Screw machine products
**PA:** X-L-Engineering Corp.
6150 W Mulford St
Niles IL 60714
847 965-3030

### (G-9821)
**Y 2 K ELECTRONICS INC**
2574 United Ln (60007-6819)
**PHONE** ............................... 847 238-9024
Nalini J Patel, *President*
Sonia Patel, *Treasurer*
Suketu Patel, *Admin Sec*
▲ **EMP:** 15 **EST:** 2000
**SQ FT:** 15,000
**SALES:** 1.5MM **Privately Held**
**SIC:** 3672 Printed circuit boards

### (G-9822)
**YE OLDE SIGN SHOPPE**
68 N Lively Blvd (60007-1317)
**PHONE** ............................... 847 228-7446
Joe Hollick, *Owner*
**EMP:** 4
**SALES (est):** 142.1K **Privately Held**
**SIC:** 3993 Signs & advertising specialties

### (G-9823)
**YEAMAN MACHINE TECH INC**
2150 Touhy Ave (60007-5325)
**PHONE** ............................... 847 758-0500
**Fax:** 847 758-9776
William Yeaman, *President*
James Daubach, *Admin Sec*
◆ **EMP:** 27
**SQ FT:** 30,000
**SALES (est):** 7.1MM **Privately Held**
**WEB:** www.yeamanmachine.net
**SIC:** 3565 Packaging machinery

### (G-9824)
**ZAPTEL CORPORATION**
836 S Arlington Hts Rd (60007-3667)
**PHONE** ............................... 847 386-8050
**Fax:** 847 483-1303
Ron Reimann, *President*
Melissa Cairns, *Manager*
▲ **EMP:** 8
**SQ FT:** 2,000
**SALES (est):** 692.9K **Privately Held**
**WEB:** www.zaptel.com
**SIC:** 2741 7389 4813 ; advertising, promotional & trade show services; local & long distance telephone communications

---

# Elkhart
*Logan County*

### (G-9825)
**ICG ILLINOIS**
781 600th St (62634-6057)
**PHONE** ............................... 217 947-2332
**EMP:** 3
**SALES (est):** 240K **Privately Held**
**SIC:** 4731 1241 Freight Transportation Arrangement Coal Mining Services

▲ = Import ▼=Export
◆ =Import/Export

# GEOGRAPHIC SECTION

Elmhurst - Dupage County (G-9852)

## Ellis Grove
### Randolph County

**(G-9826)**
**CHARTRAND EQUIPMENT CO INC**
Also Called: Chartrand Equipement Co
6760 State Route 3 (62241-1318)
PHONE...............................618 853-2314
Willie R Chartrand, *Manager*
Catherine Chartrand, *Admin Sec*
▼ **EMP:** 4
**SALES (est):** 260K **Privately Held**
**SIC:** 3531 Construction machinery

## Ellsworth
### Mclean County

**(G-9827)**
**CRUTCHER MFG**
102 S West St (61737-7541)
PHONE...............................309 724-8206
Donald E Crutcher, *Principal*
**EMP:** 2
**SALES (est):** 210.1K **Privately Held**
**SIC:** 3999 Manufacturing industries

## Elmhurst
### Dupage County

**(G-9828)**
**A J MANUFACTURING CO INC**
437 W Wrightwood Ave (60126-1011)
PHONE...............................630 832-2828
Fax: 630 832-2889
Shiv Sitaram, *Opers Mgr*
Dariusz Lachowski, *Engineer*
Joe Chrzanowski, *Branch Mgr*
**EMP:** 8
**SALES (corp-wide):** 6.6MM **Privately Held**
**SIC:** 3545 Machine tool attachments & accessories
**PA:** A J Manufacturing Co., Inc.
449 W Wrightwood Ave
Elmhurst IL
630 832-2828

**(G-9829)**
**A LIFT ABOVE INC**
699 N Walnut St Ste 1 (60126-1540)
PHONE...............................630 758-1023
Ken Vaisvila, *President*
**EMP:** 5
**SALES:** 500K **Privately Held**
**SIC:** 3537 Forklift trucks

**(G-9830)**
**ADAM TOOL & MFG CO INC**
900 N Larch Ave (60126-1115)
PHONE...............................630 530-8810
Fax: 630 530-8814
Anton Adam, *President*
Raymond Adam, *Vice Pres*
Hugh Adam, *Admin Sec*
▲ **EMP:** 12 **EST:** 1963
**SQ FT:** 24,000
**SALES:** 560.6K **Privately Held**
**WEB:** www.adam-mfg.com
**SIC:** 3599 Machine shop, jobbing & repair

**(G-9831)**
**AIM INC**
586 S Rex Blvd (60126-4259)
PHONE...............................630 941-0027
Bill Kawales, *Manager*
**EMP:** 2
**SALES (est):** 201.9K **Privately Held**
**SIC:** 3699 Electrical equipment & supplies

**(G-9832)**
**ALBERT F AMLING LLC (PA)**
Also Called: Amling's Flowerland
331 N York St (60126-2371)
PHONE...............................630 333-1720
Carl R Hayes, *President*
Dave Meyers, *General Mgr*
Douglas Aniballi, *Vice Pres*
Pat Allen, *Manager*
Michael Jinks, *Manager*
**EMP:** 176 **EST:** 1890
**SALES (est):** 25.2MM **Privately Held**
**SIC:** 5992 5261 7359 3999 Flowers, fresh; plants, potted; garden supplies & tools; fertilizer; nursery stock, seeds & bulbs; live plant rental; flowers, artificial & preserved; plants, artificial & preserved; landscape contractors

**(G-9833)**
**ALPHA CIRCUIT CORPORATION**
730 N Oaklawn Ave (60126-1406)
PHONE...............................630 617-5555
Fax: 630 617-5598
Bhagvan Vaghani, *President*
Dale Gorski, *General Mgr*
David Olson, *General Mgr*
Scott Goggans, *Opers Staff*
Ankit Dungrani, *Purchasing*
▲ **EMP:** 47
**SQ FT:** 44,000
**SALES:** 6.9MM **Privately Held**
**WEB:** www.alphacircuit.com
**SIC:** 3672 Printed circuit boards

**(G-9834)**
**ASM SENSORS INC**
650 W Grand Ave Ste 205 (60126-1025)
PHONE...............................630 832-3202
Ines Steinich, *Manager*
Fred Fiedler, *Technology*
**EMP:** 10
**SALES (est):** 1.7MM **Privately Held**
**WEB:** www.asmsensors.com
**SIC:** 3829 Measuring & controlling devices

**(G-9835)**
**AV STUMPFL USA CORP**
960 N Industrial Dr Ste 3 (60126-1119)
PHONE...............................630 359-0999
Franklin Moore, *President*
Ulli Stumpfl, *Vice Pres*
Michael Patterson, *Purch Mgr*
Reinhold Stumpfl, *CFO*
Thomas M Berichon, *Sales Mgr*
▲ **EMP:** 10
**SQ FT:** 5,000
**SALES (est):** 1.1MM **Privately Held**
**WEB:** www.avstumpfusa.com
**SIC:** 3861 Screens, projection

**(G-9836)**
**BAUMBACH MANUFACTURING**
650 W Grand Ave (60126-1043)
PHONE...............................630 941-0505
Fax: 630 941-1504
Emil Baumbach, *President*
**EMP:** 4
**SALES (est):** 220K **Privately Held**
**SIC:** 3999 3493 Manufacturing industries; steel springs, except wire

**(G-9837)**
**BB SERVICES LLC**
Also Called: UPS Store of Elmhurst, The
205 E Butterfield Rd (60126-5103)
PHONE...............................630 941-8122
Edward J Chrabaszcz,
**EMP:** 9
**SQ FT:** 2,000
**SALES (est):** 471.2K **Privately Held**
**SIC:** 4215 7334 2789 Courier services, except by air; photocopying & duplicating services; binding & repair of books, magazines & pamphlets

**(G-9838)**
**BELDEN ENERGY SOLUTIONS INC**
719 S Berkley Ave (60126-4203)
PHONE...............................800 235-3361
James Belden, *Principal*
**EMP:** 6
**SALES (est):** 511.9K **Privately Held**
**SIC:** 3643 3678 3363 Current-carrying wiring devices; electronic connectors; aluminum die-castings

**(G-9839)**
**BEMA INC**
744 N Oaklawn Ave (60126-1406)
PHONE...............................630 279-7800
Fax: 630 279-0284
Glen Galloway, *President*
Leon Tasche, *Prdtn Mgr*
Eric Kainer, *QC Mgr*
Bob Reese, *Chief Engr*
Rocco Casamassimo, *Accounting Mgr*
▲ **EMP:** 70
**SQ FT:** 37,500
**SALES (est):** 17.5MM
**SALES (corp-wide):** 18.9MM **Privately Held**
**SIC:** 3081 Unsupported plastics film & sheet
**PA:** Galloway Consolidated Holdings, Inc.
744 N Oaklawn Ave
Elmhurst IL 60126
630 279-7800

**(G-9840)**
**BLAC INC**
195 W Spangler Ave Ste A (60126-1505)
PHONE...............................630 279-6400
Fax: 630 279-1005
Phillip B Black, *President*
Lenz Counsil, *VP Opers*
Guy Hornikel, *Purchasing*
Keith McDinley, *Purchasing*
Robert Siegerdt, *QC Mgr*
▲ **EMP:** 65
**SQ FT:** 22,000
**SALES (est):** 27.2MM **Privately Held**
**WEB:** www.blacinc.com
**SIC:** 3593 Fluid power cylinders & actuators

**(G-9841)**
**BLOWERS LLC**
835 N Industrial Dr (60126-1107)
PHONE...............................708 594-1800
Sabit Inan, *CEO*
Bonnie Quine, *Manager*
Judith Smatzni, *IT/INT Sup*
**EMP:** 23 **EST:** 1951
**SQ FT:** 30,000
**SALES (est):** 1MM **Privately Held**
**WEB:** www.clementsnational.com
**SIC:** 3564 Dust or fume collecting equipment, industrial

**(G-9842)**
**BRITISH CNVRTNG SLTNS NRTH AME**
650 W Grand Ave Ste 201 (60126-1025)
PHONE...............................281 764-6651
Robert Garvey, *Vice Pres*
Simon Needham, *Sales Dir*
▲ **EMP:** 24 **EST:** 2013
**SQ FT:** 300
**SALES (est):** 2.2MM **Privately Held**
**SIC:** 3565 Packaging machinery
**HQ:** British Converting Solutions Limited
Blackburn Road
Dunstable BEDS
152 537-9359

**(G-9843)**
**BRUNNER & LAY INC**
756 N Industrial Dr (60126-1129)
PHONE...............................847 678-3232
Fax: 847 678-0642
James R Finkler, *Branch Mgr*
Michael Malget, *Manager*
R Valadez, *Director*
Frederick Klose, *Intl Dir*
R Finkler, *Administration*
**EMP:** 120
**SALES (corp-wide):** 63.7MM **Privately Held**
**WEB:** www.brunnerlay.com
**SIC:** 3545 3546 3531 Drills (machine tool accessories); hammers, portable: electric or pneumatic, chipping, etc.; construction machinery
**PA:** Brunner & Lay, Inc.
1510 N Old Missouri Rd
Springdale AR 72764
479 756-0880

**(G-9844)**
**BULLSEYE IMPRINTING & EMB**
846 N York St Ste C (60126-1239)
PHONE...............................630 834-8175
Angie Nelson, *President*
Nick Nelson, *Vice Pres*
**EMP:** 3
**SALES:** 300K **Privately Held**
**SIC:** 2395 Embroidery products, except schiffli machine

**(G-9845)**
**CARSON PROPERTIES INC (PA)**
Also Called: Closet Works Division
953 N Larch Ave (60126-1128)
PHONE...............................630 832-3322
Michael D Carson, *CEO*
**EMP:** 47
**SQ FT:** 30,000
**SALES (est):** 7.6MM **Privately Held**
**WEB:** www.closets.com
**SIC:** 2511 Wood household furniture

**(G-9846)**
**CHEMSTATION CHICAGO LLC**
934 N Oaklawn Ave Ste 1 (60126-1032)
PHONE...............................630 279-2857
Andrew Lasker, *President*
**EMP:** 24 **EST:** 2014
**SQ FT:** 25,000
**SALES:** 7.5MM **Privately Held**
**SIC:** 2841 Soap & other detergents

**(G-9847)**
**CHICAGO BRICK OVEN LLC (PA)**
559 S Kenilworth Ave (60126-4444)
PHONE...............................630 359-4793
William Pathen, *Vice Pres*
Carmen Parisi, *Mng Member*
▼ **EMP:** 4
**SALES:** 1.5MM **Privately Held**
**SIC:** 3567 Industrial furnaces & ovens

**(G-9848)**
**CHICAGO SWITCHBOARD CO INC**
470 W Wrightwood Ave (60126-1016)
PHONE...............................630 833-2266
Fax: 630 833-2277
Richard Blomquist, *President*
Bill Eder, *Vice Pres*
William Blomquist, *Treasurer*
**EMP:** 34 **EST:** 1915
**SQ FT:** 20,000
**SALES (est):** 11.4MM **Privately Held**
**WEB:** www.chiswbd.com
**SIC:** 3613 3644 Switchgear & switchboard apparatus; switchboards & parts, power; switchboard apparatus, except instruments; control panels, electric; noncurrent-carrying wiring services

**(G-9849)**
**CLOSET WORKS INC**
953 N Larch Ave (60126-1128)
PHONE...............................630 832-3322
Frank Happ, *President*
Fran Worness, *Human Res Mgr*
Andres Deavila, *Manager*
Greg Cetera, *Master*
**EMP:** 22
**SALES (est):** 3.4MM **Privately Held**
**SIC:** 2511 Wood household furniture

**(G-9850)**
**CLOSET WORKS LLC**
953 N Larch Ave (60126-1128)
PHONE...............................630 832-4422
Candace Goffrier, *Finance*
Zena Hallman, *Sales Staff*
Frank Happ, *Mng Member*
Greg Cetera, *Executive*
**EMP:** 4
**SALES (est):** 673K **Privately Held**
**SIC:** 2434 Wood kitchen cabinets

**(G-9851)**
**CMP MILLWORK CO**
601 S Il Route 83 Ste 100 (60126-4261)
PHONE...............................630 832-6462
Mark E Olson, *President*
**EMP:** 6
**SALES (est):** 530K **Privately Held**
**SIC:** 2521 5039 5031 2431 Wood office filing cabinets & bookcases; doors, sliding; windows; millwork

**(G-9852)**
**COKI FOODS LLC**
110 N Willow Rd Apt 4 (60126-2958)
PHONE...............................708 261-5758
Nancy R Vega, *Principal*
**EMP:** 6
**SALES (est):** 210K **Privately Held**
**SIC:** 2099 Food preparations

Elmhurst - Dupage County (G-9853)

**(G-9853)**
**COLOR SMITHS INC**
747 N Church Rd Ste E6 (60126-1440)
PHONE..................................708 562-0061
Calvin Hill, *President*
Lori Hill, *Vice Pres*
EMP: 20
SQ FT: 11,000
SALES: 1.4MM **Privately Held**
WEB: www.colorsmiths.com
SIC: **2796** 3555 2791 Lithographic plates, positives or negatives; color separations for printing; printing plates; typesetting

**(G-9854)**
**COMET DIE & ENGRAVING COMPANY**
909 N Larch Ave (60126-1158)
PHONE..................................630 833-5600
Fax: 630 833-2644
Terence J Donlin Jr, *President*
Mary L Donlin, *Treasurer*
Ed Foreman, *Controller*
Paul Beale, *Sales Engr*
Tony Mariniello, *Sales Engr*
▲ EMP: 65 EST: 1898
SQ FT: 35,000
SALES: 12.6MM **Privately Held**
WEB: www.cometdie.com
SIC: **3544** 3479 Industrial molds; engraving jewelry silverware, or metal

**(G-9855)**
**COMMON GOAL SYSTEMS INC**
188 W Industrial Dr # 240 (60126-1610)
PHONE..................................630 592-4200
Michael Xakellis, *President*
Chris Gauldin, *Technical Mgr*
Linda Murrin, *Accounts Exec*
Cindy Rose, *Accounts Exec*
Vicki Tieri, *Mktg Dir*
EMP: 25
SQ FT: 3,500
SALES: 2.5MM **Privately Held**
SIC: **7372** Prepackaged software

**(G-9856)**
**COPY-MOR INC**
Also Called: CMI
767 N Industrial Dr (60126-1500)
PHONE..................................312 666-4000
Fax: 312 666-4001
David Steinberg, *President*
Laura Gang, *Controller*
▲ EMP: 44 EST: 1961
SQ FT: 40,000
SALES: 15MM
SALES (corp-wide): 6.9B **Publicly Held**
WEB: www.cmiart.com
SIC: **2752** 2791 2789 Commercial printing, lithographic; typesetting; bookbinding & related work
HQ: Consolidated Graphics, Inc.
5858 Westheimer Rd # 200
Houston TX 77057
713 787-0977

**(G-9857)**
**CQ INDUSTRIES INC**
Also Called: Crazy Quilt Patch Factory
477 W Fullerton Ave (60126-1404)
PHONE..................................630 530-0177
Fax: 630 833-9503
Paul Jemmi, *President*
EMP: 5
SALES (est): 290K **Privately Held**
SIC: **2395** Emblems, embroidered

**(G-9858)**
**CRAFTWOOD INC**
889 N Larch Ave Ste 100 (60126-1109)
PHONE..................................630 758-1740
Jakub J Razniak, *President*
EMP: 16
SALES (est): 3MM **Privately Held**
SIC: **1389** Construction, repair & dismantling services

**(G-9859)**
**CROWN METAL MANUFACTURING CO (PA)**
765 S Il Route 83 (60126-4228)
PHONE..................................630 279-9800
Fax: 630 279-9807
Steven Varon, *President*

Mary Ellen Bielawski, *Human Res Mgr*
Donna Bielanski, *Human Resources*
Brad Ashton, *VP Sales*
Justin Greiner, *Regl Sales Mgr*
▲ EMP: 50
SQ FT: 140,000
SALES (est): 19.6MM **Privately Held**
SIC: **3429** Manufactured hardware (general)

**(G-9860)**
**CRUISE BOILER AND REPR CO INC**
Also Called: Delta Steel Boilers Div
824 N Addison Ave (60126-1218)
PHONE..................................630 279-7111
EMP: 12
SALES (est): 870K **Privately Held**
SIC: **7699** 3433 Boiler Repair Service And Mfg Low Pressure Heating Boilers

**(G-9861)**
**CU INFO SYSTEMS**
Also Called: Cais
100 N Addison Ave (60126-2848)
PHONE..................................630 607-0300
Clark Craig, *Prgrmr*
Scott Hermanses, *Director*
EMP: 30
SALES (est): 1.5MM **Privately Held**
SIC: **7372** Educational computer software

**(G-9862)**
**CUMMINS - ALLISON CORP**
851 N Addison Ave (60126-1217)
PHONE..................................630 833-2285
Keith Garvey, *Manager*
EMP: 18
SALES (corp-wide): 377.1MM **Privately Held**
SIC: **3579** 3519 Perforators (office machines); internal combustion engines
PA: Cummins - Allison Corp.
852 Feehanville Dr
Mount Prospect IL 60056
847 759-6403

**(G-9863)**
**EIS**
752 N Larch Ave (60126-1522)
PHONE..................................630 530-7500
Jesse Quiles, *Principal*
EMP: 3
SALES (est): 122.7K **Privately Held**
SIC: **3677** Electronic coils, transformers & other inductors

**(G-9864)**
**ELITE ACCESS SYSTEMS INC**
845 N Larch Ave (60126-1114)
PHONE..................................800 528-5880
Walodi Parsadayan, *President*
Alex Parsadayan, *Vice Pres*
Rob Verrilli, *Web Proj Mgr*
EMP: 75
SQ FT: 40,000
SALES (est): 7.8MM **Privately Held**
WEB: www.electricgate.com
SIC: **3699** Security control equipment & systems

**(G-9865)**
**ELMHURST-CHICAGO STONE COMPANY (PA)**
400 W 1st St (60126-2604)
P.O. Box 57 (60126-0057)
PHONE..................................630 832-4000
Fax: 630 832-0140
Charles Hammersmith Jr, *President*
Charles Hammersmith Sr, *Chairman*
Kenneth J Lahner, *Vice Pres*
Karen Jones, *Human Res Mgr*
Britt Lienau, *Sales Staff*
EMP: 30 EST: 1960
SQ FT: 21,000
SALES (est): 122.7MM **Privately Held**
SIC: **1442** 3273 3272 Gravel mining; ready-mixed concrete; pipe, concrete or lined with concrete

**(G-9866)**
**ENGINEERING FINSHG SYSTEMS LLC (PA)**
Also Called: Engineered Finishing Systems
202 E Bttrfield Rd Ste 20 (60126)
PHONE..................................815 893-6090
Fax: 815 459-6051
Jim McRoy, *Vice Pres*
Linda Zielinski, *Purch Agent*
Curtis Breutzmann, *Engineer*
Mike Horton, *Engineer*
Joseph Campbell, *Design Engr*
▲ EMP: 21
SQ FT: 4,900
SALES: 9MM **Privately Held**
WEB: www.kmisystemsinc.com
SIC: **3559** 8711 Paint making machinery; engineering services

**(G-9867)**
**ENTROPY INTERNATIONAL INC USA**
918 N Oaklawn Ave (60126-1015)
PHONE..................................630 834-3872
Henry Yeh, *President*
Anthony Raichel, *Vice Pres*
Thomas Welsh, *Vice Pres*
Sarah Apland, *Controller*
▲ EMP: 11
SQ FT: 5,000
SALES (est): 2.8MM **Privately Held**
WEB: www.entropy.com
SIC: **3679** Electronic circuits
PA: Entropy Precision System Inc.
6f-2, 66, Sanchong Rd.,
Taipei City TAP
226 535-536

**(G-9868)**
**ETCH-TECH INC**
494 W Wrightwood Ave (60126-1078)
PHONE..................................630 833-4234
Fax: 630 530-5960
Hans J Peskowits, *President*
Woodrow J Fisher, *Corp Secy*
EMP: 6
SQ FT: 3,300
SALES (est): 668K **Privately Held**
WEB: www.etchtech.com
SIC: **3479** 3544 Etching on metals; special dies, tools, jigs & fixtures

**(G-9869)**
**EUROVIEW ENTERPRISES LLC**
420 W Wrightwood Ave (60126-1016)
PHONE..................................630 227-3300
Duman Adam, *Principal*
Robin Krause, *Controller*
Arnie Harris, *Mng Member*
▲ EMP: 50
SALES (est): 15.4MM **Privately Held**
SIC: **5039** 3211 1793 Glass construction materials; tempered glass; construction glass; glass & glazing work

**(G-9870)**
**FANTASY COVERAGE INC**
Also Called: Big Game Software
261 N York St Ste 202 (60126-2757)
PHONE..................................630 592-8082
Brett Baker, *President*
EMP: 10 EST: 2009
SALES (est): 813.2K **Privately Held**
SIC: **7372** Prepackaged software

**(G-9871)**
**FAST HEAT INC (PA)**
Also Called: Fast Heat International
776 N Oaklawn Ave (60126-1406)
PHONE..................................630 359-6300
Fax: 630 833-0493
Tim Stojka, *President*
Dennis White, *Engineer*
Christy Zvonar, *Human Res Mgr*
George Vera, *Sales Dir*
Jeff Ashton, *Sales Mgr*
▲ EMP: 165 EST: 1957
SQ FT: 80,000
SALES (est): 26.9MM **Privately Held**
WEB: www.fastheat.com
SIC: **3567** Heating units & devices, industrial: electric

**(G-9872)**
**FIREPLACE & CHIMNEY AUTHORITY**
120 E Lake St (60126-2012)
PHONE..................................630 279-8500
Fax: 630 279-5895
Paul Loar, *President*
EMP: 30
SALES (est): 4.6MM **Privately Held**
WEB: www.chimneyauthority.com
SIC: **3271** Blocks, concrete: chimney or fireplace

**(G-9873)**
**GC DIES LLC (PA)**
877 N Larch Ave (60126-1114)
PHONE..................................630 758-4100
Jose Dones, *General Mgr*
Lisa Boyd, *Sales Dir*
Annette Irizarry, *Accounts Mgr*
Michael Tinnon, *Mng Member*
Christine Gierke, *Director*
EMP: 50 EST: 2000
SQ FT: 37,500
SALES: 5.5MM **Privately Held**
SIC: **3544** Special dies, tools, jigs & fixtures

**(G-9874)**
**GC PACKAGING LLC (PA)**
877 N Larch Ave (60126-1114)
PHONE..................................630 758-4100
Fax: 630 833-1058
Michael Tinnon, *President*
John Tinnon, *Chairman*
Steve Skalski, *Exec VP*
John Dean, *Vice Pres*
Alan Tinnon, *Purch Mgr*
▲ EMP: 55
SQ FT: 37,540
SALES: 63MM **Privately Held**
WEB: www.graphicconverting.com
SIC: **2754** 7389 Cards, except greeting: gravure printing; packaging & labeling services

**(G-9875)**
**GLASS AMERICA MIDWEST INC (PA)**
977 N Oaklawn Ave Ste 200 (60126-1028)
PHONE..................................877 743-7237
Fax: 312 781-6451
Michael G Barry, *CEO*
Bob Simpson, *General Mgr*
Ken Staples, *Regional Mgr*
Dessie Bonduris, *Business Mgr*
Nik Frye, *Vice Pres*
EMP: 6
SALES (est): 16.9MM **Privately Held**
SIC: **7536** 3231 Automotive glass replacement shops; windshields, glass: made from purchased glass

**(G-9876)**
**GLASS AMERICA MIDWEST INC**
977 N Oaklawn Ave Ste 200 (60126-1028)
PHONE..................................203 932-0248
Andre Santamaria, *Manager*
EMP: 9
SALES (corp-wide): 16.9MM **Privately Held**
SIC: **3211** Building glass, flat
PA: Glass America Midwest Inc.
977 N Oaklawn Ave Ste 200
Elmhurst IL 60126
877 743-7237

**(G-9877)**
**GLIDERA INC**
188 W Industrial Dr # 240 (60126-1623)
P.O. Box 111, Lake Forest (60045-0111)
PHONE..................................773 350-4000
David Ripley, *President*
Michael Xakellis, *Chief Engr*
EMP: 5
SALES (est): 304.7K **Privately Held**
SIC: **7372** Application computer software

**(G-9878)**
**GM LAMINATING & MOUNTING CORP**
Also Called: Suburban Map Store
1041 S Il Route 83 (60126-4973)
PHONE..................................630 941-7979
Fax: 630 941-1441

# GEOGRAPHIC SECTION
## Elmhurst - Dupage County (G-9903)

Glenn M Muzik, *President*
**EMP:** 7
**SQ FT:** 8,600
**SALES (est)** 480K **Privately Held**
**WEB:** www.gmmountlam.com
**SIC:** 2789 7389 Mounting of maps & samples; laminating service

### (G-9879)
### GRANITEX CORP (PA)
704 N Larch Ave (60126-1522)
**PHONE** ..................................... 630 888-1838
Rolandas Karinauskas, *President*
**EMP:** 4
**SALES (est)** 950.8K **Privately Held**
**SIC:** 3281 Dimension stone for buildings

### (G-9880)
### GRAPHIC CONVERTING INC
877 N Larch Ave (60126-1114)
**PHONE** ..................................... 630 758-4100
**Fax:** 630 470-4400
John R Tinnon, *President*
Stibi Skalaski, *Principal*
Joe Yaney, *CFO*
Richard McKinny, *Manager*
▲ **EMP:** 300
**SALES (est)** 91.8MM **Privately Held**
**SIC:** 2675 Die-cut paper & board

### (G-9881)
### HENKELMAN INC
493 W Fullerton Ave (60126-1404)
**PHONE** ..................................... 331 979-2013
Meike Persons, *President*
**EMP:** 7
**SALES:** 1.5MM **Privately Held**
**SIC:** 3565 Vacuum packaging machinery

### (G-9882)
### HILTI INC
135 W Diversey Ave (60126-1101)
**PHONE** ..................................... 847 364-9818
Ron Beckstrom, *Branch Mgr*
**EMP:** 6
**SALES (corp-wide):** 4.6B **Privately Held**
**SIC:** 3545 3399 Tools & accessories for machine tools; drill bits, metalworking; drills (machine tool accessories); metal fasteners
**HQ:** Hilti, Inc.
7250 Dallas Pkwy Ste 1000
Plano TX 75024
800 879-8000

### (G-9883)
### IDEK GRAPHICS LLC
926 S Prospect Ave (60126-5008)
**PHONE** ..................................... 630 530-1232
Kristine Granstrom, *Mng Member*
**EMP:** 4
**SQ FT:** 2,400
**SALES:** 100K **Privately Held**
**SIC:** 3993 Signs & advertising specialties

### (G-9884)
### IDEX MPT INC (HQ)
Also Called: Fitzpatrick Company, The
832 Indul Dr (60126)
**PHONE** ..................................... 630 530-3333
**Fax:** 630 530-0832
Bruce Manning, *President*
Kim Fields, *President*
Sam Mawley, *General Mgr*
Andrea Panico, *General Mgr*
Richard Murphy, *Exec VP*
▲ **EMP:** 100 **EST:** 1912
**SQ FT:** 100,000
**SALES (est)** 25MM
**SALES (corp-wide):** 2.1B **Publicly Held**
**WEB:** www.fitzmill.com
**SIC:** 3599 3999 1541 Amusement park equipment; barber & beauty shop equipment; pharmaceutical manufacturing plant construction
**PA:** Idex Corporation
1925 W Field Ct Ste 200
Lake Forest IL 60045
847 498-7070

### (G-9885)
### ILLINOIS TOOL WORKS INC
Also Called: I T W Chronotherm
935 N Oaklawn Ave (60126-1012)
**PHONE** ..................................... 630 993-9990
**Fax:** 630 993-9399

Michael Neenan, *Principal*
Kim Norris, *Plant Mgr*
Patrick O'Donnell, *Engineer*
Jennifer Bloom, *Human Res Mgr*
George Siepiora, *Manager*
**EMP:** 66
**SALES (corp-wide):** 13.6B **Publicly Held**
**SIC:** 3714 Heaters, motor vehicle
**PA:** Illinois Tool Works Inc.
155 Harlem Ave
Glenview IL 60025
847 724-7500

### (G-9886)
### INGERSOLL-RAND COMPANY
131 W Diversey Ave (60126-1101)
**PHONE** ..................................... 630 530-3800
**Fax:** 630 530-3908
Shaun Rigby, *Manager*
**EMP:** 50
**SQ FT:** 17,000 **Privately Held**
**WEB:** www.ingersoll-rand.com
**SIC:** 5085 5084 1081 Industrial supplies; processing & packaging equipment; metal mining services
**HQ:** Ingersoll-Rand Company
800 Beaty St Ste B
Davidson NC 28036
704 655-4000

### (G-9887)
### INLAND MIDWEST CORPORATION (HQ)
Also Called: Medtorque
612 W Lamont Rd (60126-1022)
**PHONE** ..................................... 773 775-2111
**Fax:** 773 775-4078
Steven Sundberg, *CEO*
Eric Parmacek, *Vice Pres*
Melody Austin, *Finance*
Evelyn White, *Office Mgr*
Michael Pekovitch, *Associate*
**EMP:** 49 **EST:** 1959
**SQ FT:** 25,000
**SALES (est)** 9.3MM
**SALES (corp-wide):** 3.5MM **Privately Held**
**WEB:** www.inlandmidwest.net
**SIC:** 3841 Surgical & medical instruments
**PA:** Medtorque Holdings, L.P.
1 Westminster Pl Ste 100
Lake Forest IL 60045
847 295-4410

### (G-9888)
### IRECO LLC
577 W Lamont Rd (60126-1021)
**PHONE** ..................................... 630 741-0155
Rudolph Nadherny, *Opers Mgr*
Jean Batech, *Accountant*
Rebecca Coomer, *Advt Staff*
Robert Grandy,
Robert Holden,
**EMP:** 15
**SALES (est)** 3.4MM **Privately Held**
**SIC:** 3441 Railroad car racks, for transporting vehicles; steel

### (G-9889)
### IRISH DANCING MAGAZINE
110 E Schiller St Ste 206 (60126-2822)
**PHONE** ..................................... 630 279-7521
Denise Keanegillette, *Manager*
**EMP:** 3
**SALES (est)** 217K **Privately Held**
**SIC:** 2721 Periodicals

### (G-9890)
### ITW DELTAR SEAT COMPONENT
935 N Oaklawn Ave (60126-1012)
**PHONE** ..................................... 630 993-9990
Cary Moreth, *Principal*
Fred Koller, *Manager*
◆ **EMP:** 23
**SALES (est)** 6.1MM **Privately Held**
**SIC:** 3714 Motor vehicle parts & accessories

### (G-9891)
### JINHAP US CORPORATION (HQ)
900 N Church Rd (60126-1014)
**PHONE** ..................................... 630 833-2880
Lee Young-Sup, *CEO*
**EMP:** 5 **EST:** 2013

**SALES (est)** 75.3MM
**SALES (corp-wide):** 221.2MM **Privately Held**
**SIC:** 3965 Fasteners, buttons, needles & pins
**PA:** Jinhap Co., Ltd.
42 Munpyeongseo-Ro, Daedeok-Gu
Daejeon 34302
707 430-1710

### (G-9892)
### JOHNSON CONTROLS INC
450 W Wrightwood Ave (60126-1016)
**PHONE** ..................................... 630 279-0050
Sean Margiotta, *Branch Mgr*
**EMP:** 94
**SALES (corp-wide):** 36.8B **Privately Held**
**SIC:** 2531 3714 Seats, automobile; motor vehicle body components & frame
**PA:** Johnson Controls, Inc.
5757 N Green Bay Ave
Milwaukee WI 53209
414 524-1200

### (G-9893)
### K & S SERVICE & RENTAL CORP (PA)
Also Called: All Foam Industries
471 W Monroe St (60126-4755)
**PHONE** ..................................... 630 279-4292
**Fax:** 630 279-4350
Robert W Kirchhoff, *President*
Carl Kirchhoff, *Vice Pres*
▲ **EMP:** 10
**SQ FT:** 17,000
**SALES (est)** 783.8K **Privately Held**
**SIC:** 3086 5074 Insulation or cushioning material, foamed plastic; heating equipment (hydronic)

### (G-9894)
### KAMCO REPRESENTATIVES INC
504 W Wrightwood Ave (60126-1010)
**PHONE** ..................................... 630 516-0417
Rocco Petrosino, *President*
**EMP:** 2
**SALES (est)** 202.2K **Privately Held**
**SIC:** 3432 5074 Plumbing fixture fittings & trim; plumbing & hydronic heating supplies

### (G-9895)
### KEANE GILLETTE PUBLISHING LLC
110 E Schiller St Ste 206 (60126-2822)
**PHONE** ..................................... 630 279-7521
Denise Gillette,
**EMP:** 3
**SALES (est)** 228.1K **Privately Held**
**WEB:** www.irishdancing.com
**SIC:** 2741 Miscellaneous publishing

### (G-9896)
### KEEBLER FOODS COMPANY (DH)
677 N Larch Ave (60126-1521)
**PHONE** ..................................... 630 833-2900
**Fax:** 630 833-6503
James T Willard, *Vice Pres*
E Nichol McCully, *CFO*
Roberto Stuart, *Finance Mgr*
Frank Schade, *Marketing Mgr*
Raymond Mangini, *Manager*
**EMP:** 40
**SALES (est)** 82MM
**SALES (corp-wide):** 13B **Publicly Held**
**WEB:** www.kelloggs.com
**SIC:** 2052 Cookies & crackers
**HQ:** Kellogg Usa Inc.
1 Kellogg Sq
Battle Creek MI 49017
269 961-2000

### (G-9897)
### KELLOGG COMPANY
Also Called: Kellogg's
545 W Lamont Rd (60126-1021)
**PHONE** ..................................... 630 941-0300
Frank Costanza, *Opers Mgr*
Dave Carr, *Director*
Stephanie A Anderson, *Executive Asst*
**EMP:** 160

**SALES (corp-wide):** 13B **Publicly Held**
**WEB:** www.kelloggs.com
**SIC:** 2052 2051 Cookies; cones, ice cream; crackers, dry; pretzels; bread, cake & related products
**PA:** Kellogg Company
1 Kellogg Sq
Battle Creek MI 49017
269 961-2000

### (G-9898)
### KIEFT BROS INC
837 S Riverside Dr (60126-4964)
**PHONE** ..................................... 630 832-8090
**Fax:** 630 834-5765
Patrick Spriet, *President*
Larry W Kieft, *President*
George A Smith, *President*
Shawn Bradford, *General Mgr*
Sue Owens, *Corp Secy*
**EMP:** 27 **EST:** 1948
**SQ FT:** 10,200
**SALES (est)** 8.1MM **Privately Held**
**SIC:** 3272 5032 3432 Septic tanks, concrete; manhole covers or frames, concrete; sewer pipe, clay; plumbing fixture fittings & trim

### (G-9899)
### KRUEGER AND COMPANY
Also Called: Krueger Steel & Wire
900 N Industrial Dr (60126-1181)
**PHONE** ..................................... 630 833-5650
**Fax:** 630 833-5652
Phyllis K Gillespie, *President*
David Kissel, *QC Mgr*
David Gillespie, *Sales Mgr*
Ginny Kvech, *Manager*
Sole Ofrier, *Admin Sec*
▲ **EMP:** 35 **EST:** 1946
**SQ FT:** 55,000
**SALES (est)** 18.2MM **Privately Held**
**WEB:** www.kruegersteelandwire.com
**SIC:** 3315 3316 3479 3471 Wire, steel: insulated or armored; bars, steel, cold finished, from purchased hot-rolled; coating of metals & formed products; plating & polishing

### (G-9900)
### LABELQUEST INC
493 W Fullerton Ave (60126-1404)
P.O. Box 1107 (60126-8107)
**PHONE** ..................................... 630 833-9400
Pat Vandenberg, *President*
William Sullivan, *Counsel*
Neil Vandenberg, *Vice Pres*
Maurice Carter, *Prdtn Mgr*
**EMP:** 23
**SQ FT:** 2,000
**SALES (est)** 2MM **Privately Held**
**SIC:** 2741 Miscellaneous publishing

### (G-9901)
### LHS INC
188 W Industrial Dr # 26 (60126-1623)
**PHONE** ..................................... 630 832-3875
Terry Healy, *Principal*
**EMP:** 3
**SALES (est)** 235.2K **Privately Held**
**SIC:** 3965 Fasteners

### (G-9902)
### LORETTE DIES INC
246 E 2nd St (60126-2940)
**PHONE** ..................................... 630 279-9682
Timothy Lohan, *President*
Laurel Lohan, *Vice Pres*
**EMP:** 3 **EST:** 1945
**SQ FT:** 1,500
**SALES:** 250K **Privately Held**
**SIC:** 3423 3544 Rules or rulers, metal; special dies & tools

### (G-9903)
### LOUVERS INTERNATIONAL INC
851 N Church Ct (60126-1036)
**PHONE** ..................................... 630 782-9977
**Fax:** 630 782-9991
Alfred Wall, *Ch of Bd*
Alfred J Wall, *Ch of Bd*
Peter Sheridan, *Controller*
Larry Anderson, *Manager*
Carol Wall, *Admin Sec*
▲ **EMP:** 27
**SQ FT:** 32,000

## Elmhurst - Dupage County (G-9904)

SALES (est): 7.6MM  Privately Held
SIC: 3646  Fluorescent lighting fixtures, commercial

**(G-9904)**
**M C F PRINTING COMPANY**
118 S York St Ste 212  (60126-3449)
P.O. Box 1501  (60126-8501)
PHONE.................................630 279-0301
Hal Cahill, *President*
Valerie Cahill, *Admin Sec*
EMP: 3
SALES (est): 496.3K  Privately Held
SIC: 5199  2752  Advertising specialties; commercial printing, lithographic

**(G-9905)**
**MAFOMSIC INCORPORATED**
756 N Industrial Dr  (60126-1129)
PHONE.................................630 279-2005
Fax: 630 279-2007
Jerome Cismoski, *President*
▲ EMP: 14
SQ FT: 13,000
SALES (est): 3.9MM  Privately Held
WEB: www.valachicago.com
SIC: 2891  Adhesives

**(G-9906)**
**MAHER PUBLICATIONS INC**
Also Called: Music Inc. Magazine
102 N Haven Rd  (60126-2970)
P.O. Box 906  (60126-0906)
PHONE.................................630 941-2030
Fax: 630 941-3210
Kevin Maher, *President*
Frank Alkyer, *Publisher*
Ed Enright, *Editor*
Bobby Reed, *Editor*
Ritche Deraney, *Sales Mgr*
EMP: 16  EST: 1940
SALES (est): 2.2MM  Privately Held
WEB: www.downbeat.com
SIC: 2721  Magazines: publishing only, not printed on site

**(G-9907)**
**MARK BST-PRO INC (DH)**
655 W Grand Ave Ste 220  (60126-1063)
PHONE.................................630 833-9900
Fax: 630 833-9909
Kristian Juenke, *President*
Robert Mackay, *President*
Christian Juenke, *Principal*
Allen Williams, *Opers Staff*
Ryan Florek, *Engineer*
▼ EMP: 53
SQ FT: 27,000
SALES (est): 8.7MM  Privately Held
WEB: www.bstpromark.com
SIC: 3555  Printing trades machinery
HQ: Bst Eltromat International Gmbh
    Heidsieker Heide 53
    Bielefeld  33739
    520 699-90

**(G-9908)**
**MATCON USA INC**
832 N Industrial Dr  (60126-1132)
PHONE.................................856 256-1330
▲ EMP: 13
SQ FT: 14,000
SALES (est): 5.1MM
SALES (corp-wide): 2B  Publicly Held
SIC: 3536  Mfg Hoists/Cranes/Monorails
HQ: Matcon (R & D) Limited
    Vale Park Way
    Evesham WORCS
    160 865-1666

**(G-9909)**
**MATERION BRUSH INC**
606 W Lamont Rd  (60126-1022)
PHONE.................................630 832-9650
Fax: 630 832-9657
Ginger Tripp, *Finance Mgr*
Craig Kozlow, *Branch Mgr*
EMP: 15
SALES (corp-wide): 969.2MM  Publicly Held
WEB: www.brushwellman.com
SIC: 3351  Rolled or drawn shapes: copper & copper alloy

HQ: Materion Brush Inc.
    6070 Parkland Blvd Ste 1
    Mayfield Heights OH 44124
    216 486-4200

**(G-9910)**
**MEMDEM  INC**
449 S Kenilworth Ave  (60126-3928)
PHONE.................................571 205-8778
Todd Thibodeaux, *President*
EMP: 3
SALES (est): 71.1K  Privately Held
SIC: 7372  Application computer software

**(G-9911)**
**MEXTELL INC**
459 S Cottage Hill Ave  (60126-3922)
PHONE.................................630 595-4146
Vedran Skulic, *President*
Novela Skulic, *Corp Secy*
Arna Skulic, *Manager*
EMP: 40
SQ FT: 15,000
SALES (est): 3.1MM  Privately Held
SIC: 3577  Computer peripheral equipment

**(G-9912)**
**MGSOLUTIONS INC**
451 N York St  (60126-2003)
PHONE.................................630 530-2005
Mike Grant, *Owner*
EMP: 3
SALES (est): 338K  Privately Held
SIC: 2752  Commercial printing, lithographic

**(G-9913)**
**MONARCH TOOL & DIE CO**
862 N Industrial Dr  (60126-1121)
PHONE.................................630 530-8886
Fax: 630 530-5480
Stanley Kabat, *President*
Tim Rose, *Vice Pres*
Greg Rose, *Admin Sec*
EMP: 35
SQ FT: 20,000
SALES (est): 6.1MM  Privately Held
WEB: www.monarch-tool.com
SIC: 3544  Special dies, tools, jigs & fixtures

**(G-9914)**
**N & M TYPE & DESIGN**
562 S Rex Blvd  (60126-3739)
PHONE.................................630 834-3696
Fax: 630 834-3697
Nancy Moroney, *Partner*
Mark Moroney, *Partner*
EMP: 2
SALES: 200K  Privately Held
SIC: 2791  Typesetting

**(G-9915)**
**NORTH STAR LIGHTING  LLC**
835 N Industrial Dr  (60126-1107)
PHONE.................................708 681-4330
Fax: 708 681-4006
Sabit Inan, *CEO*
Ken Cox, *Purch Agent*
Bonnie Quine, *Cust Svc Mgr*
Terry Murphy, *Director*
Judith Smatzny, *Admin Sec*
▲ EMP: 100
SQ FT: 50,000
SALES (est): 18.3MM  Privately Held
WEB: www.cameralowering.com
SIC: 3646  Commercial indusl & institutional electric lighting fixtures

**(G-9916)**
**NSA (CHI) LIQUIDATING CORP**
Also Called: Milton Division
205 E Bttrfeld Rd Ste 238  (60126)
PHONE.................................708 728-2000
Christopher Picone, *CEO*
Steve Little, *Plant Mgr*
Jeff Thibert, *Engineer*
Rick Cairo, *Project Engr*
Randy Hills, *Controller*
▲ EMP: 14
SQ FT: 200,000
SALES (est): 2.6MM  Privately Held
SIC: 3728  Gears, aircraft power transmission; aircraft power transmission equipment

**(G-9917)**
**OBERWEIS DAIRY  INC**
1018 S York St  (60126-5122)
PHONE.................................630 782-0141
Fax: 630 782-0142
Cindy Dairy, *Branch Mgr*
EMP: 15
SALES (corp-wide): 202.6MM  Privately Held
WEB: www.webfc.net
SIC: 2026  5963  5451  Milk processing (pasteurizing, homogenizing, bottling); milk delivery; milk; ice cream (packaged)
PA: Oberweis Dairy, Inc.
    951 Ice Cream Dr
    North Aurora IL 60542
    630 801-6100

**(G-9918)**
**PAN-O-GRAPHICS INC**
408 S Washington St  (60126-3938)
PHONE.................................630 834-7123
Fax: 630 834-7137
Marcella Schonta, *President*
Timothy Schonta, *Opers Mgr*
EMP: 4
SQ FT: 2,500
SALES (est): 500K  Privately Held
SIC: 3993  Signs & advertising specialties

**(G-9919)**
**PATIENTBOND  LLC**
126 N York St Ste 2  (60126-2888)
PHONE.................................312 445-8751
Anurag Juneja, *CEO*
Jonathan Phillips, *Ch of Bd*
EMP: 22
SALES (est): 549.1K  Privately Held
SIC: 7372  Application computer software

**(G-9920)**
**PATRIOT MATERIALS LLC**
750 N Industrial Dr  (60126-1129)
PHONE.................................630 501-0260
Fagan Timothy W, *Mng Member*
▲ EMP: 7
SALES (est): 804.2K  Privately Held
SIC: 3672  Printed circuit boards

**(G-9921)**
**PET CELEBRATIONS  INC**
269 N Highland Ave  (60126-2554)
PHONE.................................630 832-6549
Robin Sparacino, *President*
Thomas Sparacino, *Vice Pres*
EMP: 6
SQ FT: 2,100
SALES (est): 450K  Privately Held
WEB: www.petcelebrations.com
SIC: 2047  Dog & cat food

**(G-9922)**
**PRAIRIE DISPLAY CHICAGO INC**
758 N Industrial Dr  (60126-1129)
PHONE.................................630 834-8773
Fax: 630 834-3729
Steve Moskal, *President*
Steve Michals, *Corp Secy*
Dan Michals, *Accounts Mgr*
Marianne McGinn, *Corp Comm Staff*
EMP: 10
SALES (est): 1.4MM  Privately Held
WEB: www.prairiedisplay.com
SIC: 5046  3993  Store fixtures & display equipment; signs & advertising specialties

**(G-9923)**
**PRO-TECH METAL SPECIALTIES INC**
233 W Diversey Ave  (60126-1103)
PHONE.................................630 279-7094
Fax: 630 279-7098
Joseph R Tummillo, *President*
Mark Tummillo, *Purchasing*
Amanda Heusinkveld, *Human Resources*
Bonnie Jones, *Manager*
EMP: 28
SQ FT: 30,000
SALES (est): 5.6MM  Privately Held
WEB: www.ptechmetal.com
SIC: 3544  3469  3444  3441  Special dies, tools, jigs & fixtures; metal stampings; sheet metalwork; fabricated structural metal

**(G-9924)**
**RACEWAY ELECTRIC COMPANY INC**
270 W Saint Charles Rd  (60126-3341)
PHONE.................................630 501-1180
Kyle Rieger, *Principal*
EMP: 6  EST: 2008
SALES (est): 482K  Privately Held
SIC: 3644  Raceways

**(G-9925)**
**RANDALL MANUFACTURING LLC**
722 N Church Rd  (60126-1402)
PHONE.................................630 782-0001
Charles Carey, *Vice Pres*
Artur Zemela, *Vice Pres*
Tim Foley, *CFO*
Phillip Pick, *Controller*
Jenny Stark, *Info Tech Mgr*
◆ EMP: 60
SQ FT: 65,000
SALES (est): 19.8MM
SALES (corp-wide): 24.3MM  Privately Held
WEB: www.randallmfg.com
SIC: 3714  Motor vehicle parts & accessories
PA: Safe Fleet Investments Llc
    6800 E 163rd St
    Belton MO 64012
    844 258-8178

**(G-9926)**
**READY INC**
231 E Fremont Ave Apt 209  (60126-2469)
PHONE.................................630 501-1352
Nicole Trinidad, *Sales Mgr*
EMP: 10
SALES: 250K  Privately Held
SIC: 2759  Letterpress & screen printing

**(G-9927)**
**RED HEN BREAD INC**
745 N Larch Ave  (60126-1504)
PHONE.................................773 342-6823
Fax: 773 342-8105
Nancy T Carey, *President*
Amber McIntosh, *Manager*
Eric Mortensen, *Manager*
Robert F Carey III, *Admin Sec*
EMP: 47
SALES (est): 4.7MM
SALES (corp-wide): 6.1MM  Privately Held
WEB: www.redhenbread.com
SIC: 2051  5461  5149  Bread, cake & related products; bread; breading mixes; bakery products
PA: Red Hen Corporation
    745 N Larch Ave
    Elmhurst IL 60126
    312 433-0436

**(G-9928)**
**RED HEN CORPORATION (PA)**
Also Called: Red Hen Bread
745 N Larch Ave  (60126-1504)
PHONE.................................312 433-0436
Fax: 312 491-0410
Rober Carey III, *President*
Rose Piccetti, *Opers Staff*
Evie Copper, *Controller*
Robert E Picchietti, *Admin Sec*
EMP: 1
SALES (est): 6.1MM  Privately Held
WEB: www.redhenbread.com
SIC: 2051  Bakery: wholesale or wholesale/retail combined

**(G-9929)**
**REHLING & ASSOCIATES INC**
1010 S Swain Ave  (60126-5004)
PHONE.................................630 941-3560
William Rehling, *President*
Jim Rehling, *Vice Pres*
EMP: 3  EST: 1995
SALES: 180K  Privately Held
SIC: 3069  Fabricated rubber products

**(G-9930)**
**ROHRER GRAPHIC ARTS INC**
491 W Fullerton Ave  (60126-1476)
PHONE.................................630 832-3434
Fax: 630 832-3462

# GEOGRAPHIC SECTION

## Elmhurst - Dupage County (G-9954)

Richard A Rohrer Jr, *President*
Alice Froelich, *Manager*
Ellen Rohrer, *Shareholder*
**EMP:** 12 **EST:** 1955
**SQ FT:** 4,000
**SALES (est):** 1.2MM **Privately Held**
**SIC:** 2731 2752 2796 2791 Pamphlets: publishing & printing; lithographing on metal; platemaking services; typesetting

### (G-9931)
### ROHRER LITHO INC
487 W Fullerton Ave (60126-1404)
**PHONE** ................................... 630 833-6610
**Fax:** 630 833-1038
Eric Rohrer, *President*
Pam Nazar, *Principal*
Cindy Rohrer, *Treasurer*
**EMP:** 4
**SQ FT:** 4,000
**SALES (est):** 390K **Privately Held**
**WEB:** www.rohrerlitho.com
**SIC:** 2752 2796 2791 2789 Commercial printing, offset; platemaking services; typesetting; bookbinding & related work

### (G-9932)
### SAI ADVANCED PWR SOLUTIONS INC (PA)
Also Called: Switchboard Apparatus
618 W Lamont Rd (60126-1022)
**PHONE** ................................... 708 450-0990
Bradley K Bell, *President*
Dale Hoppensteadt, *Chairman*
David Martin, *COO*
Brian Elia, *Project Engr*
Traci Yeaton, *Design Engr*
▲ **EMP:** 26 **EST:** 1995
**SQ FT:** 50,000
**SALES:** 15.7MM **Privately Held**
**SIC:** 3613 Switchgear & switchboard apparatus; switchboards & parts, power

### (G-9933)
### SALMAN METAL
552 W Fay Ave (60126-2149)
**PHONE** ................................... 630 359-5110
Syed Iqbal, *Owner*
▼ **EMP:** 5 **EST:** 2009
**SALES (est):** 474.2K **Privately Held**
**SIC:** 3398 Metal heat treating

### (G-9934)
### SANDBAGGER LLC
Also Called: Sb Acquisition
765 S State Route 83 (60126-4228)
**PHONE** ................................... 630 876-2400
Steven Varon, *CEO*
Timothy Vandergrift, *President*
▼ **EMP:** 70
**SQ FT:** 160,000
**SALES (est):** 2.2MM **Privately Held**
**SIC:** 3599 Custom machinery

### (G-9935)
### SANDBAGGER CORP
765 S Il Route 83 (60126-4228)
P.O. Box 5798, Villa Park (60181-5309)
**PHONE** ................................... 630 876-2400
**Fax:** 630 876-8558
Timothy J Vandergrift, *President*
Kristi Hall, *Sales Staff*
Erika Thayer, *Manager*
**EMP:** 10
**SQ FT:** 2,300
**SALES:** 1MM **Privately Held**
**WEB:** www.thesandbagger.com
**SIC:** 3599 Sand riddles (hand sifting or screening apparatus)

### (G-9936)
### SEMBLEX CORPORATION (DH)
900 N Church Rd (60126-1162)
**PHONE** ................................... 630 833-2880
**Fax:** 630 941-8440
Charles D Cunningham, *President*
Jinsoo Kim, *COO*
Gregg Horath, *Mfg Mgr*
Zulma Rijos, *Purch Agent*
Eric Breidenbaugh, *Engineer*
▲ **EMP:** 95
**SQ FT:** 44,000
**SALES:** 75.3MM
**SALES (corp-wide):** 221.2MM **Privately Held**
**WEB:** www.semblex.com
**SIC:** 3452 Bolts, nuts, rivets & washers
**HQ:** Jinhap Us Corporation
900 N Church Rd
Elmhurst IL 60126
630 833-2880

### (G-9937)
### SEMBLEX CORPORATION
370 W Carol Ln (60126-1003)
**PHONE** ................................... 630 833-2880
Jose Rodriguez, *Plant Mgr*
Matt Rohde, *HR Admin*
Mark Quebbeman, *VP Sales*
Gene Simpson, *Manager*
John Grimsby, *Manager*
**EMP:** 45
**SALES (corp-wide):** 221.2MM **Privately Held**
**WEB:** www.semblex.com
**SIC:** 3452 Bolts, nuts, rivets & washers
**HQ:** Semblex Corporation
900 N Church Rd
Elmhurst IL 60126
630 833-2880

### (G-9938)
### SENTRY SEASONINGS INC
928 N Church Rd (60126-1014)
P.O. Box 1413, Park Ridge (60068-7413)
**PHONE** ................................... 630 530-5370
Carla Staniec, *President*
Wayne Staniec, *General Mgr*
**EMP:** 20
**SQ FT:** 10,000
**SALES (est):** 3.6MM **Privately Held**
**WEB:** www.sentryseasonings.com
**SIC:** 2099 Seasonings & spices

### (G-9939)
### SONGEAR HOLDING COMPANY LLC
226 N West Ave (60126-2528)
**PHONE** ................................... 630 699-1119
Robert Van Zandt,
**EMP:** 3
**SALES (est):** 290.8K **Privately Held**
**SIC:** 2389 Apparel & accessories

### (G-9940)
### SOUTH WATER SIGNS LLC
934 N Church Rd Ste B (60126-1048)
**PHONE** ................................... 630 333-4900
Thomas R Merkel, *President*
Jim Hoss, *Senior VP*
Holly Heath, *Project Mgr*
Frank Lambert, *Project Mgr*
Rob Miller, *Project Mgr*
**EMP:** 36
**SQ FT:** 50,000
**SALES:** 20.5MM **Privately Held**
**WEB:** www.southwatersigns.com
**SIC:** 3993 Signs & advertising specialties

### (G-9941)
### SPECTRUM GRAPHIC SERVICES INC
398 W Wrightwood Ave (60126-1002)
**PHONE** ................................... 630 766-7673
**Fax:** 630 766-7698
Joe Tripoli, *Owner*
Nick Menotti, *Vice Pres*
Kathy Geiken, *CFO*
Tripoli Joe, *CFO*
**EMP:** 30
**SQ FT:** 18,000
**SALES (est):** 5MM **Privately Held**
**WEB:** www.spectrumonline.com
**SIC:** 2752 Commercial printing, offset

### (G-9942)
### STENOGRAPH LLC (DH)
596 W Lamont Rd (60126-1022)
**PHONE** ................................... 630 532-5100
John Wenclawski, *President*
Reginald James, *Business Mgr*
Robert J Panfil, *Vice Pres*
Christy Mulder, *Buyer*
Vito Mangialardi, *Accounting Mgr*
**EMP:** 100
**SQ FT:** 75,000

**SALES (est):** 28.6MM
**SALES (corp-wide):** 1.3B **Privately Held**
**SIC:** 7371 3669 3579 Computer software development; intercommunication systems, electric; shorthand machines
**HQ:** Pettibone L.L.C.
27501 Bella Vista Pkwy
Warrenville IL 60555
630 353-5000

### (G-9943)
### STENOGRAPH LLC
596 W Lamont Rd (60126-1022)
**PHONE** ................................... 630 532-5100
**Fax:** 847 803-1089
John Wenclawski, *President*
**EMP:** 100 **EST:** 2010
**SALES (est):** 11.5MM
**SALES (corp-wide):** 1.7B **Privately Held**
**SIC:** 3695 Computer software tape & disks: blank, rigid & floppy
**PA:** The Heico Companies L L C
70 W Madison St Ste 5600
Chicago IL 60602
312 419-8220

### (G-9944)
### STENTECH INC
Also Called: Stentech-Chicago
853 N Industrial Dr (60126-1117)
**PHONE** ................................... 630 833-4747
Raza Khan, *Branch Mgr*
**EMP:** 4
**SALES (corp-wide):** 6.2MM **Privately Held**
**SIC:** 3952 Pencils & pencil parts, artists'
**HQ:** Stentech, Inc.
22 Manchester Rd Unit 8b
Derry NH 03038
603 505-4470

### (G-9945)
### STEVENS GROUP LLC
Also Called: Business Graphics
188 W Indl Dr Ste 428 (60126)
**PHONE** ................................... 331 209-2100
Chris Gorski, *Administration*
**EMP:** 22
**SALES (est):** 4.1MM **Privately Held**
**SIC:** 2752 Commercial printing, lithographic; offset & photolithographic printing

### (G-9946)
### SWIATEK ELECTRIC
730 N Industrial Dr (60126-1526)
**PHONE** ................................... 331 225-3052
Mario Perri, *Principal*
**EMP:** 2 **EST:** 2013
**SALES (est):** 302.7K **Privately Held**
**SIC:** 3699 Electrical equipment & supplies

### (G-9947)
### SYNSEL ENERGY INC
445 W Fullerton Ave (60126-1404)
**PHONE** ................................... 630 516-1284
Timothy Tawoda, *CEO*
Robert Brylski, *COO*
Michael Judd, *Chief Engr*
John Woodbury, *CFO*
**EMP:** 4
**SQ FT:** 1,500
**SALES (est):** 270.8K **Privately Held**
**SIC:** 2911 Diesel fuels

### (G-9948)
### TAYCORP INC
Also Called: Fay Electric Wire
752 N Larch Ave (60126-1522)
**PHONE** ................................... 630 530-7500
Phillip D Gnolfo, *Manager*
Gary Chittaro, *Manager*
Dan Diegnan, *Manager*
Luis Paez, *Manager*
**EMP:** 26
**SALES (corp-wide):** 2.7MM **Privately Held**
**WEB:** www.taylorspring.com
**SIC:** 3677 Electronic coils, transformers & other inductors
**PA:** Taycorp, Inc.
5700 W 120th St
Alsip IL 60803
708 629-0921

### (G-9949)
### TELE PRINT
494 E Atwood Ct (60126-4605)
**PHONE** ................................... 630 941-7877
Frank Troila, *Partner*
Donald Troila, *Partner*
**EMP:** 5
**SQ FT:** 1,500
**SALES:** 400K **Privately Held**
**SIC:** 2752 Commercial printing, offset

### (G-9950)
### THATCHER OAKS INC
Also Called: Thatcher Retractbles
718 N Industrial Dr (60126-1526)
**PHONE** ................................... 630 833-5700
James Patten, *President*
Nora Patten, *Pub Rel Mgr*
Kevin Eltoft, *Marketing Staff*
Nancy Nikonez, *Marketing Staff*
**EMP:** 30
**SALES (est):** 3.9MM **Privately Held**
**WEB:** www.thatcheroaks.com
**SIC:** 2394 Canvas awnings & canopies

### (G-9951)
### TREE TOWNS REPROGRAPHICS INC
Also Called: GM Mounting and Laminating
1041 N S Il Route 83 (60126-4973)
**PHONE** ................................... 630 832-0209
**Fax:** 630 832-8631
Charles W Wingard Jr, *President*
Janice Cowhey, *Managing Dir*
Bob Trimble, *Sales Staff*
Denise Wasielewski, *Office Mgr*
Tom Armstrong, *Officer*
**EMP:** 32 **EST:** 1955
**SQ FT:** 2,400
**SALES (est):** 5.7MM **Privately Held**
**WEB:** www.treetowns.com
**SIC:** 7334 7384 2752 5999 Blueprinting service; photograph developing & retouching; commercial printing, offset; drafting equipment & supplies; artists' supplies & materials; bookbinding & related work; commercial printing

### (G-9952)
### TRI VANTAGE LLC
Also Called: Geo B Carpenter Co Division
957 N Oaklawn Ave (60126-1012)
**PHONE** ................................... 630 530-5333
Ronald Paratore, *Branch Mgr*
**EMP:** 18
**SALES (corp-wide):** 746.9MM **Privately Held**
**WEB:** www.astrup.com
**SIC:** 5085 2394 Cordage; rope, except wire rope; twine; canvas & related products
**HQ:** Tri Vantage, Llc
1831 N Park Ave
Burlington NC 27217
800 786-1876

### (G-9953)
### TUTCO INC
650 W Grand Ave Ste 303 (60126-1026)
**PHONE** ................................... 630 833-5400
Ralp Homes, *Manager*
**EMP:** 180
**SALES (corp-wide):** 4.1B **Privately Held**
**WEB:** www.tutco.com
**SIC:** 3567 Heating units & devices, industrial: electric
**HQ:** Tutco, Inc.
500 Gould Dr
Cookeville TN 38506
931 432-4141

### (G-9954)
### UICO LLC
650 W Grand Ave Ste 308 (60126-1026)
**PHONE** ................................... 630 592-4400
Hiten Randhawa, *CEO*
Jason Remillard, *QC Mgr*
Scott Hoekman, *CFO*
Eric Williams, *CFO*
Teodora Filip, *Accounting Mgr*
◆ **EMP:** 50
**SQ FT:** 38,400
**SALES (est):** 11.4MM **Privately Held**
**SIC:** 3679 Electronic circuits

# Elmhurst - Dupage County (G-9955)   GEOGRAPHIC SECTION

### (G-9955)
**UNITED TECHNOLOGIES CORP**
655 W Grand Ave Ste 320 (60126-1065)
PHONE.................................630 516-3460
Cliff Akey, *Branch Mgr*
Melinda Smith, *Executive*
**EMP:** 255
**SALES (corp-wide):** 57.2B **Publicly Held**
**SIC: 3724** Aircraft engines & engine parts
**PA:** United Technologies Corporation
10 Farm Springs Rd
Farmington CT 06032
860 728-7000

### (G-9956)
**VAL-MATIC VALVE AND MFG CORP (PA)**
905 S Riverside Dr (60126-4900)
PHONE.................................630 941-7600
**Fax:** 630 941-8042
John Ballun, *CEO*
Patricia Nuter, *Ch of Bd*
Sam Dirks, *Plant Supt*
Shawn Ciombor, *Traffic Mgr*
Karen Wiencek, *Buyer*
◆ **EMP:** 115 **EST:** 1966
**SQ FT:** 118,000
**SALES (est):** 27.4MM **Privately Held**
**WEB:** www.val-matic.com
**SIC: 3491** Valves, automatic control; water works valves

### (G-9957)
**VIKING AWARDS INC**
846 N York St Ste A (60126-1239)
PHONE.................................630 833-1733
**Fax:** 630 833-9101
James Hamilton, *President*
**EMP:** 5
**SQ FT:** 4,300
**SALES (est):** 700K **Privately Held**
**SIC: 5199** 7336 3479 Advertising specialties; commercial art & graphic design; engraving jewelry silverware, or metal

### (G-9958)
**VITAL SIGNS USA**
791 N Industrial Dr (60126-1107)
PHONE.................................630 832-9600
**Fax:** 630 832-9669
Don Meyers, *President*
**EMP:** 5 **EST:** 1997
**SALES (est):** 591.6K **Privately Held**
**WEB:** www.vitalsignsusa.com
**SIC: 3993** Signs & advertising specialties

### (G-9959)
**W R S INC**
Also Called: Minuteman Press
675 W Saint Charles Rd (60126-3024)
PHONE.................................630 279-0400
William R Sturm, *President*
**EMP:** 5
**SQ FT:** 6,000
**SALES (est):** 480K **Privately Held**
**SIC: 2752** Commercial printing, lithographic

### (G-9960)
**WESCO INTERNATIONAL INC**
737 N Oaklawn Ave (60126-1405)
PHONE.................................630 513-4864
John J Engel, *CEO*
Kim Thurbush, *Financial Analy*
**EMP:** 5
**SALES (est):** 939.5K **Privately Held**
**SIC: 7361** 5063 3699 Employment agencies; electrical apparatus & equipment; electrical equipment & supplies

### (G-9961)
**WIRELESS CHAMBERLAIN PRODUCTS**
845 N Larch Ave (60126-1114)
PHONE.................................800 282-6225
Shary Nassimi, *President*
Sonia Lawhead, *Manager*
Ruth Millard, *Manager*
▲ **EMP:** 22
**SQ FT:** 15,000
**SALES (est):** 1.3MM
**SALES (corp-wide):** 1.4B **Privately Held**
**WEB:** www.chamberlaingroup.com
**SIC: 3651** 3663 3661 3669 Household audio & video equipment; television broadcasting & communications equipment; telephone & telegraph apparatus; emergency alarms
**HQ:** The Chamberlain Group Inc
300 Windsor Dr
Oak Brook IL 60523
630 279-3600

### (G-9962)
**WOODX LUMBER INC**
471 W Wrightwood Ave (60126-1011)
PHONE.................................331 979-2171
**EMP:** 3
**SALES (est):** 395K **Privately Held**
**SIC: 5031** 2426 Building materials, exterior; lumber, hardwood dimension

## Elmwood
### Peoria County

### (G-9963)
**HOME SHOPPER PUBLISHING**
208 E Hawthorne St Unit A (61529-7922)
P.O. Box 289 (61529-0289)
PHONE.................................309 742-2521
Deellda J Swindler, *Owner*
**EMP:** 7
**SALES (est):** 406.9K **Privately Held**
**SIC: 2711** Newspapers: publishing only, not printed on site

### (G-9964)
**LAMPE PUBLICATIONS**
401 W Main St (61529-9785)
P.O. Box 745 (61529-0745)
PHONE.................................309 741-9790
Jeffrey D Lampe, *Principal*
**EMP:** 2
**SALES (est):** 214.2K **Privately Held**
**SIC: 2759** Publication printing

### (G-9965)
**POWERS JOHN**
Also Called: Elmwood Locker Service
214 S Magnolia St (61529-7902)
P.O. Box 603 (61529-0603)
PHONE.................................309 742-8929
**Fax:** 309 742-7071
John Powers, *Owner*
**EMP:** 4 **EST:** 1957
**SALES (est):** 223.6K **Privately Held**
**SIC: 7299** 2013 Butcher service, processing only; sausages & other prepared meats

## Elmwood Park
### Cook County

### (G-9966)
**D & R PRESS**
7959 W Grand Ave (60707-1831)
PHONE.................................708 452-0500
David Ransom Jr, *Owner*
Daryl J Ransom, *General Mgr*
**EMP:** 8
**SQ FT:** 8,000
**SALES (est):** 1.1MM **Privately Held**
**WEB:** www.dandrpress.com
**SIC: 2759** 2752 Letterpress printing; commercial printing, offset

### (G-9967)
**ECLIPSE USA INC**
2231 N 75th Ct (60707-3034)
PHONE.................................773 816-0886
Sergio Saldana, *President*
**EMP:** 3
**SALES (est):** 344.2K **Privately Held**
**SIC: 3585** Heating & air conditioning combination units

### (G-9968)
**ELEGANT CONCEPTS LTD**
7444 W Grand Ave (60707-1911)
PHONE.................................708 456-9590
**Fax:** 708 456-9591
Joseph Faraone, *CEO*
**EMP:** 4
**SALES (est):** 1MM **Privately Held**
**SIC: 2499** Bowls, wood

### (G-9969)
**ELS ELECTRONIC LIGHTING SPC**
2715 N 77th Ave (60707-1406)
P.O. Box 423, River Grove (60171-0423)
PHONE.................................708 453-3666
Irene E Brame, *President*
James Brame, *Vice Pres*
**EMP:** 4
**SALES (est):** 350K **Privately Held**
**SIC: 3647** Vehicular lighting equipment

### (G-9970)
**FEDEX OFFICE & PRINT SVCS INC**
1720 N Harlem Ave (60707-4304)
PHONE.................................708 452-0149
George Sutton, *Manager*
**EMP:** 20
**SALES (corp-wide):** 50.3B **Publicly Held**
**WEB:** www.kinkos.com
**SIC: 7334** 2791 2789 2759 Photocopying & duplicating services; typesetting; bookbinding & related work; commercial printing
**HQ:** Fedex Office And Print Services, Inc.
7900 Legacy Dr
Plano TX 75024
214 550-7000

### (G-9971)
**FOREMOST PLASTIC PDTS CO INC**
Also Called: Foremost Plastics
7834 W Grand Ave (60707-1891)
PHONE.................................708 452-5300
**Fax:** 708 452-0446
Kenneth Muszynski, *President*
Adrian Press, *QC Dir*
Chris Fitzgerald, *Engineer*
Ken Siuba, *Sales/Mktg Mgr*
**EMP:** 44 **EST:** 1961
**SQ FT:** 37,500
**SALES (est):** 9.3MM **Privately Held**
**WEB:** www.foremostplastic.com
**SIC: 3089** Injection molded finished plastic products

### (G-9972)
**ME AND GIA INC**
7434 W North Ave (60707-4238)
PHONE.................................708 583-1111
Angelo Lollino, *Principal*
**EMP:** 5
**SALES (est):** 389.9K **Privately Held**
**SIC: 2024** Ice cream & frozen desserts

### (G-9973)
**MEDICAL LIABILITY MONITOR INC**
7234 W North Ave Ste 101 (60707-4200)
P.O. Box 680, Oak Park (60303-0680)
PHONE.................................312 944-7900
Barbara Dillard, *Principal*
James H Cunningham, *Principal*
**EMP:** 4
**SALES (est):** 261.4K **Privately Held**
**SIC: 2721** Periodicals: publishing only

### (G-9974)
**RAPID COPY & DUPLICATING CO**
7959 W Grand Ave (60707-1831)
PHONE.................................312 733-3353
**Fax:** 312 733-3635
Anthony Kara, *President*
Elissa Kara, *Corp Secy*
**EMP:** 4
**SQ FT:** 4,000
**SALES (est):** 549.2K **Privately Held**
**SIC: 2752** 7334 Commercial printing, lithographic; photocopying & duplicating services

### (G-9975)
**VAR GRAPHICS**
1743 N 75th Ct (60707-4132)
PHONE.................................708 456-2028
Orlando Vale, *President*
**EMP:** 5
**SQ FT:** 3,000
**SALES (est):** 500K **Privately Held**
**SIC: 2759** Flexographic printing

## Elsah
### Jersey County

### (G-9976)
**JACOBS REPRODUCTION**
25116 Beltrees Rd (62028-7031)
PHONE.................................618 374-2198
Stewart J Becker, *Owner*
**EMP:** 3
**SALES (est):** 120K **Privately Held**
**SIC: 2499** Decorative wood & woodwork

## Elwin
### Macon County

### (G-9977)
**ILLINOIS VALLEY PAVING CO**
Rr 51 Box S (62532)
PHONE.................................217 422-1010
Eric Roegge, *Vice Pres*
**EMP:** 37
**SQ FT:** 2,500
**SALES (corp-wide):** 10.1MM **Privately Held**
**SIC: 2951** 1611 Asphalt & asphaltic paving mixtures (not from refineries); highway & street construction
**PA:** Illinois Valley Paving Co Inc
Junction Rtes 100 & 106
Winchester IL 62694
217 742-3103

## Elwood
### Will County

### (G-9978)
**AUTOCUT MACHINE CO**
23702 S Vetter Rd (60421-9671)
PHONE.................................815 436-1900
**Fax:** 815 436-2344
Daniel R Caskey, *President*
Rita Caskey, *Corp Secy*
Maude Caskey, *Vice Pres*
**EMP:** 7 **EST:** 1967
**SQ FT:** 13,000
**SALES (est):** 918.9K **Privately Held**
**SIC: 3599** 3545 Machine shop, jobbing & repair; machine tool accessories

### (G-9979)
**BISSELL INC**
20200 Ira Morgan Dr (60421)
PHONE.................................815 423-1300
Brian Bissell, *Principal*
**EMP:** 4 **Privately Held**
**SIC: 3589** Vacuum cleaners & sweepers, electric: industrial
**HQ:** Bissell Inc.
2345 Walker Ave Nw
Grand Rapids MI 49544
616 453-4451

### (G-9980)
**EXXONMOBIL PIPELINE COMPANY**
Also Called: Joliet Refinery
Interstate 55 & Smth Brg (60421)
PHONE.................................815 423-5571
Paullette Myers, *Branch Mgr*
Raymond Duchene, *IT/INT Sup*
**EMP:** 15
**SALES (corp-wide):** 226B **Publicly Held**
**SIC: 2911** Petroleum refining
**HQ:** Exxonmobil Pipeline Company
22777 Sprngwoods Vlg Pkwy
Spring TX 77389
713 656-3636

### (G-9981)
**GEORGIA-PACIFIC LLC**
21837 W Mississippi Ave (60421-8004)
PHONE.................................815 423-9990
**EMP:** 12

# GEOGRAPHIC SECTION

**Evanston - Cook County (G-10003)**

SALES (corp-wide): 27.4B **Privately Held**
SIC: 2676 Sanitary paper products
HQ: Georgia-Pacific Llc
133 Peachtree St Ne # 4810
Atlanta GA 30303
404 652-4000

**(G-9982)**
**STEPAN COMPANY**
Also Called: Millsdale Plant
22500 Stepan Rd (60421)
PHONE..................................815 727-4944
Fax: 815 774-5376
Matthew Levinson, *Vice Pres*
Gary Traverso, *Plant Mgr*
Dennis Maskel, *Opers Mgr*
Brian Holmes, *Opers Staff*
Jim Pytlewski, *Production*
EMP: 400
SALES (corp-wide): 1.7B **Publicly Held**
WEB: www.stepan.com
SIC: 2869 2865 2821 Industrial organic chemicals; cyclic crudes & intermediates; plastics materials & resins
PA: Stepan Company
22 W Frontage Rd
Northfield IL 60093
847 446-7500

## Emden
### Logan County

**(G-9983)**
**B B MILLING CO INC**
Also Called: Bills Best Feeds
300 North St (62635-6427)
P.O. Box 289 (62635-0289)
PHONE..................................217 376-3131
Lee E Komnick, *President*
Dorothy Komnick, *Corp Secy*
EMP: 3 EST: 1942
SQ FT: 2,400
SALES (est): 100K **Privately Held**
SIC: 5191 2048 Feed; seeds: field, garden & flower; prepared feeds

## Energy
### Williamson County

**(G-9984)**
**AEROTECH INC**
403 S Pershing St (62933-3546)
P.O. Box 114 (62933-0114)
PHONE..................................618 942-5131
Terry L Griffith, *President*
Deborah H Griffith, *Corp Secy*
Frank Deutsch, *Accounting Mgr*
EMP: 59
SQ FT: 7,000
SALES: 1.8MM **Privately Held**
SIC: 3635 Household vacuum cleaners

**(G-9985)**
**CAVCO PRINTERS**
Also Called: Cavco Printers Prtg & Copy Ctr
406 N Pershing St (62933-3620)
P.O. Box 340 (62933-0340)
PHONE..................................618 988-8011
Fax: 618 988-1369
David J Normington, *Owner*
EMP: 6
SQ FT: 1,400
SALES (est): 517.5K **Privately Held**
SIC: 2752 2759 Commercial printing, offset; commercial printing

**(G-9986)**
**ENERGY CULVERT CO INC**
501 E College St (62933-3612)
P.O. Box 640 (62933-0640)
PHONE..................................618 942-7381
Fax: 618 942-7834
Ted J Kemp, *President*
Beulah Kemp, *Corp Secy*
Charles A Kemp, *Vice Pres*
EMP: 9
SQ FT: 6,000
SALES (est): 2.3MM **Privately Held**
WEB: www.energyculvert.com
SIC: 3444 5051 Culverts, sheet metal; metals service centers & offices

## Enfield
### White County

**(G-9987)**
**BIG ALS MACHINES INC**
204 Il Highway 14 (62835-2420)
P.O. Box 94 (62835-0094)
PHONE..................................618 963-2619
Allan R Kemp, *President*
Tabitha Hylton, *Administration*
EMP: 7
SALES (est): 209K **Privately Held**
SIC: 3533 Oil field machinery & equipment

## Eola
### Dupage County

**(G-9988)**
**ASBESTOS CONTROL & ENVMTL SVC**
Also Called: Storage Dem Envmtl Consulting
31 W 780 Poss Rd (60519)
P.O. Box 511, Wheaton (60187-0511)
PHONE..................................630 690-0189
Daniel Coyne, *President*
John Coyne, *Principal*
Todd Coyne, *Vice Pres*
EMP: 12
SQ FT: 9,000
SALES (est): 1MM **Privately Held**
SIC: 3292 3589 Insulation, molded asbestos; asbestos removal equipment

## Equality
### Gallatin County

**(G-9989)**
**PEABODY ARCLAR MINING LLC**
Also Called: Arclar Coal
420 Long Lane Rd (62934-2047)
P.O. Box 66846, Saint Louis MO (63166-6846)
PHONE..................................618 273-4314
John F Quinn, *Vice Pres*
James A Tichenor, *Treasurer*
Keith R Haley,
Kenneth L Wagner, *Admin Sec*
EMP: 4
SALES (est): 2.8MM
SALES (corp-wide): 4.7B **Publicly Held**
SIC: 1241 Coal mining services
PA: Peabody Energy Corporation
701 Market St
Saint Louis MO 63101
314 342-3400

**(G-9990)**
**PEABODY MIDWEST MINING LLC**
Also Called: Wildcat Hlls Cottage Grove Pit
12250 Mclain Rd (62934-2310)
PHONE..................................618 276-5006
EMP: 120
SALES (corp-wide): 5.6B **Publicly Held**
SIC: 1221 Bituminous Coal/Lignite Surface Mining
HQ: Peabody Midwest Mining, Llc
566 Dickeyville Rd
Lynnville IN 47619
812 434-8500

## Erie
### Whiteside County

**(G-9991)**
**DEINES-NITZ SOLUTIONS LLC**
721 Chase Rd (61250-9438)
PHONE..................................309 658-9985
Fax: 309 658-9986
Greg J Deines, *President*
Mark S Nitz, *Vice Pres*
Becky Kranovich, *Financial Exec*
Brian Deines, *Sales Staff*
EMP: 45
SALES (est): 9MM **Privately Held**
SIC: 2621 Packaging paper; wrapping & packaging papers; specialty or chemically treated papers

**(G-9992)**
**GOLD STAR FS INC**
9087 Moline Rd (61250-9757)
PHONE..................................309 659-2801
Fax: 309 659-2232
Jeff Wirth, *Manager*
EMP: 6
SALES (corp-wide): 224.2MM **Privately Held**
SIC: 2873 Fertilizers: natural (organic), except compost
PA: Gold Star Fs, Inc.
101 N East St
Cambridge IL 61238
309 937-3369

**(G-9993)**
**REVIEW**
Also Called: Wns Publication
910 Albany St (61250-7766)
P.O. Box 357 (61250-0357)
PHONE..................................309 659-2761
Tony Komlanc, *President*
EMP: 4
SALES (est): 179.5K **Privately Held**
SIC: 2711 Newspapers

## Eureka
### Woodford County

**(G-9994)**
**C TRI CO**
1035 W Center St (61530-9558)
PHONE..................................309 467-4715
Fax: 309 467-3667
Richard D McCollum, *President*
Richard McCollum, *President*
Sherman Brewer, *General Mgr*
Kelly Hatfield, *Business Mgr*
Kenneth Brown, *Mfg Staff*
EMP: 32
SQ FT: 21,000
SALES (est): 7.3MM **Privately Held**
WEB: www.triccompany.com
SIC: 7373 3599 3544 Computer-aided design (CAD) systems service; machine shop, jobbing & repair; special dies, tools, jigs & fixtures

**(G-9995)**
**COLUMBUS MCKINNON CORPORATION**
Also Called: Washington Equipment Company
801 W Center St (61530-9501)
PHONE..................................800 548-2930
Jeff Borders, *Branch Mgr*
EMP: 134
SALES (corp-wide): 637.1MM **Publicly Held**
WEB: www.cmworks.com
SIC: 3536 Hoists
PA: Columbus Mckinnon Corporation
205 Crosspoint Pkwy
Getzville NY 14068
716 689-5400

**(G-9996)**
**CRANE EQUIPMENT & SERVICES INC (HQ)**
Also Called: Ces Material Handling
801 W Center St (61530-9501)
PHONE..................................309 467-6262
Fax: 309 467-5118
Jeff Borders, *Opers Mgr*
Bruce Chadderton, *Opers Mgr*
Brian Overly, *Engineer*
Kim Hake, *CFO*
Sherri Boyer, *Human Res Mgr*
EMP: 30
SQ FT: 96,000
SALES: 13MM
SALES (corp-wide): 637.1MM **Publicly Held**
WEB: www.washequip.com
SIC: 5084 3536 Materials handling machinery; hoists, cranes & monorails
PA: Columbus Mckinnon Corporation
205 Crosspoint Pkwy
Getzville NY 14068
716 689-5400

**(G-9997)**
**DIE DARRELL**
106 W Burton Ave (61530-1302)
PHONE..................................309 282-9112
Darrell Dies, *Psychologist*
E Dies, *Executive Asst*
EMP: 5 EST: 2007
SALES (est): 466.1K **Privately Held**
SIC: 3544 Special dies & tools

**(G-9998)**
**EUREKA LOCKER INC**
110 4h Park Rd (61530-1706)
P.O. Box 194 (61530-0194)
PHONE..................................309 467-2731
Fax: 309 467-2731
Scott Bittner, *Owner*
EMP: 10
SQ FT: 3,000
SALES (est): 275K **Privately Held**
SIC: 2011 4222 2013 Meat packing plants; storage, frozen or refrigerated goods; sausages & other prepared meats

**(G-9999)**
**MCDOWELL INC**
809 W Center St (61530-9501)
PHONE..................................309 467-2335
William M Frederick, *President*
EMP: 6
SALES (est): 550K **Privately Held**
SIC: 3589 Sewage & water treatment equipment

**(G-10000)**
**PAUL D BURTON**
Also Called: Eureka Printing & Stationery
124 N Main St (61530-1157)
PHONE..................................309 467-2613
Fax: 309 467-2601
Paul Burton, *Owner*
EMP: 4
SQ FT: 2,000
SALES: 150K **Privately Held**
SIC: 2752 2759 Lithographing on metal; letterpress printing

## Evanston
### Cook County

**(G-10001)**
**ABRA ENTERPRISES INC**
606 Sheridan Rd Apt 1e (60202-3139)
PHONE..................................847 866-6903
Melvin S Lindberg Jr, *President*
Robert Rekowski, *Vice Pres*
EMP: 6
SQ FT: 3,000
SALES (est): 480K **Privately Held**
SIC: 3541 3672 7629 3625 Electrochemical milling machines; printed circuit boards; electrical equipment repair services; business machine repair, electric; circuit board repair; relays & industrial controls

**(G-10002)**
**ACCRUENT LLC**
500 Davis St Ste 1000 (60201-4643)
PHONE..................................847 425-3600
Fax: 847 425-1675
Lisa Thompson, *Office Mgr*
EMP: 3 **Privately Held**
SIC: 7372 Prepackaged software
HQ: Accruent, Llc
11500 Alterra Pkwy # 110
Austin TX 78758

**(G-10003)**
**ACCUITY INC**
1007 Church St Ste 600 (60201-5930)
PHONE..................................847 676-9600
Fax: 847 933-8101
Hugh M Jones IV, *President*
Jay Ryan, *Managing Dir*
Joel Lange, *Business Mgr*
Brent Newman, *Exec VP*
Ken Fogarty, *Senior VP*

# Evanston - Cook County (G-10004)

**EMP:** 294
**SQ FT:** 18,000
**SALES (est):** 49.3MM
**SALES (corp-wide):** 8.4B **Privately Held**
**SIC:** 7374 7372 Data processing service; application computer software
**PA:** Relx Plc
1-3 Strand
London WC2N
207 166-5500

### (G-10004)
### ACCUTONE HEARING AID INC
1580 Sherman Ave (60201-4465)
**PHONE** ..................773 545-3279
Stege Kim, *Principal*
**EMP:** 3
**SALES (est):** 221.2K **Privately Held**
**SIC:** 3842 Hearing aids

### (G-10005)
### AGATE PUBLISHING INC
1328 Greenleaf St (60202-1153)
**PHONE** ..................847 475-4457
Douglas Seibold, *President*
David Schlesinger, *Manager*
Suzanne Sonnier, *Director*
▲ **EMP:** 2
**SALES (est):** 249.2K **Privately Held**
**SIC:** 2741 Miscellaneous publishing

### (G-10006)
### ALEXANDER TECHNIQUE
1830 Sherman Ave Ste 302 (60201-3772)
**PHONE** ..................847 337-7926
John Henes, *Owner*
**EMP:** 3
**SALES (est):** 209.3K **Privately Held**
**SIC:** 3221 Medicine bottles, glass

### (G-10007)
### ALL FRESH FOOD PRODUCTS (PA)
2156 Green Bay Rd (60201-3046)
**PHONE** ..................847 864-5030
**Fax:** 847 869-3103
Gulshan Wadhwa, *Owner*
Anil Wadhwa, *Vice Pres*
**EMP:** 1
**SQ FT:** 15,000
**SALES (est):** 21.8MM **Privately Held**
**SIC:** 2079 Edible fats & oils

### (G-10008)
### ALLFRESH FOOD PRODUCTS INC (HQ)
2156 Green Bay Rd (60201-3046)
**PHONE** ..................847 869-3100
Gulshan Wadhwa, *President*
**EMP:** 3 **EST:** 1952
**SQ FT:** 15,000
**SALES (est):** 21.8MM **Privately Held**
**SIC:** 2079 Edible fats & oils
**PA:** All Fresh Food Products
2156 Green Bay Rd
Evanston IL 60201
847 864-5030

### (G-10009)
### AMERICAN BIOOPTICS LLC
1801 Maple Ave Ste 4316 (60201-3149)
**PHONE** ..................847 467-0628
Andrew Cittadine,
▲ **EMP:** 5
**SQ FT:** 1,500
**SALES (est):** 380K **Privately Held**
**WEB:** www.americanbiooptics.com
**SIC:** 3841 Diagnostic apparatus, medical

### (G-10010)
### ANATOMICAL WORLDWIDE LLC
Also Called: Anatomywarehouse.com
1630 Darrow Ave (60201-3418)
**PHONE** ..................312 224-4772
Thomas Stelter, *Principal*
Alicia Kull, *Finance Dir*
Liz Huff, *Mktg Dir*
Linda Jacobs, *Manager*
Adam Cordell,
▲ **EMP:** 8
**SQ FT:** 30,000
**SALES (est):** 3MM **Privately Held**
**SIC:** 3842 5961 Models, anatomical; catalog & mail-order houses

### (G-10011)
### ARLAND CLEAN FUELS LLC
630 Davis St Ste 300 (60201-4480)
**PHONE** ..................847 868-8580
Louis Stern,
**EMP:** 5
**SQ FT:** 3,000
**SALES (est):** 421.4K **Privately Held**
**SIC:** 2911 Fractionation products of crude petroleum, hydrocarbons

### (G-10012)
### ASHLEY LAUREN
Also Called: Ashley Lauren Natural Products
636 Church St Ste 701 (60201-6031)
**PHONE** ..................847 733-9470
Georgia Parker, *Owner*
**EMP:** 5
**SALES (est):** 437K **Privately Held**
**SIC:** 2841 Textile soap

### (G-10013)
### ASHTON GILL PUBLISHING LLC
Also Called: Foodservice Equipment Reports
2906 Central St Fl 1 (60201-1283)
**PHONE** ..................847 673-8675
**Fax:** 847 673-8679
Robin Ashton,
Jessica Scurlock, *Assistant*
**EMP:** 11
**SQ FT:** 1,422
**SALES (est):** 2.9MM **Privately Held**
**SIC:** 2721 Trade journals: publishing & printing

### (G-10014)
### BELGIAN CHOCOLATIER PIRON INC
509 Main St Fl A (60202-4539)
**PHONE** ..................847 864-5504
Robert F Piron, *President*
Fred Piron, *Vice Pres*
Sigfried Piron, *Vice Pres*
**EMP:** 3
**SALES (est):** 200K **Privately Held**
**WEB:** www.belgchocpiron.com
**SIC:** 5441 2064 2066 Candy, nut & confectionery stores; candy & other confectionery products; chocolate & cocoa products

### (G-10015)
### BERNARD FOOD INDUSTRIES INC (PA)
1125 Hartrey Ave (60202-1035)
P.O. Box 1497 (60204-1497)
**PHONE** ..................847 869-5222
**Fax:** 847 679-5417
Steven F Bernard, *President*
Jules F Bernard, *President*
John Zabraus, *Division Mgr*
Lou Haan, *Vice Pres*
Ed Zabraus, *Plant Mgr*
**EMP:** 89
**SQ FT:** 42,000
**SALES (est):** 18MM **Privately Held**
**WEB:** www.bernardfoods.com
**SIC:** 2099 2034 Food preparations; dehydrated fruits, vegetables, soups

### (G-10016)
### BIOSPAWN LURE CO
9332 Hamlin Ave (60203-1302)
**PHONE** ..................773 458-0752
**EMP:** 4 **EST:** 2015
**SALES (est):** 296.8K **Privately Held**
**SIC:** 3949 Lures, fishing: artificial

### (G-10017)
### BOTTI STUDIO OF ARCHITECTURAL (PA)
919 Grove St (60201-4315)
**PHONE** ..................847 869-5933
**Fax:** 847 869-5996
Ettore C Botti, *CEO*
Michael Kent, *Finance*
Magene Brady, *Administration*
**EMP:** 40 **EST:** 1864
**SQ FT:** 25,000

**SALES (est):** 7.8MM **Privately Held**
**WEB:** www.bottistudio.com
**SIC:** 3231 3446 3281 2431 Stained glass: made from purchased glass; architectural metalwork; marble, building: cut & shaped; ornamental woodwork: cornices, mantels, etc.; glass & glazing work; interior design services

### (G-10018)
### BUILDERS READY-MIX CO
2525 Oakton St (60202-2759)
**PHONE** ..................847 866-6300
**Fax:** 847 866-6313
Thomas Sobczak, *President*
Mark Ronan, *Vice Pres*
Maria Sobczak, *Treasurer*
Judy Ronan, *Admin Sec*
**EMP:** 25
**SQ FT:** 3,000
**SALES (est):** 5MM **Privately Held**
**SIC:** 3273 Ready-mixed concrete

### (G-10019)
### CATALYST PAPER
960 Grove St (60201-4316)
**PHONE** ..................224 307-2650
**EMP:** 3 **EST:** 2015
**SALES (est):** 72.1K **Privately Held**
**SIC:** 2711 Newspapers

### (G-10020)
### CHARLES SHERIDAN AND SONS
2331 Church St (60201-3940)
**PHONE** ..................847 903-7209
Charles Sheridan, *Owner*
**EMP:** 5 **EST:** 2011
**SALES:** 100K **Privately Held**
**SIC:** 3442 1611 Window & door frames; general contractor, highway & street construction

### (G-10021)
### CHARTWELL STUDIO INC
824 Sheridan Rd (60202-2513)
**PHONE** ..................847 868-8674
Jeanette McCallum, *Principal*
**EMP:** 2
**SALES (est):** 8MM **Privately Held**
**SIC:** 2621 2782 5092 Wallpaper (hanging paper); scrapbooks; arts & crafts equipment & supplies

### (G-10022)
### CHASE CORPORATION
Tapecoat Company
1527 Lyons St (60201-3551)
P.O. Box 631 (60204-9031)
**PHONE** ..................847 866-8500
**Fax:** 847 866-8596
Juan Lopez, *COO*
Kip Bennett, *Vice Pres*
Charles Heroux, *Vice Pres*
Jill Blakemore, *Accounting Mgr*
Dick Reeves, *Branch Mgr*
**EMP:** 50
**SALES (corp-wide):** 238MM **Publicly Held**
**WEB:** www.chasecorp.com
**SIC:** 2672 2891 2851 2241 Adhesive papers, labels or tapes: from purchased material; adhesives & sealants; paints & allied products; narrow fabric mills
**PA:** Chase Corporation
295 University Ave
Westwood MA 02090
508 819-4200

### (G-10023)
### CHICAGO TANK LINING SALES
3603 Hillside Rd (60201-4936)
**PHONE** ..................847 328-0500
**Fax:** 847 328-0620
Warren Brand, *President*
Kenneth Brand, *Vice Pres*
Sheila Brand, *Admin Sec*
**EMP:** 9
**SQ FT:** 3,000
**SALES:** 1.1MM **Privately Held**
**SIC:** 7699 3479 3443 Tank repair & cleaning services; tank repair; painting, coating & hot dipping; liners/lining; liners, industrial: metal plate

### (G-10024)
### CHRISTIAN NATIONAL WOMANS (PA)
Also Called: SIGNAL PRESS DIVISION
1730 Chicago Ave Ste 4585 (60201-4502)
**PHONE** ..................847 864-1396
**Fax:** 847 864-9497
Sarah F Ward, *President*
**EMP:** 3 **EST:** 1874
**SALES:** 400.2K **Privately Held**
**SIC:** 8661 2731 Religious organizations; book publishing

### (G-10025)
### DARD PRODUCTS INC
Also Called: Tag Master Line
912 Custer Ave (60201-1897)
**PHONE** ..................847 328-5000
**Fax:** 847 328-7835
Cary J Shevin, *President*
Sal Marsiglia, *General Mgr*
Eric Esz, *Opers Mgr*
Joanne Molina, *Purch Dir*
Rebecca Harris, *Purchasing*
▲ **EMP:** 200 **EST:** 1946
**SQ FT:** 75,000
**SALES (est):** 36.8MM **Privately Held**
**WEB:** www.tagmaster.net
**SIC:** 3993 7311 Signs & advertising specialties; advertising consultant

### (G-10026)
### DEAN PRSTHTIC ORTHTIC SVCS LTD
Also Called: Dean P & O Services
2530 Crawford Ave Ste 218 (60201-4959)
**PHONE** ..................847 475-7080
**Fax:** 847 475-0241
Linda Dean, *Owner*
Linda Jernigan, *Owner*
**EMP:** 5
**SQ FT:** 1,500
**SALES (est):** 277.3K **Privately Held**
**WEB:** www.deanprosthetics.com
**SIC:** 8011 3842 Specialized medical practitioners, except internal; surgical appliances & supplies

### (G-10027)
### DEPTH ACTION MARKETING GROUP
2512 Lawndale Ave (60201-1158)
**PHONE** ..................847 475-7122
Walter Holdamf, *President*
Sylvia Holdamf, *Corp Secy*
**EMP:** 4
**SALES:** 500K **Privately Held**
**SIC:** 3299 Images, small: gypsum, clay or papier mache

### (G-10028)
### DFG MERCURY CORP
Also Called: Df Goldsmith
909 Pitner Ave (60202-1550)
**PHONE** ..................847 869-7800
Robert P Goldsmith, *President*
James Moran, *Vice Pres*
Kathy Steiner, *Manager*
**EMP:** 5
**SQ FT:** 5,500
**SALES (est):** 955.7K
**SALES (corp-wide):** 6MM **Privately Held**
**WEB:** www.dfgoldsmith.com
**SIC:** 2819 Mercury, redistilled
**PA:** D. F. Goldsmith Chemical & Metal Corporation
909 Pitner Ave
Evanston IL
847 869-7800

### (G-10029)
### DOUBLETAKE MARKETING INC
54 Williamsburg Rd (60203-1813)
**PHONE** ..................845 598-3175
**EMP:** 2
**SALES (est):** 226.1K **Privately Held**
**SIC:** 2752 Commercial printing, lithographic

### (G-10030)
### ENHANCED PLASMONICS LLC
820 Davis St Ste 216 (60201-4445)
**PHONE** ..................904 238-9270
Nathan Greenelltch,
Martin Blaber,

**EMP:** 4
**SALES (est):** 250K **Privately Held**
**SIC:** 3826 Infrared analytical instruments

### (G-10031)
### ERDCO ENGINEERING CORPORATION
721 Custer Ave (60202-2200)
P.O. Box 6318 (60204-6318)
**PHONE**....................847 328-0550
**Fax:** 847 328-3535
Bruce Nesvig, *President*
Robert Jeske, *Admin Sec*
**EMP:** 50 **EST:** 1946
**SQ FT:** 21,000
**SALES (est):** 10.2MM **Privately Held**
**WEB:** www.erdco.com
**SIC:** 3823 3825 3824 3829 Industrial instrmnts msrmnt display/control process variable; flow instruments, industrial process type; instruments to measure electricity; fluid meters & counting devices; measuring & controlling devices

### (G-10032)
### EVANSTON AWNING COMPANY
2801 Central St (60201-1200)
**PHONE**....................847 864-4520
**Fax:** 847 864-5886
Edward P Hunzinger Jr, *President*
Ann Hunzinger, *Admin Sec*
**EMP:** 13
**SQ FT:** 7,200
**SALES:** 1MM **Privately Held**
**WEB:** www.evanstonawning.com
**SIC:** 2394 5999 Awnings, fabric: made from purchased materials; canvas products

### (G-10033)
### EVANSTON GRAPHIC IMAGING INC
Also Called: Allegra Print & Imaging
1255 Hartrey Ave (60202-1056)
**PHONE**....................847 869-7446
Frank Muns, *President*
Kyle Kurz, *Vice Pres*
▲ **EMP:** 9 **EST:** 1962
**SQ FT:** 47,000
**SALES (est):** 1.7MM **Privately Held**
**SIC:** 2752 3663 2759 Commercial printing, offset; digital encoders; letterpress printing

### (G-10034)
### EVANSTON SENTINEL CORPORATION
Also Called: The Evanston Sentinel Newsppr
1229 Emerson St Ste 2w (60201-3524)
P.O. Box 5683 (60204-5683)
**PHONE**....................847 492-0177
**Fax:** 847 424-1623
Bennett J Johnson, *President*
Kathleen H Lucas, *Admin Sec*
**EMP:** 8
**SALES (est):** 483.3K **Privately Held**
**SIC:** 2711 Newspapers, publishing & printing

### (G-10035)
### EVE J ALFILLE LTD
Also Called: Eve J Alfille Gallery & Studio
623 Grove St (60201-4403)
**PHONE**....................847 869-7920
**Fax:** 847 869-5451
Eve J Alfille, *President*
Diane Alfille, *Vice Pres*
Cato Heinz, *Sales Mgr*
Maurice Alfille, *Admin Sec*
**EMP:** 20
**SQ FT:** 3,600
**SALES:** 2MM **Privately Held**
**WEB:** www.alfille.com
**SIC:** 5944 3911 Jewelry, precious stones & precious metals; jewel settings & mountings, precious metal

### (G-10036)
### FEDEX OFFICE & PRINT SVCS INC
2518 Green Bay Rd (60201-2231)
**PHONE**....................847 475-8650
Lynnette Strobel, *Manager*
**EMP:** 15

**SALES (corp-wide):** 50.3B **Publicly Held**
**WEB:** www.kinkos.com
**SIC:** 7334 2791 2789 Photocopying & duplicating services; typesetting; bookbinding & related work
**HQ:** Fedex Office And Print Services, Inc.
7900 Legacy Dr
Plano TX 75024
214 550-7000

### (G-10037)
### FILMFAX MAGAZINE INC
Also Called: Outre'
1320 Oakton St (60202-2719)
**PHONE**....................847 866-7155
**Fax:** 847 866-7554
Michael Stein, *President*
**EMP:** 2
**SALES (est):** 229.6K **Privately Held**
**SIC:** 2721 5942 Magazines: publishing only, not printed on site; book stores

### (G-10038)
### FLOW VALVES INTERNATIONAL LLC
500 Davis St Ste 600 (60201-4622)
**PHONE**....................847 866-1188
George Stevenson, *Mng Member*
Cliff Deremo, *Mng Member*
**EMP:** 2
**SALES (est):** 228.5K **Privately Held**
**SIC:** 3492 Fluid power valves & hose fittings

### (G-10039)
### FRANK S JOHNSON & COMPANY
Also Called: Franks Auto Insurance A Div BR
1718 Sherman Ave Ste 211 (60201-5610)
**PHONE**....................847 492-1660
**Fax:** 847 492-1663
Frank S Johnson, *President*
John B Galbraith Jr, *Admin Sec*
Richard F Johnson, *Admin Sec*
**EMP:** 3
**SALES:** 1.3MM **Privately Held**
**WEB:** www.franksjohnsoninsurance.com
**SIC:** 2951 6411 Asphalt & asphaltic paving mixtures (not from refineries); insurance agents, brokers & service

### (G-10040)
### FRANKS MAINTENANCE & ENGRG
Also Called: Forking By Frank
945 Pitner Ave (60202-1550)
**PHONE**....................847 475-1003
Mary Stankovich, *President*
Douglas Graham, *Admin Sec*
**EMP:** 6 **EST:** 1961
**SQ FT:** 3,500
**SALES:** 400K **Privately Held**
**SIC:** 5013 3312 3751 Motorcycle parts; pipes, iron & steel; motorcycles, bicycles & parts

### (G-10041)
### GENERATION COPY INC
960 Grove St (60201-4316)
**PHONE**....................847 866-0469
**Fax:** 847 866-1871
Cornelius D Scott, *President*
Caesar Scott, *Admin Asst*
**EMP:** 6
**SQ FT:** 770
**SALES (est):** 646.4K **Privately Held**
**SIC:** 2752 Commercial printing, lithographic

### (G-10042)
### GERMANN INSTRUMENTS INC
8845 Forestview Rd (60203-1924)
**PHONE**....................847 329-9999
**Fax:** 847 329-8888
Claus Petersen, *President*
Mariana Lara, *Vice Pres*
Tom Nakaguchi, *Office Mgr*
**EMP:** 7
**SALES (est):** 1.2MM **Privately Held**
**WEB:** www.germann.org
**SIC:** 3829 Surveying & drafting equipment

### (G-10043)
### GOOSE PRINTING CO
8833 Ewing Ave (60203-1904)
**PHONE**....................847 673-1414
Stuart Garber, *Owner*
**EMP:** 3
**SALES (est):** 265.9K **Privately Held**
**SIC:** 2752 Commercial printing, lithographic

### (G-10044)
### GORDON BURKE JOHN PUBLISHER
1032 Cleveland St (60202-2113)
**PHONE**....................847 866-8625
John Gordon Burke, *President*
**EMP:** 6
**SALES (est):** 386.7K **Privately Held**
**WEB:** www.jgburkepub.com
**SIC:** 2731 Textbooks: publishing only, not printed on site

### (G-10045)
### GRANDSTAND PUBLISHING LLC
Also Called: Baseball Digest
990 Grove St Ste 400 (60201-4370)
**PHONE**....................847 491-6440
Norman Jacobs, *Publisher*
**EMP:** 7
**SQ FT:** 1,200
**SALES (est):** 433.2K **Privately Held**
**SIC:** 2721 Magazines: publishing only, not printed on site

### (G-10046)
### GRANT WOOD WORKS
2204 Green Bay Rd (60201-3027)
**PHONE**....................847 328-4349
David Trippel, *Owner*
**EMP:** 4
**SQ FT:** 2,400
**SALES:** 150K **Privately Held**
**SIC:** 2511 Wood household furniture

### (G-10047)
### GTX SURGERY INC
848 Dodge Ave Unit 384 (60202-1506)
**PHONE**....................847 920-8489
Samuel Glassenberg, *CEO*
**EMP:** 3
**SALES (est):** 78.2K **Privately Held**
**SIC:** 7372 Educational computer software

### (G-10048)
### H & H PRINTING
1800 Dempster St (60202-1003)
**PHONE**....................847 866-9520
William Holloway, *President*
**EMP:** 6 **EST:** 1970
**SQ FT:** 5,000
**SALES (est):** 487.5K **Privately Held**
**SIC:** 2759 Commercial printing

### (G-10049)
### HALPER PUBLISHING COMPANY
913 Forest Ave Apt 2s (60202-5408)
**PHONE**....................847 542-9793
**Fax:** 847 433-6602
Rick Levine, *President*
**EMP:** 4 **EST:** 1930
**SQ FT:** 1,300
**SALES (est):** 363.9K **Privately Held**
**WEB:** www.halper.com
**SIC:** 2721 2741 Magazines: publishing only, not printed on site; directories: publishing only, not printed on site

### (G-10050)
### HARRY J BOSWORTH COMPANY (PA)
820 Davis St Ste 216 (60201-4445)
**PHONE**....................847 679-3400
**Fax:** 847 679-2080
Mildred Goldstein, *President*
Martin Herbst, *General Mgr*
Herbert Pozen, *Vice Pres*
Robert Mitchell, *Purchasing*
Murray Herbest, *Sales Mgr*
▲ **EMP:** 40 **EST:** 1912
**SQ FT:** 50,000

**SALES (est):** 6.4MM **Privately Held**
**WEB:** www.bosworth.com
**SIC:** 3843 8021 2821 Dental equipment & supplies; offices & clinics of dentists; plastics materials & resins

### (G-10051)
### HINMAN SPECIALTY FUELS
825 Elmwood Ave (60202-4952)
**PHONE**....................847 868-6026
**EMP:** 3
**SALES (est):** 182.5K **Privately Held**
**SIC:** 2869 Fuels

### (G-10052)
### HOUGHTON MIFFLIN HARCOURT PUBG
909 Davis St Ste 300 (60201-3645)
**PHONE**....................847 869-2300
Kim Logue, *Sales Staff*
Caroline Chen, *Manager*
Raj Desai, *Manager*
Jennifer Raimi, *Consultant*
**EMP:** 350
**SALES (corp-wide):** 1.3B **Publicly Held**
**WEB:** www.hmco.com
**SIC:** 2731 Book publishing
**HQ:** Houghton Mifflin Harcourt Publishing Company
125 High St Ste 900
Boston MA 02110
617 351-5000

### (G-10053)
### HOUGHTON MIFFLIN HARCOURT PUBG
McDougal Littell
1560 Sherman Ave (60201-4818)
P.O. Box 1667 (60204-1667)
**PHONE**....................708 869-2300
**Fax:** 847 869-2598
Julie A Mc Gee, *President*
Toni Horner, *Database Admin*
**EMP:** 300
**SALES (corp-wide):** 1.3B **Publicly Held**
**WEB:** www.hmco.com
**SIC:** 2731 Textbooks: publishing only, not printed on site
**HQ:** Houghton Mifflin Harcourt Publishing Company
125 High St Ste 900
Boston MA 02110
617 351-5000

### (G-10054)
### HOUSE OF ATLAS LLC
1578 Sherman Ave Fl 2 (60201-4484)
**PHONE**....................847 491-1800
Matthew Berman,
Jason Moss,
**EMP:** 6
**SALES (est):** 632.7K **Privately Held**
**SIC:** 2591 Drapery hardware & blinds & shades

### (G-10055)
### INCLUSION SOLUTIONS LLC
2000 Greenleaf St Ste 3 (60202-1083)
**PHONE**....................847 869-2500
Anthony Golec, *Warehouse Mgr*
Michael De Baskin, *VP Sales*
Patrick Hughes,
Dawn Betz, *Admin Asst*
▲ **EMP:** 7
**SALES (est):** 990K **Privately Held**
**WEB:** www.inclusionsolutions.com
**SIC:** 3663 Radio & TV communications equipment

### (G-10056)
### INNOVATIONS FOR LEARNING INC
Also Called: SOFTWARE FOR SUCCESS
518 Davis St (60201-4644)
**PHONE**....................800 975-3452
Seth Weinburger, *President*
Caryn Weiner, *Editor*
Randy Burgess, *CTO*
Frank Spranze, *Info Tech Mgr*
Sandra C Jerald, *Director*
**EMP:** 5
**SALES:** 2MM **Privately Held**
**WEB:** www.innovationsforlearning.org
**SIC:** 7372 Prepackaged software

# Evanston - Cook County (G-10057) — GEOGRAPHIC SECTION

**(G-10057)**
**INNOVTIVE DESIGN GRAPHICS CORP**
Also Called: Innovative Design & Graphics
1327 Greenleaf St 1 (60202-1152)
PHONE.................847 475-7772
Fax: 847 475-7784
Tim Sonder, *President*
EMP: 4
SQ FT: 1,500
SALES (est): 656.6K **Privately Held**
WEB: www.insoftdesign.com
SIC: 2791 7336 2752 Typesetting; graphic arts & related design; commercial printing, lithographic

**(G-10058)**
**INTELLIDRAIN INC**
600 Davis St Fl 3 (60201-4488)
PHONE.................312 725-4332
Adam Piotrowski, *CEO*
Ankit Bharat MD, *Ch of Bd*
EMP: 4
SQ FT: 1,500
SALES (est): 140K **Privately Held**
SIC: 8731 3845 Medical research, commercial; respiratory analysis equipment, electromedical

**(G-10059)**
**JOHN HARDY CO**
Also Called: Hardy Company, The
1728 Brummel St (60202-3738)
PHONE.................847 864-8060
John Hardy, *President*
Charles R Goerth, *Admin Sec*
EMP: 5
SALES: 200K **Privately Held**
SIC: 3651 Audio electronic systems

**(G-10060)**
**JUST YOUR TYPE INC**
1800 Dempster St (60202-1003)
PHONE.................847 864-8890
Fax: 847 866-6466
William Holloway, *President*
EMP: 5
SQ FT: 1,500
SALES (est): 380K **Privately Held**
SIC: 7336 2791 Graphic arts & related design; typesetting

**(G-10061)**
**KIMMY COMPOST INC**
807 Oakton St (60202-2826)
PHONE.................847 372-9201
EMP: 3
SALES (est): 209.6K **Privately Held**
SIC: 2875 Compost

**(G-10062)**
**L P M INC**
Also Called: Minuteman Press
1553 Sherman Ave (60201-4421)
PHONE.................847 866-9777
Fax: 847 866-9888
Lisa Pharris Moran, *President*
Peter Moran, *Vice Pres*
Herbert Rivero, *Admin Asst*
EMP: 6
SALES (est): 540K **Privately Held**
SIC: 2752 7334 7336 Commercial printing, lithographic; photocopying & duplicating services; commercial art & graphic design

**(G-10063)**
**LAKELAND BOATING MAGAZINE**
Also Called: O'Meara/Brown Publications
630 Davis St Ste 301 (60201-4480)
PHONE.................312 276-0610
Fax: 630 276-0619
Walter B O'Meara, *President*
Linda O'Meara, *Mktg Dir*
Patti McCleery, *Manager*
Kate Bush, *Director*
Christy T Bauhs, *Art Dir*
EMP: 9
SALES (est): 1MM **Privately Held**
SIC: 2721 Magazines: publishing only, not printed on site

**(G-10064)**
**LAKESIDE PUBLISHING CO LLC**
990 Grove St Ste 400 (60201-4370)
PHONE.................847 491-6440
Barry Jacobs, *Principal*
Dale Jacobs, *Director*
Nancy Janus, *Administration*
EMP: 5
SALES (est): 420K **Privately Held**
SIC: 2721 Magazines: publishing only, not printed on site

**(G-10065)**
**LOCHMAN REF SILK SCREEN CO**
Also Called: R.E.F. Silk Screen Productions
2405 Oakton St (60202-2743)
PHONE.................847 475-6266
Fax: 847 475-1723
Adeline Hatzel, *Ch of Bd*
Phillip J Koser, *President*
Richard Magis, *Exec VP*
Dan Koser, *Vice Pres*
Robert Fuchs, *Admin Sec*
EMP: 14 EST: 1934
SQ FT: 10,000
SALES: 900K **Privately Held**
SIC: 5085 3069 3861 2396 Seals, industrial; printers' rolls & blankets: rubber or rubberized fabric; photographic processing chemicals; automotive & apparel trimmings

**(G-10066)**
**LOOP LIMITED**
Also Called: Digital Imports
825 Chicago Ave Ste C2 (60202-2377)
PHONE.................312 612-1010
Nadzieja Wieczorek, *President*
EMP: 3 EST: 2009
SALES (est): 94.5K **Privately Held**
SIC: 3572 Computer storage devices

**(G-10067)**
**M WARD MANUFACTURING CO INC**
2222-2230 Main St (60202)
PHONE.................847 864-4786
Fax: 847 864-4945
Michael Ward Jr, *President*
Tom Ward, *CFO*
EMP: 42 EST: 1943
SALES (est): 9.8MM **Privately Held**
WEB: www.wardmfgco.com
SIC: 3469 3544 Stamping metal for the trade; special dies, tools, jigs & fixtures

**(G-10068)**
**MANUFACTURERS NEWS INC**
Also Called: Mni
1633 Central St (60201-1569)
PHONE.................847 864-7000
Fax: 847 332-1100
Thomas Dubin, *President*
Mabel Burton, *Editor*
Steven Garland, *Editor*
Liliana Martinez, *Editor*
Howard S Dubin, *Chairman*
EMP: 95
SQ FT: 20,000
SALES (est): 13.3MM **Privately Held**
WEB: www.manufacturersnews.com
SIC: 7379 2741 Computer related consulting services; directories: publishing only, not printed on site

**(G-10069)**
**MARCMETALS**
2114 Central St Apt B (60201-2294)
P.O. Box 5811 (60204-5811)
PHONE.................847 905-0018
Marc Rosenbaum, *President*
EMP: 3
SALES (est): 189.1K **Privately Held**
SIC: 3441 7389 Fabricated structural metal;

**(G-10070)**
**MARKETING ANALYTICS INC**
1603 Orrington Ave A (60201-3841)
PHONE.................847 733-8459
Ross Link, *President*
Cynthia Link, *Vice Pres*
Billy Duong, *Research*
EMP: 52
SQ FT: 1,000
SALES (est): 3.6MM
SALES (corp-wide): 6.1B **Privately Held**
SIC: 8732 7372 8742 Market analysis or research; business oriented computer software; marketing consulting services
HQ: The Nielsen Company Us Llc
85 Broad St
New York NY 10004

**(G-10071)**
**MEYER GLASS DESIGN INC**
9237 Springfield Ave (60203-1517)
P.O. Box 4304, Lutherville Timonium MD (21094-4304)
PHONE.................847 675-7219
Steve Meyer, *President*
EMP: 12
SALES (est): 936.6K **Privately Held**
SIC: 3231 Products of purchased glass

**(G-10072)**
**MICHELE TERRELL**
Also Called: Premiere Distribution
230c Dodge Ave (60202-3671)
PHONE.................312 305-0876
Michele Terrell, *Owner*
EMP: 3
SALES (est): 217.1K **Privately Held**
SIC: 3677 3672 Coil windings, electronic; transformers power supply, electronic type; filtration devices, electronic; inductors, electronic; printed circuit boards

**(G-10073)**
**MINASIAN RUG CORPORATION**
1244 Chicago Ave (60202-1338)
PHONE.................847 864-1010
Armen Minasian, *President*
Minasian Carnig, *Advisor*
Carnig Minasian, *Advisor*
EMP: 3
SALES (est): 134.4K **Privately Held**
SIC: 2273 Carpets & rugs

**(G-10074)**
**MONOGRAM OF EVANSTON INC**
Also Called: Monogram Etched Crystal
2108 Jackson Ave (60201-3093)
PHONE.................847 864-8100
Fax: 847 864-8838
Philip C Holm, *President*
▲ EMP: 1
SQ FT: 11,000
SALES: 300K **Privately Held**
SIC: 3231 3479 Decorated glassware: chipped, engraved, etched, etc.; etching & engraving

**(G-10075)**
**MOTIVEQUEST LLC (HQ)**
Also Called: Lrwmotivequest
723 Chicago Ave (60202-2310)
PHONE.................847 905-6100
Fax: 847 866-1826
Colin Utley, *Engineer*
Brook Miller, *CTO*
David Rabjohns,
EMP: 15
SQ FT: 5,000
SALES (est): 6.1MM
SALES (corp-wide): 45.1MM **Privately Held**
WEB: www.motivequest.com
SIC: 8748 7372 Business consulting; business oriented computer software
PA: Lieberman Research Worldwide Inc.
1900 Ave Of The Sts 160 Ste 1600
Los Angeles CA 90067
310 553-7721

**(G-10076)**
**MP TECHNOLOGIES LLC**
1801 Maple Ave Ste 5 (60201-3150)
PHONE.................847 491-4253
Laura Bennett, *Office Mgr*
Dr Manijeh Razeghi, *Mng Member*
Dr Patrick Kung,
EMP: 6
SQ FT: 870
SALES (est): 1.3MM **Privately Held**
SIC: 8733 3674 Scientific research agency; semiconductors & related devices; ultra-violet sensors, solid state

**(G-10077)**
**NANOCYTOMICS LLC**
1801 Maple Ave Ste 19 (60201-3150)
PHONE.................847 467-2868
Maria Proenca, *General Mgr*
Radha Iyengar, *Engineer*
Vadim Backman,
EMP: 2
SALES (est): 256.1K **Privately Held**
SIC: 3845 Ultrasonic scanning devices, medical

**(G-10078)**
**NAUREX INC**
1801 Maple Ave Ste 70 (60201-5103)
PHONE.................847 871-0377
Norbert G Riedel, *CEO*
James Schulz, *President*
Derek Small, *President*
Jam Leestma, *Chief Mktg Ofcr*
Lisa Payne, *Office Mgr*
EMP: 3
SQ FT: 1,000
SALES (est): 1.1MM **Privately Held**
SIC: 8071 2834 Neurological laboratory; pharmaceutical preparations
PA: Allergan Public Limited Company
Euro House
Cork

**(G-10079)**
**NETWORKED ROBOTICS CORPORATION**
825 Chicago Ave (60202-2375)
PHONE.................847 424-8019
Mark Woodford, *President*
John Vedo, *President*
EMP: 1
SALES (est): 252.1K **Privately Held**
WEB: www.networkedrobotics.com
SIC: 3826 Environmental testing equipment

**(G-10080)**
**ODX MEDIA LLC**
848 Dodge Ave (60202-1506)
PHONE.................847 868-0548
Karla Figueroa,
EMP: 5
SALES (est): 240.9K **Privately Held**
SIC: 2741

**(G-10081)**
**OHMX CORPORATION**
1801 Maple Ave Ste 18 (60201-3150)
PHONE.................847 491-8500
Charles Rowland, *CEO*
Paul Bao, *President*
Fang Lai, *General Mgr*
Richard Parrillo Jr, *Director*
Erin Tower, *Executive*
EMP: 12
SALES (est): 2.8MM **Privately Held**
WEB: www.ohmxbio.com
SIC: 2835 In vitro & in vivo diagnostic substances

**(G-10082)**
**OLD TOWN OIL EVANSTON**
1924 Central St (60201-2228)
PHONE.................312 787-9595
John D Dine, *Principal*
EMP: 3 EST: 2011
SALES (est): 203.4K **Privately Held**
SIC: 2079 Olive oil

**(G-10083)**
**OPTICENT INC**
600 Davis St Fl 3 (60201-4488)
PHONE.................410 829-7384
Kieren Patel, *CEO*
Cheng Sun, *CTO*
Hao Zhang, *CTO*
EMP: 5
SALES (est): 206.8K **Privately Held**
SIC: 3841 Surgical & medical instruments; ophthalmic instruments & apparatus

**(G-10084)**
**ORION MEDIA LOGISTICS INC**
1619 Florence Ave (60201-4014)
PHONE.................847 866-6215
Eric Peterson, *President*
EMP: 4

SALES (est): 381.7K **Privately Held**
SIC: 3641 Electric light bulbs, complete

**(G-10085)**
**PETERSON DERMOND DESIGN LLC**
900 Grove St Ste 10 (60201-6523)
PHONE.....................414 383-5029
Fax: 414 383-8315
Susan Peterson,
Sandra Dermond,
EMP: 3
SQ FT: 8,169
SALES (est): 287.1K **Privately Held**
SIC: 2392 Hassocks, textile: made from purchased materials

**(G-10086)**
**PHALANX TRAINING INC**
617 Grove St Ste A (60201-4478)
PHONE.....................847 859-9156
Jordan Zoot, *CEO*
EMP: 3 EST: 2013
SALES (est): 207K **Privately Held**
SIC: 3484 Guns (firearms) or gun parts, 30 mm. & below

**(G-10087)**
**PINTO NOODLE & RICE**
1931 Central St (60201-2277)
PHONE.....................847 328-8881
Peter Lau, *Principal*
EMP: 4
SALES (est): 246.3K **Privately Held**
SIC: 2098 Noodles (e.g. egg, plain & water), dry

**(G-10088)**
**PM WOODWIND REPAIR INC**
822 Custer Ave (60202-2269)
PHONE.....................847 869-7049
Paul Maslin, *President*
Kevin Brant, *Office Mgr*
EMP: 8
SALES (est): 392K **Privately Held**
WEB: www.pmwoodwind.com
SIC: 7692 5099 Welding repair; musical instruments

**(G-10089)**
**PNEU FAST INC**
Also Called: Pneu-Fast
2200 Greenleaf St (60202-1030)
PHONE.....................847 866-8787
Fax: 847 866-8196
Reno Joseph, *President*
Edward Chester, *President*
Michelle Jay, *Controller*
▲ EMP: 18
SQ FT: 40,000
SALES (est): 4.8MM **Privately Held**
WEB: www.pneufast.com
SIC: 3315 Nails, spikes, brads & similar items

**(G-10090)**
**PRARIE MATERIAL SALES INC**
828 Davis St (60201-4420)
PHONE.....................847 733-8809
Jerry Krozal, *Vice Pres*
EMP: 3
SALES (est): 175.8K **Privately Held**
SIC: 3273 5211 Ready-mixed concrete; cement

**(G-10091)**
**PRINTED WORD INC**
1807 Central St (60201-1509)
PHONE.....................847 328-1511
Fax: 847 328-1579
Bernard Brady, *President*
EMP: 3 EST: 1983
SQ FT: 2,200
SALES (est): 230K **Privately Held**
WEB: www.printedwordevanston.com
SIC: 2752 7336 2791 2789 Lithographing on metal; commercial art & graphic design; typesetting; bookbinding & related work

**(G-10092)**
**PSYLOTECH INC**
1616 Payne St (60201-3032)
PHONE.....................847 328-7100
Alex Arzoumanidis, *President*
EMP: 9 EST: 2008

SQ FT: 2,000
SALES (est): 1.5MM **Privately Held**
SIC: 3829 7371 Measuring & controlling devices; computer software development & applications

**(G-10093)**
**S R BASTIEN CO**
Also Called: Retailer Watch Newsletter
600 Davis St Rear (60201-4488)
P.O. Box 5453 (60204-5453)
PHONE.....................847 858-1175
Fax: 847 491-6331
Steven R Bastien, *President*
Jackie Johnson, *Office Mgr*
EMP: 10
SQ FT: 6,000
SALES (est): 1.2MM **Privately Held**
SIC: 2731 7331 2721 Pamphlets: publishing only, not printed on site; direct mail advertising services; periodicals

**(G-10094)**
**SOCIUS INGREDIENTS LLC**
1033 University Pl # 110 (60201-3196)
PHONE.....................847 440-0156
Martin O'Donovan, *President*
Jim Gissel, *CFO*
James Gassel, *Manager*
Conor Buckley,
Kieran Lonergan,
▲ EMP: 13
SQ FT: 5,000
SALES (est): 4MM **Privately Held**
WEB: www.sociusingredients.com
SIC: 2026 Milk & cream, except fermented, cultured & flavored
PA: Lakeland Dairies Co-Operative Society Ltd
Killeshandra
Cavan

**(G-10095)**
**ST JOHNS UNITED CHURCH CHRIST**
Also Called: St John S United Church of
1136 Wesley Ave (60202-1163)
PHONE.....................847 491-6686
Charles Powell, *President*
Rev Todd Mushaney, *Pastor*
EMP: 3
SALES (est): 160K **Privately Held**
SIC: 2741 8661 Miscellaneous publishing; Church of Christ

**(G-10096)**
**STRYDE TECHNOLOGIES INC**
Also Called: Mypowr
600 Davis St Fl 3w (60201-4488)
PHONE.....................510 786-8890
Tejas Shastry, *CEO*
Michael Geier, *Co-Owner*
Alexander Smith, *Co-Owner*
EMP: 5
SALES (est): 609.4K **Privately Held**
SIC: 3677 Electronic coils, transformers & other inductors

**(G-10097)**
**STUDENTS PUBLISHING COMPANY IN**
Also Called: DAILY NORTHWESTERN NEWSPAPER
1999 Sheridan Rd (60201-2924)
PHONE.....................847 491-7206
Fax: 847 491-9905
Charles Whitaker, *Chairman*
Stacia G Campbell, *Manager*
Rebekah Abel, *Technology*
Michael Kelley, *Technology*
EMP: 2
SQ FT: 1,200
SALES: 395K **Privately Held**
SIC: 2731 2711 Books: publishing only; newspapers: publishing only, not printed on site

**(G-10098)**
**SUGAR/SPICE EXTRAORDINRY TREAT**
1205 Hartrey Ave (60202-1056)
PHONE.....................847 864-7800
Jean Kroll, *President*
EMP: 9

SALES (est): 1MM **Privately Held**
WEB: www.ilovesweets.com
SIC: 2052 Cookies

**(G-10099)**
**SURREY BOOKS INC**
1501 Madison St (60202-2033)
PHONE.....................847 475-4457
Susan Schwartz, *President*
Christine Swinko, *Asst to Pres*
EMP: 3
SQ FT: 1,000
SALES (est): 140K **Privately Held**
WEB: www.surreybooks.com
SIC: 2731 Books: publishing only

**(G-10100)**
**TAGS BAKERY INC**
Also Called: Tag's Bakery & Pastry Shop
2010 Central St (60201-2218)
PHONE.....................847 328-1200
Fax: 847 328-1299
Gregory Vetter, *President*
Donald J Vetter, *President*
Greg Vetter, *Vice Pres*
Gretchen Vetter, *Treasurer*
Jan Vetter, *Admin Sec*
EMP: 25
SQ FT: 2,500
SALES (est): 850K **Privately Held**
WEB: www.tagscakes.com
SIC: 5461 2052 2051 Bakeries; cookies & crackers; bread, cake & related products

**(G-10101)**
**TEMPERANCE BEER COMPANY LLC**
2000 Dempster St (60202-1017)
PHONE.....................847 864-1000
Josh Dildert,
EMP: 8
SALES (est): 573.6K **Privately Held**
SIC: 2041 Corn grits & flakes, for brewers' use

**(G-10102)**
**THOMAS A DOAN**
Also Called: Estima
1560 Sherman Ave Ste 1029 (60201-4803)
PHONE.....................847 864-8772
Fax: 847 864-6221
Thomas A Doan, *Owner*
EMP: 3
SQ FT: 1,800
SALES (est): 337.4K **Privately Held**
WEB: www.estima.com
SIC: 7372 7371 Business oriented computer software; custom computer programming services

**(G-10103)**
**UBERLUBE INC**
2611 Hartzell St (60201-1311)
PHONE.....................847 372-3127
Jack A Magnusen, *President*
Stephen Magnusen, *Relations*
▲ EMP: 7 EST: 2011
SALES (est): 1.3MM **Privately Held**
SIC: 2992 Lubricating oils & greases

**(G-10104)**
**UNITED PRESS INTERNATIONAL INC**
1561 Darrow Ave (60201-4075)
PHONE.....................847 864-9450
Albert Swanson, *Manager*
EMP: 3
SALES (corp-wide): 495.3MM **Privately Held**
SIC: 2741 Miscellaneous publishing
HQ: United Press International, Inc.
1133 19th St Nw Ste 800
Washington DC
202 898-8000

**(G-10105)**
**WCTU PRESS (PA)**
Also Called: Woman Christian Temperance Un
1730 Chicago Ave (60201-4502)
PHONE.....................847 864-1396
Sarah F Ward, *President*
EMP: 9
SALES: 14.6K **Privately Held**
SIC: 2732 Pamphlets: printing only, not published on site

**(G-10106)**
**WILLIAM HOLLOWAY LTD**
Also Called: Sir Speedy
1800 Dempster St (60202-1003)
PHONE.....................847 866-9520
William Holloway, *President*
EMP: 9
SQ FT: 2,400
SALES: 750K **Privately Held**
SIC: 2752 7334 2789 2759 Commercial printing, lithographic; photocopying & duplicating services; bookbinding & related work; commercial printing; coated & laminated paper

**(G-10107)**
**WONDER KIDS INC**
1719 Brummel St (60202-3737)
PHONE.....................773 437-8025
Sarah White, *Principal*
EMP: 3
SALES (est): 183.9K **Privately Held**
SIC: 3261 Bathroom accessories/fittings, vitreous china or earthenware

## Evansville
### Randolph County

**(G-10108)**
**WOLTERS CUSTOM CABINETS LLC**
8204 State Route 3 (62242-1020)
PHONE.....................618 282-3158
Glenn A Wolter, *Mng Member*
Glenn Wolter, *Mng Member*
EMP: 8
SQ FT: 6,000
SALES: 1MM **Privately Held**
SIC: 2434 Wood kitchen cabinets

## Evergreen Park
### Cook County

**(G-10109)**
**ADAMS STREET IRON INC**
9127 S Kedzie Ave (60805-1606)
PHONE.....................312 733-3229
Fax: 708 424-1764
John Magnon Sr, *President*
EMP: 12
SQ FT: 3,700
SALES (est): 2.8MM **Privately Held**
WEB: www.adams-st-iron.com
SIC: 5051 5031 3442 3441 Iron & steel (ferrous) products; rails & accessories; structural shapes, iron or steel; fencing, wood; metal doors, sash & trim; fabricated structural metal; wood kitchen cabinets; millwork

**(G-10110)**
**BELL CABINET & MILLWORK CO**
9340 S Kedzie Ave (60805-2318)
PHONE.....................708 425-1200
Joe Bellettiere, *President*
EMP: 6
SQ FT: 8,500
SALES: 800K **Privately Held**
SIC: 2434 2511 Wood kitchen cabinets; wood household furniture

**(G-10111)**
**DELTA DESIGN INC (PA)**
3140 W 92nd St (60805-1602)
PHONE.....................708 424-9400
Cynthia M Tallent, *President*
John H Gaden, *Vice Pres*
▲ EMP: 10 EST: 1976
SQ FT: 4,000
SALES: 675K **Privately Held**
WEB: www.deltadesigncorp.com
SIC: 3599 5999 3679 Machine shop, jobbing & repair; electronic parts & equipment; harness assemblies for electronic use: wire or cable

**(G-10112)**
**DELTA DESIGN INC**
3140 W 92nd St (60805-1602)
PHONE.....................708 424-9400

## Evergreen Park - Cook County (G-10113)

Cyndia Talent, *Branch Mgr*
**EMP:** 12
**SALES (corp-wide):** 675K **Privately Held**
**SIC:** 3679 3651 3672 Harness assemblies for electronic use: wire or cable; electronic kits for home assembly: radio, TV, phonograph; circuit boards, television & radio printed
**PA:** Delta Design, Inc.
3140 W 92nd St
Evergreen Park IL 60805
708 424-9400

**(G-10113)**
**ECLIPSE AWNINGS INC**
3609 W 95th St (60805-2119)
**PHONE**.................708 636-3160
**Fax:** 708 923-6361
Rey Williams, *Manager*
**EMP:** 15
**SALES (est):** 790K **Privately Held**
**SIC:** 3444 2394 5999 Awnings & canopies; canvas awnings & canopies; awnings

**(G-10114)**
**EVERGREEN MARATHON**
2755 W 87th St (60805-1104)
**PHONE**.................708 636-5700
**EMP:** 3
**SALES (est):** 153.3K **Privately Held**
**SIC:** 1389 Oil/Gas Field Services

**(G-10115)**
**EVERGREEN PRINTING**
9420 S Trumbull Ave (60805-2224)
**PHONE**.................708 499-0688
Birney Berten, *Owner*
Cindy Jones, *Co-Owner*
**EMP:** 6
**SALES (est):** 300K **Privately Held**
**SIC:** 2752 Commercial printing, lithographic

**(G-10116)**
**J GARVIN INDUSTRIES**
9628 S Harding Ave (60805-2918)
**PHONE**.................708 819-1148
Adrienne Garvin, *Principal*
**EMP:** 3
**SALES (est):** 257.6K **Privately Held**
**SIC:** 3999 Manufacturing industries

**(G-10117)**
**MENARD INC**
9100 S Western Ave (60805-2501)
**PHONE**.................708 346-9144
**EMP:** 68
**SALES (corp-wide):** 15.2B **Privately Held**
**SIC:** 2431 Millwork
**PA:** Menard, Inc.
5101 Menard Dr
Eau Claire WI 54703
715 876-5911

**(G-10118)**
**ROBERT L MURPHY**
9545 S Hamlin Ave (60805-2030)
**PHONE**.................708 424-0277
Robert Murphy, *Principal*
**EMP:** 4
**SALES (est):** 378.9K **Privately Held**
**SIC:** 3565 Vacuum packaging machinery

**(G-10119)**
**SEASONAL MAGNETS**
3133 W 102nd St (60805-3516)
**PHONE**.................708 499-3235
**EMP:** 3
**SALES (est):** 195.4K **Privately Held**
**SIC:** 3674 Mfg Semiconductors/Related Devices

### Ewing
*Franklin County*

**(G-10120)**
**K & K STORAGE BARNS LLC**
Also Called: K & K Buildings
19867 Ketterman Ln (62836-1307)
**PHONE**.................618 927-0533
Keith Ebersole, *Mng Member*
Gordon Ebersole,
**EMP:** 12
**SQ FT:** 9,600
**SALES (est):** 900K **Privately Held**
**SIC:** 2452 Prefabricated wood buildings

### Fairbury
*Livingston County*

**(G-10121)**
**AMERICAN PUBLISHING CO INC**
Also Called: Leader Union Publishing
125 W Locust St (61739-1548)
**PHONE**.................815 692-2366
Linda Blair, *Manager*
**EMP:** 3
**SALES (est):** 164.5K
**SALES (corp-wide):** 304.8MM **Privately Held**
**SIC:** 2711 Newspapers
**HQ:** Sun-Times Media Group, Inc.
350 N Orleans St Fl 10
Chicago IL 60654
312 321-2299

**(G-10122)**
**AVOCA RIDGE LTD**
Also Called: Design and Woodworks
310 S 7th St Ste 2 (61739-1687)
**PHONE**.................815 692-4772
James A Tipton, *Owner*
**EMP:** 2 **EST:** 1999
**SALES:** 250K **Privately Held**
**SIC:** 3429 Cabinet hardware

**(G-10123)**
**DOUBLE M MACHINE INC**
614 W Pine St (61739-1453)
**PHONE**.................815 692-4676
**Fax:** 815 692-4880
Jim Meister, *President*
Martin Meister, *President*
**EMP:** 12
**SQ FT:** 5,600
**SALES:** 1.7MM **Privately Held**
**WEB:** www.doublemmachine.com
**SIC:** 3544 Special dies & tools

**(G-10124)**
**FEHR CAB INTERIORS**
10116 N 1900 East Rd (61739-9265)
**PHONE**.................815 692-3355
Ron Fehr, *Owner*
Norma Fehrm, *Partner*
Loel Lanz, *Mfg Staff*
▲ **EMP:** 7
**SQ FT:** 8,100
**SALES (est):** 782.1K **Privately Held**
**WEB:** www.fehrcab.com
**SIC:** 7641 3523 Upholstery work; farm machinery & equipment

**(G-10125)**
**HOFFMAN TOOL INC**
1301 W Oak St (61739-1490)
**PHONE**.................815 692-4643
Gerald Hoffman, *President*
Jean Biefeldt, *Manager*
**EMP:** 20
**SQ FT:** 32,000
**SALES (est):** 1.7MM **Privately Held**
**SIC:** 3544 Special dies, tools, jigs & fixtures

**(G-10126)**
**HOFFMAN TOOL & DIE INC**
1303 W Oak St (61739-1490)
P.O. Box 257 (61739-0257)
**PHONE**.................815 692-2628
**Fax:** 815 692-3840
Jerry Hoffman, *President*
**EMP:** 25
**SQ FT:** 12,000
**SALES (est):** 4.7MM **Privately Held**
**WEB:** www.hoffmantool.com
**SIC:** 3544 Special dies, tools, jigs & fixtures; jigs & fixtures; forms (molds), for foundry & plastics working machinery; punches, forming & stamping

**(G-10127)**
**JENNER PRECISION INC**
8735 N 2000 East Rd (61739-9101)
**PHONE**.................815 692-6655
James L Fehr, *President*
Clint B Hohenstein, *Admin Sec*
**EMP:** 10
**SALES (est):** 471.6K **Privately Held**
**SIC:** 5999 3711 Farm equipment & supplies; truck & tractor truck assembly

**(G-10128)**
**JOHN JODA POST 54**
Also Called: FAIRBURY FAIR ASSOCIATION
600 S 3rd St (61739-1586)
P.O. Box 74 (61739-0074)
**PHONE**.................815 692-3222
Dennis Kaisner, *President*
Elmer Hallock, *Treasurer*
**EMP:** 3
**SALES:** 1.1MM **Privately Held**
**SIC:** 8641 2499 Veterans' organization; bakers' equipment, wood

**(G-10129)**
**KILGUS FARMSTEAD INC**
21471 E 670 North Rd (61739-8974)
**PHONE**.................815 692-6080
Matt Kilgus, *President*
Paul Kilgus, *Vice Pres*
**EMP:** 6
**SALES (est):** 640K **Privately Held**
**SIC:** 2026 Fluid milk

**(G-10130)**
**L & W FUELS**
5484 N 2100 East Rd (61739-9151)
**PHONE**.................815 848-8360
James Waldbeser, *Owner*
**EMP:** 3
**SALES (est):** 215.8K **Privately Held**
**SIC:** 2869 Fuels

**(G-10131)**
**PTC TUBULAR PRODUCTS LLC**
Also Called: Fairbury Division
23041 E 800 North Rd (61739-8824)
**PHONE**.................815 692-4900
**Fax:** 815 692-3513
Dan McMann, *General Mgr*
Warren Mackenzie, *Vice Pres*
Louie Ross, *Plant Mgr*
Dave Jenkins, *Chief Engr*
David McMinn, *Chief Engr*
**EMP:** 112 **Privately Held**
**SIC:** 3312 3321 3317 3498 Tubes, steel & iron; gray & ductile iron foundries; steel pipe & tubes; tube fabricating (contract bending & shaping)
**HQ:** Ptc Tubular Products Llc
1480 Nw 11th St
Richmond IN 47374
765 259-3334

**(G-10132)**
**SLAGEL DRAPERY SERVICE**
302 S 8th St (61739-1315)
**PHONE**.................815 692-3834
Judy Slagel, *Owner*
**EMP:** 3
**SALES (est):** 213.6K **Privately Held**
**SIC:** 2391 2392 Curtains & draperies; household furnishings

**(G-10133)**
**TECHNICAL METALS INC**
Also Called: TMI
1301 W Oak St (61739-1490)
P.O. Box 140 (61739-0140)
**PHONE**.................815 692-4643
**Fax:** 815 692-2085
Gerald Hoffman, *President*
Becky Hoffman, *Warehouse Mgr*
Kevin Russell, *Mfg Staff*
Rosemary Hoffman, *Treasurer*
Amber Chambers, *Manager*
**EMP:** 100
**SQ FT:** 32,000
**SALES (est):** 25.5MM **Privately Held**
**WEB:** www.technical-metals.com
**SIC:** 3469 3599 Machine parts, stamped or pressed metal; stamping metal for the trade; machine shop, jobbing & repair

**(G-10134)**
**U S CO-TRONICS CORP**
403 E Locust St (61739-1652)
P.O. Box 168 (61739-0168)
**PHONE**.................815 692-3204
**Fax:** 815 692-3520
Paul Bullard, *President*
Sharlene Bullard, *Admin Sec*
**EMP:** 40
**SQ FT:** 9,000
**SALES (est):** 6.2MM **Privately Held**
**SIC:** 3621 3677 3612 Coils, for electric motors or generators; electronic coils, transformers & other inductors; transformers, except electric

### Fairfield
*Wayne County*

**(G-10135)**
**ACE CUSTOM UPHOLSTERY & ROD SP**
200 W Delaware St (62837-1712)
**PHONE**.................618 842-2913
Amos Eckleberry, *Owner*
**EMP:** 3
**SALES (est):** 140K **Privately Held**
**SIC:** 3315 Steel wire & related products

**(G-10136)**
**BASNETTS INVESTMENTS**
Also Called: Basnett, John
215 Se 3rd St Ste 208 (62837-2172)
**PHONE**.................618 842-4040
**Fax:** 618 842-3825
John Basnett, *Partner*
Greg Basnett, *Partner*
**EMP:** 3
**SQ FT:** 600
**SALES:** 1.6MM **Privately Held**
**SIC:** 1311 Crude petroleum production

**(G-10137)**
**BULLARDS BAKERY**
906 E Main St (62837-2216)
**PHONE**.................618 842-6666
Jennifer Collins, *Owner*
**EMP:** 3
**SALES (est):** 189.1K **Privately Held**
**SIC:** 2051 Bakery: wholesale or wholesale/retail combined

**(G-10138)**
**CARDINAL CONSTRUCTION CO**
705 S 1st St (62837-1804)
**PHONE**.................618 842-5553
Melvin Clark, *President*
**EMP:** 4
**SALES (est):** 512.1K **Privately Held**
**SIC:** 3585 Room coolers, portable

**(G-10139)**
**DNOW LP**
Also Called: National Oilwell
2210 W Delaware St (62837-2367)
P.O. Box C (62837-0048)
**PHONE**.................618 842-9176
David Read, *Manager*
**EMP:** 3
**SALES (corp-wide):** 2.1B **Publicly Held**
**WEB:** www.natoil.com
**SIC:** 3533 Oil field machinery & equipment
**HQ:** Dnow L.P.
7402 N Eldridge Pkwy
Houston TX 77041
281 823-4700

**(G-10140)**
**FAIRFIELD ACID AND FRAC CO**
Hwy 15 W (62837)
**PHONE**.................618 842-9186
Jerry Friend, *Partner*
Paul Friend, *Partner*
Gary Grove, *Partner*
**EMP:** 10
**SQ FT:** 7,000
**SALES (est):** 520K **Privately Held**
**SIC:** 1389 Acidizing wells; oil field services

**(G-10141)**
**FAIRFIELD READY MIX INC**
Also Called: Garman Trucking
County Rte 45 N (62837)
P.O. Box 5 (62837-0005)
**PHONE**.................618 842-9462
Ed Musgrave, *President*
Robert Musgrave, *Corp Secy*
Robert P Musgrave, *Treasurer*
**EMP:** 5

# GEOGRAPHIC SECTION

Fairview Heights - St. Clair County (G-10168)

SQ FT: 2,200
SALES (est): 569K Privately Held
SIC: 3273 Ready-mixed concrete

**(G-10142)**
**FRIEND OIL CO**
Enterprise Rd Rr 3 (62837)
P.O. Box 545 (62837-0545)
PHONE..................................618 842-9161
Jerry Friend, *Owner*
EMP: 5
SQ FT: 1,500
SALES (est): 366.1K Privately Held
SIC: 1311 Crude petroleum production

**(G-10143)**
**GORDYS MACHINE AND TOOL INC**
1101 Sw 3rd St (62837-1866)
P.O. Box 760 (62837-0760)
PHONE..................................618 842-9331
Fax: 618 847-5521
Gordon Toombs, *President*
Robert Banks, *Vice Pres*
Dianne Toombs, *Vice Pres*
Laverna Toombs, *Vice Pres*
EMP: 15
SALES (est): 2.1MM Privately Held
SIC: 3599 Machine shop, jobbing & repair

**(G-10144)**
**J R G OIL CO INC**
306 Petroleum Blvd Te A (62837)
P.O. Box 456 (62837-0456)
PHONE..................................618 842-9131
Robert Gain, *President*
Gary Gain, *President*
Ronnie Gain, *Vice Pres*
EMP: 3
SALES: 300K Privately Held
SIC: 1311 8641 Crude petroleum production; condominium association

**(G-10145)**
**JACK WALTERS & SONS CORP**
Also Called: Walters Buildings
204 E Main St (62837-2002)
P.O. Box 455 (62837-0455)
PHONE..................................618 842-2642
Fax: 618 842-5235
Fred Gilbert, *Manager*
EMP: 20
SALES (corp-wide): 28MM Privately Held
WEB: www.waltersbuildings.com
SIC: 3448 Buildings, portable: prefabricated metal
PA: Jack Walters & Sons, Corp.
    6600 Midland Ct
    Allenton WI 53002
    262 629-5521

**(G-10146)**
**JHT ROBERTSON LUMBER INC**
408 Airport Rd (62837-1377)
PHONE..................................618 842-2004
Harold Robertson, *President*
EMP: 9
SALES (est): 1MM Privately Held
SIC: 2421 Lumber: rough, sawed or planed

**(G-10147)**
**JONES GARRISON SONS MCH WORKS**
Hwy 15 W (62837)
P.O. Box 274 (62837-0274)
PHONE..................................618 847-2161
Carroll E Garrison, *President*
EMP: 3
SQ FT: 2,400
SALES: 250K Privately Held
SIC: 7699 5999 3599 7539 Engine repair & replacement, non-automotive; agricultural equipment repair services; industrial machinery & equipment repair; engine & motor equipment & supplies; machine shop, jobbing & repair; radiator repair shop, automotive

**(G-10148)**
**LARRY MUSGRAVE LOGGING**
414 Nw 6th St (62837-1510)
PHONE..................................618 842-6386
Larry Musgrave, *Owner*
EMP: 4

SALES (est): 291.9K Privately Held
SIC: 2421 2411 Sawmills & planing mills, general; logging

**(G-10149)**
**LEGGS MANUFACTURING**
900 W Delaware St (62837-1411)
PHONE..................................618 842-9847
Fax: 618 847-4032
David Legg, *Owner*
EMP: 7
SALES (est): 440K Privately Held
SIC: 3446 Architectural metalwork

**(G-10150)**
**MID STATES SALVAGE**
Also Called: Mid States Distributing
6 Petroleum Blvd (62837)
P.O. Box 111 (62837-0111)
PHONE..................................618 842-6741
Fax: 618 842-4700
Tom Taylor, *Owner*
EMP: 8
SQ FT: 1,000
SALES (est): 1MM Privately Held
WEB: www.midstatessalvage.com
SIC: 1382 Oil & gas exploration services

**(G-10151)**
**MID-STATES SERVICES LLC**
6 Petroleum Blvd (62837)
PHONE..................................618 842-4726
Taylor Tommy J, *President*
EMP: 10
SALES (est): 237.9K Privately Held
SIC: 1389 Oil field services

**(G-10152)**
**REEF DEVELOPMENT INC**
Rr 3 (62837)
P.O. Box 666 (62837-0666)
PHONE..................................618 842-7711
Fax: 618 842-3760
Jerry E Friend, *President*
Kevin Scheuneman, *Corp Secy*
EMP: 12
SALES (est): 1MM Privately Held
SIC: 1381 Drilling oil & gas wells

**(G-10153)**
**REPUBLIC OIL CO INC**
1508 W Delaware St (62837-2333)
P.O. Box D (62837)
PHONE..................................618 842-7591
Fax: 618 842-7594
Eldon Doty, *President*
EMP: 4
SQ FT: 1,000
SALES (est): 670.2K Privately Held
SIC: 1311 Crude petroleum production

**(G-10154)**
**ROBINSON PRODUCTION INC**
108 Ne 7th St (62837-2153)
P.O. Box 131 (62837-0131)
PHONE..................................618 842-6111
Ann B Robinson, *President*
Beverly Downs, *Manager*
EMP: 5
SQ FT: 2,000
SALES (est): 446.8K Privately Held
SIC: 1311 Crude petroleum production

**(G-10155)**
**STRATA EXPLORATION INC**
201 Ne 7th St (62837-2154)
P.O. Box 401 (62837-0401)
PHONE..................................618 842-2610
John R Kinney, *President*
Sheila Kinney, *Corp Secy*
EMP: 2
SALES (est): 267.2K Privately Held
SIC: 1382 Geophysical exploration, oil & gas field

**(G-10156)**
**TIPPS CASING PULLING COMPANY**
Hc 15 (62837)
P.O. Box 247 (62837-0247)
PHONE..................................618 847-7986
Max Tipps, *Owner*
EMP: 3
SQ FT: 6,300

SALES (est): 180K Privately Held
SIC: 1311 5084 Crude petroleum production; oil well machinery, equipment & supplies

**(G-10157)**
**VAUGHN & SONS MACHINE SHOP**
Hwy 45 (62837)
Rr # 5 Box 396 (62837-4328)
PHONE..................................618 842-9048
Robert T Vaughn, *Owner*
Rosina Vaughn, *Co-Owner*
EMP: 3
SALES: 250K Privately Held
SIC: 5082 7692 3541 Oil field equipment; welding repair; machine tools, metal cutting type

**(G-10158)**
**WABASH PRODUCTION & DEV**
4 Petroleum Blvd (62837)
P.O. Box 398 (62837-0398)
PHONE..................................618 847-7401
Michael N Gooch, *President*
EMP: 7
SQ FT: 4,900
SALES (est): 651.2K Privately Held
WEB: www.wabashproduction.com
SIC: 1389 Pumping of oil & gas wells

**(G-10159)**
**WAYNE COUNTY PRESS INC**
213 E Main St (62837-2028)
P.O. Box F (62837-0149)
PHONE..................................618 842-2662
Fax: 618 842-7912
C Preston Mathews, *President*
Thomas O Mathews Jr, *Vice Pres*
Preston T Mathews, *Financial Exec*
EMP: 31 EST: 1866
SQ FT: 12,000
SALES (est): 2MM Privately Held
SIC: 2711 Commercial printing & newspaper publishing combined

**(G-10160)**
**WAYNE COUNTY WELL SURVEYS INC**
2225 Industrial Dr (62837-2719)
P.O. Box 421 (62837-0421)
PHONE..................................618 842-9116
Fax: 618 842-4002
Danny Young, *President*
David J Watson, *Admin Sec*
EMP: 13
SALES (est): 1.2MM Privately Held
SIC: 1389 Servicing oil & gas wells

**(G-10161)**
**WEB PRINTING CONTROLS CO INC**
Also Called: Baldwin Americas
600 Us Highway 45 Ste A (62837-2555)
Rr # 5 Box 430
PHONE..................................618 842-2664
Fax: 618 842-3616
Bruce Fetherling, *Vice Pres*
Trish Balding, *Purchasing*
John Legg, *Administration*
EMP: 110
SALES (corp-wide): 15.7MM Privately Held
SIC: 3555 3822 3625 Printing trades machinery; auto controls regulating residntl & coml environmt & applncs; relays & industrial controls
PA: Web Printing Controls Company Incorporated
    3350 W Salt Creek Ln # 110
    Arlington Heights IL 60005
    618 842-2664

## Fairmount
*Vermilion County*

**(G-10162)**
**DECATUR AERATION AND TEMP**
Also Called: Dat Metal Fabricating
101 N Main St (61841-6422)
P.O. Box 1757, Decatur (62525-1757)
PHONE..................................217 733-2800
Fax: 217 428-8535

J Michael Strader, *President*
Brenda Strader, *Admin Sec*
EMP: 15
SQ FT: 6,000
SALES (est): 1.2MM Privately Held
SIC: 3823 Industrial instrmnts msrmnt display/control process variable

**(G-10163)**
**FERBER GEORGE & SONS**
Also Called: Fairmount Redi-Mix
102 S Pine St (61841-7030)
P.O. Box 200 (61841-0200)
PHONE..................................217 733-2184
Fax: 217 733-2284
Kurt Ferber, *Partner*
Mike Ferber, *General Mgr*
EMP: 7 EST: 1940
SQ FT: 2,880
SALES (est): 1MM Privately Held
SIC: 3273 3272 Ready-mixed concrete; concrete products

**(G-10164)**
**P L R SALES INC**
14187 N 850 E Rd (61841)
PHONE..................................217 733-2245
Peggy Lindsey, *President*
EMP: 3
SALES: 200K Privately Held
WEB: www.plrsales.com
SIC: 3691 Storage batteries

## Fairview
*Fulton County*

**(G-10165)**
**COLUMBUS INDUSTRIES INC**
17383 E State Route 116 (61432-9677)
PHONE..................................309 245-1010
Fax: 309 245-4210
David C Donaldson, *President*
John C La Reau, *Corp Secy*
John Lareau, *Treasurer*
Dede Boyer, *Manager*
EMP: 15
SQ FT: 25,000
SALES: 3.5MM Privately Held
SIC: 3444 Sheet metalwork

## Fairview Heights
*St. Clair County*

**(G-10166)**
**BI-STATE BIKING LLC**
Also Called: Biking Life Magazine, The
807 Coral Dr (62208-2906)
PHONE..................................618 531-0432
Jim Furey, *Mng Member*
Jennifer Furey, *Manager*
EMP: 3
SALES (est): 101K Privately Held
SIC: 2721 Magazines: publishing & printing

**(G-10167)**
**EAGLE MEDICAL CONCEPTS INC**
6001 Old Collinsville Rd 4c (62208-2937)
P.O. Box 304, New Athens (62264-0304)
PHONE..................................618 475-3671
J R Dietl, *CEO*
Dr James Vest, *President*
EMP: 3 EST: 2000
SALES (est): 211.7K Privately Held
SIC: 3841 Surgical & medical instruments

**(G-10168)**
**HEIL SOUND LTD**
5800 N Illinois St (62208-3505)
PHONE..................................618 257-3000
Bob Heil, *CEO*
Sarah Heil, *President*
Gerald Lynch, *Pub Rel Mgr*
▲ EMP: 11 EST: 1966

SALES (est): 2.1MM  Privately Held
WEB: www.heilsound.com
SIC: 3663  5731  1731  3651  Radio & TV communications equipment; radio, television & electronic stores; communications specialization; cable television installation; sound equipment specialization; household audio & video equipment; current-carrying wiring devices; nonferrous wiredrawing & insulating

**(G-10169)**
**INK WELL**
10603 Lincoln Trl  (62208-1913)
PHONE..................................618 398-1427
Clark Medley, *Owner*
EMP: 4  EST: 1996
SALES (est): 250K  Privately Held
SIC: 2752  Commercial printing, lithographic

**(G-10170)**
**LENSCRAFTERS CRAFTERS**
271 Saint Clair Sq  (62208-2134)
PHONE..................................618 632-2312
Brenda Flusher, *Manager*
EMP: 16
SALES (est): 1.1MM  Privately Held
SIC: 3827  Lenses, optical: all types except ophthalmic

**(G-10171)**
**SMART CONTROLS  LLC**
10000 Saint Clair Ave  (62208-1726)
PHONE..................................618 394-0300
David Kniepkamp,
EMP: 5  EST: 2000
SALES (est): 918K  Privately Held
SIC: 3674  Integrated circuits, semiconductor networks, etc.

## Farina
### Fayette County

**(G-10172)**
**ADVANCE MANUFACTURING**
204 Through St  (62838-3751)
PHONE..................................618 245-6515
Calvin Byers, *President*
EMP: 3  EST: 2008
SALES (est): 225.2K  Privately Held
SIC: 3999  Manufacturing industries

**(G-10173)**
**B&A LIVESTOCK FEED COMPANY LLC**
201 E Jefferson Ave  (62838-1334)
PHONE..................................618 245-6422
EMP: 3
SALES (est): 184K  Privately Held
SIC: 2048  Livestock feeds

**(G-10174)**
**BLOMBERG BROS INC**
Hwy 37 S  (62838)
P.O. Box 99  (62838-0099)
PHONE..................................618 245-6321
Fax: 618 245-3344
Charles E Blomberg, *President*
Ed Blomberg, *Corp Secy*
Frank Blomberg, *Vice Pres*
Larry Daerrel, *Supervisor*
EMP: 12  EST: 1948
SQ FT: 5,600
SALES: 900K  Privately Held
SIC: 4212  3273  5191  Local trucking, without storage; ready-mixed concrete; limestone, agricultural

**(G-10175)**
**FARINA LOCKER SERVICE**
23 7 Madison St  (62838)
P.O. Box 36  (62838-0036)
PHONE..................................618 245-6491
Alan Stock, *Owner*
EMP: 8
SALES (est): 585.1K  Privately Held
SIC: 4222  2013  2011  Storage, frozen or refrigerated goods; sausages & other prepared meats; meat packing plants

**(G-10176)**
**FARINA NEWS**
109 N Walnut St  (62838-1326)
P.O. Box 245  (62838-0245)
PHONE..................................618 245-6216
Shirley Ann Quick, *Owner*
EMP: 3
SQ FT: 2,500
SALES (est): 80K  Privately Held
SIC: 2711  Job printing & newspaper publishing combined

**(G-10177)**
**QUALITY TARGETS**
204 Through St  (62838-3751)
PHONE..................................618 245-6515
EMP: 4
SALES (est): 258.1K  Privately Held
SIC: 3949  Sporting & athletic goods

## Farmer City
### De Witt County

**(G-10178)**
**BRANDT CONSOLIDATED  INC**
788 E 3070 North Rd  (61842)
PHONE..................................217 626-1123
Steve Darrett, *Branch Mgr*
EMP: 7
SALES (corp-wide): 180MM  Privately Held
WEB: www.indresgroup.com
SIC: 2875  5191  Fertilizers, mixing only; fertilizer & fertilizer materials
PA: Brandt Consolidated, Inc.
    2935 S Koke Mill Rd
    Springfield IL 62711
    217 547-5800

**(G-10179)**
**MAXWELL COUNTERS INC**
324 S Plum St  (61842-1438)
P.O. Box 234  (61842-0234)
PHONE..................................309 928-2848
Fax: 309 928-2833
Kevin Maxwell, *President*
Morgan Brackenhoff, *Accounts Mgr*
Paul Tobin, *Sales Associate*
Scott Daily, *Office Mgr*
Greg Schrock, *Manager*
EMP: 30
SALES (est): 5MM  Privately Held
WEB: www.maxwellcounters.com
SIC: 2541  2821  Counters or counter display cases, wood; plastics materials & resins

**(G-10180)**
**NEW ALLIANCE PRODUCTION LLC**
1701 N John St  (61842-1076)
P.O. Box 79  (61842-0079)
PHONE..................................309 928-3123
Fax: 309 928-3216
Cheryl Shane, *Manager*
Ronald White,
Thomas W Butler,
▼ EMP: 26
SALES (est): 2.7MM  Privately Held
SIC: 2041  0723  0115  5191  Flour & other grain mill products; crop preparation services for market; corn; seeds & bulbs

**(G-10181)**
**SALT CREEK ALPACAS INC**
3605 N 3300 East Rd  (61842-8304)
PHONE..................................309 530-7904
Dee Stielow, *Principal*
EMP: 3
SALES (est): 366.4K  Privately Held
SIC: 2231  Alpacas, mohair: woven

**(G-10182)**
**T&L INTERNATIONAL MFG/DIST INC**
25833 Hillcrest Dr  (61842-7804)
PHONE..................................309 830-7238
Thomas E Blalock, *President*
Leila Blalock, *Corp Secy*
Paris Blalock, *Vice Pres*
Nicole Vanderspool, *Vice Pres*
▲ EMP: 4
SQ FT: 18,000
SALES: 1MM  Privately Held
SIC: 3679  Electronic loads & power supplies

## Farmersville
### Montgomery County

**(G-10183)**
**CARTER PRINTING CO INC**
607 Elevator St  (62533-4414)
P.O. Box 289  (62533-0289)
PHONE..................................217 227-4464
Fax: 217 227-4140
Roy Carter Jr, *President*
Chris Holloway, *Sales Staff*
EMP: 8
SQ FT: 4,000
SALES (est): 1MM  Privately Held
WEB: www.raffle-tickets.com
SIC: 2752  2759  2791  2789  Commercial printing, offset; letterpress printing; typesetting; bookbinding & related work

**(G-10184)**
**TRANTER PHE INC**
30241 W Frontage Rd  (62533)
PHONE..................................217 227-3470
Donna Long, *Principal*
▲ EMP: 13
SALES (est): 2.2MM  Privately Held
SIC: 3443  Fabricated plate work (boiler shop)

## Farmington
### Fulton County

**(G-10185)**
**FARMINGTON LOCKER/ICE PLANT CO**
101 W Fort St  (61531-1117)
PHONE..................................309 245-4621
Michael Thurman, *Owner*
EMP: 4
SQ FT: 3,000
SALES: 300K  Privately Held
SIC: 5421  0751  2013  2011  Meat markets, including freezer provisioners; slaughtering: custom livestock services; sausages & other prepared meats; meat packing plants

**(G-10186)**
**FARMINGTON WILBERT VAULT CORP (PA)**
Also Called: Farmington Crematory
22413 E State Route 116  (61531-9452)
P.O. Box 50  (61531-0050)
PHONE..................................309 245-2133
Fax: 309 245-2132
Louis D Hecox, *President*
Janet Hecox, *Treasurer*
Karen Hecox, *Admin Sec*
EMP: 10  EST: 1954
SQ FT: 7,000
SALES (est): 1.2MM  Privately Held
SIC: 3272  Burial vaults, concrete or precast terrazzo; concrete products, precast; septic tanks, concrete

**(G-10187)**
**KITCHEN COOKED  INC (PA)**
632 N Main St  (61531-1076)
P.O. Box 200  (61531-0200)
PHONE..................................309 245-2191
Fax: 309 245-2196
Richard L Blackhurst, *President*
Paul Blackhurst, *Vice Pres*
Corey Starcevich, *Treasurer*
Lori Blackhurst, *Manager*
Mary Starcevich, *Admin Sec*
EMP: 47
SQ FT: 6,000
SALES (est): 3.5MM  Privately Held
SIC: 2096  Potato chips & other potato-based snacks

**(G-10188)**
**SAWMILL HYDRAULICS**
Also Called: Helle Sawmills
23522 W Farmington Rd  (61531-9492)
PHONE..................................309 245-2448
Fax: 309 245-5126
Verle Helle, *President*
Tom Skaggs, *Vice Pres*
Dennis Sanders, *Purch Agent*
Alice Herink, *Purchasing*
Chris Helle, *Marketing Staff*
EMP: 18
SQ FT: 26,000
SALES (est): 4.8MM  Privately Held
WEB: www.4helle.com
SIC: 3553  Sawmill machines

## Fillmore
### Montgomery County

**(G-10189)**
**S&S RECOVERY**
227 Baldknob Trl  (62032-2029)
PHONE..................................217 538-2206
Steve Bell, *Owner*
EMP: 4  EST: 2008
SALES (est): 296.2K  Privately Held
SIC: 3531  Automobile wrecker hoists

**(G-10190)**
**UNIQUE NOVELTY & MANUFACTURING**
Also Called: Unique Novelty Mfg & Sales
200 S Main St  (62032-2348)
P.O. Box 98  (62032-0098)
PHONE..................................217 538-2014
Fax: 217 538-2014
Mary Jones, *President*
EMP: 3
SALES (est): 192.6K  Privately Held
SIC: 7389  3942  Textile & apparel services; dolls & stuffed toys

## Fisher
### Champaign County

**(G-10191)**
**PRAXSYM  INC**
120 S 3rd St  (61843-9549)
P.O. Box 369  (61843-0369)
PHONE..................................217 897-1744
Fax: 217 897-6388
David Heiser, *President*
Roger Heiser, *Admin Sec*
Walter Gordon,
EMP: 12
SQ FT: 4,500
SALES: 825.7K  Privately Held
WEB: www.praxsym.com
SIC: 3829  Measuring & controlling devices

**(G-10192)**
**VESUVIUS U S A CORPORATION**
Hwy 136 E  (61843)
P.O. Box 639  (61843-0639)
PHONE..................................217 897-1145
Fax: 217 897-6532
EMP: 134
SALES (corp-wide): 2.3B  Privately Held
SIC: 3297  Mfg Nonclay Refractories Mfg Valves/Pipe Fittings Mfg Industrial Valves Nonferrous Metal Foundry
HQ: Vesuvius U S A Corporation
    1404 Newton Dr
    Champaign IL 61822
    217 402-9204

## Fithian
### Vermilion County

**(G-10193)**
**FORSYTH BROTHERS CONCRETE PDTS**
104 E North Sherman St  (61844-1000)
P.O. Box 65  (61844-0065)
PHONE..................................217 548-2770
Jeffrey Bell, *President*

## GEOGRAPHIC SECTION

Flora - Clay County (G-10218)

EMP: 3
SALES (corp-wide): 1.1MM **Privately Held**
SIC: 3272 Burial vaults, concrete or pre-cast terrazzo; septic tanks, concrete
PA: Forsyth Brothers Concrete Products Inc
4500 N Fruitridge St
Terre Haute IN 47805
812 466-4080

### Flanagan
*Livingston County*

**(G-10194)**
**HULSE EXCAVATING**
20289 N 400 East Rd (61740-8968)
PHONE...................................815 796-4106
Marlan Hulse, *Owner*
EMP: 3
SALES (est): 200K **Privately Held**
SIC: 1794 3272 Excavation work; drain tile, concrete

### Flat Rock
*Crawford County*

**(G-10195)**
**DATAFORDUMMIES**
32 N 1550th St (62427-2705)
PHONE...................................618 421-2323
EMP: 5 EST: 2010
SALES (est): 190K **Privately Held**
SIC: 7372 Prepackaged Software Services

**(G-10196)**
**RUSTIC WOODCRAFTS**
10510 E 350th Ave (62427-2019)
PHONE...................................618 584-3912
David A Raber, *Owner*
EMP: 4
SALES: 360K **Privately Held**
SIC: 2519 Household furniture

**(G-10197)**
**STAR ENERGY CORP INC**
1675 N 1200 Rd (62427)
P.O. Box 584, Lawrenceville (62439-0584)
PHONE...................................618 584-3631
Frank Ruvolo, *President*
EMP: 3
SALES (est): 267.4K **Privately Held**
SIC: 1311 Crude petroleum & natural gas

**(G-10198)**
**SUGARCREEK WOODWORKING**
1501 N 1300th St (62427-2623)
PHONE...................................618 584-3817
EMP: 4
SALES (est): 274.9K **Privately Held**
SIC: 2431 Millwork

**(G-10199)**
**WHITE OWL WINERY INCORPORATED**
Rr 1 (62427)
PHONE...................................618 928-2898
Fax: 618 928-2016
Brian Neighbors, *President*
Fred Tromley, *Plant Mgr*
Ken Neighbors, *Branch Mgr*
EMP: 4
SALES (est): 380K **Privately Held**
WEB: www.whiteowlwinery.com
SIC: 2048 Cereal-, grain-, & seed-based feeds

### Flora
*Clay County*

**(G-10200)**
**BOOTH OIL CO INC**
Rr 2 (62839-9803)
P.O. Box 158 (62839-0158)
PHONE...................................618 662-7696
Doug Pottorff, *President*
Marilyn Booth, *Vice Pres*
EMP: 6
SQ FT: 1,300
SALES: 249.8K **Privately Held**
SIC: 1311 Crude petroleum production

**(G-10201)**
**BOOTH RESOURCES INC**
Also Called: B R I Operations
7965 Old Highway 50 (62839-4106)
P.O. Box 720 (62839-0720)
PHONE...................................618 662-4955
Marcus P Booth, *President*
EMP: 9
SQ FT: 4,000
SALES (est): 1.1MM **Privately Held**
SIC: 1311 1381 Crude petroleum production; directional drilling oil & gas wells

**(G-10202)**
**CARGILL INCORPORATED**
6 Industrial Park (62839-9700)
PHONE...................................618 662-8070
Fax: 618 662-4458
Mary Henry, *QC Dir*
Jim Cartwright, *Manager*
EMP: 17
SALES (corp-wide): 107.1B **Privately Held**
WEB: www.cargill.com
SIC: 2048 Prepared feeds
PA: Cargill, Incorporated
15407 Mcginty Rd W
Wayzata MN 55391
952 742-7575

**(G-10203)**
**CLAY CNTY RHBILITATION CTR INC**
Also Called: Clay County Industries
1 Commercial Dr (62839-9000)
PHONE...................................618 662-6607
Gary White, *Branch Mgr*
EMP: 12
SALES (corp-wide): 1.8MM **Privately Held**
WEB: www.clayrhab.com
SIC: 8331 3465 Vocational rehabilitation agency; vocational training agency; job counseling; automotive stampings
PA: Clay County Rehabilitation Center, Inc.
1 Commercial Dr
Flora IL 62839
618 662-4916

**(G-10204)**
**CLAY COUNTY ADVOCATE PRESS**
Also Called: Liberty Group Pubg III Hldings
105 W North Ave (62839-1613)
P.O. Box 519 (62839-0519)
PHONE...................................618 662-6397
Fax: 618 662-2939
Ray McGrew, *Publisher*
Duane Crays, *Publisher*
Carrie Dagg, *Manager*
EMP: 4
SALES (est): 160K **Privately Held**
WEB: www.advocatepress.com
SIC: 2711 Newspapers: publishing only, not printed on site

**(G-10205)**
**CRUSADE ENTERPRISES INC**
Also Called: T Renee Productions
200 E North Ave (62839-2029)
PHONE...................................618 662-4461
Fax: 618 662-3371
Dolores Harris, *Partner*
Tammy R Pob, *Corp Secy*
EMP: 2
SQ FT: 7,500
SALES (est): 238.9K **Privately Held**
WEB: www.tammyrenee.org
SIC: 3652 8661 Pre-recorded records & tapes; religious organizations

**(G-10206)**
**FLORA BOWL**
927 W North Ave (62839-1221)
PHONE...................................618 662-4561
Steven Galloway, *President*
◆ EMP: 5 EST: 1975
SQ FT: 3,100
SALES: 130K **Privately Held**
SIC: 3949 Bowling alleys & accessories

**(G-10207)**
**FLORA READY MIX INC**
11170 Old Highway 50 (62839-3432)
PHONE...................................618 662-4818
Eddie Musgrave, *President*
William Kent Musgrave, *Vice Pres*
Robert P Musgrave, *Treasurer*
EMP: 7
SQ FT: 2,200
SALES: 1.2MM **Privately Held**
SIC: 3273 Ready-mixed concrete

**(G-10208)**
**HELLA CORPORATE CENTER USA INC**
Also Called: Hella Electronics
50 Industrial Park (62839-9700)
PHONE...................................734 414-0900
Bill Killeon, *Branch Mgr*
EMP: 350
SALES (corp-wide): 7.2B **Privately Held**
SIC: 3625 5013 5088 Relays & industrial controls; motor vehicle supplies & new parts; transportation equipment & supplies
HQ: Hella Corporate Center Usa, Inc.
43811 Plymouth Oaks Blvd
Plymouth MI 48170
586 232-4788

**(G-10209)**
**HELLA CORPORATE CENTER USA INC**
1101 Vincennes Ave (62839-3440)
P.O. Box 398 (62839-0398)
PHONE...................................618 662-4402
Bill Killion, *Plt & Fclts Mgr*
Dustin Hackney, *IT/INT Sup*
Steve Hubble, *IT/INT Sup*
EMP: 350
SALES (corp-wide): 7.2B **Privately Held**
SIC: 3625 Relays & industrial controls
HQ: Hella Corporate Center Usa, Inc.
43811 Plymouth Oaks Blvd
Plymouth MI 48170
586 232-4788

**(G-10210)**
**HELLA ELECTRONICS CORPORATION**
1101 Vincennes Ave (62839-3440)
P.O. Box 398 (62839-0398)
PHONE...................................618 662-5186
Fax: 618 662-4720
Steve Hubble, *Plant Mgr*
Bryan Hawkins, *Prdtn Mgr*
Bill Killion, *Plt & Fclts Mgr*
Mike Saltsgaver, *QC Mgr*
Brad Fruend, *Engineer*
EMP: 540
SALES (corp-wide): 7.2B **Privately Held**
SIC: 3625 Relays & industrial controls
HQ: Hella Electronics Corporation
43811 Plymouth Oaks Blvd
Plymouth MI 48170
734 414-0900

**(G-10211)**
**MEAGHER SIGN & GRAPHICS INC**
225 Hagen Dr (62839-2338)
PHONE...................................618 662-7446
Lela Meagher, *President*
Norman Meagher, *Admin Sec*
EMP: 7
SALES (est): 901.2K **Privately Held**
SIC: 3993 Signs & advertising specialties

**(G-10212)**
**NORTH AMERICAN LIGHTING INC**
Also Called: N A L
20 Industrial Park (62839-9700)
PHONE...................................618 662-4483
Fax: 618 662-8143
Mark Kinsella, *General Mgr*
Greg Conrad, *Mfg Dir*
Stan Stanford, *Opers Mgr*
Randy Flood, *Opers Staff*
Mike Frank, *Production*
EMP: 500
SALES (corp-wide): 7.4B **Privately Held**
WEB: www.nal.com
SIC: 3647 Automotive lighting fixtures

HQ: North American Lighting, Inc.
2275 S Main St
Paris IL 61944
217 465-6600

**(G-10213)**
**PACKAGING CORPORATION AMERICA**
Also Called: PCA
32 Industrial Park (62839-9700)
PHONE...................................618 662-6700
Fax: 618 662-4504
Tom Krutsinger, *Plant Mgr*
Tom Krugsinger, *Branch Mgr*
EMP: 7
SALES (corp-wide): 5.7B **Publicly Held**
WEB: www.columbuscontainer.com
SIC: 2653 Boxes, corrugated: made from purchased materials; boxes, solid fiber: made from purchased materials
PA: Packaging Corporation Of America
1955 W Field Ct
Lake Forest IL 60045
847 482-3000

**(G-10214)**
**QCIRCUITS INC**
1 Industrial Park (62839-9700)
PHONE...................................618 662-8365
Cody Keen, *Plant Mgr*
Eric Petty, *Opers Mgr*
Tom Scanlan, *Engineer*
Nancy Leak, *Office Mgr*
EMP: 40
SALES (corp-wide): 8.7MM **Privately Held**
WEB: www.bel-tronicscorp.com
SIC: 3677 3672 3612 Electronic coils, transformers & other inductors; printed circuit boards; motors & generators
PA: Qcircuits, Inc.
2775 Algonquin Rd Ste 300
Rolling Meadows IL 60008
847 797-6678

**(G-10215)**
**SHERWIN-WILLIAMS COMPANY**
14 Industrial Park (62839-9700)
PHONE...................................618 662-4415
Jim Taylor, *Manager*
Lisa Pierson, *Exec Sec*
EMP: 126
SQ FT: 34,000
SALES (corp-wide): 11.8B **Publicly Held**
WEB: www.sherwin.com
SIC: 5231 2851 Paint & painting supplies; paints & allied products
PA: The Sherwin-Williams Company
101 W Prospect Ave # 1020
Cleveland OH 44115
216 566-2000

**(G-10216)**
**SHIRT TALES**
134 W North Ave (62839-1612)
PHONE...................................618 662-4572
Rick Slaughter, *President*
Sharon Slaghtuerl, *President*
EMP: 3
SALES (est): 192.6K **Privately Held**
SIC: 2395 Embroidery products, except schiffli machine

**(G-10217)**
**SILGAN PLASTICS LLC**
2 Industrial Park (62839-9700)
PHONE...................................618 662-4471
Brian Craig, *Branch Mgr*
Robert Cohn, *Programmer Anys*
EMP: 85
SALES (corp-wide): 3.6B **Publicly Held**
WEB: www.silganplastics.com
SIC: 3089 3085 2673 Molding primary plastic; plastics bottles; bags: plastic, laminated & coated
HQ: Silgan Plastics Llc
14515 North Outer 40 Rd # 210
Chesterfield MO 63017
800 274-5426

**(G-10218)**
**SMOCO INC**
832 W North Ave Ste A1 (62839-1293)
P.O. Box 367 (62839-0367)
PHONE...................................618 662-6458
Milton Smith II, *President*

**Flora - Clay County (G-10219)**

EMP: 2
SQ FT: 1,200
SALES: 200K **Privately Held**
SIC: 1311 Crude petroleum production

**(G-10219)**
**SOUTHWIRE COMPANY LLC**
Southwire Utility Products Div
Eash Rd (62839)
P.O. Box 479 (62839-0479)
PHONE..................................618 662-8341
Fax: 618 662-8344
Chuck McLendon, *Plant Mgr*
Larry Brown, *QC Dir*
Kari Warren, *Manager*
Jim Owens, *Manager*
EMP: 72
SALES (corp-wide): 3.2B **Privately Held**
WEB: www.southwire.com
SIC: 3315 3355 Cable, steel: insulated or armored; wire, aluminum: made in rolling mills
PA: Southwire Company, Llc
   1 Southwire Dr
   Carrollton GA 30119
   770 832-4242

**(G-10220)**
**WARRIOR LOGGING & PERFORAGINE**
174 Lincoln Rd (62839-3352)
P.O. Box 51 (62839-0051)
PHONE..................................618 662-7373
EMP: 4
SALES (est): 368.9K **Privately Held**
SIC: 2411 Logging

**(G-10221)**
**WARRIOR WELL SERVICES INC**
745 Cedardom Dr (62839)
PHONE..................................618 662-7710
Brent Burgess, *President*
Tom Skinner, *Manager*
EMP: 9 EST: 1999
SQ FT: 1,000
SALES (est): 708.8K **Privately Held**
WEB: www.warriorenergyservices.com
SIC: 2411 Logging

**(G-10222)**
**WOODROW TODD**
1502 N Olive Rd (62839-2347)
PHONE..................................618 838-9105
Todd Woodrow,
EMP: 3
SALES (est): 140.1K **Privately Held**
SIC: 1382 Oil & gas exploration services

---

### Flossmoor
*Cook County*

**(G-10223)**
**CAULFIELDS RESTAURANT LTD**
Also Called: Flossmoor Station Brewing Co
1035 Sterling Ave (60422-1252)
PHONE..................................708 798-1599
Fax: 708 957-8329
F Dean Armstrong, *President*
Carolyn Armstrong, *Vice Pres*
Donna Hruska, *Info Tech Dir*
EMP: 50
SQ FT: 4,000
SALES (est): 6.9MM **Privately Held**
WEB: www.flossmoorstation.com
SIC: 2082 5812 Beer (alcoholic beverage); eating places

**(G-10224)**
**FLEETCHEM LLC (PA)**
1222 Brassie Ave Ste 19 (60422-1623)
PHONE..................................708 957-5311
Thomas J Blakemore,
Tim Thompson, *Admin Sec*
Kathy Blakemore,
Shelley Howard, *Clerk*
EMP: 1
SALES (est): 1.1MM **Privately Held**
WEB: www.fleetchem.com
SIC: 2045 Blended flour: from purchased flour

**(G-10225)**
**HANDS OF MANY LLC**
1301 Braeburn Ave (60422-1801)
P.O. Box 604 (60422-0604)
PHONE..................................917 841-9969
Christopher Casey, *Mng Member*
EMP: 3
SALES (est): 146.8K **Privately Held**
SIC: 7372 7379 Prepackaged software; computer related consulting services

**(G-10226)**
**JOLIET ORTHOTICS**
2119 Vardon Ln (60422-1372)
PHONE..................................708 798-1767
Daniel Rinella, *Principal*
EMP: 3
SALES (est): 256K **Privately Held**
SIC: 3842 Orthopedic appliances

**(G-10227)**
**PIN HSIAO & ASSOCIATES LLC**
Also Called: Zen Bakery, MA
1040 Sterling Ave (60422-1234)
PHONE..................................206 818-0155
Pin Hsiano,
EMP: 20
SALES (corp-wide): 68.8MM **Privately Held**
SIC: 2051 Bakery: wholesale or wholesale/retail combined
PA: Pin Hsiao & Associates L.L.C.
   138 105th Ave Ne
   Bellevue WA 98004
   425 637-3357

**(G-10228)**
**SNOW COMMAND INCORPORATED**
1607 Tina Ln (60422-1952)
PHONE..................................708 991-7004
Nick Eeluca, *President*
EMP: 3
SALES (est): 261.8K **Privately Held**
SIC: 2851 Removers & cleaners

**(G-10229)**
**SPRINGBOX INC**
Also Called: Ink Solution
2842 Scott Cres (60422-1724)
PHONE..................................708 921-9944
Therone Watson, *President*
EMP: 3
SALES (est): 389.2K **Privately Held**
SIC: 2893 Printing ink

**(G-10230)**
**STONE LIGHTING LLC**
2630 Flossmoor Rd Ste 102 (60422-1560)
PHONE..................................312 240-0400
Andy Stone, *Vice Pres*
Jenny Kruse, *Cust Mgr*
Ben Sanborn, *Business Anlyst*
Ronald Stone,
EMP: 19
SALES (est): 3.1MM **Privately Held**
SIC: 3645 5063 Boudoir lamps; chandeliers, residential; fluorescent lighting fixtures, residential; garden, patio, walkway & yard lighting fixtures: electric; light bulbs & related supplies; lighting fixtures, residential

**(G-10231)**
**SWEET ANNIES BAKERY INC**
19710 Governors Hwy Ste 6 (60422-2081)
PHONE..................................708 297-7066
Fax: 708 799-7956
Michele Williams, *President*
EMP: 10
SQ FT: 1,700
SALES (est): 771.5K **Privately Held**
SIC: 2051 Cakes, bakery: except frozen

---

### Foosland
*Champaign County*

**(G-10232)**
**HEDRICKS WELDING & FABRICATION**
201 Main St (61845-9403)
P.O. Box 77 (61845-0077)
PHONE..................................217 846-3230
Fax: 217 846-3921
Greg H Hedrick, *President*
Amy Hedrick, *Manager*
EMP: 3
SQ FT: 5,200
SALES (est): 250K **Privately Held**
SIC: 7692 Welding repair

---

### Ford Heights
*Cook County*

**(G-10233)**
**FORD MOTOR COMPANY**
1000 E Lincoln Hwy (60411-2997)
P.O. Box 6, Chicago Heights (60412-0020)
PHONE..................................708 757-5700
Fax: 708 681-6423
Lisa Recinella, *QC Mgr*
Steve Fugaj, *Engineer*
Randolph Griffin, *Branch Mgr*
Robert Marotta, *Manager*
R J Mielcarz, *Supervisor*
EMP: 1920
SQ FT: 2,500,000
SALES (corp-wide): 151.8B **Publicly Held**
WEB: www.ford.com
SIC: 3465 3469 Automotive stampings; metal stampings
PA: Ford Motor Company
   1 American Rd
   Dearborn MI 48126
   313 322-3000

---

### Forest Park
*Cook County*

**(G-10234)**
**ACCENTS BY FRED**
7519 Madison St (60130-1407)
PHONE..................................708 366-9850
Frederick Bryant, *Owner*
EMP: 4
SALES (est): 388.3K **Privately Held**
SIC: 3911 Jewelry, precious metal

**(G-10235)**
**BLUE MONKEY GRAPHICS INC**
7540 Roosevelt Rd Ste 4 (60130-3054)
P.O. Box 56, Lyons (60534-0056)
PHONE..................................708 488-9501
Ruben Meza, *President*
Daniel Meza, *Vice Pres*
Hector Meza, *Manager*
EMP: 3
SALES (est): 253.1K **Privately Held**
WEB: www.bluemonkeyinc.com
SIC: 3953 Screens, textile printing

**(G-10236)**
**CASA DE PUROS**
7410 Madison St (60130-1501)
PHONE..................................708 725-7180
EMP: 2
SALES (est): 233.4K **Privately Held**
SIC: 2131 Smoking tobacco

**(G-10237)**
**CHICAGO PRODUCERS INC**
Also Called: Studio Out West
7507 Madison St Ste D4 (60130-3514)
PHONE..................................312 226-6900
Fax: 312 226-6906
William Vala, *President*
Jason Gill, *Vice Pres*
Alcides Mariano Jr, *Accountant*
Michael Bambacht, *Director*
Bill Vala, *Creative Dir*
EMP: 13

SALES: 1MM **Privately Held**
WEB: www.chicagoproducers.com
SIC: 3652 2754 Pre-recorded records & tapes; visiting cards: gravure printing

**(G-10238)**
**CLARK CASTER CO**
Also Called: A & E Forge
7310 Roosevelt Rd (60130-2443)
P.O. Box 83, Cave In Rock (62919-0083)
PHONE..................................708 366-1913
Fax: 708 366-5103
James H Clark, *President*
Bernice Clark, *Admin Sec*
EMP: 5
SQ FT: 3,000
SALES (est): 853.1K **Privately Held**
WEB: www.clarkcaster.com
SIC: 5072 3537 Casters & glides; industrial trucks & tractors

**(G-10239)**
**CLASSIC SCREEN PRINTING INC**
1401 Circle Ave Ste 1n (60130-2649)
PHONE..................................708 771-9355
Fax: 708 366-0788
Robert Shaw, *President*
Laura Shaw, *Vice Pres*
EMP: 12
SQ FT: 5,400
SALES (est): 750K **Privately Held**
WEB: www.cspselect.com
SIC: 2396 Screen printing on fabric articles

**(G-10240)**
**ENERGY TEES**
1401 Circle Ave Ste 1n (60130-2649)
PHONE..................................708 771-0000
Robert Shaw, *President*
Laura Shaw, *Vice Pres*
EMP: 6
SALES: 350K **Privately Held**
SIC: 2759 7389 Screen printing; embroidering of advertising on shirts, etc.

**(G-10241)**
**ESSENTRA COMPONENTS INC**
Also Called: Essentra Components-Richco
7400 Industrial Dr (60130-2536)
PHONE..................................815 943-6487
Fax: 815 943-5510
David Decker, *Principal*
Andrew Shallcross, *Business Mgr*
William Vasa, *Facilities Mgr*
Valerie Olcott, *QC Dir*
Cheryl Cummins, *Engineer*
EMP: 150
SALES (corp-wide): 1.2B **Privately Held**
WEB: www.richco-inc.com
SIC: 3089 3544 3496 3452 Plastic processing; special dies, tools, jigs & fixtures; miscellaneous fabricated wire products; bolts, nuts, rivets & washers
HQ: Essentra Components Inc.
   2 Westbrook Corp Ctr
   Westchester IL 60154
   704 418-8692

**(G-10242)**
**ESSENTRA SPECIALTY TAPES INC**
7400 Industrial Dr (60130-2536)
PHONE..................................708 488-1025
Fax: 708 488-1215
Brett J York, *President*
John Brunner, *Vice Pres*
Gary Taylor, *Vice Pres*
Dwight Deck, *Plant Mgr*
Bill Vasa, *Opers Mgr*
▲ EMP: 116 EST: 1947
SQ FT: 152,000
SALES (est): 29.7MM
SALES (corp-wide): 1.2B **Privately Held**
WEB: www.duracoinc.com
SIC: 3069 3086 Sponge rubber & sponge rubber products; plastics foam products
HQ: Porex Technologies Corporation
   1625 Ashton Park Dr Ste A
   South Chesterfield VA 23834
   804 524-4983

**(G-10243)**
**FARMINGTON FOODS INC (PA)**
7419 Franklin St (60130-1016)
PHONE..................................708 771-3600

Fax: 708 771-4623
Anthony Dijohn, *President*
Frank A Dijohn, *President*
Michael Crangle, *Engineer*
▼ **EMP:** 155
**SQ FT:** 55,000
**SALES (est):** 96MM **Privately Held**
**WEB:** www.farmingtonfoods.com
**SIC: 2013** Prepared beef products from purchased beef; prepared pork products from purchased pork

**(G-10244)**
**FERRARA CANDY COMPANY**
Also Called: Ferrara Pan Candy Co
7301 Harrison St (60130-2083)
**PHONE**.................................630 366-0500
**EMP:** 272
**SALES (corp-wide):** 616.5MM **Privately Held**
**SIC: 2064** Candy & other confectionery products
**PA:** Ferrara Candy Company
1 Tower Ln Ste 2700
Oakbrook Terrace IL 60181
708 366-0500

**(G-10245)**
**FERRARA CANDY COMPANY**
7525 Industrial Dr (60130-2515)
**PHONE**.................................708 488-1892
Sal Ferrara, *CEO*
**EMP:** 272
**SALES (corp-wide):** 618.9MM **Privately Held**
**SIC: 2064** Candy & other confectionery products; chewing candy, not chewing gum; chocolate candy, except solid chocolate; jellybeans
**PA:** Ferrara Candy Company
1 Tower Ln Ste 2700
Oakbrook Terrace IL 60181
708 366-0500

**(G-10246)**
**FOREST PLATING CO**
930 Des Plaines Ave (60130-2199)
**PHONE**.................................708 366-2071
Fax: 708 366-2092
Walter Mc Govern, *President*
William P Mc Govern, *President*
**EMP:** 6 **EST:** 1947
**SQ FT:** 4,800
**SALES:** 566.7K **Privately Held**
**SIC: 3471** Plating of metals or formed products

**(G-10247)**
**FOREST PRINTING CO**
7214 Madison St Ste 1 (60130-3106)
P.O. Box 79 (60130-0079)
**PHONE**.................................708 366-5100
Fax: 708 366-6400
Randy Martini, *President*
Dennis Turek, *President*
Vaughn Martini, *Prdtn Mgr*
Diana Alvarez, *Manager*
Ken Turek, *Director*
**EMP:** 13
**SQ FT:** 3,000
**SALES (est):** 2.3MM **Privately Held**
**WEB:** www.forestprinting.net
**SIC: 2752** Commercial printing, lithographic

**(G-10248)**
**HEIMBURGER HOUSE PUBG CO INC**
Also Called: Scenery Unlimited
7236 Madison St (60130-1765)
**PHONE**.................................708 366-1973
Fax: 708 366-1973
Donald Heimburger, *President*
Cindy Kelley, *Admin Sec*
Marilyn Heimburger, *Assistant*
▲ **EMP:** 6
**SALES (est):** 500K **Privately Held**
**SIC: 2731** Book music: publishing only, not printed on site

**(G-10249)**
**INDEPENDENT NETWORK TV LLC**
1525 Circle Ave Ste 3 (60130-2647)
**PHONE**.................................312 953-8508
Rodger Jackson, *Mng Member*

**EMP:** 3
**SALES (est):** 71.1K **Privately Held**
**SIC: 7372** Home entertainment computer software

**(G-10250)**
**KAFKA MANUFACTURING CO**
7600 Industrial Dr (60130-2518)
**PHONE**.................................708 771-0970
Fax: 708 771-0108
Jeffrey S Kafka, *President*
Karen Kafka, *Corp Secy*
Jose Villarruel, *Project Mgr*
**EMP:** 9
**SQ FT:** 21,000
**SALES (est):** 693K **Privately Held**
**SIC: 3534** Elevators & equipment

**(G-10251)**
**NEW ARCHERY PRODUCTS LLC**
Also Called: Quikfletch
7500 Industrial Dr (60130-2516)
**PHONE**.................................708 488-2500
Fax: 708 488-2515
Greg Smith, *General Mgr*
Holger Volger, *Business Mgr*
Chris Hunter, *Plant Mgr*
Chris Kozlik, *Engineer*
David Speelman, *Controller*
▲ **EMP:** 60 **EST:** 1975
**SQ FT:** 20,000
**SALES:** 7.6MM
**SALES (corp-wide):** 11.4MM **Privately Held**
**WEB:** www.newarchery.com
**SIC: 3949** Archery equipment, general; arrows, archery
**PA:** Brs Outdoor Sports Holdings Llc
126 E 56th St Fl 29
New York NY 10022
212 521-3700

**(G-10252)**
**S & S ELECTRIC SERVICE**
447 Hannah Ave (60130-1703)
P.O. Box 486 (60130-0486)
**PHONE**.................................708 366-5800
Michael Stisevic, *Owner*
**EMP:** 4
**SALES (est):** 439.9K **Privately Held**
**SIC: 3699** Electrical equipment & supplies

**(G-10253)**
**SIEVERT ELECTRIC SVC & SLS CO**
1230 Hannah Ave (60130-2400)
**PHONE**.................................708 771-1600
Peter A Sievert, *President*
Dave Bishop, *Project Mgr*
Greg Michigan, *VP Sales*
John Gilbert, *Admin Sec*
Scott C Sievert, *Admin Sec*
**EMP:** 60
**SQ FT:** 20,000
**SALES (est):** 22.8MM **Privately Held**
**WEB:** www.sievertelectric.com
**SIC: 3536 1731** Hoists; cranes, industrial plant; general electrical contractor

**(G-10254)**
**THULE INC**
Also Called: Thule Chicago
7609 Industrial Dr (60130-2517)
**PHONE**.................................847 455-2420
Gary Vehrenkamp, *Vice Pres*
Frank Giannotta, *Purchasing*
Rich Ellinger, *Sales Staff*
Megan Morrissey, *Mktg Dir*
Donald Domanus, *Director*
**EMP:** 120
**SALES (corp-wide):** 605.7MM **Privately Held**
**WEB:** www.karriteus.com
**SIC: 3713** Truck & bus bodies
**HQ:** Thule, Inc.
42 Silvermine Rd
Seymour CT 06483
203 881-9600

**(G-10255)**
**TIFFANY STAINED GLASS LTD**
428 Des Plaines Ave Ste 1 (60130-3195)
**PHONE**.................................312 642-0680
Fax: 312 642-0701
Robert Nugent,
**EMP:** 6 **EST:** 1975

**SQ FT:** 5,000
**SALES (est):** 410K **Privately Held**
**WEB:** www.tiffanystainedglass.com
**SIC: 3231 7699** Stained glass: made from purchased glass; antique repair & restoration, except furniture, automobiles

**(G-10256)**
**VOCO TOOL & MFG INC**
1441 Circle Ave (60130-2697)
**PHONE**.................................708 771-3800
Fax: 708 771-3278
Ralph Vogel, *President*
Bob Bennett, *Managing Prtnr*
Mary Jane Bennett, *Vice Pres*
Nancy Vogel, *Treasurer*
Jim Bennett, *Manager*
**EMP:** 8 **EST:** 1960
**SQ FT:** 15,000
**SALES:** 1MM **Privately Held**
**WEB:** www.vocotool.com
**SIC: 3469 3544** Stamping metal for the trade; special dies, tools, jigs & fixtures

**(G-10257)**
**WEST FUELS INC**
7340 Harrison St (60130-2017)
**PHONE**.................................708 488-8880
Deborah Stange, *President*
**EMP:** 5
**SALES (est):** 473.2K **Privately Held**
**SIC: 2869** Fuels

### Forest View
*Cook County*

**(G-10258)**
**JDB MACHINING INC**
4635 S Harlem Ave (60402-4252)
**PHONE**.................................708 749-9596
William Dinon, *President*
Daniel Ziemkiewicz, *Treasurer*
▲ **EMP:** 5
**SQ FT:** 6,700
**SALES (est):** 602.8K **Privately Held**
**SIC: 3599** Machine & other job shop work

**(G-10259)**
**JDB MANUFACTURING COMPANY**
4635 S Harlem Ave (60402-4252)
**PHONE**.................................708 749-9596
William G Dinon, *President*
▲ **EMP:** 7
**SQ FT:** 15,000
**SALES:** 1.5MM **Privately Held**
**SIC: 3599** Machine & other job shop work

### Forrest
*Livingston County*

**(G-10260)**
**ANLIKER CUSTOM WOOD**
208 W Wabash Ave (61741-9651)
**PHONE**.................................815 657-7510
Robert Anliker, *Owner*
**EMP:** 10
**SALES (est):** 700.9K **Privately Held**
**WEB:** www.anlikercabinet.com
**SIC: 2434** Wood kitchen cabinets

**(G-10261)**
**CROSSROAD CRATING & PALLET**
27700 E 700 North Rd (61741-9468)
P.O. Box 260 (61741-0260)
**PHONE**.................................815 657-8409
Mark Haab, *President*
**EMP:** 9
**SALES:** 1.4MM **Privately Held**
**SIC: 2448** Wood pallets & skids

**(G-10262)**
**FORREST REDI-MIX INC**
321 W Krack St (61741-9368)
P.O. Box 308 (61741-0308)
**PHONE**.................................815 657-8241
Ron Steidinger, *President*
Scot Steidinger, *Vice Pres*
Pam Rieger, *CFO*

Pamela Rieger, *Admin Sec*
**EMP:** 6
**SQ FT:** 800
**SALES (est):** 1.1MM **Privately Held**
**SIC: 3273 3272** Ready-mixed concrete; concrete products

**(G-10263)**
**KNAPP INDUSTRIAL WOOD**
820 N Center St (61741-9600)
P.O. Box 543 (61741-0543)
**PHONE**.................................815 657-8854
Fax: 815 657-8151
Louie D Knapp, *Owner*
Ken Wooten, *General Mgr*
**EMP:** 12
**SALES:** 1.9MM **Privately Held**
**SIC: 2512** Upholstered household furniture

**(G-10264)**
**SELIG S LLC**
342 E Wabash Ave (61741-9500)
**PHONE**.................................815 785-2100
Andrew Kauffman,
**EMP:** 3 **EST:** 2015
**SALES (est):** 142K **Privately Held**
**SIC: 3089** Mfg Plastic Products

**(G-10265)**
**SELIG SEALING HOLDINGS INC (DH)**
342 E Wabash Ave (61741-9500)
**PHONE**.................................815 785-2100
Steve Brucker, *President*
Stephen Cassidy, *Principal*
Bill Radek, *Exec VP*
John Brown, *Vice Pres*
Randy Hart, *Buyer*
**EMP:** 8 **EST:** 2005
**SALES (est):** 33.5MM
**SALES (corp-wide):** 1.4B **Privately Held**
**SIC: 3089** Caps, plastic
**HQ:** Cc Industries Inc.
222 N La Salle St # 1000
Chicago IL 60601
312 855-4000

**(G-10266)**
**SELIG SEALING PRODUCTS INC (DH)**
342 E Wabash Ave (61741-9500)
**PHONE**.................................815 785-2100
Fax: 815 657-8578
Steve Cassidy, *CEO*
Mark Bossong, *Exec VP*
Bob Woods, *Vice Pres*
Steve Brucker, *VP Mfg*
Christiane Lant, *Purch Dir*
▲ **EMP:** 2
**SQ FT:** 128,000
**SALES:** 33.5MM
**SALES (corp-wide):** 1.4B **Privately Held**
**WEB:** www.seligsealing.com
**SIC: 2671** Paper coated or laminated for packaging
**HQ:** Selig Sealing Holdings, Inc.
342 E Wabash Ave
Forrest IL 61741
815 785-2100

**(G-10267)**
**SLAGEL MANUFACTURING INC**
Also Called: Vulcan Equipment
2911 N 2700 East Rd (61741-9333)
**PHONE**.................................815 688-3318
Mark Slagel, *President*
Christie Todd, *Office Mgr*
Sheila Howard, *Admin Sec*
Donald Slagel, *Admin Sec*
▲ **EMP:** 40
**SQ FT:** 64,000
**SALES (est):** 5.6MM **Privately Held**
**SIC: 3999** Novelties, bric-a-brac & hobby kits

### Forreston
*Ogle County*

**(G-10268)**
**DANLEE WOOD PRODUCTS INC**
207 S Chestnut St (61030-8000)
**PHONE**.................................815 938-9016
**Toll Free:**.................................888 -

# Forreston - Ogle County (G-10269)   GEOGRAPHIC SECTION

Fax: 815 938-3187
Daniel Reif, *President*
**EMP:** 2 **EST:** 1997
**SQ FT:** 3,200
**SALES:** 3MM **Privately Held**
**SIC:** 2499 Laundry products, wood

**(G-10269)**
**FORRESTON TOOL INC**
400 E Avon St (61030-7712)
P.O. Box 119 (61030-0119)
**PHONE**.................................815 938-3626
Fax: 815 938-2001
Paul W White, *President*
Danny Mc Kean, *Vice Pres*
**EMP:** 11
**SQ FT:** 4,560
**SALES:** 750K **Privately Held**
**SIC:** 3089 Injection molded finished plastic products

**(G-10270)**
**MID-AMERICA PLASTIC COMPANY**
500 E Avon St (61030-7713)
P.O. Box 667 (61030-0667)
**PHONE**.................................815 938-3110
Fax: 815 938-3172
Patricia Erdmann, *CEO*
Eric Erdmann, *President*
**EMP:** 32
**SQ FT:** 17,500
**SALES (est):** 5.6MM **Privately Held**
**WEB:** www.midamericaplastic.com
**SIC:** 3089 Injection molding of plastics

## Forsyth
### Macon County

**(G-10271)**
**REVELLE RESOURCES INC**
275 Hickory Point Ct (62535-9708)
**PHONE**.................................217 875-7336
Karen S Revelle, *President*
Brett Revelle, *Vice Pres*
Joseph Revelle, *Vice Pres*
Shelly Revelle, *Vice Pres*
Debbie Revelle, *Admin Sec*
**EMP:** 4
**SALES (est):** 339.2K **Privately Held**
**SIC:** 1311 Crude petroleum production

## Fowler
### Adams County

**(G-10272)**
**B L I TOOL & DIE INC**
1468 Highway 24 (62338-2309)
**PHONE**.................................217 434-9106
David A Ley, *President*
**EMP:** 5
**SALES (est):** 360K **Privately Held**
**SIC:** 3544 Special dies & tools

## Fox Lake
### Lake County

**(G-10273)**
**ABRASIVE RUBBER WHEEL CO**
135 S Us Highway 12 (60020-1770)
**PHONE**.................................847 587-0900
Fax: 847 587-7325
Evelynn Ortman, *President*
J Bock, *Purchasing*
**EMP:** 10 **EST:** 1943
**SQ FT:** 5,000
**SALES (est):** 1.1MM **Privately Held**
**SIC:** 3291 Wheels, abrasive

**(G-10274)**
**ALERT SCRW PRODUCTS INC**
100 Honing Rd (60020-1929)
**PHONE**.................................847 587-1360
Joe Dvorak, *President*
**EMP:** 9
**SALES (est):** 1.5MM **Privately Held**
**SIC:** 3451 Screw machine products

**(G-10275)**
**D C GROVE ELECTRIC INC**
155 Sayton Rd Ste A (60020-1844)
**PHONE**.................................847 587-0864
Marc Harris, *President*
**EMP:** 5
**SQ FT:** 1,500
**SALES (est):** 883.4K **Privately Held**
**SIC:** 3621 3694 3625 Motors & generators; starters, for motors; engine electrical equipment; relays & industrial controls

**(G-10276)**
**DIAMOND J GLASS**
498 S Us Highway 12 Ste A (60020-1908)
**PHONE**.................................847 973-2741
Fax: 847 973-8047
Steve Tunberg, *President*
Joe Reayel, *Vice Pres*
**EMP:** 3
**SALES (est):** 303K **Privately Held**
**SIC:** 3231 Products of purchased glass

**(G-10277)**
**HAMSHER LAKESIDE FUNERALS**
12 N Pistakee Lake Rd (60020-1208)
**PHONE**.................................847 587-2100
**EMP:** 3 **EST:** 2015
**SALES (est):** 146.7K **Privately Held**
**SIC:** 2396 Veils & veiling; bridal, funeral, etc.

**(G-10278)**
**MCINTYRE & ASSOCIATES**
41 Nippersink Rd Apt 3 (60020-1468)
**PHONE**.................................847 639-8050
Robert McIntyre, *Partner*
Robert Mc Intyre, *Partner*
Margo McIntyre, *Partner*
**EMP:** 3
**SALES (est):** 414.9K **Privately Held**
**SIC:** 2752 7311 Commercial printing, lithographic; advertising agencies

**(G-10279)**
**METHODS DISTRS & MFRS INC**
Also Called: Bruin Brake Cables
104 Sayton Rd (60020-1758)
**PHONE**.................................847 973-1449
Fax: 847 973-1456
Richard Gelscheit, *President*
Jessica Coari, *Vice Pres*
▲ **EMP:** 6
**SQ FT:** 9,500
**SALES:** 850K **Privately Held**
**WEB:** www.methodsmanufacturing.com
**SIC:** 3714 Motor vehicle brake systems & parts

**(G-10280)**
**NORTHERN ILLINOIS PALLET INC**
1285 Wentworth Dr (60020-3417)
**PHONE**.................................815 236-9242
Scott Ganan, *Principal*
**EMP:** 4
**SALES (est):** 246.4K **Privately Held**
**SIC:** 2448 Pallets, wood & wood with metal

**(G-10281)**
**POWERSOURCE GENERATOR RENTALS**
119 Christopher Way (60020-1732)
P.O. Box 157 (60020-0157)
**PHONE**.................................847 587-3991
Mark Anthony Rossi, *President*
**EMP:** 9
**SALES (est):** 2MM **Privately Held**
**SIC:** 3621 Generators & sets, electric

**(G-10282)**
**PRECISION CHROME INC**
105 Precision Rd (60020-1999)
**PHONE**.................................847 587-1515
Fax: 847 587-1568
Donald Hjortland, *President*
Cheryl Preece, *Admin Sec*
**EMP:** 25
**SQ FT:** 24,000
**SALES (est):** 2.6MM **Privately Held**
**SIC:** 3471 3541 3567 3398 Chromium plating of metals or formed products; grinding, polishing, buffing, lapping & honing machines; honing & lapping machines; induction heating equipment; metal heat treating

**(G-10283)**
**SIGN APPEAL INC**
20 E Grand Ave (60020-1217)
**PHONE**.................................847 587-4300
Fax: 847 587-6879
Debra Busch, *Owner*
**EMP:** 6
**SQ FT:** 4,000
**SALES (est):** 440K **Privately Held**
**WEB:** www.signappeal.com
**SIC:** 3993 Signs & advertising specialties

**(G-10284)**
**WELDING APPARATUS COMPANY**
87 Honing Rd (60020-1941)
**PHONE**.................................773 252-7670
Fax: 773 252-8378
Brant Terzic, *President*
**EMP:** 20 **EST:** 1933
**SQ FT:** 17,000
**SALES (est):** 4.2MM **Privately Held**
**SIC:** 3317 3316 Steel pipe & tubes; sheet, steel, cold-rolled; from purchased hot-rolled

## Fox River Grove
### Mchenry County

**(G-10285)**
**A D SPECIALTY SEWING**
410 Northwest Hwy (60021-1139)
**PHONE**.................................847 639-0390
Fax: 847 639-1034
Adele Migdal, *Owner*
**EMP:** 6
**SQ FT:** 6,000
**SALES:** 230K **Privately Held**
**WEB:** www.adspecialtysewing.com
**SIC:** 2391 5714 5949 5999 Draperies, plastic & textile; from purchased materials; upholstery materials; fabric stores piece goods; foam & foam products; upholstery work; household furnishings

**(G-10286)**
**FINISHERS EXCHANGE**
744 Northwest Hwy (60021-1207)
**PHONE**.................................847 462-0533
Fax: 847 462-0637
Nelson G Stevens, *Principal*
▲ **EMP:** 3
**SALES (est):** 292.9K **Privately Held**
**SIC:** 3554 Paper industries machinery

**(G-10287)**
**GROVE PLATING COMPANY INC**
400 Algonquin Rd (60021-1498)
**PHONE**.................................847 639-7651
Fax: 847 639-7764
Richard Kostner, *President*
Beverly Kostner, *Vice Pres*
Julio Rivera, *Plant Mgr*
Brian Feezel, *Manager*
Shelly K Kostner, *Manager*
**EMP:** 15
**SQ FT:** 16,000
**SALES (est):** 1.9MM **Privately Held**
**WEB:** www.spryhealthlife.com
**SIC:** 3471 Plating of metals or formed products

**(G-10288)**
**LEMAITRE VASCULAR INC**
912 Northwest Hwy Ste 106 (60021-1925)
**PHONE**.................................847 462-2191
**EMP:** 16
**SALES (corp-wide):** 89.1MM **Publicly Held**
**SIC:** 8099 3842 Blood related health services; cosmetic restorations
**PA:** Lemaitre Vascular, Inc.
 63 2nd Ave
 Burlington MA 01803
 781 221-2266

**(G-10289)**
**SALES & MARKETING RESOURCES**
Also Called: Sterling RE & Investments
21 Ashcroft Ct (60021-1864)
**PHONE**.................................847 910-9169
Rick Maningas, *Owner*
**EMP:** 4
**SALES (est):** 210K **Privately Held**
**SIC:** 7372 Prepackaged software

## Frankfort
### Will County

**(G-10290)**
**3D MANUFACTURING CORPORATION**
9218 Corsair Rd Unit 5 (60423-2566)
**PHONE**.................................815 806-9200
Patrick Dalton, *President*
Michelle Dalton, *Admin Sec*
**EMP:** 8
**SALES:** 1MM **Privately Held**
**SIC:** 3545 Machine tool attachments & accessories

**(G-10291)**
**AKRYLIX INC (PA)**
171 Ontario St (60423-1808)
**PHONE**.................................773 869-9005
Randy Janata, *President*
**EMP:** 12
**SALES (est):** 1.4MM **Privately Held**
**WEB:** www.akrylix.com
**SIC:** 2541 2821 3089 Store & office display cases & fixtures; acrylic resins; boxes, plastic

**(G-10292)**
**ALLIANCE SERVICE CO**
21200 S La Grange Rd (60423-2003)
**PHONE**.................................708 746-5026
Sandra Hall, *Principal*
**EMP:** 4
**SALES (est):** 412.6K **Privately Held**
**SIC:** 3578 Automatic teller machines (ATM)

**(G-10293)**
**ALPS GROUP INC (PA)**
Also Called: Alps Group, The
8779 W Laraway Rd (60423-9704)
**PHONE**.................................815 469-3800
**EMP:** 5
**SALES (est):** 626.5K **Privately Held**
**SIC:** 3421 Table & food cutlery, including butchers'

**(G-10294)**
**AMERICAN PERFORATOR COMPANY**
22803 S Mustang Rd Ste A (60423-2557)
**PHONE**.................................815 469-4300
Fax: 708 430-2420
Bryan Spencer, *President*
Carl V Spencer, *Corp Secy*
**EMP:** 2 **EST:** 1890
**SQ FT:** 5,000
**SALES:** 293.2K **Privately Held**
**SIC:** 3579 Perforators (office machines)

**(G-10295)**
**ANDERSON COPPER & BRASS CO LLC (DH)**
Also Called: Anderson Fittings
7231 W Laraway Rd (60423-7767)
**PHONE**.................................708 535-9030
Fax: 708 687-6945
Douglas Marciniak, *President*
Jason Jellovitz, *Opers Mgr*
Jim Radavich, *Sales Staff*
Shawn Houston, *Maintence Staff*
▲ **EMP:** 50 **EST:** 1986
**SQ FT:** 10,000
**SALES (est):** 10.9MM
**SALES (corp-wide):** 223.6B **Publicly Held**
**SIC:** 3432 Plumbing fixture fittings & trim
**HQ:** Marmon Holdings, Inc.
 181 W Madison St Ste 2600
 Chicago IL 60602
 312 372-9500

# GEOGRAPHIC SECTION

Frankfort - Will County (G-10322)

**(G-10296)**
**ANDERSON COPPER & BRASS CO LLC**
Also Called: Anderson Fittings
255 Industry Ave (60423-1640)
PHONE..................................815 469-8201
Fax: 815 806-0957
Jeff Hensley, *Branch Mgr*
EMP: 15
SALES (corp-wide): 223.6B **Publicly Held**
SIC: 3432 Plumbing fixture fittings & trim
HQ: Anderson Copper And Brass Company Llc
7231 W Laraway Rd
Frankfort IL 60423
708 535-9030

**(G-10297)**
**AREA MARKETING INC**
Also Called: Family Time Magazine
10221 W Lincoln Hwy (60423-1279)
PHONE..................................815 806-8844
Caroline O'Connell, *President*
Rex Robinson, *Editor*
Mike O'Connell, *Vice Pres*
Mike Oconnell, *Vice Pres*
Diane Mondrella, *Accounts Exec*
EMP: 7
SALES (est): 824K **Privately Held**
SIC: 2721 7389 Magazines: publishing & printing; promoters of shows & exhibitions

**(G-10298)**
**B CREATIVE SCREEN PRINT CO**
8844 W Steger Rd (60423-8077)
PHONE..................................815 806-3037
Bob Stortako, *Owner*
Bob Storako, *Owner*
EMP: 4
SALES (est): 446.6K **Privately Held**
SIC: 2759 Screen printing

**(G-10299)**
**BIMBA MANUFACTURING COMPANY**
9450 W Laraway Rd (60423-1902)
PHONE..................................708 534-8544
Dan Harris, *Marketing Staff*
EMP: 40
SQ FT: 45,000
SALES (corp-wide): 128.7MM **Privately Held**
SIC: 3593 Fluid power cylinders & actuators
PA: Bimba Manufacturing Company Inc
25150 S Governors Hwy
University Park IL 60484
708 534-8544

**(G-10300)**
**BING ENGINEERING INC**
Also Called: Bing Construction Company
20240 S Pine Hill Rd (60423-2406)
PHONE..................................708 228-8005
Daniel Bingenheimer, *President*
EMP: 150
SALES: 15MM **Privately Held**
SIC: 8711 1761 4212 3444 Engineering services; sheet metalwork; moving services; sheet metalwork; millwright

**(G-10301)**
**BLACHFORD CORPORATION**
401 Center Rd (60423-1630)
PHONE..................................815 464-2100
Fax: 815 464-2112
John L Blachford, *President*
Joe Borean, *Corp Secy*
Mark Langenderfer, *Mfg Staff*
Frank Skubic, *Administration*
▲ EMP: 25
SQ FT: 45,000
SALES (est): 6.4MM
SALES (corp-wide): 51.6MM **Privately Held**
WEB: www.blachford.com
SIC: 2841 Soap & other detergents
HQ: Blachford Enterprises, Inc.
1400 Nuclear Dr
West Chicago IL 60185
630 231-8300

**(G-10302)**
**BORGWARNER INC**
300 S Maple St (60423-1691)
PHONE..................................248 754-9200
Fax: 815 469-3116
Andy Mickus, *Plant Mgr*
Benjamin Rominski, *Engineer*
Timothy Milewski, *Associate*
EMP: 30
SALES (corp-wide): 9B **Publicly Held**
SIC: 3714 Motor vehicle parts & accessories
PA: Borgwarner Inc.
3850 Hamlin Rd
Auburn Hills MI 48326
248 754-9200

**(G-10303)**
**BORGWARNER TRANSM SYSTEMS INC**
300 S Maple St (60423-1691)
PHONE..................................815 469-7815
Fax: 815 469-7089
Ron Ames, *Plant Mgr*
Edwin Rieser, *Finance Other*
Bill Liacone, *Branch Mgr*
EMP: 450
SALES (corp-wide): 9B **Publicly Held**
SIC: 3714 Transmissions, motor vehicle
HQ: Borgwarner Transmission Systems Inc.
3800 Automation Ave # 500
Auburn Hills MI 48326
248 754-9200

**(G-10304)**
**BRADLEY INDUSTRIES INC**
Also Called: Atlantis Match Company
524 Center Rd (60423-1633)
P.O. Box 1227, Euless TX (76039-1227)
PHONE..................................815 469-2314
Fax: 815 469-7089
Jonathan Bradley, *President*
Cindy Nicholson, *Manager*
▲ EMP: 50 EST: 1970
SQ FT: 40,000
SALES (est): 4.5MM **Privately Held**
WEB: www.matchbooks.com
SIC: 3999 2759 Matches & match books; commercial printing

**(G-10305)**
**BRAGI NA LLC**
20635 Abbley Woods Ste 303 (60423)
PHONE..................................708 717-5000
David Hogan, *Owner*
EMP: 64
SQ FT: 10,000
SALES (est): 2MM **Privately Held**
SIC: 3678 Electronic connectors

**(G-10306)**
**CANVAS COMMUNICATION**
7320 W Benton Dr (60423-9102)
PHONE..................................815 464-5947
Cynthia Grobmeier, *President*
EMP: 3
SALES (est): 196.3K **Privately Held**
SIC: 2721 Periodicals

**(G-10307)**
**CARNEY FLOW TECHNICS LLC**
181 Ontario St (60423-1646)
PHONE..................................815 277-2600
Patrick Carney, *Principal*
EMP: 6
SALES (est): 681.5K **Privately Held**
SIC: 3589 Sewage & water treatment equipment

**(G-10308)**
**CARROLL DISTRG & CNSTR SUP INC**
121 Industry Ave (60423-1639)
PHONE..................................815 464-0100
Eric Burnham, *Sales Staff*
Theo Buys, *Manager*
EMP: 6
SALES (corp-wide): 75.9MM **Privately Held**
WEB: www.carrolldistributing.com
SIC: 3444 Concrete forms, sheet metal

PA: Carroll Distributing & Construction Supply, Inc.
205 S Iowa Ave
Ottumwa IA 52501
641 683-1888

**(G-10309)**
**CHEMICAL PUMP**
23233 S Center Rd (60423-9793)
P.O. Box 1627 (60423-7627)
PHONE..................................815 464-1908
John Reynhout, *Owner*
EMP: 4 EST: 2007
SALES (est): 210K **Privately Held**
SIC: 3589 Water treatment equipment, industrial

**(G-10310)**
**CLASSROOM TECHNOLOGIES LLC**
9227 Gulfstream Rd (60423-2550)
PHONE..................................708 548-1642
Milos Klipic,
EMP: 6 EST: 2013
SALES (est): 256.5K **Privately Held**
SIC: 7372 Educational computer software

**(G-10311)**
**CROWN PREMIUMS INC (PA)**
22774 Citation Rd Unit A (60423-2638)
PHONE..................................815 469-8789
Bill Maxwell, *President*
▲ EMP: 12
SALES (est): 1.2MM **Privately Held**
SIC: 3449 2821 3363 Miscellaneous metalwork; plastics materials & resins; aluminum die-castings

**(G-10312)**
**DESK & DOOR NAMEPLATE COMPANY**
9310 Gulfstream Rd (60423-2522)
PHONE..................................815 806-8670
Jay Burrichter, *President*
Beverly Burrichter, *Corp Secy*
EMP: 10 EST: 1967
SQ FT: 8,600
SALES (est): 1.2MM **Privately Held**
WEB: www.deskndoorusa.com
SIC: 3993 3469 2396 Letters for signs, metal; metal stampings; automotive & apparel trimmings

**(G-10313)**
**DJB CORPORATION**
Also Called: Vees Collectibles
9527 Corsair Rd Ste 2w (60423-2531)
PHONE..................................815 469-7533
Fax: 815 469-7590
EMP: 5
SALES (est): 502.4K **Privately Held**
SIC: 3542 Mfg Machine Tools-Forming

**(G-10314)**
**DS SERVICES OF AMERICA INC**
Also Called: Hinckley Springs
9409 Gulfstream Rd (60423-2518)
PHONE..................................815 469-7100
Dale Sjoerdsma, *Site Mgr*
Amy Gerlech, *Branch Mgr*
EMP: 26
SALES (est): 3.2B **Privately Held**
WEB: www.suntorywatergroup.com
SIC: 5499 2086 Water: distilled mineral or spring; mineral water, carbonated: packaged in cans, bottles, etc.
HQ: Ds Services Of America, Inc.
2300 Windy Ridge Pkwy Se 500n
Atlanta GA 30339
770 933-1400

**(G-10315)**
**DUNHILL CORP**
Also Called: Tuf-Guard
9218 Corsair Rd Unit 1 (60423-2566)
P.O. Box 581 (60423-0581)
PHONE..................................815 806-8600
Gary Clarke, *Principal*
▲ EMP: 10
SALES (est): 1.8MM **Privately Held**
WEB: www.tuf-guard.com
SIC: 2541 Store fixtures, wood

**(G-10316)**
**DURA-CRAFTS CORP**
9408 Gulfstream Rd (60423-2521)
PHONE..................................815 464-3561
Timothy Digrazia, *President*
Tim Digrazia, *President*
EMP: 19
SQ FT: 30,000
SALES (est): 2.1MM **Privately Held**
SIC: 3999 3842 Pet supplies; surgical appliances & supplies; orthopedic appliances

**(G-10317)**
**E-QUIP MANUFACTURING CO**
230 Industry Ave (60423-1641)
PHONE..................................815 464-0053
Fax: 815 464-0059
Millard Minyard, *President*
Michael R Ginise, *General Mgr*
Dan Minyard, *Treasurer*
Margaret A Minyard, *Admin Sec*
▲ EMP: 40
SQ FT: 35,000
SALES (est): 10.1MM **Privately Held**
SIC: 3556 Meat processing machinery

**(G-10318)**
**EAGLE BURIAL VAULT**
9535 W Steger Rd (60423-7776)
PHONE..................................815 722-8660
EMP: 6
SALES (est): 507.3K **Privately Held**
SIC: 3272 Burial vaults, concrete or precast terrazzo

**(G-10319)**
**EDISON ELECTRIC**
21851 Blue Bird Ln (60423-2292)
PHONE..................................815 464-1006
Stephen Langdon, *Principal*
EMP: 2
SALES (est): 226.1K **Privately Held**
SIC: 3699 Electrical equipment & supplies

**(G-10320)**
**EXRESS MOTOR AND LIFT PARTS**
1018 Lambrecht Dr (60423-1649)
PHONE..................................630 327-2000
Ron Cogswell, *Owner*
EMP: 6
SALES (est): 405.7K **Privately Held**
SIC: 3714 Motor vehicle parts & accessories

**(G-10321)**
**F VOGELMANN AND COMPANY**
440 Center Rd (60423-1816)
P.O. Box 324 (60423-0324)
PHONE..................................815 469-2285
Fax: 815 469-8063
Fred Vogelmann, *President*
Ilse Vogelmann, *Admin Sec*
EMP: 14 EST: 1980
SQ FT: 20,000
SALES (est): 1.3MM **Privately Held**
SIC: 1799 3441 7692 3444 Welding on site; fabricated structural metal; welding repair; sheet metalwork

**(G-10322)**
**FKM USA LLC**
21950 S La Grange Rd A (60423-9780)
PHONE..................................815 469-2473
Douglas Goetz, *General Mgr*
James S Rusczyk, *Mng Member*
Julie Boomsman, *Manager*
Ulrich Freutenberg,
▲ EMP: 11 EST: 2000
SQ FT: 200,000
SALES (est): 2.8MM
SALES (corp-wide): 5.3MM **Privately Held**
WEB: www.fkmusa.com
SIC: 3547 Steel rolling machinery
PA: Fkm Walzentechnik Dr. Freudenberg Gmbh
Stempelstr. 2-4
Duisburg 47167
203 581-805

# Frankfort - Will County (G-10323)

## (G-10323)
**FRA-MILCO CABINETS CO INC**
386 Nevada A Ct (60423-1533)
**EMP:** 8 **EST:** 1953
**SQ FT:** 8,500
**SALES:** 650K **Privately Held**
**SIC:** 5712 2541 2434 Ret Furniture Mfg Wood Partitions/Fixtures Mfg Wood Kitchen Cabinets

## (G-10324)
**FRANKFORT MACHINE & TOOLS INC**
285 Industry Ave (60423-1640)
**PHONE**.................................815 469-9902
**Fax:** 815 469-9947
Angelo Rotondi, *President*
**EMP:** 6
**SQ FT:** 14,000
**SALES (est):** 1MM **Privately Held**
**SIC:** 3544 Special dies, tools, jigs & fixtures

## (G-10325)
**GH CRANES CORPORATION**
9134 Gulfstream Rd (60423-2582)
**PHONE**.................................815 277-5328
Jose Antonio Guerra, *CEO*
John O' Toole, *Sales Mgr*
▲ **EMP:** 3
**SQ FT:** 7,200
**SALES:** 3.6MM **Privately Held**
**WEB:** www.ghsa.com
**SIC:** 3536 Cranes, overhead traveling

## (G-10326)
**H&H DIE MANUFACTURING INC**
22772 Challenger Rd A (60423-2599)
**PHONE**.................................708 479-6267
**Fax:** 708 479-6169
Andrew Mueller, *President*
Linda Mueller, *Corp Secy*
**EMP:** 9 **EST:** 1952
**SQ FT:** 11,000
**SALES (est):** 1.5MM **Privately Held**
**SIC:** 3544 3423 Special dies, tools, jigs & fixtures; hand & edge tools

## (G-10327)
**HOLSOLUTIONS INC**
21200 S La Grange Rd # 119 (60423-2003)
**PHONE**.................................888 847-5467
Johnny Holliday, *President*
**EMP:** 3
**SALES (est):** 77.9K **Privately Held**
**SIC:** 7374 7311 2741 5065 Computer graphics service; advertising agencies; miscellaneous publishing; tapes, audio & video recording

## (G-10328)
**HPP PRECISION MACHINE CO INC**
22829 S Mustang Rd (60423-2561)
**PHONE**.................................815 469-2608
Robert Harper, *President*
Lawrence Polselli, *President*
Lee Pickett, *Admin Sec*
**EMP:** 4
**SQ FT:** 5,600
**SALES (est):** 250K **Privately Held**
**SIC:** 3599 Machine shop, jobbing & repair

## (G-10329)
**ILLINOIS TOOL WORKS INC**
Also Called: Norwood Marketing Systems
250 Industry Ave (60423-1641)
**PHONE**.................................708 720-0300
Larry Kulik, *Manager*
**EMP:** 15
**SALES (corp-wide):** 13.6B **Publicly Held**
**SIC:** 3569 Filters
**PA:** Illinois Tool Works Inc.
155 Harlem Ave
Glenview IL 60025
847 724-7500

## (G-10330)
**ILLINOIS TOOL WORKS INC**
Also Called: ITW Delpro
21601 S Harlem Ave (60423-6018)
**PHONE**.................................708 720-0300
Eric Parker, *Manager*
**EMP:** 100
**SALES (corp-wide):** 13.6B **Publicly Held**
**SIC:** 3089 Plastic processing
**PA:** Illinois Tool Works Inc.
155 Harlem Ave
Glenview IL 60025
847 724-7500

## (G-10331)
**ILLINOIS TOOL WORKS INC**
ITW Deltar Fasteners
21555 S Harlem Ave (60423-6017)
**PHONE**.................................708 720-2600
Karla Dearstyne, *Director*
Rick Koscik, *Coordinator*
**EMP:** 117
**SALES (corp-wide):** 13.6B **Publicly Held**
**SIC:** 3452 Bolts, nuts, rivets & washers
**PA:** Illinois Tool Works Inc.
155 Harlem Ave
Glenview IL 60025
847 724-7500

## (G-10332)
**ILLINOIS TOOL WORKS INC**
Also Called: ITW Deltar Ipac
21701 S Harlem Ave (60423-6020)
**PHONE**.................................708 720-7070
Walter Belchine, *Principal*
**EMP:** 8
**SALES (corp-wide):** 13.6B **Publicly Held**
**SIC:** 5031 2499 Building materials, exterior; tool handles, wood
**PA:** Illinois Tool Works Inc.
155 Harlem Ave
Glenview IL 60025
847 724-7500

## (G-10333)
**ILLINOIS TOOL WORKS INC**
Norwood Marking Systems
250 Industry Ave (60423-1641)
**PHONE**.................................708 720-0300
**Fax:** 815 469-2003
Mark Lester, *Personnel*
Bhabin Vave, *Manager*
**EMP:** 36
**SALES (corp-wide):** 13.6B **Publicly Held**
**SIC:** 3565 5045 3955 2789 Packaging machinery; bag opening, filling & closing machines; bottling machinery: filling, capping, labeling; bread wrapping machinery; computers; carbon paper & inked ribbons; bookbinding & related work
**PA:** Illinois Tool Works Inc.
155 Harlem Ave
Glenview IL 60025
847 724-7500

## (G-10334)
**ILLINOIS TOOL WORKS INC**
Also Called: Deltar Body Interior
21701 S Harlem Ave (60423-6020)
**PHONE**.................................708 720-3541
**Fax:** 708 720-3961
Steve Spain, *Controller*
Carol Salas, *Branch Mgr*
**EMP:** 9
**SALES (corp-wide):** 13.6B **Publicly Held**
**SIC:** 3465 Body parts, automobile: stamped metal
**PA:** Illinois Tool Works Inc.
155 Harlem Ave
Glenview IL 60025
847 724-7500

## (G-10335)
**ITW MOTION**
21601 S Harlem Ave (60423-6018)
**PHONE**.................................708 720-7070
Adolph Galinski, *Principal*
Pan Bo, *Sales Staff*
Kristen Leidolph, *Manager*
**EMP:** 19 **EST:** 2013
**SALES (est):** 4MM **Privately Held**
**SIC:** 3822 Damper operators: pneumatic, thermostatic, electric

## (G-10336)
**JEWEL OSCO INC**
Also Called: Jewel-Osco 3052
21164 N Lagrange Rd (60423-2010)
**PHONE**.................................815 464-5352
George Rumbaugh, *Manager*
**EMP:** 125
**SALES (corp-wide):** 58.8B **Privately Held**
**WEB:** www.jewelosco.com
**SIC:** 5411 5812 5421 2051 Supermarkets, chain; eating places; meat & fish markets; bread, cake & related products
**HQ:** Jewel Osco, Inc.
150 E Pierce Rd Ste 200
Itasca IL 60143
630 948-6000

## (G-10337)
**JOFAS PRINT CORPORATION**
22856 Lkview Estates Blvd (60423)
**PHONE**.................................815 534-5725
Joseph Ayoola, *President*
**EMP:** 7
**SALES (est):** 605K **Privately Held**
**SIC:** 2752 7389 Commercial printing, lithographic;

## (G-10338)
**K&H FUEL**
22193 Clove Dr (60423-7808)
**PHONE**.................................815 405-4364
Keith Asare, *Principal*
**EMP:** 3
**SALES (est):** 194.6K **Privately Held**
**SIC:** 2869 Fuels

## (G-10339)
**KAVANAUGH ELECTRIC INC**
9511 Corsair Rd Ste B (60423-2559)
**PHONE**.................................708 503-1310
Alicia Kavanaugh, *President*
**EMP:** 4
**SALES (est):** 288.1K **Privately Held**
**SIC:** 3699 1731 Electrical equipment & supplies; electrical work

## (G-10340)
**KOSON TOOL INC**
9235 Corsair Rd Ste B (60423-2578)
**PHONE**.................................815 277-2107
Andrew A Koson, *President*
Debra A Koson, *Admin Sec*
**EMP:** 4
**SALES (est):** 575.7K **Privately Held**
**SIC:** 3544 5251 Special dies, tools, jigs & fixtures; hardware

## (G-10341)
**MACE IRON WORKS INC (PA)**
221 Industry Ave (60423-1687)
**PHONE**.................................708 479-2456
**Fax:** 708 469-6401
Casimer Macewicz Jr, *President*
Dennis Macewicz, *Vice Pres*
Mike Mace, *Info Tech Dir*
Casmier J Macewicz Sr, *Shareholder*
**EMP:** 24 **EST:** 1943
**SQ FT:** 20,000
**SALES (est):** 4MM **Privately Held**
**SIC:** 3441 Fabricated structural metal

## (G-10342)
**MIDWEST CAGE COMPANY**
9217 Gulfstream Rd # 101 (60423-2564)
**PHONE**.................................815 806-0005
**Fax:** 815 463-0310
Daniel Casey, *President*
Kathy Nicholson, *Vice Pres*
**EMP:** 9
**SQ FT:** 10,000
**SALES (est):** 1.8MM **Privately Held**
**SIC:** 3446 Gratings, tread: fabricated metal

## (G-10343)
**MIDWEST INNOVATIVE PDTS LLC**
Also Called: Twist and Seal
9370 W Laraway Rd Ste E (60423-1936)
**PHONE**.................................888 945-4545
Bryan Nooner, *President*
**EMP:** 20 **EST:** 2012
**SQ FT:** 25,000
**SALES:** 2MM **Privately Held**
**SIC:** 2821 Casein plastics

## (G-10344)
**MODERN FOOD CONCEPTS INC**
22813 Challenger Rd C (60423-2632)
**PHONE**.................................815 534-5747
James L Soper, *President*
Rudy Korosec, *Shareholder*
**EMP:** 8
**SQ FT:** 5,000
**SALES (est):** 1.4MM **Privately Held**
**SIC:** 3556 Food products machinery

## (G-10345)
**NEENAH FOUNDRY CO**
925 Lambrecht Dr (60423-1617)
**PHONE**.................................800 558-5075
Rob Klaus, *Principal*
**EMP:** 4
**SALES (est):** 378.1K **Privately Held**
**SIC:** 3325 Steel foundries

## (G-10346)
**PACTIV LLC**
437 Center Rd (60423-1630)
P.O. Box 92590, Chicago (60675-2590)
**PHONE**.................................815 469-2112
**Fax:** 815 469-3829
Brian Elshah, *Senior Buyer*
Salvador Castaneda, *Human Res Dir*
Brian Hoffman, *Manager*
Jay Krish, *Info Tech Dir*
Heather Krueger, *Admin Asst*
**EMP:** 238 **Privately Held**
**SIC:** 2673 3089 Food storage & trash bags (plastic); food storage & frozen food bags, plastic; food casings, plastic
**HQ:** Pactiv Llc
1900 W Field Ct
Lake Forest IL 60045
847 482-2000

## (G-10347)
**PAPER SPOT**
11 S White St Ste 201 (60423-4011)
**PHONE**.................................815 464-8533
Maryann Wall, *Partner*
**EMP:** 2
**SALES (est):** 273.4K **Privately Held**
**WEB:** www.papercents.com
**SIC:** 2621 Stationery, envelope & tablet papers

## (G-10348)
**PARATECH INCORPORATED (PA)**
Also Called: Femsa
1025 Lambrecht Dr (60423-1648)
P.O. Box 1000 (60423-7000)
**PHONE**.................................815 469-3911
**Fax:** 815 469-7748
Peter K Nielsen, *CEO*
Kenneth Nielsen, *President*
Cathy Connor, *Purch Mgr*
Irwin Korngoot, *Manager*
Richard Yorke, *Admin Sec*
▲ **EMP:** 71 **EST:** 1963
**SQ FT:** 30,000
**SALES (est):** 13.3MM **Privately Held**
**WEB:** www.paratech-inc.com
**SIC:** 3569 Firefighting apparatus & related equipment

## (G-10349)
**PIP PRINTING INC**
9218 Corsair Rd Unit 3 (60423-2566)
**PHONE**.................................815 464-0075
John Bitter, *President*
Dawn Bitter, *Vice Pres*
**EMP:** 2
**SQ FT:** 1,200
**SALES (est):** 300K **Privately Held**
**SIC:** 2752 7334 2791 2789 Commercial printing, offset; photocopying & duplicating services; typesetting; bookbinding & related work

## (G-10350)
**PRECISION CONVEYOR AND ERCT CO**
9511 Corsair Rd Ste E (60423-2559)
**PHONE**.................................779 324-5269
Jeff Reis, *President*
Jeffrey Reis, *Vice Pres*
**EMP:** 10
**SQ FT:** 6,000
**SALES (est):** 1.5MM **Privately Held**
**SIC:** 3535 Conveyors & conveying equipment

## (G-10351)
**PRECISION TOOL**
21200 S La Grange Rd (60423-2003)
**PHONE**.................................815 464-2428
William Pradelski, *Principal*
Ed Marshall, *Principal*

EMP: 10
SALES (est): 478K  Privately Held
SIC: 3423  Mfg Of Hand Tools

**(G-10352)**
**PREMIER PACKAGING CORP**
9424 Gulfstream Rd  (60423-2521)
PHONE..................815 469-7951
Dick Ballot, *President*
Dan Brtis, *Vice Pres*
▲ EMP: 8 EST: 1995
SQ FT: 9,000
SALES (est): 1.3MM  Privately Held
SIC: 3951  Markers, soft tip (felt, fabric, plastic, etc.)

**(G-10353)**
**PRIME MARKET TARGETING INC**
Also Called: Pmt
7777 W Lincoln Hwy Ste A  (60423-9491)
PHONE..................815 469-4555
Scott Duff, *President*
Daniel Hendrickson, *Vice Pres*
Michelle Duff, *Treasurer*
Brian Sheely, *Sales Mgr*
Steve Sirt, *Accounts Exec*
EMP: 35
SQ FT: 6,000
SALES (est): 8.6MM  Privately Held
WEB: www.pmtadvertising.com
SIC: 7311  7336  2791  3993  Advertising agencies; graphic arts & related design; typesetting; signs & advertising specialties; platemaking services

**(G-10354)**
**PRINCIPAL INSTRUMENTS INC**
845 Basswood Ln  (60423-1180)
PHONE..................815 469-8159
Michael Rosandich, *President*
Christine Rosandich, *Vice Pres*
EMP: 4
SALES: 1MM  Privately Held
SIC: 3823  Primary elements for process flow measurement

**(G-10355)**
**QUANTUM TECHNICAL SERVICES INC**
Also Called: Quantum Topping Systems
9524 Gulfstream Rd  (60423-2520)
PHONE..................815 464-1540
Fax: 815 464-1541
Mark Freudinger, *President*
Jim Machura, *Sales Mgr*
David White, *Admin Sec*
EMP: 20
SALES (est): 6MM  Privately Held
WEB: www.q-t-s.com
SIC: 3589  Commercial cooking & food-warming equipment

**(G-10356)**
**QUINCEANERABOUTIQUECOM INC**
7624 W Saint Francis Rd  (60423-6931)
PHONE..................779 324-5468
A J Solheim, *CEO*
Sylvia Solheim, *Admin Sec*
EMP: 2
SALES (est): 295.7K  Privately Held
WEB: www.quinceanera-boutique.com
SIC: 3499  Novelties & giftware, including trophies

**(G-10357)**
**REVERE METALS LLC**
21200 S La Grange Rd # 260  (60423-2003)
PHONE..................708 945-3992
Rob Lange, *Mng Member*
EMP: 2
SQ FT: 500
SALES: 2.5MM  Privately Held
SIC: 3312  Sheet or strip, steel, hot-rolled; sheet or strip, steel, cold-rolled: own hot-rolled

**(G-10358)**
**RIECO-TITAN PRODUCTS INC**
965 Lambrecht Dr  (60423-1650)
PHONE..................815 464-7400
Robert E Mc Carthy, *President*
Jan Prigden, *Purch Agent*
John Verre, *Engineer*
Doug Bakker, *Manager*
Sharon M E Mc Carthy, *Admin Sec*
▲ EMP: 35
SQ FT: 31,000
SALES (est): 5MM  Privately Held
WEB: www.riecotitan.com
SIC: 3423  3792  Jacks: lifting, screw or ratchet (hand tools); travel trailers & campers

**(G-10359)**
**ROLL-KRAFT NORTHERN INC**
9324 Gulfstream Rd Ste 1e  (60423-2541)
PHONE..................815 469-0205
EMP: 6
SALES (est): 410K  Privately Held
SIC: 3599  Machine Shop

**(G-10360)**
**S&R PRECISION MACHINE  LLC**
9305 Corsair Rd Ste A  (60423-2580)
PHONE..................815 469-6544
Alan Redman,
Bogdon Struminski,
EMP: 10
SQ FT: 12,000
SALES (est): 880K  Privately Held
SIC: 3599  3568  Machine shop, jobbing & repair; power transmission equipment

**(G-10361)**
**SANDRA E GREENE**
Also Called: Promotions Plus
228 N Locust St  (60423-1263)
PHONE..................815 469-0092
EMP: 4
SALES (est): 250K  Privately Held
SIC: 3993  7336  Mfg Signs/Advertising Specialties Commercial Art/Graphic Design

**(G-10362)**
**SHARN ENTERPRISES  INC**
22749 Citation Rd  (60423-2587)
PHONE..................815 464-9715
Roger Wandersee, *President*
Sharon Wandersee, *Vice Pres*
Greg Schelderg, *Shareholder*
James Wandersee, *Shareholder*
Roger S Wandersee, *Shareholder*
▲ EMP: 22 EST: 1976
SQ FT: 26,000
SALES (est): 5.3MM  Privately Held
WEB: www.sharndisplays.com
SIC: 3993  Signs & advertising specialties; displays & cutouts, window & lobby; displays, paint process

**(G-10363)**
**SHOCKYAVE CUSTOMS**
9565 W Lincoln Hwy Ste A  (60423-1942)
PHONE..................815 469-9141
Fax: 815 469-9148
Anthony Shockwave, *Owner*
EMP: 4
SALES (est): 408.1K  Privately Held
SIC: 3651  Audio electronic systems

**(G-10364)**
**SOLUBLEND TECHNOLOGIES LLC**
11487 Amhearst Ct  (60423-5123)
PHONE..................815 534-5778
Richard Staack, *Mng Member*
EMP: 6 EST: 2011
SALES (est): 398.9K  Privately Held
SIC: 2053  Frozen bakery products, except bread

**(G-10365)**
**STURDI IRON  INC**
22405 S Center Rd  (60423-1632)
PHONE..................815 464-1173
Gregory A Szablewski, *President*
Wendi Szablewski, *Vice Pres*
EMP: 3
SALES (est): 812.8K  Privately Held
SIC: 3441  Fabricated structural metal

**(G-10366)**
**SUSTANABLE INFRASTRUCTURES INC**
20632 Abbey Dr  (60423-3109)
PHONE..................815 341-1447
Myron Brick, *President*
George Olsen, *Admin Sec*
EMP: 6
SALES (est): 150K  Privately Held
SIC: 3699  Electrical equipment & supplies

**(G-10367)**
**T R Z MOTORSPORTS INC**
Also Called: Trz Race Cars
25045 S Center Rd  (60423-8200)
PHONE..................815 806-0838
Thomas R Zdancewicz, *Owner*
EMP: 3
SALES (est): 21.8K  Privately Held
SIC: 3465  3711  Automotive stampings; automobile assembly, including specialty automobiles

**(G-10368)**
**TARANDA SPECIALTIES INC**
8746 W Manhattan Monee Rd  (60423-9799)
PHONE..................815 469-3041
Richard M Taranda Jr, *President*
Richard M Taranda Sr Estate of, *President*
Irene Taranda, *Treasurer*
Linda Taranda, *Office Mgr*
EMP: 6
SALES (est): 450K  Privately Held
SIC: 3672  Printed circuit boards

**(G-10369)**
**THERAFIN CORPORATION**
9450 W Laraway Rd  (60423-1902)
PHONE..................708 479-7300
Fax: 708 479-1515
Todd Fink, *President*
Deanna Hnetkovsky, *General Mgr*
Julie Verbeeren, *Corp Secy*
Mike Fagan, *Project Mgr*
Jeremy Fischer, *Opers Staff*
▲ EMP: 43
SQ FT: 42,000
SALES (est): 8.4MM  Privately Held
WEB: www.therafin.com
SIC: 3842  Surgical appliances & supplies

**(G-10370)**
**TOP SHELF QUILTS INC**
10 Elwood St  (60423-1400)
PHONE..................815 806-1694
Ronald Conran, *President*
Michael Pawlisz, *Vice Pres*
EMP: 6
SALES (est): 96K  Privately Held
WEB: www.topshelfquilts.com
SIC: 2395  Quilting & quilting supplies

**(G-10371)**
**TRI-STATE CUT STONE CO**
Also Called: Tri State Cut Stone & Brick Co
10333 Vans Dr  (60423-8547)
PHONE..................815 469-7550
Gary Murino Jr, *President*
Harold Togtman, *Marketing Staff*
EMP: 40 EST: 1963
SQ FT: 30,000
SALES (est): 5.6MM  Privately Held
WEB: www.tscutstonebrick.com
SIC: 3281  5032  1422  1411  Cut stone & stone products; limestone, cut & shaped; flagstones; brick, stone & related material; masons' materials; crushed & broken limestone; dimension stone

**(G-10372)**
**TRIO WIRE PRODUCTS INC**
141 Ontario St  (60423-1646)
PHONE..................815 469-2148
Fax: 815 469-1471
Stephen Mikan, *CEO*
Adele Mikan, *Corp Secy*
John Mikan, *Shareholder*
EMP: 7
SQ FT: 5,600
SALES (est): 1.2MM  Privately Held
SIC: 3496  3469  Miscellaneous fabricated wire products; metal stampings

**(G-10373)**
**TSV ADHESIVE SYSTEMS  INC**
9411 Corsair Rd  (60423-2513)
PHONE..................815 464-5606
Fax: 815 464-5650
Edward Koziol, *President*
Eric Gut, *Sales Mgr*
Miles Shiveley, *Marketing Staff*
Cathy Albert, *Manager*
Gary Johnson, *Admin Sec*
◆ EMP: 50
SALES (est): 13MM
SALES (corp-wide): 582.1MM  Privately Held
WEB: www.instantca.com
SIC: 2891  Adhesives
PA: Royal Adhesives And Sealants Llc
2001 W Washington St
South Bend IN 46628
574 246-5000

**(G-10374)**
**VILUTIS AND CO  INC**
22535 S Center Rd  (60423-1655)
P.O. Box 10  (60423-0010)
PHONE..................815 469-2116
Fax: 815 469-0327
James M Vilutis, *President*
John Vilutis, *Treasurer*
▼ EMP: 31
SQ FT: 50,000
SALES (est): 10.1MM  Privately Held
WEB: www.vilutisinc.com
SIC: 2673  3556  Plastic bags: made from purchased materials; food products machinery

**(G-10375)**
**VINDEE INDUSTRIES  INC**
965 Lambrecht Dr  (60423-1650)
PHONE..................815 469-3300
Robert Mc Carthy, *President*
Sharon Mc Carthy, *Corp Secy*
▲ EMP: 30
SQ FT: 30,000
SALES (est): 5.4MM  Privately Held
WEB: www.vindee.com
SIC: 3498  7692  3549  3993  Tube fabricating (contract bending & shaping); welding repair; metalworking machinery; signs & advertising specialties; stamping metal for the trade

**(G-10376)**
**WARFIELD ELECTRIC COMPANY INC (PA)**
175 Industry Ave  (60423-1685)
PHONE..................815 469-4094
Fax: 815 469-4168
Jerome H Warfield, *President*
Charles Minderman, *General Mgr*
Nancy Monahan, *General Mgr*
Sandra K Warfield, *Vice Pres*
Denis J Novak, *Controller*
▲ EMP: 50 EST: 1974
SQ FT: 28,000
SALES (est): 6MM  Privately Held
SIC: 7694  3621  Rewinding stators; rebuilding motors, except automotive; coil winding service; motors, electric

**(G-10377)**
**WOOW SUSHI ORLAND PARK LLC**
Also Called: Big Tuna
19951 S Lagrange Rd  (60423-3105)
PHONE..................815 469-5189
EMP: 11
SALES (corp-wide): 966.3K  Privately Held
SIC: 2752  Commercial printing, lithographic
PA: Woow Sushi Orland Park Llc
13137 S La Grange Rd
Orland Park IL 60462
708 671-1716

### Franklin
*Morgan County*

**(G-10378)**
**COCAJO BLADES & LEATHER**
481 Oxley Rd  (62638-5031)
PHONE..................217 370-6634
EMP: 3
SALES (est): 248.6K  Privately Held
SIC: 3199  Leather goods

**(G-10379)**
**FAITH PRINTING**
Also Called: Its Easy With Jesus Printing
824 Bills Rd (62638-5144)
PHONE...................217 675-2191
Lyle Janell, *Principal*
EMP: 6
SALES (est): 440K **Privately Held**
SIC: 2752 Commercial printing, lithographic

## Franklin Park
### Cook County

**(G-10380)**
**A AND D INDUSTRIAL IGNITION**
10330 Front Ave (60131-1516)
PHONE...................773 992-4040
Doru Andronic, *Owner*
Lydda Andronic, *Co-Owner*
EMP: 3
SALES: 166.2K **Privately Held**
SIC: 3694 Motors, starting: automotive & aircraft; alternators, automotive; generators, automotive & aircraft

**(G-10381)**
**A E MICEK ENGINEERING CORP**
9239 Cherry Ave (60131-3009)
PHONE...................847 455-8181
Fax: 847 455-8080
Ronald A Micek, *President*
Robert Gruner, *General Mgr*
Wayne J Micek, *Treasurer*
EMP: 26
SQ FT: 11,000
SALES (est): 4.1MM **Privately Held**
SIC: 3451 Screw machine products

**(G-10382)**
**AARSTAR PRECISION GRINDING**
9007 Exchange Ave (60131-2815)
PHONE...................847 678-4880
Frank L Tarolla, *President*
EMP: 4 EST: 1965
SQ FT: 5,000
SALES (est): 596.1K **Privately Held**
SIC: 3599 Machine shop, jobbing & repair

**(G-10383)**
**ABILITY CABINET CO INC**
3503 Martens St (60131-2015)
PHONE...................847 678-6678
Fax: 847 678-2405
Chuck Star, *President*
Teresa Vasquez, *Vice Pres*
Ron Cruise, *Treasurer*
EMP: 8 EST: 1953
SQ FT: 6,000
SALES: 850K **Privately Held**
SIC: 2434 2541 2431 Wood kitchen cabinets; vanities, bathroom: wood; wood partitions & fixtures; millwork

**(G-10384)**
**ADVANCED METALCRAFT INC**
9128 Belden Ave (60131-3506)
PHONE...................847 451-0771
Fax: 847 451-0773
Peter Anwar, *President*
EMP: 10
SQ FT: 15,000
SALES (est): 1.8MM **Privately Held**
WEB: www.metalcrafter.com
SIC: 3444 Ducts, sheet metal

**(G-10385)**
**AERO APMC INC**
Also Called: Aero Precision Machining
411 S County Line Rd (60131-1002)
PHONE...................630 766-0910
Fax: 630 766-4372
Ark Maciaczek, *President*
Stanislaw Kapusciarz, *Vice Pres*
Lucjan Borowsky, *Treasurer*
Curtis Snyder, *Admin Sec*
EMP: 14
SQ FT: 5,000
SALES (est): 2.1MM **Privately Held**
WEB: www.aeroapmc.com
SIC: 3599 Machine shop, jobbing & repair

**(G-10386)**
**AETNA BEARING COMPANY**
1081 Sesame St (60131-1316)
PHONE...................630 694-0024
Fax: 630 694-0087
James Trauscht, *Principal*
Jim Gehrke, *Purch Mgr*
Don Koziel, *QC Mgr*
Joseph Amaro, *Engineer*
Joe Amarro, *Engineer*
▲ EMP: 23
SALES (est): 4.5MM **Privately Held**
SIC: 3366 Bushings & bearings

**(G-10387)**
**AJAX TOOL WORKS INC**
Also Called: Ajax Tools
10801 Franklin Ave (60131-1407)
PHONE...................847 455-5420
Fax: 708 455-9242
Robert J Benedict, *President*
Regina Hall, *Accountant*
Anthony Cadd, *Manager*
Steve Tisdall, *Manager*
▲ EMP: 87 EST: 1946
SQ FT: 120,000
SALES: 13MM **Privately Held**
WEB: www.ajaxtools.com
SIC: 3423 3546 3542 Hand & edge tools; power-driven handtools; mechanical (pneumatic or hydraulic) metal forming machines

**(G-10388)**
**AL GELATO CHICAGO LLC**
9133 Belden Ave (60131-3505)
PHONE...................847 455-5355
Fax: 847 455-7553
Paula Dinardo,
EMP: 9
SALES (est): 1.1MM **Privately Held**
SIC: 5169 5451 5143 2024 Gelatin; ice cream (packaged); frozen dairy desserts; ice cream & frozen desserts; ice cream, packaged: molded, on sticks, etc.; dairy based frozen desserts

**(G-10389)**
**ALL AMERICAN SPRING STAMPING**
10220 Franklin Ave (60131-1528)
PHONE...................847 928-9468
Mark Sobkowicz, *President*
Chris Sobkowicz, *Vice Pres*
Elizabeth Sobkowicz, *Admin Sec*
EMP: 8
SALES (est): 1.1MM **Privately Held**
SIC: 3495 3469 Wire springs; metal stampings

**(G-10390)**
**ALLIED ASPHALT PAVING CO INC**
10555 Waveland Ave (60131-1219)
PHONE...................847 824-2848
Fax: 847 233-9772
Larry Mack, *General Mgr*
EMP: 10
SALES (corp-wide): 5.8MM **Privately Held**
SIC: 2951 Asphalt & asphaltic paving mixtures (not from refineries)
PA: Allied Asphalt Paving Co Inc
1100 Brandt Dr
Elgin IL 60120
630 289-6080

**(G-10391)**
**AMERICAN METALCRAFT INC**
3708 River Rd Ste 800 (60131-2158)
PHONE...................800 333-9133
Fax: 708 345-5758
David Kahn, *President*
Susan Kahn, *Vice Pres*
George McFadden, *Vice Pres*
Richard K Packer, *Vice Pres*
Anthony Di Tusa, *QC Mgr*
◆ EMP: 100 EST: 1947
SQ FT: 100,000
SALES (est): 18.5MM **Privately Held**
WEB: www.amnow.com
SIC: 2599 5087 Restaurant furniture, wood or metal; restaurant supplies

**(G-10392)**
**AMERICAN PRECISION MACHINING**
11135 Franklin Ave (60131-1411)
PHONE...................847 455-1720
Fax: 847 455-0503
Naresh Patel, *President*
Ramesh Patel, *Vice Pres*
EMP: 10
SQ FT: 5,000
SALES (est): 165K **Privately Held**
WEB: www.apm-i.com
SIC: 3569 Filters, general line: industrial

**(G-10393)**
**AMERICAN SCREW MACHINE CO**
2833 N Comm St (60131)
PHONE...................847 455-4308
Stephen Kocian, *Owner*
Larry Williams, *Manager*
Sarah Alzamora, *Admin Sec*
Steve Williams,
EMP: 9 EST: 2006
SQ FT: 5,000
SALES: 800K
SALES (corp-wide): 12.5MM **Privately Held**
SIC: 3451 Screw machine products
PA: Komar Screw Corp.
7790 N Merrimac Ave
Niles IL 60714
847 965-9090

**(G-10394)**
**AMERICAN/JEBCO CORPORATION**
Also Called: Jebco" Screw" and Speciality
11330 Melrose Ave (60131-1323)
PHONE...................847 455-3150
Matthew O'Connor, *President*
▲ EMP: 130 EST: 1956
SQ FT: 40,000
SALES (est): 26.7MM **Privately Held**
WEB: www.americanjebco.com
SIC: 3451 3452 3356 Screw machine products; screws, metal; bolts, metal; rivets, metal; nonferrous rolling & drawing

**(G-10395)**
**AMMENTORP TOOL COMPANY INC**
9828 Franklin Ave (60131-1913)
PHONE...................847 671-9290
Fax: 847 671-9388
Edward Ammentorp, *President*
Dale Ammentorp, *Vice Pres*
Wayne Ammentorp, *Vice Pres*
EMP: 5
SQ FT: 5,500
SALES: 200K **Privately Held**
SIC: 3545 3544 3469 Tools & accessories for machine tools; die sets for metal stamping (presses); metal stampings

**(G-10396)**
**ANDSCOT CO INC**
9117 Medill Ave (60131-3468)
PHONE...................847 455-5800
Fax: 773 625-1242
Andrew Shaffer, *President*
J M Shaffer, *Treasurer*
EMP: 4
SQ FT: 4,000
SALES (est): 557.2K **Privately Held**
WEB: www.andscot.com
SIC: 3441 5051 Fabricated structural metal; metals service centers & offices

**(G-10397)**
**APEX WIRE PRODUCTS COMPANY INC**
9030 Gage Ave (60131-2102)
PHONE...................847 671-1830
Fax: 847 671-1673
Richard Kosowski, *President*
Carmen J Laterza, *Purch Agent*
Matthew Kosowski, *MIS Mgr*
EMP: 15 EST: 1940
SQ FT: 24,000
SALES (est): 3.3MM **Privately Held**
WEB: www.apexwireproducts.com
SIC: 3496 3469 3315 2542 Woven wire products; metal stampings; steel wire & related products; partitions & fixtures, except wood

**(G-10398)**
**ARCADIA PRESS INC**
10915 Franklin Ave Ste L (60131-1431)
PHONE...................847 451-6390
Fax: 847 451-6395
Dan Rosen, *President*
Andrew Rosen, *General Mgr*
EMP: 10 EST: 1937
SQ FT: 3,500
SALES (est): 1.3MM **Privately Held**
WEB: www.arcadiapress.net
SIC: 2754 2791 2759 2672 Labels: gravure printing; typesetting; commercial printing; coated & laminated paper; packaging paper & plastics film, coated & laminated

**(G-10399)**
**ARCHER SCREW PRODUCTS INC (PA)**
11341 Melrose Ave (60131-1322)
PHONE...................847 451-1150
Fax: 847 451-1951
Timothy Coffee, *President*
Tom Zoccoli, *Mfg Mgr*
Chuck Wolter, *Engineer*
Kelly Metcalf, *Chief Mktg Ofcr*
Jodie Coffee, *Admin Sec*
▲ EMP: 63
SQ FT: 49,000
SALES (est): 23.3MM **Privately Held**
WEB: www.archerscrew.com
SIC: 5072 3452 Screws; bolts, nuts, rivets & washers

**(G-10400)**
**ARMITAGE INDUSTRIES INC**
Also Called: Thermal-Chem
2550 Edgington St Ste A (60131-3403)
PHONE...................847 288-9090
Fax: 847 288-9091
Charles Powell, *President*
John Von Leesen, *Vice Pres*
Jack Stoecker, *Accounting Mgr*
Ed Tutas, *Sales Mgr*
Donna Steiger, *Office Mgr*
EMP: 15
SQ FT: 27,000
SALES (est): 3.3MM **Privately Held**
WEB: www.thermalchem.com
SIC: 2891 2851 Adhesives; paints & allied products

**(G-10401)**
**ART-CRAFT PRINTERS**
9108 Belden Ave (60131-3506)
PHONE...................847 455-2201
Fax: 847 455-2044
Gary Nardiello, *Owner*
Jeanmarie Nardiello, *Bookkeeper*
EMP: 2
SALES: 300K **Privately Held**
SIC: 2752 2759 Commercial printing, offset; letterpress printing

**(G-10402)**
**ASAP PALLETS INC**
480 Podlin Dr (60131-1008)
PHONE...................630 350-7689
EMP: 10
SALES (est): 92.9K **Privately Held**
SIC: 2448 Pallets, wood & wood with metal

**(G-10403)**
**ASH PALLET MANAGEMENT INC**
9400 King St (60131-2116)
PHONE...................847 473-5700
Anthony James Ash, *President*
EMP: 30
SALES (corp-wide): 9.5MM **Privately Held**
SIC: 2448 Pallets, wood & wood with metal
PA: Ash Pallet Management, Inc.
61 Mcmillen Rd
Antioch IL 60002
847 473-5700

# GEOGRAPHIC SECTION

Franklin Park - Cook County (G-10429)

**(G-10404)**
**ASSOCIATE GENERAL LABS INC**
Also Called: Rowlar Tool & Die Div
9035 Exchange Ave (60131-2815)
**PHONE**.................................847 678-2717
Arthur Schroeder III, *President*
Arthur Schroeder Jr, *General Mgr*
**EMP:** 5
**SQ FT:** 5,000
**SALES:** 250K **Privately Held**
**SIC: 3548** 8734 8731 3699 Welding & cutting apparatus & accessories; testing laboratories; commercial physical research; electrical equipment & supplies

**(G-10405)**
**AST INDUSTRIES INC**
Also Called: Anti-Seize Technology
2345 17th St (60131-3432)
**PHONE**.................................847 455-2300
Fax: 847 455-2371
John H Heydt, *President*
Allen Majeski, *Vice Pres*
Katie Niesen, *Sales Mgr*
Joe Coutee, *Manager*
Harold Heydt, *Shareholder*
▼ **EMP:** 12
**SQ FT:** 15,000
**SALES (est):** 3.8MM **Privately Held**
**WEB:** www.astinfo.com
**SIC: 2891** 2869 Sealing compounds for pipe threads or joints; industrial organic chemicals

**(G-10406)**
**AWNINGS OVER CHICAGOLAND INC**
10204 Franklin Ave (60131-1528)
**PHONE**.................................847 233-0310
James Girard, *President*
**EMP:** 5
**SQ FT:** 3,800
**SALES (est):** 596.6K **Privately Held**
**SIC: 3444** Awnings & canopies

**(G-10407)**
**B & R GRINDING CO**
459 Podlin Dr (60131-1009)
**PHONE**.................................630 595-7789
Fax: 630 595-2639
Richard Ruhl, *President*
Debbie Ruhl, *Admin Sec*
**EMP:** 4 **EST:** 1974
**SQ FT:** 3,500
**SALES (est):** 380K **Privately Held**
**WEB:** www.brgrinding.com
**SIC: 3599** Grinding castings for the trade

**(G-10408)**
**B J PLASTIC MOLDING CO (PA)**
435 S County Line Rd (60131-1092)
**PHONE**.................................630 766-3200
Fax: 630 766-1584
Robert K Jacobsen Jr, *President*
Mary M Jacobsen, *Corp Secy*
Craig L Jacobson, *Vice Pres*
Craig Jacobsen, *Plant Mgr*
Jackie Novak, *Manager*
**EMP:** 38
**SQ FT:** 35,000
**SALES (est):** 10.8MM **Privately Held**
**WEB:** www.bjplastic.com
**SIC: 3089** 2789 Injection molded finished plastic products; bookbinding & related work

**(G-10409)**
**BADGER AIR BRUSH CO**
9128 Belmont Ave (60131-2895)
**PHONE**.................................847 678-3104
Fax: 847 671-4352
Kenneth Schlotfeldt, *President*
Russ Mattes, *Purchasing*
Herman Robisch, *Engineer*
Candy Carnes, *Treasurer*
Richard Ryser, *Controller*
▲ **EMP:** 90 **EST:** 1963
**SQ FT:** 26,000
**SALES (est):** 14.5MM **Privately Held**
**WEB:** www.badgerairbrush.com
**SIC: 3952** Brushes, air, artists'; artists' materials, except pencils & leads

**(G-10410)**
**BELMONT PLATING WORKS INC (PA)**
9145 King St (60131-2109)
**PHONE**.................................847 678-0200
Fax: 847 678-0758
Mark Toni, *President*
David Toni, *Vice Pres*
**EMP:** 120 **EST:** 1947
**SQ FT:** 35,000
**SALES (est):** 15.1MM **Privately Held**
**WEB:** www.belmontplatingworks.com
**SIC: 3471** Plating of metals or formed products; polishing, metals or formed products

**(G-10411)**
**BEST REP COMPANY CORPORATION**
Also Called: Alca Industrial Instrs Svc
9224 Grand Ave Ste 2 (60131-3029)
**PHONE**.................................847 451-6644
Larry Gulik, *President*
**EMP:** 2 **EST:** 1966
**SQ FT:** 1,500
**SALES (est):** 278.6K **Privately Held**
**SIC: 3699** 7699 Appliance cords for household electrical equipment; industrial machinery & equipment repair

**(G-10412)**
**BINDER TOOL INC**
9833 Franklin Ave (60131-1912)
**PHONE**.................................847 678-4222
Hans Bittenbinder, *President*
Anna Bittenbinder, *Treasurer*
**EMP:** 7
**SQ FT:** 6,000
**SALES (est):** 1.1MM **Privately Held**
**SIC: 3544** Special dies, tools, jigs & fixtures

**(G-10413)**
**BLOCKSMOY INC**
10632 Grand Ave (60131-2211)
**PHONE**.................................847 260-9070
Wolfgang Reichelt, *CEO*
Jorg Reichelt, *President*
Lars Ullenboom, *Treasurer*
**EMP:** 13
**SALES:** 239K **Privately Held**
**SIC: 3677** Electronic coils, transformers & other inductors

**(G-10414)**
**BLUEBERRY WOODWORKING INC**
2824 Birch St (60131-3004)
**PHONE**.................................773 230-7179
Krzysztof Jagoda, *Principal*
**EMP:** 2
**SALES (est):** 224.9K **Privately Held**
**SIC: 2431** Millwork

**(G-10415)**
**BONSAL AMERICAN INC**
10352 Franklin Ave (60131-1530)
**PHONE**.................................847 678-6220
Robert Main, *Principal*
Debbie Aponte, *Personnel*
**EMP:** 70
**SALES (corp-wide):** 28.6B **Privately Held**
**WEB:** www.bonsalamerican.com
**SIC: 3272** 2952 2951 2899 Dry mixture concrete; asphalt felts & coatings; asphalt paving mixtures & blocks; chemical preparations; cement, hydraulic
**HQ:** Bonsal American, Inc.
625 Griffith Rd Ste 100
Charlotte NC 28217
704 525-1621

**(G-10416)**
**BRETFORD MANUFACTURING INC (PA)**
11000 Seymour Ave (60131-1230)
P.O. Box 92170, Elk Grove Village (60009-2170)
**PHONE**.................................847 678-2545
Fax: 847 671-9537
Chris Petrick, *CEO*
Mikel S Briggs, *President*
Ryan Madden, *Regional Mgr*
Justin Nacpil, *Business Mgr*
Phil Cloutier, *Vice Pres*
◆ **EMP:** 300 **EST:** 1948
**SQ FT:** 120,000
**SALES:** 2.9MM **Privately Held**
**SIC: 2522** 3861 2521 3651 Office furniture, except wood; photographic equipment & supplies; wood office furniture; household audio & video equipment

**(G-10417)**
**BRISTAR**
3541 Martens St Ste 304 (60131-2058)
**PHONE**.................................847 678-5000
Paul G Keefe Sr, *Owner*
Betty Lou Keefe, *Partner*
**EMP:** 3
**SALES (est):** 209.5K **Privately Held**
**SIC: 3496** Miscellaneous fabricated wire products

**(G-10418)**
**BRUNSWICK CORPORATION**
Also Called: Life Fitness Mfg Fclity
10601 Belmont Ave (60131-1545)
**PHONE**.................................847 288-3300
Joseph Pedone, *Branch Mgr*
Christopher Ratliff, *Manager*
**EMP:** 786
**SALES (corp-wide):** 4.4B **Publicly Held**
**WEB:** www.lifefitness.com
**SIC: 3949** Exercising cycles
**PA:** Brunswick Corporation
1 N Field Ct
Lake Forest IL 60045
847 735-4700

**(G-10419)**
**BRUNSWICK CORPORATION**
Also Called: Life Fitness US
10600 Belmont Ave (60131-1548)
**PHONE**.................................847 288-3300
Emil Golen, *Engineer*
Chris Clewson, *Manager*
Jerry Briggs, *Senior Mgr*
Gerald Reyes, *Admin Asst*
**EMP:** 394
**SALES (corp-wide):** 4.4B **Publicly Held**
**WEB:** www.lifefitness.com
**SIC: 3949** Gymnasium equipment
**PA:** Brunswick Corporation
1 N Field Ct
Lake Forest IL 60045
847 735-4700

**(G-10420)**
**C & F FORGE COMPANY (PA)**
9100 Parklane Ave (60131-3054)
**PHONE**.................................847 455-6609
Thomas Herbstritt Jr, *President*
Brian Herbstritt, *General Mgr*
Gregg Carlevato, *Controller*
**EMP:** 2 **EST:** 1938
**SQ FT:** 500
**SALES (est):** 4.1MM **Privately Held**
**WEB:** www.candj.com
**SIC: 3312** 3462 Forgings, iron & steel; iron & steel forgings

**(G-10421)**
**C & J METAL PRODUCTS INC**
11119 Franklin Ave (60131-1486)
**PHONE**.................................847 455-0766
Fax: 847 455-0289
Steven Dolecki, *President*
Christine Dolecki, *Treasurer*
▲ **EMP:** 16
**SQ FT:** 10,000
**SALES (est):** 3MM **Privately Held**
**SIC: 3469** 3496 Stamping metal for the trade; miscellaneous fabricated wire products

**(G-10422)**
**C/B MACHINE TOOL CORP**
9321 Schiller Blvd (60131-2949)
**PHONE**.................................847 288-1807
Fax: 847 288-1801
Stanley Barnas, *President*
Ann Barnasv, *President*
**EMP:** 5
**SQ FT:** 3,000
**SALES:** 250K **Privately Held**
**SIC: 3599** 7692 7629 3544 Machine shop, jobbing & repair; welding repair; electrical repair shops; special dies, tools, jigs & fixtures; metal heat treating

**(G-10423)**
**CALMA OPTIMA FOODS**
10915 Franklin Ave Ste A (60131-1431)
**PHONE**.................................847 962-8329
Paul Zielinski, *Principal*
**EMP:** 6 **EST:** 2012
**SALES (est):** 604.4K **Privately Held**
**SIC: 2099** Sandwiches, assembled & packaged: for wholesale market

**(G-10424)**
**CASA NOSTRA BAKERY CO INC**
3140 Mannheim Rd (60131-2375)
**PHONE**.................................847 455-5175
Mike Florio, *President*
Joe Catucci, *Treasurer*
**EMP:** 15
**SQ FT:** 10,000
**SALES (est):** 1.8MM **Privately Held**
**SIC: 2051** 2052 Bread, cake & related products; cookies & crackers

**(G-10425)**
**CASTING IMPREGNATORS INC (PA)**
11150 Addison Ave (60131-1404)
**PHONE**.................................847 455-1000
Fax: 847 455-4455
David Koehler, *President*
Michelle Koehler, *Sales Associate*
Nancy Walsdorf, *Office Mgr*
Nancy Walsdors, *Office Mgr*
James Farrington, *Manager*
**EMP:** 13 **EST:** 1950
**SQ FT:** 20,000
**SALES (est):** 2.2MM **Privately Held**
**WEB:** www.castingimpregnators.com
**SIC: 3479** Coating of metals with plastic or resins

**(G-10426)**
**CENTERLESS GRINDING CO**
2330 17th St Unit B (60131-3409)
**PHONE**.................................847 455-7660
Fax: 847 455-7044
Haribhai Patel, *President*
Mary Jones, *Admin Sec*
**EMP:** 18
**SQ FT:** 4,000
**SALES (est):** 1.3MM **Privately Held**
**SIC: 3599** Machine shop, jobbing & repair

**(G-10427)**
**CHARLES H LUCK ENVELOPE INC**
10551 Anderson Pl (60131-2301)
**PHONE**.................................847 451-1500
Timothy Kennedy, *President*
Kevin Dean, *Vice Pres*
Charles H Luck, *Personnel Exec*
Denise Kennedy, *Admin Sec*
**EMP:** 22
**SQ FT:** 24,000
**SALES (est):** 4.8MM **Privately Held**
**WEB:** www.luckenvelope.com
**SIC: 2672** Gummed paper: made from purchased materials

**(G-10428)**
**CHICAGO DIE CASTING MFG CO**
9148 King St (60131-2188)
**PHONE**.................................847 671-5010
Fax: 847 671-1355
John C Brundige III, *President*
Marie Brundige, *Vice Pres*
Rob Brundige, *Manager*
**EMP:** 30 **EST:** 1919
**SQ FT:** 40,000
**SALES (est):** 7.9MM **Privately Held**
**WEB:** www.chicagodiecasting.com
**SIC: 3568** 3364 Pulleys, power transmission; zinc & zinc-base alloy die-castings

**(G-10429)**
**CHICAGO HARDWARE AND FIX CO (PA)**
9100 Parklane Ave (60131-3066)
**PHONE**.................................847 455-6609
Fax: 847 455-0012
Thomas A Herbstritt Jr, *President*
Gregg Carlevato, *Corp Secy*
Kevin Keane, *Plant Mgr*
James Whelan, *Prdtn Mgr*
Nick Whelan, *Warehouse Mgr*
▲ **EMP:** 100 **EST:** 1914

# Franklin Park - Cook County (G-10430)  GEOGRAPHIC SECTION

**SQ FT:** 85,000
**SALES (est):** 27.1MM **Privately Held**
**WEB:** www.chicagohardware.com
**SIC:** 3429 3545 3496 3462 Manufactured hardware (general); machine tool accessories; miscellaneous fabricated wire products; iron & steel forgings; bolts, nuts, rivets & washers; copper rolling & drawing

### (G-10430)
**CHICAGOLAND METAL FABRICATORS**
10355 Franklin Ave (60131-1542)
**PHONE** ........................... 847 260-5320
Robert Szczepanik, *President*
Agnes Spiewak, *Office Mgr*
**EMP:** 5
**SALES (est):** 620K **Privately Held**
**SIC:** 1521 1542 3441 3444 Single-family housing construction; nonresidential construction; fabricated structural metal; sheet metalwork

### (G-10431)
**CHUCKING MACHINE PRODUCTS INC**
3550 Birch St (60131-2099)
**PHONE** ........................... 847 678-1192
**Fax:** 847 678-1269
Edward Allen Iverson, *President*
Jerry R Iverson, *Corp Secy*
Milton Ramos, *Maintenance Dir*
Kevin Sullivan, *Plant Mgr*
Timothy Mayo, *Production*
**EMP:** 74 **EST:** 1957
**SALES (est):** 16.6MM **Privately Held**
**WEB:** www.chucking.com
**SIC:** 3728 3714 3841 Aircraft parts & equipment; motor vehicle parts & accessories; surgical & medical instruments; ophthalmic instruments & apparatus

### (G-10432)
**CIRCLE CASTER ENGINEERING CO**
10706 Grand Ave Ste 1 (60131-2215)
**PHONE** ........................... 847 455-2206
Michael Gianelli, *President*
Jeffrey Giannelli, *Admin Sec*
▲ **EMP:** 5 **EST:** 1991
**SQ FT:** 11,000
**SALES (est):** 1MM **Privately Held**
**SIC:** 3089 Tires, plastic

### (G-10433)
**CIRCLE ENGINEERING COMPANY**
10706 Grand Ave Ste 1 (60131-2215)
**PHONE** ........................... 847 455-2204
Jeffrey A Solomon, *President*
Udelle Solomon, *Admin Sec*
▲ **EMP:** 5 **EST:** 1952
**SALES (est):** 471.9K **Privately Held**
**SIC:** 3089 Plastic processing

### (G-10434)
**CLAD-REX STEEL LLC**
11500 King St (60131-1310)
**PHONE** ........................... 847 455-7373
Davies Peter G, *Mng Member*
Mark A Bounds,
Rick Luft,
Stuart Skinner,
**EMP:** 30
**SQ FT:** 60,000
**SALES (est):** 7.5MM **Privately Held**
**WEB:** www.cladrex.com
**SIC:** 3479 Coating of metals with plastic or resins

### (G-10435)
**CLASSIC SHEET METAL INC**
1065 Sesame St (60131-1316)
**PHONE** ........................... 630 694-0300
**Fax:** 630 694-1990
Jack Lococo, *President*
Jim Lococo, *President*
Mike Lococo, *Corp Secy*
Robert Lococo, *CFO*
Diane Faust, *Manager*
**EMP:** 75
**SQ FT:** 90,000
**SALES (est):** 15.3MM **Privately Held**
**WEB:** www.classic-sheet-metal.com
**SIC:** 3444 3469 Sheet metalwork; metal stampings

### (G-10436)
**CLEAR FOCUS IMAGING INC (PA)**
9201 Belmont Ave Ste 100c (60131-2842)
**PHONE** ........................... 707 544-7990
Debbie Ross, *President*
Maria Sisson, *Manager*
▲ **EMP:** 21
**SQ FT:** 22,000
**SALES (est):** 2.2MM **Privately Held**
**WEB:** www.clearfocus.com
**SIC:** 3081 Vinyl film & sheet

### (G-10437)
**CLEAR PACK COMPANY**
Also Called: Division Sonoco Products Co
11610 Copenhagen Ct (60131-1302)
**PHONE** ........................... 847 957-6282
**Fax:** 847 957-1529
R Howard Coker, *President*
Ritchie L Bond, *Admin Sec*
**EMP:** 130
**SALES (est):** 181.6K
**SALES (corp-wide):** 4.7B **Publicly Held**
**SIC:** 3089 3081 Thermoformed finished plastic products; plastic film & sheet
**PA:** Sonoco Products Company
1 N 2nd St
Hartsville SC 29550
843 383-7000

### (G-10438)
**CLIMATE SLTION WNDOWS DORS INC**
10100 Pacific Ave (60131-1654)
**PHONE** ........................... 847 233-9800
**Fax:** 847 233-9808
Mariusz Nalepa, *President*
Violet Slowik, *Vice Pres*
Charlie Morello, *Sales Dir*
**EMP:** 30
**SQ FT:** 30,000
**SALES (est):** 6MM **Privately Held**
**SIC:** 3442 Window & door frames

### (G-10439)
**COATINGS INTERNATIONAL INC**
Also Called: Americoats
3429 Runge St (60131-1315)
**PHONE** ........................... 847 455-1400
**Fax:** 847 455-2797
Rajendra Patel, *President*
Anna Kita, *General Mgr*
Bharat Patel, *Exec VP*
Kamini Lodhavia, *Manager*
Lorena Saldana, *Clerk*
▲ **EMP:** 40
**SQ FT:** 35,000
**SALES (est):** 19MM **Privately Held**
**WEB:** www.americoats.com
**SIC:** 2851 Paints & allied products

### (G-10440)
**CONSOLIDATED ELEC WIRE & CABLE**
11044 King St (60131-1412)
**PHONE** ........................... 847 455-8830
**Fax:** 847 455-8837
Thomas A Mann, *CEO*
David J Duncan, *President*
▲ **EMP:** 60
**SQ FT:** 55,000
**SALES (est):** 13MM **Privately Held**
**WEB:** www.conwire.com
**SIC:** 3679 5065 Loads, electronic; harness assemblies for electronic use: wire or cable; electronic parts & equipment; coils, electronic; connectors, electronic

### (G-10441)
**CONTAINER SPECIALTIES INC**
10800 Belmont Ave Ste 200 (60131-1562)
**PHONE** ........................... 708 615-1400
Ralph W Johnson, *President*
Priscilla Trippi, *Admin Sec*
**EMP:** 21
**SALES (est):** 5.4MM **Privately Held**
**WEB:** www.midwestcan.com
**SIC:** 3085 Plastics bottles

### (G-10442)
**CORPORATE BUSINESS CARD LTD**
9611 Franklin Ave (60131-2703)
**PHONE** ........................... 847 455-5760
**Fax:** 847 455-5780
Patricia Letarte, *President*
Terrance H Zimmer, *Principal*
**EMP:** 20
**SQ FT:** 5,300
**SALES (est):** 2.5MM **Privately Held**
**WEB:** www.corpbuscards.com
**SIC:** 2752 2759 Business form & card printing, lithographic; commercial printing

### (G-10443)
**CORTINA COMPANIES INC**
10706 Grand Ave Ste 1 (60131-2215)
**PHONE** ........................... 847 455-2800
Jeffrey Giannelli, *President*
Micahel Giannelli, *Admin Sec*
**EMP:** 23
**SALES (est):** 3.7MM **Privately Held**
**SIC:** 3089 Injection molding of plastics

### (G-10444)
**CORTINA TOOL & MOLDING CO**
Also Called: Cortina Safety Products
10706 Grand Ave Ste 1 (60131-2215)
**PHONE** ........................... 847 455-2800
Michele Lozada, *President*
Michael Giannelli, *Principal*
Jeffrey Giannelli, *Vice Pres*
Nathan Sparkman, *Opers Mgr*
Gene Berryman, *QC Mgr*
▲ **EMP:** 200 **EST:** 1971
**SQ FT:** 125,000
**SALES (est):** 76.1MM **Privately Held**
**WEB:** www.cortinaco.com
**SIC:** 3089 Injection molding of plastics; blow molded finished plastic products

### (G-10445)
**COSMOS PLASTICS COMPANY**
3630 Wolf Rd (60131-1426)
**PHONE** ........................... 847 451-1307
**Fax:** 847 451-1308
Andrew A Park, *President*
Paul Park, *Sales Staff*
▲ **EMP:** 41
**SQ FT:** 57,000
**SALES (est):** 4MM **Privately Held**
**WEB:** www.cosmosplastics.com
**SIC:** 3993 Displays & cutouts, window & lobby

### (G-10446)
**CRM NORTH AMERICA LLC**
2308 17th St (60131-3407)
**PHONE** ........................... 708 603-3475
Pintore Luigi, *Mng Member*
**EMP:** 2
**SALES (est):** 241.5K **Privately Held**
**SIC:** 3556 Food products machinery

### (G-10447)
**CULINARY CO-PACK INC**
9140 Belden Ave (60131-3506)
**PHONE** ........................... 847 451-1551
**EMP:** 6
**SALES (est):** 655.2K **Privately Held**
**SIC:** 2099 Mfg Food Preparations

### (G-10448)
**CULINARY CO-PACK INCORPORATED**
2300 N 17th Ave (60131)
**PHONE** ........................... 847 451-1551
**Fax:** 847 451-1590
John J Capozzoli Sr, *President*
John J Capozzoli Jr, *Vice Pres*
Barbara Capozzoli, *Treasurer*
Tom Sabel, *Manager*
Stewart Riske, *Executive*
**EMP:** 20 **EST:** 1981
**SALES (est):** 4.1MM **Privately Held**
**WEB:** www.jamaicajohn.com
**SIC:** 2099 2087 Food preparations; syrups, drink

### (G-10449)
**CUSTOM DESIGNS BY GEORGIO**
9955 Pacific Ave (60131-1920)
**PHONE** ........................... 847 233-0410
**Fax:** 773 233-0413
George Spyropoulos, *President*
**EMP:** 10
**SALES (est):** 400K **Privately Held**
**WEB:** www.customdesignsbygeorgio.com
**SIC:** 2511 Wood household furniture

### (G-10450)
**CUSTOM TOOL & GAGE CO INC**
10109 Franklin Ave (60131-1819)
**PHONE** ........................... 847 671-5306
**Fax:** 847 671-5313
Franco Bianchi, *President*
Roy Bianchi, *Vice Pres*
**EMP:** 8
**SQ FT:** 4,000
**SALES (est):** 947.5K **Privately Held**
**SIC:** 3544 3545 Special dies & tools; gauges (machine tool accessories)

### (G-10451)
**CUTTING EDGE INDUSTRIES INC**
9015 Exchange Ave (60131-2815)
**PHONE** ........................... 847 678-1777
Richard Richter, *President*
Tom Javan, *Treasurer*
**EMP:** 7
**SQ FT:** 6,000
**SALES (est):** 1MM **Privately Held**
**SIC:** 3542 3544 3496 Machine tools, metal forming type; die casting & extruding machines; special dies, tools, jigs & fixtures; miscellaneous fabricated wire products

### (G-10452)
**D & N DEBURRING CO INC**
2919 Birch St (60131-3005)
**PHONE** ........................... 847 451-7702
**Fax:** 847 451-7712
Stephen Flemming, *President*
**EMP:** 9
**SQ FT:** 4,600
**SALES (est):** 860K **Privately Held**
**SIC:** 7699 3471 Industrial equipment services; plating & polishing

### (G-10453)
**D E SPECIALTY TOOL & MFG INC**
9865 Franklin Ave (60131-1912)
**PHONE** ........................... 847 678-0004
**Fax:** 847 678-0017
Joseph Fuchs, *President*
Paul Fuchs, *Vice Pres*
Tony Fuchs, *Vice Pres*
▲ **EMP:** 20
**SQ FT:** 12,000
**SALES:** 1.2MM **Privately Held**
**WEB:** www.despecialty.com
**SIC:** 3544 3599 Special dies, tools, jigs & fixtures; machine & other job shop work

### (G-10454)
**DEALER TIRE LLC**
3708 River Rd Ste 600 (60131-2158)
**PHONE** ........................... 847 671-0683
**EMP:** 7
**SALES (corp-wide):** 2.1B **Privately Held**
**SIC:** 3011 5014 Tires & inner tubes; tires & tubes
**PA:** Dealer Tire, Llc
7012 Euclid Ave
Cleveland OH 44103
216 432-0088

### (G-10455)
**DEAN FOOD PRODUCTS COMPANY**
Also Called: Mrs Weavers Salads
3600 River Rd (60131-2152)
**PHONE** ........................... 847 678-1680
**Fax:** 847 671-8744
William D Fischer, *President*
Vic Deguilio, *Senior VP*
Timothy J Bondy, *Vice Pres*
Ed Alsip, *Foreman/Supr*
Roger Westergren, *Purch Agent*
**EMP:** 20
**SQ FT:** 2,500
**SALES (est):** 4.9MM **Publicly Held**
**SIC:** 2099 Salads, fresh or refrigerated

**HQ:** Dean Holding Company
2711 N Haskell Ave
Dallas TX 75204
214 303-3200

**(G-10456)**
**DEL GREAT FRAME UP SYSTEMS INC (PA)**
9335 Belmont Ave Ste 100  (60131-2802)
PHONE..................847 808-1955
David Klitzky, *President*
Michael Kahn, *Vice Pres*
Marlowe Klitzky, *Vice Pres*
Lori Morris, *Controller*
▲ **EMP:** 19
**SQ FT:** 50,000
**SALES (est):** 3.5MM  **Privately Held**
**WEB:** www.delawarecountypabusinesses.com
**SIC:** 5999  7311  5023  3442  Art, picture frames & decorations; advertising agencies; home furnishings; metal doors, sash & trim; millwork

**(G-10457)**
**DELUXE STITCHER COMPANY INC**
Also Called: Deluxe Fixture
3747 Acorn Ln  (60131-1101)
PHONE..................847 455-4400
**Fax:** 773 777-0156
Frank P Cangelosi, *President*
Russ Gename, *Opers Mgr*
Rich Huffman, *Purchasing*
Rob Klemp, *Engineer*
Rob Ventura, *Engineer*
◆ **EMP:** 60  **EST:** 1970
**SQ FT:** 19,000
**SALES (est):** 14.4MM  **Privately Held**
**WEB:** www.deluxebostitch.com
**SIC:** 3579  3549  Binding machines, plastic & adhesive; metalworking machinery

**(G-10458)**
**DEVON PRECISION MACHINE PDTS**
10140 Pacific Ave  (60131-1647)
PHONE..................847 233-9700
**Fax:** 847 233-9733
Steve Weingart, *President*
Jose Corona, *Vice Pres*
▲ **EMP:** 11  **EST:** 1958
**SQ FT:** 8,400
**SALES (est):** 1.8MM  **Privately Held**
**WEB:** www.devonamerica.com
**SIC:** 3451  Screw machine products

**(G-10459)**
**DSIGN IN PLASTICS INC**
10915 Franklin Ave Ste J  (60131-1431)
PHONE..................847 288-8085
Rafael Carvajao, *Owner*
**EMP:** 10
**SALES (est):** 1.5MM  **Privately Held**
**SIC:** 3089  Plastics products

**(G-10460)**
**DUAL MFG CO INC**
3522 Martens St  (60131-2000)
PHONE..................773 267-4457
**Fax:** 773 267-4521
Mary E Newon, *President*
Bonnie Price, *Corp Secy*
Eric Newon, *Vice Pres*
Leonard J Newon Jr, *Vice Pres*
**EMP:** 12  **EST:** 1942
**SQ FT:** 5,200
**SALES (est):** 2.4MM  **Privately Held**
**SIC:** 3821  3829  Clinical laboratory instruments, except medical & dental; time interval measuring equipment, electric (lab type); balances, laboratory; measuring & controlling devices

**(G-10461)**
**DURABLE ENGRAVERS INC**
521 S County Line Rd  (60131-1013)
PHONE..................630 766-6420
**Fax:** 847 766-0219
Theodore Maybach, *President*
Gary Berenger, *Corp Secy*
James L Maybach, *Vice Pres*
**EMP:** 21
**SQ FT:** 10,000
**SALES (est):** 2.9MM  **Privately Held**
**WEB:** www.durableengravers.com
**SIC:** 3479  Name plates: engraved, etched, etc.

**(G-10462)**
**EAGLE FREIGHT INC**
3710 River Rd Ste 200  (60131-2162)
PHONE..................708 202-0651
Lukasz Jedrejek, *President*
**EMP:** 1
**SALES (est):** 234.9K  **Privately Held**
**SIC:** 3743  Freight cars & equipment

**(G-10463)**
**EDGARS CUSTOM CABINETS**
3315 Dora St  (60131-1815)
PHONE..................847 928-0922
Edgar Mallqui, *Principal*
**EMP:** 5
**SALES (est):** 737.6K  **Privately Held**
**SIC:** 2434  Wood kitchen cabinets

**(G-10464)**
**EKLIND TOOL CO**
11040 King St  (60131-1412)
PHONE..................847 994-8550
**Fax:** 847 288-8610
Earl Cunningham, *CEO*
Gina Cozzi, *Manager*
Larry Everett, *Manager*
Karen J Eklind, *Admin Sec*
▼ **EMP:** 125
**SQ FT:** 105,000
**SALES (est):** 34.8MM  **Privately Held**
**WEB:** www.eklindtool.net
**SIC:** 3423  Hand & edge tools

**(G-10465)**
**ERECT-O-VEYOR CORPORATION**
421 S County Line Rd  (60131-1002)
PHONE..................630 766-1200
**Fax:** 630 766-4411
John D Ulm, *President*
Julia Brunner, *Admin Sec*
**EMP:** 10  **EST:** 1954
**SQ FT:** 11,000
**SALES (est):** 1.8MM  **Privately Held**
**WEB:** www.erectoveyor.com
**SIC:** 3535  Belt conveyor systems, general industrial use

**(G-10466)**
**EVERSHARP PEN COMPANY**
9240 Belmont Ave Unit A  (60131-2849)
PHONE..................847 366-5030
Bruce J Brizzolara, *President*
Paul A Smith, *Vice Pres*
Anthony Lamantia, *CFO*
David T Fall, *VP Sales*
Christine Mear, *Admin Sec*
▲ **EMP:** 28  **EST:** 1948
**SQ FT:** 50,000
**SALES (est):** 3.2MM  **Privately Held**
**WEB:** www.eversharpproducts.com
**SIC:** 3951  Ball point pens & parts; cartridges, refill: ball point pens

**(G-10467)**
**EX-CELL KAISER LLC**
11240 Melrose Ave  (60131-1332)
PHONE..................847 451-0451
Jeffrey Speizman, *President*
Mary Peterson, *Warehouse Mgr*
Brian Carey, *Buyer*
Tom Berg, *CFO*
Lubia Barrios, *Human Res Mgr*
▲ **EMP:** 40
**SQ FT:** 70,000
**SALES (est):** 8.5MM  **Privately Held**
**SIC:** 3441  Fabricated structural metal

**(G-10468)**
**EXPRESS MACHINING & MOLDS**
456 Dominic Ct  (60131-1004)
PHONE..................630 350-8480
Steve Arnold, *Owner*
**EMP:** 2
**SALES (est):** 208.6K  **Privately Held**
**SIC:** 3599  Machine shop, jobbing & repair

**(G-10469)**
**FABTEC MANUFACTURING INC**
9896 Franklin Ave  (60131-1937)
PHONE..................847 671-4888
**Fax:** 847 671-4428
Frank Guerrero, *President*
**EMP:** 12
**SQ FT:** 16,500
**SALES (est):** 1MM  **Privately Held**
**SIC:** 3599  Machine shop, jobbing & repair

**(G-10470)**
**FLASH PRINTING INC**
9224 Grand Ave Ste 1  (60131-3029)
PHONE..................847 288-9101
**Fax:** 847 288-9102
Mary Rix, *President*
Sean Rix, *Vice Pres*
**EMP:** 4
**SQ FT:** 1,600
**SALES (est):** 300K  **Privately Held**
**SIC:** 2752  2791  2789  Commercial printing, offset; typesetting; bookbinding & related work

**(G-10471)**
**FORMEL INDUSTRIES INC**
2355 25th Ave  (60131-3504)
PHONE..................847 928-5100
**Fax:** 847 455-0572
Donald W O'Malley Jr, *President*
Sam Omalley, *Financial Exec*
Jim Zidek, *Office Mgr*
**EMP:** 40
**SQ FT:** 110,000
**SALES (est):** 9.9MM  **Privately Held**
**SIC:** 2671  Packaging paper & plastics film, coated & laminated

**(G-10472)**
**FRANKLIN PARK BUILDING MTLS**
9400 Chestnut Ave  (60131-2911)
PHONE..................847 455-3985
**Fax:** 847 455-1621
James Kusta Jr, *President*
David Kusta, *Vice Pres*
Marcy Carli, *Manager*
Nancy Kusta, *Admin Sec*
**EMP:** 6  **EST:** 1952
**SQ FT:** 900
**SALES (est):** 1.3MM  **Privately Held**
**SIC:** 5211  3273  Lumber & other building materials; ready-mixed concrete

**(G-10473)**
**G & M METAL FABRICATORS INC**
9120 Gage Ave  (60131-2191)
PHONE..................847 678-6501
**Fax:** 847 678-3099
Ralph C Disilvestro, *Ch of Bd*
Anthony Disilvestro, *Plant Mgr*
Nadia Krynski, *Accountant*
Ken Cielocha, *Mktg Dir*
Pat Prater, *Office Mgr*
**EMP:** 55
**SQ FT:** 65,000
**SALES (est):** 17.3MM  **Privately Held**
**SIC:** 3499  3469  Fire- or burglary-resistive products; stamping metal for the trade

**(G-10474)**
**G & R STAINED GLASS**
2919 Emerson St  (60131-2616)
P.O. Box 219  (60131-0219)
PHONE..................847 455-7026
M R Gordon, *Owner*
Renata Thorn, *Partner*
**EMP:** 3
**SALES (est):** 98.7K  **Privately Held**
**SIC:** 3231  Stained glass: made from purchased glass

**(G-10475)**
**GARVIN INDUSTRIES INC**
Also Called: Garvin Electrical Manufacturer
3700 Sandra St  (60131-1114)
PHONE..................847 455-0188
Barton L Garvin, *President*
Craig Watson, *Controller*
Ken Kuehn, *Sales Staff*
Michael Dougherty, *Sales Associate*
Hannah Wilson, *Marketing Mgr*
◆ **EMP:** 22  **EST:** 1980
**SQ FT:** 65,000
**SALES (est):** 15MM  **Privately Held**
**WEB:** www.garvinindustries.com
**SIC:** 3643  Outlets, electric: convenience

**(G-10476)**
**GARY POPPINS LLC**
10929 Franklin Ave Ste N  (60131-1430)
PHONE..................847 455-2200
Brian Lipner, *Mng Member*
**EMP:** 2
**SALES (est):** 403.6K  **Privately Held**
**SIC:** 2096  2064  Popcorn, already popped (except candy covered); popcorn balls or other treated popcorn products

**(G-10477)**
**GAUNT INDUSTRIES INC**
9828 Franklin Ave  (60131-1913)
PHONE..................847 671-0776
**Fax:** 847 671-0864
Wayne Ammentorp, *President*
William E Gaunt, *Owner*
Dale Ammentorp, *Vice Pres*
**EMP:** 2  **EST:** 1948
**SQ FT:** 1,800
**SALES (est):** 300K  **Privately Held**
**WEB:** www.gauntindustries.com
**SIC:** 3569  3423  Lubrication equipment, industrial; hand & edge tools

**(G-10478)**
**GEMINI TOOL & MANUFACTURING**
3541 Martens St  (60131-2058)
PHONE..................847 678-5000
**Fax:** 847 678-5809
Paul G Keefe Jr, *President*
Betty Lou Keefe, *Corp Secy*
**EMP:** 17  **EST:** 1966
**SQ FT:** 13,000
**SALES (est):** 1.9MM  **Privately Held**
**WEB:** www.geminitl.com
**SIC:** 3544  Dies & die holders for metal cutting, forming, die casting; jigs & fixtures

**(G-10479)**
**GLAZERS STOLLER DISTRG LLC**
2881 Busse Rd  (60131)
PHONE..................847 350-3200
Randy Stoller, *President*
Jay Stoller, *Senior VP*
Larry Stoller, *Senior VP*
**EMP:** 3  **EST:** 2013
**SALES (est):** 290.5K  **Privately Held**
**SIC:** 2082  2084  2023  Beer (alcoholic beverage); wines, brandy & brandy spirits; eggnog, packaged: non-alcoholic

**(G-10480)**
**GRAB BROTHERS IR WORKS CO CORP**
2302 17th St  (60131)
PHONE..................847 288-1055
Tadeusz Grab, *President*
Jozef Grab, *Admin Sec*
**EMP:** 10
**SALES (est):** 1.3MM  **Privately Held**
**SIC:** 3312  Rods, iron & steel: made in steel mills

**(G-10481)**
**GRANITE XPERTS INC**
1091 E Green St  (60131-1014)
PHONE..................847 364-1900
Vito Guarino, *President*
**EMP:** 20
**SQ FT:** 80,000
**SALES (est):** 4.5MM  **Privately Held**
**SIC:** 1799  2541  5023  Counter top installation; counter & sink tops; home furnishings

**(G-10482)**
**GRANT PARK PACKING COMPANY INC**
3434 Runge St  (60131-1315)
PHONE..................312 421-4096
**Fax:** 312 421-1484
Joe Maffei, *President*
Vince Maffei, *Vice Pres*
Lucia Maffei, *Admin Sec*
**EMP:** 45
**SQ FT:** 17,500

# Franklin Park - Cook County (G-10483)   GEOGRAPHIC SECTION

SALES (est): 11.2MM **Privately Held**
WEB: www.grantparkpacking.com
SIC: **5147** 2011 2015 5149 Meats & meat products; pork products from pork slaughtered on site; beef products from beef slaughtered on site; poultry slaughtering & processing; pizza supplies; restaurant supplies

### (G-10483)
### GRAPHIC PACKAGING CORPORATION
Also Called: Graph-Pak
11250 Addison Ave (60131-1199)
PHONE..................847 451-7400
Fax: 847 451-0520
John Hewitt, *President*
Steve Farley, *Plant Mgr*
Warren Weber, *Sales Executive*
EMP: 120
SQ FT: 93,000
SALES (est): 39.1MM **Privately Held**
SIC: **2631** 2752 Folding boxboard; commercial printing, offset

### (G-10484)
### GROVE PLASTIC INC
10352 Front Ave (60131-1540)
PHONE..................847 678-8244
Fax: 847 671-6322
Ernesto O'Rosco, *President*
Gerrik L Grove, *President*
Raul Orosco, *Vice Pres*
Jose Luis Orosco, *Treasurer*
EMP: 10 EST: 1965
SQ FT: 7,000
SALES (est): 1.1MM **Privately Held**
WEB: www.groveplastics.com
SIC: **3544** Jigs & fixtures; dies, plastics forming

### (G-10485)
### H & M THREAD ROLLING CO INC
9212 Grand Ave (60131-3002)
PHONE..................847 451-1570
Fax: 847 450-0448
Hubert Monzel, *President*
John Butchers, *Plant Mgr*
EMP: 5
SQ FT: 6,500
SALES (est): 443.7K **Privately Held**
WEB: www.hm-thread.com
SIC: **3599** 3451 Machine shop, jobbing & repair; screw machine products

### (G-10486)
### HENRY TOOL & DIE CO (PA)
Also Called: Tube Pierce Manufacturing
10012 Pacific Ave (60131-1831)
P.O. Box 1096 (60131-8096)
PHONE..................847 671-1361
Fax: 847 671-1430
Albert Gruchalski, *President*
Jadwiga Gruchalski, *Corp Secy*
EMP: 4
SQ FT: 6,800
SALES: 197K **Privately Held**
SIC: **3544** Special dies & tools

### (G-10487)
### HOME STYLE
11125 Franklin Ave (60131-1411)
PHONE..................847 455-5000
Albert Cortez, *Manager*
EMP: 3 EST: 2001
SALES (est): 120K **Privately Held**
SIC: **2099** Dessert mixes & fillings

### (G-10488)
### HONEY FOODS INC
4028 Tugwell St (60131-1216)
PHONE..................847 928-9300
Elizabeth Rosinski, *President*
Derick Rosinski, *Manager*
EMP: 5
SALES (est): 1.8MM **Privately Held**
SIC: **5146** 2011 Fish & seafoods; meat packing plants

### (G-10489)
### HOWELL WELDING CORPORATION
1071 Waveland Ave (60131-1011)
PHONE..................630 616-1100
Fax: 630 616-1102
Thomas Cipolla, *President*

Angela Cipolla, *Vice Pres*
EMP: 9 EST: 1974
SQ FT: 8,500
SALES: 310K **Privately Held**
SIC: **7692** 3544 3398 Welding repair; special dies, tools, jigs & fixtures; metal heat treating

### (G-10490)
### HOYA LENS OF CHICAGO INC
Also Called: Hoya Vision Care
3531 Martens St (60131-2058)
PHONE..................847 678-4700
Paul J Ingraffia Jr, *President*
EMP: 30
SQ FT: 2,800
SALES (est): 3.4MM
SALES (corp-wide): 4.3B **Privately Held**
WEB: www.csolab.com
SIC: **5048** 5995 3851 3842 Ophthalmic goods; eyeglasses, prescription; ophthalmic goods; surgical appliances & supplies
PA: Hoya Corporation
6-10-1, Nishishinjuku
Shinjuku-Ku TKY 160-0
369 114-811

### (G-10491)
### HUDSON TOOL & DIE CO
3845 Carnation St (60131-1201)
PHONE..................847 678-8710
Fax: 847 678-0526
Linda Hellwig-Salerno, *President*
Peter A Salerno, *Vice Pres*
Laurie Barwacz, *Manager*
Tom Lahart, *Manager*
Joe Messina, *Manager*
EMP: 18 EST: 1942
SQ FT: 45,000
SALES (est): 3.8MM **Privately Held**
SIC: **3469** 3496 Stamping metal for the trade; miscellaneous fabricated wire products

### (G-10492)
### HUNTER PANELS LLC
9201 Belmont Ave Ste 100b (60131-2842)
PHONE..................847 671-2516
Fax: 847 671-3049
Bruce Roush, *Traffic Mgr*
Vince Loiacono, *Manager*
EMP: 95
SALES (corp-wide): 3.6B **Publicly Held**
WEB: www.hpanels.com
SIC: **3086** Insulation or cushioning material, foamed plastic
HQ: Hunter Panels Llc
15 Franklin St Ste B2
Portland ME 04101
888 746-1114

### (G-10493)
### HUNTER-STEVENS COMPANY INC
4003 Fleetwood Dr (60131-1205)
PHONE..................847 671-5014
Fax: 847 671-0206
John A Zizzo, *President*
EMP: 17
SQ FT: 4,400
SALES (est): 1.2MM **Privately Held**
SIC: **3429** 3452 Metal fasteners; bolts, nuts, rivets & washers

### (G-10494)
### ILLINOIS ELECTRO DEBURRING CO (PA)
2915 Birch St (60131-3005)
PHONE..................847 678-5010
Fax: 847 678-5068
Ken Semerau, *President*
George Bull, *Treasurer*
Nancy Kurowski, *Manager*
Gary Snell, *Manager*
EMP: 12 EST: 1963
SQ FT: 6,000
SALES (est): 1.1MM **Privately Held**
WEB: www.illinoiselectro.com
SIC: **3089** 3471 3541 Injection molded finished plastic products; finishing, metals or formed products; machine tools, metal cutting type

### (G-10495)
### IMPERIAL FABRICATORS CO
9119 Medill Ave (60131-3418)
PHONE..................773 463-5522
Fax: 773 463-1744
Robert Goehrke, *President*
James Falco, *Vice Pres*
Rosley Falco, *Shareholder*
Sandra Goehrke, *Shareholder*
EMP: 25 EST: 1955
SQ FT: 15,000
SALES (est): 3.6MM **Privately Held**
SIC: **3644** 3625 3643 Terminal boards; switches, electronic applications; connectors & terminals for electrical devices

### (G-10496)
### INDILAB INC
10367 Franklin Ave (60131-1542)
PHONE..................847 928-1050
Fax: 847 928-1052
Robert Gavrick Jr, *President*
Catherine Gavrick, *COO*
Mark Espenscheid, *Vice Pres*
Robert Gavrick Sr, *Vice Pres*
Tom Griffin, *Vice Pres*
EMP: 20
SQ FT: 10,000
SALES (est): 5.3MM **Privately Held**
WEB: www.indilab.com
SIC: **5047** 2911 8021 Medical equipment & supplies; non-aromatic chemical products; dental clinic

### (G-10497)
### INDUSTRIAL FINISHING INC
2337 17th St (60131-3432)
PHONE..................847 451-4230
Fax: 847 451-4243
Stanley Styrczula, *President*
EMP: 10
SQ FT: 5,000
SALES: 900K **Privately Held**
SIC: **3479** Painting of metal products

### (G-10498)
### INDUSTRIAL GRAPHITE PRODUCTS
429 S County Line Rd (60131-1002)
P.O. Box 548, Bensenville (60106-0548)
PHONE..................630 350-0155
Fax: 630 766-0247
Ronald Machaj, *President*
Frank Machaj, *General Mgr*
EMP: 4
SQ FT: 16,000
SALES (est): 630K **Privately Held**
WEB: www.industrialgraphiteproducts.com
SIC: **3624** Electric carbons

### (G-10499)
### INTERPLEX DAYSTAR INC
11130 King St 1 (60131-1413)
PHONE..................847 455-2424
Bob Hudson, *Principal*
Dan Larcher, *Production*
Jim Cimnoy, *Controller*
Trilby Rogers, *Manager*
Jim Ciemny, *Admin Sec*
▼ EMP: 67
SQ FT: 55,000
SALES (est): 21MM **Privately Held**
SIC: **3469** 3674 Metal stampings; semiconductors & related devices
HQ: Interplex Industries, Inc.
231 Ferris Ave
Rumford RI 02916
718 961-6212

### (G-10500)
### J & I SON TOOL COMPANY INC
Also Called: J&I Tool Company
9219 Parklane Ave (60131-2837)
PHONE..................847 455-4200
John Wodzinski, *Partner*
Mike Myung, *Partner*
▲ EMP: 8
SQ FT: 8,000
SALES (est): 1.2MM **Privately Held**
SIC: **3599** 7692 3444 Machine shop, jobbing & repair; welding repair; sheet metalwork

### (G-10501)
### J AND D INSTALLERS INC
9330 Franklin Ave (60131-2831)
PHONE..................847 288-0783
Fax: 847 288-0897
Jeffrey Blazek, *President*
Dawn Blazek, *Corp Secy*
Zeb Foster, *Opers Mgr*
EMP: 6
SQ FT: 23,000
SALES: 800K **Privately Held**
SIC: **3449** Bars, concrete reinforcing; fabricated steel

### (G-10502)
### J S PALUCH CO INC (PA)
3708 River Rd Ste 400 (60131-2158)
P.O. Box 2703, Schiller Park (60176-0703)
PHONE..................847 678-9300
Fax: 847 233-2940
William J Rafferty, *President*
Patty Nowak, *General Mgr*
Israel Martinez, *Editor*
Everette Locke, *Vice Pres*
Steve Nanai, *Vice Pres*
▼ EMP: 180 EST: 1913
SQ FT: 120,000
SALES (est): 78.8MM **Privately Held**
WEB: www.jspaluch.com
SIC: **2731** 2721 7371 2741 Pamphlets: publishing & printing; periodicals; computer software development; miscellaneous publishing

### (G-10503)
### J S PRINTING INC
Also Called: Catholic Book Covers
9832 Franklin Ave (60131-1913)
PHONE..................847 678-6300
Fax: 847 678-6395
John Sammarco, *CEO*
John H Sammarco, *CEO*
Paul J Sammarco, *President*
Phillip J Sammarco, *Vice Pres*
Mary Jane Sammarco, *Treasurer*
EMP: 6 EST: 1952
SQ FT: 5,000
SALES: 390K **Privately Held**
SIC: **2752** 2759 Commercial printing, offset; letterpress printing

### (G-10504)
### JADAY INDUSTRIES
10002 Pacific Ave (60131-1831)
PHONE..................847 928-1033
Jane Park, *President*
Dan Park, *Supervisor*
EMP: 10
SQ FT: 3,000
SALES (est): 1.1MM **Privately Held**
SIC: **3599** Machine shop, jobbing & repair

### (G-10505)
### JAMCO TOOL & CAMS INC
10151 Franklin Ave (60131-1889)
PHONE..................847 678-0280
Fax: 847 678-0282
Michael Hohenzy, *President*
Joseph Hohenzy, *Vice Pres*
Arthur Hohenzy, *Treasurer*
EMP: 15
SQ FT: 3,500
SALES (est): 1.2MM **Privately Held**
SIC: **3544** 3545 Special dies & tools; machine tool accessories

### (G-10506)
### JAME ROLL FORM PRODUCTS INC
2401 Rose St (60131-3322)
PHONE..................847 455-0496
Fax: 847 455-6381
Robert P Perkaus, *President*
Larry Martin, *Vice Pres*
Jim Clark, *Sales Staff*
Bobby Rieves, *Sales Staff*
Lynn Pikrone, *Office Mgr*
EMP: 50
SQ FT: 100,000
SALES (est): 20.7MM **Privately Held**
WEB: www.jamerollform.com
SIC: **3325** Rolling mill rolls, cast steel
PA: Mars Steel Corporation
2401 25th Ave
Franklin Park IL 60131
847 455-6277

## GEOGRAPHIC SECTION
### Franklin Park - Cook County (G-10533)

**(G-10507)**
**JB MFG & SCREW MACHINE PR**
9243 Parklane Ave (60131-2838)
PHONE.................847 451-0892
Jarzi Rojincki, *Owner*
Cynthia Miller, *Finance*
**EMP:** 3
**SALES (est):** 410.2K **Privately Held**
**SIC:** 3451 Screw machine products

**(G-10508)**
**JBW MACHINING INC**
2826 Birch St (60131-3004)
PHONE.................847 451-0276
Fax: 847 451-0277
John Mroczek, *President*
Wesley Miszczyszyn, *Vice Pres*
**EMP:** 15
**SQ FT:** 10,000
**SALES (est):** 1.5MM **Privately Held**
**WEB:** www.jbwmachining.com
**SIC:** 3599 3544 Custom machinery; industrial molds

**(G-10509)**
**JOHNSON SIGN CO**
Also Called: C Johnson Sign Co
9615 Waveland Ave (60131-1792)
PHONE.................847 678-2092
John C Johnson, *Owner*
**EMP:** 8
**SQ FT:** 4,000
**SALES (est):** 957.2K **Privately Held**
**WEB:** www.johnsonsigns.com
**SIC:** 7336 7389 3993 3264 Silk screen design; sign painting & lettering shop; signs & advertising specialties; porcelain electrical supplies

**(G-10510)**
**JUST MANUFACTURING COMPANY (PA)**
9233 King St (60131-2189)
PHONE.................847 678-5151
Fax: 847 678-6817
Paul Just, *President*
Matthew E Just, *Treasurer*
Richard Berkhout, *Manager*
Elizabeth Collins, *Admin Sec*
Gertrude Just, *Admin Sec*
▲ **EMP:** 140 EST: 1933
**SQ FT:** 175,000
**SALES (est):** 28.3MM **Privately Held**
**WEB:** www.justmfg.com
**SIC:** 3431 Sinks: enameled iron, cast iron or pressed metal; plumbing fixtures: enameled iron cast iron or pressed metal

**(G-10511)**
**KAUTZMANN MACHINE WORKS INC**
9105 Belden Ave (60131-3505)
PHONE.................847 455-9105
Ted Schab, *President*
Chris Jendrzejewski, *Supervisor*
**EMP:** 4
**SQ FT:** 5,000
**SALES (est):** 517.8K **Privately Held**
**SIC:** 3541 3462 Gear cutting & finishing machines; iron & steel forgings

**(G-10512)**
**KENSEN TOOL & DIE INC**
9200 Parklane Ave (60131-2878)
PHONE.................847 455-0150
Fax: 847 455-7999
Ronald F Kenyeri, *President*
Ann Kenyeri, *Manager*
**EMP:** 15
**SQ FT:** 10,000
**SALES (est):** 2.2MM **Privately Held**
**SIC:** 3544 3469 Special dies & tools; jigs & fixtures; jigs: inspection, gauging & checking; stamping metal for the trade

**(G-10513)**
**KOEHLER ENTERPRISES INC**
Also Called: Raydyot US
2960 Hart Ct (60131-2214)
PHONE.................847 451-4966
Peter Koehler, *President*
Gail Dupuls, *Vice Pres*
▲ **EMP:** 8
**SQ FT:** 27,000
**SALES (est):** 1.4MM **Privately Held**
**SIC:** 5013 3714 Motor vehicle supplies & new parts; motor vehicle parts & accessories

**(G-10514)**
**KRAIG CORPORATION**
10253 Franklin Ave (60131-1541)
PHONE.................847 928-0630
Dennis Fontechia, *President*
**EMP:** 25
**SQ FT:** 30,000
**SALES (est):** 1MM **Privately Held**
**SIC:** 3369 3429 White metal castings (lead, tin, antimony), except die; casket hardware

**(G-10515)**
**LEGACY WOODWORK INC**
9137 Cherry Ave (60131-3007)
PHONE.................847 451-7602
**EMP:** 5
**SQ FT:** 8,000
**SALES (est):** 420K **Privately Held**
**SIC:** 2511 Mfg Wood Household Furniture

**(G-10516)**
**LIFE FITNESS INC**
10601 Belmont Ave (60131-1500)
PHONE.................847 288-3300
Fax: 847 288-3703
Cheryl Hagan, *President*
Chris Keel, *Technical Mgr*
Julie Daly, *Engineer*
Joe Gajewski, *Engineer*
Greg Joseph, *Engineer*
**EMP:** 6
**SALES (corp-wide):** 4.4B **Publicly Held**
**SIC:** 3949 Exercise equipment
**HQ:** Life Fitness, Inc.
9525 Bryn Mawr Ave Fl 6
Rosemont IL 60018
847 288-3300

**(G-10517)**
**LOREN TOOL & MANUFACTURING CO**
430 Podlin Dr (60131-1081)
PHONE.................630 595-0100
Fax: 630 595-4369
Ronald J Weirich, *President*
Dennis Berry, *Plant Mgr*
**EMP:** 8 EST: 1947
**SQ FT:** 8,900
**SALES (est):** 1.6MM **Privately Held**
**WEB:** www.lorencameron.com
**SIC:** 3544 Special dies & tools

**(G-10518)**
**LUMENITE CONTROL TECHNOLOGY**
Also Called: Lumenite Electronic
2331 17th St (60131-3432)
PHONE.................847 455-1450
Fax: 847 455-0127
Ronald V Calabrese, *President*
David Calabrese, *Marketing Staff*
Carol Calabrese, *Admin Sec*
**EMP:** 15 EST: 1934
**SQ FT:** 6,500
**SALES (est):** 3.4MM **Privately Held**
**SIC:** 3625 3873 3823 3613 Electric controls & control accessories, industrial; timing devices, electronic; watches, clocks, watchcases & parts; industrial instrmnts msrmnt display/control process variable; switchgear & switchboard apparatus

**(G-10519)**
**MAC LEAN-FOGG COMPANY**
Reliable Power Products
11411 Addison Ave (60131-1123)
PHONE.................847 288-2534
Fax: 847 455-0029
Walter Dockus, *Vice Pres*
Robert McDowell, *Vice Pres*
Robert Gignac, *Purchasing*
Jamie Hypes, *Controller*
Brendan Conley, *Regl Sales Mgr*
**EMP:** 250
**SALES (corp-wide):** 1.4B **Privately Held**
**WEB:** www.maclean-fogg.com
**SIC:** 3643 2298 3229 3699 Electric connectors; insulator pads, cordage; pressed & blown glass; electrical equipment & supplies
**PA:** Mac Lean-Fogg Company
1000 Allanson Rd
Mundelein IL 60060
847 566-0010

**(G-10520)**
**MADE RITE BEDDING COMPANY**
11221 Melrose Ave (60131-1331)
PHONE.................847 349-5886
Fax: 847 349-5880
Perry Stricker, *President*
Corey Stricker, *Vice Pres*
**EMP:** 12 EST: 1946
**SQ FT:** 15,000
**SALES (est):** 2.5MM **Privately Held**
**WEB:** www.maderitebedding.com
**SIC:** 2515 Mattresses & foundations; box springs, assembled

**(G-10521)**
**MANDEL METALS INC (PA)**
Also Called: American Aerospace Material
11419 Addison Ave (60131-1124)
PHONE.................847 455-6606
Richard Mandel, *President*
Barbara Lindstrom, *Corp Secy*
Steve Fallon, *COO*
Tom Cunniff, *Manager*
◆ **EMP:** 90
**SQ FT:** 100,000
**SALES (est):** 55.2MM **Privately Held**
**SIC:** 5051 3353 Aluminum bars, rods, ingots, sheets, pipes, plates, etc.; aluminum sheet, plate & foil

**(G-10522)**
**MANDEL METALS INC**
US Standard Sign
11400 W Addison St (60131)
PHONE.................847 455-7446
Fax: 847 455-3330
Steve Fallon, *COO*
**EMP:** 6
**SALES (corp-wide):** 55.2MM **Privately Held**
**SIC:** 3993 Signs & advertising specialties
**PA:** Mandel Metals, Inc.
11400 Addison Ave
Franklin Park IL 60131
847 455-6606

**(G-10523)**
**MATT PAK INC**
2910 Commerce St (60131-2929)
PHONE.................847 451-4018
Theodore S Kunach, *President*
Tedd Cunach, *Manager*
David Orr, *Director*
▲ **EMP:** 75
**SALES (est):** 17.5MM **Privately Held**
**WEB:** www.mattpak.com
**SIC:** 2621 8711 Packaging paper; machine tool design

**(G-10524)**
**MBS MANUFACTURING**
1100 E Green St (60131-1005)
PHONE.................630 227-0300
**EMP:** 2
**SALES (est):** 220.8K **Privately Held**
**SIC:** 3999 3544 Manufacturing industries; special dies, tools, jigs & fixtures

**(G-10525)**
**MC LAMINATED CABINETS**
3115 Dora St (60131-1811)
PHONE.................773 301-0393
**EMP:** 3
**SALES (est):** 187.9K **Privately Held**
**SIC:** 2434 Wood kitchen cabinets

**(G-10526)**
**MEADOR INDUSTRIES INC**
10031 Franklin Ave (60131-1893)
PHONE.................847 671-5042
Fax: 847 671-5126
Darla Meador, *President*
John Meador, *President*
Robert Meador, *Vice Pres*
Bob Meador, *Treasurer*
Darla Gryzwa, *Admin Sec*
**EMP:** 20 EST: 1964
**SQ FT:** 16,000
**SALES (est):** 3.9MM **Privately Held**
**SIC:** 3451 Screw machine products

**(G-10527)**
**MEIER GRANITE COMPANY**
9966 Pacific Ave (60131-1933)
PHONE.................847 678-7300
Fax: 773 678-7327
Michael Kwiatkski, *President*
**EMP:** 6 EST: 1929
**SQ FT:** 2,500
**SALES (est):** 864.2K **Privately Held**
**WEB:** www.meiergranite.com
**SIC:** 5999 3281 3253 2541 Monuments & tombstones; cut stone & stone products; ceramic wall & floor tile; wood partitions & fixtures; wood household furniture

**(G-10528)**
**MERCURYS GREEN LLC**
Also Called: Picture Frame Factory
9201 King St (60131-2111)
PHONE.................708 865-9134
Jatin J Patel, *President*
Riten Patel, *Manager*
Urmela Patel, *Admin Sec*
**EMP:** 40
**SQ FT:** 48,000
**SALES (est):** 18MM **Privately Held**
**SIC:** 5999 2499 7699 5023 Art, picture frames & decorations; picture frames, ready made; picture & mirror frames, wood; picture framing, custom; frames & framing, picture & mirror

**(G-10529)**
**METAL BOX INTERNATIONAL INC**
11600 King St (60131-1311)
P.O. Box 9002, Chicago (60609-0002)
PHONE.................847 455-8500
Bruce Saltzberg, *President*
Gary Green, *Safety Dir*
Jack Frigo, *Plant Mgr*
Judy Woz, *Purchasing*
Yale Mappa, *Finance Dir*
▲ **EMP:** 200
**SQ FT:** 115,000
**SALES (est):** 31MM **Privately Held**
**WEB:** www.edsal.com
**SIC:** 2514 3993 3444 2542 Metal bookcases & stereo cabinets; signs & advertising specialties; sheet metalwork; partitions & fixtures, except wood; office furniture, except wood

**(G-10530)**
**METAL CERAMICS INC**
9306 Belmont Ave (60131-2810)
PHONE.................847 678-2293
Fax: 847 678-2368
**EMP:** 2 EST: 2010
**SALES (est):** 200K **Privately Held**
**SIC:** 3568 Mfg Power Transmission Equipment

**(G-10531)**
**MICRO LAPPING & GRINDING CO**
2330 17th St Unit B (60131-3409)
PHONE.................847 455-5446
Haribloi Patel, *President*
Mary Jones, *Bookkeeper*
**EMP:** 25
**SALES (est):** 3.9MM **Privately Held**
**SIC:** 3541 3915 Lapping machines; grinding machines, metalworking; jewelers' materials & lapidary work

**(G-10532)**
**MIDWEST BRASS FORGING CO**
10015 Franklin Ave 21 (60131-1817)
PHONE.................847 678-7023
Fax: 847 678-8331
John Chew, *President*
Barbara Chew, *Corp Secy*
Maria Constantino, *Asst Admin*
**EMP:** 20 EST: 1946
**SQ FT:** 15,000
**SALES (est):** 3.8MM **Privately Held**
**WEB:** www.midwestbrass.com
**SIC:** 3463 Nonferrous forgings; aluminum forgings

**(G-10533)**
**MIDWEST FOODS MFG INC**
11359 Franklin Ave (60131-1117)
PHONE.................847 455-4636

# Franklin Park - Cook County (G-10534)

Amrit Patel, *President*
▲ **EMP:** 32
**SALES (est):** 7.6MM **Privately Held**
**SIC:** 3999 Fruits, artificial & preserved

### (G-10534)
### MINT MASTERS INC
9136 Belden Ave (60131-3506)
**PHONE**..................847 451-1133
**Fax:** 847 451-8636
Elke Timm, *President*
Kerstin Palumbo, *Vice Pres*
**EMP:** 20
**SALES (est):** 2.1MM **Privately Held**
**SIC:** 3999 3914 3911 3469 Badges, metal: policemen, firemen, etc.; trophies; medals, precious or semiprecious metal; metal stampings

### (G-10535)
### MIREK CABINETS
1086 Waveland Ave (60131)
**PHONE**..................630 350-8336
Mirek Cientkiewicz, *Owner*
**EMP:** 2
**SALES (est):** 263.8K **Privately Held**
**SIC:** 2434 Wood kitchen cabinets

### (G-10536)
### MLA FRANKLIN PARK INC
2925 Lucy Ln (60131-2218)
**PHONE**..................847 451-0279
**Fax:** 847 451-0379
Mike Kramer, *President*
**EMP:** 12
**SQ FT:** 13,000
**SALES (est):** 1.6MM **Privately Held**
**SIC:** 2851 Epoxy coatings; coating, air curing

### (G-10537)
### MRT SUREWAY INC (PA)
Also Called: Sureway Tool & Engineering Co
2959 Hart Ct (60131-2213)
**PHONE**..................847 801-3010
**Fax:** 847 288-0155
M Richard Tetrault, *President*
Julian Burnley, *Vice Pres*
Marcelo Buenrostro, *Mfg Dir*
Kevin Greco, *Project Mgr*
Anna Siembida, *Project Mgr*
**EMP:** 95 **EST:** 1962
**SQ FT:** 82,000
**SALES (est):** 21.4MM **Privately Held**
**SIC:** 3441 Fabricated structural metal

### (G-10538)
### NAMEPLATE ROBINSON & PRECISION
10129 Pacific Ave (60131-1623)
**PHONE**..................847 678-2255
Lu Martin, *Principal*
**EMP:** 7
**SALES (est):** 347K **Privately Held**
**SIC:** 3479 3993 3953 3949 Name plates: engraved, etched, etc.; signs & advertising specialties; marking devices; sporting & athletic goods

### (G-10539)
### NATIONAL CONCRETE PIPE CO (PA)
11825 Franklin Ave (60131-1068)
**PHONE**..................630 766-3600
**Fax:** 630 766-6197
John M Esposito, *President*
Paula Cannar, *Manager*
Jeff L Delia, *Admin Sec*
**EMP:** 35
**SQ FT:** 38,000
**SALES (est):** 6.2MM **Privately Held**
**WEB:** www.nationalconcretepipe.com
**SIC:** 3272 4212 Sewer pipe, concrete; drain tile, concrete; pipe, concrete or lined with concrete; local trucking, without storage

### (G-10540)
### NELSEN STEEL AND WIRE LP
Also Called: Nelsen Steel Company
9400 Belmont Ave (60131-2800)
**PHONE**..................847 671-9700
**Fax:** 847 671-9700
C Davis Nelsen II, *CEO*
John R Mc Vicker, *Vice Pres*
Miguel Santacruz, *Facilities Mgr*
William Lundburg, *Purchasing*
Donna Zielinski, *Bookkeeper*
▲ **EMP:** 80 **EST:** 1939
**SQ FT:** 250,000
**SALES (est):** 57.2MM **Privately Held**
**WEB:** www.nelsensteel.com
**SIC:** 3316 Bars, steel, cold finished, from purchased hot-rolled

### (G-10541)
### NESTLE USA INC
Also Called: Nestle Confections
3401 Mount Prospect Rd (60131-1304)
**PHONE**..................847 957-7850
Sandra Gray, *Purchasing*
Rick Pullman, *Purchasing*
Thomas Cygan, *Engineer*
Paul Warnecke, *Engineer*
Michael Nelson, *Branch Mgr*
**EMP:** 70
**SALES (corp-wide):** 88.4B **Publicly Held**
**WEB:** www.nestleusa.com
**SIC:** 2064 Candy & other confectionery products
**HQ:** Nestle Usa, Inc.
  800 N Brand Blvd
  Glendale CA 91203
  818 549-6000

### (G-10542)
### NOVA-CHROME INC
3200 Wolf Rd (60131-1363)
**PHONE**..................847 455-8200
**Fax:** 847 455-8323
Lynn Knoth, *President*
Jeffrey Knoth, *VP Opers*
▲ **EMP:** 11 **EST:** 1953
**SQ FT:** 7,800
**SALES (est):** 1.8MM **Privately Held**
**SIC:** 3471 Chromium plating of metals or formed products

### (G-10543)
### OMNI PUMP REPAIRS INC
9224 Chestnut Ave (60131-3014)
**PHONE**..................847 451-0000
**Fax:** 847 451-0119
Mary Moraitis, *President*
Pete Moraitis, *General Mgr*
Ana Wybriec, *Manager*
Dennis Moraitis, *Admin Sec*
Peter Moraitis, *Admin Sec*
▲ **EMP:** 12
**SQ FT:** 9,000
**SALES (est):** 770K **Privately Held**
**WEB:** www.omnipump.com
**SIC:** 7699 3561 Pumps & pumping equipment repair; industrial pumps & parts

### (G-10544)
### OPTICOTE INC
10455 Seymour Ave (60131-1234)
**PHONE**..................847 678-8900
**Fax:** 847 678-8878
Bob Sypniewski, *President*
Don Ellefsen, *Vice Pres*
Elaine A Favaro, *Admin Sec*
◆ **EMP:** 27
**SQ FT:** 16,000
**SALES (est):** 5MM **Privately Held**
**WEB:** www.opticote.com
**SIC:** 2891 3851 Adhesives & sealants; lens coating, ophthalmic

### (G-10545)
### PACTIV LLC
2607 Rose St (60131-3326)
**PHONE**..................847 451-1480
Michael Champney, *Engineer*
Mark Bradtke, *Branch Mgr*
Sandy Drummonds, *Manager*
**EMP:** 207 **Privately Held**
**SIC:** 3089 Lenses, except optical: plastic
**HQ:** Pactiv Llc
  1900 W Field Ct
  Lake Forest IL 60045
  847 482-2000

### (G-10546)
### PARK ENGINEERING INC
9227 Parklane Ave (60131-2882)
**PHONE**..................847 455-1424
**Fax:** 847 455-0206
Ed Swan, *President*
Mona Szwankowski, *Corp Secy*
Mona Swan, *Vice Pres*
**EMP:** 20
**SQ FT:** 13,000
**SALES (est):** 1.5MM **Privately Held**
**WEB:** www.lappingcarriers.com
**SIC:** 3561 3542 3599 Pump jacks & other pumping equipment; die casting & extruding machines; custom machinery

### (G-10547)
### PARTEC INC
9301 Belmont Ave (60131-2809)
**PHONE**..................847 678-9520
Brian Poklacki, *President*
Frank Rogers, *Vice Pres*
Toni Burl, *Accountant*
Tony Berra, *Manager*
Andrea Jaurigue, *Manager*
▲ **EMP:** 120
**SQ FT:** 70,000
**SALES (est):** 11.3MM **Privately Held**
**WEB:** www.partec-inc.com
**SIC:** 3581 3679 Automatic vending machines; harness assemblies for electronic use: wire or cable

### (G-10548)
### PATRICK INDUSTRIES INC
Also Called: Gravure Ink
1077 Sesame St (60131-1316)
**PHONE**..................630 595-0595
Debbie Elderkin, *Plant Mgr*
Harold Gordon, *Supervisor*
**EMP:** 93
**SALES (corp-wide):** 1.2B **Publicly Held**
**SIC:** 3275 Gypsum products
**PA:** Patrick Industries, Inc.
  107 W Franklin St
  Elkhart IN 46516
  574 294-7511

### (G-10549)
### PHOENIX WELDING CO INC
9220 Parklane Ave (60131-2836)
**PHONE**..................630 616-1700
**Fax:** 630 616-1707
Norman Gron, *President*
Susan Linch, *Manager*
**EMP:** 15
**SQ FT:** 11,000
**SALES (est):** 2.1MM **Privately Held**
**SIC:** 7692 7699 3441 Welding repair; aircraft & heavy equipment repair services; construction equipment repair; fabricated structural metal

### (G-10550)
### PICTURE FRAME FULFILLMENT LLC
9201 King St (60131-2111)
**PHONE**..................847 260-5071
Riten Patel,
**EMP:** 51
**SALES (est):** 3.7MM **Privately Held**
**SIC:** 5023 5719 2499 Wood products

### (G-10551)
### PIONEER GRINDING & MFG CO
10011 Franklin Ave (60131-1817)
**PHONE**..................847 678-6565
**Fax:** 847 678-7811
Charles Stephens, *Owner*
**EMP:** 3 **EST:** 1960
**SALES (est):** 300K **Privately Held**
**SIC:** 3599 Grinding castings for the trade

### (G-10552)
### PIONEER POWDER COATINGS LLC
9240 Belmont Ave Unit B (60131-2849)
**PHONE**..................847 671-1100
Dave Schmidt, *Opers Mgr*
Jimmy Bauchwitz, *Sales Mgr*
John Bauchwitz, *Mng Member*
John Landes, *Technical Staff*
**EMP:** 20
**SALES (est):** 5.2MM **Privately Held**
**SIC:** 2851 Paints & allied products

### (G-10553)
### PLASTIC POWER CORPORATION
4046 Tugwell St (60131-1216)
**PHONE**..................847 233-9601
Slawomir Lukasik, *President*
**EMP:** 8
**SQ FT:** 9,000
**SALES (est):** 1.3MM **Privately Held**
**SIC:** 3089 Injection molding of plastics

### (G-10554)
### PLATING INTERNATIONAL INC
11142 Addison Ave (60131-1404)
P.O. Box 81, Bensenville (60106-0081)
**PHONE**..................847 451-2101
Matthew D Pankow, *President*
David Harris, *Engineer*
Deborah Contreras, *Office Mgr*
Kristian Villarreal, *Supervisor*
Greg Pankow, *Lab Dir*
▲ **EMP:** 11 **EST:** 2007
**SQ FT:** 20,000
**SALES (est):** 9MM **Privately Held**
**SIC:** 2899 7699 3471 Plating compounds; industrial equipment services; gold plating

### (G-10555)
### POWER DISTRIBUTION EQP CO INC
3010 Willow St (60131-2835)
**PHONE**..................847 455-2500
John Gandy, *President*
**EMP:** 17 **EST:** 1997
**SQ FT:** 10,000
**SALES (est):** 4.3MM **Privately Held**
**SIC:** 3613 Switchboards & parts, power; panel & distribution boards & other related apparatus

### (G-10556)
### PRAIRIE STATE GRAPHICS INC
11100 Addison Ave (60131-1404)
**PHONE**..................847 801-3100
**Fax:** 847 801-3101
Richard A Heinzen, *President*
Dennis Soroko, *Maintenance Dir*
John Croft, *Controller*
Sandy Nelson, *Human Res Mgr*
Dunn Dougherty, *Manager*
**EMP:** 75
**SQ FT:** 40,000
**SALES (est):** 18.6MM **Privately Held**
**WEB:** www.psglabels.com
**SIC:** 2672 Gummed tape, cloth or paper base: from purchased materials

### (G-10557)
### PRAIRIE STATE IMPRESSIONS LLC
Also Called: P S G
11100 Addison Ave (60131-1404)
**PHONE**..................847 801-3100
John Kropf, *CFO*
Loucia Jastrzebsky, *Controller*
Roz Mitofsky, *Accounts Mgr*
Michelle Talko, *Manager*
Richard Heinzen,
▲ **EMP:** 70
**SALES (est):** 19.3MM **Privately Held**
**SIC:** 2672 Adhesive backed films, foams & foils

### (G-10558)
### PRECISE FINISHING CO INC
2842 Birch St (60131-3004)
**PHONE**..................847 451-2077
**Fax:** 847 451-2078
John R Rivera, *President*
Joe Padilla, *General Mgr*
Iris Rivera, *Vice Pres*
Michael Rivera, *Sales Staff*
▲ **EMP:** 25
**SQ FT:** 11,000
**SALES:** 1MM **Privately Held**
**WEB:** www.precisefinishing.com
**SIC:** 3471 Finishing, metals or formed products

### (G-10559)
### PRECISION PLASTIC BALL CO
Also Called: Robinson Name Plate
10129 Pacific Ave (60131-1623)
**PHONE**..................847 678-2255
**Fax:** 847 678-3100
Lu Martin, *Vice Pres*
**EMP:** 4
**SQ FT:** 7,000
**SALES (est):** 1.5MM **Privately Held**
**WEB:** www.precisionplasticball.com
**SIC:** 3562 Ball bearings & parts

## GEOGRAPHIC SECTION
### Franklin Park - Cook County (G-10585)

**(G-10560)**
**PRECISION STEEL WAREHOUSE INC (DH)**
3500 Wolf Rd (60131-1395)
PHONE .................................. 800 323-0740
Fax: 847 455-1341
Terry A Piper, *President*
Ron G Cornwell, *Vice Pres*
Charles Henning, *Vice Pres*
Gordon Hoppestad, *Plant Mgr*
Jim Kuta, *Maint Spvr*
▲ **EMP:** 104 **EST:** 1940
**SQ FT:** 140,000
**SALES (est):** 52.6MM
**SALES (corp-wide):** 223.6B **Publicly Held**
**WEB:** www.pbrand.com
**SIC: 5051** 3499 3451 3496 Metals service centers & offices; shims, metal; screw machine products; miscellaneous fabricated wire products
**HQ:** Wesco Financial Corporation
   301 E Colo Blvd Ste 300
   Pasadena CA 91101
   626 585-6700

**(G-10561)**
**PRINTERS PARTS INC**
2706 Edgington St Unit A (60131-3438)
PHONE .................................. 847 288-9000
James E Hughes, *President*
**EMP:** 1
**SALES (est):** 208.1K **Privately Held**
**SIC: 5084** 3555 Printing trades machinery, equipment & supplies; printing trades machinery

**(G-10562)**
**PRINTERS REPAIR PARTS INC**
Also Called: Printers Parts Store
2706 Edgington St Unit A (60131-3443)
PHONE .................................. 847 288-9000
Fax: 847 288-9010
Nikki Calhoun, *President*
Sandy Janito, *Controller*
Hugo Castro, *Sales Staff*
Elvis Salinas, *Sales Staff*
Paul Holmquist, *Sales Executive*
▼ **EMP:** 30
**SQ FT:** 3,000
**SALES (est):** 7.3MM **Privately Held**
**WEB:** www.printersrepairparts.com
**SIC: 3555** Printing presses

**(G-10563)**
**PRODUCTION CHEMICAL CO INC**
Also Called: Action Painting & Cleaning
9381 Schiller Blvd (60131-2949)
PHONE .................................. 847 455-8450
Fax: 847 455-8453
Daniel F Lane, *President*
**EMP:** 25
**SQ FT:** 70,000
**SALES (est):** 2.7MM **Privately Held**
**SIC: 3479** 3471 Painting, coating & hot dipping; plating & polishing

**(G-10564)**
**PROSPECT TOOL COMPANY LLC**
9233 King St (60131-2111)
PHONE .................................. 630 766-2200
Paul Just, *President*
Matthew Just Jr, *Mng Member*
**EMP:** 6 **EST:** 2012
**SALES:** 724.9K
**SALES (corp-wide):** 28.3MM **Privately Held**
**SIC: 3469** Metal stampings
**PA:** Just Manufacturing Company Inc
   9233 King St
   Franklin Park IL 60131
   847 678-5151

**(G-10565)**
**QC FINISHERS INC**
10244 Franklin Ave (60131-1528)
PHONE .................................. 847 678-2660
Fax: 847 678-2711
John Zeinda, *President*
Tony Warzecha, *General Mgr*
Paul Podedworney, *Corp Secy*
▲ **EMP:** 20
**SQ FT:** 25,000
**SALES (est):** 2.7MM **Privately Held**
**SIC: 3479** 7389 Painting of metal products; coating of metals & formed products; sign painting & lettering shop

**(G-10566)**
**QUALITY CLEANING FLUIDS INC**
9216 Grand Ave (60131-3002)
PHONE .................................. 847 451-1190
Fax: 847 451-6654
Vito Dellegrazie, *President*
Doris Dellegrazie, *Admin Sec*
**EMP:** 4
**SQ FT:** 3,000
**SALES:** 1MM **Privately Held**
**SIC: 5169** 3569 3564 Specialty cleaning & sanitation preparations; filters; blowers & fans

**(G-10567)**
**QUALITY TOOL INC**
9239 Parklane Ave (60131-2838)
PHONE .................................. 847 288-9330
Fax: 847 288-9331
RAO Kilani, *President*
▲ **EMP:** 1
**SALES (est):** 237K **Privately Held**
**SIC: 3599** Machine shop, jobbing & repair

**(G-10568)**
**RADIAD MANUFACTURING**
3543 Martens St (60131-2058)
PHONE .................................. 847 678-5808
Paul G Keefe, *President*
Jeff Dubow, *Accountant*
**EMP:** 5
**SQ FT:** 13,000
**SALES (est):** 373K **Privately Held**
**WEB:** www.radiadmfg.com
**SIC: 3469** Metal stampings

**(G-10569)**
**RAMAR INDUSTRIES INC**
9211 Parklane Ave (60131-2837)
PHONE .................................. 847 451-0445
Mike Roberts, *President*
John Roberts, *Human Res Mgr*
**EMP:** 4
**SQ FT:** 5,000
**SALES (est):** 1MM **Privately Held**
**SIC: 5162** 2431 Plastics materials & basic shapes; millwork

**(G-10570)**
**RAND JIG BORING INC**
10009 Franklin Ave Ste 1 (60131-1817)
PHONE .................................. 847 678-7416
Fax: 847 678-7485
Andy Bodnar, *President*
James Egers, *Vice Pres*
Deborah Bodnar, *Admin Sec*
**EMP:** 2
**SQ FT:** 2,600
**SALES:** 400K **Privately Held**
**SIC: 3599** Machine shop, jobbing & repair

**(G-10571)**
**RCM INDUSTRIES INC (PA)**
Also Called: Allied Die Casting Company III
3021 Cullerton St (60131-2204)
PHONE .................................. 847 455-1950
Fax: 630 455-1529
Robert C Marconi, *President*
Donald Kilburg, *Exec VP*
William Herrington, *Vice Pres*
Carl Rudd, *Purchasing*
Rich Nunez, *QC Mgr*
**EMP:** 250
**SQ FT:** 100,000
**SALES (est):** 170.7MM **Privately Held**
**WEB:** www.imperialdiecasting.com
**SIC: 3363** Aluminum die-castings

**(G-10572)**
**RELIABLE METAL STAMPING CO INC**
9244 Parklane Ave (60131-2836)
PHONE .................................. 773 625-1177
Fax: 847 451-9235
Clarence W Ruesch, *CEO*
Carl Ruesch, *President*
Karen Calkins, *Vice Pres*
▲ **EMP:** 14 **EST:** 1945
**SQ FT:** 20,000
**SALES (est):** 4.4MM **Privately Held**
**WEB:** www.reliablemetalstamping.com
**SIC: 3469** Stamping metal for the trade

**(G-10573)**
**RELIANCE TOOL & MFG CO**
Also Called: Mosedale Manufacturing
11333 W Melrose St (60131)
PHONE .................................. 847 455-4350
**EMP:** 45
**SALES (corp-wide):** 24.1MM **Privately Held**
**SIC: 3541** Machine tools, metal cutting type
**PA:** Reliance Tool & Mfg. Co.
   900 N State St Ste 101
   Elgin IL 60123
   847 695-1235

**(G-10574)**
**RESCO PRODUCTS CO**
9101 Belden Ave (60131-3505)
PHONE .................................. 847 455-3776
Margarette Gofell, *President*
**EMP:** 6
**SALES (est):** 1MM **Privately Held**
**SIC: 3541** Machine tools, metal cutting type

**(G-10575)**
**RINGSPANN CORPORATION**
10550 Anderson Pl (60131-2302)
PHONE .................................. 847 678-3581
Thomas L Werking, *CEO*
Jason Mears, *Regional Mgr*
Bill Nolan, *Regional Mgr*
Rich Collins, *Vice Pres*
Roger Gates, *Mfg Mgr*
▲ **EMP:** 19
**SQ FT:** 3,000
**SALES:** 10MM
**SALES (corp-wide):** 67.2MM **Privately Held**
**WEB:** www.ringspanncorp.com
**SIC: 3568** Clutches, except vehicular
**PA:** Ringspann Gmbh
   Schaberweg 30-38
   Bad Homburg 61348
   617 227-50

**(G-10576)**
**RJ CNC WORKS INC**
10134 Pacific Ave (60131-1647)
PHONE .................................. 847 671-9120
Boguslaw Janczura, *Principal*
**EMP:** 7
**SALES (est):** 921K **Privately Held**
**SIC: 3599** Machine shop, jobbing & repair

**(G-10577)**
**RRP ENTERPRISES INC**
9510 Fullerton Ave (60131-3340)
PHONE .................................. 847 455-5674
Richard Perales, *President*
Georgia Perez, *Manager*
**EMP:** 2
**SQ FT:** 3,000
**SALES (est):** 574.6K **Privately Held**
**SIC: 3561** 3643 Cylinders, pump; current-carrying wiring devices

**(G-10578)**
**RTM TREND INDUSTRIES INC**
11333 Melrose Ave (60131-1322)
PHONE .................................. 847 455-4350
Fax: 847 455-2525
Paul Knowlton, *President*
Nadine Knowlton, *Vice Pres*
Robert Sanchez, *Engineer*
Gina Sebastian, *Manager*
**EMP:** 35
**SQ FT:** 50,000
**SALES (est):** 6.7MM **Privately Held**
**SIC: 3469** Stamping metal for the trade

**(G-10579)**
**S & L TOOL CO INC**
Also Called: Aero Tool & Stamping
2324 17th St (60131-3407)
PHONE .................................. 847 455-5550
Fax: 847 455-5501
Judy Snook, *President*
**EMP:** 4 **EST:** 1964
**SQ FT:** 5,500

**SALES (est):** 363K **Privately Held**
**SIC: 3469** Machine parts, stamped or pressed metal

**(G-10580)**
**SACCO-CAMEX INC**
460 Dominic Ct (60131-1004)
PHONE .................................. 630 595-8090
Fax: 630 595-8102
Steve Sacco, *President*
**EMP:** 3
**SALES (est):** 210K **Privately Held**
**SIC: 3545** 3541 Cams (machine tool accessories); machine tools, metal cutting type

**(G-10581)**
**SANDEE MANUFACTURING CO (PA)**
10520 Waveland Ave (60131-1288)
PHONE .................................. 847 671-1335
Fax: 847 671-7127
Thomas Kunkel, *President*
James Kunkel, *Exec VP*
Jim Tavenner, *Sales Staff*
Erin Knobbe, *Manager*
Erin McLeod, *Manager*
**EMP:** 5
**SQ FT:** 35,000
**SALES:** 15.8MM **Privately Held**
**SIC: 3089** 3993 3082 3081 Extruded finished plastic products; signs & advertising specialties; unsupported plastics profile shapes; unsupported plastics film & sheet

**(G-10582)**
**SARJ USA INC**
Also Called: Picture Frame Factory
9201 King St (60131-2111)
PHONE .................................. 708 865-9134
Jatin Patel, *CEO*
Riten Patel, *Manager*
Urmela Patel, *Admin Sec*
◆ **EMP:** 48
**SQ FT:** 48,600
**SALES:** 10.7MM **Privately Held**
**SIC: 2499** 3231 5023 5999 Picture & mirror frames, wood; framed mirrors; frames & framing, picture & mirror; art, picture frames & decorations; picture framing, custom

**(G-10583)**
**SAS INDUSTRIAL MACHINERY INC**
9212 Cherry Ave (60131-3010)
PHONE .................................. 847 455-5526
Fax: 847 455-5527
Stanley Niedbalec, *President*
**EMP:** 5
**SQ FT:** 14,500
**SALES:** 600K **Privately Held**
**SIC: 3599** Machine & other job shop work

**(G-10584)**
**SCOT FORGE COMPANY**
9394 Belmont Ave (60131-2810)
PHONE .................................. 847 678-6000
Fax: 847 678-6000
Matt Blankenberger, *Maint Spvr*
Steve Hughes, *QA Dir*
Bill Berger, *Engineer*
Harry Clayton, *Manager*
Luke Hahn, *Manager*
**EMP:** 58
**SALES (corp-wide):** 145.7MM **Privately Held**
**WEB:** www.scotforge.com
**SIC: 3462** 3325 Iron & steel forgings; steel foundries
**PA:** Scot Forge Company
   8001 Winn Rd
   Spring Grove IL 60081
   815 675-1000

**(G-10585)**
**SEALTRONIX INC**
11150 Addison Ave (60131-1404)
PHONE .................................. 800 878-9864
**EMP:** 12
**SQ FT:** 6,800

# Franklin Park - Cook County (G-10586)

**SALES:** 538.5K
**SALES (corp-wide):** 2.2MM **Privately Held**
**WEB:** www.sealtronix.com
**SIC: 3479** Coating of metals & formed products
**PA:** Casting Impregnators, Inc.
 11150 Addison Ave
 Franklin Park IL 60131
 847 455-1000

### (G-10586)
### SEMLER INDUSTRIES INC
3800 Carnation St (60131-1202)
**PHONE**.................................847 671-5650
**Fax:** 847 671-7686
Loren H Semler, *Ch of Bd*
Loren W Semler, *President*
Katherine Felton, *Senior VP*
Joe Palm, *Vice Pres*
Ron Neubert, *Purchasing*
▲ **EMP:** 31 **EST:** 1905
**SQ FT:** 20,000
**SALES (est):** 27.8MM **Privately Held**
**WEB:** www.semlerindustries.com
**SIC: 5085** 5084 3823 Industrial supplies; hose, belting & packing; valves & fittings; filters, industrial; water pumps (industrial); meters, consumption registering; industrial instrmnts msrmnt display/control process variable

### (G-10587)
### SIMS RCYCL SLTONS HOLDINGS INC
3700 Runge St (60131-1112)
**PHONE**.................................847 455-8800
Robert Goable, *Manager*
**EMP:** 120 **Privately Held**
**SIC: 3341** Secondary precious metals
**PA:** Sims Recycling Solutions Holdings Inc.
 1750 Harvester Rd
 West Chicago IL 60185

### (G-10588)
### SIMS RECYCLING SOLUTIONS INC
3700 Runge St (60131-1112)
**PHONE**.................................847 455-8800
**EMP:** 3
**SALES (corp-wide):** 3.4B **Privately Held**
**SIC: 3341** Secondary precious metals
**HQ:** Sims Recycling Solutions, Inc.
 1600 Harvester Rd
 West Chicago IL 60185
 630 231-6060

### (G-10589)
### SKYLINE BEAUTY SUPPLY INC
Also Called: Nail Superstore
3804 Carnation St (60131-1202)
**PHONE**.................................773 275-6003
Kevin Bao Huynh, *President*
◆ **EMP:** 10
**SQ FT:** 20,000
**SALES (est):** 1.6MM **Privately Held**
**WEB:** www.nailsuperstore.com
**SIC: 5087** 2844 Beauty parlor equipment & supplies; cosmetic preparations

### (G-10590)
### SLOAN VALVE COMPANY (PA)
10500 Seymour Ave (60131-1259)
**PHONE**.................................847 671-4300
**Fax:** 312 453-3071
James C Allen, *President*
Charles S Allen, *Chairman*
John Aykroyd, *Exec VP*
Parthiv Amin, *Vice Pres*
Tom Coleman, *Vice Pres*
◆ **EMP:** 6
**SQ FT:** 410,000
**SALES (est):** 223.2MM **Privately Held**
**WEB:** www.sloanvalve.com
**SIC: 3494** 3432 Valves & pipe fittings; pipe fittings; plumbing fixture fittings & trim

### (G-10591)
### SONOCO PRODUCTS COMPANY
Clear Pack Company
11608 Copenhagen Ct (60131-1348)
**PHONE**.................................847 957-6282
**Fax:** 847 957-1529
**EMP:** 130

**SALES (corp-wide):** 4.9B **Publicly Held**
**SIC: 3089** 3081 Plastics Products, Nec, Nsk
**PA:** Sonoco Products Company
 1 N 2nd St
 Hartsville SC 29550
 843 383-7000

### (G-10592)
### SPECIALTY ENTERPRISES INC
1075 Waveland Ave (60131-1011)
**PHONE**.................................630 595-7808
**Fax:** 847 350-0239
John Finn III, *President*
Wayne Finn, *Vice Pres*
Lorraine Finn, *Marketing Staff*
**EMP:** 9 **EST:** 1959
**SQ FT:** 8,000
**SALES:** 900K **Privately Held**
**SIC: 3541** 3599 Machine tools, metal cutting type; machine shop, jobbing & repair

### (G-10593)
### STARK STANDARD CO
4028 Tugwell St (60131-1216)
**PHONE**.................................847 916-2636
Paul Nowotarski, *President*
**EMP:** 5 **EST:** 2014
**SQ FT:** 10,000
**SALES (est):** 394.9K **Privately Held**
**SIC: 3083** Thermosetting laminates: rods, tubes, plates & sheet

### (G-10594)
### STERIS CORPORATION
11457 Melrose Ave Ste B (60131-1303)
**PHONE**.................................847 455-2881
Harry Bala, *President*
Rebecca Aldhizer, *Manager*
**EMP:** 10
**SQ FT:** 25,000
**SALES (est):** 1.6MM **Privately Held**
**SIC: 3841** Surgical & medical instruments

### (G-10595)
### STERLING EXTRACT COMPANY INC
10929 Franklin Ave Ste V (60131-1430)
**PHONE**.................................847 451-9728
**Fax:** 847 451-9745
Craig Wakefield, *President*
Marion Wakefield, *Corp Secy*
Deborah Pavone, *Mktg Dir*
**EMP:** 6 **EST:** 1949
**SQ FT:** 4,900
**SALES:** 1.5MM **Privately Held**
**WEB:** www.sterlingextractcompany.com
**SIC: 2087** Extracts, flavoring; concentrates, flavoring (except drink)

### (G-10596)
### STUECKLEN MANUFACTURING CO
10022 Pacific Ave (60131-1837)
P.O. Box 190 (60131-0190)
**PHONE**.................................847 678-5130
**Fax:** 847 678-5168
Paul Davis, *President*
Alexandra Davis, *Vice Pres*
**EMP:** 7 **EST:** 1948
**SQ FT:** 14,500
**SALES (est):** 1MM **Privately Held**
**SIC: 3444** 3469 Sheet metalwork; spinning metal for the trade

### (G-10597)
### SUBURBAN INDUSTRIES INC
1090 E Green St (60131-1015)
**PHONE**.................................630 766-3773
**Fax:** 847 766-1364
C Kenneth Pobloske Jr, *President*
L Parrish, *Director*
**EMP:** 10
**SQ FT:** 14,000
**SALES (est):** 1.8MM **Privately Held**
**SIC: 3452** 3356 Dowel pins, metal; nonferrous rolling & drawing

### (G-10598)
### SUBURBAN METALCRAFT INC
Also Called: Decor Rv Locks
9045 Exchange Ave (60131-2815)
**PHONE**.................................847 678-7550
**Fax:** 847 678-7556
Patricia Ragon, *President*
Richard Ragon, *Vice Pres*
**EMP:** 8 **EST:** 1946
**SQ FT:** 7,500
**SALES (est):** 1.4MM **Privately Held**
**SIC: 3499** Fire- or burglary-resistive products

### (G-10599)
### SUBURBAN WELDING & STEEL LLC
9820 Franklin Ave (60131-1913)
**PHONE**.................................847 678-1264
**Fax:** 847 678-8559
Brian Kasmer, *Vice Pres*
Lakresha Johnson, *Manager*
Karen Karner,
**EMP:** 14 **EST:** 1951
**SQ FT:** 13,500
**SALES (est):** 1.3MM **Privately Held**
**WEB:** www.suburbanwelding.com
**SIC: 3444** 7692 Sheet metalwork; welding repair

### (G-10600)
### SURFACETEC CORP
471 Podlin Dr (60131-1007)
**PHONE**.................................630 521-0001
Takao Nagai, *CEO*
**EMP:** 14
**SALES (est):** 949.3K **Privately Held**
**SIC: 3544** Industrial molds

### (G-10601)
### SWINGMASTER CORPORATION
11415 Melrose Ave (60131-1324)
**PHONE**.................................847 451-1224
**Fax:** 847 451-1247
Dan Grammatis, *President*
▼ **EMP:** 22
**SALES (est):** 6.3MM **Privately Held**
**SIC: 3537** Trucks, tractors, loaders, carriers & similar equipment

### (G-10602)
### T CAT ENTERPRISE INC
9300 Franklin Ave (60131-2831)
P.O. Box 657 (60131-0657)
**PHONE**.................................630 330-6800
James R Trumbull Jr, *President*
**EMP:** 4
**SALES (est):** 1.2MM **Privately Held**
**SIC: 1081** Metal mining services

### (G-10603)
### T J ASSEMBLIES INC
10439 Franklin Ave (60131-1529)
**PHONE**.................................847 671-0060
**Fax:** 847 671-0694
Dolores Jarosz, *President*
Brian Jarosz, *Vice Pres*
Bruce Jarosz, *Vice Pres*
Don Jarosz, *Vice Pres*
Jim Jarosz, *Vice Pres*
**EMP:** 50 **EST:** 1973
**SQ FT:** 22,000
**SALES (est):** 8.4MM **Privately Held**
**WEB:** www.tjassemblies.com
**SIC: 2655** Bobbins, textile spinning: made from purchased fiber

### (G-10604)
### TASTY BREADS INTERNATIONAL INC
9445 Fullerton Ave (60131-3303)
**PHONE**.................................847 451-4000
Constanitin Bartsocas, *President*
Jorge Ferragut, *Vice Pres*
Nancy Murphy, *Vice Pres*
**EMP:** 70
**SALES (est):** 7MM **Privately Held**
**WEB:** www.tastybreads.com
**SIC: 2041** Doughs, frozen or refrigerated

### (G-10605)
### TELEGARTNER INC
411 Dominic Ct (60131-1003)
**PHONE**.................................630 616-7600
**Fax:** 630 616-6322
Ralph Souders, *President*
Jeanette Reedy, *Treasurer*
Al Ehredt, *Manager*
Peter W Mitchell, *Admin Sec*
**EMP:** 22
**SQ FT:** 7,800

**SALES:** 3.7MM **Privately Held**
**WEB:** www.telegartner.com
**SIC: 3643** 5063 Power line cable; electrical supplies

### (G-10606)
### THRIFT N SWIFT
9651 Franklin Ave (60131-2719)
**PHONE**.................................847 455-1350
**Fax:** 847 455-1305
William Denten, *President*
Christopher Denton, *Sales Mgr*
**EMP:** 7 **EST:** 1967
**SQ FT:** 2,500
**SALES (est):** 630K **Privately Held**
**WEB:** www.thriftnswift.com
**SIC: 2752** Commercial printing, offset

### (G-10607)
### TITAN TOOL COMPANY INC
10001 Pacific Ave (60131-1830)
**PHONE**.................................847 671-0045
Jim Jaroch, *President*
Anne M Jaroch, *Corp Secy*
Peter Jaroch, *Vice Pres*
Michelle Jaroch, *Office Mgr*
**EMP:** 5 **EST:** 1961
**SQ FT:** 4,000
**SALES:** 120K **Privately Held**
**SIC: 3544** 3549 Special dies & tools; industrial molds; metalworking machinery

### (G-10608)
### TOMCO DIE & KELLERING CO
10025 Franklin Ave (60131-1835)
**PHONE**.................................847 678-8113
**Fax:** 847 678-7460
Richard Fafinski, *President*
**EMP:** 3
**SQ FT:** 5,000
**SALES:** 300K **Privately Held**
**SIC: 3089** 3544 Injection molding of plastics; special dies, tools, jigs & fixtures

### (G-10609)
### TRANSCENDIA INC (PA)
9201 Belmont Ave (60131-2842)
**PHONE**.................................847 678-1800
**Fax:** 847 678-0199
Andy J Brewer, *President*
Mark Baumann, *Vice Pres*
Ruben Sanchez, *Project Mgr*
Pam Piazza, *Opers Mgr*
Alex Culafic, *Opers Staff*
◆ **EMP:** 125
**SQ FT:** 147,000
**SALES (est):** 427.9MM **Privately Held**
**WEB:** www.transilwrap.com
**SIC: 3081** 5162 Plastic film & sheet; plastics products

### (G-10610)
### TRANSCENDIA INC
Lamination/Id Securities Div
9201 Belmont Ave Ste 100a (60131-2842)
**PHONE**.................................847 678-1800
Dennis Kuta, *General Mgr*
**EMP:** 26
**SALES (corp-wide):** 427.9MM **Privately Held**
**SIC: 3083** Plastic finished products, laminated
**PA:** Transcendia, Inc.
 9201 Belmont Ave
 Franklin Park IL 60131
 847 678-1800

### (G-10611)
### TRANSILWRAP COMPANY INC
9201 Belmont Ave Ste 100a (60131-2842)
**PHONE**.................................847 678-1800
Jeff Mitchelle, *Manager*
**EMP:** 30
**SALES (corp-wide):** 427.9MM **Privately Held**
**WEB:** www.interfilm-usa.com
**SIC: 3081** Unsupported plastics film & sheet
**HQ:** Transcendia, Inc.
 127 Turningstone Ct
 Greenville SC 29611
 864 269-4690

## (G-10612)
**TRIANGLE SCREEN PRINT INC**
10353 Franklin Ave  (60131-1529)
PHONE .................................. 847 678-9200
Fax: 847 678-9685
Dan Congine, *President*
**EMP:** 14
**SALES:** 985K  **Privately Held**
**SIC:** 2759  2396  2395  Screen printing; automotive & apparel trimmings; pleating & stitching

## (G-10613)
**TRO MANUFACTURING COMPANY INC**
2610 Edgington St  (60131-3492)
P.O. Box 528  (60131-0528)
PHONE .................................. 847 455-3755
Fax: 847 455-6116
Scott Sanda, *President*
Scott D Sanda, *General Mgr*
Keith Cutts, *Sales Dir*
Patricia R Sanda, *Admin Sec*
**EMP:** 48
**SQ FT:** 68,000
**SALES (est):** 19.1MM  **Privately Held**
**WEB:** www.tromfg.com
**SIC:** 3469  Stamping metal for the trade

## (G-10614)
**TWO FIGS BAKING CO**
3849 Carnation St  (60131-1201)
PHONE .................................. 847 233-0500
Nancy Dalessio, *Principal*
**EMP:** 4 **EST:** 2010
**SALES (est):** 250.2K  **Privately Held**
**SIC:** 2051  Bakery: wholesale or wholesale/retail combined

## (G-10615)
**UNIQUE CHECKOUT SYSTEMS**
2312 17th St  (60131-3407)
PHONE .................................. 773 522-4400
Stanley Tesler, *Principal*
**EMP:** 12  **EST:** 2008
**SALES (est):** 1.8MM  **Privately Held**
**SIC:** 3444  Sheet metalwork

## (G-10616)
**UNITED ELECTRONICS CORP INC**
3615 Wolf Rd  (60131-1425)
PHONE .................................. 847 671-6034
Hemant Patel, *President*
Betty Zelcsco, *Purchasing*
Shan Nadarajah, *Engineer*
Mangesh Patel, *Treasurer*
Michael Marshall, *Sales Mgr*
▲ **EMP:** 70
**SQ FT:** 70,000
**SALES:** 7.5MM  **Privately Held**
**WEB:** www.unitedel.com
**SIC:** 3672  Printed circuit boards

## (G-10617)
**US SMOKELESS TOB MFG CO LLC**
11601 Copenhagen Ct  (60131-1301)
PHONE .................................. 804 274-2000
Fax: 847 957-8682
Greg Ray, *VP Mfg*
Steve Ryba, *Plant Supt*
Gary Kark, *Purchasing*
Bill Dunne, *QC Mgr*
Carrie Jacobs, *Engineer*
**EMP:** 22
**SALES (corp-wide):** 25.7B  **Publicly Held**
**SIC:** 2131  Chewing & smoking tobacco
**HQ:** U.S. Smokeless Tobacco Manufacturing Company Llc
800 Harrison St
Nashville TN 37203

## (G-10618)
**UST  INC**
11601 Copenhagen Ct  (60131-1301)
PHONE .................................. 847 957-5104
**EMP:** 4
**SALES (est):** 300.9K  **Privately Held**
**SIC:** 2131  Chewing & smoking tobacco

## (G-10619)
**VALMONT INDUSTRIES  INC**
Also Called: Valmont Ctngs Empire Glvnizing
10909 Franklin Ave  (60131-1409)
PHONE .................................. 773 625-0354
Brent Toller, *Managing Dir*
Gerald Hill, *Opers Mgr*
Keith Windross, *Sls & Mktg Exec*
Marylin Meade, *Controller*
Carol Schlau, *Branch Mgr*
**EMP:** 75
**SQ FT:** 65,000
**SALES (corp-wide):** 2.5B  **Publicly Held**
**WEB:** www.valmont.com
**SIC:** 3441  Fabricated structural metal
**PA:** Valmont Industries, Inc.
1 Valmont Plz Ste 500
Omaha NE 68154
402 963-1000

## (G-10620)
**VANART ENGINEERING COMPANY**
3504 River Rd  (60131-2193)
PHONE .................................. 847 678-6255
Fax: 847 678-0443
Jane Baptist, *CEO*
Daniel A Baptist, *President*
Don Noren, *Vice Pres*
Barbara Jasinski, *Manager*
**EMP:** 30  **EST:** 1949
**SQ FT:** 8,000
**SALES (est):** 5MM  **Privately Held**
**WEB:** www.vanartengineering.com
**SIC:** 3469  3544  Stamping metal for the trade; special dies, tools, jigs & fixtures

## (G-10621)
**VENUS PROCESSING & STORAGE**
2401 Rose St  (60131-3322)
PHONE .................................. 847 455-0496
Shesfield Wolk, *President*
James Mayer, *President*
**EMP:** 52
**SALES (est):** 5.3MM  **Privately Held**
**SIC:** 4225  3444  3312  General warehousing & storage; sheet metalwork; blast furnaces & steel mills

## (G-10622)
**VICARI TOOL & PLASTICS INC**
3350 Schierhorn Ct  (60131-2125)
PHONE .................................. 847 671-9430
Fax: 847 671-4434
Lou Vicari, *President*
Mark Vicari, *Treasurer*
**EMP:** 4
**SQ FT:** 5,000
**SALES:** 380K  **Privately Held**
**SIC:** 3599  Machine shop, jobbing & repair

## (G-10623)
**VORTEQ COIL FINISHERS  LLC**
11440 W Addison St  (60131)
PHONE .................................. 847 455-7200
Michael Hartenstein, *Vice Pres*
Jan Terrizzi, *Vice Pres*
Robert Tallon, *Sales Staff*
Dave Kuiz, *Branch Mgr*
**EMP:** 50
**SALES (corp-wide):** 25.8MM  **Privately Held**
**WEB:** www.wismarq.com
**SIC:** 3444  Siding, sheet metal
**PA:** Vorteq Coil Finishers, Llc
930 Armour Rd
Oconomowoc WI 53066
262 567-1112

## (G-10624)
**VPI ACQUISITION COMPANY LLC (PA)**
Also Called: Vapor Power International
551 S County Line Rd  (60131-1013)
PHONE .................................. 630 694-5500
Fax: 630 694-2230
Robert Forslund,
Jim Pawlak,
◆ **EMP:** 31
**SQ FT:** 55,000
**SALES (est):** 7.8MM  **Privately Held**
**WEB:** www.vaporpower.com
**SIC:** 3511  3443  Turbines & turbine generator sets; fabricated plate work (boiler shop)

## (G-10625)
**W N G S INC**
11415 Melrose Ave  (60131-1324)
PHONE .................................. 847 451-1224
Anthony Grammatis, *Ch of Bd*
Daniel Grammatis, *President*
Cindi Misyk, *Manager*
▼ **EMP:** 48
**SQ FT:** 25,000
**SALES (est):** 9.4MM  **Privately Held**
**WEB:** www.swingmastercorp.com
**SIC:** 3531  5084  Cranes, locomotive; loaders, shovel: self-propelled; materials handling machinery

## (G-10626)
**WALTER H JELLY & CO INC**
2822 Birch St  (60131-3074)
PHONE .................................. 847 455-4235
Fax: 847 455-4315
Susan Jelly, *Principal*
▲ **EMP:** 4
**SALES (est):** 341.5K  **Privately Held**
**SIC:** 3466  Bottle caps & tops, stamped metal

## (G-10627)
**WARDZALA INDUSTRIES INC**
9330 Grand Ave  (60131-3411)
PHONE .................................. 847 288-9909
Fax: 847 288-1581
Walter Wardzala, *President*
**EMP:** 16
**SQ FT:** 40,000
**SALES (est):** 3.2MM  **Privately Held**
**SIC:** 3542  7692  3544  3496  Machine tools, metal forming type; welding repair; special dies, tools, jigs & fixtures; miscellaneous fabricated wire products; metal stampings

## (G-10628)
**WESTERN LIGHTING INC**
2349 17th St  (60131-3432)
PHONE .................................. 847 451-7200
Fax: 847 451-7275
Norma Heen, *President*
Victor Heen Sr, *Vice Pres*
Victor Heen Jr, *Vice Pres*
**EMP:** 15
**SQ FT:** 10,000
**SALES:** 600K  **Privately Held**
**SIC:** 3993  3646  3648  3645  Electric signs; fluorescent lighting fixtures, commercial; lighting equipment; residential lighting fixtures

## (G-10629)
**WILCZAK INDUSTRIAL PARTS INC**
9220 Chestnut Ave  (60131-3014)
PHONE .................................. 708 260-5559
Fax: 708 343-9864
Eric Wilczak, *President*
Barbara Wilczak, *Admin Sec*
**EMP:** 7
**SQ FT:** 5,000
**SALES (est):** 530K  **Privately Held**
**SIC:** 3599  Machine & other job shop work

## (G-10630)
**WILLERT COMPANY**
1144 E Green St  (60131-1005)
PHONE .................................. 630 860-1620
Fax: 630 860-9789
Edward John Butler Jr, *President*
**EMP:** 3  **EST:** 1933
**SALES:** 300K  **Privately Held**
**WEB:** www.willettco.com
**SIC:** 2752  Lithographing on metal

## (G-10631)
**WORLD LIBRARY PUBLICATIONS**
3708 River Rd Ste 400  (60131-2158)
PHONE .................................. 847 678-9300
William Rafferty, *President*
Jerry Galipeau, *Editor*
Israel Martinez, *Editor*
Christine Krzystofczyk, *Regional Mgr*
John Ficarra, *Vice Pres*
**EMP:** 180
**SQ FT:** 10,000
**SALES (est):** 11.9MM  **Privately Held**
**WEB:** www.worldlibrary.net
**SIC:** 2741  Miscellaneous publishing

## (G-10632)
**YALE SECURITY INC**
Rixson
9100 Belmont Ave  (60131-2806)
PHONE .................................. 704 283-2101
Fax: 847 671-5479
Eric Tannhauser, *Manager*
Jose Lopez, *Director*
**EMP:** 75
**SQ FT:** 100,000
**SALES (corp-wide):** 7.7B  **Privately Held**
**SIC:** 3699  7629  Door opening & closing devices, electrical; security control equipment & systems; electronic equipment repair
**HQ:** Yale Security Inc.
1902 Airport Rd
Monroe NC 28110
704 283-2101

---

### Freeburg
*St. Clair County*

## (G-10633)
**BITTLE**
713 N Kristie Lynn St  (62243-1639)
PHONE .................................. 618 539-6099
Cynthia Bittle, *Owner*
**EMP:** 2
**SALES (est):** 238.2K  **Privately Held**
**SIC:** 3825  Automotive ammeters & voltmeters

## (G-10634)
**CUSTOM TOWELS INC**
6410 Hilgard Memorial Dr  (62243-2343)
PHONE .................................. 618 539-5005
Debbie Martin, *President*
Tom Martin, *Vice Pres*
**EMP:** 3
**SALES:** 1MM  **Privately Held**
**WEB:** www.towelsandblankets.com
**SIC:** 2396  Screen printing on fabric articles

## (G-10635)
**FREEBURG PRINTING & PUBLISHING**
820 S State St  (62243-1548)
P.O. Box 98  (62243-0098)
PHONE .................................. 618 539-3320
Fax: 618 593-3346
Harold Carpenter, *President*
Harold C Carpenter, *Owner*
Tom Carpenter, *Vice Pres*
Judy Carpenter, *Manager*
**EMP:** 8
**SQ FT:** 2,500
**SALES:** 185K  **Privately Held**
**WEB:** www.freeburgtribune.com
**SIC:** 2711  2759  Newspapers, publishing & printing; letterpress printing

## (G-10636)
**GENERAL MACHINE  INC**
6038 Schiermeier Rd  (62243-2012)
PHONE .................................. 618 234-1919
Fax: 618 234-1501
Joseph C Kreher Jr, *President*
Patti Kreher, *Corp Secy*
**EMP:** 22  **EST:** 1980
**SQ FT:** 18,000
**SALES (est):** 3.5MM  **Privately Held**
**WEB:** www.generalmachineinc.com
**SIC:** 3599  Machine shop, jobbing & repair

## (G-10637)
**HUBBELL WIEGMANN INC**
501 W Apple St  (62243-1389)
P.O. Box 1  (62243-0001)
PHONE .................................. 618 539-3542
Fax: 618 539-5794
Timothy H Powers, *President*
Richard W Davies, *Vice Pres*
Paul Fix, *Opers Mgr*
Charlie Rogers, *Opers Mgr*
Scott Smith, *Opers Staff*

▲ EMP: 350
SQ FT: 220,000
SALES (est): 49.2MM
SALES (corp-wide): 3.5B **Publicly Held**
WEB: www.hubbell-wiegmann.com
SIC: **3644** Junction boxes, electric
PA: Hubbell Incorporated
    40 Waterview Dr
    Shelton CT 06484
    475 882-4000

**(G-10638)**
**LEE SAUZEK**
316 Silverthorne Dr (62243-2680)
P.O. Box 36 (62243-0036)
PHONE..................................618 539-5815
Lee Sauzek, *CEO*
EMP: 4
SALES (est): 213.3K **Privately Held**
SIC: **3635** Household vacuum cleaners

**(G-10639)**
**PROFESSIONAL METAL WORKS LLC**
9 Industrial Dr (62243-3229)
PHONE..................................618 539-2214
Fax: 618 539-2216
Rhonda Kaiser, *Mng Member*
Dennis J Kaiser,
Dennis Jkaiser,
EMP: 14
SQ FT: 15,000
SALES: 4MM **Privately Held**
WEB: www.professionalmetalworks.com
SIC: **3441** 7692 Fabricated structural metal; welding repair

**(G-10640)**
**SENTINEL EMRGNCY SOLUTIONS LLC (PA)**
502 S Richland St (62243-1533)
PHONE..................................618 539-3863
EMP: 21 EST: 2008
SALES (est): 7.3MM **Privately Held**
SIC: **3711** Fire department vehicles (motor vehicles), assembly of

**(G-10641)**
**SIEMENS MANUFACTURING CO INC (PA)**
410 W Washington St (62243-1394)
P.O. Box 61 (62243-0061)
PHONE..................................618 539-3000
Fax: 618 539-6172
Joe Kaeser, *President*
John F Siemens III, *President*
Janet Siemens, *Vice Pres*
Perry Danford, *QC Dir*
Linda Abbott, *CPA*
EMP: 60 EST: 1963
SQ FT: 50,000
SALES (est): 44.8MM **Privately Held**
WEB: www.jans50.com
SIC: **3672** Printed circuit boards

**(G-10642)**
**STANDARD LABORATORIES INC**
Also Called: Standard Laboratory
8451 River King Dr (62243-2352)
PHONE..................................618 539-5836
Fax: 618 539-5839
Steve Smith, *Safety Mgr*
Richard Wilburn, *Manager*
Debbie Pritts, *Manager*
Steve Stoodley, *Manager*
Robert Veto, *Manager*
EMP: 28
SALES (corp-wide): 70.9MM **Privately Held**
WEB: www.standardlabs.com
SIC: **1221** 8734 Bituminous coal & lignite-surface mining; testing laboratories
PA: Standard Laboratories, Inc.
    147 11th Ave Ste 100
    South Charleston WV 25303
    304 744-6200

**(G-10643)**
**STAR CUSHION PRODUCTS INC**
5 Commerce Dr (62243-3228)
PHONE..................................618 539-7070
Fax: 618 539-7073
Janice Fraser, *President*
▲ EMP: 12

SQ FT: 6,700
SALES: 2.5MM **Privately Held**
WEB: www.starcushion.com
SIC: **3841** 3842 Surgical & medical instruments; ligatures, medical

## Freeport
### Stephenson County

**(G-10644)**
**ADVANCE TECHNOLOGIES INC**
430 Challenge St (61032-2540)
PHONE..................................815 297-1771
Fax: 815 297-1770
Steve Buss, *CEO*
Robert Horton, *Vice Pres*
EMP: 4
SALES: 500K **Privately Held**
WEB: www.advancetechnologies.net
SIC: **3663** Satellites, communications

**(G-10645)**
**ALTONA CO**
Also Called: Mrs Mike's Potato Chips
70 E Monterey St (61032-3347)
PHONE..................................815 232-7819
Robert L Mordick, *President*
Mordick Robert, *IT/INT Sup*
EMP: 5
SQ FT: 3,100
SALES (est): 220K **Privately Held**
WEB: www.mrsmikes.com
SIC: **2096** 5441 2099 Potato chips & similar snacks; confectionery produced for direct sale on the premises; food preparations

**(G-10646)**
**ANCHOR-HARVEY COMPONENTS LLC**
Also Called: Ah
600 W Lamm Rd (61032-9631)
PHONE..................................815 233-3833
Harold Brown Harvey, *President*
Tom Lefaivre, *President*
Laura Fitz, *Plant Mgr*
Michelle Wilcox, *Buyer*
George Mack, *Engineer*
EMP: 97 EST: 1923
SQ FT: 100,000
SALES (est): 5MM **Privately Held**
WEB: www.forgings.com
SIC: **3463** Nonferrous forgings; aluminum forgings
PA: Boler Ventures Llc
    500 Park Blvd Ste 1010
    Itasca IL 60143
    630 773-9111

**(G-10647)**
**ANDERSEN MACHINE & WELDING INC**
1731 Lincoln Dr (61032-9712)
PHONE..................................815 232-4664
Fax: 815 233-2068
Norma Andersen, *President*
Stephanie Dinderman, *Office Mgr*
EMP: 9
SQ FT: 6,000
SALES (est): 710K **Privately Held**
SIC: **3714** 3441 7692 Motor vehicle engines & parts; fabricated structural metal; welding repair

**(G-10648)**
**BEE LINE SERVICE INC**
2291 Us Highway 20 E (61032-9643)
PHONE..................................815 233-1812
Fax: 815 233-4533
Michael Bauch, *President*
Phyllis Bauch, *Vice Pres*
EMP: 5 EST: 1946
SALES: 500K **Privately Held**
SIC: **3273** Ready-mixed concrete

**(G-10649)**
**BLACKHAWK BIOFUELS LLC**
210 W Spring St Ste 1 (61032-4346)
P.O. Box 888, Ames IA (50010-0888)
PHONE..................................217 431-6600
EMP: 30

SALES (est): 2.5MM
SALES (corp-wide): 1.2B **Publicly Held**
SIC: **2911** Petroleum Refiner
HQ: Reg Biofuels, Llc
    416 S Bell Ave
    Ames IA 50010
    515 239-8000

**(G-10650)**
**CARPETS BY KUNIEJ (PA)**
1308 S Armstrong Ave (61032-2504)
PHONE..................................815 232-9060
Jeffery Kuniej, *President*
Tina Kuniej, *Vice Pres*
EMP: 4
SALES (est): 150K **Privately Held**
SIC: **3996** Asphalted-felt-base floor coverings: linoleum, carpet

**(G-10651)**
**CONMAT INC (HQ)**
2283 Us Highway 20 E (61032-9643)
PHONE..................................815 235-2200
Fax: 815 235-9590
Eric Helm, *President*
EMP: 35
SQ FT: 7,200
SALES: 6.3MM
SALES (corp-wide): 153.7MM **Privately Held**
WEB: www.helmgroup.com
SIC: **1422** 4212 0711 1794 Crushed & broken limestone; dump truck haulage; lime spreading services; excavation work
PA: Helm Group Inc
    2283 Business Us 20 E
    Freeport IL 61032
    815 235-2244

**(G-10652)**
**DANFOSS POWER SOLUTIONS US CO**
580 N Henderson Rd (61032-9017)
PHONE..................................815 233-4200
Steve Macdougall, *QC Mgr*
Bert Lohr, *Manager*
EMP: 150
SALES (corp-wide): 5.5B **Privately Held**
SIC: **3594** 3462 3714 Fluid power pumps & motors; pump, compressor & turbine forgings; motor vehicle parts & accessories
HQ: Danfoss Power Solutions (Us) Company
    2800 E 13th St
    Ames IA 50010
    515 239-6000

**(G-10653)**
**DOUGLAS GRAYBILL**
Also Called: Deerland Dairy
3693 N Dakota Rd (61032-9178)
PHONE..................................815 218-1749
Douglas Graybill, *Owner*
EMP: 4
SALES (est): 116.1K **Privately Held**
SIC: **2026** Fluid milk; fermented & cultured milk products

**(G-10654)**
**EASTRICH PRINTING & SALES**
2252 W Galena Ave (61032-3016)
PHONE..................................815 232-4216
Fax: 815 232-8773
Richard A Eastman Jr, *Owner*
EMP: 6
SQ FT: 2,700
SALES (est): 684.4K **Privately Held**
SIC: **2752** 2789 Commercial printing, offset; bookbinding & related work

**(G-10655)**
**FAMOUS FOSSIL VINYARD & WINERY**
395 W Cedarville Rd (61032-9156)
PHONE..................................815 563-4665
Pam Rosmann, *Executive*
EMP: 4
SALES (est): 348.1K **Privately Held**
SIC: **2084** Wines, brandy & brandy spirits

**(G-10656)**
**FISCHER STONE & MATERIALS LLC**
1567 N Heine Rd (61032-8402)
PHONE..................................815 233-3232
Wayne Fischer,
Joe Fischer,
EMP: 7
SALES (est): 1.1MM **Privately Held**
SIC: **3272** Cast stone, concrete

**(G-10657)**
**FNH READY MIX INC**
751 Il Route 26 N (61032-8302)
P.O. Box 747 (61032-0747)
PHONE..................................815 235-1400
Dean Briggs, *Principal*
EMP: 12
SALES (est): 2MM **Privately Held**
SIC: **3273** Ready-mixed concrete

**(G-10658)**
**FREEPORT PRESS INC**
1031 W Empire St (61032-6267)
P.O. Box 916 (61032-0916)
PHONE..................................815 232-1181
Jack Barron, *President*
Debbie Barron, *Vice Pres*
EMP: 5
SQ FT: 8,000
SALES: 200K **Privately Held**
WEB: www.yourideasinprint.com
SIC: **2759** Commercial printing

**(G-10659)**
**FURST-MCNESS COMPANY (PA)**
120 E Clark St (61032-3300)
PHONE..................................800 435-5100
Fax: 815 232-9724
Frank E Furst, *Ch of Bd*
Martha Furst, *President*
Mark Romero, *General Mgr*
Kevin Gyland, *Exec VP*
Lawrence Feaver, *Vice Pres*
◆ EMP: 63
SQ FT: 165,000
SALES: 345.2MM **Privately Held**
WEB: www.mcness.com
SIC: **2048** 5191 Feed premixes; feed

**(G-10660)**
**GAMETIME SCREEN PRINTING**
311 E South St (61032-9672)
PHONE..................................815 297-5263
Greg Gordon, *Principal*
EMP: 2 EST: 2011
SALES (est): 212.4K **Privately Held**
SIC: **2752** Commercial printing, lithographic

**(G-10661)**
**GS CUSTOM WORKS INC**
2110 Park Crest Dr (61032-3553)
PHONE..................................815 233-4724
Mark Spittler, *President*
EMP: 2
SALES (est): 200.2K **Privately Held**
SIC: **3714** 3751 3465 Gas tanks, motor vehicle; motorcycle accessories; fenders, automobile: stamped or pressed metal

**(G-10662)**
**HBP INC**
Also Called: HB Plastics
107 N Henderson Rd (61032-3335)
PHONE..................................815 235-3000
William R Bailey, *President*
Ted Neels, *General Mgr*
Lori Reed, *QC Mgr*
Heidorn Dan, *Controller*
Melissa Curry, *Human Res Mgr*
▲ EMP: 100
SQ FT: 85,000
SALES (est): 21.5MM **Privately Held**
WEB: www.hbplasticsinc.net
SIC: **3089** Molding primary plastic; thermoformed finished plastic products

**(G-10663)**
**HONEYWELL**
315 E Stephenson St (61032-3340)
PHONE..................................815 235-5500
EMP: 26
SALES (est): 3.6MM **Privately Held**
SIC: **3724** Mfg Aircraft Engines/Parts

## Freeport - Stephenson County (G-10686)

**(G-10664)**
**HONEYWELL INTERNATIONAL INC**
315 E Stephenson St  (61032-3340)
PHONE................................815 235-5500
Ronald Sieck, *Vice Pres*
Paul Murphy, *Research*
Dan McDermott, *Engineer*
Tom Ingman, *Human Res Dir*
Ron Sieck, *Branch Mgr*
**EMP:** 4
**SALES (corp-wide):** 39.3B  **Publicly Held**
**WEB:** www.honeywell.com
**SIC:** 3613  3644  3829  3822  Switchgear & switchboard apparatus; switch boxes, electric; measuring & controlling devices; auto controls regulating residntl & coml environmt & applncs; search & navigation equipment; relays & industrial controls
**PA:** Honeywell International Inc.
  115 Tabor Rd
  Morris Plains NJ 07950
  973 455-2000

**(G-10665)**
**HONEYWELL INTERNATIONAL INC**
315 E Stephenson St  (61032-3340)
P.O. Box 460, Mars Hill NC  (28754-0460)
PHONE................................815 235-5500
**EMP:** 65
**SALES (corp-wide):** 38.5B  **Publicly Held**
**SIC:** 3613  Mfg Switchgear/Switchboards
**PA:** Honeywell International Inc.
  115 Tabor Rd
  Morris Plains NJ 07950
  973 455-2000

**(G-10666)**
**HOOKER CUSTOM HARNESS INC**
Also Called: Hooker Harness
324 E Stephenson St  (61032-3341)
PHONE................................815 233-5478
**Fax:** 815 233-5479
Jack Hooker, *President*
Mike Showerman, *Vice Chairman*
Susanne Hooker, *Corp Secy*
Scott McPhillips, *Vice Pres*
**EMP:** 5
**SQ FT:** 3,500
**SALES (est):** 689.5K  **Privately Held**
**WEB:** www.hookerharness.com
**SIC:** 2399  Seat belts, automobile & aircraft

**(G-10667)**
**INERTIA MACHINE CORPORATION**
730 S Hancock Ave Ste A  (61032-5362)
P.O. Box 858  (61032-0858)
PHONE................................815 233-1619
**Fax:** 815 233-4446
Steve Fritz, *President*
Mandy Moore, *Admin Sec*
**EMP:** 34
**SALES (est):** 14.7MM  **Privately Held**
**SIC:** 3531  Construction machinery

**(G-10668)**
**INKY PRINTERS (PA)**
122 N Van Buren Ave  (61032-4105)
PHONE................................815 235-3700
James Dooley, *Owner*
**EMP:** 4
**SQ FT:** 6,000
**SALES (est):** 919.8K  **Privately Held**
**SIC:** 2752  2791  Commercial printing, offset; typesetting

**(G-10669)**
**IRWIN INDUSTRIAL TOOL COMPANY**
29 E Stephenson St  (61032-4235)
PHONE................................815 235-4171
Jon D Chamberlain, *Principal*
William Shine, *VP Sales*
Bill Cappollge, *Info Tech Dir*
Jake Loftis, *Director*
**EMP:** 150
**SALES (corp-wide):** 11.4B  **Publicly Held**
**WEB:** www.americantool.com
**SIC:** 3423  3545  3471  Screw drivers, pliers, chisels, etc. (hand tools); wrenches, hand tools; mechanics' hand tools; drill bits, metalworking; snips, tinners'
**HQ:** Irwin Industrial Tool Company
  8935 N Pointe Exec Pk Dr
  Huntersville NC 28078
  704 987-4555

**(G-10670)**
**JOURNAL STANDARD**
Also Called: Freeport Journal Standard
50 W Douglas St Ste 900  (61032-4141)
P.O. Box 330  (61032-0330)
PHONE................................815 232-1171
**Fax:** 815 232-3601
Josh Crust, *Publisher*
Julie Taulman, *Publisher*
Michele Massoth, *General Mgr*
Jillian Duchnowski, *Editor*
Pat Schneiderman, *Vice Pres*
**EMP:** 9
**SALES (est):** 687K
**SALES (corp-wide):** 614.3MM  **Publicly Held**
**WEB:** www.journalstandard.com
**SIC:** 2711  Newspapers: publishing only, not printed on site
**HQ:** Lee Publications, Inc.
  201 N Harrison St Ste 600
  Davenport IA 52801
  563 383-2100

**(G-10671)**
**K & S MANUFACTURING CO INC**
24 S Hooker Ave  (61032-5319)
P.O. Box 313  (61032-0313)
PHONE................................815 232-7519
**Fax:** 815 232-1126
Leo Krueger, *President*
Jan Wagner, *Treasurer*
Richard Krueger, *Admin Sec*
**EMP:** 11
**SQ FT:** 4,500
**SALES (est):** 1.7MM  **Privately Held**
**SIC:** 3589  Water treatment equipment, industrial

**(G-10672)**
**LEGGETT & PLATT INCORPORATED**
Also Called: Leggett & Platt 0351
1555 Il Route 75 E Ste 2  (61032-8703)
PHONE................................815 233-0022
C Hogan, *Purchasing*
Steve Ellison, *Manager*
John Brown, *Director*
Stephen Hotchkiss, *Director*
**EMP:** 60
**SALES (corp-wide):** 3.7B  **Publicly Held**
**WEB:** www.leggett.com
**SIC:** 2515  Mattresses & bedsprings
**PA:** Leggett & Platt, Incorporated
  1 Leggett Rd
  Carthage MO 64836
  417 358-8131

**(G-10673)**
**LEMANSKI HEATING & AC**
1398 S Armstrong Ave  (61032-2504)
PHONE................................815 232-4519
**Fax:** 815 235-1444
James Lemanski, *President*
**EMP:** 7
**SALES (est):** 710K  **Privately Held**
**WEB:** www.lemanskihvac.com
**SIC:** 1711  3444  Heating & air conditioning contractors; sheet metalwork

**(G-10674)**
**MODERN PLATING CORPORATION**
Also Called: Modern Pltg Coatings Finishes
701 S Hancock Ave  (61032-5300)
P.O. Box 838  (61032-0838)
PHONE................................815 235-1790
**Fax:** 815 235-4571
James R Stenberg, *President*
Lucille F Miller, *Chairman*
Don M Martin Jr, *Plant Mgr*
Colin McDonough, *CFO*
H Brian Christianson, *Sales Mgr*
▲ **EMP:** 100
**SQ FT:** 100,000
**SALES (est):** 14MM  **Privately Held**
**WEB:** www.modernplating.com
**SIC:** 3471  Electroplating of metals or formed products

**(G-10675)**
**NEWELL OPERATING COMPANY (HQ)**
29 E Stephenson St  (61032-4235)
PHONE................................815 235-4171
**Fax:** 815 233-8060
Mark D Ketchum, *President*
William A Burke III, *President*
Dale L Matschullat, *Vice Pres*
Danniel Connel, *CFO*
William Alldrege, *Financial Exec*
◆ **EMP:** 250  **EST:** 1903
**SQ FT:** 41,900
**SALES (est):** 848.8MM
**SALES (corp-wide):** 13.2B  **Publicly Held**
**SIC:** 3365  3991  3089  2591  Cooking/kitchen utensils, cast aluminum; paint rollers; paint brushes; trays, plastic; shade, curtain & drapery hardware; shade pulls, window; window shade rollers & fittings; needles, hand or machine; hooks, crochet; bathroom scales
**PA:** Newell Brands Inc.
  221 River St
  Hoboken NJ 07030
  201 610-6600

**(G-10676)**
**NOR SERVICE INC**
215 S State Ave  (61032-5150)
PHONE................................815 232-8379
**Fax:** 815 232-4108
Steven Rouse, *President*
Sharon Rouse, *Corp Secy*
Steven Roose, *Vice Pres*
Barry O Rouse, *Vice Pres*
Terry Rouse, *Vice Pres*
**EMP:** 24
**SQ FT:** 32,400
**SALES (est):** 601.8K  **Privately Held**
**WEB:** www.normaplewood.com
**SIC:** 3599  3542  3547  Machine shop, jobbing & repair; rebuilt machine tools, metal forming types; sheet metalworking machines; rolling mill machinery

**(G-10677)**
**NOVA WILDCAT AMEROCK  LLC**
Also Called: Piedmont Hardware Brands
1750 Lincoln Dr  (61032-9712)
PHONE................................815 266-6416
**EMP:** 14
**SALES (corp-wide):** 23.2MM  **Privately Held**
**SIC:** 3429  Cabinet hardware
**HQ:** Nova Wildcat Amerock, Llc
  4051 S Iowa Ave
  Saint Francis WI 53235
  704 696-5110

**(G-10678)**
**PERKINS CONSTRUCTION**
4872 W Lily Creek Rd  (61032-8877)
PHONE................................815 233-9655
Pete Perkins, *Owner*
**EMP:** 2
**SALES (est):** 200K  **Privately Held**
**SIC:** 1521  1799  2434  1751  Single-family home remodeling, additions & repairs; new construction, single-family houses; kitchen & bathroom remodeling; wood kitchen cabinets; carpentry work

**(G-10679)**
**PINNACLE METALS  INC**
Also Called: Pinnacle Real Estate Inv
611 W Lamm Rd  (61032-9630)
PHONE................................815 232-1600
Gary L Romig, *President*
William D Pigott II, *Vice Pres*
Bob McGlure, *Prdtn Mgr*
Nickolus R Pigott, *VP Sales*
▲ **EMP:** 45
**SQ FT:** 100,000
**SALES (est):** 12.1MM
**SALES (corp-wide):** 21.2MM  **Privately Held**
**SIC:** 3312  Stainless steel
**PA:** Tri Star Metals, Llc
  375 Village Dr
  Carol Stream IL 60188
  630 462-7600

**(G-10680)**
**PRECISION DRIVE & CONTROL INC**
1650 S Galena Ave  (61032-2518)
PHONE................................815 235-7595
**Fax:** 815 233-5006
Keith Jacobson, *Manager*
**EMP:** 9
**SALES (corp-wide):** 32.8MM  **Privately Held**
**WEB:** www.precisiondrive.com
**SIC:** 5063  7694  Electrical apparatus & equipment; armature rewinding shops
**PA:** Precision Drive & Control, Inc.
  504 11th St
  Monroe WI 53566
  608 328-5600

**(G-10681)**
**PROTO-CUTTER  INC**
101 S Liberty Ave Ste 1  (61032-5108)
PHONE................................815 232-2300
**Fax:** 815 233-9279
Peter P Alber, *President*
Jeff Spencer, *Opers Mgr*
Eshell Edler, *Purchasing*
Valerie Goeke, *QC Mgr*
Linda Alber, *Bookkeeper*
▼ **EMP:** 18
**SQ FT:** 16,000
**SALES (est):** 2.2MM  **Privately Held**
**WEB:** www.protocutter.com
**SIC:** 3545  5084  Reamers, machine tool; industrial machinery & equipment

**(G-10682)**
**R-SQUARED CONSTRUCTION INC**
35 N Commercial Ave  (61032-3308)
PHONE................................815 232-7433
**Fax:** 815 232-7474
Harold Rood, *President*
Robert Rood, *Vice Pres*
Dan Baldauf, *Sales Staff*
**EMP:** 7
**SQ FT:** 12,000
**SALES (est):** 1.1MM  **Privately Held**
**WEB:** www.r2components.com
**SIC:** 1521  2435  New construction, single-family houses; panels, hardwood plywood

**(G-10683)**
**RE-MAID INCORPORATED**
1440 Sylvan Ct  (61032-6642)
PHONE................................815 315-0500
Brian Potempa, *Mng Member*
**EMP:** 4
**SALES (est):** 241.2K  **Privately Held**
**SIC:** 3991  Brooms & brushes

**(G-10684)**
**RHINO PROS**
4223 Autumn Ln  (61032-8635)
PHONE................................815 235-7767
**EMP:** 3
**SALES (est):** 203.3K  **Privately Held**
**SIC:** 3465  Body parts, automobile: stamped metal

**(G-10685)**
**ROGERS PRECISION MACHINING**
5816 Us Highway 20 W  (61032-8707)
PHONE................................815 233-0065
Dorothy C Rogers, *President*
Larry Rogers, *Vice Pres*
Jim Rogers, *Prdtn Mgr*
▲ **EMP:** 10
**SALES (est):** 1.3MM  **Privately Held**
**WEB:** www.rogersrpm.com
**SIC:** 3599  3444  Machine shop, jobbing & repair; sheet metalwork

**(G-10686)**
**S & J MACHINE  INC**
2171 E Yellow Creek Rd  (61032-9696)
PHONE................................815 297-1594
**Fax:** 815 297-1375
Troy Milks, *President*
Vicki Milks, *Treasurer*
**EMP:** 5
**SQ FT:** 1,600
**SALES (est):** 200K  **Privately Held**
**SIC:** 3599  Machine shop, jobbing & repair

# Freeport - Stephenson County (G-10687)

## GEOGRAPHIC SECTION

**(G-10687)**
**SANDES QUYNETTA**
752 W American St Apt 5 (61032-4974)
**PHONE** .......... 815 275-4876
Quynnetta Sanders, *Owner*
**EMP:** 6
**SALES (est):** 240K **Privately Held**
**SIC: 3679** 7929 2732 5961 Recording heads, speech & musical equipment; popular music groups or artists; book music: printing & binding, not published on site; record &/or tape (music or video) club, mail order

**(G-10688)**
**SEAGA MANUFACTURING INC**
700 Seaga Dr (61032-9644)
**PHONE** .......... 815 297-9500
**Fax:** 815 297-1700
Steven V Chesney, *President*
Janelle Blomberg, *Controller*
Todd McPeek, *Marketing Mgr*
Joel Ruthe, *Manager*
Gary Partridge, *Director*
▲ **EMP:** 131
**SQ FT:** 104,000
**SALES (est):** 29.2MM **Privately Held**
**WEB:** www.seagamfg.com
**SIC: 3581** Automatic vending machines

**(G-10689)**
**SNAK-KING CORP**
3133 Industrial Dr (61032-9690)
**PHONE** .......... 815 232-6700
**Fax:** 815 232-0094
Dave Bull, *VP Opers*
Jorge Nava, *Plant Mgr*
Tracy Staten, *QC Mgr*
Sandy Stamps, *Human Res Dir*
Larry King, *Manager*
**EMP:** 140
**SALES (corp-wide):** 108.2MM **Privately Held**
**WEB:** www.vitners.com
**SIC: 2096** 2099 Corn chips & other corn-based snacks; food preparations
**PA:** Snak-King Corp.
  16150 Stephens St
  City Of Industry CA 91745
  626 336-7711

**(G-10690)**
**SPG INTERNATIONAL LLC**
1555 Il Route 75 E Ste 2 (61032-8703)
**PHONE** .......... 815 233-0022
Steve Ellison, *Vice Pres*
**EMP:** 20 **Privately Held**
**SIC: 3441** Fabricated structural metal
**PA:** Spg International Llc
  11230 Harland Dr Ne
  Covington GA 30014

**(G-10691)**
**STAR FORGE INC**
Also Called: Star Manufacturing Company
1801 S Ihm Blvd (61032-9737)
**PHONE** .......... 815 235-7750
**Fax:** 815 235-4813
C E Johnson, *CEO*
Clarence E Johnson Jr, *Ch of Bd*
John Lehnhard, *Vice Pres*
Dan F Johnson, *CFO*
Julie Folgate, *HR Admin*
▲ **EMP:** 75
**SQ FT:** 110
**SALES (est):** 19.8MM **Privately Held**
**WEB:** www.starmfg.com
**SIC: 3523** 3462 3444 Farm machinery & equipment; iron & steel forgings; sheet metalwork

**(G-10692)**
**TITAN TYRE CORPORATION**
3769 Us Highway 20 E (61032-9652)
**PHONE** .......... 217 228-6011
Maurice Taylor, *President*
Bill Wilson, *Purch Agent*
Deb Schurch, *Accountant*
**EMP:** 3
**SALES (est):** 334K **Privately Held**
**SIC: 3011** Tires & inner tubes

**(G-10693)**
**TREBOR ENTERPRISES LTD**
927 W Stephenson St (61032-4963)
P.O. Box 88 (61032-0088)
**PHONE** .......... 815 235-1700
**Fax:** 815 235-3900
Robert J Drucker, *President*
Jody Petta, *Controller*
**EMP:** 6
**SALES (est):** 500K **Privately Held**
**SIC: 3911** Rings, finger: precious metal

**(G-10694)**
**TRI STAR METALS LLC (HQ)**
611 W Lamm Rd (61032-9630)
**PHONE** .......... 815 232-1600
James Mandel, *President*
Jim Roach, *Exec VP*
▲ **EMP:** 31
**SALES (est):** 9MM
**SALES (corp-wide):** 21.2MM **Privately Held**
**SIC: 3914** Stainless steel ware
**PA:** Tri Star Metals, Llc
  375 Village Dr
  Carol Stream IL 60188
  630 462-7600

**(G-10695)**
**ULTRASONIC POWER CORPORATION**
239 E Stephenson St (61032-4213)
**PHONE** .......... 815 235-6020
**Fax:** 815 232-2150
Judith A Thompson, *President*
Robert F Schnoes, *Chairman*
Debora A Witcik, *Vice Pres*
Chris Sperry, *Prdtn Mgr*
Michael W Thompson, *Admin Sec*
▼ **EMP:** 30
**SQ FT:** 10,000
**SALES (est):** 7.7MM **Privately Held**
**WEB:** www.upcorp.com
**SIC: 3829** 3621 Ultrasonic testing equipment; motors & generators

**(G-10696)**
**UNITED SPORTSMENS COMPANY**
1931 Route 75 E (61032-8196)
**PHONE** .......... 815 599-5690
**Fax:** 815 232-2743
Brendan Walsh, *President*
Mary Walsh, *Admin Sec*
**EMP:** 6
**SQ FT:** 8,000
**SALES (est):** 420K **Privately Held**
**SIC: 3949** Sporting & athletic goods

**(G-10697)**
**VAN DIEST SUPPLY COMPANY**
1771 Lincoln Dr (61032-9712)
P.O. Box 855 (61032-0855)
**PHONE** .......... 815 232-6053
Bill Edwardson, *Branch Mgr*
**EMP:** 5
**SALES (corp-wide):** 632.8MM **Privately Held**
**WEB:** www.vdsc.com
**SIC: 5191** 2875 2879 Chemicals, agricultural; fertilizer & fertilizer materials; fertilizers, mixing only; agricultural chemicals
**PA:** Van Diest Supply Company
  1434 220th St
  Webster City IA 50595
  515 832-2366

**(G-10698)**
**WAGNER PRINTING CO (PA)**
Also Called: Infocomm Div
1 E Spring St (61032-4338)
P.O. Box 10047, Chicago (60610-0047)
**PHONE** .......... 630 941-7961
**Fax:** 815 235-4801
Matt Wager, *CEO*
Matthew M Wagner, *President*
Mark W Wagner, *President*
Eric Wagner, *Treasurer*
Bonnie Hale, *Manager*
**EMP:** 21 **EST:** 1912
**SQ FT:** 25,000
**SALES (est):** 4.8MM **Privately Held**
**SIC: 2789** 2752 Binding only: books, pamphlets, magazines, etc.; commercial printing, lithographic

**(G-10699)**
**WITTE KENDEL DIE & MOLD**
Also Called: Witte Kendel Die & Mold
657 Youngs Ln (61032-6856)
**PHONE** .......... 815 233-9270
**Fax:** 815 233-9590
Kendel E Witte, *Owner*
Kendel Witte, *Owner*
**EMP:** 4
**SALES (est):** 160K **Privately Held**
**SIC: 3544** Dies, plastics forming; forms (molds), for foundry & plastics working machinery

---

### Fulton
*Whiteside County*

**(G-10700)**
**FENIX MANUFACTURING LLC**
2001 9th St (61252-1385)
**PHONE** .......... 815 208-0755
Julie Boonstra, *Office Mgr*
John Benson,
Maggie Benson, *Graphic Designe*
Randall Boonstra,
James Hegner,
**EMP:** 4
**SQ FT:** 10,000
**SALES (est):** 506.9K **Privately Held**
**SIC: 3429** Manufactured hardware (general)

**(G-10701)**
**FULTON CORPORATION (PA)**
Also Called: Davies Mfg
303 8th Ave (61252-1636)
**PHONE** .......... 815 589-3211
**Fax:** 815 589-4433
Richard C Willoughby, *President*
Terry Temple, *Purch Mgr*
Audrey Willoughby, *Admin Sec*
Mrs R J Willoughby, *Admin Sec*
**EMP:** 57 **EST:** 1894
**SQ FT:** 64,800
**SALES (est):** 11.8MM **Privately Held**
**WEB:** www.fultoncorp.com
**SIC: 3469** 3545 Boxes: tool, lunch, mail, etc.: stamped metal; machine tool accessories

**(G-10702)**
**JT CULLEN CO INC**
901 31st Ave (61252-9609)
P.O. Box 311 (61252-0311)
**PHONE** .......... 815 589-2412
**Fax:** 815 589-4018
Eric N Johnson, *President*
Jennifer Dean, *Info Tech Dir*
Janis Johnson, *Admin Sec*
**EMP:** 70 **EST:** 1900
**SQ FT:** 120,000
**SALES (est):** 26.4MM **Privately Held**
**WEB:** www.jtcullenco.com
**SIC: 3443** 5051 3444 Fabricated plate work (boiler shop); iron or steel flat products; sheet metalwork

**(G-10703)**
**MB BOX INC**
1201 4th St (61252-1719)
**PHONE** .......... 815 589-3043
**Fax:** 815 589-3469
Paul G Brown, *President*
David Martinez, *Vice Pres*
▲ **EMP:** 6 **EST:** 1997
**SQ FT:** 5,000
**SALES (est):** 450K **Privately Held**
**SIC: 2657** Folding paperboard boxes

**(G-10704)**
**QUALITY READY MIX CONCRETE CO**
1415 14th Ave (61252-1185)
**PHONE** .......... 815 589-2013
Dave Poss, *Manager*
**EMP:** 4
**SALES (corp-wide):** 2.9MM **Privately Held**
**SIC: 3273** Ready-mixed concrete
**PA:** Quality Ready Mix Concrete Co.
  14849 Lyndon Rd
  Morrison IL 61270
  815 772-7181

**(G-10705)**
**RIVERSIDE CUSTOM WOODWORKING**
1225 22nd Ave (61252-2104)
**PHONE** .......... 815 589-3608
**Fax:** 815 589-2002
Mark Evers, *President*
**EMP:** 6
**SALES (est):** 550K **Privately Held**
**WEB:** www.rcwood.org
**SIC: 2434** 2426 2431 2511 Wood kitchen cabinets; furniture stock & parts, hardwood; staircases & stairs, wood; wood household furniture

**(G-10706)**
**TIMKEN DRIVES LLC (HQ)**
901 19th Ave (61252-1366)
**PHONE** .......... 815 589-2211
**Fax:** 815 589-3111
James Lamb, *Principal*
Eric Donnelly, *Regional Mgr*
Amy Swane, *Credit Mgr*
Derek Vlasaty, *Sales Mgr*
Jim Lamb, *Sales Staff*
◆ **EMP:** 133 **EST:** 1959
**SQ FT:** 301,154
**SALES (est):** 67.8MM
**SALES (corp-wide):** 2.6B **Publicly Held**
**WEB:** www.drivesinc.com
**SIC: 3462** 5072 Chains, forged steel; chains
**PA:** The Timken Company
  4500 Mount Pleasant St Nw
  North Canton OH 44720
  234 262-3000

**(G-10707)**
**VISUAL MARKETING SOLUTIONS**
Also Called: Visual Imaging
800 20th Ave (61252-1376)
**PHONE** .......... 815 589-3848
Michael J Ottens, *President*
Michael Ottens, *Corp Secy*
Eisenhauer John I, *Director*
Gary Holstein, *Shareholder*
**EMP:** 5
**SQ FT:** 5,000
**SALES (est):** 480K **Privately Held**
**SIC: 3993** Signs & advertising specialties

**(G-10708)**
**WARREN WIERSEMA SIGNS**
Also Called: Wiersema Wrren Signs Trck Tstg
1701 9th Ave (61252-1037)
P.O. Box 27 (61252-0027)
**PHONE** .......... 815 589-3001
Warren Wiersema, *Owner*
**EMP:** 3
**SALES:** 75K **Privately Held**
**SIC: 3993** Signs & advertising specialties

---

### Fults
*Monroe County*

**(G-10709)**
**F S GATEWAY INC**
Also Called: GATEWAY F. S. INC
3145 Maeystown Rd (62244-1733)
**PHONE** .......... 618 458-6588
**Fax:** 618 458-6966
Ronald Rodenberg, *Branch Mgr*
**EMP:** 5
**SALES (corp-wide):** 57.9MM **Privately Held**
**WEB:** www.gatewayfs.com
**SIC: 5191** 5153 2875 Fertilizer & fertilizer materials; grain elevators; fertilizers, mixing only
**PA:** Gateway Fs, Inc.
  221 E Pine St
  Red Bud IL 62278
  618 282-4000

**(G-10710)**
**GILBERT ELECTRIC**
3585 Kaskaskia Rd (62244-1601)
**PHONE** .......... 618 458-7235
Lisa Gilbert, *Principal*
**EMP:** 2
**SQ FT:** 2,034

---

▲ = Import ▼=Export ◆ =Import/Export

SALES (est): 254.7K Privately Held
SIC: 3699 Electrical equipment & supplies

## Galatia
### Saline County

**(G-10711)**
**AMERICAN COAL COMPANY (HQ)**
9085 Highway 34 N (62935-2344)
PHONE..........................618 268-6311
Randy Wiles, *Managing Dir*
Matt Mortis, *Safety Dir*
Rick Vaughn, *Foreman/Supr*
Cindy Bakes, *Manager*
Michael O McKown, *Admin Sec*
▲ EMP: 3
SALES (est): 678.5MM
SALES (corp-wide): 4B Privately Held
SIC: 1222 5052 Bituminous coal-underground mining; copper ore
PA: Murray Energy Corporation
46226 National Rd W
Saint Clairsville OH 43950
740 338-3100

**(G-10712)**
**MINERAL PRODUCTS INC**
1170 Telephone Rd (62935-2303)
PHONE..........................618 433-3150
Jerry Farmer, *President*
EMP: 4 EST: 2014
SALES (est): 156.9K Privately Held
SIC: 3274 3295 3531 Lime; building lime; minerals, ground or treated; barite, ground or otherwise treated; railway track equipment

**(G-10713)**
**TRI-COUNTY CHEMICAL INC**
20 Lebanon Rd (62935-2232)
PHONE..........................618 268-4318
Harry Melton, *Owner*
Steve Thorne, *Manager*
EMP: 3
SALES (corp-wide): 9.4MM Privately Held
SIC: 2879 Arsenates, arsenites (formulated)
PA: Tri-County Chemical, Inc.
2441 Public Rd
Eldorado IL 62930
618 273-2071

## Galena
### Jo Daviess County

**(G-10714)**
**A R B C INC**
Also Called: Lindstrand Balloons USA
11440 Dandar St (61036-8102)
PHONE..........................815 777-6006
Fax: 815 777-6004
Phil Thompson, *President*
Katrina Orr, *Manager*
EMP: 10
SALES: 1.5MM Privately Held
SIC: 3721 3069 Balloons, hot air (aircraft); balloons, advertising & toy: rubber

**(G-10715)**
**C & C EMBROIDERY INC**
800 Spring St Ste 201 (61036-2003)
PHONE..........................815 777-6167
Terry Carrol, *President*
Virginia Carroll, *Vice Pres*
EMP: 4
SALES (est): 258.4K Privately Held
WEB: www.candc-embroidery.com
SIC: 2395 Embroidery products, except schiffli machine

**(G-10716)**
**CAMPECHE RESTAURANT INC**
Also Called: Campeche Restaurant & Bar
230 N Commerce St (61036-2212)
PHONE..........................815 776-9950
Alex Lopez, *President*
Isidra Lopez, *Admin Sec*
EMP: 7 EST: 2010
SALES (est): 639.7K Privately Held
SIC: 2599 5812 Bar, restaurant & cafeteria furniture; eating places; Mexican restaurant

**(G-10717)**
**COMPUTERS AT WORK INC**
10890 E Golf View Dr (61036-8203)
P.O. Box 6145 (61036-6145)
PHONE..........................815 776-9470
Karl Malik, *President*
Renee Malik, *Admin Sec*
EMP: 4 EST: 1997
SQ FT: 2,400
SALES (est): 534.2K Privately Held
WEB: www.caw.cc
SIC: 3695 Computer software tape & disks: blank, rigid & floppy

**(G-10718)**
**COUNTRY CAST PRODUCTS**
7650 W Us Highway 20 (61036-9362)
PHONE..........................815 777-1070
Fax: 815 777-1170
Hans Weinert, *President*
EMP: 13
SQ FT: 7,000
SALES: 500K Privately Held
SIC: 3365 3353 3544 Aluminum & aluminum-based alloy castings; plates, aluminum; industrial molds

**(G-10719)**
**DUHACK LEHN & ASSOCIATES INC**
1228 N Blackjack Rd (61036-9400)
P.O. Box 45 (61036-0045)
PHONE..........................815 777-3460
Lehn Duhack, *President*
EMP: 2
SALES (est): 200K Privately Held
SIC: 1521 2431 Single-family housing construction; millwork

**(G-10720)**
**GALENA CELLARS WINERY (PA)**
Also Called: Lawlor Family Winery
515 S Main St (61036-2352)
P.O. Box 207 (61036-0207)
PHONE..........................815 777-3330
Fax: 815 777-3335
Christine Lawlor, *President*
Robert L Lawlor, *Corp Secy*
Rob Steger, *Manager*
EMP: 9
SQ FT: 10,000
SALES (est): 4.4MM Privately Held
SIC: 2084 5813 5182 5947 Wines; wine bar; wine; gift shop; commercial & industrial building operation

**(G-10721)**
**GALENA CELLARS WINERY**
Also Called: Lawlor Family Winery
4746 N Ford Rd (61036)
PHONE..........................815 777-3429
Christine Lawlor, *Branch Mgr*
EMP: 30
SALES (corp-wide): 4.4MM Privately Held
SIC: 2084 Wines
PA: Galena Cellars Winery
515 S Main St
Galena IL 61036
815 777-3330

**(G-10722)**
**GALENA MANUFACTURING CO INC**
100 Monroe St (61036-2336)
PHONE..........................815 777-2078
Fax: 815 777-9540
Gary Green, *President*
EMP: 8
SQ FT: 23,000
SALES (est): 680K Privately Held
SIC: 3496 3466 Miscellaneous fabricated wire products; crowns & closures

**(G-10723)**
**GALENAS KANDY KITCHEN**
100 N Main St (61036-2222)
PHONE..........................815 777-0241
Fax: 815 777-0241
George Paxton, *President*
Melissa Ettleman, *Manager*
EMP: 6
SQ FT: 2,500
SALES (est): 609K Privately Held
SIC: 5441 2064 2066 Candy; candy & other confectionery products; chocolate & cocoa products

**(G-10724)**
**GAZETTE (PA)**
716 S Bench St (61036-2502)
PHONE..........................815 777-0105
Paul Newton, *President*
Sarah Newton, *Vice Pres*
EMP: 14 EST: 1834
SALES: 800K Privately Held
WEB: www.gazette.net
SIC: 2711 2721 Newspapers: publishing only, not printed on site; periodicals

**(G-10725)**
**GREAT AMERICAN POPCORN COMPANY**
110 S Main St (61036-2225)
PHONE..........................815 777-4116
David A Lewis, *President*
Catherine Lewis, *Vice Pres*
EMP: 6
SALES (est): 670.8K Privately Held
WEB: www.greatpopcorn.com
SIC: 2096 2099 5441 Popcorn, already popped (except candy covered); popcorn, packaged: except already popped; popcorn, including caramel corn

**(G-10726)**
**HONEYWELL INTERNATIONAL INC**
11309 W Chetlain Ln (61036-9433)
PHONE..........................815 777-2780
Fax: 815 777-3603
Carl Kastning, *Plant Mgr*
Doug Valkema, *Engineer*
Russ Pilsner, *Manager*
Brenda Beschen, *Manager*
EMP: 150
SALES (corp-wide): 39.3B Publicly Held
WEB: www.honeywell.com
SIC: 3679 Electronic switches
PA: Honeywell International Inc.
115 Tabor Rd
Morris Plains NJ 07950
973 455-2000

**(G-10727)**
**J P VINCENT & SONS INC**
11340 W Us Highway 20 (61036-8210)
P.O. Box 326 (61036-0326)
PHONE..........................815 777-2365
Steven F Vincent, *President*
Patti Vincent, *Corp Secy*
Stephanie Vincent, *Vice Pres*
EMP: 8 EST: 1884
SALES (est): 1.2MM Privately Held
SIC: 5999 3272 Monuments, finished to custom order; tombstones; burial vaults, concrete or precast terrazzo; septic tanks, concrete

**(G-10728)**
**KINETIC FIT WORKS INC**
34 Lake Ridge Rd (61036-9611)
PHONE..........................630 340-5168
Andrew Carver, *CEO*
EMP: 5
SALES (est): 239.7K Privately Held
SIC: 3824 Fluid meters & counting devices

**(G-10729)**
**LEMFCO INC**
100 S Comm St (61036)
P.O. Box 316 (61036-0316)
PHONE..........................815 777-0242
Fax: 815 777-3240
John C Einsweiler, *President*
Dirk Einsweiler, *Corp Secy*
Wayne Einsweiler, *VP Finance*
EMP: 33 EST: 1912
SQ FT: 50,000
SALES (est): 7.1MM Privately Held
WEB: www.lemfco.com
SIC: 3321 3369 3714 Gray & ductile iron foundries; nonferrous foundries; motor vehicle parts & accessories

**(G-10730)**
**RJT WOOD SERVICES**
1653 S Tippett Rd (61036-9359)
PHONE..........................815 858-2081
Ron Tippett, *Principal*
EMP: 2
SALES (est): 242.5K Privately Held
SIC: 2421 Sawmills & planing mills, general

**(G-10731)**
**SIGNCRAFT SCREENPRINT INC**
100 A J Harle Dr (61036-9000)
PHONE..........................815 777-3030
Fax: 815 777-0740
Sandra Redington, *President*
Ron Redington, *Vice Pres*
Neva Schmid, *Purch Agent*
Ian Harris, *Treasurer*
Heather Fonseca, *Accounting Mgr*
EMP: 120 EST: 1947
SQ FT: 50,000
SALES (est): 22.3MM Privately Held
WEB: www.signcraftinc.com
SIC: 3993 2399 2752 2672 Name plates: except engraved, etched, etc.: metal; signs, not made in custom sign painting shops; emblems, badges & insignia: from purchased materials; commercial printing, lithographic; coated & laminated paper; automotive & apparel trimmings

**(G-10732)**
**TECHNICAL SEALANTS INC**
Also Called: T S I
11476 Technnical Dr (61036-8117)
P.O. Box 6565 (61036-6565)
PHONE..........................815 777-9797
Fax: 815 777-8080
John Sedan, *President*
▲ EMP: 15
SALES (est): 1.9MM Privately Held
WEB: www.technicalsealants.com
SIC: 2295 2241 Sealing or insulating tape for pipe: coated fiberglass; narrow fabric mills

**(G-10733)**
**VINTAJ NATURAL BRASS CO**
5140 W Us Highway 20 A (61036-9313)
PHONE..........................815 776-9300
Doug Duplessis, *Manager*
EMP: 4
SALES (est): 320K Privately Held
SIC: 3911 Jewelry apparel

**(G-10734)**
**WESTWICK FOUNDRY LTD**
200 S Main St (61036-2227)
PHONE..........................815 777-0815
Fax: 815 777-0816
William P Friede, *President*
Mary L Friede, *Corp Secy*
Donald Friede, *Plant Mgr*
Amy Shanley, *Office Mgr*
EMP: 25
SQ FT: 90,000
SALES: 1.1MM Privately Held
SIC: 3321 Gray & ductile iron foundries

**(G-10735)**
**WOODED WONDERLAND**
610 S Devils Ladder Rd (61036-9448)
PHONE..........................815 777-1223
Fax: 815 777-1223
John Eisbach, *Owner*
EMP: 3 EST: 1977
SALES: 60K Privately Held
WEB: www.woodedwonderland.com
SIC: 2421 5211 5031 7033 Sawmills & planing mills, general; lumber & other building materials; lumber: rough, dressed & finished; campgrounds; hardwood dimension & flooring mills

**(G-10736)**
**WORKSHOP (PA)**
Also Called: Jo Davies County Transit
706 S West St (61036-2544)
P.O. Box 6087 (61036-6087)
PHONE..........................815 777-2211
Mary Kay, *Manager*
Mike Bieleinva, *Exec Dir*
EMP: 23
SQ FT: 20,000

# Galesburg - Knox County (G-10737)

SALES: 2.3MM **Privately Held**
WEB: www.jdwi.org
SIC: **8331** 5947 7211 7349 Sheltered workshop; gift shop; power laundries, family & commercial; janitorial service, contract basis; building cleaning service; lawn services; screen printing

## Galesburg
### Knox County

**(G-10737)**
**ALUMINUM CASTINGS CORPORATION**
340 S Kellogg St (61401-4918)
PHONE..........................309 343-8910
Fax: 309 343-2022
Bart Markum, *President*
▲ EMP: 24
SQ FT: 27,000
SALES (est): 5.1MM **Privately Held**
SIC: **3363** Aluminum die-castings

**(G-10738)**
**BLACKBURN SAMPLING INC**
77 S Henderson St (61401-4327)
PHONE..........................309 342-8429
Fax: 309 342-0299
Bob Blackburn, *President*
EMP: 6
SQ FT: 1,900
SALES (est): 302.5K **Privately Held**
WEB: www.blackburnsi.com
SIC: **3084** 8748 Plastics pipe; environmental consultant

**(G-10739)**
**BRADLEY SMOKER USA INC**
644 Enterprise Ave (61401-5799)
PHONE..........................309 343-1124
Wade Bradley, *President*
Robert Chandler, *Plant Mgr*
Frank Cannady, *Warehouse Mgr*
Lissa Dickerson, *Cust Mgr*
Becky Good, *Manager*
EMP: 14
SALES (corp-wide): 242.5K **Privately Held**
SIC: **2861** Wood extract products
PA: Bradley Smoker Inc
   8380 River Rd
   Delta BC V4G 1
   604 946-3848

**(G-10740)**
**CANADIAN HARVEST LP**
701 W 6th St (61401-5903)
PHONE..........................309 343-7808
Elaine Thomas, *Branch Mgr*
EMP: 10 **Privately Held**
SIC: **2099** Food preparations
HQ: Canadian Harvest Lp
   16369 Us Highway 131 S
   Schoolcraft MI 49087
   952 835-6429

**(G-10741)**
**CANVAS CREATIONS INC**
1565 Meadow Lark Dr (61401-2235)
PHONE..........................309 343-5082
Fax: 309 341-3112
Joseph L Smith, *President*
EMP: 3
SALES (est): 140K **Privately Held**
SIC: **5999** 2394 Awnings; canvas & related products

**(G-10742)**
**CARDINAL ENGINEERING INC**
Also Called: Centroid and Cardinal Engrg
1640 N Kellogg St (61401-1845)
PHONE..........................309 342-7474
Fax: 309 342-3182
R W Friestad, *President*
Hershel Statham, *Vice Pres*
Lynne E Friestad, *Admin Sec*
EMP: 7
SQ FT: 15,000
SALES (est): 900.5K **Privately Held**
WEB: www.cardinaleng.com
SIC: **3469** 3499 Metal stampings; novelties & giftware, including trophies

**(G-10743)**
**CENTRAL MOUNTAIN COFFEE LLC**
520 N Chambers St (61401-3806)
PHONE..........................309 981-0094
Andres Gironza, *CEO*
Elsa Galyean, *President*
EMP: 3
SALES (est): 101.4K **Privately Held**
SIC: **2095** Roasted coffee; coffee extracts; coffee, ground: mixed with grain or chicory; freeze-dried coffee

**(G-10744)**
**CUSTOM FIBERGLASS OF ILLINOIS**
875 Enterprise Ave (61401-9362)
PHONE..........................309 344-7727
Jeannie Gumm, *President*
EMP: 2 EST: 1996
SALES (est): 217.6K **Privately Held**
SIC: **3732** Boats, fiberglass: building & repairing

**(G-10745)**
**DENTAL ARTS LABORATORIES INC**
1172 Monroe St Ste 5 (61401-2554)
P.O. Box 813 (61402-0813)
PHONE..........................309 342-3117
Steve Baker, *Branch Mgr*
EMP: 7
SALES (corp-wide): 17.9MM **Privately Held**
SIC: **8072** 3843 Dental laboratories; dental equipment & supplies
PA: Dental Arts Laboratories, Inc.
   241 Ne Perry Ave
   Peoria IL 61603
   309 674-8191

**(G-10746)**
**DERBY INDUSTRIES LLC**
Also Called: Derby Supply Chain Solutions
1033 Enterprise Ave (61401-5794)
PHONE..........................309 344-0547
Darryl Phillips, *Manager*
Carrey Bledsoe, *Manager*
EMP: 50
SALES (corp-wide): 76.8MM **Privately Held**
WEB: www.derbyllc.com
SIC: **3469** Metal stampings
HQ: Derby Industries, Llc
   4451 Robards Ln
   Louisville KY 40218
   502 451-7373

**(G-10747)**
**DICK BLICK COMPANY**
695 Us Highway 150 E (61401-8310)
P.O. Box 1267 (61402-1267)
PHONE..........................309 343-6181
John Polillo, *Exec VP*
Don Forslund, *Vice Pres*
Winnie Tuszynski, *Vice Pres*
Anthony Fritzel, *Controller*
Bill Seward, *VP Human Res*
EMP: 200
SALES (corp-wide): 150.5MM **Privately Held**
SIC: **5961** 2851 Arts & crafts equipment & supplies, mail order; paints & allied products
HQ: Dick Blick Company
   1849 Green Bay Rd Ste 310
   Highland Park IL 60035
   847 681-6800

**(G-10748)**
**DUCKYS FORMAL WEAR INC**
244 E Main St (61401-4707)
PHONE..........................309 342-5914
Fax: 309 342-5921
Diane Peters, *Branch Mgr*
EMP: 4
SALES (corp-wide): 936.4K **Privately Held**
WEB: www.duckysformalwear.com
SIC: **7299** 5611 5699 5621 Tuxedo rental; clothing accessories: men's & boys'; formal wear; bridal shops: invitation & stationery printing & engraving
PA: Ducky's Formal Wear, Inc
   1773 Copperfield Ln
   Crystal Lake IL

**(G-10749)**
**GALESBURG CASTINGS INC**
940 Avenue C St (61401-5700)
P.O. Box 390 (61402-0390)
PHONE..........................309 343-6178
John P Fox, *President*
Peggy L Fox, *Treasurer*
EMP: 60
SQ FT: 125,000
SALES (est): 6.2MM **Privately Held**
WEB: www.galesburgcastings.com
SIC: **3321** Ductile iron castings

**(G-10750)**
**GALESBURG MANUFACTURING CO (PA)**
1835 Lacon Dr (61401-9017)
P.O. Box 710 (61402-0710)
PHONE..........................309 342-3173
Fax: 309 343-6796
Steve Apsey, *President*
EMP: 42
SALES (est): 14.1MM **Privately Held**
SIC: **3589** Car washing machinery

**(G-10751)**
**GALESBURG SIGN & LIGHTING**
1518 S Henderson St (61401-5708)
PHONE..........................309 342-9798
Fax: 309 342-5799
Kenneth Pickrell, *President*
Carol Pickrell, *Vice Pres*
Jeffery Pickrell, *Treasurer*
Adam Pickrell, *Admin Sec*
EMP: 5
SQ FT: 7,524
SALES (est): 663.8K **Privately Held**
SIC: **3993** Electric signs; signs, not made in custom sign painting shops

**(G-10752)**
**GATES CORPORATION**
Also Called: Gates Rubber Co, The
630 Us Highway 150 E (61401-8311)
PHONE..........................309 342-7171
Fax: 309 345-5423
Ken Telker, *QC Dir*
Bob Atwood, *Manager*
EMP: 150 **Privately Held**
WEB: www.gates.com
SIC: **3052** 3714 Rubber hose; motor vehicle parts & accessories
HQ: The Gates Corporation
   1551 Wewatta St
   Denver CO 80202
   303 744-1911

**(G-10753)**
**GBS LIQUIDATING CORP**
Also Called: Builders Supply Co
2530 Grand Ave (61401-6633)
P.O. Box 1488 (61402-1488)
PHONE..........................309 342-4155
John Kovach, *President*
Robert Fulton, *Vice Pres*
Charlie Sams, *Finance Mgr*
EMP: 4
SQ FT: 4,000
SALES (est): 1.2MM
SALES (corp-wide): 122.9MM **Privately Held**
WEB: www.dentoncompanies.net
SIC: **5032** 3281 3273 3272 Sand, construction; gravel; concrete mixtures; sewer pipe, clay; cut stone & stone products; ready-mixed concrete; concrete products; cement, hydraulic; construction sand & gravel
HQ: Gunther Construction Co.
   816 N Henderson St
   Galesburg IL 61401
   309 343-1032

**(G-10754)**
**GENERAL MILLS INC**
1557 S Henderson St (61401-5707)
PHONE..........................309 342-9165
Fax: 309 342-6257
Courtney Padgett, *Branch Mgr*
Michael Bangert, *Manager*
Charlie Duran, *Manager*
John Paszylk, *Manager*
EMP: 50
SALES (corp-wide): 16.5B **Publicly Held**
WEB: www.generalmills.com
SIC: **2041** Flour mixes
PA: General Mills, Inc.
   1 General Mills Blvd
   Minneapolis MN 55426
   763 764-7600

**(G-10755)**
**GO VAN GOGHS TEE SHIRT**
Also Called: Galeria De Graphics
237 E Tompkins St (61401-4710)
PHONE..........................309 342-1112
Fakhry Azer, *Partner*
Patty Ross, *General Mgr*
EMP: 3
SQ FT: 4,000
SALES (est): 283.1K **Privately Held**
SIC: **7336** 5136 5699 2396 Silk screen design; shirts, men's & boys'; uniforms, men's & boys': shirts, custom made; uniforms; automotive & apparel trimmings

**(G-10756)**
**GUNTHER CONSTRUCTION CO (HQ)**
Also Called: Galesburg Builders Supply
816 N Henderson St (61401-2518)
P.O. Box 1488 (61402-1488)
PHONE..........................309 343-1032
John Kovach, *President*
Michael McGillicuddy, *Vice Pres*
EMP: 8 EST: 1923
SQ FT: 10,000
SALES: 15MM
SALES (corp-wide): 122.9MM **Privately Held**
WEB: www.dentoncompanies.net
SIC: **1611** 3273 General contractor, highway & street construction; ready-mixed concrete
PA: United Contractors Midwest, Inc.
   3151 Robbins Rd Ste A
   Springfield IL 62704
   217 546-6192

**(G-10757)**
**HARVEY BROS INC**
2181 Grand Ave (61401-6484)
PHONE..........................309 342-3137
Fax: 309 342-8629
Gary Harvey, *President*
Paul Harvey, *Treasurer*
Rick Harvey, *Manager*
Dale Harvey, *Admin Sec*
EMP: 17
SQ FT: 14,400
SALES (est): 1.1MM **Privately Held**
WEB: www.harveybrothers.com
SIC: **7694** 3694 3625 3621 Motor repair services; engine electrical equipment; relays & industrial controls; motors & generators

**(G-10758)**
**HEAT AND CONTROL INC**
Galesburg Division
1721 Us Highway 164 (61401)
PHONE..........................309 342-5518
Ron Vanwynsberg, *Plant Mgr*
Cory Silber, *Purch Dir*
Stephen Bohn, *Engineer*
Denise Leo, *Manager*
EMP: 65
SALES (corp-wide): 296.3MM **Privately Held**
WEB: www.heatandcontrol.com
SIC: **3556** Food products machinery
PA: Heat And Control, Inc.
   21121 Cabot Blvd
   Hayward CA 94545
   510 259-0500

**(G-10759)**
**HOLM INDUSTRIES**
611 S Linwood Rd (61401-9060)
PHONE..........................309 343-3332
Fax: 309 343-3345
Arthur Antoine, *Plant Mgr*
EMP: 3
SALES (est): 217K **Privately Held**
SIC: **3999** Manufacturing industries

## Galt - Whiteside County (G-10781)

**(G-10760)**
**ILPEA INDUSTRIES INC**
611 S Linwood Rd (61401-9060)
P.O. Box 190 (61402-0190)
**PHONE**.................................309 343-3332
Tom Cagney, *Plant Mgr*
Amy Greer, *Executive*
**EMP:** 72
**SALES (corp-wide):** 212.4MM **Privately Held**
**WEB:** www.holmindustries.com
**SIC:** 3089 3053 Window frames & sash, plastic; gaskets, all materials
**PA:** Ilpea Industries, Inc.
  745 S Gardner St
  Scottsburg IN 47170
  812 752-2526

**(G-10761)**
**J BRODIE MEAT PRODUCTS INC**
Also Called: Brodie's
605 W 6th St (61401-5901)
**PHONE**.................................309 342-1500
**Fax:** 309 342-5838
Kay F Johnson, *President*
John Brodie, *Vice Pres*
Virgil Frye, *Vice Pres*
Bob Waight, *Vice Pres*
Roland D Johnson, *Treasurer*
**EMP:** 15
**SQ FT:** 16,000
**SALES (est):** 2MM **Privately Held**
**SIC:** 2011 2013 Meat packing plants; pork products from pork slaughtered on site; sausages & other prepared meats

**(G-10762)**
**KCCDD INC**
Also Called: Phoenix Industries
1200 Monmouth Blvd (61401-5769)
**PHONE**.................................309 344-2030
Bob Paulsgrove, *Manager*
**EMP:** 60
**SALES (corp-wide):** 3.3MM **Privately Held**
**WEB:** www.kccdd.com
**SIC:** 2448 8331 2441 8322 Pallets, wood; sheltered workshop; work experience center; nailed wood boxes & shook; general counseling services; motor vehicle parts & accessories
**PA:** Kccdd, Inc.
  2015 Windish Dr
  Galesburg IL 61401
  309 344-2600

**(G-10763)**
**KOPPERS INDUSTRIES INC**
Koppers RR & Utility Pdts Div
Rr 41 Box S (61402)
**PHONE**.................................309 343-5157
**Fax:** 309 343-3501
Gary Ambrose, *General Mgr*
Ted Woerle, *Opers-Prdtn-Mfg*
Rob Whiteman, *Supervisor*
**EMP:** 46
**SALES (corp-wide):** 18.8MM **Privately Held**
**WEB:** www.koppers.com
**SIC:** 2491 2421 Poles, posts & pilings: treated wood; railroad cross bridges & switch ties, treated wood; railroad crossties, treated wood; sawmills & planing mills, general
**PA:** Koppers Industries, Inc
  436 7th Ave Ste 2026
  Pittsburgh PA 15219
  412 227-2001

**(G-10764)**
**L V BARNHOUSE & SONS**
49 N Prairie St Ste D (61401-4656)
**PHONE**.................................309 586-5404
Larry Barnhouse, *Owner*
**EMP:** 2
**SALES (est):** 203.8K **Privately Held**
**SIC:** 3561 5084 Pumps & pumping equipment; pumps & pumping equipment

**(G-10765)**
**LEE BROTHERS WELDING INC**
575 Lincoln St (61401-4033)
**PHONE**.................................309 342-6017
**Fax:** 309 344-4838
Robert Brown, *President*
**EMP:** 3

**SQ FT:** 7,500
**SALES (est):** 304.4K **Privately Held**
**SIC:** 7692 Welding repair

**(G-10766)**
**MARNIC INC (PA)**
Also Called: American Speedy Printing
439 N Henderson St (61401-3507)
**PHONE**.................................309 343-1418
**Fax:** 309 343-1925
Marvin Eberle, *President*
**EMP:** 4
**SQ FT:** 1,800
**SALES (est):** 368.7K **Privately Held**
**WEB:** www.marnic.com
**SIC:** 2752 Commercial printing, offset

**(G-10767)**
**MIDSTATE MANUFACTURING COMPANY**
Also Called: Steelweld Division
750 W 3rd St (61401-5829)
**PHONE**.................................309 342-9555
**Fax:** 309 342-7940
Curtis A Pitman, *President*
Russell Larson, *Vice Pres*
Wayne Rednour, *Purch Agent*
Andy King, *Engineer*
Ed Winter, *Engineer*
**EMP:** 150 **EST:** 1979
**SQ FT:** 16,000
**SALES (est):** 29.7MM **Privately Held**
**WEB:** www.midstate-mfg.com
**SIC:** 3599 5084 Machine shop, jobbing & repair; industrial machinery & equipment

**(G-10768)**
**MIDWEST HYDRA-LINE INC (HQ)**
Also Called: Bemis Hydraulics
698 Us Highway 150 E (61401-8311)
P.O. Box 1265 (61402-1265)
**PHONE**.................................309 342-6171
**Fax:** 309 342-6946
Will Stewart, *President*
David Palmer, *Vice Pres*
David M Uhlmann, *Vice Pres*
**EMP:** 11
**SQ FT:** 6,000
**SALES (est):** 3MM
**SALES (corp-wide):** 31.3MM **Privately Held**
**SIC:** 5085 3443 Hose, belting & packing; tools; cylinders, pressure: metal plate
**PA:** Minnesota Flexible Corp.
  305 Bridgepoint Dr # 400
  South Saint Paul MN 55075
  651 645-7522

**(G-10769)**
**NATIONAL COATINGS INC (PA)**
604 Us Highway 150 E (61401-8311)
P.O. Box 1314 (61402-1314)
**PHONE**.................................309 342-4184
**Fax:** 309 342-5568
James W Hillhouse, *President*
Mary Deutasch, *Accountant*
▲ **EMP:** 35 **EST:** 1980
**SQ FT:** 35,000
**SALES (est):** 9.7MM **Privately Held**
**WEB:** www.nationalcoatings.com
**SIC:** 2851 Paints & allied products; paints & paint additives

**(G-10770)**
**PEGASUS MFG INC**
1382 Enterprise Ave (61401-9380)
P.O. Box 1503 (61402-1503)
**PHONE**.................................309 342-9337
Ruth Whitehead, *President*
James Kinkade, *Director*
Lauretta Hayes, *Admin Sec*
Karen Delatorre, *Administration*
**EMP:** 15
**SQ FT:** 15,000
**SALES (est):** 2.2MM **Privately Held**
**SIC:** 3999 Atomizers, toiletry

**(G-10771)**
**PROGRESS RAIL SERVICES CORP**
618 Us Highway 150 E (61401-8311)
**PHONE**.................................309 343-6176
Billy Ainsworth, *Branch Mgr*
**EMP:** 6

**SALES (corp-wide):** 38.5B **Publicly Held**
**SIC:** 3399 Reclaiming ferrous metals from clay
**HQ:** Progress Rail Services Corporation
  1600 Progress Dr
  Albertville AL 35950
  256 593-1260

**(G-10772)**
**RBJ INC**
Also Called: Robbins Pallets
796 S Pearl St (61401-6159)
**PHONE**.................................309 344-5066
Rich L Robbins, *President*
Jason Robbins, *Vice Pres*
**EMP:** 15
**SALES (est):** 3MM **Privately Held**
**WEB:** www.robbinspallets.net
**SIC:** 2448 Wood pallets & skids

**(G-10773)**
**REGISTER-MAIL (HQ)**
Also Called: Galesburg Register Mail
140 S Prairie St (61401-4636)
P.O. Box 310 (61402-0310)
**PHONE**.................................309 343-7181
**Fax:** 309 342-5171
John Mc Connell, *President*
Don Cooper, *Publisher*
Robert Buck, *Editor*
Tom Martin, *Editor*
Mike Trueblood, *Editor*
**EMP:** 115 **EST:** 1898
**SQ FT:** 40,000
**SALES (est):** 11MM
**SALES (corp-wide):** 92.6MM **Privately Held**
**SIC:** 2711 2752 Newspapers, publishing & printing; commercial printing, lithographic
**PA:** The Copley Press Inc
  7776 Ivanhoe Ave
  La Jolla CA 92037
  858 454-0411

**(G-10774)**
**RJ RACE CARS INC**
300 N Linwood Rd (61401-3280)
**PHONE**.................................309 343-7575
**Fax:** 309 343-0886
Rick Jones, *President*
Bonnie Jones, *Treasurer*
Craig Whitaker, *Sales Mgr*
Shaun Clark, *Sales Staff*
Richard Weiss, *Branch Mgr*
**EMP:** 11
**SQ FT:** 5,000
**SALES (est):** 2MM **Privately Held**
**WEB:** www.rjracecars.com
**SIC:** 3711 3714 5531 Automobile assembly, including specialty automobiles; motor vehicle parts & accessories; speed shops, including race car supplies

**(G-10775)**
**ROYAL PUBLISHING INC**
Also Called: Royal Publishing Co
311 E Main St Ste 220 (61401-4879)
**PHONE**.................................309 343-4007
**Fax:** 309 343-4016
Nate Thomas, *Info Tech Dir*
John Nelson, *Systems Staff*
Blanche Shoup, *Exec Dir*
Pat Robert, *Executive*
**EMP:** 9
**SALES (corp-wide):** 7MM **Privately Held**
**WEB:** www.royalpublishing.com
**SIC:** 2731 7336 Pamphlets: publishing & printing; graphic arts & related design
**PA:** Royal Publishing, Inc.
  7620 N Harker Dr
  Peoria IL
  309 693-3171

**(G-10776)**
**SCHWARZ BROS MANUFACTURING CO**
584 E Brooks St (61401-5075)
**PHONE**.................................309 342-5814
Steven Gray, *President*
C Gray, *Treasurer*
**EMP:** 6 **EST:** 1940
**SQ FT:** 4,800
**SALES (est):** 858.2K **Privately Held**
**SIC:** 3544 Special dies & tools; jigs & fixtures

**(G-10777)**
**THE PARTS HOUSE**
343 S Kellogg St (61401-4969)
**PHONE**.................................309 343-0146
**Fax:** 309 343-4046
Steven Fransene, *President*
Jason Fransene, *Vice Pres*
Ed Yaeger, *Opers Mgr*
Teddi Shipp, *Treasurer*
**EMP:** 3
**SQ FT:** 23,000
**SALES (est):** 720K **Privately Held**
**SIC:** 3315 3496 Steel wire & related products; miscellaneous fabricated wire products

**(G-10778)**
**THRUSHWOOD FRMS QLTY MEATS INC**
2860 W Main St (61401-8502)
**PHONE**.................................309 343-5193
**Fax:** 309 343-1531
James Hankes, *President*
William Fugate, *Principal*
Ray Hankes, *Principal*
Kae Hankes, *Admin Sec*
**EMP:** 15
**SQ FT:** 7,500
**SALES (est):** 3.5MM **Privately Held**
**WEB:** www.thrushwoodfarms.com
**SIC:** 2011 Beef products from beef slaughtered on site

**(G-10779)**
**WESTERN ILLINOIS ENTERPRISES**
Also Called: Hansen Lumber Company
161 N Academy St (61401-3609)
P.O. Box 110 (61402-0110)
**PHONE**.................................309 342-5185
Dustin G Courson, *President*
Tammy Lufkin, *Vice Pres*
Dave Marshall, *Manager*
**EMP:** 9
**SALES (est):** 1.8MM **Privately Held**
**SIC:** 5211 2441 1751 Lumber & other building materials; millwork & lumber; planing mill products & lumber; shipping cases, wood: nailed or lock corner; cabinet & finish carpentry

**(G-10780)**
**WESTROCK CP LLC**
Also Called: Smurfit-Stone Container
775 S Linwood Rd (61401-9002)
P.O. Box 1268 (61402-1268)
**PHONE**.................................309 342-0121
**Fax:** 309 342-5554
Douglas P Hooks, *Prdtn Mgr*
Al Widman, *Manager*
Mark Grunder, *Manager*
Mark Newton, *Manager*
Rick Ivie, *Maintence Staff*
**EMP:** 130
**SALES (corp-wide):** 14.1B **Publicly Held**
**WEB:** www.smurfit-stone.com
**SIC:** 2653 2657 2631 5113 Corrugated & solid fiber boxes; folding paperboard boxes; paperboard mills; corrugated & solid fiber boxes
**HQ:** Westrock Cp, Llc
  504 Thrasher St
  Norcross GA 30071

## Galt
### Whiteside County

**(G-10781)**
**IFH GROUP INC**
5505 Anne St (61037)
**PHONE**.................................815 380-2367
**EMP:** 6
**SALES (corp-wide):** 23.3MM **Privately Held**
**SIC:** 3594 3443 Fluid power pumps; fuel tanks (oil, gas, etc.): metal plate
**PA:** The Ifh Group Inc
  3300 E Rock Falls Rd
  Rock Falls IL 61071
  800 435-7003

# Galva
*Henry County*

**(G-10782)**
**ALL-FEED PROC & PACKG INC**
717 W Division St (61434-1636)
PHONE.....................309 932-3119
Tim Shanahan, *Safety Dir*
Heather Anderson, *Branch Mgr*
**EMP:** 5
**SALES (corp-wide):** 2.1MM **Privately Held**
**WEB:** www.allfeed.com
**SIC:** 2048 Canned pet food (except dog & cat)
**PA:** All-Feed Processing And Packaging, Inc.
210 S 1st St
Alpha IL 61413
309 629-0001

**(G-10783)**
**BIG RIVER PRAIRIE GOLD LLC**
1100 Se 2nd St (61434-8907)
PHONE.....................319 753-1100
Raymond E Defenbaugh,
Andy Brader,
Roger Hubele,
Floyd Schultz,
Eugene Youngquist,
**EMP:** 5
**SALES:** 29.2K **Privately Held**
**SIC:** 2869 Industrial organic chemicals

**(G-10784)**
**BIG RIVER RESOURCES GALVA LLC**
1100 Se 2nd St (61434-8907)
PHONE.....................309 932-2033
Ray Defenbaugh, *President*
Windy Anderson, *Project Mgr*
Travis Sparks, *Production*
Jim Hall, *Finance Dir*
Les Allen,
**EMP:** 238
**SALES:** 244.9MM
**SALES (corp-wide):** 851.4MM **Privately Held**
**WEB:** www.bigriverresources.com
**SIC:** 2869 Ethyl alcohol, ethanol
**HQ:** Big River Resources West Burlington, Llc
15210 103rd St
West Burlington IA 52655
319 753-1100

**(G-10785)**
**BOB EVANS FARMS INC**
1001 Sw 2nd St (61434-1605)
PHONE.....................309 932-2194
**EMP:** 62
**SALES (corp-wide):** 1.6B **Publicly Held**
**SIC:** 2013 Mfg Prepared Meats
**PA:** Bob Evans Farms, Inc.
8111 Smiths Mill Rd
New Albany OH 43054
614 491-2225

**(G-10786)**
**BRANCHFIELD CASTING**
502 Se Industrial Ave (61434-8923)
P.O. Box 116 (61434-0116)
PHONE.....................309 932-2278
Tebie Hopping, *President*
Mark Compton, *Corp Secy*
J B Hopping, *Vice Pres*
Bonnie Rogers, *Manager*
**EMP:** 25
**SALES (est):** 3.5MM **Privately Held**
**SIC:** 3915 Jewelers' castings

**(G-10787)**
**DIXLINE CORPORATION (PA)**
Also Called: Thomson Casual Furniture Co
136 Exchange St (61434-1710)
P.O. Box 166 (61434-0166)
PHONE.....................309 932-2011
Fax: 309 932-3004
David E Thomson, *President*
David Fenton, *COO*
Martha Thomson, *Vice Pres*
Chris Kocan, *Controller*
Gale Clark, *Manager*
**EMP:** 15 **EST:** 1922
**SQ FT:** 2,000
**SALES (est):** 13.8MM **Privately Held**
**WEB:** www.dixline.com
**SIC:** 3469 3429 2514 3471 Metal stampings; casket hardware; lawn furniture: metal; finishing, metals or formed products; aluminum die-castings; miscellaneous metalwork

**(G-10788)**
**DIXLINE CORPORATION**
26 Sw 4th Ave (61434-1611)
P.O. Box 166 (61434-0166)
PHONE.....................309 932-2011
Willard Thomson, *President*
**EMP:** 80
**SALES (corp-wide):** 13.8MM **Privately Held**
**WEB:** www.dixline.com
**SIC:** 3429 3995 3471 3469 Casket hardware; burial caskets; plating & polishing; metal stampings; miscellaneous metalwork; aluminum die-castings
**PA:** Dixline Corporation
136 Exchange St
Galva IL 61434
309 932-2011

**(G-10789)**
**GALVA IRON AND METAL CO INC**
625 Se Industrial Ave (61434-8930)
P.O. Box 121 (61434-0121)
PHONE.....................309 932-3450
Fax: 309 932-2210
Jeff Schilling, *President*
Brian Kenney, *Office Mgr*
**EMP:** 7
**SQ FT:** 5,000
**SALES (est):** 930K **Privately Held**
**SIC:** 5093 5051 5072 5531 Scrap & waste materials; steel; chains; automotive & home supply stores; secondary nonferrous metals

**(G-10790)**
**J MAC METALS INC**
330 Se Industrial Ave (61434-8921)
P.O. Box 277 (61434-0277)
PHONE.....................309 822-2023
Adam Baze, *President*
Gary Baze, *Vice Pres*
**EMP:** 2
**SQ FT:** 8,000
**SALES (est):** 810K **Privately Held**
**SIC:** 3444 Metal roofing & roof drainage equipment

**(G-10791)**
**JOHN H BEST & SONS INC**
Also Called: Best Display Systems
1 Burlington Rd (61434-1481)
P.O. Box 293 (61434-0293)
PHONE.....................309 932-2127
Fax: 309 932-2127
Ronald A Pankau, *President*
Bob Hook, *CFO*
Amy Morse, *Sales Staff*
Paul Brody, *Manager*
Teresa O Pankau, *Admin Sec*
**EMP:** 38 **EST:** 1892
**SQ FT:** 45,000
**SALES (est):** 7.3MM **Privately Held**
**WEB:** www.jhbest.com
**SIC:** 2542 3599 Racks, merchandise display or storage: except wood; machine shop, jobbing & repair

**(G-10792)**
**LMT INC**
1105 Se 2nd St (61434-8911)
PHONE.....................309 932-3311
Fax: 309 932-3155
Michael Fenneman, *President*
Tim Kitterman, *Manager*
Natalie Pearson, *Admin Sec*
◆ **EMP:** 16
**SQ FT:** 33,000
**SALES (est):** 4.2MM **Privately Held**
**SIC:** 3523 Farm machinery & equipment

# Garden Prairie
*Boone County*

**(G-10793)**
**CCSI INTERNATIONAL INC**
Also Called: Garden Prrie Pool Spa Enclsres
8642 Us Highway 20 (61038-9531)
PHONE.....................815 544-8385
Russell Caldwell, *Ch of Bd*
Cynthia Caldwell, *Corp Secy*
Thomas Caldwell, *Vice Pres*
Charles Caldwel, *Shareholder*
▲ **EMP:** 30
**SQ FT:** 23,000
**SALES (est):** 4MM **Privately Held**
**WEB:** www.ccsiusa.com
**SIC:** 3949 1761 Water sports equipment; skylight installation

**(G-10794)**
**GARDEN PRAIRIE ORGANICS LLC**
11887 Us Rt 20 (61038)
PHONE.....................815 597-1318
Michael Dimucci,
Robert Dimucci,
**EMP:** 4
**SALES (est):** 386.6K **Privately Held**
**SIC:** 2875 Fertilizers, mixing only

**(G-10795)**
**MACHOLL METAL FABRICATION**
6934 Garden Prairie Rd (61038-9702)
PHONE.....................815 597-1908
Jack Macholl, *Principal*
**EMP:** 2
**SALES (est):** 233.2K **Privately Held**
**SIC:** 3499 Fabricated metal products

# Geneseo
*Henry County*

**(G-10796)**
**ALL IN STITCHES**
100 E Main St (61254-1566)
PHONE.....................309 944-4084
Fax: 309 944-2345
Jan Dahl, *Owner*
**EMP:** 8
**SQ FT:** 5,000
**SALES (est):** 746.6K **Privately Held**
**SIC:** 2395 5137 Embroidery & art needlework; embroidery products, except schiffli machine; women's & children's outerwear; women's & children's sportswear & swimsuits; women's & children's dresses, suits, skirts & blouses

**(G-10797)**
**ALLQUIP CO INC**
524 E Exchange St (61254-2108)
P.O. Box 347 (61254-0347)
PHONE.....................309 944-6153
Fax: 309 944-5148
Raymond Pribble, *President*
Lona Pribble, *Corp Secy*
**EMP:** 6
**SQ FT:** 11,000
**SALES (est):** 1MM **Privately Held**
**SIC:** 5084 3325 3444 3443 Materials handling machinery; steel foundries; sheet metalwork; fabricated plate work (boiler shop); fabricated structural metal; manufactured hardware (general)

**(G-10798)**
**AR1510 LLC**
Also Called: Armalite
745 Hanford St (61254-1603)
P.O. Box 299 (61254-0299)
PHONE.....................309 944-6939
Fax: 309 944-6949
Jared Sprunger, *General Mgr*
Rich Wanicki, *Purchasing*
Shawn Driscoll, *Comptroller*
Julie Van Overberg, *Sales Mgr*
Bob Schanen, *Marketing Staff*
**EMP:** 12
**SQ FT:** 13,000
**SALES (est):** 3.2MM **Privately Held**
**WEB:** www.armalite.com
**SIC:** 3484 5941 Machine guns & grenade launchers; sporting goods & bicycle shops
**PA:** Strategic Armory Corps, Llc
48955 Moccasin Trail Rd
Prague OK 74864

**(G-10799)**
**BRIDGE CITY MECHANICAL INC**
777 E Culver Ct (61254-1851)
P.O. Box 176 (61254-0176)
PHONE.....................309 944-4873
Martin Kauzlarich, *President*
Deborah Kauzlarich, *Treasurer*
**EMP:** 15 **EST:** 2001
**SALES (est):** 1.2MM **Privately Held**
**SIC:** 3441 Fabricated structural metal

**(G-10800)**
**CULMAC INC**
Also Called: Delta Sales
720 Hanford St Ste 2 (61254-1604)
P.O. Box 182 (61254-0182)
PHONE.....................309 944-5197
Fax: 309 944-6495
**EMP:** 21 **EST:** 1975
**SQ FT:** 6,000
**SALES (est):** 1.7MM **Privately Held**
**SIC:** 3554 3555 Paper industries machinery; printing trades machinery

**(G-10801)**
**INNOVATIVE MACHINE INC**
925 Dilenbeck Dr (61254-1650)
PHONE.....................309 945-9445
Fax: 309 945-9446
Kim M McCubbin, *President*
**EMP:** 7
**SQ FT:** 2,400
**SALES (est):** 1.2MM **Privately Held**
**SIC:** 3599 Machine shop, jobbing & repair

**(G-10802)**
**LIBERTY GROUP PUBLISHING (PA)**
Also Called: Geneseo Republic, The
108 W 1st St (61254-1342)
PHONE.....................309 944-1779
Fax: 309 944-5615
Tim Evans, *Principal*
Mindy Carls, *Advt Staff*
Cathy Terry, *Shareholder*
Karry Wheelhouse, *Admin Sec*
**EMP:** 15 **EST:** 1856
**SALES (est):** 1.6MM **Privately Held**
**WEB:** www.geneseorepublic.com
**SIC:** 2711 2741 Job printing & newspaper publishing combined; shopping news: publishing & printing

**(G-10803)**
**M & B SUPPLY INC**
208 W 1st St (61254-1344)
PHONE.....................309 944-3206
Fax: 309 944-6754
Scott Cocquit, *President*
William Heller, *Vice Pres*
**EMP:** 12
**SQ FT:** 5,600
**SALES (est):** 1.1MM **Privately Held**
**SIC:** 2721 8999 Statistical reports (periodicals): publishing only; technical manual preparation

**(G-10804)**
**SIVCO WELDING COMPANY**
624 E Prospect St (61254-1828)
PHONE.....................309 944-5171
Fax: 309 944-5172
Irvin Venter, *President*
Karen Venter, *Vice Pres*
**EMP:** 5
**SQ FT:** 10,000
**SALES (est):** 1MM **Privately Held**
**SIC:** 7692 3441 Welding repair; fabricated structural metal

**(G-10805)**
**SPRINGFIELD INC**
Also Called: Springfield Armory
420 W Main St (61254-1524)
PHONE.....................309 944-5631
Fax: 309 944-3676
Tom Reese, *President*

# GEOGRAPHIC SECTION
## Geneva - Kane County (G-10832)

Mike Doy, *Facilities Mgr*
Keith Stage, *Warehouse Mgr*
Donna Rahn, *Sls & Mktg Exec*
Ron Diekminn, *Controller*
▲ **EMP:** 170
**SQ FT:** 32,860
**SALES (est):** 80.2MM **Privately Held**
**WEB:** www.springfieldarmory.com
**SIC:** 3484 Small arms

**(G-10806)**
**SWAN MANUFACTURING CO**
62 Crestview Cir (61254-9540)
**PHONE**.....................................309 441-6985
Steven M Swan, *Owner*
**EMP:** 20
**SALES (est):** 682.5K **Privately Held**
**WEB:** www.swanmanufacturing.com
**SIC:** 3999 Manufacturing industries

## Geneva
### Kane County

**(G-10807)**
**ALL SIGNS & WONDERS CO**
1020 W Fabyan Pkwy (60134-3104)
**PHONE**.....................................630 232-9019
**Fax:** 630 232-2485
Victor Covarrubias, *Owner*
**EMP:** 2
**SALES (est):** 810K **Privately Held**
**SIC:** 5099 3993 Signs, except electric; signs & advertising specialties

**(G-10808)**
**ALLIED RIVET INC**
1172 Commerce Dr (60134-2484)
**PHONE**.....................................630 208-0120
**Fax:** 630 208-0562
Steven O Hindi, *President*
Jacquelyn J Hindi, *Vice Pres*
Brian Prodoehl, *Vice Pres*
Bernard Bauer, *Accounts Mgr*
**EMP:** 14
**SQ FT:** 17,500
**SALES (est):** 1.7MM **Privately Held**
**WEB:** www.alliedrivet.com
**SIC:** 3452 Bolts, nuts, rivets & washers

**(G-10809)**
**AMERICAN TRISTAR INC**
2089 Pillsbury Dr (60134-3731)
**PHONE**.....................................630 262-5500
John Russo, *Plant Mgr*
**EMP:** 3
**SALES (corp-wide):** 60.6B **Privately Held**
**SIC:** 2099 Food preparations
**HQ:** American Tristar, Inc.
    525 Dunham Rd
    Saint Charles IL 60174
    920 872-2181

**(G-10810)**
**ARGENTUM MEDICAL LLC**
2571 Kaneville Ct (60134-2505)
**PHONE**.....................................888 551-0188
Lynn Uvodich, *Controller*
Judy Blaeser, *Marketing Staff*
Raul Brizuela,
**EMP:** 20
**SALES (est):** 4MM **Privately Held**
**SIC:** 3842 3841 Surgical appliances & supplies; surgical & medical instruments

**(G-10811)**
**BANNON ENTERPRISES INC**
2627 Lorraine Cir (60134-4418)
**PHONE**.....................................847 529-9265
Gerald Bannon, *President*
Maureen Bannon, *Vice Pres*
**EMP:** 3
**SALES:** 100K **Privately Held**
**SIC:** 3089 Organizers for closets, drawers, etc.: plastic

**(G-10812)**
**BLUE CHIP CONSTRUCTION INC**
435 Stevens St (60134-1361)
**PHONE**.....................................630 208-5254
**EMP:** 11
**SQ FT:** 12,000
**SALES (est):** 1MM **Privately Held**
**SIC:** 2431 Architectural Woodwork

**(G-10813)**
**BURGESS-NORTON MFG CO INC (HQ)**
737 Peyton St (60134-2189)
**PHONE**.....................................630 232-4100
**Fax:** 630 232-3634
Brett E Vasseuer, *President*
Robert Douthat, *General Mgr*
David Xu, *General Mgr*
Brian Dalisay, *Business Mgr*
Brice Barker, *Vice Pres*
▲ **EMP:** 277
**SALES (est):** 145.1MM
**SALES (corp-wide):** 1.9B **Privately Held**
**SIC:** 3399 3592 3452 Powder, metal; pistons & piston rings; pins
**PA:** Amsted Industries Incorporated
    180 N Stetson Ave
    Chicago IL 60601
    312 645-1700

**(G-10814)**
**BURGESS-NORTON MFG CO INC**
500 Western Ave (60134-3083)
**PHONE**.....................................630 232-4100
Donni Hess, *Branch Mgr*
**EMP:** 25
**SALES (corp-wide):** 1.9B **Privately Held**
**SIC:** 3321 3363 3452 3463 Gray & ductile iron foundries; aluminum die-castings; bolts, nuts, rivets & washers; engine or turbine forgings, nonferrous
**HQ:** Burgess-Norton Mfg. Co., Inc.
    737 Peyton St
    Geneva IL 60134
    630 232-4100

**(G-10815)**
**BURNING LEAF CIGARS**
577 S 3rd St Ste 101 (60134-2758)
**PHONE**.....................................815 267-3570
Jamal Hussein, *Owner*
Lucinda Sanchez-Huss, *Manager*
▲ **EMP:** 2
**SQ FT:** 7,000
**SALES:** 200K **Privately Held**
**SIC:** 2121 Cigars

**(G-10816)**
**C R KESNER COMPANY**
2520 Kaneville Ct (60134-2506)
**PHONE**.....................................630 232-8118
Rudy C Kesner, *President*
**EMP:** 7
**SQ FT:** 7,500
**SALES:** 2MM **Privately Held**
**SIC:** 5047 3842 Hospital equipment & supplies; surgical appliances & supplies

**(G-10817)**
**CHRONICLE NEWSPAPERS INC**
1000 Randall Rd (60134-2590)
**PHONE**.....................................630 845-5247
**Fax:** 630 232-4962
Lee Husfeldt, *Principal*
**EMP:** 9
**SALES (est):** 459.6K **Privately Held**
**SIC:** 2711 Newspapers

**(G-10818)**
**CLC LUBRICANTS COMPANY (PA)**
0n902 Old Kirk Rd (60134)
P.O. Box 764 (60134-0764)
**PHONE**.....................................630 232-7900
**Fax:** 630 232-7915
Patrick T O'Brien, *President*
Mike O'Brien, *Vice Pres*
Gary Hartung, *Plant Mgr*
Donna Pelletier, *Purchasing*
Dan Piet, *Sales Mgr*
**EMP:** 25 **EST:** 1966
**SQ FT:** 27,000
**SALES (est):** 5.7MM **Privately Held**
**WEB:** www.clclubricants.com
**SIC:** 2992 2899 2842 Oils & greases, blending & compounding; cutting oils, blending: made from purchased materials; chemical preparations; specialty cleaning, polishes & sanitation goods

**(G-10819)**
**COACH INC**
306 Commons Dr (60134-2524)
**PHONE**.....................................630 232-0667
**Fax:** 630 232-0506
Lindsay Navarro, *Manager*
**EMP:** 15
**SALES (corp-wide):** 4.4B **Publicly Held**
**WEB:** www.coach.com
**SIC:** 3171 Handbags, women's
**PA:** Coach, Inc.
    10 Hudson Yards
    New York NY 10001
    212 594-1850

**(G-10820)**
**COILFORM COMPANY (PA)**
2571 Kaneville Ct (60134-2505)
**PHONE**.....................................630 232-8000
**Fax:** 630 232-8005
Richard M Mc Farlane, *President*
**EMP:** 4 **EST:** 1955
**SQ FT:** 25,000
**SALES (est):** 2.8MM **Privately Held**
**WEB:** www.coilform.com
**SIC:** 3677 3621 3083 Electronic coils, transformers & other inductors; motors & generators; laminated plastics plate & sheet

**(G-10821)**
**CPR PRINTING INC (PA)**
321 Stevens St Ste E (60134-1318)
**PHONE**.....................................630 377-8420
**Fax:** 630 377-8584
Pat Hofstetter, *President*
Mindy Hofstetter, *Vice Pres*
**EMP:** 10
**SQ FT:** 5,000
**SALES:** 600K **Privately Held**
**SIC:** 2752 2796 2791 2789 Commercial printing, lithographic; platemaking services; typesetting; bookbinding & related work

**(G-10822)**
**CY LASER LLC**
65 N River Ln Ste 209 (60134-2268)
**PHONE**.....................................630 208-1931
Massimo Denipoti, *Principal*
▲ **EMP:** 3
**SALES (est):** 385.4K **Privately Held**
**SIC:** 3552 Fiber & yarn preparation machinery & equipment

**(G-10823)**
**DENTAL LABORATORY INC**
Also Called: Merrimac Lab
37w391 Keslinger Rd (60134-3914)
**PHONE**.....................................630 262-3700
**Fax:** 630 262-3702
Paul I Ema, *President*
Connie Rempala, *Senior VP*
Andrea C Ema, *Admin Sec*
**EMP:** 39
**SALES (est):** 2.7MM **Privately Held**
**WEB:** www.dentallaboratory.com
**SIC:** 8072 5047 3843 Dental laboratories; dentists' professional supplies; dental equipment & supplies

**(G-10824)**
**DERMATIQUE LASER & SKIN**
407 S 3rd St Ste 240 (60134-2744)
**PHONE**.....................................630 262-2515
Gina Lesnik, *Owner*
Lora Kassaros, *Practice Mgr*
**EMP:** 11
**SALES (est):** 1.3MM **Privately Held**
**SIC:** 3845 Laser systems & equipment, medical

**(G-10825)**
**DESIGN MERCHANTS**
Also Called: Garden Impression
125 S 7th St (60134-2627)
**PHONE**.....................................630 208-1850
**Fax:** 630 208-0630
Albert J Ochsner, *Owner*
Lorraine Ochsner, *Co-Owner*
**EMP:** 3
**SALES (est):** 103.5K **Privately Held**
**WEB:** www.gardenimpressions.com
**SIC:** 3999 Artificial flower arrangements

**(G-10826)**
**DYNAWAVE CORPORATION**
2520 Kaneville Ct (60134-2587)
**PHONE**.....................................630 232-4945
**Fax:** 630 232-7042
Rudy C Kesner, *President*
Keith Kesner, *Vice Pres*
**EMP:** 10
**SQ FT:** 7,500
**SALES:** 2MM **Privately Held**
**SIC:** 3674 Solid state electronic devices

**(G-10827)**
**FONA INTERNATIONAL INC (PA)**
1900 Averill Rd (60134-1601)
**PHONE**.....................................630 578-8600
**Fax:** 630 578-8601
Joseph James Slawek, *CEO*
Luke Slawek, *COO*
Amy McDonald, *Vice Pres*
Mary Slawek, *Vice Pres*
Tj Widuch, *Vice Pres*
▲ **EMP:** 33
**SQ FT:** 82,000
**SALES (est):** 87.5MM **Privately Held**
**WEB:** www.fona.com
**SIC:** 2087 Extracts, flavoring; syrups, flavoring (except drink)

**(G-10828)**
**FONA UK LTD**
1900 Averill Rd (60134-1601)
**PHONE**.....................................331 442-5779
Joseph Slawek, *CEO*
**EMP:** 200
**SALES (corp-wide):** 87.5MM **Privately Held**
**SIC:** 2087 Extracts, flavoring; syrups, flavoring (except drink)
**HQ:** Fona Uk Ltd
    New Bridge Street House
    London

**(G-10829)**
**GALENA GARLIC CO**
318 W State St (60134-2103)
**PHONE**.....................................331 248-0342
Laszlo Marton, *Principal*
**EMP:** 2
**SALES (est):** 249.5K **Privately Held**
**SIC:** 3556 Food products machinery

**(G-10830)**
**GENEVA GLASSWORKS INC**
Also Called: Geneva Glass Works
560 Lark St Bldg C (60134-2527)
P.O. Box 76, Wasco (60183-0076)
**PHONE**.....................................630 232-1200
**Fax:** 630 232-2151
Mike Busch, *President*
**EMP:** 3
**SQ FT:** 3,000
**SALES (est):** 358.7K **Privately Held**
**SIC:** 3231 Products of purchased glass

**(G-10831)**
**GENEVA RUNNING OUTFITTERS LLC**
221 W State St (60134-2255)
**PHONE**.....................................331 248-0221
Elizabeth Ott, *Principal*
**EMP:** 6
**SALES (est):** 633.9K **Privately Held**
**SIC:** 3949 Sporting & athletic goods

**(G-10832)**
**HOUGHTON MIFFLIN HARCOURT**
1900 S Batavia Ave (60134-3310)
**PHONE**.....................................928 467-9599
**Fax:** 630 232-2568
Gary Greenwood, *Principal*
Ledbetter Mark, *Vice Pres*
Klaus Weber, *Engineer*
Rosemary Lemke, *Human Resources*
Jon Jacobs, *Program Mgr*
◆ **EMP:** 21
**SALES (est):** 1.6MM **Privately Held**
**SIC:** 2741 Miscellaneous publishing

## Geneva - Kane County (G-10833)

**(G-10833)**
**HOUGHTON MIFFLIN HARCOURT PUBG**
Holt McDougal
1900 S Batavia Ave  (60134-3310)
**PHONE** ................................ 630 208-5704
William Rader, *Editor*
Jess Toland, *Vice Pres*
Tricia Stewart, *Vice Pres*
Stephanie Mette, *Accounts Exec*
Randall Peestal, *Manager*
**EMP:** 250
**SALES (corp-wide):** 1.3B  **Publicly Held**
**WEB:** www.hmco.com
**SIC: 2731**  Textbooks; publishing & printing
**HQ:** Houghton Mifflin Harcourt Publishing Company
125 High St Ste 900
Boston MA 02110
617 351-5000

**(G-10834)**
**INDUSTRIAL HARD CHROME LTD**
501 Fluid Power Dr  (60134-1181)
**PHONE** ................................ 630 208-7000
**Fax:** 630 208-7035
C G Therkildsen, *President*
Dave Hahne, *Vice Pres*
Fred Parker, *Vice Pres*
Rich Peterson, *VP Opers*
Bruce Busse, *VP Mfg*
**EMP:** 120 **EST:** 1955
**SQ FT:** 84,000
**SALES (est):** 20.6MM  **Privately Held**
**SIC: 3471**  Electroplating of metals or formed products

**(G-10835)**
**INDUSTRIAL STEEL CNSTR INC (PA)**
413 Old Kirk Rd  (60134)
P.O. Box 323  (60134-0323)
**PHONE** ................................ 630 232-7473
**Fax:** 630 232-7492
Joseph R Hish, *President*
Michael Mariano, *Treasurer*
Dorothy Avigiano, *Admin Sec*
**EMP:** 5
**SALES (est):** 38.1MM  **Privately Held**
**WEB:** www.iscbridge.com
**SIC: 3441**  Fabricated structural metal; fabricated structural metal for bridges

**(G-10836)**
**INITIAL IMPRESSIONS INC**
405 Stevens St  (60134-1361)
**PHONE** ................................ 630 208-9399
Rick Carlson, *President*
Mary Carlson, *Vice Pres*
**EMP:** 5
**SQ FT:** 3,000
**SALES:** 400K  **Privately Held**
**WEB:** www.initialimpressions.com
**SIC: 3552**  Embroidery machines

**(G-10837)**
**INNOVA PRINT FULFILLMENT INC**
2000 S Batavia Ave # 310  (60134-3303)
**PHONE** ................................ 630 845-3215
Steve Kuhn, *President*
Richard Kennedy, *Human Res Dir*
Kim Chisholm, *Manager*
**EMP:** 6
**SALES (est):** 868.7K  **Privately Held**
**SIC: 2752**  Commercial printing, lithographic

**(G-10838)**
**INNOVATIVE MOLECULAR DIAGNOSTI**
Also Called: Imds
1436 Fargo Blvd  (60134-2979)
**PHONE** ................................ 630 845-8246
Vijai K Pasupuleti, *CEO*
**EMP:** 1
**SALES:** 260K  **Privately Held**
**SIC: 2835** 5169  In vitro & in vivo diagnostic substances; industrial chemicals

**(G-10839)**
**INTERNTNAL INGREDIENT MALL LLC**
Also Called: Fona International
1900 Averill Rd  (60134-1601)
**PHONE** ................................ 630 462-1414
Bill Slawk, *CEO*
**EMP:** 3
**SALES (est):** 210.2K  **Privately Held**
**SIC: 2087**  Flavoring extracts & syrups

**(G-10840)**
**ITS A GIRL THING**
618 W State St  (60134-2106)
**PHONE** ................................ 630 232-2778
Mary Sinacore, *Owner*
**EMP:** 10
**SALES (est):** 854.4K  **Privately Held**
**SIC: 2339**  Women's & misses' accessories

**(G-10841)**
**JAMES STREET DENTAL P C**
22 James St Ste 3  (60134-4513)
**PHONE** ................................ 630 232-9535
Laurie Slavik, *Principal*
**EMP:** 8
**SALES (est):** 797.9K  **Privately Held**
**SIC: 3843**  Enamels, dentists'

**(G-10842)**
**JOHNSON CONTRLS BTRY GROUP INC**
300 S Glengarry Dr  (60134-3803)
**PHONE** ................................ 630 232-4270
**Fax:** 630 232-4277
Ray Chandler, *Safety Mgr*
Donna Brucher, *Personnel*
Tom Kreider, *Manager*
Linda Fieldstad, *Manager*
Jack Huisingh, *Manager*
**EMP:** 325  **Privately Held**
**SIC: 3691** 5063  Storage batteries; storage batteries, industrial
**HQ:** Johnson Controls Battery Group Inc.
5757 N Green Bay Ave
Milwaukee WI 53209

**(G-10843)**
**JOHNSONS SCREEN PRINTING**
419 Stevens St Ste C  (60134-1392)
**PHONE** ................................ 630 262-8210
Tom Johnson, *Owner*
**EMP:** 4
**SALES (est):** 365.1K  **Privately Held**
**SIC: 2752**  Commercial printing, lithographic

**(G-10844)**
**LAKELAND PALLETS INC**
2080 Gary Ln Ste 3  (60134-2582)
**PHONE** ................................ 616 949-9515
Bruce Kintop, *Manager*
**EMP:** 3
**SALES (corp-wide):** 4.2MM  **Privately Held**
**SIC: 2448**  Pallets, wood & wood with metal
**PA:** Lakeland Pallets, Inc.
3801 Kraft Ave Se
Grand Rapids MI 49512
616 949-9515

**(G-10845)**
**LAMAR OWINGS**
730 Forrest Ave  (60134-3040)
**PHONE** ................................ 630 232-0564
Lamar Owings, *Owner*
**EMP:** 3
**SALES (est):** 173.7K  **Privately Held**
**SIC: 2899**  Chemical preparations

**(G-10846)**
**LION PRODUCTIONS LLC**
619 Campbell St  (60134-2636)
**PHONE** ................................ 630 845-1610
Vincent Tornatore, *Mng Member*
**EMP:** 2
**SALES (est):** 224.2K  **Privately Held**
**SIC: 3652**  Phonograph records, prerecorded

**(G-10847)**
**LUCK E STRIKE CORPORATION**
Also Called: Luck E Strike USA
2100 Enterprise Ave  (60134-4101)
**PHONE** ................................ 630 313-2408
Jeffrey Lee, *President*
Cindy Angelus, *General Mgr*
▲ **EMP:** 15
**SQ FT:** 30,000
**SALES (est):** 2.5MM  **Privately Held**
**SIC: 3949**  Lures, fishing: artificial

**(G-10848)**
**MINER ELASTOMER PRODUCTS CORP**
1200 E State St  (60134-2440)
P.O. Box 471  (60134-0471)
**PHONE** ................................ 630 232-3000
**Fax:** 630 232-3177
David W Withall, *Ch of Bd*
Richard J Beranek, *President*
Gary A Withall, *Exec VP*
Edward Hahn, *Mfg Dir*
Carrie Edwards, *Purchasing*
▲ **EMP:** 35
**SQ FT:** 22,000
**SALES (est):** 8.2MM
**SALES (corp-wide):** 69MM  **Privately Held**
**WEB:** www.minerelastomer.com
**SIC: 2821**  Elastomers, nonvulcanizable (plastics)
**PA:** Miner Enterprises Inc
1200 E State St
Geneva IL 60134
630 232-3000

**(G-10849)**
**MINER ENTERPRISES INC (PA)**
Also Called: W H Miner Div
1200 E State St  (60134-2493)
P.O. Box 471  (60134-0471)
**PHONE** ................................ 630 232-3000
**Fax:** 630 232-3123
David W Withall, *President*
John Vitkus, *Vice Pres*
Jeffrey Ballerini, *Buyer*
Tom Ekstrom, *Technical Mgr*
Ken James, *Engineer*
◆ **EMP:** 130
**SQ FT:** 211,000
**SALES (est):** 69MM  **Privately Held**
**WEB:** www.minerent.com
**SIC: 3743**  Railroad equipment

**(G-10850)**
**MINING INTERNATIONAL LLC**
719 Shady Ave  (60134-3073)
**PHONE** ................................ 630 232-4246
Kay Stoupa, *Controller*
Gerard J Keating, 
**EMP:** 18
**SQ FT:** 2,000
**SALES (est):** 1.8MM  **Privately Held**
**WEB:** www.keatingresources.com
**SIC: 1422**  Limestones, ground

**(G-10851)**
**NATIONAL BINDING SUPS EQP INC**
39w254 Sheldon Ct  (60134-6043)
**PHONE** ................................ 630 801-7600
Ken Vedder, *President*
Maureen Vedder, *Vice Pres*
**EMP:** 6
**SALES (est):** 400K  **Privately Held**
**WEB:** www.digitalprairie.com
**SIC: 2789**  Binding & repair of books, magazines & pamphlets

**(G-10852)**
**NAVIGO TECHNOLOGIES LLC**
1770 S Randall Rd Ste 161  (60134-4646)
**PHONE** ................................ 312 560-9257
Vince Lo Faso, *Principal*
**EMP:** 3
**SALES (est):** 324.7K  **Privately Held**
**SIC: 3812**  Navigational systems & instruments

**(G-10853)**
**NEW YORK & COMPANY INC**
Also Called: Lerner New York
410 Commons Dr  (60134-2518)
**PHONE** ................................ 630 232-7693
**Fax:** 630 232-7693
Melanie Towalski, *Manager*
**EMP:** 17
**SALES (corp-wide):** 929MM  **Publicly Held**
**WEB:** www.nyco.com
**SIC: 5621** 2389 5137  Women's specialty clothing stores; men's miscellaneous accessories; women's & children's clothing
**PA:** New York & Company, Inc.
330 W 34th St Fl 9
New York NY 10001
212 884-2000

**(G-10854)**
**O BRIEN BILL**
Also Called: K B Sales & Service
0n175 Alexander Dr  (60134-6023)
**PHONE** ................................ 630 980-5571
Bill O'Brien, *Owner*
**EMP:** 3
**SALES (est):** 243.9K  **Privately Held**
**SIC: 5087** 5051 3599  Cleaning & maintenance equipment & supplies; iron & steel (ferrous) products; machine shop, jobbing & repair

**(G-10855)**
**OASIS INTERNATIONAL LIMITED**
Also Called: Oak Foundation
1770 S Randall Rd Ste A  (60134-4646)
**PHONE** ................................ 630 326-0045
Mathew Eliott, *President*
Edward Elliot, *Chairman*
**EMP:** 3
**SQ FT:** 400
**SALES:** 580.8K  **Privately Held**
**WEB:** www.oasisint.net
**SIC: 2731**  Book publishing

**(G-10856)**
**OLIVE OIL STORE INC (PA)**
Also Called: Olive Mill, The
315 James St  (60134-2114)
**PHONE** ................................ 630 262-0210
Ed O Connell, *Principal*
**EMP:** 3
**SALES (est):** 18.1MM  **Privately Held**
**SIC: 2079**  Vegetable shortenings (except corn oil)

**(G-10857)**
**OLON INDUSTRIES INC (US) (HQ)**
Also Called: Olon Decoratives
411 Union St  (60134-1367)
**PHONE** ................................ 630 232-4705
Don Hambly, *President*
John Kozuch, *Vice Pres*
Greg Kavoch, *Opers Staff*
Ernie Saberieno, *CFO*
Craig Cacheson, *Controller*
▲ **EMP:** 23
**SQ FT:** 40,000
**SALES (est):** 17MM
**SALES (corp-wide):** 21.8MM  **Privately Held**
**WEB:** www.olon.com
**SIC: 3083**  Laminated plastic sheets
**PA:** Errion Group Inc
42 Armstrong Ave
Georgetown ON L7G 4
905 877-7300

**(G-10858)**
**OLON INDUSTRIES INC (US)**
411 Union St  (60134-1367)
**PHONE** ................................ 630 232-4705
Aaron Selby, *Production*
Terry L Elliott, *Sales Mgr*
Kevin Kirby, *Sales Mgr*
Richard Locke, *Branch Mgr*
**EMP:** 43
**SALES (corp-wide):** 21.8MM  **Privately Held**
**SIC: 3083** 3599 2891  Laminated plastics plate & sheet; machine & other job shop work; adhesives & sealants
**HQ:** Olon Industries Inc. (Us)
411 Union St
Geneva IL 60134
630 232-4705

**(G-10859)**
**PHILLIP C COWEN**
106 7th Pl  (60134-2100)
**PHONE** ................................ 630 208-1848
Phillip Cowen, *Owner*
**EMP:** 40

# GEOGRAPHIC SECTION

## Genoa - Dekalb County (G-10885)

SALES (est): 2.6MM **Privately Held**
SIC: 3399 3316 Primary metal products; cold finishing of steel shapes

### (G-10860)
**PROVENA RANDALWOOD OPEN MRI**
110 James St (60134-2242)
PHONE..................630 587-9917
Derrick Oregon, *Principal*
EMP: 20
SALES (est): 1MM **Privately Held**
SIC: 3841 Diagnostic apparatus, medical

### (G-10861)
**R & R CREATIVE GRAPHICS INC**
Also Called: Mid West Investors Solutions
111 N Northampton Dr (60134-1802)
PHONE..................630 208-4724
Roger Brown, *President*
▲ EMP: 2
SALES (est): 1MM **Privately Held**
SIC: 5112 5199 7389 2752 Business forms; advertising specialties; packaging & labeling services; commercial printing, offset

### (G-10862)
**RICHARDSON RFPD INC (HQ)**
1950 S Batavia Ave # 100 (60134-3332)
PHONE..................630 262-6800
Fax: 630 208-2661
Edward J Richardson, *CEO*
Paul Reilly, *President*
Eckart Seitter, *Senior VP*
Maxine McReynolds, *Buyer*
Jim Dudek, *Controller*
▲ EMP: 3
SALES (est): 2.4MM
SALES (corp-wide): 23.8B **Publicly Held**
SIC: 3629 Power conversion units, a.c. to d.c.: static-electric
PA: Arrow Electronics, Inc.
9201 E Dry Creek Rd
Centennial CO 80112
303 824-4000

### (G-10863)
**RIVER BANK LABORATORIES INC**
18 S 8th St (60134-2002)
P.O. Box 110 (60134-0110)
PHONE..................630 232-2207
Fax: 630 232-7606
Robert Swanson, *President*
Jack Martin, *Vice Pres*
Mary Robinson, *Vice Pres*
EMP: 16 EST: 1904
SALES (est): 3.2MM **Privately Held**
WEB: www.riverbanklabs.com
SIC: 3841 Surgical & medical instruments

### (G-10864)
**ROQUETTE AMERICA INC**
2211 Innovation Dr (60134-1602)
PHONE..................630 232-2157
EMP: 5 EST: 1981
SALES (est): 440K **Privately Held**
SIC: 2041 Mfg Flour/Grain Mill Prooducts

### (G-10865)
**S & N MANUFACTURING INC**
455 Stevens St (60134-1361)
PHONE..................630 232-0275
Fax: 630 232-7003
Nancy G Paganessi, *President*
Jennifer Paganessi, *Corp Secy*
Arthur B Paganessi, *Vice Pres*
EMP: 22
SQ FT: 10,000
SALES (est): 4.4MM **Privately Held**
WEB: www.snmfg.com
SIC: 3625 Solenoid switches (industrial controls)

### (G-10866)
**SHADING SOLUTIONS GROUP INC**
1770 S Randall Rd A172 (60134-4646)
PHONE..................630 444-2102
Joseph F Diffendal, *President*
Laz Szabo, *Vice Pres*
Jacqueline Diffendal, *Admin Sec*
Mary Diffendal, *Admin Sec*
EMP: 2

SALES: 200K **Privately Held**
WEB: www.cardiffindustries.com
SIC: 2394 8611 Shades, canvas: made from purchased materials; contractors' association

### (G-10867)
**SILVESTRI SWEETS INC**
Also Called: Carousel Candies
2248 Gary Ln (60134-2519)
PHONE..................630 232-2500
Fax: 630 656-0010
Mary Jane Silvestri, *President*
J Andrew Silvestri, *Principal*
Joe Silvestri, *Manager*
▲ EMP: 10
SQ FT: 12,000
SALES (est): 1.9MM **Privately Held**
WEB: www.carouselcandy.com
SIC: 2064 Candy & other confectionery products

### (G-10868)
**SMITH & RICHARDSON MFG CO**
727 May St (60134-1379)
P.O. Box 589 (60134-0589)
PHONE..................630 232-2581
Fax: 630 232-2610
Phil Cowen, *CEO*
W Richard Hoster III, *President*
Rene Schroer, *Vice Pres*
Matt Liebert, *Plant Engr*
Anna Kelley, *Accountant*
▲ EMP: 38
SQ FT: 66,000
SALES (est): 9MM **Privately Held**
WEB: www.smithandrichardson.com
SIC: 3469 Stamping metal for the trade

### (G-10869)
**STEEL MANAGEMENT INC**
716 Natwill Sq (60134-2073)
PHONE..................630 397-5083
Robert Harrington, *President*
EMP: 1 EST: 1997
SALES (est): 216K **Privately Held**
SIC: 3441 Fabricated structural metal

### (G-10870)
**STRATHMORE COMPANY**
2000 Gary Ln (60134-2500)
P.O. Box 391 (60134-0391)
PHONE..................630 232-9677
Fax: 630 232-0198
Chang Park, *President*
John Park, *VP Opers*
Guy Geiger, *Project Mgr*
Don Hoffer, *Purch Mgr*
Charles B Ong, *Controller*
EMP: 47
SQ FT: 74,000
SALES (est): 9.4MM **Privately Held**
WEB: www.strath.com
SIC: 2752 Commercial printing, lithographic; commercial printing, offset

### (G-10871)
**TEAMDANCE ILLINOIS**
215 Fulton St (60134-2747)
PHONE..................815 463-9044
Fax: 630 578-3839
Ramona Kitching, *Principal*
EMP: 4
SALES: 85.2K **Privately Held**
SIC: 3221 Medicine bottles, glass

### (G-10872)
**THRYSELIUS STAMPING INC**
28 S 8th St (60134-2002)
PHONE..................630 232-0795
Fax: 630 232-0812
Jason Thryselius, *President*
EMP: 4 EST: 1956
SQ FT: 8,500
SALES: 430K **Privately Held**
WEB: www.thryseliusstamping.com
SIC: 3469 Stamping metal for the trade

### (G-10873)
**TONJON COMPANY**
1450 Meadows Rd (60134-3254)
PHONE..................630 208-1173
Fax: 630 892-3989
Anthony Llewellyn, *Ch of Bd*
Allen Eberts, *President*
EMP: 11

SQ FT: 9,000
SALES (est): 1.7MM **Privately Held**
WEB: www.tonjon.com
SIC: 3634 3827 3231 Electric housewares & fans; hair dryers, electric; mirrors, optical; products of purchased glass

### (G-10874)
**TRI CITY SHEET METAL**
701 May St (60134-1303)
P.O. Box 51 (60134-0051)
PHONE..................630 232-4255
Fax: 630 232-0032
Ken Hiscox, *President*
Margie Hiscox, *Admin Sec*
EMP: 5
SALES (est): 610K **Privately Held**
WEB: www.foxbusiness.net
SIC: 1711 3444 Warm air heating & air conditioning contractor; sheet metalwork

## Genoa
### *Dekalb County*

### (G-10875)
**BENZINGER PRINTING**
673 Park Ave Ste 1 (60135-5408)
PHONE..................815 784-6560
Fax: 815 784-2052
Tony Benzinger Sr, *Partner*
Patrick Crosby, *Partner*
David Miller, *Partner*
EMP: 4
SQ FT: 1,200
SALES (est): 270K **Privately Held**
WEB: www.benzinger.com
SIC: 2759 7389 5999 2791 Commercial printing; engraving service; rubber stamps; typesetting; bookbinding & related work; commercial printing, lithographic

### (G-10876)
**CLEARY PALLET SALES INC**
32570 Genoa Rd (60135-8211)
P.O. Box 100 (60135-0100)
PHONE..................815 784-3048
Fax: 815 923-2160
John Cleary, *President*
John Dewindt, *Plant Mgr*
Marc Blouin, *Manager*
EMP: 25
SALES: 1.5MM **Privately Held**
SIC: 2448 Pallets, wood

### (G-10877)
**CUSTOM ALUMINUM PRODUCTS INC**
312 Eureka St (60135-1012)
PHONE..................847 717-5000
Mark Thurlby, *Branch Mgr*
EMP: 100
SALES (corp-wide): 77.1MM **Privately Held**
WEB: www.custom-aluminum.com
SIC: 3354 3442 Aluminum extruded products; metal doors, sash & trim; sash, door or window: metal
PA: Custom Aluminum Products, Inc.
414 Division St
South Elgin IL 60177
847 717-5000

### (G-10878)
**FRANKLIN SCREW PRODUCTS INC**
600 S Sycamore St Unit 1 (60135-1155)
PHONE..................815 784-8500
Fax: 815 697-2052
Dave Rice, *President*
EMP: 3
SALES (est): 353.3K **Privately Held**
WEB: www.franklinscrew.com
SIC: 3451 Screw machine products

### (G-10879)
**GREENLEE TEXTRON INC**
Also Called: Genoa Manufacturing Center
702 W Main St (60135-1034)
PHONE..................815 784-5127
Fax: 815 784-2193
Jessica Hanson, *Treasurer*
Ed Certisimo, *Financial Exec*

David Johnson, *Branch Mgr*
Danielle Watson, *Executive*
EMP: 180
SALES (corp-wide): 13.7B **Publicly Held**
SIC: 3825 Battery testers, electrical
HQ: Greenlee Textron Inc.
4455 Boeing Dr
Rockford IL 61109
815 397-7070

### (G-10880)
**INLAID WOODCRAFT CO**
Also Called: Kishwood
12814 Ellen Dr (60135-7725)
PHONE..................815 784-6386
Fax: 815 895-8287
Dale L Johnson, *President*
Margaret Johnson, *Corp Secy*
Sharon Nicklaus, *Vice Pres*
EMP: 15
SQ FT: 22,706
SALES (est): 1.8MM **Privately Held**
WEB: www.inlaidwoodcraft.com
SIC: 2499 Marquetry, wood

### (G-10881)
**NORDSON CORPORATION**
416 Holly Ct (60135-1133)
PHONE..................815 784-5025
Edward Campbell, *President*
EMP: 50
SALES (corp-wide): 1.8B **Publicly Held**
WEB: www.nordson.com
SIC: 3563 Air & gas compressors
PA: Nordson Corporation
28601 Clemens Rd
Westlake OH 44145
440 892-1580

### (G-10882)
**POLAR TECH INDUSTRIES INC (PA)**
415 E Railroad Ave (60135-1200)
PHONE..................815 784-9000
Fax: 815 784-9009
Donald Santeler, *President*
Autumn Santeler, *General Mgr*
Rob Evans, *Maint Mgr*
Cindy Nunez, *Production*
Judy Tischhauser, *Purch Mgr*
EMP: 30
SQ FT: 405,000
SALES (est): 10.8MM **Privately Held**
WEB: www.polar-tech.com
SIC: 3089 3086 Plastic containers, except foam; packaging & shipping materials, foamed plastic

### (G-10883)
**R HANSEL & SON INC**
221 N Sycamore St (60135-1071)
PHONE..................815 784-5500
Fax: 815 784-2472
Don Hansel, *President*
Robert Hansel, *President*
EMP: 6
SQ FT: 7,500
SALES: 700K **Privately Held**
SIC: 3469 Machine parts, stamped or pressed metal

### (G-10884)
**SYCAMORE PRECISION**
334 E 1st St Ste 1 (60135-1097)
PHONE..................815 784-5151
Ernest Hirn, *President*
Marylyn Smith, *Project Mgr*
Karen Hirn, *Admin Sec*
▲ EMP: 85
SQ FT: 60,000
SALES (est): 20.9MM **Privately Held**
WEB: www.sycamoreprecision.com
SIC: 3599 3491 3479 Machine shop, jobbing & repair; industrial valves; painting, coating & hot dipping

### (G-10885)
**SYCAMORE WELDING & FABG CO**
675 Park Ave (60135-1100)
PHONE..................815 784-2557
Richard J Freeman, *Owner*
EMP: 3
SQ FT: 3,150
SALES: 200K **Privately Held**
SIC: 7692 Welding repair

## Georgetown
### Vermilion County

**(G-10886)**
**GEORGETOWN WASTE WATER**
208 S Walnut St (61846-1956)
PHONE.................................217 662-2525
Ed Shirley, *Manager*
Dale Brooks, *Manager*
EMP: 3
SALES (est): 253.9K **Privately Held**
SIC: 3561 Pumps, domestic: water or sump

**(G-10887)**
**GEORGETOWN WOOD AND PALLET CO**
5781 State Route 1 (61846-6091)
P.O. Box 235 (61846-0235)
PHONE.................................217 662-2563
Fax: 217 662-5592
Gil A Winland, *President*
Eric K Winland, *Vice Pres*
Donald W Winland, *Admin Sec*
EMP: 21
SQ FT: 30,000
SALES (est): 3.7MM **Privately Held**
SIC: 2448 Pallets, wood

**(G-10888)**
**HAMMER ENTERPRISES INC**
5781 State Route 1 (61846-6091)
P.O. Box 235 (61846-0235)
PHONE.................................217 662-8225
Gil Alan Winland, *President*
EMP: 10
SQ FT: 300
SALES (est): 710K **Privately Held**
SIC: 2448 Wood pallets & skids

**(G-10889)**
**NEWPORT PALLET**
310 S Main St (61846-1825)
PHONE.................................217 662-6577
Adam Winland, *Principal*
EMP: 3
SALES (est): 150.2K **Privately Held**
SIC: 2448 Pallets, wood & wood with metal

## German Valley
### Stephenson County

**(G-10890)**
**ARCHER-DANIELS-MIDLAND COMPANY**
54 Stephenson St (61039-9003)
PHONE.................................815 362-2180
EMP: 10
SALES (corp-wide): 62.3B **Publicly Held**
SIC: 5153 2048 Grains; prepared feeds
PA: Archer-Daniels-Midland Company
 77 W Wacker Dr Ste 4600
 Chicago IL 60601
 312 634-8100

**(G-10891)**
**LA BELLA CHRSTNAS KITCHENS INC**
Also Called: Christina's Bakery
25 Church St (61039-9017)
PHONE.................................815 801-1600
Christine Hatlak, *President*
Amanda Lawton, *Business Mgr*
EMP: 8
SQ FT: 2,800
SALES (est): 210.6K **Privately Held**
SIC: 5812 2051 5149 Caterers; cakes, bakery: except frozen; pies, bakery: except frozen; bakery products

## Germantown
### Clinton County

**(G-10892)**
**KOHNENS CONCRETE PRODUCTS INC**
503 Green St (62245-2719)
P.O. Box 276 (62245-0276)
PHONE.................................618 277-2120
Fax: 618 523-4751
Gregory Wilburn, *President*
Pat Kreke, *Plant Mgr*
Kim Aubogat, *Office Mgr*
Dan Kohnen, *Manager*
Jan Wilburn, *Admin Sec*
EMP: 40 EST: 1952
SQ FT: 10,000
SALES (est): 7MM **Privately Held**
WEB: www.kohnenconcrete.com
SIC: 3272 3443 1781 Septic tanks, concrete; tanks, concrete; pipe, concrete or lined with concrete; water tanks, metal plate; water well drilling

**(G-10893)**
**LAKENBURGES MOTOR CO**
806 Walnut St (62245-2737)
P.O. Box 248 (62245-0248)
PHONE.................................618 523-4231
Roger H Lakenburges, *Partner*
Florence M Lakenburges, *Partner*
EMP: 3
SQ FT: 4,350
SALES (est): 200K **Privately Held**
SIC: 7538 5261 7699 5541 General automotive repair shops; lawnmowers & tractors; lawn mower repair shop; filling stations, gasoline; electric motor repair; automotive parts

**(G-10894)**
**WHITE STAR SILO**
8320 Wesclin Rd (62245-1614)
PHONE.................................618 523-4735
William Heimbecker, *President*
Marcy Heimbecker, *Corp Secy*
EMP: 7 EST: 1957
SALES (est): 785.6K **Privately Held**
SIC: 3272 3448 Silos, prefabricated concrete; prefabricated metal buildings

## Germantown Hills
### Woodford County

**(G-10895)**
**AUTOMOTIVE METAL SPECIALIST**
417 Schmitt Ln (61548-9087)
PHONE.................................309 383-2980
Timothy Adams, *Principal*
EMP: 2 EST: 2008
SALES (est): 227.5K **Privately Held**
SIC: 3713 3711 Truck & bus bodies; automobile bodies, passenger car, not including engine, etc.

**(G-10896)**
**WHITE OAK TECHNOLOGY**
524 Wedgewood Ter (61548-9062)
PHONE.................................309 228-4201
James W Sutton, *President*
EMP: 2
SALES (est): 245.3K **Privately Held**
SIC: 3553 Saws, power: bench & table, except portable: woodworking

## Gibson City
### Ford County

**(G-10897)**
**ALAMO GROUP (IL) INC**
Also Called: M & W Gear Company
1020 S Sangamon Ave (60936-1700)
PHONE.................................217 784-4261
Fax: 217 784-4326
Jim Sirovatka, *Safety Mgr*
Sandy Burt, *Engineer*
Scott Wolf, *Branch Mgr*
Debbie Williams, *Manager*
Jon Shiffer, *Director*
EMP: 37
SALES (corp-wide): 844.7MM **Publicly Held**
SIC: 3523 Farm machinery & equipment
HQ: Alamo Group (II) Inc.
 1627 E Walnut St
 Seguin TX 78155
 800 882-5756

**(G-10898)**
**BUNGE NORTH AMERICA FOUNDATION**
Rts 9& 47 # 9 (60936)
P.O. Box 112 (60936-0112)
PHONE.................................217 784-8261
Bill Sallee, *Superintendent*
Jeff Hopkins, *QC Dir*
Walt Powell, *Controller*
Gary Hammond, *Sales Mgr*
Mick Sullivan, *Branch Mgr*
EMP: 150 **Privately Held**
WEB: www.bungemarion.com
SIC: 2075 Soybean protein concentrates & isolates; soybean flour & grits; lecithin, soybean
HQ: Bunge North America Foundation
 11720 Borman Dr
 Saint Louis MO 63146
 314 872-3030

**(G-10899)**
**DAVIS WELDING & MANFCTG INC**
511 W 8th St (60936-1309)
P.O. Box 111 (60936-0111)
PHONE.................................217 784-5480
Fax: 217 784-4330
Mike Davis, *President*
Thomas Davis, *Corp Secy*
EMP: 10 EST: 1945
SQ FT: 18,000
SALES (est): 1.7MM **Privately Held**
SIC: 3561 3523 Cylinders, pump; barn cleaners; loaders, farm type: manure, general utility

**(G-10900)**
**DOW CHEMICAL COMPANY**
454 E 300n Rd (60936-7127)
PHONE.................................217 784-2093
Andrew N Liveris, *Branch Mgr*
EMP: 75
SALES (corp-wide): 48.1B **Publicly Held**
SIC: 2821 Thermoplastic materials
PA: The Dow Chemical Company
 2030 Dow Ctr
 Midland MI 48674
 989 636-1000

**(G-10901)**
**HEARTHSIDE FOOD SOLUTIONS LLC**
310 W 10th St (60936-1327)
PHONE.................................217 784-4238
Rich Scalise, *Branch Mgr*
EMP: 175 **Privately Held**
SIC: 3999 Barber & beauty shop equipment
PA: Hearthside Food Solutions, Llc
 3250 Lacey Rd Ste 200
 Downers Grove IL 60515

**(G-10902)**
**HI-TECH TOWERS INC**
496 N 600e Rd (60936-7218)
P.O. Box 305 (60936-0305)
PHONE.................................217 784-5212
Fax: 217 784-5899
Mark Sizemore, *President*
Gena Sizemore, *Corp Secy*
William Thompson, *Manager*
EMP: 20
SALES (est): 5.2MM **Privately Held**
WEB: www.hi-techtowers.com
SIC: 3441 Tower sections, radio & television transmission

**(G-10903)**
**HUSTEDT MANUFACTURING JEWELERS**
113 N Sangamon Ave (60936-1342)
P.O. Box 124 (60936-0124)
PHONE.................................217 784-8462
Kermit Larry Hustedt, *Owner*
Ursala Hustedt, *Manager*
EMP: 4
SALES (est): 207.8K **Privately Held**
SIC: 3911 7631 3961 Jewelry, precious metal; jewelry repair services; costume jewelry

**(G-10904)**
**LOAD REDI INC**
1124 S Sangamon Ave (60936-1762)
PHONE.................................217 784-4200
Fax: 217 784-4216
Jerry Minion, *President*
EMP: 3
SQ FT: 8,000
SALES (est): 220K **Privately Held**
SIC: 7539 3715 Trailer repair; truck trailers

**(G-10905)**
**ONE EARTH ENERGY LLC**
202 Jordan Dr (60936-2203)
PHONE.................................217 784-5321
Fax: 217 784-5332
Steven Kelly, *President*
Jack Murray, *President*
Scott Docherty, *Chairman*
Joseph Thompson, *Vice Pres*
Larry Brees, *CFO*
EMP: 48
SALES (est): 19.9MM **Privately Held**
SIC: 2869 Ethyl alcohol, ethanol

**(G-10906)**
**PRECISION PLASTIC PRODUCTS**
111 E 8th St (60936-1454)
PHONE.................................217 784-4920
Fax: 217 784-8988
William Tubbs, *Owner*
Sarah Tubbs, *Admin Sec*
EMP: 2
SALES: 1.2MM **Privately Held**
WEB: www.plastic-man.com
SIC: 3089 Windshields, plastic

**(G-10907)**
**SOLAE**
115 Jordan Dr (60936)
PHONE.................................217 784-8261
Paul Hosack, *General Mgr*
Gordon Fuoss, *Engineer*
Bill Miller, *Manager*
◆ EMP: 16
SALES (est): 2.6MM **Privately Held**
SIC: 2075 Soybean oil mills

**(G-10908)**
**SOLAE**
509 W 1st St (60936-2201)
PHONE.................................217 784-2085
Paul Hosack, *Manager*
EMP: 3 EST: 2013
SALES (est): 362.4K **Privately Held**
SIC: 2075 Soybean oil mills

**(G-10909)**
**SOLAE LLC**
124 N Rte 47 (60936)
P.O. Box 112 (60936-0112)
PHONE.................................219 261-2124
Jeff Hopkins, *QC Mgr*
Bill Miller, *Manager*
EMP: 125
SALES (corp-wide): 24.5B **Publicly Held**
WEB: www.solae.com
SIC: 2075 Soybean oil mills
HQ: Solae Llc
 4300 Duncan Ave
 Saint Louis MO 63110
 314 659-3000

# GEOGRAPHIC SECTION

## Gifford
### Champaign County

**(G-10910)**
**SPREADER INC**
2296 County Road 3000 N (61847-9725)
P.O. Box 189 (61847-0189)
**PHONE**..................217 568-7219
Armin Hesterberg, *President*
**EMP:** 7
**SQ FT:** 6,240
**SALES (est):** 1MM **Privately Held**
**WEB:** www.thespreader.com
**SIC: 3523** 3531 3494 Spreaders, fertilizer; construction machinery; valves & pipe fittings

## Gilberts
### Kane County

**(G-10911)**
**ACCURATE METAL FINISHING CO**
359 Sola Dr (60136-9006)
**PHONE**..................847 428-7705
Arnel Arias, *President*
**EMP:** 8
**SQ FT:** 6,000
**SALES (est):** 894.8K **Privately Held**
**SIC: 3471** Cleaning, polishing & finishing

**(G-10912)**
**AMRON STAIR WORKS INC (PA)**
152 Industrial Dr (60136-9752)
**PHONE**..................847 426-4800
**Fax:** 847 426-4806
Ron Thorson, *President*
Julie Anderson, *Executive*
Julie Benchley, *Administration*
**EMP:** 15
**SQ FT:** 20,000
**SALES (est):** 1.7MM **Privately Held**
**SIC: 2431** 3446 Staircases & stairs, wood; stair railings, wood; architectural metalwork

**(G-10913)**
**BLACK RHINO CONCEALMENT**
24 Center Dr Ste 6 (60136-9645)
**PHONE**..................847 783-6499
Robert E Noe, *Principal*
Robert Bottalla, *Co-Owner*
Robert Noe, *Manager*
**EMP:** 3
**SQ FT:** 1,950
**SALES (est):** 136.2K **Privately Held**
**SIC: 3089** Cases, plastic

**(G-10914)**
**BW EXHIBITS**
41 Prairie Pkwy (60136-4039)
**PHONE**..................847 697-9224
Bruce Barna, *Principal*
**EMP:** 4 **EST:** 2009
**SALES (est):** 479.6K **Privately Held**
**SIC: 3553** Cabinet makers' machinery

**(G-10915)**
**CHOICE USA LLC**
80 Industrial Dr Unit 111 (60136-9103)
**PHONE**..................847 428-2252
Zaidi Abu Torav,
Shankar S Deshmukh,
Shabnam Zaidi,
▲ **EMP:** 2
**SALES (est):** 207.8K **Privately Held**
**SIC: 5191** 3199 Saddlery; harness or harness parts

**(G-10916)**
**COMPONENT HARDWARE INC**
120 Center Dr (60136-9619)
**PHONE**..................847 458-8181
Brian Swanson, *President*
**EMP:** 3
**SQ FT:** 3,500
**SALES:** 340K **Privately Held**
**SIC: 3965** 5085 3452 Fasteners; fasteners, industrial: nuts, bolts, screws, etc.; bolts, nuts, rivets & washers

**(G-10917)**
**DONTECH INDUSTRIES INC**
76 Center Dr (60136-9712)
**PHONE**..................847 428-8222
**Fax:** 847 428-6855
Don L Catton, *President*
William Cataldo, *General Mgr*
Mark Mann, *Corp Secy*
Stephanie Richardson, *Vice Pres*
Joel Schmidt, *Mfg Spvr*
▲ **EMP:** 10
**SQ FT:** 13,500
**SALES (est):** 2.2MM **Privately Held**
**WEB:** www.dontechindustriesinc.com
**SIC: 3556** 3589 8711 1796 Food products machinery; sewage & water treatment equipment; designing: ship, boat, machine & product; machinery installation; electric lamps

**(G-10918)**
**E-Z PRODUCTS INC**
92 E End Dr (60136-9731)
**PHONE**..................847 551-9199
**Fax:** 847 551-9266
Geraldine Hall, *President*
Kurt Hall, *General Mgr*
William Hall, *Principal*
Frank Hall, *Sales/Mktg Mgr*
▲ **EMP:** 10
**SQ FT:** 10,000
**SALES (est):** 1.4MM **Privately Held**
**WEB:** www.ezplasticbags.com
**SIC: 3081** 2673 Unsupported plastics film & sheet; bags: plastic, laminated & coated

**(G-10919)**
**GATOR PRODUCTS INC**
Also Called: Microcut Engineering
80 Industrial Dr Unit 105 (60136-9103)
**PHONE**..................847 836-0581
Andrew Starrenburg, *President*
Lisa Poderys, *Admin Asst*
▲ **EMP:** 8
**SQ FT:** 4,000
**SALES (est):** 1.6MM **Privately Held**
**WEB:** www.gatorproducts.com
**SIC: 3546** 3545 Power-driven handtools; machine tool accessories

**(G-10920)**
**HARMONY METAL FABRICATION INC**
148 Industrial Dr (60136-9752)
**PHONE**..................847 426-8900
**Fax:** 708 426-8912
Robert F Farnham, *President*
Sam Farnham, *Controller*
Ronda Kenian, *Manager*
**EMP:** 25
**SQ FT:** 20,000
**SALES:** 5MM **Privately Held**
**WEB:** www.harmonymetalfab.com
**SIC: 3599** 3441 Machine shop, jobbing & repair; fabricated structural metal

**(G-10921)**
**HENDERSON PRODUCTS INC**
Also Called: Henderson Truck Equipment
124 Industrial Dr (60136-9752)
**PHONE**..................847 836-4996
Scott Gilmore, *Principal*
**EMP:** 10 **Publicly Held**
**SIC: 3531** Snow plow attachments
**HQ:** Henderson Products, Inc.
1085 S 3rd St
Manchester IA 52057
563 927-2828

**(G-10922)**
**HUESTIS PRO-TRONICS INC**
Also Called: Huestis Medical
106 Industrial Dr (60136-9752)
**PHONE**..................847 426-1055
**Fax:** 847 426-3099
Scott Gebele, *Manager*
Robert M Wadsworth, *Director*
Richard M Glenn, *Admin Sec*
**EMP:** 14
**SQ FT:** 9,500
**SALES (est):** 1.6MM
**SALES (corp-wide):** 3.8MM **Privately Held**
**SIC: 3844** X-ray apparatus & tubes

**PA:** Hmc Holding Corporation
68 Buttonwood St
Bristol RI 02809
401 253-5501

**(G-10923)**
**HUML INDUSTRIES INC**
78 E End Dr (60136-9731)
P.O. Box 95 (60136-0095)
**PHONE**..................847 426-8061
**Fax:** 847 426-4796
Alan Huml, *President*
**EMP:** 8 **EST:** 1923
**SQ FT:** 7,000
**SALES (est):** 960K **Privately Held**
**SIC: 3541** 3334 Cutoff machines (metalworking machinery); primary aluminum

**(G-10924)**
**HYPERMAX ENGINEERING INC**
255 Higgins Rd (60136-9795)
**PHONE**..................847 428-5655
**Fax:** 847 428-5682
Jerome A Lagod, *President*
Linda Lagod, *Vice Pres*
Pat Michael, *Purchasing*
Pat McMicheal, *Manager*
**EMP:** 17 **EST:** 1973
**SQ FT:** 12,000
**SALES (est):** 2.6MM **Privately Held**
**WEB:** www.hypermaxdiesel.com
**SIC: 8711** 5531 3523 Designing: ship, boat, machine & product; truck equipment & parts; farm machinery & equipment

**(G-10925)**
**J D MACHINING**
57 Center Dr Ste B (60136-9647)
**PHONE**..................847 428-8690
Jack Diehl, *Owner*
**EMP:** 5
**SQ FT:** 3,600
**SALES (est):** 516.1K **Privately Held**
**SIC: 3599** Machine shop, jobbing & repair

**(G-10926)**
**MIDWEST INTGRTED COMPANIES LLC**
Also Called: Midwest Material Management
275 Sola Dr (60136-9003)
**PHONE**..................847 426-6354
Scott Villalobos, *Manager*
Veronica Berglund, *Executive*
Steve Berglund,
Dana Stillson,
Debra Stilson,
**EMP:** 150
**SQ FT:** 100,000
**SALES (est):** 30.4MM **Privately Held**
**WEB:** www.midwestforestree.com
**SIC: 2875** 7699 2491 Compost; waste cleaning services; railroad cross-ties, treated wood

**(G-10927)**
**MIDWEST TURNED PRODUCTS LLC**
80 Prairie Pkwy (60136-4090)
**PHONE**..................847 551-4482
John Robert Lang,
**EMP:** 1
**SALES (est):** 3.3MM **Privately Held**
**SIC: 3541** Drilling & boring machines

**(G-10928)**
**N J TECH INC**
160 Industrial Dr Ste 5 (60136-9100)
P.O. Box 103 (60136-0103)
**PHONE**..................847 428-1001
**Fax:** 847 428-1015
Phounsanath Nanthanong, *President*
Douglas Jacobs, *Vice Pres*
**EMP:** 5
**SQ FT:** 8,000
**SALES (est):** 715K **Privately Held**
**WEB:** www.njtech.com
**SIC: 3599** Machine shop, jobbing & repair

**(G-10929)**
**NOLTE & TYSON INC**
24 Center Dr Ste 1 (60136-9645)
**PHONE**..................847 551-3313
**Fax:** 847 551-1897
Scott Tyson, *President*
Betty Nolte, *Vice Pres*
**EMP:** 14

**SQ FT:** 6,000
**SALES (est):** 1.8MM **Privately Held**
**WEB:** www.entertainmentstudios.com
**SIC: 2211** 5131 5021 7641 Upholstery fabrics, cotton; sheets, bedding & table cloths: cotton; upholstery fabrics, woven; beds & bedding; reupholstery & furniture repair; upholstered household furniture

**(G-10930)**
**OLIVERS HELICOPTERS INC**
726 Tipperary St (60136-8903)
**PHONE**..................847 697-7346
Darrel Oliver, *President*
Helen Oliver, *Corp Secy*
**EMP:** 4
**SQ FT:** 10,000
**SALES (est):** 392.2K **Privately Held**
**SIC: 3721** 5599 Helicopters; aircraft dealers

**(G-10931)**
**PAVER PROTECTOR INC**
57 Railroad St 171 (60136-9670)
P.O. Box 171 (60136-0171)
**PHONE**..................630 488-0069
**EMP:** 2 **EST:** 2011
**SALES (est):** 243.3K **Privately Held**
**SIC: 3531** Pavers

**(G-10932)**
**PRAXAIR INC**
330 Arrowhead Dr (60136-9602)
**PHONE**..................847 428-3405
**EMP:** 21
**SALES (corp-wide):** 10.5B **Publicly Held**
**SIC: 2813** Industrial gases
**PA:** Praxair, Inc.
10 Riverview Dr
Danbury CT 06810
203 837-2000

**(G-10933)**
**R & I ORNAMENTAL IRON INC**
Also Called: M B E
96 Center Dr (60136-9712)
**PHONE**..................847 836-6934
**Fax:** 847 836-6398
Raul Valdez Sr, *President*
Rene Valdez, *Vice Pres*
Olga Valdez, *Admin Sec*
**EMP:** 26 **EST:** 1970
**SQ FT:** 14,000
**SALES:** 6MM **Privately Held**
**SIC: 3446** 1799 Architectural metalwork; ornamental metal work

**(G-10934)**
**SAFETY SOCKET LLC**
49 Prairie Pkwy (60136-4039)
**PHONE**..................224 484-6222
**Fax:** 773 763-1610
Jim Erbs, *President*
Steven Payne, *Vice Pres*
Jessica Dishman, *Purchasing*
Steve Payne, *VP Sls/Mktg*
Bob Lukowski, *Manager*
**EMP:** 43
**SQ FT:** 40,500
**SALES:** 4.3MM **Privately Held**
**SIC: 3965** Fasteners

**(G-10935)**
**SBS STEEL BELT SYSTEMS USA INC**
59 Prairie Pkwy (60136-4039)
**PHONE**..................847 841-3300
Paolo Fasana, *President*
James Innes, *Engineer*
Terri Hill, *Accounts Mgr*
Steve Fetters, *MIS Mgr*
Teresa A Hill, *Admin Sec*
◆ **EMP:** 12
**SALES (est):** 5.8MM
**SALES (corp-wide):** 9.6MM **Privately Held**
**WEB:** www.berndorf-usa.com
**SIC: 3535** Conveyors & conveying equipment
**PA:** Sbs Steel Belt Systems Srl
Via Mattei 3
Venegono Inferiore VA 21040
033 186-4841

## Gilberts - Kane County

**(G-10936)**
**SCOTT INDUSTRIAL BLOWER CO**
15 W End Dr (60136-9657)
P.O. Box 226 (60136-0226)
PHONE.....................847 426-8800
Fax: 847 426-8068
Hermes Haralambous, *President*
James Pierce, *General Mgr*
Tom Sloan, *Vice Pres*
Marlene Haralambous, *Admin Sec*
**EMP:** 18 **EST:** 1968
**SQ FT:** 22,000
**SALES (est):** 3.5MM **Privately Held**
**SIC:** 3564 Blowers & fans; blowing fans: industrial or commercial

**(G-10937)**
**SELEE CORPORATION**
Engineered Ceramics
24 W End Dr (60136-9657)
P.O. Box 365 (60136-0365)
PHONE.....................847 428-4455
Fax: 847 428-0158
Robert Simpson, *Manager*
**EMP:** 40
**SQ FT:** 10,000
**SALES (corp-wide):** 136.2MM **Privately Held**
**WEB:** www.selee.com
**SIC:** 3251 Ceramic glazed brick, clay
**HQ:** Selee Corporation
700 Shepherd St
Hendersonville NC 28792
828 693-0256

**(G-10938)**
**THERMAL BAGS BY INGRID INC**
131 Sola Dr (60136-9748)
PHONE.....................847 836-4400
Fax: 847 836-4408
Ingrid Kosar, *President*
Mary Denicolo, *Sales Mgr*
▲ **EMP:** 18
**SQ FT:** 6,000
**SALES (est):** 3.2MM **Privately Held**
**WEB:** www.thermalbags.com
**SIC:** 2657 Food containers, folding: made from purchased material

**(G-10939)**
**TII TECHNICAL EDUCATN SYSTEMS**
56 E End Dr (60136-9731)
PHONE.....................847 428-3085
Marvin Ness, *President*
**EMP:** 5
**SQ FT:** 6,000
**SALES (est):** 1.8MM **Privately Held**
**WEB:** www.tii-tech.com
**SIC:** 3999 3823 3699 Education aids, devices & supplies; industrial instrmnts msrmnt display/control process variable; electrical equipment & supplies

**(G-10940)**
**VEGA MOLDED PRODUCTS INC**
122 Industrial Dr (60136-9752)
P.O. Box 246 (60136-0246)
PHONE.....................847 428-7761
Fax: 847 428-7764
Karl Weid, *President*
Doris Weid, *Vice Pres*
**EMP:** 7
**SALES (est):** 1MM **Privately Held**
**WEB:** www.vegamoldedproducts.com
**SIC:** 3089 3544 Injection molding of plastics; special dies, tools, jigs & fixtures

## Gillespie
*Macoupin County*

**(G-10941)**
**GILLESPIE CITY WATER**
400 Pear St (62033-1137)
PHONE.....................217 839-3279
Fax: 217 839-4626
Dan Fisher, *Mayor*
Don Shuey, *Manager*
**EMP:** 7
**SALES (est):** 561.8K **Privately Held**
**SIC:** 3589 Water treatment equipment, industrial

## Gilman
*Iroquois County*

**(G-10942)**
**GILMAN STAR INC**
203 N Central St 7 (60938-1218)
P.O. Box 7 (60938-0007)
PHONE.....................815 265-7332
Fax: 815 265-7880
John Elliott, *President*
**EMP:** 4 **EST:** 1949
**SQ FT:** 3,000
**SALES (est):** 210K **Privately Held**
**WEB:** www.gilmanil.com
**SIC:** 2711 Newspapers: publishing only, not printed on site

**(G-10943)**
**GREGORY MARTIN**
Also Called: M & D Supplies
325 E Park Ct (60938-1621)
PHONE.....................815 265-4527
Gregory Martin, *Owner*
**EMP:** 4 **EST:** 1994
**SALES (est):** 241.6K **Privately Held**
**WEB:** www.mdsupplies.com
**SIC:** 3484 Rifles or rifle parts, 30 mm. & below

**(G-10944)**
**INCOBRASA INDUSTRIES LTD**
540 E Us Highway 24 (60938-6078)
P.O. Box 98 (60938-0098)
PHONE.....................815 265-4803
Fax: 815 265-8082
R B Ribeiro D Pedro II, *President*
Rick Eshleman, *General Mgr*
Sergio Baruffi, *Plant Mgr*
Jeff Seibert, *Buyer*
Joe Czernik, *Sls & Mktg Exec*
▲ **EMP:** 120
**SALES (est):** 44MM **Privately Held**
**WEB:** www.incobrasa.com
**SIC:** 2075 Soybean oil mills

## Girard
*Macoupin County*

**(G-10945)**
**FREEMAN UNITED COAL MINING CO**
22393 Crown Two Mine Rd 2 Mine (62640)
P.O. Box 259, Farmersville (62533-0259)
PHONE.....................217 627-3411
Fax: 217 627-3411
Don Dame, *General Mgr*
Bill Hinz, *Maintence Staff*
**EMP:** 250
**SALES (corp-wide):** 31.3B **Publicly Held**
**SIC:** 1241 Coal mining services
**HQ:** Freeman United Coal Mining Company
4440 Ash Grove Dr Ste A
Springfield IL 62711
217 698-3300

**(G-10946)**
**FUNERAL REGISTER BOOKS INC**
499 Rachel Rd (62640-8652)
PHONE.....................217 627-3235
Richard R Roberts, *President*
Robert Alan Mc Intire, *Treasurer*
**EMP:** 15
**SQ FT:** 10,000
**SALES (est):** 1.3MM **Privately Held**
**SIC:** 2782 Memorandum books, printed

**(G-10947)**
**LANGHEIM READY MIX INC**
110 E Jefferson St (62640-1106)
P.O. Box 297, Pawnee (62558-0297)
PHONE.....................217 625-2351
Reese Langheim, *President*
**EMP:** 2
**SALES (est):** 246K **Privately Held**
**SIC:** 3273 1771 Ready-mixed concrete; concrete work

**(G-10948)**
**MASTER ENGRAVING INC**
499 Rachel Rd (62640-8652)
PHONE.....................217 627-3279
Fax: 217 627-3260
Rick Roberts, *President*
Alan McIntyre, *Treasurer*
**EMP:** 5
**SQ FT:** 8,000
**SALES (est):** 599.8K **Privately Held**
**SIC:** 2759 Invitation & stationery printing & engraving

**(G-10949)**
**R & R BINDERY SERVICE INC**
499 Rachel Rd (62640-8652)
PHONE.....................217 627-2143
Robert C Mullins, *President*
Robert A McIntire, *Corp Secy*
Richard Roberts, *Vice Pres*
Robert A Mc Intire, *Treasurer*
**EMP:** 180
**SQ FT:** 72,000
**SALES (est):** 22.6MM **Privately Held**
**WEB:** www.printusa.com
**SIC:** 2789 Bookbinding & related work

**(G-10950)**
**THERMAL CERAMICS INC**
1st & Mound St (62640)
P.O. Box 138 (62640-0138)
PHONE.....................217 627-2101
Alinda Hart, *Purchasing*
John Stang, *Branch Mgr*
**EMP:** 35
**SALES (corp-wide):** 1.2B **Privately Held**
**WEB:** www.thermalceramics.com
**SIC:** 3299 4225 3255 3229 Ceramic fiber; general warehousing; clay refractories; pressed & blown glass; flat glass
**HQ:** Thermal Ceramics Inc.
2102 Old Savannah Rd
Augusta GA 30906
706 796-4200

## Glasford
*Peoria County*

**(G-10951)**
**GAZETTE PRINTING CO**
Also Called: Glasford Gazette
508 W Main St (61533-9793)
PHONE.....................309 389-2811
Fax: 309 389-4949
William Watkins, *Owner*
**EMP:** 3 **EST:** 1899
**SALES (est):** 213.4K **Privately Held**
**SIC:** 2711 2752 2791 Newspapers; commercial printing, lithographic; typesetting

## Glen Carbon
*Madison County*

**(G-10952)**
**HOPCROFT ELECTRIC INC**
606 Glen Crossing Rd (62034-4065)
PHONE.....................618 288-7302
Fax: 618 288-7307
Lola Niebruegge, *President*
Paul E Niebruegge, *Treasurer*
**EMP:** 7 **EST:** 1932
**SQ FT:** 2,200
**SALES (est):** 1MM **Privately Held**
**SIC:** 7694 5063 3699 3621 Electric motor repair; motors, electric; electrical equipment & supplies; motors & generators

**(G-10953)**
**JOURNAL OF BANKING AND FIN**
4 Oxford Ln (62034-1531)
PHONE.....................618 203-9074
**EMP:** 4
**SALES (est):** 210.5K **Privately Held**
**SIC:** 2711 Newspapers, publishing & printing

**(G-10954)**
**MECHANICS PLANING MILL INC**
Also Called: Mpm Industries
1 Cottonwood Indus Park (62034-2742)
PHONE.....................618 288-3000
Fax: 618 288-0601
Jeffrey W Hanselman, *President*
Randy Happick, *Vice Pres*
Randall Hettick, *Vice Pres*
Mark Vorhies, *Vice Pres*
Kim Myatt, *Controller*
◆ **EMP:** 30
**SQ FT:** 42,000
**SALES (est):** 6.4MM **Privately Held**
**WEB:** www.mpmdistribution.com
**SIC:** 2421 3442 5072 Flooring (dressed lumber); softwood; metal doors, sash & trim; hardware

**(G-10955)**
**WOODEN NICKEL PUB AND GRILL**
171 S Main St (62034-1416)
PHONE.....................618 288-2141
Kelly Fuesting, *Officer*
**EMP:** 5
**SALES (est):** 548.2K **Privately Held**
**SIC:** 3356 Nickel

## Glen Ellyn
*Dupage County*

**(G-10956)**
**A-RELIABLE PRINTING**
604 Roosevelt Rd (60137-5737)
PHONE.....................630 790-2525
Sharon Meyer, *Owner*
Ken Meyer, *Principal*
**EMP:** 4 **EST:** 2007
**SALES (est):** 372.2K **Privately Held**
**SIC:** 2752 Commercial printing, lithographic

**(G-10957)**
**ACCUWARE INCORPORATED**
799 Roosevelt Rd 3-218 (60137-5922)
PHONE.....................630 858-8409
Steve Morris, *President*
Carrie Morris, *Treasurer*
**EMP:** 10
**SQ FT:** 1,300
**SALES (est):** 1MM **Privately Held**
**WEB:** www.accuware-inc.com
**SIC:** 7372 Prepackaged software

**(G-10958)**
**ANAMET INC (PA)**
799 Roosevelt Rd 4-313 (60137-5873)
PHONE.....................217 234-8844
Fax: 630 469-1463
Joseph Venzron, *CEO*
Allen Hoube, *Vice Pres*
David Wright, *Treasurer*
William Cady, *Director*
John Thomas, *Director*
**EMP:** 2
**SQ FT:** 2,000
**SALES (est):** 73.1MM **Privately Held**
**WEB:** www.anamet.com
**SIC:** 3599 3644 3829 3441 Hose, flexible metallic; electric conduits & fittings; vibration meters, analyzers & calibrators; expansion joints (structural shapes), iron or steel

**(G-10959)**
**ANDERSON HOUSE FOUNDATION**
258 Harwarden St (60137-5305)
PHONE.....................630 461-7254
Yuri Mezenko, *Exec Dir*
**EMP:** 1
**SALES:** 500K **Privately Held**
**SIC:** 2721 Periodicals

**(G-10960)**
**BANTIX TECHNOLOGIES LLC**
490 Pennsylvania Ave (60137-4432)
P.O. Box 2968 (60138-2968)
PHONE.....................630 446-0886
Tony Andriacchi, *Vice Pres*
Nicholas J Howard, *Mng Member*
Terra C Howard,

## Glen Ellyn - Dupage County (G-10990)

EMP: 3
SALES: 1.5MM  Privately Held
SIC: 5734  7379  7372  Computer software & accessories; computer related consulting services; prepackaged software

### (G-10961)
### BOOK POWER INC
253 Traver Ave  (60137-5328)
PHONE.....................630 790-4144
Ronald Sahara, President
EMP: 3
SALES (est): 224.1K  Privately Held
WEB: www.blacklightpower.com
SIC: 2731  2741  Textbooks: publishing only, not printed on site; miscellaneous publishing

### (G-10962)
### CHEMSONG INC
22w471 Mccarron Rd  (60137-7059)
Mike Song, President
David Song, Technology
Shirley Song, Admin Sec
EMP: 10
SQ FT: 3,000
SALES: 1MM  Privately Held
WEB: www.chemsong.com
SIC: 2899  8742  Ink or writing fluids; industrial consultant

### (G-10963)
### COLES CRAFT CORPORATION
868 Baker Ct  (60137-6104)
PHONE.....................630 858-8171
Eric Coles, President
EMP: 4
SALES (est): 334.6K  Privately Held
SIC: 3699  Appliance cords for household electrical equipment

### (G-10964)
### CONLEY PRECISION ENGINES INC
825 Duane St  (60137-4709)
PHONE.....................630 858-3160
Fax: 630 858-3199
Gary Conley, President
EMP: 10
SALES: 500K  Privately Held
WEB: www.conleyprecision.com
SIC: 3944  3519  Engines, miniature; internal combustion engines

### (G-10965)
### CPA SYSTEMS INCORPORATED
369 Birchbrook Ct  (60137-6847)
PHONE.....................630 858-3057
Jacquelyn Simoni, President
Robert Simoni, Vice Pres
Vachary Simoni, Opers Mgr
▲ EMP: 4
SQ FT: 1,200
SALES: 185K  Privately Held
SIC: 3674  Light emitting diodes

### (G-10966)
### DIAMOND INDUSTRIAL SALES LTD
175 Cortland Ct  (60137-6481)
PHONE.....................630 858-3687
Daniel Steinbach, President
EMP: 5
SALES (est): 414.1K  Privately Held
SIC: 3599  5085  Amusement park equipment; diamonds, industrial: natural, crude

### (G-10967)
### DREISILKER ELECTRIC MOTORS INC (PA)
352 Roosevelt Rd  (60137-5692)
PHONE.....................630 469-7510
Fax: 630 469-3474
Leo Dreisilker, President
Susan Muehlfelt, Vice Pres
Marlene Schneider, Vice Pres
Dave Van Horn, Vice Pres
Larry Ninis, Prdtn Mgr
EMP: 120  EST: 1965
SQ FT: 72,800

EMP: 3
SALES (est): 69.9MM  Privately Held
WEB: www.dreisilker.com
SIC: 5063  7694  Electrical apparatus & equipment; motor controls, starters & relays: electric; motors, electric; armature rewinding shops; motor repair services; electric motor repair; rewinding services

### (G-10968)
### DUPAGE CHROPRACTIC CENTRE LTD
45 S Park Blvd Ste 155  (60137-6298)
PHONE.....................630 858-9780
Sally A Pepping, Principal
EMP: 5
SALES (est): 435.9K  Privately Held
SIC: 3845  Patient monitoring apparatus

### (G-10969)
### EQES INC
Also Called: Equipment Engineering & Sales
799 Roosevelt Rd 6-208  (60137-5908)
PHONE.....................630 858-6161
Fax: 630 858-8787
Newal K Agnihotri, President
Sue Agnihotri, Publisher
Anu Agnihotri, Sales Staff
EMP: 5  EST: 1981
SQ FT: 1,600
SALES (est): 557.2K  Privately Held
WEB: www.ramayanainstitute.com
SIC: 4813  2721  ; periodicals

### (G-10970)
### FEDEX OFFICE & PRINT SVCS INC
714 Roosevelt Rd  (60137-5806)
PHONE.....................630 469-2677
Fax: 630 469-2807
Lacie Whyte, Branch Mgr
EMP: 6
SALES (corp-wide): 50.3B  Publicly Held
SIC: 2752  Commercial printing, lithographic
HQ: Fedex Office And Print Services, Inc.
7900 Legacy Dr
Plano TX 75024
214 550-7000

### (G-10971)
### FORREST CONSULTING
479 N Main St Ste 220  (60137-5174)
PHONE.....................630 730-9619
Lee S Crumbaugh, Owner
Lee F Crumbaugh, Owner
EMP: 5
SQ FT: 900
SALES (est): 319.9K  Privately Held
WEB: www.forrestcd.com
SIC: 8748  2711  8742  8743  Publishing consultant; newspapers; marketing consulting services; public relations services

### (G-10972)
### H2O POD INC
Also Called: Watermat Company
490 Pennsylvania Ave  (60137-4432)
P.O. Box 882320, Steamboat Springs CO (80488-2320)
PHONE.....................630 240-1769
Jay Croockston, Vice Pres
Robert Pole, Mng Member
EMP: 5  EST: 2015
SALES (est): 220.7K  Privately Held
SIC: 3949  Water sports equipment

### (G-10973)
### ICON CO
1s640 Sunnybrook Rd  (60137-6451)
PHONE.....................630 545-2345
Young Bahng, Owner
EMP: 7
SQ FT: 7,700
SALES (est): 458.1K  Privately Held
WEB: www.iconroller.com
SIC: 3535  Conveyors & conveying equipment

### (G-10974)
### INTERNTNAL MSCAL SUPPLIERS INC
Also Called: Lisa's Clarinet Shop
364 Pennsylvania Ave  (60137-4386)
PHONE.....................847 774-2938
Lisa Canning, President

EMP: 1
SALES (est): 1,000K  Privately Held
SIC: 3931  Clarinets & parts

### (G-10975)
### LEDRETROFITTING INC
2n138 Bernice Ave  (60137-3136)
PHONE.....................815 347-5047
EMP: 4
SALES: 100K  Privately Held
SIC: 3999  Manufacturing Ofled Retrofits

### (G-10976)
### LEYDEN LAWN SPRINKLERS
23w274 North Ave  (60137-3474)
PHONE.....................630 665-5520
Karen Lipscomb, President
EMP: 24
SALES (est): 2.6MM  Privately Held
SIC: 3432  Lawn hose nozzles & sprinklers

### (G-10977)
### LIBERTY GROVE SOFTWARE INC
189 Newton Ave Ste B  (60137-5343)
PHONE.....................630 858-7388
Karen Studebaker, President
David Studebaker, Principal
Ron Oates, Project Mgr
EMP: 2
SALES (est): 600K  Privately Held
SIC: 7372  Prepackaged software

### (G-10978)
### LOOP BELT INDUSTRIES INC
21w171 Hill Ave  (60137-4860)
PHONE.....................630 469-1300
Kevin Blake, President
Tavia Oury, Admin Sec
EMP: 9
SALES (est): 844.7K  Privately Held
SIC: 3535  Conveyors & conveying equipment

### (G-10979)
### MACHINE & DESIGN
767 Willis St  (60137-4266)
PHONE.....................630 858-6416
William Hansen, Partner
EMP: 2
SALES (est): 238K  Privately Held
SIC: 3599  3281  Machine shop, jobbing & repair; cut stone & stone products

### (G-10980)
### MATTARUSKY INC
1n272 Pleasant Ave  (60137-3751)
PHONE.....................630 469-4125
Ann M Litavsky, President
Matt Litavsky, Vice Pres
EMP: 2
SALES: 2.4MM  Privately Held
WEB: www.mattarusky.com
SIC: 5199  3229  Christmas novelties; Christmas tree ornaments, from glass produced on-site

### (G-10981)
### MIDWEST BIOFLUIDS INC
22w080 Glen Valley Dr  (60137-6854)
PHONE.....................630 790-9708
Michael W Rooney, President
EMP: 6
SALES (est): 676.3K  Privately Held
SIC: 2834  Pharmaceutical preparations

### (G-10982)
### NAKED ARMY USA LLC
Also Called: Khaki Army
582 Hillside Ave  (60137-4680)
PHONE.....................630 456-8738
Douglas Dickson, Principal
EMP: 4
SALES (est): 304.8K  Privately Held
SIC: 3499  Novelties & giftware, including trophies

### (G-10983)
### OBERWEIS DAIRY INC
651 E Roosevelt St  (60137)
PHONE.....................630 474-0284
Fax: 630 858-0234
Scott Wille, Branch Mgr
Paul Davison, Manager
Dan Martinez, Manager

EMP: 25
SALES (corp-wide): 202.6MM  Privately Held
WEB: www.webfc.net
SIC: 2026  5963  5451  Milk processing (pasteurizing, homogenizing, bottling); milk delivery; milk; ice cream (packaged)
PA: Oberweis Dairy, Inc.
951 Ice Cream Dr
North Aurora IL 60542
630 801-6100

### (G-10984)
### OLIVE AND VINNIES
449 N Main St  (60137-5123)
PHONE.....................630 534-6457
Gary Evanson, Owner
EMP: 3
SALES (est): 200K  Privately Held
SIC: 2079  5149  Olive oil; specialty food items

### (G-10985)
### PARTNERS RESOURCE INC
831 Woodland Dr  (60137-4246)
PHONE.....................630 620-9161
Gregory J Yangas, President
Richard J Yangas, President
Deborah Morelli, Office Mgr
EMP: 3
SALES (est): 469K  Privately Held
WEB: www.partnersresource.com
SIC: 2531  8742  Public building & related furniture; sales (including sales management) consultant

### (G-10986)
### PEANUT BUTTER PARTNERS LLC
564 Crescent Blvd  (60137)
PHONE.....................847 489-5322
Lawrence Hanson, Principal
EMP: 5  EST: 2012
SALES (est): 450.4K  Privately Held
SIC: 2099  Peanut butter

### (G-10987)
### PETERSON PUBLICATION SERVICES
887 Hill Ave  (60137-5250)
PHONE.....................630 469-6732
Mark Peterson, President
EMP: 2
SALES: 500K  Privately Held
SIC: 2752  7331  Promotional printing, lithographic; direct mail advertising services

### (G-10988)
### PS TOBACCO INC
434 Roosevelt Rd  (60137-5642)
PHONE.....................630 793-9823
Snehal Patel, Owner
EMP: 3
SALES (est): 275.4K  Privately Held
SIC: 2131  Smoking tobacco

### (G-10989)
### SIGN IDENTITY INC
415 Taft Ave Ste 1b  (60137-6214)
PHONE.....................630 942-1400
Fax: 630 942-8400
Tom Van Winkle, President
Steve Peterson, Production
Paul Buetell, Manager
EMP: 3
SQ FT: 2,200
SALES (est): 344.9K  Privately Held
WEB: www.signidentity.com
SIC: 3993  7389  Signs & advertising specialties; laminating service

### (G-10990)
### SPECTAPE OF MIDWEST INC
75 Tanglewood Dr  (60137-7830)
PHONE.....................630 682-8600
Bob Humpreys, Branch Mgr
EMP: 3
SALES (corp-wide): 6.4MM  Privately Held
SIC: 3652  Master records or tapes, preparation of
PA: Spectape Of The Midwest, Inc.
7821 Palace Dr
Cincinnati OH 45249
513 489-7887

# Glen Ellyn - Dupage County

**(G-10991)**
**STAR SLEIGH**
716 Crescent Blvd (60137-4208)
PHONE .................... 630 858-2576
Mike Wilson, *Owner*
**EMP:** 15
**SALES (est):** 1MM **Privately Held**
**WEB:** www.starsleigh.com
**SIC:** 3944 Child restraint seats, automotive

**(G-10992)**
**US PAVING INC**
849 N Main St (60137-3674)
PHONE .................... 630 653-4900
**Fax:** 630 653-4944
Lafayette Hugh Usry, *President*
John Usry, *Vice Pres*
Barbara Splitt, *Manager*
**EMP:** 20 **EST:** 1970
**SQ FT:** 9,000
**SALES (est):** 3MM **Privately Held**
**SIC:** 3271 Paving blocks, concrete

**(G-10993)**
**VANGUARD SOLUTIONS GROUP INC**
800 Roosevelt Rd Ste E410 (60137-5869)
PHONE .................... 630 545-1600
**Fax:** 630 545-1681
Anthony Balio, *President*
Michael Caldwell, *Vice Pres*
Dhananjay Joshi, *Vice Pres*
John Fandl, *Production*
Veena Vighuti, *Engineer*
**EMP:** 37
**SQ FT:** 8,000
**SALES (est):** 2.4MM
**SALES (corp-wide):** 229MM **Privately Held**
**SIC:** 7372 Prepackaged software
**HQ:** Exact Software North America, Llc
5455 Rings Rd Ste 100
Dublin OH 43017
978 539-6186

**(G-10994)**
**VIBRA-TECH ENGINEERS INC**
Also Called: Vibra Tech
777 Roosevelt Rd Ste 110 (60137-5911)
PHONE .................... 630 858-0681
**Fax:** 630 858-0682
Dane Tittman, *Manager*
**EMP:** 5
**SALES (corp-wide):** 11.9MM **Privately Held**
**WEB:** www.vibra-tech-inc.com
**SIC:** 3829 8711 Measuring & controlling devices; professional engineer
**PA:** Vibra-Tech Engineers, Inc.
109 E 1st St
Hazleton PA 18201
570 455-5861

**(G-10995)**
**WINFUN USA LLC**
551 Roosevelt Rd Ste 137 (60137-5734)
PHONE .................... 630 942-8464
Tom Salzmann,
**EMP:** 2
**SALES:** 1MM
**SALES (corp-wide):** 87.6MM **Privately Held**
**SIC:** 3069 Toys, rubber
**PA:** Winfat Industrial Co., Limited
Rm 903-904 9/F East Ocean Ctr
Tsim Sha Tsui East KLN
279 068-98

## Glenarm
### Sangamon County

**(G-10996)**
**LINCOLNLAND ARCHTCTRAL GRPHICS**
Also Called: Lincolnland Graphics
12 Covered Bridge Acres (62536-6529)
PHONE .................... 217 629-9009
**Fax:** 217 629-9898
Karen Moore, *President*
**EMP:** 3
**SALES (est):** 200K **Privately Held**
**SIC:** 3993 5999 Signs & advertising specialties; banners, flags, decals & posters

**(G-10997)**
**RAYS COUNTERTOP SHOP INC**
125 Robb St (62536)
P.O. Box 46 (62536-0046)
PHONE .................... 217 483-2514
**Fax:** 217 483-3876
Raymond Drendel, *CEO*
**EMP:** 12
**SQ FT:** 15,000
**SALES:** 500K **Privately Held**
**SIC:** 3131 5211 2541 5023 Counters; counter tops; wood partitions & fixtures; kitchenware; kitchen & bathroom remodeling; cabinet & finish carpentry

## Glencoe
### Cook County

**(G-10998)**
**DESIGN PACKAGING COMPANY INC**
100 Hazel Ave (60022-1731)
PHONE .................... 847 835-3327
Myron Horvitz, *President*
Gregory Horvitz, *Vice Pres*
Conrad Capulong, *Admin Sec*
▼ **EMP:** 29
**SQ FT:** 50,000
**SALES (est):** 2.7MM **Privately Held**
**SIC:** 3081 Unsupported plastics film & sheet; polypropylene film & sheet

**(G-10999)**
**ELLIOTT JSJ & ASSOCIATES INC**
Also Called: Directions Magazine
194 Green Bay Rd (60022-2126)
PHONE .................... 847 242-0412
Jane Elliot, *President*
Scott Elliot, *Owner*
Rebeckah Flowers, *Editor*
Nitin Gupta, *Vice Pres*
**EMP:** 6
**SALES (est):** 1MM **Privately Held**
**SIC:** 2721 Periodicals

**(G-11000)**
**INTERNATIONAL ICE BAGGING SYST**
234 Dennis Ln (60022-1320)
PHONE .................... 312 633-4000
David C Makowski, *Principal*
Mike Oates, *Director*
Stephen Smith, *Director*
**EMP:** 6
**SALES (est):** 898.5K **Privately Held**
**SIC:** 5078 2097 Commercial refrigeration equipment; manufactured ice; ice cubes

**(G-11001)**
**INTERNATIONAL SILVER PLATING**
Also Called: International Locksmith
364 Park Ave (60022-1553)
PHONE .................... 847 835-0705
David Hartley, *President*
Joyce Hartley, *President*
**EMP:** 3
**SALES (est):** 266.6K **Privately Held**
**WEB:** www.isilverplating.com
**SIC:** 3471 5932 Plating & polishing; plating, metals or formed products; finishing, metals or formed products; polishing, metals or formed products; art objects, antique

**(G-11002)**
**MI-TE FAST PRINTERS INC**
Also Called: Mi-Te Printing & Graphics
311 Park Ave (60022-1525)
PHONE .................... 312 236-3278
**Fax:** 847 835-8918
Susan Davis, *Manager*
Chas Howard, *Co-Mgr*
**EMP:** 5
**SALES (corp-wide):** 4MM **Privately Held**
**WEB:** www.miteweddinginvitations.com
**SIC:** 2752 Commercial printing, lithographic; commercial printing
**PA:** Mi-Te Fast Printers, Inc
180 W Washington St Fl 2
Chicago IL 60602
312 236-8352

**(G-11003)**
**NLS ANALYTICS LLC**
375 Dundee Rd (60022-1510)
PHONE .................... 312 593-0293
Sean Murdock, *CEO*
**EMP:** 2
**SALES (est):** 203.9K **Privately Held**
**SIC:** 3825 7389 Test equipment for electronic & electric measurement;

**(G-11004)**
**NON VIOLENT TOYS INC**
1179 Hohlfelder Rd (60022-1018)
PHONE .................... 847 835-9066
Phil Siegel, *President*
Maryanne Siegel, *Vice Pres*
**EMP:** 6
**SALES:** 100K **Privately Held**
**SIC:** 3944 Games, toys & children's vehicles

**(G-11005)**
**PANACHE EDITIONS LTD**
Also Called: Art of Running, The
234 Dennis Ln (60022-1320)
PHONE .................... 847 921-8574
Donna Macleod, *Partner*
Andrew Macleod, *Partner*
**EMP:** 5
**SALES (est):** 390.4K **Privately Held**
**SIC:** 2741 7389 Posters: publishing only, not printed on site; interior designer

## Glendale Heights
### Dupage County

**(G-11006)**
**A J R INTERNATIONAL INC (PA)**
300 Regency Dr (60139-2283)
PHONE .................... 800 232-3965
James Oestereich, *President*
Mark Pustil, *Vice Pres*
Steve Will, *Opers Mgr*
Barbara Chopper, *Accounting Mgr*
Dwayne Gilmore, *Manager*
**EMP:** 58
**SQ FT:** 56,000
**SALES:** 21MM **Privately Held**
**WEB:** www.ajrinternational.com
**SIC:** 7629 3629 7622 7699 Electrical repair shops; electronic generation equipment; radio & television repair; customizing services

**(G-11007)**
**ACCURATE CARRIERS INC**
Also Called: Accurate Carriers USA
500 Mitchell Rd (60139-2581)
PHONE .................... 630 790-3430
Darryl Asnaz, *President*
Cecilia Asnaz, *General Mgr*
Jay Hindersman, *Purchasing*
▲ **EMP:** 16
**SQ FT:** 23,000
**SALES (est):** 3.2MM **Privately Held**
**SIC:** 3089 Boxes, plastic

**(G-11008)**
**AMERICAN EMB & SCREEN PRTG LLC**
Also Called: American EMB & Screen Prtg
1935 Brandon Ct Ste A (60139-2199)
PHONE .................... 630 766-2825
Samuel Giliberto, *President*
**EMP:** 5
**SALES (est):** 434.6K **Privately Held**
**SIC:** 2395 Emblems, embroidered

**(G-11009)**
**ATLAS DIE LLC**
2000 Bloomingdale Rd # 235 (60139-2182)
PHONE .................... 630 351-5140
**Fax:** 630 351-5379
Ed Singleton, *Branch Mgr*
**EMP:** 56
**SALES (corp-wide):** 34.4MM **Privately Held**
**SIC:** 3423 3544 Cutting dies, except metal cutting; industrial molds
**PA:** Atlas Die, Llc
2000 Middlebury St
Elkhart IN 46516
574 295-0050

**(G-11010)**
**AUTH-FLORENCE MFG**
591 Mitchell Rd (60139-2582)
**Fax:** 630 545-1896
Dave Dailey, *President*
**EMP:** 7
**SALES (est):** 594.5K **Privately Held**
**SIC:** 3999 Manufacturing industries

**(G-11011)**
**AVANTI ENGINEERING INC (PA)**
200 W Lake Dr (60139-4825)
PHONE .................... 630 260-1333
**Fax:** 630 260-1762
Rocco Bratta, *President*
Rita J Bratta, *Corp Secy*
Nick Bratta, *Vice Pres*
Don Maxwell, *QC Mgr*
**EMP:** 10
**SQ FT:** 55,000
**SALES (est):** 2.2MM **Privately Held**
**WEB:** www.avantiengineering.com
**SIC:** 3451 Screw machine products

**(G-11012)**
**BRIDGESTONE RET OPERATIONS LLC**
Also Called: Firestone
2015 Bloomingdale Rd (60139-2166)
PHONE .................... 630 893-6336
**Fax:** 630 893-7691
Rich Verde, *Manager*
**EMP:** 12
**SALES (corp-wide):** 30.1B **Privately Held**
**WEB:** www.bfis.com
**SIC:** 5531 3011 Automotive tires; tires & inner tubes
**HQ:** Bridgestone Retail Operations, Llc
333 E Lake St Ste 300
Bloomingdale IL 60108
630 259-9000

**(G-11013)**
**CAPITAL PTTERN MODEL WORKS INC**
410 Windy Point Dr (60139-2177)
PHONE .................... 630 469-8200
**Fax:** 630 469-8201
Douglas Steffey, *President*
Lynn Steffey, *Vice Pres*
**EMP:** 8
**SQ FT:** 11,500
**SALES:** 2.3MM **Privately Held**
**WEB:** www.capitalpattern.com
**SIC:** 3999 3543 Models, general, except toy; industrial patterns

**(G-11014)**
**CARD PRSNLZATION SOLUTIONS LLC**
80 Internationale Blvd C (60139-2000)
PHONE .................... 630 543-2630
**Fax:** 630 543-4179
Jim Cooney, *General Mgr*
Arlene Rupslauk, *Manager*
Chris Fuchs, *Director*
**EMP:** 30
**SALES (corp-wide):** 24.2MM **Privately Held**
**WEB:** www.crdpersol.com
**SIC:** 2752 7331 2759 Commercial printing, lithographic; direct mail advertising services; commercial printing
**PA:** Card Personalization Solutions Co., Llc
7520 Morris Ct Ste 100
Allentown PA 18106
610 231-1860

**(G-11015)**
**CASTLE METAL PRODUCTS CORP**
1947 Quincy Ct (60139-2045)
PHONE .................... 847 806-4540
**Fax:** 847 806-4541
Gary M Castle, *President*
**EMP:** 5

# GEOGRAPHIC SECTION

## Glendale Heights - Dupage County (G-11040)

SALES (est): 871.3K **Privately Held**
WEB: www.castlemetalproducts.com
SIC: 3444 Roof deck, sheet metal

### (G-11016)
### CHOICE CABINET CHICAGO
2000 Bloomingdale Rd # 135 (60139-2100)
PHONE..................630 599-1099
Barbara Regan, *Principal*
EMP: 7
SALES (est): 990.3K **Privately Held**
SIC: 2434 Wood kitchen cabinets

### (G-11017)
### COMMUNICATION TECHNOLOGIES INC
Also Called: Data Management Center
188 Internationale Blvd (60139-2094)
PHONE..................630 384-0900
Fax: 847 397-0661
Dale Dembski, *President*
Karen Franson, *CFO*
EMP: 33
SQ FT: 20,000
SALES (est): 9MM **Privately Held**
WEB: www.dmcilink.com
SIC: 2752 7331 7389 Promotional printing, lithographic; direct mail advertising services; telemarketing services; subscription fulfillment services: magazine, newspaper, etc.

### (G-11018)
### CORNELIUS INC (DH)
101 Regency Dr (60139-2206)
PHONE..................630 539-6850
Tim Hubbard, *CEO*
Alen Duncan, *President*
Craig Heetland, *Vice Pres*
Joseph Madonia, *Administration*
◆ EMP: 300 EST: 1935
SALES: 225MM
SALES (corp-wide): 223.6B **Publicly Held**
WEB: www.imiremcor.com
SIC: 3585 3556 3586 Soda fountain & beverage dispensing equipment & parts; food products machinery; measuring & dispensing pumps
HQ: The Marmon Group Llc
181 W Madison St Ste 2600
Chicago IL 60602
312 372-9500

### (G-11019)
### CREATIVE STEEL RULE DIES INC
1935 Brandon Ct Ste D (60139-2199)
PHONE..................630 307-8880
Fax: 630 307-8884
Larry T Corriere, *President*
Marvin Cichlar, *Vice Pres*
Sandra Corriere, *Admin Sec*
EMP: 15
SQ FT: 6,000
SALES (est): 1MM **Privately Held**
SIC: 3544 Dies, steel rule

### (G-11020)
### DOUBLE IMAGE PRESS INC
151 N Brandon Dr (60139-2039)
PHONE..................630 893-6777
Fax: 630 893-3335
Carole Anderson, *President*
EMP: 10
SALES (est): 613.6K **Privately Held**
SIC: 2752 Commercial printing, lithographic

### (G-11021)
### ELMED INCORPORATED
35 N Brandon Dr (60139-2024)
PHONE..................630 543-2792
Fax: 630 543-2102
Werner Hausner, *President*
Othmar Goettel, *Marketing Mgr*
Hermine Hausner, *Shareholder*
Karl Hausner, *Shareholder*
EMP: 22
SQ FT: 25,000
SALES (est): 3.8MM **Privately Held**
WEB: www.elmed.com
SIC: 3845 3842 3841 3827 Electromedical equipment; cardiographs; surgical support systems: heart-lung machine, exc. iron lung; surgical appliances & supplies; surgical & medical instruments; optical instruments & lenses

### (G-11022)
### ENDERS PROCESS EQUIPMENT CORP
Also Called: Enders Engineering
746 Armitage Ave (60139-3356)
P.O. Box 308, Glen Ellyn (60138-0308)
PHONE..................630 469-3787
Joseph T Enders, *President*
Lisa Enders, *Sales Staff*
EMP: 6 EST: 1970
SQ FT: 250
SALES (est): 920.8K **Privately Held**
SIC: 5084 8711 3567 Pollution control equipment, air (environmental); pollution control equipment, water (environmental); consulting engineer; incinerators, metal: domestic or commercial

### (G-11023)
### FEDEX GROUND PACKAGE SYS INC
115 W Lake Dr Ste 100 (60139-4882)
PHONE..................800 463-3339
Nicki Gushes, *Branch Mgr*
EMP: 4
SALES (corp-wide): 50.3B **Publicly Held**
SIC: 2759 5099 7334 Commercial printing; signs, except electric; photocopying & duplicating services
HQ: Fedex Ground Package System, Inc.
1000 Fed Ex Dr
Coraopolis PA 15108
800 463-3339

### (G-11024)
### FORMTEC INC
180 W Lake Dr (60139-4818)
PHONE..................630 752-9700
Fax: 630 752-9917
Charles J Nemec Jr, *President*
Susan Kraus, *Corp Secy*
Brad Nemec, *VP Sales*
EMP: 29
SQ FT: 37,000
SALES: 160K **Privately Held**
SIC: 3444 Sheet metalwork

### (G-11025)
### G T L TECHNOLOGIES INC
Also Called: G.T.L. International
413 2nd Pl Ste 100 (60139-3505)
P.O. Box 42, Glen Ellyn (60138-0042)
PHONE..................630 469-9818
Brian Xue, *President*
WEI Song, *Admin Sec*
EMP: 4
SALES: 800K **Privately Held**
WEB: www.knivesandgear.com
SIC: 3469 Machine parts, stamped or pressed metal

### (G-11026)
### GATEWAY SCREW & RIVET INC
301 High Grove Blvd (60139-2256)
PHONE..................630 539-2232
Fax: 630 595-1970
Richard L Gunderson, *President*
Tom Kondrat, *Controller*
Laverne Penrod, *Sales Staff*
Randall T Gunderson, *Admin Sec*
▲ EMP: 30 EST: 1954
SALES (est): 5.5MM **Privately Held**
WEB: www.gatewayscrew.com
SIC: 3452 5072 Screws, metal; screws

### (G-11027)
### GLENDALE WOODWORKING
641 E North Ave (60139-3561)
PHONE..................630 545-1520
Ben Malekian, *Owner*
EMP: 4
SALES (est): 395.8K **Privately Held**
SIC: 2431 Millwork

### (G-11028)
### GLOBAL INDUSTRIES INC
1879 Internationale Blvd (60139-2097)
PHONE..................630 681-2818
Lynnette Poole, *Manager*
EMP: 15
SALES (corp-wide): 128.2MM **Privately Held**
SIC: 2521 Wood office furniture
PA: Global Industries, Inc.
17 W Stow Rd
Marlton NJ 08053
856 596-3390

### (G-11029)
### GODING ELECTRIC COMPANY
686 E Fullerton Ave (60139-2597)
PHONE..................630 858-7700
Fax: 630 858-8019
James M Goding, *President*
David Goding, *Vice Pres*
John Goding, *Vice Pres*
EMP: 14
SQ FT: 13,000
SALES (est): 2.9MM **Privately Held**
WEB: www.goding.com
SIC: 7694 5999 5063 Electric motor repair; motors, electric; motors, electric; motor controls, starters & relays: electric

### (G-11030)
### HOERBIGER-ORIGA CORPORATION
100 W Lake Dr (60139-4818)
PHONE..................800 283-1377
Fax: 630 871-1515
Joseph M Hughes, *President*
Joseph H Mihalko, *Corp Secy*
Larry Huetsch, *Vice Pres*
Lenard Winkeler, *Purchasing*
▲ EMP: 55 EST: 1978
SQ FT: 56,000
SALES (est): 8MM **Privately Held**
WEB: www.hoerbigeroriga.com
SIC: 3443 5084 Cylinders, pressure: metal plate; industrial machinery & equipment

### (G-11031)
### HUDAPACK MTAL TREATING ILL INC
550 Mitchell Rd (60139-2581)
PHONE..................630 793-1916
Fax: 630 858-1313
Gary Huss, *President*
Earl Pack, *Vice Pres*
EMP: 40
SQ FT: 42,000
SALES (est): 9.9MM **Privately Held**
SIC: 3398 Metal heat treating

### (G-11032)
### HURST ENTERPRISES INC
1771 English Dr (60139-2469)
PHONE..................708 344-9291
Fax: 708 344-0154
Donald Fagin, *Ch of Bd*
Bill Nordstrom, *President*
Bill Bergghold, *Corp Secy*
EMP: 3
SQ FT: 6,000
SALES: 1MM **Privately Held**
WEB: www.hurstent.com
SIC: 3599 7629 3462 Machine shop, jobbing & repair; electrical repair shops; iron & steel forgings

### (G-11033)
### ILLINOIS TOOL WORKS INC
ITW Commercial Cnstr N Amer
700 High Grove Blvd (60139-2277)
PHONE..................630 825-7900
Timm Fields, *General Mgr*
Inna Tfenver, *Controller*
EMP: 40
SALES (corp-wide): 13.6B **Publicly Held**
SIC: 3672 Printed circuit boards
PA: Illinois Tool Works Inc.
155 Harlem Ave
Glenview IL 60025
847 724-7500

### (G-11034)
### INDUSTRIAL PALLETS LLC
1462 Glen Ellyn Rd (60139-3304)
PHONE..................708 351-8783
Anwar Cantarero,
EMP: 3
SALES (est): 271.3K **Privately Held**
SIC: 2448 Pallets, wood & wood with metal

### (G-11035)
### INVENTIVE CONCEPTS INTL LLC
Also Called: ICI
500 Wall St (60139-1988)
PHONE..................847 350-6102
Young Park, *CEO*
Rick Sizemore, *President*
Gary James, *Vice Pres*
EMP: 8
SALES: 58K **Privately Held**
SIC: 2393 Bags & containers, except sleeping bags: textile

### (G-11036)
### J N R CUSTO-MATIC SCREW INC
200 W Lake Dr (60139-4825)
PHONE..................630 260-1333
Joseph J Bratta, *President*
Nicholas C Bratta, *Vice Pres*
Rocco J Bratta, *Vice Pres*
Briana Pape, *Asst Controller*
Patricia White, *Accounts Mgr*
▲ EMP: 62
SQ FT: 55,000
SALES: 12.2MM **Privately Held**
SIC: 3451 Screw machine products

### (G-11037)
### JDS PRINTING INC
1709 President St (60139-2019)
PHONE..................630 208-1195
Fax: 630 208-1207
Abdul Mandani, *President*
Mariam Mandani, *Director*
EMP: 4
SQ FT: 1,375
SALES: 100K **Privately Held**
WEB: www.jdsprintinginc.com
SIC: 2752 2791 5943 Commercial printing, offset; typesetting; office forms & supplies

### (G-11038)
### KKSP PRECISION MACHINING LLC (PA)
1688 Glen Ellyn Rd (60139-2504)
PHONE..................630 260-1735
Dave Dolan, *CEO*
Ken Duffy, *General Mgr*
Mark Murray, *Vice Pres*
Mark Murey, *CFO*
Mark Ollinger, *CFO*
▲ EMP: 100
SQ FT: 85,000
SALES (est): 60MM **Privately Held**
WEB: www.kksp.com
SIC: 3451 Screw machine products

### (G-11039)
### KRONOS FOODS CORP (PA)
1 Kronos (60139-1965)
PHONE..................773 847-2250
Fax: 224 353-5402
Howard C Eirinberg, *CEO*
Patrick Costello, *President*
Marilyn Kelly, *President*
Pete Bouloukos, *Area Mgr*
Bob Michaels, *Senior VP*
EMP: 277
SQ FT: 93,000
SALES (est): 104.9MM **Privately Held**
WEB: www.kronosproducts.com
SIC: 2013 2051 5141 5963 Prepared beef products from purchased beef; breads, rolls & buns; food brokers; food services, direct sales

### (G-11040)
### LECTRO STIK CORP
Also Called: Stikkiworks Co
1957 Quincy Ct (60139-2045)
PHONE..................630 894-1355
Fax: 630 539-5915
Penny Press Crow, *President*
Joe Cackowski, *Vice Pres*
Cindy Arendt, *Purchasing*
Pete Carter, *Finance*
Rick Wies, *Mktg Dir*
▲ EMP: 26
SQ FT: 25,000

# Glendale Heights - Dupage County (G-11041)    GEOGRAPHIC SECTION

SALES (est): 4.2MM **Privately Held**
SIC: 3952 2891 Wax, artists'; adhesives & sealants

### (G-11041)
**LIFT-ALL COMPANY INC**
1620 Fullerton Ct Ste 400 (60139-2754)
PHONE..................630 534-6860
Fax: 630 534-6864
Lori Lee, *Purch Agent*
Sam Ortiz, *Purch Agent*
Jim Platte, *Human Res Mgr*
Larry Hutchinson, *Sales Mgr*
Steve Pacilio, *Manager*
EMP: 43
SALES (corp-wide): 22.8MM **Privately Held**
WEB: www.lift-all.com
SIC: 3315 Wire & fabricated wire products
HQ: Lift-All Company, Inc.
  1909 Mcfarland Dr
  Landisville PA 17538
  717 898-6615

### (G-11042)
**LUXURY BATH LINERS INC**
1958 Brandon Ct (60139-2086)
PHONE..................630 295-9084
Fax: 630 295-9418
Mark Domanico, *CEO*
Davis Glassberg, *President*
Jacqulyn Graves,
▲ EMP: 30
SQ FT: 28,000
SALES (est): 6MM **Privately Held**
WEB: www.luxurybath.com
SIC: 3088 1521 Tubs (bath, shower & laundry), plastic; single-family housing construction

### (G-11043)
**M-WAVE INTERNATIONAL LLC**
100 High Grove Blvd (60139-2276)
PHONE..................630 562-5550
Fax: 630 562-2430
Joseph A Turek, *President*
Matt Murray, *Technical Mgr*
John Piccirilli, *Manager*
Robert Duke,
▲ EMP: 24
SALES (est): 7.4MM **Privately Held**
SIC: 3672 Printed circuit boards

### (G-11044)
**MAALDAR PUKHTOON GROUP LLC**
Also Called: Smoothie King
339 E Army Trail Rd (60139)
PHONE..................630 696-1723
Nazir Umair, *President*
EMP: 3
SALES (est): 106.8K **Privately Held**
SIC: 2037 Frozen fruits & vegetables

### (G-11045)
**MAKKAH PRINTING**
1979 Bloomingdale Rd (60139-2171)
PHONE..................630 980-2315
Mohammed Uzzaman, *Owner*
EMP: 5 EST: 2008
SQ FT: 1,500
SALES (est): 449.5K **Privately Held**
SIC: 2752 Commercial printing, lithographic

### (G-11046)
**MARSHALL MOLD INC**
Also Called: Marshall Mold & Engineering
1934 Bentley Ct Ste A (60139-4200)
PHONE..................630 582-1800
Dean Stout, *President*
Justin Stout, *Engineer*
EMP: 9 EST: 1987
SQ FT: 6,200
SALES: 1.3MM **Privately Held**
SIC: 3544 Special dies, tools, jigs & fixtures

### (G-11047)
**MEDTEC APPLICATIONS INC**
35 N Brandon Dr Ste A (60139-2024)
PHONE..................224 353-6752
Sarah Goettel, *President*
Helga Hausner, *Treasurer*
EMP: 6

SALES: 500K **Privately Held**
WEB: www.medtecapp.com
SIC: 3841 Surgical & medical instruments

### (G-11048)
**MID-AMERICA TAPING REELING INC (PA)**
Also Called: Mid-America Government Supply
121 Exchange Blvd (60139-2095)
PHONE..................630 629-6646
Barbara Pauls, *President*
Sue Lauritzen, *Vice Pres*
Ed Walton, *Vice Pres*
Baudel Uribe, *Prdtn Mgr*
Enrique Acquart, *Buyer*
▲ EMP: 80
SQ FT: 18,800
SALES (est): 9.1MM **Privately Held**
WEB: www.matr.com
SIC: 7694 Coil winding service; rewinding stators

### (G-11049)
**MOBILE AIR INC**
380 Windy Point Dr (60139-2176)
PHONE..................847 755-0586
Ryan Boyle, *Manager*
EMP: 12
SALES (corp-wide): 12.1MM **Privately Held**
SIC: 7359 3479 Equipment rental & leasing; name plates: engraved, etched, etc.
PA: Mobile Air, Inc
  1821 Northwood Dr
  Troy MI 48084
  248 545-0808

### (G-11050)
**MORRELL INCORPORATED**
340 Windy Point Dr (60139-2176)
PHONE..................630 858-4600
Fax: 630 858-6200
Rosemary Chvojka, *Editor*
Thomas Tiffany, *Engineer*
Matt Flournoy, *Sales Engr*
Robert Halladay, *Sales Engr*
Eduard Speth, *Sales Staff*
EMP: 10
SALES (corp-wide): 95.9MM **Privately Held**
WEB: www.morrellinc.com
SIC: 5084 5065 3621 3643 Hydraulic systems equipment & supplies; electronic parts; motors & generators; power line cable; metal finishing equipment for plating, etc.
PA: Morrell Incorporated
  3333 Bald Mountain Rd
  Auburn Hills MI 48326
  248 373-1600

### (G-11051)
**NESTLE PREPARED FOODS COMPANY**
601 Wall St (60139-1906)
PHONE..................630 671-3721
Scott Agan, *General Mgr*
EMP: 495
SALES (corp-wide): 88.4B **Publicly Held**
SIC: 2038 Dinners, frozen & packaged
HQ: Nestle Prepared Foods Company
  30003 Bainbridge Rd
  Solon OH 44139
  440 248-3600

### (G-11052)
**NORTHSTAR INDUSTRIES INC**
Also Called: Northstar Metal Products
591 Mitchell Rd (60139-2582)
PHONE..................630 446-7800
Fax: 630 446-7810
Linda C Boggess, *President*
Thomas Q Quine, *Principal*
Paul Caravello, *Production*
Imelda Flores, *Purchasing*
George Iwamoto, *Purchasing*
▲ EMP: 55
SQ FT: 35,000
SALES (est): 20.4MM **Privately Held**
SIC: 3444 Sheet metal specialties, not stamped

### (G-11053)
**OMNI VISION INC**
2000 Bloomingdale Rd # 245 (60139-2198)
PHONE..................630 893-1720

Fax: 630 893-9991
Thomas Fair, *President*
Howard Rhodes, *Vice Pres*
Linda Fritz, *Office Mgr*
Walt Kowalski, *Technical Staff*
▲ EMP: 42
SQ FT: 15,000
SALES (est): 5.4MM **Privately Held**
WEB: www.omnivisionusa.com
SIC: 3663 3577 Television monitors; computer peripheral equipment

### (G-11054)
**OSG USA INC (HQ)**
676 E Fullerton Ave (60139-2538)
PHONE..................630 790-1400
Fax: 630 790-3898
Gohei Osawa, *CEO*
Michael Grantham, *President*
Jeffry Tennant, *Exec VP*
Tak Kojima, *Senior VP*
Sherry Tiani, *Controller*
▲ EMP: 50
SQ FT: 37,000
SALES (est): 62.7MM
SALES (corp-wide): 1B **Privately Held**
WEB: www.osgtool.com
SIC: 5084 3541 Machine tools & metalworking machinery; machine tools, metal cutting type
PA: Osg Corporation
  3-22, Honnogahara
  Toyokawa AIC 442-0
  533 821-111

### (G-11055)
**OVAL FIRE PRODUCTS CORPORATION**
Also Called: Oval Brand Fire Products
115 W Lake Dr Ste 300 (60139-4824)
PHONE..................630 635-5000
Kevin Kozlowski, *President*
EMP: 8
SQ FT: 16,000
SALES (est): 148.1K **Privately Held**
SIC: 3999 5999 Fire extinguishers, portable; fire extinguishers; banners

### (G-11056)
**PELCO TOOL & MOLD INC**
181 Exchange Blvd (60139-2095)
PHONE..................630 871-1010
Fax: 630 871-1011
Richard Truhlar, *President*
Roger Wittersheim, *Vice Pres*
Andrea Kadow, *Manager*
Robert W Suva, *Admin Sec*
EMP: 30 EST: 1963
SQ FT: 16,000
SALES: 6.6MM **Privately Held**
WEB: www.pelcotool.com
SIC: 3544 Industrial molds

### (G-11057)
**PILKINGTON NORTH AMERICA INC**
500 Windy Point Dr (60139-2178)
PHONE..................630 545-0063
Rich Buch, *Principal*
EMP: 223
SALES (corp-wide): 5.3B **Privately Held**
SIC: 3211 Flat glass
HQ: Pilkington North America, Inc.
  811 Madison Ave Fl 1
  Toledo OH 43604
  419 247-4955

### (G-11058)
**PRECISION TECHNOLOGIES INC**
Also Called: Pcb Services
2200 Gladstone Ct Ste H (60139-1500)
PHONE..................847 439-5447
Amin Rupani, *President*
Mumtaz Jamal, *Admin Sec*
EMP: 5
SQ FT: 20,000
SALES (est): 530K **Privately Held**
SIC: 7373 3674 Computer-aided manufacturing (CAM) systems service; integrated circuits, semiconductor networks, etc.

### (G-11059)
**PREFERRED PRESS INC**
1934 Bentley Ct Ste D (60139-4200)
P.O. Box 773, Wayne (60184-0773)
PHONE..................630 980-9799

Fax: 630 980-9725
Frank Fanella, *President*
Kenneth Bork, *Admin Sec*
EMP: 6
SQ FT: 3,200
SALES (est): 607.3K **Privately Held**
WEB: www.preferredpress.com
SIC: 2752 Commercial printing, lithographic

### (G-11060)
**PRINTING SYSTEM**
1935 Brandon Ct Ste A (60139-2199)
P.O. Box 88296, Carol Stream (60188-0296)
PHONE..................630 339-5900
Ruel Lacsam, *Principal*
EMP: 3
SALES (est): 160K **Privately Held**
SIC: 2759 Commercial printing

### (G-11061)
**QUANTUM MERUIT LLC**
399 Wall St (60139-1987)
PHONE..................630 283-3555
Oberhier John H, *Principal*
EMP: 3
SALES (est): 135.4K **Privately Held**
SIC: 3572 Computer storage devices

### (G-11062)
**R C COIL SPRING MFG CO INC**
490 Mitchell Rd (60139-2580)
PHONE..................630 790-3500
Fax: 630 790-0113
Paul Sawko, *President*
Chester Sawko, *Chairman*
Gregory E Dembek, *Corp Secy*
Mitchell Sawko, *Exec VP*
Mark Sawko, *Vice Pres*
EMP: 40
SQ FT: 57,000
SALES: 3.8MM **Privately Held**
WEB: www.rccoilspring.com
SIC: 3495 3469 Wire springs; metal stampings

### (G-11063)
**RAIN CREEK BAKING CORP**
1 Sexton Dr (60139-1965)
PHONE..................559 347-9960
EMP: 4 EST: 2011
SALES (est): 231.5K **Privately Held**
SIC: 2051 Bread, cake & related products

### (G-11064)
**RIGHTWAY PRINTING INC**
Also Called: Allegra Print & Imaging
460 Windy Point Dr (60139-2177)
PHONE..................630 790-0444
Fax: 630 790-0440
Gary Blaski, *President*
Stefano Myszka, *Manager*
Cynthia Blaski, *Admin Sec*
EMP: 12
SQ FT: 6,000
SALES (est): 1.8MM **Privately Held**
SIC: 2759 2752 2791 2789 Commercial printing; commercial printing, lithographic; typesetting; bookbinding & related work

### (G-11065)
**ROBERT C WEISHEIT CO INC**
Also Called: Robert C Weisheit Company
999 Regency Dr (60139-2281)
PHONE..................630 766-1213
Fax: 630 766-1350
Robert C Weisheit Jr, *President*
Bill Brubaker, *Plant Supt*
Joe Kowal, *Research*
Bill Serritella, *Human Resources*
Alejandro Limon, *Manager*
EMP: 40 EST: 1946
SQ FT: 23,000
SALES (est): 9.2MM **Privately Held**
WEB: www.weisheit.com
SIC: 3599 Machine shop, jobbing & repair

### (G-11066)
**SCHMIT LABORATORIES INC**
500 Wall St (60139-1988)
PHONE..................773 476-0072
Fax: 773 476-7750
Robert G Schmit, *President*
Cathy Barton, *Office Mgr*
EMP: 48

## Glendale Heights - Dupage County (G-11091)

SQ FT: 100,000
SALES (est): 7.1MM **Privately Held**
SIC: **3999** 7389 2844 Hair & hair-based products; packaging & labeling services; toilet preparations

### (G-11067)
### SCHUBERT ENVIRONMENTAL EQP INC
Also Called: Replace Air
2000 Bloomingdale Rd # 115 (60139-2181)
PHONE.................................630 307-9400
Fax: 630 307-9474
John Schubert, *President*
Tom Martus, *Vice Pres*
EMP: 12 EST: 1979
SQ FT: 12,000
SALES: 1.5MM **Privately Held**
WEB: www.schubert-env.com
SIC: **3444** 3564 Sheet metalwork; air cleaning systems

### (G-11068)
### SCREWS INDUSTRIES INC
301 High Grove Blvd (60139-2256)
PHONE.................................630 539-9200
Fax: 630 539-9060
Dennis Fiedler, *President*
Jim Wormsley, *Plant Mgr*
Julie Barrow, *Purchasing*
Thomas J Kondrat, *Controller*
Arnie Berg, *Sales Mgr*
▲ EMP: 55
SQ FT: 75,000
SALES (est): 13.1MM **Privately Held**
WEB: www.screwsindustries.com
SIC: **3452** 3451 3316 Bolts, metal; nuts, metal; screws, metal; screw machine products; cold finishing of steel shapes

### (G-11069)
### SI ENTERPRISES INC
Also Called: American Fastening Systems
301 High Grove Blvd (60139-2256)
PHONE.................................630 539-9200
Dennis Fiedler, *President*
▲ EMP: 4
SALES (est): 215.2K **Privately Held**
SIC: **3452** Screws, metal

### (G-11070)
### SOUND ENHANCEMENT PRODUCTS INC
Also Called: S.E. P. I.
100 High Grove Blvd (60139-2276)
PHONE.................................847 639-4646
Fax: 847 639-4723
Randy Wright, *President*
Scott Flesher, *Vice Pres*
Ken Scott, *Vice Pres*
Bill Wenzloff, *Sales Mgr*
▲ EMP: 32
SQ FT: 38,000
SALES (est): 5.1MM **Privately Held**
WEB: www.morleypedals.com
SIC: **3651** Household audio equipment

### (G-11071)
### SPIROTHERM INC
25 N Brandon Dr (60139-2024)
PHONE.................................630 307-2662
Fax: 630 307-3773
Eric Roffelsen, *President*
Falke Bruinsma, *Exec VP*
Matt Pefley, *Manager*
Nelleke Roffelson, *Manager*
▲ EMP: 9
SQ FT: 16,000
SALES: 4MM **Privately Held**
WEB: www.spirotherm.com
SIC: **3585** 3433 Parts for heating, cooling & refrigerating equipment; heating equipment, except electric

### (G-11072)
### SPRAYING SYSTEMS CO (PA)
Also Called: Autojet Technologies
200 W North Ave (60139-3408)
P.O. Box 7900, Wheaton (60187-7900)
PHONE.................................630 665-5000
Fax: 630 260-0842
James E Bramsen, *President*
Ken Harriman, *General Mgr*
Jim McGarrey, *General Mgr*
David Yates, *Area Mgr*
Stephen Pearson, *Business Mgr*
▲ EMP: 700
SQ FT: 240,000
SALES (est): 384.3MM **Privately Held**
WEB: www.spray.com
SIC: **3499** Nozzles, spray: aerosol, paint or insecticide

### (G-11073)
### SPRAYING SYSTEMS MIDWEST INC
Also Called: Spraying Systems Co
N Ave And Schmale Rd (60139)
P.O. Box 7900, Wheaton (60187-7900)
PHONE.................................630 665-5000
John A Shoemaker Jr, *President*
Martin Baxter, *Regional Mgr*
Don Fox, *VP Mfg*
Jason Boettcher, *Engineer*
Rich Kassanits, *Engineer*
◆ EMP: 8
SALES (est): 1.7MM
SALES (corp-wide): 384.3MM **Privately Held**
SIC: **3499** Nozzles, spray: aerosol, paint or insecticide
PA: Spraying Systems Co.
200 W North Ave
Glendale Heights IL 60139
630 665-5000

### (G-11074)
### STERLING DIE INC
676 E Fullerton Ave (60139-2538)
PHONE.................................216 267-1300
EMP: 5
SALES (est): 270K **Privately Held**
SIC: **3544** Mfg Dies/Tools/Jigs/Fixtures

### (G-11075)
### STONE DESIGN INC
598 Mitchell Rd (60139-2581)
PHONE.................................630 790-5715
Jean Mitchell-Lockerbie, *Branch Mgr*
EMP: 16
SALES (corp-wide): 21.4MM **Privately Held**
SIC: **5032** 3281 Building stone; cut stone & stone products
PA: Stone Design, Inc
551 598 Mitchell Rd
Glendale Heights IL 60139
630 790-5715

### (G-11076)
### STONE DESIGN INC (PA)
551 598 Mitchell Rd (60139)
PHONE.................................630 790-5715
Jean Mitchell-Lockerbie, *President*
Steve Skroamovsky, *CFO*
Jennifer Cichy, *Sales Staff*
Jackie Patterson, *Sales Associate*
Chris Sorrell, *Marketing Staff*
▲ EMP: 49
SQ FT: 19,500
SALES (est): 21.4MM **Privately Held**
SIC: **5032** 3281 Building stone; marble building stone; cut stone & stone products

### (G-11077)
### STONE INSTALLATION & MAINT INC
598 Mitchell Rd (60139-2581)
PHONE.................................630 545-2326
William Santello, *President*
EMP: 1
SALES (est): 259K **Privately Held**
SIC: **3272** Stone, cast concrete

### (G-11078)
### SUMITOMO MACHINERY CORP AMER
175 W Lake Dr (60139-4818)
PHONE.................................630 752-0200
Fax: 630 752-0208
Steve Scott, *President*
Jeff Eggleston, *Regional Mgr*
John Gresham, *Controller*
Wade Walder, *Manager*
EMP: 25
SALES (corp-wide): 5.9B **Privately Held**
WEB: www.smcyclo.com
SIC: **5063** 3714 3625 3566 Power transmission equipment, electric; motor vehicle parts & accessories; relays & industrial controls; speed changers, drives & gears; iron & steel forgings
HQ: Sumitomo Machinery Corp Of America
4200 Holland Blvd
Chesapeake VA 23323
800 762-9256

### (G-11079)
### SUNBURST SPORTSWEAR INC (PA)
Also Called: Chicago T-Shirt Authority
95 N Brandon Dr (60139-2024)
PHONE.................................630 717-8680
Fax: 630 924-0008
Jin-Yan Lin, *President*
John Smith, *Manager*
Judy Chun Chun Yeh Lin, *Admin Sec*
EMP: 11
SQ FT: 30,000
SALES (est): 2.6MM **Privately Held**
WEB: www.sunburstsportswear.com
SIC: **7336** 2759 Silk screen design; graphic arts & related design; screen printing

### (G-11080)
### SURYA ELECTRONICS INC
Also Called: Amtex
600 Windy Point Dr (60139-3802)
PHONE.................................630 858-8000
Fax: 630 858-0103
Bharat R Patel, *President*
Bob Patel, *President*
Paul Sigler, *QC Mgr*
William Jesse, *Senior Mgr*
▲ EMP: 120
SQ FT: 60,000
SALES (est): 28.8MM **Privately Held**
WEB: www.suryaelectronics.com
SIC: **3672** 3823 Printed circuit boards; computer interface equipment for industrial process control

### (G-11081)
### SYR-TECH PERFORATING CO
325 Windy Point Dr (60139-3804)
PHONE.................................630 942-7300
Fax: 630 942-0500
Gary T Heflen Sr, *President*
Gary Heflen, *General Mgr*
Annette Heflen, *Admin Sec*
EMP: 45
SQ FT: 40,000
SALES (est): 9.2MM **Privately Held**
WEB: www.syrtech.com
SIC: **3441** Fabricated structural metal

### (G-11082)
### SYSTEMSLOGIX LLC
140 W Lake Dr (60139-4818)
PHONE.................................630 784-3113
Dennis Dicosola,
EMP: 3
SALES: 36K **Privately Held**
SIC: **7372** Prepackaged software

### (G-11083)
### TARGET PLASTICS TECH CORP
400 Windy Point Dr (60139-2177)
PHONE.................................630 545-1776
Fax: 630 545-1700
Ivan Racz, *President*
Richard Denning, *Vice Pres*
Marie Racz, *Manager*
Tony Knatt, *Admin Sec*
EMP: 68
SQ FT: 15,000
SALES: 6MM **Privately Held**
WEB: www.tarplatech.com
SIC: **3089** Plastic processing

### (G-11084)
### TIGER TOOL INC
Also Called: Tiger Tool Supply, Inc.
410 Windy Point Dr (60139-2177)
PHONE.................................888 551-4490
Jason Steffey, *Principal*
EMP: 4
SALES (est): 445.5K **Privately Held**
SIC: **3541** Machine tools, metal cutting type

### (G-11085)
### TITAN METALS INC
180 W Lake Dr (60139-4818)
PHONE.................................630 752-9700
Susan Kraus, *President*
Brad Nemec, *Corp Secy*
Colleen Martens, *Manager*
EMP: 45
SQ FT: 37,500
SALES (est): 9.9MM **Privately Held**
WEB: www.titanmetalsinc.com
SIC: **3499** Fire- or burglary-resistive products

### (G-11086)
### TRYMARK PRINT PRODUCTION LLC
155 Internationale Blvd (60139-2092)
PHONE.................................630 668-7800
Mark Nigro, *Principal*
EMP: 2 EST: 2010
SALES (est): 209.4K **Privately Held**
SIC: **2752** Commercial printing, lithographic

### (G-11087)
### UNITED STEEL PERFORATING/ARC
Also Called: Syr Tech Perforating
325 Windy Point Dr (60139-3804)
PHONE.................................630 942-7300
Gary Heflen Sr, *President*
EMP: 40 EST: 1951
SQ FT: 40,000
SALES (est): 475.4K **Privately Held**
WEB: www.syrtechperforating.com
SIC: **3469** Perforated metal, stamped

### (G-11088)
### UNIVERSAL BEAUTY PRODUCTS INC
500 Wall St (60139-1988)
PHONE.................................847 805-4100
Yong C Park, *President*
Barry Williams, *President*
Joycelyn Stephens, *Vice Pres*
Cathy Barton, *Opers Mgr*
Jeff Gorden, *CFO*
◆ EMP: 22
SQ FT: 25,000
SALES (est): 8MM **Privately Held**
WEB: www.universalbeauty.com
SIC: **2844** Shampoos, rinses, conditioners: hair

### (G-11089)
### VITA-V ENERGY CO INC
168 N Brandon Dr (60139-2025)
PHONE.................................630 999-8961
John Golat, *CEO*
EMP: 6
SQ FT: 2,000
SALES (est): 271K **Privately Held**
SIC: **2086** Fruit drinks (less than 100% juice); packaged in cans, etc.

### (G-11090)
### VR PRINTING CO INC
1979 Bloomingdale Rd (60139-2171)
PHONE.................................630 980-2315
Virgil Remot, *President*
EMP: 3
SQ FT: 700
SALES (est): 142.1K **Privately Held**
SIC: **2759** Commercial printing

### (G-11091)
### WEBSTER-HOFF CORPORATION
704 E Fullerton Ave (60139-2998)
PHONE.................................630 858-8030
Fax: 630 858-4993
Tom Zwitter, *CEO*
Jack T Webster, *Ch of Bd*
Bryan Webster, *President*
Liaquat Babul, *Vice Pres*
Mike Winograd, *QC Dir*
▲ EMP: 52
SQ FT: 17,800
SALES: 8MM **Privately Held**
WEB: www.webster-hoff.com
SIC: **3499** Friction material, made from powdered metal

## Glendale Heights - Dupage County (G-11092)

**(G-11092)**
**WHISCO COMPONENT ENGRG INC**
Also Called: Comtelco Industries
501 Mitchell Rd (60139-2582)
PHONE...................630 790-9785
Fax: 630 790-9799
Robert Scorza, *President*
Kathryn Scorza, *Corp Secy*
EMP: 16
SQ FT: 15,000
SALES: 2MM **Privately Held**
WEB: www.comtelcoantennas.com
SIC: 3812 Antennas, radar or communications

**(G-11093)**
**YORK CORRUGATED CONTAINER CORP**
120 W Lake Dr (60139-4818)
PHONE...................630 260-2900
Arthur Bostelman Jr, *President*
William F Lewis, *Vice Pres*
Ken Neuffer, *Vice Pres*
Barry Shamie, *Plant Mgr*
Tom Smith, *Opers Staff*
EMP: 75 EST: 1962
SQ FT: 58,500
SALES (est): 20.4MM **Privately Held**
WEB: www.yorkcorrugated.com
SIC: 2653 Corrugated & solid fiber boxes

## Glenview
### Cook County

**(G-11094)**
**ACRYLIC VENTURES INC**
Also Called: Pease Plastics
1857 Elmdale Ave Ste A (60026-1338)
PHONE...................847 901-4440
Patrick Pease, *President*
Jeanne Pease, *Admin Sec*
EMP: 10
SALES (est): 1.3MM **Privately Held**
WEB: www.acrylicland.com
SIC: 2511 Wood lawn & garden furniture

**(G-11095)**
**ADAMS APPLE DISTRIBUTING LP**
2301 Ravine Way (60025-7627)
PHONE...................847 832-9900
Fax: 847 832-1728
Ellis Levin, *Partner*
Allan Kandelman, *Partner*
▲ EMP: 50
SALES (est): 7.2MM **Privately Held**
WEB: www.drl-ent.com
SIC: 3089 5199 Novelties, plastic; variety store merchandise

**(G-11096)**
**ADDISON STEEL INC**
1340 Bonnie Glen Ln (60025-3137)
PHONE...................847 998-9445
James Chapman, *President*
Carol Chapman, *Admin Sec*
EMP: 2
SQ FT: 1,500
SALES (est): 274.7K **Privately Held**
SIC: 3441 Fabricated structural metal

**(G-11097)**
**ADVANCE TOOLS LLC ○**
2456 Saranac Ln (60026-1061)
PHONE...................855 685-0633
Chiencheng Liu, *Principal*
EMP: 5 EST: 2016
SALES (est): 187.6K **Privately Held**
SIC: 5072 2393 5137 3651 Hardware; duffle bags, canvas: made from purchased materials; canvas bags; handbags; loudspeakers, electrodynamic or magnetic

**(G-11098)**
**AG PRECISION INC**
2443 Fontana Dr (60025-4814)
PHONE...................847 724-7786
Fax: 847 758-9410
George Hass, *President*
Adam Hass, *Vice Pres*
Margaret Staszczak, *Office Mgr*
EMP: 4
SALES (est): 412.8K **Privately Held**
SIC: 3541 7692 Machine tool replacement & repair parts, metal cutting types; welding repair

**(G-11099)**
**AMERICAN CLLEGE CHEST PHYSCANS (PA)**
2595 Patriot Blvd (60026-8022)
PHONE...................224 521-9800
Fax: 847 498-5460
Stephen J Welch, *CEO*
Curt Sessler, *President*
Carla Miller, *Editor*
Martha Zaborowski, *Editor*
Toni Diorio, *Business Mgr*
EMP: 82
SQ FT: 48,500
SALES (est): 26.6MM **Privately Held**
SIC: 8621 2721 Medical field-related associations; periodicals

**(G-11100)**
**AMERICAN GRAPHICS NETWORK INC**
1625 Glenview Rd Unit 309 (60025-2973)
P.O. Box 869 (60025-0869)
PHONE...................847 729-7220
Wanda M Sclavenitis, *President*
Frank Sclavenitis, *Treasurer*
Kirk Guthrie, *Sales Staff*
Lynne Mappa, *Manager*
EMP: 12
SQ FT: 4,200
SALES (est): 1.7MM **Privately Held**
WEB: www.agninc.com
SIC: 2759 2791 2761 2677 Commercial printing; typesetting; manifold business forms; envelopes; packaging paper & plastics film, coated & laminated

**(G-11101)**
**ANGEL EQUIPMENT LLC**
1941 Johns Dr (60025-1615)
PHONE...................815 455-4320
Timothy Anderson,
EMP: 4
SALES (est): 172.1K **Privately Held**
SIC: 3556 Bakery machinery

**(G-11102)**
**ANIXTER INC**
2301 Patriot Blvd (60025-8020)
P.O. Box 609 (60025)
PHONE...................512 989-4254
EMP: 31
SALES (est): 11.6MM **Privately Held**
SIC: 3965 5251 Mfg Fasteners/Buttons/Pins Ret Hardware

**(G-11103)**
**ANIXTER INC**
2301 Patriot Blvd (60025-8020)
PHONE...................800 323-8167
EMP: 198
SALES (est): 104.2MM **Privately Held**
SIC: 3641 Mfg Electric Lamps

**(G-11104)**
**APPLE RUSH COMPANY**
4300 Dipaolo Ctr (60025)
PHONE...................847 730-5324
Robert J Corr, *Principal*
EMP: 4
SALES (est): 225.3K **Privately Held**
SIC: 2082 Malt beverages

**(G-11105)**
**ASAHI KASEI BIOPROCESS INC**
1855 Elmdale Ave (60026-1355)
PHONE...................847 834-0800
Osamu Matsuzaki, *President*
Nobuo Nakano, *Principal*
Tomoyuki Miyabayashi, *Vice Pres*
Christopher Nordhoff, *Vice Pres*
Kimo Sanderson, *Vice Pres*
EMP: 48
SQ FT: 24,000
SALES (est): 13.4MM
SALES (corp-wide): 16.5B **Privately Held**
SIC: 3559 5047 Pharmaceutical machinery; medical laboratory equipment
HQ: Asahi Kasei Medical Co., Ltd.
1-105, Kandajimbocho
Chiyoda-Ku TKY 101-0
332 963-785

**(G-11106)**
**BEAS BAGS**
315 Cherry Ln (60025-4507)
PHONE...................847 486-1943
Bea Cerrone, *Owner*
EMP: 3
SALES (est): 143.6K **Privately Held**
SIC: 2393 Textile bags

**(G-11107)**
**BELTONE CORPORATION (DH)**
2601 Patriot Blvd (60026-8023)
PHONE...................847 832-3300
Todd Murray, *President*
Dan Lanan, *Project Mgr*
Paul Giampaolo, *Treasurer*
Steve Erickson, *Controller*
Megan Sommer, *Human Resources*
EMP: 78
SALES (est): 61MM
SALES (corp-wide): 1.2B **Privately Held**
SIC: 3842 Hearing aids
HQ: Gn Hearing Care Corporation
8001 E Bloomington Fwy
Bloomington MN 55420
800 248-4327

**(G-11108)**
**BERGMANN ORTHOTIC LABORATORY**
1864 Johns Dr (60025-1657)
PHONE...................847 729-7923
Fax: 847 729-9020
David Bergmann, *Manager*
EMP: 3
SALES (est): 240.5K **Privately Held**
SIC: 3842 Orthopedic appliances

**(G-11109)**
**BOWS ARTS INC**
1944 Lehigh Ave Ste B (60025-1661)
PHONE...................847 501-3161
Barbara McBride, *President*
Deborah Da Silva, *Vice Pres*
Charles McBride, *Treasurer*
▲ EMP: 18
SALES: 750K **Privately Held**
SIC: 3069 7389 Rubber hair accessories;

**(G-11110)**
**BRANMARK STRATEGY GROUP LLC**
2013 Burr Oak Dr W (60025-1805)
PHONE...................847 849-9080
Richard Kerndt, *Managing Dir*
Sarah Kerndt, *Principal*
EMP: 3
SALES (est): 257.5K **Privately Held**
SIC: 3761 Guided missiles & space vehicles, research & development

**(G-11111)**
**CENTURY MOLDED PLASTICS INC**
Also Called: Soho
3120 W Lake Ave (60026-1294)
PHONE...................847 729-3455
Fax: 847 998-1085
Kenneth J Lemanski, *President*
Catherine Lemanski, *Corp Secy*
Anthony Bell, *Purchasing*
Sheryl Devorak, *Office Mgr*
Sean Lemanski, *Manager*
▲ EMP: 35 EST: 1959
SQ FT: 20,000
SALES (est): 7.6MM **Privately Held**
WEB: www.centuryplastics.com
SIC: 3089 5719 Injection molding of plastics; molding primary plastic; housewares

**(G-11112)**
**CHOCOLATE POTPOURRI LTD**
Also Called: Chicago Toffee Co
3908 Kiess Dr (60026-1083)
PHONE...................847 729-8878
Fax: 847 729-8879
Richard Gordon, *President*
Marsha Gordon, *Vice Pres*
Patty Steffen, *Manager*
Robert Gordon, *Admin Sec*
EMP: 11
SQ FT: 7,800
SALES (est): 1.9MM **Privately Held**
WEB: www.chocolatetruffles.com
SIC: 2066 2064 Chocolate & cocoa products; chocolate candy, except solid chocolate

**(G-11113)**
**CHRISTIANICA CENTER**
1807 Prairie St (60025-2921)
P.O. Box 685 (60025-0685)
PHONE...................847 657-3818
Fax: 847 657-3831
John P Gabriel, *Director*
▲ EMP: 4
SQ FT: 700
SALES: 78.3K **Privately Held**
SIC: 2731 Books: publishing only

**(G-11114)**
**CIS SYSTEMS INC**
Also Called: Ink2image
4338 Regency Dr (60025-5218)
PHONE...................847 827-0747
Anthony K Martin, *President*
Deborah Ascaridis, *Corp Secy*
EMP: 5
SQ FT: 4,000
SALES: 900K **Privately Held**
SIC: 2851 5111 5085 2893 Lacquers, varnishes, enamels & other coatings; printing paper; ink, printers'; printing ink

**(G-11115)**
**CORA LEE CANDIES INC**
1844 Waukegan Rd (60025-2112)
PHONE...................847 724-2754
Fax: 847 724-4608
James Preibe, *President*
James A Priebe, *President*
EMP: 12
SQ FT: 2,600
SALES (est): 510K **Privately Held**
SIC: 5441 5145 2066 Candy; candy; chocolate & cocoa products

**(G-11116)**
**CORNERSTONES PUBLISHING I**
3054 Crestwood Ln (60025-2622)
PHONE...................847 998-4746
Pam Mers, *Principal*
EMP: 25
SALES (est): 1.9MM **Privately Held**
SIC: 2731 Books: publishing only

**(G-11117)**
**CREATIVE CONFECTIONS INC**
1955 Johns Dr (60025-1615)
PHONE...................847 724-0990
Catherine Raffles, *President*
EMP: 2
SQ FT: 1,134
SALES (est): 258.4K **Privately Held**
WEB: www.etoffee.com
SIC: 2064 Candy & other confectionery products

**(G-11118)**
**CRYSTAL CAVE**
1946 Lehigh Ave Ste E (60026-1662)
PHONE...................847 251-1160
Fax: 847 251-1172
Joseph Puehringer, *Owner*
Sharon Pundt, *Bookkeeper*
EMP: 10 EST: 1969
SQ FT: 3,400
SALES (est): 605K **Privately Held**
WEB: www.thecrystalcave.us
SIC: 3231 5719 Cut & engraved glassware: made from purchased glass; glassware

**(G-11119)**
**DAILY MONEY MATTERS LLC**
2200 Goldenrod Ln (60026-8008)
PHONE...................847 729-8393
Wendy Freimuth, *Principal*
EMP: 3 EST: 2010
SALES (est): 126.7K **Privately Held**
SIC: 2711 Newspapers, publishing & printing

## GEOGRAPHIC SECTION
### Glenview - Cook County (G-11145)

**(G-11120)**
**DANIELS JEWELRY & MFG CO**
1436 Waukegan Rd (60025-2121)
PHONE..................847 998-5222
Fax: 847 998-0662
Albert Daniels, *President*
Esther Daniels, *Corp Secy*
Valerie Daniels, *Manager*
**EMP:** 3
**SQ FT:** 1,200
**SALES (est):** 350K **Privately Held**
**WEB:** www.danielsjewelry.net
**SIC:** 5944 3961 Jewelry, precious stones & precious metals; costume jewelry

**(G-11121)**
**DREAMWRKS GRPHIC CMMNCTONS LLC**
2323 Ravine Way (60025-7627)
PHONE..................847 679-6710
John Perkins, *Exec VP*
Jason Elsner, *Project Mgr*
Rocky Sardo, *Project Mgr*
Reno Tomasi, *Project Mgr*
Rick Steinberg, *Sales Mgr*
**EMP:** 55
**SQ FT:** 45,000
**SALES (est):** 18.2MM **Privately Held**
**WEB:** www.glginc.com
**SIC:** 2752 Commercial printing, offset

**(G-11122)**
**DUO-FAST CORPORATION (HQ)**
155 Harlem Ave (60025-4075)
PHONE..................847 944-2288
Robert Bohan, *COO*
Michael Flannery, *Vice Pres*
Craig Hindmarch, *Vice Pres*
Alan Moon, *Vice Pres*
Holly Roberts, *Vice Pres*
◆ **EMP:** 24 **EST:** 1936
**SQ FT:** 60,000
**SALES (est):** 56.3MM
**SALES (corp-wide):** 13.6B **Publicly Held**
**WEB:** www.tack.com
**SIC:** 3399 3542 3546 Staples, nonferrous metal or wire; nails: aluminum, brass or other nonferrous metal or wire; machine tools, metal forming type; power-driven handtools
**PA:** Illinois Tool Works Inc.
 155 Harlem Ave
 Glenview IL 60025
 847 724-7500

**(G-11123)**
**EIESLAND BUILDERS INC**
Also Called: Eiesland Woodwork
2041 Johns Dr (60025-1654)
PHONE..................847 998-1731
Fax: 847 998-1766
Arvid Eiesland, *President*
Lisa Eiesland, *Bookkeeper*
Brian Cloney, *Manager*
**EMP:** 20
**SALES:** 1.4MM **Privately Held**
**WEB:** www.eiesland.com
**SIC:** 1751 2431 Cabinet & finish carpentry; millwork

**(G-11124)**
**FEDEX OFFICE & PRINT SVCS INC**
1623 Waukegan Rd (60025-2107)
PHONE..................847 729-3030
David Stevens, *Principal*
**EMP:** 28
**SALES (corp-wide):** 50.3B **Publicly Held**
**WEB:** www.kinkos.com
**SIC:** 7334 2791 2789 Photocopying & duplicating services; typesetting; bookbinding & related work
**HQ:** Fedex Office And Print Services, Inc.
 7900 Legacy Dr
 Plano TX 75024
 214 550-7000

**(G-11125)**
**FITNESS WEAR INC**
1940 Lehigh Ave Ste B (60026-1659)
PHONE..................847 486-1704
Barry Brandwein, *VP Sales*
Carol Clanton, *Manager*
**EMP:** 3

**SALES (corp-wide):** 1.4MM **Privately Held**
**WEB:** www.fitnesswear.com
**SIC:** 2396 2395 Screen printing on fabric articles; pleating & stitching
**PA:** Fitness Wear Inc
 2714 Prairie Ave
 Evanston IL 60201
 847 486-1704

**(G-11126)**
**FLEET MANAGEMENT SOLUTIONS INC (DH)**
2700 Patriot Blvd Ste 200 (60026-8064)
PHONE..................805 787-0508
Tony Eales, *CEO*
Sheila Henley Roth, *CFO*
**EMP:** 22
**SALES (est):** 2.5MM **Privately Held**
**WEB:** www.fmsgps.com
**SIC:** 3663 4899 Radio & TV communications equipment; satellite earth stations
**HQ:** Teletrac Navman (Uk) Ltd
 K1 - First Floor
 Milton Keynes BUCKS MK7 6
 123 475-9131

**(G-11127)**
**G & H BALANCER SERVICE**
2212 Strawberry Ln (60026-1346)
PHONE..................773 509-1988
Fax: 847 559-1120
Gary Hildreth, *Owner*
**EMP:** 3
**SALES (est):** 192.7K **Privately Held**
**WEB:** www.ghbalancer.com
**SIC:** 3596 Industrial scales

**(G-11128)**
**GCG CORP**
Also Called: Stitchmine Custom Embroidery
4344 Regency Dr (60025-5218)
PHONE..................847 298-2285
Gary Glenn, *President*
Carolyn Glenn, *Vice Pres*
**EMP:** 2
**SALES (est):** 309.9K **Privately Held**
**SIC:** 5611 2396 Clothing accessories: men's & boys'; clothing, men's & boys': everyday, except suits & sportswear; clothing, sportswear, men's & boys'; cap fronts & visors; screen printing on fabric articles

**(G-11129)**
**GLEN PRODUCTS**
927 Harms Rd (60025-3246)
P.O. Box 956 (60025-0956)
PHONE..................847 998-1361
David Slaght, *Owner*
**EMP:** 1 **EST:** 1960
**SALES:** 250K **Privately Held**
**SIC:** 3545 Precision measuring tools

**(G-11130)**
**GLENVIEW CUSTOM CABINETS INC**
1921 Pickwick Ln (60026-1308)
PHONE..................847 345-5754
Fax: 847 724-7401
Wayne Belue, *President*
Chuck Matchen, *Office Mgr*
**EMP:** 9
**SQ FT:** 12,200
**SALES (est):** 1MM **Privately Held**
**WEB:** www.glenviewcustomcabinets.com
**SIC:** 2599 5712 2541 2434 Cabinets, factory; cabinet work, custom; wood partitions & fixtures; wood kitchen cabinets

**(G-11131)**
**GLENVIEW GRIND**
1837 Glenview Rd (60025-2909)
PHONE..................847 729-0111
**EMP:** 2
**SALES (est):** 207.4K **Privately Held**
**SIC:** 3599 Grinding castings for the trade

**(G-11132)**
**GLENVIEW SYSTEMS INC**
Also Called: Glenview Health Systems
3048 N Lake Ter (60026-1335)
PHONE..................847 724-2691
Fax: 847 724-1713
Michael Sciortino, *President*
Jeannie Sciortino, *Admin Sec*

▲ **EMP:** 10
**SQ FT:** 11,000
**SALES (est):** 1.8MM **Privately Held**
**WEB:** www.glensys.com
**SIC:** 3596 Scales & balances, except laboratory

**(G-11133)**
**GREEK ART PRINTING & PUBG CO**
Also Called: Chicago Menu Co
2921 Covert Rd (60025-4608)
PHONE..................847 724-8860
John A Damianos, *Owner*
**EMP:** 4 **EST:** 1914
**SQ FT:** 2,400
**SALES:** 900K **Privately Held**
**SIC:** 2759 2752 2732 2731 Letterpress printing; commercial printing, offset; book printing; book publishing

**(G-11134)**
**GREEN ROOF SOLUTIONS INC**
4336 Regency Dr (60025-5218)
PHONE..................847 297-7936
Kate Horvath, *President*
Brian Barry, *Opers Mgr*
John Brophy, *Accounts Mgr*
▼ **EMP:** 5
**SQ FT:** 2,500
**SALES (est):** 861.4K **Privately Held**
**WEB:** www.greenroofsolutions.com
**SIC:** 2952 Roof cement: asphalt, fibrous or plastic

**(G-11135)**
**HAMMOND PRINTING**
1622 Pickwick Ln (60025-1506)
PHONE..................847 724-1539
**EMP:** 5
**SALES (est):** 370K **Privately Held**
**SIC:** 2752 Commercial Printing

**(G-11136)**
**HENES USA INC**
125 Milwaukee Ave Ste 301 (60025)
PHONE..................312 448-6130
Kyung Kyun Min, *President*
Yung Hwa, *Vice Pres*
Leslie Charles, *Agent*
Jin Dongbang, *Asst Mgr*
▲ **EMP:** 60
**SQ FT:** 833
**SALES (est):** 5.5MM **Privately Held**
**SIC:** 3944 Children's vehicles, except bicycles

**(G-11137)**
**HERITAGE SHEET METAL INC**
2049 Johns Dr (60025-1654)
PHONE..................847 724-8449
Michael A Witt, *President*
Richard H Witt III, *Admin Sec*
**EMP:** 2
**SALES (est):** 215.9K **Privately Held**
**SIC:** 3444 Sheet metalwork

**(G-11138)**
**HUE CIRCLE INC**
4315 Regency Dr (60025-5219)
PHONE..................224 567-8116
▲ **EMP:** 3 **EST:** 2009
**SALES (est):** 232.2K **Privately Held**
**SIC:** 5087 3999 Beauty salon & barber shop equipment & supplies; barber & beauty shop equipment

**(G-11139)**
**HYGEIA INDUSTRIES INC**
1855 Elmdale Ave (60026-1355)
PHONE..................847 380-2030
Louis Bellafiore, *President*
James Sanderson, *Vice Pres*
Mark Dunn, *Engineer*
Catherine Bellafiore, *CFO*
**EMP:** 10
**SQ FT:** 3,000
**SALES (est):** 1.9MM **Privately Held**
**WEB:** www.technikrom.com
**SIC:** 3559 Pharmaceutical machinery

**(G-11140)**
**I T W INC**
155 Harlem Ave (60025-4075)
PHONE..................847 657-6171
Fax: 847 657-4790

Michael Larsen, *President*
Mike Potempa, *Vice Pres*
Mike Colwell, *Manager*
Vishal Garg, *Manager*
Belinda Quaiyoom, *Manager*
**EMP:** 199
**SALES (est):** 51.6MM
**SALES (corp-wide):** 13.6B **Publicly Held**
**SIC:** 3565 Packing & wrapping machinery
**PA:** Illinois Tool Works Inc.
 155 Harlem Ave
 Glenview IL 60025
 847 724-7500

**(G-11141)**
**ILLINOIS TOOL WORKS INC (PA)**
155 Harlem Ave (60025-4075)
PHONE..................847 724-7500
Fax: 847 657-4261
E Scott Santi, *Ch of Bd*
Randall J Scheuneman, *Vice Pres*
Michael M Larsen, *CFO*
Marcos Mihara, *Controller*
Olaf Roth, *Finance Mgr*
**EMP:** 400 **EST:** 1912
**SALES:** 13.6B **Publicly Held**
**WEB:** www.itw.com
**SIC:** 3089 3965 3499 2891 Injection molded finished plastic products; closures, plastic; synthetic resin finished products; fasteners; strapping, metal; adhesives & sealants; refrigeration & heating equipment

**(G-11142)**
**ILLINOIS TOOL WORKS INC**
3640 W Lake Ave (60026-1215)
PHONE..................847 657-4639
Arthur Malin, *Manager*
**EMP:** 4
**SALES (corp-wide):** 13.6B **Publicly Held**
**SIC:** 2621 Paper mills
**PA:** Illinois Tool Works Inc.
 155 Harlem Ave
 Glenview IL 60025
 847 724-7500

**(G-11143)**
**ILLINOIS TOOL WORKS INC**
Magnaflux
155 Harlem Ave (60025-4075)
PHONE..................847 657-5300
Fax: 847 657-5388
Steve Groeninger, *General Mgr*
Steve Henn, *Div Sub Head*
Bob Dixon, *Engineer*
David Foley, *Enginr/R&D Mgr*
Illeana Perez, *Human Res Dir*
**EMP:** 40
**SALES (corp-wide):** 13.6B **Publicly Held**
**SIC:** 3829 3825 Measuring & controlling devices; instruments to measure electricity
**PA:** Illinois Tool Works Inc.
 155 Harlem Ave
 Glenview IL 60025
 847 724-7500

**(G-11144)**
**ILLINOIS TOOL WORKS INC**
Signode Packaging Systems
3650 W Lake Ave (60026-1215)
PHONE..................847 724-6100
Fax: 847 657-4675
John Becker, *General Mgr*
Michael Loeschen, *Vice Pres*
Lary Ruud, *Controller*
Alex Popovich, *Controller*
**EMP:** 300
**SALES (corp-wide):** 13.6B **Publicly Held**
**SIC:** 3089 Injection molded finished plastic products; closures, plastic; synthetic resin finished products
**PA:** Illinois Tool Works Inc.
 155 Harlem Ave
 Glenview IL 60025
 847 724-7500

**(G-11145)**
**ILLINOIS TOOL WORKS INC**
3660 W Lake Ave (60026-1215)
PHONE..................847 657-4022
**EMP:** 92
**SALES (corp-wide):** 13.6B **Publicly Held**
**SIC:** 3089 Injection molded finished plastic products

## Glenview - Cook County (G-11146) — GEOGRAPHIC SECTION

PA: Illinois Tool Works Inc.
155 Harlem Ave
Glenview IL 60025
847 724-7500

**(G-11146)**
**IMED GLENVIEW**
1247 Milwaukee Ave (60025-2464)
PHONE....................847 298-2200
Alexander Gorodetsky, *Principal*
**EMP:** 3 **EST:** 2007
**SALES (est):** 334K **Privately Held**
**SIC:** 3826 Magnetic resonance imaging apparatus

**(G-11147)**
**INK SPOT SILK SCREEN**
84 Park Dr (60025-2721)
PHONE....................847 724-6234
**EMP:** 2
**SALES (est):** 215.9K **Privately Held**
**SIC:** 2752 Commercial printing, offset

**(G-11148)**
**INSTITUTIONAL FOODS PACKING CO**
Also Called: Leahy-Ifp Company
2350 Ravine Way Ste 200 (60025-7621)
PHONE....................847 904-5250
Timothy Leahy, *CEO*
Michael Leahy, *President*
Greg Lojkutz, *President*
Margaret Leahy, *Corp Secy*
**EMP:** 40
**SALES (est):** 3.7MM
**SALES (corp-wide):** 101.5MM **Privately Held**
**WEB:** www.ecarbotrol.com
**SIC:** 2087 Fruit juices: concentrated for fountain use
PA: Wm. H Leahy Associates, Inc.
2350 Ravine Way Ste 200
Glenview IL 60025
847 904-5250

**(G-11149)**
**INTER-MARKET INC**
1946 Lehigh Ave Ste A (60026-1644)
PHONE....................847 729-5330
**Fax:** 847 729-4849
Jerry O'Connor, *President*
Trung Nguyen, *CTO*
**EMP:** 5
**SQ FT:** 2,100
**SALES (est):** 852.9K **Privately Held**
**WEB:** www.imlec.com
**SIC:** 5063 2542 Electrical apparatus & equipment; partitions & fixtures, except wood

**(G-11150)**
**ITW BLDG COMPONENTS GROUP (HQ)**
Also Called: ITW Paslode
155 Harlem Ave (60025-4075)
PHONE....................847 634-1900
**Fax:** 708 634-6203
David B Speer, *CEO*
▲ **EMP:** 8
**SALES (est):** 1.8MM
**SALES (corp-wide):** 13.6B **Publicly Held**
**SIC:** 3999 3315 5072 Atomizers, toiletry; nails, spikes, brads & similar items; staples
PA: Illinois Tool Works Inc.
155 Harlem Ave
Glenview IL 60025
847 724-7500

**(G-11151)**
**ITW DYNATEC**
3600 W Lake Ave (60026-1215)
PHONE....................847 657-4830
Scott Santi, *CEO*
**EMP:** 3 **EST:** 2010
**SALES (est):** 204.1K **Privately Held**
**SIC:** 2891 3465 Adhesives; body parts, automobile: stamped metal

**(G-11152)**
**ITW GLOBAL INVESTMENTS INC (HQ)**
155 Harlem Ave (60025-4075)
PHONE....................847 724-7500
Randall Scheuneman, *President*
Phillip J McGovern, *Vice Pres*
Joanna B Pasek, *Vice Pres*
David O Livingston, *Treasurer*
**EMP:** 1
**SALES (est):** 4.5MM
**SALES (corp-wide):** 13.6B **Publicly Held**
**SIC:** 3714 Motor vehicle parts & accessories
PA: Illinois Tool Works Inc.
155 Harlem Ave
Glenview IL 60025
847 724-7500

**(G-11153)**
**ITW INTERNATIONAL HOLDINGS LLC (HQ)**
Also Called: I T W Affrdbl Hsing Invstments
3600 W Lake Ave (60026-1215)
PHONE....................847 724-7500
Harold Smith, *Ch of Bd*
David C Parry, *Principal*
E Scott Santi, *Principal*
Timothy J Gardner, *Vice Pres*
John R Hartnett, *Vice Pres*
**EMP:** 10
**SALES (est):** 19.4MM
**SALES (corp-wide):** 13.6B **Publicly Held**
**SIC:** 3089 Injection molded finished plastic products; closures, plastic
PA: Illinois Tool Works Inc.
155 Harlem Ave
Glenview IL 60025
847 724-7500

**(G-11154)**
**JOSEPHS PRINTING SERVICE**
1739 Chestnut Ave Ste 107 (60025-1760)
PHONE....................847 724-4429
M Terry Oswald, *President*
**EMP:** 5
**SQ FT:** 6,800
**SALES (est):** 479.4K **Privately Held**
**SIC:** 2752 7336 2791 Commercial printing, offset; graphic arts & related design; typesetting

**(G-11155)**
**K & A PRECISION MACHINE INC**
2500 Ravine Way (60025-7629)
PHONE....................847 998-1933
**Fax:** 847 832-9019
Arie Zweig, *President*
Mike Gniot, *Plant Mgr*
Hava Frenkel, *Admin Sec*
**EMP:** 55
**SQ FT:** 17,000
**SALES (est):** 6.1MM **Privately Held**
**SIC:** 3599 Machine shop, jobbing & repair

**(G-11156)**
**KOHLER CO**
Also Called: Kohler K&B Store
1180 Milwaukee Ave (60025-2418)
PHONE....................847 635-8071
Gar Trispell, *General Mgr*
**EMP:** 48
**SALES (corp-wide):** 8B **Privately Held**
**SIC:** 3431 7389 Plumbing fixtures: enameled iron cast iron or pressed metal; design services
PA: Kohler Co.
444 Highland Dr
Kohler WI 53044
920 457-4441

**(G-11157)**
**KOREA TIMES**
615 Milwaukee Ave Ste 12 (60025-3878)
PHONE....................847 626-0388
**Fax:** 847 463-2345
Yung W Kim, *Owner*
Yong Tae Park, *Systems Staff*
Khi Lee, *Admin Sec*
▲ **EMP:** 66
**SALES (est):** 4.4MM **Privately Held**
**SIC:** 2721 2791 2759 2711 Periodicals; typesetting; commercial printing; newspapers

**(G-11158)**
**KOREA TIMES CHICAGO INC**
615 Milwaukee Ave Ste 12 (60025-3878)
PHONE....................847 626-0388
John Lee, *President*
Sean Kwon, *Manager*
Jong S Lee, *Director*
**EMP:** 33
**SQ FT:** 22,000
**SALES (est):** 1.6MM
**SALES (corp-wide):** 76.7MM **Privately Held**
**WEB:** www.koreatimeshawaii.com
**SIC:** 2711 Newspapers, publishing & printing
PA: The Korea Times Los Angeles Inc
3731 Wilshire Blvd
Los Angeles CA 90010
323 692-2000

**(G-11159)**
**KRAFT FOOD INGREDIENTS CORP (HQ)**
Also Called: Kraft Foods
801 Waukegan Rd (60025-4391)
P.O. Box 398, Memphis TN (38101-0398)
PHONE....................901 381-6500
**Fax:** 847 646-5150
Robert Herron, *President*
Mark H Berling, *Exec VP*
Paul Kenny, *Vice Pres*
Ron Jones, *Opers Staff*
Catherine Powers, *Credit Mgr*
▼ **EMP:** 100
**SQ FT:** 60,000
**SALES (est):** 71.2MM
**SALES (corp-wide):** 26.4B **Publicly Held**
**WEB:** www.kraftfoodingredients.com
**SIC:** 5143 5149 2099 Cheese; dairy products, dried or canned; flavourings & fragrances; food preparations
PA: The Kraft Heinz Company
200 E Randolph St # 7300
Chicago IL 60601
412 456-5700

**(G-11160)**
**KRAFT HEINZ COMPANY**
801 Waukegan Rd (60025-4391)
PHONE....................847 646-2000
Bernardo Hees, *CEO*
Nichol Drews, *Manager*
George Logothetis, *Analyst*
**EMP:** 120
**SALES (corp-wide):** 26.4B **Publicly Held**
**SIC:** 2022 3411 2095 2043 Natural cheese; processed cheese; spreads, cheese; dips, cheese-based; food & beverage containers; coffee roasting (except by wholesale grocers); freeze-dried coffee; instant coffee; cereal breakfast foods; dressings, salad: raw & cooked (except dry mixes); powders, drink
PA: The Kraft Heinz Company
200 E Randolph St # 7300
Chicago IL 60601
412 456-5700

**(G-11161)**
**KRAFT HEINZ FOODS COMPANY**
801 Waukegan Rd (60025-4391)
PHONE....................847 646-3690
**Fax:** 847 998-2992
**EMP:** 210
**SALES (corp-wide):** 26.4B **Publicly Held**
**SIC:** 2022 Processed cheese
HQ: Kraft Heinz Foods Company
1 Ppg Pl Ste 3200
Pittsburgh PA 15222
412 456-5700

**(G-11162)**
**KRAFT HEINZ FOODS COMPANY**
801 Waukegan Rd (60025-4391)
PHONE....................847 646-2000
Catherine Chen, *QC Mgr*
Berrie Ererd, *Engineer*
Sarwat Gabriel, *Engineer*
Angela Dodge, *Senior Engr*
Maureen Taylor, *Sales Staff*
**EMP:** 203
**SALES (corp-wide):** 26.4B **Publicly Held**
**WEB:** www.kraft.com
**SIC:** 2035 Dressings, salad: raw & cooked (except dry mixes)
HQ: Kraft Heinz Foods Company
1 Ppg Pl Ste 3200
Pittsburgh PA 15222
412 456-5700

**(G-11163)**
**KRAFT PIZZA COMPANY INC (DH)**
Also Called: Kraft Foods
1 Kraft Ct (60025)
PHONE....................847 646-2000
**Fax:** 847 646-2454
David S Johnson, *President*
Peter Boyle, *President*
Barbara M Ford, *President*
Rajesh Garg, *Exec VP*
Gregory P Banks, *Vice Pres*
▼ **EMP:** 50 **EST:** 1962
**SQ FT:** 450,000
**SALES (est):** 260.9MM
**SALES (corp-wide):** 88.4B **Publicly Held**
**SIC:** 2038 Pizza, frozen; snacks, including onion rings, cheese sticks, etc.
HQ: Nestle Usa, Inc.
800 N Brand Blvd
Glendale CA 91203
818 549-6000

**(G-11164)**
**KRAM DIGITAL SOLUTIONS INC (PA)**
1717 Chestnut Ave (60025-1720)
PHONE....................312 222-0431
David Kohn, *President*
Bill Smith, *Manager*
**EMP:** 4
**SQ FT:** 1,100
**SALES (est):** 419.7K **Privately Held**
**WEB:** www.kramdigital.com
**SIC:** 2752 7334 Commercial printing, offset; photocopying & duplicating services

**(G-11165)**
**LCR HALLCREST LLC (PA)**
1911 Pickwick Ln (60026-1308)
PHONE....................847 998-8580
**Fax:** 847 998-6866
Rocco Saoienza Jr, *Vice Pres*
John Romano, *Sales Dir*
Jason Symons, *Manager*
Rocco Sapienza,
◆ **EMP:** 46
**SQ FT:** 25,000
**SALES (est):** 7.4MM **Privately Held**
**WEB:** www.liquidcrystalresources.com
**SIC:** 3829 Thermometers, liquid-in-glass & bimetal type

**(G-11166)**
**LOTTUS INC**
3216 Ronald Rd (60025-4563)
PHONE....................847 691-9464
Artemio Marquez, *Manager*
**EMP:** 4
**SALES (est):** 399.2K **Privately Held**
**SIC:** 2448 Wood pallets & skids

**(G-11167)**
**MARCH MANUFACTURING INC (PA)**
Also Called: March Pumps
1819 Pickwick Ln (60026-1306)
PHONE....................847 729-5300
**Fax:** 847 729-7062
Fredrick Zimmermann, *President*
Fritz Zimmermann, *Corp Secy*
Carl Zimmermann, *Vice Pres*
Hans Zimmermann, *Vice Pres*
Michelle Bellito, *Purch Mgr*
▲ **EMP:** 56 **EST:** 1954
**SQ FT:** 120,000
**SALES (est):** 13.1MM **Privately Held**
**SIC:** 3561 3586 Pumps & pumping equipment; measuring & dispensing pumps

**(G-11168)**
**MICROWARE INC**
2418 Swainwood Dr (60025-2744)
PHONE....................847 943-9113
William Anderson, *President*
Barbara Anderson, *Corp Secy*
**EMP:** 2
**SALES (est):** 230K **Privately Held**
**WEB:** www.mwcomputers.net
**SIC:** 3625 Control circuit relays, industrial

# GEOGRAPHIC SECTION

Glenview - Cook County (G-11195)

**(G-11169)**
**MID AMERICA INTL INC**
Also Called: Mid America Chemical
1245 Milwaukee Ave # 202 (60025-2400)
 PHONE..................................847 635-8303
 John C MA, *President*
 ▲ EMP: 6
 SALES (est): 841K  **Privately Held**
 SIC: 2899  Chemical supplies for foundries

**(G-11170)**
**MONOGRAM CREATIVE GROUP INC**
1723 Wildberry Dr Unit C (60025-1794)
 PHONE..................................312 802-1433
 Pamela Vankirk-Schmidt, *President*
 ▲ EMP: 4
 SALES (est): 83K  **Privately Held**
 SIC: 2064  Candy & other confectionery products

**(G-11171)**
**NAVMAN WIRELESS HOLDINGS LP (HQ)**
2701 Patriot Blvd Ste 200 (60026-8039)
 PHONE..................................866 527-9896
 Fax: 847 729-5988
 Tzau J Chung, *General Ptnr*
 Chris Bradley, *Vice Pres*
 Renaat Eecke, *Vice Pres*
 Adam Micek, *Controller*
 Diane Drabfcki, *Manager*
 ▲ EMP: 63
 SALES (est): 95.8MM
 SALES (corp-wide): 6.2B  **Publicly Held**
 SIC: 3812  Search & navigation equipment
 PA: Fortive Corporation
  6920 Seaway Blvd
  Everett WA 98203
  425 446-5000

**(G-11172)**
**NAVMAN WIRELESS NORTH AMER LTD**
2700 Patriot Blvd Ste 200 (60026-8064)
 PHONE..................................866 527-9896
 Tj Chung, *Principal*
 Davis Gammage, *Vice Pres*
 Mike Henn, *CFO*
 Sherry Sokol, *Accounting Mgr*
 Melissa Beeskow, *Accountant*
 ▲ EMP: 40
 SQ FT: 10,000
 SALES (est): 6MM
 SALES (corp-wide): 6.2B  **Publicly Held**
 SIC: 3812  Navigational systems & instruments
 HQ: Navman Wireless Holdings Lp
  2701 Patriot Blvd Ste 200
  Glenview IL 60026

**(G-11173)**
**NEW PANEL BRICK COMPANY OF ILL** ✪
4345 Di Paolo Ctr (60025-5202)
 PHONE..................................847 696-1686
 Zeno Popa, *Principal*
 EMP: 4  EST: 2016
 SALES (est): 297.9K  **Privately Held**
 SIC: 3271  Brick, concrete

**(G-11174)**
**NORM GORDON & ASSOCIATES INC**
3911 Kiess Dr (60026-1093)
 PHONE..................................847 564-7022
 Fax: 847 564-8022
 Norm Gordon, *President*
 Irwin Bereskin, *Principal*
 Chad Spivack, *Vice Pres*
 Dana Gordon, *Admin Sec*
 EMP: 4
 SQ FT: 800
 SALES (est): 320K  **Privately Held**
 WEB: www.ngarecycling.com
 SIC: 2611  Pulp manufactured from waste or recycled paper

**(G-11175)**
**NORTHWEST SNOW TIMBER SVC LTD**
328 Washington St (60025-5030)
P.O. Box 1296, Arlington Heights (60006-1296)
 PHONE..................................847 778-4998
 Kevin Lavin, *President*
 EMP: 3
 SALES (est): 71.6K  **Privately Held**
 SIC: 4959  2491  0781  Snowplowing; structural lumber & timber, treated wood; landscape services

**(G-11176)**
**OCEAN CLIFF CORPORATION (PA)**
3419 Ralmark Ln (60026-1552)
P.O. Box 417 (60025-0417)
 PHONE..................................847 729-9074
 David Belzer, *President*
 Rob Belzer, *VP Opers*
 Greg White, *Admin Sec*
 EMP: 1
 SQ FT: 20,000
 SALES (est): 1.1MM  **Privately Held**
 WEB: www.oceancliffcorp.com
 SIC: 2087  Extracts, flavoring; powders, flavoring (except drink)

**(G-11177)**
**ORION METALS CO**
3318 Maple Leaf Dr (60026-1127)
 PHONE..................................847 412-9532
 David Adams, *Principal*
 EMP: 4
 SALES (est): 399.3K  **Privately Held**
 SIC: 3399  Primary metal products

**(G-11178)**
**PALLET WRAPZ**
2009 Johns Dr (60025-1616)
 PHONE..................................847 729-5850
 EMP: 15
 SALES (est): 2.4MM  **Privately Held**
 SIC: 2448  Mfg Wood Pallets/Skids

**(G-11179)**
**PALLET WRAPZ INC**
2009 Johns Dr (60025-1616)
 PHONE..................................847 729-5850
 Mark Lato, *CEO*
 Vivian Lato, *CFO*
 EMP: 5
 SALES (est): 41.1K  **Privately Held**
 SIC: 2448  Pallets, wood & wood with metal

**(G-11180)**
**PASLODE CORP**
155 Harlem Ave (60025-4075)
 PHONE..................................641 672-2515
 Ian Brooks, *President*
 Paul Lord, *Regional Mgr*
 Dennis Lichui, *Plant Mgr*
 Sue Abdallah, *Design Engr*
 Daveiva Tejada, *Controller*
 ▲ EMP: 4
 SALES (est): 129.8K  **Privately Held**
 SIC: 3546  Power-driven handtools

**(G-11181)**
**PERMISSIONS GROUP INC**
1247 Milwaukee Ave # 303 (60025-2464)
 PHONE..................................847 635-6550
 Sherry Hoesly, *President*
 Cheryl Besenjack, *President*
 Heather Salus, *Project Mgr*
 Linda Teegen, *Project Mgr*
 EMP: 8
 SALES (est): 793K  **Privately Held**
 SIC: 2731  Book publishing

**(G-11182)**
**PIP PRINTING**
1220 Waukegan Rd (60025-3020)
 PHONE..................................847 998-6330
 Fax: 847 998-8619
 Alex Rozenblat, *Owner*
 EMP: 3
 SQ FT: 1,300
 SALES (est): 220K  **Privately Held**
 SIC: 2752  2789  Commercial printing, offset; binding only: books, pamphlets, magazines, etc.

**(G-11183)**
**PRACTECHAL MARKETING**
1867 Waukegan Rd (60025-2158)
 PHONE..................................847 486-8600
 April Perry, *Owner*
 EMP: 3
 SALES (est): 100K  **Privately Held**
 SIC: 3429  Manufactured hardware (general); locks or lock sets

**(G-11184)**
**PRECISION REPRODUCTIONS INC**
4316 Regency Dr (60025-5200)
 PHONE..................................847 724-0182
 Fax: 847 724-0193
 Mike Miller, *President*
 Sandy Miller, *Admin Sec*
 EMP: 14
 SQ FT: 5,000
 SALES (est): 1.2MM  **Privately Held**
 WEB: www.reproman.net
 SIC: 7334  2752  7374  Photocopying & duplicating services; blueprinting service; commercial printing, lithographic; service bureau, computer

**(G-11185)**
**QUALITY CUSTOM CLOSETS**
4304 Di Paolo Ctr (60025-5201)
 PHONE..................................773 307-1105
 EMP: 5
 SALES (est): 605.1K  **Privately Held**
 SIC: 3089  Organizers for closets, drawers, etc.: plastic

**(G-11186)**
**QUIPP INC (HQ)**
3700 W Lake Ave (60026-1217)
 PHONE..................................305 623-8700
 Cristina H Kepner, *Ch of Bd*
 Michael S Kady, *President*
 John Connors, *Vice Pres*
 John F Connors, *Vice Pres*
 Eric Bello, *CFO*
 ▲ EMP: 15
 SQ FT: 63,170
 SALES (est): 6.1MM
 SALES (corp-wide): 13.6B  **Publicly Held**
 WEB: www.quipp.com
 SIC: 3554  Paper industries machinery
 PA: Illinois Tool Works Inc.
  155 Harlem Ave
  Glenview IL 60025
  847 724-7500

**(G-11187)**
**QUIPP SYSTEMS INC**
3650 W Lake Ave (60026-1215)
 PHONE..................................305 304-1985
 EMP: 4
 SALES (corp-wide): 13.6B  **Publicly Held**
 SIC: 3555  Printing trades machinery
 HQ: Quipp Systems, Inc.
  3700 W Lake Ave
  Glenview IL 60026

**(G-11188)**
**QUIPP SYSTEMS INC (DH)**
3700 W Lake Ave (60026-1217)
 PHONE..................................305 623-8700
 Michael S Kady, *President*
 Nora Zampieri, *Controller*
 Jeremy Hyne, *Manager*
 EMP: 30
 SQ FT: 60,000
 SALES (est): 5.5MM
 SALES (corp-wide): 13.6B  **Publicly Held**
 SIC: 3555  Printing trades machinery
 HQ: Quipp, Inc.
  3700 W Lake Ave
  Glenview IL 60026
  305 623-8700

**(G-11189)**
**RAINMAKER**
1539 Palmgren Dr (60025-4341)
 PHONE..................................847 998-0838
 R Shinkle, *Principal*
 EMP: 2
 SALES (est): 240.9K  **Privately Held**
 SIC: 3569  Sprinkler systems, fire: automatic

**(G-11190)**
**RANSBURG CORPORATION**
Also Called: ITW
155 Harlem Ave (60025-4075)
 PHONE..................................847 724-7500
 W James Farrell, *President*
 Michael W Gregg, *Senior VP*
 Linda Williams, *Vice Pres*
 Michael J Robinson, *Treasurer*
 Lucy Kiolbasa, *Manager*
 ▲ EMP: 488  EST: 1946
 SQ FT: 114,000
 SALES (est): 48MM
 SALES (corp-wide): 13.6B  **Publicly Held**
 SIC: 3559  3629  Electroplating machinery & equipment; wheel balancing equipment, automotive; static elimination equipment, industrial
 PA: Illinois Tool Works Inc.
  155 Harlem Ave
  Glenview IL 60025
  847 724-7500

**(G-11191)**
**REDDI-PAC INC (HQ)**
3700 W Lake Ave (60025-1217)
 PHONE..................................847 657-5222
 Mike Loeschen, *Vice Pres*
 EMP: 13
 SQ FT: 10,000
 SALES (est): 5.1MM
 SALES (corp-wide): 13.6B  **Publicly Held**
 SIC: 2652  Setup paperboard boxes
 PA: Illinois Tool Works Inc.
  155 Harlem Ave
  Glenview IL 60025
  847 724-7500

**(G-11192)**
**REEDY INDUSTRIES INC (PA)**
2440 Ravine Way Ste 200 (60025-7649)
 PHONE..................................847 729-9450
 Fax: 847 729-0558
 Thomas W Reedy, *Ch of Bd*
 Bill Reedy, *President*
 Coleen Reedy, *Corp Secy*
 Marti Leonard, *CFO*
 Lynn Bradus, *Controller*
 EMP: 15
 SQ FT: 20,000
 SALES: 1.6K  **Privately Held**
 WEB: www.reedyequipment.com
 SIC: 5078  1711  3585  Refrigeration equipment & supplies; commercial refrigeration equipment; warm air heating & air conditioning contractor; parts for heating, cooling & refrigerating equipment

**(G-11193)**
**REPUBLIC GROUP INC (PA)**
2301 Ravine Way (60025-7627)
 PHONE..................................800 288-8888
 Donald R Levin, *CEO*
 Lynett Siron, *Controller*
 EMP: 8
 SALES (est): 33.5MM  **Privately Held**
 SIC: 2131  Smoking tobacco

**(G-11194)**
**ROCKYS BEVERAGES LLC**
1813 Elmdale Ave (60026-1355)
 PHONE..................................312 561-3182
 Lori Johnson, *Manager*
 Peter Rocky Mosele, *Principal*
 EMP: 10
 SALES (est): 1MM  **Privately Held**
 SIC: 2086  Carbonated soft drinks, bottled & canned

**(G-11195)**
**SHENGLONG INTL GROUP CORP**
1939 Waukegan Rd Ste 205 (60025-1758)
 PHONE..................................312 388-2345
 Chunxiang Zhang, *President*
 Licai Yang, *Vice Pres*
 Zhanhai Zhang, *Vice Pres*
 ◆ EMP: 7
 SQ FT: 1,200
 SALES (est): 520K  **Privately Held**
 SIC: 5047  5021  3411  Hospital equipment & furniture; office & public building furniture; food & beverage containers

## Glenview - Cook County (G-11196)

**(G-11196)**
**SHERI LYN KRAFT**
827 Wagner Rd (60025-3229)
PHONE..................847 724-4718
Sheri Lyn Kraft, *Principal*
EMP: 3
SALES (est): 169.6K **Privately Held**
SIC: 2022 Processed cheese

**(G-11197)**
**SIGNODE CORPORATION**
Also Called: Signode Ips
3600 W Lake Ave (60026-1215)
PHONE..................800 527-1499
Fax: 847 724-5910
Russell Flaum, *President*
Regis Fraval, *General Mgr*
Barry Henderson, *General Mgr*
Santosh Tandon, *General Mgr*
Gerard Young, *General Mgr*
◆ EMP: 1500
SQ FT: 72,000
SALES (est): 228.8MM
SALES (corp-wide): 2.2B **Publicly Held**
SIC: 3565 3499 Packaging machinery; strapping, metal
PA: The Carlyle Group L P
1001 Pennsylvania Ave Nw 220s
Washington DC 20004
202 729-5626

**(G-11198)**
**SIGNODE INDUSTRIAL GROUP LLC (HQ)**
Also Called: Insulated Transport Products
3650 W Lake Ave (60026-1215)
PHONE..................847 724-7500
Mark Burgess, *CEO*
Ron Kropp, *CFO*
Nils Stenger, *Treasurer*
Mark Wade, *Sales Executive*
Judy Agee, *Office Admin*
▲ EMP: 40 EST: 2013
SALES (est): 259.4MM **Privately Held**
SIC: 2671 Resinous impregnated paper for packaging; thermoplastic coated paper for packaging
PA: Signode Industrial Group Holdings (Bermuda) Ltd
C/O Conyers, Dill & Pearman
Hamilton
441 295-1422

**(G-11199)**
**SIGNODE INDUSTRIAL GROUP LLC**
Muller Lcs
3644 W Lake Ave (60026-1215)
PHONE..................847 483-1490
Mindy Perezcassar, *Accountant*
Ryan Womble, *Natl Sales Mgr*
Vic Teriaszwili, *Manager*
EMP: 45 **Privately Held**
SIC: 3565 3081 Packing & wrapping machinery; polyethylene film
HQ: Signode Industrial Group Llc
3650 W Lake Ave
Glenview IL 60026
847 724-7500

**(G-11200)**
**SIGNODE INDUSTRIAL GROUP LLC**
Also Called: Signode Consumable Plastics
3680 W Lake Ave (60026-1215)
PHONE..................847 724-6100
EMP: 39 **Privately Held**
SIC: 2671 Thermoplastic coated paper for packaging
HQ: Signode Industrial Group Llc
3650 W Lake Ave
Glenview IL 60026
847 724-7500

**(G-11201)**
**SIGNODE INDUSTRIAL GROUP LLC**
Fleetwood
3624 W Lake Ave (60026-1215)
PHONE..................630 268-9999
Fax: 630 268-9919
Terry Keehn, *Opers Mgr*
Rick Powell, *Treasurer*
Tim Alexander, *Sales Mgr*
Susan Fisher, *Cust Mgr*
Steven Martindale, *Branch Mgr*
EMP: 5 **Privately Held**
SIC: 3565 Packaging machinery
HQ: Signode Industrial Group Llc
3650 W Lake Ave
Glenview IL 60026
847 724-7500

**(G-11202)**
**SIGNODE INTL HOLDINGS LLC (HQ)**
3700 W Lake Ave (60026-1217)
PHONE..................800 648-8864
EMP: 19
SALES (est): 46.8MM **Privately Held**
SIC: 5199 2671 Industrial Packaging

**(G-11203)**
**SIGNODE PACKAGING SYSTEMS CORP**
Also Called: Signode Packing Systems
3650 W Lake Ave (60026-1215)
PHONE..................800 323-2464
David B Speer, *CEO*
Scott Eschenbrenner, *Prdtn Mgr*
Alex Popvich, *Controller*
Nicole Sladek, *Controller*
Joseph Lininger, *Manager*
▲ EMP: 100
SALES (est): 17.4MM **Privately Held**
SIC: 3089 3965 3499 Injection molded finished plastic products; fasteners; strapping, metal
HQ: Signode Industrial Group Llc
3650 W Lake Ave
Glenview IL 60026
847 724-7500

**(G-11204)**
**SOCCER HOUSE**
999 Waukegan Rd Ste A (60025-4314)
PHONE..................847 998-0088
Nora Dyjack, *Partner*
EMP: 3
SALES (est): 306.1K **Privately Held**
SIC: 3949 5941 Sporting & athletic goods; sporting goods & bicycle shops

**(G-11205)**
**SOLOMON PLUMBING**
3706 Winnetka Rd (60026-1354)
PHONE..................847 498-6388
Solomon Altez, *Owner*
EMP: 2 EST: 1998
SALES (est): 258.5K **Privately Held**
SIC: 3494 Plumbing & heating valves

**(G-11206)**
**SUBURBAN FABRICATORS INC**
1119 Depot St (60025-2905)
PHONE..................847 729-0866
Fax: 847 729-2469
Michael Nemmer, *President*
Tim Nemmer, *Corp Secy*
EMP: 3
SQ FT: 800
SALES (est): 480.8K **Privately Held**
SIC: 2541 Wood partitions & fixtures

**(G-11207)**
**SUE PETERSON**
Also Called: Sue P Knits
1100 Raleigh Rd (60025-3026)
PHONE..................847 730-3035
Sue Paterson, *Owner*
Sue Peterson, *Owner*
EMP: 3
SALES (est): 190K **Privately Held**
WEB: www.suepknits.com
SIC: 2253 Sweaters & sweater coats, knit

**(G-11208)**
**TEITELBAUM BROTHERS INC**
Also Called: Pixie Sparkle
1944 Lehigh Ave Ste D (60026-1661)
PHONE..................847 729-3490
Fax: 847 729-3492
James R Lucas, *President*
Louisa A Lucas, *Corp Secy*
EMP: 2
SQ FT: 1,100
SALES (est): 253.9K **Privately Held**
SIC: 2842 Industrial plant disinfectants or deodorants

**(G-11209)**
**TIMEOUT DEVICES INC**
2718 Covert Rd (60025-4605)
PHONE..................847 729-6543
Jim Daniel, *President*
EMP: 10
SALES (est): 250K **Privately Held**
WEB: www.timeoutdevices.com
SIC: 3577 Computer peripheral equipment

**(G-11210)**
**TOP TOBACCO LP (PA)**
Also Called: Republic Tobacco
2301 Ravine Way (60025-7627)
PHONE..................847 832-9700
Fax: 847 724-1952
Alan Kandelman, *CEO*
Donald R Levin, *President*
Seth Gold, *Exec VP*
MEI Lin, *Purch Dir*
Allan Kandelman, *CFO*
▲ EMP: 1
SQ FT: 150,000
SALES (est): 47MM **Privately Held**
SIC: 2131 Smoking tobacco

**(G-11211)**
**TWO TRIBES LLC**
3607 Lawson Rd (60026-1105)
P.O. Box 2367, Northbrook (60065-2367)
PHONE..................847 272-7711
Diana Israel, *Mng Member*
EMP: 6
SALES: 500K **Privately Held**
WEB: www.twotribes.com
SIC: 2022 Natural cheese

**(G-11212)**
**UNITED STANDARD INDUSTRIES INC**
2062 Lehigh Ave (60026-1684)
PHONE..................847 724-0350
Fax: 847 724-0397
Sherwin E Feldstein, *President*
William Gode, *Vice Pres*
Bill Richter, *Engrg Mgr*
Erna Kamin, *Manager*
Allison Schiller, *Consultant*
EMP: 63
SQ FT: 37,500
SALES (est): 14.1MM **Privately Held**
WEB: www.unitedstandard.com
SIC: 3469 Machine parts, stamped or pressed metal

**(G-11213)**
**UNITED STATES AUDIO CORP (PA)**
Also Called: US Audio
411 Crabtree Ln (60025-5114)
PHONE..................312 316-2929
John Kowalik, *President*
Frances Kowalik, *Admin Sec*
EMP: 12
SALES (est): 265K **Privately Held**
SIC: 3651 Household audio equipment

**(G-11214)**
**VINS BBQ LLC**
506 Lotus Ln (60025-4560)
PHONE..................847 302-3259
Ladonna Del Rosario, *Mng Member*
Joe Bustamante, *Manager*
EMP: 8
SALES (est): 274.2K **Privately Held**
SIC: 2033 Barbecue sauce: packaged in cans, jars, etc.

## Glenwood
### Cook County

**(G-11215)**
**CHEMIX CORP**
330 W 194th St (60425-1502)
PHONE..................708 754-2150
Fax: 708 754-2150
Arthur Danko, *President*
J Stern, *Purchasing*
Art Edwards, *Sales Staff*
Paul Danko, *Manager*
Andrienne Danko, *Admin Sec*
EMP: 15 EST: 1960
SQ FT: 3,000
SALES (est): 2.5MM **Privately Held**
WEB: www.chemix.com
SIC: 5169 3471 2992 2899 Chemicals & allied products; plating & polishing; lubricating oils & greases; chemical preparations; paints & allied products; specialty cleaning, polishes & sanitation goods

**(G-11216)**
**INK SPOTS PRTG MDIA DESIGN INC**
18300 S Halsted St (60425-1046)
PHONE..................708 754-1300
William S Tucker Jr, *General Mgr*
EMP: 3
SQ FT: 3,000
SALES (est): 75K **Privately Held**
SIC: 2759 Commercial printing

**(G-11217)**
**JAMES WALKER MFG CO**
511 W 195th St (60425-1532)
P.O. Box 467 (60425-0467)
PHONE..................708 754-4020
Fax: 708 754-4058
Peter Needham, *President*
Chris May, *General Mgr*
John Humphrey, *Managing Dir*
Peter A Tompsett, *Principal*
David Gibson, *Vice Pres*
▲ EMP: 43 EST: 1915
SQ FT: 30,000
SALES (est): 7.9MM
SALES (corp-wide): 268.1MM **Privately Held**
WEB: www.jameswalkermfg.com
SIC: 3053 3599 3492 3441 Oil seals, leather; oil seals, rubber; gaskets, all materials; bellows, industrial: metal; fluid power valves & hose fittings; fabricated structural metal; mechanical rubber goods
PA: James Walker Group Limited
Lion House
Woking GU22
148 374-6120

**(G-11218)**
**LANDAUER INC (PA)**
2 Science Rd (60425-1586)
PHONE..................708 755-7000
Fax: 708 755-7016
Michael T Leatherman, *Ch of Bd*
Michael P Kaminski, *President*
Peter Cempellin, *President*
Michael R Kennedy, *Senior VP*
G Douglas King, *Senior VP*
EMP: 148
SQ FT: 59,100
SALES: 149.2MM **Publicly Held**
SIC: 8734 5047 3829 Radiation laboratories; radiation dosimetry laboratory; instruments, surgical & medical; X-ray film & supplies; measuring & controlling devices

**(G-11219)**
**MORRISON TIMING SCREW COMPANY**
Also Called: Morrison Cont Hdlg Solutions
335 W 194th St (60425-1501)
PHONE..................708 331-6600
Fax: 708 756-6620
Nancy Wilson, *CEO*
Nick L Wilson, *President*
Chris Wilson, *Vice Pres*
Rae Lee, *Sls & Mktg Exec*
Mark Burk, *Sales Mgr*
EMP: 60
SQ FT: 30,000
SALES (est): 21.2MM **Privately Held**
WEB: www.morrisontimingscrew.com
SIC: 3535 Conveyors & conveying equipment

**(G-11220)**
**SWEET CREATION BY SHEILA**
803 N Rainbow Dr (60425-1307)
PHONE..................708 754-7938
Sheila Kimbrough, *Principal*
EMP: 3
SALES (est): 152.4K **Privately Held**
SIC: 2053 Cakes, bakery: frozen

## Godfrey
*Madison County*

**(G-11221)**
**ABBEY COPYING SUPPORT SVCS INC**
3312 Godfrey Rd (62035-2558)
**PHONE**.................................618 466-3300
Sherie Schroeder, *President*
**EMP:** 3
**SALES (est):** 261K **Privately Held**
**WEB:** www.theabbeygraphics.com
**SIC:** 2759 Commercial printing

**(G-11222)**
**ARROW SIGNS (PA)**
4545 N Alby Rd (62035-1954)
**PHONE**.................................618 466-0818
Lance De Mond, *Principal*
**EMP:** 14
**SALES (est):** 619.1K **Privately Held**
**SIC:** 3993 Signs & advertising specialties

**(G-11223)**
**DAVID L KNOCHE**
Also Called: Hgh Products
611 Armsway Blvd (62035-2734)
**PHONE**.................................618 466-7120
**Fax:** 618 466-7115
David L Knoche, *Owner*
**EMP:** 7
**SQ FT:** 2,400
**SALES (est):** 601.3K **Privately Held**
**SIC:** 3599 Custom machinery

**(G-11224)**
**DRUG TESTING SUPPLIERS INC**
421 Saint John Dr (62035-2174)
**PHONE**.................................618 208-3810
Kenneth Waggoner, *President*
Michael Balentine, *Vice Pres*
**EMP:** 4
**SALES (est):** 199.6K **Privately Held**
**SIC:** 2385 Gowns, plastic: made from purchased materials

**(G-11225)**
**HEAFNER CONTRACTING INC**
27457 Heafner Dr (62035-3635)
**PHONE**.................................618 466-3678
Michael E Heafner, *President*
**EMP:** 10
**SALES (est):** 1MM **Privately Held**
**SIC:** 1521 1389 Single-family housing construction; construction, repair & dismantling services

**(G-11226)**
**KEN ELLIOTT CO INC**
3704 Riehl Ln (62035-1064)
**PHONE**.................................618 466-8200
Kent Elliot, *President*
Kent Elliott, *President*
Gary Elliott, *Sales Staff*
**EMP:** 2 **EST:** 1952
**SQ FT:** 20,000
**SALES (est):** 241.9K **Privately Held**
**WEB:** www.elliottgears.com
**SIC:** 3462 3593 Gears, forged steel; fluid power cylinders & actuators

**(G-11227)**
**KIMMATERIALS INC**
Also Called: Lohr Quarry
9434 Godfrey Rd (62035-3046)
P.O. Box 187 (62035-0187)
**PHONE**.................................618 466-0352
**Fax:** 618 466-5283
Dave Bangert, *President*
**EMP:** 5 **EST:** 1939
**SALES (est):** 430K **Privately Held**
**SIC:** 1422 Crushed & broken limestone

**(G-11228)**
**MAX FIRE TRAINING INC**
Also Called: Max Fire Box
901 Hampton Ct (62035-1800)
**PHONE**.................................618 210-2079
Shawn Bloemker, *President*
**EMP:** 13
**SALES (est):** 516.2K **Privately Held**
**SIC:** 3441 3429 9411 Building components, structural steel; nozzles, fire fighting;

**(G-11229)**
**MIDLAND RAILWAY SUPPLY INC (PA)**
1815 W Delmar Ave (62035-1352)
**PHONE**.................................618 467-6305
John Ferenbach, *President*
Eric Ferenbach, *Vice Pres*
Dana James, *Administration*
**EMP:** 25 **EST:** 1946
**SALES (est):** 24.2MM **Privately Held**
**SIC:** 5088 3743 Railroad equipment & supplies; railroad equipment

**(G-11230)**
**NEW CENTURY PERFORMANCE INC**
3704 Riehl Ln (62035-1064)
P.O. Box 727 (62035-0727)
**PHONE**.................................618 466-6383
Lowell Bodenbach, *General Mgr*
**EMP:** 4
**SALES:** 500K **Privately Held**
**SIC:** 3334 Primary aluminum

**(G-11231)**
**OLIVE OIL MARKET PLACE**
1018 Richard Dr (62035-2574)
**PHONE**.................................618 304-3769
Safi Dani, *Branch Mgr*
**EMP:** 3
**SALES (corp-wide):** 15.1MM **Privately Held**
**SIC:** 2079 Olive oil
**PA:** Olive Oil Marketplace Inc.
108 W 3rd St
Alton IL 62002
618 304-3769

**(G-11232)**
**PROGROUP INSTRUMENT INC**
26582 Lockhaven Hl (62035-3556)
**PHONE**.................................618 466-2815
Scott A Hovey, *President*
Russell Leaker, *Vice Pres*
Candace Hovey, *Executive*
**EMP:** 8
**SQ FT:** 3,000
**SALES (est):** 1.1MM **Privately Held**
**SIC:** 3826 Analytical instruments

**(G-11233)**
**RICHARD TINDALL**
Also Called: Tindall Composites
1026 Lexington Estates Dr (62035-4172)
**PHONE**.................................618 433-8107
Richard Tindall, *Owner*
**EMP:** 2
**SALES:** 500K **Privately Held**
**WEB:** www.tindallcomposites.com
**SIC:** 3083 Laminated plastics plate & sheet

**(G-11234)**
**RINALLI BOAT CO INC**
3406 W Delmar Ave (62035-1007)
**PHONE**.................................618 467-8850
Donald B Rhodes, *President*
**EMP:** 6
**SALES:** 250K **Privately Held**
**SIC:** 3732 7389 Boats, fiberglass: building & repairing;

**(G-11235)**
**RIVIERA TAN SPA (DEL)**
Also Called: Riviera Tan Products
5114 Stiritz Ln (62035-1244)
**PHONE**.................................618 466-1012
Joyce Carroll, *President*
Harley Carroll, *Admin Sec*
**EMP:** 5
**SALES (est):** 290K **Privately Held**
**SIC:** 3999 5122 Barber & beauty shop equipment; toiletries

**(G-11236)**
**ROTARY RAM INC**
3704 Riehl Ln (62035-1064)
**PHONE**.................................618 466-2651
**Fax:** 618 466-2653
Kent Elliott, *President*
Gary Elliott, *Sales Executive*
**EMP:** 20 **EST:** 1951
**SQ FT:** 15,100
**SALES (est):** 5MM **Privately Held**
**SIC:** 3492 Control valves, fluid power: hydraulic & pneumatic

**(G-11237)**
**SCHNUCK MARKETS INC**
Also Called: Schnucks Pharmacy
2712 Godfrey Rd (62035-3311)
**PHONE**.................................618 466-0825
**Fax:** 618 467-0544
Phil Lunn, *Manager*
**EMP:** 200
**SALES (corp-wide):** 3.5B **Privately Held**
**WEB:** www.schnucks.com
**SIC:** 5411 5812 5912 7841 Supermarkets, chain; eating places; drug stores & proprietary stores; video tape rental; florists; bread, cake & related products
**PA:** Schnuck Markets, Inc.
11420 Lackland Rd
Saint Louis MO 63146
314 994-9900

**(G-11238)**
**TAW ENTERPRISES LLC**
5100 Seminole Ct (62035-1543)
**PHONE**.................................618 466-0134
Thomas Williams, *Principal*
**EMP:** 4
**SALES (est):** 449.7K **Privately Held**
**SIC:** 3714 Shock absorbers, motor vehicle

## Golconda
*Pope County*

**(G-11239)**
**HOGG HOLLOW WINERY LLC**
48 E Glendale Rd (62938-4018)
**PHONE**.................................618 695-9463
Steve Hogg, *Owner*
April Hogg, *Principal*
**EMP:** 4
**SALES (est):** 202.9K **Privately Held**
**SIC:** 2084 Wines

**(G-11240)**
**LAFARGE NORTH AMERICA INC**
Rr 1 Box 128 (62938-9608)
**PHONE**.................................773 372-1000
**EMP:** 29
**SALES (corp-wide):** 26.6B **Privately Held**
**SIC:** 3241 Cement, hydraulic
**HQ:** Lafarge North America Inc.
8700 W Bryn Mawr Ave Ll
Chicago IL 60631
703 480-3600

**(G-11241)**
**MARTIN MARIETTA MATERIALS INC**
Also Called: Rosiclare Quarry
Missouri Portland Rd (62938)
Rural Route 1 Box 128 (62938-9608)
**PHONE**.................................618 285-6267
**Fax:** 618 285-3343
Donna Robertson, *Office Mgr*
Jimmy Mc Crary, *Branch Mgr*
Angel Vaughn, *Manager*
Marcus Sunga, *Director*
Sarah Little, *Nursing Dir*
**EMP:** 15
**SALES (corp-wide):** 3.8B **Publicly Held**
**WEB:** www.martinmarietta.com
**SIC:** 1423 Crushed & broken granite
**PA:** Martin Marietta Materials Inc
2710 Wycliff Rd
Raleigh NC 27607
919 781-4550

**(G-11242)**
**SOUTHERN ILL WINE TRAIL NFP**
48 E Glendale Rd (62938-4018)
**PHONE**.................................618 695-9463
**EMP:** 4
**SALES (est):** 184K **Privately Held**
**SIC:** 2084 Winery Trail

## Good Hope
*Mcdonough County*

**(G-11243)**
**MIDWEST OIL LLC**
135 S Chestnut St (61438-5028)
**PHONE**.................................309 456-3663
**Fax:** 309 456-3587
Jerry Lewis, *President*
Cindy Bricker, *Manager*
**EMP:** 4
**SQ FT:** 4,000
**SALES:** 4MM **Privately Held**
**SIC:** 1311 Crude petroleum & natural gas

## Goodfield
*Woodford County*

**(G-11244)**
**CNH INDUSTRIAL AMERICA LLC**
Case/D M I
1498 Us Highway 150 (61742-7515)
P.O. Box 65 (61742-0065)
**PHONE**.................................309 965-2233
**Fax:** 309 965-2042
Tim Nix, *Sls & Mktg Exec*
Terry White, *Human Res Dir*
William Schmidgall, *Manager*
Ray Collins, *Data Proc Dir*
John C Nowack, *Info Tech Mgr*
**EMP:** 20
**SALES (corp-wide):** 26.3B **Privately Held**
**SIC:** 3523 3599 3714 Farm machinery & equipment; machine shop, jobbing & repair; bumpers & bumperettes, motor vehicle
**HQ:** Cnh Industrial America Llc
700 St St
Racine WI 53404
262 636-6011

**(G-11245)**
**CNH INDUSTRIAL AMERICA LLC**
600 E Peoria St (61742-9705)
P.O. Box 65 (61742-0065)
**PHONE**.................................309 965-2217
Paul Rouse, *Manager*
**EMP:** 208
**SALES (corp-wide):** 26.3B **Privately Held**
**SIC:** 3523 Farm machinery & equipment
**HQ:** Cnh Industrial America Llc
700 St St
Racine WI 53404
262 636-6011

**(G-11246)**
**DSI INC**
401 State Route 117 (61742-7520)
**PHONE**.................................309 965-5110
William Dietrich, *President*
**EMP:** 6
**SALES (est):** 794.7K **Privately Held**
**WEB:** www.dsiag.com
**SIC:** 0115 0119 3523 Corn; bean (dry field & seed) farm; farm machinery & equipment

**(G-11247)**
**MIDWEST BIO FUEL INC**
125 W Fisk St (61742-7530)
**PHONE**.................................309 965-2612
Garrett Schamberger, *Owner*
**EMP:** 3 **EST:** 2011
**SALES (est):** 170.2K **Privately Held**
**SIC:** 2869 Fuels

**(G-11248)**
**PAUL WEVER CONSTRUCTION EQP CO**
Also Called: P W C E
401 W Martin Dr (61742-7536)
P.O. Box 85 (61742-0085)
**PHONE**.................................309 965-2005
**Fax:** 309 965-2905
Paul Wever, *President*
Paul Imm, *Sales Mgr*
Alice Linn, *Office Mgr*
Karen Wever, *Admin Sec*
**EMP:** 10

SALES (est): 1.7MM **Privately Held**
WEB: www.pwce.com
SIC: 3531 3441 Construction machinery attachments; fabricated structural metal

**(G-11249)**
**TYSON FRESH MEATS INC**
Also Called: I B P
373 Hwy 117 N (61742)
P.O. Box 386 (61742-0386)
PHONE.................309 965-2565
Thad Heffren, *Manager*
EMP: 10
SALES (corp-wide): 36.8B **Publicly Held**
SIC: 2011 5154 Meat packing plants; livestock
HQ: Tyson Fresh Meats, Inc.
800 Stevens Port Dr
Dakota Dunes SD 57049
605 235-2061

### Goreville
*Johnson County*

**(G-11250)**
**CHEERS FOOD AND FUEL 240**
845 S Broadway (62939-2479)
PHONE.................618 995-9153
EMP: 3
SALES (est): 157K **Privately Held**
SIC: 2869 Fuels

**(G-11251)**
**GOREVILLE AUTO PARTS & MCH SP**
Also Called: NAPA Auto Parts
Rr 37 (62939)
P.O. Box 106 (62939-0106)
PHONE.................618 995-2375
Fax: 618 995-2375
Wendell Stokes, *Owner*
Scottsa Stokes, *Vice Pres*
EMP: 7
SALES (est): 457.5K **Privately Held**
SIC: 5531 3599 Automobile & truck equipment & parts; machine & other job shop work

**(G-11252)**
**GOREVILLE CONCRETE INC**
301 N Hubbard Ave (62939-2351)
P.O. Box 232 (62939-0232)
PHONE.................618 995-2670
Fax: 618 995-9339
Carl Henderson, *President*
Tammy Rowe, *Admin Sec*
EMP: 20 EST: 1945
SQ FT: 1,200
SALES (est): 2.3MM **Privately Held**
SIC: 3273 Ready-mixed concrete

**(G-11253)**
**GOREVILLE GAZETTE**
Also Called: Weekly Newspaper
205 S Broadway (62939-2446)
P.O. Box 70 (62939-0070)
PHONE.................618 995-9445
Don Sanders, *Owner*
EMP: 3
SALES (est): 128.8K **Privately Held**
SIC: 2711 Newspapers

### Gorham
*Jackson County*

**(G-11254)**
**JACKSON COUNTY SAND & GRAV CO**
1 Sickler Rd (62940-2109)
P.O. Box 242, Chester (62233-0242)
PHONE.................618 763-4711
Spencer F Brown, *President*
Shelby Lawder, *Corp Secy*
Bruce Brown, *Vice Pres*
EMP: 3
SQ FT: 1,000
SALES (est): 237.6K **Privately Held**
SIC: 1442 5032 Construction sand mining; brick, stone & related material

### Grafton
*Jersey County*

**(G-11255)**
**LAWRENCE ALLEN**
21031 State Highway 3 (62037-2440)
P.O. Box 113 (62037-0113)
PHONE.................618 786-3794
Allen Lawrence, *Owner*
EMP: 3
SALES (est): 401.7K **Privately Held**
SIC: 3523 Driers (farm): grain, hay & seed

### Grand Chain
*Pulaski County*

**(G-11256)**
**LAFARGE NORTH AMERICA INC**
2500 Portland Rd (62941-2306)
PHONE.................618 543-7541
Dale Smith, *Project Mgr*
Deborah McKinney, *Safety Mgr*
Alan Kerr, *Engineer*
Todd Montgomery, *Engineer*
Lynn Wehrmeier, *Finance*
EMP: 150
SALES (corp-wide): 26.6B **Privately Held**
WEB: www.lafargenorthamerica.com
SIC: 3241 Cement, hydraulic
HQ: Lafarge North America Inc.
8700 W Bryn Mawr Ave Ll
Chicago IL 60631
703 480-3600

### Grand Ridge
*Lasalle County*

**(G-11257)**
**EPIC EYE**
1869 E 19th Rd (61325-9765)
PHONE.................309 210-6212
Susan Rees, *Owner*
EMP: 3
SALES (est): 133.1K **Privately Held**
SIC: 7335 3651 Photographic studio, commercial; video camera-audio recorders, household use

### Granite City
*Madison County*

**(G-11258)**
**ACCURATE FABRICATORS INC**
Also Called: G & M Steel Fabricating
1603 Cleveland Blvd (62040-4402)
PHONE.................618 451-1886
Fax: 618 451-1887
Craig Vance, *President*
Marc Plank, *Principal*
John Carlyle, *Vice Pres*
EMP: 7
SQ FT: 20,000
SALES (est): 1.4MM **Privately Held**
SIC: 3441 Fabricated structural metal

**(G-11259)**
**ACCURATE FABRICATORS SVCS INC**
1603 Cleveland Blvd (62040-4402)
PHONE.................618 530-7883
EMP: 5 EST: 2015
SALES (est): 320K **Privately Held**
SIC: 3441 3443 Building components, structural steel; boiler shop products: boilers, smokestacks, steel tanks

**(G-11260)**
**AIR PRODUCTS AND CHEMICALS INC**
2200 Monroe St (62040-5426)
P.O. Box 695 (62040-0695)
PHONE.................618 452-5335
Fax: 618 452-5334
Carl Beck, *Plant Mgr*
Kenneth Miller, *Branch Mgr*
EMP: 25
SALES (corp-wide): 9.5B **Publicly Held**
WEB: www.airproducts.com
SIC: 2813 Industrial gases
PA: Air Products And Chemicals, Inc.
7201 Hamilton Blvd
Allentown PA 18195
610 481-4911

**(G-11261)**
**AIR PRODUCTS AND CHEMICALS INC**
35 N Gate Indus Dr (62040-6806)
PHONE.................618 451-0577
Fax: 618 451-0043
Joe Buccella, *Plant Mgr*
Tom Minor, *Branch Mgr*
EMP: 58
SALES (corp-wide): 9.5B **Publicly Held**
WEB: www.airproducts.com
SIC: 2813 5169 Industrial gases; chemicals & allied products
PA: Air Products And Chemicals, Inc.
7201 Hamilton Blvd
Allentown PA 18195
610 481-4911

**(G-11262)**
**ALL PALLET SERVICE**
1459 State St (62040-4433)
PHONE.................618 451-7545
Carrie Shrum, *Principal*
EMP: 9 EST: 2009
SALES (est): 1.4MM **Privately Held**
SIC: 2448 Pallets, wood & wood with metal

**(G-11263)**
**AMERICAN COLLOID COMPANY**
1601 Walnut St (62040-3117)
PHONE.................618 452-8143
Fax: 618 452-9554
Van Coats, *Opers Staff*
Van Coates, *Opers-Prdtn-Mfg*
Kate Ciskowski, *Financial Exec*
Terry Tinsley, *Maintence Staff*
EMP: 23
SALES (corp-wide): 1.6B **Publicly Held**
WEB: www.colloid.com
SIC: 1459 2899 Bentonite mining; chemical preparations
HQ: American Colloid Company
2870 Forbs Ave
Hoffman Estates IL 60192

**(G-11264)**
**AMSTED RAIL COMPANY INC**
1700 Walnut St (62040-3100)
PHONE.................618 452-2111
Eric Stopka, *Managing Dir*
Paul Limbach, *Vice Pres*
Terry Mills, *Buyer*
Scott Kuehnel, *Project Engr*
Diana Lopez, *Auditing Mgr*
EMP: 2000
SALES (corp-wide): 1.9B **Privately Held**
SIC: 3366 Machinery castings: copper or copper-base alloy
HQ: Amsted Rail Company, Inc.
311 S Wacker Dr Ste 5300
Chicago IL 60606

**(G-11265)**
**AMSTED RAIL COMPANY INC**
1078 19th St (62040)
PHONE.................618 225-6463
John Wories, *Branch Mgr*
Tara Semb, *Director*
EMP: 450
SALES (corp-wide): 1.9B **Privately Held**
SIC: 3743 Railroad equipment
HQ: Amsted Rail Company, Inc.
311 S Wacker Dr Ste 5300
Chicago IL 60606

**(G-11266)**
**ANYTIME BLACKTOPPING**
804 E Chain Of Rocks Rd (62040-2811)
PHONE.................618 931-6958
Bob Chaulsett, *Owner*
Jeff Chaulsett, *Manager*
EMP: 3
SALES (est): 200K **Privately Held**
SIC: 2951 Asphalt paving mixtures & blocks

**(G-11267)**
**ARIZON STRCTURES WORLDWIDE LLC**
1200 W 7th St (62040-1895)
PHONE.................618 451-7250
John A Brennan, *CFO*
EMP: 50
SALES (est): 6.1MM
SALES (corp-wide): 124.5MM **Privately Held**
SIC: 3069 Air-supported rubber structures
PA: Arizon Companies, Inc.
11880 Dorsett Rd
Maryland Heights MO 63043
314 739-0037

**(G-11268)**
**ARNETTE PATTERN CO INC**
Also Called: Midwest Machining & Fabg
3203 Missouri Ave (62040-6833)
PHONE.................618 451-7700
Gary Z Zimmer, *President*
Chuck Duckworth, *Foreman/Supr*
Mike Murphy, *Sales Engr*
Joe Stimac, *Manager*
David Zimmer, *Admin Sec*
EMP: 30
SQ FT: 30,000
SALES (est): 6.3MM **Privately Held**
WEB: www.arnettepattern.com
SIC: 3599 3543 3441 Machine shop, jobbing & repair; foundry patternmaking; fabricated structural metal

**(G-11269)**
**CEDAR CREEK LLC**
122 E Chanin Of Rocks Rd (62040)
PHONE.................618 797-1220
Fax: 618 931-7523
Mark Corso, *Branch Mgr*
EMP: 48
SALES (corp-wide): 1.2B **Privately Held**
SIC: 5031 2439 Lumber: rough, dressed & finished; trusses, wooden roof
HQ: Cedar Creek Llc
450 N Macarthur Blvd
Oklahoma City OK 73127

**(G-11270)**
**CHAULSETTS PAINTING**
804 E Chain Of Rocks Rd (62040-2811)
PHONE.................618 931-6958
Robert Chaulsett, *Principal*
EMP: 3
SALES (est): 281.7K **Privately Held**
SIC: 2951 Asphalt paving mixtures & blocks

**(G-11271)**
**CUSTOM FBRICATION COATINGS INC**
1107 22nd St (62040-3306)
PHONE.................618 452-9540
Terry Carron, *President*
Cathy Carron, *Principal*
Jim Douglas, *Purchasing*
Velvett Burns, *Manager*
EMP: 60
SQ FT: 130,000
SALES (est): 17.8MM **Privately Held**
SIC: 3441 Fabricated structural metal

**(G-11272)**
**CUSTOM SYSTEMS INC**
3660 State Route 111 (62040-6612)
P.O. Box 1738 (62040-1738)
PHONE.................314 355-4575
Robert L Stanford, *President*
Carol Stanford, *Admin Sec*
EMP: 4
SALES: 2MM **Privately Held**
SIC: 3556 3564 Bakery machinery; dust or fume collecting equipment, industrial

**(G-11273)**
**DICKEY SIGN CO**
116 Springfield Dr (62040-2831)
PHONE.................618 797-1262
Dale Dickey, *Owner*
EMP: 3
SALES: 300K **Privately Held**
SIC: 3993 Signs & advertising specialties

## GEOGRAPHIC SECTION

Granite City - Madison County (G-11297)

**(G-11274)**
**EHRHARDT TOOL & MACHINE LLC**
25 Central Industrial Dr (62040-6802)
**PHONE**..................314 436-6900
Ralph Phillips, *President*
Patrick Walsh, *Vice Pres*
Michael Walz, *Vice Pres*
Tom Werly, *CFO*
▼ **EMP:** 150
**SQ FT:** 100,000
**SALES (est):** 3.4MM **Privately Held**
**SIC: 7692** 3544 8711 Brazing; die sets for metal stamping (presses); machine tool design

**(G-11275)**
**EVOQUA WATER TECHNOLOGIES LLC**
3202 W 20th St (62040-1820)
**PHONE**..................618 451-1205
James Kopsic, *Manager*
**EMP:** 8
**SALES (corp-wide):** 1.2B **Privately Held**
**SIC: 3589** 3569 Sewage & water treatment equipment; water treatment equipment, industrial; sewage treatment equipment; water purification equipment, household type; filters, general line: industrial
**HQ:** Evoqua Water Technologies Llc
   181 Thorn Hill Rd
   Warrendale PA 15086
   724 772-0044

**(G-11276)**
**FAIRFIELD PROCESSING CORP**
1201 W 1st St (62040-1890)
**PHONE**..................618 452-8404
Demond Sosa, *Principal*
**EMP:** 28
**SALES (corp-wide):** 45.4MM **Privately Held**
**SIC: 2824** Polyester fibers
**PA:** Fairfield Processing Corp
   88 Rose Hill Ave
   Danbury CT 06810
   203 744-2090

**(G-11277)**
**FULLER ASPHALT & LANDSCAPE**
4353 Lake Dr (62040-3038)
**PHONE**..................618 797-1169
Gary W Fuller, *President*
Paula Fuller, *Admin Sec*
**EMP:** 5
**SALES (est):** 389.5K **Privately Held**
**SIC: 1771** 0782 4212 2951 Driveway contractor; parking lot construction; landscape contractors; local trucking, without storage; asphalt paving mixtures & blocks

**(G-11278)**
**G F PRINTING**
2439 Hemlock Ave (62040-2902)
**PHONE**..................618 797-0576
**Fax:** 618 877-8620
Laura Falter, *President*
Greg Falter, *Owner*
Glenn Falter, *Vice Pres*
**EMP:** 3
**SQ FT:** 4,400
**SALES (est):** 180K **Privately Held**
**WEB:** www.gfprinting.com
**SIC: 2752** 2791 2789 2759 Commercial printing, offset; typesetting; bookbinding & related work; commercial printing

**(G-11279)**
**GATEWAY PACKAGING COMPANY (PA)**
20 Central Industrial Dr (62040-6801)
**PHONE**..................618 876-4856
**Fax:** 618 876-4856
Roger D Miller, *President*
Rebecca J Miller, *Vice Pres*
Robert Tiepelman, *Prdtn Mgr*
Kathy S Harris, *Senior Buyer*
Russ Leeker, *Engineer*
▲ **EMP:** 140
**SALES (est):** 107.3MM **Privately Held**
**SIC: 2674** 2679 Bags: uncoated paper & multiwall; labels, paper: made from purchased material

**(G-11280)**
**GATEWAY PACKAGING COMPANY LLC (HQ)**
Also Called: Gateway Packaging Co Gran Cy
20 Central Industrial Dr (62040-6801)
**PHONE**..................618 415-0010
Omar Abuaita, *CEO*
David Antonini, *CFO*
▲ **EMP:** 250
**SQ FT:** 15,000
**SALES (est):** 68.4MM
**SALES (corp-wide):** 107.3MM **Privately Held**
**SIC: 2674** 3565 Bags: uncoated paper & multiwall; packaging machinery
**PA:** Gateway Packaging Company
   20 Central Industrial Dr
   Granite City IL 62040
   618 451-0010

**(G-11281)**
**GEBCO MACHINE INC**
2900 Emzee Ave (62040-1999)
**PHONE**..................618 452-6120
**Fax:** 618 452-8005
Gary Vogeller, *President*
George Vogeller, *President*
**EMP:** 12
**SQ FT:** 17,000
**SALES (est):** 1.6MM **Privately Held**
**SIC: 3599** Machine shop, jobbing & repair

**(G-11282)**
**GREG WATERS**
3477 Nameoki Rd (62040-3709)
**PHONE**..................618 798-9758
Greg Waters, *Owner*
**EMP:** 3
**SALES (est):** 208K **Privately Held**
**SIC: 3086** Packaging & shipping materials, foamed plastic

**(G-11283)**
**H&S MACHINE & TOOLS INC**
35 Central Industrial Dr (62040-6802)
**PHONE**..................618 451-0164
Richard Hollshouser, *President*
**EMP:** 9
**SALES (est):** 930.9K **Privately Held**
**SIC: 7539** 3599 Machine shop, automotive; industrial machinery

**(G-11284)**
**HEIDTMAN STEEL PRODUCTS INC**
10 Northgate Indus Dr (62040-6842)
**PHONE**..................618 451-0052
**Fax:** 618 451-0240
Tim Berra, *Branch Mgr*
**EMP:** 100
**SQ FT:** 55,000
**SALES (corp-wide):** 273MM **Privately Held**
**WEB:** www.heidtman.com
**SIC: 3312** 5051 3471 Blast furnaces & steel mills; metals service centers & offices; plating & polishing
**HQ:** Heidtman Steel Products, Inc.
   2401 Front St
   Toledo OH 43605
   419 691-4646

**(G-11285)**
**HEIDTMAN STEEL PRODUCTS INC**
10 Northgate Indus Dr (62040-6842)
**PHONE**..................618 451-0052
Allan Bates Jr, *Branch Mgr*
**EMP:** 99
**SQ FT:** 2,380
**SALES (corp-wide):** 273MM **Privately Held**
**WEB:** www.heidtman.com
**SIC: 3312** 5051 3471 Blast furnaces & steel mills; metals service centers & offices; plating & polishing
**HQ:** Heidtman Steel Products, Inc.
   2401 Front St
   Toledo OH 43605
   419 691-4646

**(G-11286)**
**HOLSHOUSER MACHINE & TOOL INC**
35 Central Industrial Dr (62040-6802)
**PHONE**..................618 451-0164
**Fax:** 618 451-0351
Richard J Holshouser, *President*
Diane Jacober, *Corp Secy*
**EMP:** 7
**SQ FT:** 6,400
**SALES (est):** 450K **Privately Held**
**SIC: 7692** 3599 Welding repair; machine shop, jobbing & repair

**(G-11287)**
**ICON MECH CNSTR & ENGRG LLC**
1616 Cleveland Blvd (62040-4401)
**PHONE**..................618 452-0035
**Fax:** 618 452-0037
Michael F Bieg, *Principal*
**EMP:** 250
**SQ FT:** 22,500
**SALES (est):** 59MM **Privately Held**
**SIC: 8711** 3498 Engineering services; fabricated pipe & fittings

**(G-11288)**
**ILLINOIS BLOCK AND TACKLE INC**
1635 W 1st St Ste 312 (62040-1883)
**PHONE**..................618 451-8696
Gary Head, *President*
**EMP:** 4
**SALES (est):** 177.3K **Privately Held**
**SIC: 3399** Laminating steel

**(G-11289)**
**KRAFT HEINZ FOODS COMPANY**
2901 Missouri Ave (62040-2032)
**PHONE**..................618 451-4820
**Fax:** 618 512-9216
Gary Roberson, *Engineer*
John Utzig, *Human Res Dir*
Patricia Riso, *Comms Dir*
Dave Peterson, *Manager*
Mark Calhoun, *Manager*
**EMP:** 324
**SALES (corp-wide):** 26.4B **Publicly Held**
**SIC: 2099** Food preparations
**HQ:** Kraft Heinz Foods Company
   1 Ppg Pl Ste 3200
   Pittsburgh PA 15222
   412 456-5700

**(G-11290)**
**KRAFT HEINZ FOODS COMPANY**
2901 Missouri Ave (62040-2032)
**PHONE**..................618 512-9100
Andy Klaas, *Vice Pres*
Don Scmitt, *Vice Pres*
Jim Price, *Human Res Mgr*
Jennifer Henion, *Branch Mgr*
**EMP:** 300
**SALES (corp-wide):** 26.4B **Publicly Held**
**WEB:** www.kraftfoods.com
**SIC: 2033** 2086 2037 Fruit juices: packaged in cans, jars, etc.; bottled & canned soft drinks; frozen fruits & vegetables
**HQ:** Kraft Heinz Foods Company
   1 Ppg Pl Ste 3200
   Pittsburgh PA 15222
   412 456-5700

**(G-11291)**
**LUMBERYARD SUPPLIERS INC**
4200 Horseshoe Lake Rd (62040-7601)
**PHONE**..................618 931-0315
Joe Mott, *Branch Mgr*
**EMP:** 10
**SALES (corp-wide):** 44MM **Privately Held**
**SIC: 2421** 1611 Building & structural materials, wood; general contractor, highway & street construction
**PA:** Lumberyard Suppliers, Inc.
   300 Pinecrest Dr
   East Peoria IL 61611
   309 694-4356

**(G-11292)**
**MAYCO MANUFACTURING LLC**
1200 16th St (62040-4444)
**PHONE**..................618 451-4400
Bob Cook, *Manager*
**EMP:** 50
**SALES (corp-wide):** 23MM **Privately Held**
**WEB:** www.maycoindustries.com
**SIC: 3339** Lead & zinc
**PA:** Mayco Manufacturing, Llc
   18 W Oxmoor Rd
   Birmingham AL 35209
   205 942-4242

**(G-11293)**
**MAYCO-GRANITE CITY INC**
1200 16th St (62040-4444)
**PHONE**..................618 451-4400
Michael Drury, *President*
Eric W Finlayson, *Corp Secy*
Robyn Richardson, *Manager*
▲ **EMP:** 40 **EST:** 1979
**SQ FT:** 186,000
**SALES (est):** 9.3MM
**SALES (corp-wide):** 476MM **Privately Held**
**WEB:** www.metalico.com
**SIC: 3356** Lead & zinc
**PA:** Metalico, Inc.
   135 Dermody St
   Cranford NJ 07016
   908 497-9610

**(G-11294)**
**MIDWEST LIFTING PRODUCTS INC**
1635 W 1st St Ste 312 (62040-1883)
**PHONE**..................214 356-7102
Sheila Bean, *President*
Radiance Bean, *Vice Pres*
Gary Head, *Admin Sec*
**EMP:** 4
**SALES (est):** 181.9K **Privately Held**
**SIC: 2499** Tackle blocks, wood

**(G-11295)**
**MIDWEST METAL COATINGS LLC**
9 Konzen Ct (62040-6855)
**PHONE**..................618 451-2971
**Fax:** 618 451-4756
Jerry Luna, *Plant Mgr*
Ben Crocker, *Controller*
Mike Dake, *Manager*
Victor Lacastro, *Manager*
Greg Taylor, *Data Proc Dir*
**EMP:** 40
**SQ FT:** 94,000
**SALES (est):** 8.4MM
**SALES (corp-wide):** 2.2B **Publicly Held**
**WEB:** www.precoatmetals.com
**SIC: 3479** Painting, coating & hot dipping
**HQ:** Precoat Metals, Inc.
   1310 Papin St Ste 300
   Saint Louis MO 63103
   314 436-7010

**(G-11296)**
**MIDWEST SUN-RAY LIGHTING & SIG**
Also Called: Midwest Sun-Ray Ltg & Sign
4762 E Chain Of Rocks Rd (62040)
**PHONE**..................618 656-2884
**Fax:** 618 656-3764
Gary Nielson, *President*
George Grindstaff, *Vice Pres*
Kevin Nowak, *Vice Pres*
**EMP:** 15
**SQ FT:** 2,000
**SALES (est):** 2.2MM **Privately Held**
**WEB:** www.midwestsunray.com
**SIC: 1799** 3993 3645 1731 Sign installation & maintenance; signs & advertising specialties; residential lighting fixtures; electrical work

**(G-11297)**
**MRC GLOBAL (US) INC**
3672 State Route 111 (62040-6612)
P.O. Box 550 (62040-0550)
**PHONE**..................314 231-3400
Rance Long, *Vice Pres*
**EMP:** 11 **Publicly Held**
**SIC: 1311** Crude petroleum & natural gas
**HQ:** Mrc Global (Us) Inc.
   1301 Mckinney St Ste 2300
   Houston TX 77010
   877 294-7574

# Granite City - Madison County (G-11298)

**(G-11298)**
**NICHOLS NET & TWINE INC**
2200 State Route 111 (62040-6581)
PHONE ..................................618 797-0211
Fax: 618 797-0212
John J Rogenski, *President*
Patrick Dillon, *Vice Pres*
Charlene Rogenski, *Admin Sec*
**EMP:** 5 **EST:** 1959
**SQ FT:** 10,000
**SALES (est):** 440K **Privately Held**
**SIC:** 2298 3949 Fishing lines, nets, seines: made in cordage or twine mills; sporting & athletic goods

**(G-11299)**
**PRAIRIE FARMS DAIRY INC**
1800 Adams St (62040-3347)
PHONE ..................................618 451-5600
Fax: 618 451-7251
Bob Kmetz, *General Mgr*
Dale Chapman, *Vice Pres*
Jim McCulloch, *Vice Pres*
Vic Fernandez, *Plant Mgr*
Charles Hays, *Controller*
**EMP:** 9
**SALES (corp-wide):** 1.8B **Privately Held**
**WEB:** www.prairiefarms.com
**SIC:** 2024 2022 2021 2026 Ice cream & frozen desserts; cheese, natural & processed; creamery butter; fluid milk
**PA:** Prairie Farms Dairy, Inc.
  1100 Broadway
  Carlinville IL 62626
  217 854-2547

**(G-11300)**
**PRECOAT METALS**
25 Northgate Indus Dr (62040-6841)
PHONE ..................................618 451-0909
Fax: 618 451-7906
Jerry Luna, *Plant Mgr*
Matt Murphy, *Plant Mgr*
Pat Copeland, *Opers Staff*
Randy Smith, *QC Dir*
Patty Schrader, *Human Res Mgr*
**EMP:** 56
**SALES (corp-wide):** 2.2B **Publicly Held**
**WEB:** www.precoatmetals.com
**SIC:** 3724 3479 Aircraft engines & engine parts; coating of metals & formed products
**HQ:** Precoat Metals, Inc.
  1310 Papin St Ste 300
  Saint Louis MO 63103
  314 436-7010

**(G-11301)**
**S & S PALLET CORP**
1459 State St (62040-4433)
P.O. Box 1387 (62040-1387)
PHONE ..................................618 219-3218
Fax: 618 219-3221
Donnye Shrum, *President*
Kim Shrum, *Admin Sec*
**EMP:** 38
**SALES (est):** 6.7MM **Privately Held**
**SIC:** 2448 Pallets, wood & wood with metal

**(G-11302)**
**SHUP TOOL & MACHINE CO**
4158 State Route 162 (62040-6607)
PHONE ..................................618 931-2596
Dennis Shup, *Owner*
**EMP:** 3 **EST:** 1974
**SQ FT:** 2,000
**SALES (est):** 251.3K **Privately Held**
**SIC:** 3544 7692 Special dies, tools, jigs & fixtures; special dies & tools; welding repair

**(G-11303)**
**SIEMENS INDUSTRY INC**
Also Called: Seamans Water Technology
3202 W 20th St (62040-1820)
P.O. Box 98 (62040-0098)
PHONE ..................................618 451-1205
Jim Kopsic, *General Mgr*
Bill Ziebold, *Accounts Mgr*
**EMP:** 10
**SALES (corp-wide):** 89.6B **Privately Held**
**SIC:** 2899 Water treating compounds
**HQ:** Siemens Industry, Inc.
  1000 Deerfield Pkwy
  Buffalo Grove IL 60089
  847 215-1000

**(G-11304)**
**SPEEDCO INC**
1201 Denham Dr (62040-4714)
PHONE ..................................618 931-1575
John Rosen, *Principal*
**EMP:** 6
**SALES (corp-wide):** 30.1B **Privately Held**
**SIC:** 2992 Lubricating oils
**HQ:** Speedco, Inc.
  535 Marriott Dr
  Nashville TN 37214

**(G-11305)**
**STEIN INC**
Also Called: Stein Still Mills
2201 Edwardsville Rd (62040-6311)
P.O. Box 1369 (62040-1369)
PHONE ..................................618 452-0836
Fax: 618 877-3281
Alan Medford, *Branch Mgr*
**EMP:** 70
**SALES (corp-wide):** 83.3MM **Privately Held**
**WEB:** www.stein.com
**SIC:** 3399 3312 5084 Iron ore recovery from open hearth slag; blast furnaces & steel mills; industrial machinery & equipment
**PA:** Stein, Inc.
  1929 E Royalton Rd Ste C
  Cleveland OH 44147
  440 526-9301

**(G-11306)**
**STRIPMASTERS ILLINOIS INC**
1107 22nd St (62040-3306)
PHONE ..................................618 452-1060
Terry Carron, *President*
Jim Douglas, *Purchasing*
Diane Valerius, *Manager*
Cathy Carron, *Admin Sec*
Heather Carron, *Administration*
**EMP:** 6
**SALES (est):** 593.5K **Privately Held**
**SIC:** 1799 3479 Sandblasting of building exteriors; painting, coating & hot dipping

**(G-11307)**
**TMS INTERNATIONAL LLC**
22nd & Edwardsville Rd (62040)
P.O. Box 398 (62040-0398)
PHONE ..................................618 451-7840
**EMP:** 55
**SALES (corp-wide):** 282.4MM **Privately Held**
**SIC:** 3295 Mfg Minerals-Ground/Treated
**HQ:** Tms International Group Llc
  12 Monongahela Ave
  Glassport PA 15045
  412 678-6141

**(G-11308)**
**TRI CITY CANVAS PRODUCTS INC (PA)**
3240 W Chain Of Rocks Rd A (62040-7065)
PHONE ..................................618 797-1662
Fax: 618 797-0410
Herman Schoeber, *Owner*
Steven Schoeber, *Manager*
**EMP:** 18
**SQ FT:** 12,000
**SALES (est):** 3.1MM **Privately Held**
**WEB:** www.tricityflatbeds.com
**SIC:** 2394 5013 Canvas & related products; tarpaulins, fabric: made from purchased materials; trailer parts & accessories

**(G-11309)**
**U S FILTER PRODUCTS**
3202 W 20th St (62040-1820)
P.O. Box 98 (62040-0098)
PHONE ..................................618 451-1205
Fax: 618 451-2576
Tom Hoyne, *Opers Mgr*
Jim Kopsic, *Manager*
**EMP:** 2
**SALES (est):** 200K **Privately Held**
**SIC:** 3569 Filters

**(G-11310)**
**UNITED STATES STEEL CORP**
Also Called: Granite City Works
1951 State St (62040-4622)
PHONE ..................................618 451-3456
Sharron Owen, *General Mgr*
Adam Radetic, *Area Mgr*
Tony Barnouski, *Engineer*
Joyce Moore, *Manager*
Michael Wilson, *Manager*
**EMP:** 100
**SALES (corp-wide):** 10.2B **Publicly Held**
**SIC:** 3312 Blast furnaces & steel mills
**PA:** United States Steel Corp
  600 Grant St Ste 468
  Pittsburgh PA 15219
  412 433-1121

**(G-11311)**
**WALTERS METAL FABRICATION INC**
3660 State Route 111 (62040-6612)
P.O. Box 1245 (62040-1245)
PHONE ..................................618 931-5551
Fax: 618 931-5557
Laurence Dittmeier, *President*
Eric Carl, *Project Mgr*
Suzanne Rodis, *Purch Mgr*
Don Porter, *Project Engr*
Keith Krause, *Sales Mgr*
**EMP:** 100 **EST:** 1985
**SQ FT:** 42,000
**SALES (est):** 39.2MM **Privately Held**
**WEB:** www.waltersmetalfab.com
**SIC:** 3441 8711 Fabricated structural metal; engineering services

## Grant Park
### Kankakee County

**(G-11312)**
**PACTIV LLC**
304 Ne Main St (60940-6001)
PHONE ..................................317 390-5306
Tom Lawson, *Principal*
**EMP:** 212 **Privately Held**
**SIC:** 2673 Food storage & trash bags (plastic)
**HQ:** Pactiv Llc
  1900 W Field Ct
  Lake Forest IL 60045
  847 482-2000

**(G-11313)**
**PEORIA PACKING LTD**
8372 N 12000e Rd (60940-5014)
PHONE ..................................815 465-9824
Fax: 815 465-0046
Eddie Lynch, *Branch Mgr*
**EMP:** 15
**SALES (corp-wide):** 11MM **Privately Held**
**SIC:** 2011 Meat packing plants
**PA:** Peoria Packing, Ltd.
  1307 W Lake St
  Chicago IL 60607
  312 226-2600

**(G-11314)**
**REYNOLDS FOOD PACKAGING**
304 Ne Main St (60940-6001)
PHONE ..................................815 465-2115
Peter Boevers, *Principal*
Deana Brezich, *Officer*
**EMP:** 13 **EST:** 2012
**SALES (est):** 2.2MM **Privately Held**
**SIC:** 3353 Foil, aluminum

**(G-11315)**
**ROYAL MACHINE WORKS INC**
204 N Stanley St (60940-7269)
P.O. Box 507 (60940-0507)
PHONE ..................................815 465-6879
Ricky Bird, *President*
Tammy Nies, *Corp Secy*
**EMP:** 2
**SQ FT:** 12,500
**SALES (est):** 200K **Privately Held**
**SIC:** 3599 Machine shop, jobbing & repair

**(G-11316)**
**TOOL-MASTERS TOOL & STAMP INC**
204 N Stanley St (60940-7269)
P.O. Box 507 (60940-0507)
PHONE ..................................815 465-6830
Fax: 815 465-6388
Tammy Nief, *President*
Rick Bird, *Admin Sec*
**EMP:** 9
**SQ FT:** 12,523
**SALES (est):** 1.8MM **Privately Held**
**SIC:** 3544 Special dies & tools

## Granville
### Putnam County

**(G-11317)**
**CONCRETE PRODUCTS**
Also Called: Concrete Products Ziano
304 E Harper Ave (61326-9719)
P.O. Box 232 (61326-0232)
PHONE ..................................815 339-6395
Fax: 815 339-6395
James Ziano, *Owner*
**EMP:** 4
**SQ FT:** 3,200
**SALES (est):** 700K **Privately Held**
**SIC:** 3272 Concrete products; septic tanks, concrete

**(G-11318)**
**J W OSSOLA COMPANY INC**
Also Called: Granville Ready Mix
502 E Harper Ave (61326-9709)
P.O. Box 346 (61326-0346)
PHONE ..................................815 339-6112
Robert Ossola, *President*
Douglas Ossola, *Vice Pres*
Jack Ossola, *Treasurer*
**EMP:** 6 **EST:** 1945
**SQ FT:** 4,000
**SALES (est):** 741.9K **Privately Held**
**SIC:** 1794 3273 Excavation work; ready-mixed concrete

**(G-11319)**
**JW OSSOLA CO INC**
Also Called: Granville Ready Mix
And Elm St Rr 71 (61326)
PHONE ..................................815 339-6113
Robert Ossola, *President*
Douglas Ossola, *Vice Pres*
Jack Ossola, *Admin Sec*
**EMP:** 6
**SALES:** 6MM **Privately Held**
**SIC:** 3273 Ready-mixed concrete

## Grayslake
### Lake County

**(G-11320)**
**ARCHITECTURAL DISTRIBUTORS**
162 Center St (60030-1533)
PHONE ..................................847 223-5800
Fax: 847 223-5826
Michael L Hoerl, *President*
Mary E Schweitzer, *Vice Pres*
**EMP:** 7
**SALES (est):** 980K **Privately Held**
**WEB:** www.archdist.com
**SIC:** 5031 3272 Building materials, interior; building materials, except block or brick; concrete

**(G-11321)**
**ASAP SPECIALTIES INC DEL**
888 E Belvidere Rd # 111 (60030-2568)
PHONE ..................................847 223-7699
Linda R Michelson, *President*
**EMP:** 6
**SALES (est):** 512.3K **Privately Held**
**WEB:** www.asapteam.com
**SIC:** 5199 5065 5136 5137 Advertising specialties; electronic parts & equipment; men's & boys' clothing; uniforms, men's & boys'; women's & children's clothing; uniforms, women's & children's; graphic arts & related design; silk screen design; embroidery & art needlework

**(G-11322)**
**BLUE SKY BIO LLC**
888 E Belvidere Rd # 212 (60030-2571)
PHONE ..................................718 376-0422
Sheldon Lerner,
Dr Albert Zickmann,
**EMP:** 2

# GEOGRAPHIC SECTION

**Grayslake - Lake County (G-11349)**

**SALES (est):** 233K  **Privately Held**
**WEB:** www.blueskybio.com
**SIC:** 3842  Implants, surgical

**(G-11323)**
**CANNY INNOVATIVE SOLUTIONS INC**
888 E Belvidere Rd # 207  (60030-2568)
**PHONE** .................................... 847 323-1271
Martin Schroeder, *President*
Ronald Schroeder, *Vice Pres*
**EMP:** 2
**SALES:** 500K  **Privately Held**
**SIC:** 3549  Metalworking machinery

**(G-11324)**
**CANNY TOOL & MOLD CORPORATION**
888 E Belvidere Rd # 207  (60030-2571)
**PHONE** .................................... 847 548-1573
Roland Schroeder, *President*
Gisela Schroeder, *Admin Sec*
▲ **EMP:** 5
**SQ FT:** 3,200
**SALES:** 600K  **Privately Held**
**SIC:** 3544  Industrial molds

**(G-11325)**
**CAREY ELECTRIC CO INC**
24809 W Chardon Rd  (60030-9518)
**PHONE** .................................... 847 949-9294
Bill Fialkowski, *Manager*
**EMP:** 4
**SALES (est):** 257.5K  **Privately Held**
**SIC:** 3699  1731  Electrical equipment & supplies; electrical work

**(G-11326)**
**CHEMPROBE INC**
888 E Belvidere Rd # 313  (60030-2576)
**PHONE** .................................... 847 231-4534
Azra Khan, *President*
Shakoor Khan, *Vice Pres*
**EMP:** 5
**SALES (est):** 678.6K  **Privately Held**
**SIC:** 2835  In vitro & in vivo diagnostic substances

**(G-11327)**
**COLLEAGUES OF BEER  INC**
Also Called: Light The Lamp Brewery
520 Laurie Ct  (60030-1572)
**PHONE** .................................... 847 727-3318
William Hermes, *CEO*
James Sheppard, *CFO*
Donald Chatten, *Admin Sec*
**EMP:** 4
**SQ FT:** 2,300
**SALES (est):** 291K  **Privately Held**
**SIC:** 2082  Ale (alcoholic beverage)

**(G-11328)**
**COMPX INTERNATIONAL INC**
715 Center St  (60030-1651)
**PHONE** .................................... 847 543-4583
Steve Willard, *Principal*
Michael Dykes, *Safety Dir*
David Burns, *Controller*
Jesse Mavromatis, *Sales Engr*
**EMP:** 5
**SALES (corp-wide):** 108.9MM  **Publicly Held**
**SIC:** 3699  Security devices
**HQ:** Compx International Inc.
   5430 Lbj Fwy Ste 1700
   Dallas TX 75240
   972 448-1400

**(G-11329)**
**COMPX SECURITY PRODUCTS INC**
Also Called: Compx Timberline
715 Center St  (60030-1651)
**PHONE** .................................... 847 234-1864
Scott C James, *President*
Gregg Walla, *Principal*
Chris Hadfield, *Manager*
Tim Peters, *Manager*
Steve Willard, *Manager*
▲ **EMP:** 85
**SQ FT:** 120,000
**SALES (est):** 18MM
**SALES (corp-wide):** 108.9MM  **Publicly Held**
**WEB:** www.nclnet.com
**SIC:** 3429  5712  Furniture hardware; furniture stores
**HQ:** Compx International Inc.
   5430 Lbj Fwy Ste 1700
   Dallas TX 75240
   972 448-1400

**(G-11330)**
**CREATIVE CLOTHING CREATED 4 U**
488 Wood Duck Ct  (60030-2794)
**PHONE** .................................... 847 543-0051
Joe Covelli, *President*
**EMP:** 6
**SQ FT:** 3,800
**SALES:** 460K  **Privately Held**
**SIC:** 2253  2396  2395  Warm weather knit outerwear, including beachwear; dresses & skirts; automotive & apparel trimmings; pleating & stitching

**(G-11331)**
**DAESAM CORPORATION**
888 E Belvidere Rd # 306  (60030-2568)
**PHONE** .................................... 917 653-2000
Lynda Kim, *President*
▲ **EMP:** 5
**SALES:** 950K  **Privately Held**
**SIC:** 3679  Electronic circuits

**(G-11332)**
**DANDELION DISTRIBUTORS INC**
Also Called: Holly Press, The
888 E Belvidere Rd # 114  (60030-2568)
P.O. Box 234  (60030-0234)
**PHONE** .................................... 815 675-9800
**Fax:** 847 223-3221
David H Gerholdt, *President*
**EMP:** 3
**SALES (est):** 444.4K  **Privately Held**
**SIC:** 2752  Commercial printing, offset

**(G-11333)**
**DISTINCTIVE SIGNS& THE NEON EX**
1868 E Belvidere Rd A  (60030-2289)
**PHONE** .................................... 847 245-7159
**Fax:** 847 395-1582
**EMP:** 2
**SALES:** 300K  **Privately Held**
**SIC:** 7389  3993  Business Services Mfg Signs/Advertising Specialties

**(G-11334)**
**ENERGY-GLAZED SYSTEMS INC**
350 Center St  (60030-1624)
**PHONE** .................................... 847 223-4500
Wayman Tidwell, *President*
**EMP:** 14
**SALES:** 950K  **Privately Held**
**SIC:** 3211  3231  Window glass, clear & colored; products of purchased glass

**(G-11335)**
**ENGINEERED MILLS  INC**
Also Called: EMI
888 E Belvidere Rd  (60030-2568)
**PHONE** .................................... 847 548-0044
**Fax:** 847 548-0099
Dave Peterson, *President*
Sherry Geisler, *Manager*
**EMP:** 5
**SQ FT:** 5,000
**SALES (est):** 805.7K  **Privately Held**
**WEB:** www.eigerus.com
**SIC:** 3541  Chemical milling machines

**(G-11336)**
**EXCEL  LTD  INC**
888 E Belvidere Rd # 105  (60030-2568)
**PHONE** .................................... 847 543-9138
**Fax:** 847 543-9230
James Bartus, *President*
Susan Eisert, *Vice Pres*
**EMP:** 6
**SALES (est):** 1.8MM  **Privately Held**
**WEB:** www.excelltdinc.com
**SIC:** 3613  Control panels, electric

**(G-11337)**
**FABRICATORS UNLIMITED INC**
55 S Barron Blvd  (60030-7825)
**PHONE** .................................... 847 223-7986
Randall E Peters, *President*
Anita Peters, *Vice Pres*
Pamela Peters, *Vice Pres*
**EMP:** 3
**SQ FT:** 8,200
**SALES:** 450K  **Privately Held**
**SIC:** 3469  1799  3599  8731  Stamping metal for the trade; welding on site; machine shop, jobbing & repair; industrial laboratory, except testing

**(G-11338)**
**FORT LOCK CORPORATION (DH)**
Also Called: Compx Fort
715 Center St  (60030-1651)
**PHONE** .................................... 708 456-1100
**Fax:** 847 752-2419
Jay A Fine, *President*
▲ **EMP:** 40  **EST:** 1954
**SQ FT:** 70,000
**SALES (est):** 31.9MM
**SALES (corp-wide):** 108.9MM  **Publicly Held**
**SIC:** 3429  Locks or lock sets
**HQ:** Compx International Inc.
   5430 Lbj Fwy Ste 1700
   Dallas TX 75240
   972 448-1400

**(G-11339)**
**GFX DYNAMIC**
32088 N Pine Ave  (60030-2543)
**PHONE** .................................... 847 543-4600
Angela Tomlinson, *Principal*
**EMP:** 2
**SALES (est):** 245.3K  **Privately Held**
**SIC:** 2759  Screen printing

**(G-11340)**
**GFX INTERNATIONAL INC (PA)**
333 Barron Blvd  (60030-1638)
**PHONE** .................................... 847 543-7179
**Fax:** 847 543-4610
Charles Huttinger, *CEO*
Jim McLaughlin, *Senior VP*
Debbie Lofchie, *Vice Pres*
Mark Taylor, *Vice Pres*
Frank Gulik, *CFO*
**EMP:** 122
**SQ FT:** 88,000
**SALES (est):** 51MM  **Privately Held**
**WEB:** www.gfxi.com
**SIC:** 7336  2759  7335  7812  Graphic arts & related design; posters, including billboards; printing; commercial photography; commercials, television: tape or film

**(G-11341)**
**GLAZED STRUCTURES  INC**
350 Center St  (60030-1624)
**PHONE** .................................... 847 223-4560
Deann Twitchel, *President*
Jeffrey Feldkamp, *Engineer*
Keith Macnaught, *Finance Mgr*
Michelle Needham, *Accounting Mgr*
J Tidwell, *Financial Exec*
**EMP:** 15
**SQ FT:** 14,000
**SALES (est):** 980K  **Privately Held**
**SIC:** 3211  3444  3231  3083  Flat glass; sheet metalwork; products of purchased glass; laminated plastics plate & sheet

**(G-11342)**
**GLUNZ FMLY WINERY CELLARS INC (PA)**
Also Called: Glunz Cellars
888 E Belvidere Rd # 107  (60030-2568)
**PHONE** .................................... 847 548-9463
**Fax:** 847 548-8038
Helen T Glunz, *President*
**EMP:** 20
**SQ FT:** 3,873
**SALES (est):** 2.5MM  **Privately Held**
**WEB:** www.gfwc.com
**SIC:** 2084  2085  Wines; distilled & blended liquors

**(G-11343)**
**GRAM COLOSSAL INC**
888 E Belvidere Rd # 113  (60030-2570)
**PHONE** .................................... 847 223-5757
**Fax:** 847 223-6191
Marilyn Schleiden, *CEO*
Bruce Schleiden, *President*
**EMP:** 3
**SALES (est):** 296.6K  **Privately Held**
**WEB:** www.colossalgram.com
**SIC:** 2771  Greeting cards

**(G-11344)**
**GRAYSLAKE FEED SALES  INC**
81 E Belvidere Rd  (60030-2438)
P.O. Box 327  (60030-0327)
**PHONE** .................................... 847 223-4855
**Fax:** 847 223-7424
Richard C De Meyer, *Manager*
**EMP:** 7
**SALES (corp-wide):** 6MM  **Privately Held**
**WEB:** www.grayslakefeed.com
**SIC:** 3568  Power transmission equipment
**PA:** Grayslake Feed Sales, Inc.
   21 N Seymour Ave
   Grayslake IL
   847 223-4855

**(G-11345)**
**HARGER  INC (PA)**
Also Called: Harger Lightning & Grounding
301 Ziegler Dr  (60030-1664)
**PHONE** .................................... 847 548-8700
**Fax:** 847 548-8755
Mark S Harger, *President*
John Salamone, *COO*
Jeffrey A Harger, *Vice Pres*
Timothy R Harger, *Vice Pres*
Barbara Lee Janowicz, *Accountant*
▲ **EMP:** 42
**SQ FT:** 50,000
**SALES (est):** 13.5MM  **Privately Held**
**WEB:** www.harger.com
**SIC:** 3643  1799  5063  Lightning protection equipment; lightning conductor erection; power transmission equipment, electric

**(G-11346)**
**HEISE INDUSTRIES INC**
Also Called: Krug-Northwest Electric Motors
123 Hawley St  (60030-1514)
**PHONE** .................................... 847 223-2410
**Fax:** 847 223-2829
Robert Heise, *President*
Andrew Heise, *Vice Pres*
**EMP:** 3  **EST:** 1971
**SQ FT:** 4,000
**SALES:** 450K  **Privately Held**
**SIC:** 7694  5063  Electric motor repair; motors, electric

**(G-11347)**
**INTERNATIONAL MOLD & PROD LLC**
Also Called: Imap
1397 Mayfair Ln  (60030-3755)
**PHONE** .................................... 313 617-5251
Leonard Koren, *President*
**EMP:** 4
**SALES (est):** 295.5K  **Privately Held**
**SIC:** 8711  3089  Engineering services; plastic containers, except foam; buckets, plastic; clothes hangers, plastic; injection molded finished plastic products

**(G-11348)**
**JAD GROUP  INC**
888 E Belvidere Rd # 213  (60030-2572)
**PHONE** .................................... 847 223-1804
Joseph Dibartolo, *CEO*
Shannon Kolek, *Manager*
Isao Kitaoka, *Director*
**EMP:** 2
**SQ FT:** 2,100
**SALES (est):** 417.5K  **Privately Held**
**WEB:** www.jadgrp.com
**SIC:** 3674  Semiconductors & related devices

**(G-11349)**
**JOINT ASIA DEV GROUP LLC**
Also Called: Divino
888 E Belvidere Rd # 213  (60030-2572)
**PHONE** .................................... 847 223-1804
Joe Dibartolo, *Mng Member*
Shannon Kolek, *Admin Asst*

# Grayslake - Lake County (G-11350)

EMP: 20
SALES (est): 2MM **Privately Held**
SIC: **2024** 5143 5812 Ice cream & frozen desserts; ice cream & ices; ice cream, soft drink & soda fountain stands

### (G-11350)
### LEGACY VULCAN LLC
Also Called: Grayslake Yard
875 S State Route 83 (60030-3509)
PHONE...................................847 548-4623
Floyd Janny, *Branch Mgr*
EMP: 5
SALES (corp-wide): 3.5B **Publicly Held**
WEB: www.vulcanmaterials.com
SIC: **1442** Construction sand & gravel
HQ: Legacy Vulcan, Llc
1200 Urban Center Dr
Vestavia AL 35242
205 298-3000

### (G-11351)
### LIQUA FIT INC (PA)
100 N Atkinson Rd Ste 102 (60030-7801)
PHONE...................................630 965-8067
Rachel Roberts, *CEO*
Maria Pawlata, *President*
EMP: 7
SQ FT: 1,400
SALES: 2.1MM **Privately Held**
SIC: **2023** Dietary supplements, dairy & non-dairy based

### (G-11352)
### LIVORSI MARINE INC
715 Center St (60030-1651)
PHONE...................................847 548-5900
Fax: 847 548-5903
Mike Livorsi, *President*
Fred Ortega, *Sales Staff*
◆ EMP: 24
SQ FT: 120,000
SALES (est): 4.9MM
SALES (corp-wide): 108.9MM **Publicly Held**
WEB: www.livorsi.com
SIC: **3829** Measuring & controlling devices
HQ: Compx Security Products Inc.
26 Old Mill Rd
Greenville SC 29607
864 286-1122

### (G-11353)
### MAGNA EXTRORS INTRORS AMER INC
414 Flanders Ln (60030-1219)
PHONE...................................847 548-9170
Jeff Henkin, *Branch Mgr*
EMP: 4
SALES (corp-wide): 36.4B **Privately Held**
WEB: www.magnaint.com
SIC: **2394** Convertible tops, canvas or boat: from purchased materials
HQ: Magna Exteriors Of America, Inc.
750 Tower Dr
Troy MI 48098
248 631-1100

### (G-11354)
### MODELS PLUS INC
888 E Belvidere Rd # 110 (60030-2569)
PHONE...................................847 231-4300
Mary Fogel, *President*
Jared Fogel, *Admin Sec*
EMP: 29
SALES (est): 2.3MM **Privately Held**
WEB: www.modelsplusinc.com
SIC: **3999** Models, except toy

### (G-11355)
### MOLD SEEKERS
319 Fairfax Ln (60030-3703)
PHONE...................................847 650-8025
Kevin Waldenstrom, *Principal*
EMP: 6
SALES (est): 634.5K **Privately Held**
SIC: **3442** Molding, trim & stripping

### (G-11356)
### NU GLO SIGN COMPANY
18880 W Gages Lake Rd (60030-1704)
PHONE...................................847 223-6160
Fax: 847 223-0129
John Samson, *Partner*
Bill Samson, *Partner*
Joan Samson, *Partner*
Tina Samson, *Partner*
EMP: 11
SQ FT: 4,500
SALES: 350K **Privately Held**
SIC: **3993** Electric signs

### (G-11357)
### NUTRITIONAL INSTITUTE LLC
100 S Atkinson Rd Ste 116 (60030-7819)
P.O. Box 7010 (60030-7010)
PHONE...................................847 223-7699
Cheryl Doros, *Pub Rel Dir*
Cheryl Doris, *Office Mgr*
Linda S Dowling,
EMP: 3
SALES (est): 250K **Privately Held**
SIC: **2833** Vitamins, natural or synthetic: bulk, uncompounded

### (G-11358)
### PAPER MOON RECYCLING INC
123 Bluff Ave (60030-2310)
PHONE...................................847 548-8875
Martin Christiansen, *Corp Secy*
Gerri Christiansen,
EMP: 2
SALES: 500K **Privately Held**
SIC: **2611** 5947 Pulp mills, mechanical & recycling processing; party favors

### (G-11359)
### PRINT BUTLER INC
674 Indian Path Rd (60030-3517)
PHONE...................................312 296-2804
Keith Andersson, *President*
EMP: 10
SALES: 2MM **Privately Held**
SIC: **2752** Commercial printing, lithographic

### (G-11360)
### QUALITY MOLDING PRODUCTS LLC
281 Frances Dr (60030-7968)
PHONE...................................224 308-4167
James Thomas, *President*
EMP: 3
SALES: 150K **Privately Held**
SIC: **3299** Moldings, architectural: plaster of paris

### (G-11361)
### RETMAP INC
34435 N Bobolink Trl (60030-2883)
PHONE...................................312 224-8938
Tamas Ban, *President*
John R Hetling, *Vice Pres*
Safa Rahmani, *Vice Pres*
EMP: 3
SALES (est): 266.4K **Privately Held**
SIC: **3845** Electromedical equipment

### (G-11362)
### RJG ENTERPRISES LTD
888 E Belvidere Rd # 222 (60030-2568)
PHONE...................................847 752-2065
Rich Gapinski, *President*
▼ EMP: 6 EST: 1985
SQ FT: 5,000
SALES (est): 1.2MM **Privately Held**
WEB: www.rjgmachinery.com
SIC: **2631** 5084 Packaging board; industrial machine parts

### (G-11363)
### SIGNARAMA
Also Called: Sign-A-Rama
1868 E Belvidere Rd A (60030-2289)
PHONE...................................847 543-4870
Fax: 847 543-4875
Mike Burcker, *President*
EMP: 4
SQ FT: 1,400
SALES (est): 330K **Privately Held**
SIC: **3993** Signs & advertising specialties

### (G-11364)
### TRI CNTY PRGNNCY PRENTING SVCS
888 E Belvidere Rd # 124 (60030-2568)
PHONE...................................847 231-4651
Scott Bryant, *Exec Dir*
Chris Wienke, *Director*
Bobbie Zamnier, *Director*
EMP: 3
SALES: 513.2K **Privately Held**
SIC: **2835** Pregnancy test kits

### (G-11365)
### TVH PARTS CO
95 S Rte 83 (60030)
PHONE...................................847 223-1000
Lon Purdy, *CFO*
Amy Castino, *Human Res Mgr*
Jim Rutkowski, *Supervisor*
Poul B Jensen, *CIO*
Joe Cernuska, *Sr Ntwrk Engine*
EMP: 22
SALES (corp-wide): 189.7MM **Privately Held**
SIC: **5084** 5013 3469 3499 Lift trucks & parts; motor vehicle supplies & new parts; metal stampings; automobile seat frames, metal; electronic circuits; lift trucks, industrial: fork, platform, straddle, etc.
PA: Tvh Parts Co.
16355 S Lone Elm Rd
Olathe KS 66062
913 829-1000

### (G-11366)
### WHYTE GATE INCORPORATED
400 S Curran Rd Ste 1 (60030-9202)
PHONE...................................847 201-7000
John Manolas, *Co-Owner*
Elli Manolas, *Co-Owner*
Karen McKee, *Finance Mgr*
EMP: 10
SQ FT: 15,000
SALES (est): 1.4MM **Privately Held**
WEB: www.whytegate.com
SIC: **3999** Pet supplies

### (G-11367)
### WINCADEMY INC
34331 N Stonebridge Ln (60030-2856)
PHONE...................................847 445-7886
Ryan Chiu, *Principal*
Jeffrey Fastow, *Principal*
Anthony Marquez, *Principal*
EMP: 3
SALES (est): 121.2K **Privately Held**
SIC: **7372** Educational computer software

### (G-11368)
### WINDSONG PRESS LTD
33403 N Greentree Rd (60030-1945)
PHONE...................................847 223-4586
Brian F Frederiksen, *President*
Arnold Jacobs, *Project Mgr*
EMP: 3
SALES: 15K **Privately Held**
WEB: www.windsongpress.com
SIC: **2731** 7929 Books: publishing only; entertainers & entertainment groups

## Grayville
### White County

### (G-11369)
### HARBISON-FISCHER INC
Also Called: Harbison Fischer Sales Co
1421 N Court St (62844-1813)
PHONE...................................618 375-3841
Wayne Middleton, *Manager*
EMP: 4
SALES (corp-wide): 6.7B **Publicly Held**
WEB: www.hfpumps.com
SIC: **3714** Oil pump, motor vehicle
HQ: Harbison-Fischer, Inc.
901 N Crowley Rd
Crowley TX 76036
817 297-2211

### (G-11370)
### HOOSIER STAMPING & MFG CORP
399 Industrial Park Dr (62844)
PHONE...................................812 426-2778
Christina Webb, *Principal*
EMP: 5
SALES (corp-wide): 16.7MM **Privately Held**
SIC: **3312** Wheels
PA: Hoosier Stamping & Mfg. Corp
1865 W Franklin St
Evansville IN 47712
812 426-2778

### (G-11371)
### HOOSIER STAMPING & MFG CORP
832 W Spring St (62844)
P.O. Box 191 (62844-0191)
PHONE...................................618 375-2057
Thomas Johnson, *Manager*
EMP: 30
SALES (corp-wide): 16.7MM **Privately Held**
WEB: www.hoosierstamping.com
SIC: **3469** 3714 3494 Metal stampings; motor vehicle parts & accessories; valves & pipe fittings
PA: Hoosier Stamping & Mfg. Corp
1865 W Franklin St
Evansville IN 47712
812 426-2778

### (G-11372)
### KASHA INDUSTRIES INC
1 Plastic Ln (62844)
P.O. Box 160 (62844-0160)
PHONE...................................618 375-2511
Fax: 618 375-5221
E Edwin Kasha Jr, *President*
James L Kasha, *Admin Sec*
EMP: 30
SQ FT: 230,000
SALES (est): 5.7MM **Privately Held**
WEB: www.kashaindustries.com
SIC: **2816** 7389 Color pigments; grinding, precision: commercial or industrial

### (G-11373)
### KASHA INDUSTRIES INC
1 Plastics Ln (62844)
PHONE...................................618 375-2511
Edwin E Kasha Jr, *President*
James L Kasha, *Admin Sec*
EMP: 10
SALES (est): 1.2MM **Privately Held**
SIC: **2816** Color pigments

### (G-11374)
### MAP OIL CO INC
139 County Road 990 E (62844)
PHONE...................................618 375-7616
Mark Peach, *Owner*
EMP: 7
SALES (est): 1MM **Privately Held**
SIC: **1389** Oil sampling service for oil companies

### (G-11375)
### MASON WELL SERVICING INC
111 S Court St (62844-1508)
P.O. Box 156 (62844-0156)
PHONE...................................618 375-4411
Max Mason, *President*
Margaret Mason, *Vice Pres*
Mike Mason, *Vice Pres*
EMP: 9
SQ FT: 1,200
SALES (est): 830K **Privately Held**
SIC: **1389** Servicing oil & gas wells

### (G-11376)
### S & R MEDIA LLC
Also Called: Navigator & Journal Register
113 N Middle St (62844-1408)
PHONE...................................618 375-7502
Patrick Seal,
Jerry Reppert,
EMP: 15
SALES (est): 536.7K **Privately Held**
SIC: **2711** Newspapers

### (G-11377)
### SIDS WELL SERVICE
1007 N Ct (62844)
P.O. Box 144 (62844-0144)
PHONE...................................618 375-5411
Sid Gross, *Owner*
Sherry Gross, *Manager*
EMP: 4
SALES: 240K **Privately Held**
SIC: **1389** Servicing oil & gas wells

## Green Valley
### Tazewell County

**(G-11378)**
**CENTRAL ILLINOIS HARDWOOD**
15634 Toboggan Ave (61534-9047)
PHONE..................309 352-2363
David Nash, *Principal*
**EMP:** 2
**SALES (est):** 261.6K **Privately Held**
**SIC:** 2426 Hardwood dimension & flooring mills

**(G-11379)**
**K D CUSTOM SAWING LOGGING**
6570 Illinois Route 29 (61534-9058)
PHONE..................309 231-4805
Steven Nash, *Principal*
**EMP:** 3 **EST:** 2010
**SALES (est):** 237.5K **Privately Held**
**SIC:** 2411 Logging

**(G-11380)**
**RLW INC**
132 Geraldine St (61534)
P.O. Box 105 (61534-0105)
PHONE..................309 352-2499
Russell L Watson, *President*
Richard Gallion, *Vice Pres*
**EMP:** 2
**SALES:** 300K **Privately Held**
**SIC:** 2411 7389 Logging;

## Greenup
### Cumberland County

**(G-11381)**
**DRUM MANUFACTURING**
804 E York Rd (62428-3559)
PHONE..................217 923-5625
David Drum, *President*
**EMP:** 10
**SALES (est):** 1.1MM **Privately Held**
**SIC:** 2821 Polyvinyl chloride resins (PVC)

**(G-11382)**
**EVAPCO INC**
Also Called: Evapco Midwest
1723 E York Rd (62428-3573)
P.O. Box 247 (62428-0247)
PHONE..................217 923-3431
Fax: 217 923-3300
Bruce Schehlein, *General Mgr*
Brett Frey, *Project Mgr*
Dave Mason, *Purch Mgr*
Heather Soccaras, *Buyer*
Walt Altman, *Branch Mgr*
**EMP:** 115
**SALES (corp-wide):** 432.8MM **Privately Held**
**WEB:** www.evapco.com
**SIC:** 3585 3443 5078 Parts for heating, cooling & refrigerating equipment; fabricated plate work (boiler shop); commercial refrigeration equipment
**PA:** Evapco, Inc.
5151 Allendale Ln
Taneytown MD 21787
410 756-2600

**(G-11383)**
**GREENUP PRESS INC**
104 E Cumberland St (62428)
P.O. Box 127 (62428-0127)
PHONE..................217 923-3704
William D McMorris, *President*
W D McMorris, *President*
Anthony McMorris, *General Mgr*
Tony McMorris, *General Mgr*
Marjorie McMorris, *Vice Pres*
**EMP:** 5
**SALES (est):** 329.3K **Privately Held**
**SIC:** 2711 2791 2752 Job printing & newspaper publishing combined; typesetting; commercial printing, lithographic

**(G-11384)**
**JALAA FIBERGLASS INC**
1654 County Road 350n (62428-3408)
P.O. Box 379, Newton (62448-0379)
PHONE..................217 923-3433
John Antrim, *President*
Louanne Antrim, *Vice Pres*
**EMP:** 3
**SALES:** 270K **Privately Held**
**SIC:** 3089 3088 2221 Plastic & fiberglass tanks; plastics plumbing fixtures; fiberglass fabrics

**(G-11385)**
**QUINN BROOM WORKS INC**
1527 Il Route 121 (62428-3222)
P.O. Box 575 (62428-0575)
PHONE..................217 923-3181
Fax: 217 923-5150
Mark Quinn, *President*
Betty Quinn, *Vice Pres*
▲ **EMP:** 22
**SQ FT:** 7,000
**SALES (est):** 2.9MM **Privately Held**
**WEB:** www.quinnbroomworks.com
**SIC:** 3991 Brooms

## Greenview
### Menard County

**(G-11386)**
**ROBERT SWAAR**
25903 Levee St (62642-9591)
PHONE..................217 968-2232
Robert Swaar, *CEO*
Sirah Jane, *President*
**EMP:** 2
**SALES:** 235K **Privately Held**
**SIC:** 3523 Driers (farm): grain, hay & seed

## Greenville
### Bond County

**(G-11387)**
**BASS-MOLLETT PUBLISHERS INC**
507 Monroe St (62246-2043)
P.O. Box 189 (62246-0189)
PHONE..................618 664-3141
Fax: 618 664-9727
John Flowers, *President*
Tad Flowers, *Vice Pres*
Duane Mollet, *Vice Pres*
Linda Flowers, *Treasurer*
David Wade, *Manager*
◆ **EMP:** 65 **EST:** 1951
**SQ FT:** 32,000
**SALES (est):** 16MM **Privately Held**
**WEB:** www.bass-mollett.com
**SIC:** 2741 2759 Miscellaneous publishing; announcements: engraved

**(G-11388)**
**BOND & FAYETTE COUNTY SHOPPER**
201 N 3rd St Ste Frnt (62246-1003)
P.O. Box 16 (62246-0016)
PHONE..................618 664-4566
Fax: 618 664-4567
Steve Holt, *Owner*
Jill Thompkins, *Marketing Staff*
**EMP:** 5
**SALES (est):** 305.8K **Privately Held**
**SIC:** 2711 Newspapers

**(G-11389)**
**BOND BROADCASTING INC**
Also Called: Wgel Radio
309 W Main St (62246-1716)
P.O. Box 277 (62246-0277)
PHONE..................618 664-3318
Fax: 618 664-3318
John Kennedy, *President*
**EMP:** 12
**SALES (est):** 672.1K **Privately Held**
**WEB:** www.wgel.com
**SIC:** 4832 2711 Radio broadcasting stations; newspapers

**(G-11390)**
**CENTRAL TOWNSHIP ROAD & BRIDGE**
920 E Bowman Dr (62246-2583)
PHONE..................618 704-5517
Mike Levinger, *Commissioner*
Dennis Lingley, *Supervisor*
**EMP:** 3
**SALES (est):** 300K **Privately Held**
**SIC:** 3531 Drags, road (construction & road maintenance equipment)

**(G-11391)**
**DEMOULIN BROTHERS & COMPANY (PA)**
1025 S 4th St (62246-2170)
PHONE..................618 664-2000
Fax: 618 664-1712
Donald R Adamski, *President*
Stan Eyman, *Purch Mgr*
Michael Coling, *CFO*
Steven Trull, *Sales Mgr*
Don Adamski, *Data Proc Mgr*
▲ **EMP:** 200
**SQ FT:** 85,000
**SALES:** 16MM **Privately Held**
**SIC:** 2389 2339 2337 2326 Band uniforms; women's & misses' outerwear; women's & misses' suits & coats; men's & boys' work clothing; men's & boys' suits & coats

**(G-11392)**
**ENERTECH GLOBAL LLC (HQ)**
2506 S Elm St (62246-2626)
PHONE..................618 664-9010
Fax: 618 664-4597
Stacia Fesler, *Accountant*
Rosie McDonald, *Bookkeeper*
Steven Smith, *Mng Member*
Kjell Ekermo,
Karen Smith,
▼ **EMP:** 49
**SQ FT:** 40,000
**SALES (est):** 11.3MM
**SALES (corp-wide):** 1.6B **Privately Held**
**SIC:** 3585 Parts for heating, cooling & refrigerating equipment
**PA:** Nibe Industrier Ab
Jarnvagsgatan 40
Markaryd 285 3
433 730-00

**(G-11393)**
**FEDERAL PRISON INDUSTRIES**
Also Called: Unicor
Us Rt 40 4th St (62246)
PHONE..................618 664-6361
John Grindstaff, *Superintendent*
**EMP:** 13 **Publicly Held**
**WEB:** www.unicor.gov
**SIC:** 2299 9223 Textile mill waste & remnant processing; correctional institutions;
**HQ:** Federal Prison Industries, Inc
320 1st St Nw
Washington DC 20534
202 305-3500

**(G-11394)**
**GREENVILLE ADVOCATE INC**
305 S 2nd St (62246-1726)
P.O. Box 9 (62246-0009)
PHONE..................618 664-3144
Jay Endress, *President*
Richard D Reeves, *Principal*
**EMP:** 8
**SQ FT:** 5,000
**SALES (est):** 577.9K **Privately Held**
**SIC:** 2711 Newspapers: publishing only, not printed on site

**(G-11395)**
**JKLEIN ENTERPRISES INC**
Also Called: Jk Installs
505a W South Ave (62246-1620)
PHONE..................618 664-4554
Jason Klein, *President*
Stephen Klein, *Vice Pres*
Doneva Klein, *Admin Sec*
**EMP:** 6
**SALES:** 52K **Privately Held**
**SIC:** 3663 1623 5731 7622 Radio & TV communications equipment; underground utilities contractor; antennas, satellite dish; radio & television receiver installation; cable television installation; subscription television services

**(G-11396)**
**JOINER SHEET METAL & ROOFING**
817 E Harris Ave (62246-2216)
PHONE..................618 664-9488
Fax: 618 664-9441
John Joiner, *Owner*
Sean Engelmann, *General Mgr*
Joseph Hamel, *General Mgr*
Marla Hamel, *Office Mgr*
Jessica Cassady, *Info Tech Mgr*
**EMP:** 8
**SALES (est):** 2MM **Privately Held**
**SIC:** 3444 1761 Sheet metalwork; roofing contractor

**(G-11397)**
**MALLINCKRODT LLC**
100 Louis Latzer Dr (62246-2154)
PHONE..................618 664-2111
Fax: 618 664-2055
Carl Evans, *Engineer*
Doug Lugge, *Manager*
Daone Pustelnik, *Manager*
**EMP:** 50 **Privately Held**
**WEB:** www.mallinckrodt.com
**SIC:** 3841 Surgical & medical instruments
**HQ:** Mallinckrodt Llc
675 Jmes S Mcdonnell Blvd
Hazelwood MO 63042
314 654-2000

**(G-11398)**
**MARCOOT JERSEY CREAMERY LLC**
526 Dudleyville Rd (62246-3801)
PHONE..................618 664-1110
Amy Marcoot, *Mng Member*
Jeffrey Tottleben,
Audrea Wall,
Beth Marcoot Young,
**EMP:** 12
**SQ FT:** 3,200
**SALES:** 600K **Privately Held**
**SIC:** 2022 0241 Natural cheese; cheese spreads, dips, pastes & other cheese products; milk production

**(G-11399)**
**MID-ILLINOIS CONCRETE INC**
Also Called: Greenville Ready Mix
1311 S 4th St (62246-2191)
PHONE..................618 664-1340
Fax: 618 664-3871
Scott Sugg, *Manager*
Rick Kohnert, *Manager*
**EMP:** 6
**SALES (corp-wide):** 17.2MM **Privately Held**
**WEB:** www.mid-illinoisconcrete.com
**SIC:** 3272 3273 Concrete products; ready-mixed concrete
**PA:** Mid-Illinois Concrete, Inc.
1805 S 4th St
Effingham IL
217 342-2115

**(G-11400)**
**NACO PRINTING CO INC**
202 S 2nd St (62246-1725)
PHONE..................618 664-0423
Fax: 618 664-0925
Larry Dieters, *President*
Steven Livingstone, *Manager*
Tracy Jeffers, *Graphic Designe*
**EMP:** 6
**SQ FT:** 8,800
**SALES (est):** 600K **Privately Held**
**WEB:** www.nacoprinting.com
**SIC:** 2752 2796 Commercial printing, lithographic; platemaking services

**(G-11401)**
**NEVCO INC (PA)**
301 E Harris Ave (62246-2193)
PHONE..................618 664-0360
Fax: 618 664-0397
Gayla Moore, *President*
Dan Phalen, *CFO*
Kelly Lamear, *Sales Staff*
▲ **EMP:** 92
**SQ FT:** 10,000
**SALES (est):** 24.1MM **Privately Held**
**WEB:** www.nevcoscoreboards.com
**SIC:** 3993 Scoreboards, electric

# Greenville - Bond County (G-11402)

**(G-11402)**
**PANTHER PRODUCTS**
102 W Main St (62246-1735)
PHONE..............................618 664-1071
Pam Craig, *Owner*
EMP: 3 EST: 1997
SQ FT: 5,000
SALES (est): 300.2K **Privately Held**
SIC: 2759 Screen printing

**(G-11403)**
**SIGNCO**
Also Called: Primeco EDS
301 E Harris Ave (62246-2193)
PHONE..............................402 474-6646
Elmer Wessel, *President*
Nicholas J Cusick, *Vice Pres*
Chris R Mannschreck, *Sales Dir*
Chris R Mannschreck, *Sales Dir*
Teresa Rathje, *Manager*
▲ EMP: 16
SQ FT: 13,481
SALES (est): 1.7MM **Privately Held**
SIC: 3993 Signs & advertising specialties
PA: Imscorp
603 L St
Lincoln NE 68508

## Gridley
### Mclean County

**(G-11404)**
**DIVERSATECH METALFAB LLC**
Also Called: Dtmf
108 S Center St (61744-4111)
PHONE..............................309 747-4159
Fax: 309 747-4177
Michael Surma, *President*
Jim Mattina, *Vice Pres*
Tom Kohl, *Purchasing*
Mike Manley, *Manager*
Lourdes Aietalo, *Admin Sec*
EMP: 30
SQ FT: 80,000
SALES (est): 10.4MM **Privately Held**
SIC: 3535 Conveyors & conveying equipment

**(G-11405)**
**GRIDLEY MEATS INC**
205 E 3rd St (61744-7715)
P.O. Box 348 (61744-0348)
PHONE..............................309 747-2120
Steve Ringger, *President*
Becky Ringger, *Manager*
EMP: 6
SALES (est): 552.7K **Privately Held**
SIC: 5421 4222 2013 2011 Meat markets, including freezer provisioners; storage, frozen or refrigerated goods; sausages & other prepared meats; meat packing plants

**(G-11406)**
**GRIDLEY WELDING INC**
Also Called: Gridley Welding Shop
116 E 3rd St (61744-7725)
P.O. Box 159 (61744-0159)
PHONE..............................309 747-2325
Charles Iverson, *President*
Laura Iverson, *Admin Sec*
EMP: 3 EST: 1959
SQ FT: 7,000
SALES (est): 334.8K **Privately Held**
SIC: 7692 Welding repair

**(G-11407)**
**JBS UNITED INC**
Also Called: Gridley Division
116 W 2nd St (61744-9783)
P.O. Box 340 (61744-0340)
PHONE..............................309 747-2196
Stephen Baner, *Vice Pres*
Jim Weber, *Maint Spvr*
John Stella, *Manager*
EMP: 40
SALES (corp-wide): 136.8MM **Privately Held**
WEB: www.jbsunited.com
SIC: 2048 5191 Livestock feeds; animal feeds

PA: Jbs United, Inc.
4310 W State Road 38
Sheridan IN 46069
317 758-4495

**(G-11408)**
**KERRY HOLDING CO**
320 W Gridley Rd (61744-8723)
PHONE..............................309 747-3534
Gary Ringger, *Division Mgr*
EMP: 66 **Privately Held**
SIC: 2099 Food preparations
HQ: Kerry Holding Co.
3330 Millington Rd
Beloit WI 53511
608 363-1200

**(G-11409)**
**KERRY INC**
320 W Gridley Rd (61744-8723)
P.O. Box 427 (61744-0427)
PHONE..............................309 747-3534
Daryl Crow, *Plant Mgr*
Marc Johnson, *Manager*
Clint Kaeb, *Info Tech Dir*
EMP: 66 **Privately Held**
WEB: www.kerryingredients.com
SIC: 5461 2099 Cookies; food preparations
HQ: Kerry Inc.
3330 Millington Rd
Beloit WI 53511
608 363-1200

**(G-11410)**
**OMNIMAX INTERNATIONAL INC**
Fabral
17904 E 3100 North Rd (61744-7547)
PHONE..............................309 747-2937
Fax: 309 747-3015
Mitchell B Lewis, *CEO*
Mike Hartsworm, *Administration*
EMP: 35
SALES (corp-wide): 854.7MM **Privately Held**
WEB: www.fabral.com
SIC: 3444 2952 Metal roofing & roof drainage equipment; asphalt felts & coatings
HQ: Omnimax International, Inc.
303 Research Dr Ste 400
Norcross GA 30092
770 449-7066

**(G-11411)**
**TRACOINSA USA**
108 S Center St (61744-4111)
PHONE..............................309 287-7046
EMP: 7
SALES (est): 688.5K **Privately Held**
SIC: 3535 Conveyors & conveying equipment

## Griggsville
### Pike County

**(G-11412)**
**HOFMEISTER WLDG & FABRICATION**
402 N Wall St (62340-1176)
P.O. Box 552 (62340-0552)
PHONE..............................217 833-2451
Roberta Hofmeister, *President*
Steven K Hofmeister, *Vice Pres*
EMP: 15
SALES: 1MM **Privately Held**
SIC: 3441 7692 5051 Fabricated structural metal; welding repair; steel

**(G-11413)**
**NATURE HOUSE INC**
30494 State Highway 107 (62340-2268)
P.O. Box 390 (62340-0390)
PHONE..............................217 833-2393
J L Wade, *President*
Frank Uram, *Sales Mgr*
EMP: 100
SQ FT: 57,000
SALES (est): 6.6MM **Privately Held**
SIC: 3999 2731 2752 3444 Pet supplies; book publishing; lithographing on metal; sheet metalwork

**(G-11414)**
**SPIRIT INDUSTRIES INC**
39920 274th Ln (62340-2216)
PHONE..............................217 285-4500
Dan Mefford, *CEO*
Anita Mefford, *President*
EMP: 4 EST: 2007
SALES (est): 464.3K **Privately Held**
SIC: 3199 Equestrian related leather articles

## Groveland
### Tazewell County

**(G-11415)**
**ELLERS CUSTOM CABINETS INC**
17956 Springfield Rd (61535-9502)
PHONE..............................309 633-0101
Fax: 309 633-9194
Wilfloyd Eller, *President*
Jim Eller, *Vice Pres*
Marlene Eller, *Admin Sec*
EMP: 15
SQ FT: 20,000
SALES (est): 1.3MM **Privately Held**
WEB: www.ellerscustomcabinets.com
SIC: 2434 5211 Wood kitchen cabinets; lumber & other building materials

## Gurnee
### Lake County

**(G-11416)**
**2D2C INC (PA)**
Also Called: Safeplug
1071 Cheswick Dr (60031-5601)
P.O. Box 250, Lincolnshire (60069)
PHONE..............................847 543-0980
Gregory Baker, *President*
Paul Schulz, *Vice Pres*
EMP: 8
SALES: 470K **Privately Held**
SIC: 3643 3699 Outlets, electric: convenience; electrical equipment & supplies

**(G-11417)**
**ABBOTT LABORATORIES**
1136 Laurel Ln (60031-5164)
PHONE..............................847 935-8130
Richard Zawadzki, *Branch Mgr*
EMP: 578
SALES (corp-wide): 20.8B **Publicly Held**
WEB: www.abbott.com
SIC: 2834 Medicines, capsuled or ampuled
PA: Abbott Laboratories
100 Abbott Park Rd
Abbott Park IL 60064
224 667-6100

**(G-11418)**
**ACTAVIS PHARMA INC**
705 Tri State Pkwy Ste B (60031-9188)
PHONE..............................847 377-5480
EMP: 4 **Privately Held**
SIC: 2834 Pharmaceutical preparations
HQ: Actavis Pharma, Inc.
400 Interpace Pkwy Ste A1
Parsippany NJ 07054
862 261-7000

**(G-11419)**
**ACTAVIS PHARMA INC**
605 Tri State Pkwy (60031-5277)
PHONE..............................847 855-0812
Robert Walter, *Project Mgr*
Jay Pichard, *Opers Mgr*
Ed Grover, *Manager*
Tim Schinkle, *Manager*
William Stewart, *Manager*
EMP: 103 **Privately Held**
WEB: www.watsonpharm.com
SIC: 2834 Pharmaceutical preparations
HQ: Actavis Pharma, Inc.
400 Interpace Pkwy Ste A1
Parsippany NJ 07054
862 261-7000

**(G-11420)**
**AGROWTEK INC**
173 Ambrogio Dr Ste A (60031-3324)
P.O. Box 1074, Waukegan (60079-1074)
PHONE..............................847 380-3009
Thomas James Theis, *President*
EMP: 3 EST: 2007
SQ FT: 1,830
SALES (est): 72.6K **Privately Held**
SIC: 3699 Electrical equipment & supplies

**(G-11421)**
**AID FOR WOMEN NORTHERN LK CNTY**
4606 Old Grand Ave Apt 2 (60031-2607)
PHONE..............................847 249-2700
Fax: 847 249-1206
Carol Walsh, *Director*
EMP: 12
SALES: 64.3K **Privately Held**
SIC: 2835 Pregnancy test kits

**(G-11422)**
**AIR DIFFUSION SYSTEMS A JOHN**
3964 Grove Ave (60031-2117)
PHONE..............................847 782-0044
Fax: 847 782-0055
John Hinde, *President*
Linda Hinde, *Corp Secy*
Bill Williams, *Manager*
EMP: 8
SQ FT: 10,000
SALES (est): 1.6MM **Privately Held**
WEB: www.airdiffusion.com
SIC: 3089 Plastic processing

**(G-11423)**
**AIR-DRIVE INC**
4070 Ryan Rd (60031-1253)
PHONE..............................847 625-0226
Fax: 847 625-7422
James H Gilford, *President*
EMP: 30
SQ FT: 45,000
SALES (est): 7.5MM **Privately Held**
WEB: www.airdrive.com
SIC: 3469 Metal stampings

**(G-11424)**
**AKHAN SEMICONDUCTOR INC**
940 Lakeside Dr (60031-2400)
PHONE..............................847 855-8400
Adam Khan, *CEO*
Christopher Fox, *Principal*
Carl Shurboff, *COO*
Kristie King, *CFO*
Craig Shaffer, *Accountant*
EMP: 8 EST: 2012
SQ FT: 18,720
SALES (est): 1.1MM **Privately Held**
SIC: 3674 Semiconductors & related devices; wafers (semiconductor devices)

**(G-11425)**
**AKORN INC**
5605 Centerpoint Ct Ste B (60031-5278)
PHONE..............................847 625-1100
Raj Rai, *Branch Mgr*
EMP: 10
SALES (corp-wide): 1.1B **Publicly Held**
SIC: 2834 5047 Pharmaceutical preparations; surgical equipment & supplies
PA: Akorn, Inc.
1925 W Field Ct Ste 300
Lake Forest IL 60045
847 279-6100

**(G-11426)**
**ALLERGAN INC**
605 Tri State Pkwy (60031-5277)
PHONE..............................714 246-4500
EMP: 3 **Privately Held**
SIC: 2834 Solutions, pharmaceutical
HQ: Allergan, Inc.
400 Interpace Pkwy Bldg D
Parsippany NJ 07054
862 261-7000

**(G-11427)**
**AMERICAN INDUSTRIAL COMPANY**
Also Called: Aic
1080 Tri State Pkwy (60031-5140)
PHONE..............................847 855-9200

## GEOGRAPHIC SECTION
### Gurnee - Lake County (G-11451)

Fax: 847 855-9300
Lynn D Dunn, *President*
Ginette Dunn, *Corp Secy*
David Dunn, *Plant Mgr*
Ron Trodler, *Purch Mgr*
Stacy Sutton, *Manager*
**EMP:** 19
**SQ FT:** 25,000
**SALES (est):** 4MM **Privately Held**
**WEB:** www.americanindust.com
**SIC:** 3469 Stamping metal for the trade

*(G-11428)*
**AMERICAN ROTORS INC**
3873 Clearview Ct (60031-1247)
**PHONE** ............................. 847 263-1300
Fax: 847 263-1303
Alan Stark, *President*
Glenn Stark, *General Mgr*
Charles Stark, *Chairman*
**EMP:** 20
**SQ FT:** 12,000
**SALES:** 1.2MM **Privately Held**
**SIC:** 3621 Rotors, for motors

*(G-11429)*
**ARTSONIA LLC**
1350 Tri State Pkwy # 106 (60031-9135)
**PHONE** ............................. 224 538-5060
James Meyers, *CEO*
Eric Meidel, *President*
Tiffany Rahn, *Education*
Kishore Swaminathan,
**EMP:** 11
**SALES (est):** 2.1MM **Privately Held**
**WEB:** www.artsonia.com
**SIC:** 2759 Screen printing

*(G-11430)*
**BASE-LINE II INC**
2001 N Delany Rd (60031-1206)
**PHONE** ............................. 847 336-8403
Fax: 847 336-8624
**EMP:** 3
**SALES (corp-wide):** 3.4MM **Privately Held**
**SIC:** 3861 Manufacture Graphic Art
**PA:** Base-Line Ii, Inc.
  30 Main St Ste 406
  Danbury CT 06810
  203 826-7031

*(G-11431)*
**BASF CONSTRUCTION CHEM LLC**
Also Called: Master Builders
1810 Northwestern Ave (60031-1216)
**PHONE** ............................. 847 249-4080
Fax: 847 249-2735
Robert Bach, *Principal*
**EMP:** 6
**SALES (corp-wide):** 60.8B **Privately Held**
**WEB:** www.basf-admixtures.com
**SIC:** 2899 2851 Concrete curing & hardening compounds; epoxy coatings; vinyl coatings, strippable
**HQ:** Basf Construction Chemicals, Llc
  23700 Chagrin Blvd
  Cleveland OH 44122
  216 831-5500

*(G-11432)*
**BUH HINES GROUP LLC**
1547 Saint Paul Ave (60031-2146)
**PHONE** ............................. 847 336-1460
Jeffrey Murphy,
Bill Buh,
Jim Buh,
John Hines,
**EMP:** 6
**SQ FT:** 1,500
**SALES (est):** 370K **Privately Held**
**SIC:** 3999 Candles

*(G-11433)*
**CINEMAQUEST INC**
5250 Grand Ave Ste 14 (60031-1877)
**PHONE** ............................. 847 603-7649
Fax: 847 589-0510
Irving S Sheldon II, *President*
**EMP:** 3
**SQ FT:** 1,000
**SALES:** 100K **Privately Held**
**SIC:** 3651 Household audio & video equipment

*(G-11434)*
**CONTROL DESIGNS INC**
4006 Grove Ave (60031-2119)
**PHONE** ............................. 847 918-9347
Fax: 847 918-9349
Robert J Ludwig, *President*
**EMP:** 6
**SQ FT:** 2,000
**SALES (est):** 350K **Privately Held**
**WEB:** www.controldesigns.com
**SIC:** 3625 Electric controls & control accessories, industrial

*(G-11435)*
**CORRIGAN CORPORATION AMERICA**
104 Ambrogio Dr (60031-3373)
**PHONE** ............................. 800 462-6478
Fax: 847 263-5944
J Michael Corrigan, *President*
Paul Jones, *Vice Pres*
Mike Corrigan, *VP Sales*
Pam Corrigan, *Manager*
**EMP:** 18
**SQ FT:** 6,700
**SALES (est):** 3.6MM **Privately Held**
**WEB:** www.corriganmist.com
**SIC:** 3556 Food products machinery

*(G-11436)*
**CUSTOM CABINET MAN INC**
3816 Grandview Ave Ste B (60031-2309)
**PHONE** ............................. 847 249-0007
Matt Pryvy, *President*
Shirley Pryvy, *Admin Sec*
**EMP:** 2
**SQ FT:** 3,000
**SALES:** 300K **Privately Held**
**SIC:** 2512 Upholstered household furniture

*(G-11437)*
**DANAHER CORPORATION**
West Control Solutions
1675 N Delany Rd (60031-1237)
**PHONE** ............................. 800 866-6659
**EMP:** 13
**SALES (corp-wide):** 16.8B **Publicly Held**
**SIC:** 3824 Controls, revolution & timing instruments; electronic totalizing counters; mechanical counters
**PA:** Danaher Corporation
  2200 Penn Ave Nw Ste 800w
  Washington DC 20037
  202 828-0850

*(G-11438)*
**DEWRICH INC**
Also Called: Signs Now
1379 Saint Paul Ave (60031-2130)
**PHONE** ............................. 847 249-7445
Douglas Groat, *President*
Jule Groat, *Vice Pres*
**EMP:** 5 **EST:** 1989
**SALES (est):** 300K **Privately Held**
**SIC:** 3993 Signs & advertising specialties

*(G-11439)*
**DOMINO AMJET INC**
4321 Lee Ave (60031-2142)
**PHONE** ............................. 847 662-3148
Fax: 847 662-4394
Neils Kruse, *Manager*
**EMP:** 50
**SQ FT:** 6,000
**SALES (corp-wide):** 6.3B **Privately Held**
**SIC:** 2899 3699 3577 2759 Ink or writing fluids; electrical equipment & supplies; computer peripheral equipment; commercial printing
**HQ:** Domino Amjet, Inc.
  1290 Lakeside Dr
  Gurnee IL 60031
  847 244-2501

*(G-11440)*
**DOMINO AMJET INC (DH)**
1290 Lakeside Dr (60031-2499)
**PHONE** ............................. 847 244-2501
Fax: 847 244-1421
Michael J Brown, *President*
David Levitan, *Engineer*
Francine D Fran, *CFO*
Josh Parks, *Credit Staff*
Lisa Swanson, *Sales Staff*
◆ **EMP:** 100
**SQ FT:** 72,000
**SALES (est):** 38.7MM
**SALES (corp-wide):** 6.3B **Privately Held**
**SIC:** 2899 2893 Printing trades machinery; ink or writing fluids

*(G-11441)*
**DOMINO HOLDINGS INC (DH)**
1290 Lakeside Dr (60031-2400)
**PHONE** ............................. 847 244-2501
Garry Havens, *CEO*
Nigel Bond, *Ch of Bd*
Richard Peterson, *Credit Mgr*
**EMP:** 100
**SQ FT:** 87,000
**SALES (est):** 32.1MM
**SALES (corp-wide):** 6.3B **Privately Held**
**SIC:** 5084 2893 Printing machinery, equipment & supplies; printing ink
**HQ:** Domino Amjet, Inc.
  1290 Lakeside Dr
  Gurnee IL 60031
  847 244-2501

*(G-11442)*
**DOMINO LASERS INC**
1290 Lakeside Dr (60031-2400)
**PHONE** ............................. 847 855-1364
Leroy Sutter Jr, *President*
Ignacio Lozano, *Corp Secy*
Paul P Lynch, *Vice Pres*
Dennise Brockway, *Materials Mgr*
Jane S Mullan, *Controller*
**EMP:** 42
**SQ FT:** 2,000
**SALES (est):** 5.4MM
**SALES (corp-wide):** 6.3B **Privately Held**
**SIC:** 3699 3845 3577 Laser systems & equipment; electromedical equipment; computer peripheral equipment
**HQ:** Domino Holdings, Inc.
  1290 Lakeside Dr
  Gurnee IL 60031
  847 244-2501

*(G-11443)*
**DYNAPAR CORPORATION (HQ)**
Also Called: Danaher Indus Sensors Contrls
1675 N Delany Rd (60031-1237)
**PHONE** ............................. 847 662-2666
Fax: 847 662-4150
Joseph Alexander, *President*
Thomas P Joyce, *Exec VP*
Chet Kwasniak, *Vice Pres*
Craig T Paulson, *Vice Pres*
Sandy Thompson, *Engineer*
▲ **EMP:** 130
**SQ FT:** 38,000
**SALES (est):** 410.7MM
**SALES (corp-wide):** 6.2B **Publicly Held**
**WEB:** www.dancon.com
**SIC:** 3824 Controls, revolution & timing instruments; electronic totalizing counters; mechanical counters
**PA:** Fortive Corporation
  6920 Seaway Blvd
  Everett WA 98203
  425 446-5000

*(G-11444)*
**ECOLOGIC INDUSTRIES LLC**
1472 Saint Paul Ave (60031-2129)
**PHONE** ............................. 847 234-5855
Fax: 847 234-5845
Andy Holley, *Senior VP*
Dan Goldman,
▲ **EMP:** 30
**SALES (est):** 6.1MM **Privately Held**
**SIC:** 3999 Chairs, hydraulic, barber & beauty shop

*(G-11445)*
**EDMIK INC**
Also Called: Edmik Plastics
3850 Grove Ave (60031-2127)
**PHONE** ............................. 847 263-0460
Fax: 847 263-0504
Haydee Knill, *President*
Donald E Knill, *Corp Secy*
Donna Crawford, *Accounts Mgr*
**EMP:** 35 **EST:** 1952
**SQ FT:** 12,000
**SALES (est):** 6.6MM **Privately Held**
**WEB:** www.edmik.com
**SIC:** 3545 3443 5162 Machine tool attachments & accessories; gauges (machine tool accessories); fabricated plate work (boiler shop); plastics sheets & rods; plastics film

*(G-11446)*
**EIRICH MACHINES INC**
Also Called: American Process Systems Div
4033 Ryan Rd (60031-1255)
**PHONE** ............................. 847 336-2444
Ralf Rohmann Postfach, *Managing Dir*
Dino Chece, *Managing Dir*
Richard Zak, *Vice Pres*
Ed Minor, *Project Mgr*
Tom Plotner, *Project Mgr*
▲ **EMP:** 100
**SQ FT:** 55,000
**SALES (est):** 39.4MM **Privately Held**
**WEB:** www.eirichusa.com
**SIC:** 3556 3559 3535 3531 Food products machinery; cement making machinery; conveyors & conveying equipment; construction machinery; fabricated plate work (boiler shop)

*(G-11447)*
**ELITE INDUSTRIES**
5710 Des Plaines Ct (60031-3204)
**PHONE** ............................. 224 433-6988
Rick Alaimo, *Owner*
**EMP:** 2
**SALES (est):** 241.5K **Privately Held**
**SIC:** 3999 Manufacturing industries

*(G-11448)*
**FLOLO CORPORATION**
1401 N Delany Rd (60031-1233)
**PHONE** ............................. 847 249-0880
Fax: 847 249-8230
Larry Layne, *Sales/Mktg Mgr*
**EMP:** 5
**SALES (corp-wide):** 15MM **Privately Held**
**WEB:** www.flolo.com
**SIC:** 5063 7694 3625 3621 Motors, electric; armature rewinding shops; relays & industrial controls; motors & generators
**PA:** Flolo Corporation
  1400 Harvester Rd
  West Chicago IL 60185
  630 595-1010

*(G-11449)*
**FOURTH QUARTER HOLDINGS INC**
Also Called: Signs Now
1379 Saint Paul Ave (60031-2130)
**PHONE** ............................. 847 249-7445
Denis Dubois, *President*
Debra Dubois, *Admin Sec*
**EMP:** 5
**SQ FT:** 3,000
**SALES (est):** 366K **Privately Held**
**SIC:** 3993 Signs & advertising specialties

*(G-11450)*
**FSP LLC**
Also Called: Federal Screw Products
245 Ambrogio Dr (60031-3374)
**PHONE** ............................. 773 992-2600
Fax: 773 478-4147
Rick Terry, *Vice Pres*
Matthew Dent, *QC Mgr*
Sabrina Defchamps, *Sales Mgr*
Kelly Jedynak, *Technology*
Kathy Novak, *Assistant*
**EMP:** 3
**SALES (est):** 25.9K **Privately Held**
**SIC:** 3451 Screw machine products

*(G-11451)*
**GALLAGHER CORPORATION**
3908 Morrison Dr (60031-1241)
**PHONE** ............................. 847 249-3440
Fax: 847 249-3473
Mary Gallagher, *Ch of Bd*
Richard J Gallagher Jr, *President*
Sharon Krawiec, *Vice Pres*
Kevin Darling, *Sales Dir*
Mia Moore, *Sales Mgr*
**EMP:** 80 **EST:** 1964
**SQ FT:** 100,000

# Gurnee - Lake County (G-11452)

SALES: 14MM  Privately Held
WEB: www.gallaghercorp.com
SIC: 2821  Plastics materials & resins

**(G-11452)**
**GATE SYSTEMS CORPORATION**
690 Chandler Rd Apt 401  (60031-3185)
PHONE .................................... 847 731-6700
Fax: 847 249-8766
John Hennessey, *President*
Sue Leverenz, *Admin Sec*
EMP: 5
SQ FT: 4,000
SALES (est): 510K  Privately Held
WEB: www.gatesystems.com
SIC: 3699  Door opening & closing devices, electrical

**(G-11453)**
**GOLD-SLVR-BRONZE MEDAL MUS INC**
Also Called: Gsb Medal Music
1442 Garnet Ct  (60031-1999)
PHONE .................................... 847 272-6854
Joseph J Giallombardo, *President*
EMP: 5
SALES (est): 343.2K  Privately Held
SIC: 2741  Music book & sheet music publishing

**(G-11454)**
**GROW MASTERS**
4641 Old Grand Ave  (60031-2623)
PHONE .................................... 224 399-9877
EMP: 3
SALES (est): 234.7K  Privately Held
SIC: 3645  Garden, patio, walkway & yard lighting fixtures: electric

**(G-11455)**
**GRUMEN MANUFACTURING  INC**
4081 Ryan Rd Ste 101  (60031-1267)
PHONE .................................... 847 473-2233
William B Lampert III, *President*
Bill Lampert, *Human Res Mgr*
Joan Lampert, *Admin Sec*
◆ EMP: 6
SQ FT: 17,000
SALES (est): 870K  Privately Held
SIC: 3053  Gaskets & sealing devices

**(G-11456)**
**H B H PRINT CO**
1400 Saint Paul Ave  (60031-2129)
PHONE .................................... 847 662-2233
Richard Haapanen, *Owner*
EMP: 10
SALES (est): 550K  Privately Held
SIC: 2752  Commercial printing, offset

**(G-11457)**
**HAAPANEN BROTHERS  INC**
1400 Saint Paul Ave  (60031-2129)
PHONE .................................... 847 662-2233
Jerry Haapanen, *President*
Jonathan Haapanen, *Vice Pres*
Matthew Haapanen, *Vice Pres*
Jamie Wiggins, *Opers Staff*
Sarah Haapanen, *Controller*
EMP: 75
SQ FT: 15,200
SALES (est): 14.4MM  Privately Held
WEB: www.hb-graphics.net
SIC: 7336  2752  Graphic arts & related design; commercial printing, lithographic

**(G-11458)**
**HANGER PROSTHETICS &**
Also Called: Hanger Clinic
35 Tower Ct Ste C  (60031-5712)
PHONE .................................... 847 623-6080
Sam Liang, *President*
Angelo Bernardi, *Manager*
EMP: 5
SALES (corp-wide): 459.1MM  Publicly Held
SIC: 5999  3842  Orthopedic & prosthesis applications; limbs, artificial
HQ: Hanger Prosthetics & Orthotics East, Inc.
33 North Ave Ste 101
Tallmadge OH 44278
330 633-9807

**(G-11459)**
**HEARING ASSOCIATES PC**
35 Tower Ct Ste A  (60031-5712)
PHONE .................................... 847 662-9300
Fax: 847 662-9360
Linda Remenssyder, *President*
EMP: 10 EST: 1980
SALES (est): 1.2MM  Privately Held
SIC: 3842  Hearing aids

**(G-11460)**
**HOLMES ASSOCIATES INC**
Also Called: Fastsigns
4949 Grand Ave Ste 2  (60031-1821)
PHONE .................................... 847 336-4515
Fax: 847 295-6133
Glenn Holmes, *President*
EMP: 3
SQ FT: 1,450
SALES (est): 451K  Privately Held
SIC: 3993  Signs & advertising specialties

**(G-11461)**
**JAMES W SMITH PRINTING COMPANY**
1573 Saint Paul Ave  (60031-2146)
PHONE .................................... 847 244-6486
Fax: 847 244-6689
James W Smith, *Ch of Bd*
Matthew J Smith, *President*
Brian Smith, *Vice Pres*
David Smith, *Treasurer*
Mark Serritella, *Planning*
▲ EMP: 45
SQ FT: 18,000
SALES (est): 12.1MM  Privately Held
SIC: 2752  Lithographing on metal

**(G-11462)**
**JETPOWER LLC**
905 Lakeside Dr Ste 2  (60031-4007)
PHONE .................................... 847 856-8359
Aaron Neff, *CEO*
Brian Tuman, *Vice Pres*
Michele Viani, *Vice Pres*
Mark Hadding,
EMP: 16
SALES (est): 620K  Privately Held
SIC: 3724  3728  Airfoils, aircraft engine; bodies, aircraft

**(G-11463)**
**K AND A GRAPHICS INC**
4090 Ryan Rd Ste A  (60031-1201)
PHONE .................................... 847 244-2345
Fax: 847 244-0038
Kenneth Echtenacher, *President*
Arlene Echtenacher, *Vice Pres*
Glenn Murphy, *Vice Pres*
Dolores Shaw, *Office Mgr*
EMP: 3
SQ FT: 3,000
SALES (est): 280K  Privately Held
SIC: 2759  3555  3993  3953  Screen printing; printing plates; signs, not made in custom sign painting shops; marking devices; automotive & apparel trimmings

**(G-11464)**
**K H M PLASTICS INC**
Also Called: Khm
4090 Ryan Rd Ste B  (60031-1201)
PHONE .................................... 847 249-4910
Fax: 847 249-4976
Dan Kloczkowski, *President*
Glenn Murphy, *Vice Pres*
Joseph Maskala, *Purchasing*
Bryan Roberts, *Manager*
EMP: 34
SQ FT: 50,000
SALES (est): 11.1MM  Privately Held
WEB: www.khmplastics.com
SIC: 3089  Molding primary plastic

**(G-11465)**
**K M J ENTERPRISES  INC**
Also Called: Frontier Soups
2001 Swanson Ct  (60031-1221)
PHONE .................................... 847 688-1200
Fax: 847 688-1206
Matt Anderson, *CEO*
Patricia Anderson, *President*
Eva Pantoja, *Prdtn Mgr*
James D Anderson, *Treasurer*
Meagan Johnson, *Manager*
EMP: 30

SQ FT: 25,000
SALES: 4.9MM  Privately Held
WEB: www.frontiersoups.com
SIC: 2034  Soup mixes

**(G-11466)**
**KALLE USA INC**
5750 Centerpoint Ct Ste B  (60031-5279)
PHONE .................................... 847 775-0781
John Lample, *CEO*
Bill Naber, *Opers Staff*
Wendy Bertolani, *Production*
Jed Hwang, *QC Mgr*
Detlev Schauwecker, *CFO*
▲ EMP: 4
SALES (est): 1.2MM  Privately Held
SIC: 3089  Plastic hardware & building products
HQ: Kalle Gmbh
Rheingaustr. 190-196
Wiesbaden  65203
611 962-07

**(G-11467)**
**LIFTEX CORPORATION**
4155 Grove Ave  (60031-2132)
PHONE .................................... 847 782-0572
Fax: 847 782-3751
John Huckner, *President*
Gerald Thiel, *Vice Pres*
Angela Orr, *Accounting Mgr*
Pamela Detine, *Marketing Mgr*
EMP: 30
SQ FT: 18,000
SALES (corp-wide): 31.6MM  Privately Held
WEB: www.liftex.com
SIC: 3536  Hoisting slings
PA: Liftex Corporation
48 Vincent Cir Ste D
Warminster PA 18974
800 478-4651

**(G-11468)**
**MAIMIN TECHNOLOGY GROUP INC**
227 Ambrogio Dr Ste B  (60031-3337)
PHONE .................................... 847 263-8200
Lance Khubchandani, *President*
Derek Khubchandani, *Vice Pres*
EMP: 28 EST: 2002
SQ FT: 28,000
SALES (est): 5.4MM  Privately Held
WEB: www.maimin.com
SIC: 3531  Construction machinery

**(G-11469)**
**MARANTEC AMERICA CORPORATION (DH)**
Also Called: M A C
5705 Centerpoint Ct  (60031-5275)
PHONE .................................... 847 596-6400
Meikel D Nagel, *President*
Michael Hoermann, *Chairman*
Robert Swieczkowski, *CFO*
Steve Hadley, *Manager*
Teresa Lechuga, *Manager*
▲ EMP: 48
SQ FT: 63,000
SALES (est): 3.6MM
SALES (corp-wide): 62.3MM  Privately Held
WEB: www.marantecamerica.com
SIC: 3699  Door opening & closing devices, electrical
HQ: Marantec Antriebs-Und Steuerungstechnik Gmbh & Co. Kg
Remser Brook 11
Marienfeld  33428
524 770-50

**(G-11470)**
**MEDICAL RESOURCE INC**
140 Ambrogio Dr  (60031-3373)
P.O. Box 7705  (60031-7003)
PHONE .................................... 847 249-0854
Robert T Moorman, *President*
John Lowrie, *Vice Pres*
EMP: 5
SALES (est): 484.4K
SALES (corp-wide): 1.1MM  Privately Held
WEB: www.lowriecoinc.com
SIC: 3069  Fabricated rubber products

PA: Lowrie & Co., Inc.
4343 Old Grand Ave
Gurnee IL
847 249-9360

**(G-11471)**
**METROPOLITAN GRAPHIC ARTS INC**
Also Called: M G A
3818 Grandville Ave  (60031-2332)
PHONE .................................... 847 566-9502
Fax: 847 566-9584
Joseph Szymanski, *President*
Brian Szymanski, *Vice Pres*
Sandy Ekern, *Executive*
EMP: 45 EST: 1963
SALES (est): 19.3MM  Privately Held
WEB: www.mgaprinting.com
SIC: 2752  7331  2791  Commercial printing, offset; mailing service; typesetting

**(G-11472)**
**MIDWEST EXCHANGE ENTPS INC**
4012 Morrison Dr  (60031-1243)
PHONE .................................... 847 599-9595
Alex Casillas, *CEO*
Marco Casillas, *General Mgr*
Vicky Vega, *Manager*
Sargon Azzo, *Director*
Nina Casillas, *Admin Sec*
▲ EMP: 45
SQ FT: 77,000
SALES (est): 16.5MM  Privately Held
SIC: 3089  Plastic processing

**(G-11473)**
**MIDWEST SIGNS & STRUCTURES INC (PA)**
4215 Grove Ave  (60031-2134)
PHONE .................................... 847 249-8398
Robert Stuckey, *President*
Diane Root, *Vice Pres*
EMP: 2
SQ FT: 450
SALES: 400K  Privately Held
SIC: 3993  Signs & advertising specialties

**(G-11474)**
**MINUTEMAN PRESS OF WAUKEGAN**
3701 Grand Ave Ste A  (60031-2966)
PHONE .................................... 847 244-6288
Fax: 847 244-6310
Karen Dzierzbicki, *President*
Martin Dzierzbicki, *Vice Pres*
EMP: 3
SQ FT: 1,100
SALES (est): 417.1K  Privately Held
SIC: 2752  2791  Commercial printing, lithographic; typesetting

**(G-11475)**
**MULTIMETAL PRODUCTS CORP**
3965 Grove Ave  (60031-2161)
PHONE .................................... 847 662-9110
Fax: 847 662-5292
Andrew Marsch, *President*
Ketie Lalyand, *Controller*
Andy Marsch, *Manager*
Dominick Stevens, *Manager*
Scott Marsch, *Admin Sec*
EMP: 28
SQ FT: 15,000
SALES (est): 7.9MM  Privately Held
WEB: www.multimetal.com
SIC: 3444  Sheet metalwork

**(G-11476)**
**NOSCO INC**
Also Called: Nosco Gurnee Mfg Site
2199 N Delany Rd  (60031-1208)
PHONE .................................... 847 336-4200
David Stephani, *Business Mgr*
Dick Leach, *Vice Pres*
John McKeough, *VP Opers*
Lee Siragusa, *Plant Mgr*
Carlos Lopez, *Project Mgr*
EMP: 90
SALES (corp-wide): 286.1MM  Privately Held
WEB: www.nosco.com
SIC: 2752  2759  Commercial printing, lithographic; commercial printing; flexographic printing; laser printing

# GEOGRAPHIC SECTION
## Gurnee - Lake County (G-11503)

HQ: Nosco, Inc
651 S Ml King Jr Ave
Waukegan IL 60085
847 336-4200

### (G-11477)
**NYPROMOLD INC**
955 Tri State Pkwy (60031-5113)
PHONE..................847 855-2200
Fax: 847 855-9058
Gordon Lankton, *President*
Robert Haag, *Mfg Mgr*
Amanda Piper, *Buyer*
Lynn Wells, *Purchasing*
Shawn Rossmann, *Engineer*
EMP: 125
SQ FT: 85,000
SALES (est): 40.8MM
SALES (corp-wide): 18.3B **Publicly Held**
WEB: www.nypro.com
SIC: 3089 Injection molded finished plastic products
HQ: Nypro Inc.
101 Union St
Clinton MA 01510
978 365-8100

### (G-11478)
**ODRA INC**
4310 Lee Ave (60031-2143)
PHONE..................847 249-2910
Fax: 847 249-2997
Hamid Bastani, *President*
Thomas M Shumate, *Accountant*
Max Bastini, *Shareholder*
EMP: 4
SQ FT: 6,000
SALES (est): 549.3K **Privately Held**
WEB: www.odra.com
SIC: 3089 2671 Injection molded finished plastic products; packaging paper & plastics film, coated & laminated

### (G-11479)
**OHIO MEDICAL LLC (DH)**
Also Called: Amvex
1111 Lakeside Dr (60031-2489)
PHONE..................847 855-0500
Fax: 847 855-6391
David Finney, *President*
Louis Manetti, *COO*
Eric Baum, *Vice Pres*
Hovy Chae, *Vice Pres*
Scott Hippensteel, *Vice Pres*
◆ EMP: 100
SQ FT: 120,000
SALES (est): 2.9MM **Privately Held**
WEB: www.ohiomedical.com
SIC: 3841 3563 Surgical & medical instruments; suction therapy apparatus; air & gas compressors
HQ: Omc Investors, Llc
1111 Lakeside Dr
Gurnee IL 60031
847 855-6220

### (G-11480)
**OMC INVESTORS LLC (HQ)**
Also Called: Ohio Medical
1111 Lakeside Dr (60031-2489)
PHONE..................847 855-6220
David Finney,
Halden Zimmerman,
EMP: 183 EST: 2014
SQ FT: 82,000
SALES (est): 13.1MM **Privately Held**
SIC: 3841 6719 Surgical & medical instruments; investment holding companies, except banks

### (G-11481)
**ONLY CHILD BREWING COMPANY LLC**
1350 Tri State Pkwy # 124 (60031-9135)
PHONE..................847 877-9822
Benjamin Rossi, *Partner*
EMP: 3
SALES (est): 234K **Privately Held**
SIC: 2082 Malt beverages

### (G-11482)
**PAYSON CASTERS INC (PA)**
2323 N Delany Rd (60031-1287)
PHONE..................847 336-6200
Harold E Sullivan, *President*
Kathy Kuroski, *Controller*
Sheile Redlin, *Credit Mgr*
Todd Larson, *Manager*
Michael J Sullivan, *Admin Sec*
▲ EMP: 105
SQ FT: 140,000
SALES (est): 29.9MM **Privately Held**
WEB: www.roll-away.com
SIC: 3562 Casters

### (G-11483)
**PAYSON CASTERS INC**
Rolla Way Conveyors
2335 N Delany Rd (60031-1212)
PHONE..................847 336-5033
Harold Sullivan, *President*
Shelia Redlin, *Finance Dir*
Dan Sullivan, *Branch Mgr*
EMP: 120
SALES (corp-wide): 29.9MM **Privately Held**
WEB: www.roll-away.com
SIC: 5084 3535 Conveyor systems; conveyors & conveying equipment
PA: Payson Casters, Inc.
2323 N Delany Rd
Gurnee IL 60031
847 336-6200

### (G-11484)
**PERFECT POWDER COATING**
16571 W Applewood Ct (60031-2471)
PHONE..................847 322-6666
Thomas K McDermott, *Principal*
EMP: 4
SALES (est): 430.5K **Privately Held**
SIC: 3399 Powder, metal

### (G-11485)
**PERFECTION EQUIPMENT INC**
4259 Lee Ave (60031-2175)
PHONE..................847 244-7200
Fax: 847 244-7205
Kay Hahn, *Ch of Bd*
Sanford Hahn, *President*
EMP: 20
SQ FT: 15,200
SALES (est): 4.6MM **Privately Held**
WEB: www.perfectequip.com
SIC: 3585 Soda fountain & beverage dispensing equipment & parts

### (G-11486)
**PLASTIC SPECIALISTS AMERICA**
4225 Tiger Lily Ln # 308 (60031-9641)
PHONE..................847 406-7547
Mitch Rabushka, *Owner*
EMP: 4
SALES (est): 289.9K **Privately Held**
SIC: 3842 3021 Personal safety equipment; protective footwear, rubber or plastic

### (G-11487)
**PPG ARCHITECTURAL FINISHES INC**
Also Called: Glidden Professional Paint Ctr
3590 Grand Ave (60031-3735)
PHONE..................847 336-2355
Fax: 847 336-2532
Joshua John, *Manager*
EMP: 4
SALES (corp-wide): 14.7B **Publicly Held**
WEB: www.gliddenpaint.com
SIC: 2891 Adhesives
HQ: Ppg Architectural Finishes, Inc.
1 Ppg Pl
Pittsburgh PA 15272
412 434-3131

### (G-11488)
**PQ CORPORATION**
1945 N Delany Rd (60031-1204)
PHONE..................847 662-8566
Robert Pickens, *Manager*
Patti Reiter, *Director*
EMP: 13
SALES (corp-wide): 1B **Privately Held**
WEB: www.pqcorp.com
SIC: 2819 Industrial inorganic chemicals
HQ: Pq Corporation
300 Lindenwood Dr
Malvern PA 19355
610 651-4429

### (G-11489)
**PRAIRIE ORTHODONTICS PC**
1475 N Dilleys Rd Ste 1 (60031-1709)
PHONE..................847 249-8800
Fax: 847 249-8869
Michael Weinberg, *President*
EMP: 10
SALES (est): 970K **Privately Held**
WEB: www.prairieortho.com
SIC: 3843 Orthodontic appliances

### (G-11490)
**PRECISION ELECTRONICS INC**
Also Called: Grommes Precision
1331 Estes St (60031-2242)
PHONE..................847 599-1799
Jeff W Franzen, *President*
William Grommes, *Founder*
Jean Feehan, *Corp Secy*
Edward Scott, *VP Engrg*
▲ EMP: 10
SQ FT: 20,000
SALES (est): 1.5MM **Privately Held**
WEB: www.grommeshifi.com
SIC: 3651 Household audio & video equipment

### (G-11491)
**PROCEQ USA INC**
4217 Grove Ave (60031-2134)
PHONE..................847 623-9570
Fax: 847 623-9580
Paul Siwek, *Sales Mgr*
Paul Ziwek, *Manager*
EMP: 3 **Privately Held**
WEB: www.procequsa.com
SIC: 3823 Industrial instrmnts msrmnt display/control process variable
HQ: Proceq Usa Inc
117 Corporation Dr
Aliquippa PA 15001
724 512-0330

### (G-11492)
**PROFORMA QUALITY BUSINESS SVCS**
Also Called: Bonnie's Slick Printing
18582 W Judy Dr (60031-1323)
PHONE..................847 356-1959
Bonnie Ross, *President*
EMP: 2 EST: 1993
SALES: 500K **Privately Held**
SIC: 2752 Promotional printing, lithographic

### (G-11493)
**PROSCO INC**
3901 Grove Ave (60031-2118)
PHONE..................847 336-1323
Stan Kubala, *President*
Andre Kubala, *Accounts Mgr*
Peter Kubala, *Manager*
Jolanta Kubala, *Admin Sec*
▲ EMP: 8
SALES (est): 1.5MM **Privately Held**
WEB: www.prosco-inc.com
SIC: 3599 Custom machinery

### (G-11494)
**PROTOTECH INDUSTRIES INC**
1479 Almaden Ln (60031-5625)
PHONE..................847 223-9808
Fax: 847 623-2096
Edwin Paff, *President*
Mary Lou Paff, *Vice Pres*
EMP: 4
SALES (est): 160K **Privately Held**
SIC: 3949 Archery equipment, general

### (G-11495)
**PURO FUTBOL NEWSPAPER**
4248 Lake Park Ave (60031-3035)
PHONE..................847 858-7493
Alberto Teran, *Principal*
EMP: 5
SALES (est): 226.8K **Privately Held**
SIC: 2711 Newspapers

### (G-11496)
**QUALITEK MANUFACTURING INC**
4240 Grove Ave (60031-2124)
PHONE..................847 336-7570
Fax: 847 336-7580
Ken Tibor, *President*
Keith Tibor, *Vice Pres*
Paulette Tibor, *Admin Sec*
EMP: 20
SQ FT: 15,000
SALES (est): 4.5MM **Privately Held**
WEB: www.qualitekmfg.com
SIC: 3544 Special dies & tools

### (G-11497)
**RADIUS MACHINE & TOOL INC**
4290 Lee Ave (60031-2164)
PHONE..................847 662-7690
Fax: 847 662-8428
Steve Fischer, *President*
Laura Fischer, *Vice Pres*
Leann Krause, *Manager*
EMP: 10
SQ FT: 6,000
SALES (est): 920K **Privately Held**
WEB: www.radiusmachine.com
SIC: 3599 3544 Machine shop, jobbing & repair; special dies & tools

### (G-11498)
**RAMPRO FACILITIES SVCS CORP** ✪
4198 Russell Ave (60031-3312)
PHONE..................224 639-6378
Rubullah Mahdee, *Principal*
EMP: 5 EST: 2016
SALES (est): 47K **Privately Held**
SIC: 7349 2899 7389 3639 Janitorial service, contract basis; fire extinguisher charges; fire extinguisher servicing; major kitchen appliances, except refrigerators & stoves; access flooring system installation

### (G-11499)
**REALWHEELS CORPORATION**
3940 Tannahill Dr (60031-1223)
PHONE..................847 662-7722
Fax: 847 662-7744
John Polka, *President*
Gregory Polka, *General Mgr*
Cheryl Polka, *Corp Secy*
Ron Tushner, *Maint Spvr*
▲ EMP: 45
SQ FT: 20,000
SALES (est): 10.8MM **Privately Held**
WEB: www.realwheels.com
SIC: 3469 3714 3443 Metal stampings; motor vehicle parts & accessories; fabricated plate work (boiler shop)

### (G-11500)
**ROLL-A-WAY CONVEYORS INC**
2335 N Delany Rd (60031-1212)
PHONE..................847 336-5033
EMP: 8
SALES (est): 620.3K **Privately Held**
SIC: 3535 7532 3999 Conveyors & conveying equipment; body shop, trucks; atomizers, toiletry

### (G-11501)
**ROQUETTE AMERICA INC**
1550 Northwestern Ave (60031-3292)
PHONE..................847 360-0886
Robert J Ireland, *Branch Mgr*
Michael Wanous, *Manager*
Jean Starr, *Senior Mgr*
Philippart Alain, *Director*
EMP: 65
SALES (corp-wide): 2.1B **Privately Held**
SIC: 2869 5169 2087 Industrial organic chemicals; chemicals, industrial & heavy; food additives & preservatives; flavoring extracts & syrups
HQ: Roquette America, Inc.
1003 S 5th St
Keokuk IA 52632
319 524-5757

### (G-11502)
**SCARS PUBLICATIONS**
829 Brian Ct (60031-3155)
PHONE..................847 281-9070
Janet Kuypers, *Owner*
EMP: 3
SALES (est): 106.4K **Privately Held**
SIC: 2741 Miscellaneous publishing

### (G-11503)
**SEXTANT COMPANY**
433 Inverness Dr (60031-5349)
PHONE..................847 680-6550

## Gurnee - Lake County (G-11504)

EMP: 3
SALES (est): 93.7K  Privately Held
SIC: 3812  Sextants

**(G-11504)**
**SIGN GIRLS INC**
Also Called: Sign-A-Rama
3608 Grand Ave Ste C  (60031-3744)
PHONE.............................847 336-4002
Fax: 847 623-4473
Neil Rosengar, *Principal*
Robin Petit, *Principal*
EMP: 5
SALES (est): 336.3K  Privately Held
SIC: 3993  Signs & advertising specialties

**(G-11505)**
**SMART SCAN MRI  LLC**
350 S Greenleaf St # 401  (60031-5709)
PHONE.............................847 623-4000
Jeffrey Rosengarten, *Mng Member*
Maria Corona, *Manager*
Robert Breit,
Frank Kalmar,
Wendy Silcox,
EMP: 8
SALES (est): 1.1MM  Privately Held
SIC: 3845 8099 3826  Ultrasonic scanning devices, medical; medical services organization; magnetic resonance imaging apparatus

**(G-11506)**
**SPEEDPRO IMAGING**
Also Called: 2 Koi
1350 Tri State Pkwy  (60031-9185)
PHONE.............................847 856-8220
Tom Kmieciak, *President*
Maureen Kmieciak, *Treasurer*
EMP: 4
SALES (est): 334K  Privately Held
SIC: 7336 2759  Graphic arts & related design; commercial printing

**(G-11507)**
**SRT PROSTHETICS ORTHOTICS LLC**
6475 Washington St # 100  (60031-4404)
PHONE.............................847 855-0030
Erin Ruxton, *Branch Mgr*
EMP: 4
SALES (corp-wide): 1,000K  Privately Held
SIC: 3842  Prosthetic appliances
PA: Srt Prosthetics & Orthotics, Llc
   408 E Washington St
   Butler IN 46721
   419 633-3961

**(G-11508)**
**STERIGENICS US  LLC**
1003 Lakeside Dr  (60031-2489)
PHONE.............................847 855-6123
Fax: 847 855-0727
Pat Hope, *Branch Mgr*
EMP: 30
SALES (corp-wide): 616.3MM  Privately Held
SIC: 7389 3821  Product sterilization service; sterilizers
HQ: Sterigenics U.S., Llc
   3 Parkway N Ste 100n
   Deerfield IL 60015
   847 607-6060

**(G-11509)**
**STERLINE MANUFACTURING CORP**
4000 Porett Dr Ste B  (60031-1209)
PHONE.............................847 244-1234
Fax: 847 244-1259
Leslie Raffel, *President*
Michael Berger, *Vice Pres*
M Raffel, *Vice Pres*
Mary Davis, *VP Opers*
Enrique Vasco, *Intl Dir*
EMP: 25  EST: 1933
SQ FT: 25,000
SALES (est): 1.7MM  Privately Held
WEB: www.barclayproducts.com
SIC: 3432 3261  Plumbers' brass goods: drain cocks, faucets, spigots, etc.; vitreous plumbing fixtures

**(G-11510)**
**SUZYS SWIRL  LLC**
6310 Grand Ave Ste 300  (60031-4519)
PHONE.............................847 855-9987
Brad Jenks, *Chairman*
EMP: 2
SALES (est): 777K  Privately Held
SIC: 2024  Ice cream & frozen desserts

**(G-11511)**
**T & T MACHINE SHOP**
4406 Lee Ave  (60031-2150)
PHONE.............................847 244-2020
Tom Olsen, *Owner*
EMP: 3
SALES (est): 322.2K  Privately Held
SIC: 3599 3714  Machine shop, jobbing & repair; motor vehicle parts & accessories

**(G-11512)**
**TABLECRAFT PRODUCTS CO INC (PA)**
801 Lakeside Dr  (60031-2489)
PHONE.............................847 855-9000
Fax: 847 855-9012
Glen Davis, *President*
Pat Arber, *President*
John Temple, *General Mgr*
Rita Davis, *Corp Secy*
David Burnside, *Exec VP*
◆ EMP: 100
SQ FT: 100,000
SALES (est): 31.6MM  Privately Held
WEB: www.tablecraft.com
SIC: 3639  Major kitchen appliances, except refrigerators & stoves

**(G-11513)**
**TECH OASIS INTERNATIONAL INC**
5652 Chapel Hl  (60031-1079)
PHONE.............................847 302-1590
Arul Veeramani, *President*
EMP: 15
SALES: 550K  Privately Held
SIC: 3674  Light emitting diodes

**(G-11514)**
**TECHNICAL SALES MIDWEST INC**
36149 N Edgewater Ct  (60031-4510)
P.O. Box 7793  (60031-7004)
PHONE.............................847 855-2457
Lj Lewis, *President*
EMP: 1
SALES: 250K  Privately Held
SIC: 3823  Industrial process measurement equipment

**(G-11515)**
**TRICEL CORPORATION**
2100 Swanson Ct  (60031-1276)
PHONE.............................847 336-1321
Fax: 847 336-1311
Blaine Loudin, *CEO*
Stephen C Loudin, *President*
Peter Toppen, *Sales Staff*
Gerry Birmingham, *Manager*
Sally Loudin, *Shareholder*
▼ EMP: 16
SQ FT: 27,400
SALES (est): 3.8MM  Privately Held
WEB: www.tricelcorp.com
SIC: 2679  Honeycomb core & board: made from purchased material

**(G-11516)**
**TRICO TECHNOLOGIES INC**
209 Ambrogio Dr  (60031-3374)
PHONE.............................847 662-9224
Philip E Cook, *President*
David B Cook, *Vice Pres*
EMP: 7
SQ FT: 15,000
SALES: 5MM  Privately Held
SIC: 2819  Industrial inorganic chemicals

**(G-11517)**
**TUXCO CORPORATION**
4300 Grove Ave  (60031-2155)
PHONE.............................847 244-2220
Fax: 847 244-7335
Oscar Blomgren Jr, *CEO*
Oscar Blomgren III, *President*
Terri Potesta, *Vice Pres*
Beryl Blomgren, *Treasurer*
Ann Coyle, *Manager*
◆ EMP: 10  EST: 1945
SQ FT: 9,000
SALES (est): 1.9MM  Privately Held
WEB: www.tuxco.com
SIC: 3714 3594 3593 3423  Motor vehicle steering systems & parts; motor vehicle wheels & parts; fluid power pumps & motors; fluid power cylinders & actuators; hand & edge tools

**(G-11518)**
**VANTAGE SPECIALTIES  INC (PA)**
3938 Porett Dr  (60031-1244)
PHONE.............................847 244-3410
Julien Steinberg, *CEO*
Patrick Brueggman, *General Mgr*
Noel Beavis, *COO*
Don Ciancio, *Exec VP*
Chris Humberstone, *Exec VP*
◆ EMP: 95
SQ FT: 1,000
SALES (est): 277.7MM  Privately Held
SIC: 4925 2869  Mixed natural & manufactured gas, distribution; fatty acid esters, aminos, etc.

**(G-11519)**
**VERDASEE SOLUTIONS  INC**
17825 W Pond Ridge Cir  (60031-1669)
PHONE.............................847 265-9441
Reuben Vasquez, *President*
Michael Vasquez, *Vice Pres*
EMP: 5  EST: 2001
SALES: 500K  Privately Held
WEB: www.verdasee.com
SIC: 3577 7371  Computer peripheral equipment; custom computer programming services

**(G-11520)**
**WEETECH INC**
1300 N Skokie Hwy Ste 104  (60031-2144)
PHONE.............................847 775-7240
Steven Mobile, *President*
Victoria Anderson, *Manager*
EMP: 3
SALES (est): 423.3K
SALES (corp-wide): 693.4K  Privately Held
SIC: 3825  Instruments to measure electricity
HQ: Weetech Gmbh
   Hafenstr. 1
   Wertheim  97877
   934 287-50

**(G-11521)**
**ZAPP TOOLING ALLOYS INC**
1528 Saint Paul Ave  (60031-2148)
PHONE.............................847 599-0351
Harry O'Brien, *General Mgr*
EMP: 4  Privately Held
SIC: 3317  Steel pipe & tubes
HQ: Zapp Tooling Alloys Inc.
   475 International Cir
   Summerville SC 29483

### Hainesville
*Lake County*

**(G-11522)**
**CLASSIC PRINTERY INC**
Also Called: Classic Management
336 W Main St  (60073-3644)
PHONE.............................847 546-6555
Fax: 847 546-6558
Mark Basel, *President*
Cynthia Kutz, *Vice Pres*
Laura L Polka, *Treasurer*
EMP: 5
SQ FT: 11,900
SALES (est): 525K  Privately Held
SIC: 2752  Commercial printing, offset

**(G-11523)**
**GROWER EQUIPMENT & SUPPLY CO**
294 E Belvidere Rd  (60030-1039)
PHONE.............................847 223-3100
Fax: 847 223-3130
Jerry De Bruyne, *President*
EMP: 13
SQ FT: 18,400
SALES: 2.8MM  Privately Held
SIC: 7699 3524 5083  Agricultural equipment repair services; lawn & garden equipment; lawn & garden machinery & equipment

**(G-11524)**
**U S MACHINE & TOOL**
331 W Main St  (60073-3645)
PHONE.............................847 740-0077
Fax: 847 740-0085
George Tieman, *President*
Frank Fedor, *Vice Pres*
Susan K Fedor, *Admin Sec*
EMP: 5
SALES (est): 500K  Privately Held
SIC: 3599 3544  Machine shop, jobbing & repair; special dies, tools, jigs & fixtures

**(G-11525)**
**WOOD CUTTERS LANE  LLC**
129 Heritage Trl  (60030-1087)
PHONE.............................847 847-2263
Rudolph Berrien III, *CEO*
Kelly Berrien, *Vice Pres*
EMP: 4
SALES (est): 208.2K  Privately Held
SIC: 2431 7389  Millwork;

### Hamburg
*Calhoun County*

**(G-11526)**
**BETTY WATTERS**
Also Called: Watters Fishmarket
Rr 1 Box 27  (62045)
PHONE.............................618 232-1150
Betty Watters, *Owner*
EMP: 2
SALES (est): 240.6K  Privately Held
SIC: 5146 2092  Fish, fresh; fresh or frozen packaged fish

**(G-11527)**
**QUILLER OUTBOARD SLS SVCS LLC**
Also Called: Quillers Outboard Kawasaki Sls
Rr 1 Box 130  (62045-9703)
PHONE.............................618 232-1218
Fax: 618 232-1321
Timothy Roth, *Principal*
EMP: 8
SQ FT: 70,000
SALES (est): 927.8K  Privately Held
SIC: 3799  All terrain vehicles (ATV)

### Hamel
*Madison County*

**(G-11528)**
**H & H SERVICES  INC**
391 N Old Route 66  (62046-1070)
P.O. Box 365  (62046-0365)
PHONE.............................618 633-2837
Fax: 618 633-2716
Kirby Harris, *President*
Kathryn Harris, *Corp Secy*
Jim Long, *Manager*
EMP: 10
SALES (est): 1.1MM  Privately Held
WEB: www.handhservices.com
SIC: 1442 7692  Construction sand & gravel; welding repair

**(G-11529)**
**HAMEL TIRE AND CONCRETE PDTS**
Also Called: Hamel Tire Service
200 Hamel Ave  (62046-1049)
P.O. Box 255  (62046-0255)
PHONE.............................618 633-2405
Howard Reising, *President*
Keith Behrhorst, *Vice Pres*
EMP: 3  EST: 1965
SQ FT: 4,800

GEOGRAPHIC SECTION                                    Hampshire - Kane County (G-11556)

SALES: 480K  Privately Held
SIC: 5531  3272  5014  Automotive tires; concrete products; tires & tubes

## Hamilton
### Hancock County

**(G-11530)**
**COOPER LAKE MILLWORKS INC**
1202 N State Highway 96  (62341-3145)
PHONE....................217 847-2681
Robin Carel, *President*
EMP: 4
SQ FT: 8,500
SALES: 500K  Privately Held
SIC: 2431  2439  2541  2517  Millwork; timbers, structural; laminated lumber; wood partitions & fixtures; wood television & radio cabinets; wood kitchen cabinets; cabinet & finish carpentry

**(G-11531)**
**CORES FOR YOU INC**
160 Industrial Park  (62341)
PHONE....................217 847-3233
Robert Harmon, *President*
Tim Neumann, *Opers Mgr*
EMP: 28
SQ FT: 52,000
SALES: 2.4MM  Privately Held
SIC: 3543  Foundry cores

**(G-11532)**
**D E ASBURY INC (PA)**
Also Called: Great River Printing
1479 Keokuk St  (62341-1135)
PHONE....................217 222-0617
Fax: 217 847-2615
Dan Asbury, *President*
EMP: 10
SQ FT: 8,000
SALES (est): 699.3K  Privately Held
SIC: 2752  2791  2789  Commercial printing, lithographic; typesetting; bookbinding & related work

**(G-11533)**
**DADANT & SONS  INC (PA)**
Also Called: American Bee Journal, The
51 S 2nd St Ste 2  (62341-1397)
PHONE....................217 847-3324
Fax: 217 847-3660
Tim C Dadant, *President*
Nicholas J Dadant, *Vice Pres*
Jerry Hayes, *Vice Pres*
Thomas G Ross, *Vice Pres*
Jon Stacey, *Cust Mgr*
◆ EMP: 60  EST: 1863
SQ FT: 45,000
SALES (est): 32.5MM  Privately Held
WEB: www.dadant.com
SIC: 3999  2721  Honeycomb foundations (beekeepers' supplies); candles; magazines: publishing only, not printed on site

**(G-11534)**
**GRAY QUARRIES INC**
Also Called: Gary Quarries
750 E County Road 1220  (62341-3140)
P.O. Box 386  (62341-0386)
PHONE....................217 847-2712
Robert Miller, *President*
Joe Richardson, *Manager*
EMP: 12
SALES (est): 1.9MM  Privately Held
SIC: 1422  Limestones, ground

**(G-11535)**
**GREAT RIVER READY MIX INC**
750 E County Road 1220  (62341-3140)
PHONE....................217 847-3515
Fax: 217 847-3921
Trent Miller, *President*
Floyd Rahn, *General Mgr*
Lloyd Rahn, *Plant Mgr*
Ralph Froman, *Manager*
EMP: 10
SQ FT: 5,000
SALES (est): 125K  Privately Held
SIC: 3273  Ready-mixed concrete

**(G-11536)**
**H & M WOODWORKS**
1610 N County Road 1200  (62341-3009)
PHONE....................608 289-3141
D Laura Mosena, *Principal*
EMP: 3
SALES (est): 179.6K  Privately Held
SIC: 2431  Millwork

**(G-11537)**
**HAMILTON CONCRETE PRODUCTS CO**
Also Called: Hamilton Construction Co
400 Windy Woods Dr  (62341-3180)
PHONE....................217 847-3118
Larry Schrader, *President*
EMP: 2  EST: 1975
SQ FT: 5,000
SALES (est): 448.2K  Privately Held
SIC: 5032  1771  1711  1794  Concrete & cinder building products; concrete work; plumbing contractors; excavation work; concrete products; concrete block & brick

**(G-11538)**
**HANCOCK COUNTY SHOPPER**
1830 Keokuk St  (62341-1144)
PHONE....................217 847-6628
Bill S Helenthal, *Partner*
Steve Helenthal, *Partner*
EMP: 6
SALES (est): 281.1K  Privately Held
WEB: www.hancockshopper.com
SIC: 2711  2741  Newspapers; miscellaneous publishing

**(G-11539)**
**PRECISION FOUNDRY TOOLING LTD**
160 Hamilton Indus Park  (62341-3169)
PHONE....................217 847-3233
Fax: 217 847-2305
Robert Harmon, *President*
Kendra Boley, *Office Mgr*
Donna Harmon, *Director*
EMP: 11
SQ FT: 5,400
SALES: 1MM  Privately Held
WEB: www.pftooling.com
SIC: 3543  Industrial patterns

**(G-11540)**
**RUSSELL FERRELL**
951 E County Road 1450  (62341-3101)
PHONE....................217 847-3954
Russell Ferrell, *Owner*
Suzanne Ferrell, *Vice Pres*
EMP: 3
SALES (est): 193.3K  Privately Held
SIC: 2411  Logging camps & contractors

**(G-11541)**
**U S FREE PRESS LLC**
950 E Us Highway 136  (62341-3159)
PHONE....................217 847-3361
James M Helenthal,
EMP: 2
SALES (est): 223.6K  Privately Held
SIC: 2741  Miscellaneous publishing

## Hampshire
### Kane County

**(G-11542)**
**BANKMARK INC**
46w299 Middleton Rd  (60140-8536)
P.O. Box 365, Burlington  (60109-0365)
PHONE....................847 683-9834
Fax: 847 683-2400
Bob Gilman, *President*
Delores Mossler, *Admin Sec*
EMP: 16
SALES (est): 3.1MM  Privately Held
WEB: www.bankmark.com
SIC: 3535  Pneumatic tube conveyor systems

**(G-11543)**
**BESTAIR PRO**
Also Called: Bestairpro
281 Keyes Ave  (60140-9449)
PHONE....................847 683-3400
Del Fields, *President*
▲ EMP: 3  EST: 1983
SALES (est): 270K  Privately Held
SIC: 3634  Humidifiers, electric: household

**(G-11544)**
**CENTER TOOL COMPANY INC**
250 Industrial Dr  (60140-7902)
PHONE....................847 683-7559
Helmut Winter, *President*
Rose Marie Winter, *Corp Secy*
EMP: 4
SQ FT: 3,000
SALES (est): 270K  Privately Held
SIC: 3544  3545  Special dies, tools, jigs & fixtures; machine tool accessories

**(G-11545)**
**COMBINED METALS CHICAGO LLC**
Also Called: El Giloy Specialty Metals
1 Hauk Rd  (60140-8239)
PHONE....................847 683-0500
Jim Darrow, *Manager*
EMP: 7  Privately Held
WEB: www.combmet.com
SIC: 3315  3316  3547  Steel wire & related products; cold finishing of steel shapes; rolling mill machinery
HQ: Combined Metals Of Chicago Llc
    2401 Grant Ave
    Bellwood IL 60104
    847 695-1900

**(G-11546)**
**DC WORKS  INC**
10n421 Burlington Rd  (60140-8734)
PHONE....................847 464-4280
Robert Warfel, *President*
Jean Warfel, *Corp Secy*
▲ EMP: 3
SALES (est): 433.8K  Privately Held
WEB: www.fakerock.com
SIC: 3086  Plastics foam products

**(G-11547)**
**DREYMILLER & KRAY INC**
140 S State St  (60140-7000)
P.O. Box 238  (60140-0238)
PHONE....................847 683-2271
Fax: 847 683-2272
Edward Reiser, *President*
EMP: 9
SQ FT: 1,200
SALES (est): 594K  Privately Held
SIC: 5421  5147  2013  Meat markets, including freezer provisioners; meats & meat products; sausages & other prepared meats

**(G-11548)**
**ELECTRO-MAX  INC**
105 Rowell Rd Ste D  (60140-9700)
PHONE....................847 683-4100
Fax: 847 683-4155
Kevin R Grant, *President*
Terry Facker, *General Mgr*
Jeremy Fawbush, *Manager*
Teri Becker, *Executive*
EMP: 22  EST: 1996
SQ FT: 24,000
SALES (est): 3.1MM  Privately Held
WEB: www.electromax-inc.com
SIC: 3471  Plating & polishing

**(G-11549)**
**ELGILOY SPECIALTY METALS**
1 Hauk Rd  (60140-8239)
PHONE....................847 683-0500
EMP: 5
SALES (est): 370.3K  Privately Held
SIC: 3356  Nickel & nickel alloy pipe, plates, sheets, etc.

**(G-11550)**
**FAIRBANKS WIRE CORPORATION**
260 Industrial Dr Ste B  (60140-7900)
PHONE....................847 683-2600
Gunther Hank Holz, *President*
Barbara Holz, *Vice Pres*
Gary Polley, *Sales Mgr*
Brent Weber, *Sales Mgr*
Jeff Holz, *Sales Staff*
EMP: 5  EST: 1948
SQ FT: 18,000
SALES: 900K  Privately Held
WEB: www.fairbankswire.com
SIC: 3315  5051  3351  Wire, steel: insulated or armored; metals service centers & offices; copper rolling & drawing

**(G-11551)**
**HYTEL GROUP  INC (PA)**
290 Industrial Dr  (60140-7907)
PHONE....................847 683-9800
Fax: 847 683-7940
Scott Johansen, *CEO*
Theophilus Green, *Opers Mgr*
Joel Acierto, *Engineer*
Renee Mazza, *Human Resources*
Jeff Green, *Program Mgr*
EMP: 38
SQ FT: 30,000
SALES (est): 3.2MM  Privately Held
SIC: 3674  3672  Hybrid integrated circuits; printed circuit boards

**(G-11552)**
**KLEHM FAMILY WINERY  LLC**
44w637 Il Route 72  (60140-8268)
PHONE....................847 609-9997
Arnold Klehm,
EMP: 6
SALES (est): 455.7K  Privately Held
SIC: 2084  Wines, brandy & brandy spirits

**(G-11553)**
**LED RITE  LLC**
120 Rowell Rd  (60140-9713)
PHONE....................847 683-8000
Yang Jean, *Principal*
Michael Yang, *Engineer*
David Scheck, *Marketing Staff*
EMP: 4
SALES (est): 498.9K  Privately Held
SIC: 3674  Light emitting diodes

**(G-11554)**
**MINERALLAC COMPANY (PA)**
100 Gast Rd  (60140-7654)
PHONE....................630 543-7080
James Hlavacek, *President*
Austin Reimers, *Business Mgr*
Warren Vickery, *Purch Mgr*
Emily Mains, *Buyer*
Lisa Mortensen, *Sales Mgr*
▲ EMP: 50
SQ FT: 135,000
SALES (est): 18.7MM  Privately Held
WEB: www.minerallac.com
SIC: 3644  3496  Noncurrent-carrying wiring services; electric conduits & fittings; staples, made from purchased wire

**(G-11555)**
**MINUTEMAN INTERNATIONAL INC**
14n845 Us Highway 20  (60140-8893)
PHONE....................847 683-5210
Fax: 847 627-1130
Dave Romke, *Facilities Mgr*
Bob Jesse, *Branch Mgr*
EMP: 65  Privately Held
WEB: www.multi-clean.com
SIC: 3589  Commercial cleaning equipment
HQ: Minuteman International, Inc.
    14n845 Us Highway 20
    Pingree Grove IL 60140
    630 627-6900

**(G-11556)**
**NUTRIAD  INC**
201 Flannigan Rd  (60140-8245)
PHONE....................847 214-4860
Keith Klanderman, *President*
Rodelo Maglente, *CFO*
◆ EMP: 20
SQ FT: 55,000
SALES: 4MM
SALES (corp-wide): 179.1MM  Privately Held
WEB: www.appliednature.com
SIC: 2048  Feed supplements
HQ: Nutri-Ad International Nv
    Hoogveld 93
    Dendermonde  9200
    145 519-90

# Hampshire - Kane County (G-11557)

**(G-11557)**
**OZINGA CONCRETE PRODUCTS INC**
401 Brier Hill Rd (60140-8103)
PHONE.................................708 479-9050
Ron Floit, *President*
**EMP:** 3
**SALES (est):** 248.3K **Privately Held**
**SIC: 3272** Concrete products

**(G-11558)**
**PET-AG INC**
Also Called: Pet AG
255 Keyes Ave (60140-9449)
PHONE.................................847 683-2288
**Fax:** 847 683-2003
Darlene A Frudakis, *President*
Lewis M Sutton, *Exec VP*
CPA D Rotolo, *Controller*
Sandra Hardcopf, *Credit Mgr*
John Nagy, *Manager*
◆ **EMP:** 40
**SQ FT:** 66,000
**SALES (est):** 11.5MM
**SALES (corp-wide):** 32.5MM **Privately Held**
**SIC: 2048** 2047 Feed supplements; dog food; cat food
**PA:** Pbi-Gordon Corporation
1217 W 12th St
Kansas City MO 64101
816 421-4070

**(G-11559)**
**POLI-FILM AMERICA INC (DH)**
1 Elgiloy Dr (60140-8238)
PHONE.................................847 453-8104
**Fax:** 847 683-7777
Dan Ulbert, *President*
John Allen, *Purch Mgr*
Mike Soares, *Engineer*
Tyson Meade, *Treasurer*
Anna Brodycz, *Marketing Mgr*
▲ **EMP:** 65
**SQ FT:** 84,000
**SALES (est):** 20.3MM **Privately Held**
**WEB:** www.poli-film.net
**SIC: 3081** Polyethylene film
**HQ:** Polifilm Gmbh
Waidmarkt 11a
Koln 50676
219 688-2990

**(G-11560)**
**POWERBOSS INC**
14n845 Us Highway 20 (60140-8893)
PHONE.................................910 944-2105
Mario Schreiber, *President*
Steve Liew, *President*
Steve Boebel, *Controller*
Donna Edge, *Accountant*
▼ **EMP:** 125
**SQ FT:** 130,000
**SALES (est):** 19.5MM **Privately Held**
**WEB:** www.minutemanpowerboss.com
**SIC: 3589** Vacuum cleaners & sweepers, electric; industrial
**HQ:** Minuteman International, Inc.
14n845 Us Highway 20
Pingree Grove IL 60140
630 627-6900

**(G-11561)**
**ROTEC INDUSTRIES INC (PA)**
270 Industrial Dr (60140-7902)
PHONE.................................630 279-3300
**Fax:** 630 279-3317
Robert F Oury, *Ch of Bd*
Alan S Ledger, *President*
William Machota, *Vice Pres*
Ken Barkhurst, *Controller*
Douglas Kline, *Manager*
◆ **EMP:** 86
**SQ FT:** 50,000
**SALES (est):** 18.8MM **Privately Held**
**WEB:** www.rotec-usa.com
**SIC: 3535** 7353 Belt conveyor systems, general industrial use; heavy construction equipment rental

**(G-11562)**
**RPS PRODUCTS INC (PA)**
Also Called: Best Air
281 Keyes Ave (60140-9463)
PHONE.................................847 683-3400
**Fax:** 847 683-3939
Richard P Schuld, *CEO*
Daniel E Schuld, *President*
Tom Myers, *Senior VP*
Bob Nelson, *Vice Pres*
Sergio Renteria, *Plant Mgr*
▲ **EMP:** 25
**SQ FT:** 80,000
**SALES (est):** 4.8MM **Privately Held**
**WEB:** www.rpsproducts.com
**SIC: 2899** 3589 3089 7389 Chemical preparations; water treating compounds; water filters & softeners, household type; plastic containers, except foam; packaging & labeling services

**(G-11563)**
**SMART INC**
41w584 Us Highway 20 (60140-8865)
PHONE.................................847 464-4160
**Fax:** 847 464-5887
Danny Smart, *President*
James Christensen, *Vice Pres*
Melisa Martinez, *Office Mgr*
▲ **EMP:** 5
**SQ FT:** 15,000
**SALES (est):** 951.3K **Privately Held**
**SIC: 3555** 5084 7629 Bookbinding machinery; printing trades machinery, equipment & supplies; electrical repair shops

**(G-11564)**
**VILLAGE HAMPSHIRE TRTMNT PLANT**
350 Mill Ave (60140)
PHONE.................................847 683-2064
Jeffrey Magnussen, *President*
**EMP:** 3
**SALES (est):** 196K **Privately Held**
**SIC: 3823** Water quality monitoring & control systems

**(G-11565)**
**WESTERN SLATE COMPANY**
Also Called: W S Hampshire
365 Keyes Ave (60140-9458)
PHONE.................................847 683-4400
Jeff Pope, *President*
Dan Jankoski, *Vice Pres*
Pat Barrett, *Purch Mgr*
Paul Bennett, *Manager*
▲ **EMP:** 55 **EST:** 1986
**SQ FT:** 140,000
**SALES:** 12MM **Privately Held**
**WEB:** www.wshampshire.com
**SIC: 3569** Assembly machines, non-metalworking

**(G-11566)**
**WHAT WE MAKE INC**
115 Mill Ave (60140-9433)
PHONE.................................331 442-4830
Dan Quinn, *President*
**EMP:** 4
**SQ FT:** 3,000
**SALES (est):** 100K **Privately Held**
**SIC: 2511** Wood household furniture

## Hanna City
### Peoria County

**(G-11567)**
**CAPTAIN HOOK INC**
5125 S Hnna Cy Glsford Rd (61536)
PHONE.................................309 565-7676
Di Wagehofp, *Principal*
**EMP:** 4
**SALES (est):** 389.7K **Privately Held**
**SIC: 3443** Dumpsters, garbage

**(G-11568)**
**ILLINOIS WELD & MACHINE INC**
123 S 2nd St (61536-8034)
PHONE.................................309 565-0533
Irwin Julin, *Manager*
**EMP:** 10
**SALES (corp-wide):** 1MM **Privately Held**
**SIC: 3312** Blast furnaces & steel mills
**PA:** Illinois Weld & Machine, Inc
101 S 2nd St
Hanna City IL 61536
309 565-0533

**(G-11569)**
**ILLINOIS WELD & MACHINE INC (PA)**
101 S 2nd St (61536)
PHONE.................................309 565-0533
Irwin Julian, *President*
Everett Frazier, *Vice Pres*
**EMP:** 1
**SQ FT:** 1,680
**SALES (est):** 1.1MM **Privately Held**
**SIC: 3312** Tool & die steel & alloys

**(G-11570)**
**RAYMOND EARL FINE WOODWORKING**
201 S Main St (61536)
P.O. Box 469 (61536-0469)
PHONE.................................309 565-7661
Earl Raymond, *Owner*
**EMP:** 2
**SQ FT:** 2,000
**SALES (est):** 213.6K **Privately Held**
**SIC: 1521** 2434 General remodeling, single-family houses; wood kitchen cabinets

## Hanover
### Jo Daviess County

**(G-11571)**
**BOURRETTE LOGGING**
1012 Blackhawk B (61041)
P.O. Box 22 (61041-0022)
PHONE.................................815 591-3761
Thomas Bourrette, *Principal*
**EMP:** 1
**SALES (est):** 205.8K **Privately Held**
**SIC: 2411** Logging

**(G-11572)**
**K D WELDING INC**
2 River Bend Dr (61041-9673)
PHONE.................................815 591-3545
Kevin C Loney, *President*
Diana Loney, *Vice Pres*
**EMP:** 9 **EST:** 1997
**SALES (est):** 923.3K **Privately Held**
**WEB:** www.jcwifi.com
**SIC: 7692** Welding repair

**(G-11573)**
**ROBERTSHAW CONTROLS COMPANY**
Also Called: Invensys Controls
107 N Washington St (61041-9620)
PHONE.................................815 591-2417
**EMP:** 24
**SALES (corp-wide):** 19.3B **Privately Held**
**SIC: 3823** Mfg Process Control Instruments
**HQ:** Robertshaw Controls Company
1222 Hamilton Pkwy
Itasca IL 60143
956 554-4107

## Hanover Park
### Cook County

**(G-11574)**
**AMPAC FLEXIBLES LLC**
825 Turnberry Ct (60133-5477)
PHONE.................................630 439-3160
Chuck Naynon, *Controller*
Lisa Rambol, *Human Resources*
Gail Bradley, *Marketing Staff*
George Thomas, *Manager*
Gary M Bell, 
▲ **EMP:** 75 **EST:** 2003
**SQ FT:** 500,000
**SALES (est):** 14.5MM
**SALES (corp-wide):** 1.3B **Privately Held**
**WEB:** www.ampaconline.com
**SIC: 2673** Bags: plastic, laminated & coated
**HQ:** Ampac Holdings, Llc
12025 Tricon Rd
Cincinnati OH 45246
513 671-1777

**(G-11575)**
**AMPAC FLEXICON LLC**
Ampac Flexibles
825 Turnberry Ct (60133-5477)
PHONE.................................630 439-3160
Joseph Beuchanan, *Manager*
**EMP:** 24
**SALES (corp-wide):** 1.3B **Privately Held**
**SIC: 2671** Plastic film, coated or laminated for packaging; paper coated or laminated for packaging
**HQ:** Ampac Flexicon, Llc
165 Chicago St
Cary IL 60013
847 639-3530

**(G-11576)**
**B/E AEROSPACE INC**
1220 Central Ave (60133-5420)
PHONE.................................561 791-5000
**EMP:** 143 **Publicly Held**
**SIC: 2531** Seats, aircraft
**HQ:** B/E Aerospace, Inc
1400 Corporate Center Way
Wellington FL 33414
561 791-5000

**(G-11577)**
**C P CONTRACTOR**
6340 Fremont Dr (60133-4946)
PHONE.................................630 235-2381
Alvaro Alcantara, *Manager*
**EMP:** 3
**SALES (est):** 135.6K **Privately Held**
**SIC: 2813** Industrial gases

**(G-11578)**
**CAMCRAFT INC (PA)**
1080 Muirfield Dr (60133-5474)
PHONE.................................630 582-6001
**Fax:** 630 582-6019
Michael Bertsche, *President*
Patrick Bertsche, *Plant Mgr*
Ray Ross, *Prdtn Mgr*
Peter Sroga, *Engineer*
Tom Kliebhan, *Controller*
**EMP:** 201 **EST:** 1950
**SQ FT:** 83,000
**SALES (est):** 44.1MM **Privately Held**
**WEB:** www.camcraft.com
**SIC: 3451** Screw machine products

**(G-11579)**
**DULCE VIDA JUICE BAR LLC**
2003 Irving Park Rd (60133-3164)
PHONE.................................224 236-5045
Gregorio Hernandez, 
**EMP:** 3
**SALES (est):** 137.9K **Privately Held**
**SIC: 2037** Fruit juices

**(G-11580)**
**FISHER SCIENTIFIC COMPANY LLC**
Also Called: Fisher Safety
4500 Turnberry Dr (60133-5491)
PHONE.................................412 490-8300
**Fax:** 630 259-4444
Amit Agarwal, *General Mgr*
Panny Swoopes, *Branch Mgr*
**EMP:** 115
**SALES (corp-wide):** 18.2B **Publicly Held**
**WEB:** www.fishersci.com
**SIC: 3826** 5049 5084 Analytical instruments; laboratory equipment, except medical or dental; safety equipment
**HQ:** Fisher Scientific Company Llc
300 Industry Dr
Pittsburgh PA 15275
412 490-8300

**(G-11581)**
**FLODYNE INC**
Also Called: Cma, Flodyne, Hydradyne
1000 Muirfield Dr (60133-5426)
PHONE.................................630 563-3600
**Fax:** 630 563-3850
Frank Machac, *President*
Dennis Okkelberg, *Warehouse Mgr*
Ingrid Hale, *Purchasing*
Kim Martino, *Purchasing*
Norman Dziedzic, *Engineer*
**EMP:** 6

SALES (est): 4.8MM **Privately Held**
SIC: 5084 3824 Hydraulic systems equipment & supplies; crushing machinery & equipment; mechanical & electromechanical counters & devices

**(G-11582)**
**FLOW CONTROL US HOLDING CORP**
1040 Muirfield Dr (60133-5468)
PHONE..................................630 307-3000
Cortney Webb, *Human Res Dir*
Jerry L Letcher, *Sales Mgr*
Rich Verson, *Marketing Mgr*
Randall J Hogan, *Branch Mgr*
EMP: 14
SALES (corp-wide): 14.5B **Publicly Held**
SIC: 3561 Pumps & pumping equipment
HQ: Flow Control Us Holding Corporation
5500 Wayzata Blvd
Minneapolis MN 55416
763 545-1730

**(G-11583)**
**INTEGRATED CIRCUITS RESEARCH**
6600 Appletree St (60133-3902)
PHONE..................................630 830-9024
Mike Rebeschini, *President*
EMP: 2
SALES: 300K **Privately Held**
WEB: www.icresearch.com
SIC: 3679 Electronic circuits

**(G-11584)**
**KAPAK COMPANY LLC**
825 Turnberry Ct (60133-5477)
PHONE..................................952 541-0730
EMP: 3 **EST:** 2015
SALES (est): 143.9K **Privately Held**
SIC: 2673 Bags: plastic, laminated & coated

**(G-11585)**
**MEDICAL SPECIALTIES DISTRS LLC**
1549 Hunter Rd (60133-6772)
PHONE..................................630 307-6200
Peter Huie, *Vice Pres*
Steve Schaudenecker, *Branch Mgr*
Philip Russo, *Supervisor*
EMP: 34
SALES (corp-wide): 463.1MM **Privately Held**
WEB: www.msdistributors.com
SIC: 3845 5047 Electromedical apparatus; electro-medical equipment
PA: Medical Specialties Distributors, Llc
800 Technology Center Dr # 3
Stoughton MA 02072
781 344-6000

**(G-11586)**
**NB CORPORATION OF AMERICA (HQ)**
930 Muirfield Dr (60133-5457)
PHONE..................................630 295-8880
Fax: 630 295-8881
Toru Yamazaki, *President*
Mitsuru Yamazaki, *President*
Larry Hensen, *General Mgr*
Masaru Funai, *Corp Secy*
Yutaka Kojima, *Vice Pres*
▲ EMP: 34
SALES (est): 6.3MM
SALES (corp-wide): 71.1MM **Privately Held**
WEB: www.nbcorporation.com
SIC: 3568 Bearings, plain
PA: Nippon Bearing Co., Ltd.
2833, Ko, Chiya
Ojiya NIG 947-0
258 825-711

**(G-11587)**
**NYPRO INC**
6325 Muirfield Dr (60133-5467)
PHONE..................................630 773-3341
Carlos Pineda, *Opers Mgr*
Jerry Siemieniuk, *Engineer*
Bharat Shah, *Director*
Ewa Marecka, *Personnel Assit*
EMP: 12
SALES (est): 1.4MM **Privately Held**
SIC: 2821 Plastics materials & resins

**(G-11588)**
**NYPRO INC**
Also Called: Nypro Hanover Park
6325 Muirfield Dr (60133-5467)
PHONE..................................630 671-2000
Mark Gomulka, *Branch Mgr*
Raymond Burg, *Program Mgr*
EMP: 50
SALES (corp-wide): 18.3B **Publicly Held**
WEB: www.nypro.com
SIC: 3089 Injection molding of plastics
HQ: Nypro Inc.
101 Union St
Clinton MA 01510
978 365-8100

**(G-11589)**
**PENTAIR FLTRTION SOLUTIONS LLC (DH)**
Also Called: Everpure
1040 Muirfield Dr (60133-5468)
PHONE..................................630 307-3000
Fax: 630 307-3030
Randall J Hogan, *CEO*
Frank Brigano, *Vice Pres*
Tim Reckinger, *Vice Pres*
Tom Kohl, *Purchasing*
N Stimburis, *Human Res Dir*
▲ EMP: 25 EST: 2007
SQ FT: 110,000
SALES (est): 55.1MM
SALES (corp-wide): 14.5B **Publicly Held**
SIC: 3589 Water purification equipment, household type; water treatment equipment, industrial
HQ: Flow Control Us Holding Corporation
5500 Wayzata Blvd
Minneapolis MN 55416
763 545-1730

**(G-11590)**
**STANDARD INDUS & AUTO EQP INC**
6211 Church Rd (60133-4802)
PHONE..................................630 289-9500
Fax: 630 289-9507
John Woitel, *President*
John F Woitel, *President*
Mike Amandes, *Engineer*
Larry Garcia, *Accounts Mgr*
Darshak Shah, *Manager*
EMP: 20 EST: 1927
SALES (est): 9.3MM **Privately Held**
WEB: www.standardus.com
SIC: 5013 2841 3569 Automotive supplies & parts; soap & other detergents; lubrication equipment, industrial

**(G-11591)**
**STANDARD LIFTS & EQUIPMENT INC**
6211 Church Rd (60133-4802)
PHONE..................................414 444-1000
John Woitel, *President*
Frank Woitel, *Vice Pres*
▲ EMP: 4
SQ FT: 20,000
SALES (est): 495.2K **Privately Held**
SIC: 5531 3586 3563 Automotive parts; oil pumps, measuring or dispensing; air & gas compressors

**(G-11592)**
**UNIDEX PACKAGING LLC**
1625 Hunter Rd B (60133-6767)
PHONE..................................630 735-7040
Charles Roy,
EMP: 14
SALES (est): 2.3MM **Privately Held**
SIC: 3111 Bag leather

### Hardin
*Calhoun County*

**(G-11593)**
**CALHOUN QUARRY INCORPORATED**
Eldred Rd (62047)
P.O. Box 68, Batchtown (62006-0068)
PHONE..................................618 576-9223
Tony Sievers, *Branch Mgr*
EMP: 8

SALES (corp-wide): 1.1MM **Privately Held**
SIC: 1422 Limestones, ground
PA: Calhoun Quarry, Incorporated
25 Main St
Batchtown IL 62006
618 396-2229

**(G-11594)**
**PLUESTERS QUALITY MEAT CO**
Batchtown Rd (62047)
Rural Route 1 Box 70 (62047-9608)
PHONE..................................618 396-2224
Irene Pluester, *President*
EMP: 8
SQ FT: 1,000
SALES: 200K **Privately Held**
SIC: 5421 0751 2011 Meat markets, including freezer provisioners; slaughtering: custom livestock services; meat packing plants

### Harmon
*Lee County*

**(G-11595)**
**J M FABRICATING INC**
214 S 1st St (61042-9400)
PHONE..................................815 359-2024
Mike Dunn, *Principal*
EMP: 4
SALES (est): 397.2K **Privately Held**
SIC: 2295 Metallizing of fabrics

### Harrisburg
*Saline County*

**(G-11596)**
**BOB BARNETT REDI-MIX INC (PA)**
Also Called: Barnett Bob Redi-Mix
285 Garden Heights Rd (62946-5200)
PHONE..................................618 252-3581
Fax: 618 252-1876
Sherry Denny, *President*
Jeff Denny, *Corp Secy*
Bret Denny, *Vice Pres*
Pete Smith, *Manager*
EMP: 15 EST: 1960
SQ FT: 2,200
SALES (est): 3.4MM **Privately Held**
SIC: 3273 4212 Ready-mixed concrete; local trucking, without storage

**(G-11597)**
**CHERRY STREET PRINTING & AWARD**
211 E Poplar St Ste 2 (62946-1544)
PHONE..................................618 252-6814
Paul Pyle, *Principal*
EMP: 2
SALES (est): 214.5K **Privately Held**
SIC: 2759 Commercial printing

**(G-11598)**
**FINITE RESOURCES LTD**
520 S Mckinley St (62946-2217)
PHONE..................................618 252-3733
Fax: 618 252-0641
Kevin Reimer, *Managing Prtnr*
EMP: 5
SALES (est): 524.7K **Privately Held**
SIC: 1389 Construction, repair & dismantling services

**(G-11599)**
**FRED HUTSON MINERAL PRODUCTS**
805 S Ledford St (62946-2808)
P.O. Box 543, Carrier Mills (62917-0543)
PHONE..................................618 994-4383
EMP: 2
SALES (est): 210K **Privately Held**
SIC: 1241 Coal mining services

**(G-11600)**
**GATEHOUSE MEDIA LLC**
Also Called: Daily Register
35 S Vine St (62946-1725)
PHONE..................................618 253-7146

Carol Rann, *Accounting Dir*
George Wilson, *Manager*
EMP: 30
SALES (corp-wide): 1.2B **Publicly Held**
WEB: www.gatehousemedia.com
SIC: 2711 Newspapers
HQ: Gatehouse Media, Llc
175 Sullys Trl Ste 300
Pittsford NY 14534
585 598-0030

**(G-11601)**
**GRAF INK PRINTING INC**
Also Called: Rocky's Advanced Printing
24 W Church St (62946-1602)
PHONE..................................618 273-4231
Christopher Beavers, *President*
EMP: 4
SQ FT: 1,080
SALES (est): 310K **Privately Held**
WEB: www.grafink.com
SIC: 2752 Commercial printing, lithographic

**(G-11602)**
**NATIONWIDE GLOVE CO INC (PA)**
925 Bauman Ln (62946-3550)
P.O. Box K (62946-5010)
PHONE..................................618 252-7192
Fax: 618 252-4497
Nathan Applebaum, *President*
Samuel Applebaum, *Vice Pres*
Annette Hubbs, *Manager*
EMP: 70 EST: 1940
SQ FT: 24,000
SALES (est): 11.2MM **Privately Held**
SIC: 2381 3151 Gloves, work: woven or knit, made from purchased materials; gloves, leather: work

**(G-11603)**
**REGISTER PUBLISHING CO**
35 S Vine St (62946-1725)
P.O. Box 617, West Frankfort (62896-0617)
PHONE..................................618 253-7146
Fax: 618 253-0863
Ken Serota, *President*
George Q Wilson, *Publisher*
Kay Brandsasse, *Business Mgr*
EMP: 25 EST: 1908
SQ FT: 10,800
SALES: 1.5MM **Privately Held**
WEB: www.dailyregister.com
SIC: 2711 Newspapers, publishing & printing

**(G-11604)**
**SOUTHERN TRUSS INC**
5510 Highway 13 W (62946-4134)
P.O. Box 275 (62946-0275)
PHONE..................................618 252-8144
Fax: 618 252-2063
Dennis J Murphy, *President*
Charles A Murphy, *Vice Pres*
Joey Heflin, *Sales Staff*
EMP: 50
SQ FT: 9,000
SALES (est): 8.9MM **Privately Held**
SIC: 2439 Trusses, wooden roof; trusses, except roof: laminated lumber

**(G-11605)**
**TISON & HALL CONCRETE PRODUCTS**
210 N Commercial St (62946-1397)
PHONE..................................618 253-7808
Fax: 618 253-7645
Sherry Denny, *President*
Wayne Mears, *General Mgr*
Brett Denny, *Vice Pres*
Frederick Denny, *Vice Pres*
Earl Miles, *Plant Mgr*
EMP: 17 EST: 1946
SQ FT: 8,000
SALES (est): 2.4MM
SALES (corp-wide): 3.4MM **Privately Held**
WEB: www.tisonandhall.com
SIC: 3271 5211 Blocks, concrete or cinder: standard; brick
PA: Bob Barnett Redi-Mix Inc
285 Garden Heights Rd
Harrisburg IL 62946
618 252-3581

**(G-11606)**
**WILSON KITCHENS INC**
Also Called: Wki
1653 S Feazel St (62946-3536)
PHONE..................................618 253-7449
Fax: 618 252-0984
Harold Wilson, *President*
Darla Martin, *Manager*
**EMP:** 54
**SQ FT:** 26,000
**SALES (est):** 10MM **Privately Held**
**WEB:** www.betterkitchens-baths.com
**SIC:** 2541 2542 5211 Cabinets, except refrigerated: show, display, etc.: wood; cabinets: show, display or storage: except wood; cabinets, kitchen

## Harristown
### Macon County

**(G-11607)**
**LEGACY VULCAN LLC**
2855 Lincoln Pkwy (62537)
PHONE..................................217 963-2196
Tom Heft, *Principal*
**EMP:** 7
**SALES (corp-wide):** 3.5B **Publicly Held**
**WEB:** www.vulcanmaterials.com
**SIC:** 1442 Construction sand & gravel
**HQ:** Legacy Vulcan, Llc
1200 Urban Center Dr
Vestavia AL 35242
205 298-3000

**(G-11608)**
**STRAIGHTLINE AG INC**
8990 W Us 36 (62537)
P.O. Box 44 (62537-0044)
PHONE..................................217 963-1270
**EMP:** 4
**SALES (est):** 317.8K **Privately Held**
**SIC:** 3523 Farm machinery & equipment

## Hartford
### Madison County

**(G-11609)**
**ADVANCED MACHINE PRODUCTS INC**
Also Called: Go Getter Racing Clutches
207 S Delmar Ave (62048-1226)
PHONE..................................618 254-4112
Fax: 618 254-4121
Gary Landolt, *President*
Beverly Landolt, *Vice Pres*
**EMP:** 4
**SQ FT:** 7,600
**SALES (est):** 250K **Privately Held**
**WEB:** www.advancedmachineauto.com
**SIC:** 3599 3714 Machine shop, jobbing & repair; clutches, motor vehicle

**(G-11610)**
**DOOLING MACHINE PRODUCTS INC (PA)**
107 N Delmar Ave (62048-1008)
P.O. Box 472, Alton (62002-0472)
PHONE..................................618 254-0724
Joseph Dooling Jr, *President*
Joseph Dooling Sr, *Corp Secy*
**EMP:** 6
**SALES (est):** 1.4MM **Privately Held**
**SIC:** 3599 7692 3549 3544 Machine shop, jobbing & repair; welding repair; metalworking machinery; special dies, tools, jigs & fixtures

**(G-11611)**
**LINDE LLC**
1200 S Delmar Ave (62048-2502)
P.O. Box 37 (62048-0037)
PHONE..................................618 251-5217
William Brown, *Branch Mgr*
**EMP:** 50
**SALES (corp-wide):** 17.9B **Privately Held**
**SIC:** 2813 Nitrogen; oxygen, compressed or liquefied
**HQ:** Linde Llc
200 Somerset Corporate Bl
Bridgewater NJ 08807
908 464-8100

**(G-11612)**
**NATIONAL MAINT & REPR INC (HQ)**
401 S Hawthorne St (62048-1052)
P.O. Box 38 (62048-0038)
PHONE..................................618 254-7451
Fax: 618 255-5743
Bruce D McGinnis, *President*
John Moren, *General Mgr*
Bill Jessie, *CFO*
Shelly Graham, *Accountant*
Duane Dawson, *VP Human Res*
▲ **EMP:** 250
**SALES (est):** 90.4MM
**SALES (corp-wide):** 147.7MM **Privately Held**
**WEB:** www.nmrinc.com
**SIC:** 3731 7699 Shipbuilding & repairing; engine repair & replacement, non-automotive
**PA:** Mcnational, Inc.
502 2nd St E
South Point OH 45680
740 377-4391

**(G-11613)**
**OMEGA PARTNERS**
1402 S Delmar Ave (62048-2501)
PHONE..................................618 254-0603
Gerald Jost, *President*
Larry Elmore, *Manager*
**EMP:** 7 **EST:** 2013
**SALES (est):** 892.9K **Privately Held**
**SIC:** 2869 Fuels

**(G-11614)**
**PHILLIPS 66**
Also Called: Hartford Lubricant Complex
2300 S Delmar Ave (62048-2520)
P.O. Box 177 (62048-0177)
PHONE..................................618 251-2800
**EMP:** 82
**SALES (corp-wide):** 85.7B **Publicly Held**
**WEB:** www.phillips66.com
**SIC:** 2911 Petroleum refining
**PA:** Phillips 66
2331 City West Blvd
Houston TX 77042
832 765-3300

## Harvard
### Mchenry County

**(G-11615)**
**A T PRODUCTS INC**
1600 S Division St (60033-9043)
P.O. Box 625 (60033-0625)
PHONE..................................815 943-3590
Fax: 815 943-3604
Mike Rose, *President*
Lynn Stoughton, *President*
Becky Zalud, *Opers Mgr*
**EMP:** 5
**SQ FT:** 4,000
**SALES (est):** 996.3K **Privately Held**
**WEB:** www.atproducts.com
**SIC:** 3661 Telephones & telephone apparatus

**(G-11616)**
**A-OK INC**
Also Called: Harvard Building Products
711 W Brown St (60033-2344)
P.O. Box 358 (60033-0358)
PHONE..................................815 943-7431
Fax: 815 943-7927
Orrin Kinney, *President*
Kathy Trumper, *Accounts Mgr*
Andy Cyrus, *Manager*
**EMP:** 45
**SQ FT:** 30,000
**SALES (est):** 10.9MM **Privately Held**
**WEB:** www.a-ok.com
**SIC:** 3442 5031 Window & door frames; doors & windows

**(G-11617)**
**ACRO MAGNETICS INC**
24005 Il Route 173 (60033-8610)
PHONE..................................815 943-5018
Fax: 815 943-8008
Neil T Schultz, *President*
Neil C Schultz, *Vice Pres*
Cynthia Schultz, *Treasurer*
Marla Schultz, *Admin Sec*
**EMP:** 5
**SQ FT:** 6,000
**SALES (est):** 892.9K **Privately Held**
**WEB:** www.acro-magnetics.com
**SIC:** 3559 3695 3535 Separation equipment, magnetic; magnetic & optical recording media; conveyors & conveying equipment

**(G-11618)**
**AERO INDUSTRIES INC**
450 Commanche Cir (60033-3110)
PHONE..................................815 943-7818
James L Clingingsmith, *President*
Steve Harkema, *General Mgr*
Gary Kinshofer, *Vice Pres*
Theresa Taylor, *Office Mgr*
▲ **EMP:** 10
**SQ FT:** 22,500
**SALES (est):** 1.7MM **Privately Held**
**SIC:** 3295 3624 Graphite, natural: ground, pulverized, refined or blended; carbon & graphite products

**(G-11619)**
**ALUM-I-TANK INC**
Also Called: Alumitank
11317 N Us Highway 14 (60033-9152)
PHONE..................................815 943-6649
Fax: 262 736-4203
Terence Kirkpatrick, *President*
Robert Kirkpatrick, *Corp Secy*
Zac Hawes, *Marketing Staff*
David Kirkpatrick, *Manager*
Kathleen Watson, *Manager*
**EMP:** 55
**SALES (est):** 13.8MM **Privately Held**
**SIC:** 3443 Fuel tanks (oil, gas, etc.): metal plate

**(G-11620)**
**AMERICAN GRINDERS INC**
3 Lincoln St Ste 3 (60033-3100)
PHONE..................................815 943-4902
Ian McHattie, *Owner*
**EMP:** 3
**SALES (est):** 513.3K **Privately Held**
**SIC:** 2952 Coating compounds, tar

**(G-11621)**
**AQUADINE INC (PA)**
Also Called: Aquadine Nutritional System
495 Commanche Cir (60033-3110)
PHONE..................................800 497-3463
Robert Weiss, *President*
Paul Butler, *CFO*
**EMP:** 5
**SALES (est):** 814.4K **Privately Held**
**WEB:** www.aquadine.com
**SIC:** 3999 5961 Pet supplies; catalog & mail-order houses

**(G-11622)**
**ATLAS MANUFACTURING LTD**
1001 W Roosevelt St (60033-1660)
PHONE..................................815 943-1400
Fax: 815 943-1490
Nick Leicht, *President*
Sandy Kerr, *Manager*
**EMP:** 15
**SQ FT:** 10,500
**SALES (est):** 2.2MM **Privately Held**
**WEB:** www.atlasmfgltd.com
**SIC:** 3599 Machine shop, jobbing & repair

**(G-11623)**
**BADGER PALLET INC**
630 W Blackman St (60033-2331)
PHONE..................................815 943-1147
**EMP:** 4
**SALES (est):** 222.5K **Privately Held**
**SIC:** 2448 Pallets, wood & wood with metal

**(G-11624)**
**BILL PETERSON**
Also Called: Peterson Farms
25007 Flat Iron Rd (60033-8942)
PHONE..................................815 378-8633
Bill Peterson, *Owner*
**EMP:** 1
**SALES (est):** 229.6K **Privately Held**
**SIC:** 3523 Driers (farm): grain, hay & seed

**(G-11625)**
**CARTEL HOLDINGS INC (PA)**
Also Called: Vincent Castillo
3 Lincoln St Ste 2a (60033-3100)
P.O. Box 151, Woodstock (60098-0151)
PHONE..................................815 334-0250
Vincent Castillo, *President*
**EMP:** 4
**SQ FT:** 3,800
**SALES (est):** 556.9K **Privately Held**
**WEB:** www.cartelproducts.com
**SIC:** 2911 2992 Fuel additives; brake fluid (hydraulic): made from purchased materials

**(G-11626)**
**CATTY CORPORATION**
6111 White Oaks Rd (60033-8307)
PHONE..................................815 943-2143
Bill Schmiederer, *Controller*
Cruce Scott, *Branch Mgr*
**EMP:** 70
**SALES (corp-wide):** 11.3MM **Privately Held**
**WEB:** www.cattycorp.com
**SIC:** 2671 Packaging paper & plastics film, coated & laminated
**PA:** Catty Corporation
6111 White Oaks Rd
Harvard IL 60033
815 943-2288

**(G-11627)**
**CINDYS POCKET KITCHEN**
23802 Chemung St (60033-8915)
PHONE..................................815 388-8385
Cynthia McGee, *President*
**EMP:** 3 **EST:** 2014
**SALES (est):** 110K **Privately Held**
**SIC:** 2099 5963 Food preparations; food service, mobile, except coffee-cart

**(G-11628)**
**CONSOLIDATED CONTAINER CO LLC**
875 W Diggins St (60033-2370)
PHONE..................................815 943-7828
Fax: 815 943-2821
Susanne Emrud, *Purchasing*
Bill Weber, *Branch Mgr*
William Weber, *Manager*
**EMP:** 120
**SALES (corp-wide):** 13.1B **Publicly Held**
**SIC:** 3089 Plastic containers, except foam
**HQ:** Consolidated Container Company, Llc
3101 Towercreek Pkwy Se
Atlanta GA 30339
678 742-4600

**(G-11629)**
**CUSTOM WINDOW ACCENTS**
900 W Diggins St (60033-2378)
P.O. Box 66 (60033-0066)
PHONE..................................815 943-7651
Fax: 815 943-3841
James Pagles, *President*
Karen Pack, *Admin Sec*
**EMP:** 19
**SQ FT:** 18,375
**SALES:** 900K **Privately Held**
**SIC:** 2591 2431 2511 2541 Window shades; ornamental woodwork: cornices, mantels, etc.; bed frames, except water bed frames: wood; headboards: wood; wood partitions & fixtures

**(G-11630)**
**DEAN FOODS COMPANY**
6303 Maxon Rd (60033-8853)
PHONE..................................815 943-7375
Fax: 815 943-5532
Tom Condon, *Opers-Prdtn-Mfg*
Rosa Honert, *Purch Agent*
Paul Hill, *QA Dir*
Jeremy Syring, *QC Mgr*
Beth Reineking, *Accountant*

EMP: 185  Publicly Held
WEB: www.deanfoods.com
SIC: 2026  Milk processing (pasteurizing, homogenizing, bottling)
PA: Dean Foods Company
2711 N Haskell Ave
Dallas TX 75204

**(G-11631)**
**DURR - ALL CORPORATION**
1001 W Diggins St Ste 2  (60033-2387)
P.O. Box 2332, Crystal Lake  (60039-2332)
PHONE.............................815 943-1032
Eric Gusakow, *President*
EMP: 3
SALES (est): 389.3K  Privately Held
SIC: 3599  3471  Machine shop, jobbing & repair; plating & polishing

**(G-11632)**
**ERECT-A-TUBE INC**
701 W Park St  (60033-2600)
P.O. Box 100  (60033-0100)
PHONE.............................815 943-4091
Fax: 800 624-9219
Susan M Wagner, *President*
Klaus H Herkert, *Vice Pres*
Randall M Kirk, *Vice Pres*
Edwin H Thurnau, *Vice Pres*
Wes Walker, *Engineer*
EMP: 45  EST: 1963
SQ FT: 60,000
SALES (est): 13.7MM  Privately Held
WEB: www.erect-a-tube.com
SIC: 1542  3442  Nonresidential construction; metal doors

**(G-11633)**
**FLOCON INC**
714 W Park St  (60033-2622)
PHONE.............................815 943-5893
Ron Kieras, *Branch Mgr*
EMP: 5
SALES (corp-wide): 4.7MM  Privately Held
SIC: 3494  Pipe fittings
PA: Flocon, Inc.
339 Cary Point Dr
Cary IL 60013
815 444-1500

**(G-11634)**
**HARVARD FACTORY AUTOMATION INC**
490 Commanche Cir  (60033-3110)
PHONE.............................815 943-1195
Charles K Weidner, *President*
Kyle J Nemetz, *Corp Secy*
Paul Stevenson, *Project Engr*
▲ EMP: 16
SQ FT: 12,000
SALES (est): 4.2MM  Privately Held
SIC: 3599  Custom machinery

**(G-11635)**
**HARVARD STATE BANK**
35 N Ayer St  (60033-2822)
PHONE.............................815 943-4400
Roger Lehmann, *Principal*
Bernard Papp, *Principal*
Anton Stricker,
Alan Yates,
EMP: 2
SALES (est): 355.7K  Privately Held
SIC: 3578  Automatic teller machines (ATM)

**(G-11636)**
**HAWK MOLDING INC**
435 Andrea Ct  (60033-7806)
PHONE.............................224 523-2888
Sean Wolfert, *Principal*
EMP: 3
SALES (est): 173.5K  Privately Held
SIC: 3089  Molding primary plastic

**(G-11637)**
**ILLINOIS CAST STONE**
343 S Division St Ste 1  (60033-3211)
PHONE.............................815 943-6050
Karen Young, *Principal*
EMP: 3
SALES (est): 304.5K  Privately Held
SIC: 3272  Concrete products

**(G-11638)**
**INDUSTRIAL GRAPHITE SALES LLC**
450 Commanche Cir  (60033-3110)
PHONE.............................815 943-5502
Marilyn Skok,
Teresa Taylor, *Admin Asst*
EMP: 2
SALES (est): 330.7K  Privately Held
SIC: 3624  Carbon & graphite products

**(G-11639)**
**JONES PACKING CO**
22701 Oak Grove Rd  (60033-8205)
PHONE.............................815 943-4488
Ray Jones, *Partner*
Robert Jones, *Partner*
Mary Ann Trebes, *Bookkeeper*
EMP: 8  EST: 1952
SQ FT: 8,000
SALES (est): 400K  Privately Held
WEB: www.jonespacking.com
SIC: 2011  5421  5147  2013  Meat packing plants; meat markets, including freezer provisioners; meats, fresh; sausages & other prepared meats

**(G-11640)**
**LOGAN ACTUATOR CO**
550 Chippewa Rd  (60033-2337)
PHONE.............................815 943-9500
Fax: 815 945-6755
George Logan, *President*
Jerald Kubasiak, *Counsel*
Scott Logan, *Vice Pres*
Adeline Logan, *Admin Sec*
EMP: 6
SALES (est): 605K  Privately Held
WEB: www.loganact.com
SIC: 3536  3532  3842  3728  Mine hoists; mining machinery; surgical appliances & supplies; aircraft parts & equipment; machine tool accessories

**(G-11641)**
**MEYER MATERIAL CO MERGER CORP**
20806 Mcguire Rd  (60033-8353)
P.O. Box 640  (60033-0640)
PHONE.............................815 943-2605
Fax: 847 943-5967
Ron Raupp, *General Mgr*
EMP: 53
SALES (corp-wide): 26.6B  Privately Held
SIC: 1422  3273  3272  Agricultural limestone, ground; ready-mixed concrete; concrete products
HQ: Meyer Material Co Merger Corp.
580 S Wolf Rd
Des Plaines IL 60016
815 331-7200

**(G-11642)**
**NORTHWEST PRINTING INC**
20 N Ayer St  (60033-2861)
PHONE.............................815 943-7977
Fax: 815 943-6076
Robert Schneider, *President*
Joy Schneider, *Corp Secy*
Jill Gaulkey, *Director*
Randy Schneider, *Director*
Rodger Schneider, *Director*
EMP: 5  EST: 1975
SQ FT: 4,000
SALES (est): 390K  Privately Held
WEB: www.nwprint.com
SIC: 2752  2791  2789  Commercial printing, offset; typesetting; bookbinding & related work

**(G-11643)**
**PEDIGREE OVENS INC**
Also Called: Pound Bakery
495 Commanche Cir  (60033-3110)
PHONE.............................815 943-8144
Fax: 815 943-8187
Kurt Stricker, *President*
Vickie Shoemaker, *Office Mgr*
▲ EMP: 20  EST: 1997
SQ FT: 5,000
SALES (est): 4.3MM  Privately Held
SIC: 2047  Dog & cat food

**(G-11644)**
**PRACTICAL BAKER EQUIPMENT**
600 Chippewa Rd  (60033-2372)
PHONE.............................815 943-8730
Fax: 815 943-9077
Tony Stricker, *Managing Prtnr*
John Stricker, *Partner*
▲ EMP: 4
SQ FT: 15,000
SALES (est): 750K  Privately Held
SIC: 3556  Bakery machinery

**(G-11645)**
**PROMMAR PLASTICS INC**
1001 W Diggins St  (60033-2386)
PHONE.............................815 770-0555
EMP: 5
SQ FT: 4,000
SALES (est): 406K  Privately Held
SIC: 3089  Plastic processing

**(G-11646)**
**ROYAL OAK FARM INC**
15908 Hebron Rd  (60033-9357)
PHONE.............................815 648-4141
Fax: 815 648-2084
Peter Bianchini, *President*
Justin Bell, *Executive*
Gloria B Bianchini, *Admin Sec*
EMP: 10
SQ FT: 12,000
SALES (est): 720.8K  Privately Held
WEB: www.royaloakfarmorchard.com
SIC: 0175  5947  2051  5812  Deciduous tree fruits; gift shop; bread, cake & related products; eating places

**(G-11647)**
**ST CHARLES SCREW PRODUCTS INC**
404 E Park St  (60033-2941)
PHONE.............................815 943-8060
Joe Adams, *President*
Joseph Michaels Adams III, *Corp Secy*
S Yvonne Adams, *Vice Pres*
EMP: 4
SQ FT: 3,500
SALES: 170K  Privately Held
SIC: 3599  3451  Machine shop, jobbing & repair; screw machine products

**(G-11648)**
**STEEL SPAN INC**
630 W Blackman St  (60033-2331)
P.O. Box 368  (60033-0368)
PHONE.............................815 943-9071
Fax: 815 943-9073
Orrin Kinney, *President*
EMP: 10  EST: 1997
SALES (est): 1.4MM  Privately Held
WEB: www.steel-span.com
SIC: 3441  3448  3444  2452  Building components, structural steel; prefabricated metal buildings; sheet metalwork; prefabricated wood buildings

## Harvey
### Cook County

**(G-11649)**
**3V PALLET**
16140 Clinton St  (60426-5909)
PHONE.............................708 333-1113
EMP: 4
SALES (est): 333.5K  Privately Held
SIC: 2448  Pallets, wood & wood with metal

**(G-11650)**
**ADVANAGE DIVERSIFIED PDTS INC**
16615 Halsted St  (60426-6112)
PHONE.............................708 331-8390
Nathan T Edwards, *President*
Arnold Bowen, *Controller*
Charles Walker, *Human Res Dir*
Diana M Byrd, *Admin Sec*
EMP: 15
SQ FT: 16,000
SALES: 1.6MM  Privately Held
SIC: 2842  3589  Disinfectants, household or industrial plant; vacuum cleaners & sweepers, electric: industrial

**(G-11651)**
**AFC CABLE SYSTEMS INC (DH)**
16100 Lathrop Ave  (60426-6021)
P.O. Box 1675  (60426-7675)
PHONE.............................508 998-1131
John P Williamson, *President*
Edward Arditte, *Vice Pres*
Carol Davidson, *Vice Pres*
John E Evard Jr, *Vice Pres*
James A Mallak, *Vice Pres*
▲ EMP: 300  EST: 1993
SQ FT: 47,250
SALES (est): 501.4MM  Publicly Held
WEB: www.afcweb.com
SIC: 3429  3444  3599  5085  Manufactured hardware (general); sheet metalwork; hose, flexible metallic; industrial supplies

**(G-11652)**
**ALLIED TUBE & CONDUIT CORP (DH)**
16100 Lathrop Ave  (60426-6021)
P.O. Box Dept Ch 10415, Palatine  (60055-0001)
PHONE.............................708 339-1610
Fax: 708 339-8392
William Taylor, *President*
Jim Hays, *Vice Pres*
Ed Kurasz, *Vice Pres*
Raymond Patterson, *Prdtn Mgr*
Charles Seaton, *Prdtn Mgr*
◆ EMP: 740
SQ FT: 500,000
SALES (est): 385.9MM  Publicly Held
WEB: www.alliedtube.com
SIC: 3317  Welded pipe & tubes

**(G-11653)**
**ALLIED TUBE AND CONDUIT**
16100 Center Ave  (60426)
PHONE.............................708 225-2955
EMP: 5
SALES (est): 261.7K  Privately Held
SIC: 3317  Steel pipe & tubes

**(G-11654)**
**ALSIP MFG INC**
16700 Carse Ave  (60426-6169)
PHONE.............................708 333-4446
Fax: 708 333-4446
Joseph Lewandowski, *President*
Mark Regan, *VP Opers*
Debbie Fentress, *Office Mgr*
Tom Lewandowski, *Office Mgr*
Judy Lewandowski, *Admin Sec*
EMP: 23
SQ FT: 6,000
SALES (est): 4.4MM  Privately Held
WEB: www.alsipmfg.com
SIC: 3599  Machine shop, jobbing & repair

**(G-11655)**
**AMERICAN FOOD DISTRS CORP**
Also Called: Skyline Foods
374 E 167th St  (60426-6102)
PHONE.............................708 331-1982
Fax: 708 331-1876
Steven Blumental, *President*
Gerry A Michalak, *Vice Pres*
Vanessa Morales, *Admin Sec*
EMP: 15
SQ FT: 22,500
SALES (est): 6.1MM  Privately Held
WEB: www.amfood.com
SIC: 5147  2011  Meats & meat products; meat packing plants

**(G-11656)**
**AMERICAN KITCHEN DELIGHTS INC**
15320 Cooper Ave  (60426-2922)
PHONE.............................708 210-3200
Fax: 708 210-3233
Shahnawaz Hasan, *President*
EMP: 100
SQ FT: 78,000
SALES (est): 16.4MM  Privately Held
WEB: www.americankitchendelights.com
SIC: 2099  2051  1541  5149  Ready-to-eat meals, salads & sandwiches; bread, cake & related products; food products manufacturing or packing plant construction; specialty food items

## Harvey - Cook County

**(G-11657)**
**ATKORE INTERNATIONAL INC (DH)**
16100 Lathrop Ave (60426-6021)
PHONE.................................708 339-1610
John P Williamson, *President*
Steve Elsdon, *President*
Ed Kurasz, *President*
Bob Pereira, *President*
Scott Crumrine, *General Mgr*
▲ **EMP:** 50
**SALES (est):** 1.1B **Publicly Held**
**SIC:** 3317 Steel pipe & tubes

**(G-11658)**
**ATKORE INTERNATIONAL GROUP INC (PA)**
16100 Lathrop Ave (60426-6021)
PHONE.................................708 339-1610
John P Williamson, *President*
Kevin P Fitzpatrick, *Vice Pres*
Keith Whisenand, *Vice Pres*
James A Mallak, *CFO*
Daniel S Kelly, *Admin Sec*
**EMP:** 3000
**SALES:** 1.5B **Publicly Held**
**SIC:** 3441 1791 3446 3448 Fabricated structural metal; structural steel erection; architectural metalwork; prefabricated metal buildings; miscellaneous fabricated wire products

**(G-11659)**
**ATKORE INTL HOLDINGS INC (HQ)**
16100 Lathrop Ave (60426-6021)
PHONE.................................708 225-2051
John Williamson, *CEO*
John P Williamson, *President*
Bob Pereira, *President*
Mike Schulte, *President*
William Waltz, *President*
**EMP:** 4
**SALES:** 1.4B **Publicly Held**
**WEB:** www.atkore.com
**SIC:** 6719 3441 1791 3446 Investment holding companies, except banks; fabricated structural metal; structural steel erection; architectural metalwork; prefabricated metal buildings; miscellaneous fabricated wire products

**(G-11660)**
**BELLA ARCHITECTURAL PRODUCTS**
16910 Lathrop Ave (60426-6033)
PHONE.................................708 339-4782
Fax: 708 339-9782
Mark Ingratta, *President*
Jason Rockhold, *Plant Mgr*
Joyce Bozzetti, *Production*
Gregg Wakefield, *Marketing Staff*
Kindy Bergman, *Manager*
▲ **EMP:** 2
**SALES (est):** 418K **Privately Held**
**SIC:** 3444 Metal housings, enclosures, casings & other containers

**(G-11661)**
**BLUE ISLAND NEWSPAPER PRTG INC**
262 W 147th St (60426-1543)
PHONE.................................708 333-1006
Fax: 708 333-6902
Gary Rice, *President*
Judy Rice, *Corp Secy*
Darleen Smith, *Manager*
Robert Ogle, *CIO*
**EMP:** 70
**SQ FT:** 25,000
**SALES (est):** 11.7MM **Privately Held**
**SIC:** 2752 Commercial printing, offset

**(G-11662)**
**BREWER COMPANY**
Also Called: Rae Supply
3852 W 159th Pl (60428-4411)
PHONE.................................708 339-9000
Fax: 708 339-9050
Mike Doelly, *President*
Anthony Ziccardi, *Marketing Staff*
**EMP:** 18
**SALES (corp-wide):** 50MM **Privately Held**
**WEB:** www.thebrewerco.com
**SIC:** 2952 5211 2813 Coating compounds, tar; lumber & other building materials; industrial gases
**PA:** The Brewer Company
1354 Us Route 50
Milford OH 45150
800 394-0017

**(G-11663)**
**CROSBY GROUP LLC**
16868 Lathrop Ave (60426-6031)
PHONE.................................708 333-3005
John Gorski, *Manager*
**EMP:** 3
**SALES (corp-wide):** 261.5MM **Privately Held**
**WEB:** www.thecrosbygroup.com
**SIC:** 3429 Manufactured hardware (general)
**PA:** The Crosby Group Llc
2801 Dawson Rd
Tulsa OK 74110
918 834-4611

**(G-11664)**
**EAM PALLETS**
15224 Dixie Hwy Ste A (60426-2932)
PHONE.................................708 333-0596
Fax: 708 331-3201
Efrain Alba, *Owner*
**EMP:** 2
**SALES (est):** 307.8K **Privately Held**
**SIC:** 2448 Pallets, wood & wood with metal

**(G-11665)**
**ENGILITY CORPORATION**
16501 Kedzie Ave Ph Rm245 (60428-5556)
PHONE.................................708 596-8245
Deanna Pammenel, *Manager*
**EMP:** 5
**SALES (corp-wide):** 2B **Publicly Held**
**SIC:** 3812 Inertial guidance systems; navigational systems & instruments
**HQ:** Engility Corporation
35 New Engld Busctr Dr200
Andover MA 01810
978 749-2100

**(G-11666)**
**FABCO ENTERPRISES INC**
16812 Lathrop Ave (60426-6031)
PHONE.................................708 333-4644
Fax: 708 333-4659
Christian G Mercedes, *President*
Jeanne Erickson, *Admin Sec*
**EMP:** 6
**SQ FT:** 9,000
**SALES:** 1MM **Privately Held**
**SIC:** 3449 7692 3441 Miscellaneous metalwork; welding repair; fabricated structural metal

**(G-11667)**
**FUCHS CORPORATION (HQ)**
Also Called: Fuchs Lubricants Co
17050 Lathrop Ave (60426-6035)
PHONE.................................800 323-7755
Steven Puffpaff, *CEO*
Pamela Watson, *Vice Pres*
John Cunningham, *Plant Mgr*
Roger Russell, *Technical Mgr*
Pam Watson, *CFO*
◆ **EMP:** 2
**SQ FT:** 180,000
**SALES:** 86.8MM
**SALES (corp-wide):** 2.4B **Privately Held**
**SIC:** 2992 5172 2899 Lubricating oils & greases; lubricating oils & greases; metal treating compounds
**PA:** Fuchs Petrolub Se
Friesenheimer Str. 17
Mannheim 68169
621 380-20

**(G-11668)**
**HARVEY CEMENT PRODUCTS INC**
16030 Park Ave (60426-5069)
PHONE.................................708 333-1910
Fax: 708 333-1900
Philipe J Steck, *President*
Frank Steck Jr, *Corp Secy*
Gorden Steck, *Vice Pres*
Scott Dahlstrom, *Opers Mgr*
Beth Steck, *Bookkeeper*
**EMP:** 12 **EST:** 1949
**SQ FT:** 22,000
**SALES (est):** 1.4MM **Privately Held**
**WEB:** www.harveycement.com
**SIC:** 3271 5032 Blocks, concrete or cinder: standard; brick, concrete; masons' materials

**(G-11669)**
**HARVEY FUELS**
2 E 159th St (60426-5004)
PHONE.................................708 339-0777
Joseph Abraham, *Principal*
**EMP:** 3
**SALES (est):** 295.9K **Privately Held**
**SIC:** 2869 Fuels

**(G-11670)**
**HOGG WELDING INC**
16201 Clinton St (60426-5910)
PHONE.................................708 339-0033
Benny Stauersboll, *President*
Carol Stauersboll, *Admin Sec*
**EMP:** 4 **EST:** 1950
**SQ FT:** 2,900
**SALES (est):** 562.7K **Privately Held**
**WEB:** www.hoggwelding.com
**SIC:** 3842 7692 3444 Wheelchairs; welding repair; sheet metalwork

**(G-11671)**
**IDEAS INC**
16131 Clinton St (60426-5908)
PHONE.................................708 596-1055
Celine Bess, *Manager*
**EMP:** 8
**SALES (corp-wide):** 2.4MM **Privately Held**
**SIC:** 2992 Lubricating oils & greases
**PA:** Ideas, Inc.
625 S Main St
Lombard IL 60148
630 620-2010

**(G-11672)**
**INDUSTRIAL WATER TRTMNT SOLTNS (HQ)**
16880 Lathrop Ave (60426-6031)
PHONE.................................708 339-1313
Christopher Dooley, *President*
Nate Vandermale, *Controller*
**EMP:** 4 **EST:** 2011
**SQ FT:** 25,000
**SALES (est):** 28.2MM **Privately Held**
**SIC:** 6719 3589 2899 Personal holding companies, except banks; water treatment equipment, industrial; chemical preparations

**(G-11673)**
**JMI CRAFTED COML MLLWK INC**
3032 W 167th St (60428-5618)
PHONE.................................708 331-6331
Fax: 708 331-6337
John R Monahan, *President*
Kathy Monahan, *Manager*
**EMP:** 14
**SALES (est):** 2.9MM **Privately Held**
**WEB:** www.jmimillwork.com
**SIC:** 2431 Millwork

**(G-11674)**
**MR T SHIRT AND DOLLAR PLUS**
75 W 159th St (60426-4956)
PHONE.................................708 596-9150
Fred Abdel, *President*
**EMP:** 5
**SALES:** 770K **Privately Held**
**SIC:** 2253 T-shirts & tops, knit

**(G-11675)**
**SOUTH SUBN LOGISTICS SUPS CORP**
16610 Finch Ave (60426-6042)
PHONE.................................312 804-3401
Tanya Johnson, *President*
**EMP:** 3
**SALES (est):** 129.3K **Privately Held**
**SIC:** 3728 Aircraft parts & equipment

**(G-11676)**
**SPECIAL SCENTS INC**
14815 Artesian Ave (60426-1364)
PHONE.................................708 596-9370
Denise Hall, *President*
**EMP:** 20
**SALES (est):** 1.1MM **Privately Held**
**SIC:** 2844 Toilet preparations

**(G-11677)**
**SUMMIT LABORATORIES INC**
17010 Halsted St (60426-6129)
PHONE.................................708 333-2995
Clyde Hammond Sr, *President*
Natalie Hutchinson, *Vice Pres*
Lynn Hutchinson, *VP Mktg*
Darlene Curry, *Director*
**EMP:** 45
**SQ FT:** 152,000
**SALES (est):** 10.4MM **Privately Held**
**WEB:** www.summitlaboratories.com
**SIC:** 2844 Hair preparations, including shampoos; cosmetic preparations

**(G-11678)**
**TRI-CITY GOLD EXCHANGE INC**
470 E 147th St (60426-2461)
PHONE.................................708 331-5995
Aaron Lake, *President*
**EMP:** 10
**SQ FT:** 900
**SALES (est):** 787K **Privately Held**
**SIC:** 5944 3911 Jewelry, precious stones & precious metals; jewelry, precious metal

**(G-11679)**
**UNISTRUT INTERNATIONAL CORP (DH)**
16100 Lathrop Ave (60426-6021)
PHONE.................................800 882-5543
John P Williamson, *President*
Nelda J Connors, *Principal*
Karl J Schmidt, *Vice Pres*
James A Mallak, *Treasurer*
Kathy Smith, *Controller*
▲ **EMP:** 127
**SALES (est):** 131.5MM **Publicly Held**
**WEB:** www.unistrutconstruction.com
**SIC:** 3441 1791 3446 3448 Fabricated structural metal; structural steel erection; partitions & supports/studs, including accoustical systems; trusses & framing: prefabricated metal; cable, uninsulated wire: made from purchased wire; manufactured hardware (general)

**(G-11680)**
**VOSS ELECTRIC INC**
15241 Commercial Ave (60426-2396)
PHONE.................................708 596-6000
Peter W Voss Jr, *President*
**EMP:** 5 **EST:** 1974
**SQ FT:** 80,000
**SALES (est):** 286.2K **Privately Held**
**SIC:** 7694 3621 Electric motor repair; motors & generators

## Harwood Heights
### Cook County

**(G-11681)**
**ADVANCED SPECIALTY LIGHTING**
Also Called: Advanced Strobe Products
7227 W Wilson Ave (60706-4705)
PHONE.................................708 867-3140
Jarold Bijak, *President*
K Beres, *Office Mgr*
▲ **EMP:** 250
**SALES (est):** 31.1MM **Privately Held**
**WEB:** www.aslamps.com
**SIC:** 3646 Commercial indusl & institutional electric lighting fixtures

**(G-11682)**
**CASEY SPRING CO INC**
4630 N Ronald St (60706-4781)
PHONE.................................708 867-7773
Fax: 708 867-8949
Dorothy M Sobczak, *President*
Donna Barone, *Vice Pres*
**EMP:** 12 **EST:** 1957
**SQ FT:** 17,000

# GEOGRAPHIC SECTION

**Hazel Crest - Cook County (G-11708)**

SALES (est): 890K  Privately Held
WEB: www.caseyspring.com
SIC: 3493  3496  Coiled flat springs; miscellaneous fabricated wire products

**(G-11683)**
**CJ ANDERSON & COMPANY**
4751 N Olcott Ave  (60706-4605)
PHONE..................................708 867-4002
Fax: 708 867-5467
Milton Sybert, *CEO*
Thomas Sybert, *President*
Joellen Toussaint, *Purch Mgr*
Jim Bjorkquist, *Sales Executive*
Jon Goode, *Manager*
EMP: 30  EST: 1910
SQ FT: 16,000
SALES: 2.6MM  Privately Held
WEB: www.cjanderson.com
SIC: 3534  Elevators & moving stairways

**(G-11684)**
**F C L GRAPHICS INC**
4600 N Olcott Ave  (60706-4604)
PHONE..................................708 867-5500
Fax: 708 867-7768
Stephen Flood, *CEO*
Michael McGuire, *CFO*
EMP: 150
SQ FT: 115,000
SALES (est): 48.8MM  Privately Held
WEB: www.fclgraphics.com
SIC: 2752  Commercial printing, offset
PA: Fcl Holding Spv, Llc
    10 S Wacker Dr Ste 2500
    Chicago IL

**(G-11685)**
**GEARS GEARS GEARS INC**
Also Called: Gear Shop, The
4615 N Ronald St  (60706-4718)
PHONE..................................708 366-6555
Fax: 708 366-6580
Gerhard Huebner, *President*
Karin Huebner, *Bookkeeper*
EMP: 6
SQ FT: 4,000
SALES (est): 510K  Privately Held
SIC: 3443  3568  3462  Metal parts; power transmission equipment; iron & steel forgings

**(G-11686)**
**LAWRENCE SCREW PRODUCTS INC (PA)**
7230 W Wilson Ave  (60706-4797)
PHONE..................................708 867-5150
Fax: 630 867-7052
Howard Levinson, *President*
Robert Hayslip, *Vice Pres*
Phil Levine, *Vice Pres*
Alan Zinger, *Vice Pres*
Bob Hayslip, *Opers Mgr*
▲ EMP: 57  EST: 1977
SQ FT: 35,000
SALES: 61.2MM  Privately Held
WEB: www.lawscrew.com
SIC: 3965  Fasteners

**(G-11687)**
**NAVITOR INC**
Consolidated Marking
7220 W Wilson Ave  (60706-4706)
PHONE..................................800 323-0253
Steve Silkaitis, *President*
Rich Williams, *Project Mgr*
Teena Lamorte, *Natl Sales Mgr*
Keith Betti, *Regl Sales Mgr*
Armando Ochoa, *Manager*
EMP: 500
SALES (corp-wide): 4.5B  Privately Held
SIC: 3953  2396  3469  3089  Marking devices; screen printing on fabric articles; metal stampings; injection molding of plastics; advertising artwork; advertising novelties; labels (unprinted), gummed: made from purchased materials
HQ: Navitor, Inc.
    1725 Roe Crest Dr
    North Mankato MN 56003
    507 625-2828

**(G-11688)**
**OFFICIAL ISSUE INC**
4640 N Oketo Ave  (60706-4601)
PHONE..................................847 795-1066

Scott Palmberg, *President*
Lisa Peiser, *Sales Mgr*
Marty Brand, *Manager*
▲ EMP: 4
SALES (est): 388.1K  Privately Held
SIC: 3949  Sporting & athletic goods

**(G-11689)**
**QCC  LLC (PA)**
Also Called: A&K C.N.C. Machining
7315 W Wilson Ave  (60706-4707)
PHONE..................................708 867-5400
Fax: 630 867-8854
Jon Goreham, *CEO*
Donald Bennett, *CFO*
Deborah Elverd, *Manager*
Keith Le Compte, *Manager*
Ronald Hailbeck, *CTO*
◆ EMP: 230  EST: 1951
SQ FT: 120,085
SALES (est): 53.8MM  Privately Held
WEB: www.qccorp.com
SIC: 3053  3451  Gaskets & sealing devices; screw machine products

**(G-11690)**
**QUALISEAL TECHNOLOGY  LLC**
7319 W Wilson Ave  (60706-4707)
PHONE..................................708 887-6080
Wes Shull, *Vice Pres*
EMP: 51
SALES (est): 1.6MM  Privately Held
SIC: 3728  Mfg Aircraft Parts/Equipment

**(G-11691)**
**TECHNETICS GROUP LLC**
Also Called: Qualiseal Technology
7319 W Wilson Ave  (60706-4707)
PHONE..................................708 887-6080
Jon Goreham, *CEO*
EMP: 7
SALES (corp-wide): 1.1B  Publicly Held
SIC: 3446  Mfg Architectural Metalwork
HQ: Technetics Group Llc
    5605 Carnegie Blvd # 500
    Charlotte NC 28209
    704 731-1500

**(G-11692)**
**WINZELER  INC**
Also Called: WINZELER GEAR
7355 W Wilson Ave  (60706-4785)
PHONE..................................708 867-7971
Fax: 708 867-7974
John Winzeler, *President*
Daniel Prysmiki, *Mfg Spvr*
Erich Fiedler, *Engineer*
Agnes Rendel, *Accountant*
Pat Nichooson, *Manager*
▲ EMP: 33  EST: 1938
SQ FT: 42,000
SALES: 14.3MM  Privately Held
WEB: www.winzelergear.com
SIC: 3089  Molding primary plastic

**(G-11693)**
**X HALE**
4811 N Olcott Ave # 504  (60706-3561)
PHONE..................................847 884-6250
Kiavash Sayar, *Principal*
EMP: 4
SALES (est): 220K  Privately Held
SIC: 2599  Bar, restaurant & cafeteria furniture

## Havana
### Mason County

**(G-11694)**
**DOWELL LYNNEA**
Also Called: Shadow Manufacturing
18937 E Cr 1800n  (62644-6328)
PHONE..................................309 543-3854
Lynnea Dowell, *Owner*
EMP: 3
SQ FT: 3,000
SALES (est): 240K  Privately Held
SIC: 1781  3533  3599  Water well drilling; irrigation equipment; machine shop, jobbing & repair

**(G-11695)**
**HAVANA PRINTING & MAILING**
Also Called: Martin Publishing Company
217 W Market St  (62644-1145)
P.O. Box 380  (62644-0380)
PHONE..................................309 543-2000
Robert Martin, *Partner*
Tim Schroll, *Partner*
Donald Clancy, *Plant Mgr*
EMP: 10
SQ FT: 7,000
SALES (est): 893.6K  Privately Held
WEB: www.havanaprint.com
SIC: 2752  7331  Offset & photolithographic printing; mailing service

**(G-11696)**
**HAVANAH FUEL**
520 E Laurel Ave  (62644-1525)
PHONE..................................309 543-2211
Brian Tracy, *Principal*
EMP: 3
SALES (est): 215.4K  Privately Held
SIC: 2869  Fuels

**(G-11697)**
**JAMES G CARTER**
Also Called: Paddlewheel The
15907 N Sr 97  (62644-6758)
PHONE..................................309 543-2634
James Carter, *Owner*
EMP: 3  EST: 1998
SALES: 200K  Privately Held
SIC: 3949  Bowling alleys & accessories

**(G-11698)**
**MARTIN PUBLISHING CO (PA)**
Also Called: Mason County Democrat
217 W Market St  (62644-1145)
P.O. Box 380  (62644-0380)
PHONE..................................309 543-2000
Fax: 309 543-6844
Robert Martin Jr, *President*
Wendy Martin, *Corp Secy*
Ruth Lynn, *Advt Staff*
EMP: 25  EST: 1849
SQ FT: 30,000
SALES (est): 2.4MM  Privately Held
WEB: www.masoncountydemocrat.com
SIC: 2711  Newspapers, publishing & printing

**(G-11699)**
**METAL CULVERTS  INC**
Also Called: Havana Metal Culverts Division
15732 Rte 97 S  (62644)
P.O. Box 350  (62644-0350)
PHONE..................................309 543-2271
Paul Fliege, *Manager*
EMP: 20
SALES (corp-wide): 36.3MM  Privately Held
WEB: www.metalculverts.com
SIC: 3444  Pipe, sheet metal
PA: Metal Culverts, Inc.
    711 Heisinger Rd
    Jefferson City MO 65109
    573 636-7312

**(G-11700)**
**OTTER CREEK SAND & GRAVEL**
4125 N Stoneyard Rd  (62644-4512)
PHONE..................................309 759-4293
Fax: 309 759-4866
David Clinard, *President*
EMP: 10
SALES (est): 667.9K  Privately Held
SIC: 1442  Construction sand & gravel

## Hawthorn Woods
### Lake County

**(G-11701)**
**ATLAS COPCO COMPTEC INC**
14 Rosewood Dr  (60047-7714)
PHONE..................................847 726-9866
Bruce Edstrand, *Manager*
EMP: 3
SALES (est): 296.3K  Privately Held
SIC: 3563  Air & gas compressors

**(G-11702)**
**FLORALSTAR ENTERPRISES**
68 Tournament Dr N  (60047-8401)
PHONE..................................847 726-0124
Debra Hillstrand, *Owner*
Barbara Howard, *Controller*
EMP: 3
SQ FT: 5,000
SALES: 340K  Privately Held
SIC: 3999  Artificial flower arrangements; Christmas trees, artificial

**(G-11703)**
**MCS MANAGEMENT CORP (PA)**
5 Keuka Ct  (60047-1905)
PHONE..................................847 680-3707
Fax: 847 680-3742
Wayne P Barto, *President*
EMP: 1
SALES: 4MM  Privately Held
WEB: www.mcsmgt.com
SIC: 5045  7372  Computer software; educational computer software

**(G-11704)**
**NATIONAL AEROSPACE CORP**
28 Sequoia Rd  (60047-1933)
PHONE..................................847 566-5834
Eric Abbott, *Owner*
EMP: 3  EST: 2015
SALES (est): 159.3K  Privately Held
SIC: 3812  Search & navigation equipment

**(G-11705)**
**T9 GROUP  LLC**
25635 N Stoney Kirk Ct  (60047-7539)
P.O. Box 777, Prospect Heights (60070-0777)
PHONE..................................847 912-8862
Steve Hadgisava,
EMP: 8
SALES: 1.2MM  Privately Held
SIC: 2822  5169  7389  Synthetic rubber; chemicals & allied products;

## Hazel Crest
### Cook County

**(G-11706)**
**A P DELI IV  INC**
1925 170th St  (60429-1361)
PHONE..................................708 335-4462
Kenneth Battee, *President*
EMP: 15
SALES (est): 1.3MM  Privately Held
SIC: 2013  Sausages & other prepared meats

**(G-11707)**
**GREENFIELD PRODUCTS  LLC (PA)**
3111 167th St  (60429-1025)
PHONE..................................708 596-5200
Fax: 708 331-3396
Niska Dennis, *Sales Mgr*
Bill Healy, *Sales Mgr*
Gustavo Anzola, *Sales Engr*
Dan Bollheimer, *Sales Staff*
Jack Lanigan, *Mng Member*
EMP: 35
SALES (est): 29.3MM  Privately Held
SIC: 3423  Jacks: lifting, screw or ratchet (hand tools)

**(G-11708)**
**HANGER PRSTHETCS & ORTHO INC**
17530 Kedzie Ave  (60429-2004)
PHONE..................................708 957-0240
Ivan Sable, *Branch Mgr*
Bill Moritz, *Manager*
EMP: 7
SALES (corp-wide): 459.1MM  Publicly Held
SIC: 3842  Limbs, artificial
HQ: Hanger Prosthetics & Orthotics, Inc.
    10910 Domain Dr Ste 300
    Austin TX 78758
    512 777-3800

# Hazel Crest - Cook County (G-11709)

**(G-11709)**
**LANCO INTERNATIONAL INC (PA)**
Also Called: Lantech Logistics
3111 167th St (60429-1025)
PHONE..................708 596-5200
John J Lanigan Jr, *President*
C Rog, *General Mgr*
Mike T Lanigan, *Exec VP*
William P Lanigan, *Exec VP*
Jack Wepfer, *Vice Pres*
▼ **EMP:** 350
**SQ FT:** 200,000
**SALES (est):** 203.3MM **Privately Held**
**WEB:** www.mi-jack.com
**SIC:** 3531 8711 5084 3536 Construction machinery; designing: ship, boat, machine & product; cranes, industrial; cranes, overhead traveling; heavy construction equipment rental; industrial trucks & tractors

**(G-11710)**
**LANIGAN HOLDINGS LLC (PA)**
3111 167th St (60429-1025)
PHONE..................708 596-5200
John J Lanigan Sr, *Ch of Bd*
John J Lanigan Jr, *President*
Mike T Lanigan, *Exec VP*
William Lanigan, *Exec VP*
Stephen J Bayers, *CFO*
**EMP:** 14
**SALES (est):** 24.9MM **Privately Held**
**SIC:** 5082 3531 7948 8743 General construction machinery & equipment; crane carriers; race track operation; promotion service

**(G-11711)**
**MI-JACK PRODUCTS INC (HQ)**
3111 167th St (60429-0975)
PHONE..................708 596-5200
**Fax:** 708 225-2312
John J Lanigan Sr, *Ch of Bd*
Michael T Lanigan, *President*
Steven Bayers, *President*
Harold Brazzale, *General Mgr*
Mike T Lanigan, *Exec VP*
◆ **EMP:** 277
**SQ FT:** 1,310
**SALES (est):** 184.8MM
**SALES (corp-wide):** 203.3MM **Privately Held**
**SIC:** 3531 8711 Construction machinery; designing: ship, boat, machine & product
**PA:** Lanco International Inc.
  3111 167th St
  Hazel Crest IL 60429
  708 596-5200

**(G-11712)**
**MI-JACK SYSTEMS & TECH LLC**
3111 167th St (60429-1025)
PHONE..................708 596-3780
Stephen J Bayers, *Principal*
Simon Fiera, *Opers Staff*
Scott Borsodi, *VP Sales*
**EMP:** 14
**SALES (est):** 2MM **Privately Held**
**SIC:** 3699 Door opening & closing devices, electrical

**(G-11713)**
**MJMC INC**
3111 167th St (60429-1025)
PHONE..................708 596-5200
John Boquist, *President*
Harvey E Schmidt, *Vice Pres*
Jerry Lynch, *Exec Dir*
Henry Gurion, *Admin Sec*
**EMP:** 36
**SALES (est):** 10.5MM **Privately Held**
**SIC:** 3531 Backhoes, tractors, cranes, plows & similar equipment

**(G-11714)**
**Q SALES LLC**
Also Called: Q Products and Services
16720 Mozart Ave Ste A (60429-1092)
PHONE..................708 271-9842
Paul Yadron, *Principal*
Tony Dellumo, *Sales Staff*
**EMP:** 2
**SALES (est):** 220K **Privately Held**
**SIC:** 3829 Thermometers & temperature sensors

## Hebron
### Mchenry County

**(G-11715)**
**BROTHERS DECORATING**
10305 Vanderkarr Rd (60034-9527)
P.O. Box 396 (60034-0396)
PHONE..................815 648-2214
Paul Musgrave, *President*
**EMP:** 2
**SALES (est):** 215.6K **Privately Held**
**SIC:** 2621 1721 Wallpaper (hanging paper); painting & paper hanging

**(G-11716)**
**CHAMPION FOODS LLC**
Also Called: Champion Pizza
9910 Main St (60034-8903)
PHONE..................815 648-2725
**Fax:** 815 648-2011
Daniel Fontana,
**EMP:** 9
**SQ FT:** 3,800
**SALES (est):** 890K **Privately Held**
**SIC:** 2038 Pizza, frozen

**(G-11717)**
**COEUR INC**
11411 Price Rd (60034-9664)
PHONE..................815 648-1093
**EMP:** 10
**SALES (corp-wide):** 13.6B **Publicly Held**
**SIC:** 3841 Surgical & medical instruments
**HQ:** Coeur, Inc.
  100 Physicians Way # 200
  Lebanon TN 37090
  615 547-7923

**(G-11718)**
**CULTIVATED ENERGY GROUP INC**
10702 Seaman Rd (60034-9535)
PHONE..................312 203-8833
Joseph E Shacter, *CEO*
**EMP:** 3
**SALES (est):** 103.9K **Privately Held**
**SIC:** 3999 Manufacturing industries

**(G-11719)**
**FILTERTEK INC (HQ)**
Also Called: ITW Flter Pdts Trnsm Fltration
11411 Price Rd (60034-8936)
PHONE..................815 648-2410
**Fax:** 815 648-2929
David F Atkinson, *CEO*
Roland Martel, *President*
Burks Law, *President*
Larry Larkin, *Vice Pres*
Vernett Blair, *Prdtn Mgr*
◆ **EMP:** 290
**SQ FT:** 100,000
**SALES (est):** 171.9MM
**SALES (corp-wide):** 13.6B **Publicly Held**
**SIC:** 3089 3564 Plastic processing; blowers & fans
**PA:** Illinois Tool Works Inc.
  155 Harlem Ave
  Glenview IL 60025
  847 724-7500

**(G-11720)**
**ILLINOIS TOOL WORKS**
Also Called: ITW Fastex
11411 Price Rd (60034-9664)
PHONE..................815 648-2416
▲ **EMP:** 27 **EST:** 2013
**SALES (est):** 9MM **Privately Held**
**SIC:** 3494 Valves & pipe fittings

**(G-11721)**
**KEYSTONE DISPLAY INC**
11916 Maple Ave (60034-8869)
P.O. Box 427 (60034-0427)
PHONE..................815 648-2456
**Fax:** 815 648-4248
James Peterson, *CEO*
John J Streit, *President*
Bruce Fiegel, *Opers Mgr*
**EMP:** 75 **EST:** 1948
**SQ FT:** 70,000
**SALES (est):** 14.5MM **Privately Held**
**SIC:** 2542 3993 Racks, merchandise display or storage: except wood; signs & advertising specialties

**(G-11722)**
**LABEL GRAPHICS CO INC**
12024 3rd Ave (60034-8923)
PHONE..................815 648-2478
**Fax:** 815 648-2902
John Korkowski, *Vice Pres*
Emil Salmons, *Manager*
**EMP:** 10
**SALES (corp-wide):** 1.6MM **Privately Held**
**SIC:** 2672 2671 Labels (unprinted), gummed: made from purchased materials; packaging paper & plastics film, coated & laminated
**PA:** Label Graphics Co., Inc.
  1225 Carnegie St Ste 104b
  Rolling Meadows IL
  847 454-1005

**(G-11723)**
**LAMINATED COMPONENTS INC**
12204 Hansen Rd (60034-8889)
PHONE..................815 648-4811
**Fax:** 815 648-2563
Mark Romme, *President*
Tammy Dawson, *General Mgr*
Sandra Romme, *Corp Secy*
Barbara Fedricks, *Accountant*
▲ **EMP:** 22
**SQ FT:** 35,000
**SALES (est):** 4.3MM **Privately Held**
**WEB:** www.laminatedcomponents.com
**SIC:** 2541 Display fixtures, wood

**(G-11724)**
**PERFECT SHUTTERS INC**
12213 Il Route 173 (60034-9610)
PHONE..................815 648-2401
**Fax:** 815 648-4510
Nikunj H Shah, *President*
Steve Schreiner, *Controller*
Kelly Sabo, *Manager*
**EMP:** 40
**SQ FT:** 100,000
**SALES (est):** 8.5MM **Privately Held**
**WEB:** www.shuttersinc.com
**SIC:** 3089 Shutters, plastic

**(G-11725)**
**POLYCAST**
10103 Main St B (60034-8905)
PHONE..................815 648-4438
**Fax:** 815 648-4439
John Moffatt, *General Mgr*
Wayne Johnson, *Treasurer*
**EMP:** 10
**SALES (est):** 1.3MM **Privately Held**
**SIC:** 2821 Polyvinylidene chloride resins

**(G-11726)**
**SHERWOOD TOOL INC**
Also Called: M J Molding
12120 Il Route 173 (60034-9619)
PHONE..................815 648-1463
**Fax:** 815 648-1473
William J Snyder, *President*
Bill Snyder, *President*
**EMP:** 12
**SALES (est):** 1.7MM **Privately Held**
**WEB:** www.sherwoodtool.com
**SIC:** 3089 Molding primary plastic

**(G-11727)**
**SIGNCRAFTERS ENTERPRISES INC**
Also Called: Signs of The Times
10714 Il Route 47 (60034-9605)
P.O. Box 368 (60034-0368)
PHONE..................815 648-4484
**Fax:** 815 648-4959
James Bryan, *President*
Sophia Bryan, *Bookkeeper*
**EMP:** 2
**SALES:** 210K **Privately Held**
**WEB:** www.signcraftersenterprises.com
**SIC:** 3993 Signs & advertising specialties

**(G-11728)**
**TRISEAL CORPORATION**
Also Called: Triseal Worldwide
11920 Price Rd (60034-8933)
PHONE..................815 648-2473
**Fax:** 815 648-2528
Patricia H Wales, *President*
Dave Paul, *Opers Mgr*
Larry Winn, *Engineer*
John L Porritt II, *CFO*
Mona Anthony, *Office Mgr*
▲ **EMP:** 35
**SQ FT:** 26,000
**SALES (est):** 6.4MM **Privately Held**
**WEB:** www.triseal.com
**SIC:** 3713 3053 Truck & bus bodies; oil seals, leather; oil seals, rubber

**(G-11729)**
**TRUE LINE MOLD AND ENGRG CORP**
12205 Hansen Rd (60034-8890)
PHONE..................815 648-2739
**Fax:** 815 648-2748
Ray Adkins, *President*
Curtis Larsen, *Vice Pres*
Amon Adkins, *Admin Sec*
**EMP:** 40 **EST:** 1965
**SQ FT:** 43,000
**SALES (est):** 2MM **Privately Held**
**WEB:** www.true-line.com
**SIC:** 3089 Molding primary plastic

**(G-11730)**
**VAUGHAN & BUSHNELL MFG CO (PA)**
11414 Maple Ave (60034)
PHONE..................815 648-2446
**Fax:** 815 648-4300
Charles S Vaughan, *President*
Howard Vaughan Jr, *Chairman*
Farlin G Caufield, *Exec VP*
Dan Caspall, *Vice Pres*
Laverne Parks, *Purchasing*
▲ **EMP:** 12 **EST:** 1869
**SQ FT:** 36,000
**SALES (est):** 40MM **Privately Held**
**WEB:** www.vbmfg.com
**SIC:** 3423 2499 3524 Hammers (hand tools); axes & hatchets; handles, wood; lawn & garden equipment

**(G-11731)**
**VILLAGE HEBRON WATER SEWAGE**
12007 Prairie Ave (60034-8892)
P.O. Box 372 (60034-0372)
PHONE..................815 648-2353
Tom Shrewsbury, *Director*
**EMP:** 1 **EST:** 2007
**SALES (est):** 239.7K **Privately Held**
**SIC:** 3823 Water quality monitoring & control systems

## Hecker
### Monroe County

**(G-11732)**
**HOTTENROTT COMPANY INC**
Also Called: Basic Industries
351 S Main St (62248)
P.O. Box 127 (62248-0127)
PHONE..................618 473-2531
**Fax:** 618 473-9393
Roger W Hottenrott, *President*
Catherine Hottenrott, *Corp Secy*
Richard Hottenrott, *Vice Pres*
Mark Wells, *Opers Mgr*
Mike Fugitt, *Finance Mgr*
**EMP:** 5
**SQ FT:** 6,336
**SALES:** 500K **Privately Held**
**WEB:** www.hottenrott.org
**SIC:** 3599 Machine shop, jobbing & repair

## Hennepin
*Putnam County*

**(G-11733)**
**D & D MANUFACTURING**
6th St Rr 26 (61327)
P.O. Box 354 (61327-0354)
PHONE..................................815 339-9100
Fax: 815 925-7579
Robert Dockins, *Owner*
EMP: 3
SALES: 300K Privately Held
SIC: 3089 3443 Plastic processing; closures, plastic; fabricated plate work (boiler shop)

**(G-11734)**
**MARQUIS ENERGY LLC**
11953 Prairie Indus Pkwy (61327-5160)
PHONE..................................815 925-7300
Mark Marquis, *CEO*
Perry Gruss, *Principal*
Walter Horst, *Principal*
Jason Marquis, *COO*
Lester Smith, *Plant Supt*
◆ EMP: 49
SALES (est): 36.2MM Privately Held
WEB: www.marquisenergy.com
SIC: 2869 Ethylene

**(G-11735)**
**WASHINGTON MILLS HENNEPIN INC**
13230 Prairie Indl Pkwy (61327)
PHONE..................................815 925-7302
Armand Ladage, *VP Mfg*
Jim Petersen, *Production*
Nancy E Gates, *Admin Sec*
▲ EMP: 60
SALES (est): 13.1MM
SALES (corp-wide): 172.6MM Privately Held
SIC: 3291 Abrasive products
PA: Washington Mills Group, Inc.
20 N Main St
North Grafton MA 01536
508 839-6511

**(G-11736)**
**WASHINGTON MILLS TONAWANDA**
City Rd 875 E (61327)
PHONE..................................815 925-7302
Armand La Dage, *Enginr/R&D Mgr*
Rebecca Haywood, *Human Res Dir*
Maria Novak, *Human Res Mgr*
Debora Urnikis, *Director*
EMP: 96
SALES (corp-wide): 172.6MM Privately Held
WEB: www.exolon.com
SIC: 3291 3295 2819 Silicon carbide abrasive; minerals, ground or treated; industrial inorganic chemicals
HQ: Washington Mills Tonawanda, Inc.
1000 E Niagara St
Tonawanda NY 14150
716 693-4550

## Henning
*Vermilion County*

**(G-11737)**
**FULL-FILL INDUSTRIES LLC**
400 N Main St (61848-8000)
PHONE..................................217 286-3532
Fax: 217 286-3683
Randy Cramer, *General Mgr*
David Clap, *Principal*
Dirk David, *QC Mgr*
Charles H Clapp Jr, *Bd of Directors*
Dave Clapp, *Executive*
EMP: 29 EST: 1999
SQ FT: 45,000
SALES (est): 16.9MM Privately Held
SIC: 2813 Aerosols

**(G-11738)**
**HENNING MACHINE & DIE WORKS**
4 N Main St (61848-8034)
PHONE..................................217 286-3393
Jenny Walters, *Owner*
EMP: 6
SQ FT: 8,000
SALES: 560K Privately Held
SIC: 3599 3544 Machine shop, jobbing & repair; special dies, tools, jigs & fixtures

## Henry
*Marshall County*

**(G-11739)**
**DERBYTEESCOM**
622 Gateway Dr (61537-1002)
PHONE..................................309 264-1033
Mark Klein, *Principal*
EMP: 3
SALES (est): 362.8K Privately Held
SIC: 2253 T-shirts & tops, knit

**(G-11740)**
**ED HARTWIG TRUCKING & EXCVTG**
Also Called: Hartwig Roll Off Containers
312 Jefferson St (61537-1322)
PHONE..................................309 364-3672
Fax: 309 364-2666
Edward Hartwig, *President*
Lori Hartwig, *Vice Pres*
Ed Saunders, *Manager*
EMP: 8
SALES (est): 1.2MM Privately Held
SIC: 1794 4213 1711 3599 Excavation work; trucking, except local; boiler & furnace contractors; machine shop, jobbing & repair; saws & sawing equipment

**(G-11741)**
**EMERALD PERFORMANCE MTLS LLC**
1550 County Road 1450 N (61537-9404)
PHONE..................................309 364-2311
Kali Dietz, *Purch Mgr*
Jeff Bolton, *Engineer*
Tom Newby, *Comptroller*
Candi Wagner, *Mng Member*
EMP: 74
SALES (corp-wide): 346.7MM Privately Held
SIC: 2821 Plastics materials & resins
PA: Emerald Performance Materials Llc
2020 Front St Ste 100
Cuyahoga Falls OH 44221
330 916-6700

**(G-11742)**
**EMERALD POLYMER ADDITIVES LLC**
1550 County Road 1450 N (61537-9404)
PHONE..................................309 364-2311
Jeff Lee, *Manager*
Leslie U Hofer, *Executive*
EMP: 81
SALES (corp-wide): 346.7MM Privately Held
SIC: 2899 Chemical preparations
HQ: Emerald Polymer Additives Llc
240 W Emerling Ave
Akron OH 44301
330 374-2424

**(G-11743)**
**HENRY NEWS REPUBLICAN**
Also Called: Wenona Index
709 3rd St (61537-1446)
P.O. Box 190 (61537-0190)
PHONE..................................309 364-3250
Fax: 309 364-3858
Doug Ziegler, *President*
EMP: 8
SALES (est): 670.7K Privately Held
SIC: 2759 2711 Newspapers: printing; newspapers

**(G-11744)**
**MEXICHEM SPECIALTY RESINS INC**
1546 County Road 1450 N (61537-9404)
PHONE..................................309 364-2154
EMP: 16
SALES (corp-wide): 5.8B Privately Held
SIC: 2822 Ethylene-propylene rubbers, EPDM polymers
HQ: Mexichem Specialty Resins Inc.
33653 Walker Rd
Avon Lake OH 44012
440 930-1435

**(G-11745)**
**OLTMAN & SONS INC**
Also Called: Oltman Ready Mix
1526 County Road 1500 E (61537)
P.O. Box 212 (61537-0212)
PHONE..................................309 364-2849
Fax: 309 364-3143
Donald Oltman, *President*
Jerry Oltman, *Vice Pres*
EMP: 5
SQ FT: 4,800
SALES: 650K Privately Held
SIC: 3273 Ready-mixed concrete

**(G-11746)**
**POLYONE CORPORATION**
1546 County Road 1450 N (61537-9404)
PHONE..................................309 364-2154
Joel Lindahl, *Branch Mgr*
EMP: 108 Publicly Held
WEB: www.polyone.com
SIC: 2821 Plastics materials & resins; polyvinyl chloride resins (PVC); vinyl resins
PA: Polyone Corporation
33587 Walker Rd
Avon Lake OH 44012

## Herod
*Pope County*

**(G-11747)**
**ILLINOIS FUEL COMPANY LLC**
920 Gape Hollow Rd (62947)
PHONE..................................618 275-4486
Kathy Smith,
John Smith Jr,
EMP: 80
SALES (est): 2.9MM Privately Held
SIC: 1221 1222 Strip mining, bituminous; bituminous coal-underground mining

## Herrin
*Williamson County*

**(G-11748)**
**FRENCH STUDIO LTD**
Also Called: Herrin News Litho
821 S Park Ave Stop 1 (62948-4174)
PHONE..................................618 942-5328
Fax: 618 942-2469
Louis A French, *President*
Becky Eaton, *Systems Staff*
Irl Eaton, *Systems Staff*
EMP: 5
SQ FT: 6,000
SALES: 150K Privately Held
SIC: 7221 2752 2791 2789 Photographer, still or video; photolithographic printing; typesetting; bookbinding & related work

**(G-11749)**
**HANGER PROSTHETICS &**
Also Called: Hanger Clinic
404 Rushing Dr (62948-3762)
PHONE..................................618 997-1451
Ivan Sabel, *President*
Sam Liang, *President*
Sheryl Price, *Director*
EMP: 4
SALES (corp-wide): 459.1MM Publicly Held
SIC: 3842 Prosthetic appliances
HQ: Hanger Prosthetics & Orthotics East, Inc.
33 North Ave Ste 101
Tallmadge OH 44278
330 633-9807

**(G-11750)**
**K R N MACHINE AND LASER CENTER**
Also Called: K R N Machine & Laser Center
516 N Park Ave (62948-3113)
P.O. Box 2065 (62948-5265)
PHONE..................................618 942-6064
Fax: 618 942-6020
Ronald P Stewart, *CEO*
Ronald Stewart, *CEO*
Randy Stewart, *Principal*
Norma Jean Stewart, *Corp Secy*
EMP: 8 EST: 1968
SQ FT: 16,000
SALES (est): 532.4K Privately Held
SIC: 3599 Machine shop, jobbing & repair

**(G-11751)**
**ODUM CONCRETE PRODUCTS INC**
201 Rushing Dr (62948-3753)
PHONE..................................618 942-4572
Fax: 618 942-5253
Scott Aud, *Branch Mgr*
EMP: 6
SALES (corp-wide): 11.6MM Privately Held
SIC: 3273 5211 Ready-mixed concrete; masonry materials & supplies
PA: Odum Concrete Products, Inc
1800 N Court St
Marion IL 62959
618 993-6211

**(G-11752)**
**ORTHOTECH SPORTS - MED EQP INC (PA)**
Also Called: Intek Strength
1211 Weaver Rd (62948-2621)
P.O. Box 430 (62948-0430)
PHONE..................................618 942-6611
Fax: 618 942-6612
Jim Vigiano, *President*
Jim Sprague, *Sales Mgr*
John Allsopp, *Sales Staff*
Justin Vancil, *Manager*
Randy Dawson, *Admin Sec*
▲ EMP: 15
SQ FT: 2,000
SALES: 6MM Privately Held
WEB: www.orthotechsports.com
SIC: 5091 3949 Fitness equipment & supplies; dumbbells & other weightlifting equipment

**(G-11753)**
**ROTH NEON SIGN COMPANY INC**
Also Called: Roth Sign Company
1100 N 13th St (62948-2813)
P.O. Box 610 (62948-0610)
PHONE..................................618 942-6378
Fax: 618 988-8850
Daniel Roth, *President*
Joy Roth, *Corp Secy*
David Roth, *Vice Pres*
EMP: 9
SQ FT: 7,000
SALES (est): 1.2MM Privately Held
SIC: 5046 1799 3993 Signs, electrical; sign installation & maintenance; signs, not made in custom sign painting shops

**(G-11754)**
**SAMUEL ROWELL**
Also Called: Rowell Pure Water
2817 S Park Ave (62948-3700)
PHONE..................................618 942-6970
Samuel Rowell, *Owner*
EMP: 3
SALES (est): 223.5K Privately Held
SIC: 2899 5999 5963 Distilled water; water purification equipment; bottled water delivery

# Herrin - Williamson County (G-11755)

**(G-11755)**
**SOLLAMI COMPANY**
1200 Weaver Rd  (62948-2626)
P.O. Box 627  (62948-0627)
PHONE.....................618 988-1521
Fax: 618 942-5367
Phillip A Sollami, *President*
Joanne Sollami, *Corp Secy*
Jim Sollami, *Vice Pres*
Julie Griffin, *Sales Staff*
▲ EMP: 20
SQ FT: 50,000
SALES (est): 4.2MM  **Privately Held**
WEB: www.sollamico.com
SIC: 3599  3546  3545  3532  Machine shop, jobbing & repair; power-driven handtools; machine tool accessories; mining machinery

**(G-11756)**
**SOUTHERN ILL WILBERT VLT CO**
2221 N Park Ave  (62948-3039)
PHONE.....................618 942-5845
Fax: 618 942-5846
Betty Humphrey, *President*
Dennis Sanders, *Vice Pres*
David Sanders, *Treasurer*
Pat King, *Admin Sec*
EMP: 17 EST: 1948
SALES (est): 1.8MM  **Privately Held**
SIC: 3272  5087  Burial vaults, concrete or precast terrazzo; concrete burial vaults & boxes

**(G-11757)**
**SOUTHERN ILLINOIS VAULT CO INC**
2221 N Park Ave  (62948-3039)
PHONE.....................270 554-4436
EMP: 5
SALES (est): 746.3K  **Privately Held**
SIC: 3272  Concrete products

**(G-11758)**
**WICOFF INC**
Also Called: Sterling Mattress Factory
3201 S Park Ave  (62948-3711)
PHONE.....................618 988-8888
Michael Wicoff, *President*
EMP: 3
SQ FT: 10,000
SALES: 450K  **Privately Held**
SIC: 5712  2515  5021  Mattresses; mattresses & foundations; mattresses

## Herscher
### Kankakee County

**(G-11759)**
**L & N STRUCTURES INC (PA)**
104 S Park Rd  (60941-9584)
P.O. Box 588  (60941-0588)
PHONE.....................815 426-2164
Leonard Tobey, *President*
Norm Riordan, *Vice Pres*
EMP: 20
SQ FT: 9,600
SALES (est): 2.8MM  **Privately Held**
SIC: 7353  3531  Heavy construction equipment rental; asphalt plant, including gravel-mix type

**(G-11760)**
**NATURAL GAS PIPELINE AMER LLC**
5611 S 12000w Rd  (60941-6031)
P.O. Box 97  (60941-0097)
PHONE.....................815 426-2151
Fax: 815 426-2350
Joe Laughlin, *Manager*
Joe McLaughlin, *Manager*
EMP: 16
SALES (corp-wide): 13B  **Publicly Held**
SIC: 4922  1311  8741  Pipelines, natural gas; storage, natural gas; natural gas production; management services
HQ: Natural Gas Pipeline Company Of America Llc
1001 Louisiana St
Houston TX 77002
713 369-9000

**(G-11761)**
**PILOT TOWNSHIP ROAD DISTRICT**
300 E Kankakee Ave  (60941-6153)
P.O. Box 394  (60941-0394)
PHONE.....................815 426-6221
Basil Kilbreth, *Vice Pres*
EMP: 6
SALES (est): 795.8K  **Privately Held**
SIC: 3531  Road construction & maintenance machinery

**(G-11762)**
**STREATOR ASPHALT INC (HQ)**
104 S Park Rd  (60941-9584)
P.O. Box 588  (60941-0588)
PHONE.....................815 426-2164
Norman C Riordan, *President*
Leonard J Tobey, *Admin Sec*
EMP: 3
SQ FT: 4,200
SALES (est): 2.5MM
SALES (corp-wide): 2.8MM  **Privately Held**
SIC: 3531  Asphalt plant, including gravel-mix type
PA: L & N Structures Inc
104 S Park Rd
Herscher IL 60941
815 426-2164

**(G-11763)**
**T & E ENTERPRISES HERSCHER INC**
Also Called: T & E Auto Haulers
80 Tobey Dr  (60941-9472)
P.O. Box 237  (60941-0237)
PHONE.....................815 426-2761
Fax: 815 426-2875
Earl Datweiler, *President*
Todd Datweiler, *Treasurer*
EMP: 15
SQ FT: 16,000
SALES (est): 2.7MM  **Privately Held**
WEB: www.tande-racetrailers.com
SIC: 3799  3537  Automobile trailer chassis; industrial trucks & tractors

## Heyworth
### Mclean County

**(G-11764)**
**ASSEMBLE AND MAIL GROUP INC**
508 S Buchanan St  (61745-7689)
P.O. Box 235  (61745-0235)
PHONE.....................309 473-2006
Lisa Gambrel, *President*
Brian Smith, *Vice Pres*
EMP: 7
SQ FT: 20,000
SALES (est): 938.6K  **Privately Held**
WEB: www.assembleandmailgroup.com
SIC: 7331  2678  2782  7389  Addressing service; mailing service; mailing list management; mailing list brokers; stationery products; blankbooks & looseleaf binders; cosmetic kits, assembling & packaging

**(G-11765)**
**RANDOLPH AGRICULTURAL SERVICES**
15125 E 625 North Rd  (61745-7567)
PHONE.....................309 473-3256
Fax: 309 473-3710
Dee Hamilton, *President*
Richard Graves, *Treasurer*
Robert Anderson, *Director*
Virgil Harbaugh, *Director*
Ted Nixon, *Director*
EMP: 8
SQ FT: 1,500
SALES (est): 2.1MM  **Privately Held**
SIC: 5191  2875  Fertilizer & fertilizer materials; chemicals, agricultural; fertilizers, mixing only

**(G-11766)**
**TATE LYLE INGRDNTS AMRICAS LLC**
Also Called: Tate and Lyle
702 S Vine St  (61745-9179)
P.O. Box 200  (61745-0200)
PHONE.....................309 473-2721
Bruce Basterd, *Branch Mgr*
EMP: 5
SALES (corp-wide): 3.4B  **Privately Held**
WEB: www.aestaley.com
SIC: 2046  2869  2048  Wet corn milling; industrial organic chemicals; poultry feeds
HQ: Tate & Lyle Ingredients Americas Llc
2200 E Eldorado St
Decatur IL 62521
217 423-4411

## Hickory Hills
### Cook County

**(G-11767)**
**BZ BEARING & POWER INC (PA)**
8731 Orchard Dr  (60457-1368)
PHONE.....................877 850-3993
Robert M Zweig, *President*
Jeanne Cloonan Zweig, *Admin Sec*
EMP: 2
SALES: 1.5MM  **Privately Held**
SIC: 5084  3641  Food industry machinery; lead-in wires, electric lamp made from purchased wire

**(G-11768)**
**CADORE-MILLER PRINTING INC**
9901 S 78th Ave  (60457-2334)
PHONE.....................708 430-7091
Fax: 708 430-5989
John Miller, *President*
Audrey Bednarz, *Vice Pres*
EMP: 10
SQ FT: 21,900
SALES (est): 1.6MM  **Privately Held**
WEB: www.cadoremiller.com
SIC: 2752  2789  Commercial printing, offset; bookbinding & related work

**(G-11769)**
**DOMINOS PASTRIES INC**
Also Called: Domino's Pastry Shop
7731 W 98th St Ste E  (60457-2371)
PHONE.....................773 889-3549
Vincent Claps, *President*
Vito Claps, *Vice Pres*
Joe Nolfi, *Accountant*
EMP: 8
SQ FT: 2,880
SALES (est): 785.6K  **Privately Held**
WEB: www.dominospastries.com
SIC: 2051  Bread, cake & related products

**(G-11770)**
**HEAVENLY ENTERPRISES**
8401 S 85th Ct  (60457-1007)
P.O. Box 116, Flossmoor  (60422-0116)
PHONE.....................773 783-2981
Marilyn Alexander, *Principal*
EMP: 2 EST: 2014
SALES (est): 205.4K  **Privately Held**
SIC: 2752  Commercial printing, lithographic

**(G-11771)**
**INFAMOUS INDUSTRIES INC**
9253 S 89th Ct  (60457-1626)
PHONE.....................708 789-2326
Vincent Matonis, *President*
EMP: 3
SALES (est): 90.5K  **Privately Held**
SIC: 3999  Manufacturing industries

**(G-11772)**
**KEVRON PRINTING & DESIGN INC**
9831 S 78th Ave Ste F  (60457-2370)
PHONE.....................708 229-7725
Kevin D Domenick, *President*
Ronald Longanecker, *Admin Sec*
EMP: 6
SQ FT: 2,400
SALES (est): 1.1MM  **Privately Held**
SIC: 2759  7331  Commercial printing; mailing service

**(G-11773)**
**MINUTEMAN PRESS**
8330 W 95th St Apt 1  (60457-3804)
PHONE.....................708 598-4915
Fax: 708 233-1273
Judy Riedel, *Owner*
EMP: 3
SALES (est): 263K  **Privately Held**
SIC: 2752  Commercial printing, lithographic

**(G-11774)**
**SMART CHOICE MOBILE INC (PA)**
Also Called: T-Mobile
7667 W 95th St Ste 300  (60457-2284)
PHONE.....................708 581-4904
Bassel Joudeh, *President*
EMP: 11
SALES (est): 5.9MM  **Privately Held**
SIC: 3661  Telephone sets, all types except cellular radio

## Highland
### Madison County

**(G-11775)**
**AIRCRAFT PLYWOOD MFG INC**
806 Cedar St  (62249-1307)
P.O. Box 133  (62249-0133)
PHONE.....................618 654-6740
Jerome Hediger, *President*
▲ EMP: 3
SQ FT: 120
SALES (est): 200K  **Privately Held**
SIC: 2435  Hardwood veneer & plywood

**(G-11776)**
**CABINET GALLERY LLC**
205 Madison St  (62249-1318)
PHONE.....................618 882-4801
Paul Ray Capelle,
Marjorie Capelle,
EMP: 4
SALES (est): 473.5K  **Privately Held**
SIC: 2521  Wood office filing cabinets & bookcases

**(G-11777)**
**CCO HOLDINGS LLC**
2762 Troxler Way  (62249-1160)
PHONE.....................618 651-6486
EMP: 3
SALES (corp-wide): 29B  **Publicly Held**
SIC: 5064  4841  3663  3651  Electrical appliances, television & radio; cable & other pay television services; radio & TV communications equipment; household audio & video equipment
HQ: Cco Holdings, Llc
400 Atlantic St
Stamford CT 06901
203 905-7801

**(G-11778)**
**CENTRAL RBR EXTRUSIONS ILL INC**
193 Woodcrest Dr Dre  (62249-1268)
PHONE.....................618 654-1171
Sharon Ammann, *President*
Steve Sanvi, *Manager*
Michael Ammann, *Admin Sec*
EMP: 3
SALES (est): 842.8K  **Privately Held**
SIC: 3069  Molded rubber products

**(G-11779)**
**CHEVRON COMMERCIAL INC**
3545 George St  (62249-2845)
P.O. Box 99  (62249-0099)
PHONE.....................618 654-5555
Fax: 618 654-6813
Bill Cunagin, *President*
Teffy Price, *Administration*
EMP: 1
SALES (est): 220K  **Privately Held**
WEB: www.chevroncommercial.com
SIC: 3537  1796  Industrial trucks & tractors; installing building equipment

## (G-11780)
### COOPER B-LINE INC (DH)
Also Called: Eaton
509 W Monroe St (62249-1331)
P.O. Box 182368, Columbus OH (43218-2368)
PHONE..................................618 654-2184
Fax: 618 654-5907
Richard H Fearon, *President*
Ken Walma, *General Mgr*
Kevin C Kissling, *Principal*
Todd Davis, *Senior VP*
David Boyer, *Vice Pres*
◆ EMP: 600 EST: 1971
SQ FT: 300,000
SALES (est): 374.7MM **Privately Held**
WEB: www.cooperbline.com
SIC: 3441 3443 3452 3444 Fabricated structural metal; cable trays, metal plate; bolts, nuts, rivets & washers; sheet metalwork; manufactured hardware (general); nonferrous rolling & drawing
HQ: Eaton Electric Holdings Llc
600 Travis St Ste 5600
Houston TX 77002
713 209-8400

## (G-11781)
### CREDIT & MANAGEMENT SYSTEMS
13648 Alpine Way (62249-5062)
PHONE..................................618 654-3500
John Sargent, *CEO*
EMP: 11
SALES (corp-wide): 2MM **Privately Held**
WEB: www.icmsglobal.com
SIC: 7372 Prepackaged software
PA: Credit & Management Systems Inc
49 Sherwood Ter Ste E
Lake Bluff IL 60044
847 735-9700

## (G-11782)
### D W MACHINE PRODUCTS INC
1111 6th St (62249-1408)
PHONE..................................618 654-2161
Donald E Weder, *President*
EMP: 6
SALES (est): 470K **Privately Held**
SIC: 3497 Metal foil & leaf

## (G-11783)
### DIGITAL ARTZ LLC
Also Called: Imageworks Creative Group
188 Woodcrest Dr (62249-1266)
PHONE..................................618 651-1500
Christian Ebl, *Exec Dir*
Chris Ebl,
Garrett Rquayate,
EMP: 6 EST: 1997
SALES (est): 605.3K **Privately Held**
WEB: www.imageworksusa.com
SIC: 3993 Signs & advertising specialties

## (G-11784)
### DOW JONES & COMPANY INC
915 Hemlock St (62249-1329)
PHONE..................................618 651-2300
Fax: 618 651-2327
Chris Galassini, *Sales/Mktg Mgr*
Tim Goldsbury, *Manager*
Dieter Holtzbrinck, *Manager*
EMP: 30
SALES (corp-wide): 8.2B **Publicly Held**
SIC: 2711 Newspapers
HQ: Dow Jones & Company, Inc.
1211 Avenue Of The Americ
New York NY 10036
609 627-2999

## (G-11785)
### ELITE POWER BOATS INC
3645 George St (62249-2865)
PHONE..................................618 654-6292
Fax: 618 654-6292
Albert Meinen Jr, *President*
Cynthia Meinen, *Treasurer*
EMP: 3 EST: 1992
SALES: 104K **Privately Held**
SIC: 3732 Boats, fiberglass: building & repairing

## (G-11786)
### GRANT J GRAPPERHAUS
470 Pike Dr E (62249-1775)
PHONE..................................618 410-4428
Grant J Grapperhaus, *Principal*
EMP: 2 EST: 2009
SALES (est): 213.5K **Privately Held**
SIC: 3537 Forklift trucks

## (G-11787)
### HIGHLAND JOURNAL PRINTING INC (PA)
1014 Laurel St (62249-1504)
P.O. Box 266 (62249-0266)
PHONE..................................618 654-4131
Fax: 618 654-7475
Keith A Federer, *President*
Kerry Federer, *Vice Pres*
Pam Schmitt, *Treasurer*
EMP: 3
SQ FT: 2,300
SALES (est): 343.2K **Privately Held**
SIC: 2759 Letterpress printing; card printing & engraving, except greeting; business forms: printing; invitation & stationery printing & engraving

## (G-11788)
### HIGHLAND MCH & SCREW PDTS CO
700 5th St (62249-1213)
PHONE..................................618 654-2103
Fax: 618 654-8016
Edwin M Frisse, *Ch of Bd*
William G Sullivan, *President*
Mike Herschbach, *Vice Pres*
Barb Bellm, *Human Res Dir*
Andy Sullivan, *Sales Associate*
EMP: 90 EST: 1944
SQ FT: 140,000
SALES (est): 18.5MM **Privately Held**
WEB: www.highlandmachine.com
SIC: 3599 3451 3594 3444 Machine shop, jobbing & repair; screw machine products; fluid power pumps & motors; sheet metalwork

## (G-11789)
### HIGHLAND MFG & SLS CO (PA)
Also Called: Highland Supply
1111 6th St (62249-1408)
PHONE..................................618 654-2161
Erwin H Weder, *Ch of Bd*
Donald E Weder, *President*
Bernard J Maliszewski, *Treasurer*
Wanda Weder, *Admin Sec*
▲ EMP: 60 EST: 1952
SQ FT: 15,000
SALES (est): 4.1MM **Privately Held**
SIC: 3081 Polyethylene film

## (G-11790)
### HIGHLAND NEWS LEADER
1 Woodcrest Prof Park (62249)
P.O. Box 427, Belleville (62222-0427)
PHONE..................................618 654-2366
Fax: 618 654-1181
Jane Dotson, *Manager*
EMP: 4
SALES (est): 220.1K **Privately Held**
SIC: 2711 Newspapers, publishing & printing

## (G-11791)
### HIGHLAND PRINTERS
907 Main St Stop 4 (62249-1549)
PHONE..................................618 654-5880
Fax: 618 654-3312
Steve Mahlandt, *Owner*
Charlie Depew, *Manager*
EMP: 2
SQ FT: 4,500
SALES: 285K **Privately Held**
SIC: 2752 2791 2789 Commercial printing, offset; typesetting; bookbinding & related work

## (G-11792)
### HIGHLAND SOUTHERN WIRE INC (PA)
Also Called: Highland Supply
1111 6th St (62249-1408)
PHONE..................................618 654-2161
Donald E Weder, *President*
Wanda M Weder, *Vice Pres*
EMP: 8
SQ FT: 75,000
SALES (est): 11.2MM **Privately Held**
SIC: 3312 3469 3496 Wire products, steel or iron; metal stampings; woven wire products

## (G-11793)
### HIGHLAND SPRING & SPECIALTY
150 Matter Dr (62249-1271)
PHONE..................................618 654-3831
Fax: 618 654-6201
Michael Kilgore, *President*
Patricia Lohman, *Opers Mgr*
Eunice Hediger, *Exec Dir*
EMP: 10
SQ FT: 10,000
SALES (est): 1.2MM **Privately Held**
SIC: 3495 3493 Wire springs; steel springs, except wire

## (G-11794)
### HIGHLAND SUPPLY CORPORATION (PA)
1111 6th St (62249-1408)
P.O. Box 1730, Redlands CA (92373-0542)
PHONE..................................618 654-2161
Fax: 618 654-3411
Donald Weder, *Ch of Bd*
Andrew Weder, *VP Opers*
Erwin Weder, *Opers Mgr*
Mike King, *Engineer*
Joe Burris, *Treasurer*
▲ EMP: 325 EST: 1937
SALES (est): 53.6MM **Privately Held**
WEB: www.hscorders.com
SIC: 3497 2672 3081 2891 Metal foil & leaf; coated & laminated paper; unsupported plastics film & sheet; adhesives & sealants; bags: plastic, laminated & coated

## (G-11795)
### HIGHLAND WIRE INC (PA)
1111 6th St (62249-1408)
PHONE..................................618 654-2161
Donald E Weder, *President*
EMP: 13
SQ FT: 15,000
SALES (est): 1.4MM **Privately Held**
SIC: 3315 Wire & fabricated wire products

## (G-11796)
### HOLT PUBLICATIONS INC
12047 Travis Ln (62249-3855)
PHONE..................................618 654-6206
Stephen L Holt, *CEO*
Terri Holt, *President*
EMP: 6
SALES: 500K **Privately Held**
SIC: 2741 Miscellaneous publishing

## (G-11797)
### HOME & LEISURE LIFESTYLES LLC
907 Washington St (62249-1644)
P.O. Box 194 (62249-0194)
PHONE..................................618 651-0358
Fax: 618 654-1328
Tom Vice,
EMP: 3
SQ FT: 4,200
SALES (est): 333.6K **Privately Held**
SIC: 3631 Barbecues, grills & braziers (outdoor cooking)

## (G-11798)
### JERRY H SIMPSON
Also Called: Jerry's Tackle Shop
604 12th St (62249-1820)
PHONE..................................618 654-3235
Fax: 618 654-5579
Jerry H Simpson, *Owner*
EMP: 3
SQ FT: 2,280
SALES: 420K **Privately Held**
SIC: 5961 5941 3949 5091 Fishing, hunting & camping equipment & supplies: mail order; bait & tackle; hunting equipment; lures, fishing: artificial; fishing equipment & supplies

## (G-11799)
### JOYCE GREINER
Also Called: Chocolate Affair
801 9th St (62249-1521)
PHONE..................................618 654-9340
Joyce Greiner, *Owner*
EMP: 5
SALES: 125K **Privately Held**
SIC: 2066 Chocolate & cocoa products

## (G-11800)
### KESSMANNS CABINET SHOP & CNSTR
Also Called: Kessmann General Construction
2679 Vulliet Rd (62249-3839)
PHONE..................................618 654-2538
Steve Kessman, *Owner*
EMP: 2
SALES (est): 200K **Privately Held**
SIC: 2434 2521 Wood kitchen cabinets; cabinets, office: wood

## (G-11801)
### KORTE MEAT PROCESSING INC
810 Deal St (62249-1313)
PHONE..................................618 654-3813
David Korte, *President*
Ruth Richter, *Vice Pres*
EMP: 9
SALES (est): 3.2MM **Privately Held**
SIC: 5147 0751 5421 4222 Meats, fresh; slaughtering: custom livestock services; meat markets, including freezer provisioners; storage, frozen or refrigerated goods; sausages & other prepared meats; meat packing plants

## (G-11802)
### MCCLATCHY NEWSPAPERS INC
Also Called: Highlandnews Leader
1 Woodcrest Prof Park (62249)
PHONE..................................618 654-2366
Mary Connors, *Senior VP*
Jane Dotson, *Branch Mgr*
EMP: 95
SALES (corp-wide): 977MM **Publicly Held**
WEB: www.sacbee.com
SIC: 2711 Newspapers
HQ: Mcclatchy Newspapers, Inc.
2100 Q St
Sacramento CA 95816
916 321-1000

## (G-11803)
### MOTOR SPORT MARKETING GROUP
Also Called: McGinley Kawasaki
7 Shamrock Blvd (62249-1174)
P.O. Box 278 (62249-0278)
PHONE..................................618 654-6750
Fax: 618 654-4560
Timothy McGinley, *President*
Tim McGinley, *Manager*
Bonnie McGinley, *Admin Sec*
EMP: 20
SALES (est): 2.2MM **Privately Held**
SIC: 5511 3699 Automobiles, new & used; electrical equipment & supplies

## (G-11804)
### MOUNT VERNON MILLS
Also Called: Regal Linen
1001 Main St (62249-1685)
PHONE..................................618 882-6300
Bill Josey, *President*
Debbie A Zobrist, *Site Mgr*
EMP: 3
SALES (est): 160.7K **Privately Held**
SIC: 2269 Embossing: linen broadwoven fabrics

## (G-11805)
### PATTY STYLE SHOP
Also Called: Patty's Style Shop
621 Broadway Apt 1 (62249-1855)
PHONE..................................618 654-2015
Pat Frey, *Owner*
EMP: 4
SQ FT: 7,000
SALES (est): 95.8K **Privately Held**
SIC: 7231 6513 3648 Cosmetology & personal hygiene salons; apartment building operators; sun tanning equipment, incl. tanning beds

# Highland - Madison County (G-11806)

**(G-11806)**
**PROINTEGRATION TECH LLC**
13348 Koch Rd (62249-4548)
PHONE.................................618 409-3233
Sheri L Eveland, *Principal*
James Eveland, *Co-Owner*
**EMP:** 1
**SALES:** 370K **Privately Held**
**SIC:** 3842 Personal safety equipment

**(G-11807)**
**QUALITY FILTER SERVICES**
14446 Baumann Rd (62249-5100)
PHONE.................................618 654-3716
Fax: 618 654-3716
Anthony Tebbe, *Owner*
**EMP:** 3
**SQ FT:** 1,000
**SALES:** 600K **Privately Held**
**SIC:** 3585 5075 Refrigeration & heating equipment; warm air heating & air conditioning; air filters

**(G-11808)**
**RED-E-MIX LLC**
405 Main St (62249-1328)
PHONE.................................618 654-2166
David Nepereny, *President*
David Howell, *Credit Mgr*
Suzanne Burns, *Services*
**EMP:** 82 **EST:** 2007
**SALES (est):** 12.8MM
**SALES (corp-wide):** 271.5MM **Privately Held**
**SIC:** 3251 Brick clay: common face, glazed, vitrified or hollow
**HQ:** Midwest Material Industries Inc.
100 Brodhead Rd Ste 230
Bethlehem PA 18017
610 882-5000

**(G-11809)**
**RED-E-MIX TRANSPORTATION LLC**
405 Main St (62249-1328)
PHONE.................................618 654-2166
David Nepereny, *President*
**EMP:** 25
**SALES (est):** 2.4MM
**SALES (corp-wide):** 271.5MM **Privately Held**
**SIC:** 3241 Portland cement
**HQ:** Midwest Material Industries Inc.
100 Brodhead Rd Ste 230
Bethlehem PA 18017
610 882-5000

**(G-11810)**
**SCHANTZ MFG INC**
13480 Us Highway 40 (62249-4852)
PHONE.................................618 654-1523
Michael Schantz, *President*
Ken Tharp, *Opers Mgr*
Lisa Schantz, *Admin Sec*
Terrie Fohne, *Admin Asst*
**EMP:** 25
**SQ FT:** 20,000
**SALES (est):** 5.3MM **Privately Held**
**SIC:** 3715 Truck trailers

**(G-11811)**
**SHOPPERS REVIEW**
1200 12th St (62249-1909)
P.O. Box 96 (62249-0096)
PHONE.................................618 654-4459
Jeff W Stratton, *Owner*
Roger Walker, *CTO*
**EMP:** 17
**SALES (est):** 705K **Privately Held**
**SIC:** 2741 Shopping news: publishing only, not printed on site

**(G-11812)**
**SOUTHERN STEEL AND WIRE INC (HQ)**
1111 6th St (62249-1408)
PHONE.................................618 654-2161
Don Weder, *President*
David Kendrick, *Vice Pres*
Joe Burris, *Treasurer*
John Culkle, *Controller*
▲ **EMP:** 5
**SQ FT:** 40,000
**SALES (est):** 11.2MM **Privately Held**
**SIC:** 3544 3312 3496 Wire drawing & straightening dies; wire products, steel or iron; woven wire products
**PA:** Highland Southern Wire, Inc
1111 6th St
Highland IL 62249
618 654-2161

**(G-11813)**
**TRI FAMILY OIL CO (PA)**
2103 Saint Michael Ct N (62249-2340)
P.O. Box 271 (62249-0271)
PHONE.................................618 654-1137
Joseph A Fennell, *President*
Deb Fennell, *Vice Pres*
Jan White, *Admin Sec*
**EMP:** 2
**SALES (est):** 500.7K **Privately Held**
**SIC:** 1311 Crude petroleum production

**(G-11814)**
**TROUW NUTRITION USA LLC**
145 Matter Dr (62249-1354)
PHONE.................................618 651-1521
Monty Barker, *General Mgr*
**EMP:** 30 **Privately Held**
**SIC:** 2048 Prepared feeds
**HQ:** Trouw Nutrition Usa, Llc
115 Executive Dr
Highland IL 62249
618 654-2070

**(G-11815)**
**TROUW NUTRITION USA LLC (DH)**
115 Executive Dr (62249-1269)
P.O. Box 219 (62249-0219)
PHONE.................................618 654-2070
Jay Clary, *Vice Pres*
Ron Sette, *Opers Mgr*
Judy Booth, *Credit Staff*
Mike Hooper, *Mktg Dir*
Lesley Burkett, *Marketing Staff*
▲ **EMP:** 40 **EST:** 2001
**SQ FT:** 10,388
**SALES (est):** 59.4MM **Privately Held**
**WEB:** www.trouw-nutritionusa.com
**SIC:** 2048 Prepared feeds
**HQ:** Nutreco N.V.
Stationsstraat 77
Amersfoort
334 226-100

**(G-11816)**
**TROUW NUTRITION USA LLC**
1 Ultraway Dr (62249-1241)
PHONE.................................618 654-2070
Karo Mikaelian, *Vice Pres*
Dan Rose, *Branch Mgr*
Thomas R Best, *Director*
**EMP:** 20
**SQ FT:** 35,000 **Privately Held**
**WEB:** www.trouw-nutritionusa.com
**SIC:** 2048 Prepared feeds
**HQ:** Trouw Nutrition Usa, Llc
115 Executive Dr
Highland IL 62249
618 654-2070

**(G-11817)**
**TROUW NUTRITION USA LLC**
145 Matter Dr (62249-1354)
PHONE.................................618 654-2070
Dan Rose, *Principal*
Sarah Furr, *Research*
**EMP:** 20
**SQ FT:** 37,000 **Privately Held**
**WEB:** www.trouw-nutritionusa.com
**SIC:** 2048 Prepared feeds
**HQ:** Trouw Nutrition Usa, Llc
115 Executive Dr
Highland IL 62249
618 654-2070

**(G-11818)**
**WESTROCK CP LLC**
501 Zschokke St (62249-1460)
P.O. Box 190 (62249-0190)
PHONE.................................618 654-2141
James Burdiss, *Vice Pres*
Dean Frey, *Plant Supt*
Dan Atterberry, *Sales Mgr*
Jerry McGraw, *Branch Mgr*
Kevin Karlson, *Manager*
**EMP:** 120
**SALES (corp-wide):** 14.1B **Publicly Held**
**WEB:** www.smurfit-stone.com
**SIC:** 2653 Corrugated & solid fiber boxes
**HQ:** Westrock Cp, Llc
504 Thrasher St
Norcross GA 30071

**(G-11819)**
**WICKS ORGAN COMPANY**
Also Called: Wicks Pipe Organ Company
416 Pine St (62249-1243)
PHONE.................................618 654-2191
Fax: 618 654-3770
Barbara Wick, *Ch of Bd*
Mark H Wick, *President*
Dorothy Kossakowski, *Controller*
Dave Ressler, *Associate*
▲ **EMP:** 29 **EST:** 1906
**SQ FT:** 140,000
**SALES (est):** 4.3MM **Privately Held**
**WEB:** www.wicks.com
**SIC:** 3931 2511 Pipes, organ; wood household furniture

## Highland Park
### Lake County

**(G-11820)**
**A LA CART INC**
1490 Old Deerfield Rd # 18 (60035-3048)
PHONE.................................847 256-4102
Fax: 847 256-0387
Wade Moyer, *President*
A J Spuria, *Chairman*
Wayne Martin, *Senior VP*
Kendra Handlon, *Vice Pres*
Bill Champion, *Engineer*
**EMP:** 20
**SQ FT:** 21,000
**SALES (est):** 2.5MM **Privately Held**
**WEB:** www.alacartinc.com
**SIC:** 3589 Commercial cooking & food-warming equipment

**(G-11821)**
**ABOUT FACE DESIGNS INC**
1510 Old Deerfield Rd # 211 (60035-3070)
PHONE.................................847 914-9040
Fax: 847 914-9041
Robert J Ricciardi, *President*
▲ **EMP:** 5
**SQ FT:** 24,200
**SALES (est):** 788.2K **Privately Held**
**WEB:** www.aboutfacedesigns.net
**SIC:** 3499 Novelties & giftware, including trophies

**(G-11822)**
**ACME AWNING CO**
1500 Old Deerfield Rd # 21 (60035-3067)
P.O. Box 23, Winnetka (60093-0023)
PHONE.................................847 446-0153
Kristopher Arends, *President*
Alyce Arends, *Vice Pres*
**EMP:** 3 **EST:** 1935
**SALES (est):** 419.8K **Privately Held**
**SIC:** 5211 2394 Roofing material; canvas & related products

**(G-11823)**
**AMER NITROGEN CO**
184 Leonard Wood S # 107 (60035-5950)
PHONE.................................847 681-1068
James Horstman, *Principal*
**EMP:** 3 **EST:** 2001
**SALES (est):** 174.6K **Privately Held**
**SIC:** 2813 Nitrogen

**(G-11824)**
**BARCOR INC**
1510 Old Deerfield Rd # 206 (60035-3071)
P.O. Box 517, Northbrook (60065-0517)
PHONE.................................847 831-2650
Judy Baria, *President*
Ed Baria, *Vice Pres*
**EMP:** 10
**SALES:** 1MM **Privately Held**
**SIC:** 3829 Measuring & controlling devices

**(G-11825)**
**BKA INC**
Also Called: Imaging Equipment Sales
1999 Castlewood Rd (60035-2907)
PHONE.................................847 831-3535
Barry Ades, *President*
**EMP:** 4
**SALES:** 230K **Privately Held**
**WEB:** www.bka.com
**SIC:** 3861 Photographic equipment & supplies

**(G-11826)**
**CAIBROS AMERICAS LLC**
116 Deere Park Ct (60035-5309)
PHONE.................................312 593-3128
Doreen Tho,
**EMP:** 3
**SALES (est):** 240K **Privately Held**
**SIC:** 2911 Fuel additives

**(G-11827)**
**CIRCLE STUDIO STAINED GLASS**
946 Central Ave (60035-5624)
PHONE.................................847 432-7249
Joseph Badalpour, *President*
**EMP:** 4
**SALES:** 300.8K **Privately Held**
**SIC:** 1793 3471 3231 Glass & glazing work; plating & polishing; products of purchased glass

**(G-11828)**
**CLIQSTER LLC**
212 Pine Point Dr (60035-5335)
PHONE.................................847 732-1457
Nicholas Wieczorek, *CEO*
**EMP:** 5
**SALES (est):** 257.7K **Privately Held**
**SIC:** 7372 Application computer software; business oriented computer software

**(G-11829)**
**CREATIVE MACHINING TECH LLC**
1949 Saint Johns Ave # 200 (60035-3105)
PHONE.................................309 755-7700
Jonathan Canel, *Managing Dir*
Scott Canel,
▲ **EMP:** 100
**SQ FT:** 115,000
**SALES (est):** 18.3MM **Privately Held**
**WEB:** www.cmtinc.us
**SIC:** 3599 Machine shop, jobbing & repair

**(G-11830)**
**EISENDRATH INC**
Also Called: Signs Now
716 Central Ave Apt B (60035-3294)
PHONE.................................847 432-3899
Sharon Eisendrath, *President*
Peter Eisendrath, *Vice Pres*
**EMP:** 6
**SALES (est):** 340K **Privately Held**
**WEB:** www.thecoinsaver.com
**SIC:** 3993 Signs & advertising specialties

**(G-11831)**
**F & F PUBLISHING INC**
144 Sheridan Rd (60035-5358)
PHONE.................................847 480-0330
Jerry Margolis, *President*
Robert Fink, *Vice Pres*
Don Nelson, *Purch Agent*
**EMP:** 4
**SALES (est):** 280K **Privately Held**
**SIC:** 2759 2741 Promotional printing; miscellaneous publishing

**(G-11832)**
**FASHION CRAFT CORPORATION**
1421 Old Deerfield Rd (60035-3025)
PHONE.................................847 998-0092
Robert Blank, *President*
Stanley Kramer, *Vice Pres*
**EMP:** 20
**SQ FT:** 4,500
**SALES (est):** 2.2MM **Privately Held**
**SIC:** 3911 Rings, finger: precious metal; earrings, precious metal; bracelets, precious metal; pins (jewelry), precious metal

## GEOGRAPHIC SECTION

### (G-11833)
**FORCERL**
1350 Forest Ave (60035-3457)
PHONE....................847 432-7588
Robert Pascal, *Principal*
**EMP: 2 EST:** 2010
**SALES (est):** 211.8K **Privately Held**
**SIC: 2752** Commercial printing, lithographic

### (G-11834)
**G-FAST DISTRIBUTION INC**
Also Called: Mrgfastman
1954 1st St 228 (60035-3104)
PHONE....................847 926-0722
**Fax:** 847 919-3855
Steve Greenberg, *President*
Suzanne Piazza, *Sls & Mktg Exec*
**EMP:** 2
**SQ FT:** 1,000
**SALES (est):** 322.6K **Privately Held**
**SIC: 3452** Bolts, nuts, rivets & washers

### (G-11835)
**GELATO ENTERPRISES LLC**
Also Called: Frost A Glato Shpp-Highland Pk
617 Central Ave (60035-3265)
PHONE....................847 432-2233
Edward G Bruksch,
**EMP:** 11
**SALES (est):** 972.1K **Privately Held**
**SIC: 2024** Ice cream & frozen desserts

### (G-11836)
**GOOD IMPRESSIONS INC**
3150 Skokie Valley Rd # 24 (60035-1079)
PHONE....................847 831-4317
Tom Lamonda, *President*
Linda Lamonda, *Vice Pres*
**EMP:** 6
**SQ FT:** 8,000
**SALES (est):** 681K **Privately Held**
**SIC: 2759** 2396 Commercial printing; automotive & apparel trimmings

### (G-11837)
**GOURMET FROG PASTRY SHOP**
316 Green Bay Rd (60035)
PHONE....................847 433-7038
Terry Lese, *Owner*
**EMP:** 5
**SALES (est):** 292K **Privately Held**
**SIC: 2051** Bread, cake & related products

### (G-11838)
**GULF COAST EXPLORATION INC**
983 Harvard Ct (60035-2377)
PHONE....................847 226-4654
Joseph L Fieger, *President*
**EMP:** 5
**SALES (est):** 550K **Privately Held**
**SIC: 1311** Crude petroleum & natural gas production

### (G-11839)
**GVW GROUP LLC (PA)**
Also Called: Gvw Holdings
625 Roger Williams Ave (60035-4807)
PHONE....................847 681-8417
Eric Schwartz, *Managing Dir*
Andrew Taitz, *Chairman*
Jim Sicking, *Vice Pres*
James Maclaughlin, *CFO*
Stracey Wallraf, *Accountant*
▲ **EMP:** 8 **EST:** 2005
**SQ FT:** 1,000
**SALES (est):** 147.8MM **Privately Held**
**WEB:** www.gvwholdings.com
**SIC: 3713** Truck bodies (motor vehicles)

### (G-11840)
**HENRY BARON ENTERPRISES INC**
940 Augusta Way Apt 105 (60035-1838)
PHONE....................847 681-2755
Henry Baron, *President*
**EMP:** 2
**SALES (est):** 200K **Privately Held**
**SIC: 3231** 5051 Mirrored glass; mirrors, truck & automobile: made from purchased glass; metals service centers & offices

### (G-11841)
**HOWARD DISPLAYS INC**
844 Auburn Ct (60035-1123)
Howard A Jacobs, *President*
Roberta Jacobs, *Corp Secy*
James S Jacobs, *Vice Pres*
**EMP:** 10
**SQ FT:** 30,000
**SALES (est):** 450K **Privately Held**
**WEB:** www.howard-displays.com
**SIC: 3993** 7389 Signs & advertising specialties; exhibit construction by industrial contractors

### (G-11842)
**I C INNOVATIONS INC**
1101 Golf Ave (60035-3637)
P.O. Box 1263, Northbrook (60065-1263)
PHONE....................847 279-7888
Donald Gaule, *President*
Ronald Yermack, *Vice Pres*
▲ **EMP:** 4
**SQ FT:** 2,500
**SALES (est):** 498.4K **Privately Held**
**WEB:** www.platepals.com
**SIC: 3829** Thermometers & temperature sensors

### (G-11843)
**ILLUMINIGHT LIGHTING LLC**
1954 1st St 394 (60035-3104)
PHONE....................312 685-4448
Scott Parrish, *Principal*
**EMP:** 10
**SALES (est):** 692.4K **Privately Held**
**SIC: 3648** 7389 Lighting equipment;

### (G-11844)
**INVITATION CREATIONS INC**
580 Roger Williams Ave # 24 (60035-4823)
PHONE....................847 432-4441
Ellen Fiely, *President*
**EMP:** 2
**SALES (est):** 202.6K **Privately Held**
**SIC: 2759** Invitation & stationery printing & engraving

### (G-11845)
**J II INC**
Also Called: Aqua Belle Manufacturing Co
1292 Old Skokie Rd (60035-3035)
P.O. Box 496 (60035-0496)
PHONE....................847 432-8979
**Fax:** 847 433-3279
Ben Israel, *President*
Randy Amir, *General Mgr*
Dov Kahana, *Vice Pres*
Eileen Siegel, *CFO*
Judy Strauss, *Marketing Mgr*
**EMP:** 91
**SQ FT:** 15,000
**SALES (est):** 8.9MM **Privately Held**
**WEB:** www.aquabelle.com
**SIC: 3589** Water filters & softeners, household type

### (G-11846)
**J K PRINTING & MAILING INC**
2090 Green Bay Rd (60035-2482)
P.O. Box 1975 (60035-7975)
PHONE....................847 432-7717
**Fax:** 847 432-7325
Robert Stoeller, *President*
**EMP:** 4
**SQ FT:** 3,300
**SALES (est):** 500K **Privately Held**
**SIC: 7331** 2752 Addressing service; mailing service; commercial printing, offset

### (G-11847)
**JBL MARKETING INC**
1473 Chantilly Ct (60035-3926)
PHONE....................847 266-1080
Judith Levin, *President*
**EMP:** 3
**SALES (est):** 300K **Privately Held**
**SIC: 2759** Commercial printing

### (G-11848)
**K A & F GROUP LLC**
2680 Greenwood Ave (60035-1354)
PHONE....................847 780-4600
Bruce Flack,
Elyse Flack,
Anim Mysorewala,
▲ **EMP:** 4
**SQ FT:** 1,200
**SALES (est):** 507.3K **Privately Held**
**SIC: 2326** Work apparel, except uniforms

### (G-11849)
**KENS QUICK PRINT INC**
1500 Old Deerfield Rd # 5 (60035-3067)
PHONE....................847 831-4410
**Fax:** 847 831-4409
Kenneth Erlander, *President*
**EMP:** 10
**SQ FT:** 2,400
**SALES (est):** 1.6MM **Privately Held**
**SIC: 2752** 2791 2789 2759 Commercial printing, offset; typesetting; bookbinding & related work; commercial printing

### (G-11850)
**KEWAUNEE SCIENTIFIC CORP**
3150 Skokie Valley Rd # 8 (60035-1079)
P.O. Box 405, Evanston (60204-0405)
PHONE....................847 675-7744
Ken Wolf, *Manager*
**EMP:** 5
**SALES (corp-wide):** 128.6MM **Publicly Held**
**WEB:** www.kewaunee.com
**SIC: 3821** 2599 2541 2542 Laboratory furniture; worktables, laboratory; laboratory apparatus, except heating & measuring; laboratory equipment: fume hoods, distillation racks, etc.; factory furniture & fixtures; work benches, factory; cabinets, except refrigerated: show, display, etc.: wood; cabinets: show, display or storage: except wood
**PA:** Kewaunee Scientific Corporation
2700 W Front St
Statesville NC 28677
704 873-7202

### (G-11851)
**LAUREL INDUSTRIES INC**
Also Called: C R L
280 Laurel Ave (60035-2620)
PHONE....................847 432-8204
**Fax:** 847 432-8243
Carl R Lambrecht Jr, *President*
Catherine A Lambrecht, *Admin Sec*
**EMP:** 50
**SQ FT:** 4,000
**SALES (est):** 7.2MM **Privately Held**
**WEB:** www.laurelindustries.com
**SIC: 3827** Optical instruments & lenses

### (G-11852)
**LILY-CANADA HOLDING CORP (PA)**
1700 Old Deerfield Rd (60035-3000)
PHONE....................847 831-4800
Robert M Korzenski, *Principal*
**EMP:** 3
**SALES (est):** 175.5K **Privately Held**
**SIC: 3089** Cups, plastic, except foam; plates, plastic; plastic containers, except foam

### (G-11853)
**MELVIN WOLF AND ASSOCIATES INC**
956 Deerfield Rd (60035-3521)
PHONE....................847 433-9098
Marilyn W Hollander, *President*
**EMP:** 3 **EST:** 1961
**SQ FT:** 1,300
**SALES (est):** 570K **Privately Held**
**SIC: 5021** 2514 Household furniture; racks; shelving; beds, including folding & cabinet, household: metal; tables, household: metal

### (G-11854)
**MENONI & MOCOGNI INC**
2160 Skokie Valley Rd (60035-1731)
P.O. Box 128 (60035-0128)
PHONE....................847 432-0850
**Fax:** 847 432-3681
Mike Miotti, *President*
Danny Loizzo, *Vice Pres*
Anthony A Loizzo, *Admin Sec*
**EMP:** 11 **EST:** 1947
**SQ FT:** 5,000
**SALES (est):** 2.8MM **Privately Held**
**WEB:** www.menoni.com
**SIC: 5211** 3273 1442 Lumber & other building materials; ready-mixed concrete; construction sand & gravel

### (G-11855)
**MIZRAHI GRILL**
215 Skokie Valley Rd (60035-4405)
PHONE....................847 831-1400
Eliyahu Mizrahi, *Principal*
**EMP:** 11
**SALES (est):** 1.2MM **Privately Held**
**SIC: 2599** Bar, restaurant & cafeteria furniture

### (G-11856)
**MOLDED DISPLAYS**
739 Old Trail Rd (60035-1359)
PHONE....................773 892-4098
**EMP:** 3
**SALES (est):** 249.9K **Privately Held**
**SIC: 3089** Molding primary plastic

### (G-11857)
**MORTON GROUP LTD**
Also Called: Great Lakes Bag & Vinyl
1510 Old Deerfield Rd (60035-3068)
P.O. Box 1075 (60035-7075)
PHONE....................847 831-2766
Harrison Kranick, *President*
Ester Kranick, *Manager*
Howard Davis, *CTO*
Philip Fayer, *Administration*
▲ **EMP:** 5
**SQ FT:** 5,000
**SALES:** 6MM **Privately Held**
**WEB:** www.glbv.com
**SIC: 3081** 5199 Vinyl film & sheet; packaging materials

### (G-11858)
**MUTUAL SVCS HIGHLAND PK INC**
Also Called: Mutual Steel
2760 Skokie Valley Rd (60035-1043)
PHONE....................847 432-3815
**Fax:** 847 432-1018
Bruno Ori, *Branch Mgr*
**EMP:** 15
**SALES (corp-wide):** 14.1MM **Privately Held**
**SIC: 5051** 3441 Structural shapes, iron or steel; fabricated structural metal
**PA:** Mutual Services Of Highland Park, Inc.
1393 Half Day Rd
Highland Park IL 60035
847 432-0026

### (G-11859)
**NERD ISLAND STUDIOS LLC**
1347 Ferndale Ave (60035-2809)
PHONE....................224 619-5361
Chris Bruce, *Principal*
Christopher Bruce, *Principal*
**EMP:** 4 **EST:** 2012
**SALES (est):** 157.9K **Privately Held**
**SIC: 7372** Educational computer software; application computer software

### (G-11860)
**OPPORTUNITY INC**
1200 Old Skokie Rd (60035-3036)
P.O. Box 1349, Deerfield (60015-6005)
PHONE....................847 831-9400
**Fax:** 847 831-9418
Lawrence Rosser, *President*
**EMP:** 75
**SQ FT:** 150,000
**SALES (est):** 9.4MM **Privately Held**
**SIC: 3842** Surgical appliances & supplies

### (G-11861)
**POLYDESIGNS LTD**
731 Orleans Dr (60035-3915)
P.O. Box 522 (60035-0522)
PHONE....................847 433-9920
Ronald Morris, *Partner*
**EMP:** 2 **EST:** 1991
**SALES (est):** 215.3K **Privately Held**
**SIC: 3089** Plastic processing

# Highland Park - Lake County (G-11862)

**(G-11862)**
**PRINCETON CHEMICALS INC**
988 Princeton Ave (60035-2380)
P.O. Box 428 (60035-0428)
PHONE.................847 975-6210
Richard Small, *President*
EMP: 1 EST: 2015
SQ FT: 300
SALES: 1.5MM **Privately Held**
SIC: 2844 Toilet preparations

**(G-11863)**
**QUANTUM LEGAL LLC**
513 Central Ave (60035-2624)
PHONE.................847 433-4500
Richard J Burke, *Principal*
EMP: 4 EST: 2015
SALES (est): 264K **Privately Held**
SIC: 3572 Computer storage devices

**(G-11864)**
**R P GROLLMAN CO INC**
1811 Lawrence Ln (60035-4326)
P.O. Box 1080 (60035-7080)
PHONE.................847 607-0294
Ronald Grollman, *President*
EMP: 3
SALES (est): 302.5K **Privately Held**
SIC: 3565 Packaging machinery

**(G-11865)**
**RIBBON PRINT COMPANY**
Also Called: Ribbon Print USA
508 Central Ave Ste 208 (60035-3271)
PHONE.................847 421-8208
Sue C Monhait, *Principal*
▲ EMP: 2
SALES (est): 261.4K **Privately Held**
SIC: 2752 Commercial printing, lithographic

**(G-11866)**
**ROSS DESIGNS LTD**
210 Skokie Valley Rd # 5 (60035-4464)
PHONE.................847 831-7669
Mark Neumann, *President*
Abby Neumann, *Vice Pres*
EMP: 1
SALES: 250K **Privately Held**
SIC: 5944 3911 Jewelry stores; jewelry, precious metal

**(G-11867)**
**SAFERSONIC US INC**
2873 Arlington Ave # 110 (60035-1115)
PHONE.................847 274-1534
Leopold Lackner, *President*
David Seitelman, *Exec Dir*
▲ EMP: 3 EST: 2012
SALES: 500K **Privately Held**
SIC: 3829 Medical diagnostic systems, nuclear

**(G-11868)**
**SENIOR CARE PHARMACY LLC**
1630 Old Deerfield Rd # 202 (60035-3031)
PHONE.................847 579-0093
Sara Kass, *Office Mgr*
Mark Kass,
EMP: 5
SQ FT: 800
SALES: 100K **Privately Held**
SIC: 2834 Pharmaceutical preparations

**(G-11869)**
**SMART CREATIONS INC**
Also Called: Chelsea's Beads
1799 Saint Johns Ave (60035-3532)
PHONE.................847 433-3451
Fax: 847 681-0681
R Dubinsky, *President*
EMP: 8
SALES (est): 590.3K **Privately Held**
SIC: 5945 3961 Arts & crafts supplies; costume jewelry

**(G-11870)**
**SOFTLABZ CORPORATION (PA)**
1180 Saint Johns Ave (60035-3423)
PHONE.................847 780-7076
Olexiy Miroshnichenko, *President*
Olena Miroshnichenko, *CFO*
EMP: 2
SQ FT: 400
SALES: 440K **Privately Held**
SIC: 7372 Prepackaged software

**(G-11871)**
**SOLARSCOPE LLC**
1360 Old Skokie Rd Ste 2n (60035-3015)
PHONE.................847 579-0024
John Ermel,
EMP: 1
SALES (est): 200K **Privately Held**
SIC: 3827 Optical instruments & lenses

**(G-11872)**
**SOLO CUP INVESTMENT CORP (HQ)**
1700 Old Deerfield Rd (60035-3000)
PHONE.................847 831-4800
Robert M Korzenski, *CEO*
Ronald Whaley, *Principal*
Hans H Heinsen, *Exec VP*
Jessie Whiting, *QC Mgr*
Robert D Koney, *CFO*
▼ EMP: 38
SALES (est): 654.2MM
SALES (corp-wide): 734.8MM **Privately Held**
SIC: 3089 2656 3421 Cups, plastic, except foam; plates, plastic; plastic containers, except foam; straws, drinking: made from purchased material; cutlery
PA: Scc Holding Company Llc
150 Saunders Rd Ste 150
Lake Forest IL 60045
847 444-5000

**(G-11873)**
**STAR INDUSTRIES INC**
Also Called: Star Industries Intl Div
2210 Skokie Valley Rd (60035-1733)
P.O. Box 178, La Grange (60525-0178)
PHONE.................708 240-4862
Fax: 847 433-0818
Robert E Morris, *President*
Jake Van Der Kooy Jr, *Vice Pres*
Laura Peterson, *Office Mgr*
EMP: 20
SQ FT: 30,000
SALES (est): 2.5MM **Privately Held**
WEB: www.starhydrodyne.com
SIC: 3589 Floor washing & polishing machines, commercial

**(G-11874)**
**SUPERB PACKAGING INC**
659 Ridge Rd (60035-4362)
PHONE.................847 579-1870
Stephen Smiley, *President*
EMP: 5
SALES: 350K **Privately Held**
SIC: 3086 Packaging & shipping materials, foamed plastic

**(G-11875)**
**SWITCHEE BANDZ USA LLC**
Also Called: Switchee USA
804 Kimballwood Ln (60035-3624)
PHONE.................312 415-1100
Michael Spatz, *Principal*
EMP: 5
SALES (est): 605.8K **Privately Held**
SIC: 3679 Electronic switches

**(G-11876)**
**T2 SITE AMENITIES INCORPORATED**
1805 Spruce St (60035-2150)
PHONE.................847 579-9003
Lori Tilkin, *President*
Stephen L Tilkin, *Vice Pres*
▼ EMP: 5
SALES (est): 1.1MM **Privately Held**
WEB: www.t2-sa.com
SIC: 5084 2449 2531 5193 Recycling machinery & equipment; planters & window boxes, wood; benches for public buildings; planters & flower pots; office chairs, benches & stools, except wood; benches, office: except wood

**(G-11877)**
**TEAM SIDER INC**
Also Called: Greater Than
158 Hastings Ave (60035-5139)
PHONE.................847 767-0107
Jon Sider, *President*
Mark Sider, *Vice Pres*
EMP: 3

SALES: 450K **Privately Held**
SIC: 2086 7389 Mineral water, carbonated: packaged in cans, bottles, etc.;

**(G-11878)**
**TOTAL DESIGN JEWELRY INC**
Also Called: Total Design Fashion Jewelry
3100 Skokie Valley Rd 1n (60035-1080)
PHONE.................847 433-5333
Fax: 847 433-5386
Jeffrey Lieb, *President*
Marlene Lieb, *Admin Sec*
EMP: 2
SALES (est): 222.8K **Privately Held**
SIC: 3961 5094 Costume jewelry, ex. precious metal & semiprecious stones; jewelry

**(G-11879)**
**VRG CONTROLS LLC**
467 Ridge Rd (60035-4368)
PHONE.................773 230-1543
James M Garvey, *Principal*
EMP: 3 EST: 2012
SALES (est): 451.7K **Privately Held**
SIC: 3492 Control valves, fluid power: hydraulic & pneumatic

**(G-11880)**
**WAND ENTERPRISES INC (PA)**
Also Called: Wand Tool Company
1029 Green Bay Rd (60035-4000)
PHONE.................847 433-0231
William N Anderson, *President*
Nancy Corbett, *Corp Secy*
Thomas Anderson, *Vice Pres*
Dan Corbett, *Accountant*
EMP: 17
SQ FT: 14,000
SALES (est): 3.3MM **Privately Held**
WEB: www.wandtool.com
SIC: 3544 3672 Special dies, tools, jigs & fixtures; printed circuit boards

**(G-11881)**
**WAND TOOL ENTERPRISE**
1029 Green Bay Rd (60035-4000)
PHONE.................847 433-0231
Todd Anderson, *President*
EMP: 3
SALES (est): 220K **Privately Held**
SIC: 3544 Special dies, tools, jigs & fixtures

**(G-11882)**
**WORKHORSE CUSTOM CHASSIS LLC**
600 Central Ave Ste 220 (60035-3256)
PHONE.................765 964-4000
Fax: 847 681-8515
Andrew Taitz, *Manager*
EMP: 5
SALES (corp-wide): 8.1B **Publicly Held**
WEB: www.workhorse.com
SIC: 3711 Chassis, motor vehicle
HQ: Workhorse Custom Chassis, Llc
1675 E Whitcomb Ave
Madison Heights MI 48071
765 964-4000

**(G-11883)**
**WORLDWIDE SHRIMP COMPANY**
430 Park Ave Ste 2a (60035-2635)
P.O. Box 640 (60035-0640)
PHONE.................847 433-3500
John W Appelbaum, *President*
William Appelbaum, *Webmaster*
William L Appelbaum, *Admin Sec*
Lulu Shrimp, *Administration*
▲ EMP: 22
SALES (est): 4.8MM **Privately Held**
SIC: 2092 Shrimp, frozen: prepared

### Highwood
*Lake County*

**(G-11884)**
**DORIS BRIDAL BOUTIQUE**
448 Sheridan Rd Ste 1 (60040-1344)
PHONE.................847 433-2575
Fax: 847 433-2659
Doris Lindqvist, *Partner*
Annette Hebel, *Partner*

EMP: 6
SQ FT: 4,000
SALES (est): 876.6K **Privately Held**
WEB: www.dorisbridal.com
SIC: 2335 5621 Bridal & formal gowns; bridal shops

**(G-11885)**
**I KUSTOM CABINETS INC**
220 Oakridge Ave (60040-1614)
PHONE.................773 343-6858
Paul Korzun, *President*
EMP: 2
SALES (est): 206.1K **Privately Held**
SIC: 2434 Wood kitchen cabinets

**(G-11886)**
**LEBOLT PRINT SERVICE INC**
802 Stables Ct E (60040-2050)
PHONE.................847 681-1210
Lynn Lebolt, *President*
Richard Lebolt, *Treasurer*
EMP: 3
SALES: 1.2MM **Privately Held**
SIC: 2752 Commercial printing, lithographic

**(G-11887)**
**PASTIFICIO INC**
122 Highwood Ave Ste 1r (60040-1547)
PHONE.................847 432-5459
Fax: 847 432-5474
Pat Galli, *President*
Elsa Amidei, *Vice Pres*
Mark Amidei, *Treasurer*
Mauro Galli, *Treasurer*
EMP: 6
SQ FT: 2,500
SALES (est): 600K **Privately Held**
WEB: www.pastificiohighwood.com
SIC: 5499 5812 2098 Gourmet food stores; eating places; macaroni & spaghetti

### Hillsboro
*Montgomery County*

**(G-11888)**
**CONTRACT ASSEMBLY PARTNERS**
Also Called: Cap
679 Washboard Trl (62049-3434)
PHONE.................217 960-3352
Dawn Clements, *President*
Mary J Niemenn, *Admin Sec*
EMP: 10
SQ FT: 7,500
SALES (est): 706.1K **Privately Held**
SIC: 1731 3489 Electronic controls installation; ordnance & accessories

**(G-11889)**
**ELITE MONUMENT CO**
Also Called: Hough General Homes
1119 School St (62049-1931)
PHONE.................217 532-6080
David Hough, *Partner*
Daniel Hough, *Partner*
Danny Hough, *Partner*
EMP: 3
SALES (est): 216.8K **Privately Held**
SIC: 3272 Monuments, concrete

**(G-11890)**
**FRITO-LAY NORTH AMERICA INC**
1400 E Tremont St (62049-1915)
PHONE.................217 532-5040
EMP: 160
SALES (corp-wide): 66.6B **Publicly Held**
SIC: 2096 Mfg Potato Chips/Snacks
HQ: Frito-Lay North America, Inc.
7701 Legacy Dr
Plano TX 75024

**(G-11891)**
**FULLER BROTHERS READY MIX**
935 Ash St (62049-1519)
PHONE.................217 532-2422
Lance Fuller, *Partner*
Harry Fuller, *Partner*
EMP: 6
SQ FT: 4,000

**GEOGRAPHIC SECTION**

**Hillside - Cook County (G-11915)**

**SALES:** 1.2MM **Privately Held**
**SIC: 3273** Ready-mixed concrete

**(G-11892)**
**HAYES ABRASIVES INC**
Smith Rd 120 (62049)
P.O. Box 237 (62049-0237)
**PHONE**..................217 532-6850
Fax: 217 532-6838
David Hayes, *President*
**EMP:** 15
**SQ FT:** 9,000
**SALES (est):** 2.1MM **Privately Held**
**WEB:** www.hayesabrasives.com
**SIC: 3291** 5085 Wheels, abrasive; industrial wheels

**(G-11893)**
**HILLERS SHEET METAL WORKS**
150 N Oak St (62049-1107)
**PHONE**..................217 532-2595
Fax: 217 532-2118
H Dennis Hiller, *Owner*
Lonna Durbin, *Admin Sec*
**EMP:** 3
**SQ FT:** 1,500
**SALES (est):** 150K **Privately Held**
**SIC: 1711** 3599 Plumbing, heating, air-conditioning contractors; machine shop, jobbing & repair

**(G-11894)**
**HILLSBORO ENERGY LLC**
925 S Main St Ste 2 (62049-1757)
P.O. Box 457 (62049-0457)
**PHONE**..................217 532-3983
Mike Beyer, *CEO*
John Mick, *CFO*
▲ **EMP:** 5
**SALES (est):** 736.8K
**SALES (corp-wide):** 875.8MM **Publicly Held**
**SIC: 1221** Bituminous coal & lignite-surface mining; bituminous coal surface mining
**HQ:** Foresight Energy Llc
1 Metropolitan Sq 211nb
Saint Louis MO 63102
314 932-6160

**(G-11895)**
**HILLSBORO JOURNAL INC**
Also Called: Sorento News, Raymond News
431 S Main St (62049-1433)
P.O. Box 100 (62049-0100)
**PHONE**..................217 532-3933
Fax: 217 532-3632
Phillip C Galer, *Vice Pres*
John Galler, *Vice Pres*
**EMP:** 40 **EST:** 1853
**SQ FT:** 4,000
**SALES (est):** 1.9MM **Privately Held**
**WEB:** www.hillsborojournal.com
**SIC: 2711** 2759 2752 Newspapers: publishing only, not printed on site; commercial printing; commercial printing, lithographic

**(G-11896)**
**JOURNAL NEWS**
425 S Main St (62049-1433)
**PHONE**..................217 532-3933
Nancy Slepicka, *Principal*
**EMP:** 3 **EST:** 2010
**SALES (est):** 179.6K **Privately Held**
**SIC: 2711** Newspapers, publishing & printing

**(G-11897)**
**PARIS FROZEN FOODS INC**
Also Called: Paris Frozen Foods Locker
305 Springfield Rd (62049-1150)
**PHONE**..................217 532-3822
Allen Hopper, *President*
Tom Compagni, *Vice Pres*
Pam Hopper, *Treasurer*
**EMP:** 5 **EST:** 1959
**SQ FT:** 4,800
**SALES (est):** 437.6K **Privately Held**
**SIC: 2011** Meat packing plants

**(G-11898)**
**PRO-BILT BUILDINGS LLC**
9181 Illinois Route 127 (62049-4117)
**PHONE**..................217 532-9331
Becky Lessman,
Barbara Bogel,
Richard Bogel,
Dean Lessman,
**EMP:** 14
**SALES (est):** 830K **Privately Held**
**SIC: 3444** Metal roofing & roof drainage equipment

**(G-11899)**
**RAVEN ENERGY LLC**
925 S Main St Ste 2 (62049-1757)
**PHONE**..................217 532-3983
Robert Boyd, *Principal*
J Matthew Fifield,
**EMP:** 4
**SALES (est):** 297.3K
**SALES (corp-wide):** 1.2B **Publicly Held**
**SIC: 2999** Coke
**HQ:** Suncoke Energy Partners, L.P.
1011 Warrenville Rd # 600
Lisle IL 60532
630 824-1000

**(G-11900)**
**SULLIVAN HOME HEALTH PRODUCTS**
311 Berry St (62049-1201)
P.O. Box 9 (62049-0009)
**PHONE**..................217 532-6366
**EMP:** 3
**SALES (corp-wide):** 555.7K **Privately Held**
**SIC: 5047** 3845 Whol Medical/Hospital Equipment Mfg Electromedical Equipment
**PA:** Sullivan Home Health Products Inc
117 W Spruce St
Gillespie IL 62033
217 839-3228

## Hillsdale
### Rock Island County

**(G-11901)**
**BOS MACHINE TOOL SERVICES INC**
621 Main St (61257-9785)
P.O. Box 96 (61257-0096)
**PHONE**..................309 658-2223
Fax: 309 658-2211
Charles Bos, *President*
Diane Bos, *Vice Pres*
Tim Marsden, *Sales Mgr*
Tim Marsdeen, *Sales Staff*
Sue Marsden, *Office Mgr*
**EMP:** 14
**SQ FT:** 30,000
**SALES:** 882.1K **Privately Held**
**WEB:** www.bosmachine.com
**SIC: 3541** 7699 Machine tools, metal cutting type; industrial machinery & equipment repair

**(G-11902)**
**NIKWOOD PRODUCTS INC**
32111 Highway 2 N (61257)
P.O. Box 214 (61257-0214)
**PHONE**..................309 658-2341
Fax: 309 658-2331
June Nicholson, *President*
Dan Nicholson, *Manager*
**EMP:** 8
**SQ FT:** 6,200
**SALES (est):** 580K **Privately Held**
**SIC: 2499** Handles, wood

**(G-11903)**
**RIVERSTONE GROUP INC**
Also Called: Midway Stone Co
2721 248th St N (61257-9622)
**PHONE**..................309 523-3159
Spud Rilling, *Branch Mgr*
**EMP:** 13
**SALES (corp-wide):** 3.9B **Privately Held**
**WEB:** www.riverstonegrp.com
**SIC: 1422** Crushed & broken limestone
**PA:** Riverstone Group, Inc.
1701 5th Ave
Moline IL 61265
309 757-8250

**(G-11904)**
**TOPPERT JETTING SERVICE INC (PA)**
510 Main St (61257-9701)
P.O. Box 838, East Moline (61244-0838)
**PHONE**..................309 755-2240
Debra Toppert, *President*
Larry Toppert, *Vice Pres*
**EMP:** 3
**SQ FT:** 150,000
**SALES (est):** 1.9MM **Privately Held**
**SIC: 7699** 7389 8999 3589 Sewer cleaning & rodding; sewer inspection service; earth science services; sewer cleaning equipment, power; excavating slush pits & cellars

**(G-11905)**
**TYSON FRESH MEATS INC**
28424 38th Ave N (61257-9656)
**PHONE**..................309 658-2291
Todd Reed, *General Mgr*
Edward Neary, *Chief Engr*
Dennis Seibel, *Plant Engr*
Craig Henkhaus, *Controller*
Al Schuetze, *Persnl Mgr*
**EMP:** 128
**SALES (corp-wide):** 36.8B **Publicly Held**
**SIC: 2011** Boxed beef from meat slaughtered on site
**HQ:** Tyson Fresh Meats, Inc.
800 Stevens Port Dr
Dakota Dunes SD 57049
605 235-2061

**(G-11906)**
**TYSON FRESH MEATS INC**
Also Called: Transcontinental Cold Storage
28424 38th Ave N (61257-9656)
**PHONE**..................309 658-3377
Steven Martet, *Branch Mgr*
**EMP:** 128
**SALES (corp-wide):** 36.8B **Publicly Held**
**SIC: 2011** Meat packing plants
**HQ:** Tyson Fresh Meats, Inc.
800 Stevens Port Dr
Dakota Dunes SD 57049
605 235-2061

## Hillside
### Cook County

**(G-11907)**
**ACE ANODIZING IMPREGNATING INC**
4161 Butterfield Rd (60162-1185)
P.O. Box 639 (60162-0639)
**PHONE**..................708 547-6680
Fax: 708 547-6682
David B Vaughn, *President*
Richard Smith, *Prdtn Mgr*
Cristal Hernandez, *Manager*
**EMP:** 60 **EST:** 1959
**SQ FT:** 36,000
**SALES (est):** 8.5MM **Privately Held**
**SIC: 3471** 2295 Anodizing (plating) of metals or formed products; coated fabrics, not rubberized

**(G-11908)**
**ACE COATING ENTERPRISES INC (PA)**
4161 Butterfield Rd (60162-1118)
P.O. Box 639 (60162-0639)
**PHONE**..................708 547-6680
David Vaughn, *President*
Nancy Burdick Vaughn, *Vice Pres*
Raquel Wenzel, *Admin Sec*
**EMP:** 19
**SQ FT:** 18,000
**SALES (est):** 3.1MM **Privately Held**
**WEB:** www.acemetalfinishing.com
**SIC: 3599** Machine & other job shop work

**(G-11909)**
**AMERIGAS**
4158 Division St (60162-1803)
**PHONE**..................708 544-1131
Patrick Arlis, *Plant Mgr*
Barbara Trentadue, *Manager*
Kelly Arlis, *Info Tech Mgr*
**EMP:** 54
**SQ FT:** 12,500

**SALES (est):** 15MM **Publicly Held**
**WEB:** www.lpg.com
**SIC: 5172** 5984 5169 2813 Gases, liquefied petroleum (propane); liquefied petroleum gas dealers; chemicals & allied products; industrial gases
**PA:** Amerigas Partners, L.P.
460 N Gulph Rd Ste 100
King Of Prussia PA 19406

**(G-11910)**
**BIO SERVICES INC**
4917 Butterfield Rd (60162-1413)
P.O. Box 6358, Villa Park (60181-5318)
**PHONE**..................630 808-2125
Shiji Chirayil, *President*
Luke Phiroeyil, *Office Mgr*
**EMP:** 4
**SALES:** 300K **Privately Held**
**SIC: 3365** Hospital utensils, cast aluminum

**(G-11911)**
**BISCO INTL INC**
543 Granville Ave (60162-1754)
**PHONE**..................708 544-6308
Michael Rizzo, *President*
**EMP:** 8
**SQ FT:** 14,000
**SALES (est):** 1.7MM **Privately Held**
**WEB:** www.biscointernational.com
**SIC: 3555** 2672 5065 Printing plates; coated & laminated paper; electronic parts

**(G-11912)**
**C2 PUBLISHING INC**
Also Called: West Suburban Living Magazine
5101 Darmstadt Rd (60162-1424)
P.O. Box 111, Elmhurst (60126-0111)
**PHONE**..................630 834-4994
Chuck Cozette, *President*
Ken Cozette, *Vice Pres*
**EMP:** 10
**SALES (est):** 620K **Privately Held**
**SIC: 2721** Magazines: publishing only, not printed on site

**(G-11913)**
**CON MOLD**
4164 May St (60162-1837)
**PHONE**..................708 442-6002
Oleg Ciubuc, *President*
**EMP:** 5
**SALES (est):** 628.9K **Privately Held**
**SIC: 3544** Industrial molds

**(G-11914)**
**DARWILL INC**
11900 Roosevelt Rd (60162-2069)
**PHONE**..................708 449-7770
Fax: 708 236-5820
Janice Van Dyke, *CEO*
Brandon Van Dyke, *President*
Howard Van Dyke, *President*
Brandon V Dyke, *Vice Pres*
Troy V Dyke, *Vice Pres*
▲ **EMP:** 150 **EST:** 1951
**SQ FT:** 60,000
**SALES:** 165.3K **Privately Held**
**WEB:** www.darwill.com
**SIC: 5963** 8748 8742 2789 Direct sales, telemarketing; communications consulting; marketing consulting services; bookbinding & related work; commercial printing

**(G-11915)**
**DYNAMIC MANUFACTURING INC**
4300 Madison St (60162-1340)
**PHONE**..................708 547-7081
John Partipilo, *President*
Olia Mlagenova, *Engineer*
Jesus Gonzalez, *Manager*
**EMP:** 100
**SALES (corp-wide):** 151.2MM **Privately Held**
**WEB:** www.dmimail.com
**SIC: 3714** 7537 7539 Transmissions, motor vehicle; automotive transmission repair shops; torque converter repair, automotive
**PA:** Dynamic Manufacturing Inc
1930 N Mannheim Rd
Melrose Park IL 60160
708 343-8753

# Hillside - Cook County (G-11916)

**(G-11916)**
**DYNAMIC MANUFACTURING INC**
Also Called: Plant 2
4211 Madison St (60162-1731)
PHONE..................708 547-9011
Fax: 708 547-9041
Tony Partipilo, *Exec VP*
Ken Hubacek, *Human Res Dir*
Sandra Landa-Puente, *Human Resources*
Mario Luperini, *Sales Executive*
Tony Portipilo, *Branch Mgr*
**EMP:** 300
**SALES (corp-wide):** 151.2MM **Privately Held**
**WEB:** www.dmimail.com
**SIC:** 3714 Motor vehicle transmissions, drive assemblies & parts
**PA:** Dynamic Manufacturing Inc
1930 N Mannheim Rd
Melrose Park IL 60160
708 343-8753

**(G-11917)**
**GPE CONTROLS INC (HQ)**
Also Called: Shand & Jurs
5911 Butterfield Rd (60162-1457)
PHONE..................708 236-6000
Fax: 708 236-6006
Louis Jannotta, *President*
Ron Davis, *Engineer*
James B Filip, *Controller*
Isaac Lim, *Sales Mgr*
Paul Smith, *Sr Project Mgr*
▼ **EMP:** 15
**SALES (est):** 12.7MM
**SALES (corp-wide):** 24.5MM **Privately Held**
**SIC:** 3829 3491 3728 3625 Gauging instruments, thickness ultrasonic; industrial valves; aircraft parts & equipment; relays & industrial controls; fluid power cylinders & actuators; fabricated plate work (boiler shop)
**PA:** L & J Holding Company, Ltd.
5911 Butterfield Rd
Hillside IL 60162
708 236-6000

**(G-11918)**
**HERFF JONES LLC**
Also Called: Replogle Globe Partners
125 Fencl Ln (60162-2040)
PHONE..................317 612-3705
Lee Tuzdal, *Plant Mgr*
Dave Reed, *Branch Mgr*
Rob N Montgomery, *Network Mgr*
**EMP:** 180
**SALES (corp-wide):** 1.1B **Privately Held**
**WEB:** www.herffjones.com
**SIC:** 2389 2384 3911 Academic vestments (caps & gowns); robes & dressing gowns; jewelry, precious metal
**HQ:** Herff Jones, Llc
4501 W 62nd St
Indianapolis IN 46268
800 419-5462

**(G-11919)**
**HIGHLAND METAL INC**
541 Hyde Park Ave (60162-1816)
PHONE..................708 544-6641
Fax: 708 544-8358
Kenneth Gerard Martin, *President*
Kathy Jones, *Manager*
**EMP:** 23 **EST:** 1943
**SQ FT:** 20,000
**SALES (est):** 4.2MM **Privately Held**
**WEB:** www.highlandmetal.com
**SIC:** 3451 3599 Screw machine products; grinding castings for the trade

**(G-11920)**
**HILLSIDE INDUSTRIES INC**
Also Called: M T H Industries
1 Mth Plz (60162-1436)
PHONE..................708 498-1100
Lyle Hill, *President*
Mike Swanberg, *Vice Pres*
Tom Swanberg, *Project Mgr*
Darshan Shah, *Project Mgr*
Evan Hickle, *Manager*
**EMP:** 130
**SQ FT:** 50,000
**SALES (est):** 17MM **Privately Held**
**SIC:** 3231 Insulating glass; made from purchased glass

**(G-11921)**
**K SYSTEMS CORPORATION**
4931 Butterfield Rd (60162-1437)
PHONE..................708 449-0400
Kent Piche, *President*
**EMP:** 6
**SQ FT:** 3,000
**SALES (est):** 883.7K **Privately Held**
**WEB:** www.ksystems.net
**SIC:** 3545 Gauges (machine tool accessories)

**(G-11922)**
**L & J ENGINEERING INC (HQ)**
Also Called: L & J Technologies
5911 Butterfield Rd (60162-1457)
PHONE..................708 236-6000
Louis J Jannotta, *President*
**EMP:** 44
**SQ FT:** 85,000
**SALES (est):** 11.6MM
**SALES (corp-wide):** 24.5MM **Privately Held**
**SIC:** 3829 5084 Measuring & controlling devices; industrial machinery & equipment
**PA:** L & J Holding Company, Ltd.
5911 Butterfield Rd
Hillside IL 60162
708 236-6000

**(G-11923)**
**L & J HOLDING COMPANY LTD (PA)**
Also Called: L & J Technologies
5911 Butterfield Rd (60162-1457)
PHONE..................708 236-6000
Louis Jannotta, *President*
Dave Dorrough, *QA Dir*
Jeff Clay, *Engineer*
Pam Senn, *CFO*
Linda Dorenbos, *Persnl Mgr*
**EMP:** 100
**SQ FT:** 85,000
**SALES (est):** 24.5MM **Privately Held**
**WEB:** www.ljtechnologies.com
**SIC:** 3829 3491 Measuring & controlling devices; gauging instruments, thickness ultrasonic; industrial valves

**(G-11924)**
**LENOVA INC (PA)**
4580 Roosevelt Rd (60162-2053)
P.O. Box 4440, Lisle (60532-9440)
PHONE..................312 733-1098
Yu Guifang, *President*
Chris Lee, *Manager*
▲ **EMP:** 5 **EST:** 2009
**SALES (est):** 982.4K **Privately Held**
**SIC:** 3431 Sinks; enameled iron, cast iron or pressed metal

**(G-11925)**
**METRITRACK INC**
4415 Harrison St Ste 230 (60162-1909)
P.O. Box 7115, Villa Park (60181-7115)
PHONE..................708 498-3578
Calin Caluser, *CEO*
**EMP:** 3
**SQ FT:** 1,400
**SALES:** 47K **Privately Held**
**SIC:** 3845 Electromedical equipment

**(G-11926)**
**MJT DESIGN AND PRTG ENTPS INC**
Also Called: Suit Plus More
4219 Butterfield Rd 1a (60162-1171)
Rural Route 4219 (60162)
PHONE..................708 240-4323
Manasses Edwards, *President*
Takiyah Baines-Edwards, *Vice Pres*
Joyce Edwards, *Admin Sec*
**EMP:** 3 **EST:** 2012
**SQ FT:** 1,200
**SALES (est):** 204.7K **Privately Held**
**SIC:** 2759 5621 5632 5699 Advertising literature; printing; women's clothing stores; women's accessory & specialty stores; T-shirts, custom printed; personal shopping service

**(G-11927)**
**MONUMENTAL MANUFACTURING CO**
Also Called: Peter Troost Monument
4300 Roosevelt Rd (60162-2030)
PHONE..................708 544-0916
Lisa Troost Kloet, *President*
Seven Swinbank, *General Mgr*
Frank Troost, *Chairman*
**EMP:** 100
**SQ FT:** 9,000
**SALES (est):** 7MM **Privately Held**
**SIC:** 3281 Monument or burial stone, cut & shaped

**(G-11928)**
**MTH ENTERPRISES LLC**
1 Mth Plz (60162-1436)
PHONE..................708 498-1100
Edwin Carey, *CFO*
Mike Swanberg,
**EMP:** 90
**SALES (est):** 15.6MM **Privately Held**
**SIC:** 3231 Products of purchased glass

**(G-11929)**
**ON TIME PRINTING AND FINISHING**
4206 Warren Ave (60162-1727)
PHONE..................708 544-4500
Fax: 708 544-4545
Dave Clark, *President*
Chris Clark, *Admin Sec*
**EMP:** 5 **EST:** 1994
**SQ FT:** 5,200
**SALES:** 1MM **Privately Held**
**SIC:** 2752 2791 2789 Commercial printing, lithographic; typesetting; bookbinding & related work

**(G-11930)**
**ORANGE CRUSH LLC (PA)**
321 Center St (60162-1814)
PHONE..................708 544-9440
Ron Bobkowski, *Superintendent*
Aaron Hoscheid, *Superintendent*
Letta Hollingsworth, *Principal*
Ryan Christensen, *Vice Pres*
Essam Abdishi, *Project Mgr*
**EMP:** 50
**SQ FT:** 20,000
**SALES (est):** 47.3MM **Privately Held**
**WEB:** www.ccagc.org
**SIC:** 2951 1795 Asphalt paving mixtures & blocks; concrete breaking for streets & highways

**(G-11931)**
**POLY FILMS INC**
4101 Washington Blvd (60162-1126)
PHONE..................708 547-7963
Randy Christie, *President*
Bob Christie, *Vice Pres*
Tom Christie, *Vice Pres*
William Christie, *Vice Pres*
**EMP:** 9
**SQ FT:** 19,000
**SALES (est):** 1.1MM **Privately Held**
**WEB:** www.polyfilms.com
**SIC:** 3081 Polyethylene film

**(G-11932)**
**RTS PACKAGING LLC**
250 N Mannheim Rd (60162-1835)
PHONE..................708 338-2800
Bob Wieck, *Purch Agent*
Mary Sachs, *Human Res Dir*
Ron Hartwig, *Branch Mgr*
**EMP:** 124
**SQ FT:** 30,000
**SALES (corp-wide):** 14.1B **Publicly Held**
**WEB:** www.rtspackaging.com
**SIC:** 2679 2675 2631 Paper products, converted; die-cut paper & board; paperboard mills
**HQ:** Rts Packaging, Llc
504 Thrasher St
Norcross GA 30071
800 558-6984

**(G-11933)**
**SHORELINE GLASS CO INC**
Also Called: Midwest Glass Co
1 Mth Plz (60162-1436)
PHONE..................312 829-9500
Jerry M Schor, *President*
Dennis Koziol, *Controller*
**EMP:** 50
**SQ FT:** 45,000
**SALES (est):** 3.6MM **Privately Held**
**SIC:** 1793 5039 5231 3442 Glass & glazing work; glass construction materials; glass; metal doors, sash & trim; products of purchased glass

## Hinckley
### Dekalb County

**(G-11934)**
**CIRCLE SYSTEMS INC (PA)**
479 W Lincoln Ave (60520-9209)
P.O. Box 1228 (60520-1228)
PHONE..................815 286-3271
Fax: 815 286-3352
R Marquiss Erlanson, *President*
Debra Shreve, *Vice Pres*
Harriet Cursio, *Treasurer*
R Steven Polachek, *Admin Sec*
**EMP:** 10
**SQ FT:** 20,000
**SALES (est):** 2.1MM **Privately Held**
**WEB:** www.circlesafe.com
**SIC:** 2819 2899 3829 Nonmetallic compounds; chemical preparations; measuring & controlling devices

**(G-11935)**
**HINCKLEY CONCRETE PRODUCTS CO**
540 W Lincoln Ave (60520-9205)
P.O. Box 1207 (60520-1207)
PHONE..................815 286-3235
Fax: 815 286-3638
Gerald C Nehring, *Owner*
Steve Nehring, *General Mgr*
Chris Burnett, *Office Mgr*
**EMP:** 8 **EST:** 1946
**SQ FT:** 16,000
**SALES (est):** 967.5K **Privately Held**
**SIC:** 3272 Septic tanks, concrete; floor slabs & tiles, precast concrete

**(G-11936)**
**LINCOLN ADVANCED TECH LLC**
161 Maple St (60520-9390)
PHONE..................815 286-3500
David Freriks,
**EMP:** 4
**SALES (est):** 307K **Privately Held**
**SIC:** 3842 Surgical appliances & supplies

**(G-11937)**
**STEP ONE STAIRWORKS INC**
201 Somonauk Rd (60520-6254)
PHONE..................815 286-7464
Fax: 815 286-7964
Gary Lambes Jr, *President*
Todd Harkness, *Plant Mgr*
Lisa Lambes, *CFO*
Brandy Vahl, *Admin Asst*
**EMP:** 12
**SQ FT:** 10,000
**SALES:** 2MM **Privately Held**
**WEB:** www.step1stairworks.com
**SIC:** 2431 Staircases, stairs & railings

## Hinsdale
### Dupage County

**(G-11938)**
**ACCURIDE CORPORATION**
201 E Ogden Ave Ste 220 (60521-3661)
PHONE..................630 568-3914
**EMP:** 243
**SALES (corp-wide):** 111.2MM **Privately Held**
**SIC:** 3714 Wheels, motor vehicle
**HQ:** Accuride Corporation
7140 Office Cir
Evansville IN 47715
812 962-5000

# GEOGRAPHIC SECTION
### Hinsdale - Dupage County (G-11969)

**(G-11939)**
**ASHLEYS INC**
Also Called: Ashley's Cutom Stationary
30 E 1st St (60521-4102)
**PHONE**....................630 794-0804
Ashley Killpack, *President*
**EMP:** 5
**SQ FT:** 600
**SALES:** 500K **Privately Held**
**SIC: 2621** 5943 Stationery, envelope & tablet papers; stationery stores

**(G-11940)**
**BADA BEANS**
215 S Monroe St (60521-3921)
**PHONE**....................630 655-0693
Richard Simon, *Mng Member*
**EMP:** 2
**SALES (est):** 215.1K **Privately Held**
**SIC: 2869** Flavors or flavoring materials, synthetic

**(G-11941)**
**BELLA CASA**
322 N Adams St (60521-3128)
**PHONE**....................630 455-5900
Mary Cashman, *Owner*
Cecil Evans, *VP Sales*
Duana Frank, *Office Mgr*
**EMP:** 3
**SALES (est):** 270K **Privately Held**
**SIC: 3999** 5199 Fire extinguishers, portable; gifts & novelties

**(G-11942)**
**BOSE CORPORATION**
Also Called: Bose Showcase Store
65 Oakbrook Ctr (60523-1809)
**PHONE**....................630 575-8044
Lee Phillips, *Branch Mgr*
**EMP:** 9
**SALES (corp-wide):** 3B **Privately Held**
**WEB:** www.bose.com
**SIC: 5731** 3651 Radio, television & electronic stores; household audio equipment
**PA:** Bose Corporation
   100 The Mountain Rd
   Framingham MA 01701
   508 879-7330

**(G-11943)**
**BUYERSVINE INC**
641 S Bodin St (60521-3916)
**PHONE**....................630 235-6804
Louis Lamoureux, *President*
**EMP:** 1
**SALES:** 200K **Privately Held**
**SIC: 7379** 7372 7389 Computer related consulting services; application computer software;

**(G-11944)**
**CHARWAT FOOD GROUP LTD**
3 Grant Sq 251 (60521-3351)
**PHONE**....................630 847-3473
Charles Waters, *Principal*
**EMP:** 3
**SALES (est):** 103.1K **Privately Held**
**SIC: 2022** 0251 5147 2013 Cheese, natural & processed; broiler, fryer & roaster chickens; meats & meat products; prepared pork products from purchased pork;

**(G-11945)**
**EVER-REDI PRINTING INC**
331 Justina St (60521-2416)
**PHONE**....................708 352-4378
Fax: 708 352-6951
Tim T Durland, *President*
Melvin T Durland, *Chairman*
Rose Durland, *Admin Sec*
**EMP:** 4 **EST:** 1948
**SQ FT:** 6,000
**SALES:** 150K **Privately Held**
**SIC: 2752** Commercial printing, offset

**(G-11946)**
**FINE GOLD MFG JEWELERS**
777 N York Rd Ste 27 (60521-3562)
**PHONE**....................630 323-9600
Jeff Rutt, *President*
Melissa Rutt, *Treasurer*
Julie Rutt, *Admin Sec*
**EMP:** 3
**SALES:** 600K **Privately Held**
**SIC: 3911** 7631 Jewel settings & mountings, precious metal; rings, finger: precious metal; necklaces, precious metal; watch, clock & jewelry repair

**(G-11947)**
**GE POLYMERS LLC**
109 Symonds Dr Unit 15 (60522-7310)
**PHONE**....................312 674-7434
Nicole Stein, *Mng Member*
Gary Kompare,
**EMP:** 6
**SQ FT:** 12,000
**SALES (est):** 2MM **Privately Held**
**SIC: 3089** Battery cases, plastic or plastic combination

**(G-11948)**
**GETEX CORPORATION**
311 Woodview Ct (60523-1527)
**PHONE**....................630 993-1300
Afsar Ali Khan, *President*
**EMP:** 4
**SALES (est):** 240K **Privately Held**
**SIC: 2841** 2899 2842 Detergents, synthetic organic or inorganic alkaline; chemical preparations; specialty cleaning, polishes & sanitation goods

**(G-11949)**
**GINGER BLISS JUICE LLC**
15 Spinning Wheel Rd (60521-2914)
**PHONE**....................773 456-0181
Donald Edwards, *Exec Dir*
**EMP:** 5 **EST:** 2013
**SALES (est):** 210.6K **Privately Held**
**SIC: 2086** Soft drinks: packaged in cans, bottles, etc.

**(G-11950)**
**GREENCAST SERVICES INC**
3 Grant Sq Ste 200 (60521-3351)
**PHONE**....................630 723-8000
Mark Smith, *President*
**EMP:** 3
**SALES (est):** 306.3K **Privately Held**
**SIC: 3645** Residential lighting fixtures

**(G-11951)**
**LUXURIOUS LATHERS LTD**
15 Spinning Wheel Rd (60521-2914)
**PHONE**....................844 877-7627
**EMP:** 3
**SQ FT:** 1,900
**SALES (est):** 78K **Privately Held**
**SIC: 5999** 2844 Ret Misc Merchandise Mfg Toilet Preparations

**(G-11952)**
**MASTERCRAFT RUG DESIGN**
838 Chestnut St (60521-3009)
**PHONE**....................630 655-3393
Rachel Lee, *President*
**EMP:** 3
**SALES:** 200K **Privately Held**
**SIC: 2273** Carpets & rugs

**(G-11953)**
**METAL RESOURCES INC (PA)**
15 Salt Creek Ln Ste 312 (60521-2964)
**PHONE**....................630 616-1850
William Wilson, *President*
**EMP:** 3
**SALES:** 3.8MM **Privately Held**
**SIC: 3312** Rods, iron & steel: made in steel mills

**(G-11954)**
**NELSON-ROSE INC**
Also Called: ARC Technologies
120 E Ogden Ave Ste 130 (60521-3683)
**PHONE**....................760 744-7400
Jonathan Friedman, *CEO*
George Dressel, *President*
Shawn Jackson, *Vice Pres*
Timothy Dressel, *Accountant*
Robert J Gerth, *Director*
**EMP:** 55
**SQ FT:** 32,000
**SALES (est):** 9.4MM **Privately Held**
**WEB:** www.arctechnologies.com
**SIC: 3599** Machine shop, jobbing & repair

**(G-11955)**
**NEVERSTRIP LLC**
111 S Hinsdale (60521)
**PHONE**....................708 588-9707
David Beedie, *President*
David Klick, *Exec VP*
Robert Peterson, *Exec VP*
John Rothschild, *Exec VP*
**EMP:** 8
**SQ FT:** 30,000
**SALES (est):** 970.5K **Privately Held**
**SIC: 2851** Epoxy coatings; polyurethane coatings; vinyl coatings, strippable

**(G-11956)**
**PETCO PETROLEUM CORPORATION (PA)**
108 E Ogden Ave Ste 100 (60521-3874)
**PHONE**....................630 654-1740
Fax: 630 325-5170
Jay D Bergman, *President*
Jay Harriman, *Admin Sec*
**EMP:** 7
**SQ FT:** 3,500
**SALES (est):** 135.9MM **Privately Held**
**WEB:** www.petcopetroleum.com
**SIC: 1389** Oil field services

**(G-11957)**
**PICCOLINO INC**
802 S Clay St (60521-4541)
**PHONE**....................708 259-2072
Dana Fort, *President*
**EMP:** 3
**SALES (est):** 210K **Privately Held**
**SIC: 2392** Pads & padding, table: except asbestos, felt or rattan

**(G-11958)**
**PIONEER NEWSPAPERS INC**
Also Called: Doings Newspaper
440 E Ogden Ave Ste 2 (60521-3691)
**PHONE**....................630 887-0600
Jim Slonoff, *Director*
**EMP:** 40
**SALES (corp-wide):** 304.8MM **Privately Held**
**WEB:** www.pioneerlocal.com
**SIC: 2711** Newspapers, publishing & printing
**HQ:** Pioneer Newspapers Inc.
   350 N Orleans St Fl 10
   Chicago IL 60654
   847 486-0600

**(G-11959)**
**PLAYGROUND POINTERS**
109 S Quincy St (60521-3012)
**PHONE**....................952 200-4168
Mistie Lucht, *Owner*
**EMP:** 4
**SALES (est):** 211.6K **Privately Held**
**SIC: 7372** Application computer software

**(G-11960)**
**R & R PRINTNSERVE INC**
7585 S Madison St (60521)
**PHONE**....................630 654-4044
Fax: 630 654-4049
Rich Jasker, *Principal*
Ron Isdonas, *Vice Pres*
Rosemary Isdonas, *Treasurer*
Nikki Jasker, *Admin Sec*
**EMP:** 4
**SQ FT:** 2,000
**SALES (est):** 872.4K **Privately Held**
**WEB:** www.rnrprint.net
**SIC: 2759** Advertising literature: printing

**(G-11961)**
**S&J FOOD MANAGEMENT CORP**
435 E 4th St (60521-4659)
**PHONE**....................630 323-9296
John Scales, *Principal*
Mark Jennings, *CFO*
**EMP:** 4
**SALES (est):** 170K **Privately Held**
**SIC: 2099** Food preparations

**(G-11962)**
**SASS-N-CLASS INC**
19 W 1st St Ste A (60521-4390)
**PHONE**....................630 655-2420
Gretchen A Wasniewski, *President*
James T Wasniewski, *Admin Sec*
**EMP:** 5
**SQ FT:** 700
**SALES (est):** 532.3K **Privately Held**
**WEB:** www.sass-n-class.com
**SIC: 2759** Invitations: printing; announcements: engraved

**(G-11963)**
**SAVINO DISPLAYS INC**
28 Bradford Ln (60523-2322)
**PHONE**....................630 574-0777
Alfred Savino, *President*
**EMP:** 3 **EST:** 1946
**SALES (est):** 190K **Privately Held**
**SIC: 3993** Signs & advertising specialties

**(G-11964)**
**SEVERSTAL US HOLDINGS II INC (HQ)**
Also Called: Esmark
907 N Elm St Ste 100 (60521-3644)
**PHONE**....................708 756-0400
James P Bouchard, *CEO*
Craig T Bouchard, *President*
Joel Mazur, *President*
David A Luptak, *Co-CEO*
Thomas A Modrowski, *Co-CEO*
◆ **EMP:** 31
**SQ FT:** 180,000
**SALES (est):** 196.3MM
**SALES (corp-wide):** 4.7B **Privately Held**
**WEB:** www.esmark.com
**SIC: 3291** Abrasive metal & steel products
**PA:** Severstal, Pao
   30 Ul. Mira
   Cherepovets 16260
   820 253-1915

**(G-11965)**
**STERLING BOOKS LIMITED**
735 S Oak St (60521-4635)
**PHONE**....................630 325-3853
Mary Sterling, *Owner*
David Sterling, *Vice Pres*
Thomas Sterling, *Vice Pres*
**EMP:** 3
**SALES (est):** 140K **Privately Held**
**SIC: 2731** Book publishing

**(G-11966)**
**TAG SALES CO INC**
1000 Jorie Blvd Ste 26 (60523-3089)
**PHONE**....................630 990-3434
Fax: 630 990-3425
Thomas E Rickleman, *President*
Tom Rickelman, *Vice Pres*
Patsy A Rickelman, *Treasurer*
Ken Clingen, *Admin Sec*
**EMP:** 4
**SQ FT:** 1,000
**SALES (est):** 350K **Privately Held**
**SIC: 3545** Tools & accessories for machine tools; cutting tools for machine tools

**(G-11967)**
**TRUDEAU APPROVED PRODUCTS INC**
3 Grant Sq 332 (60521-3351)
**PHONE**....................312 924-7230
Suneil Sant, *President*
**EMP:** 5 **EST:** 2011
**SALES (est):** 404.3K **Privately Held**
**SIC: 2834** Vitamin preparations

**(G-11968)**
**WAVETEAM LLC**
10 Hampshire West 260 S (60527)
**PHONE**....................630 323-0277
Manuel Munguia, *Mng Member*
Therese Munguia,
**EMP:** 9
**SALES (est):** 747.1K **Privately Held**
**WEB:** www.waveteam.com
**SIC: 3676** Resistor networks

**(G-11969)**
**XEROX CORPORATION**
2301 W 22nd St Ste 300 (60523-1224)
**PHONE**....................630 573-1000
Colleen Finlay, *Manager*
Dave Renaud, *Director*
**EMP:** 35

# Hodgkins - Cook County (G-11970)

SALES (corp-wide): 10.7B  Publicly Held
WEB: www.xerox.com
SIC: 3861  3577 7629 7378 Photocopy machines; computer peripheral equipment; business machine repair, electric; computer maintenance & repair; office equipment
PA: Xerox Corporation
201 Merritt 7
Norwalk CT 06851
203 968-3000

## Hodgkins
### Cook County

**(G-11970)**
**ARRO CORPORATION**
7250 Santa Fe Dr (60525-5017)
PHONE..................................708 352-8200
Patrick Gaughan, *President*
EMP: 117
SALES (corp-wide): 644MM  Privately Held
SIC: 5141  2045 4225 Groceries, general line; pancake mixes, prepared: from purchased flour; general warehousing & storage
PA: Arro Corporation
7440 Santa Fe Dr
Hodgkins IL 60525
708 352-8200

**(G-11971)**
**ARRO CORPORATION**
Also Called: Arro Liquid Division
7550 Santa Fe Dr (60525-5046)
PHONE..................................708 352-7412
Patrick Gaughan, *President*
EMP: 30
SALES (corp-wide): 644MM  Privately Held
SIC: 2045  4225 5141 Pancake mixes, prepared: from purchased flour; general warehousing & storage; groceries, general line
PA: Arro Corporation
7440 Santa Fe Dr
Hodgkins IL 60525
708 352-8200

**(G-11972)**
**CHICAGO CNC MACHINING CO**
6880 River Rd Unit 2 (60525-3417)
PHONE..................................708 352-1255
Doug Miller, *President*
Paul Julius, *Vice Pres*
Ed Montalvo, *Admin Sec*
EMP: 5
SQ FT: 3,200
SALES: 500K  Privately Held
SIC: 3541 Machine tool replacement & repair parts, metal cutting types

**(G-11973)**
**CUMMINS NPOWER LLC**
Also Called: Cummins Diesel Sales
7145 Santa Fe Dr (60525-5181)
PHONE..................................708 579-9222
Bruce Harner, *Opers Mgr*
Michael Hoehn, *Branch Mgr*
Matt Carstenbrock, *Manager*
Donna Downs, *Technology*
Sharon Steen, *Executive*
EMP: 50
SALES (corp-wide): 17.5B  Publicly Held
SIC: 5084  3519 Engines & parts, diesel; internal combustion engines
HQ: Cummins Npower Llc
1600 Buerkle Rd
White Bear Lake MN 55110
800 642-0085

**(G-11974)**
**EVENT EQUIPMENT SALES LLC**
7515 Santa Fe Dr (60525-5053)
PHONE..................................708 352-0662
Fax: 708 352-8267
Douglas Crowe, *COO*
Nicole Rediehs, *Accounts Exec*
Roberta Decillo, *Mktg Dir*
Bernard Shipper, *Mng Member*
Ed Alsweve, *Manager*
◆ EMP: 10
SQ FT: 9,000
SALES (est): 1.7MM  Privately Held
WEB: www.eventequipment.com
SIC: 2394  5021 Canvas & related products; restaurant furniture

**(G-11975)**
**GOSIA CARTAGE LTD**
6400 River Rd (60525-4256)
PHONE..................................312 613-8735
Margaret Malinin, *President*
EMP: 6
SALES (est): 728.2K  Privately Held
SIC: 4212  3991 Local trucking, without storage; street sweeping brooms, hand or machine

**(G-11976)**
**INDUSTRIAL STEEL CNSTR INC**
6120 River Rd (60525-5186)
PHONE..................................219 885-7600
Fax: 708 482-8549
Art Bustos, *General Mgr*
Fonda Ryan, *Manager*
Jon Papineau, *Manager*
EMP: 60
SALES (corp-wide): 38.1MM  Privately Held
WEB: www.iscbridge.com
SIC: 3441 Fabricated structural metal
PA: Industrial Steel Construction, Inc.
413 Old Kirk Rd
Geneva IL 60134
630 232-7473

**(G-11977)**
**JANIK CUSTOM MILLWORK INC**
6017 Lenzi Ave Ste 1 (60525-4258)
PHONE..................................708 482-4844
Fax: 708 482-4844
Stanley A Janik, *President*
Ed J Janik, *Vice Pres*
Pat Janik, *Admin Sec*
EMP: 5
SALES: 1.2MM  Privately Held
WEB: www.janikcustommillwork.com
SIC: 2431  2541 2434 Millwork; doors & door parts & trim, wood; windows & window parts & trim, wood; staircases, stairs & railings; wood partitions & fixtures; wood kitchen cabinets

**(G-11978)**
**ODM TOOL & MFG CO INC**
9550 Joliet Rd (60525-4148)
PHONE..................................708 485-6130
Fax: 708 485-6540
Gary Kautz, *Principal*
Sandra Michaelsen, *Corp Secy*
James Schwenn, *Foreman/Supr*
Chris Ericksen, *Production*
Dwayne Ford, *QC Mgr*
EMP: 75
SQ FT: 153,000
SALES (est): 18.7MM  Privately Held
WEB: www.odmtool.com
SIC: 3469  3544 Stamping metal for the trade; special dies, tools, jigs & fixtures

**(G-11979)**
**OPW FUEL MGT SYSTEMS INC (DH)**
6900 Santa Fe Dr (60525-7600)
PHONE..................................708 352-9617
Steven Trabilsy, *President*
Shaun Stroud, *Opers Mgr*
John Gray, *Engineer*
Eric Riffle, *Engineer*
Scott Burkard, *Treasurer*
▲ EMP: 1
SQ FT: 55,000
SALES (est): 559K
SALES (corp-wide): 6.7B  Publicly Held
WEB: www.opwfms.com
SIC: 3824 Gasoline dispensing meters
HQ: Opw Fluid Transfer Group
4304 Nw Mattox Rd
Kansas City MO 64150
816 741-6600

**(G-11980)**
**OPW FUELING COMPONENTS INC**
Also Called: Opw Fueling Management Systems
6900 Santa Fe Dr (60525-7600)
PHONE..................................708 485-4200
Kelly Klodell, *Mktg Coord*
EMP: 5
SALES (corp-wide): 6.7B  Publicly Held
SIC: 2899 Fuel treating compounds
HQ: Opw Fueling Components Inc.
9393 Prnceton Glendale Rd
West Chester OH 45011

**(G-11981)**
**RECONSERVE OF ILLINOIS INC**
6160 River Rd (60525-4278)
PHONE..................................708 354-4641
Fax: 708 354-5883
Meyer Luskin, *CEO*
Mark Hoffer, *Transptn Dir*
Rida Hamed, *Admin Sec*
Peggy Kaiser, *Administration*
EMP: 23
SALES (est): 6.3MM
SALES (corp-wide): 203.7MM  Privately Held
SIC: 2048 Prepared feeds
PA: Scope Industries
2811 Wilshire Blvd # 410
Santa Monica CA 90403
310 458-1574

**(G-11982)**
**SEALED AIR CORPORATION**
Packaging Products Div
7110 Santa Fe Dr (60525-5051)
PHONE..................................708 352-8700
Fax: 708 352-8713
David Reaume, *Plant Mgr*
Craig Buechel, *QC Mgr*
Randy Mazura, *Engineer*
Donna Bonder, *Human Res Mgr*
Tom Kenealy, *Marketing Staff*
EMP: 100
SALES (corp-wide): 6.7B  Publicly Held
WEB: www.sealedair.com
SIC: 3086 Packaging & shipping materials, foamed plastic
PA: Sealed Air Corporation
2415 Cascade Pointe Blvd
Charlotte NC 28208
980 221-3235

**(G-11983)**
**SILBRICO CORPORATION**
6300 River Rd (60525-5189)
PHONE..................................708 354-3350
Fax: 708 354-6698
Steven B Garnett, *President*
Christopher Mendius, *Vice Pres*
Lawrence Mendius, *Vice Pres*
James Clark, *Engineer*
Vincent Galanek, *Project Engr*
◆ EMP: 89 EST: 1946
SQ FT: 100,000
SALES (est): 24.6MM  Privately Held
WEB: www.silbrico.com
SIC: 3296 Mineral wool

**(G-11984)**
**TARA INTERNATIONAL LP**
9100 67th St (60525-5183)
PHONE..................................708 354-7050
Fax: 708 354-7065
Mark Meyer, *General Mgr*
Steve Whitescarver, *Maint Spvr*
Jackie Daily, *Office Mgr*
Amy Jensen, *Manager*
Dean Doman, *Info Tech Mgr*
EMP: 100 EST: 1978
SQ FT: 110,000
SALES (est): 13.3MM  Privately Held
WEB: www.tarainternational.com
SIC: 7389  2099 Packaging & labeling services; food preparations

**(G-11985)**
**VALSPAR CORPORATION**
6880 River Rd Unit 22 (60525-3233)
PHONE..................................708 469-7194
EMP: 100
SALES (corp-wide): 11.8B  Publicly Held
SIC: 2851 Paints & allied products
HQ: The Valspar Corporation
1101 S 3rd St
Minneapolis MN 55415
612 851-7000

**(G-11986)**
**VEE PAK LLC (PA) ✪**
6710 River Rd (60525-4310)
PHONE..................................708 482-8881
Katherine M Vennetti, *President*
Ralph S Vennetti, *President*
David Vennetti, *Vice Pres*
Mike Vennetti, *Vice Pres*
Ralph A Vennetti Jr, *Vice Pres*
EMP: 100 EST: 2017
SQ FT: 70,000
SALES: 250MM  Privately Held
SIC: 2844  4225 Cosmetic preparations; general warehousing

**(G-11987)**
**WEI-CHUAN USA INC**
6845 Santa Fe Dr (60525-7637)
PHONE..................................708 352-8886
Fax: 708 352-8884
Weiyao Sung, *Branch Mgr*
Eyao Sung, *Manager*
EMP: 13
SALES (corp-wide): 120.2MM  Privately Held
SIC: 5142  2038 Packaged frozen goods; dinners, frozen & packaged; ethnic foods, frozen
PA: Wei-Chuan U.S.A., Inc.
6655 Garfield Ave
Bell Gardens CA 90201
323 587-2101

## Hoffman
### Clinton County

**(G-11988)**
**DON ANDERSON CO**
101 S Hickory St (62250)
P.O. Box 227 (62250-0227)
PHONE..................................618 495-2511
Fax: 618 495-2511
Donald L Anderson, *President*
Vicky Anderson, *Corp Secy*
Tom Anderson, *Vice Pres*
EMP: 5 EST: 1953
SQ FT: 2,000
SALES (est): 765.4K  Privately Held
SIC: 1611  2952 2951 General contractor, highway & street construction; asphalt felts & coatings; asphalt paving mixtures & blocks

## Hoffman Estates
### Cook County

**(G-11989)**
**ACCESS FLOORING CO INC**
680 Alhambra Ln (60169-1908)
PHONE..................................847 781-0100
Peter Dudzik, *President*
EMP: 2
SALES (est): 222.4K  Privately Held
SIC: 2426 Flooring, hardwood

**(G-11990)**
**AMCOL HLTH BUTY SOLUTIONS INC (DH)**
2870 Forbs Ave (60192-3702)
PHONE..................................847 851-1300
Fax: 847 851-1210
Gary Castagna, *President*
Kevin Cureton, *Managing Dir*
Debbie Herbert, *Accounts Mgr*
Ro Oteri, *Director*
James W Ashley Jr, *Admin Sec*
▼ EMP: 12
SALES (est): 5.8MM
SALES (corp-wide): 1.6B  Publicly Held
WEB: www.amcol.com
SIC: 2821 Polymethyl methacrylate resins (plexiglass)
HQ: Amcol International Corp
2870 Forbs Ave
Hoffman Estates IL 60192
847 851-1500

## GEOGRAPHIC SECTION

Hoffman Estates - Cook County (G-12014)

**(G-11991)**
**AMCOL INTERNATIONAL CORP (HQ)**
2870 Forbs Ave (60192-3702)
PHONE .................................. 847 851-1500
Ryan F McKendrick, *President*
Thomas Stam, *Business Mgr*
Gary L Castagna, *Senior VP*
Robert C Steele, *Senior VP*
James W Ashley, *Vice Pres*
◆ EMP: 49
SALES (est): 909.7MM
SALES (corp-wide): 1.6B Publicly Held
WEB: www.amcol.com
SIC: 1459 5032 4213 4731 Bentonite mining; fuller's earth mining; clay construction materials, except refractory; trucking, except local; truck transportation brokers
PA: Minerals Technologies Inc.
622 3rd Ave Fl 38
New York NY 10017
212 878-1800

**(G-11992)**
**AMERICAN COLLOID COMPANY (DH)**
Also Called: Amcol
2870 Forbs Ave (60192-3702)
P.O. Box 95411 (60195-0411)
PHONE .................................. 847 851-1700
Fax: 847 851-1943
Gary Morrison, *President*
Bob Oliver, *Regional Mgr*
Mike Bartol, *Vice Pres*
Jim Papp, *Vice Pres*
Jeff Campbell, *Plant Mgr*
◆ EMP: 25
SQ FT: 7,300
SALES (est): 602.5MM
SALES (corp-wide): 1.6B Publicly Held
WEB: www.colloid.com
SIC: 1459 2899 Bentonite mining; chemical preparations
HQ: Amcol International Corp
2870 Forbs Ave
Hoffman Estates IL 60192
847 851-1500

**(G-11993)**
**BALLEK DIE MOLD INC**
2125 Stonington Ave (60169-2016)
PHONE .................................. 847 885-2300
Fax: 847 885-3874
Stefan Ballek, *President*
Mariane Ballek, *Corp Secy*
Steven W Ballek, *Vice Pres*
Diane Beldsoe, *Manager*
Lucy Titarchuk, *Director*
EMP: 10
SQ FT: 36,000
SALES (est): 760K Privately Held
WEB: www.ballekdiemold.com
SIC: 3544 Industrial molds

**(G-11994)**
**BEVERLY MATERIALS LLC**
1100 Brandt Dr (60192-1676)
PHONE .................................. 847 695-9300
Doug Heatherly, *Manager*
Bill Wheeler, *Manager*
David R Plote,
Daniel R Plote,
Raymond E Plote,
EMP: 3
SALES (est): 400.3K Privately Held
SIC: 1442 Construction sand & gravel

**(G-11995)**
**BI SOFTWARE INC**
808 Linden Cir (60169-3261)
PHONE .................................. 224 622-4706
Dariusz Danielewski, *President*
EMP: 3
SALES: 500K Privately Held
SIC: 7372 Prepackaged software

**(G-11996)**
**BIG KSER PRECISION TOOLING INC**
2600 Huntington Blvd (60192-1574)
PHONE .................................. 847 228-7660
Fax: 847 228-0881
Chris Kaiser, *CEO*
John Burley, *Vice Pres*

Anthony Bylina, *Sales Staff*
Hilary Schnirring, *Asst Mgr*
Kristina Bouzard, *Admin Asst*
EMP: 33
SQ FT: 13,000
SALES (est): 7.6MM
SALES (corp-wide): 153.7MM Privately Held
WEB: www.bigkaiser.com
SIC: 3545 Machine tool accessories
PA: Big Daishowa K.K.
3-3-39, Nishiishikiricho
Higashi-Osaka OSK 579-8
729 822-312

**(G-11997)**
**BOLAND HILL MEDIA LLC**
3 Golf Ctr Ste 314 (60169-4910)
PHONE .................................. 877 658-0418
Bob Jenisch, *Mng Member*
John Stewart, *Mng Member*
EMP: 2
SALES: 650K Privately Held
WEB: www.digitaltransactions.net
SIC: 2721 Magazines: publishing only, not printed on site

**(G-11998)**
**CDK GLOBAL INC (PA)**
1950 Hassell Rd (60169-6308)
PHONE .................................. 847 397-1700
Leslie A Brun, *Ch of Bd*
Brian P Macdonald, *President*
Andrew Dean, *President*
Robert N Karp, *President*
Howard Gardner, *General Mgr*
EMP: 700
SQ FT: 155,000
SALES: 2.1B Publicly Held
SIC: 7372 Business oriented computer software

**(G-11999)**
**CHICAGO BOTTLING INDUSTRIES**
2075 Stonington Ave (60169-2014)
PHONE .................................. 847 885-8093
EMP: 3
SALES (est): 68.6K Privately Held
SIC: 2086 Bottled & canned soft drinks

**(G-12000)**
**CLOVER GLOBAL HEADQUARTERS**
Also Called: Clover Wireless
2700 W Higgins Rd Ste 100 (60169-2006)
PHONE .................................. 815 431-8100
Brian Regan, *President*
Robert Kelly, *Project Mgr*
Jeffrey Schaffer, *Warehouse Mgr*
Brian Bauer, *Sales Staff*
Lauri Driscoll-Hite, *Sales Associate*
EMP: 1
SALES (est): 3.3MM Privately Held
SIC: 7389 3861 Telephone services; photographic equipment & supplies

**(G-12001)**
**CLOVER TECHNOLOGIES GROUP LLC**
2700 W Higgins Rd Ste 100 (60169-2006)
PHONE .................................. 847 885-6400
Fax: 847 885-6400
Guy Kevin, *Senior VP*
Andrew Buck, *Vice Pres*
Rick Cerkleski, *Vice Pres*
Jeff Regal, *Vice Pres*
Tanya Ware, *Vice Pres*
EMP: 17
SALES (corp-wide): 627.3MM Privately Held
SIC: 3861 Printing equipment, photographic
HQ: Clover Technologies Group, Llc
4200 Columbus St
Ottawa IL 61350

**(G-12002)**
**COLLOID ENVMTL TECH CO LLC (DH)**
Also Called: Cetco
2870 Forbs Ave (60192-3702)
PHONE .................................. 847 851-1500
Fax: 847 851-1899
Ryan F McKendrick, *President*

Pedro Abad, *General Mgr*
Patrick Carpenter, *Vice Pres*
Allen Bullock, *Sales Mgr*
Richard Heskett, *Sales Mgr*
◆ EMP: 160
SQ FT: 72,000
SALES (est): 271.2MM
SALES (corp-wide): 1.6B Publicly Held
WEB: www.amcol.com
SIC: 3259 2899 Liner brick or plates for sewer/tank lining, vitrified clay; concrete curing & hardening compounds
HQ: Amcol International Corp
2870 Forbs Ave
Hoffman Estates IL 60192
847 851-1500

**(G-12003)**
**CONVERGENT BILL ETE ORT T**
2000 W Att Center Dr Rm 4 (60192-5005)
PHONE .................................. 847 387-4059
EMP: 3
SALES (est): 210.4K Privately Held
SIC: 3674 Mfg Semiconductors/Related Devices

**(G-12004)**
**DDN INDUSTRIES INC**
2155 Stnngton Ave Ste 221 (60169)
PHONE .................................. 847 885-8595
Fax: 847 885-6116
Dian Naugle, *President*
David Naugle, *Vice Pres*
Karen Balick, *Manager*
EMP: 6
SQ FT: 1,350
SALES: 1.4MM Privately Held
WEB: www.ddn-industries.com
SIC: 2653 Boxes, corrugated: made from purchased materials

**(G-12005)**
**DMG CHARLOTTE LLC (DH)**
2400 Huntington Blvd (60192-1564)
PHONE .................................. 704 583-1193
Karen Shetty, *CFO*
Rakhee Chatterke, *Controller*
Dave Thomas, *Mng Member*
Dieter Schaefer,
Thorsten Schmidt,
▲ EMP: 18
SQ FT: 21,000
SALES: 2.4MM
SALES (corp-wide): 3.4B Privately Held
SIC: 3541 Machine tools, metal cutting type
HQ: Dmg America Inc.
2400 Huntington Blvd
Hoffman Estates IL 60192
630 227-3900

**(G-12006)**
**DMG MORI USA INC (HQ)**
Also Called: Dmg Mori Seiki U.S.a
2400 Huntington Blvd (60192-1564)
PHONE .................................. 847 593-5400
Thorsten Schmidt, *President*
Mark H Mohr, *Principal*
Brian McGirk, *Corp Secy*
Randall Harland, *Exec VP*
Marlow Knabach, *Exec VP*
▲ EMP: 100
SQ FT: 102,000
SALES: 506.1MM
SALES (corp-wide): 3.4B Privately Held
SIC: 3541 3545 Machine tools, metal cutting type; machine tool accessories
PA: Dmg Mori Co., Ltd.
2-35-16, Meieki, Nakamura-Ku
Nagoya AIC 450-0
525 871-811

**(G-12007)**
**E I P INC (PA)**
2200 W Higgins Rd Ste 355 (60169-2423)
PHONE .................................. 847 885-3615
Fax: 847 885-3616
James Karambelas, *President*
Peter Karambelas, *Principal*
Connie Karambelas, *Treasurer*
Christine Greco, *Admin Sec*
EMP: 4
SQ FT: 1,100
SALES: 2.8MM Privately Held
SIC: 3564 Blowers & fans

**(G-12008)**
**EXCLUSIVE PUBLICATIONS INC**
3830 Bordeaux Dr (60192-1616)
PHONE .................................. 847 963-0400
Christian M Jacobs, *Manager*
EMP: 3
SALES (est): 145.5K Privately Held
SIC: 2741 Miscellaneous publishing

**(G-12009)**
**FANUC AMERICA CORPORATION**
1800 Lakewood Blvd (60192-5008)
PHONE .................................. 847 898-5000
Fax: 847 898-5001
Zach Heuer, *General Mgr*
John Roemisch, *General Mgr*
James Persenaire, *District Mgr*
Mahesh Jadhwani, *Vice Pres*
Chris Hunt, *Senior Buyer*
EMP: 34
SALES (corp-wide): 4.7B Privately Held
WEB: www.fanucrobotics.com
SIC: 3559 3548 3569 Metal finishing equipment for plating, etc.; electric welding equipment; robots, assembly line: industrial & commercial
HQ: Fanuc America Corporation
3900 W Hamlin Rd
Rochester Hills MI 48309
248 377-7000

**(G-12010)**
**FMS USA INC**
2155 Stnngton Ave Ste 119 (60169)
PHONE .................................. 847 519-4400
Joerg Inhelder, *President*
Steven Leibold, *Vice Pres*
EMP: 3
SQ FT: 1,500
SALES (est): 512.4K Privately Held
SIC: 3823 Flow instruments, industrial process type

**(G-12011)**
**FORTUNE INTERNATIONAL TECH LLC**
5883 Chatham Dr (60192-4637)
PHONE .................................. 847 429-9791
Ronald Oberstar, *Mng Member*
Mary Beth Oberstar,
▲ EMP: 2
SALES (est): 332.1K Privately Held
SIC: 2816 5198 Inorganic pigments; colors & pigments

**(G-12012)**
**GANNETT STLLITE INFO NTWRK INC**
Also Called: Gannett Health Care Group
1721 Moon Lake Blvd # 540 (60169-1069)
PHONE .................................. 847 839-1700
Janet Boivin, *Publisher*
Eric Kalter, *CFO*
Brian Taback, *Sales Mgr*
EMP: 70
SALES (corp-wide): 3B Publicly Held
WEB: www.usatoday.com
SIC: 2721 Magazines: publishing only, not printed on site
HQ: Gannett Satellite Information Network, Llc
7950 Jones Branch Dr
Mc Lean VA 22102
703 854-6000

**(G-12013)**
**GENERAL ELECTRIC COMPANY**
2501 Barrington Rd (60192-2061)
PHONE .................................. 847 304-7400
John Ruf, *Branch Mgr*
EMP: 400
SALES (corp-wide): 123.6B Publicly Held
SIC: 3845 Electromedical apparatus
PA: General Electric Company
41 Farnsworth St
Boston MA 02210
617 443-3000

**(G-12014)**
**GEORGIA-PACIFIC LLC**
895 Hillcrest Blvd (60169-6949)
PHONE .................................. 847 885-3920
Jim Schmauf, *Branch Mgr*

---

(PA)=Parent Co (HQ)=Headquarters (DH)=Div Headquarters
✪ = New Business established in last 2 years

2017 Harris Illinois Industrial Directory

477

# Hoffman Estates - Cook County (G-12015)

**(G-12015 cont.)**
EMP: 90
SALES (corp-wide): 27.4B Privately Held
WEB: www.gp.com
SIC: 2431 Millwork
HQ: Georgia-Pacific Llc
133 Peachtree St Ne # 4810
Atlanta GA 30303
404 652-4000

**(G-12015)**
### HAMILTON BEACH BRANDS INC
3100 W Higgins Rd Ste 155 (60169-7244)
PHONE.................847 252-7036
Tom Galey, Branch Mgr
EMP: 38
SALES (corp-wide): 856.4MM Publicly Held
SIC: 3634 Toasters, electric: household
HQ: Hamilton Beach Brands, Inc.
4421 Waterfront Dr
Glen Allen VA 23060
804 273-9777

**(G-12016)**
### HMS TEACH INC
Also Called: Educational Resources
3150 W Higgins Rd Ste 140 (60169-7285)
PHONE.................800 624-2926
Ken Leonard, CEO
Paul Clinkscales, CFO
Nirmal Vaghasiya, Accounts Exec
EMP: 20
SALES (est): 1.7MM Privately Held
SIC: 7372 Educational computer software

**(G-12017)**
### IDEAL SIGN SOLUTIONS LLC
1275 Hunters Rdg W # 200 (60192-4528)
PHONE.................847 695-9091
Kimberly Dellert, Mng Member
EMP: 8 EST: 2010
SALES (est): 506.3K Privately Held
SIC: 3993 Signs & advertising specialties

**(G-12018)**
### INNOLUX TECHNOLOGY USA INC (HQ)
2300 Barrington Rd # 400 (60169-2082)
PHONE.................847 490-5315
Jyh-Chau Wang, President
Brant White, Vice Pres
Leah Mayseless, Finance
EMP: 1
SALES (est): 1.4MM
SALES (corp-wide): 11.2B Privately Held
SIC: 3679 Liquid crystal displays (LCD)
PA: Innolux Corporation
160, Kesyue Rd., Hsinchu Science Park,
Chunan Chen MIA 35000
375 860-00

**(G-12019)**
### INTEGRITY PRTG MCHY SVCS LLC
1650 Glen Lake Rd (60169-4025)
PHONE.................847 834-9484
Thomas Dieden, Principal
EMP: 3 EST: 2011
SALES (est): 414.3K Privately Held
SIC: 2752 Commercial printing, lithographic

**(G-12020)**
### JEWEL OSCO INC
Also Called: Jewel - Osco 3316
1071 N Roselle Rd (60169-4929)
PHONE.................847 882-6477
Fax: 847 882-5116
Charl Pecoraro, Branch Mgr
EMP: 149
SALES (corp-wide): 58.8B Privately Held
SIC: 5912 5122 2833 Drug stores; pharmaceuticals; medicinals & botanicals
HQ: Jewel Osco, Inc.
150 E Pierce Rd Ste 200
Itasca IL 60143
630 948-6000

**(G-12021)**
### KEN YOUNG CONSTRUCTION CO
Also Called: K D R Productions
1185 Ash Rd (60169-4449)
PHONE.................847 358-3026
Ken Young, Owner
EMP: 2
SALES: 500K Privately Held
SIC: 1751 3993 7389 Carpentry work; advertising novelties; recording studio, non-commercial records

**(G-12022)**
### MINERALS TECHNOLOGIES INC
2870 Forbs Ave (60192-3702)
PHONE.................847 851-1500
Jodi Lindsay, General Mgr
Leo Bringer, Manager
Jeanette Snyder, Manager
Veronica Woo, Manager
EMP: 9
SALES (corp-wide): 1.6B Publicly Held
SIC: 3295 Minerals, ground or treated
PA: Minerals Technologies Inc.
622 3rd Ave Fl 38
New York NY 10017
212 878-1800

**(G-12023)**
### MINUTE MAN PRESS
Also Called: Minuteman Press
1037 W Golf Rd (60169-1339)
PHONE.................847 839-9600
Fax: 847 839-9601
Steven Horton, Principal
Tony Hasel, Manager
EMP: 4
SALES (est): 260K Privately Held
SIC: 2752 Commercial printing, lithographic

**(G-12024)**
### MOISTURE DETECTION INC
2200 Stonington Ave (60169-2031)
PHONE.................847 426-0464
Fax: 847 934-9296
Richard Ward PHD, President
Beverly Bacher, Vice Pres
EMP: 6
SQ FT: 3,500
SALES: 300K Privately Held
SIC: 3826 Moisture analyzers

**(G-12025)**
### MOTOROLA SOLUTIONS INC
1299 E Algonquin Rd (60196-1077)
PHONE.................630 308-9394
Rick Osterloh, Branch Mgr
EMP: 139
SALES (corp-wide): 6B Publicly Held
SIC: 3663 Radio & TV communications equipment
PA: Motorola Solutions, Inc.
500 W Monroe St Ste 4400
Chicago IL 60661
847 576-5000

**(G-12026)**
### NANOCOR LLC (DH)
2870 Forbs Ave (60192-3702)
PHONE.................847 851-1900
Fax: 847 851-1919
Gary Castagna, CEO
Peter Maul, President
Tom Hotaling, Business Mgr
Anthony Tomlin, Vice Pres
Jim Edwards, Engineer
▼ EMP: 20
SQ FT: 72,000
SALES (est): 3.5MM
SALES (corp-wide): 1.6B Publicly Held
WEB: www.nanocor.com
SIC: 2821 Plastics materials & resins
HQ: Amcol International Corp
2870 Forbs Ave
Hoffman Estates IL 60192
847 851-1500

**(G-12027)**
### NATIONAL BEDDING COMPANY LLC
Also Called: Serta Mattress Company
2600 4th Ave (60192)
PHONE.................847 645-0200
Fax: 847 645-0205
Melissa Griffin, Personnel
Jim Moss, Sales Dir
Spencer Bennett, Sales Executive
Mickey Morgan, Sales Executive
Jason Parilla, Manager
EMP: 50

SALES (corp-wide): 4.2B Privately Held
WEB: www.sertanational.com
SIC: 5712 2515 Mattresses; box springs, assembled
HQ: National Bedding Company L.L.C.
2600 Forbs Ave
Hoffman Estates IL 60192
847 645-0200

**(G-12028)**
### NATIONAL BEDDING COMPANY LLC (DH)
Also Called: Serta Mattress Company
2600 Forbs Ave (60192-3723)
PHONE.................847 645-0200
Norman Axelrod, Ch of Bd
Richard E Yulman, Ch of Bd
Barbara Bradford, Senior VP
Charissa Dillard, Vice Pres
Thomas Wenholz, Vice Pres
▲ EMP: 130
SQ FT: 90,000
SALES (est): 622.3MM
SALES (corp-wide): 4.2B Privately Held
WEB: www.sertanational.com
SIC: 2515 Box springs, assembled

**(G-12029)**
### NAVRAN ADVNCD NANOPRDCTS DEV
2055 Kettering Rd Ste 101 (60169-2508)
PHONE.................847 331-0809
Shalav Kumar, Administration
EMP: 5
SALES (est): 38.2K Privately Held
SIC: 2865 5169 Cyclic crudes & intermediates; chemical additives

**(G-12030)**
### NILAN/PRIMARC TOOL & MOLD INC
Also Called: Nilan/Primarc Tool & Mold
2125 Stonington Ave (60169-2016)
PHONE.................847 885-2300
Wesley Pietrasik, CEO
Diane Pietrasik, Business Mgr
Gerald Calvacca, Opers Staff
EMP: 19
SALES (est): 1MM Privately Held
SIC: 3061 Mechanical rubber goods

**(G-12031)**
### NSK-AMERICA CORPORATION
1800 Global Pkwy (60192-1578)
PHONE.................847 843-7664
Fax: 847 843-7622
Eiichi Nakanishi, President
Hirohiko Murasi, Exec VP
Hiro Hiko, Vice Pres
Diane Kulak, Accountant
Phil Gozlan, Marketing Staff
▲ EMP: 15
SQ FT: 5,500
SALES (est): 4.2MM Privately Held
WEB: www.nskamerica.com
SIC: 3569 Filters

**(G-12032)**
### NXP USA INC
2800 W Higgins Rd Ste 600 (60169-7247)
PHONE.................847 843-6824
Robert Popper, Electrical Engi
Daniel Herdmann, Manager
EMP: 366
SALES (corp-wide): 9.5B Privately Held
WEB: www.freescale.com
SIC: 3674 Semiconductors & related devices
HQ: Nxp Usa, Inc.
6501 W William Cannon Dr
Austin TX 78735
512 933-8214

**(G-12033)**
### OMRON ELECTRONICS LLC (DH)
Also Called: O E I
2895 Greenspt Pkwy 200 (60169)
PHONE.................847 843-7900
Fax: 847 843-7787
Nigel Blakeway, CEO
Thomas F Mabrey, COO
Sho Sasaki, Research
David Dudley, Engineer
Michael Kurtz, Engineer

EMP: 106
SQ FT: 53,000
SALES (est): 98.9MM
SALES (corp-wide): 7.1B Privately Held
WEB: www.nowling.com
SIC: 5065 3699 Electronic parts; electrical equipment & supplies
HQ: Omron Management Center Of America, Inc.
2895 Greenspoint Pkwy # 100
Hoffman Estates IL 60169
224 520-7650

**(G-12034)**
### PLATT G MOSTARDI
Also Called: Mostardi Platt
5595 Trillium Blvd (60192-3405)
PHONE.................630 993-2100
Robert Platt, Owner
Anthony Decola, Administration
EMP: 12
SALES (est): 1.1MM Privately Held
SIC: 1389 Testing, measuring, surveying & analysis services

**(G-12035)**
### PLOTE CONSTRUCTION INC
Also Called: Beverly Materials
1100 Brandt Dr (60192-1676)
PHONE.................847 695-0422
Daniel R Plote, President
EMP: 50
SALES (corp-wide): 19.9MM Privately Held
WEB: www.plote.com
SIC: 1442 1611 Gravel mining; highway & street paving contractor
PA: Plote Construction Inc.
1100 Brandt Dr
Hoffman Estates IL 60192
847 695-9300

**(G-12036)**
### PLOTE CONSTRUCTION INC (PA)
Also Called: Allied Asphalt Paving Company
1100 Brandt Dr (60192-1676)
PHONE.................847 695-9300
Fax: 847 628-6113
Daniel R Plote, President
Pat Griffin, Superintendent
Ty Ziller, Superintendent
Jerry Reece, Exec VP
Richard Roi, Vice Pres
EMP: 85
SALES (est): 19.9MM Privately Held
SIC: 2951 1531 1442 6552 Asphalt paving mixtures & blocks; speculative builder, single-family houses; speculative builder, multi-family dwellings; construction sand mining; gravel mining; subdividers & developers; highway & street paving contractor; excavation & grading, building construction

**(G-12037)**
### PLOTE INC
1100 Brandt Dr (60192-1676)
PHONE.................847 695-9467
Raymond E Plote, President
Janice Plote, Corp Secy
Daniel R Plote, Vice Pres
Bob Newman, Plant Mgr
Shady Hajjar, Project Mgr
EMP: 85 EST: 1957
SALES (est): 12.9MM Privately Held
WEB: www.plote.com
SIC: 1794 2952 2951 1442 Excavation & grading, building construction; asphalt felts & coatings; asphalt paving mixtures & blocks; construction sand & gravel

**(G-12038)**
### PLUG-IN ELECTRIC CHARGE INC
1660 Nicholson Dr (60192-4512)
PHONE.................224 856-5229
Neil O'Shea, Vice Pres
EMP: 4
SALES (est): 4MM Privately Held
SIC: 3699 Electrical equipment & supplies

**(G-12039)**
### PLUM GROVE PRINTERS INC
2160 Stonington Ave (60169-7204)
PHONE.................847 882-4020

# GEOGRAPHIC SECTION
## Hoffman Estates - Cook County (G-12065)

Peter Lineal, *CEO*
Adam Haines, *Vice Pres*
Andy Grzynkowicz, *Opers Staff*
Kimberley Doreen, *Controller*
**EMP:** 27
**SQ FT:** 9,500
**SALES (est):** 6.9MM **Privately Held**
**WEB:** www.plumgroveprinters.com
**SIC:** 2752 Commercial printing, offset

### (G-12040)
### PO FOOD SPECIALISTS LTD
1800 Huntington Blvd # 610 (60169-6743)
**PHONE** ............................. 847 517-8315
**EMP:** 6
**SALES (est):** 290K **Privately Held**
**SIC:** 2099 Food Mfg/Product Development

### (G-12041)
### PRINCETON INDUSTRIAL PRODUCTS
2119 Stonington Ave (60169-2016)
**PHONE** ............................. 847 839-8500
**Fax:** 847 839-8526
Sue Schreiber, *President*
Elizabeth Lorance, *President*
Mark Huber, *Vice Pres*
Al Schreiber, *VP Opers*
**EMP:** 10
**SQ FT:** 1,400
**SALES (est):** 1.6MM **Privately Held**
**WEB:** www.princetonind.com
**SIC:** 3451 Screw machine products

### (G-12042)
### R & P FUELS
798 Barrington Rd (60169-1107)
**PHONE** ............................. 630 855-2358
**EMP:** 3
**SALES (est):** 158K **Privately Held**
**SIC:** 2869 Fuels

### (G-12043)
### RESINS INC
2200 W Higgins Rd Ste 204 (60169-2400)
**PHONE** ............................. 847 884-0025
Mark Cohen, *President*
**EMP:** 2
**SALES (est):** 378.1K **Privately Held**
**SIC:** 5162 3089 Resins; plastics resins; resins, synthetic; molding primary plastic

### (G-12044)
### ROTARY FORMS AND SYSTEMS INC
2500 W Higgins Rd # 1280 (60169-7220)
**PHONE** ............................. 847 843-8585
Jim Downs, *President*
Mary Downs, *Admin Sec*
**EMP:** 5
**SQ FT:** 700
**SALES:** 1MM **Privately Held**
**WEB:** www.rfsgraphics.com
**SIC:** 2759 Promotional printing

### (G-12045)
### ROYAL BEDDING COMPANY INC (PA)
Also Called: Serta Mattress Co
2600 Forbs Ave (60192-3723)
**PHONE** ............................. 847 645-0200
Alva Moog Jr, *President*
Christopher Shy, *Controller*
Roxanne Franklin, *Info Tech Mgr*
**EMP:** 80 **EST:** 1919
**SQ FT:** 75,000
**SALES (est):** 6.6MM **Privately Held**
**SIC:** 2515 Mattresses, innerspring or box spring; box springs, assembled

### (G-12046)
### S HIMMELSTEIN AND COMPANY
2490 Pembroke Ave (60169-2077)
P.O. Box 1134, Barrington (60011-1134)
**PHONE** ............................. 847 843-3300
**Fax:** 847 843-8488
S Himmelstein, *President*
Geraldine Shamoon, *Purch Mgr*
Allan Jacks, *Engineer*
Steven Tveter, *Sales Mgr*
Angela Woltman, *Sales Mgr*
**EMP:** 48 **EST:** 1960
**SQ FT:** 40,000
**SALES (est):** 12.7MM **Privately Held**
**WEB:** www.himmelstein.com
**SIC:** 3825 Measuring instruments & meters, electric; test equipment for electronic & electrical circuits

### (G-12047)
### S VS INDUSTRIES INC
646 Wainsford Dr (60169-4544)
P.O. Box 681532, Schaumburg (60168-1532)
**PHONE** ............................. 630 408-1083
Bob Vonschaumburg, *President*
Robert Vonschaumburg, *Principal*
Deborah Vonschaumburg, *Vice Pres*
**EMP:** 2
**SALES (est):** 1MM **Privately Held**
**SIC:** 3545 5199 7389 Machine tool attachments & accessories; packaging materials;

### (G-12048)
### SADELCO USA CORP
1120 Warwick Cir N (60169-2330)
**PHONE** ............................. 847 781-8844
Piet Zandbergen, *President*
**EMP:** 2 **EST:** 1996
**SALES (est):** 4.5MM **Privately Held**
**SIC:** 2843 Leather finishing agents

### (G-12049)
### SENSIENT FLAVORS
5115 Sedge Blvd (60192-3708)
**PHONE** ............................. 847 645-7002
Patrick Pingul, *Manager*
Lisa Abney, *Manager*
**EMP:** 140 **EST:** 2014
**SALES (est):** 24.5MM **Privately Held**
**SIC:** 2869 Flavors or flavoring materials, synthetic

### (G-12050)
### SENSIENT FLAVORS LLC (HQ)
2800 W Higgins Rd Ste 900 (60169-7288)
**PHONE** ............................. 317 243-3521
Ralph Pickles, *President*
John Wagner, *Purch Agent*
Pat Horning, *Accounts Mgr*
Rechelle Huck, *Sales Associate*
Eric Dick, *Marketing Mgr*
◆ **EMP:** 320
**SQ FT:** 200,000
**SALES (est):** 340MM
**SALES (corp-wide):** 1.3B **Publicly Held**
**SIC:** 2087 Flavoring extracts & syrups
**PA:** Sensient Technologies Corporation
777 E Wisconsin Ave # 1100
Milwaukee WI 53202
414 271-6755

### (G-12051)
### SERTA INC (DH)
Also Called: Serta International
2600 Forbs Ave (60192-3723)
**PHONE** ............................. 847 645-0200
Gary T Fazio, *CEO*
Michael Traub, *President*
Kristi Morris, *Business Mgr*
Maria Balistreri, *Vice Pres*
Susan Ebaugh, *Vice Pres*
▲ **EMP:** 140 **EST:** 1931
**SALES (est):** 950.1MM
**SALES (corp-wide):** 4.2B **Privately Held**
**WEB:** www.serta.com
**SIC:** 2515 Mattresses & foundations

### (G-12052)
### SIEMENS INDUSTRY INC
2501 Barrington Rd (60192-2061)
P.O. Box 2134, Carol Stream (60132-2134)
**PHONE** ............................. 301 419-2600
Neil Tubman, *Director*
**EMP:** 87
**SALES (corp-wide):** 89.6B **Privately Held**
**SIC:** 3822 Air conditioning & refrigeration controls
**HQ:** Siemens Industry, Inc.
1000 Deerfield Pkwy
Buffalo Grove IL 60089
847 215-1000

### (G-12053)
### SIEMENS MED SOLUTIONS USA INC
Also Called: Hoffman Nuclear Medicine Group
2501 Barrington Rd (60192-2061)
**PHONE** ............................. 847 304-7700
Jodi Kaelin, *Partner*
Praveen Nadkarni, *Business Mgr*
Michael Sigmund, *Exec VP*
Sam Brandt, *Vice Pres*
Jeff Heer, *Vice Pres*
**EMP:** 60
**SALES (corp-wide):** 89.6B **Privately Held**
**WEB:** www.siemensmedical.com
**SIC:** 3829 3845 Medical diagnostic systems, nuclear; electromedical equipment
**HQ:** Siemens Medical Solutions Usa, Inc.
40 Liberty Blvd
Malvern PA 19355
610 219-6300

### (G-12054)
### SILESIA FLAVORS INC
5250 Prairie Stone Pkwy (60192-3709)
**PHONE** ............................. 847 645-0270
**Fax:** 847 645-0266
Clemons Hanke, *President*
Philip Roman, *Purch Mgr*
Richard Bartoszewski, *Controller*
Richard Bartszewski, *Controller*
Tim Castle, *Accounts Mgr*
▲ **EMP:** 25
**SQ FT:** 26,000
**SALES (est):** 6.3MM
**SALES (corp-wide):** 113.6MM **Privately Held**
**WEB:** www.silesiafl.com
**SIC:** 2087 Extracts, flavoring
**PA:** Silesia Gerhard Hanke Gmbh & Co. Kg
Am Alten Bach 20-24
Neuss 41470
213 778-40

### (G-12055)
### SOLID SOUND INC
2400 Hassell Rd Ste 430 (60169-2041)
**PHONE** ............................. 847 490-2101
Judd Sager, *President*
Thomas Sudow, *Vice Pres*
**EMP:** 3
**SQ FT:** 2,200
**SALES (est):** 210K **Privately Held**
**SIC:** 3652 Master records or tapes, preparation of

### (G-12056)
### SOLIDYNE CORPORATION
2155 Stonington Ave # 105 (60169-2057)
**PHONE** ............................. 847 394-3333
Baha Erturk, *CEO*
**EMP:** 2 **EST:** 1980
**SALES (est):** 283.8K **Privately Held**
**SIC:** 3822 Auto controls regulating residntl & coml environmt & applncs

### (G-12057)
### SOLUTIONS MANUFACTURING INC
2109 Stonington Ave (60169-2016)
**PHONE** ............................. 847 310-4506
**Fax:** 847 310-4508
Michael Sosine, *President*
Tim Lucey, *Exec VP*
Jeff Lebelle, *Vice Pres*
Amy Lanahan, *Manager*
**EMP:** 20 **EST:** 1994
**SQ FT:** 5,000
**SALES (est):** 3.8MM **Privately Held**
**WEB:** www.solutionsmfg.net
**SIC:** 3599 Machine & other job shop work

### (G-12058)
### STAR CUTTER CO
5200 Prairie Stone Pkwy (60192-3709)
**PHONE** ............................. 231 264-5661
Ronald Peruski, *Branch Mgr*
**EMP:** 4
**SALES (corp-wide):** 228.1MM **Privately Held**
**SIC:** 3559 Sewing machines & hat & zipper making machinery
**PA:** Star Cutter Co.
23461 Industrial Park Dr
Farmington Hills MI 48335
248 474-8200

### (G-12059)
### STARFISH VENTURES INC
Also Called: Aquarium Adventure & Pet Land
11a Golf Ctr (60169-4910)
**PHONE** ............................. 847 490-9334
**Fax:** 847 490-9322
Dan Star, *President*
**EMP:** 50
**SALES (est):** 4.2MM **Privately Held**
**WEB:** www.aquariumadventure.com
**SIC:** 3999 Pet supplies

### (G-12060)
### STEVENS PLASTIC INC
Also Called: Tangler Wrangler
2125 Stonington Ave (60169-2016)
**PHONE** ............................. 847 885-2378
Steven Ballek, *President*
Christine Ballek, *Admin Sec*
**EMP:** 20 **EST:** 1976
**SQ FT:** 14,000
**SALES (est):** 4.6MM **Privately Held**
**WEB:** www.stevensmolding.com
**SIC:** 3089 Injection molding of plastics

### (G-12061)
### STRICTLY STAINLESS INC
2108 Stonington Ave (60169-2017)
**PHONE** ............................. 847 885-2890
Todd Hopp, *President*
**EMP:** 3
**SALES:** 600K **Privately Held**
**SIC:** 3312 7389 Stainless steel; artists' agents & brokers

### (G-12062)
### TANGENT SYSTEMS INC
2155 Stnngton Ave Ste 107 (60169)
**PHONE** ............................. 847 882-3833
**Fax:** 847 882-3780
Steve Mack, *President*
Dave Berkowitz, *Manager*
**EMP:** 16
**SQ FT:** 10,246
**SALES (est):** 1.7MM **Privately Held**
**WEB:** www.tansys.com
**SIC:** 7371 3577 Computer software development; magnetic ink & optical scanning devices; bar code (magnetic ink) printers; magnetic ink recognition devices; optical scanning devices

### (G-12063)
### TATE & LYLE AMERICAS LLC
5450 Prairie Stone Pkwy # 170 (60192-3403)
**PHONE** ............................. 847 396-7500
John Schnake, *Branch Mgr*
**EMP:** 21
**SALES (corp-wide):** 3.4B **Privately Held**
**SIC:** 2046 Corn & other vegetable starches
**HQ:** Tate & Lyle Americas Llc
2200 E Eldorado St
Decatur IL 62521
217 421-2964

### (G-12064)
### TEGNA INC
Also Called: Oncourse Learning
1721 Moon Lake Blvd # 540 (60169-1069)
**PHONE** ............................. 847 490-6657
Cynthia Vlasich, *Branch Mgr*
**EMP:** 120
**SALES (corp-wide):** 3.3B **Publicly Held**
**WEB:** www.gannett.com
**SIC:** 2711 2721 Commercial printing & newspaper publishing combined; periodicals
**PA:** Tegna Inc.
7950 Jones Branch Dr
Mc Lean VA 22102
703 873-6600

### (G-12065)
### THOMAS ENGINEERING INC (PA)
Also Called: Triangle Metals Div
575 W Central Rd (60192-1999)
P.O. Box 950198 (60195)
**PHONE** ............................. 847 358-5800
Brian T Casey, *Ch of Bd*

Joseph Kingsley, *Exec VP*
Jean Y Lefloc'h, *Vice Pres*
Karyn Thompson, *Vice Pres*
Thomas P Driscoll, *VP Mfg*
▲ **EMP:** 100 **EST:** 1959
**SQ FT:** 72,000
**SALES (est):** 25.2MM **Privately Held**
**WEB:** www.thomaseng.com
**SIC:** 3559 5084 Pharmaceutical machinery; industrial machinery & equipment

**(G-12066)**
**UNIVERSAL HOLDINGS INC**
2800 W Higgins Rd Ste 210 (60169-7284)
**PHONE** .................... 224 353-6198
Dean Raschke, *President*
Gloria McDonald, *Vice Pres*
John Read, *Admin Sec*
**EMP:** 18
**SALES (est):** 3.6MM **Privately Held**
**SIC:** 5084 3845 5199 Plastic products machinery; electrocardiographs; cards, plastic: unprinted

**(G-12067)**
**UPHAM & WALSH LUMBER CO**
2155 Stnngton Ave Ste 209 (60169)
**PHONE** .................... 847 519-1010
Christopher Hayden, *Owner*
Carter Hayden, *Co-Owner*
Kelly Hayden, *Purchasing*
▲ **EMP:** 6
**SQ FT:** 1,550
**SALES (est):** 685K **Privately Held**
**WEB:** www.uphamwalshlumber.com
**SIC:** 5031 2448 2441 Lumber: rough, dressed & finished; wood pallets & skids; nailed wood boxes & shook

**(G-12068)**
**VISIONARY SLEEP LLC**
1721 Moon Lake Blvd (60169-1069)
**PHONE** .................... 224 829-0440
Robert L Sherman, *CEO*
Barbara Bradford, *President*
Jayesh Patel, *COO*
Shannon Brogan, *Sales Mgr*
**EMP:** 181
**SALES (est):** 3.6MM **Privately Held**
**SIC:** 2515 Mattresses & bedsprings

**(G-12069)**
**WELLNESS CENTER USA INC (PA)**
2500 W Higgins Rd Ste 770 (60169-2047)
**PHONE** .................... 847 925-1885
**Fax:** 847 925-1859
Andrew J Kandalepas, *President*
Ricky Howard, *President*
Jay Joshi, *Admin Sec*
**EMP:** 7
**SALES:** 481.2K **Publicly Held**
**SIC:** 8099 3829 2834 Nutrition services; medical services organization; measuring & controlling devices; pharmaceutical preparations

**(G-12070)**
**ZEBRA SOFTWARE INC**
5525 Mallard Ln (60192-4564)
P.O. Box 95592 (60195-0592)
**PHONE** .................... 847 742-9110
Usama Noureldin, *CEO*
**EMP:** 7 **EST:** 1989
**SALES (est):** 200K **Privately Held**
**WEB:** www.zebrasoft.com
**SIC:** 7372 Prepackaged software

## Hoffman Estates
### Lake County

**(G-12071)**
**CSI2D INC**
4907 Turnberry Dr (60010-5678)
**PHONE** .................... 312 282-7407
Steven Kroll, *CEO*
**EMP:** 4
**SALES (est):** 180K **Privately Held**
**SIC:** 3674 Semiconductors & related devices

**(G-12072)**
**NORTHWEST MARBLE PRODUCTS (PA)**
1229 Silver Pine Dr (60010-5877)
**PHONE** .................... 630 860-2288
**Fax:** 630 860-5060
Keith Madelung, *President*
Maureen Madelung, *Corp Secy*
Kathy Parus, *Office Mgr*
**EMP:** 30
**SQ FT:** 25,000
**SALES (est):** 2.2MM **Privately Held**
**SIC:** 3088 2541 2434 Bathroom fixtures, plastic; sinks, plastic; tubs (bath, shower & laundry), plastic; shower stalls, fiberglass & plastic; wood partitions & fixtures; wood kitchen cabinets

## Homer
### Champaign County

**(G-12073)**
**ALLENS FARM QUALITY MEATS**
Rr 49 (61849)
P.O. Box 24 (61849-0024)
**PHONE** .................... 217 896-2532
Ronald D Allen, *President*
**EMP:** 5 **EST:** 1964
**SQ FT:** 11,700
**SALES (est):** 396.4K **Privately Held**
**SIC:** 5421 5147 2013 2011 Meat markets, including freezer provisioniers; meats, fresh; sausages & other prepared meats; meat packing plants

**(G-12074)**
**ALLERTON SUPPLY COMPANY**
1050 N &Amp 2600 E (61849)
**PHONE** .................... 217 896-2522
Fred Page, *Branch Mgr*
**EMP:** 12
**SALES (corp-wide):** 14.1MM **Privately Held**
**SIC:** 2875 5261 Fertilizers, mixing only; fertilizer
**PA:** Allerton Supply Company
309 E Yates
Allerton IL 61810
217 834-3301

**(G-12075)**
**HOMER VINTAGE BAKERY**
111 S Main St (61849-1232)
**PHONE** .................... 217 896-2538
Crystal Allen, *Principal*
**EMP:** 5
**SQ FT:** 2,000
**SALES (est):** 139.9K **Privately Held**
**SIC:** 2051 5812 5499 Cakes, bakery: except frozen; pies, bakery: except frozen; fast-food restaurant, independent; soft drinks

## Homer Glen
### Will County

**(G-12076)**
**ARTHUR R BAKER INC**
13507 W Oakwood Ct (60491-8157)
**PHONE** .................... 708 301-4828
**Fax:** 708 596-8230
Fred Fairfield, *President*
Cynthia Fairfield, *Corp Secy*
Betty Smith, *Vice Pres*
**EMP:** 7
**SQ FT:** 3,600
**SALES (est):** 642.8K **Privately Held**
**SIC:** 5999 2752 Architectural supplies; commercial printing, lithographic

**(G-12077)**
**DRAPERY ROOM INC**
15757 Annico Dr Ste 5 (60491-4738)
**PHONE** .................... 708 301-3374
**Fax:** 708 301-3375
Lorraine Simard, *President*
**EMP:** 10
**SQ FT:** 2,000
**SALES (est):** 800K **Privately Held**
**SIC:** 2211 2391 Draperies & drapery fabrics, cotton; curtains & draperies

**(G-12078)**
**FLOORING WAREHOUSE DIRECT INC**
14126 Camdan Rd (60491-8259)
**PHONE** .................... 815 730-6767
Jessica S Ringelsten, *President*
**EMP:** 5
**SALES (est):** 1.5MM **Privately Held**
**SIC:** 2426 Flooring, hardwood

**(G-12079)**
**FOURIER SYSTEMS INC**
12610 W Hank Ct E (60491-9294)
**PHONE** .................... 708 478-5333
Tamar Antokol, *Principal*
**EMP:** 5 **EST:** 2011
**SALES (est):** 521.3K **Privately Held**
**SIC:** 5045 3571 Computers, peripherals & software; electronic computers

**(G-12080)**
**GLITTER YOUR PALLET**
14350 S Saddle Brook Ln (60491-8567)
**PHONE** .................... 708 516-8494
Lisa Schultz, *Principal*
**EMP:** 3
**SALES (est):** 125.7K **Privately Held**
**SIC:** 2448 Pallets, wood & wood with metal

**(G-12081)**
**HOMELAND**
13910 S Mormann Ln (60491-9317)
**PHONE** .................... 708 415-4555
**EMP:** 3
**SALES (est):** 150K **Privately Held**
**SIC:** 2721 Periodicals

**(G-12082)**
**LEAS BAKING COMPANY LLC**
14660 Pebble Creek Ct (60491-9355)
**PHONE** .................... 708 710-3404
Robert Trebe, *Principal*
**EMP:** 4
**SALES (est):** 208.2K **Privately Held**
**SIC:** 2051 Bread, cake & related products

**(G-12083)**
**NAMA GRAPHICS E LLC**
15751 Annico Dr Ste 2 (60491-4739)
**PHONE** .................... 262 966-3853
Rick Smith, *Principal*
John Griffin, *Principal*
**EMP:** 3
**SALES (est):** 235.7K **Privately Held**
**SIC:** 3555 Printing trades machinery

**(G-12084)**
**OMNICARE GROUP INC**
13557 Parkland Ct (60491-7577)
**PHONE** .................... 708 949-8802
Abdullah H Darwish, *President*
**EMP:** 3
**SQ FT:** 1,800
**SALES (est):** 634.1K **Privately Held**
**SIC:** 3841 Surgical & medical instruments

**(G-12085)**
**P I W CORPORATION**
15765 Annico Dr (60491-9273)
**PHONE** .................... 708 301-5100
**Fax:** 708 301-5105
Gloria Shepherd, *President*
John D Shepherd, *Vice Pres*
Donna Throw, *Manager*
John Shepherd, *Admin Sec*
John K Shepherd, *Admin Sec*
**EMP:** 11
**SQ FT:** 35,000
**SALES (est):** 2.2MM **Privately Held**
**WEB:** www.piwcorp.com
**SIC:** 3446 Architectural metalwork

**(G-12086)**
**SHERI LAW ART GLASS LTD**
12551 W 159th St (60491-7845)
**PHONE** .................... 708 301-2800
Sharon A Law, *President*
**EMP:** 3
**SALES (est):** 344.2K **Privately Held**
**SIC:** 3231 Art glass: made from purchased glass

**(G-12087)**
**SIMPLY SALSA LLC**
12630 W 159th St (60491-7855)
**PHONE** .................... 815 514-3993
Deless Jennifer, *Mng Member*
**EMP:** 7
**SALES (est):** 550K **Privately Held**
**SIC:** 2033 2035 Tomato sauce: packaged in cans, jars, etc.; seasonings, vegetable sauces (except tomato & dry)

**(G-12088)**
**SLICK LOCKS LLC**
15959 W 143rd St (60491-8541)
**PHONE** .................... 815 838-3557
Robert J Kaminsky, *Principal*
**EMP:** 4
**SALES (est):** 432.8K **Privately Held**
**SIC:** 3429 Door locks, bolts & checks

**(G-12089)**
**ZETA MANUFACTURING COMPANY**
13338 W Oak Ct (60491-5974)
**PHONE** .................... 708 301-3766
Joyce Horvath, *President*
**EMP:** 3
**SALES (est):** 250K **Privately Held**
**SIC:** 3999 Manufacturing industries

## Homewood
### Cook County

**(G-12090)**
**AB&D CUSTOM FURNITURE INC**
Also Called: AB & D Custom Cabinets
17200 Palmer Blvd (60430-4601)
**PHONE** .................... 708 922-9061
**Fax:** 708 563-0915
Randall Agate, *President*
Patrick Stone, *Corp Secy*
Jose Lopez, *Design Engr*
Marie Agate, *Office Mgr*
Christopher Agate, *Director*
**EMP:** 25
**SQ FT:** 40,000
**SALES (est):** 4.4MM **Privately Held**
**WEB:** www.abdfurniture.com
**SIC:** 2541 2521 2511 Store & office display cases & fixtures; cabinets, lockers & shelving; wood office furniture; wood household furniture

**(G-12091)**
**APOLLO PRINTING INC**
2135 183rd St (60430-3225)
**PHONE** .................... 815 741-3065
**EMP:** 2 **EST:** 1979
**SQ FT:** 2,000
**SALES:** 320K **Privately Held**
**SIC:** 2752 7336 Commercial Lithograhic Printer & Graphic Designer

**(G-12092)**
**BOLZONI AURAMO INC**
17635 Hoffman Way (60430-2186)
**PHONE** .................... 708 957-8809
**Fax:** 708 957-8832
Roberto Scotti, *President*
Robert Lensink, *Managing Dir*
Ken Smith, *Managing Dir*
Joost Fissette, *Area Mgr*
Koen Lensink, *Area Mgr*
▲ **EMP:** 48
**SQ FT:** 40,000
**SALES (est):** 30MM
**SALES (corp-wide):** 2.5B **Publicly Held**
**WEB:** www.bolzoni-auramo.com
**SIC:** 5084 3537 Lift trucks & parts; lift trucks, industrial: fork, platform, straddle, etc.
**HQ:** Bolzoni Spa
Via I Maggio 103
Podenzano PC 29027
052 355-5511

**(G-12093)**
**CARL BUDDIG AND COMPANY (PA)**
950 175th St (60430-2027)
**PHONE** .................... 708 798-0900
**Fax:** 708 798-6709
Robert Budding, *President*

Thomas Buddig, *Co-CEO*
Timothy Buddig, *Vice Pres*
Karen Noble, *Vice Pres*
David Oyervides, *Purch Mgr*
**EMP:** 50
**SQ FT:** 15,000
**SALES (est):** 147.9MM  **Privately Held**
**SIC: 2013**  2022  Smoked meats from purchased meat; sausages from purchased meat; natural cheese

### (G-12094)
### CBS BROADCASTING INC
1055 175th St Ste 102  (60430-4615)
**PHONE**..................................708 206-2900
Walter Gray, *Manager*
**EMP:** 30
**SALES (corp-wide):** 13.1B  **Publicly Held**
**WEB:** www.cbs4.com
**SIC: 3575**  Computer terminals, monitors & components
**HQ:** Cbs Broadcasting Inc.
51 W 52nd St
New York NY 10019
212 975-4321

### (G-12095)
### DUNIGAN CUSTOM WOODWORKING
1426 Ridge Rd  (60430-1827)
**PHONE**..................................708 351-5213
Dustin Dunigan, *Principal*
**EMP:** 4
**SALES (est):** 387.8K  **Privately Held**
**SIC: 2431**  Millwork

### (G-12096)
### DZRO-BANS INTERNATIONAL INC
3011 183rd St  (60430-2804)
**PHONE**..................................779 324-2740
Emmanuel Bansa Jr, *CEO*
Connie Bansa, *President*
Melishia Bansa, *Director*
**EMP:** 4
**SQ FT:** 800
**SALES (est):** 463.3K  **Privately Held**
**SIC: 5136**  2844  5141  5137  Men's & boys' clothing; face creams or lotions; groceries, general line; women's & children's clothing; commercial art & graphic design

### (G-12097)
### ENTRIGUE DESIGNS
825 Maple Ave  (60430-2031)
**PHONE**..................................708 647-6159
Carrol Jones, *Principal*
**EMP:** 3
**SALES (est):** 168.5K  **Privately Held**
**SIC: 3089**  5932  Plastic hardware & building products; clothing & shoes, secondhand

### (G-12098)
### FEDEX OFFICE & PRINT SVCS INC
17952 Halsted St  (60430-2014)
**PHONE**..................................708 799-5323
**Fax:** 708 799-5369
Darrick Walker, *Branch Mgr*
**EMP:** 4
**SALES (corp-wide):** 50.3B  **Publicly Held**
**SIC: 2752**  Commercial printing, lithographic
**HQ:** Fedex Office And Print Services, Inc.
7900 Legacy Dr
Plano TX 75024
214 550-7000

### (G-12099)
### GALLERY OFFICE PDTS & PRTRS
18031 Dixie Hwy  (60430-1705)
**PHONE**..................................708 798-2220
**Fax:** 708 798-1562
Allen Leppellere, *Owner*
Patricia Leppellere, *Administration*
**EMP:** 5
**SQ FT:** 5,000
**SALES (est):** 490K  **Privately Held**
**WEB:** www.galleryofficepros.com
**SIC: 5943**  2752  Office forms & supplies; commercial printing, offset

### (G-12100)
### HI TECH
1551 187th St  (60430-3849)
**PHONE**..................................708 957-4210
**EMP:** 1 **EST:** 2009
**SALES:** 950K  **Privately Held**
**SIC: 3661**  2517  Mfg Telephone/Telegraph Apparatus

### (G-12101)
### HOMEWOOD-FLOSSMOOR CHRONICLE
1361 Olive Rd  (60430-2409)
**PHONE**..................................630 728-2661
Marilyn Thomas, *Principal*
Eric Crump, *Manager*
Michael Schlesinger,
**EMP:** 4 **EST:** 2015
**SALES (est):** 173.6K  **Privately Held**
**SIC: 2721**  Magazines: publishing only, not printed on site

### (G-12102)
### INK SPOTS PRTG & MEIDA DESIGN
Also Called: Isp
1131 175th St Ste B  (60430-4604)
**PHONE**..................................708 754-1300
William Tucker, *Owner*
**EMP:** 4
**SQ FT:** 1,600
**SALES:** 265K  **Privately Held**
**SIC: 2732**  2759  2752  2721  Book printing; laser printing; commercial printing, lithographic; magazines: publishing & printing

### (G-12103)
### INX GROUP LTD
1000 Maple Rd  (60430-2047)
**PHONE**..................................708 799-1993
Nicole Esposito, *Human Res Dir*
James Kochanny, *Manager*
**EMP:** 6
**SALES (corp-wide):** 1.3B  **Privately Held**
**SIC: 2893**  Printing ink
**HQ:** The Inx Group Ltd
150 N Martingale Rd # 700
Schaumburg IL 60173
630 382-1800

### (G-12104)
### MITCHLLS CNDIES ICE CREAMS INC
18211 Dixie Hwy  (60430-2205)
**PHONE**..................................708 799-3835
George E Mitchell, *President*
Mary Kay Mitchell, *Treasurer*
**EMP:** 14
**SQ FT:** 4,000
**SALES (est):** 640K  **Privately Held**
**SIC: 5441**  5812  2024  5143  Candy; ice cream stands or dairy bars; ice cream & frozen desserts; ice cream & ices

### (G-12105)
### ROSS-GAGE INC
2346 Alexander Ter  (60430-3102)
**PHONE**..................................708 347-3659
Thomas W Ross, *Branch Mgr*
**EMP:** 19
**SALES (corp-wide):** 7.2MM  **Privately Held**
**SIC: 2675**  Die-cut paper & board
**PA:** Ross-Gage Inc
8502 Brookville Rd
Indianapolis IN 46239
317 283-2323

### (G-12106)
### WALTER LAGESTEE INC
Also Called: Walts Food Center
2345 183rd St Ste 2  (60430-3141)
**PHONE**..................................708 957-2974
**Fax:** 708 957-4963
Jerry Scaffguard, *Manager*
**EMP:** 200
**SQ FT:** 4,800
**SALES (corp-wide):** 117.8MM  **Privately Held**
**WEB:** www.waltsfoods.com
**SIC: 5411**  5921  5992  5912  Grocery stores; beer (packaged); florists; drug stores & proprietary stores; cookies & crackers; bread, cake & related products
**PA:** Walter Lagestee, Inc.
16145 State St
South Holland IL 60473
708 596-3166

## Hoopeston
### *Vermilion County*

### (G-12107)
### CLINE CONCRETE PRODUCTS
438 W Thompson Ave  (60942-1067)
**PHONE**..................................217 283-5012
Gerald L Cline, *President*
Mae Dell Cline, *Vice Pres*
**EMP:** 10  **EST:** 1950
**SQ FT:** 10,000
**SALES (est):** 1.2MM  **Privately Held**
**SIC: 3272**  3523  3281  Septic tanks, concrete; monuments, concrete; tile, precast terrazzo or concrete; farm machinery & equipment; cut stone & stone products

### (G-12108)
### CRAFTSMEN PRINTING
217 Bank St  (60942-1510)
**PHONE**..................................217 283-9574
**Fax:** 217 283-9558
Daniel W De Neal, *Owner*
**EMP:** 3
**SALES:** 100K  **Privately Held**
**SIC: 2752**  2791  2789  2759  Commercial printing, offset; typesetting; bookbinding & related work; commercial printing

### (G-12109)
### DAVES ELECTRONIC SERVICE
105 E Penn St  (60942-1501)
**PHONE**..................................217 283-5010
**Fax:** 217 283-5161
David Coffman, *President*
**EMP:** 15
**SALES (est):** 791.1K  **Privately Held**
**SIC: 7699**  3931  3672  Organ tuning & repair; organ parts & materials; printed circuit boards

### (G-12110)
### EZEE ROLL MANUFACTURING CO
20 N 3000 East Rd  (60942-1473)
P.O. Box 47  (60942-0047)
**PHONE**..................................217 339-2279
Lucille Layden, *President*
Paul Layden, *Vice Pres*
Mark Layden, *Treasurer*
▲ **EMP:** 6
**SQ FT:** 700
**SALES (est):** 1.2MM  **Privately Held**
**WEB:** www.ezeeroll.com
**SIC: 3537**  3714  3548  3444  Trucks, tractors, loaders, carriers & similar equipment; motor vehicle parts & accessories; welding apparatus; sheet metalwork

### (G-12111)
### FELSTE CO INC
217 N 9th Ave  (60942-1016)
**PHONE**..................................217 283-4884
Eugene Felstehausen, *President*
Kevin Moore, *President*
**EMP:** 5
**SALES:** 270K  **Privately Held**
**SIC: 3556**  Food products machinery

### (G-12112)
### L S DIESEL REPAIR INC
220 N 10th Ave  (60942-1024)
**PHONE**..................................217 283-5537
Layton Seggebruch, *President*
Kim Seggebruch, *Corp Secy*
**EMP:** 3
**SALES (est):** 410K  **Privately Held**
**SIC: 3519**  Diesel engine rebuilding

### (G-12113)
### PERFORMANCE DIESEL SERVICE
7586 E 4200 North Rd  (60942-6299)
**PHONE**..................................217 375-4429
Robert Marshall, *President*
**EMP:** 3
**SALES (est):** 463.2K  **Privately Held**
**SIC: 3519**  Diesel, semi-diesel or duel-fuel engines, including marine

### (G-12114)
### PRODUCTION TOOLING AND AUTOMTN
Also Called: Production Tooling & Automtn
342 N Dixie Hwy  (60942-1032)
**PHONE**..................................217 283-7373
Paula Ridl, *President*
Mark Ridl, *Vice Pres*
**EMP:** 5
**SQ FT:** 4,500
**SALES:** 400K  **Privately Held**
**SIC: 3312**  Tool & die steel & alloys

### (G-12115)
### SCHUMACHER ELECTRIC CORP
1025 E Thompson Ave  (60942-1368)
**PHONE**..................................217 283-5551
**Fax:** 217 283-5991
John Waldron, *COO*
**EMP:** 35
**SALES (corp-wide):** 142.6MM  **Privately Held**
**SIC: 3629**  Battery chargers, rectifying or nonrotating
**PA:** Schumacher Electric Corporation
801 E Business Center Dr
Mount Prospect IL 60056
847 385-1600

### (G-12116)
### SILGAN CONTAINERS MFG CORP
324 W Main St  (60942-1130)
**PHONE**..................................217 283-5501
**Fax:** 217 241-6629
Jerry Northam, *Human Res Dir*
Colin Bertsch, *Branch Mgr*
**EMP:** 110
**SALES (corp-wide):** 3.6B  **Publicly Held**
**WEB:** www.silgancontainers.com
**SIC: 3411**  Can lids & ends, metal
**HQ:** Silgan Containers Manufacturing Corporation
21800 Oxnard St Ste 600
Woodland Hills CA 91367

### (G-12117)
### SILVER BROS INC
105 E Washington St  (60942-1698)
**PHONE**..................................217 283-7751
**Fax:** 217 283-5778
David Silver, *President*
Brian Silver, *Vice Pres*
Deanna Silver, *Admin Sec*
**EMP:** 6
**SQ FT:** 10,000
**SALES:** 1.1MM  **Privately Held**
**SIC: 1541**  3273  Industrial buildings, new construction; warehouse construction; ready-mixed concrete

### (G-12118)
### TEASDALE FOODS INC
Also Called: Hoopeston Foods
215 W Washington St  (60942-1145)
P.O. Box 405  (60942-0405)
**PHONE**..................................217 283-7771
Tony Rocco, *Vice Pres*
Mel Lollar, *Plant Mgr*
Kathy Norris, *Opers Staff*
Ted Goodner, *Branch Mgr*
Charles Page, *IT Specialist*
**EMP:** 82
**SALES (corp-wide):** 195.3MM  **Privately Held**
**SIC: 2032**  Beans, without meat: packaged in cans, jars, etc
**PA:** Teasdale Foods, Inc.
901 Packers St
Atwater CA 95301
209 358-5616

### (G-12119)
### TIMES REPUBLIC
Also Called: The Chronicle
308 E Main St  (60942-1505)
**PHONE**..................................217 283-5111
Kevin Armold, *Manager*
Carol Hicks, *Manager*
**EMP:** 4  **Privately Held**
**WEB:** www.communitymediagroup.com

**Hoopeston - Vermilion County (G-12120)** — GEOGRAPHIC SECTION

SIC: 2711 Newspapers, publishing & printing
HQ: The Times Republic
1492 E Walnut St
Watseka IL 60970
815 432-5227

**(G-12120)**
**TYLERS FAB & WELDING INC**
1013 W Main St (60942-1044)
PHONE..................................217 283-6855
Deborah M Tyler, *President*
Kevin E Tyler, *Vice Pres*
EMP: 2
SALES (est): 200.9K Privately Held
SIC: 7692 Welding repair

## Hopedale
### Tazewell County

**(G-12121)**
**CARROLL DISTRG & CNSTR SUP INC**
201 Ford Ave (61747-9492)
PHONE..................................309 449-6044
Dan Reed, *Branch Mgr*
EMP: 4
SALES (corp-wide): 75.9MM Privately Held
SIC: 5082 3444 Contractors' materials; concrete forms; sheet metal
PA: Carroll Distributing & Construction Supply, Inc.
205 S Iowa Ave
Ottumwa IA 52501
641 683-1888

**(G-12122)**
**J & J EQUIPMENT INC**
260 4th Ave (61747)
PHONE..................................309 449-5442
Fax: 309 449-5442
Joe Slager, *President*
Alice Slager, *Vice Pres*
EMP: 4
SQ FT: 4,000
SALES: 330K Privately Held
SIC: 3523 Farm machinery & equipment

## Hudson
### Mclean County

**(G-12123)**
**HAMILTON-MAURER INTL INC**
Also Called: H M I
14391 E 2400 North Rd (61748-7556)
PHONE..................................713 468-6805
Rolf Maurer, *President*
EMP: 5
SALES: 500K Privately Held
SIC: 3829 Physical property testing equipment

**(G-12124)**
**KONGSKILDE INDUSTRIES INC**
19500 N 1425 East Rd (61748-7630)
PHONE..................................309 452-3300
Fax: 309 820-1364
Hans Rasmussen, *President*
John L Pratt, *Principal*
Arnold McKinnis, *Purch Mgr*
Brian Rudin, *Design Engr*
Kathryn Lyssemko, *CFO*
▲ EMP: 110
SALES (est): 40.7MM
SALES (corp-wide): 6.4B Privately Held
WEB: www.kongskilde.com
SIC: 3535 3523 Pneumatic tube conveyor systems; soil preparation machinery, except turf & grounds; fertilizing machinery, farm
HQ: Kongskilde Industries A/S
Skalskorvej 64
SorO 4180
336 835-00

**(G-12125)**
**STARLIGHT SOFTWARE SYSTEM INC**
25130 Arrowhead Ln (61748-7400)
P.O. Box 37, Normal (61761-0037)
PHONE..................................309 454-7349
Lee Green, *President*
EMP: 1
SALES: 500K Privately Held
WEB: www.starlightsoftware.com
SIC: 7372 Prepackaged software

**(G-12126)**
**SUN AG INC**
108 N Shiner St (61748-9393)
P.O. Box 195 (61748-0195)
PHONE..................................309 726-1331
John Layden, *Branch Mgr*
John N Laydem, *Manager*
EMP: 5
SQ FT: 1,200
SALES (corp-wide): 29.1MM Privately Held
SIC: 2873 2874 5261 Nitrogenous fertilizers; phosphatic fertilizers; fertilizer
PA: Sun Ag, Inc.
2702 County Road 800 N
El Paso IL 61738
309 527-6500

**(G-12127)**
**WHITACRES COUNTRY OAKS SHOP**
Also Called: Whitacres Handcrafted
704 S Broadway St (61748-9162)
PHONE..................................309 726-1305
Fax: 309 726-1329
Rick Whitacre, *Owner*
Bob Brady, *Co-Owner*
Ed Brady, *Co-Owner*
William Brady, *Co-Owner*
Mike O'Grady, *Co-Owner*
EMP: 17
SQ FT: 40,000
SALES (est): 1MM Privately Held
WEB: www.whitacresfurniture.com
SIC: 5712 2511 Furniture stores; desks, household: wood

## Humboldt
### Coles County

**(G-12128)**
**BOBBIE HAYCRAFT**
Also Called: Bidwells Candies
110 Homann Ct (61931-9735)
PHONE..................................217 856-2194
Bobbie Haycraft, *Owner*
EMP: 3
SALES (est): 147.1K Privately Held
SIC: 2064 Candy & other confectionery products

**(G-12129)**
**NORTH OKAW WOODWORKING**
2409 E County Road 1700n (61931-8009)
PHONE..................................217 856-2178
Clarence Stutzman, *Owner*
EMP: 5
SALES (est): 245.6K Privately Held
SIC: 3931 Woodwind instruments & parts

**(G-12130)**
**WILLIAMS WELDING SERVICE**
14772 Cooks Mills Rd (61931-7972)
PHONE..................................217 235-1758
Fax: 217 235-1756
Barry Williams, *Owner*
EMP: 3
SALES (est): 170K Privately Held
SIC: 7692 Welding repair

## Huntley
### Mchenry County

**(G-12131)**
**ALUMAPRO INC**
1 Union Special Plz (60142-7007)
PHONE..................................224 569-3650
Ken Meyer, *President*
Matthew Honnert, *Engineer*
Tony Valene, *Manager*
▲ EMP: 9
SALES (est): 1.2MM Privately Held
WEB: www.alumapro.com
SIC: 3651 Speaker systems

**(G-12132)**
**AQUARIUS METAL PRODUCTS INC (PA)**
12795 Muir Dr (60142-7799)
PHONE..................................847 659-9266
Fax: 847 841-8424
Allen J Treml, *President*
Raympnd Ossman, *Purch Agent*
Michael Boncosky, *Sales Dir*
Judy Treml, *Admin Sec*
EMP: 13
SQ FT: 26,000
SALES (est): 1.8MM Privately Held
SIC: 3444 Sheet metalwork

**(G-12133)**
**BG DIE MOLD INC**
11520 Smith Dr (60142-9600)
PHONE..................................847 961-5861
EMP: 7
SALES (est): 610K Privately Held
SIC: 3544 Mfg Special Dies/Tools/Jigs/Fixtures

**(G-12134)**
**BUSINESS IDENTITY SPC INC**
Also Called: Bis
10418 Oxford Dr (60142-2375)
PHONE..................................847 669-1946
Terri Durham, *President*
Larry Durham, *Vice Pres*
EMP: 3
SALES (est): 231.1K Privately Held
SIC: 2759 Promotional printing

**(G-12135)**
**CELL PARTS MANUFACTURING CO**
10675 Wolf Dr (60142-7032)
PHONE..................................847 669-9690
Valerie Dorr, *President*
EMP: 3
SALES (est): 209.4K Privately Held
SIC: 3999 Manufacturing industries

**(G-12136)**
**DATA ACCESSORIES INC**
40w735 Powers Rd (60142-8043)
PHONE..................................847 669-3640
Bruce Rose, *President*
Bobbie Rose, *Admin Sec*
EMP: 4
SALES (est): 340K Privately Held
SIC: 1731 5063 3678 Computer installation; switches, except electronic; electronic connectors

**(G-12137)**
**DEAN FOODS COMPANY**
11713 Mill St (60142-7398)
PHONE..................................847 669-5123
Fax: 708 664-5236
Ranal Lentz, *Plant Supt*
Dave Dickson, *Safety Mgr*
Karen Ostrander, *Purchasing*
Terri Borrett, *Accountant*
Greg Warren, *Manager*
EMP: 130 Publicly Held
WEB: www.deanfoods.com
SIC: 2026 Milk processing (pasteurizing, homogenizing, bottling)
PA: Dean Foods Company
2711 N Haskell Ave
Dallas TX 75204

**(G-12138)**
**DOGA USA CORPORATION**
12060 Raymond Ct (60142-8069)
PHONE..................................847 669-8529
Antonio Garcia, *President*
Juan Campo, *General Mgr*
Manel Roure, *Vice Pres*
Connie McElfresh, *Manager*
Marcel Molins, *Admin Sec*
▲ EMP: 15
SQ FT: 19,000
SALES: 9.2MM Privately Held
SIC: 3714 Motor vehicle parts & accessories

**(G-12139)**
**EXTRUDE HONE LLC**
Thermoburr Illinois
10663 Wolf Dr (60142-7032)
PHONE..................................847 669-5355
Bryan Wallis, *Principal*
Seth Kessler, *Branch Mgr*
Susana Acevedo, *Admin Asst*
EMP: 25
SALES (corp-wide): 191.6MM Privately Held
WEB: www.extrudehone.com
SIC: 3541 Milling machines
HQ: Extrude Hone Llc
235 Industry Blvd
Irwin PA 15642
724 863-5900

**(G-12140)**
**GENERAL RV CENTER INC**
14000 Automall Dr (60142-8067)
PHONE..................................847 669-5570
Faraon Ocampo, *Business Mgr*
Dan Cottrell, *Parts Mgr*
Chris Stevens, *Finance Mgr*
Josh Cooper, *Manager*
Scott Roesslein, *Manager*
EMP: 191
SALES (corp-wide): 258.8MM Privately Held
SIC: 3799 Recreational vehicles
PA: General R.V. Center, Inc.
25000 Assembly Park Dr
Wixom MI 48393
248 349-0900

**(G-12141)**
**GLENRAVEN INC**
40w260 Apache Ln (60142-8000)
PHONE..................................847 515-1321
Alan Eant, *CEO*
John Von Wachenfeldt, *Principal*
EMP: 3
SALES (est): 154K Privately Held
SIC: 2299 Textile goods

**(G-12142)**
**GOING VERTICAL INC**
11175 Dundee Rd (60142-9246)
PHONE..................................847 669-3377
Ralph Scalise, *Owner*
EMP: 4
SALES (est): 442.8K Privately Held
SIC: 2591 Blinds vertical

**(G-12143)**
**H S CROCKER COMPANY INC (PA)**
12100 Smith Dr (60142-9618)
PHONE..................................847 669-3600
Fax: 630 833-9892
Ronald J Giordano, *President*
Dennis Anderson, *General Mgr*
Lisa Sulma, *General Mgr*
John C Dai, *Vice Pres*
William Linehan, *Vice Pres*
▲ EMP: 81
SQ FT: 65,000
SALES (est): 21.2MM Privately Held
SIC: 2671 2672 Packaging paper & plastics film, coated & laminated; adhesive papers, labels or tapes: from purchased material

**(G-12144)**
**HENDERSON PRODUCTS INC**
11921 Smith Dr (60142-9604)
PHONE..................................847 515-3482
EMP: 3 Publicly Held
SIC: 3537 Industrial trucks & tractors
HQ: Henderson Products, Inc.
1085 S 3rd St
Manchester IA 52057
563 927-2828

**(G-12145)**
**HUNTING NETWORK LLC**
Also Called: Bowhunting.com
11964 Oak Creek Pkwy (60142-6728)
PHONE..................................847 659-8200
Todd Graf, *President*
EMP: 8
SQ FT: 5,600
SALES (est): 612.4K Privately Held
SIC: 2741

# GEOGRAPHIC SECTION

Huntley - Mchenry County (G-12175)

**(G-12146)**
**IDEAL SUPPLY INC (PA)**
11400 Kreutzer Rd (60142-8094)
PHONE.................................847 961-5900
Fax: 847 961-5300
Elizabeth Oakes, *President*
Marc Lodi, *General Mgr*
Peggy McCune, *Manager*
▲ **EMP:** 8
**SQ FT:** 5,000
**SALES (est):** 1.6MM **Privately Held**
**SIC: 3965** Fasteners

**(G-12147)**
**IMAGE INDUSTRIES INC (PA)**
11220 Main St (60142-7369)
PHONE.................................847 659-0100
Fax: 847 659-0108
Blake Hobson, *President*
Stacia Hobson, *President*
Mike Fleury, *General Mgr*
Dan Bell, *Project Mgr*
Scott Usher, *Engineer*
▲ **EMP:** 26
**SQ FT:** 67,000
**SALES (est):** 9.6MM **Privately Held**
**SIC: 3699** 3548 3452 Welding machines & equipment, ultrasonic; welding apparatus; bolts, nuts, rivets & washers

**(G-12148)**
**IN-PLACE MACHINING CO INC**
11414 Smith Dr Unit D (60142-9635)
PHONE.................................847 669-3006
**EMP:** 8
**SALES (corp-wide):** 20.3MM **Privately Held**
**SIC: 3599** Mfg Industrial Machinery
**PA:** In-Place Machining Co., Inc.
3811 N Holton St
Milwaukee WI 53212
414 562-2000

**(G-12149)**
**INGLESE BOX CO LTD**
13851 Prime Point Rd (60142-8015)
PHONE.................................847 669-1700
Fax: 847 961-5742
Len Inglese, *President*
Calogero Inglese, *Corp Secy*
Kris Galil, *Admin Sec*
**EMP:** 28
**SQ FT:** 140,000
**SALES (est):** 16.4MM **Privately Held**
WEB: www.inglesebox.com
**SIC: 5113** 2653 Industrial & personal service paper; corrugated & solid fiber boxes; corrugated & solid fiber boxes

**(G-12150)**
**INTEGRITY MATERIAL HDLG SVCS**
11932 Oak Creek Pkwy R (60142-6728)
PHONE.................................847 669-6233
Joseph Gallagher, *President*
**EMP:** 4
**SALES (est):** 600.2K **Privately Held**
**SIC: 3537** Forklift trucks

**(G-12151)**
**INTERNATIONAL WATER WERKS INC**
11470 Kreutzer Rd (60142-8094)
PHONE.................................847 669-1902
Fax: 847 669-1937
William Tobin, *President*
Nancy Tobin, *Vice Pres*
**EMP:** 6
**SQ FT:** 10,000
**SALES (est):** 1.5MM **Privately Held**
**SIC: 5074** 3589 Water purification equipment; water treatment equipment, industrial

**(G-12152)**
**JGR COMMERCIAL SOLUTIONS INC**
11414 Smith Dr Unit G (60142-9635)
PHONE.................................847 669-7010
Ron Ludwig, *President*
Scott Dombrowski, *Manager*
**EMP:** 7
**SQ FT:** 6,000
**SALES (est):** 1MM **Privately Held**
**SIC: 3272** Door frames, concrete

**(G-12153)**
**JIM JOLLY SALES INC**
11225 Giordano Ct (60142-6805)
PHONE.................................847 669-7570
Fax: 847 669-7571
James E Jolly, *Owner*
Celeste M Jolly, *Admin Sec*
**EMP:** 2
**SALES (est):** 635.8K **Privately Held**
WEB: www.jimjollysales.com
**SIC: 5074** 3991 Plumbing & hydronic heating supplies; brushes, except paint & varnish

**(G-12154)**
**JOHNSON TOOL COMPANY**
11528 Smith Dr 3 (60142-9600)
PHONE.................................708 453-8600
Fax: 708 453-1180
Arvid I Johnson, *President*
James Carlson, *Vice Pres*
**EMP:** 4 **EST:** 1945
**SQ FT:** 10,000
**SALES (est):** 330K **Privately Held**
WEB: www.johnsontool.net
**SIC: 3469** 3496 3495 3493 Stamping metal for the trade; miscellaneous fabricated wire products; wire springs; steel springs, except wire

**(G-12155)**
**KOHLER CO**
11449 Morning Glory Ln (60142-7674)
PHONE.................................847 734-1777
Fax: 847 427-9109
Barbara Paulster, *Human Res Mgr*
Reg G Garratt, *Branch Mgr*
**EMP:** 90
**SALES (corp-wide):** 8B **Privately Held**
**SIC: 3432** 3431 3261 Plumbing fixture fittings & trim; metal sanitary ware; vitreous plumbing fixtures
**PA:** Kohler Co.
444 Highland Dr
Kohler WI 53044
920 457-4441

**(G-12156)**
**KUNDE WOODWORK INC**
11901 Smith Dr (60142)
PHONE.................................847 669-2030
Tony Kunde, *President*
**EMP:** 4
**SALES (est):** 608.7K **Privately Held**
**SIC: 2441** Cases, wood

**(G-12157)**
**LDI INDUSTRIES INC**
12901 Jim Dhamer Dr (60142-8053)
PHONE.................................847 669-7510
Mark Lukas, *Branch Mgr*
**EMP:** 70
**SALES (corp-wide):** 31.8MM **Privately Held**
WEB: www.lubedevices.com
**SIC: 3569** Lubrication equipment, industrial
**PA:** Ldi Industries, Inc.
1864 Nagle Ave
Manitowoc WI 54220
920 682-6877

**(G-12158)**
**LIFE SPINE INC**
13951 Quality Dr (60142-8099)
PHONE.................................847 884-6117
Michael S Butler, *CEO*
Rich Mueller, *COO*
Todd Fanning, *Vice Pres*
Omar Faruqi, *Vice Pres*
Jason Grumbacher, *Vice Pres*
**EMP:** 40
**SALES (est):** 12.3MM **Privately Held**
WEB: www.lifespine.com
**SIC: 3841** Medical instruments & equipment, blood & bone work

**(G-12159)**
**LIONHEART CRITICAL POW**
13151 Executive Ct (60142-8096)
PHONE.................................847 291-1413
Fax: 815 338-7143
Ken Lenhart, *President*
Pete Stunkard, *Principal*
Don Ritter, *Opers Mgr*
Mindy Olson, *Accountant*
Mike Hunter, *Marketing Mgr*
**EMP:** 45
**SQ FT:** 9,500
**SALES (est):** 10.6MM **Privately Held**
WEB: www.lionheartengineering.com
**SIC: 3621** 5063 7629 Power generators; generators; generator repair

**(G-12160)**
**MAASS MIDWEST MFG INC (PA)**
11283 Dundee Rd (60142-9247)
P.O. Box 547 (60142-0547)
PHONE.................................847 669-5135
John Surinak, *President*
Donna Surinak, *Corp Secy*
▲ **EMP:** 37
**SQ FT:** 55,000
**SALES (est):** 10.8MM **Privately Held**
WEB: www.maassmidwest.com
**SIC: 3533** Oil & gas field machinery; water well drilling equipment

**(G-12161)**
**MALL GRAPHIC INC**
Also Called: Mall Publishing
12693 Cold Springs Dr (60142-7427)
PHONE.................................847 668-7600
Ernest Mall, *President*
**EMP:** 12
**SQ FT:** 9,000
**SALES:** 1.1MM **Privately Held**
WEB: www.mallmarketing.biz
**SIC: 2752** 2789 Commercial printing, offset; bookbinding & related work

**(G-12162)**
**MANNING MATERIAL SERVICES INC**
11804 S Il Route 47 (60142-9662)
PHONE.................................847 669-5750
Tom Manning, *President*
Franz Schumacher, *Office Mgr*
**EMP:** 15
**SALES (est):** 1.3MM **Privately Held**
**SIC: 3317** Steel pipe & tubes

**(G-12163)**
**MC METALS & FABRICATING INC**
10683 Wolf Dr (60142-7032)
PHONE.................................847 961-5242
**EMP:** 4
**SALES (est):** 336.1K **Privately Held**
**SIC: 3499** Mfg Misc Fabricated Metal Products

**(G-12164)**
**NORTH AMERICAN PRESS INC**
12203 Spring Creek Dr (60142-7727)
PHONE.................................847 515-3882
Herman H Pump, *Principal*
**EMP:** 4
**SALES (est):** 271.9K **Privately Held**
**SIC: 2741** Miscellaneous publishing

**(G-12165)**
**PARADIGM COATINGS LLC**
11259 Kiley Dr (60142-6940)
PHONE.................................847 961-6466
Jim Riley,
**EMP:** 4
**SALES (est):** 275K **Privately Held**
WEB: www.paradigmcoatings.com
**SIC: 3479** 3471 Painting, coating & hot dipping; sand blasting of metal parts

**(G-12166)**
**PARTING LINE TOOL INC**
11915 Smith Ct (60142-7300)
PHONE.................................847 669-0331
Fax: 847 669-0354
Mike Hookom, *President*
**EMP:** 16
**SQ FT:** 6,400
**SALES:** 3MM **Privately Held**
**SIC: 3089** 3544 Injection molded finished plastic products; special dies, tools, jigs & fixtures

**(G-12167)**
**PHOENIX UNLIMITED LTD**
11514 Smith Dr Unit D (60142-9633)
P.O. Box 503 (60142-0503)
PHONE.................................847 515-1263
Fax: 847 515-1266
Jonathan Treubig, *President*

Jill Holgerson, *Admin Sec*
**EMP:** 6
**SQ FT:** 5,500
**SALES:** 350K **Privately Held**
WEB: www.phoenixunlimited.com
**SIC: 3085** 7389 Plastics bottles; packaging & labeling services

**(G-12168)**
**PRELLA TECHNOLOGIES INC**
11408 Kiley Dr (60142-6988)
PHONE.................................630 400-0626
**EMP:** 4
**SALES (est):** 335.8K **Privately Held**
**SIC: 3531** Construction machinery

**(G-12169)**
**QUALITY CONVERTING INC**
10611 Wolf Dr (60142-7032)
P.O. Box 99, Woodstock (60098-0099)
PHONE.................................847 669-9094
Guy Spinelli, *Principal*
**EMP:** 5
**SALES (est):** 734.2K **Privately Held**
**SIC: 3554** Paper industries machinery

**(G-12170)**
**QUANTUM MECHANICAL LLC**
11182 Victoria Ln (60142-2451)
PHONE.................................773 480-8200
Allo Scott, *Principal*
**EMP:** 3
**SALES (est):** 272.1K **Privately Held**
**SIC: 3572** Computer storage devices

**(G-12171)**
**R M ARMSTRONG & SON INC**
11006 Bakley St (60142-7125)
P.O. Box 56 (60142-0056)
PHONE.................................847 669-3988
Fax: 847 669-5899
Leon E Tripp, *President*
**EMP:** 4
**SQ FT:** 4,500
**SALES:** 500K **Privately Held**
**SIC: 3599** Machine shop, jobbing & repair

**(G-12172)**
**RAM PLASTIC CORP**
11414 Smith Dr Unit B (60142-9635)
PHONE.................................847 669-8003
Fax: 847 669-9819
Robert Anderson, *President*
**EMP:** 2 **EST:** 1971
**SALES:** 250K **Privately Held**
WEB: www.ramplastic.com
**SIC: 3089** Injection molding of plastics

**(G-12173)**
**REVOLUTION BRANDS LLC**
12327 Bartelt Ct (60142-6062)
PHONE.................................847 902-3320
Ian Abbott,
Glenn Backus,
**EMP:** 3 **EST:** 2014
**SALES:** 400K **Privately Held**
**SIC: 2099** 7389 Food preparations;

**(G-12174)**
**ROHRER CORPORATION**
Also Called: Gateway Printing
13701 George Bush Ct (60142)
P.O. Box 248 (60142-0248)
PHONE.................................847 961-5920
Fax: 847 961-5925
Mark Skradski, *Superintendent*
Robert Grelck, *Purch Mgr*
Jean Laramie, *Human Resources*
George Colletti, *Branch Mgr*
Dennis McCaffrey, *Info Tech Mgr*
**EMP:** 80
**SALES (corp-wide):** 130.6MM **Privately Held**
WEB: www.rohrer.com
**SIC: 3089** 2675 Blister or bubble formed packaging, plastic; die-cut paper & board
**PA:** Rohrer Corporation
717 Seville Rd
Wadsworth OH 44281
330 335-1541

**(G-12175)**
**RONCIN CUSTOM DESIGN**
11514 Smith Dr Unit B (60142-9633)
PHONE.................................847 669-0260
Fax: 847 669-0262

# Huntley - Mchenry County (G-12176)

Ronald Ludwig, *President*
Cynthia Ludwig, *Admin Sec*
**EMP:** 5
**SQ FT:** 4,500
**SALES:** 750K **Privately Held**
**SIC:** 2434 2511 2541 2517 Wood kitchen cabinets; wood household furniture; wood partitions & fixtures; wood television & radio cabinets

### (G-12176)
### SERVICE PRINTING CORPORATION
11960 Oak Creek Pkwy (60142-6728)
**PHONE**....................847 669-9620
**Fax:** 847 669-9630
Henry T Goers, *President*
Kevin Goers, *Vice Pres*
**EMP:** 7
**SQ FT:** 7,700
**SALES (est):** 1MM **Privately Held**
**WEB:** www.serviceprintingcorp.com
**SIC:** 2752 2789 Commercial printing, offset; bookbinding & related work

### (G-12177)
### SPECTRA JET
10611 Wolf Dr (60142-7032)
P.O. Box 99, Woodstock (60098-0099)
**PHONE**....................847 669-9094
Guy Spinelli, *President*
**EMP:** 2
**SALES (est):** 250K **Privately Held**
**SIC:** 2679 Paper products, converted

### (G-12178)
### TAMPOTECH DECORATING INC
10901 Union Special Plz (60142-7020)
**PHONE**....................847 515-2968
Karin Kleist, *President*
Egon Kleist, *Treasurer*
**EMP:** 8
**SQ FT:** 15,000
**SALES (est):** 3.1MM **Privately Held**
**WEB:** www.tampoinc.com
**SIC:** 5084 3569 Printing trades machinery, equipment & supplies; robots, assembly line: industrial & commercial

### (G-12179)
### THERMFORM ENGINEERED QULTY LLC (HQ)
Also Called: T E Q
11320 Main St (60142-7396)
P.O. Box 68 (60142-0068)
**PHONE**....................847 669-5291
**Fax:** 847 669-2720
Randall Loga, *President*
Paule Sepe, *Vice Pres*
Jackie Kangas, *Purch Agent*
Herbert Knight, *Engineer*
Kris Scczesiak, *Controller*
▼ **EMP:** 65
**SQ FT:** 90,000
**SALES (est):** 27.1MM
**SALES (corp-wide):** 571.4MM **Publicly Held**
**SIC:** 3089 Plastic kitchenware, tableware & houseware
**PA:** Esco Technologies Inc.
9900 Clayton Rd Ste A
Saint Louis MO 63124
314 213-7200

### (G-12180)
### TRAXCO INC
11416 Kiley Dr (60142-7136)
**PHONE**....................847 669-1545
Rose Marie Traxler, *President*
Lisa Modich, *Admin Sec*
▲ **EMP:** 4
**SQ FT:** 6,000
**SALES:** 850K **Privately Held**
**WEB:** www.traxco.com
**SIC:** 3599 Machine & other job shop work

### (G-12181)
### UNICHEM INTERNATIONAL INC
11530 Smith Dr (60142-9600)
**PHONE**....................847 669-6552
Khaleeq Ahmed, *President*
**EMP:** 22
**SQ FT:** 160,000
**SALES:** 3.7MM **Privately Held**
**SIC:** 2834 Vitamin, nutrient & hematinic preparations for human use

### (G-12182)
### UNION SPECIAL LLC
1 Union Special Plz (60142-7007)
**PHONE**....................847 669-5101
**Fax:** 847 669-5179
Ken Waser, *Mfg Spvr*
Bobby Turner, *Engineer*
Scott Ziegler, *Engineer*
Jim Davis, *Info Tech Mgr*
Scott Hester, *Technology*
▲ **EMP:** 110 **EST:** 1881
**SQ FT:** 400,000
**SALES (est):** 24.9MM **Privately Held**
**WEB:** www.unionspecial.com
**SIC:** 3559 5084 5131 5063 Sewing machines & attachments, industrial; sewing machines, industrial; industrial machine parts; sewing accessories; motors, electric; sewing machine repair shop

### (G-12183)
### WEBER-STEPHEN PRODUCTS LLC
11811 Oak Creek Pkwy (60142-6704)
**PHONE**....................847 669-4916
**Fax:** 847 669-4916
Bill Geid, *General Mgr*
Barbara Casimere, *Purchasing*
Barb Mark, *Human Res Dir*
Pam Key, *Manager*
**EMP:** 18
**SALES (corp-wide):** 1.2B **Privately Held**
**SIC:** 3631 Barbecues, grills & braziers (outdoor cooking)
**PA:** Weber-Stephen Products Llc
1415 S Roselle Rd
Palatine IL 60067
847 934-5700

## INA
### Jefferson County

### (G-12184)
### CRAFT PALLET INC
1620 N Benton Ln (62846-2209)
**PHONE**....................618 437-5382
Bill Kniffen, *President*
Susan Kniffen, *Admin Sec*
**EMP:** 8 **EST:** 1992
**SALES (est):** 937.9K **Privately Held**
**SIC:** 2448 Pallets, wood & wood with metal

## Indian Creek
### Lake County

### (G-12185)
### CASH HOUSE MUSIC GROUP LLC
1320 Laci Ct (60061-3279)
**PHONE**....................847 471-7401
Yan Gusinsky,
Dylan L Clay,
Omar R Edwards,
Craig D Jordan,
Dominique M Turner,
**EMP:** 5
**SALES (est):** 167K **Privately Held**
**SIC:** 2741 7389 Music books: publishing & printing;

## Ingleside
### Lake County

### (G-12186)
### AMERICAN TOTAL ENGINE CO
Also Called: Ateco Automotive
27840 W Concrete Dr Ste B (60041-9317)
**PHONE**....................847 623-2737
**Fax:** 847 623-2752
William Lawson, *Owner*
**EMP:** 5
**SQ FT:** 4,000
**SALES (est):** 473.2K **Privately Held**
**WEB:** www.ateco.org
**SIC:** 3599 3621 3544 Machine shop, jobbing & repair; motors & generators; special dies, tools, jigs & fixtures

### (G-12187)
### BETTER GASKETS INC
Also Called: Better Gaskets Sealing Systems
26218 W Ingleside Ave (60041-9656)
**PHONE**....................847 276-7635
Sandy Gordon, *President*
Robert L Gordon, *Admin Sec*
**EMP:** 7
**SQ FT:** 5,000
**SALES:** 125K **Privately Held**
**SIC:** 3053 Gaskets, packing & sealing devices

### (G-12188)
### CUSTOM CANVAS LLC
26463 W Grand Ave (60041-9785)
**PHONE**....................847 587-0225
**Fax:** 847 587-0261
Roy Gundelach,
Marie Gundelach,
**EMP:** 6 **EST:** 1974
**SQ FT:** 8,000
**SALES:** 365K **Privately Held**
**WEB:** www.customcanvas.com
**SIC:** 2394 5999 5065 7532 Convertible tops, canvas or boat: from purchased materials; awnings, fabric: made from purchased materials; telephone & communication equipment; telephone equipment; upholstery & trim shop, automotive

### (G-12189)
### FIBERTEX NONWOVENS LLC
27981 W Concrete Dr (60041-8835)
**PHONE**....................815 349-3200
Lars Bertelsen, *COO*
Mark Schultz, *Opers Mgr*
Clayton Carter, *CFO*
Alan Zenner, *Controller*
Henrik Kjeldsen, *Sales Staff*
▲ **EMP:** 60
**SQ FT:** 100,000
**SALES:** 34MM **Privately Held**
**SIC:** 2297 Nonwoven fabrics

### (G-12190)
### IDENTCO INTERNATIONAL CORP (PA)
28164 W Concrete Dr (60041-8836)
**PHONE**....................815 385-0011
Scott B Lucas, *President*
Bruce Hupfer, *Manager*
**EMP:** 85
**SQ FT:** 20,000
**SALES (est):** 34.9MM **Privately Held**
**WEB:** www.identco.com
**SIC:** 2672 Coated & laminated paper

### (G-12191)
### IDENTCO WEST LLC
28164 W Concrete Dr (60041-8836)
**PHONE**....................815 385-0011
**Fax:** 815 385-0359
Scott Lucas, *President*
Rick Brizek, *Opers Mgr*
Kim Couture, *Human Res Mgr*
**EMP:** 2 **EST:** 1999
**SALES (est):** 552.8K **Privately Held**
**SIC:** 2679 Converted paper products

### (G-12192)
### LAKE SHORE STAIR CO INC (PA)
28090 W Concrete Dr (60041-9329)
**PHONE**....................815 363-7777
**Fax:** 815 363-7778
Christopher M Jensen, *President*
Peter Jensen, *Admin Sec*
**EMP:** 39 **EST:** 1931
**SQ FT:** 5,200
**SALES:** 3.5MM **Privately Held**
**WEB:** www.lakeshorestair.com
**SIC:** 2431 Staircases, stairs & railings; staircases & stairs, wood; stair railings, wood

### (G-12193)
### MAJESTY CASES INC
34550 N Wilson Rd (60041-9247)
**PHONE**....................847 546-2558
Adam Button, *President*
**EMP:** 20
**SALES (est):** 2.4MM **Privately Held**
**SIC:** 3537 Containers (metal), air cargo

### (G-12194)
### MIX FOODS LLC
25635 W Venetian Dr (60041-9589)
**PHONE**....................224 338-0377
William George McCoy, *Principal*
**EMP:** 4
**SALES (est):** 235.7K **Privately Held**
**SIC:** 3273 Ready-mixed concrete

### (G-12195)
### NEOLIGHT LABS LLC
34768 N Elm St (60041-9103)
**PHONE**....................312 242-1773
Momir Milinovich, *Principal*
Peter Dragic, *Manager*
**EMP:** 3
**SALES (est):** 152.1K **Privately Held**
**SIC:** 3229 Fiber optics strands

### (G-12196)
### NEOLIGHT TECHNOLOGIES LLC
34768 N Elm St (60041-9103)
**PHONE**....................773 561-1410
Momir Milinovich,
**EMP:** 2
**SALES:** 200K **Privately Held**
**SIC:** 3357 Nonferrous wiredrawing & insulating

### (G-12197)
### ONLINE MERCHANT SYSTEMS LLC
35453 N Indian Ln (60041-9689)
**PHONE**....................847 973-2337
Samuel H Wright, *Manager*
**EMP:** 3
**SALES (est):** 210.3K **Privately Held**
**SIC:** 3999 Framed artwork

### (G-12198)
### SHORELINE GRAPHICS INC
415 Washington St (60041-9291)
**PHONE**....................847 587-4804
Harold D Pfuehler, *President*
**EMP:** 4
**SALES (est):** 358.4K **Privately Held**
**SIC:** 7336 2791 2789 2752 Graphic arts & related design; typesetting; bookbinding & related work; commercial printing, lithographic

## Ingraham
### Clay County

### (G-12199)
### ARTHUR LEO KUHL
Also Called: Kuhl's Trailer Sales
1023 N 500th St (62434-2122)
**PHONE**....................618 752-5473
Phyllis Prosser, *Owner*
Larry Prosser, *Owner*
**EMP:** 4
**SQ FT:** 1,400
**SALES (est):** 42.8K **Privately Held**
**SIC:** 3792 7033 0191 Camping trailers & chassis; campgrounds; general farms, primarily crop

## Inverness
### Cook County

### (G-12200)
### AERODINE MAGAZINE
1514 Banbury Rd (60067-4285)
P.O. Box 247, Palatine (60078-0247)
**PHONE**....................847 358-4355
Kenneth Keifer, *President*
**EMP:** 3
**SALES (est):** 170K **Privately Held**
**SIC:** 2741 Directories: publishing only, not printed on site

### (G-12201)
### ALMACEN INC
927 Kirkwood Dr (60067-4235)
**PHONE**....................847 934-7955
Lloyd Wolf, *Principal*
**EMP:** 4

SALES: 1,000K **Privately Held**
SIC: 2521 2522 Wood office furniture; office furniture, except wood

**(G-12202)**
**ANTHOS AND CO LLC**
2010 Dundee Rd (60067-1801)
PHONE..................................773 744-6813
Tammy Stergio,
EMP: 7
SALES (est): 369.7K **Privately Held**
SIC: 3961 7389 5999 Rosaries & small religious articles, except precious metal; decoration service for special events; religious goods

**(G-12203)**
**EXTENTEL WRLESS COMMUNICATIONS**
90 Dirleton Ln (60067-4877)
PHONE..................................847 809-3131
Michael Ghadaksaz, *Principal*
EMP: 4
SALES (est): 205.4K **Privately Held**
SIC: 3669 Communications equipment

**(G-12204)**
**GENERAL EXHIBITS AND DISPLAYS**
1425 Appleby Rd (60067-4428)
PHONE..................................847 934-1943
Gerhard Stegemann, *President*
Philip Kedzie, *Vice Pres*
George Stegemann, *Vice Pres*
Robert Murray, *Purch Mgr*
John Concannon, *Controller*
EMP: 90 EST: 1937
SQ FT: 320,000
SALES (est): 3.8MM **Privately Held**
SIC: 7389 3993 Exhibit construction by industrial contractors; displays & cutouts, window & lobby; displays, paint process

**(G-12205)**
**MEI REALTY LTD**
1601 W Colonial Pkwy (60067-4732)
PHONE..................................847 358-5000
Fax: 847 358-3488
Paul W Ziegler, *CEO*
Irene Ziegler, *Treasurer*
Linda Schutz, *Admin Sec*
EMP: 5
SQ FT: 45,000
SALES (est): 804K **Privately Held**
WEB: www.meirealty.com
SIC: 6512 3677 Commercial & industrial building operation; electronic transformers

**(G-12206)**
**T L SWINT INDUSTRIES INC**
2211 Banbury Rd (60067-4213)
P.O. Box 277, Palatine (60078-0277)
PHONE..................................847 358-3834
Thomas L Swint, *President*
EMP: 3
SQ FT: 2,000
SALES (est): 405.6K **Privately Held**
SIC: 3089 Injection molding of plastics

## Inverness
### Lake County

**(G-12207)**
**CARGO SUPPORT INDUSTRIES INC**
242 Willow St (60010-5812)
EMP: 3
SALES (est): 288.5K **Privately Held**
SIC: 3999 Manufacturing industries

**(G-12208)**
**ENGELHARDT ENTERPRISES INC**
710 Bradwell Rd (60010-5601)
PHONE..................................847 277-7070
Dean Englehardt, *President*
EMP: 2
SALES (est): 350K **Privately Held**
WEB: www.gearman.com
SIC: 3462 Gear & chain forgings

**(G-12209)**
**MASON ENGINEERING & DESIGNING**
Also Called: Cloud 9 Division
505 W Lancaster Ct (60010-5664)
PHONE..................................630 595-5000
Fax: 630 595-5902
Jon Spranger, *President*
Jerry Ladin, *Sales Staff*
Fred Green, *Marketing Staff*
EMP: 45
SQ FT: 19,000
SALES (est): 6.3MM **Privately Held**
WEB: www.4cloud9.com
SIC: 3564 Air purification equipment

**(G-12210)**
**PROMOTIONAL CO OF ILLINOIS**
2222 Shetland Rd (60010-5412)
PHONE..................................847 382-0239
Jay Morgan, *Owner*
EMP: 5 EST: 1990
SALES: 500K **Privately Held**
SIC: 3993 Advertising novelties

**(G-12211)**
**ROSERI BUSINESS FORMS INC**
2236 Harrow Gate Dr (60010-5426)
PHONE..................................847 381-8012
Sam Roseri, *President*
EMP: 1
SQ FT: 5,000
SALES: 200K **Privately Held**
SIC: 5112 2759 Business forms; commercial printing

## Island Lake
### Lake County

**(G-12212)**
**AJS PUBLICATIONS**
229 Brier Ct (60042-9750)
PHONE..................................847 526-5027
Alex J Schmidt, *Owner*
EMP: 3 EST: 1998
SALES (est): 163K **Privately Held**
SIC: 2731 Book publishing

**(G-12213)**
**CARGILL COCOA & CHOCOLATE INC**
217 Tulip Cir. (60042-8512)
PHONE..................................815 578-2000
Joe Sofia, *Branch Mgr*
EMP: 3
SALES (corp-wide): 107.1B **Privately Held**
SIC: 2066 Chocolate; cocoa & cocoa products
HQ: Cargill Cocoa & Chocolate, Inc.
15407 Mcginty Rd W
Wayzata MN 55391
952 742-7575

**(G-12214)**
**DEAN PRINTING SYSTEMS**
4358 Shooting Star Dr (60042-8220)
PHONE..................................847 526-9545
David Dean, *Owner*
EMP: 2
SALES (est): 232.6K **Privately Held**
SIC: 2752 Commercial printing, lithographic

**(G-12215)**
**G & W TECHNICAL CORPORATION**
578 E Burnett Rd (60042-9203)
PHONE..................................847 487-0990
Waclaw Wanduch, *President*
EMP: 2
SQ FT: 2,000
SALES (est): 561K **Privately Held**
SIC: 3569 Assembly machines, non-metalworking

**(G-12216)**
**G&R MACHINING INC**
3205 Poplar Dr (60042-9484)
P.O. Box 585 (60042-0585)
PHONE..................................847 526-7364
George Rudolph, *Principal*

EMP: 2 EST: 2007
SALES (est): 207.5K **Privately Held**
SIC: 3599 Machine shop, jobbing & repair

**(G-12217)**
**KNIGHT PRTG & LITHO SVC LTD**
Also Called: Knight Printing and Litho Svcs
706 E Burnett Rd (60042-9236)
PHONE..................................847 487-7700
Fax: 847 487-0802
John A Hansen, *President*
Candy Hansen, *Office Mgr*
EMP: 8
SQ FT: 13,000
SALES (est): 1.1MM **Privately Held**
SIC: 2752 2759 2672 Commercial printing, lithographic; commercial printing; coated & laminated paper

**(G-12218)**
**SENSORY ESSENCE INC**
209 Brier Ct (60042-9750)
P.O. Box 87 (60042-0087)
PHONE..................................847 526-3645
Jan Salko, *President*
EMP: 2
SALES (est): 270K **Privately Held**
SIC: 2899 Essential oils

**(G-12219)**
**STANCY WOODWORKING CO INC**
301 Fern Dr (60042-9456)
PHONE..................................847 526-0252
Teresa J Vazouez-Stancy, *President*
Craig Stancy, *Manager*
EMP: 10
SALES: 220K **Privately Held**
SIC: 2499 2511 2434 2431 Decorative wood & woodwork; wood household furniture; wood kitchen cabinets; millwork

**(G-12220)**
**VULCAN LADDER USA LLC**
Also Called: G P International
710 Wood Creek Ct (60042-9590)
PHONE..................................847 526-6321
David Briggs, *Mng Member*
Candy Power, *Executive*
Michael Lee,
▲ EMP: 5 EST: 2008
SALES (est): 110K **Privately Held**
SIC: 3499 7389 Metal ladders;

**(G-12221)**
**WAGNERS CUSTOM WOOD DESIGN**
4035 Roberts Rd (60042-8505)
P.O. Box 283 (60042-0283)
PHONE..................................847 487-2788
William Wagner, *President*
Christopher Wagner, *Admin Sec*
EMP: 2
SQ FT: 1,600
SALES (est): 291.1K **Privately Held**
SIC: 5712 2431 1751 Cabinet work, custom; panel work, wood; cabinet & finish carpentry

## Itasca
### Dupage County

**(G-12222)**
**ABBOTT LABEL INC**
1414 Norwood Ave (60143-1129)
PHONE..................................630 773-3614
Jose Garcia, *General Mgr*
Ken Young, *Opers Mgr*
EMP: 10
SALES (corp-wide): 25.3MM **Privately Held**
SIC: 2759 Labels & seals: printing
PA: Abbott Label, Inc.
11440 Hillguard Rd
Dallas TX 75243
866 228-0100

**(G-12223)**
**ABS GRAPHICS INC (PA)**
Also Called: ABS Equipment Division
900 N Rohlwing Rd (60143-1161)
PHONE..................................630 495-2400
Fax: 630 495-5729

Kenneth Vander Veen, *President*
Steven Vanderveen, *Corp Secy*
Mark Biernacki, *Controller*
Steve Burkhardt, *Controller*
Marion Degroot, *Human Res Dir*
▼ EMP: 120
SQ FT: 70,000
SALES (est): 34.7MM **Privately Held**
WEB: www.absgraphics.com
SIC: 2752 2789 2759 Commercial printing, lithographic; bookbinding & related work; commercial printing

**(G-12224)**
**AGS PARTNERS LLC**
905 W Irving Park Rd (60143-2023)
PHONE..................................630 446-7777
EMP: 53
SALES (corp-wide): 36.2MM **Privately Held**
SIC: 3944 Mfg Games/Toys
PA: Ags Partners, Llc
6680 Amelia Earhart Ct # 50
Las Vegas NV 89118
702 294-0440

**(G-12225)**
**ALLMETAL INC (PA)**
1 Pierce Pl Ste 900 (60143-1253)
P.O. Box 850, Bensenville (60106-0850)
PHONE..................................630 250-8090
Jeff Andresen, *General Mgr*
Philip C Colin, *General Mgr*
Bill Innis, *General Mgr*
Philip Collin, *Principal*
Eugene Guichu, *Plant Mgr*
▼ EMP: 60 EST: 1915
SQ FT: 8,300
SALES (est): 92.9MM **Privately Held**
WEB: www.allmetalinc.com
SIC: 3699 3089 Laser welding, drilling & cutting equipment; injection molding of plastics

**(G-12226)**
**AMADA AMERICA INC**
1091 W Hawthorn Dr (60143-2057)
PHONE..................................877 262-3287
Mike Zordan, *Branch Mgr*
EMP: 6
SALES (corp-wide): 2.6B **Privately Held**
WEB: www.metalsoft.com
SIC: 7372 Prepackaged software
HQ: Amada America, Inc.
7025 Firestone Blvd
Buena Park CA 90621
714 739-2111

**(G-12227)**
**AMCOR RIGID PLASTICS USA LLC**
750 Expressway Dr (60143-1322)
PHONE..................................630 773-3235
Dave Clark, *Plant Mgr*
Curt Crogan, *Plant Mgr*
Yessenia Valle, *Buyer*
Eric Ferguson, *Engineer*
Bryan Wilson, *Engineer*
EMP: 100
SALES (corp-wide): 9.4B **Privately Held**
WEB: www.slpcamericas.com
SIC: 3085 Plastics bottles
HQ: Amcor Rigid Plastics Usa, Llc
935 Technology Dr Ste 100
Ann Arbor MI 48108

**(G-12228)**
**AMERICAN SUPPLY ASSOCIATION (PA)**
Also Called: ASA
1200 N Arlngton Hts 150 (60143-3178)
PHONE..................................630 467-0000
Fax: 312 464-0091
Don Maloney, *Ch of Bd*
John Hester, *President*
Inge Calderon, *General Mgr*
Polina Baklashev, *Accountant*
Barbara Burdiak, *Mktg Dir*
EMP: 14
SQ FT: 7,500
SALES: 2.5MM **Privately Held**
WEB: www.asa.net
SIC: 8611 2731 Trade associations; book publishing

## (G-12229)
### AMERISUN INC
1141 W Bryn Mawr Ave  (60143-1568)
PHONE .................................... 800 791-9458
Bill Godwin, *President*
Jim Weiskircher, *Admin Sec*
▲ **EMP:** 10
**SQ FT:** 58,000
**SALES (est):** 7.2MM
**SALES (corp-wide):** 10.3MM  **Privately Held**
**SIC:** 5083  3524  Mowers, power; snowblowers & throwers, residential
**PA:** Zhejiang Dobest Power Tools Co., Ltd.
No.9, Huacheng West Road,
Huachuan Industrial Zone
Yongkang
579 892-8632

## (G-12230)
### ARCHITCTRAL BLDRS HDWR MFG INC
Also Called: Abh Manufacturing
1222 Ardmore Ave  (60143-1141)
PHONE .................................... 630 875-9900
**Fax:** 630 437-9918
Kurt Shah, *President*
Raxa Shah, *Treasurer*
▲ **EMP:** 26
**SQ FT:** 20,000
**SALES (est):** 7.1MM  **Privately Held**
**WEB:** www.abhmfg.com
**SIC:** 3429  Builders' hardware

## (G-12231)
### ARMSTRONG AEROSPACE INC
1377 Industrial Dr  (60143-1847)
PHONE .................................... 847 250-5132
Jack Cotugno, *Principal*
Matt Harrison, *Buyer*
**EMP:** 3  **EST:** 2013
**SALES (est):** 280K  **Privately Held**
**SIC:** 3812  Aircraft/aerospace flight instruments & guidance systems

## (G-12232)
### ARMSTRONG AEROSPACE INC
1437 Harmony Ct  (60143-1850)
PHONE .................................... 630 285-0200
**Fax:** 630 782-6401
Robert Abbinante, *President*
Matt Dunham, *Engineer*
Robert Louis, *Design Engr*
Krunal Patel, *Design Engr*
Rachel Wright, *Design Engr*
**EMP:** 100
**SQ FT:** 20,000
**SALES (est):** 19.3MM
**SALES (corp-wide):** 633.1MM  **Publicly Held**
**WEB:** www.armstrongaerospace.com
**SIC:** 8711  3728  Consulting engineer; aircraft parts & equipment
**PA:** Astronics Corporation
130 Commerce Way
East Aurora NY 14052
716 805-1599

## (G-12233)
### BAMBERGER POLYMERS INC
1 Pierce Pl Ste 255c  (60143-2613)
PHONE .................................... 630 773-8626
**Fax:** 630 773-8696
Michael Pignataro, *Manager*
**EMP:** 10
**SALES (corp-wide):** 262.1MM  **Privately Held**
**SIC:** 5162  2822  Resins; synthetic rubber
**HQ:** Bamberger Polymers, Inc.
2 Jericho Plz Ste 109
Jericho NY 11753

## (G-12234)
### BANDO USA INC (HQ)
1149 W Bryn Mawr Ave  (60143-1508)
PHONE .................................... 630 773-6600
Joseph Laudadio, *President*
John Allessio, *General Mgr*
Minoru Fukuda, *Chairman*
Jack Harrington, *Vice Pres*
Saburo Araki, *CFO*
◆ **EMP:** 35
**SALES (est):** 48.2MM
**SALES (corp-wide):** 777.7MM  **Privately Held**
**SIC:** 3052  Rubber belting
**PA:** Bando Chemical Industries, Ltd.
4-6-6, Minatojimaminamimachi, Chuo-Ku
Kobe HYO 650-0
783 042-923

## (G-12235)
### BARON MANUFACTURING CO LLC
730 Baker Dr  (60143-1308)
PHONE .................................... 630 628-9110
**Fax:** 630 628-9141
Robert A McKinney Sr, *President*
Robert A Mc Kinney Jr, *VP Sales*
◆ **EMP:** 20  **EST:** 1964
**SQ FT:** 16,217
**SALES (est):** 4.3MM  **Privately Held**
**WEB:** www.baronsnaps.com
**SIC:** 3429  Manufactured hardware (general)

## (G-12236)
### BOLER COMPANY (PA)
500 Park Blvd Ste 1010  (60143-1285)
PHONE .................................... 630 773-9111
**Fax:** 630 773-9121
Matthew J Boler, *President*
Nancy B Coons, *Exec VP*
Michael J Boler, *Vice Pres*
David Templeton, *VP Human Res*
James Colley, *Admin Sec*
◆ **EMP:** 15  **EST:** 1980
**SQ FT:** 7,000
**SALES (est):** 1B  **Privately Held**
**SIC:** 3714  3493  Motor vehicle parts & accessories; axles, motor vehicle; bumpers & bumperettes, motor vehicle; leaf springs: automobile, locomotive, etc.

## (G-12237)
### BOLER VENTURES LLC (PA)
500 Park Blvd Ste 1010  (60143-2608)
PHONE .................................... 630 773-9111
Matthew Boler, *Partner*
James Boler, *Partner*
Michael Boler, *Partner*
Jeffrey Gunnlaugson, *Manager*
**EMP:** 9
**SQ FT:** 6,000
**SALES (est):** 5MM  **Privately Held**
**SIC:** 3463  Nonferrous forgings; aluminum forgings

## (G-12238)
### BUDAPEST TOOL
1300 Industrial Dr Ste A  (60143-1876)
PHONE .................................... 630 250-0711
**Fax:** 630 250-0711
Karoly Nemeth, *Owner*
**EMP:** 2
**SQ FT:** 2,500
**SALES:** 450K  **Privately Held**
**SIC:** 3599  Machine shop, jobbing & repair

## (G-12239)
### BULAW WELDING & ENGINEERING CO
Also Called: Aero Vac Brazing Heat Treating
750 N Rohlwing Rd  (60143-1347)
PHONE .................................... 630 228-8300
**Fax:** 630 467-1614
Jay Bulaw, *President*
Michael Bulaw, *Vice Pres*
Teresa Archambault, *Manager*
**EMP:** 70  **EST:** 1935
**SQ FT:** 37,500
**SALES (est):** 2.5MM  **Privately Held**
**SIC:** 1799  7692  3398  Welding on site; welding repair; metal heat treating

## (G-12240)
### CANON SOLUTIONS AMERICA INC
1800 Bruning Dr W  (60143-1061)
PHONE .................................... 630 351-1227
William E Mayer, *Senior VP*
John H Forbes, *Vice Pres*
Chuck Jacobson, *Vice Pres*
Steve Frank, *VP Opers*
Mary Magowen, *Human Res Dir*
**EMP:** 95
**SALES (corp-wide):** 30.7B  **Privately Held**
**SIC:** 3861  7371  Photographic film, plate & paper holders; custom computer programming services
**HQ:** Canon Solutions America, Inc.
1 Canon Park
Melville NY 11747
631 330-5000

## (G-12241)
### CARDINAL COLORPRINT PRTG CORP
1270 Ardmore Ave  (60143-1141)
PHONE .................................... 630 467-1000
Partick A Lebeau, *President*
Michael J Lebeau, *Corp Secy*
Arthur Le Beau, *Vice Pres*
Daniel Mathisen, *Accounts Exec*
Mary Baker, *Sales Staff*
**EMP:** 46  **EST:** 1947
**SQ FT:** 50,000
**SALES:** 10.5MM  **Privately Held**
**WEB:** www.cardinalcolorprint.com
**SIC:** 2752  2796  2791  2789  Commercial printing, lithographic; platemaking services; typesetting; bookbinding & related work

## (G-12242)
### CARL MANUFACTURING USA INC
100 E Pierce Rd Ste 100  (60143-2665)
PHONE .................................... 847 884-2842
**Fax:** 847 956-0701
Yuichi Mori, *Ch of Bd*
Alex Martinez, *President*
Dave McGrory, *Sales Staff*
▲ **EMP:** 12
**SQ FT:** 6,000
**SALES:** 5MM
**SALES (corp-wide):** 5.1MM  **Privately Held**
**SIC:** 2678  Stationery products
**HQ:** Carl Manufacturing Co., Ltd.
3-7-9, Tateishi
Katsushika-Ku TKY 124-0
336 952-501

## (G-12243)
### CHARLOTTE DMG INC
265 Spring Lake Dr  (60143-3203)
PHONE .................................... 630 227-3900
Thorsten Schmidt, *President*
Thomas Bone, *President*
Rakhee Chatterjee, *Controller*
John Stiff, *CIO*
Dan Wohlbruck, *Info Tech Dir*
**EMP:** 9
**SALES (est):** 473.6K
**SALES (corp-wide):** 3.4B  **Privately Held**
**WEB:** www.dmgamerica.com
**SIC:** 3541  3699  Machine tools, metal cutting type; laser welding, drilling & cutting equipment
**HQ:** Dmg Charlotte Llc
2400 Huntington Blvd
Hoffman Estates IL 60192

## (G-12244)
### CHURCH STREET BREWING CO LLC
1480 Industrial Dr Ste C  (60143-1857)
PHONE .................................... 630 438-5725
Lisa Gregor MD, *Principal*
Gregor Joseph H, *Business Mgr*
**EMP:** 8
**SALES (est):** 1.5MM  **Privately Held**
**SIC:** 5181  2082  Beer & ale; ale (alcoholic beverage)

## (G-12245)
### CIRCUIT WORLD INC
751 Hilltop Dr  (60143-1325)
PHONE .................................... 630 250-1100
**Fax:** 630 238-2523
Vipan Patel, *President*
Kanti Sanghani, *Vice Pres*
Jagdish Metha, *Treasurer*
▲ **EMP:** 42
**SQ FT:** 25,000
**SALES (est):** 7.7MM  **Privately Held**
**WEB:** www.circuitw.com
**SIC:** 3672  Printed circuit boards

## (G-12246)
### CONCENTRIC ITASCA INC
800 Hollywood Ave  (60143-1353)
PHONE .................................... 630 268-1528
David Woolley, *CEO*
Len Mason, *President*
Joe Garlick, *Vice Pres*
John Magee, *Project Mgr*
Martin Moesgaard, *Mfg Mgr*
▲ **EMP:** 87
**SQ FT:** 50,000
**SALES (est):** 26.5MM
**SALES (corp-wide):** 216.3MM  **Privately Held**
**WEB:** www.concentric-pumps.com
**SIC:** 3519  5084  Governors, pump, for diesel engines; engines & parts, diesel
**HQ:** Concentric Birmingham Limited
3 The Archway
Birmingham W MIDLANDS B24 8

## (G-12247)
### CONTINENTAL WEB PRESS INC (PA)
1430 Industrial Dr  (60143-1858)
PHONE .................................... 630 773-1903
**Fax:** 630 773-8770
Diane K Field, *President*
Ken Field Jr, *General Mgr*
Jim Arnold, *Exec VP*
Al Hardy, *Opers Mgr*
Al Gervais, *Opers Staff*
▲ **EMP:** 125
**SQ FT:** 230,000
**SALES (est):** 58.5MM  **Privately Held**
**WEB:** www.continentalweb.com
**SIC:** 2752  Commercial printing, offset

## (G-12248)
### CONTINENTAL WEB PRESS KY INC
1430 Industrial Dr  (60143-1858)
PHONE .................................... 630 773-1903
W R Burgess, *Director*
**EMP:** 129  **Privately Held**
**SIC:** 2752  Commercial printing, offset
**PA:** Continental Web Press Of Kentucky, Inc.
1430 Industrial Dr
Itasca IL 60143

## (G-12249)
### CONTINENTAL WEB PRESS KY INC (PA)
1430 Industrial Dr  (60143-1858)
PHONE .................................... 859 485-1500
Diane K Field, *President*
Jim Arnold, *COO*
Ken Field Jr, *Vice Pres*
Kenneth W Field, *Vice Pres*
Bill Scarpaci, *Manager*
▲ **EMP:** 56
**SQ FT:** 225,000
**SALES:** 38.4MM  **Privately Held**
**SIC:** 2752  Commercial printing, offset

## (G-12250)
### DICE MOLD & ENGINEERING INC
75 N Prospect Ave  (60143-1867)
PHONE .................................... 630 773-3595
**Fax:** 630 773-4005
Raymond Dierking, *President*
Sergio Ciscolini, *Treasurer*
Kevin Dirking, *Technology*
**EMP:** 20
**SQ FT:** 8,000
**SALES (est):** 3.8MM  **Privately Held**
**WEB:** www.dicemold.com
**SIC:** 3089  3544  Injection molding of plastics; special dies & tools

## (G-12251)
### DIES PLUS INC
1425 Industrial Dr  (60143-1803)
PHONE .................................... 630 285-1065
Gerald Dohe, *President*
Craig Dohe, *Vice Pres*
Neil Dohe, *Vice Pres*
Jerry Dohe, *Manager*
Candice Dohe, *Systems Mgr*
**EMP:** 10
**SQ FT:** 13,000
**SALES (est):** 1.3MM  **Privately Held**
**WEB:** www.diesplus.com
**SIC:** 3544  Special dies, tools, jigs & fixtures; special dies & tools

## GEOGRAPHIC SECTION
## Itasca - Dupage County (G-12278)

**(G-12252)**
**DIVERSFIED LBLING SLUTIONS INC (PA)**
Also Called: D L S
1285 Hamilton Pkwy (60143-1150)
PHONE..................630 625-1225
Bob Hakman, *President*
Herb Troyer, *General Mgr*
Ken Bozelka, *Plant Mgr*
Daniel Petersen, *Plant Mgr*
Tommy Highton, *Prdtn Mgr*
EMP: 100
SQ FT: 140,000
SALES (est): 32.1MM **Privately Held**
WEB: www.teamdlsolutions.com
SIC: 2679 2672 Labels, paper: made from purchased material; tape, pressure sensitive: made from purchased materials; labels (unprinted), gummed: made from purchased materials

**(G-12253)**
**DPCAC LLC**
Also Called: Dwyer Products & Services
1345 Norwood Ave (60143-1126)
PHONE..................630 741-7900
Paula Sund, *Controller*
Frank San Roman, *Mng Member*
EMP: 12
SALES (est): 940K **Privately Held**
SIC: 2434 2514 3264 2541 Wood kitchen cabinets; kitchen cabinets: metal; porcelain electrical supplies; wood partitions & fixtures

**(G-12254)**
**DPM SOLUTIONS LLC**
1521 Industrial Dr (60143-1849)
PHONE..................630 285-1170
Alexander Robledo, *Mng Member*
EMP: 3 EST: 2009
SALES (est): 245.9K **Privately Held**
SIC: 3999 Atomizers, toiletry

**(G-12255)**
**DU PONT DELAWARE INC**
Also Called: Dupont
500 Park Blvd Ste 545 (60143-1267)
PHONE..................630 285-2700
EMP: 5
SALES (corp-wide): 24.5B **Publicly Held**
SIC: 2879 Agricultural chemicals
HQ: Du Pont Delaware, Inc.
974 Centre Rd Chestnut
Wilmington DE 19805
302 774-1000

**(G-12256)**
**EBWAY INDUSTRIES INC**
1201 Ardmore Ave (60143-1187)
PHONE..................630 860-5959
Alan Jardis, *President*
David Hansen, *Controller*
Gary Klawinski, *Sales Staff*
EMP: 40
SQ FT: 22,750
SALES (est): 9.2MM **Privately Held**
WEB: www.jardis.com
SIC: 3555 Printing trades machinery
PA: Jardis Industries, Inc.
1201 Ardmore Ave
Itasca IL 60143
630 860-5959

**(G-12257)**
**ELEMATEC USA CORPORATION**
500 Park Blvd Ste 760 (60143-2623)
PHONE..................847 466-1451
Kenichi Oshiva, *Branch Mgr*
EMP: 5
SALES (corp-wide): 69.6B **Privately Held**
SIC: 3676 Electronic resistors
HQ: Elematec Usa Corporation
7220 Trade St Ste 215
San Diego CA 92121
858 527-1700

**(G-12258)**
**ELLIS CORPORATION (PA)**
1400 W Bryn Mawr Ave (60143-1384)
PHONE..................630 250-9222
Fax: 630 250-9241
Robert H Fesmire Jr, *President*
Jim Shaw, *Senior VP*
Alan Burleson, *Engineer*
Dan Noltin, *Design Engr*
Harry Manos, *Electrical Engi*
▲ EMP: 60 EST: 1931
SQ FT: 64,800
SALES (est): 12.8MM **Privately Held**
SIC: 3582 3589 Commercial laundry equipment; water treatment equipment, industrial

**(G-12259)**
**ENVIRONMENTAL SPECIALTIES INC**
Also Called: E S I
1600 Glenlake Ave (60143-1005)
PHONE..................630 860-7070
Michael T Miske, *President*
▲ EMP: 5
SQ FT: 24,000
SALES (est): 520K **Privately Held**
WEB: www.environmentalspecialties.com
SIC: 3625 3555 2899 2893 Industrial controls: push button, selector switches, pilot; printing trades machinery; chemical preparations; printing ink

**(G-12260)**
**ERGO-TECH INCORPORATED**
217 Catalpa Ave (60143-2027)
P.O. Box 8, Urbana (61803-0008)
PHONE..................630 773-2222
Neal T Lilly, *President*
Matthew Leahy, *Vice Pres*
Brian P Lilly, *Admin Sec*
EMP: 3
SALES (est): 380K **Privately Held**
SIC: 3491 Water works valves

**(G-12261)**
**EXCEL GROUP HOLDINGS INC (PA)**
800 Baker Dr (60143-1310)
PHONE..................630 773-1815
Fax: 630 775-0100
John R Iacono, *President*
Scott Blazzak, *Vice Pres*
Shawn Sanders, *Vice Pres*
Joe Dalessio, *Sales Staff*
▲ EMP: 24
SALES (est): 4MM **Privately Held**
WEB: www.exceldowel.com
SIC: 2499 Dowels, wood

**(G-12262)**
**FELLOWES TRADING COMPANY**
1789 Norwood Ave (60143-1059)
PHONE..................630 893-1600
EMP: 5 EST: 1999
SALES (est): 29.7K **Privately Held**
SIC: 2522 Office furniture, except wood

**(G-12263)**
**FILTER MONKEY LLC**
424 S Lombard Rd (60143-2566)
PHONE..................630 773-4402
Timothy D Krause,
EMP: 2
SALES (est): 212.8K **Privately Held**
SIC: 3569 Filters

**(G-12264)**
**FITZ CHEM CORPORATION**
450 E Devon Ave Ste 175 (60143-1261)
PHONE..................630 467-8383
Fax: 630 467-1183
Donald Deihs, *President*
Robert Becker, *Chairman*
Edward Croco, *Exec VP*
Christy Marcuccelli, *Cust Mgr*
▲ EMP: 39 EST: 1984
SQ FT: 5,300
SALES (est): 43.4MM **Privately Held**
WEB: www.fitzchem.com
SIC: 5169 2821 2891 Chemicals, industrial & heavy; plastics materials & resins; adhesives & sealants

**(G-12265)**
**FLEXERA HOLDINGS LP**
300 Park Blvd Ste 500 (60143-2635)
PHONE..................847 466-4000
EMP: 3
SALES: 236.4MM **Privately Held**
SIC: 7371 7372 Computer software development; prepackaged software
PA: Flexera Software Llc
300 Park Blvd Ste 500
Itasca IL 60143

**(G-12266)**
**FLEXERA SOFTWARE LLC (PA)**
300 Park Blvd Ste 500 (60143-2635)
PHONE..................800 374-4353
Fax: 847 619-0788
Jim Ryan, *President*
Mark Bishof, *Principal*
Art Middlekauff, *Senior VP*
Richard Northing, *Senior VP*
Peter Prestele, *Senior VP*
EMP: 403
SALES (est): 245MM **Privately Held**
SIC: 7371 7372 Computer software development; prepackaged software

**(G-12267)**
**FPM HEAT TREATMENT**
1349 W Bryn Mawr Ave (60143-1313)
PHONE..................847 274-7269
EMP: 6
SALES (est): 461.8K **Privately Held**
SIC: 3398 Metal heat treating

**(G-12268)**
**GENESIS PRESS INC**
1270 Ardmore Ave (60143-1141)
PHONE..................630 467-1000
Robert Moore, *President*
Paul Bauman, *Corp Secy*
Ken Ford, *Production*
Steve Brewster, *Director*
EMP: 4
SQ FT: 51,000
SALES (est): 741.2K **Privately Held**
WEB: www.genesispressinc.com
SIC: 2752 Offset & photolithographic printing

**(G-12269)**
**GEORGE VAGGELATOS**
Also Called: Apple Print
400 W Center St (60143-1710)
PHONE..................847 361-3880
George Vaggelatos, *Principal*
EMP: 2
SALES (est): 203.2K **Privately Held**
SIC: 2752 Commercial printing, lithographic

**(G-12270)**
**GIVAUDAN FLAVORS CORPORATION**
880 W Thorndale Ave (60143-1341)
PHONE..................630 773-8484
Fax: 630 773-8794
Charles Faraci, *Purch Mgr*
Tom Grant, *Branch Mgr*
EMP: 50
SALES (corp-wide): 1.1B **Privately Held**
SIC: 2869 2087 Flavors or flavoring materials, synthetic; flavoring extracts & syrups
HQ: Givaudan Flavors Corporation
1199 Edison Dr
Cincinnati OH 45216
513 948-8000

**(G-12271)**
**GOGO INTERMEDIATE HOLDINGS LLC (HQ)**
1250 N Arlington Rd (60143)
PHONE..................630 647-1400
EMP: 5 EST: 2012
SALES (est): 300.8MM
SALES (corp-wide): 596.5MM **Publicly Held**
SIC: 3663 Radio & TV communications equipment
PA: Gogo Inc.
111 N Canal St Ste 1500
Chicago IL 60606
312 517-5000

**(G-12272)**
**GRAPHIC TOOL CORP**
1211 Norwood Ave (60143-1124)
PHONE..................630 250-9800
Fax: 630 250-0761
Charles Gonzalez, *President*
Richard Burman, *President*
Clifford Kroening, *Vice Pres*
Don Smith, *Plant Mgr*
Tim Bandurske, *Foreman/Supr*
▲ EMP: 26
SQ FT: 17,500
SALES (est): 5.9MM **Privately Held**
WEB: www.graphictool.com
SIC: 3089 Injection molding of plastics

**(G-12273)**
**GRINDAL COMPANY**
1551 Industrial Dr (60143-1861)
PHONE..................630 250-8950
Fax: 630 250-7082
Janice E Spooner, *President*
Wayne D Domke, *General Mgr*
Jorge Chinchilla, *QC Mgr*
Joyce Whipple, *Manager*
Bob Taylor, *CTO*
▲ EMP: 20
SQ FT: 20,000
SALES (est): 4.3MM **Privately Held**
WEB: www.grindal.com
SIC: 3541 Grinding machines, metalworking

**(G-12274)**
**HENDRICKSON USA LLC (HQ)**
500 Park Blvd Ste 450 (60143-3153)
PHONE..................630 874-9700
Nancy Coons, *VP Admin*
Jim Colley, *Vice Pres*
Wayne Goble, *Vice Pres*
Rick Johnson, *Vice Pres*
Mike Keeler, *Vice Pres*
EMP: 174
SALES (est): 98.8MM
SALES (corp-wide): 1B **Privately Held**
SIC: 3537 Industrial trucks & tractors
PA: The Boler Company
500 Park Blvd Ste 1010
Itasca IL 60143
630 773-9111

**(G-12275)**
**HOUGHTON MIFFLIN HARCOURT CO**
Also Called: Hmh
761 District Dr (60143-1319)
PHONE..................630 467-6049
EMP: 3
SALES (corp-wide): 1.3B **Publicly Held**
SIC: 3999 2731 Education aids, devices & supplies; book publishing
PA: Houghton Mifflin Harcourt Company
125 High St Ste 900
Boston MA 02110
617 351-5000

**(G-12276)**
**HOUGHTON MIFFLIN HARCOURT PUBG**
Also Called: Riverside Publishing
425 Spring Lake Dr (60143-2076)
PHONE..................630 467-6095
Fax: 630 467-7191
John Laramy, *President*
Argy Anargyros, *Manager*
Eric Blackledge, *Info Tech Dir*
Rose Lattuca, *Recruiter*
EMP: 300
SALES (corp-wide): 1.3B **Publicly Held**
WEB: www.hmco.com
SIC: 2731 Book publishing
HQ: Houghton Mifflin Harcourt Publishing Company
125 High St Ste 900
Boston MA 02110
617 351-5000

**(G-12277)**
**HYUNDAI WIA MACHINE AMER CORP**
265 Spring Lake Dr (60143-3203)
PHONE..................201 636-5600
Peter Youm, *Office Mgr*
EMP: 35
SALES (corp-wide): 6B **Privately Held**
SIC: 3541 Lathes, metal cutting & polishing
HQ: Hyundai Wia Machine America, Corp.
265 Spring Lake Dr
Itasca IL 60143
201 636-5600

**(G-12278)**
**ICP INDUSTRIAL INC (PA)**
Also Called: National Industrial Coatings
1600 Glenlake Ave (60143-1005)
P.O. Box 809137, Chicago (60680-9137)
PHONE..................630 227-1692

# Itasca - Dupage County (G-12279) — GEOGRAPHIC SECTION

Chuck Turnbull, *President*
Doug Bigford, *Senior VP*
Jorge Hasbun, *Vice Pres*
Dave Lorey, *CFO*
David Lorey, *CFO*
◆ **EMP:** 35
**SQ FT:** 75,000
**SALES (est):** 11.3MM **Privately Held**
**WEB:** www.nicoat.com
**SIC: 2851** Lacquers, varnishes, enamels & other coatings

### (G-12279)
### IFS NORTH AMERICA INC (HQ)
300 Park Blvd Ste 555 (60143-2635)
**PHONE** .................................. 888 437-4968
Cindy Jaudon, *CEO*
Jan Brunaes, *Vice Pres*
Ronny Frey, *Vice Pres*
Mitch Dwight, *CFO*
Rodney Caroll, *Controller*
**EMP:** 50
**SQ FT:** 15,888
**SALES (est):** 68.3MM
**SALES (corp-wide):** 388.2MM **Privately Held**
**WEB:** www.ifsworld.com
**SIC: 7372** 7379 8243 Prepackaged software; data processing consultant; software training, computer
**PA:** Industrial And Financial Systems, Ifs Ab
Lindhagensgatan 116
Stockholm 112 5
858 784-500

### (G-12280)
### ILLINOIS TOOL WORKS INC
HI Cone Div
1140 W Bryn Mawr Ave (60143-1509)
**PHONE** .................................. 630 773-9300
**Fax:** 630 773-3015
Tim Gardner, *Vice Pres*
Tom Slaters, *Engineer*
Michael Kuschel, *Controller*
Jay Hiller, *Sales Staff*
Elizabeth Sheaffer, *Mktg Dir*
**EMP:** 30
**SALES (corp-wide):** 13.6B **Publicly Held**
**SIC: 3089** Pallets, plastic
**PA:** Illinois Tool Works Inc.
155 Harlem Ave
Glenview IL 60025
847 724-7500

### (G-12281)
### ILLINOIS TOOL WORKS INC
ITW Commercial Cnstr N Amer
1349 W Bryn Mawr Ave (60143-1313)
**PHONE** .................................. 630 595-3500
**Fax:** 630 595-3569
Timm Fields, *General Mgr*
Inna Tfenver, *Controller*
Inna Tsenver, *Controller*
Jim Paulsen, *Manager*
Jeff Wilcox, *Manager*
**EMP:** 227
**SALES (corp-wide):** 13.6B **Publicly Held**
**SIC: 3452** 3542 Bolts, nuts, rivets & washers; machine tools, metal forming type
**PA:** Illinois Tool Works Inc.
155 Harlem Ave
Glenview IL 60025
847 724-7500

### (G-12282)
### ILLINOIS TOOL WORKS INC
Also Called: Hi-Cone Division
1140 W Bryn Mawr Ave (60143-1509)
**PHONE** .................................. 630 773-9301
**Fax:** 630 773-9315
Phil Robertson, *Plant Mgr*
Andy Mazurek, *Controller*
Carole Dohse, *Analyst*
**EMP:** 53
**SALES (corp-wide):** 13.6B **Publicly Held**
**SIC: 3089** Plastic containers, except foam
**PA:** Illinois Tool Works Inc.
155 Harlem Ave
Glenview IL 60025
847 724-7500

### (G-12283)
### IMAGING SYSTEMS INC (PA)
Also Called: Integrated Document Tech
1009 W Hawthorn Dr (60143-2057)
**PHONE** .................................. 630 875-1100
**Fax:** 630 875-1101
Paul E Szemplinski, *Ch of Bd*
Michael Nolfo, *President*
John Dobbins, *Exec VP*
Scott Burns, *Vice Pres*
Joe Caldarone, *Vice Pres*
**EMP:** 14
**SQ FT:** 5,700
**SALES (est):** 3.6MM **Privately Held**
**WEB:** www.idt-inc.com
**SIC: 7371** 5045 7372 7374 Computer software writers, freelance; computer software; application computer software; business oriented computer software; data processing & preparation

### (G-12284)
### IMCP INC
900 N Arlington (60143)
P.O. Box 9 (60143-0009)
**PHONE** .................................. 630 477-8600
Patrick Grant, *President*
Bob Lorenz, *Manager*
Mark Ward, *CTO*
Barry Hamilton, *Director*
**EMP:** 3
**SQ FT:** 2,000
**SALES (est):** 452.1K **Privately Held**
**WEB:** www.imcp.com
**SIC: 7379** 7372 Computer related consulting services; prepackaged software

### (G-12285)
### INDUSTRIAL FINANCE SYSTEMS
300 Park Blvd (60143-2682)
**PHONE** .................................. 847 592-0200
**Fax:** 847 592-0201
Bengt G Nilsson, *Principal*
Mitch Dwight, *CFO*
Steve Andrew, *Director*
**EMP:** 8
**SALES (est):** 627.7K **Privately Held**
**SIC: 7372** Prepackaged software

### (G-12286)
### INTERNATIONAL PAPER COMPANY
1225 W Bryn Mawr Ave (60143-1311)
**PHONE** .................................. 630 250-1300
Clare Anderson, *General Mgr*
Walter Rivera, *Manager*
**EMP:** 25
**SALES (corp-wide):** 21B **Publicly Held**
**WEB:** www.internationalpaper.com
**SIC: 2621** 2611 Paper mills; pulp mills
**PA:** International Paper Company
6400 Poplar Ave
Memphis TN 38197
901 419-9000

### (G-12287)
### IRETIRED LLC
700 District Dr (60143-1320)
**PHONE** .................................. 630 285-9500
**Fax:** 630 285-9501
Seufina Kotnaur, *Project Mgr*
Andrea Miller, *Project Mgr*
Tracey Oconnor, *Sales Mgr*
Mary Levi, *Accounts Exec*
Zach Stock, *Accounts Exec*
▲ **EMP:** 34
**SQ FT:** 49,000
**SALES (est):** 8.1MM **Privately Held**
**WEB:** www.ionexhibits.com
**SIC: 5046** 2542 Display equipment, except refrigerated; partitions & fixtures, except wood

### (G-12288)
### J-TEC METAL PRODUCTS INC
1320 Ardmore Ave (60143-1105)
**PHONE** .................................. 630 875-1300
**Fax:** 630 875-1200
Jesus Garza, *President*
Raymond Bogosh, *Sales Executive*
Francisca Garza, *Admin Sec*
**EMP:** 18
**SALES (est):** 5.1MM **Privately Held**
**WEB:** www.jtecmetal.com
**SIC: 3353** 3469 3444 Aluminum sheet & strip; metal stampings; sheet metalwork

### (G-12289)
### JARDIS INDUSTRIES INC (PA)
Also Called: Bachi Company Div
1201 Ardmore Ave (60143-1187)
**PHONE** .................................. 630 860-5959
Alan W Jardis, *President*
Wayne Eggebrecht, *Purchasing*
Dave Hansen, *Controller*
David Hanson, *Financial Exec*
Art Langosch, *Sales Mgr*
▲ **EMP:** 42
**SQ FT:** 32,500
**SALES (est):** 9.2MM **Privately Held**
**WEB:** www.bachiwinder.com
**SIC: 3555** 5084 Printing trades machinery; industrial machinery & equipment

### (G-12290)
### JARDIS INDUSTRIES INC
Bachi Company
1201 Ardmore Ave (60143-1187)
**PHONE** .................................. 630 773-5600
**Fax:** 630 773-5621
Robert Labarre, *Chief Engr*
David Hansen, *Branch Mgr*
**EMP:** 10
**SALES (corp-wide):** 9.2MM **Privately Held**
**WEB:** www.bachiwinder.com
**SIC: 3549** 5084 3699 3621 Coil winding machines for springs; printing trades machinery, equipment & supplies; electrical equipment & supplies; motors & generators
**PA:** Jardis Industries, Inc.
1201 Ardmore Ave
Itasca IL 60143
630 860-5959

### (G-12291)
### JEWEL OSCO INC (DH)
150 E Pierce Rd Ste 200 (60143-1224)
P.O. Box 210379, Dallas TX (75211-0379)
**PHONE** .................................. 630 948-6000
Shane Sampson, *President*
Mike Withers, *President*
William Emmons, *Principal*
Gerald D Bay, *Senior VP*
Sherry M Smith, *Senior VP*
**EMP:** 200 **EST:** 1899
**SALES (est):** 2.8B
**SALES (corp-wide):** 58.8B **Privately Held**
**WEB:** www.jewelosco.com
**SIC: 5411** 2834 Supermarkets, chain; proprietary drug products
**HQ:** New Albertson's, Inc.
250 E Parkcenter Blvd
Boise ID 83706
208 395-6200

### (G-12292)
### KEEPER CORP
1345 Industrial Dr (60143-1894)
**PHONE** .................................. 630 773-9393
**Fax:** 630 773-3323
Edward Kryger, *President*
Ronald Kryger, *Vice Pres*
Tom Kryger, *Vice Pres*
**EMP:** 7
**SQ FT:** 10,500
**SALES (est):** 1.1MM **Privately Held**
**WEB:** www.keepercorp.com
**SIC: 3599** Machine & other job shop work

### (G-12293)
### KESTER INC
940 W Thorndale Ave (60143-1339)
**PHONE** .................................. 630 616-6882
**EMP:** 6
**SALES (corp-wide):** 13.6B **Publicly Held**
**SIC: 3356** Solder: wire, bar, acid core, & rosin core
**HQ:** Kester, Inc
800 W Thorndale Ave
Itasca IL 60143
630 616-4000

### (G-12294)
### KESTER INC (HQ)
800 W Thorndale Ave (60143-1341)
**PHONE** .................................. 630 616-4000
**Fax:** 847 699-5548
Steven L Martindale, *President*
Roger Savage, *President*
Carmelle Giblin, *General Mgr*
Scott Karels, *Engineer*
Ken Datko, *Controller*
◆ **EMP:** 230
**SALES (est):** 95.1MM
**SALES (corp-wide):** 13.6B **Publicly Held**
**WEB:** www.kester.com
**SIC: 3356** Solder: wire, bar, acid core, & rosin core
**PA:** Illinois Tool Works Inc.
155 Harlem Ave
Glenview IL 60025
847 724-7500

### (G-12295)
### KNOWLES CORPORATION (PA)
1151 Maplewood Dr (60143-2058)
**PHONE** .................................. 630 250-5100
Jean-Pierre M Ergas, *Ch of Bd*
Jeffrey S Niew, *President*
Paul M Dickinson, *President*
Mike Polacek, *President*
**EMP:** 59 **EST:** 2013
**SALES:** 859.3MM **Publicly Held**
**SIC: 3651** 3675 Household audio & video equipment; audio electronic systems; microphones; speaker systems; electronic capacitors

### (G-12296)
### KNOWLES ELEC HOLDINGS INC
1151 Maplewood Dr (60143-2058)
**PHONE** .................................. 630 250-5100
**Fax:** 630 250-0575
Jean-Pierre M Ergas, *Ch of Bd*
Michael A Adell, *President*
Jeffrey S Niew, *President*
John J Zei, *Principal*
Raymond D Cabrera, *Senior VP*
**EMP:** 2420 **EST:** 1954
**SQ FT:** 60,000
**SALES (est):** 228.8MM
**SALES (corp-wide):** 859.3MM **Publicly Held**
**SIC: 3679** 3625 3651 8731 Transducers, electrical; headphones, radio; solenoid switches (industrial controls); sound reproducing equipment; engineering laboratory, except testing; commercial research laboratory; loan institutions, general & industrial
**PA:** Knowles Corporation
1151 Maplewood Dr
Itasca IL 60143
630 250-5100

### (G-12297)
### KNOWLES ELECTRONICS LLC (HQ)
1151 Maplewood Dr (60143-2071)
**PHONE** .................................. 630 250-5100
Jeffrey Niew, *President*
Pete Loeppert, *President*
Charles King, *Vice Chairman*
John Anderson, *Senior VP*
Mike Adell, *Vice Pres*
▲ **EMP:** 2418
**SQ FT:** 60,000
**SALES (corp-wide):** 859.3MM **Publicly Held**
**WEB:** www.emkayproducts.com
**SIC: 3679** 3842 Transducers, electrical; hearing aids
**PA:** Knowles Corporation
1151 Maplewood Dr
Itasca IL 60143
630 250-5100

### (G-12298)
### KODIAK CONCRETE FORMS INC
Also Called: Allenform Con Forming Pdts
1320 Industrial Dr Ste C (60143-1863)
**PHONE** .................................. 630 773-9339
**Fax:** 630 773-9227
Jim Bissing, *President*
Joe Joaillier, *Corp Secy*
**EMP:** 4
**SQ FT:** 3,000
**SALES (est):** 454.8K **Privately Held**
**SIC: 3272** 3443 Building materials, except block or brick: concrete; fabricated plate work (boiler shop)

### (G-12299)
### KWIK PRINT INC
206 W Irving Park Rd (60143-2041)
**PHONE** .................................. 630 773-3225
**Fax:** 630 773-3254

# GEOGRAPHIC SECTION

Itasca - Dupage County (G-12321)

Gary F Roback, *President*
Julie Roback, *Corp Secy*
Jeanette Roback, *Admin Sec*
**EMP:** 4
**SALES (est):** 503.1K **Privately Held**
**SIC:** 2752 2789 2759 Commercial printing, offset; bookbinding & related work; commercial printing

**(G-12300)**
**L & W TOOL & SCREW MCH PDTS**
1447 Ardmore Ave (60143-1142)
**PHONE**.....................847 238-1212
**Fax:** 847 238-1254
Walter Sowa, *President*
Joseph Sowa, *Admin Sec*
**EMP:** 25
**SQ FT:** 15,000
**SALES (est):** 5.1MM **Privately Held**
**SIC:** 3451 Screw machine products

**(G-12301)**
**LAB EQUIPMENT INC (PA)**
1549 Ardmore Ave (60143-1108)
**PHONE**.....................630 595-4288
Phil Roberto, *CEO*
William Noonan, *President*
Elsie Markioplis, *Purchasing*
Kimberly Grumbos, *Manager*
Kurt Wolf, *Manager*
▲ **EMP:** 24
**SQ FT:** 26,000
**SALES (est):** 4MM **Privately Held**
**WEB:** www.noonanmachine.com
**SIC:** 3825 3559 Lab standards, electric: resistance, inductance, capacitance; rubber working machinery, including tires

**(G-12302)**
**LEMKO CORPORATION**
1 Pierce Pl Ste 700w (60143-2606)
**PHONE**.....................630 948-3025
Nicholas Labun, *Ch of Bd*
Robert Condon, *President*
Bohdan Pyskir, *President*
Joseph Barr, *CFO*
Jason Osborne, *VP Sales*
**EMP:** 35
**SQ FT:** 22,000
**SALES (est):** 6.8MM **Privately Held**
**WEB:** www.lemko.com
**SIC:** 7371 3663 Computer software development; cellular radio telephone

**(G-12303)**
**LENS LENTICLEAR LENTICULAR**
Also Called: Jacobsen Lenticu
19w030 Marino Ct (60143-1208)
P.O. Box 4289 (60143-4289)
**PHONE**.....................630 467-0900
Gary A Jacobsen, *President*
James R Schirott, *Vice Pres*
**EMP:** 11
**SQ FT:** 11,000
**SALES:** 2MM **Privately Held**
**WEB:** www.lenticlearlens.com
**SIC:** 3089 3542 3827 3544 Engraving of plastic; extruding machines (machine tools), metal; lenses, optical: all types except ophthalmic; forms (molds), for foundry & plastics working machinery

**(G-12304)**
**LIFELINE SCIENTIFIC INC (PA)**
1 Pierce Pl Ste 475w (60143-2618)
**PHONE**.....................847 294-0300
**Fax:** 847 294-0301
David Kravitz, *President*
Becky Lyne, *Controller*
**EMP:** 20
**SALES (est):** 3.4MM **Privately Held**
**SIC:** 3845 Electromedical equipment

**(G-12305)**
**LILLY AIR SYSTEMS CO INC**
217 Catalpa Ave (60143-2027)
P.O. Box 173 (60143-0173)
**PHONE**.....................630 773-2225
**Fax:** 630 773-3443
Tim Lilly, *President*
John Lilly, *President*
Brian Lilly, *Engineer*
**EMP:** 10
**SQ FT:** 700

**SALES (est):** 1.6MM **Privately Held**
**WEB:** www.darbydrug.com
**SIC:** 3564 Filters, air: furnaces, air conditioning equipment, etc.

**(G-12306)**
**LILLY INDUSTRIES INC**
Also Called: Lilly Steam Trap
427 W Irving Park Rd (60143-2039)
P.O. Box 173 (60143-0173)
**PHONE**.....................630 773-2222
Timothy Lilly, *President*
Jane Lorenz, *Office Mgr*
John R Lilly, *Admin Sec*
▲ **EMP:** 10
**SQ FT:** 6,000
**SALES (est):** 1.1MM **Privately Held**
**SIC:** 3491 3494 Steam traps; valves & pipe fittings

**(G-12307)**
**LITHO RESEARCH INCORPORATED**
1600 Glenlake Ave (60143-1005)
**PHONE**.....................630 860-7070
Michael T Miske, *President*
Brian Miske, *General Mgr*
**EMP:** 8
**SQ FT:** 25,000
**SALES:** 124.6K
**SALES (corp-wide):** 11.3MM **Privately Held**
**WEB:** www.lithoresearch.com
**SIC:** 5169 2899 5085 5084 Chemicals & allied products; chemical preparations; industrial supplies; industrial machinery & equipment
**PA:** Icp Industrial, Inc.
1600 Glenlake Ave
Itasca IL 60143
630 227-1692

**(G-12308)**
**MADMAXMAR GROUP INC**
1 Pierce Pl Ste 510w (60143-2630)
**PHONE**.....................630 320-3700
Michael B Messina, *President*
**EMP:** 25 **EST:** 2006
**SALES (est):** 3.2MM **Privately Held**
**SIC:** 2759 Commercial printing

**(G-12309)**
**MAJOR DIE & ENGINEERING CO**
1352 Industrial Dr (60143-1804)
**PHONE**.....................630 773-3444
**Fax:** 630 773-3111
James Fett Sr, *President*
James Fett Jr, *Vice Pres*
**EMP:** 11 **EST:** 1956
**SQ FT:** 15,000
**SALES (est):** 2.5MM **Privately Held**
**SIC:** 3469 3544 Stamping metal for the trade; special dies, tools, jigs & fixtures

**(G-12310)**
**MANUFACTURERS INV GROUP LLC**
Also Called: Mrl Industries
690 Hilltop Dr (60143-1326)
**PHONE**.....................630 285-0800
**Fax:** 630 285-0807
Andrew Sandberg, *CEO*
James Soderquist, *President*
Patrick Irwin, *General Mgr*
George Pillion, *Info Tech Mgr*
▼ **EMP:** 35 **EST:** 1964
**SQ FT:** 40,000
**SALES (est):** 9.1MM **Privately Held**
**WEB:** www.magrad.com
**SIC:** 3499 Magnetic shields, metal

**(G-12311)**
**MARTY LUNDEEN**
311 Willow St (60143-1760)
**PHONE**.....................630 250-8917
Marty Lundeen, *Executive*
**EMP:** 3
**SALES (est):** 118.7K **Privately Held**
**SIC:** 3511 Turbines & turbine generator sets

**(G-12312)**
**MASTER SPRING & WIRE FORM CO**
1340 Ardmore Ave (60143-1105)
**PHONE**.....................708 453-2570
**Fax:** 708 453-6420
Jeff Burda, *President*
Steve Skolozynski, *Vice Pres*
Sherry Anton, *QC Mgr*
Bob Turk, *Marketing Staff*
Toni La Fonti, *Manager*
**EMP:** 25
**SQ FT:** 20,000
**SALES (est):** 4.5MM **Privately Held**
**WEB:** www.masterspring.com
**SIC:** 3496 3495 Miscellaneous fabricated wire products; wire springs

**(G-12313)**
**MEI LLC**
315 N Linden St (60143-1839)
**PHONE**.....................630 285-1505
Darin Edgecomb,
**EMP:** 1
**SALES (est):** 217K **Privately Held**
**SIC:** 2671 Thermoplastic coated paper for packaging

**(G-12314)**
**METAL STRIP BUIDING PRODUCTS**
1345 Norwood Ave (60143-1126)
**PHONE**.....................847 742-8500
**Fax:** 630 458-0405
Frank San Roman, *President*
Edward Swantek, *Corp Secy*
Gerald Pines, *Vice Pres*
Julie Geniesse, *Controller*
Jeanne Peterson, *Manager*
**EMP:** 6 **EST:** 1946
**SQ FT:** 8,000
**SALES (est):** 901.5K
**SALES (corp-wide):** 65MM **Privately Held**
**SIC:** 3499 3449 3444 Novelties & specialties, metal; miscellaneous metalwork; sheet metalwork
**PA:** Millenia Products Group, Inc.
1345 Norwood Ave
Itasca IL 60143
630 458-0401

**(G-12315)**
**MICROCHIP TECHNOLOGY INC**
333 W Pierce Rd Ste 180 (60143-3120)
**PHONE**.....................630 285-0071
**Fax:** 630 285-0075
Shane Crandall, *Engineer*
Ron Mathius, *Engineer*
Rob Ostapiuk, *Engineer*
Steve Rusnock, *Regl Sales Mgr*
James Green, *Sales Engr*
**EMP:** 27
**SALES (corp-wide):** 3.4B **Publicly Held**
**WEB:** www.microchip.com
**SIC:** 3674 Integrated circuits, semiconductor networks, etc.
**PA:** Microchip Technology Inc
2355 W Chandler Blvd
Chandler AZ 85224
480 792-7200

**(G-12316)**
**MICROS SYSTEMS INC**
2 Pierce Pl Ste 1700 (60143-3124)
**PHONE**.....................443 285-6000
**Fax:** 847 439-5003
Jeff Wooden, *Business Mgr*
Carroll Johnson, *Exec VP*
Steven Freitag, *Vice Pres*
John Cameron, *Opers Mgr*
Biswajit Ganguly, *Engineer*
**EMP:** 17
**SALES (est):** 37B **Publicly Held**
**WEB:** www.micros.com
**SIC:** 3578 5044 3577 Point-of-sale devices; cash registers; computer peripheral equipment
**HQ:** Micros Systems, Inc.
7031 Columbia Gateway Dr # 1
Columbia MD 21046
443 285-6000

**(G-12317)**
**MILLENIA METALS LLC**
Also Called: Ravinia Metals
1345 Norwood Ave (60143-1126)
**PHONE**.....................630 458-0401
James Carroll, *CFO*
Frank San Roman, *Mng Member*
Gerald Pines,
Edward Swantek,
**EMP:** 100
**SALES (est):** 5.3MM
**SALES (corp-wide):** 65MM **Privately Held**
**SIC:** 3469 5051 Metal stampings; iron & steel (ferrous) products
**PA:** Millenia Products Group, Inc.
1345 Norwood Ave
Itasca IL 60143
630 458-0401

**(G-12318)**
**MILLENIA PRODUCTS GROUP INC (PA)**
Also Called: Mill Tek Metals
1345 Norwood Ave (60143-1126)
**PHONE**.....................630 458-0401
**Fax:** 630 741-7974
Frank San Roman, *CEO*
Patrick Milet, *Vice Pres*
John Gallo, *Production*
Gerald Pines, *Treasurer*
Marlon Carney, *Controller*
▲ **EMP:** 130
**SQ FT:** 110,000
**SALES:** 65MM **Privately Held**
**SIC:** 3499 3469 Fire- or burglary-resistive products; machine bases, metal; metal stampings

**(G-12319)**
**MILLENIA SPECIALTY METALS LLC**
1345 Norwood Ave (60143-1126)
**PHONE**.....................630 458-0401
Frank San Roman, *CEO*
Gerald Pines, *Chairman*
Patrick Milet, *Vice Pres*
James Carroll, *CFO*
Edward Swantek,
**EMP:** 5
**SALES (est):** 328.2K
**SALES (corp-wide):** 65MM **Privately Held**
**SIC:** 5051 3499 3469 Iron or steel flat products; machine bases, metal; metal stampings
**PA:** Millenia Products Group, Inc.
1345 Norwood Ave
Itasca IL 60143
630 458-0401

**(G-12320)**
**MILLENIA TRUCKING LLC**
1345 Norwood Ave (60143-1126)
**PHONE**.....................630 458-0401
James Carroll, *CFO*
Frank San Roman, *Mng Member*
Gerald Pines,
Edward Swantek,
**EMP:** 20 **EST:** 2012
**SALES (est):** 230.1K
**SALES (corp-wide):** 65MM **Privately Held**
**SIC:** 5051 3499 3469 Iron or steel flat products; machine bases, metal; metal stampings
**PA:** Millenia Products Group, Inc.
1345 Norwood Ave
Itasca IL 60143
630 458-0401

**(G-12321)**
**MILPLEX CIRCUITS INC**
1301 Ardmore Ave (60143-1104)
**PHONE**.....................630 250-1580
**Fax:** 630 250-1590
Bhupendra R Patel, *President*
Rajani Patel, *Vice Pres*
Shashi Patel, *Vice Pres*
Kan Patel, *Opers Mgr*
Bhasker Patel, *Treasurer*
**EMP:** 120
**SQ FT:** 40,000
**SALES (est):** 15.5MM **Privately Held**
**WEB:** www.milplex.com
**SIC:** 3672 Printed circuit boards

# Itasca - Dupage County (G-12322)

### (G-12322)
**MOONS INDUSTRIES AMERICA INC**
1113 N Prospect Ave (60143-1401)
PHONE..................630 833-5940
James Chang, *President*
William Chen, *General Mgr*
Robert Wester, *Opers Mgr*
Richard Lenzing, *Mktg Dir*
Karen Ostendof, *Office Mgr*
▲ **EMP:** 520
**SQ FT:** 2,800
**SALES (est):** 71.3MM **Privately Held**
**WEB:** www.moons.com.cn
**SIC:** 3621 Motors, electric

### (G-12323)
**N HENRY & SON INC**
900 N Rohlwing Rd (60143-1161)
PHONE..................847 870-0797
**Fax:** 773 385-6322
Ben I Wolf, *President*
Alfred B Henry, *Chairman*
**EMP:** 85
**SQ FT:** 60,000
**SALES (est):** 9.4MM **Privately Held**
**WEB:** www.nhenryandson.com
**SIC:** 2399 Banners, pennants & flags

### (G-12324)
**NATIONAL SAFETY COUNCIL (PA)**
Also Called: Nsc
1121 Spring Lake Dr (60143-3201)
PHONE..................630 285-1121
**Fax:** 630 775-2285
Kent McElhattan, *Ch of Bd*
John Surma, *Ch of Bd*
Mark P Vergnano, *Vice Ch Bd*
Deborah AP Hersman, *President*
Joseph Ucciferro, *President*
**EMP:** 275
**SQ FT:** 90,200
**SALES (est):** 54.9MM **Privately Held**
**SIC:** 8399 2721 1731 5084 Health & welfare council; periodicals: publishing only; safety & security specialization; safety equipment

### (G-12325)
**NATIONAL TRACKWORK INC**
1500 Industrial Dr (60143-1848)
PHONE..................630 250-0600
Michelle Sargis, *President*
Melissa Sargis, *Admin Sec*
▲ **EMP:** 40
**SALES (est):** 6MM **Privately Held**
**WEB:** www.nationaltrackwork.com
**SIC:** 3743 Railroad equipment

### (G-12326)
**NCAB GROUP USA INC**
1300 Norwood Ave (60143-1127)
PHONE..................630 562-5550
Berry Zielke, *Branch Mgr*
**EMP:** 14
**SALES (corp-wide):** 3.6MM **Privately Held**
**SIC:** 3672 Circuit boards, television & radio printed; wiring boards
**PA:** Ncab Group Usa, Inc.
10 Starwood Dr
Hampstead NH 03841
603 329-4551

### (G-12327)
**NEC DISPLAY SOLUTIONS AMER INC**
500 Park Blvd Ste 1100 (60143-2602)
PHONE..................630 467-5000
Tammy Long, *Purch Dir*
Timothy Trojan, *Manager*
**EMP:** 5
**SALES (corp-wide):** 23.4B **Privately Held**
**SIC:** 3678 Electronic connectors
**HQ:** Nec Display Solutions Of America, Inc.
500 Park Blvd Ste 1100
Itasca IL 60143
630 467-3000

### (G-12328)
**NEC DISPLAY SOLUTIONS AMER INC (DH)**
500 Park Blvd Ste 1100 (60143-2602)
PHONE..................630 467-3000
**Fax:** 630 467-3050
Todd Bouman, *President*
Harry Salna, *General Mgr*
Sean Dolan, *Senior VP*
Jean Dubois, *Senior VP*
Douglas Albert, *Vice Pres*
◆ **EMP:** 140
**SQ FT:** 45,000
**SALES (est):** 49.2MM
**SALES (corp-wide):** 23.4B **Privately Held**
**SIC:** 3575 Computer terminals, monitors & components
**HQ:** Nec Display Solutions, Ltd.
1-4-28, Mita
Minato-Ku TKY 108-0
354 465-300

### (G-12329)
**NEOPOST R MEADOWS**
1200 N Arlington Hts Rd (60143-1284)
PHONE..................630 467-0604
**Fax:** 630 981-9117
**EMP:** 4 **EST:** 2006
**SALES (est):** 370K **Privately Held**
**SIC:** 3579 Mfg Office Machines

### (G-12330)
**NESTLE USA INC**
Also Called: Willy Wonka Candy Factory
1445 Norwood Ave (60143-1128)
PHONE..................630 773-2090
**Fax:** 630 773-1467
Leida Hartman, *Human Res Mgr*
Louise Defalco, *Manager*
John Archambo, *Manager*
Robert Rooney, *Manager*
**EMP:** 139
**SALES (corp-wide):** 88.4B **Publicly Held**
**WEB:** www.nestleusa.com
**SIC:** 2023 Evaporated milk
**HQ:** Nestle Usa, Inc.
800 N Brand Blvd
Glendale CA 91203
818 549-6000

### (G-12331)
**NIDEC-SHIMPO AMERICA CORP (DH)**
1701 Glenlake Ave (60143-1072)
PHONE..................630 924-7138
T Nishimoto, *President*
Jeff Williams, *General Mgr*
Arthur Morales, *Engineer*
Doug Pitchford, *Human Res Mgr*
Douglas Pitchford, *Human Res Mgr*
▲ **EMP:** 30
**SQ FT:** 35,000
**SALES (est):** 13MM
**SALES (corp-wide):** 10B **Privately Held**
**WEB:** www.shimpoinst.com
**SIC:** 5085 3566 5084 3825 Power transmission equipment & apparatus; speed changers, drives & gears; industrial machinery & equipment; instruments to measure electricity; ceramic products, excluding refractory
**HQ:** Nidec-Shimpo Corporation
1, Terada, Kotari
Nagaokakyo KYO 617-0
759 583-606

### (G-12332)
**NNT ENTERPRISES INCORPORATED**
1320 Norwood Ave (60143-1127)
PHONE..................630 875-9600
David Nyc, *President*
Michael Nyc, *Vice Pres*
▲ **EMP:** 32
**SQ FT:** 30,000
**SALES (est):** 9.9MM **Privately Held**
**WEB:** www.nntcorp.com
**SIC:** 5084 3546 3545 3541 Industrial machinery & equipment; metalworking tools (such as drills, taps, dies, files); power-driven handtools; machine tool accessories; machine tools, metal cutting type; industrial inorganic chemicals

### (G-12333)
**NORTHROP GRMMN SPCE & MSSN SYS**
1131 W Bryn Mawr Ave (60143-1508)
PHONE..................630 773-6900
Arthur Karsel, *Branch Mgr*
**EMP:** 10 **Publicly Held**

**WEB:** www.trw.com
**SIC:** 3694 Distributors, motor vehicle engine
**HQ:** Northrop Grumman Space & Mission Systems Corp.
6379 San Ignacio Ave
San Jose CA 95119
703 280-2900

### (G-12334)
**OFFICEMAX INCORPORATED**
800 W Bryn Mawr Ave (60143-1503)
PHONE..................877 969-6629
**EMP:** 3
**SALES (corp-wide):** 11B **Publicly Held**
**SIC:** 2599 Boards: planning, display, notice
**HQ:** Officemax Incorporated
6600 N Military Trl
Boca Raton FL 33496
630 438-7800

### (G-12335)
**OMEGA DOOR FRAME PRODUCTS**
1222 Ardmore Ave (60143-1141)
PHONE..................630 773-9900
Kurt Shah, *President*
Kristi Olson, *Accountant*
**EMP:** 40
**SALES (est):** 1.9MM **Privately Held**
**SIC:** 3999 Manufacturing industries

### (G-12336)
**ORACLE CORPORATION**
17th Fl 2 Pierce Pl (60143)
PHONE..................630 931-6400
**Fax:** 630 285-8752
Kathy Martin, *Branch Mgr*
Joseph Baksha, *Manager*
Denise Cowan, *Director*
**EMP:** 302
**SALES (corp-wide):** 37B **Publicly Held**
**SIC:** 7372 Business oriented computer software
**PA:** Oracle Corporation
500 Oracle Pkwy
Redwood City CA 94065
650 506-7000

### (G-12337)
**ORGAN RECOVERY SYSTEMS INC**
1 Pierce Pl Ste 475w (60143-2618)
PHONE..................847 824-2600
David Kravitz, *President*
Peter Demuylder, *Vice Pres*
Tim Govin, *VP Opers*
Kayla Andalina, *QC Mgr*
Kerrie Trebonsky, *Controller*
▲ **EMP:** 10 **EST:** 1998
**SQ FT:** 3,000
**SALES (est):** 1.3MM **Privately Held**
**SIC:** 3841 Surgical & medical instruments
**PA:** Lifeline Scientific, Inc.
1 Pierce Pl Ste 475w
Itasca IL 60143

### (G-12338)
**OVERHEAD DOOR CORPORATION**
Also Called: Genie Pro Sales Center
295 S Prospect Ave (60143-2337)
PHONE..................630 775-9118
**Fax:** 630 775-9130
Glenn Kerley, *Branch Mgr*
**EMP:** 7
**SALES (corp-wide):** 3.1B **Privately Held**
**WEB:** www.overheaddoor.com
**SIC:** 3442 2431 Garage doors, overhead: metal; doors, wood
**HQ:** Overhead Door Corporation
2501 S State Hwy 121 Ste
Lewisville TX 75067
469 549-7100

### (G-12339)
**PHOENIX CONVERTING LLC**
1251 Ardmore Ave (60143-1103)
PHONE..................630 285-1500
**Fax:** 630 773-9450
Samantha Miletic, *Cust Mgr*
Vanessa Budzinski, *Office Mgr*
Stanley Budzinski, *Mng Member*
▲ **EMP:** 15

**SALES (est):** 4MM **Privately Held**
**SIC:** 3825 Analog-digital converters, electronic instrumentation type

### (G-12340)
**PIONEER INDUSTRIES INTL INC (PA)**
500 Park Blvd Ste 250 (60143-2623)
PHONE..................630 543-7676
Shawn Lavin, *President*
▼ **EMP:** 3 **EST:** 2014
**SALES (est):** 6.8MM **Privately Held**
**SIC:** 3999 Manufacturing industries

### (G-12341)
**PITNEY BOWES INC**
1025 Hilltop Dr (60143-1118)
PHONE..................800 784-4224
Koying Kim, *Branch Mgr*
**EMP:** 35
**SALES (corp-wide):** 3.4B **Publicly Held**
**SIC:** 3579 7359 3661 8744 Mailing machines; postage meters; forms handling equipment; business machine & electronic equipment rental services; facsimile equipment; facilities support services; prepackaged software
**PA:** Pitney Bowes Inc.
3001 Summer St Ste 3
Stamford CT 06905
203 356-5000

### (G-12342)
**PLEXUS CORP**
1550 W Bryn Mawr Ave (60143-1318)
PHONE..................630 250-1074
**EMP:** 3 **EST:** 2015
**SALES (est):** 146.4K **Privately Held**
**SIC:** 3672 Printed circuit boards

### (G-12343)
**POLYBILT BODY COMPANY LLC (PA)**
325 Spring Lake Dr (60143-2072)
PHONE..................708 345-8050
Timothy S Dean, *President*
Paul Danielson, *Safety Dir*
Dennis Harp, *Opers Mgr*
Peter Darley, *Mng Member*
Daniel Owen, *Mng Member*
**EMP:** 3
**SALES (est):** 342.8K **Privately Held**
**SIC:** 2821 Plastics materials & resins

### (G-12344)
**PPG ARCHITECTURAL FINISHES INC**
Also Called: Glidden Professional Paint Ctr
880 W Thorndale Ave (60143-1341)
PHONE..................630 773-8484
Ed Loreto, *Principal*
Edward Ford, *Branch Mgr*
Young Kang, *Manager*
**EMP:** 50
**SQ FT:** 3,000
**SALES (corp-wide):** 14.7B **Publicly Held**
**WEB:** www.gliddenpaint.com
**SIC:** 2891 Adhesives
**HQ:** Ppg Architectural Finishes, Inc.
1 Ppg Pl
Pittsburgh PA 15272
412 434-3131

### (G-12345)
**PRECISION TOOL WELDING**
1300 Industrial Dr Ste B (60143-1821)
PHONE..................630 285-9844
Gary Welther, *Owner*
**EMP:** 4
**SALES (est):** 377.8K **Privately Held**
**SIC:** 7692 Welding repair

### (G-12346)
**QUALITAS MANUFACTURING INC (PA)**
Also Called: Qmi Roll Shutter Supply
1661 Glenlake Ave (60143-1004)
PHONE..................630 529-7111
**Fax:** 630 980-6364
James V Miller, *President*
Pritesh Gandhi, *General Mgr*
Stephen Miller, *Vice Pres*
Kathy Newell, *Controller*
Andre Terblanche, *Manager*
◆ **EMP:** 78

# GEOGRAPHIC SECTION
## Itasca - Dupage County (G-12370)

SQ FT: 20,000
SALES (est): 22MM **Privately Held**
WEB: www.qmiusa.com/home.aspx
SIC: 3442 3089 Shutters, door or window: metal; shutters, plastic

### (G-12347)
### RDI GROUP INC
Also Called: Chicago Slitter
1025 W Thorndale Ave (60143-1336)
PHONE...................................630 773-4900
Fax: 630 875-1201
Curtis Maas, *Ch of Bd*
Fred Kestler, *President*
Herm Ilag, *VP Opers*
Andy Walkowicz, *Plant Mgr*
Pietro D'Ambrosio, *Project Mgr*
▲ EMP: 120 EST: 1902
SQ FT: 120,000
SALES (est): 64MM
SALES (corp-wide): 735K **Privately Held**
WEB: www.therdigroup.com
SIC: 3531 Roofing equipment
PA: Reichel & Drews Gmbh
    Am Weichselgarten 28
    Erlangen 91058

### (G-12348)
### ROBERTS SWISS INC
1387 Ardmore Ave (60143-1104)
PHONE...................................630 467-9100
Fax: 630 467-9106
Robert C Armitage, *President*
Fernando Ortiz Jr, *Vice Pres*
John Makris, *Materials Mgr*
Lawrence Rutan, *QC Mgr*
Pat Morrison, *Accountant*
EMP: 48
SQ FT: 12,200
SALES (est): 9.5MM **Privately Held**
SIC: 3451 3562 3541 3452 Screw machine products; ball & roller bearings; machine tools, metal cutting type; bolts, nuts, rivets & washers

### (G-12349)
### ROBERTSHAW CONTROLS COMPANY (HQ)
1222 Hamilton Pkwy (60143-1160)
PHONE...................................630 260-3400
Mark Balcunas, *President*
Ramiro Vargas, *Vice Pres*
Rick Delvaux, *QC Mgr*
Mauricio Vargas, *QC Mgr*
Ray Bambule, *Engineer*
◆ EMP: 150
SALES (est): 805.2MM
SALES (corp-wide): 18.5B **Privately Held**
SIC: 3823 3822 3492 Industrial instrmnts msrmnt display/control process variable; auto controls regulating residntl & coml environmt & applncs; control valves, aircraft: hydraulic & pneumatic
PA: Sun Capital Partners, Inc.
    5200 Town Center Cir # 600
    Boca Raton FL 33486
    561 962-3400

### (G-12350)
### ROLL SOURCE PAPER
900 N Arlington Heights R (60143-2805)
PHONE...................................630 875-0308
Sue Kiewert, *Manager*
Glen Grigoletti, *Manager*
EMP: 9
SALES (est): 1.2MM **Privately Held**
SIC: 2621 5113 5111 Paper mills; paperboard & products; writing paper

### (G-12351)
### ROYALE INNOVATION GROUP LTD
794 Willow Ct (60143-2864)
P.O. Box 479 (60143-0479)
PHONE...................................312 339-1406
Lisa Liarakos, *President*
Nicholas Liarakos, *Vice Pres*
EMP: 2
SALES: 1MM **Privately Held**
SIC: 3432 8711 7389 Plumbing fixture fittings & trim; engineering services

### (G-12352)
### SAI INFO USA
Also Called: Service Provider
183 Bay Dr (60143-1259)
PHONE...................................630 773-3335
Latha Damarapati, *Owner*
EMP: 2
SALES: 200K **Privately Held**
SIC: 7372 Prepackaged software

### (G-12353)
### SHIMA AMERICAN CORPORATION
Also Called: Performance Material Division
500 Park Blvd Ste 725 (60143-3146)
PHONE...................................630 760-4330
Fax: 630 285-1045
Shima Koshi, *Ch of Bd*
Shinichiro Taki, *President*
Charlie Hatano, *Vice Pres*
Motoyasu Momoki, *Vice Pres*
Tony Glowinski, *Accountant*
▲ EMP: 18 EST: 1963
SQ FT: 23,000
SALES (est): 22.3MM
SALES (corp-wide): 355.2MM **Privately Held**
WEB: www.shimarollers.com
SIC: 5013 2992 5085 Automotive supplies & parts; lubricating oils & greases; industrial supplies; bearings; industrial tools; industrial wheels
PA: Shima Trading Co., Ltd.
    2-12-14, Ginza
    Chuo-Ku TKY 104-0
    335 423-111

### (G-12354)
### SMART SOLUTIONS INC
211 Catalpa Ave (60143-2027)
P.O. Box 568 (60143-0568)
PHONE...................................630 775-1517
Fax: 630 775-9492
Brian Lilly, *President*
EMP: 5
SALES (est): 447.1K **Privately Held**
SIC: 3061 Mechanical rubber goods

### (G-12355)
### SOLBERG INTERNATIONAL LTD (PA)
1151 Ardmore Ave (60143-1305)
PHONE...................................630 616-4400
Charles H Solberg, *President*
Joyce C Solberg, *Vice Pres*
▲ EMP: 5
SALES (est): 955.5K **Privately Held**
SIC: 3564 Filters, air: furnaces, air conditioning equipment, etc.

### (G-12356)
### SOLBERG MFG INC (PA)
1151 Ardmore Ave (60143-1387)
P.O. Box 5988, Carol Stream (60197-5988)
PHONE...................................630 616-4400
Fax: 630 773-0727
Charles H Solberg Jr, *CEO*
Arnold Tor Solberg, *President*
Marguerite B Solberg, *Corp Secy*
Guillermo Reyes, *Plant Mgr*
Troy Kole, *Purch Agent*
◆ EMP: 60 EST: 1968
SQ FT: 97,000
SALES (est): 19.9MM **Privately Held**
WEB: www.solbergmfg.com
SIC: 3564 Filters, air: furnaces, air conditioning equipment, etc.

### (G-12357)
### SOLBERG MFG INC
680 Baker Dr (60143-1346)
PHONE...................................630 773-1363
Charles Solberg Jr, *President*
EMP: 30
SALES (corp-wide): 19.9MM **Privately Held**
WEB: www.solbergmfg.com
SIC: 3564 Filters, air: furnaces, air conditioning equipment, etc.
PA: Solberg Mfg., Inc
    1151 Ardmore Ave
    Itasca IL 60143
    630 616-4400

### (G-12358)
### SPRING BROOK NATURE CENTER
Also Called: Village Itasca Nature Center
411 N Prospect Ave (60143-1605)
PHONE...................................630 773-5572
Fax: 630 773-2239
Fred Maier, *Director*
EMP: 6
SALES: 500K **Privately Held**
SIC: 3822 Auto controls regulating residntl & coml environmt & applncs

### (G-12359)
### STANDARD REGISTER INC
1 Pierce Pl Ste 270c (60143-2621)
PHONE...................................630 467-8300
EMP: 18
SALES (corp-wide): 3.8B **Privately Held**
SIC: 2754 Printing
HQ: Standard Register, Inc.
    600 Albany St
    Dayton OH 45417
    937 221-1000

### (G-12360)
### STERIGENICS US LLC
Also Called: Steripro Laboratories
1500 W Thorndale Ave (60143-1133)
PHONE...................................630 285-9121
Mike Rahn, *Branch Mgr*
Mike Rahan, *Manager*
EMP: 25
SALES (corp-wide): 616.3MM **Privately Held**
SIC: 3826 Thermal analysis instruments, laboratory type
HQ: Sterigenics U.S., Llc
    3 Parkway N Ste 100n
    Deerfield IL 60015
    847 607-6060

### (G-12361)
### SUBARU OF AMERICA INC
Also Called: Great Lakes Region
500 Park Blvd Ste 255c (60143-3126)
PHONE...................................630 250-4740
Fax: 630 285-1100
Drew Watson, *Regional Mgr*
Linda Walter, *Administration*
EMP: 23
SALES (corp-wide): 29.2B **Privately Held**
SIC: 5511 8741 3711 Automobiles, new & used; management services; motor vehicles & car bodies
HQ: Subaru Of America, Inc.
    2235 Rte 70 W
    Cherry Hill NJ 08002
    856 488-8500

### (G-12362)
### SYSTEMATICS SCREEN PRINTING
1625 Norwood Ave (60143-1009)
PHONE...................................630 521-1123
Govind Sanghani, *President*
Nalini Sanghani, *Vice Pres*
Matt Campione, *Accounts Mgr*
Nino Makasarashvili, *Sales Staff*
Andy Sanghani, *Sales Executive*
EMP: 12
SQ FT: 15,000
SALES (est): 2.2MM **Privately Held**
SIC: 2759 Screen printing

### (G-12363)
### SYSTEMS UNLIMITED INC
1350 W Bryn Mawr Ave (60143-1314)
PHONE...................................630 285-0010
Fax: 630 285-0084
Russell S Omuro, *President*
Ammie Doll, *Manager*
▲ EMP: 140
SQ FT: 107,000
SALES (est): 14.3MM **Privately Held**
WEB: www.systemsunlimitedinc.com
SIC: 1799 2521 Home/office interiors finishing, furnishing & remodeling; office furniture installation; desks, office: wood; chairs, office: padded, upholstered or plain: wood

### (G-12364)
### TARCO PRINTING INC
1270 Ardmore Ave (60143-1141)
PHONE...................................630 467-1000
Fax: 630 467-0317
Jeff Reckards, *Principal*
EMP: 3
SALES (est): 348.9K **Privately Held**
SIC: 2752 Commercial printing, lithographic

### (G-12365)
### TECH-MAX MACHINE INC
1170 Ardmore Ave (60143-1306)
PHONE...................................630 875-0054
Fax: 630 875-0056
Richard Malek, *President*
Ted Morawa, *Exec VP*
EMP: 20
SQ FT: 40,000
SALES (est): 4.3MM **Privately Held**
WEB: www.tech-max.com
SIC: 3599 Machine shop, jobbing & repair

### (G-12366)
### TELCOM INNOVATIONS GROUP LLC
125 N Prospect Ave (60143-1811)
PHONE...................................630 350-0700
Jo Splinter, *Controller*
Cheri Beatty, *Accounts Exec*
Shannon Carroll, *Sales Staff*
Shannon Dykema, *Sales Staff*
Randall Borchardt, *Mng Member*
EMP: 50
SQ FT: 25,000
SALES (est): 12.6MM **Privately Held**
WEB: www.telcominnovations.com
SIC: 4813 3825 8999 7389 Telephone communication, except radio; network analyzers; communication services; design services

### (G-12367)
### TRADE LABEL & DECAL (PA)
1285 Hamilton Pkwy (60143-1150)
P.O. Box 821 (60143-0821)
PHONE...................................630 773-0447
Harry Blecker, *President*
Catherine Blecker, *Admin Sec*
EMP: 8
SQ FT: 1,000
SALES (est): 659.7K **Privately Held**
WEB: www.tradelabeldecal.com
SIC: 2679 Labels, paper: made from purchased material

### (G-12368)
### TRIVIAL DEVELOPMENT CORP
1035 Hilltop Dr (60143-1118)
PHONE...................................630 860-2500
Lawrence J Balsamo, *President*
Charles Schmelzer, *Vice Pres*
▲ EMP: 25
SQ FT: 15,000
SALES (est): 6.7MM **Privately Held**
WEB: www.tdcgames.com
SIC: 5092 3944 Toys & games; board games, puzzles & models, except electronic

### (G-12369)
### TWO FOUR SEVEN METAL LASER
1428 Norwood Ave (60143-1129)
PHONE...................................847 250-5199
EMP: 2
SALES (est): 220.2K **Privately Held**
SIC: 3499 Welding tips, heat resistant: metal

### (G-12370)
### UNITED STEEL & FASTENERS INC
1500 Industrial Dr (60143-1800)
PHONE...................................630 250-0900
Isaac Sargis, *President*
Bill Albert, *Opers Mgr*
Jesline Sargis, *Controller*
Angela Hedger, *Accounting Mgr*
Robert Fiorio, *Sales Mgr*
▲ EMP: 41
SQ FT: 60,000

## Itasca - Dupage County (G-12371)

SALES (est): 9.9MM **Privately Held**
WEB: www.unitedsteelandfasteners.com
SIC: 3429 Metal fasteners

**(G-12371)**
**VORNE INDUSTRIES INC**
1445 Industrial Dr (60143-1849)
PHONE..................................630 250-9378
Fax: 630 875-3609
Ramon Vorne, *President*
Ana Castaneda, *Buyer*
Andrew Gorny, *Engineer*
Scott Kirkpatrick, *Engineer*
Adam Moran, *Sales Mgr*
EMP: 25
SQ FT: 12,000
SALES: 9.7MM **Privately Held**
WEB: www.vorne.com
SIC: 3823 Industrial process measurement equipment

**(G-12372)**
**W S DARLEY & CO**
Also Called: Odin Foam
325 Spring Lake Dr (60143-2072)
PHONE..................................630 735-3500
Jim Guse, *Manager*
EMP: 17
SALES (corp-wide): 169.1MM **Privately Held**
WEB: www.darley.com
SIC: 3561 Pumps & pumping equipment
PA: W. S. Darley & Co.
 325 Spring Lake Dr
 Itasca IL 60143
 630 735-3500

**(G-12373)**
**WEIDENMILLER CO**
1464 Industrial Dr (60143-1848)
PHONE..................................630 250-2500
Fax: 630 250-2525
Kim Schulte, *Accountant*
Thomas E Weidenmiller Sr, *Admin Sec*
▲ EMP: 16 EST: 1903
SQ FT: 25,000
SALES (est): 3.8MM **Privately Held**
WEB: www.weidenmiller.com
SIC: 3556 Biscuit cutting dies

**(G-12374)**
**WERNER CO**
850 N Arlington Hts Rd (60143-1411)
PHONE..................................847 455-8001
Craig Werner, *President*
Marty Young, *Purchasing*
James Ingram, *Personnel*
Eric Hull, *Admin Asst*
EMP: 800 **Privately Held**
SIC: 3353 3446 3354 Aluminum sheet, plate & foil; architectural metalwork; aluminum extruded products
HQ: Werner Co
 93 Werner Rd
 Greenville PA 16125
 724 588-2000

**(G-12375)**
**XERTREX INTERNATIONAL INC (PA)**
Also Called: Tabbies
1530 Glenlake Ave (60143-1171)
PHONE..................................630 773-4020
Fax: 630 285-1876
Dennis W Cunningham, *President*
Cheri Miroballi, *Corp Secy*
Christopher Cunningham, *Vice Pres*
Pete Martel, *CFO*
Chris Cunningham, *Treasurer*
▲ EMP: 40 EST: 1955
SQ FT: 42,000
SALES (est): 8.4MM **Privately Held**
WEB: www.tabbies.com
SIC: 2679 5943 Tags & labels, paper; office forms & supplies

**(G-12376)**
**YES EQUIPMENT & SERVICES LLC**
1151 W Bryn Mawr Ave (60143-1508)
PHONE..................................866 799-7743
Cliff Anglewicz, *CEO*
EMP: 2
SALES (est): 534.3K **Privately Held**
SIC: 3537 Lift trucks, industrial: fork, platform, straddle, etc.

### Ivesdale
*Champaign County*

**(G-12377)**
**DAVID MARTIN**
Also Called: Martin Machine Co
504 E 4th St (61851)
P.O. Box 25 (61851-0025)
PHONE..................................217 564-2440
Fax: 217 564-2440
David Martin, *Owner*
Sue Martin, *Co-Owner*
EMP: 3
SALES (est): 180K **Privately Held**
SIC: 3821 Laboratory apparatus & furniture

### Jacksonville
*Morgan County*

**(G-12378)**
**BILL WEST ENTERPRISES INC**
2170 Arcadia Rd (62650-6082)
PHONE..................................217 886-2591
William C West Sr, *President*
Kathy West, *Vice Pres*
EMP: 1
SQ FT: 5,500
SALES: 900K **Privately Held**
SIC: 7948 3694 3621 3444 Stock car racing; automotive electrical equipment; starting equipment, street cars; sheet metalwork; motor vehicles & car bodies

**(G-12379)**
**BIRDSELL MACHINE & ORNA INC**
531 W Independence Ave (62650-1311)
P.O. Box 100 (62651-0100)
PHONE..................................217 243-5849
Kevin Birdsell, *President*
Doug Birdsell, *Corp Secy*
EMP: 5
SALES (est): 440K **Privately Held**
SIC: 3441 3446 Fabricated structural metal; grillwork, ornamental metal

**(G-12380)**
**BRAHLERS TRUCKERS SUPPLY INC (DH)**
21 Harold Cox Dr (62650-6771)
PHONE..................................217 243-6471
Richard William Brahler, *President*
Rita Williams, *CFO*
Steve Wardlow, *Manager*
Mary C Brahler, *Admin Sec*
▲ EMP: 30
SQ FT: 80,000
SALES: 28.5MM
SALES (corp-wide): 42.8B **Privately Held**
SIC: 3011 Retreading materials, tire
HQ: Continental Tire The Americas, Llc
 1830 Macmillan Park Dr
 Fort Mill SC 29707
 800 450-3187

**(G-12381)**
**BRANSTITER PRINTING CO**
217 E Morgan St (62650-2508)
PHONE..................................217 245-6533
Fax: 217 245-1392
Glenn Kafer, *Owner*
Janet Kay Kafer, *Co-Owner*
EMP: 7 EST: 1897
SQ FT: 1,800
SALES (est): 735.6K **Privately Held**
SIC: 2752 2791 2789 2759 Commercial printing, lithographic; commercial printing, offset; typesetting; bookbinding & related work; commercial printing

**(G-12382)**
**CCK AUTOMATIONS INC**
500 Capitol Way (62650-1092)
PHONE..................................217 243-6040
J J Richardson, *President*
Tyler Aring, *COO*
Mike Allan, *Opers Staff*
Janet Lewis, *QC Mgr*
Lucas McPherson, *Accounting Mgr*
▲ EMP: 49
SALES (est): 26.9MM **Privately Held**
WEB: www.cckautomations.com
SIC: 3672 Printed circuit boards

**(G-12383)**
**CENVEO INC**
Also Called: Production Press
320 E Morton Ave (62650-3064)
PHONE..................................217 243-4258
Fax: 217 243-1181
Ronald Weaver, *General Mgr*
Brian McBride, *Manager*
EMP: 5 **Publicly Held**
WEB: www.mail-well.com
SIC: 2752 2791 2789 2759 Commercial printing, offset; typesetting; bookbinding & related work; commercial printing; coated & laminated paper
PA: Cenveo, Inc.
 200 First Stamford Pl # 200
 Stamford CT 06902

**(G-12384)**
**CIVITAS MEDIA LLC**
Also Called: Jacksonville Journal-Courier
235 W State St (62650-2001)
P.O. Box 1048 (62651-1048)
PHONE..................................217 245-6121
Fax: 217 245-1226
John Power, *Publisher*
Dennis Mathes, *Editor*
Jeff Lonergan, *Prdtn Mgr*
Karen Walker, *Adv Dir*
David Bauer, *Manager*
EMP: 100
SALES (corp-wide): 1.3B **Privately Held**
WEB: www.freedom.com
SIC: 2711 Newspapers: publishing only, not printed on site
PA: Civitas Media, Llc
 130 Harbour Place Dr # 300
 Davidson NC 28036
 704 897-6020

**(G-12385)**
**COMMUNITY READYMIX INC**
710 Brooklyn Ave (62650-3072)
PHONE..................................217 245-6668
Fax: 217 245-6518
Jay Beltman, *President*
EMP: 20
SALES: 2.8MM **Privately Held**
SIC: 3273 Ready-mixed concrete

**(G-12386)**
**CREATIVE IDEAS INC**
Also Called: Theatre In The Park
4 Sunnydale Ave (62650-2656)
PHONE..................................217 245-1378
EMP: 4 EST: 1994
SALES (est): 170K **Privately Held**
SIC: 2741 Misc Publishing

**(G-12387)**
**FREEDOM COMMUNICATIONS INC**
Also Called: Journal-Courier
235 W State St (62650-2001)
PHONE..................................217 245-6121
Fax: 217 243-7659
Jonathan Segal, *President*
EMP: 5
SALES (est): 327.3K **Privately Held**
SIC: 2711 Newspapers

**(G-12388)**
**GAITHER TOOL CO**
21 Harold Cox Dr (62650-6771)
PHONE..................................217 245-0545
Richard Brahler, *President*
Jeff Alexander, *Vice Pres*
▲ EMP: 6
SQ FT: 6,000
SALES: 1.7MM **Privately Held**
WEB: www.gaithertool.com
SIC: 3559 Automotive related machinery

**(G-12389)**
**GIRLS IN WHITE SATIN**
300 E State St (62650-2030)
Rural Route 3 Box 285, Roodhouse (62082-9556)
PHONE..................................217 245-5400
Deb Lash, *Principal*
EMP: 4

SALES (est): 473.9K **Privately Held**
SIC: 2221 Satins

**(G-12390)**
**HANNA HOPPER TRLR SLS & RV CTR**
Also Called: Hopper Trailer Sales & Service
298 Moeller Rd (62650-6532)
PHONE..................................217 243-3374
Fax: 217 245-6303
William Hopper, *Owner*
EMP: 8 EST: 1970
SQ FT: 10,800
SALES (est): 921.6K **Privately Held**
SIC: 3792 Travel trailers & campers

**(G-12391)**
**HOLE IN THE WALL SCREEN ARTS**
112 Park St (62650-2308)
PHONE..................................217 243-9100
James Jamison, *President*
Gary Goodwin, *Treasurer*
John Carpenter, *Admin Sec*
EMP: 3
SQ FT: 2,400
SALES: 120K **Privately Held**
SIC: 5699 2396 2759 T-shirts, custom printed; automotive & apparel trimmings; screen printing

**(G-12392)**
**I T R INC**
21 Harold Cox Dr (62650-6771)
PHONE..................................217 245-4478
Richard W Brahler III, *President*
▲ EMP: 30
SALES (est): 3.1MM **Privately Held**
WEB: www.itr.com
SIC: 3559 Automotive related machinery

**(G-12393)**
**ILLINOIS ROAD CONTRACTORS INC (PA)**
520 N Webster Ave (62650-1115)
P.O. Box 1060 (62651-1060)
PHONE..................................217 245-6181
Fax: 217 243-0604
Devon Davidsmeyer, *CEO*
Jeffry Davidsmeyer, *President*
R Thomas Slayback, *Corp Secy*
Thomas L Atkins, *Exec VP*
Earl L Forrer, *Treasurer*
EMP: 40 EST: 1925
SQ FT: 2,500
SALES (est): 36.8MM **Privately Held**
SIC: 1611 2951 4213 Highway & street maintenance; asphalt & asphaltic paving mixtures (not from refineries); trucking, except local

**(G-12394)**
**ILMO PRODUCTS COMPANY (PA)**
7 Eastgate Dr (62650-6761)
P.O. Box 790 (62651-0790)
PHONE..................................217 245-2183
Fax: 217 243-7634
Linda Standley, *CEO*
Brad Floreth, *President*
Terry Jack, *Store Mgr*
Penny McCormick, *Store Mgr*
John Damaro, *CFO*
◆ EMP: 45 EST: 1913
SQ FT: 40,000
SALES (est): 37.3MM **Privately Held**
WEB: www.ilmo.com
SIC: 5084 2813 Welding machinery & equipment; industrial gases

**(G-12395)**
**JACKSONVILLE ART GLASS INC**
54 N Central Park Plz (62650-2024)
PHONE..................................217 245-0500
John Krol, *President*
Ron Weaver, *General Mgr*
Julie Krol, *Vice Pres*
EMP: 7
SQ FT: 5,400
SALES: 224.8K **Privately Held**
SIC: 3211 Flat glass

# GEOGRAPHIC SECTION

Jerseyville - Jersey County (G-12422)

**(G-12396)**
**JACKSONVILLE MACHINE INC**
2265 W Morton Ave (62650-2626)
PHONE..................217 243-1119
Fax: 217 243-3631
Jeff Rodems, *President*
Robert Rodems, *Vice Pres*
Mike Theivagt, *Foreman/Supr*
James Byus, *Purch Mgr*
Eva Rodems, *Treasurer*
**EMP:** 60 **EST:** 1919
**SQ FT:** 35,000
**SALES:** 6MM **Privately Held**
**WEB:** www.jmimachine.com
**SIC:** 3599 7692 Machine shop, jobbing & repair; machine & other job shop work; welding repair

**(G-12397)**
**JACKSONVILLE MONUMENT CO**
330 E State St (62650-2030)
PHONE..................217 245-2514
Fax: 217 243-3739
Andy Burington, *Owner*
John Mahoney, *General Mgr*
**EMP:** 5
**SQ FT:** 3,000
**SALES (est):** 372.5K **Privately Held**
**SIC:** 5999 3281 Monuments, finished to custom order; cut stone & stone products

**(G-12398)**
**JESS ELECTRIC**
2360 Mound Rd (62650-2242)
PHONE..................217 243-7946
Scott Jess, *Principal*
**EMP:** 4 **EST:** 2009
**SALES (est):** 454K **Privately Held**
**SIC:** 3699 Electrical equipment & supplies

**(G-12399)**
**JOHNNYS LITTLE LLC**
1848 Mound Rd (62650-2265)
PHONE..................217 243-2570
Fax: 217 291-0499
Ron Boerema,
**EMP:** 3 **EST:** 1999
**SALES (est):** 339.6K **Privately Held**
**SIC:** 2842 Sanitation preparations

**(G-12400)**
**LONELINO SIGN COMPANY INC**
2122 E Morton Ave (62650-6431)
PHONE..................217 243-2444
Thomas Lonelino, *President*
**EMP:** 3
**SALES (est):** 90K **Privately Held**
**SIC:** 3993 Signs & advertising specialties

**(G-12401)**
**MARK LAHEY**
107 S Johnson St (62650-2542)
PHONE..................217 243-4433
Fax: 217 243-3666
Mark Lahey, *Owner*
**EMP:** 3
**SQ FT:** 5,400
**SALES:** 500K **Privately Held**
**WEB:** www.netjax.com
**SIC:** 3599 7692 Machine shop, jobbing & repair; welding repair

**(G-12402)**
**MOELLER READY MIX INC**
Rr 67 Box S (62650)
P.O. Box 1086 (62651-1086)
PHONE..................217 243-7471
Fax: 217 243-6576
Arminda Moeller, *President*
Cheryl Moeller, *Admin Sec*
**EMP:** 13
**SALES (est):** 1.8MM **Privately Held**
**SIC:** 3273 Ready-mixed concrete

**(G-12403)**
**NESTLE USA INC**
Also Called: Nestle Beverage Division
1111 Carnation Dr (62650-1144)
PHONE..................217 243-9175
Fax: 217 479-2280
Ryan Johnston, *Branch Mgr*
**EMP:** 135
**SALES (corp-wide):** 88.4B **Publicly Held**
**WEB:** www.nestleusa.com
**SIC:** 2023 Evaporated milk
**HQ:** Nestle Usa, Inc.
 800 N Brand Blvd
 Glendale CA 91203
 818 549-6000

**(G-12404)**
**PACTIV LLC**
2230 E Morton Ave (62650)
PHONE..................217 479-1144
Jeff Phillips, *Manager*
**EMP:** 238 **Privately Held**
**WEB:**
**SIC:** 2673 3497 3089 2621 Food storage & trash bags (plastic); trash bags (plastic film): made from purchased materials; food storage & frozen food bags, plastic; metal foil & leaf; plastic containers, except foam; plastic kitchenware, tableware & houseware; pressed & molded pulp & fiber products; molded pulp products
**HQ:** Pactiv Llc
 1900 W Field Ct
 Lake Forest IL 60045
 847 482-2000

**(G-12405)**
**PACTIV LLC**
500 E Superior Ave (62650-3355)
PHONE..................217 243-3311
Carl Gunterman, *Area Mgr*
Mike Troedel, *Business Mgr*
James Oaf, *Plant Mgr*
Scott Szwejbka, *Plant Mgr*
Jerry Winnett, *Project Mgr*
**EMP:** 400 **Privately Held**
**WEB:** www.pactiv.com
**SIC:** 2673 Plastic & pliofilm bags
**HQ:** Pactiv Llc
 1900 W Field Ct
 Lake Forest IL 60045
 847 482-2000

**(G-12406)**
**PALLET REPAIR SYSTEMS INC**
Also Called: P R S
2 Eastgate Dr (62650-6268)
PHONE..................217 291-0009
Fax: 217 291-0008
Carolyn Williams, *President*
Jeff Williams, *Vice Pres*
Thomas Locher, *Engineer*
Andrea Martin, *Controller*
▲ **EMP:** 16
**SQ FT:** 25,000
**SALES:** 4.5MM **Privately Held**
**WEB:** www.pallet-repair.com
**SIC:** 3537 Palletizers & depalletizers

**(G-12407)**
**PETRI WELDING & PROP REPR INC**
2253 W Morton Ave (62650-2626)
PHONE..................217 243-1748
Jeff Petri, *President*
Kim Petri, *Corp Secy*
**EMP:** 9
**SQ FT:** 17,500
**SALES:** 130K **Privately Held**
**WEB:** www.bluffsnet.com
**SIC:** 7692 Welding repair

**(G-12408)**
**PRAIRIE FARMS DAIRY INC**
1105 W Walnut St (62650-1130)
PHONE..................217 245-4413
Eric Bien, *Branch Mgr*
**EMP:** 16
**SALES (corp-wide):** 1.8B **Privately Held**
**WEB:** www.prairiefarms.com
**SIC:** 2026 0241 Fluid milk; milk production
**PA:** Prairie Farms Dairy, Inc.
 1100 Broadway
 Carlinville IL 62626
 217 854-2547

**(G-12409)**
**PRODUCTION PRESS INC (PA)**
307 E Morgan St (62650-2546)
P.O. Box 940 (62651-0940)
PHONE..................217 243-3353
Fax: 217 245-0400
Joseph Racey, *President*
Steve Reveal, *Production*
Brad Wade, *Purch Agent*
Anthony Hall, *CFO*
Shelly Whewell, *Human Res Dir*
**EMP:** 40 **EST:** 1998
**SALES (est):** 6.7MM **Privately Held**
**WEB:** www.productionpress.net
**SIC:** 2752 Commercial printing, offset

**(G-12410)**
**PROGRESSIVE RECYCLING SYSTEMS**
2 Eastgate Dr (62650-6268)
PHONE..................217 291-0009
Carolyn Williams, *President*
**EMP:** 3 **EST:** 2010
**SALES (est):** 202.4K **Privately Held**
**SIC:** 2448 Wood pallets & skids

**(G-12411)**
**REYNOLDS CONSUMER PRODUCTS LLC**
500 E Superior Ave (62650-3355)
PHONE..................217 479-1126
Shelly Murphy, *Safety Mgr*
Mark Struble, *Safety Mgr*
Reynolds Howard, *Branch Mgr*
**EMP:** 21 **Privately Held**
**SIC:** 3353 Foil, aluminum
**HQ:** Reynolds Consumer Products Llc
 1900 W Field Ct
 Lake Forest IL 60045
 847 482-3500

**(G-12412)**
**REYNOLDS CONSUMER PRODUCTS LLC**
2226 E Morton Ave (62650-6204)
PHONE..................217 479-1466
**EMP:** 8 **Privately Held**
**SIC:** 3353 Foil, aluminum
**HQ:** Reynolds Consumer Products Llc
 1900 W Field Ct
 Lake Forest IL 60045
 847 482-3500

**(G-12413)**
**RUTLAND INC**
Also Called: Rutland Products
7 Crabtree Rd (62650-1785)
P.O. Box 1175 (62651-1175)
PHONE..................217 245-7810
▲ **EMP:** 35 **EST:** 1961
**SALES (est):** 6.9MM
**SALES (corp-wide):** 6.9MM **Privately Held**
**WEB:** www.rutland.com
**SIC:** 3429 Manufactured hardware (general)
**PA:** Rutland Fire Clay Co.
 8 Madison St
 Rutland VT 05701
 802 775-5519

**(G-12414)**
**SECRETARY OF STATE ILLINOIS**
901 E Morton Ave (62650-3003)
PHONE..................217 243-4327
**EMP:** 5 **Privately Held**
**SIC:** 3469 Automobile license tags, stamped metal
**HQ:** Secretary Of State, Illinois
 213 State House
 Springfield IL 62706
 217 782-2201

**(G-12415)**
**UNITED GILSONITE LABORATORIES**
550 Capitol Way (62650-1092)
PHONE..................217 243-7878
Fax: 217 245-1292
George Crolly, *Branch Mgr*
**EMP:** 30
**SQ FT:** 34,000
**SALES (corp-wide):** 55MM **Privately Held**
**WEB:** www.ugl.com
**SIC:** 2851 2899 2891 2821 Varnishes; stains: varnish, oil or wax; chemical preparations; adhesives & sealants; plastics materials & resins; paints
**PA:** United Gilsonite Laboratories
 1396 Jefferson Ave
 Scranton PA 18509
 570 344-1202

## Jerseyville
### Jersey County

**(G-12416)**
**A STUCKI COMPANY**
Also Called: American Inds A Div A Stucki
27128 Crystal Lake Rd (62052-7089)
PHONE..................618 498-4442
**EMP:** 20
**SALES (corp-wide):** 23.7MM **Privately Held**
**SIC:** 3999 Barber & beauty shop equipment
**PA:** A. Stucki Company
 360 Wright Brothers Dr
 Coraopolis PA 15108
 412 424-0560

**(G-12417)**
**ASSOCIATED AGRI-BUSINESS INC**
Also Called: Simfax Agri-Services
100 S State St (62052-1853)
PHONE..................618 498-2977
Connie Blackorby, *Manager*
**EMP:** 3
**SALES (corp-wide):** 468.9K **Privately Held**
**SIC:** 6331 7372 Federal crop insurance corporation; prepackaged software
**PA:** Associated Agri-Business, Inc.
 229 Elm St
 Eldred IL 62027
 618 498-2977

**(G-12418)**
**ATLAS BUILDING COMPONENTS INC**
Also Called: A B C Truss
5 Industrial Dr (62052-3612)
PHONE..................618 639-0222
Fax: 618 498-6473
Robert M Higgins, *President*
**EMP:** 20
**SALES:** 2MM **Privately Held**
**SIC:** 2439 Trusses, wooden roof; trusses, except roof: laminated lumber

**(G-12419)**
**CAMPBELL PUBLISHING CO INC**
Also Called: Jersey County Journal
832 S State St (62052-2343)
P.O. Box 407 (62052-0407)
PHONE..................618 498-1234
Bruce Campbell, *Branch Mgr*
**EMP:** 10
**SALES (corp-wide):** 2MM **Privately Held**
**SIC:** 2711 Newspapers
**PA:** Campbell Publishing Co Inc
 310 S County Rd
 Hardin IL
 618 576-2345

**(G-12420)**
**CUSTOM CHROME & POLISHING**
18416 Stagecoach Rd (62052-6987)
PHONE..................618 885-9499
Bill Sheck, *Manager*
**EMP:** 5 **EST:** 2008
**SALES (est):** 280K **Privately Held**
**SIC:** 3471 Chromium plating of metals or formed products

**(G-12421)**
**EXTREME FORCE VALVE INC**
515 Mound St (62052-2843)
PHONE..................618 494-5795
Mark Willmore, *President*
Eric Linder, *Vice Pres*
**EMP:** 4
**SALES (est):** 204.5K **Privately Held**
**SIC:** 3592 7699 Valves; valve repair, industrial

**(G-12422)**
**GORMAN BROTHERS READY MIX INC**
Also Called: Gorman Ready Mix
721 S State St (62052-2357)
PHONE..................618 498-2173
Fax: 618 498-6974
Jane Leonhardt, *President*

# Jerseyville - Jersey County (G-12423)

Eric W Leonhardt, *Vice Pres*
**EMP**: 18
**SQ FT**: 100,000
**SALES**: 2.3MM **Privately Held**
**SIC**: **3273** 2951 1794 5211 Ready-mixed concrete; asphalt & asphaltic paving mixtures (not from refineries); excavation work; lumber & other building materials; local trucking, without storage

*(G-12423)*
## HANSEN PACKING CO
807 State Highway 16 (62052-2813)
**PHONE**..................618 498-3714
**Fax**: 618 498-5507
Dave Hansen, *President*
David Hansen, *Vice Pres*
Ryan Hansen, *Manager*
Terrie Perry, *Manager*
**EMP**: 8
**SQ FT**: 3,700
**SALES (est)**: 572K **Privately Held**
**WEB**: www.hansenpackingmeats.com
**SIC**: **2011** 5147 2013 Meat packing plants; meats, fresh; sausages & other prepared meats

*(G-12424)*
## HENDERSON WATER DISTRICT
1004 State Highway 16 (62052-2826)
**PHONE**..................618 498-6418
Don Miller, *Owner*
Mary Blotna, *General Mgr*
Sarah Harding, *Info Tech Mgr*
**EMP**: 2
**SALES**: 481.8K **Privately Held**
**SIC**: **2086** Pasteurized & mineral waters, bottled & canned

*(G-12425)*
## PHILLIP GRIGALANZ
Also Called: Grigalanz Software Enterprises
114 N Washington St (62052-1603)
**PHONE**..................219 628-6706
Phillip Grigalanz, *Owner*
**EMP**: 3 **EST**: 2015
**SALES (est)**: 84.7K **Privately Held**
**SIC**: **7371** 7372 7373 Computer software systems analysis & design, custom; computer software development & applications; business oriented computer software; utility computer software; computer integrated systems design

*(G-12426)*
## SMITH BROTHERS FABRICATING
Also Called: Smith Bros Engineering
406 Maple Ave (62052-2218)
**PHONE**..................618 498-5612
John N Smith, *President*
**EMP**: 3
**SQ FT**: 2,000
**SALES (est)**: 230K **Privately Held**
**WEB**: www.sboe.com
**SIC**: **3441** Fabricated structural metal

*(G-12427)*
## UNIQUE CONCRETE CONCEPTS INC
Also Called: Ingram Vault Co
26860 State Highway 16 (62052-6555)
P.O. Box 188 (62052-0188)
**PHONE**..................618 466-0700
**Fax**: 618 466-2072
Carol Spencer, *Owner*
**EMP**: 10
**SQ FT**: 6,000
**SALES**: 1.5MM **Privately Held**
**SIC**: **3272** 7699 Manhole covers or frames, concrete; septic tanks, concrete; septic tank cleaning service

*(G-12428)*
## W A RICE SEED COMPANY
1108 W Carpenter St (62052-1363)
**PHONE**..................618 498-5538
**Fax**: 618 498-5530
William A Rice, *President*
Pamela Rice Weber, *Admin Sec*
▲ **EMP**: 6 **EST**: 1898
**SQ FT**: 9,000
**SALES (est)**: 1MM **Privately Held**
**WEB**: www.wariceseed.com
**SIC**: **5191** 3523 Seeds: field, garden & flower; cleaning machines for fruits, grains & vegetables

*(G-12429)*
## WEBE INK
103 Lincoln Ave (62052-1455)
**PHONE**..................618 498-7620
Marty Baker, *Owner*
**EMP**: 3
**SALES**: 170K **Privately Held**
**SIC**: **2759** Screen printing

## Johnsburg
### Mchenry County

*(G-12430)*
## ARBORTECH CORPORATION
3607 Chapel Hill Rd Ste M (60051-2515)
**PHONE**..................847 462-1111
Raymond J Graffia, *President*
Thomas Huemann, *Engineer*
**EMP**: 4
**SALES (est)**: 440K **Privately Held**
**WEB**: www.arbortech.com
**SIC**: **5074** 3589 Water purification equipment; water treatment equipment, industrial

*(G-12431)*
## C & S FABRICATION SERVICES INC
Also Called: C&S Services
5390 Fieldstone Way (60051-7403)
**PHONE**..................815 363-8510
Chris Nicolay, *Owner*
**EMP**: 5
**SALES (est)**: 456.4K **Privately Held**
**SIC**: **3441** 2899 Fabricated structural metal; fluxes: brazing, soldering, galvanizing & welding

*(G-12432)*
## CDC ENTERPRISES INC
1512 River Terrace Dr (60051-7568)
P.O. Box 202, Ringwood (60072-0202)
**PHONE**..................815 790-4205
Paul Pieper, *President*
**EMP**: 3
**SALES (est)**: 280K **Privately Held**
**SIC**: **3699** 7373 3822 Electrical equipment & supplies; systems integration services; incinerator control systems, residential & commercial type

*(G-12433)*
## CURRENT WORKS INC
Also Called: Quizworks Company, The
1395 Horizon Dr (60051-8420)
P.O. Box 203, Ringwood (60072-0203)
**PHONE**..................847 497-9650
Robert Schroyer, *President*
Patricia Sullivan-Schroyer, *Treasurer*
Rick McGuire, *Director*
**EMP**: 5
**SQ FT**: 10,000
**SALES**: 510K **Privately Held**
**WEB**: www.currentworks.com
**SIC**: **3577** 3672 Computer peripheral equipment; printed circuit boards

*(G-12434)*
## FOCUS MARKETING GROUP INC
3320 Rocky Beach Rd (60051-9669)
**PHONE**..................815 363-2525
Mary Lou Hutchinson, *President*
**EMP**: 3
**SQ FT**: 900
**SALES (est)**: 300K **Privately Held**
**SIC**: **3429** Furniture hardware

*(G-12435)*
## GROVE INDUSTRIAL
3915 Spring Grove Rd (60051-5906)
**PHONE**..................815 385-4800
Wendel Dschida, *Partner*
Martin Dschida, *Partner*
**EMP**: 5
**SQ FT**: 3,000
**SALES (est)**: 80K **Privately Held**
**SIC**: **3545** Boring machine attachments (machine tool accessories)

*(G-12436)*
## ILLINOIS INSTRUMENTS INC
2401 Hiller Rdg Ste A (60051-7451)
**PHONE**..................815 344-6212
Bryan Cummings, *President*
Richard Smith, *President*
Michael Buckley, *Engineer*
Victor Kofman, *Engineer*
Donna Palmer, *Office Mgr*
**EMP**: 20
**SQ FT**: 10,000
**SALES (est)**: 4.7MM **Privately Held**
**WEB**: www.illinoisinstruments.com
**SIC**: **3826** Analytical instruments

*(G-12437)*
## JDI MOLD AND TOOL LLC
2510 Hiller Rdg (60051-7447)
**PHONE**..................815 759-5646
**Fax**: 815 759-5646
Bill Reinherz, *Vice Pres*
Clinton Renji, *VP Opers*
Debra Jurinak, *Manager*
James T Jurinak,
Richard D Minehart Jr,
**EMP**: 15
**SQ FT**: 16,000
**SALES (est)**: 2.6MM **Privately Held**
**WEB**: www.jdimolds.com
**SIC**: **3089** Plastic processing

*(G-12438)*
## MURPHY USA
2901 N Richmond Rd (60051-5436)
Less Than, *Principal*
**EMP**: 4
**SALES (est)**: 168.9K **Privately Held**
**SIC**: **5541** 1311 Gasoline service stations; gas & hydrocarbon liquefaction from coal

*(G-12439)*
## NANAS KITCHEN INC
1313 Old Bay Rd (60051-9652)
**PHONE**..................815 363-8500
Sargon Boudakh, *President*
**EMP**: 7
**SQ FT**: 1,200
**SALES**: 2MM **Privately Held**
**SIC**: **2099** Seasonings & spices

*(G-12440)*
## ON-LINE COMPRESSOR INC
Also Called: Compressor Services
5723 Weatherstone Way (60051-8431)
**PHONE**..................847 497-9750
Michael Britt, *President*
Gina Britt, *Admin Sec*
**EMP**: 8
**SALES (est)**: 650K **Privately Held**
**SIC**: **3563** Air & gas compressors

*(G-12441)*
## REMINGTON INDUSTRIES INC
3521 Chapel Hill Rd (60051-2504)
**PHONE**..................815 385-1987
**Fax**: 815 385-1987
Tom Liston, *Owner*
**EMP**: 15
**SQ FT**: 1,500
**SALES**: 1.6MM **Privately Held**
**SIC**: **3549** Coiling machinery

*(G-12442)*
## SONIC LOW VOLTAGE
3218 N Richmond Rd Unit 3 (60051-5441)
**PHONE**..................815 790-4400
Sean Geraty, *Owner*
**EMP**: 1
**SALES**: 750K **Privately Held**
**SIC**: **3651** Video camera-audio recorders, household use

*(G-12443)*
## TURTLE ISLAND INC
1910 Bay Rd (60051-9616)
**PHONE**..................815 759-9000
**Fax**: 815 759-9100
Janice Berger, *President*
Terry Berger, *Vice Pres*
**EMP**: 15
**SALES (est)**: 2.2MM **Privately Held**
**WEB**: www.turtleislandsoups.com
**SIC**: **2034** 5149 Dried & dehydrated soup mixes; soups, except frozen

*(G-12444)*
## WOOD LABELING SYSTEMS INC
4906 Brorson Ln (60051-6907)
**PHONE**..................815 344-8733
Walter Wood, *Principal*
**EMP**: 4
**SALES (est)**: 443.3K **Privately Held**
**SIC**: **2752** Commercial printing, lithographic

## Johnston City
### Williamson County

*(G-12445)*
## SATELLINK INC
724 W 15th St (62951-2012)
**PHONE**..................618 983-5555
Hugh Durham, *Owner*
Kay Durham, *Co-Owner*
**EMP**: 5
**SALES (est)**: 290K **Privately Held**
**SIC**: **3679** Antennas, satellite: household use

*(G-12446)*
## SOUTHERN MOLD FINISHING INC
500 Follis Ave (62951-1432)
P.O. Box 228 (62951-0228)
**PHONE**..................618 983-5049
**Fax**: 618 983-5791
James Oxendine, *President*
Sharon Beltz, *Corp Secy*
Shannon Oxedine, *Vice Pres*
**EMP**: 15
**SQ FT**: 8,000
**SALES**: 1.4MM **Privately Held**
**SIC**: **5031** 3544 Molding, all materials; special dies, tools, jigs & fixtures

*(G-12447)*
## SOUTHERN PLATING INC
500 Follis Ave (62951-1432)
**PHONE**..................618 983-6350
Mark Willingham, *President*
Ted Oxendine, *Principal*
**EMP**: 3
**SALES (est)**: 207.8K **Privately Held**
**WEB**: www.southernmold.com
**SIC**: **3471** Plating of metals or formed products

*(G-12448)*
## US FABG & MINE SVCS INC
11196 Illinois Steel Rd (62951-2614)
**PHONE**..................618 983-7850
Kenneth Cobb, *President*
Bill Cobb, *President*
**EMP**: 4
**SQ FT**: 1,000
**SALES**: 200K **Privately Held**
**SIC**: **3441** Fabricated structural metal

## Joliet
### Will County

*(G-12449)*
## AAA GALVANIZING - JOLIET INC (HQ)
Also Called: A Z Z
625 Mills Rd (60433-2842)
**PHONE**..................815 723-5000
**Fax**: 815 723-5008
David Dindus, *President*
Rodolfo Navarro, *Plant Mgr*
Lydia Jordan, *Manager*
Bob Shireman, *Manager*
▲ **EMP**: 60
**SQ FT**: 100,000
**SALES (est)**: 26.1MM
**SALES (corp-wide)**: 858.9MM **Publicly Held**
**SIC**: **3479** Hot dip coating of metals or formed products; coating of metals & formed products

## Joliet - Will County (G-12474)

PA: Azz Inc.
3100 W 7th St Ste 500
Fort Worth TX 76107
817 810-0095

### (G-12450)
### ADVANTAGE COMPONENTS INC
2240 Oak Leaf St (60436-1868)
**PHONE**.................815 725-8644
Kevin O'Sullivan, *President*
Timothy Kucera, *Vice Pres*
Mike Burman, *Engineer*
▲ **EMP:** 50
**SQ FT:** 14,000
**SALES (est):** 12.9MM **Privately Held**
**WEB:** www.advantagecomponentsinc.com
**SIC:** 3496 3678 Cable, uninsulated wire: made from purchased wire; electronic connectors

### (G-12451)
### AGRESEARCH INC
1 Genstar Ln (60435-2674)
**PHONE**.................815 726-0410
**Fax:** 815 726-0521
John Gribble, *Admin Sec*
▲ **EMP:** 15
**SQ FT:** 20,000
**SALES (est):** 3.1MM **Privately Held**
**WEB:** www.agresearch.com
**SIC:** 2048 Prepared feeds

### (G-12452)
### AMERICAN CHUTE SYSTEMS INC
Also Called: Nicor Products
603 E Washington St (60433-1135)
**PHONE**.................815 723-7632
**Fax:** 815 723-7652
Frank Stephens, *President*
Connie Gossar, *Manager*
Bonnie Reynolds, *Admin Sec*
Mary Kay, *Administration*
**EMP:** 5
**SALES (est):** 790.4K **Privately Held**
**WEB:** www.americanchutesystems.com
**SIC:** 3444 3443 Sheet metalwork; chutes & troughs

### (G-12453)
### AMERIPLATE INC
600 Joyce Rd (60436-1814)
P.O. Box 2129 (60434-2129)
**PHONE**.................815 744-8585
**Fax:** 815 744-2400
Douglas I McCallister, *President*
Mark Friend, *General Mgr*
Betty Wittenbrj, *General Mgr*
Kathleen McCallister, *Vice Pres*
**EMP:** 20
**SQ FT:** 30,000
**SALES (est):** 2.4MM **Privately Held**
**WEB:** www.ameriplate.com
**SIC:** 3471 Electroplating & plating

### (G-12454)
### ANDREW CORPORATION
2700 Ellis Rd (60433-8459)
**PHONE**.................779 435-6000
**EMP:** 24
**SALES (est):** 6.3MM **Publicly Held**
**SIC:** 3357 Nonferrous Wiredrawing/Insulating
**HQ:** Commscope Technologies Llc
4 Westbrook Corporate Ctr
Westchester IL 60154
708 236-6600

### (G-12455)
### ANDREW INTERNATIONAL SVCS CORP
2700 Ellis Rd (60433-8459)
**PHONE**.................779 435-6000
Marvin S Edwards, *President*
Ralph Faison, *President*
**EMP:** 1400
**SQ FT:** 571,000
**SALES (est):** 106.8MM **Publicly Held**
**SIC:** 3663 Microwave communication equipment
**HQ:** Commscope Technologies Llc
4 Westbrook Corporate Ctr
Westchester IL 60154
708 236-6600

### (G-12456)
### APEX MATERIAL TECHNOLOGIES LLC
10 Industry Ave (60435-2652)
**PHONE**.................815 727-3010
Lee Welgs, *Mng Member*
**EMP:** 8
**SALES (est):** 1.5MM **Privately Held**
**SIC:** 3312 Chemicals & other products derived from coking

### (G-12457)
### AVE INC
Also Called: Mr. Rooter Plumbing
126 S Des Plaines St (60436)
**PHONE**.................815 727-0153
Adam Erickson, *CEO*
Joe Fitzgerald, *Office Mgr*
**EMP:** 3
**SQ FT:** 7,000
**SALES (est):** 2.5MM **Privately Held**
**SIC:** 7699 1711 1081 Sewer cleaning & rodding; plumbing contractors; heating & air conditioning contractors; draining or pumping of metal mines

### (G-12458)
### AVSEC PRINTING INC
825 Plainfield Rd Ste 1 (60435-5974)
**PHONE**.................815 722-2961
**Fax:** 815 722-3469
Elaine Vroman, *President*
Susan Lyons, *Manager*
Glen C Davis, *Admin Sec*
**EMP:** 4
**SQ FT:** 2,000
**SALES:** 150K **Privately Held**
**SIC:** 2752 Commercial printing, lithographic

### (G-12459)
### AZZ INCORPORATED
625 Mills Rd (60433-2842)
**PHONE**.................815 723-5000
Laxman Alreja, *Branch Mgr*
**EMP:** 62
**SALES (corp-wide):** 858.9MM **Publicly Held**
**SIC:** 3699 Electrical equipment & supplies
PA: Azz Inc.
3100 W 7th St Ste 500
Fort Worth TX 76107
817 810-0095

### (G-12460)
### BAR STOOL DEPOTCOM
Also Called: In Focus Restaurant & Bar Sup
816 Caton Ave (60435-5906)
**PHONE**.................815 727-7294
Ursala Martin, *President*
**EMP:** 6
**SALES:** 230K **Privately Held**
**WEB:** www.barstooldepot.com
**SIC:** 2711 5021 2542 Newspapers, publishing & printing; bar furniture; partitions & fixtures, except wood

### (G-12461)
### BARNETT-BATES CORPORATION
500 Mills Rd (60433-2795)
**PHONE**.................815 726-5223
Robert H Barnett, *President*
Thomas C Barnett, *Vice Pres*
Janet Barnett, *Marketing Mgr*
Shayla Gallinger, *Manager*
Krista Andersen, *Director*
▲ **EMP:** 18 **EST:** 1926
**SQ FT:** 20,000
**SALES (est):** 4.4MM **Privately Held**
**WEB:** www.barnettbates.com
**SIC:** 3446 5085 Gratings, tread: fabricated metal; valves & fittings

### (G-12462)
### BARNEYS ALUMINUM SPECIALTIES
340 Ruby St (60435-6272)
**PHONE**.................815 723-5341
**Fax:** 815 723-3443
William Barney, *President*
**EMP:** 1
**SQ FT:** 1,000
**SALES (est):** 229.4K **Privately Held**
**SIC:** 5211 3442 Doors, storm: wood or metal; windows, storm: wood or metal; metal doors, sash & trim

### (G-12463)
### BEAVER CREEK ENTERPRISES INC (PA)
Also Called: Beaver Creek Golf Carts
801 Rowell Ave (60433-2524)
**PHONE**.................815 723-9455
**Fax:** 815 726-9916
William Rulien, *President*
Bonnie Rulien, *Corp Secy*
Warner Rulien, *Vice Pres*
**EMP:** 11
**SQ FT:** 8,500
**SALES (est):** 1.6MM **Privately Held**
**WEB:** www.beavercreektrailers.com
**SIC:** 7692 3443 Welding repair; fabricated plate work (boiler shop)

### (G-12464)
### BERGERON GROUP INC
Also Called: Cedar Rustic Fence Co.
99 Republic Ave (60435-6513)
**PHONE**.................815 741-1635
**Fax:** 815 741-7059
James Bergeron, *CEO*
Gregory Bergeron, *President*
Michael O'Lena, *Opers Staff*
**EMP:** 35
**SQ FT:** 86,000
**SALES (est):** 6.4MM **Privately Held**
**SIC:** 2499 1799 1531 3496 Fencing, wood; fence construction; patio & deck construction & repair; miscellaneous fabricated wire products

### (G-12465)
### BERGSTROM INC
4060 Mound Rd (60436-8901)
**PHONE**.................847 394-4013
Sharon Asche, *Opers Staff*
Regina Tomaszewski, *Human Res Mgr*
Gus Anton, *Manager*
**EMP:** 100
**SALES (corp-wide):** 455.3MM **Privately Held**
**WEB:** www.bergstrominc.com
**SIC:** 3714 3711 Heaters, motor vehicle; air conditioner parts, motor vehicle; motor vehicles & car bodies
PA: Bergstrom Inc.
2390 Blackhawk Rd
Rockford IL 61109
815 874-7821

### (G-12466)
### BIOBLEND LUBRICANTS INTL
2439 Reeves Rd (60436-9538)
**PHONE**.................630 227-1800
Gary Dyal, *President*
David Gaulke, *VP Sales*
John Peters, *Manager*
Douglas Haugh, *Director*
**EMP:** 7 **EST:** 2001
**SQ FT:** 3,000
**SALES (est):** 930K **Privately Held**
**WEB:** www.bioblend.com
**SIC:** 2992 Lubricating oils & greases

### (G-12467)
### BROCK INDUSTRIAL SERVICES LLC
United
2210 Oak Leaf St (60436-1894)
**PHONE**.................815 730-3350
Mike Gantz, *Branch Mgr*
**EMP:** 30 **Privately Held**
**WEB:** www.unitedanco.com
**SIC:** 3599 Bellows, industrial: metal
**HQ:** Brock Industrial Services, Llc
2210 Oak Leaf St
Joliet IL 60436
815 730-3350

### (G-12468)
### BUZZI UNICEM USA INC
450 Railroad St (60436-2704)
**PHONE**.................815 768-3660
Scott Richardson, *Manager*
**EMP:** 23
**SALES (corp-wide):** 271.5MM **Privately Held**
**SIC:** 3241 Cement, hydraulic

**HQ:** Buzzi Unicem Usa Inc.
100 Brodhead Rd Ste 230
Bethlehem PA 18017
610 882-5000

### (G-12469)
### C & C PUBLICATIONS
Also Called: Joliet Times Weekly
254 E Cass St (60433-1813)
P.O. Box 2277 (60434-2277)
**PHONE**.................815 723-0325
**Fax:** 815 723-0326
Jayme Cain, *President*
Karen Sorensen, *Editor*
Laura Halloway, *Manager*
**EMP:** 7
**SALES (est):** 483.3K **Privately Held**
**SIC:** 2711 Newspapers

### (G-12470)
### C & S CHEMICALS INC
Also Called: C & R Industries
1306 Mckinley St (60436-2915)
P.O. Box 2877 (60434-2877)
**PHONE**.................815 722-6671
**EMP:** 5
**SALES (corp-wide):** 7.6MM **Privately Held**
**SIC:** 2819 2836 3842 3841 Mfg Indstl Inorgan Chem Mfg Biological Products Mfg Surgical Appliances Mfg Surgical/Med Instr Mfg Ophthalmic Goods
PA: C & S Chemicals, Inc.
4180 Providence Rd # 310
Marietta GA 30062
770 977-2669

### (G-12471)
### CATERPILLAR INC
540 Joyce Rd (60436-1812)
P.O. Box 504 (60434-0504)
**PHONE**.................815 729-5511
**Fax:** 815 729-5586
Robert Macier, *Vice Pres*
Ken Hayslett, *Project Mgr*
W L Goben, *Purchasing*
G D Hall, *Engineer*
Roger Simmons, *Engineer*
**EMP:** 355
**SALES (corp-wide):** 38.5B **Publicly Held**
**WEB:** www.cat.com
**SIC:** 3531 3823 3822 3625 Construction machinery; industrial instrmnts msrmnt display/control process variable; auto controls regulating residntl & coml environmt & applncs; relays & industrial controls; fluid power pumps & motors; valves & pipe fittings
PA: Caterpillar Inc.
100 Ne Adams St
Peoria IL 61629
309 675-1000

### (G-12472)
### CHICAGO BLIND COMPANY
20607 Burl Ct (60433-9713)
**PHONE**.................815 553-5525
Mark Sims, *President*
Kelly Philbin, *Office Mgr*
Allen Sims, *Admin Sec*
**EMP:** 3
**SQ FT:** 2,800
**SALES (est):** 548.9K **Privately Held**
**SIC:** 2591 Window blinds

### (G-12473)
### CHROME CRANKSHAFT COMPANY LLC
4166 Mound Rd (60436-9009)
**PHONE**.................815 725-9030
**Fax:** 815 725-9990
Diane Bell, *Finance Mgr*
William F Walen,
▲ **EMP:** 15
**SQ FT:** 22,500
**SALES (est):** 2.5MM **Privately Held**
**WEB:** www.chromecrankshaft.com
**SIC:** 3599 Crankshafts & camshafts, machining

### (G-12474)
### CMA INC
929 Kelly Ave (60435-4648)
**PHONE**.................847 848-0674
Robert Johnson, *Principal*
**EMP:** 45 **Privately Held**

# Joliet - Will County (G-12475)   GEOGRAPHIC SECTION

SIC: 2499 Insulating material, cork
PA: Cma, Inc.
19 Stonehill Rd
Oswego IL 60543

### (G-12475)
### CMC AMERICA CORPORATION
Also Called: C M C
208 S Center St (60436-2202)
PHONE.................................815 726-4337
Edward Fay, President
Michael Baron, Plant Mgr
Joel Swidergal, Project Engr
John Madia, Sales Dir
Mary Moore, Office Mgr
▲ EMP: 15 EST: 1993
SQ FT: 40,000
SALES (est): 4.6MM Privately Held
WEB: www.cmc-america.com
SIC: 3556 Bakery machinery

### (G-12476)
### COMMSCOPE TECHNOLOGIES LLC
Also Called: Andrew Solutions
2700 Ellis Rd (60433-8459)
PHONE.................................779 435-6000
Stan Catey, General Mgr
Roger Blaylock, Senior VP
Connie Doles, Vice Pres
Norman McMullen, Engineer
Ronald Brandau, Design Engr
EMP: 260 Publicly Held
WEB:
SIC: 3663 3357 3679 3577 Microwave communication equipment; coaxial cable, nonferrous; waveguides & fittings; computer peripheral equipment
HQ: Commscope Technologies Llc
4 Westbrook Corporate Ctr
Westchester IL 60154
708 236-6600

### (G-12477)
### CORSETTI STRUCTURAL STEEL INC
2515 New Lenox Rd (60433-9718)
PHONE.................................815 726-0186
Fax: 815 726-0186
Nino Corsetti, President
Edward Corsetti, Corp Secy
Anthony Corsetti, Vice Pres
Brenda Grant, Controller
Silvana Corsetti, Admin Sec
EMP: 20
SQ FT: 17,000
SALES: 11.7MM Privately Held
SIC: 1791 3441 Structural steel erection; fabricated structural metal

### (G-12478)
### COVIDIEN LP
Also Called: Medical Supplies
3901 Rock Creek Blvd (60431-8988)
PHONE.................................815 744-3766
Erick Smrt, Branch Mgr
Patrick Mazanec, Supervisor
EMP: 200 Privately Held
WEB: www.tycohealthcare.com
SIC: 3291 5047 Abrasive products; medical & hospital equipment
HQ: Covidien Lp
15 Hampshire St
Mansfield MA 02048
508 261-8000

### (G-12479)
### CROWN EQUIPMENT CORPORATION
Also Called: Crown Lift Trucks
4100 Olympic Blvd (60431-7942)
PHONE.................................815 773-0022
Fax: 708 354-0331
Scott Furlow, Principal
Gary Intres, Sales Mgr
Fred Morrone, Systems Staff
EMP: 133
SQ FT: 5,000
SALES (corp-wide): 5.5B Privately Held
SIC: 3537 Lift trucks, industrial: fork, platform, straddle, etc.
PA: Crown Equipment Corporation
44 S Washington St
New Bremen OH 45869
419 629-2311

### (G-12480)
### CUSTOM FABRICATING HTG & COOLG
1120 Manhattan Rd (60433-8533)
PHONE.................................815 726-0477
Donald Lauth, Principal
EMP: 2
SALES (est): 207.4K Privately Held
SIC: 3444 1711 Sheet metalwork; heating & air conditioning contractors

### (G-12481)
### CUSTOM WOOD & LAMINATE LTD
1102 Davison St (60433-8512)
PHONE.................................815 727-4168
EMP: 2 EST: 2001
SQ FT: 4,000
SALES (est): 200K Privately Held
SIC: 2599 Mfg Furniture/Fixtures

### (G-12482)
### DAILY KRATOM
4010 Brenton Dr (60431-9264)
PHONE.................................815 768-7104
Kevin Murdaugh, Principal
EMP: 3
SALES (est): 163.5K Privately Held
SIC: 2711 Newspapers, publishing & printing

### (G-12483)
### DAVID NELSON EXQUISITE JEWELRY
1312 W Jefferson St Ste 2 (60435-6888)
PHONE.................................815 741-4702
Fax: 815 741-4736
David Nelson, President
Ann Marie Nelson, Vice Pres
EMP: 6
SQ FT: 3,000
SALES (est): 700K Privately Held
SIC: 5944 3911 7631 Jewelry stores; rings, finger: precious metal; watch, clock & jewelry repair

### (G-12484)
### DAVIS MACHINE COMPANY INC
312 Henderson Ave (60432-2537)
PHONE.................................815 723-9121
Richard L Davis, President
Dan M Davis, Corp Secy
EMP: 7
SQ FT: 4,000
SALES: 500K Privately Held
SIC: 3599 3544 Machine & other job shop work; special dies & tools

### (G-12485)
### DIETRICH INDUSTRIES INC
3901 Olympic Blvd (60431-7947)
PHONE.................................815 207-0110
Andy Rybowiak, Branch Mgr
EMP: 25
SALES (corp-wide): 2.8B Publicly Held
WEB: www.dietrichmetalframing.com
SIC: 3441 Building components, structural steel
HQ: Dietrich Industries, Inc.
200 W Old Wilson Brdge Rd
Worthington OH 43085
800 873-2604

### (G-12486)
### E & F TOOL COMPANY INC
213 Amendodge Dr (60404-9362)
PHONE.................................815 729-1305
Fax: 815 729-3913
Wilhelm Engelsbel, CEO
Margaret Engelsbel, President
Diane Engelsbel, Purch Agent
▲ EMP: 12
SQ FT: 17,000
SALES: 1.1MM Privately Held
WEB: www.e-ftool.com
SIC: 3599 Machine & other job shop work

### (G-12487)
### E Z LUBE
1984 Essington Rd (60435-1628)
PHONE.................................815 439-3980
Fax: 815 439-6990
Henry Ales, Principal
EMP: 3
SALES (est): 358.2K Privately Held
SIC: 2911 Oils, lubricating

### (G-12488)
### ECOLAB INC
Also Called: Johnson Contrls Authorized Dlr
3001 Channahon Rd (60436-9581)
PHONE.................................815 729-7334
Fax: 815 729-7303
Debi Moore, Purch Mgr
Paul Anderson, Branch Mgr
Tom Bowes, Director
Francisco Reyes, Director
EMP: 38
SALES (corp-wide): 13.1B Publicly Held
WEB: www.ecolab.com
SIC: 2842 5075 Specialty cleaning, polishes & sanitation goods; warm air heating & air conditioning
PA: Ecolab Inc.
1 Ecolab Pl
Saint Paul MN 55102
800 232-6522

### (G-12489)
### ELLWOOD GROUP INC
4166 Mound Rd (60436-9009)
PHONE.................................815 725-9030
Brian Taylor, President
Tyler Kissick, General Mgr
EMP: 15
SQ FT: 30,000
SALES (corp-wide): 774.9MM Privately Held
SIC: 3471 Chromium plating of metals or formed products
PA: Ellwood Group, Inc.
600 Commercial Ave
Ellwood City PA 16117
724 752-3680

### (G-12490)
### EMC INNOVATIONS INC
1252 Woodland Ct (60436-1926)
PHONE.................................815 741-2546
Wayne B Barnett, Owner
▲ EMP: 6
SALES (est): 571.9K Privately Held
WEB: www.barndtsbakery.com
SIC: 3089 Plastic kitchenware, tableware & houseware

### (G-12491)
### ENGINEERED PLUMBING SPC LLC
Also Called: Kamflex, LLC
2312 Oak Leaf St (60436-1065)
PHONE.................................630 682-1555
Michael Whiteside, President
Grant Branch, General Mgr
John Tomaka, Vice Pres
Luis Mejia, Accounts Mgr
EMP: 30
SQ FT: 60,000
SALES (est): 10.3MM Privately Held
WEB: www.kamflex.com
SIC: 3535 Conveyors & conveying equipment
PA: Mifab, Inc.
1321 W 119th St
Chicago IL 60643
773 341-3030

### (G-12492)
### FAST PRINTING OF JOLIET INC
842 Plainfield Rd (60435-4686)
PHONE.................................815 723-0080
Fax: 815 723-5160
Jim Studer, President
Kenneth Studer Sr, Vice Pres
Kenneth Studer Jr, Vice Pres
Christopher M Studer, Treasurer
Denise Studer, Treasurer
EMP: 9
SALES (est): 1.2MM Privately Held
WEB: www.fastprintingofjoliet.com
SIC: 7334 2752 2789 Photocopying & duplicating services; commercial printing, offset; bookbinding & related work

### (G-12493)
### FAST SIGNS
Also Called: Fastsigns
1920 Plainfield Rd (60403-1940)
PHONE.................................815 730-7828
Fax: 815 730-7829
Bob Meyer, Branch Mgr
EMP: 3
SALES (corp-wide): 2.5MM Privately Held
SIC: 3993 Signs & advertising specialties
PA: Fast Signs
8373 Southwest Fwy
Houston TX 77074
713 771-5586

### (G-12494)
### FILTRATION GROUP CORPORATION (PA)
912 E Washington St Ste 1 (60433-1286)
PHONE.................................815 726-4600
George Nolen, President
Howard Sims, General Mgr
Bill Huber, Senior VP
Tim McCarty, CFO
Gary Wexler, Sales Staff
EMP: 53 EST: 2010
SALES (est): 185.3MM Privately Held
SIC: 3564 Blowers & fans

### (G-12495)
### FILTRATION GROUP LLC
912 E Washington St Ste 1 (60433-1286)
PHONE.................................815 726-4600
Lawrence Ost, CEO
EMP: 50
SALES (corp-wide): 287MM Privately Held
WEB: www.filtrationgroup.com
SIC: 3564 Blowers & fans
PA: Filtration Group Llc
912 E Washington St Ste 1
Joliet IL 60433
815 726-4600

### (G-12496)
### FORCE AMERICA INC
500 Brookforest Ave (60404-9706)
PHONE.................................815 730-3600
Fax: 815 323-4605
Jack Donovan, Sales Mgr
Dan Larsson, Sales Staff
Mike Taylor, Marketing Staff
Jack Donvanan, Manager
EMP: 10
SALES (corp-wide): 166MM Privately Held
WEB: www.forceamerica.com
SIC: 5084 3568 Hydraulic systems equipment & supplies; drives, chains & sprockets
PA: Force America Inc.
501 Cliff Rd E Ste 100
Burnsville MN 55337
952 707-1300

### (G-12497)
### FREEDOM AIR FILTRATION INC
1712 Arden Pl (60435-5784)
P.O. Box 3742 (60434-3742)
PHONE.................................815 744-8999
Linda Freveletti, President
EMP: 1
SALES: 350K Privately Held
SIC: 3564 Blowers & fans

### (G-12498)
### FRENCH QRTER PROF OFF BLDG LLC
21625 S Mattox Ln (60404-8971)
PHONE.................................815 972-0681
Jun Ja Kim, Principal
EMP: 3
SALES (est): 201.9K Privately Held
SIC: 3131 Quarters

### (G-12499)
### GALLEON INDUSTRIES INC
Also Called: Galleon Printing Co
16714 Cherry Creek Ct (60433-8466)
PHONE.................................708 478-5444
Paul Turay, President
Craig Turay, Vice Pres
Jeff Turay, Vice Pres
EMP: 5
SQ FT: 4,500
SALES (est): 540K Privately Held
WEB: www.galleonindustries.com
SIC: 2759 7389 Commercial printing; printing broker

# GEOGRAPHIC SECTION

Joliet - Will County (G-12526)

**(G-12500)**
**GAYTAN SIGNS & CO INC**
317 Mcdonough St (60436-2235)
PHONE..............................815 726-2975
Pedro Garcia, *President*
Mayra Garcia, *Corp Secy*
**EMP:** 4 **EST:** 2001
**SQ FT:** 900
**SALES (est):** 300K **Privately Held**
**SIC:** 3993 Signs & advertising specialties

**(G-12501)**
**GEORGE W PIERSON COMPANY**
Also Called: Norwalk Tank Co
2121 Maple Rd (60432-9642)
PHONE..............................815 726-3351
Fax: 815 726-2945
Ronald Pierson, *President*
Chris Scholp, *General Mgr*
**EMP:** 35 **EST:** 1961
**SQ FT:** 9,000
**SALES (est):** 7.2MM **Privately Held**
**SIC:** 3272 3084 Septic tanks, concrete; plastics pipe

**(G-12502)**
**GIER RADIO & TELEVISION INC**
201 E Cail St Ste 1 (60432)
PHONE..............................815 722-8514
Gary E Gier, *President*
Timothy Gier, *Vice Pres*
**EMP:** 5
**SQ FT:** 11,500
**SALES (est):** 610K **Privately Held**
**SIC:** 3651 7622 5722 Television receiving sets; radio repair shop; television repair shop; electric household appliances

**(G-12503)**
**GRATE SIGNS INC**
4044 Mcdonough St (60431-8816)
P.O. Box 2788 (60434-2788)
PHONE..............................815 729-9700
Fax: 815 729-3355
Anton Grate, *President*
James Bowman, *Controller*
Linda Stuart, *Manager*
**EMP:** 25 **EST:** 1948
**SQ FT:** 50,000
**SALES (est):** 3.2MM **Privately Held**
**WEB:** www.gratesigns.com
**SIC:** 3993 7359 7389 Electric signs; equipment rental & leasing; sign painting & lettering shop

**(G-12504)**
**GREG SIGNS**
1201 N Broadway St (60435-4313)
PHONE..............................815 726-5655
Fax: 815 726-0436
Gregory Minarich, *Owner*
**EMP:** 3
**SQ FT:** 2,100
**SALES (est):** 227.2K **Privately Held**
**SIC:** 7389 3993 Lettering & sign painting services; neon signs

**(G-12505)**
**GROOVY LOGISTICS INC**
1120 Manhattan Rd (60433-8533)
PHONE..............................847 946-1491
Marta Gawel, *President*
Radoslaw Stoklosa, *Admin Sec*
**EMP:** 5
**SQ FT:** 1,100
**SALES (est):** 788.6K **Privately Held**
**SIC:** 3715 Truck trailers

**(G-12506)**
**GUYS HI-DEF INC**
1948 Essington Rd Ste C (60435-1615)
PHONE..............................708 261-7487
Bajram Memishofski, *President*
**EMP:** 4
**SALES (est):** 410K **Privately Held**
**SIC:** 3651 Speaker monitors

**(G-12507)**
**HANGER PROSTHETICS &**
Also Called: Hanger Clinic
694 Essington Rd Unit B (60435-4904)
PHONE..............................815 937-0241
Sam Liang, *President*
Vinit Asar, *Principal*
James Murphy, *Branch Mgr*
Sheryl Price, *Director*
**EMP:** 18
**SALES (corp-wide):** 459.1MM **Publicly Held**
**SIC:** 3842 Surgical appliances & supplies
**HQ:** Hanger Prosthetics & Orthotics East, Inc.
33 North Ave Ste 101
Tallmadge OH 44278
330 633-9807

**(G-12508)**
**HANGER PRSTHETCS & ORTHO INC**
694 Essington Rd Unit B (60435-4904)
PHONE..............................815 744-9944
Karen Gamble, *Principal*
Lodi Gill, *Manager*
Robert Picken, *Manager*
**EMP:** 3
**SALES (corp-wide):** 459.1MM **Publicly Held**
**SIC:** 3842 Prosthetic appliances
**HQ:** Hanger Prosthetics & Orthotics, Inc.
10910 Domain Dr Ste 300
Austin TX 78758
512 777-3800

**(G-12509)**
**HEADCO INDUSTRIES INC**
Also Called: Bearing Headquarters Co
2104 Oak Leaf St Unit D (60436-1875)
PHONE..............................815 729-4016
Jennifer Thomas, *Manager*
Mark Barkus, *Manager*
**EMP:** 5
**SALES (corp-wide):** 145.7MM **Privately Held**
**WEB:** www.his-tech.com
**SIC:** 5085 5084 3599 Bearings, bushings, wheels & gears; bearings; sprockets; hydraulic systems equipment & supplies; machine shop, jobbing & repair
**PA:** Headco Industries, Inc.
2601 Parkes Dr
Broadview IL 60155
708 681-4400

**(G-12510)**
**HENDRICKSON INTERNATIONAL CORP**
Hendrickson Stamping Division
501 Caton Farm Rd (60434)
P.O. Box 458 (60434-0458)
PHONE..............................815 727-4031
Fax: 815 727-9697
Jeff Zawacki, *Opers Mgr*
Bob Grah, *Purch Agent*
Gary Smith, *Engrg Mgr*
Nav Sharma, *Engineer*
Ron Seposs, *Controller*
**EMP:** 200
**SQ FT:** 100,000
**SALES (corp-wide):** 1B **Privately Held**
**SIC:** 3714 3429 Bumpers & bumperettes, motor vehicle; manufactured hardware (general)
**HQ:** Hendrickson International Corporation
500 Park Blvd Ste 450
Itasca IL 60143
630 874-9700

**(G-12511)**
**HOME CUT DONUTS INC**
1317 E Washington St (60433-1354)
PHONE..............................815 726-2132
William Ruhak, *Owner*
**EMP:** 4
**SALES (corp-wide):** 2.3MM **Privately Held**
**SIC:** 2051 Doughnuts, except frozen
**PA:** Home Cut Donuts Inc
815 W Jefferson St
Joliet IL 60435
815 727-3511

**(G-12512)**
**HUDDLESTUN CREAMERY INC**
Also Called: Coldstone
1153 Brookforest Ave (60404-8845)
PHONE..............................815 609-1893
**EMP:** 12
**SALES (corp-wide):** 685.3K **Privately Held**
**SIC:** 2024 Ice cream & frozen desserts
**PA:** Huddlestun Creamery Inc
72 S Weber Rd
Romeoville IL 60446
815 886-5714

**(G-12513)**
**ILLCO INC**
Also Called: Johnson Contrls Authorized Dlr
2106 Mcdonough St (60436-1840)
PHONE..............................815 725-9100
Fax: 815 725-9145
Mike Dauner, *Principal*
Wally Kott, *Sales Staff*
**EMP:** 4
**SALES (corp-wide):** 40MM **Privately Held**
**SIC:** 3498 5075 Pipe fittings, fabricated from purchased pipe; warm air heating & air conditioning
**PA:** Illco, Inc.
535 S River St
Aurora IL 60506
630 892-7904

**(G-12514)**
**IMPRESS PRINTING & DESIGN INC**
1325 W Jefferson St (60435-6862)
PHONE..............................815 730-9440
Richard Lozano, *President*
Katie Kosiek, *Graphic Designe*
**EMP:** 2
**SALES (est):** 228.4K **Privately Held**
**SIC:** 2759 Commercial printing

**(G-12515)**
**IN AAW HAIR EMPORIUM LLC**
423 Buell Ave 1 (60435-7021)
PHONE..............................779 227-1450
Akilah Williams, *Principal*
**EMP:** 3
**SALES (est):** 88.9K **Privately Held**
**SIC:** 3999 Barber & beauty shop equipment

**(G-12516)**
**INCLINE CONSTRUCTION INC**
Also Called: Incline Welding & Construction
131 Airport Dr Unit H (60431-4792)
P.O. Box 377, Plainfield (60544-0377)
PHONE..............................815 577-8881
Val Curlee, *President*
**EMP:** 1
**SALES (est):** 403.7K **Privately Held**
**SIC:** 7692 Welding repair

**(G-12517)**
**INEOS SILICAS AMERICAS LLC**
111 Ingalls Ave (60435-4373)
PHONE..............................815 727-3651
Fax: 815 774-2804
Sheryl Jarsombeck, *Controller*
Diana Sroka, *Accountant*
Daniel J Bush, *Mng Member*
William J Lutz, *Mng Member*
Patrick T Murphy, *Mng Member*
▼ **EMP:** 94 **EST:** 2001
**SALES (est):** 18.7MM
**SALES (corp-wide):** 1B **Privately Held**
**WEB:** www.pqcorp.com
**SIC:** 2821 Plastics materials & resins
**HQ:** Pq Corporation
300 Lindenwood Dr
Malvern PA 19355
610 651-4429

**(G-12518)**
**INTERACTIVE BLDG SOLUTIONS LLC**
1919 Cherry Hill Rd (60433-8440)
P.O. Box 186, New Lenox (60451-0186)
PHONE..............................815 724-0525
Milton Woo, *Sls & Mktg Exec*
Carol Hill, *Controller*
Pam Melvin, *Office Admin*
Joseph Jovsa,
**EMP:** 14
**SALES:** 950K **Privately Held**
**SIC:** 3822 Temperature controls, automatic

**(G-12519)**
**J H BOTTS LLC**
Also Called: J.H. Botts
253 Bruce St (60432-1281)
P.O. Box 128 (60434-0128)
PHONE..............................815 726-5885
Fax: 815 726-5994
Monica Hickey, *Vice Pres*
Michael Friel, *Mng Member*
Hickey Jim, *Manager*
Patrick Sheffield, *Director*
**EMP:** 39
**SQ FT:** 51,000
**SALES (est):** 15.5MM **Privately Held**
**WEB:** www.jhbotts.com
**SIC:** 3441 3452 3446 3443 Fabricated structural metal; bolts, metal; architectural metalwork; fabricated plate work (boiler shop)

**(G-12520)**
**J L M PLASTICS CORPORATION**
1012 Collins St (60432-1215)
PHONE..............................815 722-0066
Fax: 815 722-0535
Frank C Mitchell, *President*
**EMP:** 16 **EST:** 1979
**SQ FT:** 37,000
**SALES (est):** 3.9MM **Privately Held**
**SIC:** 2821 Plastics materials & resins

**(G-12521)**
**JANS**
321 Richards St (60433-1859)
PHONE..............................815 722-9360
John Hickman IV, *Owner*
**EMP:** 3
**SQ FT:** 2,500
**SALES (est):** 200K **Privately Held**
**SIC:** 3161 5712 Clothing & apparel carrying cases; furniture stores

**(G-12522)**
**JETIN SYSTEMS INC**
800 Railroad St (60436-9524)
PHONE..............................815 726-4686
Stephen M Jacak, *President*
Becky Dunlop, *Vice Pres*
Thomas Gajcak, *Vice Pres*
Walter Gajzak, *Vice Pres*
Judy Hise, *Manager*
**EMP:** 12
**SQ FT:** 10,000
**SALES (est):** 1.7MM **Privately Held**
**SIC:** 3589 3582 High pressure cleaning equipment; commercial laundry equipment

**(G-12523)**
**JOLIET HERALD NEWSPAPER**
Also Called: Shaw Media
2175 Oneida St (60435-6560)
PHONE..............................815 280-4100
Bob Wall, *Administration*
**EMP:** 20
**SALES (est):** 590K **Privately Held**
**SIC:** 2711 7379 Newspapers; computer related services

**(G-12524)**
**JOLIET PALLETS**
111 Bissel St (60432-3001)
**EMP:** 6
**SALES (est):** 456.7K **Privately Held**
**SIC:** 2448 Pallets, wood & wood with metal

**(G-12525)**
**JSN PRINTING INC**
Also Called: Minuteman Press
1400 Essington Rd (60435-2886)
PHONE..............................815 582-4014
Fax: 815 609-6941
Scott Nelson, *President*
Frank Judd, *Manager*
**EMP:** 5
**SALES (est):** 573.9K **Privately Held**
**SIC:** 2752 Commercial printing, lithographic

**(G-12526)**
**KAMFLEX CONVEYOR CORPORATION** ✪
2312 Oak Leaf St (60436-1065)
PHONE..............................630 682-1555
Roderick Barbee, *Principal*
**EMP:** 6 **EST:** 2016
**SQ FT:** 4,800
**SALES (est):** 325K **Privately Held**
**SIC:** 3535 Conveyors & conveying equipment

## Joliet - Will County (G-12527)   GEOGRAPHIC SECTION

**(G-12527)**
**KLEINHOFFER MANUFACTURING INC**
1852 Terry Dr (60436-8541)
PHONE................815 725-3638
Fax: 815 531-1002
Dale Kleinhoffer, *President*
**EMP:** 4
**SALES:** 450K **Privately Held**
**SIC:** 3714 5531 Motor vehicle parts & accessories; truck equipment & parts

**(G-12528)**
**KNAUER INDUSTRIES LTD**
19505 Ne Frontage Rd (60404-3567)
PHONE................815 725-0246
Fax: 815 725-8296
Conrad Knauer Sr, *CEO*
Robert Knauer, *President*
Louis Knauer, *Treasurer*
Chris Griffen, *Office Mgr*
**EMP:** 20
**SQ FT:** 7,500
**SALES (est):** 3.6MM **Privately Held**
**SIC:** 3272 Burial vaults, concrete or precast terrazzo

**(G-12529)**
**L SURGES CUSTOM WOODWORK**
225 Maple St (60432-3040)
PHONE................815 774-9663
L Surges, *Owner*
**EMP:** 2
**SALES (est):** 382.1K **Privately Held**
**SIC:** 2431 1751 Millwork; cabinet & finish carpentry

**(G-12530)**
**L T P LLC**
Also Called: Premier Laundry Technologies
490 Mills Rd (60433-2734)
PHONE................815 723-9400
Jerry E Lewin,
**EMP:** 120
**SALES (est):** 10.4MM **Privately Held**
**SIC:** 3582 8748 Commercial laundry equipment; business consulting

**(G-12531)**
**LA NUEVA MICHOACANA**
30 Ohio St (60432-4045)
PHONE................815 722-3720
Dora Sanchez, *Principal*
**EMP:** 4
**SALES (est):** 243.9K **Privately Held**
**SIC:** 2024 Ice cream, bulk

**(G-12532)**
**LAMONS GASKET COMPANY**
3305 Corporate Dr (60431-7915)
PHONE................815 744-3902
David Denison, *Manager*
**EMP:** 4
**SALES (corp-wide):** 794MM **Publicly Held**
**SIC:** 3053 Gaskets, all materials
**HQ:** Lamons Gasket Company
   7300 Airport Blvd
   Houston TX 77061
   713 547-9527

**(G-12533)**
**LEGACY VULCAN LLC**
Midwest Division
595 W Laraway Rd (60436-8560)
PHONE................815 726-6900
Fax: 815 726-6987
Bob Tota, *Plant Mgr*
William Glusac, *Branch Mgr*
**EMP:** 15
**SALES (corp-wide):** 3.5B **Publicly Held**
**WEB:** www.vulcanmaterials.com
**SIC:** 1442 Construction sand & gravel
**HQ:** Legacy Vulcan, Llc
   1200 Urban Center Dr
   Vestavia AL 35242
   205 298-3000

**(G-12534)**
**LUB-TEK PETROLEUM PRODUCTS (PA)**
2439 Reeves Rd (60436-9538)
PHONE................815 741-0414
Fax: 815 741-0451
William Nehart, *President*
**EMP:** 7
**SQ FT:** 1,000
**SALES:** 9MM **Privately Held**
**WEB:** www.lub-tek.com
**SIC:** 2992 2911 Lubricating oils & greases; gases & liquefied petroleum gases

**(G-12535)**
**MAHONEY ENVIRONMENTAL INC (PA)**
712 Essington Rd (60435-4912)
PHONE................815 730-2087
Fax: 815 730-2087
John Mahoney, *President*
Rick Sabol, *President*
Dave Ciarlette, *Exec VP*
Robert Amicon, *Vice Pres*
Vito Dipietra, *Vice Pres*
**EMP:** 30
**SQ FT:** 5,000
**SALES (est):** 53.8MM **Privately Held**
**WEB:** www.mahoneyenvironmental.com
**SIC:** 2079 Shortening & other solid edible fats

**(G-12536)**
**MANCUSO CHEESE COMPANY**
612 Mills Rd Ste 1 (60433-2897)
PHONE................815 722-2475
Fax: 815 722-1302
Michael Berta, *President*
Phillip Falbo, *Vice Pres*
**EMP:** 19 **EST:** 1917
**SQ FT:** 20,000
**SALES (est):** 3.7MM **Privately Held**
**WEB:** www.mancusocheese.com
**SIC:** 2022 5149 2033 Cheese, natural & processed; pizza supplies; canned fruits & specialties

**(G-12537)**
**MARSHA LEGA STUDIO INC**
Also Called: Marsha Lega Gallery 28
28 W Crowley Ave (60432-4003)
Marsha Lega, *President*
**EMP:** 3
**SQ FT:** 2,000
**SALES (est):** 369.5K **Privately Held**
**WEB:** www.marshalega.com
**SIC:** 3449 3444 Miscellaneous metalwork; sheet metalwork

**(G-12538)**
**MASTERMOLDING INC**
1715 Terry Dr (60436-8543)
PHONE................815 741-1230
Fax: 815 741-2965
Ray Steinhart, *President*
Kenneth R Steinhart, *Vice Pres*
Joe Grenda, *QC Mgr*
Paul Kwak, *Sales Mgr*
Kirsten Reinje, *Office Mgr*
▼ **EMP:** 34
**SQ FT:** 13,000
**SALES (est):** 8.8MM **Privately Held**
**WEB:** www.mastermolding.com
**SIC:** 3089 Injection molding of plastics

**(G-12539)**
**MATHESON TRI-GAS INC**
200 Alessio Dr (60433-2975)
PHONE................815 727-2202
Don Ramlow, *President*
Anthony Purefoy, *Opers Mgr*
G Cantrella, *Personnel*
W Kroll, *Marketing Staff*
C J Van, *Manager*
**EMP:** 26
**SALES (corp-wide):** 32.6B **Privately Held**
**WEB:** www.matheson-trigas.com
**SIC:** 2813 5084 2911 Industrial gases; welding machinery & equipment; petroleum refining
**HQ:** Matheson Tri-Gas, Inc.
   150 Allen Rd Ste 302
   Basking Ridge NJ 07920
   908 991-9200

**(G-12540)**
**MEYER SYSTEMS**
25035 W Black Rd (60404-8600)
PHONE................815 436-7077
Fax: 815 436-8736
Bruce Meyer, *Owner*
**EMP:** 1
**SQ FT:** 2,000
**SALES:** 300K **Privately Held**
**WEB:** www.meyersystemsonline.com
**SIC:** 8711 3625 Consulting engineer; control equipment, electric

**(G-12541)**
**MID-AMERICAN ELEVATOR CO INC**
Also Called: USA Hoist Company
1000 Sak Dr Unit A (60403-2562)
PHONE................815 740-1204
Tom Haas, *Manager*
**EMP:** 35
**SALES (corp-wide):** 48.3MM **Privately Held**
**WEB:** www.spacesaverparking.com
**SIC:** 1796 7699 3823 3535 Elevator installation & conversion; elevators: inspection, service & repair; controllers for process variables, all types; conveyors & conveying equipment; elevators & moving stairways
**PA:** Mid-American Elevator Company, Inc.
   820 N Wolcott Ave
   Chicago IL 60622
   773 486-6900

**(G-12542)**
**MILANO BAKERY INC**
433 S Chicago St (60436-2268)
PHONE................815 727-2253
Fax: 815 727-3116
Mario De Benedetti III, *President*
Darin De Benedetti, *Vice Pres*
Darin De Benedetti, *Vice Pres*
Mario De Benedetti Sr, *Shareholder*
**EMP:** 50 **EST:** 1915
**SQ FT:** 30,000
**SALES (est):** 15.1MM **Privately Held**
**WEB:** www.milanobakery.com
**SIC:** 5149 2051 5461 Bakery products; bread, cake & related products; bread

**(G-12543)**
**MINING INTERNATIONAL LLC**
1955 Patterson Rd (60436-9303)
PHONE................815 722-0900
Alec Burnham, *Director*
**EMP:** 50
**SALES (est):** 1.6MM **Privately Held**
**SIC:** 1422 Agricultural limestone, ground

**(G-12544)**
**MRC GLOBAL (US) INC**
Also Called: M R C
4026 Mound Rd (60436-8901)
PHONE................815 729-7742
Fax: 815 729-7741
Craig Shear, *President*
**EMP:** 10 **Publicly Held**
**SIC:** 3494 Pipe fittings
**HQ:** Mrc Global (Us) Inc.
   1301 Mckinney St Ste 2300
   Houston TX 77010
   877 294-7574

**(G-12545)**
**NAVISTAR INC**
2700 Haven Ave (60433-8469)
PHONE................331 332-5000
Fax: 815 293-2881
Tom Barker, *Branch Mgr*
Gene Hillard, *Manager*
**EMP:** 140
**SALES (corp-wide):** 8.1B **Publicly Held**
**WEB:** www.internationaldelivers.com
**SIC:** 3711 Motor vehicles & car bodies
**HQ:** Navistar, Inc.
   2701 Navistar Dr
   Lisle IL 60532
   331 332-5000

**(G-12546)**
**NORTHERN ILLINOIS GAS COMPANY**
Also Called: Nicor Gas
3000 E Cass St (60432-9713)
PHONE................815 693-3907
Fax: 815 740-1235
Mike Hancock, *Project Mgr*
Richard Stutzman, *Branch Mgr*
**EMP:** 133
**SALES (corp-wide):** 19.9B **Publicly Held**
**WEB:** www.nicor.com
**SIC:** 4924 1382 4923 Natural gas distribution; oil & gas exploration services; gas transmission & distribution
**HQ:** Northern Illinois Gas Company
   1844 W Ferry Rd
   Naperville IL 60563
   630 983-8676

**(G-12547)**
**NYCOR PRODUCTS INC**
603 E Washington St (60433-1135)
PHONE................815 727-9883
Lawrence Nyquist, *President*
**EMP:** 5
**SALES:** 230K **Privately Held**
**SIC:** 3993 2542 Signs & advertising specialties; racks, merchandise display or storage: except wood

**(G-12548)**
**OMNI GEAR AND MACHINE CORP**
90 Bissel St (60432-3052)
PHONE................815 723-4327
John Hall, *President*
Valerie Franck, *Admin Sec*
Keith Mellen, *Admin Sec*
**EMP:** 10
**SQ FT:** 11,000
**SALES (est):** 1.2MM **Privately Held**
**WEB:** www.omnigearandmachine.com
**SIC:** 3566 5085 Speed changers, drives & gears; gears

**(G-12549)**
**PAPMPERED PUPS**
2011 Essington Rd (60435-1629)
PHONE................815 782-8383
Rachell Tomswell, *Partner*
**EMP:** 3
**SALES:** 100K **Privately Held**
**SIC:** 0752 2047 Grooming services, pet & animal specialties; dog food

**(G-12550)**
**PETER PERELLA & CO**
600 N Scott St (60432-1758)
PHONE................815 727-4526
Fax: 815 727-0945
Jack Perella, *President*
John M Perella, *Corp Secy*
Steve Bruno, *Project Mgr*
Judy Kuiken, *Manager*
**EMP:** 10
**SQ FT:** 6,000
**SALES (est):** 3.6MM **Privately Held**
**SIC:** 3444 1711 Sheet metalwork; plumbing contractors; heating & air conditioning contractors

**(G-12551)**
**PETRAK INDUSTRIES INCORPORATED**
17250 New Lenox Rd (60433-9758)
PHONE................815 483-2290
Fax: 815 483-2295
Thomas J Petrak, *President*
Janice Petrak, *Corp Secy*
Christoher Petrak, *Vice Pres*
▲ **EMP:** 21
**SQ FT:** 12,000
**SALES (est):** 5.3MM **Privately Held**
**WEB:** www.petrakinc.com
**SIC:** 3542 Machine tools, metal forming type

**(G-12552)**
**POWER HOUSE TOOL INC**
626 Nicholson St (60435-6114)
PHONE................815 727-6301
Fax: 815 727-4835
Laura Patterson, *CEO*
Michael W Kelly, *President*
Travis Bachman, *Sales Mgr*
▲ **EMP:** 25
**SQ FT:** 4,000
**SALES (est):** 4.1MM **Privately Held**
**WEB:** www.porta-safe.com
**SIC:** 3544 3829 3677 3612 Special dies, tools, jigs & fixtures; measuring & controlling devices; electronic coils, transformers & other inductors; transformers, except electric; hand & edge tools

## Joliet - Will County (G-12582)

**(G-12553)**
**PRECISION GRINDING AND MCH INC**
16664 Cherry Creek Ct (60433-8458)
David H Pluister, *President*
Deanna Larrabee, *General Mgr*
Andrew Meckler, *Admin Sec*
**EMP:** 4
**SQ FT:** 1,400
**SALES:** 316K **Privately Held**
**SIC:** 3599 Air intake filters, internal combustion engine, except auto

**(G-12554)**
**PRIME TIME COMPUTER SERVICES**
2249 Highland Park Dr (60432-2245)
**PHONE**..................................815 553-0300
Robert Clemp Jr, *President*
**EMP:** 6
**SALES (est):** 340K **Privately Held**
**WEB:** www.ptcsi.com
**SIC:** 7372 Business oriented computer software

**(G-12555)**
**PRINTING CRAFTSMEN OF JOLIET**
2101 New Port Dr (60431-0604)
**PHONE**..................................815 254-3982
**Fax:** 815 726-8139
Reed Mott, *President*
**EMP:** 6
**SQ FT:** 35,500
**SALES (est):** 975.1K **Privately Held**
**SIC:** 2752 2791 2789 2759 Commercial printing, lithographic; commercial printing, offset; typesetting; bookbinding & related work; commercial printing

**(G-12556)**
**PRINTING PRESS OF JOLIET INC**
1920 Donmaur Dr (60403-1905)
**PHONE**..................................815 725-0018
**Fax:** 815 725-3585
Mary Minarich, *President*
**EMP:** 8
**SQ FT:** 5,000
**SALES (est):** 997.8K **Privately Held**
**SIC:** 2759 2791 2789 2752 Commercial printing; typesetting; bookbinding & related work; commercial printing, lithographic

**(G-12557)**
**PROTEK**
315 Airport Dr (60431-4894)
**PHONE**..................................815 773-2280
Jay White, *Owner*
**EMP:** 3
**SALES (est):** 125K **Privately Held**
**SIC:** 3399 Powder, metal

**(G-12558)**
**PRY-BAR COMPANY**
18542 Nw Frontage Rd (60404-9654)
**PHONE**..................................815 436-3383
**Fax:** 815 439-2429
Leonard F Baran, *President*
Scott Baran, *Vice Pres*
**EMP:** 16
**SQ FT:** 14,000
**SALES (est):** 3.9MM **Privately Held**
**SIC:** 2653 5113 3993 2675 Corrugated boxes, partitions, display items, sheets & pad; corrugated & solid fiber boxes; signs & advertising specialties; die-cut paper & board

**(G-12559)**
**QUAD PLUS LLC (PA)**
1921 Cherry Hill Rd (60435-8507)
**PHONE**..................................815 740-0860
**Fax:** 815 740-0864
John Crosetto, *CEO*
Tom Engel, *President*
Steve Chasten, *Project Mgr*
Jim Watson, *Project Mgr*
Erich E Lauer, *Opers Mgr*
**EMP:** 39
**SQ FT:** 10,000
**SALES (est):** 19MM **Privately Held**
**WEB:** www.quadplus.com
**SIC:** 3566 Speed changers, drives & gears

**(G-12560)**
**QUALITY QUICKPRINT INC**
2405 Caton Farm Rd (60403-1302)
**PHONE**..................................815 439-3430
**EMP:** 10
**SALES (corp-wide):** 1.3MM **Privately Held**
**SIC:** 2752 2791 2789 Lithographic Commercial Printing Typesetting Services Bookbinding/Related Work
**PA:** Quality Quickprint Inc
1258 Cronin Ct
Lemont IL 60439
815 723-0941

**(G-12561)**
**QUANTUM SERVICES INC**
8115 Bluestem Ave (60431-4001)
**PHONE**..................................815 230-5893
Melissa Williams, *CEO*
**EMP:** 5
**SALES (est):** 410K **Privately Held**
**SIC:** 3535 Bulk handling conveyor systems

**(G-12562)**
**R-SIGNS SERVICE AND DESIGN INC**
720 Collins St Ste D (60432-1628)
**PHONE**..................................815 722-0283
Ruben Franchini, *President*
Rosa M Esparza, *Admin Sec*
**EMP:** 5
**SALES (est):** 460K **Privately Held**
**SIC:** 3993 Signs & advertising specialties

**(G-12563)**
**RAPID LINE INDUSTRIES INC**
455 N Ottawa St Ste 1 (60432-1714)
**PHONE**..................................815 727-4362
Thomas S Papesh, *President*
**EMP:** 10
**SQ FT:** 12,000
**SALES:** 1MM **Privately Held**
**WEB:** www.rapidline.com
**SIC:** 3559 Frame straighteners, automobile (garage equipment)

**(G-12564)**
**RAVCO INCORPORATED**
1313 Colorado Ave (60435-3704)
**PHONE**..................................815 725-9095
Joseph Filisko, *President*
**EMP:** 2
**SALES (est):** 215.5K **Privately Held**
**SIC:** 3544 3423 Special dies, tools, jigs & fixtures; hand & edge tools

**(G-12565)**
**RELAY SYSTEMS AMERICA INC**
Also Called: Paul Bjekich, President
3225 Corporate Dr (60431-7961)
**PHONE**..................................815 730-0100
**Fax:** 815 730-0107
Paul Bjekich, *President*
Theresa Stanick, *Vice Pres*
Steve Stanick, *Director*
**EMP:** 10 **EST:** 2010
**SQ FT:** 4,000
**SALES (est):** 1.6MM **Privately Held**
**SIC:** 3651 Home entertainment equipment, electronic

**(G-12566)**
**REMIN LABORATORIES INC**
Also Called: Remin Kart A Bag
510 Manhattan Rd (60433-3099)
**PHONE**..................................815 723-1940
**Fax:** 815 723-2495
Eugene A Kazmark Jr, *President*
Barbara Starner, *Vice Pres*
Mary Bruskotter, *Treasurer*
Vivcky Valadaz, *Manager*
▲ **EMP:** 60
**SQ FT:** 5,000
**SALES (est):** 9.7MM **Privately Held**
**WEB:** www.kart-a-bag.com
**SIC:** 3496 3429 3444 Miscellaneous fabricated wire products; luggage hardware; sheet metalwork

**(G-12567)**
**RESIST-A-LINE INDUSTRIES INC**
214 Elm St (60433-2432)
**PHONE**..................................815 650-3177
Ron M Pinzker, *President*
Sandra M Pinkzer, *Admin Sec*
▲ **EMP:** 7 **EST:** 2000
**SALES:** 600K **Privately Held**
**WEB:** www.resist-a-line.com
**SIC:** 3443 Liners/lining

**(G-12568)**
**RHO CHEMICAL COMPANY INC**
30 Industry Ave (60435-2688)
P.O. Box 55 (60434-0055)
**PHONE**..................................815 727-4791
Robert Rolih, *President*
Lorraine Rolih, *Corp Secy*
Mark Rolih, *Vice Pres*
▲ **EMP:** 13 **EST:** 1960
**SQ FT:** 100,000
**SALES (est):** 3.3MM **Privately Held**
**WEB:** www.rhochem.com
**SIC:** 2869 Industrial organic chemicals

**(G-12569)**
**ROBERT E BOLTON**
3021 Theodore St Unit E (60435-8526)
**PHONE**..................................815 725-7120
Robert E Bolton, *Owner*
Bert Bolton, *Principal*
**EMP:** 5
**SALES (est):** 230.8K **Privately Held**
**SIC:** 2591 Window blinds

**(G-12570)**
**ROBOTICS TECHNOLOGIES INC**
20655 Burl Ct (60433-9713)
**PHONE**..................................815 722-7650
**Fax:** 815 722-7665
Allan Roberts, *President*
Tom Mavec, *CFO*
▲ **EMP:** 26
**SQ FT:** 16,600
**SALES (est):** 3.9MM **Privately Held**
**WEB:** www.roboticstech.com
**SIC:** 3861 3613 3651 Cameras & related equipment; control panels, electric; household audio & video equipment

**(G-12571)**
**ROSE LABORATORIES INC**
660 Collins St Unit 2 (60432-1855)
**PHONE**..................................815 740-1121
Rose Kuchar, *President*
Mike Field, *Shareholder*
**EMP:** 30
**SQ FT:** 30,000
**SALES (est):** 1.9MM **Privately Held**
**WEB:** www.roselab.com
**SIC:** 7389 2844 Packaging & labeling services; toilet preparations

**(G-12572)**
**ROVANCO PIPING SYSTEMS INC**
20535 Se Frontage Rd (60431-9357)
**PHONE**..................................815 741-6700
**Fax:** 815 741-4229
Larry Stonitsch, *President*
Derek Lindsey, *President*
Richard Stonitsch, *Vice Pres*
Drew Kobus, *Engineer*
Charles Ray, *CFO*
▲ **EMP:** 88
**SQ FT:** 56,000
**SALES:** 18MM **Privately Held**
**WEB:** www.rovanco.com
**SIC:** 3498 Piping systems for pulp paper & chemical industries

**(G-12573)**
**SATELLITE CERTIFIED INC**
216 Jessie St (60433-1431)
**PHONE**..................................815 230-3877
Paul Benavides, *President*
**EMP:** 6
**SALES (est):** 557.1K **Privately Held**
**SIC:** 3663 Satellites, communications

**(G-12574)**
**SHARP BULLET RESISTANT PDTS**
1933 Cherry Hill Rd (60433-8507)
**PHONE**..................................815 726-2626
**Fax:** 815 726-3514
Roland Metzger, *President*
Ann Metzger, *Manager*
**EMP:** 7 **EST:** 1993

**SALES (est):** 855.7K **Privately Held**
**WEB:** www.sharpbulletresistant.com
**SIC:** 3231 Safety glass: made from purchased glass

**(G-12575)**
**SIGN O RAMA**
1107 Essington Rd (60435-2870)
**PHONE**..................................815 744-8702
Joren Apiquian, *President*
**EMP:** 3
**SQ FT:** 1,400
**SALES (est):** 210K **Privately Held**
**WEB:** www.sarjoliet.com
**SIC:** 3993 Signs & advertising specialties

**(G-12576)**
**SMOLICH BROS**
760 Theodore St (60403-2380)
**PHONE**..................................815 727-2144
Rudy Smolich, *Owner*
**EMP:** 2
**SQ FT:** 1,500
**SALES (est):** 200K **Privately Held**
**SIC:** 2013 Sausages from purchased meat

**(G-12577)**
**SNOOK EQUIPMENT CRANE INC**
2139 Maxim Dr (60436-9012)
**PHONE**..................................815 223-0003
Paul Snook, *General Mgr*
**EMP:** 4
**SALES (est):** 415K **Privately Held**
**SIC:** 3531 Cranes

**(G-12578)**
**STANDARD TRUCK PARTS INC (PA)**
566 N Chicago St (60432-1779)
**PHONE**..................................815 726-4486
John M Jones Jr, *President*
Brian Lagner, *Manager*
**EMP:** 3 **EST:** 1955
**SQ FT:** 21,000
**SALES (est):** 1.9MM **Privately Held**
**WEB:** www.standardtruckparts.com
**SIC:** 5013 3492 3429 Truck parts & accessories; fluid power valves & hose fittings; manufactured hardware (general)

**(G-12579)**
**SULZER PUMP SERVICES (US) INC**
Also Called: Sulzer Midwest Service Center
2600 Citys Edge Dr (60436-4554)
**PHONE**..................................815 600-7355
Mike Ostrowski, *Principal*
**EMP:** 13
**SQ FT:** 750 **Privately Held**
**WEB:** www.sulzerpumps.com
**SIC:** 7692 Welding repair
**HQ:** Sulzer Pump Services (Us) Inc.
1255 Enclave Pkwy Ste 300
Houston TX 77077
281 934-6061

**(G-12580)**
**SUPERIOR BAKING STONE INC**
926 Plainfield Rd (60435-4473)
**PHONE**..................................815 726-4610
**EMP:** 4
**SALES (est):** 212.1K **Privately Held**
**SIC:** 2051 Bread, cake & related products

**(G-12581)**
**SYSTEMS SERVICE & SUPPLY**
10 Fairlane Dr (60435-5484)
**PHONE**..................................815 725-1836
**EMP:** 2
**SALES (est):** 252.4K **Privately Held**
**SIC:** 2782 Bank checkbooks & passbooks

**(G-12582)**
**TJA HEALTH LLC**
2501-2505 Reeves Rd (60436)
Ben Vaziri, *Branch Mgr*
**EMP:** 7
**SQ FT:** 10,000
**SALES (corp-wide):** 1MM **Privately Held**
**SIC:** 2844 Oral preparations; denture cleaners; toothpastes or powders, dentifrices; toilet preparations

## Joliet - Will County (G-12583)

**PA:** Tja Health, Llc
10075 S Jog Rd Ste 308
Boynton Beach FL 33437
561 866-6684

**(G-12583)**
**TOPZ DAIRY PRODUCTS CO**
Also Called: Chellino Cheese Co
505 Bennett Ave (60433-2301)
P.O. Box 721 (60434-0721)
**PHONE**.................815 726-5700
**Fax:** 815 726-6441
Fred S Cemeno, *President*
Tom Cemeno, *Corp Secy*
Fred Chellino, *Manager*
**EMP:** 15 **EST:** 1919
**SQ FT:** 4,000
**SALES (est):** 2MM **Privately Held**
**SIC:** 2022 Natural cheese

**(G-12584)**
**UNITED GRANITE & MARBLE**
321 Airport Dr (60431-4894)
**PHONE**.................815 582-3345
Maria Ochoa, *Principal*
**EMP:** 3
**SALES (est):** 204K **Privately Held**
**SIC:** 3281 Granite, cut & shaped

**(G-12585)**
**UNITED UNIVERSAL INDS INC**
20620 Burl Ct Ste 1 (60433-9707)
**PHONE**.................815 727-4445
**Fax:** 815 727-4490
Edward B Smith, *President*
Diana Smith, *Corp Secy*
Nancy Gayhart, *Manager*
**EMP:** 25
**SQ FT:** 10,000
**SALES (est):** 3.5MM **Privately Held**
**WEB:** www.uniteduniversal.com
**SIC:** 3643 3699 3678 3577 Current-carrying wiring devices; electrical equipment & supplies; electronic connectors; computer peripheral equipment; nonferrous wiredrawing & insulating

**(G-12586)**
**VALLEY CONCRETE INC**
19515 Ne Frontage Rd (60404-3567)
**PHONE**.................815 725-2422
**Fax:** 815 725-2488
Tom Huiner, *President*
Bill Pommerening, *Vice Pres*
William Pommerening, *Vice Pres*
**EMP:** 60
**SALES (est):** 684.1K **Privately Held**
**SIC:** 3273 Ready-mixed concrete

**(G-12587)**
**VISTA WOODWORKING**
500 Joyce Rd Unit B (60436-1879)
**PHONE**.................815 922-2297
Nancy Quattrochi, *President*
**EMP:** 5
**SALES (est):** 420.9K **Privately Held**
**SIC:** 2431 Millwork

**(G-12588)**
**WEIGH RIGHT AUTOMATIC SCALE CO**
612a Mills Rd (60433)
**PHONE**.................815 726-4626
**Fax:** 815 726-7638
Stephen N Almberg, *President*
Steve Walmberg, *Engineer*
John Greenan, *Design Engr*
Mike Phillips, *Mktg Dir*
**EMP:** 9 **EST:** 1932
**SQ FT:** 11,500
**SALES (est):** 2.1MM **Privately Held**
**WEB:** www.weighrightasc.com
**SIC:** 3565 Packaging machinery

**(G-12589)**
**WILTON BRANDS INC**
Also Called: Wilton Industries
21350 Sw Frontage Rd (60404-4702)
**PHONE**.................815 823-8547
**EMP:** 10
**SALES (est):** 1.1MM **Privately Held**
**SIC:** 3999 Manufacturing industries

**(G-12590)**
**WUNDERLICH DOORS INC**
300 Allen St (60436-1797)
**PHONE**.................815 727-6430
**Fax:** 815 727-8880
Russell Wunderlich, *President*
Gary Steinberg, *General Mgr*
Kelly Jones, *Human Resources*
Brian Bednarkiewicz, *Sales Staff*
Matthew Klancnik, *Sales Staff*
**EMP:** 20
**SQ FT:** 16,000
**SALES (est):** 4.2MM **Privately Held**
**WEB:** www.wunderlichdoors.com
**SIC:** 3442 Metal doors, sash & trim

### Jonesboro
*Union County*

**(G-12591)**
**G & C ENTERPRISES INC**
18837 County Line Rd (62952-5002)
**PHONE**.................618 747-2272
Conrad Shepard, *President*
Glenda Shepard, *Corp Secy*
**EMP:** 4
**SALES (est):** 405.1K **Privately Held**
**SIC:** 2411 Logging

### Joy
*Mercer County*

**(G-12592)**
**ROBIN L BARNHOUSE**
Also Called: G1 Industries Co
1106 120th Ave (61260-8558)
**PHONE**.................309 737-5431
Robin L Barnhouse, *Owner*
Mike Barnhouse, *Principal*
**EMP:** 3
**SALES:** 50K **Privately Held**
**SIC:** 3499 Fabricated metal products

### Junction
*Gallatin County*

**(G-12593)**
**BARNETT REDI-MIX INC**
11300 Highway 1 (62954-2103)
P.O. Box 207, Equality (62934-0207)
**PHONE**.................618 276-4298
Shery Denny, *President*
Mike Bardos, *Manager*
**EMP:** 3
**SALES (est):** 197.8K **Privately Held**
**SIC:** 3273 Ready-mixed concrete

### Justice
*Cook County*

**(G-12594)**
**ABILITY PLASTICS INC**
8721 Industrial Dr (60458-1765)
**PHONE**.................708 458-4480
**Fax:** 708 458-7750
Michael L Nuzzo, *President*
Ted Kraus, *General Mgr*
Donna Nuzzo, *Human Res Mgr*
**EMP:** 35 **EST:** 1973
**SQ FT:** 15,000
**SALES (est):** 12.3MM **Privately Held**
**WEB:** www.abilityplastics.com
**SIC:** 5162 3993 Plastics products; signs, not made in custom sign painting shops

**(G-12595)**
**CLASSIC ROADLINER CORPORATION**
8027 Marion Dr Apt 1e (60458-1641)
**PHONE**.................708 769-0666
Shadi Alnadi, *President*
**EMP:** 4
**SALES (est):** 330K **Privately Held**
**SIC:** 3715 Truck trailers

**(G-12596)**
**CZARNIK MEMORIALS INC**
7300 Archer Rd (60458-1141)
P.O. Box 333, Summit Argo (60501-0333)
**PHONE**.................708 458-4443
**Fax:** 708 458-4444
Carrie Sewcyck, *President*
Irene Bucher, *Corp Secy*
**EMP:** 3 **EST:** 1920
**SALES (est):** 382.9K **Privately Held**
**SIC:** 5999 3281 Monuments & tombstones; tombstones; cut stone & stone products

**(G-12597)**
**DEMETRIOS TAILOR INC**
8444 S 88th Ave (60458-1761)
**PHONE**.................708 974-0304
Demetrios Georgantoni, *President*
**EMP:** 2
**SALES (est):** 240K **Privately Held**
**SIC:** 2325 5699 2339 Trousers, dress (separate): men's, youths' & boys'; slacks, dress: men's, youths' & boys'; custom tailor; slacks: women's, misses' & juniors'

**(G-12598)**
**E C MACHINING INC**
8267 S 86th Ct (60458-1767)
**PHONE**.................708 496-0116
**Fax:** 708 496-3401
Edward A Czorniak, *President*
Jessica Gutkoska, *Office Mgr*
**EMP:** 27
**SQ FT:** 7,500
**SALES (est):** 4.5MM **Privately Held**
**WEB:** www.ecmachining.com
**SIC:** 3599 Machine shop, jobbing & repair

### Kaneville
*Kane County*

**(G-12599)**
**ELMHURST-CHICAGO STONE COMPANY**
45 W 371 Main (60144)
P.O. Box 149 (60144-0149)
**PHONE**.................630 557-2446
Glen Ulery, *Superintendent*
**EMP:** 15
**SALES (corp-wide):** 122.7MM **Privately Held**
**SIC:** 3272 1442 Concrete products; construction sand & gravel
**PA:** Elmhurst-Chicago Stone Company
400 W 1st St
Elmhurst IL 60126
630 832-4000

**(G-12600)**
**NEEDHAM SHOP INC**
46 W 840 Main (60144)
**PHONE**.................630 557-9019
Bart Needham, *President*
**EMP:** 7
**SQ FT:** 6,000
**SALES:** 400K **Privately Held**
**SIC:** 7692 7699 Welding repair; farm machinery repair

### Kankakee
*Kankakee County*

**(G-12601)**
**ADCRAFT PRINTERS INC**
1355 W Jeffery St (60901-4626)
**PHONE**.................815 932-6432
**Fax:** 815 932-8792
Dallas Wheeler, *President*
Erik Wheeler, *Corp Secy*
**EMP:** 17 **EST:** 1940
**SQ FT:** 8,500
**SALES:** 900K **Privately Held**
**SIC:** 2752 2791 2789 Commercial printing, offset; typesetting; bookbinding & related work

**(G-12602)**
**ADVANCED LUBRICATION INC (PA)**
4517 E 2000n Rd (60901-7501)
**PHONE**.................815 932-3288
David Ward, *President*
Mary Pawlak, *Manager*
**EMP:** 3
**SALES:** 1.8MM **Privately Held**
**WEB:** www.advancedlubrication.com
**SIC:** 1389 Oil consultants

**(G-12603)**
**BASF CORPORATION**
Kankakee Manufacturing Plant
2525 S Kensington Ave (60901-8243)
**PHONE**.................815 932-9863
Kevin Hird, *Mfg Staff*
Alan Pranica, *Mfg Staff*
Ronald Miller, *Finance Other*
Denny Ohomansiek, *Manager*
Mark Egler, *Manager*
**EMP:** 400
**SALES (corp-wide):** 60.8B **Privately Held**
**WEB:** www.na.cognis.com
**SIC:** 2869 2899 2821 Industrial organic chemicals; chemical preparations; plastics materials & resins
**HQ:** Basf Corporation
100 Park Ave
Florham Park NJ 07932
973 245-6000

**(G-12604)**
**BERENS INC**
1650 E Sheridan St (60901-5662)
**PHONE**.................815 932-0913
**Fax:** 815 427-6929
Mark Berens, *President*
Elvira Berens, *Corp Secy*
**EMP:** 6
**SALES (est):** 552.1K **Privately Held**
**WEB:** www.berens.com
**SIC:** 3429 Clamps, metal

**(G-12605)**
**COCA-COLA REFRESHMENTS USA INC**
1220 Harvard Dr (60901-9468)
**PHONE**.................815 933-2653
**Fax:** 815 933-2149
Jeff Chambers, *Manager*
**EMP:** 32
**SALES (corp-wide):** 41.8B **Publicly Held**
**WEB:** www.cokecce.com
**SIC:** 2086 Bottled & canned soft drinks
**HQ:** Coca-Cola Refreshments Usa, Inc.
2500 Windy Ridge Pkwy Se
Atlanta GA 30339
770 989-3000

**(G-12606)**
**COMMERCIAL METALS COMPANY**
780 Eastgate Indus Pkwy (60901-2889)
**PHONE**.................815 928-9600
**EMP:** 5
**SALES (corp-wide):** 4.6B **Publicly Held**
**SIC:** 3441 3312 5051 Fabricated structural metal; blast furnaces & steel mills; metals service centers & offices
**PA:** Commercial Metals Company
6565 N Mcarthr Blvd # 800
Irving TX 75039
214 689-4300

**(G-12607)**
**DAYTON SUPERIOR CORPORATION**
2150b S Us Highway 45 52 (60901-7200)
**PHONE**.................219 476-4106
**EMP:** 40
**SALES (corp-wide):** 2.8B **Privately Held**
**SIC:** 3315 3452 Mfg Steel Wire/Related Products Mfg Bolts/Screws/Rivets
**PA:** Dayton Superior Corporation
1125 Byers Rd
Miamisburg OH 45342
937 866-0711

## GEOGRAPHIC SECTION

Kankakee - Kankakee County (G-12632)

**(G-12608)**
**DAYTON SUPERIOR CORPORATION**
Also Called: Block Heavy and Highway Pdts
2150b S Us Highway 45 52 (60901-7200)
PHONE .................................. 219 476-4106
Steve Marak, *Manager*
**EMP:** 40 **Publicly Held**
**SIC:** 3449 3441 Bars, concrete reinforcing; fabricated steel; fabricated structural metal
**HQ:** Dayton Superior Corporation
1125 Byers Rd
Miamisburg OH 45342
937 866-0711

**(G-12609)**
**DAYTON SUPERIOR CORPORATION**
American Highway Technology
2150 W Jeffery St (60901-8221)
PHONE .................................. 815 936-3300
Jesus Valdez, *Branch Mgr*
**EMP:** 150 **Publicly Held**
**WEB:** www.daytonsuperior.com
**SIC:** 3315 3452 3462 3089 Steel wire & related products; dowel pins, metal; construction or mining equipment forgings, ferrous; plastic hardware & building products; chemical preparations; miscellaneous fabricated wire products
**HQ:** Dayton Superior Corporation
1125 Byers Rd
Miamisburg OH 45342
937 866-0711

**(G-12610)**
**DOW CHEMICAL COMPANY**
1400 Harvard Dr (60901-9462)
PHONE .................................. 815 933-8900
Gary Farland, *Plant Mgr*
William Williamson, *Purchasing*
Craig Rosenow, *QC Dir*
Gary Mc Farland, *Manager*
Rich Kustwein, *Director*
**EMP:** 75
**SALES (corp-wide):** 48.1B **Publicly Held**
**SIC:** 2819 2821 Industrial inorganic chemicals; plastics materials & resins
**HQ:** The Dow Chemical Company
25500 Whitesell St
Hayward CA 94545
510 786-0100

**(G-12611)**
**DOW CHEMICAL COMPANY**
550 N Hobbie Ave (60901-2612)
PHONE .................................. 815 933-5514
Kurt Shei, *Mfg Staff*
William Williamson, *Purchasing*
Alan Clodi, *QC Dir*
Robert Shier, *Manager*
**EMP:** 46
**SQ FT:** 15,000
**SALES (corp-wide):** 48.1B **Publicly Held**
**WEB:** www.dow.com
**SIC:** 2879 3714 Fungicides, herbicides; motor vehicle parts & accessories
**PA:** The Dow Chemical Company
2030 Dow Ctr
Midland MI 48674
989 636-1000

**(G-12612)**
**ELECTRON BEAM TECHNOLOGIES INC**
1275 Harvard Dr (60901-9471)
PHONE .................................. 815 935-2211
Fax: 815 935-8605
Paul Wlos, *President*
Michael Murtha, *Vice Pres*
Bob Tokoly, *CFO*
Robert Tokoly, *Admin Sec*
▲ **EMP:** 116
**SQ FT:** 100,000
**SALES (est):** 27.6MM **Privately Held**
**WEB:** www.electronbeam.com
**SIC:** 3548 3541 7699 Welding wire, bare & coated; plasma process metal cutting machines; industrial equipment services

**(G-12613)**
**EMD MILLIPORE CORPORATION**
195 W Birch St (60901-2346)
PHONE .................................. 815 937-8270
Linda Cooper, *Purchasing*
Dyann Nowman, *Engineer*
Dave Leppert, *Manager*
Joseph Montalto, *Admin Mgr*
**EMP:** 180
**SALES (corp-wide):** 15.8B **Privately Held**
**WEB:** www.millipore.com
**SIC:** 3826 Analytical instruments
**HQ:** Emd Millipore Corporation
290 Concord Rd
Billerica MA 01821
781 533-6000

**(G-12614)**
**EMD MILLIPORE CORPORATION**
2407 Eastgate Pkwy (60901)
PHONE .................................. 815 932-9017
**EMP:** 317
**SALES (corp-wide):** 13.8B **Publicly Held**
**SIC:** 3826 Mfg Analytical Instruments
**HQ:** Emd Millipore Corporation
290 Concord Rd
Billerica MA 01821
781 533-6000

**(G-12615)**
**FAST SIGNS 590**
Also Called: Fastsigns
601a N 5th Ave (60901-2344)
PHONE .................................. 815 937-1855
**EMP:** 4 **EST:** 2011
**SALES (est):** 307.2K **Privately Held**
**SIC:** 3993 Signs & advertising specialties

**(G-12616)**
**FIBRE DRUM COMPANY**
1650 E Sheridan St (60901-5662)
P.O. Box 349 (60901-0349)
PHONE .................................. 815 933-3222
Fax: 815 933-5326
Mark Berens, *President*
Jennifer Riojas, *Office Mgr*
Arnold C Berens, *Admin Sec*
**EMP:** 28 **EST:** 1946
**SQ FT:** 45,000
**SALES:** 6MM **Privately Held**
**WEB:** www.fibredrumco.com
**SIC:** 2655 Drums, fiber: made from purchased material

**(G-12617)**
**FOOD SERVICE**
1501 E Maple St (60901-4371)
PHONE .................................. 815 933-0725
Cathy Breeck, *Director*
**EMP:** 70
**SALES (est):** 3.9MM **Privately Held**
**SIC:** 2099 Food preparations

**(G-12618)**
**FRIENDLY SIGNS INC**
1281 N Schuyler Ave (60901-2108)
PHONE .................................. 815 933-7070
Dave Whitlow, *Partner*
Francis Gullquist, *Partner*
**EMP:** 4
**SALES:** 300K **Privately Held**
**SIC:** 1799 3993 Sign installation & maintenance; signs & advertising specialties

**(G-12619)**
**GROFF TESTING CORPORATION**
1410 Stanford Dr (60901-9474)
PHONE .................................. 815 939-1153
Fax: 815 939-7398
Ron Groff, *President*
**EMP:** 4
**SQ FT:** 4,800
**SALES:** 500K **Privately Held**
**SIC:** 3546 Drills & drilling tools

**(G-12620)**
**HANGER PRSTHETCS & ORTHO INC**
450 N Kennedy Dr Ste 2 (60901-2900)
PHONE .................................. 815 937-0241
Fax: 815 937-0471
Bill Moritz, *Branch Mgr*
Bill Morris, *Manager*
**EMP:** 7
**SALES (corp-wide):** 459.1MM **Publicly Held**
**SIC:** 3842 Prosthetic appliances

**HQ:** Hanger Prosthetics & Orthotics, Inc.
10910 Domain Dr Ste 300
Austin TX 78758
512 777-3800

**(G-12621)**
**HEARTLAND HARVEST INC**
2401 Eastgate Indus Pkwy (60901-2856)
PHONE .................................. 815 932-2100
Warren Ouwenga, *President*
Dennis Bunck, *Vice Pres*
▲ **EMP:** 2
**SALES (est):** 656.4K **Privately Held**
**SIC:** 2038 Frozen specialties
**HQ:** Bunge North America, Inc.
11720 Borman Dr
Saint Louis MO 63146
314 292-2000

**(G-12622)**
**HOSTMANN STEINBERG INC (HQ)**
2850 Festival Dr (60901-8937)
PHONE .................................. 502 968-5961
Fax: 815 929-0412
Winfred Gleue, *President*
Purvish Masrani, *Opers Mgr*
Steve Moore, *Maint Spvr*
Ernie Meyer, *Engineer*
Venkat Subramanian, *CFO*
**EMP:** 18
**SALES (est):** 9MM
**SALES (corp-wide):** 1.3MM **Privately Held**
**WEB:** www.hostmann-steinberg.com
**SIC:** 2893 Printing ink
**PA:** Michael Huber Ohg
Bahnhofstr. 3
Bergen 83346
866 280-52

**(G-12623)**
**HUBERGROUP USA INC (DH)**
2850 Festival Dr (60901-8937)
PHONE .................................. 815 929-9293
Martin Weber, *CEO*
Thomas Hensel, *President*
Michel Aubry, *Regional Mgr*
Bob Yontz, *Regional Mgr*
Aniruddha Joshi, *Vice Pres*
▲ **EMP:** 90
**SQ FT:** 264,000
**SALES (est):** 50.5MM
**SALES (corp-wide):** 879.3MM **Privately Held**
**WEB:** www.hostmann-steinberg.us
**SIC:** 2893 Printing ink
**HQ:** Hubergroup India Private Limited
Plot No.808/E, Phase - Ii
Valsad GUJ 39619
260 304-8000

**(G-12624)**
**IKO MIDWEST INC**
235 W South Tec Dr (60901-8426)
PHONE .................................. 815 936-9600
David Koschitzky, *President*
Ronald Healey, *Treasurer*
Michael Pinder, *Chief Acct*
Audrey Pilbean, *Human Res Mgr*
Daniel Lindehl, *Manager*
▲ **EMP:** 65
**SALES (est):** 22.6MM
**SALES (corp-wide):** 42.6MM **Privately Held**
**WEB:** www.iko.com
**SIC:** 2429 Shingle & shingle mills
**PA:** Goldis Enterprises, Inc.
120 Hay Rd
Wilmington DE 19809
302 764-3100

**(G-12625)**
**INLAND PLASTICS INC**
1310 E Birch St (60901-2621)
P.O. Box 803 (60901-0803)
PHONE .................................. 815 933-3500
John W Goudy, *President*
Lorna E Goudy, *Admin Sec*
▲ **EMP:** 6
**SQ FT:** 30,000
**SALES (est):** 495K **Privately Held**
**SIC:** 3089 Molding primary plastic

**(G-12626)**
**INSYNC MANUFACTURING LLC**
601a N 5th Ave (60901-2344)
PHONE .................................. 815 304-6300
Gregory Yates,
Terrance Yates,
▲ **EMP:** 10 **EST:** 2008
**SQ FT:** 450,000
**SALES (est):** 2.4MM **Privately Held**
**SIC:** 3599 Machine shop, jobbing & repair

**(G-12627)**
**J R SHORT MILLING COMPANY (PA)**
1580 Grinnell Rd (60901-8246)
PHONE .................................. 815 937-2635
Fax: 815 937-8806
Jon E Luikar, *President*
Craig R Petray, *Principal*
Nick Ladin, *VP Opers*
Richard Cochran, *Finance Other*
Janet Ivanic, *Human Res Mgr*
▲ **EMP:** 5 **EST:** 1910
**SALES (est):** 28.9MM **Privately Held**
**WEB:** www.shortmill.com
**SIC:** 2041 5149 Flour; corn grits & flakes, for brewers' use; hominy grits (except breakfast food); baking supplies

**(G-12628)**
**J R SHORT MILLING COMPANY**
Bunge Milling
1580 Grinnell Rd (60901-8246)
PHONE .................................. 815 937-2633
Bernard Sloan, *Division Mgr*
Dennis Bunck, *General Mgr*
Louis Johnson, *Superintendent*
Raleigh Wilkinson, *Vice Pres*
Patrick Mullady, *Maintenance Dir*
**EMP:** 120
**SALES (corp-wide):** 28.9MM **Privately Held**
**WEB:** www.shortmill.com
**SIC:** 2041 Flour & other grain mill products
**PA:** J. R. Short Milling Company
1580 Grinnell Rd
Kankakee IL 60901
815 937-2635

**(G-12629)**
**J&A MTCHELL STL FBRICATORS INC**
2524 S 8000w Rd (60901-7932)
PHONE .................................. 815 939-2144
Adam J Mitchell, *President*
Jeremy Mitchell, *Vice Pres*
David Mitchell, *Manager*
Lisa Walsh, *Admin Sec*
**EMP:** 8
**SQ FT:** 1,200
**SALES (est):** 500K **Privately Held**
**SIC:** 3499 Aerosol valves, metal

**(G-12630)**
**JOES AUTOMOTIVE INC**
560 S Washington Ave (60901-3746)
PHONE .................................. 815 937-9281
Larry Nottke, *President*
Maurice Marcotte, *Vice Pres*
**EMP:** 9
**SQ FT:** 150
**SALES (est):** 1.2MM **Privately Held**
**SIC:** 3694 7694 5531 5013 Automotive electrical equipment; electric motor repair; automotive accessories; automotive supplies

**(G-12631)**
**JOSEPH B PIGATO MD LTD**
375 N Wall St Ste P630 (60901-3495)
PHONE .................................. 815 937-2122
Dr Joseph B Pigato, *Principal*
**EMP:** 9 **EST:** 2014
**SALES (est):** 884.8K **Privately Held**
**SIC:** 2834 Drugs acting on the gastrointestinal or genitourinary system

**(G-12632)**
**KANKAKEE DAILY JOURNAL CO LLC (HQ)**
Also Called: Daily Journal, The
8 Dearborn Sq (60901-3945)
PHONE .................................. 815 937-3300
Mario Sebastiani, *General Mgr*
Brenda Montogomery, *Human Res Mgr*

---

(PA)=Parent Co  (HQ)=Headquarters  (DH)=Div Headquarters
✪ = New Business established in last 2 years

2017 Harris Illinois Industrial Directory

# Kankakee - Kankakee County (G-12633)

Nancy Ghiotto, *Manager*
Douglas McAvoy, *Manager*
Rob Small, *Manager*
**EMP:** 220 **EST:** 1853
**SQ FT:** 15,000
**SALES (est):** 21.9MM
**SALES (corp-wide):** 168.9MM **Privately Held**
**WEB:** www.daily-journal.com
**SIC:** 2711 Newspapers, publishing & printing
**PA:** Small Newspaper Group
8 Dearborn Sq
Kankakee IL 60901
815 937-3300

### (G-12633)
### KANKAKEE SPRING AND ALIGNMENT
Also Called: Kankakee Alignment
88 W Issert Dr (60901-7131)
**PHONE**.................................815 932-6718
**Fax:** 815 932-3492
Bart Azzarelli, *President*
**EMP:** 8 **EST:** 1947
**SQ FT:** 20,000
**SALES (est):** 980K **Privately Held**
**SIC:** 5531 7539 3493 Automotive parts; automotive springs, rebuilding & repair; steel springs, except wire

### (G-12634)
### KANKAKEE TENT & AWNING CO
679b W 2000s Rd (60901-7838)
**PHONE**.................................815 932-8000
**Fax:** 815 932-8020
Lee E Fredrickson, *Owner*
**EMP:** 4
**SALES (est):** 466.2K **Privately Held**
**SIC:** 7359 2394 5999 Tent & tarpaulin rental; awnings, fabric: made from purchased materials; awnings

### (G-12635)
### KEY PRINTING
111 E Court St (60901-3823)
**PHONE**.................................815 933-1800
Norman Strasma, *Owner*
**EMP:** 5
**SQ FT:** 2,420
**SALES (est):** 444K **Privately Held**
**SIC:** 3334 2789 2752 Photocopying & duplicating services; bookbinding & related work; commercial printing, lithographic

### (G-12636)
### KOERNER AVIATION INC
1520 S State Route 115 (60901-7792)
**PHONE**.................................815 932-4222
**Fax:** 815 932-1208
Roger Koerner Sr, *President*
**EMP:** 4
**SALES:** 100K **Privately Held**
**SIC:** 3599 8249 5088 7692 Machine shop, jobbing & repair; aviation school; aircraft equipment & supplies; welding repair

### (G-12637)
### LEGACY VULCAN CORP
Also Called: South Midwest Division
1277 S 7000w Rd (60901-7923)
**PHONE**.................................815 937-7928
**Fax:** 815 937-7926
Ron Baron, *Superintendent*
Kjell Oliverson, *Vice Pres*
Steve Novak, *Opers-Prdtn-Mfg*
Mike Boyda, *Sales Executive*
Tiffany Wegner, *Sales Executive*
**EMP:** 28
**SALES (corp-wide):** 3.5B **Publicly Held**
**WEB:** www.vulcanmaterials.com
**SIC:** 1442 Construction sand & gravel
**HQ:** Legacy Vulcan, Llc
1200 Urban Center Dr
Vestavia AL 35242
205 298-3000

### (G-12638)
### METZKA INC
Also Called: Woody's Ems
431 S Washington Ave (60901-3743)
**PHONE**.................................815 932-6363
**Fax:** 815 932-5474
Ronald Metzka, *President*
**EMP:** 6

**SQ FT:** 7,250
**SALES:** 450K **Privately Held**
**SIC:** 7694 5063 Electric motor repair; motors, electric

### (G-12639)
### MURPHY USA INC
503 Riverstone Pkwy (60901-7227)
**PHONE**.................................815 936-6144
**EMP:** 53 **Publicly Held**
**SIC:** 5541 1311 Gasoline service stations; crude petroleum & natural gas production
**PA:** Murphy Usa Inc.
200 E Peach St
El Dorado AR 71730

### (G-12640)
### NORTHERN ILLINOIS GAS COMPANY
Also Called: Nicor Gas
2704 Festival Dr (60901-8953)
**PHONE**.................................630 983-8676
**Fax:** 815 939-2995
Richard Stutzman, *Manager*
**EMP:** 48
**SALES (corp-wide):** 19.9B **Publicly Held**
**WEB:** www.nicor.com
**SIC:** 4924 1382 4923 Natural gas distribution; oil & gas exploration services; gas transmission & distribution
**HQ:** Northern Illinois Gas Company
1844 W Ferry Rd
Naperville IL 60563
630 983-8676

### (G-12641)
### OFFKO TOOL INC
1995 S Kensington Ave (60901-8244)
P.O. Box 1826 (60901-1826)
**PHONE**.................................815 933-9477
**Fax:** 815 933-9477
Wayne H Offerman, *President*
Charlotte Offerman, *Corp Secy*
Howard Offerman, *Manager*
**EMP:** 8
**SQ FT:** 6,000
**SALES (est):** 704K **Privately Held**
**SIC:** 3312 3469 Tool & die steel; metal stampings

### (G-12642)
### OPTECH ORTHO & PROSTH SVCS (PA)
119 E Court St Ste 100 (60901-3823)
**PHONE**.................................815 932-8564
Martin B McNab, *Principal*
**EMP:** 8
**SALES (est):** 1.3MM **Privately Held**
**SIC:** 3842 Orthopedic appliances

### (G-12643)
### PROVENA ENTERPRISES INC (HQ)
555 W Court St Ste 414 (60901-3675)
**PHONE**.................................708 478-3230
Ray Dewitte, *President*
Carol Karnitsky, *Vice Pres*
Terry S Solem, *Vice Pres*
Wendell Provest, *Human Res Dir*
Cynthia Ortiz, *Supervisor*
**EMP:** 20
**SALES (est):** 97.7K
**SALES (corp-wide):** 311K **Privately Held**
**SIC:** 2752 Commercial printing, offset
**PA:** Provena Ventures, Inc
200 E Court St Ste 200
Kankakee IL
815 933-4452

### (G-12644)
### RINGWOOD CONTAINERS LP
Also Called: Ring Can
1825 American Way (60901-9400)
**PHONE**.................................815 939-7270
Clarence Heber, *Plant Mgr*
Ronald Owen, *Branch Mgr*
Paul Simmons, *Manager*
Delores Hedge, *Exec Dir*
John Southe, *Maintence Staff*
**EMP:** 23 **Privately Held**
**SIC:** 3085 Plastics bottles
**PA:** Ringwood Containers, L.P.
1 Industrial Park
Oakland TN 38060

### (G-12645)
### RIVERSIDE MEDI-CENTER INC
Also Called: Pharmacy Store
400 N Wall St Ste 1 (60901-2965)
**PHONE**.................................815 932-6632
**Fax:** 815 935-4358
Tom Marcotte, *Manager*
**EMP:** 4
**SALES (corp-wide):** 340.2MM **Privately Held**
**SIC:** 2834 Druggists' preparations (pharmaceuticals)
**HQ:** Riverside Medi-Center, Inc
350 N Wall St
Kankakee IL 60901
815 933-1671

### (G-12646)
### ROHM AND HAAS COMPANY
Also Called: Dow Chemical
1400 Harvard Dr (60901-9462)
**PHONE**.................................815 935-7725
**Fax:** 815 933-2357
Tracy Willis, *Maintence Staff*
**EMP:** 80
**SALES (corp-wide):** 48.1B **Publicly Held**
**SIC:** 2821 Plastics materials & resins
**HQ:** Rohm And Haas Company
100 N Independence Mall W
Philadelphia PA 19106
215 592-3000

### (G-12647)
### RYAN METAL PRODUCTS INC
Also Called: Stor-Loc
880 N Washington Ave (60901-2004)
**PHONE**.................................815 936-0700
**Fax:** 815 936-0767
Michael J Ryan, *President*
Patrick Ryan, *Corp Secy*
**EMP:** 35
**SQ FT:** 12,200
**SALES (est):** 9MM **Privately Held**
**WEB:** www.storloc.com
**SIC:** 2542 Partitions & fixtures, except wood; cabinets: show, display or storage: except wood

### (G-12648)
### SHOUP MANUFACTURING CO INC
3 Stuart Dr (60901-8947)
**PHONE**.................................815 933-4439
**Fax:** 815 933-9597
Raymond Lovell, *President*
Cheryl Baber, *Vice Pres*
Bruce Smith, *Admin Sec*
◆ **EMP:** 43
**SALES (est):** 20.7MM **Privately Held**
**WEB:** www.shoupparts.com
**SIC:** 3523 5083 Farm machinery & equipment; farm equipment parts & supplies

### (G-12649)
### SIGNODE INDUSTRIAL GROUP LLC
Also Called: Plastic Packaging Systems
2150 S Us Highway 45 52 (60901-7200)
**PHONE**.................................815 939-6192
**EMP:** 39 **Privately Held**
**SIC:** 2671 Resinous impregnated paper for packaging
**HQ:** Signode Industrial Group Llc
3650 W Lake Ave
Glenview IL 60026
847 724-7500

### (G-12650)
### SIGNODE INDUSTRIAL GROUP LLC
Also Called: Angleboard
2150m S Us Highway 45 52 (60901-7200)
**PHONE**.................................815 939-0033
Lawrance Peck, *Manager*
Keith Anderson, *Manager*
**EMP:** 50 **Privately Held**
**SIC:** 2679 2631 Paper products, converted; paperboard mills
**HQ:** Signode Industrial Group Llc
3650 W Lake Ave
Glenview IL 60026
847 724-7500

### (G-12651)
### SMALL NEWSPAPER GROUP
Also Called: Daily Journal The
8 Dearborn Sq (60901-3909)
P.O. Box 250, Peotone (60468-0250)
**PHONE**.................................708 258-3410
Mary Baskerville, *Manager*
**EMP:** 3
**SALES (corp-wide):** 168.9MM **Privately Held**
**SIC:** 2711 Newspapers
**PA:** Small Newspaper Group
8 Dearborn Sq
Kankakee IL 60901
815 937-3300

### (G-12652)
### SMALL NEWSPAPER GROUP (PA)
Also Called: Journal
8 Dearborn Sq (60901-3909)
P.O. Box 632 (60901-0632)
**PHONE**.................................815 937-3300
**Fax:** 815 937-3301
Len R Small, *President*
Bryan Corbin, *Sls & Mktg Exec*
Joseph Lacaeyse, *Treasurer*
Edward Yucis, *Controller*
Douglas McAvoy, *Manager*
**EMP:** 200
**SQ FT:** 15,000
**SALES (corp-wide):** 168.9MM **Privately Held**
**SIC:** 2711 2791 2752 Newspapers, publishing & printing; typesetting; commercial printing, lithographic

### (G-12653)
### STARMONT MANUFACTURING CO
655 S Harrison Ave (60901-5107)
**PHONE**.................................815 939-1041
Arthur W Schumacher, *President*
Tamara K Diorio, *Corp Secy*
**EMP:** 7
**SQ FT:** 17,000
**SALES (est):** 420K **Privately Held**
**SIC:** 3444 3599 3469 Concrete forms, sheet metal; machine shop, jobbing & repair; metal stampings

### (G-12654)
### STEELFAB INC
2045 S Kensington Ave (60901-7100)
**PHONE**.................................815 935-6540
Matt McLaren, *President*
Martha McLaren, *Vice Pres*
Celeste Noel, *Manager*
**EMP:** 20
**SQ FT:** 40,000
**SALES (est):** 6.1MM **Privately Held**
**SIC:** 3441 Fabricated structural metal

### (G-12655)
### SUN CHEMICAL CORPORATION
3200 Festival Dr (60901-8945)
**PHONE**.................................815 939-0136
**Fax:** 815 939-9833
Carl Donaldson, *Opers Mgr*
Jeff Gallis Torfer, *Manager*
**EMP:** 52
**SALES (corp-wide):** 6.7B **Privately Held**
**WEB:** www.sunchemical.com
**SIC:** 2893 Printing ink
**HQ:** Sun Chemical Corporation
35 Waterview Blvd Ste 100
Parsippany NJ 07054
973 404-6000

### (G-12656)
### TAIT MACHINE TOOL INC
417 S Schuyler Ave (60901-5131)
P.O. Box 134 (60901-0134)
**PHONE**.................................815 932-2011
**Fax:** 815 932-2011
Louis Schuh, *President*
Eric Thompson, *Vice Pres*
**EMP:** 6
**SQ FT:** 4,800
**SALES (est):** 550K **Privately Held**
**WEB:** www.tmadeproducts.com
**SIC:** 3599 7692 Machine shop, jobbing & repair; welding repair

# GEOGRAPHIC SECTION

**(G-12657)**
**VALSPAR CORPORATION**
901 N Greenwood Ave (60901-2100)
**PHONE**..................................815 933-5561
**Fax:** 815 936-7811
Forrest Davis, *Production*
Annelies Esch, *Purch Mgr*
Michael Sawayda, *Purch Mgr*
Shane Ponton, *Buyer*
Nathan Kuhlemeier, *Engineer*
**EMP:** 160
**SALES (corp-wide):** 11.8B **Publicly Held**
**SIC: 2851** Paints & allied products
**HQ:** The Valspar Corporation
  1101 S 3rd St
  Minneapolis MN 55415
  612 851-7000

**(G-12658)**
**WEST LABORATORIES INC**
1305 Harvard Dr (60901-9473)
**PHONE**..................................815 935-1630
**Fax:** 815 935-9934
Gary West, *President*
Scott West, *Vice Pres*
Jay West, *Treasurer*
Debbie Jensen, *Manager*
Dana West, *Admin Sec*
▼ **EMP:** 22
**SQ FT:** 20,000
**SALES:** 4.9MM **Privately Held**
**SIC: 2836** Plasmas; serums

## Kansas
### Edgar County

**(G-12659)**
**CROP PRODUCTION SERVICES INC**
3240 Il Highway 16 (61933-6220)
**PHONE**..................................217 466-5430
Bob Calles, *Manager*
Robert Calles, *Manager*
**EMP:** 9
**SALES (corp-wide):** 13.6B **Privately Held**
**WEB:** www.cropproductionservices.com
**SIC: 2879** Agricultural chemicals
**HQ:** Crop Production Services, Inc.
  3005 Rocky Mountain Ave
  Loveland CO 80538
  970 685-3300

## Keensburg
### Wabash County

**(G-12660)**
**ALPHA NATURAL RESOURCES INC**
Also Called: Wabash Mines
1000 Beall Woods Dr (62852)
**PHONE**..................................618 298-2394
**Fax:** 618 298-2620
Randall Scott, *Div Sub Head*
William A Kelly, *Manager*
**EMP:** 205
**SALES (corp-wide):** 186.9MM **Privately Held**
**SIC: 1221** 1222 Bituminous coal & lignite-surface mining; bituminous coal-underground mining
**HQ:** Alpha Natural Resources, Inc. Anr, Inc
  1989 E Stone Dr
  Kingsport TN 37660
  423 723-8900

## Kempton
### Ford County

**(G-12661)**
**ADVENTURES UNLIMITED (PA)**
Also Called: World Explorer
303 Main St (60946-4115)
P.O. Box 74 (60946-0074)
**PHONE**..................................815 253-6390
**Fax:** 815 253-6300
David Childress, *Owner*
Jennifer Bolm, *Co-Owner*
**EMP:** 5
**SALES (est):** 450K **Privately Held**
**SIC: 2731** 5961 Books: publishing only; books, mail order (except book clubs)

## Kenilworth
### Cook County

**(G-12662)**
**C2 WATER INC**
732 Cummings Ave (60043-1013)
**PHONE**..................................312 550-1159
Kevin Buzard, *President*
**EMP:** 4
**SALES:** 822.2K **Privately Held**
**SIC: 3589** Water treatment equipment, industrial

**(G-12663)**
**SHERWIN-WILLIAMS COMPANY**
Also Called: Sherwin Williams Paint Store
614 Green Bay Rd (60043-1003)
**PHONE**..................................847 251-6115
**Fax:** 847 251-6177
**EMP:** 4
**SALES (corp-wide):** 11.8B **Publicly Held**
**SIC: 5231** 3991 Paint & painting supplies; push brooms
**PA:** The Sherwin-Williams Company
  101 W Prospect Ave # 1020
  Cleveland OH 44115
  216 566-2000

## Kenney
### De Witt County

**(G-12664)**
**SCHNEIDER PIPE ORGANS INC**
104 S Johnston St (61749-9615)
P.O. Box 137 (61749-0137)
**PHONE**..................................217 871-4807
**Fax:** 217 668-2232
Richard M Schneider, *President*
Joan Schneider, *Admin Sec*
**EMP:** 6 **EST:** 1976
**SQ FT:** 20,000
**SALES (est):** 350K **Privately Held**
**WEB:** www.schneiderpipeorgans.com
**SIC: 3931** 7699 Musical instruments, electric & electronic; organ tuning & repair

## Kent
### Stephenson County

**(G-12665)**
**B T BROWN MANUFACTURING**
14871 E Airport Rd (61044-9707)
**PHONE**..................................815 947-3633
Brian T Brown, *Owner*
**EMP:** 3
**SALES:** 200K **Privately Held**
**SIC: 7692** 3523 Welding repair; farm machinery & equipment

**(G-12666)**
**NUESTRO QUESO LLC**
752 N Kent Rd (61044-9636)
P.O. Box 101 (61044-0101)
**PHONE**..................................815 443-2100
Anthony Andrate, *Branch Mgr*
**EMP:** 135 **Privately Held**
**SIC: 2022** Cheese, natural & processed
**PA:** Nuestro Queso, Llc
  9500 Bryn Mawr Ave
  Rosemont IL 60018

## Kewanee
### Henry County

**(G-12667)**
**ACCESSING YOUR ABILITIES INC**
733 S Chestnut St (61443-2809)
**PHONE**..................................309 761-4016
George Giesenhagen, *CEO*
Gerard Rux, *President*
Louis Little, *Vice Pres*
Dean Tetty, *Vice Pres*
John Kolata, *CFO*
**EMP:** 6 **EST:** 2007
**SQ FT:** 22,000
**SALES (est):** 520K **Privately Held**
**SIC: 3841** Surgical & medical instruments

**(G-12668)**
**ADVANCE METALWORKING COMPANY**
Also Called: Lo Riser Trailers
3726 Us Highway 34 (61443-8315)
**PHONE**..................................309 853-3387
**Fax:** 309 853-3389
Leonard Kull, *Ch of Bd*
Richard D Kull, *President*
Annette K Kull, *Corp Secy*
Denis Shenaut, *Purch Mgr*
Lucretia Sloan, *Technology*
▲ **EMP:** 20 **EST:** 1955
**SQ FT:** 33,000
**SALES (est):** 4.5MM **Privately Held**
**WEB:** www.hdm-tamco.com
**SIC: 3799** Trailers & trailer equipment

**(G-12669)**
**AMERICAN STEEL CARPORTS INC**
832 N East St (61443-1516)
**PHONE**..................................800 487-4010
**Fax:** 309 853-1805
Melton Castillo, *Manager*
**EMP:** 15
**SALES (corp-wide):** 25.2MM **Privately Held**
**SIC: 3448** Carports: prefabricated metal
**PA:** American Steel Carports, Inc.
  457 N Brwy St
  Joshua TX 76058
  866 471-8761

**(G-12670)**
**BAILLEU & BAILLEU PRINTING INC**
Also Called: B & B Printing
214 S Main St Ste A (61443-4006)
**PHONE**..................................309 852-2517
**Fax:** 309 854-7748
Robert Bailleu, *President*
Leann Bailleu, *Admin Sec*
**EMP:** 8 **EST:** 1978
**SQ FT:** 10,000
**SALES (est):** 1.4MM **Privately Held**
**SIC: 2752** 2759 2791 2789 Commercial printing, offset; screen printing; typesetting; bookbinding & related work; automotive & apparel trimmings

**(G-12671)**
**BLUE CHIP INDUSTRIES INC**
Also Called: International Polymers
1134 W South St (61443-8357)
P.O. Box 383 (61443-0383)
**PHONE**..................................309 854-7100
**Fax:** 309 854-7300
Larry R Van Daele, *President*
Tammy Johnson, *Purch Mgr*
Toni Wells, *Office Mgr*
**EMP:** 10
**SALES (est):** 660K **Privately Held**
**WEB:** www.bluechip-il.com
**SIC: 3599** Machine shop, jobbing & repair

**(G-12672)**
**BOSS BALLOON COMPANY INC**
1221 Page St (61443-3241)
**PHONE**..................................309 852-2131
Bruce Lancaster, *President*
Steve Pont, *Vice Pres*
**EMP:** 5
**SQ FT:** 15,700
**SALES (est):** 403.5K **Publicly Held**
**WEB:** www.bossballoon.com
**SIC: 3069** Balloons, advertising & toy: rubber
**HQ:** Boss Manufacturing Company Inc
  1221 Page St
  Kewanee IL 61443
  309 852-2131

**(G-12673)**
**BOSS HOLDINGS INC (PA)**
1221 Page St (61443-3241)
**PHONE**..................................309 852-2131
**Fax:** 309 852-0260
G Louis Graziadio III, *Ch of Bd*
John Wicker, *Vice Pres*
Sumner Cohen, *Purchasing*
Steven G Pont, *VP Finance*
Josh Miskinis, *Mktg Dir*
▲ **EMP:** 70
**SQ FT:** 70,000
**SALES (est):** 68.3MM **Publicly Held**
**WEB:** www.bossholdings.com
**SIC: 2381** 3151 2385 3069 Gloves, work: woven or knit, made from purchased materials; gloves, leather: work; waterproof outerwear; balloons, advertising & toy: rubber

**(G-12674)**
**BOSS MANUFACTURING COMPANY (DH)**
1221 Page St (61443-3241)
**PHONE**..................................309 852-2131
**Fax:** 309 852-0848
G Louis Graziadio III, *President*
Steven Pont, *Vice Pres*
John Wohlrav, *Plant Mgr*
Dave Oliesger, *Controller*
Diane Ogorcaled, *VP Finance*
▲ **EMP:** 80
**SQ FT:** 80,000
**SALES (est):** 60.5MM **Publicly Held**
**WEB:** www.bossgloves.com
**SIC: 3151** Gloves, leather: work
**HQ:** Boss Manufacturing Holdings Inc
  1221 Page St
  Kewanee IL 61443
  309 852-2781

**(G-12675)**
**BOSS MANUFACTURING HOLDINGS (HQ)**
1221 Page St (61443-3241)
**PHONE**..................................309 852-2781
Bruce Lancaster, *CFO*
Beverly Williams, *Manager*
▲ **EMP:** 10
**SALES (est):** 60.5MM **Publicly Held**
**SIC: 2381** 3151 3842 3949 Fabric dress & work gloves; leather gloves & mittens; gloves, safety; gloves, sport & athletic: boxing, handball, etc.; waterproof outerwear; boot or shoe products, plastic

**(G-12676)**
**BOSS MANUFACTURING HOLDINGS**
Warren Pet Products
1221 Page St (61443-3241)
**PHONE**..................................309 852-2131
Bruce Lancaster, *President*
Diana Ogorzalek, *Administration*
**EMP:** 4 **Publicly Held**
**SIC: 3999** Pet supplies
**HQ:** Boss Manufacturing Holdings Inc
  1221 Page St
  Kewanee IL 61443
  309 852-2781

**(G-12677)**
**BREEDLOVE SPORTING GOODS INC (PA)**
Also Called: Breedlove's
123 W 2nd St (61443-2259)
**PHONE**..................................309 852-2434
**Fax:** 309 852-3333
William Breedlove, *President*
Debbie Breedlove, *Corp Secy*
Daniel Breedlove, *Vice Pres*
Catherine E Breedlove, *Shareholder*
**EMP:** 10
**SQ FT:** 3,500
**SALES (est):** 3.3MM **Privately Held**
**SIC: 5941** 2396 Sporting goods & bicycle shops; screen printing on fabric articles

**(G-12678)**
**BREEDLOVE SPORTING GOODS INC**
215 W 2nd St (61443-2149)
**PHONE**..................................309 852-2434
William Breedlove, *President*
**EMP:** 10
**SALES (corp-wide):** 3.3MM **Privately Held**
**SIC: 5941** 2396 Sporting goods & bicycle shops; screen printing on fabric articles

# Kewanee - Henry County (G-12679)

PA: Breedlove Sporting Goods, Inc.
123 W 2nd St
Kewanee IL 61443
309 852-2434

### (G-12679)
### DIERZEN-KEWANEE HEAVY INDS
101 Franklin St (61443-2608)
P.O. Box 524 (61443-0524)
**PHONE**.................309 853-2316
Louie Dierzen, *Owner*
**EMP:** 80
**SALES (est):** 2MM **Privately Held**
**SIC:** 7532 3711 Truck painting & lettering; truck tractors for highway use, assembly of

### (G-12680)
### DOOLEY BROTHERS PLUMBING & HTG
306 N Tremont St (61443-2240)
P.O. Box 312 (61443-0312)
**PHONE**.................309 852-2720
**Fax:** 309 852-2777
Patrick J Dooley, *President*
Dorothy Ann Dooley, *Vice Pres*
Irene Dooley, *Manager*
**EMP:** 8
**SALES (est):** 1.4MM **Privately Held**
**SIC:** 3494 7539 Plumbing & heating valves; electrical services

### (G-12681)
### ELM STREET INDUSTRIES INC
Also Called: R & T Enterprises
206 W 4th St (61443-2132)
**PHONE**.................309 854-7000
Fred Butcher, *Manager*
**EMP:** 14
**SALES (corp-wide):** 4.7MM **Privately Held**
**SIC:** 2441 2449 5731 2653 Boxes, wood; food containers, wood: wirebound; sound equipment, automotive; corrugated & solid fiber boxes; wood television & radio cabinets
**PA:** Elm Street Industries, Inc.
1310 Elm Pl
Kelso WA
360 423-1840

### (G-12682)
### EXCELLED SHEEPSKIN & LEA COAT
1700 Burlington Ave (61443-3200)
**PHONE**.................309 852-3341
Phil Dubow, *Division Mgr*
Dennis Carreau, *Manager*
Sharon Russell, *Manager*
Leatha Moon, *Executive*
**EMP:** 130
**SALES (corp-wide):** 81.2MM **Privately Held**
**WEB:** www.leathercoatsetc.com
**SIC:** 2386 3111 2311 Coats & jackets, leather & sheep-lined; leather tanning & finishing; men's & boys' suits & coats
**PA:** Excelled Sheepskin & Leather Coat Corp
1400 Broadway Fl 31
New York NY 10018
212 594-5843

### (G-12683)
### EXCELLED SHEEPSKIN & LEA COAT
1700 Burlington Ave (61443-3200)
**PHONE**.................309 852-3341
Dennis Carreau, *Branch Mgr*
**EMP:** 20
**SALES (corp-wide):** 81.2MM **Privately Held**
**WEB:** www.leathercoatsetc.com
**SIC:** 2386 2371 Coats & jackets, leather & sheep-lined; fur goods
**PA:** Excelled Sheepskin & Leather Coat Corp
1400 Broadway Fl 31
New York NY 10018
212 594-5843

### (G-12684)
### FLEX COURT INTERNATIONAL INC
Also Called: Flex Court Electronic
4328 Us Highway 34 (61443-8317)
P.O. Box 741 (61443-0741)
**PHONE**.................309 852-0899
**Fax:** 309 852-2499
Mats Jonmarker, *President*
Teri Jonmarker, *Vice Pres*
Robyn Resch, *Accountant*
▼ **EMP:** 12
**SQ FT:** 10,000
**SALES (est):** 1.2MM **Privately Held**
**WEB:** www.flexcourt.com
**SIC:** 3949 Sporting & athletic goods

### (G-12685)
### FRED STOLLENWERK
Also Called: Central Welding Shop
801 Elmwood Ave (61443-3039)
**PHONE**.................309 852-3794
Fred Stollenwerk, *Owner*
**EMP:** 1
**SALES:** 360K **Privately Held**
**SIC:** 7692 Welding repair

### (G-12686)
### GATEHOUSE MEDIA LLC
Also Called: Kewanee Star Courier
105 E Central Blvd (61443-2245)
P.O. Box A (61443-0836)
**PHONE**.................309 852-2181
**Fax:** 309 852-0010
Stu Griffith, *Principal*
Mike Landis, *Editor*
Margi Washburn, *Editor*
Janice Nugent, *Marketing Staff*
Mike Berry, *Assoc Editor*
**EMP:** 15
**SALES (corp-wide):** 1.2B **Publicly Held**
**WEB:** www.gatehousemedia.com
**SIC:** 2711 Newspapers: publishing only, not printed on site
**HQ:** Gatehouse Media, Llc
175 Sullys Trl Ste 300
Pittsford NY 14534
585 598-0030

### (G-12687)
### GREAT DANE LIMITED PARTNERSHIP
324 N Main St (61443-2226)
P.O. Box 364 (61443-0364)
**PHONE**.................309 854-0407
Nick Johnson, *Manager*
**EMP:** 175
**SALES (corp-wide):** 1.4B **Privately Held**
**WEB:** www.greatdanetrailers.com
**SIC:** 3715 Semitrailers for truck tractors
**HQ:** Great Dane Limited Partnership
222 N Lasalle St Ste 920
Chicago IL 60601

### (G-12688)
### GREAT DANE LIMITED PARTNERSHIP
Also Called: Great Dane Trlrs-Kewanee Plant
2006 Kentville Rd (61443-1714)
**PHONE**.................309 854-0407
Chris Stolfe, *Manager*
**EMP:** 309
**SALES (corp-wide):** 1.4B **Privately Held**
**SIC:** 3715 Truck trailers; demountable cargo containers
**HQ:** Great Dane Limited Partnership
222 N Lasalle St Ste 920
Chicago IL 60601

### (G-12689)
### GREAT DANE LIMITED PARTNERSHIP
Also Called: Pines Trailer
2006 Kentville Rd (61443-1714)
**PHONE**.................773 254-5533
**Fax:** 309 853-1546
Brady Jones, *Plant Mgr*
Chris Stolfe, *Manager*
Chuck Kunz, *Manager*
David Wates, *Manager*
**EMP:** 81
**SALES (corp-wide):** 1.4B **Privately Held**
**WEB:** www.greatdanetrailers.com
**SIC:** 3715 5511 Semitrailers for truck tractors; trucks, tractors & trailers: new & used
**HQ:** Great Dane Limited Partnership
222 N Lasalle St Ste 920
Chicago IL 60601

### (G-12690)
### HEARTFELT GIFTS INC
Also Called: Heartfelt Framing Gallery
224 N Main St (61443-2224)
**PHONE**.................309 852-2296
**Fax:** 309 856-5904
Susan Sagmoen, *President*
**EMP:** 4
**SQ FT:** 4,500
**SALES (est):** 200K **Privately Held**
**SIC:** 5947 2253 5999 Gift shop; knit outerwear mills; picture frames, ready made

### (G-12691)
### K D INDUSTRIES ILLINOIS INC
1134 W South St (61443-8357)
P.O. Box 383 (61443-0383)
**PHONE**.................309 854-7100
Roy J Carver Jr, *President*
Melanie Stabler, *General Mgr*
Larry Van Daele, *Principal*
**EMP:** 8
**SALES (est):** 250K **Privately Held**
**SIC:** 3599 Machine & other job shop work

### (G-12692)
### L & M MANUFACTURING INC
101 Franklin St (61443-2608)
**PHONE**.................309 734-3009
Thomas Lawson, *President*
**EMP:** 12 **EST:** 1995
**SALES:** 2MM **Privately Held**
**SIC:** 3713 Specialty motor vehicle bodies

### (G-12693)
### MIDWEST TRAILER MFG LLC
2000 Kentville Rd (61443-1714)
**PHONE**.................309 897-8216
James Hunt, *President*
Adam T Endress, *Principal*
**EMP:** 5 **EST:** 2015
**SALES (est):** 244.7K **Privately Held**
**SIC:** 3792 Trailer coaches, automobile

### (G-12694)
### RHINO TOOL COMPANY
Also Called: Ground Cover Marketing
620 Andrews Ave (61443-3809)
P.O. Box 111 (61443-0111)
**PHONE**.................309 853-5555
**Fax:** 309 856-5905
James Martin, *President*
Herb Whitmer, *Mfg Staff*
Ruth Appleton, *Bookkeeper*
R B Matin, *Data Proc Staff*
Julie Martin, *Admin Sec*
▲ **EMP:** 11 **EST:** 1975
**SQ FT:** 10,000
**SALES (est):** 3.9MM **Privately Held**
**WEB:** www.rhinotool.com
**SIC:** 3531 3594 3566 3546 Construction machinery; fluid power pumps & motors; speed changers, drives & gears; power-driven handtools; industrial valves; hand & edge tools

### (G-12695)
### TRIANGLE CONCRETE CO INC
Also Called: Kewanee Triangle Concrete
1201 New St (61443-1841)
**PHONE**.................309 853-4334
Thomas Ratliff, *President*
Tom Kazubowski, *Plant Mgr*
William Leaf, *Admin Sec*
**EMP:** 4 **EST:** 1961
**SQ FT:** 1,300
**SALES:** 200K **Privately Held**
**SIC:** 3273 Ready-mixed concrete

## Keyesport
### Clinton County

### (G-12696)
### KEYESPORT MANUFACTURING INC
1610 Mulberry St (62253-2140)
**PHONE**.................618 749-5510
**Fax:** 618 749-5572
Charlie Kern, *President*
Glenda Kern, *Treasurer*
**EMP:** 5
**SQ FT:** 18,360
**SALES (est):** 639.6K **Privately Held**
**SIC:** 3993 Electric signs

## Kilbourne
### Mason County

### (G-12697)
### HARDWOOD LUMBER PRODUCTS CO
21046 E Cr 800n (62655-6547)
**PHONE**.................309 538-4411
**Fax:** 309 538-4279
Gary Hodgson, *Partner*
Todd Hodgson, *Partner*
**EMP:** 5
**SALES:** 1MM **Privately Held**
**SIC:** 2448 2426 Pallets, wood; furniture dimension stock, hardwood

### (G-12698)
### SUNRISE AG SERVICE COMPANY
Rr 1 (62655)
**PHONE**.................309 538-4287
Mike Willing, *Manager*
**EMP:** 7
**SALES (corp-wide):** 96.9MM **Privately Held**
**SIC:** 2873 Nitrogenous fertilizers
**PA:** Sunrise Ag Service Company
104 S 1st St
Easton IL 62633
309 562-7296

## Kildeer
### Lake County

### (G-12699)
### DRYWEAR APPAREL LLC
21231 W Brandon Rd (60047-8619)
**PHONE**.................847 687-8540
Peter Durment,
**EMP:** 6
**SALES (est):** 352.3K **Privately Held**
**SIC:** 2321 7389 Men's & boys' sports & polo shirts;

### (G-12700)
### INTEREXPO LTD
Also Called: Mobileskin Imaging
22438 N Clayton Ct (60047-7947)
**PHONE**.................847 489-7056
George Webb, *President*
**EMP:** 16 **EST:** 2007
**SALES:** 700K **Privately Held**
**SIC:** 3845 5047 5999 Electromedical equipment; electro-medical equipment; medical apparatus & supplies

### (G-12701)
### LBE LTD
21038 N Andover Rd (60047-8604)
P.O. Box 1852, Palatine (60078-1852)
**PHONE**.................847 907-4959
Loyd Bostic, *President*
Claudia Bostic, *Admin Sec*
**EMP:** 4
**SQ FT:** 1,000
**SALES:** 100K **Privately Held**
**SIC:** 7372 7389 Utility computer software; financial services

# GEOGRAPHIC SECTION

**La Grange - Cook County (G-12726)**

**(G-12702)**
**MARKET CONNECT INC**
21616 Cambridge Dr (60047-2978)
PHONE.................847 726-6788
James F Meister Jr, *President*
EMP: 3
SALES (est): 288.7K Privately Held
SIC: 2759 5199 Advertising literature: printing; packaging materials

**(G-12703)**
**SANCO INDUSTRIES INC**
21800 N Andover Rd (60047-8523)
PHONE.................847 243-8675
Fax: 847 634-9920
Edwin Sanchez, *President*
Edward Sanchez, *President*
Dina E Pine, *Accounts Mgr*
EMP: 15
SQ FT: 14,000
SALES (est): 2MM Privately Held
WEB: www.sanco.com
SIC: 3965 3495 5072 3496 Fasteners; wire springs; bolts; nuts (hardware); rivets; miscellaneous fabricated wire products; bolts, nuts, rivets & washers

**(G-12704)**
**SHOELACE INC**
20505 Rand Rd Ste 218 (60047-3004)
PHONE.................847 854-2500
Robert J Guss, *President*
EMP: 6
SALES (corp-wide): 388.5K Privately Held
SIC: 2241 Narrow fabric mills
PA: Shoelace, Inc.
23 N Williams St
Crystal Lake IL 60014
847 854-2500

## Kings
*Ogle County*

**(G-12705)**
**SPRING SPECIALIST CORPORATION**
14400 E Dutch Rd (61068-4535)
PHONE.................815 562-7991
John Nichols, *President*
Wesley Nichols, *Vice Pres*
Nancy G Nichols, *Admin Sec*
EMP: 8
SQ FT: 5,000
SALES (est): 1.2MM Privately Held
WEB: www.springspecialists.com
SIC: 3495 3496 3493 Mechanical springs; precision; miscellaneous fabricated wire products; steel springs, except wire

## Kingston
*Dekalb County*

**(G-12706)**
**DECAL WORKS LLC**
2021 Johnson Ct (60145-8345)
PHONE.................815 784-4000
Ron Joynt, *President*
Ken Decalmx, *Opers Staff*
▲ EMP: 25
SQ FT: 12,000
SALES (est): 3.3MM Privately Held
SIC: 2759 Screen printing

**(G-12707)**
**NEWERA SOFTWARE INC**
9505 Wolf Rd (60145-8169)
PHONE.................815 784-3345
Glennon Bagsby, *President*
Mary King, *Office Mgr*
EMP: 9
SALES (est): 554.2K Privately Held
WEB: www.newera.com
SIC: 7372 Prepackaged software

**(G-12708)**
**US CHROME CORP ILLINOIS**
United States Chrome
305 Herbert Rd (60145-7008)
PHONE.................815 544-3487
John Leahy, *Manager*
EMP: 20
SALES (corp-wide): 30.4MM Privately Held
SIC: 3471 Electroplating of metals or formed products; chromium plating of metals or formed products
HQ: U.S. Chrome Corporation Of Illinois
175 Garfield Ave
Stratford CT
203 378-9622

## Kinmundy
*Marion County*

**(G-12709)**
**DEEP ROCK ENERGY CORPORATION**
7601 Oleary Rd (62854-2621)
PHONE.................618 548-2779
Benny D Webster, *President*
EMP: 20
SALES (est): 1.6MM Privately Held
SIC: 1389 Building oil & gas well foundations on site

**(G-12710)**
**GESELL OIL WELL SERVICE LLC**
101 S Adams St (62854-1987)
P.O. Box 127 (62854-0127)
PHONE.................618 547-7114
Connie Chasteen, *Mng Member*
Teresa Rankin,
EMP: 6
SALES (est): 444.6K Privately Held
SIC: 1389 Cleaning wells; servicing oil & gas wells

## Kirkland
*Dekalb County*

**(G-12711)**
**DIVISION 5 METALS INC**
2314 Old State Rd (60146-8724)
P.O. Box 52, Esmond (60129-0052)
PHONE.................815 901-5001
Timothy Gulotta, *President*
EMP: 8
SALES (est): 1.2MM Privately Held
SIC: 3531 Construction machinery

**(G-12712)**
**F LEE CHARLES & SONS INC**
1473 Flora Church Rd (60146-8122)
PHONE.................815 547-7141
Fax: 815 544-0035
Eunice V Lee, *President*
Clara L Chilson, *Admin Sec*
EMP: 7
SQ FT: 200
SALES (est): 625.7K Privately Held
SIC: 1771 1794 1411 3281 Blacktop (asphalt) work; excavation & grading, building construction; dimension stone; cut stone & stone products

**(G-12713)**
**IL GREEN PASTURES FIBER CO-OP**
28668 Bell Rd (60146-8736)
PHONE.................815 751-0887
Connie Gustafson, *Treasurer*
EMP: 3
SALES (est): 198.2K Privately Held
SIC: 3661 Fiber optics communications equipment

**(G-12714)**
**KIRKLAND SAWMILL INC**
606 W Main St (60146)
P.O. Box 245 (60146-0245)
PHONE.................815 522-6150
Ronald Sester, *President*
Gayle Sester, *Vice Pres*
Thomas Michael, *Treasurer*
Ronald Michael, *Admin Sec*
EMP: 3
SQ FT: 18,800
SALES (est): 274.8K Privately Held
SIC: 2421 Sawmills & planing mills, general

**(G-12715)**
**NESTEROWICZ & ASSOCIATES INC**
313 W Main St (60146-8438)
P.O. Box 50 (60146-0050)
PHONE.................815 522-4469
Fax: 815 522-4468
Phillip A Nesterowicz, *President*
Nancy S Nesterowicz, *Corp Secy*
EMP: 6
SQ FT: 8,000
SALES (est): 1MM Privately Held
SIC: 1761 3444 Architectural sheet metal work; sheet metalwork

**(G-12716)**
**R B MANUFACTURING INC**
140 North St (60146-8610)
P.O. Box 490 (60146-0490)
PHONE.................815 522-3100
Fax: 815 522-3131
Don Nichols, *President*
Norma Allen, *Plant Mgr*
▲ EMP: 20
SQ FT: 4,200
SALES (est): 429K Privately Held
WEB: www.rbmanufacturing.com
SIC: 3672 3679 Printed circuit boards; parametric amplifiers

**(G-12717)**
**RB MANUFACTURING & ELECTRONICS**
Also Called: Edge Electronics
140 North St (60146-8610)
P.O. Box 490 (60146-0490)
PHONE.................815 522-3100
Donald J Nichols, *President*
Sonya Monnie, *Office Mgr*
▲ EMP: 31
SQ FT: 5,000
SALES: 4MM Privately Held
SIC: 3672 Circuit boards, television & radio printed

**(G-12718)**
**SHAPE-MASTER TOOL CO**
801 W Main St (60146-8465)
P.O. Box 520 (60146-0520)
PHONE.................815 522-6186
Fax: 815 522-6229
Don Spolum Jr, *President*
Glenn Spolum, *Vice Pres*
Scott Chambers, *Purch Dir*
Brett Young, *Natl Sales Mgr*
▲ EMP: 30
SALES (est): 5.5MM Privately Held
WEB: www.shapemastertool.com
SIC: 3545 Diamond cutting tools for turning, boring, burnishing, etc.

**(G-12719)**
**TAMMS INDUSTRIES INC**
3835 Il Route 72 (60146-8635)
PHONE.................815 522-3394
Fax: 815 522-3257
M Thomas McCall, *President*
Moorman Scott, *Exec VP*
Jackie Ray, *Vice Pres*
Stephen Scarpinato, *Vice Pres*
Doug White, *Plant Mgr*
EMP: 63
SQ FT: 80,000
SALES (est): 12.3MM Privately Held
WEB: www.tamms.com
SIC: 2851 2899 5211 Paints & allied products; waterproofing compounds; masonry materials & supplies

**(G-12720)**
**THE EUCLID CHEMICAL COMPANY**
Also Called: Epoxy Chemicals
3835 State Route 72 (60146-8635)
PHONE.................815 522-2308
Brad Nemunaitis, *Principal*
Ralph Gosorn, *Controller*
Heath Morrall, *Sales Staff*
Stephen Scarpinato, *VP Mktg*
Doug Cole, *Info Tech Mgr*
EMP: 11
SALES (corp-wide): 4.8B Publicly Held
WEB: www.epoxychemicals.com
SIC: 2899 Chemical preparations; concrete curing & hardening compounds
HQ: The Euclid Chemical Company
19218 Redwood Rd
Cleveland OH 44110
800 321-7628

## Knoxville
*Knox County*

**(G-12721)**
**KASER POWER EQUIPMENT INC**
480 Henderson Rd (61448-1066)
P.O. Box 216 (61448-0216)
PHONE.................309 289-2176
Fax: 309 289-8909
David Kaser, *President*
Carla Kaser, *Vice Pres*
EMP: 5
SQ FT: 1,680
SALES (est): 450K Privately Held
WEB: www.kaserglassstudio.com
SIC: 5261 7699 5251 5084 Garden supplies & tools; general household repair services; door locks & lock sets; engines, gasoline; saws & sawing equipment

**(G-12722)**
**OLD BLUE ILLINOIS INC**
Also Called: Old Blue Construction
1277 Knox Road 1600 N (61448-9565)
PHONE.................309 289-7921
Laura Collins, *Principal*
Matt Jenkins, *Vice Pres*
Justin Bush, *Treasurer*
Rick Collins, *Admin Sec*
EMP: 15
SQ FT: 1,750
SALES (est): 2MM Privately Held
WEB: www.trilliumdell.com
SIC: 1521 2511 0782 Single-family housing construction; wood household furniture; landscape contractors

**(G-12723)**
**RING SHEET METAL HEATING & AC**
213 Grove St (61448-1227)
PHONE.................309 289-4213
Jon Nelson, *Owner*
EMP: 3 EST: 2001
SALES (est): 242.6K Privately Held
SIC: 1711 3585 Warm air heating & air conditioning contractor; ventilation & duct work contractor; refrigeration & heating equipment

## La Grange
*Cook County*

**(G-12724)**
**ADVANCED WELDING SERVICES**
8250 School St (60525-5227)
PHONE.................630 759-3334
Fax: 708 246-9516
Skip Meyers, *President*
EMP: 7
SALES (est): 270.5K Privately Held
SIC: 7692 Welding repair

**(G-12725)**
**ANDREWS CONVERTING LLC**
707 E 47th St (60525-3069)
PHONE.................708 352-2555
James Andrews, *President*
Scott Andrews, *Vice Pres*
Debbie Ballard, *Manager*
EMP: 38
SQ FT: 33,000
SALES: 4.7MM Privately Held
SIC: 2675 Die-cut paper & board

**(G-12726)**
**BLUE PEARL STONE TECH LLC**
333 Washington Ave (60525-6831)
PHONE.................708 698-5700
Fax: 708 698-5689

# La Grange - Cook County (G-12727)

John Ervin, *Mfg Staff*
Terresa Fister, *Mng Member*
Fister Terresa, *Manager*
**EMP:** 5
**SALES (est):** 471.7K **Privately Held**
**SIC:** 8731 1411 3272 Commercial physical research; granite dimension stone; art marble, concrete

## (G-12727)
### BOYER CORPORATION
9600 W Ogden Ave (60525)
**PHONE** .................. 708 352-2553
Harold Hurwitz, *President*
**EMP:** 2
**SQ FT:** 5,000
**SALES (est):** 263.7K **Privately Held**
**WEB:** www.boyercorporation.com
**SIC:** 2842 2992 2819 Specialty cleaning preparations; cleaning or polishing preparations; drain pipe solvents or cleaners; lubricating oils & greases; industrial inorganic chemicals

## (G-12728)
### BUDGET SIGN
930 S Kensington Ave (60525-2711)
**PHONE** .................. 708 354-7512
Lawrence Guenther, *Principal*
**EMP:** 3
**SALES (est):** 201.1K **Privately Held**
**SIC:** 3993 Signs & advertising specialties

## (G-12729)
### CONNOMAC CORPORATION
340 Washington Ave (60525-6869)
**PHONE** .................. 708 482-3434
**Fax:** 708 352-3067
Gregory McDonnell, *President*
Bridget Mushrush, *Marketing Mgr*
**EMP:** 34 **EST:** 1977
**SALES (est):** 1MM **Privately Held**
**SIC:** 3643 Connectors & terminals for electrical devices

## (G-12730)
### CONSUMER VINEGAR AND SPICE
745 S Ashland Ave (60525-2816)
**PHONE** .................. 708 354-1144
Stan Zarnowiecki, *President*
**EMP:** 3
**SALES (est):** 228.3K **Privately Held**
**SIC:** 2099 Vinegar

## (G-12731)
### EZ BLINDS AND DRAPERY INC (PA)
Also Called: Eddie Z'S
1 Raquel Way (60525-3073)
**PHONE** .................. 708 246-6600
James E Zakoor, *President*
Craig Duff, *President*
Mark Lokanc, *CFO*
James Zakoor, *Agent*
Gabe Courey, *Admin Sec*
▲ **EMP:** 15
**SQ FT:** 528
**SALES (est):** 48.3MM **Privately Held**
**SIC:** 5023 2591 Window furnishings; window blinds

## (G-12732)
### FRENCH CORPORATION
Also Called: Connomac
340 Washington Ave (60525-6869)
**PHONE** .................. 708 354-9000
Thomas F Kearney, *President*
**EMP:** 25
**SALES (est):** 5.3MM **Privately Held**
**WEB:** www.connomac.com
**SIC:** 3643 Connectors & terminals for electrical devices

## (G-12733)
### GOALGETTERS INC
639 S La Grange Rd Fl 2 (60525-5604)
**PHONE** .................. 708 579-9800
**Fax:** 708 579-9813
Al Zuffrano, *President*
**EMP:** 10
**SALES (est):** 1.5MM **Privately Held**
**WEB:** www.goalgettersinc.com
**SIC:** 2752 3993 2759 Commercial printing, lithographic; signs & advertising specialties; commercial printing

## (G-12734)
### GRAYHILL INC (PA)
561 W Hillgrove Ave (60525-5997)
**PHONE** .................. 708 354-1040
**Fax:** 708 354-2820
Gene R Hill, *CEO*
Brian May, *President*
Lisa Audino, *Business Mgr*
Jeffrey Sherry, *Business Mgr*
Jamie Dobravec, *Vice Pres*
▲ **EMP:** 500 **EST:** 1940
**SQ FT:** 175,000
**SALES (est):** 160.6MM **Privately Held**
**WEB:** www.grayhill.com
**SIC:** 3613 3625 3679 3643 Switches, electric power except snap, push button, etc.; switches, electric power; switches, electronic applications; electronic switches; electric switches; keyboards, computer, office machine

## (G-12735)
### HANDLING SYSTEMS INC
408 E Cossitt Ave (60525-2514)
P.O. Box 626 (60525-0626)
**PHONE** .................. 708 352-1213
**Fax:** 708 352-6593
James Chereskin, *President*
Gregory Kwoleck, *President*
Mark F Rehor, *Vice Pres*
**EMP:** 20
**SQ FT:** 33,000
**SALES (est):** 14.7MM **Privately Held**
**WEB:** www.handlingsystemsintl.com
**SIC:** 5084 3536 3537 Hoists; materials handling machinery; cranes, industrial plant; industrial trucks & tractors

## (G-12736)
### HOLTON FOOD PRODUCTS COMPANY
500 W Burlington Ave (60525-2227)
**PHONE** .................. 708 352-5599
**Fax:** 708 352-3788
Ross Holton, *President*
John E Holton, *Exec VP*
David Holton, *Vice Pres*
Chris Miotk, *VP Mfg*
Dawn Brabec, *Manager*
**EMP:** 12
**SQ FT:** 2,000
**SALES (est):** 2.4MM
**SALES (corp-wide):** 4.8B **Publicly Held**
**WEB:** www.hfpglobal.com
**SIC:** 2099 Dessert mixes & fillings
**HQ:** Mantrose-Haeuser Co., Inc.
1175 Post Rd E Ste 3b
Westport CT 06880
203 454-1800

## (G-12737)
### ID ADDITIVES INC
512 W Burlington Ave # 208 (60525-2245)
**PHONE** .................. 708 588-0081
Nicholas Sotos, *President*
Ronald Bishop, *Technical Mgr*
Rob Koehn, *Accounts Mgr*
Damon Wickmann, *Accounts Mgr*
**EMP:** 3
**SALES (est):** 599.7K **Privately Held**
**SIC:** 2821 Plastics materials & resins

## (G-12738)
### IMPACT SIGNS & GRAPHICS INC
Also Called: Impact Bronze Plaques
26 E Burlington Ave (60525-2430)
**PHONE** .................. 708 469-7178
**Toll Free:** .................. 866 -
**Fax:** 708 492-0136
Ammar Moosabhoy, *President*
Shabbir Moosabhoy, *Vice Pres*
**EMP:** 5 **EST:** 1999
**SQ FT:** 1,400
**SALES (est):** 430K **Privately Held**
**WEB:** www.impactsigns.com
**SIC:** 3993 Signs & advertising specialties

## (G-12739)
### K & N LABORATORIES INC
633 S La Grange Rd (60525-6741)
P.O. Box 7226, Deerfield (60015-7226)
**PHONE** .................. 708 482-3240
June Sabin, *President*
**EMP:** 13

**SALES (est):** 1.6MM **Privately Held**
**SIC:** 2679 Converted paper products

## (G-12740)
### NATURAL PACKAGING INC
550 Hillgrove Ave Ste 518 (60525)
**PHONE** .................. 708 246-3420
Jack B Rolff, *President*
**EMP:** 4 **EST:** 2005
**SALES (est):** 270K **Privately Held**
**SIC:** 2673 Bags: plastic, laminated & coated

## (G-12741)
### ONE WAY SAFETY LLC
418 Shawmut Ave Ste B (60525)
**PHONE** .................. 708 579-0229
Meg Shanley,
**EMP:** 5
**SALES (est):** 1.2MM **Privately Held**
**SIC:** 7389 3851 Safety inspection service; goggles: sun, safety, industrial, underwater, etc.

## (G-12742)
### PMB INDUSTRIES INC
8072 53rd St (60525)
**PHONE** .................. 708 442-4515
Paul Boburka Sr, *President*
**EMP:** 8
**SALES (est):** 453K **Privately Held**
**WEB:** www.pmbindustries.com
**SIC:** 7389 3599 Design, commercial & industrial; custom machinery

## (G-12743)
### RLC INDUSTRIES INC
715 S 10th Ave (60525-3061)
**PHONE** .................. 708 837-7300
Raymond J Strack Jr, *President*
**EMP:** 3 **EST:** 2010
**SALES (est):** 346K **Privately Held**
**SIC:** 3613 Control panels, electric

## (G-12744)
### SERGIO BARAJAS
Also Called: SBA
205 Washington Ave (60525-2569)
**PHONE** .................. 708 238-7614
Sergio Barajas, *Owner*
**EMP:** 5
**SALES (est):** 175K **Privately Held**
**SIC:** 3432 Plastic plumbing fixture fittings, assembly

## (G-12745)
### SIBOR EXPRESS LTD
1030 S La Grange Rd # 24 (60525-2899)
**PHONE** .................. 773 499-8707
Milos Siroteic, *President*
**EMP:** 3
**SQ FT:** 900
**SALES (est):** 500K **Privately Held**
**SIC:** 3531 Trucks, off-highway

## (G-12746)
### SOTISH LTD
23 S La Grange Rd Ste 1 (60525-2519)
**PHONE** .................. 708 476-2017
Susan Rearden, *President*
Timothy Reardan, *Admin Sec*
**EMP:** 7
**SALES (est):** 300K **Privately Held**
**WEB:** www.sotish.com
**SIC:** 3229 5812 Art, decorative & novelty glassware; cafe

## (G-12747)
### TOM CROWN MUTE CO
130 N La Grange Rd # 315 (60525-2004)
**PHONE** .................. 708 352-1039
Tom Crown, *President*
William Camp, *Vice Pres*
**EMP:** 4
**SALES (est):** 254.1K **Privately Held**
**SIC:** 3931 Musical instruments

## (G-12748)
### UPS AUTHORIZED RETAILER
106 W Calendar Ave (60525-2325)
**PHONE** .................. 708 354-8772
Jinit Patel, *President*
**EMP:** 5
**SQ FT:** 2,200

**SALES (est):** 301.2K **Privately Held**
**SIC:** 2759 Package delivery, vehicular; commercial printing

---

## La Grange Highlands
### Cook County

## (G-12749)
### D2 LIGHTING LLC
5718 Harvey Ave (60525-7008)
**PHONE** .................. 708 243-9059
David E Doubek, *Principal*
**EMP:** 5 **EST:** 2008
**SALES (est):** 610.3K **Privately Held**
**SIC:** 3648 Lighting equipment

## (G-12750)
### QUALITY SLEEP SHOP INC (PA)
1519 W 55th St (60525-7014)
**PHONE** .................. 708 246-2224
Timothy W Masters, *President*
◆ **EMP:** 6
**SQ FT:** 4,000
**SALES (est):** 425K **Privately Held**
**WEB:** www.qualitysleepshop.com
**SIC:** 2515 Mattresses & foundations

---

## La Grange Park
### Cook County

## (G-12751)
### ABET INDUSTRIES CORPORATION
111 Kemman Ave (60526-6007)
**PHONE** .................. 708 482-8282
**Fax:** 708 482-8228
Cindy V Mottl, *President*
Susan Summers, *Vice Pres*
Paul Tomac, *Plant Mgr*
Eileen Votava, *Treasurer*
Barb Molina, *Manager*
**EMP:** 5
**SQ FT:** 8,300
**SALES (est):** 744.2K **Privately Held**
**WEB:** www.production-edm.com
**SIC:** 3599 Electrical discharge machining (EDM)

## (G-12752)
### ALPHADIGITAL INC
Also Called: AlphaGraphics
417 N La Grange Rd (60526-5623)
**PHONE** .................. 708 482-4488
**Fax:** 708 482-4499
Albert Schnell, *President*
Janet Schnell, *Corp Secy*
Michael A Schnell, *Vice Pres*
**EMP:** 6
**SQ FT:** 3,800
**SALES (est):** 926.6K **Privately Held**
**WEB:** www.alphadigital.com
**SIC:** 2752 7334 2791 2789 Commercial printing, lithographic; photocopying & duplicating services; typesetting; bookbinding & related work

## (G-12753)
### CJJ INDUSTRIES INC
211 Community Dr (60526-5304)
P.O. Box 1286 (60526-9386)
**PHONE** .................. 708 921-9290
Susan A Jeffries, *Principal*
**EMP:** 3
**SALES (est):** 224.3K **Privately Held**
**SIC:** 3999 Manufacturing industries

## (G-12754)
### DESLAURIERS INC (PA)
1245 Barnsdale Rd (60526-1276)
**PHONE** .................. 708 544-4455
Gary Workman, *President*
Philip Cozza, *Vice Pres*
Paul Cozza, *CFO*
Conrad Graff, *Sales Staff*
Gary Yaccino, *Manager*
▲ **EMP:** 40 **EST:** 1888
**SQ FT:** 620,000
**SALES (est):** 12.8MM **Privately Held**
**WEB:** www.deslinc.com
**SIC:** 3089 5051 Washers, plastic; forms, concrete construction (steel)

# GEOGRAPHIC SECTION
## La Salle - Lasalle County (G-12778)

**(G-12755)**
**DIE SPECIALTY CO**
1510 Cleveland Ave (60526-1308)
PHONE..................................312 303-5738
Harold W Langeland, *President*
Glenn E Langeland, *Vice Pres*
**EMP:** 6 **EST:** 1946
**SQ FT:** 5,000
**SALES (est):** 587.9K **Privately Held**
**SIC:** 3544  3545  Special dies, tools, jigs & fixtures; machine tool accessories

**(G-12756)**
**G G PREMIER PRECISION INC**
500 Shawmut Ave (60526-2072)
PHONE..................................708 588-1234
Glenn Grozich, *President*
Paula Grozich, *Office Mgr*
**EMP:** 25 **EST:** 1957
**SQ FT:** 100,000
**SALES (est):** 3MM **Privately Held**
**WEB:** www.billetspecialties.com
**SIC:** 3599  Machine shop, jobbing & repair

**(G-12757)**
**INTERNATIONAL MOLDING MCH CO**
1201 Barnsdale Rd Ste 1 (60526-1285)
P.O. Box 1366 (60526-9466)
PHONE..................................708 354-1380
Tyrrell B Eichler Jr, *President*
Robert Eichler, *Corp Secy*
William Lavery, *Vice Pres*
**EMP:** 6 **EST:** 1891
**SQ FT:** 46,000
**SALES:** 1MM **Privately Held**
**WEB:** www.internationalmolding.com
**SIC:** 3559  Foundry machinery & equipment

**(G-12758)**
**MARCY ENTERPRISES INC**
Also Called: MEI
250 Kings Ct (60526-5307)
P.O. Box 1322 (60526-9422)
PHONE..................................708 352-7220
Fax: 708 352-0557
Marcy K Britigan, *President*
Stuart Goldsand, *Corp Secy*
Cathy Briggs, *Accountant*
**EMP:** 5
**SQ FT:** 3,000
**SALES:** 2MM **Privately Held**
**WEB:** www.mei-systems.com
**SIC:** 5078  2521  2541  Refrigeration equipment & supplies; wood office furniture; cabinets, except refrigerated: show, display, etc.: wood

**(G-12759)**
**PRO-QUIP INCORPORATED**
418 Shawmut Ave Ste A (60526-2085)
PHONE..................................708 352-5732
Fax: 708 352-6389
Robert S Lefley III, *CEO*
David Lefley, *President*
Robert S Lefley IV, *Vice Pres*
Don Edwards, *Accounting Mgr*
Dale Kitchell, *Sales Engr*
**EMP:** 10
**SQ FT:** 10,000
**SALES (est):** 8.7MM **Privately Held**
**WEB:** www.proquip.com
**SIC:** 5084  3625  3494  Industrial machinery & equipment; controlling instruments & accessories; relays & industrial controls; valves & pipe fittings

## La Salle
### Lasalle County

**(G-12760)**
**AGRI-NEWS PUBLICATIONS INC (HQ)**
Also Called: Www.agrinews-Pubs.com
426 2nd St (61301-2334)
PHONE..................................815 223-2558
Fax: 815 223-5997
Peter Miller, *President*
Lynn Barker, *Publisher*
Craig Baker, *Accounting Mgr*
Ginny Parnisari, *Executive*
**EMP:** 53
**SALES (est):** 13.3MM
**SALES (corp-wide):** 36MM **Privately Held**
**WEB:** www.country-news.com
**SIC:** 2711  Newspapers
**PA:** Daily News Tribune, Inc
  426 2nd St
  La Salle IL 61301
  815 223-2558

**(G-12761)**
**AIR PRODUCTS AND CHEMICALS INC**
Civic Rd Industrial Park (61301)
P.O. Box 1249 (61301-3249)
PHONE..................................815 223-2924
Fax: 815 224-3060
John Hardy, *Plant Mgr*
Susan Mennie, *Office Mgr*
**EMP:** 50
**SALES (corp-wide):** 9.5B **Publicly Held**
**WEB:** www.airproducts.com
**SIC:** 2813  Industrial gases
**PA:** Air Products And Chemicals, Inc.
  7201 Hamilton Blvd
  Allentown PA 18195
  610 481-4911

**(G-12762)**
**AMERICAN BARE CONDUCTOR INC**
2969 Chartres St (61301-1085)
PHONE..................................815 224-3422
Fax: 815 895-7007
Marcos C Ramalho, *President*
Jorge Kawamura, *Vice Pres*
Patti Mutehart, *Marketing Staff*
Leslie McKee, *Manager*
Ricardo Kawamura, *Shareholder*
**EMP:** 35
**SQ FT:** 80,000
**SALES (est):** 10.4MM **Privately Held**
**WEB:** www.abcwire.com
**SIC:** 3351  3643  3366  Wire, copper & copper alloy; current-carrying wiring devices; copper foundries

**(G-12763)**
**ANBEK INC**
222 3rd St (61301-2336)
PHONE..................................815 672-6087
James C Olmsted, *Principal*
**EMP:** 8
**SALES (corp-wide):** 1.2MM **Privately Held**
**SIC:** 3993  Signs & advertising specialties
**PA:** Anbek, Inc
  104 W Madison St
  Ottawa IL 61350
  815 434-7340

**(G-12764)**
**ANBEK INC**
Also Called: Designs and Signs By Anderson
222 3rd St (61301-2336)
PHONE..................................815 223-0734
**EMP:** 12
**SALES (corp-wide):** 1.3MM **Privately Held**
**SIC:** 3993  Mfg Signs/Advertising Specialties
**PA:** Anbek, Inc
  104 W Madison St
  Ottawa IL 61350
  815 434-7340

**(G-12765)**
**ARROW SALES & SERVICE INC**
3101 E 3rd Rd (61301-9722)
PHONE..................................815 223-0251
Alma McCabe, *President*
Mike Fauth, *President*
**EMP:** 2
**SALES (est):** 208.1K **Privately Held**
**SIC:** 3999  Fire extinguishers, portable

**(G-12766)**
**CARUS CORPORATION**
Also Called: Carus Chemical Company
1500 8th St (61301-1978)
P.O. Box 1500 (61301-0150)
PHONE..................................815 223-1500
Fax: 815 433-1724
Dave Covey, *Plant Mgr*
Barbie Smith, *Marketing Staff*
Sandi Grubich, *Branch Mgr*
Regina Mitchell, *Admin Sec*
**EMP:** 123
**SALES (corp-wide):** 150.6MM **Privately Held**
**SIC:** 2819  Industrial inorganic chemicals
**HQ:** Carus Corporation
  315 5th St
  Peru IL 61354
  815 223-1500

**(G-12767)**
**CARUS CORPORATION**
1500 8th St (61301-1978)
PHONE..................................815 223-1565
**EMP:** 94
**SALES (corp-wide):** 157.4MM **Privately Held**
**SIC:** 2819  Mfg Industrial Inorganic Chemicals
**HQ:** Carus Corporation
  315 5th St
  Peru IL 61354
  815 223-1500

**(G-12768)**
**CHRISTYS KITCHEN**
2203 Aplington St (61301-1127)
PHONE..................................815 735-6791
Christopher Kuhn, *Principal*
**EMP:** 8
**SALES (est):** 586.8K **Privately Held**
**SIC:** 2051  Bakery: wholesale or wholesale/retail combined

**(G-12769)**
**CYCLOPS WELDING CO**
11 Joliet St (61301-2593)
PHONE..................................815 223-0685
Fax: 815 223-0874
Joseph R Piano, *President*
**EMP:** 7
**SQ FT:** 5,000
**SALES (est):** 1.1MM **Privately Held**
**SIC:** 3441  7692  3444  3443  Fabricated structural metal; welding repair; sheet metalwork; fabricated plate work (boiler shop)

**(G-12770)**
**DAILY NEWS TRIBUNE  INC (PA)**
426 2nd St (61301-2334)
P.O. Box 128 (61301)
PHONE..................................815 223-2558
Fax: 815 223-2543
Joyce T McCullough, *President*
Joe Zokal, *Editor*
Bob Vickrey, *Vice Pres*
Lynn Ridder, *Prdtn Mgr*
Robert Vickrey, *Sales Mgr*
**EMP:** 150
**SQ FT:** 11,700
**SALES (est):** 36MM **Privately Held**
**WEB:** www.newstrib.com
**SIC:** 2711  Newspapers, publishing & printing

**(G-12771)**
**ELECTRO-GLO DISTRIBUTION INC**
316 Raccuglia Dr (61301-9778)
P.O. Box 596, Princeton (61356-0596)
PHONE..................................815 224-4030
Jack Downey, *President*
Larry Castelli, *Vice Pres*
Randy Vecchia, *Vice Pres*
**EMP:** 3
**SALES (est):** 236.6K **Privately Held**
**SIC:** 3471  2842  3559  3291  Polishing, metals or formed products; finishing, metals or formed products; metal polish; metal finishing equipment for plating, etc.; abrasive products

**(G-12772)**
**FAST PIPE LINING INC**
320 Raccuglia Dr (61301-9723)
P.O. Box 1521 (61301-3521)
PHONE..................................815 712-8646
**EMP:** 5
**SALES (est):** 586.2K **Privately Held**
**SIC:** 3321  Sewer pipe, cast iron

**(G-12773)**
**FORTE INCORPORATED**
601 2nd St Ste 3 (61301-8850)
P.O. Box 10, Ladd (61329-0010)
PHONE..................................815 224-8300
Jim Love, *President*
Bernie Victor, *Vice Pres*
Rebecca Sondgeroth, *Engineer*
**EMP:** 7
**SALES:** 1.2MM **Privately Held**
**WEB:** www.forteeng.com
**SIC:** 7372  Operating systems computer software

**(G-12774)**
**HARVEST VALLEY BAKERY  INC**
348 Civic Rd (61301-9710)
PHONE..................................815 224-9030
Fax: 815 224-9033
Nancy Norton, *CEO*
Debra L Sobut, *Vice Pres*
Joe Laffin, *Director*
◆ **EMP:** 20 **EST:** 1990
**SQ FT:** 44,000
**SALES:** 2MM **Privately Held**
**WEB:** www.harvestvalleybakery.com
**SIC:** 2052  Cookies

**(G-12775)**
**ILLINOIS AGRINEWS INC**
426 2nd St (61301-2334)
PHONE..................................815 223-7448
Kevin Conerton, *Principal*
**EMP:** 4
**SALES (est):** 197.1K **Privately Held**
**SIC:** 2711  Newspapers, publishing & printing

**(G-12776)**
**ILLINOIS CEMENT COMPANY LLC (HQ)**
1601 Rockwell Rd (61301-9600)
P.O. Box 442 (61301-0442)
PHONE..................................815 224-2112
Fax: 815 224-4358
Steven R Rowley, *President*
Wayne Emmer, *Mng Member*
Frank Koeppel,
▲ **EMP:** 149
**SQ FT:** 4,000
**SALES (est):** 37MM
**SALES (corp-wide):** 1.2B **Publicly Held**
**SIC:** 3241  5032  Masonry cement; cement
**PA:** Eagle Materials Inc.
  3811 Turtle Creek Blvd # 1100
  Dallas TX 75219
  214 432-2000

**(G-12777)**
**INDIANA AGRI-NEWS INC**
420 2nd St (61301-2334)
PHONE..................................317 726-5391
Fax: 309 223-5997
Peter Miller III, *Vice Pres*
Craig Baker, *Accountant*
Lynn Barker, *Director*
S C Miller, *Admin Sec*
**EMP:** 3
**SQ FT:** 1,600
**SALES (est):** 261.6K
**SALES (corp-wide):** 36MM **Privately Held**
**WEB:** www.newstrib.com
**SIC:** 2711  Newspapers, publishing & printing
**PA:** Daily News Tribune, Inc
  426 2nd St
  La Salle IL 61301
  815 223-2558

**(G-12778)**
**INMAN ELECTRIC MOTORS  INC**
314 Civic Rd (61301-9710)
P.O. Box 1108 (61301-3108)
PHONE..................................815 223-2288
Fax: 815 223-7108
David Inman, *President*
Celeste Inman, *Corp Secy*
Heather Salley, *Accountant*
**EMP:** 27
**SQ FT:** 75,000

**La Salle - Lasalle County (G-12779)** — GEOGRAPHIC SECTION

SALES (est): 7.2MM **Privately Held**
WEB: www.inmanelectric.com
SIC: **7694** 5063 3621 3613 Electric motor repair; rebuilding motors, except automotive; motors, electric; motors & generators; coils, for electric motors or generators; switchgear & switchboard apparatus; industrial pumps & parts

**(G-12779)**
**JANE STODDEN BRIDALS**
955 Marquette St (61301-1869)
PHONE..............................815 223-2091
Jane Stodden, *Owner*
EMP: 3
SALES: 8K **Privately Held**
SIC: **2335** 5621 5947 Wedding gowns & dresses; bridal shops; greeting cards

**(G-12780)**
**KEY OUTDOOR INC**
2968 Saint Vincent Ave (61301-9707)
PHONE..............................815 224-4742
Fax: 815 224-3765
Ann Salz, *Sales/Mktg Mgr*
EMP: 4
SALES (corp-wide): 6.1MM **Privately Held**
WEB: www.keyoutdoor.com
SIC: **7312** 3993 Outdoor advertising services; signs & advertising specialties
PA: Key Outdoor Inc
1873 Armour Rd
Bourbonnais IL 60914
815 933-3333

**(G-12781)**
**NEW CIE INC**
Also Called: Special Products Division
85 Chartres St (61301-2313)
P.O. Box 529 (61301)
PHONE..............................815 224-1485
Fax: 815 224-3405
Donald Boken, *President*
Bob Baker, *Manager*
Ken Cappeni, *Systems Mgr*
EMP: 12
SQ FT: 10,000
SALES (corp-wide): 11.4MM **Privately Held**
SIC: **3613** 3625 7694 5063 Switchgear & switchboard apparatus; relays & industrial controls; armature rewinding shops; electrical apparatus & equipment
PA: New Cie, Inc.
1220 Wenzel Rd
Peru IL 61354
815 224-1510

**(G-12782)**
**QUALITY LIQUID FEEDS INC**
75 Creve Coeur St (61301-2319)
PHONE..............................815 224-1553
Fax: 815 224-1590
Joe Saini, *Branch Mgr*
EMP: 10
SALES (corp-wide): 213.7MM **Privately Held**
WEB: www.qlf.com
SIC: **2048** Feed supplements
PA: Quality Liquid Feeds, Inc.
3586 State Road 23
Dodgeville WI 53533
608 935-2345

**(G-12783)**
**REMURIATE LLC (PA)**
Also Called: Remuriate Technologies
654 1st St Ste 200 (61301-2484)
PHONE..............................815 220-5050
Paul Carus, *CEO*
Hildi Grivetti, *CFO*
Lashica Oliver, *Director*
EMP: 4 EST: 2013
SALES: 3.2MM **Privately Held**
SIC: **2819** Hydrochloric acid

**(G-12784)**
**RS DUCTLESS TECHNICAL SUPPORT**
227 Bucklin St (61301-2343)
PHONE..............................815 223-7949
Michael Porkup, *Owner*
EMP: 7

SALES (est): 223.1K **Privately Held**
SIC: **2741** Technical manuals: publishing & printing

### Lacon
*Marshall County*

**(G-12785)**
**BILLY & RACHEL POIGNANT**
237 Crossover Rd (61540-8855)
PHONE..............................309 713-5500
Billy Poignant, *Principal*
EMP: 3
SALES (est): 214.7K **Privately Held**
SIC: **2411** Logging

**(G-12786)**
**DJH INDUSTRIES INC**
400 N Commercial St (61540-1764)
PHONE..............................309 246-8456
Fax: 309 246-3117
Dale Hardin, *President*
Tim Fishel, *Manager*
Jenny Medress, *Manager*
EMP: 37
SQ FT: 50,000
SALES (est): 7.8MM **Privately Held**
WEB: www.hardin-inc.com
SIC: **3621** Electric motor & generator parts

**(G-12787)**
**HARDIN INDUSTRIES LLC** ◉
400 N Commercial St (61540-1764)
PHONE..............................309 246-8456
Becki Salmon, *President*
EMP: 38 EST: 2016
SALES (est): 1.2MM **Privately Held**
SIC: **3621** Motors & generators

**(G-12788)**
**MCKEAN PALLET CO**
1046 State Route 26 (61540-8906)
PHONE..............................309 246-7543
Frank McKean, *Owner*
EMP: 3
SALES (est): 314.5K **Privately Held**
SIC: **2448** Wood pallets & skids

**(G-12789)**
**META TEC DEVELOPMENT INC (PA)**
125 N Commercial St (61540-8820)
PHONE..............................309 246-2960
David Suffren, *President*
Rita Ann Suffern, *Admin Sec*
▲ EMP: 3
SALES (est): 2.6MM **Privately Held**
WEB: www.metatecinc.com
SIC: **7699** 3599 Industrial equipment services; machine shop, jobbing & repair

**(G-12790)**
**META TEC OF ILLINOIS INC**
125 N Commercial St (61540-8820)
PHONE..............................309 246-2960
David Suffren, *President*
John Brackney, *General Mgr*
Rita Ann Suffern, *Admin Sec*
EMP: 85
SQ FT: 17,200
SALES (est): 15.1MM **Privately Held**
SIC: **3321** 3599 Gray iron castings; custom machinery

**(G-12791)**
**POIGNANT LOGGING**
857 State Route 26 (61540-8903)
PHONE..............................309 246-5647
Leroy Poignant, *Owner*
EMP: 4
SALES (est): 219.1K **Privately Held**
SIC: **2411** Logging

### Ladd
*Bureau County*

**(G-12792)**
**TEE GROUP FILMS INC**
605 N Mn Ave (61329)
P.O. Box 425 (61329-0425)
PHONE..............................815 894-2331
Thomas H Malpass, *President*
Dave Bejster, *Opers Mgr*
Brad Gill, *Prdtn Mgr*
Bob Lund, *Opers Staff*
Neil Hammerich, *Engineer*
▲ EMP: 60
SQ FT: 60,000
SALES (est): 20.1MM **Privately Held**
WEB: www.tee-group.com
SIC: **3081** Polyethylene film

### Lafox
*Kane County*

**(G-12793)**
**BI-TORQ VALVE AUTOMATION INC**
1n046 Linlar Dr (60147)
P.O. Box 309 (60147-0309)
PHONE..............................630 208-9343
Brent Showalter, *Principal*
Beth Bitner, *Opers Mgr*
Dan Eckel, *CFO*
Timothy Filipovits, *Accounting Mgr*
EMP: 7
SALES (est): 268.1K
SALES (corp-wide): 12MM **Privately Held**
SIC: **3494** Valves & pipe fittings
PA: Strahman Valves, Inc.
2801 Baglyos Cir Lhgh Vly
Bethlehem PA 18020
877 787-2462

**(G-12794)**
**LAFOX MANUFACTURING CORP**
1 N 278 Lafox Rd (60147)
P.O. Box 399 (60147-0399)
PHONE..............................630 232-0266
Fax: 630 208-8351
Kurt Kranz, *President*
Mike Zoch, *Vice Pres*
EMP: 7
SALES: 1.3MM **Privately Held**
SIC: **3498** Pipe fittings, fabricated from purchased pipe

**(G-12795)**
**RICHARDSON ELECTRONICS LTD**
Canvys
40 W 267 Keslinger Rd (60147)
P.O. Box 393 (60147-0393)
PHONE..............................630 208-2278
Fax: 630 208-2553
Kevin Kardian, *QC Mgr*
Doug Hopkins, *Sales Mgr*
Ryan Peterson, *Sales Mgr*
Michael Ryan, *Sales Mgr*
Karina Macholz, *Marketing Staff*
EMP: 250
SALES (corp-wide): 142MM **Publicly Held**
SIC: **5046** 3679 3577 7371 Display equipment, except refrigerated; liquid crystal displays (LCD); data conversion equipment, media-to-media: computer; decoders, computer peripheral equipment; encoders, computer peripheral equipment; graphic displays, except graphic terminals; computer software systems analysis & design, custom; computer software development & applications
PA: Richardson Electronics, Ltd.
40w267 Keslinger Rd
Lafox IL 60147
630 208-2200

**(G-12796)**
**RICHARDSON ELECTRONICS LTD (PA)**
40w267 Keslinger Rd (60147)
P.O. Box 393 (60147-0393)
PHONE..............................630 208-2200
Fax: 630 208-2550
Edward J Richardson, *Ch of Bd*
Jerome Czajkowski, *General Mgr*
Wendy S Diddell, *COO*
Gregory J Peloquin, *Exec VP*
Kathleen M McNally, *Senior VP*
EMP: 191 EST: 1947
SQ FT: 242,000
SALES: 142MM **Publicly Held**
WEB: www.rell.com
SIC: **5065** 7373 3671 Electronic parts & equipment; electronic tubes: receiving & transmitting or industrial; semiconductor devices; closed circuit television; computer integrated systems design; value-added resellers, computer systems; electronic tube parts, except glass blanks

**(G-12797)**
**STRAHMAN VALVES INC**
Also Called: Bi-Torq Valve Automation
1n046 Linlar Dr (60147)
P.O. Box 309 (60147-0309)
PHONE..............................630 208-9343
Dan Eckel, *CFO*
Timothy Filipovits, *Accounting Mgr*
EMP: 24
SALES (corp-wide): 12MM **Privately Held**
SIC: **3491** 3494 Automatic regulating & control valves; valves & pipe fittings
PA: Strahman Valves, Inc.
2801 Baglyos Cir Lhgh Vly
Bethlehem PA 18020
877 787-2462

### Lake Barrington
*Lake County*

**(G-12798)**
**AEROMAX INDUSTRIES INC**
28 W079 Industrial Ave (60010)
PHONE..............................847 756-4085
Mark Levine, *President*
Sean Schipper, *COO*
Mel Davis, *VP Mktg*
Jared Heidenreich, *Office Mgr*
▲ EMP: 6
SQ FT: 2,000
SALES: 3MM **Privately Held**
WEB: www.aeromaxtoys.com
SIC: **3944** Games, toys & children's vehicles

**(G-12799)**
**AMBER SOFT INC**
28214 W Northwest Hwy (60010-2324)
PHONE..............................630 377-6945
H Wayne Roby, *President*
Doris Roby, *Corp Secy*
EMP: 12
SQ FT: 3,000
SALES (est): 1.6MM **Privately Held**
WEB: www.ambersoft.com
SIC: **3589** 5999 7359 Water filters & softeners, household type; water purification equipment, household type; water treatment equipment, industrial; water purification equipment; equipment rental & leasing

**(G-12800)**
**BARRINGTON MILLWORK LLC**
27214 W Henry Ln (60010-2304)
PHONE..............................847 304-0791
Mike Proksa,
Walter Proksa,
William Proksa,
EMP: 7
SQ FT: 8,000
SALES (est): 714.3K **Privately Held**
WEB: www.barringtonmillwork.com
SIC: **1751** 2431 Cabinet building & installation; millwork

# GEOGRAPHIC SECTION
## Lake Barrington - Lake County (G-12826)

**(G-12801)**
**C B FERRARI INCORPORATED**
22179 N Pepper Rd (60010-2461)
**PHONE**................................847 756-4100
Josef Blechner, *President*
▲ **EMP:** 2
**SALES (est):** 258.4K **Privately Held**
**SIC: 3549** Wiredrawing & fabricating machinery & equipment, ex. die

**(G-12802)**
**COLE-PARMER INSTRUMENT CO LLC**
28092 W Commercial Ave (60010-2443)
**PHONE**................................847 381-7050
Larry Jones, *Manager*
**EMP:** 140 **Privately Held**
**SIC: 3821** Laboratory equipment: fume hoods, distillation racks, etc.
**HQ:** Cole-Parmer Instrument Company Llc
625 Bunker Ct
Vernon Hills IL 60061
847 549-7600

**(G-12803)**
**CROWN GYM MATS INC**
27929 W Industrial Ave (60010-2455)
**PHONE**................................847 381-8282
**Fax:** 847 381-8297
Judy Eckert, *President*
Holly Chevopulos, *General Mgr*
Jon Eckert, *Corp Secy*
**EMP:** 10 **EST:** 1945
**SQ FT:** 14,000
**SALES (est):** 1.6MM **Privately Held**
**WEB:** www.crowngymmats.com
**SIC: 3949** 7699 Gymnasium equipment; recreational sporting equipment repair services

**(G-12804)**
**CTI INDUSTRIES CORPORATION (PA)**
22160 N Pepper Rd (60010-2301)
**PHONE**................................847 382-1000
**Fax:** 847 382-1219
John H Schwan, *Ch of Bd*
Stephen M Merrick, *President*
Jana Schwan, *Vice Pres*
Rahul P Deshmukh, *VP Mfg*
Timothy Patterson, *CFO*
▲ **EMP:** 172
**SQ FT:** 68,000
**SALES (est):** 64.2MM **Publicly Held**
**WEB:** www.ctiindustries.com
**SIC: 3089** 3069 Plastic containers, except foam; tubs, plastic (containers); plastic kitchenware, tableware & houseware; balloons, metal foil laminated with rubber; balloons, advertising & toy: rubber; balls, rubber

**(G-12805)**
**D S ARMS INCORPORATED**
Also Called: D S A
27 W 990 Indl Ave (60010)
P.O. Box 370, Barrington (60011-0370)
**PHONE**................................847 277-7258
**Fax:** 847 277-7259
Dave Selvaggio, *President*
Mike Fowler, *Sales Mgr*
Jennifer Koranek, *Executive*
**EMP:** 17
**SQ FT:** 22,000
**SALES (est):** 4.7MM **Privately Held**
**SIC: 3484** 5199 5099 5961 Small arms; general merchandise, non-durable; firearms & ammunition, except sporting; mail order house

**(G-12806)**
**FLAME GUARD USA LLC**
4 Hillview Dr Units A&B (60010)
**PHONE**................................815 219-4074
Joseph Kuesis,
James Mackey,
**EMP:** 6
**SQ FT:** 5,000
**SALES (est):** 502.2K **Privately Held**
**SIC: 3999** 5099 5063 5087 Fire extinguishers, portable; fire extinguishers; fire alarm systems; firefighting equipment; sprinkler systems, fire: automatic

**(G-12807)**
**FRANZ STATIONERY COMPANY INC**
Also Called: Franz Discount Office Products
81 Vista Ln (60010-1944)
**PHONE**................................847 593-0060
**Fax:** 847 593-0070
Richard J Franzese, *President*
James Franzese, *Vice Pres*
**EMP:** 10 **EST:** 1928
**SQ FT:** 21,000
**SALES:** 1.7MM **Privately Held**
**WEB:** www.franzop.com
**SIC: 5943** 5112 2752 5021 Office forms & supplies; writing supplies; office supplies; commercial printing, offset; office furniture; mail order house; furniture & furnishings, mail order

**(G-12808)**
**GUARDIAN ROLLFORM LLC**
27951 W Industrial Ave (60010-2455)
**PHONE**................................847 382-8074
Maurice Loeffel, *Manager*
**EMP:** 55
**SALES (est):** 5.4MM **Privately Held**
**SIC: 3356** Nonferrous rolling & drawing

**(G-12809)**
**HOWW MANUFACTURING COMPANY INC**
28020 W Commercial Ave (60010-2443)
P.O. Box 276, Barrington (60011-0276)
**PHONE**................................847 382-4380
**Fax:** 847 382-4383
M P Kalamaras, *President*
Glenn Greenwood, *VP Sales*
Jim Kalamaras, *VP Sales*
Michelle Roth-Smoot, *Creative Dir*
James Kalamaras, *Admin Sec*
▲ **EMP:** 25
**SALES (est):** 3.8MM **Privately Held**
**SIC: 3231** Novelties, glass: fruit, foliage, flowers, animals, etc.

**(G-12810)**
**HUNZINGER WILLIAMS INC**
27w982 Commercial Ave (60010)
**PHONE**................................847 381-1878
**Fax:** 847 381-2063
Lee J Ford, *President*
William Hunzinger, *Vice Pres*
Debbie Hunzinger, *Treasurer*
**EMP:** 11
**SALES (est):** 1.1MM **Privately Held**
**SIC: 2394** Awnings, fabric: made from purchased materials; canopies, fabric: made from purchased materials

**(G-12811)**
**JOHN C GRAFFT (PA)**
Also Called: Foreclosure Report
28045 Roberts Rd (60010-1139)
**PHONE**................................847 842-9200
**Fax:** 847 381-0253
John C Grafft, *Owner*
**EMP:** 12
**SALES (est):** 250K **Privately Held**
**WEB:** www.midwestforeclosures.com
**SIC: 2721** 6531 2741 8748 Magazines: publishing only, not printed on site; real estate agents & managers; miscellaneous publishing; publishing consultant

**(G-12812)**
**JOHN F MATE CO**
27930 W Industrial Ave # 5 (60010-2531)
**PHONE**................................847 381-8131
**Fax:** 847 381-2013
John C Mate, *Partner*
Russell Mate, *Partner*
**EMP:** 2 **EST:** 1962
**SQ FT:** 2,400
**SALES (est):** 250K **Privately Held**
**WEB:** www.tmcscsi.com
**SIC: 3585** 3446 2541 Cabinets, show & display, refrigerated; architectural metalwork; wood partitions & fixtures

**(G-12813)**
**JONEM GRP INC DBA SIGN A RAMA**
28039 W Coml Ave Ste 9 (60010)
**PHONE**................................224 848-4620
**EMP:** 2

**SALES (est):** 236.1K **Privately Held**
**SIC: 3993** Signs & advertising specialties

**(G-12814)**
**K C PRINTING SERVICES INC**
22292 N Pepper Rd Ste A (60010-2544)
**PHONE**................................847 382-8822
Phillip Claps, *President*
Paul Claps, *Vice Pres*
**EMP:** 10
**SQ FT:** 3,000
**SALES (est):** 2.5MM **Privately Held**
**WEB:** www.kcprint.com
**SIC: 2621** 5111 7389 Printing paper; printing & writing paper; advertising, promotional & trade show services

**(G-12815)**
**K&R ENTERPRISES I INC**
28128 Gray Barn Ln (60010-1895)
**PHONE**................................847 502-3371
Karl Renner, *President*
Robert Renner, *General Mgr*
Hilde Renner, *Treasurer*
Howard Renner, *Controller*
**EMP:** 80
**SQ FT:** 38,000
**SALES (est):** 3.3MM **Privately Held**
**SIC: 7692** 3599 3441 Welding repair; brazing; machine shop, jobbing & repair; fabricated structural metal

**(G-12816)**
**KANETIC INC**
22102 N Pepper Rd Ste 107 (60010-2550)
**PHONE**................................847 382-9922
Joseph Kane, *President*
Laurie Kane, *Vice Pres*
**EMP:** 40
**SQ FT:** 35,000
**SALES (est):** 3.7MM **Privately Held**
**WEB:** www.kanetic.com
**SIC: 3535** Conveyors & conveying equipment

**(G-12817)**
**LAKE PROCESS SYSTEMS INC**
27930 W Commercial Ave (60010-2442)
**PHONE**................................847 381-7663
**Fax:** 847 381-7688
Paul Harris, *President*
Rebecca A Harris, *Treasurer*
Holly Harris, *Office Mgr*
**EMP:** 20
**SQ FT:** 11,100
**SALES (est):** 5MM **Privately Held**
**WEB:** www.lakeprocess.com
**SIC: 3443** 1623 5085 8711 Tanks, standard or custom fabricated: metal plate; pipe laying construction; valves, pistons & fittings; designing: ship, boat, machine & product; mechanical contractor

**(G-12818)**
**MATTSN/WITT PRECISION PDTS INC**
28005 W Industrial Ave (60010-2454)
**PHONE**................................847 382-7810
Jeffrey Witt, *President*
Kevin Graff, *Opers Staff*
James Meyer, *Engineer*
Ron Cope, *Supervisor*
Faith Witt, *Admin Sec*
▲ **EMP:** 20 **EST:** 1957
**SQ FT:** 28,000
**SALES (est):** 3.7MM **Privately Held**
**SIC: 3599** Machine shop, jobbing & repair

**(G-12819)**
**MCLEAN MANUFACTURING COMPANY**
Also Called: McLean Machine Tools
28040 W Industrial Ave (60010-2454)
**PHONE**................................847 277-9912
**Fax:** 847 277-9915
John Cherney, *President*
Susan Mueller, *Admin Sec*
▲ **EMP:** 5 **EST:** 1945
**SALES (est):** 804K **Privately Held**
**WEB:** www.mcleanmfg.com
**SIC: 3499** 5084 Strapping, metal; metalworking machinery

**(G-12820)**
**MK TEST SYSTEMS AMERICAS INC**
22102 N Pepper Rd Ste 116 (60010-2548)
**PHONE**................................773 569-3778
Arturo Nasarre, *Sales Engr*
Joseph Kane, *Admin Sec*
**EMP:** 2
**SALES:** 2MM
**SALES (corp-wide):** 5.3MM **Privately Held**
**SIC: 3679** Harness assemblies for electronic use: wire or cable
**HQ:** M.K. Test Systems Ltd.
Orchard Court
Wellington TA21
182 366-1100

**(G-12821)**
**NORMAN P MOELLER**
Also Called: Universal Instrument Company
372 Rolling Wood Ln Apt D (60010-1789)
P.O. Box 2776, Glenview (60025-6776)
**PHONE**................................847 991-3933
**Fax:** 847 991-3971
Norman Moeller, *Owner*
**EMP:** 8 **EST:** 1936
**SQ FT:** 3,000
**SALES (est):** 1.1MM **Privately Held**
**WEB:** www.uicoglass.com
**SIC: 3829** 3821 3231 3229 Hydrometers, except industrial process type; thermometers, including digital: clinical; laboratory apparatus & furniture; products of purchased glass; pressed & blown glass

**(G-12822)**
**PHOENIX TRADING CHICAGO INC**
26809 W Lakeridge Dr (60010-1980)
**PHONE**................................847 304-5181
Stephen Grafrath, *President*
Katherine Gregory, *Corp Secy*
**EMP:** 2
**SALES:** 4.3MM **Privately Held**
**SIC: 3462** Iron & steel forgings

**(G-12823)**
**S & S INTERNATIONAL INC ILL**
27996 W Industrial Ave # 8 (60010-2532)
**PHONE**................................847 304-1890
**Fax:** 847 304-1891
Mike D'Agostino, *President*
Greg Norton, *Vice Pres*
**EMP:** 5
**SQ FT:** 5,000
**SALES (est):** 809.5K **Privately Held**
**SIC: 3965** Fasteners, buttons, needles & pins

**(G-12824)**
**STRUT & SUPPLY INC**
28005 W Commercial Ave (60010-2443)
**PHONE**................................847 756-4337
Mike Dagostino, *President*
Jim Romano, *VP Sales*
▲ **EMP:** 2
**SALES (est):** 276.9K **Privately Held**
**SIC: 3429** Clamps, metal

**(G-12825)**
**T J M & ASSOCIATES INC**
Also Called: Reflections In Glass
22292 N Pepper Rd Ste D (60010-2544)
**PHONE**................................847 382-1993
Tim Meade, *President*
**EMP:** 7
**SQ FT:** 3,700
**SALES (est):** 1.1MM **Privately Held**
**SIC: 3431** 5039 5231 1793 Shower stalls, metal; exterior flat glass: plate or window; glass, leaded or stained; glass & glazing work

**(G-12826)**
**U R ON IT**
22172 N Hillview Dr (60010-2317)
**PHONE**................................847 382-0182
**Fax:** 847 382-3122
Ralph Gualano, *Owner*
**EMP:** 3

# Lake Bluff - Lake County (G-12827)

## GEOGRAPHIC SECTION

SALES (est): 115K **Privately Held**
WEB: www.uronit.com
SIC: **5699** 7389 5231 2395 Miscellaneous apparel & accessories; business services; glass, leaded or stained; embroidery products, except schiffli machine; trophies & plaques

## Lake Bluff
### Lake County

### (G-12827)
**ADVANGENE CONSUMABLES INC**
21 N Skokie Hwy Ste 104 (60044-1777)
PHONE ............................. 847 283-9780
Shau-Zou Lu, *President*
EMP: 6
SALES: 150K **Privately Held**
WEB: www.advangene.com
SIC: **3089** Plastics products

### (G-12828)
**AGRIPLASTICS LLC**
11 N Skokie Hwy (60044-1796)
PHONE ............................. 847 604-8847
Robert L Broten, *Principal*
EMP: 5
SALES (est): 379K **Privately Held**
SIC: **3089** Plastics products

### (G-12829)
**AMERICAN MEDICAL INDUSTRIES**
Also Called: European American Industries
28915 N Herky Dr Ste 107 (60044-1466)
PHONE ............................. 847 918-9800
Amit Helmer, *Vice Pres*
Jim Fiocchi, *Director*
EMP: 6
SALES (corp-wide): 1.6MM **Privately Held**
WEB: www.americanmedicalindustries.com
SIC: **3841** Surgical & medical instruments; veterinarians' instruments & apparatus
PA: American Medical Industries Inc
   330 E 3rd St Ste 2
   Dell Rapids SD 57022
   605 428-4683

### (G-12830)
**AMERICAN METAL FIBERS INC (PA)**
Also Called: Amfi
13420 Rockland Rd (60044-1469)
PHONE ............................. 847 295-8166
Fax: 847 362-7494
Rose Marie Carlson, *President*
Robert Carlson, *Treasurer*
Arnold M Schili, *Admin Sec*
◆ EMP: 50
SQ FT: 57,000
SALES (est): 10.9MM **Privately Held**
WEB: www.amfi-usa.com
SIC: **3399** Metal powders, pastes & flakes

### (G-12831)
**ANATOL EQUIPMENT MFG CO**
919 Sherwood Dr (60044-2203)
PHONE ............................. 847 367-9760
Anatol Topolewski, *President*
Andrew Peisker, *General Mgr*
Adam Koleno, *Sales Mgr*
Matt Short, *Regl Sales Mgr*
Michael Jirasek, *Manager*
◆ EMP: 40
SALES (est): 6.6MM **Privately Held**
WEB: www.anatol.com
SIC: **2759** Screen printing

### (G-12832)
**APPAREL WORKS INTL LLC**
51 Sherwood Ter Ste G (60044-2232)
PHONE ............................. 224 235-4240
Gregg Pavalon, *Managing Prtnr*
◆ EMP: 4
SALES: 3MM **Privately Held**
SIC: **2326** 2331 Industrial garments, men's & boys'; women's & misses' blouses & shirts

### (G-12833)
**ARCHER-DANIELS-MIDLAND COMPANY**
Also Called: Caterina Foods
927 N Shore Dr (60044-2201)
PHONE ............................. 224 544-5980
Edward Pinkowski, *Opers Mgr*
Tina Smith, *Admin Asst*
EMP: 60
SALES (corp-wide): 62.3B **Publicly Held**
SIC: **2099** Pasta, uncooked; packaged with other ingredients
PA: Archer-Daniels-Midland Company
   77 W Wacker Dr Ste 4600
   Chicago IL 60601
   312 634-8100

### (G-12834)
**AUTOMATED SYSTEMS & CONTROL CO**
11 N Skokie Hwy Ste 115 (60044-1776)
P.O. Box 7592, Algonquin (60102-7592)
PHONE ............................. 847 735-8310
William Schrieber, *President*
Keith Schrieber, *Purch Mgr*
EMP: 3
SALES (est): 330K **Privately Held**
SIC: **3625** 3577 8711 3613 Relays & industrial controls; computer peripheral equipment; engineering services; switchgear & switchboard apparatus

### (G-12835)
**BAKER MANUFACTURING LLC**
1349 Rockland Rd (60044-1435)
PHONE ............................. 847 362-3663
Arthur M Baker II, *Principal*
▲ EMP: 2
SALES (est): 281.8K **Privately Held**
SIC: **3999** Manufacturing industries

### (G-12836)
**BERRY GLOBAL INC**
Also Called: Covalence Plastics
495 Green Bay Rd (60044-2340)
EMP: 3
SALES (corp-wide): 6.4B **Publicly Held**
WEB: www.6sens.com
SIC: **3089** Bottle caps, molded plastic
HQ: Berry Global, Inc.
   101 Oakley St
   Evansville IN 47710
   812 424-2904

### (G-12837)
**BRANDT ASSOC**
1002 Muir Ave (60044-1538)
PHONE ............................. 847 362-0556
Dixon Brandt, *Partner*
Don Bitters, *Consultant*
EMP: 2
SALES (est): 307K **Privately Held**
SIC: **3825** Network analyzers

### (G-12838)
**BRAVURA MOULDING COMPANY**
28915 N Herky Dr Ste 103 (60044-1466)
PHONE ............................. 262 633-1882
Kent Parco, *President*
EMP: 5
SQ FT: 5,000
SALES: 1MM **Privately Held**
SIC: **2499** Picture frame molding, finished

### (G-12839)
**CORKEN INC (HQ)**
105 Albrecht Dr (60044-2252)
PHONE ............................. 405 946-5576
Art Laszio, *President*
Dave Misterson, *General Mgr*
◆ EMP: 3
SQ FT: 67,000
SALES: 40MM
SALES (corp-wide): 2.1B **Publicly Held**
WEB: www.idexcorp.com
SIC: **3563** 3561 3491 Air & gas compressors; pumps & pumping equipment; gas valves & parts, industrial
PA: Idex Corporation
   1925 W Field Ct Ste 200
   Lake Forest IL 60045
   847 498-7070

### (G-12840)
**DORMA USA INC**
Crane Revolving Door Company
924 Sherwood Dr (60044-2204)
PHONE ............................. 847 295-2700
Wartman Ron, *Financial Exec*
Andy Chapman, *Sales Mgr*
Angus Macmillan, *Branch Mgr*
Emma Rentell, *Payroll Mgr*
Ron Wartman, *Manager*
EMP: 70 **Privately Held**
SIC: **3442** 3231 Metal doors, sash & trim; products of purchased glass
HQ: Dorma Usa, Inc.
   100 Dorma Dr
   Reamstown PA 17567
   717 336-3881

### (G-12841)
**DUROWELD COMPANY INC**
Also Called: Arctic Blast Co
1565 Rockland Rd (60044-1455)
PHONE ............................. 847 680-3064
Fax: 847 816-8082
Stephen R Austin, *President*
Richard Austin, *Vice Pres*
Joe Smith, *Manager*
Claudia Austin, *Admin Sec*
EMP: 30
SALES (est): 6.3MM **Privately Held**
WEB: www.duroweld.net
SIC: **3449** 3842 3648 3471 Bars, concrete reinforcing: fabricated steel; wheelchairs; lighting equipment; cleaning, polishing & finishing; welding repair; sheet metalwork

### (G-12842)
**F G LIGHTING INC**
1111 Foster Ave (60044-1405)
PHONE ............................. 847 295-0445
Harold Holth, *Principal*
EMP: 3
SALES (est): 294.5K **Privately Held**
SIC: **3648** Lighting equipment

### (G-12843)
**FBM GALAXY INC**
1301 Laura Ln (60044-1427)
PHONE ............................. 847 362-0925
Fax: 847 362-7889
Keith J Artelt, *Manager*
EMP: 30
SQ FT: 20,000
SALES (corp-wide): 656.8MM **Publicly Held**
WEB: www.spi-co.com
SIC: **3296** Fiberglass insulation; insulation: rock wool, slag & silica minerals; glass wool
HQ: Fbm Galaxy, Inc.
   1650 Manheim Pike Ste 202
   Lancaster PA 17601
   717 569-3900

### (G-12844)
**FLUID MANUFACTURING SERVICES**
105 Albrecht Dr (60044-2252)
PHONE ............................. 800 458-5262
Frederick Wacker, *Owner*
EMP: 2
SALES (est): 207.3K **Privately Held**
SIC: **3829** Measuring & controlling devices

### (G-12845)
**GENETICS DEVELOPMENT CORP**
21 N Skokie Hwy Ste 104 (60044-1777)
PHONE ............................. 847 283-9780
K Y Chiu, *President*
EMP: 3
SALES: 10K **Privately Held**
SIC: **3999** Manufacturing industries

### (G-12846)
**GEORGE DROWNE CABINET SAND**
517 Lincoln Ave (60044-2419)
PHONE ............................. 847 234-1487
George Drowne, *Principal*
EMP: 4
SALES (est): 481K **Privately Held**
SIC: **2431** Millwork

### (G-12847)
**GPI MANUFACTURING INC**
Also Called: Gpi Prototype & Mfg Svcs
940 W North Shore Dr (60044-2202)
PHONE ............................. 847 615-8900
Fax: 847 615-8920
Scott Galloway, *CEO*
Adam Galloway, *President*
Sara Bilancia, *Vice Pres*
Jonathan Green, *VP Mfg*
Scott Volk, *VP Mfg*
▲ EMP: 35
SQ FT: 40,000
SALES (est): 9.6MM **Privately Held**
WEB: www.gpianatomicals.com
SIC: **3499** Friction material, made from powdered metal

### (G-12848)
**HELIO PRECISION PRODUCTS INC (PA)**
Also Called: Hn Precision
601 N Skokie Hwy Ste B (60044-1500)
PHONE ............................. 847 473-1300
Fax: 847 473-1306
Daniel Nash, *President*
Joe Tuzzolino, *Production*
Andrew Szatkowski, *QC Mgr*
Carl Drake, *Project Engr*
Paul Ainsworth, *CFO*
▲ EMP: 135
SQ FT: 155,000
SALES (est): 29.6MM **Privately Held**
WEB: www.helioprecision.com
SIC: **3592** Valves, engine

### (G-12849)
**HOMEWERKS WORLDWIDE LLC**
55 Albrecht Dr (60044-2226)
PHONE ............................. 877 319-3757
Peter Berkman, *President*
Art Wilkins, *Warehouse Mgr*
Richard Wild, *CFO*
Erik Stoesser, *Manager*
Ben Mills, *Senior Mgr*
▲ EMP: 25
SQ FT: 75,000
SALES: 50MM **Privately Held**
WEB: www.homewerksww.com
SIC: **5074** 3564 Plumbing & hydronic heating supplies; exhaust fans: industrial or commercial

### (G-12850)
**ILLINOIS TOOL WORKS INC**
Buehler
41 Waukegan Rd (60044-1691)
PHONE ............................. 847 295-6500
Fax: 847 295-7929
David Rollings, *Vice Pres*
Peter Wllner, *Vice Pres*
Joe Breslin, *Opers Mgr*
Tracy Putnam, *Branch Mgr*
EMP: 180
SALES (corp-wide): 13.6B **Publicly Held**
SIC: **5049** 3821 3829 3827 Optical goods; sample preparation apparatus; measuring & controlling devices; optical instruments & lenses; analytical instruments; instruments to measure electricity
PA: Illinois Tool Works Inc.
   155 Harlem Ave
   Glenview IL 60025
   847 724-7500

### (G-12851)
**JESSUP MANUFACTURING COMPANY**
1701 Rockland Rd (60044-1450)
PHONE ............................. 847 362-0961
Fax: 847 362-1070
Richard T Merle, *Exec VP*
Richard Merle, *Exec VP*
Bill Gagainis, *Vice Pres*
Vilnis Gagainis, *VP Opers*
Dan Moen, *Prdtn Mgr*
EMP: 35
SALES (corp-wide): 17.2MM **Privately Held**
SIC: **3069** 2295 Sponge rubber & sponge rubber products; coated fabrics, not rubberized

# GEOGRAPHIC SECTION

## Lake Forest - Lake County (G-12875)

**PA:** Jessup Manufacturing Company Inc
2815 W Rte 120
Mchenry IL 60051
815 385-6650

### (G-12852)
### L R GREGORY AND SON INC
1233 Rockland Rd (60044-1433)
**PHONE**..................847 247-0216
**Fax:** 847 247-0364
Jim Gregory, *President*
Jeff Fortin, *Manager*
Gwen Gregory, *Admin Sec*
Dennis Valentini, *Administration*
**EMP:** 20
**SQ FT:** 10,000
**SALES (est):** 2.2MM **Privately Held**
**WEB:** www.lrgregory.com
**SIC: 1711** 1761 3444 Warm air heating & air conditioning contractor; ventilation & duct work contractor; roofing contractor; sheet metalwork; sheet metalwork

### (G-12853)
### LEGACY VULCAN LLC
29821 N Skokie Hwy (60044-1117)
**PHONE**..................847 578-9622
**Fax:** 847 578-9714
Mike McCollum, *Manager*
**EMP:** 6
**SALES (corp-wide):** 3.5B **Publicly Held**
**WEB:** www.vulcanmaterials.com
**SIC: 1442** Construction sand & gravel
**HQ:** Legacy Vulcan, Llc
1200 Urban Center Dr
Vestavia AL 35242
205 298-3000

### (G-12854)
### LINDEMANN CHIMNEY SERVICE INC (PA)
Also Called: Lindemann Chimney Co
110 Albrecht Dr (60044-2247)
**PHONE**..................847 918-7994
**Fax:** 847 549-7995
Robert Lindemann, *President*
Gary Lindeman, *Treasurer*
Jeanne Smith, *Manager*
Mike Largen, *Technician*
▲ **EMP:** 10
**SQ FT:** 5,000
**SALES (est):** 3.5MM **Privately Held**
**WEB:** www.lindemannchimney.com
**SIC: 3444** 5087 7349 Ducts, sheet metal; cleaning & maintenance equipment & supplies; chimney cleaning

### (G-12855)
### LIQUID CONTROLS LLC (HQ)
105 Albrecht Dr (60044-2252)
**PHONE**..................847 295-1050
**Fax:** 847 295-1057
Fred Niemeier, *General Mgr*
Rob Rose, *Regional Mgr*
Mike Deren, *Engineer*
Dave Vaughn, *Engineer*
Teri Gulke, *Project Engr*
▲ **EMP:** 190
**SQ FT:** 69,000
**SALES (est):** 39.3MM
**SALES (corp-wide):** 2.1B **Publicly Held**
**WEB:** www.lcmeter.com
**SIC: 3824** Positive displacement meters
**PA:** Idex Corporation
1925 W Field Ct Ste 200
Lake Forest IL 60045
847 498-7070

### (G-12856)
### MASTER CONTROL SYSTEMS INC (PA)
910 N Shore Dr (60044-2295)
P.O. Box 276 (60044-0276)
**PHONE**..................847 295-1010
**Fax:** 847 295-0704
Jon Beckstrand, *CEO*
William Stelter, *President*
Yamari Aviles, *Purchasing*
Dana Conway, *Purchasing*
James S Nasby, *Engineer*
▼ **EMP:** 30

**SALES (est):** 4.4MM **Privately Held**
**WEB:** www.mastercontrols.com
**SIC: 3823** 3629 3625 Industrial instrmnts msrmnt display/control process variable; battery chargers, rectifying or nonrotating; control circuit devices, magnet & solid state

### (G-12857)
### MEYER MATERIAL CO MERGER CORP
30288 N Skokie Hwy (60044)
**PHONE**..................847 689-9200
Steve Wernke, *General Mgr*
**EMP:** 40
**SALES (corp-wide):** 26.6B **Privately Held**
**SIC: 3273** Ready-mixed concrete
**HQ:** Meyer Material Co Merger Corp.
580 S Wolf Rd
Des Plaines IL 60016
815 331-7200

### (G-12858)
### NATURAL STONE INC
611 Rockland Rd Ste 208 (60044-2000)
**PHONE**..................847 735-1129
Paul Piwowarczyk, *President*
Anna Piwowarczyk, *Admin Sec*
**EMP:** 7
**SQ FT:** 5,000
**SALES (est):** 727.1K **Privately Held**
**SIC: 3281** Marble, building: cut & shaped; granite, cut & shaped

### (G-12859)
### NORTH SHORE STAIRS
100 N Skokie Hwy Ste D (60044-1790)
**PHONE**..................847 295-7906
Steve Ehlert, *General Mgr*
Joan Boulet Lynch, *Principal*
**EMP:** 5
**SALES (est):** 550.6K **Privately Held**
**SIC: 3534** Elevators & moving stairways

### (G-12860)
### NORTH SHORE TRUCK & EQUIPMENT
29800 N Skokie Hwy Ste B (60044-1101)
**PHONE**..................847 887-0200
**Fax:** 847 887-0229
Mike Bicanic, *President*
**EMP:** 5
**SALES (est):** 771.7K **Privately Held**
**SIC: 7538** 7699 7692 5012 General truck repair; industrial equipment services; welding repair; automobiles & other motor vehicles; sheet metalwork

### (G-12861)
### PETER BAKER & SON CO (PA)
1349 Rockland Rd (60044-1498)
P.O. Box 187 (60044-0187)
**PHONE**..................847 362-3663
**Fax:** 847 362-0707
Arthura Baker II, *President*
Arthur M Baker II, *President*
John Brunner, *President*
John G Broecker, *Exec VP*
Michael Dieck, *Foreman/Supr*
**EMP:** 100 **EST:** 1915
**SQ FT:** 6,000
**SALES (est):** 22.2MM **Privately Held**
**WEB:** www.peterbaker.com
**SIC: 2951** 3272 1611 Asphalt paving mixtures & blocks; paving materials, prefabricated concrete; highway & street paving contractor; resurfacing contractor

### (G-12862)
### PHARMANUTRIENTS INC
37 Sherwood Ter Ste 109 (60044-2200)
**PHONE**..................847 234-2334
Mark A Nottoli, *President*
Betsy Moreno, *Office Mgr*
Artemis Lisserman, *Webmaster*
**EMP:** 5
**SALES (est):** 784K **Privately Held**
**SIC: 2834** Pharmaceutical preparations

### (G-12863)
### PLC CORP
220 Baker Rd (60044-1442)
P.O. Box 67 (60044-0067)
**PHONE**..................847 247-1900
**Fax:** 847 247-1902
Roger Risher, *President*

**EMP:** 6 **EST:** 1967
**SQ FT:** 6,000
**SALES (est):** 1.2MM **Privately Held**
**SIC: 2842** 2841 Cleaning or polishing preparations; automobile polish; sanitation preparations, disinfectants & deodorants; soap & other detergents

### (G-12864)
### PROFILE PLASTICS INC
Also Called: Safety Security Products Co
65 Waukegan Rd (60044-1665)
**PHONE**..................847 256-1623
**Fax:** 847 604-8030
Stephen R Murrill, *President*
Paul Stubitsch, *COO*
**EMP:** 80
**SALES (est):** 21.9MM **Privately Held**
**WEB:** www.vacform.com
**SIC: 3089** Thermoformed finished plastic products

### (G-12865)
### RONDOUT IRON & METAL CO INC
1501 Rockland Rd (60044-1446)
**PHONE**..................847 362-2750
**Fax:** 847 251-8821
Bob Miller, *President*
Steve Nadeluk, *Manager*
**EMP:** 7
**SQ FT:** 5,000
**SALES (est):** 830.4K **Privately Held**
**SIC: 5093** 3341 Ferrous metal scrap & waste; secondary nonferrous metals

### (G-12866)
### SEXTON WIND POWER LLC
49 Sherwood Ter Ste A (60044-2231)
**PHONE**..................224 212-1250
Arthur Daniels, *Principal*
**EMP:** 3
**SALES (est):** 253K **Privately Held**
**SIC: 3621** Windmills, electric generating

### (G-12867)
### TERLATO WINE GROUP LTD (PA)
Also Called: Local Wine Tours
900 Armour Dr (60044-1926)
**PHONE**..................847 604-8900
**Fax:** 847 236-0848
Anthony J Terlato, *Ch of Bd*
William A Terlato, *President*
Laurent Gallais-Pradal, *District Mgr*
Liz Barrett, *Vice Pres*
Rob Carruthers, *Vice Pres*
▲ **EMP:** 25
**SQ FT:** 26,000
**SALES (est):** 189MM **Privately Held**
**WEB:** www.rutherfordhills.com
**SIC: 5182** 2084 8743 Wine; wines; promotion service

### (G-12868)
### UNITED EDUCATORS INC (PA)
Also Called: Book House For Children Div
900 W North Shore Dr # 279 (60044-2243)
**PHONE**..................847 234-3700
**Fax:** 847 234-8705
Remo D Piazzi, *President*
Anthony Sacramento, *Vice Pres*
**EMP:** 15 **EST:** 1931
**SQ FT:** 6,000
**SALES (est):** 3.9MM **Privately Held**
**WEB:** www.theunitededucators.com
**SIC: 2731** Book publishing

### (G-12869)
### US FIREPLACE PRODUCTS INC
110 Albrecht Dr (60044-2247)
**PHONE**..................888 290-8181
Robert Lindemann, *President*
**EMP:** 5
**SALES (est):** 269.8K **Privately Held**
**SIC: 3272** Fireplace & chimney material; concrete

### (G-12870)
### WEC WELDING AND MACHINING LLC (DH)
Also Called: Westinghouse
1 Energy Dr (60044-1453)
**PHONE**..................847 680-8100
**Fax:** 847 362-6441

Jimmy Morgan, *President*
Tim Hanson, *Safety Mgr*
Thomas Panzilius, *Senior Engr*
**EMP:** 1
**SALES (est):** 43.5MM
**SALES (corp-wide):** 48.4B **Privately Held**
**SIC: 3398** 3541 1799 Metal heat treating; machine tools, metal cutting type; welding on site
**HQ:** Westinghouse Electric Company Llc
1000 Westinghouse Dr
Cranberry Township PA 16066
412 374-4111

### (G-12871)
### WECO TRADING INC (PA)
21 N Skokie Hwy Ste 101 (60044-1777)
**PHONE**..................847 615-1020
Walter L Roth, *CEO*
W Theodore Roth, *President*
Robert F Roth, *Vice Pres*
**EMP:** 7
**SQ FT:** 1,000
**SALES (est):** 20MM **Privately Held**
**SIC: 5093** 3341 Ferrous metal scrap & waste; secondary nonferrous metals

### (G-12872)
### WISCONSIN WILDERNESS FOOD PDTS
11 N Skokie Hwy Ste 207 (60044-1776)
**PHONE**..................847 735-8661
Margaret B Gunn, *President*
Robert Loveman, *Treasurer*
Neil Gunn, *Shareholder*
Reed Eberly, *Admin Sec*
Marsha Nusslock, *Asst Sec*
**EMP:** 5
**SQ FT:** 22,000
**SALES (est):** 480K **Privately Held**
**WEB:** www.wisconsinwilderness.com
**SIC: 2035** 2096 7389 2099 Pickles, sauces & salad dressings; potato chips & similar snacks; packaging & labeling services; food preparations; canned fruits & specialties

### (G-12873)
### WOODLAND ENGINEERING COMPANY
122 Baker Rd (60044-1424)
P.O. Box 632, Libertyville, (60048-0632)
**PHONE**..................847 362-0110
**Fax:** 847 362-5130
David Englund, *President*
Donald Englund, *Admin Sec*
**EMP:** 9 **EST:** 1960
**SQ FT:** 16,000
**SALES:** 810K **Privately Held**
**SIC: 3089** 3423 Injection molding of plastics; hand & edge tools

---

## Lake Forest
### Lake County

### (G-12874)
### ADAZON INC
1485 N Western Ave (60045-1218)
**PHONE**..................847 235-2700
**Fax:** 847 604-8364
John Barth, *President*
Jill Barth, *CFO*
Rachel Snyder, *Accounts Mgr*
**EMP:** 4
**SALES (est):** 1.4MM **Privately Held**
**WEB:** www.adazonusa.com
**SIC: 5131** 3577 Piece goods & notions; computer peripheral equipment

### (G-12875)
### ADVANCED AUDIO DEVICES LLC
725 N Mckinley Rd Ste 102 (60045-1850)
P.O. Box 769 (60045-0769)
**PHONE**..................847 604-9630
Peter Keller,
John Lahr,
**EMP:** 4
**SALES (est):** 260K **Privately Held**
**WEB:** www.advaudiodev.com
**SIC: 3651** Audio electronic systems

---

(PA)=Parent Co (HQ)=Headquarters (DH)=Div Headquarters
✪ = New Business established in last 2 years

# Lake Forest - Lake County (G-12876)  GEOGRAPHIC SECTION

**(G-12876)**
**AKORN INC (PA)**
1925 W Field Ct Ste 300 (60045-4862)
PHONE..................................847 279-6100
Raj Rai, *CEO*
John N Kapoor, *Ch of Bd*
Bruce Kutinsky, *COO*
Joseph Bonaccorsi, *Exec VP*
Jonathan Kafer, *Exec VP*
▲ **EMP:** 124
**SQ FT:** 58,000
**SALES:** 1.1B Publicly Held
**WEB:** www.akorn.com
**SIC:** 2834 5047 Pharmaceutical preparations; surgical equipment & supplies

**(G-12877)**
**ALBERTI ENTERPRISES INC**
825 S Waukegan Rd A8151 (60045-2696)
PHONE..................................847 810-7610
Tony Alberti, *Principal*
▲ **EMP:** 6
**SALES (est):** 599K Privately Held
**WEB:** www.albertienterprises.com
**SIC:** 3556 5078 Beverage machinery; refrigerated beverage dispensers

**(G-12878)**
**AMERICAN NURSERYMAN PUBG CO**
1696 Oak Knoll Dr (60045-3710)
PHONE..................................847 234-5867
Allen Seidel, *Ch of Bd*
Wayne Siatte, *General Mgr*
Les Gage, *Sls & Mktg Exec*
Jennifer Misek, *Manager*
Donald W Shields, *Manager*
**EMP:** 20 **EST:** 1904
**SQ FT:** 6,400
**SALES (est):** 2.4MM Privately Held
**WEB:** www.amernursery.com
**SIC:** 2721 2731 Magazines: publishing & printing; book publishing

**(G-12879)**
**AMITY DIE AND STAMPING CO**
Also Called: ADS
13870 W Polo Trail Dr (60045-5102)
PHONE..................................847 680-6600
**Fax:** 847 680-6677
Evelyn Westphal, *President*
Patrick Stevens, *President*
Glen Westphal, *Vice Pres*
Brian Westphal, *Treasurer*
Vince Addante, *Sales Mgr*
**EMP:** 30
**SQ FT:** 30,000
**SALES (est):** 6.8MM Privately Held
**WEB:** www.amitydie.com
**SIC:** 3469 3544 Stamping metal for the trade; die sets for metal stamping (presses)

**(G-12880)**
**ARNDT ENTERPRISE LTD**
674 Timber Ln Ste 200 (60045-3118)
PHONE..................................847 234-5736
Raymond Puszczewicz, *President*
◆ **EMP:** 3
**SALES:** 100K Privately Held
**SIC:** 7699 7692 Picture framing, custom; welding repair

**(G-12881)**
**ASSOCIATED RESEARCH INC**
13860 W Laurel Dr (60045-4531)
PHONE..................................847 367-4077
**Fax:** 847 367-4080
Richard Inman, *Ch of Bd*
Michael Braverman, *President*
Peter Stevens, *General Mgr*
Joseph Guerriero, *Vice Pres*
Eric Snow, *Opers Mgr*
▲ **EMP:** 35 **EST:** 1936
**SALES (est):** 10.9MM
**SALES (corp-wide):** 16.5MM Privately Held
**WEB:** www.asresearch.com
**SIC:** 3825 Test equipment for electronic & electric measurement
**PA:** Ikonix Group, Inc
  28105 N Keith Dr
  Lake Forest IL 60045
  847 367-4671

**(G-12882)**
**ATCH INC (PA)**
825 S Waukegan Rd Pmb 157 (60045-2696)
PHONE..................................847 295-5055
Kate Sackman, *President*
Paul Pesek, *Chairman*
Chris Coffin, *Director*
**EMP:** 1
**SALES (est):** 418.8K Privately Held
**SIC:** 3841 Diagnostic apparatus, medical

**(G-12883)**
**AUTOPARTS HOLDINGS LTD**
1900 W Field Ct (60045-4828)
PHONE..................................203 830-7800
Gregory Allen Cole, *Mng Member*
**EMP:** 2400
**SALES (est):** 105.3MM Privately Held
**SIC:** 3714 Motor vehicle parts & accessories

**(G-12884)**
**BARRIERSAFE SOLUTIONS INTL INC (HQ)**
Also Called: Bssi
150 N Field Dr Ste 210 (60045-4853)
PHONE..................................847 735-0163
Michael Mattos, *President*
Brian Moore, *Vice Pres*
Steven Olechny, *Vice Pres*
Jim Tao, *Vice Pres*
Joseph H Kubicek, *Treasurer*
▲ **EMP:** 20
**SALES (est):** 45.2MM
**SALES (corp-wide):** 1.5B Privately Held
**WEB:** www.barriersafe.com
**SIC:** 3069 Laboratory sundries: cases, covers, funnels, cups, etc.; medical sundries, rubber
**PA:** Ansell Limited
  L 3 678 Victoria St
  Richmond VIC 3121
  130 085-0505

**(G-12885)**
**BEAVER-VISITEC INTL HOLDINGS**
272 E Deerpath Ste 328 (60045-1947)
PHONE..................................847 739-3219
Tom Kapfer, *President*
Michele Szot, *Executive Asst*
**EMP:** 343
**SALES (est):** 18.3MM Privately Held
**SIC:** 3841 Ophthalmic instruments & apparatus

**(G-12886)**
**BEAVER-VISITEC INTL INC**
272 E Deerpath Ste 328 (60045-1947)
PHONE..................................847 739-3219
Tom Kapfer, *President*
Michele Szot, *Admin Asst*
**EMP:** 8
**SALES (corp-wide):** 304.8MM Privately Held
**SIC:** 3841 Surgical knife blades & handles
**HQ:** Beaver-Visitec International, Inc.
  411 Waverley Oaks Rd # 227
  Waltham MA 02452
  781 906-8080

**(G-12887)**
**BLISSFUL BROWNIES INC**
619 Highview Ter (60045-3226)
P.O. Box 949 (60045-0949)
PHONE..................................541 308-0226
Ambler Fitzsimons, *President*
**EMP:** 5
**SQ FT:** 2,500
**SALES (est):** 342.5K Privately Held
**SIC:** 5441 2052 5149 Candy, nut & confectionery stores; bakery products, dry; cookies

**(G-12888)**
**BRUNSWICK CORPORATION (PA)**
1 N Field Ct (60045-4811)
PHONE..................................847 735-4700
**Fax:** 847 735-4765
Mark D Schwabero, *Ch of Bd*
Huw S Bower, *Vice Pres*
Christopher F Dekker, *Vice Pres*
Jaime A Irick, *Vice Pres*
John C Pfeifer, *Vice Pres*
◆ **EMP:** 339 **EST:** 1845
**SALES:** 4.4B Publicly Held
**WEB:** www.brunswick.com
**SIC:** 3519 3732 3949 7933 Outboard motors; marine engines; boats, fiberglass: building & repairing; motorboats, inboard or outboard: building & repairing; sporting & athletic goods; reels, fishing; rods & rod parts, fishing; bowling alleys & accessories; bowling centers; billiard equipment & supplies

**(G-12889)**
**BRUNSWICK INTERNATIONAL LTD (HQ)**
Also Called: B I L
1 N Field Ct (60045-4811)
PHONE..................................847 735-4700
Judith Zelisko, *Vice Pres*
Fred Florjanick, *Vice Pres*
Yozoh Tetsa, *Vice Pres*
Richard O'Brien, *Treasurer*
Leslie Harling, *Manager*
**EMP:** 7
**SALES (est):** 9MM
**SALES (corp-wide):** 4.4B Publicly Held
**SIC:** 3519 3732 3949 3728 Outboard motors; marine engines; boats, fiberglass: building & repairing; motorboats, inboard or outboard: building & repairing; reels, fishing; rods & rod parts, fishing; bowling alleys & accessories; aircraft body assemblies & parts; airframe assemblies, except for guided missiles; navigational systems & instruments
**PA:** Brunswick Corporation
  1 N Field Ct
  Lake Forest IL 60045
  847 735-4700

**(G-12890)**
**CARROLL INTERNATIONAL CORP (PA)**
55 N Mayflower Rd (60045-2420)
PHONE..................................630 983-5979
Barry J Carroll, *President*
James M Elsen, *CFO*
**EMP:** 10
**SQ FT:** 6,000
**SALES (est):** 9.5MM Privately Held
**WEB:** www.carrollhomes.com
**SIC:** 3444 3532 Metal ventilating equipment; mineral beneficiation equipment

**(G-12891)**
**CINDYS NAIL & HAIR CARE**
Also Called: Bella Salon
950 N Western Ave Ste G (60045-1734)
PHONE..................................847 234-0780
Cindy Schultz, *Owner*
**EMP:** 3
**SALES (est):** 84.7K Privately Held
**SIC:** 7231 3999 Beauty shops; hair curlers, designed for beauty parlors

**(G-12892)**
**COLBERT PACKAGING CORPORATION (PA)**
Also Called: C P
28355 N Bradley Rd (60045-1173)
PHONE..................................847 367-5990
**Fax:** 847 367-4403
James B Hamilton, *President*
Nancy C Macdougall, *Vice Pres*
Jerry Franklin, *Plant Mgr*
Marilyn Calhoun, *Opers Mgr*
Belinda Charleston, *Opers Mgr*
▲ **EMP:** 155 **EST:** 1959
**SQ FT:** 95,000
**SALES (est):** 62.9MM Privately Held
**WEB:** www.colbertpkg.com
**SIC:** 2657 2652 Folding paperboard boxes; setup paperboard boxes

**(G-12893)**
**COLBORNE ACQUISITION CO LLC**
28495 N Ballard Dr (60045-4510)
PHONE..................................847 371-0101
Rich Hoskins, *Sls & Mktg Exec*
Patrice Painchaud, *Sales Mgr*
Rich Stepanian, *Manager*
Page Thomas, *Manager*
Rick Hoskins, *Director*
**EMP:** 30 **EST:** 2009
**SALES (est):** 8.1MM Privately Held
**SIC:** 3556 Food products machinery

**(G-12894)**
**CORETECHS CORP**
245 Butler Dr (60045-3009)
PHONE..................................847 295-3720
Dr Nelson L Levy, *President*
Louisa Levy, *Admin Sec*
**EMP:** 17
**SQ FT:** 600
**SALES (est):** 1.4MM Privately Held
**SIC:** 2834 Pharmaceutical preparations

**(G-12895)**
**DEERPATH PUBLISHING CO INC**
692 Linden Ave (60045-3926)
PHONE..................................847 234-3385
Clark Schmitz, *President*
Ronda Schmitz, *Corp Secy*
Eugene Jones, *Vice Pres*
**EMP:** 3
**SALES (est):** 125.3K Privately Held
**SIC:** 2731 Book publishing

**(G-12896)**
**DISTRIBUTION ENTERPRISES INC**
Also Called: Graphic Marking Systems
28457 N Ballard Dr Ste A1 (60045-4545)
PHONE..................................847 582-9276
Marjorie Mc Cullough, *President*
Doug Goodloe, *Vice Pres*
Paul Kolodzik, *Technical Staff*
**EMP:** 10
**SQ FT:** 18,000
**SALES:** 4MM Privately Held
**WEB:** www.distributionenterprises.com
**SIC:** 3555 5084 Printing trades machinery; printing trades machinery, equipment & supplies

**(G-12897)**
**ENVISION INC**
40 N Ahwahnee Rd (60045)
PHONE..................................847 735-0789
Eric Arnson, *Principal*
**EMP:** 5
**SALES (est):** 451.9K Privately Held
**SIC:** 2673 Bags: plastic, laminated & coated

**(G-12898)**
**EXCEL SPECIALTY CORP**
Also Called: National Multi Products Co
28101 N Ballard Dr Ste A (60045-4544)
PHONE..................................773 262-7575
**Fax:** 773 262-1330
Robert Kopf, *CEO*
Paul Kopf, *President*
Michelle Kopf, *Corp Secy*
▲ **EMP:** 25 **EST:** 1949
**SQ FT:** 20,000
**SALES (est):** 4.3MM Privately Held
**WEB:** www.excelspecialty.com
**SIC:** 3679 3694 3644 3643 Harness assemblies for electronic use: wire or cable; engine electrical equipment; noncurrent-carrying wiring services; current-carrying wiring devices; nonferrous wiredrawing & insulating; steel wire & related products

**(G-12899)**
**FRAM GROUP OPERATIONS LLC (HQ)**
Also Called: Fram Group Limited
1900 W Field Ct (60045-4828)
PHONE..................................800 890-2075
Bruce Zorich, *President*
Ike Petersen, *Vice Pres*
George Dirado, *CFO*
Mark Wikingstad, *CIO*
Brenda James, *Analyst*
◆ **EMP:** 277
**SALES (est):** 998MM Privately Held
**SIC:** 3694 3714 Engine electrical equipment; motor vehicle parts & accessories
**PA:** Rank Group Limited
  Fl 9 148 Quay St
  Auckland
  936 662-59

## GEOGRAPHIC SECTION
## Lake Forest - Lake County (G-12924)

**(G-12900)**
**GIVAUDAN FRAGRANCES CORP**
1720 N Waukegan Rd (60045-1155)
PHONE.....................847 735-0221
Fax: 847 735-0602
Christopher Johnson, *Vice Pres*
EMP: 5
SALES (corp-wide): 1.1B Privately Held
SIC: 5149 2844 Flavourings & fragrances; colognes
HQ: Givaudan Fragrances Corporation
1199 Edison Dr Ste 1-2
Cincinnati OH 45216
513 948-3428

**(G-12901)**
**GLASER USA INC**
14181 W Hawthorne Ave (60045-1086)
PHONE.....................847 362-7878
Peter Glaser, *President*
Harry Haack, *Admin Sec*
Melanie Reinmuller, *Admin Sec*
EMP: 3
SALES: 200K Privately Held
WEB: www.glaser-usa.com
SIC: 3541 Buffing & polishing machines

**(G-12902)**
**GOHEAR LLC**
100 Saunders Rd (60045-2502)
PHONE.....................847 574-7829
EMP: 3
SALES (est): 257.2K Privately Held
SIC: 3842 5047 8099 Hearing aids; hearing aids; hearing testing service

**(G-12903)**
**GOODHOME FOODS INC**
100 Saunders Rd (60045-2502)
PHONE.....................847 816-6832
Dalyn L Dye, *President*
EMP: 2 EST: 2011
SALES (est): 358.3K Privately Held
SIC: 5149 5141 2034 Groceries & related products; groceries, general line; dehydrated fruits, vegetables, soups

**(G-12904)**
**GREGOR JONSSON ASSOCIATES INC**
13822 W Laurel Dr (60045-4529)
PHONE.....................847 247-4200
Fax: 847 247-4272
Frank Heurich, *President*
Beth Dancy, *Vice Pres*
Elizabeth Dancy, *Vice Pres*
Scott Heurich, *Opers Mgr*
Laura Pegoraro, *Purchasing*
EMP: 25 EST: 1956
SQ FT: 13,600
SALES (est): 5.9MM Privately Held
WEB: www.jonsson.com
SIC: 3556 Fish & shellfish processing machinery

**(G-12905)**
**HOOGWEGT US INC**
100 Saunders Rd Ste 200 (60045-2502)
PHONE.....................847 680-6143
Fax: 847 680-6143
Dalyn L Dye, *CEO*
Jill De Lio, *Vice Pres*
Arjen Opt Hof, *Vice Pres*
Jill Lio, *VP Opers*
Arjen Opthof, *Opers Mgr*
▼ EMP: 62
SQ FT: 14,000
SALES (est): 35.4MM
SALES (corp-wide): 2.4B Privately Held
WEB: www.hoogwegtus.com
SIC: 2021 2022 2023 Creamery butter; cheese, natural & processed; powdered buttermilk; powdered cream; powdered milk; powdered skim milk
PA: Hoogwegt Group B.V.
Groningensingel 1
Arnhem
263 884-802

**(G-12906)**
**HORIZON PHARMA INC (HQ)**
150 Saunders Rd Ste 400 (60045-2523)
PHONE.....................224 383-3000
Fax: 224 383-3001
Timothy P Walbert, *President*
Fabian Chapur, *District Mgr*
Gary Geraghty, *District Mgr*
Lance Martin, *District Mgr*
Jeremy Nye, *District Mgr*
EMP: 79
SQ FT: 34,460
SALES: 296.9MM Privately Held
SIC: 2834 Pharmaceutical preparations

**(G-12907)**
**HORIZON THERAPEUTICS INC**
Also Called: Ravicti
150 Saunders Rd Ste 150 (60045-2523)
PHONE.....................224 383-3000
Timothy P Walbert, *President*
Ashley Gould, *Senior VP*
Tony Brew, *Facilities Mgr*
Paul W Hoelscher, *CFO*
Natalie Svaldi, *CPA*
EMP: 54
SALES: 113.5MM Privately Held
WEB: www.hyperiontx.com
SIC: 2834 Pharmaceutical preparations
HQ: Horizon Pharma, Inc.
150 Saunders Rd Ste 400
Lake Forest IL 60045

**(G-12908)**
**HOSPIRA INC (HQ)**
275 N Field Dr (60045-2510)
PHONE.....................224 212-2000
F Michael Ball, *CEO*
Peter Brigida, *Counsel*
Royce R Bedward, *Senior VP*
Richard Davies, *Senior VP*
John B Elliot, *Senior VP*
◆ EMP: 700
SALES: 4.4B
SALES (corp-wide): 52.8B Publicly Held
WEB: www.abbotthpd.com
SIC: 2834 3841 Pharmaceutical preparations; proprietary drug products; tablets, pharmaceutical; diagnostic apparatus, medical; medical instruments & equipment, blood & bone work; IV transfusion apparatus
PA: Pfizer Inc.
235 E 42nd St
New York NY 10017
212 733-2323

**(G-12909)**
**HOSPIRA INC**
375 N Field Dr Bldg H3 (60045-2513)
PHONE.....................224 212-6244
Jean Kirkeleit Davis, *Manager*
EMP: 154
SALES (corp-wide): 52.8B Publicly Held
WEB: www.abbotthpd.com
SIC: 2834 3841 Druggists' preparations (pharmaceuticals); emulsions, pharmaceutical; proprietary drug products; tablets, pharmaceutical; diagnostic apparatus, medical; medical instruments & equipment, blood & bone work; IV transfusion apparatus
HQ: Hospira, Inc.
275 N Field Dr
Lake Forest IL 60045
224 212-2000

**(G-12910)**
**HOSPIRA WORLDWIDE LLC (DH)**
275 N Field Dr (60045-2510)
PHONE.....................224 212-2000
F Michael Ball, *CEO*
Christopher Begley, *CEO*
John C Staley, *Ch of Bd*
Royce R Bedward, *Senior VP*
Richard Davies, *Senior VP*
◆ EMP: 2
SALES (est): 1.1MM
SALES (corp-wide): 52.8B Publicly Held
SIC: 3841 Diagnostic apparatus, medical
HQ: Hospira, Inc.
275 N Field Dr
Lake Forest IL 60045
224 212-2000

**(G-12911)**
**HUNTER MANUFACTURING GROUP INC**
227 Northgate St Ste 3 (60045-1884)
PHONE.....................859 254-7573
Jack C Smith, *President*
EMP: 2
SALES (est): 211.8K Privately Held
SIC: 3231 Products of purchased glass

**(G-12912)**
**HUNTER MFG LLP (PA)**
227 Northgate St Ste 3 (60045-1884)
PHONE.....................859 254-7573
Fax: 859 254-7614
Mark Shepherd, *CEO*
Will Harward, *CFO*
▲ EMP: 90
SQ FT: 255,262
SALES (est): 17.5MM Privately Held
WEB: www.huntermfg.com
SIC: 3229 3949 3999 3942 Novelty glassware; sporting & athletic goods; pet supplies; stuffed toys, including animals

**(G-12913)**
**HZNP USA INC**
150 Saunders Rd Ste 200 (60045-2523)
PHONE.....................224 383-3000
Tim Walbert, *CEO*
Brian Jennette, *Controller*
Stephanie Kupsky, *Director*
Natalie Svaldi, *Analyst*
EMP: 18
SALES (est): 2.5MM Privately Held
WEB: www.vidararx.com
SIC: 2834 Pharmaceutical preparations
PA: Vidara Therapeutics Holdings Llc
1000 Holcomb Woods Pkwy
Roswell GA 30076
678 205-5444

**(G-12914)**
**IDENTIFICATION PRODUCTS MFG CO (PA)**
13777 W Laurel Dr (60045-4530)
PHONE.....................847 367-6452
Fax: 847 367-7004
Michael Klainos, *CEO*
Sandra Klainos, *Corp Secy*
Mark Klainos, *Vice Pres*
Gary Bendfeldt, *Sales Staff*
Nikki Klainos, *Manager*
▲ EMP: 8
SQ FT: 5,000
SALES (est): 1.8MM Privately Held
WEB: www.identification-products.com
SIC: 3089 3579 Identification cards, plastic; laminating of plastic; binding machines, plastic & adhesive

**(G-12915)**
**IDEX CORPORATION (PA)**
1925 W Field Ct Ste 200 (60045-4862)
PHONE.....................847 498-7070
Andrew K Silvernail, *Ch of Bd*
Eric D Ashleman, *COO*
Denise R Cade, *Senior VP*
James Maclennan, *Senior VP*
Moez Adatia, *Vice Pres*
EMP: 277
SQ FT: 36,588
SALES: 2.1B Publicly Held
WEB: www.idexcorp.com
SIC: 3561 3563 3594 Industrial pumps & parts; air & gas compressors; fluid power pumps & motors

**(G-12916)**
**IKONIX GROUP INC (PA)**
Also Called: Electrical Safety Testing Eqp
28105 N Keith Dr (60045-4528)
PHONE.....................847 367-4671
Fax: 847 367-4625
Michael R Braverman, *President*
Graner Eva, *Human Res Dir*
Adam Mikos, *Sales Mgr*
Jim Kenesie, *Mktg Dir*
Adam Braverman, *Marketing Mgr*
▲ EMP: 5
SQ FT: 12,000
SALES (est): 16.5MM Privately Held
SIC: 3679 Power supplies, all types: static

**(G-12917)**
**INITIAL CHOICE**
226 E Westminster (60045-1840)
PHONE.....................847 234-5884
Fax: 847 234-5894
Margaret H Lambrecht, *Partner*
Sarah Lambrecht, *Partner*
EMP: 10
SQ FT: 1,500
SALES (est): 704.9K Privately Held
WEB: www.theinitialchoice.com
SIC: 5947 5641 2395 Gift shop; children's wear; infants' wear; pleating & stitching

**(G-12918)**
**INNOWARE PLASTIC INC**
150 Saunders Rd Ste 150 (60045-2523)
PHONE.....................678 690-5100
Chuck Woodward, *President*
Tracy Garrett, *Credit Mgr*
Dan Brunner, *Accounts Mgr*
▲ EMP: 160
SALES (est): 11.4MM Privately Held
WEB: www.innowareinc.com
SIC: 3089 Plastic kitchenware, tableware & houseware; trays, plastic

**(G-12919)**
**INTERSECT HEALTHCARE SYSTEMS**
230 Northgate St Unit 145 (60045-5606)
PHONE.....................847 457-2159
Larry Rine, *President*
EMP: 3
SALES (est): 153.2K Privately Held
SIC: 7372 Application computer software

**(G-12920)**
**KIRBY LESTER LLC (HQ)**
13700 W Irma Lee Ct (60045-5123)
PHONE.....................847 984-3377
Gary Zage, *President*
Karen Bergendorf, *COO*
Dave Johnson, *Vice Pres*
Christopher Thomsen, *Vice Pres*
Kay Benedict, *Office Mgr*
▲ EMP: 70
SQ FT: 15,000
SALES (est): 19.3MM
SALES (corp-wide): 47.7MM Privately Held
WEB: www.kirbylester.com
SIC: 3559 Pharmaceutical machinery
PA: Capsa Solutions Llc
4253 Ne 189th Ave
Portland OR 97230
503 766-2324

**(G-12921)**
**KLAI-CO IDNTIFICATION PDTS INC**
13777 W Laurel Dr (60045-4530)
PHONE.....................847 573-0375
Mark Klainos, *President*
Gary Bendfeldt, *Manager*
◆ EMP: 23
SQ FT: 20,000
SALES (est): 4.6MM Privately Held
SIC: 3555 3579 5044 5112 Bookbinding machinery; binding machines, plastic & adhesive; office equipment; office supplies; business machines & equipment

**(G-12922)**
**LAMINTING BNDING SOLUTIONS INC ✪**
27885 Irma Lee Cir (60045-5110)
PHONE.....................847 573-0375
John Moorehouse, *President*
Amy Beth Moorehouse, *Vice Pres*
EMP: 9 EST: 2016
SQ FT: 6,000
SALES: 7.5MM Privately Held
SIC: 3579 Binding machines, plastic & adhesive

**(G-12923)**
**LANA UNLIMITED CO (PA)**
Also Called: Lana Jewelry
736 N Western Ave Ste 308 (60045-1820)
PHONE.....................312 226-7050
Fax: 312 492-6516
Lana Fertelmeister, *President*
Naum Fertelmeister, *Vice Pres*
Kristen Zivic, *Sales Dir*
EMP: 8
SALES (est): 626.5K Privately Held
SIC: 3911 Jewelry, precious metal

**(G-12924)**
**MASTER CONTAINERS INC**
1900 W Field Ct (60045-4828)
P.O. Box 586, Mulberry FL (33860-0586)
PHONE.....................863 425-5571

# Lake Forest - Lake County (G-12925)     GEOGRAPHIC SECTION

Elaine Kurau, *Sales Mgr*
**EMP:** 11 **Privately Held**
**SIC:** 3086 Cups & plates, foamed plastic
**HQ:** Master Containers, Inc.
   200 Brickstone Sq Ste G05
   Andover MA 01810
   800 881-6847

### (G-12925)
### MAYNE PHARMA USA INC
275 N Field Dr (60045-2579)
**PHONE** ............................ 224 212-2660
Stuart Hinchen, *President*
**EMP:** 3
**SALES (est):** 245.5K **Privately Held**
**SIC:** 2834 Pharmaceutical preparations

### (G-12926)
### MIDWEST RESEARCH LABS LLC (PA)
476 Oakwood Ave (60045-1927)
**PHONE** ............................ 847 283-9176
James L Yeager, *Partner*
Nadir Buyuktimkim, *Partner*
Servet Buyuktimkim, *Partner*
Jean Yeager, *Partner*
**EMP:** 5
**SQ FT:** 1,000
**SALES (est):** 546.6K **Privately Held**
**SIC:** 2834 Pharmaceutical preparations

### (G-12927)
### MJM GRAPHICS
433 Greenwood Ave (60045-3917)
**PHONE** ............................ 847 234-1802
Michael J Mc Kiernan, *Owner*
Michael J McKiernan, *Owner*
**EMP:** 5 **EST:** 1979
**SALES:** 1MM **Privately Held**
**WEB:** www.mjmgraphics.com
**SIC:** 2752 2759 Commercial printing, offset; commercial printing

### (G-12928)
### MPD INC
13795 W Polo Trail Dr A (60045-5142)
**PHONE** ............................ 847 489-7705
**Fax:** 847 367-0711
Joe Hajnos, *President*
Bo Shapich, *Vice Pres*
Dave Cohen, *Engineer*
Eva Hajnos, *Manager*
◆ **EMP:** 28
**SQ FT:** 30,000
**SALES:** 10.1MM **Privately Held**
**SIC:** 3089 Injection molded finished plastic products

### (G-12929)
### NEPTUN LIGHT INC
13950 W Bus Ctr Dr (60045)
**PHONE** ............................ 847 735-8330
**Fax:** 847 789-7189
Andrew Bobel, *President*
Marzenna Bobel, *CFO*
Marzenna Neptun, *CFO*
Matthew Jarosz, *Sales Associate*
◆ **EMP:** 4
**SALES (est):** 1.4MM **Privately Held**
**WEB:** www.neptunlight.com
**SIC:** 3646 Commercial indusl & institutional electric lighting fixtures

### (G-12930)
### NORTH AMRCN HERB SPICE LTD LLC
13900 W Polo Trail Dr (60045-5103)
P.O. Box 4885, Buffalo Grove (60089-4885)
**PHONE** ............................ 847 367-6070
Jennifer Bilotti, *Manager*
Angelo Camp, *Manager*
Lelia Davis, *Manager*
Bill Gray, *Manager*
Judy Kay Gray, *Manager*
▲ **EMP:** 14
**SQ FT:** 30,000
**SALES (est):** 3.3MM **Privately Held**
**SIC:** 2833 Drugs & herbs: grading, grinding & milling

### (G-12931)
### NORTHWOODS WREATHS COMPANY
450 W Deerpath (60045-1618)
P.O. Box 682 (60045-0682)
**PHONE** ............................ 847 615-9491
Andy Barrie, *Owner*
**EMP:** 30
**SALES (est):** 1.9MM **Privately Held**
**SIC:** 3999 5961 Wreaths, artificial; catalog & mail-order houses

### (G-12932)
### OMRON HEALTHCARE INC (DH)
1925 W Field Ct (60045-4862)
**PHONE** ............................ 847 680-6200
**Fax:** 800 680-6269
Ranndy Kellogg, *CEO*
Karen Stenseth, *General Mgr*
Jim LI, *Business Mgr*
Michelle Misialek, *Senior VP*
Helen Reetz, *Vice Pres*
◆ **EMP:** 80 **EST:** 1974
**SQ FT:** 145,000
**SALES (est):** 52.2MM
**SALES (corp-wide):** 7.1B **Privately Held**
**WEB:** www.omronhealthcare.com
**SIC:** 5047 3845 3841 3829 Hospital equipment & supplies; surgical equipment & supplies; electromedical equipment; surgical & medical instruments; measuring & controlling devices; industrial instrmnts msrmnt display/control process variable
**HQ:** Omron Healthcare Co.,Ltd.
   53, Kyunotsubo, Teradocho
   Muko KYO 617-0
   759 252-000

### (G-12933)
### PACKAGING CORPORATION AMERICA (PA)
Also Called: PCA
1955 W Field Ct (60045-4824)
**PHONE** ............................ 847 482-3000
**Fax:** 847 482-4532
Mark W Kowlzan, *Ch of Bd*
Thomas A Hassfurther, *Exec VP*
Charles J Carter, *Senior VP*
Kent A Pflederer, *Senior VP*
Thomas W H Walton, *Senior VP*
▲ **EMP:** 200
**SALES:** 5.7B **Publicly Held**
**WEB:** www.packagingcorp.com
**SIC:** 2631 2653 Container board; container, packaging & boxboard; corrugated & solid fiber boxes

### (G-12934)
### PACTIV INTL HOLDINGS INC (DH)
1900 W Field Ct (60045-4828)
**PHONE** ............................ 847 482-2000
James D Morris, *President*
David P Brush, *Vice Pres*
James D Butler, *Vice Pres*
Daniel G Carr, *Vice Pres*
Bradley W Early, *Vice Pres*
**EMP:** 9
**SALES (est):** 737.5K **Privately Held**
**WEB:** www.pactiv.com
**SIC:** 2621 3089 2673 Paper mills; plastic processing; bags: plastic, laminated & coated
**HQ:** Pactiv Llc
   1900 W Field Ct
   Lake Forest IL 60045
   847 482-2000

### (G-12935)
### PACTIV LLC (DH)
1900 W Field Ct (60045-4828)
P.O. Box 5040 (60045-5040)
**PHONE** ............................ 847 482-2000
Richard L Wambold, *CEO*
Jacquelyne Huerta, *CEO*
Adolfo Salinas, *Principal*
Jason Dennis, *Exec Officer*
Deirdre Brekke, *Counsel*
◆ **EMP:** 550 **EST:** 1965
**SALES (est):** 10.5B **Privately Held**
**WEB:** www.pactiv.com
**SIC:** 5113 3089 2673 Containers, paper & disposable plastic; food casings, plastic; food storage & frozen food bags, plastic

**HQ:** Reynolds Group Holdings Limited
   L 9 148 Quay St
   Auckland 1010
   935 912-68

### (G-12936)
### PACTIV LLC
Also Called: Pactiv Molded Products
1900 W Field Ct (60045-4828)
**PHONE** ............................ 219 924-4120
Sharon Asche, *Plant Mgr*
John Paul, *Buyer*
Murday Celeste, *Financial Exec*
Liz Schofield, *Cust Mgr*
Ronald Bullock, *Branch Mgr*
**EMP:** 150 **Privately Held**
**WEB:** www.pactiv.com
**SIC:** 2656 Sanitary food containers
**HQ:** Pactiv Llc
   1900 W Field Ct
   Lake Forest IL 60045
   847 482-2000

### (G-12937)
### PACTIV LLC
1900 W Field Ct (60045-4828)
**PHONE** ............................ 847 482-2000
Dana Nead, *President*
Adam Patrick, *Purch Mgr*
Ted Beveridge, *Director*
**EMP:** 50 **Privately Held**
**WEB:** www.pactiv.com
**SIC:** 3353 3497 Foil, aluminum; metal foil & leaf
**HQ:** Pactiv Llc
   1900 W Field Ct
   Lake Forest IL 60045
   847 482-2000

### (G-12938)
### PACTIV LLC
1900 W Field Ct (60045-4828)
**PHONE** ............................ 715 723-4181
Win Clemmons, *General Mgr*
Mark Kohls, *Prdtn Mgr*
Tim Sheehan, *Mfg Spvr*
Robin Jaenke, *Purchasing*
Ray Peterson, *Financial Exec*
**EMP:** 320 **Privately Held**
**WEB:** www.pactiv.com
**SIC:** 3089 2821 Plastic processing; plastics materials & resins
**HQ:** Pactiv Llc
   1900 W Field Ct
   Lake Forest IL 60045
   847 482-2000

### (G-12939)
### PARTNER HEALTH LLC
736 Nw Ave Ste 326 (60045)
**PHONE** ............................ 847 208-6074
Lynne Grenier, *Vice Pres*
Bob Aydt, *VP Finance*
Karen Curtiss, *Mng Member*
**EMP:** 7 **EST:** 2011
**SALES (est):** 400K **Privately Held**
**SIC:** 2731 Book publishing

### (G-12940)
### PCA CORRUGATED AND DISPLAY LLC
1955 W Field Ct (60045-4824)
**PHONE** ............................ 847 482-3000
**EMP:** 4
**SALES (est):** 251.4K **Privately Held**
**SIC:** 2631 Container, packaging & boxboard

### (G-12941)
### PCA INTERNATIONAL INC (HQ)
1955 W Field Ct (60045-4824)
**PHONE** ............................ 847 482-3000
**EMP:** 2 **EST:** 2001
**SALES (est):** 280.3K
**SALES (corp-wide):** 5.7B **Publicly Held**
**SIC:** 2653 Corrugated & solid fiber boxes
**PA:** Packaging Corporation Of America
   1955 W Field Ct
   Lake Forest IL 60045
   847 482-3000

### (G-12942)
### PERFECT CIRCLE PROJECTILES LLC
Also Called: Ato Systems
28101 N Ballard Dr Ste C (60045-4544)
**PHONE** ............................ 847 367-8960
Gary Gibson, *Mng Member*
**EMP:** 15
**SALES:** 900K **Privately Held**
**SIC:** 3081 Tile, unsupported plastic

### (G-12943)
### PHARMDIUM HLTHCARE HLDINGS INC
2 Conway Prk 150 N (60045)
**PHONE** ............................ 800 523-7749
William R Spalding, *CEO*
Matthew D Anderson, *CFO*
Ted Krueger, *Database Admin*
**EMP:** 3
**SALES (est):** 131.7K
**SALES (corp-wide):** 146.8B **Publicly Held**
**SIC:** 2834 6719 Adrenal pharmaceutical preparations; personal holding companies, except banks
**PA:** Amerisourcebergen Corporation
   1300 Morris Dr Ste 100
   Chesterbrook PA 19087
   610 727-7000

### (G-12944)
### PHARMEDIUM HEALTHCARE CORP (PA)
150 N Field Dr Ste 350 (60045-2506)
**PHONE** ............................ 847 457-2300
David N Jonas, *CEO*
Richard Kruzynski, *President*
William R Spalding, *Exec VP*
Jennifer Adams, *Vice Pres*
Tom Cosentino, *Vice Pres*
**EMP:** 25
**SALES (est):** 24.1MM **Privately Held**
**SIC:** 5912 2834 Drug stores; pharmaceutical preparations

### (G-12945)
### PHOSPHATE RESOURCE PTRS
100 Saunders Rd Ste 300 (60045-2508)
**PHONE** ............................ 847 739-1200
J Reid Porter, *CEO*
**EMP:** 2972
**SALES (est):** 154.2MM **Publicly Held**
**WEB:** www.phosplp.com
**SIC:** 2874 1311 1475 2819 Phosphatic fertilizers; phosphoric acid; superphosphates, ammoniated or not ammoniated; crude petroleum production; phosphate rock; sulfuric acid, oleum; uranium ore mining
**HQ:** Mosaic Global Holdings Inc.
   3033 Campus Dr Ste E490
   Minneapolis MN 55441
   763 577-2700

### (G-12946)
### PLASTIC BINDING LAMINATING INC
27885 Irma Lee Cir # 105 (60045-5110)
**PHONE** ............................ 847 573-0375
Frederick Nief, *President*
John Moorehouse, *General Mgr*
Laurie Hanson, *Manager*
Garry Bendfeldt, *Administration*
▲ **EMP:** 9
**SQ FT:** 7,000
**SALES:** 7.5MM **Privately Held**
**WEB:** www.laminator.com
**SIC:** 3579 Binding machines, plastic & adhesive

### (G-12947)
### POLYURTHANE ENGRG TCHNQUES INC (PA)
Also Called: Petco
28041 N Bradley Rd (60045-1163)
**PHONE** ............................ 847 362-1820
**Fax:** 847 362-1833
Russell S Smith, *President*
Dale Smith, *Vice Pres*
Gregory Smith, *Vice Pres*
William F Smith III, *Vice Pres*
Julie Mellon, *Accountant*
**EMP:** 47
**SQ FT:** 37,000

# GEOGRAPHIC SECTION
## Lake Forest - Lake County (G-12969)

**SALES (est):** 13.4MM **Privately Held**
**SIC:** 3555 Printing trades machinery

**(G-12948)**
### PRESTONE PRODUCTS CORPORATION
1900 W Field Ct (60045-4828)
**PHONE**..................203 731-8185
Tim Shipley, *Vice Pres*
**EMP:** 4
**SALES (corp-wide):** 496.1K **Privately Held**
**SIC:** 2899 Antifreeze compounds
**HQ:** Prestone Products Corporation
1900 W Field Ct
Lake Forest IL 60045

**(G-12949)**
### PRESTONE PRODUCTS CORPORATION (DH)
1900 W Field Ct (60045-4828)
**PHONE**..................847 482-2045
Steven Clancy, *President*
David Lundstedt, *COO*
Leonard A Dececchis, *Exec VP*
Glen Skola, *Opers Staff*
Dennis Smithyman, *Opers Staff*
▼ **EMP:** 157
**SQ FT:** 25,000
**SALES (est):** 123MM
**SALES (corp-wide):** 496.1K **Privately Held**
**WEB:** www.honeywell.com
**SIC:** 2899 Antifreeze compounds

**(G-12950)**
### RAMPART LLC
28101 N Ballard Dr Ste C (60045-4544)
**PHONE**..................847 367-8960
Mary Gibson, *CFO*
Gary Gibson Mang,
Gary Gibson,
Tom Kotsiopoulos,
Steve Rosa,
**EMP:** 4 **EST:** 2001
**SALES (est):** 301.6K **Privately Held**
**WEB:** www.ramparts-nw.com
**SIC:** 3082 3482 Unsupported plastics profile shapes; small arms ammunition

**(G-12951)**
### RENAISSANCE SSP HOLDINGS INC (HQ)
272 E Deerpath Ste 350 (60045-5326)
**PHONE**..................210 476-8194
Pierre Frechette, *President*
Glenn Kues, *Vice Pres*
Christine Woolgar, *Treasurer*
Kyle Jaster, *Controller*
David Koo, *Asst Sec*
**EMP:** 4 **EST:** 2012
**SQ FT:** 5,000
**SALES (est):** 217.3MM
**SALES (corp-wide):** 737.1MM **Privately Held**
**SIC:** 2834 Pharmaceutical preparations
**PA:** Renaissance Acquisition Holdings, Llc
272 E Deerpath Ste 206
Lake Forest IL 60045
847 283-7772

**(G-12952)**
### REYNOLDS CONSUMER PRODUCTS LLC (DH)
Also Called: Reynolds Consumer Products Co
1900 W Field Ct (60045-4828)
P.O. Box 5040 (60045-5040)
**PHONE**..................847 482-3500
Lance Mitchell, *President*
Thomas J Degnan, *President*
Thomas Degnan, *President*
David Watson, *Principal*
Paul Thomas, *Senior VP*
◆ **EMP:** 277
**SALES (est):** 613.8MM **Privately Held**
**SIC:** 3353 Foil, aluminum
**HQ:** Reynolds Consumer Products Holdings Inc.
1900 W Field Ct
Lake Forest IL 60045
847 482-3050

**(G-12953)**
### REYNOLDS FOOD PACKAGING LLC
1900 W Field Ct (60045-4828)
P.O. Box 1128, Grove City PA (16127-5128)
**PHONE**..................847 482-3500
Ken Lane, *Vice Pres*
Matthew Maurer, *Marketing Mgr*
Rick Holbrook, *Manager*
Casella Okulaja, *Manager*
Boyd Selby, *Manager*
**EMP:** 232 **Privately Held**
**WEB:** www.reynoldsfoodpackaging.ca
**SIC:** 3081 Unsupported plastics film & sheet
**HQ:** Reynolds Food Packaging Llc
6601 W Broad St
Richmond VA 23230
800 446-3020

**(G-12954)**
### ROUNDTBLE HLTHCARE PARTNERS LP (PA)
272 E Deerpath Ste 350 (60045-5326)
**PHONE**..................847 482-9275
**Fax:** 847 482-9215
Lester Knight, *Managing Prtnr*
David Koo, *Senior Partner*
Joseph Damico, *Partner*
Leonard G Kuhr, *Partner*
Jack McGinley, *Partner*
**EMP:** 21
**SALES (est):** 304.8MM **Privately Held**
**WEB:** www.roundtablehp.com
**SIC:** 6722 3699 2834 Management investment, open-end; electrical equipment & supplies; pills, pharmaceutical

**(G-12955)**
### SALIBA INDUSTRIES INC
13885 W Laurel Dr (60045-4530)
**PHONE**..................847 680-2266
**Fax:** 847 680-2288
Frank Saliba, *President*
Mike Gregg, *Opers Mgr*
Denise Heelan, *Manager*
Danielle Saliba, *Admin Asst*
**EMP:** 7
**SQ FT:** 5,000
**SALES (est):** 1.2MM **Privately Held**
**WEB:** www.salibaindustries.com
**SIC:** 3599 Machine shop, jobbing & repair

**(G-12956)**
### SALTER LABS
272 E Deerpath Ste 302 (60045-1981)
**PHONE**..................661 854-3166
Jane Kiernan, *President*
Angie Leonard, *Regl Sales Mgr*
George Gedeon, *Sales Staff*
Eva Iaccino, *Senior Mgr*
**EMP:** 4
**SALES (corp-wide):** 304.8MM **Privately Held**
**SIC:** 3841 Surgical & medical instruments
**HQ:** Salter Labs
272 E Deerpath Ste 302
Lake Forest IL 60045
847 739-3224

**(G-12957)**
### SALTER LABS (HQ)
272 E Deerpath Ste 302 (60045-1981)
**PHONE**..................847 739-3224
Jane Kiernan, *CEO*
Gnell Babb, *General Mgr*
Mark Landon, *Vice Pres*
Lorelee Goehle, *Project Mgr*
Oscar Rodriguez, *Project Mgr*
◆ **EMP:** 35 **EST:** 1976
**SQ FT:** 100,000
**SALES (est):** 50.9MM
**SALES (corp-wide):** 304.8MM **Privately Held**
**WEB:** www.salterlabs.com
**SIC:** 3841 Surgical & medical instruments
**PA:** Roundtable Healthcare Partners, Lp
272 E Deerpath Ste 350
Lake Forest IL 60045
847 482-9275

**(G-12958)**
### SCC HOLDING COMPANY LLC (PA)
150 Saunders Rd Ste 150 (60045-2523)
**PHONE**..................847 444-5000
Jeff Goldberg,
John F Hulseman,
Robert L Hulseman,
**EMP:** 8000
**SALES (est):** 734.8MM **Privately Held**
**SIC:** 3089 2656 3421 Cups, plastic, except foam; straws, drinking: made from purchased material; cutlery

**(G-12959)**
### SHERMAN MEDIA COMPANY INC
222 E Wisconsin Ave Ste 7 (60045-1701)
**PHONE**..................312 335-1962
Harry Sherman, *President*
Andrew Sherman, *Corp Secy*
Lison Sherman, *Vice Pres*
**EMP:** 3
**SALES (est):** 19.6K **Privately Held**
**SIC:** 2721 Magazines: publishing only, not printed on site; magazines

**(G-12960)**
### SLAUGHTER COMPANY INC
28105 N Keith Dr (60045-4528)
**PHONE**..................847 932-3662
Eve Gramer, *President*
Peter Stevens, *General Mgr*
▲ **EMP:** 35
**SALES (est):** 5.3MM
**SALES (corp-wide):** 16.5MM **Privately Held**
**WEB:** www.ikonixgroup.com
**SIC:** 3629 Electronic generation equipment
**PA:** Ikonix Group, Inc
28105 N Keith Dr
Lake Forest IL 60045
847 367-4671

**(G-12961)**
### SPHEROTECH INC
27845 Irma Lee Cir # 101 (60045-5100)
**PHONE**..................847 680-8922
Andrew Wang, *President*
Angela Gloria, *QC Mgr*
Amy Wang, *CFO*
Cindy Wang, *CFO*
Robert Wijas, *Manager*
**EMP:** 13
**SQ FT:** 15,000
**SALES (est):** 1.6MM **Privately Held**
**WEB:** www.spherotech.com
**SIC:** 2836 Biological products, except diagnostic

**(G-12962)**
### SPIRIT FOODSERVICE INC
Also Called: Spirit Brands/ Zoo Piks
1900 W Field Ct (60045-4828)
**PHONE**..................214 634-1393
**EMP:** 125 **Privately Held**
**SIC:** 3089 Mfg Plastic Products
**HQ:** Spirit Foodservice, Llc
200 Brickstone Sq Ste G05
Andover MA 01810
978 964-1551

**(G-12963)**
### SRM INDUSTRIES INC (PA)
1009 S Green Bay Rd (60045-4041)
**PHONE**..................847 735-0077
Jay Jacobsen Jr, *Vice Pres*
**EMP:** 2
**SALES (est):** 270.9K **Privately Held**
**SIC:** 2221 Nylon broadwoven fabrics

**(G-12964)**
### SUNSET FOOD MART INC
825 S Waukegan Rd Ste A8 (60045-2665)
**PHONE**..................847 234-0854
**Fax:** 847 234-6927
Steve Davis, *Manager*
Oather Davis, *Manager*
William Tarpe, *Manager*
**EMP:** 150
**SALES (corp-wide):** 172.6MM **Privately Held**
**SIC:** 5411 5992 5912 2051 Grocery stores; florists; drug stores & proprietary stores; bread, cake & related products; bakeries
**PA:** Sunset Food Mart, Inc.
777 Central Ave Ste 2
Highland Park IL 60035
847 234-8380

**(G-12965)**
### TENNECO AUTOMOTIVE OPER CO INC (HQ)
500 N Field Dr (60045-2595)
**PHONE**..................847 482-5000
Gregg Sherrill, *CEO*
James B Harrington, *Exec VP*
Richard Schneider, *Senior VP*
Tony Melo, *Opers Mgr*
Kenneth R Trammell, *CFO*
▼ **EMP:** 150 **EST:** 1916
**SQ FT:** 90,000
**SALES (est):** 4.5B
**SALES (corp-wide):** 8.6B **Publicly Held**
**WEB:** www.quiet-flow.com
**SIC:** 3714 3699 Shock absorbers, motor vehicle; electrical equipment & supplies
**PA:** Tenneco Inc.
500 N Field Dr
Lake Forest IL 60045
847 482-5000

**(G-12966)**
### TENNECO GLOBAL HOLDINGS INC (DH)
500 N Field Dr (60045-2595)
**PHONE**..................847 482-5000
Gregg Sherrill, *Ch of Bd*
Hari N Nair, *COO*
Josep Fornos, *Exec VP*
Tim Jackson, *Exec VP*
Kenneth R Trammell, *CFO*
**EMP:** 10
**SALES (est):** 10.5MM
**SALES (corp-wide):** 8.6B **Publicly Held**
**SIC:** 3714 Motor vehicle engines & parts; shock absorbers, motor vehicle
**HQ:** Tenneco International Holding Corp.
500 N Field Dr
Lake Forest IL 60045
847 482-5000

**(G-12967)**
### TENNECO INC (PA)
500 N Field Dr (60045-2595)
**PHONE**..................847 482-5000
**Fax:** 847 482-5940
Gregg M Sherrill, *Ch of Bd*
Brian J Kesseler, *COO*
Peng Guo, *Exec VP*
Martin Hendricks, *Exec VP*
Henry Hummel, *Exec VP*
◆ **EMP:** 80
**SALES:** 8.6B **Publicly Held**
**WEB:** www.tenneco-automotive.com
**SIC:** 3714 Motor vehicle parts & accessories; motor vehicle engines & parts; shock absorbers, motor vehicle

**(G-12968)**
### TENNECO INTL HOLDG CORP (DH)
500 N Field Dr (60045-2595)
**PHONE**..................847 482-5000
Gregg Sherrill, *CEO*
Brian Kesseler, *COO*
Josep Fornos, *Exec VP*
Tim Jackson, *Exec VP*
Kenneth R Trammell, *CFO*
**EMP:** 7
**SALES (est):** 10.5MM
**SALES (corp-wide):** 8.6B **Publicly Held**
**SIC:** 3714 3743 3711 Shock absorbers, motor vehicle; locomotives & parts; automobile bodies, passenger car, not including engine, etc.
**HQ:** Tenneco Automotive Operating Company, Inc.
500 N Field Dr
Lake Forest IL 60045
847 482-5000

**(G-12969)**
### TENNECO PACKAGING
1900 W Field Ct (60045-4828)
**PHONE**..................847 482-2000
**Fax:** 847 482-4738
Dana G Mead, *Principal*
Warren Hazleton, *Vice Pres*
Dennis Ruddy, *Vice Pres*
Bob Schneider, *Vice Pres*

Tony Zalewski, *Vice Pres*
EMP: 9
SALES (est): 1.4MM  Privately Held
SIC: 2821  Polystyrene resins

**(G-12970)**
**THE UNITED GROUP INC**
Also Called: Ergonomic Office Chairs
13700 W Polo Trail Dr  (60045-5101)
PHONE.................................847 816-7100
Fax: 847 816-7102
Paul Monfardini, *President*
Scott Radtke, *President*
Kara Heather, *General Mgr*
Dawn Jordan, *General Mgr*
Sharon Leinbach, *General Mgr*
◆ EMP: 32
SQ FT: 33,000
SALES (est): 6.6MM  Privately Held
WEB: www.buytruckstuff.com
SIC: 2531  Seats, automobile

**(G-12971)**
**TPF LIQUIDATION CO**
28160 Keith Rd  (60045)
PHONE.................................847 362-0028
Cheryl Zatz, *Vice Pres*
EMP: 75
SALES (corp-wide): 1.1B  Publicly Held
SIC: 2096  2099 Popcorn, already popped (except candy covered); popcorn, packaged: except already popped
HQ: Tpf Acquisition Co.
13970 W Laurel Dr
Lake Forest IL 60045
847 362-0028

**(G-12972)**
**TRIUMPH PACKAGING GEORGIA LLC**
736 N Western Ave Ste 352  (60045-1820)
PHONE.................................312 251-9600
Connelly Roberts,
Michael Roberts,
EMP: 35
SALES: 950K  Privately Held
SIC: 2671  Packaging paper & plastics film, coated & laminated

**(G-12973)**
**TRIUMPH PACKAGING GROUP**
736 N Western Ave Ste 352  (60045-1820)
PHONE.................................312 251-9600
Connelly Roberts, *Principal*
EMP: 35
SALES: 950K  Privately Held
SIC: 2671  Packaging paper & plastics film, coated & laminated

**(G-12974)**
**TRIWATER HOLDINGS LLC**
1915 Windridge Dr  (60045-4613)
PHONE.................................847 457-1812
EMP: 4
SALES (est): 246.9K  Privately Held
SIC: 3589  Water treatment equipment, industrial

**(G-12975)**
**UCI INTERNATIONAL INC**
Also Called: UCI-Fram Autobrands
1900 W Field Ct  (60045-4828)
PHONE.................................847 941-0965
Bruce Zorich, *CEO*
Joe Doolan, *Vice Pres*
Daniel Johnston, *Vice Pres*
Keith A Zar, *Vice Pres*
Keith Zar, *Vice Pres*
▲ EMP: 46
SALES (est): 510MM  Privately Held
SIC: 3714  Motor vehicle parts & accessories
HQ: Uci Acquisition Holdings (No 1) Corp
14601 Highway 41 N
Evansville IN 47725

**(G-12976)**
**UNICORN DESIGNS**
659 N Bank Ln  (60045-1826)
PHONE.................................847 295-5230
Lisa Bennett, *Owner*
EMP: 3
SALES (est): 180K  Privately Held
SIC: 5944  7631 3911 Jewelry, precious stones & precious metals; jewelry repair services; jewelry, precious metal

**(G-12977)**
**UNITED COMPONENTS LLC (DH)**
Also Called: UCI
1900 W Field Ct  (60045-4828)
PHONE.................................812 867-4516
Ian I Fujiyama, *Principal*
Paul R Lederer, *Principal*
Gregory S Ledford, *Principal*
Raymond A Ranelli, *Principal*
John C Ritter, *Principal*
◆ EMP: 50
SALES (est): 686.2MM  Privately Held
WEB: www.ucinc.com
SIC: 5013  3714 Automotive supplies & parts; motor vehicle parts & accessories
HQ: Uci Holdings (No.1) Limited
Floor 9, 148 Quay Street
Auckland,1010
936 662-59

**(G-12978)**
**UNITED TACTICAL SYSTEMS LLC (PA)**
Also Called: Pepperball
28101 N Ballard Dr Ste F  (60045-4544)
PHONE.................................877 887-3773
George Eurick, *CEO*
Cal Stuart, *CFO*
◆ EMP: 20
SALES (est): 17.1MM  Privately Held
SIC: 3489  Ordnance & accessories

**(G-12979)**
**VELOCITY INTERNATIONAL INC**
100 N Field Dr Ste 160  (60045-4844)
PHONE.................................773 570-6441
James Krogman, *President*
Saumil Sheth, *Director*
EMP: 4
SALES (est): 364.6K  Privately Held
SIC: 3462  Construction or mining equipment forgings, ferrous
PA: Vulcan Industrial Engineering Company Limited
A-2/440, G.I.D.C.
Anand GUJ 38812

**(G-12980)**
**WILMAR GROUP LLC**
818 Larchmont Ln  (60045-1647)
PHONE.................................847 421-6595
Bruce Rylance,
EMP: 3
SALES (est): 200K  Privately Held
SIC: 3674  Semiconductors & related devices

---

**Lake In The Hills**
*Mchenry County*

**(G-12981)**
**ABITZY INC**
2921 Hillsboro Ln  (60156-5686)
PHONE.................................847 800-8666
Maria Medema, *Principal*
EMP: 2
SALES (est): 207.5K  Privately Held
SIC: 3441  Fabricated structural metal

**(G-12982)**
**ACCURATE SECURITY & LOCK CORP**
5533 Danbury Cir  (60156-6376)
PHONE.................................815 455-0133
Bian D Nelson, *President*
EMP: 2
SALES (est): 200K  Privately Held
SIC: 3699  1731 Security devices; fire detection & burglar alarm systems specialization

**(G-12983)**
**ADVANCED FLXBLE COMPOSITES INC (PA)**
Also Called: A F C
14 Walter Ct  (60156-1586)
PHONE.................................847 658-3938
Fax: 847 336-3938
W Christopher Lewis, *President*
Robert Ward, *CFO*
Janis Kolberg, *Controller*
Dale Lewis, *Human Resources*
Michael Baker, *VP Sales*
▲ EMP: 90
SQ FT: 60,000
SALES: 20MM  Privately Held
WEB: www.afconline.com
SIC: 2296  2295 Fabric for reinforcing industrial belting; coated fabrics, not rubberized

**(G-12984)**
**AG MEDICAL SYSTEMS INC**
Also Called: AMS
13 Prosper Ct Ste B  (60156-9603)
PHONE.................................847 458-3100
Fax: 847 658-0497
James M Conroy, *President*
Don Nommensen, *Marketing Staff*
Lori Nommensen, *Office Mgr*
EMP: 11
SALES: 2.4MM  Privately Held
SIC: 3339  Primary nonferrous metals

**(G-12985)**
**AMS STORE AND SHRED LLC**
13 Prosper Ct Ste B  (60156-9603)
PHONE.................................847 458-3100
James M Conroy, *President*
Carol Bein, *Project Mgr*
Ashley Delavane, *Marketing Staff*
Denise Hammer, *Manager*
EMP: 11 EST: 2013
SALES (est): 1.6MM  Privately Held
SIC: 3339  Primary nonferrous metals

**(G-12986)**
**AXON ELECTRIC LLC**
9114 Virginia Rd Ste 105  (60156-9605)
PHONE.................................630 834-4090
Bruce Dewey,
Robert Evans,
Richard Kessler,
EMP: 7 EST: 2003
SALES (est): 1.1MM
SALES (corp-wide): 482.1MM  Privately Held
PA: Mestek, Inc.
260 N Elm St
Westfield MA 01085
413 568-9571

**(G-12987)**
**BARRINGTON AUTOMATION LTD**
Also Called: Frame World
9116 Virginia Rd  (60156-9600)
PHONE.................................847 458-0900
Al Mueller, *President*
Wanda Lashaure, *Purch Mgr*
Michael Mueller, *VP Sales*
Richard Stampnick, *Sales Mgr*
Roy Smith, *Sales Staff*
EMP: 25
SQ FT: 23,000
SALES (est): 7.3MM  Privately Held
WEB: www.barrington-atn.com
SIC: 3535  3469 3569 3494 Pneumatic tube conveyor systems; machine parts, stamped or pressed metal; assembly machines, non-metalworking; valves & pipe fittings

**(G-12988)**
**BARRINGTON FINANCIAL SERVICES**
3 Sunvalley Ct  (60156-4473)
PHONE.................................847 404-1767
Dennis Coll, *President*
EMP: 1
SALES: 1,000K  Privately Held
SIC: 3715  Truck trailers

**(G-12989)**
**BLIND CONNECTION INC**
3763 Sonoma Cir  (60156-6742)
PHONE.................................630 728-6275
Mark Alpert, *Principal*
EMP: 4
SALES (est): 445.7K  Privately Held
SIC: 2591  Window blinds

**(G-12990)**
**DOBRATZ SALES COMPANY INC**
5945 Lucerne Ln  (60156-6746)
PHONE.................................224 569-3081
Walter G Dobratz, *President*
Nola K Dobratz, *Vice Pres*
EMP: 7
SALES (est): 1.2MM  Privately Held
SIC: 5085  3423 Hose, belting & packing; tools; rubber goods, mechanical; hammers (hand tools)

**(G-12991)**
**EMISSIONS SYSTEMS INCORPORATED**
Also Called: E M S
480 Wright Dr  (60156-6234)
P.O. Box 7086, Algonquin  (60102-7086)
PHONE.................................847 669-8044
Jon Palek, *President*
EMP: 3
SALES (est): 493.1K  Privately Held
WEB: www.emsgas.com
SIC: 3829  Aircraft & motor vehicle measurement equipment

**(G-12992)**
**EMMEL INC**
13 Baldwin Ct  (60156-6718)
PHONE.................................847 254-5178
Katherine Emmel, *Principal*
EMP: 3
SALES: 3MM  Privately Held
WEB: www.emmel.net
SIC: 2013  Sausages & other prepared meats

**(G-12993)**
**FSG CREST LLC**
770 Parc Ct  (60156-5634)
PHONE.................................708 210-0800
William Dustin, *Mng Member*
Steve Colen,
EMP: 10
SQ FT: 26,000
SALES (est): 1.1MM  Privately Held
SIC: 2771  5112 Greeting cards; greeting cards

**(G-12994)**
**GENERAL PRODUCTS INTL LTD**
Also Called: G P I
9245 S Il Route 31  (60156-1670)
PHONE.................................847 458-6357
Edward Mack, *President*
Karen Hess, *Manager*
▲ EMP: 6
SALES: 10MM  Privately Held
SIC: 3469  3366 Metal stampings; machinery castings: copper or copper-base alloy

**(G-12995)**
**GRAPHIC SOURCE GROUP INC**
Also Called: American Apparels & Promotions
1119 W Algonquin Rd Ste B  (60156-3560)
PHONE.................................847 854-2670
Sharon Meyer, *President*
Sue Halvorson, *Manager*
EMP: 4
SALES (est): 540K  Privately Held
WEB: www.graphicsourcegroup.com
SIC: 5112  2752 Office supplies; commercial printing, lithographic

**(G-12996)**
**JODI MAURER**
Also Called: Ebk Containers
5001 Princeton Ln  (60156-6393)
PHONE.................................847 961-5347
Jodi Maurer, *Owner*
EMP: 2
SALES (est): 206.6K  Privately Held
SIC: 3089  3443 Plastic containers, except foam; industrial vessels, tanks & containers

**(G-12997)**
**KOLD-BAN INTERNATIONAL LTD**
8390 Pingree Rd  (60156-9671)
PHONE.................................847 658-8561
Fax: 847 658-9280
James W Burke, *President*
James O Burke, *Vice Pres*
Matthew Burke, *Engineer*
Richard Burke, *Treasurer*
James Burk, *VP Sales*
▼ EMP: 21
SQ FT: 14,200

# GEOGRAPHIC SECTION

## Lake Villa - Lake County (G-13026)

**SALES (est):** 5MM **Privately Held**
**WEB:** www.koldban.com
**SIC:** 3694 Engine electrical equipment

### (G-12998)
### LITH LIQURE
461 N Randall Rd (60156-6335)
**PHONE**..................847 458-5180
Sangeeta Patel, *Principal*
**EMP:** 4
**SALES (est):** 312.1K **Privately Held**
**SIC:** 2752 Commercial printing, lithographic

### (G-12999)
### MURRAYS DISC AUTO STORES INC
108 N Randall Rd (60156-4471)
**PHONE**..................847 458-7179
Courtney Hurley, *Branch Mgr*
**EMP:** 5 **Publicly Held**
**SIC:** 7699 7694 5531 3714 Engine repair & replacement, non-automotive; rebuilding motors, except automotive; automotive parts; motor vehicle parts & accessories
**HQ:** Murray's Discount Auto Stores, Inc.
8080 Haggerty Rd
Belleville MI 48111
734 957-8080

### (G-13000)
### MW HOPKINS & SONS INC
Also Called: Hopkins Grease Company
9150 Pyott Rd (60156-9765)
P.O. Box 7722 (60102-7722)
**PHONE**..................847 458-1010
Michael A Hopkins, *President*
Timothy Hopkins, *Vice Pres*
**EMP:** 3 **EST:** 1997
**SALES (est):** 344K **Privately Held**
**SIC:** 2077 Rendering

### (G-13001)
### NORTH STAR STAMPING & TOOL INC
1264 Industrial Dr (60156-1500)
**PHONE**..................847 658-9400
**Fax:** 847 658-2610
Catherine O'Brien, *CEO*
Fran Smead, *General Mgr*
William Love, *Opers Mgr*
**EMP:** 11
**SQ FT:** 15,000
**SALES (est):** 1.8MM **Privately Held**
**WEB:** www.northstarstampingandtool.com
**SIC:** 3469 Metal stampings

### (G-13002)
### ON-TARGET SPORTS MARKETING
9117 Trinity Dr (60156-1668)
P.O. Box 7012, Algonquin (60102-7012)
**PHONE**..................847 458-9360
James Taege, *President*
Pamela Taege, *Admin Sec*
**EMP:** 2
**SALES (est):** 750K **Privately Held**
**WEB:** www.on-targetsales.com
**SIC:** 2329 Riding clothes:, men's, youths' & boys'

### (G-13003)
### PARKVIEW SAND & GRAVEL INC (PA)
41 Walter Ct (60156-1586)
P.O. Box 313, Fox River Grove (60021-0313)
**PHONE**..................262 534-4347
Patrick Loppnow, *President*
Felicia Loppnow, *Vice Pres*
Paul Loppnow, *Manager*
**EMP:** 2 **EST:** 1962
**SALES:** 1.2MM **Privately Held**
**SIC:** 1442 Construction sand mining; gravel mining

### (G-13004)
### REDI-WELD & MFG CO INC
8711 Pyott Rd (60156-9722)
**PHONE**..................815 455-4460
Guy Overlees Jr, *President*
**EMP:** 5
**SQ FT:** 3,100

**SALES (est):** 780.1K **Privately Held**
**SIC:** 3441 7692 7538 3444 Fabricated structural metal; welding repair; general automotive repair shops; sheet metalwork; fabricated plate work (boiler shop)

### (G-13005)
### SCOTT LIND OWNER
9182 Trinity Dr (60156-1666)
**PHONE**..................847 323-9140
Scott Lind, *Principal*
**EMP:** 2 **EST:** 2011
**SALES (est):** 209.8K **Privately Held**
**SIC:** 2431 Millwork

### (G-13006)
### SEAT TRANS INC
620 Joseph St (60156-5200)
**PHONE**..................224 522-1007
Petya I Marinova, *President*
**EMP:** 3
**SALES:** 220K **Privately Held**
**SIC:** 3715 7389 Truck trailers;

### (G-13007)
### SERVICE KING PLBG HTG COLG ELC
720 White Pine Ct (60156-4606)
**PHONE**..................847 458-8900
**EMP:** 2
**SALES (est):** 200.6K **Privately Held**
**SIC:** 3699 1711 Electrical equipment & supplies; heating systems repair & maintenance

### (G-13008)
### TOUR INDUSTRIES INC (PA)
1188 Starwood Pass (60156-4892)
**PHONE**..................847 854-9400
Greg Squires, *President*
Donna Squires, *Admin Sec*
**EMP:** 8
**SALES (est):** 14MM **Privately Held**
**SIC:** 3452 Bolts, nuts, rivets & washers

### (G-13009)
### VERTISSE INC
9244 Trinity Dr (60156-1664)
**PHONE**..................224 532-5145
Geneva Savage, *President*
**EMP:** 3
**SALES:** 2MM **Privately Held**
**SIC:** 2521 2522 5712 5021 Wood office furniture; office furniture, except wood; office furniture; office furniture

## Lake Villa
### Lake County

### (G-13010)
### ALLAN BROOKS & ASSOCIATES INC
Also Called: Brooks Allan
413 Park Ave (60046-6530)
**PHONE**..................847 537-7500
Deborah L Dunne, *President*
Joseph Dunne, *CFO*
Stacy Riley, *Administration*
**EMP:** 13
**SQ FT:** 10,000
**SALES (est):** 3.2MM **Privately Held**
**WEB:** www.brooks-allan.com
**SIC:** 5112 2759 Business forms; commercial printing

### (G-13011)
### BUMPER SCUFFS
37254 N Piper Ln (60046-7363)
**PHONE**..................847 489-7926
Ryan Mendoza, *CEO*
**EMP:** 2
**SALES (est):** 214.6K **Privately Held**
**SIC:** 2842 Automobile polish

### (G-13012)
### C & F PACKING CO INC
Also Called: Arco Brand
515 Park Ave (60046-6512)
P.O. Box 209 (60046-0209)
**PHONE**..................847 245-2000
**Fax:** 847 245-2100
Joseph A Freda, *President*
Mark Freda, *Vice Pres*

Michael P Stock, *Vice Pres*
Becky Fanchi, *Bookkeeper*
Maria Solis, *Manager*
**EMP:** 130 **EST:** 1945
**SQ FT:** 120,000
**SALES (est):** 33.2MM **Privately Held**
**WEB:** www.cfpacking.com
**SIC:** 2013 5147 Sausages from purchased meat; meats, fresh

### (G-13013)
### FORCE MANUFACTURING INC
266 Park Ave (60046-8915)
**PHONE**..................847 265-6500
Russell Valin, *President*
Bob Anderson, *Plant Mgr*
**EMP:** 7
**SALES (est):** 1.4MM **Privately Held**
**WEB:** www.forcemfg.com
**SIC:** 3469 7692 Machine parts, stamped or pressed metal; welding repair

### (G-13014)
### GALLIMORE INDUSTRIES INC
200 Park Ave Ste B (60046-8903)
P.O. Box 158 (60046-0158)
**PHONE**..................847 356-3331
**Fax:** 847 356-6224
Claris C Gallimore, *President*
Kent Gallimore, *VP Engrg*
Dorothea J Gallimore, *Treasurer*
Dottie Gallimore, *Treasurer*
Mark Gallimore, *VP Mktg*
**EMP:** 15
**SQ FT:** 19,000
**SALES (est):** 2.4MM **Privately Held**
**WEB:** www.gallimoreindustriesinc.com
**SIC:** 2759 Coupons: printing

### (G-13015)
### HANSEN CUSTOM CABINET INC
23418 W Apollo Ct (60046-9699)
**PHONE**..................847 356-1100
**Fax:** 847 356-1663
Keith Hansen, *President*
Fredrick Hansen, *Vice Pres*
**EMP:** 5 **EST:** 1956
**SQ FT:** 4,000
**SALES:** 450K **Privately Held**
**WEB:** www.hansencustomcabinets.com
**SIC:** 5712 2541 2434 Cabinet work, custom; wood partitions & fixtures; wood kitchen cabinets

### (G-13016)
### ID LABEL INC (PA)
425 Park Ave (60046-6540)
**PHONE**..................847 265-1200
**Fax:** 847 265-9681
Neil P Johnston, *President*
Jim Nauseda, *Business Mgr*
Tom Morgan, *Vice Pres*
Jeff Chandler, *CFO*
James Frice, *Finance*
**EMP:** 35
**SQ FT:** 40,000
**SALES (est):** 9.7MM **Privately Held**
**WEB:** www.idlabelinc.com
**SIC:** 2759 Flexographic printing

### (G-13017)
### JACK & LIDIAS RESORT INC
3610 N Edgewood St (60046)
**PHONE**..................847 356-1389
Jack Krupka, *President*
Lidia Oleksy, *Vice Pres*
**EMP:** 2
**SALES (est):** 207.5K **Privately Held**
**SIC:** 3949 7011 Fishing equipment; hotels & motels

### (G-13018)
### M & G SIMPLICITEES
39420 N Il Route 59 # 4 (60046-8141)
**PHONE**..................224 372-7426
Gary Matthews, *Partner*
Marc Thompson, *Partner*
**EMP:** 3
**SALES (est):** 331.7K **Privately Held**
**SIC:** 2253 7389 T-shirts & tops, knit; design services

### (G-13019)
### MACKIN GROUP LLC
447 Red Cedar Rd (60046-8627)
**PHONE**..................847 245-4201

Mona Mustafa,
**EMP:** 3
**SALES (est):** 200K **Privately Held**
**SIC:** 3944 Structural toy sets

### (G-13020)
### MATRIX CIRCUITS LLC (PA)
37575 N Il Route 59 (60046-9148)
**PHONE**..................319 367-5000
Paul Krumenacher,
Mike Forseen,
**EMP:** 4 **EST:** 2008
**SQ FT:** 6,000
**SALES:** 600K **Privately Held**
**SIC:** 3679 7373 Electronic circuits; computer integrated systems design

### (G-13021)
### MIDWEST CARPET RECYCLING INC
38334 N Munn Rd (60046-8816)
**PHONE**..................855 406-8600
Nicholas Fiore, *President*
**EMP:** 32 **EST:** 2012
**SALES (est):** 3.3MM **Privately Held**
**SIC:** 2299 Carpet lining: felt, except woven

### (G-13022)
### PICTURE PERFECT PUZZLES LLC
39721 N Beck Rd (60046-7414)
**PHONE**..................847 838-0848
Victor Giampietro, *President*
**EMP:** 3
**SALES (est):** 157.8K **Privately Held**
**SIC:** 3944 5092 Puzzles; puzzles

### (G-13023)
### PRINT SOURCE FOR BUSINESS INC
38966 N Deep Lake Rd (60046-6705)
P.O. Box 368 (60046-0368)
**PHONE**..................847 356-0190
George Richter, *President*
James Richter, *Corp Secy*
**EMP:** 6
**SQ FT:** 4,200
**SALES (est):** 685.8K **Privately Held**
**WEB:** www.printsourceinc.com
**SIC:** 2752 Commercial printing, offset

### (G-13024)
### PRO PATCH SYSTEMS INC
25704 W Lehmann Blvd (60046-9717)
**PHONE**..................847 356-8100
Dennis Hoffmann, *President*
Linda Hoffman, *Vice Pres*
Brad W Sherr, *Manager*
**EMP:** 2
**SALES:** 1MM **Privately Held**
**WEB:** www.proenhance.com
**SIC:** 5032 2672 Drywall materials; adhesive backed films, foams & foils

### (G-13025)
### R+D CUSTOM AUTOMATION INC
23411 W Wall St (60046-8140)
P.O. Box 228 (60046-0228)
**PHONE**..................847 395-3330
**Fax:** 847 395-3376
Loren Esch, *President*
Jim Marron, *Project Mgr*
Kraig Carlson, *Engineer*
Eric Holme, *Engineer*
Timothy Roshko, *Engineer*
▼ **EMP:** 31
**SQ FT:** 20,000
**SALES (est):** 7.6MM **Privately Held**
**WEB:** www.rd-tool.com
**SIC:** 3549 7373 8742 Assembly machines, including robotic; systems integration services; automation & robotics consultant

### (G-13026)
### SHEAS IRON WORKS INC
735 N Milwaukee Ave A (60046-8567)
P.O. Box 730 (60046-0730)
**PHONE**..................847 356-2922
**Fax:** 847 356-9380
Judy Shea, *President*
Ryan Shea, *Corp Secy*
**EMP:** 30
**SQ FT:** 10,000

# Lake Villa - Lake County (G-13027)    GEOGRAPHIC SECTION

SALES (est): 6.2MM **Privately Held**
SIC: 3441 7389 7692 3446 Building components, structural steel; crane & aerial lift service; welding repair; architectural metalwork; sheet metalwork

**(G-13027)**
**STRATEGIC APPLICATIONS INC**
Also Called: SAI
278 Park Ave (60046-8915)
PHONE.................................847 680-9385
Fax: 847 680-9837
Steven C Denault, *President*
**EMP:** 2 **EST:** 1996
**SALES:** 1.6MM **Privately Held**
WEB: www.strategicapplications.com
SIC: 2834 8748 Pharmaceutical preparations; business consulting

**(G-13028)**
**TRI-TECH MOLDING**
21547 W Morton Dr (60046-8246)
PHONE.................................847 263-7769
Keith Rosedall, *Co-Owner*
Jeff Jones, *Co-Owner*
Rob Regel, *Co-Owner*
**EMP:** 5
**SALES (est):** 280K **Privately Held**
SIC: 3089 Molding primary plastic

**(G-13029)**
**VONCO PRODUCTS LLC**
201 Park Ave (60046-8999)
PHONE.................................847 356-2323
Fax: 847 356-8630
Keith Smith, *President*
**EMP:** 30 **EST:** 2012
**SALES (est):** 8.9MM **Privately Held**
SIC: 2673 Plastic bags: made from purchased materials

**(G-13030)**
**WARMING SYSTEMS**
7706 Industrial Dr Unit D (60046)
PHONE.................................800 663-7831
Mark Bowernan, *CEO*
**EMP:** 6
**SALES (est):** 388.6K **Privately Held**
SIC: 3625 Flow actuated electrical switches

**(G-13031)**
**WORKS IN PROGRESS FOUNDATION**
24978 W Lakeview Dr (60046-9618)
PHONE.................................847 997-8338
Daniela Gorsuch, *President*
Matthew Gorsuch, *Admin Sec*
**EMP:** 3
**SALES (est):** 190K **Privately Held**
SIC: 3312 Primary finished or semifinished shapes

---
## Lake Zurich
### Lake County
---

**(G-13032)**
**ACCO BRANDS INC**
4 Corporate Dr (60047-8997)
PHONE.................................847 541-9500
Fax: 847 419-4127
Robert J Keller, *President*
David Campbell, *President*
John Moynihan, *Counsel*
Neal V Fenwick, *Exec VP*
Thomas Tedford, *Exec VP*
▲ **EMP:** 1484
**SALES (est):** 177.5MM
**SALES (corp-wide):** 1.5B **Publicly Held**
WEB: www.acco.com
SIC: 2542 Fixtures: display, office or store: except wood
PA: Acco Brands Corporation
   4 Corporate Dr
   Lake Zurich IL 60047
   847 541-9500

**(G-13033)**
**ACCO BRANDS CORPORATION (PA)**
4 Corporate Dr (60047-8997)
PHONE.................................847 541-9500
Fax: 847 541-5750
Boris Elisman, *Ch of Bd*
Ralph P Hargrow, *Senior VP*
Kathleen D Schnaedter, *Senior VP*
Pamela R Schneider, *Senior VP*
Neal V Fenwick, *CFO*
◆ **EMP:** 600 **EST:** 1970
**SALES:** 1.5B **Publicly Held**
WEB: www.acco.com
SIC: 2782 3083 2761 2672 Looseleaf binders & devices; paper ruling; laminated plastic sheets; computer forms, manifold or continuous; adhesive papers, labels or tapes: from purchased material

**(G-13034)**
**ACCO BRANDS USA LLC (HQ)**
4 Corporate Dr (60047-8997)
P.O. Box 1342, Brentwood NY (11717-0718)
PHONE.................................800 222-6462
Boris Elisman, *President*
Mike Vogel, *Exec VP*
Christopher Franey, *Vice Pres*
Jed Peters, *Vice Pres*
Thomas Tedford, *Vice Pres*
◆ **EMP:** 400 **EST:** 1925
**SALES (est):** 1B
**SALES (corp-wide):** 1.5B **Publicly Held**
WEB: www.accobrands.com
SIC: 3089 2761 3496 2675 Injection molding of plastics; manifold business forms; clips & fasteners, made from purchased wire; folders, filing, die-cut: made from purchased materials
PA: Acco Brands Corporation
   4 Corporate Dr
   Lake Zurich IL 60047
   847 541-9500

**(G-13035)**
**ACME AWNING CO INC**
325 Pebblecreek Dr (60047-2755)
P.O. Box 23, Winnetka (60093-0023)
PHONE.................................847 446-0153
Kristopher Arands, *President*
**EMP:** 4
**SALES:** 125K **Privately Held**
SIC: 3089 5039 Awnings, fiberglass & plastic combination; awnings

**(G-13036)**
**AFCO PRODUCTS INCORPORATED**
1030 Commerce Dr (60047-1545)
PHONE.................................847 299-1055
Fax: 847 299-8455
Kenneth A Klancnik, *President*
Chris Klancnik, *Vice Pres*
Rob Klancnik, *Vice Pres*
Bill Brunelli, *Plant Mgr*
Ronald Strentz, *QC Mgr*
**EMP:** 35 **EST:** 1940
**SQ FT:** 40,000
**SALES (est):** 8.8MM **Privately Held**
WEB: www.afco-products.com
SIC: 3451 Screw machine products

**(G-13037)**
**AFFIRMED LLC**
280a N Rand Rd Ste A (60047-2282)
PHONE.................................847 550-0170
Terrence Canning, *Mng Member*
Nick Canning,
**EMP:** 7
**SALES (est):** 334.5K **Privately Held**
SIC: 2844 Manicure preparations

**(G-13038)**
**ALL RITE INDUSTRIES INC**
470 Oakwood Rd (60047-1515)
P.O. Box 189 (60047-0189)
PHONE.................................847 540-0300
Fax: 847 540-0340
Edward Bilik, *President*
Mary Bilik, *Corp Secy*
Kathy Muncer, *Vice Pres*
Chad Genengels, *VP Sls/Mktg*
Mark Andreasik, *Manager*
**EMP:** 38
**SQ FT:** 40,000
**SALES (est):** 9.4MM **Privately Held**
WEB: www.allriteindustries.com
SIC: 3496 Woven wire products

**(G-13039)**
**ALPHA BEDDING LLC**
Also Called: Alpha Tekniko
1290 Ensell Rd (60047-1537)
PHONE.................................847 550-5110
Ted Lazakis, *CEO*
Lorri Lunak, *Accounts Mgr*
Tia Lazakis,
**EMP:** 11
**SQ FT:** 10,000
**SALES (est):** 2.4MM **Privately Held**
SIC: 3634 2211 Bedcoverings, electric; bed sheeting, cotton

**(G-13040)**
**ANCIENT GRAFFITI INC**
300 E Il Route 22 (60047-2572)
PHONE.................................847 726-5800
Ron Zisman, *President*
Brad Emalfarb, *Vice Pres*
◆ **EMP:** 20 **EST:** 2000
**SALES (est):** 3.1MM **Privately Held**
SIC: 3446 Architectural metalwork

**(G-13041)**
**ANDERSON MSNRY REFR SPCIALISTS**
Also Called: Anderson Msnry Refr Spcalist I
25675 N Stoney Kirk Ct (60047-6701)
PHONE.................................847 540-8885
Fax: 847 540-6409
Cynthia L Anderson, *President*
Alan R Anderson, *Vice Pres*
**EMP:** 6
**SQ FT:** 500
**SALES (est):** 730K **Privately Held**
SIC: 4953 3567 5085 Incinerator operation; industrial furnaces & ovens; refractory material

**(G-13042)**
**APEX DENTAL MATERIALS INC**
330 Telser Rd (60047-6701)
PHONE.................................847 719-1133
Scott Lamerand, *Admin Sec*
**EMP:** 4
**SALES (est):** 493K **Privately Held**
SIC: 3843 Dental equipment & supplies

**(G-13043)**
**ARDAGH CONVERSION SYSTEMS INC**
570 Telser Rd Ste B (60047-1529)
PHONE.................................847 438-4100
John-Marc Legresy, *President*
Amy Ban, *Accountant*
John G Boyas, *Admin Sec*
**EMP:** 8 **EST:** 2010
**SQ FT:** 10,000
**SALES (est):** 1.1MM **Privately Held**
SIC: 3542 Machine tools, metal forming type

**(G-13044)**
**ASTRON DENTAL CORPORATION**
815 Oakwood Rd Ste G (60047-6704)
PHONE.................................847 726-8787
Fax: 847 726-8793
Dr Robert E Muller Sr, *President*
Robert E Muller Jr, *Vice Pres*
Douglas Muller, *VP Opers*
Lori Jones, *Plant Supt*
▲ **EMP:** 15
**SQ FT:** 3,000
**SALES (est):** 2.3MM **Privately Held**
WEB: www.astrondental.com
SIC: 3843 Denture materials

**(G-13045)**
**BASEMENT FLOOD PROTECTOR INC**
707 Rose Rd (60047-1542)
PHONE.................................847 438-6770
Fax: 847 726-3007
Hollie Sloss, *President*
Jeffery Sloss, *Owner*
Louis Sloss, *Controller*
▲ **EMP:** 10
**SQ FT:** 5,000
**SALES (est):** 730K **Privately Held**
WEB: www.basementfloodprotector.com
SIC: 7699 3561 Pumps & pumping equipment repair; battery service & repair; pumps, domestic: water or sump; industrial pumps & parts

**(G-13046)**
**BISH CREATIVE DISPLAY INC**
945 Telser Rd (60047-6752)
PHONE.................................847 438-1500
Fax: 847 438-1508
Jerrold E Fox, *President*
Dawn Barchus, *Accounting Mgr*
Diana Anderson, *Director*
Pam Riley, *Admin Sec*
◆ **EMP:** 20
**SALES:** 22.7MM **Privately Held**
WEB: www.bishdisplay.com
SIC: 3993 Displays & cutouts, window & lobby

**(G-13047)**
**BRIGHT LIGHT SIGN COMPANY INC**
310 Telser Rd (60047-6701)
PHONE.................................847 550-8902
Fax: 847 550-6383
William Holley, *President*
**EMP:** 9
**SALES (est):** 1.3MM **Privately Held**
WEB: www.brightlightsign.com
SIC: 3993 Signs & advertising specialties

**(G-13048)**
**C M HOLDING CO INC**
800 Ela Rd (60047-2340)
PHONE.................................847 438-2171
Mark Faber, *CEO*
Michael F Jenkins, *Vice Pres*
Richard D Barton, *VP Sales*
Suzanne Saxman, *Admin Sec*
**EMP:** 4
**SQ FT:** 300,000
**SALES:** 439.2K
**SALES (corp-wide):** 36.1MM **Privately Held**
SIC: 6512 3469 3497 Commercial & industrial building operation; cooking ware, except porcelain enamelled; foil containers for bakery goods & frozen foods
PA: R And R Brokerage Co.
   800 Ela Rd
   Lake Zurich IL 60047
   847 438-4600

**(G-13049)**
**C M INDUSTRIES INC**
505 Oakwood Rd Ste 120 (60047-1534)
PHONE.................................847 550-0033
Fax: 847 550-0444
Z Zenny Kukich, *President*
David Kukich, *Project Engr*
Ken Pratt, *VP Sls/Mktg*
Emil Vasek, *Sales Dir*
Ed May, *Cust Mgr*
▲ **EMP:** 36
**SQ FT:** 75,000
**SALES (est):** 7.7MM **Privately Held**
SIC: 3548 Gas welding equipment

**(G-13050)**
**CATALYTIC PRODUCTS INTL INC**
980 Ensell Rd (60047-1557)
PHONE.................................847 438-0334
Fax: 847 438-0944
Julia Lincoln, *CEO*
Dennis W Lincoln, *President*
Mark A Betz, *Vice Pres*
Scott Shaver, *Vice Pres*
Francis Costanzo, *Project Mgr*
◆ **EMP:** 28
**SQ FT:** 10,000
**SALES (est):** 12.9MM **Privately Held**
WEB: www.cpilink.com
SIC: 3822 3567 2819 3564 Auto controls regulating residntl & coml environmt & applncs; ; catalysts, chemical; blowers & fans

**(G-13051)**
**CCTY USA BEARING CO**
1111 Rose Rd (60047-1533)
PHONE.................................847 540-8196
Fax: 847 540-9130
Evan Poulakidas, *President*

▲ = Import ▼=Export
◆ =Import/Export

# GEOGRAPHIC SECTION
## Lake Zurich - Lake County (G-13076)

Traci Fritz, *Controller*
David Olsen, *Admin Sec*
▲ **EMP:** 7
**SALES (est):** 1MM **Privately Held**
**WEB:** www.ccvi.com
**SIC:** 5085 3562 Bearings; roller bearings & parts

### (G-13052)
### CHAMPION MEDICAL TECH INC
765 Ela Rd Ste 200 (60047-6305)
**PHONE** ............................ 866 803-3720
Peter I Casady, *President*
Steve Coloia, *Vice Pres*
Jay Rudman, *Vice Pres*
Jim Sipe, *Vice Pres*
Brent Dobsch, *CFO*
**EMP:** 32
**SALES (est):** 4.5MM **Privately Held**
**SIC:** 7372 Application computer software

### (G-13053)
### CHELSEA FRAMING PRODUCTS INC
333 Enterprise Pkwy (60047-6733)
**PHONE** ............................ 847 550-5556
Min Han, *Principal*
**EMP:** 4
**SALES (est):** 458.7K **Privately Held**
**SIC:** 3795 Tanks & tank components

### (G-13054)
### CLAY VOLLMAR PRODUCTS CO
124 N Buesching Rd (60047-1569)
**PHONE** ............................ 847 540-5850
**Fax:** 847 540-5852
Kurt Schulberg, *Manager*
**EMP:** 6
**SALES (corp-wide):** 3.1MM **Privately Held**
**WEB:** www.vollmar.com
**SIC:** 5032 3272 7699 Brick, stone & related material; concrete products; septic tank cleaning service
**PA:** Clay Vollmar Products Co
5835 W Touhy Ave
Chicago IL 60646
773 774-1234

### (G-13055)
### COBRACO MANUFACTURING INC (PA)
300 E Il Route 22 (60047-2572)
**PHONE** ............................ 847 726-5800
**Fax:** 847 726-0330
Sy Emalfarb, *CEO*
Brad Emalfarb, *President*
▲ **EMP:** 20
**SQ FT:** 106,000
**SALES (est):** 2.3MM **Privately Held**
**WEB:** www.cobraco.com
**SIC:** 3999 5083 Coin-operated amusement machines; lawn & garden machinery & equipment

### (G-13056)
### COMPREHENSIVE CONVGNT SOLUT
830 W Il Route 22 Ste 51 (60047-2560)
**PHONE** ............................ 847 558-1401
Louis J Pace, *President*
George Karp, *Vice Pres*
**EMP:** 10
**SQ FT:** 1,200
**SALES:** 250K **Privately Held**
**SIC:** 3661 Telephone & telegraph apparatus

### (G-13057)
### COORDINATED KITCHEN DEV INC
Also Called: Ckd
1525 Coral Reef Way (60047-2921)
**PHONE** ............................ 847 847-7692
Martin J Aimone, *President*
**EMP:** 1
**SALES:** 300K **Privately Held**
**SIC:** 2541 Cabinets, lockers & shelving

### (G-13058)
### CRD ENTERPRISES INC
549 Capital Dr (60047-6711)
**PHONE** ............................ 847 438-4299
**Fax:** 847 438-4323
Charles R Davidson, *President*

▼ **EMP:** 3
**SQ FT:** 3,000
**SALES:** 1.2MM **Privately Held**
**WEB:** www.crdco.net
**SIC:** 5084 3542 Machine tools & metalworking machinery; die casting machines

### (G-13059)
### CREATIVE CONVENIENCES BY K&E
55 N Buesching Rd Apt 312 (60047-6110)
P.O. Box 759 (60047-0759)
**PHONE** ............................ 847 975-8526
Karen Rafalowitz, *President*
Ellen Jakubicek, *Vice Pres*
**EMP:** 4
**SALES:** 50K **Privately Held**
**SIC:** 3089 Automotive parts, plastic

### (G-13060)
### CTI INDUSTRIES CORPORATION
800 Church St (60047-1573)
**PHONE** ............................ 800 284-5605
Dorothy Gates, *CFO*
**EMP:** 75
**SALES (corp-wide):** 64.2MM **Publicly Held**
**SIC:** 3089 3069 Plastic containers, except foam; tubs, plastic (containers); plastic kitchenware, tableware & houseware; balloons, advertising & toy: rubber; balloons, metal foil laminated with rubber; balls, rubber
**PA:** Cti Industries Corporation
22160 N Pepper Rd
Lake Barrington IL 60010
847 382-1000

### (G-13061)
### D&W FINE PACK LLC
800 Ela Rd (60047-2340)
**PHONE** ............................ 800 323-0422
**EMP:** 4
**SALES (corp-wide):** 711.5MM **Privately Held**
**SIC:** 3089 Plastic kitchenware, tableware & houseware
**HQ:** D&W Fine Pack Llc
1900 Pratt Blvd
Elk Grove Village IL 60007

### (G-13062)
### DEVIL DOG ARMS INC
650 Telser Rd (60047-1528)
**PHONE** ............................ 847 790-4004
**Fax:** 847 996-2131
Joseph J Lucania III, *President*
**EMP:** 2
**SALES (est):** 272.8K **Privately Held**
**SIC:** 3484 3489 5091 5941 Guns (firearms) or gun parts, 30 mm. & below; guns or gun parts, over 30 mm.; guns, howitzers, mortars & related equipment; firearms, sporting; firearms

### (G-13063)
### DMS INC
1120 Ensell Rd (60047-6718)
**PHONE** ............................ 847 726-2828
**Fax:** 847 726-9292
David Polkinghorne, *President*
Duane Polkinghorne, *Vice Pres*
John Powers, *Facilities Mgr*
Robert Kaplan, *CFO*
Cassandra LI, *Controller*
**EMP:** 17
**SQ FT:** 12,000
**SALES (est):** 4.2MM **Privately Held**
**WEB:** www.dmsdies.com
**SIC:** 3555 3544 Printing trades machinery; die sets for metal stamping (presses)

### (G-13064)
### ECHO INCORPORATED (HQ)
400 Oakwood Rd (60047-1564)
**PHONE** ............................ 847 540-8400
**Fax:** 847 540-8413
Dan Obringer, *President*
John Harkins, *Business Mgr*
Wayne Thomsen, *Vice Pres*
Manny Ruiz, *Mfg Spvr*
Phillip Steinhauer, *Purch Agent*
◆ **EMP:** 830 **EST:** 1972
**SQ FT:** 400,000

**SALES (est):** 289.2MM
**SALES (corp-wide):** 985MM **Privately Held**
**SIC:** 3524 Lawn & garden equipment
**PA:** Yamabiko Corporation
1-7-2, Suehirocho
Ome TKY 198-0
428 326-111

### (G-13065)
### ECHO INCORPORATED
1000 Rose Rd (60047)
**PHONE** ............................ 847 540-3500
Dan Obringer, *Branch Mgr*
**EMP:** 47
**SALES (corp-wide):** 985MM **Privately Held**
**SIC:** 3524 Lawn & garden equipment
**HQ:** Echo, Incorporated
400 Oakwood Rd
Lake Zurich IL 60047
847 540-8400

### (G-13066)
### ELECTRONIC DESIGN & MFG INC
Also Called: E D M
1225 Flex Ct (60047-1578)
**PHONE** ............................ 847 550-1912
Anthony Trocano, *President*
Sandra Trocano, *Principal*
Sherry Dixon, *Sales & Mktg St*
Annette Anderson, *Controller*
**EMP:** 100
**SQ FT:** 24,000
**SALES (est):** 12.9MM **Privately Held**
**WEB:** www.edminc.net
**SIC:** 3672 3679 Printed circuit boards; power supplies, all types: static

### (G-13067)
### ELEGANT EMBROIDERY INC
100 Oakwood Rd Ste C (60047-1524)
**PHONE** ............................ 847 540-8003
**Fax:** 847 540-8477
Nancy Solomon, *President*
Andrew Malinowski, *Manager*
**EMP:** 6
**SALES (est):** 477.4K **Privately Held**
**SIC:** 2395 2759 Embroidery & art needlework; screen printing

### (G-13068)
### ELEVATORS USA INCORPORATED
Also Called: USA Elevators
932 Donata Ct (60047-5025)
**PHONE** ............................ 847 847-1856
Waleed Etawi, *President*
**EMP:** 2 **EST:** 2012
**SALES (est):** 218.8K **Privately Held**
**SIC:** 3534 Elevators & equipment

### (G-13069)
### EOE INC
590 Telser Rd Ste A (60047-1584)
**PHONE** ............................ 847 550-1665
Jim Hnilo, *President*
Alice Hnilo, *VP Finance*
▼ **EMP:** 10
**SQ FT:** 12,000
**SALES (est):** 1.7MM **Privately Held**
**SIC:** 3565 Packaging machinery

### (G-13070)
### ERI AMERICA INC
353 Enterprise Pkwy (60047-6733)
**PHONE** ............................ 847 550-9710
**Fax:** 847 550-9716
Frank Fullone, *President*
▲ **EMP:** 3
**SALES (est):** 586.9K **Privately Held**
**WEB:** www.eri-america.com
**SIC:** 3545 Tool holders

### (G-13071)
### FAIRCHILD INDUSTRIES INC
475 Capital Dr (60047-6732)
**PHONE** ............................ 847 550-9580
Robert W Schauer, *President*
Kathryn Schauer, *President*
Joel Schauer, *Admin Sec*
Suzan Sarvady, *Administration*
▲ **EMP:** 22
**SQ FT:** 20,000

**SALES (est):** 10MM **Privately Held**
**WEB:** www.fairchildind.com
**SIC:** 5199 3061 Foams & rubber; mechanical rubber goods
**PA:** Mcclure Associates Inc
475 Capital Dr
Lake Zurich IL 60047
847 550-9570

### (G-13072)
### FENWAL INC (DH)
3 Corporate Dr Ste 300 (60047-8930)
**PHONE** ............................ 847 550-2300
Dean A Gregory, *President*
Anthony Orsini, *COO*
William H Cork, *Senior VP*
Angie Goodwin, *Senior VP*
Emilio Gonzalez, *Mfg Mgr*
▲ **EMP:** 450
**SQ FT:** 25,000
**SALES (est):** 694.5MM
**SALES (corp-wide):** 31.1B **Privately Held**
**WEB:** www.fenwalinc.com
**SIC:** 5047 3069 Medical equipment & supplies; medical & laboratory rubber sundries & related products

### (G-13073)
### FENWAL HOLDINGS INC (DH)
3 Corporate Dr Ste 300 (60047-8930)
**PHONE** ............................ 847 550-2300
Ron K Labrum, *President*
William H Cork, *Senior VP*
Geoffrey D Fenton, *Senior VP*
Angela Goodwin, *Senior VP*
Dean A Gregory, *Senior VP*
▲ **EMP:** 400
**SQ FT:** 25,000
**SALES (est):** 694.5MM
**SALES (corp-wide):** 31.1B **Privately Held**
**SIC:** 3069 5047 Medical & laboratory rubber sundries & related products; medical equipment & supplies
**HQ:** Fresenius Kabi Deutschland Gmbh
Else-Kroner-Str. 1
Bad Homburg
617 268-60

### (G-13074)
### FM WOODWORKING
325 Red Bridge Rd (60047-2643)
**PHONE** ............................ 847 533-1545
Filip Macon, *Principal*
**EMP:** 4 **EST:** 2011
**SALES (est):** 478.3K **Privately Held**
**SIC:** 2431 Millwork

### (G-13075)
### FOOD EQUIPMENT TECHNOLOGIES CO (PA)
Also Called: Fetco
600 Rose Rd (60047-1560)
P.O. Box 429 (60047-0429)
**PHONE** ............................ 847 719-3000
**Fax:** 847 719-3001
Christopher Nowak, *President*
Michael Ferrusquia, *Mfg Dir*
Adam Sieprawski, *Plant Mgr*
Les Wroblewski, *Research*
Dennis Adamczyk, *Engineer*
▲ **EMP:** 159
**SQ FT:** 160,000
**SALES (est):** 30.7MM **Privately Held**
**WEB:** www.fetco.com
**SIC:** 3589 Cooking equipment, commercial; food warming equipment, commercial; coffee brewing equipment

### (G-13076)
### FRESENIUS KABI USA INC (DH)
3 Corporate Dr Ste 300 (60047-8930)
**PHONE** ............................ 847 969-2700
John Ducker, *CEO*
Bruce J Wendel, *Exec VP*
Sharon Schwartz, *Purch Mgr*
Jason Ashbury, *Engineer*
Patrick Whitehead, *Engineer*
▲ **EMP:** 277
**SQ FT:** 36,200
**SALES (est):** 601.8MM
**SALES (corp-wide):** 31.1B **Privately Held**
**WEB:** www.appdrugs.com
**SIC:** 2834 Pharmaceutical preparations

# Lake Zurich - Lake County (G-13077)    GEOGRAPHIC SECTION

HQ: Fresenius Kabi Ag
Else-Kroner-Str. 1
Bad Homburg 61352
617 268-60

### (G-13077)
### FRESENIUS KABI USA LLC (DH)
3 Corporate Dr Ste 300 (60047-8930)
PHONE.....................847 550-2300
Fax: 847 413-2653
John Ducker, *President*
Steven J Adams, *Exec VP*
Jack Silhavy, *Exec VP*
Alexandr Gonzalez, *Vice Pres*
David Bowman, *VP Prdtn*
▲ EMP: 1500 EST: 2007
SALES (est): 583.2MM
SALES (corp-wide): 31.1B  Privately Held
SIC: 2834  Pharmaceutical preparations
HQ: Fresenius Kabi Usa, Inc.
3 Corporate Dr Ste 300
Lake Zurich IL 60047
847 969-2700

### (G-13078)
### FRESENIUS KABI USA LLC
3 Corporate Dr Ste 300 (60047-8930)
PHONE.....................847 550-2300
EMP: 35
SALES (corp-wide): 31.1B  Privately Held
WEB: www.appdrugs.com
SIC: 2834  Pharmaceutical preparations
HQ: Fresenius Kabi Usa, Llc
3 Corporate Dr Ste 300
Lake Zurich IL 60047
847 550-2300

### (G-13079)
### GOUDIE TOOL AND ENGRG DEL
Also Called: Goudie Tool & Engineering
480 Telser Rd (60047-1588)
PHONE.....................847 438-5597
Fax: 847 438-5641
Edward Goudie, *President*
Susan Goudie, *Vice Pres*
EMP: 10
SQ FT: 5,300
SALES: 800K  Privately Held
SIC: 3089  Injection molding of plastics

### (G-13080)
### GPM MFG INC
1199 Flex Ct (60047-1578)
PHONE.....................847 550-8200
Fax: 847 550-8204
Ted Godek, *President*
Augustyna Godek, *Corp Secy*
EMP: 15
SQ FT: 6,800
SALES: 2MM  Privately Held
SIC: 3599  Machine shop, jobbing & repair

### (G-13081)
### H BORRE & SONS INC
617 Cortland Dr (60047-2366)
PHONE.....................847 524-8890
Jeff Borre, *President*
EMP: 3
SALES (est): 386.6K  Privately Held
SIC: 3599  1751  1522  Machine shop, jobbing & repair; carpentry work; residential construction

### (G-13082)
### HARRIS AND DISCOUNT SUPPLIES
450 E Il Route 22 (60047-2575)
PHONE.....................847 726-3800
Deborah Delana, *President*
EMP: 4 EST: 1998
SALES (est): 212.7K  Privately Held
SIC: 3843  Gold, dental; dental metal; orthodontic appliances

### (G-13083)
### HEIDTS AUTOMOTIVE LLC
Also Called: Heidt's Hot Rod Shop
800 Oakwood Rd (60047-1522)
PHONE.....................847 487-0150
Fax: 847 487-0156
Wallace Leyshon, *CEO*
Gary Heidt, *President*
Matt Stahl, *Engineer*
Nancy Keyser, *Manager*
Scott Schroeder, *Manager*
EMP: 38

SQ FT: 25,000
SALES (est): 7.5MM  Privately Held
WEB: www.heidts.com
SIC: 3089  Automotive parts, plastic

### (G-13084)
### HPL STAMPINGS INC (PA)
425 Enterprise Pkwy (60047-6710)
PHONE.....................847 540-1400
Roger E Hedberg Jr, *President*
Gene Jasionowski, *Plant Mgr*
Rich Suvak, *Engineer*
Dave Duginski, *Controller*
Mary Romano, *Credit Mgr*
EMP: 49
SQ FT: 79,000
SALES: 5.5MM  Privately Held
WEB: www.hplstampings.com
SIC: 3444  3469  Sheet metalwork; stamping metal for the trade

### (G-13085)
### HUNTLEY & ASSOCIATES INC
47 Carolyn Ct (60047-1506)
PHONE.....................224 381-8500
Craig Herriges, *President*
EMP: 3
SALES (est): 242.8K  Privately Held
SIC: 8742  3441  3442  Management consulting services; fabricated structural metal; molding, trim & stripping

### (G-13086)
### INDUSTRIAL WIRE & CABLE CORP
66 N Buesching Rd (60047-1514)
PHONE.....................847 726-8910
Carl Calabrese, *CEO*
Christine Graham, *Vice Pres*
Stephanie Hadzima, *Human Resources*
Thomas M Lacalamita, *Sales Mgr*
▲ EMP: 29
SQ FT: 110
SALES (est): 7.6MM  Privately Held
WEB: www.industwire.com
SIC: 3357  3496  Nonferrous wiredrawing & insulating; cable, uninsulated wire: made from purchased wire

### (G-13087)
### INDUSTRIAL WIRE CABLE II CORP
66 N Buesching Rd (60047-1514)
PHONE.....................847 726-8910
Fax: 847 726-7544
Carl Calabrese, *President*
Christine A Graham, *Exec VP*
Stephanie Hadzima, *Human Resources*
▲ EMP: 16
SQ FT: 10,000
SALES (est): 3.9MM  Privately Held
SIC: 3357  3351  Coaxial cable, nonferrous; appliance fixture wire, nonferrous; wire, copper & copper alloy

### (G-13088)
### INSIDE BEVERAGES
635 Oakwood Rd (60047-1518)
PHONE.....................847 438-1338
Andy Burke, *President*
Rich Ply, *Vice Pres*
Geoff Huenerfauth, *Purchasing*
EMP: 110
SQ FT: 87,000
SALES (est): 14.8MM  Privately Held
SIC: 2045  2087  2066  Cake mixes, prepared: from purchased flour; powders, drink; instant cocoa

### (G-13089)
### INSIGHT BEVERAGES INC
750 Oakwood Rd (60047-1519)
PHONE.....................847 438-1598
EMP: 3  Privately Held
SIC: 2087  Beverage bases
HQ: Insight Beverages, Inc.
750 Oakwood Rd
Lake Zurich IL 60047
847 438-1598

### (G-13090)
### INSIGHT BEVERAGES INC (DH)
750 Oakwood Rd (60047-1519)
PHONE.....................847 438-1598
Fax: 847 438-1236
Andrew F Burke, *CEO*

Gerard A Behan, *President*
Claudio Marasti, *Business Mgr*
Richard Bruner, *Vice Pres*
Donald Lillard, *Vice Pres*
▼ EMP: 13
SQ FT: 196,000
SALES (est): 52.5MM  Privately Held
SIC: 2087  2095  2099  5499  Beverage bases; coffee extracts; tea blending; beverage stores
HQ: Kerry Inc.
3330 Millington Rd
Beloit WI 53511
608 363-1200

### (G-13091)
### JAY ELKA
Also Called: Dunkin' Donuts
1180 Heather Dr (60047-6707)
PHONE.....................847 540-7776
Fax: 847 540-2183
Jay Patel, *President*
EMP: 15
SQ FT: 3,400
SALES (est): 780K  Privately Held
SIC: 5461  2051  Doughnuts; doughnuts, except frozen

### (G-13092)
### JLJ CORP
Also Called: Georges Printwear
250 Telser Rd Ste D (60047-1543)
PHONE.....................847 726-9795
John George, *President*
EMP: 3
SALES: 250K  Privately Held
SIC: 2759  Commercial printing

### (G-13093)
### JOHNSON BAG CO INC
1166 Flex Ct (60047-1578)
PHONE.....................847 438-2424
Robert L Johnson, *President*
Doreen Johnson-Taylor, *Corp Secy*
Dan Johnson, *Vice Pres*
EMP: 10 EST: 1952
SQ FT: 12,000
SALES (est): 1.5MM  Privately Held
WEB: www.johnsonbag.com
SIC: 3089  Plastic processing

### (G-13094)
### JPMORGAN CHASE BANK NAT ASSN
1289 S Rand Rd (60047-2960)
PHONE.....................847 726-4000
Fax: 847 726-3383
Jack Reck, *Branch Mgr*
EMP: 6
SALES (corp-wide): 105.4B  Publicly Held
SIC: 3578  Automatic teller machines (ATM)
HQ: Jpmorgan Chase Bank, National Association
1111 Polaris Pkwy
Columbus OH 43240
614 436-3055

### (G-13095)
### LEGEND PROMOTIONS
Also Called: Legend Creative Group
815 Oakwood Rd Ste B (60047-6704)
PHONE.....................847 438-3528
Fax: 847 438-3526
David Voitik, *President*
Donhesscell Hess, *Credit Mgr*
EMP: 6
SQ FT: 500
SALES (est): 604.9K  Privately Held
WEB: www.legendpro.com
SIC: 7336  2791  2759  2752  Commercial art & graphic design; typesetting; commercial printing; commercial printing, lithographic; advertising consultant

### (G-13096)
### LOCH PRECISION TECHNOLOGIES
Also Called: L P T
1215 Berkley Rd (60047-1827)
PHONE.....................847 438-1400
Fax: 847 438-1401
Terry Loch, *Owner*
Kathleen A Loch, *Nurse*
EMP: 6

SALES (est): 310K  Privately Held
SIC: 3462  Gear & chain forgings

### (G-13097)
### M P V INC
214 Fairway Rd (60047-2136)
PHONE.....................847 234-3960
Marco Polo Valladolid, *President*
Juli Lehman, *Senior VP*
EMP: 4
SALES (est): 320K  Privately Held
SIC: 3699  Accelerating waveguide structures

### (G-13098)
### MAG DADDY LLC
1155 Rose Rd (60047-1547)
PHONE.....................847 719-5600
Jonathan Winnie, *Sales Mgr*
William R Smith,
▲ EMP: 2
SALES (est): 310.3K  Privately Held
SIC: 3714  5531  Motor vehicle parts & accessories; automotive & home supply stores

### (G-13099)
### MARIE GERE CORPORATION
1275 Ensell Rd (60047-1532)
PHONE.....................847 540-1154
Fax: 847 540-1189
James G Schultz, *President*
Sheri Principato, *Vice Pres*
Alvaro Hinestrosa, *Production*
Cory Peltzer, *Purch Agent*
Doug Erdman, *Engineer*
EMP: 170 EST: 1997
SQ FT: 165,000
SALES (est): 55.9MM  Privately Held
SIC: 3479  7379  8711  Aluminum coating of metal products; computer related consulting services; consulting engineer

### (G-13100)
### MEAD PRODUCTS LLC
4 Corporate Dr (60047-8924)
PHONE.....................847 541-9500
Robert J Keller, *CEO*
Boris Elisman, *President*
Neal V Fenwick, *CFO*
▲ EMP: 9
SALES: 1MM
SALES (corp-wide): 1.5B  Publicly Held
SIC: 3542  3441  Machine tools, metal forming type; fabricated structural metal
PA: Acco Brands Corporation
4 Corporate Dr
Lake Zurich IL 60047
847 541-9500

### (G-13101)
### MELON INK SCREEN PRINT
100 Oakwood Rd Ste B (60047-1524)
PHONE.....................847 726-0003
EMP: 1
SALES: 500K  Privately Held
SIC: 2759  Commercial Printing

### (G-13102)
### METROM LLC (NOT LLC)
904 Donata Ct (60047-5025)
PHONE.....................847 847-7233
Tony Scala,
FL Griffin,
EMP: 3
SALES (est): 265.9K  Privately Held
SIC: 3545  Scales, measuring (machinists' precision tools)

### (G-13103)
### MIKRON DESIGNS INC
705 Rose Rd (60047-1542)
PHONE.....................847 726-3990
Fax: 847 726-3998
Ronald Zaar, *President*
Mary Zaar, *Vice Pres*
Mark Zaar, *Treasurer*
Eric Zaar, *Admin Sec*
EMP: 7
SQ FT: 5,000
SALES: 850K  Privately Held
SIC: 2542  Counters or counter display cases: except wood

# GEOGRAPHIC SECTION

Lake Zurich - Lake County (G-13131)

**(G-13104)**
**MILLENNIUM MOLD & TOOL**
1194 Heather Dr (60047-6707)
PHONE.................................847 438-5600
Irene Gorney, *Principal*
**EMP:** 5
**SALES (est):** 652.7K **Privately Held**
**SIC:** 3544 Industrial molds

**(G-13105)**
**MINDFUL MIX**
15 Maple Ave (60047-2323)
PHONE.................................847 284-4404
Claire Slattery, *President*
Lora Rampino, *Consultant*
**EMP:** 8
**SALES (est):** 853.6K **Privately Held**
**SIC:** 3273 Ready-mixed concrete

**(G-13106)**
**MORGAN BRONZE PRODUCTS INC**
340 E Il Route 22 (60047-2572)
PHONE.................................847 526-6000
Fax: 847 526-3960
Ron Rogers, *President*
Scott Doorn, *General Mgr*
Dave Eakins, *Prdtn Mgr*
Paul Swanson, *Safety Mgr*
Fred Talbot, *Maint Spvr*
▲ **EMP:** 85
**SQ FT:** 70,000
**SALES:** 20.6MM **Privately Held**
**WEB:** www.morganbronze.com
**SIC:** 3599 5051 Machine shop, jobbing & repair; metals service centers & offices

**(G-13107)**
**MTECH CNC MACHINING INC**
1154 Rose Rd (60047-1567)
PHONE.................................224 848-0818
Witold Zbierowski, *President*
**EMP:** 9
**SQ FT:** 6,000
**SALES:** 1.4MM **Privately Held**
**SIC:** 3599 Machine shop, jobbing & repair

**(G-13108)**
**NATIONAL BUSHING & MFG**
505 Oakwood Rd Ste 240 (60047-1534)
PHONE.................................847 847-1553
Fax: 847 847-1554
John Carr, *President*
Lesley Carr, *Admin Sec*
**EMP:** 4
**SQ FT:** 2,000
**SALES (est):** 165K **Privately Held**
**WEB:** www.natbushing.com
**SIC:** 3545 Drill bushings (drilling jig)

**(G-13109)**
**NORTH STAR PICKLE LLC**
968 Donata Ct (60047-5025)
PHONE.................................847 970-5555
Jeff Oziemkowski,
Mike Alexander,
Steve Spector,
**EMP:** 10
**SALES (est):** 1.1MM **Privately Held**
**SIC:** 2035 Pickles, vinegar

**(G-13110)**
**NORTHSTAR GROUP INC**
577 Capital Dr (60047-6711)
PHONE.................................847 726-0880
Karl Heerdegen, *President*
Frank Novy, *Project Mgr*
**EMP:** 10
**SALES (est):** 2.1MM **Privately Held**
**WEB:** www.northstargroup.com
**SIC:** 5112 2752 Stationery & office supplies; color lithography

**(G-13111)**
**OLIVET WOODWORKING**
316 Hickory Rd (60047-2142)
PHONE.................................773 505-5225
**EMP:** 4
**SALES (est):** 232.4K **Privately Held**
**SIC:** 2431 Millwork

**(G-13112)**
**PERFECTION PROBES INC**
24241 W Rose Ave (60047-9362)
PHONE.................................847 726-8868
Paul Christensen, *President*
**EMP:** 4
**SQ FT:** 1,400
**SALES:** 260K **Privately Held**
**SIC:** 3829 Physical property testing equipment

**(G-13113)**
**PERFORMANCE DESIGN INC**
Also Called: Pdi
238 Telser Rd (60047-1525)
PHONE.................................847 719-1535
Fax: 847 719-1537
John A Fioretto, *President*
Deborah Fioretto, *Admin Sec*
**EMP:** 5
**SQ FT:** 7,000
**SALES (est):** 108K **Privately Held**
**SIC:** 3549 8711 3544 Assembly machines, including robotic; designing: ship, boat, machine & product; special dies, tools, jigs & fixtures

**(G-13114)**
**PIXEL PUSHERS INCORPORATED**
1050 Ensell Rd Ste 108 (60047-6709)
P.O. Box 1067, Palatine (60078-1067)
PHONE.................................847 550-6560
Ryan Burke, *President*
**EMP:** 6
**SALES (est):** 513.3K **Privately Held**
**SIC:** 3545 Pushers

**(G-13115)**
**POINTE INTERNATIONAL COMPANY**
234 Oakwood Rd (60047-1508)
PHONE.................................847 550-7001
Sheila Liao, *President*
▲ **EMP:** 16 **EST:** 1997
**SQ FT:** 34,000
**SALES:** 3.4MM **Privately Held**
**SIC:** 2522 2531 Office furniture, except wood; school furniture

**(G-13116)**
**POWERNAIL COMPANY**
1300 Rose Rd (60047-1554)
PHONE.................................800 323-1653
David A Anstett, *President*
Tom Anstett, *President*
Thomas Anstett, *Sales Executive*
Sue Krieskey, *Manager*
Todd Janstett, *Admin Sec*
▲ **EMP:** 50
**SALES (est):** 25.7MM **Privately Held**
**WEB:** www.powernail.com
**SIC:** 5084 3546 3315 Machine tools & metalworking machinery; power-driven handtools; steel wire & related products

**(G-13117)**
**PROTIDE PHARMACEUTICALS INC**
220 Telser Rd (60047-1525)
PHONE.................................847 726-3100
Fax: 847 726-3110
Milo R Polovina, *Ch of Bd*
Gayle Polovina, *Vice Pres*
**EMP:** 3
**SQ FT:** 9,500
**SALES (est):** 411.3K **Privately Held**
**WEB:** www.protidepharma.com
**SIC:** 2836 Biological products, except diagnostic

**(G-13118)**
**PSYTRONICS INC**
545 Capital Dr (60047-6711)
PHONE.................................847 719-1371
Noel H Simon, *President*
Wayne Simon, *Office Mgr*
Marianne Simon, *Admin Sec*
**EMP:** 3
**SQ FT:** 1,500
**SALES (est):** 370K **Privately Held**
**WEB:** www.psytronicstvss.com
**SIC:** 5063 3612 Electrical apparatus & equipment; transformers, except electric

**(G-13119)**
**PURSUIT BEVERAGE COMPANY LLC**
500 E Il Route 22 (60047-2592)
PHONE.................................888 606-3353
Dominick Voso, *President*
Richard Atkinson, *Vice Pres*
**EMP:** 9
**SALES (est):** 1.2MM **Privately Held**
**SIC:** 2086 Bottled & canned soft drinks

**(G-13120)**
**QUARTER MASTER INDUSTRIES INC**
510 Telser Rd (60047-1500)
PHONE.................................847 540-8999
Fax: 847 540-0526
Ron Weinberg, *President*
Mike Levin, *Plant Mgr*
Karen Ciochon, *Buyer*
Colleen Dunkel, *Asst Controller*
Jeff Weigert, *Sales Staff*
**EMP:** 24
**SQ FT:** 12,000
**SALES (est):** 5.8MM
**SALES (corp-wide):** 42.4MM **Privately Held**
**SIC:** 3714 Drive shafts, motor vehicle
**PA:** Competition Cams, Inc.
 3406 Democrat Rd
 Memphis TN 38118
 901 795-2400

**(G-13121)**
**R AND R BROKERAGE CO (PA)**
Also Called: C M Products
800 Ela Rd (60047-2340)
PHONE.................................847 438-4600
Fax: 847 438-1812
Dave Randall, *President*
Mark Faber, *President*
Richard D Barton, *Vice Pres*
Michael F Jenkins, *Vice Pres*
Kevin Scelander, *CFO*
◆ **EMP:** 140 **EST:** 1982
**SQ FT:** 300,000
**SALES (est):** 36.1MM **Privately Held**
**WEB:** www.cmprod.com
**SIC:** 3497 3089 Foil containers for bakery goods & frozen foods; tubs, plastic (containers)

**(G-13122)**
**REYCO PRECISION WELDING INC (PA)**
320 E Il Route 22 (60047-2572)
PHONE.................................847 593-2947
Fax: 847 593-3518
Jose Reyes, *President*
Daniel Reyes, *Opers Mgr*
Marciala Reyes, *Admin Sec*
**EMP:** 14
**SQ FT:** 15,000
**SALES (est):** 1.7MM **Privately Held**
**WEB:** www.reycoprecision.com
**SIC:** 3599 1799 Machine shop, jobbing & repair; welding on site

**(G-13123)**
**ROBBINS HDD LLC**
1221 Flex Ct (60047-1578)
PHONE.................................847 955-0050
Stanislav Rozenbaum, *Purchasing*
Oleg Raskin, *Mng Member*
Alexander Murovanny,
**EMP:** 11
**SALES (est):** 4.2MM **Privately Held**
**SIC:** 3541 Machine tools, metal cutting type; drilling & boring machines

**(G-13124)**
**ROMED INDUSTRIES CORPORATION**
320 E Il Route 22 (60047-2572)
PHONE.................................847 362-3900
Oliver Osterhues, *President*
Mark Osterhues, *General Mgr*
Inam Khan, *CFO*
**EMP:** 7
**SQ FT:** 10,000
**SALES (est):** 1.7MM **Privately Held**
**SIC:** 3599 Custom machinery

**(G-13125)**
**SCHAFF INTERNATIONAL LLC**
Also Called: Schaff Piano Supply
451 Oakwood Rd (60047-1516)
PHONE.................................847 438-4560
Fax: 847 438-4615
Mike Donovan, *Plant Mgr*
Peggy Lenz, *Controller*
Kevin Dwyer, *Sales Executive*
Chas Hoyt, *Director*
Stephen L Johnson,
▲ **EMP:** 40 **EST:** 1867
**SQ FT:** 80,000
**SALES (est):** 8.7MM **Privately Held**
**WEB:** www.schaffinternational.com
**SIC:** 3495 3931 3496 Wire springs; musical instruments; miscellaneous fabricated wire products

**(G-13126)**
**SCHNEIDER GRAPHICS INC**
885 Telser Rd (60047-1536)
PHONE.................................847 550-4310
Gregory Schneider, *President*
Anne Schneider, *Controller*
Justin Hess, *VP Human Res*
**EMP:** 25
**SQ FT:** 35,000
**SALES (est):** 5.8MM **Privately Held**
**SIC:** 2752 Commercial printing, lithographic

**(G-13127)**
**SCHWEITZER ENGRG LABS INC**
Also Called: E O Schweitzer Manufacturing
450 Enterprise Pkwy (60047-6722)
PHONE.................................847 540-3037
Edmund O Schweitzer III, *CEO*
Daniel Clifford, *General Mgr*
Gloria Guillen, *Opers Staff*
Jim Duros, *Design Engr*
Susan Menn, *Marketing Mgr*
**EMP:** 30 **EST:** 1992
**SALES (est):** 5.7MM **Privately Held**
**SIC:** 3829 Temperature sensors, except industrial process & aircraft

**(G-13128)**
**SCHWEITZER ENGRG LABS INC**
Fault Indicator & Sensor Div
450 Enterprise Pkwy (60047-6722)
PHONE.................................847 362-8304
Jim Loris, *Plant Mgr*
**EMP:** 100
**SALES (corp-wide):** 1B **Privately Held**
**SIC:** 3825 Indicating instruments, electric
**PA:** Schweitzer Engineering Laboratories Inc.
 2440 Ne Hopkins Ct
 Pullman WA 99163
 509 332-1890

**(G-13129)**
**SCRUBAIR SYSTEMS INC**
1200 Ensell Rd (60047-1537)
PHONE.................................847 550-8061
Fax: 847 550-8062
Thomas O'Connor, *President*
Vanessa Tweten, *Office Mgr*
Bill Vaughan, *Supervisor*
**EMP:** 30
**SQ FT:** 25,000
**SALES:** 11MM **Privately Held**
**SIC:** 3564 Air purification equipment

**(G-13130)**
**SESHIN USA INC**
Also Called: Hiwood USA
333 Enterprise Pkwy (60047-6733)
PHONE.................................847 550-5556
Brian Moon, *President*
Max Hahn, *Vice Pres*
Julie John, *Manager*
◆ **EMP:** 6 **EST:** 1997
**SALES (est):** 1.1MM **Privately Held**
**WEB:** www.seshinbikes.com
**SIC:** 5023 2671 Frames & framing, picture & mirror; packaging paper & plastics film, coated & laminated

**(G-13131)**
**SIGNSCAPES INC**
884 S Rand Rd Ste D (60047-3412)
PHONE.................................847 719-2610
Fax: 847 719-2613
Richard Palmblad, *President*

# Lake Zurich - Lake County (G-13132)   GEOGRAPHIC SECTION

Gloria Palmblad, *Corp Secy*
**EMP**: 3
**SALES (est)**: 200K **Privately Held**
**SIC**: 3993 Signs & advertising specialties

**(G-13132)**
**SMALLEY STEEL RING CO (PA)**
555 Oakwood Rd (60047-1558)
**PHONE** .................... 847 537-7600
**Fax**: 847 719-5999
Michael A Greenhill, *President*
Charles Greenhill, *President*
Ramona Cristea, *General Mgr*
Mark A Greenhill, *Vice Pres*
Michael Greenhill, *Vice Pres*
▲ **EMP**: 110 **EST**: 1918
**SALES (est)**: 53.1MM **Privately Held**
**WEB**: www.smalley.com
**SIC**: 3493 3495 Steel springs, except wire; wire springs

**(G-13133)**
**SPIROLOX INC**
555 Oakwood Rd (60047-1558)
**PHONE** .................... 847 719-5900
Mark Reno, *President*
**EMP**: 450
**SALES (est)**: 13.2K
**SALES (corp-wide)**: 53.1MM **Privately Held**
**SIC**: 3493 3495 Steel springs, except wire; wire springs
**PA**: Smalley Steel Ring Co.
555 Oakwood Rd
Lake Zurich IL 60047
847 537-7600

**(G-13134)**
**STANDARD CONTAINER CO OF EDGAR (PA)**
Also Called: Badger Basket Co
717 N Old Rand Rd (60047-2209)
**PHONE** .................... 847 438-1510
Gary Rasmussen, *President*
Janet Rasmussen, *Vice Pres*
Sara Logan, *Manager*
▲ **EMP**: 23
**SQ FT**: 1,000
**SALES (est)**: 19.7MM **Privately Held**
**WEB**: www.standardcontainer.com
**SIC**: 2519 3944 5719 Wicker furniture: padded or plain; doll carriages & carts; bedding (sheets, blankets, spreads & pillows); bath accessories

**(G-13135)**
**STANICK TOOL MANUFACTURING CO**
1190 Heather Dr (60047-6707)
**PHONE** .................... 847 726-7090
Stanley S Kosjer, *President*
Edie Kosjer, *Principal*
**EMP**: 3
**SALES (est)**: 220K **Privately Held**
**SIC**: 3544 Special dies, tools, jigs & fixtures

**(G-13136)**
**SWB INC**
529 Capital Dr (60047-6711)
**PHONE** .................... 847 438-1800
Scot Braunling, *President*
▲ **EMP**: 4
**SALES (est)**: 520K **Privately Held**
**WEB**: www.swbinc.net
**SIC**: 3313 3672 3496 Electrometallurgical products; printed circuit boards; miscellaneous fabricated wire products

**(G-13137)**
**TERMAX CORPORATION (PA)**
1155 Rose Rd Ste A (60047-1547)
**PHONE** .................... 847 519-1500
Wes Gardocki, *President*
Michael Smith, *Co-CEO*
William R Smith, *Co-CEO*
Ken Bird, *Opers Staff*
Jon Spencer, *Production*
▲ **EMP**: 156
**SALES (est)**: 54MM **Privately Held**
**WEB**: www.termax.com
**SIC**: 3429 Metal fasteners

**(G-13138)**
**TREDEGAR FILM PRODUCTS CORP**
351 Oakwood Rd (60047-1509)
**PHONE** .................... 847 438-2111
Bryan Matte, *Prdtn Mgr*
Brian Wall, *Engineer*
Brian Pesch, *Controller*
Dennis Beard, *Manager*
**EMP**: 170
**SALES (corp-wide)**: 830.7MM **Publicly Held**
**WEB**: www.tredegar.com
**SIC**: 3081 3089 Polyethylene film; plastic processing
**HQ**: Tredegar Film Products Corporation
1100 Boulders Pkwy # 200
North Chesterfield VA 23225
804 330-1000

**(G-13139)**
**TUF-TITE INC**
1200 Flex Ct (60047-1578)
**PHONE** .................... 847 550-1011
**Fax**: 847 550-8004
Theodore W Meyers, *President*
John Kullman, *Plant Mgr*
Wayne Huerth, *Opers Mgr*
Urszula Pyskaty, *Sales Staff*
◆ **EMP**: 12
**SQ FT**: 40,000
**SALES (est)**: 5.1MM **Privately Held**
**WEB**: www.tuf-tite.com
**SIC**: 3089 Plastic hardware & building products

**(G-13140)**
**UNIVERSAL HRZNTAL DRCTNAL DRLG**
Also Called: Universal Hdd
1221 Flex Ct (60047-1578)
**PHONE** .................... 847 847-3300
Alex Murovanny, *CEO*
Roman Petryshyn, *Prdtn Mgr*
George Kolcan, *Purch Agent*
Michael Fry, *Sales Mgr*
Alexender Veytsman, *Manager*
▲ **EMP**: 2
**SALES (est)**: 854.8K **Privately Held**
**SIC**: 1381 Directional drilling oil & gas wells

**(G-13141)**
**VS MFG CO**
715 Rose Rd (60047-1542)
**PHONE** .................... 224 475-1190
**EMP**: 3
**SALES (est)**: 195.7K **Privately Held**
**SIC**: 3999 Manufacturing industries

**(G-13142)**
**W & W ASSOCIATES INC**
704 Telser Rd (60047-1576)
**PHONE** .................... 847 719-1760
**Fax**: 847 719-1766
Walter Toben, *President*
Katherine Toben, *Corp Secy*
**EMP**: 8
**SQ FT**: 1,620
**SALES (est)**: 2.4MM **Privately Held**
**WEB**: www.wnwinc.com
**SIC**: 5131 2241 Sewing supplies & notions; labels, woven

## Lakemoor
### Mchenry County

**(G-13143)**
**COMPETITIVE EDGE OPPORTUNITIES**
Also Called: High Performance Packaging
426 Scotland Rd Unit A (60051-8672)
**PHONE** .................... 815 322-2164
Ron Crews, *President*
Roula Crews, *VP Sales*
**EMP**: 5
**SALES (est)**: 1.5MM **Privately Held**
**WEB**: www.hp-packaging.com
**SIC**: 5521 7389 3565 Used car dealers; labeling bottles, cans, cartons, etc.; packaging machinery

**(G-13144)**
**ILLINOIS RACK ENTERPRISES INC**
480 Scotland Rd Ste A (60051-3001)
**PHONE** .................... 815 385-5750
**Fax**: 815 385-5760
Brian Mooney, *President*
Jorge Martinez, *Vice Pres*
**EMP**: 20
**SQ FT**: 9,000
**SALES**: 1.4MM **Privately Held**
**SIC**: 2542 3443 Racks, merchandise display or storage: except wood; fabricated plate work (boiler shop)

**(G-13145)**
**PETERSEN SAND & GRAVEL INC**
914 Rand Rd Ste A (60051-8709)
**PHONE** .................... 815 344-1060
**Fax**: 815 344-6252
Raymond J Petersen, *President*
Dennis Petersen, *Vice Pres*
Rosalee Hoskins, *Bookkeeper*
**EMP**: 13 **EST**: 1950
**SQ FT**: 200
**SALES (est)**: 1.2MM **Privately Held**
**SIC**: 1442 5211 Gravel mining; lumber & other building materials

**(G-13146)**
**PRECISION GROUND**
548 Herbert Rd Ste 2 (60051-8829)
**PHONE** .................... 815 578-2613
Kurt Suda, *President*
Ken Royce, *Vice Pres*
**EMP**: 12
**SALES (est)**: 1.7MM **Privately Held**
**WEB**: www.precisiongroundinc.com
**SIC**: 3599 Grinding castings for the trade

**(G-13147)**
**PRINTING IMPRESSION DIREC**
31704 N Clearwater Dr (60051-2203)
**PHONE** .................... 815 385-6688
James Maczko, *Owner*
Regia Maczko, *Vice Pres*
**EMP**: 6
**SALES (est)**: 505.3K **Privately Held**
**SIC**: 2752 Commercial printing, lithographic

**(G-13148)**
**STONECRAFTERS INC**
430 W Wegner Rd (60051-8653)
**PHONE** .................... 815 363-8730
**Fax**: 815 363-5907
David Hammerl, *President*
▲ **EMP**: 45
**SQ FT**: 15,000
**SALES (est)**: 10.9MM **Privately Held**
**WEB**: www.stonecrafters.com
**SIC**: 5031 5719 5999 3281 Kitchen cabinets; bath accessories; monuments & tombstones; marble, building: cut & shaped; granite, cut & shaped; marble installation, interior

## Lanark
### Carroll County

**(G-13149)**
**ACRES OF SKY COMMUNICATIONS**
Also Called: Prairie Advocate Newspaper
446 S Broad St (61046-1245)
P.O. Box 84 (61046-0084)
**PHONE** .................... 815 493-2560
Thomas Kocal, *Owner*
Lynn Kocal, *Vice Pres*
Tammi Burkholder, *Sales/Mktg Mgr*
**EMP**: 7 **EST**: 1937
**SALES (est)**: 355.1K **Privately Held**
**WEB**: www.prairie-advocate-news.com
**SIC**: 2711 2752 2759 2791 Newspapers; commercial printing, offset; letterpress printing; typesetting; bookbinding & related work

**(G-13150)**
**ALDO-SHANE CORPORATION**
Also Called: Phylrich International
105 N Rochester St (61046-1149)
**PHONE** .................... 714 361-4830

Alfred R Dubin, *President*
**EMP**: 90
**SALES (est)**: 6.8MM **Privately Held**
**WEB**: www.phylrich.com
**SIC**: 3431 Bathroom fixtures, including sinks

**(G-13151)**
**CARROLL COUNTY LOCKER**
122 E Carroll St (61046-1144)
**PHONE** .................... 815 493-2370
Nancy Byington, *Owner*
**EMP**: 6
**SQ FT**: 1,800
**SALES (est)**: 500K **Privately Held**
**SIC**: 4222 2013 Warehousing, cold storage or refrigerated; sausages & other prepared meats

**(G-13152)**
**EASTLAND FABRICATION LLC**
14273 Il Route 73 (61046-8860)
**PHONE** .................... 815 493-8399
Roger Coultherd, *Mng Member*
Terry Blair,
**EMP**: 4
**SQ FT**: 6,800
**SALES (est)**: 410K **Privately Held**
**SIC**: 3443 Tanks, standard or custom fabricated: metal plate

**(G-13153)**
**ELKAY MANUFACTURING COMPANY**
Water Cooler Division
105 N Rochester St (61046-1149)
**PHONE** .................... 815 493-8850
**Fax**: 815 493-2187
Ed Perz, *Opers-Prdtn-Mfg*
Kraig Kniss, *QC Mgr*
Bruce Lake, *Human Res Dir*
Phyliss Roth, *Personnel*
**EMP**: 250
**SALES (corp-wide)**: 1.1B **Privately Held**
**SIC**: 3585 Coolers, milk & water: electric
**PA**: Elkay Manufacturing Company Inc
2222 Camden Ct
Oak Brook IL 60523
630 574-8484

**(G-13154)**
**FORSTER PRODUCTS INC**
310 Se Lanark Ave (61046-9704)
**PHONE** .................... 815 493-6360
**Fax**: 815 493-2371
Rodney P Hartman, *President*
Robert R Ruch, *CFO*
**EMP**: 21 **EST**: 1933
**SQ FT**: 22,000
**SALES (est)**: 2.9MM **Privately Held**
**WEB**: www.forsterproducts.com
**SIC**: 3544 3545 Special dies & tools; precision tools, machinists'

**(G-13155)**
**HYGIENIC FABRICS & FILTERS INC (PA)**
Also Called: Bandage, The Div
118 S Broad St (61046-1204)
P.O. Box 34 (61046-0034)
**PHONE** .................... 815 493-2502
**Fax**: 815 493-1098
John F Wilson Jr, *President*
Tom Laiken, *Vice Pres*
Kelly Leight, *Office Mgr*
Robert Krier, *Manager*
**EMP**: 9 **EST**: 1959
**SQ FT**: 3,000
**SALES (est)**: 2MM **Privately Held**
**WEB**: www.hyfab.com
**SIC**: 2211 Filter cloth, cotton; bags & bagging, cotton

## Lansing
### Cook County

**(G-13156)**
**AMERICAN CAST PRODUCTS INC**
Also Called: Beverly Fndry Prcsion McHining
17730 Chicago Ave Frnt (60438-1964)
**PHONE** .................... 708 895-5152
**Fax**: 708 895-5288

## GEOGRAPHIC SECTION

Lansing - Cook County (G-13182)

Gordon W Fortier, *President*
▲ **EMP:** 12
**SALES (est):** 1.6MM **Privately Held**
**SIC: 3364** Nonferrous die-castings except aluminum

**(G-13157)**
### BEDFORD RAKIM
Also Called: Passco Parts & Electronics
3022 Bernice Ave Apt 3s (60438-1396)
**PHONE** .................................. 773 749-3086
Rakim Bedford, *Owner*
**EMP:** 3
**SALES (est):** 102.7K **Privately Held**
**SIC: 3599** Air intake filters, internal combustion engine, except auto

**(G-13158)**
### CALUMET MOTORSPORTS INC
3441 Washington St (60438-2317)
**PHONE** .................................. 708 895-0398
Thomas Milton, *President*
**EMP:** 3
**SALES (est):** 210K **Privately Held**
**WEB:** www.calumetair.com
**SIC: 3721** Aircraft

**(G-13159)**
### CHICAGOS FINEST IRONWORKS
17564 Chicago Ave (60438-1925)
**PHONE** .................................. 708 895-4484
John Micun, *President*
Bryan Hardy, *Vice Pres*
**EMP:** 6
**SALES (est):** 590K **Privately Held**
**SIC: 3446** 3496 2514 2511 Ornamental metalwork; miscellaneous fabricated wire products; metal household furniture; wood household furniture

**(G-13160)**
### DMS INDUSTRIES INC (PA)
Also Called: Deny Machine Shop
1925 177th St (60438-1566)
**PHONE** .................................. 708 895-8000
**Fax:** 708 895-8189
Steve Cirjakovich, *President*
**EMP:** 10
**SQ FT:** 3,500
**SALES (est):** 1.9MM **Privately Held**
**SIC: 3599** Machine shop, jobbing & repair

**(G-13161)**
### EENIGENBURG MFG INC
19530 Burnham Ave (60438)
P.O. Box 286 (60438-0286)
**PHONE** .................................. 708 474-0850
**Fax:** 708 474-4631
Robert Eenigenburg, *President*
Randall Eenigenburg, *Vice Pres*
Drew Eenigenburg, *Engineer*
**EMP:** 7 **EST:** 1947
**SQ FT:** 5,840
**SALES (est):** 1.3MM **Privately Held**
**SIC: 3599** 7692 Machine shop, jobbing & repair; welding repair

**(G-13162)**
### FORZA CUSTOMS
17809 Torrence Ave (60438-1835)
**PHONE** .................................. 708 474-6625
**EMP:** 2
**SALES (est):** 273.8K **Privately Held**
**SIC: 3312** Wheels

**(G-13163)**
### GAYETY CANDY CO INC (PA)
Also Called: Gayetys Chocolates & Ice Cream
3306 Ridge Rd (60438-3112)
**PHONE** .................................. 708 418-0062
**Fax:** 708 418-3237
James L Flessor, *President*
Jim Flessor, *President*
Nick Flessor, *Principal*
Elias Flessor, *Vice Pres*
**EMP:** 20 **EST:** 1920
**SALES:** 1.5MM **Privately Held**
**SIC: 5441** 5812 2066 2024 Candy; ice cream stands or dairy bars; chocolate & cocoa products; ice cream & frozen desserts

**(G-13164)**
### GOOSE ISLAND MFG & SUPPLY CORP
Also Called: National Excelsior Company
17725 Volbrecht Rd Ste 1 (60438-4543)
**PHONE** .................................. 708 343-4225
John Brady, *President*
Dave Kerber, *General Mgr*
William Cotugno, *Corp Secy*
Tom Milostan, *Exec VP*
Mike Boris Jr, *Vice Pres*
**EMP:** 1 **EST:** 1886
**SQ FT:** 120,000
**SALES (est):** 10.5MM
**SALES (corp-wide):** 102.6MM **Privately Held**
**WEB:** www.excelsior-hvac.com
**SIC: 3444** 5075 3585 3564 Furnace casings, sheet metal; warm air heating equipment & supplies; air conditioning & ventilation equipment & supplies; refrigeration & heating equipment; blowers & fans; architectural metalwork; heating equipment, except electric
**HQ:** Temperature Equipment Corporation
17725 Volbrecht Rd Ste 1
Lansing IL 60438
708 418-0900

**(G-13165)**
### HADADY MACHINING COMPANY INC (PA)
16730 Chicago Ave (60438-1113)
**PHONE** .................................. 708 474-8620
**Fax:** 708 474-0899
Peter Lanman, *President*
Charlotte Stapke, *Office Mgr*
Hal Chadwick, *Manager*
John Walker, *Supervisor*
Larry Hunt, *Info Tech Mgr*
**EMP:** 12 **EST:** 1947
**SQ FT:** 16,000
**SALES (est):** 6MM **Privately Held**
**WEB:** www.hadadyinc.com
**SIC: 3599** 3823 3593 Machine shop, jobbing & repair; industrial instrmnts msrmnt display/control process variable; fluid power cylinders & actuators

**(G-13166)**
### INNOVATIVE AUTOMATION
3116 192nd St (60438-3724)
**PHONE** .................................. 708 418-8720
Ronald Carine, *Owner*
Karen Carine, *Admin Sec*
**EMP:** 1
**SALES:** 310K **Privately Held**
**SIC: 5084** 3053 Robots, industrial; packing materials

**(G-13167)**
### KAMSTRA DOOR SERVICE INC
2007 Thornton Lansing Rd (60438-2111)
**PHONE** .................................. 708 895-9990
Bruce Kamstra, *President*
Linda Kamstra, *Admin Sec*
**EMP:** 2
**SQ FT:** 2,000
**SALES (est):** 250K **Privately Held**
**SIC: 5211** 3699 Door & window products; door opening & closing devices, electrical

**(G-13168)**
### KINGERY STEEL FABRICATORS INC
16895 Chicago Ave (60438-1197)
**PHONE** .................................. 708 474-6665
**Fax:** 708 474-2201
David R Ash Jr, *President*
Patricia Yackanich, *Manager*
Joanne Ash, *Admin Sec*
**EMP:** 36
**SQ FT:** 10,000
**SALES (est):** 15.3MM **Privately Held**
**SIC: 3441** Fabricated structural metal

**(G-13169)**
### LAND OFROST INC (PA)
16850 Chicago Ave (60438-1115)
**PHONE** .................................. 708 474-7100
**Fax:** 708 474-9295
Donna Van Eekeren, *Ch of Bd*
David Van Eekeren, *President*
John Butts, *Vice Pres*
John Horton, *Vice Pres*
Barb Hagen, *Transptn Dir*
▲ **EMP:** 225
**SQ FT:** 100,000
**SALES:** 7.5MM **Privately Held**
**SIC: 2013** 2099 Sausages & other prepared meats; smoked meats from purchased meat; prepared beef products from purchased beef; ready-to-eat meals, salads & sandwiches

**(G-13170)**
### LANSING CUT STONE CO
3125 Glenwood Lansing Rd (60438)
P.O. Box 5178 (60438-5178)
**PHONE** .................................. 708 474-7515
**Fax:** 708 474-7565
John Boersma, *President*
Darlene Boersma, *Admin Sec*
**EMP:** 10
**SQ FT:** 7,000
**SALES (est):** 1.5MM **Privately Held**
**WEB:** www.lansingcutstone.com
**SIC: 5032** 3281 Building stone; cut stone & stone products

**(G-13171)**
### LANSING WINGS INC
3720 Ridge Rd (60438-3319)
**PHONE** .................................. 708 895-3300
Alan D Krygier, *President*
**EMP:** 3
**SALES (est):** 141.9K **Privately Held**
**SIC: 2087** Beverage bases

**(G-13172)**
### LIFETIME CREATIONS
17838 Chappel Ave (60438-4523)
**PHONE** .................................. 708 895-2770
Pat Jensen, *President*
**EMP:** 4
**SALES (est):** 455.7K **Privately Held**
**SIC: 3479** Etching on metals

**(G-13173)**
### LITHO TYPE LLC
16710 Chicago Ave (60438-1118)
P.O. Box 332 (60438-0332)
**PHONE** .................................. 708 895-3720
Edward Dewitt, *Vice Pres*
Kathleen Wajda, *Project Mgr*
Shelley Hendrickson, *Accountant*
Vincent Pellettiere, *Human Res Mgr*
Victor Arana, *Supervisor*
**EMP:** 50
**SQ FT:** 27,000
**SALES (est):** 8.1MM **Privately Held**
**SIC: 2752** Commercial printing, lithographic

**(G-13174)**
### LIVE LOVE HAIR
17734 Commercial Ave (60438-4822)
**PHONE** .................................. 530 554-2471
McNair Grant, *Managing Prtnr*
Cynthia Jemison, *Partner*
**EMP:** 4
**SALES (est):** 223K **Privately Held**
**SIC: 3999** 5621 7389 Hair curlers, designed for beauty parlors; hair & hair-based products; women's specialty clothing stores;

**(G-13175)**
### MAGNUM INTERNATIONAL INC
1965 Bernice Rd Ste 2se (60438-6052)
P.O. Box 1727, Calumet City (60409-7727)
**PHONE** .................................. 708 889-9999
**Fax:** 708 889-1090
David Creech, *President*
Melissa Otis, *Accounts Mgr*
Thomas S Eisner, *Admin Sec*
▲ **EMP:** 6
**SQ FT:** 2,600
**SALES (est):** 1.9MM **Privately Held**
**SIC: 2851** 5162 5169 Coating, air curing; plastics materials; chemicals, industrial & heavy

**(G-13176)**
### MEDICAL CMMNCTIONS SYSTEMS INC (PA)
17595 Paxton Ave (60438-1514)
**PHONE** .................................. 708 895-4500
William P Wilson, *President*
Ray Christner, *Vice Pres*
**EMP:** 3
**SQ FT:** 7,500
**SALES:** 2MM **Privately Held**
**SIC: 1731** 3661 Communications specialization; telephone & telegraph apparatus

**(G-13177)**
### MINUTEMAN PRESS OF LANSING
17930 Torrence Ave Ste A (60438-1987)
**PHONE** .................................. 708 895-0505
Karen E Kleine, *Owner*
Judith Hojnicki, *Manager*
**EMP:** 6 **EST:** 1978
**SQ FT:** 1,700
**SALES (est):** 490K **Privately Held**
**SIC: 2752** Commercial printing, lithographic

**(G-13178)**
### MORTON NIPPON COATINGS
2701 E 170th St (60438-1107)
**PHONE** .................................. 708 868-7403
**Fax:** 708 868-7484
**EMP:** 5
**SALES (est):** 635.2K
**SALES (corp-wide):** 4.2B **Privately Held**
**SIC: 2851** Paints & allied products
**PA:** Nippon Paint Holdings Co., Ltd.
2-1-2, Oyodokita, Kita-Ku
Osaka OSK 531-0
664 581-111

**(G-13179)**
### NB COATINGS INC (DH)
2701 E 170th St (60438-1107)
**PHONE** .................................. 800 323-3224
Kristina Nelson, *CEO*
Mitsuo Yamada, *Chairman*
Hidefumi Morita, *Corp Secy*
Takashi Tohi, *Exec VP*
Ron Krause, *Plant Mgr*
▲ **EMP:** 250 **EST:** 1945
**SQ FT:** 160,000
**SALES (est):** 107.8MM
**SALES (corp-wide):** 4.2B **Privately Held**
**WEB:** www.nbcoatings.com
**SIC: 2851** 2865 Plastics base paints & varnishes; coating, air curing; color pigments, organic
**HQ:** Nippon Paint (Usa) Inc.
300 Frank W Burr Blvd # 10
Teaneck NJ 07666
201 692-1111

**(G-13180)**
### PRINTMEISTERS INC
3240 Ridge Rd (60438-3193)
**PHONE** .................................. 708 474-8400
**Fax:** 708 474-8443
Christine Widstrand, *President*
**EMP:** 4
**SQ FT:** 1,250
**SALES (est):** 290K **Privately Held**
**SIC: 2752** 7334 2791 2789 Commercial printing, offset; photocopying & duplicating services; typesetting; bookbinding & related work; commercial printing

**(G-13181)**
### QUICK QUALITY PRINTING INC
Also Called: Sign-A-Rama
17332 Torrence Ave (60438-1019)
**PHONE** .................................. 708 895-5885
**Fax:** 708 895-5757
Virginia Jokubauskas, *President*
Peter Jokubauskas, *Vice Pres*
**EMP:** 3
**SQ FT:** 2,000
**SALES:** 300K **Privately Held**
**SIC: 3993** Signs & advertising specialties

**(G-13182)**
### SEALS & COMPONENTS INC
Also Called: Seal Jet Unlimited
17955 Chappel Ave (60438-4526)
**PHONE** .................................. 708 895-5222
Barbara Baney, *President*
Michael Baney, *Treasurer*
Janice Clark, *Director*
John Clark, *Director*
**EMP:** 5
**SQ FT:** 2,000

# Lansing - Cook County (G-13183)

SALES (est): 540K  Privately Held
SIC: 3053  3089  3492  Gaskets, packing & sealing devices; extruded finished plastic products; fluid power valves & hose fittings

**(G-13183)**
**SECURECOM INC**
3338 E 170th St  (60438-1142)
P.O. Box 5302  (60438-5302)
PHONE...................................219 314-4537
Michael Banach, *President*
EMP: 2
SALES: 200K  Privately Held
SIC: 3669  Communications equipment

**(G-13184)**
**SILVER LINE BUILDING PDTS LLC**
Also Called: Silverline Windows
16801 Exchange Ave Ste 2  (60438-6040)
PHONE...................................708 474-9100
Fax: 708 474-4055
Ken Silverman, *CEO*
Justin Schwarz, *Engineer*
Stephen J Marley, *Human Res Mgr*
Danny Hall, *Sales Staff*
Dave Siciarz, *Sales Staff*
EMP: 500
SALES (corp-wide): 2.7B  Privately Held
WEB: www.silverlinewindow.com
SIC: 3089  3442  Window screening, plastic; metal doors, sash & trim
HQ: Silver Line Building Products Llc
1 Silverline Dr
North Brunswick NJ 08902
732 435-1000

**(G-13185)**
**STANDARD PRECISION GRINDING CO**
2800 Bernice Rd Ste 1  (60438-1282)
PHONE...................................708 474-1211
Fax: 708 474-7655
Cynthia Bauer, *President*
Christy Kats, *Manager*
▲ EMP: 12
SQ FT: 20,000
SALES (est): 2MM  Privately Held
SIC: 3463  Bearing & bearing race forgings, nonferrous

**(G-13186)**
**STATE LINE INTERNATIONAL INC**
18107 Torrence Ave  (60438-2157)
PHONE...................................708 251-5772
Jamel Mitchell, *Vice Pres*
EMP: 6
SALES (est): 320.6K  Privately Held
SIC: 3569  5331  Robots, assembly line: industrial & commercial; variety stores

**(G-13187)**
**STEEL SERVICES ENTERPRISES**
17500 Paxton Ave  (60438-1696)
PHONE...................................708 259-1181
Stephen H Leeson, *President*
Josh Leeson, *Vice Pres*
Lisa Hickey, *Manager*
EMP: 30
SQ FT: 3,000
SALES: 18MM  Privately Held
SIC: 1791  7692  3444  Iron work, structural; storage tanks, metal: erection; welding repair; sheet metalwork

**(G-13188)**
**SUPERIOR METALCRAFT  INC**
17655 Chappel Ave  (60438-4544)
PHONE...................................708 418-8940
Joshua A Lesson, *President*
Charles Brent, *Vice Pres*
EMP: 14
SALES: 3.8MM  Privately Held
SIC: 3449  Bars, concrete reinforcing: fabricated steel

**(G-13189)**
**TARTE CUPCAKERY COMPANY**
18509 School St  (60438-2966)
PHONE...................................312 898-2103
EMP: 4

SALES (est): 177.7K  Privately Held
SIC: 2051  Bread, cake & related products

**(G-13190)**
**TOTH AUTOMOTIVE**
1621 Thornton Lansing Rd  (60438-1595)
PHONE...................................708 474-5137
Fax: 708 895-1621
James Toth, *Owner*
EMP: 10
SQ FT: 7,200
SALES (est): 1.7MM  Privately Held
SIC: 5013  3599  Automotive supplies & parts; machine shop, jobbing & repair

**(G-13191)**
**V & C CONVERTERS**
3511 Illinois St  (60438-3393)
PHONE...................................708 251-5635
EMP: 3
SALES (est): 222.1K  Privately Held
SIC: 3535  Conveyors & conveying equipment

**(G-13192)**
**VECTOR ENGINEERING & MFG CORP**
17506 Chicago Ave  (60438-1925)
PHONE...................................708 474-3900
Fax: 708 474-3939
Daryl P Sullivan, *President*
Phillip Fisher, *Vice Pres*
▲ EMP: 20
SQ FT: 21,600
SALES (est): 3.3MM  Privately Held
SIC: 3599  3536  Machine shop, jobbing & repair; hoists, cranes & monorails

**(G-13193)**
**ZEGERS  INC**
16727 Chicago Ave  (60438-1196)
PHONE...................................708 474-7700
Fax: 708 474-7704
William H Zegers, *President*
Nancy Z Mitros, *Vice Pres*
Nanacy Nitros, *Vice Pres*
Nancy Zegers, *Vice Pres*
EMP: 15
SQ FT: 65,000
SALES (est): 2MM  Privately Held
WEB: www.zegers.com
SIC: 3479  Coating of metals & formed products

## Lawrenceville
### Lawrence County

**(G-13194)**
**AMBRAW ASPHALT MATERIALS INC**
S 15th St  (62439)
P.O. Box 551  (62439-0551)
PHONE...................................618 943-4716
Fax: 618 943-4149
Kenneth Kavanaugh, *President*
John B Kavanaugh, *Corp Secy*
Shirley Kavanaugh, *Vice Pres*
Troy Zeigler, *Project Mgr*
EMP: 25  EST: 1954
SQ FT: 6,000
SALES (est): 3.8MM  Privately Held
SIC: 1611  2951  General contractor, highway & street construction; asphalt paving mixtures & blocks

**(G-13195)**
**ASPHALT PRODUCTS INC**
Also Called: Amberaw Asphalt Materials
6574 Akin Rd  (62439-4062)
P.O. Box 551  (62439-0551)
PHONE...................................618 943-4716
Kenneth Kavanaugh, *President*
John B Kavanaugh, *Corp Secy*
Shirley K Kavanaugh, *Vice Pres*
EMP: 25
SALES (est): 4.2MM  Privately Held
WEB: www.asphaltproducts.com
SIC: 2951  Asphalt & asphaltic paving mixtures (not from refineries)

**(G-13196)**
**CENTRAL INDUSTRIES OF INDIANA**
Rr 4 Box 200  (62439-9673)
Rural Route Box 200
PHONE...................................618 943-2311
Fax: 618 943-6913
Terry Silver, *President*
EMP: 3  EST: 2008
SALES (est): 219.4K  Privately Held
SIC: 3679  Harness assemblies for electronic use: wire or cable

**(G-13197)**
**CUSTOM GRAIN SYSTEMS  LLC**
15733 Gollyville Rd  (62439-4703)
Rr # 2 Box 252
PHONE...................................812 881-8175
Tim Gartner, *President*
EMP: 1
SALES (est): 700K  Privately Held
SIC: 3523  Grain stackers

**(G-13198)**
**DAILY LAWRENCEVILLE RECORD**
Also Called: The Daily Record
1209 State St  (62439-2332)
P.O. Box 559  (62439-0559)
PHONE...................................618 943-2331
Mike Vandorn, *Editor*
Mike Van Dorn, *Manager*
EMP: 12
SALES (corp-wide): 827.6K  Privately Held
SIC: 2711  Newspapers: publishing only, not printed on site
PA: Daily Lawrenceville Record Inc
302 S Cross St
Robinson IL 62454
618 544-2101

**(G-13199)**
**EMULSIONS INC**
1105 Adams St  (62439-2614)
P.O. Box 147  (62439-0147)
PHONE...................................618 943-2615
Fax: 618 943-7511
Earl Kavanaugh, *President*
Robert Kizer, *Admin Sec*
EMP: 7
SQ FT: 2,000
SALES (est): 1MM  Privately Held
WEB: www.emulsions.com
SIC: 2951  Asphalt & asphaltic paving mixtures (not from refineries)

**(G-13200)**
**FRANKLIN WELL SERVICES INC**
10483 May Chapel Rd  (62439-4791)
P.O. Box 237, Vincennes IN  (47591-0237)
PHONE...................................812 494-2800
Donald E Jones Jr, *President*
Brent Jones, *President*
Jerry Robinson, *Sales Mgr*
Andria Strange, *Manager*
Mark A Jones, *Admin Sec*
EMP: 55
SALES (est): 6MM  Privately Held
WEB: www.franklinwell.net
SIC: 1389  Servicing oil & gas wells

**(G-13201)**
**HALTER MACHINE SHOP  INC**
9452 Peachtree Rd  (62439-4812)
P.O. Box 867  (62439-0867)
PHONE...................................618 943-2224
Fax: 618 943-2848
Patrick Halter, *President*
Renee Halter, *Admin Sec*
EMP: 4  EST: 1975
SQ FT: 9,000
SALES: 500K  Privately Held
SIC: 3599  7692  Machine shop, jobbing & repair; welding repair

**(G-13202)**
**HERMAN L LOEB LLC**
Also Called: Loeb Oil
600 Country Club Rd  (62439-3369)
P.O. Box 838  (62439-0838)
PHONE...................................618 943-2227
Fax: 618 943-2220
Jesse Middagh, *Opers Staff*
Janette Loeb, *Mng Member*
Diane Lebovitz,
Laura Loeb,
EMP: 50
SQ FT: 1,800
SALES (est): 50MM  Privately Held
SIC: 1311  Crude petroleum production

**(G-13203)**
**NU-LIFE INC OF ILLINOIS**
Hwy 1 S  (62439)
P.O. Box 450  (62439-0450)
PHONE...................................618 943-4500
Fax: 618 943-2819
Herman Brinkley, *President*
Frances Brinkley, *Admin Sec*
EMP: 7
SQ FT: 24,500
SALES (est): 750K  Privately Held
SIC: 2389  Men's miscellaneous accessories

**(G-13204)**
**SWEET TS  LLC**
12061 Indian Creek Blvd  (62439-4138)
PHONE...................................618 943-5729
Daniel Powell,
EMP: 1
SALES (est): 218.1K  Privately Held
SIC: 2759  Letterpress & screen printing

**(G-13205)**
**TOYOTA BOSHOKU ILLINOIS LLC**
Also Called: A T S
100 Trim Masters Dr  (62439-9501)
PHONE...................................618 943-5300
Akira Furusawa, *CEO*
Shuhei Toyoda, *President*
Barry Derousse, *General Mgr*
Stephanie Stitt, *General Mgr*
Shigetoshi Miyoshi, *COO*
▲ EMP: 470
SQ FT: 209,000
SALES (est): 122.6MM
SALES (corp-wide): 12.1B  Privately Held
SIC: 3714  Motor vehicle parts & accessories
HQ: Toyota Boshoku America, Inc.
1360 Dolwick Rd Ste 125
Erlanger KY 41018
859 817-4000

**(G-13206)**
**TRACY ELECTRIC  INC**
Also Called: T-P Electric & Manufacturing
1308 Jefferson St  (62439-2418)
PHONE...................................618 943-6205
Fax: 618 943-3368
Robert W Tracy, *President*
Angie Sweeten, *Admin Sec*
EMP: 33
SQ FT: 12,200
SALES (est): 6.2MM  Privately Held
WEB: www.tracyelectric.com
SIC: 1731  1711  7694  3621  General electrical contractor; refrigeration contractor; rewinding services; electric motor repair; phase or rotary converters (electrical equipment)

## Le Roy
### Mclean County

**(G-13207)**
**DEN GRAPHIX INC**
111 S Chestnut St  (61752-1782)
PHONE...................................309 962-2000
Bill Frautchi, *President*
EMP: 15
SALES (est): 1.2MM  Privately Held
SIC: 2261  Screen printing of cotton broadwoven fabrics

**(G-13208)**
**OMNI-TECH SYSTEMS INC**
Also Called: Permabilt of Illinois
7 Demma Dr  (61752-9792)
PHONE...................................309 962-2281
Fax: 309 962-6216
Richard Janko, *President*
Dominic Pasquale, *Vice Pres*
Michael Janko, *Treasurer*
Leanna Bane, *Bookkeeper*

Nicki Harvin, *Office Mgr*
**EMP:** 20
**SQ FT:** 12,000
**SALES (est):** 2.2MM **Privately Held**
**WEB:** www.permabiltil.com
**SIC:** 2452 Prefabricated buildings, wood

### (G-13209)
### PIONEER HI-BRED INTL INC
28857 E 200 North Rd (61752-7596)
**PHONE**............................309 962-2931
**Fax:** 309 962-2399
Van Luck, *President*
Terence Whitsitt, *Opers Mgr*
Joseph C Bandy, *Branch Mgr*
Mark Mead, *Info Tech Mgr*
**EMP:** 17
**SALES (corp-wide):** 24.5B **Publicly Held**
**WEB:** www.pioneer.com
**SIC:** 8734 2075 5191 Seed testing laboratory; soybean oil mills; seeds & bulbs
**HQ:** Pioneer Hi-Bred International, Inc.
7100 Nw 62nd Ave
Johnston IA 50131
515 535-3200

## Leaf River
### Ogle County

### (G-13210)
### ENGLE MANUFACTURING CO
214 Main St (61047-9797)
P.O. Box 220 (61047-0220)
**PHONE**............................815 738-2282
**Fax:** 815 738-2281
Jeffery Engle, *Managing Prtnr*
Lester Engle, *Partner*
**EMP:** 10 **EST:** 1965
**SQ FT:** 16,000
**SALES (est):** 1.5MM **Privately Held**
**SIC:** 3599 Machine shop, jobbing & repair

### (G-13211)
### GLORIUS RENDITIONS
508 E Third St (61047-4500)
**PHONE**............................815 315-0177
Patricia Marie Mitchell, *Partner*
Sharon Mitchell, *Partner*
**EMP:** 6
**SALES (est):** 241.8K **Privately Held**
**SIC:** 2741 Miscellaneous publishing

## Lebanon
### St. Clair County

### (G-13212)
### CHRIST BROS PRODUCTS LLC
820 S Fritz St (62254-1720)
P.O. Box 158 (62254-0158)
**PHONE**............................618 537-6174
Mark Christ,
**EMP:** 6
**SALES:** 770K **Privately Held**
**SIC:** 2951 Asphalt paving mixtures & blocks

### (G-13213)
### CUSTOM COATING INNOVATIONS INC
30 Commerce Dr (62254-2541)
**PHONE**............................618 808-0500
Kyle McCarter, *President*
Susan D Carlos, *General Mgr*
Sue Doncarlos, *Business Mgr*
Joe Behnken, *Vice Pres*
Mike Hill, *Vice Pres*
**EMP:** 15
**SQ FT:** 6,000
**SALES (est):** 2.1MM **Privately Held**
**SIC:** 2295 Tape, varnished: plastic & other coated (except magnetic)

### (G-13214)
### CUSTOM PRODUCT INNOVATIONS
40 Commerce Dr (62254-2541)
**PHONE**............................618 628-0111
**Fax:** 618 628-0222
Kyle Mc Carter, *President*
Victoria McCarter, *Vice Pres*

Carol Ashcraft, *Office Mgr*
▲ **EMP:** 7
**SQ FT:** 16,000
**SALES (est):** 1.7MM **Privately Held**
**SIC:** 3069 Rubber coated fabrics & clothing

### (G-13215)
### GOLDEN STATE FOODS CORP
Also Called: Gsf St. Louis
720 W Mc Allister St (62254-2642)
**PHONE**............................618 537-6121
Scott Thomas, *Vice Pres*
**EMP:** 160
**SALES (corp-wide):** 338.8MM **Privately Held**
**SIC:** 2099 Food preparations
**PA:** Golden State Foods Corp.
18301 Von Karman Ave # 1100
Irvine CA 92612
949 247-8000

### (G-13216)
### PRESCRIPTION PLUS LTD (PA)
Also Called: True Value
753 True Value Dr (62254-1593)
**PHONE**............................618 537-6202
**Fax:** 618 537-4534
Louis Schlaefer, *President*
Jackie Schlaefer, *Admin Sec*
**EMP:** 13 **EST:** 1979
**SQ FT:** 10,000
**SALES (est):** 4.2MM **Privately Held**
**SIC:** 5251 5912 2851 5021 Hardware; drug stores; paints & allied products; outdoor & lawn furniture

## Lee
### Lee County

### (G-13217)
### FMC CORPORATION
100 E Lee Rd (60530-3102)
**PHONE**............................815 824-2153
Bob Setter, *Branch Mgr*
**EMP:** 100
**SALES (corp-wide):** 3.2B **Publicly Held**
**WEB:** www.fmc.com
**SIC:** 3325 Steel foundries
**PA:** Fmc Corporation
2929 Walnut St
Philadelphia PA 19104
215 299-6668

## Leland
### Lasalle County

### (G-13218)
### BILT-RITE METAL PRODUCTS INC
Also Called: Bilt-Rite Metal Products
100 E North St (60531-3138)
P.O. Box 97 (60531-0097)
**PHONE**............................815 495-2211
**Fax:** 815 495-2251
Linda Thomas, *President*
Marilyn Ellerby, *Vice Pres*
Anita Raines, *Purch Agent*
**EMP:** 30 **EST:** 1950
**SQ FT:** 65,000
**SALES (est):** 2.8MM **Privately Held**
**WEB:** www.biltritemetalproducts.com
**SIC:** 3444 3648 3469 2542 Sheet metalwork; metal housings, enclosures, casings & other containers; restaurant sheet metalwork; lighting equipment; metal stampings; partitions & fixtures, except wood

### (G-13219)
### CALCON MACHINE INC
210 E Lincoln Ave (60531-9748)
P.O. Box 9 (60531-0009)
**PHONE**............................815 495-9227
**Fax:** 815 495-9226
Victor J Brown Jr, *President*
Phil Brown, *Vice Pres*
Thomas Brown, *Marketing Staff*
Irma Brown, *Admin Sec*
**EMP:** 8
**SQ FT:** 10,000

**SALES:** 500K **Privately Held**
**SIC:** 3451 Screw machine products

### (G-13220)
### PRODUCTION STAMPINGS INC
1864 N 4253rd Rd (60531-9772)
**PHONE**............................815 495-2800
Michael E Mayton, *President*
**EMP:** 7 **EST:** 1993
**SQ FT:** 6,500
**SALES:** 330K **Privately Held**
**SIC:** 3469 Metal stampings

## Lemont
### Cook County

### (G-13221)
### A BARR FTN BEVERAGE SLS & SVC
16300 103rd St (60439-9666)
**PHONE**............................708 442-2000
Thomas Barc, *President*
**EMP:** 60
**SALES (est):** 5.5MM **Privately Held**
**SIC:** 2087 Syrups, drink

### (G-13222)
### A&B RELIABLE
190 Munster Rd (60439-4452)
**PHONE**............................708 228-6148
Vilma Ratkeviciute, *Principal*
**EMP:** 2 **EST:** 2008
**SALES (est):** 232.7K **Privately Held**
**SIC:** 3822 Water heater controls

### (G-13223)
### AMERICAN CAST STONE
14563 136th St (60439-7925)
**PHONE**............................630 291-0250
Robert Blaho, *Principal*
**EMP:** 10
**SALES (est):** 710K **Privately Held**
**SIC:** 3272 Concrete products

### (G-13224)
### AMFAB LLC
1385 101st St Ste A (60439-9631)
**PHONE**............................630 783-2570
David A Oestermeyer,
▼ **EMP:** 8
**SALES (est):** 2.5MM **Privately Held**
**SIC:** 3743 Railroad locomotives & parts, electric or nonelectric

### (G-13225)
### ASHTON DIVERSIFIED ENTERPRISES
19w442 Deerpath Ln (60439-8898)
**PHONE**............................630 739-0981
Lina J Schade, *President*
**EMP:** 6
**SALES (est):** 392.5K **Privately Held**
**SIC:** 2452 Farm & agricultural buildings, prefabricated wood

### (G-13226)
### B&L SERVICES INC
1042 Florence St (60439-3941)
**PHONE**............................630 257-1688
Willard J Luzzo, *Principal*
**EMP:** 4
**SALES (est):** 188.4K **Privately Held**
**SIC:** 2051 Bread, cake & related products

### (G-13227)
### BARTECH PRECISION MACHINING CO
16135 New Ave Ste 3 (60439-2648)
**PHONE**............................630 243-9068
**Fax:** 630 243-9078
Abdul Labaran, *President*
Bart Hypta, *Vice Pres*
**EMP:** 15
**SQ FT:** 5,000
**SALES (est):** 1.5MM **Privately Held**
**WEB:** www.bartechprecision.com
**SIC:** 3599 Machine shop, jobbing & repair

### (G-13228)
### BROMBEREKS FLAGSTONE CO INC (PA)
910 Singer Ave (60439-3929)
**PHONE**............................630 257-0686
Ronald Bromberek, *President*
Larry Bromberek, *Vice Pres*
**EMP:** 9
**SALES (est):** 882.9K **Privately Held**
**WEB:** www.bromberekflagstone.com
**SIC:** 3281 Stone, quarrying & processing of own stone products

### (G-13229)
### CARROLL DISTRG & CNSTR SUP INC
13087 Main St (60439-9373)
**PHONE**............................630 243-0272
Mike Petkovich, *Branch Mgr*
**EMP:** 4
**SALES (corp-wide):** 75.9MM **Privately Held**
**SIC:** 5082 3444 Contractors' materials; concrete forms, sheet metal
**PA:** Carroll Distributing & Construction Supply, Inc.
205 S Iowa Ave
Ottumwa IA 52501
641 683-1888

### (G-13230)
### CCI MANUFACTURING IL CORP
Also Called: CCI Manufacturing Illinois
15550 Canal Bank Rd (60439-3885)
P.O. Box 339 (60439-0339)
**PHONE**............................630 685-7534
Okabe Shuji, *CEO*
Tetsuya Okabe, *President*
Koji Momiyama, *Controller*
◆ **EMP:** 38
**SQ FT:** 30,000
**SALES (est):** 17MM **Privately Held**
**SIC:** 2899 Chemical preparations

### (G-13231)
### CHALON WOOD PRODUCTS INC
12670 111th St (60439-9327)
**PHONE**............................630 243-9793
**EMP:** 3 **EST:** 2003
**SALES:** 360K **Privately Held**
**SIC:** 2435 Mfg Hardwood Veneer/Plywood

### (G-13232)
### CHICAGO MATERIALS CORPORATION
13769 Main St (60439-9371)
**PHONE**............................630 257-5600
George Krug Jr, *President*
Mark Smiegowski, *CFO*
Robert W Krug, *Admin Sec*
**EMP:** 35
**SALES (est):** 6.3MM
**SALES (corp-wide):** 72.9MM **Privately Held**
**WEB:** www.k-five.net
**SIC:** 3531 Asphalt plant, including gravel-mix type
**PA:** K-Five Construction Corporation
999 Oakmont Plaza Dr # 200
Westmont IL 60559
630 257-5600

### (G-13233)
### CITGO PETROLEUM CORPORATION
13500 New Ave (60439-3655)
**PHONE**............................847 734-7611
**Fax:** 847 734-7677
Douglas Lawrence, *Principal*
Raymond Boutt, *Project Mgr*
**EMP:** 18
**SALES (est):** 2.7MM **Privately Held**
**WEB:** www.douglaslawrence.com
**SIC:** 5541 2911 Filling stations, gasoline; petroleum refining

### (G-13234)
### D & B FABRICATORS & DISTRS
16w065 Jeans Rd (60439-8894)
**PHONE**............................630 325-3811
John D Young Jr, *President*
**EMP:** 15

# Lemont - Cook County (G-13235)  GEOGRAPHIC SECTION

SALES (est): 1.7MM **Privately Held**
WEB: www.dbfabricators.com
SIC: 3411 3531 3523 3469 Metal cans; construction machinery; farm machinery & equipment; metal stampings; metal barrels, drums & pails

**(G-13235)**
**FGC PLASMA SOLUTIONS LLC**
9700 S Case Ave Bldg 203 (60439)
PHONE .................. 954 591-1429
Felipe Gomez Del Campo,
Joe Scott,
EMP: 5
SQ FT: 80
SALES (est): 222.4K **Privately Held**
SIC: 3728 Aircraft parts & equipment

**(G-13236)**
**IDI FABRICATION INC**
1385 101st St (60439-9630)
PHONE .................. 630 783-2246
Scott Doll, *Branch Mgr*
Alejandro Garcia, *Executive Asst*
EMP: 20 **Privately Held**
SIC: 3567 Induction & dielectric heating equipment
PA: Idi Fabrication, Inc.
     14444 Herriman Blvd
     Noblesville IN 46060

**(G-13237)**
**KEY COLONY INC**
Also Called: Red Parrot Juices
16300 103rd St (60439-9666)
PHONE .................. 630 783-8572
James Behrens, *President*
Robert Brennan, *Sales Mgr*
Theresa Barc, *Manager*
Janice Baisden, *Admin Sec*
EMP: 6
SALES (est): 693.8K **Privately Held**
SIC: 2087 2086 2037 2033 Fruit juices: concentrated for fountain use; bottled & canned soft drinks; frozen fruits & vegetables; canned fruits & specialties

**(G-13238)**
**KROMRAY HYDRAULIC MCHY INC**
870 Kromray Rd (60439-6107)
P.O. Box 595 (60439-0595)
PHONE .................. 630 257-8655
Anita Kromray, *President*
Paul Kromray Jr, *Vice Pres*
EMP: 1
SALES (est): 200.4K **Privately Held**
SIC: 3694 Automotive electrical equipment

**(G-13239)**
**LEMONT SCRAP PROCESSING**
16229 New Ave (60439-3684)
PHONE .................. 630 257-6532
Leslie A Dudek, *President*
EMP: 8
SALES (est): 2.1MM **Privately Held**
SIC: 5093 3341 Ferrous metal scrap & waste; metal scrap & waste materials; secondary nonferrous metals

**(G-13240)**
**MACHINING TECHNOLOGY INC**
Also Called: Grem Machining Division
418 Keepataw Dr (60439-4341)
PHONE .................. 815 469-0400
Tom Guimont, *President*
▼ EMP: 4
SQ FT: 4,500
SALES (est): 380K **Privately Held**
SIC: 3599 Machine shop, jobbing & repair

**(G-13241)**
**MENO STONE CO INC**
10800 Route 83 (60439-4700)
PHONE .................. 630 257-9220
Michael Meno, *President*
Joseph Meno Jr, *Corp Secy*
Terry Chandler, *Office Mgr*
EMP: 35
SQ FT: 32,000
SALES (est): 6.8MM **Privately Held**
SIC: 3441 1741 3281 3271 Fabricated structural metal; stone masonry; cut stone & stone products; concrete block & brick

**(G-13242)**
**MISSION SIGNS INC**
1415 Chestnut Xing (60439-7488)
PHONE .................. 630 243-6731
Fax: 708 226-8119
EMP: 2
SALES (est): 265.6K **Privately Held**
SIC: 3993 Mfg Signs/Advertising Specialties

**(G-13243)**
**MORRIS INDUSTRIES INC**
11237 Joliet Rd (60439-8887)
PHONE .................. 630 739-1502
Peter Morris, *Principal*
EMP: 3
SALES (est): 225.1K **Privately Held**
SIC: 3999 Manufacturing industries

**(G-13244)**
**NORTHERN ILLINOIS REAL ESTATE**
1244 State St Ste 351 (60439-4489)
PHONE .................. 630 257-2480
Fax: 630 257-5042
Roger Krieg, *President*
Maryann Krieg, *Sales Dir*
Mary Ann Wilke, *Sales Mgr*
Maryann Wilke, *Advt Staff*
EMP: 7
SALES: 400K **Privately Held**
WEB: www.niremag.com
SIC: 2721 Magazines: publishing & printing

**(G-13245)**
**OAKRIDGE CORPORATION**
Also Called: Oakridge Hobbies
15800 New Ave (60439-3680)
P.O. Box 247 (60439-0247)
PHONE .................. 630 435-5900
Terrance Robb, *President*
EMP: 4
SQ FT: 6,500
SALES (est): 553.8K **Privately Held**
SIC: 3944 5945 Trains & equipment, toy: electric & mechanical; hobby, toy & game shops

**(G-13246)**
**OUTDOOR NOTEBOOK PUBLISHING**
14805 131st St (60439-7444)
PHONE .................. 630 257-6534
Fax: 630 257-8455
Robert A Maciulis, *President*
EMP: 10
SQ FT: 1,200
SALES (est): 600K **Privately Held**
SIC: 2721 Magazines: publishing only, not printed on site

**(G-13247)**
**OXBOW CARBON LLC**
Also Called: Oxbow Midwest
12308 New Ave (60439-3686)
PHONE .................. 630 257-7751
Brett Wiltshire, *Branch Mgr*
EMP: 22
SALES (corp-wide): 1.1B **Privately Held**
SIC: 2911 Coke, petroleum
HQ: Oxbow Carbon Llc
    1601 Forum Pl Ste 1400
    West Palm Beach FL 33401
    561 907-5400

**(G-13248)**
**OXBOW MIDWEST CALCINING LLC**
12308 New Ave (60439-3686)
PHONE .................. 630 257-7751
Steve Fried, *President*
Rich Callahan, *Vice Pres*
Eric Johnson, *Vice Pres*
Raymond Baran, *Purch Mgr*
Zachery Shipley, *CFO*
EMP: 75
SALES (est): 11.2MM
SALES (corp-wide): 1.1B **Privately Held**
SIC: 2911 Coke, petroleum
HQ: Oxbow Carbon Llc
    1601 Forum Pl Ste 1400
    West Palm Beach FL 33401
    561 907-5400

**(G-13249)**
**PARTY PLATE LLC**
5 Martin Ct (60439-8100)
P.O. Box 784, Flossmoor (60422-0784)
PHONE .................. 708 268-4571
Ophelia Smith, *Director*
Gregory Evans,
EMP: 2
SQ FT: 2,000
SALES (est): 250K **Privately Held**
SIC: 2656 Plates, paper: made from purchased material

**(G-13250)**
**PATRICK IMPRESSIONS LLC**
Also Called: Rainbow Printing
16135 New Ave Ste 1a (60439-2605)
PHONE .................. 630 257-9336
Fax: 630 257-1669
Patrick O'Neil,
EMP: 3
SALES (est): 384.1K **Privately Held**
SIC: 2752 2791 2789 2759 Commercial printing, lithographic; typesetting; bookbinding & related work; commercial printing

**(G-13251)**
**PATTI GROUP INCORPORATED (PA)**
12301 New Ave Ste A (60439-3676)
PHONE .................. 630 243-6320
Dale Patti, *President*
Nick Patti, *Vice Pres*
Robert Wise, *Manager*
▲ EMP: 10
SQ FT: 3,000
SALES (est): 2.1MM **Privately Held**
WEB: www.pattigroup.com
SIC: 2653 Solid fiber boxes, partitions, display items & sheets

**(G-13252)**
**PAWZ & KLAWZ**
447 Talcott Ave (60439-3744)
PHONE .................. 630 257-0245
Norb Siwek, *President*
EMP: 5
SALES (est): 381.5K **Privately Held**
WEB: www.pawzandklawz.com
SIC: 3999 Pet supplies

**(G-13253)**
**PC SUCCESSOR INC**
Also Called: PC Aquisition
1005 101st St Ste A (60439-9628)
PHONE .................. 630 783-2400
John Semmelhack, *President*
Brian Hyvy, *VP Finance*
Anna Dolder, *Executive Asst*
◆ EMP: 160
SQ FT: 170,000
SALES (est): 13.1MM **Privately Held**
SIC: 3999 Boutiquing: decorating gift items with sequins, fruit, etc.

**(G-13254)**
**PDV MIDWEST REFINING LLC**
Also Called: Citgo Refinery
135th St New Ave (60439)
PHONE .................. 630 257-7761
Jenny Allums, *President*
Carlos Jorda,
Oswaldo Contreras Maza,
Andres Riera,
EMP: 540
SALES (est): 124MM **Privately Held**
SIC: 2992 2911 5171 4213 Lubricating oils & greases; petroleum refining; petroleum bulk stations & terminals; trucking, except local
PA: Pdv America, Inc.
    1293 Eldridge Pkwy
    Houston TX 77077

**(G-13255)**
**PHOENIX INKS AND COATINGS LLC**
20w267 101st St (60439-9672)
PHONE .................. 630 972-2500
Sheryl A Desanto, *Principal*
EMP: 19
SALES (est): 4.3MM **Privately Held**
SIC: 2899 Ink or writing fluids

**(G-13256)**
**PODHALÁNSKA LLC**
1304 Oakmont Dr Unit 10 (60439-6444)
P.O. Box 16135 (60439)
PHONE .................. 630 247-9256
Rene T Skorusa,
EMP: 8
SALES (est): 464.9K **Privately Held**
SIC: 2085 Vodka (alcoholic beverage)

**(G-13257)**
**PRESS DOUGH INC**
22 Longwood Way (60439-4479)
PHONE .................. 630 243-6900
James Bartley, *Principal*
EMP: 4
SALES (est): 210K **Privately Held**
SIC: 2741 Miscellaneous publishing

**(G-13258)**
**QUALITY QUICKPRINT INC (PA)**
Also Called: Quick Print
1258 Cronin Ct (60439-8579)
PHONE .................. 815 723-0941
Fax: 815 723-0431
Janet Fisher, *President*
Jean Henry, *Branch Mgr*
Jeffery Fisher, *Admin Sec*
EMP: 7
SALES (est): 1.2MM **Privately Held**
SIC: 2752 7334 Commercial printing, offset; photocopying & duplicating services

**(G-13259)**
**QUANTUM MARKETING LLC**
12305 New Ave Ste H (60439-2613)
PHONE .................. 630 257-7012
Patrick Gardner, *Principal*
EMP: 14
SALES (est): 2.7MM **Privately Held**
SIC: 3572 Computer storage devices

**(G-13260)**
**ROUTE 66 ASPHALT COMPANY**
13769 Main St (60439-9371)
PHONE .................. 630 739-6633
James Fiala, *President*
Terry Burgel, *Manager*
EMP: 3
SALES (est): 739.7K **Privately Held**
SIC: 2951 Asphalt paving mixtures & blocks

**(G-13261)**
**SALCO PRODUCTS INC (PA)**
1385 101st St Ste A (60439-9631)
PHONE .................. 630 783-2570
Fax: 630 783-2580
David Oestermeyer, *President*
Brian Putnam, *Vice Pres*
Thomas Wilcox, *Opers Mgr*
Lonnie Horne, *Research*
David E Clauter, *Controller*
EMP: 60
SQ FT: 51,735
SALES (est): 54.5MM **Privately Held**
SIC: 5013 5088 3743 Truck parts & accessories; railroad equipment & supplies; railroad equipment

**(G-13262)**
**SENECA PETROLEUM CO INC**
12460 New Ave (60439-3669)
P.O. Box 219 (60439-0219)
PHONE .................. 630 257-2268
Fax: 630 257-2520
Bob Krissik, *Manager*
EMP: 50
SALES (corp-wide): 22.1MM **Privately Held**
SIC: 2951 Asphalt & asphaltic paving mixtures (not from refineries)
PA: Seneca Petroleum Co., Inc.
    13301 Cicero Ave
    Crestwood IL 60445
    708 396-1100

**(G-13263)**
**SOLAR TRAFFIC SYSTEMS INC**
16135 New Ave Ste 2 (60439-2605)
PHONE .................. 331 318-8500
Ray Gal, *Treasurer*
EMP: 4
SQ FT: 3,100
SALES (est): 125.8K **Privately Held**
SIC: 3993 Electric signs

# GEOGRAPHIC SECTION

Lewistown - Fulton County (G-13290)

**(G-13264)**
**SUPERIOR PRINT SERVICES INC**
12305 New Ave Ste H (60439-2613)
**PHONE**..................630 257-7012
**Fax:** 630 257-8055
Patrick Gardner, *President*
Suzanne Gardner, *Treasurer*
Dave Hanley, *Director*
**EMP:** 8
**SALES (est):** 610K **Privately Held**
**SIC:** 2752 Commercial printing, lithographic

**(G-13265)**
**SWEET SPECIALTY SOLUTIONS LLC**
1005 101st St Ste B (60439-9628)
**PHONE**..................630 739-9151
Chris Schweizer, *Plant Mgr*
William Bergin, *Controller*
John B Yonover,
**EMP:** 40
**SALES (est):** 9.9MM **Privately Held**
**SIC:** 2063 Beet sugar

**(G-13266)**
**TOMKO MACHINE WORKS INC**
20w067 Pleasantdale Dr (60439-9618)
**PHONE**..................630 244-0902
John C Tomaskovic, *President*
Patricia J Tomaskovic, *Treasurer*
Judy Tomaskovic, *Admin Sec*
**EMP:** 9
**SQ FT:** 10,000
**SALES (est):** 876.9K **Privately Held**
**SIC:** 3599 7692 3462 3312 Machine shop, jobbing & repair; welding repair; iron & steel forgings; blast furnaces & steel mills

**(G-13267)**
**VENEER SPECIALTIES INC**
1385 101st St Ste F (60439-9631)
**PHONE**..................630 754-8550
**Fax:** 630 754-8560
Ralph Zuiker, *Principal*
Carole Cullotta, *Sales Executive*
**EMP:** 14
**SALES (est):** 1.9MM **Privately Held**
**SIC:** 2435 Hardwood veneer & plywood

**(G-13268)**
**VIVA SOLUTIONS INC** ✪
2 E Illinois St (60439-3608)
**PHONE**..................312 332-8882
Renaldas Budrys, *President*
Roland Rauduve, *Treasurer*
**EMP:** 3 **EST:** 2017
**SALES (est):** 79.7K **Privately Held**
**SIC:** 7373 7379 7372 7371 Systems software development services; ; business oriented computer software; computer software systems analysis & design, custom

**(G-13269)**
**WEST SIDE MACHINE INC**
11201 S Boyer St (60439-8769)
P.O. Box 426 (60439-0426)
**PHONE**..................630 243-1069
**Fax:** 630 243-1469
Casey Sularski, *President*
Andy Wilczek, *General Mgr*
Andy J Wilczek, *Admin Sec*
▲ **EMP:** 17
**SQ FT:** 20,000
**SALES (est):** 3.6MM **Privately Held**
**WEB:** www.westsidemachine.net
**SIC:** 3599 Machine shop, jobbing & repair

**(G-13270)**
**WILLOW FARM PRODUCTS INC**
20w114 97th St (60439-9680)
**PHONE**..................630 430-7491
Sharon Polivka, *President*
**EMP:** 3
**SALES (est):** 292.8K **Privately Held**
**SIC:** 3545 3441 Machine tool accessories; fabricated structural metal

**(G-13271)**
**XCELL INTERNATIONAL CORP**
16400 103rd St (60439-9667)
P.O. Box 452, Westmont (60559-0452)
**PHONE**..................630 323-0107
Dean J Henning, *President*
Dean Henning, *Principal*
Carrie Novak, *Facilities Mgr*
Brian Misevich, *Warehouse Mgr*
Scott Henning, *Research*
▲ **EMP:** 100
**SQ FT:** 44,000
**SALES (est):** 21.1MM **Privately Held**
**WEB:** www.xcellint.com
**SIC:** 3089 5023 Jars, plastic; kitchenware

### Lena
*Stephenson County*

**(G-13272)**
**ADKINS ENERGY LLC**
4350 W Galena Rd (61048-8504)
P.O. Box 227 (61048-0227)
**PHONE**..................815 369-9173
**Fax:** 815 369-2043
Ray Baker, *General Mgr*
Chris Posey, *Safety Mgr*
Joan Strong, *Controller*
Eric Lockart, *Manager*
Joan Humphrey,
**EMP:** 35
**SALES (est):** 10.5MM **Privately Held**
**SIC:** 2869 Ethyl alcohol, ethanol

**(G-13273)**
**BUSS BOYZ CUSTOMS INC**
216 S Center St (61048-8708)
P.O. Box 750 (61048-0750)
**PHONE**..................815 369-2803
Ryan Buss, *President*
**EMP:** 2
**SALES (est):** 313.3K **Privately Held**
**WEB:** www.bussboyz.com
**SIC:** 3699 Automotive driving simulators (training aids), electronic

**(G-13274)**
**CENTRAL RADIATOR CABINET CO (PA)**
8857 N 5 Corners Rd (61048-9761)
**PHONE**..................773 539-1700
Jeffrey Bishop, *President*
**EMP:** 5 **EST:** 1932
**SQ FT:** 3,000
**SALES:** 1MM **Privately Held**
**WEB:** www.eradiatorcovers.com
**SIC:** 3444 3469 2522 Radiator shields or enclosures, sheet metal; metal stampings; office furniture, except wood

**(G-13275)**
**KOLB-LENA INC**
Also Called: Kolb-Lena Bresse Bleu, Inc.
3990 N Sunnyside Rd (61048-9613)
**PHONE**..................815 369-4577
**Fax:** 815 369-4914
Jim Williams, *President*
Stephen Bouchayer, *Corp Secy*
Jones Kaldy, *Manager*
Leisa Hubb, *Director*
▲ **EMP:** 65
**SQ FT:** 60,000
**SALES (est):** 11.4MM **Privately Held**
**SIC:** 2022 Natural cheese
**HQ:** Zausner Foods Corp.
400 S Custer Ave
New Holland PA 17557
717 355-8505

**(G-13276)**
**KRAFTY KABINETS**
106 W Provost St (61048-9112)
**PHONE**..................815 369-5250
Chuck Kraft, *Principal*
**EMP:** 2
**SALES (est):** 215.8K **Privately Held**
**SIC:** 2434 Wood kitchen cabinets

**(G-13277)**
**LENA AJS MAID MEATS**
500 W Main St (61048-9726)
**PHONE**..................815 369-4522
**Fax:** 815 369-2075
Kevin Koning, *CEO*
Marcia Pax, *Owner*
**EMP:** 14
**SQ FT:** 10,000
**SALES (est):** 820K **Privately Held**
**WEB:** www.lenamaidmeats.com
**SIC:** 7299 2011 5147 5142 Butcher service, processing only; meat packing plants; meats & meat products; packaged frozen goods; sausages & other prepared meats

**(G-13278)**
**LENA MERCANTILE**
101 W Railroad St (61048-9038)
P.O. Box 188 (61048-0188)
**PHONE**..................815 369-9955
Larry Maedge, *Principal*
**EMP:** 15
**SALES (est):** 1.6MM **Privately Held**
**WEB:** www.lenamercantile.com
**SIC:** 2599 Restaurant furniture, wood or metal

**(G-13279)**
**LENA SIGN SHOP**
109 W Railroad St (61048-9038)
P.O. Box 188 (61048-0188)
**PHONE**..................815 369-9090
**Fax:** 815 369-9092
Larry Maedge, *Owner*
**EMP:** 3
**SALES (est):** 241.6K **Privately Held**
**WEB:** www.lenasignshop.com
**SIC:** 3993 Signs & advertising specialties

**(G-13280)**
**LINGLE DESIGN GROUP INC**
158 W Main St (61048-9247)
**PHONE**..................815 369-4495
**Fax:** 815 369-4495
Carl Lingle, *President*
Tony Bolotnik, *Vice Pres*
Lisa Donmeyer, *Project Mgr*
**EMP:** 20
**SALES (est):** 3.2MM **Privately Held**
**SIC:** 2211 8712 Crepes & other crinkled texture fabrics, cotton; architectural services

**(G-13281)**
**MAHONEY PUBLISHING INC**
707 Maple St (61048-9370)
P.O. Box 95 (61048-0095)
**PHONE**..................815 369-5384
Mark Mahoney, *President*
**EMP:** 7
**SALES (est):** 198.8K **Privately Held**
**SIC:** 2711 Newspapers

**(G-13282)**
**NORTHWESTERN ILLINOIS FARMER**
119 W Railroad St (61048-9038)
**PHONE**..................815 369-2811
**Fax:** 815 369-2816
Norman Templin, *Owner*
Connie Kempel, *Manager*
**EMP:** 3
**SALES (est):** 108.1K **Privately Held**
**SIC:** 2711 2759 Newspapers, publishing & printing; commercial printing

**(G-13283)**
**SAVENCIA CHEESE USA LLC**
3990 N Sunnyside Rd (61048-9613)
**PHONE**..................815 369-4577
Dino Constantine, *Technical Mgr*
Rachel Bull, *Human Res Mgr*
Kay Larsen, *Branch Mgr*
Fred Demeter, *Manager*
**EMP:** 3 **Privately Held**
**SIC:** 5143 2022 Dairy products, except dried or canned; cheese, natural & processed
**HQ:** Savencia Cheese Usa Llc
400 S Custer Ave
New Holland PA 17557
717 355-8500

**(G-13284)**
**SHOPPERS GUIDE**
Also Called: Scope, The
213 S Center St (61048-8711)
**PHONE**..................815 369-4112
**Fax:** 815 369-9093
Pete Kruger, *President*
Jack Kruger, *President*
Cyndi Jensen, *Controller*
Lori Tanley, *Manager*
**EMP:** 6
**SALES (est):** 237.9K **Privately Held**
**WEB:** www.davisshopper.com
**SIC:** 2711 2752 2741 Newspapers: publishing only, not printed on site; lithographing on metal; miscellaneous publishing

### Leonore
*Lasalle County*

**(G-13285)**
**BRIAN BURCAR**
Also Called: Double R Manufacturing Co
310 Walnut St (61332)
**PHONE**..................815 856-2271
**Fax:** 815 856-2270
Brian Burcar, *Owner*
**EMP:** 4
**SQ FT:** 10,000
**SALES (est):** 390.9K **Privately Held**
**SIC:** 3523 3599 3596 3444 Farm machinery & equipment; planting machines, agricultural; cattle feeding, handling & watering equipment; machine shop, jobbing & repair; scales & balances, except laboratory; sheet metalwork; hand & edge tools

**(G-13286)**
**MARETA RAVIOLI INC**
Also Called: Mareta Ravioli & Noodle
303 Gary St (61332)
P.O. Box 163 (61332-0163)
**PHONE**..................815 856-2621
**Fax:** 815 856-2621
Martha Mareta, *President*
Michael Villareal, *Vice Pres*
Esteban Villareal, *Admin Sec*
**EMP:** 10
**SQ FT:** 3,500
**SALES:** 300K **Privately Held**
**SIC:** 2098 Macaroni products (e.g. alphabets, rings & shells), dry

### Lerna
*Coles County*

**(G-13287)**
**JAKES WORLD DESIGN**
2736 N County Road 1100e (62440-2311)
**PHONE**..................217 348-3043
Jake Kuhn, *Owner*
**EMP:** 3
**SALES (est):** 337.6K **Privately Held**
**WEB:** www.jakesworld.biz
**SIC:** 2821 Vinyl resins

**(G-13288)**
**M J KULL LLC**
1911 3rd St (62440-1100)
**PHONE**..................217 246-5952
Mark E Kull,
**EMP:** 5
**SALES (est):** 345.6K **Privately Held**
**SIC:** 2611 Pulp manufactured from waste or recycled paper

### Lewistown
*Fulton County*

**(G-13289)**
**GOODMAN SAWMILL**
114 N Broadway St (61542-1202)
**PHONE**..................309 547-3597
David Goodman, *Owner*
**EMP:** 3
**SALES:** 100K **Privately Held**
**SIC:** 2421 Sawmills & planing mills, general

**(G-13290)**
**L T D INDUSTRIES INC**
14310 E Back Rd (61542-9387)
**PHONE**..................309 547-3251

# Lexington - Mclean County (G-13291) — GEOGRAPHIC SECTION

Fax: 309 547-3984
C Lee Duncan, *President*
Karen Duncan, *Vice Pres*
John Kline, *Purch Mgr*
Keith Lehman, *Engineer*
Rita Linn, *Office Mgr*
**EMP:** 29
**SQ FT:** 34,000
**SALES (est):** 4MM **Privately Held**
**SIC:** 3599 Machine shop, jobbing & repair

## Lexington
### Mclean County

**(G-13291)**
**BRANDT CONSOLIDATED INC**
610 W Main St (61753-1226)
P.O. Box 107 (61753-0107)
**PHONE**.................309 365-7201
Dennis Myer, *Manager*
**EMP:** 7
**SALES (corp-wide):** 180MM **Privately Held**
**SIC:** 2875 5191 Fertilizers, mixing only; farm supplies
**PA:** Brandt Consolidated, Inc.
2935 S Koke Mill Rd
Springfield IL 62711
217 547-5800

**(G-13292)**
**H & H MACHINING**
500 S Spencer St (61753-1615)
P.O. Box 116 (61753-0116)
**PHONE**.................309 365-7010
Fax: 309 365-7011
Steve Hoselton, *President*
Stuart Hoselton, *Corp Secy*
**EMP:** 3
**SQ FT:** 7,000
**SALES (est):** 434K **Privately Held**
**WEB:** www.hnhmachining.com
**SIC:** 3599 Machine & other job shop work

**(G-13293)**
**SCHUMAKER PUBLICATIONS INC**
Rr 2 Box 72a (61753)
**PHONE**.................309 365-7105
Roland Schumaker II, *Owner*
Sharla Ishmael, *Editor*
Ammie McGraw, *Director*
Amber Martin, *Creative Dir*
**EMP:** 3
**SALES (est):** 195.8K **Privately Held**
**WEB:** www.theshowcircuit.com
**SIC:** 2741 Miscellaneous publishing

**(G-13294)**
**THATS SO SWEET**
429 W Main St (61753-1258)
**PHONE**.................903 331-7221
Lindsay Bachman, *Owner*
**EMP:** 3
**SALES (est):** 149.6K **Privately Held**
**SIC:** 2051 Cakes, bakery: except frozen

## Liberty
### Adams County

**(G-13295)**
**ELLIOTT PUBLISHING INC**
Also Called: Liberty Bee
103 E Hannibal St (62347-1055)
**PHONE**.................217 645-3033
Fax: 217 645-3083
James Elliott, *President*
**EMP:** 8
**SQ FT:** 1,200
**SALES (est):** 527.3K **Privately Held**
**SIC:** 2711 2789 2759 2752 Newspapers, publishing & printing; bookbinding & related work; commercial printing; commercial printing, lithographic

**(G-13296)**
**LIBERTY FEED MILL**
203 Richfield Rd (62321-1014)
**PHONE**.................217 645-3441
Fax: 217 645-3802
Brad Kroencke, *President*
Cheryl Ann Kroencke, *Treasurer*
**EMP:** 12
**SQ FT:** 5,000
**SALES (est):** 2.5MM **Privately Held**
**SIC:** 5191 5153 2048 Feed; grains; prepared feeds

## Libertyville
### Lake County

**(G-13297)**
**A-S MEDICATION SOLUTIONS LLC (PA)**
2401 Commerce Dr (60048-4464)
**PHONE**.................847 680-3515
Walter Hoff, *CEO*
Sherry Gregor, *Senior VP*
Chris Zirzow, *Vice Pres*
Dawn Powless, *QC Mgr*
Lauren McElroy, *VP Mktg*
**EMP:** 75
**SALES (est):** 19.5MM **Privately Held**
**SIC:** 2834 Pharmaceutical preparations

**(G-13298)**
**ABBOTT LABORATORIES**
279 Adler Dr (60048-3922)
**PHONE**.................224 330-0271
Kevin Dcluff, *Branch Mgr*
**EMP:** 752
**SALES (corp-wide):** 20.8B **Publicly Held**
**SIC:** 2834 Pharmaceutical preparations
**PA:** Abbott Laboratories
100 Abbott Park Rd
Abbott Park IL 60064
224 667-6100

**(G-13299)**
**ABSOLUTE PROCESS INSTRUMENTS (PA)**
1220 American Way (60048-3936)
**PHONE**.................847 918-3510
William Sawyer, *President*
Jeanette Ehrlich, *Corp Secy*
Robert Magnus, *Engineer*
**EMP:** 32
**SQ FT:** 12,000
**SALES (est):** 5.8MM **Privately Held**
**WEB:** www.api-usa.com
**SIC:** 3679 Electronic circuits

**(G-13300)**
**ALDRIDGE ELECTRIC INC (PA)**
844 E Rockland Rd (60048-3358)
**PHONE**.................847 680-5200
Fax: 847 680-9738
Steven Rivi, *CEO*
Ken Aldridge, *Ch of Bd*
Tom McLinden, *President*
Randy Farmer, *Division Mgr*
Anthony Hill, *Superintendent*
▲ **EMP:** 475 **EST:** 1952
**SALES (est):** 273.5MM **Privately Held**
**SIC:** 2899 4789 3643 Drilling mud; cargo loading & unloading services; power line cable

**(G-13301)**
**ALLFORM MANUFACTURING CO**
342 4th St (60048-2312)
**PHONE**.................847 680-0144
Fax: 847 680-0235
Deno Alexakos, *President*
**EMP:** 2
**SALES:** 500K **Privately Held**
**SIC:** 3315 3496 Steel wire & related products; miscellaneous fabricated wire products

**(G-13302)**
**AMERICAN CUSTOM PUBLISHING**
Also Called: Natl Senior Hlth & Fitnes Day
328 W Lincoln Ave (60048-2725)
**PHONE**.................847 816-8660
Gary W Ford, *President*
Ronald Baughman, *Vice Pres*
Patricia Henze Ford, *Vice Pres*
Brad Neville, *Treasurer*
Patricia Henze, *Exec Dir*
**EMP:** 9
**SQ FT:** 4,000
**SALES (est):** 970.7K **Privately Held**
**WEB:** www.fitnessday.com
**SIC:** 2741 2721 Miscellaneous publishing; newsletter publishing; periodicals

**(G-13303)**
**ANDREWS CARAMEL APPLES INC**
5471 River Park Dr (60048-4201)
**PHONE**.................773 286-2224
Fax: 773 286-2258
Daniel Demarco, *President*
Daniel De Marco, *President*
Sylvia Schuman, *Corp Secy*
Mary De Marco, *Vice Pres*
**EMP:** 15 **EST:** 1955
**SQ FT:** 14,700
**SALES (est):** 2MM **Privately Held**
**SIC:** 2064 Candy & other confectionery products

**(G-13304)**
**ARIA CORPORATION**
29471 N Northwoods Dr (60048-1629)
**PHONE**.................847 918-9329
John Perlick, *President*
**EMP:** 3
**SQ FT:** 1,500
**SALES (est):** 269.9K **Privately Held**
**WEB:** www.ariacorp.com
**SIC:** 8711 3679 Electrical or electronic engineering; electronic circuits

**(G-13305)**
**AUSTINS SALOON & EATERY**
481 Peterson Rd (60048-1009)
**PHONE**.................847 549-1972
Mark Khayat, *Principal*
Gregg Kalble, *Manager*
**EMP:** 3
**SALES (est):** 382.8K **Privately Held**
**SIC:** 2869 Fuels

**(G-13306)**
**BACH PLASTIC WORKS INC**
1711 Young Dr B (60048-3902)
**PHONE**.................847 680-4342
James A Herchenbach, *President*
**EMP:** 4
**SQ FT:** 2,000
**SALES:** 42.3K **Privately Held**
**SIC:** 3087 5162 Custom compound purchased resins; plastics materials & basic shapes

**(G-13307)**
**BCI ACRYLIC INC (PA)**
Also Called: B C I
1800 Industrial Dr (60048-9439)
**PHONE**.................847 963-8827
Fax: 847 358-4710
Scott Rosenbach, *President*
Rick Hirschhaut, *Senior VP*
Tom Barzantny, *Vice Pres*
Jim Crutchfield, *Engineer*
Eric Peschke, *Marketing Mgr*
**EMP:** 3
**SQ FT:** 50,000
**SALES (est):** 7.4MM **Privately Held**
**WEB:** www.bciacrylic.com
**SIC:** 3088 Plastics plumbing fixtures

**(G-13308)**
**BEACHWAVER**
408 N Milwaukee Ave # 202 (60048-2213)
**PHONE**.................224 513-5817
Erin Wall, *President*
**EMP:** 29
**SALES (est):** 2.8MM **Privately Held**
**SIC:** 3999 Hair & hair-based products

**(G-13309)**
**BOX ENCLSRES ASSEMBLY SVCS INC (PA)**
14092 W Lambs Ln (60048-9505)
**PHONE**.................847 932-4700
John Fiocchi, *President*
▲ **EMP:** 6
**SQ FT:** 5,300
**SALES (est):** 1.9MM **Privately Held**
**WEB:** www.boxenclosures.com
**SIC:** 3089 Molding primary plastic

**(G-13310)**
**BRILLIANT COLOR CORP**
14044 W Petronella Dr # 3 (60048-9656)
**PHONE**.................847 367-3300
Fax: 847 367-3315
James D Ozga, *President*
Joseph D Ozga, *Vice Pres*
Lauren Ozga, *Office Mgr*
**EMP:** 8
**SQ FT:** 5,000
**SALES (est):** 1MM **Privately Held**
**WEB:** www.brcolor.com
**SIC:** 2752 2741 2796 Color lithography; miscellaneous publishing; platemaking services

**(G-13311)**
**BURGESS MANUFACTURING INC**
1911 Industrial Dr (60048-9731)
**PHONE**.................847 680-1724
Allen J Bassel Sr, *President*
Ann Bassel, *Corp Secy*
Kathy Thompson, *Manager*
**EMP:** 15 **EST:** 1973
**SQ FT:** 15,000
**SALES (est):** 2.4MM **Privately Held**
**SIC:** 3599 7692 Machine shop, jobbing & repair; welding repair

**(G-13312)**
**CCL DISPENSING SYSTEMS LLC**
901 Technology Way (60048-5348)
**PHONE**.................847 816-9400
Phil Gwinn, *President*
Boris Savoibskiy, *Manager*
Peter Gamoff,
Kevin Shelander,
▲ **EMP:** 90 **EST:** 2001
**SQ FT:** 68,000
**SALES (est):** 11.5MM **Privately Held**
**SIC:** 3085 Plastics bottles

**(G-13313)**
**CECOMP ELECTRONICS INC**
1220 American Way (60048-3936)
**PHONE**.................847 918-3510
Jan Ehrlich, *Admin Sec*
**EMP:** 32
**SALES (est):** 3.3MM
**SALES (corp-wide):** 5.8MM **Privately Held**
**WEB:** www.cecomp-usa.com
**SIC:** 3699 Electrical equipment & supplies
**PA:** Absolute Process Instruments, Inc
1220 American Way
Libertyville IL 60048
847 918-3510

**(G-13314)**
**CHICAGO TAG & LABEL INC**
2501 Commerce Dr (60048-2495)
**PHONE**.................847 362-5100
Fax: 847 362-5140
Francis P Valenti Jr, *CEO*
Miriam Tovar, *General Mgr*
Chris Valenti, *COO*
Dan Hedger, *Vice Pres*
Pete Mezyk, *Vice Pres*
▲ **EMP:** 76
**SQ FT:** 72,000
**SALES (est):** 34.8MM **Privately Held**
**WEB:** www.chicagotag.com
**SIC:** 2679 Tags & labels, paper

**(G-13315)**
**CLASSIC WINDOWS INC**
750 Liberty Dr (60048-2343)
**PHONE**.................847 362-3100
Fax: 847 362-3173
Tom Davis, *President*
**EMP:** 15
**SQ FT:** 75,000
**SALES (est):** 3.6MM **Privately Held**
**WEB:** www.classicwindows.net
**SIC:** 2431 Window sashes, wood

**(G-13316)**
**COLOR4**
28100 N Ashley Cir Ste 10 (60048-9478)
**PHONE**.................847 996-6880
Fax: 847 996-6881
Steve Rokicki,
**EMP:** 10

# GEOGRAPHIC SECTION
## Libertyville - Lake County (G-13342)

**SALES (est):** 1.1MM **Privately Held**
**WEB:** www.color4.com
**SIC: 2759** Commercial printing

*(G-13317)*
### COMBINED TECHNOLOGIES INC (PA)
Also Called: CTI
732 Florsheim Dr Ste 14 (60048-3722)
**PHONE** ............................. 847 968-4855
Jerry Thompson, *President*
Steve Jambi, *Manager*
**EMP:** 9
**SQ FT:** 160,000
**SALES:** 4MM **Privately Held**
**WEB:** www.ctipack.com
**SIC: 2631** 2657 2653 3565 Container, packaging & boxboard; folding paperboard boxes; corrugated & solid fiber boxes; bottling machinery: filling, capping, labeling; bag opening, filling & closing machines; carton packing machines; sugar; confectionery

*(G-13318)*
### CULLIGAN INTERNATIONAL COMPANY
1520 Harris Rd (60048-2433)
**PHONE** ............................. 847 430-1338
Greg Hinners, *Principal*
**EMP:** 20 **Privately Held**
**SIC: 3589** Sewage & water treatment equipment
**HQ:** Culligan International Company
9399 W Higgins Rd # 1100
Rosemont IL 60018
847 430-2800

*(G-13319)*
### DESSERTWERKS INC (PA)
1421 Allyson Ct (60048-1401)
**PHONE** ............................. 847 487-8239
Raymond L King, *President*
**EMP:** 5
**SALES (est):** 951.1K **Privately Held**
**WEB:** www.dessertwerks.com
**SIC: 2051** 5145 Cakes, pies & pastries; snack foods

*(G-13320)*
### E-Z CUFF INC
1840 Industrial Dr # 260 (60048-9467)
**PHONE** ............................. 847 549-1550
Lisa Kohn, *Owner*
**EMP:** 7
**SALES (est):** 694.1K **Privately Held**
**WEB:** www.ezcuff.com
**SIC: 3842** Restraints, patient

*(G-13321)*
### EWAB ENGINEERING INC
1971 Kelley Ct (60048-9639)
**PHONE** ............................. 847 247-0015
**Fax:** 847 247-0098
W Tom Lebiedz, *President*
Adilson Lepchak, *General Mgr*
Chris Bates, *Managing Dir*
Stephane Bui, *Managing Dir*
Sonia Gimeno, *Managing Dir*
▲ **EMP:** 20
**SQ FT:** 35,000
**SALES (est):** 9.9MM **Privately Held**
**WEB:** www.ewab.com
**SIC: 3535** Unit handling conveying systems
**HQ:** Ewab Engineering Ab
Kungs Starbyvagen 8
Vadstena 592 4
143 750-00

*(G-13322)*
### EYE SURGEONS OF LIBERTYVILLE
1880 W Winchester Rd # 105 (60048-5321)
**PHONE** ............................. 847 362-3811
Sara Vegh, *President*
**EMP:** 8
**SALES (est):** 619.2K **Privately Held**
**SIC: 3851** 8042 Eyes, glass & plastic; offices & clinics of optometrists

*(G-13323)*
### FASTSIGNS
1350 S Milwaukee Ave (60048-3795)
**PHONE** ............................. 847 680-7446
**Fax:** 847 680-7459
Larry Kilpatrick, *Owner*
**EMP:** 5
**SQ FT:** 2,500
**SALES (est):** 706.4K **Privately Held**
**SIC: 3993** Signs & advertising specialties

*(G-13324)*
### FIRM OF JOHN DICKINSON (PA)
2000 Hollister Dr (60048-3746)
**PHONE** ............................. 847 680-1000
V George Maliekel, *President*
Alan F Herbert, *Principal*
Sam Brilliant, *CFO*
Melissa G Brunette, *Admin Sec*
Jerome A Saxon, *Admin Sec*
◆ **EMP:** 20
**SQ FT:** 200,000
**SALES (est):** 9.7MM **Privately Held**
**SIC: 3842** Surgical appliances & supplies

*(G-13325)*
### FOULDS INC
520 E Church St (60048-2329)
**PHONE** ............................. 414 964-1428
**Fax:** 847 362-6658
Christopher J Bradley, *President*
Carolyn Calderone, *Sls & Mktg Exec*
Jon Zemanek, *Maintence Staff*
**EMP:** 49 **EST:** 1974
**SALES (est):** 10.4MM **Privately Held**
**WEB:** www.foulds.net
**SIC: 2099** Packaged combination products: pasta, rice & potato

*(G-13326)*
### GENESIS MOLD CORP
854 Liberty Dr Ste C (60048-2330)
**PHONE** ............................. 847 573-9431
Mike Robison, *President*
**EMP:** 4
**SALES:** 328.1K **Privately Held**
**SIC: 3089** Injection molding of plastics

*(G-13327)*
### GREAT IMPRESSIONS INC
19071 W Casey Rd (60048-1078)
**PHONE** ............................. 847 367-6725
**Fax:** 847 816-0024
**EMP:** 4 **EST:** 1983
**SQ FT:** 2,500
**SALES:** 450K **Privately Held**
**SIC: 2752** Offset Commercial Printer

*(G-13328)*
### H AND D DISTRIBUTION INC
28045 N Ashley Cir Unit 1 (60048-9658)
**PHONE** ............................. 847 247-2011
Christopher Hogstrom, *President*
John Daniels, *Vice Pres*
**EMP:** 3
**SQ FT:** 4,300
**SALES (est):** 199.7K **Privately Held**
**SIC: 3999** Dock equipment & supplies, industrial

*(G-13329)*
### HANDI PRODUCTS INC
Also Called: Handi-Ramp
510 North Ave (60048-2025)
**PHONE** ............................. 847 816-7525
**Fax:** 847 816-8866
Thomas Disch, *CEO*
Leyla Anderfuren, *Opers Staff*
Chris Siskovic, *Chief Engr*
Jerry Graybosch, *Controller*
Jeff Mann, *Sales Mgr*
▲ **EMP:** 32
**SQ FT:** 27,000
**SALES (est):** 22.4MM **Privately Held**
**WEB:** www.handiramp.com
**SIC: 5084** 3446 Metalworking machinery; architectural metalwork

*(G-13330)*
### HERITAGE PRESS INC
312 Peterson Rd (60048-1008)
**PHONE** ............................. 847 362-9699
**Fax:** 847 367-0886
Connie Fiorelli, *President*
Paul Fiorelli, *Vice Pres*
Cathleen Frank, *Manager*
**EMP:** 5
**SQ FT:** 2,000
**SALES (est):** 700.2K **Privately Held**
**SIC: 2752** 2791 2789 Commercial printing, offset; typesetting; bookbinding & related work

*(G-13331)*
### HERITAGE SIGNS LTD
1840 Industrial Dr # 240 (60048-9400)
**PHONE** ............................. 847 549-1942
**Fax:** 847 549-1944
Cynthia Fitzpatrick, *Owner*
**EMP:** 4
**SQ FT:** 1,000
**SALES (est):** 300K **Privately Held**
**SIC: 3993** Signs & advertising specialties

*(G-13332)*
### HOLLAND SAFETY EQUIPMENT INC
726 Mckinley Ave (60048-2640)
**PHONE** ............................. 847 680-9930
Gary Holland, *President*
Kathleen Holland, *Admin Sec*
Scott Holland, *Administration*
▲ **EMP:** 4
**SQ FT:** 750
**SALES:** 1.7MM **Privately Held**
**SIC: 3822** Air flow controllers, air conditioning & refrigeration

*(G-13333)*
### HOLLISTER INCORPORATED (PA)
2000 Hollister Dr (60048-3781)
**PHONE** ............................. 847 680-1000
**Fax:** 847 680-2123
George Maliekel, *President*
Klaus Grunau, *Managing Dir*
Denis R Chevaleau, *Vice Pres*
Holly Crandell, *Vice Pres*
Robert A Crowe, *Vice Pres*
◆ **EMP:** 350 **EST:** 1959
**SQ FT:** 200,000
**SALES (est):** 725.2MM **Privately Held**
**WEB:** www.hollister.com
**SIC: 3841** 3842 Surgical & medical instruments; surgical appliances & supplies

*(G-13334)*
### HOLLISTER WOUND CARE LLC
1580 S Milwaukee Ave # 405 (60048-3775)
**PHONE** ............................. 847 996-6000
J Locey, *Manager*
Karen McKenzie, *Manager*
Mary Regan, *Director*
Joseph Tokarz,
**EMP:** 3
**SALES (est):** 538.1K
**SALES (corp-wide):** 725.2MM **Privately Held**
**SIC: 3842** Bandages & dressings
**PA:** Hollister Incorporated
2000 Hollister Dr
Libertyville IL 60048
847 680-1000

*(G-13335)*
### HURLETRON INCORPORATED
1820 Tempel Dr (60048-9729)
P.O. Box 712, Lincolnshire (60069-0712)
**PHONE** ............................. 847 680-7022
**Fax:** 847 680-7338
Ricky A Brainin, *President*
Thomas Halpin, *Controller*
Leonard Chen, *Office Mgr*
Gary Tracy, *Admin Sec*
**EMP:** 20
**SQ FT:** 27,500
**SALES:** 3.5MM
**SALES (corp-wide):** 62.6MM **Privately Held**
**WEB:** www.altaircorp.net
**SIC: 3625** Control equipment, electric
**HQ:** Altair Corporation (Del)
350 Barclay Blvd
Lincolnshire IL 60069
847 634-9540

*(G-13336)*
### IGM SOLUTIONS INC
1900 Enterprise Ct (60048-9737)
**PHONE** ............................. 847 918-1790
Paul Kelly, *President*
Jane Mohapp, *CFO*
Edward J Kelly, *Admin Sec*
▲ **EMP:** 50
**SQ FT:** 55,000
**SALES (est):** 25.4MM **Privately Held**
**WEB:** www.igmsolutions.com
**SIC: 3441** Fabricated structural metal

*(G-13337)*
### ILLINOIS TOOL WORKS INC
14050 W Lambs Ln Unit 1 (60048-9505)
**PHONE** ............................. 847 918-6473
Jeff Ford, *Branch Mgr*
**EMP:** 15
**SALES (corp-wide):** 13.6B **Publicly Held**
**SIC: 3531** Roofing equipment
**PA:** Illinois Tool Works Inc.
155 Harlem Ave
Glenview IL 60025
847 724-7500

*(G-13338)*
### IRONWOOD INDUSTRIES INC
115 S Bradley Rd (60048-9509)
**PHONE** ............................. 847 362-8681
**Fax:** 847 362-9190
Robert Grala, *Principal*
Michael Stuart, *Plant Mgr*
Rita Wolins, *Purchasing*
Kim Albrecht, *Controller*
▲ **EMP:** 70
**SQ FT:** 51,000
**SALES (est):** 18.2MM **Privately Held**
**SIC: 3089** Injection molded finished plastic products

*(G-13339)*
### ISM MACHINERY INCORPORATED
1915 Enterprise Ct (60048-9764)
P.O. Box 680, Grayslake (60030-0680)
**PHONE** ............................. 847 231-8002
Brian J Timmerman, *President*
John J Gaines, *Admin Sec*
▲ **EMP:** 6
**SQ FT:** 4,000
**SALES (est):** 1.2MM **Privately Held**
**SIC: 3531** Construction machinery

*(G-13340)*
### JASON INCORPORATED
1530 Artaius Pkwy (60048-3789)
P.O. Box 399 (60048-0399)
**PHONE** ............................. 847 362-8300
Robert C Birk, *Vice Pres*
Steve Targos, *Plant Mgr*
Greg Maksudian, *Purchasing*
Hughes John, *Sales Executive*
**EMP:** 102
**SALES (corp-wide):** 705.5MM **Publicly Held**
**WEB:** www.jasoninc.com
**SIC: 3449** 3339 Miscellaneous metalwork; primary nonferrous metals
**HQ:** Jason Incorporated
E Michigan St Ste 900
Milwaukee WI 53202
414 277-9300

*(G-13341)*
### LAKE COUNTY GRADING CO LLC (PA)
32901 N Milwaukee Ave (60048-9710)
P.O. Box L (60048-4912)
**PHONE** ............................. 847 362-2590
**Fax:** 847 362-9460
Tom Rosenquist, *President*
Richard Keller, *General Mgr*
Ron Russell, *General Mgr*
Bob Keegan, *Superintendent*
Dan Hubbard, *Vice Pres*
**EMP:** 30
**SQ FT:** 2,000
**SALES (est):** 18.1MM **Privately Held**
**SIC: 1794** 1442 1623 1795 Excavation work; gravel mining; water main construction; sewer line construction; wrecking & demolition work

*(G-13342)*
### LIBERTY CLASSICS INC
1860 W Winchester Rd # 103 (60048-5312)
**PHONE** ............................. 847 367-1288
**Fax:** 847 367-1295
Erick J Stoneman, *President*
John E Stoneman, *Chairman*

# Libertyville - Lake County (G-13343)  GEOGRAPHIC SECTION

Arlene Stoneman, *Corp Secy*
Paul Stoneman, *Vice Pres*
▲ **EMP:** 5
**SQ FT:** 3,500
**SALES:** 1MM **Privately Held**
**WEB:** www.libertyclassics.com
**SIC:** 3944 Banks, toy

### (G-13343)
### LIBERTYVILLE BREWING COMPANY
Also Called: Mickey Finns Brewery
345 N Milwaukee Ave (60048-2237)
**PHONE** ...................................847 362-6688
**Fax:** 847 362-3121
Brian Grano, *President*
Bill Sugars, *President*
Kristen Christensen, *Relations*
**EMP:** 75
**SQ FT:** 12,000
**SALES (est):** 2.5MM **Privately Held**
**WEB:** www.mickeyfinnsbrewery.com
**SIC:** 5812 5813 2082 American restaurant; cocktail lounge; malt beverages

### (G-13344)
### LIGHTSCAPE INC
342 4th St (60048-2312)
**PHONE** ...................................847 247-8800
**Fax:** 847 247-8802
Steven Achtemeier, *President*
Alejandro Martinez, *Vice Pres*
Karen Achtemeier, *Admin Sec*
**EMP:** 20
**SQ FT:** 1,200
**SALES (est):** 3.6MM **Privately Held**
**WEB:** www.lsilighting.net
**SIC:** 3648 1731 Outdoor lighting equipment; electrical work

### (G-13345)
### LUCTA U S A INC
950 Technology Way # 110 (60048-5361)
**PHONE** ...................................847 996-3400
**Fax:** 847 996-3401
Carlos Ventos, *CEO*
Carlos Prada, *Chairman*
James Bouc, *CFO*
▲ **EMP:** 7
**SQ FT:** 43,000
**SALES (est):** 1.4MM
**SALES (corp-wide):** 91.1MM **Privately Held**
**WEB:** www.lucta.com
**SIC:** 2869 2087 5149 Perfumes, flavorings & food additives; chloroethylenes; flavoring extracts & syrups; flavourings & fragrances
**PA:** Lucta, Sa
Calle De Can Parellada 28
Montornes Del Valles 08170
938 458-888

### (G-13346)
### MARJO GRAPHICS INC
1510 Bull Creek Dr (60048-1028)
P.O. Box Q (60048-4917)
**PHONE** ...................................847 367-1305
**Fax:** 847 367-8582
Adam Kimpler, *President*
Margaret Kimpler, *Vice Pres*
**EMP:** 2
**SALES:** 350K **Privately Held**
**SIC:** 2752 Commercial printing, lithographic

### (G-13347)
### MARYTOWN
Also Called: Knights of Immaculata
1600 W Park Ave (60048-2563)
**PHONE** ...................................847 367-7800
**Fax:** 847 367-7831
Kathy Caspary, *Manager*
Mrs Marcia O Connor, *Manager*
Stephen McKinley, *Director*
**EMP:** 21
**SQ FT:** 87,000
**SALES (est):** 1.8MM **Privately Held**
**WEB:** www.consecration.com
**SIC:** 8661 2731 Monastery; shrines; books: publishing only; pamphlets: publishing only, not printed on site

### (G-13348)
### MATTHEWS-GERBAR LTD (PA)
Also Called: Matthews Fan Company
1881 Industrial Dr (60048-9783)
**PHONE** ...................................847 680-9043
Chuck Matthews, *President*
▲ **EMP:** 5
**SQ FT:** 10,000
**SALES (est):** 1.4MM **Privately Held**
**WEB:** www.matthewsgerbar.com
**SIC:** 3634 Ceiling fans

### (G-13349)
### MATTHEWSGERBAR LTD
Also Called: Mathews Fan Company
1881 Industrial Dr (60048-9783)
**PHONE** ...................................847 680-9043
Charles Matthews, *Principal*
Dean Hunting, *Vice Pres*
**EMP:** 7
**SALES (corp-wide):** 1.4MM **Privately Held**
**SIC:** 3634 Ceiling fans
**PA:** Matthews-Gerbar, Ltd
1881 Industrial Dr
Libertyville IL 60048
847 680-9043

### (G-13350)
### MAXXSONICS USA INC
Also Called: MB Quart Entertainment
851 E Park Ave (60048-2980)
**PHONE** ...................................847 540-7700
Alden Stiefel, *President*
Sherri Sawyer, *Vice Pres*
Bryan Walter, *Sales Staff*
▲ **EMP:** 25
**SQ FT:** 65,000
**SALES (est):** 5.8MM **Privately Held**
**SIC:** 3651 Audio electronic systems

### (G-13351)
### MCCARTHY ENTERPRISES INC
15060 W Clover Ln (60048-1437)
**PHONE** ...................................847 367-5718
Mayo McCarthy Jr, *President*
**EMP:** 3
**SALES (est):** 268.5K **Privately Held**
**SIC:** 3469 3315 Metal stampings; wire products, ferrous/iron: made in wiredrawing plants

### (G-13352)
### MEDLINE INDUSTRIES INC
1501 Harris Rd (60048-2433)
**PHONE** ...................................847 557-2400
Michael G Lee, *President*
Brandon Reeder, *Opers Mgr*
Will Ingalls, *Opers Staff*
Jay Brehm, *Supervisor*
**EMP:** 14
**SALES (corp-wide):** 5.6B **Privately Held**
**SIC:** 3999 Barber & beauty shop equipment
**PA:** Medline Industries, Inc.
3 Lakes Dr
Northfield IL 60093
847 949-5500

### (G-13353)
### MEKTRONIX TECHNOLOGY INC
530 N Milwaukee Ave Ste B (60048-2008)
**PHONE** ...................................847 680-3300
Gregory Mayworm, *President*
Suzanne Quinn, *Treasurer*
**EMP:** 5
**SALES (est):** 645.7K **Privately Held**
**SIC:** 3625 3672 Controls for adjustable speed drives; printed circuit boards

### (G-13354)
### METALEX CORPORATION (DH)
1530 Artaius Pkwy (60048-3789)
P.O. Box 399 (60048-0399)
**PHONE** ...................................847 362-8300
**Fax:** 847 362-0533
Bob Birk, *Vice Pres*
Rick Mathys, *Opers Mgr*
Ted Dohse, *Sales Mgr*
Jim Desonia, *Director*
▲ **EMP:** 105
**SALES (est):** 35MM
**SALES (corp-wide):** 705.5MM **Publicly Held**
**SIC:** 3449 3469 Lath, expanded metal; perforated metal, stamped
**HQ:** Jason Incorporated
E Michigan St Ste 900
Milwaukee WI 53202
414 277-9300

### (G-13355)
### METALEX CORPORATION
700 Liberty Dr (60048-2343)
**PHONE** ...................................847 362-5400
**EMP:** 105
**SALES (corp-wide):** 705.5MM **Publicly Held**
**SIC:** 3446 3444 Gratings, open steel flooring; sheet metalwork
**HQ:** Metalex Corporation
1530 Artaius Pkwy
Libertyville IL 60048
847 362-8300

### (G-13356)
### MFRONTIERS LLC
1631 Northwind Blvd (60048-9613)
**PHONE** ...................................224 513-5312
Daniel Pahng, *Principal*
Michael Ottoman, *Exec VP*
Walter Sloan, *Vice Pres*
**EMP:** 4
**SALES (est):** 126.8K **Privately Held**
**SIC:** 5734 7372 Software, business & non-game; application computer software

### (G-13357)
### MGS GROUP NORTH AMERICA INC
14050 W Lambs Ln Ste 4 (60048-9505)
**PHONE** ...................................847 371-1158
Craig Hall, *CEO*
Steve Paul, *Plant Mgr*
**EMP:** 100
**SALES (corp-wide):** 258.6MM **Privately Held**
**SIC:** 3089 Plastic processing
**HQ:** Mgs Group North America, Inc.
W190n11701 Moldmakers Way
Germantown WI 53022
262 250-2950

### (G-13358)
### MGS MFG GROUP INC
Also Called: Tecstar Mfg Company III Div
14050 Lands Ln Ste 2 (60048)
**PHONE** ...................................847 968-4335
**Fax:** 847 968-4336
Chris Navratil, *Vice Pres*
Chris Nevratil, *Manager*
**EMP:** 45
**SALES (corp-wide):** 258.6MM **Privately Held**
**WEB:** www.mgstech.com
**SIC:** 3089 Plastic kitchenware, tableware & houseware
**PA:** Mgs Mfg. Group, Inc.
W188n11707 Maple Rd
Germantown WI 53022
262 255-5790

### (G-13359)
### MOTOROLA SOLUTIONS INC
622 N Us Highway 45 (60048-1286)
**PHONE** ...................................847 523-5000
Fred Kuznik, *General Mgr*
Tonya Luniak, *Project Mgr*
Gregory Skillman, *Engineer*
Anuranjan Gulati, *Manager*
Jason Christensen, *Software Engr*
**EMP:** 4
**SALES (corp-wide):** 6B **Publicly Held**
**WEB:** www.motorola.com
**SIC:** 3661 Telephones & telephone apparatus
**PA:** Motorola Solutions, Inc.
500 W Monroe St Ste 4400
Chicago IL 60661
847 576-5000

### (G-13360)
### MOTOROLA SOLUTIONS INC
1200 Technology Way (60048-5369)
**PHONE** ...................................847 523-5000
**EMP:** 7
**SALES (corp-wide):** 6B **Publicly Held**
**WEB:** www.motorola.com
**SIC:** 3663 Radio & TV communications equipment
**PA:** Motorola Solutions, Inc.
500 W Monroe St Ste 4400
Chicago IL 60661
847 576-5000

### (G-13361)
### MRK INDUSTRIES INC
1821 Industrial Dr (60048-9727)
**PHONE** ...................................847 362-8720
**Fax:** 847 537-8790
Michael Schaefer, *President*
Daniela Schaefer, *Vice Pres*
Matthew Rozycki, *Program Mgr*
▲ **EMP:** 40
**SQ FT:** 45,000
**SALES:** 7.1MM **Privately Held**
**SIC:** 3446 Acoustical suspension systems, metal

### (G-13362)
### NOISE BARRIERS LLC
2001 Kelley Ct (60048-9610)
**PHONE** ...................................847 843-0500
Steve Mitchell, *Managing Dir*
Ariel Reyes, *Plant Mgr*
John Wilson, *Prdtn Mgr*
Michael Daut, *Engineer*
Mark Herdman, *Engineer*
**EMP:** 50
**SALES (est):** 18.9MM **Privately Held**
**WEB:** www.noisebarriers.com
**SIC:** 3499 Fire- or burglary-resistive products; barricades, metal

### (G-13363)
### NORTH SHORE DISTILLERY LLC
13990 W Rockland Rd (60048-9724)
P.O. Box 279, Lake Bluff (60044-0279)
**PHONE** ...................................847 574-2499
Sonja Kassalbaum, *Mktg Dir*
Sonja Kassebaum, *Mng Member*
Derek Kassebaum,
**EMP:** 9
**SQ FT:** 5,000
**SALES (est):** 560.8K **Privately Held**
**SIC:** 2085 Cocktails, alcoholic

### (G-13364)
### NORTH SHORE SIGN COMPANY
1925 Industrial Dr (60048-9731)
**PHONE** ...................................847 816-7020
**Fax:** 847 816-7145
Duane Laska, *President*
Patrick Dooley, *Vice Pres*
Kevin Laska, *Vice Pres*
Petra Osborn, *Accounting Mgr*
William Konkol, *Accountant*
**EMP:** 35
**SQ FT:** 17,000
**SALES:** 2.2MM **Privately Held**
**WEB:** www.northshoresign.com
**SIC:** 3993 1799 Electric signs; sign installation & maintenance

### (G-13365)
### PADDOCK PUBLICATIONS INC
Also Called: Daily Herald
1795 N Butterfield Rd # 100 (60048-1212)
**PHONE** ...................................847 680-5800
Peter Nenni, *General Mgr*
**EMP:** 30
**SALES (corp-wide):** 122.6MM **Privately Held**
**WEB:** www.dailyherald.com
**SIC:** 2711 2741 Newspapers; miscellaneous publishing
**PA:** Paddock Publications, Inc.
155 E Algonquin Rd
Arlington Heights IL 60005
847 427-4300

### (G-13366)
### PERFORMANCE MAILING & PRTG INC
777 N Milwaukee Ave (60048-1913)
**PHONE** ...................................847 549-0500
**Fax:** 847 549-0343
Marianne Wilson, *Owner*
Jenett New, *Assistant*
**EMP:** 3
**SALES:** 330K **Privately Held**
**SIC:** 2752 Commercial printing, lithographic

## Libertyville - Lake County (G-13396)

**(G-13367)**
**PHARMASYN INC**
1840 Industrial Dr # 140 (60048-9400)
PHONE.................847 752-8405
John Pierpont III, *President*
Glenn Norley, *Exec VP*
**EMP:** 4
**SQ FT:** 5,000
**SALES:** 500K **Privately Held**
**WEB:** www.pharmasyn.com
**SIC:** 2819 8731 Chemicals, high purity: refined from technical grade; commercial physical research

**(G-13368)**
**PIERCE CRANDELL & CO INC**
14047 W Petronella Dr # 103 (60048-9429)
PHONE.................847 549-6015
Roy Crandall Sr, *Ch of Bd*
Roy L Crandall Jr, *President*
Steve Crandall, *Research*
Roy L Crandall III, *Admin Sec*
**EMP:** 7
**SALES (est):** 711.1K **Privately Held**
**WEB:** www.crandallpierce.com
**SIC:** 2721 2741 Statistical reports (periodicals): publishing only; miscellaneous publishing

**(G-13369)**
**PIPER PLASTICS INC (PA)**
1840 Enterprise Ct (60048-9445)
P.O. Box 536, Mundelein (60060-0536)
PHONE.................847 367-0110
Fax: 847 367-0566
Randall W Wojtysiak, *President*
Bruce White, *Vice Pres*
Mike Wiza, *Safety Mgr*
Matt Engler, *Opers Staff*
Amy Krueger, *Production*
▲ **EMP:** 52
**SQ FT:** 34,000
**SALES (est):** 30.7MM **Privately Held**
**WEB:** www.piperplastics.com
**SIC:** 3599 5162 3081 Machine shop, jobbing & repair; plastics film; plastics sheets & rods; plastic film & sheet; film base, cellulose acetate or nitrocellulose plastic

**(G-13370)**
**PLATIT INC**
1840 Industrial Dr # 220 (60048-9412)
PHONE.................847 680-5270
Bo Torp, *President*
Goran Bulaja, *General Mgr*
▲ **EMP:** 2
**SALES (est):** 470.1K **Privately Held**
**WEB:** www.platitusa.com
**SIC:** 3554 Coating & finishing machinery, paper

**(G-13371)**
**PRECISION METAL CRAFTERS INC**
1840 Industrial Dr # 340 (60048-9466)
PHONE.................847 816-3244
**EMP:** 14
**SQ FT:** 9,500
**SALES (est):** 1.1MM **Privately Held**
**SIC:** 3599 Precision Machine Shop

**(G-13372)**
**PW MASONRY INC**
1230 Hunters Ln (60048-3408)
PHONE.................847 573-0510
Piotr Wyszkowski, *President*
**EMP:** 3
**SALES (est):** 270K **Privately Held**
**SIC:** 2381 Fabric dress & work gloves

**(G-13373)**
**R R DONNELLEY & SONS COMPANY**
Moore Computer Supplies
850 Technology Way (60048-5350)
PHONE.................847 393-3000
Fax: 847 393-2971
Hank Hamner, *Vice Pres*
Jim Rowe, *Asst Treas*
**EMP:** 120
**SQ FT:** 28,000
**SALES (corp-wide):** 6.9B **Publicly Held**
**WEB:** www.moore.com
**SIC:** 2741 Catalogs: publishing only, not printed on site

**PA:** R. R. Donnelley & Sons Company
35 W Wacker Dr Ste 3650
Chicago IL 60601
312 326-8000

**(G-13374)**
**RAILSHOP INC**
902 Wexford Ct (60048-3059)
P.O. Box 7400 (60048-7400)
PHONE.................847 816-0925
**EMP:** 4
**SALES (est):** 382K **Privately Held**
**SIC:** 3089 Mfg Plastic Products

**(G-13375)**
**REIN ELECTRIC**
700 E Park Ave (60048-2907)
PHONE.................224 433-6936
Anthony Rein, *Principal*
Michael Malinowski, *Manager*
**EMP:** 5
**SALES (est):** 424.3K **Privately Held**
**SIC:** 3699 Electrical equipment & supplies

**(G-13376)**
**RHOPAC FABRICATED PRODUCTS LLC**
1819 Industrial Dr (60048-9727)
P.O. Box 83008, Chicago (60691-3010)
PHONE.................847 362-3300
Fax: 847 362-3433
Gregory Nemecek, *President*
Philip B Langlois, *Vice Pres*
Barbara Dettman, *Controller*
Susan Sponsler, *Admin Sec*
**EMP:** 40 **EST:** 1932
**SQ FT:** 40,000
**SALES (est):** 10.7MM **Privately Held**
**WEB:** www.rhopac.com
**SIC:** 3053 2891 2821 2675 Gaskets, all materials; adhesives & sealants; plastics materials & resins; die-cut paper & board

**(G-13377)**
**SAMSUNG SIGN CORP**
1840 Industrial Dr # 230 (60048-9412)
PHONE.................847 816-1374
Brandon Chin, *President*
**EMP:** 5
**SALES:** 200K **Privately Held**
**SIC:** 3993 Signs & advertising specialties

**(G-13378)**
**SEC DESIGN TECHNOLOGIES INC**
1800 Tempel Dr (60048-9443)
PHONE.................847 680-0439
Fax: 847 680-0449
Rory Gahart, *President*
Robert Luehrsen, *Engineer*
Kevin Johnson, *Manager*
Ellen Gahart, *Admin Sec*
**EMP:** 14
**SQ FT:** 6,000
**SALES (est):** 3.7MM **Privately Held**
**WEB:** www.secdesign.com
**SIC:** 3599 Custom machinery

**(G-13379)**
**SERRA LASER PRECISION LLC**
2400 Commerce Dr (60048-4462)
PHONE.................847 367-0282
Fax: 847 367-0236
Victor Martinez, *VP Mfg*
Doug Camerer, *QC Mgr*
Jason Ming, *Engineer*
Jeff Adams, *Mng Member*
**EMP:** 75
**SQ FT:** 60,000
**SALES (est):** 28MM **Privately Held**
**SIC:** 3499 Machine bases, metal

**(G-13380)**
**SHERWIN-WILLIAMS COMPANY**
1618 S Milwaukee Ave (60048-3751)
PHONE.................847 573-0240
Fax: 847 573-0362
**EMP:** 4
**SALES (corp-wide):** 11.8B **Publicly Held**
**SIC:** 5231 5198 2851 Paint & painting supplies; paints, varnishes & supplies; wood fillers or sealers
**PA:** The Sherwin-Williams Company
101 W Prospect Ave # 1020
Cleveland OH 44115
216 566-2000

**(G-13381)**
**SIGNS & WONDERS UNLIMITED LLC**
28318 N Oak Ln (60048-9762)
PHONE.................847 816-9734
Nancy Powers,
**EMP:** 3
**SALES (est):** 151.1K **Privately Held**
**SIC:** 7372 Application computer software

**(G-13382)**
**SMART SOLAR INC**
Also Called: Smart Living Home & Garden
1203 Loyola Dr (60048-1290)
PHONE.................813 343-5770
James Bologeorges, *President*
▲ **EMP:** 15
**SALES (est):** 2.2MM **Privately Held**
**SIC:** 5719 3799 5261 3645 Lamps & lamp shades; pushcarts; fountains, outdoor; garden, patio, walkway & yard lighting fixtures: electric; hammocks: metal or fabric & metal combination

**(G-13383)**
**SPECTRIS HOLDINGS INC**
732 Florsheim Dr Ste 11 (60048-3722)
PHONE.................847 680-3709
R Stephens, *President*
**EMP:** 19
**SALES (est):** 2.5MM
**SALES (corp-wide):** 1.6B **Privately Held**
**SIC:** 3545 Micrometers
**HQ:** Spectris Us Holdings Limited
Heritage House Church Road
Egham
178 447-0470

**(G-13384)**
**STAREX INC**
1880 W Winchester Rd # 206 (60048-5336)
PHONE.................847 918-5555
James Yan, *President*
▲ **EMP:** 6
**SQ FT:** 2,000
**SALES:** 10MM **Privately Held**
**WEB:** www.starexinc.com
**SIC:** 3624 Electrodes, thermal & electrolytic uses: carbon, graphite

**(G-13385)**
**STRUCTURAL DESIGN CORP**
1133 Claridge Dr (60048-1240)
PHONE.................847 816-3816
William Vanni, *President*
Deborah Vanni, *Admin Sec*
**EMP:** 6
**SQ FT:** 400
**SALES (est):** 470K **Privately Held**
**SIC:** 8711 3441 Structural engineering; consulting engineer; fabricated structural metal

**(G-13386)**
**SWANSON WATER TREATMENT INC (PA)**
509 E Park Ave Ste 101 (60048-2873)
P.O. Box 675, Mundelein (60060-0675)
PHONE.................847 680-1113
Fax: 847 680-1130
Murner Swanson, *President*
Diane Desbiens, *Opers Mgr*
**EMP:** 1
**SQ FT:** 1,500
**SALES:** 300K **Privately Held**
**SIC:** 2899 Water treating compounds

**(G-13387)**
**T J BROOKS CO**
804 E Park Ave Ste 104 (60048-2901)
PHONE.................847 680-0350
**EMP:** 2 **EST:** 2009
**SALES (est):** 200K **Privately Held**
**SIC:** 3593 Mfg Fluid Power Cylinders

**(G-13388)**
**TALOC USA INC**
1915 Enterprise Ct (60048-9764)
PHONE.................847 665-8222
Bryan Timmerman, *President*
**EMP:** 6

**SALES (est):** 637.3K **Privately Held**
**SIC:** 3579 1761 8999 Canceling machinery, post office; architectural sheet metal work; actuarial consultant

**(G-13389)**
**TAYLOR ENTERPRISES INC**
5510 Fairmont Rd Ste A (60048-4806)
PHONE.................847 367-1032
Dr Wayne A Taylor, *Chairman*
Dr Wayne Taylor, *Chairman*
Ann Taylor, *Treasurer*
**EMP:** 2
**SALES:** 800K **Privately Held**
**WEB:** www.variation.com
**SIC:** 2731 Book publishing

**(G-13390)**
**THERAPEUTIC ENVISIONS INC**
Also Called: Braceunder
151 Blueberry Rd (60048-2161)
PHONE.................720 323-7032
Charles Hodges, *CEO*
**EMP:** 5
**SALES (est):** 240K **Privately Held**
**SIC:** 3842 Braces, orthopedic

**(G-13391)**
**TOUCHPOINTCARE LLC**
215 E Park Ave Ste D (60048-2870)
PHONE.................866 713-6590
David Anderson, *Principal*
**EMP:** 6
**SALES (est):** 517.2K **Privately Held**
**WEB:** www.touchpointcare.com
**SIC:** 3845 Patient monitoring apparatus

**(G-13392)**
**TRI R**
1921 Industrial Dr (60048-9731)
PHONE.................224 399-7786
Rory Hebel, *Principal*
**EMP:** 8
**SALES (est):** 1MM **Privately Held**
**SIC:** 3842 Welders' hoods

**(G-13393)**
**ULTRASONIC BLIND CO**
342 4th St (60048-2312)
PHONE.................847 579-8084
Mike Dzsak, *President*
**EMP:** 2
**SALES:** 500K **Privately Held**
**SIC:** 2591 7699 Blinds vertical; window blind repair services

**(G-13394)**
**UNIQUE INDOOR COMFORT**
624 2nd St (60048-2076)
PHONE.................847 362-1910
Fax: 847 362-4043
Judy Henrich, *Owner*
Josh Henrich, *Opers Mgr*
Kelly Covert, *Sales Executive*
**EMP:** 15
**SQ FT:** 3,500
**SALES (est):** 1.7MM **Privately Held**
**SIC:** 1711 5063 3639 3561 Heating & air conditioning contractors; generators; hot water heaters, household; pumps, domestic: water or sump; geothermal drilling

**(G-13395)**
**US ACRYLIC LLC**
1320 Harris Rd (60048-2413)
PHONE.................847 837-4800
Fax: 847 837-1955
Anne O' Connel, *Controller*
Hsu,
Monique Hsu,
Tina Hsu,
Jerry Lee,
▲ **EMP:** 56
**SQ FT:** 85,000
**SALES (est):** 12.2MM **Privately Held**
**WEB:** www.usacrylic.com
**SIC:** 3089 Plastic kitchenware, tableware & houseware; novelties, plastic

**(G-13396)**
**USG CORPORATION**
Also Called: Research & Technology Center
700 N Us Highway 45 (60048-1268)
P.O. Box 982600, El Paso TX (79998-2126)
PHONE.................847 970-5200

# Libertyville - Lake County (G-13397)

Fax: 847 362-4871
Michael Shake, *Research*
**EMP:** 19
**SALES (corp-wide):** 3B **Publicly Held**
**SIC:** 3275 3296 Gypsum products; gypsum board; gypsum plaster; insulating plaster, gypsum; mineral wool insulation products; acoustical board & tile, mineral wool
**PA:** Usg Corporation
550 W Adams St
Chicago IL 60661
312 436-4000

## (G-13397)
### VALENT BIOSCIENCES CORPORATION (DH)
Also Called: Valent USA
870 Technology Way # 100 (60048-5350)
**PHONE** ............................ 847 968-4700
**Fax:** 847 968-4802
Masayo Tada, *CEO*
Michael D Donaldson, *President*
Andrew Lee, *President*
Geoff Quick, *President*
Gonzalo Maturana, *General Mgr*
◆ **EMP:** 80
**SQ FT:** 20,000
**SALES (est):** 49.6MM
**SALES (corp-wide):** 17.2B **Privately Held**
**WEB:** www.valentbiosciences.com
**SIC:** 2879 Agricultural chemicals
**HQ:** Valent U.S.A. Llc
1600 Riviera Ave Ste 200
Walnut Creek CA 94596
925 256-2700

## (G-13398)
### VIDASYM INC
1673 Cedar Glen Dr (60048-3924)
**PHONE** ............................ 847 680-6072
Kinfun Wong,
Allen Lau,
Jin Tian,
**EMP:** 8
**SALES (est):** 933.6K **Privately Held**
**SIC:** 2833 Medicinals & botanicals

## (G-13399)
### VILLAGE PRESS INC
124 E Church St (60048-2218)
**PHONE** ............................ 847 362-1856
**Fax:** 847 362-1931
Stuart Pyle, *President*
Elizabeth Pyle, *Corp Secy*
Howard Pyle, *Vice Pres*
Elizabeth Goering, *Admin Sec*
**EMP:** 6
**SQ FT:** 1,200
**SALES:** 400K **Privately Held**
**SIC:** 2752 3953 2759 2675 Commercial printing, lithographic; screens, textile printing; commercial printing; die-cut paper & board; printing broker; platemaking services

## (G-13400)
### WEBER METALS INC
1076 E Park Ave (60048-2951)
P.O. Box 8045, Gurnee (60031-7009)
**PHONE** ............................ 847 951-7920
**Fax:** 847 362-1375
Joseph Woldhuis Jr, *President*
**EMP:** 9
**SQ FT:** 9,000
**SALES (est):** 1.3MM **Privately Held**
**WEB:** www.webmetals.com
**SIC:** 3446 Architectural metalwork

## (G-13401)
### WILLIAM FRICK & COMPANY
2600 Commerce Dr (60048-2494)
**PHONE** ............................ 847 918-3700
**Fax:** 847 918-3701
William G Frick, *CEO*
Jeffrey H Brandt, *President*
Evie Bennett, *Vice Pres*
Chad Svastisalee, *Opers Staff*
James Heidner, *Controller*
◆ **EMP:** 34
**SQ FT:** 30,333
**SALES (est):** 10.1MM **Privately Held**
**WEB:** www.fricknet.com
**SIC:** 3993 7389 Signs, not made in custom sign painting shops; design, commercial & industrial

## (G-13402)
### WILLIAM W MEYER AND SONS (PA)
1700 Franklin Blvd (60048-4407)
**PHONE** ............................ 847 918-0111
**Fax:** 847 918-8183
Gregory R Buric, *President*
Steven Ansai, *Draft/Design*
Kenneth A Nowak, *Controller*
Mitchell Wolin, *Mktg Coord*
Mike Doorey, *Manager*
▲ **EMP:** 90
**SQ FT:** 60,000
**SALES (est):** 17.3MM **Privately Held**
**WEB:** www.wmwmeyer.com
**SIC:** 3535 3589 3564 3537 Bulk handling conveyor systems; vacuum cleaners & sweepers, electric: industrial; blowers & fans; industrial trucks & tractors; air & gas compressors

## (G-13403)
### ZELLER PLASTIK USA INC (HQ)
1515 Franklin Blvd (60048-4458)
**PHONE** ............................ 847 247-7900
**Fax:** 847 247-7901
Christian Voegeli, *President*
Sharon Pierce, *Principal*
Jorge Loza, *Business Mgr*
Christopher Ray, *Mfg Dir*
Peter Goshorn, *Sales Dir*
◆ **EMP:** 126
**SALES (est):** 43MM **Privately Held**
**SIC:** 3089 Closures, plastic

# Lincoln
## *Logan County*

## (G-13404)
### ARCHER-DANIELS-MIDLAND COMPANY
Also Called: ADM Animal Nutrition
2250 5th St (62656-9611)
P.O. Box 827 (62656-0827)
**PHONE** ............................ 217 732-6678
Jon Cornelius, *Engineer*
Ken Hunter, *Branch Mgr*
**EMP:** 11
**SALES (corp-wide):** 62.3B **Publicly Held**
**WEB:** www.admalliancenutrition.com
**SIC:** 2048 Prepared feeds
**PA:** Archer-Daniels-Midland Company
77 W Wacker Dr Ste 4600
Chicago IL 60601
312 634-8100

## (G-13405)
### ARDAGH GLASS INC
1200 N Logan St (62656-1707)
**PHONE** ............................ 217 732-1796
Brian Houger, *Plant Mgr*
Glenn Miller, *Prdtn Mgr*
Stanley Konazeski, *Opers Staff*
Tara Costa, *Purch Agent*
Ed Block, *Personnel*
**EMP:** 200 **Privately Held**
**WEB:** www.sgcontainers.com
**SIC:** 3221 Bottles for packing, bottling & canning: glass
**HQ:** Ardagh Glass Inc.
10194 Crosspoint Blvd
Indianapolis IN 46256

## (G-13406)
### BALL FOSTER GLASS CONTAINER CO
1200 N Logan St (62656-1707)
**PHONE** ............................ 217 735-1511
Chris Bering, *Manager*
**EMP:** 3
**SALES (est):** 144.6K **Privately Held**
**SIC:** 3221 Glass containers

## (G-13407)
### CONTRACTORS READY-MIX INC (PA)
601 S Kickapoo St (62656-3007)
P.O. Box 56 (62656-0056)
**PHONE** ............................ 217 735-2565
**Fax:** 217 735-1099
Dan Curry, *President*
Jessie Butler, *Corp Secy*
Jim Curry, *Vice Pres*
Sue Curry, *Vice Pres*
**EMP:** 15
**SALES (est):** 3.4MM **Privately Held**
**SIC:** 3273 3272 Ready-mixed concrete; concrete products

## (G-13408)
### COPLEY PRESS INC
Courier, The
2201 Woodlawn Rd (62656-9645)
P.O. Box 740 (62656-0740)
**PHONE** ............................ 217 732-2101
Bill Welt, *Editor*
Karen Hargis, *Advt Staff*
Richard Johnston, *Branch Mgr*
John Clarke, *Director*
**EMP:** 10
**SQ FT:** 20,000
**SALES (corp-wide):** 92.6MM **Privately Held**
**WEB:** www.copleynewspapers.com
**SIC:** 2711 Newspapers: publishing only, not printed on site
**PA:** The Copley Press Inc
7776 Ivanhoe Ave
La Jolla CA 92037
858 454-0411

## (G-13409)
### EATON CORPORATION
Eaton Electrical
1725 1200th Ave (62656-5040)
**PHONE** ............................ 217 732-3131
**Fax:** 217 732-3131
Vladimir Salazar, *Plant Mgr*
Mark Gunter, *Mfg Staff*
Jack Detjer, *Purchasing*
Robert Duvall, *Engineer*
Syed Karim, *Engineer*
**EMP:** 700 **Privately Held**
**WEB:** www.eaton.com
**SIC:** 3613 3644 Switchgear & switchboard apparatus; noncurrent-carrying wiring services
**HQ:** Eaton Corporation
1000 Eaton Blvd
Cleveland OH 44122
216 523-5000

## (G-13410)
### HERITAGE PACKAGING LLC
Also Called: H P
2350 5th St (62656-9628)
**PHONE** ............................ 217 735-4406
Rick Washam, *Manager*
Terry Shea, *Director*
Gregory Basford,
Steve Douglass,
**EMP:** 29
**SQ FT:** 39,000
**SALES (est):** 5MM **Privately Held**
**SIC:** 2653 5113 Boxes, corrugated: made from purchased materials; shipping supplies

## (G-13411)
### INTERNATIONAL PAPER COMPANY
1601 5th St (62656-9128)
**PHONE** ............................ 217 735-1221
Debbie Conlin, *Branch Mgr*
**EMP:** 160
**SALES (corp-wide):** 21B **Publicly Held**
**SIC:** 2621 2653 2656 2631 Paper mills; printing paper; text paper; bristols; boxes, corrugated: made from purchased materials; food containers (liquid tight), including milk cartons; cartons, milk: made from purchased material; container, packaging & boxboard; container board; packaging board; pulp mills
**PA:** International Paper Company
6400 Poplar Ave
Memphis TN 38197
901 419-9000

## (G-13412)
### LAWRENCE SCREW PRODUCTS INC
437 8th St (62656-2561)
**PHONE** ............................ 217 735-1230
Richard Schmidt, *Branch Mgr*
Dick Schmidt, *Manager*
**EMP:** 6
**SALES (corp-wide):** 61.2MM **Privately Held**
**WEB:** www.lawscrew.com
**SIC:** 3451 Screw machine products
**PA:** Lawrence Screw Products, Inc.
7230 W Wilson Ave
Harwood Heights IL 60706
708 867-5150

## (G-13413)
### LINCOLN PRINTERS INC
711 Broadway St (62656-2837)
**PHONE** ............................ 217 732-3121
**Fax:** 217 732-3122
Mike Dykman, *President*
Rachel Stroud, *Office Mgr*
Noah Atkinson, *Manager*
**EMP:** 4
**SQ FT:** 3,600
**SALES (est):** 563.4K **Privately Held**
**SIC:** 2752 Commercial printing, offset

## (G-13414)
### LINCOLNDAILYNEWSCOM
601 Keokuk St (62656-1730)
**PHONE** ............................ 217 732-7443
Jim Youngquist, *Owner*
**EMP:** 6 **EST:** 2000
**SALES (est):** 169.4K **Privately Held**
**WEB:** www.lincolndailynews.com
**SIC:** 2711 Newspapers

## (G-13415)
### MENTAL HEALTH CTRS CENTL ILL
Also Called: Logan Mason Rehabilitation
760 S Postville Dr (62656-2237)
**PHONE** ............................ 217 735-1413
**Fax:** 217 735-5780
Gene Frioli, *Manager*
Brenda Diedrich, *Manager*
**EMP:** 100
**SALES (corp-wide):** 14.8MM **Privately Held**
**SIC:** 8093 8331 2448 8399 Mental health clinic, outpatient; job training & vocational rehabilitation services; wood pallets & skids; community development groups
**PA:** Mental Health Centers Of Central Illinois
710 N 8th St
Springfield IL 62702
217 525-4777

## (G-13416)
### NEALS TRAILER SALES
1670 1100th St (62656-5027)
**PHONE** ............................ 217 792-5136
**Fax:** 217 792-5869
Donny Neal, *Owner*
**EMP:** 3
**SALES (est):** 237.4K **Privately Held**
**SIC:** 5013 7692 Trailer parts & accessories; welding repair

## (G-13417)
### NEW HERALD NEWS LLC
727 Galena St (62656-1811)
**PHONE** ............................ 217 651-8064
Hoagland Ann R, *Principal*
**EMP:** 3
**SALES (est):** 118.8K **Privately Held**
**SIC:** 2711 Newspapers, publishing & printing

## (G-13418)
### PRECISION PRODUCTS INC
316 Limit St (62656-2943)
**PHONE** ............................ 217 735-1590
Mort Kay, *President*
Renee Work, *Vice Pres*
Rick Clayton, *Prdtn Mgr*
Les Jannings, *QC Mgr*
Becky Juilfs, *Human Res Mgr*
◆ **EMP:** 200
**SQ FT:** 650,000
**SALES (est):** 48.3MM **Privately Held**
**WEB:** www.precisionprodinc.com
**SIC:** 3423 3524 Hand & edge tools; lawn & garden equipment

## (G-13419)
### SHEWS CUSTOM WOODWORKING
1441 1200th St (62656-5049)
**PHONE** ............................ 217 737-5543

# GEOGRAPHIC SECTION
## Lincolnshire - Lake County (G-13442)

Fax: 217 732-6566
Mark Shew, *Owner*
**EMP:** 3
**SQ FT:** 1,872
**SALES:** 125K **Privately Held**
**SIC:** 2434  2511  Wood kitchen cabinets; wood household furniture

### (G-13420)
### SIEBS DIE CUTTING SPECIALTY CO
Also Called: Sieb's Die Cutting Specialties
912 Clinton St  (62656-3111)
**PHONE** ................................. 217 735-1432
Paul Dumser, *Owner*
Pat Chadwick, *Officer*
**EMP:** 1
**SQ FT:** 14,000
**SALES:** 350K **Privately Held**
**SIC:** 2675  2653  2631  Cutouts, cardboard, die-cut: from purchased materials; boxes, corrugated: made from purchased materials; paperboard mills

### (G-13421)
### VERNON MICHEAL
Also Called: Hardball Chemical Co
1100 Home Ave  (62656-3056)
**PHONE** ................................. 217 735-4005
Michael Vernon, *Owner*
**EMP:** 7
**SALES (est):** 370K **Privately Held**
**WEB:** www.michaelvernon.com
**SIC:** 2819  Industrial inorganic chemicals

## Lincolnshire
### Lake County

### (G-13422)
### 1883 PROPERTIES INC (HQ)
Also Called: E H Wachs Company
600 Knightsbridge Pkwy  (60069-3617)
**PHONE** ................................. 847 537-8800
Edward H Wachs, *Ch of Bd*
Ken Morency, *President*
Nathan Miller, *General Mgr*
Craig Lewandowski, *Vice Pres*
Tim Sheehan, *Vice Pres*
▲ **EMP:** 70
**SQ FT:** 80,000
**SALES (est):** 42.1MM
**SALES (corp-wide):** 13.6B **Publicly Held**
**WEB:** www.wachsco.com
**SIC:** 1799  3541  Welding on site; machine tools, metal cutting type; pipe cutting & threading machines
**PA:** Illinois Tool Works Inc.
 155 Harlem Ave
 Glenview IL 60025
 847 724-7500

### (G-13423)
### ACCO BRANDS USA LLC
500 Bond St  (60069-4207)
**PHONE** ................................. 847 272-3700
Victor Finch, *Director*
**EMP:** 100
**SALES (corp-wide):** 1.5B **Publicly Held**
**WEB:** www.gbc.com
**SIC:** 3089  2761  3496  2675  Injection molding of plastics; manifold business forms; clips & fasteners, made from purchased wire; letters, cardboard, die-cut: from purchased materials
**HQ:** Acco Brands Usa Llc
 4 Corporate Dr
 Lake Zurich IL 60047
 800 222-6462

### (G-13424)
### ADCO GLOBAL INC (HQ)
100 Tri State Intl # 135  (60069-4425)
**PHONE** ................................. 847 282-3485
Fax: 847 282-3481
John Knox, *Principal*
Michael Graf, *Vice Pres*
Peter Paulsen, *CFO*
Suanne Stevens, *Controller*
◆ **EMP:** 3

**SALES (est):** 290.1MM
**SALES (corp-wide):** 582.1MM **Privately Held**
**WEB:** www.adcoglobal.com
**SIC:** 2891  Adhesives & sealants
**PA:** Royal Adhesives And Sealants Llc
 2001 W Washington St
 South Bend IN 46628
 574 246-5000

### (G-13425)
### AKSYS LTD
2 Marriott Dr  (60069-3700)
**PHONE** ................................. 847 229-2020
Fax: 847 229-2080
Howard J Lewin, *President*
Dennis Erwin, *Senior VP*
Jerry D Fisher, *Senior VP*
Richard P Goldhaber, *Senior VP*
Lawrence A Rohrer, *Senior VP*
**EMP:** 87
**SQ FT:** 41,500
**SALES (est):** 10.2MM **Privately Held**
**SIC:** 3841  Hemodialysis apparatus

### (G-13426)
### ALTAIR CORPORATION (DEL) (HQ)
350 Barclay Blvd  (60069-3643)
**PHONE** ................................. 847 634-9540
Fax: 847 634-2627
Garry Brainin, *CEO*
Steven Siler, *COO*
Eric Brainin, *Production*
M J Coate, *Treasurer*
Eugene Kaydanovsky, *Information Mgr*
**EMP:** 39 **EST:** 1937
**SQ FT:** 17,000
**SALES (est):** 58.7MM
**SALES (corp-wide):** 62.6MM **Privately Held**
**WEB:** www.altaircorp.net
**SIC:** 3555  3564  2048  Printing trades machinery; air purification equipment; livestock feeds
**PA:** Chatham Corporation
 350 Barclay Blvd
 Lincolnshire IL 60069
 847 634-5506

### (G-13427)
### AMPHENOL CORPORATION
Amphenol Mechconect
100 Tristate Intl  (60069-4403)
**PHONE** ................................. 847 478-5600
**EMP:** 3
**SALES (corp-wide):** 6.2B **Publicly Held**
**SIC:** 3678  Electronic connectors
**PA:** Amphenol Corporation
 358 Hall Ave
 Wallingford CT 06492
 203 265-8900

### (G-13428)
### AMPHENOL T&M ANTENNAS INC (HQ)
100 Tri State Intl # 255  (60069-4405)
**PHONE** ................................. 847 478-5600
Edward Jepson, *CFO*
Jim Adams, *Controller*
Jeff Chow, *Sales Mgr*
Lauren Devine, *Manager*
▲ **EMP:** 10
**SQ FT:** 1,100
**SALES (est):** 2.2MM
**SALES (corp-wide):** 6.2B **Publicly Held**
**WEB:** www.tmantennas.com
**SIC:** 3663  Antennas, transmitting & communications
**PA:** Amphenol Corporation
 358 Hall Ave
 Wallingford CT 06492
 203 265-8900

### (G-13429)
### ANYWAVE COMMUNICATION TECH INC
300 Knightsbridge Pkwy  (60069-3625)
**PHONE** ................................. 847 415-2258
Wenhua LI, *Ch of Bd*
Jingsong Xia, *President*
Frank Massa, *Sales Mgr*
**EMP:** 10
**SALES (est):** 1.6MM **Privately Held**
**SIC:** 3663  Studio equipment, radio & television broadcasting

**HQ:** Anywave Communication Technologies Co., Ltd.
 No.900, Yishan Road, Xuhui District
 Shanghai 20023
 216 432-0796

### (G-13430)
### B&W TECHNOLOGIES INC
405 Barclay Blvd  (60069-3609)
**PHONE** ................................. 888 749-8878
Carl Johnson, *President*
Cindy Kennedy, *Vice Pres*
Don Malaker, *Opers Mgr*
Kadar Ajmeri, *Engineer*
Dan Austin, *Engineer*
▲ **EMP:** 7 **EST:** 1993
**SALES (est):** 2.1MM
**SALES (corp-wide):** 39.3B **Publicly Held**
**SIC:** 3829  Gas detectors
**HQ:** Bw Technologies Ltd
 2840 2 Ave Se
 Calgary AB T2A 7
 403 248-9226

### (G-13431)
### BARCLAY BUSINESS GROUP INC
Also Called: The Intelligent Office
250 Parkway Dr Ste 150  (60069-4340)
**PHONE** ................................. 847 325-5555
Keith Drew, *President*
**EMP:** 6
**SQ FT:** 7,000
**SALES (est):** 521.4K **Privately Held**
**SIC:** 7372  Prepackaged software

### (G-13432)
### BAXTER HEALTHCARE CORPORATION
75 Tri State Intl  (60069-4428)
**PHONE** ................................. 847 948-4251
David Miller, *Principal*
**EMP:** 260
**SALES (corp-wide):** 10.1B **Publicly Held**
**SIC:** 2834  Pharmaceutical preparations
**HQ:** Baxter Healthcare Corporation
 1 Baxter Pkwy
 Deerfield IL 60015
 224 948-2000

### (G-13433)
### BURGHOF ENGINEERING & MFG CO
16051 W Deerfield Pkwy # 1  (60069-9629)
**PHONE** ................................. 847 634-0737
Fax: 847 634-3790
Kaspar Kammerer, *President*
Richard M Kammerer, *Technical Staff*
**EMP:** 20
**SQ FT:** 10,000
**SALES (est):** 4.8MM **Privately Held**
**SIC:** 3565  Packaging machinery

### (G-13434)
### CEC INDUSTRIES LTD
599 Bond St  (60069-4226)
**PHONE** ................................. 847 821-1199
Fax: 847 821-1133
Warren Wen Lai, *President*
Wen Hsin Lai, *President*
Sidney Liu, *General Mgr*
Michael Kwan, *COO*
Pearl Lai, *Controller*
▲ **EMP:** 50
**SALES (est):** 9.9MM **Privately Held**
**SIC:** 3641  Electric lamps

### (G-13435)
### CENTRAL MACHINES INC
645 Margate Dr  (60069-4248)
**PHONE** ................................. 847 634-6900
Fax: 847 634-6901
Gerhard M Kendler, *President*
Ulla Kendler, *Corp Secy*
Peter Kendler, *Vice Pres*
Mark Ziocchi, *Project Engr*
Jack Quillin, *Design Engr*
**EMP:** 25
**SQ FT:** 15,000
**SALES (est):** 6.7MM **Privately Held**
**WEB:** www.centralmachines.com
**SIC:** 3549  Assembly machines, including robotic

### (G-13436)
### CHATHAM CORPORATION (PA)
350 Barclay Blvd  (60069-3606)
**PHONE** ................................. 847 634-5506
Garry Brainin, *President*
Thomas Morthorst, *Vice Pres*
Eric Sundin, *CTO*
**EMP:** 17
**SALES (est):** 62.6MM **Privately Held**
**SIC:** 3555  3559  3564  2048  Printing trades machinery; foundry machinery & equipment; air purification equipment; feeds, specialty: mice, guinea pig, etc.

### (G-13437)
### CHEMICAL PROCESSING & ACC
175 Old Hlf Day Rd 140-10  (60069-3087)
P.O. Box 6475, Libertyville  (60048-6475)
**PHONE** ................................. 847 793-2387
Rich Podolski, *Owner*
**EMP:** 7
**SALES (est):** 865.1K **Privately Held**
**WEB:** www.chemicalprocessingandaccessories.com
**SIC:** 2899  5084  Chemical preparations; metal refining machinery & equipment

### (G-13438)
### CO-RECT PRODUCTS INC (PA)
Also Called: Co-Rect Bar Products
300 Knightsbridge Pkwy # 400  (60069-3668)
**PHONE** ................................. 763 542-9200
Fax: 612 542-9205
Michael B Pierce, *President*
Steve Ess, *Vice Pres*
Greg Loffler, *Vice Pres*
Michael Vinston, *Sales Mgr*
▲ **EMP:** 30
**SQ FT:** 45,000
**SALES:** 8MM **Privately Held**
**WEB:** www.co-rectproducts.com
**SIC:** 5046  2599  Restaurant equipment & supplies; bar, restaurant & cafeteria furniture

### (G-13439)
### CONDOMINIUMS NORTHBROOK CORT 1
Also Called: Condominiums Northbrook Court
830 Audubon Way Apt 217  (60069-3846)
**PHONE** ................................. 847 498-1640
David Levine, *President*
**EMP:** 5 **EST:** 1980
**SALES (est):** 190K **Privately Held**
**SIC:** 8641  3273  Condominium association; ready-mixed concrete

### (G-13440)
### COUPLINGS COMPANY INC
570 Bond St  (60069-4223)
**PHONE** ................................. 847 634-8990
Fax: 847 634-9282
Lewis Kwate, *President*
Steven Kwate, *Vice Pres*
▲ **EMP:** 15
**SQ FT:** 40,000
**SALES (est):** 3.2MM **Privately Held**
**WEB:** www.couplingscompany.com
**SIC:** 3494  3432  Valves & pipe fittings; plumbers' brass goods: drain cocks, faucets, spigots, etc.

### (G-13441)
### CREATIVE MERCHANDISING SYSTEMS
425 Village Grn Unit 307  (60069-3098)
**PHONE** ................................. 847 955-9990
Fax: 847 955-9994
Norman E Topping, *Owner*
Joan S Topping, *CFO*
**EMP:** 5
**SALES:** 1.3MM **Privately Held**
**SIC:** 3578  5046  Point-of-sale devices; display equipment, except refrigerated; store fixtures

### (G-13442)
### DECAMS CABINETS INC
23431 N Elm Rd  (60069-2201)
**PHONE** ................................. 847 360-4970
**EMP:** 3
**SALES (est):** 206.4K **Privately Held**
**SIC:** 2434  Wood kitchen cabinets

# Lincolnshire - Lake County (G-13443)

### (G-13443)
**DIGI TRAX CORPORATION**
650 Heathrow Dr  (60069-4205)
PHONE..................847 613-2100
Richard Kriozere, *CEO*
Jeff Kriozere, *President*
Larry Cullen, *Vice Pres*
Jeff Kriozer, *Vice Pres*
Tess Cullen, *Finance Mgr*
**EMP:** 26
**SQ FT:** 15,000
**SALES (est):** 5MM  **Privately Held**
**WEB:** www.digi-trax.com
**SIC:** 7371  7372  5734  Computer software systems analysis & design, custom; business oriented computer software; printers & plotters: computers

### (G-13444)
**DOUGHNUT BOY**
Also Called: Little Miss Muffin
250 Parkway Dr Ste 270  (60069-4346)
PHONE..................773 463-6328
Fax: 773 463-7101
**EMP:** 40
**SALES (est):** 6.7MM  **Privately Held**
**SIC:** 2051  Mfg Bread/Related Products

### (G-13445)
**DYNOMAX  INC**
640 Heathrow Dr  (60069-4205)
PHONE..................224 542-1031
**EMP:** 50
**SALES (corp-wide):** 33.9MM  **Privately Held**
**SIC:** 3679  Antennas, receiving
**PA:** Dynomax, Inc.
  1535 Abbott Dr
  Wheeling IL 60090
  847 680-8833

### (G-13446)
**E H WACHS**
600 Knightsbridge Pkwy  (60069-3617)
PHONE..................815 943-4785
David B Speer, *Principal*
Mark Wozniak, *Manager*
**EMP:** 7
**SALES (est):** 1.2MM  **Privately Held**
**SIC:** 3541  Saws & sawing machines

### (G-13447)
**FAXITRON X-RAY LLC**
575 Bond St  (60069-4226)
PHONE..................847 465-9729
Chris Donovan, *Sales Dir*
Allan Little, *Mng Member*
Luois Guerrero, *Manager*
Kelley Lamping, *Manager*
Efrain Mondragon, *Manager*
**EMP:** 20
**SQ FT:** 10,000
**SALES (est):** 3.5MM  **Privately Held**
**WEB:** www.faxitron.com
**SIC:** 5047  3844  Hospital equipment & furniture; X-ray apparatus & tubes

### (G-13448)
**FIRE SENTRY CORPORATION**
405 Barclay Blvd  (60069-3609)
PHONE..................714 694-0823
Mark Levy, *President*
Olden Carr, *Vice Pres*
Theodore Lapp, *Vice Pres*
John J Tus, *Treasurer*
Michelle Cabbell, *Controller*
▲ **EMP:** 25
**SQ FT:** 12,000
**SALES (est):** 4.4MM
**SALES (corp-wide):** 39.3B  **Publicly Held**
**WEB:** www.firesentry.com
**SIC:** 3669  Fire detection systems, electric
**HQ:** Honeywell Analytics Inc.
  405 Barclay Blvd
  Lincolnshire IL 60069
  847 955-8200

### (G-13449)
**FORMS SPECIALIST INC**
Also Called: FSI Print
131 Camden Ct  (60069-3429)
PHONE..................847 298-2868
Fax: 847 298-5335
Robert M Alsteen, *President*
Tom Navratil, *Accounts Exec*
Sandi Sacco, *Office Mgr*
**EMP:** 9  **EST:** 1972
**SALES (est):** 1MM  **Privately Held**
**WEB:** www.fsiprint.com
**SIC:** 2759  2752  2761  Business forms: printing; commercial printing, lithographic; manifold business forms

### (G-13450)
**GOOD SAM ENTERPRISES  LLC (DH)**
Also Called: GSE
250 Parkway Dr Ste 270  (60069-4346)
PHONE..................847 229-6720
Stephen Adams, *Ch of Bd*
Marcus A Lemonis, *President*
Ronald Epstein, *Publisher*
Stuart Bourdon, *Editor*
Robert Filla, *Editor*
**EMP:** 24
**SALES:** 481.4MM
**SALES (corp-wide):** 1.4B  **Privately Held**
**SIC:** 5561  7997  2721  Recreational vehicle parts & accessories; membership sports & recreation clubs; magazines: publishing only, not printed on site
**HQ:** Affinity Group Holding, Llc
  2750 Park View Ct Ste 240
  Oxnard CA 93036
  805 667-4100

### (G-13451)
**GREAT LAKES MECH SVCS INC**
100 Tri State Intl  (60069-4403)
PHONE..................708 672-5900
Gary Lombardi, *CEO*
Chris Lombardi, *President*
Bill Brigham, *Sales Executive*
**EMP:** 12
**SQ FT:** 10,000
**SALES (est):** 1.3MM  **Privately Held**
**SIC:** 7699  1796  7692  Metal reshaping & replating services; mechanical instrument repair; installing building equipment; welding repair

### (G-13452)
**HANGER PROSTHETICS &**
Also Called: Hanger Clinic
300 Village Grn Ste 205  (60069-3079)
PHONE..................847 478-8154
Sam Liang, *President*
Angelo Bernardi, *Manager*
Sheryl Price, *Director*
**EMP:** 5
**SALES (corp-wide):** 459.1MM  **Publicly Held**
**SIC:** 3842  Orthopedic appliances
**HQ:** Hanger Prosthetics & Orthotics East, Inc.
  33 North Ave Ste 101
  Tallmadge OH 44278
  330 633-9807

### (G-13453)
**HCS HAHN CALIBRATION SERVICE**
20575 N William Ave  (60069-9602)
PHONE..................847 567-2500
William Hahn, *President*
Laurie Hahn, *Vice Pres*
**EMP:** 1
**SALES (est):** 226.7K  **Privately Held**
**SIC:** 3821  Calibration tapes for physical testing machines

### (G-13454)
**HONEYWELL ANALYTICS INC (HQ)**
405 Barclay Blvd  (60069-3609)
PHONE..................847 955-8200
Fax: 847 955-8210
Carl Johnson, *President*
Cesar Cabanzo, *Business Mgr*
Thomas Cinko, *Business Mgr*
Todd Smith, *Business Mgr*
Paul H Brownstein, *Vice Pres*
▲ **EMP:** 175
**SALES (est):** 178.6MM
**SALES (corp-wide):** 39.3B  **Publicly Held**
**WEB:** www.honeywell.com
**SIC:** 3491  3829  Process control regulator valves; gas detectors
**PA:** Honeywell International Inc.
  115 Tabor Rd
  Morris Plains NJ 07950
  973 455-2000

### (G-13455)
**HYDRAFORCE  INC (PA)**
500 Barclay Blvd  (60069-4314)
PHONE..................847 793-2300
Fax: 847 793-0087
James Brizzolara, *President*
Chuck Kloser, *Managing Dir*
Craig Sinnott, *Regional Mgr*
Greg Balog, *Vice Pres*
Bernhard Biederma, *Vice Pres*
▲ **EMP:** 252
**SQ FT:** 130,000
**SALES (est):** 197.3MM  **Privately Held**
**WEB:** www.hydraforce.com
**SIC:** 3492  Control valves, fluid power: hydraulic & pneumatic

### (G-13456)
**ICD PUBLICATIONS INC**
Also Called: Home World Business
175 Old Hlf Day Rd # 240  (60069-3063)
PHONE..................847 913-8295
Fax: 847 913-9202
Stefani O'Connor, *Editor*
Michael Reckling, *Sales Mgr*
Cyndi Evans, *Manager*
Allen Rolleri, *Director*
**EMP:** 3
**SALES (corp-wide):** 3.5MM  **Privately Held**
**WEB:** www.icdnet.com
**SIC:** 8743  2721  Sales promotion; periodicals
**PA:** Icd Publications Inc
  1377 Motor Pkwy Ste 410
  Islandia NY 11749
  631 246-9300

### (G-13457)
**ILLINOIS TOOL WORKS INC**
600 Knightsbridge Pkwy  (60069-3617)
PHONE..................847 537-8800
Chris Bauer, *Opers Mgr*
William Pence, *Accounts Mgr*
Ten Morency, *Manager*
**EMP:** 75
**SALES (corp-wide):** 13.6B  **Publicly Held**
**SIC:** 3644  Insulators & insulation materials, electrical
**PA:** Illinois Tool Works Inc.
  155 Harlem Ave
  Glenview IL 60025
  847 724-7500

### (G-13458)
**KIEFFER HOLDING CO (PA)**
585 Bond St  (60069-4226)
PHONE..................877 543-3337
Matthew Mele, *President*
Jeffrey Fuhrmann, *VP Mfg*
Mark Steffen, *Treasurer*
Larry Caracciolo, *VP Sales*
Stella Chaves, *Admin Sec*
**EMP:** 5  **Privately Held**
**SIC:** 3993  Electric signs

### (G-13459)
**KLEIN PLASTICS COMPANY LLC**
450 Bond St  (60069-4225)
PHONE..................616 863-9900
Jay Bylsma, *Controller*
Mathias Klein,
Ken Trupke,
**EMP:** 85
**SQ FT:** 70,000
**SALES (est):** 10.7MM  **Privately Held**
**SIC:** 3089  Injection molded finished plastic products

### (G-13460)
**KLEIN TOOLS  INC (PA)**
450 Bond St  (60069-4225)
P.O. Box 1418  (60069-1418)
PHONE..................847 821-5500
Fax: 847 478-0625
Mark Klein, *President*
Thomas R Klein Jr, *President*
Ryan Wojtkiewicz, *General Mgr*
Thomas R Klein, *Chairman*
David Inman, *District Mgr*
◆ **EMP:** 380  **EST:** 1958
**SQ FT:** 210,000
**SALES (est):** 344.9MM  **Privately Held**
**WEB:** www.kleintools.com
**SIC:** 3423  3199  Hand & edge tools; belting for machinery: solid, twisted, flat, etc.: leather; safety belts, leather

### (G-13461)
**KLEIN TOOLS  INC**
450 Bond St  (60069-4225)
PHONE..................847 821-5500
**EMP:** 48
**SALES (corp-wide):** 346.8MM  **Privately Held**
**SIC:** 3423  3199  3469  2899  Mfg Hand Edge Tools Leather Goods Metal Stampings And Chemical Preparation
**PA:** Klein Tools, Inc.
  450 Bond St
  Lincolnshire IL 60069
  847 821-5500

### (G-13462)
**LG INNOTEK USA INC**
2000 Millbrook Dr  (60069-3630)
PHONE..................847 941-8713
Patrick M Kang, *Marketing Staff*
**EMP:** 3
**SALES (corp-wide):** 4.5B  **Privately Held**
**SIC:** 3812  Defense systems & equipment
**HQ:** Lg Innotek Usa Inc
  2540 N 1st St Ste 400
  San Jose CA 95131
  408 955-0364

### (G-13463)
**LIBERTY MACHINERY COMPANY**
111 Schelter Rd  (60069-3603)
PHONE..................847 276-2761
Peter Sonneborn, *President*
▼ **EMP:** 10  **EST:** 1996
**SQ FT:** 23,000
**SALES (est):** 2MM  **Privately Held**
**WEB:** www.libertymachinery.com
**SIC:** 3441  5084  Fabricated structural metal; industrial machinery & equipment

### (G-13464)
**MCALLISTER EQUIPMENT CO**
100 Tri State Intl # 215  (60069-4427)
PHONE..................217 789-0351
Dave Piehler, *Marketing Staff*
Dave Peters, *Manager*
**EMP:** 28
**SALES (corp-wide):** 19.1MM  **Privately Held**
**SIC:** 3053  Packing: steam engines, pipe joints, air compressors, etc.
**PA:** Mcallister Equipment Co.
  12500 S Cicero Ave
  Alsip IL 60803
  708 389-7700

### (G-13465)
**MIDMARK CORPORATION**
Progeny
675 Heathrow Dr  (60069-4206)
PHONE..................847 415-9800
Edwin J McDonough, *Branch Mgr*
**EMP:** 69
**SALES (corp-wide):** 390MM  **Privately Held**
**WEB:** www.midmark.com
**SIC:** 3844  X-ray apparatus & tubes
**PA:** Midmark Corporation
  60 Vista Dr
  Versailles OH 45380
  937 526-3662

### (G-13466)
**MOLEX  LLC**
Woodhead
333 Knightsbridge Pkwy # 200  (60069-3662)
PHONE..................847 353-2500
Fax: 847 883-8732
Philippe Lemaitre, *CEO*
Joe Murphy, *Engineer*
**EMP:** 15
**SALES (corp-wide):** 27.4B  **Privately Held**
**SIC:** 3678  Electronic connectors
**HQ:** Molex, Llc
  2222 Wellington Ct
  Lisle IL 60532
  630 969-4550

# GEOGRAPHIC SECTION
## Lincolnshire - Lake County (G-13490)

**(G-13467)**
**NICHOLS ALUMINUM LLC**
200 Schelter Rd (60069-3635)
P.O. Box 1401 (60069-1401)
PHONE..................847 634-3150
Sean M Stack, *CEO*
Dave Sallander, *Info Tech Mgr*
**EMP:** 106 **Privately Held**
**WEB:** www.nicholsal.com
**SIC:** 3354 3353 Shapes, extruded aluminum; aluminum sheet, plate & foil
**HQ:** Nichols Aluminum Llc
25825 Science Park Dr # 400
Beachwood OH 44122

**(G-13468)**
**NILES AUTO PARTS**
20734 N Elizabeth Ave (60069-9631)
PHONE..................847 215-2549
Paul Mitsui, *President*
Sheryl Mitsui, *Admin Sec*
**EMP:** 4 **EST:** 1968
**SQ FT:** 2,800
**SALES:** 550K **Privately Held**
**SIC:** 5531 5013 3694 3625 Automotive parts; automotive supplies & parts; engine electrical equipment; relays & industrial controls

**(G-13469)**
**PACTIV LLC**
605 Heathrow Dr (60069-4206)
**EMP:** 150 **Privately Held**
**SIC:** 2631 2673 3714 3731 Mfg Packaging Products Data Processing Preparation
**HQ:** Pactiv Llc
1900 W Field Ct
Lake Forest IL 60045
847 482-2000

**(G-13470)**
**PAPER GRAPHICS INC**
612 Heathrow Dr (60069-4205)
PHONE..................847 276-2727
Craig Funk, *President*
**EMP:** 3
**SALES (est):** 194.1K **Privately Held**
**SIC:** 2893 Printing ink

**(G-13471)**
**PARALLELDIRECT LLC**
Also Called: Magic Mist, The
103 Schelter Rd Ste 20 (60069-3657)
PHONE..................847 748-2025
Guru Charan,
Amit Aggarwal,
Sanjay Veerkar,
**EMP:** 7 **EST:** 2011
**SALES:** 400.8K **Privately Held**
**SIC:** 2131 7389 Smoking tobacco;

**(G-13472)**
**PARKER-HANNIFIN CORPORATION**
Also Called: Hydralic Cartridge Systems Div
595 Schelter Rd Ste 100 (60069-4220)
PHONE..................847 955-5000
**Fax:** 847 821-7600
Peggy Barr, *Vice Pres*
Boris Peysin, *Engineer*
Antonio Morales, *Manager*
Chuck Divincenzo, *Manager*
Robert Nelson, *Manager*
**EMP:** 200
**SALES (corp-wide):** 11.3B **Publicly Held**
**WEB:** www.parker.com
**SIC:** 3594 Fluid power pumps
**PA:** Parker-Hannifin Corporation
6035 Parkland Blvd
Cleveland OH 44124
216 896-3000

**(G-13473)**
**PERFORMANCE MILITARY GROUP INC**
300 Knightsbridge Pkwy # 116 (60069-3663)
PHONE..................847 325-4450
Gary Weisbaum, *President*
Lenore Kelly, *Director*
**EMP:** 8
**SALES (est):** 750.1K **Privately Held**
**WEB:** www.performancemilitarygroup.com
**SIC:** 3711 Military motor vehicle assembly

**(G-13474)**
**PHENOME TECHNOLOGIES INC**
23220 N Indian Creek Rd (60069-2925)
PHONE..................847 962-1273
Michael J Wellems, *President*
Debbie A Masloskie, *Vice Pres*
**EMP:** 3
**SALES:** 350K **Privately Held**
**WEB:** www.phenometechnologies.com
**SIC:** 3841 Surgical & medical instruments

**(G-13475)**
**SAPUTO CHEESE USA INC**
1 Overlook Pt Ste 300 (60069-4327)
PHONE..................847 267-1100
John Schneider, *Branch Mgr*
**EMP:** 160
**SALES (corp-wide):** 85.7K **Privately Held**
**SIC:** 2022 Natural cheese
**HQ:** Saputo Cheese Usa Inc.
1 Overlook Pt Ste 300
Lincolnshire IL 60069
847 267-1100

**(G-13476)**
**SAPUTO CHEESE USA INC (DH)**
1 Overlook Pt Ste 300 (60069-4327)
PHONE..................847 267-1100
Lino A Saputo Jr, *President*
Terry Brockman, *Vice Pres*
Ernie Carreiro, *Vice Pres*
Dominique Delugeau, *Vice Pres*
Chris Sandretti, *Vice Pres*
▲ **EMP:** 100
**SALES (est):** 8B
**SALES (corp-wide):** 85.7K **Privately Held**
**SIC:** 2022 Cheese spreads, dips, pastes & other cheese products
**HQ:** Saputo Inc
6869 Boul Metropolitain E
Saint-Leonard QC H1P 1
514 328-6662

**(G-13477)**
**SENTRAL ASSEMBLIES LLC (HQ)**
Also Called: Conectec International
595 Bond St (60069-4226)
PHONE..................847 478-9720
**Fax:** 847 478-9740
Edward Kus, *Opers Staff*
John Graham, *Engineer*
Andy Workman, *Project Engr*
Debbie Kemsley, *Accounting Mgr*
Veronica Lopez, *Hum Res Coord*
**EMP:** 100
**SQ FT:** 40,000
**SALES (est):** 25.5MM
**SALES (corp-wide):** 26.3MM **Privately Held**
**WEB:** www.sentral.com
**SIC:** 3679 Harness assemblies for electronic use; wire or cable
**PA:** Sentral Group Llc
595 Bond St
Lincolnshire IL 60069
847 478-9720

**(G-13478)**
**SENTRAL GROUP LLC (PA)**
595 Bond St (60069-4226)
PHONE..................847 478-9720
Sandra Fletcher, *Sales Associate*
Randall Olech,
John Carretta,
**EMP:** 6 **EST:** 2011
**SALES (est):** 26.3MM **Privately Held**
**SIC:** 3679 3694 6719 Harness assemblies for electronic use: wire or cable; harness wiring sets, internal combustion engines; investment holding companies, except banks

**(G-13479)**
**SF HOLDINGS GROUP INC (HQ)**
Also Called: Solo Cup
300 Tr State Intl Ste 200 (60069)
PHONE..................847 831-4800
**Fax:** 847 831-0424
Robert M Korzenski, *CEO*
Julie Harvey, *COO*
Robert D Koney Jr, *Exec VP*
Robert Koney, *Exec VP*
Susan Marks, *Exec VP*
▼ **EMP:** 71

**SALES (est):** 77.6MM
**SALES (corp-wide):** 1.3B **Privately Held**
**SIC:** 2656 Plates, paper: made from purchased material; food containers (liquid tight), including milk cartons
**PA:** Solo Cup Company Llc
300 Tri State Intl # 200
Lincolnshire IL 60069
847 444-5000

**(G-13480)**
**SOLO CUP COMPANY (HQ)**
300 Tri State Intl # 200 (60069-4415)
PHONE..................847 831-4800
**Fax:** 847 579-3245
Robert M Korzenski, *President*
Pete Mendola, *Senior VP*
Mike Northington, *Warehouse Mgr*
Ludmila Piskoun, *Buyer*
Susan Davis, *Human Res Mgr*
▼ **EMP:** 187 **EST:** 2004
**SALES (est):** 701.5MM
**SALES (corp-wide):** 1.3B **Privately Held**
**WEB:** www.solocup.com
**SIC:** 3089 3421 2656 Cups, plastic, except foam; plates, plastic; plastic containers, except foam; cutlery; straws, drinking: made from purchased material

**(G-13481)**
**SOLO CUP COMPANY LLC (PA)**
300 Tri State Intl # 200 (60069-4415)
PHONE..................847 444-5000
Robert C Dart, *CEO*
Steve Jungmann, *Senior VP*
Jan Stern Reed, *Vice Pres*
Ronald E Wesel, *Vice Pres*
Chris Koenig, *Project Mgr*
▲ **EMP:** 150
**SQ FT:** 133,218
**SALES (est):** 1.3B **Privately Held**
**SIC:** 3089 2656 3421 Cups, plastic, except foam; plates, plastic; plastic containers, except foam; straws, drinking: made from purchased material; cutlery

**(G-13482)**
**SOLO CUP OPERATING CORPORATION (DH)**
300 Tr State Intl Ste 200 (60069)
PHONE..................847 444-5000
Robert C Dart, *President*
Jim Kallikragas, *COO*
James W Nellen, *CFO*
Linda Ridgley, *Treasurer*
Gary Gobeli, *Controller*
▼ **EMP:** 100
**SALES (est):** 11.9MM
**SALES (corp-wide):** 1.3B **Privately Held**
**WEB:** www.sweetheart.com
**SIC:** 3089 2656 3556 Plastic kitchenware, tableware & houseware; cups, plastic, except foam; plates, plastic; plastic containers, except foam; paper cups, plates, dishes & utensils; cups, paper: made from purchased material; plates, paper: made from purchased material; straws, drinking: made from purchased material; food products machinery
**HQ:** Sf Holdings Group, Inc.
300 Tr State Intl Ste 200
Lincolnshire IL 60069
847 831-4800

**(G-13483)**
**SWIRLCUP**
255 Parkway Dr Ste B (60069-4311)
PHONE..................847 229-2200
**EMP:** 8
**SALES (est):** 250K **Privately Held**
**SIC:** 2051 Mfg Bread/Related Products

**(G-13484)**
**SYSMEX AMERICA INC (HQ)**
577 Aptakisic Rd (60069-4325)
PHONE..................847 996-4500
**Fax:** 847 996-4559
John Kershaw, *President*
Cathleen Fuhrman, *Business Mgr*
Jeffrey Hawkins, *Business Mgr*
Robert Degnan, *Exec VP*
Andre Ezers, *Exec VP*

▼ **EMP:** 125
**SQ FT:** 55,000
**SALES:** 280.3MM
**SALES (corp-wide):** 2.1B **Privately Held**
**WEB:** www.sysmex.com
**SIC:** 5047 3841 Instruments, surgical & medical; medical instruments & equipment, blood & bone work
**PA:** Sysmex Corporation
1-5-1, Wakinohamakaigandori, Chuo-Ku
Kobe HYO 651-0
782 650-500

**(G-13485)**
**TENNECO AUTOMOTIVE OPER CO INC**
605 Heathrow Dr (60069-4206)
PHONE..................847 821-0757
Ken Wengzen, *Purchasing*
Dave Shanaberger, *Branch Mgr*
Masoud Mobli, *Manager*
Tom Schaid, *CTO*
Frank Monteleone, *Exec Dir*
**EMP:** 204
**SALES (corp-wide):** 8.6B **Publicly Held**
**WEB:** www.tenneco-automotive.com
**SIC:** 3714 Motor vehicle parts & accessories
**HQ:** Tenneco Automotive Operating Company, Inc.
500 N Field Dr
Lake Forest IL 60045
847 482-5000

**(G-13486)**
**TRADEMARK CABINET CORPORATION**
101 Schelter Rd Ste 201b (60069-3656)
PHONE..................847 478-9393
Mark Elsesser, *President*
**EMP:** 2
**SALES (est):** 325.6K **Privately Held**
**WEB:** www.tmcc.net
**SIC:** 2434 Wood kitchen cabinets

**(G-13487)**
**UNITED PRESS INC (DEL)**
211 Northampton Ln (60069-2400)
PHONE..................847 482-0597
**Fax:** 847 482-0624
Robert Deer, *President*
Michael Deer, *Prgrmr*
**EMP:** 16
**SALES:** 1MM **Privately Held**
**SIC:** 2752 2771 2657 Commercial printing, offset; greeting cards; folding paperboard boxes

**(G-13488)**
**VAREX IMAGING CORPORATION**
425 Barclay Blvd (60069-3609)
PHONE..................847 279-5121
Barry Smith, *Manager*
**EMP:** 21
**SALES (corp-wide):** 3.2B **Publicly Held**
**SIC:** 3844 X-ray apparatus & tubes
**HQ:** Varex Imaging Corporation
1678 S Pioneer Rd
Salt Lake City UT 84104
801 972-5000

**(G-13489)**
**VICTOR CONSULTING**
42 Cumberland Dr 2a (60069-3109)
PHONE..................847 267-8012
Barry Tauber, *Principal*
Catherine Tauber, *Principal*
**EMP:** 9
**SALES:** 250K **Privately Held**
**SIC:** 7372 Educational computer software

**(G-13490)**
**WOODHEAD INDUSTRIES LLC (DH)**
333 Knightsbridge Pkwy # 200 (60069-3662)
PHONE..................847 353-2500
Philippe Lemaitre, *Ch of Bd*
Gregory Baker, *Vice Pres*
Michael Gies, *Vice Pres*
Robert A Moulton, *Vice Pres*
John Newark, *Vice Pres*
▲ **EMP:** 500
**SQ FT:** 11,600

# Lincolnshire - Lake County (G-13491)

SALES (est): 113.8MM
SALES (corp-wide): 27.4B **Privately Held**
WEB: www.woodhead.com
SIC: **3678** 3679 3643 3357 Electronic connectors; electronic switches; electronic circuits; connectors & terminals for electrical devices; communication wire; fiber optic cable (insulated)
HQ: Molex, Llc
2222 Wellington Ct
Lisle IL 60532
630 969-4550

**(G-13491)**
**XFPG LLC**
300 Knightsbridge Pkwy (60069-3625)
PHONE.................................224 513-2010
Fax: 847 968-3899
Eric Lockwood, *COO*
Mike Cobb, *Vice Pres*
Lacey Devereaux, *Vice Pres*
Phil Noga, *Vice Pres*
Marybeth Reiff, *Vice Pres*
◆ EMP: 388
SALES (est): 752.8K **Privately Held**
SIC: **5023** 5064 3634 Kitchenware; electric household appliances; housewares, excluding cooking appliances & utensils

**(G-13492)**
**ZAH GROUP INC (PA)**
450 Bond St (60069-4225)
P.O. Box 1418 (60069-1418)
PHONE.................................847 821-5500
Thomas R Klein, *President*
EMP: 1
SALES (est): 284.2K **Privately Held**
SIC: **3423** Hand & edge tools

**(G-13493)**
**ZEBRA ENTP SOLUTIONS CORP (HQ)**
3 Overlook Pt (60069-4302)
PHONE.................................847 634-6700
Michael Terzich, *CEO*
David Wisherd, *Ch of Bd*
Bill Walch, *Principal*
Megan Carroll, *Project Mgr*
Michael Smiley, *CFO*
EMP: 40
SQ FT: 20,000
SALES (est): 11.7MM
SALES (corp-wide): 3.5B **Publicly Held**
WEB: www.wherenet.com
SIC: **3812** Navigational systems & instruments
PA: Zebra Technologies Corporation
3 Overlook Pt
Lincolnshire IL 60069
847 634-6700

**(G-13494)**
**ZEBRA TECHNOLOGIES CORPORATION (PA)**
3 Overlook Pt (60069-4302)
PHONE.................................847 634-6700
Fax: 847 634-1830
Anders Gustafsson, *CEO*
Michael A Smith, *Ch of Bd*
William Burns, *Senior VP*
Michael Cho, *Senior VP*
Hugh K Gagnier, *Senior VP*
▲ EMP: 265
SALES: 3.5B **Publicly Held**
WEB: www.zebra.com
SIC: **3577** 2672 2679 5045 Bar code (magnetic ink) printers; adhesive papers, labels or tapes: from purchased material; labels (unprinted); gummed: made from purchased materials; tags, paper (unprinted): made from purchased paper; computers, peripherals & software

**(G-13495)**
**ZEBRA TECHNOLOGIES INTL LLC (HQ)**
3 Overlook Pt (60069-4302)
PHONE.................................847 634-6700
Philip Gerskovich, *Principal*
Donald F Oshea, *Vice Pres*
Joe Weadick, *Engineer*
Bruce Alph, *VP Human Res*
Ken Pywell, *Sales Staff*
◆ EMP: 6

SALES (est): 7.7MM
SALES (corp-wide): 3.5B **Publicly Held**
SIC: **3577** Bar code (magnetic ink) printers
PA: Zebra Technologies Corporation
3 Overlook Pt
Lincolnshire IL 60069
847 634-6700

**(G-13496)**
**ZENITH ELECTRONICS CORPORATION (DH)**
2000 Millbrook Dr (60069-3630)
PHONE.................................847 941-8000
Fax: 847 941-8177
Tok Joo Lee, *Ch of Bd*
Michael K Ahn, *Senior VP*
Ron Snaidauf, *Vice Pres*
Beverley Wyckoff, *Vice Pres*
Paul Krutiak, *Purch Dir*
EMP: 46 EST: 1918
SALES (est): 138.2MM
SALES (corp-wide): 24.3B **Privately Held**
WEB: www.zenith.com
SIC: **3651** 3671 3663 3674 Household audio & video equipment; television receiving sets; video cassette recorders/players & accessories; television tubes; television broadcasting & communications equipment; cable television equipment; microcircuits, integrated (semiconductor); television cabinets, wood; television cabinets, plastic
HQ: Lg Electronics U.S.A., Inc.
1000 Sylvan Ave
Englewood Cliffs NJ 07632
201 816-2000

**(G-13497)**
**ZIH CORP (HQ)**
3 Overlook Pt (60069-4302)
PHONE.................................847 634-6700
Anders Gustafsson, *CEO*
Gerhard Cless, *Exec VP*
Michael C Smiley, *CFO*
▲ EMP: 8
SQ FT: 154,300
SALES (est): 1MM
SALES (corp-wide): 3.5B **Publicly Held**
SIC: **3577** 2672 Bar code (magnetic ink) printers; adhesive papers, labels or tapes: from purchased material; labels (unprinted); gummed: made from purchased materials
PA: Zebra Technologies Corporation
3 Overlook Pt
Lincolnshire IL 60069
847 634-6700

**(G-13498)**
**ZIH CORP**
Also Called: Zebra
3 Overlook Pt (60069-4302)
PHONE.................................847 634-6700
EMP: 26
SALES (est): 5.5MM
SALES (corp-wide): 3.6B **Publicly Held**
SIC: **3577** Mfg Computer Peripheral Equipment
PA: Zebra Technologies Corporation
3 Overlook Pt
Lincolnshire IL 60069
847 634-6700

## Lincolnwood
### Cook County

**(G-13499)**
**ABCT CORPORATION**
3924 W Devon Ave Ste 300 (60712-1040)
PHONE.................................773 427-1010
EMP: 5 **Privately Held**
SIC: **5999** 3499 Art, picture frames & decorations; picture frames, metal
PA: Abct Corporation
1809 W Webster Ave
Chicago IL

**(G-13500)**
**ADA METAL PRODUCTS INC**
7120 N Capitol Dr (60712-2702)
PHONE.................................847 673-1190
Fax: 847 673-1162
Peter Barkules, *President*

Byron Barkules, *Vice Pres*
Rene Campos, *Production*
Jon Croskey, *Buyer*
William Barkules, *Treasurer*
EMP: 38 EST: 1945
SQ FT: 63,000
SALES (est): 8.4MM **Privately Held**
WEB: www.adametal.com
SIC: **3465** Automotive stampings

**(G-13501)**
**ADVANCED PLASTIC CORP**
3725 W Lunt Ave (60712-2615)
PHONE.................................847 674-2070
Fax: 847 674-2072
Harold Koenig, *President*
James Stoesser, *Vice Pres*
Jim Stoesser, *Vice Pres*
Lewis Kirkwood, *Purch Agent*
Tom Spear, *Sales Mgr*
▲ EMP: 80 EST: 1981
SQ FT: 75,000
SALES (est): 24.6MM **Privately Held**
WEB: www.advancedplastic.com
SIC: **3082** Rods, unsupported plastic; tubes, unsupported plastic

**(G-13502)**
**ALL CONTAINER INC**
7060 N Lawndale Ave (60712-2610)
PHONE.................................847 677-2100
Linda Worley, *Manager*
EMP: 8 EST: 1968
SALES (est): 796.4K **Privately Held**
SIC: **3411** Metal cans

**(G-13503)**
**BROWN WOOD PRODUCTS COMPANY (PA)**
Also Called: Gavel Company Div, The
7040 N Lawndale Ave (60712-2610)
P.O. Box 598052, Chicago (60659-8052)
PHONE.................................847 673-4780
Fax: 847 673-7381
Terry D Gross, *President*
Todd Dennison, *General Mgr*
Amy Mikal, *Vice Pres*
Dano Pinkham, *Vice Pres*
Kathryn Constantine, *VP Sls/Mktg*
▲ EMP: 14 EST: 1927
SQ FT: 18,000
SALES (est): 3.2MM **Privately Held**
WEB: www.brownwoodinc.com
SIC: **2499** 2431 5199 Carved & turned wood; interior & ornamental woodwork & trim; advertising specialties

**(G-13504)**
**BUSTER SNOW INC**
7356 N Kildare Ave (60712-1918)
PHONE.................................847 673-4275
Louis Napravnik, *Owner*
EMP: 3
SALES (est): 252.8K **Privately Held**
SIC: **2851** Removers & cleaners

**(G-13505)**
**CORPORATE TEXTILES INC**
6529 N Lincoln Ave 5 (60712-3925)
PHONE.................................847 433-4111
Arnold L Kapp, *President*
EMP: 2
SQ FT: 1,000
SALES (est): 240K **Privately Held**
WEB: www.shop4ties.com
SIC: **2323** Neckties, men's & boys': made from purchased materials

**(G-13506)**
**DANZIGER KOSHER CATERING INC**
Also Called: Classic Foods
3910 W Devon Ave (60712-1099)
PHONE.................................847 982-1818
Fax: 847 982-1168
Stuart Morginstin, *President*
Kathy Ramos, *Sales Mgr*
Gerhart Asanger, *Manager*
Howard Wax, *Director*
▲ EMP: 30 EST: 1948
SQ FT: 30,000
SALES (est): 1.6MM **Privately Held**
SIC: **5812** 2038 Caterers; frozen specialties

**(G-13507)**
**DENTAL TECHNOLOGIES INC**
6901 N Hamlin Ave (60712-2553)
PHONE.................................847 677-5500
Stephen Erickson, *President*
Alfonso Zepeda, *Marketing Staff*
Paula Erickson, *Admin Sec*
Kyle Kudelka, *Representative*
▲ EMP: 70
SQ FT: 40,000
SALES (est): 21MM **Privately Held**
WEB: www.dentaltechno.com
SIC: **2834** 3843 Pharmaceutical preparations; dental equipment & supplies

**(G-13508)**
**DYNAMIC AUTOMATION INC**
3445 W Arthur Ave (60712-3841)
PHONE.................................312 782-8555
Fax: 312 782-8808
Shaun Nejati, *President*
EMP: 6
SALES (est): 420K **Privately Held**
WEB: www.dynamicgear.com
SIC: **8711** 3541 Mechanical engineering; screw machines, automatic; tapping machines

**(G-13509)**
**FASTSIGNS**
3450 W Devon Ave (60712-1304)
PHONE.................................847 675-1600
Fax: 847 675-1614
Elizabeth Oconnor, *President*
David Spaeth, *General Mgr*
EMP: 5
SQ FT: 1,800
SALES (est): 569.9K **Privately Held**
SIC: **3993** 8712 Signs & advertising specialties; architectural services

**(G-13510)**
**FEDEX OFFICE & PRINT SVCS INC**
6829 N Lincoln Ave (60712-2623)
PHONE.................................847 329-9464
Tomhugo Demenn, *Manager*
Tamika Longstreet, *Admin Mgr*
EMP: 12
SALES (corp-wide): 50.3B **Publicly Held**
WEB: www.kinkos.com
SIC: **7334** 2791 2789 2672 Photocopying & duplicating services; typesetting; bookbinding & related work; coated & laminated paper
HQ: Fedex Office And Print Services, Inc.
7900 Legacy Dr
Plano TX 75024
214 550-7000

**(G-13511)**
**FREESHOPPER AD PAPER INC**
7301 N Lincoln Ave # 185 (60712-1736)
PHONE.................................847 675-2783
Rich Schwartz, *President*
EMP: 9
SALES (est): 375.5K **Privately Held**
WEB: www.freeshopper.com
SIC: **2711** Newspapers

**(G-13512)**
**GAGE ASSEMBLY CO**
3771 W Morse Ave (60712-2684)
PHONE.................................847 679-5180
Fax: 847 679-5190
Daniel Plodzeen, *President*
Brad Plodzeen, *COO*
Dawn Wittig, *Human Res Mgr*
EMP: 55 EST: 1953
SQ FT: 23,000
SALES (est): 9.6MM **Privately Held**
SIC: **3545** Gauges (machine tool accessories); threading tools (machine tool accessories)

**(G-13513)**
**GENERAL CUTNG TL SVC & MFG INC**
6440 N Ridgeway Ave (60712-4028)
PHONE.................................847 677-8770
Fax: 847 677-8786
Les J Kasperek, *President*
Joseph Carone, *Vice Pres*
Robert Kasperek, *Mktg Dir*
Yolanda Kasperek, *Admin Sec*

## GEOGRAPHIC SECTION
## Lincolnwood - Cook County (G-13537)

**EMP:** 18 **EST:** 1978
**SQ FT:** 7,500
**SALES (est):** 6.3MM **Privately Held**
**WEB:** www.gencuttingtool.com
**SIC:** 5085 3545 Industrial tools; machine knives, metalworking; precision tools, machinists'; shaping tools (machine tool accessories)

### (G-13514)
### GERALD GRAFF
Also Called: Aaron Co
6818 N Kildare Ave (60712-4726)
**PHONE**..................312 343-2612
Gerald Graff, *Owner*
**EMP:** 20
**SALES (est):** 1.1MM **Privately Held**
**SIC:** 2451 Mobile homes

### (G-13515)
### GLENAIR INC
Also Called: Microway Systems Div Glenair
7000 N Lawndale Ave (60712-2610)
**PHONE**..................847 679-8833
Donald Carroll, *Branch Mgr*
**EMP:** 48
**SALES (corp-wide):** 331.6MM **Privately Held**
**SIC:** 3678 Electronic connectors
**PA:** Glenair, Inc.
  1211 Air Way
  Glendale CA 91201
  818 247-6000

### (G-13516)
### JBSMWG CORP
7170 N Ridgeway Ave (60712-2622)
**PHONE**..................847 675-1865
**Fax:** 847 675-3345
Basil Jacobson, *President*
Frank Guihan, *Vice Pres*
Ann Trujillo, *Financial Exec*
Ann Trujillo, *Manager*
Michael Shade, *Admin Sec*
▲ **EMP:** 10
**SALES (est):** 1.3MM **Privately Held**
**WEB:** www.icd-sales.com
**SIC:** 3675 Electronic capacitors

### (G-13517)
### JVI INC
7131 N Ridgeway Ave (60712-2621)
**PHONE**..................847 675-1560
James Voss, *President*
Rafael Resendez, *Sales Staff*
▼ **EMP:** 20
**SQ FT:** 12,000
**SALES (est):** 3.4MM **Privately Held**
**WEB:** www.jvi-inc.com
**SIC:** 3069 Hard rubber & molded rubber products

### (G-13518)
### K CHAE CORP
Also Called: Modern Card Co
3630 W Pratt Ave (60712-3724)
**PHONE**..................847 763-0077
Kris Chae, *President*
**EMP:** 10
**SALES (est):** 1.1MM **Privately Held**
**WEB:** www.novocard.net
**SIC:** 2771 2752 Greeting cards; commercial printing, offset

### (G-13519)
### KIM TIFFANI INSTITUTE LLC
3926 W Touhy Ave 310 (60712-1028)
**PHONE**..................312 260-9000
**Fax:** 312 260-9096
Jackie Kim, *Principal*
Jason Bussel, *Acupuncture*
▲ **EMP:** 80
**SALES (est):** 7.9MM **Privately Held**
**SIC:** 3999 7231 Hair, dressing of, for the trade; beauty shops

### (G-13520)
### LA SWEET INC
4433 W Touhy Ave Ste 207 (60712-1833)
**PHONE**..................252 340-0390
Stacy Katsibaros, *CEO*
**EMP:** 12 **EST:** 2013
**SQ FT:** 12,500
**SALES (est):** 460K **Privately Held**
**SIC:** 2064 Candy & other confectionery products

### (G-13521)
### LIPSNER SMITH CO
Also Called: RGI Group
4700 W Chase Ave (60712-1608)
**PHONE**..................847 677-3000
**Fax:** 847 677-1311
Jonathan Banks, *President*
Calvin Hasselbring, *Purch Agent*
William Deiker, *Regl Sales Mgr*
**EMP:** 5
**SQ FT:** 52,500
**SALES (est):** 487.6K
**SALES (corp-wide):** 7MM **Privately Held**
**WEB:** www.lipsner.com
**SIC:** 3861 Photographic processing equipment & chemicals
**PA:** Research Technology International Company
  4700 W Chase Ave
  Lincolnwood IL 60712
  847 677-3000

### (G-13522)
### LL DISPLAY GROUP LTD
7085 N Ridgeway Ave (60712-2619)
**PHONE**..................847 982-0231
**Fax:** 847 982-1519
Justin Malczynski, *Purchasing*
Tom Ferraro, *Accountant*
Scott Durham, *VP Sales*
Robert Aleman, *Manager*
**EMP:** 35
**SQ FT:** 25,000
**SALES (est):** 8.4MM **Privately Held**
**WEB:** www.lldisplay.com
**SIC:** 2821 Molding compounds, plastics

### (G-13523)
### LOGAN SQUARE ALUMINUM SUP INC
Also Called: Studio 41
4767 W Touhy Ave (60712-1622)
**PHONE**..................847 676-4767
**Fax:** 847 677-8701
Evaristo Roman, *Branch Mgr*
**EMP:** 10
**SALES (corp-wide):** 101.1MM **Privately Held**
**WEB:** www.remodelerssupply.com
**SIC:** 3442 Window & door frames
**PA:** Logan Square Aluminum Supply, Inc.
  2500 N Pulaski Rd
  Chicago IL 60639
  773 235-2500

### (G-13524)
### MARC BUSINESS FORMS INC
6416 N Ridgeway Ave (60712-4028)
**PHONE**..................847 568-9200
**Fax:** 847 568-9272
Barbara Faermark, *President*
Charlotte Marcuse, *Corp Secy*
Edith Wittner, *Office Mgr*
**EMP:** 10
**SQ FT:** 2,400
**SALES (est):** 1.4MM **Privately Held**
**WEB:** www.marcprint.com
**SIC:** 5112 2761 2752 Business forms; manifold business forms; commercial printing, lithographic

### (G-13525)
### MICROWAY SYSTEMS INC
7000 N Lawndale Ave (60712-2610)
**PHONE**..................847 679-8833
Richard Zic, *President*
**EMP:** 44
**SQ FT:** 24,000
**SALES (est):** 6.6MM **Privately Held**
**SIC:** 3678 Electronic connectors

### (G-13526)
### NEW METAL CRAFTS INC
6453 N Kilpatrick Ave (60712-3416)
**PHONE**..................312 787-6991
**Fax:** 773 342-5733
James R Neumann, *President*
Sol Biewiess, *Corp Secy*
Noel O'Brien, *Controller*
Paul Jurkschat, *Manager*
▲ **EMP:** 50
**SQ FT:** 40,000
**SALES (est):** 6.3MM **Privately Held**
**WEB:** www.newmetalcrafts.com
**SIC:** 3646 3645 5063 7349 Ornamental lighting fixtures, commercial; residential lighting fixtures; lighting fixtures, commercial & industrial; lighting fixtures, residential; building maintenance services

### (G-13527)
### NIGHT VISION CORPORATION
4324 W Chase Ave (60712-1915)
**PHONE**..................847 677-7611
**Fax:** 847 329-1358
Danny Filipovich, *President*
Thomas J Karacic, *Vice Pres*
**EMP:** 5
**SQ FT:** 2,200
**SALES (est):** 820.2K **Privately Held**
**SIC:** 8732 3851 Commercial nonphysical research; ophthalmic goods

### (G-13528)
### NYLOK FASTENER CORPORATION
Also Called: Nylok Chicago
6465 N Proesel Ave (60712-3916)
**PHONE**..................847 674-9680
**Fax:** 847 674-1269
Pete Henley, *Vice Pres*
Emina Jimenez, *Sales Associate*
**EMP:** 75
**SALES (corp-wide):** 223.6B **Publicly Held**
**SIC:** 3452 Screws, metal
**HQ:** Nylok Fastener Corporation
  15260 Hallmark Ct
  Macomb MI 48042
  586 786-0100

### (G-13529)
### PEERLESS CONFECTION COMPANY (PA)
7383 N Lincoln Ave # 100 (60712-1734)
**PHONE**..................773 281-6100
**Fax:** 773 281-5812
Kathleen Picken, *Ch of Bd*
Richard C Lyman, *President*
Judy Criniti, *Regional Mgr*
Jo Ann Pickett, *Vice Pres*
Alan Hamann, *Facilities Mgr*
**EMP:** 100
**SQ FT:** 175,000
**SALES (est):** 7.1MM **Privately Held**
**WEB:** www.peerlesscandy.com
**SIC:** 2064 Candy & other confectionery products

### (G-13530)
### QUALIFRESH LLC
7301 N Lincoln Ave # 180 (60712-1709)
**PHONE**..................847 337-1483
Phillip Skaff, *President*
Jim Schwab, *Vice Pres*
Vicky Danelski, *Admin Sec*
Issam Maatouk, 
**EMP:** 25
**SQ FT:** 35,000
**SALES:** 10MM **Privately Held**
**SIC:** 2099 Ready-to-eat meals, salads & sandwiches

### (G-13531)
### QUAY CORPORATION INC (PA)
Also Called: Mgr Imports
7101 N Capitol Dr (60712-2701)
**PHONE**..................847 676-4233
Victor Cuellar, *Ch of Bd*
Gerardo Fitz, *President*
Margaret Cuellar, *Vice Pres*
Hector Cuellar, *Shareholder*
▲ **EMP:** 16
**SQ FT:** 20,000
**SALES (est):** 5.1MM **Privately Held**
**SIC:** 2032 5149 5147 Mexican foods: packaged in cans, jars, etc.; dairy products, dried or canned; meats & meat products

### (G-13532)
### RESEARCH TECHNOLOGY INTL CO (PA)
Also Called: R T I
4700 W Chase Ave (60712-1608)
**PHONE**..................847 677-3000
Ray L Short Jr, *President*
Tom Boyle, *Senior VP*
Bill Wolavka, *Vice Pres*
Calvin Hasselbring, *Plant Mgr*
Richard Seidener, *Prdtn Mgr*
**EMP:** 40
**SQ FT:** 54,000
**SALES (est):** 7MM **Privately Held**
**WEB:** www.tapechek.com
**SIC:** 3861 Photographic equipment & supplies; motion picture apparatus & equipment

### (G-13533)
### RF MAU CO
7140 N Lawndale Ave (60712-2612)
**PHONE**..................847 329-9731
**Fax:** 847 673-4295
Bruce Mau, *President*
Brian J Adams, *President*
Steve Nitschneider, *Safety Dir*
Tony Gemignani, *Prdtn Mgr*
Cliff Garcia, *Mfg Mgr*
**EMP:** 15
**SQ FT:** 10,000
**SALES (est):** 4.1MM **Privately Held**
**WEB:** www.rfmau.com
**SIC:** 3494 3451 3599 Couplings, except pressure & soil pipe; screw machine products; tubing, flexible metallic

### (G-13534)
### ROLFS PATISSERIE INC
4343 W Touhy Ave (60712-1908)
**PHONE**..................847 675-6565
**Fax:** 847 329-7653
Lloyd Culbertson, *President*
Karon Leyva, *Manager*
Marisol Pagan, *Admin Mgr*
Ford Culbertson, *Admin Sec*
**EMP:** 110
**SQ FT:** 20,000
**SALES (est):** 13.5MM **Privately Held**
**WEB:** www.rolfspatisserie.com
**SIC:** 2051 Bakery: wholesale or wholesale/retail combined; pastries, e.g. danish: except frozen; cakes, bakery: except frozen; pies, bakery: except frozen

### (G-13535)
### RUTGERS ENTERPRISES INC (PA)
Also Called: MSI Southland
6511 W Proesel Ave (60712-3918)
**PHONE**..................847 674-7666
Rachel Grunfeld, *CEO*
Aaron Grunfeld, *President*
**EMP:** 5 **Privately Held**
**SIC:** 3053 3069 Gaskets & sealing devices; molded rubber products

### (G-13536)
### SAFE TRAFFIC SYSTEM INC
6600 N Lincoln Ave (60712-3620)
**PHONE**..................847 233-0365
**Fax:** 847 329-8112
Hyun Kim, *CEO*
Moon Kim, *Ch of Bd*
Hoon Y Kim, *President*
Paul Kim, *President*
Andrew Kim, *Mktg Dir*
▲ **EMP:** 5
**SQ FT:** 1,200
**SALES (est):** 450K **Privately Held**
**SIC:** 3944 Child restraint seats, automotive

### (G-13537)
### SHANIN COMPANY
6454 N Kimball Ave (60712-3814)
P.O. Box 577909, Chicago (60657-7341)
**PHONE**..................847 676-1200
Milton H Shanin, *President*
Raymond Shanin, *Vice Pres*
Greg Shanin, *Office Mgr*
Rose Shanin, *Office Mgr*
Jeffrey Shanin, *Admin Sec*
**EMP:** 60
**SALES (est):** 4.4MM **Privately Held**
**SIC:** 2752 2761 2759 Commercial printing, offset; business forms, lithographed; manifold business forms; commercial printing

# Lincolnwood - Cook County (G-13538)

**(G-13538)**
**SHARIN TOY COMPANY**
6460 N Lincoln Ave (60712-4038)
P.O. Box 597604, Chicago (60659-7604)
PHONE..................847 676-1200
Fax: 773 676-1254
Jeffrey Shanin, *President*
EMP: 50
SALES (est): 3.2MM **Privately Held**
SIC: 3944 Games, toys & children's vehicles; board games, children's & adults'; books, toy: picture & cutout; craft & hobby kits & sets

**(G-13539)**
**TERRANEO MERCHANTS INC**
6525 W Proesel Ave (60712-3918)
PHONE..................312 753-9134
Sasha Burekovic, *President*
EMP: 4
SQ FT: 2,000
SALES (est): 134.8K **Privately Held**
SIC: 2084 Wines

**(G-13540)**
**TRIM-TEX INC (PA)**
3700 W Pratt Ave (60712-2500)
PHONE..................847 679-3000
Fax: 847 679-3017
Joseph Koenig Jr, *President*
Leo Budzik, *COO*
William Dunn, *Vice Pres*
Katie Koenig, *VP Opers*
Linda Khalil, *Prdtn Mgr*
▲ EMP: 100
SQ FT: 218,000
SALES (est): 16.9MM **Privately Held**
WEB: www.trim-tex.com
SIC: 3089 Extruded finished plastic products

**(G-13541)**
**VOSS BELTING & SPECIALTY CO**
6965 N Hamlin Ave Ste 1 (60712-2598)
PHONE..................847 673-8900
Richard A Voss, *President*
Albert Craiss, *Vice Pres*
Dennis Johnson, *Plant Mgr*
Bruce Herr, *Controller*
Mike Covich, *Sales Mgr*
EMP: 45 EST: 1934
SQ FT: 48,000
SALES: 9MM **Privately Held**
WEB: www.vossbelting.com
SIC: 3052 3069 2822 2821 Rubber belting; hard rubber products; silicone rubbers; polytetrafluoroethylene resins (teflon); coated & laminated paper; narrow fabric mills

**(G-13542)**
**VOSS ENGINEERING INC**
6965 N Hamlin Ave Ste 1 (60712-2549)
PHONE..................847 673-8900
Fax: 847 673-1408
Richard A Voss, *President*
Bruce Herr, *Controller*
A D Martin, *Sales Mgr*
EMP: 45 EST: 1956
SQ FT: 25,500
SALES (est): 6.9MM **Privately Held**
WEB: www.vossengineering.com
SIC: 3463 5085 Bearing & bearing race forgings, nonferrous; bearings; rubber goods, mechanical

**(G-13543)**
**WHITE STOKES COMPANY INC**
4433 W Touhy Ave Ste 207 (60712-1833)
P.O. Box 9623, Chicago (60609-0623)
PHONE..................773 254-5000
Fax: 773 523-0767
Irene Tzakis, *President*
Marilyn Tzakis, *Controller*
Dino Collaros, *Manager*
Joanne Smith, *Director*
EMP: 40
SQ FT: 80,000
SALES (est): 6MM **Privately Held**
SIC: 2064 2087 Cake ornaments, confectionery; syrups, flavoring (except drink)

**(G-13544)**
**YAZDAN ESSIE**
Also Called: Laminate Craft
3730 W Morse Ave (60712-2618)
PHONE..................847 675-7916
Fax: 847 675-7930
Essie Yazdan, *Owner*
EMP: 2
SALES (est): 467.5K **Privately Held**
WEB: www.laminatecraft.com
SIC: 3553 Cabinet makers' machinery

## Lindenhurst
### Lake County

**(G-13545)**
**ABBOTT LABORATORIES**
445 Red Rock Dr (60046-8807)
PHONE..................847 921-9455
Julie Orpano, *Principal*
EMP: 5
SALES (est): 523.2K **Privately Held**
SIC: 2834 Pharmaceutical preparations

**(G-13546)**
**CROSSWIND PRINTING**
588 Crosswind Ln (60046-6743)
PHONE..................847 356-1009
Robert Clausing, *Owner*
EMP: 2
SALES: 525K **Privately Held**
SIC: 2752 Commercial printing, lithographic

**(G-13547)**
**MEDIMMUNE LLC**
839 Colony Ct (60046-8768)
PHONE..................847 356-3274
Peter McDonald, *Manager*
EMP: 5
SALES (corp-wide): 23B **Privately Held**
SIC: 5122 2833 Pharmaceuticals; medicinals & botanicals
HQ: Medimmune, Llc
1 Medimmune Way
Gaithersburg MD 20878
301 398-1200

**(G-13548)**
**MOONBEAM BABIES**
259 Thrush Cir (60046-7949)
PHONE..................847 245-7371
Teresa Dethloff, *Partner*
Christine Fluhler, *Partner*
EMP: 2
SQ FT: 2,436
SALES (est): 210.8K **Privately Held**
WEB: www.moonbeambabies.com
SIC: 2369 Buntings, infants'

**(G-13549)**
**SITEXPEDITE LLC**
430 N Crooked Lake Ln (60046-6429)
PHONE..................847 245-2185
Vinh Diep, *VP Opers*
John McDade,
EMP: 27
SQ FT: 5,000
SALES: 2.2MM **Privately Held**
SIC: 7629 3449 Telecommunication equipment repair (except telephones); miscellaneous metalwork

**(G-13550)**
**WATSON FOODS CO INC**
1711 E Grand Ave (60046-7815)
PHONE..................847 245-8404
EMP: 63
SALES (corp-wide): 60.5MM **Privately Held**
SIC: 2045 Mfg Prepared Flour Mixes
PA: Watson Foods Co., Inc.
301 Heffernan Dr
West Haven CT 06516
203 932-3000

## Lindenwood
### Ogle County

**(G-13551)**
**SWENSON SPREADER LLC**
Also Called: Swensen's
127 S Walnut St (61049-7702)
PHONE..................815 393-4455
Fax: 815 393-4964
Stephen Paul, *Ch of Bd*
Andrew Outcalt, *President*
Eric Larsen, *General Mgr*
William Hintzsche, *Director*
Linda Pirkle, *Admin Sec*
▲ EMP: 125
SQ FT: 130,154
SALES: 43.7MM
SALES (corp-wide): 78.3MM **Privately Held**
WEB: www.swensonspreader.com
SIC: 3531 Aggregate spreaders
PA: The Louis Berkman Company
600 Grant St Ste 3230
Pittsburgh PA 15219
740 283-3722

## Lisle
### Dupage County

**(G-13552)**
**AAIS SERVICES CORPORATION**
701 Wrrnvlle Rd Ste 100 (60532)
PHONE..................630 457-3263
Edmund Kelly, *CEO*
Joan Zerkovich, *COO*
Michael Peters, *CFO*
EMP: 4
SQ FT: 11,000
SALES: 13.9K
SALES (corp-wide): 11.9MM **Privately Held**
WEB: www.aais.org
SIC: 6411 5112 2721 Professional standards services, insurance; business forms; trade journals: publishing only, not printed on site
PA: American Association Of Insurance Services
701 Warrenville Rd # 100
Lisle IL 60532
630 681-8347

**(G-13553)**
**ADVANTAGE PRESS INC**
3033 Ogden Ave Ste 110 (60532-1976)
P.O. Box 3025 (60532-8025)
PHONE..................630 960-5305
William Rowland, *President*
Rick Windsor, *Treasurer*
EMP: 8
SALES (est): 542.2K **Privately Held**
SIC: 2731 8748 Books: publishing & printing; business consulting

**(G-13554)**
**ALLEGRA PRINT & IMAGING**
2200 Ogden Ave Ste 500a (60532-1972)
PHONE..................630 963-9100
Wayne Muhs, *Owner*
EMP: 10
SALES (est): 1.2MM **Privately Held**
SIC: 2752 Commercial printing, offset

**(G-13555)**
**ALPHAGRAPHICS PRINTSHOPS**
1997 Ohio St Ste B (60532-4131)
PHONE..................630 964-9600
Fax: 630 964-9253
Lynn McKenzie, *President*
Danielle Gregor, *Marketing Staff*
Susan McKenzie Vice President, *Admin Sec*
EMP: 4
SQ FT: 1,734
SALES (est): 551.5K **Privately Held**
SIC: 2752 7334 2791 2789 Commercial printing, lithographic; photocopying & duplicating services; typesetting; bookbinding & related work

**(G-13556)**
**ALTMAN MANUFACTURING CO INC**
1990 Ohio St (60532-2145)
PHONE..................630 963-0031
Fax: 630 963-0089
Paul C Altman, *President*
Kathleen Altman, *Corp Secy*
Brian Altman, *VP Sales*
▲ EMP: 10 EST: 1942
SQ FT: 4,800
SALES (est): 979K **Privately Held**
WEB: www.altmanmfg.com
SIC: 3544 3542 Special dies & tools; machine tools, metal forming type

**(G-13557)**
**AMERICAN ASSN INSUR SVCS (PA)**
701 Warrenville Rd # 100 (60532-1371)
PHONE..................630 681-8347
Fax: 630 681-8356
Edmund Kelly, *CEO*
Joan Zerkovich, *COO*
Tom Claude, *Vice Pres*
Robert Guevara, *Vice Pres*
Joyce Tigino, *Vice Pres*
EMP: 50
SQ FT: 11,500
SALES: 11.9MM **Privately Held**
WEB: www.aais.org
SIC: 6411 5112 2721 Professional standards services, insurance; business forms; trade journals: publishing only, not printed on site

**(G-13558)**
**AMERICAN COMM & NETWORKS**
Also Called: Acnc
1958 Ohio St (60532-2145)
PHONE..................630 241-2800
Pao-Fan Liu, *Ch of Bd*
Paul Liu, *President*
▲ EMP: 40
SALES (est): 4.9MM **Privately Held**
SIC: 5045 3661 Computers, peripherals & software; telephones & telephone apparatus

**(G-13559)**
**AMPHENOL CORPORATION**
Amphenol Fiber Optic Products
2100 Western Ct Ste 300 (60532-1971)
PHONE..................800 944-6446
Fax: 630 810-5600
Thomas J Ricko, *General Mgr*
Stuart Abelson, *General Mgr*
Jenny Anguiano, *Purch Mgr*
James Turner, *Finance*
Melissa Sarlea, *Human Res Dir*
EMP: 83
SALES (corp-wide): 6.2B **Publicly Held**
SIC: 3678 Electronic connectors
PA: Amphenol Corporation
358 Hall Ave
Wallingford CT 06492
203 265-8900

**(G-13560)**
**AMPHENOL FIBER OPTIC PRODUCTS**
2100 Western Ct Ste 300 (60532-1971)
PHONE..................630 960-1010
Fax: 630 810-5600
▲ EMP: 25
SALES (est): 6.4MM
SALES (corp-wide): 5.5B **Publicly Held**
SIC: 3678 Mfg Electronic Connectors
PA: Amphenol Corporation
358 Hall Ave
Wallingford CT 06492
203 265-8900

**(G-13561)**
**ANHEUSER-BUSCH LLC**
1011 Warrenville Rd # 350 (60532-0934)
PHONE..................630 512-9002
Kevin Feehan, *Vice Pres*
EMP: 162 **Privately Held**
SIC: 2082 Beer (alcoholic beverage)
HQ: Anheuser-Busch, Llc
1 Busch Pl
Saint Louis MO 63118
314 632-6777

# GEOGRAPHIC SECTION

**Lisle - Dupage County (G-13584)**

**(G-13562)**
**ARIBA INC**
3333 Warrenville Rd # 130 (60532-1498)
**PHONE**................................630 649-7600
Christine Morrissey, *Manager*
**EMP:** 5
**SALES (corp-wide):** 23.3B **Privately Held**
**WEB:** www.ariba.com
**SIC:** 7372 Prepackaged software
**HQ:** Ariba, Inc.
   3420 Hillview Ave Bldg 3
   Palo Alto CA 94304

**(G-13563)**
**ARMOUR-ECKRICH MEATS LLC (DH)**
4225 Naperville Rd # 600 (60532-3699)
**PHONE**................................630 281-5000
**Fax:** 630 281-7670
Michael Brown, *President*
Larry Hawley, *District Mgr*
Yolanda Johnson, *Business Mgr*
Steve France, *Senior VP*
Ray Fairbanks, *Transptn Dir*
▼ **EMP:** 277
**SALES (est):** 66.2MM **Privately Held**
**SIC:** 3556 Meat, poultry & seafood processing machinery
**HQ:** Morrell John & Co
   805 E Kemper Rd
   Cincinnati OH 45246
   513 782-3800

**(G-13564)**
**ARRIS GROUP INC**
2400 Ogden Ave Ste 180 (60532-3999)
**PHONE**................................630 281-3000
**Fax:** 630 281-3362
Ken Russman, *Principal*
Mark Ruettiger, *Manager*
**EMP:** 25
**SALES (corp-wide):** 6.8B **Privately Held**
**WEB:** www.arrisgroup.com
**SIC:** 3661 3663 5063 3357 Modems; radio & TV communications equipment; cable television equipment; television broadcasting & communications equipment; satellites, communications; lighting fixtures; fiber optic cable (insulated); coaxial cable, nonferrous
**HQ:** Arris Group, Inc.
   3871 Lakefield Dr Ste 300
   Suwanee GA 30024
   678 473-2907

**(G-13565)**
**ASTA SERVICE INC**
5821 Iris Ln (60532-2731)
**PHONE**................................630 271-0960
Curt Willeford, *President*
Susan Willeford, *Vice Pres*
**EMP:** 2
**SALES (est):** 641.1K **Privately Held**
**WEB:** www.astaservice.com
**SIC:** 5051 3559 Foundry products; foundry machinery & equipment

**(G-13566)**
**AUTOMATED LOGIC CORPORATION**
Also Called: Automated Logic Chicago
2400 Ogden Ave Ste 100 (60532-3933)
**PHONE**................................630 852-1700
George Biskup, *Branch Mgr*
**EMP:** 18
**SALES (corp-wide):** 57.2B **Publicly Held**
**SIC:** 3823 Water quality monitoring & control systems
**HQ:** Automated Logic Corporation
   1150 Roberts Blvd Nw
   Kennesaw GA 30144
   770 429-3000

**(G-13567)**
**B GUNTHER & CO**
4742 Main St (60532-1724)
**PHONE**................................630 969-5595
**Fax:** 630 969-5768
Jeanne Brommer, *President*
Fran Oleksy, *Project Mgr*
Michael Brommer, *Treasurer*
**EMP:** 14
**SQ FT:** 5,400
**SALES:** 1.3MM **Privately Held**
**WEB:** www.bgunther.com
**SIC:** 5999 5199 5046 3993 Trophies & plaques; advertising specialties; store fixtures & display equipment; signs & advertising specialties

**(G-13568)**
**BIG JOES SEALCOATI**
6563 Fernwood Dr (60532-3451)
**PHONE**................................630 935-7032
Eric Rasmussen, *Principal*
**EMP:** 3
**SALES (est):** 217.1K **Privately Held**
**SIC:** 3679 Hermetic seals for electronic equipment

**(G-13569)**
**BISHOP ENGINEERING COMPANY (PA)**
6495 Bannister Ct (60532-3342)
**PHONE**................................630 305-9538
Samuel Bishop, *President*
Jackie Bishop, *Admin Sec*
**EMP:** 12
**SQ FT:** 6,000
**SALES (est):** 1.2MM **Privately Held**
**SIC:** 8711 3672 2741 5734 Electrical or electronic engineering; printed circuit boards; technical manuals: publishing & printing; computer software & accessories

**(G-13570)**
**BLUE LIGHT INC**
1440 Maple Ave Ste 5b (60532-4136)
P.O. Box 1121, Westmont (60559-8321)
**PHONE**................................630 400-4539
Robert Bevis, *CEO*
**EMP:** 20
**SALES (est):** 2MM **Privately Held**
**SIC:** 2842 Specialty cleaning preparations; sanitation preparations

**(G-13571)**
**BOLINGBROOK COMMUNICATIONS INC**
Also Called: CPI Satcom Division- Lisle
1938 University Ln Ste C (60532-2314)
**PHONE**................................630 759-9500
**Fax:** 630 759-5018
Howard Hausman, *President*
Frank Mack, *General Mgr*
Mike Longsdorf, *Sr Corp Ofcr*
Kim Craddock, *Vice Pres*
John Harrington, *Opers Staff*
▲ **EMP:** 510
**SQ FT:** 120,000
**SALES (est):** 73.2MM
**SALES (corp-wide):** 10.5B **Publicly Held**
**WEB:** www.mcl.com
**SIC:** 3825 3663 3812 3621 Instruments to measure electricity; satellites, communications; search & navigation equipment; motors & generators
**PA:** L3 Technologies, Inc.
   600 3rd Ave Fl 34
   New York NY 10016
   212 697-1111

**(G-13572)**
**CA INC**
3333 Warrenville Rd # 800 (60532-4554)
**PHONE**................................631 342-6000
David Geltner, *Research*
Albert Zhong, *Engineer*
Sanjay Kumar, *Branch Mgr*
Bill Veber, *Manager*
Maheswaran Ramu, *Info Tech Mgr*
**EMP:** 84
**SQ FT:** 212,000
**SALES (corp-wide):** 4B **Publicly Held**
**WEB:** www.cai.com
**SIC:** 7372 7371 Prepackaged software; custom computer programming services
**PA:** Ca, Inc.
   520 Madison Ave Fl 22
   New York NY 10022
   800 225-5224

**(G-13573)**
**CANNON BALL MARKETING INC**
Also Called: Press Express
701 59th St (60532-3116)
**PHONE**................................630 971-2127
James Cannon, *President*
Stan Scazepink, *Manager*
Maureen Cannon, *Admin Sec*
**EMP:** 3
**SQ FT:** 2,000
**SALES:** 450K **Privately Held**
**SIC:** 2752 2759 2789 Commercial printing, offset; commercial printing; bookbinding & related work

**(G-13574)**
**CHAS LEVY CIRCULATING CO**
815 Ogden Ave (60532-1337)
**PHONE**................................630 353-2500
Katey Snider, *VP Human Res*
**EMP:** 4
**SALES (corp-wide):** 117.2MM **Privately Held**
**WEB:** www.nationwidemidwest.com
**SIC:** 2721 Periodicals
**PA:** Chas. Levy Circulating Co.
   1930 George St Ste 4
   Melrose Park IL 60160
   708 356-3600

**(G-13575)**
**COGNIZANT TECH SOLUTIONS CORP**
3333 Warrenville Rd # 350 (60532-1157)
**PHONE**................................630 955-0617
**Fax:** 630 955-0618
John Trux, *Sales Dir*
Rajcan Surface, *Marketing Staff*
David Althoff, *Manager*
Deborah Okopski, *Executive Asst*
**EMP:** 23
**SALES (est):** 13.4B **Publicly Held**
**WEB:** www.cognizant.com
**SIC:** 7371 7372 Computer software development & applications; prepackaged software
**PA:** Cognizant Technology Solutions Corporation
   500 Frank W Burr Blvd
   Teaneck NJ 07666
   201 801-0233

**(G-13576)**
**CONCORDE LABORATORIES INC**
4504 Concorde Pl (60532-3707)
**PHONE**................................630 717-5300
Bonnie Metallo, *President*
**EMP:** 9 **EST:** 1996
**SALES (est):** 1.1MM **Privately Held**
**SIC:** 3991 Brooms & brushes

**(G-13577)**
**CORPORATE PROMOTIONS INC**
4712 Main St Ste 202 (60532-1969)
**PHONE**................................630 964-5000
Richard J Maag, *President*
**EMP:** 2
**SQ FT:** 1,000
**SALES:** 800K **Privately Held**
**WEB:** www.corp-promo.com
**SIC:** 2759 Promotional printing

**(G-13578)**
**CTS AUTOMOTIVE LLC (HQ)**
2375 Cabot Dr (60532-3631)
**PHONE**................................630 614-7201
**Fax:** 630 577-8894
Troy Herold, *Engineer*
Steve Street, *Engineer*
Larry Swensck, *Branch Mgr*
Raphael Caballero, *Mng Member*
David Hartley,
▲ **EMP:** 146 **EST:** 1998
**SQ FT:** 50,000
**SALES (est):** 24.1MM
**SALES (corp-wide):** 396.6MM **Publicly Held**
**WEB:** www.d-r-t.com
**SIC:** 3625 3845 3714 3674 Switches, electronic applications; electromedical apparatus; motor vehicle parts & accessories; semiconductors & related devices; current-carrying wiring devices; blow molded finished plastic products
**PA:** Cts Corporation
   2375 Cabot Dr
   Lisle IL 60532
   630 577-8800

**(G-13579)**
**CTS CORPORATION (PA)**
2375 Cabot Dr (60532-3631)
**PHONE**................................630 577-8800
Kieran O'Sullivan, *Ch of Bd*
Luis Francisco Machado, *Vice Pres*
Ashish Agrawal, *CFO*
Raj Patel, *Director*
▲ **EMP:** 110 **EST:** 1896
**SQ FT:** 37,300
**SALES:** 396.6MM **Publicly Held**
**WEB:** www.ctscorp.com
**SIC:** 3678 3829 3676 3679 Electronic connectors; measuring & controlling devices; aircraft & motor vehicle measurement equipment; resistor networks; electronic switches; switches, stepping; semiconductors & related devices

**(G-13580)**
**CTS ELECTRONIC COMPONENTS INC (HQ)**
2375 Cabot Dr (60532-3631)
**PHONE**................................630 577-8800
**Fax:** 630 295-6601
Vinod Khilnani, *CEO*
Kieran M O Sullivan, *President*
Dave Holmes, *Vice Pres*
David Fleischman, *Buyer*
Anna Lu, *Controller*
▲ **EMP:** 71
**SALES (est):** 199.1MM
**SALES (corp-wide):** 396.6MM **Publicly Held**
**SIC:** 3724 Research & development on aircraft engines & parts
**PA:** Cts Corporation
   2375 Cabot Dr
   Lisle IL 60532
   630 577-8800

**(G-13581)**
**D B M SERVICES CORP**
Also Called: Dbm Tubecutting Service
1996 University Ln (60532-2152)
**PHONE**................................630 964-5678
**Fax:** 630 724-9745
**EMP:** 5
**SQ FT:** 10,000
**SALES (est):** 400K **Privately Held**
**SIC:** 7389 3498 Metal slitting & shearing; fabricated pipe & fittings

**(G-13582)**
**DANA AUTO SYSTEMS GROUP LLC**
Dana Sealing Products
1945 Ohio St (60532-2169)
**PHONE**................................630 960-4200
Charlie Olfig, *Vice Pres*
Tim Plona, *Finance*
Rich Kozerski, *Branch Mgr*
Richard Kozerski, *Manager*
**EMP:** 100
**SQ FT:** 10,000
**SALES (corp-wide):** 5.8B **Publicly Held**
**SIC:** 3714 Motor vehicle parts & accessories
**HQ:** Dana Automotive Systems Group, Llc
   3939 Technology Dr
   Maumee OH 43537
   419 887-3000

**(G-13583)**
**DEMATIC CORP**
750 Warrenville Rd # 101 (60532-0901)
**PHONE**................................630 852-9200
Prashant Ranade, *President*
Robert F Bork, *Vice Pres*
Jeffrey R Heinze, *Admin Sec*
**EMP:** 10
**SALES (est):** 706.7K **Privately Held**
**SIC:** 3535 Conveyors & conveying equipment
**HQ:** Dematic Corp.
   507 Plymouth Ave Ne
   Grand Rapids MI 49505
   678 695-4500

**(G-13584)**
**E & J GALLO WINERY**
4225 Naperville Rd # 330 (60532-3656)
**PHONE**................................630 505-4000
**Fax:** 630 505-7017
Jeremy Cutler, *Sales Dir*

## Lisle - Dupage County (G-13585)

Peter Makris, *Sales Dir*
Brandon Scott, *Sales Dir*
Geoff Smith, *Sales Mgr*
Molly Swopes, *Marketing Staff*
**EMP:** 25
**SALES (corp-wide):** 4.1B **Privately Held**
**WEB:** www.gallo.com
**SIC:** 5182 5149 2086 Wine; groceries & related products; bottled & canned soft drinks
**PA:** E. & J. Gallo Winery
600 Yosemite Blvd
Modesto CA 95354
209 341-3111

### (G-13585)
### EMC CORPORATION
4225 Naperville Rd # 500 (60532-3699)
**PHONE**..................630 505-3273
**Fax:** 630 505-3290
Rick Hoffman, *Principal*
Jan Zeidel, *Accounts Mgr*
Jon Egan, *Accounts Exec*
Manish Jain, *Manager*
Diki Trikha, *Consultant*
**EMP:** 100
**SALES (corp-wide):** 67.2B **Publicly Held**
**SIC:** 7372 Prepackaged software
**HQ:** Emc Corporation
176 South St
Hopkinton MA 01748
508 435-1000

### (G-13586)
### ENDEPTH VISION SYSTEMS LLC
2497 Sun Valley Rd (60532-3450)
**PHONE**..................630 329-7909
Pu-Lan Wang,
**EMP:** 3
**SALES (est):** 282.8K **Privately Held**
**SIC:** 3841 Surgical & medical instruments

### (G-13587)
### ENERSYS
801 Warrenville Rd # 250 (60532-4336)
**PHONE**..................630 455-4872
John D Craig, *Ch of Bd*
**EMP:** 88
**SALES (corp-wide):** 2.3B **Publicly Held**
**SIC:** 3691 5063 Storage batteries; electrical apparatus & equipment
**PA:** Enersys
2366 Bernville Rd
Reading PA 19605
610 208-1991

### (G-13588)
### FCA US LLC
Also Called: Midwest Business Center
901 Warrenville Rd # 550 (60532-4301)
**PHONE**..................630 724-2321
Phil Scroggin, *Branch Mgr*
**EMP:** 4
**SALES (corp-wide):** 117.3B **Privately Held**
**SIC:** 3711 3714 Motor vehicles & car bodies; automobile assembly, including specialty automobiles; truck & tractor truck assembly; bus & other large specialty vehicle assembly; motor vehicle parts & accessories; motor vehicle engines & parts
**HQ:** Fca Us Llc
1000 Chrysler Dr
Auburn Hills MI 48326

### (G-13589)
### FORMTEK INC (HQ)
711 Ogden Ave (60532-1845)
**PHONE**..................630 285-1500
John E Reed, *Ch of Bd*
Bruce Dewey, *President*
Don Hill, *Exec VP*
Edward J Kay, *Vice Pres*
Victor Malespina, *Vice Pres*
▲ **EMP:** 15
**SALES (est):** 40.4MM
**SALES (corp-wide):** 482.1MM **Privately Held**
**WEB:** www.formtekinc.com
**SIC:** 3542 Machine tools, metal forming type
**PA:** Mestek, Inc.
260 N Elm St
Westfield MA 01085
413 568-9571

### (G-13590)
### FOX METER INC
5403 Patton Dr Ste 218 (60532-4625)
**PHONE**..................630 968-3635
Lila Grant, *President*
John Grant, *Vice Pres*
Bob Holmes, *Sales Mgr*
**EMP:** 6
**SQ FT:** 4,800
**SALES:** 500K **Privately Held**
**WEB:** www.foxmeter.com
**SIC:** 3825 Test equipment for electronic & electric measurement

### (G-13591)
### G T LABORATORIES INC
3333 Warrenville Rd # 200 (60532-1157)
**PHONE**..................847 998-4776
Sam Tripas, *President*
Judith Tripas, *Corp Secy*
Vicki Landon, *Sales Staff*
Chizuko Hadaka, *Office Mgr*
**EMP:** 5
**SQ FT:** 7,500
**SALES (est):** 516K **Privately Held**
**SIC:** 3851 Ophthalmic goods

### (G-13592)
### GATEWAY CABLE INC (PA)
1998 Ohio St Ste 100 (60532-2147)
**PHONE**..................630 766-7969
Kenneth Flerlage, *President*
Donald Flerlage, *Vice Pres*
**EMP:** 6
**SQ FT:** 11,000
**SALES (est):** 1.9MM **Privately Held**
**SIC:** 3643 Connectors & terminals for electrical devices

### (G-13593)
### GE INTELLIGENT PLATFORMS INC
Also Called: Smartsignal
901 Warrenville Rd # 300 (60532-4301)
**PHONE**..................630 829-4000
Chad Stoecker, *Project Engr*
Robert Krzyzak, *Accountant*
Craig Lawson, *Sales Staff*
Cynthia Stone, *Marketing Mgr*
Daphne Mischel, *Mktg Coord*
**EMP:** 75
**SALES (corp-wide):** 123.6B **Publicly Held**
**SIC:** 7372 7373 Prepackaged software; computer integrated systems design
**HQ:** Ge Intelligent Platforms, Inc.
2500 Austin Dr
Charlottesville VA 22911

### (G-13594)
### GENERAL MILLS INC
2441 Warrenville Rd # 610 (60532-3664)
**PHONE**..................630 577-3800
**Fax:** 630 577-0085
Cathey Johnsen, *Manager*
**EMP:** 15
**SALES (corp-wide):** 16.5B **Publicly Held**
**WEB:** www.generalmills.com
**SIC:** 2043 2041 Rice: prepared as cereal breakfast food; flour mixes
**PA:** General Mills, Inc.
1 General Mills Blvd
Minneapolis MN 55426
763 764-7600

### (G-13595)
### GERB VIBRATION CONTROL SYSTEMS
1950 Ohio St (60532-2145)
**PHONE**..................630 724-1660
**Fax:** 630 724-1664
Victor Salcedo, *President*
Dr Frank Barutzki, *Vice Pres*
Mark Kulaga, *Opers Mgr*
Christoff Von Waldow, *Treasurer*
Laurie Eklund, *Manager*
▲ **EMP:** 7
**SQ FT:** 6,000
**SALES:** 1.5MM
**SALES (corp-wide):** 129MM **Privately Held**
**WEB:** www.gerb.com
**SIC:** 3495 8711 Mechanical springs, precision; industrial engineers

**HQ:** Gerb Holding Gmbh
Roedernallee 174-176
Berlin
304 191-0

### (G-13596)
### GKN AEROSPACE INC
550 Warrenville Rd # 400 (60532-4308)
**PHONE**..................630 737-1456
Capri L Pelshaw, *Principal*
**EMP:** 6
**SALES (est):** 583.6K **Privately Held**
**SIC:** 3812 Search & navigation equipment

### (G-13597)
### GRAPHICS PLUS INC
1808 Ogden Ave (60532-1501)
**PHONE**..................630 968-9073
**Fax:** 630 963-7887
Richard J Hejna, *President*
Marco Incrocci, *Vice Pres*
Michael Jais, *Vice Pres*
Mona Hurt, *Office Mgr*
John Lord, *Manager*
**EMP:** 12 **EST:** 1966
**SQ FT:** 21,000
**SALES (est):** 1.8MM **Privately Held**
**WEB:** www.graphicsplusinc.com
**SIC:** 2791 2796 2752 7336 Typesetting; lithographic plates, positives or negatives; commercial printing, offset; commercial art & graphic design

### (G-13598)
### H2O FILTER INC
4407 Chelsea Ave (60532-1314)
**PHONE**..................630 963-3303
Greg Johnson, *Principal*
**EMP:** 2
**SALES (est):** 242.4K **Privately Held**
**SIC:** 3569 Filters

### (G-13599)
### HERA CNSLTNG INTERNTNL OPRATN
4307 Westerhoff Dr (60532-4190)
**PHONE**..................630 515-8819
Hemant Koritala, *President*
**EMP:** 10
**SALES:** 300K **Privately Held**
**WEB:** www.hcicorp.com
**SIC:** 7372 Prepackaged software

### (G-13600)
### HILSCHER NORTH AMERICA INC
2525 Cabot Dr Ste 200 (60532-3628)
**PHONE**..................630 505-5301
**Fax:** 630 505-7532
Philip Marshall, *CEO*
Norine Mosele, *Office Mgr*
Craig Lentzkow, *Manager*
Terry Tirko, *Sr Software Eng*
**EMP:** 15
**SQ FT:** 1,500
**SALES (est):** 885.6K
**SALES (corp-wide):** 46.7MM **Privately Held**
**WEB:** www.hilscher.com
**SIC:** 3549 Assembly machines, including robotic
**PA:** Hilscher Gesellschaft Fur Systemautomation Mit Beschrankter Haftung
Rheinstr. 15
Hattersheim Am Main 65795
619 099-070

### (G-13601)
### HUNTER MARKETING INC
Also Called: Unique Targets
6523 Royal Glen Ct (60532-3321)
**PHONE**..................630 541-8480
Todd Moxley, *President*
**EMP:** 3
**SALES (est):** 21.2K **Privately Held**
**SIC:** 3949 Sporting & athletic goods

### (G-13602)
### INDUSTRIES PUBLICATION INC
4412 Black Partridge Ln (60532-1035)
P.O. Box 441 (60532-0441)
**PHONE**..................630 357-5269
Leonard Butler, *President*
**EMP:** 38

**SALES (est):** 1.6MM **Privately Held**
**SIC:** 3433 Heating equipment, except electric

### (G-13603)
### INEOS AMERICAS LLC
Also Called: Ineos Technologies
3030 Warrenville Rd # 650 (60532-1000)
**PHONE**..................630 857-7000
Joshua Hartley, *Engineer*
Martin Olavesen, *CFO*
Dana Hall, *Manager*
Todd Kruse, *Manager*
Gregory Novak, *Manager*
**EMP:** 3
**SALES (corp-wide):** 40B **Privately Held**
**SIC:** 2899 Chemical preparations
**HQ:** Ineos Americas Llc
2600 S Shore Blvd Ste 500
League City TX 77573
281 535-6600

### (G-13604)
### INEOS BIO USA LLC (DH)
Also Called: Ineos Bio Americas
3030 Warrenville Rd # 650 (60532-1000)
**PHONE**..................630 857-7000
**Fax:** 630 857-7369
Peter Williams, *CEO*
Keith Connors, *Project Engr*
Bob Sokol, *CFO*
Vickie Funk, *Financial Exec*
Debbie Johnson, *Sales Staff*
▼ **EMP:** 38
**SALES (est):** 6.5MM
**SALES (corp-wide):** 40B **Privately Held**
**SIC:** 2821 Plastics materials & resins
**HQ:** Ineos Bio Sa
Avenue Des Uttins 3
Rolle VD
216 241-721

### (G-13605)
### INEOS NEW PLANET BIOENERGY LLC
3030 Warrenville Rd # 650 (60532-1000)
**PHONE**..................630 857-7143
Dan Cummings, *President*
Tex Carter, *Vice Pres*
Mark Niederschulte,
David King,
**EMP:** 75
**SALES (est):** 10.5MM **Privately Held**
**SIC:** 2821 Plastics materials & resins

### (G-13606)
### INFOSYS LIMITED
2300 Cabot Dr Ste 250 (60532-4619)
**PHONE**..................630 482-5000
Matt Dhillon, *Business Mgr*
Steve Jeffries, *VP Human Res*
Puneet Sharma, *Sales Mgr*
Paneesh Murthy, *Branch Mgr*
Amit Kumar, *Program Mgr*
**EMP:** 50
**SALES (corp-wide):** 7.9B **Privately Held**
**SIC:** 7371 7379 7372 Computer software development; computer related consulting services; prepackaged software
**HQ:** Infosys Limited
6100 Tennyson Pkwy # 200
Plano TX 75024
469 229-9400

### (G-13607)
### INTERFACE PROTEIN TECH INC
Also Called: Ipt
5401 Patton Dr Ste 110 (60532-4503)
**PHONE**..................630 963-8809
Han Xiao-Qing, *President*
Mindy Liu, *Vice Pres*
▲ **EMP:** 100
**SQ FT:** 2,000
**SALES:** 10MM **Privately Held**
**WEB:** www.iproteintech.com
**SIC:** 2869 8071 Enzymes; biological laboratory

### (G-13608)
### INVISION SOFTWARE INC
Also Called: Invision Software AG
3333 Warrenville Rd # 200 (60532-1157)
**PHONE**..................312 474-7767
Peter Bollenbeck, *President*
Craig Shambaugh, *Vice Pres*
Klaus U Thiedmann, *Admin Sec*

## GEOGRAPHIC SECTION
### Lisle - Dupage County (G-13629)

EMP: 10
SQ FT: 4,000
SALES (est): 1.4MM
SALES (corp-wide): 13.1MM **Privately Held**
SIC: 3572 Computer storage devices
PA: Invision Ag
    Speditionstr. 5
    Dusseldorf 40221
    211 781-7816

### (G-13609)
### ISOPRIME CORPORATION
505 Warrenville Rd # 104 (60532-1669)
P.O. Box 3751 (60532-8751)
PHONE.................................630 737-0963
Kenneth Modaff, *President*
Adam Steinmetz, *Sr Software Eng*
EMP: 7
SALES: 100K **Privately Held**
WEB: www.isoprime.com
SIC: 7371 7372 Computer software development; prepackaged software

### (G-13610)
### JEWELL RESOURCES CORPORATION (HQ)
1011 Warrenville Rd # 600 (60532-0903)
PHONE.................................276 935-8810
Charles Ellis, *President*
Jack Allison, *Treasurer*
Kenneth Ritchie, *Admin Sec*
EMP: 3
SALES (est): 59.4MM
SALES (corp-wide): 1.2B **Publicly Held**
SIC: 1222 Bituminous coal-underground mining
PA: Suncoke Energy, Inc.
    1011 Warrenville Rd # 600
    Lisle IL 60532
    630 824-1000

### (G-13611)
### JORDAN SERVICES
2100 Scarlet Oak Ln (60532-2855)
PHONE.................................630 416-6701
Michael G Jordan, *Owner*
EMP: 5
SALES (est): 340K **Privately Held**
SIC: 3531 Asphalt plant, including gravel-mix type

### (G-13612)
### JOSTENS INC
5980 State Route 53 Ste A (60532-3389)
P.O. Box 3500 (60532-8500)
PHONE.................................630 963-3500
Pat Buschette, *Branch Mgr*
EMP: 46
SALES (corp-wide): 13.2B **Publicly Held**
SIC: 3911 Jewelry, precious metal
HQ: Jostens, Inc.
    3601 Minnesota Dr Ste 400
    Minneapolis MN 55435
    952 830-3300

### (G-13613)
### KENNAMETAL INC
2150 Western Ct Ste 300 (60532-1973)
PHONE.................................630 963-2910
Thomas Nicholls, *Manager*
EMP: 21
SALES (corp-wide): 2.1B **Publicly Held**
WEB: www.kennametal.com
SIC: 3545 Machine tool accessories
PA: Kennametal Inc.
    600 Grant St Ste 5100
    Pittsburgh PA 15219
    412 248-8200

### (G-13614)
### KONE INC (HQ)
4225 Naperville Rd # 400 (60532-3699)
PHONE.................................630 577-1650
Fax: 309 743-5469
Larry Wash, *CEO*
Michael Williams, *Managing Dir*
Wayne Dowty, *District Mgr*
Dennis Gerard, *Senior VP*
Nicole Manzo, *Senior VP*
▲ EMP: 580 EST: 1956
SQ FT: 527,000
SALES (est): 692.4MM
SALES (corp-wide): 650.6MM **Privately Held**
WEB: www.us.kone.com
SIC: 7699 3534 1796 Elevators: inspection, service & repair; escalators, passenger & freight; walkways, moving; dumbwaiters; elevator installation & conversion
PA: Kone Oyj
    Keilasatama 3
    Espoo 02150
    204 751-

### (G-13615)
### KRAFT HEINZ FOODS COMPANY
3030 Warrenville Rd # 200 (60532-1000)
PHONE.................................630 505-0170
Fax: 630 505-0177
Ralph Latagliata, *Branch Mgr*
EMP: 25
SALES (corp-wide): 26.4B **Publicly Held**
SIC: 2033 Catsup: packaged in cans, jars, etc.
HQ: Kraft Heinz Foods Company
    1 Ppg Pl Ste 3200
    Pittsburgh PA 15222
    412 456-5700

### (G-13616)
### KWIKSET CORPORATION
4225 Naperville Rd # 340 (60532-3656)
PHONE.................................630 577-0500
EMP: 5
SALES (corp-wide): 5.9B **Publicly Held**
SIC: 3429 Mfg Hardware
HQ: Kwikset Corporation
    19701 Da Vinci
    Foothill Ranch CA 92610
    949 672-4000

### (G-13617)
### LEECO STEEL PRODUCTS
1011 Warrenville Rd # 500 (60532-0933)
PHONE.................................630 427-2100
Bob Pepoff, *President*
EMP: 8
SALES (est): 2.4MM **Privately Held**
SIC: 3312 Blast furnaces & steel mills

### (G-13618)
### MANNA ORGANICS LLC
4650 Western Ave (60532-1543)
PHONE.................................630 795-0500
Markus Schramm, *CEO*
Shanti Schramm, *CFO*
▲ EMP: 13
SALES: 2MM **Privately Held**
SIC: 2051 Bakery: wholesale or wholesale/retail combined

### (G-13619)
### MANROLAND WEB SYSTEMS INC
2150 Western Ct Ste 420 (60532-1973)
PHONE.................................630 920-5850
Greg Blue, *President*
Roland Ortbach, *VP Sales*
Denise Lease, *Marketing Staff*
John Regan, *Admin Sec*
▲ EMP: 25
SALES (est): 5.4MM **Privately Held**
SIC: 3555 Printing trades machinery

### (G-13620)
### MCCAIN FOODS USA INC (DH)
2275 Cabot Dr (60532-3653)
P.O. Box 2464, Carol Stream (60132-2464)
PHONE.................................630 955-0400
Frank Finn, *President*
Dirk Van De Put, *COO*
Ian Mitchell, *Counsel*
Michael Campbell, *Vice Pres*
Patrick Davis, *Vice Pres*
◆ EMP: 275 EST: 1952
SQ FT: 100,000
SALES (est): 1.2B
SALES (corp-wide): 3.5B **Privately Held**
WEB: www.mccainusa.com
SIC: 2037 Potato products, quick frozen & cold pack; vegetables, quick frozen & cold pack, excl. potato products
HQ: Mccain Usa, Inc.
    2275 Cabot Dr
    Lisle IL 60532
    800 938-7799

### (G-13621)
### MCCAIN USA INC (DH)
2275 Cabot Dr (60532-3653)
PHONE.................................800 938-7799
Gilles Lessard, *President*
Randy A Myles, *Corp Secy*
Cheryl Mavoy, *Controller*
Cheryl Navoy, *Controller*
Valerie Hargrett, *Manager*
▼ EMP: 250
SQ FT: 50,000
SALES (est): 1.2B
SALES (corp-wide): 3.5B **Privately Held**
SIC: 2037 2038 5411 Potato products, quick frozen & cold pack; fruit juices; pizza, frozen; grocery stores
HQ: Mccain Foods Limited
    439 King St W Suite 500
    Toronto ON M5V 1
    416 955-1700

### (G-13622)
### METRASENS INC
2150 Western Ct Ste 360 (60532-1973)
PHONE.................................603 541-6509
Simon Goodyear, *CEO*
Dennis Cook, *President*
Rob Young, *Regional Mgr*
Harry Schultz, *Opers Staff*
Greg Hinds, *Sales Mgr*
▲ EMP: 25
SALES (est): 5MM
SALES (corp-wide): 5.8MM **Privately Held**
SIC: 3812 Magnetic field detection apparatus
PA: Metrasens Limited
    8 Beauchamp Business Centre
    Malvern WORCS WR14
    168 421-9000

### (G-13623)
### MIDDLETOWN COKE COMPANY LLC
1011 Warrenville Rd # 600 (60532-0903)
PHONE.................................630 284-1755
Matt Schwarz, *Principal*
EMP: 1
SALES (est): 6.3MM
SALES (corp-wide): 1.2B **Publicly Held**
SIC: 3312 Blast furnaces & steel mills
PA: Suncoke Energy, Inc.
    1011 Warrenville Rd # 600
    Lisle IL 60532
    630 824-1000

### (G-13624)
### MINELAB AMERICAS INC
1938 University Ln Ste A (60532-2314)
PHONE.................................630 401-8150
Fax: 630 401-8151
Peter Charlesworth, *President*
David Shields McGurk, *President*
Gary Schafer, *General Mgr*
Julieann Telford, *Corp Secy*
Maria Gabriela Olivarez, *Controller*
▲ EMP: 17
SQ FT: 10,000
SALES (est): 3.8MM
SALES (corp-wide): 124.5MM **Privately Held**
WEB: www.minelab.com
SIC: 3669 Metal detectors
HQ: Minelab Electronics Pty. Limited
    Technology Park 2 Second Ave
    Mawson Lakes SA 5095
    882 380-888

### (G-13625)
### MOLEX LLC (HQ)
2222 Wellington Ct (60532-1682)
PHONE.................................630 969-4550
Fax: 630 512-8638
Martin P Slark, *CEO*
Graham Brock, *President*
Jeses Amarilla, *General Mgr*
J Michael Nauman, *Division Pres*
Larry Schultz, *Business Mgr*
▲ EMP: 1100
SALES (est): 11.2B
SALES (corp-wide): 27.4B **Privately Held**
WEB: www.molex.com
SIC: 3679 3643 3357 Antennas, receiving; electronic circuits; connectors & terminals for electrical devices; communication wire; fiber optic cable (insulated)
PA: Koch Industries, Inc.
    4111 E 37th St N
    Wichita KS 67220
    316 828-5500

### (G-13626)
### MOLEX LLC
Also Called: Logistic Department
2200 Wellington Ct (60532-3831)
PHONE.................................630 527-4357
Jim Kicher, *Principal*
EMP: 3
SALES (corp-wide): 27.4B **Privately Held**
SIC: 3678 Electronic connectors
HQ: Molex, Llc
    2222 Wellington Ct
    Lisle IL 60532
    630 969-4550

### (G-13627)
### MOLEX INTERNATIONAL INC (DH)
2222 Wellington Ct (60532-1682)
PHONE.................................630 969-4550
Martin P Slark, *President*
Liam McCarthy, *Vice Pres*
David Johnson, *Treasurer*
Jan Maritz, *Manager*
Miles Shearer, *Manager*
▲ EMP: 10
SQ FT: 20,000
SALES (est): 1.7MM
SALES (corp-wide): 27.4B **Privately Held**
SIC: 3678 3679 3643 3357 Electronic connectors; electronic switches; electronic circuits; connectors & terminals for electrical devices; communication wire; fiber optic cable (insulated)
HQ: Molex, Llc
    2222 Wellington Ct
    Lisle IL 60532
    630 969-4550

### (G-13628)
### MOLEX PREMISE NETWORKS INC
2222 Wellington Ct (60532-1682)
PHONE.................................866 733-6659
Fax: 630 813-9770
Liam McCarthy, *President*
Brian Hauge, *General Mgr*
Todd Hester, *General Mgr*
Larry Schultz, *Business Mgr*
William Spink, *Business Mgr*
▲ EMP: 10001
SALES (est): 126.8MM **Privately Held**
SIC: 3679 3643 3357 Antennas, receiving; electronic circuits; connectors & terminals for electrical devices; communication wire; fiber optic cable (insulated)

### (G-13629)
### NAVISTAR INC (HQ)
2701 Navistar Dr (60532-3637)
P.O. Box 1488, Warrenville (60555-7488)
PHONE.................................331 332-5000
Fax: 630 753-2192
Troy A Clarke, *CEO*
Bill Kozek, *President*
Persio V Lisboa, *President*
Persio Lisboa, *President*
Rudi Von Meister, *President*
◆ EMP: 200 EST: 1965

# Lisle - Dupage County (G-13630)

SALES: 124.2MM
SALES (corp-wide): 8.1B **Publicly Held**
WEB: www.internationaldelivers.com
SIC: **3711** 3714 3519 6153 Motor vehicles & car bodies; chassis, motor vehicle; motor vehicle parts & accessories; engines, diesel & semi-diesel or dual-fuel; financing of dealers by motor vehicle manufacturers organ.; purchasers of accounts receivable & commercial paper; buying of installment notes; truck finance leasing; finance leasing, vehicles: except automobiles & trucks; property damage insurance; fire, marine & casualty insurance: stock
PA: Navistar International Corporation
2701 Navistar Dr
Lisle IL 60532
331 332-5000

### (G-13630)
### NAVISTAR INC
2701 Navistar Dr (60532-3637)
PHONE..................................331 332-5000
EMP: 64
SALES (corp-wide): 10.1B **Publicly Held**
SIC: **3711** Manufacturing Of Motor Vehicle Bodies
HQ: Navistar, Inc.
2701 Navistar Dr
Lisle IL 60532
331 332-5000

### (G-13631)
### NAVISTAR INC
2701 Navistar Dr (60532-3637)
PHONE..................................662 494-3421
Rick Robertson, *Branch Mgr*
EMP: 353
SALES (corp-wide): 8.1B **Publicly Held**
SIC: **3713** Truck & bus bodies
HQ: Navistar, Inc.
2701 Navistar Dr
Lisle IL 60532
331 332-5000

### (G-13632)
### NAVISTAR DEFENSE LLC (HQ)
2701 Navistar Dr (60532-3637)
P.O. Box 1488, Warrenville (60555-7488)
PHONE..................................331 332-3500
Tom High, *General Mgr*
Joyce Privitt, *Accounts Mgr*
Michael Lyons, *Manager*
Eleanor Cabrere, *Director*
◆ EMP: 41
SALES (est): 9.4MM
SALES (corp-wide): 8.1B **Publicly Held**
SIC: **3812** Defense systems & equipment
PA: Navistar International Corporation
2701 Navistar Dr
Lisle IL 60532
331 332-5000

### (G-13633)
### NAVISTAR INTERNATIONAL CORP (PA)
2701 Navistar Dr (60532-3637)
PHONE..................................331 332-5000
Fax: 630 753-2305
Troy A Clarke, *Ch of Bd*
Phil Christman, *President*
William R Kozek, *President*
William V McMenamin, *President*
Steven K Covey, *Senior VP*
◆ EMP: 1000
SALES: 8.1B **Publicly Held**
WEB: www.navistar.com
SIC: **3711** 3714 3713 3519 Truck & tractor truck assembly; chassis, motor vehicle; motor homes, self-contained, assembly of; motor vehicle parts & accessories; truck & bus bodies; engines, diesel & semi-diesel or dual-fuel; automobile finance leasing

### (G-13634)
### NUCLEAR POWER OUTFITTERS LLC
1955 University Ln (60532-2161)
PHONE..................................630 963-0320
Michael Fern, *Mng Member*
Jesica Popps, *Administration*
EMP: 12

SALES (est): 2MM
SALES (corp-wide): 13.8MM **Privately Held**
WEB: www.eichrom.com
SIC: **3356** Lead & lead alloy bars, pipe, plates, shapes, etc.
HQ: Eichrom Technologies Llc
1955 University Ln
Lisle IL 60532
630 963-0320

### (G-13635)
### OAG AVIATION WORLDWIDE LLC (DH)
801 Warrenville Rd # 555 (60532-4345)
PHONE..................................630 515-5300
Fax: 630 515-5301
John Grant, *Exec VP*
Angela McGovern, *Exec VP*
Bart Haasbeek, *Vice Pres*
Jan Wood, *Vice Pres*
Dave Hopkins, *Safety Mgr*
▼ EMP: 2
SALES (est): 1.8MM **Privately Held**
SIC: **2741** Guides: publishing & printing;
HQ: Joc Group Inc.
2 Penn Plz E Fl 12
Newark NJ 07105
973 776-8660

### (G-13636)
### ON TIME CIRCUITS INC
3121 Ridgeland Ave (60532-3311)
P.O. Box 3212 (60532-8212)
PHONE..................................630 955-1110
Aijaz Lakhani, *President*
Joe Cane, *Principal*
Mary Lou, *CFO*
May Lakhani, *Admin Sec*
EMP: 25
SALES (est): 2.6MM **Privately Held**
WEB: www.ontimepcb.com
SIC: **3679** 3672 Electronic circuits; printed circuit boards

### (G-13637)
### ONX USA LLC
1001 Warrenville Rd (60532-1391)
PHONE..................................630 343-8940
Brandon Harris, *VP Sales*
Alexandra Pladys, *Accounts Exec*
Mike Cox, *Branch Mgr*
Nicole Wayne, *Manager*
EMP: 45
SALES (corp-wide): 3.6B **Privately Held**
SIC: **7379** 7372 Computer related consulting services; business oriented computer software
HQ: Onx Usa Llc
5910 Landerbrook Dr # 250
Cleveland OH 44124

### (G-13638)
### PADDOCK PUBLICATIONS INC
Also Called: Daily Herald
4300 Commerce Ct Ste 100 (60532-3698)
PHONE..................................630 955-3500
Jim Davis, *General Mgr*
Ernie Schweit, *Editor*
Jim Cook, *Info Tech Mgr*
Mike Borta, *Education*
Sherry Lacerra, *Exec Sec*
EMP: 65
SALES (corp-wide): 122.6MM **Privately Held**
WEB: www.dailyherald.com
SIC: **5192** 2711 Newspapers; newspapers
PA: Paddock Publications, Inc.
155 E Algonquin Rd
Arlington Heights IL 60005
847 427-4300

### (G-13639)
### PHYSICIAN SOFTWARE SYSTEMS LLC
3333 Warrenville Rd # 200 (60532-1157)
PHONE..................................630 717-8192
Lewis Mitchell, *CEO*
Roelaf Boonstra, *Chief*
Christopher Logel, *Technology*
Matt Stiegert, *Software Engr*
Mike Botsch, *Director*
EMP: 12
SQ FT: 1,500
SALES (est): 600K **Privately Held**
SIC: **7372** Application computer software

### (G-13640)
### PITNEY BOWES INC
2200 Western Ct Ste 100 (60532-3618)
PHONE..................................630 435-7476
Elizabeth Martucci, *Vice Pres*
Clint Dally, *Vice Pres*
Linda Lego, *Project Mgr*
Peter Mayley, *Manager*
Ved Prakash, *Software Engr*
EMP: 80
SALES (corp-wide): 3.4B **Publicly Held**
SIC: **3579** 7359 Postage meters; business machine & electronic equipment rental services
PA: Pitney Bowes Inc.
3001 Summer St Ste 3
Stamford CT 06905
203 356-5000

### (G-13641)
### PITNEY BOWES INC
750 Warrenville Rd # 300 (60532-0901)
PHONE..................................630 435-7500
Micheal Cooper, *Principal*
Nathan Fineberg, *VP Sales*
Sheri Peterson, *Info Tech Mgr*
EMP: 100
SQ FT: 20,000
SALES (corp-wide): 3.4B **Publicly Held**
SIC: **3579** 7359 Postage meters; business machine & electronic equipment rental services
PA: Pitney Bowes Inc.
3001 Summer St Ste 3
Stamford CT 06905
203 356-5000

### (G-13642)
### PIX2DOC LLC
1968 Pleasant Hill Ln (60532-2827)
PHONE..................................312 925-4010
Asif Ahmed, *Manager*
EMP: 4
SALES (est): 191K **Privately Held**
SIC: **7372** 7389 Business oriented computer software;

### (G-13643)
### PRECISION CONTROL SYSTEMS
1980 University Ln (60532-4015)
PHONE..................................630 521-0234
William B Gushurst, *President*
Gena Gabel, *Manager*
Andrew J Arnold, *Admin Sec*
EMP: 58
SQ FT: 8,000
SALES (est): 19.7MM **Privately Held**
WEB: www.pcsoc.com
SIC: **3822** Temperature controls, automatic

### (G-13644)
### PRECISION SOFTWARE LIMITED
1011 Warrenville Rd # 210 (60532-0903)
PHONE..................................312 239-1630
Fax: 312 238-1631
Greg Lloyd, *CEO*
Angela Magee, *Project Mgr*
Creary Pat, *Sales Staff*
Melanie Leung, *Marketing Staff*
Chalotte Rantis, *Office Mgr*
EMP: 24
SALES (est): 1.9MM **Privately Held**
WEB: www.precisionsoftware.com
SIC: **7372** Prepackaged software
HQ: Precision Software Limited
Castlewood House
Dublin 6

### (G-13645)
### PRIME INDUSTRIES INC
4611 Main St Ste A (60532-1260)
PHONE..................................630 833-6821
Robert Antonio, *President*
Karen M Antonio, *Corp Secy*
Barbara Arnold, *Vice Pres*
◆ EMP: 50
SALES (est): 7.4MM **Privately Held**
WEB: www.primeindustriesinc.com
SIC: **3821** Laboratory furniture

### (G-13646)
### PYLON PLASTICS INC
2111 Ogden Ave (60532-1508)
P.O. Box 505 (60532-0505)
PHONE..................................630 968-6374
Fax: 630 968-6403

Debora Kolzow, *President*
Frank Charles Brand, *Vice Pres*
S Vainowski, *Sales Staff*
EMP: 6
SQ FT: 16,700
SALES (est): 814.4K **Privately Held**
SIC: **3089** 3953 Plastic containers, except foam; planters, plastic; marking devices

### (G-13647)
### QAD INC
1011 Warrenville Rd # 210 (60532-0929)
PHONE..................................630 964-4030
Chris Parsons, *Branch Mgr*
Charlotte Rantis, *Admin Asst*
EMP: 5
SALES (corp-wide): 277.9MM **Publicly Held**
SIC: **7372** Prepackaged software
PA: Qad Inc.
100 Innovation Pl
Santa Barbara CA 93108
805 566-6000

### (G-13648)
### R S BACON VENEER COMPANY (PA)
Also Called: Bvc Veneer
770 Front St (60532-2207)
PHONE..................................630 323-1414
Fax: 630 323-1499
James McCracken, *President*
George Wilhelm, *Shareholder*
Nancy McCracken, *Admin Sec*
◆ EMP: 117
SQ FT: 7,000
SALES (est): 13.7MM **Privately Held**
WEB: www.baconveneer.com
SIC: **2499** 2435 5031 Decorative wood & woodwork; veneer stock, hardwood; veneer

### (G-13649)
### R S BACON VENEER COMPANY
770 Front St (60532-2207)
PHONE..................................331 777-4762
Dan Meyerson, *Sales/Mktg Mgr*
EMP: 3
SALES (corp-wide): 13.7MM **Privately Held**
WEB: www.baconveneer.com
SIC: **2435** Hardwood plywood, prefinished
PA: R. S. Bacon Veneer Company
770 Front St
Lisle IL 60532
630 323-1414

### (G-13650)
### REDLINE PRESS
1613 Ogden Ave (60532-1229)
PHONE..................................630 690-9828
John Belton, *Owner*
EMP: 5
SALES (est): 400K **Privately Held**
WEB: www.redlinepress.com
SIC: **2752** 2791 2789 Commercial printing, lithographic; typesetting; bookbinding & related work

### (G-13651)
### RELCO LOCOMOTIVES INC (PA)
1001 Warrenville Rd # 201 (60532-1393)
P.O. Box 647 (60532-0647)
PHONE..................................630 968-0670
Donald L Bachman, *CEO*
Howard W Clark III, *President*
Mark Bachman, *COO*
Eric C Bachman, *Vice Pres*
Daniel P Mc Gowan, *Vice Pres*
EMP: 80
SALES (est): 21.9MM **Privately Held**
SIC: **4741** 3743 5088 Rental of railroad cars; railroad car cleaning, icing, ventilating & heating; locomotives & parts; railroad equipment & supplies

### (G-13652)
### RMCIS CORPORATION
4300 Commerce Ct Ste 320 (60532-3698)
PHONE..................................630 955-1310
David S Dickson, *President*
Kathy Bartheit, *Vice Pres*
Sue Buchelt, *Mktg Coord*
Stepheny Ricca, *Manager*
EMP: 20
SQ FT: 5,000

# Lisle - Dupage County (G-13676)

SALES: 2MM **Privately Held**
WEB: www.rmcis.com
SIC: **7372** 5045 Prepackaged software; computers; computer software

## (G-13653)
### RR DONNELLEY & SONS COMPANY
Also Called: R R Donnelley
750 Warrenville Rd (60532-0901)
PHONE................................630 588-5000
Fax: 630 810-5233
Jim Graham, *Manager*
EMP: 468
SALES (corp-wide): 6.9B **Publicly Held**
WEB: www.rrdonnelley.com
SIC: **2732** 2754 2759 Books: printing & binding; commercial printing, gravure; magazines: gravure printing, not published on site; catalogs: gravure printing, not published on site; directories: gravure printing, not published on site; letterpress printing
PA: R. R. Donnelley & Sons Company
35 W Wacker Dr Ste 3650
Chicago IL 60601
312 326-8000

## (G-13654)
### SARDEE INDUSTRIES INC (PA)
5100 Academy Dr Ste 400 (60532-4208)
PHONE................................630 824-4200
Steven R Sarovich, *President*
Ana Sarovich, *Controller*
Laura L Maran, *Admin Sec*
▲ EMP: 4
SQ FT: 4,500
SALES (est): 15MM **Privately Held**
WEB: www.sardee.com
SIC: **1796** 3565 5084 3537 Machinery installation; packaging machinery; conveyor systems; industrial trucks & tractors; conveyors & conveying equipment

## (G-13655)
### SEAGON INC
1960 Ohio St (60532-2145)
PHONE................................630 541-5460
Fax: 630 964-2890
Elaine Seamon, *President*
George J Simon, *Treasurer*
EMP: 4
SQ FT: 5,000
SALES: 1.2MM **Privately Held**
WEB: www.seagon-inc.com
SIC: **5162** 3679 Plastics products; electronic circuits

## (G-13656)
### SLEEPING BEAR INC
5401 Patton Dr Ste 115 (60532-4532)
PHONE................................630 541-7220
Robert Kasinecz, *President*
Rebecca Wing, *Principal*
EMP: 8
SALES: 500K **Privately Held**
WEB: www.sleepingbear.net
SIC: **1751** 2434 Cabinet building & installation; wood kitchen cabinets

## (G-13657)
### SMART SURVEILLANCE INC
6444 Coach House Rd (60532-3215)
PHONE................................630 968-5075
Douglas Meyer, *President*
EMP: 3
SALES (est): 230K **Privately Held**
SIC: **7382** 3613 1731 3625 Security systems services; control panels, electric; standby or emergency power specialization; energy management controls; electric controls & control accessories, industrial

## (G-13658)
### SMARTSIGNAL CORPORATION
901 Warrenville Rd # 300 (60532-4301)
PHONE................................630 829-4000
Fax: 630 829-4001
James Gagnard, *President*
Wayne Jurgerson, *Project Mgr*
Vivek Shah, *Project Mgr*
Bhaskar Balu, *QA Dir*
George Cerny, *QC Mgr*
EMP: 75

SALES (est): 5.9MM **Privately Held**
WEB: www.smartsignal.com
SIC: **7372** 7373 Prepackaged software; computer integrated systems design

## (G-13659)
### SMITHFIELD GLOBAL PRODUCTS INC (DH)
4225 Naperville Rd # 600 (60532-3656)
PHONE................................630 281-5000
Kevin Keenan, *President*
Susan Solomon, *Finance*
Ling Xie, *Manager*
Arnie Silver, *Director*
▲ EMP: 4
SALES (est): 1.5MM **Privately Held**
SIC: **2011** Hams & picnics from meat slaughtered on site
HQ: Armour-Eckrich Meats Llc
4225 Naperville Rd # 600
Lisle IL 60532
630 281-5000

## (G-13660)
### SPIRAX SARCO INC
1500 Eisenhower Ln # 600 (60532-2135)
PHONE................................630 493-4525
Pierre Schmidt, *Branch Mgr*
EMP: 10
SALES (corp-wide): 932.4MM **Privately Held**
WEB: www.spiraxsarco-usa.com
SIC: **3491** 3494 3561 Steam traps; pressure valves & regulators, industrial; line strainers, for use in piping systems; pumps & pumping equipment
HQ: Spirax Sarco, Inc.
1150 Northpoint Blvd
Blythewood SC 29016
803 714-2000

## (G-13661)
### SSAB ENTERPRISES LLC (DH)
801 Warrenville Rd # 800 (60532-1396)
PHONE................................630 810-4800
Chuck Schmitt, *President*
Helena Stalnert, *Exec VP*
Michele Klebuc-Simes, *Vice Pres*
Greg Maindonald, *Vice Pres*
Phillip Marusarz, *CFO*
▲ EMP: 40
SALES: 2B
SALES (corp-wide): 5.9B **Privately Held**
WEB: www.ipscoenterprises.com
SIC: **3312** Blast furnaces & steel mills

## (G-13662)
### SSAB US HOLDING INC (HQ)
801 Warrenville Rd # 800 (60532-1396)
PHONE................................630 810-4800
David Britten, *President*
Michele Klebuc-Simes, *Vice Pres*
Phillip Marusarz, *CFO*
Gregory Burnett, *Treasurer*
Eric Kroeger, *CIO*
EMP: 1
SALES (est): 2B
SALES (corp-wide): 5.9B **Privately Held**
SIC: **3312** Blast furnaces & steel mills
PA: Ssab Ab
Klarabergsviadukten 70
Stockholm 111 6
845 457-00

## (G-13663)
### STANLEY SECURITY SOLUTIONS INC
2150 Western Ct Ste 300 (60532-1973)
PHONE................................630 724-3600
EMP: 13
SALES (corp-wide): 11.4B **Publicly Held**
SIC: **3699** Security control equipment & systems
HQ: Stanley Security Solutions, Inc.
9998 Crosspoint Blvd # 3
Indianapolis IN 46256
317 849-2555

## (G-13664)
### STONE CENTER INC
2127 Ogden Ave (60532-1508)
PHONE................................630 971-2060
Charles Joseph Plasil, *President*
Arlene Plasil, *Admin Sec*
Becky Zar, *Administration*
EMP: 7

SQ FT: 4,000
SALES (est): 458.2K **Privately Held**
WEB: www.stonecenterlisle.com
SIC: **0781** 5032 3281 Landscape architects; brick, except refractory; stone, crushed or broken; cut stone & stone products

## (G-13665)
### SUN COKE INTERNATIONAL INC (HQ)
Also Called: Sun Coke Energy
1011 Warrenville Rd # 600 (60532-0904)
PHONE................................630 824-1000
Michael J Thomson, *President*
Cleo Boyd, *Vice Pres*
Mark Maccormick, *Vice Pres*
▲ EMP: 79
SQ FT: 5,692
SALES (est): 38.3MM
SALES (corp-wide): 1.2B **Publicly Held**
SIC: **1222** 3312 1221 Bituminous coal-underground mining; blast furnaces & steel mills; bituminous coal & lignite-surface mining
PA: Suncoke Energy, Inc.
1011 Warrenville Rd # 600
Lisle IL 60532
630 824-1000

## (G-13666)
### SUNCOKE ENERGY INC (PA)
1011 Warrenville Rd # 600 (60532-0903)
PHONE................................630 824-1000
Frederick A Henderson, *Ch of Bd*
P Michael Hardesty, *Senior VP*
Mark Newman, *Senior VP*
Gary P Yeaw, *Senior VP*
Allison S Lausas, *Vice Pres*
EMP: 277
SALES: 1.2B **Publicly Held**
SIC: **3312** 1241 Blast furnaces & steel mills; coal mining services

## (G-13667)
### SUNCOKE ENERGY PARTNERS LP (DH)
1011 Warrenville Rd # 600 (60532-0903)
PHONE................................630 824-1000
Frederick A Henderson, *Ch of Bd*
Suncoke E LLC, *General Ptnr*
Fay West, *CFO*
EMP: 11 EST: 2012
SALES: 779.7MM
SALES (corp-wide): 1.2B **Publicly Held**
SIC: **3312** Blast furnaces & steel mills; coke oven products (chemical recovery); coal gas derived from chemical recovery coke ovens

## (G-13668)
### SUNCOKE TECHNOLOGY AND DEV LLC
1011 Warrenville Rd Fl 6 (60532-0903)
PHONE................................630 824-1000
Michael J Thomson,
Mark Newman,
EMP: 2
SALES (est): 334.6K
SALES (corp-wide): 1.2B **Publicly Held**
SIC: **3312** Blast furnaces & steel mills
PA: Suncoke Energy, Inc.
1011 Warrenville Rd # 600
Lisle IL 60532
630 824-1000

## (G-13669)
### TALARIS INC (DH)
3333 Warrenville Rd # 310 (60532-9831)
PHONE................................630 577-1000
Fax: 630 369-5999
Joseph P Patten, *President*
John Mouser, *Engineer*
E Leslie, *Manager*
Dean Shaw, *Director*
▲ EMP: 250
SALES (est): 243.5MM
SALES (corp-wide): 1.9B **Privately Held**
WEB: www.delarue.com
SIC: **3578** 3499 Banking machines; safes & vaults, metal; safe deposit boxes or chests, metal

## (G-13670)
### TECHNICAL POWER SYSTEMS INC
4642 Western Ave (60532-1543)
P.O. Box 606 (60532-0606)
PHONE................................630 719-1471
Fax: 630 719-1416
Joseph G Giovanatto, *President*
Kurt Padera, *Vice Pres*
John R Bophy, *CFO*
John R Brophy, *CFO*
Najib Habiby, *Sales Mgr*
▲ EMP: 20
SQ FT: 8,000
SALES (est): 4.8MM **Privately Held**
WEB: www.technicalpowersystems.com
SIC: **3691** 3999 Batteries, rechargeable; barber & beauty shop equipment

## (G-13671)
### THOMAS PROESTLER
5400 Patton Dr Ste 2c (60532-4003)
PHONE................................630 971-0185
John Drousias, *Owner*
Scott Barnewolt, *Vice Pres*
EMP: 3
SALES (est): 114.7K **Privately Held**
SIC: **2099** 5141 Food preparations; groceries, general line

## (G-13672)
### TIANHE STEM CELL
6398 Holly Ct (60532-3312)
PHONE................................630 723-1968
Yong Zhao, *President*
EMP: 17
SALES (est): 587K **Privately Held**
SIC: **3841** Medical instruments & equipment, blood & bone work

## (G-13673)
### TRIBUNE MEDIA COMPANY
3333 Warrenville Rd # 750 (60532-1157)
PHONE................................708 498-0584
Ted Biedron, *Manager*
EMP: 3
SALES (corp-wide): 1.9B **Publicly Held**
SIC: **2711** Newspapers, publishing & printing
PA: Tribune Media Company
435 N Michigan Ave # 600
Chicago IL 60611
212 210-2786

## (G-13674)
### VALID SECURE SOLUTIONS LLC
1011 Warrenville Rd # 450 (60532-0903)
PHONE................................260 633-0728
Dean Warner, *President*
Ron Stott, *Vice Pres*
Bob Zick, *Vice Pres*
Suzanne Ybarra, *Controller*
EMP: 19
SQ FT: 62,000
SALES (est): 394.7K **Privately Held**
SIC: **8999** 2759 Communication services; commercial printing

## (G-13675)
### VALID USA INC (HQ)
1011 Warrenville Rd # 450 (60532-0903)
PHONE................................630 852-8200
Carlos Alfonso Seigneur, *CEO*
Carlos Alfonso Seigneur D'Albu, *CEO*
Doug Bensing, *Vice Pres*
Steve Hill, *Vice Pres*
Joseph J Taylor, *Vice Pres*
EMP: 1
SQ FT: 106,000
SALES (est): 193MM **Privately Held**
SIC: **2752** Commercial printing, lithographic

## (G-13676)
### VARGYAS NETWORKS INC
Also Called: Baltic Networks
2200 Ogden Ave Ste 240 (60532-1972)
PHONE................................630 929-3610
Brian K Vargyas, *President*
Brian Vargyas, *President*
Eva Ernest Vargyas, *Treasurer*
Jennifer Mason, *Accounting Mgr*
Eva Vargyas, *Sales Mgr*
◆ EMP: 11

# Lisle - Dupage County (G-13677)

## GEOGRAPHIC SECTION

**SQ FT:** 10,000
**SALES (est):** 3.4MM **Privately Held**
**SIC: 3315** 7371 Wire & fabricated wire products; custom computer programming services

### (G-13677)
**VAULT SHOP**
2827 Sun Valley Rd (60532-3440)
**PHONE**.................630 699-0307
Shanshan Zhu, *Principal*
**EMP:** 3
**SALES (est):** 223.3K **Privately Held**
**SIC: 3272** Burial vaults, concrete or pre-cast terrazzo

### (G-13678)
**VERITAS STEEL LLC (PA)**
2300 Cabot Dr Ste 425 (60532-4611)
**PHONE**.................630 423-8708
**Fax:** 630 505-0868
Henrik Jensen, *Ch of Bd*
Tracy Glende, *President*
Jim Uptain, *General Mgr*
Richard Phillips, *Principal*
Mike Sobieski, *COO*
**EMP:** 216 **EST:** 2013
**SALES:** 86.4MM **Privately Held**
**SIC: 3441** Fabricated structural metal for bridges

### (G-13679)
**ZEMAN MFG CO**
1996 University Ln (60532-2152)
**PHONE**.................630 960-2300
**Fax:** 708 724-9745
Robert Zeman, *President*
Matty Trujillo, *Sales Associate*
Dave Zeman, *Marketing Staff*
Leslie Finch, *Manager*
◆ **EMP:** 25 **EST:** 1936
**SQ FT:** 15,000
**SALES (est):** 3.7MM **Privately Held**
**WEB:** www.zemanmfg.com
**SIC: 3498** 3567 Tube fabricating (contract bending & shaping); heating units & devices, industrial: electric

## Litchfield
### Montgomery County

### (G-13680)
**ALPLY INSULATED PANELS LLC**
1401 Eilerman Ave (62056-3001)
**PHONE**.................217 324-6700
**EMP:** 9
**SALES (est):** 2MM **Privately Held**
**SIC: 2452** Prefabricated buildings, wood

### (G-13681)
**AMERITEX INDUSTRIES INC**
14 Litchfield Plz Ste 1a (62056-1095)
P.O. Box 305 (62056-0305)
**PHONE**.................217 324-4044
**Fax:** 217 324-3404
Jerry L Ruckman, *President*
Aaron Ruckman, *Vice Pres*
Carrie Barnes, *Project Mgr*
Randi Howart, *Manager*
**EMP:** 10
**SQ FT:** 10,000
**SALES (est):** 1.2MM **Privately Held**
**WEB:** www.ameritexindustries.com
**SIC: 2392** Napkins, fabric & nonwoven: made from purchased materials; tablecloths: made from purchased materials; table mats, plastic & textile

### (G-13682)
**BRAKE PARTS INC LLC**
725 Mckinley Ave (62056-2701)
P.O. Box 725 (62056-0725)
**PHONE**.................217 324-2161
Jeff Dempsey, *Mfg Staff*
Jake Jacobson, *Personnel*
Debbie Duff, *Exec Dir*
**EMP:** 6
**SALES (corp-wide):** 600MM **Privately Held**
**WEB:** www.raybestosracing.com
**SIC: 5013** 3714 3593 Automotive brakes; motor vehicle parts & accessories; fluid power cylinders & actuators

**HQ:** Brake Parts Inc Llc
4400 Prime Pkwy
Mchenry IL 60050
815 363-9000

### (G-13683)
**COUNTY TOOL & DIE**
1400 W Hudson Dr (62056-3016)
P.O. Box 186 (62056-0186)
**PHONE**.................217 324-6527
**Fax:** 217 324-3234
Jim Garrett, *Owner*
**EMP:** 3 **EST:** 1974
**SALES (est):** 276.4K **Privately Held**
**SIC: 3544** 7692 7389 3599 Special dies & tools; welding repair; personal service agents, brokers & bureaus; amusement park equipment

### (G-13684)
**FISHER & LUDLOW INC**
1501 Eilerman Ave Ste 400 (62056-3005)
**PHONE**.................217 324-6106
Brian Rutter, *President*
Douglas Deighton, *Admin Sec*
**EMP:** 7
**SALES (est):** 1.4MM **Privately Held**
**SIC: 3324** Steel Investment Foundry

### (G-13685)
**FISHER & LUDLOW INC**
1501 Eilerman Ave (62056-3005)
**PHONE**.................217 324-6106
Carl Orourke, *Plant Mgr*
Thomas Clinard, *Production*
Michelle Paulos, *Human Res Dir*
Carol Lee, *Data Proc Dir*
Carl O'Roake, *Systems Mgr*
**EMP:** 56 **Privately Held**
**SIC: 3441** 3446 Structural Metal Fabrication Mfg Architectural Metalwork

### (G-13686)
**GARTECH MANUFACTURING CO**
1400 W Hudson Dr (62056-3016)
P.O. Box 186 (62056-0186)
**PHONE**.................217 324-6527
Janet Garrett, *President*
Jim Garrett, *Vice Pres*
Rhonda Braden, *Marketing Staff*
**EMP:** 30
**SQ FT:** 10,500
**SALES (est):** 4.9MM **Privately Held**
**SIC: 3423** 3599 3316 Knives, agricultural or industrial; machine shop, jobbing & repair; cold finishing of steel shapes

### (G-13687)
**GEORGE PRESS INC**
905 N Old Route 66 (62056-1071)
**PHONE**.................217 324-2242
**Fax:** 217 324-5866
Robert Corrado, *Owner*
**EMP:** 7
**SQ FT:** 9,000
**SALES (est):** 1MM **Privately Held**
**WEB:** www.thegeorgepress.com
**SIC: 2759** 3571 2752 Letterpress printing; invitation & stationery printing & engraving; computers, digital, analog or hybrid; commercial printing, lithographic; advertising posters, lithographed

### (G-13688)
**INTERNATIONAL FILTER MFG CORP**
Also Called: Ifm
713 W Columbian Blvd S (62056-3027)
P.O. Box 549 (62056-0099)
**PHONE**.................217 324-2303
**Fax:** 217 532-6554
Cecilia Ewing, *President*
James R Hayes, *Vice Pres*
Cecilia Hayes, *Marketing Mgr*
Tracey Crow, *Manager*
Tracy Crow, *Exec Sec*
**EMP:** 18
**SQ FT:** 20,000
**SALES (est):** 4.7MM **Privately Held**
**SIC: 3569** Filters, general line: industrial

### (G-13689)
**ITW BLDING CMPONENTS GROUP INC**
ITW Alpine
7 Skyview Dr (62056-4654)
**PHONE**.................217 324-0303
Robbin Huffman, *Plant Mgr*
Ufgy Bratt, *Branch Mgr*
**EMP:** 40
**SALES (corp-wide):** 13.6B **Publicly Held**
**WEB:** www.alpineengineeredproducts.com
**SIC: 3443** 3446 3441 Truss plates, metal; architectural metalwork; fabricated structural metal
**HQ:** Itw Building Components Group, Inc.
13389 Lakefront Dr
Earth City MO 63045
314 344-9121

### (G-13690)
**JOURNAL NEWS**
510 N State St (62056-1568)
**PHONE**.................217 324-6604
Nancy Slepicka, *Principal*
**EMP:** 3
**SALES (est):** 127.3K **Privately Held**
**SIC: 2711** Newspapers, publishing & printing

### (G-13691)
**KRANOS CORPORATION (PA)**
Also Called: Schutt Sports
710 Industrial Dr (62056-3030)
**PHONE**.................217 324-3978
Robert Erb, *CEO*
Drew Harcharik, *Business Mgr*
Omare Lowe, *Business Mgr*
Brady Pisano, *Business Mgr*
Arrietta Lemon, *Vice Pres*
▲ **EMP:** 69
**SALES (est):** 40.2MM **Privately Held**
**SIC: 3949** Masks: hockey, baseball, football, etc.; baseball equipment & supplies, general; baseball, softball & cricket sports equipment; football equipment & supplies, general

### (G-13692)
**LAMBOO INC**
311 W Edwards St (62056-1904)
P.O. Box 195 (62056-0195)
**PHONE**.................866 966-2999
▲ **EMP:** 20
**SALES (est):** 3.9MM **Privately Held**
**SIC: 2421** Sawmill/Planing Mill

### (G-13693)
**LAMBOO TECHNOLOGIES LLC**
311 W Edwards St (62056-1904)
**PHONE**.................866 966-2999
Gary Harvey, *CEO*
Luke D Schuette, *COO*
Jeran Hammann, *Exec VP*
**EMP:** 4
**SQ FT:** 17,000
**SALES (est):** 310.6K
**SALES (corp-wide):** 22MM **Privately Held**
**SIC: 2439** Timbers, structural: laminated lumber
**PA:** Af Holding Co.
811 S Hamilton St
Sullivan IL 61951
217 728-8388

### (G-13694)
**LITCHFIELD NEWS HERALD INC**
112 E Ryder St (62056-2031)
P.O. Box 160 (62056-0160)
**PHONE**.................217 324-2121
**Fax:** 217 324-2122
John C Hanafin, *President*
Fred Jones, *Advt Staff*
Michelle Romanus, *Admin Sec*
**EMP:** 10 **EST:** 1856
**SQ FT:** 5,000
**SALES (est):** 792.4K **Privately Held**
**SIC: 2711** Newspapers: publishing only, not printed on site; job printing & newspaper publishing combined

### (G-13695)
**QUALITY PLUS**
Also Called: Supportstoreus
901 S Old Route 66 (62056-1879)
**PHONE**.................618 779-4931

John D Shaw, *Owner*
**EMP:** 10
**SALES (est):** 50K **Privately Held**
**SIC: 2499** Wood products

### (G-13696)
**RIVER BEND PRINTING**
60 Flat School Ln (62056-4546)
**PHONE**.................217 324-6056
Sam Weller, *Owner*
**EMP:** 4
**SALES:** 200K **Privately Held**
**SIC: 2752** 2791 2789 Commercial printing, lithographic; typesetting; bookbinding & related work

### (G-13697)
**SARCO HYDRAULICS INC (PA)**
216 N Old Route 66 (62056-2626)
P.O. Box 248 (62056-0248)
**PHONE**.................217 324-6577
Richard Sarver, *President*
Aaron Mike, *Opers Mgr*
Verla I Sarver, *Treasurer*
◆ **EMP:** 30 **EST:** 1975
**SQ FT:** 50,000
**SALES (est):** 3.2MM **Privately Held**
**WEB:** www.sarcohyd.com
**SIC: 7699** 3593 Hydraulic equipment repair; fluid power cylinders & actuators

### (G-13698)
**SIERRA INTERNATIONAL LLC (PA)**
Also Called: Teleflex Marine
1 Sierra Pl (62056-3029)
**PHONE**.................217 324-9400
**Fax:** 217 324-2461
Joe Holtschulte, *President*
Yvan Cote, *Vice Pres*
Joseph Holtschulte, *Vice Pres*
Scott Voumard, *Opers Staff*
Tom Youngless, *Human Res Mgr*
▲ **EMP:** 155
**SQ FT:** 175,000
**SALES (est):** 108.1MM **Privately Held**
**WEB:** www.sierramarine.com
**SIC: 5088** 3519 Marine crafts & supplies; parts & accessories, internal combustion engines

### (G-13699)
**W A M COMPUTERS INTERNATIONAL**
211 N State St (62056-2036)
P.O. Box 261 (62056-0261)
**PHONE**.................217 324-6926
**Fax:** 217 324-6938
William A Morgan Jr, *Owner*
Monte Govaia, *Vice Pres*
**EMP:** 5
**SQ FT:** 7,000
**SALES (est):** 346.9K **Privately Held**
**WEB:** www.wamcomputers.com
**SIC: 8611** 7372 Business associations; prepackaged software

## Lockport
### Will County

### (G-13700)
**A & S STEEL SPECIALTIES INC**
1001 Clinton St Ste A (60441-4838)
P.O. Box 97 (60441-0097)
**PHONE**.................815 838-8188
**EMP:** 20 **EST:** 1964
**SQ FT:** 50,000
**SALES (est):** 208.2K **Privately Held**
**SIC: 3449** 3792 3743 3715 Mfg Misc Structural Mtl Mfg Trailers/Campers Mfg Railroad Equipment Mfg Truck Trailers Structural Metal Fabrctn

### (G-13701)
**AA RIGONI BROTHERS INC**
112 Connor Ave (60441-4736)
**PHONE**.................815 838-9770
**Fax:** 815 838-9772
Doug Rigoni, *President*
Mark Rigoni, *Admin Sec*
**EMP:** 20

# GEOGRAPHIC SECTION

Lockport - Will County (G-13729)

SALES (est): 2.7MM **Privately Held**
SIC: 3281 Granite, cut & shaped; marble, building: cut & shaped

**(G-13702)**
**AFTERDARK OUTDOOR LIGHTING**
15451 Nolan Ct (60491-7429)
PHONE.............................708 243-1228
Dean Likas, *President*
Robert Likas, *Vice Pres*
EMP: 3
SALES (est): 266.7K **Privately Held**
SIC: 3648 Outdoor lighting equipment

**(G-13703)**
**AMERI ROLLS AND GUIDES**
337 Clover Ridge Dr (60441-3299)
PHONE.............................815 588-0486
Frank Di Falco, *President*
EMP: 1 EST: 2008
SALES: 200K **Privately Held**
SIC: 3325 Rolling mill rolls, cast steel

**(G-13704)**
**ATMI DYNACORE LLC (PA)**
551 S Independence Blvd (60441-4042)
PHONE.............................815 838-9492
John B Armbruster, *Mng Member*
James K Armbruster,
John Cordogan,
EMP: 2 EST: 1998
SALES (est): 6.5MM **Privately Held**
SIC: 3272 Concrete products, precast

**(G-13705)**
**AXELENT INC**
14503 S Gougar Rd # 900 (60491-6402)
PHONE.............................708 745-3128
Magnus Lundberg, *President*
Marcel Darroch-Davies, *Manager*
Doug Ashton, *Admin Mgr*
EMP: 10
SALES (est): 1.7MM **Privately Held**
SIC: 3496 Miscellaneous fabricated wire products

**(G-13706)**
**BENDING SPECIALISTS LLC**
Also Called: Wil Lan Company
3051 S State St (60441-5024)
PHONE.............................815 726-6281
Greg Radecki, *President*
Mark Sorby, *General Mgr*
EMP: 20
SQ FT: 12,000
SALES (est): 2.9MM **Privately Held**
WEB: www.bendingspecialists.com
SIC: 3354 Shapes, extruded aluminum

**(G-13707)**
**BINZEL INDUSTRIES LLC**
3051 S State St (60441-5024)
PHONE.............................847 506-0003
Julian Lawitz, *Purch Mgr*
Anthony Ditommaso,
Greg Radecki,
EMP: 2 EST: 2011
SALES (est): 294.3K **Privately Held**
SIC: 3399 Metal powders, pastes & flakes

**(G-13708)**
**BYRNE & SCHAEFER INC**
1061 Caton Farm Rd (60441-6517)
P.O. Box 453, Lisle (60532-0453)
PHONE.............................815 727-5000
Fax: 630 963-6005
Timothy K Byrne, *President*
EMP: 3
SALES (est): 169.7K **Privately Held**
SIC: 3599 Air intake filters, internal combustion engine, except auto

**(G-13709)**
**CHEMTECH SERVICES INC**
20648 Gaskin Dr (60446-1910)
PHONE.............................815 838-4800
John Hart, *President*
Steve Coccaro, *Manager*
Monika Hart, *Admin Sec*
EMP: 15
SQ FT: 15,000
SALES (est): 4.6MM **Privately Held**
WEB: www.chemtechservicesinc.com
SIC: 2819 3559 Chemicals, high purity: refined from technical grade; refinery, chemical processing & similar machinery

**(G-13710)**
**DONALDSON & ASSOCIATES INC**
12141 W 159th St Ste A (60491-7804)
PHONE.............................708 633-1090
Fax: 708 633-1094
Dave Donaldson, *President*
EMP: 9
SQ FT: 1,100
SALES (est): 1.2MM **Privately Held**
SIC: 5091 3949 Fishing equipment & supplies; hunting equipment & supplies; fishing equipment; hunting equipment

**(G-13711)**
**DOVE PRODUCTS INC**
3357 S State St (60441-5251)
P.O. Box 717 (60441-0717)
PHONE.............................815 727-4683
EMP: 25
SQ FT: 16,000
SALES (est): 240K **Privately Held**
SIC: 3089 Mfg Molded Plastic Parts

**(G-13712)**
**DOVE STEEL INC**
16035 W Red Cloud Dr (60441-4597)
PHONE.............................815 588-3772
Dan Blankenship, *President*
Beverly Blankenship, *Director*
EMP: 10
SALES (est): 1.2MM **Privately Held**
SIC: 3498 Tube fabricating (contract bending & shaping)

**(G-13713)**
**DVORAKS CREATIONS INC**
1521 Daviess Ave (60441-2890)
PHONE.............................815 838-2214
Gary Dvorak, *President*
EMP: 4
SQ FT: 6,300
SALES (est): 462.4K **Privately Held**
WEB: www.dvorakscreations.com
SIC: 2434 Wood kitchen cabinets

**(G-13714)**
**DYNAMICSIGNALS LLC (PA)**
900 N State St (60441-2230)
PHONE.............................815 838-0005
Andre Lareau, *President*
Patrick Cassady, *General Mgr*
Patricia Ramazinski, *General Mgr*
Wayne Coppe, *Opers Staff*
Ben Copeland, *Buyer*
▼ EMP: 40 EST: 1970
SQ FT: 60,000
SALES (est): 18.6MM **Privately Held**
WEB: www.dynamicsignals.com
SIC: 3829 Measuring & controlling devices

**(G-13715)**
**ENVIRONETICS INC**
1201 Commerce St (60441-2879)
PHONE.............................815 838-8331
Fax: 815 838-8336
Raymond Winters, *Chairman*
Steve S Kett, *Opers Mgr*
Larry Kjeldsen, *Purch Mgr*
Mark Mirro, *Sales Staff*
Rosemary Winters, *Manager*
EMP: 10
SALES (est): 1.9MM **Privately Held**
WEB: www.environeticsinc.com
SIC: 3081 2394 Unsupported plastics film & sheet; canvas & related products

**(G-13716)**
**GAGE APPLIED TECHNOLOGIES LLC**
900 N State St (60441-2230)
PHONE.............................815 838-0005
Eric Gillas, *General Mgr*
Ricky Goldstein, *Software Dev*
William A Boston,
Patrick A Cassady,
Eric Schroeder,
EMP: 40

SALES (est): 6.9MM
SALES (corp-wide): 18.6MM **Privately Held**
WEB: www.dynamicsignals.com
SIC: 3678 Electronic connectors
PA: Dynamicsignals Llc
    900 N State St
    Lockport IL 60441
    815 838-0005

**(G-13717)**
**GENERAL MACHINE AND TOOL INC (PA)**
348 Caton Farm Rd (60441-9535)
PHONE.............................815 727-4342
Fax: 815 727-9380
Matt Gregurich, *President*
Toni Gregurich, *Office Mgr*
EMP: 2
SQ FT: 1,200
SALES: 4MM **Privately Held**
SIC: 3599 Custom machinery; machine shop, jobbing & repair

**(G-13718)**
**GOLF GAZETTE**
428 S Washington St (60441-3037)
PHONE.............................815 838-0184
Joann North, *Principal*
EMP: 3
SALES (est): 158.6K **Privately Held**
SIC: 2711 Newspapers

**(G-13719)**
**GREIF INC**
Industrial Container Division
1225 Daviess Ave (60441-2804)
PHONE.............................815 838-7210
Fax: 815 838-8521
Dean Babcock, *Manager*
Amadeo Lopez, *Manager*
Jose Arreguin, *Maintence Staff*
EMP: 50
SALES (corp-wide): 3.3B **Publicly Held**
WEB: www.greif.com
SIC: 3089 Plastic containers, except foam
PA: Greif, Inc.
    425 Winter Rd
    Delaware OH 43015
    740 549-6000

**(G-13720)**
**GRIFFIN JOHN**
15751 Annico Dr Ste 2 (60491-4739)
PHONE.............................708 301-2316
John Griffin, *Owner*
Joyce Koster, *Manager*
EMP: 3
SALES (est): 98.5K **Privately Held**
SIC: 2759 Commercial printing

**(G-13721)**
**HOLLINGWORTH CANDIES INC**
926 N State St (60441-2230)
PHONE.............................815 838-2275
Fax: 815 838-2275
Wendy Carver, *President*
Margaret Carlson, *Corp Secy*
EMP: 23
SALES (est): 2.3MM **Privately Held**
WEB: www.hollingworthtoffee.com
SIC: 2064 Candy & other confectionery products

**(G-13722)**
**HUDSON BOILER & TANK COMPANY**
3101 S State St (60441-5053)
PHONE.............................312 666-4780
Fax: 312 666-5145
Edward Hoveke, *President*
Brent Tillman, *Vice Pres*
Hank Klein, *Project Mgr*
EMP: 15
SQ FT: 20,000
SALES: 5MM **Privately Held**
WEB: www.hudsonboiler.com
SIC: 3443 1791 1711 Boiler & boiler shop work; structural steel erection; boiler maintenance contractor; boiler setting contractor

**(G-13723)**
**INTERNATIONAL TITANIUM POWDER**
20634 Gaskin Dr (60446-1910)
PHONE.............................815 834-2112
Fax: 630 324-4808
Paul Shields, *Sales Mgr*
Richard Anderson, *Executive*
EMP: 9
SALES (est): 993K **Privately Held**
SIC: 3356 Titanium

**(G-13724)**
**JOLIET CABINET COMPANY INC**
405 Caton Farm Rd (60441-6513)
PHONE.............................815 727-4096
Fax: 815 727-4099
Daryl Del Sasso, *President*
Rosemary P Del Sasso, *Corp Secy*
Robert Ostapkowicz, *Vice Pres*
Colleen Ford, *Administration*
EMP: 40
SQ FT: 33,000
SALES (est): 6.4MM **Privately Held**
WEB: www.jolietcabinet.com
SIC: 2434 2511 Wood kitchen cabinets; vanities, bathroom: wood; wood household furniture

**(G-13725)**
**LA DOLCE BELLA CUPCAKES**
1228 Newbridge Ave (60441-2782)
PHONE.............................847 987-3738
Nicole Pacione, *Principal*
EMP: 4
SALES (est): 193.1K **Privately Held**
SIC: 2051 Bread, cake & related products

**(G-13726)**
**LINDE NORTH AMERICA INC**
810 E Romeo Rd (60441-5804)
P.O. Box 7068, Romeoville (60446-0968)
PHONE.............................630 257-3612
Jim Bates, *Branch Mgr*
EMP: 21
SALES (corp-wide): 17.9B **Privately Held**
WEB: www.bocsureflow.com
SIC: 2813 8711 Industrial gases; engineering services
HQ: Linde North America, Inc.
    200 Somerset Corporate Bl
    Bridgewater NJ 08807
    908 464-8100

**(G-13727)**
**LOCKPORT FISH PANTRY**
604 E 9th St (60441-3604)
P.O. Box 42 (60441-0042)
PHONE.............................815 588-3543
Sylvia Wynveen, *Principal*
EMP: 2 EST: 2010
SALES: 405.9K **Privately Held**
SIC: 2048 Fish food

**(G-13728)**
**LOCKPORT STEEL FABRICATORS LLC**
3051 S State St (60441-5024)
PHONE.............................815 726-6281
Greg Radecki, *President*
Bob Neff, *Purch Agent*
Dan Wiesbrock, *CFO*
Mike Kerrigan, *Marketing Staff*
Vincent Ditommaso, *Supervisor*
EMP: 80
SQ FT: 75,000
SALES (est): 29.5MM **Privately Held**
SIC: 3449 Bars, concrete reinforcing: fabricated steel

**(G-13729)**
**M R GLENN ELECTRIC INC**
200 W 6th St (60441-2990)
PHONE.............................708 479-9200
Fax: 708 479-4760
Michael R Glenn, *President*
EMP: 30
SALES (est): 4.1MM **Privately Held**
WEB: www.geminicompanies.com
SIC: 7694 5063 3621 Rebuilding motors, except automotive; motors, electric; motors & generators

## Lockport - Will County (G-13730)

**(G-13730)**
**MAGENTA LLC (PA)**
15160 New Ave (60441-2244)
PHONE.................................773 777-5050
Fax: 773 777-4055
Russell A Steele, *President*
Tony Colletti, *COO*
Selso Alvarado, *Prdtn Mgr*
Mike Witek, *Opers Staff*
Russell Burzych, *Purch Mgr*
**EMP:** 96 **EST:** 2008
**SQ FT:** 120,000
**SALES (est):** 30MM **Privately Held**
**SIC:** 3089 Injection molding of plastics

**(G-13731)**
**MARTIN DENTAL LABORATORY INC**
411 New Ave Unit 2 (60441-2213)
PHONE.................................708 597-8880
Martin Buchtenkirch Jr, *President*
**EMP:** 17
**SQ FT:** 5,200
**SALES (est):** 1.3MM **Privately Held**
**SIC:** 3843 8072 Teeth, artificial (not made in dental laboratories); dental laboratories

**(G-13732)**
**METAL PRODUCTS SALES CORP**
15700 S Parker Rd (60491-5969)
PHONE.................................708 301-6850
Fax: 708 301-6850
William H Rehr, *President*
**EMP:** 6 **EST:** 1962
**SQ FT:** 6,264
**SALES (est):** 705.6K **Privately Held**
**SIC:** 5211 5039 5031 3442 Doors, storm: wood or metal; windows, storm: wood or metal; doors, wood or metal, except storm; doors, sliding; glass construction materials; windows; metal doors, sash & trim; products of purchased glass; millwork

**(G-13733)**
**MONTY BURCENSKI**
1213 S Lincoln St (60441-3655)
PHONE.................................815 838-0934
Monty Burcenski, *President*
**EMP:** 6
**SALES (est):** 365.7K **Privately Held**
**SIC:** 3999 Manufacturing industries

**(G-13734)**
**MY BED INC**
14040 S Shoshoni Dr (60491-8906)
PHONE.................................800 326-9233
Frank G Cavazos, *President*
Judy Cavazos, *Admin Sec*
**EMP:** 10
**SQ FT:** 68,000
**SALES (est):** 930K **Privately Held**
WEB: www.mybed.com
**SIC:** 2515 Mattresses, containing felt, foam rubber, urethane, etc.

**(G-13735)**
**NETGAIN MOTORS INC**
800 S State St Ste 4 (60441-3434)
PHONE.................................630 243-9100
George Hamstra, *President*
**EMP:** 7
**SALES (est):** 550K **Privately Held**
**SIC:** 3621 Motors & generators

**(G-13736)**
**OMNI CRAFT INC**
411 New Ave Unit 1 (60441-2213)
PHONE.................................815 838-1285
Fax: 815 838-7852
Preston Wakeland, *President*
**EMP:** 6 **EST:** 1973
**SALES (est):** 477.4K **Privately Held**
**SIC:** 2541 2791 Cabinets, except refrigerated: show, display, etc.: wood; typesetting

**(G-13737)**
**PANDUIT CORP**
16530 W 163rd St (60441-7607)
PHONE.................................815 836-1800
Fax: 815 836-1811
Jack Caveney, *President*
Mark Acklin, *Division Mgr*
Robert Fitzpatrick, *Engineer*
Dale Twietmeyer, *Credit Mgr*
Tom Cullen, *Human Res Dir*
**EMP:** 50
**SALES (corp-wide):** 1B **Privately Held**
WEB: www.panduit.com
**SIC:** 3644 3643 5063 3699 Electric conduits & fittings; connectors & terminals for electrical devices; electrical apparatus & equipment; electrical equipment & supplies
**PA:** Panduit Corp.
18900 Panduit Dr
Tinley Park IL 60487
708 532-1800

**(G-13738)**
**PANEL AUTHORITY INC**
411 New Ave Unit 1 (60441-2213)
PHONE.................................815 838-0488
Preston Wakeland, *President*
Penelope Wendel, *Vice Pres*
**EMP:** 12 **EST:** 1994
**SQ FT:** 5,000
**SALES (est):** 1.1MM **Privately Held**
WEB: www.panelauthority.com
**SIC:** 3613 Control panels, electric

**(G-13739)**
**PRINTING PLUS**
Also Called: A Arbec Company
15751 Annico Dr Ste 5 (60491-4739)
PHONE.................................708 301-3900
Fax: 708 301-4060
Beth Mc Lane, *President*
Roger Wulff, *Vice Pres*
**EMP:** 5
**SQ FT:** 4,000
**SALES (est):** 470K **Privately Held**
**SIC:** 2752 7331 2789 Commercial printing, offset; mailing service; bookbinding & related work

**(G-13740)**
**QUALITY QUICKPRINT INC**
909 E 9th St (60441-3216)
PHONE.................................815 838-1784
**EMP:** 10
**SALES (corp-wide):** 1.4MM **Privately Held**
**SIC:** 2752 7334 2791 2789 Lithographic Coml Print Photocopying Service Typesetting Services Bookbinding/Related Work
**PA:** Quality Quickprint Inc
1258 Cronin Ct
Lemont IL 60439
815 723-0941

**(G-13741)**
**REDING OPTICS INC**
Also Called: Homer Township Vision Center
13231 W 143rd St Ste 101 (60491-6668)
PHONE.................................708 301-2020
Fax: 708 301-0884
Jeanine L Reding, *President*
Mary Statis, *Manager*
**EMP:** 8
**SQ FT:** 2,400
**SALES (est):** 1MM **Privately Held**
WEB: www.homervision.com
**SIC:** 3851 Frames, lenses & parts, eyeglass & spectacle

**(G-13742)**
**REGAL CONVERTING CO INC**
14503 S Gougar Rd Unit 1 (60491-6402)
P.O. Box 723 (60441-0723)
PHONE.................................630 257-3581
George E Gross, *President*
Matt Prim, *Opers Staff*
Bob Schmidt, *Treasurer*
Cecil Archbold, *Sales Staff*
Pam Neper, *Sales Staff*
▲ **EMP:** 15
**SALES (est):** 1.5MM **Privately Held**
**SIC:** 1011 Iron ores

**(G-13743)**
**S & S MFG SOLUTIONS LLC**
15509 Weber Rd # 3 (60446-3566)
PHONE.................................815 838-1960
**EMP:** 3
**SALES (est):** 200.8K **Privately Held**
**SIC:** 3999 Manufacturing industries

**(G-13744)**
**SIGNAGE PLUS LTD**
17908 S Parker Rd (60491-8296)
PHONE.................................815 485-0300
Fax: 815 485-0436
Les Jansto, *President*
**EMP:** 2
**SALES:** 250K **Privately Held**
**SIC:** 1721 1799 3993 Commercial painting; sign installation & maintenance; signs & advertising specialties

**(G-13745)**
**SIMON BOX MFG CO**
355 Caton Farm Rd (60441-6512)
PHONE.................................815 722-6661
Fax: 815 722-6662
Paul Hischier, *President*
Jacqueline Edmonson, *Admin Sec*
**EMP:** 7
**SQ FT:** 12,000
**SALES (est):** 1.3MM **Privately Held**
**SIC:** 2631 Folding boxboard

**(G-13746)**
**SIMPSON WELL & PUMP COMPANY**
14823 W North Creek Ct (60491-9338)
PHONE.................................708 301-0826
Roger A Simpson, *President*
Pamela Simpson, *Admin Sec*
**EMP:** 4
**SALES (est):** 530K **Privately Held**
**SIC:** 3561 Pumps & pumping equipment

**(G-13747)**
**SOURCE SOFTWARE INC (PA)**
16525 W 159th St 200 (60441-7900)
PHONE.................................815 922-7717
Thomas Weinberger, *President*
Alex Kantas, *Principal*
Kevin Schmidt, *Vice Pres*
Christine Weinberger, *Sls & Mktg Exec*
Mick Cairns, *Marketing Staff*
**EMP:** 3
**SQ FT:** 500
**SALES (est):** 216.3K **Privately Held**
WEB: www.sourcesoft.com
**SIC:** 7299 3577 Personal document & information services; computer peripheral equipment

**(G-13748)**
**STARHOUSE INC**
1312 Enterprise Dr (60446-4077)
PHONE.................................630 679-0979
Todd Chang, *Principal*
▲ **EMP:** 8
**SALES (est):** 914.8K **Privately Held**
WEB: www.starhouseinc.com
**SIC:** 3823 Digital displays of process variables

**(G-13749)**
**TOYAL AMERICA INC (DH)**
17401 Broadway St (60441-6508)
PHONE.................................815 740-3000
Bud Loprest, *President*
Stephen Fugulsang, *Vice Pres*
Dennis Debrodt, *Engineer*
◆ **EMP:** 85
**SQ FT:** 3,000
**SALES (est):** 18MM
**SALES (corp-wide):** 3.9B **Privately Held**
**SIC:** 2816 3399 Inorganic pigments; powder, metal
**HQ:** Toyo Aluminium K.K.
3-6-8, Kyutaromachi, Chuo-Ku
Osaka OSK 541-0
662 713-151

**(G-13750)**
**WHEATON CABINETRY**
17238 Weber Rd (60441-6525)
PHONE.................................815 729-1085
Ken Wheaton, *Owner*
**EMP:** 8
**SALES (est):** 1MM **Privately Held**
**SIC:** 2434 Wood kitchen cabinets

## Loda
### Iroquois County

**(G-13751)**
**HYDRA FOLD AUGER INC**
931 N 1600e Rd (60948-9428)
PHONE.................................217 379-2614
Wayne Niewold, *President*
Douglas Niewold, *Vice Pres*
Janet Niewold, *Treasurer*
Grace J Funk, *Manager*
Grace Funk, *Director*
**EMP:** 3
**SQ FT:** 1,000
**SALES:** 500K **Privately Held**
WEB: www.hydrafoldauger.com
**SIC:** 3532 5084 3423 Auger mining equipment; industrial machinery & equipment; hand & edge tools

**(G-13752)**
**LODA ELECTRONICS CO**
307 S Elm St (60948)
P.O. Box 207 (60948-0207)
PHONE.................................217 386-2554
Jack Sandford, *Partner*
Bruce Komadina, *Partner*
**EMP:** 4
**SALES (est):** 514.5K **Privately Held**
WEB: www.lodaelectronics.com
**SIC:** 3679 8711 3625 Electronic circuits; engineering services; relays & industrial controls

**(G-13753)**
**MIDWEST POULTRY SERVICES LP**
Also Called: Hi-Grade Egg Producers
Hwy 45 N Ste 2 (60948)
P.O. Box 69 (60948-0069)
PHONE.................................217 386-2313
Fax: 217 386-2686
David Garrelts, *Manager*
**EMP:** 60
**SQ FT:** 40,000
**SALES (corp-wide):** 174.9MM **Privately Held**
**SIC:** 2015 Poultry slaughtering & processing
**PA:** Midwest Poultry Services, L.P.
9951 W State Road 25
Mentone IN 46539
574 353-7232

**(G-13754)**
**POWER PLANTER INC**
931 N 1600e Rd (60948-9428)
PHONE.................................217 379-2614
Gregory Niewold, *President*
**EMP:** 4
**SALES (est):** 167.2K **Privately Held**
**SIC:** 1221 Auger mining, bituminous

## Logan
### Franklin County

**(G-13755)**
**T & T CARBIDE**
17409 Lowry Ave (62856-2205)
P.O. Box 13 (62856-0013)
PHONE.................................618 439-7253
Fax: 618 435-4347
Rick Thomas, *Owner*
Adam Thomas, *Vice Pres*
Nancy Thomas, *Office Mgr*
Kelly Flanagan, *Executive Asst*
▲ **EMP:** 2
**SQ FT:** 8,500
**SALES (est):** 2MM **Privately Held**
WEB: www.tandtcarbide.com
**SIC:** 5084 3546 Drilling bits; oil refining machinery, equipment & supplies; power-driven handtools

## Lombard
*Dupage County*

**(G-13756)**
**A K TOOL & MANUFACTURING INC**
260 Cortland Ave Ste 4 (60148-1223)
PHONE.....................630 889-9220
John Asan, *President*
Mike Kirch, *Vice Pres*
**EMP:** 4
**SQ FT:** 3,500
**SALES (est):** 516.2K **Privately Held**
**SIC: 3599** 3544 Machine shop, jobbing & repair; special dies, tools, jigs & fixtures

**(G-13757)**
**ABITZY INC**
1041 N Lombard Rd (60148-1238)
PHONE.....................847 659-9228
**EMP:** 9 **EST:** 2013
**SALES (est):** 1.1MM **Privately Held**
**SIC: 2541** Wood partitions & fixtures

**(G-13758)**
**ACE METAL REFINISHERS INC (PA)**
978 N Dupage Ave (60148)
PHONE.....................630 778-9200
Fax: 630 778-9287
Gordon R Swanson, *President*
▲ **EMP:** 18
**SQ FT:** 12,000
**SALES (est):** 3.3MM **Privately Held**
**SIC: 3471** Finishing, metals or formed products; polishing, metals or formed products

**(G-13759)**
**ADDITION TECHNOLOGY INC**
820 Oak Creek Dr (60148-6405)
PHONE.....................847 297-8419
Pedro Salazar, *CEO*
Daniel Salazar, *General Mgr*
Richard Rudy, *Info Tech Mgr*
**EMP:** 10
**SQ FT:** 2,500
**SALES (est):** 1.4MM **Privately Held**
**WEB:** www.additiontechinc.com
**SIC: 3841** 0752 Surgical & medical instruments; animal specialty services

**(G-13760)**
**ADVANTAGE PRINTING INC**
1920 S Highland Ave # 300 (60148-6149)
PHONE.....................630 627-7468
Shiv Mendiratta, *President*
**EMP:** 2
**SQ FT:** 20,000
**SALES:** 274K **Privately Held**
**SIC: 2621** 2752 2771 Business form paper; commercial printing, lithographic; greeting cards

**(G-13761)**
**AEROSTAR GLOBAL LOGISTICS INC (PA)**
Also Called: Aerostar Technical Services
901 Oak Creek Dr (60148-6408)
PHONE.....................630 396-7890
Anthony V Fiacchino, *CEO*
Anthony D Fiacchino, *President*
Michael Sorden, *CFO*
Eliseo Arredondo, *Broker*
Todd Lipinski, *Finance*
◆ **EMP:** 15
**SQ FT:** 20,000
**SALES:** 27MM **Privately Held**
**WEB:** www.aerostarglobal.com
**SIC: 4731** 4225 3482 Freight transportation arrangement; general warehousing & storage; shotgun ammunition: empty, blank or loaded

**(G-13762)**
**AESPHEPTICS MEDICAL LTD**
Also Called: Skin and Laser Aesheptics
477 E Bttrfeld Rd Ste 408 (60148)
PHONE.....................630 416-1400
Fax: 630 416-7833
Selma Arain, *Principal*
**EMP:** 3
**SALES (est):** 260K **Privately Held**
**SIC: 3845** Laser systems & equipment, medical

**(G-13763)**
**AKZO NOBEL COATINGS INC**
931 N Du Page Ave (60148-1214)
PHONE.....................630 792-1619
Fax: 630 792-1670
**EMP:** 20
**SALES (corp-wide):** 15B **Privately Held**
**SIC: 2851** 5198 2821 Paints: oil or alkyd vehicle or water thinned; lacquer: bases, dopes, thinner; varnishes; paints; plastics materials & resins
**HQ:** Akzo Nobel Coatings Inc.
8220 Mohawk Dr
Strongsville OH 44136
440 297-5100

**(G-13764)**
**AMTEX CHEMICALS LLC**
450 E 22nd St Ste 164 (60148-6175)
PHONE.....................630 268-0085
Nicolas Leyva, *Sales Mgr*
David Gazzera, *Sales Staff*
▲ **EMP:** 2
**SALES (est):** 230.5K **Privately Held**
**SIC: 2869** 5169 Industrial organic chemicals; industrial chemicals

**(G-13765)**
**AT&T CORP**
851 Oak Creek Dr (60148-6426)
PHONE.....................630 693-5000
Fax: 630 693-5228
Dave Lobianco, *Branch Mgr*
**EMP:** 222
**SALES (corp-wide):** 163.7B **Publicly Held**
**SIC: 2741** Telephone & other directory publishing
**HQ:** At&T Corp.
1 At&T Way
Bedminster NJ 07921
800 403-3302

**(G-13766)**
**BALDWIN GRAPHIC SYSTEMS INC**
Baldwin Web Controls
1051 N Main St Ste B (60148-1350)
P.O. Box 901, Shelton CT (06484-0941)
PHONE.....................630 261-9180
Fax: 630 261-9186
Ron Callan, *Principal*
**EMP:** 25
**SQ FT:** 13,000
**SALES (est):** **Privately Held**
**SIC: 3861** Graphic arts plates, sensitized
**HQ:** Baldwin Graphic Systems, Inc.
14600 W 106th St
Lenexa KS 66215
913 888-9800

**(G-13767)**
**BEAR MTAL WLDG FABRICATION INC**
948 N Ridge Ave (60148-1209)
PHONE.....................630 261-9353
Dean Mormino, *President*
Melisa Mormino, *Corp Secy*
**EMP:** 6
**SALES:** 400K **Privately Held**
**WEB:** www.bearmetalwelding.com
**SIC: 7692** Welding repair

**(G-13768)**
**BIG LIFT LLC (PA)**
Also Called: Big Joe Forklift
1060 N Garfield St (60148-1336)
PHONE.....................630 916-2600
Dan Rosskamm, *President*
Kevin Pletch, *Sales Mgr*
Bill Pedriana, *Director*
Jim Clark,
Sang Tian,
▲ **EMP:** 12
**SALES (est):** 6.7MM **Privately Held**
**SIC: 3537** Industrial trucks & tractors

**(G-13769)**
**BIGTIME FANTASY SPORTS INC**
149 W Washington Blvd (60148-2544)
PHONE.....................630 605-7544
Joe Ream, *President*
**EMP:** 4

**SALES (est):** 375.2K **Privately Held**
**SIC: 3577** 7371 Computer peripheral equipment; computer software development

**(G-13770)**
**BILZ TOOL COMPANY**
1140 N Main St (60148-1362)
PHONE.....................630 495-3996
Timothy Fara, *Managing Dir*
Tim Drumheller, *Branch Mgr*
**EMP:** 18 **Privately Held**
**SIC: 3541** Machine tools, metal cutting type
**HQ:** Bilz Tool Company
1351 Brummel Ave
Elk Grove Village IL 60007
847 734-9390

**(G-13771)**
**BIOMERIEUX INC**
1105 N Main St (60148-1360)
PHONE.....................630 628-6055
Douglas Maxwell, *Vice Pres*
Ted Walsh, *Info Tech Dir*
Kelly Martin, *Technology*
Janice Sowinski, *Executive Asst*
**EMP:** 30 **Privately Held**
**WEB:** www.biomerieux-usa.com
**SIC: 2833** 8734 8071 3231 Medicinals & botanicals; testing laboratories; medical laboratories; products of purchased glass
**HQ:** Biomerieux , Inc.
100 Rodolphe St
Durham NC 27712
919 620-2000

**(G-13772)**
**BLOOMING COLOR INC**
230 Eisenhower Ln N (60148-5403)
PHONE.....................630 705-9200
Fax: 630 705-1212
Valji Patel, *President*
John R Lehman, *President*
Alyssa King, *Project Mgr*
Nicole Rutkowski, *Project Mgr*
Neil Penvly, *Purch Agent*
**EMP:** 45
**SQ FT:** 30,700
**SALES (est):** 2.6MM **Privately Held**
**SIC: 2796** Color separations for printing

**(G-13773)**
**BOWTIE INC**
477 E Bttrfeld Rd Ste 200 (60148)
PHONE.....................630 515-9493
Tina Pelletier, *Manager*
**EMP:** 9 **Privately Held**
**WEB:** www.bowtieinc.com
**SIC: 2721** Periodicals
**HQ:** Bowtie, Inc.
500 N Brand Blvd Ste 600
Glendale CA 91203
213 385-2222

**(G-13774)**
**BUSINESSMINE LLC**
Also Called: Pledgemine
784 Oak Creek Dr (60148-6403)
PHONE.....................630 541-8480
Todd Moxley, *President*
**EMP:** 4 **EST:** 2009
**SALES (est):** 175.4K **Privately Held**
**SIC: 2741** 4813 Business service newsletters: publishing & printing;

**(G-13775)**
**CHEM-TAINER INDUSTRIES INC**
2 N 225 Grace (60148)
PHONE.....................630 932-7778
Fax: 630 932-0150
Rick Straub, *Branch Mgr*
**EMP:** 5
**SQ FT:** 10,000
**SALES (corp-wide):** 55.5MM **Privately Held**
**WEB:** www.chemtainer.com
**SIC: 3089** Pallets, plastic
**PA:** Chem-Tainer Industries Inc.
361 Neptune Ave
West Babylon NY 11704
631 422-8300

**(G-13776)**
**CHEMI-FLEX LLC**
1040 N Ridge Ave (60148-1211)
PHONE.....................630 627-9650
Fax: 630 627-9655
Maryann Morrell, *Managing Dir*
Luke Beausoleil, *Prdtn Mgr*
Mark Tobias, *QC Mgr*
Jim Creek, *Accounts Mgr*
Henery Kowalewski, *Manager*
**EMP:** 45
**SQ FT:** 45,000
**SALES (est):** 8.8MM **Privately Held**
**SIC: 3052** Plastic belting

**(G-13777)**
**CHICAGO ROLL CO INC**
970 N Lombard Rd (60148-1231)
PHONE.....................630 627-8888
Fax: 630 629-8858
Chuck Gehrisch, *CEO*
San Gy Shing, *President*
Jeffrey George, *General Mgr*
Frank Deangelis, *Plant Supt*
Arjana Bebo, *Design Engr*
**EMP:** 25
**SQ FT:** 48,000
**SALES (est):** 4.9MM
**SALES (corp-wide):** 22.2MM **Privately Held**
**WEB:** www.chicagoroll.com
**SIC: 3544** 3547 Dies & die holders for metal cutting, forming, die casting; rolling mill machinery
**PA:** Rki, Inc.
8901 Tyler Blvd
Mentor OH 44060
888 953-9400

**(G-13778)**
**CHROMETEC LLC**
820 N Ridge Ave Ste I (60148-1236)
P.O. Box 733 (60148-0733)
PHONE.....................630 792-8777
Brian Skerik, *Mng Member*
**EMP:** 3
**SALES:** 500K **Privately Held**
**SIC: 2441** Packing cases, wood: nailed or lock corner

**(G-13779)**
**CINCH CNNCTIVITY SOLUTIONS INC (HQ)**
1700 S Finley Rd (60148-4884)
PHONE.....................847 739-0300
Fax: 847 739-0301
Pete Bittner, *President*
Matt Meares, *General Mgr*
Steve Armstrong, *Vice Pres*
Kent Schultz, *Opers Mgr*
Robert Leppert, *CFO*
▲ **EMP:** 174
**SQ FT:** 100,000
**SALES:** 800MM
**SALES (corp-wide):** 500.1MM **Publicly Held**
**WEB:** www.aimelectronics.net
**SIC: 3678** 3679 Electronic connectors; harness assemblies for electronic use: wire or cable
**PA:** Bel Fuse Inc.
206 Van Vorst St
Jersey City NJ 07302
201 432-0463

**(G-13780)**
**CINCH CONNECTORS INC (HQ)**
1700 S Finley Rd (60148-4890)
PHONE.....................630 705-6001
Fax: 630 705-6055
Michael Murray, *President*
Larry Stanley, *General Mgr*
Bob Cwynar, *Vice Pres*
Michael Stewart, *Buyer*
David Chuchro, *Engineer*
**EMP:** 100
**SALES:** 156.7MM
**SALES (corp-wide):** 500.1MM **Publicly Held**
**WEB:** www.cinch.com
**SIC: 3643** 3678 Connectors & terminals for electrical devices; electronic connectors

**Lombard - Dupage County (G-13781)**      **GEOGRAPHIC SECTION**

---

**PA:** Bel Fuse Inc.
206 Van Vorst St
Jersey City NJ 07302
201 432-0463

**(G-13781)**
**CINCH CONNECTORS INC**
1700 S Finley Rd (60148-4890)
PHONE..................................630 705-6001
Bill Humes, *Branch Mgr*
**EMP:** 350
**SALES (corp-wide):** 500.1MM **Publicly Held**
**WEB:** www.cinch.com
**SIC: 3643** Electric connectors
**HQ:** Cinch Connectors Inc.
1700 S Finley Rd
Lombard IL 60148
630 705-6001

**(G-13782)**
**COMET NEON**
1120 N Ridge Ave (60148-1213)
PHONE..................................630 668-6366
Peter Wolak, *Owner*
**EMP:** 9
**SALES:** 1MM **Privately Held**
**SIC: 3641** Lamps, incandescent filament, electric

**(G-13783)**
**COMPUTHINK INC**
151 E 22nd St (60148-6226)
PHONE..................................630 705-9050
**Fax:** 630 705-9065
James Sivis, *President*
Donna Barrington, *Publisher*
John Stelmach, *CFO*
Jim Ducharme, *Regl Sales Mgr*
Randall Chrisman, *Sales Staff*
**EMP:** 33
**SALES (est):** 4.7MM **Privately Held**
**WEB:** www.computhink.com
**SIC: 7372 3089** Publishers' computer software; identification cards, plastic

**(G-13784)**
**CONTRACTORS REGISTER INC**
Also Called: Blue Book of Building & Cnstr
555 Waters Edge Ste 150 (60148-7046)
PHONE..................................630 519-3480
**Fax:** 847 297-0429
Chris Haden, *Accounts Mgr*
Todd Brown, *Manager*
**EMP:** 10
**SALES (corp-wide):** 74MM **Privately Held**
**WEB:** www.constrnet.com
**SIC: 2731** Book publishing
**PA:** Contractors Register, Inc.
800 E Main St
Jefferson Valley NY 10535
914 245-0200

**(G-13785)**
**COUNTER CFT SVC SYSTEMS & PDTS**
720 Concord Ln (60148-3719)
PHONE..................................630 629-7336
Phyllis C Whitlock, *President*
Ed Kring, *Corp Secy*
**EMP:** 3
**SALES (est):** 125K **Privately Held**
**SIC: 2782** Looseleaf binders & devices

**(G-13786)**
**CUSTOM CALENDAR CORP**
Also Called: Custom Calender
875 E 22nd St Apt 202 (60148-5025)
P.O. Box 912, Oak Park (60303-0912)
PHONE..................................708 547-6191
Patrick Schumann, *President*
**EMP:** 3
**SQ FT:** 1,000
**SALES:** 1.5MM **Privately Held**
**SIC: 2752** Calendars, lithographed

**(G-13787)**
**CUSTOM CULINARY INC (DH)**
2505 S Finley Rd Ste 100 (60148-4867)
PHONE..................................630 928-4898
Dean L Griffith, *Ch of Bd*
T C Chatterjee, *President*
Herve De La Vauvre, *President*
Mark Mason, *Regional Mgr*
Tom Nemanich, *Business Mgr*
**EMP:** 80
**SQ FT:** 75,000
**SALES (est):** 19.4MM
**SALES (corp-wide):** 756.3MM **Privately Held**
**WEB:** www.customculinary.com
**SIC: 2034 2099** Soup mixes; gravy mixes, dry; seasonings: dry mixes
**HQ:** Griffith Foods Inc.
12200 S Central Ave
Alsip IL 60803
708 371-0900

**(G-13788)**
**DE AMERTEK CORPORATION INC (PA)**
2000 S Finley Rd (60148-4825)
PHONE..................................630 572-0800
**Fax:** 630 572-1183
Jack C Chen, *President*
David Dzhang, *Purchasing*
Cash Colbert, *CFO*
Theresa Chen, *Admin Sec*
▲ **EMP:** 50
**SQ FT:** 140,000
**SALES:** 30MM **Privately Held**
**WEB:** www.deamertek.com
**SIC: 3679** Electronic circuits; electronic crystals; oscillators

**(G-13789)**
**DELTA STRUCTURES INC**
18w675 18th St (60148-5076)
PHONE..................................630 694-8700
Maria Chambers, *President*
Thomas Chambers, *Vice Pres*
Joshua Chambers, *Finance Mgr*
▲ **EMP:** 19
**SQ FT:** 15,000
**SALES (est):** 3.3MM **Privately Held**
**WEB:** www.deltastructures.com
**SIC: 3441** Fabricated structural metal

**(G-13790)**
**DIE CUT GROUP INC**
850 N Du Page Ave Ste 5 (60148-1250)
PHONE..................................630 629-9211
**Fax:** 630 629-9214
Marvin A Cichlar, *President*
**EMP:** 10
**SQ FT:** 20,000
**SALES:** 2.5MM **Privately Held**
**SIC: 3544** Dies, steel rule

**(G-13791)**
**DIGITAL IGNITE LLC (DH)**
101 W 22nd St Ste 104 (60148-4997)
P.O. Box 9272 (60148-9272)
PHONE..................................630 317-7904
Tamer Ali, *CEO*
Christina Turner, *Vice Pres*
Nayela Hoda, *Project Mgr*
John Sun, *CTO*
**EMP:** 9
**SQ FT:** 10,000
**SALES (est):** 1MM
**SALES (corp-wide):** 3.6B **Privately Held**
**SIC: 7372** Educational computer software
**HQ:** Yourmembership.Com, Inc.
9620 Exec Ctr N 200
Saint Petersburg FL 33702
727 827-0046

**(G-13792)**
**DIGITAL PRTG & TOTAL GRAPHICS**
123 Eisenhower Ln N (60148)
PHONE..................................630 627-7400
Gary Johnson, *President*
Andrew Jeakel, *Admin Sec*
**EMP:** 6
**SQ FT:** 3,000
**SALES (est):** 710K **Privately Held**
**WEB:** www.digitalprinting1.com
**SIC: 2759 7336** Commercial printing; commercial art & graphic design

**(G-13793)**
**EA MACKAY ENTERPRISES INC**
Also Called: Speak Out
104 N West Rd (60148-2120)
PHONE..................................630 627-7010
**Fax:** 630 627-7027
Scott D Mackay, *President*
Marguerite Micken, *Sales Staff*
Bonnie Mackay, *Admin Sec*
**EMP:** 20
**SQ FT:** 2,500
**SALES (est):** 1.2MM **Privately Held**
**SIC: 2711 2741** Newspapers: publishing only, not printed on site; miscellaneous publishing

**(G-13794)**
**EASTGATE CLEANERS**
837 Westmore-Myers Rd A10 (60148-3777)
PHONE..................................630 627-9494
Yun D Shim, *Owner*
**EMP:** 3
**SALES:** 200K **Privately Held**
**SIC: 3633 7216** Household laundry machines, including coin-operated; cleaning & dyeing, except rugs

**(G-13795)**
**ELECTRONIC RESOURCES CORP**
920 N Ridge Ave Ste A8 (60148-1226)
PHONE..................................630 620-0725
Michaela V Barrios, *President*
Ruben Barrios, *Admin Sec*
**EMP:** 5
**SALES (est):** 820.9K **Privately Held**
**SIC: 3672** Printed circuit boards

**(G-13796)**
**EMPIRE BRONZE CORP**
1130 N Ridge Ave (60148-1213)
PHONE..................................630 916-9722
Luciano Mordini, *President*
Ed Bandola, *Vice Pres*
▲ **EMP:** 16 **EST:** 1958
**SQ FT:** 12,000
**SALES (est):** 2.7MM **Privately Held**
**SIC: 3914 3446 3351** Ecclesiastical ware; architectural metalwork; copper rolling & drawing

**(G-13797)**
**EXCELL FASTENER SOLUTIONS INC**
920 N Ridge Ave Ste A7 (60148-1226)
PHONE..................................630 424-3360
**EMP:** 6
**SALES (est):** 641.8K **Privately Held**
**SIC: 3965** Fasteners

**(G-13798)**
**EXIDE TECHNOLOGIES**
Also Called: GNB Industrial Global Business
829 Parkview Blvd (60148-3230)
PHONE..................................678 566-9000
Bob Twidle, *Sls & Mktg Exec*
John Bondy, *Branch Mgr*
**EMP:** 86
**SALES (est):** 2.5B **Privately Held**
**SIC: 3691 3692** Lead acid batteries (storage batteries); primary batteries, dry & wet
**PA:** Exide Technologies
13000 Deerfield Pkwy # 200
Milton GA 30004
678 566-9000

**(G-13799)**
**FLOWSERVE CORPORATION**
10 Eisenhower Ln N (60148-5414)
PHONE..................................630 435-9596
James Baker, *Manager*
**EMP:** 25
**SALES (corp-wide):** 3.9B **Publicly Held**
**SIC: 3561** Pumps & pumping equipment
**PA:** Flowserve Corporation
5215 N Oconnor Blvd Connor
Irving TX 75039
972 443-6500

**(G-13800)**
**FLOYDWARE LLC**
1020 Parkview Blvd (60148-3238)
PHONE..................................630 469-1078
John Bertorelli, *VP Sales*
James Bower, *Manager*
Ron Guarisco, *CTO*
**EMP:** 2
**SALES (est):** 238.8K **Privately Held**
**SIC: 7372** Business oriented computer software

**(G-13801)**
**FOOT LOCKER RETAIL INC**
Also Called: Champs Sports
112 Yorktown Ctr (60148-5527)
PHONE..................................630 678-0155
Bogdan Babek, *Branch Mgr*
Brandon Kelvey, *Manager*
**EMP:** 8
**SALES (corp-wide):** 7.7B **Publicly Held**
**WEB:** www.venatorgroup.com
**SIC: 5661 2329** Footwear, athletic; athletic (warmup, sweat & jogging) suits: men's & boys'
**HQ:** Foot Locker Retail, Inc.
112 W 34th St Frnt 1
New York NY 10120

**(G-13802)**
**FRANK R WALKER COMPANY**
Also Called: Callahan Industries
700 Springer Dr (60148-6411)
PHONE..................................630 613-9312
Eugene Callahan, *President*
Scott Siddens, *Editor*
Doreen Saddler, *Sales Mgr*
**EMP:** 6
**SQ FT:** 5,000
**SALES (est):** 523.3K **Privately Held**
**WEB:** www.frankrwalker.com
**SIC: 2741 2731 2761 2721** Miscellaneous publishing; books: publishing only; manifold business forms; periodicals

**(G-13803)**
**FSI TECHNOLOGIES INC**
Also Called: Fork Standards
668 E Western Ave (60148-2005)
PHONE..................................630 932-9380
**Fax:** 630 932-0016
W Scott Tobey, *President*
Paul Curatolo, *Treasurer*
Ferd Turek, *Officer*
Gloria Tobey, *Admin Sec*
James Brown, *Technician*
**EMP:** 20
**SQ FT:** 5,500
**SALES (est):** 3.5MM **Privately Held**
**WEB:** www.fsinet.com
**SIC: 3825 3625 3823 3812** Oscillators, audio & radio frequency (instrument types); solenoid switches (industrial controls); industrial instrmnts msrmnt display/control process variable; search & navigation equipment; semiconductors & related devices; radio & TV communications equipment

**(G-13804)**
**FUEL RESEARCH & INSTRUMENT CO**
1919 S Highland Ave (60148-6153)
PHONE..................................630 953-2459
**EMP:** 3
**SALES (est):** 195.7K **Privately Held**
**SIC: 2869** Fuels

**(G-13805)**
**GRANADINO FOOD SERVICES CORP**
260 Cortland Ave Ste 11 (60148-1224)
PHONE..................................708 717-2930
Arturo Orozco, *President*
**EMP:** 15
**SQ FT:** 3,000
**SALES (est):** 581.4K **Privately Held**
**SIC: 2099** Seasonings & spices

**(G-13806)**
**GREAT LAKES SERVICE CHICAGO**
52 Eisenhower Ln N (60148-5414)
PHONE..................................630 627-4022
William Reedy, *President*
**EMP:** 4 **EST:** 2001
**SALES (est):** 873.4K **Privately Held**
**WEB:** www.greatlakesservice.com
**SIC: 3556** Food products machinery

**(G-13807)**
**GRIMM METAL FABRICATORS INC**
1121 N Garfield St (60148-1336)
PHONE..................................630 792-1710
**Fax:** 630 791-1714
Warren Buesching, *President*

▲ = Import ▼=Export
◆ =Import/Export

Kathleen Buesching, *Vice Pres*
Bud Buesching, *Manager*
Dianne Buesching, *Manager*
**EMP:** 21
**SQ FT:** 20,000
**SALES (est):** 5.7MM **Privately Held**
**SIC:** 3441 7692 3444 Fabricated structural metal; welding repair; sheet metalwork

**(G-13808)**
### HELANDER METAL SPINNING CO
931 N Ridge Ave (60148-1208)
P.O. Box 1824 (60148-8824)
**PHONE**..................630 268-9292
**Fax:** 630 268-9393
Samuel A Ibrahim, *President*
Siham Ibrahim, *CFO*
Judi White, *Sales Mgr*
Bharthi Patel, *Manager*
Don Szady, *Manager*
▲ **EMP:** 29
**SQ FT:** 30,000
**SALES (est):** 7.3MM **Privately Held**
**WEB:** www.helandermetal.com
**SIC:** 3444 3469 Sheet metalwork; metal stampings; spinning metal for the trade

**(G-13809)**
### HK AMERICA INC
Also Called: Hankwang U S A Incorporated
1120 N Garfield St (60148-1336)
**PHONE**..................630 916-0200
Jay Kay, *CEO*
Robert Won, *Vice Pres*
Young Kim, *Technical Mgr*
▲ **EMP:** 8
**SQ FT:** 9,000
**SALES (est):** 1.2MM **Privately Held**
**SIC:** 3699 Laser welding, drilling & cutting equipment

**(G-13810)**
### HOUSE OF RATTAN INC (PA)
18w375 Roosevelt Rd (60148-4167)
**PHONE**..................630 627-8160
Richard Sanders, *President*
Joann Sanders, *Treasurer*
Elizabeth Leonard, *Admin Sec*
▼ **EMP:** 3
**SALES (est):** 1.8MM **Privately Held**
**SIC:** 2519 5719 Rattan furniture: padded or plain; wicker, rattan or reed home furnishings

**(G-13811)**
### ICONN SYSTEMS LLC
1110 N Garfield St (60148-1336)
**PHONE**..................630 827-6000
Richard M Regole, *CEO*
Anthony Czyz, *Vice Pres*
Robert Smith, *VP Opers*
Jorge Villagran, *QC Mgr*
Ron Prokup, *VP Sls/Mktg*
▲ **EMP:** 30
**SQ FT:** 10,000
**SALES (est):** 7.1MM **Privately Held**
**SIC:** 3678 Electronic connectors

**(G-13812)**
### IDEAS INC (PA)
625 S Main St (60148-3341)
**PHONE**..................630 620-2010
**Fax:** 630 620-2014
Todd Ressa, *President*
Francis Ressa, *Corp Secy*
Carole M Ressa, *Vice Pres*
▲ **EMP:** 5
**SALES (est):** 2.4MM **Privately Held**
**SIC:** 2992 Lubricating oils & greases

**(G-13813)**
### J K CUSTOM COUNTERTOPS
820 N Ridge Ave Ste A (60148-1236)
**PHONE**..................630 495-2324
**Fax:** 630 495-2324
Gary McKenna, *Owner*
**EMP:** 3
**SQ FT:** 3,000
**SALES (est):** 173K **Privately Held**
**SIC:** 3231 2434 2431 2521 Furniture tops, glass: cut, beveled or polished; wood kitchen cabinets; doors & door parts & trim, wood; wood office furniture; wood partitions & fixtures

**(G-13814)**
### JAMES J SANDOVAL
Also Called: JMS Auto Electric
333 N Grace St (60148-1817)
**PHONE**..................734 717-7555
James J Sandoval, *Owner*
**EMP:** 4
**SALES (est):** 200K **Privately Held**
**SIC:** 5999 3699 Miscellaneous retail stores; electrical equipment & supplies

**(G-13815)**
### JODAAT INC
Also Called: Signs Now
18w333 Roosevelt Rd Ste 1 (60148-4180)
**PHONE**..................630 916-7776
**Fax:** 630 916-4950
Lori Pastuszak, *President*
**EMP:** 5
**SQ FT:** 2,200
**SALES (est):** 746.9K **Privately Held**
**SIC:** 3993 Signs & advertising specialties

**(G-13816)**
### KLEAN-KO INC
960 N Lombard Rd Ste A (60148-1261)
**PHONE**..................630 620-1860
**Fax:** 630 620-1429
Daniel E Marsh, *President*
Mary Lou Gregorio, *Vice Pres*
Vanda Marsh, *Shareholder*
Robert L Marsh, *Admin Sec*
**EMP:** 60
**SQ FT:** 5,000
**SALES (est):** 2.2MM **Privately Held**
**SIC:** 7349 2819 Janitorial service, contract basis; industrial inorganic chemicals

**(G-13817)**
### KOI COMPUTERS INC
200 W North Ave (60148-1205)
**PHONE**..................630 627-8811
**Fax:** 630 627-8877
Fanny Ho, *President*
Stan Ho, *Engineer*
Ayde Chavez, *Marketing Staff*
Rita Guillen, *Manager*
Catherine Ho, *Manager*
**EMP:** 6
**SQ FT:** 3,500
**SALES (est):** 2.3MM **Privately Held**
**SIC:** 7373 3571 5045 5734 Computer integrated systems design; electronic computers; computers, peripherals & software; computer peripheral equipment

**(G-13818)**
### KORMEX METAL CRAFT INC
961 Dupage Ave (60148)
**PHONE**..................630 953-8856
**Fax:** 630 953-8857
Chul Y Whang, *President*
Grace B Whang, *President*
Bok S Whang, *Vice Pres*
Rick Sansone, *Opers Mgr*
Grace Whang, *Human Res Dir*
**EMP:** 30
**SQ FT:** 22,000
**SALES (est):** 6.4MM **Privately Held**
**SIC:** 3444 3599 3549 Sheet metalwork; machine shop, jobbing & repair; metalworking machinery

**(G-13819)**
### LINE CRAFT INC
10 W North Ave (60148-1263)
**PHONE**..................630 932-1182
**EMP:** 15
**SALES (est):** 3.7MM **Privately Held**
**SIC:** 2672 Coated & laminated paper

**(G-13820)**
### LINE CRAFT TOOL COMPANY INC
Also Called: Amstadt Industries
10 W North Ave (60148-1263)
**PHONE**..................630 932-1182
**Fax:** 630 932-1195
Jakob Amstadt, *President*
Jack W Amstadt, *President*
Hildegard Amstadt, *Admin Sec*
**EMP:** 170 **EST:** 1976

**SALES (est):** 20.4MM **Privately Held**
**SIC:** 3599 5251 5084 3714 Machine shop, jobbing & repair; tools; machine tools & accessories; motor vehicle parts & accessories

**(G-13821)**
### LIQUITECH INC
421 Eisenhower Ln S (60148-5706)
**PHONE**..................630 693-0500
**Fax:** 630 693-0505
Steve Schira, *Chairman*
Tory Schira, *COO*
Mark Desanto, *Director*
Chuck Maw, *Director*
Joe Smith, *Director*
▲ **EMP:** 19
**SALES (est):** 5.1MM **Privately Held**
**SIC:** 3589 Water filters & softeners, household type

**(G-13822)**
### LSA UNITED INC
1020 E Emerson Ave (60148-3142)
**PHONE**..................773 476-7439
**Fax:** 773 476-2750
Richard W Gessner, *Ch of Bd*
Robert Brani, *Vice Pres*
Hal Miller, *Plant Mgr*
Connie Rae Wimmermark, *Admin Sec*
▲ **EMP:** 140
**SQ FT:** 47,000
**SALES (est):** 15.7MM **Privately Held**
**WEB:** www.lsaunited.net
**SIC:** 3469 Stamping metal for the trade

**(G-13823)**
### MACKS WOOD WORKING
544 S Highland Ave (60148-3053)
**PHONE**..................630 953-2559
Thomas A Macks, *Owner*
**EMP:** 3 **EST:** 2001
**SALES (est):** 229K **Privately Held**
**SIC:** 2499 Decorative wood & woodwork

**(G-13824)**
### MEDTRONIC INC
1 E 22nd St Ste 407 (60148-6159)
**PHONE**..................630 627-6677
**Fax:** 630 627-6705
Don Schoening, *Branch Mgr*
**EMP:** 25 **Privately Held**
**WEB:** www.medtronic.com
**SIC:** 3841 Surgical & medical instruments
**HQ:** Medtronic, Inc.
710 Medtronic Pkwy
Minneapolis MN 55432
763 514-4000

**(G-13825)**
### METAL IMPROVEMENT COMPANY LLC
E/M Coatings Solutions
129 Eisenhower Ln S (60148-5408)
**PHONE**..................630 620-6808
Don Breivik, *Prdtn Mgr*
Dan Tomasik, *Branch Mgr*
**EMP:** 36
**SALES (corp-wide):** 2.1B **Publicly Held**
**SIC:** 3443 Plate work for the nuclear industry
**HQ:** Metal Improvement Company, Llc
80 E State Rt 4 Ste 310
Paramus NJ 07652
201 843-7800

**(G-13826)**
### MIDWEST ENERGY MANAGEMENT INC
10 E 22nd St Ste 111 (60148-6107)
**PHONE**..................630 759-6007
Lonnie Samples, *President*
Thomas Samples, *Vice Pres*
Mark Brown, *Manager*
**EMP:** 6
**SQ FT:** 1,500
**SALES (est):** 1.1MM **Privately Held**
**WEB:** www.midwestenergymgmt.com
**SIC:** 3823 Industrial process measurement equipment

**(G-13827)**
### MINUTEMAN PRESS
347 W Eugenia St (60148-2236)
**PHONE**..................630 279-0438
Bob Peickert, *President*

Frank Esposito, *Owner*
**EMP:** 3
**SQ FT:** 1,800
**SALES (est):** 321.3K **Privately Held**
**SIC:** 2752 2791 2789 Commercial printing, lithographic; typesetting; bookbinding & related work

**(G-13828)**
### MOLDS & TOOLING
Also Called: Mitsuboshi Chem. Corporation
1040 N Ridge Ave (60148-1211)
**PHONE**..................630 627-9650
James Hennessy, *President*
**EMP:** 9
**SQ FT:** 40,000
**SALES (est):** 1MM
**SALES (corp-wide):** 584.2MM **Privately Held**
**WEB:** www.chemiflex.com
**SIC:** 3052 Plastic belting
**PA:** Mitsuboshi Belting Ltd.
4-1-21, Hamazoedori, Nagata-Ku
Kobe HYO 653-0
786 715-071

**(G-13829)**
### MONARCH MANUFACTURING
118 E Goebel Dr (60148-1736)
**PHONE**..................630 519-4580
Dave Petrucci, *Owner*
**EMP:** 3 **EST:** 1958
**SQ FT:** 3,000
**SALES (est):** 300K **Privately Held**
**SIC:** 3544 Forms (molds), for foundry & plastics working machinery; industrial molds

**(G-13830)**
### MUNTONS MALTED INGREDIENTS INC
2505 S Finley Rd Ste 130 (60148-4867)
**PHONE**..................630 812-1600
Giselle Mu, *Sales Mgr*
Simon Scott, *Sales Mgr*
Hannah Cappleman, *Cust Mgr*
Jake Mortiboys, *Sales Staff*
Katie Richardson, *Sales Staff*
**EMP:** 5 **EST:** 2009
**SALES (est):** 110.5K **Privately Held**
**SIC:** 2083 Malt

**(G-13831)**
### NANOLUBE INC
9 N Main St Ste 2 (60148-2351)
**PHONE**..................630 706-1250
Christopher Arnold, *President*
Marijean Arnold, *Corp Secy*
Richard Nagel, *Vice Pres*
▼ **EMP:** 3
**SALES (est):** 240K **Privately Held**
**SIC:** 2992 Lubricating oils & greases

**(G-13832)**
### NATURE S AMERICAN CO
665 W North Ave Ste 105 (60148-1134)
**PHONE**..................630 246-4776
Jason Samatas, *CEO*
Tyler Page, *General Mgr*
**EMP:** 2
**SALES:** 800K **Privately Held**
**SIC:** 2064 Granola & muesli, bars & clusters

**(G-13833)**
### NEXT GERNERATION
1052 N Du Page Ave (60148-1246)
**PHONE**..................630 261-1477
Stuart Fishman, *Owner*
**EMP:** 10
**SALES (est):** 1.4MM **Privately Held**
**SIC:** 2759 Commercial printing

**(G-13834)**
### NOVAK BUSINESS FORMS INC
20 Eisenhower Ln N (60148-5414)
**PHONE**..................630 932-9850
Mae Novak, *President*
Edward Novak, *Corp Secy*
**EMP:** 31
**SQ FT:** 10,000
**SALES (est):** 3.3MM **Privately Held**
**SIC:** 2752 2761 Business form & card printing, lithographic; manifold business forms

## Lombard - Dupage County (G-13835)

**(G-13835)**
**OLYMPIC SIGNS INC**
1130 N Garfield St (60148-1336)
PHONE..................630 424-6100
Fax: 630 424-6120
Rob Whitehead, *President*
Bill Pyter, *Vice Pres*
Rob Burgner, *Project Dir*
Tom Byers, *Accountant*
Guy Dragisic, *Accounts Mgr*
**EMP:** 48
**SQ FT:** 35,000
**SALES (est):** 7.9MM **Privately Held**
**WEB:** www.olysigns.com
**SIC:** 3993 Signs & advertising specialties

**(G-13836)**
**OLYMPUS AMERICA INC**
1900 Springer Dr (60148-6419)
PHONE..................630 953-2080
Fax: 630 953-2066
Ann Berry, *Manager*
Ann Kroupa, *Manager*
**EMP:** 14
**SQ FT:** 7,700
**SALES (corp-wide):** 6.5B **Privately Held**
**SIC:** 5043 3845 Cameras & photographic equipment; electromedical equipment
**HQ:** Olympus America Inc
3500 Corporate Pkwy
Center Valley PA 18034
484 896-5000

**(G-13837)**
**OMIOTEK COIL SPRING CO (PA)**
833 N Ridge Ave (60148-1286)
PHONE..................630 495-4056
Fax: 630 495-4073
Mike Omiotek, *President*
Diane Omiotek, *Vice Pres*
Edward Omiotek, *Vice Pres*
Victor Omiotek, *Vice Pres*
Mario Reglewski, *Manager*
▲ **EMP:** 60
**SQ FT:** 32,000
**SALES (est):** 8.5MM **Privately Held**
**SIC:** 3493 3469 3549 Coiled flat springs; stamping metal for the trade; metalworking machinery

**(G-13838)**
**ONYX ENVIRONMENTAL SVCS LLC (DH)**
700 E Bttrfeld Rd Ste 201 (60148)
PHONE..................630 218-1500
Jim Bell, *CEO*
Melanie Free, *General Mgr*
Wieneke Amos, *Business Mgr*
Mark Dennis, *Vice Pres*
Greig Siedor, *Vice Pres*
**EMP:** 20
**SQ FT:** 13,000
**SALES (est):** 351.1MM
**SALES (corp-wide):** 452.1MM **Privately Held**
**WEB:** www.onyxes.com
**SIC:** 8711 4953 2869 1799 Engineering services; hazardous waste collection & disposal; solvents, organic; asbestos removal & encapsulation; power plant construction
**HQ:** Veolia Environmental Services North America Corp.
200 E Randolph St # 7900
Chicago IL 60601
312 552-2800

**(G-13839)**
**ORORA NORTH AMERICA**
Also Called: Landsberg Chicago
100 E Progress Rd (60148-1333)
PHONE..................630 613-2600
Fax: 847 629-9700
Linda Caswick, *Senior Buyer*
Dan Sajdak, *Technical Mgr*
Michael Brawley, *Sales Mgr*
Jim Recher, *Sales Mgr*
Gary Loll, *Marketing Staff*
**EMP:** 80
**SALES (corp-wide):** 2.8B **Privately Held**
**SIC:** 5113 2653 Paper & products, wrapping or coarse; boxes, corrugated: made from purchased materials
**HQ:** Orora Packaging Solutions
6600 Valley View St
Buena Park CA 90620
714 562-6000

**(G-13840)**
**PACRIMSON FIRE RISK SVCS INC**
920 N Ridge Ave Ste C7 (60148-1226)
PHONE..................630 424-3400
Anna Grezenko, *Treasurer*
**EMP:** 1
**SALES (est):** 283.2K **Privately Held**
**SIC:** 3569 Firefighting apparatus & related equipment

**(G-13841)**
**PANZER TOOL CORP**
920 N Ridge Ave Ste A2 (60148-1226)
PHONE..................630 519-5214
Fax: 630 628-8508
Earl Proball, *President*
Charles Proball, *Vice Pres*
**EMP:** 4 **EST:** 1964
**SQ FT:** 9,000
**SALES:** 700K **Privately Held**
**SIC:** 3544 Special dies & tools; industrial molds

**(G-13842)**
**PARTEX MARKING SYSTEMS INC**
1155 N Main St (60148-1360)
PHONE..................630 516-0400
Fax: 630 833-7631
Barbara Susmilch, *Project Mgr*
Lennart Anderdahl, *Export Mgr*
Viveca Blomquist, *Export Mgr*
Janet Torres, *Manager*
**EMP:** 4
**SALES (est):** 1.4MM
**SALES (corp-wide):** 23.2MM **Privately Held**
**WEB:** www.partex-marking.com
**SIC:** 5063 3496 Wire & cable; cable conduit; miscellaneous fabricated wire products
**HQ:** Partex Marking Systems Ab
Tore Loofs Gata 2
Gullspang 547 3
551 280-00

**(G-13843)**
**PATE COMPANY INC**
245 Eisenhower Ln S (60148-5407)
PHONE..................630 705-1920
Micheal Pylypczak, *President*
John R Gritis, *Vice Pres*
Joseph Valente, *Treasurer*
Leon Richlak, *Natl Sales Mgr*
Tom Sauer, *Sales Mgr*
**EMP:** 35 **EST:** 1963
**SQ FT:** 45,000
**SALES (est):** 8.2MM **Privately Held**
**WEB:** www.patecurbs.com
**SIC:** 3444 Roof deck, sheet metal

**(G-13844)**
**PRECISION PRINTING INC**
230 Eisenhower Ln N (60148-5403)
P.O. Box 427 (60148-0427)
PHONE..................630 737-0075
Kevin Bauman, *Principal*
**EMP:** 5 **EST:** 2010
**SALES (est):** 689.2K **Privately Held**
**SIC:** 2752 Commercial printing, lithographic

**(G-13845)**
**PRESS BRAKES**
260 Cortland Ave Ste 6 (60148-1224)
PHONE..................630 916-1494
John Pekny, *President*
**EMP:** 6
**SALES (est):** 305.6K **Privately Held**
**SIC:** 3542 Press brakes

**(G-13846)**
**PRS INC**
434 S Ahrens Ave (60148-3006)
PHONE..................630 620-7259
Paul Sanko, *President*
**EMP:** 2 **EST:** 2000
**SALES (est):** 233K **Privately Held**
**SIC:** 3543 Foundry patternmaking

**(G-13847)**
**QC COMPONENTS & SALES INC**
260 Cortland Ave Ste 9 (60148-1224)
PHONE..................630 268-0644
James McGuire, *President*
**EMP:** 12
**SQ FT:** 4,000
**SALES (est):** 1.5MM **Privately Held**
**SIC:** 3599 Custom machinery

**(G-13848)**
**ROTO-DIE COMPANY INC**
Also Called: Roto Die Company
1054 N Du Page Ave (60148-1246)
PHONE..................630 932-8605
**EMP:** 3
**SALES (corp-wide):** 183.5MM **Privately Held**
**SIC:** 3544 Special dies, tools, jigs & fixtures
**PA:** Roto-Die Company, Inc.
800 Howerton Ln
Eureka MO 63025
636 587-3600

**(G-13849)**
**S A W CO**
376 E Saint Charles Rd # 5 (60148-2376)
P.O. Box 233, Addison (60101-0233)
PHONE..................630 678-5400
Sylvester Wetle, *Owner*
**EMP:** 3
**SALES (est):** 170K **Privately Held**
**SIC:** 3641 Electric lamps & parts for generalized applications

**(G-13850)**
**SAF-T-LOK INTERNATIONAL CORP**
Also Called: Saf-T-Eze
300 Eisenhower Ln N (60148-5405)
PHONE..................630 495-2001
Fax: 630 495-8813
Helen C Sherry, *President*
Neal Sherry, *Purch Mgr*
Andrew Merrill, *Regl Sales Mgr*
Shaun Sherry, *Mktg Dir*
Madonna Lawrence, *Office Mgr*
**EMP:** 20
**SQ FT:** 25,000
**SALES (est):** 4.6MM **Privately Held**
**WEB:** www.saftlok.com
**SIC:** 2891 Adhesives & sealants

**(G-13851)**
**SAFETY COMPOUND CORPORATION**
Also Called: Saftey Glass
300 Eisenhower Ln N (60148-5405)
PHONE..................630 953-1515
James Wendell Sherry, *President*
Helen C Sherry, *Admin Sec*
**EMP:** 20
**SALES (est):** 2.9MM **Privately Held**
**SIC:** 2891 2899 Sealants; corrosion preventive lubricant

**(G-13852)**
**SEAMLESS GUTTER CORP**
Also Called: A Seamless Gutters
601 E Saint Charles Rd (60148-2099)
PHONE..................630 495-9800
Fax: 630 495-9864
Robert G Carter, *President*
Brian Carter, *Vice Pres*
Scott Carter, *Vice Pres*
Nancy Hull, *Office Admin*
Marlene Carter, *Admin Sec*
**EMP:** 50
**SALES (est):** 5MM **Privately Held**
**SIC:** 1761 3444 3429 Siding contractor; gutter & downspout contractor; sheet metalwork; manufactured hardware (general)

**(G-13853)**
**SIGNWISE INC**
208 W North Ave (60148-1205)
PHONE..................630 932-3204
Fax: 630 932-3205
Kevin Nolan, *President*
Tom Nolan, *Vice Pres*
**EMP:** 5
**SQ FT:** 800
**SALES (est):** 466.4K **Privately Held**
**SIC:** 3993 Signs, not made in custom sign painting shops

**(G-13854)**
**SPECIALIZED WOODWORK INC**
Also Called: Plastic Art
74 Eisenhower Ln N (60148-5414)
PHONE..................630 627-0450
Fax: 630 627-0452
**EMP:** 3 **EST:** 1956
**SQ FT:** 2,500
**SALES:** 400K **Privately Held**
**SIC:** 3089 2541 2511 2434 Mfg Plastic Products Mfg Wood Partitions/Fixt Mfg Wood Household Furn Mfg Wood Kitchen Cabinet

**(G-13855)**
**SPECIALTY FOODS HOLDINGS INC**
Also Called: Scott Petersen & Company
477 E Bttrfeld Rd Ste 410 (60148)
PHONE..................630 599-5900
Jim Bolnius, *Manager*
**EMP:** 5 **Privately Held**
**SIC:** 2013 2011 Prepared beef products from purchased beef; meat packing plants
**PA:** Specialty Foods Holdings, Inc.
6 Dublin Ln
Owensboro KY 42301

**(G-13856)**
**SPECTRACRAFTS LTD**
Also Called: All Spun Metal Products
931 N Ridge Ave (60148-1208)
PHONE..................847 824-4117
Fax: 847 824-0419
Gianfranco Isaia, *President*
John Horstmann, *Controller*
Maria Isaia, *Admin Sec*
**EMP:** 9
**SQ FT:** 10,000
**SALES (est):** 1MM **Privately Held**
**SIC:** 3469 3441 Spinning metal for the trade; fabricated structural metal

**(G-13857)**
**SPEEDPRO OF DUPAGE**
441 Eisenhower Ln S (60148-5706)
PHONE..................630 812-5080
Jim Delaney, *Owner*
**EMP:** 4 **EST:** 2010
**SALES (est):** 438K **Privately Held**
**SIC:** 3577 Printers & plotters

**(G-13858)**
**STALEX INC**
1051 N Main St Ste A (60148-1350)
PHONE..................630 627-9401
Alex A Muchajer, *President*
William R Wilson, *Vice Pres*
Lori Nielsen, *Office Mgr*
**EMP:** 8
**SQ FT:** 10,000
**SALES (est):** 830K **Privately Held**
**WEB:** www.stalexinc.com
**SIC:** 3549 Coilers (metalworking machines)

**(G-13859)**
**STANLEY SECURITY SOLUTIONS INC**
Also Called: Best Access Systems
840 Oak Creek Dr (60148-6405)
PHONE..................877 476-4968
Mark Slingerland, *Manager*
**EMP:** 15
**SALES (corp-wide):** 11.4B **Publicly Held**
**WEB:** www.bestlock.com
**SIC:** 3429 Keys, locks & related hardware
**HQ:** Stanley Security Solutions, Inc.
9998 Crosspoint Blvd # 3
Indianapolis IN 46256
317 849-2255

**(G-13860)**
**STEVES CIGARETTES**
1247 S Main St (60148-4535)
PHONE..................630 827-0820
Sam Jaber, *President*
**EMP:** 2
**SALES:** 950K **Privately Held**
**SIC:** 2111 Cigarettes

## GEOGRAPHIC SECTION — Long Grove - Lake County (G-13886)

**(G-13861)**
**STURTEVANT INC**
Also Called: Fcm Mills
959 N Garfield St (60148-1336)
PHONE..................630 613-8968
Tomas Johansson, *Branch Mgr*
**EMP:** 4
**SALES (corp-wide):** 8MM **Privately Held**
**SIC:** 3999 Custom pulverizing & grinding of plastic materials
**PA:** Sturtevant, Inc.
    348 Circuit St Ste 1
    Hanover MA 02339
    781 829-6501

**(G-13862)**
**SUPERIOR BUMPERS INC**
920 N Ridge Ave Ste C3 (60148-1226)
PHONE..................630 932-4910
John Lindquist, *President*
**EMP:** 5
**SALES:** 1MM **Privately Held**
**WEB:** www.superiorbumpers.com
**SIC:** 3069 Medical & laboratory rubber sundries & related products

**(G-13863)**
**T G AUTOMOTIVE**
901 N Ridge Ave Ste 1 (60148-1228)
P.O. Box 395 (60148-0395)
PHONE..................630 916-7818
Fax: 630 916-1138
Greg Soulides, *President*
Frank Novelli, *Vice Pres*
Paul Jackson, *QC Mgr*
**EMP:** 30
**SQ FT:** 1,600
**SALES (est):** 1MM **Privately Held**
**WEB:** www.tgautomotive.com
**SIC:** 3714 7536 5531 Motor vehicle parts & accessories; motor vehicle wheels & parts; automotive glass replacement shops; automotive & home supply stores

**(G-13864)**
**TASSOS METAL INC**
950 N Lombard Rd (60148-1231)
PHONE..................630 953-1333
Fax: 630 953-9893
Tassos Dafnis, *President*
Kathryn Dafnis, *Admin Sec*
▲ **EMP:** 30
**SQ FT:** 30,000
**SALES (est):** 5.5MM **Privately Held**
**SIC:** 3444 Sheet metalwork

**(G-13865)**
**TAURUS SAFETY PRODUCTS INC**
39 S Glenview Ave (60148-2463)
P.O. Box 1002 (60148-8002)
PHONE..................630 620-7940
Joseph Wimberly, *President*
Deborah Wimberly, *Admin Sec*
**EMP:** 7
**SALES (est):** 711K **Privately Held**
**SIC:** 3272 3644 Chimney caps, concrete; noncurrent-carrying wiring services

**(G-13866)**
**TEC REP CORPORATION**
1919 S Highland Ave 330a (60148-4979)
PHONE..................630 627-9110
Ronald Kleinschmidt, *President*
Barbara Simone, *Vice Pres*
**EMP:** 11
**SALES (est):** 43.5K **Privately Held**
**SIC:** 3825 Test equipment for electronic & electric measurement

**(G-13867)**
**TELLA TOOL & MFG CO (PA)**
Also Called: Tella Technology Div
1015 N Ridge Ave Ste 1 (60148-1258)
PHONE..................630 495-0545
Fax: 630 495-3056
Scott Prince, *President*
Daniel M Provenzano, *Corp Secy*
Scott Kaurin, *Project Mgr*
Richard Wagy, *Opers Mgr*
Ed Hurtig, *Purch Mgr*
**EMP:** 100
**SQ FT:** 65,000
**SALES (est):** 33.7MM **Privately Held**
**SIC:** 3544 3444 Special dies, tools, jigs & fixtures; sheet metal specialties, not stamped

**(G-13868)**
**THERAPEUTIC SKIN CARE**
21w221 Hemstead Rd (60148-5148)
PHONE..................630 244-1833
Susie Fricano, *President*
**EMP:** 6
**SALES:** 266K **Privately Held**
**SIC:** 2834 Dermatologicals

**(G-13869)**
**TORNOS TECHNOLOGIES US CORP (PA)**
840 Parkview Blvd (60148-3200)
PHONE..................630 812-2040
Jon Dobosenski, *Vice Pres*
▲ **EMP:** 8
**SALES (est):** 1.2MM **Privately Held**
**SIC:** 3545 Machine tool attachments & accessories

**(G-13870)**
**TOWER PRINTING & DESIGN**
2211 S Highland Ave 5a (60148-5333)
PHONE..................630 495-1976
John Wimmer, *Owner*
**EMP:** 3
**SQ FT:** 2,000
**SALES:** 250K **Privately Held**
**SIC:** 2752 2791 2789 Commercial printing, lithographic; typesetting; bookbinding & related work

**(G-13871)**
**TRICOR INTERNATIONAL INC**
678 E Western Ave (60148-2005)
P.O. Box 367 (60148-0367)
PHONE..................630 629-1213
Fax: 630 629-1230
Tom J Hebda, *President*
Eric Ebert, *Manager*
T K Hebda, *Admin Sec*
**EMP:** 20
**SQ FT:** 7,000
**SALES (est):** 3.5MM **Privately Held**
**WEB:** www.tcisales.com
**SIC:** 3699 Door opening & closing devices, electrical

**(G-13872)**
**TRIMARK SCREEN PRINTING INC**
710 E Western Ave Ste C (60148-2005)
PHONE..................630 629-2823
Debbie Martin, *President*
Keith Martin, *Vice Pres*
**EMP:** 5
**SQ FT:** 900
**SALES:** 200K **Privately Held**
**SIC:** 2759 2396 2395 Screen printing; automotive & apparel trimmings; pleating & stitching

**(G-13873)**
**TRP ACQUISITION CORP (PA)**
Also Called: Room Place, The
1000 N Rohlwing Rd Ste 46 (60148-1187)
PHONE..................630 261-2380
Joe Connolly, *CEO*
▲ **EMP:** 4
**SALES (est):** 157.8MM **Privately Held**
**SIC:** 2512 Living room furniture: upholstered on wood frames

**(G-13874)**
**TRUE LACROSSE LLC**
131 Eisenhower Ln N (60148-5413)
PHONE..................630 359-3857
Ryan Covert, *Managing Dir*
Flannery Posner, *Mktg Dir*
Dan Catzere, *Director*
Colin Davis, *Director*
Giuseppe Palermo, *Director*
**EMP:** 4
**SALES:** 78.2K **Privately Held**
**SIC:** 3949 Lacrosse equipment & supplies, general

**(G-13875)**
**UDCE LIMITED**
Also Called: Universal Drilling and Cutting
974 N Du Page Ave (60148-1244)
PHONE..................630 495-9940
Michael Hatfield, *Vice Pres*
**EMP:** 8
**SQ FT:** 10,000
**SALES:** 4.5MM
**SALES (corp-wide):** 173.4K **Privately Held**
**SIC:** 3545 Cutting tools for machine tools
**HQ:** Universal Drilling & Cutting Equipment Limited
    43 Catley Road
    Sheffield S9 5J
    114 291-1000

**(G-13876)**
**UNCOMMON USA INC (PA)**
1146 N Main St (60148-1362)
PHONE..................630 268-9672
Mark Erickson, *President*
Ed Reeder, *Vice Pres*
Phil Snidf, *Sales Mgr*
Celina Klein, *Manager*
▲ **EMP:** 10
**SQ FT:** 13,000
**SALES (est):** 4.9MM **Privately Held**
**WEB:** www.uncommonusa.com
**SIC:** 3446 Flagpoles, metal

**(G-13877)**
**VELOCITY SOFTWARE LLC**
1042 E Maple St (60148)
PHONE..................800 351-6893
Brian Kramer, *Principal*
David D O'Sullivan, *Principal*
Colin Finn, *Accounts Mgr*
**EMP:** 12
**SALES:** 1.3MM **Privately Held**
**SIC:** 7372 Prepackaged software

**(G-13878)**
**VERTIV GROUP CORPORATION**
995 Oak Creek Dr (60148-6408)
PHONE..................630 579-5000
Michael Bax, *Vice Pres*
Kevin Bailey, *Branch Mgr*
John Russer, *Manager*
Karthik Kailasam, *Director*
Paul Misar, *Director*
**EMP:** 39 **Privately Held**
**SIC:** 3661 3644 Telephone & telegraph apparatus; noncurrent-carrying wiring services
**HQ:** Vertiv Group Corporation
    1050 Dearborn Dr
    Columbus OH 43085
    614 888-0246

**(G-13879)**
**VISKASE COMPANIES INC (HQ)**
333 E Butterfield Rd # 400 (60148-5679)
PHONE..................630 874-0700
Fax: 630 455-2158
Thomas D Davis, *Ch of Bd*
Jean-Luc Tillon, *President*
Gonzalo Valdez, *General Mgr*
Maurice J Ryan, *Senior VP*
Michael M Blecic, *Vice Pres*
◆ **EMP:** 100
**SALES:** 343.5MM
**SALES (corp-wide):** 16.3B **Publicly Held**
**WEB:** www.viskase.com
**SIC:** 3089 Celluloid products; cases, plastic; battery cases, plastic or plastic combination
**PA:** Icahn Enterprises L.P.
    767 5th Ave Ste 4700
    New York NY 10153
    212 702-4300

**(G-13880)**
**VISKASE CORPORATION (DH)**
333 E Bttrfield Rd Ste 400 (60148)
PHONE..................630 874-0700
Fax: 630 874-0178
F Edward Gustafson, *Ch of Bd*
John F Weber, *President*
Gordon S Donovan, *Vice Pres*
Pat Glarrow, *Plant Mgr*
Kimberly Diddia, *Office Mgr*
▼ **EMP:** 80
**SQ FT:** 45,000
**SALES (est):** 234.9MM
**SALES (corp-wide):** 16.3B **Publicly Held**
**SIC:** 3089 Celluloid products
**HQ:** Viskase Companies, Inc.
    333 E Butterfield Rd # 400
    Lombard IL 60148
    630 874-0700

**(G-13881)**
**WE LOVE SOY INC**
Also Called: Chicago Soy Dairy
905 N Ridge Ave Ste 8 (60148-1227)
P.O. Box 666, Glen Ellyn (60138-0666)
PHONE..................630 629-9667
Ryan D Howard, *President*
Joe Conway, *Plant Mgr*
Daniel Ziegler, *Admin Sec*
**EMP:** 8
**SQ FT:** 4,400
**SALES (est):** 490.6K **Privately Held**
**WEB:** www.welovesoy.com
**SIC:** 2024 2064 2022 Ice cream & frozen desserts; marshmallows; imitation cheese

**(G-13882)**
**WELCH PACKAGING LLC**
Also Called: Go Packaging
1000 N Main St (60148-1361)
PHONE..................630 916-8090
Kyle Hawkins, *Branch Mgr*
**EMP:** 5
**SALES (corp-wide):** 160.2MM **Privately Held**
**SIC:** 2621 5999 Wrapping & packaging papers; packaging materials: boxes, padding, etc.
**HQ:** Welch Packaging, Llc
    1020 Herman St
    Elkhart IN 46516
    574 295-2460

**(G-13883)**
**WESTMORE SUPPLY CO**
250 Westmore Meyers Rd (60148-3088)
PHONE..................630 627-0278
Fax: 630 627-0613
John A Bielenda, *President*
Mark Bielenda, *Vice Pres*
**EMP:** 10
**SQ FT:** 75,000
**SALES:** 1.6MM **Privately Held**
**WEB:** www.westmoresupply.com
**SIC:** 5983 3273 Fuel oil dealers; ready-mixed concrete

**(G-13884)**
**WHALE MANUFACTURING INC**
870 N Ridge Ave (60148-1215)
PHONE..................847 357-9192
Ron Lepinski, *President*
**EMP:** 4
**SQ FT:** 2,000
**SALES (est):** 250K **Privately Held**
**SIC:** 3599 Custom machinery

**(G-13885)**
**YORKE PRINTE SHOPPE INC**
930 N Lombard Rd (60148-1231)
PHONE..................630 627-4960
Fax: 630 627-4965
Bradley P Scull, *President*
Sharon L Scull, *Vice Pres*
Gerald Wheeler, *Plant Mgr*
Philip E Scull, *Treasurer*
Michele Willis-Rosso, *Marketing Mgr*
**EMP:** 41 **EST:** 1969
**SQ FT:** 20,500
**SALES (est):** 9.9MM **Privately Held**
**WEB:** www.yorkeprinte.com
**SIC:** 2752 Commercial printing, offset

## Long Grove
### Lake County

**(G-13886)**
**BENTLEYS PET STUFF LLC**
4196 Illinois Rte 83 (60047)
PHONE..................847 793-0500
**EMP:** 14
**SALES (corp-wide):** 1.4MM **Privately Held**
**SIC:** 3999 Animal specialty services

# Long Grove - Lake County (G-13887) — GEOGRAPHIC SECTION

**HQ:** Bentley's Pet Stuff, Llc
4192 Ill Rte 83 Ste C
Long Grove IL 60047
224 567-4700

### (G-13887)
### BENTLEYS PET STUFF LLC (HQ)
4192 Ill Rte 83 Ste C  (60047)
**PHONE**.................224 567-4700
Marcus Lemonis, *Mng Member*
**EMP:** 2
**SALES (est):** 1.3MM
**SALES (corp-wide):** 1.4MM  Privately Held
**SIC:** 3999  Pet supplies
**PA:** Bentley's Corner Barkery, Ltd.
12 S Dunton Ave
Arlington Heights IL 60005
224 735-2160

### (G-13888)
### BROKEN EARTH WINERY
219 Rbert Prker Coffin Rd  (60047-9616)
**PHONE**.................847 383-5052
Melissa Forsythe, *Principal*
**EMP:** 10
**SALES (est):** 305.1K  Privately Held
**SIC:** 2084  Wines

### (G-13889)
### CONTROL SYSTEMS INC
3603 Crestview Dr  (60047-5231)
**PHONE**.................847 438-6228
Gerhard Maier, *President*
Susanne Maier, *Corp Secy*
**EMP:** 7  **EST:** 2000
**SALES (est):** 1.3MM  Privately Held
**WEB:** www.electroniccontrol.com
**SIC:** 3625  Control equipment, electric

### (G-13890)
### CUSTOM INNOVATION LLC
4634 Twin Lakes Ln  (60047-5279)
**PHONE**.................847 847-7100
Steven Hoffman, *Mng Member*
◆ **EMP:** 2
**SALES (est):** 235.7K  Privately Held
**SIC:** 3585  Parts for heating, cooling & refrigerating equipment

### (G-13891)
### INTEL CORP
1 Corporate Dr Ste 310  (60047-8954)
**PHONE**.................847 602-1170
**EMP:** 5
**SALES (est):** 285.9K  Privately Held
**SIC:** 3674  Microprocessors

### (G-13892)
### INTERNATIONAL DRUG DEV CONS
Also Called: Iddc
1549 Rfd  (60047-9532)
**PHONE**.................847 634-9586
**Fax:** 847 634-3349
Esam Dajani, *President*
**EMP:** 5
**SALES (est):** 377.1K  Privately Held
**SIC:** 2834  Druggists' preparations (pharmaceuticals)

### (G-13893)
### LORDAHL MANUFACTURING CO
Also Called: Lordahl Engineering
1571 Rfd  (60047-9789)
**PHONE**.................847 244-0448
Var Lordahl, *Owner*
Frank O'Sullivan, *Vice Pres*
Scott Koepsel, *Engrg Mgr*
**EMP:** 59
**SALES (corp-wide):** 7.8MM  Privately Held
**SIC:** 4225  5074  3089  General warehousing; plumbing & hydronic heating supplies; molding primary plastic
**PA:** Lordahl Manufacturing Co.
1001 S Lewis Ave
Waukegan IL 60085
847 244-0448

### (G-13894)
### MANGEL AND CO
Also Called: Long Grove Apple Haus
230 Rbert Prker Coffin Rd  (60047-9539)
**PHONE**.................847 634-0730
**Fax:** 847 634-0730
John Blyth, *Manager*
**EMP:** 10
**SALES (corp-wide):** 6.3MM  Privately Held
**SIC:** 5149  2099  2051  5499  Bakery products; food preparations; bread, cake & related products; juices, fruit or vegetable
**PA:** Mangel And Co.
333 Lexington Dr
Buffalo Grove IL 60089
847 459-3100

### (G-13895)
### MAT CAPITAL LLC (PA)
6700 Wildlife Way  (60047)
**PHONE**.................847 821-9630
Steve Wang,
**EMP:** 3
**SALES (est):** 542.3K  Privately Held
**SIC:** 3089  3999  5141  6719  Plastic kitchenware, tableware & houseware; straw goods; food brokers; investment holding companies, except banks

### (G-13896)
### MAT ENGINE TECHNOLOGIES LLC (DH)
6700 Wildlife Way  (60047)
**PHONE**.................847 821-9630
Greg Purse, *CFO*
Steve Wang,
▲ **EMP:** 1
**SALES (est):** 19.7MM  Privately Held
**SIC:** 3694  Engine electrical equipment
**HQ:** Mat Industries, Llc
6700 Wildlife Way
Long Grove IL 60047
847 821-9630

### (G-13897)
### MAT HOLDINGS INC (PA)
Also Called: MAT-AUTOMOTIVE
6700 Wildlife Way  (60047)
**PHONE**.................847 821-9630
Steve Wang, *CEO*
George Ruhl, *President*
Charles Walker, *Senior VP*
Darin Aprati, *Vice Pres*
Grace Chang, *Vice Pres*
◆ **EMP:** 100
**SALES:** 1.4B  Privately Held
**SIC:** 2842  3714  3563  Specialty cleaning, polishes & sanitation goods; motor vehicle parts & accessories; air & gas compressors including vacuum pumps

### (G-13898)
### MAT INDUSTRIES LLC (HQ)
6700 Wildlife Way  (60047)
**PHONE**.................847 821-9630
Greg Purse,
◆ **EMP:** 4
**SALES:** 107.1MM  Privately Held
**SIC:** 3563  Air & gas compressors

### (G-13899)
### NATIONAL SCHOOL SERVICES INC
3254 Mayflower Ln  (60047-5019)
**PHONE**.................847 438-3859
Norman Olson, *President*
**EMP:** 30
**SQ FT:** 3,000
**SALES (est):** 1.9MM  Privately Held
**WEB:** www.n-s-s.com
**SIC:** 7373  7313  2731  5999  Computer integrated systems design; radio, television, publisher representatives; textbooks: publishing only, not printed on site; education aids, devices & supplies

### (G-13900)
### PATTERSON AVENUE TOOL COMPANY
6515 High Meadow Ct  (60047-5109)
**PHONE**.................847 949-8100
James M Clarke, *President*
Karen Ann Keane, *Corp Secy*
Margo M Clarke, *Vice Pres*
▲ **EMP:** 3
**SALES:** 120K  Privately Held
**SIC:** 3423  Hand & edge tools

### (G-13901)
### SHERWIN-WILLIAMS COMPANY
Also Called: Sherwin Williams
4194 Il Route 83  (60047-9563)
**PHONE**.................847 478-0677
Shawn Faulkner, *Site Mgr*
**EMP:** 4
**SALES (corp-wide):** 11.8B  Publicly Held
**SIC:** 5231  5198  2851  Paint & painting supplies; paints, varnishes & supplies; wood fillers or sealers
**PA:** The Sherwin-Williams Company
101 W Prospect Ave # 1020
Cleveland OH 44115
216 566-2000

### (G-13902)
### TIGER ACCESSORY GROUP LLC (HQ)
Also Called: MAT-AUTOMOTIVE
6700 Wildlife Way  (60047)
**PHONE**.................847 821-9630
Steve Wang, *Owner*
Terry Obrien, *CFO*
Susan Nustra, *Director*
Mary Ann, *Executive Asst*
George Ruhl,
▲ **EMP:** 5
**SQ FT:** 2,500
**SALES:** 45.1MM  Privately Held
**WEB:** www.midwest-air.com
**SIC:** 2842  2259  3647  Specialty cleaning preparations; towels, knit; motor vehicle lighting equipment

### (G-13903)
### TOM ZOSEL ASSOCIATES LTD
Also Called: Tza Consulting
3880 Salem Lake Dr Ste B  (60047-5292)
**PHONE**.................847 540-6543
Thomas W Zosel, *CEO*
Evan Danner, *President*
Lisa Danner, *Vice Pres*
Chase Sowden, *Vice Pres*
Rob Weiland, *Vice Pres*
◆ **EMP:** 60
**SQ FT:** 10,000
**SALES (est):** 8.1MM  Privately Held
**WEB:** www.tzaconsulting.com
**SIC:** 8742  7372  Management consulting services; prepackaged software

### (G-13904)
### VALENTINO VINEYARDS INC
Also Called: Valentino Vineyards & Winery
5175 Aptakisic Rd  (60047-5186)
**PHONE**.................847 634-2831
Rudolph Valentino, *President*
**EMP:** 3
**SALES (est):** 173.5K  Privately Held
**SIC:** 2084  Wines

### (G-13905)
### WEILAND FAST TRAC INC
3386 Rfd  (60047-9724)
P.O. Box 1059, Lake Zurich  (60047-1059)
**PHONE**.................847 438-7996
David Weiland, *President*
Terry Weiland, *Vice Pres*
Kathy Weiland, *Treasurer*
Norma Weiland, *Admin Sec*
**EMP:** 4
**SALES (est):** 382K  Privately Held
**SIC:** 3069  5571  3061  Hard rubber & molded rubber products; motorcycle dealers; mechanical rubber goods

---

## Lostant
### Lasalle County

### (G-13906)
### HART ELECTRIC LLC
102 S Main St  (61334-9004)
P.O. Box 230  (61334-0230)
**PHONE**.................815 368-3341
**Fax:** 815 368-3341
Milton Hartenbower,
Catherine Hartenbower,
Milton Fred Hartenbower,
**EMP:** 45
**SQ FT:** 10,000
**SALES (est):** 10.6MM  Privately Held
**WEB:** www.accesselectronicsinc.com
**SIC:** 3679  Harness assemblies for electronic use: wire or cable

### (G-13907)
### PHOENIX PAPER PRODUCTS INC
1652 N Us Highway 251  (61334-9628)
**PHONE**.................815 368-3343
**Fax:** 815 368-3428
Terry Havens, *President*
Sam J Morris, *Vice Pres*
James Dale, *Admin Sec*
**EMP:** 13
**SQ FT:** 30,000
**SALES (est):** 4.3MM  Privately Held
**WEB:** www.greenchoice.com
**SIC:** 2679  Paper products, converted

### (G-13908)
### PORCH ELECTRIC LLC
205 N Main St  (61334-9017)
**PHONE**.................815 368-3230
Janet Porch,
Eric Porch,
**EMP:** 2
**SALES (est):** 347.8K  Privately Held
**SIC:** 3643  Current-carrying wiring devices

---

## Louisville
### Clay County

### (G-13909)
### R & W OIL COMPANY
6166 Bible Grove Ln  (62858-2468)
**PHONE**.................618 686-3084
**Fax:** 618 686-3085
Stanley Kincaid, *President*
**EMP:** 5
**SQ FT:** 2,000
**SALES:** 171.8K  Privately Held
**SIC:** 1311  Crude petroleum production

### (G-13910)
### SIMS COMPANY INC
1431 Panther Creek Ln  (62858-2573)
P.O. Box 129  (62858-0129)
**PHONE**.................618 665-3901
Scott Sims, *President*
Lori Sims, *Admin Sec*
**EMP:** 2
**SQ FT:** 5,500
**SALES:** 400K  Privately Held
**SIC:** 1389  Chemically treating wells

---

## Loves Park
### Winnebago County

### (G-13911)
### A-L-L EQUIPMENT COMPANY
5619 Pike Rd  (61111-4710)
P.O. Box 909, Moline  (61266-0909)
**PHONE**.................815 877-7000
Erick Welser, *Manager*
**EMP:** 7
**SALES (corp-wide):** 6MM  Privately Held
**WEB:** www.a-l-lequipment.com
**SIC:** 5084  5075  3561  Pumps & pumping equipment; compressors, except air conditioning; compressors, air conditioning; pumps & pumping equipment
**PA:** A-L-L Equipment Company
204 38th St
Moline IL 61265
309 762-8096

### (G-13912)
### ADVANCED AUTOMATION SYSTEMS
5318 Forest Hills Ct  (61111-8319)
**PHONE**.................815 877-1075
**Fax:** 815 877-1284
John Haulotte, *Owner*
**EMP:** 4  **EST:** 2000
**SQ FT:** 3,000

# GEOGRAPHIC SECTION
## Loves Park - Winnebago County (G-13939)

SALES (est): 275K **Privately Held**
SIC: 3491 Automatic regulating & control valves

### (G-13913)
### ADVANCED HEAT TREATING INC
980 Industrial Ct (61111-7512)
PHONE.....................815 877-8593
Fax: 815 877-8605
Gloria Stuhr Pernacciaro, *CEO*
Chuck Pernacciaro, *President*
Jerry Otterson, *Plant Mgr*
Bill Hawker, *Manager*
Doug Colson, *Director*
EMP: 25
SALES (est): 5.8MM **Privately Held**
WEB: www.advancedheattreat.com
SIC: 3398 Metal heat treating

### (G-13914)
### AERO ALEHOUSE
6164 E Riverside Blvd (61111-4468)
PHONE.....................815 977-5602
Pendergrass Matthew,
EMP: 4
SALES (est): 203K **Privately Held**
SIC: 2082 5812 Ale (alcoholic beverage); eating places

### (G-13915)
### AGI CORP
6075 Material Ave Ste 100 (61111-4242)
P.O. Box 2506 (61132-2506)
PHONE.....................815 708-0502
Christopher C Weber, *President*
EMP: 10 EST: 2013
SALES (est): 926K **Privately Held**
SIC: 2851 Polyurethane coatings

### (G-13916)
### AIRCRAFT GEAR CORPORATION (PA)
Also Called: Rockford Acromatic Products
611 Beacon St (61111-5902)
P.O. Box 2066 (61130-0066)
PHONE.....................815 877-7473
Fax: 815 877-1218
Dean A Olson II, *Ch of Bd*
James N Olson, *President*
Rick G Grimes, *Vice Pres*
Lynn Stohlglen, *Vice Pres*
Ron Barlow, *Opers Mgr*
▲ EMP: 65 EST: 1965
SQ FT: 50,000
SALES (est): 32.3MM **Privately Held**
WEB: www.rockfordacromatic.com
SIC: 3714 3728 Universal joints, motor vehicle; gears, aircraft power transmission

### (G-13917)
### ALERT TUBING FABRICATORS INC
8019 Commercial Ave (61111-2702)
PHONE.....................815 633-5065
Kevin Coffey, *President*
Roberto Cardenas III, *Opers Staff*
Sarah Lingel, *Office Mgr*
EMP: 8
SALES (est): 1.7MM **Privately Held**
SIC: 3498 Tube fabricating (contract bending & shaping)

### (G-13918)
### ALLIED SCORING TABLES INC
5417 Forest Hills Ct (61111-8318)
P.O. Box 833, Roscoe (61073-0833)
PHONE.....................815 654-8807
Fax: 815 654-8819
John Rygh, *President*
John Riygh, *COO*
Nancy Moate, *Sales Executive*
EMP: 6
SQ FT: 4,800
SALES: 1MM **Privately Held**
SIC: 3949 Basketball equipment & supplies, general

### (G-13919)
### AMERICAN BOTTLING COMPANY
Also Called: 7-Up-The American Bottling Co
5300 Forest Hills Rd (61111-5210)
PHONE.....................815 877-7777
Fax: 815 877-7798
Larry Heck, *Manager*

EMP: 50
SALES (corp-wide): 6.4B **Publicly Held**
WEB: www.cs-americas.com
SIC: 2086 Bottled & canned soft drinks
HQ: The American Bottling Company
5301 Legacy Dr
Plano TX 75024

### (G-13920)
### AMV INTERNATIONAL INC
7814 Forest Hills Rd (61111-3310)
PHONE.....................815 282-9990
Fax: 815 282-4275
Jean-Thierry Catrice, *President*
▲ EMP: 11
SALES (est): 1.3MM **Privately Held**
WEB: www.amvinternational.com
SIC: 3425 Saw blades for hand or power saws

### (G-13921)
### ARACHNID 360 LLC (PA)
6212 Material Ave (61111-4244)
P.O. Box 2901 (61132-2901)
PHONE.....................815 654-0212
Fax: 815 654-9082
Ron Gieseke, *Treasurer*
Joe Ullrich, *Controller*
Becky Cantele, *Accountant*
John Bauk, *CIO*
Anthony P Beall,
◆ EMP: 50 EST: 1970
SQ FT: 35,000
SALES: 10MM **Privately Held**
WEB: www.arachnidinc.com
SIC: 3949 Dartboards & accessories

### (G-13922)
### ARCHITECTURAL METALS LLC
6200 Forest Hills Rd (61111-4763)
PHONE.....................815 654-2370
Fax: 815 654-2399
Ivone Place, *Vice Pres*
Vicki Walker, *Manager*
Michael Messinnk,
David Wendler,
Jason Wendler,
EMP: 12
SALES (est): 1.3MM **Privately Held**
SIC: 3446 Architectural metalwork

### (G-13923)
### AUDIO INSTALLERS INC
Also Called: A I Satellite Distributing
5061 Contractors Dr (61111-1907)
PHONE.....................815 969-7500
Michael Roncke, *President*
Jeanette M Roncke, *Vice Pres*
▲ EMP: 10
SQ FT: 4,900
SALES (est): 1.5MM **Privately Held**
WEB: www.aisatellite.com
SIC: 5731 5064 5063 1731 Radios, two-way, citizens' band, weather, short-wave, etc.; high fidelity stereo equipment; antennas, satellite dish; radios, motor vehicle; high fidelity equipment; burglar alarm systems; antennas, receiving, satellite dishes; telephone & telephone equipment installation; electronic kits for home assembly: radio, TV, phonograph

### (G-13924)
### BEST PALLET COMPANY LLC
Also Called: Great Lakes Pallet Company
1110 Widsor Rd (61111)
PHONE.....................815 637-1500
Mike Faas, *Manager*
EMP: 14
SALES (corp-wide): 2.8MM **Privately Held**
SIC: 2448 Pallets, wood & wood with metal
PA: Best Pallet Company Llc
166 W Washington St # 300
Chicago IL 60602
312 242-4009

### (G-13925)
### COLORWAVE GRAPHICS LLC
2024 Windsor Rd (61111-3963)
PHONE.....................815 397-4293
Fax: 815 397-7009
Karla Lombardo, *Sales Staff*
Michael Lombardo, *Mng Member*
Karry Kleemann, *Manager*
EMP: 6

SQ FT: 2,100
SALES: 825K **Privately Held**
WEB: www.colorwavegraphics.com
SIC: 7336 2752 Commercial art & graphic design; commercial printing, lithographic

### (G-13926)
### CORPRO SCREEN TECH INC
5129 Forest Hills Ct (61111-8305)
PHONE.....................815 633-1201
Jeffrey Foster, *President*
Scott Gesner, *Treasurer*
Mike White, *Admin Sec*
EMP: 8
SQ FT: 4,000
SALES (est): 1.2MM **Privately Held**
SIC: 3993 Advertising artwork

### (G-13927)
### COVACHEM LLC
6260 E Riverside Blvd (61111-4418)
PHONE.....................815 714-8421
Tony Nooner, *Managing Dir*
Anthony Nooner,
EMP: 10 EST: 2012
SALES (est): 1.2MM **Privately Held**
SIC: 2869 High purity grade chemicals, organic; laboratory chemicals, organic

### (G-13928)
### CRAFT WORLD INC
Also Called: Alpine Imports
6836 Forest Hills Rd (61111-4367)
PHONE.....................800 654-6114
Fax: 815 654-2746
Terry W King, *President*
Carol A King, *Admin Sec*
EMP: 4 EST: 1974
SQ FT: 10,000
SALES (est): 399.9K **Privately Held**
SIC: 3944 Craft & hobby kits & sets; automobiles, children's, pedal driven

### (G-13929)
### CRANDALL STATS AND SENSORS INC
1354 Clifford Ave (61111-4729)
P.O. Box 10189 (61131-0189)
PHONE.....................815 979-3340
Mike Crandall, *President*
Kathleen Crandall, *Human Resources*
EMP: 22
SALES (est): 5MM **Privately Held**
SIC: 3822 Temperature sensors for motor windings; hydronic pressure or temperature controls; surface burner controls, temperature

### (G-13930)
### CRYSTAL PRECISION DRILLING
5122 Torque Rd (61111-7165)
PHONE.....................815 633-5460
Fax: 815 633-5336
Norman Fisher, *President*
Bruce N Fisher, *Prdtn Mgr*
EMP: 7
SALES (est): 720K **Privately Held**
SIC: 1381 3469 Drilling oil & gas wells; machine parts, stamped or pressed metal

### (G-13931)
### CUSTOM CUTTING TOOLS INC
5405 Forest Hills Ct (61111-8318)
PHONE.....................815 986-0320
Fax: 815 636-8422
William J Mc Kenzie, *President*
Prudence M Mc Kenzie, *Treasurer*
Prudence McKenzie, *Treasurer*
EMP: 4 EST: 1961
SQ FT: 6,000
SALES (est): 300K **Privately Held**
SIC: 3423 3546 3545 3541 Edge tools for woodworking: augers, bits, gimlets, etc.; power-driven handtools; machine tool accessories; machine tools, metal cutting type; cutlery

### (G-13932)
### CUSTOM FEEDER CO OF ROCKFORD
6207 Material Ave Ste 1 (61111-4284)
P.O. Box 2802 (61132-2802)
PHONE.....................815 654-2444
Fax: 815 654-3630
James Stamm, *President*
Michael J Stamm, *Treasurer*

Ryan Meseck, *Sales Mgr*
EMP: 20
SQ FT: 20,000
SALES (est): 3.5MM **Privately Held**
WEB: www.customfeeder.com
SIC: 3545 3441 Hopper feed devices; fabricated structural metal

### (G-13933)
### D & S MANUFACTURING INC
5604 Pike Rd (61111-4711)
PHONE.....................815 637-8889
Fax: 815 637-8899
Eric Johnson, *President*
John Rodz, *Vice Pres*
EMP: 8
SQ FT: 5,000
SALES (est): 600K **Privately Held**
SIC: 3599 Machine shop, jobbing & repair

### (G-13934)
### D MACHINE INC
921 River Ln (61111-4712)
PHONE.....................815 877-5991
Fax: 815 877-6032
Vern Meyer, *President*
Linda Meyer, *Admin Sec*
EMP: 5
SQ FT: 15,000
SALES (est): 834.5K **Privately Held**
WEB: www.dmachine-inc.com
SIC: 3599 Machine shop, jobbing & repair

### (G-13935)
### DANFOSS INC
7500 Beverage Blvd (61111-5601)
PHONE.....................815 639-8600
Jan Ryholl, *Director*
▲ EMP: 4
SALES (est): 746.8K **Privately Held**
SIC: 3625 Motor controls & accessories

### (G-13936)
### DANFOSS LLC
Also Called: Danfoss Power Electronics
4401 N Bell School Rd (61111-2603)
PHONE.....................888 326-3677
Fax: 815 639-8000
Michael Reckamp, *Business Mgr*
Susanne B Jensen, *Project Mgr*
Grzegorz Neubauer, *Project Mgr*
Senthil K Palani, *Project Mgr*
Kuno B Richard, *Project Mgr*
EMP: 182
SALES (corp-wide): 5.5B **Privately Held**
WEB: www.danfoss.us
SIC: 3625 3823 Motor controls & accessories; industrial instrmnts msrmnt display/control process variable
HQ: Danfoss, Llc
11655 Crossroads Cir A
Baltimore MD 21220
410 931-8250

### (G-13937)
### DRIVNN LLC
Also Called: Spartan Energy
6355 Commonwealth Dr (61111-8650)
PHONE.....................815 222-4447
Wilfred M Ramirez,
EMP: 4
SALES (est): 260K **Privately Held**
SIC: 2086 Fruit drinks (less than 100% juice): packaged in cans, etc.

### (G-13938)
### DURA FEED INC
7542 Forest Hills Rd (61111-3304)
PHONE.....................815 395-1115
John Lapour, *President*
Henry Aniszewski, *General Mgr*
EMP: 2
SALES (est): 220K **Privately Held**
WEB: www.durafeed.com
SIC: 3599 Machine & other job shop work

### (G-13939)
### EKLUND METAL TREATING INC
721 Beacon St (61111-5993)
PHONE.....................815 877-7436
Fax: 815 877-2759
Henry Adamski Sr, *President*
Todd Alton, *Vice Pres*
Cheryl Adamski, *Admin Sec*
EMP: 25
SQ FT: 26,500

## Loves Park - Winnebago County (G-13940)

**SALES (est):** 5.4MM **Privately Held**
**SIC:** 3398 Metal heat treating

**(G-13940)**
**EQUSTOCK LLC**
Also Called: Guardian Horse Bedding
8179 Starwood Dr Ste 1 (61111-5718)
**PHONE** .................... 866 962-4686
Claire Brant, *Managing Prtnr*
Jonathan Brant, *Managing Prtnr*
Jim Peterson, *Opers Mgr*
Pammy Oozzio, *Receptionist*
▼ **EMP:** 10
**SQ FT:** 2,500
**SALES (est):** 3.2MM **Privately Held**
**WEB:** www.guardianhorsebedding.com
**SIC:** 2499 2448 Carved & turned wood; pallets, wood

**(G-13941)**
**FORD TOOL & MACHINING INC (PA)**
Also Called: Lathom Pin - Div
2205 Range Rd (61111-2724)
P.O. Box 2211 (61131-0211)
**PHONE** .................... 815 633-5727
**Fax:** 815 633-0380
Thomas Chustak, *President*
Robert Ford, *President*
David P Beto, *Chairman*
Judy Miller, *Purch Mgr*
Ronald Roling, *CFO*
**EMP:** 75
**SQ FT:** 39,000
**SALES (est):** 18.5MM **Privately Held**
**WEB:** www.fordtool.com
**SIC:** 3544 Special dies, tools, jigs & fixtures

**(G-13942)**
**FOREST CITY COUNTER TOPS INC**
6050 Broadcast Pkwy (61111-4486)
**PHONE** .................... 815 633-8602
**Fax:** 815 633-8616
Charles Markese, *President*
Joanne Markese, *Corp Secy*
Thomas Markese, *Vice Pres*
Kevin Huckabee, *Purch Agent*
**EMP:** 11
**SALES (est):** 1.1MM **Privately Held**
**SIC:** 2541 2542 2434 Table or counter tops, plastic laminated; partitions & fixtures, except wood; wood kitchen cabinets

**(G-13943)**
**FOREST CITY INDUSTRY INC**
6100 Material Ave (61111-4242)
P.O. Box 2105 (61130-0105)
**PHONE** .................... 815 877-4084
Michael A Gaffney, *President*
**EMP:** 18 **EST:** 1966
**SQ FT:** 30,000
**SALES (est):** 1.2MM **Privately Held**
**SIC:** 3452 Bolts, nuts, rivets & washers

**(G-13944)**
**GKN ROCKFORD INC**
1200 Windsor Rd (61111-4250)
**PHONE** .................... 815 633-7460
Einar K Forsman, *President*
William Heffernan, *President*
Heidi M Garner, *COO*
Rhonda Brunette, *Vice Pres*
David Carter, *Vice Pres*
◆ **EMP:** 203
**SQ FT:** 621,000
**SALES (est):** 59.6MM
**SALES (corp-wide):** 10.8B **Privately Held**
**WEB:** www.rockfordpowertrain.com
**SIC:** 3714 Motor vehicle transmissions, drive assemblies & parts; clutches, motor vehicle; drive shafts, motor vehicle; universal joints, motor vehicle
**HQ:** Gkn America Corp.
2715 Davey Rd Ste 300
Woodridge IL 60517
630 972-5200

**(G-13945)**
**GRAFCOR PACKAGING INC**
1030 River Ln (61111-4715)
**PHONE** .................... 815 639-2380
William E Hall, *Vice Pres*
**EMP:** 10

**SALES (corp-wide):** 5.9MM **Privately Held**
**SIC:** 2631 3412 2653 Paperboard mills; metal barrels, drums & pails; corrugated & solid fiber boxes
**PA:** Grafcor Packaging, Inc.
121 Loomis St
Rockford IL 61101
815 963-1300

**(G-13946)**
**HI-TECH POLYMERS INC**
7967 Crest Hills Dr (61111-8301)
**PHONE** .................... 815 282-2272
**Fax:** 815 282-9772
Larry Phippen, *President*
Steven Wilke, *Vice Pres*
**EMP:** 14
**SQ FT:** 10,800
**SALES (est):** 2.4MM **Privately Held**
**SIC:** 3089 Casting of plastic

**(G-13947)**
**IMAGE SIGNS INC**
7323 N Alpine Rd (61111-3901)
**PHONE** .................... 815 282-4141
**Fax:** 815 282-4157
Bob Baker, *President*
Joann Baker, *Vice Pres*
Debbie Hurm, *Office Mgr*
**EMP:** 10
**SQ FT:** 5,000
**SALES (est):** 1.3MM **Privately Held**
**SIC:** 3993 7532 5999 1799 Signs & advertising specialties; electric signs; truck painting & lettering; banners; sign installation & maintenance

**(G-13948)**
**INDEV GAUGING SYSTEMS INC**
6830 Forest Hills Rd (61111-4367)
**PHONE** .................... 815 282-4463
Dan Hanrahan, *President*
Dave Smalley, *Opers Mgr*
Mark Woodworth, *Treasurer*
**EMP:** 5
**SALES (est):** 1.2MM **Privately Held**
**WEB:** www.indevsystems.com
**SIC:** 3823 Draft gauges, industrial process type

**(G-13949)**
**J-INDUSTRIES INC**
5129 Forest Hills Ct (61111-8305)
**PHONE** .................... 815 654-0055
Jeffrey L Foster, *President*
**EMP:** 10
**SQ FT:** 3,500
**SALES (est):** 1MM **Privately Held**
**SIC:** 2782 3161 3172 Library binders, looseleaf; briefcases; wallets

**(G-13950)**
**JANSSEN MACHINE INC**
Also Called: Janssen, Ron
985 Industrial Ct (61111-7512)
**PHONE** .................... 815 877-9901
Ron J Janssen, *President*
Jeff Reisetter, *Vice Pres*
**EMP:** 12
**SALES:** 907K **Privately Held**
**SIC:** 3599 Machine & other job shop work

**(G-13951)**
**JAVAMANIA COFFEE ROASTERY INC**
8179 Starwood Dr Ste 4 (61111-5718)
**PHONE** .................... 815 885-3654
**Fax:** 815 885-4662
Sandy Keller, *President*
William Keller, *Vice Pres*
**EMP:** 3
**SALES (est):** 215.1K **Privately Held**
**WEB:** www.javamaniacoffeeroastery.com
**SIC:** 5812 2095 Coffee shop; roasted coffee

**(G-13952)**
**JEFCO SCREW MACHINE PRODUCTS**
6203 Material Ave (61111-4282)
P.O. Box 2625 (61132-2625)
**PHONE** .................... 815 282-2000
**Fax:** 815 282-1328
Bruce C Mayer, *President*
Dorothy Townsmned, *Manager*

Taysha Warner, *Manager*
**EMP:** 16 **EST:** 1960
**SQ FT:** 9,000
**SALES (est):** 3.4MM **Privately Held**
**WEB:** www.jefco-inc.com
**SIC:** 3451 Screw machine products

**(G-13953)**
**JOHN & HELEN INC**
988 Industrial Ct (61111-7512)
**PHONE** .................... 815 654-1070
**Fax:** 815 654-2094
John Czaczkowski, *President*
Helen Czaczkowski, *Vice Pres*
Brad Arabia, *Mfg Mgr*
**EMP:** 16
**SQ FT:** 8,000
**SALES (est):** 2.7MM **Privately Held**
**WEB:** www.jcmilling.com
**SIC:** 3599 Machine shop, jobbing & repair

**(G-13954)**
**JOHNSON & JOHNSON**
5500 Forest Hills Rd (61111-5213)
**PHONE** .................... 815 282-5671
Patricia Murrin, *Principal*
**EMP:** 79
**SALES (corp-wide):** 71.8B **Publicly Held**
**SIC:** 2834 Pharmaceutical preparations
**PA:** Johnson & Johnson
1 Johnson And Johnson Plz
New Brunswick NJ 08933
732 524-0400

**(G-13955)**
**JRM INTERNATIONAL INC**
5701 Industrial Ave (61111-4706)
**PHONE** .................... 815 282-9330
James R Mattox, *President*
Lisa Giedd, *Accountant*
▲ **EMP:** 9
**SQ FT:** 32,000
**SALES (est):** 3.8MM **Privately Held**
**SIC:** 5084 3545 Hydraulic systems equipment & supplies; vises, machine (machine tool accessories)

**(G-13956)**
**KOMAX SYSTEMS ROCKFORD INC**
4608 Interstate Blvd (61111-5702)
**PHONE** .................... 815 885-8800
Eugene Haffely, *President*
Alan Stone, *Principal*
William Hoff, *Principal*
Greg Raschke, *Principal*
Dave Hoshaw, *Project Dir*
**EMP:** 77
**SQ FT:** 55,861
**SALES (est):** 8.9MM
**SALES (corp-wide):** 368.7MM **Privately Held**
**WEB:** www.sibosprime.com
**SIC:** 3569 Liquid automation machinery & equipment; robots, assembly line: industrial & commercial
**PA:** Komax Holding Ag
Industriestrasse 6
Dierikon LU
414 550-455

**(G-13957)**
**L M SHEET METAL INC**
6727 Elm Ave (61111-3817)
**PHONE** .................... 815 654-1837
**Fax:** 815 654-0007
C Sue Middleton, *President*
Bruce Middleton, *Treasurer*
Susan Middleton, *Office Mgr*
Susan L Middleton, *Admin Sec*
**EMP:** 20
**SQ FT:** 19,500
**SALES (est):** 3.7MM **Privately Held**
**WEB:** www.lmsheetmetalinc.com
**SIC:** 1711 3444 Warm air heating & air conditioning contractor; sheet metalwork

**(G-13958)**
**LAH INC**
Also Called: Luthers Form Grinding Company
6309 Material Ave Ste 2 (61111-4286)
**PHONE** .................... 815 282-4939
**Fax:** 815 282-4941
Lewis A Hiilstad, *President*
Brandon Hillstad, *Manager*
**EMP:** 2

**SQ FT:** 1,600
**SALES:** 200K **Privately Held**
**SIC:** 3544 Special dies, tools, jigs & fixtures

**(G-13959)**
**LASER ENERGY SYSTEMS**
4924 Torque Rd (61111-7163)
**PHONE** .................... 815 282-8200
Steve Schaede, *President*
**EMP:** 2 **EST:** 1998
**SALES (est):** 294.4K **Privately Held**
**SIC:** 3699 Laser systems & equipment

**(G-13960)**
**LEGIBLE SIGNS GROUP CORP**
2221 Nimtz Rd (61111-3928)
**PHONE** .................... 815 654-0100
Dorthy Drummond, *President*
Rick Collins, *Sales Staff*
**EMP:** 15
**SQ FT:** 11,000
**SALES (est):** 1.7MM **Privately Held**
**WEB:** www.legiblesigns.com
**SIC:** 3993 Signs, not made in custom sign painting shops; name plates: except engraved, etched, etc.: metal

**(G-13961)**
**LIFETOUCH SERVICES INC**
5126 Forest Hills Ct (61111-8304)
**PHONE** .................... 815 633-3881
Chris Kamler, *Engineer*
Arlyn Poppen, *Finance Mgr*
June Ramer, *Human Res Dir*
Kris Elliott, *Sales Staff*
Doug Phillips, *Mktg Dir*
**EMP:** 200
**SALES (corp-wide):** 803MM **Privately Held**
**SIC:** 2741 2731 Yearbooks: publishing & printing; book publishing
**HQ:** Lifetouch Services Inc.
11000 Viking Dr
Eden Prairie MN 55344

**(G-13962)**
**LSL PRECISION MACHINING INC**
Also Called: Long Screw
2210 Nimtz Rd (61111-3929)
P.O. Box 2093 (61130-0093)
**PHONE** .................... 815 633-4701
**Fax:** 815 633-4954
Brian Long, *President*
Bradley Long, *Vice Pres*
Norman J Long, *Treasurer*
Donna Long, *Accountant*
Dwayne E Long, *Admin Sec*
**EMP:** 23 **EST:** 1962
**SQ FT:** 30,000
**SALES:** 1.9MM **Privately Held**
**SIC:** 3492 3451 Fluid power valves & hose fittings; screw machine products

**(G-13963)**
**MANNER PLATING INC**
926 River Ln (61111-4795)
**PHONE** .................... 815 877-7791
**Fax:** 815 877-7971
John Gruner, *President*
**EMP:** 5
**SQ FT:** 10,000
**SALES:** 400K **Privately Held**
**SIC:** 3471 Plating of metals or formed products

**(G-13964)**
**MERIDIAN**
8173 Starwood Dr (61111-5704)
**PHONE** .................... 815 885-4646
Mark Terry, *Principal*
Jake Chanson, *Principal*
Shelley Hart, *Principal*
Mary Terry, *Principal*
Bruce Vorel, *Vice Pres*
**EMP:** 32
**SALES (est):** 5.2MM **Privately Held**
**SIC:** 2759 Commercial printing

**(G-13965)**
**METHOD MOLDS INC**
5085 Contractors Dr (61111-1907)
**PHONE** .................... 815 877-0191
**Fax:** 815 877-7390
M C Moore, *President*
Joanne L Moore, *Admin Sec*

EMP: 4
SQ FT: 7,000
SALES (est): 550K **Privately Held**
SIC: 3544 7692 3545 Forms (molds), for foundry & plastics working machinery; industrial molds; welding repair; machine tool accessories

### (G-13966)
### MICROGRAMS INC
Also Called: Micrograms Software
5615 Jensen Dr (61111-4621)
P.O. Box 2603 (61132-2603)
PHONE..................................815 877-4455
Fax: 815 877-1482
Richard Shelain, *President*
Kent Holden, *Vice Pres*
Maxine Shelain, *Manager*
EMP: 5
SALES (est): 340.4K **Privately Held**
WEB: www.micrograms.com
SIC: 7372 7371 Prepackaged software; custom computer programming services

### (G-13967)
### MINUTEMAN PRESS OF ROCKFORD
5128 N 2nd St (61111-5002)
PHONE..................................815 633-2992
Fax: 815 633-9125
Eugene D Syring, *President*
Patricia L Syring, *Admin Sec*
EMP: 8
SQ FT: 2,500
SALES (est): 1.2MM **Privately Held**
SIC: 2752 2791 2789 Commercial printing, lithographic; typesetting; bookbinding & related work

### (G-13968)
### MONDELEZ GLOBAL LLC
Also Called: Cadbury
5500 Forest Hills Rd (61111-5213)
PHONE..................................815 877-8081
David Brown, *Project Mgr*
EMP: 190 **Publicly Held**
SIC: 2064 Candy & other confectionery products
HQ: Mondelez Global Llc
3 Parkway N Ste 300
Deerfield IL 60015
847 943-4000

### (G-13969)
### NATIONAL METAL WORKS INC
916 River Ln (61111-4713)
PHONE..................................815 282-5533
Mary Kisting, *President*
David Kisting, *Admin Sec*
EMP: 7
SQ FT: 6,600
SALES: 1.4MM **Privately Held**
WEB: www.nationalmetalworks.com
SIC: 3444 1711 Sheet metalwork; heating & air conditioning contractors

### (G-13970)
### OLE SALTYS OF ROCKFORD INC (PA)
1920 E Riverside Blvd (61111-4900)
P.O. Box 8433, Rockford (61126-8433)
PHONE..................................815 637-2447
Al Domico, *President*
Karen Albornoz, *Train & Dev Mgr*
EMP: 3
SQ FT: 2,000
SALES (est): 1.1MM **Privately Held**
WEB: www.olesaltys.com
SIC: 2096 Potato chips & other potato-based snacks

### (G-13971)
### ONSITE WOODWORK CORPORATION (PA)
4100 Rock Valley Pkwy (61111-4472)
PHONE..................................815 633-6400
Fax: 815 633-6477
Ralph E Peterson, *Chairman*
Joy Peterson, *Corp Secy*
Mark Peterson, *Exec VP*
Ryan Ramsey, *Project Mgr*
Carol Peterson, *Office Mgr*
EMP: 68
SQ FT: 40,000
SALES (est): 16.6MM **Privately Held**
WEB: www.onsitewoodwork.com
SIC: 2431 Woodwork, interior & ornamental

### (G-13972)
### PARK LICENSE SERVICE INC
6402 N 2nd St (61111-4110)
PHONE..................................815 633-5511
Fax: 815 633-6825
Hazel Lindblade, *President*
EMP: 6
SALES: 150K **Privately Held**
SIC: 3711 Cars, electric, assembly of

### (G-13973)
### PHILLIP RODGERS
Also Called: Precise Tool & Manufacturing
5366 Forest Hills Ct (61111-8319)
PHONE..................................815 877-5461
Phillip Rodgers, *Owner*
Debra Rodgers, *Co-Owner*
EMP: 2
SQ FT: 4,000
SALES: 300K **Privately Held**
SIC: 3599 Custom machinery

### (G-13974)
### PIERCE PACKAGING CO (PA)
Also Called: Pierce Distribution Svcs Co
2028 E Riverside Blvd (61111-4804)
P.O. Box 15600 (61132-5600)
PHONE..................................815 636-5650
Fax: 815 636-5660
Kevin Hogan, *President*
Dino McNabb, *Vice Pres*
Kristi Taylor, *Vice Pres*
Anthony Chiodini, *CFO*
Tony Chiobini, *VP Finance*
EMP: 10
SQ FT: 3,500
SALES (est): 62.2MM **Privately Held**
WEB: www.piercedistribution.com
SIC: 4783 2441 Packing goods for shipping; crating goods for shipping; containerization of goods for shipping; boxes, wood

### (G-13975)
### PIERCE PACKAGING CO
1200 Windsor Rd (61111-4250)
PHONE..................................815 636-5656
Judy Spitson, *Branch Mgr*
EMP: 10
SALES (corp-wide): 62.2MM **Privately Held**
SIC: 4783 2441 Packing goods for shipping; crating goods for shipping; containerization of goods for shipping; boxes, wood
PA: Pierce Packaging Co.
2028 E Riverside Blvd
Loves Park IL 61111
815 636-5650

### (G-13976)
### PLANET EARTH ANTIFREEZE INC
6307 Material Ave (61111-4245)
PHONE..................................815 282-2463
Cynthia A Bloyer, *President*
Donald Bloyer, *Vice Pres*
EMP: 5 **EST:** 1996
SQ FT: 4,500
SALES (est): 791.1K **Privately Held**
SIC: 2899 Antifreeze compounds

### (G-13977)
### PRO ARC INC
7440 Forest Hills Rd (61111-3971)
P.O. Box 15007 (61132-5007)
PHONE..................................815 877-1804
Fax: 815 877-0184
Denny J Forni, *President*
Angela Forni, *Corp Secy*
Mike Daugherty, *Project Mgr*
Rigina Sniper, *Manager*
EMP: 32
SQ FT: 25,000
SALES (est): 6.2MM **Privately Held**
WEB: www.proarc.net
SIC: 3599 Machine & other job shop work

### (G-13978)
### PRO MACHINING INC
2131 Harlem Rd (61111-2751)
PHONE..................................815 633-4140
John McMullin, *President*
Ashley McMullin, *Office Mgr*
EMP: 13
SALES (est): 959.5K **Privately Held**
SIC: 3469 1799 Machine parts, stamped or pressed metal; welding on site

### (G-13979)
### PROGRESSIVE STEEL TREATING INC
922 Lawn Dr (61111-5192)
PHONE..................................815 877-2571
Fax: 815 877-7922
James R Simonovich, *President*
Richard Freiman, *Controller*
Richard J Simonovich, *Manager*
Rick Freiman, *Administration*
Healy Genus, *Administration*
EMP: 25 **EST:** 1956
SQ FT: 45,000
SALES (est): 6.2MM **Privately Held**
WEB: www.progressivesteeltreating.com
SIC: 3398 Metal heat treating; annealing of metal; brazing (hardening) of metal

### (G-13980)
### QUANTUM DESIGN INC (PA)
8400 E Riverside Blvd (61111-5721)
PHONE..................................815 885-1300
Fax: 815 885-1370
Danny S Pearse, *President*
David Culvey, *Exec VP*
Peter Geisser, *Vice Pres*
Nevagay Abel, *Engineer*
Marc J Glas, *Engineer*
EMP: 63
SQ FT: 19,500
SALES (est): 17.8MM **Privately Held**
WEB: www.quantumdi.com
SIC: 3613 Control panels, electric

### (G-13981)
### RELIANCE TOOL INC
946 River Ln (61111-4713)
PHONE..................................815 636-2770
Larry Dilillo Esq, *President*
EMP: 5
SALES (est): 579.1K **Privately Held**
SIC: 3599 Machine shop, jobbing & repair

### (G-13982)
### RICHARD KING AND SONS
6735 Elm Ave (61111-3817)
PHONE..................................815 654-0226
Fax: 815 654-0262
Richard King, *President*
Wanetta King, *Corp Secy*
Dave King, *Vice Pres*
Tracy King, *Vice Pres*
EMP: 6
SQ FT: 6,500
SALES: 250K **Privately Held**
WEB: www.king-and-sons.com
SIC: 2431 2434 Millwork; doors, wood; trim, wood; ornamental woodwork: cornices, mantels, etc.; wood kitchen cabinets; vanities, bathroom: wood

### (G-13983)
### ROCK VALLEY OIL & CHEMICAL CO (PA)
1911 Windsor Rd (61111-4293)
PHONE..................................815 654-2400
Fax: 815 654-2428
Roger L Schramm, *President*
John Price, *Vice Pres*
Jessica Osborne, *Plant Mgr*
Ron Stone, *Plant Mgr*
Ron Starks, *Opers Staff*
EMP: 50 **EST:** 1970
SALES (est): 16.8MM **Privately Held**
WEB: www.rockvalleyoil.com
SIC: 2992 5169 4953 Lubricating oils & greases; cutting oils, blending: made from purchased materials; brake fluid (hydraulic): made from purchased materials; chemicals & allied products; chemical detoxification

### (G-13984)
### ROCKFORD METAL POLISHING CO
5700 Industrial Ave (61111-7503)
PHONE..................................815 282-4448
Fax: 815 282-4449
Howard M Feldman, *President*
John Gagliano, *General Mgr*
Barbara A Gagliano, *Vice Pres*
Dave Moore, *Plant Mgr*
EMP: 8
SQ FT: 5,000
SALES: 1MM **Privately Held**
SIC: 3471 Buffing for the trade; finishing, metals or formed products; polishing, metals or formed products

### (G-13985)
### ROCKFORD MOLDED PRODUCTS INC
5600 Pike Rd (61111-4711)
PHONE..................................815 637-0585
Fax: 815 637-0590
Wayne Rasner Jr, *CEO*
Gerald G Gustafson, *President*
Barbara Pearson, *QC Mgr*
Tom Thome, *Controller*
Norman Sadler, *Manager*
EMP: 60 **EST:** 1943
SQ FT: 45,000
SALES (est): 14.8MM **Privately Held**
WEB: www.rockfordmolded.com
SIC: 3089 Injection molded finished plastic products; thermoformed finished plastic products

### (G-13986)
### ROCKFORD SAND & GRAVEL CO (HQ)
5290 Nimtz Rd (61111-3932)
P.O. Box 2071 (61130-0071)
PHONE..................................815 654-4700
Myron Rafferty, *President*
Dan Fisher, *Vice Pres*
Neil Maloney, *Treasurer*
Charles Howard, *Director*
Wayne Schwalen, *Admin Sec*
EMP: 25
SALES (est): 3.7MM
SALES (corp-wide): 172MM **Privately Held**
SIC: 5211 1442 Sand & gravel; construction sand & gravel
PA: William Charles, Ltd.
1401 N 2nd St
Rockford IL 61107
815 963-7400

### (G-13987)
### ROCKFORD SEWER CO INC
Also Called: Aqua Marine Pools
6204 Forest Hills Rd (61111-4763)
PHONE..................................815 877-9060
Fax: 815 877-9105
Nicholas J Migliore, *President*
Audrey A Migliore, *Corp Secy*
EMP: 9 **EST:** 1962
SQ FT: 5,500
SALES (est): 1.1MM **Privately Held**
SIC: 3272 1711 7699 5999 Septic tanks, concrete; septic system construction; plumbing contractors; sewer cleaning & rodding; septic tank cleaning service; swimming pools, above ground; swimming pool chemicals, equipment & supplies; swimming pool construction

### (G-13988)
### ROTHENBERGER USA INC
7130 Clinton Rd (61111-3872)
PHONE..................................815 397-7617
Fax: 815 633-0879
Glen Schlueter, *Manager*
EMP: 40 **Privately Held**
WEB: www.rothenberger-usa.com
SIC: 3541 Pipe cutting & threading machines
HQ: Rothenberger Usa, Inc.
110 Washington St
Winneconne WI 54986

## Loves Park - Winnebago County (G-13989)

**(G-13989)**
**RRB FABRICATION INC**
Also Called: Welding Fabrication
5430 Forest Hills Ct (61111-8317)
PHONE..................815 977-5603
Fax: 815 629-2400
Sharon Brunson, *President*
Robin Brunson, *President*
EMP: 12
SQ FT: 4,200
SALES: 250K **Privately Held**
SIC: 3441 Fabricated structural metal

**(G-13990)**
**S & B JIG GRINDING**
6820 Forest Hills Rd (61111-4367)
PHONE..................815 654-7907
Fax: 815 654-7908
Carl Bradberry, *President*
Melba Bradberry, *Admin Sec*
EMP: 6
SQ FT: 4,500
SALES: 500K **Privately Held**
WEB: www.s-b-jiggrinding.com
SIC: 3599 Grinding castings for the trade

**(G-13991)**
**SEROLA BIOMECHANICS INC**
5406 Forest Hills Ct (61111-8317)
PHONE..................815 636-2780
Rick Serola, *President*
Lowell Gillia, *Principal*
Melody Serola, *Vice Pres*
Thomas Person, *VP Opers*
Matt Johnson, *VP Sales*
EMP: 10
SALES (est): 1.9MM **Privately Held**
WEB: www.serolabio.com
SIC: 3842 5047 8041 Orthopedic appliances; orthopedic equipment & supplies; offices & clinics of chiropractors

**(G-13992)**
**SERVICE MACHINE COMPANY INC**
6205 Material Ave (61111-4243)
P.O. Box 2183 (61130-0183)
PHONE..................815 654-2310
Fax: 815 654-2426
Arthur L Kneller Jr, *President*
Pete Basile, *General Mgr*
Frances Kneller, *Corp Secy*
EMP: 18
SQ FT: 18,500
SALES (est): 3.5MM **Privately Held**
WEB: www.sermach.com
SIC: 3599 Machine shop, jobbing & repair

**(G-13993)**
**SOUTHERN IMPERIAL INC**
7135 Clinton Rd (61111-3871)
PHONE..................815 877-7041
EMP: 4
SALES (corp-wide): 137MM **Privately Held**
SIC: 3452 Screw eyes & hooks
PA: Southern Imperial, Inc.
   1400 Eddy Ave
   Rockford IL 61103
   815 877-7041

**(G-13994)**
**STEINER IMPRESSIONS INC**
5596 E Riverside Blvd # 2 (61111-4950)
P.O. Box 2430 (61132-0430)
PHONE..................815 633-4135
David Steiner, *President*
EMP: 5
SALES (est): 420K **Privately Held**
SIC: 2752 Commercial printing, offset

**(G-13995)**
**SUPERIOR METAL FINISHING**
Also Called: Northern Star Plating Division
962 Industrial Ct (61111-7512)
PHONE..................815 282-8888
Fax: 815 282-3127
Larry Walsh, *President*
Kellie Walsh, *Office Mgr*
Ken Wescott, *Manager*
EMP: 16
SALES (est): 1.2MM **Privately Held**
SIC: 3471 Plating of metals or formed products; sand blasting of metal parts; tumbling (cleaning & polishing) of machine parts

**(G-13996)**
**TADS**
10 E Riverside Blvd (61111-4500)
PHONE..................815 654-3500
Therese Dobson, *Owner*
Therese Dobson, *Principal*
EMP: 4 EST: 2008
SALES (est): 309.6K **Privately Held**
SIC: 2599 Bar, restaurant & cafeteria furniture

**(G-13997)**
**TAPCO CUTTING TOOLS INC**
5605 Pike Rd (61111-4710)
PHONE..................815 877-4039
Terry Brewster, *President*
Jackie Brewster, *Admin Sec*
EMP: 4
SALES (est): 403.7K **Privately Held**
SIC: 3545 Taps, machine tool

**(G-13998)**
**TAPCO USA INC**
5605 Pike Rd (61111-4710)
PHONE..................815 877-4039
Fax: 815 877-6143
Jackie Brewster, *Opers Mgr*
Susan Hickey, *Controller*
John A Cotton, *Manager*
EMP: 6 EST: 1969
SQ FT: 10,000
SALES: 750K **Privately Held**
WEB: www.tapcousa.com
SIC: 3545 5085 3546 3544 Taps, machine tool; industrial tools; power-driven handtools; special dies, tools, jigs & fixtures

**(G-13999)**
**TEMCO GRINDING INC**
1002 River Ln (61111-4715)
PHONE..................815 282-9405
Fax: 815 282-1205
Mike Mahoney, *President*
Dan Mahoney, *Vice Pres*
EMP: 12
SQ FT: 25,000
SALES: 750K **Privately Held**
SIC: 3599 Machine shop, jobbing & repair

**(G-14000)**
**TH FOODS INC**
2154 Harlem Rd (61111-2752)
PHONE..................702 565-2816
Dennis Mower, *Branch Mgr*
EMP: 3
SALES (corp-wide): 59.1B **Privately Held**
SIC: 2052 Crackers, dry
HQ: Th Foods, Inc.
   2134 Harlem Rd
   Loves Park IL 61111
   800 896-2396

**(G-14001)**
**TH FOODS INC (DH)**
2134 Harlem Rd (61111)
PHONE..................800 896-2396
Mark Tanabe, *Ch of Bd*
Terry Jessen, *President*
Rick Lutzow, *Business Mgr*
Derrick Tatis, *Business Mgr*
Jeff Baldwin, *Vice Pres*
▲ EMP: 250
SQ FT: 200,000
SALES: 101.4MM
SALES (corp-wide): 59.1B **Privately Held**
WEB: www.thfoods.com
SIC: 2052 Crackers, dry
HQ: Mitsubishi International Corporation
   655 3rd Ave
   New York NY 10017
   212 605-2000

**(G-14002)**
**TOP DOLLAR SLOTS**
6590 N Alpine Rd (61111-4353)
PHONE..................779 210-4884
Frank Laudicina, *Owner*
EMP: 8
SALES (est): 120.1K **Privately Held**
SIC: 5812 3999 Italian restaurant; slot machines

**(G-14003)**
**TRI STATE ALUMINUM PRODUCTS**
Also Called: Tri-State Alum & Vinyl Pdts
6300 Forest Hills Rd (61111-4761)
P.O. Box 2614 (61132-2614)
PHONE..................815 877-6081
Fax: 815 877-6119
James Heidenreich, *President*
Norman Heidenreich, *Corp Secy*
Lawrence Heidenreich, *Vice Pres*
Michael Heidenreich, *Shareholder*
EMP: 10 EST: 1961
SQ FT: 43,000
SALES (est): 2.1MM **Privately Held**
WEB: www.tristatealuminum.com
SIC: 5031 5039 3442 3444 Metal doors, sash & trim; windows; awnings; screen & storm doors & windows; awnings, sheet metal; roofing, siding & insulation; millwork

**(G-14004)**
**TRIWIRE INC**
Also Called: Ford-Tool
2201 Range Rd (61111-2724)
P.O. Box 2211 (61131-0211)
PHONE..................815 633-7707
Fax: 815 633-7797
David P Beto, *CEO*
Ginger Elsasser, *General Mgr*
Ronald Roling, *CFO*
EMP: 3
SQ FT: 5,000
SALES: 650K
SALES (corp-wide): 18.5MM **Privately Held**
WEB: www.triwire.com
SIC: 3599 Machine shop, jobbing & repair
PA: Ford Tool & Machining, Inc.
   2205 Range Rd
   Loves Park IL 61111
   815 633-5727

**(G-14005)**
**UNITED TOOLERS OF ILLINOIS**
7203 Clinton Rd (61111-3806)
PHONE..................779 423-0548
Daniel Baumann, *Principal*
EMP: 10
SALES (est): 1.4MM **Privately Held**
SIC: 3312 Stainless steel

**(G-14006)**
**WARD CNC MACHINING**
7480 Forest Hills Rd (61111-3971)
PHONE..................815 637-1490
Doug Sosnowskik, *Owner*
EMP: 6 EST: 2000
SQ FT: 3,600
SALES: 188K **Privately Held**
SIC: 3448 Prefabricated metal components

**(G-14007)**
**WILLIAM CHARLES CNSTR CO LLC (HQ)**
5290 Nimtz Rd (61111-3932)
P.O. Box 2071 (61130-0071)
PHONE..................815 654-4700
Charles J Howard, *Ch of Bd*
Ben Holmstrom, *President*
Jeff Potter, *CFO*
Wayne L Schwalen, *Treasurer*
David Casey, *Sr Project Mgr*
EMP: 97 EST: 1940
SQ FT: 15,000
SALES (est): 46.1MM
SALES (corp-wide): 172MM **Privately Held**
SIC: 1611 1623 1629 1794 Highway & street paving contractor; resurfacing contractor; highway & street maintenance; grading; sewer line construction; water main construction; drainage system construction; excavation & grading, building construction; asphalt paving mixtures & blocks; construction sand & gravel
PA: William Charles, Ltd.
   1401 N 2nd St
   Rockford IL 61107
   815 963-7400

**(G-14008)**
**WOODWARD INC**
1 Woodward (61111-7700)
P.O. Box 7001, Rockford (61125-7001)
PHONE..................815 877-7441
Sagar A Patel, *President*
Marla Newman, *Purchasing*
James Keclik, *Engineer*
Angie Moe, *Engineer*
Kim Plaziak, *Engineer*
EMP: 468
SALES (corp-wide): 2B **Publicly Held**
SIC: 3728 Aircraft parts & equipment
PA: Woodward, Inc.
   1081 Woodward Way
   Fort Collins CO 80524
   970 482-5811

**(G-14009)**
**WOODWARD INC**
5001 N 2nd St (61111-5808)
P.O. Box 7001, Rockford (61125-7001)
PHONE..................815 877-7441
Fax: 815 639-5119
Pat Kirane, *COO*
Mary Cox, *Vice Pres*
Christopher Fawzy, *Vice Pres*
Martin V Glass, *Vice Pres*
Ann Kreutziger, *Project Mgr*
EMP: 1200
SALES (corp-wide): 2B **Publicly Held**
WEB: www.woodward.com
SIC: 3724 Aircraft engines & engine parts
PA: Woodward, Inc.
   1081 Woodward Way
   Fort Collins CO 80524
   970 482-5811

**(G-14010)**
**WOODWARD INTERNATIONAL INC (HQ)**
5001 N 2nd St (61111-5808)
PHONE..................815 877-7441
Sagar Patel, *President*
Harlan Barkely, *Vice Pres*
John Hallbrook, *Opers Mgr*
Russell Poppe, *Materials Mgr*
Mike Nevicosi, *Facilities Mgr*
EMP: 3
SALES: 38.7MM
SALES (corp-wide): 2B **Publicly Held**
SIC: 3724 Turbines, aircraft type
PA: Woodward, Inc.
   1081 Woodward Way
   Fort Collins CO 80524
   970 482-5811

**(G-14011)**
**ZNL CORPORATION**
Also Called: Window Coverings
2120 Harlem Rd (61111-2752)
PHONE..................815 654-0870
Fax: 815 654-1099
William Lapins, *Vice Pres*
EMP: 6
SALES (corp-wide): 48.3MM **Privately Held**
SIC: 2591 Window blinds
HQ: Znl Corporation
   1 Raquel Way
   Hodgkins IL 60525

## Lovington
*Moultrie County*

**(G-14012)**
**REEVES LURE CO**
4165 Shaw Rd (61937-9777)
PHONE..................217 864-3493
Pam Reeves, *Owner*
EMP: 8
SALES: 45K **Privately Held**
SIC: 3949 Lures, fishing: artificial

## Lyndon
### Whiteside County

**(G-14013)**
**C & D MACHINING INC**
207 E Commercial St (61261-7766)
P.O. Box 308 (61261-0308)
PHONE..................................815 778-4946
Fax: 815 778-4913
Keith Crady, *President*
Brian Dolieslager, *Vice Pres*
EMP: 10
SALES (est): 500K  Privately Held
WEB: www.freelabs.com
SIC: 3599  Machine shop, jobbing & repair

**(G-14014)**
**PHILLIPS & JOHNSTON  INC**
Also Called: Rock River Fabrication
900 E Commercial St (61261-7767)
P.O. Box 338 (61261-0338)
PHONE..................................815 778-3355
Fax: 815 778-4969
Brandon Eads, *Office Mgr*
EMP: 11
SALES (corp-wide): 481.7MM Privately Held
SIC: 3312  Tubes, steel & iron
HQ: Phillips & Johnston, Inc.
    21w179 Hill Ave
    Glen Ellyn IL 60137
    630 469-8150

## Lynn Center
### Henry County

**(G-14015)**
**CALMER CORN HEADS  INC**
3056 N 700th Ave (61262-9581)
P.O. Box 9, Alpha (61413-0009)
PHONE..................................309 629-9000
Fax: 309 629-9001
Marion Calmer, *President*
▲ EMP: 23
SALES (est): 5.6MM  Privately Held
SIC: 3523  Farm machinery & equipment

**(G-14016)**
**DARLING INGREDIENTS INC**
202 Bengston St (61262-7703)
P.O. Box 40 (61262-0040)
PHONE..................................309 476-8111
Keith Fulton, *Manager*
EMP: 20
SALES (corp-wide): 3.4B  Publicly Held
WEB: www.darlingii.com
SIC: 2077  2048  Animal & marine fats & oils; prepared feeds
PA: Darling Ingredients Inc.
    251 Oconnor Ridge Blvd
    Irving TX 75038
    972 717-0300

## Lynwood
### Cook County

**(G-14017)**
**AVAN PRECAST CONCRETE PDTS INC**
3201 211th St (60411-8788)
PHONE..................................708 757-6200
Fax: 708 757-6270
Ann Vandergenugten, *CEO*
Roger Vandergenugten, *President*
Brian Vandergenugten, *Admin Sec*
EMP: 15
SQ FT: 8,500
SALES (est): 1.5MM  Privately Held
SIC: 3272  Concrete products, precast; steps, prefabricated concrete; slabs, crossing; concrete

**(G-14018)**
**BEHR PROCESS CORPORATION**
21399 Torrence Ave Ste 1 (60411-8709)
PHONE..................................708 753-1820
Jeffrey D Filley, *Branch Mgr*
EMP: 62
SALES (corp-wide): 7.3B  Publicly Held
SIC: 2851  Paints & paint additives
HQ: Behr Process Corporation
    3400 W Segerstrom Ave
    Santa Ana CA 92704

**(G-14019)**
**DDU MAGNETICS  INC**
20152 Cypress Ave (60411-6809)
PHONE..................................708 325-6587
Douglas Richard, *President*
Clara Richard, *Admin Sec*
EMP: 2
SALES (est): 248.8K  Privately Held
SIC: 3621  8748  Motors, electric; testing services

**(G-14020)**
**KOSWELL PATTERN WORKS INC**
3149 Glenwood Dyer Rd H (60411-9747)
PHONE..................................708 757-5225
James Koselke, *President*
EMP: 4
SQ FT: 1,500
SALES (est): 350K  Privately Held
SIC: 3543  Industrial patterns

**(G-14021)**
**LANS PRINTING INC**
2581 Glenwd Lansing Rd A (60411-1682)
PHONE..................................708 895-6226
Joe Jiampaulo, *President*
EMP: 3
SQ FT: 2,000
SALES (est): 393.6K  Privately Held
SIC: 2752  2759  2791  2789  Commercial printing, offset; screen printing; typesetting; bookbinding & related work

**(G-14022)**
**ON TARGET GRINDING AND MFG**
2250 199th St Ste 3 (60411-9606)
PHONE..................................708 418-3905
Barry Bridgeford, *President*
Mal Dixon, *Vice Pres*
EMP: 2
SQ FT: 1,500
SALES (est): 300K  Privately Held
WEB: www.on-target-mfg.com
SIC: 3449  Bars, concrete reinforcing: fabricated steel

**(G-14023)**
**POUR IT AGAIN SAM INC**
2200 198th Pl (60411-8501)
PHONE..................................708 474-1744
EMP: 3
SALES (est): 144.5K  Privately Held
SIC: 2084  Wines

**(G-14024)**
**QUALITY CIRCLE MACHINE INC**
2250 199th St Ste 3 (60411-9606)
PHONE..................................708 474-1160
Kenneth E Casner Jr, *President*
EMP: 2
SQ FT: 1,000
SALES (est): 201.1K  Privately Held
SIC: 3599  8734  Machine shop, jobbing & repair; metallurgical testing laboratory

**(G-14025)**
**ROGAN GRANITINDUSTRIE INC (HQ)**
21550 E Lincoln Hwy (60411-8744)
PHONE..................................708 758-0050
Thomas R Rogan, *President*
Bernice Rogan, *Treasurer*
▲ EMP: 2
SALES (est): 606.3K  Privately Held
WEB: www.rogangranite.com
SIC: 3281  2434  Monuments, cut stone (not finishing or lettering only); building stone products; furniture, cut stone; wood kitchen cabinets

**(G-14026)**
**S & S MACHINING SERVICES INC**
3151 Glenwood Dyer Rd 1c (60411-9760)
PHONE..................................708 758-8300
William Sisk, *President*
EMP: 8
SALES (est): 1.1MM  Privately Held
SIC: 3599  Machine & other job shop work

**(G-14027)**
**SCHEPEL SIGNS INC**
Also Called: Woodmaster Graphics
3149 Glenwood Dyer Rd I (60411-9747)
PHONE..................................708 758-1441
Fax: 708 758-1322
Charles L Schepel, *President*
EMP: 3 EST: 1971
SQ FT: 5,200
SALES (est): 373.4K  Privately Held
WEB: www.woodmastergraphics.com
SIC: 3993  Signs, not made in custom sign painting shops

## Lyons
### Cook County

**(G-14028)**
**A BARR FTN BEVERAGE SLS & SVC**
4424 Prescott Ave (60534-1932)
PHONE..................................708 442-2000
Thomas Barc, *Manager*
EMP: 5
SALES (est): 288K  Privately Held
SIC: 5149  2087  2086  Beverages, except coffee & tea; flavoring extracts & syrups; bottled & canned soft drinks

**(G-14029)**
**ACCUSHIM INC (PA)**
4601 Lawndale Ave (60534-1730)
P.O. Box 73 (60534-0073)
PHONE..................................708 442-6448
Fax: 708 442-6918
Daniel Mottl, *President*
George Hurtado, *General Mgr*
Gary Mottl, *Vice Pres*
Glen Mottl, *Vice Pres*
EMP: 5
SQ FT: 1,000
SALES (est): 1.2MM  Privately Held
WEB: www.accushim.com
SIC: 3825  5084  Instruments to measure electricity; machine tools & metalworking machinery

**(G-14030)**
**ART CRYSTAL II ENTERPRISES INC**
7852 47th St (60534-1852)
PHONE..................................630 739-0222
Patrick Dorgan, *President*
Albert Dorgan, *Vice Pres*
Steven Stone, *Consultant*
▼ EMP: 20
SQ FT: 13,500
SALES (est): 2.4MM  Privately Held
WEB: www.artcrystalltd.com
SIC: 3231  Cut & engraved glassware: made from purchased glass

**(G-14031)**
**ATLAS TOOL & DIE WORKS  INC**
4633 Lawndale Ave (60534-1724)
P.O. Box 32 (60534-0032)
PHONE..................................708 442-1661
Fax: 708 442-0016
Daniel J Mottl, *President*
Gary R Mottl, *Vice Pres*
Zack Mottl, *Purch Mgr*
Robert Lapat, *Engineer*
Rose K Mottl, *Treasurer*
▲ EMP: 55 EST: 1918
SQ FT: 50,000
SALES (est): 13.9MM  Privately Held
WEB: www.atlas-tool.com
SIC: 3469  3544  3443  Metal stampings; special dies, tools, jigs & fixtures; fabricated plate work (boiler shop)

**(G-14032)**
**BOND BROTHERS & CO**
7826 47th St (60534-1852)
PHONE..................................708 442-5510
Fax: 708 442-5894
Buddi Byinsky, *President*
Bruce Jobb, *Vice Pres*
Scott Jobb, *Vice Pres*
Joseph W Moore, *Vice Pres*
Robert Murray, *Vice Pres*
EMP: 12
SQ FT: 15,000
SALES (est): 1.8MM  Privately Held
WEB: www.bondbrothers.net
SIC: 2759  2791  2752  Letterpress printing; typesetting; commercial printing, lithographic

**(G-14033)**
**BUELL MANUFACTURING COMPANY**
Also Called: Buell Airhorns
8125 47th St (60534-1835)
PHONE..................................708 447-6320
Fax: 708 447-6387
Gary Buell, *President*
Rudy Andrew, *CFO*
EMP: 6 EST: 1912
SALES (est): 1.2MM  Privately Held
WEB: www.buellairhorns.com
SIC: 3714  3669  3585  3563  Horns, motor vehicle; marine horns, electric; compressors for refrigeration & air conditioning equipment; air & gas compressors

**(G-14034)**
**C E R MACHINING & TOOLING LTD**
8214 47th St (60534-1715)
PHONE..................................708 442-9614
Fax: 708 442-9450
David Spencer Sr, *President*
EMP: 5
SQ FT: 4,000
SALES: 450K  Privately Held
SIC: 3599  3825  3469  7692  Machine & other job shop work; instruments to measure electricity; metal stampings; welding repair; metalworking machinery

**(G-14035)**
**CHOICE TREAT EQUIPMENT MFG**
8130 47th St (60534-1836)
PHONE..................................708 442-2004
Fax: 708 447-9353
Dorothy Conley, *President*
Theresa Lyons, *Corp Secy*
Mickey Rigney, *Manager*
EMP: 6
SQ FT: 10,000
SALES (est): 629K  Privately Held
SIC: 3556  Beverage machinery

**(G-14036)**
**DRIVE SHAFT UNLIMITED INC**
4323 Joliet Rd (60534-1986)
PHONE..................................708 447-2211
Fax: 708 447-2211
Dan Swain, *President*
Karen Swain, *Vice Pres*
EMP: 4
SQ FT: 3,000
SALES: 550K  Privately Held
WEB: www.driveshaftsunlimited.com
SIC: 3714  Drive shafts, motor vehicle

**(G-14037)**
**FILTER KLEEN INC**
8432 44th Pl (60534-1744)
PHONE..................................708 447-4666
Fax: 708 447-4588
William Buckholtz, *President*
Natalie Buckholtz, *Corp Secy*
EMP: 8
SALES (est): 931.5K  Privately Held
WEB: www.filterkleen.com
SIC: 5085  2992  Filters, industrial; lubricating oils & greases

**(G-14038)**
**FRASER MILLWORK INC**
8109 Ogden Ave (60534-1125)
P.O. Box 95 (60534-0095)
PHONE..................................708 447-3262
Gale W Fraser, *President*
Mark Fraser, *Superintendent*
Marilyn Fraser, *Corp Secy*
Barbara Uhlich, *Accountant*
EMP: 4
SALES (est): 371.5K  Privately Held
SIC: 2434  2431  2421  Wood kitchen cabinets; millwork; sawmills & planing mills, general

## Lyons - Cook County (G-14039)

**(G-14039)**
**G & P PRODUCTS INC**
4215 Lawndale Ave (60534-1131)
P.O. Box 720 (60534-0720)
PHONE.....................708 442-9667
Fax: 708 442-6928
Donald Grossman, *President*
Linda Grossman, *Corp Secy*
▲ **EMP:** 20 **EST:** 1978
**SQ FT:** 14,000
**SALES (est):** 1.9MM **Privately Held**
**WEB:** www.gpproducts.com
**SIC: 2326** Work apparel, except uniforms

**(G-14040)**
**GROSSE&SONS HTG &SHEET MET INC**
4236 Elm Ave (60534-1428)
PHONE.....................708 447-8397
Fax: 708 447-8453
Phillip Grosse, *President*
Gene Grosse, *Treasurer*
Arthur Grosse, *Shareholder*
**EMP:** 6
**SQ FT:** 1,200
**SALES (est):** 460K **Privately Held**
**SIC: 1711** 1761 3444 Warm air heating & air conditioning contractor; gutter & downspout contractor; sheet metalwork

**(G-14041)**
**HOSPITAL HLTH CARE SYSTEMS INC (PA)**
7830 47th St Ste 1 (60534-1870)
PHONE.....................708 863-3400
Albert J Paveza, *President*
Albertas Simokaitis, *Vice Pres*
Ron Banaszak, *Treasurer*
Hermann Reutter, *Admin Sec*
**EMP:** 20
**SQ FT:** 20,000
**SALES:** 3MM **Privately Held**
**SIC: 2679** Tags & labels, paper

**(G-14042)**
**NJC MACHINE CO**
8338 47th St (60534-1761)
PHONE.....................708 442-6004
Fax: 708 442-1343
Mladen Curcija, *President*
Marcia Curcija, *Corp Secy*
**EMP:** 14
**SQ FT:** 10,000
**SALES (est):** 2.1MM **Privately Held**
**SIC: 3599** 7692 Machine shop, jobbing & repair; welding repair

**(G-14043)**
**PATT SUPPLY CORPORATION**
8111 47th St (60534-1835)
PHONE.....................708 442-3901
Fax: 708 442-3907
Craig Behrendt, *Principal*
George Yurkovich, *Principal*
**EMP:** 11 **EST:** 1929
**SQ FT:** 10,000
**SALES (est):** 1.7MM **Privately Held**
**WEB:** www.pattcorp.com
**SIC: 5072** 3993 7389 Security devices, locks; displays & cutouts, window & lobby; packaging & labeling services

**(G-14044)**
**SPECIALTY TAPE & LABEL CO INC**
7830 47th St (60534-1869)
PHONE.....................708 863-3800
Brian D Gale, *President*
Rick Paveza, *Opers Mgr*
**EMP:** 20
**SQ FT:** 7,500
**SALES (est):** 2.2MM **Privately Held**
**SIC: 2672** Tape, pressure sensitive: made from purchased materials; labels (unprinted), gummed: made from purchased materials
**PA:** I.D. Images Llc
2991 Interstate Pkwy
Brunswick OH 44212

**(G-14045)**
**STAIRSLAND**
8001 47th St Fl 4 (60534-1833)
PHONE.....................708 853-9593
Douglas Wojnicz, *Owner*

**EMP:** 8
**SALES (est):** 482.6K **Privately Held**
**SIC: 2431** 1751 Staircases & stairs, wood; cabinet & finish carpentry

**(G-14046)**
**STEVE BORTMAN**
Also Called: Minuteman Press
7937 Ogden Ave (60534-1337)
PHONE.....................708 442-1669
Steve Bortman, *Owner*
**EMP:** 5
**SQ FT:** 1,500
**SALES (est):** 520K **Privately Held**
**SIC: 2752** 2791 2789 Commercial printing, lithographic; typesetting; bookbinding & related work

### Macedonia
*Hamilton County*

**(G-14047)**
**SENECA REBUILD LLC**
11550 N Thompsonville Rd (62860-1175)
PHONE.....................618 435-9445
John Neal, *General Mgr*
Jonathan Zimmerle, *Engineer*
Dana Wilkerson, *Mng Member*
**EMP:** 16
**SALES (est):** 766.8K
**SALES (corp-wide):** 875.8MM **Publicly Held**
**SIC: 1241** Anthracite mining services, contract basis
**HQ:** Foresight Energy Llc
1 Metropolitan Sq 211nb
Saint Louis MO 63102
314 932-6160

### Machesney Park
*Winnebago County*

**(G-14048)**
**ABBACUS INC**
Also Called: ABBACUS INJECTION MOLDING
1248 Shappert Dr (61115-1418)
PHONE.....................815 637-9222
Fax: 815 877-2770
Judith A Beall, *President*
Paul F Beall, *General Mgr*
**EMP:** 27
**SQ FT:** 24,000
**SALES:** 4.3K **Privately Held**
**SIC: 3089** 3949 Injection molding of plastics; darts & table sports equipment & supplies

**(G-14049)**
**ABBACUS INJECTION MOLDING INC**
1248 Shappert Dr (61115-1418)
PHONE.....................815 637-9222
Judith A Beall, *Principal*
Tony Beall, *Principal*
**EMP:** 33
**SALES (est):** 2.7MM **Privately Held**
**SIC: 3089** Injection molding of plastics

**(G-14050)**
**ABILITY TOOL CO**
9816 Norman Ave (61115-1606)
PHONE.....................815 633-5909
Bradley Schutt, *President*
Don Martain, *Manager*
**EMP:** 21 **EST:** 1964
**SQ FT:** 21,000
**SALES (est):** 1.9MM **Privately Held**
**SIC: 3544** 3545 Special dies & tools; punches, forming & stamping; precision tools, machinists'

**(G-14051)**
**ACCURATE BUSINESS CONTROLS INC**
7846 Burden Rd (61115-8201)
P.O. Box 2244, Loves Park (61131-0244)
PHONE.....................815 633-5500
Fax: 815 633-5506
Frank J Moran, *President*

Timothy B Moran, *Vice Pres*
**EMP:** 2 **EST:** 1969
**SQ FT:** 1,600
**SALES:** 850K **Privately Held**
**SIC: 2752** 5112 Commercial printing, lithographic; business forms

**(G-14052)**
**AIRGAS USA LLC**
10853 N 2nd St (61115-1460)
PHONE.....................815 289-1928
Grant Sandberg, *Manager*
**EMP:** 12
**SALES (corp-wide):** 163.9MM **Privately Held**
**WEB:** www.riws.com
**SIC: 7692** Welding repair
**HQ:** Airgas Usa, Llc
259 N Radnor Chester Rd # 100
Radnor PA 19087
610 687-5253

**(G-14053)**
**AKD CONTROLS INC**
10340 Product Dr (61115-1439)
PHONE.....................815 633-4586
Fax: 815 633-8860
Andy Ballinger, *President*
Kathleen Ballinger, *Corp Secy*
**EMP:** 7
**SQ FT:** 4,500
**SALES (est):** 800K **Privately Held**
**WEB:** www.akdcontrols.com
**SIC: 3613** Panelboards & distribution boards, electric

**(G-14054)**
**AL MITE MANUFACTURING CO INC**
1215 Shappert Dr (61115-1417)
PHONE.....................815 654-0720
Fax: 815 654-0743
Curtis Navickis, *President*
**EMP:** 3 **EST:** 2010
**SALES (est):** 216.3K **Privately Held**
**SIC: 3999** Manufacturing industries

**(G-14055)**
**ALDI INC**
1545 W Lane Rd (61115-1903)
PHONE.....................815 877-0861
**EMP:** 11 **Privately Held**
**SIC: 2082** Mfg Malt Beverages
**HQ:** Aldi Inc.
1200 N Kirk Rd
Batavia IL 60510
630 879-8100

**(G-14056)**
**ANDERSON AWNING & SHUTTER**
Also Called: Anderson Limousine
8414 N 2nd St (61115-2413)
PHONE.....................815 654-1155
Fax: 815 654-1196
James H Anderson, *Owner*
Sandra Anderson, *Co-Owner*
**EMP:** 3
**SALES:** 250K **Privately Held**
**SIC: 5999** 5039 3444 3443 Awnings; awnings; sheet metalwork; fabricated plate work (boiler shop); millwork

**(G-14057)**
**APPLIED PRODUCTS INC**
12000 Product Dr (61115-1479)
P.O. Box 10229, Loves Park (61131-3129)
PHONE.....................815 633-3825
Fax: 815 633-2385
Steven R Nethery, *President*
Elizabeth A Nethery, *Corp Secy*
Jack Nethery, *Vice Pres*
Liz Nethery, *Financial Exec*
**EMP:** 30 **EST:** 1967
**SQ FT:** 50,000
**SALES (est):** 10MM **Privately Held**
**SIC: 2671** Packaging paper & plastics film, coated & laminated

**(G-14058)**
**ARMOR COATED TECHNOLOGY CORP**
1190 Anvil Rd (61115-1483)
PHONE.....................815 636-7200
Randal G Loomis, *President*

Mike Zimmerman, *Opers Mgr*
**EMP:** 4
**SALES (est):** 490K **Privately Held**
**WEB:** www.zipfastener.net
**SIC: 3356** Titanium & titanium alloy: rolling, drawing or extruding

**(G-14059)**
**ASTRO-PHYSICS INC**
11250 Forest Hills Rd (61115-8238)
PHONE.....................815 282-1513
Fax: 815 282-9847
Roland Christen, *President*
Marjorie Christen, *Vice Pres*
Tony Stevens, *Mfg Staff*
Christene Schmidt, *Manager*
Alice Thompson, *Admin Asst*
**EMP:** 18 **EST:** 1975
**SQ FT:** 11,000
**SALES (est):** 4.4MM **Privately Held**
**WEB:** www.astro-physics.com
**SIC: 3827** Telescopes: elbow, panoramic, sighting, fire control, etc.; lens mounts

**(G-14060)**
**BOWL DOCTORS INC**
7664 Hawks Rdg (61115-8269)
PHONE.....................815 282-6009
Jim Egert, *President*
Tanya Egert, *Vice Pres*
**EMP:** 7
**SQ FT:** 6,000
**SALES (est):** 1.3MM **Privately Held**
**SIC: 3569** Liquid automation machinery & equipment

**(G-14061)**
**BUSINESS CARD SYSTEMS INC**
Also Called: B C T
11025 Raleigh Ct (61115-1416)
P.O. Box 2002, Loves Park (61130-0002)
PHONE.....................815 877-0990
Fax: 815 877-2696
Thomas G Mc Neany, *President*
Jeri A Mc Neany, *Corp Secy*
**EMP:** 15
**SQ FT:** 4,000
**SALES (est):** 3MM **Privately Held**
**SIC: 2752** Commercial printing, lithographic

**(G-14062)**
**BUSINESS CARDS TOMORROW**
Also Called: B C T
11025 Raleigh Ct (61115-1416)
PHONE.....................815 877-0990
Kenneth Johnson, *President*
Mary Johnson, *Vice Pres*
**EMP:** 14
**SALES (est):** 920K **Privately Held**
**SIC: 2752** 2759 Commercial printing, lithographic; thermography

**(G-14063)**
**BY DOZEN BAKERY INC**
8324 N 2nd St (61115-2470)
PHONE.....................815 636-0668
Fax: 815 636-3910
Martha Nelson, *President*
Brent Nelson, *Opers Mgr*
**EMP:** 7
**SALES (est):** 769.5K **Privately Held**
**SIC: 2051** Doughnuts, except frozen

**(G-14064)**
**CHAMFERMATIC INC**
7842 Burden Rd (61115-8201)
PHONE.....................815 636-5082
Fax: 815 636-0075
Michael Magee, *President*
Dixie Magee, *Vice Pres*
**EMP:** 3
**SALES (est):** 250K **Privately Held**
**WEB:** www.chamfermatic.com
**SIC: 3599** Machine shop, jobbing & repair

**(G-14065)**
**CLINTON TOPPER NEWSPAPER**
Also Called: Rockberry Publishing
11512 N 2nd St (61115-1101)
P.O. Box 443, Clinton WI (53525-0443)
PHONE.....................815 654-4850
Pete Cruger, *CEO*
Randy Johnson, *Manager*
Celeste Thompson, *Director*
**EMP:** 50

**SALES (est):** 224.8K  Privately Held
**SIC: 2711**  Newspapers

**(G-14066)**
### CLUTCH SYSTEMS INC
10901 N 2nd St (61115-1461)
P.O. Box 15130, Loves Park (61132-5130)
**PHONE**.................................815 282-7960
Dan Lemmons, *President*
**EMP:** 3
**SQ FT:** 18,000
**SALES (est):** 387.2K  Privately Held
**SIC: 3714  7371**  Clutches, motor vehicle; custom computer programming services

**(G-14067)**
### COCA-COLA REFRESHMENTS USA INC
10400 N 2nd St (61115-1497)
**PHONE**.................................815 636-7300
**Fax:** 815 636-7340
Les Lankanship, *Sales/Mktg Mgr*
**EMP:** 100
**SQ FT:** 207,000
**SALES (corp-wide):** 41.8B  Publicly Held
**WEB:** www.cokecce.com
**SIC: 2086**  Bottled & canned soft drinks
**HQ:** Coca-Cola Refreshments Usa, Inc.
2500 Windy Ridge Pkwy Se
Atlanta GA 30339
770 989-3000

**(G-14068)**
### CURTIS METAL FINISHING COMPANY
Also Called: Curtis Thermal Processing
10911 N 2nd St (61115-1461)
**PHONE**.................................815 282-1433
Matt Heystek, *Branch Mgr*
**EMP:** 13
**SALES (corp-wide):** 24.8MM  Privately Held
**SIC: 3398**  Metal heat treating
**HQ:** Curtis Metal Finishing Company
6645 Sims Dr
Sterling Heights MI 48313
586 939-2850

**(G-14069)**
### CURTIS METAL FINISHING COMPANY
9917 N Alpine Rd (61115-8212)
**PHONE**.................................815 633-6693
**Fax:** 815 633-9220
Steve Wasson, *President*
**EMP:** 70
**SALES (corp-wide):** 24.8MM  Privately Held
**WEB:** www.curtismetal.com
**SIC: 3479  3471**  Coating of metals & formed products; plating & polishing
**HQ:** Curtis Metal Finishing Company
6645 Sims Dr
Sterling Heights MI 48313
586 939-2850

**(G-14070)**
### D & D COUNTER TOPS CO INC
9710 Forest Hills Rd (61115-8214)
**Fax:** 815 654-1563
Robert Adams, *President*
James Stromquist, *Treasurer*
Al Kooling, *Office Mgr*
**EMP:** 4
**SQ FT:** 9,100
**SALES (est):** 528.9K  Privately Held
**SIC: 2434  2541**  Wood kitchen cabinets; vanities, bathroom: wood; counter & sink tops; sink tops, plastic laminated; table or counter tops, plastic laminated

**(G-14071)**
### DIABLO FURNACES LLC ✪
7723 Burden Rd (61115-8219)
**PHONE**.................................815 636-7502
Sue Harrod,
**EMP:** 12 EST: 2017
**SALES:** 1MM  Privately Held
**SIC: 3564**  Filters, air: furnaces, air conditioning equipment, etc.

**(G-14072)**
### ELECTROFORM COMPANY (PA)
11070 Raleigh Ct (61115-1416)
**PHONE**.................................815 633-1113
**Fax:** 815 633-3710
Wade Clark, *President*
Marcy Loven, *Manager*
Brian Smith, *Manager*
▲ **EMP:** 27
**SQ FT:** 9,000
**SALES (est):** 4.5MM  Privately Held
**WEB:** www.injectionmoldmaking.com
**SIC: 3089  3599**  Injection molding of plastics; electrical discharge machining (EDM)

**(G-14073)**
### FERRELLGAS  LP
10522 N 2nd St (61115-1405)
**PHONE**.................................815 877-7333
**Fax:** 815 877-9716
Gregory West, *Branch Mgr*
**EMP:** 3  Publicly Held
**SIC: 5984  1321**  Propane gas, bottled; natural gas liquids
**HQ:** Ferrellgas, L.P.
7500 College Blvd # 1000
Overland Park KS 66210

**(G-14074)**
### FERRELLGAS  LP
10522 N 2nd St (61115-1405)
**PHONE**.................................815 599-8967
**Fax:** 815 233-3184
Mike Rentminster, *Manager*
**EMP:** 6  Publicly Held
**SIC: 1321**  Propane (natural) production
**HQ:** Ferrellgas, L.P.
7500 College Blvd # 1000
Overland Park KS 66210

**(G-14075)**
### FIRST HEADER DIE INC
1313 Anvil Rd (61115-1463)
**PHONE**.................................815 282-5161
**Fax:** 815 282-5295
Mark Gritzmacher, *President*
Kathy Gritzmacher, *Vice Pres*
Deedee Hecker, *Office Mgr*
**EMP:** 21
**SQ FT:** 2,500
**SALES (est):** 2.7MM  Privately Held
**WEB:** www.fhdinc.com
**SIC: 3542  3544**  Headers; special dies, tools, jigs & fixtures

**(G-14076)**
### FORTE AUTOMATION SYSTEMS INC
8155 Burden Rd (61115-8208)
**PHONE**.................................815 316-6247
**Fax:** 815 633-7131
Toby Henderson, *President*
Jim Deemer, *Vice Pres*
Tami Henderson, *Vice Pres*
Steve Smith, *Opers Mgr*
Ed Wilson, *Engineer*
▲ **EMP:** 50
**SQ FT:** 50,000
**SALES (est):** 22.1MM  Privately Held
**WEB:** www.forteautomation.com
**SIC: 3552  3535**  Textile machinery; conveyors & conveying equipment

**(G-14077)**
### G & E AUTOMATIC
10462 Product Dr Ste B (61115-1465)
**PHONE**.................................815 654-7766
**Fax:** 815 654-7795
Kevin Merkle, *Owner*
**EMP:** 4
**SALES (est):** 493.4K  Privately Held
**SIC: 3451**  Screw machine products

**(G-14078)**
### HENNIG INC (HQ)
9900 N Alpine Rd (61115-8211)
**PHONE**.................................815 636-9900
**Fax:** 815 636-9737
Willy Goellner, *Ch of Bd*
Dietmar Goellner, *President*
Dietmar Goellner, *President*
Marika Mertz, *Corp Secy*
Greg Champion, *Vice Pres*
▲ **EMP:** 4
**SQ FT:** 73,000
**SALES (est):** 25.3MM
**SALES (corp-wide):** 115.6MM  Privately Held
**SIC: 3444**  Machine guards, sheet metal

**PA:** Goellner, Inc.
2500 Latham St
Rockford IL 61103
815 962-6076

**(G-14079)**
### HI-FIVE SPORTSWEAR INC
7836 N 2nd St (61115-2822)
P.O. Box 10139, Loves Park (61131-0139)
**PHONE**.................................815 637-6044
**Fax:** 815 637-4912
Phil Staley, *President*
Wendy Williams, *Admin Sec*
**EMP:** 2
**SQ FT:** 4,000
**SALES:** 270K  Privately Held
**SIC: 2759  5699  2396  2395**  Screen printing; sports apparel; automotive & apparel trimmings; pleating & stitching

**(G-14080)**
### ILLINOIS TOOL WORKS INC
Also Called: I T W Shakeproof Indus Pdts
10818 N 2nd St (61115-1406)
**PHONE**.................................815 654-1510
Keith Gasiorowski, *Plant Mgr*
Walt Stalker, *Manager*
**EMP:** 50
**SQ FT:** 24,000
**SALES (corp-wide):** 13.6B  Publicly Held
**SIC: 3451**  Screw machine products
**PA:** Illinois Tool Works Inc.
155 Harlem Ave
Glenview IL 60025
847 724-7500

**(G-14081)**
### ILLINOIS TOOL WORKS INC
Also Called: ITW Shake Proof Auto Division
10818 N 2nd St (61115-1406)
**PHONE**.................................815 654-1510
Mike Campbell, *Manager*
Eric Schliker, *Supervisor*
**EMP:** 12
**SALES (corp-wide):** 13.6B  Publicly Held
**SIC: 3452**  Screws, metal
**PA:** Illinois Tool Works Inc.
155 Harlem Ave
Glenview IL 60025
847 724-7500

**(G-14082)**
### INSTRUMENT SERVICES INC
4075 Steele Dr (61115-8358)
**PHONE**.................................815 623-2993
**Fax:** 815 316-2926
Chuck Cruse, *President*
Lynn Nocifora, *Controller*
**EMP:** 8
**SQ FT:** 40,000
**SALES (est):** 930K  Privately Held
**WEB:** www.clocksandgauges.com
**SIC: 5013  3873  5944**  Automotive supplies & parts; clocks, assembly of; clocks

**(G-14083)**
### INTERSTATE GRAPHICS  INC
7817 Burden Rd (61115-8241)
**PHONE**.................................815 877-6777
**Fax:** 815 654-7221
John Norwood Jr, *President*
John V Norwood Sr, *President*
Jim Norwood, *Treasurer*
Polly Ralston, *Manager*
Diane Ratcliff, *Admin Sec*
**EMP:** 21
**SQ FT:** 23,500
**SALES (est):** 4.5MM  Privately Held
**WEB:** www.interstategraphicsinc.com
**SIC: 2759**  Screen printing

**(G-14084)**
### KANNEBERG CUSTOM KITCHENS INC
1242 Shappert Dr (61115-1499)
**PHONE**.................................815 654-1110
**Fax:** 815 654-3944
Roger E Kanneberg, *Owner*
Frederick Cook, *Vice Pres*
**EMP:** 6
**SQ FT:** 4,000
**SALES (est):** 515.1K  Privately Held
**SIC: 2434**  Wood kitchen cabinets

**(G-14085)**
### KERNEL KUTTER INC
10509 Tartan Ct (61115-1373)
**PHONE**.................................815 877-1515
Patricia Caccia, *President*
Cathy Caccia, *President*
Craig Wassel, *General Mgr*
Dan Caccia, *Corp Secy*
**EMP:** 3
**SQ FT:** 5,000
**SALES (est):** 220K  Privately Held
**WEB:** www.corn-pineapple-cutters.com
**SIC: 3469  5812  3421**  Utensils, household: metal, except cast; eating places; cutlery

**(G-14086)**
### KLEIN TOOLS  INC
9929 N Alpine Rd (61115-8212)
**PHONE**.................................815 282-0530
**EMP:** 3
**SALES (corp-wide):** 344.9MM  Privately Held
**SIC: 3545**  Cutting tools for machine tools
**PA:** Klein Tools, Inc.
450 Bond St
Lincolnshire IL 60069
847 821-5500

**(G-14087)**
### LAB TEN LLC
5029 Willow Creek Rd (61115-8218)
**PHONE**.................................815 877-1410
Matt Smith, *Business Mgr*
Smith Clifford, *Mng Member*
Bye Patrick, *Mng Member*
Chris Rubert, *Manager*
Duane Wingate,
**EMP:** 40
**SQ FT:** 16,000
**SALES (est):** 5.6MM  Privately Held
**SIC: 3451  5084**  Screw machine products; industrial machinery & equipment

**(G-14088)**
### LAMINATED DESIGNS COUNTERTOPS
9731 N 2nd St (61115-1617)
**PHONE**.................................815 877-7222
**EMP:** 5
**SALES (est):** 296.8K  Privately Held
**SIC: 2541**  Wood partitions & fixtures

**(G-14089)**
### LLOYD MIDWEST GRAPHICS
7103 N 2nd St (61115-3709)
**PHONE**.................................815 282-8828
**Fax:** 815 282-8840
Deborah Swain, *President*
**EMP:** 5
**SALES (est):** 434.5K  Privately Held
**SIC: 2759  7336  2796  2791**  Commercial printing; graphic arts & related design; platemaking services; typesetting; commercial printing, lithographic; automotive & apparel trimmings

**(G-14090)**
### MARK POWER INTERNATIONAL
7897 Burden Rd (61115-8220)
**PHONE**.................................815 877-5984
Greg Powers, *Owner*
Carrie Myers, *Manager*
▲ **EMP:** 15
**SALES (est):** 1.2MM  Privately Held
**WEB:** www.powermarkint.com
**SIC: 3089**  Injection molded finished plastic products

**(G-14091)**
### MIDLAND PLASTICS  INC
Also Called: Midland Industrial Plastics
7861 Burden Rd (61115-8220)
**PHONE**.................................815 282-4079
**Fax:** 815 282-4776
Cris Shick, *Branch Mgr*
**EMP:** 3
**SALES (corp-wide):** 70.1MM  Privately Held
**WEB:** www.midlandplastic.com
**SIC: 3089**  Plastic processing
**PA:** Midland Plastics, Inc.
5405 S Westridge Ct
New Berlin WI 53151
262 938-7000

## Machesney Park - Winnebago County (G-14092)

**(G-14092)**
**MIDWEST AERO SUPPORT INC**
1303 Turret Dr (61115-1452)
PHONE ............................................ 815 398-9202
Brent R Johnson, *President*
Lynn Breed, *General Mgr*
Mike Lubbs, *COO*
Barbara Johnson, *Vice Pres*
John Oller, *Mfg Staff*
**EMP:** 29
**SQ FT:** 14,400
**SALES (est):** 5.3MM **Privately Held**
**WEB:** www.midwestaerosupport.com
**SIC:** 7699 3812 3679 3694 Aircraft & heavy equipment repair services; aircraft control systems, electronic; electronic circuits; harness wiring sets, internal combustion engines

**(G-14093)**
**MIDWEST PACKAGING & CONT INC**
9718 Forest Hills Rd (61115-8214)
PHONE ............................................ 815 633-6800
Terry Young, *President*
Leslie Young, *Vice Pres*
Robert Young, *Vice Pres*
James Waller, *Admin Sec*
**EMP:** 70
**SQ FT:** 92,500
**SALES (est):** 19MM **Privately Held**
**WEB:** www.midpack.com
**SIC:** 2653 7389 Boxes, corrugated: made from purchased materials; packaging & labeling services

**(G-14094)**
**MIDWEST TOOL & MANUFACTURING**
7864 Burden Rd (61115-8201)
PHONE ............................................ 815 282-6754
Larry Shelley, *President*
Robert Shelley, *Vice Pres*
Carol Stai, *Admin Sec*
**EMP:** 5
**SQ FT:** 6,000
**SALES:** 300.3K **Privately Held**
**SIC:** 3545 Cutting tools for machine tools

**(G-14095)**
**PARKER-HANNIFIN CORPORATION**
Also Called: Hydraulic Accumulator
10711 N 2nd St (61115-1459)
PHONE ............................................ 815 636-4100
Charles Kokesh, *Engineer*
Bob Rajabi, *Engineer*
Rafael Toledo, *Engineer*
Rick Philibin, *Marketing Staff*
Mark Gagnon, *Manager*
**EMP:** 80
**SQ FT:** 20,000
**SALES (corp-wide):** 11.3B **Publicly Held**
**WEB:** www.parker.com
**SIC:** 3593 Fluid power cylinders, hydraulic or pneumatic
**PA:** Parker-Hannifin Corporation
6035 Parkland Blvd
Cleveland OH 44124
216 896-3000

**(G-14096)**
**PDQ MACHINE INC**
7909b Burden Rd (61115-8277)
PHONE ............................................ 815 282-7575
Fax: 815 282-7577
Chris Eickstead, *General Mgr*
Paul Zingg, *Manager*
**EMP:** 8
**SALES:** 750K **Privately Held**
**SIC:** 3599 3545 Machine & other job shop work; machine tool accessories

**(G-14097)**
**PLASTIC PARTS INTL INC**
1248 Shappert Dr (61115-1418)
PHONE ............................................ 815 637-9222
Anthony Beall, *President*
Chris Beall, *VP Sales*
▲ **EMP:** 24
**SQ FT:** 23,000
**SALES (est):** 6.9MM **Privately Held**
**SIC:** 3089 Injection molding of plastics

**(G-14098)**
**POLY PLASTICS FILMS CORP**
334 Northway Park Rd # 3 (61115-4040)
P.O. Box 427, Grand Island NY (14072-0427)
PHONE ............................................ 815 636-0821
Merle Wilson, *President*
**EMP:** 7
**SQ FT:** 6,000
**SALES (est):** 773K **Privately Held**
**SIC:** 5113 2673 Bags, paper & disposable plastic; plastic & pliofilm bags

**(G-14099)**
**PRECISION DYNAMICS INC**
5029 Willow Creek Rd (61115-8218)
PHONE ............................................ 815 877-1592
William Brook, *Vice Pres*
Robert Becker, *Vice Pres*
**EMP:** 12
**SALES (est):** 580K **Privately Held**
**SIC:** 3599 Crankshafts & camshafts, machining

**(G-14100)**
**PREMIER PRINTING & PROMOTIONS**
1338 Turret Dr Ste B (61115-3405)
P.O. Box 596, Roscoe (61073-0596)
PHONE ............................................ 815 282-3890
Fax: 815 282-3895
Ron Einsel, *Owner*
**EMP:** 11
**SALES (est):** 1MM **Privately Held**
**SIC:** 2759 Commercial printing

**(G-14101)**
**PRINTJET CORPORATION**
7816 Burden Rd (61115-8201)
PHONE ............................................ 815 877-7511
Fax: 815 877-7621
Pedro Sotelo, *President*
Susan Sotelo, *Admin Sec*
▲ **EMP:** 15
**SQ FT:** 11,000
**SALES (est):** 4.6MM **Privately Held**
**WEB:** www.printjet.net
**SIC:** 3577 Bar code (magnetic ink) printers

**(G-14102)**
**ROCK VALLEY PALLET COMPANY**
3511 Mildred Ct (61115-3877)
PHONE ............................................ 815 654-4850
James A Webb, *Principal*
**EMP:** 3
**SALES (est):** 131.9K **Privately Held**
**SIC:** 2448 Pallets, wood & wood with metal

**(G-14103)**
**ROCK VALLEY PUBLISHING LLC (PA)**
Also Called: Gazette Newspapers
11512 N 2nd St (61115-1101)
PHONE ............................................ 815 467-6397
Pete Cruger, *President*
R Johnson, *General Mgr*
Todd Nielson, *Editor*
Cyndi Jensen, *Finance Other*
Jack Crueger,
**EMP:** 20 **EST:** 1966
**SQ FT:** 3,000
**SALES (est):** 4.5MM **Privately Held**
**WEB:** www.rvpublishing.com
**SIC:** 2711 Newspapers: publishing only, not printed on site

**(G-14104)**
**ROCKFORD AIR DEVICES INC**
1201 Turret Dr (61115-1451)
P.O. Box 2497, Loves Park (61132-2497)
PHONE ............................................ 815 654-3330
Fax: 815 654-0847
Scott Bosi, *President*
Scott J Bosi, *President*
Laura Bosi, *Finance Other*
**EMP:** 10
**SQ FT:** 20,000
**SALES (est):** 3MM **Privately Held**
**SIC:** 3443 Cylinders, pressure: metal plate

**(G-14105)**
**ROCKFORD COMMERCIAL WHSE INC**
Also Called: STC International
8105 Burden Rd (61115-8208)
P.O. Box 140, Roscoe (61073-0140)
PHONE ............................................ 815 623-8400
Adam Clayton, *President*
▲ **EMP:** 7
**SQ FT:** 16,000
**SALES (est):** 2.6MM **Privately Held**
**WEB:** www.rockford-intl.com
**SIC:** 5072 3546 Hand tools; miscellaneous fasteners; grinders, portable: electric or pneumatic

**(G-14106)**
**RUSCO MANUFACTURING INC**
1304 Anvil Rd (61115-1409)
PHONE ............................................ 815 654-3930
Russell Winters Jr, *Owner*
Carol Winters, *Vice Pres*
Craig Valore, *QC Mgr*
Michelle Stothert, *Office Mgr*
**EMP:** 14
**SQ FT:** 55,000
**SALES (est):** 3.3MM **Privately Held**
**SIC:** 3599 Machine shop, jobbing & repair

**(G-14107)**
**SHAWCRAFT SIGN CO**
7727 Burden Rd (61115-8219)
PHONE ............................................ 815 282-4105
Fax: 815 282-4147
Jay A Schoepski, *President*
**EMP:** 4
**SQ FT:** 3,120
**SALES (est):** 467.1K **Privately Held**
**WEB:** www.shawcraft.com
**SIC:** 2499 3993 Signboards, wood; signs & advertising specialties

**(G-14108)**
**SPARTACUS GROUP INC**
Also Called: Spartaclean
925 Colonial Dr (61115-3801)
PHONE ............................................ 815 637-1574
Clayton Balmes, *Director*
**EMP:** 10
**SALES (est):** 950K **Privately Held**
**SIC:** 2992 Lubricating oils & greases

**(G-14109)**
**SUPERIOR JOINING TECH INC**
Also Called: Sjti
1260 Turret Dr (61115-1442)
PHONE ............................................ 815 282-7581
Fax: 815 282-7583
Teresa L Beach-Shelow, *President*
Thomas A Shelow, *Treasurer*
**EMP:** 26
**SQ FT:** 55,000
**SALES (est):** 2.5MM **Privately Held**
**WEB:** www.superiorjt.com
**SIC:** 7692 3444 3724 8734 Welding repair; culverts, flumes & pipes; aircraft engines & engine parts; product testing laboratories; fabricated structural metal; steel wool

**(G-14110)**
**SWEBCO MFG INC**
7909 Burden Rd (61115-8277)
PHONE ............................................ 815 636-7160
Fax: 815 636-7166
Kirk Schwebke, *President*
Daniel Schwebke, *Vice Pres*
Patricia Schwebke, *Vice Pres*
Rick St Clair, *Opers Mgr*
Shauna Schwebke, *Purchasing*
**EMP:** 50
**SQ FT:** 34,000
**SALES (est):** 7.2MM **Privately Held**
**WEB:** www.swebco.com
**SIC:** 3451 3599 Screw machine products; machine & other job shop work

**(G-14111)**
**T R JONES MACHINE CO INC**
3040 Hamlin Dr (61115-7637)
PHONE ............................................ 815 356-5000
Fax: 815 356-5033
Richard G Elwell, *President*
David Elwell, *Corp Secy*
Robert Jones, *Vice Pres*
Laura Kunold, *Finance Mgr*
**EMP:** 6 **EST:** 1969
**SQ FT:** 7,500
**SALES:** 500K **Privately Held**
**WEB:** www.trjonesmachine.com
**SIC:** 3451 3544 Screw machine products; special dies & tools

**(G-14112)**
**TOWER TOOL & ENGINEERING INC**
11052 Raleigh Ct (61115-1416)
PHONE ............................................ 815 654-1115
Fax: 815 654-1175
Daniel Noe, *President*
Gordon Akey, *Vice Pres*
**EMP:** 13
**SQ FT:** 10,000
**SALES:** 1.8MM **Privately Held**
**SIC:** 3544 3599 Special dies & tools; custom machinery

**(G-14113)**
**TRD MANUFACTURING INC**
10914 N 2nd St (61115-1400)
PHONE ............................................ 815 654-7775
Jeffrey Brown, *President*
Mr Kerry Reinhardt, *General Mgr*
James S Meldeau, *Admin Sec*
**EMP:** 45
**SQ FT:** 75,000
**SALES (est):** 12.2MM
**SALES (corp-wide):** 128.7MM **Privately Held**
**WEB:** www.trdmfg.com
**SIC:** 3561 Cylinders, pump
**PA:** Bimba Manufacturing Company Inc
25150 S Governors Hwy
University Park IL 60484
708 534-8544

**(G-14114)**
**TRI-PART SCREW PRODUCTS INC**
10739 N 2nd St (61115-1459)
PHONE ............................................ 815 654-7311
Fax: 815 654-0468
Donald Schuur, *President*
Mark C Lender, *President*
Robert Flaningam, *Corp Secy*
Jackie Wedler, *Manager*
**EMP:** 45 **EST:** 1982
**SQ FT:** 16,600
**SALES (est):** 9.3MM **Privately Held**
**WEB:** www.tri-part.com
**SIC:** 3451 Screw machine products

**(G-14115)**
**UNIVERSAL DIE CAST CORPORATION**
11500 Summerwood Dr (61115-8338)
PHONE ............................................ 815 633-1702
Harold Winebaugh, *President*
Edward Palsgrove, *Vice Pres*
**EMP:** 6
**SQ FT:** 10,000
**SALES (est):** 882.5K **Privately Held**
**SIC:** 3364 Zinc & zinc-base alloy die-castings

**(G-14116)**
**UNIVERSAL FEEDER INC**
5299 Irving Blvd (61115-8274)
PHONE ............................................ 815 633-0752
Fax: 815 633-6338
Harold Winebaugh, *President*
Edward Polsgrove, *President*
**EMP:** 7
**SALES (est):** 614.5K **Privately Held**
**WEB:** www.universalmfg.net
**SIC:** 7389 3545 3537 Design, commercial & industrial; hopper feed devices; industrial trucks & tractors

**(G-14117)**
**UNLIMITED SVCS WISCONSIN INC**
Also Called: Kenwood Electrical Systems
10108 Forest Hills Rd (61115-8234)
P.O. Box 170, Oconto WI (54153-0170)
PHONE ............................................ 815 399-0282
William Kessenich, *President*
**EMP:** 20

# GEOGRAPHIC SECTION

Madison - Madison County (G-14143)

SALES (corp-wide): 81MM **Privately Held**
WEB: www.us-wire-harness.com
SIC: **3679** 3643 Harness assemblies for electronic use: wire or cable; current-carrying wiring devices
PA: Unlimited Services Of Wisconsin, Inc.
170 Evergreen Rd
Oconto WI 54153
920 834-4418

## Mackinaw
### Tazewell County

**(G-14118)**
**PLAYING WITH FUSION INC**
31201 State Route 9 (61755-8758)
PHONE..................309 258-7259
Justin Steinlage, *President*
EMP: 3
SALES (est): 253.5K **Privately Held**
SIC: **3599** Amusement park equipment

**(G-14119)**
**US CONVEYOR TECH MFG INC**
30000 State Route 9 (61755-9571)
PHONE..................309 359-4088
Fax: 309 359-6040
Kent Graves, *President*
Larry Sninebby, *Admin Sec*
EMP: 34
SQ FT: 50,000
SALES (est): 9.6MM **Privately Held**
WEB: www.usconveyor.net
SIC: **3535** Conveyors & conveying equipment

**(G-14120)**
**US CONVEYOR TECHNOLOGIES**
30000 State Route 9 (61755-9571)
PHONE..................309 359-4088
Kent Graves, *Principal*
◆ EMP: 18
SALES (est): 5.2MM **Privately Held**
SIC: **3535** Conveyors & conveying equipment

## Macomb
### Mcdonough County

**(G-14121)**
**CHALLENGE PUBLICATIONS L T D**
Also Called: Palaestra
1948 Riverview Dr (61455-1277)
P.O. Box 269, Bushnell (61422-0269)
PHONE..................309 421-0392
Dr David Beaver, *President*
Joseph Huver, *Vice Pres*
Ann Modrcin, *Admin Sec*
EMP: 6
SALES: 25MM **Privately Held**
WEB: www.palaestra.com
SIC: **2721** Periodicals

**(G-14122)**
**CLUGSTON TIBBITTS FUNERAL HOME (PA)**
Also Called: Clugston-Tibbots Monument Co
303 E Washington St (61455-2341)
PHONE..................309 833-2188
Steve Tibbitts, *President*
EMP: 4 EST: 1926
SALES: 500K **Privately Held**
SIC: **7261** 3281 Funeral home; funeral director; cut stone & stone products

**(G-14123)**
**CROOKED CREEK OUTDOORS**
1025 W Grant St (61455-2620)
PHONE..................309 837-3000
EMP: 2
SALES (est): 203.7K **Privately Held**
SIC: **3949** Sporting & athletic goods

**(G-14124)**
**DESIGNED FOR JUST FOR YOU**
106 Pam Ln (61455-3304)
PHONE..................309 221-2667
Gloria Castle, *Owner*

EMP: 3
SALES (est): 145K **Privately Held**
SIC: **3648** Lanterns: electric, gas, carbide, kerosene or gasoline

**(G-14125)**
**HILLYER INC**
Also Called: Hillyer's U-Store-It
1420 E Carroll St (61455-1819)
P.O. Box 728 (61455-0728)
PHONE..................309 837-6434
Fax: 309 837-6435
William H Hillyer Sr, *President*
Michael Hillyer, *Corp Secy*
David Hillyer, *Vice Pres*
William H Hillyer Jr, *Vice Pres*
Sara Chance, *Accountant*
EMP: 85
SQ FT: 2,000
SALES (est): 9.3MM **Privately Held**
WEB: www.hillyer.com
SIC: **1611** 1622 1794 1623 Surfacing & paving; bridge construction; excavation & grading, building construction; water main construction; sewer line construction; asphalt paving mixtures & blocks

**(G-14126)**
**JOURNAL STAR-PEORIA**
1432 E Jackson St (61455-2573)
PHONE..................309 833-2449
Fax: 309 837-1981
George Guzzardo, *Principal*
EMP: 3 EST: 2010
SALES (est): 103.4K **Privately Held**
SIC: **2711** Newspapers, publishing & printing

**(G-14127)**
**NTN BEARING CORPORATION**
Also Called: NTN Warehouse
1805 E University Dr (61455-1842)
PHONE..................847 298-7500
EMP: 5
SALES (est): 397.3K **Privately Held**
SIC: **3562** Roller bearings & parts

**(G-14128)**
**NTN-BOWER CORPORATION (DH)**
711 Bower Rd (61455-2511)
PHONE..................309 837-0440
Fax: 309 837-0438
Kunio Kamo, *President*
Mike Lawson, *Opers Mgr*
Dean Curley, *Prdtn Mgr*
Tammy Dalbello, *Safety Mgr*
Bob Donnell, *Engineer*
◆ EMP: 5
SQ FT: 20,000
SALES: 172MM
SALES (corp-wide): 6B **Privately Held**
WEB: www.ntnbower.com
SIC: **3562** Roller bearings & parts
HQ: Ntn Usa Corporation
1600 Bishop Ct
Mount Prospect IL 60056
847 298-4652

**(G-14129)**
**NTN-BOWER CORPORATION**
711 Bower Rd (61455-2511)
PHONE..................309 837-0322
Tim Daudelin, *Purchasing*
Richard Metzner, *Purchasing*
James Hare, *Engineer*
Lee A Hare, *Engineer*
Steve Hensley, *Controller*
EMP: 550
SALES (corp-wide): 6B **Privately Held**
WEB: www.ntn.co.jp
SIC: **3562** 3568 Roller bearings & parts; power transmission equipment
PA: Ntn Corporation
1-3-17, Kyomachibori, Nishi-Ku
Osaka OSK 550-0
664 435-001

**(G-14130)**
**QUICKPRINTERS**
Also Called: Signs Express
1120 E Jackson St (61455-2522)
PHONE..................309 833-5250
Fax: 309 833-3123
Tammie Speer, *President*
Tim Speer, *Vice Pres*

EMP: 4
SQ FT: 2,000
SALES: 362K **Privately Held**
SIC: **2752** 2759 2791 2789 Commercial printing, offset; commercial printing; typesetting; bookbinding & related work

**(G-14131)**
**RICHARDSON ENTERPRISES**
Also Called: Pipe Scraper Div
830 W Jackson St (61455-2014)
PHONE..................309 833-5395
Fax: 309 833-5201
Nancy Richardson, *President*
Lori Richardson, *Admin Sec*
EMP: 4
SALES: 100K **Privately Held**
SIC: **3423** Plumbers' hand tools

**(G-14132)**
**ROYAL HAEGER LAMP CO**
1300 W Piper St (61455-2741)
P.O. Box 218 (61455-0218)
PHONE..................309 837-9966
Fax: 309 837-5267
Nicholas Estes, *President*
Irwin Breinin, *Sales Mgr*
David Estes, *Data Proc Mgr*
▼ EMP: 30
SQ FT: 130,000
SALES (est): 3.8MM **Privately Held**
WEB: www.royalhaegerlamp.com
SIC: **3645** 3641 Table lamps; electric lamps

**(G-14133)**
**TNE MCDONOUGH DEMOCRAT INC**
833 N Lafayette St (61455-7337)
PHONE..................309 837-3343
Brian Morris, *Manager*
EMP: 1
SALES (est): 143K **Privately Held**
SIC: **2711** Newspapers, publishing & printing

**(G-14134)**
**WAYLAND READY MIX CONCRETE SVC**
1343 W Jackson St (61455-1929)
P.O. Box 207 (61455-0207)
PHONE..................309 833-2064
Fax: 309 837-2259
Champ H Wayland, *President*
Pauline Wayland, *Treasurer*
Larry Wayland, *Admin Sec*
EMP: 13
SQ FT: 2,400
SALES (est): 2.1MM **Privately Held**
SIC: **3273** 1442 Ready-mixed concrete; construction sand & gravel

**(G-14135)**
**WESTERN ILINOIS OPTICAL INC**
909 E Grant St (61455-3371)
PHONE..................309 837-2000
Gary Distin, *President*
Dr David Anderson, *Vice Pres*
Dr Gary Crosby, *Treasurer*
Dr Dan Doyle, *Admin Sec*
EMP: 3
SQ FT: 2,000
SALES (est): 390.3K **Privately Held**
SIC: **3851** 5048 Frames & parts, eyeglass & spectacle; lenses, ophthalmic; ophthalmic goods

**(G-14136)**
**WHALEN MANUFACTURING COMPANY**
1270 E Murray St (61455-1800)
PHONE..................309 836-1438
Fax: 309 836-2645
Bernard F Whalen, *President*
Patrick T Whalen, *Admin Sec*
▲ EMP: 1
SQ FT: 30,000
SALES (est): 326.2K
SALES (corp-wide): 30.7MM **Privately Held**
SIC: **3523** Farm machinery & equipment
PA: Yetter Manufacturing Company Inc
109 S Mcdonough St
Colchester IL 62326
309 776-3222

**(G-14137)**
**YEAST PRINTING INC**
319 N Lafayette St (61455-1598)
PHONE..................309 833-2845
Fax: 309 837-7468
Robert Yeast, *President*
John S Yeast, *Corp Secy*
Steve Yeast, *Vice Pres*
EMP: 5
SQ FT: 9,000
SALES: 500K **Privately Held**
SIC: **2752** 7334 2791 Commercial printing, offset; photocopying & duplicating services; typesetting

**(G-14138)**
**YETTER MANUFACTURING COMPANY**
1270 E Murray St (61455-1800)
P.O. Box 15, Colchester (62326-0015)
PHONE..................309 833-1445
Brian Concannon, *Principal*
EMP: 32
SALES (corp-wide): 30.7MM **Privately Held**
SIC: **3999** Atomizers, toiletry
PA: Yetter Manufacturing Company Inc
109 S Mcdonough St
Colchester IL 62326
309 776-3222

## Madison
### Madison County

**(G-14139)**
**BEELMAN SLAG SALES**
2000 Edwardsville Rd (62060-1349)
PHONE..................618 452-8120
Sam Beelman, *President*
EMP: 500
SALES (est): 20.2MM **Privately Held**
SIC: **3295** Slag, crushed or ground

**(G-14140)**
**BLAST PRODUCTS INC**
224 State St (62060-1114)
PHONE..................618 452-4700
Kent Newell, *President*
Carol B Newell, *Vice Pres*
EMP: 4
SQ FT: 20,000
SALES: 600K **Privately Held**
SIC: **2841** Soap & other detergents

**(G-14141)**
**DAMCO PRODUCTS INC**
Also Called: Blast Products
224 State St (62060-1114)
PHONE..................618 452-4700
Mark J Fleming, *President*
Dave Altman, *Admin Sec*
EMP: 4 EST: 2010
SALES (est): 526.6K **Privately Held**
SIC: **2841** 2842 Soap & other detergents; specialty cleaning, polishes & sanitation goods

**(G-14142)**
**DIAMOND PLATING COMPANY INC**
5 Caine Dr (62060-1574)
P.O. Box 129 (62060-0129)
PHONE..................618 451-7740
Fax: 618 451-7756
Loretta Clark, *President*
Robert Cox, *Vice Pres*
Gina Scaturro, *Treasurer*
EMP: 35
SQ FT: 20,000
SALES (est): 4MM **Privately Held**
WEB: www.diamondwheelinc.com
SIC: **3471** Plating of metals or formed products

**(G-14143)**
**DYNO MANUFACTURING INC**
2 Fox Industrial Dr (62060-1155)
PHONE..................618 451-6609
Larry Dittmeier, *Principal*
EMP: 4
SALES (est): 249.6K **Privately Held**
SIC: **3999** Manufacturing industries

# Madison - Madison County (G-14144)

**(G-14144)**
**ELEKTRON N MAGNESIUM AMER INC (DH)**
1001 College St (62060-1084)
P.O. Box 258 (62060-0258)
PHONE..................618 452-5190
Fax: 618 452-7929
Chris Barnes, *Exec VP*
Ken Clark, *Vice Pres*
Mike Hall, *Purch Mgr*
Howard Kaplan, *VP Sls/Mktg*
Tony Keller, *Controller*
◆ **EMP**: 82
**SQ FT**: 538,900
**SALES (est)**: 17.4MM
**SALES (corp-wide)**: 414.8MM **Privately Held**
**WEB**: www.magnesium-elektron.com
**SIC**: 3356 Magnesium; magnesium & magnesium alloy bars, sheets, shapes, etc.; magnesium & magnesium alloy: rolling, drawing or extruding

**(G-14145)**
**FALL PROTECTION SYSTEMS INC (PA)**
2901 Old Nickel Plate Rd (62060-1673)
P.O. Box 229 (62060-0229)
PHONE..................618 452-7000
Thomas Morhaus, *President*
Thomas Kolosike, *Controller*
Matthew Proctor, *Sales Dir*
Pat Cleveland, *Marketing Staff*
Thomas Kolosieke, *Technology*
**EMP**: 22
**SQ FT**: 5,000
**SALES (est)**: 4.6MM **Privately Held**
**WEB**: www.fallprotectionsystems.com
**SIC**: 3842 Personal safety equipment

**(G-14146)**
**GATEWAY RAIL SERVICES INC**
1980 3rd St (62060-1556)
P.O. Box 9 (62060-0009)
PHONE..................618 451-0100
Roger J Verbeeren Jr, *President*
Clyde Hetz, *President*
George Williams, *Admin Sec*
**EMP**: 15
**SQ FT**: 740,520
**SALES**: 1.4MM **Privately Held**
**SIC**: 3743 Railroad car rebuilding

**(G-14147)**
**GREEN PLAINS MADISON LLC**
395 Bissell St (62060-1177)
PHONE..................618 451-8195
**EMP**: 4
**SALES (corp-wide)**: 3.4B **Publicly Held**
**SIC**: 2869 Ethyl alcohol, ethanol
**HQ**: Green Plains Madison Llc
450 Regency Pkwy Ste 400
Omaha NE 68114
402 884-8700

**(G-14148)**
**GREEN PLAINS PARTNERS LP**
395 Bissell St (62060-1177)
PHONE..................618 451-4420
**EMP**: 14
**SALES (corp-wide)**: 50.9MM **Publicly Held**
**SIC**: 2869 Mfg Industrial Organic Chemicals
**PA**: Green Plains Partners Lp
450 Regency Pkwy Ste 400
Omaha NE 68114
402 884-8700

**(G-14149)**
**HB COATINGS LLC**
932 Fairway Park Dr (62060-1900)
PHONE..................618 215-8161
Jason Hunsaker, *President*
Ashley Hunsaker, *CFO*
**EMP**: 6 EST: 2015
**SQ FT**: 30,000
**SALES (est)**: 285.1K **Privately Held**
**SIC**: 7692 7699 Welding repair; industrial machinery & equipment repair; aircraft & heavy equipment repair services

**(G-14150)**
**ILLINOIS TRANSIT ASSEMBLY CORP**
1980 3rd St (62060-1556)
P.O. Box 9 (62060-0009)
PHONE..................618 451-8934
Fax: 618 451-8934
Leslie Kasten, *President*
▲ **EMP**: 18
**SQ FT**: 7,000
**SALES**: 1.5MM **Privately Held**
**SIC**: 3743 Railroad car rebuilding

**(G-14151)**
**KIENSTRA PIPE & PRECAST LLC**
1072 Eagle Park Rd (62060-1666)
PHONE..................618 482-3283
Chris Kienstra, *President*
Ron Voss, *General Mgr*
Steve Peery, *Sales Staff*
**EMP**: 26
**SALES (est)**: 3MM **Privately Held**
**SIC**: 3272 Precast terrazo or concrete products

**(G-14152)**
**MB STEEL COMPANY INC**
9 Fox Industrial Dr (62060-1170)
PHONE..................618 877-7000
Fax: 618 877-0955
Mark A Benz, *President*
Andy Matt, *Plant Mgr*
Brooke Ante, *Office Mgr*
Heather Yates, *Manager*
**EMP**: 15
**SQ FT**: 100,000
**SALES (est)**: 4.4MM **Privately Held**
**SIC**: 3449 Miscellaneous metalwork

**(G-14153)**
**SLSB LLC**
Also Called: St Louis Screw & Bolt
2000 Access Rd (62060-1083)
P.O. Box 260 (62060-0260)
PHONE..................618 219-4115
Fax: 618 219-4128
Chris O'Daniel, *Controller*
Michael Friel, *Mng Member*
◆ **EMP**: 52
**SQ FT**: 120,000
**SALES (est)**: 12.2MM **Privately Held**
**SIC**: 3452 5072 Bolts, nuts, rivets & washers; bolts

**(G-14154)**
**TRONOX INCORPORATED**
2 Washington Ave (62060-1463)
P.O. Box 166 (62060-0166)
PHONE..................203 705-3704
Mike Rauh, *Vice Pres*
John Falcone, *Branch Mgr*
**EMP**: 30
**SALES (corp-wide)**: 2B **Privately Held**
**WEB**: www.tieandtimber.com
**SIC**: 2491 2421 Wood products, creosoted; sawmills & planing mills, general
**HQ**: Tronox Incorporated
1 Stamford Plz
Stamford CT 06901
203 705-3800

**(G-14155)**
**U S STORAGE GROUP LLC**
915 Fairway Park Dr (62060-1902)
PHONE..................618 482-8000
James Lauer,
▲ **EMP**: 12
**SALES (est)**: 2.2MM **Privately Held**
**SIC**: 2449 Wood containers

**(G-14156)**
**WESTWOOD LANDS INC**
4 Caine Dr (62060-1574)
PHONE..................618 877-4990
Peter O'Dovero, *President*
James O'Dovero, *Vice Pres*
Joe O'Dovero, *Vice Pres*
Gayla Salani, *Manager*
**EMP**: 4
**SALES (est)**: 400K **Privately Held**
**WEB**: www.westwoodlands.com
**SIC**: 3312 Blast furnaces & steel mills

## Mahomet
### Champaign County

**(G-14157)**
**AMERICAN DECK & SUNROOM C**
2603 Appaloosa Ln (61853-9773)
PHONE..................217 586-4840
Thomas Parker, *Manager*
**EMP**: 8
**SALES (est)**: 812K **Privately Held**
**SIC**: 3448 Prefabricated metal buildings

**(G-14158)**
**F & L ELECTRONICS LLC**
103 N Prairieview Rd (61853-7031)
P.O. Box 19 (61853-0019)
PHONE..................217 586-2132
Fax: 217 586-5733
Frank Luksander,
Louis Lucksander,
**EMP**: 10
**SALES (est)**: 600K **Privately Held**
**SIC**: 3671 Electron tubes, transmitting

**(G-14159)**
**ILLINOIS VALLEY PRESS EAST**
Also Called: Muhammed Citizens
303 E Main St Ste D (61853-7448)
P.O. Box 919 (61853-0919)
PHONE..................217 586-2512
Steve Hoffman, *General Mgr*
Berry Winterland, *Principal*
**EMP**: 5
**SALES (est)**: 173.4K **Privately Held**
**SIC**: 2711 Newspapers

**(G-14160)**
**LL ELECTRONICS**
103 S Prairieview Rd (61853)
PHONE..................217 586-6477
Louis A Luksander, *Owner*
**EMP**: 6
**SALES (est)**: 330K **Privately Held**
**SIC**: 3663 Transmitter-receivers, radio

**(G-14161)**
**MID-AMERICA SAND & GRAVEL (PA)**
Also Called: Mid America Recycling
250 County Rd 2050 N (61853)
P.O. Box 290 (61853-0290)
PHONE..................217 586-4536
Fax: 217 586-4726
Hugh Gallivan, *President*
William Booker, *Vice Pres*
Karen O'Neil, *Vice Pres*
**EMP**: 7
**SQ FT**: 900
**SALES (est)**: 2MM **Privately Held**
**SIC**: 1442 Sand mining; gravel mining

## Makanda
### Jackson County

**(G-14162)**
**BLUE SKY VINEYARD**
3150 S Rocky Comfort Rd (62958-4062)
PHONE..................618 995-9463
Barrett Rochman, *Owner*
Jim Ewers, *General Mgr*
**EMP**: 7
**SALES (est)**: 650.1K **Privately Held**
**SIC**: 2084 Wine cellars, bonded: engaged in blending wines

**(G-14163)**
**KINSER WOODWORKS**
120 Old Lower Cobden Rd (62958)
P.O. Box 14 (62958-0014)
PHONE..................618 549-4540
Kyler Kinser, *Owner*
**EMP**: 3
**SALES (est)**: 135.6K **Privately Held**
**SIC**: 2511 Wood household furniture

## Malden
### Bureau County

**(G-14164)**
**METAL COMPONENT MACHINING**
1900 N County Rd (61337)
P.O. Box 181 (61337-0181)
PHONE..................815 643-2207
Fax: 815 643-2207
Gary J Crockett, *Owner*
**EMP**: 12
**SQ FT**: 5,200
**SALES (est)**: 1MM **Privately Held**
**WEB**: www.metalcomponentmachining.com
**SIC**: 3599 Machine shop, jobbing & repair

## Malta
### Dekalb County

**(G-14165)**
**BEE DESIGNS EMBROIDERY & SCREE**
24637 Esmond Rd (60150-8502)
PHONE..................815 393-4593
Barbara Eychaner, *Principal*
**EMP**: 3
**SALES (est)**: 224.4K **Privately Held**
**WEB**: www.beedesigns.biz
**SIC**: 2395 2759 5941 Embroidery products, except schiffli machine; screen printing; sporting goods & bicycle shops

**(G-14166)**
**NEILAND CUSTOM PRODUCTS**
400 Il Route 38 (60150-9590)
P.O. Box 96 (60150-0096)
PHONE..................815 825-2233
Neil Anderson, *Owner*
**EMP**: 3
**SALES**: 40K **Privately Held**
**SIC**: 3479 3471 Painting, coating & hot dipping; coating of metals & formed products; finishing, metals or formed products

## Manhattan
### Will County

**(G-14167)**
**AEROPRES CORPORATION**
100 S Park Rd (60442)
P.O. Box 42 (60442-0042)
PHONE..................815 478-3266
Michael Barron, *Superintendent*
**EMP**: 6
**SALES (corp-wide)**: 40.1MM **Privately Held**
**WEB**: www.aeropres.com
**SIC**: 2813 Industrial gases
**PA**: Aeropres Corporation
1324 N Hearne Ave Ste 200
Shreveport LA 71107
318 429-6744

**(G-14168)**
**BOLHUIS WOODWORKING CO**
14250 W Joliet Rd (60442-8199)
P.O. Box 1109, South Holland (60473-7109)
PHONE..................708 333-5100
Fax: 708 333-5140
Steve Couch, *Owner*
Jean Bolhuis, *Bookkeeper*
**EMP**: 9 EST: 1970
**SQ FT**: 4,000
**SALES (est)**: 849.8K **Privately Held**
**SIC**: 5712 2541 2434 Cabinet work, custom; wood partitions & fixtures; wood kitchen cabinets

**(G-14169)**
**ERBECK ONE CHEM & LAB SUP INC**
15607 W Waterford Ln (60442-9163)
PHONE..................312 203-0078
Stephen Erbeck, *President*
**EMP**: 1

# GEOGRAPHIC SECTION
## Manteno - Kankakee County (G-14194)

SALES: 700K **Privately Held**
SIC: 5169 3677 Silicon lubricants; filtration devices, electronic

**(G-14170)**
**RESPECT INCORPORATED**
15555 Tyndall Ct (60442-6227)
PHONE..................................815 806-1907
Kent Mast, *President*
EMP: 5
SALES (est): 440K **Privately Held**
WEB: www.respectincorporated.com
SIC: 2731 Textbooks: publishing only, not printed on site

**(G-14171)**
**WINNING COLORS**
345 Jan St Unit C (60442-9284)
PHONE..................................815 462-4810
Mark Cryer, *Owner*
EMP: 4
SALES (est): 400.9K **Privately Held**
SIC: 3399 7532 Metal powders, pastes & flakes; top & body repair & paint shops

### Manito
*Mason County*

**(G-14172)**
**CJS PRINTING**
118 N Broadway St (61546-9321)
PHONE..................................309 968-6585
Fax: 309 968-6881
Ellen Lee, *Owner*
Brad Lee, *Co-Owner*
EMP: 4
SQ FT: 640
SALES: 105K **Privately Held**
SIC: 2752 2791 2789 Commercial printing, offset; typesetting; bookbinding & related work

**(G-14173)**
**DEL MONTE FOODS INC**
812 S Adams St (61546-9397)
PHONE..................................309 968-7033
Fax: 309 968-7362
Gary Molid, *Manager*
EMP: 3
SALES (corp-wide): 2.2B **Privately Held**
SIC: 2033 Vegetables & vegetable products in cans, jars, etc.
HQ: Del Monte Foods, Inc.
  3003 Oak Rd Ste 600
  Walnut Creek CA 94597
  925 949-2772

**(G-14174)**
**DONS MEAT MARKET**
203 W Market St (61546-9386)
PHONE..................................309 968-6026
Don Wilson, *Owner*
EMP: 4
SQ FT: 1,680
SALES (est): 250.6K **Privately Held**
SIC: 3556 2013 Meat, poultry & seafood processing machinery; sausages & other prepared meats

**(G-14175)**
**RICKARD PUBLISHING**
106 N Broadway St (61546-9321)
P.O. Box 560 (61546-0560)
PHONE..................................309 968-6705
Lois Rickard, *Owner*
Victor J Rickard, *Principal*
EMP: 4
SALES (est): 117K **Privately Held**
SIC: 2711 Newspapers

**(G-14176)**
**SENECA FOODS CORPORATION**
7757 Airport Rd (61546-8706)
PHONE..................................309 545-2233
Bob Held, *Manager*
EMP: 50
SALES (corp-wide): 1.2B **Publicly Held**
SIC: 2099 Food preparations
PA: Seneca Foods Corporation
  3736 S Main St
  Marion NY 14505
  315 926-8100

**(G-14177)**
**WILLETTS WINERY & CELLAR**
105 E Market St (61546-9205)
PHONE..................................309 968-7070
Cris Willett, *Executive*
EMP: 4
SALES (est): 265.3K **Privately Held**
SIC: 2084 Wines, brandy & brandy spirits

### Mansfield
*Piatt County*

**(G-14178)**
**PIATT COUNTY SERVICE CO**
1070 Old Us 150 (61854-6835)
PHONE..................................217 489-2411
Fax: 217 489-2971
Richard M Buckingham, *Opers Mgr*
Keith Niemeier, *Opers-Prdtn-Mfg*
EMP: 5
SALES (corp-wide): 29MM **Privately Held**
WEB: www.piattfs.com
SIC: 5999 5261 2875 Insecticides; fertilizer; fertilizers, mixing only
PA: Piatt County Service Co (Inc)
  427 W Marion St Ste 2
  Monticello IL 61856
  217 762-2133

### Manteno
*Kankakee County*

**(G-14179)**
**AAMSTRAND ROPES & TWINES INC**
711 N Grove St (60950-9347)
PHONE..................................815 468-2100
Fax: 815 468-2117
James G Dunne, *CEO*
James David Dunne, *President*
Frederick A Cone, *Agent*
▲ EMP: 16
SQ FT: 60,000
SALES (est): 1.7MM **Privately Held**
WEB: www.aamstrand.com
SIC: 2298 Cordage & twine; rope, except asbestos & wire; cordage: abaca, sisal, henequen, hemp, jute or other fiber; twine

**(G-14180)**
**ABC COATING COMPANY INC**
Also Called: ABC Coating Company Illinois
1160 N Boudreau Rd (60950-3028)
PHONE..................................708 258-9633
Fax: 708 258-9637
Fred Rocha, *Plant Mgr*
Tom Greenfield, *Branch Mgr*
EMP: 20
SALES (corp-wide): 8MM **Privately Held**
WEB: www.abccoating.com
SIC: 3479 Coating of metals with plastic or resins
PA: Abc Coating Company, Inc.
  2236 S Yukon Ave
  Tulsa OK 74107
  918 585-2587

**(G-14181)**
**BIMBA MANUFACTURING COMPANY**
500 S Spruce St (60950-9473)
PHONE..................................708 534-7997
Dave Rademacher, *Manager*
EMP: 50
SALES (corp-wide): 128.7MM **Privately Held**
SIC: 3593 Fluid power cylinders & actuators
PA: Bimba Manufacturing Company Inc
  25150 S Governors Hwy
  University Park IL 60484
  708 534-8544

**(G-14182)**
**CORNERSTONE MEDIA**
450 S Spruce St Unit H (60950-9415)
PHONE..................................779 529-0108
Mike Russell, *Manager*
EMP: 3

SALES (est): 116.7K **Privately Held**
SIC: 2711 Newspapers

**(G-14183)**
**F WEBER PRINTING CO INC**
450 N Locust St (60950-1225)
PHONE..................................815 468-6152
Fax: 815 468-6202
Franklin Weber, *President*
Anna Weber, *Corp Secy*
EMP: 9
SQ FT: 5,000
SALES (est): 670K **Privately Held**
SIC: 2752 2759 7336 2791 Commercial printing, offset; letterpress printing; commercial art & graphic design; typesetting; bookbinding & related work

**(G-14184)**
**FRITO-LAY NORTH AMERICA INC**
450 N Grove St (60950)
PHONE..................................815 468-7576
Fax: 815 468-3940
Don Middleton, *District Mgr*
EMP: 15
SALES (corp-wide): 62.8B **Publicly Held**
WEB: www.fritolay.com
SIC: 2099 5145 Food preparations; potato chips
HQ: Frito-Lay North America, Inc.
  7701 Legacy Dr
  Plano TX 75024

**(G-14185)**
**HIGH PERFORMANCE LUBR LLC**
500 S Spruce St (60950-9473)
PHONE..................................815 468-3535
EMP: 8
SALES (est): 1.1MM **Privately Held**
SIC: 2992 Lubricating oils

**(G-14186)**
**LEGACY VULCAN LLC**
Also Called: Manteno Quarry
6141 N Rte 50 (60950-3491)
PHONE..................................815 468-8141
Fax: 815 468-1733
Dave Szymski, *Superintendent*
Jerry Roth, *Manager*
Joseph Moran, *Supervisor*
Rich Laurence, *Director*
EMP: 23
SALES (corp-wide): 3.5B **Publicly Held**
WEB: www.vulcanmaterials.com
SIC: 1442 1422 Construction sand & gravel; crushed & broken limestone
HQ: Legacy Vulcan, Llc
  1200 Urban Center Dr
  Vestavia AL 35242
  205 298-3000

**(G-14187)**
**LLC URBAN FARMER**
655 Mulberry St (60950-9219)
PHONE..................................815 468-7200
Beth Jacobson, *Office Admin*
Ryan Sparrow,
Warren Ouwenga,
▲ EMP: 15
SALES (est): 3MM **Privately Held**
SIC: 2041 Pizza dough, prepared

**(G-14188)**
**MERISANT US INC**
1551 N Boudreau Rd (60950-9386)
PHONE..................................815 929-2700
Douglas Owensby, *Materials Mgr*
Jason Sowles, *Controller*
Debbie Adams, *Human Res Mgr*
Kathy Wybourn, *Branch Mgr*
EMP: 200 **Privately Held**
WEB: www.merisant.com
SIC: 2869 2063 Sweeteners, synthetic; beet sugar
HQ: Merisant Us, Inc.
  125 S Wacker Dr Ste 3150
  Chicago IL 60606
  312 840-6000

**(G-14189)**
**PERFORMANCE AUTO SALON INC**
17 E Sixth St (60950-1210)
PHONE..................................815 468-6882
Thomas Kopp, *President*
EMP: 20
SALES (est): 1.3MM **Privately Held**
SIC: 3471 Finishing, metals or formed products

**(G-14190)**
**PLOCHMAN INC**
1333 N Boudreau Rd (60950-9384)
PHONE..................................815 468-3434
Fax: 815 468-8755
Carl Plochman III, *President*
David Nicholson, *President*
Markus Kahr, *Principal*
Carl M Plochman Jr, *Chairman*
Vince Hungerford, *Vice Pres*
EMP: 50 EST: 1852
SQ FT: 106,000
SALES: 13MM
SALES (corp-wide): 365.7MM **Privately Held**
WEB: www.plochman.com
SIC: 2035 5812 Mustard, prepared (wet); eating places
PA: Haco Holding Ag
  Worbstrasse 262
  Muri Bei Bern BE 3074
  319 501-111

**(G-14191)**
**R S CRYO EQUIPMENT INC**
629 N Grove St (60950-9345)
PHONE..................................815 468-6115
Ronald L Stluka, *President*
Bob Adams, *Purchasing*
Michele Stluka, *Treasurer*
▲ EMP: 8
SQ FT: 32,000
SALES (est): 1.8MM **Privately Held**
WEB: www.rscryo.com
SIC: 3556 Smokers, food processing equipment

**(G-14192)**
**REYNOLDS PACKAGING KAMA INC**
1050 W Sycamore Rd (60950-9326)
PHONE..................................815 468-8300
Michael Williamson, *Maint Spvr*
David Reifsteck, *Branch Mgr*
Robert Stasicky, *CIO*
EMP: 111 **Privately Held**
WEB: www.kamacorp.com
SIC: 3334 Primary aluminum
HQ: Reynolds Packaging Kama Inc.
  100 W 7th St
  Richmond VA 23224
  804 281-2000

**(G-14193)**
**SONO ITALIANO CORPORATION**
Also Called: True Sun Dried Tomatoes
655 Mulberry St (60950-9219)
PHONE..................................817 472-8903
EMP: 4
SALES (est): 300K **Privately Held**
SIC: 2034 2099 Mfg Dehydrated Fruits/Vegetables Mfg Food Preparations

**(G-14194)**
**SOUTHFIELD CORPORATION**
Also Called: Prairie North Central Mtls
8215c N Us Highway 45 52 (60950-3381)
PHONE..................................815 468-8700
Fax: 815 468-8745
Jim Purdy, *Manager*
EMP: 15
SALES (corp-wide): 273.9MM **Privately Held**
WEB: www.prairiegroup.com
SIC: 1422 Crushed & broken limestone
PA: Southfield Corporation
  8995 W 95th St
  Palos Hills IL 60465
  708 344-1000

# Manteno - Kankakee County (G-14195)

**(G-14195)**
**STEVENSON FABRICATION SVCS INC**
680 Mulberry St (60950-9218)
P.O. Box 713 (60950-0713)
PHONE..................................815 468-7941
Mark Stevenson, *President*
Elizabeth Stevenson, *President*
**EMP:** 4
**SQ FT:** 6,000
**SALES (est):** 607.3K **Privately Held**
**SIC:** 3441 7692 3446 Fabricated structural metal; welding repair; architectural metalwork

## Maple Park
### Kane County

**(G-14196)**
**A & P GRAIN SYSTEMS INC**
410 S County Line Rd (60151-8005)
PHONE..................................815 827-3079
David Altepeter, *President*
Melessa Brady, *Corp Secy*
**EMP:** 12 **EST:** 1996
**SQ FT:** 2,000
**SALES:** 7.2MM **Privately Held**
**SIC:** 3523 Farm machinery & equipment

**(G-14197)**
**ACQUAVIVA WINERY LLC**
47 W 614 Rr 38 (60151)
PHONE..................................630 365-0333
Vito Brandonisio, *Principal*
**EMP:** 7
**SALES (est):** 799.9K **Privately Held**
**SIC:** 2084 Wines

**(G-14198)**
**BORK INDUSTRIES**
44w508 Ic Trl (60151-8725)
PHONE..................................630 365-5517
**EMP:** 5 **EST:** 2015
**SALES (est):** 426.9K **Privately Held**
**SIC:** 3999 Manufacturing industries

**(G-14199)**
**C A LARSON & SON INC**
Also Called: Old World Millworks
5n200 Wooley Rd (60151-8303)
PHONE..................................847 717-6010
**Fax:** 630 365-6767
Robert Larson, *President*
Mary Stancy, *Office Mgr*
Bruce Woodbridge, *Manager*
Claudia Larson, *Admin Sec*
**EMP:** 35
**SQ FT:** 120,000
**SALES (est):** 6.5MM **Privately Held**
**WEB:** www.oldworldmillworks.com
**SIC:** 2431 Newel posts, wood; stair railings, wood

**(G-14200)**
**INDUSTRIAL VACUUM**
21694 Oak Ln (60151-5037)
P.O. Box 219 (60151-0219)
PHONE..................................630 357-7700
**EMP:** 2 **EST:** 2013
**SALES (est):** 238.1K **Privately Held**
**SIC:** 3563 Vacuum pumps, except laboratory

**(G-14201)**
**LINEAR KINETICS INC**
48 W 989 Rr 64 (60151)
PHONE..................................630 365-0075
Todd E Bruhl, *President*
Jay D Bruhl, *CFO*
**EMP:** 5
**SQ FT:** 7,500
**SALES (est):** 715.6K **Privately Held**
**WEB:** www.linearkinetics.com
**SIC:** 3569 3441 Robots, assembly line: industrial & commercial; fabricated structural metal

**(G-14202)**
**MAPLE PARK TRUCKING INC**
Also Called: Maple Park Landscape Supplies
50w 363 Isle Rr 64 (60151)
PHONE..................................815 899-1958
Connie J Meyer, *President*
Alana Meyer, *Treasurer*
Jodi Meyer, *Bookkeeper*
Deborah Meyer, *Admin Sec*
**EMP:** 6
**SQ FT:** 2,500
**SALES (est):** 872.9K **Privately Held**
**SIC:** 3715 0782 Truck trailers; landscape contractors

**(G-14203)**
**STOVERS FINE WOODWORKING INC**
474 Harter Rd (60151)
PHONE..................................630 557-0072
Mike Stover, *Principal*
**EMP:** 2
**SALES (est):** 210.3K **Privately Held**
**SIC:** 2431 Millwork

**(G-14204)**
**TOWER WORKS INC**
47w543 Perry Rd (60151-9797)
PHONE..................................630 557-2221
Steven Svestha, *President*
Eddy Finley, *Vice Pres*
▼ **EMP:** 15
**SALES (est):** 3MM **Privately Held**
**SIC:** 3663 Receivers, radio communications

## Mapleton
### Peoria County

**(G-14205)**
**CATERPILLAR INC**
8826 W Us Highway 24 (61547-7503)
PHONE..................................309 633-8788
Brian Callear, *Business Mgr*
David Goodman, *Plant Mgr*
D Hill, *Mfg Staff*
Baltasar R Weiss, *Purch Mgr*
Sherry Blackmore, *Buyer*
**EMP:** 650
**SALES (corp-wide):** 38.5B **Publicly Held**
**WEB:** www.cat.com
**SIC:** 3321 Gray & ductile iron foundries
**PA:** Caterpillar Inc.
  100 Ne Adams St
  Peoria IL 61629
  309 675-1000

**(G-14206)**
**CATERPILLAR INC**
8826 W Us Highway 24 (61547-7503)
PHONE..................................706 779-4620
Doug Hampton, *Manager*
**EMP:** 120
**SALES (corp-wide):** 38.5B **Publicly Held**
**WEB:** www.cat.com
**SIC:** 3369 Castings, except die-castings, precision
**PA:** Caterpillar Inc.
  100 Ne Adams St
  Peoria IL 61629
  309 675-1000

**(G-14207)**
**CHEMICAL SPECIALTIES MFG CORP**
8316 W Route 24 (61547-7500)
PHONE..................................309 697-5400
Jan Pribble, *Branch Mgr*
Michael Banks, *Business Dir*
**EMP:** 3
**SALES (corp-wide):** 4.8B **Publicly Held**
**WEB:** www.chemspecworld.com
**SIC:** 2842 Cleaning or polishing preparations
**HQ:** Chemical Specialties Manufacturing Corporation
  901 N Newkirk St
  Baltimore MD 21205
  410 675-4800

**(G-14208)**
**COMMON SCENTS MOM**
10812 W Timber Rd (61547-9478)
PHONE..................................309 389-3216
**EMP:** 3
**SALES (est):** 187.8K **Privately Held**
**SIC:** 2844 Toilet preparations

**(G-14209)**
**EVONIK CORPORATION**
8300 W Route 24 (61547-7500)
P.O. Box 9 (61547-0009)
PHONE..................................309 697-6220
Micki Gifford, *QC Mgr*
Darrell Munton, *Engineer*
Jeffrey Ralph, *Financial Exec*
Dan Guzzi, *Human Res Mgr*
Carl Sima, *Branch Mgr*
**EMP:** 250
**SALES (corp-wide):** 2.3B **Privately Held**
**SIC:** 2869 Industrial organic chemicals
**HQ:** Evonik Corporation
  299 Jefferson Rd
  Parsippany NJ 07054
  973 929-8000

**(G-14210)**
**INGREDION INCORPORATED**
8310 W Rte 24 (61547-7500)
PHONE..................................309 550-9136
Bill Coyle, *Principal*
Matthew Beier, *Technical Mgr*
**EMP:** 100
**SALES (corp-wide):** 5.7B **Publicly Held**
**SIC:** 2046 Wet corn milling; corn starch; corn oil products; corn sugars & syrups
**PA:** Ingredion Incorporated
  5 Westbrook Corporate Ctr # 500
  Westchester IL 60154
  708 551-2600

**(G-14211)**
**LANXESS SOLUTIONS US INC**
8220 W Route 24 (61547-7509)
PHONE..................................309 633-9480
Don Stahlberg, *Manager*
**EMP:** 19
**SQ FT:** 60,000
**SALES (corp-wide):** 8.1B **Privately Held**
**WEB:** www.cromptoncorp.com
**SIC:** 2821 Plastics materials & resins
**HQ:** Lanxess Solutions Us Inc.
  199 Benson Rd
  Middlebury CT 06762
  203 573-2000

**(G-14212)**
**LONZA INC**
8316 W Rte 24 (61547-7500)
P.O. Box 105 (61547-0105)
PHONE..................................309 697-7200
**Fax:** 309 697-7250
Tom Scheel, *Regional Mgr*
Guidry Allendale, *Prdtn Mgr*
Jacob Neuenschwander, *Safety Mgr*
Jim Steiner, *Maint Spvr*
Eric Daly, *Engineer*
**EMP:** 95
**SALES (corp-wide):** 4B **Privately Held**
**WEB:** www.riversidecap.com
**SIC:** 2833 2869 2819 Medicinals & botanicals; industrial organic chemicals; industrial inorganic chemicals
**HQ:** Lonza Inc.
  90 Boroline Rd Ste 1
  Allendale NJ 07401
  201 316-9200

**(G-14213)**
**MATHESON TRI-GAS INC**
7700 W Wheeler Rd (61547-9302)
PHONE..................................309 697-1933
Mike Boock, *Branch Mgr*
**EMP:** 15
**SALES (corp-wide):** 32.6B **Privately Held**
**WEB:** www.mgindustries.com
**SIC:** 2813 5084 Industrial gases; nitrogen; oxygen, compressed or liquefied; argon; welding machinery & equipment; safety equipment
**HQ:** Matheson Tri-Gas, Inc.
  150 Allen Rd Ste 302
  Basking Ridge NJ 07920
  908 991-9200

**(G-14214)**
**UPPERCASE LIVING - INDEPNDENT**
4415 S Newcastle Ct (61547-9557)
PHONE..................................309 657-3054
Peggy Edwards, *Principal*
**EMP:** 3
**SALES (est):** 203.7K **Privately Held**
**SIC:** 3131 Uppers

## Maquon
### Knox County

**(G-14215)**
**CHOPPER MM LLC**
500 Knox Road 900 E (61458-9392)
PHONE..................................309 875-3544
Andrea Scharfenberg, *Principal*
**EMP:** 3
**SALES (est):** 291.1K **Privately Held**
**SIC:** 3751 Motorcycles & related parts

**(G-14216)**
**CUSTOM LUMBERMILL WORKS**
221 E St (61458-5097)
PHONE..................................309 875-3534
James Donsbach, *Principal*
**EMP:** 3
**SALES (est):** 212.9K **Privately Held**
**SIC:** 2421 Custom sawmill

## Marengo
### Mchenry County

**(G-14217)**
**ALAN MANUFACTURING CORP**
Also Called: Alan Stamping
5017 Ritz Rd (60152-9128)
PHONE..................................815 568-6836
**Fax:** 815 568-8696
Lyle Elyea, *Owner*
**EMP:** 5
**SQ FT:** 4,000
**SALES (est):** 398.8K **Privately Held**
**SIC:** 3469 3643 3542 3452 Metal stampings; current-carrying wiring devices; machine tools, metal forming type; bolts, nuts, rivets & washers; manufactured hardware (general)

**(G-14218)**
**ARNOLD ENGINEERING CO (DH)**
300 N West St (60152-2192)
PHONE..................................815 568-2000
**Fax:** 815 568-2365
Gordon McNeil, *Ch of Bd*
Tim Wilson, *President*
Rob Strahs, *Vice Pres*
Sheila Blackwell, *Purchasing*
Aaron Williams, *Engineer*
▲ **EMP:** 100 **EST:** 1905
**SQ FT:** 90,000
**SALES (est):** 21.6MM
**SALES (corp-wide):** 978.3MM **Publicly Held**
**SIC:** 3677 Electronic coils, transformers & other inductors
**HQ:** Arnold Magnetic Technologies Corporation
  770 Linden Ave
  Rochester NY 14625
  585 385-9010

**(G-14219)**
**ARNOLD MAGNETIC TECH CORP**
300 N West St (60152-2103)
PHONE..................................815 568-2000
Norb Jarosch, *Managing Dir*
Roy Hollon, *Branch Mgr*
Mike Leavy, *Technology*
**EMP:** 26
**SALES (corp-wide):** 978.3MM **Publicly Held**
**SIC:** 3264 Magnets, permanent: ceramic or ferrite
**HQ:** Arnold Magnetic Technologies Corporation
  770 Linden Ave
  Rochester NY 14625
  585 385-9010

**(G-14220)**
**B & D MURRAY MANUFACTURING CO**
3911 N Il Route 23 (60152-8629)
P.O. Box 102 (60152-0102)
PHONE..................................815 568-6176
Bobby D Murray, *President*

David Murray, *Vice Pres*
Evelyn Murray, *Treasurer*
**EMP:** 3 **EST:** 1975
**SQ FT:** 5,000
**SALES:** 500K **Privately Held**
**SIC:** 3544 3469 Special dies, tools, jigs & fixtures; metal stampings

**(G-14221)**
**CAISSON INDUSTRIES INC (PA)**
Also Called: Dia Packaging
20020 E Grant Hwy (60152-8239)
**PHONE**................................815 568-6554
Dana T Richardson, *President*
Robert Selleck, *General Mgr*
**EMP:** 12
**SQ FT:** 28,000
**SALES (est):** 8.2MM **Privately Held**
**WEB:** www.diapkg.com
**SIC:** 2449 Rectangular boxes & crates, wood

**(G-14222)**
**CONSOLIDATED MATERIALS INC (PA)**
Also Called: Coral Lake
8920 S Rt 23 (60152)
**PHONE**................................815 568-1538
Thomas A Lee, *President*
Thomas Kelecius, *Admin Sec*
**EMP:** 3
**SALES (est):** 971.9K **Privately Held**
**SIC:** 1442 Construction sand & gravel

**(G-14223)**
**COUNTER CREATIONS LLC**
22521 W Grant Hwy (60152-9660)
P.O. Box 314 (60152-0314)
**PHONE**................................815 568-1000
Mark Evans, *COO*
**EMP:** 4
**SALES (est):** 552K **Privately Held**
**WEB:** www.countercreations.net
**SIC:** 3131 Counters

**(G-14224)**
**DAN HORENBERGER**
Also Called: Brass Ring Entertainment
1004 N Taylor St (60152-2367)
**PHONE**................................818 394-0028
Dan Horenberger, *Owner*
Dan Hornberger, *Executive*
**EMP:** 15
**SALES:** 2.5MM **Privately Held**
**WEB:** www.carousel.com
**SIC:** 3599 Carousels (merry-go-rounds)

**(G-14225)**
**DANAHER CORPORATION**
1300 N State St (60152-2204)
**PHONE**................................815 568-8001
Al Wroblaski, *Production*
C L Galloway, *Product Mgr*
Ron Wendel, *Manager*
Scott Evans, *Info Tech Mgr*
James Julison, *Info Tech Mgr*
**EMP:** 225
**SALES (corp-wide):** 16.8B **Publicly Held**
**SIC:** 3823 Industrial instrmnts msrmnt display/control process variable; liquid level instruments, industrial process type
**PA:** Danaher Corporation
2200 Penn Ave Nw Ste 800w
Washington DC 20037
202 828-0850

**(G-14226)**
**ENGINEERED POLYMR SOLUTIONS INC (DH)**
1400 N State St (60152-2206)
**PHONE**................................815 568-4205
**Fax:** 815 568-4145
J R Benites, *President*
Steve Lindberg, *President*
Gary Pierce, *Vice Pres*
Brian Kolar, *Safety Mgr*
Stacey Young, *Purch Mgr*
▲ **EMP:** 50
**SALES (est):** 60.7MM
**SALES (corp-wide):** 11.8B **Publicly Held**
**SIC:** 2295 Resin or plastic coated fabrics
**HQ:** The Valspar Corporation
1101 S 3rd St
Minneapolis MN 55415
612 851-7000

**(G-14227)**
**EPSCCA**
1400 N State St (60152-2206)
**PHONE**................................815 568-3020
Steve Lindberg, *CEO*
Kim Keefer, *Cust Mgr*
**EMP:** 50
**SALES (est):** 3.2MM **Privately Held**
**SIC:** 3479 Coating of metals with plastic or resins

**(G-14228)**
**FANPLASTIC MOLDING CO**
10704 Harmony Hill Rd (60152-9483)
**PHONE**................................815 923-6950
Steve Moorhouse, *Principal*
**EMP:** 4 **EST:** 2007
**SALES (est):** 364K **Privately Held**
**SIC:** 3089 Plastic processing

**(G-14229)**
**GLOBAL CMPNENT TECH AMRCAS INC**
Also Called: Nissan Forklift
19720 E Grant Hwy (60152-9493)
P.O. Box 116 (60152-0116)
**PHONE**................................815 568-4507
Hiroshi Kakinuma, *President*
Peter Kruse, *CFO*
Sandy Klinger, *Accountant*
Bernard Schulte, *Admin Sec*
Brandon J Nierhoff, *Internal Med*
▲ **EMP:** 22
**SALES (est):** 5MM
**SALES (corp-wide):** 104.1B **Privately Held**
**SIC:** 3519 Engines, diesel & semi-diesel or dual-fuel
**HQ:** Nissan Kohki Co.,Ltd.
6-6-1, Okada, Samukawamachi
Koza-Gun KNG 253-0
467 751-711

**(G-14230)**
**HYPERSTITCH**
117 W Prairie St (60152-2134)
**PHONE**................................815 568-0590
Paticia Lawlor, *President*
**EMP:** 12
**SALES (est):** 768.1K **Privately Held**
**WEB:** www.hyperstitch.com
**SIC:** 2395 Embroidery & art needlework

**(G-14231)**
**IN A BIND ASSEMBLY FULFILLMENT**
4104 Millstream Rd (60152-9496)
**PHONE**................................815 568-6952
**Fax:** 630 529-1575
Michelle Greco, *President*
Jack Meagher, *Vice Pres*
Paul Tenerelli, *Vice Pres*
Dave Lapash, *VP Opers*
Shawn Broda, *Marketing Staff*
**EMP:** 40
**SQ FT:** 52,000
**SALES (est):** 4.4MM
**SALES (corp-wide):** 9MM **Privately Held**
**WEB:** www.inabindassembly.com
**SIC:** 2789 Bookbinding & related work
**PA:** Id Commerce & Logistics Llc
80 Internationale Blvd A
Glendale Heights IL 60139
630 694-7200

**(G-14232)**
**J & M FAB METALS INC**
6710 S Grant Hwy (60152-9441)
P.O. Box 427 (60152-0427)
**PHONE**................................815 758-0354
Keane Paradiso, *President*
**EMP:** 2
**SQ FT:** 5,000
**SALES:** 250K **Privately Held**
**SIC:** 7692 3444 Welding repair; sheet metalwork

**(G-14233)**
**K TROX SALES INC**
6807 Paulson Dr (60152-9361)
**PHONE**................................815 568-1521
Debra Troxell, *President*
Tom Troxell, *Admin Sec*
▲ **EMP:** 2
**SALES:** 1MM **Privately Held**
**SIC:** 3672 Printed circuit boards

**(G-14234)**
**KOZIN WOODWORK US**
3911 N Il Route 23 (60152-8629)
**PHONE**................................815 568-8918
Dave Kozin, *Principal*
**EMP:** 4
**SALES (est):** 410.4K **Privately Held**
**SIC:** 2431 Millwork

**(G-14235)**
**LINDSAY METAL MADNESS INC**
711 W Grant Hwy (60152-3075)
**PHONE**................................815 568-4560
**EMP:** 2
**SALES (est):** 224.5K **Privately Held**
**SIC:** 5051 3399 3499 Metals Service Center Mfg Primary Metal Products Mfg Misc Fabricated Metal Products

**(G-14236)**
**MARENGO TOOL & DIE WORKS INC**
201 E Railroad St (60152-3133)
P.O. Box 100 (60152-0100)
**PHONE**................................815 568-7411
**Fax:** 815 568-8730
Gilbert Tauck, *CEO*
Fred Struckmeier, *President*
Robert Rosulek, *Corp Secy*
**EMP:** 45
**SQ FT:** 70,000
**SALES (est):** 7.7MM **Privately Held**
**SIC:** 3469 3452 3544 Metal stampings; bolts, nuts, rivets & washers; special dies, tools, jigs & fixtures

**(G-14237)**
**MARENGO UNION TIMES**
709 Lura Ln (60152-3382)
**PHONE**................................815 568-5400
Jennifer Blais, *Principal*
**EMP:** 3
**SALES (est):** 157.5K **Privately Held**
**SIC:** 2711 Newspapers, publishing & printing

**(G-14238)**
**PAVELOC INDUSTRIES INC**
8302 S Il Route 23 (60152-9317)
**PHONE**................................815 568-4700
**Fax:** 815 568-1210
Mike Corteen, *President*
Bradley Le Gare, *Vice Pres*
Mike Corten, *Manager*
**EMP:** 15
**SALES (est):** 1.9MM **Privately Held**
**WEB:** www.paveloc.com
**SIC:** 3271 5032 Paving blocks, concrete; brick, stone & related material

**(G-14239)**
**PORK KING PACKING INC**
8808 S Il Route 23 (60152-9383)
P.O. Box 253 (60152-0253)
**PHONE**................................815 568-8024
**Fax:** 815 568-9054
Tom Miles, *President*
Frank Faso, *Vice Pres*
Su Pajerski, *Opers Staff*
Joe Maffei, *Treasurer*
Mary Faso, *Manager*
**EMP:** 200
**SQ FT:** 57,000
**SALES (est):** 36.5MM **Privately Held**
**WEB:** www.porkkingpacking.com
**SIC:** 2011 Meat packing plants; pork products from pork slaughtered on site

**(G-14240)**
**PRAIRIE PURE CHEESE**
1405 N State St (60152-2215)
**PHONE**................................815 568-5000
Brian Gerloff, *Principal*
**EMP:** 5
**SALES (est):** 327.5K **Privately Held**
**SIC:** 2022 5143 Cheese, natural & processed; dairy products, except dried or canned

**(G-14241)**
**SWIFT TECHNOLOGIES INC**
8601 S Hill Rd (60152-8251)
**PHONE**................................815 568-8402
John Bussert, *President*
Patricia Bussert, *Vice Pres*
**EMP:** 9
**SALES (est):** 900K **Privately Held**
**WEB:** www.swiftorder.com
**SIC:** 7372 7373 5045 Prepackaged software; value-added resellers, computer systems; computers, peripherals & software

**(G-14242)**
**TEMPO WOOD PRODUCTS INC**
Also Called: Tempo Components
641 W Washington St (60152-2157)
**PHONE**................................815 568-7315
**Fax:** 815 522-7730
Stephen Kannaka, *President*
Mike Hotopp, *Manager*
▲ **EMP:** 70
**SQ FT:** 24,000
**SALES (est):** 3.8MM **Privately Held**
**WEB:** www.tempocomponents.com
**SIC:** 2439 Trusses, wooden roof

**(G-14243)**
**THOMSON LINEAR LLC**
1300 N State St (60152-2204)
**PHONE**................................815 568-8001
Russ Cline, *Purch Agent*
Len Ejma, *CFO*
Peggie Angelkort, *Accounting Mgr*
Diane Baedke, *Manager*
Brock Etherton, *Manager*
▲ **EMP:** 146
**SALES (est):** 66.3MM **Privately Held**
**SIC:** 3562 3625 Ball & roller bearings; actuators, industrial

**(G-14244)**
**UNICARRIERS AMERICAS CORP (DH)**
Also Called: Nissan Forklift
240 N Prospect St (60152-3235)
**PHONE**................................800 871-5438
**Fax:** 815 568-0179
James J Radous II, *President*
Derek Robson, *General Mgr*
James Radous, *Exec VP*
Steve Cianci, *Vice Pres*
Dan Domberg, *Vice Pres*
◆ **EMP:** 274 **EST:** 1966
**SQ FT:** 450,000
**SALES (est):** 118.2MM
**SALES (corp-wide):** 34.4B **Privately Held**
**WEB:** www.nissanforklift.com
**SIC:** 3537 3519 5084 Lift trucks, industrial: fork, platform, straddle, etc.; gasoline engines; lift trucks & parts; engines, gasoline
**HQ:** Unicarriers Corporation
1-2, Shin-Ogura, Saiwai-Ku
Kawasaki KNG 212-0
443 309-001

**(G-14245)**
**YOUR SUPPLY DEPOT LIMITED**
Also Called: Army Navy Supply Depot
207 E Grant Hwy (60152-3339)
**PHONE**................................815 568-4115
**Fax:** 847 640-7782
Robert Stewart, *President*
Thomas Stewart, *Sales Mgr*
▲ **EMP:** 4
**SQ FT:** 1,200
**SALES (est):** 680.4K **Privately Held**
**WEB:** www.yoursupply.com
**SIC:** 3579 5961 Embossing machines for store & office use; catalog & mail-order houses

## Marine
### Madison County

**(G-14246)**
**HESS MACHINE INC**
10724 Pocahontas Rd (62061-1232)
**PHONE**................................618 887-4444
Timothy Hess, *President*
Shelley Hess, *Admin Sec*
**EMP:** 7
**SQ FT:** 3,150
**SALES (est):** 976.3K **Privately Held**
**SIC:** 3599 Custom machinery

## Marion
*Williamson County*

**(G-14247)**
**ADVANCED MBILITY SOLUTIONS LLC**
3205 W Commercial Rd (62959-5508)
**PHONE**.................618 658-8580
**EMP:** 2
**SALES (est):** 291.5K  Privately Held
**SIC:** 3842 Surgical appliances & supplies

**(G-14248)**
**AISIN ELECTRONICS ILLINOIS LLC**
11000 Redco Dr (62959-5889)
**PHONE**.................618 997-9800
Yutaka Iguchi, *President*
Naoki Niimi, *Corp Secy*
Shane Moore, *Controller*
Maylan Hallum, *Director*
◆ **EMP:** 118
**SALES (est):** 34.4MM
**SALES (corp-wide):** 27.7B  Privately Held
**SIC:** 3714 Instrument board assemblies, motor vehicle
**HQ:** Aisin Holdings Of America, Inc.
   1665 E 4th Street Rd
   Seymour IN 47274
   812 524-8144

**(G-14249)**
**AISIN LIGHT METALS  LLC**
11000 Redco Dr (62959-5889)
**PHONE**.................618 997-7900
**Fax:** 618 997-1550
Fumihiko Sugiura, *President*
Yukio AMI,
**EMP:** 5
**SALES (est):** 1.8MM
**SALES (corp-wide):** 27.7B  Privately Held
**SIC:** 3675 Electronic capacitors
**HQ:** Aisin Holdings Of America, Inc.
   1665 E 4th Street Rd
   Seymour IN 47274
   812 524-8144

**(G-14250)**
**AISIN MFG ILLINOIS  LLC**
1100 Glenn Clarida Dr (62959)
**PHONE**.................618 998-8333
Patty Clark, *Branch Mgr*
**EMP:** 70
**SALES (corp-wide):** 27.7B  Privately Held
**SIC:** 3714 Motor vehicle parts & accessories
**HQ:** Aisin Mfg. Illinois, Llc
   11000 Redco Dr
   Marion IL 62959
   618 998-8333

**(G-14251)**
**AISIN MFG ILLINOIS  LLC (DH)**
11000 Redco Dr (62959-5889)
**PHONE**.................618 998-8333
**Fax:** 618 998-8383
Hiroyuki Kato, *President*
Glenn Edwards, *Exec VP*
Abigail Miesner, *Engineer*
Naoki Niimi, *Treasurer*
Diane Bybee, *Finance*
▲ **EMP:** 650
**SQ FT:** 160,000
**SALES (est):** 132.8MM
**SALES (corp-wide):** 27.7B  Privately Held
**WEB:** www.aisinusa.com
**SIC:** 3714 Motor vehicle parts & accessories
**HQ:** Aisin U.S.A. Mfg., Inc.
   1700 E 4th Street Rd
   Seymour IN 47274
   812 523-1969

**(G-14252)**
**ALPHA SERVICES II  INC**
1806 N Court St (62959-4558)
P.O. Box 1045 (62959-7545)
**PHONE**.................618 997-9999
**Fax:** 618 998-9940
Richard Elliott, *President*
Vickilyn Elliott, *Corp Secy*
Eric Elliott, *Purch Mgr*
Greg Summery, *Manager*
**EMP:** 28
**SALES (est):** 4.2MM  Privately Held
**WEB:** www.alphaservicesinc.com
**SIC:** 7699 3532 Aircraft & heavy equipment repair services; shuttle cars, underground

**(G-14253)**
**AMERICAN MONUMENT CO**
306 S Court St (62959-2710)
**PHONE**.................618 993-8968
**Fax:** 618 993-8969
Edward Patterson, *President*
Tammy Patterson, *Vice Pres*
**EMP:** 8
**SALES (est):** 800.7K  Privately Held
**WEB:** www.americanmonument.com
**SIC:** 3281 5999 Monument or burial stone, cut & shaped; monuments & tombstones

**(G-14254)**
**ASSOCIATE COMPUTER SYSTEMS**
211 N Market St Ste A (62959-2427)
**PHONE**.................618 997-3653
**Fax:** 618 997-0519
Patrick L Devine, *Partner*
Doug Camden, *Partner*
Pat Devine, *Partner*
**EMP:** 4
**SQ FT:** 1,200
**SALES (est):** 700K  Privately Held
**SIC:** 5734 7372 Computer & software stores; prepackaged software

**(G-14255)**
**BIKER THREADS INC**
500 S Court St (62959-2802)
**PHONE**.................618 993-3046
John B Cox, *President*
Linda Cox, *Admin Sec*
**EMP:** 3
**SALES (est):** 323.9K  Privately Held
**SIC:** 3751 Motorcycles, bicycles & parts

**(G-14256)**
**BUCKET MART  INC**
300 W Longstreet Rd (62959-5327)
P.O. Box 1240 (62959-7740)
**PHONE**.................813 390-8626
Jack Johnson, *President*
**EMP:** 2
**SALES (est):** 230K  Privately Held
**SIC:** 3536 Hoists, cranes & monorails

**(G-14257)**
**CRISP CONTAINER CORPORATION**
Also Called: Pepsi Midamerica
700 Skyline Dr (62959-4871)
**PHONE**.................618 998-0400
**Fax:** 618 993-6483
Harry Crisp, *President*
Evelyn Clayton, *Exec VP*
Bryan Springvloed, *VP Opers*
Jeffery Hames, *Human Res Mgr*
Sam Hood, *Human Res Mgr*
**EMP:** 55
**SQ FT:** 100,000
**SALES (est):** 9.4MM  Privately Held
**SIC:** 2086 Carbonated soft drinks, bottled & canned

**(G-14258)**
**DANIEL & SONS MECH CONTRS INC**
105 Hilltop Ln (62959-7027)
P.O. Box 126, Carterville (62918-0126)
**PHONE**.................618 997-2822
**Fax:** 618 997-2855
Daniel Sloam, *President*
**EMP:** 10
**SALES (est):** 982.5K  Privately Held
**SIC:** 3444 Ducts, sheet metal

**(G-14259)**
**FAST PRINT SHOP**
501 W Deyoung St Ste 7 (62959-1676)
**PHONE**.................618 997-1976
**Fax:** 618 997-1976
Lisa Mc Raven, *Partner*
Mitch McRaven, *Partner*
**EMP:** 4
**SQ FT:** 1,200
**SALES (est):** 360K  Privately Held
**SIC:** 2752 5943 2761 2759 Commercial printing, offset; office forms & supplies; manifold business forms; commercial printing

**(G-14260)**
**FRITO-LAY NORTH AMERICA INC**
5309 Meadowland Pkwy (62959-5893)
**PHONE**.................618 997-2865
Bill Parrish, *Manager*
**EMP:** 20
**SALES (corp-wide):** 62.8B  Publicly Held
**WEB:** www.fritolay.com
**SIC:** 2096 Potato chips & similar snacks
**HQ:** Frito-Lay North America, Inc.
   7701 Legacy Dr
   Plano TX 75024

**(G-14261)**
**GENERAL DYNAMICS ORDNANCE**
6658 Route 148 (62959-6389)
P.O. Box 278 (62959-0278)
**PHONE**.................618 985-8211
**Fax:** 618 993-9233
Dennis Diehl, *Mfg Staff*
Mark Doss, *Engineer*
Steve Preston, *Personnel*
Hank Gross, *Marketing Mgr*
Jim Price, *Manager*
**EMP:** 235
**SALES (corp-wide):** 31.3B  Publicly Held
**SIC:** 2892 3489 3483 Explosives; ordnance & accessories; ammunition, except for small arms
**HQ:** General Dynamics Ordnance And Tactical Systems, Inc.
   11399 16th Ct N Ste 200
   Saint Petersburg FL 33716
   727 578-8100

**(G-14262)**
**GL DOWNS INC**
1805 Wolff Dr (62959-1427)
P.O. Box 1164, Benton (62812-5164)
**PHONE**.................618 993-9777
Glen L Downs II, *President*
**EMP:** 1
**SQ FT:** 2,000
**SALES (est):** 213.6K  Privately Held
**SIC:** 5169 5087 5099 3299 Chemicals & allied products; janitors' supplies; signs, except electric; mica products

**(G-14263)**
**GOLDEN EAGLE DISTRIBUTING LLC (PA)**
2713 Merchant St (62959-4922)
P.O. Box 1810 (62959-8010)
**PHONE**.................618 993-8900
**Fax:** 618 993-1855
R E Pugh,
Beverly Pugh,
**EMP:** 10
**SQ FT:** 6,000
**SALES (est):** 1.4MM  Privately Held
**SIC:** 2082 Beer (alcoholic beverage)

**(G-14264)**
**HAUHINCO LP**
Also Called: Tiesenbach
810 Skyline Dr (62959-4874)
**PHONE**.................618 993-5399
Bennie Manion, *Exec VP*
**EMP:** 20
**SALES (corp-wide):** 23MM  Privately Held
**WEB:** www.hauhinco.com
**SIC:** 4011 4899 3823 3643 Railroads, line-haul operating; communication signal enhancement network system; industrial instrmnts msrmnt display/control process variable; current-carrying wiring devices; electronic generation equipment; relays & industrial controls
**HQ:** Hauhinco, L.P.
   1325 Evans City Rd
   Evans City PA 16033
   724 789-7050

**(G-14265)**
**HORIZON PUBLICATIONS  INC (PA)**
1120 N Carbon St Ste 100 (62959-1055)
**PHONE**.................618 993-1711
**Fax:** 618 997-5209
David Radler, *President*
Roland McBride, *CFO*
Steve Jones, *MIS Dir*
Daren Youngblood, *Executive*
**EMP:** 194
**SALES (est):** 78.5MM  Privately Held
**WEB:** www.malvern-online.com
**SIC:** 2711 Newspapers

**(G-14266)**
**HORIZON PUBLICATIONS (2003) (PA)**
1120 N Carbon St Ste 100 (62959-1055)
**PHONE**.................618 993-1711
David Radler, *President*
Roland McBride, *Exec VP*
Mark Kipnis, *Vice Pres*
**EMP:** 3
**SQ FT:** 7,000
**SALES (est):** 29MM  Privately Held
**WEB:** www.horizonpublicationsinc.com
**SIC:** 2711 Newspapers

**(G-14267)**
**HOSPITAL & PHYSICIAN PUBG**
Also Called: Hospital Physician
6116 N Chamnesstown Rd (62959)
**PHONE**.................618 997-9375
**Fax:** 618 997-9376
Gary Lee Stanley, *President*
Shirley J Stanley, *Admin Sec*
**EMP:** 7
**SALES (est):** 477.7K  Privately Held
**SIC:** 2741 Technical manuals: publishing only, not printed on site

**(G-14268)**
**HPC OF PENNSYLVANIA INC**
1120 N Carbon St Ste 100 (62959-1055)
**PHONE**.................618 993-1711
David Radler, *President*
Roland McBride, *Exec VP*
Leslie Carson, *Controller*
**EMP:** 100
**SQ FT:** 7,000
**SALES (est):** 2.8MM
**SALES (corp-wide):** 29MM  Privately Held
**WEB:** www.horizonpublicationsinc.com
**SIC:** 2711 Newspapers
**PA:** Horizon Publications (2003) Inc
   1120 N Carbon St Ste 100
   Marion IL 62959
   618 993-1711

**(G-14269)**
**ILLINOIS TOOL WORKS INC**
Also Called: Diagraph MSP & ITW Company
5307 Meadowland Pkwy (62959-5893)
**PHONE**.................618 997-1716
**Fax:** 618 997-1766
Robert Quarles, *Branch Mgr*
Kathy Halstead, *Manager*
**EMP:** 65
**SQ FT:** 66,000
**SALES (corp-wide):** 13.6B  Publicly Held
**SIC:** 3953 3577 3565 3549 Marking devices; computer peripheral equipment; packaging machinery; metalworking machinery
**PA:** Illinois Tool Works Inc.
   155 Harlem Ave
   Glenview IL 60025
   847 724-7500

**(G-14270)**
**LEE ENTERPRISES INCORPORATED**
Also Called: Southern Illinoisan
3000 W Deyoung St Ste 336 (62959-4893)
**PHONE**.................618 998-8499
Tom Woolf, *Manager*
**EMP:** 4
**SALES (corp-wide):** 614.3MM  Publicly Held
**WEB:** www.lee.net
**SIC:** 2711 Newspapers, publishing & printing

# GEOGRAPHIC SECTION
## Mark - Putnam County (G-14298)

**PA:** Lee Enterprises, Incorporated
201 N Harrison St Ste 600
Davenport IA 52801
563 383-2100

**(G-14271)**
**MACH MINING  LLC**
16468 Liberty School Rd  (62959-7537)
**PHONE**..................................618 983-3020
David Jude,
Maxine Jude, *Admin Sec*
**EMP:** 8
**SALES (est):** 576.8K  **Privately Held**
**SIC: 1241**  Coal mining services

**(G-14272)**
**MARION FIRE SPRNKLR ALARM INC**
1820 N Court St  (62959-4558)
P.O. Box 386  (62959-0386)
**PHONE**..................................618 889-9106
Andrew Allen, *CEO*
**EMP:** 12
**SQ FT:** 100,000
**SALES (est):** 2.6MM  **Privately Held**
**SIC: 3569**  Sprinkler systems, fire: automatic

**(G-14273)**
**MARY E FISHER**
Also Called: Melco Insulation
5679 Wards Mill Rd  (62959-6153)
P.O. Box 176  (62959-0176)
**PHONE**..................................618 964-1528
**Fax:** 618 964-1768
Mary E Fisher, *Owner*
Melvin Fisher, *General Mgr*
**EMP:** 6
**SQ FT:** 12,000
**SALES (est):** 260K  **Privately Held**
**SIC: 3296**  Fiberglass insulation

**(G-14274)**
**MINOVA USA INC**
809 Skyline Dr  (62959-4875)
**PHONE**..................................618 993-2611
William Resnik, *Branch Mgr*
**EMP:** 52
**SALES (corp-wide):** 3.9B  **Privately Held**
**SIC: 2821**  Plastics materials & resins
**HQ:** Minova Usa Inc.
150 Summer Ct
Georgetown KY 40324
502 863-6800

**(G-14275)**
**ODUM CONCRETE PRODUCTS INC (PA)**
1800 N Court St  (62959-5433)
P.O. Box 248  (62959-0248)
**PHONE**..................................618 993-6211
**Fax:** 618 997-3085
Tim Odum, *President*
**EMP:** 25 **EST:** 1921
**SQ FT:** 4,500
**SALES (est):** 11.6MM  **Privately Held**
**SIC: 3273**  Ready-mixed concrete

**(G-14276)**
**PARKS INDUSTRIES  LLC**
Also Called: HP2000 APU
15460 Crabtree School Rd  (62959-6420)
**PHONE**..................................618 997-9608
L Dianne Parks, *Mng Member*
Dianne Parks,
Gary Parks,
**EMP:** 10
**SQ FT:** 18,000
**SALES (est):** 2.1MM  **Privately Held**
**SIC: 3585**  Compressors for refrigeration & air conditioning equipment

**(G-14277)**
**PEPSI MIDAMERICA CO (PA)**
2605 W Main St  (62959-4932)
P.O. Box 1070  (62959-7570)
**PHONE**..................................618 997-1377
**Fax:** 618 998-3247
Harry L Crisp III, *President*
Harry L Crisp II, *Chairman*
John Rains, *COO*
Jeff McGee, *Opers Mgr*
Bobby Deppen, *Purchasing*
**EMP:** 695
**SQ FT:** 312,000
**SALES (est):** 285.5MM  **Privately Held**
**WEB:** www.pepsimidamerica.com
**SIC: 2086**  Carbonated soft drinks, bottled & canned

**(G-14278)**
**PERMA-TREAT OF ILLINOIS  INC**
Also Called: Permatreat Lumber
1800 Permatreat Dr  (62959-1048)
P.O. Box 99  (62959-0099)
**PHONE**..................................618 997-5646
**Fax:** 618 993-8680
Sara R Bond, *President*
Dana Yates, *Manager*
**EMP:** 12
**SQ FT:** 22,500
**SALES (est):** 1.1MM  **Privately Held**
**SIC: 5031** 5211 2491  Lumber: rough, dressed & finished; lumber & other building materials; wood preserving

**(G-14279)**
**PIECES OF LEARNING  INC**
1112 N Carbon St Unit A  (62959-1075)
**PHONE**..................................618 964-9426
Tyler Young, *President*
**EMP:** 4
**SQ FT:** 6,400
**SALES (est):** 731.6K  **Privately Held**
**WEB:** www.piecesoflearning.com
**SIC: 2731** 8748 7812  Books: publishing only; educational consultant; video tape production

**(G-14280)**
**PINTSCH TIEFENBACH US  INC**
810 Skyline Dr  (62959-4874)
**PHONE**..................................618 993-8513
Bennie Manion, *President*
**EMP:** 5
**SALES (est):** 607.5K  **Privately Held**
**SIC: 3679** 7371 3743  Static power supply converters for electronic applications; computer software development & applications; railroad equipment; railroad locomotives & parts, electric or nonelectric

**(G-14281)**
**PORTERVILLE RECORDER INC**
1120 N Carbon St Ste 100  (62959-1055)
**PHONE**..................................559 784-5000
Melanie Walsh, *CEO*
**EMP:** 4 **EST:** 2013
**SALES (est):** 174.3K  **Privately Held**
**SIC: 2711**  Newspapers: publishing only, not printed on site

**(G-14282)**
**POS PLUS LLC**
1001 W Central St  (62959-1803)
P.O. Box 1907  (62959-8107)
**PHONE**..................................618 993-7587
Paula Grace, *Accountant*
Bob Satterfield,
**EMP:** 15
**SQ FT:** 10,000
**SALES (est):** 1.8MM  **Privately Held**
**SIC: 3577** 3578  Magnetic ink & optical scanning devices; point-of-sale devices

**(G-14283)**
**PRECISION MACHINE AND**
410 N Pentecost Dr  (62959)
**PHONE**..................................618 997-8795
Tony Burdin, *President*
**EMP:** 14
**SALES (est):** 1.8MM  **Privately Held**
**SIC: 3599**  Machine shop, jobbing & repair

**(G-14284)**
**PRO CABINETS INC**
11123 Skyline Dr  (62959-8380)
**PHONE**..................................618 993-0008
Cody Stacey, *President*
**EMP:** 1
**SALES (est):** 297.3K  **Privately Held**
**SIC: 2434**  Wood kitchen cabinets

**(G-14285)**
**REVIEW**
Also Called: Horizon, The
1120 N Carbon St Ste 100  (62959-1055)
P.O. Box 111  (62959-0111)
**PHONE**..................................618 997-2222
**EMP:** 4
**SALES (est):** 216.1K  **Privately Held**
**SIC: 2711**  Newspapers-Publishing/Printing

**(G-14286)**
**SHEW BROTHERS INC**
Also Called: Ron Shew Welding & Fabricating
812 W Longstreet Rd  (62959-5421)
**PHONE**..................................618 997-4414
Ronald D Shew, *President*
**EMP:** 9
**SALES (est):** 800K  **Privately Held**
**SIC: 3441** 5084 3498 3444  Fabricated structural metal; welding machinery & equipment; fabricated pipe & fittings; sheet metalwork; fabricated plate work (boiler shop)

**(G-14287)**
**SIGLEY PRINTING & OFF SUP CO**
Also Called: Hill Printing and Office Sup
110 N Print Ave  (62959-2412)
**PHONE**..................................618 997-5304
**Fax:** 618 997-2776
Rita Sigley, *President*
Earl Sigley, *Vice Pres*
Tim Nation, *Accounting Dir*
**EMP:** 6 **EST:** 1998
**SQ FT:** 4,000
**SALES (est):** 787.2K  **Privately Held**
**SIC: 2752** 5943 2791 2789  Commercial printing, offset; office forms & supplies; typesetting; bookbinding & related work; commercial printing

**(G-14288)**
**SOUTHERN IL RACEWAY**
11682 Macie Dr  (62959-1386)
**PHONE**..................................618 201-0500
**EMP:** 3 **EST:** 2014
**SALES (est):** 112.2K  **Privately Held**
**SIC: 3644**  Raceways

**(G-14289)**
**SOUTHERN ILLINOIS MINERS**
1000 Miners Dr  (62959-5080)
**PHONE**..................................618 969-8506
Kyle Bass, *Principal*
Mike Pinto, *COO*
Meghan Obrien, *Marketing Staff*
Rachel Stroud, *Manager*
Chris Hagstrom, *Director*
**EMP:** 14
**SALES (est):** 1.6MM  **Privately Held**
**SIC: 3949**  Bases, baseball

**(G-14290)**
**SOUTHERN ILLINOIS REDIMIX INC (PA)**
11039 Skyline Dr  (62959-8371)
**PHONE**..................................618 993-3600
**Fax:** 618 997-8035
Sherri Denny, *President*
Bret Denny, *Vice Pres*
Jeff Denny, *Treasurer*
**EMP:** 10
**SQ FT:** 1,100
**SALES (est):** 866.2K  **Privately Held**
**SIC: 3273** 5211 3272  Ready-mixed concrete; masonry materials & supplies; concrete products, precast

**(G-14291)**
**TIME RECORDS PUBLISHING AND BO**
2537 Wards Mill Rd  (62959-8621)
**PHONE**..................................618 996-3803
Bobby Martin, *President*
Tabitha Martin, *Exec VP*
Marjalea Martin, *Vice Pres*
**EMP:** 3
**SALES (est):** 230K  **Privately Held**
**SIC: 7313** 3089 7929  Radio, television, publisher representatives; cases, plastic; musical entertainers; gospel singers; popular music groups or artists

**(G-14292)**
**TONDINIS WRECKER SERVICE**
2200 S Court St  (62959-3630)
**PHONE**..................................618 997-9884
**Fax:** 618 993-6257
Kevin Pondini, *Owner*
Kevin Tondini, *Owner*
**EMP:** 4
**SALES (est):** 364.1K  **Privately Held**
**SIC: 7549** 3713  Towing services; automobile wrecker truck bodies

**(G-14293)**
**VESTIBULAR TECHNOLOGIES LLC (PA)**
1207 Early Bird Ln  (62959-3794)
**PHONE**..................................618 993-7561
Elena Oggero, *Vice Pres*
Guido Pagnacco, *Vice Pres*
Bob Henderson,
**EMP:** 2 **EST:** 1996
**SALES (est):** 450.1K  **Privately Held**
**WEB:** www.vestibtech.com
**SIC: 3845**  Electromedical equipment

**(G-14294)**
**WARREN OIL MGT CO IL LLC**
201 N 4th St  (62959-4704)
**PHONE**..................................618 997-5951
▲ **EMP:** 3
**SALES (est):** 210K  **Privately Held**
**SIC: 1311**  Crude Petroleum/Natural Gas Production

**(G-14295)**
**WILLIAMSON ENERGY  LLC**
18624 Liberty School Rd  (62959)
**PHONE**..................................618 983-3020
**Fax:** 618 993-8906
Thomas Workman, *Controller*
Anthony Webb, *Mng Member*
**EMP:** 30
**SQ FT:** 7,500
**SALES (est):** 13.9MM
**SALES (corp-wide):** 875.8MM  **Publicly Held**
**SIC: 1241**  Bituminous coal mining services, contract basis
**PA:** Foresight Energy Lp
211 N Broadway Ste 2600
Saint Louis MO 63102
314 932-6160

### Marissa
*St. Clair County*

**(G-14296)**
**MIDWEST METALS  INC**
1296 Green Diamond Rd  (62257-2518)
**PHONE**..................................618 295-3444
Vicky L Neuwirth, *President*
**EMP:** 4
**SQ FT:** 8,400
**SALES (est):** 551.9K  **Privately Held**
**SIC: 3441**  Fabricated structural metal

**(G-14297)**
**QUAD-COUNTY READY MIX CORP**
655 Wshngton Cnty Line Rd  (62257)
**PHONE**..................................618 295-3000
Amy Birkalo, *Principal*
**EMP:** 6
**SALES (corp-wide):** 18.9MM  **Privately Held**
**SIC: 5211** 3273  Sand & gravel; ready-mixed concrete
**PA:** Quad-County Ready Mix Corp.
300 W 12th St
Okawville IL 62271
618 243-6430

### Mark
*Putnam County*

**(G-14298)**
**MARK DEVELOPMENT CORPORATION**
Mennie Dr Rr 71  (61340)
**PHONE**..................................815 339-2226
Hubert J Mennie, *President*
Cheryl Mennie, *Admin Sec*
**EMP:** 180
**SQ FT:** 200,000
**SALES (est):** 17.2MM  **Privately Held**
**SIC: 3469**  Machine parts, stamped or pressed metal

**(G-14299)**
**MENNIES MACHINE COMPANY (PA)**
Also Called: MMC Armory
Mennie Dr Rr 71 (61340)
P.O. Box 110 (61340-0110)
PHONE..................................815 339-2226
Richard Cavaletto, *General Mgr*
David Mennie, *Vice Pres*
Bill Mennie, *Vice Pres*
William Mennie, *Vice Pres*
Mark Stengel, *Vice Pres*
▲ **EMP:** 193
**SALES (est):** 91MM **Privately Held**
**SIC: 3544** 8742 Special dies, tools, jigs & fixtures; materials mgmt. (purchasing, handling, inventory) consultant

**(G-14300)**
**TAYLOR MADE MACHINING INC**
W Mark Indus Park Rr 71 (61340)
P.O. Box 177 (61340-0177)
PHONE..................................815 339-6267
Frank Niewinski, *President*
Julie Niewinski, *Admin Sec*
**EMP:** 5
**SQ FT:** 6,300
**SALES (est):** 676.7K **Privately Held**
**SIC: 3599** Machine shop, jobbing & repair

## Markham
### Cook County

**(G-14301)**
**CATLYST REACTION LLC**
16624 Marshfield Ave (60428-5844)
P.O. Box 214, Hazel Crest (60429-0214)
PHONE..................................708 941-4616
Robert Young,
**EMP:** 3
**SALES (est):** 330K **Privately Held**
**SIC: 2821** Molding compounds, plastics

**(G-14302)**
**CITY BEVERAGE LLC**
2064 W 167th St (60428-5605)
PHONE..................................708 333-4360
Cecil Troutwine, *Principal*
Jeff Wiley, *Sales Staff*
Rob Fehling, *Marketing Staff*
Pat Mercer, *Manager*
**EMP:** 90
**SALES (est):** 14.1MM **Privately Held**
**SIC: 2082** Malt beverages

**(G-14303)**
**KEN DON LLC**
Also Called: Heimlich Jones
2222 W 162nd St (60428-5604)
PHONE..................................708 596-4910
Fax: 708 596-9019
Donald N Carvalho,
**EMP:** 4
**SQ FT:** 34,000
**SALES (est):** 270K **Privately Held**
**SIC: 2671** 4225 Packaging paper & plastics film, coated & laminated; general warehousing

**(G-14304)**
**RACO STEEL COMPANY**
2100 W 163rd Pl (60428-5649)
PHONE..................................708 339-2958
Fax: 708 596-0313
Denny Erickson, *President*
David B Daly, *President*
Dennis Erickson, *President*
Diane Rogers, *General Mgr*
Robert Bruce, *Vice Pres*
▲ **EMP:** 50 **EST:** 1953
**SQ FT:** 120,000
**SALES (est):** 15.2MM **Privately Held**
**WEB:** www.racosteel.com
**SIC: 3312** 5051 3544 Blast furnaces & steel mills; metals service centers & offices; special dies, tools, jigs & fixtures

## Maroa
### Macon County

**(G-14305)**
**HARBACH GILLAN & NIXON INC**
Also Called: Maroa AG
40 Ag Rd (61756)
P.O. Box 679 (61756-0679)
PHONE..................................217 794-5117
Fax: 217 794-5532
Tim Wolfe, *Manager*
Jeff Toohill, *Manager*
**EMP:** 5
**SALES (corp-wide):** 16.7MM **Privately Held**
**SIC: 5191** 2873 Fertilizer & fertilizer materials; nitrogenous fertilizers
**PA:** Harbach, Gillan & Nixon, Inc.
618 W Van Buren St
Clinton IL 61727
217 935-8378

**(G-14306)**
**MASHBURN WELL DRILLING**
214 N Pine St (61756-9240)
P.O. Box 45 (61756-0045)
PHONE..................................217 794-3728
Robert Edwin Mashburn, *Owner*
**EMP:** 2
**SALES (est):** 228.6K **Privately Held**
**SIC: 1381** 1781 Drilling water intake wells; water well drilling

**(G-14307)**
**PERFORMANCE WELDING LLC**
10333 W Washington St Rd (61756-9116)
P.O. Box 388 (61756-0388)
PHONE..................................217 412-5722
Grey Hale Jr,
**EMP:** 2
**SALES (est):** 275.6K **Privately Held**
**SIC: 7692** Welding repair

## Marseilles
### Lasalle County

**(G-14308)**
**EXELON CORPORATION**
2602 N 21st Rd (61341)
PHONE..................................815 357-6761
David B Wozniak, *Vice Pres*
Susan Landahl, *Plant Mgr*
David P Rhoades, *Manager*
Nathan Darrow, *Info Tech Mgr*
**EMP:** 800
**SALES (corp-wide):** 31.3B **Publicly Held**
**SIC: 3462** Nuclear power plant forgings, ferrous
**PA:** Exelon Corporation
10 S Dearborn St Fl 53
Chicago IL 60603
800 483-3220

**(G-14309)**
**GLEN-GERY CORPORATION**
1401 Broadway St (61341-2067)
PHONE..................................815 795-6911
Eric Efchleman, *CFO*
**EMP:** 78 **Privately Held**
**WEB:** www.glengerybrick.com
**SIC: 3271** 5211 Brick, concrete; brick
**HQ:** Glen-Gery Corporation
1166 Spring St
Reading PA 19610
610 374-4011

**(G-14310)**
**ICON POWER ROLLER INC**
2882 E 24th Rd (61341-9624)
P.O. Box 216 (61341-0216)
PHONE..................................630 545-2345
Eunice Kim, *Principal*
▲ **EMP:** 20
**SALES (est):** 1.5MM **Privately Held**
**SIC: 3469** Machine parts, stamped or pressed metal

**(G-14311)**
**INDEPENDENCE TUBE CORPORATION**
1201 Broadway St (61341-2000)
PHONE..................................815 795-4400
Fax: 815 795-6378
John Koschwanez, *Vice Pres*
Rick Cook, *Warehouse Mgr*
Jim Hollingsworth, *Production*
Chuck Moore, *Purch Agent*
Bart Vaughn, *Engineer*
**EMP:** 63
**SALES (corp-wide):** 16.2B **Publicly Held**
**WEB:** www.independencetube.com
**SIC: 3317** Steel pipe & tubes
**HQ:** Independence Tube Corporation
6226 W 74th St
Chicago IL 60638
708 496-0380

**(G-14312)**
**INVENERGY**
2192 E 25th Rd (61341-9752)
PHONE..................................815 795-4964
Mark Geibel, *Principal*
Linda Pierce, *Admin Asst*
**EMP:** 6
**SALES (est):** 917.8K **Privately Held**
**SIC: 3511** Turbines & turbine generator sets

**(G-14313)**
**MACHINE TECHNOLOGY INC (PA)**
Also Called: Machine Tech Services
1020 Broadway St (61341-2038)
PHONE..................................815 795-6818
Fax: 815 795-6535
George Sandorat, *President*
Tony Sandorat, *Vice Pres*
**EMP:** 15
**SALES (est):** 2.5MM **Privately Held**
**WEB:** www.mtipowerservices.com
**SIC: 3541** 3599 Machine tools, metal cutting type; machine shop, jobbing & repair

**(G-14314)**
**MAGIC SLEEP MATTRESS CO INC**
Also Called: Marr-Sales Factory Outlet
220 Commercial St (61341-1808)
PHONE..................................815 795-6942
Fax: 815 795-2178
Sam Carlino Sr, *President*
Sam Carlino, *President*
Frank Carlino, *Vice Pres*
Sam Carlino Jr, *Treasurer*
**EMP:** 20
**SQ FT:** 37,000
**SALES (est):** 2.3MM **Privately Held**
**SIC: 2515** Mattresses & bedsprings

**(G-14315)**
**P & H PATTERN INC**
225 Lincoln St (61341-1904)
PHONE..................................815 795-2449
Fax: 815 795-6456
Michael Garrison, *President*
Vicky Garrison, *Vice Pres*
**EMP:** 4 **EST:** 1962
**SQ FT:** 3,000
**SALES (est):** 300K **Privately Held**
**SIC: 3543** Industrial patterns

**(G-14316)**
**PCS PHOSPHATE COMPANY INC**
2660 E Us Highway 6 (61341-9401)
P.O. Box 88 (61341-0088)
PHONE..................................815 795-5111
Don Jackson, *Purchasing*
Robert Startzer, *Manager*
**EMP:** 38
**SALES (corp-wide):** 4.4B **Privately Held**
**WEB:** www.potashcorp.com
**SIC: 2048** 5191 Prepared feeds; animal feeds
**HQ:** Pcs Phosphate Company, Inc.
1101 Skokie Blvd Ste 400
Northbrook IL 60062
847 849-4200

**(G-14317)**
**RIVER REDI MIX INC**
2195 E Bluff St (61341-9200)
PHONE..................................815 795-2025
Fax: 815 795-2442
Michael Dearth, *President*
Steven Dearth, *Corp Secy*
**EMP:** 7
**SALES (est):** 500K **Privately Held**
**SIC: 3273** Ready-mixed concrete

## Marshall
### Clark County

**(G-14318)**
**BIG CREEK FORESTRY & LOGGING L**
75 Archer Ave (62441-1065)
PHONE..................................217 822-8282
Mark Strait, *Principal*
**EMP:** 3
**SALES (est):** 220K **Privately Held**
**SIC: 2411** Logging

**(G-14319)**
**CHARLES INDUSTRIES LTD**
Also Called: Coil Sales and Manufacturing
16265 E National Rd (62441-4287)
P.O. Box 319 (62441-0319)
PHONE..................................217 826-2318
Fax: 217 826-8352
Cheryl Sanders, *Plant Mgr*
Larry Stepp, *Opers Staff*
Trebbie Thome, *Production*
David Brown, *Purch Agent*
Linda Phillips, *Purch Agent*
**EMP:** 100
**SQ FT:** 44,000
**SALES (corp-wide):** 131.6MM **Privately Held**
**WEB:** www.charlesmarine.com
**SIC: 3661** 8741 3677 3621 Telephone & telegraph apparatus; administrative management; electronic coils, transformers & other inductors; motors & generators; nonferrous wiredrawing & insulating
**PA:** Charles Industries, Ltd.
5600 Apollo Dr
Rolling Meadows IL 60008
847 806-6300

**(G-14320)**
**CUSTOM FILMS INC**
1400 Archer Ave (62441-4437)
PHONE..................................217 826-2326
Fax: 217 826-2012
Larry Bender, *President*
Richard Bernardoni, *Vice Pres*
Kim Bender, *Office Mgr*
**EMP:** 19
**SQ FT:** 10,000
**SALES:** 2MM **Privately Held**
**SIC: 2821** 3089 3083 3082 Polyurethane resins; synthetic resin finished products; laminated plastics plate & sheet; unsupported plastics profile shapes; unsupported plastics film & sheet

**(G-14321)**
**DORIC PRODUCTS INC (PA)**
201 W Us Highway 40 (62441)
P.O. Box 10 (62441-0010)
PHONE..................................217 826-6302
Fax: 217 826-6444
Steven F Vincent, *President*
Michael C Crummitt, *Vice Pres*
James R Wiens, *Treasurer*
Denise Cox, *Accountant*
Jeanie Walker, *Comp Spec*
**EMP:** 67
**SQ FT:** 44,000
**SALES (est):** 13.6MM **Privately Held**
**SIC: 3995** Burial vaults, fiberglass

**(G-14322)**
**G & S ASPHALT INC**
16870 N Quality Lime Rd (62441-4442)
PHONE..................................217 826-2421
Fax: 217 826-2629
Gary Peak, *President*
Nancy Peak, *Admin Sec*
**EMP:** 12

GEOGRAPHIC SECTION　　　　　　　　　　　　　　　　　　　　　　　　　　　　　　　　　　Maryville - Madison County (G-14347)

SALES: 1.2MM **Privately Held**
SIC: 1611 2951 Resurfacing contractor; asphalt paving mixtures & blocks

**(G-14323)**
**HEARTLAND LABELS INC**
17135 N Quality Lime Rd (62441-4460)
P.O. Box 299 (62441-0299)
PHONE..................................217 826-8324
Fax: 217 826-8215
James J Withrow, *President*
Janice Withrow, *Treasurer*
Phil Freeman, *Sales Staff*
Crystal Smitley, *Sales Staff*
EMP: 20
SALES (est): 1MM **Privately Held**
SIC: 2759 Labels & seals: printing

**(G-14324)**
**KEMPER INDUSTRIES**
1017 Clarksville Rd (62441-3822)
P.O. Box 117 (62441-0117)
PHONE..................................217 826-5712
Fax: 217 826-2726
Lloyd Kemper, *Owner*
EMP: 6 EST: 1944
SQ FT: 4,800
SALES (est): 627.8K **Privately Held**
WEB: www.kemperindustries.com
SIC: 3599 3441 7692 3444 Machine shop, jobbing & repair; fabricated structural metal; welding repair; sheet metalwork; manufactured hardware (general); rubber & plastics hose & beltings

**(G-14325)**
**KIMCO USA INC**
Also Called: Kimco U S A
118 E Trefz Dr (62441-3974)
PHONE..................................800 788-1133
Fax: 217 826-8848
Max Coffey, *President*
Kimberly Coffey, *Corp Secy*
Melissa Steadville, *Manager*
EMP: 12
SALES: 4MM **Privately Held**
SIC: 3535 Conveyors & conveying equipment

**(G-14326)**
**MJ SNYDER IRONWORKS INC**
15640 E National Rd (62441-4293)
P.O. Box 357 (62441-0357)
PHONE..................................217 826-6440
Julie Snyder, *President*
Abigail Snyder, *Vice Pres*
Mark Snyder, *Treasurer*
EMP: 9
SALES (est): 440K **Privately Held**
SIC: 7699 3531 3446 3444 Industrial machinery & equipment repair; construction machinery; architectural metalwork; sheet metalwork; fabricated plate work (boiler shop); fabricated structural metal

**(G-14327)**
**PEPSI MID AMERICA**
202 Vine St (62441-1848)
PHONE..................................217 826-8118
Kenneth Cannady, *Principal*
EMP: 4
SALES (est): 213.3K **Privately Held**
SIC: 2086 Carbonated soft drinks, bottled & canned

**(G-14328)**
**QUALITY LIME COMPANY**
Also Called: Quality Line
14915 N Quality Lime Rd (62441)
P.O. Box 439 (62441-0439)
PHONE..................................217 826-2343
Fax: 217 826-2345
Jerald Tarble, *President*
John Tarble, *Vice Pres*
EMP: 15
SQ FT: 1,000
SALES: 5MM **Privately Held**
SIC: 1422 Limestones, ground

**(G-14329)**
**STROHM NEWSPAPERS INC**
Also Called: Marshall Advocate
610 Archer Ave (62441-1268)
P.O. Box 433 (62441-0433)
PHONE..................................217 826-3600
Fax: 217 826-3700

Gary Strohm, *President*
Melody Strohm, *Corp Secy*
EMP: 2
SALES (est): 405K **Privately Held**
SIC: 2711 Newspapers

**(G-14330)**
**TRW AUTOMOTIVE US LLC**
Also Called: TRW Active Passive Safety Tech
902 S 2nd St (62441-1854)
PHONE..................................217 826-3011
Joseph Smitley, *Mfg Mgr*
John Welborn, *Facilities Mgr*
Daniel Connell, *Engineer*
Andy Rutledge, *Human Res Mgr*
Mary Wilson, *Branch Mgr*
EMP: 500 **Privately Held**
WEB: www.trw.mediaroom.com
SIC: 3469 3679 Metal stampings; electronic loads & power supplies
HQ: Trw Automotive U.S. Llc
　　12001 Tech Center Dr
　　Livonia MI 48150
　　734 855-2600

**(G-14331)**
**YARGUS MANUFACTURING INC**
Also Called: Layco
12285 E Main St (62441-4127)
P.O. Box 238 (62441-0238)
PHONE..................................217 826-6352
Larry D Yargus, *President*
Jeff Ivan, *President*
Anne Sheehey, *Senior VP*
Anne Sheehy, *Senior VP*
Tammie Benoit, *Vice Pres*
▼ EMP: 26
SQ FT: 80,000
SALES: 15MM
SALES (corp-wide): 393.2MM **Privately Held**
WEB: www.yargus.com
SIC: 3523 Fertilizing machinery, farm
PA: Ag Growth International Inc
　　198 Commerce Dr
　　Winnipeg MB R3P 0
　　204 489-1855

### Martinsville
*Clark County*

**(G-14332)**
**BEEMAN & SONS INC**
5815 E Snake Trail Rd (62442-2635)
PHONE..................................217 232-4268
Larry L Beeman, *President*
EMP: 15
SALES (est): 1.8MM **Privately Held**
SIC: 2411 Logging

**(G-14333)**
**COLORKRAFT ROLL PRODUCTS INC (PA)**
1 Harry Glynn Dr (62442-2247)
P.O. Box N (62442-0169)
PHONE..................................217 382-4967
Scott Ware, *CEO*
Tom Parking, *President*
▲ EMP: 20
SQ FT: 120,000
SALES (est): 2.9MM **Privately Held**
SIC: 2621 Paper mills

**(G-14334)**
**E ROWE FOUNDRY & MACHINE CO**
147 W Cumberland St (62442-1192)
P.O. Box 130 (62442-0130)
PHONE..................................217 382-4135
Fax: 217 382-4615
Ellen Norton, *President*
Larry Norton, *Vice Pres*
Bill Toner, *Safety Dir*
Kelly Norton, *Treasurer*
Tony Williams, *Admin Sec*
EMP: 87 EST: 1898
SQ FT: 107,000
SALES: 16.5MM **Privately Held**
WEB: www.rowefoundry.com
SIC: 3596 3321 Scales & balances, except laboratory; gray iron castings

**(G-14335)**
**EVERGREEN MANUFACTURING INC**
1 Harry Glynn Dr (62442-2247)
PHONE..................................217 382-5108
Scott Ware, *President*
Tom Hoffman, *Vice Pres*
Heidi Buck, *Sales Executive*
Judy Drater, *Manager*
EMP: 25
SALES (est): 4.1MM **Privately Held**
SIC: 2676 Towels, napkins & tissue paper products

**(G-14336)**
**HELENA CHEMICAL COMPANY**
9666 E Angling Rd (62442-2837)
PHONE..................................217 382-4241
Michael Zachary, *Branch Mgr*
EMP: 15
SALES (corp-wide): 62.7B **Privately Held**
SIC: 2819 Industrial inorganic chemicals
HQ: Helena Chemical Company
　　255 Schilling Blvd # 200
　　Collierville TN 38017
　　901 761-0050

**(G-14337)**
**KELLER UNITED ELC & MCH CO**
12 S York St (62442-1239)
P.O. Box Q (62442-0317)
PHONE..................................217 382-4521
EMP: 4
SQ FT: 1,000
SALES (est): 260K **Privately Held**
SIC: 1731 7694 General electrical contractor; electric motor repair

**(G-14338)**
**MID-ILLINOIS CONCRETE INC**
Also Called: Clark County Ready Mix
1001 N Ridgelawn Rd (62442-2548)
P.O. Box 386 (62442-0386)
PHONE..................................217 382-6650
Fax: 217 382-4760
Floyd Spraker, *Branch Mgr*
EMP: 4
SALES (corp-wide): 17.2MM **Privately Held**
WEB: www.mid-illinoisconcrete.com
SIC: 3272 3273 Concrete products, precast; ready-mixed concrete
PA: Mid-Illinois Concrete, Inc.
　　1805 S 4th St
　　Effingham IL
　　217 342-2115

**(G-14339)**
**PAP-R PRODUCTS COMPANY (PA)**
Also Called: Counting House
1 Harry Glynn Dr (62442-2247)
P.O. Box N (62442-0169)
PHONE..................................775 828-4141
Fax: 217 382-4242
K Scott Ware, *President*
Clayton Huckaba, *Engineer*
Jerome Williams, *CFO*
Lori Turner, *Human Res Mgr*
Randy Weaver, *Sales Mgr*
▲ EMP: 90 EST: 1964
SALES (est): 21.5MM **Privately Held**
WEB: www.paprproducts.com
SIC: 2679 2752 Wrappers, paper (unprinted): made from purchased material; commercial printing, lithographic

### Maryville
*Madison County*

**(G-14340)**
**COLLINSVILLE CUSTOM KITCHENS**
6 Schiber Ct (62062-5625)
P.O. Box 528 (62062-0528)
PHONE..................................618 288-2000
Fax: 618 288-2929
Fred Fish, *President*
Shirley Fish, *Corp Secy*
Doug Fish, *Plant Mgr*
EMP: 15 EST: 1960
SQ FT: 10,000

SALES: 900K **Privately Held**
SIC: 2541 Counters or counter display cases, wood

**(G-14341)**
**HANGER PROSTHETICS & ORTHOTICS**
2118 Vadalabene Dr (62062-5632)
PHONE..................................618 288-8920
John Klutz, *CEO*
William Johnson III, *President*
Brian Karban, *Manager*
EMP: 25
SQ FT: 7,400
SALES: 2.1MM **Privately Held**
SIC: 3842 Prosthetic appliances; orthopedic appliances

**(G-14342)**
**JH CHOPPERS LLC**
3 Hungate Ln (62062-1930)
PHONE..................................618 420-2500
Joel P Harrison, *Principal*
EMP: 2 EST: 2009
SALES (est): 201.7K **Privately Held**
SIC: 3751 Motorcycles & related parts

**(G-14343)**
**KURTS CARSTAR COLLISION CTR**
1 Mueller Dr (62062-6854)
PHONE..................................618 345-4519
Fax: 618 344-9266
Kurt Mueller, *Principal*
Kurt Nathan Mueller, *Principal*
EMP: 15
SALES (est): 1.1MM **Privately Held**
SIC: 7532 3713 3711 Body shop, automotive; truck & bus bodies; automobile bodies, passenger car, not including engine, etc.

**(G-14344)**
**MIDWEST RAILCAR CORPORATION (HQ)**
4949 Autumn Oaks Dr Ste B (62062-8557)
PHONE..................................618 288-2233
Fax: 618 288-2871
Rich Murphy, *President*
Joseph Barbieri, *Assistant VP*
Alan Willaredt, *Vice Pres*
Jon Sparks, *VP Opers*
Amber Saathoff, *Opers Staff*
EMP: 14
SALES (est): 4.8MM
SALES (corp-wide): 62.7B **Privately Held**
SIC: 3743 Railroad equipment
PA: Marubeni Corporation
　　2-7-1, Nihombashi
　　Chuo-Ku TKY 103-0
　　332 822-111

**(G-14345)**
**NEW STEP ORTHOTIC LAB INC**
Also Called: Allison's Comfort Shoes
14 Schiber Ct (62062-5625)
P.O. Box 669 (62062-0669)
PHONE..................................618 208-4444
Joshua Allison, *President*
EMP: 13
SQ FT: 4,752
SALES: 875.6K **Privately Held**
SIC: 5661 3842 Shoe stores; supports: abdominal, ankle, arch, kneecap, etc.

**(G-14346)**
**PISTOLEERCOM LLC**
12 Schiber Ct (62062-5625)
PHONE..................................618 288-4649
Peter J Wahle,
EMP: 3
SALES: 500K **Privately Held**
WEB: www.pistoleer.com
SIC: 3949 Target shooting equipment

**(G-14347)**
**VILLA MARIE WINE & BANQUET CTR**
6633 E Main St (62062-5463)
PHONE..................................618 345-3100
Al Cline, *Principal*
Al Cusanelli, *Manager*
Carol Bierbaum, *Admin Asst*
EMP: 7

Mascoutah - St. Clair County (G-14348)  GEOGRAPHIC SECTION

SALES (est): 640K Privately Held
SIC: 2084 Wines, brandy & brandy spirits

## Mascoutah
### St. Clair County

**(G-14348)**
**BETTER NEWS PAPERS INC (PA)**
Also Called: Mascoutah Herald
314 E Church St Ste 1 (62258-2100)
PHONE..............................618 566-8282
Cleon Birkemeyer, Ch of Bd
Greg Hoskins, President
EMP: 9
SQ FT: 4,500
SALES (est): 3MM Privately Held
SIC: 2711 7331 Newspapers; newspapers, publishing & printing; mailing service

**(G-14349)**
**BOBS TSHIRT STORE**
419 Jackson St (62258-1043)
P.O. Box 63 (62258-0063)
PHONE..............................618 567-1730
Robert Schubert, Owner
EMP: 1
SQ FT: 2,000
SALES: 300K Privately Held
SIC: 2759 Screen printing

**(G-14350)**
**CABLOFIL INC**
Also Called: Cablofil/Legrand
8319 State Route 4 (62258-2824)
PHONE..............................618 566-3230
Fax: 618 566-3250
Timothy Place, President
Robert Julian, Vice Pres
Wendy Childress, Engineer
Jim Kramer, CFO
James Laperriere, Treasurer
▲ EMP: 500
SQ FT: 80,000
SALES (est): 142.1MM
SALES (corp-wide): 16.3MM Privately Held
WEB: www.cablofil.com
SIC: 3443 Cable trays, metal plate
HQ: Legrand Holding, Inc.
  60 Woodlawn St
  West Hartford CT 06110
  860 233-6251

**(G-14351)**
**CONTINENTAL TIRE AMERICAS LLC**
10075 Progress Pkwy (62258-2825)
PHONE..............................618 246-2585
EMP: 5
SALES (corp-wide): 42.8B Privately Held
SIC: 3011 Tires & inner tubes
HQ: Continental Tire The Americas, Llc
  1830 Macmillan Park Dr
  Fort Mill SC 29707
  800 450-3187

**(G-14352)**
**HASSEBROCK ASPHALT SEALING**
111 W Poplar St (62258-1312)
PHONE..............................618 566-7214
EMP: 4 EST: 1998
SALES: 200K Privately Held
SIC: 2951 Mfg Asphalt Mixtures/Blocks

**(G-14353)**
**HERALD PUBLICATIONS (PA)**
Also Called: Fairview Heights Tribune
314 E Church St Ste 1 (62258-2100)
P.O. Box C (62258-0189)
PHONE..............................618 566-8282
Fax: 618 566-8283
Greg Hoskins, President
Lynn Maberry, Publisher
EMP: 11
SQ FT: 4,320
SALES: 310K Privately Held
SIC: 2711 7331 Newspapers, publishing & printing; mailing service

**(G-14354)**
**JOSEPH B KRISHER**
9950 Drum Hill Rd (62258-4532)
PHONE..............................618 677-2016
Joseph Krisher, Principal
EMP: 4
SALES (est): 307.2K Privately Held
SIC: 2448 Pallets, wood & wood with metal

**(G-14355)**
**KASKASKIA MECHANICAL INSUL CO**
6606 State Route 15 (62258-5128)
PHONE..............................618 768-4526
Jill Oeltjen, President
EMP: 6
SALES (est): 660K Privately Held
SIC: 2611 Mechanical pulp, including groundwood & thermomechanical

**(G-14356)**
**MID-WEST MILLWORK WHOLESALE**
9 W Green St (62258-2037)
PHONE..............................618 407-5940
Harry Horstman, Owner
EMP: 2
SALES (est): 417.9K Privately Held
SIC: 5031 3541 Millwork; milling machines

**(G-14357)**
**MIDWEST RECUMBENT BICYCLES**
Also Called: Mwrbents
109 W George St (62258-2310)
PHONE..............................618 343-1885
Carolee Wright, Owner
EMP: 3
SALES: 154K Privately Held
SIC: 3751 Motorcycles, bicycles & parts

**(G-14358)**
**N W HORIZONTAL BORING**
8100 Summerfield South Rd (62258-3010)
PHONE..............................618 566-9117
R Friederich, CEO
EMP: 4
SALES (est): 519.3K Privately Held
SIC: 3541 Drilling & boring machines

**(G-14359)**
**PURCHASING SERVICES LTD INC**
602 Industrial St (62258-1724)
PHONE..............................618 566-8100
Tracey Vernier, President
EMP: 25
SQ FT: 10,000
SALES: 900K Privately Held
WEB: www.purchasingserviceslimited.com
SIC: 3565 Packaging machinery

**(G-14360)**
**TRIPLE B MANUFACTURING CO INC**
620 Industrial St (62258)
P.O. Box 139 (62258-0139)
PHONE..............................618 566-2888
Fax: 618 566-2888
Steve Beimfohr, President
Janis Beimfohr, Corp Secy
Jeff Beimfour, Corp Secy
Bruce Mueller, Vice Pres
EMP: 3 EST: 1954
SQ FT: 7,500
SALES: 300K Privately Held
SIC: 3799 3537 Trailers & trailer equipment; industrial trucks & tractors

## Mason
### Effingham County

**(G-14361)**
**MARVIN SUCKOW**
5267 N 700th St (62443-2001)
PHONE..............................618 483-5570
Marvin Suckow, Owner
EMP: 4 EST: 1927
SALES (est): 250K Privately Held
SIC: 0115 0116 2421 Corn; soybeans; sawmills & planing mills, general

## Mason City
### Mason County

**(G-14362)**
**CONTRACTORS READY-MIX INC**
Also Called: Curry Ready Mix of Mason City
210 E Elm St (62664-1435)
PHONE..............................217 482-5530
Bob Harrison, Manager
EMP: 4
SALES (corp-wide): 3.4MM Privately Held
SIC: 3273 3496 3281 3271 Ready-mixed concrete; miscellaneous fabricated wire products; cut stone & stone products; concrete block & brick; construction sand & gravel
PA: Contractor's Ready-Mix Inc
  601 S Kickapoo St
  Lincoln IL 62656
  217 735-2565

**(G-14363)**
**DARLING INGREDIENTS INC**
1000 S Main St (62664-1522)
P.O. Box 192 (62664-0192)
PHONE..............................217 482-3261
Dave Riley, Controller
Robert L Griffin, Branch Mgr
EMP: 50
SALES (corp-wide): 3.4B Publicly Held
WEB: www.darlingii.com
SIC: 2077 4953 2992 2079 Meat meal & tankage, except as animal feed; grease rendering, inedible; refuse systems; lubricating oils & greases; edible fats & oils
PA: Darling Ingredients Inc.
  251 Oconnor Ridge Blvd
  Irving TX 75038
  972 717-0300

**(G-14364)**
**GROSCH IRRIGATION COMPANY**
Also Called: Grosch Well Drilling
13590 Sr 29 (62664-7364)
PHONE..............................217 482-5479
Fax: 217 482-3863
Richard Klassen, Branch Mgr
EMP: 14
SALES (corp-wide): 14.3MM Privately Held
WEB: www.groschirrigation.com
SIC: 1381 Drilling water intake wells
PA: Grosch Irrigation Company
  119 N 4th St
  Oneill NE 68763
  402 336-1438

**(G-14365)**
**MASON CITY BANNER TIMES**
Also Called: W H A M
126 N Tonica St (62664-1115)
P.O. Box 71 (62664-0071)
PHONE..............................217 482-3276
Lois Lee Rickard, Owner
EMP: 14 EST: 1920
SALES (est): 530.5K Privately Held
SIC: 2711 2791 2789 2759 Job printing & newspaper publishing combined; typesetting; bookbinding & related work; commercial printing; commercial printing, lithographic

**(G-14366)**
**RICKARD PUBLISHING**
126 N Tonica St (62664-1115)
P.O. Box 71 (62664-0071)
PHONE..............................217 482-3276
Lois Rickard, Owner
EMP: 15
SALES (est): 793.1K Privately Held
SIC: 2741 Miscellaneous publishing

## Matherville
### Mercer County

**(G-14367)**
**SLAVISH INC**
309 1st St (61263-9010)
P.O. Box 641 (61263-0641)
PHONE..............................309 754-8233
Paul Slavish, President
Kristen Slavish, Vice Pres
EMP: 5 EST: 1940
SQ FT: 5,000
SALES (est): 899.4K Privately Held
SIC: 3272 Burial vaults, concrete or precast terrazzo; septic tanks, concrete

## Matteson
### Cook County

**(G-14368)**
**BRITE ONE INC**
21649 Richmond Rd (60443-2615)
PHONE..............................708 481-8005
Kevin Zara, President
EMP: 3
SALES (est): 175.8K Privately Held
SIC: 3471 Cleaning, polishing & finishing

**(G-14369)**
**CUSTOM GOLF BY TANIS**
Also Called: Tanis Custom Golf
21750 Main St Unit 17 (60443-3717)
PHONE..............................708 481-4433
Richard L Tanis, President
EMP: 3
SQ FT: 900
SALES (est): 291.5K Privately Held
SIC: 3949 5941 7699 Golf equipment; golf goods & equipment; golf club & equipment repair

**(G-14370)**
**DATA LINK COMMUNICATIONS**
21153 Kildare Ave (60443-2305)
PHONE..............................815 405-2856
Bryan Bramson, Principal
EMP: 2
SALES (est): 201.8K Privately Held
WEB: www.waynesweb.com
SIC: 7372 Prepackaged software

**(G-14371)**
**E & H GRAPHIC SERVICE**
21750 Main St Unit 21 (60443-3716)
PHONE..............................708 748-5656
Fax: 708 481-4717
Errol Outarsingh, Owner
EMP: 2 EST: 1982
SALES (est): 256.4K Privately Held
SIC: 2759 7699 5084 2791 Commercial printing; industrial machinery & equipment repair; printing trades machinery, equipment & supplies; typesetting; bookbinding & related work; commercial printing, lithographic

**(G-14372)**
**HANGER INC**
4525 Lincoln Hwy (60443-2318)
PHONE..............................708 679-1006
EMP: 23
SALES (corp-wide): 459.1MM Publicly Held
SIC: 3842 Orthopedic appliances
PA: Hanger, Inc.
  10910 Domain Dr Ste 300
  Austin TX 78758
  512 777-3800

**(G-14373)**
**IMAGINE THAT CANDLE CO**
4107 Applewood Ln (60443-1902)
PHONE..............................708 481-6370
Joseph L Franklin, Principal
EMP: 3
SALES (est): 172.7K Privately Held
SIC: 3999 Candles

**(G-14374)**
**JORH FRAME & MOULDING CO INC**
21750 Main St Ste 14&15 (60443-3702)
PHONE..............................708 747-3440
Fax: 708 747-2291
Gordon N Harrington Jr, President
Patricia Harrington, Corp Secy
EMP: 5
SQ FT: 7,000
SALES (est): 564.3K Privately Held
SIC: 2499 Picture frame molding, finished

# GEOGRAPHIC SECTION

**Mattoon - Coles County (G-14399)**

**(G-14375)**
**KONZEN CHEMICALS INC**
Also Called: Kci Chemical
4248 Oakwood Ln (60443-1923)
PHONE.................................708 878-7636
Fax: 708 748-0136
Bernard Konzen, *President*
James Konzen, *Vice Pres*
Mark Konzen, *Vice Pres*
**EMP:** 18
**SQ FT:** 4,000
**SALES (est):** 2.9MM **Privately Held**
**SIC:** 2992 2819 Oils & greases, blending & compounding; industrial inorganic chemicals

**(G-14376)**
**LLC ETHERSONIC TECHNO**
4203 Oakwood Ln (60443-1922)
PHONE.................................708 441-4730
Jerrold F Jackson Jr, *Principal*
**EMP:** 4
**SALES (est):** 303.5K **Privately Held**
**SIC:** 2869 Ethers

**(G-14377)**
**OAK TECHNICAL LLC (PA)**
600 Holiday Plaza Dr # 130 (60443-2241)
PHONE.................................931 455-7011
Nathan Buchanan, *President*
Dan Marshall, *Manager*
▲ **EMP:** 6
**SALES (est):** 3.4MM **Privately Held**
**WEB:** www.oakgloves.com
**SIC:** 3089 Gloves or mittens, plastic

**(G-14378)**
**SENSIENT TECHNOLOGIES CORP**
810 Carnation Ln (60443-1946)
PHONE.................................708 481-0910
Richard Koenig, *Branch Mgr*
**EMP:** 37
**SALES (corp-wide):** 1.3B **Publicly Held**
**WEB:** www.sensient-tech.com
**SIC:** 2087 2099 Flavoring extracts & syrups; beverage bases; food colorings; yeast; seasonings & spices; chili pepper or powder; seasonings: dry mixes
**PA:** Sensient Technologies Corporation
777 E Wisconsin Ave # 1100
Milwaukee WI 53202
414 271-6755

**(G-14379)**
**SPIKE NANOTECH INC**
1008 Donnington Dr (60443-2290)
PHONE.................................847 504-6273
Patty Fu-Giles, *Principal*
Cary Giles, *Admin Sec*
**EMP:** 3
**SALES (est):** 174K **Privately Held**
**SIC:** 2844 Toilet preparations

**(G-14380)**
**VALSPAR CORPORATION**
21901 Central Ave (60443-2801)
PHONE.................................708 720-0600
Fax: 708 720-0696
Thomas Daly, *General Mgr*
Dale S Johnson, *Project Mgr*
Jerald West, *Project Mgr*
Stacey Sanders, *QC Mgr*
David Coker, *Plant Engr*
**EMP:** 190
**SQ FT:** 260,000
**SALES (corp-wide):** 11.8B **Publicly Held**
**SIC:** 2851 Paints & allied products
**HQ:** The Valspar Corporation
1101 S 3rd St
Minneapolis MN 55415
612 851-7000

**(G-14381)**
**WEI TO ASSOCIATES INC**
21750 Main St Unit 27 (60443-3716)
PHONE.................................708 747-6660
Fax: 708 747-6639
Richard Daniel Smith, *President*
**EMP:** 6 **EST:** 1972
**SQ FT:** 3,600
**SALES (est):** 952K **Privately Held**
**WEB:** www.weito.com
**SIC:** 3559 Chemical machinery & equipment

## Mattoon
### Coles County

**(G-14382)**
**ANAMET ELECTRICAL INC**
1000 Broadway Ave E (61938-4677)
P.O. Box 39 (61938-0039)
PHONE.................................217 234-8844
Fax: 217 234-8856
William Cady, *President*
Terrall L Steward, *Vice Pres*
Nicholas Houser, *Purch Agent*
Badrinarayan Belur, *Engineer*
Gilbert Henning, *Engineer*
▲ **EMP:** 120
**SQ FT:** 231,000
**SALES (est):** 35.6MM **Privately Held**
**WEB:** www.anacondasealtite.com
**SIC:** 3644 3498 Electric conduits & fittings; fabricated pipe & fittings

**(G-14383)**
**AUDIBEL HEARING AID SERVICES**
Also Called: Audibel Hearing Aid Center
408 Country Club Rd (61938-9269)
PHONE.................................217 234-6426
Fax: 217 235-5210
Dennis Stevens, *Owner*
**EMP:** 6 **EST:** 1977
**SQ FT:** 1,500
**SALES (est):** 280K **Privately Held**
**SIC:** 7372 5999 Prepackaged software; hearing aids

**(G-14384)**
**BOCKS CATTLE-IDENTI CO INC**
Also Called: Bock's Identi Co.
3101 Cedar Ave (61938-3612)
P.O. Box 614 (61938-0614)
PHONE.................................217 234-6634
Fax: 217 234-8520
Craig Salak, *President*
Brook Weemer, *Manager*
▼ **EMP:** 7
**SQ FT:** 15,000
**SALES (est):** 751.5K **Privately Held**
**WEB:** www.bocksid.com
**SIC:** 3999 Identification tags, except paper

**(G-14385)**
**BRIGHTON CABINETRY INC**
2908 Lake Land Blvd (61938-9522)
PHONE.................................217 235-1978
Fax: 217 235-1988
John Mikk, *Branch Mgr*
**EMP:** 11
**SALES (corp-wide):** 2.5MM **Privately Held**
**SIC:** 2434 Wood kitchen cabinets
**PA:** Brighton Cabinetry, Inc.
1095 Industrial Park Ave
Neoga IL 62447
217 895-3000

**(G-14386)**
**COMMERCIAL RFRGN CENTL ILL INC**
2020 Prairie Ave (61938-2836)
PHONE.................................217 235-5016
Fax: 217 235-5011
Joe Gillette, *President*
Debbie Parkerson, *Admin Sec*
**EMP:** 23
**SALES (est):** 5.3MM **Privately Held**
**SIC:** 3585 Refrigeration & heating equipment

**(G-14387)**
**COOK PRINTING CO INC**
921 S 19th St (61938-5218)
PHONE.................................217 345-2514
Fax: 217 348-7990
Robert Taylor, *President*
**EMP:** 4
**SALES (est):** 374.8K **Privately Held**
**SIC:** 2752 2759 Commercial printing, lithographic; commercial printing

**(G-14388)**
**DEDICA ENERGY CORPORATION**
104 N 11th St (61938-4114)
P.O. Box 1034 (61938-1034)
PHONE.................................217 235-9191
Debra Heller, *President*
Carol Zuhone, *Vice Pres*
William Heller, *Manager*
William Hone, *Manager*
William Zuhone, *Manager*
**EMP:** 2
**SQ FT:** 1,000
**SALES:** 1MM **Privately Held**
**SIC:** 1311 Crude petroleum production

**(G-14389)**
**GENERAL ELECTRIC COMPANY**
1501 S 19th St (61938-5900)
PHONE.................................217 235-4081
Fax: 217 258-9204
Joshua Smith, *Plant Mgr*
Joe Lagermasini, *Engineer*
Chuck Hicky, *Branch Mgr*
Thomas Ladendecker, *Manager*
Stephanie Miller, *Manager*
**EMP:** 250
**SALES (corp-wide):** 123.6B **Publicly Held**
**SIC:** 3641 Photoflash & photoflood lamps
**PA:** General Electric Company
41 Farnsworth St
Boston MA 02210
617 443-3000

**(G-14390)**
**HARRIS METALS & RECYCLING**
1213 N 11th St (61938-3156)
PHONE.................................217 235-1808
Toni Harris, *President*
**EMP:** 5
**SQ FT:** 12,000
**SALES (est):** 685.9K **Privately Held**
**SIC:** 3559 5051 Recycling machinery; nonferrous metal sheets, bars, rods, etc.

**(G-14391)**
**HELENA CHEMICAL COMPANY**
3559 E County Road 1000n (61938-6658)
PHONE.................................217 234-2726
Randy Parman, *Branch Mgr*
**EMP:** 9
**SALES (corp-wide):** 62.7B **Privately Held**
**SIC:** 5191 2819 Farm supplies; industrial inorganic chemicals
**HQ:** Helena Chemical Company
255 Schilling Blvd # 200
Collierville TN 38017
901 761-0050

**(G-14392)**
**HI-DEF COMMUNICATIONS**
3116 Pine Ave (61938-3633)
PHONE.................................217 258-6679
Toby Ferris, *Owner*
Sara Ferris, *Owner*
**EMP:** 5
**SALES:** 500K **Privately Held**
**SIC:** 3663 Satellites, communications

**(G-14393)**
**HOWELL ASPHALT COMPANY (PA)**
Also Called: Howell Paving
1020 N 13th St (61938-3022)
P.O. Box 1009 (61938-1009)
PHONE.................................217 234-8877
Fax: 217 234-4226
Holly A Bailey, *President*
Jamie Callison, *General Mgr*
Larry Leitch, *Senior VP*
Charles A Adams, *Vice Pres*
Dan Lindsey, *Engineer*
**EMP:** 6 **EST:** 1951
**SQ FT:** 2,600
**SALES (est):** 3.5MM **Privately Held**
**SIC:** 2951 Asphalt & asphaltic paving mixtures (not from refineries)

**(G-14394)**
**J L LAWRENCE & CO**
Also Called: Lawrence J L & Co Dental Labs
1921 Richmond Ave (61938-2843)
P.O. Box 728 (61938-0728)
PHONE.................................217 235-3622
Jimmy R Lawrence, *Owner*
**EMP:** 4
**SALES (est):** 312.1K **Privately Held**
**SIC:** 8072 3843 Dental laboratories; dental equipment & supplies

**(G-14395)**
**JELENIZ**
1414 Broadway Ave (61938-4014)
PHONE.................................217 235-6789
Jeff Eaton, *Principal*
**EMP:** 2
**SALES (est):** 225.7K **Privately Held**
**SIC:** 2599 Bar, restaurant & cafeteria furniture

**(G-14396)**
**JUSTRITE MANUFACTURING CO LLC**
Also Called: Justrite Mfg
3921 Dewitt Ave (61938-6618)
PHONE.................................217 234-7486
Fax: 217 234-7632
Ken Shead, *Div Sub Head*
Keith Lynch, *Purch Mgr*
Jim Lamar, *Buyer*
Stephaine Hanks, *Human Res Mgr*
John Norman, *Manager*
**EMP:** 150
**SQ FT:** 150,000
**SALES (corp-wide):** 69.6MM **Privately Held**
**WEB:** www.justritemfg.com
**SIC:** 3411 Metal cans
**PA:** Justrite Manufacturing Company, L.L.C.
2454 E Dempster St # 300
Des Plaines IL 60016
847 298-9250

**(G-14397)**
**KELLOGG COMPANY**
3801 Dewitt Ave (61938-6616)
PHONE.................................217 258-3251
**EMP:** 10
**SALES (corp-wide):** 13B **Publicly Held**
**WEB:** www.kelloggs.com
**SIC:** 2043 Cereal breakfast foods
**PA:** Kellogg Company
1 Kellogg Sq
Battle Creek MI 49017
269 961-2000

**(G-14398)**
**LUCO MOP COMPANY**
Also Called: American Broom Company
1200 Moultrie Ave (61938-3123)
PHONE.................................217 235-1992
Fax: 217 234-9180
Clarence Gillespie, *Manager*
**EMP:** 7
**SALES (corp-wide):** 5.3MM **Privately Held**
**WEB:** www.lucomop.com
**SIC:** 3991 5719 Brooms; brooms
**PA:** Luco Mop Company
3345 Morganford Rd
Saint Louis MO 63116
314 772-5656

**(G-14399)**
**MATTOON PRECISION MFG**
2408 S 14th St (61938-5748)
PHONE.................................217 235-6000
Fax: 217 235-6010
Robert Shamdin, *President*
Noriyoshi Nishida, *Chairman*
Takesi Nakani, *Corp Secy*
Trent Packer, *Prdtn Mgr*
Corde Ayers, *QC Mgr*
▲ **EMP:** 160
**SQ FT:** 134,000
**SALES:** 58.8MM
**SALES (corp-wide):** 106.6MM **Privately Held**
**WEB:** www.mpmiusa.com
**SIC:** 3714 3363 Axles, motor vehicle; motor vehicle brake systems & parts; aluminum die-castings
**PA:** Nukabe Corporation
2457-2, Kuraganomachi
Takasaki GNM 370-1
273 461-201

## Mattoon - Coles County (G-14400)

**(G-14400)**
**MATTOON PRINTING CENTER**
212 N 20th St  (61938-2851)
PHONE...................217 234-3100
Fax: 217 234-3100
Bruce Cavitt, *President*
Kathy Cavitt, *Admin Sec*
EMP: 4  EST: 1963
SQ FT: 3,700
SALES (est): 340K  Privately Held
SIC: 2752  2791 2789 2759 Commercial printing, offset; typesetting; bookbinding & related work; commercial printing

**(G-14401)**
**MATTSON LAMP PLANT**
1501 S 19th St  (61938-5956)
PHONE...................217 258-9390
Bonnie Gravil, *Purchasing*
▲ EMP: 2
SALES (est): 308.3K  Privately Held
SIC: 3641  Electric lamps

**(G-14402)**
**MERVIS INDUSTRIES INC**
Also Called: General Steel & Materials
612 N Logan St  (61938-3505)
P.O. Box 8  (61938-0008)
PHONE...................217 235-5575
Fax: 217 235-5591
Lou Mervis, *President*
Michael Smith, *Treasurer*
Paul Garrett, *Manager*
EMP: 10
SQ FT: 3,000
SALES (corp-wide): 140.2MM  Privately Held
SIC: 5093  3341 Ferrous metal scrap & waste; secondary nonferrous metals
PA: Mervis Industries, Inc.
    3295 E Main St Ste C
    Danville IL 61834
    217 442-5300

**(G-14403)**
**METZGER WELDING SERVICE**
Also Called: Metzger Welding & Machine
2900 Marshall Ave  (61938-4912)
PHONE...................217 234-2851
Fax: 217 234-2851
EMP: 4  EST: 1979
SQ FT: 7,900
SALES (est): 210K  Privately Held
SIC: 7692  5521 Welding Shop And Ret Used Cars

**(G-14404)**
**MID-ILLINOIS CONCRETE INC**
Also Called: Mattoon-Charleston Ready Mix
1413 Dewitt Ave E  (61938-3533)
PHONE...................217 235-5858
Fax: 217 234-7429
Bud Ervin, *Manager*
Joe Fillpot, *Asst Mgr*
EMP: 20
SALES (corp-wide): 17.2MM  Privately Held
WEB: www.mid-illinoisconcrete.com
SIC: 3273  3272 Ready-mixed concrete; concrete products
PA: Mid-Illinois Concrete, Inc.
    1805 S 4th St
    Effingham IL
    217 342-2115

**(G-14405)**
**MONITOR SIGN CO**
316 N Division St  (61938-4540)
P.O. Box 61  (61938-0061)
PHONE...................217 234-2412
Fax: 217 234-2312
David Cornell, *President*
Dennis Creasy, *Vice Pres*
William Creasy, *Vice Pres*
Cindy Cornell, *Accounts Mgr*
EMP: 18
SQ FT: 12,000
SALES (est): 1.3MM  Privately Held
WEB: www.monitorsign.com
SIC: 3993  1799 Electric signs; displays, paint process; sign installation & maintenance

**(G-14406)**
**PINNACLE FOODS GROUP LLC**
Lenders Bagels
3801 Dewitt Ave  (61938-6616)
PHONE...................217 235-3181
Brad Sam, *Manager*
Brad Sams, *Manager*
EMP: 350
SALES (corp-wide): 2.5B  Publicly Held
WEB: www.aurorafoods.com
SIC: 2051  5461 Bagels, fresh or frozen; bagels
HQ: Pinnacle Foods Group Llc
    399 Jefferson Rd
    Parsippany NJ 07054

**(G-14407)**
**RR DONNELLEY & SONS COMPANY**
Also Called: R R Donnelley
6821 E County Road 1100n  (61938-3478)
PHONE...................217 258-2675
Fax: 217 258-2817
Isabell Day, *Manager*
Vallie Witherspoon, *Manager*
John Karpus, *Info Tech Mgr*
EMP: 40
SALES (corp-wide): 6.9B  Publicly Held
WEB: www.rrdonnelley.com
SIC: 2754  Commercial printing, gravure
PA: R. R. Donnelley & Sons Company
    35 W Wacker Dr Ste 3650
    Chicago IL 60601
    312 326-8000

**(G-14408)**
**RR DONNELLEY PRINTING CO LP**
Manufacturing Division
6821 E County Road 1100n  (61938-3478)
P.O. Box 1668  (61938-1668)
PHONE...................217 235-0561
Vallie Witherspoon, *Purchasing*
Joyce Lindsay, *Human Res Dir*
Daon Knotts, *Branch Mgr*
EMP: 960
SALES (corp-wide): 6.9B  Publicly Held
SIC: 2754  2752 Commercial printing, gravure; letters, circular or form: lithographed
HQ: R.R. Donnelley Printing Company L.P.
    111 S Wacker Dr Ste 3500
    Chicago IL 60606
    312 326-8000

**(G-14409)**
**SPECTRUM MEDIA INC**
921 S 19th St  (61938-5218)
P.O. Box 611  (61938-0611)
PHONE...................217 234-2044
Fax: 217 234-2163
Kyle Jansen, *President*
EMP: 3
SQ FT: 4,200
SALES (est): 318.7K  Privately Held
SIC: 2759  Commercial printing

**(G-14410)**
**THAI NOODLE**
1418 Broadway Ave  (61938-4014)
PHONE...................217 235-5584
EMP: 4
SALES (est): 281.4K  Privately Held
SIC: 2098  Noodles (e.g. egg, plain & water), dry

**(G-14411)**
**U S SOY LLC**
Also Called: US Soy
2808 Thomason Dr  (61938-9277)
PHONE...................217 235-1020
Fax: 217 235-1006
Tom Condron, *Plant Mgr*
Jake Florey,
Larry Nichols,
▼ EMP: 16
SALES (est): 2.3MM  Privately Held
WEB: www.ussoy.com
SIC: 2041  Flour & other grain mill products

**(G-14412)**
**UNITED GRAPHICS LLC**
2916 Marshall Ave  (61938-4912)
P.O. Box 559  (61938-0559)
PHONE...................217 235-7161
Fax: 217 234-6274
Jeffery Scrimager, *Exec VP*
Kerry Considine, *Vice Pres*
Erica Stollard, *Treasurer*
▲ EMP: 130
SQ FT: 75,000
SALES (est): 31.7MM  Privately Held
WEB: www.unitedgraphicsinc.com
SIC: 2732  Book printing

**(G-14413)**
**UNITED GRAPHICS INDIANA INC**
2916 Marshall Ave  (61938-4912)
PHONE...................217 235-7161
EMP: 12
SQ FT: 16,000
SALES: 914.7K  Privately Held
SIC: 2752  Commercial printing, offset

---

### Maywood
### Cook County

**(G-14414)**
**ALECTO INDUSTRIES INC**
148 S 8th Ave  (60153-1330)
PHONE...................708 344-1488
Marta Szwaya, *President*
Darren Musial, *General Mgr*
James Szwaya, *Sales Executive*
James E Szway, *Admin Sec*
EMP: 29
SALES: 6.7MM  Privately Held
WEB: www.alecto.biz
SIC: 3496  Miscellaneous fabricated wire products

**(G-14415)**
**ALLIANCE TOOL & MANUFACTURING**
91 Wilcox St  (60153-2397)
PHONE...................708 345-5444
Fax: 708 345-4004
Carl Uzgiris, *President*
Ramesh Gandhi, *General Mgr*
Carol Runtke, *Accounting Dir*
Carol Ruhnke, *Finance Mgr*
EMP: 16  EST: 1945
SQ FT: 10,000
SALES (est): 2MM  Privately Held
SIC: 3541  3545 Machine tools, metal cutting: exotic (explosive, etc.); machine tool accessories

**(G-14416)**
**APPLE EXPRESS**
1701 S 1st Ave Ste 307  (60153-2419)
PHONE...................708 483-8168
EMP: 2
SALES (est): 239.7K  Privately Held
SIC: 3571  Personal computers (microcomputers)

**(G-14417)**
**AVW EQUIPMENT COMPANY INC**
105 S 9th Ave  (60153-1340)
PHONE...................708 343-7738
Fax: 708 343-9065
Milovan Vidakovich, *President*
Mira Djordjevic, *Admin Sec*
▲ EMP: 25
SQ FT: 25,400
SALES (est): 7.6MM  Privately Held
WEB: www.avwequipment.com
SIC: 3589  Car washing machinery

**(G-14418)**
**BECKER BROTHERS GRAPHITE CORP**
39 Legion St  (60153-2321)
PHONE...................708 410-0700
Cheryl Ivanovich, *President*
EMP: 7
SALES: 325K  Privately Held
WEB: www.beckergraphite.com
SIC: 3624  Carbon specialties for electrical use

**(G-14419)**
**BEST INSTITUTIONAL SUPPLY CO**
Also Called: Seaway Supply Co
15 N 9th Ave  (60153-1180)
PHONE...................708 216-0000
Fax: 708 216-0100
Thomas Engoren, *President*
Jorge Saenz, *General Mgr*
Gary Cumbo, *Sales Mgr*
EMP: 8
SQ FT: 12,500
SALES (est): 2.1MM  Privately Held
SIC: 2676  Sanitary paper products

**(G-14420)**
**BOST CORPORATION (PA)**
601 Saint Charles Rd  (60153-1315)
P.O. Box 698  (60153-0698)
PHONE...................708 344-7023
Fax: 708 343-6754
Bogdan Lodyga, *President*
Stefan Kaminski, *Vice Pres*
Kinga Pamkowska, *Office Mgr*
EMP: 20
SQ FT: 12,000
SALES (est): 5.2MM  Privately Held
SIC: 3564  3535 Dust or fume collecting equipment, industrial; conveyors & conveying equipment

**(G-14421)**
**BROWNS GLOBAL EXCHANGE**
1928 S 21st Ave  (60153-2916)
PHONE...................708 345-0955
Maurice Brown, *Owner*
EMP: 99
SALES: 500K  Privately Held
SIC: 2389  Apparel & accessories

**(G-14422)**
**CHEM-PLATE INDUSTRIES INC**
30 N 8th Ave  (60153-1319)
PHONE...................708 345-3588
Fax: 708 343-0911
Octavio Nava, *Branch Mgr*
EMP: 25
SALES (corp-wide): 56.1MM  Privately Held
WEB: www.chemplateindustries.com
SIC: 3398  3471 Metal heat treating; plating of metals or formed products
PA: Chem-Plate Industries, Inc
    1800 Touhy Ave
    Elk Grove Village IL 60007
    847 640-1600

**(G-14423)**
**CHICAGO PALLET SERVICE INC**
1305 S 1st Ave  (60153-2405)
PHONE...................847 439-8330
Araceli Rodriguez, *Vice Pres*
EMP: 28
SALES (corp-wide): 8.4MM  Privately Held
SIC: 3537  Pallets, metal
HQ: Chicago Pallet Service, Inc.
    1875 Greenleaf Ave
    Elk Grove Village IL 60007
    847 439-8754

**(G-14424)**
**DAN DE TASH KNITS**
1118 S 2nd Ave  (60153-2223)
PHONE...................708 970-6238
Teann Walker, *Owner*
EMP: 3
SALES (est): 96.8K  Privately Held
SIC: 3961  2284 5949 7389 Costume jewelry; crochet thread; hand knitting thread; sewing & needlework;

**(G-14425)**
**DELLEMAN ASSOCIATES & CORP**
8 N 6th Ave  (60153-1310)
PHONE...................708 345-9520
Dan Delleman, *Owner*
EMP: 3
SALES (est): 261.4K  Privately Held
SIC: 2499  Decorative wood & woodwork

## Mc Cook - Cook County (G-14450)

**(G-14426)**
**JSN INC**
Also Called: Wire Cloth Filter Mfg
611 Saint Charles Rd (60153-1315)
PHONE....................708 410-1800
Fax: 708 410-1807
Suryakant B Patel, *President*
Urvasht S Patel, *Admin Sec*
▲ EMP: 28
SQ FT: 17,000
SALES (est): 5.3MM  Privately Held
SIC: 3496 3493 3714 3728 3469 Wire cloth & woven wire products; filters: oil, fuel & air, motor vehicle; aircraft body & wing assemblies & parts; metal stampings; gaskets, packing & sealing devices

**(G-14427)**
**KRAMER WINDOW CO**
1219 Orchard Ave (60153-2330)
P.O. Box 576 (60153-0576)
PHONE....................708 343-4780
Fax: 708 343-1053
James Scolaro, *President*
Diane Scolaro, *Vice Pres*
EMP: 8  EST: 1955
SQ FT: 5,500
SALES: 850K  Privately Held
SIC: 3442 5031 Storm doors or windows, metal; metal doors; doors & windows

**(G-14428)**
**MACKENZIE JOHNSON**
Also Called: Sunshine Products
1826 S 10th Ave (60153-3102)
PHONE....................630 244-2367
Mackenzie Johnson, *Owner*
EMP: 2
SALES (est): 210K  Privately Held
WEB: www.likesunshine.com
SIC: 2842 Specialty cleaning, polishes & sanitation goods

**(G-14429)**
**MORRIS MEAT PACKING CO INC**
1406 S 5th Ave (60153-2129)
PHONE....................708 865-8566
Frank Masellis, *Manager*
EMP: 6
SALES (corp-wide): 1.5MM  Privately Held
SIC: 2011 2013 Meat packing plants; sausages & other prepared meats
PA: Morris Meat Packing Company, Inc.
1611 N Division St
Morris IL
815 942-9284

**(G-14430)**
**NATIONAL CYCLE INC**
Also Called: Barry Electric Div
2200 S Maywood Dr (60153-1783)
P.O. Box 158 (60153-0158)
PHONE....................708 343-0400
Barry Willey, *President*
Gordon B Willey, *Vice Pres*
Rudy Flores, *Production*
Zulma Side, *Senior Buyer*
John Kuta, *Purch Agent*
▲ EMP: 200  EST: 1937
SQ FT: 160,000
SALES (est): 31.4MM  Privately Held
WEB: www.nationalcycle.com
SIC: 3714 3751 3451 3441 Motor vehicle parts & accessories; motorcycle accessories; screw machine products; fabricated structural metal

**(G-14431)**
**NPC SEALANTS**
1208 S 8th Ave (60153-1906)
P.O. Box 645 (60153-0645)
PHONE....................708 681-1040
Angie Thompson, *Human Res Dir*
EMP: 18
SALES (est): 3.9MM  Privately Held
SIC: 2891 Sealants

**(G-14432)**
**NS PRECISION LATHE INC**
519 Lake St (60153-1651)
PHONE....................708 867-5023
Fax: 708 343-8224
Nicolas Sacarelos, *President*
Alfredo Santos,
EMP: 7
SQ FT: 5,000
SALES: 600K  Privately Held
SIC: 3599 Machine shop, jobbing & repair

**(G-14433)**
**NU-PUTTIE CORPORATION**
Also Called: Npc Sealants
1208 S 8th Ave (60153-1995)
P.O. Box 645 (60153-0645)
PHONE....................708 681-1040
Fax: 708 681-1424
Stephen F Stefely, *President*
Helen Walsh, *Vice Pres*
Angela Thompson, *Manager*
Helen A Stefely, *Admin Sec*
EMP: 35
SQ FT: 20,000
SALES (est): 9.4MM  Privately Held
WEB: www.npcsealants.com
SIC: 2851 2952 2891 Putty; asphalt felts & coatings; adhesives & sealants

**(G-14434)**
**OJEDAS WELDING  CO**
312 S 3rd Ave (60153-1640)
PHONE....................708 595-3799
Cristino Ojeda, *Principal*
Jose Ojeda, *Mng Member*
EMP: 6
SALES: 209K  Privately Held
SIC: 3499 Ladder assemblies, combination workstand: metal

**(G-14435)**
**TECH UPGRADERS**
2007 S 9th Ave (60153-3232)
PHONE....................877 324-8940
Elijah Goodwin, *Principal*
EMP: 8  EST: 2010
SALES: 350K  Privately Held
SIC: 7378 3651 Computer maintenance & repair; household audio & video equipment

**(G-14436)**
**TRY OUR PALLETS INC**
37 S 9th Ave (60153-1364)
P.O. Box 1571, Melrose Park (60161-1571)
PHONE....................708 343-0166
Fax: 708 343-0198
Jose Trujillo, *President*
Dawn Trujillo, *Vice Pres*
EMP: 9
SALES (est): 1.6MM  Privately Held
WEB: www.tryourpallets.com
SIC: 2448 4953 Wood pallets & skids; refuse systems

**(G-14437)**
**WELDON CORPORATION**
Also Called: Van Bergen & Greener
1818 Madison St (60153-1710)
PHONE....................708 343-4700
Fax: 708 343-9425
Paul J Weldon, *President*
Eleanor Voeltz, *Manager*
EMP: 45  EST: 1919
SQ FT: 45,000
SALES (est): 9.2MM  Privately Held
WEB: www.solenoids.net
SIC: 3621 3679 3566 Frequency converters (electric generators); solenoids for electronic applications; speed changers, drives & gears

### Mazon
*Grundy County*

**(G-14438)**
**ILLINOIS TOOL WORKS INC**
ITW Filtration Products Div
804 Commercial Dr (60444-6203)
PHONE....................815 448-7300
Fax: 815 448-2066
Cynthia Hagemaster, *Manager*
John Seibert, *Manager*
EMP: 125
SALES (corp-wide): 13.6B  Publicly Held
SIC: 3089 3714 Injection molding of plastics; motor vehicle parts & accessories
PA: Illinois Tool Works Inc.
155 Harlem Ave
Glenview IL 60025
847 724-7500

**(G-14439)**
**MUELLER CUSTOM CABINETRY INC**
4730 S Old Mazon Rd (60444-6264)
PHONE....................815 448-5448
Daniel Mueller, *Executive*
EMP: 4
SALES (est): 452.9K  Privately Held
SIC: 2434 Wood kitchen cabinets

**(G-14440)**
**PERITUS PLASTICS LLC**
804 Commercial Dr (60444-6203)
PHONE....................815 448-2005
Timothy Clasby, *President*
James Macier, *Vice Pres*
EMP: 20
SQ FT: 25,000
SALES (est): 737.9K  Privately Held
SIC: 3089 Injection molding of plastics

**(G-14441)**
**WILLOUGHBYS AUTO & MCH SP**
615 East St (60444-6043)
P.O. Box 330 (60444-0330)
PHONE....................815 448-2281
Berton Willoughby, *Owner*
EMP: 5
SALES (est): 474.5K  Privately Held
SIC: 3599 Machine shop, jobbing & repair

### Mc Connell
*Stephenson County*

**(G-14442)**
**CONNELL MC MACHINE & WELDING**
8934 N Korth Rd (61050-9705)
PHONE....................815 868-2275
Fax: 815 868-2275
Roger Klontz, *Owner*
EMP: 6
SQ FT: 300
SALES (est): 100K  Privately Held
SIC: 7692 3599 Welding repair; machine shop, jobbing & repair

### Mc Cook
*Cook County*

**(G-14443)**
**A&S MACHINING & WELDING INC**
Also Called: Asmw
4828 Lawndale Ave Ste 3 (60525-3106)
PHONE....................708 442-4544
Fax: 708 442-4313
Stanley Rafacz, *President*
Mary Rafacz, *Admin Sec*
EMP: 20
SQ FT: 23,000
SALES (est): 3.9MM  Privately Held
WEB: www.asmw.com
SIC: 3599 1799 7692 3544 Machine shop, jobbing & repair; welding on site; welding repair; special dies, tools, jigs & fixtures; sheet metalwork

**(G-14444)**
**ACCURATE PARTITIONS CORP**
8000 Joliet Rd (60525-3254)
P.O. Box 287, Lyons (60534-0287)
PHONE....................708 442-6801
Fax: 708 442-7439
Michael F Rolla, *President*
Peter Rolla, *President*
Carl Liggett, *General Mgr*
Jim Povejsil, *General Mgr*
Rey Salvador, *Opers Mgr*
▲ EMP: 7
SQ FT: 65,000
SALES (est): 2.1MM
SALES (corp-wide): 167.6MM  Privately Held
WEB: www.accuratepartitions.com
SIC: 3446 3083 2542 Partitions & supports/studs, including accoustical systems; laminated plastics plate & sheet; laminated plastic sheets; partitions & fixtures, except wood
PA: Itr Industries, Inc
441 Saw Mill River Rd
Yonkers NY 10701
914 964-7063

**(G-14445)**
**BARTELL GRINDING AND MCH LLC**
8312 Joliet Rd Unit 9 (60525-3103)
PHONE....................708 408-1700
Larry Ray Sr,
EMP: 2
SALES (est): 203.4K  Privately Held
SIC: 3441 Fabricated structural metal

**(G-14446)**
**CAPITOL WHOLESALE MEATS INC**
Also Called: Fontanini Itln Meats Sausages
8751 W 50th St (60525-3132)
PHONE....................708 485-4800
Fax: 708 485-9600
Eugene Fontanini, *CEO*
Joanne Fontanini, *President*
Charles L Brown, *General Mgr*
Jose Salas, *QA Dir*
Steve Fradkin, *CFO*
▲ EMP: 414
SQ FT: 188,000
SALES (est): 162.7MM  Privately Held
WEB: www.fontanini.com
SIC: 2013 Frozen meats from purchased meat; prepared pork products from purchased pork

**(G-14447)**
**CORR-PAK CORPORATION**
8000 Joliet Rd Ste 100 (60525-3256)
PHONE....................708 442-7806
Fax: 708 442-0467
Hal Taylor, *President*
Henry O Taylor, *President*
Mary Ikorn, *Manager*
Anne Taylor, *Shareholder*
EMP: 24
SQ FT: 46,000
SALES (est): 5.9MM  Privately Held
WEB: www.corr-pak.com
SIC: 2653 7336 7389 2448 Boxes, corrugated: made from purchased materials; display items, solid fiber: made from purchased materials; silk screen design; package design; packaging & labeling services; pallets, wood & wood with metal; freight transportation arrangement; general warehousing & storage

**(G-14448)**
**GPA INC**
8740 W 50th St (60525-3149)
PHONE....................773 650-2020
Michael Ratcliff, *CEO*
◆ EMP: 6
SALES (est): 1.3MM  Privately Held
SIC: 3861 Graphic arts plates, sensitized

**(G-14449)**
**K & K IRON WORKS  LLC (PA)**
5100 Lawndale Ave Ste 7 (60525-3311)
PHONE....................708 924-0000
Fax: 708 924-1240
Bob Sullivan, *President*
Paul Wendt, *Project Mgr*
Clark Roemmich, *CFO*
Steve Thackson, *Controller*
Mary Lang, *Bookkeeper*
EMP: 73
SQ FT: 35,000
SALES (est): 24.4MM  Privately Held
WEB: www.kkironworks.com
SIC: 3441 3446 Fabricated structural metal; stairs, staircases, stair treads: prefabricated metal; railings, prefabricated metal

**(G-14450)**
**LEGACY VULCAN  LLC**
Midwest Division
5500 Joliet Rd (60525-3113)
PHONE....................708 485-6602
Audrey Rogers, *Opers Staff*
Melissa Traynere, *Sales Executive*
Jeff May, *Manager*
Dennis Passow, *Supervisor*
Brad Susala, *Supervisor*
EMP: 75

## Mc Cook - Cook County (G-14451)

SALES (corp-wide): 3.5B **Publicly Held**
WEB: www.vulcanmaterials.com
SIC: **1442** Construction sand & gravel
HQ: Legacy Vulcan, Llc
1200 Urban Center Dr
Vestavia AL 35242
205 298-3000

**(G-14451)**
**MATERIAL SERVICE CORPORATION**
9101 W 47th St (60525-3306)
PHONE..................................708 485-8211
Fax: 708 485-8212
James Goldberg, *Superintendent*
EMP: 60
SALES (corp-wide): 16B **Privately Held**
WEB: www.materialservice.com
SIC: **1411** Limestone, dimension-quarrying
HQ: Material Service Corporation
2235 Entp Dr Ste 3504
Westchester IL 60154
708 731-2600

**(G-14452)**
**MCCOOK COLD STORAGE CORP**
8801 W 50th St (60525-6003)
PHONE..................................708 387-2585
Fax: 708 387-2446
Tony Kucharski, *President*
James Nowak, *General Mgr*
Freddie Ocampo, *Manager*
▲ EMP: 50
SALES (est): 12.3MM **Privately Held**
SIC: **2673** Food storage & frozen food bags, plastic

**(G-14453)**
**MICHAEL LEWIS COMPANY (HQ)**
Also Called: Simon Products Co
8900 W 50th St (60525-6005)
PHONE..................................708 688-2200
Fax: 708 688-2880
Craig Simon, *President*
Bob Frye, *Managing Dir*
Michael L Simon, *Principal*
Sheldon L Rosen, *Vice Pres*
Jim Kleinert, *Opers Staff*
◆ EMP: 210
SQ FT: 400,000
SALES: 412MM **Privately Held**
WEB: www.mlco.com
SIC: **5113** 5141 5142 2782 Industrial & personal service paper; groceries, general line; packaged frozen goods; looseleaf binders & devices; menus: printing; packaging paper
PA: Simu Ltd.
201 Mittel Dr
Wood Dale IL 60191
630 350-1060

**(G-14454)**
**NORTH AMERICAN REFINING CO**
7601 W 47th St (60525-3203)
PHONE..................................708 762-5117
Lowell D Aughenbaugh, *President*
Laurie Witter, *Manager*
EMP: 3
SALES (est): 365.3K **Privately Held**
SIC: **2911** Oils, partly refined: sold for re-running

**(G-14455)**
**PELRON CORPORATION**
7847 W 47th St (60525-3204)
P.O. Box 6, Lyons (60534-0006)
PHONE..................................708 442-9100
Fax: 708 442-0213
Floy Pelletier, *President*
Eric Lasey, *General Mgr*
Edward L Eubank, *Vice Pres*
Michele Eubank, *Vice Pres*
Donna McClelland, *Purch Agent*
◆ EMP: 34
SQ FT: 33,000
SALES (est): 10.6MM **Privately Held**
SIC: **2833** Organic medicinal chemicals: bulk, uncompounded

**(G-14456)**
**PROGRESS RAIL LOCOMOTIVE INC (DH)**
Also Called: Electro Motive Diesel
9301 W 55th St (60525-3214)
P.O. Box 689, La Grange (60525-0689)
PHONE..................................800 255-5355
Fax: 708 387-6665
William P Ainsworth, *CEO*
Keri Harkne, *COO*
Marc N Buncher, *Senior VP*
Duane Cantrell, *Senior VP*
Paul Denton, *Senior VP*
◆ EMP: 1850
SQ FT: 790,000
SALES (est): 914.6MM
SALES (corp-wide): 38.5B **Publicly Held**
WEB: www.emdiesels.com
SIC: **3621** 3519 3647 Motors & generators; internal combustion engines; locomotive & railroad car lights
HQ: Progress Rail Services Corporation
1600 Progress Dr
Albertville AL 35950
256 593-1260

**(G-14457)**
**PROGRESS RAIL LOCOMOTIVE INC**
Also Called: EMD
9301 W 55th St (60525-3214)
P.O. Box 2377, La Grange (60525-8477)
PHONE..................................708 387-5510
EMP: 13
SALES (corp-wide): 38.5B **Publicly Held**
SIC: **3621** 3519 3647 Motors & generators; internal combustion engines; vehicular lighting equipment
HQ: Progress Rail Locomotive Inc.
9301 W 55th St
Mc Cook IL 60525
800 255-5355

**(G-14458)**
**SKYLINE**
9200 W 55th St (60525-3654)
PHONE..................................312 300-4700
Mary Crowe, *Principal*
EMP: 2
SALES (est): 237.8K **Privately Held**
SIC: **2759** Screen printing

**(G-14459)**
**SUMMIT TANK & EQUIPMENT CO**
7801 W 47th St (60525-3204)
P.O. Box 9, Summit Argo (60501-0009)
PHONE..................................708 594-3040
Al Majeres, *President*
Peter Majeres, *Vice Pres*
EMP: 15
SQ FT: 15,000
SALES: 1MM **Privately Held**
WEB: www.tankfarmvendor.com
SIC: **7699** 3715 3713 Tank repair; truck trailers; truck & bus bodies

**(G-14460)**
**UOP LLC**
Also Called: Mc Cook Manufacturing Plant
8400 Joliet Rd Ste 100 (60525-3310)
PHONE..................................708 442-7400
Fax: 708 442-8082
EMP: 75
SALES (corp-wide): 38.5B **Publicly Held**
SIC: **2833** 2819 1311 Mfg Medicinal/Botanicals Mfg Indstl Inorgan Chem Petro/Natural Gas Prodn
HQ: Uop Llc
25 E Algonquin Rd
Des Plaines IL 60016
847 391-2000

**(G-14461)**
**WERTHEIMER BOX & PAPER CORP**
7950 Joliet Rd Ste 100 (60525-3206)
PHONE..................................312 829-4545
Douglas Wertheimer, *President*
John Soukup, *Plant Mgr*
Maria Deizman, *Project Mgr*
EMP: 100 EST: 1939
SQ FT: 180,000

SALES (est): 31.7MM **Privately Held**
WEB: www.wertheimerbox.com
SIC: **2653** Boxes, corrugated: made from purchased materials

### Mc Henry
*Mchenry County*

**(G-14462)**
**PETER BAKER & SON CO**
Also Called: Plant 6
914 W Illinois Rte 120 (60050)
PHONE..................................815 344-1640
Fax: 815 344-1653
Arthura Baker II, *Branch Mgr*
EMP: 10
SALES (corp-wide): 22.2MM **Privately Held**
WEB: www.peterbaker.com
SIC: **3531** 1611 Asphalt plant, including gravel-mix type; highway & street construction
PA: Peter Baker & Son Co.
1349 Rockland Rd
Lake Bluff IL 60044
847 362-3663

### Mc Lean
*Mclean County*

**(G-14463)**
**MILLER WHITESIDE WOOD WORKING**
Also Called: Miller-Whiteside Woodworking
3645 N 400 East Rd (61754-7511)
PHONE..................................309 827-6470
Kent Whiteside, *Owner*
Dorothy Huffington, *Bookkeeper*
EMP: 4 EST: 1987
SQ FT: 6,000
SALES (est): 621.5K **Privately Held**
SIC: **5712** 2491 2541 2511 Cabinet work, custom; millwork, treated wood; wood partitions & fixtures; wood household furniture; wood kitchen cabinets; millwork

### Mc Leansboro
*Hamilton County*

**(G-14464)**
**EAGLE ENTERPRISES INC**
Also Called: Eagle Seal
Hc 14 Box E (62859)
P.O. Box 283 (62859-0283)
PHONE..................................618 643-2588
Gary C Bruce, *President*
Paula Young, *Corp Secy*
William Gwaltney, *Vice Pres*
Robert Young, *Vice Pres*
Kermit Webb, *Director*
EMP: 5
SALES (est): 571.7K **Privately Held**
WEB: www.eerecycling.com
SIC: **2891** Sealants

**(G-14465)**
**HAMILTON COUNTY CONCRETE CO**
Ollie St (62859)
P.O. Box 454 (62859-0454)
PHONE..................................618 643-4333
Glen Zeller, *President*
Gary Hook, *Admin Sec*
EMP: 7
SQ FT: 2,000
SALES (est): 1.1MM **Privately Held**
SIC: **3273** Ready-mixed concrete

**(G-14466)**
**NEWSPAPER HOLDING INC**
Also Called: Times-Leader
200 S Washington St Ste 1 (62859)
PHONE..................................618 643-2387
Fax: 618 643-3426
Erin Smith, *Business Mgr*
Brenda Carrolton, *Manager*
EMP: 3
SQ FT: 8,000 **Privately Held**

WEB: www.clintonnc.com
SIC: **2711** Newspapers
HQ: Newspaper Holding, Inc.
425 Locust St
Johnstown PA 15901
814 532-5102

**(G-14467)**
**SOUTHERN IL PRECISION**
310 W Randolph St (62859-1278)
PHONE..................................618 643-3340
EMP: 2
SALES (est): 217.4K **Privately Held**
SIC: **3599** Industrial machinery

**(G-14468)**
**STC INC**
Also Called: Sun Transformer
1201 W Randolph St (62859-2028)
PHONE..................................618 643-2555
Fax: 618 643-2316
Brad Cross, *President*
Lynn Vines, *Purch Dir*
Angie Calkin, *QC Mgr*
Les Vaughn, *Design Engr*
Kezya Newman, *Financial Exec*
▼ EMP: 30
SQ FT: 27,000
SALES: 5MM **Privately Held**
WEB: www.suntransformer.com
SIC: **3677** 3663 Electronic coils, transformers & other inductors;

**(G-14469)**
**TRADE INDUSTRIES**
Rr 5 (62859-9805)
P.O. Box 5 (62859-0005)
PHONE..................................618 643-4321
Fax: 618 643-4230
John Dean, *President*
Mark Auten, *Business Mgr*
Tammy Bowman, *Business Mgr*
EMP: 30 EST: 1967
SQ FT: 8,000
SALES: 1.6MM **Privately Held**
SIC: **8331** 2448 2441 Vocational training agency; wood pallets & skids; nailed wood boxes & shook

**(G-14470)**
**WUEBBELS REPAIR & SALES LLC**
505 W Market St (62859-1069)
P.O. Box Rr3 184 (62859)
PHONE..................................618 648-2227
Shelly A Wuebbels, *Principal*
EMP: 3
SALES (est): 150K **Privately Held**
SIC: **3519** Parts & accessories, internal combustion engines

### McCullom Lake
*Mchenry County*

**(G-14471)**
**FILTER RENEW TECNOLOGIES**
3205 Lakeside Ct (60050-1514)
PHONE..................................815 344-2200
John T Colomer, *Principal*
EMP: 2
SALES (est): 285.6K **Privately Held**
SIC: **3569** Filters

**(G-14472)**
**SASSY PRIMITIVES LTD**
3202 Lakeside Ct Unit 2 (60050-1512)
PHONE..................................815 385-9302
Wendy Patchett, *President*
Lisbeth Nielson, *Principal*
EMP: 2
SALES (est): 215.9K **Privately Held**
SIC: **3999** Candles

### McHenry
*Mchenry County*

**(G-14473)**
**A FISCHER PHASE DRIVES**
4615 Prime Pkwy (60050-7001)
PHONE..................................815 759-6928

## McHenry
### Mchenry County

**(G-14474)**
**A YARD MATERIALS CO**
Ringwood Rd (60051)
P.O. Box 75, McHenry (60051-9001)
PHONE.................................815 385-4560
Fax: 815 385-4568
EMP: 3 EST: 2001
SALES (est): 268.3K Privately Held
SIC: 3524 Lawn & garden equipment

## McHenry
### Mchenry County

**(G-14475)**
**ACCURATE SPRING TECH INC**
Also Called: Hill Design
5801 W Hill St (60050-7445)
PHONE.................................815 344-3333
Fax: 815 344-6333
Ken Fullick, President
EMP: 13
SALES (est): 920K Privately Held
SIC: 3542 Spring winding & forming machines

**(G-14476)**
**ACE ENGRAVING & SPECIALTIES CO**
4204 Ponca St (60050-5340)
PHONE.................................815 759-2093
Brenda Singleton, President
Morris Singleton, Vice Pres
EMP: 3 EST: 1975
SQ FT: 3,000
SALES: 400K Privately Held
SIC: 3479 Engraving jewelry silverware, or metal

**(G-14477)**
**ADAMS STEEL SERVICE INC**
2022 S Il Route 31 Ste A (60050-8211)
PHONE.................................815 385-9100
Fax: 815 385-8382
Mike Chambers, President
Pete Kasper, General Mgr
EMP: 22
SQ FT: 11,000
SALES (est): 6.1MM Privately Held
WEB: www.edsdoors.com
SIC: 3441 7692 3548 Fabricated structural metal; welding repair; welding apparatus

**(G-14478)**
**AJI CUSTOM CABINETS**
5720 Wilmot Rd (60051-8400)
PHONE.................................847 312-7847
EMP: 4 EST: 2013
SALES (est): 206.7K Privately Held
SIC: 2434 Wood kitchen cabinets

**(G-14479)**
**ALLIED DIE CASTING CORPORATION**
3923 W West Ave (60050-4395)
PHONE.................................815 385-9330
Fax: 815 385-9338
Michael J Albanese Jr, President
Adam Albanese, Vice Pres
Gayle Albanese, Treasurer
Jack Dahlman, Sales Staff
▲ EMP: 20
SQ FT: 20,000
SALES (est): 3.8MM Privately Held
WEB: www.allieddiecasting.net
SIC: 3364 3993 Zinc & zinc-base alloy die-castings; signs & advertising specialties

Henry Fischer, Principal
EMP: 2
SALES (est): 210.7K Privately Held
SIC: 3568 Power transmission equipment

**(G-14480)**
**AMERICAN CONVENIENCE INC**
Also Called: Riverside Chocolate Factory
2102 W Il Route 120 (60051-4759)
PHONE.................................815 344-6040
Fax: 815 344-6268
Robert B Hunter, President
Diana Hunter, Corp Secy
Tabitha Deibler, Manager
EMP: 12
SQ FT: 1,500
SALES (est): 886.8K Privately Held
SIC: 5441 2064 2066 Candy; confectionery; candy & other confectionery products; fudge (candy); chocolate & cocoa products

**(G-14481)**
**APTARGROUP INC**
Aptar and Cary Illinois
4900 Prime Pkwy (60050-7019)
PHONE.................................847 462-3900
Bill Ostrow, Branch Mgr
EMP: 50
SALES (corp-wide): 2.3B Publicly Held
SIC: 3089 Injection molded finished plastic products
PA: Aptargroup, Inc.
    475 W Terra Cotta Ave E
    Crystal Lake IL 60014
    815 477-0424

**(G-14482)**
**BLACK MOUNTAIN PRODUCTS INC**
1412 Ridgeview Dr (60050-7022)
PHONE.................................224 655-5955
Daniel Borak, President
Julie Weidener, Principal
Patricia Weidener, Principal
Thomas Wiznerowicz, Sales Dir
▲ EMP: 6
SQ FT: 4,500
SALES (est): 600K Privately Held
SIC: 3499 Stabilizing bars (cargo), metal

**(G-14483)**
**BPI HOLDINGS INTERNATIONAL INC (PA)**
4400 Prime Pkwy (60050-7003)
PHONE.................................815 363-9000
David Overbeeke, President
Mike Caruso, Vice Pres
Phil Cutting, CFO
Stephanie Flatkin, Admin Sec
EMP: 200 EST: 2012
SQ FT: 100,000
SALES: 600MM Privately Held
SIC: 3714 Motor vehicle brake systems & parts

**(G-14484)**
**BRAKE PARTS INC INDIA LLC (DH)**
4400 Prime Pkwy (60050-7033)
PHONE.................................815 363-9000
Christian Robbins, Controller
Josh Russell, Marketing Staff
Terry R McCormack, Mng Member
Suzie Stuart, Admin Sec
◆ EMP: 16
SALES (est): 49.9MM
SALES (corp-wide): 185.8K Privately Held
WEB: www.affiniagroup.com
SIC: 5013 3714 Automotive supplies & parts; motor vehicle brake systems & parts
HQ: Mann+Hummel Filtration Technology Group Inc.
    1 Wix Way
    Gastonia NC 28054
    704 869-3300

**(G-14485)**
**BRAKE PARTS INC LLC (HQ)**
4400 Prime Pkwy (60050-7033)
PHONE.................................815 363-9000
Fax: 815 363-9303
H David Overbeeke, President
Don Boeckenstedt, Vice Pres
Kevin Judge, Vice Pres
Ross Hinrichsen, Purchasing
Dennis Toby, Engineer
◆ EMP: 125

SQ FT: 40,000
SALES (est): 546.2MM
SALES (corp-wide): 600MM Privately Held
WEB: www.raybestosracing.com
SIC: 3714 Motor vehicle brake systems & parts; brake drums, motor vehicle
PA: Bpi Holdings International, Inc.
    4400 Prime Pkwy
    Mchenry IL 60050
    815 363-9000

**(G-14486)**
**CHROMOLD PLATING INC**
1631 Oak Dr (60050-0305)
PHONE.................................815 344-8644
Eric Coulter, President
EMP: 3
SALES (est): 248.5K Privately Held
SIC: 3471 Plating of metals or formed products

**(G-14487)**
**CLASSIC PRODUCTS INC**
Also Called: Mastercoil Spring
4010 W Albany St (60050-8301)
PHONE.................................815 344-0051
Fax: 815 344-0071
Catherine Musielak Miller, President
Paul Weisinger, Maint Spvr
Sean Wolfert, Opers Staff
Cathy M Musielak, Purch Mgr
Linda Meyer, Accountant
▲ EMP: 45
SQ FT: 45,000
SALES (est): 9.9MM Privately Held
WEB: www.mastercoil.com
SIC: 3493 Coiled flat springs

**(G-14488)**
**CONCORDE MFG & FABRICATION INC**
1620 S Schroeder Ln (60050-8251)
PHONE.................................815 344-3788
Fax: 815 344-8621
John West, President
John Silberbauer, Vice Pres
Janine McQuiddy, Manager
EMP: 19
SQ FT: 12,000
SALES (est): 3.9MM Privately Held
WEB: www.concordetools.com
SIC: 3599 Machine shop, jobbing & repair

**(G-14489)**
**CORPORATE DISK COMPANY (PA)**
Also Called: Disk.com
4610 Prime Pkwy (60050-7005)
PHONE.................................800 634-3475
Fax: 815 331-6030
William Mahoney, President
Alan Gault, President
David Gimbel, Exec VP
Cheryl Coyle, Senior VP
Joseph Foley, Vice Pres
EMP: 90
SQ FT: 60,000
SALES (est): 18.8MM Privately Held
WEB: www.disk.com
SIC: 3652 Compact laser discs, prerecorded

**(G-14490)**
**CPM CO INC**
1805 Dot St (60050-6586)
P.O. Box 250 (60051-0250)
PHONE.................................815 385-7700
Fax: 815 385-2494
Scott Smith, CEO
John Smith, Owner
Randall Smith, Vice Pres
Kelly Stanger, Comms Dir
Ken Gaylord, Manager
▼ EMP: 29 EST: 1970
SQ FT: 54,900
SALES (est): 5.2MM Privately Held
WEB: www.millerformless.com
SIC: 3531 Construction machinery

**(G-14491)**
**CREATIVE CURRICULA INC**
1621 Park St (60050-4440)
PHONE.................................815 363-9419
EMP: 7 EST: 1998

SALES: 250K Privately Held
SIC: 8299 2731 School/Educational Services Books-Publishing/Printing

**(G-14492)**
**CRYSTAL NAILS MCHENRY**
2030 N Richmond Rd (60051-5419)
PHONE.................................815 363-5498
Giang Ta, Owner
EMP: 5
SALES (est): 301.4K Privately Held
SIC: 3999 Fingernails, artificial

**(G-14493)**
**CTS AUTOMOTIVE LLC**
Also Called: Fabrick Molded Plastic Div
5213 Prime Pkwy (60050-7034)
PHONE.................................815 385-9480
Seth Wagner, Branch Mgr
EMP: 50
SALES (corp-wide): 396.6MM Publicly Held
WEB: www.d-r-t.com
SIC: 3625 3089 Switches, electronic applications; boxes, plastic
HQ: Cts Automotive, Llc
    2375 Cabot Dr
    Lisle IL 60532
    630 614-7201

**(G-14494)**
**DEATAK INC**
Also Called: Frederick P Schall
4004 W Dayton St (60050-8376)
PHONE.................................815 322-2013
Frederick P Schall, President
Michael Schall, Vice Pres
Carol Ann Schall, Admin Sec
▲ EMP: 10
SQ FT: 10,000
SALES (est): 2.2MM Privately Held
SIC: 3829 Measuring & controlling devices

**(G-14495)**
**DENTAL USA INC**
Also Called: Power Dental U.S.A.
5005 Mccullom Lake Rd (60050-1509)
PHONE.................................815 363-8003
Fax: 815 363-3545
Jang Lim, President
Sabino Orozco, Sales Staff
David Berrard, Marketing Staff
Kathy Rettig, Office Mgr
▲ EMP: 13
SQ FT: 7,500
SALES (est): 1.5MM Privately Held
WEB: www.mydentalusa.com
SIC: 3843 Dental equipment & supplies

**(G-14496)**
**DIVERSIFIED FLEET MGT INC**
776 Ridgeview Dr (60050-7054)
PHONE.................................815 578-1051
Robert Ozimek, President
EMP: 28
SALES (est): 3.8MM Privately Held
SIC: 8741 3535 Business management; robotic conveyors

**(G-14497)**
**DONS DRAPERY SERVICE**
Also Called: Don's Custom Draperies
2210 Orchard Beach Rd (60050-2850)
PHONE.................................815 385-4759
Donald Welch, Owner
EMP: 2
SALES (est): 350K Privately Held
SIC: 5023 1799 2591 2391 Draperies; drapery track installation; drapery hardware & blinds & shades; curtains & draperies

**(G-14498)**
**DREWRYS BREWING COMPANY**
5402 Brittany Dr (60050-3354)
PHONE.................................815 385-9115
Francis Manzo, Principal
EMP: 4
SALES (est): 246K Privately Held
SIC: 2082 Malt beverages

**(G-14499)**
**DURA WAX COMPANY**
4101 W Albany St (60050-4807)
PHONE.................................815 385-5000
Brian Schwerman, President

# McHenry - Mchenry County (G-14500)

Mark P Chianakas, *Admin Sec*
Cindy Schwerman, *Admin Sec*
▼ **EMP**: 12
**SQ FT**: 16,000
**SALES (est)**: 2.7MM **Privately Held**
**SIC**: 2842 5087 3291 Floor waxes; janitors' supplies; abrasive products

### (G-14500)
### E & J PRECISION MACHINING INC
4215 W Orleans St (60050-3999)
**PHONE**..................815 363-2522
Ed Prealkowski, *President*
Joy Prealkowski, *Vice Pres*
**EMP**: 10 **EST**: 2008
**SALES (est)**: 1.7MM **Privately Held**
**SIC**: 3599 Machine shop, jobbing & repair

### (G-14501)
### ELECTROHONE TECHNOLOGIES INC
4615 Prime Pkwy (60050-7001)
P.O. Box 317, Crystal Lake (60039-0317)
**PHONE**..................815 363-5536
George Bull, *President*
**EMP**: 3
**SALES (est)**: 235.9K **Privately Held**
**SIC**: 3471 Finishing, metals or formed products

### (G-14502)
### EMERALD PRINTING & PROMOTIONS
1009 Bay Rd Lot 8 (60051-9683)
**PHONE**..................815 344-3303
Cyndy Lawrence, *President*
**EMP**: 4
**SQ FT**: 3,000
**SALES**: 1MM **Privately Held**
**SIC**: 2752 Commercial printing, lithographic

### (G-14503)
### ENGINRED MOLDING SOLUTIONS INC
4913 Prime Pkwy (60050-7016)
**PHONE**..................815 363-9600
Mike Jacobs, *President*
**EMP**: 26 **EST**: 1996
**SQ FT**: 25,000
**SALES (est)**: 5.3MM **Privately Held**
**WEB**: www.moldingsolutions.com
**SIC**: 3089 Injection molding of plastics

### (G-14504)
### EVSCO INC
2309 N Ringwood Rd Ste M (60050-1313)
**PHONE**..................847 362-7068
**Fax**: 847 362-7501
Michael Barrett, *President*
Ann Barrett, *Admin Sec*
**EMP**: 10
**SALES (est)**: 1.2MM **Privately Held**
**WEB**: www.evsco.com
**SIC**: 3491 3494 Industrial valves; valves & pipe fittings

### (G-14505)
### FABRIK INDUSTRIES INC
Also Called: Fabrik Molded Plastics
5213 Prime Pkwy (60050-7038)
**PHONE**..................815 385-9480
**Fax**: 815 385-9614
Seth Wagner, *President*
Keith Wagner, *President*
Deb Madoni, *Vice Pres*
Tony Wancket, *Vice Pres*
Mark Badgley, *Engineer*
▲ **EMP**: 280
**SQ FT**: 120,000
**SALES (est)**: 85.2MM **Privately Held**
**SIC**: 3089 3544 Injection molding of plastics; special dies & tools

### (G-14506)
### FEDERAL-MOGUL CORPORATION
Also Called: Federal-Mogul Motorparts
4500 Prime Pkwy (60050-2136)
**PHONE**..................815 271-9600
Rainer Jueckstock, *Co-CEO*
**EMP**: 140
**SALES (corp-wide)**: 16.3B **Publicly Held**
**SIC**: 3677 3714 Filtration devices, electronic; motor vehicle parts & accessories
**HQ**: Federal-Mogul Llc
27300 W 11 Mile Rd
Southfield MI 48034

### (G-14507)
### FOLLETT SCHOOL SOLUTIONS INC
1340 Ridgeview Dr (60050-7047)
**PHONE**..................815 759-1700
Tom Schenck, *President*
Simona Rollinson, *Vice Pres*
Timothy Henrichs, *Treasurer*
Patrick Rivers, *Asst Treas*
R Mark Sproat, *Admin Sec*
**EMP**: 200
**SALES (est)**: 19.3MM
**SALES (corp-wide)**: 6.3B **Privately Held**
**SIC**: 7371 7372 5999 5192 Computer software development & applications; educational computer software; educational aids & electronic training materials; books
**HQ**: Follett School Solutions, Inc.
1391 Corporate Dr
Mchenry IL 60050
708 884-5000

### (G-14508)
### GARRELTS & SONS INC
Also Called: Garrelts & Sons Water Trtmnt
2309 N Ringwood Rd Ste A (60050-1313)
P.O. Box 295 (60051-9004)
**PHONE**..................815 385-3821
**Fax**: 815 385-3892
Jim Garrelts, *President*
**EMP**: 2
**SALES (est)**: 310.8K **Privately Held**
**SIC**: 3589 Sewage & water treatment equipment

### (G-14509)
### GEITEK AUTOMATION INC
4615 Prime Pkwy (60050-7001)
**PHONE**..................815 385-3500
David F Geiser, *President*
**EMP**: 65
**SQ FT**: 39,000
**SALES (est)**: 5.4MM **Privately Held**
**SIC**: 3621 3566 3625 Motors, electric; reduction gears & gear units for turbines, except automotive; controls for adjustable speed drives; electric controls & control accessories, industrial

### (G-14510)
### GLASS HAUS
2412 S Justen Rd (60050-8180)
**PHONE**..................815 459-5849
Leonard Wilson, *Owner*
Carolyn Wilson, *Owner*
**EMP**: 3
**SALES**: 150K **Privately Held**
**WEB**: www.theglasshaus.com
**SIC**: 2653 3231 3221 Sheets, solid fiber: made from purchased materials; novelties, glass: fruit, foliage, flowers, animals, etc.; glass containers

### (G-14511)
### HANGER INC
649 Ridgeview Dr (60050-7012)
**PHONE**..................847 695-6955
Tracey Moore, *Office Mgr*
**EMP**: 23
**SALES (corp-wide)**: 459.1MM **Publicly Held**
**SIC**: 3842 Prosthetic appliances; orthopedic appliances
**PA**: Hanger, Inc.
10910 Domain Dr Ste 300
Austin TX 78758
512 777-3800

### (G-14512)
### HANGER PROSTHETICS &
Also Called: Hanger Clinic
649 Ridgeview Dr (60050-7012)
**PHONE**..................815 344-3070
Sam Liang, *President*
James Stilenen, *Manager*
**EMP**: 5

**SALES (corp-wide)**: 459.1MM **Publicly Held**
**WEB**: www.hanger.com
**SIC**: 3842 Surgical appliances & supplies
**HQ**: Hanger Prosthetics & Orthotics East, Inc.
33 North Ave Ste 101
Tallmadge OH 44278
330 633-9807

### (G-14513)
### HILL DESIGN PRODUCTS INC
5801 W Hill St (60050-7445)
**PHONE**..................815 344-3333
Ken Fullick, *President*
Tom Kraus, *Vice Pres*
Dian Blebson, *Manager*
**EMP**: 15
**SALES (est)**: 2.4MM **Privately Held**
**SIC**: 2431 Windows & window parts & trim, wood

### (G-14514)
### I P C AUTOMATION INC
4615 Prime Pkwy (60050-7001)
**PHONE**..................815 759-3934
David F Geiser, *President*
Gerald Warnke, *COO*
Bill Soltmann, *Vice Pres*
Steven Plump, *Sales Mgr*
Susan Ryan, *Accounts Mgr*
▲ **EMP**: 6
**SQ FT**: 15,000
**SALES (est)**: 1.4MM **Privately Held**
**WEB**: www.ipcautomation.com
**SIC**: 3625 3825 Electric controls & control accessories, industrial; instruments to measure electricity
**HQ**: Bluffton Motor Works Llc
410 E Spring St
Bluffton IN 46714
800 579-8527

### (G-14515)
### JARR PRINTING CO
5435 Bull Valley Rd # 300 (60050-7436)
**PHONE**..................815 363-5435
**Fax**: 847 546-8147
Dennis C Jarr, *Owner*
Greg Jarr, *Marketing Staff*
**EMP**: 13
**SQ FT**: 4,000
**SALES (est)**: 650K **Privately Held**
**WEB**: www.jarrprinting.com
**SIC**: 2752 Commercial printing, lithographic

## Mchenry
### *Mchenry County*

### (G-14516)
### JEDI CORPORATION
4450 Bull Valley Rd Ste 2 (60050-7495)
P.O. Box 459 (60051-9007)
**PHONE**..................815 344-5334
Robert Karolewski, *President*
Edward Karolewski, *Vice Pres*
Denise Karolewski, *Admin Sec*
**EMP**: 4
**SALES**: 500K **Privately Held**
**WEB**: www.jedica.com
**SIC**: 3451 Screw machine products

### (G-14517)
### JESSUP MANUFACTURING COMPANY (PA)
2815 W Rte 120 (60051)
P.O. Box 366, McHenry (60051-0366)
**PHONE**..................815 385-6650
**Fax**: 815 385-0079
Robert A Jessup, *President*
Heidi Gluchman, *General Mgr*
Jeff Harvey, *Business Mgr*
Michael Kilkenny, *Business Mgr*
Mike Richardson, *Business Mgr*
▲ **EMP**: 60 **EST**: 1956
**SQ FT**: 55,000
**SALES (est)**: 17.2MM **Privately Held**
**WEB**: www.jessupmfg.com
**SIC**: 3089 Battery cases, plastic or plastic combination

## McHenry
### *Mchenry County*

### (G-14518)
### KREISCHER OPTICS LTD
1729 Oak Dr (60050-0306)
**PHONE**..................815 344-4220
**Fax**: 815 344-4221
Cody Kreischer, *President*
John Taylor, *General Mgr*
Daniel Charland, *Sales Staff*
Tina Kreischer, *Mktg Dir*
Debbie Trexler, *Office Mgr*
**EMP**: 18
**SQ FT**: 8,400
**SALES**: 3MM **Privately Held**
**WEB**: www.kreischer.com
**SIC**: 3827 Optical elements & assemblies, except ophthalmic

### (G-14519)
### KWIK MARK INC
4071 W Albany St (60050-8390)
**PHONE**..................815 363-8268
Emil Cindric, *President*
Michelle Morin, *Manager*
**EMP**: 6
**SALES (est)**: 670K **Privately Held**
**WEB**: www.kwikmark.com
**SIC**: 3542 Marking machines

### (G-14520)
### LENCO ELECTRONICS INC
1330 S Belden St (60050-8381)
**PHONE**..................815 344-2900
**Fax**: 815 344-2730
Lenard J Duncan, *President*
Bruce Thackwray, *General Mgr*
Brad Schwagerman, *Safety Mgr*
Lauretta Montgomery, *Purch Dir*
Erik Johnson, *CPA*
▲ **EMP**: 40 **EST**: 1971
**SQ FT**: 22,000
**SALES (est)**: 9.7MM **Privately Held**
**WEB**: www.lenco-elect.com
**SIC**: 3612 3677 Transformers, except electric; electronic transformers

### (G-14521)
### LIBERTY LIMESTONE INC
430 W Wegner Rd (60051-8653)
**PHONE**..................815 385-5011
Dave Hammerl, *President*
**EMP**: 7
**SALES**: 350K **Privately Held**
**SIC**: 3281 Limestone, cut & shaped

### (G-14522)
### LIMITLESS INNOVATIONS INC
4800 Metalmaster Dr (60050-7017)
**PHONE**..................855 843-4828
Michael V Smeja, *Principal*
Daniel F Smeja, *Principal*
Rock M Smeja, *Principal*
Jessica Coari, *Accountant*
▲ **EMP**: 20
**SQ FT**: 100,000
**SALES (est)**: 2.2MM **Privately Held**
**SIC**: 3679 5065 5023 3089 Electronic loads & power supplies; electronic parts & equipment; decorative home furnishings & supplies; kitchenware, plastic

### (G-14523)
### LINCOLNSHIRE PRINTING INC
4004 W Dayton St (60050-8376)
**PHONE**..................815 578-0740
**Fax**: 815 566-3420
John Kunath, *President*
Bill Kunath, *Software Engr*
**EMP**: 9 **EST**: 1977
**SALES (est)**: 1.2MM **Privately Held**
**WEB**: www.omrscan.com
**SIC**: 2752 2759 Commercial printing, offset; commercial printing

### (G-14524)
### M S —ACTION MACHINING CORP
4061 W Dayton St (60050-8377)
**PHONE**..................815 344-3770
**Fax**: 815 344-2122
Norman Stengel, *President*

Ralph Stengel, *Vice Pres*
Fred Compisano, *Manager*
Maureen Schmidt, *Manager*
**EMP:** 35 **EST:** 1966
**SQ FT:** 12,000
**SALES (est):** 6.7MM **Privately Held**
**WEB:** www.ms-action.com
**SIC:** 3599 Machine shop, jobbing & repair

**(G-14525)**
**M-1 TOOL WORKS INC**
1419 S Belden St (60050-8399)
**PHONE** ............................ 815 344-1275
**Fax:** 815 344-1950
Martin Ryba, *President*
Karin Peter, *Corp Secy*
Sandy Miller, *Manager*
**EMP:** 40
**SQ FT:** 15,000
**SALES (est):** 9.6MM **Privately Held**
**WEB:** www.m1toolworks.com
**SIC:** 3544 3625 Special dies, tools, jigs & fixtures; control equipment, electric

**(G-14526)**
**MANN+HUMMEL FILTRATION TECH**
4500 Prime Pkwy (60050-2136)
**PHONE** ............................ 800 407-9263
**EMP:** 19
**SALES (corp-wide):** 3.4B **Privately Held**
**SIC:** 3714 5013 Mfg Vechicle Replacement Parts
**HQ:** Mann+Hummel Filtration Technology Group Inc.
1 Wix Way
Gastonia NC 28054
704 869-3300

**(G-14527)**
**MANN+HUMMEL FILTRATION TECHNOL**
1380 Corporate Dr (60050-7044)
**PHONE** ............................ 815 759-7744
Pat Keane, *Branch Mgr*
**EMP:** 7
**SALES (corp-wide):** 185.8K **Privately Held**
**WEB:** www.affiniagroup.com
**SIC:** 3714 Motor vehicle parts & accessories
**HQ:** Mann+Hummel Filtration Technology Group Inc.
1 Wix Way
Gastonia NC 28054
704 869-3300

**(G-14528)**
**MASTER TECH TOOL INC**
4539 Prime Pkwy (60050-7000)
**PHONE** ............................ 815 363-4001
Kathy Farwick, *Treasurer*
Glenn Farwick, *Treasurer*
**EMP:** 2
**SQ FT:** 2,500
**SALES (est):** 200K **Privately Held**
**WEB:** www.mastertechtoolinc.com
**SIC:** 3544 Special dies, tools, jigs & fixtures

**(G-14529)**
**MC HENRY SCREW PRODUCTS INC**
4515 Prime Pkwy (60050-7000)
**PHONE** ............................ 815 344-4638
Ronald Wenk, *President*
**EMP:** 3
**SQ FT:** 1,900
**SALES (est):** 181.5K **Privately Held**
**SIC:** 3451 Screw machine products

**(G-14530)**
**MECC ALTE INC**
1229 Adams Dr (60051-4562)
**PHONE** ............................ 815 344-0530
Pom Weber, *CEO*
Nikolay Bogvanov, *Manager*
Kevin Schroeder, *Manager*
◆ **EMP:** 11 **EST:** 2008
**SQ FT:** 20,000
**SALES (est):** 2.2MM **Privately Held**
**SIC:** 3621 Generating apparatus & parts, electrical; generators & sets, electric

**(G-14531)**
**MEDELA LLC (DH)**
1101 Corporate Dr (60050-7006)
P.O. Box 660 (60051-0660)
**PHONE** ............................ 800 435-8316
**Fax:** 815 363-6031
Carolin Archibald, *President*
Karen Csech, *President*
Bonnie Voigt, *General Mgr*
Donald Alexander, *Vice Pres*
Patrik Bosshard, *Vice Pres*
◆ **EMP:** 153
**SQ FT:** 135,000
**SALES (est):** 155.2MM **Privately Held**
**WEB:** www.medela.com
**SIC:** 5047 3596 Medical & hospital equipment; scales & balances, except laboratory; baby scales
**HQ:** Medela Ag
Lattichstrasse 4b
Baar ZG
417 695-151

**(G-14532)**
**MFS HOLDINGS LLC**
Also Called: Miller Formers Co
1805 Dot St (60050-6586)
**PHONE** ............................ 815 385-7700
Scott Smith, *CEO*
**EMP:** 35 **EST:** 2015
**SQ FT:** 85,000
**SALES (est):** 7MM **Privately Held**
**SIC:** 3531 Drags, road (construction & road maintenance equipment)

**(G-14533)**
**MIDWEST INNOVATIONS INC**
4137 W Orleans St (60050-3973)
P.O. Box 221 (60051-9003)
**PHONE** ............................ 815 578-1401
Lindsay Trax, *President*
**EMP:** 2 **EST:** 2009
**SALES:** 1MM **Privately Held**
**SIC:** 3559 Plastics working machinery

**(G-14534)**
**MIDWEST WATER GROUP INC**
Also Called: Red Arrow Sales
4410 S Hi Point Rd (60050-8389)
**PHONE** ............................ 866 526-6558
Michelle Harrod, *President*
Jeffrey Blindt, *Principal*
**EMP:** 3
**SQ FT:** 1,800
**SALES (est):** 506.6K **Privately Held**
**SIC:** 3491 Water works valves

**(G-14535)**
**MILLENNIUM MOLD DESIGN INC**
3513 W Elm St (60050-4401)
P.O. Box 159, Ringwood (60072-0159)
**PHONE** ............................ 815 344-9790
**Fax:** 815 344-9792
David Quinn, *President*
**EMP:** 3
**SQ FT:** 1,400
**SALES (est):** 500.5K **Privately Held**
**WEB:** www.mmdi.net
**SIC:** 3089 8711 3544 Injection molding of plastics; consulting engineer; special dies, tools, jigs & fixtures

**(G-14536)**
**MITCHELL AIRCRAFT PRODUCTS**
2309 N Ringwood Rd Ste U (60050-1313)
**PHONE** ............................ 815 331-8609
Bob Woasecki, *Principal*
**EMP:** 5 **EST:** 2013
**SALES (est):** 537.7K **Privately Held**
**SIC:** 3728 Aircraft parts & equipment

**(G-14537)**
**MJF WOODWORKING**
5250 W Flanders Rd (60050-3414)
**PHONE** ............................ 815 679-6700
**EMP:** 2
**SALES (est):** 217.2K **Privately Held**
**SIC:** 2431 Millwork

**(G-14538)**
**OAKRIDGE PRODUCTS LLC**
Also Called: Oak Ridge Molded Products
4612 Century Ct (60050-7018)
**PHONE** ............................ 815 363-4700
Conor O'Malley, *President*
Andrew Kovari, *Exec VP*
▲ **EMP:** 7
**SQ FT:** 17,000
**SALES (est):** 1.6MM
**SALES (corp-wide):** 893.7K **Privately Held**
**WEB:** www.mrchips.net
**SIC:** 3089 Caps, plastic
**PA:** Mr. Chips, Inc.
1380 Gateway Dr Ste 7
Elgin IL 60124
847 468-9000

**(G-14539)**
**OMNI PRODUCTS INC (PA)**
3911 W Dayton St (60050-8377)
**PHONE** ............................ 815 344-3100
**Fax:** 815 344-5086
William E Cook, *President*
John Hart, *Corp Secy*
James Clark, *CFO*
Jack Clark, *Controller*
Christine Johnson, *Manager*
**EMP:** 6
**SALES (est):** 5.1MM **Privately Held**
**SIC:** 3069 Molded rubber products

**(G-14540)**
**ONLINE INC**
4071 W Albany St (60050-8390)
**PHONE** ............................ 815 363-8008
**Fax:** 815 363-8089
Emil Cindric, *President*
Nada Cindric, *Accountant*
Michelle Morin, *Marketing Mgr*
**EMP:** 12
**SQ FT:** 10,000
**SALES (est):** 3MM **Privately Held**
**WEB:** www.online.net
**SIC:** 3569 Liquid automation machinery & equipment

**(G-14541)**
**PAN AMERICA ENVIRONMENTAL INC**
2309 N Ringwood Rd Ste G (60050-1313)
**PHONE** ............................ 847 487-9166
Scott Spalding, *President*
Dorota Szkopnicka, *Purchasing*
▲ **EMP:** 4
**SALES:** 848K **Privately Held**
**WEB:** www.panamenv.com
**SIC:** 3823 8748 Water quality monitoring & control systems; environmental consultant

**(G-14542)**
**PAPYS FOODS INC**
4131 W Albany St (60050-8390)
**PHONE** ............................ 815 385-3313
**Fax:** 815 385-3367
David L Gallimore, *Ch of Bd*
Matt Gallimore, *President*
Elizabeth Olson, *Controller*
**EMP:** 25
**SQ FT:** 65,000
**SALES (est):** 3.9MM **Privately Held**
**WEB:** www.papys.com
**SIC:** 7389 2099 Packaging & labeling services; seasonings: dry mixes

**(G-14543)**
**PAW OFFICE MACHINES INC**
816 Madison Ave (60050-2414)
**PHONE** ............................ 815 363-9780
**EMP:** 2
**SALES (est):** 200K **Privately Held**
**SIC:** 3555 Mfg Printing Trades Machinery

**(G-14544)**
**PINNACLE WOOD PRODUCTS INC**
1703 S Schroeder Ln (60050-7028)
**PHONE** ............................ 815 385-0792
Wayne Lyons, *President*
Tracey Christinson, *Office Mgr*
Martha Kornak, *Manager*
Norman Evan, *Shareholder*
**EMP:** 7
**SQ FT:** 10,000
**SALES (est):** 700K **Privately Held**
**WEB:** www.pinnaclewood.net
**SIC:** 2431 Millwork

**(G-14545)**
**PIONEER PAVERS INC**
4910 Pioneer Rd (60051-8571)
**PHONE** ............................ 847 833-9866
**EMP:** 4
**SALES (est):** 340K **Privately Held**
**SIC:** 3531 Pavers

**(G-14546)**
**PLASPROS INC (PA)**
1143 Ridgeview Dr (60050-7013)
**PHONE** ............................ 815 430-2300
**Fax:** 815 430-2260
Norm Dusenberry, *President*
David Georgi, *President*
Phyllis Nelson, *COO*
Mark Doner, *Plant Mgr*
Sue Haraway, *Plant Mgr*
◆ **EMP:** 100
**SQ FT:** 76,500
**SALES (est):** 30.4MM **Privately Held**
**WEB:** www.plaspros.com
**SIC:** 3089 Injection molded finished plastic products

**(G-14547)**
**POINT READY MIX LLC (PA)**
5435 Bull Valley Rd # 130 (60050-7434)
**PHONE** ............................ 815 578-9100
David Lapointe, *President*
**EMP:** 4 **EST:** 2014
**SALES (est):** 861.2K **Privately Held**
**SIC:** 3273 Ready-mixed concrete

**(G-14548)**
**POLYONE CORPORATION**
GLS Thrmplstic Elstmers N Amer
833 Ridgeview Dr (60050-7050)
**PHONE** ............................ 815 385-8500
Walter Ripple, *Manager*
**EMP:** 75 **Publicly Held**
**SIC:** 2821 3087 Thermoplastic materials; custom compound purchased resins
**PA:** Polyone Corporation
33587 Walker Rd
Avon Lake OH 44012

**(G-14549)**
**PROSTHETICS ORTHOTICS HAN**
620 S II Route 31 Ste 7 (60050-3134)
**PHONE** ............................ 847 695-6955
Tracy Moore, *Manager*
**EMP:** 1
**SALES (est):** 184.5K **Privately Held**
**SIC:** 3842 Prosthetic appliances

**(G-14550)**
**REHOBOT INC**
3980 W Albany St Ste 1 (60050-8397)
**PHONE** ............................ 815 385-7777
Kjell-Roger Holmstrom, *Ch of Bd*
Magnus Johnson, *Principal*
Trish Simpson, *Administration*
▲ **EMP:** 3
**SALES (est):** 274.7K **Privately Held**
**SIC:** 1799 3569 3593 3492 Hydraulic equipment, installation & service; jacks, hydraulic; fluid power actuators, hydraulic or pneumatic; fluid power valves & hose fittings; pumps, hydraulic power transfer

**(G-14551)**
**RELIABLE SAND AND GRAVEL CO**
Also Called: Drr Construction
2121 S River Rd Ste B (60051-9228)
P.O. Box 707, Island Lake (60042-0707)
**PHONE** ............................ 815 385-5020
**Fax:** 815 385-5030
Donald R Roberts, *President*
**EMP:** 8 **EST:** 1966
**SQ FT:** 600
**SALES (est):** 1.1MM **Privately Held**
**SIC:** 1442 Common sand mining; gravel mining

**(G-14552)**
**RIVERSIDE BAKE SHOP**
1309 N Riverside Dr (60050-4509)
**PHONE** ............................ 815 385-0044
**Fax:** 815 385-0772
Charles B Rice, *President*
Carol Rice, *Corp Secy*
**EMP:** 40 **EST:** 1973
**SQ FT:** 1,200

# McHenry - Mchenry County (G-14553)

**SALES (est):** 1.7MM  **Privately Held**
**WEB:** www.riversidebakeshop.com
**SIC:** 5461 5149 2051  Bakeries; bakery products; bread, cake & related products

### (G-14553)
### RUSH PRINTING ON OAK
1627 Oak Dr  (60050-0305)
**PHONE** ............................ 815 344-8880
**Fax:** 815 344-8882
John De Fabio, *President*
**EMP:** 4
**SALES (est):** 377.3K  **Privately Held**
**SIC:** 2752  Commercial printing, lithographic

### (G-14554)
### SCHOMMER INC
Also Called: Minuteman Press
3410 W Elm St  (60050-4433)
**PHONE** ............................ 815 344-1404
**Fax:** 815 344-9552
Tom Schommer, *President*
**EMP:** 8
**SQ FT:** 2,500
**SALES (est):** 750K  **Privately Held**
**WEB:** www.schommer.com
**SIC:** 2752 2791 2789  Commercial printing, lithographic; typesetting; bookbinding & related work

### (G-14555)
### SNO GEM INC
Also Called: Sno Gem Snow Guards
4800 Metalmaster Dr  (60050-7017)
**PHONE** ............................ 888 766-4367
Michael V Smeja, *Principal*
James Carpenter, *Vice Pres*
David Kozial, *Controller*
Jim Carpenter, *Marketing Staff*
**EMP:** 13
**SQ FT:** 100,000
**SALES (est):** 3.5MM  **Privately Held**
**WEB:** www.888snogems.com
**SIC:** 3354 3089 3446  Aluminum extruded products; plastic hardware & building products; architectural metalwork

### (G-14556)
### STANDARD SAFETY EQUIPMENT CO
1407 Ridgeview Dr  (60050-7023)
P.O. Box 189 (60051-9003)
**PHONE** ............................ 815 363-8565
**Fax:** 815 363-8633
Scott R Olson, *President*
Steven A Medves, *Exec VP*
Cindy Burger, *Vice Pres*
Kim Jebens, *Mfg Staff*
Rosalio Gonzalez, *Sales Mgr*
**EMP:** 32  **EST:** 1921
**SQ FT:** 35,000
**SALES (est):** 5.9MM  **Privately Held**
**WEB:** www.standardsafety.com
**SIC:** 3842 2826 3021 2326  Personal safety equipment; welders' hoods; clothing, fire resistant & protective; environmental testing equipment; rubber & plastics footwear; men's & boys' work clothing

### (G-14557)
### SULLIVANS INC
5508 W Chasefield Cir  (60050-5133)
**PHONE** ............................ 815 331-8347
**EMP:** 10
**SALES (corp-wide):** 17.6MM  **Privately Held**
**SIC:** 5131 3965  Notions; fasteners, buttons, needles & pins
**PA:** Sullivans, Inc.
121 Franklin St
Hanson MA
781 293-9430

### (G-14558)
### SUMMIT PLASTICS INC
1207 Adams Dr  (60051-4562)
**PHONE** ............................ 815 578-8700
Michael Stekl, *President*
Michelle L Martin, *Vice Pres*
Rob Gumpf, *Sales Mgr*
Ron Vandiver, *Sales Staff*
Sarah Dopke, *Office Mgr*
▲ **EMP:** 5
**SQ FT:** 4,500

**SALES (est):** 794.9K  **Privately Held**
**SIC:** 3081  Unsupported plastics film & sheet

### (G-14559)
### SUMMIT TOOLING INC
1207 Adams Dr  (60051-4562)
**PHONE** ............................ 815 385-7500
**Fax:** 815 385-7520
Dan Martin, *President*
Al Linden, *Foreman/Supr*
Dale Christensen, *Engineer*
Michelle Martin, *CFO*
**EMP:** 18
**SQ FT:** 3,000
**SALES (est):** 4.8MM  **Privately Held**
**SIC:** 3542  Machine tools, metal forming type

### (G-14560)
### SUPER AGGREGATES INC (HQ)
Also Called: Super Mix
5435 Bull Valley Rd # 330  (60050-7434)
**PHONE** ............................ 815 385-8000
Jack Pease, *President*
Karl Skathum, *Project Mgr*
Patty Peterson, *Mktg Dir*
Andrea Jones, *Admin Sec*
**EMP:** 8
**SALES (est):** 2.2MM
**SALES (corp-wide):** 15.2MM  **Privately Held**
**SIC:** 1442  Sand mining; gravel mining
**PA:** J. Pease Construction Co., Inc.
1001 Williams Rd
Genoa City WI 53128
815 790-1293

### (G-14561)
### SUPER MIX INC
5435 Bull Valley Rd # 130  (60050-7433)
**PHONE** ............................ 815 544-9100
Steve Seabold, *Manager*
**EMP:** 25
**SALES (corp-wide):** 15.7MM  **Privately Held**
**SIC:** 3273  Ready-mixed concrete
**PA:** Super Mix, Inc.
5435 Bull Valley Rd # 130
Mchenry IL 60050
815 578-9100

### (G-14562)
### SUPER MIX INC (PA)
Also Called: Negative
5435 Bull Valley Rd # 130  (60050-7433)
**PHONE** ............................ 815 578-9100
Jack Pease, *President*
Thomas Ziemba, *General Mgr*
Tory Pease, *Principal*
Margaret Bower, *Accounting Mgr*
Shelly Denkov, *Manager*
**EMP:** 57
**SALES (est):** 15.7MM  **Privately Held**
**SIC:** 3273  Ready-mixed concrete

### (G-14563)
### SUPER MIX CONCRETE LLC
5435 Bull Valley Rd # 130  (60050-7433)
**PHONE** ............................ 262 742-2892
**EMP:** 4
**SALES (est):** 177.1K  **Privately Held**
**SIC:** 3273  Ready-mixed concrete

### (G-14564)
### SUPER MIX OF WISCONSIN INC
5435 Bull Valley Rd # 130  (60050-7433)
**PHONE** ............................ 262 859-9000
Robert Epping, *President*
**EMP:** 3
**SALES (est):** 357K  **Privately Held**
**SIC:** 3272  Concrete products, precast

### (G-14565)
### SUPER MIX OF WISCONSIN INC
5435 Bull Valley Rd # 130  (60050-7433)
**PHONE** ............................ 815 578-9100
Jack Pease, *President*
Michael Anderson, *Principal*
Margaret Bower, *Accounting Mgr*
**EMP:** 12
**SALES (est):** 1.8MM  **Privately Held**
**SIC:** 3273  Ready-mixed concrete

### (G-14566)
### T AND T CABINET CO
5505 W Chasefield Cir  (60050-5134)
**PHONE** ............................ 815 245-6322
Mike Heinz, *Owner*
**EMP:** 3
**SALES (est):** 241.6K  **Privately Held**
**SIC:** 2434  Wood kitchen cabinets

### (G-14567)
### T J VAN DER BOSCH & ASSOCIATES
430 W Wegner Rd  (60051-8653)
P.O. Box 340, Wauconda (60084-0340)
**PHONE** ............................ 815 344-3210
**Fax:** 815 344-3211
Thomas J Van Der Bosch, *President*
Cornelia M Van Der Bosch, *Treasurer*
**EMP:** 20
**SQ FT:** 15,000
**SALES (est):** 1.3MM  **Privately Held**
**SIC:** 3711 3714 3088 2522  Automobile bodies, passenger car, not including engine, etc.; motor vehicle parts & accessories; plastics plumbing fixtures; office furniture, except wood

### (G-14568)
### VANDERBOSCH TJ & ASSOC INC
1614 S River Rd  (60051-9251)
**PHONE** ............................ 815 344-3210
Thomas Der Bosch, *President*
**EMP:** 3
**SALES (est):** 243.6K  **Privately Held**
**SIC:** 3711  Automobile bodies, passenger car, not including engine, etc.

### (G-14569)
### VESTERGAARD COMPANY INC (PA)
1721 Oak Dr  (60050-0306)
P.O. Box 280 (60051-9004)
**PHONE** ............................ 815 759-9102
**Fax:** 815 759-9103
Godfrey Vestergaard, *President*
Stefan Vestergaard, *Vice Pres*
Brock Crocker, *Manager*
**EMP:** 6
**SQ FT:** 10,000
**SALES (est):** 549.7K  **Privately Held**
**WEB:** www.g-vestergaard.com
**SIC:** 3728  Aircraft parts & equipment

### (G-14570)
### W M PLASTICS INC
Also Called: Novation Industries
5151 Bolger Ct  (60050-7015)
**PHONE** ............................ 815 578-8888
**Fax:** 815 639-8096
Chris Metz, *Ch of Bd*
Scott Baxter, *President*
David Butt, *President*
John Snyder, *President*
Scott A Baxter, *COO*
▲ **EMP:** 87  **EST:** 1966
**SQ FT:** 105,000
**SALES (est):** 30.4MM  **Privately Held**
**WEB:** www.wmplastics.com
**SIC:** 3089  Injection molding of plastics

### (G-14571)
### WIRFS INDUSTRIES INC
4021 Main St  (60050-5244)
P.O. Box 2049 (60051-9034)
**PHONE** ............................ 815 344-0635
**Fax:** 815 344-0635
Timothy Wirfs, *President*
Marita Buss, *Office Mgr*
**EMP:** 10
**SQ FT:** 6,500
**SALES (est):** 1.4MM  **Privately Held**
**SIC:** 7538 7692 3444  General truck repair; welding repair; sheet metalwork

## Mchenry
### Mchenry County

### (G-14572)
### WORTH DOOR COMPANY
Also Called: Moving Up Garage Door Company
4203 W Orleans St  (60050-3999)
**PHONE** ............................ 877 379-4947
Chris Filskov, *President*
**EMP:** 5  **EST:** 2012
**SALES (est):** 980.6K  **Privately Held**
**SIC:** 3674  Microprocessors

## McHenry
### Mchenry County

### (G-14573)
### WRIGHT TOOL & DIE INC
4829 Prime Pkwy  (60050-7002)
**PHONE** ............................ 815 669-2020
Dan Peterson, *President*
Lind Calabrese, *Manager*
**EMP:** 12
**SQ FT:** 9,000
**SALES (est):** 1.1MM  **Privately Held**
**WEB:** www.wrighttoolanddie.com
**SIC:** 3544  Forms (molds), for foundry & plastics working machinery; special dies & tools

## Mechanicsburg
### Sangamon County

### (G-14574)
### PRYCO INC (PA)
3rd And Garvey  (62545)
P.O. Box 108 (62545-0108)
**PHONE** ............................ 217 364-4467
**Fax:** 217 364-4494
Marjorie Bernhal, *President*
Marjorie Zeno-Bassard, *Vice Pres*
Rolla Womack, *CIO*
Marjorie Bernahl, *MIS Dir*
▼ **EMP:** 30
**SQ FT:** 30,000
**SALES (est):** 3.8MM  **Privately Held**
**SIC:** 3714 5661 3443  Fuel systems & parts, motor vehicle; men's boots; women's boots; fabricated plate work (boiler shop)

### (G-14575)
### QUANTUM HEALING
809 Timber Ridge Rd  (62545-8101)
**PHONE** ............................ 217 414-2412
Donna Kirby, *Principal*
**EMP:** 3
**SALES (est):** 171.9K  **Privately Held**
**SIC:** 3572  Computer storage devices

## Medinah
### Dupage County

### (G-14576)
### INGENIOUS CONCEPTS INC
22w313 Temple Dr  (60157-9707)
**PHONE** ............................ 630 539-8059
Robert L Cucchi, *President*
Karen Cucchi, *Vice Pres*
**EMP:** 3
**SQ FT:** 500
**SALES (est):** 281.7K  **Privately Held**
**SIC:** 8711 3542  Machine tool design; machine tools, metal forming type

## Melrose Park
### Cook County

### (G-14577)
### A & L CONSTRUCTION INC
1951 Cornell Ave  (60160-1001)
**PHONE** ............................ 708 343-1660

▲ = Import  ▼ = Export
◆ = Import/Export

# GEOGRAPHIC SECTION

Melrose Park - Cook County (G-14603)

Fax: 708 343-4014
Angela Cook, *CEO*
Brice Schweitzer, *Real Est Agnt*
**EMP:** 30
**SALES (est):** 3.9MM **Privately Held**
**WEB:** www.alconcrete.com
**SIC:** 3273 Ready-mixed concrete

**(G-14578)**
**A & Z SAS EXPRESS INC**
3051 Lee St (60164-1240)
**PHONE**...................847 451-0851
Zbigniew Sasinowski, *President*
**EMP:** 2
**SALES (est):** 215.9K **Privately Held**
**SIC:** 3715 Truck trailers

**(G-14579)**
**A-1 TOOL CORPORATION**
1425 Armitage Ave Ste 2 (60160-1424)
**PHONE**...................708 345-5000
Fax: 708 345-2089
Geoffrey Luther, *President*
Michael Schillaci, *Project Mgr*
Monica Lucero, *Purch Agent*
Tom Otoole, *Chief Engr*
Ken Trenhaile, *Engineer*
▲ **EMP:** 80
**SQ FT:** 50,000
**SALES (est):** 17MM
**SALES (corp-wide):** 43.4MM **Privately Held**
**WEB:** www.a1toolco.com
**SIC:** 3544 Forms (molds), for foundry & plastics working machinery
**PA:** Triangle Tool Corporation
8609 W Port Ave
Milwaukee WI 53224
414 357-7117

**(G-14580)**
**ABLE BARMILLING & MFG CO INC**
1310 Main St (60160-4020)
**PHONE**...................708 343-5666
Fax: 708 343-5668
Ronald Spears, *President*
Laura Spears, *Vice Pres*
Kristin Kaese, *Manager*
**EMP:** 10
**SQ FT:** 10,000
**SALES (est):** 1.7MM **Privately Held**
**WEB:** www.ablebar.com
**SIC:** 3469 Machine parts, stamped or pressed metal

**(G-14581)**
**ABOVE & BEYOND BLACK OXIDING**
1029 N 27th Ave (60160-2940)
P.O. Box 1724 (60161-1724)
**PHONE**...................708 345-7100
Fax: 708 345-7148
Jack Cooper, *President*
**EMP:** 4
**SALES (est):** 487.7K **Privately Held**
**SIC:** 3541 Brushing machines (metalworking machinery)

**(G-14582)**
**ABRAXIS BIOSCIENCE LLC**
2020 N Ruby St (60160-1112)
**PHONE**...................310 883-1300
Barbara Relation, *Branch Mgr*
**EMP:** 4
**SALES (corp-wide):** 11.2B **Publicly Held**
**SIC:** 2834 Pharmaceutical preparations
**HQ:** Abraxis Bioscience, Llc
11755 Wilshire Blvd Fl 20
Los Angeles CA 90025

**(G-14583)**
**ACCRO PRECISION GRINDING INC**
2080 N Hawthorne Ave (60160-1174)
**PHONE**...................708 681-0520
Fax: 708 681-0567
Marshall Klenske, *President*
Kristin Klenske, *Vice Pres*
**EMP:** 8 **EST:** 1964
**SQ FT:** 10,000
**SALES (est):** 600K **Privately Held**
**SIC:** 3599 Machine shop, jobbing & repair

**(G-14584)**
**ACCU-CHEM INDUSTRIES INC**
1930 George St Ste 3 (60160-1501)
**PHONE**...................708 344-0900
Richard Ponx, *President*
**EMP:** 3
**SQ FT:** 12,000
**SALES:** 1.5MM **Privately Held**
**SIC:** 3555 Printing trades machinery

**(G-14585)**
**ALIN MACHINING COMPANY INC (PA)**
Also Called: Power Plant Services
3131 W Soffel Ave (60160-1718)
**PHONE**...................708 681-1043
Fax: 708 345-9181
Manish Gandhi, *CEO*
Philip Sexauer, *President*
Sanjay Shah, *Business Mgr*
Jozef Kyezel, *Vice Pres*
Richard Phillips, *Vice Pres*
▲ **EMP:** 130
**SQ FT:** 100,000
**SALES:** 50MM **Privately Held**
**WEB:** www.ppsvcs.com
**SIC:** 3621 Electric motor & generator parts; power generators; electric motor & generator auxillary parts

**(G-14586)**
**ALL AMERICAN CHEMICAL CO INC**
1701 N 33rd Ave (60160-1707)
**PHONE**...................847 297-2840
Samuel J Saltzman, *President*
▲ **EMP:** 23
**SQ FT:** 18,000
**SALES (est):** 6.4MM **Privately Held**
**WEB:** www.allamericanchemical.com
**SIC:** 2899 Chemical preparations

**(G-14587)**
**ALL STYLE AWNING CORPORATION**
2100 W Lake St Ste A (60160-3649)
**PHONE**...................708 343-2323
Fax: 708 343-2343
Richard Jeskey, *President*
Gloria Jeskey, *Admin Sec*
**EMP:** 2 **EST:** 1959
**SQ FT:** 2,000
**SALES:** 275K **Privately Held**
**WEB:** www.allstyleawning.com
**SIC:** 5999 3444 3442 Awnings; sheet metalwork; metal doors, sash & trim

**(G-14588)**
**ALLOY WELDING CORP**
2033 Janice Ave (60160-1076)
**PHONE**...................708 345-6756
Fax: 708 345-6776
John Troccoli, *President*
Mark Nausieda, *Design Engr*
Kathy Hicks, *Manager*
Santo Urso, *Shareholder*
Elizabeth Schultz, *Admin Sec*
**EMP:** 30
**SQ FT:** 35,000
**SALES (est):** 5.8MM **Privately Held**
**WEB:** www.alloywelding.com
**SIC:** 3444 7692 Sheet metalwork; welding repair

**(G-14589)**
**ALM DISTRIBUTORS LLC**
Also Called: Racconto
2060 Janice Ave (60160-1011)
**PHONE**...................708 865-8000
Andrea J Mugnolo, *Mng Member*
Steve Listecki,
Lee Mugnolo,
▲ **EMP:** 3
**SALES (est):** 606.3K **Privately Held**
**SIC:** 2032 Italian foods: packaged in cans, jars, etc.

**(G-14590)**
**ALOIS BOX CO INC**
2000 N Mannheim Rd (60160-1092)
**PHONE**...................708 681-4090
Fax: 708 681-4389
David G Jones, *President*
Bruna J Granato, *Vice Pres*
George Hurd, *Purchasing*

**EMP:** 50 **EST:** 1953
**SQ FT:** 55,000
**SALES (est):** 13.8MM **Privately Held**
**WEB:** www.aloisbox.com
**SIC:** 2653 Boxes, corrugated: made from purchased materials; display items, corrugated: made from purchased materials

**(G-14591)**
**ALRO STEEL CORPORATION**
Also Called: Alro Group
4501 James Pl (60160-1006)
**PHONE**...................708 202-3200
Al Glick, *CEO*
**EMP:** 30
**SALES (corp-wide):** 1.6B **Privately Held**
**SIC:** 1099 Aluminum & beryllium ores mining
**PA:** Alro Steel Corporation
3100 E High St
Jackson MI 49203
517 787-5500

**(G-14592)**
**ALTERNATIVE TECHNOLOGIES**
123 N 10th Ave (60160-4142)
P.O. Box 831, Bensenville (60106-0831)
**PHONE**...................888 858-4678
Dean Myer, *President*
Alton Files, *Business Anlyst*
Jonathan Siegle, *Director*
**EMP:** 7
**SQ FT:** 10,000
**SALES:** 600K **Privately Held**
**WEB:** www.delta-equipment.com
**SIC:** 3621 Generating apparatus & parts, electrical

**(G-14593)**
**AMERICAN STEEL FABRICATORS INC**
1985 Anson Dr (60160-1018)
**PHONE**...................847 807-4200
Mary Ann Parker, *President*
Terry Stoll, *Director*
**EMP:** 11 **EST:** 2005
**SQ FT:** 1,500
**SALES (est):** 4.7MM **Privately Held**
**SIC:** 5051 3449 Structural shapes, iron or steel; miscellaneous metalwork

**(G-14594)**
**AP MACHINE INC**
1975 N 17th Ave (60160-1348)
**PHONE**...................708 450-1010
Peter Konieczny, *CEO*
**EMP:** 19
**SALES (est):** 3.3MM **Privately Held**
**WEB:** www.apmachine.com
**SIC:** 3599 Machine & other job shop work

**(G-14595)**
**APACHE SUPPLY**
324 La Porte Ave (60164-1713)
**PHONE**...................708 409-1040
Douglas Macpherson, *Owner*
▲ **EMP:** 3
**SALES:** 100K **Privately Held**
**SIC:** 3631 Barbecues, grills & braziers (outdoor cooking)

**(G-14596)**
**ATHENIAN FOODS CO**
Also Called: Athenian Pastries & Food
1814 N 15th Ave (60160-2112)
**PHONE**...................708 343-6700
Kostas Thanopoulos, *President*
Bobby Thanopoulos, *Manager*
Polyxeni Thanopoulos, *Admin Sec*
**EMP:** 10
**SALES (est):** 4.2MM **Privately Held**
**SIC:** 5149 5461 2099 2051 Bakery products; bakeries; food preparations; bread, cake & related products

**(G-14597)**
**AUTOMATION SYSTEMS INC**
2001 N 17th Ave (60160-1347)
**PHONE**...................847 671-9515
Fax: 847 671-1241
Carl Schanstra, *President*
Jim Menendez, *Vice Pres*
Hart Boyajian, *Plant Mgr*
Jim Lentz, *QC Dir*
Jim Elarde, *Finance Mgr*
**EMP:** 20 **EST:** 1960

**SQ FT:** 12,000
**SALES (est):** 3.2MM **Privately Held**
**SIC:** 8711 3569 3451 3549 Designing; ship, boat, machine & product; assembly machines, non-metalworking; screw machine products; metalworking machinery

**(G-14598)**
**AVLON INDUSTRIES INC**
1999 N 15th Ave (60160-1402)
**PHONE**...................708 344-0709
Ali N Syed, *President*
Tomasz Lachiewicz, *Purchasing*
Jasmine Mathew, *Research*
Gilles Verboom, *Research*
Khadijeh Saad, *Engineer*
◆ **EMP:** 90
**SQ FT:** 60,000
**SALES (est):** 56.7MM **Privately Held**
**WEB:** www.avlon.com
**SIC:** 5122 2844 5131 Cosmetics; hair preparations; toilet preparations; hair preparations, including shampoos; piece goods & notions

**(G-14599)**
**BALEY ENTERPRISES INC**
1206 N 31st Ave (60160-2969)
**PHONE**...................708 681-0900
Fax: 708 544-3204
James Baley, *President*
Jim Baley, *Owner*
Norma Baley, *Corp Secy*
**EMP:** 5
**SQ FT:** 6,000
**SALES:** 750K **Privately Held**
**SIC:** 3599 5084 7692 Machine shop, jobbing & repair; industrial machinery & equipment; welding repair

**(G-14600)**
**BILLY CASH FOR GOLD INC**
101 N 19th Ave (60160-3702)
**PHONE**...................773 905-2447
Aqel Harb, *Owner*
**EMP:** 3
**SALES (est):** 149.1K **Privately Held**
**SIC:** 1041 Gold ores

**(G-14601)**
**BODYCOTE THERMAL PROC INC**
1975 N Ruby St (60160-1109)
**PHONE**...................708 236-5360
Tim Veenbaas, *Branch Mgr*
William Iancau, *Director*
**EMP:** 63
**SQ FT:** 150,000
**SALES (corp-wide):** 739.3MM **Privately Held**
**SIC:** 3398 Metal heat treating
**HQ:** Bodycote Thermal Processing, Inc.
12700 Park Central Dr # 700
Dallas TX 75251
214 904-2420

**(G-14602)**
**BORGWARNER TRANSM SYSTEMS INC**
2437 W North Ave (60160-1120)
**PHONE**...................708 731-4540
Darlene Baldridge, *Branch Mgr*
**EMP:** 19
**SALES (corp-wide):** 9B **Publicly Held**
**SIC:** 3694 Distributors, motor vehicle engine
**HQ:** Borgwarner Transmission Systems Inc.
3800 Automation Ave # 500
Auburn Hills MI 48326
248 754-9200

**(G-14603)**
**BOST CORPORATION**
Also Called: Tax Collector
2780 Thomas St (60160-2900)
**PHONE**...................708 450-9234
Fax: 708 450-1241
Stefan Kiminski, *Manager*
**EMP:** 10
**SALES (corp-wide):** 5.2MM **Privately Held**
**SIC:** 3564 Blowers & fans
**PA:** Bost Corporation
601 Saint Charles Rd
Maywood IL 60153
708 344-7023

# Melrose Park - Cook County (G-14604)   GEOGRAPHIC SECTION

**(G-14604)**
**BOYCE INDUSTRIES INC**
4915 Division St (60160-2653)
PHONE.................................708 345-0455
Fax: 708 345-0476
Robert L Boyce, *President*
Donna Lawver, *Manager*
EMP: 13
SQ FT: 10,000
SALES: 1.3MM **Privately Held**
SIC: 3498 3714 Tube fabricating (contract bending & shaping); motor vehicle parts & accessories; frames, motor vehicle; exhaust systems & parts, motor vehicle

**(G-14605)**
**CARTERS INC**
1312 Winston Plz (60160-1508)
PHONE.................................708 345-6680
EMP: 9
SALES (corp-wide): 3.2B **Publicly Held**
SIC: 2361 Girls' & children's dresses, blouses & shirts
PA: Carter's, Inc.
3438 Peachtree Rd Ne # 1800
Atlanta GA 30326
678 791-1000

**(G-14606)**
**CATCHING HYDRAULICS CO LTD**
1733 N 25th Ave (60160-1823)
PHONE.................................708 344-2334
Inderjit Sundal, *President*
Juanita B Sundal, *Corp Secy*
Ronald Arreola, *Engineer*
EMP: 20
SQ FT: 1,000
SALES: 1MM **Privately Held**
WEB: www.catchingengineering.com
SIC: 3593 3494 3511 Fluid power cylinders, hydraulic or pneumatic; plumbing & heating valves; turbines & turbine generator sets

**(G-14607)**
**CELGENE CORPORATION**
2045 Cornell Ave (60160-1002)
PHONE.................................908 673-9000
Brooke Raphael, *Business Mgr*
Mitchall Clark, *Senior VP*
Joseph Hogan, *Vice Pres*
Joseph Ivan, *Opers Mgmr*
Amar Singh, *Treasurer*
EMP: 20
SALES (corp-wide): 11.2B **Publicly Held**
SIC: 2834 Pharmaceutical preparations
PA: Celgene Corporation
86 Morris Ave
Summit NJ 07901
908 673-9000

**(G-14608)**
**CHASE FASTENERS INC**
1539 N 25th Ave (60160-1821)
PHONE.................................708 345-0335
Fax: 708 345-9462
Kennith Chadwick, *CEO*
EMP: 40
SQ FT: 40,000
SALES (est): 9.1MM **Privately Held**
WEB: www.chasefasteners.com
SIC: 3316 3451 3452 5085 Cold finishing of steel shapes; screw machine products; screws, metal; industrial supplies

**(G-14609)**
**CHICAGO ENCLOSURES**
1975 N 17th Ave (60160-1348)
PHONE.................................708 344-6600
Angela P Caulfield, *Principal*
EMP: 4
SALES (est): 604.6K **Privately Held**
SIC: 3448 Screen enclosures

**(G-14610)**
**CHICAGO GRINDING & MACHINE CO**
1950 N 15th Ave (60160-1403)
PHONE.................................708 681-4087
Fax: 708 681-4087
Leonard D Kreplin, *Principal*
Glen Micek, *Site Mgr*
Mike Kreplin, *CFO*
EMP: 47 EST: 1920
SQ FT: 22,000
SALES (est): 8.8MM **Privately Held**
WEB: www.chicagogrinding.com
SIC: 3599 3541 3441 3423 Machine shop, jobbing & repair; machine tools, metal cutting type; fabricated structural metal; hand & edge tools

**(G-14611)**
**CONSUMERS PACKING CO INC**
1301 Carson Dr (60160-2970)
PHONE.................................708 344-0047
William Schutz, *President*
EMP: 73 EST: 1953
SQ FT: 14,000
SALES (est): 45.2MM **Privately Held**
WEB: www.consumerspacking.com
SIC: 5147 5812 2013 2011 Meats & meat products; eating places; sausages & other prepared meats; meat packing plants

**(G-14612)**
**CSL PLASMA INC**
1977 N Mannheim Rd (60160-1012)
PHONE.................................708 343-8845
Veartis Phillips, *Training Spec*
EMP: 44
SALES (corp-wide): 5.9B **Privately Held**
SIC: 2836 Plasmas
HQ: Csl Plasma Inc.
900 Broken Sound Pkwy # 4
Boca Raton FL 33487
561 981-3700

**(G-14613)**
**CURTO-LIGONIER FOUNDRIES CO**
1215 N 31st Ave (60160-2905)
PHONE.................................708 345-2250
Fax: 708 345-1184
Mark Borneman, *President*
Robert Krencik, *Vice Pres*
Darleen Helig, *Manager*
Holly N Borneman, *Admin Sec*
Stephen Payne, *Admin Sec*
EMP: 50 EST: 1946
SQ FT: 40,000
SALES: 6MM **Privately Held**
SIC: 3364 3365 3363 3543 Magnesium & magnesium-base alloy die-castings; aluminum foundries; aluminum die-castings; industrial patterns; nonferrous foundries

**(G-14614)**
**DELAIR PUBLISHING COMPANY INC**
2085 Cornell Ave (60160-1002)
PHONE.................................708 345-7000
Dan P Genovese, *President*
Ralph P Genovese, *President*
Mike Leaver, *Purch Mgr*
Robert Flatow, *Admin Sec*
EMP: 250
SALES (est): 11.7MM **Privately Held**
SIC: 2731 Books: publishing only

**(G-14615)**
**DEMCO INC**
2975 W Soffel Ave (60160-1714)
PHONE.................................708 345-4822
Fax: 708 681-2547
Daniel Spata, *President*
Tara Dee, *Manager*
EMP: 10
SQ FT: 4,500
SALES (est): 1MM **Privately Held**
SIC: 3444 Sheet metalwork; metal ventilating equipment

**(G-14616)**
**DETREX CORPORATION**
Solvents & Envmtl Svcs Div
2537 W Le Moyne St (60160-1830)
PHONE.................................708 345-3806
Fax: 708 345-3903
David Cody, *Branch Mgr*
EMP: 5
SALES (corp-wide): 58.3MM **Publicly Held**
WEB: www.detrex.com
SIC: 3589 2842 Commercial cleaning equipment; drain pipe solvents or cleaners
PA: Detrex Corporation
1000 Belt Line Ave
Cleveland OH 44109

**(G-14617)**
**DIAMOND BLAST CORPORATION**
1741 N 30th Ave (60160-1787)
PHONE.................................708 681-2640
Fax: 708 681-0390
David Collignon, *President*
Bob Bulgarelli, *General Mgr*
EMP: 13 EST: 1958
SQ FT: 11,000
SALES (est): 1.8MM **Privately Held**
WEB: www.diamondblast.com
SIC: 3471 Cleaning & descaling metal products

**(G-14618)**
**DIESEL RADIATOR CO (PA)**
1990 Janice Ave (60160-1077)
PHONE.................................708 345-2839
Brian P Cahill, *President*
Humberto Suarez, *Principal*
Lisa Burkhart, *Vice Pres*
Brian Light, *CFO*
◆ EMP: 40
SQ FT: 18,000
SALES (est): 28.9MM **Privately Held**
SIC: 3519 Radiators, stationary engine

**(G-14619)**
**DIESEL RADIATOR CO**
3030 W Hirsch St (60160-1793)
PHONE.................................708 865-7299
Wayne Gorham, *Manager*
EMP: 75
SALES (corp-wide): 28.9MM **Privately Held**
SIC: 3443 3519 Air coolers, metal plate; radiators, stationary engine
PA: Diesel Radiator Co.
1990 Janice Ave
Melrose Park IL 60160
708 345-2839

**(G-14620)**
**DIVERSIFIED CNSTR SVCS LLC**
Also Called: DCS
2001 Cornell Ave (60160-1029)
PHONE.................................708 344-4900
Franklin Colon, *Mng Member*
EMP: 5 EST: 2008
SALES: 698.8K **Privately Held**
SIC: 5082 8711 3444 Scaffolding; engineering services; canopies; sheet metal

**(G-14621)**
**DOUBLE-DISC GRINDING CORP**
2041 Janice Ave (60160-1010)
PHONE.................................708 410-1770
Mike Patel, *Principal*
James Gallos, *Exec VP*
EMP: 11
SQ FT: 17,000
SALES (est): 1.6MM **Privately Held**
SIC: 3599 Machine shop, jobbing & repair

**(G-14622)**
**DUNE MANUFACTURING COMPANY**
1800 N 15th Ave (60160-2112)
PHONE.................................708 681-2905
Fax: 708 681-2907
Denis Colht, *President*
EMP: 10 EST: 1980
SQ FT: 12,500
SALES (est): 1.8MM **Privately Held**
SIC: 3451 Screw machine products

**(G-14623)**
**DYNAMIC MANUFACTURING INC (PA)**
1930 N Mannheim Rd (60160-1013)
PHONE.................................708 343-8753
Fax: 708 343-8768
Nancy Partipilo, *President*
Tony Falco, *General Mgr*
John Paukovits, *General Mgr*
Gary R Noel, *Chairman*
Tony Partipilo, *Exec VP*
▲ EMP: 70
SQ FT: 14,000
SALES (est): 151.2MM **Privately Held**
WEB: www.dmimail.com
SIC: 3714 Transmissions, motor vehicle

**(G-14624)**
**DYNAMIC MANUFACTURING INC**
1800 N 30th Ave Ste 1 (60160-1700)
PHONE.................................708 681-0682
Fax: 708 345-5246
Dominic Bellantuono, *Empl Rel Mgr*
Beronica Garibay, *Human Resources*
Mark Woday, *Branch Mgr*
Chad Richardson, *Senior Mgr*
EMP: 85
SALES (corp-wide): 151.2MM **Privately Held**
SIC: 3714 Transmissions, motor vehicle
PA: Dynamic Manufacturing Inc
1930 N Mannheim Rd
Melrose Park IL 60160
708 343-8753

**(G-14625)**
**DYNAMIC MANUFACTURING INC**
Also Called: Dynamic Mfg Torque Converters
1930 N Mannheim Rd (60160-1013)
PHONE.................................708 343-8753
Gary Noel, *Branch Mgr*
EMP: 36
SALES (corp-wide): 151.2MM **Privately Held**
WEB: www.dmimail.com
SIC: 3714 Transmissions, motor vehicle
PA: Dynamic Manufacturing Inc
1930 N Mannheim Rd
Melrose Park IL 60160
708 343-8753

**(G-14626)**
**DYNAMIC MANUFACTURING INC**
1801 N 32nd Ave (60160-1043)
PHONE.................................708 343-8753
Fax: 708 343-5843
Dale Nickos, *Engineer*
Tony Falco, *Manager*
Rocky Primavera, *Manager*
EMP: 29
SALES (corp-wide): 151.2MM **Privately Held**
WEB: www.dmimail.com
SIC: 4225 3566 General warehousing & storage; speed changers, drives & gears
PA: Dynamic Manufacturing Inc
1930 N Mannheim Rd
Melrose Park IL 60160
708 343-8753

**(G-14627)**
**ECONOMIC PLASTIC COATING INC**
Also Called: Economic Coating
1829 Gardner Rd (60160)
P.O. Box 254, Winfield (60190-0254)
PHONE.................................708 343-2216
Fax: 708 343-2218
Christos Marinos, *President*
Sophia Langguth, *Office Mgr*
EMP: 16
SQ FT: 46,500
SALES (est): 1.4MM **Privately Held**
SIC: 3479 Coating of metals with plastic or resins

**(G-14628)**
**ECONOMY IRON INC**
3132 W Hirsch St (60160-1741)
PHONE.................................708 343-1777
Fax: 708 343-1816
Donna Johnston, *President*
Dan Johnston, *Vice Pres*
EMP: 15
SQ FT: 6,000
SALES (est): 1MM **Privately Held**
WEB: www.economyiron.com
SIC: 3312 3496 3446 Hot-rolled iron & steel products; miscellaneous fabricated wire products; architectural metalwork

**(G-14629)**
**EDGEWATER PRODUCTS COMPANY INC**
3315 W North Ave (60160-1016)
P.O. Box 8484 (60161-8484)
PHONE.................................708 345-9200
Fax: 708 345-5446
Edward D Rolf, *President*

▲ = Import ▼ = Export
◆ = Import/Export

# GEOGRAPHIC SECTION

## Melrose Park - Cook County (G-14653)

Dave Rolf, *VP Sales*
Bob Smith, *Manager*
Lois J Rolf, *Admin Sec*
▲ **EMP:** 18 **EST:** 1947
**SQ FT:** 14,000
**SALES (est):** 3.2MM **Privately Held**
**WEB:** www.edgewaterproducts.com
**SIC:** 3069 2499 Rubber hardware; washers, rubber; cork & cork products

### (G-14630)
### EDGEWELL PER CARE BRANDS LLC
5000 Proviso Dr (60163-1360)
**PHONE**.................................708 544-5550
Sue Eggersdorfer, *Manager*
**EMP:** 300
**SALES (corp-wide):** 2.3B **Publicly Held**
**WEB:** www.eveready.com
**SIC:** 3421 Razor blades & razors
**HQ:** Edgewell Personal Care Brands, Llc
6 Research Dr
Shelton CT 06484
203 944-5500

### (G-14631)
### EJ SOMERVILLE PLATING CO
Also Called: E J Somerville
1305 N 31st Ave (60160-2907)
**PHONE**.................................708 345-5100
**Fax:** 708 345-5102
Ralph Hauslein, *President*
Randy Hauslein, *Corp Secy*
Lori Cushion, *Bookkeeper*
**EMP:** 9 **EST:** 1955
**SQ FT:** 6,000
**SALES:** 800K **Privately Held**
**SIC:** 3471 Chromium plating of metals or formed products

### (G-14632)
### ELM TOOL AND MANUFACTURING CO
10257 Dickens Ave (60164-1912)
**PHONE**.................................847 455-6805
**EMP:** 3
**SALES (est):** 180K **Privately Held**
**SIC:** 3544 Mfg Dies/Tools/Jigs/Fixtures

### (G-14633)
### EN-CHRO PLATING INC
2755 W Lake St (60160-3041)
**PHONE**.................................708 450-1250
**Fax:** 708 681-6393
Milan Pecharich, *President*
▲ **EMP:** 50
**SQ FT:** 85,000
**SALES (est):** 6.5MM **Privately Held**
**WEB:** www.enchro.com
**SIC:** 3471 Electroplating of metals or formed products

### (G-14634)
### ENVIRO TECH INTERNATIONAL INC
1800 N 25th Ave (60160-1869)
**PHONE**.................................708 343-6641
**Fax:** 708 343-4633
Rich Morford, *CEO*
Salvatore Lamantia, *President*
▲ **EMP:** 9
**SALES (est):** 3.1MM **Privately Held**
**WEB:** www.ensolv.com
**SIC:** 2899 Chemical preparations

### (G-14635)
### FANNIE MAY CNFCTONS BRANDS INC (HQ)
Also Called: Fannie May Fine Chocolate
2457 W North Ave (60160-1120)
**PHONE**.................................773 693-9100
**Fax:** 773 693-9600
David Taiclet, *CEO*
Terry Mitchell, *President*
Alan Petrik, *COO*
Cheryl Philips, *Human Res Mgr*
Jamie Turner, *Accounts Mgr*
**EMP:** 15
**SALES (est):** 146MM
**SALES (corp-wide):** 156.7MM **Privately Held**
**SIC:** 2064 5441 Candy & other confectionery products; candy, nut & confectionery stores

**PA:** Ferrero International Sa
Rue De Treves
Sandweiler
349 711-1

### (G-14636)
### FASTRON CO
2040 Janice Ave (60160-1011)
**PHONE**.................................630 766-5000
**Fax:** 630 766-6251
Tracy Martin, *President*
▲ **EMP:** 25 **EST:** 1942
**SQ FT:** 40,000
**SALES (est):** 5.6MM **Privately Held**
**WEB:** www.fastron.com
**SIC:** 3452 Screws, metal; bolts, metal

### (G-14637)
### FEDEX OFFICE & PRINT SVCS INC
2509 W North Ave (60160-1121)
**PHONE**.................................708 345-0984
**Fax:** 708 345-0995
**EMP:** 6
**SALES (corp-wide):** 50.3B **Publicly Held**
**SIC:** 2752 Commercial printing, lithographic
**HQ:** Fedex Office And Print Services, Inc.
7900 Legacy Dr
Plano TX 75024
214 550-7000

### (G-14638)
### FEEDER CORPORATION OF AMERICA
4429 James Pl (60160-1004)
**PHONE**.................................708 343-4900
**Fax:** 708 343-0057
Theodore Francis Jr, *President*
Pat E Francis, *Vice Pres*
Katherine Zell, *Office Mgr*
**EMP:** 10 **EST:** 1965
**SQ FT:** 5,000
**SALES (est):** 890K **Privately Held**
**SIC:** 3523 3549 Feed grinders, crushers & mixers; assembly machines, including robotic

### (G-14639)
### FOREST ELECTRIC COMPANY
Also Called: Felco
1301 Armitage Ave Ste B (60160-1423)
**PHONE**.................................708 681-0180
**Fax:** 708 681-0609
Charles C Meeks Jr, *President*
Alan Spindler, *General Mgr*
EER Loof, *Principal*
Carmen Rompala, *Purchasing*
Jorge Alvarez, *Engrg Mgr*
**EMP:** 22 **EST:** 1946
**SQ FT:** 25,000
**SALES (est):** 4.6MM
**SALES (corp-wide):** 757.7MM **Publicly Held**
**WEB:** www.forestelectric.com
**SIC:** 3677 3612 Electronic coils, transformers & other inductors; transformers, except electric
**HQ:** Kemet Electronics Corporation
2835 Kemet Way
Simpsonville SC 29681
864 963-6700

### (G-14640)
### FRESENIUS KABI USA INC
2020 N Ruby St (60160-1112)
**PHONE**.................................708 450-7500
Steve Weltler, *Manager*
**EMP:** 400
**SALES (corp-wide):** 31.1B **Privately Held**
**WEB:** www.appdrugs.com
**SIC:** 5122 2834 Pharmaceuticals; pharmaceutical preparations
**HQ:** Fresenius Kabi Usa, Inc.
3 Corporate Dr Ste 300
Lake Zurich IL 60047
847 969-2700

### (G-14641)
### FRESENIUS KABI USA INC
2020 N Ruby St (60160-1112)
**PHONE**.................................708 410-4761
Joanna Jablonski, *Engineer*
Virgil Derencius, *Branch Mgr*
Steve Weltler, *Manager*
**EMP:** 166

**SALES (corp-wide):** 31.1B **Privately Held**
**SIC:** 2834 Pharmaceutical preparations
**HQ:** Fresenius Kabi Usa, Inc.
3 Corporate Dr Ste 300
Lake Zurich IL 60047
847 969-2700

### (G-14642)
### FRESENIUS KABI USA INC
2020 N Ruby St (60160-1112)
**PHONE**.................................708 450-7509
Steven Nowicki, *Vice Pres*
John Fitzgerald, *Site Mgr*
Bobby Grigoropoulos, *QC Mgr*
James Akstulewicz, *Manager*
Eric Hernandez, *Controller*
**EMP:** 166
**SALES (corp-wide):** 31.1B **Privately Held**
**SIC:** 2834 Pharmaceutical preparations
**HQ:** Fresenius Kabi Usa, Inc.
3 Corporate Dr Ste 300
Lake Zurich IL 60047
847 969-2700

### (G-14643)
### FRESENIUS KABI USA INC
American Pharmaceutical
2020 N Ruby St (60160-1112)
**PHONE**.................................708 345-6170
**Fax:** 708 450-7563
Sam Trippie, *Principal*
Peter Ponterio, *Training Spec*
**EMP:** 200
**SALES (corp-wide):** 31.1B **Privately Held**
**WEB:** www.appdrugs.com
**SIC:** 2834 Pharmaceutical preparations
**HQ:** Fresenius Kabi Usa, Inc.
3 Corporate Dr Ste 300
Lake Zurich IL 60047
847 969-2700

### (G-14644)
### FRESENIUS KABI USA LLC
2045 Cornell Ave (60160-1002)
**PHONE**.................................708 343-6100
Steven Nowicki, *VP Mfg*
Malik Ali, *Opers Mgr*
Evan Darrow, *Research*
Agnes Fekete, *Manager*
Jianfeng Hong, *Manager*
**EMP:** 35
**SALES (corp-wide):** 31.1B **Privately Held**
**WEB:** www.appdrugs.com
**SIC:** 2834 Pharmaceutical preparations
**HQ:** Fresenius Kabi Usa, Llc
3 Corporate Dr Ste 300
Lake Zurich IL 60047
847 550-2300

### (G-14645)
### FRIGID FLUID COMPANY
11631 W Grand Ave (60164-1302)
**PHONE**.................................708 836-1215
**Fax:** 708 836-1247
Robert Yeazel, *President*
John Yeazel, *Principal*
Marilyn Yeazel, *Chairman*
▲ **EMP:** 30 **EST:** 1892
**SQ FT:** 40,400
**SALES (est):** 4.1MM **Privately Held**
**WEB:** www.frigidfluidco.com
**SIC:** 2869 5087 Embalming fluids; cemetery & funeral directors' equipment & supplies

### (G-14646)
### GENERAL MANUFACTURING LLC
1725 N 33rd Ave (60160-1707)
**PHONE**.................................708 345-8600
Shailja Gandhi, *CEO*
Earl Kaminski, *General Mgr*
Mike Netuik, *Principal*
Philip Sexauer, *Vice Pres*
Anthony McGee, *CFO*
▲ **EMP:** 70 **EST:** 2011
**SALES:** 16MM **Privately Held**
**SIC:** 3621 Motors & generators

### (G-14647)
### GLASS DIMENSIONS INC
Also Called: Extreme Glass
1942 N 15th Ave (60160-1403)
**PHONE**.................................708 410-2305
DOE Corsei, *President*
Haxsan Boyd, *Info Tech Mgr*

**EMP:** 15
**SALES (est):** 1.3MM **Privately Held**
**SIC:** 3231 Products of purchased glass

### (G-14648)
### GRAPHIC ARTS FINISHING COMPANY
Also Called: Gafco
1990 N Mannheim Rd (60160-1013)
**PHONE**.................................708 345-8484
**Fax:** 708 345-8494
William J Quinn, *President*
Mary Pat Quinn-Headley, *Corp Secy*
Robert D Quinn, *Vice Pres*
Dave Mikolajczak, *Cust Mgr*
Steve Souvannasot, *Accounts Exec*
▲ **EMP:** 51 **EST:** 1945
**SQ FT:** 57,500
**SALES (est):** 12.4MM **Privately Held**
**WEB:** www.GAFCO.com
**SIC:** 2675 Paper die-cutting; paperboard die-cutting

### (G-14649)
### GRO-MAR INDUSTRIES INC
2725 Thomas St (60160-2934)
P.O. Box 1649 (60161-1649)
**PHONE**.................................708 343-5901
George E Molitor, *President*
Parb Fultz, *Manager*
**EMP:** 18
**SQ FT:** 20,000
**SALES (est):** 4.6MM **Privately Held**
**SIC:** 2679 Paper products, converted

### (G-14650)
### H J M P CORP (HQ)
Also Called: Home Juice Co of Memphis
1930 George St Ste 2 (60160-1501)
**PHONE**.................................708 345-5370
Stan Sheraton, *President*
Mike Hoeppel, *President*
Allen Domzalski, *Vice Pres*
Alan Weinstein, *Project Mgr*
Jim Bodam, *Opers Staff*
**EMP:** 150
**SQ FT:** 65,000
**SALES (est):** 587.3MM
**SALES (corp-wide):** 704.7MM **Publicly Held**
**WEB:** www.nationalbeverage.com
**SIC:** 2033 5149 0174 2037 Fruit juices: packaged in cans, jars, etc.; beverages, except coffee & tea; juices; orange grove; frozen fruits & vegetables
**PA:** National Beverage Corp.
8100 Sw 10th St Ste 4000
Plantation FL 33324
954 581-0922

### (G-14651)
### HARRIS EQUIPMENT CORPORATION
2040 N Hawthorne Ave (60160-1106)
**PHONE**.................................708 343-0866
**Fax:** 708 343-0995
Gary Pollack, *President*
Phil Kruger, *General Mgr*
John Pearson, *Vice Pres*
Cindy Johnson, *Opers Mgr*
Ted Manzano, *Sales Engr*
◆ **EMP:** 42
**SALES (est):** 12.7MM **Privately Held**
**SIC:** 3563 Air & gas compressors

### (G-14652)
### HECKMANN BUILDING PRODUCTS INC
1501 N 31st Ave (60160-2911)
**PHONE**.................................708 865-2403
**Fax:** 708 865-2640
Paul M Curtis, *CEO*
Paul G Curtis, *President*
David Sanchez, *VP Mktg*
▲ **EMP:** 20
**SQ FT:** 45,000
**SALES (est):** 3.8MM **Privately Held**
**WEB:** www.heckmannbuildingprods.com
**SIC:** 3429 5039 Builders' hardware; joists

### (G-14653)
### HEF CORPORATION
2010 N Ruby St (60160-1112)
**PHONE**.................................708 343-0866
Gary Pollack, *President*

# Melrose Park - Cook County (G-14654)

Jeff Levin, *Vice Pres*
Walter McHugh, *Engineer*
Shaun Davis, *Manager*
Maria Dipierro, *Manager*
▲ **EMP**: 30
**SQ FT**: 25,000
**SALES (est)**: 5MM **Privately Held**
**WEB**: www.harrisequipment.com
**SIC**: 3443 5084 Fabricated plate work (boiler shop); industrial machinery & equipment

### (G-14654)
### HOME JUICE CORP
1930 George St Ste 2 (60160-1501)
**PHONE** .................... 708 681-2678
**EMP**: 5
**SALES (est)**: 2.9MM
**SALES (corp-wide)**: 704.7MM **Publicly Held**
**SIC**: 2086 Iced tea & fruit drinks, bottled & canned
**PA**: National Beverage Corp.
8100 Sw 10th St Ste 4000
Plantation FL 33324
954 581-0922

### (G-14655)
### IMPAC GROUP INC
1950 N Ruby St (60160-1110)
**PHONE** .................... 708 344-9100
Richard Block, *President*
**EMP**: 1526
**SALES (est)**: 63.4MM
**SALES (corp-wide)**: 14.1B **Publicly Held**
**WEB**: www.meadwestvaco.com
**SIC**: 2657 Folding paperboard boxes
**HQ**: Westrock Mwv, Llc
501 S 5th St
Richmond VA 23219
804 444-1000

### (G-14656)
### INDAR VENTURES LLC
4429 James Pl (60160-1004)
**PHONE** .................... 708 343-4900
Carlos Artola, *President*
Mark Bulanda, *Vice Pres*
**EMP**: 10
**SALES (est)**: 856.6K **Privately Held**
**WEB**: www.indarventures.com
**SIC**: 3599 Industrial machinery

### (G-14657)
### INDUSTRIAL FIBERGLASS INC
Also Called: I F I
1100 Main St (60160-4130)
**PHONE** .................... 708 681-2707
**Fax**: 708 681-5983
Daryl Johnson, *President*
Dennis Johnson, *Admin Sec*
**EMP**: 10
**SQ FT**: 12,000
**SALES**: 1MM **Privately Held**
**WEB**: www.industrialfiberglass.com
**SIC**: 3229 3564 3088 Glass fiber products; blowers & fans; plastics plumbing fixtures

### (G-14658)
### INDUSTRIAL SERVICE PALLET INC
1505 Hawk Ave (60160-2611)
**PHONE** .................... 708 655-4963
**EMP**: 3
**SALES (est)**: 150.2K **Privately Held**
**SIC**: 2448 Pallets, wood & wood with metal

### (G-14659)
### INTERLAKE MECALUX INC (DH)
1600 N 25th Ave (60160-1868)
**PHONE** .................... 708 344-9999
**Fax**: 708 343-9788
Angel De Arriba, *President*
Rick Jones, *Project Mgr*
Jaime Diaz, *Purchasing*
Bryan Leist, *Purchasing*
Ron Rhodes, *QC Dir*
◆ **EMP**: 289
**SQ FT**: 285,000
**SALES (est)**: 340MM
**SALES (corp-wide)**: 16.2K **Privately Held**
**WEB**: www.mecalux.com
**SIC**: 5084 2542 Industrial machinery & equipment; partitions & fixtures, except wood

**HQ**: Mecalux, Sa
Calle Silici, 1 -5
Cornella De Llobregat 08940
932 616-900

### (G-14660)
### INTERNATIONAL CUTTING DIE INC
2030 Janice Ave (60160-1027)
**PHONE** .................... 708 343-3333
Kevin McHenry, *President*
Maritta Koczwara, *Controller*
Timothy McEnery, *Admin Sec*
**EMP**: 30
**SQ FT**: 23,000
**SALES (est)**: 6.2MM **Privately Held**
**WEB**: www.internationalcuttingdie.com
**SIC**: 3544 Special dies & tools

### (G-14661)
### J & S MACHINE WORKS INC
1733 N 25th Ave (60160-1823)
**PHONE** .................... 708 344-2101
Juanita B Sundal, *President*
Singh Sundal, *General Mgr*
**EMP**: 6
**SALES (est)**: 470K **Privately Held**
**SIC**: 3599 Machine & other job shop work

### (G-14662)
### JKS VENTURES INC (PA)
2035 Indian Boundry Dr (60160-1136)
**PHONE** .................... 708 345-9344
Josephine Difronzo, *President*
**EMP**: 5
**SALES (est)**: 4.6MM **Privately Held**
**WEB**: www.jksventures.com
**SIC**: 1411 Limestone & marble dimension stone

### (G-14663)
### JKS VENTURES INC
3800 W Lake St (60160-2710)
**PHONE** .................... 708 338-3408
Josephine Di Fronzo, *President*
**EMP**: 8
**SALES (corp-wide)**: 4.6MM **Privately Held**
**WEB**: www.jksventures.com
**SIC**: 2611 Pulp manufactured from waste or recycled paper
**PA**: Jks Ventures Inc
2035 Indian Boundry Dr
Melrose Park IL 60160
708 345-9344

### (G-14664)
### JOHN J MONACO PRODUCTS CO INC
3120 W Lake St (60160-2920)
**PHONE** .................... 708 344-3333
**Fax**: 708 344-3512
Louis Monaco, *President*
▼ **EMP**: 40 **EST**: 1959
**SALES (est)**: 6.6MM **Privately Held**
**WEB**: www.monaco-packaging.com
**SIC**: 2653 Boxes, solid fiber: made from purchased materials; partitions, solid fiber: made from purchased materials

### (G-14665)
### JT PRODUCTS CO
1515 N 25th Ave (60160-1821)
**PHONE** .................... 773 378-4550
Thomas Schweihs, *Principal*
**EMP**: 3
**SALES (est)**: 136.5K **Privately Held**
**SIC**: 3451 Screw machine products

### (G-14666)
### KERRY INC
Also Called: Kerry Ingredients
3141 W North Ave (60160-1108)
**PHONE** .................... 708 450-3260
Philip Rizzo, *Production*
Jim Braglia, *Purchasing*
Sara Camacho, *Human Res Dir*
Jess Meyer, *Manager*
Don Fanning, *Consultant*
**EMP**: 100 **Privately Held**
**WEB**: www.kerryingredients.com
**SIC**: 2045 2099 Bread & bread type roll mixes: from purchased flour; food preparations

**HQ**: Kerry Inc.
3330 Millington Rd
Beloit WI 53511
608 363-1200

### (G-14667)
### KP PERFORMANCE INC
5000 Proviso Dr Ste 2 (60163-1360)
**PHONE** .................... 780 809-1908
Justin Graham, *Manager*
**EMP**: 3 **EST**: 2015
**SALES (est)**: 142.8K **Privately Held**
**SIC**: 3679 Antennas, receiving

### (G-14668)
### KREG MEDICAL INC
1940 Janice Ave (60160-1009)
**PHONE** .................... 312 829-8904
Craig Poulos, *President*
Oscar Lopez, *Supervisor*
▲ **EMP**: 120
**SQ FT**: 5,000
**SALES (est)**: 12.1MM **Privately Held**
**SIC**: 2599 Hospital beds

### (G-14669)
### LAKE BOOK MANUFACTURING INC
2085 Cornell Ave (60160-1002)
**PHONE** .................... 708 345-7000
**Fax**: 708 345-1544
Ralph P Genovese, *CEO*
Dan Genovese, *President*
Robert Flatow, *Vice Pres*
Bill Richards, *Vice Pres*
Nick Vergoth, *Vice Pres*
◆ **EMP**: 300
**SQ FT**: 400,000
**SALES (est)**: 66.7MM **Privately Held**
**WEB**: www.lakebook.com
**SIC**: 2732 Books: printing & binding

### (G-14670)
### LEE FOSS ELECTRIC MOTOR SVC
3418 W North Ave (60165-1043)
**PHONE** .................... 708 681-5335
**Fax**: 708 681-6147
Charles Fossen, *President*
Terry Likens, *Corp Secy*
**EMP**: 4
**SQ FT**: 5,000
**SALES (est)**: 754.9K **Privately Held**
**WEB**: www.leefoss.net
**SIC**: 7694 Electric motor repair

### (G-14671)
### MECH-TRONICS CORPORATION (PA)
1635 N 25th Ave (60160-1860)
**PHONE** .................... 708 344-9823
Eugene R Demuro, *President*
Michael Miller, *Purchasing*
George Regino, *QC Mgr*
Dong Qiu, *Engineer*
Irv Reimer, *Controller*
▼ **EMP**: 98 **EST**: 1948
**SQ FT**: 50,000
**SALES**: 12.8MM **Privately Held**
**SIC**: 3444 3823 Sheet metalwork; industrial instrmnts msrmnt display/control process variable

### (G-14672)
### MECH-TRONICS CORPORATION
Also Called: Mech-Tronics Nuclesuer Div
1701 N 25th Ave (60160-1823)
**PHONE** .................... 708 344-0202
**Fax**: 708 344-0067
Vince Campobasso, *Manager*
**EMP**: 6
**SALES (corp-wide)**: 12.8MM **Privately Held**
**SIC**: 4225 3829 General warehousing & storage; measuring & controlling devices
**PA**: Mech-Tronics Corporation
1635 N 25th Ave
Melrose Park IL 60160
708 344-9823

### (G-14673)
### MIDWEST CAN COMPANY (PA)
1950 N Mannheim Rd (60160-1037)
**PHONE** .................... 708 615-1400
**Fax**: 708 615-0381

John Trippi, *President*
John Evans, *Sales Mgr*
◆ **EMP**: 37
**SALES (est)**: 8.7MM **Privately Held**
**SIC**: 3443 Gas holders, metal plate

### (G-14674)
### MILLWOOD INC
Also Called: Chep/Millwood
5000 Proviso Dr Ste 1 (60163-1360)
**PHONE** .................... 708 343-7341
Brad Arnold, *Vice Pres*
Jayson Rhodes, *Branch Mgr*
Mike Brown, *Manager*
Lee Evans III, *Manager*
Judy Gaither, *Manager*
**EMP**: 17 **Privately Held**
**SIC**: 3565 Packaging machinery
**PA**: Millwood, Inc.
3708 International Blvd
Vienna OH 44473

### (G-14675)
### NAVISTAR INC
10400 W North Ave (60160-1028)
**Fax**: 708 865-4043
Tim Dany, *Branch Mgr*
**EMP**: 150
**SALES (corp-wide)**: 8.1B **Publicly Held**
**WEB**: www.internationaldelivers.com
**SIC**: 3519 Internal combustion engines
**HQ**: Navistar, Inc.
2701 Navistar Dr
Lisle IL 60532
331 332-5000

### (G-14676)
### NAVISTAR INC
10400 W North Ave (60160-1028)
**PHONE** .................... 317 352-4500
Sergio Sgarbi, *Branch Mgr*
Sonny Painter, *Director*
**EMP**: 290
**SALES (corp-wide)**: 8.1B **Publicly Held**
**WEB**: www.internationaldelivers.com
**SIC**: 3519 Internal combustion engines
**HQ**: Navistar, Inc.
2701 Navistar Dr
Lisle IL 60532
331 332-5000

### (G-14677)
### NB FINISHING INC
3131 W Soffel Ave (60160-1718)
**PHONE** .................... 847 364-7500
**Fax**: 847 895-0999
Bruce Nichols, *President*
Dave Nichols, *Purchasing*
**EMP**: 10
**SQ FT**: 6,000
**SALES**: 2MM **Privately Held**
**SIC**: 7389 3471 Grinding, precision: commercial or industrial; plating & polishing

### (G-14678)
### NORKOL CONVERTING CORPORATION (PA)
11650 W Grand Ave (60164-1300)
**PHONE** .................... 708 531-1000
**Fax**: 708 531-0030
Lawrence Kolinski, *President*
Michael Maloy, *President*
Mary Ellen Kolinski, *Corp Secy*
Ellen Rehm, *Senior VP*
Richard Harris, *Vice Pres*
◆ **EMP**: 125
**SQ FT**: 270,000
**SALES (est)**: 79.2MM **Privately Held**
**SIC**: 2621 Printing paper

### (G-14679)
### OTAK INTERNATIONAL INC
2080 N 16th Ave (60160)
**PHONE** .................... 630 373-9229
Taher Elashry, *President*
▼ **EMP**: 3
**SQ FT**: 46,000
**SALES**: 1.7MM **Privately Held**
**SIC**: 3824 5082 Mechanical & electromechanical counters & devices; general construction machinery & equipment

# GEOGRAPHIC SECTION

Melrose Park - Cook County (G-14704)

### (G-14680)
**P & M ORNAMENTAL IR WORKS INC**
1200 N 31st Ave (60160-2906)
**PHONE**................................708 267-2868
**Fax:** 708 345-4655
Michael Iovane, *President*
**EMP:** 15
**SALES (est):** 2.3MM **Privately Held**
**SIC:** 3446 Architectural metalwork

### (G-14681)
**PARAGON MANUFACTURING INC**
2001 N 15th Ave (60160-1404)
**PHONE**................................708 345-1717
**Fax:** 708 345-1721
Peter J Wright, *President*
Sheila Wright, *Corp Secy*
Sandy Bovilsky, *Manager*
Jennifer Wright, *Administration*
**EMP:** 60
**SQ FT:** 36,000
**SALES (est):** 26.3MM **Privately Held**
**WEB:** www.paragonmanufacturing.com
**SIC:** 3089 Plastic containers, except foam

### (G-14682)
**PARK MANUFACTURING CORP INC**
Also Called: Park Industries
1819 N 30th Ave (60160-1701)
**PHONE**................................708 345-6090
Larry K Warren, *President*
George Radcliff, *Engineer*
George Radcliffe, *Engineer*
Cynthia Bell, *Manager*
**EMP:** 12
**SQ FT:** 13,560
**SALES (est):** 2.4MM **Privately Held**
**WEB:** www.parkindustriesinc.com
**SIC:** 3493 3496 3469 Flat springs, sheet or strip stock; woven wire products; metal stampings

### (G-14683)
**PRECISE LAPPING GRINDING CORP**
2041 Janice Ave (60160-1010)
**PHONE**................................708 615-0240
**Fax:** 708 615-0333
Balwant Patel, *President*
Mike Patel, *Vice Pres*
Upendra Patel, *Admin Sec*
▲ **EMP:** 16
**SQ FT:** 7,200
**SALES (est):** 3.1MM **Privately Held**
**WEB:** www.preciselapping.com
**SIC:** 3541 3915 Deburring machines; grinding machines, metalworking; lapping machines; diamond cutting & polishing

### (G-14684)
**PRIDE MACHINE & TOOL CO INC**
1821 N 30th Ave (60160-1798)
**PHONE**................................708 343-7190
**Fax:** 708 343-2170
John Ilczyszyn, *President*
Paul Ciochon, *QC Mgr*
Wally Ciochon, *Manager*
Teodora Kulikowska, *Manager*
**EMP:** 14 **EST:** 1951
**SQ FT:** 16,500
**SALES:** 4.5MM **Privately Held**
**WEB:** www.pridemachinetool.com
**SIC:** 3599 Machine & other job shop work

### (G-14685)
**RAPID ELECTROPLATING PROCESS**
2901 W Soffel Ave (60160-1714)
**PHONE**................................708 344-2504
**Fax:** 708 344-2514
Richard Rapids, *President*
Pauline Glinka, *Vice Pres*
Arlene Mickols, *Admin Sec*
**EMP:** 5 **EST:** 1938
**SQ FT:** 6,700
**SALES:** 600K **Privately Held**
**WEB:** www.rapidelectroplating.com
**SIC:** 3559 Electroplating machinery & equipment

### (G-14686)
**REPUBLIC DRILL**
2058 N 15th Ave (60160-1405)
P.O. Box 1606 (60161-1606)
**PHONE**................................708 865-7666
**Fax:** 708 865-1042
Luke Branchaw, *Mktg Dir*
Donald Consitt, *Manager*
Joseph Houck, *Manager*
Gary Poteshman, *Manager*
Tom Strohmayer, *Manager*
**EMP:** 2
**SALES (est):** 202K **Privately Held**
**SIC:** 3544 Jigs & fixtures

### (G-14687)
**ROMEL PRESS INC**
1747 N 20th Ave (60160-1905)
**PHONE**................................708 343-6090
Robert Zamboni, *President*
Laura Zamboni, *Treasurer*
**EMP:** 3 **EST:** 1967
**SQ FT:** 1,600
**SALES (est):** 404.4K **Privately Held**
**WEB:** www.timelogic.com
**SIC:** 2752 2399 Commercial printing, offset; banners, pennants & flags

### (G-14688)
**ROMERO STEEL COMPANY INC**
1300 Main St (60160-4020)
**PHONE**................................708 216-0001
**Fax:** 708 216-0002
Jose G Romero, *President*
Jose Romero Jr, *Treasurer*
Jesse Jay Martinez, *Admin Sec*
▼ **EMP:** 30
**SQ FT:** 55,000
**SALES (est):** 9.2MM **Privately Held**
**WEB:** www.romerosteel.com
**SIC:** 3441 Fabricated structural metal

### (G-14689)
**ROYAL MACHINING CORPORATION**
1617 N 31st Ave (60160-1837)
**PHONE**................................708 338-3387
Bob Branko, *President*
Branko Dragojlovich, *President*
Milka Dragojlovich, *Vice Pres*
Vladimir Dragojlovich, *Manager*
**EMP:** 4
**SQ FT:** 10,000
**SALES (est):** 580K **Privately Held**
**WEB:** www.royalmachiningcorp.com
**SIC:** 3451 Screw machine products

### (G-14690)
**SALTZMAN PRINTERS INC**
Also Called: Combo Color
2150 N 15th Ave Ste C (60160-1411)
**PHONE**................................708 344-4500
Lewis Saltzman, *President*
Ira Saltzman, *Corp Secy*
Jack Saltzman, *Senior VP*
Tashawn Burnett, *Manager*
Alex Schubow, *Info Tech Mgr*
**EMP:** 30 **EST:** 1945
**SQ FT:** 128,000
**SALES (est):** 4.4MM **Privately Held**
**WEB:** www.saltz.com
**SIC:** 2796 2752 2721 Color separations for printing; commercial printing, lithographic; magazines: publishing only, not printed on site

### (G-14691)
**SAND-RITE MANUFACTURING CO**
3080 W Soffel Ave (60160-1717)
**PHONE**................................312 997-2200
**Fax:** 312 997-2407
Meyer S Kaplan, *President*
Marcus Kaplan, *Vice Pres*
Sharon Barrera, *Admin Sec*
▲ **EMP:** 6
**SQ FT:** 5,000
**SALES:** 1MM **Privately Held**
**WEB:** www.sand-rite.com
**SIC:** 3553 3291 Sanding machines, except portable floor sanders: woodworking; abrasive products

### (G-14692)
**SCHILKE MUSIC PRODUCTS INC**
4520 James Pl (60160-1007)
**PHONE**................................708 343-8858
**Fax:** 708 343-8912
Andrew Naumann, *President*
Julie Neuman, *Vice Pres*
Pat Hund, *Opers Staff*
Phil Baughman, *Finance Mgr*
Elizabeth Nowak, *Human Resources*
**EMP:** 31 **EST:** 1950
**SQ FT:** 12,000
**SALES:** 1MM **Privately Held**
**WEB:** www.schilkemusic.com
**SIC:** 3931 7699 Musical instruments; musical instrument repair services

### (G-14693)
**SCHRAM ENTERPRISES INC**
5017 W Lake St (60160-2754)
**PHONE**................................708 345-2252
Mark F Schram, *President*
Lorraine Schram, *Vice Pres*
Pam Schram, *Office Mgr*
**EMP:** 35
**SQ FT:** 15,000
**SALES (est):** 7.1MM **Privately Held**
**WEB:** www.acegrinding.com
**SIC:** 3599 3541 3291 Machine shop, jobbing & repair; machine tools, metal cutting type; abrasive products

### (G-14694)
**SOUTHFIELD CORPORATION**
Also Called: Patrone Ready Mix
5300 W Lake St (60160-2713)
**PHONE**................................708 345-0030
**Fax:** 708 345-6592
Chester Jobe, *Manager*
**EMP:** 100
**SALES (corp-wide):** 273.9MM **Privately Held**
**WEB:** www.prairiegroup.com
**SIC:** 3273 8741 Ready-mixed concrete; management services
**PA:** Southfield Corporation
8995 W 95th St
Palos Hills IL 60465
708 344-1000

### (G-14695)
**SQUARE 1 PRECISION LTG INC**
4300 W North Ave (60165-1038)
**PHONE**................................708 343-1500
Donna Franco, *Manager*
Jon Mead, *Director*
**EMP:** 5
**SALES (corp-wide):** 2.4MM **Privately Held**
**WEB:** www.sq1pl.com
**SIC:** 5063 3993 3648 3646 Electrical apparatus & equipment; signs & advertising specialties; lighting equipment; commercial indusl & institutional electric lighting fixtures; fabricated structural metal
**PA:** Square 1 Precision Lighting Inc.
4300 W North Ave
Stone Park IL 60165
708 343-1500

### (G-14696)
**STAIRS & RALES INC**
1200 Main St (60160-4059)
**PHONE**................................708 216-0078
Robert Srachta, *Principal*
**EMP:** 4
**SALES (est):** 300K **Privately Held**
**SIC:** 3441 Fabricated structural metal

### (G-14697)
**SUBURBAN LAMINATING INC**
908 W Lake St (60160-4145)
**PHONE**................................708 389-6106
**Fax:** 708 389-6599
John Dixon, *President*
Michael Twohill, *Vice Pres*
**EMP:** 9
**SQ FT:** 5,800
**SALES (est):** 940K **Privately Held**
**SIC:** 3083 2541 2511 Plastic finished products, laminated; wood partitions & fixtures; wood household furniture

### (G-14698)
**SUNSCAPE TIME INC**
Also Called: Pets Stop
2001 Janice Ave (60160-1046)
P.O. Box 1975, Bolingbrook (60440-7711)
**PHONE**................................708 345-8791
Hemant K Bhandari, *President*
Milan Bhandari, *Vice Pres*
▲ **EMP:** 7 **EST:** 2001
**SALES (est):** 592.1K **Privately Held**
**SIC:** 3999 0782 Pet supplies; lawn & garden services

### (G-14699)
**T & K PRECISION GRINDING**
1301 Armitage Ave Ste C (60160-1423)
**PHONE**................................708 450-0565
Chris Czapka, *Partner*
Ted Niepsuj, *Partner*
John Coleman, *Manager*
**EMP:** 2
**SALES (est):** 254.2K **Privately Held**
**SIC:** 3599 Grinding castings for the trade

### (G-14700)
**TARNOW LOGISTICS INC**
1001 N 16th Ave (60160-3327)
**PHONE**................................773 844-3203
Artur Tendera, *Owner*
**EMP:** 1 **EST:** 2015
**SALES:** 200K **Privately Held**
**SIC:** 3537 Trucks: freight, baggage, etc.: industrial, except mining

### (G-14701)
**TECHNICAL COATINGS CO**
2525 W North Ave (60160-1121)
**PHONE**................................708 343-6000
**Fax:** 708 343-6061
**EMP:** 40
**SALES (corp-wide):** 223.6B **Publicly Held**
**SIC:** 2851 Paints & allied products
**HQ:** Technical Coatings Co
360 Us Highway 206
Flanders NJ 07836
973 927-8600

### (G-14702)
**TONE PRODUCTS INC**
2129 N 15th Ave (60160-1406)
**PHONE**................................708 681-3660
Tim Evon, *President*
Jerry Christopoulos, *Vice Pres*
Tom Evon, *Vice Pres*
William H Hamen, *CFO*
▼ **EMP:** 45 **EST:** 1947
**SQ FT:** 72,000
**SALES (est):** 11MM **Privately Held**
**WEB:** www.toneproducts.com
**SIC:** 2087 Syrups, drink; fruit juices: concentrated for fountain use; extracts, flavoring

### (G-14703)
**UNITED CONVEYOR SUPPLY COMPANY**
2025 N 15th Ave (60160-1404)
**PHONE**................................708 344-8050
**Fax:** 708 344-2135
Michael E Connor, *Prdtn Mgr*
Christine Hunter, *Purchasing*
James Howell, *Engineer*
Priya Patel, *Engineer*
Zdravka Vassileva, *Engineer*
**EMP:** 50
**SALES (corp-wide):** 162.4MM **Privately Held**
**WEB:** www.unitedconveyorsupply.com
**SIC:** 3441 3446 3444 3443 Fabricated structural metal; architectural metalwork; sheet metalwork; fabricated plate work (boiler shop); secondary nonferrous metals
**HQ:** United Conveyor Supply Company
2100 Norman Dr
Waukegan IL 60085

### (G-14704)
**VALLEY FASTENER GROUP LLC**
Forgo Fastener Division
3302 Bloomingdale Ave (60160-1030)
**PHONE**................................708 343-2496
**Fax:** 708 343-2498

## Melrose Park - Cook County (G-14705)

Ed Belson, *Plant Mgr*
Edward Belsan, *Manager*
**EMP:** 10
**SALES (corp-wide):** 21.6MM **Privately Held**
**WEB:** www.valleyrivet.com
**SIC: 3452** Screws, metal; rivets, metal
**PA:** Valley Fastener Group, Llc
1490 Mitchell Rd
Aurora IL 60505
630 299-8910

### (G-14705)
### VEECO MANUFACTURING INC
Also Called: Pet Groom Products Div
1930 George St Ste A (60160-1501)
**PHONE** .................................. 312 666-0900
Leonard S Cohen, *President*
Laurie Cohen, *Vice Pres*
David Davis, *Sales Dir*
Marcy Turner, *Marketing Staff*
Tania Samaras, *Office Mgr*
◆ **EMP:** 20 **EST:** 1944
**SQ FT:** 50,000
**SALES (est):** 3.2MM **Privately Held**
**WEB:** www.veecomanufacturing.com
**SIC: 3999** 5021 Barber & beauty shop equipment; furniture

### (G-14706)
### WAGNER ZIP-CHANGE INC
3100 W Hirsch St (60160-1741)
**PHONE** .................................. 708 681-4100
**Fax:** 800 243-4924
Georgene A Bercier, *President*
Gary Delaquila, *Vice Pres*
Paul Mauersberger, *Purch Mgr*
Donald Kolkebeck, *Treasurer*
Jim Leone, *Sales Mgr*
▲ **EMP:** 40
**SQ FT:** 33,000
**SALES (est):** 12.9MM **Privately Held**
**WEB:** www.wagnerzip.com
**SIC: 5099** 3993 3953 3444 Signs, except electric; letters for signs, metal; marking devices; sheet metalwork; nonferrous rolling & drawing; automotive & apparel trimmings

### (G-14707)
### WALLYS PRECISION MACHINING
1025 N 27th Ave (60160-2940)
**PHONE** .................................. 708 205-2950
**Fax:** 708 338-9471
Wally Gorny, *President*
**EMP:** 5
**SQ FT:** 2,000
**SALES:** 500K **Privately Held**
**SIC: 3599** Machine shop, jobbing & repair

### (G-14708)
### WESTROCK CNSMR PACKG GROUP LLC
1950 N Ruby St (60160-1110)
**PHONE** .................................. 804 444-1000
Rita Foley, *Mng Member*
Tina Vieira, *Executive*
Jacqueline M Barry,
John A Luke Jr,
Gretta Martinez,
◆ **EMP:** 799
**SQ FT:** 257,000
**SALES (est):** 734.9K
**SALES (corp-wide):** 14.1B **Publicly Held**
**WEB:** www.agiinc.com
**SIC: 2671** Packaging paper & plastics film, coated & laminated
**HQ:** Westrock Mwv, Llc
501 S 5th St
Richmond VA 23219
804 444-1000

### (G-14709)
### WESTROCK RKT COMPANY
1945 Cornell Ave (60160-1005)
**PHONE** .................................. 847 649-9231
**Fax:** 708 344-9794
Sam Perez, *Branch Mgr*
**EMP:** 161
**SALES (corp-wide):** 14.1B **Publicly Held**
**SIC: 2653** Corrugated & solid fiber boxes
**HQ:** Westrock Rkt Company
504 Thrasher St
Norcross GA 30071
770 448-2193

### (G-14710)
### WISCON CORP (PA)
Also Called: Wisconsin Cheese
2050 N 15th Ave (60160-1405)
P.O. Box 5008 (60161-5008)
**PHONE** .................................. 708 450-0074
**Fax:** 708 450-1670
Pasquale Caputo, *CEO*
Natale Caputo, *President*
Anna Luu, *Controller*
Jenny Venhuizen, *Director*
Caterina Caputo, *Admin Sec*
◆ **EMP:** 30
**SQ FT:** 40,000
**SALES (est):** 86.5MM **Privately Held**
**WEB:** www.wisconcorp.com
**SIC: 5143** 2022 Cheese; cheese, natural & processed

### (G-14711)
### WISCON CORP
Also Called: Wisconsin Cheese
1931 N 15th Ave (60160-1402)
**PHONE** .................................. 708 450-0074
Natale Caputo, *President*
Jennifer Hurtuk, *Mktg Dir*
**EMP:** 39
**SALES (corp-wide):** 86.5MM **Privately Held**
**WEB:** www.wisconcorp.com
**SIC: 2022** 5451 Cheese, natural & processed; dairy products stores
**PA:** Wiscon Corp.
2050 N 15th Ave
Melrose Park IL 60160
708 450-0074

### (G-14712)
### YOUR CUSTOM CABINETRY CORP
1609 N 31st Ave (60160-1837)
**PHONE** .................................. 773 290-7247
Kacarzyna Pacholczyk, *President*
**EMP:** 2
**SALES:** 200K **Privately Held**
**SIC: 3553** Cabinet makers' machinery

### (G-14713)
### ZAGONE STUDIO LLC
Also Called: Be Something Studio
4533 W North Ave (60160-1022)
**PHONE** .................................. 773 509-0610
**Fax:** 773 509-0613
Phil Zagone, *President*
Margret Omano, *Vice Pres*
▲ **EMP:** 27 **EST:** 1972
**SQ FT:** 17,000
**SALES (est):** 616K **Privately Held**
**SIC: 2389** Masquerade costumes

## Mendota
### Lasalle County

### (G-14714)
### ADVANCED DRAINAGE SYSTEMS INC
1600 Industrial Dr (61342-9409)
**PHONE** .................................. 815 539-2160
Miro Medvedec, *Engineer*
Joseph Chlapaty, *Manager*
**EMP:** 14
**SALES (corp-wide):** 1.2B **Publicly Held**
**WEB:** www.ads-pipe.com
**SIC: 3089** Plastic hardware & building products
**PA:** Advanced Drainage Systems, Inc.
4640 Trueman Blvd
Hilliard OH 43026
614 658-0050

### (G-14715)
### AMERICAN MACHINE
215 E 12th St (61342-1878)
**PHONE** .................................. 815 539-6558
Michael Schuhler, *Owner*
**EMP:** 4
**SQ FT:** 4,000
**SALES:** 750K **Privately Held**
**SIC: 3499** Welding tips, heat resistant: metal

### (G-14716)
### ANDOVER JUNCTION PUBLICATIONS
467 N 46th Rd (61342-9552)
P.O. Box 500 (61342-0500)
**PHONE** .................................. 815 538-3060
Stephen A Esposito, *Managing Prtnr*
Michael Schafer, *Partner*
**EMP:** 4
**SQ FT:** 2,000
**SALES (est):** 318.2K **Privately Held**
**WEB:** www.andoverjunction.com
**SIC: 2732** 2721 7812 Book printing; magazines: publishing & printing; video tape production

### (G-14717)
### BLACK BROS CO (PA)
501 9th Ave (61342-1927)
P.O. Box 410 (61342-0410)
**PHONE** .................................. 815 539-7451
**Fax:** 815 538-2451
Matthew B Carroll, *President*
Skip Stachlewitz, *COO*
Bob Shaw, *Vice Pres*
Walter Weiland, *Vice Pres*
Brian Schultz, *Plant Mgr*
▲ **EMP:** 51
**SQ FT:** 225,000
**SALES (est):** 10.6MM **Privately Held**
**WEB:** www.blackbros.com
**SIC: 3553** 3549 3554 3559 Woodworking machinery; metalworking machinery; paper industries machinery; plastics working machinery

### (G-14718)
### CLASSIC METAL COMPANY INC
115 16th St (61342-1315)
**PHONE** .................................. 815 252-0104
**EMP:** 3
**SALES (est):** 195.9K **Privately Held**
**SIC: 3471**

### (G-14719)
### DAILY NEWS TRIBUNE INC
Also Called: News-Tribune
900 Washington St (61342-1621)
**PHONE** .................................. 815 539-5200
**Fax:** 815 539-5200
Jenny Parnisari, *Manager*
**EMP:** 3
**SALES (corp-wide):** 36MM **Privately Held**
**WEB:** www.newstrib.com
**SIC: 2711** Newspapers
**PA:** Daily News Tribune, Inc
426 2nd St
La Salle IL 61301
815 223-2558

### (G-14720)
### E N P INC (PA)
Also Called: Smith Greenhouse & Supplies
603 14th St (61342-1219)
P.O. Box 618 (61342-0618)
**PHONE** .................................. 800 255-4906
**Fax:** 815 538-6981
Thomas J Smith, *President*
**EMP:** 5
**SQ FT:** 6,400
**SALES (est):** 668.3K **Privately Held**
**WEB:** www.fertilegrower.com
**SIC: 2873** 2879 2875 Nitrogenous fertilizers; agricultural chemicals; fertilizers, mixing only

### (G-14721)
### E N P INC
2001 E Main St (61342)
P.O. Box 618 (61342-0618)
**PHONE** .................................. 815 539-7471
Thomas Smith, *Branch Mgr*
**EMP:** 5
**SALES (corp-wide):** 668.3K **Privately Held**
**WEB:** www.fertilegrower.com
**SIC: 2873** 2875 Nitrogenous fertilizers; fertilizers, mixing only
**PA:** E N P Inc
603 14th St
Mendota IL 61342
800 255-4906

### (G-14722)
### HCC INC
1501 1st Ave (61342-1385)
P.O. Box 952 (61342-0952)
**PHONE** .................................. 815 539-9371
**Fax:** 815 539-7331
Donald Bickel, *Ch of Bd*
Bryan Nelson, *President*
Jim Register, *Vice Pres*
Jef Fields, *Opers Mgr*
Robert Glessner, *Materials Mgr*
◆ **EMP:** 200
**SQ FT:** 150,000
**SALES (est):** 62.5MM **Privately Held**
**WEB:** www.hccincorporated.com
**SIC: 3523** Farm machinery & equipment; combines (harvester-threshers)

### (G-14723)
### KUNZ ENGINEERING INC
2100 Welland Rd (61342-9139)
**PHONE** .................................. 815 539-6954
Gary L Kunz, *President*
Matthew A Kunz, *Vice Pres*
Frederick Kunz, *Engineer*
Wanda M Kunz, *Admin Sec*
▼ **EMP:** 3
**SALES (est):** 521.3K **Privately Held**
**WEB:** www.kunzeng.com
**SIC: 3524** Lawnmowers, residential: hand or power

### (G-14724)
### MENDOTA AGRI-PRODUCTS INC (PA)
448 N 3973rd Rd (61342-9305)
**PHONE** .................................. 815 539-5633
**Fax:** 815 539-7943
John T Mahoney, *President*
Scott Miller, *Corp Secy*
Randy Churchill, *Controller*
**EMP:** 33
**SQ FT:** 40,000
**SALES (est):** 6.1MM **Privately Held**
**WEB:** www.mendotaagriproducts.com
**SIC: 2077** 2048 Animal fats, oils & meals; prepared feeds

### (G-14725)
### MENDOTA MONUMENT CO
606 Main St (61342-1983)
P.O. Box 63 (61342-0063)
**PHONE** .................................. 815 539-7276
Eric Schmitt, *Partner*
Ronald Schmitt, *Partner*
Stephen Schmitt, *Partner*
**EMP:** 3 **EST:** 1913
**SQ FT:** 2,000
**SALES (est):** 254.6K **Privately Held**
**WEB:** www.mendotamonument.com
**SIC: 5999** 3281 Monuments, finished to custom order; cut stone & stone products

### (G-14726)
### MENDOTA REPORTER
Also Called: Reporter Money Saver
703 Illinois Ave (61342-1637)
P.O. Box 300 (61342-0300)
**PHONE** .................................. 815 539-9396
**Fax:** 815 539-7862
John Tompkins, *President*
Kip Cheek, *Publisher*
Mark Elston, *General Mgr*
Kip Sheek, *Principal*
Jennifer Sommer, *Editor*
**EMP:** 11
**SALES (est):** 882.6K **Privately Held**
**WEB:** www.mendotareporter.com
**SIC: 2711** 2741 Newspapers, publishing & printing; miscellaneous publishing
**HQ:** Rochelle Newspapers Inc
211 E Il Route 38
Rochelle IL 61068
815 562-2061

### (G-14727)
### MENDOTA WELDING & MFG
1605 One Half 13th Ave (61342)
**PHONE** .................................. 815 539-6944
**Fax:** 815 539-9042
Mark E Wujek, *Owner*
Debra Wujek, *Co-Owner*
**EMP:** 4
**SQ FT:** 4,000

# GEOGRAPHIC SECTION

**Metamora - Woodford County (G-14751)**

SALES (est): 469.1K **Privately Held**
SIC: 7692 3714 3444 3443 Welding repair; bumpers & bumperettes, motor vehicle; sheet metalwork; fabricated plate work (boiler shop)

**(G-14728)**
**MINNESOTA DIVERSIFIED PDTS INC**
Also Called: Diversifoam Products
1101 Lori Ln (61342-9232)
P.O. Box 619 (61342-0619)
PHONE...................................815 539-3106
Fax: 815 539-3433
Jim Pestula, *Plant Mgr*
Randy Markowitz, *Sales Staff*
Jim Postula, *Manager*
Joe Kaiser, *Manager*
Ben Sachs, *Data Proc Exec*
EMP: 30
SALES (corp-wide): 19.6MM **Privately Held**
WEB: www.diversifoam.com
SIC: 3086 Insulation or cushioning material, foamed plastic
PA: Minnesota Diversified Products, Inc.
 9091 County Road 50
 Rockford MN 55373
 763 477-5854

**(G-14729)**
**NORTHERN ILLINOIS GAS COMPANY**
Also Called: Nicor Gas
169 N 36th Rd (61342-9611)
PHONE...................................815 223-8097
Fax: 815 223-9440
Mike Fugate, *Branch Mgr*
Kari Sennes, *Admin Asst*
EMP: 18
SALES (corp-wide): 19.9B **Publicly Held**
WEB: www.nicor.com
SIC: 4924 1382 Natural gas distribution; oil & gas exploration services
HQ: Northern Illinois Gas Company
 1844 W Ferry Rd
 Naperville IL 60563
 630 983-8676

**(G-14730)**
**PLANO MOLDING COMPANY LLC**
1800 Hume Dr (61342-8906)
P.O. Box 440 (61342-0440)
PHONE...................................815 538-3111
Fax: 815 538-2246
Ron Jergenson, *Principal*
Andrew Huss, *Accountant*
Michelle McNeil, *Manager*
John Clark, *Maintence Staff*
Jose Medina, *Maintence Staff*
EMP: 170
SALES (corp-wide): 44MM **Privately Held**
WEB: www.planomolding.com
SIC: 3089 3469 Molding primary plastic; metal stampings
HQ: Plano Molding Company, Llc
 431 E South St
 Plano IL 60545
 630 552-3111

**(G-14731)**
**PRAIRIE LAND MLLWRGHT SVCS INC**
617 E Us Highway 34 (61342-9207)
PHONE...................................815 538-3085
Fax: 815 538-3087
Duane Chaon, *President*
Curt Chaon, *Corp Secy*
Marcia Johnson, *Manager*
EMP: 18 EST: 1997
SQ FT: 30,000
SALES (est): 4.4MM **Privately Held**
SIC: 3523 Planting, haying, harvesting & processing machinery

**(G-14732)**
**ROYAL SMOKE SHOP**
1001 Main St (61342-1604)
PHONE...................................815 539-3499
Mike Ashour, *Owner*
EMP: 2
SALES (est): 212.9K **Privately Held**
SIC: 2111 Cigarettes

**(G-14733)**
**SPARTAN TOOL LLC (DH)**
1506 Division St (61342-2426)
PHONE...................................815 539-7411
Fax: 815 539-9786
Tom Pranka, *President*
Aaron Yoder, *Production*
Ross Wilson, *Engineer*
Kevin Dineen, *Project Engr*
Marvin Little, *Sls & Mktg Exec*
▲ EMP: 25
SQ FT: 100,000
SALES (est): 19.5MM
SALES (corp-wide): 1.3B **Privately Held**
WEB: www.spartantool.com
SIC: 3589 Sewer cleaning equipment, power
HQ: Pettibone L.L.C.
 27501 Bella Vista Pkwy
 Warrenville IL 60555
 630 353-5000

## Meredosia
### Morgan County

**(G-14734)**
**PPG ARCHITECTURAL FINISHES INC**
Also Called: Glidden Professional Paint Ctr
S Washington St (62665)
P.O. Box 500 (62665-0500)
PHONE...................................217 584-1323
Frank Mastria, *Dir Ops-Prd-Mfg*
Robbie N Sage, *Engineer*
Vithal Ayyagari, *Enginr/R&D Mgr*
EMP: 268
SALES (corp-wide): 14.7B **Publicly Held**
WEB: www.gliddenpaint.com
SIC: 2821 2891 Plastics materials & resins; adhesives & sealants
HQ: Ppg Architectural Finishes, Inc.
 1 Ppg Pl
 Pittsburgh PA 15272
 412 434-3131

**(G-14735)**
**TARPS MANUFACTURING INC**
1000 State Highway 104 (62665-7165)
PHONE...................................217 584-1900
Jeff Davidsmeyer, *CEO*
P Devon Davidsmeyer, *President*
Tom Atkins, *Vice Pres*
Richard Ott, *Opers Mgr*
R Thomas Slayback, *Treasurer*
EMP: 10
SQ FT: 28,000
SALES: 661.9K
SALES (corp-wide): 36.8MM **Privately Held**
WEB: www.tarpall.com
SIC: 2394 Tarpaulins, fabric: made from purchased materials
PA: Illinois Road Contractors, Inc.
 520 N Webster Ave
 Jacksonville IL 62650
 217 245-6181

## Merrionette Park
### Cook County

**(G-14736)**
**BEVEL GRANITE CO INC**
11849 S Kedzie Ave (60803-4518)
PHONE...................................708 388-9060
Fax: 708 371-2782
James Rogan, *President*
Thomas Rogan, *Vice Pres*
David Antkiewicz, *Controller*
▲ EMP: 75 EST: 1927
SQ FT: 5,000
SALES (est): 9.3MM **Privately Held**
WEB: www.bevelgranite.com
SIC: 3281 5999 Monuments, cut stone (not finishing or lettering only); granite, cut & shaped; monuments, finished to custom order

**(G-14737)**
**ROGAN GRANITINDUSTRIE INC**
Also Called: Bevel Granite
11849 S Kedzie Ave (60803-4518)
PHONE...................................708 758-0050
James Rogan, *Manager*
EMP: 4 **Privately Held**
WEB: www.rogangranite.com
SIC: 3281 Monuments, cut stone (not finishing or lettering only); building stone products; furniture, cut stone
HQ: Rogan Granitindustrie Inc
 21550 E Lincoln Hwy
 Lynwood IL 60411
 708 758-0050

**(G-14738)**
**ROGAN GROUP INC (PA)**
11849 S Kedzie Ave (60803-4518)
PHONE...................................708 371-4191
James R Rogan, *President*
Thomas R Rogan, *Treasurer*
EMP: 7
SALES (est): 15.7MM **Privately Held**
SIC: 3281 5999 5082 5087 Building stone products; tombstones, cut stone (not finishing or lettering only); gravestones, finished; construction & mining machinery; service establishment equipment

## Metamora
### Woodford County

**(G-14739)**
**ARTS TAMALES**
1453 Hickory Point Rd (61548-7803)
PHONE...................................309 367-2850
David Chinuge, *Owner*
Ruby Dirks, *Opers Staff*
EMP: 6 EST: 1935
SQ FT: 4,200
SALES: 180K **Privately Held**
SIC: 2099 2035 2013 Food preparations; pickles, sauces & salad dressings; sausages & other prepared meats

**(G-14740)**
**BENCHMARK ELECTRONICS INC**
388 Riverview Blf (61548-9075)
PHONE...................................309 822-8587
Philip Bumbalough, *Principal*
EMP: 276
SALES (corp-wide): 2.3B **Publicly Held**
SIC: 3672 Printed circuit boards
PA: Benchmark Electronics, Inc.
 3000 Technology Rd
 Angleton TX 77515
 979 849-6550

**(G-14741)**
**CENTRAL ILLINOIS GLASS &**
506 W Mount Vernon St (61548-7006)
P.O. Box 80 (61548-0080)
PHONE...................................309 367-4242
Fax: 309 367-4245
Cristy Mooney, *Owner*
EMP: 8
SALES (est): 836.8K **Privately Held**
SIC: 3231 Products of purchased glass

**(G-14742)**
**HONEYWELL INTERNATIONAL INC**
539 Justa Rd (61548-7833)
PHONE...................................309 383-4045
EMP: 673
SALES (corp-wide): 39.3B **Publicly Held**
SIC: 3724 Aircraft engines & engine parts
PA: Honeywell International Inc.
 115 Tabor Rd
 Morris Plains NJ 07950
 973 455-2000

**(G-14743)**
**LOGO WEAR UNLIMITED INC**
104 S Menard St (61548-7097)
P.O. Box 861 (61548-0861)
PHONE...................................309 367-2333
Andrew Martin, *CEO*
EMP: 2

SALES (est): 216.1K **Privately Held**
SIC: 2759 Screen printing

**(G-14744)**
**MCBRIDE & SHOFF INC**
723 N Wiedman St (61548-9614)
P.O. Box 650 (61548-0650)
PHONE...................................309 367-4193
Fax: 309 367-2552
Clifford D Shoff, *President*
Michael W Shoff, *Vice Pres*
Ryan Shoff, *Vice Pres*
Scott Shoff, *Vice Pres*
Willis Bachman, *Purchasing*
EMP: 50
SQ FT: 109,000
SALES (est): 8.4MM **Privately Held**
WEB: www.mcbrideandshoff.com
SIC: 3599 Machine shop, jobbing & repair

**(G-14745)**
**METAMORA INDUSTRIES LLC**
723 N Wiedman St (61548-9614)
P.O. Box 650 (61548-0650)
PHONE...................................309 367-2368
Fax: 309 367-2946
Willis Bachman, *Purchasing*
Cliff Shoff, *Mng Member*
Shoff Clifford D,
Mike Shoff,
Ryan Shoff,
▲ EMP: 40 EST: 1965
SQ FT: 50,000
SALES (est): 10.2MM **Privately Held**
WEB: www.metamoraindustries.com
SIC: 3441 3498 Fabricated structural metal; tube fabricating (contract bending & shaping)

**(G-14746)**
**OLD MILL VINEYARD LLC**
700 Coon Creek Rd (61548-7416)
PHONE...................................309 258-9954
Grohsmeyer Kurt, *Principal*
EMP: 4 EST: 2015
SALES (est): 206.6K **Privately Held**
SIC: 2084 Wines, brandy & brandy spirits

**(G-14747)**
**PEORIA WILBERT VAULT CO INC**
510 Townhall Rd (61548-9405)
P.O. Box 27 (61548-0027)
PHONE...................................309 383-2882
Fax: 309 383-3182
William Buren, *President*
Bryant Defrance, *President*
EMP: 10
SALES (est): 1MM **Privately Held**
SIC: 3272 Burial vaults, concrete or pre-cast terrazzo

**(G-14748)**
**ROY WINNETT**
303 W Pine St (61548-9687)
PHONE...................................309 367-4867
Roy Winnett, *Principal*
EMP: 3
SALES (est): 252.8K **Privately Held**
SIC: 2836 Toxins, viruses & similar substances, including venom

**(G-14749)**
**SAND & GRAVEL SERVICE**
305 Murphy Ln (61548-9183)
PHONE...................................309 648-4585
EMP: 3
SALES (est): 105.3K **Privately Held**
SIC: 1442 Construction sand & gravel

**(G-14750)**
**SIMPLY SIGNS**
1001 W Mount Vernon St D (61548-8411)
PHONE...................................309 849-9016
Nathan Connelly, *Principal*
EMP: 2 EST: 2011
SALES (est): 227.6K **Privately Held**
SIC: 3993 Signs & advertising specialties

**(G-14751)**
**UNIT STEP COMPANY OF PEORIA**
510 Townhall Rd (61548-9405)
PHONE...................................309 674-4392
Fax: 309 674-0154

## Metropolis
### Massac County

**(G-14752)**
**BROWN & MEYERS INC**
Also Called: South Paw Donuts
1400 W 10th St (62960-2429)
PHONE..................................618 524-3838
Glena Brown, *President*
EMP: 5
SALES: 90K **Privately Held**
SIC: 2051 Doughnuts, except frozen

**(G-14753)**
**GLOBAL MAINTENANCE LLC**
654 Kennedy Dr (62960-2623)
PHONE..................................270 933-1281
James S Scourick, *Mng Member*
Steven Hibner,
Jason Mc Kendree,
EMP: 16
SALES (est): 3.2MM **Privately Held**
SIC: 3498 Fabricated pipe & fittings

**(G-14754)**
**HONEYWELL INTERNATIONAL INC**
2768 N Us Hwy 45 N (62960)
P.O. Box 430 (62960-0430)
PHONE..................................618 524-2111
Mark J Byrne, *President*
Dave Edwards, *Plant Mgr*
Jno Bernard, *Controller*
Gayley Hester, *Human Res Dir*
Mark McPhee, *Human Res Mgr*
EMP: 400
SALES (corp-wide): 39.3B **Publicly Held**
SIC: 2819 2869 Industrial inorganic chemicals; industrial organic chemicals
PA: Honeywell International Inc.
115 Tabor Rd
Morris Plains NJ 07950
973 455-2000

**(G-14755)**
**HONEYWELL INTERNATIONAL INC**
704 E 5th St (62960-2183)
PHONE..................................618 940-0401
Bernard Bass, *Engineer*
Ernie Roberson, *Engineer*
Don Sawyer, *Branch Mgr*
EMP: 147
SALES (corp-wide): 39.3B **Publicly Held**
SIC: 3823 Industrial instrmnts msrmnt display/control process variable
PA: Honeywell International Inc.
115 Tabor Rd
Morris Plains NJ 07950
973 455-2000

**(G-14756)**
**MARCAL ROPE & RIGGING INC**
5357 Industrial Park Dr (62960-4170)
PHONE..................................618 462-0172
Ray Henderson, *Manager*
EMP: 3
SALES (corp-wide): 8.4MM **Privately Held**
WEB: www.marcalrigging.com
SIC: 3496 Miscellaneous fabricated wire products
PA: Marcal Rope & Rigging, Inc.
1862 E Broadway
Alton IL 62002
618 462-0172

**(G-14757)**
**METRO SERVICE CENTER**
103 W 10th St Ste Ba (62960-1571)
PHONE..................................618 524-8583
Fax: 618 524-5069
David Christian, *Owner*
EMP: 2
SALES (est): 212.9K **Privately Held**
SIC: 3663 Satellites, communications

Michael J Kelley, *Owner*
Linda Kelley, *Co-Owner*
EMP: 3
SALES (est): 306.3K **Privately Held**
SIC: 3272 5999 Concrete products, precast; concrete products, pre-cast

**(G-14758)**
**METROPOLIS READY MIX INC (PA)**
Also Called: Kotter Ready Mix
1200 E 2nd St (62960-2289)
P.O. Box 107 (62960-0107)
PHONE..................................618 524-8221
Fax: 618 524-5410
Karl Kotter, *President*
Mary Kotter, *Accountant*
Rick Kotter, *Admin Sec*
EMP: 25 EST: 1950
SQ FT: 1,800
SALES (est): 2.2MM **Privately Held**
WEB: www.metropolischamber.com
SIC: 3273 4491 4222 4212 Ready-mixed concrete; loading vessels; unloading vessels; refrigerated warehousing & storage; local trucking, without storage

**(G-14759)**
**MICHAELS EQUIPMENT CO**
Also Called: Kubota Authorized Dealer
5481 Illinois 145 Rd (62960-3634)
PHONE..................................618 524-8560
Fax: 618 524-1325
Michael Reames, *Partner*
Rebecca Reames, *Partner*
EMP: 5
SQ FT: 3,600
SALES (est): 487.5K **Privately Held**
SIC: 5999 3546 5083 Farm equipment & supplies; saws & sawing equipment; farm & garden machinery

**(G-14760)**
**NEWS METROPOLIS**
111 E 5th St (62960-2108)
PHONE..................................618 524-2141
EMP: 3
SALES (est): 107.3K **Privately Held**
SIC: 2711 Newspapers, publishing & printing

**(G-14761)**
**R&R MEAT CO**
5156 Old Marion Rd (62960-3527)
PHONE..................................270 898-6296
Len Rudd, *Owner*
EMP: 5
SQ FT: 3,000
SALES: 600K **Privately Held**
SIC: 2013 Sausages & other prepared meats

## Mettawa
### Lake County

**(G-14762)**
**ABBOTT LABORATORIES**
26525 N Riverwoods Blvd (60045-3440)
PHONE..................................847 735-0573
EMP: 817
SALES (corp-wide): 20.8B **Publicly Held**
SIC: 2834 Pharmaceutical preparations
PA: Abbott Laboratories
100 Abbott Park Rd
Abbott Park IL 60064
224 667-6100

**(G-14763)**
**ABBVIE INC**
26525 N Riverwoods Blvd (60045-3440)
PHONE..................................847 735-0573
EMP: 6
SALES (est): 644.7K **Privately Held**
SIC: 2834 Pharmaceutical preparations

**(G-14764)**
**VYAIRE MEDICAL INC (PA)** ◆
26125 N Riverwoods Blvd (60045-3401)
PHONE..................................847 362-8088
Dave Mowry, *CEO*
Marilyn Frank, *Manager*
EMP: 17 EST: 2016
SALES (est): 22.8MM **Privately Held**
SIC: 3841 Surgical & medical instruments

## Midlothian
### Cook County

**(G-14765)**
**CHICAGO PREPRESS COLOR INC**
14650 Kostner Ave (60445-2662)
PHONE..................................708 385-3465
Larry Sargis, *President*
EMP: 3
SALES (est): 200K **Privately Held**
SIC: 2796 Color separations for printing

**(G-14766)**
**FIX IT FAST LTD**
14922 Lawndale Ave (60445-3533)
PHONE..................................708 401-8320
Shawn Fuller, *President*
William Fuller, *Vice Pres*
EMP: 12 EST: 2012
SALES (est): 1.3MM **Privately Held**
SIC: 3442 1799 Fire doors, metal; dock equipment installation, industrial

**(G-14767)**
**MARKHAM CABINET WORKS INC**
4235 151st St (60445-3316)
PHONE..................................708 687-3074
Gerhardt Reichel, *President*
Jack Reichel, *Vice Pres*
Sandra Reichel, *Controller*
Alice Reichel, *Admin Sec*
EMP: 6 EST: 1946
SQ FT: 7,000
SALES: 300K **Privately Held**
SIC: 2434 2541 5211 Wood kitchen cabinets; table or counter tops, plastic laminated; cabinets, kitchen; counter tops

**(G-14768)**
**SECRETARY OF STATE ILLINOIS**
14434 Pulaski Rd (60445-2895)
PHONE..................................708 388-9199
EMP: 3 **Privately Held**
SIC: 3469 Automobile license tags, stamped metal
HQ: Secretary Of State, Illinois
213 State House
Springfield IL 62706
217 782-2201

**(G-14769)**
**SOUTHWEST MESSENGER PRESS INC**
Also Called: Alsip Express Newspaper
3840 147th St (60445-3452)
PHONE..................................708 388-2425
Fax: 708 385-7811
Margaret D Lysen, *President*
Walter H Lysen, *President*
Margaret O Lysen, *Corp Secy*
Don Talac, *Vice Pres*
George Brown, *Purchasing*
EMP: 46 EST: 1929
SQ FT: 3,750
SALES (est): 2.3MM **Privately Held**
SIC: 2711 Newspapers: publishing only, not printed on site

**(G-14770)**
**TITANIUM INSULATION INC**
14533 Turner Ave (60445-3029)
PHONE..................................708 932-5927
Cesar Garcia, *President*
EMP: 1
SALES (est): 260.2K **Privately Held**
SIC: 3356 Titanium

**(G-14771)**
**UNIVERSAL DIGITAL PRINTING**
3314 147th St (60445-3612)
PHONE..................................708 389-0133
EMP: 3
SALES (est): 259K **Privately Held**
SIC: 2759 Commercial printing

## Milan
### Rock Island County

**(G-14772)**
**ADVANCED BATTERY LLC**
Also Called: Advanced Battery Systems
1410 11th St W (61264-2264)
PHONE..................................309 755-7775
John Mitchell, *Controller*
Edward Lampo,
Alexander Anthony,
Robert W Stucker,
▲ EMP: 10 EST: 2012
SQ FT: 5,000
SALES: 3MM **Privately Held**
SIC: 3691 Batteries, rechargeable
PA: Lynco Distribution, Inc.
1410 11th St W
Milan IL 61264

**(G-14773)**
**AGUSTA MILL WORKS**
Also Called: Carver Custom Woodworks
117 17th St E (61264-2650)
PHONE..................................309 787-4616
Ronald F Carver, *President*
Jan Carver, *President*
Rod Carver, *President*
EMP: 2 EST: 1946
SALES: 200K **Privately Held**
SIC: 2431 5211 5031 Moldings, wood: unfinished & prefinished; doors, wood; window frames, wood; lumber & other building materials; lumber, plywood & millwork

**(G-14774)**
**ANTLER INN MANUFACTORY INC**
7501 50th St (61264-3207)
PHONE..................................309 799-1132
Jeffery Desmet, *President*
EMP: 3
SALES: 250K **Privately Held**
SIC: 3599 Machine shop, jobbing & repair

**(G-14775)**
**BELLOTA AGRSLTIONS TLS USA LLC**
1421 11th St W (61264-2262)
PHONE..................................309 787-2491
Jose Hidalgo, *Managing Dir*
Patricio Echeverria,
▼ EMP: 24 EST: 2008
SALES (est): 6.8MM **Privately Held**
SIC: 3469 3523 Metal stampings; planting, haying, harvesting & processing machinery

**(G-14776)**
**BMS MANUFACTURING COMPANY INC**
651 8th Ave W (61264-2332)
PHONE..................................309 787-3158
Victoria J Bennett, *President*
Thomas Bennet, *Vice Pres*
Daniel M Bennett, *Vice Pres*
EMP: 25
SQ FT: 26,000
SALES (est): 9.5MM **Privately Held**
SIC: 3565 Packaging machinery

**(G-14777)**
**BOHL MACHINE & TOOL COMPANY**
4405 78th Ave (61264-3214)
PHONE..................................309 799-5122
Theodore C Bohl Jr, *President*
Carolyn Bohl, *Corp Secy*
Tim Bohl, *Manager*
EMP: 28
SALES (est): 5.2MM **Privately Held**
WEB: www.bohlmt.com
SIC: 3542 3544 Machine tools, metal forming type; special dies, tools, jigs & fixtures

**(G-14778)**
**CHARNOR INC**
1711 1st Ave E (61264-2610)
PHONE..................................309 787-2427
Fax: 309 787-9410

Josh Hamilton, *Principal*
Anthony Stanley, *CFO*
Ray Inman, *Mktg Coord*
Doreen Braden, *CTO*
▲ **EMP:** 52 **EST:** 2010
**SALES:** 6MM **Privately Held**
**SIC: 3823** Industrial process control instruments

**(G-14779)**
**CHICAGO TUBE AND IRON COMPANY**
Also Called: Quad Cities Plant
1040 11th St W (61264-2243)
P.O. Box 1070 (61264-1070)
**PHONE**..................................309 787-4947
**Fax:** 309 787-7939
Randy Happ, *Purchasing*
James W Glackin, *Finance Other*
Ed Epperson, *Manager*
**EMP:** 40
**SQ FT:** 30,000
**SALES (corp-wide):** 1B **Publicly Held**
**WEB:** www.chicagotube.com
**SIC: 5051** 4225 3498 Tubing, metal; pipe & tubing, steel; general warehousing; fabricated pipe & fittings
**HQ:** Chicago Tube And Iron Company
1 Chicago Tube Dr
Romeoville IL 60446
815 834-2500

**(G-14780)**
**COLLINSON STONE CO (PA)**
Also Called: Milan Stone Quarry
225 1st St E (61264-2509)
P.O. Box 290 (61264-0290)
**PHONE**..................................309 787-7983
**Fax:** 309 787-1402
Kenneth Collinson, *President*
R Deschepper, *Manager*
Robert Collinson, *Admin Sec*
**EMP:** 15
**SQ FT:** 1,500
**SALES (est):** 2MM **Privately Held**
**SIC: 1422** Crushed & broken limestone

**(G-14781)**
**COUNTRY STONE INC (PA)**
6300 75th Ave Ste A (61264-3267)
P.O. Box 1160 (61264-1160)
**PHONE**..................................309 787-1744
Ronald D Bjustrom, *Owner*
Jane Kenny, *Office Mgr*
Shawn P Larson, *Manager*
**EMP:** 35
**SQ FT:** 1,000
**SALES (est):** 148MM **Privately Held**
**SIC: 2499** 2875 3273 3281 Mulch, wood & bark; potting soil, mixed; ready-mixed concrete; cut stone & stone products

**(G-14782)**
**DAVENPORT TRACTOR INC**
11115 Knoxville Rd (61264-5256)
**PHONE**..................................309 781-8305
Allen Jarosz, *General Mgr*
**EMP:** 3
**SALES (corp-wide):** 1.2MM **Privately Held**
**SIC: 3523** Farm machinery & equipment
**PA:** Davenport Tractor, Inc.
318 E 2nd St
Davenport IA 52801
563 323-2295

**(G-14783)**
**DEL-CO-WEST INC**
7507 50th St (61264-3207)
**PHONE**..................................309 799-7543
**Fax:** 309 799-3464
Tim A Honert, *President*
Jeanette Orr, *Manager*
**EMP:** 13
**SQ FT:** 8,000
**SALES (est):** 2.2MM **Privately Held**
**WEB:** www.delcowest.com
**SIC: 3545** 3541 Machine tool accessories; machine tools, metal cutting type

**(G-14784)**
**EDWARDS CREATIVE SERVICES LLC**
435 1st St E (61264-2740)
**PHONE**..................................309 756-0199
**Fax:** 309 756-0224
Cathy Edwards, *Sales Dir*
Tiffany Stott, *Marketing Mgr*
Matt Nielsen, *Graphic Designe*
Steve Edwards,
**EMP:** 14
**SQ FT:** 14,000
**SALES (est):** 1.2MM **Privately Held**
**SIC: 7336** 7312 7319 7311 Graphic arts & related design; outdoor advertising services; transit advertising services; advertising agencies; commercial printing

**(G-14785)**
**ELLIOTT AVIATION ARCFT SLS INC**
6601 74th Ave (61264-3203)
P.O. Box 100, Moline (61266-0100)
**PHONE**..................................309 799-3183
**Fax:** 309 799-9893
Wynn Elliott, *CEO*
Richard Baeder, *Vice Pres*
Rick Michalski, *Vice Pres*
Greg Sahr, *Vice Pres*
Joe Smith, *Vice Pres*
**EMP:** 2
**SALES (est):** 210K **Privately Held**
**SIC: 8711** 7389 3553 Building construction consultant; interior design services; woodworking machinery

**(G-14786)**
**EXPORT PACKAGING CO INC (PA)**
Also Called: Xpac
525 10th Ave E (61264-3117)
**PHONE**..................................309 756-4288
**Fax:** 309 787-0448
Donald Ruggles, *CEO*
Gregory A Ruggies, *President*
John Beck, *Vice Pres*
Bob Smith, *Plant Mgr*
Byron Fernald, *CFO*
**EMP:** 800 **EST:** 1962
**SQ FT:** 1,500,000
**SALES (est):** 112.1MM **Privately Held**
**SIC: 4783** 2448 2441 Packing & crating; pallets, wood; shipping cases, wood: nailed or lock corner

**(G-14787)**
**GETT INDUSTRIES LTD**
Also Called: Machine Job Shop
7307 50th St (61264-3259)
**PHONE**..................................309 799-5131
**Fax:** 309 799-5773
Patricia Edwards, *President*
Timothy Edwards, *President*
Karla Lee, *Manager*
Pam Swemline, *Administration*
**EMP:** 55
**SQ FT:** 45,000
**SALES:** 12MM **Privately Held**
**WEB:** www.gettindustries.com
**SIC: 3599** Machine shop, jobbing & repair

**(G-14788)**
**GROUP O INC**
Also Called: Group O Supply Chain Solution
7300 50th St (61264-3200)
P.O. Box 1220 (61264-1220)
**PHONE**..................................309 736-8660
Stan Rutland, *QC Mgr*
Ambrose Capell, *Branch Mgr*
Bonnie J Haack, *Administration*
**EMP:** 90
**SALES (corp-wide):** 541.7MM **Privately Held**
**SIC: 3648** Decorative area lighting fixtures
**PA:** Group O, Inc.
4905 77th Ave E
Milan IL 61264
309 736-8100

**(G-14789)**
**GROUP O INC**
Group O Supply Chain Solutions
120 4th Ave E (61264-2803)
**PHONE**..................................309 736-8311
Gregg Ontiveros, *Vice Pres*
Robert Ontiveros, *Manager*
**EMP:** 280
**SALES (corp-wide):** 541.7MM **Privately Held**
**SIC: 5085** 5013 3479 Industrial supplies; bearings; automotive supplies; painting of metal products

PA: Group O, Inc.
4905 77th Ave E
Milan IL 61264
309 736-8100

**(G-14790)**
**GROUP O INC**
Group O Direct Marketing Div
4905 77th Ave E (61264-3250)
**PHONE**..................................309 736-8100
Gregg Ontiveros, *Branch Mgr*
**EMP:** 40
**SALES (corp-wide):** 541.7MM **Privately Held**
**SIC: 7331** 7389 2789 8732 Direct mail advertising services; telephone answering service; binding only: books, pamphlets, magazines, etc.; commercial nonphysical research
**PA:** Group O, Inc.
4905 77th Ave E
Milan IL 61264
309 736-8100

**(G-14791)**
**HURST MANUFACTURING CO**
823 9th St W (61264-2214)
P.O. Box 708 (61264-0708)
**PHONE**..................................309 756-9960
Todd Hurst, *President*
William R Hurst, *President*
Peggy Merchie, *Controller*
John Goodwin, *Manager*
**EMP:** 13
**SQ FT:** 10,000
**SALES (est):** 4.3MM **Privately Held**
**SIC: 3492** Hose & tube fittings & assemblies, hydraulic/pneumatic

**(G-14792)**
**LEWIS MACHINE & TOOL CO**
1305 11th St W (61264-2260)
**PHONE**..................................309 787-7151
**Fax:** 309 787-7193
Karl R Lewis, *President*
Neal Hohl, *Mfg Staff*
Mary Henkel, *Comptroller*
▼ **EMP:** 75
**SQ FT:** 22,000
**SALES (est):** 17.1MM **Privately Held**
**WEB:** www.lewismachine.net
**SIC: 3599** Machine shop, jobbing & repair

**(G-14793)**
**MIDAMERICA INDUSTRIES INC**
1519 1st Ave E (61264-2607)
**PHONE**..................................309 787-5119
**Fax:** 309 787-5484
Jeffrey J Leech, *President*
**EMP:** 3
**SQ FT:** 10,000
**SALES:** 300K **Privately Held**
**SIC: 3714** 7532 5561 Motor vehicle parts & accessories; body shop, automotive; recreational vehicle dealers

**(G-14794)**
**MILL CREEK MINING INC**
700 4th St W (61264-2725)
**PHONE**..................................309 787-1414
Beau Brandt, *Exec VP*
**EMP:** 6 **EST:** 2015
**SALES (est):** 406.4K **Privately Held**
**SIC: 1422** Crushed & broken limestone; dolomite, crushed & broken-quarrying

**(G-14795)**
**MOLINE WELDING INC (PA)**
3603 78th Ave (61264-3217)
**PHONE**..................................309 756-0643
**Fax:** 309 756-0225
James Swinburn, *President*
Marilyn Swinburn, *President*
**EMP:** 17 **EST:** 1916
**SQ FT:** 36,000
**SALES (est):** 2.2MM **Privately Held**
**WEB:** www.molinewelding.com
**SIC: 3469** 7692 3441 Metal stampings; welding repair; fabricated structural metal

**(G-14796)**
**MOLINE WELDING INC**
3603 78th Ave (61264-3217)
**PHONE**..................................309 756-0643
James Swinburn, *Owner*
**EMP:** 8

**SALES (corp-wide):** 2.2MM **Privately Held**
**WEB:** www.molinewelding.com
**SIC: 3469** 7692 Metal stampings; welding repair
**PA:** Moline Welding, Inc
3603 78th Ave
Milan IL 61264
309 756-0643

**(G-14797)**
**MORRISON WEIGHING SYSTEMS INC**
7605 50th St (61264-3272)
P.O. Box 860 (61264-0860)
**PHONE**..................................309 799-7311
**Fax:** 309 799-7313
Donald G Morrison, *President*
Janice R Morrison, *Admin Sec*
**EMP:** 9
**SQ FT:** 8,600
**SALES:** 1.2MM **Privately Held**
**WEB:** www.morrison-weighing.com
**SIC: 3596** Weighing machines & apparatus

**(G-14798)**
**POOLS WELDING INC**
816 10th Ave W (61264-2314)
**PHONE**..................................309 787-2083
**Fax:** 309 787-8389
Doyle E Pool, *CFO*
**EMP:** 6 **EST:** 1973
**SQ FT:** 6,642
**SALES (est):** 800.8K **Privately Held**
**WEB:** www.poolswelding.com
**SIC: 1799** 3441 3713 3537 Welding on site; fabricated structural metal; truck & bus bodies; industrial trucks & tractors; sheet metalwork; fabricated plate work (boiler shop)

**(G-14799)**
**QUAD CITIES CONCRETE PDTS LLC**
636 10th Ave W (61264-2309)
**PHONE**..................................309 787-4919
Michael Banks,
Gregory Banks,
Jason Banks,
**EMP:** 9 **EST:** 2014
**SQ FT:** 24,172
**SALES (est):** 1.1MM **Privately Held**
**SIC: 3272** Burial vaults, concrete or precast terrazzo

**(G-14800)**
**R & O SPECIALTIES INCORPORATED (HQ)**
120 4th Ave E (61264-2803)
P.O. Box 1220 (61264-1220)
**PHONE**..................................309 736-8660
**Fax:** 309 736-8661
Gregg Ontiveros, *CEO*
Robert Ontiveros, *President*
Kim Fox, *Vice Pres*
Alfred Ramirez, *Vice Pres*
Bob Marriott, *CFO*
**EMP:** 55
**SQ FT:** 300,000
**SALES (est):** 144.4MM
**SALES (corp-wide):** 541.7MM **Privately Held**
**SIC: 5085** 5013 3479 Industrial supplies; bearings; automotive supplies; painting of metal products
**PA:** Group O, Inc.
4905 77th Ave E
Milan IL 61264
309 736-8100

**(G-14801)**
**R C INDUSTRIAL INC**
Also Called: Rci
255 5th Ave W (61264-2709)
**PHONE**..................................309 756-3724
Clayton H Weissenborn, *President*
Brenda Weisenborn, *Treasurer*
Tara Weisenborn, *Officer*
**EMP:** 7 **EST:** 2006
**SQ FT:** 5,280
**SALES:** 400K **Privately Held**
**SIC: 1796** 3441 Machinery installation; fabricated structural metal

## Milan - Rock Island County

**(G-14802)**
**REFLEX FITNESS PRODUCTS INC**
1130 15th Ave W (61264-2263)
PHONE................................309 756-1050
Fax: 309 756-1052
Mike Adolphson, *President*
Craig Askam, *Vice Pres*
Dan Gluba, *Marketing Staff*
Bryce Adolphson, *Manager*
EMP: 15
SALES: 1.5MM **Privately Held**
SIC: 3949 Exercise equipment; gymnasium equipment

**(G-14803)**
**REYNOLDS MANUFACTURING COMPANY**
630 4th St W (61264-2736)
PHONE................................309 787-8600
Fax: 309 787-7164
Larry Wilson, *General Mgr*
Larry E Wilson, *General Mgr*
Keith Thompson, *Project Engr*
Gary Burrows, *Sales Staff*
Souk Kongkousonh, *Manager*
EMP: 43
SALES (corp-wide): 11.5MM **Privately Held**
WEB: www.reynoldsmfg.com
SIC: 3544 3599 3369 3366 Special dies, tools, jigs & fixtures; machine shop, jobbing & repair; nonferrous foundries; copper foundries; aluminum foundries; gray & ductile iron foundries
PA: Reynolds Manufacturing Company
501 38th St
Rock Island IL 61201
309 788-7443

**(G-14804)**
**RIVERSTONE GROUP INC**
Also Called: Allied Stone
601 Us Route 67 N (61264-2116)
PHONE................................309 787-3141
Fax: 309 787-3752
Matt Aonjevich, *Superintendent*
Jody Pace, *Manager*
EMP: 20
SALES (corp-wide): 4.3B **Privately Held**
WEB: www.riverstonegrp.com
SIC: 5032 1422 Stone, crushed or broken; crushed & broken limestone
PA: Riverstone Group, Inc.
1701 5th Ave
Moline IL 61265
309 757-8250

**(G-14805)**
**ROY E ROTH COMPANY (PA)**
Also Called: Roth's Pump Co.
6th Ave And 4th St (61264)
PHONE................................309 787-1791
Peter P Roth, *CEO*
Ed McRoberts, *Chancellor*
Correen Montgomery, *Mfg Staff*
Ed Mc Roberts, *Sales Mgr*
Dale Klapperich, *Admin Sec*
EMP: 3 EST: 1932
SQ FT: 98,700
SALES (est): 15.9MM **Privately Held**
SIC: 3561 5084 Pump jacks & other pumping equipment; pumps & pumping equipment

**(G-14806)**
**TICKLE ASPHALT CO LTD**
700 4th St W (61264-2725)
PHONE................................309 787-1308
Fax: 309 787-7527
Charles Brandt, *President*
Dennis Heggen, *Plant Mgr*
Todd Brandt, *Treasurer*
Terrence Brandt, *Admin Sec*
EMP: 4
SALES (est): 580K
SALES (corp-wide): 10.3MM **Privately Held**
WEB: www.brandtconstructionco.com
SIC: 3272 Paving materials, prefabricated concrete
PA: Brandt Construction Co.
700 4th St W
Milan IL 61264
309 787-4644

**(G-14807)**
**WALMAN OPTICAL COMPANY**
1280 11th St W (61264-2234)
PHONE................................309 787-0000
Rhonda Whitcomb, *Branch Mgr*
Dan Senatra, *Lab Dir*
EMP: 41
SALES (corp-wide): 356.2MM **Privately Held**
SIC: 3851 Ophthalmic goods
PA: The Walman Optical Company
801 12th Ave N Ste 1
Minneapolis MN 55411
612 520-6000

**(G-14808)**
**WHIPPLES PRINTING PRESS INC**
Also Called: Printing Press The
2410 119th Avenue Ct W (61264-4687)
PHONE................................309 787-3538
Christine D Whipple, *President*
EMP: 4
SALES (est): 270K **Privately Held**
SIC: 2752 Commercial printing, lithographic

**(G-14809)**
**WILBERT VAULT COMPANY**
Also Called: Milan, Wilbert Vault Co
636 10th Ave W (61264-2309)
PHONE................................309 787-5281
Fax: 309 787-7189
Michael Peterson, *President*
Susan Anthony, *Admin Sec*
EMP: 10
SQ FT: 3,000
SALES (est): 1.2MM **Privately Held**
SIC: 3272 Burial vaults, concrete or precast terrazzo

**(G-14810)**
**WINDWARD PRINT STAR INC**
801 1st St E (61264-3102)
PHONE................................309 787-8853
Jiji Korah, *Manager*
EMP: 6
SALES (corp-wide): 89.1MM **Privately Held**
WEB: www.adplex.com
SIC: 2752 Commercial printing, offset
PA: Windward Print Star, Inc.
650 Century Plaza Dr # 120
Houston TX 77073
281 821-5522

## Milford
### Iroquois County

**(G-14811)**
**CLOSET CONCEPT**
1881 E 300 North Rd (60953-6323)
PHONE................................217 375-4214
Fax: 217 375-4214
EMP: 3
SALES (est): 208.6K **Privately Held**
SIC: 2673 Mfg Bags-Plastic/Coated Paper

**(G-14812)**
**FIM ENGINEERING LLC**
2199 E 1120 North Rd (60953-6106)
PHONE................................773 880-8841
Marc Harris, *General Mgr*
EMP: 3
SALES (est): 157.4K **Privately Held**
SIC: 3484 Guns (firearms) or gun parts, 30 mm. & below

**(G-14813)**
**ILLIANA REAL LOG HOMES INC**
107 N Fritz Dr (60953-1017)
PHONE................................815 471-4004
Steven W Cross, *President*
EMP: 5
SALES: 373.4K **Privately Held**
SIC: 2411 Logging

**(G-14814)**
**ROBERT DAVIS & SON INC**
Also Called: Davis Welding
832 N State Route 1 (60953-6347)
PHONE................................815 889-4168
Fax: 815 889-4390
John Davis, *President*
Barbara Davis, *Manager*
EMP: 6 EST: 1928
SQ FT: 6,400
SALES (est): 620K **Privately Held**
WEB: www.fieldpup.com
SIC: 3715 7692 Truck trailers; automotive welding

**(G-14815)**
**WAGNERS LLC**
2812 E 1100 North Rd (60953-6053)
PHONE................................815 889-4101
James Lundquist Jr, *Opers-Prdtn-Mfg*
EMP: 20
SALES (corp-wide): 50MM **Privately Held**
WEB: www.wagnerproducts.com
SIC: 2048 5199 Bird food, prepared; pet supplies
PA: Wagner's, Llc
366 N Broadway Ste 402
Jericho NY 11753
516 933-6580

## Milledgeville
### Carroll County

**(G-14816)**
**CARROLL INDUSTRIAL MOLDS INC**
Also Called: Carroll Industrial Coatings
202 N Washington St (61051-9274)
P.O. Box 429 (61051-0429)
PHONE................................815 225-7250
Fax: 815 225-7260
Craig Dusing, *President*
Kaye A Dusing, *Corp Secy*
Mike Scribner, *Purchasing*
EMP: 19
SQ FT: 36,000
SALES (est): 3.4MM **Privately Held**
WEB: www.carrollmolds.com
SIC: 3544 3543 Industrial molds; industrial patterns

**(G-14817)**
**JSP MOLD**
404 E 4th St (61051-9104)
P.O. Box 669 (61051-0669)
PHONE................................815 225-7110
Fax: 815 225-7272
Paul Sandefer, *General Mgr*
Bob Frederick, *COO*
Phyllis Deal, *Purch Agent*
Kevin Maag, *Financial Exec*
Tami Smith, *Human Res Dir*
EMP: 3
SALES (est): 625K
SALES (corp-wide): 4.9B **Privately Held**
SIC: 3544 3543 3365 Industrial molds; industrial patterns; aluminum foundries
HQ: Jsp International Llc
1285 Drummers Ln Ste 301
Wayne PA 19087
610 651-8600

**(G-14818)**
**SHANKS VETERINARY EQUIPMENT**
505 E Old Mill St (61051-9264)
P.O. Box 397 (61051-0397)
PHONE................................815 225-7700
Fax: 815 225-5130
Mark Dettman, *President*
Al Dettman, *General Mgr*
Jennifer Dettman, *Corp Secy*
EMP: 8
SQ FT: 18,400
SALES: 955.3K **Privately Held**
WEB: www.shanksvet.com
SIC: 3841 7692 Veterinarians' instruments & apparatus; welding repair

## Millington
### Kendall County

**(G-14819)**
**KVK FOUNDRY INC**
302 Vine St (60537-1095)
P.O. Box 159 (60537-0159)
PHONE................................815 695-5212
Fax: 815 695-5218
Angela M Bejarano, *President*
Donald R Garcia, *Vice Pres*
Louise Delcruz, *Treasurer*
EMP: 10
SALES (est): 880K **Privately Held**
SIC: 3365 3366 Aluminum foundries; brass foundry

## Millstadt
### St. Clair County

**(G-14820)**
**ACE GREASE SERVICE INC (PA)**
9035 State Route 163 (62260-3239)
PHONE................................618 781-1207
Fax: 618 337-2248
Mike Costenak, *President*
Michael Kostelac III, *President*
Mike Kostelac, *President*
Chris Pendegraft, *Sales Staff*
Shaun Johnston, *Marketing Staff*
EMP: 3
SALES (est): 4.2MM **Privately Held**
WEB: www.acegrease.com
SIC: 2077 Animal & marine fats & oils

**(G-14821)**
**ACE GREASE SERVICE INC**
9011 State Route 163 (62260-3251)
PHONE................................618 337-0974
Mike Kostelack, *Manager*
EMP: 6 **Privately Held**
WEB: www.acegrease.com
SIC: 2077 Rendering
PA: Ace Grease Service, Inc.
9035 State Route 163
Millstadt IL 62260

**(G-14822)**
**CRUSHED GRAPES LTD**
10 Greenfield Dr (62260-1265)
PHONE................................618 659-3530
Arlene I Scaturro, *President*
Len Scaturro, *Vice Pres*
EMP: 2
SALES (est): 200K **Privately Held**
WEB: www.crushedgrapesltd.com
SIC: 2084 2095 2082 5149 Wines; roasted coffee; beer (alcoholic beverage); wine makers' equipment & supplies

**(G-14823)**
**DOUBLE NICKEL LLC**
Also Called: Detonics Defense Technologies
609 S Breese St Ste 101 (62260-2003)
PHONE................................618 476-3200
Bruce Siddle, *Principal*
EMP: 3
SALES (est): 170K **Privately Held**
SIC: 7382 3484 Security systems services; machine guns & grenade launchers

**(G-14824)**
**DOUBLE NICKEL HOLDINGS LLC**
609 S Breese St Ste 101 (62260-2003)
PHONE................................618 476-3200
Bruce Siddle, *Principal*
EMP: 3
SALES (est): 198.7K **Privately Held**
SIC: 3356 Nickel

**(G-14825)**
**HASTINGS MANUFACTURING INC**
3708 Thorne Briar Ct (62260-2627)
PHONE................................800 338-8688
Robert Hastings, *President*
Christine Hastings, *Vice Pres*
Tracy Walsh, *Opers Mgr*
Rose Brightfield, *Purch Mgr*

Richard Zwiernikowski, *Controller*
**EMP:** 20
**SQ FT:** 1,200
**SALES (est):** 3.9MM  **Privately Held**
**WEB:** www.hastingsmfg.net
**SIC:** 3542  3559  3544  Presses: hydraulic & pneumatic, mechanical & manual; plastics working machinery; special dies, tools, jigs & fixtures

**(G-14826)**
**HUMAN FACTOR RES GROUP INC**
609 Suth Brese St Ste 101  (62260)
**PHONE** .................................. 618 476-3200
Bruce K Siddle, *CEO*
Tracy Donnelly, *General Mgr*
**EMP:** 8
**SALES (est):** 634.5K  **Privately Held**
**SIC:** 2731  Book publishing

**(G-14827)**
**INLAND TECH HOLDINGS LLC**
609 S Breese St  (62260-2003)
**PHONE** .................................. 618 476-7678
Rick Schmidt, *Vice Pres*
**EMP:** 20 EST: 2015
**SQ FT:** 21,600
**SALES (est):** 1.4MM  **Privately Held**
**SIC:** 3613  3674  Control panels, electric; modules, solid state

**(G-14828)**
**ITS SOLAR  LLC**
609 S Breese St  (62260-2003)
**PHONE** .................................. 618 476-7678
Richard Schmidt Sr, *Mng Member*
Joy Vougt, *Assistant*
**EMP:** 3
**SALES (est):** 121.3K  **Privately Held**
**SIC:** 3613  Control panels, electric

**(G-14829)**
**METRO PRINTING & PUBG INC**
Also Called: Record Printing & Publishing
109 W Washington St  (62260-1155)
**PHONE** .................................. 618 476-9587
**Fax:** 618 476-9588
Paul Adrignola, *President*
**EMP:** 12
**SQ FT:** 11,500
**SALES (est):** 2.5MM  **Privately Held**
**WEB:** www.recordprinting.biz
**SIC:** 2752  2791  2789  2721  Commercial printing, lithographic; typesetting; bookbinding & related work; periodicals

**(G-14830)**
**MIDWEST RADIANT OIL AND GAS**
3668 Lake Ln  (62260-2117)
**PHONE** .................................. 618 476-1303
Jasper N Peters, *President*
**EMP:** 1
**SALES (est):** 729K  **Privately Held**
**SIC:** 1311  Crude petroleum & natural gas

**(G-14831)**
**MILLSTADT TOWNSHIP**
Also Called: Road District
18 E Harrison St  (62260-2006)
P.O. Box 274  (62260-0274)
**PHONE** .................................. 618 476-3592
Stan Jarvis, *Commissioner*
**EMP:** 3  **Privately Held**
**WEB:** www.millstadt.org
**SIC:** 3531  Road construction & maintenance machinery
**PA:** Millstadt Township
  820 S Jefferson St
  Millstadt IL 62260

**(G-14832)**
**PLAS-CO INC**
Also Called: Plastic Laminate Speciality Co
1475 B And H Indus Ct  (62260-2051)
**PHONE** .................................. 618 476-1761
**Fax:** 618 476-1854
George Baur, *President*
Jack Matthews, *Vice Pres*
Gina Mathews, *Treasurer*
John Heil, *Manager*
**EMP:** 15
**SQ FT:** 15,000
**SALES:** 1.5MM  **Privately Held**
**WEB:** www.plas-co.com
**SIC:** 2542  2434  Cabinets: show, display or storage: except wood; counters or counter display cases: except wood; wood kitchen cabinets

---

### Minier
*Tazewell County*

**(G-14833)**
**LAUGHING DOG GRAPHICS**
Also Called: Sudden Impact Sports
207 N Main Ave  (61759-7524)
P.O. Box 889  (61759-0889)
**PHONE** .................................. 309 392-3330
**Fax:** 309 392-3156
Kenny Williams, *Owner*
**EMP:** 3
**SQ FT:** 3,500
**SALES (est):** 44K  **Privately Held**
**SIC:** 2759  Screen printing

---

### Minonk
*Woodford County*

**(G-14834)**
**SMF  INC (PA)**
1550 N Industrial Park Rd  (61760-9700)
**PHONE** .................................. 309 432-2586
**Fax:** 309 432-2390
Brian Brown, *CEO*
Terry Manning, *Vice Pres*
Ken Bauer, *Opers Mgr*
Paul Halvorsen, *Purchasing*
Paul J Halvorsen, *CFO*
**EMP:** 186
**SQ FT:** 160,000
**SALES (est):** 50.2MM  **Privately Held**
**WEB:** www.smf-inc.com
**SIC:** 3441  Fabricated structural metal

**(G-14835)**
**ZARC INTERNATIONAL  INC**
529 S Petri Dr  (61760-7646)
P.O. Box 108  (61760-0108)
**PHONE** .................................. 309 807-2565
David T Froelich, *President*
**EMP:** 17
**SQ FT:** 15,000
**SALES:** 1.4MM  **Privately Held**
**SIC:** 3949  3999  Bags, golf; chairs, hydraulic, barber & beauty shop

---

### Minooka
*Grundy County*

**(G-14836)**
**APPLETON RACK & PINIONS INC**
110 Industrial Dr Unit E  (60447-9152)
**PHONE** .................................. 815 467-9583
**Fax:** 815 467-1179
Fred Appleton, *President*
Frances Appleton, *Admin Sec*
**EMP:** 10
**SQ FT:** 2,000
**SALES (est):** 1.1MM  **Privately Held**
**SIC:** 3714  Motor vehicle steering systems & parts

**(G-14837)**
**BUILDERS UNITED SALES CO INC**
713 Briarcliff Dr  (60447-8827)
**PHONE** .................................. 815 467-2224
Dennis Murnighan Jr, *President*
Patrick Murnighan, *Chairman*
Dennis Murnighan Sr, *Vice Pres*
**EMP:** 4 EST: 1932
**SQ FT:** 2,000
**SALES (est):** 550K  **Privately Held**
**WEB:** www.buildersunitedsales.com
**SIC:** 2542  Partitions & fixtures, except wood

**(G-14838)**
**DOLLS LETTERING INC**
110 Industrial Dr Unit A  (60447-9130)
**PHONE** .................................. 815 467-8000
Jeffrey A Doll, *President*
**EMP:** 5
**SALES (est):** 333.6K  **Privately Held**
**WEB:** www.dollslettering.com
**SIC:** 2759  Screen printing

**(G-14839)**
**DYNE INC**
7280 E Us Highway 6  (60447-9144)
P.O. Box 848  (60447-0848)
**PHONE** .................................. 815 521-1111
Roy Breaudoin, *President*
Shawan Breaudoin, *Manager*
▲ **EMP:** 8
**SQ FT:** 100,000
**SALES (est):** 1MM  **Privately Held**
**WEB:** www.dyneproducts.com
**SIC:** 2221  Upholstery, tapestry & wall covering fabrics

**(G-14840)**
**ELCON INC (PA)**
600 Twin Rail Dr  (60447-9465)
P.O. Box 910  (60447-0910)
**PHONE** .................................. 815 467-9500
Frank J Garrone Jr, *President*
Steven E Holic, *CFO*
Joe Defazio, *Manager*
Bob Mason, *Manager*
Lorraine Garrone, *Admin Sec*
**EMP:** 50 EST: 1988
**SQ FT:** 25,000
**SALES (est):** 9MM  **Privately Held**
**WEB:** www.elconinc.net
**SIC:** 3625  7629  3829  3822  Control equipment, electric; electronic equipment repair; measuring & controlling devices; auto controls regulating residntl & coml environmt & applncs; printed circuit boards; switchgear & switchboard apparatus

**(G-14841)**
**LAB SOFTWARE INC**
2021 Holt Rd  (60447-8698)
**PHONE** .................................. 815 521-9116
David J Meyer, *President*
**EMP:** 5
**SQ FT:** 7,200
**SALES (est):** 437K  **Privately Held**
**WEB:** www.inkjetkit.com
**SIC:** 7372  7371  7373  Prepackaged software; custom computer programming services; systems software development services

**(G-14842)**
**METALSTAMP INC**
6800 E Minooka Rd  (60447-9445)
**PHONE** .................................. 815 467-7800
**Fax:** 815 467-7838
Leroy Hutchinson, *President*
Kathy F Hutchinson, *Vice Pres*
Tom Skibinski, *Opers Mgr*
Jack Gockman, *Prdtn Mgr*
Steve Benson, *Engineer*
▲ **EMP:** 50
**SQ FT:** 12,000
**SALES (est):** 13.6MM  **Privately Held**
**WEB:** www.metalstampinc.com
**SIC:** 3469  Metal stampings

**(G-14843)**
**MIDWEST DETENTION SYSTEMS INC**
105 Industrial Dr  (60447-9558)
**PHONE** .................................. 815 521-4580
Ron Coose, *President*
Dennis Price, *Vice Pres*
**EMP:** 5
**SALES (est):** 646.9K  **Privately Held**
**SIC:** 3442  Window & door frames

**(G-14844)**
**NARVICK BROS LUMBER CO INC**
Also Called: Narvick Bros Ready Mix
801 Rail Way Ct  (60447-9242)
**PHONE** .................................. 815 521-1773
**Fax:** 815 521-0986
Tim Hardy, *Manager*
**EMP:** 20
**SALES (corp-wide):** 10.8MM  **Privately Held**
**WEB:** www.narvickbrothers.net
**SIC:** 3273  Ready-mixed concrete
**PA:** Narvick Bros. Lumber Co., Inc.
  1037 Armstrong St
  Morris IL 60450
  815 942-1173

**(G-14845)**
**OAK COURT CREATIONS**
202 Oak Ct  (60447-9148)
**PHONE** .................................. 815 467-7676
Beverly Sievers, *President*
**EMP:** 3
**SALES (est):** 344.1K  **Privately Held**
**WEB:** www.oakcourtcreations.com
**SIC:** 2844  Bath salts

**(G-14846)**
**PROMPT USA INC**
1502 Red Top Ln  (60447-8261)
**PHONE** .................................. 309 660-0222
Constantin Tenea, *Owner*
**EMP:** 3
**SALES (est):** 206.8K  **Privately Held**
**SIC:** 3799  Carriages, horse drawn

**(G-14847)**
**SHIELD ELECTRONICS LLC**
512 Twin Rail Dr Ste 220  (60447-9353)
P.O. Box 6131, Lindenhurst  (60046-6131)
**PHONE** .................................. 815 467-4134
Camden Jerup, *Mng Member*
Tim Louis,
**EMP:** 4 EST: 2015
**SQ FT:** 1,400
**SALES (est):** 150K  **Privately Held**
**SIC:** 3699  8748  Security control equipment & systems; telecommunications consultant

**(G-14848)**
**UMT WIND DOWN CO**
105 Indl Dr  (60447)
**PHONE** .................................. 815 467-7900
**Fax:** 815 467-7989
Dennis Price, *President*
**EMP:** 36 EST: 1979
**SALES (est):** 37.7K
**SALES (corp-wide):** 9MM  **Privately Held**
**SIC:** 3541  Machine tool replacement & repair parts, metal cutting types
**PA:** Elcon, Inc
  600 Twin Rail Dr
  Minooka IL 60447
  815 467-9500

---

### Mode
*Shelby County*

**(G-14849)**
**IOLA QUARRY INC**
Also Called: Brush Creek Quarry
2671 County Hwy 6  (62444)
**PHONE** .................................. 217 682-3865
**Fax:** 217 682-3877
Bryan Hood, *President*
**EMP:** 10
**SALES (corp-wide):** 111.1MM  **Privately Held**
**SIC:** 1422  Limestones, ground
**HQ:** Iola Quarry Inc
  202 W Main St Ste A
  Salem IL
  618 548-1585

---

### Mokena
*Will County*

**(G-14850)**
**ALINE INTERNATIONAL LLC**
9100 W 191st St Ste 103  (60448-8773)
**PHONE** .................................. 708 478-2471
Liang Ruquan,
▲ **EMP:** 8
**SALES (est):** 1.1MM
**SALES (corp-wide):** 23.1MM  **Privately Held**
**SIC:** 2599  Cabinets, factory

# Mokena - Will County (G-14851)

**PA:** Shouguang Sanyang Wood Industry Co Ltd
West End Of Anqian St., Economic And Technology Development Zone
Shouguang  26270
536 578-7705

### (G-14851)
### ALPHA LASER OF CHICAGO
9632 194th Pl (60448-9344)
**PHONE**..................................708 478-0464
Jack McCallum, *Owner*
**EMP:** 2
**SQ FT:** 800
**SALES:** 250K  **Privately Held**
**SIC:** 3861  Toners, prepared photographic (not made in chemical plants)

### (G-14852)
### AMERICAN MACHINE PDTS & SVCS
11863 W Josephine Dr (60448-8480)
**PHONE**..................................708 743-9088
Edward C Richerme, *President*
**EMP:** 3
**SALES (est):** 227.2K  **Privately Held**
**SIC:** 3451  Screw machine products

### (G-14853)
### APPLIED ARTS & SCIENCES INC
Also Called: Hangerjack
21432 Prestancia Dr (60448-8404)
P.O. Box 3814, Winter Park FL (32790-3814)
**PHONE**..................................407 288-8228
Jack A Fugett, *President*
Dina Fugett, *Vice Pres*
Mark Fugett, *Vice Pres*
**EMP:** 4
**SQ FT:** 5,000
**SALES (est):** 344K  **Privately Held**
**SIC:** 3089  Clothes hangers, plastic

### (G-14854)
### ARCHITCTURAL GRILLES SUNSHADES
9950 W 190th St (60448-5600)
**PHONE**..................................708 479-9458
John Trainor, *CEO*
**EMP:** 10
**SQ FT:** 5,000
**SALES (est):** 3.8MM  **Privately Held**
**WEB:** www.agsinc.org
**SIC:** 3354  Aluminum extruded products

### (G-14855)
### ASPEN CARPET DESIGNS
11335 Stratford Rd (60448-2007)
**PHONE**..................................815 483-8501
Gerald Krull, *Principal*
**EMP:** 3
**SALES (est):** 202.2K  **Privately Held**
**WEB:** www.aspencarpetdesigns.com
**SIC:** 2273  Carpets & rugs

### (G-14856)
### CALUMET SCREW MACHINE PRODUCTS
19600 97th Ave (60448-9388)
**PHONE**..................................708 479-1660
**Fax:** 708 479-1682
Louis J Bertoletti, *President*
**EMP:** 70
**SQ FT:** 48,000
**SALES (est):** 15.7MM  **Privately Held**
**WEB:** www.calscrew.com
**SIC:** 3451  Screw machine products

### (G-14857)
### CHICAGO FASTENER  INC
10902 Walnut Ln (60448-1652)
**PHONE**..................................708 479-9770
**Fax:** 708 479-9450
Evelyn Vujevich, *President*
Ron Rodeghero, *VP Opers*
▲ **EMP:** 10
**SQ FT:** 22,000
**SALES (est):** 2.5MM  **Privately Held**
**WEB:** www.chicagofastener.com
**SIC:** 3452  Bolts, metal

### (G-14858)
### CHICAP PIPE LINE COMPANY
18401 Wolf Rd (60448-9016)
**PHONE**..................................708 479-1219
**Fax:** 708 479-9208
Jack Howes, *District Mgr*
**EMP:** 12
**SALES (est):** 1.3MM  **Privately Held**
**SIC:** 1311  Crude petroleum & natural gas

### (G-14859)
### CITIZENPRIME LLC
Also Called: Firepenny
8940 W 192nd St Ste I (60448-8137)
**PHONE**..................................708 995-1241
Brian Moke, *Mng Member*
**EMP:** 1
**SQ FT:** 1,600
**SALES (est):** 225K  **Privately Held**
**SIC:** 5023  3569  Fireplace equipment & accessories; firefighting apparatus & related equipment

### (G-14860)
### DETAILS ETC
19256 85th Ct (60448-8854)
**PHONE**..................................708 932-5543
Phyllis Bauer, *President*
**EMP:** 16
**SALES (est):** 1.2MM  **Privately Held**
**WEB:** www.detailsetc.net
**SIC:** 3272  Concrete products

### (G-14861)
### FIRE SYSTEMS HOLDINGS  INC
Also Called: Automatic Fire Controls
8940 W 192nd St Ste M (60448-8137)
**PHONE**..................................708 333-4130
Charles S Cebula, *CEO*
Tom Hughes, *Opers Mgr*
**EMP:** 15
**SALES (est):** 2.8MM  **Privately Held**
**SIC:** 3569  Sprinkler systems, fire: automatic

### (G-14862)
### FORMAX  INC
9150 W 191st St (60448-1394)
P.O. Box 3 (60448-0003)
**PHONE**..................................708 479-3000
**Fax:** 708 479-3598
Mel Cohen, *President*
Carl Bueschel, *Maint Spvr*
Bill Dickover, *Cust Mgr*
Michael Kamp, *Administration*
**EMP:** 44
**SALES (est):** 10.8MM
**SALES (corp-wide):** 1.4B  **Privately Held**
**SIC:** 3556  Food products machinery
**HQ:** Provisur Technologies, Inc.
9150 W 191st St
Mokena IL 60448
708 479-3500

### (G-14863)
### FRANK MILLER & SONS INC (PA)
Also Called: Fms of Wisconsin Div
10002 W 190th Pl (60448-8752)
P.O. Box 8215, South Bend IN (46660-8215)
**PHONE**..................................708 201-7200
Richard Miller, *President*
James A Miller Jr, *Vice Pres*
Johanna McInerney, *Admin Sec*
**EMP:** 30 **EST:** 1889
**SQ FT:** 87,000
**SALES (est):** 5MM  **Privately Held**
**WEB:** www.icemelt.com
**SIC:** 2842  2869  2879  2819  Sweeping compounds, oil or water absorbent, clay or sawdust; cleaning or polishing preparations; chemical preparations; fungicides, herbicides; industrial inorganic chemicals

### (G-14864)
### FREEDOM DESIGN & DECALS INC
18811 90th Ave Ste G (60448-8030)
**PHONE**..................................815 806-8172
Julie Raduen, *Owner*
**EMP:** 3
**SALES (est):** 270K  **Privately Held**
**SIC:** 2759  Decals: printing

### (G-14865)
### FUTURE ENVIRONMENTAL INC (PA)
19701 97th Ave (60448-9391)
**PHONE**..................................708 479-6900
**Fax:** 708 479-6890
Steven A Lempera, *President*
Ryan Fruendt, *CPA*
Carolyn Murphy, *Office Mgr*
Jackie Porch, *Administration*
**EMP:** 110
**SQ FT:** 24,000
**SALES (est):** 55.9MM  **Privately Held**
**WEB:** www.futureenvironmental.com
**SIC:** 2842  4953  Specialty cleaning preparations; recycling, waste materials

### (G-14866)
### GALLASI CUT STONE & MARBLE LLC
10001 191st St (60448-8361)
P.O. Box 2848, Orland Park (60462-1097)
**PHONE**..................................708 479-9494
Paul Glassi, *Safety Mgr*
Paul Gallasi,
**EMP:** 22
**SQ FT:** 13,000
**SALES (est):** 2.7MM  **Privately Held**
**SIC:** 5032  3281  Stone, crushed or broken; cut stone & stone products

### (G-14867)
### GEORGE PAGELS COMPANY
9910 W 190th St Ste H (60448-5607)
**PHONE**..................................708 478-7036
Richard Pagel, *CEO*
**EMP:** 3
**SALES (est):** 356.5K  **Privately Held**
**SIC:** 3272  Columns, concrete

### (G-14868)
### GERBER MANUFACTURING (GM) LLC
Also Called: GM Lighting
9830 W 190th St Ste F (60448-5603)
**PHONE**..................................708 478-0100
Steve Ceseretti, *Sales Mgr*
Dennise Ziegler, *Manager*
Sylvan Gerber,
Rob Gerber,
David Meyer,
▲ **EMP:** 11
**SQ FT:** 5,000
**SALES (est):** 1.2MM  **Privately Held**
**SIC:** 3645  Residential lighting fixtures

### (G-14869)
### HUSKY INJECTION MOLDING
8845 W 192nd St Ste B (60448-8455)
**PHONE**..................................708 479-9049
Rick Tustin, *Manager*
**EMP:** 17
**SALES (est):** 2.9MM  **Privately Held**
**SIC:** 3089  Injection molding of plastics

### (G-14870)
### HYDRIVE SALES
8808 Clare Ave (60448-8612)
**PHONE**..................................708 478-8194
Debbie Partington, *Principal*
**EMP:** 4 **EST:** 2000
**SALES (est):** 214.7K  **Privately Held**
**SIC:** 2086  Carbonated beverages, nonalcoholic: bottled & canned

### (G-14871)
### ILLIANA MACHINE & MFG CORP
19700 97th Ave (60448-9396)
**PHONE**..................................708 479-1333
**Fax:** 708 479-1361
Tito T Mattera, *President*
Anthony U Mattera, *Corp Secy*
▲ **EMP:** 60
**SQ FT:** 34,500
**SALES (est):** 7.9MM  **Privately Held**
**SIC:** 3599  Machine shop, jobbing & repair

### (G-14872)
### ILLINOIS TOOL WORKS INC
Also Called: ITW Engineered Components
9629 197th St (60448-9351)
**PHONE**..................................708 342-6000
**Fax:** 708 479-7212
Pat Allie, *Branch Mgr*
**EMP:** 132
**SALES (corp-wide):** 13.8B  **Publicly Held**
**SIC:** 3965  3499  2821  Fasteners; strapping, metal; adhesives & sealants
**PA:** Illinois Tool Works Inc.
155 Harlem Ave
Glenview IL 60025
847 724-7500

### (G-14873)
### ILLINOIS TOOL WORKS INC
ITW Deltar Fuel Systems Div
9629 197th St (60448-9351)
**PHONE**..................................708 479-7200
Judy Lake, *Human Resources*
Denise Morris, *Manager*
Brian Peeck, *Manager*
Bob Belcher, *Info Tech Mgr*
Robert Belcher, *Technology*
**EMP:** 200
**SQ FT:** 50,000
**SALES (corp-wide):** 13.8B  **Publicly Held**
**SIC:** 3089  3714  3544  Plastic hardware & building products; motor vehicle parts & accessories; special dies, tools, jigs & fixtures
**PA:** Illinois Tool Works Inc.
155 Harlem Ave
Glenview IL 60025
847 724-7500

### (G-14874)
### INDUSTRIAL MAINTENANCE & MCHY
9618 194th Pl (60448-9344)
**PHONE**..................................815 726-0030
**Fax:** 815 726-0050
Leo Kienig, *President*
Anna Kienig, *Vice Pres*
**EMP:** 5
**SQ FT:** 30,000
**SALES:** 400K  **Privately Held**
**SIC:** 3599  7692  3443  Machine shop, jobbing & repair; welding repair; fabricated plate work (boiler shop)

### (G-14875)
### INTEGRITY SIGN COMPANY
18770 88th Ave Unit A (60448-8777)
**PHONE**..................................708 532-5038
Ken Becvar, *President*
Keith Hlad, *Vice Pres*
**EMP:** 12
**SALES (est):** 1.2MM  **Privately Held**
**SIC:** 3993  Signs & advertising specialties

### (G-14876)
### JCL SPECIALTY PRODUCTS  INC
19106 S Blackhawk Pkwy (60448-8985)
**PHONE**..................................815 806-2202
Joan Kujawa, *President*
Thomas Kujawa, *Vice Pres*
Lisa Rubin, *Treasurer*
**EMP:** 4
**SALES (est):** 708.8K  **Privately Held**
**SIC:** 2992  Lubricating oils & greases

### (G-14877)
### JOHNSON DIARIES
Also Called: Johnson Editorial Limited
9850 W 190th St Ste E (60448-5606)
**PHONE**..................................708 478-2882
Dale Rettker, *President*
▲ **EMP:** 2
**SALES (est):** 214.3K  **Privately Held**
**SIC:** 2782  Diaries

### (G-14878)
### LANDQUIST & SON  INC
Also Called: Magiglide
9850 W 190th St Ste L (60448-5606)
**PHONE**..................................847 674-6600
**Fax:** 847 674-6674
Dennis Box, *President*
Leanne Davis, *Treasurer*
**EMP:** 20 **EST:** 1893
**SQ FT:** 3,000
**SALES (est):** 3.2MM  **Privately Held**
**SIC:** 2431  Doors, wood; interior & ornamental woodwork & trim

### (G-14879)
### LETTERMEN SIGNAGE INC
19912 Wolf Rd (60448-1318)
**PHONE**..................................708 479-5161
**Fax:** 708 479-4748
Lawrence W Hansen, *President*

John Hansen, *Vice Pres*
**EMP:** 7
**SQ FT:** 1,800
**SALES:** 800K  **Privately Held**
**WEB:** www.lettermensign.com
**SIC:** 7389  3993  Sign painting & lettering shop; signs & advertising specialties

**(G-14880)**
**LIGHTING DESIGN BY MICHAEL ANT**
9840 Forestview Dr  (60448-7774)
**PHONE**..................................708 289-4783
Michael Gandy, *Owner*
**EMP:** 3
**SALES:** 200K  **Privately Held**
**SIC:** 3646  8748  Commercial indusl & institutional electric lighting fixtures; lighting consultant

**(G-14881)**
**LIGO PRODUCTS INC**
9100 W 191st St Ste 101  (60448-8773)
**PHONE**..................................708 478-1800
Ss Lee, *President*
Su-Tsen Lee, *Admin Sec*
▲ **EMP:** 34
**SQ FT:** 350,000
**SALES (est):** 4.6MM  **Privately Held**
**WEB:** www.ligoproducts.com
**SIC:** 2519  5021  Fiberglass furniture, household: padded or plain; household furniture

**(G-14882)**
**M H DETRICK COMPANY**
9400 Bormet Dr Ste 10  (60448-7402)
**PHONE**..................................708 479-5085
Fax: 708 479-1030
R J Pena, *President*
Eric Bloom, *Vice Pres*
K L Farrell, *Vice Pres*
Roger L Hosbein, *Vice Pres*
Jim Neely, *VP Sales*
▲ **EMP:** 31  **EST:** 1914
**SALES (est):** 11.3MM  **Privately Held**
**WEB:** www.mhdetrick.com
**SIC:** 3567  8711  3322  3321  Industrial furnaces & ovens; engineering services; malleable iron foundries; gray & ductile iron foundries; nonclay refractories; ceramic wall & floor tile

**(G-14883)**
**MARLEY CANDLES**
12525 187th St  (60448-8278)
**PHONE**..................................815 485-6604
Fax: 815 485-1067
Alice Fixari, *Owner*
**EMP:** 20
**SQ FT:** 4,784
**SALES (est):** 849.4K  **Privately Held**
**WEB:** www.marleycandles.com
**SIC:** 5947  5999  3999  Gift shop; candle shops; candles

**(G-14884)**
**MAX RESOURCES INC**
9951 W 190th St Ste G  (60448-8336)
**PHONE**..................................708 478-5656
James Derose, *President*
▲ **EMP:** 7
**SALES (est):** 1.1MM  **Privately Held**
**SIC:** 2541  Window backs, store or lunchroom, prefabricated: wood

**(G-14885)**
**METRIC FELT CO**
10201 191st St Bldg 3  (60448-8358)
**PHONE**..................................708 479-7979
Fax: 708 479-4177
James Duhig, *President*
Ann Duhig, *Marketing Staff*
Kathy Duhig, *Office Mgr*
▲ **EMP:** 8
**SQ FT:** 6,500
**SALES (est):** 1.2MM  **Privately Held**
**WEB:** www.metricfelt.com
**SIC:** 2299  Felts & felt products

**(G-14886)**
**MJ WORKS HOSE & FITTING LLC (PA)**
11122 W 189th Pl Bldg C1  (60448-8963)
**PHONE**..................................708 995-5723
Fax: 708 479-9310

Marty Martin, *Mng Member*
Lisa Martin,
**EMP:** 3
**SQ FT:** 1,500
**SALES:** 285K  **Privately Held**
**SIC:** 5085  3492  Valves & fittings; fluid power valves & hose fittings

**(G-14887)**
**NORCHEM INC**
Also Called: Norchem Industries, A Division
8910 W 192nd St Ste O  (60448-8111)
**PHONE**..................................708 478-4777
Fax: 708 478-4776
Dennis G Pardikes, *President*
Wayne Wise, *Controller*
**EMP:** 12
**SQ FT:** 8,000
**SALES (est):** 3.2MM  **Privately Held**
**WEB:** www.norchem.com
**SIC:** 3559  Chemical machinery & equipment

**(G-14888)**
**NORTH AMERICAN SAFETY PRODUCTS**
8910 W 192nd St Ste C  (60448-8111)
**PHONE**..................................815 469-1144
Martin Mobeck, *President*
Nicole Pfeiffer, *Manager*
Janelle Wozniak, *Technical Staff*
Cynthia Ruzon, *Director*
▲ **EMP:** 6
**SQ FT:** 12,000
**SALES (est):** 2.7MM  **Privately Held**
**WEB:** www.versa-guard.com
**SIC:** 5084  5999  3499  Safety equipment; safety supplies & equipment; barricades, metal

**(G-14889)**
**OZINGA BROS INC (PA)**
19001 Old Lagrange Rd # 30  (60448-8012)
**PHONE**..................................708 326-4200
Martin Ozinga III, *Ch of Bd*
James A Ozinga, *Vice Pres*
Brent Dyk, *Treasurer*
Tim Nelson, *Controller*
Bryan Vankampen, *Business Anlyst*
**EMP:** 20  **EST:** 1928
**SALES (est):** 221.8MM  **Privately Held**
**SIC:** 3273  5032  Ready-mixed concrete; brick, stone & related material

**(G-14890)**
**OZINGA INDIANA RDYMX CON INC**
19001 Old Lagrange Rd  (60448-8012)
**PHONE**..................................708 479-9050
Fax: 708 326-4201
**EMP:** 4
**SALES (est):** 460.3K  **Privately Held**
**SIC:** 3273  Ready-mixed concrete

**(G-14891)**
**OZINGA MATERIALS INC**
19001 Old Lagrange Rd  (60448-8012)
**PHONE**..................................309 364-3401
Martin Ozinga III, *President*
Barry N Voorn, *Admin Sec*
**EMP:** 13
**SALES (est):** 2.1MM  **Privately Held**
**SIC:** 3273  Ready-mixed concrete

**(G-14892)**
**OZINGA READY MIX CONCRETE INC**
19001 Old Lagrange Rd # 300  (60448-8012)
**PHONE**..................................708 326-4200
Justin Ozinga, *President*
Martin Ozinga, *President*
Barry N Voorn, *Admin Sec*
**EMP:** 33
**SALES (est):** 9.5MM  **Privately Held**
**SIC:** 8711  3272  5999  3273  Building construction consultant; concrete products; concrete products, pre-cast; ready-mixed concrete

**(G-14893)**
**OZINGA S SUBN RDYMX CON INC**
18825 Old Lagrange Rd  (60448-8350)
**PHONE**..................................708 479-3080

Thomas Kerkstra, *Branch Mgr*
**EMP:** 10
**SALES (corp-wide):** 221.8MM  **Privately Held**
**WEB:** www.ozinga.com
**SIC:** 3273  Ready-mixed concrete
**HQ:** Ozinga South Suburban Ready Mix Concrete, Inc.
  19001 Old Lagrange Rd # 300
  Mokena IL 60448

**(G-14894)**
**OZINGA S SUBN RDYMX CON INC (HQ)**
Also Called: Ozinga South Suburban RMC
19001 Old Lagrange Rd # 300  (60448-8012)
**PHONE**..................................708 326-4201
Fax: 708 478-2949
Justin Ozinga, *President*
Mark Ronan, *General Mgr*
Amit Arifi, *Administration*
Kent Bratt, *Administration*
**EMP:** 55
**SALES (est):** 30.6MM
**SALES (corp-wide):** 221.8MM  **Privately Held**
**WEB:** www.ozinga.com
**SIC:** 3273  Ready-mixed concrete
**PA:** Ozinga Bros., Inc.
  19001 Old Lagrange Rd # 30
  Mokena IL 60448
  708 326-4200

**(G-14895)**
**PHOENIX INDUSTRIES INC**
10601 Saint John Dr  (60448-1744)
**PHONE**..................................708 478-5474
James Taylor-Gurley, *Principal*
▲ **EMP:** 3
**SALES (est):** 249.5K  **Privately Held**
**SIC:** 3999  Manufacturing industries

**(G-14896)**
**POLYENVIRO LABS INC**
9960 191st St Ste K  (60448-8642)
**PHONE**..................................708 489-0195
Vishnu Gor, *President*
Kanak Gor, *Treasurer*
Allen Resnick, *Admin Sec*
**EMP:** 4
**SQ FT:** 11,000
**SALES (est):** 673K  **Privately Held**
**SIC:** 2992  2869  3471  2899  Lubricating oils & greases; industrial organic chemicals; plating & polishing; chemical preparations

**(G-14897)**
**PRINTERS QUILL INC**
Also Called: AlphaGraphics
19135 S Blackhawk Pkwy  (60448-8986)
**PHONE**..................................708 429-3636
Fax: 708 429-7776
Thomas Kane, *President*
Margaret Kane, *Admin Sec*
**EMP:** 6
**SQ FT:** 2,500
**SALES:** 780K  **Privately Held**
**SIC:** 2752  Commercial printing, lithographic

**(G-14898)**
**PRINTING BY JOSEPH**
19640 S La Grange Rd  (60448-9321)
**PHONE**..................................708 479-2669
Fax: 708 479-4706
Joseph Koszulinski, *Owner*
**EMP:** 3
**SQ FT:** 500
**SALES (est):** 343.6K  **Privately Held**
**WEB:** www.photoworkshop.com
**SIC:** 2752  2791  2789  Commercial printing, offset; typesetting; bookbinding & related work

**(G-14899)**
**PURIFIED LUBRICANTS INC**
9629 194th St  (60448-9301)
**PHONE**..................................708 478-3500
Fax: 708 478-3504
Robert J Maloney, *President*
**EMP:** 22
**SQ FT:** 6,000

**SALES (est):** 2.3MM  **Privately Held**
**WEB:** www.purifiedlubricants.com
**SIC:** 1389  Construction, repair & dismantling services

**(G-14900)**
**ROTOSPRAY MFG INC**
Also Called: Roto Spray Manufacturing
10315 Aileen Ave  (60448-3331)
**PHONE**..................................708 478-3307
Joseph R Kral, *President*
**EMP:** 4
**SALES (est):** 233.8K  **Privately Held**
**WEB:** www.rotospray.com
**SIC:** 7699  3569  Tool repair services; general industrial machinery

**(G-14901)**
**RRR GRAPHICS & FILM CORP**
Also Called: Triple R Graphics
19759 Westminster Dr  (60448-2404)
**PHONE**..................................708 478-4573
**EMP:** 8
**SALES (est):** 1MM  **Privately Held**
**SIC:** 2752  2791  2789  Lithographic Commercial Printing Typesetting Services Bookbinding/Related Work

**(G-14902)**
**RYAN INDUSTRIES**
9515 191st St  (60448-8349)
P.O. Box 164  (60448-0164)
**PHONE**..................................708 479-7600
David Susay, *Principal*
**EMP:** 3
**SALES (est):** 213.1K  **Privately Held**
**SIC:** 3999  Manufacturing industries

**(G-14903)**
**SMS TECHNICAL SERVICES LLC**
19700 97th Ave  (60448-9390)
**PHONE**..................................708 479-1333
Marie Muhr, *Purch Agent*
Tito T Mattera, *Branch Mgr*
**EMP:** 3  **Privately Held**
**SIC:** 3559  Sewing machines & hat & zipper making machinery
**HQ:** Sms Technical Services Llc
  210 W Kensinger Dr # 300
  Cranberry Township PA 16066
  724 553-3420

**(G-14904)**
**SPECIFIC PRESS BRAKE DIES INC**
9439 Enterprise Dr  (60448-8319)
**PHONE**..................................708 478-1776
Janett Pelech, *President*
Lynda Crites, *Vice Pres*
Bruno Pelech, *Vice Pres*
Bruno J Pelech, *Manager*
**EMP:** 11  **EST:** 1996
**SQ FT:** 3,200
**SALES (est):** 1.7MM  **Privately Held**
**WEB:** www.specificbrakedies.com
**SIC:** 3544  Special dies, tools, jigs & fixtures

**(G-14905)**
**STORE 409 INC**
Also Called: Image 360 - Mokena
9981 W 190th St Ste K  (60448-5613)
**PHONE**..................................708 478-5751
Fax: 708 478-5752
Fred Osborne, *President*
Jon Osborne, *Vice Pres*
Jonathan Osborne, *Vice Pres*
**EMP:** 10
**SQ FT:** 5,000
**SALES (est):** 1.1MM  **Privately Held**
**SIC:** 3993  Signs & advertising specialties

**(G-14906)**
**SUBURBAN MACHINE & TOOL**
8119 189th St  (60448-8840)
**PHONE**..................................815 469-2221
Fax: 815 469-9381
Alan Pokrzywa, *Owner*
**EMP:** 5  **EST:** 1977
**SQ FT:** 7,000
**SALES (est):** 492.8K  **Privately Held**
**SIC:** 3599  Machine shop, jobbing & repair

### (G-14907)
**SURFACE SOLUTIONS ILLINOIS INC**
9615 194th Pl (60448-9317)
PHONE..................................708 571-3449
Fax: 708 571-3445
Sandra Acosta, *President*
Mark Mercado, *General Mgr*
**EMP:** 4 **EST:** 2014
**SQ FT:** 11,200
**SALES (est):** 1.2MM **Privately Held**
**SIC:** 1799 2541 1741 Counter top installation; counter & sink tops; masonry & other stonework

### (G-14908)
**SUSTAINABLE SOURCING LLC**
19633 S La Grange Rd (60448-9360)
PHONE..................................815 714-8055
John T Mahoney, *Mng Member*
**EMP:** 11
**SALES (est):** 1.8MM **Privately Held**
**SIC:** 2077 Animal & marine fats & oils

### (G-14909)
**SWEET COMPANY**
18707 Hickory St (60448-8283)
PHONE..................................815 462-4586
Jeff Mattson, *Owner*
**EMP:** 10
**SALES (est):** 227.7K **Privately Held**
**SIC:** 5812 2095 2064 Ice cream stands or dairy bars; instant coffee; candy & other confectionery products

### (G-14910)
**TANYA SHIPLEY**
Also Called: Decorators Vault
11344 Abbey Rd (60448-2437)
PHONE..................................708 476-0433
Tanya Shipley, *Principal*
**EMP:** 3
**SALES (est):** 197.8K **Privately Held**
**SIC:** 3272 Burial vaults, concrete or precast terrazzo

### (G-14911)
**TIMKEN GEARS & SERVICES INC**
Also Called: Philadelphia Gear
8529 192nd St (60448-8874)
PHONE..................................708 720-9400
Terry Dempsey, *Manager*
**EMP:** 10
**SALES (corp-wide):** 2.6B **Publicly Held**
**WEB:** www.philagear.com
**SIC:** 3566 Speed changers, drives & gears
**HQ:** Timken Gears & Services Inc.
901 E 8th Ave Ste 100
King Of Prussia PA 19406

### (G-14912)
**TOMSONS PRODUCTS INC**
Also Called: Tomson Railings
18800 Wolf Rd (60448-8933)
PHONE..................................708 479-7030
Fax: 708 479-7027
Thomas Wisinski, *President*
Mark Wisinski, *Vice Pres*
**EMP:** 4
**SALES (corp-wide):** 500K **Privately Held**
**WEB:** www.tomsonchem.com
**SIC:** 3599 Machine shop, jobbing & repair
**PA:** Tomson's Products Inc
13210 S 85th Ave
Orland Park IL

### (G-14913)
**TORRENCE MACHINE & TOOL CO**
18830 82nd Ave (60448-9724)
PHONE..................................815 469-1850
Fax: 815 469-6862
Scott Evans, *President*
▲ **EMP:** 9
**SQ FT:** 10,000
**SALES (est):** 451K **Privately Held**
**WEB:** www.torrencemachine.com
**SIC:** 3599 7692 Machine shop, jobbing & repair; welding repair

### (G-14914)
**UNITED SYSTEMS INCORPORATED**
9704 194th St (60448-9456)
PHONE..................................708 479-1450
Fax: 708 479-1533
Radovan Ilic, *President*
Mike Ilic, *Exec VP*
**EMP:** 16
**SQ FT:** 20,000
**SALES (est):** 4.2MM **Privately Held**
**SIC:** 3535 Conveyors & conveying equipment

### (G-14915)
**VOLFLEX INC**
10838 Walnut Ln (60448-1651)
PHONE..................................708 478-1117
Joseph A Bunch, *President*
Richard Bunch, *Co-Owner*
David Bunch, *Vice Pres*
Brian Meyer, *Production*
Tim Schoolman, *Sales Mgr*
▲ **EMP:** 28
**SQ FT:** 27,000
**SALES (est):** 7.8MM **Privately Held**
**SIC:** 3086 Packaging & shipping materials, foamed plastic

---

## Moline
### Rock Island County

### (G-14916)
**A 1 MARKING PRODUCTS**
Also Called: Des Moines Stamp Mfg Co
1801 5th Ave (61265-7902)
PHONE..................................309 762-6096
Fax: 309 762-3039
Sheila Chess, *General Mgr*
Pam Talley, *Manager*
**EMP:** 4 **EST:** 1918
**SALES (est):** 329.8K **Privately Held**
**SIC:** 5943 3953 Stationery stores; marking devices

### (G-14917)
**AMERICAN SPEED ENTERPRISES**
3006 Avenue Of The Cities (61265-4364)
PHONE..................................309 764-3601
Fax: 309 764-2786
Gail Trent, *President*
**EMP:** 2 **EST:** 1973
**SQ FT:** 6,500
**SALES:** 350K **Privately Held**
**WEB:** www.amerspeed.com
**SIC:** 3714 5961 3519 Motor vehicle engines & parts; automotive supplies & equipment, mail order; internal combustion engines

### (G-14918)
**ANP INC**
1515 5th Ave Ste 428 (61265-1367)
PHONE..................................309 757-0372
Monte Bottens, *President*
Dawn Bull, *President*
Robyn Botten, *Treasurer*
Christina Nantz, *Director*
**EMP:** 8
**SQ FT:** 900
**SALES:** 5.9MM **Privately Held**
**SIC:** 2875 Fertilizers, mixing only

### (G-14919)
**BIMBO BAKERIES USA INC**
5205 22nd Ave (61265-3626)
PHONE..................................309 797-4968
Harrold Nelson, *Branch Mgr*
**EMP:** 24
**SALES (corp-wide):** 12.3B **Privately Held**
**SIC:** 2051 Bakery: wholesale or wholesale/retail combined
**HQ:** Bimbo Bakeries Usa, Inc
255 Business Center Dr # 200
Horsham PA 19044
215 347-5500

### (G-14920)
**CAR SHOP INC**
421 12th St (61265-1266)
PHONE..................................309 797-4188
Fax: 309 764-1987
Tim Ryherd, *Vice Pres*
**EMP:** 6
**SQ FT:** 7,000
**SALES (est):** 782.8K **Privately Held**
**WEB:** www.carshopinc.com
**SIC:** 5531 3599 Speed shops, including race car supplies; automotive parts; automotive accessories; machine shop, jobbing & repair

### (G-14921)
**CENTRAL STONE COMPANY (HQ)**
1701 5th Ave (61265-7908)
PHONE..................................309 757-8250
James Ellis, *President*
Charles C Ellis, *Vice Pres*
Larry Roland, *Vice Pres*
Gregory C Eckman, *Treasurer*
Nancy A Devriese, *Asst Treas*
**EMP:** 90
**SQ FT:** 30,000
**SALES:** 47.9MM
**SALES (corp-wide):** 3.9B **Privately Held**
**SIC:** 1422 5032 Limestones, ground; sand, construction
**PA:** Riverstone Group, Inc.
1701 5th Ave
Moline IL 61265
309 757-8250

### (G-14922)
**CLEAN ENERGY RENEWABLES LLC**
4709 15th Street A (61265-7083)
PHONE..................................309 797-4844
Bas Mattingly, *CEO*
Matthew Cumberworth Sr, *President*
**EMP:** 22
**SQ FT:** 7,500
**SALES:** 4MM **Privately Held**
**SIC:** 8748 8711 3829 3823 Energy conservation engineering; energy conservation consultant

### (G-14923)
**DAVENPORT DRYER L L C**
600 River Dr (61265-1122)
PHONE..................................309 786-1500
Kevin Mueller, *CEO*
Robert L Bateman, *Vice Pres*
Robert Bateman, *Vice Pres*
Rob Feller, *Sales Mgr*
**EMP:** 5
**SALES (est):** 1.1MM **Privately Held**
**WEB:** www.davenportdryer.com
**SIC:** 3556 Dehydrating equipment, food processing

### (G-14924)
**DAVID HALL**
1529 46th Ave (61265-7084)
PHONE..................................309 797-9721
David Hall, *Owner*
**EMP:** 50
**SALES (est):** 1.5MM **Privately Held**
**SIC:** 3949 Swimming pools, except plastic

### (G-14925)
**DEERE & COMPANY (PA)**
1 John Deere Pl (61265-8098)
PHONE..................................309 765-8000
Fax: 309 765-5889
Samuel R Allen, *Ch of Bd*
James M Field, *President*
Max A Guinn, *President*
John C May, *President*
Cory J Reed, *President*
**EMP:** 1400 **EST:** 1837
**SALES:** 26.6B **Publicly Held**
**WEB:** www.deere.com
**SIC:** 3523 3531 3524 6159 Farm machinery & equipment; tractors, farm; harrows: disc, spring, tine, etc.; plows, agricultural: disc, moldboard, chisel, listers, etc.; construction machinery; tractors, crawler; dozers, tractor mounted: material moving; bulldozers (construction machinery); lawn & garden tractors & equipment; lawnmowers, residential: hand or power; rollers, lawn; agricultural credit institutions

### (G-14926)
**DEERE & COMPANY**
3800 Avenue Of The Cities # 108 (61265-4424)
P.O. Box 9109 (61265-9109)
PHONE..................................309 748-0580
Fax: 309 748-0625
Michael R Pasold, *Branch Mgr*
Gary Parker, *Manager*
Lynn Toney, *Manager*
Mark Robbins, *Consultant*
Anna Impens, *Administration*
**EMP:** 712
**SALES (corp-wide):** 26.6B **Publicly Held**
**SIC:** 3523 Farm machinery & equipment
**PA:** Deere & Company
1 John Deere Pl
Moline IL 61265
309 765-8000

### (G-14927)
**DEERE & COMPANY**
Also Called: John Deere
400 19th St (61265-1373)
PHONE..................................309 765-3177
Chris Trapkus, *President*
Scott Cline, *Vice Pres*
Tauseef Ahmed, *Project Mgr*
Jack Guzzo, *Project Mgr*
Kevin Koenig, *Project Mgr*
**EMP:** 40
**SALES (corp-wide):** 26.6B **Publicly Held**
**WEB:** www.deere.com
**SIC:** 3523 Farm machinery & equipment
**PA:** Deere & Company
1 John Deere Pl
Moline IL 61265
309 765-8000

### (G-14928)
**DEERE & COMPANY**
15 S 80th St (61266)
PHONE..................................309 765-8000
**EMP:** 712
**SALES (corp-wide):** 26.6B **Publicly Held**
**SIC:** 3523 Farm machinery & equipment
**PA:** Deere & Company
1 John Deere Pl
Moline IL 61265
309 765-8000

### (G-14929)
**DEERE & COMPANY**
Also Called: John Deere Accounts Payble
3400 80th St (61265-5884)
P.O. Box 8808 (61266-8808)
PHONE..................................309 765-8275
Chuck Needham, *Sales Mgr*
Erin Tennant, *Program Mgr*
Darrell Hess, *Manager*
Marci Driskell, *Manager*
Rebecca Jaska, *Manager*
**EMP:** 60
**SALES (corp-wide):** 26.6B **Publicly Held**
**WEB:** www.deere.com
**SIC:** 3523 Combines (harvester-threshers)
**PA:** Deere & Company
1 John Deere Pl
Moline IL 61265
309 765-8000

### (G-14930)
**DEERE & COMPANY**
Also Called: John Deere
909 River Dr (61265-1202)
PHONE..................................309 765-8000
Bill Anderson, *General Mgr*
Dale Johnson, *Managing Dir*
Don Tholl, *Managing Dir*
Kevin Ford, *COO*
Cory Reed, *Vice Pres*
**EMP:** 25
**SALES (corp-wide):** 26.6B **Publicly Held**
**WEB:** www.deere.com
**SIC:** 3443 Fabricated plate work (boiler shop)
**PA:** Deere & Company
1 John Deere Pl
Moline IL 61265
309 765-8000

### (G-14931)
**DEERE & COMPANY**
3400 80th St Swob (61265)
PHONE..................................309 748-8260
Martin Wilkinson, *Vice Pres*

Jeffrey Garbin, *Branch Mgr*
David Hanson, *Manager*
Gregory Kinman, *Manager*
John Menard, *Manager*
**EMP:** 25
**SALES (corp-wide):** 26.6B **Publicly Held**
**WEB:** www.deere.com
**SIC: 3523** Farm machinery & equipment
**PA:** Deere & Company
　　1 John Deere Pl
　　Moline IL 61265
　　309 765-8000

**(G-14932)**
## DEERE & COMPANY
Also Called: John Deere Waterloo Works
3400 80th St (61265-5884)
P.O. Box 8808 (61266-8808)
**PHONE** ............................ 309 765-8000
Tom Phan, *President*
Will Hubbard, *Vice Pres*
Christie Riek, *Project Mgr*
Norman Hayes, *QC Mgr*
Matthew Reif, *Engineer*
**EMP:** 17
**SALES (corp-wide):** 26.6B **Publicly Held**
**WEB:** www.deere.com
**SIC: 3523** Farm machinery & equipment; tractors, farm
**PA:** Deere & Company
　　1 John Deere Pl
　　Moline IL 61265
　　309 765-8000

**(G-14933)**
## DEERE & COMPANY
1 John Deere Pl (61265-8098)
**PHONE** ............................ 309 765-2960
**EMP:** 30
**SALES (corp-wide):** 36B **Publicly Held**
**SIC: 3829** Mfg Measuring/Controlling Devices
**PA:** Deere & Company
　　1 John Deere Pl
　　Moline IL 61265
　　309 765-8000

**(G-14934)**
## DEERE & COMPANY
1 John Deere Pl (61265-8098)
P.O. Box 8808 (61266-8808)
**PHONE** ............................ 309 765-8277
Antonio Madero, *Branch Mgr*
**EMP:** 689
**SALES (corp-wide):** 26.6B **Publicly Held**
**WEB:** www.deere.com
**SIC: 3523** Farm machinery & equipment; tractors, farm; harrows: disc, spring, tine, etc.; plows, agricultural: disc, moldboard, chisel, listers, etc.
**PA:** Deere & Company
　　1 John Deere Pl
　　Moline IL 61265
　　309 765-8000

**(G-14935)**
## DEERE & COMPANY
Also Called: John Deere Seeding Group
501 River Dr (61265-1121)
**PHONE** ............................ 309 765-7310
**Fax:** 309 765-7283
Jim Steinbach, *Division Mgr*
David Deveault, *General Mgr*
Zach Waters, *Safety Dir*
Robert Rauh, *Project Mgr*
Dric Windeknecht, *Design Engr*
**EMP:** 25
**SALES (corp-wide):** 26.6B **Publicly Held**
**WEB:** www.deere.com
**SIC: 3523** Planting, haying, harvesting & processing machinery
**PA:** Deere & Company
　　1 John Deere Pl
　　Moline IL 61265
　　309 765-8000

**(G-14936)**
## EAGLE PRINTING COMPANY
2957 12th Ave (61265-3302)
**PHONE** ............................ 309 762-0771
**Fax:** 309 762-7705
**EMP:** 5
**SQ FT:** 2,300
**SALES:** 400K **Privately Held**
**SIC: 5112** 2752 Whol Business Forms & Offset Printing

**(G-14937)**
## EVAC SYSTEMS FIRE & RESCUE
400 24th St (61265-1552)
P.O. Box 771 (61266-0771)
**PHONE** ............................ 309 764-7812
**Fax:** 309 764-7813
Laurel McCune, *President*
Harold Defrieze, *Vice Pres*
Ginny Defrieze, *Marketing Staff*
Joan Mc Court, *Office Mgr*
Judy Finnessy, *Manager*
**EMP:** 12
**SQ FT:** 3,000
**SALES:** 805.5K **Privately Held**
**WEB:** www.evacsystems.com
**SIC: 3569** Firefighting apparatus & related equipment

**(G-14938)**
## FARISS JOHN
Also Called: Fariss Step & Railing Co
3700 N Shore Dr (61265-6465)
**PHONE** ............................ 815 433-3803
John Fariss, *Owner*
Tom Buck, *Owner*
**EMP:** 3
**SALES (est):** 140K **Privately Held**
**SIC: 3446** Architectural metalwork

**(G-14939)**
## FCA LLC (PA)
Also Called: FCA Packaging
7601 John Deere Pkwy (61265-8028)
P.O. Box 758 (61266-0758)
**PHONE** ............................ 309 792-3444
David Wilsted, *President*
Todd Wrobbel, *Business Mgr*
Jenny Dormire, *Vice Pres*
Brent Lindstrom, *Vice Pres*
Dale Ryder, *Plant Supt*
**EMP:** 23
**SQ FT:** 3,000
**SALES (est):** 159.6MM **Privately Held**
**WEB:** www.fcamfg.com
**SIC: 4783** 5031 5085 2448 Packing goods for shipping; composite board products, woodboard; industrial supplies; pallets, wood

**(G-14940)**
## FOSBINDER FABRICATION INC
130 35th St (61265-1742)
**PHONE** ............................ 309 764-0913
**Fax:** 309 736-2402
Mike Fosbinder, *President*
▼ **EMP:** 23
**SQ FT:** 23,000
**SALES (est):** 4MM **Privately Held**
**WEB:** www.fosbinderfab.com
**SIC: 3599** 3544 Machine shop, jobbing & repair; special dies, tools, jigs & fixtures

**(G-14941)**
## GBA SYSTEMS INTEGRATORS LLC
1701 River Dr Ste 100 (61265-1384)
**PHONE** ............................ 913 492-0400
Michael L Smith, *CEO*
Shaun Kotwitz, *CFO*
Jane Robnett, *Manager*
Candy Rivelli, *Network Analyst*
Doug Pershall, *Business Dir*
**EMP:** 6
**SALES (est):** 893.6K **Privately Held**
**SIC: 3674** 4899 Integrated circuits, semiconductor networks, etc.; communication signal enhancement network system

**(G-14942)**
## HARRINGTON SIGNAL INC
Also Called: Commercial Product Group
2519 4th Ave (61265-1527)
P.O. Box 590 (61266-0590)
**PHONE** ............................ 309 762-0731
**Fax:** 309 768-8215
Roy J Carver, *Ch of Bd*
Richard D Eisenlauer, *President*
Julie Olson, *Credit Mgr*
Megan Randoll, *Human Res Mgr*
Cathy Drake, *VP Mktg*
▲ **EMP:** 50
**SQ FT:** 55,000
**SALES:** 12MM **Privately Held**
**WEB:** www.harringtonems.com
**SIC: 3669** 3625 Fire alarm apparatus, electric; electric controls & control accessories, industrial

**(G-14943)**
## INN INTL NEWSPAPER NETWORK
1521 47th Ave (61265-7022)
**PHONE** ............................ 309 764-5314
**Fax:** 309 743-0830
Marc Wilson, *CEO*
**EMP:** 3
**SALES (est):** 160.8K **Privately Held**
**SIC: 2711** Newspapers, publishing & printing

**(G-14944)**
## INN PARTNERS LLC
Also Called: Accudata L.L.C.
1510 47th Ave (61265-7021)
**PHONE** ............................ 309 743-0800
Spiro Dokolas, *Regional Mgr*
Linda Rowlee, *Regional Mgr*
Loren Widrick, *Regional Mgr*
Dave Demeyer, *Regional Mgr*
Chris Edmonds, *Opers Mgr*
**EMP:** 93
**SALES:** 3MM **Privately Held**
**SIC: 2741**

**(G-14945)**
## INVISIBLE FENCING OF QUAD CITY
5202 38th Ave Ste 2 (61265-6722)
**PHONE** ............................ 309 797-1688
Phil Vromen, *Owner*
**EMP:** 3
**SALES (est):** 228.3K **Privately Held**
**SIC: 1799** 3699 Fence construction; electric fence chargers

**(G-14946)**
## JOHN DEERE AG HOLDINGS INC
1 John Deere Pl (61265-8010)
**PHONE** ............................ 309 765-8000
Samuel R Allen, *CEO*
**EMP:** 5 **EST:** 1996
**SALES:** 357.7K
**SALES (corp-wide):** 26.6B **Publicly Held**
**SIC: 3523** 3531 3524 6159 Farm machinery & equipment; tractors, farm; harrows: disc, spring, tine, etc.; plows, agricultural: disc, moldboard, chisel, listers, etc.; construction machinery; tractors, crawler; dozers, tractor mounted; material moving; bulldozers (construction machinery); lawn & garden tractors & equipment; lawnmowers, residential: hand or power; rollers, lawn; agricultural credit institutions
**PA:** Deere & Company
　　1 John Deere Pl
　　Moline IL 61265
　　309 765-8000

**(G-14947)**
## JOHN DEERE CNSTR & FOR CO
1515 5th Ave Ste 200 (61265-1397)
P.O. Box 8806 (61266-8806)
**PHONE** ............................ 309 765-8000
David Gordon, *Business Mgr*
Louise Davis, *Project Mgr*
Mike Fitzgerald, *Facilities Mgr*
Bryan Forrest, *Engineer*
Michael Schlax, *Engineer*
**EMP:** 10
**SALES (corp-wide):** 26.6B **Publicly Held**
**SIC: 3523** Farm machinery & equipment
**HQ:** John Deere Construction & Forestry Company
　　1 John Deere Pl
　　Moline IL 61265
　　309 765-8000

**(G-14948)**
## JOSEPH TAYLOR INC
708 18th Avenue A (61265-3845)
**PHONE** ............................ 309 762-5323
Joseph Taylor, *Principal*
**EMP:** 3
**SALES (est):** 321.5K **Privately Held**
**SIC: 3421** Table & food cutlery, including butchers'

**(G-14949)**
## K R O ENTERPRISES LTD
Also Called: Printing Unlimited
1806 15th Street Pl (61265-3963)
**PHONE** ............................ 309 797-2213
**Fax:** 309 797-1325
Karen Osterhaus, *President*
**EMP:** 6
**SQ FT:** 1,500
**SALES (est):** 876.9K **Privately Held**
**WEB:** www.printingunlimited.com
**SIC: 2752** 3993 2791 2789 Commercial printing, offset; signs & advertising specialties; typesetting; bookbinding & related work; manifold business forms

**(G-14950)**
## KONE ELEVATOR (DH)
1 Kone Ct (61265-1380)
**PHONE** ............................ 309 764-6771
David Jensen, *Human Res Mgr*
Ty Jewell, *Sales Mgr*
Becker Edward, *Sales Staff*
Matt Delks, *Sales Associate*
Carolyn Rodriguez, *Admin Asst*
▲ **EMP:** 200
**SALES:** 76.2MM
**SALES (corp-wide):** 650.6MM **Privately Held**
**SIC: 7699** 3534 Elevators: inspection, service & repair; elevators & equipment
**HQ:** Kone Holland B.V.
　　Rijn 10
　　's-Gravenhage
　　703 171-000

**(G-14951)**
## L & W BEDDING INC
1211 16th Ave (61265-3035)
**PHONE** ............................ 309 762-6019
John A Wheatley, *President*
**EMP:** 3
**SQ FT:** 35,000
**SALES:** 393.7K **Privately Held**
**SIC: 2392** 5712 Mattress pads; mattresses; bedding & bedsprings

**(G-14952)**
## LAMCO SLINGS & RIGGING INC
4960 41st Street Ct (61265-7586)
**PHONE** ............................ 309 764-7400
**Fax:** 309 764-1105
Charles Lambrecht, *CEO*
Ted King, *Vice Pres*
Chuck Lambrecht, *Vice Pres*
**EMP:** 24
**SALES (est):** 13.8MM **Privately Held**
**WEB:** www.lamcoinc.com
**SIC: 5084** 3496 3444 Industrial machinery & equipment; hoists; slings; lifting: made from purchased wire; wire chain; sheet metalwork

**(G-14953)**
## LE CLAIRE INVESTMENT INC (HQ)
1701 5th Ave (61265-7908)
**PHONE** ............................ 309 757-8250
**Fax:** 309 757-7825
Charles C Ellis, *President*
Gregory C Eckman, *Corp Secy*
James O'Keith Ellis, *Vice Pres*
Gregory C Ekman, *Treasurer*
Nancy A Devriese, *Asst Treas*
**EMP:** 9
**SQ FT:** 30,000
**SALES:** 1.9MM
**SALES (corp-wide):** 3.9B **Privately Held**
**SIC: 6799** 1422 1442 Real estate investors, except property operators; crushed & broken limestone; construction sand & gravel
**PA:** Riverstone Group, Inc.
　　1701 5th Ave
　　Moline IL 61265
　　309 757-8250

**(G-14954)**
## LEE ENTERPRISES INCORPORATED
1521 47th Ave (61265-7022)
**PHONE** ............................ 309 743-0800
Darcy Heist, *Manager*
**EMP:** 20

## Moline - Rock Island County (G-14955)

SALES (corp-wide): 614.3MM **Publicly Held**
WEB: www.lee.net
SIC: 2711 Newspapers
PA: Lee Enterprises, Incorporated
  201 N Harrison St Ste 600
  Davenport IA 52801
  563 383-2100

### (G-14955)
### MCLAUGHLIN BODY CO (PA)
2430 River Dr (61265-1500)
PHONE...................................309 762-7755
Fax: 309 762-2823
Raymond L Mc Laughlin, *Ch of Bd*
Robert Lillicrap, *President*
John Mann, *President*
Randy Frederick, *General Mgr*
Jason Wilson, *General Mgr*
▲ **EMP:** 60
**SQ FT:** 277,000
**SALES (est):** 14.8MM **Privately Held**
WEB: www.mclbody.com
SIC: 3713 3441 3559 3523 Truck & bus bodies; fabricated structural metal; frame straighteners, automobile (garage equipment); farm machinery & equipment

### (G-14956)
### MEGA INTERNATIONAL LTD
506 16th St (61265-2110)
PHONE...................................309 764-5310
Thomas Pham, *President*
C Stanley Uskavitch, *Vice Pres*
**EMP:** 4
**SQ FT:** 1,225
**SALES:** 1MM **Privately Held**
WEB: www.megaintl.net
SIC: 5083 5084 3523 2085 Farm & garden machinery; industrial machinery & equipment; turf equipment, commercial; distillers' dried grains & solubles & alcohol; winches

### (G-14957)
### MIDLAND DAVIS CORPORATION (PA)
Also Called: MIDLAND PAPER & PRODUCTS
3301 4th Ave (61265-1605)
PHONE...................................309 637-4491
Fax: 309 764-6729
Martin H Davis, *President*
Mitchell L Davis, *Vice Pres*
Leonard Zeid, *Director*
Eric Davis, *Admin Sec*
▼ **EMP:** 51 **EST:** 1892
**SQ FT:** 75,000
**SALES:** 30.2MM **Privately Held**
WEB: www.midland-davis.com
SIC: 5093 2679 3341 Scrap & waste materials; pressed & molded pulp products, purchased material; pressed fiber products from wood pulp; from purchased goods; secondary nonferrous metals

### (G-14958)
### MOLINE CONSUMERS CO
200 23rd Ave (61265-4616)
PHONE...................................309 757-8289
Fax: 309 757-8254
**EMP:** 13
**SALES (est):** 1.5MM **Privately Held**
SIC: 3273 Ready-mixed concrete

### (G-14959)
### MOLINE DISPATCH PUBLISHING CO (HQ)
Also Called: Rock Island Argus
1720 5th Ave (61265-7907)
PHONE...................................309 764-4344
Fax: 309 757-4992
Linda Bridgeford, *Credit Mgr*
Jessica Avants, *Sales Staff*
Judy Holder, *Sales Staff*
Faith Hrncirik, *Sales Staff*
Jessica Licko, *Sales Staff*
**EMP:** 2
**SQ FT:** 60,000
**SALES (est):** 79.9MM
**SALES (corp-wide):** 168.9MM **Privately Held**
WEB: www.qconline.com
SIC: 2711 2752 Newspapers, publishing & printing; commercial printing, lithographic

PA: Small Newspaper Group
  8 Dearborn Sq
  Kankakee IL 60901
  815 937-3300

### (G-14960)
### MOLINE FORGE INC
4101 4th Ave (61265-1997)
PHONE...................................309 762-5506
Fax: 309 762-5508
Michael Schmooke, *CEO*
Michael H Schmooke, *Exec VP*
Keith Scrowther, *Opers Mgr*
Tiffany McDaniel, *Treasurer*
Tiffany Thieme, *Office Mgr*
▲ **EMP:** 65
**SQ FT:** 80,000
**SALES (est):** 11.6MM **Privately Held**
WEB: www.molineforge.com
SIC: 3462 Iron & steel forgings

### (G-14961)
### PARR INSTRUMENT COMPANY (PA)
211 53rd St (61265-1770)
PHONE...................................309 762-7716
Fax: 309 762-9453
Michael R Steffenson, *President*
James Nelson, *COO*
Jeffrey Wood, *Vice Pres*
Randy Steining, *CFO*
Michel Torregrossa, *Mktg Dir*
▼ **EMP:** 98 **EST:** 1899
**SQ FT:** 48,184
**SALES:** 27.5MM **Privately Held**
WEB: www.parrinst.com
SIC: 3821 3826 Calorimeters; laboratory measuring apparatus; analytical instruments

### (G-14962)
### PLASTIC PRODUCTS COMPANY INC
4610 44th St (61265-7501)
PHONE...................................309 762-6532
Scott Bolster, *Engineer*
Richard Klim, *Branch Mgr*
Heather Sanderson, *Manager*
Terri Cooley, *Executive*
Paul Tanghe, *Maintence Staff*
**EMP:** 125
**SALES (corp-wide):** 170MM **Privately Held**
WEB: www.plasticproductsco.com
SIC: 3089 3544 Injection molded finished plastic products; industrial molds
PA: Plastic Products Company, Inc.
  30355 Akerson St
  Lindstrom MN 55045
  651 257-5980

### (G-14963)
### PURE ELEMENT
915 33rd Ave (61265-7117)
PHONE...................................309 269-7823
**EMP:** 3
**SALES (est):** 213.6K **Privately Held**
SIC: 2819 Mfg Industrial Inorganic Chemicals

### (G-14964)
### QCFEC LLC
4401 44th Ave (61265-6753)
PHONE...................................309 517-1158
Frank Miroballi, *Principal*
**EMP:** 4
**SALES (est):** 220K **Privately Held**
SIC: 3949 Bowling alleys & accessories

### (G-14965)
### QUAD CITY PRESS
1325 15th St (61265-4059)
PHONE...................................309 764-8142
Fax: 309 764-9603
Daniel Brieser, *Owner*
Betty Brieser, *Bookkeeper*
**EMP:** 10
**SQ FT:** 3,000
**SALES (est):** 790K **Privately Held**
SIC: 2752 2791 2789 Commercial printing, offset; typesetting; bookbinding & related work

### (G-14966)
### QUAD CITY ULTRALIGHT AIRCRAFT
3810 34th St (61265-5300)
P.O. Box 370 (61266-0370)
PHONE...................................309 764-3515
Fax: 309 762-3920
Dave Goulet, *President*
William Ehlers, *Vice Pres*
Charles R Hamilton Sr, *Shareholder*
**EMP:** 12
**SQ FT:** 8,000
**SALES:** 1MM **Privately Held**
WEB: www.quadcitychallenger.com
SIC: 3728 3721 Aircraft parts & equipment; aircraft

### (G-14967)
### RIVERSTONE GROUP INC
200 23rd Ave (61265-4616)
PHONE...................................309 757-8297
L Poell, *Marketing Staff*
Chuck Ellis, *Branch Mgr*
**EMP:** 5
**SALES (corp-wide):** 4.3B **Privately Held**
WEB: www.riverstonegrp.com
SIC: 3273 Ready-mixed concrete
PA: Riverstone Group, Inc.
  1701 5th Ave
  Moline IL 61265
  309 757-8250

### (G-14968)
### SALES MIDWEST PRTG & PACKG INC
426 37th St (61265-1629)
PHONE...................................309 764-5544
Fax: 309 764-5595
Jeffrey Wood, *President*
**EMP:** 4
**SQ FT:** 4,000
**SALES (est):** 77.7K **Privately Held**
SIC: 2752 3086 2675 Commercial printing, offset; packaging & shipping materials, foamed plastic; die-cut paper & board

### (G-14969)
### SEDONA INC (HQ)
Also Called: Sedona Group, The
612 Valley View Dr (61265-6100)
PHONE...................................309 736-4104
Fax: 309 765-7999
Richard C John Jr, *President*
Bill Wheatley, *Business Mgr*
Larry John, *Vice Pres*
Tim John, *Vice Pres*
Jennifer Sharer, *Project Mgr*
**EMP:** 120
**SQ FT:** 4,000
**SALES:** 20MM **Privately Held**
SIC: 7372 7379 Business oriented computer software; computer related consulting services

### (G-14970)
### SENTRY POOL & CHEMICAL SUPPLY
Also Called: Polar Paint Systems
1529 46th Ave Ste 1 (61265-7084)
PHONE...................................309 797-9721
David E Hall, *President*
Sharon K Hall, *Corp Secy*
Darrell Harper, *Sales Dir*
**EMP:** 37
**SQ FT:** 18,500
**SALES (est):** 8MM **Privately Held**
WEB: www.polarpaint.com
SIC: 5999 3949 5075 Swimming pool chemicals, equipment & supplies; air purification equipment; swimming pools, plastic; air filters

### (G-14971)
### SMITH FILTER CORPORATION
5000 41st Street Ct (61265-7583)
PHONE...................................309 764-8324
Fax: 309 764-6816
Jana Lecander, *President*
Roger O Smith, *Principal*
Sharilyn Solis, *Corp Secy*
June Beres, *Vice Pres*
Diane Baumeister, *Plant Mgr*
▲ **EMP:** 44 **EST:** 1939
**SQ FT:** 72,000

**SALES (est):** 10.3MM **Privately Held**
WEB: www.smithfilter.com
SIC: 1711 3564 Plumbing, heating, air-conditioning contractors; filters, air: furnaces, air conditioning equipment, etc.

### (G-14972)
### STANDARD MACHINE & TOOL CORP
206 43rd St (61265-1930)
PHONE...................................309 762-6431
Fax: 309 762-7504
Martin C Frederickson, *President*
Allen L Frederickson, *Vice Pres*
**EMP:** 18
**SQ FT:** 15,000
**SALES:** 1.2MM **Privately Held**
SIC: 3599 3544 Machine shop, jobbing & repair; grinding castings for the trade; special dies & tools

### (G-14973)
### SUMMIT GRAPHICS INC
6810 34th Street Ct (61265-9756)
PHONE...................................309 799-5100
Fax: 309 799-5104
David Deem, *President*
Deb Deem, *Vice Pres*
Debra Deem, *Office Mgr*
**EMP:** 10 **EST:** 1979
**SQ FT:** 7,000
**SALES (est):** 800K **Privately Held**
WEB: www.summitgraphics.com
SIC: 3552 5137 Silk screens for textile industry; women's & children's outerwear

### (G-14974)
### US GOLF MANUFACTURING
1612 7th St (61265-3711)
PHONE...................................309 797-9820
Scott Cristianson, *Owner*
**EMP:** 6
**SALES (est):** 322.1K **Privately Held**
SIC: 3949 Golf equipment

### (G-14975)
### VAN LANCKER STEVEN
Also Called: Model Printers
310 15th St (61265-1308)
PHONE...................................309 764-2221
Fax: 309 764-4441
Steven Van Lancker, *Owner*
Christine Van Lancker, *Co-Owner*
**EMP:** 4
**SQ FT:** 2,000
**SALES:** 245K **Privately Held**
SIC: 2752 2759 Offset & photolithographic printing; commercial printing, offset; commercial printing

### (G-14976)
### VEEDER-ROOT COMPANY
4926 5th Ave (61265-1923)
PHONE...................................309 797-1762
**EMP:** 3
**SALES (corp-wide):** 6.2B **Publicly Held**
SIC: 3823 Industrial instrmnts msrmnt display/control process variable
HQ: Veeder-Root Company
  125 Powder Forest Dr
  Weatogue CT 06089
  860 651-2700

### (G-14977)
### WILLIAMS WHITE & COMPANY
600 River Dr (61265-1178)
PHONE...................................309 797-7650
Fax: 309 797-7677
Sunder Subbaroyan, *CEO*
David Takes, *President*
David Nesbitt, *Vice Pres*
Scott Law, *Project Mgr*
Brian Danner, *Purch Mgr*
**EMP:** 130
**SQ FT:** 7,200
**SALES (est):** 40.3MM **Privately Held**
SIC: 3542 Mechanical (pneumatic or hydraulic) metal forming machines; presses: hydraulic & pneumatic, mechanical & manual; presses: forming, stamping, punching, sizing (machine tools); shearing machines, power

## Momence
### Kankakee County

**(G-14978)**
**APPLIED MECHANICAL TECH LLC**
135 Industrial Dr (60954-3903)
P.O. Box 530 (60954-0530)
**PHONE**.................................815 472-2700
**Fax:** 815 472-2930
Linda Lynch, *Financial Exec*
Carey Krefft, *VP Sales*
Steven Wolf, *Sales Mgr*
Alexander Sherrie, *Mng Member*
Patrick Lynch, *Mng Member*
**EMP:** 20
**SQ FT:** 8,450
**SALES (est):** 4.4MM **Privately Held**
**WEB:** www.appliedmechtech.com
**SIC:** 3621 8711 Motors & generators; consulting engineer

**(G-14979)**
**D & J MACHINE SHOP INC**
2120 N 11250e Rd (60954-3329)
**PHONE**.................................815 472-6057
**Fax:** 815 472-6087
Donald Haut, *President*
Tim Haut, *Vice Pres*
**EMP:** 5
**SQ FT:** 10,000
**SALES:** 600K **Privately Held**
**SIC:** 3599 3544 3469 Machine shop, jobbing & repair; special dies, tools, jigs & fixtures; metal stampings

**(G-14980)**
**FLANDERS CORPORATION**
Also Called: Flanders Precisionaire
11360 E State Rte 114 (60954)
P.O. Box 706 (60954-0706)
**PHONE**.................................815 472-4230
**Fax:** 815 472-0018
Donna Osteen, *Manager*
**EMP:** 120
**SALES (corp-wide):** 17.9B **Privately Held**
**WEB:** www.precisionaire.com
**SIC:** 3564 Filters, air: furnaces, air conditioning equipment, etc.
**HQ:** Flanders Corporation
531 Flanders Filter Rd
Washington NC 27889

**(G-14981)**
**GEMINI STEEL INC (PA)**
1450 N 11250e Rd (60954-3326)
**PHONE**.................................815 472-4462
INA Toma, *President*
Raymond J Toma, *Vice Pres*
**EMP:** 2
**SQ FT:** 1,500
**SALES:** 725K **Privately Held**
**WEB:** www.geministeel.com
**SIC:** 3446 3441 Architectural metalwork; fabricated structural metal

**(G-14982)**
**HURLEY CHICAGO COMPANY INC**
601 Hill St (60954-1055)
**PHONE**.................................815 472-0087
**Fax:** 815 388-9271
Gus Losos, *President*
Sylvia Losos, *Vice Pres*
John De Vries, *Admin Sec*
**EMP:** 4
**SQ FT:** 7,500
**SALES (est):** 721.4K **Privately Held**
**WEB:** www.hurleychicago.com
**SIC:** 3589 Water purification equipment, household type

**(G-14983)**
**LEE GILSTER-MARY CORPORATION**
305 E Washington St (60954-1615)
**PHONE**.................................815 472-6456
Mark Simpkins, *Warehouse Mgr*
Lisa Tosh, *Purchasing*
Gary Schultz, *Manager*
Valerie Latham, *Manager*
**EMP:** 84
**SALES (corp-wide):** 1.1B **Privately Held**
**WEB:** www.gilstermarylee.com
**SIC:** 2098 2046 2099 2045 Macaroni products (e.g. alphabets, rings & shells), dry; wet corn milling; popcorn, packaged: except already popped; blended flour: from purchased flour; plastic containers, except foam; bottled & canned soft drinks
**HQ:** Gilster-Mary Lee Corporation
1037 State St
Chester IL 62233
618 826-2361

**(G-14984)**
**MOMENCE PACKING CO**
334 W North St (60954-1157)
**PHONE**.................................815 472-6485
**Fax:** 815 472-2459
Robert Salzwedel, *President*
Dennis Sherwood, *Purchasing*
**EMP:** 300
**SQ FT:** 66,000
**SALES (est):** 38.2MM **Privately Held**
**SIC:** 2013 2011 Sausages & other prepared meats; meat packing plants

**(G-14985)**
**MOMENCE PALLET CORPORATION**
11414 E State Route 114 (60954-3882)
P.O. Box 708 (60954-0708)
**PHONE**.................................815 472-6451
**Fax:** 815 472-6453
Andrew Cryer, *President*
Patrick Cryer, *Vice Pres*
**EMP:** 40
**SQ FT:** 40,000
**SALES (est):** 6.3MM **Privately Held**
**SIC:** 2448 Pallets, wood

**(G-14986)**
**PROGRESS REPORTER INC**
Also Called: Progress Reporter Press
110 W River St (60954-1516)
**PHONE**.................................815 472-2000
**Fax:** 815 472-3877
Anita Allison, *President*
Marilyn Lincoln, *Treasurer*
**EMP:** 5 **EST:** 1900
**SQ FT:** 3,000
**SALES (est):** 444.9K **Privately Held**
**SIC:** 2711 Commercial printing & newspaper publishing combined; job printing & newspaper publishing combined

**(G-14987)**
**R J VAN DRUNEN & SONS INC (PA)**
Also Called: Van Drunen Farms
300 W 6th St (60954-1136)
**PHONE**.................................815 472-3100
**Fax:** 815 472-3850
Kevin Van Drunen, *President*
Michael Ciadella, *Purch Mgr*
Jeffrey Van Drunen, *Treasurer*
Debra Dobben, *Admin Sec*
◆ **EMP:** 52 **EST:** 1880
**SQ FT:** 30,000
**SALES (est):** 101.5MM **Privately Held**
**WEB:** www.vandrunenfarms.com
**SIC:** 2034 2037 0161 2099 Dried & dehydrated vegetables; frozen fruits & vegetables; rooted vegetable farms; seasonings & spices

**(G-14988)**
**R J VAN DRUNEN & SONS INC**
Also Called: Van Drunen Farms
214 Mechanic St (60954-1151)
**PHONE**.................................830 422-2167
Kevin Van Drunen, *President*
**EMP:** 28
**SALES (corp-wide):** 101.5MM **Privately Held**
**SIC:** 2034 0161 0175 2099 Dried & dehydrated vegetables; rooted vegetable farms; deciduous tree fruits; seasonings & spices; frozen fruits & vegetables
**PA:** R. J. Van Drunen & Sons, Inc.
300 W 6th St
Momence IL 60954
815 472-3100

**(G-14989)**
**R J VAN DRUNEN & SONS INC**
3878 N Vincennes Trl (60954-3288)
**PHONE**.................................815 472-3211
Jeff Van Drunen, *President*
**EMP:** 100
**SALES (corp-wide):** 101.5MM **Privately Held**
**WEB:** www.vandrunenfarms.com
**SIC:** 2037 2099 0191 2034 Frozen fruits & vegetables; food preparations; general farms, primarily crop; dehydrated fruits, vegetables, soups
**PA:** R. J. Van Drunen & Sons, Inc.
300 W 6th St
Momence IL 60954
815 472-3100

## Monee
### Will County

**(G-14990)**
**A PLUS SIGNS INC**
25807 S Governors Hwy (60449-8650)
P.O. Box 508 (60449-0508)
**PHONE**.................................708 534-2030
Joe Grasser, *Manager*
**EMP:** 3
**SALES (est):** 292.7K **Privately Held**
**SIC:** 3993 Signs & advertising specialties

**(G-14991)**
**ADVANCED MOBILITY &**
Also Called: Amst
6370 W Emerald Pkwy # 107 (60449-2405)
**PHONE**.................................708 235-2800
**Fax:** 708 235-2002
Larry Sodomire, *CEO*
Robert Bachman, *President*
Kim Panozzo, *Manager*
**EMP:** 30
**SALES (est):** 11.5MM
**SALES (corp-wide):** 6.1B **Publicly Held**
**SIC:** 3715 Truck trailers
**HQ:** R. C. Tway Company
7201 Logistics Dr
Louisville KY 40258
502 637-2551

**(G-14992)**
**AQUAGREEN DISPOSITIONS LLC**
25731 S Bristol Ln (60449-7207)
**PHONE**.................................708 606-0211
Ryan Cattoni, *Principal*
**EMP:** 4
**SALES (est):** 500.8K **Privately Held**
**SIC:** 3569 Cremating ovens

**(G-14993)**
**ENTERPRISE PRODUCTS COMPANY**
23313 S Ridgeland Ave (60449-9293)
**PHONE**.................................708 534-6266
**EMP:** 4
**SALES (est):** 380.7K **Privately Held**
**SIC:** 1321 Natural gas liquids

**(G-14994)**
**FAS-TRAK INDUSTRIES INC**
4654 W Crocus Ave (60449-8771)
P.O. Box 757 (60449-0757)
**PHONE**.................................708 570-0650
Mark Feldmeier, *President*
Mark Seldmeier, *President*
Julie Velasco, *Manager*
**EMP:** 8
**SALES (est):** 670K **Privately Held**
**SIC:** 2269 Finishing plants

**(G-14995)**
**FUNK LINKO GROUP INC**
26815 S Winfield Rd (60449-9229)
**PHONE**.................................708 757-7421
James Dichristofano, *President*
**EMP:** 13
**SQ FT:** 30,000
**SALES (est):** 687.1K **Privately Held**
**SIC:** 3441 Fabricated structural metal

**(G-14996)**
**G K ENTERPRISES INC (PA)**
26000 S Whiting Way Ste 2 (60449-8162)
**PHONE**.................................708 587-2150
Kenneth Hoving, *President*
Jeffrey Kahn, *President*
Gene Kreider, *Principal*
Matthew Banevich, *Electrical Engi*
Marilyn Platter, *Treasurer*
▲ **EMP:** 5
**SQ FT:** 200,000
**SALES (est):** 100.7MM **Privately Held**
**SIC:** 3743 3443 3559 3556 Railroad equipment; fabricated plate work (boiler shop); cupolas, metal plate; towers (bubble, cooling, fractionating, etc.): metal plate; ladles, metal plate; chemical machinery & equipment; food products machinery; hoists, cranes & monorails; cranes, overhead traveling; hoists

**(G-14997)**
**HUGH COURTRIGHT & CO LTD**
26749 S Governors Hwy (60449-9144)
**PHONE**.................................708 534-8400
Patricia S Schoenbeck, *President*
Wayne Kozak, *Mktg Dir*
Ted Bachand, *Director*
**EMP:** 10 **EST:** 1930
**SQ FT:** 6,000
**SALES (est):** 2.9MM **Privately Held**
**SIC:** 5113 6794 5049 5084 Pressure sensitive tape; patent buying, licensing, leasing; laboratory equipment, except medical or dental; industrial machinery & equipment; coated & laminated paper

**(G-14998)**
**K-MET INDUSTRIES INC**
25911 S Ridgeland Ave (60449-9125)
**PHONE**.................................708 534-3300
**Fax:** 708 534-3350
Carol Kranz, *President*
Steve Kranz, *Plant Mgr*
Sandra Putz, *Treasurer*
Gunther Kranz, *Admin Sec*
**EMP:** 18
**SQ FT:** 16,000
**SALES (est):** 9.2MM **Privately Held**
**WEB:** www.k-met.com
**SIC:** 5051 3441 Metals service centers & offices; fabricated structural metal

**(G-14999)**
**RAINBOW FARMS ENTERPRISES INC**
25715 S Ridgeland Ave (60449-8963)
**PHONE**.................................708 534-1070
Jacqueline Musch, *President*
**EMP:** 5
**SALES (est):** 500K **Privately Held**
**SIC:** 2499 Mulch, wood & bark

**(G-15000)**
**REPLAY S DISC COOK-KANKAEE LLC**
25526 S Devonshire Ln (60449-1606)
**PHONE**.................................312 371-5018
Charles D Connolley,
**EMP:** 19
**SALES:** 950K **Privately Held**
**SIC:** 3652 Pre-recorded records & tapes

**(G-15001)**
**SIGNALMASTERS INC**
26120 S Governors Hwy (60449-8585)
**PHONE**.................................708 534-3330
Ty Beoo, *President*
**EMP:** 12
**SQ FT:** 4,000
**SALES (est):** 1.2MM **Privately Held**
**SIC:** 3669 Railroad signaling devices, electric

**(G-15002)**
**SOUTH HOLLAND MET FINSHG INC**
26100 S Whiting Way (60449-8058)
**PHONE**.................................708 235-0842
**Fax:** 708 235-0840
Robert Meagher, *President*
Deborah Jackson, *Vice Pres*
James Meagher, *Prdtn Mgr*
Don Troy, *Opers Staff*
Craig Sklrood, *CFO*

EMP: 54
SQ FT: 90,000
SALES (est): 8.6MM  Privately Held
WEB: www.shmf.com
SIC: 3471  Electroplating of metals or formed products

**(G-15003)**
**SWENSON TECHNOLOGY INC**
Also Called: Swensen's
26000 S Whiting Way  (60449-8060)
PHONE.................................708 587-2300
Fax: 708 587-2225
Timothy K Nordahl, *President*
Robert Turner, *Vice Pres*
Gary Cervak, *Facilities Mgr*
Eddie Taylor, *Draft/Design*
Kyle Hiatt, *Engineer*
EMP: 19
SALES (est): 3.6MM
SALES (corp-wide): 100.7MM  **Privately Held**
WEB: www.swensontech.com
SIC: 8741  3821  7389  8731  Industrial management; evaporation apparatus, laboratory type; personal service agents, brokers & bureaus; commercial physical research; chemical supplies for foundries
PA: G. K. Enterprises, Inc.
   26000 S Whiting Way Ste 2
   Monee IL 60449
   708 587-2150

**(G-15004)**
**TRITON MANUFACTURING CO INC (PA)**
5700 W Triton Way  (60449-8025)
P.O. Box 623, Bedford Park  (60499-0623)
PHONE.................................708 587-4000
Fax: 708 534-1417
Michael Edwards Sr, *CEO*
Kyle Edwards, *President*
Lee Cassidy, *Vice Pres*
Heather Hepworth, *Production*
Nancy Salin, *Purch Mgr*
EMP: 87
SQ FT: 96,000
SALES (est): 23.8MM  **Privately Held**
WEB: www.triton-mfg.com
SIC: 3643  3679  Bus bars (electrical conductors); harness assemblies for electronic use: wire or cable

**(G-15005)**
**VINCOR LTD (PA)**
5652 W Monee Manhattan Rd (60449-9611)
PHONE.................................708 534-0008
Fax: 708 534-0117
Jeanne C Vinezeano, *CEO*
Anthony D Vinezeano, *President*
Clyde T Bade, *Vice Pres*
David E Basile, *Vice Pres*
Mark S Vinezeano, *Vice Pres*
EMP: 17
SQ FT: 14,000
SALES (est): 3.4MM  **Privately Held**
WEB: www.vincor.com
SIC: 3663  4812  1799  5065  Satellites, communications; radio telephone communication; antenna installation; electronic parts & equipment; video tape rental; radio, television & electronic stores

**(G-15006)**
**VOORTMAN USA CORP**
26200 S Whiting Way Ste 1  (60449-8096)
PHONE.................................815 468-6300
Fax: 815 935-2201
Adrian Morrall, *President*
Ben Morrall, *Sales Mgr*
Tiffany Castongia, *Office Mgr*
Dennis T Harmsel, *Manager*
Stephanie Diedrich, *Info Tech Mgr*
▲ EMP: 10
SQ FT: 20,000
SALES (est): 2.2MM  **Privately Held**
WEB: www.voortmancorp.com
SIC: 3541  Machine tools, metal cutting type

**(G-15007)**
**WHITING CORPORATION (HQ)**
26000 S Whiting Way Ste 1  (60449-8161)
PHONE.................................708 587-2000
Toll Free:.................................888  -
Fax: 708 587-2001
Jeff Kahn, *President*
Warren Jones, *General Mgr*
Michael Williams, *General Mgr*
Alan J Burke, *Vice Pres*
Casimir J Skorpinski, *Vice Pres*
◆ EMP: 150  EST: 1983
SQ FT: 192,500
SALES (est): 73.7MM
SALES (corp-wide): 100.7MM  **Privately Held**
SIC: 3536  3441  3743  3443  Hoists, cranes & monorails; cranes, overhead traveling; hoists; fabricated structural metal; railroad equipment; fabricated plate work (boiler shop); cupolas, metal plate; vessels, process or storage (from boiler shops): metal plate; ladles, metal plate
PA: G. K. Enterprises, Inc.
   26000 S Whiting Way Ste 2
   Monee IL 60449
   708 587-2150

**(G-15008)**
**WILLE BROS CO (PA)**
Also Called: Do It Best
11303 Manhattan Monee Rd  (60449-9658)
PHONE.................................708 535-4101
Fax: 708 388-6558
Curt Wille, *President*
Richard Shadle, *Vice Pres*
Richard E Wille, *Vice Pres*
Kris Ernest, *Human Res Dir*
Mark Tews, *Sales Executive*
EMP: 55
SQ FT: 35,000
SALES (est): 16.5MM  **Privately Held**
WEB: www.willebrothers.com
SIC: 5211  3531  Millwork & lumber; bituminous, cement & concrete related products & equipment

**(G-15009)**
**WILLE BROS CO**
Also Called: Ready Mix Concrete
11301 W Mnee Manhattan Rd  (60449)
PHONE.................................815 464-1300
Wayne Pasquarella, *Branch Mgr*
Bob Free, *Info Tech Mgr*
EMP: 21
SALES (corp-wide): 16.5MM  **Privately Held**
WEB: www.willebrothers.com
SIC: 3273  Ready-mixed concrete
PA: Wille Bros., Co.
   11303 Manhattan Monee Rd
   Monee IL 60449
   708 535-4101

## Monmouth
### Warren County

**(G-15010)**
**BIG RVER RSRCES W BRLNGTON LLC**
Also Called: Monmouth Grain & Dryer
903 S Sunny Ln  (61462-2516)
P.O. Box 768  (61462-0768)
PHONE.................................309 734-8423
Raymond Defenbaugh, *Branch Mgr*
EMP: 8
SALES (corp-wide): 851.4MM  **Privately Held**
WEB: www.bigriverresources.com
SIC: 2869  Fuels
HQ: Big River Resources West Burlington, Llc
   15210 103rd St
   West Burlington IA 52655
   319 753-1100

**(G-15011)**
**CUSTOM MILLERS SUPPLY INC**
511 S 3rd St  (61462-2235)
PHONE.................................309 734-6312
Fax: 309 734-7466
Howard White, *President*
Wanda White, *Treasurer*
EMP: 5
SQ FT: 6,000
SALES (est): 702.1K  **Privately Held**
SIC: 3523  5063  3599  3799  Feed grinders, crushers & mixers; transformers & transmission equipment; machine shop, jobbing & repair; trailers & trailer equipment; automobile tires & tubes

**(G-15012)**
**FORMAN CO INC**
Also Called: Orion Enterprises
609 W Broadway  (61462-1620)
PHONE.................................309 734-3413
Fax: 309 734-7430
Gary Judy, *President*
Robert Forman, *Chairman*
Marcia Judy, *Vice Pres*
Steve Andrews, *Sales/Mktg Mgr*
EMP: 4  EST: 1856
SQ FT: 3,500
SALES (est): 110K  **Privately Held**
WEB: www.theformancompany.com
SIC: 2789  7389  Binding only: books, pamphlets, magazines, etc.; microfilm recording & developing service

**(G-15013)**
**GATEHOUSE MEDIA LLC**
Also Called: Oquawka Cross Current Newsppr
400 S Main St  (61462-2164)
PHONE.................................309 734-3164
Tony Scott, *General Mgr*
Ken Gudiatis, *Sales Staff*
EMP: 30
SALES (corp-wide): 1.2B  **Publicly Held**
WEB: www.gatehousemedia.com
SIC: 2711  Newspapers: publishing only, not printed on site
HQ: Gatehouse Media, Llc
   175 Sullys Trl Ste 300
   Pittsford NY 14534
   585 598-0030

**(G-15014)**
**IMI MCR INC**
1301 N Main St Ste 3  (61462-5223)
PHONE.................................309 734-6282
Tim Hubbard, *President*
▲ EMP: 32
SALES (est): 11.7MM
SALES (corp-wide): 2B  **Privately Held**
SIC: 3556  Beverage machinery
PA: Imi Plc
   4060 Lakeside
   Birmingham W MIDLANDS B37 7
   121 717-3700

**(G-15015)**
**JIM COKEL WELDING**
Also Called: Cokel Jim Prtble Wldg Sp Servi
204 E 6th Ave  (61462-2612)
PHONE.................................309 734-5063
James Cokel, *Owner*
EMP: 2
SQ FT: 3,000
SALES (est): 200K  **Privately Held**
SIC: 7692  Welding repair

**(G-15016)**
**KELLOGG PRINTING CO**
95 Public Sq  (61462-1772)
PHONE.................................309 734-8388
Fax: 309 734-8083
Buster L Kellogg Jr, *Owner*
Caroline Taylor, *Office Mgr*
EMP: 12  EST: 1924
SQ FT: 3,200
SALES (est): 1.3MM  **Privately Held**
SIC: 2752  3953  2761  2759  Commercial printing, offset; marking devices; manifold business forms; commercial printing; book printing

**(G-15017)**
**KIM GOUGH**
Also Called: Metal Crafters
1201 N Main St Ste 2  (61462-5221)
PHONE.................................309 734-3511
Kim Gough, *Owner*
Jason Allen, *General Mgr*
EMP: 6
SALES (est): 240K  **Privately Held**
SIC: 3441  7692  3444  Fabricated structural metal; welding repair; sheet metalwork

**(G-15018)**
**KIRKMAN COMPOSITES**
1201 N Main St Ste 2  (61462-5221)
PHONE.................................309 734-5606
Mark D Kirkman, *Owner*
EMP: 8
SALES (est): 680.2K  **Privately Held**
SIC: 3624  Carbon & graphite products

**(G-15019)**
**MIDWESTERN PET FOODS INC**
Also Called: Wells Pet Stores
617 S D St  (61462-2157)
P.O. Box 677  (61462-0677)
PHONE.................................309 734-3121
Fax: 309 734-7420
Ed Cooper, *Branch Mgr*
EMP: 50
SALES (corp-wide): 12.8MM  **Privately Held**
WEB: www.propacpetfood.com
SIC: 2047  5199  Dog & cat food; pet supplies
PA: Midwestern Pet Foods Inc
   9634 Hedden Rd
   Evansville IN 47725
   812 867-7466

**(G-15020)**
**MONMOUTH METAL CULVERT CO**
706 W 3rd Ave Ste 708  (61462-2022)
P.O. Box 325  (61462-0325)
PHONE.................................309 734-7723
Fax: 309 734-7830
John B Decker, *Partner*
Robert D Decker, *Partner*
EMP: 8
SQ FT: 10,000
SALES: 571K  **Privately Held**
SIC: 3444  Culverts, sheet metal

**(G-15021)**
**MONMOUTH READY MIX CORP**
620 S 2nd St  (61462-2708)
P.O. Box 1488, Galesburg  (61402-1488)
PHONE.................................309 734-3211
John Kovak, *President*
Bob Fulton, *Vice Pres*
Mike Trevor, *Plant Mgr*
EMP: 5
SQ FT: 3,200
SALES (est): 628.4K
SALES (corp-wide): 122.9MM  **Privately Held**
WEB: www.dentoncompanies.net
SIC: 3273  3271  5211  Ready-mixed concrete; concrete block & brick; masonry materials & supplies
HQ: Gunther Construction Co.
   816 N Henderson St
   Galesburg IL 61401
   309 343-1032

**(G-15022)**
**MONMOUTH STONE CO (PA)**
1420 N Main St  (61462-5224)
PHONE.................................309 734-7951
Dan G Kistler, *President*
John Pratt, *Vice Pres*
James Howe, *Admin Sec*
EMP: 12  EST: 1935
SQ FT: 15,000
SALES (est): 1.3MM  **Privately Held**
SIC: 1429  Igneous rock, crushed & broken-quarrying

**(G-15023)**
**SMITHFIELD FARMLAND CORP**
1220 N 6th St  (61462-9674)
PHONE.................................309 734-5353
Dennis Simpson, *Purchasing*
Jan Asbury, *QC Dir*
Robin Scanlan, *Engineer*
Michelle Reyburn, *Human Res Dir*
Michelle McMurl, *Personnel*
EMP: 600  **Privately Held**
WEB: www.farmlandfoods.com
SIC: 2011  5147  2013  Meat packing plants; meats & meat products; sausages & other prepared meats
HQ: Smithfield Farmland Corp.
   111 Commerce St
   Smithfield VA 23430
   757 357-3131

# GEOGRAPHIC SECTION

**(G-15024)**
**WS INCORPORATED OF MANMOUTH (PA)**
Also Called: Western Stoneware
220 W Franklin Ave (61462-1163)
PHONE ................................ 309 734-2161
Dong SOO Chong, *President*
Dave Bates, *Vice Pres*
**EMP:** 10
**SQ FT:** 180,000
**SALES (est):** 1MM **Privately Held**
**WEB:** www.westernstoneware.com
**SIC:** 3269 Stoneware pottery products

## Monroe Center
### Ogle County

**(G-15025)**
**WITTWER BROTHERS INC**
33462 W County Line Rd (61052-9507)
PHONE ................................ 815 522-3589
Tim Wittwer, *President*
Mark Wittwer, *Admin Sec*
**EMP:** 2
**SALES (est):** 307.4K **Privately Held**
**SIC:** 0115 0116 7692 7699 Corn; soybeans; welding repair; agricultural equipment repair services; welding on site

## Montgomery
### Kendall County

**(G-15026)**
**A LAKIN & SONS INC (PA)**
Also Called: Lakin General
2001 Greenfield Rd (60538-1183)
PHONE ................................ 773 871-6360
Fax: 773 871-6675
Ken Lakin, *President*
Lewis G Lakin, *Chairman*
Rob Grammer, *Corp Secy*
Richard Gust, *Vice Pres*
Gib Younger, *Vice Pres*
▲ **EMP:** 30
**SQ FT:** 124,000
**SALES (est):** 38.2MM **Privately Held**
**SIC:** 5014 3069 5013 Tires, used; rubber automotive products; motor vehicle supplies & new parts

**(G-15027)**
**AURORA BEARING COMPANY**
901 Aucutt Rd (60538-1338)
PHONE ................................ 630 897-8941
Jesse F Maberry, *Ch of Bd*
David Richard, *President*
Harvey Sterkel, *Vice Pres*
Tim Orr, *Engineer*
Dave Richard, *Engineer*
▲ **EMP:** 252
**SQ FT:** 206,000
**SALES (est):** 99.7MM **Privately Held**
**WEB:** www.aurorabearing.com
**SIC:** 3568 Bearings, plain

**(G-15028)**
**AURORA METALS DIVISION LLC**
1995 Greenfield Rd (60538-1140)
PHONE ................................ 630 844-4900
Fax: 630 844-6839
Jack Kalal, *Foreman/Supr*
Dave Bumbar, *Mfg Staff*
Alan Degarmo, *Engineer*
Brian Davis, *Manager*
Jeff Mihalka, *Manager*
◆ **EMP:** 120
**SQ FT:** 90,000
**SALES (est):** 32MM **Privately Held**
**WEB:** www.aurorametals.com
**SIC:** 3366 3599 Copper foundries; machine shop, jobbing & repair

**(G-15029)**
**AUSTIN-WESTRAN LLC**
Viking Metal Cabinet Company
420 N Main St (60538-1367)
PHONE ................................ 815 234-2811
Troy Berg, *Branch Mgr*
Lisa Carpenter, *Administration*
**EMP:** 103
**SALES (corp-wide):** 37.8MM **Privately Held**
**SIC:** 3499 3444 2522 2514 Fire- or burglary-resistive products; sheet metalwork; office furniture, except wood; metal household furniture; wood kitchen cabinets
**PA:** Austin-Westran Llc
602 E Blackhawk Dr
Byron IL 61010
815 234-2811

**(G-15030)**
**BINKS INDUSTRIES INC**
1997a Aucutt Rd (60538-1135)
PHONE ................................ 630 801-1100
Fax: 630 801-0819
James D Calkins, *President*
Robert Wiersbe, *Purch Mgr*
Carol Shroka, *Manager*
▲ **EMP:** 4 **EST:** 1962
**SQ FT:** 5,000
**SALES:** 350K **Privately Held**
**SIC:** 3812 Search & detection systems & instruments

**(G-15031)**
**BIOLOGOS INC**
2235 Cornell Ave (60538-3201)
PHONE ................................ 630 801-4740
Fax: 630 801-4766
Dennis Raine, *President*
**EMP:** 9 **EST:** 1976
**SQ FT:** 15,000
**SALES (est):** 1.6MM **Privately Held**
**WEB:** www.biologos.com
**SIC:** 2836 Biological products, except diagnostic

**(G-15032)**
**BOC GLOBAL HELIUM INC**
1998 Albright Rd (60538-1158)
PHONE ................................ 630 897-1900
Fax: 630 897-1919
Mike Totteleer, *Principal*
Kirk Phelps, *Manager*
**EMP:** 149
**SALES (est):** 13.8MM
**SALES (corp-wide):** 17.9B **Privately Held**
**WEB:** www.boc.com
**SIC:** 2813 5169 Helium; industrial gases
**HQ:** Linde Gas Usa Llc
200 Somset Cor B Ste 7000
Bridgewater NJ 08807
908 464-8100

**(G-15033)**
**BRAEBURN SYSTEMS LLC**
2215 Cornell Ave (60538-3201)
PHONE ................................ 866 268-8892
Fax: 630 844-2497
Glenn Moore, *President*
George Schleder, *Accounts Mgr*
Amy Igelman, *Sales Executive*
Robert Rados, *Manager*
Glenn A Moore, *Manager*
▲ **EMP:** 11
**SALES (est):** 2.4MM **Privately Held**
**SIC:** 3822 Thermostats & other environmental sensors

**(G-15034)**
**BUSATIS INC**
1755 Aucutt Rd (60538-3025)
P.O. Box 1962, Arlington Heights (60006-1962)
PHONE ................................ 630 844-9803
Reinhard Jordan, *President*
Stephen Peck, *Admin Sec*
▲ **EMP:** 4
**SALES (est):** 310K **Privately Held**
**SIC:** 3444 8748 Sheet metalwork; agricultural consultant

**(G-15035)**
**BUTTERBALL LLC**
2125 Rochester Rd (60538-1066)
PHONE ................................ 800 575-3365
Ralph Caballero Sr, *President*
**EMP:** 375
**SALES (corp-wide):** 1.8B **Privately Held**
**SIC:** 2011 Meat packing plants
**PA:** Butterball, Llc
1 Butterball Ln
Garner NC 27529
919 255-7900

**(G-15036)**
**CATERPILLAR INC**
325 S Rte 31 (60538)
P.O. Box 348, Aurora (60507-0348)
PHONE ................................ 630 859-5000
Fax: 630 859-5494
Dave Peterson, *Opers Mgr*
Larry Reddish, *Opers Mgr*
James L Cromer, *Controller*
Gerald Palmer, *Manager*
Mike Miller, *Analyst*
**EMP:** 3500
**SALES (corp-wide):** 38.5B **Publicly Held**
**WEB:** www.cat.com
**SIC:** 3531 3537 Construction machinery; excavators: cable, clamshell, crane, derrick, dragline, etc.; loaders, shovel: self-propelled; industrial trucks & tractors
**PA:** Caterpillar Inc.
100 Ne Adams St
Peoria IL 61629
309 675-1000

**(G-15037)**
**CHICAGO FLAMEPROOF WD SPC CORP (PA)**
Also Called: Wisconsin Flameproof Shop
1200 S Lake St (60538-1400)
PHONE ................................ 630 859-0009
Fax: 630 859-1736
Vince Mancini, *President*
Maddy Rossobillo, *Vice Pres*
Vince Lundy, *Plant Supt*
Bob Bagato, *Sales Mgr*
Matt Woodcock, *Sales Staff*
**EMP:** 30
**SQ FT:** 80,000
**SALES (est):** 48.3MM **Privately Held**
**WEB:** www.chicagoflameproof.com
**SIC:** 5031 2491 Building materials, exterior; building materials, interior; wood preserving

**(G-15038)**
**CIPHER TECHNOLOGY SOLUTION**
Also Called: Cipher Tech Solutions
1556 Crescent Lake Dr (60538-1243)
PHONE ................................ 630 892-2355
Eric Light, *Principal*
Joe McElroy, *Opers Staff*
Dan Martin, *Office Mgr*
**EMP:** 9
**SALES (est):** 1.8MM **Privately Held**
**SIC:** 3699 7382 Security devices; security systems services

**(G-15039)**
**COMERS WELDING SERVICE INC**
1105 S Lake St (60538-1258)
P.O. Box 317 (60538-0317)
PHONE ................................ 630 892-0168
Gary Comer, *President*
Kay Comer, *Vice Pres*
Tom Comer, *Vice Pres*
William Comer, *Treasurer*
**EMP:** 8
**SALES (est):** 1MM **Privately Held**
**SIC:** 7692 Welding repair

**(G-15040)**
**COMFORTS HOME SERVICES INC**
1551 Aucutt Rd (60538-1235)
PHONE ................................ 847 856-8002
Brad Martin, *President*
Daniel Fischer, *Sales Mgr*
Cara Martin, *Admin Sec*
▼ **EMP:** 7
**SQ FT:** 14,000
**SALES (est):** 2MM **Privately Held**
**WEB:** www.cohsi.com
**SIC:** 3448 Prefabricated metal buildings

**(G-15041)**
**DIAL CORPORATION**
2000 Aucutt Rd (60538-1192)
PHONE ................................ 630 892-4381
Fax: 630 892-5635
Dan Ahearn, *Purchasing*
Tom Hebert, *QC Dir*
Will Jensen, *Human Res Dir*
Byron Rimm, *Branch Mgr*
Linda Kavois, *Manager*
**EMP:** 200
**SALES (corp-wide):** 19.7B **Privately Held**
**WEB:** www.dialcorp.com
**SIC:** 2841 2844 2842 2032 Soap & other detergents; soap: granulated, liquid, cake, flaked or chip; detergents, synthetic organic or inorganic alkaline; dishwashing compounds; toilet preparations; deodorants, personal; hair preparations, including shampoos; face creams or lotions; specialty cleaning, polishes & sanitation goods; bleaches, household: dry or liquid; ammonia, household; fabric softeners; canned specialties; chili with or without meat: packaged in cans, jars, etc.; spaghetti: packaged in cans, jars, etc.; detergents & soaps, except specialty cleaning
**HQ:** The Dial Corporation
7201 E Henkel Way
Scottsdale AZ 85255
480 754-3425

**(G-15042)**
**ELECTRIC GRAND**
2252 Cornell Ave (60538-3200)
PHONE ................................ 630 363-8893
**EMP:** 4
**SALES (est):** 399.4K **Privately Held**
**SIC:** 3699 Electrical equipment & supplies

**(G-15043)**
**FOX VALLEY PRINTING CO INC**
1810 Fox Mead Cir (60538-2953)
PHONE ................................ 419 232-3348
George E Kook, *President*
Colleen Kook, *Corp Secy*
Heather Janicki, *Sales Staff*
**EMP:** 10 **EST:** 1962
**SQ FT:** 10,000
**SALES (est):** 930K **Privately Held**
**SIC:** 2752 2759 2657 Commercial printing, lithographic; commercial printing; folding paperboard boxes

**(G-15044)**
**GCS STEEL INSTALLERS INC**
2256 Margaret Dr (60538-5014)
PHONE ................................ 630 487-6736
Jorge Alcantara, *President*
**EMP:** 3
**SALES (est):** 127.8K **Privately Held**
**SIC:** 1791 3441 Precast concrete structural framing or panels, placing of; fabricated structural metal

**(G-15045)**
**GENERAL MILLS INC**
1370 Orchard Rd (60538-1065)
PHONE ................................ 630 844-1125
Fax: 630 896-4990
John Pascylk, *Marketing Mgr*
Mason Austin, *Branch Mgr*
Austin Mason, *Branch Mgr*
**EMP:** 75
**SALES (corp-wide):** 16.5B **Publicly Held**
**WEB:** www.generalmills.com
**SIC:** 2043 Cereal breakfast foods
**PA:** General Mills, Inc.
1 General Mills Blvd
Minneapolis MN 55426
763 764-7600

**(G-15046)**
**HERTZ CORPORATION**
1375 Bohr Ave (60538-1190)
PHONE ................................ 630 897-0956
**EMP:** 5
**SALES (corp-wide):** 8.8B **Publicly Held**
**SIC:** 7513 5012 3711 Truck rental, without drivers; automobiles & other motor vehicles; truck & tractor truck assembly
**HQ:** The Hertz Corporation
8501 Williams Rd
Estero FL 33928
239 301-7000

**(G-15047)**
**HORMANN LLC (HQ)**
5050 Baseline Rd (60538-1125)
PHONE ................................ 877 654-6762
Frank Weber, *President*
Camron Rudd, *Opers Staff*
Michael Adam, *Purch Mgr*
Steve Koehl, *Engineer*
Bagher Dorch, *CFO*

# Montgomery - Kendall County (G-15048)

**GEOGRAPHIC SECTION**

▲ **EMP:** 240
**SQ FT:** 181,000
**SALES (est):** 67.1MM
**SALES (corp-wide):** 85.6MM **Privately Held**
**WEB:** www.hoermann-gadco.com
**SIC:** 3442 Garage doors, overhead: metal
**PA:** Hormann Kg Verkaufsgesellschaft
Upheider Weg 94-98
Steinhagen 33803
520 491-50

### (G-15048)
### HORMANN LLC
5050 Baseline Rd (60538-1125)
**PHONE** .................. 630 859-3000
Shelly Lanaville, *Branch Mgr*
Jim Campbell, *Branch Mgr*
**EMP:** 8
**SALES (corp-wide):** 85.6MM **Privately Held**
**SIC:** 5211 3442 Garage doors, sale & installation; garage doors, overhead: metal
**HQ:** Hormann Llc
5050 Baseline Rd
Montgomery IL 60538
877 654-6762

### (G-15049)
### IDENTI-GRAPHICS INC
101 Knell St (60538-1248)
**PHONE** .................. 630 801-4845
Terry Strong, *President*
Selena Semeraro, *Admin Sec*
**EMP:** 6
**SALES (est):** 899K **Privately Held**
**SIC:** 2759 2679 Flexographic printing; labels, paper: made from purchased material

### (G-15050)
### INTERNATIONAL PAPER COMPANY
1001 Knell St (60538-1299)
**PHONE** .................. 630 896-2061
Janet Drury, *Personnel*
Jeff Novack, *Sales Staff*
Vito Goztziewicz, *Branch Mgr*
**EMP:** 125
**SALES (corp-wide):** 21B **Publicly Held**
**WEB:** www.internationalpaper.com
**SIC:** 2653 Corrugated & solid fiber boxes
**PA:** International Paper Company
6400 Poplar Ave
Memphis TN 38197
901 419-9000

### (G-15051)
### L & D GROUP INC
Also Called: Lyon & Dittrich Holding Co
420 N Main St (60538-1367)
P.O. Box 671, Aurora (60507-0671)
**PHONE** .................. 630 892-8941
**Fax:** 630 264-4542
R Peter Washington, *Ch of Bd*
Douglas M Harrison, *COO*
Bob Miller, *COO*
Charles Sekerak, *Vice Pres*
Frank Butler, *Controller*
**EMP:** 500
**SQ FT:** 25,000
**SALES (est):** 42.6K **Privately Held**
**WEB:** www.ldgroup.com
**SIC:** 2542 2522 2599 Shelving, office & store: except wood; lockers (not refrigerated): except wood; fixtures, office: except wood; desks, office: except wood; work benches, factory; stools, factory; cabinets, factory; tool stands, factory

### (G-15052)
### L & M SCREW MACHINE PRODUCTS
321 Webster St (60538-1252)
**PHONE** .................. 630 801-0455
**Fax:** 630 801-0468
Louis Galarza, *President*
Dick Macula, *Accountant*
**EMP:** 10
**SQ FT:** 6,000
**SALES:** 350K **Privately Held**
**SIC:** 3965 3714 3545 3452 Fasteners; motor vehicle parts & accessories; machine tool accessories; bolts, nuts, rivets & washers

### (G-15053)
### LABORATORY MEDIA CORPORATION
1731 Commerce Dr (60538-1232)
**PHONE:** 630 897-8000
**Fax:** 630 897-7990
Daniel Micek, *President*
John Gawecki, *Vice Pres*
**EMP:** 15
**SQ FT:** 17,000
**SALES:** 1.3MM **Privately Held**
**SIC:** 2836 5049 Culture media; laboratory equipment, except medical or dental

### (G-15054)
### LAKIN GENERAL CORPORATION
2001 Greenfield Rd (60538-1183)
**PHONE** .................. 773 871-6360
Lewis Lakin, *President*
Rob Grammer, *CFO*
**EMP:** 90
**SALES:** 20MM
**SALES (corp-wide):** 38.2MM **Privately Held**
**SIC:** 5014 3069 Tires, used; rubber automotive products
**PA:** A. Lakin & Sons, Inc.
2001 Greenfield Rd
Montgomery IL 60538
773 871-6360

### (G-15055)
### LAKONE COMPANY
1003 Aucutt Rd (60538-1176)
**PHONE** .................. 630 892-4251
**Fax:** 630 892-2816
Bruce Rhoades, *President*
Jennifer Patti, *Purchasing*
Tracy Frieders, *Human Resources*
Kris Nelson, *Manager*
▲ **EMP:** 100 **EST:** 1944
**SQ FT:** 51,000
**SALES (est):** 22.4MM **Privately Held**
**WEB:** www.lakoneco.com
**SIC:** 3089 3083 Molding primary plastic; laminated plastics plate & sheet

### (G-15056)
### LION ORNAMENTAL CONCRETE PDTS
111 N Railroad St (60538-1214)
**PHONE** .................. 630 892-7304
**Fax:** 630 892-6980
Scott Neuprt, *Owner*
**EMP:** 3 **EST:** 2004
**SALES (est):** 230K **Privately Held**
**SIC:** 5199 3272 3271 5211 Statuary; concrete products; concrete block & brick; masonry materials & supplies

### (G-15057)
### LYON LLC (HQ)
420 N Main St (60538-1367)
P.O. Box 671, Aurora (60507-0671)
**PHONE** .................. 630 892-8941
**Fax:** 800 367-6681
Louise E Berg, *CEO*
Bill Countryman, *District Mgr*
Roy Talyor, *District Mgr*
William Guo, *Exec VP*
Matthew Zakaras, *Exec VP*
▲ **EMP:** 141 **EST:** 2013
**SALES (est):** 110.6MM **Privately Held**
**SIC:** 2542 Shelving, office & store: except wood
**PA:** Echelon Capital Llc
121 W Wacker Dr
Chicago IL 60601
312 263-0263

### (G-15058)
### LYON WORKSPACE PRODUCTS INC
420 N Main St (60538-1367)
**PHONE** .................. 630 892-8941
R Peter Washington, *President*
**EMP:** 5 **EST:** 2013
**SALES (est):** 616.6K **Privately Held**
**SIC:** 2542 Partitions & fixtures, except wood

### (G-15059)
### MAMATA ENTERPRISES INC (HQ)
2275 Cornell Ave (60538-3201)
**PHONE** .................. 941 205-0227
Dharmisth Patel, *President*
Varun Patel, *Vice Pres*
Harshad Desai, *Admin Sec*
▲ **EMP:** 6
**SQ FT:** 5,000
**SALES:** 8MM
**SALES (corp-wide):** 8.7MM **Privately Held**
**WEB:** www.mamatausa.com
**SIC:** 3559 3565 Plastics working machinery; packaging machinery
**PA:** Mamata Machinery Private Limited
Survey No. 423 / P,
Ahmedabad GUJ 38244
271 730-0700

### (G-15060)
### MARJAN INC
Also Called: Marjan Hot Tinning
1801 Albright Rd (60538-1194)
**PHONE** .................. 630 906-0053
Bill Strobel, *Vice Pres*
William Strobel, *Vice Pres*
**EMP:** 8
**SALES (est):** 1MM **Privately Held**
**WEB:** www.marjan.com
**SIC:** 3471 Plating & polishing

### (G-15061)
### MKC ELECTRIC
1791 Commerce Dr (60538-1232)
**PHONE** .................. 630 844-9700
Micheal Catich, *Owner*
**EMP:** 3
**SALES (est):** 453.4K **Privately Held**
**SIC:** 3699 Electrical equipment & supplies

### (G-15062)
### MULTIPLEX INDUSTRIES INC
1650 Se River Rd (60538-1500)
**PHONE** .................. 630 906-9780
Ronald Potter, *President*
**EMP:** 2
**SQ FT:** 1,250
**SALES (est):** 350K **Privately Held**
**SIC:** 5051 3316 3312 Steel; cold finishing of steel shapes; blast furnaces & steel mills

### (G-15063)
### MURPHY USA INC
1927 Us Route 30 (60538-7100)
**PHONE** .................. 630 801-4950
Less Than, *Branch Mgr*
**EMP:** 21 **Publicly Held**
**SIC:** 1382 Oil & gas exploration services
**PA:** Murphy Usa Inc.
200 E Peach St
El Dorado AR 71730

### (G-15064)
### NORTHERN ILLINOIS LUMBER SPC
1200 S Lake St (60538-1400)
P.O. Box 318 (60538-0318)
**PHONE** .................. 630 859-3226
**EMP:** 35
**SQ FT:** 75,000
**SALES:** 300K **Privately Held**
**SIC:** 2491 Wood Preserving, Nsk

### (G-15065)
### PROFORMA AWARDS PRINT & PROMOT
15 Ridgefield Rd (60538-2744)
**PHONE** .................. 630 897-9848
**Fax:** 630 390-7403
Gregory Siebert, *Principal*
**EMP:** 2
**SALES (est):** 339K **Privately Held**
**SIC:** 2752 Commercial printing, lithographic

### (G-15066)
### ROCHESTER MIDLAND CORPORATION
2200 Rochester Rd (60538-1068)
**PHONE** .................. 630 896-8543
John Schultz, *Principal*
Paula Parrish, *Sls & Mktg Exec*
Lorrie Covarrubias, *Financial Exec*
Laurie Gutierrez, *Human Res Mgr*
Tim Bulthuis, *Manager*
**EMP:** 40
**SALES (corp-wide):** 126.6MM **Privately Held**
**WEB:** www.rochestermidland.com
**SIC:** 2844 Toilet preparations
**PA:** Rochester Midland Corporation
155 Paragon Dr
Rochester NY 14624
585 336-2200

### (G-15067)
### TOGO PACKING CO INC
2125 Rochester Rd (60538-1066)
**PHONE** .................. 800 575-3365
**Fax:** 630 896-9698
▼ **EMP:** 500
**SQ FT:** 244,000
**SALES (est):** 97.4MM **Privately Held**
**WEB:** www.gustopack.com
**SIC:** 2011 Meat packing plants

### (G-15068)
### TRIO FOUNDRY INC (PA)
Also Called: Sandwich Casting & Machine Div
1985 Aucutt Rd (60538-1135)
**PHONE** .................. 630 892-1676
Scott Rayfield, *President*
Ford Rayfield, *General Mgr*
Neil Hambly, *Plant Mgr*
Keith Koch, *Marketing Staff*
Susie Abraham, *Manager*
**EMP:** 38 **EST:** 1909
**SQ FT:** 70,000
**SALES (est):** 6.9MM **Privately Held**
**SIC:** 3366 3365 3369 Brass foundry; aluminum foundries; nonferrous foundries

### (G-15069)
### VIKING METAL CABINET CO LLC
420 N Main St (60538-1367)
**PHONE** .................. 800 776-7767
Bill Wilcoxson, *President*
Lisa Carpenter, *Director*
**EMP:** 90
**SALES (est):** 2.9MM **Privately Held**
**SIC:** 3499 3444 2522 2514 Fabricated metal products; sheet metalwork; office furniture, except wood; metal household furniture; wood kitchen cabinets

### (G-15070)
### VIKING METAL CABINET COMPANY
Also Called: A Divison of Da
420 N Main St (60538-1367)
**PHONE** .................. 630 863-7234
**Fax:** 708 594-1028
Eugene Berg, *CEO*
Troy Berg, *President*
Jim Willis, *President*
David Bakutis, *COO*
Jeff Musielak, *Opers Staff*
**EMP:** 100 **EST:** 2010
**SQ FT:** 70,000
**SALES (est):** 19.4MM **Privately Held**
**WEB:** www.vikingmetal.com
**SIC:** 3499 3444 2522 2514 Fire- or burglary-resistive products; sheet metalwork; office furniture, except wood; metal household furniture; wood kitchen cabinets

### (G-15071)
### VVF ILLINOIS SERVICES LLC
2000 Aucutt Rd (60538-1133)
**PHONE** .................. 630 892-4381
Rebecca Belmer, *Principal*
Larry Hagemeyer, *Engineer*
Sharon Horvat, *Project Engr*
Fred Baier, *Accountant*
Jeanne Keach, *Executive*
▲ **EMP:** 450
**SALES (est):** 188.1MM
**SALES (corp-wide):** 5.7MM **Privately Held**
**SIC:** 2841 Soap & other detergents
**PA:** V V F Limited
Plot No-109
Mumbai MH 40002
982 111-8281

# GEOGRAPHIC SECTION

**Morris - Grundy County (G-15097)**

**(G-15072)**
**WATER & OIL TECHNOLOGIES INC**
52 Eastfield Rd (60538-2402)
PHONE .................................. 630 892-2007
Fax: 630 892-7472
Edward Laurent, *President*
Patricia Laurent, *Vice Pres*
**EMP:** 6
**SALES (est):** 1MM **Privately Held**
**SIC: 2869** 8748 Industrial organic chemicals; environmental consultant

**(G-15073)**
**WORKSPACE LYON PRODUCTS LLC**
420 N Main St (60538-1367)
P.O. Box 671, Aurora (60507-0671)
PHONE .................................. 630 892-8941
Robert Brossell, *District Mgr*
Douglas M Harrison, *COO*
Mike Pine, *Plant Mgr*
◆ **EMP:** 500 **EST:** 2015
**SALES (est):** 96MM **Privately Held**
**SIC: 2542** Shelving, office & store: except wood; lockers (not refrigerated): except wood; cabinets: show, display or storage: except wood

## Monticello
*Piatt County*

**(G-15074)**
**B AND A SCREEN PRINTING**
350 W Burnside Rd (61856-9574)
PHONE .................................. 217 762-2632
Fax: 217 762-2012
Alan Arney, *Owner*
**EMP:** 4
**SQ FT:** 10,000
**SALES (est):** 459.7K **Privately Held**
**SIC: 2261** 5137 5136 2396 Fire resistance finishing of cotton broadwoven fabrics; sportswear, women's & children's; sportswear, men's & boys'; automotive & apparel trimmings

**(G-15075)**
**BLUE RIDGE LAND AND CATTLE**
1068 E 1765 North Rd (61856-8406)
P.O. Box 505 (61856-0505)
PHONE .................................. 217 762-9652
Fax: 217 817-0705
Steve Koss, *Partner*
Mindy Romano, *Manager*
**EMP:** 5
**SALES (est):** 615.4K **Privately Held**
**SIC: 3523** Driers (farm): grain, hay & seed

**(G-15076)**
**COUNTY OF PIATT**
Also Called: Piatt County Clerk Recorder
101 W Washington St # 214 (61856-1672)
PHONE .................................. 217 762-7009
Fax: 217 762-7563
Pat Rhodes, *Principal*
**EMP:** 5 **Privately Held**
**SIC: 3823** Panelboard indicators, recorders & controllers: receiver
**PA:** County Of Piatt
1020 N Market St
Monticello IL 61856
217 762-4002

**(G-15077)**
**H2O LTD (PA)**
Also Called: Fasprint of Central Illinois
119 E Washington St Ste 1 (61856-1695)
P.O. Box 55 (61856-0055)
PHONE .................................. 217 762-7441
Fax: 217 762-3461
M Scott Hudson, *President*
Pat Howard, *Vice Pres*
**EMP:** 2
**SQ FT:** 4,000
**SALES (est):** 1.3MM **Privately Held**
**WEB:** www.fasprintonline.biz
**SIC: 2752** Commercial printing, lithographic

**(G-15078)**
**LUMBER SPECIALISTS INC**
Also Called: Piatt County Journal Repub
118 E Washington St (61856-1641)
PHONE .................................. 217 762-2511
Fax: 217 352-1722
Dennis Kaster, *Publisher*
Morgan Polito, *General Mgr*
Ken Hartman, *Principal*
Maggie Schwartzentraub, *Editor*
**EMP:** 4
**SALES (corp-wide):** 63.7MM **Privately Held**
**SIC: 2711** Newspapers
**PA:** The News-Gazette Inc
15 E Main St
Champaign IL 61820
217 351-5252

**(G-15079)**
**MCSHARES INC**
Also Called: Viobin USA
226 W Livingston St (61856-1632)
PHONE .................................. 217 762-2561
Fax: 217 762-2489
Paul Hooper, *Warehouse Mgr*
Suzy Morton, *Corp Comm Staff*
Roger Mohr, *Branch Mgr*
Whitney Bauman, *Manager*
James Oliver, *Manager*
**EMP:** 45
**SALES (corp-wide):** 25.3MM **Privately Held**
**WEB:** www.mcshares.com
**SIC: 2041** 2819 2077 2032 Flour; peroxides, hydrogen peroxide; animal & marine fats & oils; canned specialties
**PA:** Mcshares, Inc.
1835 E N St
Monticello IL 61856
217 762-2561

**(G-15080)**
**MCSHARES INC (PA)**
Also Called: Research Flour Service Pdts Co
1835 E N St (61856)
P.O. Box 1460, Salina KS (67402-1460)
PHONE .................................. 217 762-2561
Monte White, *President*
Roger Mohr, *General Mgr*
William L Edison, *Chairman*
William Gambel, *Exec VP*
Doris Chase, *Vice Pres*
◆ **EMP:** 46
**SQ FT:** 75,000
**SALES (est):** 25.3MM **Privately Held**
**WEB:** www.mcshares.com
**SIC: 2041** Flour; wheat germ

**(G-15081)**
**MONTICELLO DESIGN & MFG**
822 Old Route 47 (61856-8114)
PHONE .................................. 217 762-8551
Fax: 217 762-7522
Bruce Erb, *President*
Nancy Prevett, *Corp Secy*
Patric Tyroll, *Vice Pres*
**EMP:** 4
**SQ FT:** 10,000
**SALES:** 500K **Privately Held**
**WEB:** www.monticello-design.com
**SIC: 2431** 2541 2517 2434 Millwork; wood partitions & fixtures; wood television & radio cabinets; wood kitchen cabinets

**(G-15082)**
**OBRIEN SCNTFIC GL BLOWING LLC**
750 W Railroad St (61856-8180)
P.O. Box 495 (61856-0495)
PHONE .................................. 217 762-3636
Anne O'Brien-Murphy, *Mng Member*
**EMP:** 3
**SALES:** 150K **Privately Held**
**SIC: 3229** 3821 3231 Scientific glassware; laboratory apparatus & furniture; products of purchased glass

**(G-15083)**
**PRAIRIE FIRE GLASS INC**
217 W Washington St (61856-1683)
PHONE .................................. 217 762-3332
Jim Downey, *President*
**EMP:** 3
**SALES (est):** 296.8K **Privately Held**
**WEB:** www.prairiefireglass.com
**SIC: 3229** Pressed & blown glass

**(G-15084)**
**SEBENS BACKHOE SERVICE INC**
903 Madison St (61856-2239)
PHONE .................................. 217 762-7365
**EMP:** 2 **EST:** 2014
**SALES (est):** 242.1K **Privately Held**
**SIC: 3531** Backhoes

**(G-15085)**
**SOY CITY SOCK CO INC**
1086 S Market St (61856-1842)
PHONE .................................. 217 762-2157
David Camfield, *President*
Rhonda Camfield, *Admin Sec*
**EMP:** 15
**SALES (est):** 1.6MM **Privately Held**
**SIC: 2252** Socks

**(G-15086)**
**SUPERIOR FABRICATION & MACHINE**
1144 E 1600 North Rd (61856-8447)
P.O. Box 191 (61856-0191)
PHONE .................................. 217 762-5512
Fred Doty, *President*
Jeff Janezewski, *Administration*
**EMP:** 5
**SALES:** 250K **Privately Held**
**SIC: 3441** 3444 3443 Fabricated structural metal; sheet metalwork; fabricated plate work (boiler shop)

**(G-15087)**
**TOSHWARE INC**
111 E Lafayette St (61856-1953)
PHONE .................................. 217 896-2437
Bruce Vetter, *President*
Kate Boyer, *Office Mgr*
**EMP:** 25
**SALES:** 1.7MM **Privately Held**
**SIC: 3172** Leather money holders

**(G-15088)**
**TRACK MY FORECLOSURES LLC**
Also Called: Bpo Assistant
107 N State St Ste 1 (61856)
PHONE .................................. 877 782-8187
Stacy Hall, *Principal*
**EMP:** 6
**SALES (est):** 146.4K **Privately Held**
**SIC: 7372** Business oriented computer software

## Montrose
*Effingham County*

**(G-15089)**
**MEINHART GRAIN FARM INC**
3546 E 1900th Ave (62445-2217)
PHONE .................................. 217 683-2692
Keith Meinhart, *President*
Denise Meinhart, *Admin Sec*
**EMP:** 2
**SALES (est):** 211.3K **Privately Held**
**SIC: 3523** Driers (farm): grain, hay & seed

## Morris
*Grundy County*

**(G-15090)**
**ADVERT DISPLAY PRODUCTS INC**
3727 N Division St (60450-9355)
PHONE .................................. 815 513-5432
Gary Chapman, *CEO*
**EMP:** 4
**SALES:** 362.5K **Privately Held**
**SIC: 2542** 5046 3089 Cabinets: show, display or storage: except wood; store fixtures & display equipment; molding primary plastic

**(G-15091)**
**AKSHAR LIMITED**
70 Gore Rd (60450-9379)
PHONE .................................. 815 942-1433
Jeimi Emim, *General Mgr*
**EMP:** 4
**SALES (est):** 206K **Privately Held**
**SIC: 2389** Lodge costumes

**(G-15092)**
**ALLIANCE PIPELINE INC**
6155 E Us Route 6 (60450-9020)
PHONE .................................. 815 941-5874
Terrance Kutryk, *President*
Greg Devens, *General Mgr*
Derek Riphagen, *Vice Pres*
George Pluemeck, *Project Mgr*
**EMP:** 3
**SALES (est):** 283.6K **Privately Held**
**SIC: 1321** Natural gasoline production

**(G-15093)**
**ARS MARINE INC EAST LOCATION**
1142 Cemetery Rd (60450-7313)
PHONE .................................. 815 942-2600
George Pataki, *Owner*
**EMP:** 3
**SALES (est):** 283.8K **Privately Held**
**SIC: 3732** Boat building & repairing

**(G-15094)**
**ATHLETIC OUTFITTERS INC**
409 Liberty St (60450-2132)
PHONE .................................. 815 942-6696
Fax: 815 942-6698
Eric Gronski, *President*
Karen Gronski, *Admin Sec*
**EMP:** 5
**SQ FT:** 7,500
**SALES (est):** 773.9K **Privately Held**
**WEB:** www.athleticoutfitters.com
**SIC: 5661** 2395 5999 5632 Footwear, athletic; embroidery & art needlework; trophies & plaques; apparel accessories

**(G-15095)**
**AUX SABLE LIQUID PRODUCTS LP (PA)**
6155 E Us Route 6 (60450-9020)
PHONE .................................. 815 941-5800
Fax: 815 941-5874
William McAdam, *Partner*
Katherine Dodds, *Partner*
Jeff White, *COO*
Dave Skaggs, *Safety Dir*
Dean Hudson, *Plant Mgr*
▲ **EMP:** 30
**SQ FT:** 10,000
**SALES (est):** 96MM **Privately Held**
**WEB:** www.auxsable.com
**SIC: 1321** Natural gas liquids production

**(G-15096)**
**AUX SABLE MIDSTREAM LLC**
Also Called: Aux Sable Liquid Products
6155 E Us Route 6 (60450-9020)
PHONE .................................. 815 941-5800
Tim Stauft,
**EMP:** 50
**SALES (est):** 4.7MM
**SALES (corp-wide):** 25.5B **Publicly Held**
**SIC: 1321** Natural gas liquids production
**PA:** Enbridge Inc
425 1 St Sw Suite 200
Calgary AB T2P 3
403 231-3900

**(G-15097)**
**BANNER EQUIPMENT CO**
1370 Bungalow Rd (60450-8929)
PHONE .................................. 815 941-9600
Fax: 815 941-9700
James K Groh, *President*
John Kanaski, *Vice Pres*
Mike Tannhauser, *Vice Pres*
Carol Schull, *Purch Dir*
Jordan Krugel, *CFO*
▲ **EMP:** 40 **EST:** 1933
**SQ FT:** 10,000
**SALES (est):** 9.3MM **Privately Held**
**WEB:** www.bannerbeer.com
**SIC: 3585** 5078 Beer dispensing equipment; refrigerated beverage dispensers

## Morris - Grundy County (G-15098)

### (G-15098)
**BLUE GEM COMPUTERS INC**
822 East St (60450-2040)
PHONE.................................708 562-5524
David Latimer, *President*
Lori Latimer, *Vice Pres*
**EMP:** 2
**SALES (est):** 210K  **Privately Held**
**SIC:** 3575  7378  Computer terminals, monitors & components; computer maintenance & repair

### (G-15099)
**CARGILL INCORPORATED**
301 Griggs St (60450-2276)
PHONE.................................815 942-0932
**Fax:** 815 942-0983
Shane Cuddy, *Branch Mgr*
**EMP:** 6
**SALES (corp-wide):** 107.1B  **Privately Held**
**SIC:** 5153  2075  Grain & field beans; soybean oil, cake or meal
**PA:** Cargill, Incorporated
15407 Mcginty Rd W
Wayzata MN 55391
952 742-7575

### (G-15100)
**CARROLL DISTRG & CNSTR SUP INC**
460 Briscoe Dr (60450-6855)
PHONE.................................815 941-1548
Chuck Frazer, *Branch Mgr*
**EMP:** 3
**SALES (corp-wide):** 75.9MM  **Privately Held**
**SIC:** 5082  3444  Contractors' materials; concrete forms, sheet metal
**PA:** Carroll Distributing & Construction Supply, Inc.
205 S Iowa Ave
Ottumwa IA 52501
641 683-1888

### (G-15101)
**CENTRAL LIMESTONE COMPANY INC**
16805 Quarry Rd (60450-9211)
PHONE.................................815 736-6341
**Fax:** 815 736-6979
John A Shaw, *President*
Kay M Shaw, *Corp Secy*
**EMP:** 13
**SQ FT:** 2,000
**SALES (est):** 1.5MM  **Privately Held**
**SIC:** 1422  Limestones, ground

### (G-15102)
**CGK ENTERPRISES INC**
Also Called: Tri-State Asphalt Emulsions
1362 Bungalow Rd (60450-8929)
P.O. Box 470 (60450-0470)
PHONE.................................815 942-0080
Todd Weist, *CEO*
Jared Hicks, *Controller*
Charles Kline, *Branch Mgr*
**EMP:** 24  **Privately Held**
**WEB:** www.il-asphalt.org
**SIC:** 2951  Asphalt paving mixtures & blocks

### (G-15103)
**CROWN CONCEPTS CORPORATION**
7080 Lisbon Rd (60450-8663)
PHONE.................................815 941-1081
**Fax:** 815 941-1086
James Sharwarko, *President*
Steven Sandstron, *Corp Secy*
**EMP:** 21
**SQ FT:** 16,500
**SALES (est):** 4.7MM  **Privately Held**
**WEB:** www.crownconcepts.net
**SIC:** 3444  Sheet metalwork

### (G-15104)
**CROWN CUSTOM CABINETRY INC**
1110 E Washington St (60450-2082)
PHONE.................................815 942-0432
**Fax:** 815 942-9278
Daniel Mueller, *President*
**EMP:** 4
**SALES (est):** 441.6K  **Privately Held**
**SIC:** 2434  Wood kitchen cabinets

### (G-15105)
**D G BRANDT INC**
Also Called: Brandt Printing
901 Liberty St (60450-1508)
PHONE.................................815 942-4064
**Fax:** 815 942-4084
Doug Brandt, *President*
**EMP:** 6
**SQ FT:** 4,000
**SALES (est):** 632.6K  **Privately Held**
**SIC:** 2759  2789  2752  Commercial printing; visiting cards (including business); printing; bookbinding & related work; commercial printing, lithographic

### (G-15106)
**DESIGNER DECKS BY MJ INC**
270 E Minooka Rd (60450-9109)
PHONE.................................815 744-7914
James Siegel, *President*
**EMP:** 5
**SQ FT:** 2,500
**SALES (est):** 150K  **Privately Held**
**SIC:** 2431  Porch work, wood

### (G-15107)
**EQUA STAR CHEMICAL CORP**
8805 Tabler Rd (60450-9153)
PHONE.................................815 942-7011
Glenn Clarke, *President*
Ken Jacobson, *Purch Mgr*
George Davis, *Purch Agent*
Pam Nickel, *Manager*
Tom Nunheimer, *Manager*
**EMP:** 3
**SALES (est):** 386.1K  **Privately Held**
**SIC:** 2819  Catalysts, chemical

### (G-15108)
**EVENSON EXPLOSIVES LLC**
2019 Dunn Rd (60450-8335)
PHONE.................................815 942-5800
**Fax:** 815 942-2025
Ron Evenson,
**EMP:** 45  **EST:** 1996
**SALES (est):** 5.7MM  **Privately Held**
**SIC:** 2892  Explosives

### (G-15109)
**FRESH LOOK & SONS**
406 E Main St (60450-2231)
PHONE.................................815 325-9692
Larry Caroline, *Owner*
**EMP:** 3
**SALES (est):** 120K  **Privately Held**
**SIC:** 3479  Painting, coating & hot dipping

### (G-15110)
**HB FULLER ADHESIVES LLC**
7440 W Dupont Rd (60450-8375)
PHONE.................................815 357-6726
John Raney II, *Branch Mgr*
**EMP:** 50
**SALES (corp-wide):** 2B  **Publicly Held**
**SIC:** 2891  Adhesives
**HQ:** H.B. Fuller Adhesives, Llc
1200 Willow Lake Blvd
Saint Paul MN 55110
651 236-5823

### (G-15111)
**JC METALCRAFTERS INC**
1360 East St (60450-1978)
PHONE.................................815 942-9891
Joseph Kapt, *President*
**EMP:** 3
**SALES:** 200K  **Privately Held**
**SIC:** 3449  Miscellaneous metalwork

### (G-15112)
**LAFARGE AUX SABLE LLC**
Also Called: Aux Sable Sand & Gravel
4225 Dellos Rd (60450-9469)
P.O. Box 150 (60450-0150)
PHONE.................................815 941-1423
Nathan Creech,
**EMP:** 3
**SALES (est):** 392K
**SALES (corp-wide):** 2.8MM  **Privately Held**
**SIC:** 1442  Construction sand & gravel
**PA:** Western Sand & Gravel Co. Llc
400 Old North Rd
Spring Valley IL
815 664-2341

### (G-15113)
**LOGO WORKS**
824 Liberty St (60450-1854)
PHONE.................................815 942-4700
Dave Wiers, *Owner*
**EMP:** 7
**SALES (est):** 310K  **Privately Held**
**SIC:** 2759  Screen printing

### (G-15114)
**LYONDELL CHEMICAL COMPANY**
Also Called: Equistar
8805 Tabler Rd (60450-9153)
PHONE.................................815 942-7011
**Fax:** 815 942-7943
John Grimmenga, *Safety Dir*
Ed Barry, *Opers Mgr*
Carol Leschewski, *Purchasing*
D Misener, *Purchasing*
Brian Brown, *QA Dir*
**EMP:** 312
**SALES (corp-wide):** 29.2B  **Privately Held**
**WEB:** www.lyondell.com
**SIC:** 2869  3087  2821  Industrial organic chemicals; custom compound purchased resins; plastics materials & resins
**HQ:** Lyondell Chemical Company
1221 Mckinney St Ste 300
Houston TX 77010
713 309-7200

### (G-15115)
**MASTERBLEND INTERNATIONAL LLC**
Also Called: Tyler Enterprises
4673 Weitz Rd (60450-8714)
PHONE.................................815 423-5551
**Fax:** 815 423-6331
James McClurg, *CEO*
A Kuebel, *General Mgr*
Mark Jeffries, *COO*
Grant Rundblade, *Accounts Mgr*
◆ **EMP:** 15
**SQ FT:** 50,000
**SALES (est):** 4.9MM  **Privately Held**
**WEB:** www.masterblend.com
**SIC:** 2875  Fertilizers, mixing only

### (G-15116)
**MICRO SURFACE CORPORATION**
465 Briscoe Dr (60450-6802)
P.O. Box 788 (60450-0788)
PHONE.................................815 942-4221
**Fax:** 815 942-4265
Ed Fabiszak, *President*
Bryan Fabiszak, *VP Opers*
Cheryl Howe, *Office Mgr*
▲ **EMP:** 17
**SQ FT:** 12,800
**SALES (est):** 2MM  **Privately Held**
**WEB:** www.microsurfacecorp.com
**SIC:** 3471  2899  2077  Plating & polishing; chemical preparations; animal & marine fats & oils

### (G-15117)
**MID RIVER MINERALS INC**
4675 Weitz Rd (60450-8714)
PHONE.................................815 941-7524
Anthony Augius, *President*
Paul Augius, *Vice Pres*
Dee Wheeler, *Accountant*
▲ **EMP:** 9
**SQ FT:** 40,000
**SALES (est):** 1.2MM  **Privately Held**
**WEB:** www.midriverminerals.com
**SIC:** 3295  Slag, crushed or ground

### (G-15118)
**MIDWEST MOTOR SPECIALISTS INC**
421 W Illinois Ave (60450-1726)
P.O. Box 673 (60450-0673)
PHONE.................................815 942-0083
James Corrick, *President*
Maria Corrick, *Treasurer*
**EMP:** 2
**SQ FT:** 2,000
**SALES (est):** 207.2K  **Privately Held**
**SIC:** 7694  Electric motor repair; rewinding stators

### (G-15119)
**MIDWEST SIGNWORKS**
307 Bedford Rd (60450-1339)
PHONE.................................815 942-3517
**Fax:** 815 942-9068
Rose Grossi, *Owner*
**EMP:** 4
**SQ FT:** 3,250
**SALES:** 200K  **Privately Held**
**WEB:** www.southmorstudios.com
**SIC:** 7389  3993  Sign painting & lettering shop; signs & advertising specialties

### (G-15120)
**MORRIS PUBLISHING COMPANY**
Also Called: Morris Daily Herald Publisher
1802 N Div St Ste 314 (60450)
PHONE.................................815 942-3221
**Fax:** 815 942-0988
Thomas D Shaw, *CEO*
Bob Wall, *General Mgr*
Kevin Rouse, *Purch Dir*
Patrick Graziano, *Engineer*
Phil Metka, *CFO*
**EMP:** 516
**SQ FT:** 13,000
**SALES (est):** 24MM
**SALES (corp-wide):** 83.1MM  **Privately Held**
**WEB:** www.morrisdailyherald.com
**SIC:** 2711  Newspapers
**PA:** The B F Shaw Printing Company
444 Pine Hill Dr
Dixon IL
815 284-4000

### (G-15121)
**NARVICK BROS LUMBER CO INC (PA)**
Also Called: Narvick Bros Construction
1037 Armstrong St (60450-1922)
PHONE.................................815 942-1173
**Fax:** 815 942-3892
Arthur Narvick, *President*
**EMP:** 5
**SQ FT:** 55,000
**SALES (est):** 10.8MM  **Privately Held**
**WEB:** www.narvickbrothers.com
**SIC:** 5211  3273  1542  7359  Lumber & other building materials; ready-mixed concrete; commercial & office building contractors; equipment rental & leasing

### (G-15122)
**NATURAL CEDAR PRODUCTS INC**
1600 Edgewater Dr (60450-2475)
PHONE.................................815 416-0223
Pamela Mueller, *President*
**EMP:** 5
**SALES (est):** 330.3K  **Privately Held**
**SIC:** 3949  Playground equipment

### (G-15123)
**NORTHFIELD BLOCK COMPANY**
3400 Bungalow Rd (60450-8945)
PHONE.................................815 941-4100
Max Hunt, *Branch Mgr*
**EMP:** 35
**SALES (corp-wide):** 28.6B  **Privately Held**
**WEB:** www.northfieldblock.com
**SIC:** 3271  Blocks, concrete or cinder: standard
**HQ:** Northfield Block Company
1 Hunt Ct
Mundelein IL 60060
847 816-9000

### (G-15124)
**NORTHWESTERN CORPORATION**
922 Armstrong St (60450-1921)
P.O. Box 490 (60450-0490)
PHONE.................................815 942-1300
**Fax:** 815 942-4417
Richard K Bolen, *President*
Carol Barry, *Persnl Dir*
Diane Olson, *Sales Mgr*
Nancy Spampaneto, *Manager*
Nancy Spampanato, *MIS Dir*
◆ **EMP:** 50

# GEOGRAPHIC SECTION

Morrisonville - Christian County (G-15150)

SQ FT: 70,000
**SALES (est):** 8.2MM  **Privately Held**
**SIC:** 3581 3469 3441 Automatic vending machines; metal stampings; fabricated structural metal

**(G-15125)**
**ORICA USA INC**
Also Called: Orica Nitrogen
7700 W Dupont Rd  (60450-8375)
**PHONE**............................815 357-8711
Ben Vanveckhoves, *Principal*
Debbie Williamson, *Purchasing*
Chris Clackley, *Manager*
**EMP:** 45
**SALES (corp-wide):** 3.9B  **Privately Held**
**SIC:** 5169 2892 2819  Explosives; explosives; industrial inorganic chemicals
**HQ:** Orica Usa Inc.
33101 E Quincy Ave
Watkins CO 80137

**(G-15126)**
**PRINT SHOP OF MORRIS**
1836 Unit B N Division St  (60450)
**PHONE**............................815 710-5030
**EMP:** 3
**SQ FT:** 1,500
**SALES (est):** 120K  **Privately Held**
**SIC:** 2759  Commercial Printing

**(G-15127)**
**PROFESSIONAL METERS INC**
3605 N State Route 47 D  (60450-8218)
P.O. Box 506  (60450-0506)
**PHONE**............................815 942-7000
Robert T Dullard, *President*
Vickie Sajnaj, *General Mgr*
Aaron Bailey, *Opers Mgr*
John R Cummings, *Admin Sec*
**EMP:** 130  **EST:** 1999
**SQ FT:** 15,000
**SALES (est):** 16.5MM  **Privately Held**
**SIC:** 1799 3825 3824  Hydraulic equipment, installation & service; digital panel meters, electricity measuring; gasoline dispensing meters

**(G-15128)**
**PROPPANT FRAC SAND LLC**
130 W Illinois Ave  (60450-2269)
**PHONE**............................815 942-2467
Wayne McFarland,
**EMP:** 4
**SALES:** 400K  **Privately Held**
**SIC:** 3533  Oil & gas field machinery

**(G-15129)**
**SANDERS INC**
2250 Wahoo Dr  (60450-9424)
**PHONE**............................815 634-4611
Scott Sanders, *President*
Deborah Sanders, *Admin Sec*
▲ **EMP:** 20
**SALES (est):** 2.2MM  **Privately Held**
**SIC:** 3564  Air purification equipment

**(G-15130)**
**SOUTH WEST OIL INC**
7080 Highland Dr  (60450-8649)
**PHONE**............................815 416-0400
Gary Guster, *CEO*
**EMP:** 10
**SALES (est):** 988.3K  **Privately Held**
**SIC:** 2911  Petroleum refining

**(G-15131)**
**SPONGE-CUSHION INC**
Also Called: SCI
902 Armstrong St  (60450-1921)
P.O. Box 709  (60450-0709)
**PHONE**............................815 942-2300
**Fax:** 815 942-9636
Scott S Douglas, *President*
Hugh McLaren, *General Mgr*
Gino Mancini, *Controller*
Robert Anderson, *VP Sales*
Bob Anderson, *Chief Mktg Ofcr*
◆ **EMP:** 67
**SQ FT:** 144,000
**SALES (est):** 15.6MM
**SALES (corp-wide):** 3.7B  **Publicly Held**
**WEB:** www.sponge-cushion.com
**SIC:** 3069  Sponge rubber & sponge rubber products

**PA:** Leggett & Platt, Incorporated
1 Leggett Rd
Carthage MO 64836
417 358-8131

**(G-15132)**
**STOCKDALE BLOCK SYSTEMS LLC**
4675 Weitz Rd  (60450-8714)
**PHONE**............................815 416-1030
Jon Marks, *Principal*
Paul Auguis, *Principal*
**EMP:** 2
**SALES:** 1MM  **Privately Held**
**WEB:** www.stockdaleblock.com
**SIC:** 5032 5999 3272  Concrete building products; concrete products, pre-cast; concrete products

**(G-15133)**
**SUBSTRATE TECHNOLOGY INC**
1384 Bungalow Rd  (60450-8929)
**PHONE**............................815 941-4800
Lynn Jones, *President*
Julie Finger, *Office Mgr*
▲ **EMP:** 10
**SALES (est):** 1.1MM  **Privately Held**
**SIC:** 1771 3559  Flooring contractor; concrete products machinery

**(G-15134)**
**T H DAVIDSON & CO INC**
Also Called: Welsch Ready Mix
1350 Bungalow Rd  (60450-8929)
**PHONE**............................815 941-0280
Michael J Dejong, *President*
Richard Chobar, *Admin Sec*
**EMP:** 5
**SALES (est):** 380.6K  **Privately Held**
**SIC:** 3273  Ready-mixed concrete

**(G-15135)**
**TORBLO INC**
Also Called: Quality Millwork and Trim
7075 Lisbon Rd  (60450-7640)
**PHONE**............................815 941-2684
**Fax:** 815 941-2871
Frank Olbrot, *President*
Brian Olbrot, *Admin Sec*
**EMP:** 4
**SQ FT:** 12,000
**SALES (est):** 620.8K  **Privately Held**
**SIC:** 2431  Doors, wood; windows, wood; window frames, wood

**(G-15136)**
**TRI-STATE ASPHALT LLC**
1362 Bungalow Rd  (60450-8929)
P.O. Box 470  (60450-0470)
**PHONE**............................815 942-0080
**Fax:** 815 942-5221
Todd Weist,
**EMP:** 3
**SALES (est):** 333.1K  **Privately Held**
**SIC:** 2951  Asphalt & asphaltic paving mixtures (not from refineries)

**(G-15137)**
**TUMINELLO ENTERPRIZES INC (PA)**
Also Called: Quality Glass Block & Win Co
1351 East St  (60450-1977)
**PHONE**............................815 416-1007
**Fax:** 708 532-8146
Jennifer L Tuminello, *President*
Chris Danek, *General Mgr*
Ray Tuminello, *Marketing Staff*
Raymond Tuminello, *Admin Sec*
▼ **EMP:** 20
**SQ FT:** 3,000
**SALES (est):** 1.9MM  **Privately Held**
**WEB:** www.qualitywindow.net
**SIC:** 5211 1793 3231  Windows, storm: wood or metal; glass & glazing work; products of purchased glass

**(G-15138)**
**TUMINELLO ENTERPRIZES INC**
Also Called: Quality Glass Block
1351 East St  (60450-1977)
**PHONE**............................815 416-1007
Dejah Woronowicz, *Sales Staff*
Chris Danek, *Branch Mgr*
**EMP:** 4

**SALES (corp-wide):** 1.9MM  **Privately Held**
**SIC:** 5211 1793 3231  Windows, storm: wood or metal; glass & glazing work; products of purchased glass
**PA:** Tuminello Enterprizes Inc.
1351 East St
Morris IL 60450
815 416-1007

**(G-15139)**
**UNION TANK CAR COMPANY**
8805 Tabler Rd  (60450-9153)
**PHONE**............................815 942-7391
**EMP:** 3
**SALES (corp-wide):** 223.6B  **Publicly Held**
**SIC:** 3743  Train cars & equipment, freight or passenger; railroad car rebuilding
**HQ:** Union Tank Car Company
175 W Jackson Blvd # 2100
Chicago IL 60604
312 431-3111

**(G-15140)**
**UTILITY CONCRETE PRODUCTS LLC**
Also Called: Ucp
2495 Bungalow Rd  (60450-9038)
**PHONE**............................815 416-1000
Thomas Heraty, *Vice Pres*
Eric Carncross, *Plant Mgr*
Patrick Larson, *Project Mgr*
Vince Polera, *Project Mgr*
Joseph Price, *Foreman/Supr*
**EMP:** 50
**SQ FT:** 30,000
**SALES (est):** 14MM  **Privately Held**
**WEB:** www.utilityconcrete.com
**SIC:** 3272  Concrete products, precast

## Morrison
### Whiteside County

**(G-15141)**
**AMERICAN PIPING GROUP INC**
Also Called: Vegter Steel Fabrication
800 French Creek Rd  (61270-9815)
**PHONE**............................815 772-7470
Mike Vegter, *President*
Steve Schoon, *Controller*
Kay McGarvey, *Exec Sec*
**EMP:** 60
**SQ FT:** 30,000
**SALES (est):** 22.9MM  **Privately Held**
**WEB:** www.americanpiping.com
**SIC:** 3498 3441  Piping systems for pulp paper & chemical industries; fabricated structural metal

**(G-15142)**
**CANDLE-LICIOUS**
634 E Lincolnway  (61270-2964)
**PHONE**............................847 488-9982
Sue Davey, *Principal*
**EMP:** 3
**SALES (est):** 223.6K  **Privately Held**
**SIC:** 3999  Candles

**(G-15143)**
**CLIMCO COILS COMPANY**
701 Klimstra Ct  (61270-3000)
**PHONE**............................815 772-3717
**Fax:** 815 772-3030
Scott Salmon, *President*
Christy Gallentine, *Purchasing*
Chad Vonholten, *Electrical Engi*
Sherry Widener, *Human Res Mgr*
▲ **EMP:** 130
**SALES (est):** 44.2MM  **Privately Held**
**WEB:** www.climco.com
**SIC:** 3353  Coils, sheet aluminum

**(G-15144)**
**HYPONEX CORPORATION**
9349 Garden Plain Rd  (61270-9631)
**PHONE**............................815 772-2167
**Fax:** 815 772-2423
Steven Williams, *Opers-Prdtn-Mfg*
Linda Vanderlaan, *Manager*
**EMP:** 25

**SALES (corp-wide):** 2.8B  **Publicly Held**
**SIC:** 2873 3524 3423 2875  Plant foods, mixed: from plants making nitrog. fertilizers; lawn & garden equipment; hand & edge tools; fertilizers, mixing only
**HQ:** Hyponex Corporation
14111 Scottslawn Rd
Marysville OH 43040
937 644-0011

**(G-15145)**
**KRUM KREATIONS**
22585 Carroll Rd  (61270-9407)
**PHONE**............................815 772-8296
Mark Krum, *Owner*
**EMP:** 3
**SALES:** 250K  **Privately Held**
**SIC:** 3446  Brasswork, ornamental: structural

**(G-15146)**
**MARKMAN PEAT CORP**
13161 Fenton Rd  (61270-9224)
**PHONE**............................815 772-4014
**Fax:** 815 772-4015
Bobby Terry, *Manager*
Bobby Cherry, *Manager*
**EMP:** 25
**SALES (corp-wide):** 50.8MM  **Privately Held**
**SIC:** 1499 5261  Peat grinding; top soil
**PA:** Markman Peat Corp.
900 Eagle Ridge Rd
Le Claire IA 52753
563 289-3478

**(G-15147)**
**QUALITY READY MIX CONCRETE CO (PA)**
14849 Lyndon Rd  (61270-9549)
**PHONE**............................815 772-7181
**Fax:** 815 772-3660
Randy Holesinger, *President*
Dawn Bush, *Admin Sec*
**EMP:** 12
**SQ FT:** 8,000
**SALES (est):** 2.9MM  **Privately Held**
**SIC:** 3273  Ready-mixed concrete

**(G-15148)**
**SHAWVER PRESS INC (PA)**
120 E Lincolnway  (61270-2623)
P.O. Box 31  (61270-0031)
**PHONE**............................815 772-4700
**Fax:** 815 772-2676
Ben Wolf, *President*
Darcy Houseman, *Vice Pres*
Mary Brackemyer, *Purchasing*
**EMP:** 6  **EST:** 1923
**SQ FT:** 5,520
**SALES (est):** 601.3K  **Privately Held**
**SIC:** 2752 3953 2791 2789  Commercial printing, offset; marking devices; typesetting; bookbinding & related work; commercial printing

**(G-15149)**
**WNS PUBLICATIONS INC**
Also Called: Review, The
100 E Main St  (61270-2638)
P.O. Box 31  (61270-0031)
**PHONE**............................815 772-7244
**Fax:** 815 772-4105
Tony Komlanc, *President*
Mary Brackemyer, *Purch Agent*
**EMP:** 21
**SQ FT:** 4,000
**SALES (est):** 950K  **Privately Held**
**SIC:** 2711  Newspapers: publishing only, not printed on site

## Morrisonville
### Christian County

**(G-15150)**
**BAIRD INC**
577 Illinois Route 48  (62546-6371)
**PHONE**............................217 526-3407
Jim Baird, *President*
**EMP:** 4
**SALES (est):** 358.4K  **Privately Held**
**SIC:** 3531  Construction machinery attachments

## Morrisonville - Christian County (G-15151)

**(G-15151)**
**LOUIS MARSCH INC**
601 Carlin St (62546-6457)
P.O. Box 42 (62546-0042)
PHONE..................217 526-3723
Fax: 217 526-3729
Kirk Vocks, *President*
James Renner, *Vice Pres*
EMP: 20
SQ FT: 2,400
SALES: 12MM **Privately Held**
SIC: 2951 1611 Asphalt & asphaltic paving mixtures (not from refineries); highway & street maintenance

## Morton
### Tazewell County

**(G-15152)**
**360 YIELD CENTER LLC**
Also Called: Yield360
180 Detroit Ave (61550-1532)
PHONE..................309 263-4360
Heather Steiner, *Accountant*
Jeff Neihouser, *Exec Dir*
EMP: 40
SQ FT: 6,000
SALES (est): 7.8MM **Privately Held**
SIC: 3523 Fertilizing, spraying, dusting & irrigation machinery; soil sampling machines

**(G-15153)**
**AUTONOMOUSTUFF LLC**
306 Erie Ave (61550-9600)
PHONE..................314 270-2123
Jill Hambrick,
Robert Hambrick,
◆ EMP: 6
SALES (est): 390K **Privately Held**
SIC: 3714 5063 5013 Motor vehicle electrical equipment; signaling equipment, electrical; testing equipment, electrical: automotive

**(G-15154)**
**BIG DOG TREESTAND INC**
120 Detroit Pkwy (61550-1857)
P.O. Box 952 (61550-0952)
PHONE..................309 263-6800
Douglas N Smith, *President*
◆ EMP: 7
SQ FT: 2,000
SALES (est): 858.7K **Privately Held**
WEB: www.bigdogtreestands.com
SIC: 3949 Hunting equipment

**(G-15155)**
**CENTRAL ILLINOIS GRANITE INC**
909 Detroit Ct (61550-3700)
PHONE..................309 263-6880
Sandra Glover, *President*
Troy Glover, *Treasurer*
Janet Stein, *Manager*
▲ EMP: 8
SALES: 730K **Privately Held**
SIC: 3281 Table tops, marble

**(G-15156)**
**D & D EMBROIDERY**
140 S Main St (61550-2030)
PHONE..................309 266-7092
Janna Grimm, *Owner*
EMP: 3
SALES (est): 229.5K **Privately Held**
WEB: www.ddembroidery.com
SIC: 2395 Embroidery & art needlework

**(G-15157)**
**DESIGN SYSTEMS INC**
361 Erie Ave (61550-9607)
PHONE..................309 263-7706
Anthony Dennis, *President*
Chad Seltvelt, *Vice Pres*
Philip L Graves, *Treasurer*
Barbara Bean, *Office Mgr*
Harry Murphy, *Info Tech Mgr*
EMP: 35
SQ FT: 27,500
SALES (est): 5.7MM **Privately Held**
SIC: 8711 3545 3544 Machine tool design; machine tool accessories; special dies, tools, jigs & fixtures

**(G-15158)**
**ENGINEERING DESIGN & DEV INC**
Also Called: Engineering Design & Dev
1001 W Jefferson St (61550-1503)
PHONE..................309 266-6298
Fax: 309 263-2067
Eric Jenkins, *President*
Scott Crank, *Vice Pres*
Linda Jenkins, *Vice Pres*
Janet Coots, *Treasurer*
EMP: 25 EST: 1977
SQ FT: 12,000
SALES (est): 4.5MM **Privately Held**
SIC: 3599 3544 Machine shop, jobbing & repair; special dies, tools, jigs & fixtures

**(G-15159)**
**G&D INTEGRATED SERVICES INC**
50 Commerce Dr (61550-9196)
PHONE..................309 284-6700
P Joseph O'Neill, *President*
Charles T Purcell, *Vice Pres*
Chris B Sanders, *Treasurer*
EMP: 46
SALES (est): 5.2MM **Privately Held**
SIC: 3532 Mining machinery

**(G-15160)**
**G&D INTGRTED MFG LOGISTICS INC**
50 Commerce Dr (61550-9196)
PHONE..................309 284-6700
P Joseph O'Neill, *President*
Frank McCloud, *COO*
Charles T Purcell, *Vice Pres*
Patrick Roesler, *CFO*
Becki Salmon, *CFO*
▲ EMP: 486
SQ FT: 15,000
SALES (est): 53.2MM **Privately Held**
SIC: 3531 Construction machinery

**(G-15161)**
**IRON-A-WAY LLC**
220 W Jackson St (61550-1588)
PHONE..................309 266-7232
Fax: 309 266-5088
Reginald R Smidt,
Cignet LLC,
Lawrence Francetti,
William Lianos,
EMP: 30
SQ FT: 15,000
SALES (est): 5.6MM **Privately Held**
WEB: www.ironaway.com
SIC: 3633 Household laundry equipment

**(G-15162)**
**MARION TOOL & DIE INC**
Also Called: Morton Machining
701 Flint Ave (61550-3603)
PHONE..................309 266-6551
Tamara Marion, *President*
Tom Schatsiek, *General Mgr*
David Nicholson, *VP Sales*
EMP: 70 **Privately Held**
SIC: 3599 Machine & other job shop work
PA: Marion Tool & Die, Inc.
1126 W National Ave
West Terre Haute IN 47885

**(G-15163)**
**MATCOR MTAL FBRICATION ILL INC (HQ)**
Also Called: Matcor Metal Fabrication Group
1021 W Birchwood St (61550-9617)
PHONE..................309 263-1707
Galliano Tiberin, *President*
Scott Piercy, *Safety Mgr*
Mary Scheffert, *HR Admin*
Todd Bannet, *Sales Mgr*
Elaine Pace II, *Admin Asst*
▲ EMP: 50
SALES (est): 17.1MM
SALES (corp-wide): 62MM **Privately Held**
SIC: 3441 Fabricated structural metal

PA: Matsu Manufacturing Inc
7657 Bramalea Rd
Brampton ON L6T 5
905 291-5000

**(G-15164)**
**MMC PRECISION HOLDINGS CORP (PA)**
1021 W Birchwood St (61550-9617)
PHONE..................309 266-7176
Frank C Lukacs, *President*
EMP: 8
SQ FT: 284,000
SALES (est): 110.5MM **Privately Held**
SIC: 3449 Miscellaneous metalwork

**(G-15165)**
**MODERN METHODS LLC**
408 N Nebraska Ave (61550-1740)
PHONE..................309 263-4100
Dan Martin, *Owner*
EMP: 2 EST: 2008
SALES (est): 231.5K **Privately Held**
SIC: 2759 Commercial printing

**(G-15166)**
**MORTON AUTOMATIC ELECTRIC CO**
Also Called: General Methods Co
641 W David St (61550-1529)
PHONE..................309 263-7577
Fax: 309 263-2969
Alan Rumbold, *President*
Alan J Rumbold, *President*
Deryl Nafziger, *Opers Staff*
Wendy Miller, *Office Mgr*
EMP: 9 EST: 1973
SQ FT: 5,544
SALES (est): 1.1MM **Privately Held**
WEB: www.mortonautomatic.com
SIC: 3613 3625 Control panels, electric; relays & industrial controls

**(G-15167)**
**MORTON INDUSTRIAL GROUP INC (HQ)**
1021 W Birchwood St (61550-9617)
PHONE..................309 266-7176
William D Morton, *Ch of Bd*
Frank C Lukacs, *President*
Brian Doolittle, *Senior VP*
Brian Geiger, *Senior VP*
Daryl R Lindemann, *Senior VP*
▲ EMP: 100 EST: 1998
SQ FT: 284,000
SALES (est): 110.5MM **Privately Held**
WEB: www.mortonindustrialgroup.com
SIC: 3449 Miscellaneous metalwork
PA: Mmc Precision Holdings Corp.
1021 W Birchwood St
Morton IL 61550
309 266-7176

**(G-15168)**
**MORTON INDUSTRIES LLC**
70 Commerce Dr (61550-9198)
PHONE..................309 263-2590
Fax: 309 263-0862
Justin Barnewolt, *Engineer*
Gary Schmitt, *Engineer*
Jan Christiansan, *CFO*
Brodie Hall, *Controller*
Elaine Swigart, *Human Res Mgr*
▲ EMP: 400
SQ FT: 225,000
SALES (est): 106.4MM **Privately Held**
WEB: www.mortonwelding.com
SIC: 3498 Fabricated pipe & fittings
PA: Nelson Global Products, Inc.
1560 Williams Dr
Stoughton WI 53589

**(G-15169)**
**MORTON METALCRAFT CO PA**
1021 W Birchwood St (61550-9617)
PHONE..................309 266-7176
Fax: 309 263-1866
Frank Lukacs, *President*
David Stratton, *Vice Pres*
Robb Herbig, *Opers Staff*
Tina Marks, *Purchasing*
Donald Shippy, *Asst Controller*
EMP: 22

SALES (est): 3.7MM **Privately Held**
SIC: 3449 3444 Miscellaneous metalwork; sheet metalwork

**(G-15170)**
**MULTAX CORPORATION**
424 W Edgewood Ct (61550-2499)
P.O. Box 266 (61550-0266)
PHONE..................309 266-9765
Fax: 309 266-5541
Don E Bigger, *President*
Doug Myers, *Vice Pres*
Will Compton, *Engineer*
Mildred R Bigger, *Admin Sec*
▲ EMP: 63
SQ FT: 66,000
SALES (est): 10.1MM **Privately Held**
WEB: www.multaxcorporation.com
SIC: 3599 3728 Machine shop, jobbing & repair; aircraft parts & equipment

**(G-15171)**
**NELSON GLOBAL PRODUCTS INC**
231 Detroit Ave (61550-1533)
PHONE..................309 263-8914
Steven Belser, *President*
EMP: 13 **Privately Held**
SIC: 3317 Steel pipe & tubes
PA: Nelson Global Products, Inc.
1560 Williams Dr
Stoughton WI 53589

**(G-15172)**
**NESTLE USA INC**
Nestle Confections Factory
216 N Morton Ave (61550-1830)
P.O. Box 198 (61550-0198)
PHONE..................309 263-2651
Fax: 309 263-2133
Terry Teske, *Controller*
Larry Popp, *Branch Mgr*
EMP: 200
SALES (corp-wide): 88.4B **Publicly Held**
WEB: www.nestleusa.com
SIC: 2023 Evaporated milk
HQ: Nestle Usa, Inc.
800 N Brand Blvd
Glendale CA 91203
818 549-6000

**(G-15173)**
**P-AMERICAS LLC**
Also Called: Pepsico
801 W Birchwood St (61550-9613)
PHONE..................309 266-2400
Fax: 309 263-5506
Lawrence Skehan, *Vice Pres*
Randy Lyons, *Sales Staff*
Randy Ravens, *Branch Mgr*
EMP: 130
SALES (corp-wide): 62.8B **Publicly Held**
SIC: 2086 5149 Soft drinks: packaged in cans, bottles, etc.; carbonated beverages, nonalcoholic: bottled & canned; soft drinks
HQ: P-Americas Llc
1 Pepsi Way
Somers NY

**(G-15174)**
**PARKER FABRICATION INC (PA)**
501 E Courtland St (61550-9043)
PHONE..................309 266-8413
Fax: 309 266-7231
Patrick A Parker, *President*
Matthew Parker, *Vice Pres*
Chuck Heerde, *Purch Agent*
Bonnie Parker, *Treasurer*
Bryan Clifton, *Marketing Mgr*
EMP: 35
SQ FT: 26,000
SALES (est): 5.4MM **Privately Held**
WEB: www.parkerfab.com
SIC: 3498 3714 7692 3444 Tube fabricating (contract bending & shaping); exhaust systems & parts, motor vehicle; welding repair; sheet metalwork

**(G-15175)**
**PARKER-HANNIFIN CORPORATION**
Also Called: Parker Hnnfin Elctrnic Contrls
1651 N Main St (61550-9058)
PHONE..................309 266-2200
Carl Murray, *General Mgr*

## GEOGRAPHIC SECTION

Pat Friend, *Vice Pres*
Tim Harris, *Safety Mgr*
Jerry Peterson, *Research*
Mike Baker, *Engineer*
**EMP:** 130
**SALES (corp-wide):** 11.3B **Publicly Held**
**WEB:** www.parker.com
**SIC:** 3625 Control equipment, electric
**PA:** Parker-Hannifin Corporation
  6035 Parkland Blvd
  Cleveland OH 44124
  216 896-3000

*(G-15176)*
### PEORIA TUBE FORMING CORP
Also Called: Ngp
231 Detroit Ave (61550-1533)
**PHONE** ................................. 309 822-0274
**Fax:** 309 822-0196
Thomas Gosnell, *CEO*
Rodger Butler, *President*
Doug Dole, *Vice Pres*
Joseph Freeman, *Vice Pres*
Kris Radhakrishnan, *CFO*
▲ **EMP:** 80
**SQ FT:** 60,000
**SALES (est):** 11.8MM **Privately Held**
**WEB:** www.peoria-tube.com
**SIC:** 3498 Tube fabricating (contract bending & shaping); manifolds, pipe: fabricated from purchased pipe
**PA:** Nelson Global Products, Inc.
  1560 Williams Dr
  Stoughton WI 53589

*(G-15177)*
### PIECE WORKS SPECIALISTS INC
300 W Adams St (61550-1988)
**PHONE** ................................. 309 266-7016
**Fax:** 309 266-5019
Charles Glover, *President*
Arlene Winter, *Bookkeeper*
**EMP:** 18
**SQ FT:** 6,000
**SALES (est):** 1.6MM **Privately Held**
**SIC:** 2448 Pallets, wood

*(G-15178)*
### PRO-FAB INC
1050 W Jefferson St Ste A (61550-1585)
P.O. Box 449 (61550-0449)
**PHONE** ................................. 309 263-8454
**Fax:** 309 263-1464
Stephen R Kopetz, *President*
Phil Young, *President*
Jess Wallace, *Vice Pres*
Laura Woodard, *CFO*
Jess Wallis, *VP Sales*
**EMP:** 45
**SQ FT:** 30,000
**SALES (est):** 15MM **Privately Held**
**SIC:** 3443 Fabricated plate work (boiler shop)

*(G-15179)*
### QUALITY TRAILER SALES INC
1701 N Main St (61550-9208)
**PHONE** ................................. 630 739-2495
Jeff Hendricks, *Manager*
**EMP:** 3
**SALES (corp-wide):** 30.2MM **Privately Held**
**WEB:** www.qualitytrailersales.net
**SIC:** 3715 Semitrailers for truck tractors
**PA:** Quality Trailer Sales, Inc
  1601 1st Ave E
  Milan IL 61264
  309 787-2179

*(G-15180)*
### ROCKFORD RIGGING INC
1480 S Main St Ste A (61550-4513)
**PHONE** ................................. 309 263-0566
Brent Hart, *Manager*
**EMP:** 5
**SALES (corp-wide):** 9.4MM **Privately Held**
**SIC:** 3531 Construction machinery attachments
**PA:** Rockford Rigging, Inc.
  5401 Mainsail Dr
  Roscoe IL 61073
  309 263-0566

*(G-15181)*
### SOUTHFIELD CORPORATION
Also Called: Morton Ready Mix Concrete
775 W Birchwood St (61550-9605)
**PHONE** ................................. 309 676-6121
Dave Minor, *Manager*
**EMP:** 57
**SALES (corp-wide):** 273.9MM **Privately Held**
**WEB:** www.prairiegroup.com
**SIC:** 3273 Ready-mixed concrete
**PA:** Southfield Corporation
  8995 W 95th St
  Palos Hills IL 60465
  708 344-1000

*(G-15182)*
### SPL SOFTWARE ALLIANCE LLC
Also Called: Caterpillar Authorized Dealer
500 N Morton Ave (61550-1527)
P.O. Box 474 (61550-0474)
**PHONE** ................................. 309 266-0304
Mary Bell, *President*
Steven Pesha, *Manager*
Angie Knoll, *Administration*
**EMP:** 2
**SALES (est):** 1MM **Privately Held**
**SIC:** 7372 5082 Prepackaged software; construction & mining machinery

*(G-15183)*
### SYNERGETIC INDUSTRIES
1484 S Main St (61550-2822)
**PHONE** ................................. 309 321-8145
Jake Ludeman, *Principal*
**EMP:** 2
**SALES (est):** 253.2K **Privately Held**
**SIC:** 3999 Manufacturing industries

*(G-15184)*
### TAZEWELL FLOOR COVERING INC
419 W Jefferson St (61550-1896)
**PHONE** ................................. 309 266-6371
**Fax:** 309 266-9812
Thomas Zimmerman, *President*
Steven Zimmerman, *Vice Pres*
**EMP:** 15
**SQ FT:** 11,000
**SALES (est):** 2.2MM **Privately Held**
**SIC:** 5713 5231 2391 Carpets; linoleum; floor tile; paint, glass & wallpaper; curtains & draperies

*(G-15185)*
### YINLUN USA INC
77 Commerce Dr (61550-9197)
P.O. Box 5077 (61550-5077)
**PHONE** ................................. 309 291-0843
Xiaomin Xu, *President*
Marco Lambert, *Vice Pres*
Saul Torres, *Manager*
▲ **EMP:** 5
**SALES (est):** 2.3MM
**SALES (corp-wide):** 135.1MM **Privately Held**
**SIC:** 3443 5075 Heat exchangers: coolers (after, inter), condensers, etc.; heat exchangers
**PA:** Zhejiang Yinlun Machinery Co., Ltd.
  No.8, Shifeng East Road, Tiantai Industry Park
  Taizhou 31720
  576 839-3825

---
### Morton Grove
### Cook County
---

*(G-15186)*
### ALFA MFG INDUSTRIES INC
Also Called: Alfa Tools
7845 Merrimac Ave (60053-2710)
**PHONE** ................................. 847 470-9595
Diljit S Ahluwalia, *President*
Mohina A Sends, *Exec VP*
Shaan Ahluwalia, *Vice Pres*
**EMP:** 21
**SQ FT:** 12,000
**SALES (est):** 4.4MM **Privately Held**
**WEB:** www.alfatools.com
**SIC:** 3545 5084 Cutting tools for machine tools; metalworking tools (such as drills, taps, dies, files)

*(G-15187)*
### ALYCE DESIGNS INC (PA)
7901 Caldwell Ave (60053-2701)
**PHONE** ................................. 847 966-6933
**Fax:** 847 966-9207
Jean Paul Hamm, *President*
Phoebe Tsao, *Marketing Staff*
▲ **EMP:** 30 **EST:** 1955
**SQ FT:** 97,000
**SALES (est):** 2.7MM **Privately Held**
**WEB:** www.alycedesigns.com
**SIC:** 2335 Wedding gowns & dresses; gowns, formal; ensemble dresses: women's, misses' & juniors'; dresses, paper: cut & sewn

*(G-15188)*
### AMERALLOY STEEL CORPORATION
7848 Merrimac Ave (60053-2737)
**PHONE** ................................. 847 967-0600
**Fax:** 847 967-0643
Richard D Steele, *President*
Michael Molnar, *General Mgr*
Jeff Johnson, *Manager*
Dale C Altmin, *Admin Sec*
**EMP:** 50
**SQ FT:** 22,600
**SALES (est):** 33.7MM **Privately Held**
**WEB:** www.ameralloy.com
**SIC:** 5051 3443 Steel; plate work for the metalworking trade

*(G-15189)*
### BESTPYSANKY INC
6212 Madison Ct (60053-3218)
**PHONE** ................................. 877 797-2659
Sergiy Lishchuk, *CEO*
▲ **EMP:** 9
**SQ FT:** 4,000
**SALES (est):** 869.3K **Privately Held**
**SIC:** 5947 3999 5199 Gift, novelty & souvenir shop; boutiquing: decorating gift items with sequins, fruit, etc.; gifts & novelties

*(G-15190)*
### BUNZL RETAIL LLC
Also Called: Cdw Merchants
8338 Austin Ave (60053-3209)
**PHONE** ................................. 847 733-1469
John Henry Flerx, *Manager*
**EMP:** 18
**SALES (corp-wide):** 9.1B **Privately Held**
**SIC:** 2542 Racks, merchandise display or storage: except wood
**HQ:** Bunzl Retail, L.L.C.
  1 Cityplace Dr
  Saint Louis MO 63141
  314 997-5959

*(G-15191)*
### C & V GRANITE INC
9120 Cherry Ave (60053-2331)
**PHONE** ................................. 847 966-0275
Cvetan Staletovic, *President*
Vesha Staletovic, *Admin Sec*
**EMP:** 6 **EST:** 2007
**SALES (est):** 456.5K **Privately Held**
**SIC:** 1411 Granite dimension stone

*(G-15192)*
### CHARGER WATER CONDITIONING INC (HQ)
8150 Lehigh Ave Ste A (60053-2600)
**PHONE** ................................. 847 967-9558
Sig Feiger, *President*
Steve Feiger, *Vice Pres*
▲ **EMP:** 16
**SQ FT:** 3,500
**SALES (est):** 5MM
**SALES (corp-wide):** 126.9MM **Privately Held**
**SIC:** 3589 Water treatment equipment, industrial
**PA:** The Crawford Supply Group Inc
  8150 Lehigh Ave Ste A
  Morton Grove IL 60053
  847 967-0550

*(G-15193)*
### DAILY DOLLAR SAVINGS LLC
9448 Skokie Blvd (60053)
**PHONE** ................................. 860 883-0351
Lababidi Michael, *Principal*

**EMP:** 5
**SALES (est):** 258.6K **Privately Held**
**SIC:** 2711 Newspapers, publishing & printing

*(G-15194)*
### DOT SHARPER PRINTING INC
8120 River Dr Ste 1 (60053-2613)
**PHONE** ................................. 847 581-9033
**Fax:** 847 581-9047
Steven R Clark, *President*
Jim Dravecky, *Admin Sec*
**EMP:** 6
**SALES (est):** 610K **Privately Held**
**WEB:** www.sharperdotprinting.com
**SIC:** 2752 Commercial printing, lithographic

*(G-15195)*
### ELAN FURS
Also Called: Barth Wind Elan Furs
3841 E 82nd St (60053)
**PHONE** ................................. 317 255-6100
John Mitropoulos, *Owner*
Anna Miraupoulos, *Co-Owner*
**EMP:** 12
**SALES (est):** 362.5K **Privately Held**
**SIC:** 3999 5651 Furs; unisex clothing stores

*(G-15196)*
### ENJOYLIFE INC
8244 Lehigh Ave (60053-2615)
P.O. Box 118, Lake Zurich (60047-0118)
**PHONE** ................................. 847 966-3377
**Fax:** 847 966-2288
Marie-France Russell, *President*
Steven Russell, *Vice Pres*
▲ **EMP:** 8
**SQ FT:** 5,000
**SALES (est):** 1MM **Privately Held**
**WEB:** www.enjoylifeinc.com
**SIC:** 3949 Sporting & athletic goods

*(G-15197)*
### FASTSIGNS INTERNATIONAL
7911 Golf Rd (60053-1040)
**PHONE** ................................. 847 967-7222
**Fax:** 847 967-7257
Richard Goldberg, *President*
Janet Goldberg, *Admin Sec*
**EMP:** 7
**SQ FT:** 1,900
**SALES (est):** 1.5MM **Privately Held**
**SIC:** 3993 Signs & advertising specialties

*(G-15198)*
### FLUID HANDLING LLC
Also Called: Bell & Gossett
8200 Austin Ave (60053-3205)
**PHONE** ................................. 773 267-1600
**Fax:** 847 965-3142
Ken Napolitano, *President*
**EMP:** 500 **Publicly Held**
**SIC:** 3561 Pumps & pumping equipment
**HQ:** Fluid Handling, Llc
  175 Standard Pkwy
  Cheektowaga NY 14227
  716 897-2800

*(G-15199)*
### GRAPHIC PRESS INC
6511 Oakton St (60053-2728)
**PHONE** ................................. 847 272-6000
Ronald Levine, *President*
**EMP:** 8
**SQ FT:** 10,000
**SALES (est):** 400K **Privately Held**
**SIC:** 2759 Commercial printing

*(G-15200)*
### HOWLAND TECHNOLOGY INC
Also Called: Evergreen Drive Systems
8129 Austin Ave (60053-3204)
**PHONE** ................................. 847 965-9808
Thomas P Howland, *President*
Stephania Holland, *Vice Pres*
Britta Franck, *Marketing Staff*
Gaby Mancuso, *Marketing Staff*
Jonas Urlaub, *Manager*
▲ **EMP:** 10
**SQ FT:** 5,000
**SALES:** 10MM **Privately Held**
**WEB:** www.globalepower.com
**SIC:** 3621 3799 Motors, electric; recreational vehicles

# Morton Grove - Cook County (G-15201)

## GEOGRAPHIC SECTION

**(G-15201)**
**ILLINI COOLANT MANAGEMENT CORP (PA)**
8011 Parkside Ave (60053-3543)
**PHONE**............................847 966-1079
John Bailey, *President*
▲ **EMP**: 16
**SALES**: 2MM **Privately Held**
**SIC**: 2992 Cutting oils, blending; made from purchased materials

**(G-15202)**
**INDECOR INC**
8222 Lehigh Ave (60053-2615)
**PHONE**............................773 561-7670
**Fax**: 773 561-5469
Thomas A Welch, *President*
Cathie Calderon, *Controller*
Jeffrey Hunt, *Director*
**EMP**: 14
**SQ FT**: 8,000
**SALES (est)**: 2.5MM
**SALES (corp-wide)**: 10MM **Privately Held**
**WEB**: www.indecorinc.com
**SIC**: 2391 Curtains & draperies
**PA**: Tana Tex, Inc.
2243 W Belmont Ave Ste 1
Chicago IL 60618
773 561-9270

**(G-15203)**
**INTERNATIONAL SPRING COMPANY**
Also Called: I S C O
7901 Nagle Ave (60053-2714)
**PHONE**............................847 470-8170
**Fax**: 847 470-8179
Joseph H Goldberg, *President*
Brett Nudelman, *Vice Pres*
Earl Peterson, *CFO*
**EMP**: 100 **EST**: 1920
**SQ FT**: 45,000
**SALES (est)**: 15.5MM **Privately Held**
**WEB**: www.internationalspring.com
**SIC**: 3495 3469 Instrument springs, precision; stamping metal for the trade

**(G-15204)**
**ITT BELL & GOSSETT**
8200 Austin Ave (60053-3283)
P.O. Box 1389 (60053-7389)
**PHONE**............................847 966-3700
**Fax**: 847 966-8366
John Waterfield, *CEO*
Yuriy Levit, *Engineer*
Robert Arentsen, *Associate*
**EMP**: 33
**SALES (est)**: 15MM **Privately Held**
**SIC**: 3561 Pumps & pumping equipment

**(G-15205)**
**ITT WATER & WASTEWATER USA INC**
Also Called: Xylem
8200 Austin Ave (60053-3205)
**PHONE**............................847 966-3700
Henry Moerlien, *Manager*
Mark Pondel, *Manager*
**EMP**: 6
**SALES (corp-wide)**: 2.4B **Publicly Held**
**SIC**: 3621 3613 3674 3511 Motors & generators; switchgear & switchboard apparatus; semiconductors & related devices; turbines & turbine generator sets
**HQ**: Itt Water & Wastewater U.S.A., Inc.
14125 S Bridge Cir
Charlotte NC 28273
704 409-9700

**(G-15206)**
**J & D INSTANT SIGNS**
5614 Dempster St (60053-3108)
**PHONE**............................847 965-2800
**Fax**: 847 965-2805
John Swanson, *President*
**EMP**: 3
**SQ FT**: 2,500
**SALES (est)**: 240K **Privately Held**
**SIC**: 7389 3993 2672 2396 Lettering & sign painting services; signs & advertising specialties; coated & laminated paper; automotive & apparel trimmings

**(G-15207)**
**JOHN CRANE INC**
6400 Oakton St (60053-2725)
P.O. Box 91502, Chicago (60693-1502)
**PHONE**............................847 967-2400
**EMP**: 7
**SALES (corp-wide)**: 4.1B **Privately Held**
**WEB**: www.johncrane.com
**SIC**: 3053 Gaskets & sealing devices; packing materials
**HQ**: John Crane Inc.
227 W Monroe St Ste 1800
Chicago IL 60606
312 605-7800

**(G-15208)**
**K & B MACHINING**
6206 Madison Ct (60053-3218)
**PHONE**............................847 663-9534
**Fax**: 847 663-9535
Robert J Zuttermeister Jr, *President*
Kurt Ericsson, *Vice Pres*
**EMP**: 6
**SQ FT**: 2,300
**SALES (est)**: 300K **Privately Held**
**SIC**: 3599 3544 Machine shop, jobbing & repair; special dies, tools, jigs & fixtures

**(G-15209)**
**KEENPAC LLC (HQ)**
Also Called: Bunzel
8338 Austin Ave (60053-3209)
**PHONE**............................845 291-8680
Fran Finnin, *Controller*
▲ **EMP**: 5
**SQ FT**: 1,900
**SALES (est)**: 1.9MM
**SALES (corp-wide)**: 9.1B **Privately Held**
**WEB**: www.keenpac.com
**SIC**: 2673 Cellophane bags, unprinted: made from purchased materials
**PA**: Bunzl Public Limited Company
York House, 45 Seymour Street
London W1H 7
207 725-5000

**(G-15210)**
**KROTO INC**
Also Called: Icanvasart
8280 Austin Ave (60053-3207)
**PHONE**............................800 980-1089
Leon Oks, *President*
Guy Lvovski, *Mktg Dir*
Elizabeth Lvovski, *Director*
Alex Goldman, *Business Dir*
▲ **EMP**: 29 **EST**: 2006
**SALES (est)**: 5.8MM **Privately Held**
**SIC**: 2394 Canvas & related products

**(G-15211)**
**LASALLE CHEMICAL & SUPPLY CO**
Also Called: Lasalle Chemical Co.
6108 Madison Ct (60053-3216)
**PHONE**............................847 470-1234
**Fax**: 847 470-1441
John Bravos, *President*
**EMP**: 11
**SQ FT**: 3,800
**SALES (est)**: 1.7MM **Privately Held**
**WEB**: www.lasallechemical.com
**SIC**: 5169 2842 2841 Chemicals & allied products; specialty cleaning, polishes & sanitation goods; soap & other detergents

**(G-15212)**
**LICHTNWALD - JOHNSTON IR WORKS**
Also Called: L J Iron Works
7840 Lehigh Ave (60053-2707)
P.O. Box 1328 (60053-7328)
**PHONE**............................847 966-1100
**Fax**: 847 966-1159
Ira Rosenberg, *President*
Patrick Cansler, *Vice Pres*
Paul Rosenberg, *Consultant*
**EMP**: 25
**SQ FT**: 120,000
**SALES (est)**: 863.9K **Privately Held**
**SIC**: 3441 1791 Expansion joints (structural shapes), iron or steel; structural steel erection

**(G-15213)**
**LIFEWAY FOODS INC (PA)**
6431 Oakton St (60053-2727)
**PHONE**............................847 967-1010
Ludmila Smolyansky, *Ch of Bd*
Julie Smolyansky, *President*
Edward P Smolyansky, *COO*
John P Waldron, *CFO*
Craig Stout, *Manager*
▲ **EMP**: 268
**SALES**: 123.8MM **Publicly Held**
**WEB**: www.lifeway.net
**SIC**: 2023 2026 Dry, condensed, evaporated dairy products; fluid milk; kefir; yogurt; fermented & cultured milk products

**(G-15214)**
**LIGHTWORKS COMMUNCATION INC**
Also Called: Monthly Aspectarian, The
5632 Carol Ave (60053-3101)
**PHONE**............................847 966-1110
Guy Spiro, *President*
Christian Ryan, *Administration*
**EMP**: 6
**SALES (est)**: 335.1K **Privately Held**
**SIC**: 2721 Periodicals

**(G-15215)**
**MAGRABAR LLC**
6100 Madison Ct (60053-3216)
**PHONE**............................847 965-7550
**Fax**: 847 965-7553
Ravi Joshi, *President*
Colin J Hoather, *Vice Pres*
Brian Kaupas, *Controller*
Jeffrey Conrad, *Info Tech Dir*
**EMP**: 16 **EST**: 1981
**SALES**: 15MM
**SALES (corp-wide)**: 142MM **Privately Held**
**SIC**: 2819 Industrial inorganic chemicals
**HQ**: Munzing North America Lp
1455 Broad St Ste 3
Bloomfield NJ 07003
973 279-1306

**(G-15216)**
**MAIERS BAKERY**
9328 Waukegan Rd (60053-1312)
**PHONE**............................847 967-8042
Gregg H Maier, *President*
John Koester, *Vice Pres*
**EMP**: 9
**SQ FT**: 1,800
**SALES (est)**: 480K **Privately Held**
**WEB**: www.maiersbakery.com
**SIC**: 2051 2052 Bakery: wholesale or wholesale/retail combined; cookies & crackers

**(G-15217)**
**MAIN STREET VISUALS INC**
Also Called: Sign One
8340 Callie Ave Unit 110 (60053-3714)
**PHONE**............................847 869-7446
**Fax**: 847 869-7494
Henry Funkenbusch, *President*
Phyllis Funkenbusch, *Vice Pres*
**EMP**: 5
**SALES (est)**: 380K **Privately Held**
**WEB**: www.signone.com
**SIC**: 3993 Signs & advertising specialties

**(G-15218)**
**MEDAOWVIEW VENTURES II INC (PA)**
8350 Lehigh Ave (60053-2616)
**PHONE**............................847 965-1700
Michael Brown, *President*
Robin Mc Vey, *Senior VP*
Monique Ware, *Planning*
**EMP**: 30
**SALES (est)**: 3.4MM **Privately Held**
**SIC**: 3911 Jewelry, precious metal

**(G-15219)**
**MEDIFIX INC**
8727 Narragansett Ave (60053-2847)
**PHONE**............................847 965-1898
George Albulescu, *President*
**EMP**: 5
**SALES (est)**: 772.8K **Privately Held**
**WEB**: www.medifixinc.com
**SIC**: 3841 5047 Surgical instruments & apparatus; hospital equipment & furniture

**(G-15220)**
**MGP HOLDING CORP**
6451 Main St (60053-2633)
**PHONE**............................847 967-5600
Frank Leo, *CEO*
Brian Tambi, *Ch of Bd*
William Goldberg, *President*
Rick Lopatin, *Controller*
▲ **EMP**: 260
**SALES (est)**: 38.8MM
**SALES (corp-wide)**: 509MM **Privately Held**
**SIC**: 2834 Pharmaceutical preparations
**PA**: Gtcr Golder Rauner, L.L.C.
300 N La Salle Dr # 5600
Chicago IL 60654
312 329-0225

**(G-15221)**
**MINUTEMAN PRESS MORTON GROVE**
6038 Dempster St (60053-2942)
**PHONE**............................847 470-0212
**Fax**: 847 470-0232
Ken Lipski, *Owner*
Bea Lipski, *Co-Owner*
Lisa Williams, *Supervisor*
**EMP**: 4 **EST**: 1979
**SALES**: 140K **Privately Held**
**WEB**: www.minutemanmortongrove.com
**SIC**: 2752 2789 Commercial printing, lithographic; bookbinding & related work

**(G-15222)**
**MORTON GROVE MED IMAGING LLC (PA)**
Also Called: 3t Imaging Center
9000 Waukegan Rd Ste 110 (60053-2128)
**PHONE**............................847 213-2700
**Fax**: 847 213-2709
Jennifer Kaszuk, *General Mgr*
Richard Kim, *Managing Dir*
Shawn Kempa, *Info Tech Mgr*
**EMP**: 25
**SALES (est)**: 8.1MM **Privately Held**
**SIC**: 3826 Magnetic resonance imaging apparatus

**(G-15223)**
**MORTON GROVE PHRMCEUTICALS INC**
6451 Main St (60053-2633)
**PHONE**............................847 967-5600
Sunil Khera, *President*
Prakash Chainani, *Sr Corp Ofcr*
Ninva Orta, *Buyer*
Aleksandra Djakovic, *Research*
Agnes Wong, *Engineer*
▲ **EMP**: 300
**SQ FT**: 125,000
**SALES**: 69.1MM **Privately Held**
**SIC**: 2834 Pharmaceutical preparations
**HQ**: Wockhardt Limited
Wockhardt Towers,
Mumbai MH
226 708-6014

**(G-15224)**
**NEW AVON LLC**
6901 Golf Rd (60053-1346)
**PHONE**............................847 966-0200
**Fax**: 847 470-5557
Reena Banga, *Project Mgr*
Dennis Fogarty, *Facilities Mgr*
Carlos Martiz, *Mfg Staff*
Shawnn Zaremba, *Purch Agent*
Joe Gonzalez, *Buyer*
**EMP**: 600
**SALES (corp-wide)**: 36B **Publicly Held**
**WEB**: www.avon.com
**SIC**: 2844 Cosmetic preparations
**HQ**: New Avon Llc
777 3rd Ave Fl 8
New York NY 10017
212 282-8500

**(G-15225)**
**OCEANAIRE INC**
6228 Oakton St (60053-2721)
**PHONE**............................847 583-0311

# GEOGRAPHIC SECTION

Mossville - Peoria County (G-15250)

Terry Schaul, *Owner*
Peter Baffes, *Owner*
Carlos Morales, *Owner*
Edward Groperg, *Controller*
**EMP:** 15
**SQ FT:** 20,000
**SALES (est):** 3.5MM **Privately Held**
**WEB:** www.oceanaire-inc.com
**SIC:** 3585 Air conditioning equipment, complete

**(G-15226)**
**PDSS CONSTRUCTION**
7516 Davis St (60053-1708)
**PHONE**.................847 980-6090
Sahir Isho, *Principal*
**EMP:** 10
**SALES (est):** 370K **Privately Held**
**SIC:** 1442 Construction sand & gravel

**(G-15227)**
**PEARL PERFECT INC**
8220 Austin Ave (60053-3207)
**PHONE**.................847 679-6251
Robert Gluck, *President*
Leah Gluck, *Admin Sec*
**EMP:** 26
**SALES (est):** 4MM **Privately Held**
**WEB:** www.pearlperfect.com
**SIC:** 5094 3961 Jewelry & precious stones; pearls; costume jewelry

**(G-15228)**
**PRINTING SOURCE INC**
Also Called: ASAP Printing
8120 River Dr Ste 2 (60053-2613)
**PHONE**.................773 588-2930
**Fax:** 773 588-1854
David S Solomon, *President*
Priscilla Solomon, *Vice Pres*
**EMP:** 5
**SQ FT:** 2,500
**SALES (est):** 712.1K **Privately Held**
**SIC:** 2752 2791 2789 Commercial printing, offset; typesetting; bookbinding & related work

**(G-15229)**
**PUBLICATIONS INTERNATIONAL LTD (PA)**
Also Called: Consumer Guide
8140 Lehigh Ave (60053-2627)
**PHONE**.................847 676-3470
**Fax:** 847 676-3671
Louis Weber, *President*
Ann Taylor, *President*
Frank Peiler, *Publisher*
Barbara Rittenhouse, *Publisher*
Damon Bell, *Editor*
◆ **EMP:** 380
**SQ FT:** 125,000
**SALES (est):** 84.1MM **Privately Held**
**WEB:** www.pubint.com
**SIC:** 2731 2721 Books: publishing only; magazines: publishing only, not printed on site

**(G-15230)**
**PURE N NATURAL SYSTEMS INC**
5836 Lincoln Ave Ste 100 (60053-3351)
P.O. Box 1137, Streamwood (60107-8137)
**PHONE**.................630 372-9681
**Fax:** 847 470-1686
Joseph A Roy Jr, *Principal*
Jim Woods, *Accounting Mgr*
**EMP:** 10
**SALES:** 1MM **Privately Held**
**WEB:** www.purennatural.com
**SIC:** 3585 3589 5075 Humidifiers & dehumidifiers; water filters & softeners, household type; air filters

**(G-15231)**
**QUANTUM COLOR GRAPHICS LLC**
6511 Oakton St (60053-2728)
**PHONE**.................847 967-3600
Frank Springer, *COO*
James Campise, *Exec VP*
Ira Shapiro, *Exec VP*
Andrew Dodge, *Vice Pres*
Taylor Kobey, *Vice Pres*
**EMP:** 155
**SQ FT:** 125,000
**SALES (est):** 62.3MM **Privately Held**
**SIC:** 2752 8741 7382 7389 Commercial printing, lithographic; management services; security systems services; finishing services

**(G-15232)**
**REGIS TECHNOLOGIES INC**
Also Called: Regis Chemical Company
8210 Austin Ave (60053-3205)
**PHONE**.................847 967-6000
**Fax:** 847 967-5876
Louis Glunz III, *CEO*
Sue Lye, *General Mgr*
Jelena Kocergin, *Business Mgr*
Rebecca Centko, *Project Mgr*
Michelle B Fritts, *Safety Mgr*
**EMP:** 53
**SQ FT:** 30,000
**SALES (est):** 18MM **Privately Held**
**WEB:** www.registech.com
**SIC:** 3826 2835 2869 2819 Analytical instruments; in vitro & in vivo diagnostic substances; industrial organic chemicals; industrial inorganic chemicals

**(G-15233)**
**RELIABLE APPLIANCE AND REF**
7443 Emerson St (60053-1146)
**PHONE**.................847 581-9520
**EMP:** 2
**SALES (est):** 209.1K **Privately Held**
**SIC:** 3822 Appliance controls except air-conditioning & refrigeration

**(G-15234)**
**SANDTECH INC**
Also Called: ALFA TOOLS
7845 Merrimac Ave (60053-2710)
**PHONE**.................847 470-9595
Dilgit S Ahluwalia, *President*
Jocelyn Glynn, *Vice Pres*
Josclyn Glynn, *Vice Pres*
Mohina Ahluwalia, *Treasurer*
Shaan Ahluwalia, *VP Sales*
▲ **EMP:** 13
**SQ FT:** 40,000
**SALES:** 48.7K **Privately Held**
**SIC:** 3545 3291 Cutting tools for machine tools; abrasive products

**(G-15235)**
**SCHWARZ PAPER COMPANY LLC (HQ)**
Also Called: Semper/Exeter
8338 Austin Ave (60053-3209)
P.O. Box 1239 (60053-7239)
**PHONE**.................847 966-2550
**Fax:** 847 966-1271
Christopher J Donnelly Jr, *CEO*
Tom Micalizzi, *General Mgr*
Mike Monteleone, *General Mgr*
Andrew Mc Kenna, *Chairman*
Bruce B Barton, *Senior VP*
◆ **EMP:** 200 **EST:** 1907
**SALES (est):** 207.9MM
**SALES (corp-wide):** 9.1B **Privately Held**
**WEB:** www.schwarz.com
**SIC:** 2621 5199 4225 Packaging paper; packaging materials; general warehousing
**PA:** Bunzl Public Limited Company
York House, 45 Seymour Street
London W1H 7
207 725-5000

**(G-15236)**
**SERVICE PACKAGING DESIGN INC**
6238 Lincoln Ave (60053-2852)
**PHONE**.................847 966-6592
Norman Croft, *President*
**EMP:** 5
**SQ FT:** 2,500
**SALES (est):** 363.7K **Privately Held**
**SIC:** 2752 7389 2679 2672 Decals, lithographed; tag, ticket & schedule printing: lithographic; packaging & labeling services; tags & labels, paper; adhesive papers, labels or tapes: from purchased material

**(G-15237)**
**STANDARD CONDENSER CORPORATION**
5412 Keeney St (60053-3512)
**PHONE**.................847 965-2722
Bryan Mc Lean, *CEO*
Richard T Mc Lean, *President*
Marilynn Mc Lean, *Corp Secy*
Brian McLean, *Vice Pres*
**EMP:** 10
**SQ FT:** 10,000
**SALES (est):** 940K **Privately Held**
**SIC:** 3675 Electronic capacitors

**(G-15238)**
**STEVEN BROWNSTEIN**
Also Called: Background Investigator, The
5830 Lincoln Ave Unit A (60053-3304)
**PHONE**.................847 909-6677
Steven Brownstein, *Owner*
Dennis Brownstein, *Opers Mgr*
Ana Brownstein, *Marketing Staff*
**EMP:** 3
**SALES (est):** 105.5K **Privately Held**
**SIC:** 2711 Newspapers: publishing only, not printed on site

**(G-15239)**
**STRANGE ENGINEERING INC**
8300 Austin Ave (60053-3209)
**PHONE**.................847 663-1701
**Fax:** 847 663-1702
Henry R Stange, *President*
Michael Stange, *Controller*
Glenn Cope, *Director*
Jeffrey Stange, *Admin Sec*
▲ **EMP:** 55
**SQ FT:** 50,000
**SALES (est):** 13.8MM **Privately Held**
**WEB:** www.strangeengineering.net
**SIC:** 3714 Axles, motor vehicle; motor vehicle brake systems & parts; steering mechanisms, motor vehicle; drive shafts, motor vehicle

**(G-15240)**
**SUCCESS JOURNAL CORP**
Also Called: Harmony House
7848 Foster St (60053-1034)
**PHONE**.................847 583-9000
Chris Witting, *President*
**EMP:** 5
**SALES (est):** 327K **Privately Held**
**WEB:** www.successjournal.com
**SIC:** 2711 Newspapers, publishing & printing

**(G-15241)**
**TOP ACE INC**
8440 Callie Ave Unit 612 (60053-5014)
**PHONE**.................847 581-0550
▲ **EMP:** 3 **EST:** 2007
**SALES (est):** 160K **Privately Held**
**SIC:** 2254 Knit Underwear Mill

**(G-15242)**
**UNLIMITED WARES INC**
6216 Oakton St (60053-2721)
**PHONE**.................773 234-4867
Yang Yiang, *President*
▲ **EMP:** 13
**SALES (est):** 1.3MM **Privately Held**
**SIC:** 3949 Archery equipment, general

**(G-15243)**
**VERLO MAT OF SKOKIE-EVANSTON**
Also Called: Verlo Mattress Factory
7927 Golf Rd (60053-1040)
**PHONE**.................847 966-9988
**Fax:** 847 966-4221
**EMP:** 7
**SQ FT:** 6,000
**SALES (est):** 994.4K **Privately Held**
**SIC:** 5712 2515 Mfg Mattresses And Ret Bedding And Accessories

**(G-15244)**
**W R TYPESETTING CO**
Also Called: W.R. Typesetting Co.
8120 River Dr Ste 2 (60053-2613)
**PHONE**.................847 966-1315
**Fax:** 847 966-8382
Bob Rubino, *President*
Maureen Rubino, *Corp Secy*
**EMP:** 8
**SQ FT:** 2,900
**SALES (est):** 978.9K **Privately Held**
**WEB:** www.wrmusicservice.com
**SIC:** 2791 7374 Typesetting; service bureau, computer

**(G-15245)**
**WATTCORE INC**
6208 Oakton St (60053-2721)
**PHONE**.................571 482-6777
Chanty Khek, *President*
◆ **EMP:** 8
**SQ FT:** 3,000
**SALES (est):** 708.6K **Privately Held**
**SIC:** 3677 Electronic coils, transformers & other inductors

**(G-15246)**
**WOCKHARDT HOLDING CORP**
6451 Main St (60053-2633)
**PHONE**.................847 967-5600
Kurt Orlofski, *President*
**EMP:** 301
**SALES (est):** 41.8MM **Privately Held**
**SIC:** 2834 Pharmaceutical preparations
**HQ:** Wockhardt Limited
Wockhardt Towers,
Mumbai MH
226 708-6014

**(G-15247)**
**XYLEM INC**
Bell & Gossett
8200 Austin Ave (60053-3205)
**PHONE**.................847 966-3700
**Fax:** 847 965-8379
Stan Gorka, *Superintendent*
Andy Kiolbasa, *Sr Corp Ofcr*
Diana Cardenas, *Purchasing*
Larry Reyes, *QA Dir*
Stanley Evans, *Engineer*
**EMP:** 58 **Publicly Held**
**WEB:** www.ittind.com
**SIC:** 3625 Control equipment, electric
**PA:** Xylem Inc.
1 International Dr
Rye Brook NY 10573

## Mossville
*Peoria County*

**(G-15248)**
**CATERPILLAR INC**
1900 E Old Galena Rd (61552)
**PHONE**.................309 266-4294
Gifford Parsons, *Branch Mgr*
**EMP:** 355
**SALES (corp-wide):** 38.5B **Publicly Held**
**SIC:** 3531 Construction machinery
**PA:** Caterpillar Inc.
100 Ne Adams St
Peoria IL 61629
309 675-1000

**(G-15249)**
**CATERPILLAR INC**
14009 Old Galena Rd (61552-7523)
**PHONE**.................903 712-4505
Charles Cray, *Branch Mgr*
**EMP:** 330
**SALES (corp-wide):** 38.5B **Publicly Held**
**SIC:** 3531 Construction machinery
**PA:** Caterpillar Inc.
100 Ne Adams St
Peoria IL 61629
309 675-1000

**(G-15250)**
**CATERPILLAR INC**
Old Galena Rd Ste H (61552)
P.O. Box 4000 (61552-4000)
**PHONE**.................309 578-2473
Mark Pflederer, *Principal*
Michael Simmons, *Technology*
**EMP:** 700
**SALES (corp-wide):** 38.5B **Publicly Held**
**WEB:** www.cat.com
**SIC:** 3531 3429 3052 Construction machinery; manufactured hardware (general); rubber & plastics hose & beltings

**Mossville - Peoria County (G-15251)**

**PA:** Caterpillar Inc.
100 Ne Adams St
Peoria IL 61629
309 675-1000

**(G-15251)**
**CATERPILLAR INC**
Illinois Rte 29 (61552)
P.O. Box 610 (61552-6100)
**PHONE**.................................309 675-6223
Mark Pflederer, *Branch Mgr*
**EMP:** 764
**SALES (corp-wide):** 38.5B **Publicly Held**
**WEB:** www.cat.com
**SIC: 1081** Metal mining services
**PA:** Caterpillar Inc.
100 Ne Adams St
Peoria IL 61629
309 675-1000

**(G-15252)**
**CENTRAL ILLINOIS COUNTER TOPS (PA)**
Also Called: C I C
11001 State St (61552-7539)
P.O. Box 415 (61552-0415)
**PHONE**.................................309 579-3550
Terry Hampton, *President*
Larry Hampton, *Vice Pres*
Bob Travers, *Vice Pres*
**EMP:** 2
**SQ FT:** 24,000
**SALES (est):** 1MM **Privately Held**
**SIC: 2541** Table or counter tops, plastic laminated

**(G-15253)**
**KENNAMETAL INC**
Olglena Rd (61552)
P.O. Box 610 (61552-6100)
**PHONE**.................................309 578-1888
Cat C Oltman, *Manager*
**EMP:** 14
**SALES (corp-wide):** 2.1B **Publicly Held**
**WEB:** www.kennametal.com
**SIC: 3545** Machine tool accessories
**PA:** Kennametal Inc.
600 Grant St Ste 5100
Pittsburgh PA 15219
412 248-8200

**(G-15254)**
**PERKINS ENGINES INC (DH)**
N4 Ac6160 # 6160 (61552)
**PHONE**.................................309 578-7364
Frank Perkins, *Principal*
Laurie J Huxtable, *Admin Sec*
▲ **EMP:** 50 **EST:** 1932
**SALES (est):** 6.4MM **Privately Held**
**WEB:** www.perkinsengines.net
**SIC: 3519** Internal combustion engines
**HQ:** Perkins Engines Company Limited
Frank Perkins Way
Peterborough CAMBS PE1 5
173 358-3000

**(G-15255)**
**WASHINGTON URS DIV**
14009 Old Galena Rd (61552-7547)
**PHONE**.................................309 578-8113
Gordon Birt, *Principal*
**EMP:** 4 **EST:** 2009
**SALES (est):** 453.4K **Privately Held**
**SIC: 3531** Tractors, construction

### Mound City
*Pulaski County*

**(G-15256)**
**CRAIN ENTERPRISES INC**
100 Ohio Ave (62963-1152)
P.O. Box 80 (62963-0080)
**PHONE**.................................618 748-9227
Steve Crain, *President*
Reda Crain, *Vice Pres*
Linda Kekow, *Office Mgr*
▲ **EMP:** 60 **EST:** 1945
**SQ FT:** 20,000
**SALES (est):** 9MM **Privately Held**
**WEB:** www.gopherpole.com
**SIC: 3829** Surveying & drafting equipment

**(G-15257)**
**SECO**
100 Ohio Ave (62963-1152)
**PHONE**.................................618 748-9227
Lynn Whitworth, *President*
▲ **EMP:** 4
**SALES (est):** 441.2K **Privately Held**
**SIC: 2221** Fiberglass fabrics

### Mounds
*Pulaski County*

**(G-15258)**
**CAMO CLAD INC**
471 Camo Clad Dr (62964-2240)
**PHONE**.................................618 342-6860
**Fax:** 618 342-6960
Joseph Warner, *President*
**EMP:** 12
**SQ FT:** 13,000
**SALES:** 1.1MM **Privately Held**
**WEB:** www.camoclad.com
**SIC: 3081** Vinyl film & sheet

**(G-15259)**
**OIL-DRI CORPORATION AMERICA**
700 Industrial Park Rd (62964-2153)
**PHONE**.................................618 745-6881
Bruce Modicue, *Purchasing*
Clarissa Merriweather, *Personnel*
Wayne Gibson, *Manager*
James Warden, *Maintence Staff*
**EMP:** 88
**SALES (corp-wide):** 262.3MM **Publicly Held**
**WEB:** www.oildri.com
**SIC: 1459** 3295 2842 Clays, except kaolin & ball; minerals, ground or treated; specialty cleaning, polishes & sanitation goods
**PA:** Oil-Dri Corporation Of America
410 N Michigan Ave # 400
Chicago IL 60611
312 321-1515

### Mount Carmel
*Wabash County*

**(G-15260)**
**B & D INDEPENDENCE INC**
1024 Empire St (62863-5101)
**PHONE**.................................618 262-7117
**Fax:** 618 263-3904
John Evans, *President*
**EMP:** 20 **EST:** 1980
**SQ FT:** 20,000
**SALES (est):** 3.7MM **Privately Held**
**SIC: 3842** 3444 Surgical appliances & supplies; sheet metalwork

**(G-15261)**
**B & G MACHINE INC**
421 W 9th St (62863-1366)
**PHONE**.................................618 262-2269
Greg Odom, *President*
Brady Cox, *Corp Secy*
Greg Ruehl, *Vice Pres*
Brad Ruehl, *Accountant*
**EMP:** 8
**SQ FT:** 4,800
**SALES (est):** 1.7MM **Privately Held**
**SIC: 3599** Machine & other job shop work

**(G-15262)**
**CEG SUBSIDIARY LLC (PA)**
Also Called: Pacific Press Technologies
714 N Walnut St (62863-1466)
**PHONE**.................................618 262-8666
**Fax:** 618 262-7000
Brian Evans, *Plant Mgr*
Brent Weir, *Sls & Mktg Exec*
Tim Johnson, *Accounting Mgr*
Chris Robinson, *Sales Mgr*
Becky Majors, *Sales Staff*
▲ **EMP:** 77
**SQ FT:** 150,000
**SALES (est):** 13.2MM **Privately Held**
**WEB:** www.pacific-press.com
**SIC: 3542** Press brakes; presses: forming, stamping, punching, sizing (machine tools); shearing machines, power

**(G-15263)**
**CORWIN PRINTING**
1004 Landes St (62863-1345)
**PHONE**.................................618 263-3936
Kyle Day, *Owner*
Connie Day, *Owner*
**EMP:** 3
**SQ FT:** 2,450
**SALES:** 160K **Privately Held**
**WEB:** www.corwin-printing.com
**SIC: 2752** 2791 2759 Commercial printing, offset; typesetting; commercial printing

**(G-15264)**
**DEE DRILLING CO (PA)**
431 N Market St (62863-1526)
P.O. Box 7 (62863-0007)
**PHONE**.................................618 262-4136
**Fax:** 618 262-4710
J Roy Dee III, *President*
Jean Dee Fischer, *Treasurer*
**EMP:** 30 **EST:** 1949
**SALES (est):** 7.9MM **Privately Held**
**SIC: 1381** Drilling oil & gas wells

**(G-15265)**
**F L BEARD SERVICE CORP**
800 Stokes St (62863-1284)
**PHONE**.................................618 262-5193
**Fax:** 618 262-5194
Kevin Baize, *President*
**EMP:** 24
**SQ FT:** 6,000
**SALES (est):** 2.7MM **Privately Held**
**SIC: 1381** 1389 Drilling oil & gas wells; oil field services

**(G-15266)**
**HAGGARD WELL SERVICES INC**
1309 Poplar St (62863-1214)
**PHONE**.................................618 262-5060
Barry Haggard, *President*
**EMP:** 6
**SALES (est):** 600K **Privately Held**
**SIC: 1389** Haulage, oil field

**(G-15267)**
**HOCKING OIL COMPANY INC**
123 W 4th St Ste 103 (62863-1562)
P.O. Box 162 (62863-0162)
**PHONE**.................................618 263-3258
**Fax:** 618 262-8998
Andy G Hocking, *President*
Patsy Hocking, *Vice Pres*
Perry Case, *Sales Executive*
Andrea M Richardson, *Admin Sec*
**EMP:** 8
**SQ FT:** 3,000
**SALES (est):** 360K **Privately Held**
**SIC: 1311** Crude petroleum production

**(G-15268)**
**HOWARD ENERGY CORPORATION**
519 W 3rd St (62863-1752)
P.O. Box 693 (62863-0693)
**PHONE**.................................618 263-3000
Craig J Howard, *President*
Margaret Howard, *Admin Sec*
**EMP:** 3
**SQ FT:** 2,800
**SALES:** 300K **Privately Held**
**WEB:** www.howardenergycorp.com
**SIC: 1382** 1311 1389 Geological exploration, oil & gas field; crude petroleum production; oil consultants

**(G-15269)**
**J & J QUALITY PALLETS INC**
226 W 11th St (62863-1407)
**PHONE**.................................618 262-6426
John Burton, *CEO*
**EMP:** 5
**SALES (est):** 195.6K **Privately Held**
**SIC: 2448** Wood pallets & skids

**(G-15270)**
**JACKSON OIL CORPORATION**
809 W 9th St (62863-2414)
P.O. Box 95 (62863-0095)
**PHONE**.................................618 263-6521
Fred Jackson, *President*
**EMP:** 3
**SQ FT:** 7,200
**SALES:** 200K **Privately Held**
**WEB:** www.jacksonoil.net
**SIC: 1381** 5084 Directional drilling oil & gas wells; oil well machinery, equipment & supplies

**(G-15271)**
**KEEPES FUNERAL HOME INC**
1500 N Cherry St (62863-1879)
**PHONE**.................................618 262-5200
Shaun Keepes, *President*
**EMP:** 10
**SALES:** 100K **Privately Held**
**SIC: 7261** 3281 Funeral home; monument or burial stone, cut & shaped

**(G-15272)**
**LAWRENCE OIL COMPANY INC**
801 W 9th St Rm 208 (62863-2446)
P.O. Box 251 (62863-0251)
**PHONE**.................................618 262-4138
**EMP:** 5
**SQ FT:** 300
**SALES (est):** 540K **Privately Held**
**SIC: 1311** Crude Oil Production

**(G-15273)**
**M & S OIL WELL CEMENTING CO (PA)**
Hwy 1 N (62863)
P.O. Box 344 (62863-0344)
**PHONE**.................................618 262-7962
John D Morgan, *CEO*
Jeff Morgan, *President*
Teri Ewald, *Corp Secy*
Branda Morgan, *Corp Secy*
Patrick Morgan, *Vice Pres*
**EMP:** 3 **EST:** 1949
**SQ FT:** 5,000
**SALES:** 720K **Privately Held**
**SIC: 1389** Cementing oil & gas well casings

**(G-15274)**
**MILLER TESTING SERVICE**
1125 W 3rd St (62863-1722)
P.O. Box 661 (62863-0661)
**PHONE**.................................618 262-5911
Tim Schuler, *Owner*
**EMP:** 20
**SQ FT:** 4,000
**SALES (est):** 950K **Privately Held**
**SIC: 1389** Testing, measuring, surveying & analysis services

**(G-15275)**
**MT CARMEL MACHINE SHOP INC**
10011 N 1250th Blvd (62863)
**PHONE**.................................618 262-4591
**Fax:** 618 263-3293
David M Partee, *President*
Stephen F Partee, *Vice Pres*
**EMP:** 14 **EST:** 1931
**SQ FT:** 6,000
**SALES (est):** 2.1MM **Privately Held**
**SIC: 3599** 3443 Machine shop, jobbing & repair; tanks, lined: metal plate

**(G-15276)**
**MT CARMEL REGISTER CO INC**
Also Called: Daily Republican Register
117 E 4th St (62863-2110)
**PHONE**.................................618 262-5144
**Fax:** 618 263-4437
Bill Brehm, *President*
Mark Short, *Vice Pres*
A Philip Tofani, *Vice Pres*
Jeff Johnson, *Treasurer*
Sally Voigt, *Advt Staff*
**EMP:** 20
**SQ FT:** 10,000

**SALES (est):** 1.2MM
**SALES (corp-wide):** 220.6MM **Privately Held**
**WEB:** www.tristate-media.com
**SIC:** 2711 2752 Newspapers, publishing & printing; commercial printing, offset
**PA:** Brehm Communications, Inc.
16644 W Bernardo Dr # 300
San Diego CA 92127
858 451-6200

*(G-15277)*
**MT CRMEL STBLZATION GROUP INC (PA)**
1611 College Dr (62863-2614)
P.O. Box 458 (62863-0458)
**PHONE**.................................618 262-5118
**Fax:** 618 263-4084
Mike McPherson, *President*
Greg Acree, *Superintendent*
Ryan Day, *Superintendent*
Tom Silvernale, *Superintendent*
Phil Hipsher, *Corp Secy*
**EMP:** 30 **EST:** 1928
**SQ FT:** 7,200
**SALES (est):** 92.4MM **Privately Held**
**WEB:** www.mtcsg.com
**SIC:** 1611 3273 Highway & street construction; ready-mixed concrete

*(G-15278)*
**NEW TRIANGLE OIL COMPANY**
Also Called: Southern Triangle Oil Co
600 Chestnut St (62863-1453)
P.O. Box 427 (62863-0427)
**PHONE**.................................618 262-4131
Lester D Moore, *Partner*
**EMP:** 2 **EST:** 1955
**SQ FT:** 1,500
**SALES (est):** 3.3MM **Privately Held**
**SIC:** 1311 Crude petroleum production

*(G-15279)*
**OMNI MATERIALS INC**
Also Called: MOUNT CARMEL STABILIZATION
1611 College Dr (62863-2614)
P.O. Box 458 (62863-0458)
**PHONE**.................................618 262-5118
Michael McPherson, *President*
Phil Hipsher, *Corp Secy*
Doug McPherson, *Exec VP*
Neil Ryan, *Vice Pres*
**EMP:** 20
**SALES (est):** 24.3MM **Privately Held**
**SIC:** 1422 Crushed & broken limestone

*(G-15280)*
**PACIFIC PRESS TECHNOLOGIES LP**
714 N Walnut St (62863-1466)
**PHONE**.................................618 262-8666
David Strothers, *Principal*
Michael Stein, *Plant Mgr*
John Jaranowski, *Electrical Engi*
Shirley Wright, *Admin Asst*
**EMP:** 8
**SALES (est):** 881.8K **Privately Held**
**SIC:** 2741 Miscellaneous publishing

*(G-15281)*
**PPT INDUSTRIAL MACHINES INC**
Also Called: Pacific Press
714 N Walnut St (62863-1466)
**PHONE**.................................800 851-3586
Richard Drexler, *CEO*
David A Somers, *President*
Tim Johnson, *Accounting Mgr*
Sheila Baumgart, *Info Tech Mgr*
TAC D Kensler, *Admin Sec*
**EMP:** 50
**SALES (est):** 4.1MM
**SALES (corp-wide):** 24MM **Privately Held**
**SIC:** 3542 3541 Machine tools, metal forming type; machine tools, metal cutting type
**PA:** Quality Products, Inc.
2222 S 3rd St
Columbus OH 43207
614 228-0185

*(G-15282)*
**SOUTHERN TRIANGLE OIL COMPANY**
600 Chestnut St (62863-1453)
P.O. Box 427 (62863-0427)
**PHONE**.................................618 262-4131
Lester D Moore, *President*
Charley Campbell, *Treasurer*
Lynette Wiles, *Admin Sec*
**EMP:** 14
**SQ FT:** 2,000
**SALES (est):** 2.2MM **Privately Held**
**SIC:** 1311 1381 Crude petroleum production; directional drilling oil & gas wells

*(G-15283)*
**SPARTAN PETROLEUM COMPANY**
328 N Market St (62863-1519)
P.O. Box 70 (62863-0070)
**PHONE**.................................618 262-4197
James Capin, *President*
Carolyn Burwer, *Manager*
**EMP:** 2
**SQ FT:** 800
**SALES (est):** 235.9K **Privately Held**
**SIC:** 1381 1311 Drilling oil & gas wells; crude petroleum production

*(G-15284)*
**TRANSCEDAR LIMITED**
916 Empire St (62863-5102)
P.O. Box 667 (62863-0667)
**PHONE**.................................618 262-4153
Mordi Fishman, *Principal*
Dan Young, *Vice Pres*
Melissa Duncan, *Controller*
▲ **EMP:** 26
**SALES (est):** 4.1MM **Privately Held**
**SIC:** 3599 3714 5531 Flexible metal hose, tubing & bellows; thermostats, motor vehicle; automotive parts

*(G-15285)*
**TRI KOTE INC**
1126 W 3rd St (62863-1798)
P.O. Box 661 (62863-0661)
**PHONE**.................................618 262-4156
Tim Schuler, *President*
**EMP:** 7 **EST:** 1965
**SALES (est):** 300K **Privately Held**
**SIC:** 1389 Oil field services

*(G-15286)*
**VIGO COAL OPERATING CO INC**
7790 Highway 15 (62863-4517)
**PHONE**.................................618 262-7022
Ron Will, *Manager*
Ubelhor Korre, *Asst Director*
**EMP:** 133
**SALES (corp-wide):** 95.9MM **Privately Held**
**SIC:** 1481 6211 Nonmetallic mineral services; oil & gas lease brokers
**PA:** Vigo Coal Operating Co., Inc.
250 N Cross Pointe Blvd
Evansville IN 47715
812 759-8446

*(G-15287)*
**WABASH CONTAINER CORPORATION**
1015 W 9th St (62863-2437)
P.O. Box 127 (62863-0127)
**PHONE**.................................618 263-3586
**Fax:** 618 263-3476
Steve Burton, *President*
Bill Stopher, *Prdtn Mgr*
Matthew Burton, *Production*
Dave Randall, *Marketing Staff*
Jack Fowler, *Admin Sec*
**EMP:** 30
**SQ FT:** 2,000
**SALES (est):** 8.5MM **Privately Held**
**WEB:** www.wabashcontainer.com
**SIC:** 2652 Setup paperboard boxes

*(G-15288)*
**WHITE LAND & MINERAL INC**
526 N Market St (62863-1558)
P.O. Box 308 (62863-0308)
**PHONE**.................................618 262-5102
**Fax:** 618 262-8235
Shad White, *President*
Clint White, *Corp Secy*
**EMP:** 6
**SQ FT:** 2,000
**SALES (est):** 1.5MM **Privately Held**
**SIC:** 1311 0191 Crude petroleum production; general farms, primarily crop

*(G-15289)*
**ZANETIS OIL COMPANY**
319 E 8th St (62863-2014)
P.O. Box 1026 (62863-1026)
**PHONE**.................................618 262-4593
**EMP:** 4
**SALES (est):** 258.6K **Privately Held**
**SIC:** 1311 Crude petroleum & natural gas

## Mount Carroll
### Carroll County

*(G-15290)*
**CHARLES ELECTRONICS LLC**
Also Called: Maco Antennas
302 S East St (61053-1448)
**PHONE**.................................815 244-7981
Thomas Charles, *Mng Member*
Nola Charles, *Admin Sec*
**EMP:** 6
**SQ FT:** 4,400
**SALES (est):** 330K **Privately Held**
**WEB:** www.gizmotchy.com
**SIC:** 3663 Antennas, transmitting & communications

*(G-15291)*
**HEISLER STONE CO INC**
Also Called: Stone Quarry
18463 Cyclone Ridge Rd (61053-9259)
**PHONE**.................................815 244-2685
Hazel Heisler, *Owner*
**EMP:** 3 **EST:** 1955
**SALES (est):** 125K **Privately Held**
**SIC:** 3281 3274 1422 Stone, quarrying & processing of own stone products; lime; crushed & broken limestone

*(G-15292)*
**MIRROR-DEMOCRAT**
Also Called: Savanna Times-Journal
308 N Main St (61053-1024)
P.O. Box 191 (61053-0191)
**PHONE**.................................815 244-2411
**Fax:** 815 244-2965
Robert Watson, *Owner*
Bob Watson, *Owner*
**EMP:** 8
**SQ FT:** 12,000
**SALES (est):** 374.9K **Privately Held**
**SIC:** 2711 Newspapers: publishing only, not printed on site

*(G-15293)*
**TEAM PRODUCTS INC**
636 S East St (61053-1459)
**PHONE**.................................815 244-6100
**Fax:** 815 244-6205
David R Johnston, *President*
▲ **EMP:** 14
**SALES (est):** 2MM **Privately Held**
**WEB:** www.teamproductsinc.com
**SIC:** 3052 Rubber & plastics hose & beltings

## Mount Erie
### Wayne County

*(G-15294)*
**UNION DRAINAGE DISTRICT**
Rr 1 (62446)
**PHONE**.................................618 445-2843
Robert Anniss, *Chairman*
**EMP:** 3
**SALES:** 72.1K **Privately Held**
**SIC:** 2843 Surface active agents

## Mount Morris
### Ogle County

*(G-15295)*
**CUSTOM SEAL & RUBBER PRODUCTS**
112 E Hitt St (61054-1220)
**PHONE**.................................888 356-2966
**Fax:** 815 946-3252
Brenda Getzendaner, *CEO*
Michael L Getzendaner, *President*
▼ **EMP:** 8
**SQ FT:** 8,500
**SALES:** 500K **Privately Held**
**WEB:** www.customsealandrubber.com
**SIC:** 3069 3061 2822 Molded rubber products; mechanical rubber goods; synthetic rubber

*(G-15296)*
**EXPRESSION WEAR INC**
2781 W Mud Creek Rd (61054-9768)
**PHONE**.................................815 732-1556
**Fax:** 815 732-1506
Anders Arvigo, *President*
Kristin Arvigo, *Admin Sec*
**EMP:** 5
**SQ FT:** 6,300
**SALES:** 450K **Privately Held**
**SIC:** 2759 2261 Letterpress & screen printing; finishing plants, cotton

*(G-15297)*
**QUAD/GRAPHICS INC**
404 N Wesley Ave (61054-1199)
**PHONE**.................................815 734-4121
Jeff Warren, *Engineer*
Tom Teresinski, *Controller*
David Miller, *Branch Mgr*
**EMP:** 509
**SALES (corp-wide):** 4.3B **Publicly Held**
**WEB:** www.qwdys.com
**SIC:** 2754 2752 2789 2759 Commercial printing, gravure; commercial printing, lithographic; bookbinding & related work; commercial printing; book printing
**PA:** Quad/Graphics Inc.
N61w23044 Harrys Way
Sussex WI 53089
414 566-6000

*(G-15298)*
**QUEBECOR WRLD MT MORRIS II LLC**
404 N Wesley Ave (61054-1150)
**PHONE**.................................815 734-4121
**Fax:** 815 734-8234
**EMP:** 11
**SALES (est):** 1.2MM **Privately Held**
**SIC:** 2752 Commercial printing, lithographic

*(G-15299)*
**RESEARCH AND TESTING WORX INC**
112 E Hitt St (61054-1220)
**PHONE**.................................815 734-7346
William H McKay III, *President*
Jill Millhouse, *Manager*
**EMP:** 5
**SALES (est):** 450K **Privately Held**
**SIC:** 7389 3592 Inspection & testing services; valves

*(G-15300)*
**SPECTRUM PREFERRED MEATS INC**
6194 W Pines Rd (61054-9755)
**PHONE**.................................815 946-3816
**Fax:** 815 946-2333
Kevin Rude, *President*
James Sklavanitis, *Plant Mgr*
Jeremy Castle, *Maint Spvr*
Ashley Rude, *Office Admin*
**EMP:** 60
**SQ FT:** 10,000
**SALES (est):** 10.9MM **Privately Held**
**SIC:** 2011 Meat packing plants; sausages & other prepared meats

# Mount Olive - Macoupin County (G-15301)

## GEOGRAPHIC SECTION

### Mount Olive
*Macoupin County*

**(G-15301)**
**COMPANIA BRASILEIRA DE T**
Also Called: Cbt
21218 Sunset St (62069)
PHONE..................................319 550-6440
Jim Helfrich, *CEO*
Karl Ragland, *Project Mgr*
David Brockes, *CFO*
Hank Trojack,
**EMP:** 4
**SALES (est):** 59.6K **Privately Held**
**SIC:** 4953 2869 5082 Recycling, waste materials; ethylene glycols; construction & mining machinery

**(G-15302)**
**GEORGIA-PACIFIC LLC**
900 S Old Route 66 (62069-1559)
PHONE..................................217 999-2511
Fax: 217 999-2571
Larry Erickson, *Personnel*
Mike Augustine, *Branch Mgr*
**EMP:** 146
**SALES (corp-wide):** 27.4B **Privately Held**
WEB: www.gp.com
**SIC:** 2653 5113 Corrugated & solid fiber boxes; corrugated & solid fiber boxes
HQ: Georgia-Pacific Llc
133 Peachtree St Ne # 4810
Atlanta GA 30303
404 652-4000

**(G-15303)**
**HERALD MOUNT OLIVE**
Also Called: Journal Fabrication
102 E Main St (62069-1702)
PHONE..................................217 999-3941
Fax: 217 999-5105
John Galer, *Owner*
**EMP:** 4
**SALES (est):** 160K **Privately Held**
**SIC:** 2711 Newspapers

**(G-15304)**
**IDEAL FABRICATORS INC**
621 S Main St (62069-2712)
PHONE..................................217 999-7017
Fax: 217 999-2510
Mark Subick, *President*
Steve Subick, *Vice Pres*
**EMP:** 12
**SQ FT:** 900
**SALES (est):** 1.8MM **Privately Held**
**SIC:** 3443 3441 3411 Trash racks; metal plate; fabricated structural metal; metal cans

**(G-15305)**
**MENNEL MILLING CO**
415 E Main St (62069-1709)
P.O. Box 255 (62069-0255)
PHONE..................................217 999-2161
Fax: 217 999-2272
Donald L Mennel, *President*
Mark Hall, *Controller*
Susan Six, *Office Mgr*
Doug Metz, *IT/INT Sup*
**EMP:** 12
**SALES (est):** 5MM
**SALES (corp-wide):** 69.4MM **Privately Held**
WEB: www.troyelevator.com
**SIC:** 2041 Wheat flour
PA: The Mennel Milling Company
320 Findlay St
Fostoria OH 44830
419 435-8151

**(G-15306)**
**NBS SYSTEMS INC (PA)**
1000 S Old Route 66 (62069-1560)
PHONE..................................217 999-3472
Bill Gascon, *President*
Gina Henrichs, *Accounts Mgr*
**EMP:** 35 **EST:** 1963
**SQ FT:** 26,000
**SALES (est):** 6.8MM **Privately Held**
WEB: www.nbschecks.com
**SIC:** 2761 2759 Continuous forms, office & business; commercial printing

**(G-15307)**
**RSB FUELS INC**
701 W Main St (62069-1554)
PHONE..................................217 999-4409
**EMP:** 5
**SALES (est):** 391.2K **Privately Held**
**SIC:** 2869 Fuels

### Mount Prospect
*Cook County*

**(G-15308)**
**ADVERTISING PREMIUMS INC**
Also Called: Steakhouse Premium
800 W Central Rd Ste 162 (60056-6512)
PHONE..................................888 364-9710
Charles Feldman, *President*
Steven Goldstein, *Vice Pres*
**EMP:** 5
**SQ FT:** 2,500
**SALES (est):** 500K **Privately Held**
**SIC:** 5147 5961 3993 Meats & meat products; food, mail order; signs & advertising specialties

**(G-15309)**
**ALDEN & OTT PRINTING INKS CO**
2050 S Carboy Rd (60056-5750)
PHONE..................................847 364-6817
Keith Elumann, *Branch Mgr*
**EMP:** 10
**SALES (corp-wide):** 879.3MM **Privately Held**
WEB: www.aldenottink.com
**SIC:** 2893 Printing ink
HQ: Alden & Ott Printing Inks Co.
616 E Brook Dr
Arlington Heights IL 60005
847 956-6830

**(G-15310)**
**ARROW ROAD CONSTRUCTION CO (PA)**
3401 S Busse Rd (60056-5588)
P.O. Box 334 (60056-0334)
PHONE..................................847 437-0700
Fax: 847 437-0779
Wayne E Healy, *Ch of Bd*
John F Healy, *President*
Eileen Healy, *Vice Pres*
Michael J Salmon, *Vice Pres*
Tim McCarty, *Plant Mgr*
**EMP:** 125 **EST:** 1925
**SQ FT:** 10,000
**SALES (est):** 41.2MM **Privately Held**
WEB: www.arrowroad.com
**SIC:** 1611 2951 Highway & street paving contractor; asphalt & asphaltic paving mixtures (not from refineries)

**(G-15311)**
**ATLAS MATERIAL TSTG TECH LLC (HQ)**
Also Called: South Florida Test Service Div
1500 Bishop Ct (60056-6039)
PHONE..................................773 327-4520
Joergen Olsson, *President*
Larry Bond, *General Mgr*
Tom Kulawiak, *Vice Pres*
Elliott Lamont, *Project Mgr*
Allen Manojlovic, *Mfg Mgr*
▲ **EMP:** 150 **EST:** 1917
**SQ FT:** 75,000
**SALES (est):** 118.4MM
**SALES (corp-wide):** 3.8B **Publicly Held**
WEB: www.atlas-mts.com
**SIC:** 3823 3569 3599 8734 Temperature measurement instruments, industrial; testing chambers for altitude, temperature, ordnance, power; machine shop, jobbing & repair; product testing laboratory, safety or performance; instruments to measure electricity; laboratory apparatus & furniture
PA: Ametek, Inc.
1100 Cassatt Rd
Berwyn PA 19312
610 647-2121

**(G-15312)**
**AVERY DENNISON CORPORATION**
902 Feehanville Dr (60056-6003)
PHONE..................................847 824-7450
Dave Heuck, *Senior Buyer*
Nikhil Agashe, *Engineer*
Eric Shafer, *Branch Mgr*
**EMP:** 115
**SALES (corp-wide):** 6B **Publicly Held**
WEB: www.avery.com
**SIC:** 2672 Coated paper, except photographic, carbon or abrasive
PA: Avery Dennison Corporation
207 N Goode Ave Fl 6
Glendale CA 91203
626 304-2000

**(G-15313)**
**BRAUN MANUFACTURING CO INC**
1350 Feehanville Dr (60056-6021)
PHONE..................................847 635-2050
Fax: 847 635-7655
Charles R Braun, *President*
Angel Carlos, *CFO*
Grace Majdzik, *Accountant*
Gloria Vasquez, *Human Resources*
Joseph Vlna, *Sales Mgr*
**EMP:** 30
**SQ FT:** 62,000
**SALES (est):** 5.5MM **Privately Held**
WEB: www.hinge1.com
**SIC:** 3429 3469 Manufactured hardware (general); stamping metal for the trade

**(G-15314)**
**C BECKY & COMPANY INC**
Also Called: Crash Candles
708 S Na Wa Ta Ave (60056-3608)
PHONE..................................847 818-1021
Becky Corzilius, *President*
Robert Clauss, *Admin Sec*
**EMP:** 2
**SQ FT:** 1,300
**SALES (est):** 250K **Privately Held**
**SIC:** 5199 5112 3999 Gifts & novelties; greeting cards; candles

**(G-15315)**
**C LINE PRODUCTS INC (PA)**
1100 E Business Center Dr (60056-6053)
PHONE..................................847 827-6661
James E Krumwiede, *Ch of Bd*
Thomas E Robertson, *Exec VP*
Judi Krumwiede, *Vice Pres*
Susan Travis, *Asst Treas*
Nancy Defranscio, *Accounts Mgr*
▲ **EMP:** 69 **EST:** 1949
**SQ FT:** 108,000
**SALES (est):** 11.7MM **Privately Held**
WEB: www.c-lineproducts.com
**SIC:** 3089 3083 Holders: paper towel, grocery bag, etc.: plastic; laminated plastics plate & sheet

**(G-15316)**
**CARTERS INC**
12 E Randhurst Village Rd (60056)
PHONE..................................847 870-0185
Fax: 847 870-0182
Carter Searcy, *Branch Mgr*
**EMP:** 9
**SALES (corp-wide):** 3.2B **Publicly Held**
**SIC:** 2361 Dresses: girls', children's & infants'
PA: Carter's, Inc.
3438 Peachtree Rd Ne # 1800
Atlanta GA 30326
678 791-1000

**(G-15317)**
**CONCEPT AND DESIGN SERVICES**
807 S Golfview Pl (60056-4330)
PHONE..................................847 259-1675
Fax: 847 259-1675
John S Glinka, *President*
**EMP:** 5
**SALES (est):** 757.5K **Privately Held**
**SIC:** 3569 8711 Assembly machines, non-metalworking; professional engineer; consulting engineer

**(G-15318)**
**CONCEPTS MAGNET**
515 S Edward St (60056-3909)
PHONE..................................847 253-3351
Louis Piazza, *President*
**EMP:** 3 **EST:** 2012
**SALES (est):** 153K **Privately Held**
**SIC:** 7389 3993 Design services; advertising novelties

**(G-15319)**
**CRESTWOOD ASSOCIATES LLC**
240 E Lincoln St (60056-3244)
PHONE..................................847 394-8820
Brian J McGuckin,
Timothy J Thompson,
Peter Fricke, *Sr Consultant*
**EMP:** 16
**SALES (est):** 2.3MM **Privately Held**
WEB: www.crestwood.com
**SIC:** 7372 Business oriented computer software

**(G-15320)**
**CUMMINS - ALLISON CORP (PA)**
852 Feehanville Dr (60056-6001)
P.O. Box 339 (60056-0339)
PHONE..................................847 759-6403
Fax: 847 299-4939
William J Jones, *Ch of Bd*
Douglas U Mennie, *President*
John E Jones, *Chairman*
James Stearns, *Exec VP*
Tim Minor, *Senior VP*
◆ **EMP:** 400 **EST:** 1887
**SQ FT:** 110,000
**SALES (est):** 377.1MM **Privately Held**
WEB: www.gsb.com
**SIC:** 3578 3519 Automatic teller machines (ATM); internal combustion engines

**(G-15321)**
**CUMMINS - ALLISON CORP**
891 Feehanville Dr (60056-6098)
PHONE..................................847 299-9550
John Mc Mc Nichols, *Engineer*
John Peklo, *Engineer*
William J Jones, *Branch Mgr*
**EMP:** 64
**SALES (corp-wide):** 377.1MM **Privately Held**
**SIC:** 3579 3519 Perforators (office machines); paper cutters, trimmers & punches; check writing, endorsing or signing machines; internal combustion engines
PA: Cummins - Allison Corp.
852 Feehanville Dr
Mount Prospect IL 60056
847 759-6403

**(G-15322)**
**CUMMINS - ALLISON CORP**
851 Feehanville Dr (60056-6002)
PHONE..................................847 299-9550
Douglas Mennie, *President*
**EMP:** 200
**SALES (corp-wide):** 377.1MM **Privately Held**
**SIC:** 3579 3519 Perforators (office machines); internal combustion engines
PA: Cummins - Allison Corp.
852 Feehanville Dr
Mount Prospect IL 60056
847 759-6403

**(G-15323)**
**CUMMINS-AMERICAN CORP**
852 Feehanville Dr (60056-6001)
PHONE..................................847 299-9550
John E Jones, *CEO*
John Diedrich, *CFO*
**EMP:** 2 **EST:** 1957
**SALES (est):** 329.1K **Privately Held**
**SIC:** 6163 3519 Mortgage brokers arranging for loans, using money of others; internal combustion engines

**(G-15324)**
**CUSTOM MOLD SERVICES**
1605 W Algonquin Rd (60056-5503)
PHONE..................................847 364-6589
Fax: 847 364-6625
John Majdzik, *Principal*
Ron Jackson, *Financial Exec*
**EMP:** 23

# Mount Prospect - Cook County (G-15351)

SALES (est): 4.5MM **Privately Held**
SIC: 3544 Industrial molds

### (G-15325)
### CYBER INNOVATION LABS LLC
Also Called: Cloud In A Vault
1221 E Business Center Dr (60056-2182)
PHONE...................847 804-4724
William J Michael, *CEO*
Jack Pressman, *Chairman*
Jorge Fernandez, *Exec VP*
Isabel Piedra, *Office Admin*
EMP: 2
SALES (est): 312.9K **Privately Held**
SIC: 3825 7389 Network analyzers;

### (G-15326)
### DT METRONIC INC
1860 S Elmhurst Rd (60056-5711)
PHONE...................847 593-0945
Rolf Klausmann, *CEO*
EMP: 4
SALES (est): 365.7K **Privately Held**
SIC: 3479 Metal coating & allied service

### (G-15327)
### E J SELF FURNITURE (PA)
516 E Northwest Hwy (60056-3306)
PHONE...................847 394-0899
Fax: 847 394-0042
Arthur H Self Sr, *President*
Barbara Bruhn, *Vice Pres*
Loretta Self, *Treasurer*
EMP: 7 EST: 1960
SQ FT: 5,000
SALES: 750K **Privately Held**
SIC: 2391 2512 2511 Draperies, plastic & textile; from purchased materials; chairs: upholstered on wood frames; tables, household: wood

### (G-15328)
### F & S ENGRAVING INC
1620 W Central Rd (60056-2269)
PHONE...................847 870-8400
Fax: 847 870-8414
James C Fromm, *President*
Clifford Fromm, *Chairman*
John Zimmer, *Sales Mgr*
David Mackey, *Director*
Scott E Fromm, *Admin Sec*
EMP: 29 EST: 1922
SQ FT: 21,000
SALES: 5.6MM **Privately Held**
SIC: 3556 2759 3544 Food products machinery; cracker making machines; commercial printing; dies, steel rule; industrial molds

### (G-15329)
### FEDEX OFFICE & PRINT SVCS INC
1 W Rand Rd Ste F (60056-1137)
PHONE...................847 670-7283
Fax: 847 670-7322
Ramabhai Patel, *Branch Mgr*
EMP: 4
SALES (corp-wide): 50.3B **Publicly Held**
WEB: www.fedex.com
SIC: 2759 7334 5099 Commercial printing; photocopying & duplicating services; signs, except electric
HQ: Fedex Office And Print Services, Inc.
7900 Legacy Dr
Plano TX 75024
214 550-7000

### (G-15330)
### FLEXXSONIC CORPORATION
1516 N Elmhurst Rd (60056-1011)
PHONE...................847 452-7226
Anna Ghazvini, *President*
EMP: 3
SALES (est): 210K **Privately Held**
SIC: 2834 3841 7389 Proprietary drug products; surgical & medical instruments;

### (G-15331)
### GAM ENTERPRISES INC
Also Called: Gam Gear
901 E Business Center Dr (60056-2181)
PHONE...................847 649-2500
Gary A Michalek, *CEO*
Craig Van Den Avont, *President*
Rebecca K Michalek, *Admin Sec*
EMP: 20

SQ FT: 8,000
SALES (est): 5.3MM **Privately Held**
WEB: www.gamweb.com
SIC: 3566 Reduction gears & gear units for turbines, except automotive

### (G-15332)
### GAMMERLER US CORP
431 Lakeview Ct Ste B (60056-6048)
PHONE...................941 465-4400
Gunter Gammerler, *Principal*
EMP: 26
SALES (est): 5.9MM **Privately Held**
SIC: 3535 Conveyors & conveying equipment

### (G-15333)
### GOOD EARTH LIGHTING INC
Also Called: Eco-Light
1400 E Business Center Dr # 104 (60056-6071)
PHONE...................847 808-1133
Fax: 847 808-0838
Marvin J Feig, *President*
Susan A Febles, *Principal*
Margaret M Hetzer, *Vice Pres*
Alexander Kowalenko, *Vice Pres*
Barbara Holden, *Controller*
▲ EMP: 23
SQ FT: 8,400
SALES (est): 9.5MM **Privately Held**
WEB: www.goodearthlighting.com
SIC: 5063 3648 Lighting fixtures; lighting equipment

### (G-15334)
### GROVAK INSTANT PRINTING CO
Also Called: Super Press Instant Prtg Co
701 S Meier Rd (60056-3546)
PHONE...................847 675-2414
Jeff Grovak, *Exec VP*
June Grovak, *Vice Pres*
EMP: 7
SQ FT: 2,000
SALES: 1.1MM **Privately Held**
SIC: 2752 2789 Commercial printing, offset; bookbinding & related work

### (G-15335)
### HOBSOURCE
834 E Rand Rd Ste 2 (60056-2569)
PHONE...................847 229-9120
Fax: 847 229-9015
Andrea Mazur, *Manager*
EMP: 2
SALES (est): 226.5K **Privately Held**
WEB: www.hobsource.com
SIC: 3541 Machine tools, metal cutting type

### (G-15336)
### IDEAL/MIKRON INC
Also Called: Digital Palace
130 S Waverly Pl (60056-2937)
PHONE...................847 873-0254
Neal Bradley, *President*
EMP: 5
SQ FT: 3,000
SALES (est): 471.5K **Privately Held**
WEB: www.digitalpalace.com
SIC: 2791 7336 2796 Typesetting, computer controlled; graphic arts & related design; platemaking services

### (G-15337)
### INDIGO TIME
800 W Central Rd Ste 162 (60056-6512)
PHONE...................847 255-4818
Dean Resnekov, *Owner*
Katy Kuzensky, *Manager*
EMP: 6
SALES (est): 699K **Privately Held**
WEB: www.indigowatch.com
SIC: 3873 Watches, clocks, watchcases & parts

### (G-15338)
### INTEL EAST
660 W Pickwick Ct Apt 1w (60056-5315)
PHONE...................312 725-2014
EMP: 3 EST: 2012
SALES (est): 185.3K **Privately Held**
SIC: 3674 Microprocessors

### (G-15339)
### INTER-CONTINENTAL TRDG USA INC
1601 W Algonquin Rd (60056-5503)
PHONE...................847 640-1777
Shrujal Patel, *President*
▲ EMP: 80
SQ FT: 20,000
SALES (est): 6.4MM **Privately Held**
SIC: 2131 Chewing & smoking tobacco

### (G-15340)
### JENCO METAL PRODUCTS INC
1690 W Imperial Ct (60056-5574)
PHONE...................847 956-0550
Fax: 847 956-0821
Gregory D Jensen, *President*
Mark D Jensen, *Corp Secy*
Larry Everett, *Design Engr*
Laurel Huyvaert, *Controller*
EMP: 12 EST: 1954
SQ FT: 16,000
SALES (est): 2.2MM **Privately Held**
WEB: www.jencometal.com
SIC: 3544 3469 3496 Die sets for metal stamping (presses); stamping metal for the trade; wire winding

### (G-15341)
### JOHN HAUTER DREMEL
1800 W Central Rd (60056-2230)
PHONE...................800 437-3635
John Dremel, *Principal*
EMP: 3
SALES (est): 335.6K **Privately Held**
SIC: 3679 Oscillators

### (G-15342)
### KL WATCH SERVICE INC
800 W Central Rd Ste 103 (60056-2383)
PHONE...................847 368-8780
Ken Kaczynski, *President*
EMP: 2
SALES (est): 219.2K **Privately Held**
SIC: 2754 3873 Circulars: gravure printing; watches & parts, except crystals & jewels

### (G-15343)
### KOREA TRIBUNE INC ✪
1699 Wall St Ste 201 (60056-5781)
PHONE...................847 956-9101
EMP: 3 EST: 2016
SALES (est): 76.2K **Privately Held**
SIC: 2711 Newspapers

### (G-15344)
### LUTHERAN GENERAL PRINTING SVCS
799 Biermann Ct Ste 130 (60056-6059)
PHONE...................847 298-8040
Fax: 847 298-8047
James Skogsbergh, *Principal*
Eric Neilson, *Director*
EMP: 4
SALES (est): 300K **Privately Held**
SIC: 2752 Commercial printing, lithographic

### (G-15345)
### MAILBOX PLUS
1516 N Elmhurst Rd (60056-1011)
PHONE...................847 577-1737
Fax: 847 577-1739
Donna Wolf, *Owner*
EMP: 3
SQ FT: 1,000
SALES (est): 249.3K **Privately Held**
SIC: 3086 Packaging & shipping materials, foamed plastic

### (G-15346)
### MARCRES MANUFACTURING INC
Also Called: Marcres Metal Works
600 W Carboy Rd (60056-5763)
PHONE...................847 439-1808
Fax: 847 439-0553
Marlene Palmer, *President*
Helen Ruetsche, *Vice Pres*
Andrew Peontke, *Engineer*
Helen King, *Office Mgr*
Helen Marks, *Manager*
EMP: 25
SQ FT: 22,500

SALES: 3MM **Privately Held**
WEB: www.marcres.com
SIC: 3444 Sheet metal specialties, not stamped

### (G-15347)
### MIZKAN AMERICA INC (DH)
Also Called: Nakano Foods
1661 Feehanville Dr # 200 (60056-6087)
PHONE...................847 590-0059
Koichi Yuki, *CEO*
Kevin Ponticelli, *President*
Craig Smith, *President*
Mike Smith, *Exec VP*
Matt Moore, *Senior VP*
◆ EMP: 50 EST: 1902
SQ FT: 13,000
SALES (est): 194.2MM **Privately Held**
SIC: 2099 2035 Vinegar; dressings, salad: raw & cooked (except dry mixes); mustard, prepared (wet)
HQ: Mizkan America Holdings, Inc
1661 Feehanville Dr # 300
Mount Prospect IL 60056
847 590-0059

### (G-15348)
### MIZKAN AMERICA HOLDINGS INC (HQ)
Also Called: Nakano Foods
1661 Feehanville Dr # 300 (60056-6087)
PHONE...................847 590-0059
Fax: 847 590-0638
Hiroyasu Nakano, *President*
Jack Kichura, *Business Mgr*
Kevin Ponticelli, *COO*
Paul Callahan, *Senior VP*
Jayne Hoover, *Vice Pres*
◆ EMP: 2
SALES (est): 794.6MM **Privately Held**
SIC: 2099 Vinegar
PA: Mizkan J Plus Holdings Co.,Ltd.
2-6, Nakamuracho
Handa AIC
569 213-331

### (G-15349)
### MJSRF INC
1864 S Elmhurst Rd (60056-5711)
PHONE...................888 677-6175
Scott Fohrman, *CEO*
Kevin Hess, *President*
Victoria Plotkin, *Manager*
▲ EMP: 17 EST: 1956
SQ FT: 10,000
SALES (est): 1.5MM **Privately Held**
WEB: www.milmour.com
SIC: 3089 Injection molded finished plastic products

### (G-15350)
### MONOTYPE IMAGING INC
1699 Wall St Ste 420 (60056-5786)
PHONE...................847 718-0400
Satoshi Asari, *Marketing Mgr*
Desi Leyba, *Branch Mgr*
EMP: 3
SALES (corp-wide): 203.4MM **Publicly Held**
SIC: 7372 7371 Prepackaged software; custom computer programming services
HQ: Monotype Imaging Inc.
600 Unicorn Park Dr
Woburn MA 01801

### (G-15351)
### MORTON SUGGESTION COMPANY LLC
800 W Central Rd Ste 101 (60056-2383)
P.O. Box 76 (60056-0076)
PHONE...................847 255-4770
Scott Kouri, *Sales Staff*
Marshall Smith,
Charles Marshall Smith,
Craig Smith,
▲ EMP: 8 EST: 1914
SQ FT: 35,000
SALES (est): 1.3MM **Privately Held**
WEB: www.mortonsuggestion.com
SIC: 5199 2752 7336 Gifts & novelties; posters, lithographed; commercial art & illustration

# Mount Prospect - Cook County (G-15352)  GEOGRAPHIC SECTION

### (G-15352)
**MULTI-PACK SOLUTIONS LLC (PA)**
Also Called: Multi-Pack Chicago
1804 W Central Rd (60056-2230)
**PHONE**.................847 635-6772
Les Teague, *Partner*
Brian McInerney, *Partner*
Steve Crass, *Exec VP*
Keith Wyatt, *Vice Pres*
Chris Benitez, *Maint Spvr*
**EMP:** 74
**SQ FT:** 48,000
**SALES (est):** 79.5MM **Privately Held**
**SIC:** 7389 2844 Packaging & labeling services; towelettes, premoistened

### (G-15353)
**NATIONAL SPORTING GOODS ASSN**
Also Called: Nsga Retail Focus
1601 Feehanville Dr # 300 (60056-6035)
**PHONE**.................847 296-6742
**Fax:** 847 391-9827
Matthew Carlson, *CEO*
Matt Carlson, *CEO*
Paul Prince, *Vice Pres*
Dustin Dobrin, *Research*
Dan Wiersma, *CFO*
**EMP:** 18 **EST:** 1929
**SQ FT:** 9,697
**SALES (est):** 2.2MM **Privately Held**
**SIC:** 8611 2721 8742 Trade associations; magazines: publishing only, not printed on site; business consultant

### (G-15354)
**NELCO COIL SUPPLY COMPANY**
1500 E Ironwood Dr (60056-1526)
**PHONE**.................847 259-7517
Joanne Nelson Sime, *President*
Lester Piotcowski, *Prdtn Mgr*
**EMP:** 20
**SQ FT:** 14,000
**SALES:** 2MM **Privately Held**
**SIC:** 3677 3621 Coil windings, electronic; motors & generators

### (G-15355)
**NOVA PRINTING AND LITHO CO**
1621 E Dogwood Ln (60056-1519)
**PHONE**.................773 486-8500
**Fax:** 773 486-1513
Jamie Thompson, *President*
Robert Ardisana, *Vice Pres*
John Turner, *Prdtn Mgr*
Jim Smetana, *Technology*
**EMP:** 19
**SQ FT:** 13,000
**SALES (est):** 3MM **Privately Held**
**WEB:** www.novaprinting.net
**SIC:** 2752 Commercial printing, offset; lithographing on metal

### (G-15356)
**NOVOMATIC AMERICAS SALES LLC**
1050 E Business Center Dr (60056-2180)
**PHONE**.................224 802-2974
Rick Meitzler, *President*
Jakob Rothwangl, *CFO*
**EMP:** 7 **EST:** 2012
**SALES (est):** 512.1K
**SALES (corp-wide):** 2.7B **Privately Held**
**SIC:** 3944 Electronic game machines, except coin-operated
**HQ:** Novomatic Ag
Wiener Straße 158
Gumpoldskirchen 2352
225 260-60

### (G-15357)
**NTN USA CORPORATION (HQ)**
1600 Bishop Ct (60056-6055)
P.O. Box 7604 (60056-7604)
**PHONE**.................847 298-4652
Masaaki Ayano, *President*
Linda Neuman, *Credit Mgr*
William Hess, *Risk Mgmt Dir*
Makoto Kikukawa, *Admin Sec*
▼ **EMP:** 111
**SQ FT:** 88,000
**SALES (est):** 678.6MM
**SALES (corp-wide):** 6B **Privately Held**
**SIC:** 5085 3562 3568 Bearings; ball bearings & parts; roller bearings & parts; joints, swivel & universal, except aircraft & automotive
**PA:** Ntn Corporation
1-3-17, Kyomachibori, Nishi-Ku
Osaka OSK 550-0
664 435-001

### (G-15358)
**OAKLAND INDUSTRIES LTD**
Also Called: E-T-A Circuit Breakers
1551 Bishop Ct (60056-6039)
**PHONE**.................847 827-7600
William Stewart, *President*
H Ellenberger, *Principal*
E Poensgen, *Principal*
William Sell, *Principal*
Todd Delerich, *VP Sales*
**EMP:** 46
**SQ FT:** 34,000
**SALES (est):** 16.2MM **Privately Held**
**WEB:** www.e-t-a.com
**SIC:** 5063 3823 3613 Circuit breakers; industrial instrmnts msrmnt display/control process variable; switchgear & switchboard apparatus

### (G-15359)
**ORCHARD PRODUCTS INC**
500 W Huntington Commons (60056-5253)
**PHONE**.................847 818-6760
Betsy Ginocopolis, *Manager*
Sharon Geanakoplos, *Admin Sec*
**EMP:** 4
**SALES (est):** 240K **Privately Held**
**WEB:** www.orchardproducts.com
**SIC:** 2833 Medicinals & botanicals

### (G-15360)
**P M ARMOR INC**
237 E Prospect Ave (60056-3236)
**PHONE**.................847 797-9940
**Fax:** 847 797-0510
Wilson Paul Mirza, *President*
Karl Sauer, *Corp Secy*
Joseph Mirza, *Vice Pres*
**EMP:** 32
**SQ FT:** 6,000
**SALES (est):** 5.7MM **Privately Held**
**SIC:** 3599 Machine shop, jobbing & repair

### (G-15361)
**PARENTI & RAFFAELLI LTD**
215 E Prospect Ave (60056-3236)
**PHONE**.................847 253-5550
**Fax:** 847 253-6055
Robert Parenti, *President*
Robert G Parenti Jr, *Vice Pres*
Rob Naurath, *Project Mgr*
John Uwe, *Safety Mgr*
Barbara Naurth, *Purchasing*
**EMP:** 170 **EST:** 1952
**SQ FT:** 45,000
**SALES (est):** 30.7MM **Privately Held**
**WEB:** www.parentiwoodwork.com
**SIC:** 2431 2434 Woodwork, interior & ornamental; wood kitchen cabinets

### (G-15362)
**PERFECTION SPRING STMPING CORP**
1449 E Algonquin Rd (60056)
P.O. Box 275 (60056-0275)
**PHONE**.................847 437-3900
**Fax:** 800 638-2524
David Kahn, *President*
Connie Nassif, *COO*
Ken McLaren, *Opers Mgr*
Don Fuller, *Purch Dir*
Marty McKean, *QA Dir*
▲ **EMP:** 100
**SQ FT:** 70,000
**SALES (est):** 21.9MM **Privately Held**
**WEB:** www.pss-corp.com
**SIC:** 3465 3469 3495 3496 Automotive stampings; electronic enclosures, stamped or pressed metal; precision springs; miscellaneous fabricated wire products

### (G-15363)
**PFIZER INC**
700 E Business Center Dr (60056-2176)
**PHONE**.................847 506-8895
Pichai Pirakitikulr, *Principal*
**EMP:** 146
**SALES (corp-wide):** 52.8B **Publicly Held**
**SIC:** 2834 Pharmaceutical preparations
**PA:** Pfizer Inc.
235 E 42nd St
New York NY 10017
212 733-2323

### (G-15364)
**PHI GROUP INC**
Also Called: Edoc Communications
555 E Business Center Dr (60056-2175)
**PHONE**.................847 824-5610
**Fax:** 847 824-5720
Michael Frank, *President*
Micheal Frank, *President*
Brian Bending, *Vice Pres*
Glenn Grendzinsi, *Opers Mgr*
Lisa White, *Controller*
**EMP:** 128
**SQ FT:** 35,000
**SALES:** 20MM **Privately Held**
**WEB:** www.edoccommunications.com
**SIC:** 2759 Commercial printing

### (G-15365)
**PICTURE STONE INC**
108 N Kenilworth Ave (60056-2234)
**PHONE**.................773 875-5021
Tomasz Parys, *Principal*
**EMP:** 3
**SALES (est):** 201.6K **Privately Held**
**SIC:** 1411 Granite dimension stone

### (G-15366)
**QUALITY GLASS AND MIRROR INC**
601 W Carboy Rd (60056-5707)
**PHONE**.................847 290-1707
**Fax:** 847 297-6105
Stanley Rydzewski, *President*
▲ **EMP:** 6
**SQ FT:** 10,000
**SALES:** 800K **Privately Held**
**SIC:** 3231 Mirrored glass

### (G-15367)
**R&B FOODS INC (DH)**
1661 Feehanville Dr # 200 (60056-6045)
**PHONE**.................847 590-0059
Ichizo Kobayashi, *President*
David Wacnik, *Controller*
Brandy Lewellen, *Accountant*
▼ **EMP:** 50
**SALES (est):** 35.2MM **Privately Held**
**SIC:** 2033 Spaghetti & other pasta sauce: packaged in cans, jars, etc.
**HQ:** Mizkan America, Inc.
1661 Feehanville Dr # 200
Mount Prospect IL 60056
847 590-0059

### (G-15368)
**R&R RESEARCH CO**
300 N Prospect Manor Ave (60056-2334)
**PHONE**.................847 345-5051
Randy R Hauslein, *Owner*
**EMP:** 8
**SALES (est):** 574.7K **Privately Held**
**WEB:** www.rrresearch.com
**SIC:** 3471 Chromium plating of metals or formed products

### (G-15369)
**ROBERT BOSCH TOOL CORPORATION (DH)**
Also Called: Garden Watering
1800 W Central Rd (60056-2230)
**PHONE**.................224 232-2000
**Fax:** 224 222-2628
Heiko Fischer, *President*
David Klein, *Vice Pres*
Peter Nueman, *Vice Pres*
Tariq Hasan, *Project Mgr*
Donna Wolf, *Opers Mgr*
◆ **EMP:** 600
**SQ FT:** 220,000
**SALES (est):** 1.4B
**SALES (corp-wide):** 236.4MM **Privately Held**
**WEB:** www.vermontamerican.com
**SIC:** 3546 Cartridge-activated hand power tools
**HQ:** Scintilla Ag
Luterbachstrasse 10
Zuchwil SO
326 863-111

### (G-15370)
**ROBERTS DRAPERIES CENTER INC**
504 E Northwest Hwy (60056-3306)
**PHONE**.................847 255-4040
**Fax:** 847 255-7687
Robert Lee Byers, *President*
Edith Byers, *Vice Pres*
Cheryl Lindholm, *Vice Pres*
**EMP:** 4 **EST:** 1950
**SQ FT:** 1,500
**SALES (est):** 370K **Privately Held**
**SIC:** 5714 5719 5231 2591 Draperies; window furnishings; wallpaper; drapery hardware & blinds & shades; curtains & draperies

### (G-15371)
**SAATI AMERICAS CORPORATION**
Also Called: Saatiprint Div
901 E Business Center Dr (60056-2181)
**PHONE**.................847 296-5090
**EMP:** 14
**SALES (corp-wide):** 16.4MM **Privately Held**
**SIC:** 2261 2262 3555 Cotton Finishing Plant Manmade Fiber & Silk Finishing Plant Mfg Printing Trades Machinery
**PA:** Saati Americas Corporation
201 Fairview Street Ext
Fountain Inn SC 29644
864 601-8300

### (G-15372)
**SCHUMACHER ELECTRIC CORP (PA)**
801 E Business Center Dr (60056-2179)
**PHONE**.................847 385-1600
**Fax:** 847 298-1698
Donald A Schumacher, *Ch of Bd*
John Waldron, *President*
Cory Watkins, *President*
Thomas Slinkard, *Purch Agent*
Marvin Hartley, *Engineer*
◆ **EMP:** 80
**SQ FT:** 37,200
**SALES (est):** 142.6MM **Privately Held**
**WEB:** www.batterychargers.com
**SIC:** 3629 3677 Battery chargers, rectifying or nonrotating; transformers power supply, electronic type

### (G-15373)
**SETTIMA USA INC**
1759 S Linneman Rd (60056-5100)
**PHONE**.................630 812-1433
Michael E Williams, *Principal*
**EMP:** 3 **EST:** 2015
**SALES (est):** 130.5K **Privately Held**
**SIC:** 3594 Pumps, hydraulic power transfer

### (G-15374)
**SIMPEX MEDICAL INC**
401 E Prospect Ave (60056-3366)
**PHONE**.................847 757-9928
Richard Gorski, *President*
**EMP:** 3
**SALES (est):** 266.2K **Privately Held**
**SIC:** 3841 5047 Surgical & medical instruments; medical equipment & supplies

### (G-15375)
**STERGO ROOFING**
172 W Golf Rd Ste 299 (60056)
**PHONE**.................312 640-9008
Steven Stergo, *President*
**EMP:** 36 **EST:** 2010
**SALES:** 5MM **Privately Held**
**SIC:** 2621 Building & roofing paper, felts & insulation siding

▲ = Import ▼=Export
◆ =Import/Export

GEOGRAPHIC SECTION                                                                 Mount Vernon - Jefferson County (G-15401)

**(G-15376)**
**SUN PROCESS CONVERTING INC**
1660 W Kenneth Dr  (60056-5515)
PHONE..............................847 593-5656
Fax: 847 593-0207
Michael J Moravectz, *President*
Bonnie Moravectz, *Vice Pres*
Diana Pilch, *Credit Mgr*
Kim Scafidi, *Human Res Mgr*
Kate Liewald, *VP Mktg*
▲ **EMP:** 100 **EST:** 1981
**SQ FT:** 138,000
**SALES (est):** 23.9MM **Privately Held**
**WEB:** www.sunprocess.com
**SIC: 3081** 3083  Vinyl film & sheet; laminated plastic sheets

**(G-15377)**
**SURETINT TECHNOLOGIES  LLC**
411 E Bus Ctr Dr Ste 104  (60056)
PHONE..............................847 509-3625
Mitchell H Saranow, *Principal*
Judy Guliuzzo, *Executive Asst*
**EMP:** 13
**SALES (est):** 2.9MM **Privately Held**
**SIC: 2844**  Toilet preparations

**(G-15378)**
**TECHNOTRANS AMERICA INC (HQ)**
1441 E Business Center Dr  (60056-2182)
PHONE..............................847 227-9200
Fax: 847 227-9400
Jeffrey Schneider, *President*
Steve Lopez, *General Mgr*
Majid Esfahani, *COO*
Tom Carbery, *Vice Pres*
Michael Reckamp, *Vice Pres*
▲ **EMP:** 38
**SQ FT:** 35,000
**SALES:** 12MM
**SALES (corp-wide):** 160.5MM **Privately Held**
**SIC: 3555**  Printing trades machinery
**PA:** Technotrans Ag
   Robert-Linnemann-Str. 17
   Sassenberg  48336
   258 330-1100

**(G-15379)**
**TRI-TECH SLTONS CONSULTING INC**
259 N Woodland Dr  (60056-1936)
PHONE..............................847 941-0199
Dong Zhu, *President*
**EMP:** 3
**SALES:** 250K **Privately Held**
**SIC: 7372**  Prepackaged software

**(G-15380)**
**U KEEP US IN STITCHES**
1420 S Redwood Dr  (60056-5018)
PHONE..............................847 427-8127
Cliff Higley, *Owner*
Diane Higley, *Co-Owner*
**EMP:** 4
**SALES (est):** 264.8K **Privately Held**
**WEB:** www.ukeepusinstitches.com
**SIC: 2395**  Embroidery products, except schiffli machine

**(G-15381)**
**UNITEL TECHNOLOGIES  INC**
479 E Bus Ctr Dr Ste 105  (60056)
PHONE..............................847 297-2265
Serge Randhava, *CEO*
Ravi Randhava, *President*
John Conroy, *Vice Pres*
Todd Harvey, *Vice Pres*
Richard KAO, *Vice Pres*
**EMP:** 15 **EST:** 1990
**SQ FT:** 3,500
**SALES (est):** 3.7MM **Privately Held**
**WEB:** www.uniteltech.com
**SIC: 3559**  8711  Petroleum refinery equipment; petroleum, mining & chemical engineers

**(G-15382)**
**VANGUARD TOOL & ENGINEERING CO**
555 W Carboy Rd  (60056-5706)
PHONE..............................847 981-9595
Fax: 847 981-0368

Gary Donaldson, *President*
Kurt Donaldson, *Vice Pres*
Gertrude Slowik, *Office Mgr*
Richard Donaldson, *Director*
**EMP:** 20
**SQ FT:** 8,000
**SALES (est):** 3MM **Privately Held**
**WEB:** www.vanguard-tool.com
**SIC: 3451**  3545  Screw machine products; machine tool accessories

**(G-15383)**
**VINS & VIGNOBLES  LLC**
40 E Northwest Hwy # 211  (60056-3214)
PHONE..............................312 375-7656
Taoufik Matty Iqbal,
**EMP:** 3
**SALES (est):** 68.6K **Privately Held**
**SIC: 2084**  5182  Wines; neutral spirits

**(G-15384)**
**WIREFORMERS  INC**
500 W Carboy Rd  (60056-5771)
PHONE..............................847 718-1920
Fax: 847 486-4645
Louis Lischko, *President*
Susan Kanellis, *Corp Secy*
Horst Lang, *Exec VP*
John Kanellis, *Vice Pres*
**EMP:** 20 **EST:** 1960
**SQ FT:** 15,000
**SALES (est):** 3.2MM **Privately Held**
**WEB:** www.wireformers.com
**SIC: 3469**  3544  3496  Stamping metal for the trade; die sets for metal stamping (presses); miscellaneous fabricated wire products

**(G-15385)**
**WOOJIN PLAIMM  INC**
1693 W Imperial Ct  (60056-5554)
PHONE..............................708 606-5536
Ick Whan Kim, *President*
Paul Hokkanen, *Technical Staff*
**EMP:** 10
**SQ FT:** 10,000
**SALES (est):** 433K **Privately Held**
**SIC: 3089**  Injection molding of plastics

**(G-15386)**
**XTTRIUM LABORATORIES  INC (PA)**
1200 E Business Center Dr # 100  (60056-6041)
PHONE..............................773 268-5800
Fax: 773 924-6002
Kevin S Creevy, *President*
Joan Bartosz, *Vice Pres*
Alan Pinkowski, *Maint Spvr*
Joe Scalise, *QC Dir*
Vijay Verma, *CFO*
▲ **EMP:** 83 **EST:** 1939
**SQ FT:** 35,000
**SALES:** 39MM **Privately Held**
**WEB:** www.xttrium.com
**SIC: 2834**  Pharmaceutical preparations

**(G-15387)**
**YS HEALTH CORPORATION**
Also Called: Young Shin Honey Farm
411 Kingston Ct Ste A  (60056-6022)
PHONE..............................847 391-9122
David Choi, *President*
Jae Heo, *Vice Pres*
Steve Yun, *Manager*
Jiwon Song, *Graphic Designe*
▲ **EMP:** 14
**SQ FT:** 9,000
**SALES (est):** 2.9MM **Privately Held**
**WEB:** www.yshealth.com
**SIC: 2099**  2833  Honey, strained & bottled; vitamins, natural or synthetic: bulk, uncompounded

## Mount Pulaski
### Logan County

**(G-15388)**
**GRO ALLIANCE LLC**
247 1500th Ave  (62548-6508)
PHONE..............................217 792-3355
Jason Thomas, *President*
**EMP:** 32

**SALES (corp-wide):** 12MM **Privately Held**
**SIC: 2046**  Corn milling by-products
**PA:** Gro Alliance Llc
   613 N Randolph St
   Cuba City WI 53807
   608 744-7333

**(G-15389)**
**INLAND TOOL COMPANY**
727 N Topper Dr  (62548-6074)
P.O. Box 137  (62548-0137)
PHONE..............................217 792-3206
Kirk Evans, *President*
Suzie Maxheimer, *Office Mgr*
Susan Evans, *Admin Sec*
**EMP:** 50 **EST:** 1974
**SQ FT:** 70,000
**SALES (est):** 18MM **Privately Held**
**WEB:** www.inlandtool.net
**SIC: 3545**  3469  3465  3544  Machine tool accessories; metal stampings; automotive stampings; special dies, tools, jigs & fixtures

## Mount Sterling
### Brown County

**(G-15390)**
**BRUCE MCCULLOUGH**
Also Called: Precision Oil Field Cnstr
1161 980n Ave  (62353-4425)
PHONE..............................217 773-3130
Bruce McCullough, *Owner*
**EMP:** 2
**SALES (est):** 283.9K **Privately Held**
**SIC: 1311**  Crude petroleum production

**(G-15391)**
**CLINARD READY MIX  INC**
Rr 24 Box West  (62353)
P.O. Box 112  (62353-0112)
PHONE..............................217 773-3965
Fax: 217 773-3613
David Clinard, *President*
**EMP:** 40
**SQ FT:** 3,000
**SALES (est):** 4.4MM **Privately Held**
**SIC: 3273**  Ready-mixed concrete

**(G-15392)**
**DEMOCRAT MESSAGE**
Also Called: Colson Publications
123 W Main St  (62353-1223)
P.O. Box 71  (62353-0071)
PHONE..............................217 773-3371
Fax: 217 773-3369
Warren Colson, *President*
Joan Coulson, *Publisher*
Misha Hull, *Manager*
**EMP:** 4
**SALES (est):** 160.4K **Privately Held**
**SIC: 2711**  Newspapers

**(G-15393)**
**R & D OIL PRODUCERS**
709 N Capitol Ave  (62353-1107)
PHONE..............................217 773-9299
Cloyd Drennan, *Principal*
**EMP:** 3
**SALES (est):** 213.9K **Privately Held**
**SIC: 1311**  Crude petroleum & natural gas production

**(G-15394)**
**SCHROCKS WOOD SHOP**
356 650n Ave  (62353-1718)
P.O. Box 4  (62353-0004)
PHONE..............................217 773-3842
Ray Schrock, *Owner*
**EMP:** 3
**SALES (est):** 210K **Privately Held**
**SIC: 2452**  Prefabricated wood buildings

**(G-15395)**
**TWO RIVERS OIL & GAS CO INC**
116 S Capitol Ave  (62353-1502)
PHONE..............................217 773-3356
Edward B Tucker, *President*
Judith Tucker, *Treasurer*
**EMP:** 3
**SQ FT:** 1,000

**SALES (est):** 280.2K **Privately Held**
**SIC: 1311**  Crude petroleum production; natural gas production

## Mount Vernon
### Jefferson County

**(G-15396)**
**A AND K PRTG & GRAPHIC DESIGN**
605 S 10th St  (62864-5308)
PHONE..............................618 244-3525
Kent Bean, *Owner*
Michael Stern, *Production*
**EMP:** 3
**SQ FT:** 1,800
**SALES:** 140K **Privately Held**
**SIC: 2752**  7331  2791  Commercial printing, offset; direct mail advertising services; typesetting

**(G-15397)**
**ACCURATE AUTO MANUFACTURING CO**
1804 S 8th St  (62864-6108)
P.O. Box 847  (62864-0017)
PHONE..............................618 244-0727
Clarence Bonifacius, *Owner*
**EMP:** 5
**SQ FT:** 3,700
**SALES (est):** 240K **Privately Held**
**SIC: 3714**  7692  Cylinder heads, motor vehicle; motor vehicle engines & parts; welding repair

**(G-15398)**
**AS FABRICATING  INC**
15518 N Il Highway 37  (62864-7856)
PHONE..............................618 242-7438
Fax: 618 242-7463
Addison Sharpe, *President*
Patricia Sharpe, *Corp Secy*
**EMP:** 5
**SQ FT:** 2,000
**SALES:** 220K **Privately Held**
**SIC: 7692**  3446  3444  3443  Welding repair; architectural metalwork; sheet metalwork; fabricated plate work (boiler shop); fabricated structural metal

**(G-15399)**
**AZUSA INC**
Also Called: Azusa Printing
1406 Salem Rd  (62864-3241)
PHONE..............................618 244-6591
Fax: 618 242-0184
Debi Trotter, *President*
**EMP:** 9
**SQ FT:** 3,160
**SALES:** 880K **Privately Held**
**WEB:** www.azusaprinting.com
**SIC: 2752**  3993  2791  2761  Commercial printing, offset; signs & advertising specialties; typesetting; manifold business forms

**(G-15400)**
**BEELMAN READY-MIX  INC**
13425 N Shiloh Dr  (62864-7390)
PHONE..............................618 244-9600
Fax: 618 244-9618
Sam Beelman, *Owner*
Earl Robinson, *Manager*
Tom Smith, *Manager*
**EMP:** 9 **Privately Held**
**WEB:** www.beelmanrm.com
**SIC: 3273**  Ready-mixed concrete
**PA:** Beelman Ready-Mix, Inc.
   1 Racehorse Dr
   East Saint Louis IL 62205

**(G-15401)**
**BENNETT METAL PRODUCTS INC**
700 Rackaway St  (62864)
P.O. Box 34  (62864-0001)
PHONE..............................618 244-1911
Fax: 618 244-1995
James C Bennett, *CEO*
Jim Stowers, *President*
Carl Galiher, *Plant Mgr*
Dale Winkeler, *Project Mgr*
Eugene Fruend, *Sales/Mktg Dir*

## Mount Vernon - Jefferson County (G-15402)

EMP: 58
SQ FT: 36,000
SALES: 6MM **Privately Held**
WEB: www.bennettmetal.com
SIC: 3544 Special dies & tools

**(G-15402)**
**BREHM OIL INC (PA)**
Also Called: Beau-Brehm L Ranches
1915 Broadway St (62864-2980)
P.O. Box 648 (62864-0014)
PHONE..............................618 242-4620
Fax: 618 242-4640
Deborah Zielonki, *President*
Deborah Zielonkl, *President*
Micheal Alexander, *Vice Pres*
Carolyn Hayes, *Manager*
Jennifer Lauflin, *Manager*
EMP: 12
SQ FT: 6,000
SALES (est): 2.5MM **Privately Held**
SIC: 1311 Crude petroleum production

**(G-15403)**
**CENTRALIA PRESS LTD**
Also Called: Mount Vernon Zone
1808 Broadway St (62864-2905)
PHONE..............................618 246-2000
Fax: 618 246-9902
Tesa Culli, *Manager*
EMP: 10
SALES (corp-wide): 10.9MM **Privately Held**
WEB: www.morningsentinel.com
SIC: 2711 Newspapers
PA: Centralia Press, Ltd
 232 E Broadway
 Centralia IL 62801
 618 532-5604

**(G-15404)**
**COLLINS BROTHERS OIL CORP (PA)**
Also Called: Collins Bros
218 N 9th St (62864-3937)
P.O. Box 689 (62864-0014)
PHONE..............................618 244-1093
Fax: 618 244-1096
Michael O'Dea, *Manager*
EMP: 2
SQ FT: 5,000
SALES (est): 882.6K **Privately Held**
SIC: 1311 Crude petroleum & natural gas production

**(G-15405)**
**CONTINENTAL RESOURCES ILL INC (PA)**
830 Il Highway 15 E (62864)
P.O. Box 749 (62864-0015)
PHONE..............................618 242-1717
Richard Straeter, *President*
Richard Strader, *Financial Exec*
▲ EMP: 25
SQ FT: 5,300
SALES (est): 5.1MM **Privately Held**
WEB: www.contresofil.com
SIC: 1311 Crude petroleum production

**(G-15406)**
**CONTINENTAL TIRE AMERICAS LLC**
Also Called: Continental General Tire
11525 N Il Highway 142 (62864-6600)
P.O. Box 1029 (62864-0022)
PHONE..............................618 246-2466
Roger Neal, *Project Dir*
Scott Bendorf, *Engineer*
Ronald Cross, *Engineer*
Greg Peterson, *Engineer*
Ivan Prada, *Engineer*
EMP: 2200
SALES (corp-wide): 42.8B **Privately Held**
WEB: www.continentaltire.com
SIC: 5531 3011 Automotive tires; tires & inner tubes
HQ: Continental Tire The Americas, Llc
 1830 Macmillan Park Dr
 Fort Mill SC 29707
 800 450-3187

**(G-15407)**
**CONTINENTAL TIRE AMERICAS LLC**
Hwy 142 S (62864)
P.O. Box 1029 (62864-0022)
PHONE..............................618 242-7100
Adam Sepanski, *Opers Mgr*
Craig Stowers, *QC Dir*
Henry Esinga, *Manager*
Danny Chow, *Manager*
EMP: 5
SALES (corp-wide): 42.8B **Privately Held**
WEB: www.continentaltire.com
SIC: 3011 Tires & inner tubes
HQ: Continental Tire The Americas, Llc
 1830 Macmillan Park Dr
 Fort Mill SC 29707
 800 450-3187

**(G-15408)**
**DECATUR CUSTOM TOOL INC**
Also Called: Dct Mount Vernon
5101 Lake Ter Ne (62864-9666)
PHONE..............................618 244-4078
Fax: 618 244-3746
Stacy Greenwalt, *Branch Mgr*
EMP: 5
SALES (corp-wide): 24MM **Privately Held**
SIC: 3546 Saws & sawing equipment
PA: Decatur Custom Tool, Inc.
 410 N Jasper St
 Decatur IL 62521
 217 423-3639

**(G-15409)**
**DECATUR INDUSTRIAL ELC INC**
Also Called: Mt Vernon Electric
1313 Harlan Rd (62864-6014)
P.O. Box 1548 (62864-0030)
PHONE..............................618 244-1066
Fax: 618 244-4722
Mike Scott, *Branch Mgr*
Susan Bundy, *Director*
EMP: 35
SALES (corp-wide): 47.8MM **Privately Held**
WEB: www.decaturindustrialelectric.com
SIC: 7694 5571 Motor repair services; motorcycle dealers
PA: Decatur Industrial Electric, Inc.
 1650 E Garfield Ave
 Decatur IL 62526
 217 428-6621

**(G-15410)**
**DENNIS CARNES**
Also Called: Cartec
2118 Brownsville Rd (62864-6074)
PHONE..............................618 244-1770
Dennis A Carnes, *Owner*
EMP: 3
SQ FT: 2,800
SALES (est): 314.2K **Privately Held**
SIC: 3069 Foam rubber

**(G-15411)**
**HERMANN GENE SIGNS & SERVICE**
12436 E Lakewood Dr (62864-1925)
PHONE..............................618 244-3681
Fax: 618 244-9601
Gene Herrmann, *Owner*
EMP: 3
SALES (est): 155.4K **Privately Held**
SIC: 3993 Signs & advertising specialties

**(G-15412)**
**HERRMANN SIGNS & SERVICE**
12436 E Lakewood Dr (62864-1925)
PHONE..............................618 246-6537
Gene Herrmann, *Owner*
EMP: 3
SALES (est): 223.1K **Privately Held**
SIC: 3993 Electric signs

**(G-15413)**
**IBT INC**
601 S 10th St (62864-5308)
PHONE..............................618 244-5353
Russ Kanus, *Manager*
Steve McDonald, *Manager*
Tom Capps, *Info Tech Dir*
EMP: 6

SALES (corp-wide): 157.9MM **Privately Held**
WEB: www.ibtinc.com
SIC: 3612 Transmission & distribution voltage regulators
PA: Ibt, Inc.
 9400 W 55th St
 Shawnee Mission KS 66203
 913 677-3151

**(G-15414)**
**ILLINOI EYE SURGNS/QUANTM VISN**
3000 Broadway St (62864-2340)
PHONE..............................618 315-6560
EMP: 3 EST: 2014
SALES (est): 196.4K **Privately Held**
SIC: 3572 Computer storage devices

**(G-15415)**
**INNOTECH MANUFACTURING LLC**
915 S 13th St (62864-4818)
P.O. Box 963 (62864-0020)
PHONE..............................618 244-6261
Dan Black,
EMP: 20
SALES (est): 4MM **Privately Held**
SIC: 3441 Fabricated structural metal

**(G-15416)**
**JACK R PHILLIPS**
Also Called: Phillips Granite Industries
2015 Broadway St (62864-2910)
P.O. Box 1448 (62864-0029)
PHONE..............................618 242-8411
Fax: 618 242-8469
Jack Phillips, *Owner*
EMP: 5
SQ FT: 8,000
SALES (est): 280K **Privately Held**
WEB: www.ameth.org
SIC: 3281 Monument or burial stone, cut & shaped

**(G-15417)**
**JACKSON MARKING PRODUCTS CO**
9105 N Rainbow Ln (62864-6407)
PHONE..............................618 242-7901
Fax: 618 242-7732
Coy Jackson, *President*
Sandra Jackson, *Treasurer*
Gerald Mayo, *Manager*
Tom Jackson, *Admin Sec*
◆ EMP: 14
SQ FT: 6,400
SALES (est): 1.9MM **Privately Held**
WEB: www.rubber-stamp.com
SIC: 3953 2899 Marking devices; chemical preparations

**(G-15418)**
**JAX ASPHALT COMPANY INC**
1800 Waterworks Rd (62864)
P.O. Box 1725 (62864-0034)
PHONE..............................618 244-0500
Fax: 618 244-0833
Robert Metcalf, *President*
Sue Metcalf, *Treasurer*
EMP: 12
SQ FT: 1,500
SALES (est): 1.6MM **Privately Held**
SIC: 1731 4212 2952 2951 Communications specialization; fiber optic cable installation; sound equipment specialization; local trucking, without storage; asphalt felts & coatings; asphalt paving mixtures & blocks

**(G-15419)**
**JOY TECHNOLOGIES INC**
4111 N Water Tower Pl B (62864-6566)
PHONE..............................618 242-3650
Fax: 618 242-8509
Jim Brannon, *Plant Mgr*
William Irmen, *Mfg Staff*
Diana Crawford, *Purchasing*
Sharon Whipple, *Persnl Mgr*
Jim Folkerts, *Sales Staff*
EMP: 25
SQ FT: 100,000
SALES (corp-wide): 15.8B **Privately Held**
SIC: 3535 Bucket type conveyor systems

HQ: Joy Global Underground Mining Llc
 40 Pennwood Pl Ste 100
 Warrendale PA 15086
 724 779-4500

**(G-15420)**
**KM ENTERPRISES INC**
Also Called: Entrac Systems
320 S 11th St Ste 2 (62864-4200)
PHONE..............................618 204-0888
Rodney K Morgan, *President*
EMP: 13
SQ FT: 15,000
SALES: 7.5MM **Privately Held**
SIC: 3669 Pedestrian traffic control equipment

**(G-15421)**
**LAYS MINING SERVICE INC**
1121 S 10th St (62864-5401)
PHONE..............................618 244-6570
Fax: 618 244-6830
James T Mellott, *President*
David G Mellott, *Admin Sec*
EMP: 35
SQ FT: 25,000
SALES: 6.2MM **Privately Held**
SIC: 3599 Machine & other job shop work

**(G-15422)**
**LEE ELECTRIC**
11689 E Il Highway 148 (62864-6474)
PHONE..............................618 244-6810
Bobby Lee, *Principal*
EMP: 2
SALES (est): 219.3K **Privately Held**
SIC: 3699 Electrical equipment & supplies

**(G-15423)**
**MAGNUM STEEL WORKS INC**
200 Shiloh Dr (62864-8347)
PHONE..............................618 244-5190
Fax: 618 244-5191
Jim Czerwinski, *President*
Angela Czerwinski, *Corp Secy*
▲ EMP: 82
SALES: 9.5MM **Privately Held**
SIC: 3549 Metalworking machinery

**(G-15424)**
**MAIN STREET RECORDS**
313 S 10th St (62864-4206)
PHONE..............................618 244-2737
John Ellis, *Owner*
EMP: 3
SQ FT: 288
SALES (est): 352.1K **Privately Held**
SIC: 2253 T-shirts & tops, knit

**(G-15425)**
**MICHEL FERTILIZER & EQUIPMENT**
1313 Shawnee St (62864-5457)
PHONE..............................618 242-6000
Fax: 618 242-6026
Chris Michel, *Owner*
EMP: 6
SQ FT: 23,000
SALES (est): 1.3MM **Privately Held**
SIC: 5191 2873 Seeds & bulbs; chemicals, agricultural; fertilizer & fertilizer materials; nitrogenous fertilizers

**(G-15426)**
**MIDWESTERN MCH HYDRAULICS INC**
17265 N Timberline Ln (62864-8414)
P.O. Box 765 (62864-0015)
PHONE..............................618 246-9440
Fax: 618 246-9442
Robin Stowers, *President*
James Stowers, *Corp Secy*
Darrin Sargent, *Manager*
EMP: 11 EST: 1997
SQ FT: 30,000
SALES (est): 1.8MM **Privately Held**
SIC: 3599 7699 Machine shop, jobbing & repair; hydraulic equipment repair

**(G-15427)**
**MILANO RAILCAR SERVICES LLC**
510 S 6th St (62864-5300)
PHONE..............................618 242-4004
Mary C Burgan, *Principal*

# GEOGRAPHIC SECTION
## Mount Zion - Macon County (G-15450)

EMP: 4
SALES (est): 226.9K **Privately Held**
SIC: 3743 Railroad equipment

**(G-15428)**
**MOUNT VERNON IRON WORKS LLC**
10950 N Cactus Ln (62864-8260)
PHONE...................................618 244-2313
David P Black, *Partner*
David R Black, *Partner*
Dave Black, *Principal*
EMP: 6 EST: 2013
SALES (est): 787.7K **Privately Held**
SIC: 3399 Iron, powdered

**(G-15429)**
**MOUNT VERNON NEON SIGN CO**
1 Neon Dr (62864-6723)
PHONE...................................618 242-0645
Bill Fritz, *President*
David Meador, *Plant Mgr*
Joe Fryza, *Project Mgr*
Jon Oliger, *Project Engr*
David Heger, *Treasurer*
EMP: 125
SQ FT: 70,000
SALES (est): 18.8MM
SALES (corp-wide): 223.5MM **Privately Held**
WEB: www.everbrite.com
SIC: 3993 Neon signs
PA: Everbrite, Llc
   4949 S 110th St
   Greenfield WI 53228
   414 529-3500

**(G-15430)**
**MOUNTAIN VALLEY SPRING CO LLC**
423 S 8th St (62864-5355)
P.O. Box 271 (62864-0053)
PHONE...................................618 242-4963
EMP: 685
SALES (corp-wide): 505.9MM **Privately Held**
WEB: www.mountainvalleyspring.com
SIC: 2086 Pasteurized & mineral waters, bottled & canned
PA: Mountain Valley Spring Company, Llc
   283 Mountain Vly Wtr Pl
   Hot Springs Village AR 71909
   501 520-2148

**(G-15431)**
**MT VERNON MOLD WORKS INC**
15 Industrial Dr (62864)
P.O. Box 1761 (62864-0055)
PHONE...................................618 242-6040
Fax: 618 242-9539
Steve Zoumberakis, *President*
Diane Echols, *Manager*
Rodney Neuhaus, *Manager*
EMP: 21
SALES (est): 3.8MM
SALES (corp-wide): 86.9MM **Privately Held**
WEB: www.qualitymold.com
SIC: 3544 7692 Special dies, tools, jigs & fixtures; welding repair
PA: Quality Mold, Inc.
   2200 Massillon Rd
   Akron OH 44312
   330 645-6653

**(G-15432)**
**NATIONAL RAILWAY EQUIPMENT CO**
1100 Shawnee St (62864-5454)
P.O. Box B (62864)
PHONE...................................618 242-6590
Scott Beal, *Manager*
EMP: 200
SALES (corp-wide): 324.9MM **Privately Held**
WEB: www.nationalrailway.com
SIC: 3743 5088 Locomotives & parts; railroad equipment & supplies
PA: National Railway Equipment Co.
   1100 Shawnee St
   Mount Vernon IL 62864
   618 242-6590

**(G-15433)**
**NATIONAL RAILWAY EQUIPMENT CO**
908 Shawnee St (62864-5451)
PHONE...................................618 241-9270
EMP: 3
SALES (corp-wide): 324.9MM **Privately Held**
SIC: 5088 3743 Commercial equipment
PA: National Railway Equipment Co.
   1100 Shawnee St
   Mount Vernon IL 62864
   618 242-6590

**(G-15434)**
**NEWSPAPER HOLDING INC**
Also Called: Mt. Vernon Register News
911 Broadway St (62864-4008)
P.O. Box 489 (62864-0010)
PHONE...................................618 242-0113
Fax: 618 242-8286
Bob Dennis, *Principal*
Sherie Copple, *Sls & Mktg Exec*
Mary Karnes, *Accounts Exec*
Greg Sargent, *Network Mgr*
EMP: 60 **Privately Held**
WEB: www.clintonnc.com
SIC: 2711 Newspapers
HQ: Newspaper Holding, Inc.
   425 Locust St
   Johnstown PA 15901
   814 532-5102

**(G-15435)**
**NUTHERM INTERNATIONAL INC**
501 S 11th St (62864-4876)
PHONE...................................618 244-6000
Fax: 618 244-6641
Judy Hinson, *CEO*
Dave Massey, *President*
Tom Sterbis, *General Mgr*
Wade Bowlin, *Principal*
Jeff Ballantyne, *Project Mgr*
▼ EMP: 33
SQ FT: 30,000
SALES (est): 10.6MM **Privately Held**
WEB: www.nutherm.com
SIC: 3613 Time switches, electrical switchgear apparatus; control panels, electric; distribution boards, electric; metering panels, electric

**(G-15436)**
**ORION PETRO CORPORATION (PA)**
125 N 11th St Rear (62864-4024)
P.O. Box 609 (62864-0013)
PHONE...................................618 244-2370
Wayne L Krehbiel, *President*
Oliver Harris, *Vice Pres*
Sherry Hutchison, *Manager*
EMP: 3
SQ FT: 3,000
SALES (est): 1.2MM **Privately Held**
SIC: 1311 Crude petroleum production; natural gas production

**(G-15437)**
**PEACOCK PRINTING INC**
Also Called: Peacock Printing & Silk Screen
1112 Jordan St (62864-3817)
PHONE...................................618 242-3157
Fax: 618 242-3177
Mark Smith, *President*
Carrie Smith, *Vice Pres*
Ashley Coark, *Manager*
EMP: 8 EST: 1946
SALES (est): 550K **Privately Held**
WEB: www.peacockprinting.com
SIC: 2752 2759 Commercial printing, offset; letterpress printing

**(G-15438)**
**PEP DRILLING CO (PA)**
123 S 10th St Ste 210 (62864-4025)
P.O. Box 824 (62864-0017)
PHONE...................................618 242-2205
Fax: 618 242-0812
Pursie E Pipes, *Owner*
Lisa Hart, *Office Mgr*
EMP: 3 EST: 1950
SQ FT: 1,800
SALES (est): 5.3MM **Privately Held**
SIC: 1381 Directional drilling oil & gas wells

**(G-15439)**
**PEPSI MIDAMERICA**
205 N Davidson St (62864-8338)
PHONE...................................618 242-6285
Fax: 618 242-6285
Eileen Sutherland, *Mktg Dir*
Randy Wright, *Manager*
EMP: 5
SALES (est): 246.3K **Privately Held**
SIC: 2086 Soft drinks: packaged in cans, bottles, etc.

**(G-15440)**
**PETCO PETROLEUM CORPORATION**
123 S 10th St Ste 505 (62864-4028)
PHONE...................................618 242-8718
Marshall Daniel, *Branch Mgr*
EMP: 99
SALES (corp-wide): 135.9MM **Privately Held**
WEB: www.petcopetroleum.com
SIC: 1311 Crude petroleum & natural gas production
PA: Petco Petroleum Corporation
   108 E Ogden Ave Ste 100
   Hinsdale IL 60521
   630 654-1740

**(G-15441)**
**PHOENIX MODULAR ELEVATOR INC**
4800 Phoenix Dr (62864-4212)
PHONE...................................618 244-2314
Allison Allgaier, *President*
Peggy Black, *Vice Pres*
Cindy Hernandez, *Purch Agent*
Tim House, *Design Engr*
Kathy Benefiel, *Admin Sec*
EMP: 10
SQ FT: 32,000
SALES (est): 2.1MM **Privately Held**
SIC: 3534 Elevators & moving stairways

**(G-15442)**
**QUAD-COUNTY READY MIX CORP**
Also Called: Jefferson County Ready Mix
9240 Sahara Rd (62864-1924)
PHONE...................................618 244-6973
Fax: 618 244-6981
Herbert Hustedde, *Manager*
EMP: 20
SALES (corp-wide): 18.9MM **Privately Held**
SIC: 3273 Ready-mixed concrete
PA: Quad-County Ready Mix Corp.
   300 W 12th St
   Okawville IL 62271
   618 243-6430

**(G-15443)**
**SA NAT INDUSTRIAL CNSTR CO INC**
103 E Perkins Ave (62864-5215)
P.O. Box 807 (62864-0017)
PHONE...................................618 246-9402
Fax: 618 246-9350
Mel Brookman, *President*
Cindy Brookman, *Office Mgr*
EMP: 28
SQ FT: 9,600
SALES (est): 6.9MM **Privately Held**
SIC: 3535 Conveyors & conveying equipment

**(G-15444)**
**SCI BOX LLC**
515 S 1st St (62864-5202)
PHONE...................................618 244-7244
Teresa Althoff, *Sales Executive*
Denise Wilson, *Mng Member*
Mike Nave, *Consultant*
EMP: 50
SQ FT: 100,000
SALES (est): 15MM **Privately Held**
SIC: 2653 Corrugated & solid fiber boxes

**(G-15445)**
**SHAPIRO BROS OF ILLINOIS INC**
Also Called: Milano Metals & Recycling
510 S 6th St (62864-5300)
P.O. Box 1327 (62864-0027)
PHONE...................................618 244-3168
Gino Federici, *President*
Mike Federici, *General Mgr*
Mary Burgan, *Vice Pres*
Mia Barker, *Treasurer*
Loretta Federici, *Treasurer*
EMP: 35
SQ FT: 14,000
SALES: 8.6MM **Privately Held**
SIC: 5093 3341 3312 Metal scrap & waste materials; secondary nonferrous metals; blast furnaces & steel mills

**(G-15446)**
**STEWART PRODUCERS INC (PA)**
Also Called: Stewart Well Service
301 N 27th St (62864-2943)
P.O. Box 546 (62864-0012)
PHONE...................................618 244-3754
J Russell Stewart, *CEO*
Robert G Stewart, *President*
EMP: 5 EST: 1951
SQ FT: 1,500
SALES (est): 1.1MM **Privately Held**
SIC: 1389 1311 Servicing oil & gas wells; crude petroleum production

**(G-15447)**
**ULTRON INC**
6 Fountain Pl (62864-6142)
P.O. Box 872 (62864-0018)
PHONE...................................618 244-3303
Fax: 618 244-9655
Derrell Whiteside, *President*
Justin Mulch, *Opers Mgr*
EMP: 11
SALES (est): 1.5MM **Privately Held**
WEB: www.ultroninc.com
SIC: 1081 Metal mining exploration & development services

**(G-15448)**
**VANEX INC**
Also Called: Vanex Color
1700 Shawnee St (62864-5572)
P.O. Box 987 (62864-0020)
PHONE...................................618 244-1413
Fax: 618 244-1461
Jim W Montgomery, *President*
Kenneth Brandt, *Vice Pres*
Christina Campbell, *Vice Pres*
W Ray Grubb, *VP Mfg*
EMP: 25 EST: 1962
SQ FT: 40,000
SALES (est): 7.6MM
SALES (corp-wide): 14.7B **Publicly Held**
WEB: www.vanex.com
SIC: 2851 Paints: oil or alkyd vehicle or water thinned; enamels; epoxy coatings; undercoatings, paint
PA: Ppg Industries, Inc.
   1 Ppg Pl
   Pittsburgh PA 15272
   412 434-3131

**(G-15449)**
**WOOD ENERGY INC**
3007 Broadway St (62864-2361)
P.O. Box 828 (62864-0017)
PHONE...................................618 244-1590
Charles P Wood, *President*
Velma R Wood, *Corp Secy*
J Nelson Wood, *Vice Pres*
EMP: 3 EST: 1949
SQ FT: 2,000
SALES (est): 936.2K **Privately Held**
SIC: 1311 Crude petroleum production

---

**Mount Zion**
*Macon County*

---

**(G-15450)**
**EDWARD HULL CABINET SHOP**
1310 N State Highway 121 (62549-1226)
PHONE...................................217 864-3011
Fax: 217 864-2551
Edward Hull, *Owner*

# Mount Zion - Macon County (G-15451) — GEOGRAPHIC SECTION

Franz Jones, *General Mgr*
**EMP**: 7
**SALES**: 1MM **Privately Held**
**SIC**: 5211 2434 Cabinets, kitchen; wood kitchen cabinets

## (G-15451)
### GIBSON INSURANCE INC
Also Called: Auto-Owners Insurance
300 N State Highway 121 (62549-1513)
**PHONE**.................................217 864-4877
**Fax**: 217 864-4511
Jeffrey Gibson, *President*
Elaine Gibson, *Vice Pres*
**EMP**: 2
**SALES (est)**: 200K **Privately Held**
**SIC**: 6411 6311 5261 3599 Insurance agents, brokers & service; life insurance; lawnmowers & tractors; machine shop, jobbing & repair; saws & sawing equipment

## (G-15452)
### GREEN VALLEY MFG ILL INC
100 Green Valley Dr (62549-1775)
**PHONE**.................................217 864-4125
**Fax**: 217 864-4275
Robert W Curry, *President*
Jonathan Simmons, *Admin Sec*
**EMP**: 26
**SQ FT**: 34,000
**SALES**: 2.5MM **Privately Held**
**WEB**: www.greenvalleyinc.com
**SIC**: 3537 Industrial trucks & tractors

## (G-15453)
### JORDAN INDUSTRIAL CONTROLS INC
215 Casa Park Dr (62549-1289)
P.O. Box 108 (62549-0108)
**PHONE**.................................217 864-4444
**Fax**: 217 864-6178
Joseph Jordan, *President*
Scott Klinger, *Opers Mgr*
Craig Kietzman, *Engineer*
Roger Fatheree, *Accounts Mgr*
**EMP**: 22
**SQ FT**: 5,000
**SALES (est)**: 5.7MM **Privately Held**
**WEB**: www.jordanici.com
**SIC**: 3829 Measuring & controlling devices

## (G-15454)
### LIAISON HOME AUTOMATION LLC
111 E Ashland Ave (62549-1272)
**PHONE**.................................888 279-1235
Steven Weber, *President*
Matt Saxhaug, *Director*
**EMP**: 9
**SALES (est)**: 884.2K **Privately Held**
**SIC**: 7372 Home entertainment computer software

## (G-15455)
### PRECISION TOOL & DIE COMPANY
445 W Main St (62549-1329)
P.O. Box 355 (62549-0355)
**PHONE**.................................217 864-3371
**Fax**: 217 864-3232
Bruce Harshman, *President*
John Harshman, *Treasurer*
Carrie Perry, *Admin Sec*
**EMP**: 16
**SQ FT**: 5,500
**SALES (est)**: 2.8MM **Privately Held**
**SIC**: 3544 3549 3545 3541 Special dies & tools; jigs & fixtures; metalworking machinery; machine tool accessories; machine tools, metal cutting type

## (G-15456)
### SALES SPECIALTY METAL
355 Secretariat Pl (62549-9710)
**PHONE**.................................217 864-1496
Don Hittmeier, *Principal*
**EMP**: 3
**SALES (est)**: 196K **Privately Held**
**SIC**: 3399 Primary metal products

## (G-15457)
### VILLAGE OF MT ZION
Also Called: Atwoot Herald
433 N State Route 121 (62549-1514)
**PHONE**.................................217 864-4212
Don Robinson, *Branch Mgr*
**EMP**: 19 **Privately Held**
**SIC**: 2711 Newspapers
**PA**: Village Of Mt Zion
1400 Mt Zion Pkwy
Mount Zion IL 62549
217 864-4012

## Moweaqua
### Christian County

## (G-15458)
### MOWEAQUA PACKING PLANT
601 N Main St (62550-3695)
**PHONE**.................................217 768-4714
Jerry Morehouse, *Owner*
Larry Baker, *Partner*
Jerry John Morehouse, *Principal*
**EMP**: 6 **EST**: 1964
**SQ FT**: 2,700
**SALES (est)**: 320K **Privately Held**
**SIC**: 0751 5147 5421 2013 Slaughtering: custom livestock services; meats, fresh; meat markets, including freezer provisioners; sausages & other prepared meats; meat packing plants

## Mulberry Grove
### Bond County

## (G-15459)
### EAGLE PANEL SYSTEM INC
127 N Maple St (62262)
P.O. Box 247 (62262-0247)
**PHONE**.................................618 326-7132
**Fax**: 618 326-7132
Kenneth Disch, *President*
Vicki Disch, *Vice Pres*
Josephine Chew, *Manager*
**EMP**: 7
**SQ FT**: 60,000
**SALES**: 750K **Privately Held**
**WEB**: www.eaglepanelsystems.com
**SIC**: 3086 Insulation or cushioning material, foamed plastic

## Mundelein
### Lake County

## (G-15460)
### 1717 CHEMALL CORPORATION
222 Terrace Dr (60060-3827)
**PHONE**.................................224 864-4180
**Fax**: 847 281-9855
WEI Xu, *President*
**EMP**: 2
**SALES (est)**: 880.1K **Privately Held**
**WEB**: www.3bsc.com
**SIC**: 5169 2834 8733 Chemicals & allied products; chlorination tablets & kits (water purification); scientific research agency

## (G-15461)
### 4 ELEMENTS COMPANY
520 Cardinal Pl (60060-2636)
**PHONE**.................................773 236-2284
Charise Cowan-Leroy, *Principal*
Travis Leroy, *Co-Owner*
**EMP**: 2 **EST**: 2012
**SALES (est)**: 246.5K **Privately Held**
**SIC**: 5122 2844 7389 Toilet soap; toilet preparations;

## (G-15462)
### A J KAY CO
304 Washington Blvd (60060-3106)
**PHONE**.................................224 475-0370
**Fax**: 773 545-2587
Robert Schweda, *President*
Paul Kiscellus, *Corp Secy*
John Kiscellus, *Vice Pres*
Karen Melzer, *Assistant*
**EMP**: 12 **EST**: 1963
**SQ FT**: 4,500
**SALES**: 660K **Privately Held**
**WEB**: www.ajkay.com
**SIC**: 3493 3496 3495 3452 Cold formed springs; coiled flat springs; miscellaneous fabricated wire products; wire springs; bolts, nuts, rivets & washers

## (G-15463)
### ACCESS ASSEMBLY LLC
1047 E High St (60060-3117)
**PHONE**.................................847 894-1047
Guenther Berg, *Business Mgr*
Sam Reman, *Business Mgr*
Jon Babii, *Mng Member*
Daniel Darla, *Info Tech Mgr*
▲ **EMP**: 5
**SALES**: 450K **Privately Held**
**SIC**: 3679 Electronic circuits

## (G-15464)
### ADLER NORCO INC
2331 Creekwood Dr (60060-5803)
**PHONE**.................................847 473-3600
**Fax**: 847 473-3956
Leonard Degand, *President*
**EMP**: 18 **EST**: 1934
**SQ FT**: 12,000
**SALES (est)**: 1.8MM **Privately Held**
**SIC**: 3444 7692 3469 Sheet metalwork; welding repair; metal stampings

## (G-15465)
### AERUS ELECTROLUX
900 N Lake St Ste 100 (60060-1359)
**PHONE**.................................847 949-4222
Tom Campanella, *Manager*
**EMP**: 6
**SALES (est)**: 357.7K **Privately Held**
**SIC**: 5722 3635 Vacuum cleaners; electric sweeper

## (G-15466)
### AGRITECH WORLDWIDE INC (PA)
1011 Campus Dr (60060-3834)
**PHONE**.................................847 549-6002
Edward Smith III, *CEO*
Edward B Smith III, *CEO*
Morris Garfinkle, *Ch of Bd*
Donald Wittmer, *CFO*
▲ **EMP**: 11
**SQ FT**: 44,000
**SALES**: 1.1MM **Publicly Held**
**WEB**: www.ztrim.com
**SIC**: 2099 2041 Food preparations; flour & other grain mill products; corn flour

## (G-15467)
### ALEF SAUSAGE INC
1026 Campus Dr (60060-3831)
**PHONE**.................................847 968-2533
Alec Mikhaylov, *CEO*
Lyubob Mikhaylov, *Vice Pres*
**EMP**: 17
**SQ FT**: 40,000
**SALES (est)**: 1.5MM **Privately Held**
**SIC**: 2013 Sausages & other prepared meats

## (G-15468)
### ALL AMERICAN WASHER WERKS INC
912 E High St (60060-3120)
**PHONE**.................................847 566-9091
**Fax**: 847 566-8381
Fred Nuemann, *President*
Michael Nuemann, *Vice Pres*
Beula Long, *Manager*
Mary Jane Neumann, *Admin Sec*
**EMP**: 24
**SQ FT**: 44,000
**SALES (est)**: 6.4MM **Privately Held**
**WEB**: www.allamericanwasherwerks.com
**SIC**: 3452 3469 3053 Bolts, nuts, rivets & washers; metal stampings; gaskets & sealing devices

## (G-15469)
### AMERI-TEX
1520 Mccormick Blvd (60060-4447)
**PHONE**.................................847 247-0777
**Fax**: 847 949-8699
Larry Pasquesi, *President*
**EMP**: 9
**SALES (est)**: 681.8K **Privately Held**
**SIC**: 7389 2395 Embroidering of advertising on shirts, etc.; emblems, embroidered

## (G-15470)
### ANTHONY COLLINS
287 N Lake St (60060-2252)
**PHONE**.................................847 566-5350
Anthony Collins, *Principal*
**EMP**: 2
**SALES (est)**: 272.1K **Privately Held**
**SIC**: 3843 Enamels, dentists'

## (G-15471)
### ARJAY INSTANT PRINTING
25785 N Hillview Ct (60060-9437)
**PHONE**.................................847 438-9059
Rick Fedor, *President*
Tim Carlson, *Vice Pres*
**EMP**: 3
**SALES**: 500K **Privately Held**
**SIC**: 2759 Commercial printing

## (G-15472)
### AUDIO SUPPLY INC
1367 Wilhelm Rd (60060-4488)
**PHONE**.................................847 549-6086
Cathleen Raasch, *President*
Lauren Mateja, *Vice Pres*
Mark Mateja, *Admin Sec*
**EMP**: 5
**SQ FT**: 6,000
**SALES (est)**: 600K **Privately Held**
**WEB**: www.audiosupply.com
**SIC**: 3651 Audio electronic systems

## (G-15473)
### AUTONICS USA INC
1353 Armour Blvd (60060-4401)
**PHONE**.................................847 680-8160
**Fax**: 847 680-8155
Simon Park, *President*
Luis Kwon, *Sales Staff*
▲ **EMP**: 5 **EST**: 2001
**SQ FT**: 5,000
**SALES**: 1.4MM
**SALES (corp-wide)**: 88.7MM **Privately Held**
**SIC**: 3829 Measuring & controlling devices
**PA**: Autonics Corporation
18 Bansong-Ro 513beon-Gil, Haeundae-Gu
Busan 48002
515 193-000

## (G-15474)
### BARCODING INC
Also Called: Miles Technologies
333 E Il Route 83 Ste 201 (60060-4279)
**PHONE**.................................847 726-7777
Jay Steinmetz, *President*
**EMP**: 12
**SALES (corp-wide)**: 18.6MM **Privately Held**
**SIC**: 5734 7371 7372 Computer & software stores; custom computer programming services; business oriented computer software
**PA**: Barcoding, Inc.
2220 Boston St
Baltimore MD 21231
888 412-7226

## (G-15475)
### BARDS PRODUCTS INC (PA)
1427 Armour Blvd (60060-4403)
**PHONE**.................................800 323-5499
**Fax**: 847 680-8670
John Campbell, *President*
Heather Campbell, *Admin Sec*
▲ **EMP**: 15
**SQ FT**: 15,000
**SALES (est)**: 2.1MM **Privately Held**
**WEB**: www.bardspro.com
**SIC**: 3231 2541 3993 Novelties, glass: fruit, foliage, flowers, animals, etc.; ornamental glass: cut, engraved or otherwise decorated; wood partitions & fixtures; signs & advertising specialties

## (G-15476)
### BELLE-AIRE FRAGRANCES INC (PA)
1600 Baskin Rd (60060-4602)
**PHONE**.................................847 816-3500
**Fax**: 847 816-7695

# GEOGRAPHIC SECTION

Mundelein - Lake County (G-15500)

Donald Conover, *President*
Charles S David, *Vice Pres*
Richard David, *Vice Pres*
Jessica Clegg, *Production*
Stacey David, *Marketing Staff*
**EMP:** 50 **EST:** 1982
**SQ FT:** 22,000
**SALES:** 23.2MM **Privately Held**
**WEB:** www.belle-aire.com
**SIC: 2869** 2844 Perfume materials, synthetic; flavors or flavoring materials, synthetic; toilet preparations

### (G-15477)
### BIO PACKAGING FILMS LLC
909 Tower Rd (60060-3811)
**PHONE** ............................ 847 566-4444
Gerald Swatek, *Manager*
Gennadiy Krivoruchko,
Alexandre Zemliakov,
**EMP:** 15
**SALES (est):** 2.4MM **Privately Held**
**SIC: 3952** Boxes, sketching & paint

### (G-15478)
### BIO-LOGIC SYSTEMS CORP
1 Bio Logic Plz (60060-3708)
**PHONE** ............................ 847 949-0456
**Fax:** 847 949-8615
James B Hawkins, *President*
Michael J Hanley, *Controller*
Chuck Lovely, *Manager*
Anu Parameswaran, *Technology*
Kenneth Ludlum, *Director*
**EMP:** 80
**SQ FT:** 26,000
**SALES (est):** 8.9MM
**SALES (corp-wide):** 381.8MM **Publicly Held**
**WEB:** www.biologicsupplies.com
**SIC: 3845** 3571 3841 Electromedical equipment; electronic computers; surgical & medical instruments
**PA:** Natus Medical Incorporated
6701 Koll Center Pkwy # 150
Pleasanton CA 94566
925 223-6700

### (G-15479)
### BOLCHAZY-CARDUCCI PUBLISHERS
1570 Baskin Rd (60060-4474)
**PHONE** ............................ 847 526-4344
**Fax:** 847 526-2867
Marie J Bolchazy, *President*
Marie C Bolchazy, *President*
Connor Hart, *Editor*
Allan Bolchazy, *Vice Pres*
Jody Cull, *Production*
▲ **EMP:** 13
**SQ FT:** 3,600
**SALES (est):** 1.8MM **Privately Held**
**WEB:** www.bolchazy.com
**SIC: 2731** Books: publishing only; textbooks: publishing only, not printed on site

### (G-15480)
### BUTTERFIELD CLEANERS
1420 S Butterfield Rd (60060-9424)
**PHONE** ............................ 847 816-7060
Yong Ho Lee, *Owner*
**EMP:** 2
**SALES (est):** 227.8K **Privately Held**
**SIC: 3589** Servicing machines, except dry cleaning, laundry: coin-oper.

### (G-15481)
### C & C ELECTRONICS INC
25719 N Hillview Ct (60060-9437)
**PHONE** ............................ 847 550-0177
**Fax:** 847 550-0179
Cheryl Oulehla, *President*
John McDonald, *Vice Pres*
Cathy Kocsis, *Treasurer*
John Kocsis, *Admin Sec*
**EMP:** 15
**SQ FT:** 10,000
**SALES (est):** 2.3MM **Privately Held**
**SIC: 3672** 3679 4783 Printed circuit boards; harness assemblies for electronic use: wire or cable; packing goods for shipping

### (G-15482)
### CAMPBELL MANAGEMENT SERVICES
Also Called: Signs Now
1500 S Lake St Ste A (60060-4255)
**PHONE** ............................ 847 566-9020
Bruce J Campbell, *President*
**EMP:** 4
**SQ FT:** 2,500
**SALES (est):** 250K **Privately Held**
**SIC: 3993** Signs & advertising specialties

### (G-15483)
### CARRERA STONE SYSTEMS OF CHICA
675 Tower Rd (60060-3819)
**PHONE** ............................ 847 566-2277
Roberto Contreras, *President*
Gary Manning, *General Mgr*
Rebecca Garcia, *Manager*
**EMP:** 50
**SALES (est):** 6MM
**SALES (corp-wide):** 4.9MM **Privately Held**
**SIC: 3281** 1799 Granite, cut & shaped; counter top installation
**HQ:** Stone Suppliers, Inc.
13124 Trinity Dr
Stafford TX
281 494-7277

### (G-15484)
### CARTER HOFFMANN LLC
1551 Mccormick Blvd (60060-4491)
**PHONE** ............................ 847 362-5500
**Fax:** 847 367-8981
Bob Fortmann, *President*
David ABI, *President*
Karl Hartung, *Production*
Janet Benes, *Buyer*
Jeremy Hillis, *Buyer*
▲ **EMP:** 110
**SQ FT:** 80,000
**SALES (est):** 33MM
**SALES (corp-wide):** 2.2B **Publicly Held**
**SIC: 3589** Food warming equipment, commercial
**HQ:** Marshall Middleby Inc
1400 Toastmaster Dr
Elgin IL 60120
847 289-0204

### (G-15485)
### CERTIFIED POWER INC
Driveline Division
970 Campus Dr (60060-3803)
**PHONE** ............................ 847 573-3800
Jerry Boast, *President*
Butch Miller, *Prdtn Mgr*
**EMP:** 32
**SALES (corp-wide):** 133MM **Privately Held**
**WEB:** www.certifiedpower.com
**SIC: 5084** 3561 3494 Hydraulic systems equipment & supplies; pumps & pumping equipment; valves & pipe fittings
**PA:** Certified Power, Inc.
970 Campus Dr
Mundelein IL 60060
847 573-3800

### (G-15486)
### CHED MARKAY INC
1065 E High St (60060-3117)
**PHONE** ............................ 847 566-3307
**Fax:** 847 566-2328
Garrett Holg, *President*
Lorraine M Holg, *Corp Secy*
Julie Holg, *Vice Pres*
**EMP:** 8
**SQ FT:** 2,260
**SALES (est):** 650K **Privately Held**
**SIC: 3843** Dental equipment & supplies

### (G-15487)
### CIRCLE K INDUSTRIES INC
25563 N Gilmer Rd (60060-9410)
**PHONE** ............................ 847 949-0363
**Fax:** 847 566-7309
**EMP:** 10
**SQ FT:** 14,000
**SALES (est):** 690K **Privately Held**
**SIC: 3496** 3523 2842 Mfg Misc Fabricated Wire Products Mfg Farm Machinery/Equipment Mfg Polish/Sanitation Goods

### (G-15488)
### CLARK WIRE & CABLE CO INC
408 Washington Blvd Ste A (60060-3102)
**PHONE** ............................ 847 949-9944
**Fax:** 847 949-9595
Shane Collins, *President*
Patricia Collins, *Vice Pres*
Karen Tunison, *Purchasing*
Ken Bernd, *Natl Sales Mgr*
Dan Collins, *Sales Dir*
**EMP:** 22
**SALES (est):** 10.1MM **Privately Held**
**WEB:** www.clarkwire.com
**SIC: 5063** 2298 Wire & cable; cable, fiber

### (G-15489)
### CLINERE PRODUCTS INC
28977 N Lemon Rd (60060-9605)
**PHONE** ............................ 847 837-4020
Richard C Olson, *President*
**EMP:** 3
**SQ FT:** 1,200
**SALES (est):** 270K **Privately Held**
**WEB:** www.clinere.com
**SIC: 3842** Swabs, sanitary cotton

### (G-15490)
### COMMERCIAL PLASTICS COMPANY (PA)
800 Allanson Rd (60060-3799)
Rural Route 72072, Chicago (60679)
**PHONE** ............................ 847 566-1700
**Fax:** 847 566-4737
Matt O'Connor, *President*
Helmuth Fendel, *Prdtn Mgr*
William G O'Connor, *Admin Sec*
Rafal Zuber, *Maintence Staff*
▲ **EMP:** 127 **EST:** 1942
**SQ FT:** 100,000
**SALES (est):** 53.3MM **Privately Held**
**WEB:** www.ecommercialplastics.com
**SIC: 3089** Injection molding of plastics; thermoformed finished plastic products

### (G-15491)
### CONNECTOR CONCEPTS INC
1530 Mccormick Blvd (60060-4447)
**PHONE** ............................ 847 541-4020
Kevin Berry, *Manager*
**EMP:** 13
**SQ FT:** 8,500
**SALES (est):** 4.9MM **Privately Held**
**SIC: 3643** Current-carrying wiring devices

### (G-15492)
### CRESTWOOD INDUSTRIES INC
1345 Wilhelm Rd (60060-4488)
**PHONE** ............................ 847 680-9088
**Fax:** 847 680-9089
Paul Langer, *President*
Dale Langer, *Treasurer*
Marie Langer, *Admin Sec*
**EMP:** 16
**SQ FT:** 20,000
**SALES (est):** 3.4MM **Privately Held**
**WEB:** www.crestwoodind.com
**SIC: 3089** Injection molding of plastics

### (G-15493)
### DESIGN WOODWORKS
27266 N Owens Rd (60060-9512)
**PHONE** ............................ 847 566-6603
Tim Mayer, *Owner*
Kate Tekampe, *Office Mgr*
**EMP:** 3
**SALES (est):** 175.9K **Privately Held**
**WEB:** www.designwoodworks.com
**SIC: 1751** 2541 2434 Cabinet & finish carpentry; wood partitions & fixtures; wood kitchen cabinets

### (G-15494)
### DESIGNATION INC
1352 Armour Blvd Ste A (60060-4499)
**PHONE** ............................ 847 367-9100
**Fax:** 847 816-6333
Margaret Hercek, *President*
Paul Brunette, *Principal*
Jerome Brunette, *Vice Pres*
Vivian Brunette, *Vice Pres*
**EMP:** 11
**SQ FT:** 26,000
**SALES (est):** 2.7MM **Privately Held**
**WEB:** www.designationprinting.com
**SIC: 5112** 2752 Business forms; office supplies; commercial printing, lithographic; business forms, lithographed

### (G-15495)
### DUVAL GROUP LTD
Also Called: Duradek
452 Morris Ave (60060-1929)
**PHONE** ............................ 847 949-7001
**Fax:** 847 949-7004
Edward F Wood, *President*
Janice Wood, *Vice Pres*
**EMP:** 2 **EST:** 1970
**SALES (est):** 700K **Privately Held**
**WEB:** www.duvalgroup.com
**SIC: 3334** Primary aluminum

### (G-15496)
### DVA METAL FABRICATION INC
1656 Brighton Dr (60060-4506)
**PHONE** ............................ 224 577-8217
Dimitar Atanassov, *Principal*
**EMP:** 2
**SALES (est):** 202.4K **Privately Held**
**SIC: 3499** Fabricated metal products

### (G-15497)
### DYNACO USA INC (HQ)
Also Called: Dynaco Door
935 Campus Dr (60060-3830)
**PHONE** ............................ 847 562-4910
Olivier Coune, *CEO*
Bryan Gregory, *President*
Dirk Wouters, *Admin Sec*
▲ **EMP:** 30
**SQ FT:** 20,000
**SALES (est):** 5.9MM
**SALES (corp-wide):** 7.7B **Privately Held**
**WEB:** www.dynacodoor.us
**SIC: 3442** Rolling doors for industrial buildings or warehouses, metal
**PA:** Assa Abloy Ab
Klarabergsviadukten 90
Stockholm 111 6
850 648-500

### (G-15498)
### ECOMED SOLUTIONS LLC
214 Terrace Dr (60060-3827)
**PHONE** ............................ 866 817-7114
David Yurek, *CEO*
**EMP:** 20 **EST:** 2012
**SQ FT:** 3,400
**SALES (est):** 1.1MM **Privately Held**
**SIC: 3842** Surgical appliances & supplies

### (G-15499)
### ENCOMPASS GROUP LLC
955 Campus Dr (60060-3830)
**PHONE** ............................ 847 680-3388
Lizz Morris, *Purch Agent*
Michael Green, *Branch Mgr*
Tom Shaw, *Info Tech Dir*
**EMP:** 48
**SALES (corp-wide):** 166.9MM **Privately Held**
**WEB:** www.pillowfactory.net
**SIC: 2392** Pillows, bed: made from purchased materials
**HQ:** Encompass Group, L.L.C.
615 Macon St
Mcdonough GA 30253
770 957-3981

### (G-15500)
### FIBERGEL TECHNOLOGIES INC
1011 Campus Dr (60060-3834)
**PHONE** ............................ 847 549-6002
Greg Halpern, *CEO*
Michael Theriult, *COO*
Dana Babney, *CFO*
**EMP:** 3
**SQ FT:** 22,000
**SALES (est):** 116.3K **Publicly Held**
**SIC: 2099** Fat substitutes
**PA:** Agritech Worldwide, Inc.
1011 Campus Dr
Mundelein IL 60060

Mundelein - Lake County (G-15501)  GEOGRAPHIC SECTION

**(G-15501)**
**FLATOUT GROUP LLC**
Also Called: Flatout Gaskets
668 Tower Rd (60060-3820)
PHONE .................. 847 837-9200
Fax: 847 837-9628
Mark J Adelizzi, *President*
Venessa Watkins, *Office Mgr*
**EMP:** 3 **EST:** 2008
**SQ FT:** 10,000
**SALES (est):** 370K **Privately Held**
**WEB:** www.flatoutgroup.com
**SIC: 3053** Gaskets, packing & sealing devices

**(G-15502)**
**FLODEN ENTERPRISES**
Also Called: Minuteman Press
674 E Hawley St (60060-1946)
PHONE .................. 847 566-7898
Douglas Floden,
**EMP:** 4
**SALES (est):** 635.6K **Privately Held**
**SIC: 2752** 2789 2759 Commercial printing, lithographic; bookbinding & related work; commercial printing

**(G-15503)**
**GRANITE WORKS LLC**
1150 Allanson Rd (60060-3806)
PHONE .................. 847 837-1688
Frank F Chen, *Mng Member*
Ming Xing Wu,
Ding Qing Xu,
Min Zheng,
▲ **EMP:** 5
**SQ FT:** 20,000
**SALES:** 1MM **Privately Held**
**SIC: 3281** Cut stone & stone products

**(G-15504)**
**GREGS FROZEN CUSTARD COMPANY**
1490 S Lake St (60060-4260)
PHONE .................. 847 837-4175
George Orfanos, *President*
**EMP:** 8
**SALES (est):** 771K **Privately Held**
**SIC: 2024** Custard, frozen

**(G-15505)**
**GURMAN FOOD CO**
906 Tower Rd (60060-3812)
PHONE .................. 847 837-1100
Larisa Mikhailov, *President*
**EMP:** 13
**SALES:** 2.5MM **Privately Held**
**SIC: 2013** Sausages from purchased meat

**(G-15506)**
**H & R BLOCK INC**
1527 S Lake St (60060-4210)
PHONE .................. 847 566-5557
Sue Elliot, *Branch Mgr*
**EMP:** 12
**SALES (corp-wide):** 3B **Publicly Held**
**SIC: 7291** 6794 7372 4822 Tax return preparation services; franchises, selling or licensing; application computer software; electronic mail
**PA:** H&R Block, Inc.
1 H&R Block Way
Kansas City MO 64105
816 854-3000

**(G-15507)**
**HAMPSTER INDUSTRIES INC**
Also Called: Big Time Bats
26400 N Pheasant Run (60060-9514)
PHONE .................. 866 280-2287
Margaret Obie, *CEO*
John Obie, *President*
**EMP:** 3
**SALES (est):** 1.8MM **Privately Held**
**SIC: 3949** 7389 Baseball, softball & cricket sports equipment;

**(G-15508)**
**IFA INTERNATIONAL INC**
Also Called: Alef Sausage & Deli
354356 Townline Rd (60060)
PHONE .................. 847 566-0003
Fax: 847 566-2210
Alex Mikhaylov, *President*
Lyubov Mikhaylov, *Vice Pres*

▲ **EMP:** 14 **EST:** 2000
**SQ FT:** 4,900
**SALES (est):** 1.9MM **Privately Held**
**SIC: 2013** 5812 Sausages & related products, from purchased meat; delicatessen (eating places)

**(G-15509)**
**IN THE ATTIC INC**
Also Called: Attic Gifts
1955 Buckingham Rd (60060-1461)
PHONE .................. 847 949-5077
Kimberly I Kelly, *President*
William P Kelly, *CFO*
**EMP:** 2
**SQ FT:** 500
**SALES (est):** 206.3K **Privately Held**
**SIC: 7699** 5947 5945 3269 Bicycle repair shop; gift shop; models, toy & hobby; art & ornamental ware, pottery; lawn ornaments

**(G-15510)**
**INDUSTRIAL MOLDED PRODUCTS**
800 Allanson Rd (60060-3711)
PHONE .................. 847 358-2160
Lee Benson, *Principal*
**EMP:** 2
**SALES (est):** 256K **Privately Held**
**SIC: 3544** Industrial molds

**(G-15511)**
**INNERWELD COVER CO**
21227 W Coml Dr Ste E (60060)
PHONE .................. 847 497-3009
Tim Interrante, *President*
Jennifer Garza, *Office Mgr*
**EMP:** 10
**SALES (est):** 1.3MM **Privately Held**
**SIC: 3533** 3429 3499 Water well drilling equipment; fireplace equipment, hardware: andirons, grates, screens; metal ladders

**(G-15512)**
**IVANHOE INDUSTRIES INC (PA)**
26267 N Hickory Rd (60060-3323)
PHONE .................. 847 566-7170
Fax: 847 566-7090
Robert Wiese, *President*
Bob Wiese, *Human Res Mgr*
Jerry McInerney, *Cust Mgr*
Dan Hamlet, *Manager*
Teri Popp, *Manager*
▲ **EMP:** 2
**SQ FT:** 7,000
**SALES (est):** 11.1MM **Privately Held**
**WEB:** www.ivanhoeind.com
**SIC: 2899** 2843 Corrosion preventive lubricant; emulsifiers, except food & pharmaceutical

**(G-15513)**
**J STONE INC**
Also Called: Endoplus
750 Tower Rd Ste A (60060-3818)
PHONE .................. 847 325-5660
Fax: 847 325-5661
Matthew Gudeman, *President*
Matt Latawiec, *Engineer*
Rob Meister, *Shareholder*
John Schwab, *Admin Sec*
▲ **EMP:** 20
**SQ FT:** 10,000
**SALES:** 2MM **Privately Held**
**WEB:** www.endoplususa.com
**SIC: 3841** Surgical & medical instruments

**(G-15514)**
**JAY RS STEEL & WELDING INC**
Also Called: Jay R Steel and Welding
840 Tower Rd (60060-3810)
PHONE .................. 847 949-9353
Fax: 847 949-9228
Ronald R Nally, *President*
Randy Nally, *Corp Secy*
Roger Nally, *Vice Pres*
**EMP:** 7
**SQ FT:** 6,300
**SALES (est):** 1.6MM **Privately Held**
**SIC: 3441** 3599 8734 Fabricated structural metal; machine shop, jobbing & repair; welded joint radiography

**(G-15515)**
**JMR PRECISION MACHINING INC**
630 S Wheeling Rd (60060)
PHONE .................. 847 279-3982
Jose Marie Y Gonzales, *President*
Rowena Gonzales, *Admin Sec*
**EMP:** 2
**SALES (est):** 253.3K **Privately Held**
**SIC: 3599** Machine shop, jobbing & repair

**(G-15516)**
**KING MIDAS SEAFOOD ENTPS INC**
309 N Lake St Ste 200 (60060-2253)
PHONE .................. 847 566-2192
Fax: 847 680-6407
Leon Trammell, *CEO*
Michael Meehan, *President*
**EMP:** 3
**SQ FT:** 800
**SALES:** 8MM **Privately Held**
**SIC: 2092** Chowders, fish & seafood: frozen

**(G-15517)**
**LAKELAND PLASTICS INC**
1550 Mccormick Blvd (60060-4447)
PHONE .................. 847 680-1550
Fax: 847 766-4084
Christopher Arendt, *President*
Phillip Duncan, *Vice Pres*
Hans Karnstedt, *Plant Mgr*
Sheryl Kurishy, *Office Mgr*
**EMP:** 30
**SQ FT:** 32,000
**SALES:** 5MM **Privately Held**
**WEB:** www.lakelandplastics.com
**SIC: 3089** Ducting, plastic; casting of plastic

**(G-15518)**
**LAKESHORE LIGHTING LLC**
25741 N Hillview Ct (60060-9437)
PHONE .................. 847 989-5843
Betzold Nick, *Mng Member*
**EMP:** 3
**SALES (est):** 2MM **Privately Held**
**SIC: 3648** 5063 Lighting equipment; lighting fixtures

**(G-15519)**
**LARSEN MANUFACTURING LLC (PA)**
1201 Allanson Rd (60060-3807)
PHONE .................. 847 970-9600
Fax: 847 970-9733
Al Manges, *Opers Mgr*
Ken Sien, *Purch Mgr*
Bob Kalicki, *CFO*
Jeff Dec, *Manager*
George Gaulke, *Manager*
▲ **EMP:** 125
**SQ FT:** 65,000
**SALES:** 43MM **Privately Held**
**WEB:** www.larsenmfg.net
**SIC: 3469** Electronic enclosures, stamped or pressed metal

**(G-15520)**
**LIFESAFETY POWER INC**
750 Tower Rd Unit B (60060-3818)
PHONE .................. 224 324-4240
Larry Ye, *President*
Joe Holland, *Vice Pres*
Guang Liu, *Vice Pres*
Michael Bone, *Opers Staff*
Cindy Hu, *Accounting Mgr*
**EMP:** 14
**SALES (est):** 3MM **Privately Held**
**SIC: 3679** Electronic loads & power supplies

**(G-15521)**
**MAC LEAN-FOGG COMPANY (PA)**
Also Called: Maclean Fasteners
1000 Allanson Rd (60060-3804)
PHONE .................. 847 566-0010
Fax: 847 566-0026
Duncan A L Maclean, *President*
Tom Macdonald, *Vice Pres*
Rob Whiteny, *Vice Pres*
Rob Whitney, *Vice Pres*
Terry Hartman, *Materials Mgr*

◆ **EMP:** 92 **EST:** 1925
**SQ FT:** 3,500
**SALES (est):** 1.4B **Privately Held**
**WEB:** www.maclean-fogg.com
**SIC: 3678** 3452 3089 3061 Electronic connectors; nuts, metal; bolts, metal; screws, metal; plastic processing; automotive rubber goods (mechanical); fluid power valves & hose fittings; screw machine products

**(G-15522)**
**MADDEN VENTURES INC**
1045 Campus Dr Ste A (60060-3802)
PHONE .................. 847 487-0644
Fax: 847 487-0912
Joseph Madden, *Principal*
Thomas Madden, *Principal*
**EMP:** 5
**SQ FT:** 28,000
**SALES:** 3MM **Privately Held**
**SIC: 5084** 3599 Machine tools & accessories; metalworking machinery; machine shop, jobbing & repair

**(G-15523)**
**MARK TWAIN PRESS INC**
3312 Sheridan Ln (60060-6029)
PHONE .................. 847 255-2700
Fax: 847 255-2768
Linda Sloan, *President*
Jim Sloan, *Vice Pres*
**EMP:** 6
**SQ FT:** 4,800
**SALES:** 450K **Privately Held**
**SIC: 2752** 2791 2789 Commercial printing, offset; typesetting; bookbinding & related work

**(G-15524)**
**MASTER MECHANIC MFG INC**
970 Campus Dr (60060-3803)
PHONE .................. 847 573-3812
Fax: 847 573-3836
Jerry Bost, *President*
**EMP:** 3
**SALES (est):** 201.4K **Privately Held**
**SIC: 2621** 5084 Catalog paper; hydraulic systems equipment & supplies

**(G-15525)**
**MBA MANUFACTURING INC**
1248 Allanson Rd (60060-3808)
PHONE .................. 847 566-2555
Otto Wolters, *President*
Gertraud Wolters, *Corp Secy*
**EMP:** 8
**SQ FT:** 3,500
**SALES (est):** 690K **Privately Held**
**SIC: 3471** Anodizing (plating) of metals or formed products

**(G-15526)**
**MBA MARKETING INC**
1248 Allanson Rd (60060-3808)
PHONE .................. 847 566-2555
Gertraud Wolters, *President*
H Otto Wolters, *Admin Sec*
**EMP:** 5
**SQ FT:** 3,000
**SALES:** 600K **Privately Held**
**WEB:** www.mbamanufacturing.com
**SIC: 3356** Titanium

**(G-15527)**
**MEDCAL SALES LLC**
1 Medline Pl (60060-4485)
PHONE .................. 847 837-2771
Freda Boid, *Manager*
Bob Kievert,
**EMP:** 2
**SALES (est):** 500.7K **Privately Held**
**SIC: 2782** Receipt, invoice & memorandum books

**(G-15528)**
**MEDLINE INDUSTRIES INC**
1200 Townline Rd (60060-4494)
PHONE .................. 847 949-2056
Fax: 847 949-3126
Charles Mills, *President*
Dmitry Dukhan, *Vice Pres*
Asta Ladavicius, *Project Mgr*
Samantha Melchor, *QA Dir*
Lanell White, *QC Mgr*
**EMP:** 500

# GEOGRAPHIC SECTION
## Mundelein - Lake County (G-15553)

SQ FT: 420,000
SALES (corp-wide): 5.6B Privately Held
WEB: www.medline.com
SIC: 3841 Surgical & medical instruments
PA: Medline Industries, Inc.
3 Lakes Dr
Northfield IL 60093
847 949-5500

**(G-15529)**
**MEDLINE INDUSTRIES INC**
Medcrest Textiles
1 Medline Pl (60060-4486)
PHONE .................................. 847 949-5500
Rhonda Hinks, *Manager*
EMP: 40
SALES (corp-wide): 5.6B Privately Held
SIC: 3842 Surgical appliances & supplies
PA: Medline Industries, Inc.
3 Lakes Dr
Northfield IL 60093
847 949-5500

**(G-15530)**
**MERRY WALKER CORPORATION**
21350 W Sylvan Dr S (60060-9442)
PHONE .................................. 847 837-9580
Fax: 847 678-3399
Mary M Harroun, *President*
EMP: 2
SQ FT: 5,000
SALES: 500K Privately Held
WEB: www.merrywalker.com
SIC: 3842 Surgical appliances & supplies

**(G-15531)**
**METFORM LLC (HQ)**
1000 Allanson Rd (60060-3804)
PHONE .................................. 847 566-0010
Dennis Keesey, *Vice Pres*
Gary Sullo, *Vice Pres*
Robert Whitney, *Vice Pres*
Thomas M Pruden, *Treasurer*
Daniel J Joyce,
▲ EMP: 5
SQ FT: 180,000
SALES (est): 78.6MM
SALES (corp-wide): 1.4B Privately Held
SIC: 3462 Iron & steel forgings
PA: Mac Lean-Fogg Company
1000 Allanson Rd
Mundelein IL 60060
847 566-0010

**(G-15532)**
**MILANO DIRECT**
823 E Orchard St (60060-3019)
PHONE .................................. 847 566-1387
Albert Baiocchi, *Principal*
EMP: 3
SALES (est): 180K Privately Held
SIC: 3281 Cut stone & stone products

**(G-15533)**
**MULCH IT INC**
19738 W Martin Dr (60060-3445)
PHONE .................................. 847 566-9372
EMP: 5
SALES (est): 382.1K Privately Held
SIC: 1499 Miscellaneous nonmetallic minerals

**(G-15534)**
**MUNTZ INDUSTRIES INC**
Also Called: Afc Machining Division
710 Tower Rd (60060-3818)
PHONE .................................. 847 949-8280
Fax: 847 949-8284
David Muntz, *President*
Steven Muntz, *Vice Pres*
Ray Prokop, *Chief Engr*
Jean Ann Muntz, *Admin Sec*
◆ EMP: 50
SQ FT: 17,000
SALES (est): 36.5MM Privately Held
SIC: 5084 3677 Metalworking machinery; electronic coils, transformers & other inductors

**(G-15535)**
**MURDOCK COMPANY INC**
Also Called: Plasmag Pump Div
936 Turret Ct (60060-3821)
PHONE .................................. 847 566-0050
Fax: 847 566-0057
Frank J Olk, *President*
Betty R Olk, *Corp Secy*
John Olk, *Sales Staff*
EMP: 6
SQ FT: 12,000
SALES (est): 1.1MM Privately Held
WEB: www.murdockcompany.com
SIC: 3564 3561 3443 5085 Filters, air: furnaces, air conditioning equipment, etc.; industrial pumps & parts; housings, pressure; filters, industrial; pumps & pumping equipment; industrial inorganic chemicals

**(G-15536)**
**NATUS MEDICAL INCORPORATED**
Also Called: Bio-Logic Systems
1 Bio Logic Plz (60060-3708)
PHONE .................................. 847 949-5200
Kenneth Pawlak, *Engineer*
Horvat Joe, *Branch Mgr*
Constance D Kemmerer, *Manager*
Frank Mancuso, *Sr Ntwrk Engine*
John Skeens, *Sr Software Eng*
EMP: 14
SALES (corp-wide): 381.8MM Publicly Held
SIC: 3845 Electromedical equipment
PA: Natus Medical Incorporated
6701 Koll Center Pkwy # 150
Pleasanton CA 94566
925 223-6700

**(G-15537)**
**NETWORK PRINTING INC**
109 Alexandra Ct (60060-2647)
PHONE .................................. 847 566-4146
Fax: 847 388-5200
Mike Murrow, *President*
EMP: 2
SALES (est): 260.1K Privately Held
SIC: 2752 Commercial printing, lithographic

**(G-15538)**
**NORTHFIELD BLOCK COMPANY (DH)**
1 Hunt Ct (60060-4487)
PHONE .................................. 847 816-9000
Fax: 847 816-9062
Craig M Belasco, *President*
Weigh Wright, *Vice Pres*
Doug Yound, *Vice Pres*
Mike Chiappetta, *CFO*
Jerry Kniery, *CFO*
▼ EMP: 218
SQ FT: 3,200
SALES (est): 54MM
SALES (corp-wide): 28.6B Privately Held
WEB: www.northfieldblock.com
SIC: 3271 Blocks, concrete or cinder: standard
HQ: Oldcastle Architectural, Inc.
900 Ashwood Pkwy Ste 600
Atlanta GA 30338
770 804-3363

**(G-15539)**
**NORTHFIELD BLOCK COMPANY**
1455 Leighton Tower Rd (60060-4409)
PHONE .................................. 847 949-3600
EMP: 35
SALES (corp-wide): 28.6B Privately Held
SIC: 3271 Concrete block & brick
HQ: Northfield Block Company
1 Hunt Ct
Mundelein IL 60060
847 816-9000

**(G-15540)**
**PACKAGING CORPORATION AMERICA**
Also Called: PCA Tech Center
250 S Shaddle Ave (60060-3114)
PHONE .................................. 847 388-6000
M A Conley, *Plant Mgr*
Dale Works, *Plant Mgr*
Eugene Foster, *Opers Mgr*
Randy Cooley, *Prdtn Mgr*
Robert Spencer, *Prdtn Mgr*
EMP: 14
SALES (corp-wide): 5.7B Publicly Held
WEB: www.packagingcorp.com
SIC: 2653 Corrugated & solid fiber boxes

PA: Packaging Corporation Of America
1955 W Field Ct
Lake Forest IL 60045
847 482-3000

**(G-15541)**
**PARKER TOOL & DIE CO**
20844 W Park Ave (60060-9109)
PHONE .................................. 847 566-2229
Fax: 847 566-2560
Tim Parker, *Owner*
EMP: 8
SQ FT: 4,000
SALES (est): 530K Privately Held
SIC: 3599 3544 Machine shop, jobbing & repair; special dies, tools, jigs & fixtures

**(G-15542)**
**PARTY FANTASY**
390 Townline Rd Ste 7150 (60060-4225)
PHONE .................................. 847 837-0010
EMP: 7
SALES (est): 899.3K Privately Held
SIC: 3644 Raceways

**(G-15543)**
**PATRICIA LOCKE LTD**
817 E Orchard St (60060-3019)
PHONE .................................. 847 949-2303
Fax: 847 949-2305
Patricia Locke, *President*
Ruta Jones, *Accountant*
Janet McDermott, *Manager*
EMP: 18
SQ FT: 3,000
SALES (est): 2.4MM Privately Held
WEB: www.patricialocke.com
SIC: 3911 Jewelry apparel

**(G-15544)**
**PET FACTORY INC**
845 E High St (60060-3100)
PHONE .................................. 847 281-8054
Tom Miller, *President*
Doug Vantreek, *Managing Dir*
Marco Corsi, *Vice Pres*
Jeff Boeing, *Natl Sales Mgr*
▲ EMP: 200
SQ FT: 117,000
SALES (est): 34.7MM Privately Held
SIC: 2047 Dog food

**(G-15545)**
**PHARMA LOGISTICS**
1050 E High St (60060-3118)
PHONE .................................. 847 388-3104
Ryan Fandel, *President*
Nicholas Fassbinder, *President*
Michael Zaccaro, *Owner*
David Malecki, *COO*
Jen Mikulski, *Vice Pres*
▲ EMP: 68
SALES (est): 11MM Privately Held
SIC: 2834 Pharmaceutical preparations

**(G-15546)**
**PHOENIX MARKETING SERVICES**
104 Terrace Dr (60060-3826)
PHONE .................................. 630 616-8000
Lynn Gulbranson, *President*
Ann Sawicki, *Corp Secy*
Lynn Guldranson, *Webmaster*
EMP: 12
SALES (est): 1.7MM Privately Held
SIC: 7336 2759 Graphic arts & related design; screen printing

**(G-15547)**
**PRECITEC CORPORATION**
Also Called: Poly-Clip Systems
1000 Tower Rd (60060-3816)
PHONE .................................. 847 949-2800
Nicholas D Brasile, *President*
Gilbert Williams, *Principal*
Amin Abushamma, *Plant Mgr*
Cindie Walker, *Credit Mgr*
Eric Carr, *Regl Sales Mgr*
▲ EMP: 70
SQ FT: 35,000
SALES (est): 19.1MM
SALES (corp-wide): 193MM Privately Held
SIC: 3496 Clips & fasteners, made from purchased wire

PA: Process-Pack Gmbh & Co. Kg
Niedeckerstr. 1
Hattersheim Am Main 65795
619 088-860

**(G-15548)**
**PREMIER PACKAGING SYSTEMS INC**
304 Terrace Dr (60060-3836)
PHONE .................................. 847 996-6860
Erik Spracklen, *President*
Kathy Spracklen, *Admin Sec*
▲ EMP: 5
SALES (est): 617K Privately Held
WEB: www.premierpackaging.org
SIC: 2653 Display items, solid fiber: made from purchased materials

**(G-15549)**
**PRINT TECH INC**
Also Called: Printing Factory, The
407 Wshington Blvd Unit C (60060)
PHONE .................................. 847 949-5400
Fax: 847 949-5455
Brad Kington, *President*
John Petrovskis, *Corp Secy*
Kim Flood, *Manager*
Fran Stephens, *Graphic Designe*
EMP: 12
SQ FT: 6,400
SALES (est): 1.2MM Privately Held
WEB: www.tpfprinting.com
SIC: 2759 Commercial printing

**(G-15550)**
**PRINT-O-TAPE INC**
755 Tower Rd (60060-3817)
P.O. Box 308, Libertyville (60048-0308)
PHONE .................................. 847 362-6433
Fax: 847 949-7449
Carl Walliser, *President*
Jon Barrere, *Vice Pres*
Ron Cuba, *Vice Pres*
Husun Ovaice, *Human Res Mgr*
Dennis May, *Sales Mgr*
EMP: 43 EST: 1947
SQ FT: 84,000
SALES (est): 23.1MM Privately Held
WEB:
SIC: 2672 Tape, pressure sensitive: made from purchased materials; labels (unprinted), gummed: made from purchased materials

**(G-15551)**
**RAINBOW MANUFACTURING INC**
Also Called: Rainbow Graphics, Inc.
933 Tower Rd (60060-3811)
PHONE .................................. 847 824-9600
Claude Koszuta, *CEO*
Jeff Koszuta, *President*
Scott Camble, *General Mgr*
Scott Campbell, *Vice Pres*
Claude Koszuta Jr, *Vice Pres*
EMP: 44
SQ FT: 50,000
SALES (est): 15MM Privately Held
WEB: www.rainbowgraphics.com
SIC: 2752 Commercial printing, offset

**(G-15552)**
**RKB DISTRIBUTORS**
216 Terrace Dr (60060-3827)
PHONE .................................. 847 970-6880
Barry Schuster, *Owner*
EMP: 3
SALES (est): 443.6K Privately Held
SIC: 2499 Kitchen, bathroom & household ware: wood

**(G-15553)**
**ROSE CUSTOM CABINETS INC**
Also Called: Rose Custom Builders
408 Washington Blvd Ste C (60060-3102)
PHONE .................................. 847 816-4800
Fax: 847 816-1418
Brian Rosenberg, *President*
Maria Gadjeva, *Manager*
EMP: 28
SQ FT: 26,000
SALES (est): 2.1MM Privately Held
SIC: 5712 2511 Cabinet work, custom; wood household furniture

## Mundelein - Lake County (G-15554)

**(G-15554)**
**ROSES MOULDING BY DESIGN INC**
408 Washington Blvd Ste C  (60060-3102)
PHONE.................................847 549-9200
Tom Troush, *President*
Terry Allen, *Manager*
**EMP:** 30
**SALES (est):** 1MM  **Privately Held**
**SIC:** 3999  Manufacturing industries

**(G-15555)**
**SENJU COMTEK CORP**
1322 Armour Blvd  (60060-4402)
PHONE.................................847 549-5690
Fax: 847 549-5699
Ryoichi Suzuki, *Branch Mgr*
**EMP:** 6  **Privately Held**
**WEB:** www.senjucomtek.com
**SIC:** 3399  Paste, metal
**HQ:** Senju Comtek Corp.
2989 San Ysidro Way
Santa Clara CA 95051
408 963-5300

**(G-15556)**
**SENSOR 21 INC**
19541 W University Dr  (60060-3485)
PHONE.................................847 561-6233
**EMP:** 5
**SALES (est):** 450K  **Privately Held**
**SIC:** 3826  R&D Optical Sensor Systems

**(G-15557)**
**SHEET METAL SUPPLY LTD**
262 S Shaddle Ave  (60060-3114)
PHONE.................................847 478-8500
Fax: 847 478-9500
Harriet Sloma, *President*
Ben Kweton, *Vice Pres*
Phillip Kweton, *Vice Pres*
**EMP:** 7
**SQ FT:** 13,000
**SALES (est):** 2.8MM  **Privately Held**
**WEB:** www.sheetmetalsupply.com
**SIC:** 3444  3441  2952  Sheet metalwork; fabricated structural metal; asphalt felts & coatings

**(G-15558)**
**SOMMERS FARE LLC**
1301 Allanson Rd  (60060-3835)
PHONE.................................877 377-9797
Jessica Cohen, *Supervisor*
Dimitrios Apostolopoulos, *Director*
Walter Sommers,
Lenny Lebovich,
**EMP:** 30
**SALES (est):** 3.9MM  **Privately Held**
**WEB:** www.sommersfare.com
**SIC:** 2011  Canned meats (except baby food), meat slaughtered on site

**(G-15559)**
**SPEC CHECK LLC**
910 Raleigh Rd  (60060-1231)
P.O. Box 1146, Medford OR  (97501-0085)
PHONE.................................773 270-0003
James E Manfredi, *Mng Member*
**EMP:** 8
**SALES (est):** 653.7K  **Privately Held**
**SIC:** 3537  3599  Forklift trucks; amusement park equipment

**(G-15560)**
**SPHERE INC**
Also Called: Signal Graphics Printing
316 Washington Blvd  (60060-3106)
PHONE.................................847 566-4800
Fax: 847 566-4884
Diane C Donovan, *President*
Kevin M Donovan, *Vice Pres*
**EMP:** 3
**SQ FT:** 2,160
**SALES (est):** 490.2K  **Privately Held**
**SIC:** 2752  Commercial printing, offset

**(G-15561)**
**STUART MOORE RACING LTD**
Also Called: SMR Components
831 E Orchard St  (60060-3019)
PHONE.................................847 949-9100
Fax: 847 949-9101
Stuart Alan Moore, *President*
Patricia Shrader, *CFO*
**EMP:** 8
**SQ FT:** 5,000
**SALES (est):** 1.1MM  **Privately Held**
**WEB:** www.smrcomponents.com
**SIC:** 3599  Machine shop, jobbing & repair

**(G-15562)**
**SYNERGISTIC TECH SOLUTIONS INC**
750 Tower Rd Unit B  (60060-3818)
PHONE.................................224 360-6165
Larry Ye, *President*
John Olliver, *Vice Pres*
Cindy Hu, *Manager*
Guang Liu, *Admin Sec*
▲ **EMP:** 5
**SQ FT:** 2,000
**SALES (est):** 3MM  **Privately Held**
**WEB:** www.sts-power.com
**SIC:** 3629  3669  Power conversion units, a.c. to d.c.: static-electric; fire alarm apparatus, electric

**(G-15563)**
**TE CONNECTIVITY CORPORATION**
Also Called: Corcom
620 S Butterfield Rd  (60060-9457)
PHONE.................................847 680-7400
**EMP:** 85
**SALES (corp-wide):** 12.2B  **Privately Held**
**SIC:** 3677  3678  Filtration devices, electronic; electronic connectors
**HQ:** Te Connectivity Corporation
1050 Westlakes Dr
Berwyn PA 19312
610 893-9800

**(G-15564)**
**TEXMAC INC**
224 Terrace Dr  (60060-3827)
PHONE.................................630 244-4702
Bill Mahon, *Manager*
**EMP:** 3
**SALES (corp-wide):** 42.5B  **Privately Held**
**SIC:** 3571  Electronic computers
**HQ:** Texmac Inc.
3001 Stafford Dr
Charlotte NC 28208
704 394-0314

**(G-15565)**
**ULTIMATE DISTRIBUTING INC**
Also Called: Ultimate Screen Printing
300 E Park St  (60060-1968)
PHONE.................................847 566-2250
Don Hermestroff, *President*
Tracy Hermestroff, *Principal*
**EMP:** 6
**SALES (est):** 831.1K  **Privately Held**
**SIC:** 2262  2759  2396  2395  Screen printing: manmade fiber & silk broadwoven fabrics; screen printing; promotional printing; automotive & apparel trimmings; pleating & stitching

**(G-15566)**
**WANDFLUH OF AMERICA INC**
909 E High St  (60060-3119)
PHONE.................................847 566-5700
Fax: 847 566-5733
James R Brooks, *President*
Hansrudolph Wandfluh, *Vice Pres*
Dawn Wells, *Purch Agent*
Tony Zingman, *Engineer*
Bruno Dollar, *Asst Treas*
▲ **EMP:** 15
**SQ FT:** 6,600
**SALES (est):** 2.9MM  **Privately Held**
**WEB:** www.wandfluh-us.com
**SIC:** 3492  3599  Control valves, fluid power; hydraulic & pneumatic; hydraulic equipment, installation & service

**(G-15567)**
**WILSON PRINTING INC**
309 N Lake St Ste 202  (60060-2253)
PHONE.................................847 949-7800
Fax: 847 949-7807
Gary Wilson, *President*
Cindy Wilson, *Admin Sec*
**EMP:** 9  EST: 1951
**SQ FT:** 5,000
**SALES:** 4MM  **Privately Held**
**SIC:** 2752  Commercial printing, lithographic; commercial printing, offset

**(G-15568)**
**WW DISPLAYS INC**
Also Called: Wood & Wire
401 Wshington Blvd Ste 10  (60060)
PHONE.................................847 566-6979
Fax: 847 566-3526
William J Scarim, *President*
Jacqueline Scarim, *Corp Secy*
Robert Miller, *Executive*
**EMP:** 16
**SQ FT:** 56,000
**SALES (est):** 3.1MM  **Privately Held**
**SIC:** 2541  1751  2542  Display fixtures, wood; carpentry work; partitions & fixtures, except wood

**(G-15569)**
**Z AUTOMATION COMPANY**
163 N Archer Ave  (60060-2301)
PHONE.................................847 357-0120
Fax: 847 483-0121
Zoran Momich, *President*
Vesna Momich, *Vice Pres*
Stojan Bajich, *Purch Mgr*
Allen Coover, *Electrical Engi*
Tyng Wu, *Marketing Staff*
◆ **EMP:** 48
**SQ FT:** 56,000
**SALES (est):** 13MM  **Privately Held**
**WEB:** www.zautomation.com
**SIC:** 3565  Packaging machinery

### Murphysboro
*Jackson County*

**(G-15570)**
**ADVANCED CUSTOM SHAPES**
550 N 19th St  (62966-1704)
P.O. Box 384  (62966-0384)
PHONE.................................618 684-2222
Fax: 618 684-2200
**EMP:** 18
**SALES (est):** 600K  **Privately Held**
**SIC:** 2673  Mfg Bags-Plastic/Coated Paper

**(G-15571)**
**ALSTAT WOOD PRODUCTS**
456 Highway 4  (62966-4205)
PHONE.................................618 684-5167
Dan Alstat, *Owner*
Sara Alstat, *Manager*
**EMP:** 10  EST: 1985
**SALES (est):** 1.4MM  **Privately Held**
**SIC:** 2421  Sawmills & planing mills, general

**(G-15572)**
**BLUFFS VINEYARD & WINERY L L C**
1505 Business Highway 13  (62966-2972)
PHONE.................................618 763-4447
Steve Ellis, *Principal*
**EMP:** 4
**SALES (est):** 113.8K  **Privately Held**
**SIC:** 2084  Wines

**(G-15573)**
**BREES STUDIO INC**
430 S 19th St  (62966-2401)
PHONE.................................618 687-3331
Gary Brees, *President*
Megan Barrett, *General Mgr*
Deborah Brees, *General Mgr*
Ashley Gierke, *Manager*
Nelson Knapp, *Manager*
**EMP:** 10
**SQ FT:** 18,000
**SALES (est):** 940K  **Privately Held**
**WEB:** www.breesstudio.com
**SIC:** 3999  Artificial trees & flowers

**(G-15574)**
**BURKE WHISTLES INC**
389 Wells St  (62966-7023)
PHONE.................................618 534-7953
Michael D Burke, *President*
Susan P Burke, *Admin Sec*
**EMP:** 2
**SQ FT:** 800
**SALES (est):** 240K  **Privately Held**
**SIC:** 3999  Whistles

**(G-15575)**
**CMT INTERNATIONAL INC**
1400 N Wood Rd  (62966-6290)
P.O. Box 3254, Carbondale  (62902-3254)
PHONE.................................618 549-1829
Fax: 618 549-7090
Ming-Tsang Chang, *President*
Monica Lien, *Corp Secy*
Lori Arend, *Human Res Mgr*
Sharon Fletcher, *Manager*
Wu Samuel, *Manager*
▲ **EMP:** 6
**SQ FT:** 1,300
**SALES (est):** 6.3MM  **Privately Held**
**WEB:** www.cmtint.com
**SIC:** 3089  Plastic processing

**(G-15576)**
**HARTMANN**
29 Steven Dr  (62966-4236)
PHONE.................................618 684-6814
Beth Hartmann, *Principal*
**EMP:** 3
**SALES (est):** 250.1K  **Privately Held**
**SIC:** 3161  Wardrobe bags (luggage)

**(G-15577)**
**JACOBS TRUCKING**
3191 W Harrison Rd  (62966-4408)
P.O. Box 371  (62966-0371)
PHONE.................................618 687-3578
Fax: 618 684-8481
Greg Jacob, *Owner*
**EMP:** 7
**SALES (est):** 660.5K  **Privately Held**
**WEB:** www.jacobstrucking.sdcoxmail.com
**SIC:** 4212  3274  5032  4959  Dump truck haulage; lime; stone, crushed or broken; snowplowing; driveway contractor; top soil

**(G-15578)**
**MARLOW HILL DRILLING INC**
107 Old Kimmel Bridge Rd  (62966-4677)
PHONE.................................618 867-2978
Tony Dowdy, *President*
**EMP:** 14
**SALES (est):** 1MM  **Privately Held**
**SIC:** 1389  Mud service, oil field drilling

**(G-15579)**
**PENN ALUMINUM INTL LLC (DH)**
1117 N 2nd St  (62966-3332)
PHONE.................................618 684-2146
Fax: 618 684-3866
Bruce Hoffman, *Business Mgr*
Bruce Castan, *Vice Pres*
Michelle Dailey, *Materials Mgr*
Adam Boss, *Safety Mgr*
Paul Crawford, *Safety Mgr*
**EMP:** 226
**SQ FT:** 200,000
**SALES (est):** 42.6MM
**SALES (corp-wide):** 223.6B  **Publicly Held**
**WEB:** www.pennaluminum.com
**SIC:** 3354  3334  3312  5051  Tube, extruded or drawn, aluminum; primary aluminum; blast furnaces & steel mills; aluminum bars, rods, ingots, sheets, pipes, plates, etc.
**HQ:** Marmon Group Llc
181 W Madison St Ste 2600
Chicago IL 60602
312 372-9500

**(G-15580)**
**POPULAR RIDGE MACHINE MET CFT**
134 S Jungle Rd  (62966-6329)
PHONE.................................618 687-1656
Michael Collins, *Principal*
**EMP:** 3
**SALES (est):** 235K  **Privately Held**
**SIC:** 3599  Machine shop, jobbing & repair

**(G-15581)**
**QUALITY COVE**
1 Apple City Ctr  (62966-4685)
PHONE.................................618 684-5900
Roger Twenhafel, *Principal*
**EMP:** 4
**SALES (est):** 501.8K  **Privately Held**
**SIC:** 3553  Cabinet makers' machinery

## GEOGRAPHIC SECTION
### Naperville - Dupage County (G-15609)

**(G-15582)**
**SCHULZE & SCHULZE INC**
3198 Town Creek Rd (62966-5375)
PHONE..................................618 687-1106
David Schulze, *President*
EMP: 5
SALES (est): 594.1K **Privately Held**
WEB: www.egyptiansealcoating.com
SIC: **2951** 1629 1611 Asphalt paving mixtures & blocks; tennis court construction; highway & street construction

**(G-15583)**
**SILKWORM INC**
Also Called: Silkworm Screen Printing
102 S Sezmore Dr (62966-7046)
P.O. Box 340 (62966-0340)
PHONE..................................618 687-4077
Fax: 618 684-4515
Robert Chambers, *President*
Cheryl Endres, *Vice Pres*
Thomas Henderson, *Opers Staff*
Julie Sellers, *Accounts Mgr*
Mike Bergman, *Accounts Exec*
EMP: 56
SQ FT: 31,000
SALES (est): 7.4MM **Privately Held**
WEB: www.silkwormink.com
SIC: **2759** Screen printing

**(G-15584)**
**SOUTHERN BLOOMS LLC**
550 E Industrial Park Rd # 17 (62966-3951)
PHONE..................................618 565-1111
Rowena K Redden, *Owner*
EMP: 5
SALES: 8MM **Privately Held**
SIC: **3999** Flowers, artificial & preserved

**(G-15585)**
**THIRTEEN RF INC**
Also Called: 13rf Rental & Fabrication
10 Alliance Ave (62966)
P.O. Box 1556 (62966-5056)
PHONE..................................618 687-1313
Nancy Fricke, *President*
Renee Moniger, *Accountant*
Randall Fricke, *Admin Sec*
EMP: 30
SALES: 2.3MM **Privately Held**
SIC: **3449** Bars, concrete reinforcing: fabricated steel

**(G-15586)**
**WILDLIFE MATERIALS INC**
1202 Walnut St (62966-2124)
PHONE..................................618 687-3505
William Liao, *CEO*
Richard Blanchard, *President*
Bridget Walsh, *Manager*
▲ EMP: 45
SQ FT: 15,000
SALES (est): 7.2MM **Privately Held**
WEB: www.wildlifematerials.com
SIC: **3699** Electrical equipment & supplies

### Naperville
### Dupage County

**(G-15587)**
**AC NALCO CHEMICAL CO**
1601 W Diehl Rd (60563-0130)
PHONE..................................630 305-1000
Randall Christner, *Plant Mgr*
Katie Townsend, *Auditing Mgr*
James Gage, *Manager*
Steve Paulson, *Manager*
EMP: 10
SALES (est): 30.2K **Privately Held**
SIC: **3589** Water treatment equipment, industrial

**(G-15588)**
**ACCURATE REPRO INC**
2368 Corporate Ln Ste 100 (60563-9631)
PHONE..................................630 428-4433
Fax: 630 428-4449
Michael A Pavetto, *President*
Michael J Merle, *Vice Pres*
Mike Pavetti, *Credit Mgr*
Scott Ladendorf, *Accounts Mgr*
Celeste Chaney, *Office Mgr*
EMP: 14
SQ FT: 10,000
SALES (est): 1.5MM **Privately Held**
SIC: **7334** 3993 Photocopying & duplicating services; blueprinting service; signs & advertising specialties

**(G-15589)**
**ACE GRAPHICS INC**
2052 Corporate Ln (60563-9691)
PHONE..................................630 357-2244
Fax: 630 357-2266
Rodney Kranz, *President*
Kaitlyn Battey, *Project Mgr*
Jessica Martin, *Project Mgr*
Beth Kranz, *Treasurer*
Chris Synal, *Manager*
▲ EMP: 20
SQ FT: 22,000
SALES (est): 4.5MM **Privately Held**
WEB: www.acegraphics.com
SIC: **2752** Commercial printing, lithographic

**(G-15590)**
**ADAMS MACHINE SHOP**
1223 Arthur Rd (60540-6901)
PHONE..................................630 851-6060
Casimir Adams, *Owner*
EMP: 4 EST: 1944
SQ FT: 5,000
SALES: 60K **Privately Held**
SIC: **3429** Piano hardware

**(G-15591)**
**ADVANCED ROBOTICS RESEARCH**
791 Sigmund Rd (60563-1391)
PHONE..................................630 544-0040
Bruce Taneja, *Principal*
Meena Taneja, *Principal*
EMP: 4
SALES (est): 180K **Privately Held**
SIC: **3549** 8733 7389 Assembly machines, including robotic; scientific research agency;

**(G-15592)**
**ADVANTAGE OPTICS INC**
Also Called: Interoptic
1555 Bond St Ste 115 (60563-0138)
PHONE..................................630 548-9870
Timothy Dixon, *CEO*
Anthony Masella, *Vice Pres*
Mary Masella, *Vice Pres*
Catherine Wundsam, *Vice Pres*
EMP: 12
SALES (est): 2.2MM **Privately Held**
WEB: www.advantageoptics.com
SIC: **3661** Fiber optics communications equipment

**(G-15593)**
**ALBRIGHT ENTERPRISES INC**
Also Called: Signs Now
426 W 5th Ave (60563-2985)
PHONE..................................630 357-2300
Stan Albright, *President*
Theresa Goss, *Office Mgr*
Scott Milgrom, *Manager*
Rachel Albright, *Admin Sec*
EMP: 8
SQ FT: 1,900
SALES (est): 610K **Privately Held**
SIC: **3993** Signs & advertising specialties

**(G-15594)**
**ALCATEL-LUCENT USA INC**
2000 Lucent Ln (60563-1443)
PHONE..................................630 979-0210
Kenneth Peluso, *Branch Mgr*
EMP: 20
SALES (corp-wide): 13.4B **Privately Held**
WEB: www.lucent.com
SIC: **3661** Telephone & telegraph apparatus
HQ: Alcatel-Lucent Usa Inc.
600 Mountain Ave Ste 700
New Providence NJ 07974

**(G-15595)**
**ALE USA INC**
1960 Nperville Wheaton Rd (60563-1594)
PHONE..................................630 713-5194
Karen Plonty, *Technical Mgr*
Daisy Su, *Marketing Mgr*
Tom Giers, *Manager*
Lawrence Algee, *Director*
EMP: 5
SALES (est): 324.4K **Privately Held**
SIC: **3663** Radio & TV communications equipment

**(G-15596)**
**ALL STAR CUSTOM AWARDS**
1203 Hidden Spring Dr (60540-4113)
PHONE..................................630 428-1515
Rick Belle, *Owner*
EMP: 1
SALES: 230K **Privately Held**
SIC: **3499** Novelties & giftware, including trophies

**(G-15597)**
**ALL STAR PUBLISHING**
1203 Hidden Spring Dr (60540-4113)
PHONE..................................630 428-1515
Rick Belle, *Principal*
EMP: 3
SALES (est): 144.9K **Privately Held**
SIC: **2711** Newspapers: publishing only, not printed on site

**(G-15598)**
**ALSTOM TRANSPORTATION INC**
1001 Frontenac Rd (60563-1746)
PHONE..................................630 369-2201
Jerome Wallut, *Principal*
Michael Carrato, *Principal*
Diana Zeno, *Buyer*
Justin Bulpitt, *Controller*
Ian Brodie, *Manager*
EMP: 28
SALES (est): 15.4MM **Privately Held**
SIC: **3321** Railroad car wheels & brake shoes, cast iron

**(G-15599)**
**ARCAM CAD TO METAL INC**
55 Shuman Blvd Ste 850 (60563-7917)
PHONE..................................630 357-5700
Glen Liddell, *Admin Sec*
▲ EMP: 3
SALES (est): 320K **Privately Held**
SIC: **3549** Metalworking machinery

**(G-15600)**
**ARCH CHEMICALS INC**
940 E Diehl Rd Ste 110 (60563-4810)
P.O. Box 2557 (60567-2557)
PHONE..................................630 955-0401
Lorena O'Neill, *Marketing Staff*
EMP: 12
SALES (corp-wide): 4B **Privately Held**
WEB: www.archchemicals.com
SIC: **2819** 2899 Industrial inorganic chemicals; chemical preparations
HQ: Arch Chemicals, Inc.
1200 Bluegrass Lakes Pkwy
Alpharetta GA 30004
678 624-5800

**(G-15601)**
**ASPEN PRINTING SERVICES LLC**
405 S River Rd (60540-5036)
PHONE..................................630 357-3203
Mark Botos, *Mng Member*
Justin Botos, *Manager*
EMP: 2
SALES (est): 313.7K **Privately Held**
WEB: www.aspenprint.net
SIC: **2759** Commercial printing

**(G-15602)**
**BAKER LA RUSSO**
Also Called: Baker's Custom Lettering
911 Joan Ct (60540-1931)
PHONE..................................630 788-5108
La Russo Baker, *Owner*
EMP: 4
SALES (est): 170K **Privately Held**
SIC: **2759** Screen printing

**(G-15603)**
**BEARD ENTERPRISES INC**
Also Called: Fastsigns
931 E Ogden Ave Ste 127 (60563-4852)
PHONE..................................630 357-3278
Fax: 630 357-5117
John Cornbleet, *President*
Mike Bowers, *Asst Mgr*
EMP: 5
SQ FT: 1,500
SALES (est): 750.9K **Privately Held**
SIC: **3993** Signs & advertising specialties

**(G-15604)**
**BECTON DICKINSON AND COMPANY**
Also Called: B D Medical Systems-Injection
5 E 14th Ave (60563-2716)
PHONE..................................630 428-3499
EMP: 5
SALES (corp-wide): 12.4B **Publicly Held**
SIC: **2834** Drugs affecting neoplasms & endocrine systems
PA: Becton, Dickinson And Company
1 Becton Dr
Franklin Lakes NJ 07417
201 847-6800

**(G-15605)**
**BERNARD CFFEY VTRANS FUNDATION**
1634 Mulligan Dr (60563-1786)
PHONE..................................630 687-0033
Bernard Coffey, *CEO*
EMP: 6
SALES (est): 434.7K **Privately Held**
SIC: **1521** 3272 3585 7997 Single-family housing construction; housing components, prefabricated concrete; heating & air conditioning combination units; indoor/outdoor court clubs

**(G-15606)**
**BITZER PRODUCTS COMPANY**
2222 Allegany Dr (60565-3415)
P.O. Box 6599, Maywood (60155-6599)
PHONE..................................708 345-0795
Fax: 708 345-2791
Roger Zlotoff, *CEO*
Raymond Coopman, *President*
Steve May, *Plant Mgr*
Don Koziel, *Sales Mgr*
Dorris Uccardi, *Manager*
EMP: 20
SQ FT: 7,800
SALES (est): 2.5MM **Privately Held**
WEB: www.bitzerproducts.com
SIC: **3599** Machine shop, jobbing & repair

**(G-15607)**
**BONECO NORTH AMERICA CORP**
Also Called: Plaston
1801 N Mill St Ste A (60563-4869)
PHONE..................................630 983-3294
Fax: 630 983-5620
Pavel Reimann, *President*
▲ EMP: 2
SALES (est): 463K **Privately Held**
SIC: **3634** Air purifiers, portable

**(G-15608)**
**BP AMOCO CHEMICAL COMPANY**
150 W Warrenville Rd (60563-8473)
PHONE..................................630 420-5111
N C Dunn, *President*
L M Sierra, *President*
Judy Ventura, *President*
David Hwang, *Top Exec*
Anne Cody, *Senior VP*
◆ EMP: 260
SQ FT: 50,000
SALES (est): 6.7MM
SALES (corp-wide): 183B **Privately Held**
SIC: **2221** 2821 2869 2819 Broadwoven fabric mills, manmade; styrene resins; industrial organic chemicals; industrial inorganic chemicals; cyclic organic crudes
HQ: Bp Corporation North America Inc.
501 Westlake Park Blvd
Houston TX 77079
281 366-2000

**(G-15609)**
**BP PRODUCTS NORTH AMERICA INC**
Also Called: Amoco
150 W Warrenville Rd (60563-8473)
PHONE..................................630 420-4300
Fax: 630 420-3698
Tom Bond, *Manager*
Charles Damianides, *Manager*

# Naperville - Dupage County (G-15610) — GEOGRAPHIC SECTION

Thomas Gebhard, *Manager*
Alison Tyler, *Senior Mgr*
Mary Kelly, *MIS Mgr*
**EMP:** 5
**SALES (corp-wide):** 183B **Privately Held**
**WEB:** www.bpproductsnorthamerica.com
**SIC:** 2911 5171 5541 4612 Petroleum refining; petroleum bulk stations & terminals; gasoline service stations; crude petroleum pipelines; refined petroleum pipelines; crude petroleum & natural gas
**HQ:** Bp Products North America Inc.
501 Westlake Park Blvd
Houston TX 77079
281 366-2000

## (G-15610)
### BP SHIPPING
150 W Warrenville Rd (60563-8473)
**PHONE**.................................630 393-1032
John Rigway, *President*
Patricia Clayton, *Manager*
Creg Larkin, *Manager*
◆ **EMP:** 14
**SALES (est):** 1.7MM **Privately Held**
**SIC:** 2441 Shipping cases, wood: nailed or lock corner

## (G-15611)
### BP SOLAR INTERNATIONAL INC
150 W Warrenville Rd (60563-8473)
**PHONE**.................................301 698-4200
Reyad Fezzani, *CEO*
Richard Bartlett, *Vice Pres*
Eric Daniels, *Vice Pres*
Andy Dutschmann, *Vice Pres*
Mark Kerstens, *Vice Pres*
▲ **EMP:** 585
**SQ FT:** 100,000
**SALES (est):** 52.5MM
**SALES (corp-wide):** 183B **Privately Held**
**WEB:** www.bpsolar.com
**SIC:** 3674 3433 Solar cells; silicon wafers, chemically doped; heating equipment, except electric
**HQ:** Amoco Technology Company (Del)
200 E Randolph St # 2100
Chicago IL 60601
312 861-6000

## (G-15612)
### BRAD FOOTE GEAR WORKS INC
47 E Chicago Ave Ste 332 (60540-5360)
**PHONE**.................................708 298-1100
**EMP:** 3
**SALES (corp-wide):** 180.8MM **Publicly Held**
**SIC:** 3566 Speed changers, drives & gears
**HQ:** Brad Foote Gear Works, Inc.
3250 S Central Ave
Cicero IL 60804
708 298-1100

## (G-15613)
### C H HANSON COMPANY (PA)
2000 N Aurora Rd (60563-8793)
**PHONE**.................................630 848-2000
**Fax:** 630 848-2515
Craig F Hanson, *President*
Kimberly M Bork, *Corp Secy*
Gordon A Vogel, *VP Mfg*
Philip C Hanson, *Asst Treas*
Tom Browne, *Sales Staff*
▲ **EMP:** 75 **EST:** 1866
**SALES (est):** 25.1MM **Privately Held**
**WEB:** www.chhanson.com
**SIC:** 3953 5085 5099 5112 Marking devices; stencils, painting & marking; date stamps, hand: rubber or metal; cancelling stamps, hand: rubber or metal; adhesives, tape & plasters; signs, except electric; pens &/or pencils; piece goods & other fabrics; identification tags, except paper

## (G-15614)
### C H HANSON COMPANY
2000 N Aurora Rd (60563-8793)
**PHONE**.................................630 848-2000
Jeff Ceres, *Branch Mgr*
**EMP:** 11
**SALES (corp-wide):** 25.1MM **Privately Held**
**WEB:** www.chhanson.com
**SIC:** 3953 Marking devices

**PA:** The C H Hanson Company
2000 N Aurora Rd
Naperville IL 60563
630 848-2000

## (G-15615)
### CALL POTENTIAL LLC
24047 W Lockport St (60540)
**PHONE**.................................877 552-2557
John Murphy, *Mng Member*
**EMP:** 13 **EST:** 2011
**SQ FT:** 2,000
**SALES (est):** 316K **Privately Held**
**SIC:** 7372 Business oriented computer software

## (G-15616)
### CARGILL INCORPORATED
400 E Diehl Rd Ste 330 (60563-3533)
**PHONE**.................................630 505-7788
Pete Richter, *Manager*
Sreeram Reddy, *Supervisor*
**EMP:** 25
**SALES (corp-wide):** 107.1B **Privately Held**
**WEB:** www.cargill.com
**SIC:** 2046 0723 Wet corn milling; corn milling by-products; grain milling, custom services
**PA:** Cargill, Incorporated
15407 Mcginty Rd W
Wayzata MN 55391
952 742-7575

## (G-15617)
### CARLIN MFG A DIV GRS HOLDG LLC
131 W Jefferson Ave # 223 (60540-4682)
**PHONE**.................................559 276-0123
Kari Franz, *Manager*
Ralph H Goldbeck,
Ralph Goldbeck,
Steven Rubin,
Frederick Stowell,
**EMP:** 25
**SALES:** 3.5MM **Privately Held**
**SIC:** 2451 Mobile buildings: for commercial use

## (G-15618)
### CAROL ANDRZEJEWSKI
Also Called: Designer Blinds
2339 Kalamazoo Dr (60565-6361)
**PHONE**.................................630 369-9711
Carol Andrzejewski, *Principal*
**EMP:** 4 **EST:** 2010
**SALES (est):** 391K **Privately Held**
**SIC:** 2591 Window blinds

## (G-15619)
### CARROLL DISTRG & CNSTR SUP INC
1700 Quincy Ave (60540-4176)
**PHONE**.................................630 369-6520
Mike Kozacek, *Branch Mgr*
**EMP:** 18
**SALES (est):** 75.9MM **Privately Held**
**SIC:** 5082 3444 Contractors' materials; concrete forms, sheet metal
**PA:** Carroll Distributing & Construction Supply, Inc.
205 S Iowa Ave
Ottumwa IA 52501
641 683-1888

## (G-15620)
### CASTROL INDUSTRIAL N AMER INC (DH)
150 W Warrenville Rd (60563-8473)
**PHONE**.................................877 641-1600
Dave Feurst, *President*
Keith Campbell, *General Mgr*
Carl Paulsen, *Vice Pres*
Chuck Kosner, *Purchasing*
Ray Sweeney, *Finance*
◆ **EMP:** 225
**SQ FT:** 40,000
**SALES (est):** 74.2MM
**SALES (corp-wide):** 183B **Privately Held**
**WEB:** www.lubecon.com
**SIC:** 2992 2899 Lubricating oils & greases; corrosion preventive lubricant; rust resisting compounds

**HQ:** Bp America Inc
4101 Winfield Rd Ste 200
Warrenville IL 60555
630 420-5111

## (G-15621)
### CATALYTIC INC ◆
23 W Jefferson Ave Fl 2 (60540-8416)
**PHONE**.................................312 927-8750
Sean Chou, *CEO*
**EMP:** 8 **EST:** 2016
**SQ FT:** 700
**SALES (est):** 218K **Privately Held**
**SIC:** 7372 Business oriented computer software

## (G-15622)
### CCS CONTRACTOR EQP & SUP INC (PA)
Also Called: Just Rite Rental
1567 Frontenac Rd (60563-1754)
**PHONE**.................................630 393-9020
Ray Barthyolomae, *President*
Lorri Buss, *Manager*
Thomas Fahey, *Admin Sec*
▲ **EMP:** 33
**SQ FT:** 20,000
**SALES (est):** 27MM **Privately Held**
**SIC:** 5032 5082 7359 3444 Concrete building products; concrete processing equipment; equipment rental & leasing; concrete forms, sheet metal

## (G-15623)
### CDA INDUSTRIES INC
1228 Jane Ave (60540-5638)
**PHONE**.................................630 357-7654
Mark Goralski, *Corp Comm Staff*
**EMP:** 3
**SALES (corp-wide):** 16.7MM **Privately Held**
**SIC:** 3496 Miscellaneous fabricated wire products
**PA:** Cda Industries Inc
1055 Squires Beach Rd
Pickering ON L1W 4
905 686-7000

## (G-15624)
### CENTRAL NEWSPAPER INCORPORATED
40 Shuman Blvd Ste 305 (60563-8656)
**PHONE**.................................630 416-4191
Michael D Haddad, *Principal*
**EMP:** 3
**SALES (est):** 164.4K **Privately Held**
**SIC:** 2711 Newspapers

## (G-15625)
### CHICAGO CHINESE TIMES
424 Fort Hill Dr Ste 100 (60540-3909)
**PHONE**.................................630 717-4567
Danny Lee, *President*
Jwo Hwa Lee, *President*
Wea Lee, *Shareholder*
▲ **EMP:** 5
**SALES (est):** 390.2K **Privately Held**
**WEB:** www.chicagochinesenews.com
**SIC:** 2711 Newspapers, publishing & printing

## (G-15626)
### CHICAGO CONTRACT BRIDGE ASSN (PA)
1624 Masters Ct (60563-1781)
P.O. Box 2858 (60567-2858)
**PHONE**.................................630 355-5560
Jackie Addis, *President*
Sue Weinstein, *Admin Sec*
**EMP:** 5
**SALES:** 199.8K **Privately Held**
**WEB:** www.bridgeinchicago.com
**SIC:** 2678 3944 Stationery: made from purchased materials; games, toys & children's vehicles

## (G-15627)
### CHICAGO RIVET & MACHINE CO (PA)
901 Frontenac Rd (60563-1744)
P.O. Box 3061 (60566-7061)
**PHONE**.................................630 357-8500
**Fax:** 630 983-9314
John A Morrissey, *Ch of Bd*
Michael J Bourg, *President*

**EMP:** 131
**SALES:** 37MM **Publicly Held**
**WEB:** www.chicagorivetsw.com
**SIC:** 3452 3542 7359 3451 Rivets, metal; riveting machines; equipment rental & leasing; screw machine products

## (G-15628)
### CHILD EVNGELISM FELLOWSHIP INC
365 Du Pahze St (60565-3052)
**PHONE**.................................630 983-7708
Joshua Chang, *Branch Mgr*
**EMP:** 41
**SALES (corp-wide):** 28.6MM **Privately Held**
**SIC:** 2752 Commercial printing, lithographic
**PA:** Child Evangelism Fellowship Incorporated
17482 Highway M
Warrenton MO 63383
636 456-4321

## (G-15629)
### CHINA YING INC
1567 N Aurora Rd Ste 139 (60563-0727)
**PHONE**.................................630 428-2638
Tony Ou, *Owner*
**EMP:** 5
**SALES (est):** 194.3K **Privately Held**
**SIC:** 2741 Miscellaneous publishing

## (G-15630)
### CLOYES GEAR AND PRODUCTS INC
Also Called: Mesh Company
1152 Frontenac Rd (60563-1749)
**PHONE**.................................630 420-0900
Haun Porter, *Branch Mgr*
**EMP:** 40
**SALES (corp-wide):** 3.9B **Publicly Held**
**WEB:** www.cloyes.com
**SIC:** 3714 Gears, motor vehicle
**HQ:** Cloyes Gear And Products, Inc.
7800 Ball Rd
Fort Smith AR 72908
479 646-1662

## (G-15631)
### COGNEX CORPORATION
800 E Diehl Rd Ste 125 (60563-7871)
**PHONE**.................................630 505-9990
**EMP:** 3
**SALES (corp-wide):** 486.2MM **Publicly Held**
**SIC:** 3823 Mfg Process Control Instruments
**PA:** Cognex Corporation
1 Vision Dr
Natick MA 01760
508 650-3000

## (G-15632)
### COLBERTS CUSTOM FRAMING
1283 S Naper Blvd (60540-8300)
**PHONE**.................................630 717-1448
Kevin Colbert, *Owner*
**EMP:** 11
**SQ FT:** 2,000
**SALES (est):** 610K **Privately Held**
**SIC:** 2499 5999 Picture & mirror frames, wood; picture frames, ready made

## (G-15633)
### CONAGRA BRANDS INC
Also Called: Hunt Foods Company
750 E Diehl Rd Ste 111 (60563-4804)
**PHONE**.................................630 857-1000
**Fax:** 630 955-0828
**EMP:** 173
**SALES (corp-wide):** 11.6B **Publicly Held**
**SIC:** 2099 2038 2013 Food preparations; dessert mixes & fillings; seasonings & spices; ready-to-eat meals, salads & sandwiches; frozen specialties; dinners, frozen & packaged; lunches, frozen & packaged; sausages & other prepared meats
**PA:** Conagra Brands, Inc.
222 Merchandise Mart Plz
Chicago IL 60654
312 549-5000

▲ = Import ▼ = Export
◆ = Import/Export

## GEOGRAPHIC SECTION
## Naperville - Dupage County (G-15661)

**(G-15634)**
**CONCRETE 1 INC**
Also Called: R & J Ready Mix
429 E 8th Ave (60563-3205)
**PHONE**..................630 357-1329
Richard Downs, *President*
Jakeda J Downs, *Admin Sec*
**EMP:** 7 **EST:** 1999
**SALES (est):** 656.4K **Privately Held**
**SIC:** 3273 Ready-mixed concrete

**(G-15635)**
**COOKIE DOUGH CREATIONS CO**
22 W Chicago Ave Ste H (60540-8541)
**PHONE**..................630 369-4833
James W Bewersdorf, *President*
**EMP:** 20
**SQ FT:** 1,400
**SALES (est):** 2.9MM **Privately Held**
**WEB:** www.cookiedoughcreations.com
**SIC:** 2051 5947 5149 2052 Bakery: wholesale or wholesale/retail combined; gift, novelty & souvenir shop; crackers, cookies & bakery products; cookies & crackers

**(G-15636)**
**CORIANT OPERATIONS INC (PA)**
1415 W Diehl Rd (60563-2349)
P.O. Box 3220 (60566-7220)
**PHONE**..................847 382-8817
Shaygan Kheradpir, *Ch of Bd*
Pat Dipietro, *Vice Ch Bd*
Ken Craft, *Exec VP*
Tarcisio Ribeiro, *Exec VP*
Thomas Cooke, *Senior VP*
▲ **EMP:** 20
**SQ FT:** 850,000
**SALES (est):** 803.8MM **Privately Held**
**WEB:** www.tellabsoperations.com
**SIC:** 3661 Telephone & telegraph apparatus

**(G-15637)**
**CORYDON CONVERTING COMPANY INC**
1350 Shore Rd Ste 120 (60563-1099)
**PHONE**..................630 898-9896
Fax: 630 898-7731
William Dunbar, *Manager*
**EMP:** 12
**SALES (corp-wide):** 6.1MM **Privately Held**
**WEB:** www.corydonconverting.com
**SIC:** 2679 Paper products, converted
**PA:** Corydon Converting Company, Inc.
1350 Shore Rd Ste 120
Naperville IL 60563
630 983-1900

**(G-15638)**
**CORYDON CONVERTING COMPANY INC (PA)**
1350 Shore Rd Ste 120 (60563-1099)
P.O. Box 1388, Aurora (60507-1388)
**PHONE**..................630 983-1900
William Dunbar, *President*
Robert McCaffrey, *Vice Pres*
Sergio Gimenec, *Plant Mgr*
Robert Stratman, *Project Mgr*
Kris Soucie, *Office Mgr*
◆ **EMP:** 25
**SQ FT:** 35,000
**SALES (est):** 6.1MM **Privately Held**
**WEB:** www.corydonconverting.com
**SIC:** 2679 Paper products, converted

**(G-15639)**
**COZENT LLC**
2135 City Gate Ln Ste 300 (60563-3066)
**PHONE**..................630 781-2822
Al Kannan,
**EMP:** 9
**SQ FT:** 16,000
**SALES:** 1.4MM **Privately Held**
**SIC:** 7372 Prepackaged software

**(G-15640)**
**CYMATICS INC**
31w280 Diehl Rd Ste 104 (60563-1066)
P.O. Box 448 (60566-0448)
**PHONE**..................630 420-7117
Nancy Mikyska, *President*
Glenn E Mikyska, *President*
Lynn Mikyska, *Vice Pres*
**EMP:** 6
**SQ FT:** 5,000
**SALES (est):** 886.5K **Privately Held**
**WEB:** www.cymaticsinc.com
**SIC:** 3612 3613 3825 Electronic meter transformers; control panels, electric; laboratory equipment: fume hoods, distillation racks, etc.; test equipment for electronic & electrical circuits

**(G-15641)**
**DALCO MARKETING SERVICES**
Also Called: Connections Company
216 Durham Ct (60540-5613)
**PHONE**..................630 961-3366
David A Lindblade, *Owner*
**EMP:** 5
**SALES (est):** 528.5K **Privately Held**
**SIC:** 5063 3679 Electrical apparatus & equipment; electronic circuits

**(G-15642)**
**DALEY AUTOMATION LLC (PA)**
1111 S Washington St (60540-7953)
**PHONE**..................630 384-9900
Gregory T Mizen, *Principal*
Tom McKevitt, *Marketing Staff*
Gregory Mizen,
Kurt Richardson,
**EMP:** 5 **EST:** 2015
**SQ FT:** 1,000
**SALES (est):** 576.3K **Privately Held**
**SIC:** 3599 3544 Custom machinery; special dies & tools

**(G-15643)**
**DALY ENGINEERED FILTRATION INC**
942 E Hillside Rd (60540-6809)
**PHONE**..................708 355-1550
William R Daly, *President*
**EMP:** 3
**SALES (est):** 367.1K **Privately Held**
**SIC:** 3677 Filtration devices, electronic

**(G-15644)**
**DAMIEN CORPORATION**
6s204 Cohasset Rd (60540-3535)
**PHONE**..................630 369-3549
Suzan N Anthaney, *President*
**EMP:** 5
**SALES (est):** 404.8K **Privately Held**
**WEB:** www.qdex.com
**SIC:** 2721 2741 2731 Periodicals: publishing only; miscellaneous publishing; book publishing

**(G-15645)**
**DIAMOND READY MIX INC**
27w742 North Ln (60540-6437)
**PHONE**..................630 355-5414
Robert Worley, *President*
**EMP:** 12
**SALES (est):** 1.7MM **Privately Held**
**SIC:** 3273 Ready-mixed concrete

**(G-15646)**
**DIEHL CONTROLS NORTH AMER INC**
1813 N Mill St Ste A (60563-4872)
**PHONE**..................630 955-9055
Ian Burman, *CEO*
Brent Wagner, *Engineer*
Shannon Carey, *Manager*
Rick Oppor, *Director*
**EMP:** 34
**SQ FT:** 12,266
**SALES (est):** 4.6MM
**SALES (corp-wide):** 3.3B **Privately Held**
**WEB:** www.diehlako.com
**SIC:** 7372 5064 Application computer software; appliance parts, household
**HQ:** Borg Instruments Inc.
701 Enterprise Dr
Delavan WI 53115

**(G-15647)**
**DIGITAL REALTY INC**
303 N Mill St (60540-4051)
**PHONE**..................630 428-7979
Ken Carn, *President*
Cristen M Carn, *Admin Sec*
**EMP:** 25
**SALES (est):** 2MM **Privately Held**
**SIC:** 7372 6531 Prepackaged software; real estate agents & managers

**(G-15648)**
**DOW AGROSCIENCES LLC**
1323 Dunrobin Rd (60540-8287)
**PHONE**..................630 428-8494
**EMP:** 100
**SALES (corp-wide):** 48.1B **Publicly Held**
**SIC:** 2879 Agricultural chemicals
**HQ:** Dow Agrosciences Llc
9330 Zionsville Rd
Indianapolis IN 46268
317 337-3000

**(G-15649)**
**E I T INC**
Also Called: Mark Promotions
2593 Arcadia Cir (60540-8394)
**PHONE**..................630 359-3543
Fax: 630 279-3420
Earl I Tobor, *Ch of Bd*
Mark Tobor, *President*
Beth Tobor, *Vice Pres*
Lucille S Tobor, *Admin Sec*
▲ **EMP:** 8
**SQ FT:** 15,000
**SALES:** 800K **Privately Held**
**SIC:** 3993 2399 5199 5131 Signs & advertising specialties; flags, fabric; advertising specialties; flags & banners; sales (including sales management) consultant

**(G-15650)**
**ECODYNE WATER TREATMENT LLC**
1270 Frontenac Rd (60563-1700)
P.O. Box 64420, Saint Paul MN (55164-0420)
**PHONE**..................630 961-5043
Fax: 630 671-8846
Ed Oneil, *Manager*
Patrick Oneill,
◆ **EMP:** 20 **EST:** 1957
**SQ FT:** 40,000
**SALES (est):** 4.1MM
**SALES (corp-wide):** 223.6B **Publicly Held**
**SIC:** 3589 Water treatment equipment, industrial; sewage treatment equipment
**HQ:** Marmon Holdings, Inc.
181 W Madison St Ste 2600
Chicago IL 60602
312 372-9500

**(G-15651)**
**EDGAR H FEY JEWELERS INC (PA)**
Also Called: Fey & Company
833 N Washington St (60563-3168)
**PHONE**..................708 352-4115
Fax: 708 352-7514
Thomas Fey, *President*
Marti Tracy, *Sales Mgr*
Edgar H Fey III, *Admin Sec*
**EMP:** 25
**SALES (est):** 4.8MM **Privately Held**
**SIC:** 3911 5944 5094 Jewelry, precious metal; jewelry, precious stones & precious metals; jewelry & precious stones

**(G-15652)**
**ELITEGEN CORP**
1112 Sheldon Ct (60540-1306)
**PHONE**..................630 637-6917
Ken Chou, *President*
Minhui KAO, *Consultant*
**EMP:** 14
**SALES (est):** 1.5MM **Privately Held**
**WEB:** www.elitegen.com
**SIC:** 7372 Prepackaged software

**(G-15653)**
**EMINENT TECHNOLOGIES LLC**
215 Shuman Blvd Ste 403 (60563-5100)
**PHONE**..................630 416-2311
**EMP:** 3
**SALES:** 950K **Privately Held**
**SIC:** 3582 Mfg Commercial Laundry Equipment

**(G-15654)**
**ENTRUST SERVICES LLC (PA)**
608 S Washington St (60540-6663)
**PHONE**..................630 699-9132
F Edward Gustafson, *President*
Steven Schuster, *Vice Pres*
J S Corcoran, *CFO*
Rosy Willson, *Admin Sec*
**EMP:** 7
**SQ FT:** 4,000
**SALES (est):** 40.5MM **Privately Held**
**WEB:** www.cgholdings.com
**SIC:** 2051 2819 2869 Bread, cake & related products; industrial inorganic chemicals; industrial organic chemicals

**(G-15655)**
**EVERGREEN RESOURCE INC**
3404 Frankstowne Dr 5 (60565-3550)
**PHONE**..................630 428-9077
Pei Wang, *President*
Xiao Zhong Geng, *Admin Sec*
▲ **EMP:** 3
**SALES (est):** 361.5K **Privately Held**
**SIC:** 3086 Packaging & shipping materials, foamed plastic

**(G-15656)**
**EXTREME TOOLS INC**
740 Frontenac Rd (60563-1709)
**PHONE**..................630 202-8324
Larry Greta, *President*
Larry Grela, *President*
Randy Cramer, *Manager*
▲ **EMP:** 4
**SQ FT:** 15,000
**SALES (est):** 1.3MM **Privately Held**
**WEB:** www.extremetools.net
**SIC:** 2441 Boxes, wood

**(G-15657)**
**FCA US LLC**
1980 High Grove Ln (60540-3934)
**PHONE**..................630 637-3000
Fax: 630 637-3050
**EMP:** 1126
**SALES (corp-wide):** 117.3B **Privately Held**
**SIC:** 3714 Motor vehicle parts & accessories
**HQ:** Fca Us Llc
1000 Chrysler Dr
Auburn Hills MI 48326

**(G-15658)**
**FINORIC LLC**
1263 Chalet Rd Apt 211n (60563-8997)
**PHONE**..................773 829-5811
Ambrish Kamdar,
▲ **EMP:** 4
**SALES (est):** 602K **Privately Held**
**SIC:** 2819 Industrial inorganic chemicals

**(G-15659)**
**FOOD PURVEYORS LOGISTICS**
760 Inland Cir Apt 101 (60563-0213)
**PHONE**..................630 229-6168
Andre Thomas, *Partner*
**EMP:** 15
**SQ FT:** 102,000
**SALES (est):** 1MM **Privately Held**
**SIC:** 2013 Smoked meats from purchased meat

**(G-15660)**
**FORECAST FIVE**
2135 City Gate Ln (60563-3018)
**PHONE**..................630 657-6400
Vladimir Dragosavljevic, *Principal*
Dan M Romano, *Senior VP*
Brad Richman, *Accounts Exec*
Dan Colbert, *Manager*
Jason Schoenleber, *Manager*
**EMP:** 3
**SALES (est):** 230.9K **Privately Held**
**SIC:** 7372 Business oriented computer software

**(G-15661)**
**G T C INDUSTRIES INC**
609 Sara Ln (60565-1611)
P.O. Box 2493 (60567-2493)
**PHONE**..................708 369-9815
Greg Weber, *President*
**EMP:** 4
**SQ FT:** 2,400

# Naperville - Dupage County (G-15662)

**SALES:** 200K **Privately Held**
**WEB:** www.missmarymusic.com
**SIC: 3679** 8748 3651 3564 Electronic circuits; business consulting; household audio & video equipment; blowers & fans

### (G-15662)
### GEA FARM TECHNOLOGIES INC (DH)
1880 Country Farm Dr (60563-1089)
**PHONE**.................................630 548-8200
Vern Foster, *President*
Matt Daley, *President*
Sanjeev Kaul, *General Mgr*
Ambrosini Angie, *Opers Staff*
Monica Jones, *Purch Mgr*
◆ **EMP:** 125 EST: 1906
**SQ FT:** 36,000
**SALES (est):** 199.3MM
**SALES (corp-wide):** 4.7B **Privately Held**
**WEB:** www.westfaliasurge.com
**SIC: 5083** 3523 2841 2842 Dairy machinery & equipment; dairy equipment (farm); detergents, synthetic organic or inorganic alkaline; sanitation preparations
**HQ:** Gea Westfalia Separator, Inc.
  100 Fairway Ct
  Northvale NJ 07647
  201 767-3900

### (G-15663)
### GELATO ENTERPRISES LLC
Also Called: Frost A Glato Shpp-Highland Pk
50 S Main St Ste 138 (60540-5485)
**PHONE**.................................630 210-8457
Edward G Bruksch,
**EMP:** 11
**SALES (est):** 1.1MM **Privately Held**
**SIC: 2024** Ice cream & frozen desserts

### (G-15664)
### GREIF INC
5s220 Frontenac Rd (60563-1711)
**PHONE**.................................630 961-9786
**Fax:** 630 961-1944
Harold Seacrest, *Plant Mgr*
Gail Crossen, *Personnel*
Harold Sechresst, *Manager*
**EMP:** 50
**SALES (corp-wide):** 3.3B **Publicly Held**
**SIC: 2655** 5085 Fiber cans, drums & similar products; commercial containers
**PA:** Greif, Inc.
  425 Winter Rd
  Delaware OH 43015
  740 549-6000

### (G-15665)
### GREIF INC
5 S 220 Frontenace Rd (60540)
**PHONE**.................................630 961-1842
Harold Sechrest, *Manager*
Harold Sechresst, *Manager*
**EMP:** 48
**SALES (corp-wide):** 3.3B **Publicly Held**
**WEB:** www.greif.com
**SIC: 2655** Drums, fiber: made from purchased material
**PA:** Greif, Inc.
  425 Winter Rd
  Delaware OH 43015
  740 549-6000

### (G-15666)
### GRS HOLDING LLC (PA)
Also Called: Kitchens To Go Built By Carlin
131 W Jefferson Ave # 223 (60540-4682)
**PHONE**.................................630 355-1660
Stevin Rubin, *Partner*
Steven Rubin, *Principal*
Frederick Stowell,
**EMP:** 9
**SALES (est):** 4.5MM **Privately Held**
**SIC: 3799** 1541 2452 6512 Trailers & trailer equipment; industrial buildings, new construction; prefabricated buildings, wood; commercial & industrial building operation; truck rental & leasing, no drivers; equipment rental & leasing

### (G-15667)
### GULFSTREAM AEROSPACE CORP
472 Quail Dr (60565-4162)
**PHONE**.................................630 470-9146
Jim Guerin, *Branch Mgr*
**EMP:** 1303
**SALES (corp-wide):** 31.3B **Publicly Held**
**SIC: 3721** Aircraft
**HQ:** Gulfstream Aerospace Corporation
  500 Gulfstream Rd
  Savannah GA 31408
  912 965-3000

### (G-15668)
### H K TELLABS LIMITED
1415 W Diehl Rd (60563-2349)
**PHONE**.................................630 445-5333
**EMP:** 3
**SALES (est):** 179.3K **Privately Held**
**SIC: 3661** Telephone & telegraph apparatus

### (G-15669)
### HAKWOOD
55 S Main St Ste 355 (60540-5381)
**PHONE**.................................630 219-3388
Robert Hak, *Principal*
Hans Alberts, *Director*
Peter Alejandro, *Director*
▲ **EMP:** 7 EST: 2012
**SALES (est):** 753.4K **Privately Held**
**SIC: 2426** 5023 Flooring, hardwood; floor coverings
**HQ:** Hakwood B.V.
  Leemansstraat 2
  Werkendam
  183 504-266

### (G-15670)
### HEMMERLE JR IRVIN
Also Called: Caid Tronics
1526 Treeline Ct (60565-2013)
**PHONE**.................................630 334-4392
Mary Hemmerle, *President*
**EMP:** 2
**SALES:** 200K **Privately Held**
**SIC: 3089** Identification cards, plastic

### (G-15671)
### I T C W INC
Also Called: Artganiks
584 Beaconsfield Ave (60565-4316)
**PHONE**.................................630 305-8849
Margaret Thomas, *President*
Dan Thomas, *Director*
**EMP:** 330
**SALES (est):** 13.5MM **Privately Held**
**WEB:** www.artganiks.com
**SIC: 8742** 3999 Management consulting services; framed artwork

### (G-15672)
### I2C LLC
1708 Chepstow Ct (60540-0395)
**PHONE**.................................630 281-2330
Datta Ajjampur,
**EMP:** 5
**SALES:** 200K **Privately Held**
**SIC: 7372** Prepackaged software

### (G-15673)
### INEOS AMERICAS LLC
150 W Warrenville Rd (60563-8473)
**PHONE**.................................630 857-7463
Martin Olavesen, *CFO*
Peter Grant, *Director*
John McNally, *Director*
**EMP:** 3
**SALES (corp-wide):** 40B **Privately Held**
**SIC: 2899** Chemical preparations
**HQ:** Ineos Americas Llc
  2600 S Shore Blvd Ste 500
  League City TX 77573
  281 535-6600

### (G-15674)
### INFOGIX INC (PA)
1240 E Diehl Rd Ste 400 (60563-4802)
**PHONE**.................................630 505-1800
Sumit Nijhawan, *President*
Angsuman Dutta, *Exec VP*
Greg McTee, *Exec VP*
Paul Skordilis, *Exec VP*
Thomas Penner, *Engineer*
**EMP:** 155
**SQ FT:** 42,000
**SALES (est):** 64.1MM **Privately Held**
**WEB:** www.infogix.com
**SIC: 7372** 8742 Business oriented computer software; management consulting services

### (G-15675)
### INNOVATIVE CUSTOM SOFTWARE INC
Also Called: Qt9 Software
1323 Bond St Ste 103 (60563-2368)
**PHONE**.................................630 892-5022
Brant Engelhart, *President*
Heather Engelhart, *Admin Sec*
**EMP:** 2
**SALES (est):** 393.9K **Privately Held**
**SIC: 7372** Prepackaged software

### (G-15676)
### INPLEX CUSTOM EXTRUDERS LLC
1657 Frontenac Rd (60563-1756)
**PHONE**.................................847 827-7046
**Fax:** 847 827-8015
Robert Anderson, *CEO*
Michael Long, *Plant Mgr*
Stan Stanton, *Site Mgr*
Mitchell Piecuch, *Controller*
Joe Tremback, *Controller*
**EMP:** 58
**SQ FT:** 36,000
**SALES (est):** 12.5MM **Privately Held**
**WEB:** www.inplexllc.com
**SIC: 3089** Plastic processing

### (G-15677)
### INTRATHERM LLC
1212 S Naper Blvd 119-221 (60540-8360)
**PHONE**.................................630 333-5419
Jerry Mraz,
**EMP:** 7
**SALES:** 150K **Privately Held**
**WEB:** www.intratherm.com
**SIC: 3841** Surgical & medical instruments

### (G-15678)
### IRONSAFE LLC
1807 W Diehl Rd (60563-1890)
P.O. Box 241352, Apple Valley MN (55124-1352)
**PHONE**.................................877 297-1833
Rick Ronchak, *CEO*
**EMP:** 4
**SALES (est):** 98.3K **Privately Held**
**SIC: 7372** Prepackaged software

### (G-15679)
### IRONWOOD MFG INC
Also Called: Hammer Source, The
24w260 Hemlock Ln (60540-9537)
**PHONE**.................................630 778-8963
Jennifer Ayers, *CEO*
Andrew A Ayers, *President*
◆ **EMP:** 2
**SQ FT:** 500
**SALES (est):** 242.8K **Privately Held**
**WEB:** www.hammersource.com
**SIC: 3423** 3999 Hammers (hand tools); barber & beauty shop equipment

### (G-15680)
### J REAM MANUFACTURING
31w280 Diehl Rd Ste 101 (60563-9624)
**PHONE**.................................630 983-6945
**Fax:** 630 983-6957
John R Fouser, *President*
Ken Cagle, *Engineer*
**EMP:** 5
**SQ FT:** 5,000
**SALES (est):** 1.2MM **Privately Held**
**SIC: 3624** 5063 Brushes & brush stock contacts, electric; motors, electric

### (G-15681)
### JEWEL OSCO INC
Also Called: Jewel-Osco 3059
1759 W Ogden Ave Ste A (60540-4205)
**PHONE**.................................630 355-2172
**Fax:** 630 637-1759
Jim Davis, *Manager*
Cindy Bienik, *Manager*
Tim Cesario, *Manager*
**EMP:** 152
**SALES (corp-wide):** 58.8B **Privately Held**
**WEB:** www.jewelosco.com
**SIC: 5411** 5912 2052 2051 Supermarkets, chain; drug stores & proprietary stores; cookies & crackers; bread, cake & related products
**HQ:** Jewel Osco, Inc.
  150 E Pierce Rd Ste 200
  Itasca IL 60143
  630 948-6000

### (G-15682)
### K & J PHILLIPS CORPORATION
Also Called: Sir Speedy
526 W 5th Ave (60563-2901)
**PHONE**.................................630 355-0660
**Fax:** 630 355-0779
Kent Phillips, *President*
Julie Phillips, *Vice Pres*
**EMP:** 5
**SQ FT:** 3,500
**SALES (est):** 600K **Privately Held**
**SIC: 2752** Commercial printing, lithographic

### (G-15683)
### K-C TOOL CO
552 S Washington St (60540-6658)
**PHONE**.................................630 983-5960
**Fax:** 630 983-5967
George Stockin, *President*
**EMP:** 8
**SALES (est):** 590K **Privately Held**
**SIC: 3546** 3545 3423 Power-driven handtools; machine tool accessories; hand & edge tools

### (G-15684)
### KOBAWALA POLY-PACK INC
800 W 5th Ave Ste 212 (60563-4949)
**PHONE**.................................312 664-3810
Ravindra Kobawala, *President*
Survi Kobawala, *Accounting Mgr*
Ashwin Shah, *CTO*
Rupak Kobawala, *Director*
Nehao Shah, *Director*
▲ **EMP:** 20
**SQ FT:** 120,000
**SALES (est):** 3.7MM **Privately Held**
**SIC: 2221** Polypropylene broadwoven fabrics

### (G-15685)
### L D REDMER SCREW PRODUCTS
448 Du Pahze St (60565-3100)
**PHONE**.................................630 787-0507
Walter Cofey, *Principal*
**EMP:** 3
**SALES (est):** 165.3K **Privately Held**
**SIC: 3451** Screw machine products

### (G-15686)
### LASER TECHNOLOGIES INC
1120 Frontenac Rd (60563-1749)
**PHONE**.................................630 761-1200
**Fax:** 630 761-1250
Keri L Foster, *President*
Jeffrey Foster, *Vice Pres*
Stanley Bourey, *Controller*
John Kus, *Sales Engr*
Keri Alwin, *Marketing Mgr*
▲ **EMP:** 147
**SQ FT:** 160,000
**SALES (est):** 36.2MM **Privately Held**
**WEB:** www.lasertechnologiesinc.com
**SIC: 3541** Machine tool replacement & repair parts, metal cutting types; numerically controlled metal cutting machine tools

### (G-15687)
### LEGACY VULCAN LLC
Midwest Division
1000 E Warrenville Rd (60563-1867)
**PHONE**.................................630 955-8500
Rob Vogl, *President*
William Glusac, *Div Sub Head*
David Danskin, *Engineer*
Ann Davidson, *Engineer*
Steve Merritt, *Senior Engr*
**EMP:** 85
**SALES (corp-wide):** 3.5B **Publicly Held**
**WEB:** www.vulcanmaterials.com
**SIC: 1442** Construction sand & gravel
**HQ:** Legacy Vulcan, Llc
  1200 Urban Center Dr
  Vestavia AL 35242
  205 298-3000

# GEOGRAPHIC SECTION
## Naperville - Dupage County (G-15710)

**(G-15688)**
**LIAM BREX**
222 S Main St (60540-5350)
PHONE..................630 848-0222
Liam Brex, *Principal*
EMP: 2
SALES (est): 271.1K Privately Held
SIC: 2542 Cabinets: show, display or storage: except wood

**(G-15689)**
**LIFETIME ROOFTILE COMPANY (PA)**
Also Called: Lifetime Roof Tile
1805 High Grove Ln (60540-3931)
PHONE..................630 355-7922
Richard Wehrli, *President*
Robert L Hammerschmidt, *Admin Sec*
EMP: 3
SALES (est): 1.4MM Privately Held
SIC: 3272 2952 Roofing tile & slabs, concrete; asphalt felts & coatings

**(G-15690)**
**LIGHTFOOT TECHNOLOGIES INC**
Also Called: Bluesun Hitech
2135 City Gate Ln Ste 300 (60563-3066)
PHONE..................331 302-1297
Shankar Krishnamoorthy, *President*
EMP: 6
SQ FT: 600
SALES (est): 1.2MM Privately Held
SIC: 3575 7371 Computer terminals; software programming applications

**(G-15691)**
**LIGHTNER PUBLISHING CORP (PA)**
Also Called: Antiques Cllecting Hobbies Mag
1849 Syracuse Rd (60565-6763)
PHONE..................312 939-4767
Fax: 312 939-0053
Dale K Graham, *President*
Frances Graham, *Corp Secy*
Greg Graham, *Vice Pres*
EMP: 10 EST: 1931
SQ FT: 5,000
SALES (est): 915.3K Privately Held
WEB: www.acmagazine.com
SIC: 2721 6512 Magazines: publishing only, not printed on site; commercial & industrial building operation

**(G-15692)**
**LINDE LLC**
Boc Gases
1751 W Diehl Rd Ste 300 (60563-4800)
PHONE..................630 515-2576
Fax: 630 515-2529
Ed Snype, *Plant Mgr*
Jay Slaughter, *Sales & Mktg St*
Andy Harder, *Manager*
EMP: 25
SALES (corp-wide): 17.9B Privately Held
SIC: 2813 Industrial gases
HQ: Linde Llc
200 Somerset Corporate Bl
Bridgewater NJ 08807
908 464-8100

**(G-15693)**
**LSSP CORPORATION**
109 S Stauffer Dr (60540-4133)
PHONE..................630 428-0099
Patrick Caruso, *President*
EMP: 6
SALES (est): 640K Privately Held
SIC: 3695 Computer software tape & disks: blank, rigid & floppy

**(G-15694)**
**LUBRIZOL CORPORATION**
40 Shuman Blvd Ste 264 (60563-7960)
PHONE..................630 355-3605
Alan Laning, *Manager*
EMP: 19
SALES (corp-wide): 223.6B Publicly Held
WEB: www.lubrizol.com
SIC: 2899 Oil treating compounds
HQ: The Lubrizol Corporation
29400 Lakeland Blvd
Wickliffe OH 44092
440 943-4200

**(G-15695)**
**MAUL ASPHALT SEALCOATING INC**
1111 Carmel Ct (60540-4105)
P.O. Box 9207 (60567-0207)
PHONE..................630 420-8765
Eric Maul, *President*
Chris Maul, *VP Sales*
EMP: 22
SALES: 1MM Privately Held
SIC: 2951 Asphalt paving mixtures & blocks

**(G-15696)**
**MERIDIAN PARTS INC**
445 Jackson Ave Ste 202 (60540-5258)
PHONE..................630 718-1995
Zhang Quan, *President*
Wang Yuhong, *Admin Sec*
▲ EMP: 3
SALES: 1.7MM Privately Held
SIC: 3469 Machine parts, stamped or pressed metal

**(G-15697)**
**MICRODYNAMICS CORPORATION (PA)**
Also Called: Microdynamics Group
1400 Shore Rd (60563-8765)
PHONE..................630 276-0527
Fax: 630 527-8440
Thomas Harter Sr, *CEO*
Jerry Carpenter, *Senior VP*
Thomas Harter Jr, *Senior VP*
Ivana Best, *Vice Pres*
Rick Schaltegger, *Vice Pres*
EMP: 144
SQ FT: 31,400
SALES (est): 56.5MM Privately Held
WEB: www.microdg.com
SIC: 7374 7389 2759 2752 Data processing & preparation; data processing service; microfilm recording & developing service; laser printing; commercial printing, lithographic

**(G-15698)**
**MOLEX INCORPORATED**
Also Called: Molex Inc. Switch Division
1750 Country Farm Dr (60563-9175)
PHONE..................630 969-4550
Fax: 630 505-0049
Garry Thompson, *General Mgr*
Laverne Zollinoffer, *Buyer*
Dave English, *Project Engr*
Mukesh Patel, *Project Engr*
David Schmidgall, *Design Engr*
EMP: 14
SALES (corp-wide): 27.4B Privately Held
WEB: www.molex.com
SIC: 3678 Electronic connectors
HQ: Molex, Llc
2222 Wellington Ct
Lisle IL 60532
630 969-4550

**(G-15699)**
**MONDELEZ GLOBAL LLC**
Also Called: Kraft Foods
1555 W Ogden Ave (60540-3966)
PHONE..................630 369-1909
Fax: 630 717-9645
Judy Czurylo, *Plant Mgr*
Charles Tongklub, *Project Mgr*
Steve Phonhoff, *Manager*
Jeffrey Schelinski, *Administration*
EMP: 300 Publicly Held
WEB: www.kraftfoods.com
SIC: 2043 2052 Cereal breakfast foods; cookies & crackers
HQ: Mondelez Global Llc
3 Parkway N Ste 300
Deerfield IL 60015
847 943-4000

**(G-15700)**
**MONONA HOLDINGS LLC (HQ)**
1952 Mc Dowell Rd Ste 207 (60563-6506)
PHONE..................630 946-0630
Dan Hurley, *MIS Mgr*
Steven R Brown, *Director*
Neal Kayes, *Director*
David Schnadig, *Director*
Roger Malatt,
EMP: 9
SQ FT: 2,550
SALES (est): 194.2MM
SALES (corp-wide): 662.1MM Publicly Held
SIC: 3694 5063 Harness wiring sets, internal combustion engines; wire & cable
PA: Commercial Vehicle Group, Inc.
7800 Walton Pkwy
New Albany OH 43054
614 289-5360

**(G-15701)**
**MTS PUBLISHING CO**
Also Called: Crosswords Club, The
800 W 5th Ave Ste 204a (60563-4925)
P.O. Box 928, Oswego (60543-0928)
PHONE..................630 955-9750
Stephen Shumate, *President*
Lisa Glueck, *Marketing Staff*
Robert Quigley, *Shareholder*
Louise Lapointe, *Admin Asst*
EMP: 15
SQ FT: 3,500
SALES (est): 1.4MM Privately Held
WEB: www.mtspbl.com
SIC: 2721 Periodicals

**(G-15702)**
**MUDLARK PAPERS INC**
1031 Shimer Ct (60565-3454)
PHONE..................630 717-7616
Doug Hamilton, *President*
Kim Hamilton, *Treasurer*
Diane Swanney, *Accountant*
▲ EMP: 20
SQ FT: 32,000
SALES (est): 3.3MM Privately Held
WEB: www.mudlark.com
SIC: 2678 2679 Stationery products; gift wrap & novelties, paper

**(G-15703)**
**NALCO COMPANY LLC (HQ)**
Also Called: Nalco Champion - An Ecolab Co
1601 W Diehl Rd (60563-1198)
PHONE..................630 305-1000
Fax: 630 305-2900
Daniel Fee, *President*
Michael Noyes, *President*
Alina Parast, *President*
Stewart Lamp, *General Mgr*
Douglas M Baker, *Chairman*
◆ EMP: 1155
SQ FT: 417,000
SALES (est): 4.6B
SALES (corp-wide): 13.1B Publicly Held
WEB: www.nalco.com
SIC: 3559 2899 2992 2891 Chemical machinery & equipment; corrosion preventive lubricant; lubricating oils; adhesives
PA: Ecolab Inc.
1 Ecolab Pl
Saint Paul MN 55102
800 232-6522

**(G-15704)**
**NALCO COMPANY LLC**
Also Called: Ecolab
1601 W Diehl Rd (60563-1198)
Doug Baker, *President*
Lee Josey, *President*
Michael P Murphy, *General Mgr*
Ana Leme, *Regional Mgr*
Jakub Cech, *District Mgr*
EMP: 3
SALES (corp-wide): 13.1B Publicly Held
WEB: www.nalco.com
SIC: 3589 Water treatment equipment, industrial
HQ: Nalco Company Llc
1601 W Diehl Rd
Naperville IL 60563
630 305-1000

**(G-15705)**
**NALCO COMPANY LLC**
Also Called: Treated Water Outsourcing
1 Nalco Ctr (60563-1198)
PHONE..................630 305-2451
Fax: 630 305-1898
Kurt Kirchof, *President*
James R Scott, *President*
Stan Gibson, *General Mgr*
Mike Chmelovski, *Manager*
Paula Tabor, *Manager*
EMP: 3
SALES (corp-wide): 13.1B Publicly Held
WEB: www.nalco.com
SIC: 3559 Chemical machinery & equipment
HQ: Nalco Company Llc
1601 W Diehl Rd
Naperville IL 60563
630 305-1000

**(G-15706)**
**NALCO HOLDING COMPANY (HQ)**
1601 W Diehl Rd (60563-1198)
PHONE..................630 305-1000
J Erik Fyrwald, *Ch of Bd*
David E Flitman, *President*
Terrence M Gallagher, *President*
Kristi Pegues, *Principal*
Dave Grasser, *District Mgr*
◆ EMP: 66
SALES (est): 2.7B
SALES (corp-wide): 13.1B Publicly Held
SIC: 2899 2992 Chemical preparations; corrosion preventive lubricant; water treating compounds; lubricating oils & greases
PA: Ecolab Inc.
1 Ecolab Pl
Saint Paul MN 55102
800 232-6522

**(G-15707)**
**NALCO HOLDINGS LLC (DH)**
1601 W Diehl Rd (60563-1198)
PHONE..................630 305-1000
Richard Bendure, *President*
David Flitman, *President*
David Johnson, *President*
Eric Melin, *President*
Steve Taylor, *President*
▲ EMP: 800
SALES (est): 431.7MM
SALES (corp-wide): 13.1B Publicly Held
SIC: 2899 2992 3559 Corrosion preventive lubricant; water treating compounds; antiscaling compounds, boiler; lubricating oils; chemical machinery & equipment
HQ: Nalco Holding Company
1601 W Diehl Rd
Naperville IL 60563
630 305-1000

**(G-15708)**
**NANOCHEM SOLUTIONS INC (PA)**
1701 Quincy Ave Ste 10 (60540-6687)
PHONE..................708 563-9200
Daniel O'Brien, *President*
Grace Fan, *Marketing Mgr*
Joseph Prochaska, *Info Tech Mgr*
▲ EMP: 9
SALES (est): 2.3MM Privately Held
WEB: www.nanochemsolutions.com
SIC: 2819 Industrial inorganic chemicals

**(G-15709)**
**NAPER DENTAL**
300 E 5th Ave Ste 400 (60563-3354)
PHONE..................630 369-6818
Fax: 630 369-7067
Ezra Chan, *Principal*
EMP: 2
SALES (est): 324.5K Privately Held
SIC: 3843 Enamels, dentists'

**(G-15710)**
**NAPERSOFT INC**
40 Shuman Blvd Ste 293 (60563-8670)
PHONE..................630 420-1515
Fax: 630 548-4050
Bart Carlson, *President*
Edward Hebda, *Vice Pres*
David Hinrichsen, *Vice Pres*
Michael J D'Onofrio, *CFO*
Bob Ingersoll, *VP Mktg*
EMP: 10
SQ FT: 9,500
SALES (est): 1.1MM Privately Held
WEB: www.napersoft.com
SIC: 7372 Business oriented computer software

# Naperville - Dupage County (G-15711)    GEOGRAPHIC SECTION

**(G-15711)**
**NESTLE USA INC**
Also Called: Chicago Sales
650 E Diehl Rd Ste 100 (60563-7855)
PHONE...................630 505-5387
Dave Peace, *Manager*
EMP: 24
SALES (corp-wide): 88.4B **Publicly Held**
WEB: www.nestleusa.com
SIC: 2023 Evaporated milk
HQ: Nestle Usa, Inc.
800 N Brand Blvd
Glendale CA 91203
818 549-6000

**(G-15712)**
**NETGEAR INC**
1000 E Warrenville Rd (60563-1867)
PHONE...................630 955-0080
EMP: 4 **Publicly Held**
SIC: 3661 Mfg Networking Solution Products
PA: Netgear, Inc.
350 E Plumeria Dr
San Jose CA 95134

**(G-15713)**
**NEW VISION PRINT & MARKETING**
31w280 Diehl Rd Ste 104 (60563-1066)
▲ EMP: 37
PHONE...................630 406-0509
Michael Frank, *Principal*
EMP: 9 **EST**: 2007
SALES (est): 989.7K **Privately Held**
SIC: 2752 Commercial printing, lithographic

**(G-15714)**
**NEWF LLC (PA)**
Also Called: Delta Waseca
608 Driftwood Ct (60540-3200)
PHONE...................630 330-5462
Dee Kapur, *President*
EMP: 4
SALES (est): 3.4MM **Privately Held**
SIC: 3713 Truck bodies & parts

**(G-15715)**
**NHANCED SEMICONDUCTORS INC** ◆
1415 Bond St Ste 155 (60563-2769)
PHONE...................408 759-4060
Robert Patti, *President*
EMP: 10 **EST**: 2016
SQ FT: 2,500
SALES: 2MM **Privately Held**
SIC: 3674 Semiconductor circuit networks

**(G-15716)**
**NOKIA SLUTIONS NETWORKS US LLC**
Also Called: Nokia Networks
2000 Lucent Ln (60563-1443)
PHONE...................630 979-9572
EMP: 3
SALES (corp-wide): 13.4B **Privately Held**
SIC: 3663 Radio broadcasting & communications equipment
HQ: Nokia Solutions And Networks Us Llc
6000 Connection Dr
Irving TX 75039
972 374-3000

**(G-15717)**
**NU-WORLD AMARANTH INC (PA)**
Also Called: Nu-World Foods
552 S Washington St # 120 (60540-6658)
PHONE...................630 369-6819
Fax: 630 369-9857
Susan Walters Flood, *President*
Paul Kerr, *Plant Mgr*
Jim Behling, *CFO*
Laura Hahne, *Natl Sales Mgr*
Marissa Kopp, *Marketing Staff*
▼ EMP: 6
SQ FT: 13,200
SALES (est): 29.7MM **Privately Held**
WEB: www.nuworldfoods.com
SIC: 2099 2041 Food preparations; flour & other grain mill products

**(G-15718)**
**OBERTHUR TECH AMER CORP**
2764 Golfview Rd (60563-9156)
PHONE...................630 551-0792
Ron Takacs, *General Mgr*
Ned Drinker, *Tax Mgr*
Alvin Lee, *Analyst*
Douglas Henk, *Training Spec*
Larry Hardy, *Coordinator*
EMP: 100
SALES (corp-wide): 4.2B **Privately Held**
WEB: www.oberthurcs.com
SIC: 3083 3089 Plastic finished products, laminated; identification cards, plastic
HQ: Oberthur Technologies Of America Corp.
4250 Pleasant Valley Rd
Chantilly VA 20151
703 263-0100

**(G-15719)**
**OROCHEM TECHNOLOGIES INC**
340 Shuman Blvd (60563-1268)
PHONE...................630 210-8300
Fax: 630 916-0250
Asha A Oroskar, *President*
Michelle Chen, *Engineer*
Thomas Clisham, *Engineer*
Sangharsh Dongre, *Engineer*
Anil Oroskar, *CFO*
▲ EMP: 37
SQ FT: 250,000
SALES: 7MM **Privately Held**
WEB: www.orochem.com
SIC: 3823 Chromatographs, industrial process type

**(G-15720)**
**P N K VENTURES INC**
Also Called: Sign-A-Rama
1701 Quincy Ave Ste 24 (60540-6685)
PHONE...................630 527-0500
Pat Sweeney, *President*
EMP: 4
SQ FT: 1,200
SALES: 500K **Privately Held**
SIC: 3993 7389 7336 Signs & advertising specialties; lettering & sign painting services; commercial art & graphic design

**(G-15721)**
**PALM INTERNATIONAL INC (PA)**
1159 Palmetto Ct Ste B (60540-6347)
P.O. Box 3923 (60567-3923)
PHONE...................630 357-1437
Brian Palm, *President*
Donna Palm, *Principal*
EMP: 5
SALES (est): 401.6K **Privately Held**
WEB: www.palmintl.com
SIC: 2741 7373 7379 8742 Miscellaneous publishing; computer integrated systems design; computer related maintenance services; ; marketing consulting services; market analysis, business & economic research

**(G-15722)**
**PAYLOCITY HOLDING CORPORATION**
27w675 South Ln (60540-6413)
PHONE...................331 701-7975
EMP: 217
SALES (corp-wide): 230.7MM **Publicly Held**
SIC: 7372 Prepackaged software
PA: Paylocity Holding Corporation
3850 N Wilke Rd
Arlington Heights IL 60004
847 463-3200

**(G-15723)**
**PELBO AMERICAS INC**
1701 Quincy Ave Ste 12 (60540-6687)
PHONE...................630 395-7788
James Nipper, *Vice Pres*
▲ EMP: 4
SALES (est): 343.9K **Privately Held**
SIC: 2015 Egg processing

**(G-15724)**
**PERLE & SONS JEWELERS INC**
8 W Jefferson Ave (60540-5309)
PHONE...................630 357-3357
Janine Perle, *President*
Dean Perle, *Vice Pres*
EMP: 3
SQ FT: 600
SALES: 800K **Privately Held**
SIC: 5944 3911 Jewelry, precious stones & precious metals; jewelry, precious metal

**(G-15725)**
**PFEIFER INDUSTRIES LLC**
2180 Corp Ln Unit 104 (60563)
PHONE...................630 596-9000
James Danovan,
Fredrick Meyers,
Brian Nass,
▲ EMP: 3
SQ FT: 7,000
SALES: 1MM **Privately Held**
SIC: 3545 Precision tools, machinists'

**(G-15726)**
**PHILIP REINISCH COMPANY**
1555 Naperville Wheaton R (60563-8448)
PHONE...................312 644-6776
Fax: 312 644-9803
Stanford J Reinisch, *President*
David Urbanick, *President*
Steve Reinisch, *Vice Pres*
Poe Nelson, *Controller*
▲ EMP: 11 **EST**: 1933
SQ FT: 5,000
SALES (est): 1.1MM **Privately Held**
WEB: www.philip-reinisch.com
SIC: 2511 Wood household furniture

**(G-15727)**
**PHILLIPS PHARMACEUTICALS INC**
710 E Ogden Ave Ste 207 (60563-8602)
PHONE...................630 328-0016
Dr A G Phillips, *President*
Dr A G Phillip, *President*
Dean Snyder, *Admin Sec*
EMP: 4
SALES (est): 248.7K **Privately Held**
SIC: 2834 Pharmaceutical preparations

**(G-15728)**
**PNC FINANCIAL SVCS GROUP INC**
1308 S Naper Blvd (60540-8362)
PHONE...................630 420-8400
Fax: 630 420-9048
Kelley Washington, *Manager*
EMP: 3
SALES (corp-wide): 16.4B **Publicly Held**
SIC: 3578 Automatic teller machines (ATM)
PA: The Pnc Financial Services Group Inc
300 5th Ave
Pittsburgh PA 15222
888 762-2265

**(G-15729)**
**POND ALLIANCE INC**
2764 Golfview Rd (60563-9156)
PHONE...................877 377-8131
Aaron Powers, *President*
Anna M Powers, *Vice Pres*
EMP: 7
SQ FT: 9,000
SALES: 950K **Privately Held**
SIC: 3589 Water treatment equipment, industrial

**(G-15730)**
**POWER-IO INC**
537 Braemar Ave (60563-1372)
PHONE...................630 717-7335
Mary Ellen Cahill, *President*
Jack Anderson, *Manager*
EMP: 50
SALES: 2MM **Privately Held**
WEB: www.power-io.com
SIC: 3625 Relays & industrial controls

**(G-15731)**
**POWERTRONICS SURGITECH USA INC**
2240 Pontiac Cir (60565-3296)
PHONE...................630 305-4261
Longtang Lin, *President*
▲ EMP: 2
SALES (est): 270.9K **Privately Held**
SIC: 5049 3545 Precision tools; precision tools, machinists'

**(G-15732)**
**PROCESS MECHANICAL INC**
2208 Pontiac Cir (60565-3206)
PHONE...................630 416-7021
John Pizzo, *President*
EMP: 1
SALES (est): 303.8K **Privately Held**
SIC: 5084 3823 Industrial machinery & equipment; industrial process measurement equipment

**(G-15733)**
**PROFESSIONAL METAL COMPANY**
Also Called: Prometco
951 Frontenac Rd (60563-1713)
PHONE...................630 983-9777
Matthew Steagall, *Branch Mgr*
EMP: 30
SALES (corp-wide): 18.1MM **Privately Held**
WEB: www.prometco.net
SIC: 3444 Awnings, sheet metal
PA: Professional Metal Company, Inc
390 River Ridge Dr
Elgin IL 60123
847 879-0200

**(G-15734)**
**PRP WINE INTERNATIONAL INC**
Also Called: Golden Grape Estate
1323 Bond St Ste 179 (60563-2368)
PHONE...................630 995-4500
Pad Bobbitt, *Branch Mgr*
EMP: 11 **Privately Held**
WEB: www.wineshippers.com
SIC: 2084 Wines
HQ: Prp Wine International, Inc.
1323 Bond St Ste 179
Naperville IL 60563
630 995-4500

**(G-15735)**
**QUALITY MSREMENT SOLUTIONS INC**
1600 Shore Rd Ste I (60563-1059)
P.O. Box 452, Batavia (60510-0452)
PHONE...................630 406-1618
Michelle Hartzell, *President*
Jeffrey Hartzell, *Vice Pres*
Sara Hartzell, *Treasurer*
David Hartzell, *Sales Mgr*
EMP: 4
SQ FT: 2,000
SALES (est): 330K **Privately Held**
SIC: 3827 Optical instruments & lenses

**(G-15736)**
**R R STREET & CO INC (PA)**
Also Called: Street's
215 Shuman Blvd Ste 403 (60563-5100)
PHONE...................630 416-4244
Fax: 630 416-4150
L Ross Beard, *CEO*
J L Mayberry III, *Chairman*
Don Danner, *Vice Pres*
Dave Dawson, *Vice Pres*
Ross Beard, *Persnl Mgr*
EMP: 25
SQ FT: 20,000
SALES (est): 42.2MM **Privately Held**
WEB: www.4streets.com
SIC: 2842 Rug, upholstery, or dry cleaning detergents or spotters

**(G-15737)**
**RADIO FREQUENCY SYSTEMS INC**
Also Called: RADIO FREQUENCY SYSTEMS,INC
2000 Nperville Wheaton Rd (60563-1443)
PHONE...................800 321-4700
Carrrie Lenkart, *Branch Mgr*
EMP: 25
SALES (corp-wide): 13.4B **Privately Held**
WEB: www.rfsworld.com
SIC: 3663 Radio & TV communications equipment
HQ: Radio Frequency Systems, Inc.
200 Pond View Dr
Meriden CT 06450
203 630-3311

# GEOGRAPHIC SECTION

**Naperville - Dupage County (G-15764)**

**(G-15738)**
**RAMONA SEDIVY**
Also Called: Chickens & Things
1840 Auburn Ave (60565-6700)
PHONE.................................630 983-1902
Ramona Sedivy, *Owner*
**EMP:** 3
**SALES:** 30K **Privately Held**
**SIC: 3999** Novelties, bric-a-brac & hobby kits

**(G-15739)**
**RAYMOND ALSTOM**
2151 Fisher Dr (60563-1784)
PHONE.................................630 369-3700
Raymond Alstom, *Principal*
▲ **EMP:** 2
**SALES (est):** 354.9K **Privately Held**
**SIC: 3541** Grinding, polishing, buffing, lapping & honing machines

**(G-15740)**
**REILLY FOAM CORP**
920 Frontenac Rd (60563-1745)
PHONE.................................630 392-2680
Michael Ernt, *Design Engr*
Rob Quier, *Manager*
**EMP:** 42
**SALES (corp-wide):** 34.1MM **Privately Held**
**SIC: 3069** 5199 Foam rubber; foam rubber
**PA:** Reilly Foam Corp.
2525 Monroe Blvd Ste B
Eagleville PA 19403
610 834-1900

**(G-15741)**
**RF COMMUNICATIONS INC**
424 Fort Hill Dr Ste 142 (60540-3912)
P.O. Box 2256 (60567-2256)
PHONE.................................630 420-8882
Fax: 630 420-8883
Robert Frantik, *President*
Harold Frantik, *Vice Pres*
Jeanne Frantik, *Admin Sec*
**EMP:** 15
**SALES (est):** 1.6MM **Privately Held**
**WEB:** www.rfcinc.com
**SIC: 5999** 3651 Telephone & communication equipment; audio electronic systems

**(G-15742)**
**ROBERT STERN INDUSTRIES INC**
2330 University Ct (60565-4011)
PHONE.................................630 983-9765
**EMP:** 3
**SALES (est):** 188.1K **Privately Held**
**SIC: 2221** Broadwoven fabric mills, man-made

**(G-15743)**
**ROCK SOLID IMPORTS LLC**
1004 Creekside Cir (60563-2420)
PHONE.................................331 472-4522
Mark Warwick, *Mng Member*
▲ **EMP:** 1
**SALES:** 250K **Privately Held**
**SIC: 3291** Stones, abrasive

**(G-15744)**
**ROGER FRITZ & ASSOCIATES INC**
1113 N Loomis St (60563-2745)
PHONE.................................630 355-2614
Roger J Fritz, *President*
Kathryn Fritz, *Admin Sec*
**EMP:** 3
**SQ FT:** 1,000
**SALES (est):** 290K **Privately Held**
**WEB:** www.rogerfritz.com
**SIC: 8742** 2732 2741 Management consulting services; corporation organizing; book printing; miscellaneous publishing

**(G-15745)**
**SADANNAH GROUP LLC**
Also Called: Signs Now Naperville
426 W 5th Ave (60563-2985)
PHONE.................................630 357-2300
David Groth, *Owner*
John Kelsheimer, *Owner*
**EMP:** 2
**SALES (est):** 200K **Privately Held**
**SIC: 3993** 7336 7389 Signs & advertising specialties; graphic arts & related design; design services

**(G-15746)**
**SHERMAN PLASTICS CORP (PA)**
1650 Shore Rd (60563-8769)
PHONE.................................630 369-6170
Lawrence Markin, *President*
Anthony Boose, *Vice Pres*
Cindy Solovy, *Manager*
Cynthia Solovy, *Admin Sec*
▲ **EMP:** 27
**SQ FT:** 50,000
**SALES (est):** 32.4MM **Privately Held**
**WEB:** www.shermanplasticscorp.com
**SIC: 5162** 2821 Plastics materials; plastics materials & resins

**(G-15747)**
**SMT LLC**
Also Called: Smt Molding
2768 Golfview Rd (60563-9156)
PHONE.................................630 961-3000
Fax: 630 961-3709
Mathias Buchmann, *Project Mgr*
Ron Bakes, *Mfg Mgr*
Yves Buchmann, *QC Mgr*
Cynthia Notariano, *CFO*
Monique Buchmann, *Controller*
**EMP:** 40
**SQ FT:** 15,000
**SALES (est):** 8.8MM **Privately Held**
**WEB:** www.smt.com
**SIC: 3089** Injection molding of plastics

**(G-15748)**
**SOLAR TURBINES INCORPORATED**
40 Shuman Blvd Ste 350 (60563-7973)
PHONE.................................630 527-1700
Fax: 630 527-1997
Russle Bruno, *President*
Mike Masters, *Manager*
**EMP:** 25
**SALES (corp-wide):** 38.5B **Publicly Held**
**WEB:** www.esolar.cat.com
**SIC: 3511** Gas turbine generator set units, complete
**HQ:** Solar Turbines Incorporated
2200 Pacific Hwy
San Diego CA 92101
619 544-5000

**(G-15749)**
**SOLVAIR LLC**
215 Shuman Blvd Ste 403 (60563-5100)
PHONE.................................630 416-4244
L Ross Beard,
Leslie Beard,
**EMP:** 10
**SALES (est):** 1.1MM **Privately Held**
**SIC: 3582** Drycleaning equipment & machinery, commercial

**(G-15750)**
**SONNE INDUSTRIES LLC**
5s528 Arlington Ave (60540-3819)
PHONE.................................630 235-6734
William Dorn, *CEO*
**EMP:** 2
**SALES (est):** 236.5K **Privately Held**
**SIC: 3822** Appliance controls except air-conditioning & refrigeration; energy cutoff controls, residential or commercial types

**(G-15751)**
**SOURCEBOOKS INC (PA)**
1935 Brookdale Rd Ste 139 (60563-7994)
P.O. Box 4410 (60567-4410)
PHONE.................................630 961-3900
Fax: 630 961-2168
Dominique Raccah, *President*
Mary Altman, *Editor*
Susie Benton, *Editor*
Sarah Cardillo, *Editor*
Todd Green, *Editor*
▲ **EMP:** 70
**SQ FT:** 14,000
**SALES (est):** 68.7MM **Privately Held**
**SIC: 2731** Book publishing

**(G-15752)**
**SPECTRAGEN INCORPORATED**
1005 Royal Blackheath Ct (60563-2305)
PHONE.................................847 982-0481
Richard Jarman, *President*
Joshua Zavelovich, *Admin Sec*
**EMP:** 6
**SQ FT:** 2,000
**SALES (est):** 390K **Privately Held**
**SIC: 3229** Optical glass

**(G-15753)**
**SPELL IT WITH COLOR INC**
Also Called: Allegra Mktg Print Mail Inc.
1644 Swallow St (60565-2332)
PHONE.................................630 961-5617
Thomas Wilhelm, *President*
Daniel Spell, *Principal*
**EMP:** 3
**SALES (est):** 315.7K **Privately Held**
**SIC: 2752** Commercial printing, offset

**(G-15754)**
**SPRING (USA) CORPORATION**
127 Ambassador Dr Ste 147 (60540-4079)
PHONE.................................630 527-8600
Fax: 630 527-8677
Tom Brija, *President*
Metsi Thomas, *Sales Staff*
▲ **EMP:** 11
**SALES (est):** 1.6MM **Privately Held**
**WEB:** www.springusa.com
**SIC: 3262** Dishes, commercial or household: vitreous china; tableware, vitreous china

**(G-15755)**
**STREAMLINX LLC**
40 Shuman Blvd Ste 140 (60563-8648)
PHONE.................................630 864-3043
Jeff Seifert, *Mng Member*
Mike Seifert, *Mng Member*
**EMP:** 12
**SALES:** 2.8MM **Privately Held**
**SIC: 7372** Prepackaged software

**(G-15756)**
**SUBURBAN CHICAGO NEWSPAPERS**
1500 W Ogden Ave (60540-3919)
PHONE.................................847 336-7000
Lois Mayer, *Mktg Dir*
**EMP:** 3
**SALES (est):** 114.7K **Privately Held**
**SIC: 2711** Newspapers

**(G-15757)**
**SUNCRAFT TECHNOLOGIES INC (PA)**
1301 Frontenac Rd (60563-1710)
PHONE.................................630 369-7900
Fax: 630 639-7070
Ronald F Desanto Sr, *President*
Russell Babka, *Vice Pres*
Eulalia Desanto, *Vice Pres*
Lia Santo, *Vice Pres*
Anthony Bartelli, *Plant Mgr*
**EMP:** 110
**SQ FT:** 72,000
**SALES (est):** 34.9MM **Privately Held**
**WEB:** www.suncraft-tech.com
**SIC: 2752** Commercial printing, lithographic

**(G-15758)**
**SUNEMCO TECHNOLOGIES INC**
500 Braemar Ave (60563-1369)
PHONE.................................630 369-8947
Liang Hu, *President*
Hong Xue, *Treasurer*
Evelyn Lin, *Admin Sec*
**EMP:** 3
**SALES (est):** 317.6K **Privately Held**
**SIC: 2821** 7379 Plastics materials & resins;

**(G-15759)**
**T C W F INC**
Also Called: Minuteman Press
1577 Nperville Wheaton Rd (60563-1556)
PHONE.................................630 369-1360
Fax: 630 369-2849
Kevin Brahler, *President*
Ray Kinney, *Vice Pres*
Paul Yerges, *Purchasing*
James Kelly, *Treasurer*
Tim Hoffman, *Sales Mgr*
**EMP:** 28
**SQ FT:** 7,200
**SALES (est):** 4.5MM **Privately Held**
**WEB:** www.m2pnaper.com
**SIC: 2752** Commercial printing, lithographic

**(G-15760)**
**TBC CORPORATION**
915 E Ogden Ave (60563-2836)
PHONE.................................630 428-2233
Christopher Cruz, *Manager*
**EMP:** 4
**SALES (corp-wide):** 35.1B **Privately Held**
**SIC: 3011** Tires, cushion or solid rubber
**HQ:** Tbc Corporation
4300 Tbc Way
Palm Beach Gardens FL 33410
561 227-0955

**(G-15761)**
**TEKNO INDUSTRIES INC (PA)**
1250 Shore Rd (60563-8761)
PHONE.................................630 766-6960
Ernest C Karras, *President*
Joseph Vodraska, *Vice Pres*
Nancy Solarz, *Accounting Mgr*
Samuel Galler, *VP Sales*
John G Karones, *Admin Sec*
**EMP:** 16
**SQ FT:** 15,000
**SALES (est):** 4.1MM **Privately Held**
**SIC: 3661** Telephone & telegraph apparatus

**(G-15762)**
**TELLABS INC (HQ)**
1415 W Diehl Rd (60563-9950)
PHONE.................................630 798-8800
Fax: 630 798-2000
Daniel P Kelly, *President*
Woody Waters, *Counsel*
John M Brots, *Exec VP*
Kenneth G Craft, *Exec VP*
Thomas J Gruenwald, *Exec VP*
▲ **EMP:** 20
**SALES (est):** 637.3MM
**SALES (corp-wide):** 3.6B **Privately Held**
**WEB:** www.tellabs.com
**SIC: 3661** 1731 Telephones & telephone apparatus; multiplex equipment, telephone & telegraph; communications specialization
**PA:** Marlin Equity Partners, Llc
338 Pier Ave
Hermosa Beach CA 90254
310 364-0100

**(G-15763)**
**TELLABS MEXICO INC (DH)**
1415 W Diehl Rd (60563-9950)
PHONE.................................630 445-5333
Michael Birck, *President*
Brian Jackman, *Exec VP*
John Kohler, *Vice Pres*
Harvey Scull, *Vice Pres*
Peter Guglielmi, *Treasurer*
**EMP:** 10
**SALES:** 3.6MM
**SALES (corp-wide):** 3.6B **Privately Held**
**SIC: 3661** Telephones & telephone apparatus
**HQ:** Tellabs, Inc.
1415 W Diehl Rd
Naperville IL 60563
630 798-8800

**(G-15764)**
**THE LIFEGUARD STORE INC**
1212 S Naper Blvd Ste 109 (60540-8399)
PHONE.................................630 548-5500
Art Eosseman, *Owner*
**EMP:** 8
**SALES (corp-wide):** 8.1MM **Privately Held**
**SIC: 2253** Bathing suits & swimwear, knit
**PA:** The Lifeguard Store Inc
2012 W College Ave
Normal IL 61761
309 451-5858

# Naperville - Dupage County (G-15765) — GEOGRAPHIC SECTION

**(G-15765)**
**THRIFT MEDICAL PRODUCTS**
1701 Quincy Ave (60540-3955)
PHONE................................630 857-3548
EMP: 3 EST: 2014
SALES (est): 198.4K Privately Held
SIC: 3841 Surgical & medical instruments

**(G-15766)**
**TOYAL AMERICA INC**
1717 N Naper Blvd Ste 201 (60563-8838)
PHONE................................630 505-2160
Bud Loprest, Vice Pres
Trish Wolf, Director
EMP: 6
SALES (corp-wide): 3.9B Privately Held
SIC: 2816 3399 2819 Inorganic pigments; powder, metal; industrial inorganic chemicals
HQ: Toyal America, Inc.
   17401 Broadway St
   Lockport IL 60441
   815 740-3000

**(G-15767)**
**TRACTRONICS**
1212 S Naper Blvd (60540-8360)
PHONE................................630 527-0000
Fax: 630 526-6207
Richard Weyand, CEO
EMP: 3
SALES (est): 159.8K Privately Held
SIC: 3944 Electronic toys

**(G-15768)**
**TRIZETTO CORPORATION**
1240 E Diehl Rd Ste 200 (60563-4802)
PHONE................................630 369-5300
Fax: 630 368-5028
Jude Dieterman, President
Rob Schleicher, Assistant VP
Marion Olson, Purch Agent
Kim Anderson, Accounting Mgr
Barb Davis, Manager
EMP: 200
SALES (corp-wide): 13.4B Publicly Held
WEB: www.trizetto.com
SIC: 7372 Prepackaged software
HQ: Trizetto Corporation
   9655 Maroon Cir
   Englewood CO 80112
   303 495-7000

**(G-15769)**
**TWOCANOES SOFTWARE INC**
34 W Chicago Ave Ste A (60540-5397)
PHONE................................630 305-9601
Timothy Perfitt, President
Sarah Burgess, Marketing Staff
Dave Lebbing, Web Dvlpr
EMP: 3
SQ FT: 1,200
SALES (est): 313.6K Privately Held
SIC: 7372 Application computer software

**(G-15770)**
**UBERLOOP INC**
1812 High Grove Ln # 101 (60540-9116)
PHONE................................630 707-0567
Joshua Dean, CEO
EMP: 5 EST: 2012
SALES (est): 247.3K Privately Held
SIC: 7372 Prepackaged software

**(G-15771)**
**UPM-KYMMENE INC**
Also Called: Upm North America
55 Shuman Blvd Ste 400 (60563-8248)
PHONE................................630 922-2500
Fax: 630 850-3322
Angelo Lamantia, General Mgr
Riitta Savonlahti, Exec VP
Matts Weckstrom, Vice Pres
Joseph Rolston, Treasurer
Rebecca Norris, Finance Dir
▲ EMP: 90 EST: 1978
SALES (est): 60.7MM
SALES (corp-wide): 10.3B Privately Held
WEB: www.upm-kymmene.com
SIC: 2621 5111 Paper mills; printing & writing paper
PA: Upm-Kymmene Oyj
   Alvar Aallon Katu 1
   Helsinki 00100
   204 151-11

**(G-15772)**
**VALLEY FASTENER GROUP LLC**
Also Called: Valley Fasteners Group
5s250 Frontenac Rd (60563-1711)
PHONE................................630 548-5679
EMP: 30
SALES (corp-wide): 21.6MM Privately Held
SIC: 3452 Bolts, nuts, rivets & washers
PA: Valley Fastener Group, Llc
   1490 Mitchell Rd
   Aurora IL 60505
   630 299-8910

**(G-15773)**
**VANGUARD ENERGY SERVICES LLC**
850 E Diehl Rd Ste 142 (60563-8236)
PHONE................................630 955-1500
Fax: 630 955-0989
John F Wier,
Paul Bougadis,
EMP: 28
SALES: 129.3MM
SALES (corp-wide): 3.2B Privately Held
WEB: www.vanguardenergy.net
SIC: 3822 Energy cutoff controls, residential or commercial types
PA: Continuum Energy, L.L.C.
   1323 E 71st St Ste 300
   Tulsa OK 74136
   918 492-2840

**(G-15774)**
**VEJ HOLDINGS LLC**
1717 N Naper Blvd Ste 108 (60563-8837)
PHONE................................630 219-1582
Vincent Jackson, President
EMP: 3
SALES (est): 828K Privately Held
SIC: 5142 5149 5147 2673 Frozen fish, meat & poultry; spices & seasonings; meats & meat products; food storage & frozen food bags, plastic; insurance agents, brokers & service

**(G-15775)**
**VENTURE DESIGN INCORPORATED**
2250 Allegany Dr (60565-3415)
PHONE................................630 369-1148
George Pullos, President
Sheila Pullos, Admin Sec
EMP: 12
SQ FT: 5,280
SALES (est): 1.2MM Privately Held
WEB: www.venturedesignpanels.com
SIC: 3613 8711 Control panels, electric; designing: ship, boat, machine & product

**(G-15776)**
**VERTEX INC**
40 Shuman Blvd Ste 160 (60563-8650)
PHONE................................630 328-2600
Madhavi Ganaham, Branch Mgr
EMP: 7
SALES (corp-wide): 207MM Privately Held
SIC: 7372 Business oriented computer software
PA: Vertex, Inc.
   2301 Renaissance Blvd
   King Of Prussia PA 19406
   610 640-4200

**(G-15777)**
**VITAL CHEMICALS USA LLC**
280 Shuman Blvd Ste 145 (60563-2500)
PHONE................................630 778-0330
Dustin Docter, Vice Pres
Ron Rong, Supervisor
Michael Xiong,
▲ EMP: 5
SALES (est): 1MM Privately Held
SIC: 2819 Industrial inorganic chemicals
PA: Qingyuan Xiandao Investment Co., Ltd.
   4f,Incubator Building,High-Tech Enterprises,Hi-Tech Zone
   Qingyuan

**(G-15778)**
**VORTEX MEDIA GROUP INC**
1118 Knoll Dr (60565-2735)
PHONE................................630 717-9541
James Vondruska, President
EMP: 6
SALES (est): 729K Privately Held
SIC: 2741

**(G-15779)**
**VULCAN CONSTRUCTION MTLS LLC**
1000 E Warrenville Rd # 100 (60563-2044)
PHONE................................630 955-8500
Lenny Novak, Manager
EMP: 25
SALES (corp-wide): 3.5B Publicly Held
SIC: 1422 Crushed & broken limestone
HQ: Vulcan Construction Materials, Llc
   1200 Urban Center Dr
   Vestavia AL 35242
   205 298-3000

**(G-15780)**
**VULCAN MATERIALS COMPANY**
1000 E Warrenville Rd # 100 (60563-2044)
PHONE................................262 639-2803
Christopher Franklin, Electrical Engi
Christopher Zapka, Electrical Engi
Roger Gagliano, Branch Mgr
Alan Berkey, Manager
Leon Montgomery, Manager
EMP: 17
SALES (corp-wide): 3.5B Publicly Held
SIC: 1422 Crushed & broken limestone
PA: Vulcan Materials Company
   1200 Urban Center Dr
   Vestavia AL 35242
   205 298-3000

**(G-15781)**
**WASHBURN GRAFICOLOR INC**
1255 E Bailey Rd (60565-1646)
PHONE................................630 596-0880
Fax: 630 596-0881
Gregory G Washburn, President
Sarah Washburn, Admin Sec
EMP: 5
SQ FT: 1,350
SALES (est): 450K Privately Held
WEB: www.washburngraficolor.com
SIC: 2752 7336 2791 Commercial printing, offset; graphic arts & related design; typesetting

**(G-15782)**
**WEBB-MASON INC**
280 Shuman Blvd Ste 200 (60563-3187)
PHONE................................630 428-5838
Dan Cahill, Branch Mgr
EMP: 10
SALES (corp-wide): 140.1MM Privately Held
SIC: 2752 Commercial printing, lithographic
PA: Webb-Mason, Inc.
   10830 Gilroy Rd
   Hunt Valley MD 21031
   410 785-1111

**(G-15783)**
**WEHRLI EQUIPMENT CO INC**
1805 High Grove Ln # 117 (60540-3987)
PHONE................................630 717-4150
Fax: 630 355-6906
Scott Wehrli, President
EMP: 10
SALES (est): 821.5K Privately Held
SIC: 3531 7699 5084 Bituminous, cement & concrete related products & equipment; industrial equipment services; industrial machinery & equipment

**(G-15784)**
**WEYERHAEUSER COMPANY**
Also Called: Weyerhauser
220 Brookshire Ct (60540-3911)
PHONE................................630 778-7070
Fax: 630 778-7575
EMP: 60
SALES (corp-wide): 7B Publicly Held
SIC: 2611 Paper Mill
PA: Weyerhaeuser Company
   33663 Weyerhaeuser Way S
   Federal Way WA 98104
   253 924-2345

**(G-15785)**
**XEROX CORPORATION**
1435 Foxhill Rd (60563-2102)
PHONE................................630 983-0172
Chuck Sabino, Branch Mgr
EMP: 74
SALES (corp-wide): 10.7B Publicly Held
WEB: www.xerox.com
SIC: 3861 Photographic equipment & supplies
PA: Xerox Corporation
   201 Merritt 7
   Norwalk CT 06851
   203 968-3000

**(G-15786)**
**XINGFA USA CORPORATION**
418 W 5th Ave (60563-2985)
PHONE................................360 720-9256
Yong Zhao, President
▲ EMP: 7 EST: 2011
SALES (est): 820.7K Privately Held
SIC: 2819 Hydrochloric acid; sodium & potassium compounds, exc. bleaches, alkalies, alum.

**(G-15787)**
**YHLSOFT INC**
625 S Wright St (60540-6733)
PHONE................................630 355-8033
Hailin LI, CEO
Hannah LI, Admin Sec
EMP: 10 EST: 2012
SALES (est): 582.3K Privately Held
SIC: 7372 Business oriented computer software

**(G-15788)**
**YUENGER WOOD MOULDING INC**
Also Called: Yuenger, Wm Mfg Co
847 Santa Maria Dr (60540-7420)
PHONE................................773 735-7100
Paul Singelyn, President
Nancy Singelyn, Corp Secy
EMP: 8 EST: 1920
SQ FT: 26,000
SALES: 1MM Privately Held
WEB: www.yuenger.com
SIC: 2431 Moldings, wood: unfinished & prefinished

## Naperville — Will County

**(G-15789)**
**AGILE HEALTH TECHNOLOGIES INC**
2728 Forgue Dr Ste 106 (60564-4192)
PHONE................................630 247-5565
Sasikant Gandhamaneni, President
Bhaskara R Katiki, Vice Pres
Dibyajyothi Mahanta, Vice Pres
Ravindran Nithyanandam, Vice Pres
EMP: 35
SALES (est): 206.4K Privately Held
SIC: 7373 7371 7372 Computer integrated systems design; systems integration services; computer software development & applications; business oriented computer software

**(G-15790)**
**AIKNOW INC**
2243 Gloucestern Ln (60564-8475)
PHONE................................312 391-9452
Zuyi LI, CEO
Mengmeng Zhuang, COO
WEI Tian, Vice Pres
Zhen Bao, Chief Engr
EMP: 10
SALES (est): 454.5K Privately Held
SIC: 3825 Instruments to measure electricity

**(G-15791)**
**AIM SCREEN PRINTING SUPPLY LLC**
2731 Willow Ridge Dr (60564-8951)
P.O. Box 9645 (60567-0645)
PHONE................................630 357-4293
Ben Goldstein, Mng Member

## GEOGRAPHIC SECTION

## Naperville - Will County (G-15820)

▲ EMP: 7
SQ FT: 3,000
SALES: 1.5MM  Privately Held
SIC: 2759  Screen printing

**(G-15792)**
**ALL LINE INC**
31w310 91st St  (60564-5615)
PHONE .................................. 630 820-1800
Alfonso Monraz, *Purch Mgr*
EMP: 5
SALES (corp-wide): 1.8MM  Privately Held
SIC: 2298  3357  Cordage: abaca, sisal, henequen, hemp, jute or other fiber; aluminum wire & cable
PA: All Line Inc.
16851 E Parkview Ave # 201
Fountain Hills AZ 85268
480 306-6001

**(G-15793)**
**ALL STAR INJECTION MOLDERS INC**
24w959 Ramm Dr Unit 5  (60564-3611)
PHONE .................................. 630 978-4046
Michael Tropinski, *President*
Marsha Tropinski, *Admin Sec*
EMP: 4
SALES (est): 487.2K  Privately Held
WEB: www.allstarco.com
SIC: 3089  Injection molding of plastics

**(G-15794)**
**AMERICAN WATERSOURCE LLC**
1228 Bards Ave  (60564-3158)
P.O. Box 9548  (60567-0548)
PHONE .................................. 630 778-9900
Tom Sorensen, *Mng Member*
EMP: 50
SALES (est): 3MM  Privately Held
SIC: 3589  7389  Water treatment equipment, industrial; water softener service

**(G-15795)**
**AMERINET OF MICHIGAN INC**
3909 White Eagle Dr W  (60564-8283)
PHONE .................................. 708 466-0110
Mark Katsis, *Branch Mgr*
EMP: 4
SALES (corp-wide): 24MM  Privately Held
WEB: www.amerinet.com
SIC: 3825  8999  Network analyzers; technical manual preparation
PA: Amerinet Of Michigan, Inc.
1241 S Maple Rd
Ann Arbor MI 48103
734 995-1233

**(G-15796)**
**ANYTIME HEATING & AC**
10s264 Schoger Dr Ste 2  (60564-8264)
PHONE .................................. 630 851-6696
Fax: 630 851-6749
Gary Murphy Sr, *President*
Gary Murphy Jr, *Corp Secy*
Michael Murphy, *Vice Pres*
Morine Robertson, *Manager*
EMP: 10  EST: 1973
SQ FT: 3,000
SALES: 2.5MM  Privately Held
SIC: 1711  5075  3444  Warm air heating & air conditioning contractor; air conditioning & ventilation equipment & supplies; sheet metalwork

**(G-15797)**
**ARBA RETAIL SYSTEMS CORP**
Also Called: Arba Retail Systems Copr
2760 Forgue Dr Ste 106  (60564-4174)
PHONE .................................. 630 620-8566
Fax: 630 396-3300
William F Hochmuth, *President*
Sandra J Mc Lain, *Vice Pres*
Theresa Meisinger, *Controller*
EMP: 8
SQ FT: 1,500
SALES (est): 1.4MM  Privately Held
WEB: www.arbapro.com
SIC: 3577  3695  Computer peripheral equipment; magnetic & optical recording media

**(G-15798)**
**AVANTI MOTOR CARRIERS INC**
4440 White Ash Ln  (60564-1102)
PHONE .................................. 630 313-9160
EMP: 3
SALES (est): 306.4K  Privately Held
SIC: 3531  Crane carriers

**(G-15799)**
**AVEC INC**
Also Called: Goldy Metals Trading
3027 English Row Ave # 205  (60564-5107)
PHONE .................................. 217 670-0439
Christopher Dandrow, *President*
EMP: 2
SALES (est): 232.1K  Privately Held
SIC: 3291

**(G-15800)**
**CALX TRADING CORPORATION**
1245 Amaranth Dr  (60564-9336)
PHONE .................................. 630 456-6721
Mohsen Abdelati, *CEO*
EMP: 25
SALES: 695K  Privately Held
SIC: 3699  Security control equipment & systems

**(G-15801)**
**CONTEMPRARY ENRGY SLUTIONS LLC**
2951 Beth Ln  (60564-4398)
PHONE .................................. 630 768-3743
Antonio Vlastelica, *Mng Member*
EMP: 12
SALES (est): 2.6MM  Privately Held
SIC: 3646  1731  Commercial indusl & institutional electric lighting fixtures; energy management controls

**(G-15802)**
**DKB INDUSTRIES LLC**
3940 White Eagle Dr  (60564-9708)
PHONE .................................. 630 450-4151
Daryll Bryant,
EMP: 10
SALES: 1MM  Privately Held
SIC: 2099  Food preparations

**(G-15803)**
**EDGO TECHNICAL SALES INC**
9s131 Skylane Dr  (60564-9450)
PHONE .................................. 630 961-8398
Fax: 630 961-8393
Edwin A Goebel Jr, *President*
Ellen M Goebel, *Admin Sec*
EMP: 2
SALES (est): 255.8K  Privately Held
SIC: 3672  Printed circuit boards

**(G-15804)**
**ELECTROSTATIC CONCEPTS INC**
Also Called: Creative Iron Solutions
31w335 Schoger Dr  (60564-5657)
PHONE .................................. 630 585-5080
Mel Drendel, *President*
Doug Lanphear, *General Mgr*
Catie Drendel, *Admin Sec*
EMP: 15
SQ FT: 17,000
SALES (est): 2.5MM  Privately Held
WEB: www.electrocoatings.net
SIC: 3446  3479  Fences or posts, ornamental iron or steel; painting of metal products

**(G-15805)**
**ENSEMBLES INC**
2320 Flambeau Pl  (60564-9653)
P.O. Box 9046  (60567-0046)
PHONE .................................. 630 527-0004
Evelyn Rivera-Brutto, *Principal*
EMP: 2
SALES (est): 240.2K  Privately Held
SIC: 2591  5023  5714  Shade, curtain & drapery hardware; window covering parts & accessories; curtains

**(G-15806)**
**FLURIDA GROUP INC**
2439 Haider Ave  (60564-5392)
PHONE .................................. 310 513-0888
Jeff Ding, *President*
EMP: 5  **Publicly Held**
SIC: 3632  Household refrigerators & freezers
PA: Flurida Group, Inc.
11220 Rojas Dr Ste C3
El Paso TX 79935

**(G-15807)**
**GLASSTEK INC**
10s059 Schoger Dr Unit 40  (60564-3601)
PHONE .................................. 630 978-9897
Fax: 630 978-9881
Torrence Caniglia, *President*
Robert Mortinsen, *Vice Pres*
Torry Coniglia, *Manager*
EMP: 9  EST: 1992
SALES (est): 1.1MM  Privately Held
WEB: www.glasstek.com
SIC: 3089  Awnings, fiberglass & plastic combination

**(G-15808)**
**GUARDIAN CONSTRUCTION PDTS INC**
10s359 Normantown Rd  (60564-5632)
PHONE .................................. 630 820-8899
Fax: 630 820-1460
Gerald J Husarik, *President*
David Husarik, *Vice Pres*
Kathleen Husarik, *Treasurer*
Betty Piltrowfki, *Manager*
Phillip Husarik, *Admin Sec*
▲ EMP: 28
SQ FT: 18,900
SALES (est): 4.7MM  Privately Held
SIC: 1791  3312  Structural steel erection; structural & rail mill products

**(G-15809)**
**HIDALGO FINE CABINETRY**
8952 Hanslik Ct Ste 22  (60564-5847)
PHONE .................................. 630 753-9323
C Hidalgo, *Owner*
EMP: 3
SALES (est): 339.6K  Privately Held
SIC: 2434  Wood kitchen cabinets

**(G-15810)**
**HONEYWELL INTERNATIONAL INC**
4412 Buttermilk Ct  (60564-7107)
PHONE .................................. 630 922-0138
Daniel Picchi, *Branch Mgr*
Ganesh Ayer, *Manager*
EMP: 694
SALES (corp-wide): 39.3B  **Publicly Held**
SIC: 3724  Aircraft engines & engine parts
PA: Honeywell International Inc.
115 Tabor Rd
Morris Plains NJ 07950
973 455-2000

**(G-15811)**
**INLET & PIPE PROTECTION INC**
24137 111th St Ste A  (60564-8316)
PHONE .................................. 630 355-3288
James Ringenbach, *President*
▲ EMP: 3  EST: 2004
SALES (est): 881K
SALES (corp-wide): 1.2B  **Publicly Held**
SIC: 5084  3589  3569  Industrial machinery & equipment; sewer cleaning equipment, power; filters
PA: Advanced Drainage Systems, Inc.
4640 Trueman Blvd
Hilliard OH 43026
614 658-0050

**(G-15812)**
**KING S COURT EXTERIOR**
2328 Skylane Dr  (60564-8529)
PHONE .................................. 630 904-4305
EMP: 3  EST: 2002
SALES (est): 180K  Privately Held
SIC: 3671  Mfg Electron Tubes

**(G-15813)**
**LARCKERS RECYCLING SVCS INC**
3119 Reflection Dr  (60564-4690)
P.O. Box 2287  (60567-2287)
PHONE .................................. 630 922-0759
Gene Larcker, *President*
EMP: 13
SALES (est): 2.5MM  Privately Held
SIC: 2611  Pulp manufactured from waste or recycled paper

**(G-15814)**
**LESSY MESSY LLC**
Also Called: Sourcing Solutions
3143 Aviara Ct  (60564-4617)
PHONE .................................. 708 790-7589
Shoaib S Khadri, *President*
Keith J Geitner,
EMP: 10
SALES: 6MM  Privately Held
SIC: 2273  Mats & matting

**(G-15815)**
**MACH MECHANICAL GROUP LLC**
28w016 Country View Dr  (60564-9643)
PHONE .................................. 630 674-6224
Amy Reiser,
EMP: 1
SQ FT: 1,750
SALES: 250K  Privately Held
SIC: 1711  3443  Heating & air conditioning contractors; ducting, metal plate

**(G-15816)**
**MEDIA UNLIMITED INC**
Also Called: Cygnet Midwest
5024 Ace Ln Ste 112  (60564-8103)
PHONE .................................. 630 527-0900
Fax: 630 527-0999
Laura Adamski, *President*
David Bartneick, *Manager*
Colin Pritchard, *Art Dir*
John Adamski, *Real Est Agnt*
EMP: 8
SALES (est): 1.4MM  Privately Held
WEB: www.cygnetmidwest.com
SIC: 7311  7336  7334  5999  Advertising agencies; commercial art & graphic design; photocopying & duplicating services; banners, flags, decals & posters; poster & decal printing, lithographic

**(G-15817)**
**MIDWEST STAIR PARTS**
31w335 Schoger Dr  (60564-5657)
PHONE .................................. 630 723-3991
EMP: 3
SALES (est): 259.3K  Privately Held
SIC: 3446  Stairs, staircases, stair treads: prefabricated metal

**(G-15818)**
**NATIONAL DEF INTELLIGENCE INC**
Also Called: Alicom
2863 95th St 143-380  (60564-9005)
PHONE .................................. 630 757-4007
Daniel Sproul, *President*
Greg Castora, *Principal*
EMP: 7
SALES (est): 942.4K  Privately Held
WEB: www.alicominc.com
SIC: 7373  1731  7381  7379  Local area network (LAN) systems integrator; voice, data & video wiring contractor; detective services; computer related consulting services; rockets, space & military, complete; personal investigation service

**(G-15819)**
**NAVIPOINT GENOMICS LLC**
2515 Dewes Ln  (60564-8473)
PHONE .................................. 630 464-8013
EMP: 5
SALES (est): 117.2K  Privately Held
SIC: 7372  Business oriented computer software

**(G-15820)**
**NU-RECYCLING TECHNOLOGY INC**
Also Called: Ecolo-Mid West
10364 Book Rd  (60564-8319)
PHONE .................................. 630 904-5237
Fax: 630 904-5239
Howard Perrine, *President*
James F Gessner, *Vice Pres*
Donald Weckel, *Controller*
EMP: 10

**Naperville - Will County (G-15821)**

SALES (est): 1.4MM **Privately Held**
WEB: www.ecoloofillinois.com
SIC: 3559  8748  5084  Recycling machinery; business consulting; recycling machinery & equipment

**(G-15821)**
**PANELSHOPNET INC**
3460 Ohara Ter  (60564-8167)
PHONE..................................630 692-0214
Gregory Schoeck, *President*
EMP: 1
SALES (est): 217.5K **Privately Held**
WEB: www.panelshop.net
SIC: 3613  Control panels, electric

**(G-15822)**
**PLUS SIGNS & BANNERS INC**
10s187 Schoger Dr Ste 51  (60564-4678)
PHONE..................................630 236-6917
Fax: 630 236-6940
Rita Mondrala, *CEO*
EMP: 3
SALES: 203K **Privately Held**
WEB: www.plussigns.com
SIC: 3993  5099  5999  Signs & advertising specialties; signs, except electric; banners, flags, decals & posters

**(G-15823)**
**PRESTIGE MOTOR WORKS INC**
11258 S Route 59 1  (60564-8090)
PHONE..................................630 780-6439
Alex Tovstanovsky, *Principal*
EMP: 6 EST: 2011
SQ FT: 10,000
SALES (est): 1.4MM **Privately Held**
SIC: 5599  3089  3069  3714  Automotive dealers; automotive parts, plastic; battery boxes, jars or parts, hard rubber; motor vehicle parts & accessories; motor vehicle engines & parts; high performance auto repair & service

**(G-15824)**
**RKC CLEANER I CORP**
4071 S Route 59  (60564-5802)
PHONE..................................630 904-0477
EMP: 15
SQ FT: 1,500
SALES (est): 241.7K
SALES (corp-wide): 729.1K **Privately Held**
SIC: 7216  3582  Drycleaning plants, except rugs; ironers, commercial laundry & drycleaning
PA: Rkc Holding Corp
    4071 S Route 59
    Naperville IL 60564
    630 904-0477

**(G-15825)**
**SCREEN PRINT PLUS INC**
8815 Ramm Dr Ste A  (60564-9347)
PHONE..................................630 236-0260
Robert Frances Jr, *President*
EMP: 2 EST: 1997
SQ FT: 3,600
SALES (est): 236.7K **Privately Held**
SIC: 2752  Commercial printing, lithographic

**(G-15826)**
**SECOND CHANCE INC**
Also Called: Craig Alan Salon
5320 Switch Grass Ln  (60564-5369)
PHONE..................................630 904-5955
EMP: 12
SALES (est): 730K **Privately Held**
SIC: 2395  Pleating/Stitching Services

**(G-15827)**
**SHARPEDGE SOLUTIONS  INC**
2728 Forgue Dr Ste 106  (60564-4192)
PHONE..................................630 792-9639
Fax: 630 792-9636
Bhaskara Katiki, *President*
Srinivasa Dullam, *General Mgr*
EMP: 17
SALES (est): 1.6MM **Privately Held**
WEB: www.esharpedge.com
SIC: 7372  Prepackaged software

**(G-15828)**
**SPRINTER COML PRINT LABEL CORP**
Also Called: Proforma Coml Print Group
4820 Fesseneva Ln  (60564-5769)
PHONE..................................630 460-3492
Kevin J Springer, *President*
EMP: 6 EST: 2003
SALES (est): 706.3K **Privately Held**
SIC: 2752  Commercial printing, lithographic

**(G-15829)**
**SUGAR MONKEY CUPCAKES INC**
2728 Wild Timothy Rd  (60564-4357)
PHONE..................................630 527-1869
Neda Darwish, *Owner*
EMP: 8 EST: 2008
SALES (est): 700.2K **Privately Held**
SIC: 2051  Cakes, bakery: except frozen

**(G-15830)**
**TINEX TECHNOLOGY CORP**
4759 Clearwater Ln  (60564-5389)
PHONE..................................630 904-5368
Fred Liu, *President*
Shirley Liu, *Controller*
Louis Liu, *Manager*
▲ EMP: 5
SALES (est): 552K **Privately Held**
SIC: 3089  Injection molding of plastics

**(G-15831)**
**VICTORIA AMPLIFIER COMPANY**
1504 Newman Ct  (60564-4132)
PHONE..................................630 369-3527
Fax: 630 527-2221
Mark A Baier, *President*
Maureen Baier, *CFO*
EMP: 10
SALES: 1MM **Privately Held**
WEB: www.victoriaamp.com
SIC: 3651  3699  Amplifiers: radio, public address or musical instrument; electric sound equipment

**(G-15832)**
**WILTEK INC**
3819 Grassmere Rd  (60564-8227)
P.O. Box 9330  (60567-0330)
PHONE..................................630 922-9200
Richard Wilinski, *President*
EMP: 3 EST: 1996
SALES: 280K **Privately Held**
WEB: www.wiltek.net
SIC: 3444  Sheet metalwork

## Nashville
### *Washington County*

**(G-15833)**
**ANTOLIN INTERIORS USA  INC**
Also Called: Nashville Interior Systems Div
18355 Enterprise Ave  (62263-1600)
PHONE..................................618 327-4416
Tim Staley, *Safety Mgr*
Cheryl Cook, *Purch Agent*
Joseph Heimbuecher, *Engineer*
John Wall, *Engineer*
Mark Deterding, *Design Engr*
EMP: 291
SALES (corp-wide): 2.8MM **Privately Held**
WEB: www.atreum.com
SIC: 3714  3429  Motor vehicle parts & accessories; manufactured hardware (general)
HQ: Antolin Interiors Usa, Inc.
    1700 Atlantic Blvd
    Auburn Hills MI 48326
    248 373-1749

**(G-15834)**
**BEELMAN READY-MIX INC**
Also Called: Plant 06
17558 Mockingbird Rd  (62263-3406)
PHONE..................................618 478-2044
Mike Hocking, *Manager*
EMP: 5 **Privately Held**
WEB: www.beelmanrm.com
SIC: 5211  3273  Masonry materials & supplies; ready-mixed concrete
PA: Beelman Ready-Mix, Inc.
    1 Racehorse Dr
    East Saint Louis IL 62205

**(G-15835)**
**EVANS TALAIHA**
550 W Saint Louis St  (62263-1110)
P.O. Box 287  (62263-0287)
PHONE..................................618 327-8200
Talaiha Evans, *Owner*
EMP: 3
SALES (est): 238K **Privately Held**
SIC: 1311  Crude petroleum production

**(G-15836)**
**GATEWAY SEED COMPANY  INC (PA)**
5517 Van Buren Rd  (62263-4812)
PHONE..................................618 327-8000
Fax: 618 327-9330
James Lutz, *President*
Dan Hish, *Vice Pres*
Matthew Heggemeier, *Admin Sec*
EMP: 4
SALES (est): 740.5K **Privately Held**
SIC: 3999  Seeds, coated or treated, from purchased seeds

**(G-15837)**
**MAGNA EXTERIORS AMERICA INC**
18310 Enterprise Ave  (62263-1619)
PHONE..................................618 327-4381
Art Stolle, *Purch Mgr*
EMP: 1000
SALES (corp-wide): 36.4B **Privately Held**
SIC: 3714  Bumpers & bumperettes, motor vehicle
HQ: Magna Exteriors Of America, Inc.
    750 Tower Dr
    Troy MI 48098
    248 631-1100

**(G-15838)**
**MAGNA EXTRORS INTRORS AMER INC**
Innertech - Nashville
18355 Enterprise Ave  (62263-1600)
PHONE..................................618 327-2136
Tosha Jasper, *Materials Mgr*
Bob Shchwab, *Branch Mgr*
Brian Mense, *CIO*
EMP: 350
SALES (corp-wide): 36.4B **Privately Held**
SIC: 3714  Motor vehicle parts & accessories
HQ: Magna Exteriors Of America, Inc.
    750 Tower Dr
    Troy MI 48098
    248 631-1100

**(G-15839)**
**MARION OELZE (PA)**
Also Called: Bits of Gold Jewelry
11872 County Highway 27 # 3  (62263-2606)
PHONE..................................618 327-9224
Marion Oelze, *Owner*
EMP: 8
SALES (est): 2.4MM **Privately Held**
WEB: www.bitsofgold.com
SIC: 1381  5084  5944  5812  Drilling oil & gas wells; oil well machinery, equipment & supplies; jewelry stores; eating places

**(G-15840)**
**NASCOTE INDUSTRIES  INC (HQ)**
18310 Enterprise Ave  (62263-1619)
PHONE..................................618 327-3286
Fax: 618 327-3566
Andrew Barban, *President*
Alan J Power, *President*
Art Stolle, *Materials Dir*
Carolyn Detering, *Senior Buyer*
Sue Brammeier, *Purch Agent*
▲ EMP: 600
SALES (est): 285.5MM
SALES (corp-wide): 36.4B **Privately Held**
SIC: 3714  Bumpers & bumperettes, motor vehicle
PA: Magna International Inc
    337 Magna Dr
    Aurora ON L4G 7
    905 726-2462

**(G-15841)**
**NASCOTE INDUSTRIES  INC**
17582 Mockingbird Rd  (62263-3406)
PHONE..................................618 478-2092
Lee Suedmeyer, *Branch Mgr*
EMP: 200
SALES (corp-wide): 36.4B **Privately Held**
SIC: 3714  Bumpers & bumperettes, motor vehicle
HQ: Nascote Industries, Inc.
    18310 Enterprise Ave
    Nashville IL 62263
    618 327-3286

**(G-15842)**
**NASCOTE INDUSTRIES INC**
18355 Enterprise Ave  (62263-1600)
PHONE..................................618 327-3286
EMP: 3
SALES (est): 107.6K **Privately Held**
SIC: 3999  Atomizers, toiletry

**(G-15843)**
**NASHVILLE MEMORIAL CO**
542 E Saint Louis St  (62263-1706)
PHONE..................................618 327-8492
Fax: 618 327-8492
Jerome Lager, *President*
EMP: 3
SALES (est): 320K **Privately Held**
SIC: 3281  Monument or burial stone, cut & shaped

**(G-15844)**
**NASHVILLE NEWS**
Also Called: Nashville News, The
211 W Saint Louis St  (62263-1161)
P.O. Box 47  (62263-0047)
PHONE..................................618 327-3411
Fax: 618 327-3299
Richard Tomaszewski, *President*
Constance Tomaszewski, *Treasurer*
EMP: 10
SALES (est): 440K **Privately Held**
SIC: 2711  Newspapers, publishing & printing

**(G-15845)**
**OELZE EQUIPMENT COMPANY LLC**
11800 County Highway 27  (62263-2606)
P.O. Box 325  (62263-0325)
PHONE..................................618 327-9111
Kim Oelze,
Elmer Dean Oelze,
Jeffery E Oelze,
Wiliam A Oelze,
EMP: 25
SQ FT: 1,500
SALES (est): 2.2MM **Privately Held**
SIC: 1389  1311  Oil field services; crude petroleum & natural gas production

**(G-15846)**
**QUAD-COUNTY READY MIX CORP**
1050 N Washington St  (62263-1000)
PHONE..................................618 327-3748
Fax: 618 327-3748
Herb Husteddi, *Manager*
EMP: 13
SALES (corp-wide): 18.9MM **Privately Held**
SIC: 3273  Ready-mixed concrete
PA: Quad-County Ready Mix Corp.
    300 W 12th St
    Okawville IL 62271
    618 243-6430

**(G-15847)**
**SISCO CORPORATION (PA)**
Also Called: Southern Illinois State Cont
1520 S Mill St  (62263-2077)
P.O. Box 51  (62263-0051)
PHONE..................................618 327-3066
Fax: 618 327-3201
Ronald D Whitener, *President*
Larry Zeitler, *General Mgr*
Emanuel Whitener, *Corp Secy*
Joel Whitener, *Vice Pres*
Jeanne Restrick, *Manager*
EMP: 45
SQ FT: 80,000

SALES (est): 11.8MM **Privately Held**
WEB: www.siscobox.com
SIC: 2653 3081 Boxes, corrugated: made from purchased materials; packing materials, plastic sheet

*(G-15848)*
**STITCH TEC CO INC (PA)**
887 N Washington St (62263-1050)
P.O. Box 253 (62263-0253)
PHONE..................................618 327-8054
H J Jones, *President*
Pat Jones, *Treasurer*
Tammy Jones, *Manager*
EMP: 6
SQ FT: 40,000
SALES (est): 1.6MM **Privately Held**
SIC: 2653 4225 Boxes, solid fiber: made from purchased materials; general warehousing & storage

## National Stock Yards
### St. Clair County

*(G-15849)*
**BAILY INTERNATIONAL INC (PA)**
1122 State Route 3 (62071)
PHONE..................................618 451-8878
Max Tsai, *Vice Pres*
Sandy Tsai, *Vice Pres*
Ted Jackson, *Human Resources*
Mike Neuhaus, *Director*
George Tsai, *Officer*
▲ EMP: 65
SQ FT: 45,000
SALES (est): 78.3MM **Privately Held**
WEB: www.bailyinc.com
SIC: 2098 Noodles (e.g. egg, plain & water), dry

*(G-15850)*
**DARLING INGREDIENTS INC**
2 Exchange Ave (62071-1003)
P.O. Box 55 (62071-0055)
PHONE..................................618 271-8190
Fax: 618 874-1001
Garry Bryd, *Manager*
EMP: 42
SALES (corp-wide): 3.4B **Publicly Held**
WEB: www.darlingii.com
SIC: 2077 3111 Tallow rendering, inedible; leather tanning & finishing
PA: Darling Ingredients Inc.
   251 Oconnor Ridge Blvd
   Irving TX 75038
   972 717-0300

*(G-15851)*
**PACKERS BY PRODUCTS INC**
1087 Rte 3 N (62071)
PHONE..................................618 271-0660
Fax: 618 271-9822
Ralph Schaefer, *President*
Chris Muetze, *Vice Pres*
EMP: 10
SQ FT: 100,000
SALES (est): 755.5K **Privately Held**
SIC: 2048 Feather meal, prepared as animal feed

## Nauvoo
### Hancock County

*(G-15852)*
**BAXTER VINEYARDS**
2010 Parley St (62354-1355)
P.O. Box 342 (62354-0342)
PHONE..................................217 453-2528
Fax: 217 453-6600
Brenda Logan, *Owner*
Kelly Logan, *Owner*
EMP: 3 EST: 1857
SALES (est): 210.2K **Privately Held**
WEB: www.nauvoowinery.com
SIC: 2084 0172 0175 0111 Wines; grapes; apple orchard; pear orchard; wheat

*(G-15853)*
**MISSOURI WOOD CRAFT INC**
Also Called: Allyn House, The
1400 Mulholland St (62354-1006)
PHONE..................................217 453-2204
Fax: 217 453-6001
Charles Allen, *President*
Debbie Allen, *Corp Secy*
EMP: 4
SALES: 300K **Privately Held**
SIC: 5947 2431 Gift shop; millwork

*(G-15854)*
**NAUVOO MILL & BAKERY**
1530 Mulholland St (62354-1152)
PHONE..................................217 453-6734
Paul Brown, *Managing Prtnr*
Carol Brown, *Partner*
EMP: 7
SALES: 250K **Privately Held**
SIC: 0723 2051 2041 Flour milling custom services; bread, cake & related products; flour & other grain mill products

*(G-15855)*
**NAUVOO PRODUCTS INC**
1420 Mulholland St (62354-1006)
P.O. Box 176 (62354-0176)
PHONE..................................217 453-2817
Fax: 217 453-6074
Rose Poppe, *President*
Matthew Poppe, *Exec VP*
David Poppe, *Director*
Jamie Poppe, *Director*
Sheila Poppe, *Director*
EMP: 11
SQ FT: 4,000
SALES: 1.3MM **Privately Held**
SIC: 2822 Synthetic rubber

*(G-15856)*
**OUTLAW TEES**
85 N Iowa St (62354-2350)
P.O. Box 145 (62354-0145)
PHONE..................................217 453-2359
John Mc Carty, *President*
EMP: 9
SALES (est): 550K **Privately Held**
WEB: www.outlawtees.com
SIC: 2396 Screen printing on fabric articles

## Neoga
### Cumberland County

*(G-15857)*
**BRIGHTON CABINETRY INC (PA)**
1095 Industrial Park Ave (62447-2421)
PHONE..................................217 895-3000
Fax: 217 895-3005
John Mikk, *President*
Tony Creek, *Vice Pres*
Randy Beltz, *Controller*
Erin Ledbetter, *Marketing Staff*
Dale Stuart, *Supervisor*
EMP: 17
SQ FT: 16,000
SALES (est): 2.5MM **Privately Held**
WEB: www.brightoncabinetry.com
SIC: 2434 Wood kitchen cabinets

*(G-15858)*
**GOLDA INC**
Also Called: Leading Lady Company
100 Trowbridge Rd (62447-1120)
P.O. Box 850 (62447-0850)
PHONE..................................217 895-3602
Fax: 217 895-3766
Jerry Maddox, *Branch Mgr*
Lila Johnson, *Asst Mgr*
EMP: 108
SALES (corp-wide): 20.3MM **Privately Held**
SIC: 2342 5621 2339 Maternity bras & corsets; maternity wear; maternity clothing
PA: Golda Inc.
   24050 Commerce Park
   Cleveland OH 44122
   216 464-5490

## Neponset
### Bureau County

*(G-15859)*
**MARTIN ENGINEERING COMPANY (PA)**
1 Martin Pl (61345-9766)
PHONE..................................309 852-2384
Fax: 309 594-2432
Scott E Hutter, *President*
Edward Peterson, *General Mgr*
Michael Hengl, *Managing Dir*
Bill Shukla, *Managing Dir*
Edwin Peterson, *Chairman*
◆ EMP: 235
SQ FT: 130,000
SALES (est): 175.3MM **Privately Held**
SIC: 3829 3532 Measuring & controlling devices; mining machinery; flotation machinery (mining machinery); cleaning machinery, mineral

## New Athens
### St. Clair County

*(G-15860)*
**KASKASKIA TOOL AND MACHINE INC**
107 S Benton St (62264-1311)
PHONE..................................618 475-3301
Fax: 618 475-2447
Roy Lee Albert, *President*
Dan Albert, *Vice Pres*
Cathy Ruhmann, *Buyer*
EMP: 24
SQ FT: 15,000
SALES (est): 2.5MM **Privately Held**
WEB: www.kaskaskia.com
SIC: 3599 3544 3469 Machine shop, jobbing & repair; special dies, tools, jigs & fixtures; metal stampings

*(G-15861)*
**SIEMENS MANUFACTURING CO INC**
500 N Johnson St (62264-1157)
PHONE..................................618 475-3325
Fax: 618 475-3334
Dennis Allschied, *Manager*
EMP: 198
SALES (corp-wide): 44.8MM **Privately Held**
WEB: www.jans50.com
SIC: 3672 Printed circuit boards
PA: Siemens Manufacturing Co. Inc.
   410 W Washington St
   Freeburg IL 62243
   618 539-3000

## New Baden
### Clinton County

*(G-15862)*
**KITBUILDERS MAGAZINE LLC**
1117 Harvey Ln (62265-2031)
PHONE..................................618 588-5232
EMP: 3 EST: 2010
SALES (est): 144.9K **Privately Held**
SIC: 2721 Periodicals

*(G-15863)*
**QUAD-COUNTY READY MIX CORP**
Also Called: Quad County Rdymx New Baden
7415 State Route 160 (62265-2713)
P.O. Box 18 (62265-0018)
PHONE..................................618 588-4656
Fax: 618 588-3236
Darrell Hewlett, *Branch Mgr*
EMP: 15
SALES (corp-wide): 18.9MM **Privately Held**
SIC: 3273 Ready-mixed concrete
PA: Quad-County Ready Mix Corp.
   300 W 12th St
   Okawville IL 62271
   618 243-6430

*(G-15864)*
**RELOAD SALES INC**
Also Called: Roof Structures
418 Plum Ln (62265-1147)
PHONE..................................618 588-2866
Mike Rehkamper, *President*
Sandy Rehkamper, *Admin Sec*
EMP: 30
SALES (est): 4.4MM **Privately Held**
SIC: 3531 Roofing equipment

*(G-15865)*
**SPAETH WELDING INC**
321 W Missouri St (62265-1741)
PHONE..................................618 588-3596
Fax: 618 588-3824
Marvin J Spaeth, *President*
Darlene Spaeth, *Admin Sec*
EMP: 15 EST: 1974
SQ FT: 35,000
SALES (est): 1.8MM **Privately Held**
SIC: 7692 Welding repair

## New Berlin
### Sangamon County

*(G-15866)*
**THOMAS TEES INC**
210 S Oak St (62670-6468)
P.O. Box 47 (62670-0047)
PHONE..................................217 488-2288
Gregory A Thomas, *President*
Denise Thomas, *Corp Secy*
EMP: 6
SALES (est): 654.9K **Privately Held**
SIC: 2759 Commercial printing

## New Boston
### Mercer County

*(G-15867)*
**WILDER FARMS**
271 140th Ave (61272-8529)
PHONE..................................309 537-3218
Maurice Wilder, *Owner*
EMP: 4 EST: 2000
SALES (est): 325K **Privately Held**
SIC: 3523 Driers (farm): grain, hay & seed

## New Canton
### Pike County

*(G-15868)*
**GOLDEN ROAD PRODUCTIONS**
27652 County Highway 13 (62356-3409)
PHONE..................................217 335-2606
Charles Dolbeare, *Owner*
EMP: 5
SQ FT: 6,400
SALES (est): 200K **Privately Held**
SIC: 3648 7359 Stage lighting equipment; sound & lighting equipment rental

## New Lenox
### Will County

*(G-15869)*
**ALPHA MACHINE CORP**
1742 Ferro Dr (60451-3501)
PHONE..................................708 532-2313
Fax: 708 532-1238
Kevin Ekert, *President*
EMP: 23 EST: 1966
SQ FT: 19,000
SALES (est): 4.3MM **Privately Held**
SIC: 3599 Machine shop, jobbing & repair

*(G-15870)*
**ARLEN-JACOB MANUFACTURING CO**
2 Ford Dr Ste H (60451-4529)
PHONE..................................815 485-4777
Fax: 815 485-4782
Keith Czaja, *President*
Robyn Robeets, *Manager*

# New Lenox - Will County (G-15871)

Donald Johnson, *Admin Sec*
**EMP:** 22
**SQ FT:** 10,000
**SALES (est):** 3.9MM **Privately Held**
**SIC: 2431** Stair railings, wood; staircases & stairs, wood

### (G-15871)
### CLASSICAL STATUARY & DECOR
21621 S Schoolhouse Rd (60451-3714)
**PHONE**.................................815 462-3408
**Fax:** 815 462-3409
Timothy Haggerty, *President*
Debra A Haggerty, *Vice Pres*
**EMP:** 8
**SQ FT:** 5,400
**SALES (est):** 550K **Privately Held**
**SIC: 3272** Concrete products

### (G-15872)
### COOLER CONCEPTS INC
21753 S Center Ave (60451-2803)
P.O. Box 1247, Frankfort (60423-7247)
**PHONE**.................................815 462-3866
William J Dunnett Jr, *President*
Diane Dunnett, *Vice Pres*
**EMP:** 6
**SQ FT:** 5,000
**SALES:** 1MM **Privately Held**
**SIC: 3411** Metal cans

### (G-15873)
### CREST CHEMICAL INDUSTRIES LTD
Also Called: Crest Industries
1066 Industry Rd Ste A (60451-2601)
P.O. Box 85 (60451-0085)
**PHONE**.................................815 485-2138
**Fax:** 815 485-2190
James Lee, *President*
Richard Sleckman, *Vice Pres*
Kathy Wehrman, *Manager*
**EMP:** 8 **EST:** 1947
**SQ FT:** 6,000
**SALES (est):** 2.6MM **Privately Held**
**WEB:** www.crest-industries.com
**SIC: 2851** Lacquers, varnishes, enamels & other coatings

### (G-15874)
### D ME TO ME
14001 W Illinois Hwy (60451-3282)
**PHONE**.................................815 485-3632
William Downs, *Owner*
**EMP:** 12
**SALES (est):** 802.2K **Privately Held**
**SIC: 3842** Wheelchairs

### (G-15875)
### DESIGN GRAPHICS INC
1309 S Schoolhouse Rd # 3 (60451-3748)
**PHONE**.................................815 462-3323
Edward Gramza, *President*
Marlene Gramza, *Corp Secy*
Kathy Gramza, *Vice Pres*
**EMP:** 6
**SQ FT:** 4,800
**SALES (est):** 618.9K **Privately Held**
**WEB:** www.midwestaccurate.net
**SIC: 2752** 2791 2789 2759 Commercial printing, offset; typesetting; bookbinding & related work; commercial printing

### (G-15876)
### DIRECT MAIL EQUIPMENT SERVICES
14460 W Edison Dr Ste D (60451-3776)
**PHONE**.................................815 485-7010
Gary Cullen, *Owner*
**EMP:** 2
**SQ FT:** 1,500
**SALES (est):** 250K **Privately Held**
**SIC: 3579** Mailing machines

### (G-15877)
### DUNHAM DESIGNS INC
1024 S Cedar Rd (60451-2646)
**PHONE**.................................815 462-0100
George Carroll, *President*
Mary Sanchez, *Office Mgr*
**EMP:** 6
**SQ FT:** 6,000
**SALES:** 200K **Privately Held**
**WEB:** www.dunhamdesigns.com
**SIC: 3089** Thermoformed finished plastic products

### (G-15878)
### DYNAMIC NUTRITIONALS INC
Also Called: Cyclone Energy Shot
1014 S Cooper Rd (60451-2679)
**PHONE**.................................815 545-9171
Craig Buske, *President*
Ray Grzesike, *Vice Pres*
**EMP:** 5
**SALES (est):** 370K **Privately Held**
**SIC: 2086** Bottled & canned soft drinks

### (G-15879)
### EJ USA INC
310 Garnet Dr (60451-3502)
**PHONE**.................................815 740-1640
**Fax:** 815 740-1633
Thomas Drown, *Manager*
**EMP:** 15 **Privately Held**
**WEB:** www.ejiw.com
**SIC: 3321** Manhole covers, metal
**HQ:** Ej Usa, Inc.
301 Spring St
East Jordan MI 49727
800 874-4100

### (G-15880)
### EMBROID ME
2399 E Joliet Hwy (60451-2578)
**PHONE**.................................815 485-4155
**Fax:** 815 485-4166
Bill Garrigan, *Owner*
**EMP:** 6
**SALES (est):** 610.8K **Privately Held**
**SIC: 2759** 5949 7319 7999 Screen printing; sewing & needlework; advertising; amusement & recreation

### (G-15881)
### EWW ENTERPRISE INC
1311 S Schoolhouse Rd # 2 (60451-3279)
**PHONE**.................................815 463-9607
**Fax:** 815 463-9615
Edward W Weiher, *President*
**EMP:** 5
**SALES (est):** 836.2K **Privately Held**
**WEB:** www.ewwenterpriseinc.com
**SIC: 3599** Machine & other job shop work

### (G-15882)
### GADGE SIGNS INC
215 E Otto Dr Ste A (60451-2649)
**PHONE**.................................815 462-4490
**Fax:** 708 599-4495
James Gajdorus, *President*
Virginia Gajdorus, *Admin Sec*
**EMP:** 3
**SQ FT:** 2,350
**SALES (est):** 326.1K **Privately Held**
**SIC: 7389** 3993 3953 Sign painting & lettering shop; signs & advertising specialties; marking devices

### (G-15883)
### GALMAR ENTERPRISES INC
Also Called: Humid-A-Mist
14408 W Edison Dr Ste F (60451-4501)
P.O. Box 437 (60451)
**PHONE**.................................815 463-9826
Gus Gallas, *President*
**EMP:** 3
**SALES (est):** 361.2K **Privately Held**
**SIC: 3585** Humidifying equipment, except portable

### (G-15884)
### GRANITE MOUNTAIN INC
538 E Illinois Hwy Ste A (60451-2661)
**PHONE**.................................708 774-1442
Lisa Ritter, *President*
Mark Ritter, *General Mgr*
**EMP:** 5
**SQ FT:** 4,000
**SALES (est):** 226.7K **Privately Held**
**SIC: 5211** 3281 Counter tops; granite, cut & shaped

### (G-15885)
### INNOVATION SPECIALISTS INC
2328 E Lincoln Hwy # 356 (60451-9533)
**PHONE**.................................815 372-9001
Christopher Gambino, *President*
**EMP:** 5
**SQ FT:** 9,000
**SALES (est):** 722.5K **Privately Held**
**SIC: 3496** 3694 Miscellaneous fabricated wire products; engine electrical equipment

### (G-15886)
### INSIGNIA STONE
1901 Howell Dr Ste 1 (60451-3222)
**PHONE**.................................815 463-9802
Mike Bajork, *Owner*
**EMP:** 2
**SALES (est):** 205K **Privately Held**
**SIC: 3281** Curbing, granite or stone

### (G-15887)
### INTEGRITY MANUFACTURING INC
612 Schoolgate Ct (60451-3212)
**PHONE**.................................815 514-8230
Cheryl Wellman, *CEO*
**EMP:** 3
**SALES (est):** 114.3K **Privately Held**
**SIC: 3469** Metal stampings

### (G-15888)
### JDA AQUA CUTTING INC
22037 Howell Dr Ste B (60451-3727)
**PHONE**.................................815 485-8028
Gary Lee, *President*
Josh Lee, *Vice Pres*
Lisa Lee, *Sales Staff*
**EMP:** 4
**SQ FT:** 12,000
**SALES (est):** 400K **Privately Held**
**WEB:** www.jdaaqua.com
**SIC: 3599** Machine & other job shop work

### (G-15889)
### JPMORGAN CHASE BANK NAT ASSN
500 W Maple St Ste 2 (60451-2952)
**PHONE**.................................815 462-2800
William Las, *Office Mgr*
Jason Seltz, *Branch Mgr*
**EMP:** 6
**SALES (corp-wide):** 105.4B **Publicly Held**
**SIC: 3578** Automatic teller machines (ATM)
**HQ:** Jpmorgan Chase Bank, National Association
1111 Polaris Pkwy
Columbus OH 43240
614 436-3055

### (G-15890)
### KRAFT CUSTOM DESIGN INC
22032 Howell Dr (60451-3708)
**PHONE**.................................815 485-5506
**Fax:** 815 485-5854
Laura Fleischhauer, *Principal*
Klaus Fleischhauer, *Principal*
**EMP:** 7
**SALES (est):** 610K **Privately Held**
**SIC: 2541** 2434 Counter & sink tops; wood kitchen cabinets

### (G-15891)
### LIGHTHOUSE PRINTING INC
21754 S Center Ave (60451-2843)
**PHONE**.................................708 479-7776
Mary J Rex, *President*
John D Rex, *Corp Secy*
**EMP:** 4
**SQ FT:** 100
**SALES (est):** 1.5MM **Privately Held**
**SIC: 2759** 7389 Commercial printing; printing broker

### (G-15892)
### MAGNETIC OCCASIONS & MORE INC
21605 S Schoolhouse Rd (60451-3714)
**PHONE**.................................815 462-4141
Kevin Petrie, *President*
Cynthia Petrie, *Vice Pres*
**EMP:** 5
**SQ FT:** 1,200
**SALES:** 259K **Privately Held**
**SIC: 2824** 3695 Vinyl fibers; magnetic & optical recording media

### (G-15893)
### MELISSA A MILLER
Also Called: Dynamic Indus Solution Solvers
13957 W Illinois Hwy # 4 (60451-3226)
Rural Route 420, Momence (60954)
**PHONE**.................................708 529-7786
Melissa Miller, *Owner*
Eric Fandrey, *Vice Pres*
**EMP:** 5
**SALES (est):** 281.8K **Privately Held**
**SIC: 3548** 5084 7699 1711 Electrodes, electric welding; food product manufacturing machinery; industrial machinery & equipment repair; process piping contractor

### (G-15894)
### MERIT EMPLYMENT ASSSSMENT SVCS
Also Called: Tyler, Thomas A PHD
342 Alana Dr (60451-1784)
P.O. Box 193, Flossmoor (60422-0193)
**PHONE**.................................815 320-3680
**Fax:** 708 957-9894
Thomas A Tyler, *President*
Thomas A Tyler Jr, *Vice Pres*
Carol Tyler, *Admin Sec*
**EMP:** 3
**SQ FT:** 700
**SALES (est):** 310.8K **Privately Held**
**SIC: 2741** 8742 Miscellaneous publishing; human resource consulting services

### (G-15895)
### METRIE
2200 W Haven Ave (60451-2542)
**PHONE**.................................815 717-2660
Ted Eisses, *Principal*
▲ **EMP:** 24
**SALES (est):** 6.7MM **Privately Held**
**SIC: 2431** Millwork

### (G-15896)
### MIDWEST COATINGS INC
21765 S Center Ave (60451-2803)
**PHONE**.................................815 717-8914
Dennis Stemper, *Vice Pres*
**EMP:** 2 **EST:** 2013
**SQ FT:** 3,200
**SALES (est):** 226.8K **Privately Held**
**SIC: 3479** Coating of metals & formed products

### (G-15897)
### MILLER PURCELL CO INC
244 W 3rd Ave (60451-1729)
P.O. Box 215 (60451-0215)
**PHONE**.................................815 485-2142
**Fax:** 815 485-2143
David Dyer, *President*
Donald Cordano, *Admin Sec*
**EMP:** 2 **EST:** 1922
**SALES:** 425K **Privately Held**
**SIC: 2952** 3297 2899 2891 Asphalt felts & coatings; nonclay refractories; chemical preparations; adhesives & sealants; cyclic crudes & intermediates; paints & allied products

### (G-15898)
### OGORMAN SON CARPENTRY CONTRS
1930 Airway Ct (60451-2701)
**PHONE**.................................815 485-8997
**Fax:** 815 485-4231
Raymond O'Gorman, *President*
Patricia O'Gorman, *Vice Pres*
**EMP:** 22
**SQ FT:** 18,000
**SALES (est):** 2.2MM **Privately Held**
**SIC: 1751** 2541 2434 Cabinet building & installation; wood partitions & fixtures; wood kitchen cabinets

### (G-15899)
### PARKVIEW ORTHOPAEDIC GROUP
688 Cedar Crossings Dr (60451-5200)
**PHONE**.................................815 727-3030
Patty Hoeksma, *Manager*
**EMP:** 16
**SALES (corp-wide):** 12.4MM **Privately Held**
**SIC: 3842** Surgical appliances & supplies

## GEOGRAPHIC SECTION

### New Lenox - Will County (G-15928)

**PA:** Parkview Orthopaedic Group
7600 W College Dr Ste 3
Palos Heights IL 60463
708 361-0600

**(G-15900)**
**PEG N REDS**
Also Called: Ramseys News Agency
212 S Main St  (60451)
**PHONE**..................................618 586-2015
Rebecca Ramsey, *Owner*
**EMP:** 3
**SQ FT:** 1,600
**SALES (est):** 130K  **Privately Held**
**SIC:** 2711  Newspapers

**(G-15901)**
**PERMA GRAPHICS PRINTERS**
216 N Marley Rd  (60451-2096)
**PHONE**..................................815 485-6955
**Fax:** 815 485-6987
Gene Ludvik, *Owner*
**EMP:** 5
**SALES (est):** 490K  **Privately Held**
**SIC:** 2752  2791  2789  Commercial printing, offset; typesetting; bookbinding & related work

**(G-15902)**
**PREFERRED BUS PUBLICATIONS INC**
1938 E Lincoln Hwy # 216  (60451-3835)
**PHONE**..................................815 717-6399
Joseph Farneti, *President*
**EMP:** 5
**SALES (est):** 352.9K  **Privately Held**
**SIC:** 2721  Periodicals

**(G-15903)**
**QUEN-TEL COMMUNICATION SVC INC**
2759 Meadow Path  (60451-1808)
**PHONE**..................................815 463-1800
Thomas J Quenzel, *President*
**EMP:** 6
**SALES (est):** 550K  **Privately Held**
**SIC:** 3661  Carrier equipment, telephone or telegraph

**(G-15904)**
**R A E TOOL AND MANUFACTURING**
1910 Clearing Ct Ste 2  (60451-3729)
**PHONE**..................................815 485-2506
**Fax:** 815 485-2635
Ron Abbott, *President*
Ed Dieringer, *Vice Pres*
**EMP:** 8  **EST:** 1996
**SQ FT:** 3,200
**SALES (est):** 1.3MM  **Privately Held**
**SIC:** 3599  Machine shop, jobbing & repair

**(G-15905)**
**R S CORCORAN CO**
500 N Vine St  (60451-2918)
**PHONE**..................................815 485-2156
**Fax:** 815 485-5840
William J Kramer, *President*
Joel Cramer, *General Mgr*
Gail K Swinson, *Treasurer*
Jerry Horvath, *Bookkeeper*
Joel Kramer, *Sales Associate*
**EMP:** 21  **EST:** 1945
**SQ FT:** 27,000
**SALES:** 4.5MM  **Privately Held**
**WEB:** www.corcoranpumps.com
**SIC:** 3561  Pumps & pumping equipment

**(G-15906)**
**RINELLA ORTHOTICS INC**
1890 Silver Cross Blvd # 445  (60451-9622)
**PHONE**..................................815 717-8970
Daniel P Rinella, *Principal*
**EMP:** 3
**SALES (est):** 315.2K  **Privately Held**
**SIC:** 3842  Orthopedic appliances

**(G-15907)**
**RISER MACHINE CORP**
1744 Ferro Dr  (60451-3501)
**PHONE**..................................708 532-2313
Chris Lira, *President*
Gina Williams, *Opers Mgr*
April Haffner, *Office Mgr*
**EMP:** 12

**SQ FT:** 8,000
**SALES (est):** 799.9K  **Privately Held**
**SIC:** 3599  Crankshafts & camshafts, machining; electrical discharge machining (EDM)

**(G-15908)**
**RIVERTON CABINET COMPANY**
Also Called: Rivertoncabinets
22000 S Schoolhouse Rd  (60451-3713)
**PHONE**..................................815 462-5300
**Fax:** 815 462-5304
Keith Hinshaw, *President*
Kristy Deboer, *Sales Staff*
Kimberley Smith, *Manager*
▲ **EMP:** 31
**SQ FT:** 50,000
**SALES (est):** 4MM  **Privately Held**
**WEB:** www.rivertoncabinets.com
**SIC:** 1751  5712  2434  Cabinet building & installation; furniture stores; wood kitchen cabinets

**(G-15909)**
**SACO  DPS/MORRIS WAX**
441 Degroate Rd  (60451-2912)
**PHONE**..................................815 462-0939
Gayle Erickson, *Manager*
**EMP:** 1
**SALES (est):** 207.3K
**SALES (corp-wide):** 485.9K  **Privately Held**
**SIC:** 2911  Mineral waxes, natural
**PA:** Kws Holdings Llc
17309 W 84th Ter
Lenexa KS 66219
815 462-0939

**(G-15910)**
**SENDRA SERVICE CORP**
309 Garnet Dr  (60451-3503)
P.O. Box 957, Mokena  (60448-0957)
**PHONE**..................................815 462-0061
Gary Sendra, *President*
Robert A Raycroft, *Admin Sec*
**EMP:** 1
**SALES (est):** 250.7K  **Privately Held**
**SIC:** 3585  3443  Air conditioning equipment, complete; boilers: industrial, power, or marine

**(G-15911)**
**SIMPLE ASSEMBLIES  INC**
22542 S Fernview  (60451)
**PHONE**..................................708 212-7494
Jeffrey Ondrejka, *President*
▲ **EMP:** 2
**SALES (est):** 232.2K  **Privately Held**
**SIC:** 3643  Current-carrying wiring devices

**(G-15912)**
**SPEEDWAY**
570 E Laraway Rd  (60451-3144)
P.O. Box 70, Frankfort  (60423-0070)
**PHONE**..................................815 463-0840
Linda Malmborg, *Principal*
**EMP:** 6
**SALES (est):** 534.4K  **Privately Held**
**SIC:** 2869  Fuels

**(G-15913)**
**STURDEE METAL PRODUCTS INC**
1060 Grand Mesa Ave  (60451-3133)
**PHONE**..................................773 523-3074
Howard Groves, *President*
Jeff Groves, *Vice Pres*
Thomas Kaliski, *Vice Pres*
Eileen Groves, *Admin Sec*
**EMP:** 7
**SQ FT:** 10,000
**SALES:** 1MM  **Privately Held**
**SIC:** 3441  3444  Fabricated structural metal; sheet metalwork

**(G-15914)**
**SUPERHEAT FGH SERVICES INC**
313 Garnet Dr  (60451-3503)
**PHONE**..................................618 251-9450
**EMP:** 6  **Privately Held**
**SIC:** 3569  Heaters, swimming pool: electric
**HQ:** Superheat Fgh Services, Inc.
313 Garnet Dr
New Lenox IL 60451
708 478-0205

**(G-15915)**
**SUPERHEAT FGH SERVICES INC (HQ)**
313 Garnet Dr  (60451-3503)
**PHONE**..................................708 478-0205
Miles Brown, *President*
Joe Borror, *Vice Pres*
Allan Pearson, *Finance*
Sandra Hofmann, *Accounts Mgr*
Craig Topping, *Marketing Staff*
**EMP:** 1
**SQ FT:** 10,000
**SALES (est):** 12.1MM  **Privately Held**
**SIC:** 3398  Metal heat treating

**(G-15916)**
**SUPERTECH HOLDINGS INC (PA)**
Also Called: Superheat Fgh
313 Garnet Dr  (60451-3503)
**PHONE**..................................708 478-0205
Norm Mac Arthur, *CEO*
Miles Brown, *President*
Brad Hennig, *Regional Mgr*
Bernie Auer, *VP Opers*
Patrick Carter, *Project Mgr*
**EMP:** 2
**SALES (est):** 77.4MM  **Privately Held**
**SIC:** 3398  Metal heat treating

**(G-15917)**
**TEC SYSTEMS  INC**
Also Called: Nutec Manufacturing
908 Garnet Ct  (60451-3569)
**PHONE**..................................815 722-2800
**Fax:** 815 722-2831
Zibe Gibson, *CEO*
Virginia Cagwin, *CFO*
**EMP:** 17
**SALES (est):** 4.2MM  **Privately Held**
**WEB:** www.nutecmfg.com
**SIC:** 3556  Meat processing machinery

**(G-15918)**
**TEDDS CSTM INSTALLATIONS INC**
Also Called: Tedds Custom Installations
21719 S Center Ave Ste A  (60451-2818)
**PHONE**..................................815 485-6800
Tedd Vinciguerra, *CEO*
Heodore Vinciquerra, *President*
**EMP:** 3
**SALES (est):** 270K  **Privately Held**
**SIC:** 3679  Antennas, receiving

**(G-15919)**
**TEES INK**
1215 Revere Ct  (60451-3172)
**PHONE**..................................815 462-7300
Tim Opitz, *Principal*
**EMP:** 3
**SALES (est):** 219.4K  **Privately Held**
**SIC:** 2759  Screen printing

**(G-15920)**
**TITAN STEEL CORPORATION**
2201 W Haven Ave  (60451-2595)
**PHONE**..................................815 726-4900
**Fax:** 815 726-0967
Mark Hunt, *Managing Dir*
Carol Barz, *Human Res Dir*
Jim Hartley, *Sales Staff*
Larry Long, *Manager*
Julie Stiles, *Manager*
**EMP:** 50
**SALES (corp-wide):** 49.2MM  **Privately Held**
**SIC:** 3441  Fabricated structural metal
**HQ:** Titan Steel Corporation
2500b Broening Hwy
Baltimore MD 21224
410 631-5200

**(G-15921)**
**TOYO PUMP NORTH AMERICA**
1520 Monarch Ave  (60451-2562)
**PHONE**..................................815 806-1414
Richard Wynn, *Design Engr*
Don Lorenz, *Manager*
**EMP:** 4  **EST:** 2007
**SALES (est):** 451.3K  **Privately Held**
**SIC:** 3561  5084  Pumps & pumping equipment; pumps & pumping equipment

**(G-15922)**
**TRI STAR CABINET & TOP CO INC (PA)**
1000 S Cedar Rd  (60451-2646)
P.O. Box 338  (60451-0338)
**PHONE**..................................815 485-2564
**Fax:** 815 485-5747
Joseph E Wilda Jr, *President*
James H Thomas, *President*
Kathleen Lenci, *Vice Pres*
Cosmo Misischia, *Admin Sec*
**EMP:** 62
**SQ FT:** 85,000
**SALES:** 9MM  **Privately Held**
**WEB:** www.tristarcabinets.com
**SIC:** 2434  Wood kitchen cabinets

**(G-15923)**
**TRIAD OIL INC**
1613 Andrea Dr  (60451-2303)
**PHONE**..................................815 485-9535
Gary Shipley, *Principal*
**EMP:** 3
**SALES (est):** 295.2K  **Privately Held**
**SIC:** 3533  Oil & gas field machinery

**(G-15924)**
**TRIPLEX MARINE LTD**
1110 E Haven Ave  (60451-4001)
**PHONE**..................................815 485-0202
**Fax:** 815 485-0777
Robert Gryczewski Jr, *President*
Donna Gryczewski, *Corp Secy*
**EMP:** 5
**SQ FT:** 5,000
**SALES (est):** 650.6K  **Privately Held**
**SIC:** 3731  Shipbuilding & repairing

**(G-15925)**
**URPOINT  LLC**
2089 Edgeview Dr  (60451-4823)
**PHONE**..................................773 919-9002
Margaret Fitzpatrick, *Owner*
James McLaughlin, *Owner*
**EMP:** 3
**SALES (est):** 240.3K  **Privately Held**
**SIC:** 3089  5092  7389  Holders: paper towel, grocery bag, etc.: plastic; toy novelties & amusements;

**(G-15926)**
**V J MATTSON COMPANY**
713 Jennifer Ct  (60451-1300)
**PHONE**..................................708 479-1990
**Fax:** 708 479-1115
Thomas E Morack, *President*
Robert Morack, *Exec VP*
Donna Kampic, *Manager*
**EMP:** 100
**SQ FT:** 5,500
**SALES (est):** 8.6MM  **Privately Held**
**WEB:** www.vjmattson.com
**SIC:** 1741  3255  Masonry & other stonework; refractory or acid brick masonry; clay refractories

**(G-15927)**
**WEST END TOOL & DIE  INC**
22020 Howell Dr  (60451-3708)
**PHONE**..................................815 462-3040
Michael J Zambon, *President*
Robert W Lipka, *Admin Sec*
**EMP:** 3  **EST:** 1999
**SALES (est):** 643.8K  **Privately Held**
**SIC:** 3544  7692  Special dies & tools; welding repair

**(G-15928)**
**WILL COUNTY WELL & PUMP CO INC (PA)**
1200 S Cedar Rd Ste 1a  (60451-4400)
**PHONE**..................................815 485-2413
**Fax:** 708 942-6387
Jacqueline Rob, *President*
Correy Rob, *Admin Sec*
**EMP:** 9
**SQ FT:** 4,000
**SALES (est):** 1.2MM  **Privately Held**
**SIC:** 3589  1781  Water treatment equipment, industrial; water well drilling

## New Windsor
*Mercer County*

**(G-15929)**
**ANR PIPELINE COMPANY**
296 N 600th Ave  (61465-9433)
PHONE..................................309 667-2158
Fax: 309 667-2855
Tim Treece, *Manager*
EMP: 5
SALES (corp-wide): 9.2B **Privately Held**
SIC: 4922 1389 Pipelines, natural gas; gas compressing (natural gas) at the fields
HQ: Anr Pipeline Company
   700 Louisiana St Ste 700
   Houston TX 77002
   832 320-2000

**(G-15930)**
**DONALDSON COMPANY INC**
3230 65th Ave  (61465-9350)
PHONE..................................309 667-2885
EMP: 238
SALES (corp-wide): 2.2B **Publicly Held**
SIC: 3599 Amusement park equipment
PA: Donaldson Company, Inc.
   1400 W 94th St
   Minneapolis MN 55431
   952 887-3131

**(G-15931)**
**ERICSON S LOG & LUMBER CO (PA)**
11 State Highway 17  (61465-9452)
P.O. Box 37  (61465-0037)
PHONE..................................309 667-2147
Fax: 309 667-2140
Sam E Ericson, *Owner*
EMP: 7
SQ FT: 800
SALES (est): 916.5K **Privately Held**
SIC: 2421 5099 2426 2411 Sawmills & planing mills, general; logs, hewn ties, posts & poles; hardwood dimension & flooring mills; logging

## Newark
*Kendall County*

**(G-15932)**
**BALLOON ART BY DJ**
231 W Joliet St  (60541-9373)
PHONE..................................815 736-6123
Gerald Conner, *Owner*
EMP: 2
SALES (est): 205.6K **Privately Held**
SIC: 3069 Balloons, advertising & toy: rubber; atomizer bulbs, rubber

**(G-15933)**
**DIERZEN TRAILER CO**
101 N Fayette St  (60541)
P.O. Box 272  (60541-0272)
PHONE..................................815 695-5291
Louis Dierzen, *President*
Floyd Dierzen, *Vice Pres*
EMP: 60
SQ FT: 46,000
SALES (est): 11.3MM **Privately Held**
SIC: 3713 Dump truck bodies

**(G-15934)**
**RYAN MANUFACTURING INC**
11610 N La Salle Rd  (60541-9626)
PHONE..................................815 695-5310
Gilbert Jacobs, *President*
Carol Jacobs, *Bookkeeper*
Ryan Jacobs, *Manager*
EMP: 5
SQ FT: 12,000
SALES: 400K **Privately Held**
SIC: 3443 3563 3524 Weldments; air & gas compressors; lawn & garden equipment

**(G-15935)**
**SPEED BLEEDER PRODUCTS CO**
13140 Apakesha Rd  (60541-9708)
P.O. Box 192  (60541-0192)
PHONE..................................815 736-6296
Fax: 815 736-6297
Mike Sulwuer, *Owner*
EMP: 3 EST: 1997
SALES: 300K **Privately Held**
WEB: www.speedbleeder.com
SIC: 3559 Automotive maintenance equipment

## Newton
*Jasper County*

**(G-15936)**
**ADVANCED PLBG & PIPE FITTING**
15498 N 1590th St  (62448-3329)
PHONE..................................618 554-2677
Justin Griffith, *Principal*
EMP: 3
SALES (est): 232.3K **Privately Held**
SIC: 3494 Pipe fittings

**(G-15937)**
**ARNDTS STORES INC (PA)**
Also Called: Arndt's Hallmark Shop
106 W Washington St  (62448-1256)
PHONE..................................618 783-2511
Fax: 618 783-2183
Tony B Arndt, *President*
William P Arndt, *Corp Secy*
Glenda Arndt, *Vice Pres*
EMP: 6
SQ FT: 12,000
SALES (est): 1.1MM **Privately Held**
WEB: www.fudgery.com
SIC: 2064 Fudge (candy)

**(G-15938)**
**BN NATIONAL TRAIL**
8810 Commercial Ave  (62448-4091)
PHONE..................................618 783-8709
EMP: 8
SALES (est): 540K **Privately Held**
SIC: 2836 Mfg Biological Products

**(G-15939)**
**DON LEVENTHAL GROUP LLC**
Also Called: Newton Broom & Brush Co
1508 W Jourdan St  (62448-2006)
P.O. Box 358  (62448-0358)
PHONE..................................618 783-4424
Fax: 618 783-2442
Becky Shamhart, *Manager*
Donald Leventhal,
▲ EMP: 28 EST: 1954
SQ FT: 26,000
SALES: 2MM **Privately Held**
SIC: 3991 2392 Brooms & brushes; mops, floor & dust

**(G-15940)**
**GATEHOUSE MEDIA LLC**
Also Called: Newton Press Mentor
700 W Washington St  (62448-1129)
P.O. Box 151  (62448-0151)
PHONE..................................618 783-2324
Fax: 618 783-2325
Lynne Campbell, *President*
Vanette King, *Editor*
EMP: 2
SALES (corp-wide): 1.2B **Publicly Held**
WEB: www.gatehousemedia.com
SIC: 2711 Newspapers
HQ: Gatehouse Media, Llc
   175 Sullys Trl Ste 300
   Pittsford NY 14534
   585 598-0030

**(G-15941)**
**HEARTLAND CLASSICS INC**
1705 W Jourdan St  (62448-2022)
P.O. Box 227  (62448-0227)
PHONE..................................618 783-4444
Toll Free:..........................................877  -
Fax: 618 783-2516
Anthony Griffith, *President*
EMP: 8
SALES (est): 1.1MM **Privately Held**
WEB: www.hclassics.com
SIC: 3711 5521 5531 7532 Reconnaissance cars, assembly of; antique automobiles; automotive accessories; upholstery & trim shop, automotive

**(G-15942)**
**JESSE B HOLT INC**
Also Called: Holt Building
13 Hillcrest Dr  (62448-1524)
PHONE..................................618 783-3075
Fax: 618 783-3916
Ronald Lee Holt, *President*
EMP: 75
SQ FT: 20,000
SALES (est): 7.1MM **Privately Held**
WEB: www.holtbuilding.com
SIC: 2439 5211 Trusses, wooden roof; lumber & other building materials

**(G-15943)**
**NEWTON IMPLEMENT PARTNERSHIP**
9460 E State Highway 33  (62448-3916)
PHONE..................................618 783-8716
Fax: 618 783-2892
Jerry Newlin, *Partner*
Dennis Frichtl, *Partner*
EMP: 22
SALES (est): 14MM **Privately Held**
SIC: 3523 Farm machinery & equipment

**(G-15944)**
**NEWTON READY MIX INC**
Also Called: Ssi
8560 N State Highway 130  (62448-4067)
P.O. Box 40, Olney  (62450-0040)
PHONE..................................618 783-8611
Fax: 618 783-2749
Terry Schrey, *President*
EMP: 10
SQ FT: 700
SALES (est): 1.3MM **Privately Held**
SIC: 3273 3281 1442 Ready-mixed concrete; cut stone & stone products; construction sand & gravel

**(G-15945)**
**NOVANTA INC**
106 Marshall Dr  (62448-4093)
PHONE..................................781 266-5700
EMP: 4
SALES (corp-wide): 384.7MM **Publicly Held**
SIC: 3699 Laser systems & equipment
PA: Novanta Inc.
   125 Middlesex Tpke
   Bedford MA 01730
   781 266-5700

**(G-15946)**
**PETRON OIL PRODUCTION INC (PA)**
Also Called: Marathon One Stop Shop
405 E Jourdan St Apt 3  (62448-1580)
P.O. Box 232  (62448-0232)
PHONE..................................618 783-4486
Fax: 618 783-2145
Ruth Parrish, *President*
Arlene Parrish Snyder, *Exec VP*
Carol Lyon, *Vice Pres*
Ilene Johnson, *Treasurer*
EMP: 6 EST: 1965
SQ FT: 3,500
SALES (est): 2.2MM **Privately Held**
SIC: 1311 7538 5531 Crude petroleum & natural gas production; general automotive repair shops; automotive tires

**(G-15947)**
**RAYMOND D WRIGHT**
35 Homestead Dr  (62448-2004)
PHONE..................................618 783-2206
Raymond Wright, *Owner*
EMP: 1
SALES: 316K **Privately Held**
SIC: 2911 Petroleum refining

**(G-15948)**
**REX VAULT CO**
E Rte 33  (62448)
P.O. Box 323  (62448-0323)
PHONE..................................618 783-2416
Fax: 618 783-3867
Mark A Bolander, *President*
Keith Kocher, *Sales Mgr*
Carol Benefiel, *Office Mgr*
EMP: 17
SQ FT: 4,000
SALES (est): 2.2MM **Privately Held**
WEB: www.rexvault.com
SIC: 3272 6553 Burial vaults, concrete or precast terrazzo; septic tanks, concrete; cemetery subdividers & developers

**(G-15949)**
**ST PIERRE OIL COMPANY INC**
Also Called: Saint Pierre Oil
102 N Van Buren St  (62448-1410)
P.O. Box 380  (62448-0380)
PHONE..................................618 783-4441
Joseph E Stpierre, *President*
Shirley Homfeditz, *Manager*
EMP: 5
SQ FT: 1,400
SALES (est): 451.5K **Privately Held**
SIC: 1311 Crude petroleum & natural gas production

**(G-15950)**
**TPS ENTERPRISES INC**
Also Called: Total Printing Systems
201 S Gregory Dr  (62448-2111)
P.O. Box 375  (62448-0375)
PHONE..................................618 783-2978
Fax: 618 783-8407
Richard Lindemann II, *President*
Loretta Hall, *Opers Staff*
Amber Lindeman, *Human Res Mgr*
Charlie Tlapa, *Natl Sales Mgr*
Darrin Sappenfield, *Sales Mgr*
▲ EMP: 44
SQ FT: 60,000
SALES: 5.5MM **Privately Held**
WEB: www.tps1.com
SIC: 2732 Textbooks: printing & binding, not publishing

**(G-15951)**
**TROJAN OIL INC**
Also Called: Scott Oil
953 N 1300th St  (62448-4939)
PHONE..................................618 754-3474
Larry L Scott, *Owner*
EMP: 3 EST: 1960
SALES (est): 250K **Privately Held**
SIC: 1311 Crude petroleum production

## Niles
*Cook County*

**(G-15952)**
**7 MILE SOLUTIONS INC**
Also Called: Maxant Technologies
7540 N Caldwell Ave  (60714-3808)
PHONE..................................847 588-2280
Fax: 847 588-1920
Robert Curran, *President*
Kathleen Muncer, *Controller*
Angela Witt, *Accountant*
John Ambrose, *Sales Mgr*
Pat Matos, *Office Mgr*
▲ EMP: 31
SQ FT: 25,000
SALES (est): 9.5MM **Privately Held**
SIC: 3829 3844 3625 Nuclear radiation & testing apparatus; X-ray apparatus & tubes; electric controls & control accessories, industrial

**(G-15953)**
**9161 CORPORATION**
Also Called: Vertical Blinds Factory
9161 N Milwaukee Ave  (60714-1538)
PHONE..................................847 470-8828
Rosa Yaker, *President*
Barbara Finn, *Vice Pres*
EMP: 7
SQ FT: 2,500
SALES: 1.2MM **Privately Held**
SIC: 2591 5719 3429 Blinds vertical; window furnishings; venetian blinds; window shades; manufactured hardware (general)

**(G-15954)**
**A W H SALES**
6001 W Gross Point Rd  (60714-4027)
PHONE..................................847 869-0950
Fax: 847 869-1618

# GEOGRAPHIC SECTION

## Niles - Cook County (G-15979)

Tony Aimone, *General Mgr*
Art Harris, *Principal*
**EMP:** 2
**SALES (est):** 207.4K **Privately Held**
**SIC: 3949** Skateboards

### (G-15955)
### ABRASIC 90 INC
Also Called: Camel Grinding Wheels
7525 N Oak Park Ave (60714-3819)
**PHONE**.................................800 447-4248
Fax: 847 647-1861
Joseph O'Mera, *President*
John Eisner, *Vice Pres*
Ken Jelinek, *Opers Mgr*
Terry Voss, *Purch Mgr*
Will Jones, *QC Mgr*
▲ **EMP:** 44
**SQ FT:** 55,000
**SALES (est):** 7.9MM
**SALES (corp-wide):** 56.9MM **Privately Held**
**WEB:** www.cgwcamel.com
**SIC: 3291** 5085 Abrasive products; abrasives
**PA:** Gamel Operated Grinding Sarid Ltd.
   Kibbutz
   Sarid 36589
   465 075-81

### (G-15956)
### ACCUQUEST HEARING CENTER INC
7317 N Harlem Ave (60714-4252)
**PHONE**.................................847 588-1895
Brian Highfill, *President*
**EMP:** 4
**SALES (corp-wide):** 52.3MM **Privately Held**
**SIC: 3842** Hearing aids
**PA:** Accuquest Hearing Center, Inc.
   2800 W Higgins Rd Ste 895
   Hoffman Estates IL 60169
   847 843-1900

### (G-15957)
### ACCURATE METAL COMPONENTS INC
Also Called: Columbia Tool & Gage Co.
7540 N Caldwell Ave (60714-3808)
**PHONE**.................................847 520-5900
Fax: 847 520-5775
Victor Herrera, *President*
Richard Tessitore, *Vice Pres*
Iris Tessitore, *Admin Sec*
**EMP:** 12
**SQ FT:** 14,000
**SALES (est):** 2.6MM **Privately Held**
**WEB:** www.columbiatoolandgage.com
**SIC: 3599** Machine shop, jobbing & repair

### (G-15958)
### AFFY TAPPLE LLC
6300 W Gross Point Rd (60714-3916)
**PHONE**.................................773 338-1100
Fax: 847 588-0392
Stuart Sorkin, *CEO*
Mario Solano, *Safety Mgr*
Carmel A Cooke, *CFO*
Bill Henry, *CFO*
Denise Perdziak, *Treasurer*
▲ **EMP:** 50 **EST:** 1948
**SQ FT:** 47,000
**SALES (est):** 18.6MM **Privately Held**
**SIC: 2064** Fruits: candied, crystallized, or glazed; fruit, chocolate covered (except dates)

### (G-15959)
### ALVA/AMCO PHARMACAL COMPANIES
7711 N Merrimac Ave (60714-3423)
**PHONE**.................................847 663-0700
Fax: 773 663-1400
Jeffery H Gerchenson, *President*
Emile H Gerchenson, *Chairman*
Thomas Burlew, *Senior VP*
Terrence Riddel, *Senior VP*
Thomas Clark, *Vice Pres*
**EMP:** 50 **EST:** 1940
**SALES (est):** 12.9MM **Privately Held**
**WEB:** www.alva-amco.com
**SIC: 2834** Druggists' preparations (pharmaceuticals); diuretics; tranquilizers or mental drug preparations

### (G-15960)
### AMERICAN REPROGRAPHICS CO LLC
Skokie Valley Reproductions
6328 W Gross Point Rd (60714-3916)
**PHONE**.................................847 647-1131
Dan Golab, *Branch Mgr*
**EMP:** 77
**SALES (corp-wide):** 406.3MM **Publicly Held**
**WEB:** www.e-arc.com
**SIC: 7334** 2752 Photocopying & duplicating services; blueprinting service; commercial printing, lithographic
**HQ:** American Reprographics Company, L.L.C.
   1981 N Broadway Ste 385
   Walnut Creek CA 94596
   925 949-5100

### (G-15961)
### ARBY GRAPHIC SERVICE INC
6019 W Howard St (60714-4801)
**PHONE**.................................847 763-0900
Richard Baruch, *CEO*
**EMP:** 12 **EST:** 1956
**SQ FT:** 9,000
**SALES (est):** 1.1MM **Privately Held**
**WEB:** www.imaginegraphicsgroup.com
**SIC: 7389** 2791 2752 Brokers' services; typesetting; commercial printing, lithographic

### (G-15962)
### AVERY DENNISON CORPORATION
7542 N Natchez Ave (60714-3804)
**PHONE**.................................877 214-0909
Yasuhiro Masaka, *Manager*
Dan Zampa, *Manager*
Rob Hampton, *Exec Dir*
**EMP:** 80
**SALES (corp-wide):** 6B **Publicly Held**
**SIC: 3081** 2672 Unsupported plastics film & sheet; coated & laminated paper
**PA:** Avery Dennison Corporation
   207 N Goode Ave Fl 6
   Glendale CA 91203
   626 304-2000

### (G-15963)
### BANKIER COMPANIES INC
6151 W Gross Point Rd (60714-3911)
**PHONE**.................................847 647-6565
Fax: 847 647-7575
Jack D Bankier, *President*
Alfonso Vazquez, *QC Mgr*
Terry Mitchell, *Controller*
Lori Moros, *Human Res Dir*
Dominic Greco, *Accounts Mgr*
▲ **EMP:** 135
**SQ FT:** 52,000
**SALES (est):** 28.9MM **Privately Held**
**WEB:** www.bankier.com
**SIC: 3089** 7389 Injection molding of plastics; packaging & labeling services

### (G-15964)
### BAXTER V MUELLER
7280 N Caldwell Ave (60714-4502)
**PHONE**.................................847 774-6800
Lyman Lance, *President*
**EMP:** 2
**SALES (est):** 205.8K **Privately Held**
**SIC: 3841** Surgical & medical instruments

### (G-15965)
### BEE SALES COMAPNY (PA)
Also Called: Riah Hair
6330 W Touhy Ave (60714-4624)
**PHONE**.................................847 600-4400
Yong H Kim, *President*
Steve Ahn, *General Mgr*
Hae Kyung Kim, *Admin Sec*
▲ **EMP:** 60
**SQ FT:** 70,000
**SALES (est):** 14.3MM **Privately Held**
**WEB:** www.beesales.com
**SIC: 2353** 5199 2252 5087 Baseball caps; general merchandise, non-durable; socks; beauty salon & barber shop equipment & supplies; girls' & children's outerwear; women's hosiery, except socks

### (G-15966)
### CANDY MFG CO INC
Also Called: Candy Controls
5633 W Howard St (60714-4011)
**PHONE**.................................847 588-2639
Fax: 847 588-0055
Sarah Hendershot, *President*
Jacob Minan, *Engineer*
Jacob Ninan, *Engineer*
Christopher Duval, *Sales Mgr*
Lisa Chou, *Manager*
▲ **EMP:** 10
**SQ FT:** 11,880
**SALES (est):** 1.8MM **Privately Held**
**WEB:** www.candycontrols.com
**SIC: 3822** Candy controls regulating residntl & coml environmt & applncs

### (G-15967)
### CARNATION ENTERPRISES
8630 N National Ave (60714-2137)
**PHONE**.................................847 804-5928
Simeon Khazin, *President*
Benjamin Glozman, *CFO*
▲ **EMP:** 5
**SALES (est):** 304.4K **Privately Held**
**WEB:** www.carnation-inc.com
**SIC: 5044** 3694 Office equipment; automotive electrical equipment

### (G-15968)
### CHOICE CAP INC
6310 W Touhy Ave Ste 111 (60714-4622)
**PHONE**.................................847 588-3443
Su Park, *Principal*
**EMP:** 4
**SALES (est):** 140K **Privately Held**
**SIC: 2353** Hats & caps

### (G-15969)
### CISLAK MANUFACTURING INC
Also Called: Zoll-Dental
7450 N Natchez Ave (60714-3802)
**PHONE**.................................847 647-1819
Fax: 847 729-2447
Karl Zoll, *President*
Ken Zoll, *Vice Pres*
Gino Sohn, *Sales Staff*
**EMP:** 24 **EST:** 1950
**SQ FT:** 3,800
**SALES (est):** 2.5MM **Privately Held**
**SIC: 2836** 3843 Veterinary biological products; dental hand instruments

### (G-15970)
### COCA COLA FLEET SERVICE
Also Called: Coca-Cola
7500 N Oak Park Ave (60714-3820)
**PHONE**.................................847 600-2279
**EMP:** 3 **EST:** 2013
**SALES (est):** 134.7K **Privately Held**
**SIC: 2086** Bottled & canned soft drinks

### (G-15971)
### COCA-COLA BTLG WISCONSIN DEL
7400 N Oak Park Ave (60714-3818)
**PHONE**.................................847 647-0200
Marvin J Herb, *President*
Arnold Foster, *Manager*
John Hayskar, *Director*
**EMP:** 400 **EST:** 2007
**SALES (est):** 54.4MM
**SALES (corp-wide):** 41.8B **Publicly Held**
**WEB:** www.cokecce.com
**SIC: 2086** Bottled & canned soft drinks
**HQ:** Coca-Cola Refreshments Usa, Inc.
   2500 Windy Ridge Pkwy Se
   Atlanta GA 30339
   770 989-3000

### (G-15972)
### COCA-COLA COMPANY
7400 N Oak Park Ave (60714-3818)
**PHONE**.................................847 647-0200
Fax: 847 490-3256
Roger Ruark, *Manager*
Mike Carroll, *Manager*
**EMP:** 70
**SALES (corp-wide):** 41.8B **Publicly Held**
**WEB:** www.cocacola.com
**SIC: 2086** Bottled & canned soft drinks
**PA:** The Coca-Cola Company
   1 Coca Cola Plz Nw
   Atlanta GA 30313
   404 676-2121

### (G-15973)
### COCA-COLA REFRESHMENTS USA INC
7425 W Oak Park Ave (60714-3817)
**PHONE**.................................847 647-0200
Fax: 312 647-9660
David Huelsman, *Vice Pres*
Michael Garrity, *Sales Dir*
Jim Skarb, *Director*
**EMP:** 70
**SALES (corp-wide):** 41.8B **Publicly Held**
**WEB:** www.cokecce.com
**SIC: 2086** Bottled & canned soft drinks
**HQ:** Coca-Cola Refreshments Usa, Inc.
   2500 Windy Ridge Pkwy Se
   Atlanta GA 30339
   770 989-3000

### (G-15974)
### D & J INTERNATIONAL INC
Also Called: Sharp Trading
7793 N Caldwell Ave (60714-3318)
**PHONE**.................................847 966-9260
Jennifer Min, *President*
Don Min, *Vice Pres*
▲ **EMP:** 13 **EST:** 1996
**SALES (est):** 484K **Privately Held**
**SIC: 2395** Embroidery & art needlework

### (G-15975)
### DOVE DENTAL STUDIO
6201 W Howard St Ste 202 (60714-3435)
**PHONE**.................................847 679-2434
Michael Aiello, *Owner*
**EMP:** 3
**SALES (est):** 200K **Privately Held**
**SIC: 8021** 3843 Offices & clinics of dentists; dental equipment & supplies

### (G-15976)
### ED GARVEY AND COMPANY (PA)
Also Called: Garvey Group, The
7400 N Lehigh Ave (60714-4024)
**PHONE**.................................847 647-1900
Edward J Garvey Jr, *President*
Mike Leonard, *CFO*
Dave Arnone, *Manager*
Tom Creutz, *Manager*
**EMP:** 49 **EST:** 1939
**SQ FT:** 100,000
**SALES (est):** 31.6MM **Privately Held**
**WEB:** www.edgarvey.com
**SIC: 2752** Offset & photolithographic printing; promotional printing, lithographic

### (G-15977)
### EINSTEIN CREST
9347 N Milwaukee Ave (60714-1303)
**PHONE**.................................847 965-7791
Brian Borowski, *President*
Raymond Borowski, *Vice Pres*
Ray Charles, *Purch Agent*
Charles Raymond, *Manager*
**EMP:** 4
**SQ FT:** 2,500
**SALES:** 285K **Privately Held**
**SIC: 2752** 2791 2789 Photo-offset printing; typesetting; bookbinding & related work

### (G-15978)
### EMBROIDERY SERVICES INC
6287 W Howard St (60714-3403)
**PHONE**.................................847 588-2660
John Reppert, *President*
Mark Reppert, *Vice Pres*
**EMP:** 4
**SQ FT:** 4,000
**SALES:** 350K **Privately Held**
**SIC: 2395** Embroidery & art needlework

### (G-15979)
### FORT DEARBORN COMPANY
6035 W Gross Point Rd (60714-4045)
**PHONE**.................................773 774-4321
Fax: 773 774-9105
Michael Anderson, *CEO*
Margaret Hug, *Opers Staff*
Lanny Martin, *Production*
Thom Capps, *Manager*
Lisa Young, *Associate*
**EMP:** 130 **Privately Held**
**SIC: 2759** Commercial printing

# Niles - Cook County (G-15980)
## GEOGRAPHIC SECTION

HQ: Fort Dearborn Company
1530 Morse Ave
Elk Grove Village IL 60007
847 357-9500

**(G-15980)**
**FRANCIS SCREW PRODUCTS CO INC**
7400 N Milwaukee Ave (60714-3708)
PHONE..................847 647-9462
Fax: 847 647-9462
John Francis, *President*
Charles Francis, *Corp Secy*
**EMP:** 1 **EST:** 1947
**SQ FT:** 3,000
**SALES:** 200K **Privately Held**
**SIC:** 3451 Screw machine products

**(G-15981)**
**GARDNER DENVER INC**
Welch-Ilmac
5621 W Howard St (60714-4011)
PHONE..................847 676-8800
John Balamuta, *Branch Mgr*
**EMP:** 20
**SALES (corp-wide):** 1.9B **Publicly Held**
**SIC:** 3821 Laboratory apparatus & furniture; vacuum pumps, laboratory
HQ: Gardner Denver, Inc.
222 E Erie St Ste 500
Milwaukee WI 53202

**(G-15982)**
**GEO T SCHMIDT INC (PA)**
Also Called: Schmidt Marking Systems
6151 W Howard St (60714-3401)
P.O. Box 480390 (60714-0390)
PHONE..................847 647-7117
Fax: 800 934-3437
Neal J O'Connor, *President*
Byrum Dickes, *Chairman*
David Lacosse, *Plant Mgr*
Dave McPhee, *Plant Mgr*
Bob Allardice, *Purchasing*
▲ **EMP:** 60
**SQ FT:** 45,000
**SALES:** 11.6MM **Privately Held**
**WEB:** www.gtschmidt.com
**SIC:** 3544 3542 3599 Special dies & tools; marking machines; machine & other job shop work

**(G-15983)**
**GHP GROUP INC (PA)**
6440 W Howard St (60714-3302)
PHONE..................847 324-5900
Gus Haramaras, *President*
Andy Galombeck, *Vice Pres*
Lauren Mack, *Controller*
Erick Tafel, *Accounting Mgr*
Aparna Madassery, *Natl Sales Mgr*
▲ **EMP:** 41
**SQ FT:** 66,000
**SALES (est):** 8.6MM **Privately Held**
**WEB:** www.ghpgroup.com
**SIC:** 3299 Tubing for electrical purposes, quartz

**(G-15984)**
**GREAT LAKES GL & MIRROR CORP**
6261 W Howard St (60714-3403)
PHONE..................847 647-1036
Robert Ginsburg, *President*
Marcy Nessenson, *Vice Pres*
**EMP:** 3
**SQ FT:** 2,500
**SALES (est):** 274.6K **Privately Held**
**WEB:** www.greatlakesglassblock.com
**SIC:** 3211 Flat glass

**(G-15985)**
**GREENWOOD ASSOCIATES INC**
6280 W Howard St (60714-3433)
PHONE..................847 579-5500
Ronald W Kaplan, *President*
Blair Greenwood, *COO*
Michael P Gard, *Admin Sec*
▲ **EMP:** 10
**SQ FT:** 2,000
**SALES (est):** 1.4MM **Privately Held**
**WEB:** www.greenwoodassociates.com
**SIC:** 2037 Fruit juice concentrates, frozen

**(G-15986)**
**HALF PRICE BKS REC MGZINES INC**
5605 W Touhy Ave (60714-4019)
PHONE..................847 588-2286
Kent Hedtke, *Branch Mgr*
**EMP:** 26
**SALES (corp-wide):** 250.9MM **Privately Held**
**SIC:** 2721 5932 Magazines: publishing & printing; book stores, secondhand
PA: Half Price Books, Records, Magazines, Incorporated
5803 E Northwest Hwy
Dallas TX 75231
214 379-8000

**(G-15987)**
**IMAGININGS 3 INC**
Also Called: Flix Candy
6401 W Gross Point Rd (60714-4507)
PHONE..................847 647-1370
Sidney Diamond, *President*
Debbie Diamond, *Vice Pres*
Jeff Grossman, *Vice Pres*
Nancy Cederquist, *CFO*
Gayle Hutten, *Manager*
▲ **EMP:** 25
**SQ FT:** 55,000
**SALES (est):** 6MM **Privately Held**
**WEB:** www.flixcandy.com
**SIC:** 2064 Candy & other confectionery products

**(G-15988)**
**IMBERT CONSTRUCTION INDS INC**
7030 N Austin Ave (60714-4602)
PHONE..................847 588-3170
John Grzeskowski, *President*
Lisa Acosta, *Controller*
William S Toth, *Admin Sec*
**EMP:** 4
**SQ FT:** 4,800
**SALES (est):** 272.5K **Privately Held**
**SIC:** 1752 3443 Access flooring system installation; floating covers, metal plate

**(G-15989)**
**INSIGHT ADVERTISING INC**
6954 W Touhy Ave Ste 101 (60714-4535)
PHONE..................847 647-0004
Fax: 847 647-1097
Andrew Berk, *President*
**EMP:** 2
**SALES:** 300K **Privately Held**
**WEB:** www.insightadv.com
**SIC:** 8743 5199 3993 Sales promotion; advertising specialties; advertising novelties

**(G-15990)**
**INVENTIVE DISPLAY GROUP LLC**
Also Called: Inventex Medical
7415 N Melvina Ave (60714-3907)
PHONE..................847 588-1100
Alex Dunn, *Project Mgr*
Rick Greenspan, *Accounts Exec*
Alex KAC, *Manager*
Seth Bankir,
Seth Bankier,
▲ **EMP:** 10
**SALES (est):** 1.1MM **Privately Held**
**WEB:** www.inventivedisplay.com
**SIC:** 2542 Office & store showcases & display fixtures

**(G-15991)**
**JERON ELECTRONIC SYSTEMS INC**
7501 N Natchez Ave (60714-3803)
PHONE..................773 275-1900
Jerome J Chesnul, *President*
Michael Faden, *General Mgr*
Matthew Chesnul, *Vice Pres*
Bill Braeckman, *Opers Mgr*
Tom Herrick, *Technical Mgr*
▲ **EMP:** 75 **EST:** 1964
**SQ FT:** 52,328
**SALES:** 15MM **Privately Held**
**WEB:** www.jeron.com
**SIC:** 3669 Emergency alarms

**(G-15992)**
**JOHNS-BYRNE COMPANY (PA)**
Also Called: Johnsbyrne
6701 W Oakton St (60714-3917)
PHONE..................847 583-3100
Corey Gustafson, *President*
John Gustafson Jr, *COO*
James Pate Gustafson, *Exec VP*
Michael J Gustafson, *Exec VP*
Michael Difranco, *VP Mktg*
**EMP:** 100 **EST:** 1959
**SQ FT:** 40,000
**SALES (est):** 26.9MM **Privately Held**
**SIC:** 2752 2791 2789 Commercial printing, lithographic; typesetting; bookbinding & related work

**(G-15993)**
**JOHNSBYRNE GRAPHIC TECH CORP**
6701 W Oakton St (60714-3032)
PHONE..................847 583-3100
Fax: 847 470-4400
Corey Gustafson, *President*
Mike Gonzales, *General Mgr*
Jack Gustafson Jr, *COO*
John Schlichting, *VP Opers*
Mark Golstab, *Opers Staff*
**EMP:** 1
**SALES (est):** 382.7K
**SALES (corp-wide):** 26.9MM **Privately Held**
**SIC:** 2752 Commercial printing, lithographic
PA: Johns-Byrne Company
6701 W Oakton St
Niles IL 60714
847 583-3100

**(G-15994)**
**JPMORGAN CHASE BANK NAT ASSN**
7007 W Dempster St (60714-2130)
PHONE..................847 663-1235
Mirela Davorija, *Branch Mgr*
**EMP:** 6
**SALES (corp-wide):** 105.4B **Publicly Held**
**SIC:** 3578 Banking machines
HQ: Jpmorgan Chase Bank, National Association
1111 Polaris Pkwy
Columbus OH 43240
614 436-3055

**(G-15995)**
**KOMAR SCREW CORP (PA)**
7790 N Merrimac Ave (60714-3424)
PHONE..................847 965-9090
Fax: 847 965-8988
Marvin Kocian, *President*
Norm Young, *Safety Mgr*
Chad Huebner, *Purch Agent*
Barbara Schroeder, *Purch Agent*
Jerry Schneider, *Engineer*
▲ **EMP:** 50
**SQ FT:** 40,000
**SALES:** 12.5MM **Privately Held**
**WEB:** www.komarscrew.com
**SIC:** 5072 3452 Screws; nuts (hardware); bolts; screws, metal

**(G-15996)**
**LEWIS SPRING AND MFG COMPANY (PA)**
7500 N Natchez Ave (60714-3804)
PHONE..................847 588-7030
Fax: 847 647-8600
James Robertson, *President*
Larry Gutowsky, *Vice Pres*
Melissa McCluskey, *Safety Mgr*
Luis Rodriguez, *Safety Mgr*
John Bold, *CFO*
**EMP:** 30
**SQ FT:** 60,000
**SALES (est):** 5.5MM **Privately Held**
**WEB:** www.lewisspring.com
**SIC:** 3495 3469 3496 3493 Instrument springs, precision; stamping metal for the trade; miscellaneous fabricated wire products; steel springs, except wire

**(G-15997)**
**M & S TECHNOLOGIES INC**
5715 W Howard St (60714-4012)
PHONE..................847 763-0500
Fax: 847 763-9170
Joseph Marino, *President*
Karen Waller, *General Mgr*
Junet Marino, *Bookkeeper*
Carolyn Crabb, *Marketing Staff*
Lynn Henry, *Office Mgr*
▲ **EMP:** 16
**SQ FT:** 7,000
**SALES (est):** 2.2MM **Privately Held**
**SIC:** 3851 5045 Ophthalmic goods; computer peripheral equipment

**(G-15998)**
**M R O SOLUTIONS LLC**
5645 W Howard St (60714-4011)
PHONE..................847 588-2480
Fax: 847 588-2477
Rob Burke, *Webmaster*
James Gajewski,
Rob Burk,
Kevin Murphy,
Glen Stampnick,
◆ **EMP:** 20 **EST:** 1998
**SALES (est):** 3.9MM **Privately Held**
**WEB:** www.mrosolutions.com
**SIC:** 2899 Corrosion preventive lubricant

**(G-15999)**
**MAG TAG**
7113 N Austin Ave (60714-4617)
PHONE..................847 647-6255
Fax: 847 647-6605
Yves Khoury, *Principal*
**EMP:** 4
**SALES (est):** 270K **Privately Held**
**SIC:** 2752 Business form & card printing, lithographic

**(G-16000)**
**MARIAS CHICKEN ATI ATIHAN**
9054 W Golf Rd (60714-5805)
PHONE..................847 699-3113
**EMP:** 3
**SALES (est):** 142.9K **Privately Held**
**SIC:** 3312 Stainless steel

**(G-16001)**
**MARVIN FEIG & ASSOCIATES INC**
5707 W Howard St (60714-4012)
PHONE..................773 384-5228
Fax: 773 384-5005
Marvin Feig, *President*
Paula Mendoza, *Manager*
Carlyn Gomberg, *Admin Sec*
▲ **EMP:** 10
**SQ FT:** 11,000
**SALES (est):** 1.5MM **Privately Held**
**WEB:** www.marvinfeig.com
**SIC:** 2591 2391 Blinds vertical; window shades; draperies, plastic & textile: from purchased materials

**(G-16002)**
**MEDICAL SCREENING LABS INC**
5727 W Howard St (60714-4012)
PHONE..................847 647-7911
Michael E Bagan, *President*
Kenneth J Bagan, *Director*
**EMP:** 28
**SQ FT:** 2,000
**SALES (est):** 1.9MM **Privately Held**
**WEB:** www.medscreening.com
**SIC:** 3841 8099 Blood pressure apparatus; health screening service

**(G-16003)**
**METAL SPRMARKETS CHICAGO NILES**
6285 W Howard St (60714-3403)
PHONE..................847 647-2423
Dan Cahill, *Owner*
**EMP:** 3
**SQ FT:** 7,500
**SALES:** 200K **Privately Held**
**SIC:** 1081 Metal mining exploration & development services

## Niles - Cook County (G-16027)

**(G-16004)**
**MICHELS FRAME SHOP**
Also Called: Michel's Frame Shop & Gallery
7120 W Touhy Ave (60714-4526)
PHONE..................847 647-7366
Fax: 847 647-7378
Margaret Michel, *Owner*
Maragaret Michel, *Principal*
Diane Hunn, *Manager*
EMP: 3
SALES: 200K **Privately Held**
SIC: 2499 5999 5023 7389 Picture & mirror frames, wood; picture frames, ready made; frames & framing, picture & mirror; interior designer

**(G-16005)**
**MICROLINK DEVICES INC**
6457 W Howard St (60714-3301)
PHONE..................847 588-3001
Fax: 847 588-3002
Dr Noren Pan, *CEO*
Glen Hillier, *Principal*
Dr Mark Osowski, *Vice Pres*
Gautham Ragunathan, *Research*
George Gonzalez, *Engineer*
EMP: 22
SQ FT: 30,000
SALES (est): 5.8MM **Privately Held**
WEB: www.mldevices.com
SIC: 3674 Semiconductor circuit networks

**(G-16006)**
**MIDWESCO FILTER RESOURCES INC**
309 Braddock St (60714)
PHONE..................540 773-4780
Stephen Buck, *President*
Joe Marcinski, *Vice Pres*
Bill Stewart, *CFO*
Herb Sturm, *Manager*
Marian Flynn, *Director*
◆ EMP: 213
SQ FT: 97,500
SALES (est): 21.1MM
SALES (corp-wide): 98.8MM **Publicly Held**
WEB: www.mfri.com
SIC: 2393 2674 Textile bags; bags: uncoated paper & multiwall
PA: Perma-Pipe International Holdings, Inc.,
     6410 W Howard St
     Niles IL 60714
     847 966-1000

**(G-16007)**
**MIDWEST COLOR**
Also Called: Hudson Color Concentrates
6240 W Gross Point Rd (60714-3914)
PHONE..................847 647-1364
Fax: 847 647-2123
Lloyd Watt, *Owner*
David Seevers, *Treasurer*
EMP: 10
SALES (est): 1.1MM **Privately Held**
SIC: 3496 Concrete reinforcing mesh & wire

**(G-16008)**
**MILWAUKEE ELECTRIC TOOL CORP**
6310 W Gross Point Rd (60714-3916)
PHONE..................847 588-3356
Keith Boulanger, *Engineer*
Peter Weisell, *Branch Mgr*
EMP: 282
SALES (corp-wide): 5B **Privately Held**
WEB: www.mil-electric-tool.com
SIC: 3546 3425 Power-driven handtools; saw blades & handsaws
HQ: Milwaukee Electric Tool Corporation
     13135 W Lisbon Rd
     Brookfield WI 53005
     800 729-3878

**(G-16009)**
**MOTR GRAFX LLC**
7430 N Lehigh Ave (60714-4024)
PHONE..................847 600-5656
Lissette Hern, *Partner*
Paul Literno, *Partner*
Delia Saboya, *Partner*
EMP: 8 EST: 2011

SALES: 15MM **Privately Held**
SIC: 2752 2759 7336 Commercial printing, lithographic; promotional printing; commercial art & graphic design

**(G-16010)**
**MPC PRODUCTS CORPORATION (HQ)**
Also Called: Woodward Mpc, Inc.
6300 W Howard St (60714-3406)
PHONE..................847 673-8300
Fax: 847 673-7144
Thomas Gendron, *CEO*
Martin Glass, *President*
William Leitzke, *Engineer*
Ganga Jayaraman, *Senior Engr*
Robert Webber Jr, *CFO*
◆ EMP: 867 EST: 1962
SQ FT: 100,000
SALES: 171MM
SALES (corp-wide): 2B **Publicly Held**
SIC: 3728 3621 3676 3812 Aircraft body & wing assemblies & parts; aircraft assemblies, subassemblies & parts; motors & generators; electronic resistors; aircraft/aerospace flight instruments & guidance systems; relays & industrial controls
PA: Woodward, Inc.
     1081 Woodward Way
     Fort Collins CO 80524
     970 482-5811

**(G-16011)**
**MPC PRODUCTS CORPORATION**
5600 W Jarvis Ave (60714-4016)
PHONE..................847 673-8300
EMP: 4
SALES (corp-wide): 2B **Publicly Held**
SIC: 3728 3625 3676 3812 Aircraft body & wing assemblies & parts; relays & industrial controls; electronic resistors; aircraft/aerospace flight instruments & guidance systems; motors & generators; fluid power cylinders & actuators
HQ: Mpc Products Corporation
     6300 W Howard St
     Niles IL 60714
     847 673-8300

**(G-16012)**
**MPC PRODUCTS CORPORATION**
6300 W Howard St (60714-3406)
PHONE..................847 673-8300
Thomas A Gendron, *CEO*
EMP: 5
SALES (corp-wide): 2B **Publicly Held**
SIC: 3625 3643 3613 Industrial electrical relays & switches; switches, electric power; switches, electronic applications; solenoid switches (industrial controls); current-carrying wiring devices; switchgear & switchboard apparatus
HQ: Mpc Products Corporation
     6300 W Howard St
     Niles IL 60714
     847 673-8300

**(G-16013)**
**NATURES SOURCES LLC**
5665 W Howard St (60714-4011)
PHONE..................847 663-9168
Fax: 847 647-9101
John Zapfel, *CEO*
Barbara Shah, *Human Res Mgr*
Lee Frank, *Manager*
EMP: 5
SALES: 575.2K **Privately Held**
WEB: www.naturessources.com
SIC: 5499 2869 5122 Vitamin food stores; enzymes; vitamins & minerals

**(G-16014)**
**ORORA VISUAL TX LLC**
7400 N Lehigh Ave (60714-4024)
PHONE..................847 647-1900
EMP: 320
SALES (corp-wide): 2.8B **Privately Held**
SIC: 2752 Commercial printing, lithographic
HQ: Orora Visual Tx Llc
     3210 Innovative Way
     Mesquite TX 75149
     972 289-0705

**(G-16015)**
**PEELMASTER PACKAGING CORP**
Also Called: Peelmaster Medical Packaging
6153 W Mulford St (60714-3413)
PHONE..................847 966-6161
Fax: 847 966-6168
William Sieck, *Principal*
Steve McCarty, *Plant Mgr*
Alfredo Cruz, *QC Mgr*
Steven Whitney, *Human Res Mgr*
Jim Bassing, *Sales Staff*
EMP: 30
SQ FT: 16,700
SALES (est): 5.6MM **Privately Held**
SIC: 2673 Cellophane bags, unprinted: made from purchased materials

**(G-16016)**
**PENCO ELECTRIC**
7153 N Austin Ave (60714-4617)
PHONE..................847 423-2159
Judy Paul, *Principal*
EMP: 4
SALES (est): 734.4K **Privately Held**
SIC: 3699 Electrical equipment & supplies

**(G-16017)**
**PERFECTION CUSTOM CLOSETS & CO**
7183 N Austin Ave (60714-4617)
PHONE..................847 647-6461
Fax: 773 647-7150
Timothy Ohagan, *President*
Andy Humann, *Sales Mgr*
Timothy O'Hagan, *Manager*
Tamara Spenny, *Manager*
EMP: 17
SALES (est): 3.5MM **Privately Held**
WEB: www.aperfectcloset.com
SIC: 2599 2541 Cabinets, factory; wood partitions & fixtures

**(G-16018)**
**PERMA-PIPE INC (HQ)**
Also Called: Permalert E S P
7720 N Lehigh Ave (60714-3416)
PHONE..................847 966-2190
Fax: 847 470-1204
David Mansfield, *CEO*
Robert Maffei, *Exec VP*
Mike Bennett, *Vice Pres*
John Carusiello, *Manager*
Frank Lau, *Manager*
▲ EMP: 40
SQ FT: 130,000
SALES (est): 24.7MM
SALES (corp-wide): 98.8MM **Publicly Held**
WEB: www.permapipe.com
SIC: 3498 Fabricated pipe & fittings
PA: Perma-Pipe International Holdings, Inc.,
     6410 W Howard St
     Niles IL 60714
     847 966-1000

**(G-16019)**
**PERMA-PIPE INTL HOLDINGS INC (PA)**
6410 W Howard St (60714-3302)
PHONE..................847 966-1000
David S Barrie, *Ch of Bd*
David J Mansfield, *President*
John Carusiello, *Senior VP*
Karl J Schmidt, *CFO*
Wayne Bosch, *Officer*
◆ EMP: 174
SQ FT: 23,400
SALES: 98.8MM **Publicly Held**
WEB: www.mfri.com
SIC: 3677 3564 3569 Filtration devices, electronic; blowers & fans; filters & strainers, pipeline

**(G-16020)**
**POLA COMPANY**
8901 N Milwaukee Ave A (60714-1889)
PHONE..................847 470-1182
Grace Pola, *Owner*
EMP: 3
SALES (est): 215.5K **Privately Held**
SIC: 2339 Women's & misses' accessories

**(G-16021)**
**POLYSCIENCE INC**
5709 W Howard St (60714-4012)
PHONE..................847 647-0611
Phillip Preston, *CEO*
◆ EMP: 100
SALES (est): 12.4MM **Privately Held**
SIC: 3585 Refrigeration & heating equipment

**(G-16022)**
**PRESTON INDUSTRIES INC**
Also Called: Polyscience
6600 W Touhy Ave (60714-4516)
PHONE..................847 647-2900
S Tinley Preston III, *President*
Philip K Preston, *President*
Nicoletta Eshbaugh, *Vice Pres*
S Tinsley Preston, *Vice Pres*
Tinsley S Preton, *Vice Pres*
◆ EMP: 152
SQ FT: 60,000
SALES (est): 47.1MM **Privately Held**
WEB: www.prestonpub.com
SIC: 3821 2731 Laboratory apparatus & furniture; book publishing

**(G-16023)**
**QUALITY ELEVATOR PRODUCTS INC**
7760 N Merrimac Ave (60714-3424)
PHONE..................847 581-0085
Fax: 847 581-0095
Joe Kawa, *Vice Pres*
▲ EMP: 33
SQ FT: 32,000
SALES (est): 9.1MM **Privately Held**
WEB: www.qualityelev.com
SIC: 3534 Elevators & equipment

**(G-16024)**
**R & D ELECTRONICS INC**
7948 W Oakton St (60714-2457)
PHONE..................847 583-9080
Ernie Ruby, *President*
EMP: 2
SQ FT: 900
SALES: 200K **Privately Held**
SIC: 3625 3822 3433 Control equipment, electric; auto controls regulating residntl & coml environmt & applncs; heating equipment, except electric

**(G-16025)**
**R Z TOOL INC**
5691 W Howard St (60714-4011)
PHONE..................847 647-2350
Fax: 847 647-2327
Samantha Jaber, *President*
Greg Sallecki, *Admin Sec*
Pam Smith, *Administration*
EMP: 14
SQ FT: 6,500
SALES (est): 1.5MM **Privately Held**
WEB: www.rztool.com
SIC: 3469 Machine parts, stamped or pressed metal

**(G-16026)**
**R-B INDUSTRIES INC**
6366 W Gross Point Rd (60714-3916)
PHONE..................847 647-4020
Ronald R Baade, *Ch of Bd*
Kris Baade, *Vice Pres*
Jeffrey Fertel, *Sales Mgr*
Marsha K Baade, *Admin Sec*
◆ EMP: 25
SQ FT: 28,000
SALES: 5.1MM **Privately Held**
WEB: www.rbi-usa.com
SIC: 5072 3965 Miscellaneous fasteners; fasteners, buttons, needles & pins

**(G-16027)**
**RICH PRODUCTS CORPORATION**
6200 W Mulford St (60714-3430)
PHONE..................847 581-1749
Fax: 847 581-1764
A Bogan, *Vice Pres*
Federico Reyes, *Opers Mgr*
Freddy Medina, *Opers Staff*
Val Hardway, *Purch Mgr*
Will Flanagan, *Engineer*
EMP: 76

# Niles - Cook County (G-16028) — GEOGRAPHIC SECTION

**SALES (corp-wide):** 3.2B **Privately Held**
**WEB:** www.richs.com
**SIC:** 2023 2092 2026 Dry, condensed, evaporated dairy products; whipped topping, dry mix; cream substitutes; fresh or frozen packaged fish; shrimp, frozen: prepared; shellfish, frozen: prepared; fluid milk
**PA:** Rich Products Corporation
1 Robert Rich Way
Buffalo NY 14213
716 878-8000

## (G-16028)
### RICO INDUSTRIES INC (PA)
Also Called: Rico Industries Tag Express
7000 N Austin Ave (60714-4602)
**PHONE** .................................. 312 427-0313
**Fax:** 847 427-1887
Cary S Schack, *President*
Bernard Schack, *Treasurer*
Ruth Schack, *Asst Sec*
▲ **EMP:** 60
**SQ FT:** 55,000
**SALES (est):** 87.4MM **Privately Held**
**WEB:** www.ricoinc.com
**SIC:** 5199 3172 2396 3993 Leather goods, except footwear, gloves, luggage, belting; wallets; checkbook covers; key cases; automotive & apparel trimmings; signs & advertising specialties

## (G-16029)
### ROYAL KITCHEN & BATHROOM CABIN (PA)
7727 N Milwaukee Ave (60714-4733)
**PHONE** .................................. 847 588-0011
Chris Hanusiak, *Vice Pres*
**EMP:** 3
**SALES (est):** 1.7MM **Privately Held**
**SIC:** 3429 Cabinet hardware

## (G-16030)
### RV ENTERPRISES LTD
8926 N Greenwood Ave (60714-5163)
**PHONE** .................................. 847 509-8710
Linda L Vaccaro, *President*
**EMP:** 15
**SALES (est):** 1.5MM **Privately Held**
**SIC:** 2759 Promotional printing

## (G-16031)
### SERBIAN YELLOW PAGES INC
7400 N Waukegan Rd # 210 (60714-4353)
**PHONE** .................................. 847 588-0555
**Fax:** 847 588-0333
Goran Veselinovic, *President*
Dusan Delic, *Vice Pres*
**EMP:** 16
**SALES (est):** 978.7K **Privately Held**
**WEB:** www.serbianyellowpages.com
**SIC:** 2741 Telephone & other directory publishing

## (G-16032)
### SHERWOOD INDUSTRIES INC
7800 N Merrimac Ave (60714-3426)
**PHONE** .................................. 847 626-0300
**Fax:** 847 626-0600
William Russin Sr, *Ch of Bd*
Robert Russin, *President*
Carole Studenroth, *Vice Pres*
Annette Ashbacher, *CFO*
Lorraine Russin Sr, *Shareholder*
▲ **EMP:** 10
**SQ FT:** 33,000
**SALES:** 4MM **Privately Held**
**SIC:** 5085 3826 2512 Packing, industrial; analytical instruments; upholstered household furniture

## (G-16033)
### SHEVICK SALES CORP
Also Called: Sleep On Latex
5620 W Jarvis Ave (60714-4016)
**PHONE** .................................. 312 487-2865
Karl Shevick, *President*
▲ **EMP:** 5
**SALES (est):** 366K **Privately Held**
**SIC:** 2515 Mattresses & bedsprings

## (G-16034)
### SMITHEREEN COMPANY
Also Called: Smithereen Pest Management
7400 N Melvina Ave (60714-3908)
**PHONE** .................................. 800 340-1888
**Fax:** 847 647-0606
Jack R Jennings, *President*
Nick Filantres, *General Mgr*
David Harris, *Vice Pres*
Hans Nielsen, *Opers Mgr*
Danny Biron, *Sales Mgr*
**EMP:** 60
**SQ FT:** 12,000
**SALES:** 8MM **Privately Held**
**SIC:** 7342 2879 Pest control in structures; agricultural chemicals

## (G-16035)
### SMITHEREEN COMPANY DEL (PA)
Also Called: Smithereen Exterminating Co
7400 N Melvina Ave (60714-3908)
**PHONE** .................................. 847 675-0010
Richard E Jennings, *President*
Angela Tucker, *Training Dir*
**EMP:** 60 EST: 1888
**SQ FT:** 1,200
**SALES (est):** 8MM **Privately Held**
**WEB:** www.pied-piper.com
**SIC:** 7342 2879 Exterminating & fumigating; agricultural chemicals

## (G-16036)
### SPECIALTY PROMOTIONS INC (PA)
Also Called: Specialty Printing Company
6019 W Howard St (60714-4801)
**PHONE** .................................. 847 588-2580
**Fax:** 847 588-2146
Paul B Lefebvre, *CEO*
Adam M Lefebvre, *President*
William Mattran, *Senior VP*
Teresa Frederick, *Vice Pres*
Ray Hoshell, *Vice Pres*
▲ **EMP:** 259
**SQ FT:** 103,000
**SALES (est):** 148.4MM **Privately Held**
**WEB:** www.specialtyprintcomm.com
**SIC:** 2752 Commercial printing, lithographic

## (G-16037)
### SRH HOLDINGS INC
6100 N Howard St (60714-3402)
**PHONE** .................................. 847 583-2295
Scott Harris, *President*
Meredith Balenske, *Comms Dir*
Vicky Maldonado, *Office Admin*
Cathy Spencer, *Admin Sec*
Minh Luu, *Analyst*
▲ **EMP:** 5
**SQ FT:** 2,000
**SALES (est):** 890K **Privately Held**
**WEB:** www.revolutiondance.com
**SIC:** 2339 Women's & misses' athletic clothing & sportswear

## (G-16038)
### SUMMIT INDUSTRIES LLC
7555 N Caldwell Ave (60714-3807)
**PHONE** .................................. 773 353-4000
**Fax:** 773 588-3424
Thomas Boon, *President*
Sparky Copaev, *President*
Joe Flies, *President*
Don Matson, *Vice Pres*
Kurt Peterson, *CFO*
◆ **EMP:** 77
**SQ FT:** 25,000
**SALES:** 26MM **Privately Held**
**WEB:** www.summitindustries.net
**SIC:** 3844 X-ray apparatus & tubes

## (G-16039)
### TALK-A-PHONE CO
7530 N Natchez Ave (60714-3804)
**PHONE** .................................. 773 539-1100
Zvie Liberman, *President*
Samuel Shanes, *Chairman*
James Hartney, *Opers Mgr*
Steve Liberman, *Chief Engr*
Jyoti Gianani, *Engineer*
**EMP:** 90 EST: 1927
**SQ FT:** 34,000
**SALES (est):** 19.4MM **Privately Held**
**WEB:** www.talkaphone.com
**SIC:** 3669 Intercommunication systems, electric

## (G-16040)
### TETRA MEDICAL SUPPLY CORP
6364 W Gross Point Rd (60714-3916)
**PHONE** .................................. 847 647-0590
**Fax:** 847 647-9034
Constance Shier, *President*
James A Shier Jr, *President*
Barb Hoffman, *Vice Pres*
Ollie Jackson, *Admin Sec*
▲ **EMP:** 12
**SQ FT:** 15,000
**SALES (est):** 1.4MM **Privately Held**
**WEB:** www.tetramed.com
**SIC:** 3842 5047 Surgical appliances & supplies; surgical equipment & supplies

## (G-16041)
### THERMAL CARE INC
5680 W Jarvis Ave (60714-3408)
**PHONE** .................................. 847 966-2260
Christopher S Keller, *Ch of Bd*
Lee Sobocinski, *President*
Jim Haden, *Buyer*
Yuri Khazanov, *Engineer*
Bryan Matias, *Engineer*
◆ **EMP:** 120 EST: 1965
**SQ FT:** 135,227
**SALES:** 28MM
**SALES (corp-wide):** 165.3MM **Privately Held**
**WEB:** www.thermalcare.com
**SIC:** 3585 3555 Refrigeration & heating equipment; printing trades machinery
**PA:** Sewickley Capital Inc
501 Silverside Rd Ste 67
Wilmington DE 19809
302 793-4964

## (G-16042)
### THERMAL CARE INC
6125 W Mulford St (60714-3427)
**PHONE** .................................. 847 929-1207
Jeanette Sierra, *Manager*
**EMP:** 12
**SALES (est):** 1.9MM **Privately Held**
**SIC:** 3585 Refrigeration & heating equipment

## (G-16043)
### TMB PUBLISHING INC
Also Called: Plumbing Engineer Magazine
6201 W Howard St Ste 201 (60714-3435)
**PHONE** .................................. 847 564-1127
**Fax:** 847 564-1264
Tom M Brown Jr, *President*
Tom Klemens, *Editor*
James Schaible, *Editor*
Kate Brown, *Prdtn Mgr*
Danielle Galian, *Production*
**EMP:** 7
**SALES (est):** 958.5K **Privately Held**
**WEB:** www.tmbpublishing.com
**SIC:** 2721 Periodicals

## (G-16044)
### TRIDENT SOFTWARE CORP
1183 S Scoville Ave (60714)
**PHONE** .................................. 847 219-8777
Ramesh Vashi, *President*
**EMP:** 2
**SALES:** 204K **Privately Held**
**SIC:** 7372 Prepackaged software

## (G-16045)
### UMF CORPORATION
Also Called: Perfect Clean
5721 W Howard St (60714-4012)
**PHONE** .................................. 224 251-7822
Kim Roman, *Branch Mgr*
**EMP:** 3
**SALES (corp-wide):** 5MM **Privately Held**
**SIC:** 2842 3589 5087 Specialty cleaning, polishes & sanitation goods; commercial cleaning equipment; cleaning & maintenance equipment & supplies
**PA:** Umf Corporation
4709 Golf Rd Ste 300a
Skokie IL 60076
847 920-0370

## (G-16046)
### WELLS LAMONT INDUST GROUP LLC
6640 W Touhy Ave (60714-4587)
**PHONE** .................................. 800 247-3295
Jean Crespin, *General Mgr*
Trainer William, *Principal*
Thomas J Palzer, *Vice Pres*
David F Rehm, *Vice Pres*
Jace Suttner, *Vice Pres*
**EMP:** 1400
**SQ FT:** 82,000
**SALES (est):** 57.4MM
**SALES (corp-wide):** 223.6B **Publicly Held**
**WEB:** www.wellslamontindustry.com
**SIC:** 2381 Gloves, work: woven or knit, made from purchased materials
**HQ:** Marmon Industrial Llc
181 W Madison St Fl 26
Chicago IL 60602
312 372-9500

## (G-16047)
### WHITNEY PRODUCTS INC
Also Called: Whitney Medical Solutions
6153 W Mulford St Ste C (60714-3419)
**PHONE** .................................. 847 966-6161
Steven Whitney, *President*
Michael Whitney, *Assistant VP*
Lisa Gyori, *Vice Pres*
Carolyn Jacobazzi, *Manager*
James Thompson, *Webmaster*
**EMP:** 18
**SQ FT:** 16,700
**SALES (est):** 2.9MM **Privately Held**
**WEB:** www.whitneyproducts.com
**SIC:** 3842 3841 3085 Surgical appliances & supplies; surgical & medical instruments; plastics bottles

## (G-16048)
### X-L-ENGINEERING CORP (PA)
6150 W Mulford St (60714-3489)
**PHONE** .................................. 847 965-3030
**Fax:** 847 967-6373
Paul T Prikos, *President*
Paul L Prikos, *Vice Pres*
Sam Crooms, *Plant Mgr*
Keith Grabski, *Design Engr*
Kathy Wendhack, *Manager*
**EMP:** 40
**SQ FT:** 18,000
**SALES (est):** 15.6MM **Privately Held**
**WEB:** www.xleng.com
**SIC:** 3451 Screw machine products

---

# Noble
## *Richland County*

## (G-16049)
### BILL CHANDLER FARMS
5182 Bucktown Ln (62868-3013)
**PHONE** .................................. 618 752-7551
William R Chandler, *Owner*
**EMP:** 2
**SALES:** 900K **Privately Held**
**SIC:** 0212 0115 0116 0213 Beef cattle except feedlots; corn; soybeans; hogs; agricultural machinery & equipment; bird food, prepared

## (G-16050)
### CLARENCE HANCOCK SAWMILL INC
1191 E White Ln (62868-2709)
**PHONE** .................................. 618 854-2232
Dennis Hancock, *President*
**EMP:** 9
**SALES (est):** 530K **Privately Held**
**SIC:** 2421 Sawmills & planing mills, general

## (G-16051)
### HITES HARDWOOD LUMBER INC
364 E Il 250 (62868)
**PHONE** .................................. 618 723-2136
**Fax:** 618 723-2136
Paul Hites, *President*
Margery Hites, *Treasurer*
Blaine Hites, *Admin Sec*
**EMP:** 12
**SALES (est):** 1.1MM **Privately Held**
**SIC:** 2421 Sawmills & planing mills, general

# GEOGRAPHIC SECTION

Normal - Mclean County (G-16076)

**(G-16052)**
**MUHS FUNITURE MANUFACTURING**
Also Called: Muhs Cabinet Creation
4808 N Passport Rd (62868-2101)
**PHONE**.................................618 723-2590
Von Muhs, *Owner*
Anjie Muhs, *Co-Owner*
**EMP:** 4
**SALES:** 210K  **Privately Held**
**SIC:** 2511  Wood household furniture

**(G-16053)**
**PATTERSON PRODUCTS**
580 E Antioch Ln (62868-2221)
**PHONE**.................................618 723-2688
Gary Patterson, *Owner*
**EMP:** 7
**SALES (est):** 726.9K  **Privately Held**
**SIC:** 3281  Table tops, marble

**(G-16054)**
**SOUTHERN ILLINOIS SCALE SERVC**
430 W South Ave (62868-1804)
**PHONE**.................................618 723-2303
Brad Fryburger, *President*
Susan Fryburger, *Vice Pres*
**EMP:** 5  **EST:** 1997
**SQ FT:** 1,340
**SALES:** 1.1MM  **Privately Held**
**SIC:** 7699  3596  Scale repair service; truck (motor vehicle) scales

## Nokomis
### *Montgomery County*

**(G-16055)**
**ALL PRECISION MFG LLC**
Also Called: A P M
153 N 5th St (62075-1753)
P.O. Box 220 (62075-0220)
**PHONE**.................................217 563-7070
**Fax:** 217 563-7060
Sharon Huddleston, *Manager*
Jeffrey Howell,
Ralph Peifer,
**EMP:** 16
**SQ FT:** 20,000
**SALES:** 1.1MM  **Privately Held**
**SIC:** 3822  Water heater controls

**(G-16056)**
**FREE PRESS PROGRESS INC**
112 W State St (62075-1657)
P.O. Box 130 (62075-0130)
**PHONE**.................................217 563-2115
**Fax:** 217 563-7464
Tom Phillips, *President*
Doris Phillip, *Treasurer*
Cynthia Hayes, *Sales Staff*
**EMP:** 2
**SQ FT:** 6,250
**SALES (est):** 214.7K
**SALES (corp-wide):** 1.8MM  **Privately Held**
**WEB:** www.pananews.com
**SIC:** 2721  2711  Periodicals: publishing & printing; newspapers
**PA:** Pana News Inc
   205 S Locust St
   Pana IL 62557
   217 562-2111

**(G-16057)**
**HENRY A ENGELHART**
1626 E 27nd Rd (62075)
P.O. Box 213 (62075-0213)
**PHONE**.................................217 563-2176
Henry Engelhart, *Owner*
**EMP:** 2
**SALES (est):** 203.6K  **Privately Held**
**SIC:** 3523  Farm machinery & equipment

**(G-16058)**
**MATERIAL SERVICE CORPORATION**
Also Called: Material Service Yard 12
22283 Taylorville Rd (62075-3812)
P.O. Box 6 (62075-0006)
**PHONE**.................................217 563-2531
**Fax:** 217 563-2330
Rich Ellis, *Manager*
**EMP:** 30
**SALES (corp-wide):** 16B  **Privately Held**
**WEB:** www.materialservice.com
**SIC:** 1422  Limestones, ground
**HQ:** Material Service Corporation
   2235 Entp Dr Ste 3504
   Westchester IL 60154
   708 731-2600

**(G-16059)**
**NOKOMIS QUARRY COMPANY**
23311 Taylorville Rd (62075-3813)
P.O. Box 90 (62075-0090)
**PHONE**.................................217 563-2011
**Fax:** 217 563-2017
James A Dougherty, *President*
James H Prosser, *Corp Secy*
Ron Oke, *Manager*
**EMP:** 15
**SQ FT:** 1,000
**SALES (est):** 2.7MM  **Privately Held**
**SIC:** 1411  1422  Limestone, dimension-quarrying; crushed & broken limestone

**(G-16060)**
**PROCESS SYSTEMS INC**
316 E State St (62075-1324)
P.O. Box 188 (62075-0188)
**PHONE**.................................217 563-2872
Ralph Jones, *Manager*
**EMP:** 5  **Privately Held**
**SIC:** 3089  Plastic processing
**PA:** Process Systems Inc.
   9160 Fishtrap Rd
   Crossroads TX 76227

**(G-16061)**
**RONK ELECTRICAL INDUSTRIES INC (PA)**
106 E State St (62075-1340)
P.O. Box 160 (62075-0160)
**PHONE**.................................217 563-8333
**Fax:** 217 563-8336
Daniel Dungan, *President*
Danny D Brady, *President*
Charlie O'Malley, *Controller*
Tom Giordano, *Sales Mgr*
Linda Hinton, *Marketing Staff*
**EMP:** 40  **EST:** 1950
**SQ FT:** 8,400
**SALES:** 6MM  **Privately Held**
**SIC:** 3621  3613  Phase or rotary converters (electrical equipment); power switching equipment; panelboards & distribution boards, electric

**(G-16062)**
**RONK ELECTRICAL INDUSTRIES INC**
106 E State St (62075-1340)
P.O. Box 160 (62075-0160)
**PHONE**.................................217 563-8333
H A Ronk, *CEO*
**EMP:** 25
**SALES (corp-wide):** 6MM  **Privately Held**
**SIC:** 3621  Motors & generators
**PA:** Ronk Electrical Industries, Inc.
   106 E State St
   Nokomis IL 62075
   217 563-8333

## Normal
### *Mclean County*

**(G-16063)**
**ALL-BRITE SIGN CO INC**
1803 Marina Dr (61761-9340)
**PHONE**.................................309 829-1551
**Fax:** 309 828-2225
Larry Olson, *President*
Kim Olson, *Vice Pres*
**EMP:** 12  **EST:** 1934
**SQ FT:** 7,000
**SALES (est):** 1.2MM  **Privately Held**
**WEB:** www.allbritesign.com
**SIC:** 1799  3993  7336  3953  Sign installation & maintenance; electric signs; graphic arts & related design; marking devices

**(G-16064)**
**AUTOMATIC FIRE SPRINKLER LLC**
1809 Industrial Park Dr (61761-4319)
**PHONE**.................................309 862-2724
**Fax:** 309 862-2914
Tim Bell,
Mery Otto, *Assistant*
**EMP:** 12
**SALES (est):** 4.7MM  **Privately Held**
**SIC:** 3569  Sprinkler systems, fire: automatic

**(G-16065)**
**BLOOM-NORM PRINTING INC**
Also Called: P I P
100 N University St # 242 (61761-4402)
**PHONE**.................................309 663-8545
**Fax:** 309 663-8546
Scott Cochran, *President*
Jerry Siadek, *Treasurer*
Andrew Siadek, *Manager*
Bruce Lang, *Consultant*
Ellen Centers, *Admin Sec*
**EMP:** 7
**SQ FT:** 1,460
**SALES (est):** 443.2K  **Privately Held**
**SIC:** 2752  7334  Commercial printing, offset; photocopying & duplicating services

**(G-16066)**
**BRIDGESTONE AMERICAS**
Also Called: Firestone
1600 Fort Jesse Rd (61761-2200)
**PHONE**.................................309 452-4411
**EMP:** 19
**SALES (corp-wide):** 30.1B  **Privately Held**
**SIC:** 3011  5531  Tires & inner tubes; automotive tires
**HQ:** Bridgestone Americas Tire Operations, Llc
   535 Marriott Dr
   Nashville TN 37214
   615 937-1000

**(G-16067)**
**CINTAS CORPORATION**
Also Called: Automatic Fire Sprinkler
1809 Industrial Park Dr (61761-4319)
**PHONE**.................................309 821-1920
**Toll Free:**...........................888   -
**Fax:** 309 821-1819
Will Conkel, *General Mgr*
**EMP:** 30
**SALES (corp-wide):** 4.9B  **Publicly Held**
**WEB:** www.cintas-corp.com
**SIC:** 3569  1711  Sprinkler systems, fire: automatic; plumbing, heating, air-conditioning contractors
**PA:** Cintas Corporation
   6800 Cintas Blvd
   Cincinnati OH 45262
   513 459-1200

**(G-16068)**
**CUMMINS CROSSPOINT LLC**
450 W Northtown Rd (61761-4743)
**PHONE**.................................309 452-4454
David McClure, *Opers Mgr*
Paul Krueger, *Sales/Mktg Mgr*
Matt Garvin, *Sales Executive*
Dennis Dewerff, *Branch Mgr*
Tim Tackett, *Manager*
**EMP:** 40
**SALES (corp-wide):** 17.5B  **Publicly Held**
**SIC:** 5084  7538  3519  Engines & parts, diesel; diesel engine repair: automotive; internal combustion engines
**HQ:** Cummins Crosspoint, Llc
   2601 Fortune Cir E 300c
   Indianapolis IN 46241
   317 243-7979

**(G-16069)**
**DIVERSIFIED ADTEE INC**
1200 Fort Jesse Rd (61761-1836)
P.O. Box 927 (61761-0927)
**PHONE**.................................309 454-2555
**Fax:** 309 454-3013
Robert Lipic, *President*
Michael Liss, *Manager*
▲ **EMP:** 30
**SQ FT:** 5,000
**SALES (est):** 2.6MM  **Privately Held**
**WEB:** www.diversified-adtee.com
**SIC:** 3993  5199  Signs & advertising specialties; advertising specialties

**(G-16070)**
**DOLL FURNITURE CO INC**
400 N Beech St (61761-1815)
**PHONE**.................................309 452-2606
**Fax:** 309 452-2606
David Shutt, *President*
Nancy Shutt, *Vice Pres*
Jeff Shutt, *Treasurer*
James Shutt, *Admin Sec*
**EMP:** 3
**SQ FT:** 5,000
**SALES (est):** 276.1K  **Privately Held**
**WEB:** www.dollfurniturecompany.com
**SIC:** 7641  5712  3553  7513  Furniture refinishing; furniture stores; woodworking machinery; truck rental & leasing, no drivers

**(G-16071)**
**FRAME MART INC**
Also Called: Wonderlin Galleries
1211 Silver Oak Cir (61761-9401)
**PHONE**.................................309 452-0658
**Fax:** 309 454-4406
**EMP:** 4
**SALES (est):** 294.6K  **Privately Held**
**SIC:** 2499  5999  Mfg Wood Products Ret Misc Merchandise

**(G-16072)**
**HARLAN VANCE COMPANY**
1741 Hovey Ave (61761-4322)
**PHONE**.................................309 888-4804
**Fax:** 309 888-4807
Teresa J Vance, *President*
Drew S Vance, *Vice Pres*
Joe Marcotte, *Marketing Staff*
Keith Jenkins, *Art Dir*
Thomas Hayslett, *Shareholder*
**EMP:** 12  **EST:** 1960
**SQ FT:** 11,000
**SALES:** 3.2MM  **Privately Held**
**WEB:** www.harlanvance.com
**SIC:** 5112  2395  2752  Stationery & office supplies; looseleaf binders; blank books; embroidery products, except schiffli machine; commercial printing, lithographic

**(G-16073)**
**IDENTITY OPTICAL LAB**
2221 W College Ave (61761-2375)
**PHONE**.................................309 807-3160
Peter Kimerling, *Director*
**EMP:** 3
**SALES (est):** 420.6K  **Privately Held**
**SIC:** 3827  Magnifying instruments, optical

**(G-16074)**
**JLM WOODWORKING**
500 Orlando Ave (61761-1233)
**PHONE**.................................309 275-8259
Joshua Moyer, *Principal*
**EMP:** 4
**SALES (est):** 314.3K  **Privately Held**
**SIC:** 2431  Millwork

**(G-16075)**
**LUTZ CORP**
208 N Parkside Rd (61761-2346)
**PHONE**.................................800 203-7740
Lee Lutz, *President*
**EMP:** 3
**SALES (est):** 316.5K  **Privately Held**
**SIC:** 3524  Lawn & garden equipment

**(G-16076)**
**MEYER ELECTRONIC MFG SVCS INC**
Also Called: Meyer E M S
440 Wylie Dr (61761-5405)
**PHONE**.................................309 808-4100
Gregory Meyer, *President*
Marsha Meyer, *Vice Pres*
**EMP:** 8
**SQ FT:** 1,000
**SALES:** 1MM  **Privately Held**
**SIC:** 3625  Relays & industrial controls

## Normal - Mclean County (G-16077)

**(G-16077)**
**MIRUS RESEARCH**
618 E Lincoln St (61761-1889)
PHONE .................................. 309 828-3100
Matt Hughes, *Owner*
**EMP:** 25
**SALES (est):** 2.3MM **Privately Held**
**WEB:** www.mirusresearch.com
**SIC:** 7372 Prepackaged software

**(G-16078)**
**MMMA**
2601 W College Ave Ste A (61761-5920)
PHONE .................................. 309 888-8765
Fax: 309 888-8202
Chuck Madis, *General Mgr*
Gerald Berwanger, *Senior VP*
Greg Wilcox, *Engineer*
Cindy Kirby, *VP Finance*
Andy Whaley, *Accounting Mgr*
**EMP:** 15
**SALES (est):** 2.7MM **Privately Held**
**SIC:** 3465 Body parts, automobile: stamped metal

**(G-16079)**
**NORMAL CORNBELTERS**
1000 W Raab Rd (61761-9578)
PHONE .................................. 309 451-3432
Ashlynne Solvie, *Manager*
Jeff Holtke, *Manager*
Zachary Kerby, *Manager*
Michael Petrini, *Asst Mgr*
**EMP:** 6
**SALES (est):** 560.8K **Privately Held**
**SIC:** 3949 Bases, baseball

**(G-16080)**
**NORMALITE NEWSPAPER**
1702 W College Ave Ste G (61761-2793)
P.O. Box 67 (61761-0067)
PHONE .................................. 309 454-5476
Ed Pyne, *Owner*
**EMP:** 10
**SALES (est):** 362.5K **Privately Held**
**WEB:** www.normalite.com
**SIC:** 2711 Newspapers

**(G-16081)**
**NUAIR FILTER COMPANY LLC (HQ)**
2219 W College Ave (61761-2375)
PHONE .................................. 309 888-4331
Fax: 309 452-1336
Jamie Harding, *Vice Pres*
Michael Busick, *Engineer*
Jim Franz, *Controller*
Tony Bianco, *Manager*
John Van Den Bossche, *Manager*
**EMP:** 15
**SQ FT:** 105,000
**SALES (est):** 19.9MM
**SALES (corp-wide):** 151.8MM **Privately Held**
**WEB:** www.nuair.net
**SIC:** 5085 3443 5075 Industrial supplies; metal parts; air filters
**PA:** Superior Consolidated Industries, Inc.
801 Sw Jefferson Ave
Peoria IL 61605
309 677-5980

**(G-16082)**
**OLDCASTLE PRECAST INC**
1204 Aurora Way (61761-1260)
PHONE .................................. 309 661-4608
Brent Anderson, *Treasurer*
**EMP:** 15
**SALES (corp-wide):** 28.6B **Privately Held**
**WEB:** www.oldcastle-precast.com
**SIC:** 3446 Open flooring & grating for construction
**HQ:** Oldcastle Precast, Inc.
1002 15th St Sw Ste 110
Auburn WA 98001
253 833-2777

**(G-16083)**
**PEORIA MIDWEST EQUIPMENT INC**
2150 W College Ave (61761-2372)
PHONE .................................. 309 454-6800
Steve Meyer, *Principal*
**EMP:** 6
**SALES (corp-wide):** 6.7MM **Privately Held**
**SIC:** 7699 5261 5063 3546 Lawn mower repair shop; lawnmowers & tractors; generators; saws & sawing equipment
**PA:** Peoria Midwest Equipment, Inc.
4826 W Farmington Rd
Peoria IL
309 676-5855

**(G-16084)**
**PRAIRIE SIGNS INC**
1215 Warriner St (61761-3334)
PHONE .................................. 309 452-0463
Fax: 309 454-8741
Andrew R Carby, *CEO*
Cassandra Mocilan, *President*
Diana Bubenik, *Treasurer*
Thomas Campana, *Marketing Staff*
Andrew Carby, *Manager*
**EMP:** 13
**SQ FT:** 14,000
**SALES (est):** 2.4MM **Privately Held**
**WEB:** www.prairiesigns.com
**SIC:** 3993 Signs & advertising specialties; electric signs

**(G-16085)**
**PROSTHETIC ORTHOTIC SPECIALIST (PA)**
303 Landmark Dr Ste 5a (61761-6164)
PHONE .................................. 309 454-8733
Fax: 309 452-3520
Kenneth W Ferencik, *President*
Rosemary D Ferencik, *Treasurer*
**EMP:** 5
**SQ FT:** 1,200
**SALES (est):** 45K **Privately Held**
**SIC:** 5999 3842 Orthopedic & prosthesis applications; orthopedic appliances

**(G-16086)**
**R B WHITE INC**
2011 Eagle Rd (61761-1001)
P.O. Box 538 (61761-0538)
PHONE .................................. 309 452-5816
Fax: 309 829-2252
Michael White, *President*
Robert White, *Chairman*
Stella White, *Vice Pres*
Dallas Wickenhauser, *Vice Pres*
Vijay Patibandla, *Purchasing*
**EMP:** 40
**SALES (est):** 6.6MM **Privately Held**
**SIC:** 2542 3469 3444 Shelving, office & store: except wood; shelving angles or slotted bars: except wood; metal stampings; sheet metalwork

**(G-16087)**
**RUSSELL BRANDS LLC**
2015 Eagle Rd (61761-1001)
P.O. Box 9 (61761-0009)
PHONE .................................. 309 454-6737
Fax: 309 454-5765
Dan Jurczak, *Branch Mgr*
**EMP:** 100
**SALES (corp-wide):** 223.6B **Publicly Held**
**WEB:** www.russellcorp.com
**SIC:** 2253 Jerseys, knit; jogging & warm-up suits, knit; T-shirts & tops, knit; pants, slacks or trousers, knit
**HQ:** Russell Brands, Llc
1 Fruit Of The Loom Dr
Bowling Green KY 42103
270 781-6400

**(G-16088)**
**SCADAWARE INC**
2023 Eagle Rd (61761-1001)
PHONE .................................. 309 665-0135
Fax: 309 665-0975
Richard J Caldwell, *President*
Neal Clark, *COO*
Morgan Steffens, *Corp Comm Staff*
Jennifer Skaggs, *Manager*
Melissa Sheet, *Administration*
**EMP:** 15 **EST:** 2000
**SQ FT:** 5,400
**SALES (est):** 4.2MM **Privately Held**
**WEB:** www.scadaware.com
**SIC:** 3577 7371 Input/output equipment, computer; computer software development & applications

**(G-16089)**
**STAR TEST DYNAMOMETER INC**
712 Thistlewood Cc Ct (61761-5301)
PHONE .................................. 309 452-0371
Michael E Barclay, *Principal*
**EMP:** 2
**SALES (est):** 233.4K **Privately Held**
**SIC:** 3829 Dynamometer instruments

**(G-16090)**
**TWIN CITIES READY MIX INC**
1324 Fort Jesse Rd (61761-1869)
PHONE .................................. 309 862-1500
Steve Maxheimer, *President*
**EMP:** 10
**SALES (est):** 748K **Privately Held**
**SIC:** 3273 Ready-mixed concrete

**(G-16091)**
**TWIN CITY AWARDS**
1531 Fort Jesse Rd Ste 5b (61761-4742)
PHONE .................................. 309 452-9291
Fax: 309 452-9291
William M McGivern Jr, *Partner*
Carol McGivern, *Partner*
**EMP:** 2
**SQ FT:** 1,800
**SALES (est):** 200K **Privately Held**
**WEB:** www.twincityawards.com
**SIC:** 5999 5947 3993 Trophies & plaques; gift shop; signs & advertising specialties

**(G-16092)**
**UNIQUE DESIGNS**
408 Lumbertown Rd (61761-4744)
PHONE .................................. 309 454-1226
Mark Fagerland, *Owner*
**EMP:** 6
**SQ FT:** 12,000
**SALES (est):** 900K **Privately Held**
**SIC:** 3083 5712 1751 Plastic finished products, laminated; cabinet work, custom; custom made furniture, except cabinets; cabinet & finish carpentry

**(G-16093)**
**VUTEQ USA INC**
2222 W College Ave (61761-2374)
PHONE .................................. 309 452-9933
Fax: 309 452-9362
Shingi Yanagawa, *Vice Pres*
Takebumi Sekiguchi, *Plant Mgr*
Ruth La Rose, *Human Res Mgr*
John Sciutto, *Manager*
**EMP:** 110
**SALES (corp-wide):** 402.5MM **Privately Held**
**WEB:** www.vuteqil.com
**SIC:** 3711 3714 5013 Motor vehicles & car bodies; motor vehicle parts & accessories; automotive supplies & parts
**HQ:** Vuteq Usa, Inc.
100 Carley Dr
Georgetown KY 40324
502 863-6322

## Norridge
*Cook County*

**(G-16094)**
**ACCU-CUT DIAMOND BORE SIZING (HQ)**
4238 N Sayre Ave (60706-7107)
PHONE .................................. 708 457-8800
Stanley Domanski, *CEO*
Christine Domanski, *President*
Cary Turner, *CFO*
Terrence W Moloney, *Accountant*
John Wagner, *Technology*
**EMP:** 10
**SQ FT:** 20,000
**SALES (est):** 997K
**SALES (corp-wide):** 10MM **Privately Held**
**SIC:** 3542 Presses: forming, stamping, punching, sizing (machine tools)
**PA:** Accu-Cut Diamond Tool Company, Inc
423840 N Sayre Ave
Norridge IL 60706
708 457-8800

**(G-16095)**
**ACCU-CUT DIAMOND TOOL COMPANY (PA)**
423840 N Sayre Ave (60706)
P.O. Box 56186, Chicago (60656-0186)
PHONE .................................. 708 457-8800
Fax: 708 457-8061
Stan Domanski, *CEO*
Christine Domanski, *President*
Carey Turner, *CFO*
Aneta Jankowska, *Marketing Staff*
Glenn Miller, *Director*
**EMP:** 19
**SQ FT:** 20,000
**SALES (est):** 10MM **Privately Held**
**WEB:** www.accucutdiamond.com
**SIC:** 3545 Diamond cutting tools for turning, boring, burnishing, etc.

**(G-16096)**
**APPLIANCE REPAIR**
4911 N Delphia Ave (60706-2808)
PHONE .................................. 708 456-1020
Jim Gagliano, *Owner*
**EMP:** 3 **EST:** 2007
**SALES (est):** 268.1K **Privately Held**
**SIC:** 3639 5064 7629 Major kitchen appliances, except refrigerators & stoves; electrical appliances, major; electrical household appliance repair

**(G-16097)**
**BUTERA FINER FOODS INC**
Also Called: Butera Markets
4411 N Cumberland Ave (60706-4220)
PHONE .................................. 708 456-5939
Fax: 708 456-0705
Vito Trioa, *Manager*
**EMP:** 100
**SALES (corp-wide):** 77.9MM **Privately Held**
**WEB:** www.buterafinerfoods.com
**SIC:** 5411 2051 Grocery stores; bread, cake & related products
**PA:** Butera Finer Foods, Inc.
1 Clock Tower Plz Ste A
Elgin IL 60120
847 741-1010

**(G-16098)**
**CAST PRODUCTS INC**
Also Called: CPI
4200 N Nordica Ave (60706-1392)
PHONE .................................. 708 457-1500
Ron Paquet, *CEO*
Zoltan Salata, *President*
Helen Salata, *COO*
Jeff Adams, *Opers Mgr*
Paul Menzel, *Opers Mgr*
▲ **EMP:** 115 **EST:** 1966
**SQ FT:** 65,000
**SALES (est):** 30.4MM **Privately Held**
**WEB:** www.castproducts.com
**SIC:** 3364 Zinc & zinc-base alloy die-castings

**(G-16099)**
**DEE CONCRETE ACCESSORIES**
7350 W Montrose Ave (60706-1158)
PHONE .................................. 708 452-0250
Fax: 708 452-7220
Barbara Skoniecizny, *Treasurer*
Terry Borys, *Human Res Dir*
▼ **EMP:** 13 **EST:** 1965
**SALES (est):** 1.7MM **Privately Held**
**WEB:** www.deeconcrete.com
**SIC:** 3444 3443 Concrete forms, sheet metal; fabricated plate work (boiler shop)

**(G-16100)**
**DISCO MACHINE & MFG INC**
7327 W Agatite Ave (60706-4703)
PHONE .................................. 708 456-0835
Zbigniew Brzostowski, *President*
Margaret Brzostowski, *Manager*
Helena Brzostowski, *Admin Sec*
**EMP:** 35
**SQ FT:** 13,500
**SALES (est):** 5.7MM **Privately Held**
**SIC:** 3599 Machine shop, jobbing & repair

**(G-16101)**
**EXPRESS LLC**
4122 N Harlem Ave (60706-1257)
PHONE .................................. 708 453-0566
Fax: 708 453-0821

Luz Camacho, *Manager*
**EMP:** 30  **Publicly Held**
**SIC: 5621**  2329  Women's clothing stores; men's & boys' sportswear & athletic clothing
**HQ:** Express, Llc
1 Express Dr
Columbus OH 43230
800 934-4437

**(G-16102)**
**IGGYS AUTO PARTS**
7230 W Montrose Ave (60706-1217)
**PHONE** ...................708 452-9790
Mike Ignoffo, *Owner*
**EMP:** 10
**SALES (est):** 928.1K  **Privately Held**
**SIC: 3714**  5531  Motor vehicle parts & accessories; automobile & truck equipment & parts

**(G-16103)**
**JOSEPH RINGELSTEIN**
Also Called: Gamma Quality
4110 1/2 N Octavia Ave (60706-1208)
P.O. Box 56356, Chicago (60656-0356)
**PHONE** ...................708 955-7467
Joseph Ringelstein, *Owner*
**EMP:** 3
**SALES (est):** 178.3K  **Privately Held**
**SIC: 3829**  Medical diagnostic systems, nuclear

**(G-16104)**
**LEONARD PUBLISHING CO**
7508 W Belle Plaine Ave (60706-1101)
**PHONE** ...................773 486-2737
Dean Leonard, *Owner*
**EMP:** 12 EST: 1908
**SQ FT:** 3,000
**SALES (est):** 520K  **Privately Held**
**SIC: 2741**  2759  2752  Guides: publishing & printing; maps: publishing & printing; commercial printing; commercial printing, lithographic

**(G-16105)**
**MAJOR WIRE INCORPORATED**
7014 W Cullom Ave (60706-1397)
**PHONE** ...................708 457-0121
**Fax:** 708 457-0616
Kenneth G Michonski, *President*
Barbara Sirovi, *Manager*
Donald Michonski, *Director*
Martin Michonski, *Director*
**EMP:** 10
**SQ FT:** 13,600
**SALES (est):** 1.1MM  **Privately Held**
**WEB:** www.majorwire.com
**SIC: 3315**  3357  3694  Steel wire & related products; wire & fabricated wire products; wire products, ferrous/iron: made in wire-drawing plants; nonferrous wiredrawing & insulating; engine electrical equipment

**(G-16106)**
**MAKRAY MANUFACTURING COMPANY (PA)**
4400 N Harlem Ave (60706-4774)
**PHONE** ...................708 456-7100
**Fax:** 773 456-7178
Paul Makray Jr, *President*
Antoinette Tonelli, *Purch Mgr*
Patty Van Derpluym, *Persnl Mgr*
Sebastian Cabrera, *Manager*
Darin Lewis, *Info Tech Mgr*
▲ **EMP:** 64
**SQ FT:** 100,000
**SALES (est):** 19.4MM  **Privately Held**
**SIC: 3089**  3544  Injection molded finished plastic products; special dies, tools, jigs & fixtures

**(G-16107)**
**OLTENIA INC**
4905 N Opal Ave (60706-3219)
**PHONE** ...................773 987-2888
**EMP:** 3
**SALES (est):** 184.7K  **Privately Held**
**SIC: 2421**  Flooring (dressed lumber), softwood

**(G-16108)**
**SIGNA DEVELOPMENT GROUP INC (PA)**
4641 N Oriole Ave (60706-4538)
**PHONE** ...................773 418-4506
John Signa, *President*
**EMP:** 2
**SALES:** 458.5K  **Privately Held**
**WEB:** www.signadg.com
**SIC: 3448**  1541  1542  7389  Buildings, portable: prefabricated metal; prefabricated building erection, industrial; commercial & office buildings, renovation & repair;

**(G-16109)**
**TESKO WELDING & MFG CO**
Also Called: Tesko Enterprises
7350 W Montrose Ave (60706-1158)
**PHONE** ...................708 452-0045
**Fax:** 708 452-0112
Zbigniew Skonieczny, *President*
Theresa Borys, *Vice Pres*
Barbara Skonieczny, *Treasurer*
Stella Skonieczny, *Admin Sec*
**EMP:** 70
**SQ FT:** 53,000
**SALES (est):** 10.9MM  **Privately Held**
**WEB:** www.teskoenterprises.com
**SIC: 2542**  2514  3498  Fixtures, store: except wood; showcases (not refrigerated): except wood; household furniture: upholstered on metal frames; fabricated pipe & fittings

**(G-16110)**
**TRANSFORMER MANUFACTURERS INC**
Also Called: TMI
7051 W Wilson Ave (60706-4784)
**PHONE** ...................708 457-1200
**Fax:** 773 457-2266
Alec K Gianaras Sr, *Ch of Bd*
Alexander Gianaras Jr, *President*
Alexander A Gianaras Jr, *President*
Katherine A Gianaras, *Vice Pres*
Viena P Gianaras, *Vice Pres*
▲ **EMP:** 20
**SQ FT:** 25,000
**SALES (est):** 4.8MM  **Privately Held**
**WEB:** www.tmitransformers.com
**SIC: 3612**  3825  3677  3621  Specialty transformers; instruments to measure electricity; electronic coils, transformers & other inductors; motors & generators

### Norris City
### White County

**(G-16111)**
**B & B TANK TRUCK CONSTRUCTION (PA)**
Also Called: Eastern Services
760 Us Highway 45 (62869-3001)
P.O. Box 276 (62869-0276)
**PHONE** ...................618 378-3337
**Fax:** 618 378-3338
William R Becker, *President*
William Becker, *President*
Phillys Becker, *Treasurer*
**EMP:** 10 EST: 1964
**SQ FT:** 3,000
**SALES (est):** 1.8MM  **Privately Held**
**SIC: 1389**  Acidizing wells; haulage, oil field; pumping of oil & gas wells; servicing oil & gas wells

**(G-16112)**
**CATERPILLAR GLOBAL MINING LLC**
635 Il Highway 1 (62869-3417)
**PHONE** ...................618 378-3441
Carrier Mills, *Manager*
**EMP:** 25
**SALES (corp-wide):** 38.5B  **Publicly Held**
**SIC: 3531**  Construction machinery
**HQ:** Caterpillar Global Mining Llc
1100 Milwaukee Ave
South Milwaukee WI 53172
414 762-0376

**(G-16113)**
**D R WALTERS**
65 County Road 300 N (62869-3844)
**PHONE** ...................618 926-6337
D R Walters, *Principal*
**EMP:** 3
**SALES (est):** 277.9K  **Privately Held**
**SIC: 3131**  Rands

**(G-16114)**
**FABICK MINING LLC**
635 Illinois Highway 1 (62869)
**PHONE** ...................618 982-9000
Douglas R Fabick, *President*
**EMP:** 12 EST: 2014
**SALES (est):** 1.4MM  **Privately Held**
**SIC: 1231**  Underground mining, anthracite

**(G-16115)**
**KINOCO INC**
230 County Road 500 E (62869-3924)
P.O. Box 150 (62869-0150)
**PHONE** ...................618 378-3802
Richard Kingston, *President*
**EMP:** 5
**SALES (est):** 419.9K  **Privately Held**
**SIC: 1381**  Drilling oil & gas wells

**(G-16116)**
**WILLIAM R BECKER**
Also Called: Brent Pumps Supply
760 Route 45 N (62869)
P.O. Box 276 (62869-0276)
**PHONE** ...................618 378-3337
William R Becker, *Owner*
Phyllis Becker, *Corp Secy*
**EMP:** 15
**SQ FT:** 3,000
**SALES:** 1MM  **Privately Held**
**SIC: 1311**  5084  Crude petroleum production; oil well machinery, equipment & supplies

### North Aurora
### Kane County

**(G-16117)**
**ABELEI INC**
194 Alder Dr (60542-1485)
**PHONE** ...................630 859-1410
**Fax:** 630 859-1448
Karen R Criss, *President*
Troy Gooding, *President*
Marcia Criss, *Vice Pres*
Shelley Hendreson, *Opers Mgr*
Shelley Henderson, *Opers Staff*
**EMP:** 10
**SQ FT:** 12,000
**SALES (est):** 3.7MM  **Privately Held*
**WEB:** www.abelei.com
**SIC: 5149**  2099  2087  Seasonings, sauces & extracts; food preparations; flavoring extracts & syrups

**(G-16118)**
**ARCH PRINTING**
710 Morton Ave (60542)
**PHONE** ...................630 896-6610
Tony Arch, *Owner*
Mary Arch, *Co-Owner*
**EMP:** 5
**SALES (est):** 500K  **Privately Held**
**SIC: 2759**  Commercial printing

**(G-16119)**
**AURORA PACKING COMPANY INC**
125 S Grant St (60542-1603)
P.O. Box 209 (60542-0209)
**PHONE** ...................630 897-0551
**Fax:** 630 897-0647
Marvin Fagel, *Ch of Bd*
Bob Harris, *Purch Mgr*
Michael Fagel, *Admin Sec*
**EMP:** 250 EST: 1939
**SQ FT:** 105,000
**SALES (est):** 48.6MM  **Privately Held**
**SIC: 2011**  Boxed beef from meat slaughtered on site

**(G-16120)**
**BELSON OUTDOORS LLC (DH)**
111 N River Rd (60542-1324)
**PHONE** ...................630 897-8489
**Fax:** 630 897-0573
John Hauptman, *CEO*
Dennis Iverson, *Controller*
Brenda Wilmsen, *Cust Mgr*
Jill Watson, *Sales Staff*
Gavin McHugh, *Manager*
◆ **EMP:** 32
**SQ FT:** 50,000
**SALES (est):** 8.2MM
**SALES (corp-wide):** 221.4MM  **Privately Held**
**WEB:** www.belson.com
**SIC: 3631**  2531  3536  Barbecues, grills & braziers (outdoor cooking); picnic tables or benches, park; trash compactors, household
**HQ:** Playcore Wisconsin, Inc.
401 Chestnut St Ste 410
Chattanooga TN 37402
423 265-7529

**(G-16121)**
**BUDD AA INC**
1310 Turnberry Dr (60542-9027)
**PHONE** ...................630 879-1740
James Budzynski, *President*
**EMP:** 3
**SALES (est):** 276.7K  **Privately Held**
**SIC: 3944**  Toy guns

**(G-16122)**
**CALO CORPORATION**
Also Called: Recora Company
197 Alder Dr (60542-1471)
**PHONE** ...................630 879-2202
**Fax:** 630 406-9797
Balan Menon, *President*
Sophia Meza, *Purch Agent*
Julie Ross, *Manager*
**EMP:** 25 EST: 1946
**SQ FT:** 55,000
**SALES (est):** 4.4MM  **Privately Held**
**WEB:** www.recora-co.com
**SIC: 3613**  Switches, electric power except snap, push button, etc.

**(G-16123)**
**CON-TEMP CABINETS INC**
201 Poplar Pl (60542-1406)
**PHONE** ...................630 892-7300
**Fax:** 630 892-7641
Joe Marino, *President*
Brett Doranski, *Vice Pres*
Bob Burnett, *Foreman/Supr*
Diane Lee, *Office Mgr*
**EMP:** 15
**SQ FT:** 12,500
**SALES (est):** 1.3MM  **Privately Held**
**WEB:** www.con-tempcabinets.com
**SIC: 2541**  2434  Cabinets, except refrigerated: show, display, etc.: wood; wood kitchen cabinets

**(G-16124)**
**DACO INCORPORATED (PA)**
609 Airport Rd (60542-1467)
P.O. Box 1250, Sugar Grove (60554-1250)
**PHONE** ...................630 897-8797
**Fax:** 630 897-4076
Bruce E Lindgren, *President*
John T Metz, *Corp Secy*
Stephen F Lindgren, *Vice Pres*
Richard Lanute, *Opers Staff*
Thomas Kozlowski, *Engineer*
▲ **EMP:** 19 EST: 1930
**SQ FT:** 90,000
**SALES (est):** 2.3MM  **Privately Held**
**WEB:** www.dacoinc.com
**SIC: 3599**  Machine & other job shop work

**(G-16125)**
**DACO PRODUCTS LLC**
609 Airport Rd (60542-1467)
P.O. Box 1250, Sugar Grove (60554-1250)
**PHONE** ...................630 373-2245
Stephen Lindgren, *Principal*
**EMP:** 5
**SALES (est):** 361.1K  **Privately Held**
**SIC: 3537**  Cars & trucks, for industrial mining

## North Aurora - Kane County (G-16126)

**(G-16126)**
**DART CONTAINER CORP ILLINOIS (PA)**
310 Evergreen Dr
P.O. Box 500, Mason MI (48854-0500)
PHONE..........................630 896-4631
Fax: 630 896-7124
Kenneth B Dart, *President*
Chuck Hird, *Opers Mgr*
Jennifer Pesch, *Executive*
James D Lammers, *Admin Sec*
Keith Blaylock, *Maintence Staff*
EMP: 81 EST: 1966
SQ FT: 50,000
SALES (est): 29.4MM **Privately Held**
WEB: www.dartbiz.com
SIC: 3086 Cups & plates, foamed plastic

**(G-16127)**
**DART CONTAINER CORP ILLINOIS**
310 Evergreen Dr (60542-1702)
PHONE..........................630 896-4631
Ron Haldeman, *Plant Mgr*
Jennifer Pesch, *Personnel Exec*
Mike Powell, *Manager*
EMP: 200
SALES (corp-wide): 29.4MM **Privately Held**
WEB: www.dartbiz.com
SIC: 3086 Cups & plates, foamed plastic
PA: Dart Container Corporation Of Illinois
310 Evergreen Dr
North Aurora IL 60542
630 896-4631

**(G-16128)**
**EARTHGRAINS**
321 Airport Rd (60542-1476)
PHONE..........................630 859-8782
Fax: 630 859-8732
Richard Kline, *Executive*
EMP: 3
SALES (est): 180K **Privately Held**
SIC: 2032 Beans, baked without meat: packaged in cans, jars, etc.

**(G-16129)**
**FAIRBANKS MORSE PUMP CORP (PA)**
800 Airport Rd (60542-1403)
PHONE..........................630 859-7000
John Kucharik, *President*
Dave Angelo, *Vice Pres*
Jeff Darbut, *Vice Pres*
Phil Fivecoat, *Controller*
Jack Orlowski, *Controller*
◆ EMP: 300
SQ FT: 300,000
SALES (est): 29.4MM **Privately Held**
SIC: 3561 Pumps & pumping equipment

**(G-16130)**
**FAR WEST PRINT SOLUTIONS LLC**
714 Fairfield Way (60542-8918)
PHONE..........................630 879-9500
Rebecca Dhuse, *Principal*
EMP: 6
SALES (est): 491.3K **Privately Held**
SIC: 2752 Commercial printing, lithographic

**(G-16131)**
**FOX VALLEY MACHINING CO INC**
198 Poplar Pl (60542-1405)
PHONE..........................630 859-0700
Fax: 630 859-0703
Joseph P Kawa, *President*
Joseph Marek, *Vice Pres*
Kimberly Powell, *Manager*
EMP: 20
SQ FT: 20,000
SALES (est): 4.1MM **Privately Held**
SIC: 3599 Machine shop, jobbing & repair

**(G-16132)**
**GENEVA CONSTRUCTION COMPANY**
216 Butterfield Rd (60542-1316)
PHONE..........................630 892-6536
Don Antich, *Branch Mgr*
EMP: 5
SALES (corp-wide): 4.2MM **Privately Held**
SIC: 1611 2951 Highway & street paving contractor; grading; asphalt paving mixtures & blocks
PA: Geneva Construction Company
1350 Aurora Ave
Aurora IL 60505
630 892-4357

**(G-16133)**
**HARNERS BAKERY RESTAURANT**
10 W State St (60542-1620)
PHONE..........................630 892-5545
Fax: 630 892-7170
Darryl Harner, *President*
Sue Lavford, *General Mgr*
Karen Johnson, *Manager*
EMP: 90
SQ FT: 6,000
SALES (est): 2MM **Privately Held**
SIC: 5812 5461 2051 Restaurant, family: independent; ice cream stands or dairy bars; bakeries; bread, cake & related products

**(G-16134)**
**INSPIRA INDUSTRIES INC**
1455 Carlson Ct (60542-8978)
PHONE..........................630 907-2123
Erik Wirjan, *Principal*
▲ EMP: 3 EST: 2007
SALES (est): 248.1K **Privately Held**
SIC: 3999 Manufacturing industries

**(G-16135)**
**IYA FOODS LLC**
Also Called: Naija Foods
348 Smoketree Bsn Dr (60542-1720)
PHONE..........................630 854-7107
Oluwatoyin Kolawole, *President*
EMP: 3
SALES (est): 178.8K **Privately Held**
SIC: 5149 2033 5141 Natural & organic foods; specialty food items; tomato products: packaged in cans, jars, etc.; groceries, general line

**(G-16136)**
**JANSSEN AVENUE BOYS INC**
Also Called: Fast Color
200 Alder Dr A (60542-1400)
PHONE..........................630 627-0202
Angela Muschong, *President*
Joe Muschong, *General Mgr*
Jeffrey Vitter, *Vice Pres*
Diane Cuzzo, *Sales Staff*
EMP: 5
SQ FT: 3,700
SALES: 500K **Privately Held**
SIC: 2752 Commercial printing, lithographic

**(G-16137)**
**LAFARGE NORTH AMERICA INC**
105 Conco St (60542-1601)
PHONE..........................630 892-1616
EMP: 29
SALES (corp-wide): 26.6B **Privately Held**
SIC: 3241 Cement, hydraulic
HQ: Lafarge North America Inc.
8700 W Bryn Mawr Ave Ll
Chicago IL 60631
703 480-3600

**(G-16138)**
**LEGGETT & PLATT INCORPORATED**
Also Called: Leggett & Platt 0n09
241 Airport Rd (60542-1816)
PHONE..........................630 801-0609
Fax: 630 879-1039
Tom Adams, *QC Dir*
James Zaerr, *Branch Mgr*
EMP: 30
SQ FT: 106,000
SALES (corp-wide): 3.7B **Publicly Held**
WEB: www.leggett.com
SIC: 2515 2511 Bedsprings, assembled; wood household furniture
PA: Leggett & Platt, Incorporated
1 Leggett Rd
Carthage MO 64836
417 358-8131

**(G-16139)**
**ORBIS RPM LLC**
261 Airport Rd (60542-1816)
PHONE..........................630 844-9255
David Joley, *Branch Mgr*
EMP: 16
SALES (corp-wide): 1.8B **Privately Held**
SIC: 2653 Sheets, corrugated: made from purchased materials
HQ: Orbis Rpm, Llc
1055 Corporate Center Dr
Oconomowoc WI 53066
262 560-5000

**(G-16140)**
**PENTAIR FLOW TECHNOLOGIES LLC**
Also Called: Aurora Pump
800 Airport Rd (60542-1403)
PHONE..........................630 859-7000
Fax: 630 859-7030
Frank Hoban, *Opers Staff*
Dan Rotta, *Engineer*
Dana Sisson, *Engineer*
John Heiberger, *Indstl Engineer*
Vicki Swaine, *Human Res Mgr*
EMP: 200
SALES (corp-wide): 14.5B **Publicly Held**
WEB: www.aurorapump.com
SIC: 3561 Pumps & pumping equipment
HQ: Pentair Flow Technologies, Llc
1101 Myers Pkwy
Ashland OH 44805
419 289-1144

**(G-16141)**
**PERFTECH INC**
251 Airport Rd (60542-1816)
PHONE..........................630 554-0010
Gerald Sullivan, *President*
Chris Jilka, *VP Opers*
Paul Devine, *Sales Staff*
Ken Gill, *Chief Mktg Ofcr*
Nigel Jayson, *Manager*
▲ EMP: 31
SQ FT: 57,000
SALES (est): 5.1MM **Privately Held**
SIC: 2761 Manifold business forms

**(G-16142)**
**PILLAR ENTERPRISES INC**
121 S Lincolnway Ste 103 (60542-5117)
PHONE..........................630 966-2566
Fax: 630 566-5973
Raymond Pillar, *President*
EMP: 3
SALES (est): 260K **Privately Held**
SIC: 3299 Ceramic fiber

**(G-16143)**
**PRECISE STAMPING INC**
202 Poplar Pl (60542-1407)
PHONE..........................630 897-6477
Fax: 630 897-6880
Christopher Goblet, *President*
Robert Goblet, *Admin Sec*
EMP: 28
SQ FT: 20,000
SALES (est): 6.5MM **Privately Held**
WEB: www.precisestamping.com
SIC: 3469 3312 Stamping metal for the trade; tool & die steel

**(G-16144)**
**SOUND SEAL INC**
IAC Acoustics
401 Airport Rd (60542-1818)
PHONE..........................630 844-1999
Mark Rubino, *General Mgr*
Darren Riley, *Sales Staff*
EMP: 31
SALES (corp-wide): 42.7MM **Privately Held**
SIC: 3625 Noise control equipment
HQ: Sound Seal, Inc.
50 Almgren Dr S
Agawam MA 01001
413 789-1770

**(G-16145)**
**SPECIALTY BOX CORP**
366 Smoketree Bsn Dr Pa (60542-1720)
PHONE..........................630 897-7278
Alan Vagoren, *President*
Bonnie L Zagoren, *Admin Sec*
EMP: 13

SALES (est): 1.4MM **Privately Held**
SIC: 2441 2657 2653 Boxes, wood; folding paperboard boxes; corrugated & fiber boxes

**(G-16146)**
**STEPHENS PIPE & STEEL LLC**
603 Oak Crest Dr (60542-9002)
PHONE..........................800 451-2612
EMP: 41
SALES (corp-wide): 2.9B **Privately Held**
SIC: 5051 3315 3523 Pipe & tubing, steel; chain link fencing; cattle feeding, handling & watering equipment
HQ: Stephens Pipe & Steel, Llc
2224 E Highway 619
Russell Springs KY 42642
270 866-3331

**(G-16147)**
**TELEHEALTH SENSORS LLC**
197 Alder Dr (60542-1471)
PHONE..........................630 879-3101
Menon Balan, *President*
EMP: 25 EST: 2010
SALES (est): 2.9MM **Privately Held**
SIC: 3674 Infrared sensors, solid state

**(G-16148)**
**TUU DUC LE INC (PA)**
Also Called: Aurora Orthopedic Laboratories
110 John St (60542-1632)
PHONE..........................630 897-6363
Fax: 630 897-7663
Tuu D Lee, *President*
Charles Grantham, *Manager*
Missy Best, *Admin Sec*
EMP: 5
SQ FT: 2,400
SALES: 750K **Privately Held**
SIC: 3842 Limbs, artificial; braces, orthopedic

**(G-16149)**
**VINYL LIFE NORTH**
661 Dewig Ct (60542-9149)
PHONE..........................630 906-9686
Emil Kaderabek, *Owner*
EMP: 3
SALES (est): 211.9K **Privately Held**
SIC: 2599 2512 Bar, restaurant & cafeteria furniture; upholstered household furniture

**(G-16150)**
**WILLIAMSBURG PRESS INC**
454 Fox Crossing Ave (60542-1797)
PHONE..........................630 229-0228
Bertram W Halley, *President*
Rosemary A Halley, *Corp Secy*
EMP: 6
SQ FT: 10,000
SALES: 600K **Privately Held**
SIC: 2752 2759 Commercial printing, offset; commercial printing

## North Barrington
### Lake County

**(G-16151)**
**HEALTHCARE LABELS INC**
245 Honey Lake Ct (60010-6534)
PHONE..........................847 382-3993
Ronald F Gagnier, *President*
Constance Gagnier, *Corp Secy*
EMP: 19
SALES (est): 2.2MM **Privately Held**
SIC: 2672 Labels (unprinted), gummed: made from purchased materials

**(G-16152)**
**HUFF & PUFF INDUSTRIES LTD**
125 Arrowhead Ln (60010-6970)
PHONE..........................847 381-8255
Elaine Silets, *President*
EMP: 3
SALES (est): 336.9K **Privately Held**
SIC: 3944 Railroad models: toy & hobby

**(G-16153)**
**MURRAY INC (PA)**
Also Called: Medical Murray
400 N Rand Rd (60010-1496)
PHONE..........................847 620-7990

Fax: 847 620-7995
Phillip M Leopold, *President*
Paul Maoka, *Vice Pres*
Andrew R Leopold, *Admin Sec*
Annette F Kroll, *Real Est Agnt*
**EMP:** 99
**SQ FT:** 10,000
**SALES (est):** 18.6MM **Privately Held**
**SIC: 3841** Medical instruments & equipment, blood & bone work

**(G-16154)**
**MY KONJAC SPONGE INC**
300 Lake View Pl (60010-1613)
**PHONE**...................630 345-3653
Jimmy Setyo, *President*
**EMP:** 10
**SALES (est):** 778.2K **Privately Held**
**SIC: 2392** Washcloths & bath mitts: made from purchased materials

**(G-16155)**
**TRADE-MARK COFFEE CORPORATION (PA)**
8 Lakeside Ln (60010-6954)
**PHONE**...................847 382-4200
**Fax:** 847 382-4229
Mark M Lessert, *President*
Terry E Lessert, *Vice Pres*
**EMP:** 12
**SALES (est):** 1.5MM **Privately Held**
**SIC: 2095** Roasted coffee

**(G-16156)**
**WILKES & MCLEAN LTD**
17 Lakeside Ln (60010-6956)
**PHONE**...................847 381-3872
Roy G Wilkes, *President*
Clarence McLean, *Vice Pres*
▲ **EMP:** 4
**SALES (est):** 4MM **Privately Held**
**SIC: 3625** Noise control equipment

## North Chicago
### Lake County

**(G-16157)**
**ABBOTT HEALTH PRODUCTS INC (HQ)**
100 Abbott Park Rd (60064-3502)
**PHONE**...................847 937-6100
Miles D White, *CEO*
Thomas C Freyman, *CFO*
Jay Dunigan, *Sales Dir*
Jorge Cubero, *Sales Mgr*
Cedrick Lafleur, *Sales Mgr*
▲ **EMP:** 100 **EST:** 1970
**SQ FT:** 7,500
**SALES (est):** 49.7MM
**SALES (corp-wide):** 20.8B **Publicly Held**
**SIC: 2834** Pharmaceutical preparations
**PA:** Abbott Laboratories
    100 Abbott Park Rd
    Abbott Park IL 60064
    224 667-6100

**(G-16158)**
**ABBOTT LABORATORIES**
100 Abbott Park Rd (60064-3500)
**PHONE**...................224 667-6100
**EMP:** 617
**SALES (corp-wide):** 20.8B **Publicly Held**
**SIC: 2834** Pharmaceutical preparations
**PA:** Abbott Laboratories
    100 Abbott Park Rd
    Abbott Park IL 60064
    224 667-6100

**(G-16159)**
**ABBOTT LABORATORIES**
100 Abbott Park Rd (60064-3500)
**PHONE**...................847 937-7970
Lawtence Blyn PHD, *Branch Mgr*
**EMP:** 588
**SALES (corp-wide):** 20.8B **Publicly Held**
**SIC: 2834** Pharmaceutical preparations
**PA:** Abbott Laboratories
    100 Abbott Park Rd
    Abbott Park IL 60064
    224 667-6100

**(G-16160)**
**ABBOTT LABORATORIES**
Also Called: Receiving D84v K2 Complex Mlk Jr Dr Rr 41 (60064)
**PHONE**...................847 937-6100
**EMP:** 628
**SALES (corp-wide):** 20.8B **Publicly Held**
**SIC: 2834** Pharmaceutical preparations
**PA:** Abbott Laboratories
    100 Abbott Park Rd
    Abbott Park IL 60064
    224 667-6100

**(G-16161)**
**ABBOTT LABORATORIES**
100 Abbott Park Rd (60064-3500)
**PHONE**...................847 937-6100
Michele Bielawski, *Manager*
**EMP:** 180
**SALES (corp-wide):** 20.8B **Publicly Held**
**WEB:** www.abbott.com
**SIC: 2834 8731** Pharmaceutical preparations; commercial physical research
**PA:** Abbott Laboratories
    100 Abbott Park Rd
    Abbott Park IL 60064
    224 667-6100

**(G-16162)**
**ABBOTT LABORATORIES**
100 Abbott Park Rd (60064-3500)
**PHONE**...................847 935-5509
Miles White, *Manager*
**EMP:** 500
**SALES (corp-wide):** 20.8B **Publicly Held**
**WEB:** www.abbott.com
**SIC: 3841** Diagnostic apparatus, medical
**PA:** Abbott Laboratories
    100 Abbott Park Rd
    Abbott Park IL 60064
    224 667-6100

**(G-16163)**
**ABBOTT LABORATORIES**
Also Called: Gpo Reference Standards
1401 Sheridan Rd (60064-4000)
**PHONE**...................847 938-8717
**Fax:** 847 937-3679
Larry Dolnik, *Superintendent*
Robert S Morris, *Business Mgr*
Sandra Klatt, *Plant Mgr*
Dawn Alexander, *Project Mgr*
John Ellis, *Project Mgr*
**EMP:** 617
**SALES (corp-wide):** 20.8B **Publicly Held**
**WEB:** www.abbott.com
**SIC: 2834 3844 2835 3841** Pharmaceutical preparations; X-ray apparatus & tubes; in vitro & in vivo diagnostic substances; surgical & medical instruments; analytical instruments; dry, condensed, evaporated dairy products
**PA:** Abbott Laboratories
    100 Abbott Park Rd
    Abbott Park IL 60064
    224 667-6100

**(G-16164)**
**ABBOTT LABORATORIES**
Also Called: Abbott Labortories Purchasing
100 Abbott Park Rd (60064-3500)
**PHONE**...................847 937-6100
**EMP:** 617
**SALES (corp-wide):** 20.8B **Publicly Held**
**SIC: 2834 2844 2835** Pharmaceutical preparations; druggists' preparations (pharmaceuticals); vitamin, nutrient & hematinic preparations for human use; vitamin preparations; toilet preparations; shampoos, rinses, conditioners: hair; in vitro & in vivo diagnostic substances; blood derivative diagnostic agents; hemotology diagnostic agents; microbiology & virology diagnostic products
**PA:** Abbott Laboratories
    100 Abbott Park Rd
    Abbott Park IL 60064
    224 667-6100

**(G-16165)**
**ABBOTT LABORATORIES PCF LTD (HQ)**
100 Abbott Park Rd (60064-3500)
P.O. Box 3020 (60064-9320)
**PHONE**...................847 937-6100
**Fax:** 847 935-5165

Miles D White, *CEO*
Robert Parkinson Jr, *President*
Vincent Ng, *General Mgr*
Kimberly Small, *Managing Dir*
Brian Dennis, *Editor*
◆ **EMP:** 15
**SALES (est):** 15.6MM
**SALES (corp-wide):** 20.8B **Publicly Held**
**SIC: 2834** Pharmaceutical preparations
**PA:** Abbott Laboratories
    100 Abbott Park Rd
    Abbott Park IL 60064
    224 667-6100

**(G-16166)**
**ABBVIE INC (PA)**
1 N Waukegan Rd (60064-1802)
**PHONE**...................847 932-7900
Richard A Gonzalez, *Ch of Bd*
Fanny Gonzalez, *Superintendent*
Carlos Alban, *Exec VP*
Henry O Gosebruch, *Exec VP*
Laura J Schumacher, *Exec VP*
◆ **EMP:** 277
**SALES:** 25.6B **Publicly Held**
**SIC: 2834 2836** Pharmaceutical preparations; druggists' preparations (pharmaceuticals); biological products, except diagnostic

**(G-16167)**
**ABBVIE INC**
1401 Sheridan Rd (60064-1803)
**PHONE**...................847 932-7900
Miles D White, *Ch of Bd*
James Foster, *Fire Chief*
Julie Porcelius, *Project Mgr*
Thomas Rezak, *Project Mgr*
Mark Hess, *Technical Mgr*
**EMP:** 51
**SALES (corp-wide):** 25.6B **Publicly Held**
**SIC: 2834** Pharmaceutical preparations; druggists' preparations (pharmaceuticals); vitamin, nutrient & hematinic preparations for human use; vitamin preparations
**PA:** Abbvie Inc.
    1 N Waukegan Rd
    North Chicago IL 60064
    847 932-7900

**(G-16168)**
**ABBVIE INC**
1675 Lakeside Ave J23 (60064)
**PHONE**...................847 938-2042
James Erker, *Branch Mgr*
Tim Verbeten, *Manager*
Krista Kleidon, *Director*
Gulden Mesara, *Director*
**EMP:** 7
**SALES (corp-wide):** 25.6B **Publicly Held**
**SIC: 2834** Pharmaceutical preparations
**PA:** Abbvie Inc.
    1 N Waukegan Rd
    North Chicago IL 60064
    847 932-7900

**(G-16169)**
**ABBVIE PRODUCTS LLC**
100 Abbott Park Rd (60064-3502)
**PHONE**...................847 937-6100
Eduardo L Pinzon, *General Mgr*
Mayra C Medina, *Editor*
Erik Axelson, *Counsel*
Daniel Zhang, *Counsel*
Anil Salpekar PHD, *Vice Pres*
**EMP:** 462 **EST:** 2014
**SALES (est):** 60.7MM
**SALES (corp-wide):** 25.6B **Publicly Held**
**SIC: 2834** Proprietary drug products
**PA:** Abbvie Inc.
    1 N Waukegan Rd
    North Chicago IL 60064
    847 932-7900

**(G-16170)**
**ABBVIE RESPIRATORY LLC**
100 Abbott Park Rd (60064-3502)
**PHONE**...................847 937-6100
**EMP:** 4 **EST:** 2014
**SALES (est):** 244.3K
**SALES (corp-wide):** 25.6B **Publicly Held**
**SIC: 2834** Drugs acting on the respiratory system

**PA:** Abbvie Inc.
    1 N Waukegan Rd
    North Chicago IL 60064
    847 932-7900

**(G-16171)**
**ABBVIE US LLC**
1 N Waukegan Rd (60064-1802)
**PHONE**...................800 255-5162
Richard A Gonzalez, *CEO*
Christine Shuler, *District Mgr*
Robert Vinson, *District Mgr*
Laura J Schumacher, *Exec VP*
John Duffey, *Vice Pres*
▲ **EMP:** 178
**SALES (est):** 44MM
**SALES (corp-wide):** 25.6B **Publicly Held**
**SIC: 2836 2834** Biological products, except diagnostic; pharmaceutical preparations
**PA:** Abbvie Inc.
    1 N Waukegan Rd
    North Chicago IL 60064
    847 932-7900

**(G-16172)**
**ACM INC**
2254 Commonwealth Ave (60064-3304)
**PHONE**...................847 473-1991
**Fax:** 847 473-1912
Art Zrimsek, *President*
Rita Zrimsek, *Corp Secy*
Martin Christoffel, *Vice Pres*
**EMP:** 9
**SQ FT:** 7,000
**SALES (est):** 500K **Privately Held**
**SIC: 2851** Paints & allied products

**(G-16173)**
**ADM INTERNATIONAL INC**
1900 Marquette St (60064-2242)
**PHONE**...................773 774-2400
**Fax:** 773 774-2099
Tom Chapman, *President*
Gary Raphael, *Vice Pres*
Francine Waldron, *Treasurer*
**EMP:** 16 **EST:** 1929
**SQ FT:** 20,000
**SALES (est):** 11MM **Privately Held**
**WEB:** www.admintl.com
**SIC: 5021 5023 2391** Furniture; public building furniture; draperies; curtains & draperies

**(G-16174)**
**AEROPHARM TECHNOLOGY LLC**
100 Abbott Park Rd (60064-3502)
**PHONE**...................847 937-6100
Chadwick Munz, *Principal*
**EMP:** 5
**SALES (est):** 330.1K
**SALES (corp-wide):** 25.6B **Publicly Held**
**SIC: 2834** Proprietary drug products
**PA:** Abbvie Inc.
    1 N Waukegan Rd
    North Chicago IL 60064
    847 932-7900

**(G-16175)**
**BLACKJACK CUSTOMS**
2920 Frontenac St (60064-3421)
**PHONE**...................847 361-5225
Quentin Jackson, *Owner*
**EMP:** 5
**SALES (est):** 321.5K **Privately Held**
**SIC: 3711** Automobile assembly, including specialty automobiles

**(G-16176)**
**C & M RECYCLING INC**
1600 Morrow Ave (60064-3224)
**PHONE**...................847 578-1066
**Fax:** 847 578-1071
Michael Braus, *President*
Jennifer Turchany, *Human Res Dir*
Josh Braus, *Manager*
Carole A Braus, *Admin Sec*
**EMP:** 25
**SALES (est):** 10.2MM **Privately Held**
**WEB:** www.cmrecycle.com
**SIC: 5093 4953 3341 2611** Waste paper; ferrous metal scrap & waste; refuse systems; secondary nonferrous metals; pulp mills

## North Chicago - Lake County (G-16177)

**(G-16177)**
**E & E PATTERN WORKS INC**
1209 Morrow Ave  (60064-3297)
PHONE.................................847 689-1088
**Fax:** 847 689-1168
Jim Hora, *President*
James Horra, *President*
**EMP:** 5 **EST:** 1932
**SQ FT:** 8,100
**SALES:** 350K **Privately Held**
**SIC: 3543** Industrial patterns

**(G-16178)**
**EMCO CHEMICAL DISTRIBUTORS INC**
2100 Commonwealth Ave  (60064-2725)
PHONE.................................262 427-0400
**Fax:** 847 689-8470
Michael A Wolfe, *General Mgr*
William Adams, *Area Mgr*
Jake Knolmayer, *Business Mgr*
Joe Lukanich, *Vice Pres*
Ronald Kaplan, *Project Mgr*
**EMP:** 150
**SALES (corp-wide):** 589.1MM **Privately Held**
**SIC: 5169** 7389 2819 Industrial chemicals; packaging & labeling services; industrial inorganic chemicals
**PA:** Emco Chemical Distributors, Inc.
    8601 95th St
    Pleasant Prairie WI 53158
    262 427-0400

**(G-16179)**
**F K PATTERN & FOUNDRY COMPANY**
1400 Morrow Ave  (60064-3220)
PHONE.................................847 578-5260
Frank Konigseder, *Principal*
**EMP:** 4
**SALES (est):** 563.6K **Privately Held**
**SIC: 3441** Fabricated structural metal

**(G-16180)**
**GILLETTE COMPANY**
3500 16th St  (60064-1599)
PHONE.................................847 689-3111
**Fax:** 847 689-0021
John Kwak, *Engineer*
Lalu Thomas, *Engineer*
Vernon Murdock, *Executive*
**EMP:** 65
**SALES (corp-wide):** 65.3B **Publicly Held**
**WEB:** www.gillette.com
**SIC: 2899** Chemical preparations
**HQ:** The Gillette Company
    1 Gillette Park
    Boston MA 02127
    617 421-7000

**(G-16181)**
**GOELITZ CONFECTIONERY COMPANY**
1501 Morrow Ave  (60064-3200)
PHONE.................................847 689-2225
**Fax:** 847 689-0667
Herman G Rowland Sr, *Ch of Bd*
William H Kelley, *President*
Val Abrahamson, *QC Dir*
Tom Wabik, *Controller*
**EMP:** 180 **EST:** 1898
**SQ FT:** 96,000
**SALES (est):** 24.6MM
**SALES (corp-wide):** 219.2MM **Privately Held**
**WEB:** www.jellybelly.com
**SIC: 2064** Candy & other confectionery products; jellybeans
**PA:** Jelly Belly Candy Company
    1 Jelly Belly Ln
    Fairfield CA 94533
    707 428-2800

**(G-16182)**
**HMT MANUFACTURING INC**
2323 Commonwealth Ave  (60064-3390)
PHONE.................................847 473-2310
**Fax:** 847 473-2349
Burton Bucher, *President*
Frank Corley, *General Mgr*
Glen J Bennett, *Plant Mgr*
Tim Bucher, *Office Mgr*
Sharon Dokoly, *Office Mgr*
▲ **EMP:** 25 **EST:** 1972
**SQ FT:** 30,500
**SALES (est):** 6MM **Privately Held**
**WEB:** www.hmtmfg.com
**SIC: 3559** 3089 Plastics working machinery; laminating of plastic

**(G-16183)**
**JELLY BELLY CANDY COMPANY**
1501 Morrow Ave  (60064-3221)
PHONE.................................847 689-2225
Jim McGovern, *Plant Mgr*
Mary Plebanek, *Manager*
Richard Paddock, *Manager*
**EMP:** 200
**SALES (corp-wide):** 219.2MM **Privately Held**
**WEB:** www.jellybelly.com
**SIC: 5441** 2064 Candy, nut & confectionery stores; candy & other confectionery products
**PA:** Jelly Belly Candy Company
    1 Jelly Belly Ln
    Fairfield CA 94533
    707 428-2800

**(G-16184)**
**LIBERTY COACH  INC**
1400 Morrow Ave  (60064-3220)
PHONE.................................847 578-4600
**Fax:** 847 578-1053
Frank Konigseder, *President*
Tom Williams, *Owner*
Kurt Konigseder, *Corp Secy*
Jan Hodgson, *Controller*
Carol Quinn, *Human Resources*
**EMP:** 68 **EST:** 1972
**SQ FT:** 12,000
**SALES (est):** 18.4MM **Privately Held**
**WEB:** www.libertycoach.com
**SIC: 3711** Motor buses, except trackless trollies, assembly of

**(G-16185)**
**NORTH CHICAGO IRON WORKS INC**
1305 Morrow Ave  (60064-3217)
P.O. Box 813  (60064-0813)
PHONE.................................847 689-2000
**Fax:** 847 689-1042
Mary Elaine Gallagher, *President*
John T Gallagher, *Vice Pres*
Mark Gallagher, *Vice Pres*
Jean Marie Humbrecht, *Vice Pres*
**EMP:** 25 **EST:** 1966
**SQ FT:** 12,000
**SALES (est):** 5.4MM **Privately Held**
**WEB:** www.northchicagoiron.com
**SIC: 1791** 3441 3446 Structural steel erection; fabricated structural metal; architectural metalwork

**(G-16186)**
**R MADERITE  INC**
2306 Commonwealth Ave  (60064-3306)
PHONE.................................847 785-0875
**Fax:** 847 785-0876
Rebecca Mellinger, *President*
Robert Engelthaler, *Controller*
**EMP:** 5
**SQ FT:** 12,000
**SALES (est):** 702K **Privately Held**
**SIC: 2511** Wood household furniture

**(G-16187)**
**STEVE O INC**
Also Called: Steve Olson Printing & Design
1550 Green Bay Rd  (60064-1522)
PHONE.................................847 473-4466
Steve Olson, *President*
Deborah Olson, *Corp Secy*
Michael Bez, *Opers Staff*
Jim Dietmeyer, *Manager*
Darius Haring, *Graphic Designe*
**EMP:** 5 **EST:** 1941
**SQ FT:** 4,400
**SALES (est):** 902.3K **Privately Held**
**WEB:** www.steveoprinting.com
**SIC: 2752** Commercial printing, offset

**(G-16188)**
**TI INTERNATIONAL  LTD**
2260 Commonwealth Ave  (60064-3304)
P.O. Box 670  (60064-0670)
PHONE.................................847 689-0233
**Fax:** 847 689-0238
Judith Krotz, *President*
Randy Krotz, *Treasurer*
**EMP:** 8 **EST:** 1914
**SQ FT:** 9,500
**SALES:** 950K **Privately Held**
**WEB:** www.tiinternational.com
**SIC: 3728** Aircraft assemblies, subassemblies & parts

**(G-16189)**
**WEAKLEY PRINTING & SIGN SHOP**
1550 Green Bay Rd  (60064-1522)
PHONE.................................847 473-4466
**Fax:** 847 473-4465
Michael Weakley, *President*
**EMP:** 5 **EST:** 1949
**SQ FT:** 5,400
**SALES (est):** 430K **Privately Held**
**SIC: 2752** 2759 3993 3953 Commercial printing, offset; letterpress printing; signs & advertising specialties; marking devices; typesetting; bookbinding & related work

**(G-16190)**
**WESTROCK CP  LLC**
1900 Foss Park Ave  (60064-2232)
PHONE.................................847 689-4200
**Fax:** 847 689-1590
James Wills, *Div Sub Head*
Anthony Ahlers, *Purch Mgr*
Richard Kelman, *Persnl Mgr*
Gordon Gerber, *Branch Mgr*
**EMP:** 230
**SALES (corp-wide):** 14.1B **Publicly Held**
**WEB:** www.smurfit-stone.com
**SIC: 2653** 3412 Boxes, corrugated: made from purchased materials; metal barrels, drums & pails
**HQ:** Westrock Cp, Llc
    504 Thrasher St
    Norcross GA 30071

**(G-16191)**
**WINNETKA SIGN CO INC (PA)**
3338 Berwyn Ave Unit 93  (60064-3418)
PHONE.................................847 473-9378
Tom Gerhart, *President*
**EMP:** 2
**SALES (est):** 663.9K **Privately Held**
**SIC: 5099** 2759 Containers: glass, metal or plastic; decals: printing

## North Pekin
### Tazewell County

**(G-16192)**
**AMEREX CORPORATION**
Getz Manufacturing
540 S Main St  (61554-1165)
P.O. Box 81, Trussville AL  (35173-0081)
PHONE.................................309 382-4389
Michael Golden, *Purchasing*
Dan Sights, *Sales Staff*
Kevin Rednour, *Branch Mgr*
**EMP:** 20
**SALES (corp-wide):** 1.1B **Privately Held**
**WEB:** www.amerex-fire.com
**SIC: 3999** 3829 3714 3711 Fire extinguishers, portable; measuring & controlling devices; motor vehicle parts & accessories; motor vehicles & car bodies
**HQ:** Amerex Corporation
    7595 Gadsden Hwy
    Trussville AL 35173
    205 655-3271

**(G-16193)**
**PEKIN WELDORS  INC**
1525 Edgewater Dr  (61554-7823)
P.O. Box 442, Pekin  (61555-0442)
PHONE.................................309 382-3627
**Fax:** 309 382-3669
James T Carter, *CEO*
Carol J Carter, *President*
Gerald W Carter, *Vice Pres*
**EMP:** 14
**SQ FT:** 15,000
**SALES (est):** 1.1MM **Privately Held**
**WEB:** www.pekinweldors.com
**SIC: 7692** 7699 Automotive welding; welding equipment repair

## Northbrook
### Cook County

**(G-16194)**
**22ND CENTURY MEDIA**
60 Revere Dr  (60062-1563)
PHONE.................................847 272-4565
Orland P Adam, *Director*
**EMP:** 5
**SALES (corp-wide):** 4.5MM **Privately Held**
**SIC: 2711** Newspapers: publishing only, not printed on site
**PA:** 22nd Century Media
    11516 W 183rd St U Sw 3
    Orland Park IL 60467
    708 326-9170

**(G-16195)**
**A M LEE INC**
Also Called: Charles Selon Associates
2778 Dundee Rd  (60062-2609)
PHONE.................................847 291-1777
**Fax:** 847 291-1786
Albert Lee, *President*
Madiz Lee, *Corp Secy*
**EMP:** 3
**SQ FT:** 1,500
**SALES (est):** 315.9K **Privately Held**
**SIC: 3911** 5944 Jewelry, precious metal; jewelry, precious stones & precious metals

**(G-16196)**
**ACME ALLIANCE  LLC (HQ)**
Also Called: Acmealliance
3610 Commercial Ave  (60062-1823)
PHONE.................................847 272-9520
**Fax:** 847 272-7542
Jason Belec, *General Mgr*
Denic Decman, *Asst Controller*
Matthew Lovejoy,
▲ **EMP:** 110
**SQ FT:** 75,000
**SALES (est):** 28.8MM
**SALES (corp-wide):** 45.9MM **Privately Held**
**WEB:** www.acmealliance.com
**SIC: 3363** Aluminum die-castings
**PA:** Lovejoy Industries, Inc
    3610 Commercial Ave
    Northbrook IL 60062
    859 873-6828

**(G-16197)**
**ACME DIE CASTING LLC**
3610 Commercial Ave  (60062-1823)
PHONE.................................847 272-9520
**Fax:** 847 272-7542
Chris Vazzana, *Vice Pres*
Roy Dusell, *Controller*
Denise Decman, *Manager*
Cari Hemmerling, *Manager*
Jesus Martinez, *Manager*
▲ **EMP:** 4
**SALES (est):** 1MM
**SALES (corp-wide):** 45.9MM **Privately Held**
**WEB:** www.acmediecasting.com
**SIC: 3363** 3364 3369 3365 Aluminum die-castings; zinc & zinc-base alloy die-castings; nonferrous foundries; aluminum foundries
**PA:** Lovejoy Industries, Inc
    3610 Commercial Ave
    Northbrook IL 60062
    859 873-6828

**(G-16198)**
**ADDAX SOUND COMPANY**
Also Called: Bi Audio Headsets
3647 Woodhead Dr  (60062-1816)
PHONE.................................847 412-0000
Chris Gantz, *President*
**EMP:** 15
**SALES (est):** 1MM **Privately Held**
**SIC: 3661** Headsets, telephone

**(G-16199)**
**ADVANCED EMR SOLUTIONS INC**
5 Revere Dr Ste 430  (60062-1583)
PHONE.................................877 327-6160

Barry Ring, *CEO*
Carol Ring, *Human Resources*
**EMP:** 6
**SQ FT:** 1,500
**SALES (est):** 272.2K **Privately Held**
**SIC:** 7372 Application computer software

**(G-16200)**
**ADVERTISING ADVICE INC (PA)**
Also Called: Reklama
3000 Dundee Rd Ste 108 (60062-2424)
**PHONE** .................................. 847 272-0707
Vlad Verevkin, *President*
Vlad Veren, *Administration*
**EMP:** 10
**SQ FT:** 1,500
**SALES (est):** 1.3MM **Privately Held**
**SIC:** 2711 Newspapers

**(G-16201)**
**AGROCHEM INC**
Also Called: Nature's Touch
3703 Pebble Beach Rd (60062-3111)
**PHONE** .................................. 847 564-1304
Donald Arenberg, *President*
Betty Beller, *Corp Secy*
Donna Arenberg, *Vice Pres*
**EMP:** 11
**SQ FT:** 10,000
**SALES (est):** 990K **Privately Held**
**SIC:** 2879 8734 Plant hormones; soil conditioners; testing laboratories

**(G-16202)**
**ALL GEAR INC**
3675 Commercial Ave (60062-1822)
**PHONE** .................................. 847 564-9016
**Fax:** 847 564-9017
Thomas Daly, *President*
**EMP:** 4
**SQ FT:** 4,000
**SALES (est):** 558.1K **Privately Held**
**WEB:** www.allgearinc.com
**SIC:** 2298 Rope, except asbestos & wire

**(G-16203)**
**AMERICAN SPCALTY ADVG PRTG CO**
Also Called: Dolores Shingleur Advertising
899 Skokie Blvd Ste 112 (60062-4021)
**PHONE** .................................. 847 272-5255
Mark Isenstein, *President*
Barry Siegel, *Sales Mgr*
Herman Levin, *Sales Executive*
Sharline Newmann, *Office Mgr*
**EMP:** 3
**SQ FT:** 600
**SALES (est):** 436K **Privately Held**
**WEB:** www.americanspec.net
**SIC:** 2759 Promotional printing

**(G-16204)**
**AMPLIVOX SOUND SYSTEMS LLC (PA)**
Also Called: Amplivox Prtable Sound Systems
650 Anthony Trl Ste D (60062-2512)
**PHONE** .................................. 800 267-5486
**Fax:** 847 498-6691
Don Roth, *President*
Ron Stelzer, *Controller*
Bill Gamber, *Sales Dir*
Merle Davis, *Cust Mgr*
Denny Porter, *Director*
▲ **EMP:** 23 **EST:** 1995
**SQ FT:** 18,000
**SALES:** 5.3MM **Privately Held**
**WEB:** www.ampli.com
**SIC:** 3663 5065 3651 Amplifiers, RF power & IF; sound equipment, electronic; household audio & video equipment

**(G-16205)**
**ASTELLAS PHARMA INC**
1 Astellas Way (60062-6111)
**PHONE** .................................. 800 695-4321
Kevin O'Toole, *President*
Marcia Marconi, *Vice Pres*
Kevin Otoole, *Vice Pres*
Karen Meurer, *Research*
Scott Aladeen, *Branch Mgr*
**EMP:** 28
**SALES (corp-wide):** 11.7B **Privately Held**
**SIC:** 2834 Pharmaceutical preparations
**PA:** Astellas Pharma Inc.
2-5-1, Nihombashihoncho
Chuo-Ku TKY 103-0
332 443-000

**(G-16206)**
**ASTELLAS US HOLDING INC (HQ)**
1 Astellas Way (60062-6111)
**PHONE** .................................. 224 205-8800
Yoshihiko Hatanaka, *CEO*
**EMP:** 46
**SALES (est):** 978MM
**SALES (corp-wide):** 11.7B **Privately Held**
**SIC:** 2834 Pharmaceutical preparations
**PA:** Astellas Pharma Inc.
2-5-1, Nihombashihoncho
Chuo-Ku TKY 103-0
332 443-000

**(G-16207)**
**ATLANTIC BEVERAGE COMPANY INC (PA)**
1033 Skokie Blvd Ste 600 (60062-4101)
**PHONE** .................................. 847 412-6200
**Fax:** 847 412-9766
Merrick M Elfman, *Ch of Bd*
Thomas M Dalton, *President*
Dean Egerter, *Managing Dir*
Richard Federico, *Managing Dir*
Steve Englander, *Exec VP*
**EMP:** 6
**SALES (est):** 81.5MM **Privately Held**
**WEB:** www.blueribbonsausage.com
**SIC:** 5147 5149 2013 Meats & meat products; meats, cured or smoked; beverages, except coffee & tea; juices; mineral or spring water bottling; soft drinks; sausages & other prepared meats; sausages & related products, from purchased meat; smoked meats from purchased meat

**(G-16208)**
**ATLAS FIBRE COMPANY (PA)**
3411 Woodhead Dr (60062-1812)
**PHONE** .................................. 847 674-1234
**Fax:** 847 674-1723
Richard Welch, *President*
John Petti, *Division Mgr*
Howard Natal, *Vice Pres*
Robert Degoerge, *Controller*
Mark Russel, *VP Sales*
▲ **EMP:** 53 **EST:** 1959
**SQ FT:** 42,000
**SALES:** 9MM **Privately Held**
**WEB:** www.atlasfibre.com
**SIC:** 3083 5162 3082 2821 Thermoplastic laminates: rods, tubes, plates & sheet; plastics materials & basic shapes; unsupported plastics profile shapes; plastics materials & resins

**(G-16209)**
**AUSTIN TOOL & DIE CO (PA)**
3555 Woodhead Dr (60062-1814)
**PHONE** .................................. 847 509-5800
James R Archer, *President*
**EMP:** 55
**SQ FT:** 70,000
**SALES:** 9.2MM **Privately Held**
**SIC:** 3599 3469 3544 Machine shop, jobbing & repair; metal stampings; special dies & tools

**(G-16210)**
**BAR LIST PUBLISHING CO**
2900 Macarthur Blvd (60062-2005)
P.O. Box 948 (60065-0948)
**PHONE** .................................. 847 498-0100
**Fax:** 847 498-6695
Bruce E Rodgers, *President*
Leslie Rodgers, *Office Mgr*
Susan M Rodgers, *Admin Sec*
**EMP:** 9
**SALES (est):** 730K **Privately Held**
**WEB:** www.barlist.com
**SIC:** 2731 2741 Books: publishing only; miscellaneous publishing

**(G-16211)**
**BARILLA AMERICA INC (DH)**
885 Sunset Ridge Rd (60062-4006)
**PHONE** .................................. 515 956-4400
Jean Pierre Comte, *President*
Giannella Alvarez, *President*
Sandy Everett, *COO*
Bill Nunn, *Vice Pres*
Sergio Periera, *Vice Pres*
▲ **EMP:** 75
**SQ FT:** 45,000
**SALES (est):** 94.2MM **Privately Held**
**SIC:** 2045 Prepared flour mixes & doughs

**(G-16212)**
**BARON-BLAKESLEE SFC INC**
2900 Macarthur Blvd (60062-2005)
**PHONE** .................................. 847 796-0822
Jacob H Berg, *President*
**EMP:** 25
**SALES (est):** 5.4MM **Privately Held**
**SIC:** 3441 Fabricated structural metal

**(G-16213)**
**BELL FLAVORS & FRAGRANCES INC (PA)**
Also Called: Bell Aromatics
500 Academy Dr (60062-2497)
**PHONE** .................................. 847 291-8300
**Fax:** 847 291-1217
James H Heinz, *President*
Raymond J Heinz, *Exec VP*
Aaron Graham, *Vice Pres*
Michael Heinz, *Vice Pres*
Simon Poppelsdorf, *Vice Pres*
◆ **EMP:** 130
**SQ FT:** 100,000
**SALES (est):** 62.2MM **Privately Held**
**WEB:** www.bellff.com
**SIC:** 2869 Perfumes, flavorings & food additives

**(G-16214)**
**BERNHARD WOODWORK LTD**
3670 Woodhead Dr (60062-1817)
**PHONE** .................................. 847 291-1040
**Fax:** 847 291-1184
Herta Bernhard, *CEO*
Mark Bernhard, *President*
Brian Lowry, *Project Mgr*
Michael Kieny, *Sales Staff*
Barbara Cassidy, *Office Mgr*
▲ **EMP:** 50
**SQ FT:** 100,000
**SALES (est):** 9.6MM **Privately Held**
**WEB:** www.bernhardwoodwork.com
**SIC:** 2541 2431 5712 Store fixtures, wood; woodwork, interior & ornamental; planing mill, millwork; customized furniture & cabinets

**(G-16215)**
**BRUCE KLAPMAN INC**
1955 Raymond Dr Ste 105 (60062-6731)
**PHONE** .................................. 847 657-8880
Bruce Klapman, *President*
**EMP:** 4
**SALES (est):** 599.2K **Privately Held**
**SIC:** 2611 Pulp manufactured from waste or recycled paper

**(G-16216)**
**CAMPUS CARDBOARD**
600 Waukegan Rd (60062-1258)
**PHONE** .................................. 847 373-7673
Matthew Pope, *Principal*
**EMP:** 3
**SALES (est):** 312.3K **Privately Held**
**SIC:** 2631 Cardboard

**(G-16217)**
**CAROLS COOKIES INC**
3184 Macarthur Blvd (60062-1904)
**PHONE** .................................. 847 831-4500
**Fax:** 847 831-4504
Carol Goldman, *President*
Jeff Goldman, *Vice Pres*
**EMP:** 5
**SQ FT:** 2,000
**SALES (est):** 665.5K **Privately Held**
**WEB:** www.carolscookies.com
**SIC:** 2052 5149 Cookies; cookies

**(G-16218)**
**CASTINO & ASSOCIATES INC** ✪
Also Called: Fastsigns
3065 Dundee Rd (60062-2401)
**PHONE** .................................. 847 291-7446
**Fax:** 847 291-7450
Deborah Castino, *President*
Josh Sacchetti, *General Mgr*
Thomas Castino, *Vice Pres*
**EMP:** 9 **EST:** 2016
**SALES (est):** 323.4K **Privately Held**
**SIC:** 3993 Signs & advertising specialties

**(G-16219)**
**CHASE GROUP LLC**
305 Era Dr (60062-1801)
**PHONE** .................................. 847 564-2000
**Fax:** 847 564-1313
Robert Chase Jr, *Mng Member*
Caroline Smith, *Administration*
▲ **EMP:** 14
**SALES (est):** 1.6MM **Privately Held**
**WEB:** www.ventisgroup.com
**SIC:** 2741 5199 8999 Art copy: publishing & printing; art goods; artists & artists' studios

**(G-16220)**
**CHESLEY LIMITED**
3170 Macarthur Blvd (60062-1904)
**PHONE** .................................. 847 562-9292
Robert Chase, *Mng Member*
**EMP:** 8
**SQ FT:** 5,000
**SALES (est):** 700K **Privately Held**
**WEB:** www.chesley.net
**SIC:** 2741 Art copy: publishing only, not printed on site

**(G-16221)**
**CHICAGO CUTTING DIE CO**
3555 Woodhead Dr (60062-1814)
**PHONE** .................................. 847 509-5800
**Fax:** 847 509-0355
Newton L Archer Jr, *President*
Kyle Archer, *Vice Pres*
James Stuper, *VP Mfg*
Ryan Archer, *Purch Agent*
Jeff Hopper, *Purchasing*
▲ **EMP:** 71 **EST:** 1923
**SQ FT:** 60,000
**SALES (est):** 9.2MM **Privately Held**
**SIC:** 3544 3469 Dies & die holders for metal cutting, forming, die casting; stamping metal for the trade
**PA:** Austin Tool & Die Co
3555 Woodhead Dr
Northbrook IL 60062
847 509-5800

**(G-16222)**
**CHRIS INDUSTRIES INC (PA)**
2810 Old Willow Rd (60062-6809)
P.O. Box 8206, Northfield (60093-8206)
**PHONE** .................................. 847 729-9292
**Fax:** 847 729-0340
Creighton R Helms, *President*
Judy Muncer, *President*
Christy Helms, *Corp Secy*
▲ **EMP:** 20
**SQ FT:** 38,000
**SALES (est):** 9MM **Privately Held**
**WEB:** www.chrisind.com
**SIC:** 5051 3444 Copper products; sheets, metal; sheet metalwork

**(G-16223)**
**CHRIS PLATING INC**
2810 Old Willow Rd (60062-6809)
**PHONE** .................................. 847 729-9271
Christy Helms, *Principal*
Ray Deckert, *Manager*
Brian K Riley, *Manager*
**EMP:** 28
**SALES (est):** 2.6MM **Privately Held**
**WEB:** www.chrisplating.com
**SIC:** 3471 Electroplating & plating

**(G-16224)**
**CIM BAR CODE TECHNOLOGY INC**
350 Pfingsten Rd Ste 102 (60062-2032)
P.O. Box 537, Lincolnshire (60069-0537)
**PHONE** .................................. 847 559-9776
**Fax:** 847 559-9098
William Dempsey, *President*
**EMP:** 6
**SQ FT:** 2,500
**SALES (est):** 610K **Privately Held**
**WEB:** www.cimbarcode.com
**SIC:** 3577 Bar code (magnetic ink) printers

## Northbrook - Cook County (G-16225)

**(G-16225)**
**CLARUS THERAPEUTICS INC**
555 Skokie Blvd Ste 340 (60062-2854)
PHONE................................847 562-4300
Robert E Dudley, *President*
John P Gargiulo, *COO*
Stanley Penzotti, *Vice Pres*
Wael A Salameh, *Vice Pres*
Patrick Shea, *Ch Credit Ofcr*
**EMP:** 8
**SALES (est):** 1.1MM **Privately Held**
**WEB:** www.clarustherapeutics.com
**SIC:** 8733 2834 Medical research; pharmaceutical preparations

**(G-16226)**
**CLASSIC PACKAGING CORPORATION**
3390 Commercial Ave (60062-1909)
PHONE................................224 723-5157
Fax: 224 273-5192
Stuart Rosen, *CEO*
Ira Rosen, *President*
**EMP:** 2
**SQ FT:** 750
**SALES (est):** 468.9K **Privately Held**
**SIC:** 2675 Egg cartons, die-cut: made from purchased materials

**(G-16227)**
**CLOWN GLOBAL BRANDS LLC**
3184 Doolittle Dr (60062-2409)
PHONE................................847 564-5950
Fax: 847 564-9076
Mary Ellen Cahill, *CEO*
Martin Haver, *COO*
Ni-Del Shubin, *Director*
**EMP:** 6
**SQ FT:** 2,000
**SALES (est):** 350K **Privately Held**
**SIC:** 2099 5411 3999 Food preparations; grocery stores; barber & beauty shop equipment

**(G-16228)**
**CO-ORDINATED PACKAGING INC**
Also Called: Coordinated Packaging
726 Anthony Trl (60062-2542)
PHONE................................847 559-8877
Fax: 847 559-8895
Beverly Wolf, *President*
Greg Wolf, *Vice Pres*
Dianne Dabe, *Purchasing*
Mark Lantz, *Treasurer*
▲ **EMP:** 10
**SQ FT:** 12,000
**SALES (est):** 2.4MM **Privately Held**
**WEB:** www.co-ordinatedpackaging.com
**SIC:** 5113 3086 3081 Boxes, paperboard & disposable plastic; packaging & shipping materials, foamed plastic; unsupported plastics film & sheet

**(G-16229)**
**COBIUS HALTHCARE SOLUTIONS LLC**
853 Sanders Rd Ste 313 (60062-2901)
PHONE................................847 656-8700
Doug Weinberg, *Mng Member*
**EMP:** 9
**SALES (est):** 996K **Privately Held**
**WEB:** www.cobius.com
**SIC:** 3577 Computer peripheral equipment

**(G-16230)**
**CONCEP MACHINE CO INC**
1800 Holste Rd (60062-7703)
PHONE................................847 498-9740
Fax: 847 498-9780
Jefferey Fischer, *President*
Dave Schwind, *Project Mgr*
Reginald Lualhati, *Engineer*
Bob Wolf, *Engineer*
Steve French, *Electrical Engi*
**EMP:** 22
**SQ FT:** 13,000
**SALES (est):** 5.9MM **Privately Held**
**WEB:** www.concepmachine.com
**SIC:** 3569 Lubrication machinery, automatic

**(G-16231)**
**CONSERVATION TECH ILL LLC**
Also Called: Contech Lighting
725 Landwehr Rd (60062-2349)
PHONE................................847 559-5500
John Ranshaw, *President*
Tim Brennan, *Vice Pres*
**EMP:** 6
**SALES (est):** 129.4K
**SALES (corp-wide):** 1.5B **Privately Held**
**SIC:** 3646 Commercial indusl & institutional electric lighting fixtures
**PA:** Leviton Manufacturing Co., Inc.
201 N Service Rd
Melville NY 11747
631 812-6000

**(G-16232)**
**CONSERVATION TECHNOLOGY LTD**
Also Called: Con-Tech
725 Landwehr Rd (60062-2349)
PHONE................................847 559-5505
Fax: 847 559-5505
John D Ranshaw, *President*
Mark Groenke, *Vice Pres*
Glenn Konieczny, *Vice Pres*
Brandon Wilson, *Design Engr*
Tim Brennan, *VP Sales*
◆ **EMP:** 92
**SALES (est):** 29.6MM **Privately Held**
**WEB:** www.con-techlighting.com
**SIC:** 3646 3564 Commercial indusl & institutional electric lighting fixtures; ventilating fans: industrial or commercial

**(G-16233)**
**COUR PHARMACEUTICALS DEV**
2215 Sanders Rd Ste 428 (60062-6126)
PHONE................................773 621-3241
John Tu, *President*
Samuel Magnuson, *Principal*
**EMP:** 4 **EST:** 2012
**SALES (est):** 320.8K **Privately Held**
**SIC:** 2834 Pharmaceutical preparations

**(G-16234)**
**CREATIVE GRAPHIC ARTS INC**
3690 Oak Ave (60062-4917)
PHONE................................847 498-2678
Kathy Barnes, *President*
**EMP:** 4
**SALES (est):** 260K **Privately Held**
**SIC:** 2752 Commercial printing, offset

**(G-16235)**
**CRYSTAL PRODUCTIONS CO**
3701 Coml Ave Ste 10 (60062)
PHONE................................847 657-8144
Fax: 847 657-8149
Thomas N Hubbard, *CEO*
Amy Woodworth, *President*
Loretta Hubbard, *Vice Pres*
▲ **EMP:** 15
**SALES (est):** 1.8MM **Privately Held**
**WEB:** www.crystalproductions.com
**SIC:** 2731 7812 Book publishing; video tape production

**(G-16236)**
**D D G INC (PA)**
1955 Shermer Rd Ste 300 (60062-5363)
PHONE................................847 412-0277
Fax: 847 714-0403
E A Goodman, *Ch of Bd*
Dd Goodman, *President*
▲ **EMP:** 4
**SQ FT:** 6,000
**SALES (est):** 226.7MM **Privately Held**
**SIC:** 3317 2511 6512 Steel pipe & tubes; wood bedroom furniture; nonresidential building operators

**(G-16237)**
**D KERSEY CONSTRUCTION CO**
4130 Timberlane Dr (60062-6123)
PHONE................................847 919-4980
Doug Kersey, *President*
Virginia Ann Kersey, *Admin Sec*
**EMP:** 3
**SALES (est):** 344.3K **Privately Held**
**SIC:** 1389 1542 Construction, repair & dismantling services; nonresidential construction; institutional building construction

**(G-16238)**
**DAITO PHARMACEUTICALS AMER INC**
633 Skokie Blvd Ste 210 (60062-2824)
PHONE................................847 205-0800
Kenji Fujita, *President*
Masamichi Oishi, *Admin Sec*
◆ **EMP:** 2
**SQ FT:** 1,500
**SALES (est):** 329.9K
**SALES (corp-wide):** 335MM **Privately Held**
**SIC:** 5122 2834 2833 Drugs & drug proprietaries; pharmaceutical preparations; medicinals & botanicals
**PA:** Daito Pharmaceutical Co.,Ltd.
326, Yokamachi
Toyama TYM 939-8
764 215-665

**(G-16239)**
**DAMICO ASSOCIATES INC**
Also Called: Fastsigns
3065 Dundee Rd (60062-2401)
PHONE................................847 291-7446
Richard D'Amico, *President*
Saja D'Amico, *Vice Pres*
Josh Sacchetti, *Info Tech Mgr*
**EMP:** 8
**SALES (est):** 1MM **Privately Held**
**SIC:** 3993 2542 Signs & advertising specialties; partitions & fixtures, except wood

**(G-16240)**
**DEC ART DESIGNS INC**
2970 Maria Ave Ste 226 (60062-2024)
PHONE................................312 329-0553
Fax: 312 329-9106
Gerald R Levy, *President*
Margaret Deshon, *Corp Secy*
Gloria Levy, *Vice Pres*
▲ **EMP:** 4
**SQ FT:** 2,000
**SALES (est):** 518.7K **Privately Held**
**WEB:** www.decartdesigns.com
**SIC:** 2211 Bedspreads, cotton

**(G-16241)**
**DFG CONFECTIONARY LLC (PA)**
60 Revere Dr Ste 750 (60062-1593)
PHONE................................847 412-1961
Phillip Gay, *COO*
Lawrence Gould,
**EMP:** 300
**SALES (est):** 39.3MM **Privately Held**
**SIC:** 2038 2099 5141 Frozen specialties; ready-to-eat meals, salads & sandwiches; groceries, general line

**(G-16242)**
**DIAMOND CELLOPHANE PDTS INC**
Also Called: Diamond Bag & Print Co
2855 Shermer Rd (60062-7710)
PHONE................................847 418-3000
Fax: 847 418-3010
Howard Diamond, *President*
Robin Diamond, *Principal*
Chad Stonecipher, *Plant Mgr*
Marion Diamond, *Admin Sec*
▲ **EMP:** 50
**SQ FT:** 85,000
**SALES (est):** 16.8MM **Privately Held**
**WEB:** www.diamondbag-print.com
**SIC:** 2673 3083 Plastic bags: made from purchased materials; laminated plastic sheets

**(G-16243)**
**DIGITAL CHECK CORP (PA)**
Also Called: Digital Check Technologies
630 Dundee Rd Ste 210 (60062-2792)
PHONE................................847 446-2285
Thomas Anderson, *President*
John Gainer, *Vice Pres*
Alex Trombetta, *Vice Pres*
Thomas Mason, *CFO*
▲ **EMP:** 20
**SQ FT:** 6,000
**SALES (est):** 17.9MM **Privately Held**
**SIC:** 3577 Optical scanning devices

**(G-16244)**
**DIVERSIFIED METAL PRODUCTS INC**
Also Called: Dispense-Rite
2205 Carlson Dr (60062-6705)
PHONE................................847 753-9595
Fax: 847 753-9648
Anton Gapp, *President*
Kevin Gapp, *Vice Pres*
Robert Gapp, *Vice Pres*
Donald Hitchcock, *Plant Mgr*
Paul Gapp, *CFO*
▲ **EMP:** 25
**SALES (est):** 4.4MM **Privately Held**
**WEB:** www.dispense-rite.com
**SIC:** 2542 Cabinets: show, display or storage: except wood; office & store showcases & display fixtures

**(G-16245)**
**EASYSHOW LLC**
450 Skokie Blvd Ste 1200 (60062-7920)
PHONE................................847 480-7177
Chris Huizenga, *Marketing Staff*
Michael Gazdzik, *Info Tech Mgr*
Terese Penza,
Adam White, *Education*
Greg Sossin,
**EMP:** 8 **EST:** 2008
**SALES (est):** 399K **Privately Held**
**SIC:** 2542 Mail racks & lock boxes, postal service: except wood

**(G-16246)**
**ECF HOLDINGS LLC**
Also Called: Encore Fastners
3550 Woodhead Dr (60062-1815)
PHONE................................224 723-5524
Don Ayres, *Mng Member*
▲ **EMP:** 3 **EST:** 2006
**SQ FT:** 6,200
**SALES (est):** 577.7K **Privately Held**
**SIC:** 3965 3399 Fasteners; metal fasteners

**(G-16247)**
**ECO-TECH PLASTICS LLC**
1519 Woodlark Dr (60062-4731)
PHONE................................262 539-3811
Joseph Sadlier, *President*
Harry Frank, *Vice Pres*
Julie A Sadlier, *Admin Sec*
**EMP:** 40 **EST:** 1993
**SALES (est):** 9.7MM **Privately Held**
**SIC:** 3089 Plastic processing

**(G-16248)**
**EGG CREAM AMERICA INC (PA)**
Also Called: Jeff's Soda
633 Skokie Blvd Ste 200 (60062-2824)
PHONE................................847 559-2700
Fax: 847 559-2709
John Beslow, *CEO*
Adam Kurlander, *President*
**EMP:** 2
**SQ FT:** 1,200
**SALES (est):** 502.2K **Privately Held**
**SIC:** 2086 Soft drinks: packaged in cans, bottles, etc.

**(G-16249)**
**ELONGATED PLASTICS INC**
677 Alice Dr (60062-2517)
PHONE................................224 456-0559
Kwang W Moon, *Principal*
▲ **EMP:** 4 **EST:** 2010
**SALES (est):** 531.3K **Privately Held**
**SIC:** 3086 Packaging & shipping materials, foamed plastic

**(G-16250)**
**ER&R INC**
Also Called: Equipment Rent and Royalty
800 Midway Rd Apt 2n (60062-3959)
PHONE................................847 791-5671
Florence Berg, *President*
Stanley Berg, *Production*
**EMP:** 6
**SALES (est):** 918.6K **Privately Held**
**SIC:** 3559 Recycling machinery

## Northbrook - Cook County (G-16279)

**(G-16251)**
**ERA DEVELOPMENT GROUP INC**
Also Called: Exclusive Wood Group
2224 Greenview Rd (60062-6631)
PHONE.................708 252-6979
Ruslanas Andrejevas, *President*
EMP: 50
SALES (est): 2.1MM **Privately Held**
SIC: 1542 2431 5031 Nonresidential construction; commercial & office building, new construction; custom builders, non-residential; storm windows, wood; doors & windows

**(G-16252)**
**EUROMARKET DESIGNS INC (DH)**
Also Called: Crate & Barrel
1250 Techny Rd (60062-5419)
PHONE.................847 272-2888
Steve Woodward, *President*
Dave Widmer, *Business Mgr*
Kasey Hooper, *Vice Pres*
Suzanne Muellman, *Vice Pres*
Susan Soldin, *Vice Pres*
◆ EMP: 600 EST: 1962
SQ FT: 190,000
SALES (est): 1.9B **Privately Held**
WEB: www.crateandbarrel.com
SIC: 5719 5947 5712 5961 Kitchenware; beddings & linens; gift shop; furniture stores; mail order house; boards: planning, display, notice
HQ: Otto (Gmbh & Co Kg)
Werner-Otto-Str. 1-7
Hamburg 22179
406 461-0

**(G-16253)**
**EXPRESS PRTG & PROMOTIONS INC**
1537 Windy Hill Dr (60062-3833)
PHONE.................847 498-9640
Fax: 847 498-2976
Mark Sterne, *President*
EMP: 7
SALES (est): 890K **Privately Held**
WEB: www.express-print.com
SIC: 5112 2752 5199 Business forms; computer paper; marking devices; envelopes; commercial printing, lithographic; advertising specialties

**(G-16254)**
**EYEWEARPLANET COM INC**
3150 Commercial Ave (60062-1906)
PHONE.................847 513-6203
EMP: 3 EST: 2010
SALES (est): 170K **Privately Held**
SIC: 3851 Eyes, glass & plastic

**(G-16255)**
**F C D INC**
Also Called: The Label and Packaging Co
1925 Holste Rd (60062-7704)
PHONE.................847 498-3711
Fax: 847 498-3862
Kerry Craig, *President*
John Daniels, *Vice Pres*
Mike Pollizze, *Purch Agent*
Patricia Murlas, *VP Finance*
Linda Mayo, *MIS Staff*
EMP: 32
SQ FT: 18,000
SALES (est): 3.6MM **Privately Held**
SIC: 2759 3565 Flexographic printing; labeling machines, industrial

**(G-16256)**
**FAVORITE FOODS**
4226 Yorkshire Ln (60062-2923)
PHONE.................847 401-7126
EMP: 6
SALES (est): 475K **Privately Held**
SIC: 2099 Food preparations

**(G-16257)**
**FIELD HOLDINGS LLC (PA)**
400 Skokie Blvd Ste 860 (60062-7936)
PHONE.................847 509-2250
Lawrence I Field, *President*
Devin Carter, *Manager*
EMP: 1
SQ FT: 5,000
SALES (est): 16.1MM **Privately Held**
SIC: 2754 Labels: gravure printing

**(G-16258)**
**FIELD VENTURES LLC**
400 Skokie Blvd Ste 860 (60062-7936)
PHONE.................847 509-2250
Joseph Kaplin, *President*
EMP: 51
SALES (est): 3.5MM
SALES (corp-wide): 16.1MM **Privately Held**
SIC: 3083 Plastic finished products, laminated
PA: Field Holdings, Llc
400 Skokie Blvd Ste 860
Northbrook IL 60062
847 509-2250

**(G-16259)**
**FILE SYSTEM LABS LLC**
3387 Commercial Ave (60062)
PHONE.................617 431-4313
Robert Swartz,
Elan Pavlov,
EMP: 15
SALES (est): 1.2MM **Privately Held**
SIC: 3572 Computer storage devices

**(G-16260)**
**FLINN & DREFFEIN ENGRG CO**
4025 Micheline Ln (60062-2144)
PHONE.................847 272-6374
J K Balaz, *President*
Rich Koomjian, *Vice Pres*
Tom Kelly, *Purch Mgr*
EMP: 30 EST: 1907
SQ FT: 30,000
SALES (est): 5.3MM **Privately Held**
WEB: www.flinndreffein.com
SIC: 3585 Heating equipment, complete

**(G-16261)**
**FREDA CUSTOM FOODS INC**
2900 Shermer Rd (60062-7717)
PHONE.................847 412-5900
Fax: 847 412-5901
EMP: 250
SALES (est): 40.3MM **Privately Held**
SIC: 2013 Sausages & other prepared meats

**(G-16262)**
**GAIL MCGRATH & ASSOCIATES INC**
Also Called: Chicago Wedding Resouce
3453 Commercial Ave (60062-1818)
PHONE.................847 770-4620
Gail McGrath, *President*
Sheldon Levin, *Vice Pres*
Rand Brichta, *Accounts Mgr*
Mike Hedge, *Marketing Mgr*
David Strouse, *Marketing Staff*
EMP: 11
SALES (est): 2.3MM **Privately Held**
SIC: 2721 Magazines: publishing & printing

**(G-16263)**
**GAMEPLAN INC**
5 Revere Dr Ste 103 (60062-1567)
PHONE.................877 284-9180
Steve Mandel, *President*
Steven T Mandell, *President*
EMP: 3
SQ FT: 2,000
SALES (est): 19.7K **Privately Held**
SIC: 3944 5092 Board games, puzzles & models, except electronic; toys & games

**(G-16264)**
**GEMWORLD INTERNATIONAL INC**
2640 Patriot Blvd Ste 240 (60062)
PHONE.................847 657-0555
Fax: 847 657-0550
Richard Drucker, *President*
David Bucks, *Vice Pres*
Stuart Robertson, *Research*
Susan Drucker, *Treasurer*
Cigdem Lule, *Manager*
EMP: 6
SALES (est): 847.2K **Privately Held**
SIC: 2721 Periodicals

**(G-16265)**
**GLASS ARTISTRY**
1908 Janke Dr (60062-6707)
PHONE.................847 998-5800
Fax: 847 998-8077
Robert Helge, *Partner*
Ardith Harris, *Partner*
EMP: 4 EST: 2000
SALES (est): 260K **Privately Held**
SIC: 2519 5947 7231 Fiberglass furniture, household: padded or plain; gift, novelty & souvenir shop; beauty shops

**(G-16266)**
**GRAPHTEK LLC (PA)**
Also Called: Pennsylvania Carbon Products
600 Academy Dr Ste 100 (60062-2408)
PHONE.................847 279-1925
Vladimir Novokhovsky,
Karina Novokhovsky,
◆ EMP: 12
SQ FT: 30,000
SALES (est): 2.2MM **Privately Held**
WEB: www.graphtekllc.com
SIC: 3624 Carbon & graphite products

**(G-16267)**
**GY PACKAGING LLC**
3215 Commercial Ave (60062-1920)
PHONE.................847 272-8803
Stephen Linen,
EMP: 15
SQ FT: 20,000
SALES (est): 2.4MM **Privately Held**
SIC: 3089 3554 Plastic containers, except foam; tubs, plastic (containers); cases, plastic; trays, plastic; paper mill machinery: plating, slitting, waxing, etc.

**(G-16268)**
**HARRIS POTTERIES LP (PA)**
Also Called: American Bakeware
707 Skokie Blvd Ste 220 (60062-2837)
PHONE.................847 564-5544
Robert S Harris, *President*
Lynn Wolfe, *Controller*
▲ EMP: 3 EST: 1975
SQ FT: 1,000
SALES (est): 17.5MM **Privately Held**
SIC: 3229 Cooking utensils, glass or glass ceramic

**(G-16269)**
**HAUSSERMANN USA LLC**
425 Huehl Rd Bldg 10 (60062-2322)
PHONE.................847 272-9850
Dale Haase,
EMP: 6
SALES (est): 490K **Privately Held**
SIC: 3559 Automotive related machinery

**(G-16270)**
**HIGHLAND BAKING COMPANY INC**
2301 Shermer Rd (60062-6721)
PHONE.................847 677-2789
James Rosen, *President*
Danny Cintron, *Safety Mgr*
Steve Barnhart, *Research*
Arlene Salas, *Human Rsrc Mgr*
Cheryl Rosen, *Human Resources*
EMP: 635
SQ FT: 38,000
SALES (est): 151.2MM **Privately Held**
WEB: www.highlandbaking.com
SIC: 5149 2051 Bakery products; bread, cake & related products

**(G-16271)**
**HOOKSET ENTERPRISES LLC**
Also Called: Decoplate
710 Landwehr Rd Ste B (60062-2337)
PHONE.................224 374-1936
William Rychel, *Owner*
EMP: 6
SQ FT: 5,500
SALES (est): 448.6K **Privately Held**
SIC: 3953 Screens, textile printing

**(G-16272)**
**ILLINOIS GLOVE COMPANY**
650 Anthony Trl Ste A (60062-2512)
PHONE.................800 342-5458
Fax: 217 323-2169
Louis Shade, *Branch Mgr*
EMP: 4
SALES (corp-wide): 3.6MM **Privately Held**
SIC: 2381 5699 Gloves, woven or knit: made from purchased materials; mittens, woven or knit: made from purchased materials; work clothing
PA: Illinois Glove Company
650 Anthony Trl Ste A
Northbrook IL 60062
847 291-1700

**(G-16273)**
**IMADA INC**
3100 Dundee Rd Ste 707 (60062-2442)
PHONE.................847 562-0834
Fax: 847 562-0839
Akira Morita, *President*
EMP: 48
SQ FT: 5,000
SALES (est): 8.9MM **Privately Held**
WEB: www.imadainc.com
SIC: 3823 Industrial instrmnts msrmnt display/control process variable

**(G-16274)**
**IMAGES ALIVE LTD**
638 Anthony Trl (60062-2540)
PHONE.................847 498-5550
Ellen Robinson, *President*
Stacy Goldsmith, *Sales Mgr*
EMP: 6
SQ FT: 3,500
SALES (est): 660K **Privately Held**
WEB: www.imagesalive.com
SIC: 3993 Signs & advertising specialties

**(G-16275)**
**IMPOSSIBLE OBJECTS LLC**
3455 Commercial Ave (60062-1818)
PHONE.................847 400-9582
Lawrence Kaplan, *CEO*
Robert Swartz, *CTO*
EMP: 10
SALES (est): 1.3MM **Privately Held**
SIC: 2752 Offset & photolithographic printing

**(G-16276)**
**INDUSTRIAL DIAMOND PRODUCTS**
3045 Macarthur Blvd (60062-1901)
PHONE.................847 272-7840
Vladimir Kompon, *President*
Michael Tobin, *Natl Sales Mgr*
▲ EMP: 20
SALES (est): 1.5MM **Privately Held**
SIC: 3545 Dressers, abrasive wheel: diamond point or other

**(G-16277)**
**INDUSTRIAL TITANIUM CORP**
3045 Commercial Ave (60062-1997)
PHONE.................847 272-2730
Fax: 847 498-3392
Richard Leopold, *President*
EMP: 5
SALES (est): 598.9K **Privately Held**
SIC: 3356 Titanium & titanium alloy bars, sheets, strip, etc.

**(G-16278)**
**INSTRUMENTALISTS INC**
Also Called: Claviers Piano Explorer
1838 Techny Ct (60062-5474)
PHONE.................847 446-5000
Fax: 847 446-6263
James T Rohner, *President*
EMP: 10
SALES (est): 1.2MM **Privately Held**
WEB: www.instrumentalistmagazine.com
SIC: 2721 Magazines: publishing & printing

**(G-16279)**
**INTERNTIONAL CMPT CONCEPTS INC**
300 Wainwright Dr (60062-1911)
PHONE.................847 808-7789
Raisa Stolyar, *President*
Chimere Brown, *Managing Dir*
Ilya Stolyar, *Vice Pres*
Daniel Goldman, *Sales Mgr*
Barry Craven, *Sales Executive*
EMP: 30
SQ FT: 41,000

SALES: 30MM **Privately Held**
WEB: www.icc-usa.com
SIC: 3571 3572 Electronic computers; computers, digital, analog or hybrid; mainframe computers; computer storage devices

**(G-16280)**
**J F WAGNER PRINTING CO**
3004 Commercial Ave (60062-1913)
PHONE.................................847 564-0017
Fax: 847 564-3312
John F Wagner, *Owner*
Laura Wagner, *Controller*
EMP: 5
SQ FT: 4,000
SALES (est): 602.7K **Privately Held**
WEB: www.print911.com
SIC: 2752 2791 2789 2759 Commercial printing, offset; typesetting; bookbinding & related work; commercial printing

**(G-16281)**
**J H ROBISON & ASSOCIATES LTD (PA)**
905 Voltz Rd (60062-4714)
PHONE.................................847 559-9662
John H Robison, *President*
EMP: 3
SQ FT: 1,300
SALES (est): 348.3K **Privately Held**
SIC: 1382 1381 Oil & gas exploration services; drilling oil & gas wells

**(G-16282)**
**JADA SPECIALTIES INC**
3834 Normandy Ln (60062-2120)
P.O. Box 753 (60065-0753)
PHONE.................................847 272-7799
Fax: 847 272-7774
David W Jacobson, *President*
EMP: 2
SALES (est): 259.9K **Privately Held**
SIC: 2869 Perfumes, flavorings & food additives; flavors or flavoring materials, synthetic

**(G-16283)**
**JAMES INJECTION MOLDING CO**
300 Pfingsten Rd (60062-2031)
PHONE.................................847 564-3820
Fax: 847 564-3965
Martin Silovich Jr, *President*
Christopher M Reiser, *Corp Secy*
EMP: 40
SQ FT: 23,400
SALES: 1.9MM **Privately Held**
SIC: 3089 3083 Injection molding of plastics; laminated plastics plate & sheet

**(G-16284)**
**KAPSTONE KRAFT PAPER CORP (HQ)**
1101 Skokie Blvd Ste 300 (60062-4124)
PHONE.................................252 533-6000
Timothy Keneally, *President*
Tim Keneally, *Vice Pres*
John Gasson, *Purch Mgr*
Jim Piette, *Marketing Staff*
Mark Mitchell, *Manager*
▼ EMP: 10
SALES (est): 253.3MM
SALES (corp-wide): 3B **Publicly Held**
SIC: 2621 Packaging paper
PA: Kapstone Paper And Packaging Corporation
1101 Skokie Blvd Ste 300
Northbrook IL 60062
847 239-8800

**(G-16285)**
**KAPSTONE PAPER AND PACKG CORP (PA)**
1101 Skokie Blvd Ste 300 (60062-4124)
PHONE.................................847 239-8800
Fax: 847 205-7551
Roger W Stone, *Ch of Bd*
Matthew Kaplan, *President*
Randy J Nebel, *President*
Kathryn D Ingraham, *Vice Pres*
Wilbur G Kessinger, *Vice Pres*
▼ EMP: 100
SALES: 3B **Publicly Held**
SIC: 2621 Paper mills

**(G-16286)**
**KEP WOODWORKING**
3240 Techny Rd (60062-6353)
PHONE.................................847 480-9545
Kenneth E Papciak, *Owner*
EMP: 10
SALES (est): 660K **Privately Held**
SIC: 2431 1521 Millwork; single-family home remodeling, additions & repairs

**(G-16287)**
**KINGPORT INDUSTRIES LLC**
1912 Shermer Rd (60062-5320)
PHONE.................................847 480-5745
Fax: 847 446-5663
Claudia Chisholm, *Mng Member*
Anyuan Chang,
▲ EMP: 5
SALES (est): 835.2K **Privately Held**
SIC: 3161 Traveling bags; suitcases; cases, carrying

**(G-16288)**
**KMP TOOL GRINDING INC**
1808 Janke Dr Ste J (60062-6703)
PHONE.................................847 205-9640
Fax: 847 205-9680
Walt Mirco, *President*
Albert Koshaba, *Vice Pres*
EMP: 3
SQ FT: 2,400
SALES (est): 424.5K **Privately Held**
SIC: 3541 7699 3545 Grinding machines, metalworking; industrial tool grinding; machine tool accessories

**(G-16289)**
**KOREAN MEDIA GROUP LLC**
3520 Milwaukee Ave Fl 2 (60062-7130)
PHONE.................................847 391-4112
Ju Kyong,
▲ EMP: 12
SALES (est): 406.9K **Privately Held**
SIC: 2711 Newspapers

**(G-16290)**
**KRAFT HEINZ FOODS COMPANY**
2301 Shermer Rd (60062-6721)
PHONE.................................847 291-3900
Joe Demarco, *Division Mgr*
Don Koerner, *Division Mgr*
Haruo Abe, *General Mgr*
Michael Doherty, *General Mgr*
Justin Lambeth, *General Mgr*
EMP: 200
SALES (corp-wide): 26.4B **Publicly Held**
SIC: 2033 2047 2091 2032 Canned fruits & specialties; dog & cat food; canned & cured fish & seafoods; canned specialties; frozen fruits & vegetables; frozen specialties
HQ: Kraft Heinz Foods Company
1 Ppg Pl Ste 3200
Pittsburgh PA 15222
412 456-5700

**(G-16291)**
**KYJEN COMPANY LLC**
Also Called: Outward Houndraise The Woof
333 Skokie Blvd Ste 104 (60062-1621)
PHONE.................................847 504-4010
Kyle Hansen, *President*
EMP: 15 **Privately Held**
SIC: 3999 Pet supplies
PA: The Kyjen Company Llc
15514 E Hinsdale Cir A
Centennial CO 80112

**(G-16292)**
**LANE INDUSTRIES INC (PA)**
1200 Shermer Rd Ste 400 (60062-4561)
PHONE.................................847 498-6650
Fax: 847 498-2104
Forrest Schneider, *President*
William Keating, *Vice Pres*
Eva Wloch, *Finance*
Linda Datz, *Human Resources*
EMP: 31
SQ FT: 12,000
SALES (est): 58.9MM **Privately Held**
WEB: www.lanehospitality.com
SIC: 3579 3589 7011 1731 Binding machines, plastic & adhesive; shredders, industrial & commercial; hotels & motels; safety & security specialization

**(G-16293)**
**LANMAR INC**
3160 Doolittle Dr (60062-2409)
PHONE.................................800 233-5520
Fax: 847 564-4682
Martin Jacobs, *President*
Paul Siegal, *Sales Staff*
EMP: 5
SQ FT: 1,800
SALES (est): 450K **Privately Held**
WEB: www.lanmarinc.com
SIC: 2295 5085 3052 Tape, varnished: plastic & other coated (except magnetic); adhesives, tape & plasters; hose, belting & packing; rubber & plastics hose & beltings

**(G-16294)**
**LEONARDS BAKERY**
2776 Dundee Rd (60062-2609)
PHONE.................................847 564-4977
Mark Becker, *Owner*
EMP: 7
SALES (est): 746.5K **Privately Held**
SIC: 2051 Bakery: wholesale or wholesale/retail combined

**(G-16295)**
**LIBRARY FURNITURE INTL**
Also Called: L F I
1945 Techny Rd Ste 10 (60062-5306)
PHONE.................................847 564-9497
Scott Fairbanks, *Owner*
Amy Fairbanks, *Co-Owner*
EMP: 4
SALES (est): 290K **Privately Held**
WEB: www.libraryfurniture-intl.com
SIC: 2531 Library furniture

**(G-16296)**
**LIGHT TO FORM LLC**
Also Called: Ltf
2905 Macarthur Blvd (60062-2004)
PHONE.................................847 498-5832
Atur Ivan, *President*
Robert Mak, *Sales Staff*
Frank Laum, *Director*
William Nethelhorst, *Director*
▲ EMP: 30
SALES (est): 4.7MM **Privately Held**
SIC: 3679 3612 Electronic loads & power supplies; distribution transformers, electric

**(G-16297)**
**LJM EQUIPMENT CO**
205 Huehl Rd (60062-1914)
PHONE.................................847 291-0162
Helen L Rivkin, *President*
EMP: 5
SQ FT: 81,000
SALES (est): 510K **Privately Held**
SIC: 3069 Rubber coated fabrics & clothing

**(G-16298)**
**LOVE ME TENDERS LLC**
2863 Woodmere Dr (60062-6446)
PHONE.................................847 564-2533
EMP: 3
SALES (est): 208.8K **Privately Held**
SIC: 2015 Chicken, processed: frozen

**(G-16299)**
**LOVEJOY INDUSTRIES INC (PA)**
3610 Commercial Ave (60062-1823)
PHONE.................................859 873-6828
Walter R Lovejoy, *Ch of Bd*
Matthew Lovejoy, *President*
Daniel Crea, *Vice Pres*
Mark Kepf, *CFO*
Catherine Mooney, *Sales Staff*
EMP: 4
SQ FT: 1,500
SALES (est): 45.9MM **Privately Held**
WEB: www.lovejoyindustries.com
SIC: 3364 3363 3544 Zinc & zinc-base alloy die-castings; aluminum die-castings; special dies, tools, jigs & fixtures

**(G-16300)**
**LUCKY GAMES INC (PA)**
574 Alice Dr (60062-2516)
PHONE.................................773 549-9051
Fax: 773 549-5267
Heidi Sonen, *President*

David Sonen, *Corp Secy*
EMP: 7
SQ FT: 7,000
SALES (est): 1.7MM **Privately Held**
SIC: 2679 Pressed fiber & molded pulp products except food products

**(G-16301)**
**LUCKY GAMES INC**
574 Alice Dr (60062-2516)
PHONE.................................773 549-9051
David Sonen, *President*
EMP: 10
SALES (corp-wide): 1.7MM **Privately Held**
SIC: 2679 Pressed fiber & molded pulp products except food products
PA: Lucky Games Inc
574 Alice Dr
Northbrook IL 60062
773 549-9051

**(G-16302)**
**LUND INDUSTRIES INC**
3175 Macarthur Blvd (60062-1903)
PHONE.................................847 459-1460
Fax: 847 459-1569
Paul A Lundberg, *President*
Mark J Lundberg, *Vice Pres*
Mary A Klein, *Admin Sec*
▼ EMP: 30
SQ FT: 16,000
SALES (est): 6.1MM **Privately Held**
WEB: www.lund-industries.com
SIC: 3669 Sirens, electric: vehicle, marine, industrial & air raid; signaling apparatus, electric

**(G-16303)**
**M I T FINANCIAL GROUP INC**
Also Called: General Lrng Communications
900 Skokie Blvd Ste 200 (60062-4031)
PHONE.................................847 205-3000
Fax: 847 564-8197
John E Cimba, *President*
Peggy Kane, *President*
David Husman, *Chairman*
Edward Conner, *Exec VP*
Dorothy Small, *Manager*
EMP: 45
SQ FT: 15,000
SALES (est): 6.6MM **Privately Held**
WEB: www.glcomm.com
SIC: 2721 Magazines: publishing only, not printed on site

**(G-16304)**
**MACKAY MITCHELL ENVELOPE CO**
707 Skokie Blvd Ste 600 (60062-2841)
PHONE.................................847 418-3866
Mike Becker, *Principal*
EMP: 3
SALES (est): 109.8K **Privately Held**
SIC: 2677 Envelopes

**(G-16305)**
**MACLEE CHEMICAL COMPANY INC**
1316 Edgewood Ln (60062-4716)
PHONE.................................847 480-0953
Fax: 773 929-1622
Joe Lee, *President*
Sam Eng, *Sales Mgr*
George Sajic, *Sales Staff*
▲ EMP: 3
SQ FT: 90,000
SALES (est): 403.9K **Privately Held**
SIC: 2819 Industrial inorganic chemicals

**(G-16306)**
**MARBLE EMPORIUM INC**
2200 Carlson Dr (60062-6728)
PHONE.................................847 205-4000
Fax: 847 205-4001
Louiza Kourkouvis, *President*
Yasna Jurisic, *Opers Staff*
▲ EMP: 20
SQ FT: 19,000
SALES (est): 4.4MM **Privately Held**
WEB: www.marblemporium.com
SIC: 5032 1743 3281 Marble building stone; granite building stone; marble installation, interior; marble, building: cut & shaped

# GEOGRAPHIC SECTION

**Northbrook - Cook County (G-16333)**

**(G-16307)**
**MAYLINE INVESTMENTS INC (PA)**
555 Skokie Blvd  (60062-2812)
PHONE.................847 948-9340
Charles Barancik, *Ch of Bd*
Paul Simons, *President*
Chris Mc Namee, *Exec VP*
Eric Volcheff, *Exec VP*
Don Clements, *Vice Pres*
◆ **EMP:** 3
**SQ FT:** 2,200
**SALES (est):** 97MM **Privately Held**
**SIC: 2522** 2521 Office furniture, except wood; office cabinets & filing drawers: except wood; panel systems & partitions, office: except wood; wood office furniture

**(G-16308)**
**MCKNIGHTS LONG TERM CARE NEWS**
Also Called: McKnight's Assisted Living
900 Skokie Blvd Ste 114  (60062-4014)
PHONE.................847 559-2884
**Fax:** 847 784-9346
William Pecover, *CEO*
Denise Devito, *Sr Corp Ofcr*
Jim Berklan, *Manager*
**EMP:** 7
**SALES (est):** 665.9K **Privately Held**
**WEB:** www.mltcn.com
**SIC: 2759** 8051 Publication printing; skilled nursing care facilities

**(G-16309)**
**MEDIARECALL HOLDINGS LLC**
3363 Commercial Ave  (60062-1908)
PHONE.................847 513-6710
Scott Smith, *Mng Member*
Ryan E Kirch,
**EMP:** 5
**SQ FT:** 3,200
**SALES:** 500K **Privately Held**
**SIC: 3577** Data conversion equipment, media-to-media: computer

**(G-16310)**
**MEMORABLE INC**
3336 Commercial Ave  (60062-1909)
PHONE.................847 272-8207
Eugene Gekhter, *CEO*
**EMP:** 6
**SQ FT:** 3,000
**SALES:** 30K **Privately Held**
**SIC: 7371** 7372 Computer software development & applications; application computer software

**(G-16311)**
**MICHAEL ZIMMERMAN**
Also Called: PIP Printing
3364 Commercial Ave  (60062-1909)
PHONE.................847 272-5560
**Fax:** 847 272-5829
Michael Zimmerman, *Owner*
**EMP:** 5
**SALES (est):** 300K **Privately Held**
**WEB:** www.pipnorthbrook.com
**SIC: 2752** 2789 2791 Commercial printing, offset; bookbinding & related work; typographic composition, for the printing trade

**(G-16312)**
**MOBILE ENDOSCOPIX LLC**
3330 Dundee Rd Ste C1  (60062-2328)
PHONE.................847 380-8992
Roth Elizabeth C, *Principal*
**EMP:** 3
**SALES (est):** 188.7K **Privately Held**
**SIC: 3845** Endoscopic equipment, electromedical

**(G-16313)**
**MOOG INC**
3650 Woodhead Dr  (60062-1817)
PHONE.................770 987-7550
John R Scannell, *CEO*
**EMP:** 49
**SALES (corp-wide):** 2.4B **Publicly Held**
**SIC: 7382** 3699 Confinement surveillance systems maintenance & monitoring; security control equipment & systems
**PA:** Moog Inc.
400 Jamison Rd Plant26
Elma NY 14059
716 652-2000

**(G-16314)**
**MOOG INC**
3650 Woodhead Dr  (60062-1817)
PHONE.................847 498-0700
Frank Diana, *Safety Mgr*
Elvira Mendez, *Opers Staff*
Rudy Merz, *Purch Agent*
Jonathan Grayson, *Engineer*
Derek Kowal, *Engineer*
**EMP:** 102
**SALES (corp-wide):** 2.4B **Publicly Held**
**SIC: 3861** Cameras & related equipment; tripods, camera & projector; cameras, still & motion picture (all types)
**PA:** Moog Inc.
400 Jamison Rd Plant26
Elma NY 14059
716 652-2000

**(G-16315)**
**MOSAIC CONSTRUCTION**
Also Called: Charlie
425 Huehl Rd Bldg 15b  (60062-2323)
PHONE.................847 504-0177
Aaron Frazin, *CEO*
**EMP:** 6 **EST:** 2012
**SALES (est):** 539.4K **Privately Held**
**SIC: 7372** 7389 Application computer software; business oriented computer software; interior designer

**(G-16316)**
**MOTOROLA SOLUTIONS INC**
2835 Farmington Rd  (60062-6911)
PHONE.................847 538-6959
Thomas Lee, *President*
**EMP:** 148
**SALES (corp-wide):** 6B **Publicly Held**
**WEB:** www.motorola.com
**SIC: 3663** Mobile communication equipment
**PA:** Motorola Solutions, Inc.
500 W Monroe St Ste 4400
Chicago IL 60661
847 576-5000

**(G-16317)**
**NATURAL PRODUCTS INC**
3555 Woodhead Dr  (60062-1814)
PHONE.................847 509-5835
**Fax:** 847 509-0360
Newton L Archer Jr, *President*
Sean Nash, *Prdtn Mgr*
James R Archer, *Admin Sec*
**EMP:** 15 **EST:** 1963
**SQ FT:** 10,000
**SALES (est):** 1.9MM
**SALES (corp-wide):** 9.2MM **Privately Held**
**WEB:** www.naturaproducts.com
**SIC: 3599** 3544 3469 Machine shop, jobbing & repair; special dies & tools; metal stampings
**PA:** Austin Tool & Die Co
3555 Woodhead Dr
Northbrook IL 60062
847 509-5800

**(G-16318)**
**ND INDUSTRIES INC**
N-D Industries Div
1840 Raymond Dr  (60062-6779)
PHONE.................847 498-3600
**Fax:** 847 498-1582
Norm Nunamaker, *Purchasing*
John J Thramann, *Manager*
Lee Woods, *Manager*
**EMP:** 30
**SALES (corp-wide):** 90.9MM **Privately Held**
**WEB:** www.ndindustries.com
**SIC: 3452** 2891 Bolts, nuts, rivets & washers; adhesives & sealants
**PA:** Nd Industries, Inc.
1000 N Crooks Rd
Clawson MI 48017
248 288-0000

**(G-16319)**
**NEWMEDICAL TECHNOLOGY INC**
310 Era Dr  (60062-1834)
PHONE.................847 412-1000
Amer Michael Hanna, *Ch of Bd*
Mercer Miller, *Managing Dir*
Michelle Brandon, *Marketing Staff*
▲ **EMP:** 24
**SQ FT:** 17,000
**SALES (est):** 250K **Privately Held**
**WEB:** www.newmedical.com
**SIC: 3842** 3841 Bandages & dressings; tape, adhesive: medicated or non-medicated; surgical & medical instruments; operating tables

**(G-16320)**
**NUCLIN DIAGNOSTICS INC**
3322 Commercial Ave  (60062-1909)
P.O. Box 1062, Lake Zurich  (60047-1062)
PHONE.................847 498-5210
**Fax:** 847 498-5211
**EMP:** 8
**SQ FT:** 5,000
**SALES (est):** 440K **Privately Held**
**SIC: 2835** 3841 In vitro & in vivo diagnostic substances; surgical & medical instruments

**(G-16321)**
**O CHILLI FROZEN FOODS INC**
1251 Shermer Rd  (60062-4599)
PHONE.................847 562-1991
**Fax:** 847 562-1822
Jeffrey L Rothschild, *President*
Odis Rothschild, *Admin Sec*
**EMP:** 27
**SQ FT:** 50,000
**SALES:** 3MM **Privately Held**
**SIC: 2038** 2099 2013 Frozen specialties; food preparations; sausages & other prepared meats

**(G-16322)**
**OCEANIC FOOD EXPRESS INC**
1715 Longvalley Dr  (60062-5117)
PHONE.................847 480-7217
Yefim Mayzenberg, *Principal*
**EMP:** 3
**SALES (est):** 221.2K **Privately Held**
**SIC: 2048** Fish food

**(G-16323)**
**OFFICERS PRINTING INC**
Also Called: Allegra Print & Imaging
710 Landwehr Rd Ste B  (60062-2337)
PHONE.................847 480-4663
Alan Wener, *President*
**EMP:** 4
**SQ FT:** 4,400
**SALES (est):** 368.5K **Privately Held**
**SIC: 2752** Commercial printing, offset

**(G-16324)**
**OLD WORLD GLOBAL LLC**
4065 Commercial Ave  (60062-1828)
PHONE.................800 323-5440
Bryan Emrich, *Vice Pres*
▲ **EMP:** 4
**SALES (est):** 371.5K **Privately Held**
**SIC: 2819** Industrial inorganic chemicals

**(G-16325)**
**OLD WORLD INDS HOLDINGS LLC**
4065 Commercial Ave  (60062-1828)
PHONE.................800 323-5440
Leonard Gazin, *Principal*
**EMP:** 5 **EST:** 2012
**SALES (est):** 673.1K **Privately Held**
**SIC: 2819** Industrial inorganic chemicals

**(G-16326)**
**ONE PLUS CORP**
3182 Macarthur Blvd  (60062-1904)
PHONE.................847 498-0955
**Fax:** 847 498-1570
Jay Simon, *President*
M Sion, *Vice Pres*
Chester Majsterek, *Engng Exec*
Morris Simon, *Treasurer*
Shirley Mankoff, *Manager*
**EMP:** 20
**SQ FT:** 15,000
**SALES (est):** 5.2MM **Privately Held**
**WEB:** www.onepluscorp.com
**SIC: 3829** Measuring & controlling devices

**(G-16327)**
**ONSRUD MACHINE CORP**
3926 Russett Ln  (60062-4235)
PHONE.................847 520-5300
**Fax:** 847 520-5423
Lawrence D Levine, *President*
**EMP:** 25
**SALES (est):** 3.3MM **Privately Held**
**SIC: 3553** 3541 3549 Woodworking machinery; machine tools, metal cutting type; metalworking machinery

**(G-16328)**
**OUTDOOR SOLUTIONS TEAM INC**
1315 Southwind Dr  (60062-4225)
PHONE.................312 446-4220
John Reeves, *President*
Robert Neff, *Admin Sec*
**EMP:** 25
**SQ FT:** 13,000
**SALES (est):** 1.6MM **Privately Held**
**SIC: 3993** Signs & advertising specialties

**(G-16329)**
**OZONOLOGY INC**
1515 Paddock Dr  (60062-6812)
PHONE.................847 998-8808
Allen Morr, *President*
**EMP:** 3
**SQ FT:** 5,600
**SALES (est):** 600K **Privately Held**
**WEB:** www.ozonology.com
**SIC: 3559** Ozone machines

**(G-16330)**
**PANEK PRECISION PRODUCTS CO**
455 Academy Dr  (60062-2416)
PHONE.................847 291-9755
**Fax:** 847 291-0360
Gregg Panek, *President*
Josephine Panek, *Corp Secy*
Brian Panek, *COO*
Jesse Gomez, *Warehouse Mgr*
Felix Vazquez, *QC Mgr*
**EMP:** 178 **EST:** 1945
**SQ FT:** 109,000
**SALES (est):** 48.5MM **Privately Held**
**SIC: 3499** Bank chests, metal

**(G-16331)**
**PCBL RETAIL HOLDINGS LLC**
Also Called: Polaroid Store
5 Revere Dr Ste 206  (60062-1568)
PHONE.................610 761-4838
Jeff Branman, *Chairman*
**EMP:** 2
**SALES:** 3MM **Privately Held**
**SIC: 2759** Commercial printing

**(G-16332)**
**PCS NITROGEN INC (HQ)**
1101 Skokie Blvd Ste 400  (60062-4123)
PHONE.................847 849-4200
Tom Regan, *President*
Lee Gooch, *Vice Pres*
Nathan Dixon, *Warehouse Mgr*
Doug Whitcomb, *Project Engr*
Michelle Polito, *Controller*
◆ **EMP:** 90
**SALES:** 394.7MM
**SALES (corp-wide):** 4.4B **Privately Held**
**SIC: 2873** 2874 Nitrogenous fertilizers; ammonia & ammonium salts; urea; ammonium nitrate, ammonium sulfate; phosphatic fertilizers
**PA:** Potash Corporation Of Saskatchewan Inc
122 1st Ave S Suite 500
Saskatoon SK S7K 7
306 933-8500

**(G-16333)**
**PCS NITROGEN FERTILIZER LP**
1101 Skokie Blvd Ste 400  (60062-4123)
PHONE.................847 849-4200
Larry Obrien, *Partner*
Wayne R Brownley, *Partner*
G David Delaney, *Partner*
Rick Harnung, *Partner*
Brian E Johnson, *Partner*

# Northbrook - Cook County (G-16334)  GEOGRAPHIC SECTION

**EMP:** 10
**SALES (est):** 3.5MM
**SALES (corp-wide):** 4.4B **Privately Held**
**SIC:** 2873 Nitrogenous fertilizers
**PA:** Potash Corporation Of Saskatchewan Inc
  122 1st Ave S Suite 500
  Saskatoon SK S7K 7
  306 933-8500

### (G-16334)
**PCS NITROGEN TRINIDAD CORP**
1101 Skokie Blvd Ste 400 (60062-4123)
**PHONE**.................................847 849-4200
Jim Dietz, *President*
Jim Heppel, *Vice Pres*
**EMP:** 180 **EST:** 1993
**SALES (est):** 15.5MM
**SALES (corp-wide):** 4.4B **Privately Held**
**SIC:** 2873 Ammonia & ammonium salts; urea
**HQ:** Pcs Nitrogen, Inc.
  1101 Skokie Blvd Ste 400
  Northbrook IL 60062
  847 849-4200

### (G-16335)
**PCS NTRGEN FRTLZER OPRTONS INC (DH)**
1101 Skokie Blvd Ste 400 (60062-4123)
**PHONE**.................................847 849-4200
Brett Heimann, *President*
Bryan E Johnson, *Corp Secy*
David Delaney, *COO*
Fritz Bertz, *Vice Pres*
Wayne R Brownlee, *Treasurer*
▲ **EMP:** 100
**SALES (est):** 102.4MM
**SALES (corp-wide):** 4.4B **Privately Held**
**SIC:** 2873 Nitrogenous fertilizers
**HQ:** Pcs Nitrogen, Inc.
  1101 Skokie Blvd Ste 400
  Northbrook IL 60062
  847 849-4200

### (G-16336)
**PCS PHOSPHATE COMPANY INC (HQ)**
Also Called: Pcs Sales
1101 Skokie Blvd Ste 400 (60062-4123)
**PHONE**.................................847 849-4200
Brent Heimann, *President*
Thomas J Regan Jr, *President*
Richard C Atwood, *General Mgr*
Paul Straughan, *Manager*
Joseph Podwika, *Admin Sec*
◆ **EMP:** 80 **EST:** 1981
**SQ FT:** 66,000
**SALES (est):** 12.5MM
**SALES (corp-wide):** 4.4B **Privately Held**
**WEB:** www.potashcorp.com
**SIC:** 1475 1474 2874 2819 Phosphate rock; potash mining; phosphatic fertilizers; phosphates, except fertilizers: defluorinated & ammoniated
**PA:** Potash Corporation Of Saskatchewan Inc
  122 1st Ave S Suite 500
  Saskatoon SK S7K 7
  306 933-8500

### (G-16337)
**PEN AT HAND**
4120 Terri Lyn Ln (60062-4939)
**PHONE**.................................847 498-9174
Ronnie Horrowitz, *Owner*
**EMP:** 5
**SALES (est):** 635.3K **Privately Held**
**WEB:** www.penathand.com
**SIC:** 2621 Writing paper

### (G-16338)
**PINGOTOPIA INC**
Also Called: Pingoworld
3334 Commercial Ave (60062-1909)
**PHONE**.................................847 503-9333
Alexander Holden, *CFO*
**EMP:** 10
**SQ FT:** 5,000
**SALES:** 1MM **Privately Held**
**SIC:** 2754 5023 Post cards, picture: gravure printing; decorative home furnishings & supplies

### (G-16339)
**POTASH CORP SSKTCHEWAN FLA INC (HQ)**
1101 Skokie Blvd Ste 400 (60062-4123)
**PHONE**.................................847 849-4200
**Fax:** 847 849-4695
William Doyle, *CEO*
Stephen F Dowdle, *President*
Steven Beckel, *COO*
Denita Stann, *Vice Pres*
Brooke Beres, *Hum Res Coord*
▼ **EMP:** 101
**SALES (est):** 54.9MM
**SALES (corp-wide):** 4.4B **Privately Held**
**SIC:** 2873 2874 2819 Nitrogenous fertilizers; phosphatic fertilizers; potash alum
**PA:** Potash Corporation Of Saskatchewan Inc
  122 1st Ave S Suite 500
  Saskatoon SK S7K 7
  306 933-8500

### (G-16340)
**POTASH CORP SSKTCHEWAN FLA INC**
1101 Skokie Blvd Ste 400 (60062-4123)
**PHONE**.................................847 849-4200
Thomas Regan, *Branch Mgr*
**EMP:** 200
**SALES (corp-wide):** 4.4B **Privately Held**
**SIC:** 1475 1474 2874 2819 Phosphate rock; potash mining; phosphatic fertilizers; phosphates, except fertilizers: defluorinated & ammoniated; nitrogenous fertilizers
**HQ:** Potash Corporation Of Saskatchewan (Florida) Inc.
  1101 Skokie Blvd Ste 400
  Northbrook IL 60062
  847 849-4200

### (G-16341)
**POTASH HOLDING COMPANY INC**
1101 Skokie Blvd Ste 400 (60062-4123)
**PHONE**.................................847 849-4200
William J Bill Doyle, *President*
Wayne R Brownlee, *Vice Pres*
G David Delaney, *Vice Pres*
**EMP:** 2
**SALES (est):** 419.1K
**SALES (corp-wide):** 4.4B **Privately Held**
**SIC:** 5191 3999 Fertilizer & fertilizer materials; atomizers, toiletry
**PA:** Potash Corporation Of Saskatchewan Inc
  122 1st Ave S Suite 500
  Saskatoon SK S7K 7
  306 933-8500

### (G-16342)
**PRAIRIE STATE SCREW & BOLT CO**
4219 Kayla Ln (60062-2167)
**PHONE**.................................847 858-9551
Joseph Schyman, *President*
▲ **EMP:** 10
**SALES (est):** 80.2K **Privately Held**
**SIC:** 3452 Bolts, nuts, rivets & washers; screws, metal

### (G-16343)
**PRIME PUBLISHING LLC**
Also Called: Ilikecrochet.com
3400 Dundee Rd Ste 220 (60062-2338)
**PHONE**.................................847 205-9375
Stuart Hochwert, *President*
Keith Kousins, *President*
Jeanette Benoit, *Editor*
Megan Boedecker, *Editor*
Jesse Carpender, *Editor*
**EMP:** 75
**SALES (est):** 7.6MM **Privately Held**
**SIC:** 2741 Miscellaneous publishing

### (G-16344)
**PRINT AND MKTG SOLUTIONS GROUP**
1537 Windy Hill Dr (60062-3833)
**PHONE**.................................847 498-9640
Mark Sterne, *President*
**EMP:** 50
**SALES (est):** 166.1K **Privately Held**
**SIC:** 8742 2752 Marketing consulting services; commercial printing, lithographic

### (G-16345)
**PRINTLINK ENTERPRISES INC**
3636 Torrey Pines Pkwy (60062-3104)
**PHONE**.................................847 753-9800
Patricia Burdett-Neiberg, *President*
Jerry Neiberg, *Admin Sec*
**EMP:** 2
**SALES:** 300K **Privately Held**
**SIC:** 2759 Commercial printing

### (G-16346)
**PRISMATEC INC**
1964 Raymond Dr (60062-6715)
**PHONE**.................................847 562-9022
Erwin Gugolz, *President*
**EMP:** 4
**SALES:** 700K **Privately Held**
**SIC:** 2759 Publication printing

### (G-16347)
**PRODUCTWORKS LLC**
610 Academy Dr (60062-2421)
**PHONE**.................................224 406-8810
Alan Cohn, *Vice Pres*
Peter Pergament, *Vice Pres*
Patrick Banach, *Accounts Mgr*
Erika Schneider, *Accounts Mgr*
Carrie Zaleski, *Director*
▲ **EMP:** 6
**SALES (est):** 1.2MM **Privately Held**
**WEB:** www.productworksllc.com
**SIC:** 3645 3646 3648 Residential lighting fixtures; commercial indusl & institutional electric lighting fixtures; lighting equipment

### (G-16348)
**PROTECT ASSOC**
2165 Shermer Rd Ste C (60062-6734)
**PHONE**.................................847 446-8664
Earl Bauer, *President*
**EMP:** 5
**SALES (est):** 406.6K **Privately Held**
**SIC:** 2273 Floor coverings, textile fiber

### (G-16349)
**PURITY SELECT INC**
125 Revere Dr (60062-1555)
**PHONE**.................................847 275-3821
**EMP:** 3 **EST:** 2010
**SALES (est):** 383.2K **Privately Held**
**SIC:** 3732 Boat building & repairing

### (G-16350)
**QUICKSET INTERNATIONAL INC (HQ)**
Also Called: Moog Quickset
3650 Woodhead Dr (60062-1817)
P.O. Box 405806, Atlanta GA (30384-5800)
**PHONE**.................................847 498-0700
**Fax:** 847 498-1258
John Scannell, *President*
Raymond Bratton, *President*
Brian Halstrom, *Vice Pres*
Steve Wyatt, *Vice Pres*
Brian Hallstrom, *VP Opers*
**EMP:** 92
**SQ FT:** 40,000
**SALES (est):** 11.9MM
**SALES (corp-wide):** 2.4B **Publicly Held**
**WEB:** www.quickset.com
**SIC:** 3861 Cameras & related equipment; tripods, camera & projector; cameras, still & motion picture (all types)
**PA:** Moog Inc.
  400 Jamison Rd Plant26
  Elma NY 14059
  716 652-2000

### (G-16351)
**RAINBO SPORTS LLC (PA)**
1440 Paddock Dr (60062-6811)
**PHONE**.................................847 998-1000
John Roscoe, *Manager*
Theodore D Greene, 
**EMP:** 22
**SALES (est):** 2.3MM **Privately Held**
**WEB:** www.rainbosports.com
**SIC:** 3949 Ice skates, parts & accessories

### (G-16352)
**RAINBOW LIGHTING**
3545 Commercial Ave (60062-1820)
**PHONE**.................................847 480-1136
**Fax:** 847 480-7315
Mike Stern, *President*
Steve Kalish, *Vice Pres*
Keith Tucker, *Vice Pres*
Julie Smith, *Controller*
Nodl M Roudaut, *Human Res Dir*
◆ **EMP:** 20
**SQ FT:** 35,000
**SALES (est):** 5.3MM **Privately Held**
**WEB:** www.rainbowlightinginc.com
**SIC:** 5719 3646 Lamps & lamp shades; commercial indusl & institutional electric lighting fixtures

### (G-16353)
**RAMCEL ENGINEERING CO**
2926 Macarthur Blvd (60062-2085)
**PHONE**.................................847 272-6980
**Fax:** 847 272-7196
Rocco Palmi, *President*
Craig Mengarelli, *Vice Pres*
Dale Mengarelli, *Vice Pres*
Mark Loehndorf, *Project Mgr*
Christopher York, *Engineer*
**EMP:** 62 **EST:** 1956
**SQ FT:** 64,000
**SALES:** 29.1MM **Privately Held**
**WEB:** www.ramcel.com
**SIC:** 3469 Stamping metal for the trade

### (G-16354)
**REGIONAL EMRGNCY DISPATCH CTR**
Also Called: Red Center
1842 Shermer Rd (60062-5318)
**PHONE**.................................847 498-5748
**Fax:** 847 498-5968
Jim Clausen, *Exec Dir*
**EMP:** 17
**SALES (est):** 1.6MM **Privately Held**
**SIC:** 3669 Emergency alarms

### (G-16355)
**RICAR INDUSTRIES INC**
2468 Greenview Rd (60062-7030)
**PHONE**.................................847 914-9083
Phil Bernstein, *CEO*
Rick Bernstein, *President*
Jacqueline Bernstein, *Treasurer*
**EMP:** 3
**SQ FT:** 500
**SALES:** 1.5MM **Privately Held**
**SIC:** 3441 Fabricated structural metal

### (G-16356)
**RICHCO GRAPHICS INC**
1500 Skokie Blvd Ste 204 (60062-4113)
**PHONE**.................................847 367-7277
Richard Lachman, *President*
**EMP:** 3
**SALES (est):** 389.4K **Privately Held**
**WEB:** www.richcographics.com
**SIC:** 2759 Letterpress printing; screen printing

### (G-16357)
**ROBKO FLOCK COATING COMPANY**
1935 Stanley St (60062-5324)
**PHONE**.................................847 272-6202
**Fax:** 847 272-6210
Alison Kotlarz, *President*
Tracy Kotlarz, *Vice Pres*
Robert Callero, *Accountant*
Marcella Kotlarz, *Admin Sec*
**EMP:** 5
**SQ FT:** 7,000
**SALES:** 750K **Privately Held**
**WEB:** www.robkoco.com
**SIC:** 3569 3564 Filters, general line: industrial; blowers & fans

### (G-16358)
**ROSENTHAL MANUFACTURING CO INC**
Also Called: Smart-Slitters
1840 Janke Dr (60062-6704)
**PHONE**.................................847 714-0404
**Fax:** 847 714-0440
Lorelei Rosenthal, *President*
David Rosenthal, *Exec VP*
Michael Rosenthal, *Exec VP*
June Norton, *Bookkeeper*
▲ **EMP:** 33 **EST:** 1926
**SQ FT:** 45,000

# GEOGRAPHIC SECTION
## Northbrook - Cook County (G-16388)

SALES (est): 10MM  **Privately Held**
**WEB:** www.rosenthalmfg.com
**SIC: 3554**  3565  Cutting machines, paper; packaging machinery

**(G-16359)**
### SCHOOL TOWN  LLC
1340 Shermer Rd Ste 245  (60062-4598)
**PHONE** ..................................847 943-9115
Matt Hochstein, *Marketing Staff*
Michael Kritzman,
**EMP:** 7
**SALES:** 600K  **Privately Held**
**SIC: 7372**  Prepackaged software

**(G-16360)**
### SEALMASTER INC
425 Huehl Rd Bldg 11b  (60062-2340)
**PHONE** ..................................847 480-7325
Hannah Malin, *President*
**EMP:** 16
**SQ FT:** 2,300
**SALES (est):** 1.7MM  **Privately Held**
**SIC: 2951**  5713  Asphalt paving mixtures & blocks; floor covering stores

**(G-16361)**
### SELLERS COMMERCE LLC
633 Skokie Blvd Ste 490  (60062-2826)
**PHONE** ..................................858 345-1212
Ashook Reddy, *President*
Rick Levine, *Vice Pres*
David Sykes,
**EMP:** 12
**SQ FT:** 2,300
**SALES:** 2.5MM  **Privately Held**
**SIC: 7372**  Application computer software

**(G-16362)**
### SERVICE ENVELOPE CORPORATION
1925 Holste Rd  (60062-7704)
**PHONE** ..................................847 559-0004
**Fax:** 847 559-0007
Thomas Washburn, *President*
Marilyn Washburn, *Corp Secy*
Jim Washburn, *Vice Pres*
**EMP:** 25
**SALES (est):** 4.8MM  **Privately Held**
**WEB:** www.serviceenvelope.com
**SIC: 2677**  Envelopes

**(G-16363)**
### SKYLINE PRINTING SALES
3004 Commercial Ave  (60062-1913)
P.O. Box 4854, Buffalo Grove  (60089-4854)
**PHONE** ..................................847 412-1931
**Fax:** 847 412-1933
Jeff Schultz, *President*
**EMP:** 4
**SALES (est):** 310K  **Privately Held**
**SIC: 2759**  Commercial printing

**(G-16364)**
### SNAGLET LLC
2101 Crabtree Ln  (60062-3552)
**PHONE** ..................................404 449-6394
Jamie D Silva, *CEO*
Amber K Aggarwal,
Jeffrey W Steffgen,
**EMP:** 3
**SALES (est):** 108.2K  **Privately Held**
**SIC: 7372**  Prepackaged software

**(G-16365)**
### SOBOT TOOL & MANUFACTURING CO
3975 Commercial Ave  (60062-1827)
**PHONE** ..................................847 480-0560
**Fax:** 847 480-9248
Steven Sobot, *President*
Mark Sobot, *Vice Pres*
Maggie Walsh, *Manager*
Zofia Sobot, *Admin Sec*
**EMP:** 20
**SQ FT:** 48,000
**SALES (est):** 3.5MM  **Privately Held**
**WEB:** www.sobottool.com
**SIC: 3599**  Machine shop, jobbing & repair

**(G-16366)**
### SOCIAL QNECT  LLC
666 Dundee Rd Ste 1904  (60062-2739)
**PHONE** ..................................847 997-0077
Gary Scheier,
**EMP:** 1 EST: 2012
**SALES:** 200K  **Privately Held**
**SIC: 7372**  Application computer software

**(G-16367)**
### SOUTH BEND SPORTING GOODS INC (PA)
Also Called: Big Game International
1910 Techny Rd  (60062-5308)
**PHONE** ..................................847 715-1400
**Fax:** 847 715-1411
Jory Katlin, *President*
Elton Allen, *Vice Pres*
▲ **EMP:** 35
**SQ FT:** 80,000
**SALES (est):** 4.2MM  **Privately Held**
**SIC: 3949**  Fishing tackle, general

**(G-16368)**
### SPENCER WELDING SERVICE INC
3215 Doolittle Dr  (60062-2410)
**PHONE** ..................................847 272-0580
Steven C Spencer, *President*
**EMP:** 5
**SQ FT:** 3,000
**SALES (est):** 366.1K  **Privately Held**
**SIC: 7692**  Welding repair

**(G-16369)**
### SPORT ELECTRONICS INC
Also Called: Hass and Associates
4121 Rutgers Ln  (60062-2911)
**PHONE** ..................................847 564-5575
Debra M Hass, *President*
Joanne Meyerhoff, *Treasurer*
**EMP:** 4
**SALES (est):** 310K  **Privately Held**
**SIC: 3999**  Stereographs, photographic

**(G-16370)**
### SPURT  INC
4033 Dana Ct  (60062-3025)
**PHONE** ..................................847 571-6497
Mark Polin, *President*
**EMP:** 5
**SALES:** 900K  **Privately Held**
**SIC: 3699**  3648  8711  Electrical equipment & supplies; lighting equipment; electrical or electronic engineering

**(G-16371)**
### ST IMAGING INC
630 Dundee Rd Ste 210  (60062-2792)
**PHONE** ..................................847 501-3344
Tom Anderson, *President*
**EMP:** 13
**SALES (est):** 950K  **Privately Held**
**WEB:** www.stimaging.com
**SIC: 3826**  Photomicrographic apparatus

**(G-16372)**
### STRATEGIC MFG PARTNER LLC (PA)
Also Called: Jsa Tool & Engineering
3145 Elder Ct  (60062-5831)
**PHONE** ..................................262 878-5213
Debra Mettry, *Purch Dir*
Paul Yost, *Mng Member*
Joseph A Dipietro,
Jim Hendrickson,
**EMP:** 5
**SQ FT:** 10,000
**SALES (est):** 5.7MM  **Privately Held**
**WEB:** www.jsatool.com
**SIC: 3599**  Machine shop, jobbing & repair

**(G-16373)**
### STRYTECH ADHESIVES
707 Skokie Blvd Ste 600  (60062-2841)
**PHONE** ..................................847 509-7566
Howard Neal, *Owner*
**EMP:** 3
**SALES (est):** 2.2MM  **Privately Held**
**SIC: 2891**  Adhesives

**(G-16374)**
### SUNBIRD SOLAR  LLC
3140 Whisperwoods Ct  (60062-6400)
**PHONE** ..................................847 509-8888
Ronald Lachman, *Principal*
**EMP:** 3
**SALES (est):** 178.6K  **Privately Held**
**SIC: 3433**  Solar heaters & collectors

**(G-16375)**
### T HASEGAWA USA INC
Also Called: Chicago Culinary Center
3100 Dundee Rd Ste 701  (60062-2442)
**PHONE** ..................................847 559-6060
**Fax:** 847 559-6464
Christopher Langbein, *Manager*
**EMP:** 3
**SALES (corp-wide):** 473.7MM  **Privately Held**
**WEB:** www.thasegawa.com
**SIC: 2087**  Flavoring extracts & syrups
**HQ:** T. Hasegawa U.S.A. Inc.
14017 183rd St
Cerritos CA 90703
714 670-1586

**(G-16376)**
### TDY INDUSTRIES  LLC
Also Called: ATI Wah Chang
700 Landwehr Rd  (60062-2310)
**PHONE** ..................................847 564-0700
**EMP:** 100
**SQ FT:** 14,000  **Publicly Held**
**WEB:** www.midwestlaboratory.com
**SIC: 3312**  Blast furnaces & steel mills
**HQ:** Tdy Industries, Llc
1000 Six Ppg Pl
Pittsburgh PA 15222
412 394-2896

**(G-16377)**
### TECHNY PLASTICS CORP
1919 Techny Rd  (60062-5383)
**PHONE** ..................................847 498-2212
**Fax:** 847 498-1522
Roger D Mann, *President*
Charles Elterman, *Vice Pres*
Tim Smith, *Plant Mgr*
Robert W Jorgensen, *Treasurer*
Jill Brdecka, *Admin Sec*
**EMP:** 35
**SQ FT:** 10,000
**SALES (est):** 4.9MM  **Privately Held**
**WEB:** www.technyplastics.com
**SIC: 3089**  Injection molding of plastics

**(G-16378)**
### UK ABRASIVES  INC
3045 Macarthur Blvd  (60062-1901)
**PHONE** ..................................847 291-3566
Vladimir Kompan, *President*
Mark Gorelik, *CFO*
Vitaly Slobodky, *Info Tech Dir*
Vitaly Slobodsky, *Admin Sec*
▲ **EMP:** 21
**SQ FT:** 35,000
**SALES (est):** 3.8MM  **Privately Held**
**SIC: 3291**  Abrasive products

**(G-16379)**
### UNDERGROUND DEVICES  INC
420 Academy Dr  (60062-2417)
**PHONE** ..................................847 205-9000
**Fax:** 847 205-9004
Adrienne Greene, *President*
Jennifer Greene, *Controller*
**EMP:** 17
**SQ FT:** 11,000
**SALES (est):** 5.3MM  **Privately Held**
**WEB:** www.udevices.com
**SIC: 2821**  Molding compounds, plastics

**(G-16380)**
### UNITROL ELECTRONICS INC
702 Landwehr Rd  (60062-2310)
**PHONE** ..................................847 480-0115
**Fax:** 847 480-0932
Roger Hirsch, *President*
Carol Hirsch, *Exec VP*
Ronald Leibovitz, *Vice Pres*
Ron Liebowitz, *Vice Pres*
Arman Leonar, *Research*
**EMP:** 20
**SQ FT:** 12,000
**SALES:** 2MM  **Privately Held**
**WEB:** www.unitrol-electronics.com
**SIC: 3625**  3822  Control equipment, electric; water heater controls

**(G-16381)**
### USA INDUSTRIAL EXPORT CORP
Also Called: Industrialexport.net
707 Skokie Blvd Ste 600  (60062-2841)
**PHONE** ..................................312 391-5552
Charles Poremba, *CEO*
**EMP:** 2
**SQ FT:** 200,000
**SALES (est):** 227.2K  **Privately Held**
**SIC: 3599**  Custom machinery

**(G-16382)**
### VAN CLEAVE WOODWORKING INC
1919 Milton Ave  (60062-3622)
**PHONE** ..................................847 424-8200
James Van Cleave, *President*
**EMP:** 3
**SQ FT:** 1,500
**SALES:** 310K  **Privately Held**
**SIC: 2434**  2511  Wood kitchen cabinets; wood household furniture

**(G-16383)**
### VARISPORT INC
3386 Commercial Ave  (60062-1909)
**PHONE** ..................................847 480-1366
Barry Slotnick, *President*
Mitchell Slotnick, *Corp Secy*
Natalie Slotnick, *Admin Sec*
**EMP:** 5
**SQ FT:** 1,000
**SALES:** 285K  **Privately Held**
**WEB:** www.varisport.com
**SIC: 3949**  Exercise equipment

**(G-16384)**
### WE INNOVEX INC
Also Called: Metal Works
3045 Macarthur Blvd  (60062-1901)
**PHONE** ..................................847 291-3553
Vladimir Kompan, *President*
▲ **EMP:** 3
**SQ FT:** 22,000
**SALES (est):** 330K  **Privately Held**
**WEB:** www.ukabrasives.com
**SIC: 3541**  Machine tools, metal cutting type

**(G-16385)**
### WEDGWORTHS INC (PA)
Also Called: Florida Favorite Fertilizer
1101 Skokie Blvd Ste 400  (60062-4123)
P.O. Box 2076, Belle Glade FL  (33430-7076)
**PHONE** ..................................863 682-2153
George H Wedgworth, *Ch of Bd*
Helen J Boynton, *Vice Pres*
**EMP:** 25
**SQ FT:** 6,000
**SALES (est):** 15.1MM  **Privately Held**
**SIC: 2875**  Mfg Fertilizers-Mix Only

**(G-16386)**
### WEXFORD HOME CORP
707 Skokie Blvd  (60062-2857)
**PHONE** ..................................847 922-5738
John McGuire, *President*
Feng Xu, *Admin Asst*
▲ **EMP:** 4
**SQ FT:** 1,000
**SALES:** 500K  **Privately Held**
**SIC: 2679**  Wallboard, decorated: made from purchased material

**(G-16387)**
### WILLIS STEIN & PARTNERS MANAGE (PA)
1033 Skokie Blvd Ste 360  (60062-4137)
**PHONE** ..................................312 422-2400
Avy Stein, *Managing Prtnr*
Philip B Pool, *Managing Dir*
Todd Smith, *CFO*
Christopher Larson, *Controller*
David Mills, *Accountant*
**EMP:** 25
**SQ FT:** 22,180
**SALES (est):** 200.8MM  **Privately Held**
**SIC: 6799**  3479  2721  8721  Investors; painting of metal products; magazines: publishing & printing; payroll accounting service

**(G-16388)**
### WINDOW TECH INC
1351 Shermer Rd  (60062-4546)
**PHONE** ..................................847 272-0739
**Fax:** 847 272-1527
Timothy J Becker, *President*
Craig Ferguson, *General Mgr*
Sherri Becker, *Vice Pres*

**Northbrook - Cook County (G-16389)** — **GEOGRAPHIC SECTION**

EMP: 4
SQ FT: 2,500
SALES (est): 425K **Privately Held**
SIC: 2591 Window blinds

**(G-16389)**
**XSHREDDERS INC (PA)**
2855 Shermer Rd (60062-7710)
PHONE .................................. 847 205-1875
Fax: 847 205-1710
David Klein, *President*
Lou Gantz, *Accountant*
Bridgett Siefert, *Office Mgr*
Helen McJohan, *Manager*
Howard Diamond, *Shareholder*
▲ EMP: 60
SQ FT: 84,000
SALES (est): 15.7MM **Privately Held**
SIC: 2671 Paper coated or laminated for packaging

## Northfield
### Cook County

**(G-16390)**
**APAC UNLIMITED INC**
790 W Frontage Rd Ste 214 (60093-1204)
PHONE .................................. 847 441-4282
Saretta Joyner, *President*
EMP: 3
SALES (est): 268.9K **Privately Held**
SIC: 2653 Corrugated & solid fiber boxes

**(G-16391)**
**ASA INC**
Also Called: Advertising/Displays/Printing
723 Happ Rd (60093-1114)
PHONE .................................. 847 446-1856
Mark Gantner, *President*
Bill Hughes, *Vice Pres*
Mark Schreiber, *Vice Pres*
Ted Magura, *Manager*
EMP: 22
SQ FT: 17,000
SALES (est): 2MM **Privately Held**
WEB: www.asapop.com
SIC: 2752 Commercial printing, lithographic

**(G-16392)**
**BERGMANN ORTHOTIC LAB INC**
1730 Holder Ln (60093-3307)
PHONE .................................. 847 446-3616
Fax: 847 446-3079
John N Bergmann, *President*
Susan C Simonetti, *Treasurer*
Dave Bergmann, *Manager*
EMP: 3
SQ FT: 4,000
SALES (est): 1.2MM **Privately Held**
SIC: 3842 Surgical appliances & supplies

**(G-16393)**
**BODINE ELECTRIC COMPANY (PA)**
201 Northfield Rd (60093-3311)
PHONE .................................. 773 478-3515
Fax: 773 478-3232
John R Bodine, *President*
Archelle Manliguez, *General Mgr*
Jeffrey Bodine, *Exec VP*
Rich Meserve, *Vice Pres*
Waldo Alvarez, *Project Mgr*
▲ EMP: 250 EST: 1905
SQ FT: 40,000
SALES (est): 132.5MM **Privately Held**
WEB: www.bodine-electric.com
SIC: 5063 3625 3621 Motors, electric; motor controls, electric; motors, electric

**(G-16394)**
**BW DALLAS LLC**
1 Northfield Plz Ste 521 (60093-1216)
PHONE .................................. 847 441-1892
Benjamin West, *Branch Mgr*
EMP: 3
SALES (corp-wide): 1.4MM **Privately Held**
SIC: 2519 Lawn & garden furniture, except wood & metal

PA: Bw Dallas, Llc
17814 Davenport Rd # 115
Dallas TX 75252
972 407-9950

**(G-16395)**
**CAP TODAY**
325 Waukegan Rd (60093-2719)
PHONE .................................. 847 832-7377
Fax: 847 832-8873
Robert McGonnagel, *Publisher*
EMP: 12
SALES (est): 376.5K **Privately Held**
SIC: 2721 Magazines: publishing & printing

**(G-16396)**
**CERTIFIED ASPHALT PAVING**
540 W Frontage Rd # 3175 (60093-1281)
P.O. Box 8363 (60093-8363)
PHONE .................................. 847 441-5000
Anthony G Harris, *President*
EMP: 7
SQ FT: 200
SALES (est): 2MM **Privately Held**
SIC: 2951 1794 1795 Asphalt & asphaltic paving mixtures (not from refineries); excavation work; demolition, buildings & other structures

**(G-16397)**
**CHICAGO MLTLINGUA GRAPHICS INC (PA)**
Also Called: Multi-Lngua Communications
550 W Frontage Rd # 2700 (60093-1202)
PHONE .................................. 847 386-7187
Fax: 847 864-3202
Lizhe Sun, *President*
Yi Han, *Vice Pres*
Jane Zhang, *Office Mgr*
Yong Wu, *Manager*
EMP: 10
SQ FT: 8,000
SALES (est): 1.4MM **Privately Held**
WEB: www.multilingua.com
SIC: 7389 7336 2752 2791 Translation services; graphic arts & related design; commercial printing, lithographic; typesetting

**(G-16398)**
**CITRIX SYSTEMS INC**
540 W Frontage Rd # 3100 (60093-1250)
PHONE .................................. 847 716-4797
EMP: 3
SALES (corp-wide): 3.4B **Publicly Held**
SIC: 7372 Prepackaged software
PA: Citrix Systems, Inc.
851 W Cypress Creek Rd
Fort Lauderdale FL 33309
954 267-3000

**(G-16399)**
**FRANK S BENDER INC**
Also Called: Frank Bender Jewels
316 Happ Rd (60093-3419)
PHONE .................................. 847 441-7370
Fax: 847 441-7372
Frank S Bender, *President*
Mona Bender, *Corp Secy*
Edward Rubin, *Vice Pres*
EMP: 3
SQ FT: 850
SALES (est): 450K **Privately Held**
SIC: 5944 3911 Jewelry, precious stones & precious metals; jewelry, precious metal

**(G-16400)**
**GREENCYCLE OF INDIANA INC (HQ)**
400 Central Ave Ste 115 (60093-3024)
PHONE .................................. 847 441-6606
Caroline Repenning, *President*
David Wagner, *Corp Secy*
EMP: 3
SQ FT: 1,899
SALES (est): 2.6MM **Privately Held**
SIC: 4953 2499 Recycling, waste materials; mulch or sawdust products, wood; mulch, wood & bark

**(G-16401)**
**H HAL KRAMER CO (PA)**
1865 Old Willow Rd # 231 (60093-2954)
PHONE .................................. 847 441-0213
Ilene Kramer, *President*
Peter Horwitz, *Vice Pres*

▲ EMP: 1 EST: 1962
SALES: 200K **Privately Held**
SIC: 3999 Plaques, picture, laminated

**(G-16402)**
**IMPACT POLYMER LLC** ◆
790 W Frontage Rd (60093-1204)
PHONE .................................. 847 441-2394
Adriano Pedrelli,
EMP: 4 EST: 2016
SALES (est): 220K **Privately Held**
SIC: 3272 Concrete products, precast

**(G-16403)**
**IONIT TECHNOLOGIES INC**
2311 Dorina Dr (60093-2705)
PHONE .................................. 847 205-9651
Fax: 847 205-9689
James Talbot, *CEO*
Tim Irwin, *President*
David Wedel, *Exec VP*
Brent Hamacheck, *CFO*
EMP: 30
SQ FT: 8,000
SALES (est): 5.2MM **Privately Held**
WEB: www.ionitusa.com
SIC: 3651 8711 5065 Video cassette recorders/players & accessories; engineering services; security control equipment & systems

**(G-16404)**
**KARLIN FOODS CORP**
1845 Oak St Ste 19 (60093-3022)
P.O. Box 8488 (60093-8488)
PHONE .................................. 847 441-8330
Fax: 847 446-2040
Mitchell Karlin, *President*
Vince Klemm, *QC Mgr*
Donna Hastings, *Treasurer*
Litsa Kokkinias, *Accountant*
Lita Kokias, *Human Res Mgr*
▼ EMP: 17 EST: 1977
SQ FT: 9,000
SALES (est): 128.8MM **Privately Held**
WEB: www.karlinfoods.com
SIC: 2034 Dehydrated fruits, vegetables, soups

**(G-16405)**
**KELLER GROUP INC (PA)**
1 Northfield Plz Ste 510 (60093-1216)
PHONE .................................. 847 446-7550
John P Keller, *Ch of Bd*
David Spada, *Vice Pres*
Carol Gudbrandsen, *Manager*
Kenneth Dachman, *Info Tech Mgr*
Jon Schepke, *Info Tech Mgr*
EMP: 350
SQ FT: 2,700
SALES (est): 90.3MM **Privately Held**
WEB: www.kellergroupinc.com
SIC: 3462 1221 1222 Iron & steel forgings; bituminous coal & lignite-surface mining; bituminous coal-underground mining

**(G-16406)**
**KRAFT FODS LTIN AMER HOLDG LLC (PA)**
3 Lakes Dr (60093-2753)
PHONE .................................. 847 646-2000
Irene Rosenfeld, *CEO*
Lachlan Grave, *Managing Dir*
EMP: 10
SALES (est): 2MM **Privately Held**
SIC: 2022 Cheese, natural & processed

**(G-16407)**
**KRAFT HEINZ FOODS COMPANY**
3 Lakes Dr 2b (60093-2753)
PHONE .................................. 847 646-2000
Bob Cole, *Opers-Prdtn-Mfg*
Liz Henningah Hendghan, *Manager*
Liz Hendghan, *Manager*
Brian Miller, *Manager*
Ricardo Ochoa, *Supervisor*
EMP: 225
SALES (corp-wide): 26.4B **Publicly Held**
WEB: www.kraftfoods.com
SIC: 2022 Cheese, natural & processed
HQ: Kraft Heinz Foods Company
1 Ppg Pl Ste 3200
Pittsburgh PA 15222
412 456-5700

**(G-16408)**
**MCILVAINE CO**
191 Waukegan Rd Ste 208 (60093-2743)
PHONE .................................. 847 784-0012
Fax: 847 784-0061
Robert Mc Ilvaine, *President*
Brian Walker, *Regional Mgr*
Peter Waanders, *Vice Pres*
Michael Cabrera, *Chief Engr*
Paul Farber, *Engineer*
EMP: 40 EST: 1974
SQ FT: 6,000
SALES: 2MM **Privately Held**
WEB: www.mcilvainecompany.com
SIC: 2741 8748 8732 8742 Technical manuals: publishing only, not printed on site; catalogs: publishing only, not printed on site; newsletter publishing; guides: publishing only, not printed on site; business consulting; market analysis or research; management consulting services

**(G-16409)**
**MEDLINE INDUSTRIES INC (PA)**
3 Lakes Dr (60093-2753)
PHONE .................................. 847 949-5500
Fax: 847 949-2633
Charles N Mills, *CEO*
Julia Downey, *President*
Pete Herbrand, *President*
Andrew Mills, *President*
Jeff Rubel, *President*
◆ EMP: 1300 EST: 1977
SQ FT: 716,000
SALES (est): 5.6B **Privately Held**
WEB: www.medline.com
SIC: 3841 5047 5999 Surgical & medical instruments; instruments, surgical & medical; medical apparatus & supplies

**(G-16410)**
**MULTICOPY CORP**
1739 Harding Rd (60093-3305)
PHONE .................................. 847 446-7015
Fax: 847 446-7017
Mike Semmerling, *President*
Judi Semmerling, *Office Mgr*
Terry Jackson, *Admin Sec*
EMP: 9 EST: 1951
SQ FT: 25,000
SALES (est): 1.7MM **Privately Held**
SIC: 2752 2796 2791 2789 Commercial printing, lithographic; platemaking services; typesetting; bookbinding & related work

**(G-16411)**
**NEAT-OH INTERNATIONAL LLC**
790 W Frontage Rd Ste 303 (60093-1204)
PHONE .................................. 847 441-4290
Meiling Chen, *Finance Dir*
Wayne H Rothschild, *Mng Member*
Sandi Washer, *Manager*
▲ EMP: 12
SALES (est): 1.3MM **Privately Held**
SIC: 3944 Games, toys & children's vehicles

**(G-16412)**
**NORTHERN PALLET AND SUPPLY CO (PA)**
464 Central Ave Ste 18 (60093-3030)
P.O. Box 8129 (60093-8129)
PHONE .................................. 847 716-1400
Fax: 847 716-1308
Steven E Schultz, *President*
Craige Schultz, *Vice Pres*
Shabnam Khan, *Accounts Mgr*
EMP: 10 EST: 1954
SQ FT: 600
SALES (est): 7MM **Privately Held**
WEB: www.northernpalletsupply.com
SIC: 5031 2448 Pallets, wood; pallets, wood

**(G-16413)**
**NV BUSINESS PUBLISHERS CORP**
540 W Frontage Rd # 3124 (60093-1230)
PHONE .................................. 847 441-5645
Tom Vilardi, *President*
EMP: 5 EST: 1984
SALES (est): 410K **Privately Held**
SIC: 2721 Periodicals

# GEOGRAPHIC SECTION

**Northlake - Cook County (G-16438)**

**(G-16414)**
**ONE WAY SOLUTIONS LLC**
400 Central Ave Ste 320 (60093-3024)
**PHONE**.................................847 446-0872
Brian Pigott,
Lindsey Pigott,
▼ **EMP:** 3
**SQ FT:** 1,200
**SALES (est):** 646.2K **Privately Held**
**WEB:** www.oneway-solutions.com
**SIC:** 3089 Pallets, plastic

**(G-16415)**
**ORREN PICKELL BUILDERS INC**
Also Called: Cabinetwerks
550 W Frontage Rd # 3800 (60093-1202)
**PHONE**.................................847 572-5200
Orren Pickell, *Owner*
**EMP:** 16
**SALES (corp-wide):** 0 **Privately Held**
**WEB:** www.cabinetwerks.com
**SIC:** 2499 5031 1751 Decorative wood & woodwork; kitchen cabinets; cabinet & finish carpentry
**PA:** Orren Pickell Builders, Incorporated
550 W Frontage Rd # 3800
Northfield IL 60093
847 572-5200

**(G-16416)**
**RAINBO SPORTS LLC**
790 W Frontage Rd Ste 705 (60093-1204)
**PHONE**.................................847 784-9857
Kevin Kasmar, *Branch Mgr*
**EMP:** 4
**SALES (corp-wide):** 2.3MM **Privately Held**
**WEB:** www.oldwillowpartners.com
**SIC:** 3949 Ice skates, parts & accessories
**PA:** Rainbo Sports, Llc
1440 Paddock Dr
Northbrook IL 60062
847 998-1000

**(G-16417)**
**SIGNA GROUP INC (PA)**
540 W Frontage Rd # 2105 (60093-1250)
**PHONE**.................................847 386-7639
Go Sugiura, *Ch of Bd*
William Henry, *CFO*
Drew Pehrson, *Controller*
**EMP:** 2
**SQ FT:** 2,000
**SALES (est):** 23.3MM **Privately Held**
**SIC:** 3354 Aluminum extruded products

**(G-16418)**
**SIMPLEMENT INC (PA)**
1 Northfield Plz Ste 300 (60093-1214)
**PHONE**.................................702 560-5332
Robert Maclain, *CEO*
Marjorie Zander, *President*
**EMP:** 2
**SALES (est):** 1.9MM **Privately Held**
**SIC:** 7372 8742 Business oriented computer software; business consultant

**(G-16419)**
**STEPAN COMPANY (PA)**
22 W Frontage Rd (60093-3470)
**PHONE**.................................847 446-7500
**Fax:** 847 501-2443
F Quinn Stepan Jr, *Ch of Bd*
Scott R Behrens, *Vice Pres*
Jennifer A Hale, *Vice Pres*
Scott C Mason, *Vice Pres*
Arthur W Mergner, *Vice Pres*
◆ **EMP:** 363 **EST:** 1932
**SALES:** 1.7B **Publicly Held**
**WEB:** www.stepan.com
**SIC:** 2843 2821 2087 2865 Surface active agents; sulfonated oils, fats or greases; emulsifiers, except food & pharmaceutical; polyurethane resins; phthalic anhydride resins; extracts, flavoring; cyclic organic intermediates

**(G-16420)**
**STEPAN SPECIALTY PRODUCTS LLC**
22 W Frontage Rd (60093-3407)
**PHONE**.................................847 446-7500
**EMP:** 4
**SALES (corp-wide):** 1.7B **Publicly Held**
**SIC:** 2099 Food preparations

**HQ:** Stepan Specialty Products, Llc
100 W Hunter Ave
Maywood NJ 07607
201 845-3030

**(G-16421)**
**TOWERS MEDIA HOLDINGS INC**
Also Called: Towers Holdings
1 Northfield Plz Ste 300 (60093-1214)
**PHONE**.................................312 993-1550
Jonathan Towers, *President*
Adam Salasek, *Opers Staff*
George Wilen, *Treasurer*
Jerry Pointer, *Accounts Mgr*
Mark Joslyn, *Manager*
▲ **EMP:** 78
**SALES (est):** 11MM **Privately Held**
**WEB:** www.towersproductions.com
**SIC:** 3652 7812 7819 Pre-recorded records & tapes; motion picture & video production; video tape or disk reproduction

**(G-16422)**
**TRMG LLP**
790 W Frontage Rd Ste 416 (60093-1204)
**PHONE**.................................847 441-4122
Alisdair Martin, *Managing Prtnr*
Johnathon Fellows,
Amanda Stevens,
Andrew Stevens,
Peter West,
**EMP:** 10
**SQ FT:** 2,000
**SALES:** 1.2MM
**SALES (corp-wide):** 11.2MM **Privately Held**
**SIC:** 2721 Magazines: publishing only, not printed on site
**PA:** Trmg Limited
Winchester Court
Hatfield HERTS AL10
170 727-3999

**(G-16423)**
**ZECO INC**
256 Lagoon Dr (60093-3511)
P.O. Box 8482 (60093-8482)
**PHONE**.................................847 446-1413
Clifford Zelinsky, *President*
Allen Zelinsky, *Vice Pres*
**EMP:** 5
**SQ FT:** 15,000
**SALES (est):** 470K **Privately Held**
**SIC:** 3599 Machine & other job shop work

## Northlake
### Cook County

**(G-16424)**
**ABC BEVERAGE MFG INC**
400 N Wolf Rd Ste A (60164-1659)
**PHONE**.................................708 449-2600
Roger Collins, *Principal*
**EMP:** 3
**SALES (est):** 355K **Privately Held**
**SIC:** 3999 Manufacturing industries

**(G-16425)**
**ALL-BRITE ANODIZING CO INC (PA)**
100 W Lake St (60164-2426)
**PHONE**.................................708 562-0502
Martin W Nieman, *President*
Chris Bateman, *Sales Staff*
Sherry W King, *Office Mgr*
Bryan Bateman, *Admin Sec*
**EMP:** 30 **EST:** 1968
**SQ FT:** 7,500
**SALES:** 2.5MM **Privately Held**
**SIC:** 3471 Anodizing (plating) of metals or formed products

**(G-16426)**
**AMERICAN BOTTLING COMPANY**
401 N Railroad Ave (60164-1666)
**PHONE**.................................708 947-5000
**Fax:** 708 562-0223
Brad Troutman, *Manager*
Dean English, *Manager*
Jenny Smrz, *Manager*
**EMP:** 320

**SALES (corp-wide):** 6.4B **Publicly Held**
**WEB:** www.cs-americas.com
**SIC:** 2086 5149 Soft drinks: packaged in cans, bottles, etc.; groceries & related products
**HQ:** The American Bottling Company
5301 Legacy Dr
Plano TX 75024

**(G-16427)**
**AMERICAN CHEMICAL & EQP INC**
128 W Lake St 130 (60164-2428)
P.O. Box 407, Ingleside (60041-0407)
**PHONE**.................................815 675-9199
**Fax:** 708 531-1978
Charles Connon, *President*
▲ **EMP:** 5
**SQ FT:** 31,000
**SALES (est):** 1MM **Privately Held**
**WEB:** www.amerchem.com
**SIC:** 2899 5084 Chemical preparations; metal refining machinery & equipment

**(G-16428)**
**ARYZTA LLC**
La Francaise Bakery Div
111 Northwest Ave (60164-1603)
**PHONE**.................................708 498-2300
**Fax:** 708 562-0373
Daniel Scales, *Branch Mgr*
**EMP:** 176
**SALES (corp-wide):** 4.3B **Privately Held**
**WEB:** www.pennantfoods.com
**SIC:** 2053 Rolls, sweet: frozen; pastries (danish): frozen; croissants, frozen
**HQ:** Aryzta Llc
6080 Center Dr Ste 900
Los Angeles CA 90045
310 417-4700

**(G-16429)**
**BOX USA**
401 Northwest Ave (60164-1698)
**PHONE**.................................708 562-6000
Jim McNeill, *Principal*
**EMP:** 5
**SALES (est):** 684.7K **Privately Held**
**SIC:** 2653 Corrugated & solid fiber boxes

**(G-16430)**
**BRISTOL HOSE & FITTING INC**
Also Called: Hydraulic Hoses & Fittings
1 W Lake St (60164-2423)
**PHONE**.................................708 492-3456
**Fax:** 708 492-0261
Michael Tuminaro, *CEO*
Carol Tuminaro, *Vice Pres*
Peter Tuminaro, *Vice Pres*
Phillip Tuminaro, *Admin Sec*
**EMP:** 23
**SQ FT:** 32,000
**SALES:** 6MM **Privately Held**
**SIC:** 5074 3492 3052 Plumbing fittings & supplies; fluid power valves & hose fittings; automobile hose, plastic

**(G-16431)**
**BRISTOL TRANSPORT INC**
Also Called: Bristol Towing & Transport
1 W Lake St (60164-2423)
**PHONE**.................................708 343-6411
**Fax:** 708 343-9828
Philip Tuminaro, *President*
Michael Tuminaro, *Vice Pres*
Peter Tuminaro, *Vice Pres*
Carol Tuminaro, *Admin Sec*
**EMP:** 26
**SQ FT:** 6,000
**SALES (est):** 3.6MM **Privately Held**
**SIC:** 4212 3492 3052 Local trucking, without storage; fluid power valves & hose fittings; rubber & plastics hose & beltings

**(G-16432)**
**BWT LLC**
Also Called: Bluewater Thermal Solutions
75 E Lake St (60164-2419)
**PHONE**.................................708 410-8000
**Fax:** 708 410-8200
Tyrone Pearson, *General Mgr*
Deborah Smith, *Human Res Dir*
**EMP:** 25 **Privately Held**
**SIC:** 3398 Metal heat treating

**HQ:** Bwt Llc
201 Brookfield Pkwy
Greenville SC 29607
864 990-0050

**(G-16433)**
**DELTA-UNIBUS CORP**
515 N Railroad Ave (60164-1652)
**PHONE**.................................708 409-1200
Tom Burtnst, *President*
Perry Weyant, *General Mgr*
Ed Peters, *Engineer*
Chris Wild, *Engineer*
Reza Mehdipour, *Sales Associate*
▲ **EMP:** 250
**SALES (est):** 60.8MM
**SALES (corp-wide):** 565.2MM **Publicly Held**
**WEB:** www.deltaunibus.com
**SIC:** 3629 Electronic generation equipment
**PA:** Powell Industries, Inc.
8550 Mosley Rd
Houston TX 77075
713 944-6900

**(G-16434)**
**DR PEPPER SNAPPLE GROUP INC**
401 N Railroad Ave (60164-1666)
**PHONE**.................................708 947-5000
Ron Summers, *Regional Mgr*
Linda Lumpkin, *Vice Pres*
Dan Graham, *Plant Mgr*
David Vicik, *Parts Mgr*
Bob Bryan, *Controller*
**EMP:** 100
**SALES (corp-wide):** 6.4B **Publicly Held**
**SIC:** 2086 Bottled & canned soft drinks
**PA:** Dr Pepper Snapple Group, Inc.
5301 Legacy Dr
Plano TX 75024
972 673-7000

**(G-16435)**
**DYNA-BURR CHICAGO INC**
65 E Lake St (60164-2483)
**PHONE**.................................708 250-6744
**Fax:** 708 345-0778
Patrick McKenna, *President*
Bob Bea, *Vice Pres*
Robert Bea, *Vice Pres*
Warren H Dickinson, *Shareholder*
**EMP:** 15 **EST:** 1968
**SQ FT:** 15,000
**SALES (est):** 1.4MM **Privately Held**
**SIC:** 3471 Plating of metals or formed products; finishing, metals or formed products

**(G-16436)**
**FHP INC**
505 N Railroad Ave (60164-1652)
**PHONE**.................................708 452-4100
Gary Brown, *Sales Dir*
Nancy Gaul, *Mktg Dir*
Tim Molek, *Marketing Staff*
Stefan Roehrig, *Info Tech Dir*
Steve Barber, *Executive*
**EMP:** 6
**SALES (est):** 516.8K **Privately Held**
**SIC:** 3471 Plating & polishing

**(G-16437)**
**G T EXPRESS LTD**
165 W Lake St (60164-2427)
**PHONE**.................................708 338-0303
**EMP:** 8
**SALES (est):** 1.3MM **Privately Held**
**SIC:** 2655 Fiber shipping & mailing containers

**(G-16438)**
**HEADHUNTER2000 INC**
328 Major Dr (60164-1819)
**PHONE**.................................708 533-3769
Scott Judge, *President*
Frank Judge, *Vice Pres*
**EMP:** 4
**SQ FT:** 2,800
**SALES:** 700K **Privately Held**
**SIC:** 3449 Bars, concrete reinforcing: fabricated steel

# Northlake - Cook County (G-16439) — GEOGRAPHIC SECTION

**(G-16439)**
**HOWARD PRESS PRINTING INC**
303 E North Ave Lowr 100 (60164-2699)
P.O. Box 1186, Riverside (60546-0586)
PHONE...............................708 345-7437
Donald Baumruck, *President*
Shirley Phillips, *Corp Secy*
Howard Baumruck, *Vice Pres*
Martha Baumruck, *Admin Sec*
**EMP:** 5
**SALES (est):** 569.3K **Privately Held**
**SIC:** 2759 2752 Commercial printing; commercial printing, lithographic

**(G-16440)**
**INTERNATIONAL PAPER COMPANY**
401 Northwest Ave (60164-1605)
PHONE...............................708 562-6000
Jim McNeill, *Principal*
Fred Berg, *Prdtn Mgr*
Kieth Wilhem, *Facilities Mgr*
Wes Molter, *Sales Mgr*
John Masariu, *Sales Staff*
**EMP:** 100
**SQ FT:** 180,000
**SALES (corp-wide):** 21B **Publicly Held**
**WEB:** www.internationalpaper.com
**SIC:** 2653 Corrugated & solid fiber boxes
**PA:** International Paper Company
6400 Poplar Ave
Memphis TN 38197
901 419-9000

**(G-16441)**
**KIMBERLY-CLARK CORPORATION**
505 Northwest Ave Ste C (60164-1662)
PHONE...............................708 409-8500
John Musich, *Manager*
**EMP:** 30
**SALES (corp-wide):** 18.2B **Publicly Held**
**WEB:** www.kimberly-clark.com
**SIC:** 2621 Paper mills
**PA:** Kimberly-Clark Corporation
351 Phelps Dr
Irving TX 75038
972 281-1200

**(G-16442)**
**MICROSOFT CORPORATION**
601 Northwest Ave (60164-1301)
PHONE...............................708 409-4759
**EMP:** 100
**SALES (corp-wide):** 85.3B **Publicly Held**
**SIC:** 7372 Prepackaged software
**PA:** Microsoft Corporation
1 Microsoft Way
Redmond WA 98052
425 882-8080

**(G-16443)**
**MURNANE PACKAGING CORPORATION**
Also Called: Murpack
607 Northwest Ave (60164-1301)
PHONE...............................708 449-1200
Frank J Murnane Sr, *Ch of Bd*
Frank J Murnane Jr, *President*
Patrick Murnane, *Vice Pres*
▼ **EMP:** 45 **EST:** 1919
**SQ FT:** 76,000
**SALES (est):** 11.7MM **Privately Held**
**WEB:** www.murnanecompanies.com
**SIC:** 2675 Cardboard cut-outs, panels & foundations: die-cut; food container products & parts, from die-cut paper

**(G-16444)**
**MURNANE SPECIALTIES INC (PA)**
607 Northwest Ave (60164-1301)
P.O. Box 631, Hinsdale (60522-0631)
PHONE...............................708 449-1200
Frank J Murnane Jr, *President*
Thomas Hanson, *President*
Patrick J Murnane, *Exec VP*
Frank J Murnane Sr, *Treasurer*
James D Firek, *Controller*
▲ **EMP:** 25
**SQ FT:** 76,000
**SALES (est):** 3.3MM **Privately Held**
**SIC:** 2653 Corrugated boxes, partitions, display items, sheets & pad

**(G-16445)**
**NORKOL INC**
11650 W Grand Ave (60164-1300)
PHONE...............................708 531-1000
Lawrence Kolinski, *Ch of Bd*
Denise M Callahan, *President*
Eric Holzer, *General Mgr*
Mary E Kolinski, *Corp Secy*
James Lindquist, *Vice Pres*
**EMP:** 175
**SQ FT:** 310,000
**SALES (est):** 124.9MM **Privately Held**
**SIC:** 2679 Book covers, paper

**(G-16446)**
**OCTAPHARMA PLASMA INC**
17 W North Ave (60164-2311)
PHONE...............................708 409-0900
**EMP:** 6
**SALES (corp-wide):** 1.4B **Privately Held**
**SIC:** 2836 Plasmas
**HQ:** Octapharma Plasma, Inc.
10644 Westlake Dr
Charlotte NC 28273
704 654-4600

**(G-16447)**
**POWELL ELECTRICAL SYSTEMS INC**
Delta-Unibus Division
515 N Railroad Ave (60164-1652)
PHONE...............................708 409-1200
Allen Haske, *Buyer*
Ernie Lang, *Purchasing*
Blain Steh, *Design Engr*
Michael Bales, *Manager*
Scott Scelfo, *Manager*
**EMP:** 200
**SALES (corp-wide):** 565.2MM **Publicly Held**
**WEB:** www.powl.com
**SIC:** 3629 Electronic generation equipment
**HQ:** Powell Electrical Systems, Inc.
8550 Mosley Rd
Houston TX 77075
708 409-1200

**(G-16448)**
**POWELL ELECTRICAL SYSTEMS INC**
Delta-Unibus
515 N Railroad Ave (60164-1652)
PHONE...............................708 409-1200
**EMP:** 250
**SALES (corp-wide):** 565.2MM **Publicly Held**
**SIC:** 3629 Electronic generation equipment
**HQ:** Powell Electrical Systems, Inc.
8550 Mosley Rd
Houston TX 77075
708 409-1200

**(G-16449)**
**POWELL INDUSTRIES INC**
515 N Railroad Ave (60164-1652)
PHONE...............................708 409-1200
Art Zimecki, *Materials Mgr*
Wendt Sharon, *Production*
Bill McGrew, *Controller*
Manda Nadkarni, *Manager*
Reza Mehdipour, *Manager*
**EMP:** 11
**SALES (corp-wide):** 565.2MM **Publicly Held**
**SIC:** 3612 Power & distribution transformers
**PA:** Powell Industries, Inc.
8550 Mosley Rd
Houston TX 77075
713 944-6900

**(G-16450)**
**SCHOLLE IPN CORPORATION (PA)**
Also Called: Scholle Packaging
200 W North Ave (60164-2402)
PHONE...............................708 562-7290
Leon Gianneschi, *CEO*
Thomas Bickford, *President*
Richard B Heath, *Vice Pres*
Kevin Mekaru, *Opers Mgr*
Brian Snavely, *Opers Staff*
◆ **EMP:** 14
**SQ FT:** 3,000
**SALES (est):** 564.9MM **Privately Held**
**WEB:** www.scholle.com
**SIC:** 2819 3081 2821 3089 Industrial inorganic chemicals; packing materials, plastic sheet; cellulose derivative materials; plastic processing

**(G-16451)**
**SCHOLLE IPN PACKAGING INC (HQ)**
Also Called: Scholle Packaging
200 W North Ave (60164-2402)
PHONE...............................708 562-7290
Thomas Bickford, *President*
Alec Marketos, *Senior VP*
Melania Craddock, *Vice Pres*
Richard Heath, *Vice Pres*
David Mondrus, *Vice Pres*
◆ **EMP:** 354
**SQ FT:** 44,000
**SALES (est):** 236.4MM
**SALES (corp-wide):** 564.9MM **Privately Held**
**WEB:** www.scholle.com
**SIC:** 3089 Plastic processing
**PA:** Scholle Ipn Corporation
200 W North Ave
Northlake IL 60164
708 562-7290

**(G-16452)**
**SCHOLLE PACKAGING INC**
120 N Railroad Ave (60164-1607)
PHONE...............................708 273-3792
Leon Gianneschi, *President*
**EMP:** 6 **EST:** 2005
**SALES (est):** 756.5K **Privately Held**
**SIC:** 3089 Plastic processing

**(G-16453)**
**STEVENS SIGN CO INC**
57 E Fullerton Ave (60164-1441)
PHONE...............................708 562-4888
Michael Stevens, *President*
**EMP:** 2
**SQ FT:** 3,000
**SALES:** 400K **Privately Held**
**WEB:** www.stevenssignco.com
**SIC:** 7389 3993 2396 Sign painting & lettering shop; signs & advertising specialties; automotive & apparel trimmings

**(G-16454)**
**SUN CHEMICAL CORPORATION**
General Printing Ink Division
135 W Lake St Ste 2 (60164-2496)
PHONE...............................708 562-0550
Fax: 708 562-5093
Robert Lorenz, *President*
Mike Murphy, *Vice Pres*
Tony Renzi, *Vice Pres*
Lyle Douthitt, *Plant Mgr*
Bruce Marx, *Mfg Staff*
**EMP:** 165
**SQ FT:** 160,000
**SALES (corp-wide):** 6.7B **Privately Held**
**WEB:** www.sunchemical.com
**SIC:** 2893 Printing ink
**HQ:** Sun Chemical Corporation
35 Waterview Blvd Ste 100
Parsippany NJ 07054
973 404-6000

**(G-16455)**
**THREE GUYS PASTA LLC**
11225 W Grand Ave (60164-1036)
PHONE...............................708 932-5555
Carl Mazzone,
Cosmo Sansone,
**EMP:** 21
**SALES (est):** 699.7K **Privately Held**
**SIC:** 2099 Noodles, fried (Chinese); packaged combination products: pasta, rice & potato; pasta, uncooked: packaged with other ingredients

**(G-16456)**
**TRI STATE RECYCLING SERVICE**
301 W Lake St Frnt 1 (60164-2403)
PHONE...............................708 865-9939
Frank Ward, *President*
Brent Fifer, *Plant Mgr*
Anthony Cbsibby, *Manager*
Gertrude Ward, *Admin Sec*
**EMP:** 25
**SALES (est):** 2.1MM **Privately Held**
**WEB:** www.tsrsi.com
**SIC:** 2611 Pulp manufactured from waste or recycled paper

**(G-16457)**
**TRU-WAY INC**
36 W Lake St (60164-2424)
P.O. Box 346127, Chicago (60634-6127)
PHONE...............................708 562-3690
Fax: 708 562-3695
Stan Mastalerz, *President*
Robert Cyran, *Accountant*
Carol Sweeney, *Office Mgr*
**EMP:** 20
**SQ FT:** 10,000
**SALES (est):** 4.1MM **Privately Held**
**WEB:** www.tru-way.com
**SIC:** 3469 3444 Metal stampings; sheet metalwork

**(G-16458)**
**VACUMET CORP**
200 W North Ave (60164-2402)
PHONE...............................708 562-7290
William Scholle, *President*
Martin Bell, *Admin Sec*
**EMP:** 15
**SALES (est):** 2.6MM **Privately Held**
**SIC:** 3081 2819 2821 2295 Packing materials, plastic sheet; industrial inorganic chemicals; cellulose derivative materials; metallizing of fabrics

## O Fallon
*St. Clair County*

**(G-16459)**
**AAA TOOL AND MACHINE CO**
230 Obernuefemann Rd (62269-7105)
PHONE...............................618 632-6718
Fax: 618 632-0987
Brian Wort, *President*
**EMP:** 9 **EST:** 1969
**SQ FT:** 13,000
**SALES:** 1.3MM **Privately Held**
**SIC:** 3599 Machine shop, jobbing & repair

**(G-16460)**
**ACN INDPNDENT BUS RPRSENTATIVE**
Also Called: Reliable Delivery Solutions
820 Cardiff Ct (62269-6878)
PHONE...............................618 623-4238
Benita Arceneaux, *Owner*
**EMP:** 5
**SALES (est):** 223.7K **Privately Held**
**SIC:** 3661 Telephone & telegraph apparatus

**(G-16461)**
**ANDRIAS FOOD GROUP INC (PA)**
Also Called: Andria's Steak Sauce
6805 Old Collinsville Rd (62269-6916)
PHONE...............................618 632-4866
Fax: 618 632-7801
Larry Kenison, *President*
Sam Andria, *Vice Pres*
**EMP:** 35
**SQ FT:** 3,000
**SALES (est):** 1.5MM **Privately Held**
**WEB:** www.andrias.com
**SIC:** 5812 5813 2035 2033 Steak restaurant; drinking places; seasonings, meat sauces (except tomato & dry); barbecue sauce: packaged in cans, jars, etc.; spices & herbs; sauces

**(G-16462)**
**ANDRIAS FOOD GROUP INC**
Also Called: Andria's Steak Sauce
6813 Old Collinsville Rd (62269-6916)
PHONE...............................618 632-3118
Larry Kenison, *Owner*
**EMP:** 4
**SALES (corp-wide):** 1.5MM **Privately Held**
**WEB:** www.andrias.com
**SIC:** 2035 2033 Seasonings, meat sauces (except tomato & dry); barbecue sauce: packaged in cans, jars, etc.

## GEOGRAPHIC SECTION

## Oak Brook - Dupage County (G-16488)

PA: Andria's Food Group, Inc.
  6805 Old Collinsville Rd
  O Fallon IL 62269
  618 632-4866

*(G-16463)*
### ARINC INCORPORATED
8 Eagle Ctr Ste 4 (62269-1963)
PHONE..........................800 633-6882
Carol Laporte, *General Mgr*
**EMP: 20 Publicly Held**
WEB: www.arinc.com
SIC: 8711 3812 Engineering services; search & navigation equipment
HQ: Arinc Incorporated
  2551 Riva Rd
  Annapolis MD 21401
  410 266-4000

*(G-16464)*
### C & C SPORT STOP
115 N Lincoln Ave (62269-1414)
PHONE..........................618 632-7812
Cathy Portell, *Owner*
Wayne Portell, *Co-Owner*
**EMP: 3**
**SQ FT: 1,000**
**SALES (est): 202.8K Privately Held**
SIC: 2396 5941 2395 7389 Screen printing on fabric articles; sporting goods & bicycle shops; pleating & stitching; embroidering of advertising on shirts, etc.

*(G-16465)*
### CENTURY PRINTING
510 Pepperwood Ct (62269-3059)
PHONE..........................618 632-2486
Fax: 618 235-3460
Gary Weldbacher, *President*
**EMP: 3**
**SQ FT: 4,000**
**SALES (est): 418.3K Privately Held**
SIC: 2752 7334 2791 2789 Commercial printing, lithographic; photocopying & duplicating services; typesetting; bookbinding & related work; commercial printing

*(G-16466)*
### DEMOND SIGNS INC
93 Betty Ln (62269-2234)
P.O. Box 414 (62269-0414)
PHONE..........................618 624-7260
Fax: 618 624-8240
Sue Demond, *President*
**EMP: 10**
**SQ FT: 2,800**
**SALES (est): 1.4MM Privately Held**
WEB: www.demondsigns.com
SIC: 3993 1799 Electric signs; sign installation & maintenance

*(G-16467)*
### EAT INVESTMENTS LLC
Also Called: Chocolate Chocolate Chocolate
3960 Green Mt (62269)
PHONE..........................618 624-5350
Fax: 618 624-5351
Tyler Tschannen, *Mng Member*
**EMP: 20 EST: 2012**
**SALES (est): 1.4MM Privately Held**
SIC: 2064 Candy bars, including chocolate covered bars

*(G-16468)*
### JARVIS ELECTRIC
1017 Hartman Ln (62269-7207)
PHONE..........................618 806-2767
**EMP: 3**
**SALES (est): 106.9K Privately Held**
SIC: 3699 Electrical equipment & supplies

*(G-16469)*
### KVD ENTERPRISES LLC
Also Called: Kvd Sewer
1392 Frontage Rd Ste 10 (62269-2086)
PHONE..........................618 726-5114
Raymond Kelly,
**EMP: 3 EST: 2008**
**SALES (est): 261.7K Privately Held**
SIC: 1623 3531 1794 Water & sewer line construction; plows: construction, excavating & grading; excavation & grading, building construction

*(G-16470)*
### LICKENBROCK & SONS INC
328 W State St (62269-1199)
PHONE..........................618 632-4977
Gary H Lickenbrock, *President*
Craig Lickenbrock, *Corp Secy*
**EMP: 4 EST: 1946**
**SQ FT: 4,000**
**SALES: 100K Privately Held**
SIC: 5051 5084 3446 3441 Iron & steel (ferrous) products; welding machinery & equipment; architectural metalwork; fabricated structural metal

*(G-16471)*
### METROEAST MOTORSPORTS INC
1714 Frontage Rd (62269-1845)
PHONE..........................618 628-2466
Ladonna Boyd, *Co-Owner*
Bret Boyd, *Co-Owner*
**EMP: 8**
**SQ FT: 5,000**
**SALES (est): 101.3K Privately Held**
SIC: 7694 5561 5571 7699 Motor repair services; recreational vehicle dealers; motorcycle dealers; motorcycle repair service; engine repair & replacement, non-automotive

*(G-16472)*
### OFALLON PRESSURE CAST CO
1418 Frontage Rd (62269-1807)
PHONE..........................618 632-8694
Fax: 618 632-9239
Raymond Leveling, *Owner*
Carolyn Leveling, *Treasurer*
Douglas Leveling, *Manager*
**EMP: 5 EST: 1979**
**SQ FT: 2,920**
**SALES (est): 842.2K Privately Held**
SIC: 3363 Aluminum die-castings

*(G-16473)*
### PET OFALLON LLC
610 E State St (62269-1538)
P.O. Box 940 (62269-0940)
PHONE..........................618 628-3300
Leonard O Jackson, *Mng Member*
Tammy Vernier, *Info Tech Mgr*
Eric Blanchard,
Robert D Dunn,
Neil Finerty,
**EMP: 72**
**SALES (est): 26.1MM Publicly Held**
WEB: www.deanfoods.com
SIC: 2026 Fluid milk
PA: Dean Foods Company
  2711 N Haskell Ave
  Dallas TX 75204

*(G-16474)*
### PLUMBERS SUPPLY CO ST LOUIS
6700 Old Collinsville Rd (62269-1883)
PHONE..........................618 624-5151
John Dubuque, *Manager*
**EMP: 6**
**SALES (corp-wide): 57.3MM Privately Held**
SIC: 3432 Plumbing fixture fittings & trim
PA: Plumbers Supply Company Of St Louis
  12012 Manchester Rd
  Saint Louis MO 63131
  314 984-0440

*(G-16475)*
### PPG INDUSTRIES INC
Also Called: PPG 4611
1333 Central Park Dr # 135 (62269-1775)
PHONE..........................618 206-2250
Hirchel Hill, *Branch Mgr*
**EMP: 4**
**SALES (corp-wide): 14.7B Publicly Held**
WEB: www.ppg.com
SIC: 2851 Paints & allied products
PA: Ppg Industries, Inc.
  1 Ppg Pl
  Pittsburgh PA 15272
  412 434-3131

*(G-16476)*
### PRAIRIE FARMS DAIRY INC
400 W Highway 50 (62269-2403)
P.O. Box 338 (62269-0338)
PHONE..........................618 632-3632
Fax: 618 632-9828
Rich McClain, *QA Dir*
Pat Hedger, *Branch Mgr*
Timothy Adair, *Prgrmr*
Mike Mennerick, *Director*
**EMP: 34**
**SALES (corp-wide): 1.8B Privately Held**
WEB: www.prairiefarms.com
SIC: 2026 2024 Milk processing (pasteurizing, homogenizing, bottling); ice cream & frozen desserts
PA: Prairie Farms Dairy, Inc.
  1100 Broadway
  Carlinville IL 62626
  217 854-2547

*(G-16477)*
### SAMS WEST INC
Also Called: Sams Pharmacy
1350 W Highway 50 (62269-1615)
PHONE..........................618 622-0507
Fax: 618 632-8002
David D Glass, *President*
**EMP: 8**
**SALES (est): 840K Privately Held**
SIC: 2834 Pharmaceutical preparations

*(G-16478)*
### SECURE DATA INC
640 Pierce Blvd Ste 200 (62269-2584)
PHONE..........................618 726-5225
Fax: 618 622-0419
Raymond Kelly, *President*
Chris Nazetta, *President*
Brad Howton, *Software Engr*
Aaron Broyles, *Admin Sec*
Jeff Berling, *Administration*
**EMP: 13**
**SQ FT: 5,000**
**SALES (est): 2MM Privately Held**
SIC: 7371 8741 7372 Custom computer programming services; business management; application computer software

*(G-16479)*
### SPRECTRA GRAPHICS INC
115 N Lincoln Ave (62269-1414)
PHONE..........................618 624-6776
Wayne Portell, *President*
**EMP: 5**
**SALES (est): 212.2K Privately Held**
SIC: 2759 Screen printing

*(G-16480)*
### ST CLAIR TENNIS CLUB LLC
Also Called: Saint Clair Tennis Club
733 Hartman Ln (62269-1729)
P.O. Box 1034 (62269-8034)
PHONE..........................618 632-1400
Fax: 618 632-1500
David T Threlkeld,
Carolyn M Mc Laughlin,
William R Rusick,
**EMP: 6 EST: 1969**
**SQ FT: 40,000**
**SALES (est): 240K Privately Held**
SIC: 7997 5941 7999 2951 Tennis club, membership; tennis goods & equipment; tennis courts, outdoor/indoor: non-membership; asphalt paving mixtures & blocks

*(G-16481)*
### TRI-COR INDUSTRIES INC
1035 Eastgate Dr Ste 2 (62269-3749)
PHONE..........................618 589-9890
Fax: 618 632-9805
Scott Parker, *Branch Mgr*
**EMP: 100**
**SALES (corp-wide): 33.1MM Privately Held**
WEB: www.tricorind.com
SIC: 7373 7374 3571 3577 Systems integration services; data processing service; electronic computers; computer peripheral equipment
PA: Tri-Cor Industries, Inc.
  2850 Eisenhower Ave # 300
  Alexandria VA 22314
  571 458-3824

*(G-16482)*
### ZAPP NOODLE
1407 W Highway 50 Ste 106 (62269-1672)
PHONE..........................618 979-8863
**EMP: 4 EST: 2010**
**SALES (est): 264K Privately Held**
SIC: 2098 Noodles (e.g. egg, plain & water), dry

## Oak Brook
### *Dupage County*

*(G-16483)*
### 2000PLUS GROUPS INC
2607 W 22nd St Ste 39 (60523-1231)
PHONE..........................630 528-3220
Ahmad A Adam, *President*
**EMP: 5**
**SALES (corp-wide): 26.1MM Privately Held**
SIC: 2015 Poultry slaughtering & processing; duck slaughtering & processing; poultry sausage, luncheon meats & other poultry products
PA: 2000plus Groups, Inc.
  4343 W 44th Pl
  Chicago IL 60632
  800 939-6268

*(G-16484)*
### ACE METAL REFINISHERS INC
2001 Spring Rd (60523-1812)
PHONE..........................800 323-7147
Gordon R Swanson, *Branch Mgr*
**EMP: 12**
**SALES (corp-wide): 3.3MM Privately Held**
SIC: 3471 Cleaning & descaling metal products
PA: Ace Metal Refinishers, Inc.
  978 N Dupage Ave
  Lombard IL 60148
  630 778-9200

*(G-16485)*
### ALAN ROCCA LTD
Also Called: Alan Rocca Fine Jewelry
3824 York Rd Ste B (60523-2753)
PHONE..........................630 323-5800
Alan Rocca, *President*
Greta Cucarese, *Engineer*
Jeff Liebich, *Manager*
**EMP: 20**
**SQ FT: 1,800**
**SALES: 3MM Privately Held**
WEB: www.alanrocca.com
SIC: 3911 5944 Jewelry, precious metal; jewelry, precious stones & precious metals

*(G-16486)*
### ALEX AND ANI LLC
100 Oakbrook Ctr (60523-1838)
PHONE..........................630 574-2329
**EMP: 7 Privately Held**
SIC: 3915 Jewelers' materials & lapidary work
PA: Alex And Ani, Llc
  2000 Chapel View Blvd # 360
  Cranston RI 02920

*(G-16487)*
### ALPINE ENERGY SYSTEMS LLC
700 Commerce Dr Ste 500 (60523-8736)
PHONE..........................630 581-4840
Ben Leung, *CTO*
Michael Wood,
**EMP: 3**
**SALES (est): 104.1K Privately Held**
SIC: 7372 Utility computer software

*(G-16488)*
### AMERICAN ELECTRONIC PDTS INC
2001 Midwest Rd Ste 105 (60523-1377)
PHONE..........................630 889-9977
Bo Zhang, *Ch of Bd*
▲ **EMP: 10**
**SQ FT: 1,100**

# Oak Brook - Dupage County (G-16489)  GEOGRAPHIC SECTION

**SALES (est):** 1.1MM **Privately Held**
**SIC:** 3594 3621 3629 3321 Fluid power pumps & motors; torque motors, electric; capacitors, a.c., for motors or fluorescent lamp ballasts; gray iron castings; aluminum die-castings

### (G-16489)
### ART OF SHAVING - FL LLC
100 Oakbrook Ctr (60523-1838)
**PHONE**..................630 684-0277
**EMP:** 3
**SALES (corp-wide):** 65.3B **Publicly Held**
**SIC:** 2844 Toilet preparations
**HQ:** The Art Of Shaving - Fl Llc
6100 Blue Lagoon Dr # 150
Miami FL 33126

### (G-16490)
### AUDIO TECH BUS BK SUMMARIES
1314 Kensington Rd # 4953 (60523-2131)
**PHONE**..................630 734-0500
**Fax:** 630 734-0600
Fred Rogers, *President*
Sue Carman, *Accountant*
**EMP:** 5
**SQ FT:** 4,000
**SALES:** 750K **Privately Held**
**WEB:** www.businessbooksummaries.com
**SIC:** 2731 Books: publishing only

### (G-16491)
### BAY VALLEY FOODS LLC
2021 Spring Rd Ste 600 (60523-1860)
**PHONE**..................708 409-5300
Harry Welsch, *Manager*
Diane Griesbach, *Manager*
**EMP:** 48
**SALES (corp-wide):** 6.1B **Publicly Held**
**SIC:** 2099 Food preparations
**HQ:** Bay Valley Foods, Llc
3200 Riverside Dr Ste A
Green Bay WI 54301
800 558-4700

### (G-16492)
### BENESSERE VINEYARD INC (PA)
2100 Clearwater Dr # 250 (60523-1927)
**PHONE**..................708 560-9840
John J Benish Jr, *CEO*
Marco Marino, *Vice Pres*
**EMP:** 1
**SALES (est):** 748.5K **Privately Held**
**WEB:** www.benesserevineyards.com
**SIC:** 2084 Wines

### (G-16493)
### BLISTEX INC (PA)
1800 Swift Dr (60523-1574)
**PHONE**..................630 571-2870
**Fax:** 630 571-3437
David C Arch, *Ch of Bd*
Michael J Donnantuono, *President*
Phillip J Hoolehan, *Vice Pres*
Michael A Wojcik, *Vice Pres*
Beatrice Spaine, *Research*
◆ **EMP:** 175 EST: 1947
**SQ FT:** 87,500
**SALES (est):** 57.4MM **Privately Held**
**WEB:** www.blistex.com
**SIC:** 2834 Ointments; lip balms; antiseptics, medicinal

### (G-16494)
### BLISTEX INC
100 Windsor Dr (60523-1506)
**PHONE**..................630 571-2870
Jackie Elliott, *Manager*
**EMP:** 4
**SALES (corp-wide):** 57.4MM **Privately Held**
**SIC:** 2834 Ointments
**PA:** Blistex Inc.
1800 Swift Dr
Oak Brook IL 60523
630 571-2870

### (G-16495)
### BUHLWORK DESIGN GUILD
320 Luthin Rd (60523-2791)
**PHONE**..................630 325-5340
Russell A Bulin, *President*
Russell Bulin, *President*
Ronald J Bulin, *Corp Secy*
Jeff Bulin, *Vice Pres*

Ross Pagliaro, *Purchasing*
**EMP:** 2
**SQ FT:** 7,600
**SALES:** 500K **Privately Held**
**SIC:** 2599 7389 Restaurant furniture, wood or metal; hotel furniture; bowling establishment furniture; interior design services

### (G-16496)
### BUZZFIRE INCORPORATED
2625 Bttrfeld Rd Ste 230s (60523)
**PHONE**..................630 572-9200
Randal Zahora, *President*
**EMP:** 15
**SQ FT:** 10,000
**SALES:** 2.9MM **Privately Held**
**SIC:** 1731 4813 5099 5999 Voice, data & video wiring contractor; telephone/video communications; video & audio equipment; audio-visual equipment & supplies; audio electronic systems; tapes, audio & video recording

### (G-16497)
### C B E INC
110 Oak Brook Rd (60523-2314)
**PHONE**..................630 571-2610
Clair Buffardi, *President*
Louis Buffardi,
**EMP:** 3
**SALES (est):** 493.3K **Privately Held**
**SIC:** 5199 2299 General merchandise, non-durable; gifts & novelties; fabrics: linen, jute, hemp, ramie

### (G-16498)
### CHAMBERLAIN GROUP INC
300 Windsor Dr (60523-1510)
**PHONE**..................630 833-0618
**EMP:** 7
**SALES (corp-wide):** 1.4B **Privately Held**
**SIC:** 3699 Door opening & closing devices, electrical
**HQ:** The Chamberlain Group Inc
300 Windsor Dr
Oak Brook IL 60523
630 279-3600

### (G-16499)
### CHAMBERLAIN GROUP INC (DH)
Also Called: Liftmaster
300 Windsor Dr (60523-1510)
**PHONE**..................630 279-3600
Joanna Sohovich, *CEO*
Craig J Duchossois, *Ch of Bd*
Robert I Baker, *President*
James J Roberts, *President*
Don Dombkowski, *Regional Mgr*
▲ **EMP:** 340
**SQ FT:** 62,000
**SALES:** 1.2B
**SALES (corp-wide):** 1.4B **Privately Held**
**WEB:** www.chamberlaingroup.com
**SIC:** 3699 Door opening & closing devices, electrical
**HQ:** Chamberlain Manufacturing Corporation
300 Windsor Dr
Oak Brook IL 60523
630 279-3600

### (G-16500)
### CHAMBERLAIN MANUFACTURING CORP (HQ)
300 Windsor Dr (60523-1510)
**PHONE**..................630 279-3600
Merton L Townsend, *Principal*
Richard L Duchossois, *Chairman*
Craig J Duchossois, *Vice Pres*
Alex Parsadayan, *Vice Pres*
Lee E Johnson, *CFO*
◆ **EMP:** 865
**SQ FT:** 62,000
**SALES (est):** 1.3B
**SALES (corp-wide):** 1.4B **Privately Held**
**WEB:** www.chamberlin.com
**SIC:** 3651 3625 3699 Household audio & video equipment; relays & industrial controls; door opening & closing devices, electrical
**PA:** The Duchossois Group Inc
300 Windsor Dr
Oak Brook IL 60523
630 279-3600

### (G-16501)
### CHICOR INC
2021 Midwest Rd Ste 200 (60523-1370)
**PHONE**..................630 953-6154
Jeff Chimienti, *Principal*
**EMP:** 2 EST: 1999
**SALES (est):** 237.7K **Privately Held**
**SIC:** 2211 Apparel & outerwear fabrics, cotton

### (G-16502)
### CONTECH ENGNERED SOLUTIONS LLC
1200 Harger Rd Ste 707 (60523-1821)
**PHONE**..................630 573-1110
**Fax:** 630 573-0079
A J Margetis, *Sales/Mktg Mgr*
**EMP:** 6 **Privately Held**
**SIC:** 3444 Pipe, sheet metal
**HQ:** Contech Engineered Solutions Llc
9025 Ctr Pinte Dr Ste 400
West Chester OH 45069
513 645-7000

### (G-16503)
### CSP INFORMATION GROUP INC
Also Called: CSP Magazine
1100 Jorie Blvd Ste 260 (60523-4431)
**PHONE**..................630 574-5075
**Fax:** 630 574-5175
Drayden McLane, *CEO*
Paul Reuder, *President*
Christine Lavelle, *Editor*
Rex Canon, *Exec VP*
Lynda Hislop, *Vice Pres*
**EMP:** 31
**SQ FT:** 3,200
**SALES (est):** 3.8MM
**SALES (corp-wide):** 5MM **Privately Held**
**WEB:** www.cspnet.com
**SIC:** 2721 Magazines: publishing only, not printed on site
**PA:** Ideal Media, Llc
200 E Randolph St # 7000
Chicago IL 60601
312 456-2822

### (G-16504)
### DUCHOSSOIS INDUSTRIES INC NON
300 Windsor Dr (60523-1510)
**PHONE**..................630 279-3600
**EMP:** 1
**SALES:** 8.5MM **Privately Held**
**SIC:** 3999 Manufacturing industries

### (G-16505)
### EDRINGTON GROUP USA LLC
1600 16th St (60523-1302)
**PHONE**..................630 701-9202
**EMP:** 38
**SALES (corp-wide):** 10.2MM **Privately Held**
**SIC:** 2084 Wines, brandy & brandy spirits
**PA:** The Edrington Group Usa Llc
150 5th Ave Fl 11
New York NY 10011
212 352-6000

### (G-16506)
### ELITE FIBER OPTICS LLC
616 Enterprise Dr Ste 102 (60523-4225)
**PHONE**..................630 225-9454
Helliwell John A, *Mng Member*
**EMP:** 21 EST: 2014
**SQ FT:** 6,000
**SALES (est):** 268.6K **Privately Held**
**SIC:** 3229 3661 Fiber optics strands; fiber optics communications equipment

### (G-16507)
### ELKAY PLUMBING PRODUCTS CO (HQ)
2222 Camden Ct (60523-1248)
**PHONE**..................630 574-8484
Timothy J Jahnke, *CEO*
Ronald C Katz, *Ch of Bd*
David Locklear, *Engineer*
John E Graves, *Admin Sec*
▲ **EMP:** 51
**SQ FT:** 90,000

**SALES (est):** 347.8MM
**SALES (corp-wide):** 1.1B **Privately Held**
**WEB:** www.elkayusa.com
**SIC:** 3431 Sinks: enameled iron, cast iron or pressed metal
**PA:** Elkay Manufacturing Company Inc
2222 Camden Ct
Oak Brook IL 60523
630 574-8484

### (G-16508)
### ELKAY VRGNIA DCRATIVE SURFACES
2222 Camden Ct (60523-1248)
**PHONE**..................630 574-8484
Tim Jahnke, *President*
**EMP:** 18
**SALES (est):** 1.2MM
**SALES (corp-wide):** 1.1B **Privately Held**
**SIC:** 3469 Kitchen fixtures & equipment, porcelain enameled
**PA:** Elkay Manufacturing Company Inc
2222 Camden Ct
Oak Brook IL 60523
630 574-8484

### (G-16509)
### ENGHOUSE INTERACTIVE INC
700 Commerce Dr Ste 100 (60523-1552)
**PHONE**..................630 472-9669
David McCrabb, *CEO*
Justin Phillips, *Technology*
Richard Briske, *Director*
**EMP:** 7
**SALES (corp-wide):** 236.6MM **Privately Held**
**SIC:** 3571 Electronic computers
**HQ:** Enghouse Interactive Inc.
2095 W Pinnacle Peak Rd # 110
Phoenix AZ 85027
602 789-2800

### (G-16510)
### FEDERAL SIGNAL CORPORATION (PA)
1415 W 22nd St Ste 1100 (60523-2004)
**PHONE**..................630 954-2000
**Fax:** 630 954-2030
Dennis J Martin, *Ch of Bd*
Jennifer L Sherman, *President*
Kevin Bruszewski, *Regional Mgr*
Matthew B Brady, *Senior VP*
Samuel E Miceli, *Senior VP*
◆ **EMP:** 54
**SALES:** 707.9MM **Publicly Held**
**WEB:** www.federalsignal.com
**SIC:** 3711 3647 3669 3559 Motor vehicles & car bodies; fire department vehicles (motor vehicles), assembly of; chassis, motor vehicle; ambulances (motor vehicles), assembly of; motor vehicle lighting equipment; dome lights, automotive; flasher lights, automotive; sirens, electric: vehicle, marine, industrial & air raid; parking facility equipment & supplies; special dies & tools; die sets for metal stamping (presses); punches, forming & stamping; cutting tools for machine tools

### (G-16511)
### FEDERAL SIGNAL CREDIT CORP
1415 W 22nd St Ste 1100 (60523-2004)
**PHONE**..................630 954-2000
**EMP:** 2
**SALES (est):** 202.9K **Privately Held**
**SIC:** 3711 Motor vehicles & car bodies

### (G-16512)
### FILTRATION GROUP LLC
600 W 22nd St Ste 300 (60523-1949)
**PHONE**..................630 968-1563
John Zyck, *General Mgr*
Reggie Murray, *Opers Staff*
Laura Deblasio, *Manager*
**EMP:** 58
**SALES (corp-wide):** 287MM **Privately Held**
**SIC:** 3564 Filters, air: furnaces, air conditioning equipment, etc.
**PA:** Filtration Group Llc
912 E Washington St Ste 1
Joliet IL 60433
815 726-4600

## GEOGRAPHIC SECTION

### Oak Brook - Dupage County (G-16536)

**(G-16513)**
**FIVECUBITS INC (HQ)**
Also Called: Bmg Seltec
1315 W 22nd St Ste 300 (60523-2062)
PHONE....................630 749-4182
John Jazwiec, *President*
Troy Carriker, *Managing Dir*
Judy Guenther, *Managing Dir*
Tim Conroy, *Exec VP*
Rob Getz, *Vice Pres*
**EMP:** 2
**SQ FT:** 3,800
**SALES (est):** 8.1MM
**SALES (corp-wide):** 91.7MM **Privately Held**
**WEB:** www.fivecubits.com
**SIC:** 7372 Business oriented computer software
**PA:** Command Alkon Incorporated
   1800 Intl Pk Dr Ste 400
   Birmingham AL 35243
   205 879-3282

**(G-16514)**
**FIVECUBITS INC**
1315 W 22nd St Ste 300 (60523-2062)
PHONE....................925 273-1862
Bob Bratt, *Branch Mgr*
**EMP:** 12
**SALES (corp-wide):** 91.7MM **Privately Held**
**SIC:** 3625 Electric controls & control accessories, industrial
**HQ:** Fivecubits Inc.
   1315 W 22nd St Ste 300
   Oak Brook IL 60523
   630 749-4182

**(G-16515)**
**FLYERINC CORPORATION**
Also Called: Chicago Direct Mail
700 Commerce Dr Ste 500 (60523-8736)
PHONE....................630 655-3400
Scott Jonlich, *President*
Dan Jonlich, *Vice Pres*
**EMP:** 7
**SQ FT:** 1,200
**SALES (est):** 690.5K **Privately Held**
**SIC:** 2752 7331 8742 Promotional printing, lithographic; direct mail advertising services; marketing consulting services

**(G-16516)**
**FORESTREE INC**
Also Called: Alliance Commodities Illinois
2021 Midwest Rd Ste 200 (60523-1370)
PHONE....................708 598-8789
Carmen C Lay, *President*
Ray W Lay, *Vice Pres*
▲ **EMP:** 5
**SQ FT:** 1,000
**SALES (est):** 11.3MM **Privately Held**
**SIC:** 2671 Plastic film, coated or laminated for packaging

**(G-16517)**
**G & K BAKING LLC**
16 Olympia Ct (60523-1618)
PHONE....................630 415-8687
Meyer Kathleen T, *Principal*
**EMP:** 4
**SALES (est):** 230.1K **Privately Held**
**SIC:** 2051 Bread, cake & related products

**(G-16518)**
**G & S PALLETS**
66 Windsor Dr (60523-2365)
PHONE....................630 574-2741
**EMP:** 4 **EST:** 2011
**SALES (est):** 234.8K **Privately Held**
**SIC:** 2448 Pallets, wood & wood with metal

**(G-16519)**
**GENERAL ELECTRIC COMPANY**
2015 Spring Rd Ste 400 (60523-1865)
PHONE....................630 334-0054
David Chiesa, *Manager*
**EMP:** 50
**SALES (corp-wide):** 123.6B **Publicly Held**
**SIC:** 3613 Switches, electric power except snap, push button, etc.; circuit breakers, air; power circuit breakers
**PA:** General Electric Company
   41 Farnsworth St
   Boston MA 02210
   617 443-3000

**(G-16520)**
**GRAND SPECIALTIES CO**
110 Oakbrook Ctr (60523-1808)
PHONE....................630 629-8000
Anthony M Sasgen Jr, *President*
George Sundheim, *Admin Sec*
**EMP:** 13 **EST:** 1920
**SQ FT:** 12,000
**SALES (est):** 920K **Privately Held**
**WEB:** www.grandspecialties.com
**SIC:** 3537 3429 3594 Lift trucks, industrial: fork, platform, straddle, etc.; cranes, industrial truck; builders' hardware; fluid power pumps & motors

**(G-16521)**
**HICKMAN WILLIAMS & COMPANY**
2015 Spring Rd Ste 715 (60523-1897)
P.O. Box 5225 (60522-5225)
PHONE....................630 574-2150
**Fax:** 630 574-2376
Steve Stark, *General Mgr*
William Snyder, *Principal*
John Jennings, *Sales Engr*
Amanda Brown, *Sales Associate*
Angela Pruitt, *Sales Associate*
**EMP:** 12
**SALES (corp-wide):** 195.8MM **Privately Held**
**WEB:** www.hicwilco.com
**SIC:** 3313 5051 Alloys, additive, except copper: not made in blast furnaces; metals service centers & offices
**PA:** Hickman, Williams & Company
   250 E 5th St Ste 300
   Cincinnati OH 45202
   513 621-1946

**(G-16522)**
**HS TECHNOLOGY INC**
900 Jorie Blvd Ste 195 (60523-0944)
PHONE....................630 572-7650
**Fax:** 630 572-7653
Peter Cox, *Managing Dir*
Tim Young, *Manager*
Simpson Mark, *Info Tech Mgr*
John Staiano, *Director*
**EMP:** 3
**SALES (est):** 397.6K
**SALES (corp-wide):** 8.3MM **Privately Held**
**WEB:** www.harlandsimon.com
**SIC:** 2711 3699 Newspapers; security control equipment & systems
**PA:** Harland Simon Public Limited Company
   Bond Avenue
   Milton Keynes BUCKS MK1 1
   190 827-6700

**(G-16523)**
**HYDROPHI TECH GROUP INC**
1000 Jorie Blvd Ste 250 (60523-2233)
PHONE....................630 981-0098
Nikola Zaric, *President*
Sagiv Israeli, *COO*
**EMP:** 2 **EST:** 2010
**SALES (est):** 278K **Privately Held**
**SIC:** 2911 Fuel additives

**(G-16524)**
**IBS CONVERSIONS INC**
2625 Bttrfeld Rd Ste 114w (60523)
PHONE....................630 571-9100
**Fax:** 630 571-0723
Daniel Williams, *CEO*
Frank Carroll, *Controller*
Roger Byrnes, *Director*
**EMP:** 88
**SALES (est):** 7.3MM
**SALES (corp-wide):** 64.2MM **Privately Held**
**WEB:** www.ibs.com
**SIC:** 3577 7378 Data conversion equipment, media-to-media: computer; computer maintenance & repair
**PA:** Interactive Business Systems, Inc.
   2625 Bttrfeld Rd Ste 114w
   Oak Brook IL 60523
   630 571-9100

**(G-16525)**
**INTEGRATED MDSG SYSTEMS LLC**
Also Called: Group II Communications
1111 W 22nd St Ste 600 (60523-1986)
PHONE....................630 571-2020
Tim Leahy, *Vice Pres*
Ann Okeefe, *Branch Mgr*
**EMP:** 55
**SALES (corp-wide):** 15.4B **Publicly Held**
**SIC:** 3993 Signs & advertising specialties
**HQ:** Integrated Merchandising Systems Llc
   8338 Austin Ave
   Morton Grove IL 60053
   847 583-3800

**(G-16526)**
**INTERNTIONAL EQP SOLUTIONS LLC (HQ)**
Also Called: Ies
2211 York Rd Ste 320 (60523-4030)
PHONE....................630 570-6880
Steve Andrews, *CEO*
Deanna Roll, *Vice Pres*
Steve Klyn, *CFO*
Jeff Dawson, *Controller*
Erin Crawford, *Human Resources*
▲ **EMP:** 66
**SALES (est):** 626.7MM
**SALES (corp-wide):** 2.3B **Privately Held**
**SIC:** 3531 Cabs, for construction machinery
**PA:** Kps Capital Partners, Lp
   485 Lexington Ave Fl 31
   New York NY 10017
   212 338-5100

**(G-16527)**
**JOHNSON CONTROLS INC**
78 Oakbrook Ctr (60523-1874)
PHONE....................630 573-0897
Dan Ellis, *Manager*
**EMP:** 91
**SALES (corp-wide):** 36.8B **Privately Held**
**SIC:** 2531 Seats, automobile
**PA:** Johnson Controls, Inc.
   5757 N Green Bay Ave
   Milwaukee WI 53209
   414 524-1200

**(G-16528)**
**JONES MEDICAL INSTRUMENT CO**
200 Windsor Dr Ste A (60523-1597)
PHONE....................630 571-1980
**Fax:** 630 571-2023
Bill Jones, *President*
Scott Jones, *Purch Mgr*
**EMP:** 20 **EST:** 1919
**SQ FT:** 20,000
**SALES (est):** 3.2MM **Privately Held**
**SIC:** 3841 3845 3829 Surgical & medical instruments; electromedical equipment; measuring & controlling devices

**(G-16529)**
**JRB ATTACHMENTS LLC**
Also Called: Paladin
2211 York Rd Ste 320 (60523-4030)
PHONE....................319 378-3696
Dave Burdakin, *Manager*
**EMP:** 9
**SALES (est):** 2.2MM **Privately Held**
**SIC:** 3531 Construction machinery

**(G-16530)**
**KANAN FASHIONS INC (PA)**
1010 Jorie Blvd Ste 324 (60523-2241)
PHONE....................630 240-1234
**Fax:** 630 833-1237
Mehul R Shah, *President*
Paresh R Joshi, *CFO*
Juanita Pacheco, *Merchandise Mgr*
▲ **EMP:** 25
**SQ FT:** 8,588
**SALES (est):** 2MM **Privately Held**
**WEB:** www.kananfashions.com
**SIC:** 2325 Men's & boys' trousers & slacks

**(G-16531)**
**KELLOGG COMPANY**
700 Commerce Dr Ste 400 (60523-1554)
PHONE....................630 820-9457
Carlos Gutierrez, *CEO*
Jeff Boser, *Vice Pres*
Tammy Sherer, *Manager*
**EMP:** 28
**SALES (corp-wide):** 13B **Publicly Held**
**SIC:** 2043 Cereal breakfast foods
**PA:** Kellogg Company
   1 Kellogg Sq
   Battle Creek MI 49017
   269 961-2000

**(G-16532)**
**L & H COMPANY INC (PA)**
Also Called: Meade Electric Co
2215 York Rd Ste 304 (60523-4004)
PHONE....................630 571-7200
John S Lizzadro, *President*
Maribel Gariday, *Accountant*
Rose Naegele, *Manager*
Alan L Shulman, *Admin Sec*
**EMP:** 10 **EST:** 1980
**SQ FT:** 18,000
**SALES (est):** 350.2MM **Privately Held**
**WEB:** www.lhcompany.com
**SIC:** 1731 1611 1623 3621 Electrical work; lighting contractor; general contractor, highway & street construction; oil & gas pipeline construction; motors, electric

**(G-16533)**
**LEARNING CURVE INTERNATIONAL (DH)**
1111 W 22nd St Ste 320 (60523-1935)
PHONE....................630 573-7200
**Fax:** 630 573-7575
Richard E Rothcopf, *Ch of Bd*
Peter Henseler, *President*
Greg Kilrea, *COO*
Richard Rothkopf, *Exec VP*
Tom Knaggs, *Vice Pres*
◆ **EMP:** 50
**SQ FT:** 15,000
**SALES (est):** 21.9MM
**SALES (corp-wide):** 1.3B **Privately Held**
**WEB:** www.learningcurve.com
**SIC:** 5092 2389 Educational toys; costumes
**HQ:** Tomy International, Inc.
   2021 9th St Se
   Dyersville IA 52040
   563 875-2000

**(G-16534)**
**LEVOLOR WINDOW FURNISHINGS INC**
Also Called: Newell
2707 Butterfield Rd (60523-1278)
PHONE....................800 346-3278
**EMP:** 3 **Privately Held**
**SIC:** 2591 Window blinds
**HQ:** Levolor Window Furnishings, Inc.
   1 Blue Hill Plz
   Pearl River NY 10965

**(G-16535)**
**LEX HOLDING CO**
1400 16th St Ste 250 (60523-8802)
PHONE....................708 594-9200
Robert S Douglass, *CEO*
Tim McFarland, *President*
Paul Douglass, *COO*
**EMP:** 6 **EST:** 2013
**SALES (est):** 523.6K **Privately Held**
**SIC:** 3317 Steel pipe & tubes

**(G-16536)**
**LEXINGTON STEEL CORPORATION**
Also Called: Lexcentral Steel
1400 16th St Ste 250 (60523-8802)
PHONE....................708 594-9200
**Fax:** 708 594-5233
Robert S Douglass, *CEO*
Timothy M McFarland, *President*
Mr William Douglass, *General Mgr*
Mr Robert Blumenschein, *Vice Pres*
Mr William Huyser, *Vice Pres*
**EMP:** 85
**SQ FT:** 94,000
**SALES (est):** 68MM **Privately Held**
**WEB:** www.lexsteel.com
**SIC:** 5051 3312 Steel; blast furnaces & steel mills

## Oak Brook - Dupage County (G-16537)

**(G-16537)**
**LIFTSEAT CORPORATION**
2001 Midwest Rd Ste 204  (60523-4308)
PHONE..................................630 424-2840
Gregory C Kilgore, *Principal*
**EMP:** 20
**SQ FT:** 4,000
**SALES (est):** 3.2MM  Privately Held
**WEB:** www.liftseat.com
**SIC:** 2499  Seats, toilet

**(G-16538)**
**MADE AS INTENDED INC**
Also Called: MAI Apparel
3423 Spring Rd  (60523-2739)
PHONE..................................630 789-3494
Ray Sproug, *CEO*
Heather Reizner, *Opers Mgr*
Ray Sprong, *CFO*
**EMP:** 11
**SALES (est):** 830K  Privately Held
**SIC:** 3911  7389  Jewelry, precious metal;

**(G-16539)**
**MC ADAMS MULTIGRAPHICS INC**
900 Jorie Blvd Ste 26  (60523-3852)
PHONE..................................630 990-1707
**Fax:** 630 990-1730
Dennis Mc Adams, *President*
Nancy Mc Adams, *Vice Pres*
Nancy McAdams, *Vice Pres*
**EMP:** 8
**SQ FT:** 2,500
**SALES:** 750K  Privately Held
**WEB:** www.mcadamsmultigraphics.com
**SIC:** 2752  2791  Commercial printing, offset; typesetting

**(G-16540)**
**MEDCORE INTERNATIONAL LLC**
900 Jorie Blvd Ste 220  (60523-3846)
PHONE..................................630 645-9900
Allison Deboer, *President*
**EMP:** 9
**SQ FT:** 4,200
**SALES (est):** 782.8K  Privately Held
**SIC:** 8741  8742  7372  Management services; hospital & health services consultant; educational computer software

**(G-16541)**
**MEDPLAST GROUP INC**
1520 Kensington Rd # 313  (60523-2139)
PHONE..................................630 706-5500
**Fax:** 630 706-5510
John Mitchell, *General Mgr*
Mat Langton, *VP Sales*
Matthew Strebe, *CIO*
**EMP:** 425
**SALES (corp-wide):** 455.3MM  Privately Held
**WEB:** www.unitedplasticsgroup.com
**SIC:** 3089  Injection molded finished plastic products
**PA:** Medplast Group, Inc.
      7865 Northcourt Rd # 100
      Houston TX 77040
      480 553-6400

**(G-16542)**
**METAL CENTER NEWS**
1100 Jorie Blvd Ste 207  (60523-4423)
PHONE..................................630 571-1067
Nancy Hartley, *Principal*
Tim Triplett, *Editor*
Carol Davies, *Art Dir*
**EMP:** 12
**SALES (est):** 700.5K  Privately Held
**SIC:** 2721  Magazines: publishing & printing

**(G-16543)**
**MICHAELS ROSS AND COLE INC (PA)**
Also Called: M R C
2001 Midwest Rd Ste 310  (60523-1340)
PHONE..................................630 916-0662
**Fax:** 630 916-0663
Joseph Stangarone, *President*
Steve Hansen, *Mktg Dir*
Brian Duffey, *Consultant*
Tracy Paulauski, *Network Mgr*
**EMP:** 13
**SALES (est):** 3.4MM  Privately Held
**WEB:** www.mrc-productivity.com
**SIC:** 5045  7372  Computer software; prepackaged software

**(G-16544)**
**MICRON INDUSTRIES CORPORATION (PA)**
Also Called: Micron Power
1211 W 22nd St Ste 200  (60523-3226)
PHONE..................................630 516-1222
Donald R Clark, *President*
David Long, *Vice Pres*
Mark Castonguay, *Opers Staff*
Dale Wagner, *QC Mgr*
Eric Mickelson, *Engineer*
▲ **EMP:** 16
**SQ FT:** 12,000
**SALES (est):** 23.4MM  Privately Held
**WEB:** www.microntransformers.com
**SIC:** 3612  Control transformers; power transformers, electric; specialty transformers

**(G-16545)**
**MINUTEMAN PRESS INTL INC**
1301 W 22nd St Ste 709  (60523-2070)
PHONE..................................630 574-0090
Thomas E Davis, *Manager*
**EMP:** 3
**SALES (corp-wide):** 23.4MM  Privately Held
**SIC:** 2752  Commercial printing, lithographic
**PA:** Minuteman Press International, Inc.
      61 Executive Blvd
      Farmingdale NY 11735
      631 249-1370

**(G-16546)**
**MOTOROLA SOLUTIONS INC**
2301 W 22nd St Ste 102  (60523-1222)
PHONE..................................847 341-3485
Gary Birkland, *Branch Mgr*
**EMP:** 5
**SALES (corp-wide):** 6B  Publicly Held
**WEB:** www.motorola.com
**SIC:** 3663  3674  3571  3812  Radio & TV communications equipment; semiconductors & related devices; electronic computers; search & navigation equipment
**PA:** Motorola Solutions, Inc.
      500 W Monroe St Ste 4400
      Chicago IL 60661
      847 576-5000

**(G-16547)**
**NORTH AMERICA PACKAGING CORP (DH)**
Also Called: Nampac
1515 W 22nd St Ste 550  (60523-8742)
PHONE..................................630 203-4100
Tom Linton, *President*
Danny Byrne, *Vice Pres*
Suzanne Bruen, *Manager*
▼ **EMP:** 24
**SQ FT:** 8,100
**SALES (est):** 208.1MM
**SALES (corp-wide):** 831.7MM  Privately Held
**WEB:** www.nampac.com
**SIC:** 3089  Plastic containers, except foam
**HQ:** Bway Corporation
      8607 Roberts Dr Ste 250
      Atlanta GA 30350
      770 645-4800

**(G-16548)**
**NOVIPAX LLC (HQ)**
2215 York Rd Ste 504  (60523-2379)
PHONE..................................630 686-2735
Bob Larson, *CEO*
Jeffrey Williams, *CFO*
Brian Bezanson, *Controller*
**EMP:** 16  **EST:** 2015
**SQ FT:** 10,000
**SALES (est):** 140.2MM
**SALES (corp-wide):** 1.7B  Privately Held
**SIC:** 2821  2299  Polystyrene resins; padding & wadding, textile
**PA:** Atlas Holdings, Llc
      100 Northfield St
      Greenwich CT 06830
      203 622-9138

**(G-16549)**
**NOVO SURGICAL INC**
700 Comme Dr Ste 500 No 1  (60523)
PHONE..................................877 860-6686
Abed Moiduddin, *President*
**EMP:** 10
**SQ FT:** 7,500
**SALES (est):** 1.9MM  Privately Held
**SIC:** 3841  Instruments, microsurgical: except electromedical

**(G-16550)**
**NRR CORP**
Also Called: Augustan
705 Deer Trail Ln  (60523-2782)
PHONE..................................630 915-8388
N A Naidu, *President*
N Athimoolan Naidu, *President*
Rajiv Naidu, *Vice Pres*
Renu Naidu, *Vice Pres*
▲ **EMP:** 12  **EST:** 1990
**SQ FT:** 13,000
**SALES (est):** 2.1MM  Privately Held
**WEB:** www.augustanusa.com
**SIC:** 5199  7213  2253  Bags, textile; apron supply; T-shirts & tops, knit

**(G-16551)**
**OEM SOLUTIONS INC**
Also Called: Oems
700 Commerce Dr Ste 500  (60523-8736)
PHONE..................................708 574-8893
Alejandro Mota, *Principal*
**EMP:** 5
**SALES (est):** 125K  Privately Held
**SIC:** 5065  3663  Sound equipment, electronic;

**(G-16552)**
**OFFICE SNAX INC**
125 Windsor Dr Ste 105  (60523-4075)
PHONE..................................630 789-1783
Todd Elmers, *CEO*
William Baker, *Exec VP*
Susan Burns, *Manager*
▲ **EMP:** 5  **EST:** 2001
**SQ FT:** 1,500
**SALES (est):** 438.8K  Privately Held
**WEB:** www.office.pricegrabber.com
**SIC:** 2064  Candy & other confectionery products

**(G-16553)**
**ORBIT ENTERPRISES INC**
3525 S Cass Ct Unit T3n  (60523-3727)
PHONE..................................630 469-3405
**Fax:** 630 469-4895
Joseph S Beda, *President*
**EMP:** 3
**SQ FT:** 1,300
**SALES (est):** 200K  Privately Held
**WEB:** www.digitize.com
**SIC:** 7372  3993  Utility computer software; signs & advertising specialties

**(G-16554)**
**PALADIN BRANDS INTERNATIONAL H**
2211 York Rd Ste 320  (60523-4030)
PHONE..................................319 378-3696
Jeff Winters, *Principal*
▲ **EMP:** 6
**SALES (est):** 1.5MM  Privately Held
**SIC:** 3531  Construction machinery

**(G-16555)**
**POWBAB INC**
1314 Kensington Rd # 3205  (60523-2131)
PHONE..................................630 481-6140
Tina Chan, *President*
**EMP:** 3  **EST:** 2012
**SALES (est):** 81.8K  Privately Held
**SIC:** 2834  Pharmaceutical preparations

**(G-16556)**
**PROCON PACIFIC LLC**
1200 Jorie Blvd Ste 235  (60523-2262)
PHONE..................................630 575-0551
Steven Dry, *CEO*
Adam Ruckh, *General Mgr*
Vanessa Rodriguez, *Manager*
Vanessa Rogriguez, *Manager*
▲ **EMP:** 11
**SALES (est):** 3.1MM  Privately Held
**SIC:** 2673  Plastic & pliofilm bags

**(G-16557)**
**PURECIRCLE USA INC**
915 Harger Rd Ste 250  (60523-1492)
PHONE..................................866 960-8242
**Fax:** 630 361-0384
Magomet Malsagov, *CEO*
Peter Milsted, *President*
Gordi Ferre, *COO*
Jordi Ferre, *Vice Pres*
William Mitchell, *CFO*
▲ **EMP:** 30
**SQ FT:** 7,000
**SALES:** 101MM  Privately Held
**SIC:** 2869  Sweeteners, synthetic
**HQ:** Purecircle Sdn. Bhd.
      Pt 23419 Lengkuk Technology Techpark
      Seremban NSB 71760

**(G-16558)**
**RANA MEAL SOLUTIONS LLC (HQ)**
Also Called: Giovanni Rana
1400 16th St Ste 275  (60523-8801)
PHONE..................................630 581-4100
Angelo Iantosca, *President*
Barbara Cola, *Corp Secy*
Alexis Ytell, *Finance*
▲ **EMP:** 209
**SQ FT:** 125,000
**SALES (est):** 140.4MM
**SALES (corp-wide):** 362.9MM  Privately Held
**SIC:** 2033  Spaghetti & other pasta sauce: packaged in cans, jars, etc.
**PA:** Pastificio Rana Spa
      Via Antonio Pacinotti 25
      San Giovanni Lupatoto VR 37057
      045 858-7311

**(G-16559)**
**RICHARDSON & EDWARDS INC**
303 Hambletonian Dr  (60523-2619)
PHONE..................................630 543-1818
**Fax:** 630 543-1887
Edward Kolodziej, *President*
Chris Klauser, *Vice Pres*
Michael Long, *Vice Pres*
Marie Long, *Admin Sec*
Kim Leffew, *Representative*
**EMP:** 38  **EST:** 1946
**SQ FT:** 48,000
**SALES (est):** 4.4MM
**SALES (corp-wide):** 44.3MM  Privately Held
**WEB:** www.richanded.com
**SIC:** 2752  Commercial printing, offset
**PA:** Transparent Container Co., Inc.
      325 S Lombard Rd
      Addison IL 60101
      708 449-8520

**(G-16560)**
**ROGER CANTU & ASSOCS**
1100 Jorie Blvd Ste 215  (60523-3025)
PHONE..................................630 573-9215
Roger Cantu, *President*
John Miceli, *Vice Pres*
**EMP:** 5
**SALES (est):** 450K  Privately Held
**WEB:** www.rcantu.com
**SIC:** 7372  Prepackaged software

**(G-16561)**
**STANDARD REGISTER INC**
900 Jorie Blvd Ste 238  (60523-3838)
P.O. Box 238, Hinsdale  (60522-0238)
PHONE..................................630 368-0336
David Caqatto, *Branch Mgr*
**EMP:** 9
**SALES (corp-wide):** 4.5B  Privately Held
**WEB:** www.stdreg.com
**SIC:** 2761  Manifold business forms
**HQ:** Standard Register, Inc.
      600 Albany St
      Dayton OH 45417
      937 221-1000

**(G-16562)**
**SYMANTEC CORPORATION**
2015 Spring Rd Ste 400  (60523-1865)
PHONE..................................630 706-4700
Bruce D Sprangers, *Principal*
Arya Barirani, *Manager*
**EMP:** 150

SALES (corp-wide): 4B **Publicly Held**
**WEB:** www.symantec.com
**SIC:** 7372 Prepackaged software
**PA:** Symantec Corporation
350 Ellis St
Mountain View CA 94043
650 527-8000

**(G-16563)**
**TAYLOR PRECISION PRODUCTS INC (HQ)**
2311 W 22nd St Ste 200 (60523-4100)
**PHONE** .................................630 954-1250
**Fax:** 630 954-1275
Rob Kay, *President*
Donald Robinson, *COO*
Patrick Bridges, *Vice Pres*
Jay Rabinowitz, *Vice Pres*
Shawn Kovach, *Credit Mgr*
▲ **EMP:** 18
**SQ FT:** 1,700
**SALES (est):** 46MM
**SALES (corp-wide):** 886.7MM **Privately Held**
**WEB:** www.taylorusa.com
**SIC:** 3829 3596 3823 Thermometers & temperature sensors; hydrometers, except industrial process type; barometers, mercury & aneroid types; humidity instruments, except industrial process type; scales & balances, except laboratory; industrial instrmnts msrmnt display/control process variable
**PA:** Centre Partners Management Llc
825 3rd Ave Fl 40
New York NY 10022
212 332-5800

**(G-16564)**
**TREBOR SALES CORPORATION (PA)**
2021 Midwest Rd Ste 307 (60523-4349)
**PHONE** .................................630 434-0040
John J Aprea, *President*
Michael Logan, *CFO*
Linda L Aprea, *Admin Sec*
◆ **EMP:** 16
**SQ FT:** 5,000
**SALES:** 10.3MM **Privately Held**
**SIC:** 3565 Packaging machinery

**(G-16565)**
**TREEHOUSE FOODS INC (PA)**
2021 Spring Rd Ste 600 (60523-1860)
**PHONE** .................................708 483-1300
**Fax:** 708 409-1062
Sam K Reed, *Ch of Bd*
Robert B Aiken, *President*
Rachel Bishop, *President*
Dennis F Riordan, *President*
Thomas E O'Neill, *Exec VP*
**EMP:** 277
**SALES:** 6.1B **Publicly Held**
**SIC:** 2035 2023 2032 2033 Pickles, sauces & salad dressings; cream substitutes; puddings, except meat: packaged in cans, jars, etc.; soups & broths: canned, jarred, etc.; jams, jellies & preserves: packaged in cans, jars, etc.; powders, drink

**(G-16566)**
**TWIN SUPPLIES LTD**
1010 Jorie Blvd Ste 124 (60523-4447)
**PHONE** .................................630 590-5138
Chris Skokna, *President*
**EMP:** 18
**SALES (est):** 1.9MM **Privately Held**
**SIC:** 1731 3646 3648 Electrical work; commercial indusl & institutional electric lighting fixtures; lighting equipment

**(G-16567)**
**VECTOR USA INC (HQ)**
Also Called: Vector Packaging
2021 Midwest Rd Ste 307 (60523-4349)
**PHONE** .................................630 434-0040
Peter Lancaster, *CEO*
Charlie Evert, *COO*
Sandra Lancaster, *Vice Pres*
Liz Ventrella, *Controller*
Stephanie Waldschmidt, *Finance*
◆ **EMP:** 15
**SQ FT:** 7,500
**SALES:** 24.1MM **Privately Held**
**SIC:** 3089 Food casings, plastic

**PA:** Vector International Sa
Rue De Beggen 8
Luxembourg
878 182-

**(G-16568)**
**VERTEX INTERNATIONAL INC**
2015 Spring Rd Ste 215 (60523-2073)
**PHONE** .................................312 242-1864
Ahmad Tayeh, *President*
**EMP:** 5
**SQ FT:** 1,008
**SALES (est):** 1.9MM **Privately Held**
**SIC:** 5136 5139 5087 2311 Uniforms, men's & boys'; footwear; firefighting equipment; military uniforms, men's & youths': purchased materials; field jackets, military

**(G-16569)**
**WESTERN PECE DYERS FNSHERS INC**
122 W 22nd St (60523-1598)
**PHONE** .................................773 523-7000
**Fax:** 773 523-0965
George J Renaldi III, *President*
George J Renaldi Jr, *Chairman*
Matt Novak, *Controller*
**EMP:** 2 **EST:** 1919
**SQ FT:** 140,000
**SALES (est):** 250K **Privately Held**
**WEB:** www.westernpiecedyers.com
**SIC:** 2261 Finishing plants, cotton; fire resistance finishing of cotton broadwoven fabrics; water repellency finishing of cotton broadwoven fabrics

**(G-16570)**
**XEROX CORPORATION**
2301 W 22nd St Ste 300 (60523-1224)
**PHONE** .................................630 573-0200
**Fax:** 630 572-9448
Christine Piemonte, *Human Resources*
Terry Lewis, *Mktg Dir*
Kevin Malone, *Manager*
**EMP:** 75
**SALES (corp-wide):** 10.7B **Publicly Held**
**WEB:** www.xerox.com
**SIC:** 3861 Photographic equipment & supplies
**PA:** Xerox Corporation
201 Merritt 7
Norwalk CT 06851
203 968-3000

## Oak Forest
### Cook County

**(G-16571)**
**3D FLIGHT SIMULATION CO**
15025 Ridgewood Dr (60452-1759)
**PHONE** .................................708 560-0701
**EMP:** 3
**SALES (est):** 204K **Privately Held**
**SIC:** 3443 Space simulation chambers, metal plate

**(G-16572)**
**ALABASTER BOX CREATIONS LLC**
15301 Kenton Ave (60452-2505)
**PHONE** .................................708 473-6880
Maritza Medernach, *Mng Member*
**EMP:** 3 **EST:** 2010
**SALES (est):** 169.7K **Privately Held**
**SIC:** 2064 Granola & muesli, bars & clusters

**(G-16573)**
**AMERICAN BLUE RBBON HLDNGS LLC**
Also Called: Legendary Baking
16425 Kilbourne Ave (60452-4602)
**PHONE** .................................708 687-7650
Randy Stone, *General Mgr*
Jill Stubbs, *Prdtn Mgr*
William Grifo, *Engineer*
Justin Mishler, *Sales Associate*
Chris Szekely, *Office Admin*
**EMP:** 87
**SALES (corp-wide):** 9.5B **Publicly Held**
**SIC:** 2051 Bakery: wholesale or wholesale/retail combined

**HQ:** American Blue Ribbon Holdings, Llc
3038 Sidco Dr
Nashville TN 37204

**(G-16574)**
**AWI / TITANIUM**
15146 Geoffrey Rd (60452-2022)
**PHONE** .................................708 263-9970
**EMP:** 3
**SALES (est):** 193.8K **Privately Held**
**SIC:** 3356 Titanium

**(G-16575)**
**CABINET DESIGNS**
15537 New England Ave (60452-1592)
**PHONE** .................................708 614-8603
Richard Vanderwarren, *President*
**EMP:** 3
**SQ FT:** 1,500
**SALES:** 400K **Privately Held**
**SIC:** 2434 2542 2541 Wood kitchen cabinets; vanities, bathroom: wood; counters or counter display cases: except wood; wood partitions & fixtures

**(G-16576)**
**CITY SPORTS & STAGE DOOR DANCE**
15801 Oak Park Ave (60452-1581)
**PHONE** .................................708 687-9950
Tom Starppeti, *Owner*
**EMP:** 20
**SALES (est):** 328.4K **Privately Held**
**SIC:** 7911 3949 Dance studios, schools & halls; sporting & athletic goods

**(G-16577)**
**DANS PRINTING & OFF SUPS INC**
Also Called: Daniels Printing & Office Sup
14800 Cicero Ave Ste 101 (60452-1458)
**PHONE** .................................708 687-3055
**Fax:** 708 687-9035
Pamela Vaclav, *President*
Daniel Vaclav Jr, *Corp Secy*
Bill Collins, *Senior VP*
**EMP:** 10
**SQ FT:** 8,800
**SALES:** 1.2MM **Privately Held**
**SIC:** 5943 2752 2759 5999 Office forms & supplies; writing supplies; commercial printing, offset; letterpress printing; business machines & equipment

**(G-16578)**
**E Z SIGN CO INC**
15347 Cicero Ave Rear (60452-2555)
**PHONE** .................................815 469-4080
**Fax:** 708 687-4081
Madelon Meents, *President*
Frederick Meents, *Corp Secy*
**EMP:** 5
**SQ FT:** 3,200
**SALES:** 400K **Privately Held**
**SIC:** 3993 7389 Signs & advertising specialties; sign painting & lettering shop; engraving service

**(G-16579)**
**ELIA DAY SPA**
5251 147th St Ste 3 (60452-1327)
**PHONE** .................................708 535-1450
**Fax:** 708 535-7611
**EMP:** 18
**SALES (est):** 800K **Privately Held**
**SIC:** 3999 5087 Mfg Misc Products Whol Service Establishment Equipment

**(G-16580)**
**EMERSON PROCESS MANAGEMENT**
4320 166th Ave (60452-4607)
**PHONE** .................................708 535-5120
Rich Perez, *Manager*
Pat Stickle, *Web Dvlpr*
▲ **EMP:** 60
**SALES (est):** 6.2MM **Privately Held**
**SIC:** 3491 3494 Gas valves & parts, industrial; valves & pipe fittings

**(G-16581)**
**FERNWOOD PRINTERS LTD**
14955 Mission Ave (60452-1308)
**PHONE** .................................630 964-9449
**Fax:** 773 233-4580

Thomas Gregor, *President*
Marie Gregor, *Admin Sec*
**EMP:** 4
**SQ FT:** 1,500
**SALES (est):** 290K **Privately Held**
**SIC:** 2752 2789 Commercial printing, offset; bookbinding & related work

**(G-16582)**
**FRITO-LAY NORTH AMERICA INC**
4170 166th St (60452-4600)
**PHONE** .................................708 331-7200
**Fax:** 708 331-7348
Denise Starcovic, *Opers Mgr*
Lino Carrillo, *Sales Mgr*
Pete Fiore, *Info Tech Mgr*
**EMP:** 200
**SALES (corp-wide):** 62.8B **Publicly Held**
**WEB:** www.fritolay.com
**SIC:** 5149 5145 2099 Pet foods; confectionery; food preparations
**HQ:** Frito-Lay North America, Inc.
7701 Legacy Dr
Plano TX 75024

**(G-16583)**
**IMPRESSION PRINTING**
4901 Lorin Ln (60452-1445)
**PHONE** .................................708 614-8660
**Fax:** 708 614-8008
Katherine Drechsel, *Owner*
Kathryn Drechsel, *Owner*
Ron Drechsel, *General Mgr*
Mary Kotnour, *Manager*
**EMP:** 10
**SQ FT:** 4,100
**SALES (est):** 1.3MM **Privately Held**
**SIC:** 2752 2759 2796 2789 Commercial printing, lithographic; letterpress printing; screen printing; platemaking services; bookbinding & related work; die-cut paper & board

**(G-16584)**
**IN-PRINT GRAPHICS INC (PA)**
Also Called: COPY WORKS
4201 166th St (60452-4608)
**PHONE** .................................708 396-1010
Joseph Racine Sr, *President*
John Vanderwey, *Principal*
Michael Ojermark, *COO*
Joseph Racine II, *Vice Pres*
John Rinozzi, *Vice Pres*
**EMP:** 30 **EST:** 1973
**SQ FT:** 20,000
**SALES:** 3.7MM **Privately Held**
**WEB:** www.in-printgraphics.com
**SIC:** 2752 7334 2789 2732 Commercial printing, offset; photocopying & duplicating services; bookbinding & related work; book printing

**(G-16585)**
**INSTRUMENT & VALVE SERVICES CO**
Also Called: Emerson
4320 166th St (60452-4607)
**PHONE** .................................708 535-5120
Reilly Patrick, *Director*
Jeff Acquaviva, *Director*
**EMP:** 54
**SALES (corp-wide):** 14.5B **Publicly Held**
**SIC:** 3494 Valves & pipe fittings
**HQ:** Instrument & Valve Services Company
205 S Center St
Marshalltown IA 50158
641 754-3011

**(G-16586)**
**KINGSBURY ENTERPRISES INC**
15007 Moorings Ln (60452-6016)
**PHONE** .................................708 535-7590
Lynn Kingsbury, *President*
Thomas Kingsbury, *Vice Pres*
**EMP:** 2
**SALES (est):** 200K **Privately Held**
**SIC:** 2752 5199 Commercial printing, lithographic; advertising specialties

**(G-16587)**
**PERFECT SMILES (PA)**
6056 159th St (60452-2904)
**PHONE** .................................708 687-6100
Kathy Bidrowski, *Manager*
**EMP:** 4

# Oak Forest - Cook County (G-16588)

SALES (est): 454.6K **Privately Held**
SIC: 3843 Enamels, dentists'

### (G-16588)
### SINGLETON PALLETS CO
15603 Waverly Ave (60452-3613)
P.O. Box 526 (60452-0526)
PHONE..................708 687-7006
Joseph Singleton, *Principal*
**EMP:** 3 **EST:** 2011
SALES (est): 153.4K **Privately Held**
SIC: 2448 Pallets, wood & wood with metal

### (G-16589)
### STANDARD REGISTER INC
4849 167th St Ste 201 (60452-4551)
PHONE..................708 560-7600
Fax: 708 560-7980
David Caquatto, *Branch Mgr*
**EMP:** 8
SALES (corp-wide): 4.5B **Privately Held**
WEB: www.stdreg.com
SIC: 2761 Manifold business forms
HQ: Standard Register, Inc.
600 Albany St
Dayton OH 45417
937 221-1000

### (G-16590)
### SYSTEMS EQUIPMENT SERVICES
4314 166th St (60452-4607)
PHONE..................708 535-1273
Fax: 708 535-1465
Robert Otterbacher, *President*
Susan Otterbacher, *Admin Sec*
**EMP:** 4 **EST:** 1978
**SQ FT:** 26,000
SALES (est): 520K **Privately Held**
SIC: 3537 5084 Forklift trucks; lift trucks & parts

### (G-16591)
### T H DAVIDSON & CO INC (PA)
Also Called: Davidson Redi-Mix Concrete
4243 166th St (60452-4608)
PHONE..................815 464-2000
Thomas W Davidson, *CEO*
Michael J Dejong, *President*
John Albinger, *President*
Joyce Warzynski, *Bookkeeper*
Richard Chobar, *Admin Sec*
**EMP:** 20
**SQ FT:** 3,000
SALES (est): 6.2MM **Privately Held**
WEB: www.davidsonreadymix.com
SIC: 3273 5032 Ready-mixed concrete; stone, crushed or broken; gravel; sand, construction

### (G-16592)
### TRIPLETT ENTEREPRISES INC
16613 Kilbourne Ave (60452-4621)
PHONE..................708 333-9421
Timothy Triplett, *CEO*
**EMP:** 2
SALES (est): 326.5K **Privately Held**
SIC: 4724 7692 4959 Travel agencies; tourist agency arranging transport, lodging & car rental; welding repair; environmental cleanup services

### (G-16593)
### WE CLEAN
Also Called: Maria Salazar Rivas
5845 Victoria Dr (60452-2863)
PHONE..................708 574-2551
Maria Salazar Rivas, *Owner*
**EMP:** 3
SALES: 40K **Privately Held**
SIC: 3589 Service industry machinery

## Oak Lawn
### Cook County

### (G-16594)
### ABSOLUTE WINDOWS INC
9630 S 76th Ave (60457-6625)
PHONE..................708 599-9191
Fax: 708 237-0952
Ronald Baker, *President*
Larry Czachor, *Corp Secy*
Carl Maturo, *Vice Pres*
Gregory Seeber, *Shareholder*
**EMP:** 24
**SQ FT:** 15,000
SALES (est): 1.9MM **Privately Held**
WEB: www.tristatewholesale.com
SIC: 2431 5031 Windows & window parts & trim, wood; doors & windows

### (G-16595)
### ACCURATE CSTM SASH MLLWK CORP
5516 W 110th St Ste 1 (60453-4764)
PHONE..................708 423-0423
Mark Sirvin, *President*
Patricia Sirvin, *Admin Sec*
**EMP:** 3 **EST:** 1981
**SQ FT:** 1,600
SALES (est): 360K **Privately Held**
WEB: www.accuratesash.com
SIC: 5211 2431 Doors, storm: wood or metal; windows, storm: wood or metal; millwork & lumber; sash, wood or metal; doors, wood; moldings, wood: unfinished & prefinished

### (G-16596)
### ACCURATE METALLIZING INC
5340 W 111th St Ste 2 (60453-5573)
PHONE..................708 424-7747
Fax: 708 424-9378
Donald Vander Meulen, *President*
Shirley Vander Meulen, *Corp Secy*
**EMP:** 5
**SQ FT:** 9,000
SALES: 800K **Privately Held**
WEB: www.accuratemetallizing.com
SIC: 3599 3479 Machine shop, jobbing & repair; painting, coating & hot dipping

### (G-16597)
### ACCUSOL INCORPORATED
9632 S Kildare Ave (60453-3225)
PHONE..................773 283-4686
David Anderson, *President*
**EMP:** 5
SALES (est): 424K **Privately Held**
SIC: 2899 Chemical preparations

### (G-16598)
### ACTIVE TOOL AND MACHINE INC
8445 Beloit Ave (60455-1717)
PHONE..................708 599-0022
Fax: 708 599-0310
Phillip D Nienhouse, *President*
Sherry A Nienhouse, *Corp Secy*
**EMP:** 12
**SQ FT:** 8,000
SALES (est): 1.9MM **Privately Held**
WEB: www.activetoolrepair.com
SIC: 3621 3568 Armatures, industrial; power transmission equipment

### (G-16599)
### ALL-AMERICAN SIGN CO INC
5501 W 109th St Ste 1 (60453-2479)
PHONE..................708 422-2203
Richard P Santucci, *President*
Dave Monahan, *Vice Pres*
Dave Monihan, *Sales Executive*
Kevin Monahan, *Manager*
Andy Wong, *Manager*
▲ **EMP:** 20
**SQ FT:** 14,000
SALES (est): 2.8MM **Privately Held**
SIC: 3993 Electric signs

### (G-16600)
### ALPINE AMUSEMENT CO INC
8037 Neva Ave (60459-1616)
PHONE..................708 233-9131
Donald Massie III, *President*
Donald Massie Jr, *Treasurer*
**EMP:** 3
SALES (est): 310K **Privately Held**
SIC: 3599 7999 Carnival machines & equipment, amusement park; exhibition & carnival operation services

### (G-16601)
### AMBIENT LIGHTNING AND ELECTRIC
10033 Menard Ave (60453-3753)
PHONE..................708 529-3434
Lisa Quick, *President*
**EMP:** 4 **EST:** 2008
SALES (est): 511K **Privately Held**
SIC: 3699 Electrical equipment & supplies

### (G-16602)
### AMERIKOS LIETUVIS CORP
7950 W 99th St (60457-2319)
PHONE..................708 924-0403
Bronius Abrutis, *President*
Giedre Eleksyte, *Administration*
**EMP:** 4
SALES (est): 193.3K **Privately Held**
SIC: 2711 Newspapers

### (G-16603)
### ARCO AUTOMOTIVE ELEC SVC CO
Also Called: Arco Automobile
10707 S Cicero Ave (60453-5401)
PHONE..................708 422-2976
Frank Malinowski Jr, *President*
Rich Malinowski, *Corp Secy*
**EMP:** 7
**SQ FT:** 3,200
SALES: 500K **Privately Held**
SIC: 5013 7539 5531 3714 Automotive supplies & parts; automotive repair shops; automotive & home supply stores; motor vehicle parts & accessories

### (G-16604)
### ART CLAY WORLD USA INC
4535 Southwest Hwy (60453-1820)
PHONE..................708 857-8800
Jackie Truty, *President*
Barbara McGuire, *Publisher*
Mike Wilk, *Office Mgr*
**EMP:** 9
SALES (est): 824K **Privately Held**
WEB: www.artclayworld.com
SIC: 3479 Engraving jewelry silverware, or metal

### (G-16605)
### AUTOMOTION INC
11000 Lavergne Ave (60453-5500)
PHONE..................708 229-3700
Fax: 708 229-3798
Merle Davis, *President*
William D Moyer Jr, *Principal*
John J Dillon Jr, *Vice Pres*
John Heimanowski, *Vice Pres*
Julie Vitos, *Human Res Mgr*
◆ **EMP:** 152 **EST:** 1967
**SQ FT:** 135,000
SALES: 58.6MM
SALES (corp-wide): 2.8B **Privately Held**
WEB: www.automotionconveyors.com
SIC: 3535 Conveyors & conveying equipment
HQ: Wynright Corporation
2500 York Rd
Elk Grove Village IL 60007
847 595-9400

### (G-16606)
### BEFCO MANUFACTURING CO INC
Also Called: G N F
5555 W 109th St (60453-5001)
PHONE..................708 424-4170
Ron K Bais, *President*
**EMP:** 12 **EST:** 2000
SALES (est): 2.2MM **Privately Held**
WEB: www.gandf.com
SIC: 3443 Boiler shop products: boilers, smokestacks, steel tanks

### (G-16607)
### C L VAULT & SAFE SRV
6754 W 89th Pl (60453-1028)
PHONE..................708 237-0039
Carlos Lopez, *Principal*
**EMP:** 3
SALES (est): 279.3K **Privately Held**
SIC: 3272 Burial vaults, concrete or precast terrazzo

### (G-16608)
### C M J ASSOCIATES INC
10745 S Kolmar Ave (60453-5348)
P.O. Box 661 (60454-0661)
PHONE..................708 636-2995
James W Gilboy, *President*
Colleen Gilboy, *Corp Secy*
Michael Gilboy, *Vice Pres*
**EMP:** 1
SALES: 300K **Privately Held**
SIC: 5112 2752 Business forms; commercial printing, offset

### (G-16609)
### CABLE ELECTRIC COMPANY INC
7640 Archer Rd (60458-1144)
PHONE..................708 458-8900
David Goacher, *President*
Susan Goacher, *Admin Sec*
**EMP:** 6
**SQ FT:** 5,000
SALES (est): 1.2MM **Privately Held**
SIC: 1731 3613 Electrical work; control panels, electric

### (G-16610)
### CHICAGO CARDINAL COMMUNICATION
Also Called: Video Surveillance
10232 S Kenton Ave (60453-4250)
PHONE..................708 424-1446
Kevin Bulger, *Owner*
**EMP:** 10
**SQ FT:** 1,500
SALES (est): 774K **Privately Held**
SIC: 4813 3679 4812 Telephone/video communications; hermetic seals for electronic equipment; paging services

### (G-16611)
### CINTAS CORPORATION
Working Class Uniforms
9525 S Cicero Ave (60453-3136)
PHONE..................708 424-4747
Nancy Armstrong, *Manager*
**EMP:** 10
SALES (corp-wide): 4.9B **Publicly Held**
SIC: 2326 Work uniforms
PA: Cintas Corporation
6800 Cintas Blvd
Cincinnati OH 45262
513 459-1200

### (G-16612)
### CINTAS CORPORATION NO 2
9525 S Cicero Ave (60453-3136)
PHONE..................708 424-4747
Nancy Armstrong, *Store Mgr*
**EMP:** 3
SALES (corp-wide): 4.9B **Publicly Held**
SIC: 2337 Uniforms, except athletic: women's, misses' & juniors'
HQ: Cintas Corporation No. 2
6800 Cintas Blvd
Mason OH 45040

### (G-16613)
### CUSTOM RAILZ & STAIRS INC
7808 La Crosse Ave (60459-1521)
PHONE..................773 592-7210
Andrei Pop, *Principal*
**EMP:** 3
SALES (est): 350.4K **Privately Held**
SIC: 3446 Stairs, staircases, stair treads: prefabricated metal

### (G-16614)
### CZARNIK PRECISION GRINDING MCH
5530 W 110th St Ste 8 (60453-2473)
PHONE..................708 229-9639
Wieslaw Czarnik, *CEO*
**EMP:** 2
SALES (est): 294.8K **Privately Held**
SIC: 3531 Grinders, stone: portable

### (G-16615)
### D & D PRINTING INC
9737 Southwest Hwy (60453-3614)
PHONE..................708 425-2080
Fax: 708 425-2206
Dan Perrino Jr, *President*
**EMP:** 2
**SQ FT:** 1,200
SALES (est): 332.7K **Privately Held**
SIC: 2752 Commercial printing, lithographic

### (G-16616)
### DEMCO PRODUCTS INC
4644 W 92nd St (60453-1802)
PHONE..................708 636-6240

# GEOGRAPHIC SECTION
## Oak Lawn - Cook County (G-16643)

**Fax:** 708 636-6251
Robert Dempster, *President*
Robert C Dempster, *Vice Pres*
Dave Rhoads, *Engineer*
Stephanie Dempster, *Treasurer*
Valerie Austra, *Bookkeeper*
**EMP:** 12 **EST:** 1950
**SQ FT:** 15,300
**SALES (est):** 3MM **Privately Held**
**WEB:** www.demcoproducts.com
**SIC:** 3451 3351 3321 Screw machine products; copper rolling & drawing; gray & ductile iron foundries

### (G-16617)
### EASTCO INC
5500 W 111th St (60453-5012)
**PHONE**...........................708 499-1701
Earl A Silverman, *President*
George Pollack, *President*
David Martinez, *Opers Mgr*
▲ **EMP:** 4
**SQ FT:** 28,000
**SALES (est):** 1.2MM **Privately Held**
**WEB:** www.eastcocorp.com
**SIC:** 3678 3643 Electronic connectors; electric connectors

### (G-16618)
### F & A INDUSTRIES COMPANY LLC
9204 S Pulaski Rd Apt 2e (60453-1960)
**PHONE**...........................630 504-9839
Rodriguez Francisco, *Principal*
**EMP:** 3 **EST:** 2015
**SALES (est):** 133K **Privately Held**
**SIC:** 3999 Manufacturing industries

### (G-16619)
### F H LEINWEBER CO INC (PA)
9812 S Cicero Ave (60453-3104)
**PHONE**...........................708 424-7000
**Fax:** 708 424-9914
Fred H Leinweber Sr, *President*
Fred H Leinweber, *Vice Pres*
Lillian Leinweber, *Treasurer*
Peggy Leinweber, *Office Mgr*
Kip Nance, *Director*
**EMP:** 4
**SQ FT:** 1,000
**SALES:** 1.7MM **Privately Held**
**SIC:** 2891 1752 Sealants; floor laying & floor work

### (G-16620)
### FORMS ETC BY MARTY WALSH
9205 S Keating Ave Ste 3 (60453-2583)
**PHONE**...........................708 499-6767
**Fax:** 708 499-6769
Martin T Walsh, *Owner*
▲ **EMP:** 2
**SQ FT:** 600
**SALES:** 400K **Privately Held**
**WEB:** www.formsetc.net
**SIC:** 5112 2761 Business forms; manifold business forms

### (G-16621)
### G & F MANUFACTURING CO INC
Also Called: Befco Manufactoring Co.
5555 W 109th St (60453-5070)
**PHONE**...........................708 424-4170
**Fax:** 708 424-4922
Ron Bias, *Principal*
Kiran Bais, *Family Practiti*
▼ **EMP:** 20
**SQ FT:** 14,000
**SALES:** 12MM **Privately Held**
**SIC:** 3613 3441 Panelboards & distribution boards, electric; fabricated structural metal

### (G-16622)
### G & M WOODWORKING INC
5656 W 88th Pl (60453-1215)
**PHONE**...........................708 425-4013
Gene Marcinkowski, *Principal*
**EMP:** 3
**SALES (est):** 338K **Privately Held**
**SIC:** 2431 Millwork

### (G-16623)
### GENERAL MACHINING SERVICE INC
5521 W 110th St Ste 6 (60453-2604)
**PHONE**...........................708 636-4848
Dennis Musial, *President*
Henry K Sziler, *Corp Secy*
**EMP:** 5
**SALES:** 800K **Privately Held**
**SIC:** 3599 Machine shop, jobbing & repair

### (G-16624)
### HANGER PROSTHETICS &
Also Called: Hanger Clinic
10837 S Cicero Aveste 100 (60453)
**PHONE**...........................708 371-9999
Sam Liang, *President*
Sheryl Price, *Director*
Vinit Asar, *Director*
**EMP:** 99
**SALES (corp-wide):** 459.1MM **Publicly Held**
**SIC:** 3842 Limbs, artificial
**HQ:** Hanger Prosthetics & Orthotics East, Inc.
33 North Ave Ste 101
Tallmadge OH 44278
330 633-9807

### (G-16625)
### HERFF JONES LLC
6305 W 95th St Ste 1w (60453-2780)
**PHONE**...........................708 425-0130
Jim Cranley, *Manager*
**EMP:** 4
**SALES (corp-wide):** 1.1B **Privately Held**
**WEB:** www.herffjones.com
**SIC:** 3911 Rings, finger: precious metal
**HQ:** Herff Jones, Llc
4501 W 62nd St
Indianapolis IN 46268
800 419-5462

### (G-16626)
### INTERSTATE BATTERY SYSTEM INTL
10336 S Cicero Ave (60453-4702)
**PHONE**...........................708 424-2288
**Fax:** 815 464-1577
Ted Golebiowski, *Branch Mgr*
**EMP:** 8 **Privately Held**
**SIC:** 5531 5063 3691 Batteries, automotive & truck; batteries; storage batteries
**PA:** Interstate Battery System International, Inc.
12770 Merit Dr Ste 1400
Dallas TX 75251

### (G-16627)
### J AND K PRINTING
5629 W 84th Pl (60459-2629)
**PHONE**...........................708 229-9558
Joseph Lorusso, *Owner*
**EMP:** 3
**SALES:** 85K **Privately Held**
**SIC:** 2752 6221 Commercial printing, lithographic; commodity contracts brokers, dealers

### (G-16628)
### JORDAN GOLD INC
Also Called: Ramallah Jewelry
8741 Ridgeland Ave (60453-1001)
**PHONE**...........................708 430-7008
Elias Mseeh, *President*
Lina Mseeh, *Treasurer*
**EMP:** 3
**SALES (est):** 270K **Privately Held**
**WEB:** www.ramallahjewelry.com
**SIC:** 5944 3961 Jewelry stores; costume jewelry

### (G-16629)
### KITCHY KOO GOURMET CO
7845 Lamon Ave (60459-1522)
**PHONE**...........................708 499-5236
Sunai Limpanathon, *Principal*
**EMP:** 2
**SALES (est):** 248.8K **Privately Held**
**SIC:** 3556 Dehydrating equipment, food processing

### (G-16630)
### L A D SPECIALTIES
9010 Beloit Ave Ste F (60455-2611)
**PHONE**...........................708 430-1588
**Fax:** 708 430-1694
Donald Grenier, *President*
Scott Greiner, *Project Mgr*
**EMP:** 3
**SALES (est):** 432.8K **Privately Held**
**WEB:** www.ladspec.com
**SIC:** 3053 Gaskets & sealing devices

### (G-16631)
### LMPL MANAGEMENT CORPORATION
5757 W 95th St Ste 3 (60453-2385)
**PHONE**...........................708 636-2443
Paul Lausch, *President*
**EMP:** 7
**SALES (est):** 440K **Privately Held**
**SIC:** 8021 8072 3843 Dental clinics & offices; dental laboratories; dental equipment & supplies

### (G-16632)
### LO-KO PERFORMANCE COATINGS
5340 W 111th St Ste 1 (60453-5573)
**PHONE**...........................708 424-7863
Donald Vander Meulen, *President*
**EMP:** 8
**SALES (est):** 866.1K **Privately Held**
**WEB:** www.lo-ko.com
**SIC:** 3479 5571 Coating of metals & formed products; motorcycle dealers

### (G-16633)
### MASTER PRINT
5533 W 109th St Ste 220 (60453-2462)
**PHONE**...........................708 499-4037
**Fax:** 708 499-4039
Don Charles, *Owner*
**EMP:** 2
**SALES (est):** 213.3K **Privately Held**
**SIC:** 2759 Commercial printing

### (G-16634)
### MEYER TOOL & MANUFACTURING INC
4601 Southwest Hwy (60453-1822)
**PHONE**...........................708 425-9080
**Fax:** 708 425-2612
Eileen Cunningham, *President*
Mike Tortorello, *General Mgr*
Kathryn M Meyer, *Chairman*
Edward Bonnema, *Vice Pres*
Bernadette Schnitzenbaumer, *Purch Agent*
**EMP:** 28 **EST:** 1969
**SQ FT:** 35,000
**SALES (est):** 9.2MM **Privately Held**
**WEB:** www.mtm-inc.com
**SIC:** 3563 Air & gas compressors including vacuum pumps

### (G-16635)
### MIDWEST IMPERIAL STEEL
5555 W 109th St (60453-5001)
**PHONE**...........................815 469-1072
Ron Bais, *Mng Member*
**EMP:** 18
**SALES (est):** 4MM **Privately Held**
**SIC:** 3443 Fabricated plate work (boiler shop)

### (G-16636)
### N P D INC
Also Called: Printmart
4720 W 103rd St (60453-4706)
**PHONE**...........................708 424-6788
**Fax:** 708 424-0410
Nick Hederman, *President*
Dawn Hederman, *Vice Pres*
Brian Jany, *Manager*
**EMP:** 3 **EST:** 1978
**SQ FT:** 1,600
**SALES (est):** 547.6K **Privately Held**
**WEB:** www.npd.net
**SIC:** 2752 2791 2789 Commercial printing, offset; typesetting; bookbinding & related work

### (G-16637)
### OFFICE ASSISTANTS INC
9722 S Cicero Ave (60453-3103)
**PHONE**...........................708 346-0505
**Fax:** 708 346-0579
M Sidney De Ruiter, *Ch of Bd*
Robert Deruiter, *President*
**EMP:** 4
**SQ FT:** 1,500
**SALES (est):** 483.9K **Privately Held**
**SIC:** 7363 2752 2791 2789 Temporary help service; commercial printing, lithographic; typesetting; bookbinding & related work

### (G-16638)
### PARK LAWN ASSOCIATION INC
5040 W 111th St (60453-5008)
**PHONE**...........................708 425-7377
**Fax:** 708 425-7899
Frank Portada, *Manager*
**EMP:** 10
**SALES (corp-wide):** 1.4MM **Privately Held**
**SIC:** 7389 8331 3565 Packaging & labeling services; job training & vocational rehabilitation services; packaging machinery
**PA:** Park Lawn Association Inc
10833 Laporte Ave
Oak Lawn IL 60453
708 425-6867

### (G-16639)
### PERMACOR INC
9540 Tulley Ave (60453-3089)
**PHONE**...........................708 422-3353
**Fax:** 708 422-9637
Peter Tsoutsas, *President*
Peter Parthenis, *Vice Pres*
Kirk Tsoutsas, *Purch Mgr*
George Geogamas, *Treasurer*
Fran Tsoutsas, *Controller*
**EMP:** 36
**SQ FT:** 22,000
**SALES (est):** 4.9MM **Privately Held**
**WEB:** www.permacor.com
**SIC:** 3264 3399 3677 Ferrite & ferrite parts; powder, metal; electronic coils, transformers & other inductors

### (G-16640)
### PETERS MACHINE WORKS INC
8277 S 86th Ct (60458-1767)
**PHONE**...........................708 496-3005
**Fax:** 708 496-8606
Delbert Peters, *President*
Ivy Taebel, *Manager*
**EMP:** 10
**SQ FT:** 9,000
**SALES:** 349.2K **Privately Held**
**SIC:** 3599 Custom machinery

### (G-16641)
### PRINT KING INC
7818 S Cicero Ave (60459-1584)
P.O. Box 1027, Plainfield (60544-1027)
**PHONE**...........................708 499-3777
**Fax:** 708 499-3802
Dan Bowen, *President*
Dennis Cramer, *Admin Sec*
Michael Kreil, *Administration*
**EMP:** 15
**SQ FT:** 4,800
**SALES:** 1.5MM **Privately Held**
**WEB:** www.print-king.com
**SIC:** 2752 2791 2789 Commercial printing, offset; typesetting; bookbinding & related work

### (G-16642)
### QUALITY MACHINE
5530 W 110th St Ste 8 (60453-2473)
**PHONE**...........................708 499-0021
Chris Ren, *Owner*
**EMP:** 3
**SALES (est):** 311K **Privately Held**
**SIC:** 3599 Machine shop, jobbing & repair

### (G-16643)
### REEL MATE MFG CO
10113 Buell Ct (60453-3802)
P.O. Box 871 (60454-0871)
**PHONE**...........................708 423-8005
**Fax:** 708 423-8005
Joseph Landgraf, *Partner*
Patricia A Landgraf, *Partner*
**EMP:** 4
**SALES (est):** 254.5K **Privately Held**
**SIC:** 2395 Embroidery & art needlework

# Oak Lawn - Cook County (G-16644) — GEOGRAPHIC SECTION

**(G-16644)**
**SOUTHFIELD CORPORATION**
A 1 Express & Cartage Co Div
7601 W 79th St (60455-1115)
**PHONE** .................... 708 458-0400
John Zoback, *Manager*
**EMP:** 50
**SALES (corp-wide):** 273.9MM **Privately Held**
**WEB:** www.prairiegroup.com
**SIC:** 5211 3273 5032 3271 Lumber & other building materials; ready-mixed concrete; stone, crushed or broken; concrete block & brick
**PA:** Southfield Corporation
8995 W 95th St
Palos Hills IL 60465
708 344-1000

**(G-16645)**
**STRAIGHTLINE ERECTORS INC**
7812 W 91st St (60457-2006)
**PHONE** .................... 708 430-5426
Don Engstrom, *President*
**EMP:** 3
**SALES (est):** 380K **Privately Held**
**SIC:** 3542 Sheet metalworking machines

**(G-16646)**
**VAN CRAFT INDUSTRY OF DEL EDEL (DH)**
8938 Ridgeland Ave (60453-1000)
**PHONE** .................... 708 430-6670
Norman Klein, *President*
Helene Jones, *Admin Sec*
**EMP:** 3
**SQ FT:** 100
**SALES (est):** 384.7K
**SALES (corp-wide):** 82.1MM **Privately Held**
**WEB:** www.deck2systems.com
**SIC:** 3429 Manufactured hardware (general)
**HQ:** Freight Consolidation Services Inc
8938 Ridgeland Ave # 200
Oak Lawn IL 60453
708 430-6670

**(G-16647)**
**VAN NORMAN MOLDING COMPANY LLC**
9615 S 76th Ave (60455-2373)
**PHONE** .................... 708 430-4343
**Fax:** 708 430-4775
Bob Andre, *VP Opers*
Frank Wenciker, *Accounts Mgr*
Rich Andre, *Sales Executive*
Kathleen Rice, *Manager*
Jim Hager, *Supervisor*
**EMP:** 32
**SQ FT:** 30,000
**SALES (est):** 8.2MM **Privately Held**
**WEB:** www.vannormanmolding.com
**SIC:** 3089 Injection molded finished plastic products; molding primary plastic

## Oak Park
*Cook County*

**(G-16648)**
**ACTIVE SIMULATIONS INC**
312 S Lombard Ave (60302-3524)
**PHONE** .................... 630 747-8393
Milos Zefran, *CEO*
Arnold Steinberg, *CFO*
**EMP:** 3
**SALES (est):** 63.5K **Privately Held**
**SIC:** 7371 7372 Computer software development & applications; educational computer software

**(G-16649)**
**ADVANCED RETINAL INSTITUTE INC**
1123 N Oak Park Ave (60302-1222)
**PHONE** .................... 617 821-5597
Calvin A Grant, *President*
**EMP:** 4
**SQ FT:** 2,000
**SALES:** 600K **Privately Held**
**SIC:** 3841 Retinoscopes

**(G-16650)**
**AIR CADDY**
Also Called: Shipbikes.com
310 Lake St Ste 8 (60302-2641)
**PHONE** .................... 708 383-5541
Robert Lickton, *President*
Levana Lickton, *Treasurer*
**EMP:** 5
**SALES (est):** 527.3K **Privately Held**
**SIC:** 3444 Metal housings, enclosures, casings & other containers

**(G-16651)**
**AJ WELDING SERVICES**
1017 S Oak Park Ave (60304-1924)
**PHONE** .................... 708 843-2701
Alejandro Jaimes, *Owner*
**EMP:** 3
**SALES:** 10K **Privately Held**
**SIC:** 3446 Architectural metalwork

**(G-16652)**
**ALTAMIRA ART GLASS**
202 And A Half S Mrion St (60302)
**PHONE** .................... 708 848-3799
Paul Damkoehler, *Owner*
**EMP:** 2
**SQ FT:** 1,000
**SALES:** 120K **Privately Held**
**WEB:** www.altamiraglass.com
**SIC:** 5719 3229 Glassware; art, decorative & novelty glassware

**(G-16653)**
**ARBETMAN & ASSOCIATES**
635 S Humphrey Ave (60304-1714)
**PHONE** .................... 708 386-8586
Jay S Arbetman, *Owner*
**EMP:** 2
**SALES:** 250K **Privately Held**
**SIC:** 2396 Apparel findings & trimmings

**(G-16654)**
**BAKER ELEMENTS INC**
159 N Marion St (60301-1032)
**PHONE** .................... 630 660-8100
Paul Baker, *CEO*
**EMP:** 10
**SALES (est):** 1.1MM **Privately Held**
**SIC:** 2431 1751 2599 Millwork; cabinet building & installation; window & door installation & erection; bar, restaurant & cafeteria furniture; hotel furniture

**(G-16655)**
**C E DIENBERG PRINTING COMPANY**
114 Madison St Lowr 1 (60302-4252)
**PHONE** .................... 708 848-4406
**EMP:** 4
**SQ FT:** 3,000
**SALES:** 300K **Privately Held**
**SIC:** 2752 2759 Lithographic Commercial Printing Commercial Printing

**(G-16656)**
**CAROLINE ROSE INC**
741 Madison St (60302-4419)
**PHONE** .................... 708 386-1011
**Fax:** 708 386-1011
Rose Becker, *CEO*
Caroline Becker, *President*
Maura Flood, *Coordinator*
**EMP:** 7
**SQ FT:** 12,000
**SALES (est):** 1.1MM **Privately Held**
**WEB:** www.carolinerose.com
**SIC:** 2339 2335 Sportswear, women's; women's, juniors' & misses' dresses

**(G-16657)**
**CHARLES CHAUNCEY WELLS INC**
Also Called: Wells Printing Co
735 N Grove Ave (60302-1551)
**PHONE** .................... 708 524-0695
Charles C Wells, *President*
Susan Austin Wells, *Admin Sec*
**EMP:** 2
**SALES (est):** 239.1K **Privately Held**
**WEB:** www.wells1.com
**SIC:** 2752 Commercial printing, lithographic

**(G-16658)**
**CHERYL & CO**
Also Called: Cheryl's
1018 Lake St (60301-1102)
**PHONE** .................... 708 386-1255
**EMP:** 153
**SALES (corp-wide):** 1.1B **Publicly Held**
**SIC:** 2052 Cookies & crackers
**HQ:** Cheryl & Co.
646 Mccorkle Blvd
Westerville OH 43082
614 776-1500

**(G-16659)**
**DIGITAL LIVING INC**
410 Madison St (60302-4012)
**PHONE** .................... 708 434-1197
Shireesh Reddy, *President*
**EMP:** 5
**SQ FT:** 2,000
**SALES:** 800K **Privately Held**
**SIC:** 3651 Home entertainment equipment, electronic

**(G-16660)**
**DOODY ENTERPRISES INC**
1100 Lake St Ste Ll25 (60301-1099)
**PHONE** .................... 312 239-6226
Dan Doody, *President*
**EMP:** 2
**SQ FT:** 1,500
**SALES:** 500K **Privately Held**
**WEB:** www.doodyenterprises.com
**SIC:** 2741 Miscellaneous publishing

**(G-16661)**
**DREHER ORTHOPEDIC INDUSTRIES (PA)**
214 Chicago Ave Ste 1 (60302-2310)
**PHONE** .................... 708 848-4646
**Fax:** 708 848-1341
Peter Dreher Jr, *President*
**EMP:** 8
**SQ FT:** 2,000
**SALES:** 1.1MM **Privately Held**
**SIC:** 3842 Orthopedic appliances

**(G-16662)**
**EARTHCOMBER LLC**
110 N Marion St (60301-1005)
**PHONE** .................... 708 366-1600
James Brady, *President*
Dana Sohr, *Vice Pres*
**EMP:** 10
**SALES (est):** 750K **Privately Held**
**WEB:** www.earthcomber.com
**SIC:** 2741 Miscellaneous publishing

**(G-16663)**
**FRAME HOUSE INC**
Also Called: Frame House Passport Photos
163 S Oak Park Ave (60302-2901)
**PHONE** .................... 708 383-1616
**Fax:** 708 383-4343
**EMP:** 9
**SQ FT:** 4,200
**SALES:** 620K **Privately Held**
**SIC:** 2499 5023 5999 Mfg Whol And Ret Picture Frames

**(G-16664)**
**FREITAS P SABAH**
Also Called: Lessabah Arts Center
6105 1/2 North Ave (60302-1124)
**PHONE** .................... 708 386-8934
Freitas P Sabah, *Owner*
**EMP:** 4
**SALES (est):** 219.2K **Privately Held**
**SIC:** 5092 3999 Arts & crafts equipment & supplies; manufacturing industries

**(G-16665)**
**FUNQUILTS INC**
719 Iowa St (60302-1639)
**PHONE** .................... 708 445-9871
Bill Kerr, *President*
Weeks Ringle, *Principal*
**EMP:** 3
**SALES (est):** 271.8K **Privately Held**
**WEB:** www.funquilts.com
**SIC:** 2221 Comforters & quilts, manmade fiber & silk

**(G-16666)**
**GENISYS DECISION CORPORATION**
1150 S Taylor Ave Ste 200 (60304-2234)
P.O. Box 714 (60303-0714)
**PHONE** .................... 708 524-5100
David J Towne, *President*
Susan Towne, *Admin Sec*
**EMP:** 3
**SALES:** 500K **Privately Held**
**SIC:** 7372 Prepackaged software

**(G-16667)**
**H J MOHR & SONS COMPANY**
915 S Maple Ave (60304-1893)
**PHONE** .................... 708 366-0338
**Fax:** 708 386-2881
Dolly Mohr, *President*
Steven E Mohr, *Vice Pres*
Karen Richards, *Vice Pres*
Marlene Mohr, *Manager*
**EMP:** 15 EST: 1893
**SQ FT:** 33,000
**SALES (est):** 6.3MM **Privately Held**
**SIC:** 5031 5211 3273 Building materials, exterior; building materials, interior; lumber & other building materials; ready-mixed concrete

**(G-16668)**
**HEARTLAND HOUSE DESIGNS**
741 N Oak Park Ave (60302-1536)
**PHONE** .................... 708 383-2278
Pat Henek, *Partner*
John Henek, *Partner*
**EMP:** 2
**SALES (est):** 211.1K **Privately Held**
**WEB:** www.heartlandhouse.com
**SIC:** 3999 5949 Sewing kits, novelty; sewing, needlework & piece goods

**(G-16669)**
**HUMAGINARIUM LLC**
325 S Grove Ave (60302-3501)
**PHONE** .................... 312 788-7719
Robert Becker, *CEO*
**EMP:** 5
**SALES (est):** 117.2K **Privately Held**
**SIC:** 7372 Educational computer software

**(G-16670)**
**I A E INC**
837 N Harlem Ave Apt 1n (60302-1673)
**PHONE** .................... 219 882-2400
Ramamurty Talluri, *President*
Peter Thayer, *Admin Sec*
**EMP:** 3 EST: 1975
**SQ FT:** 1,800
**SALES (est):** 231.6K **Privately Held**
**SIC:** 2873 8711 Urea; civil engineering; structural engineering; sanitary engineers

**(G-16671)**
**KAP HOLDINGS LLC**
Also Called: Partscription
137 N Oak Park Ave # 214 (60301-1344)
**PHONE** .................... 708 948-0226
Kevin Price, *Mng Member*
**EMP:** 10
**SALES (est):** 203.9K **Privately Held**
**SIC:** 3585 3564 3621 Refrigeration & heating equipment; blower filter units (furnace blowers); filters, air: furnaces, air conditioning equipment, etc.; electric motor & generator parts

**(G-16672)**
**KATYS LLC (PA)**
Also Called: Katy's Goodness
1040 S Maple Ave (60304-1805)
P.O. Box 6364, River Forest (60305-6364)
**PHONE** .................... 708 522-9814
Kathleen Frantz, *Mng Member*
**EMP:** 2
**SALES:** 5MM **Privately Held**
**SIC:** 2052 5149 7389 Cookies & crackers; crackers, cookies & bakery products;

**(G-16673)**
**KRUGER NORTH AMERICA INC**
1033 South Blvd Ste 200 (60302-2823)
**PHONE** .................... 708 851-3670
Micheal De Vootd, *President*
Anton Straughan, *Vice Pres*
Laurie Bunkers, *Dir Ops-Prd-Mfg*

Kristin Lugar, *Finance Dir*
**EMP:** 10
**SQ FT:** 35,000
**SALES:** 9.8MM
**SALES (corp-wide):** 1.6B  **Privately Held**
**SIC:** 2066 2087 2099 Chocolate & cocoa products; instant cocoa; powdered cocoa; chocolate coatings & syrup; powders, drink; syrups, drink; food preparations
**PA:** Kruger Gmbh & Co. Kg
Senefelderstr. 44
Bergisch Gladbach 51469
220 210-50

*(G-16674)*
**LAURENCELESTE INC**
230 Clinton Ave (60302-3114)
**PHONE** .................... 708 383-3432
Lauren Murphy, *President*
Celeste Bayer, *Vice Pres*
**EMP:** 3
**SALES (est):** 210K  **Privately Held**
**WEB:** www.laurenceleste.com
**SIC:** 2369 Girls' & children's outerwear

*(G-16675)*
**MINUTEMAN PRESS**
6949 North Ave (60302-1046)
**PHONE** .................... 708 524-4940
Fax: 708 524-4945
Laurie Freeman, *Owner*
**EMP:** 4  **EST:** 2009
**SALES (est):** 520.2K  **Privately Held**
**SIC:** 2752 Commercial printing, lithographic

*(G-16676)*
**NEW MILLENNIUM INVESTMENT**
1100 Rossell Ave (60302-1102)
**PHONE** .................... 708 358-1512
Shelia Hasley, *Partner*
Lise Cheers, *Partner*
**EMP:** 9
**SALES (est):** 480K  **Privately Held**
**SIC:** 2741 Miscellaneous publishing

*(G-16677)*
**NORTHERN LIGHTING & POWER INC**
1138 Woodbine Ave (60302-1212)
**PHONE** .................... 708 383-9926
Fax: 847 671-9817
**EMP:** 3
**SALES (est):** 280K  **Privately Held**
**SIC:** 3648 Mfg Lighting Equipment

*(G-16678)*
**OBERWEIS DAIRY INC**
124 N Oak Park Ave (60301-1304)
**PHONE** .................... 708 660-1350
Fax: 708 660-1348
Patti Buchholv, *Branch Mgr*
**EMP:** 20
**SALES (corp-wide):** 202.6MM  **Privately Held**
**WEB:** www.webfc.net
**SIC:** 2026 5963 5451 Milk processing (pasteurizing, homogenizing, bottling); milk delivery; milk; ice cream (packaged)
**PA:** Oberweis Dairy, Inc.
951 Ice Cream Dr
North Aurora IL 60542
630 801-6100

*(G-16679)*
**PIONEER NEWSPAPERS INC**
1010 Lake St Ste 104 (60301-1106)
**PHONE** .................... 708 383-3200
Fax: 708 383-3678
Douglas Rector, *Controller*
Rick Behren, *Advt Staff*
Jennifer Clark, *Branch Mgr*
Beth Burmahl, *Manager*
**EMP:** 20
**SALES (corp-wide):** 304.8MM  **Privately Held**
**WEB:** www.pioneerlocal.com
**SIC:** 2711 Newspapers, publishing & printing
**HQ:** Pioneer Newspapers Inc.
350 N Orleans St Fl 10
Chicago IL 60654
847 486-0600

*(G-16680)*
**POYNTING PRODUCTS INC**
1011 Madison St (60302-4404)
P.O. Box 1564 (60304-0564)
**PHONE** .................... 708 386-2139
Fax: 708 386-2517
**EMP:** 3
**SQ FT:** 3,000
**SALES:** 680.6K  **Privately Held**
**SIC:** 7371 3577 Custom Computer Programing Mfg Computer Peripheral Equipment

*(G-16681)*
**PRINTING STORE INC**
621 Madison St (60302-4408)
**PHONE** .................... 708 383-3638
Fax: 708 383-3982
Philip Barry, *President*
Paul Barry, *General Mgr*
Raymond Barry, *Chairman*
Marge Barry, *Admin Sec*
**EMP:** 12
**SQ FT:** 2,000
**SALES (est):** 1MM  **Privately Held**
**WEB:** www.theprintingstore.com
**SIC:** 2752 5999 Commercial printing, offset; banners, flags, decals & posters

*(G-16682)*
**ROOKIE LLC**
545 S Scolville Ave (60304)
**PHONE** .................... 708 278-1628
Steven Gevinson,
**EMP:** 5
**SALES:** 612K  **Privately Held**
**SIC:** 2721 2731 Magazines: publishing only, not printed on site; book clubs: publishing & printing

*(G-16683)*
**SCHECK & SIRESS**
401 Harrison St (60304-1427)
**PHONE** .................... 708 383-2257
Fax: 708 383-0739
John Angelico, *Manager*
**EMP:** 2
**SALES (est):** 206.9K  **Privately Held**
**SIC:** 3842 Surgical appliances & supplies

*(G-16684)*
**SCHECK SIRESS PROSTHETICS INC**
401 Harrison St (60304-1427)
**PHONE** .................... 630 424-0392
James Kaiser, *CEO*
Ryan Caldwell, *Vice Pres*
Tomi Lancaster, *Opers Staff*
Dan Hasso, *Bd of Directors*
Robin D Spencer, *Bd of Directors*
**EMP:** 120
**SALES (corp-wide):** 11.6MM  **Privately Held**
**WEB:** www.scheckandsiress.com
**SIC:** 3842 Limbs, artificial
**PA:** Scheck & Siress Prosthetics, Inc
1 S 376 Summit Ave Ct E
Oakbrook Terrace IL
708 383-2257

*(G-16685)*
**SHEDRAIN CORPORATION**
715 Lake St Ste 269 (60301-1411)
**PHONE** .................... 708 848-5212
Greg Liebreich, *Principal*
**EMP:** 9
**SALES (corp-wide):** 30.7MM  **Privately Held**
**SIC:** 3999 5136 Umbrellas, canes & parts; umbrellas, men's & boys'
**PA:** Shedrain Corporation
8303 Ne Killingsworth St
Portland OR 97220
503 255-2200

*(G-16686)*
**SIGN EXPRESS INC**
900 S Oak Park Ave Ste 1 (60304-1936)
**PHONE** .................... 708 524-8811
Fax: 708 524-1211
Bill David, *President*
**EMP:** 4
**SQ FT:** 850
**SALES:** 250K  **Privately Held**
**SIC:** 3993 Signs & advertising specialties

*(G-16687)*
**SPANNUTH BOILER CO**
264 Madison St (60302-4112)
**PHONE** .................... 708 386-1882
Fax: 708 386-2133
Keith Golz, *President*
Kirk Golz, *Vice Pres*
Scott Golz, *Admin Sec*
**EMP:** 7  **EST:** 1936
**SQ FT:** 2,500
**SALES (est):** 730K  **Privately Held**
**SIC:** 7699 7692 1542 Boiler repair shop; welding repair; nonresidential construction

*(G-16688)*
**SWEET THYME SOAPS**
808 S Elmwood Ave (60304-1417)
**PHONE** .................... 708 848-0234
Dianne Alexander, *Manager*
**EMP:** 3
**SALES:** 15K  **Privately Held**
**SIC:** 2841 Soap & other detergents

*(G-16689)*
**TOLAR GROUP LLC**
641 S Humphrey Ave (60304-1714)
**PHONE** .................... 847 668-9485
Eric Tolar,
**EMP:** 50
**SQ FT:** 3,500
**SALES (est):** 440.6K  **Privately Held**
**SIC:** 0181 3995 4212 5087 Florists' greens & flowers; burial caskets; delivery service, vehicular; cemetery & funeral directors' equipment & supplies; monuments & grave markers

*(G-16690)*
**UNITEX INDUSTRIES INC (PA)**
Also Called: Fashionaire
7001 North Ave Ste 203 (60302-1025)
**PHONE** .................... 708 524-0664
Fax: 630 985-4690
Robert C Sassetti, *President*
**EMP:** 5
**SQ FT:** 1,000
**SALES (est):** 2.4MM  **Privately Held**
**WEB:** www.unitexindustries.com
**SIC:** 2391 2392 2591 5023 Draperies, plastic & textile: from purchased materials; bedspreads & bed sets: made from purchased materials; drapery hardware & blinds & shades; vertical blinds

*(G-16691)*
**WEDNESDAY JOURNAL INC**
Also Called: Chicago Parent News Magazine
141 S Oak Park Ave Ste 1 (60302-2972)
**PHONE** .................... 708 386-5555
Fax: 708 524-0447
Dan Haley, *Publisher*
Timothy Inklebarger, *Editor*
Graham Johnston, *Editor*
Tamara Oshaughnessy, *Editor*
Lourdes Nicholls, *Area Mgr*
**EMP:** 80
**SQ FT:** 6,500
**SALES (est):** 6.7MM  **Privately Held**
**WEB:** www.chicagoparent.com
**SIC:** 2711 Newspapers, publishing & printing

*(G-16692)*
**WEINER OPTICAL INC**
1100 Lake St Ste 180 (60301-1028)
**PHONE** .................... 708 848-4040
Joan Winitz- Leon, *Branch Mgr*
**EMP:** 5
**SALES (corp-wide):** 1.2MM  **Privately Held**
**SIC:** 3851 5995 Ophthalmic goods; optical goods stores
**PA:** Weiner Optical Inc
1100 Lake St Ste 180
Oak Park IL 60301
708 848-4040

## Oakbrook Terrace
*Dupage County*

*(G-16693)*
**AARDVARK PHARMA LLC**
Also Called: Aardvark Pharmaceuticals
2 Mid America Plz Ste 800 (60181-4727)
**PHONE** .................... 630 248-2380
Rajiv Khatau, *Mng Member*
◆ **EMP:** 32
**SQ FT:** 2,000
**SALES (est):** 1.5MM  **Privately Held**
**SIC:** 2834 Druggists' preparations (pharmaceuticals)

*(G-16694)*
**ALPHAGRAPHICS**
17w703 Butterfield Rd A (60181-4280)
**PHONE** .................... 630 261-1227
Fax: 630 261-1237
Aaron Grohs, *President*
Sreenu Tadavarthy, *President*
Sheila Tadavarthy, *Vice Pres*
Tommy E Auger, *CFO*
Gay Burke, *Exec Dir*
**EMP:** 10
**SQ FT:** 3,750
**SALES (est):** 900K  **Privately Held**
**SIC:** 2752 2759 7334 2789 Commercial printing, lithographic; laser printing; photocopying & duplicating services; binding only: books, pamphlets, magazines, etc.; typesetting

*(G-16695)*
**AMANI FROYO LLC**
2005 S Meyers Rd Apt 316 (60181-5268)
**PHONE** .................... 941 744-1111
Malik Mustansir, *Principal*
**EMP:** 6
**SALES (est):** 340.5K  **Privately Held**
**SIC:** 2024 Yogurt desserts, frozen

*(G-16696)*
**AMEDICO LABORATORIES LLC**
Also Called: Maylan Skincare
17w173 16th St (60181-4034)
**PHONE** .................... 347 857-7546
Winnie Chan,
**EMP:** 4
**SALES (est):** 384.4K  **Privately Held**
**SIC:** 2844 Toilet preparations

*(G-16697)*
**AMIGO MOBILITY CENTER**
Also Called: Mobility Center of Chicago
17w620 14th St Ste 101 (60181-3700)
**PHONE** .................... 630 268-8670
**EMP:** 5
**SALES (est):** 33.3K  **Privately Held**
**SIC:** 3845 Mfg Electromedical Equipment

*(G-16698)*
**BALDWIN RICHARDSON FOODS CO (PA)**
1 Tower Ln (60181-4671)
**PHONE** .................... 815 464-9994
Fax: 815 283-1822
Eric Johnson, *President*
Pamela Johnson, *Vice Pres*
Karen Condello, *Senior Buyer*
Rachael Elrod, *QA Dir*
Andrew Patterson, *QA Dir*
**EMP:** 7
**SALES (est):** 88.5MM  **Privately Held**
**WEB:** www.brfoods.com
**SIC:** 2024 Dairy based frozen desserts

*(G-16699)*
**BIO-BRIDGE SCIENCE INC**
1801 S Meyers Rd Ste 220 (60181-5265)
P.O. Box 168081, Chicago (60616-8071)
**PHONE** .................... 630 328-0213
Fax: 630 203-6088
Liang Qiao, *Ch of Bd*
**EMP:** 23
**SQ FT:** 2,203
**SALES (est):** 2.4MM  **Privately Held**
**WEB:** www.bio-bridge-science.com
**SIC:** 2834 Pharmaceutical preparations

# Oakbrook Terrace - Dupage County (G-16700)

## (G-16700)
**CARDIAC IMAGING INC**
2 Transam Plaza Dr # 420 (60181-4290)
PHONE...................................630 834-7100
Sam Kancherlapalli, *Director*
EMP: 16
SALES (est): 2.7MM **Privately Held**
SIC: 3845 Surgical support systems: heart-lung machine, exc. iron lung

## (G-16701)
**CHICAGO TECHNICAL SALES INC**
17w755 Butterfield Rd (60181-4253)
PHONE...................................630 889-7121
James Moynihan, *President*
Thomas Bell, *Vice Pres*
Adam Straus, *Administration*
EMP: 2
SQ FT: 400
SALES (est): 3MM **Privately Held**
WEB: www.ctsalesinc.com
SIC: 3679 5063 Electronic switches; electrical apparatus & equipment

## (G-16702)
**CIMC LEASING USA INC**
Also Called: Cimc Capital
2 Transam Plaza Dr # 320 (60181-4823)
PHONE...................................630 785-6875
Jeffrey Walker, *CEO*
Si Feng, *COO*
Kempten Taylor, *Administration*
▲ EMP: 6
SALES (est): 1MM
SALES (corp-wide): 1.5B **Privately Held**
SIC: 2448 Cargo containers, wood & metal combination
HQ: China International Marine Containers (Group) Co., Ltd.
Cimc R&D Center, No.2 Gangwan Avenue,Shekou Industrial Zone,Nans Shenzhen 51806
755 266-9113

## (G-16703)
**COINSTAR PROCUREMENT LLC**
1 Tower Ln Ste 900 (60181-4623)
PHONE...................................630 424-4788
EMP: 4 EST: 2011
SALES (est): 281.5K **Privately Held**
SIC: 3674 3829 Modules, solid state; nuclear instrument modules

## (G-16704)
**COLSON GROUP HOLDINGS LLC (PA)**
1815 S Meyers Rd Ste 750 (60181-5280)
PHONE...................................630 613-2941
Tom Blashill, *CEO*
Dennis Byrd, *Treasurer*
EMP: 3
SALES (est): 1.2MM **Privately Held**
SIC: 3325 Railroad car wheels, cast steel

## (G-16705)
**CREATE USA MODEM EIGHT**
1801 S Meyers Rd (60181-5242)
PHONE...................................630 519-3403
Norma F Rosenhain, *Principal*
EMP: 3
SALES (est): 183.9K **Privately Held**
SIC: 3661 Modems

## (G-16706)
**ECOLOGIC LLC (PA)**
18w140 Butterfield Rd # 1180 (60181-4845)
P.O. Box 477, Downers Grove (60515-0477)
PHONE...................................630 869-0495
James J Rooney,
EMP: 13
SALES (est): 1.3MM **Privately Held**
SIC: 2821 Plastics materials & resins

## (G-16707)
**FERRARA CANDY COMPANY (PA)**
1 Tower Ln Ste 2700 (60181-4641)
PHONE...................................708 366-0500
Fax: 708 366-5921
Todd Siwak, *CEO*
Jim Nicketta, *President*
Thomas P Polke, *President*
Bernie Woziwodzki, *President*
Cynthia Hiskes, *Chairman*
◆ EMP: 450 EST: 1908
SQ FT: 300,000
SALES (est): 616.5MM **Privately Held**
WEB: www.ferrarapan.com
SIC: 2064 Candy & other confectionery products; chewing candy, not chewing gum; chocolate candy, except solid chocolate; jellybeans

## (G-16708)
**GATEHOUSE MEDIA LLC**
Also Called: Metropolitan Newspapers, The
18w140 Butterfield Rd # 450 (60181-4857)
PHONE...................................585 598-0030
Fax: 630 368-0538
Christopher Biondi, *Editor*
Jean Hodges, *Editor*
Toni Mann, *Manager*
Bill Casey, *Manager*
Kalpana Ramanathan, *Manager*
EMP: 100
SALES (corp-wide): 1.2B **Publicly Held**
WEB: www.gatehousemedia.com
SIC: 2711 Newspapers, publishing & printing
HQ: Gatehouse Media, Llc
175 Sullys Trl Ste 300
Pittsford NY 14534
585 598-0030

## (G-16709)
**HEAT TRANSFER LABORATORIES**
2 Mid America Plz Ste 800 (60181-4727)
PHONE...................................708 715-4300
Bruce Green, *President*
EMP: 2
SALES (est): 207.8K **Privately Held**
WEB: www.heattransferlabs.com
SIC: 3589 Sewage & water treatment equipment

## (G-16710)
**HENG TUO USA INC (PA)**
Also Called: Nci Technology
1 Transam Plaza Dr # 545 (60181-4822)
PHONE...................................630 705-1898
Weilong LI, *Principal*
James Xu, *Principal*
▲ EMP: 8
SQ FT: 4,800
SALES (est): 1.1MM **Privately Held**
SIC: 3823 3621 3596 Temperature measurement instruments, industrial; industrial process measurement equipment; storage battery chargers, motor & engine generator type; baby scales; industrial scales

## (G-16711)
**HICX SOLUTIONS INC**
1 Tower Ln Ste 1700 (60181-4631)
PHONE...................................630 560-3640
Douglas Markle, *Exec VP*
EMP: 45 **Privately Held**
SIC: 7372 Application computer software
PA: Hicx Solutions Limited
Crusader House
London
203 544-5033

## (G-16712)
**HIPSKIND TECH SLTONS GROUP INC**
17w220 22nd St Ste 450 (60181-4471)
PHONE...................................630 920-0960
Fax: 630 920-0794
Stephen W Hipskind, *President*
EMP: 41
SALES (est): 9.3MM **Privately Held**
WEB: www.d1corp.com
SIC: 7373 3825 7382 Value-added resellers, computer systems; network analyzers; security systems services

## (G-16713)
**KANBO INTERNATIONAL (US) INC**
2 Mid America Plz Ste 800 (60181-4727)
PHONE...................................630 873-6320
Jianxin LI, *President*
James Hinkle, *Vice Pres*
Aling LI, *Administration*
EMP: 3
SALES (est): 91.3K **Privately Held**
SIC: 2099 Mfg Food Preparations

## (G-16714)
**LEDCOR CONSTRUCTION INC**
18w140 Butterfield Rd (60181-4843)
PHONE...................................630 916-1200
Fax: 630 916-1500
John Helliwell, *Manager*
Steven Cullen, *Director*
Kristen Roberts, *Executive Asst*
EMP: 10
SALES (corp-wide): 64.7MM **Privately Held**
SIC: 3661 Fiber optics communications equipment
PA: Ledcor Construction, Inc.
16000 Christensen Rd
Tukwila WA 98188

## (G-16715)
**LODAAT LLC (PA)**
Also Called: Nutraceuticals and Pharma Tls
2 Mid America Plz Ste 800 (60181-4727)
PHONE...................................630 248-2380
Yogeeta Khatau, *Opers Staff*
Ramila Khatau, *Mng Member*
EMP: 9 EST: 2007
SQ FT: 500,000
SALES (est): 50MM **Privately Held**
SIC: 2834 Extracts of botanicals: powdered, pilular, solid or fluid

## (G-16716)
**MAC GRAPHICS GROUP INC**
17w703 Butterfield Rd D (60181-4280)
P.O. Box 537, Elmhurst (60126-0537)
PHONE...................................630 620-7200
Fax: 630 620-7299
Robert J Cronin Jr, *President*
Bob Geiger, *Principal*
EMP: 8
SQ FT: 2,500
SALES (est): 690K **Privately Held**
WEB: www.macgraphicsgrp.com
SIC: 2759 7331 2752 7336 Commercial printing; publication printing; direct mail advertising services; commercial printing, lithographic; commercial art & graphic design

## (G-16717)
**NEXX BUSINESS SOLUTIONS INC**
17w727 Butterfield Rd (60181-4278)
PHONE...................................708 252-1958
Victoria Gatling, *CEO*
EMP: 4
SQ FT: 1,500
SALES (est): 286.8K **Privately Held**
SIC: 3151 Mittens, leather

## (G-16718)
**PTC INC**
1815 S Meyers Rd Ste 220 (60181-5227)
PHONE...................................630 827-4900
Fax: 630 536-1871
Howard Heppelmann, *Manager*
EMP: 25
SALES (corp-wide): 1.1B **Publicly Held**
WEB: www.ptc.com
SIC: 7372 Application computer software
PA: Ptc Inc.
140 Kendrick St
Needham MA 02494
781 370-5000

## (G-16719)
**PUMP SOLUTIONS GROUP (HQ)**
1815 S Meyers Rd Ste 670 (60181-5262)
PHONE...................................630 487-2240
John D Allen, *President*
EMP: 79
SALES (est): 147.6MM
SALES (corp-wide): 6.7B **Publicly Held**
SIC: 3561 Pumps & pumping equipment
PA: Dover Corporation
3005 Highland Pkwy # 200
Downers Grove IL 60515
630 541-1540

## (G-16720)
**S G C M CORP**
Also Called: Spot Printing & Office Sups
1s171 Summit Ave (60181-3904)
PHONE...................................630 953-2428
Sue Mehta, *President*
G C Mehta, *Vice Pres*
EMP: 4
SQ FT: 1,500
SALES (est): 583.7K **Privately Held**
SIC: 2752 5112 Commercial printing, offset; office supplies

## (G-16721)
**VASCO DATA SECURITY INC (DE)**
1901 S Meyers Rd Ste 210 (60181-5206)
PHONE...................................630 932-8844
Kendall Hunt, *CEO*
T Kendall Hunt, *CEO*
John C Haggard, *President*
Mario Houthooft, *President*
Jo Pelsmaeker, *Manager*
▲ EMP: 6
SALES (est): 1.2MM
SALES (corp-wide): 192.3MM **Publicly Held**
SIC: 3699 Security control equipment & systems
PA: Vasco Data Security International, Inc.
1901 S Meyers Rd Ste 210
Oakbrook Terrace IL 60181
630 932-8844

## (G-16722)
**VAUTO INC (DH)**
1901 S Meyers Rd Ste 700 (60181-5211)
PHONE...................................630 590-2000
Keith Jezek, *President*
Morrie Eisenberg, *Vice Pres*
John Griffin, *Vice Pres*
Randy Kobat, *Vice Pres*
Jill Tyson, *VP Finance*
EMP: 30
SALES (est): 10.4MM
SALES (corp-wide): 32.8B **Privately Held**
SIC: 7372 Prepackaged software
HQ: Autotrader.Com, Inc.
3003 Summit Blvd Fl 200
Brookhaven GA 30319
404 568-8000

## (G-16723)
**WOZNIAK INDUSTRIES INC (PA)**
Also Called: Gmp Metal Products
2 Mid America Plz Ste 700 (60181-4796)
PHONE...................................630 954-3400
Sandra Wozniak, *Ch of Bd*
Michael Wozniak, *President*
Michael Powers, *CFO*
Jason Komenda, *Controller*
Robert Gamboa, *Info Tech Mgr*
◆ EMP: 9
SQ FT: 3,000
SALES (est): 135MM **Privately Held**
WEB: www.wozniakindustries.com
SIC: 3469 3444 3462 Metal stampings; sheet metalwork; iron & steel forgings

---

## Oakland
### Coles County

## (G-16724)
**OAKLAND NOODLE COMPANY**
10 W Main St (61943-7182)
P.O. Box 644 (61943-0644)
PHONE...................................217 346-2322
Todd Ethington, *President*
EMP: 4
SALES (est): 399.8K **Privately Held**
SIC: 2099 8322 Noodles, fried (Chinese); geriatric social service

# Oakwood
## Vermilion County

**(G-16725)**
**JAMESON STEEL FABRICATION INC**
19965 Newtown Rd (61858-6272)
**PHONE**.................................217 354-2205
Fax: 217 354-4053
Doug Cunningham, *President*
Terry McElwain, *Vice Pres*
Michael Smith, *Controller*
Diana Jameson, *Manager*
Douglas Cunningham, *Info Tech Mgr*
**EMP:** 8
**SALES (est):** 2.5MM **Privately Held**
**SIC:** 3441 Fabricated structural metal

**(G-16726)**
**KEY CAR STEREO**
12078 Us Route 150 (61858-6146)
**PHONE**.................................217 446-4556
Bradley Key, *Owner*
**EMP:** 3
**SQ FT:** 2,500
**SALES:** 300K **Privately Held**
**WEB:** www.keycarstereo.com
**SIC:** 5731 3651 Sound equipment, automotive; amplifiers: radio, public address or musical instrument

# Oakwood Hills
## Mchenry County

**(G-16727)**
**NEIWEEM INDUSTRIES INC (PA)**
21 Greenview Rd (60013-1061)
**PHONE**.................................847 487-1239
Fax: 815 759-1377
Kurt Neiweem, *President*
**EMP:** 8
**SQ FT:** 4,000
**SALES (est):** 620K **Privately Held**
**WEB:** www.neiweemindustries.com
**SIC:** 3446 3441 1796 Fences or posts, ornamental iron or steel; fabricated structural metal; millwright

**(G-16728)**
**SIMON ZELIKMAN**
106 Meadow Ln (60013-1151)
P.O. Box 151, Cary (60013-0151)
**PHONE**.................................847 338-8031
Simon Zelikman, *Owner*
**EMP:** 3
**SALES:** 100K **Privately Held**
**SIC:** 3911 7631 Jewelry, precious metal; jewelry repair services

# Oblong
## Crawford County

**(G-16729)**
**BULLETIN**
103 W Main St Ste 4 (62449-1165)
P.O. Box 687, Olney (62450-0687)
**PHONE**.................................618 553-9764
**EMP:** 4
**SALES (est):** 243.2K **Privately Held**
**SIC:** 2711 Newspapers, publishing & printing

**(G-16730)**
**CORTELYOU MACHINE & WELDING**
511 E Main St (62449-1420)
P.O. Box 99 (62449-0099)
**PHONE**.................................618 592-3961
Fax: 618 592-4339
James E French, *President*
Lois Ikemire, *Admin Sec*
**EMP:** 6
**SQ FT:** 8,300
**SALES (est):** 798.2K **Privately Held**
**SIC:** 3599 7629 3533 3441 Machine shop, jobbing & repair; electrical repair shops; oil & gas field machinery; fabricated structural metal

**(G-16731)**
**CROSS OIL & WELL SERVICE INC**
104 E Missouri St (62449-1456)
**PHONE**.................................618 592-4609
John O Cross, *President*
**EMP:** 11
**SALES:** 1MM **Privately Held**
**SIC:** 1389 Oil field services

**(G-16732)**
**DEPENDABLE ELECTRIC**
728 E State Hwy 33 (62449)
P.O. Box 202 (62449-0202)
**PHONE**.................................618 592-3314
Phillip Rich, *Owner*
**EMP:** 2
**SQ FT:** 6,000
**SALES (est):** 200K **Privately Held**
**SIC:** 7694 5999 Electric motor repair; motors, electric

**(G-16733)**
**ROSS OIL CO INC**
11172 N 450th St (62449-2902)
**PHONE**.................................618 592-3808
Curtis Ross, *President*
Sandra Ross, *Admin Sec*
**EMP:** 4
**SALES (est):** 450K **Privately Held**
**SIC:** 1311 5172 Crude petroleum production; petroleum products

**(G-16734)**
**SCHAEFFER ELECTRIC CO (PA)**
400 S Taylor St (62449)
P.O. Box 52 (62449-0052)
**PHONE**.................................618 592-3231
Gary Plumber, *Owner*
**EMP:** 3
**SQ FT:** 10,000
**SALES (est):** 1.4MM **Privately Held**
**SIC:** 7694 Electric motor repair

**(G-16735)**
**T GRAPHICS**
701 S Range St (62449-1606)
**PHONE**.................................618 592-4145
Tony Madlem, *Owner*
**EMP:** 3
**SQ FT:** 5,000
**SALES (est):** 275K **Privately Held**
**SIC:** 2759 3993 2395 Screen printing; signs & advertising specialties; embroidery & art needlework

**(G-16736)**
**THIRD DAY OIL & GAS LLC**
210 S Range St (62449-1225)
P.O. Box 81, Casey (62420-0081)
**PHONE**.................................618 553-5538
Danny Sheridan, *Mng Member*
David Sheridan,
**EMP:** 4
**SALES (est):** 183.3K **Privately Held**
**SIC:** 1382 7389 Oil & gas exploration services;

**(G-16737)**
**WILLOWBROOK SAWMILL**
1469 E 1600th Ave (62449-4704)
**PHONE**.................................618 592-3806
**EMP:** 3
**SALES (est):** 196.4K **Privately Held**
**SIC:** 2421 Sawmills & planing mills, general

# Odin
## Marion County

**(G-16738)**
**AAA TRASH**
408 S Merritt St (62870-1190)
**PHONE**.................................618 775-1365
V Stull, *Principal*
**EMP:** 4
**SALES (est):** 330.6K **Privately Held**
**SIC:** 3089 Garbage containers, plastic

**(G-16739)**
**CITATION OIL & GAS CORP**
2302 Hoots Chapel Rd (62870-2527)
**PHONE**.................................618 548-2331
Fax: 618 548-2349
Michael Gorden, *Chief*
**EMP:** 18
**SALES (est):** 881.8K **Privately Held**
**SIC:** 1389 Oil field services

**(G-16740)**
**JJS HIGH TEC MACHINING INC**
103 N Everett St (62870-1008)
P.O. Box 213 (62870-0213)
**PHONE**.................................618 775-8840
John C January, *President*
**EMP:** 3 **EST:** 1997
**SALES (est):** 324.2K **Privately Held**
**SIC:** 3544 Special dies, tools, jigs & fixtures

**(G-16741)**
**ODIN FIRE PROTECTION DISTRICT**
100 Perkins St (62870-1262)
P.O. Box 223 (62870-0223)
**PHONE**.................................618 775-8292
Greg Miller, *Chief*
**EMP:** 25
**SALES (est):** 2.4MM **Privately Held**
**SIC:** 3711 Fire department vehicles (motor vehicles), assembly of

**(G-16742)**
**WILSON & WILSON MONUMENT CO**
406 W Poplar St (62870-1293)
P.O. Box 247 (62870-0247)
**PHONE**.................................618 775-6488
Lindel Adams, *President*
**EMP:** 15 **EST:** 1946
**SQ FT:** 1,200
**SALES (est):** 1.1MM **Privately Held**
**SIC:** 3281 5999 Cut stone & stone products; gravestones, finished; monuments, finished to custom order

# Ogden
## Champaign County

**(G-16743)**
**OGDEN METALWORKS INC**
301 N Marilyn St (61859-5813)
P.O. Box 128 (61859-0128)
**PHONE**.................................217 582-2552
Fax: 217 582-2746
Jeffrey L Mohr, *President*
Debbie Unzicker, *Manager*
▲ **EMP:** 15
**SQ FT:** 20,000
**SALES (est):** 3.6MM **Privately Held**
**WEB:** www.ogdenmetalworks.com
**SIC:** 3523 Farm machinery & equipment

**(G-16744)**
**SHAPE MASTER INC**
108 E Main St (61859-9527)
P.O. Box 372 (61859-0372)
**PHONE**.................................217 582-2638
Kenneth Cooley, *CEO*
Pamela Cooley, *Corp Secy*
Brian Holden, *Warehouse Mgr*
Andy Seibring, *Manager*
**EMP:** 8
**SALES (est):** 1.5MM **Privately Held**
**SIC:** 3082 Unsupported plastics profile shapes

**(G-16745)**
**SPORT REDI-MIX LLC**
401 Wilbur Ave (61859)
P.O. Box 292, Champaign (61824-0292)
**PHONE**.................................217 582-2555
Mile Ducey, *Owner*
**EMP:** 7
**SALES (corp-wide):** 4.3MM **Privately Held**
**WEB:** www.sportredimix.com
**SIC:** 3241 Cement, hydraulic
PA: Sport Redi-Mix, L.L.C.
401 Wilbur Ave
Champaign IL 61822
217 355-4222

# Oglesby
## Lasalle County

**(G-16746)**
**BADGE-A-MINIT LTD (HQ)**
345 N Lewis Ave (61348-1628)
**PHONE**.................................815 883-8822
Malcolm Roebuck, *Ch of Bd*
Cindy Kurkowski, *President*
Karen Sydlowski, *Controller*
◆ **EMP:** 21
**SQ FT:** 85,000
**SALES (est):** 15MM
**SALES (corp-wide):** 21.4MM **Privately Held**
**WEB:** www.badgeaminit.com
**SIC:** 5199 3999 Advertising specialties; badges, metal: policemen, firemen, etc.
PA: Malcolm Group, Inc
429 E North Water St
Chicago IL
815 883-8822

**(G-16747)**
**COOKIE KINGDOM INC**
1201 E Walnut St (61348-1344)
**PHONE**.................................815 883-3331
Fax: 815 883-3332
Quentin G Pierce, *Ch of Bd*
Clifford A Sheppard, *President*
**EMP:** 100
**SQ FT:** 38,000
**SALES (est):** 19.4MM **Privately Held**
**SIC:** 2052 Cookies

**(G-16748)**
**FIRST IMPRESSION**
211 S Columbia Ave (61348-1415)
**PHONE**.................................815 883-3357
Bill Quick, *Partner*
Robert Zetlis, *Partner*
**EMP:** 6
**SALES (est):** 100K **Privately Held**
**SIC:** 2395 2759 Embroidery & art needlework; commercial printing

**(G-16749)**
**HI-TECH ELCTRONIC PDTS MFG INC**
25 Hi Tech Dr (61348-9532)
**PHONE**.................................815 220-1543
Michael Johnson, *President*
Helen Letourneau, *Purch Mgr*
Sue Nickel, *Controller*
Kathy Johnson, *Human Res Mgr*
▲ **EMP:** 25
**SQ FT:** 33,000
**SALES:** 5.2MM **Privately Held**
**SIC:** 3679 Electronic circuits

**(G-16750)**
**JASIEK MOTOR REBUILDING INC**
451 E State Route 71 (61348-9720)
**PHONE**.................................815 883-3678
Fax: 815 883-9885
Jeff Jasiek, *President*
Jerry Jasiek, *Corp Secy*
Bonnie Jasiek, *Vice Pres*
**EMP:** 7
**SALES:** 300K **Privately Held**
**SIC:** 7539 7694 7692 3714 Machine shop, automotive; armature rewinding shops; welding repair; motor vehicle parts & accessories; motors & generators; internal combustion engines

**(G-16751)**
**LONE STAR INDUSTRIES INC**
490 Portland Ave (61348-1334)
P.O. Box 130 (61348-0130)
**PHONE**.................................815 883-3173
Fax: 815 883-3329
Mark Hubinsky, *Purchasing*
Richard Zimmell, *Manager*
**EMP:** 7

# Oglesby - Lasalle County (G-16752)

**SALES (corp-wide):** 271.5MM **Privately Held**
**SIC: 3241** Portland cement
**HQ:** Lone Star Industries Inc
10401 N Meridian St # 400
Indianapolis IN 46290
317 706-3314

**(G-16752)**
**WIRE MESH LLC**
42 Marquette Ave (61348-1461)
**PHONE**...............................815 579-8597
Rafael Barrenechea, *Mng Member*
**EMP:** 6
**SALES (est):** 842.1K **Privately Held**
**SIC: 3496** Miscellaneous fabricated wire products

## Ohio
### Bureau County

**(G-16753)**
**SISLER DAIRY PRODUCTS COMPANY**
Also Called: Sisler's Ice & Ice Cream Co
102 S Grove St (61349)
**PHONE**...............................815 376-2913
William M Sisler, *President*
Karen Anderson, *Corp Secy*
Daniel G Thompson, *Shareholder*
**EMP:** 5 **EST:** 1907
**SQ FT:** 10,500
**SALES (est):** 649.7K **Privately Held**
**WEB:** www.sislers.com
**SIC: 2097** 2024 Ice cubes; ice cream, packaged: molded, on sticks, etc.

## Okawville
### Washington County

**(G-16754)**
**OKAWVILLE TIMES**
Also Called: Putt and Times
109 E Walnut St (62271-1883)
**PHONE**...............................618 243-5563
**Fax:** 618 243-5563
Gary Stricker, *Owner*
**EMP:** 3 **EST:** 1893
**SALES (est):** 219.9K **Privately Held**
**SIC: 2711** 7999 2791 Commercial printing & newspaper publishing combined; miniature golf course operation; typesetting

**(G-16755)**
**QUAD-COUNTY READY MIX CORP (PA)**
300 W 12th St (62271-2137)
P.O. Box 158 (62271-0158)
**PHONE**...............................618 243-6430
**Fax:** 618 243-6300
Herbert Hustedde, *President*
Carol Hustedde, *Vice Pres*
**EMP:** 17 **EST:** 1952
**SQ FT:** 1,500
**SALES (est):** 18.9MM **Privately Held**
**SIC: 3273** Ready-mixed concrete

## Old Mill Creek
### Lake County

**(G-16756)**
**TEMPEL STEEL COMPANY**
Also Called: Tempel Farms
17000 W Wadsworth Rd (60083-9761)
**PHONE**...............................847 244-5330
**Fax:** 773 244-5069
Jill West, *Bookkeeper*
Larry Leffingwell, *Manager*
Jodi Inger, *IT/INT Sup*
**EMP:** 15
**SQ FT:** 1,500
**SALES (corp-wide):** 714.1MM **Privately Held**
**SIC: 3313** Electrometallurgical products
**PA:** Tempel Steel Company
5500 N Wolcott Ave
Chicago IL 60640
773 250-8000

## Olmsted
### Pulaski County

**(G-16757)**
**AFCO INDUSTRIES INC**
8161 State Highway 37 (62970-2240)
**PHONE**...............................618 742-6469
**EMP:** 9
**SALES (corp-wide):** 91.4MM **Privately Held**
**SIC: 3354** Aluminum extruded products
**PA:** Afco Industries, Inc.
3400 Roy Ave
Alexandria LA 71302
318 448-1651

## Olney
### Richland County

**(G-16758)**
**ALLANS WELDING & MACHINE INC**
3815 E Ilinois Hwy 250 (62450)
P.O. Box 343 (62450-0343)
**PHONE**...............................618 392-3708
**Fax:** 618 393-4208
Allan May, *President*
Rhonda May, *Vice Pres*
**EMP:** 8
**SQ FT:** 200
**SALES (est):** 1.4MM **Privately Held**
**SIC: 7692** 3599 Welding repair; machine shop, jobbing & repair

**(G-16759)**
**AMERICAN CIPS**
4978 N Il 130 (62450-3740)
**PHONE**...............................618 393-5641
Ron Bailey, *Principal*
**EMP:** 3
**SALES (est):** 140K **Privately Held**
**SIC: 3612** Voltage regulators, transmission & distribution

**(G-16760)**
**ANGEL ROSE ENERGY LLC**
4368 N Holly Rd (62450-3318)
**PHONE**...............................618 392-3700
Cody Heer, *Mng Member*
**EMP:** 4 **EST:** 2007
**SALES (est):** 390K **Privately Held**
**SIC: 1382** Oil & gas exploration services

**(G-16761)**
**BAKER HGHES OLFLD OPRTIONS INC**
Also Called: Baker Atlas
930 S West St (62450-1319)
**PHONE**...............................618 393-2919
Donald Lapalne, *Manager*
**EMP:** 16
**SALES (corp-wide):** 9.8B **Privately Held**
**WEB:** www.bakeratlas.com
**SIC: 1382** 1389 1381 Oil & gas exploration, seismograph surveys; oil field services; well logging; drilling oil & gas wells
**HQ:** Baker Hughes Oilfield Operations, Inc.
17021 Aldine Westfield Rd
Houston TX 77073
713 879-1000

**(G-16762)**
**BENCHMARK PROPERTIES LTD**
Also Called: Blumthal Gas Geologist
5076 N Il 130 (62450-3742)
P.O. Box 419 (62450-0419)
**PHONE**...............................618 395-7023
**Fax:** 618 395-8647
James Blumthal, *President*
**EMP:** 2
**SQ FT:** 2,400
**SALES (est):** 250K **Privately Held**
**SIC: 1382** Oil & gas exploration services

**(G-16763)**
**BILLS MACHINE & POWER TRANSM (PA)**
Also Called: Bm Machine & Fabrication
4678 Weinmann Dr Ste B (62450-1845)
**PHONE**...............................618 392-2500
**Fax:** 618 392-2559
James Harmon, *President*
Timothy Berry, *Vice Pres*
Sherry Inyart, *Treasurer*
Kieth Barber, *Office Mgr*
William Barber, *Director*
▲ **EMP:** 21
**SQ FT:** 12,000
**SALES (est):** 3.2MM **Privately Held**
**WEB:** www.billsmachine.com
**SIC: 3599** Machine shop, jobbing & repair

**(G-16764)**
**CONCORD OIL & GAS CORPORATION**
1712 S Whittle Ave (62450-3426)
**PHONE**...............................618 393-2124
Greg Gibson, *President*
Peter A Morse Sr, *Incorporator*
**EMP:** 20
**SALES (est):** 1.1MM **Privately Held**
**SIC: 1389** Oil field services; servicing oil & gas wells

**(G-16765)**
**CONCORD WELL SERVICE INC**
1102 N East St (62450-2489)
P.O. Box 448 (62450-0448)
**PHONE**...............................618 395-4405
Peter Morse, *President*
Kate Blackford, *Office Mgr*
**EMP:** 5
**SALES (est):** 500K **Privately Held**
**SIC: 1311** Crude petroleum & natural gas

**(G-16766)**
**FEHRENBACHER READY-MIX INC**
1401 S Whittle Ave (62450-3444)
**PHONE**...............................618 395-2306
**Fax:** 618 395-2306
Tom Fehrenbacher, *President*
Barbara Miller, *Manager*
**EMP:** 5
**SALES (est):** 495.4K **Privately Held**
**SIC: 3273** Ready-mixed concrete

**(G-16767)**
**FLOYDS WELDING SERVICE**
3519 N Union Dr (62450-5141)
**PHONE**...............................618 395-2414
Darrell Fehrenbacher, *Owner*
**EMP:** 4 **EST:** 1946
**SQ FT:** 3,200
**SALES (est):** 407.4K **Privately Held**
**SIC: 7692** Automotive welding

**(G-16768)**
**FOX CREEK VINEYARDS**
5502 N Fox Rd (62450-3734)
**PHONE**...............................618 395-3325
**Fax:** 618 392-0418
Gordon Schnepper, *President*
Della Schnepper, *Vice Pres*
Marlene Schnepper, *Vice Pres*
**EMP:** 3
**SALES (est):** 221.5K **Privately Held**
**WEB:** www.foxcreekwinery.com
**SIC: 2084** Wines

**(G-16769)**
**GATEHOUSE MEDIA LLC**
Also Called: Olney Daily Reporter
206 S Whittle Ave (62450-2251)
P.O. Box 340 (62450-0340)
**PHONE**...............................618 393-2931
**Fax:** 618 392-2953
Carol Garison, *General Mgr*
**EMP:** 24
**SALES (corp-wide):** 1.2B **Publicly Held**
**WEB:** www.gatehousemedia.com
**SIC: 2711** Newspapers
**HQ:** Gatehouse Media, Llc
175 Sullys Trl Ste 300
Pittsford NY 14534
585 598-0030

**(G-16770)**
**GLOVER OIL FIELD SERVICE INC**
4993 N Il 130 (62450-3741)
**PHONE**...............................618 395-3624
**Fax:** 618 392-3919
Carmon L Glover Jr, *President*
Robert Swinson, *Manager*
**EMP:** 11 **EST:** 1960
**SQ FT:** 5,000
**SALES (est):** 500K **Privately Held**
**SIC: 1381** 1389 1311 Drilling oil & gas wells; cementing oil & gas well casings; crude petroleum & natural gas production

**(G-16771)**
**HOUPT REVOLVING CUTTERS INC**
516 W Butler St (62450-1407)
**PHONE**...............................618 395-1913
**Fax:** 618 392-6100
Kenneth D Houpt, *President*
Katherine Houpt, *Treasurer*
Patricia Houpt, *Admin Sec*
**EMP:** 1
**SQ FT:** 3,200
**SALES (est):** 213.4K **Privately Held**
**SIC: 3556** Cutting, chopping, grinding, mixing & similar machinery

**(G-16772)**
**IMPERIAL TRAILER MFG INC**
3519 N Union Dr (62450-5141)
**PHONE**...............................618 395-2414
**Fax:** 618 392-3338
Darrell Fehrenbacher, *President*
Mimi Fehrenbacher, *Admin Sec*
**EMP:** 14
**SQ FT:** 12,000
**SALES (est):** 2.3MM **Privately Held**
**SIC: 3715** Truck trailers

**(G-16773)**
**JABAT INC**
715 N West St (62450-1033)
P.O. Box 38 (62450-0038)
**PHONE**...............................618 392-3010
**Fax:** 618 392-3812
Stanley Kulkaski, *President*
Aaron Ackman, *Vice Pres*
Rita Kman, *Vice Pres*
Tom Simmering, *Vice Pres*
Sandy French, *Accountant*
**EMP:** 50
**SQ FT:** 75,000
**SALES (est):** 11.9MM **Privately Held**
**WEB:** www.jabat.com
**SIC: 3082** Tubes, unsupported plastic

**(G-16774)**
**JOE HUNT**
1911 E Main St (62450-3312)
**PHONE**...............................618 392-2000
Joe Hunt, *Principal*
▲ **EMP:** 3
**SALES (est):** 327.2K **Privately Held**
**SIC: 3751** 5091 8748 Motorcycles, bicycles & parts; bicycle equipment & supplies; business consulting

**(G-16775)**
**KABINET KRAFT**
536 E Cherry St (62450-2727)
**PHONE**...............................618 395-1047
Bob Buscher, *President*
**EMP:** 15
**SALES (est):** 1.8MM **Privately Held**
**SIC: 5031** 5211 2541 2434 Lumber, plywood & millwork; cabinets, kitchen; wood partitions & fixtures; wood kitchen cabinets; millwork

**(G-16776)**
**KAPP COMPANY LLC**
3600 E White Ln (62450-5537)
**PHONE**...............................618 676-1000
**Fax:** 618 676-1384
Chesleigh Kapp,
**EMP:** 3
**SALES (est):** 310K **Privately Held**
**SIC: 1381** Drilling oil & gas wells

# GEOGRAPHIC SECTION

**(G-16777)**
**LIQUID RESIN INTERNATIONAL**
4295 N Holly Rd (62450-4813)
P.O. Box 760 (62450-0760)
PHONE ............................... 618 392-3590
James Pottor, *President*
Thomas F Sloan, *Vice Pres*
Anthony Reed, *Manager*
**EMP:** 20
**SQ FT:** 7,800
**SALES (est):** 3.6MM **Privately Held**
**WEB:** www.liquidresins.com
**SIC:** 5169 2869 Chemicals & allied products; industrial organic chemicals

**(G-16778)**
**M & L WELL SERVICE INC**
3648 N Illinois 130 (62450)
P.O. Box 670 (62450-0670)
PHONE ............................... 618 393-7144
**EMP:** 20 **EST:** 1978
**SALES (est):** 930K **Privately Held**
**SIC:** 1389 Oil/Gas Field Services

**(G-16779)**
**M & L WELL SERVICE INC**
800 E Main St (62450-2620)
P.O. Box 670 (62450-0670)
PHONE ............................... 618 395-4538
**Fax:** 618 395-4538
Harold Murbarger, *President*
George Lambird, *Treasurer*
**EMP:** 9
**SQ FT:** 4,000
**SALES:** 600K **Privately Held**
**SIC:** 1389 1761 Servicing oil & gas wells; roofing, siding & sheet metal work

**(G-16780)**
**MASTER-HALCO INC**
4633 E Radio Tower Ln (62450-4742)
PHONE ............................... 618 395-4365
**Fax:** 618 392-3125
Mike Uhl, *Manager*
**EMP:** 50
**SALES (corp-wide):** 42.5B **Privately Held**
**WEB:** www.fenceonline.com
**SIC:** 3315 5031 3496 Chain link fencing; lumber, plywood & millwork; miscellaneous fabricated wire products
**HQ:** Master-Halco, Inc.
3010 Lbj Fwy Ste 800
Dallas TX 75234
972 714-7300

**(G-16781)**
**MIDWEST DESIGN & AUTOMTN INC**
302 N Walnut St (62450-2103)
PHONE ............................... 618 392-2892
Gary Kallenbach, *President*
Steve Sterchi, *Vice Pres*
**EMP:** 6
**SQ FT:** 6,000
**SALES:** 300K **Privately Held**
**SIC:** 3599 7699 7629 Machine shop, jobbing & repair; motorcycle repair service; electrical repair shops

**(G-16782)**
**MOLDING SERVICES ILLINOIS INC**
126 N West St (62450-1107)
PHONE ............................... 618 395-3888
Anthony King, *CEO*
Andy Scheutz, *Vice Pres*
Debbie King, *Manager*
▲ **EMP:** 28
**SALES (est):** 6MM **Privately Held**
**SIC:** 3089 Injection molding of plastics

**(G-16783)**
**MURVIN & MEIR OIL CO**
1102 N East St (62450-2489)
P.O. Box 396 (62450-0396)
PHONE ............................... 618 395-4405
**Fax:** 618 395-3207
Don Runyon, *Corp Secy*
Peter Morse, *Exec VP*
Kate M Blackford, *Vice Pres*
David W Meier Sr, *Director*
**EMP:** 7 **EST:** 1964
**SALES (est):** 839.8K **Privately Held**
**SIC:** 1311 Crude petroleum & natural gas

**(G-16784)**
**MURVIN OIL COMPANY**
1712 S Whittle Ave (62450-3426)
P.O. Box 297 (62450-0297)
PHONE ............................... 618 393-2124
Gregg C Gibson, *President*
Anthony C Gibson, *Vice Pres*
**EMP:** 22
**SALES (est):** 4.4MM **Privately Held**
**SIC:** 1311 Crude petroleum production

**(G-16785)**
**NATIONAL VINEGAR CO**
203 W South Ave (62450-1776)
PHONE ............................... 618 395-1011
**Fax:** 618 393-4502
Steve Wilson, *Manager*
**EMP:** 11 **Privately Held**
**SIC:** 2099 Vinegar

**(G-16786)**
**OLDE PRINT SHOPPE INC**
Also Called: Print Shoppe Inc The Olde
1314 E Main St (62450-2630)
PHONE ............................... 618 395-3833
Max Balding, *President*
Velda Balding, *Treasurer*
Greg Balding, *Manager*
**EMP:** 8
**SQ FT:** 5,100
**SALES (est):** 986.2K **Privately Held**
**SIC:** 2752 2759 2789 Commercial printing, offset; letterpress printing; typesetting; bookbinding & related work

**(G-16787)**
**OLNEY DAILY MAIL**
206 S Whittle Ave (62450-2251)
PHONE ............................... 618 393-2931
Kerry Kocher, *Owner*
**EMP:** 50 **EST:** 2010
**SALES (est):** 1.5MM **Privately Held**
**SIC:** 2741 Miscellaneous publishing

**(G-16788)**
**OLNEY MACHINE & DESIGN INC**
4632 E Radio T (62450)
P.O. Box 66 (62450-0066)
PHONE ............................... 618 392-6634
Doug Walker, *President*
**EMP:** 10
**SQ FT:** 6,400
**SALES (est):** 2.1MM **Privately Held**
**SIC:** 3599 Machine & other job shop work

**(G-16789)**
**PACIFIC CYCLE INC**
4730 E Radio Tower Ln (62450-4743)
P.O. Box 344 (62450-0344)
PHONE ............................... 618 393-2508
**Fax:** 618 393-2396
Mike Fritz, *Vice Pres*
Bernie Kotlier, *Vice Pres*
Jim Slattery, *Vice Pres*
Howard Atkison, *VP Opers*
Barbara Smith, *Branch Mgr*
**EMP:** 200
**SQ FT:** 1,000,000
**SALES (corp-wide):** 2.6B **Privately Held**
**WEB:** www.pacific-cycle.com
**SIC:** 3751 3944 Bicycles & related parts; sleds, children's; wagons: coaster, express & play: children's
**HQ:** Pacific Cycle Inc.
4902 Hammersley Rd
Madison WI 53711
608 268-2468

**(G-16790)**
**PINNACLE EXPLORATION CORP**
510 E Lafayette St (62450-2914)
P.O. Box 428 (62450-0428)
PHONE ............................... 618 395-8100
**Fax:** 618 395-8100
George Hagan, *President*
Jmaes Hagan, *Vice Pres*
Carletta Hagan, *Admin Sec*
**EMP:** 4
**SQ FT:** 5,000
**SALES (est):** 351.1K **Privately Held**
**SIC:** 1389 Oil field services

**(G-16791)**
**PRAIRIE FARMS DAIRY INC**
217 W Main St (62450-1532)
P.O. Box 128 (62450-0128)
PHONE ............................... 618 392-2128
**Fax:** 618 392-2668
Ron Wilke, *Plant Mgr*
Terry Michaels, *Office Mgr*
Kenny Kuhn, *Manager*
**EMP:** 60
**SALES (corp-wide):** 1.8B **Privately Held**
**WEB:** www.prairiefarms.com
**SIC:** 2026 Milk processing (pasteurizing, homogenizing, bottling)
**PA:** Prairie Farms Dairy, Inc.
1100 Broadway
Carlinville IL 62626
217 854-2547

**(G-16792)**
**PRECISION PLUGGING AND SLS INC**
108 Linn St (62450-4538)
P.O. Box 22 (62450-0022)
PHONE ............................... 618 395-8510
John L Runyon, *President*
Jonathan Runyon, *Vice Pres*
Elizabeth Fore, *Admin Sec*
**EMP:** 10
**SALES (est):** 1.3MM **Privately Held**
**SIC:** 1389 Well plugging & abandoning, oil & gas

**(G-16793)**
**PRINTFORCE INC**
1409 E Main St (62450-3162)
PHONE ............................... 618 395-7746
**Fax:** 618 395-7746
Bob McClenatham, *President*
**EMP:** 4
**SALES:** 200K **Privately Held**
**SIC:** 2759 Commercial printing

**(G-16794)**
**RUNYON OIL PRODUCTION INC**
208 Linn St (62450)
P.O. Box 22 (62450-0022)
PHONE ............................... 618 395-8510
John Runyon, *President*
**EMP:** 4
**SALES (est):** 570.8K **Privately Held**
**SIC:** 1381 Drilling oil & gas wells

**(G-16795)**
**RUNYON OIL TOOLS INC**
331 Herman Dr (62450-4766)
PHONE ............................... 618 395-5045
Steven E Runyon, *President*
**EMP:** 8
**SQ FT:** 4,500
**SALES (est):** 490K **Privately Held**
**SIC:** 1389 Grading oil & gas well foundations

**(G-16796)**
**SANSUI AMERICA INC**
3471 N Union Dr (62450-5142)
PHONE ............................... 618 392-7000
Edward Beller, *Branch Mgr*
**EMP:** 133
**SALES (corp-wide):** 46.1MM **Privately Held**
**WEB:** www.orionsalesinc.com
**SIC:** 5064 3651 Electrical appliances, television & radio; household audio & video equipment
**PA:** Sansui America, Inc.
28 W Grand Ave Ste 2
Montvale NJ 07645
201 587-8900

**(G-16797)**
**STEVEN A ZANETIS**
1060 W Main St (62450-1100)
P.O. Box 99 (62450-0099)
PHONE ............................... 618 393-2176
Steven A Zanetis, *Owner*
**EMP:** 5
**SALES (est):** 262.6K **Privately Held**
**SIC:** 1311 Crude petroleum & natural gas production

**(G-16798)**
**TRI-STATE PRODUCING DEVELOPING**
1060 W Main St (62450-1100)
P.O. Box 99 (62450-0099)
PHONE ............................... 618 393-2176
Steven A Zanetis, *President*
L Ronald Schwarzlose, *Vice Pres*
**EMP:** 5
**SQ FT:** 3,000
**SALES (est):** 707.9K **Privately Held**
**SIC:** 1311 Crude petroleum production

**(G-16799)**
**U S WEIGHT INC**
Also Called: Escalade Sports
4594 E Radio Tower Ln (62450-4748)
PHONE ............................... 618 392-0408
Robert E Griffin, *President*
Bob Quinn, *Director*
Deborah Meinert, *Admin Sec*
▲ **EMP:** 35
**SQ FT:** 100,000
**SALES:** 9MM
**SALES (corp-wide):** 167.6MM **Publicly Held**
**SIC:** 3949 Dumbbells & other weightlifting equipment
**HQ:** Indian Industries Inc
817 Maxwell Ave
Evansville IN 47711
812 467-1200

**(G-16800)**
**WABASH VALLEY SERVICE CO**
Also Called: Rich-Law
1201 S Whittle Ave (62450-3437)
P.O. Box 403 (62450-0403)
PHONE ............................... 618 393-2971
**Fax:** 618 392-3842
Ben Anderson, *Manager*
**EMP:** 10
**SALES (corp-wide):** 57.7MM **Privately Held**
**WEB:** www.wabashvalleyrodders.com
**SIC:** 5171 5191 5199 5083 Petroleum bulk stations & terminals; feed; plant food; farm & garden machinery; fertilizers, mixing only
**PA:** Wabash Valley Service Co
909 N Court St
Grayville IL 62844
888 869-8127

**(G-16801)**
**XENIA MFG INC**
1915 Miller Dr (62450-4744)
P.O. Box 237, Xenia (62899-0237)
PHONE ............................... 618 392-7212
**Fax:** 618 392-2504
Yancey Glassford, *Manager*
**EMP:** 40
**SALES (corp-wide):** 22MM **Privately Held**
**WEB:** www.xmiharness.com
**SIC:** 3694 Harness wiring sets, internal combustion engines
**PA:** Xenia Mfg., Inc.
1507 Church St
Xenia IL 62899
618 678-2218

**(G-16802)**
**YOCKEY OIL INCORPORATED**
1043 W Main St (62450-1156)
P.O. Box 70 (62450-0070)
PHONE ............................... 618 393-6236
Carolyn Ledtka-Crow, *President*
James Blumthal, *Vice Pres*
Donald Quillen, *Vice Pres*
Connie Shafer, *Treasurer*
**EMP:** 2 **EST:** 1968
**SALES (est):** 305.6K **Privately Held**
**SIC:** 1311 Crude petroleum production

## Olympia Fields
### Cook County

**(G-16803)**
**NAS MEDIA GROUP INC (PA)**
424 Brookwood Ter 2 (60461-1539)
PHONE ............................... 312 371-7499
Michael Gardner, *CEO*

Brandi McGhee, *CFO*
**EMP:** 6
**SALES (est)** 1.3MM **Privately Held**
**SIC:** 2741  8748  Business service newsletters: publishing & printing; business consulting

**(G-16804)**
**OFGD INC**
2401 Lincoln Hwy  (60461-1901)
**PHONE** ................................. 708 283-7101
George Nediyakalayil, *President*
**EMP:** 2
**SALES (est):** 248.9K **Privately Held**
**SIC:** 1382  Oil & gas exploration services

**(G-16805)**
**REFINERS HOUSE**
20227 Overland Trl  (60461-1138)
**PHONE** ................................. 708 922-0772
Katrina Laquanda Harris, *Principal*
**EMP:** 3
**SALES (est):** 155.8K **Privately Held**
**SIC:** 3339  Primary nonferrous metals

**(G-16806)**
**TIA TYNETTE DESIGNS INC**
2600 Troy Cir  (60461-1951)
**PHONE** ................................. 219 440-2859
Tia Rogers, *President*
**EMP:** 2 **EST:** 2008
**SALES (est):** 213.2K **Privately Held**
**SIC:** 3172  5094  Cases, jewelry; jewelry & precious stones

## Omaha
### Gallatin County

**(G-16807)**
**HAYDEN MILLS INC**
Also Called: Omaha Grain & Fertilizer
119 Washington Ave  (62871)
P.O. Box 98  (62871-0098)
**PHONE** ................................. 618 962-3136
**Fax:** 618 962-3411
David Sutton, *President*
Richard Sutton, *Vice Pres*
**EMP:** 33
**SQ FT:** 3,000
**SALES:** 10MM **Privately Held**
**SIC:** 5191  2875  2041  Farm supplies; fertilizers, mixing only; flour & other grain mill products

## Onarga
### Iroquois County

**(G-16808)**
**ANGEL WIND ENERGY INC**
113 N Pine St  (60955-1081)
**PHONE** ................................. 815 471-2020
Michael Harroun, *President*
Ben Harroun, *Vice Pres*
Benjamin Harroun, *Vice Pres*
Will Harroun, *Project Mgr*
**EMP:** 3 **EST:** 2008
**SALES (est):** 293.6K **Privately Held**
**SIC:** 3511  Turbines & turbine generator sets

**(G-16809)**
**PROCOMM INC HOOPESTON ILLINOIS**
209 W Grant Ave  (60955-1117)
P.O. Box 149  (60955-0149)
**PHONE** ................................. 815 268-4303
James M Bennett, *President*
Tondra Bennett, *Co-Owner*
Karen Small, *Finance Dir*
▲ **EMP:** 34 **EST:** 1999
**SQ FT:** 25,000
**SALES (est):** 4.9MM **Privately Held**
**SIC:** 3669  5999  Intercommunication systems, electric; communication equipment

## Opdyke
### Jefferson County

**(G-16810)**
**CROOKED TRAILS SAWMILL**
18058 E Il Highway 142  (62872-2405)
**PHONE** ................................. 618 244-1547
David Mast, *Owner*
**EMP:** 3 **EST:** 2008
**SALES:** 130K **Privately Held**
**SIC:** 2421  Sawmills & planing mills, general

**(G-16811)**
**T HAM SIGN INC (PA)**
7699 N Goshen Ln  (62872-2707)
P.O. Box 155, Mount Vernon  (62864-0004)
**PHONE** ................................. 618 242-2010
**Fax:** 618 242-2016
Todd Ham, *President*
Carmen Ham, *Vice Pres*
John Dungan, *Marketing Staff*
Jennifer Vineyard, *Admin Sec*
Jason Suchomski, *Graphic Designe*
**EMP:** 15 **EST:** 1954
**SQ FT:** 3,800
**SALES (est):** 2.4MM **Privately Held**
**WEB:** www.thamsign.com
**SIC:** 1799  3993  Sign installation & maintenance; signs & advertising specialties

## Oquawka
### Henderson County

**(G-16812)**
**OQUAWKA BOATS AND FABRICATIONS**
1312 E State Highway 164  (61469-7017)
**PHONE** ................................. 309 867-2213
**Fax:** 309 867-2211
Carmen Thompson, *President*
**EMP:** 5
**SQ FT:** 9,000
**SALES (est):** 864.2K **Privately Held**
**WEB:** www.oquawkaboats.com
**SIC:** 3732  7699  Boat building & repairing; boat repair

**(G-16813)**
**PRO FUEL NINE INC**
101 S 8th St  (61469-9531)
**PHONE** ................................. 309 867-3375
Sean Chinna, *Principal*
**EMP:** 4 **EST:** 2011
**SALES (est):** 307.5K **Privately Held**
**SIC:** 2869  Fuels

## Orangeville
### Stephenson County

**(G-16814)**
**COREFX INGREDIENTS LLC**
12495 N Pleasant Hill Rd  (61060-9758)
**PHONE** ................................. 773 271-2663
Michael Ernster, *Branch Mgr*
**EMP:** 15 **Privately Held**
**SIC:** 2023  Dry, condensed, evaporated dairy products
**HQ:** Corefx Ingredients Llc
4725 W North Ave Ste 240
Chicago IL 60639
773 271-2663

**(G-16815)**
**HOGBACK HAVEN MAPLE FARM**
Also Called: Hogback Hardwoods
13800 N Hogback Rd  (61060-9794)
**PHONE** ................................. 815 291-9440
Scott E Elsasser, *Owner*
**EMP:** 9
**SALES (est):** 379.2K **Privately Held**
**SIC:** 2099  Sugar, industrial maple

## Oreana
### Macon County

**(G-16816)**
**AKERS PACKAGING SOLUTIONS INC**
Also Called: Akers Packg Solutions Decatur
7573 N State Route 48  (62554)
P.O. Box 248  (62554-0248)
**PHONE** ................................. 217 468-2396
David Econie, *General Mgr*
**EMP:** 28
**SALES (corp-wide):** 11.9MM **Privately Held**
**SIC:** 2653  Corrugated & solid fiber boxes
**PA:** Akers Packaging Solutions, Inc.
2820 Lefferson Rd
Middletown OH 45044
513 422-6312

**(G-16817)**
**GREIF INC**
7573 N Rte 48  (62554)
P.O. Box 248  (62554-0248)
**PHONE** ................................. 217 468-2396
Jean Myers, *Purchasing*
David Econie, *Manager*
Paul J Smith, *Manager*
**EMP:** 56
**SALES (corp-wide):** 3.3B **Publicly Held**
**WEB:** www.greif.com
**SIC:** 2653  Boxes, corrugated: made from purchased materials; boxes, solid fiber: made from purchased materials
**PA:** Greif, Inc.
425 Winter Rd
Delaware OH 43015
740 549-6000

## Oregon
### Ogle County

**(G-16818)**
**ART CASTING OF IL INC**
5 Madison St  (61061-1852)
P.O. Box 394  (61061-0394)
**PHONE** ................................. 815 732-7777
Karlyn K Spell, *President*
Harry Spell, *Vice Pres*
**EMP:** 9
**SALES (est):** 790K **Privately Held**
**WEB:** www.harryspell.com
**SIC:** 3366  Castings (except die): bronze

**(G-16819)**
**B F SHAW PRINTING COMPANY**
Also Called: Ogle County Newspaper
121 S 4th St Ste A  (61061-1628)
P.O. Box 8  (61061-0008)
**PHONE** ................................. 815 732-6166
**Fax:** 815 732-4238
Earleen Hinton, *Manager*
Jim Harrison, *Manager*
Bob Wendt, *Director*
**EMP:** 8
**SALES (corp-wide):** 83.1MM **Privately Held**
**WEB:** www.bcrnews.com
**SIC:** 2711  Newspapers
**PA:** The B F Shaw Printing Company
444 Pine Hill Dr
Dixon IL
815 284-4000

**(G-16820)**
**COILCRAFT INCORPORATED**
9 Clay St  (61061-2030)
**PHONE** ................................. 815 732-6834
**Fax:** 815 732-2735
Lupe Angeles, *QC Mgr*
Phil Devers, *Engineer*
Vickie Berner, *Sales Staff*
Paul Slonsky, *Manager*
Brent Kruger, *Manager*
**EMP:** 100
**SALES (corp-wide):** 476.5K **Privately Held**
**SIC:** 3677  Coil windings, electronic; electronic transformers; filtration devices, electronic
**PA:** Coilcraft, Incorporated
1102 Silver Lake Rd
Cary IL 60013
847 639-2361

**(G-16821)**
**DAYTON SUPERIOR CORPORATION**
Also Called: Dayton Richmond
402 S 1st St  (61061-1836)
**PHONE** ................................. 815 732-3136
**Fax:** 815 732-2866
John Farrenkopf, *Mfg Staff*
Kevin Miller, *Purchasing*
**EMP:** 20 **Publicly Held**
**WEB:** www.daytonsuperior.com
**SIC:** 2899  3496  Concrete curing & hardening compounds; miscellaneous fabricated wire products
**HQ:** Dayton Superior Corporation
1125 Byers Rd
Miamisburg OH 45342
937 866-0711

**(G-16822)**
**ED ETNYRE & CO**
Also Called: Oci Manufacturing Company
1333 S Daysville Rd  (61061-9778)
**PHONE** ................................. 815 732-2116
Roger L Etnyre, *President*
Sharon Engel, *Vice Pres*
**EMP:** 375
**SQ FT:** 225,000
**SALES (est):** 56MM
**SALES (corp-wide):** 88.5MM **Privately Held**
**WEB:** www.etnyre.com
**SIC:** 3531  3711  3537  Road construction & maintenance machinery; chip spreaders, self-propelled; motor vehicles & car bodies; industrial trucks & tractors
**PA:** Etnyre International, Ltd.
1333 S Daysville Rd
Oregon IL 61061
815 732-2116

**(G-16823)**
**ETNYRE INTERNATIONAL LTD (PA)**
1333 S Daysville Rd  (61061-9783)
**PHONE** ................................. 815 732-2116
**Fax:** 815 732-7400
Roger L Etnyre, *Ch of Bd*
Thomas Brown, *President*
Tim Krueger, *General Mgr*
Brian Horner, *Regional Mgr*
Dennis Muse, *Regional Mgr*
◆ **EMP:** 300
**SQ FT:** 250,000
**SALES (est):** 88.5MM **Privately Held**
**WEB:** www.etnyre.com
**SIC:** 3531  Road construction & maintenance machinery

**(G-16824)**
**F N SMITH CORPORATION**
1200 S 2nd St  (61061-2330)
P.O. Box 179  (61061-0179)
**PHONE** ................................. 815 732-2171
**Fax:** 815 732-6173
Fred N Smith, *CEO*
Ed N Smith, *President*
Louise M Smith, *Corp Secy*
Gary Reding, *Plant Mgr*
Julie Kelly, *Purch Mgr*
**EMP:** 45
**SQ FT:** 20,000
**SALES (est):** 10.5MM **Privately Held**
**WEB:** www.fnsmithcorp.com
**SIC:** 3599  Custom machinery

**(G-16825)**
**GENWOODS HOLDCO LLC**
2606 S Il Route 2  (61061-9685)
P.O. Box 1000  (61061-1000)
**PHONE** ................................. 815 732-2141
Greg Malicki, *Vice Pres*
Mike Goldberg, *CFO*
Fred Korndorf,
**EMP:** 1250
**SQ FT:** 420,000
**SALES (est):** 258.9MM
**SALES (corp-wide):** 828.5MM **Privately Held**
**SIC:** 3523  Farm machinery & equipment

HQ: Blount International, Inc.
   4909 Se International Way
   Portland OR 97222
   503 653-8881

**(G-16826)**
**HA-INTERNATIONAL LLC**
1449 W Devils Backbone Rd (61061-9583)
PHONE..................................815 732-3898
J Ebens, *Branch Mgr*
**EMP:** 30 **Privately Held**
**SIC:** 2869 Industrial organic chemicals
HQ: Ha-International, Llc
   630 Oakmont Ln
   Westmont IL 60559
   630 575-5700

**(G-16827)**
**LARRY PONTNACK**
Also Called: Mo-Par City
6309 E Brick Rd (61061-9623)
PHONE..................................815 732-7751
Larry Pontnack, *Owner*
**EMP:** 3
**SALES (est):** 321.9K **Privately Held**
**WEB:** www.moparcity.com
**SIC:** 7538 3714 General automotive repair shops; motor vehicle engines & parts

**(G-16828)**
**MYERS CONCRETE & CONSTRUCTION**
1100 Bennett Dr (61061-2140)
P.O. Box 96 (61061-0096)
PHONE..................................815 732-2591
Robert Diehl, *Owner*
**EMP:** 5 **EST:** 1936
**SALES (est):** 330K **Privately Held**
**SIC:** 3273 1771 4212 1794 Ready-mixed concrete; concrete work; dump truck haulage; excavation work; general warehousing

**(G-16829)**
**OGLE COUNTY LIFE**
311 Washington St (61061-1621)
PHONE..................................815 732-2156
**Fax:** 815 732-6154
Mike Feltes, *General Mgr*
Tina Ketter, *Principal*
John Shank, *CTO*
**EMP:** 4
**SALES (est):** 176.4K **Privately Held**
**SIC:** 2711 Newspapers, publishing & printing

**(G-16830)**
**OREGON FIRE PROTECTION DST**
106 S 1st St (61061-1618)
PHONE..................................815 732-7214
Richard Little, *President*
**EMP:** 30
**SALES (est):** 4.1MM **Privately Held**
**SIC:** 3569 Firefighting apparatus

**(G-16831)**
**ROGERS READY MIX & MTLS INC**
Also Called: Byron Ready Mix
201 E Washington St (61061-9562)
P.O. Box 250, Byron (61010-0250)
PHONE..................................815 234-8044
**Fax:** 815 732-9033
Roger Corbitt, *Manager*
**EMP:** 4
**SALES (corp-wide):** 14.3MM **Privately Held**
**SIC:** 3273 Ready-mixed concrete
**PA:** Rogers Ready Mix & Materials, Inc.
   8128 N Walnut St
   Byron IL 61010
   815 234-8212

**(G-16832)**
**SPEECO INCORPORATED**
Also Called: Special Products Company
2606 S Illinois Route 2 (61061)
PHONE..................................303 279-5544
Paul Valas, *President*
Ken Lehman, *CFO*
◆ **EMP:** 140
**SQ FT:** 120,000
**SALES (est):** 29MM
**SALES (corp-wide):** 828.5MM **Privately Held**
**SIC:** 3523 3531 Farm machinery & equipment; log splitters
HQ: Blount International, Inc.
   4909 Se International Way
   Portland OR 97222
   503 653-8881

**(G-16833)**
**UNIMIN CORPORATION**
1446 W Devils Backbone Rd (61061-9583)
P.O. Box 156 (61061-0156)
PHONE..................................815 732-2121
**Fax:** 815 732-6363
Craig Johnson, *Marketing Staff*
Ken Smith, *Manager*
**EMP:** 40
**SALES (corp-wide):** 117.6MM **Privately Held**
**WEB:** www.unimin.com
**SIC:** 1446 Industrial sand
HQ: Unimin Corporation
   258 Elm St
   New Canaan CT 06840
   203 966-8880

**(G-16834)**
**WOODS EQUIPMENT COMPANY**
Gannon Manufacturing
2606 S Il Route 2 (61061-9685)
PHONE..................................815 732-2141
Tom Sieper, *Marketing Staff*
Eric Ritchie, *Manager*
Judy Navarrete, *Director*
**EMP:** 80
**SQ FT:** 80,883
**SALES (corp-wide):** 828.5MM **Privately Held**
**WEB:** www.woodsonline.com
**SIC:** 3531 3412 5083 Construction machinery attachments; backhoe mounted, hydraulically powered attachments; buckets, excavating; clamshell, concrete, dragline, etc.; metal barrels, drums & pails; tractors, agricultural
HQ: Woods Equipment Company
   2606 S Il Route 2
   Oregon IL 61061
   815 732-2141

## Orion
### Henry County

**(G-16835)**
**ORION TOOL DIE & MACHINE CO**
1400 16th St (61273-7795)
P.O. Box 278 (61273-0278)
PHONE..................................309 526-3303
**Fax:** 309 526-3304
William Lange, *President*
Cory Lange, *General Mgr*
Sandra K Lange, *COO*
Mike Engelkens, *Plant Mgr*
Randy Fransene, *Sales Mgr*
**EMP:** 23
**SQ FT:** 14,000
**SALES (est):** 3.8MM **Privately Held**
**SIC:** 3599 Machine shop, jobbing & repair

## Orland Park
### Cook County

**(G-16836)**
**22ND CENTURY MEDIA (PA)**
11516 W 183rd St U Sw 3 (60467)
PHONE..................................708 326-9170
Andrew Nicks, *Principal*
Eric Degrechie, *Editor*
Fouad Egbaria, *Editor*
Jamie Ferguson, *Editor*
Colin Hanner, *Editor*
**EMP:** 31
**SALES (est):** 4.5MM **Privately Held**
**SIC:** 2711 Newspapers: publishing only, not printed on site

**(G-16837)**
**ACORN DIVERSIFIED INC**
17809 New Jersey Ct # 14 (60467-9326)
PHONE..................................708 478-1051
Ralph McCurdy Jr, *President*
Karen McCurdy, *Admin Sec*
**EMP:** 12
**SALES (est):** 1.1MM **Privately Held**
**WEB:** www.acorndiversified.com
**SIC:** 2671 Plastic film, coated or laminated for packaging

**(G-16838)**
**ADVANCE AWNAIR CORP**
15418 S 70th Ct (60462-5133)
PHONE..................................708 422-2730
**Fax:** 708 422-2742
Joseph Jochheim, *President*
Billie Jochheim, *Vice Pres*
**EMP:** 10 **EST:** 1952
**SQ FT:** 10,000
**SALES (est):** 1.2MM **Privately Held**
**SIC:** 3444 Awnings, sheet metal; canopies, sheet metal

**(G-16839)**
**AEMM A ELECTRIC**
8448 Camelia Ln (60462-4003)
PHONE..................................708 403-6700
Mark Czubiak, *Owner*
**EMP:** 2
**SALES (est):** 212.6K **Privately Held**
**SIC:** 3699 1731 Electrical equipment & supplies; electrical work

**(G-16840)**
**AIRBRAKE PRODUCTS INC**
10334 Alveston St (60462-3072)
PHONE..................................708 594-1110
**Fax:** 708 594-3280
George Gajc, *President*
Richard J Murawski, *Corp Secy*
Peter Pasdach, *Vice Pres*
Ted Chasse, *Plant Mgr*
**EMP:** 15
**SQ FT:** 17,000
**SALES (est):** 1.5MM **Privately Held**
**SIC:** 3714 Air brakes, motor vehicle

**(G-16841)**
**ALL-WAYS QUICK PRINT**
14609 Birch St (60462-2619)
PHONE..................................708 403-8422
Bill Griffin, *President*
**EMP:** 1
**SALES (est):** 250K **Privately Held**
**SIC:** 2752 2791 2789 Commercial printing, offset; typesetting; bookbinding & related work

**(G-16842)**
**AMERICAN ASP SURFC RECYCL INC**
13301 Southwest Hwy Ste H (60462-1313)
PHONE..................................708 448-9540
Cheryl Jager, *President*
**EMP:** 13
**SALES (est):** 2.3MM **Privately Held**
**SIC:** 2952 Sheathing, asphalt saturated

**(G-16843)**
**ANDREW NEW ZEALAND INC**
10500 W 153rd St (60462-3071)
PHONE..................................708 873-3507
**Fax:** 708 349-5510
Jim Giacobazzi, *Vice Pres*
George Goldyn, *Info Tech Mgr*
Martin Zimmerman, *Analyst*
**EMP:** 40
**SALES (est):** 5.8MM **Publicly Held**
**WEB:** www.andrew.com
**SIC:** 3663 3357 3679 3812 Microwave communication equipment; antennas, transmitting & communications; television antennas (transmitting) & ground equipment; receiver-transmitter units (transceiver); coaxial cable, nonferrous; waveguides & fittings; search & navigation equipment; radar systems & equipment; computer peripheral equipment
HQ: Commscope Technologies Llc
   4 Westbrook Corporate Ctr
   Westchester IL 60154
   708 236-6600

**(G-16844)**
**ARKADIAN GAMING LLC**
11227 Distinctive Dr (60467-9458)
PHONE..................................708 377-5656
Nick Karounos,
Sam A Cappas,
**EMP:** 3
**SALES (est):** 234.1K **Privately Held**
**SIC:** 3944 Electronic game machines, except coin-operated

**(G-16845)**
**CALUTECH INC**
15646 S 70th Ct 1 (60462-5108)
PHONE..................................708 614-0228
Doug Freitag, *President*
**EMP:** 8
**SQ FT:** 5,000
**SALES (est):** 998.5K **Privately Held**
**WEB:** www.calutech.com
**SIC:** 5999 3564 7375 Air purification equipment; air purification equipment; on-line data base information retrieval

**(G-16846)**
**CAM TEK LUBRICANTS INC**
9540 W 144th Pl Ste 2a (60462-2554)
PHONE..................................708 477-3000
**EMP:** 4
**SALES (est):** 262.6K **Privately Held**
**SIC:** 2992 Lubricating oils

**(G-16847)**
**CLEAR VIEW SHADE INC**
Also Called: Alan and Assoc
15430 S 70th Ct 32 (60462-5133)
PHONE..................................708 535-8631
**Fax:** 708 535-8630
Alan Hardt, *President*
▲ **EMP:** 12 **EST:** 1946
**SQ FT:** 7,500
**SALES (est):** 1MM **Privately Held**
**SIC:** 2591 Window shades

**(G-16848)**
**COACH INC**
432 Orland Square Dr (60462-3215)
PHONE..................................708 349-1053
**Fax:** 708 349-1054
Mike Tucci, *Manager*
**EMP:** 25
**SALES (corp-wide):** 4.4B **Publicly Held**
**WEB:** www.coach.com
**SIC:** 3171 Handbags, women's
**PA:** Coach, Inc.
   10 Hudson Yards
   New York NY 10001
   212 594-1850

**(G-16849)**
**CONVEYORS PLUS INC**
13301 Southwest Hwy Ste J (60462-1313)
P.O. Box 1038 (60462-8038)
PHONE..................................708 361-1512
**Fax:** 708 361-4372
Herbert Zimmermann, *President*
Helen Zimmerman, *Treasurer*
**EMP:** 5
**SQ FT:** 3,600
**SALES (est):** 1MM **Privately Held**
**WEB:** www.conveyorsplus.net
**SIC:** 3535 3537 Conveyors & conveying equipment; industrial trucks & tractors

**(G-16850)**
**COOPER OIL CO**
9500 W 159th St (60467-5504)
PHONE..................................708 349-2893
**Fax:** 708 349-2897
Bill Cooper, *Principal*
**EMP:** 8
**SALES (est):** 927.2K **Privately Held**
**SIC:** 2869 Fuels

**(G-16851)**
**CREATIVE CABINETRY INC**
9632 W 143rd St (60462-2002)
PHONE..................................708 460-2900
**Fax:** 708 460-2967
Mark W Costigan, *President*
Robin D Costigan, *Admin Sec*
**EMP:** 4

# Orland Park - Cook County (G-16852)

SALES (est): 497.5K **Privately Held**
SIC: **2434** 5211 5712 1751 Wood kitchen cabinets; lumber & other building materials; cabinet work, custom; cabinet building & installation; cut stone & stone products; wood partitions & fixtures

### (G-16852)
**DAX STEEL RULE DIES INC**
13250 Jean Creek Dr (60462-1410)
PHONE ............................... 708 448-4436
Fax: 708 496-1825
Patricia Sczopanski, *President*
Leon Sczopanski, *Vice Pres*
EMP: 6
SALES (est): 570K **Privately Held**
SIC: **3544** Dies, steel rule

### (G-16853)
**DEADY BRIAN RFG INC**
10457 Venice Ln (60467-8218)
PHONE ............................... 708 479-8249
Brian Deady, *Owner*
EMP: 4 EST: 2010
SALES (est): 271.3K **Privately Held**
SIC: **2393** 7389 Duffle bags, canvas: made from purchased materials;

### (G-16854)
**DIAGRIND INC**
Also Called: T J Martin & Co Division
10491 164th Pl (60462-5438)
PHONE ............................... 708 460-4333
Fax: 708 460-8842
Donald Sommer, *President*
Michael Sommer, *Project Mgr*
EMP: 13
SQ FT: 10,000
SALES (est): 2MM **Privately Held**
WEB: www.diagrind.com
SIC: **3291** 5085 Wheels, abrasive; industrial wheels

### (G-16855)
**DONSON MACHINE**
15440 S 70th Ct (60462-5133)
PHONE ............................... 708 468-8392
Nick Knowski, *Principal*
EMP: 2
SALES (est): 201.5K **Privately Held**
SIC: **3599** Machine shop, jobbing & repair

### (G-16856)
**DS PRODUCTION LLC**
16101 108th Ave (60467-5305)
PHONE ............................... 708 873-3142
Derick Turl, *Director*
EMP: 5
SALES (est): 266.8K **Privately Held**
SIC: **2273** Carpets & rugs

### (G-16857)
**DUNKIN DONUTS**
14461 S La Grange Rd (60462-2505)
PHONE ............................... 708 460-3088
John C Grivas, *President*
Roula Boorazanes, *Corp Secy*
Bill Boorazanes, *Vice Pres*
EMP: 22
SALES (est): 958.7K **Privately Held**
SIC: **5461** 2051 Doughnuts; doughnuts, except frozen

### (G-16858)
**DUO PLEX GLASS LTD (PA)**
15626 S 70th Ct (60462-5108)
PHONE ............................... 708 532-4422
Fax: 708 532-4429
Edward J Wytrwal, *President*
Cynthia M Wytrwal, *Corp Secy*
EMP: 3
SALES (est): 419.6K **Privately Held**
SIC: **3231** 5231 3211 Insulating glass: made from purchased glass; glass; flat glass

### (G-16859)
**EMBASSY SECURITY GROUP INC**
11535 183rd Pl Ste 107 (60467-4901)
PHONE ............................... 800 627-1325
Kenneth Boudreau, *CEO*
Mark Delia, *CEO*
EMP: 44 EST: 1995
SQ FT: 3,000
SALES: 170K **Privately Held**
SIC: **7381** 7372 Guard services; prepackaged software

### (G-16860)
**GEORGE ELECTRONICS INC**
11625 Hidden Valley Cv (60467-1319)
PHONE ............................... 708 331-1983
Gary Tarnopol, *President*
Cindy Cockrell, *Sales Staff*
Jim Hernandez, *Technical Staff*
Sarah Finney, *Representative*
EMP: 4 EST: 1959
SQ FT: 10,000
SALES: 600K **Privately Held**
SIC: **5065** 5045 3571 Electronic parts & equipment; computers, peripherals & software; electronic computers

### (G-16861)
**GLOBAL GREEN PRODUCTS LLC (PA)**
8617 Golfview Dr (60462-2852)
PHONE ............................... 708 341-3670
Larry P Koskan,
▲ EMP: 6 EST: 2004
SALES (est): 1.3MM **Privately Held**
SIC: **3822** Auto controls regulating residntl & coml environmt & applncs

### (G-16862)
**GLOBAL WATER TECHNOLOGY INC**
14604 John Humphrey Dr (60462-2642)
PHONE ............................... 708 349-9991
Maria Villarreal, *President*
EMP: 26
SALES: 950K **Privately Held**
WEB: www.globalwatertechnology.com
SIC: **8711** 2869 2899 5169 Engineering services; industrial organic chemicals; antiscaling compounds, boiler; industrial chemicals; swimming pool & spa chemicals; air, water or soil test kits

### (G-16863)
**GRAPHIC SCREEN PRINTING INC**
15640 S 70th Ct (60462-5108)
PHONE ............................... 708 429-3330
Fax: 708 429-5137
Michael C Ahern, *President*
Mary Ahern, *Admin Sec*
EMP: 9
SQ FT: 2,000
SALES (est): 1.1MM **Privately Held**
SIC: **2759** 2396 Screen printing; automotive & apparel trimmings

### (G-16864)
**HALANICK ENTERPRISES INC**
Also Called: Eva's Bridal
14428 John Humphrey Dr (60462-2638)
PHONE ............................... 708 403-3334
Fax: 708 403-3341
Hala Samiri, *Owner*
Nick Ghusein, *Principal*
EMP: 20
SALES (est): 1.6MM **Privately Held**
SIC: **2335** 2384 Wedding gowns & dresses; robes & dressing gowns

### (G-16865)
**HMK MATTRESS HOLDINGS LLC**
15840 S Harlem Ave (60462-5212)
PHONE ............................... 708 429-0704
EMP: 3
SALES (corp-wide): 1.6B **Privately Held**
SIC: **2515** Mattresses & foundations
HQ: Hmk Mattress Holdings Llc
1000 S Oyster Bay Rd
Hicksville NY 11801
800 934-6848

### (G-16866)
**ICI FIBERITE**
14342 Beacon Ave (60462-2422)
PHONE ............................... 708 403-3788
Susan Gonzalez, *Principal*
EMP: 3
SALES (est): 204.4K **Privately Held**
SIC: **3089** Plastics products

### (G-16867)
**IMPERIAL TECHNICAL SERVICES**
14001 Thomas Dr (60462-2038)
PHONE ............................... 708 403-1564
Diane Riley, *President*
Donald Riley, *Manager*
EMP: 12
SQ FT: 1,400
SALES: 1.5MM **Privately Held**
WEB: www.imperialtsi.com
SIC: **3695** Instrumentation type tape, blank

### (G-16868)
**INK SMART INC**
9979 W 151st St (60462-3113)
PHONE ............................... 708 349-9555
Tim Brown, *President*
EMP: 1
SALES: 200K **Privately Held**
SIC: **2899** Ink or writing fluids

### (G-16869)
**INSTAR AUTO CARRIERS LLC** ◯
15255 S 94th Ave Ste 500 (60462-3895)
PHONE ............................... 708 428-6318
Sharrieff Rowell,
EMP: 5 EST: 2016
SALES (est): 210.2K **Privately Held**
SIC: **3713** Car carrier bodies

### (G-16870)
**JCW INVESTMENTS INC**
Also Called: Tekky Toys
11415 183rd Pl Ste E (60462-5011)
PHONE ............................... 708 478-7323
James Wirt, *CEO*
Collette Hostert, *Office Mgr*
Erika Demith, *Admin Sec*
◆ EMP: 5
SALES (est): 764.3K **Privately Held**
WEB: www.tekkytoys.com
SIC: **3944** 5092 Electronic toys; toy novelties & amusements

### (G-16871)
**K&G MENS COMPANY INC**
Also Called: K & G Men's Superstore
180 Orland Park Pl (60462-3854)
PHONE ............................... 708 349-2579
Fax: 708 349-2817
Harvey Pearlstein, *Manager*
Tina Bogacki, *Manager*
EMP: 6
SALES (corp-wide): 3.3B **Publicly Held**
WEB: www.kgstores.com
SIC: **2389** Men's miscellaneous accessories
HQ: K&G Men's Company Inc.
6380 Rogerdale Rd
Houston TX 77072
281 776-7000

### (G-16872)
**K-TRON INC**
9704 Hummingbird Hill Dr (60467-5557)
PHONE ............................... 708 460-2128
Frank S Kasper, *President*
EMP: 3 EST: 1990
SALES (est): 250K **Privately Held**
SIC: **7372** Prepackaged software

### (G-16873)
**LIDS CORPORATION**
416 Orland Square Dr (60462-3215)
PHONE ............................... 708 873-9606
Robert Fiore, *Office Mgr*
Bob Fiore, *Manager*
EMP: 7
SALES (corp-wide): 2.8B **Publicly Held**
WEB: www.hatworld.com
SIC: **2353** 5661 Hats & caps; men's shoes
HQ: Lids Corporation
7555 Woodland Dr
Indianapolis IN 46278

### (G-16874)
**MC MECHANICAL CONTRACTORS INC**
15774 S La Grange Rd # 245 (60462-4766)
PHONE ............................... 708 460-0075
Marcel Cairo Jr, *President*
Jamie B Penwitt, *Admin Sec*
EMP: 2 EST: 2010

SALES (est): 289K **Privately Held**
SIC: **2499** Cooling towers, wood or wood & sheet metal combination

### (G-16875)
**MIDWEST NAMEPLATE CORP**
15127 S 73rd Ave Ste H (60462-3437)
PHONE ............................... 708 614-0606
Fax: 708 614-0696
Douglas Holgate, *President*
Susan Holgate, *Treasurer*
EMP: 5
SALES (est): 446.6K **Privately Held**
SIC: **3999** 3993 3479 3469 Manufacturing industries; signs & advertising specialties; metal coating & allied service; metal stampings

### (G-16876)
**MOSTERT & FERGUSON SIGNS**
Also Called: Artisan Signs
15617 S 71st Ct (60462-5135)
PHONE ............................... 815 485-1212
Fax: 708 841-4433
John F Mostert, *Owner*
Pete McKenzie, *Human Res Mgr*
Mary Cahill, *Officer*
EMP: 8
SQ FT: 10,000
SALES (est): 779.8K **Privately Held**
SIC: **3993** Electric signs; neon signs

### (G-16877)
**MUHAMMAD SOTAVIA**
9601 165th St (60467-5660)
PHONE ............................... 708 966-2262
Sotavia Muhammad, *Principal*
EMP: 3
SALES (est): 305.9K **Privately Held**
SIC: **2835** Microbiology & virology diagnostic products

### (G-16878)
**MUSIC CONNECTION INC**
10751 165th St Ste 104 (60467-8702)
PHONE ............................... 708 364-7590
Janet Kuester, *Executive Asst*
EMP: 3
SALES (est): 250.9K **Privately Held**
SIC: **3931** Musical instruments

### (G-16879)
**NEXT DAY TONER SUPPLIES INC**
11411 183rd St Ste A (60467-9451)
PHONE ............................... 708 478-1000
Jeff Bollman, *President*
Beverly Bollman, *Vice Pres*
Tom Kosloskus, *Vice Pres*
EMP: 22 EST: 1998
SALES (est): 7.8MM **Privately Held**
SIC: **5112** 3955 Photocopying supplies; laserjet supplies; print cartridges for laser & other computer printers

### (G-16880)
**OPTECH ORTHO & PROSTH SVCS**
18016 Wolf Rd (60467-5407)
PHONE ............................... 708 364-9700
Gail Simpson, *Branch Mgr*
EMP: 9 **Privately Held**
SIC: **3842** Mfg Surgical Appliances/Supplies
PA: Optech Orthotics & Prosthetics Services, Ltd.
119 E Court St Ste 100
Kankakee IL 60901

### (G-16881)
**ORLAND PARK BAKERY LTD**
14850 S La Grange Rd (60462-3229)
PHONE ............................... 708 349-8516
Thomas Major, *President*
Kathleen Major, *Admin Sec*
EMP: 27
SQ FT: 2,000
SALES (est): 1.6MM **Privately Held**
WEB: www.orlandparkbakery.com
SIC: **5461** 2051 Bakeries; bread, cake & related products

# GEOGRAPHIC SECTION
## Oswego - Kendall County (G-16911)

**(G-16882)**
**PANDUIT CORP**
Panduit Network Systems Div
10500 W 167th St (60467-4523)
PHONE.................708 460-1800
Royal Jenner, *Mfg Mgr*
Fred Dorman, *Engineer*
Rick Fallbacher, *Engineer*
Gary Frigo, *Engineer*
Erik Homerding, *Engineer*
**EMP:** 200
**SALES (corp-wide):** 1B **Privately Held**
**WEB:** www.panduit.com
**SIC:** 3644 Electric conduits & fittings
**PA:** Panduit Corp.
18900 Panduit Dr
Tinley Park IL 60487
708 532-1800

**(G-16883)**
**PAPENDIK INC**
8711 Robinhood Dr (60462-5601)
PHONE.................708 492-6230
Charles Papendik, *President*
Denise Papendik, *Vice Pres*
**EMP:** 4
**SQ FT:** 5,000
**SALES:** 350K **Privately Held**
**SIC:** 7692 Welding repair

**(G-16884)**
**PELLEGRINI ENTERPRISES INC**
Also Called: Artisan Signs & Lighting
15417 S 71st Ct (60462-5135)
PHONE.................815 717-6408
Ruth Pelegrini, *President*
**EMP:** 4
**SALES:** 200K **Privately Held**
**SIC:** 3993 Electric signs

**(G-16885)**
**PRO-ORTHOTICS INC**
11508 183rd Pl (60467-9487)
PHONE.................708 326-1554
**Fax:** 708 326-1556
John Parise, *President*
**EMP:** 3
**SALES (est):** 179.1K **Privately Held**
**SIC:** 3842 Prosthetic appliances

**(G-16886)**
**PROTECTIVE COATINGS & WATERPRO**
9320 136th St (60462-1344)
P.O. Box 127 (60462-0127)
PHONE.................708 403-7650
Curtis Neeley, *Principal*
**EMP:** 2
**SALES (est):** 280K **Privately Held**
**SIC:** 1522 1799 3479 Residential construction; waterproofing; painting, coating & hot dipping

**(G-16887)**
**REMMERT STUDIOS INC**
8834 W 140th St Unit 1b (60462-9220)
PHONE.................815 933-4867
Stephen A Remmert, *President*
**EMP:** 3
**SALES:** 285K **Privately Held**
**SIC:** 2431 Millwork

**(G-16888)**
**ROSELAND II LLC**
18410 115th Ave (60467-9488)
PHONE.................708 479-5010
David M Lautenbach, *Principal*
**EMP:** 4 **EST:** 2010
**SALES (est):** 496.3K **Privately Held**
**SIC:** 2431 Staircases, stairs & railings

**(G-16889)**
**RUTLEDGE PRINTING CO**
11415 183rd Pl Ste C (60467-5011)
PHONE.................708 479-8282
Richard W Marks, *President*
Linda Marks, *Corp Secy*
Debbie Sprouse, *Manager*
**EMP:** 12 **EST:** 1923
**SQ FT:** 2,800
**SALES (est):** 1.1MM **Privately Held**
**SIC:** 2752 Commercial printing, offset

**(G-16890)**
**SENSIBLE DESIGNS ONLINE INC**
10556 Great Egret Dr (60467-8509)
PHONE.................708 267-8924
Gintautas Burokas, *President*
▲ **EMP:** 7
**SQ FT:** 1,500
**SALES (est):** 801.7K **Privately Held**
**SIC:** 3634 Housewares, excluding cooking appliances & utensils

**(G-16891)**
**SIR SPEEDY PRINTING CNTR 6129**
9412 W 143rd St (60462-2031)
PHONE.................708 349-7789
**Fax:** 708 349-7199
Gary Grohovena, *Owner*
**EMP:** 4
**SQ FT:** 1,500
**SALES (est):** 332.8K **Privately Held**
**SIC:** 2752 Commercial printing, lithographic

**(G-16892)**
**SNOW CONTROL INC**
7245 W 151st St (60462-2967)
PHONE.................708 670-6269
**EMP:** 3
**SALES (est):** 230.1K **Privately Held**
**SIC:** 2851 Removers & cleaners

**(G-16893)**
**SOUTH SIDE BLER WLDG WORKS INC**
Also Called: South Side Boiler & Wldg Work
10811 Minnesota Ct (60467-9341)
PHONE.................708 478-1714
Edward Haavig, *President*
William Haavig, *Corp Secy*
**EMP:** 8
**SALES:** 750K **Privately Held**
**SIC:** 7699 7692 Boiler repair shop; welding repair

**(G-16894)**
**SOUTHWEST TOOL & MACHINE**
15600 116th Ct (60467-5884)
PHONE.................708 349-4441
John Rekart, *Owner*
**EMP:** 4
**SALES (est):** 236.8K **Privately Held**
**SIC:** 3599 Machine shop, jobbing & repair

**(G-16895)**
**SPIRIT WARRIOR INC**
Also Called: New Life Screen Printing
15519 S 70th Ct (60462-5105)
P.O. Box 871 (60462-0871)
PHONE.................708 614-0020
Richard Ryan, *President*
Nancy Jo Ryan, *Vice Pres*
Lisa Jenrich, *Office Mgr*
**EMP:** 8
**SQ FT:** 2,700
**SALES (est):** 1MM **Privately Held**
**SIC:** 2759 5961 7389 Screen printing; mail order house; embroidering of advertising on shirts, etc.

**(G-16896)**
**SURFACE SHIELDS INC (PA)**
10457 163rd Pl (60467-5442)
PHONE.................708 226-9810
Kyle W Behringer, *President*
Shelly Steinhauer, *HR Admin*
Mark Hilke, *Sales Mgr*
Todd Rosica, *Regl Sales Mgr*
Daniel Berger, *Sales Staff*
◆ **EMP:** 40
**SQ FT:** 21,000
**SALES (est):** 10.8MM **Privately Held**
**WEB:** www.surfaceshields.com
**SIC:** 3996 Hard surface floor coverings

**(G-16897)**
**SWISSTRONICS CORP**
16308 107th Ave Ste 8 (60467-4559)
PHONE.................708 403-8877
**EMP:** 5 **EST:** 1966
**SQ FT:** 5,000
**SALES:** 450K **Privately Held**
**SIC:** 3451 3541 Mfg Screw Machine Products Mfg Machine Tools-Cutting

**(G-16898)**
**TINDALL ASSOCIATES INC**
Also Called: Tai
10727 Winterset Dr (60467-1106)
PHONE.................708 403-7775
**Fax:** 708 403-7801
John Carroll, *President*
Tim Kuhn, *COO*
Mitchell Ocampo, *Exec VP*
**EMP:** 15
**SALES (est):** 1.1MM **Privately Held**
**WEB:** www.taire.com
**SIC:** 7379 7372 Computer related consulting services; prepackaged software

## Osco
### Henry County

**(G-16899)**
**HELFTER ENTERPRISES INC**
Also Called: Advanced Biological Concepts
301 Main St (61274-7001)
P.O. Box 27 (61274-0027)
PHONE.................309 522-5505
**Fax:** 309 522-5570
Kendra Helfter, *President*
James Helfter, *Vice Pres*
**EMP:** 19
**SQ FT:** 135,000
**SALES (est):** 2.6MM **Privately Held**
**WEB:** www.helfterfeeds.com
**SIC:** 2048 Prepared feeds

**(G-16900)**
**NOSTALGIA PYROTECHNICS INC**
Also Called: Nostalgia Fireworks
119 South St (61274-7005)
P.O. Box 207 (61274-0207)
PHONE.................309 522-5136
Tom Krawiec, *President*
▲ **EMP:** 4
**SQ FT:** 2,500
**SALES (est):** 431.1K **Privately Held**
**SIC:** 2899 Fireworks

## Oswego
### Kendall County

**(G-16901)**
**ACQUAMED TECHNOLOGIES INC**
195 Kendall Point Dr # 16 (60543-8884)
PHONE.................630 728-4014
**Fax:** 630 761-3081
Hugh Palmer, *COO*
**EMP:** 8
**SALES (est):** 986.6K **Privately Held**
**SIC:** 3843 Dental equipment & supplies

**(G-16902)**
**AERO-CABLES CORP**
Also Called: S & M Products
114 Kirkland Cir Ste A (60543-8067)
PHONE.................815 609-6600
Russell Coblentz, *President*
Susan Coblentz, *CFO*
▼ **EMP:** 4
**SQ FT:** 1,500
**SALES:** 370K **Privately Held**
**SIC:** 3724 Aircraft engines & engine parts

**(G-16903)**
**ALIN MACHINING COMPANY INC**
Also Called: Power Plant Repair Services
80 Kendall Point Dr (60543-8802)
PHONE.................708 345-8600
Manny Gandhi, *President*
Charles Vollmer, *Manager*
**EMP:** 58
**SALES (corp-wide):** 50MM **Privately Held**
**SIC:** 3599 Machine shop, jobbing & repair
**PA:** Alin Machining Company, Inc.
3131 W Soffel Ave
Melrose Park IL 60160
708 681-1043

**(G-16904)**
**ANFINSEN PLASTIC MOULDING INC**
445b Treasure Dr Unit B (60543-7945)
PHONE.................630 554-4100
Steve La Ham, *President*
Kim Burks, *CFO*
Carol Lancols, *Manager*
▲ **EMP:** 25 **EST:** 1935
**SQ FT:** 40,000
**SALES (est):** 7.7MM **Privately Held**
**SIC:** 3089 3999 Molding primary plastic; barber & beauty shop equipment

**(G-16905)**
**BLUE CHIP MFG LLC**
37 Stonehill Rd (60543-9449)
PHONE.................630 553-6321
Ronald K Gates, *President*
Su Gates,
**EMP:** 3
**SQ FT:** 2,000
**SALES (est):** 245K **Privately Held**
**SIC:** 3469 Machine parts, stamped or pressed metal

**(G-16906)**
**CA CUSTOM WOODWORKING**
254 Main St (60543-8533)
PHONE.................630 201-6154
Chris Ammenhauser, *Principal*
**EMP:** 4
**SALES (est):** 236.3K **Privately Held**
**SIC:** 2431 Millwork

**(G-16907)**
**CHRISTOPHER WAGNER**
563 Cardinal Ave (60543-7741)
PHONE.................630 205-9200
Christopher Wagner, *Principal*
**EMP:** 6
**SALES (est):** 707.8K **Privately Held**
**SIC:** 2752 Commercial printing, lithographic

**(G-16908)**
**CLASSIC IMPRESSIONS INC**
150 Kendall Point Dr B (60543-8332)
Robert A Depaul, *Principal*
Lynn Hillier, *Admin Sec*
**EMP:** 5
**SQ FT:** 5,000
**SALES (est):** 430K **Privately Held**
**WEB:** www.classicstationery.com
**SIC:** 2759 Embossing on paper

**(G-16909)**
**CMA INC (PA)**
19 Stonehill Rd (60543-9449)
PHONE.................630 551-3100
William Schultz, *CEO*
Jim Reinsdorff, *General Mgr*
Marvin Peplo, *CFO*
**EMP:** 25
**SALES (est):** 10.8MM **Privately Held**
**WEB:** www.cmainc.net
**SIC:** 2499 Insulating material, cork

**(G-16910)**
**COMPU DOC INC**
105 Theodore Dr Ste A (60543-6031)
PHONE.................630 554-5800
**Fax:** 630 554-5885
James Mellema, *CEO*
Carol Mellema, *Admin Sec*
**EMP:** 5
**SQ FT:** 1,800
**SALES (est):** 669.3K **Privately Held**
**WEB:** www.c-doc.com
**SIC:** 3679 Electronic components

**(G-16911)**
**CONSOLIDATED DISPLAYS CO INC**
1210 Us Highway 34 (60543-8939)
PHONE.................630 851-8666
**Fax:** 630 851-8756
Sebastian Puccio, *President*
Anthony Puccio, *Vice Pres*
David L Miller, *CFO*
Rachael Puccio, *Treasurer*
**EMP:** 9
**SQ FT:** 13,000

## Oswego - Kendall County (G-16912)

SALES: 1MM  Privately Held
WEB: www.letitsnow.com
SIC: 3993  3999  2542  Displays & cutouts, window & lobby; theatrical scenery; partitions & fixtures, except wood

**(G-16912)**
**CUSTOM CULINARY INC**
Also Called: Custom Food Products
2100 Wiesbrook Rd  (60543-8309)
PHONE................................630 299-0500
Fax: 630 906-0298
Bob Whealan, *Finance Mgr*
Rob Pellicano, *Marketing Mgr*
Sargon Boudakh, *Branch Mgr*
William Potter, *Manager*
George Neill, *Director*
EMP: 70
SALES (corp-wide): 756.3MM  Privately Held
WEB: www.customculinary.com
SIC: 5141  2099  2087  Food brokers; food preparations; flavoring extracts & syrups
HQ: Custom Culinary, Inc.
    2505 S Finley Rd Ste 100
    Lombard IL 60148
    630 928-4898

**(G-16913)**
**DISA HOLDING CORP (DH)**
80 Kendall Point Dr  (60543-8802)
PHONE................................630 820-3000
Mike Lewis, *President*
Russel Dobney, *General Mgr*
Timothy Bates, *Exec VP*
William H Sager Jr, *Production*
Bob Grezlik, *Buyer*
▲ EMP: 5
SALES (est): 30.5MM
SALES (corp-wide): 16.3MM  Privately Held
SIC: 3569  3559  5084  Blast cleaning equipment, dustless; foundry machinery & equipment; industrial machinery & equipment
HQ: Disa Holding Ag
    Kasernenstrasse 1
    BachenbUlach ZH
    448 154-000

**(G-16914)**
**DQM INC**
Also Called: Sealtech
120 Kendall Point Dr  (60543-8803)
PHONE................................630 692-0633
Fax: 630 898-0633
Charles Herrera, *President*
Carla Herrera, *Vice Pres*
EMP: 11
SQ FT: 40,000
SALES (est): 1.2MM  Privately Held
SIC: 3643  Current-carrying wiring devices

**(G-16915)**
**EMPOWERED PRESS LLC**
139 Pineridge Dr S  (60543-7579)
PHONE................................630 400-3127
Michael L Redd,
Kerri Redd,
EMP: 5
SALES: 75K  Privately Held
SIC: 2731  Books: publishing only

**(G-16916)**
**ESSENTIAL FLOORING INC**
566 Lincoln Station Dr  (60543-8137)
PHONE................................630 788-3121
Thomas Nguyen, *President*
EMP: 5  EST: 2014
SQ FT: 100
SALES: 250K  Privately Held
SIC: 3446  Open flooring & grating for construction

**(G-16917)**
**EUGENE EWBANK**
Also Called: Flexo Prepress Solutions
118 Kirkland Cir Ste B  (60543-8069)
PHONE................................630 705-0400
Gene Ewbank, *Owner*
EMP: 4
SALES (est): 320K  Privately Held
SIC: 2752  2796  2759  Commercial printing, lithographic; platemaking services; commercial printing

**(G-16918)**
**FOX RIDGE STONE CO**
6275 State Route 71  (60543-9698)
PHONE................................630 554-9101
Donald Hamman, *Partner*
Carol Hamman, *Partner*
Roger Lorang, *Office Mgr*
EMP: 4
SQ FT: 7,200
SALES (est): 250K  Privately Held
SIC: 1442  Gravel mining

**(G-16919)**
**FOX VALLEY WINERY INC**
5600 Us Highway 34  (60543-9169)
PHONE................................630 554-0404
Richard A Faltz, *President*
Karen Thompson, *Vice Pres*
Wine Club, *Sales Staff*
Christine C Fatz, *Admin Sec*
EMP: 7
SALES (est): 658.2K  Privately Held
WEB: www.foxvalleywinery.com
SIC: 2084  Wines

**(G-16920)**
**GREEN MOUNTAIN FLAVORS INC**
442 Treasure Dr  (60543-7936)
PHONE................................630 554-9530
Stan Sitton, *President*
EMP: 10
SALES (est): 1.1MM  Privately Held
WEB: www.greenmountainflavors.com
SIC: 2087  Flavoring extracts & syrups

**(G-16921)**
**HONEYWELL INTERNATIONAL INC**
637 Salem Cir  (60543-8667)
PHONE................................630 554-5342
Joe Idzo, *Branch Mgr*
EMP: 4
SALES (corp-wide): 39.3B  Publicly Held
WEB: www.honeywell.com
SIC: 2899  Antifreeze compounds
PA: Honeywell International Inc.
    115 Tabor Rd
    Morris Plains NJ 07950
    973 455-2000

**(G-16922)**
**INTEX SYSTEMS CORP**
22 Crestview Dr  (60543-9512)
PHONE................................630 636-6594
Allen W Hametta, *Principal*
EMP: 3
SALES (est): 235.9K  Privately Held
SIC: 3812  Detection apparatus: electronic/magnetic field, light/heat

**(G-16923)**
**JAMES A FREUND LLC**
Also Called: Fish Window Cleaning
26 Longford Ct  (60543-8881)
PHONE................................630 664-7692
James A Freund, *Mng Member*
EMP: 4
SALES: 100K  Privately Held
SIC: 7349  3589  Window cleaning; high pressure cleaning equipment

**(G-16924)**
**JANIN GROUP INC**
43 Crestview Dr  (60543-9500)
P.O. Box 21717, Waco TX  (76702-1717)
PHONE................................630 554-8906
John A Navis, *President*
Irene Navis, *Vice Pres*
EMP: 3
SQ FT: 5,000
SALES (est): 495.4K  Privately Held
WEB: www.medigroupinc.com
SIC: 3841  Surgical & medical instruments

**(G-16925)**
**LARES TECHNOLOGIES LLC**
748 Charismatic Dr  (60543-7003)
PHONE................................630 408-4368
Kevin L Hartman, *Manager*
Kevin Hartman,
EMP: 1
SALES: 600K  Privately Held
WEB: www.larestechnologies.com
SIC: 3669  Communications equipment

**(G-16926)**
**MEDIGROUP INC**
14a Stonehill Rd  (60543-9400)
P.O. Box 950  (60543-0950)
PHONE................................630 554-5533
Fax: 630 554-5535
EMP: 2
SALES (est): 262.4K  Privately Held
SIC: 3841  Mfg Surgical/Medical Instruments

**(G-16927)**
**MOLOR PRODUCTS COMPANY**
110 Kirkland Cir Ste K  (60543-8068)
P.O. Box 897  (60543-0897)
PHONE................................630 375-5999
Fax: 630 375-5995
Vance Lorenzana, *President*
Phyllis Rusnock, *Office Mgr*
▲ EMP: 11
SQ FT: 50,000
SALES (est): 1.4MM  Privately Held
WEB: www.molor.com
SIC: 3999  3089  3714  Pet supplies; plastic kitchenware, tableware & houseware; plastic processing; motor vehicle parts & accessories

**(G-16928)**
**OBERWEIS DAIRY INC**
2274 Us Highway 30  (60543-8972)
PHONE................................630 906-6455
Fax: 630 906-6456
Steven Storey, *Accountant*
Darlene George, *Branch Mgr*
EMP: 21
SALES (corp-wide): 202.6MM  Privately Held
WEB: www.webfc.net
SIC: 2026  5963  5451  Milk processing (pasteurizing, homogenizing, bottling); milk delivery; milk; ice cream (packaged)
PA: Oberweis Dairy, Inc.
    951 Ice Cream Dr
    North Aurora IL 60542
    630 801-6100

**(G-16929)**
**Q C H INCORPORATED**
230 Kendall Point Dr  (60543-8150)
PHONE................................630 820-5550
Fax: 630 820-5549
Blair Pasternak, *President*
Carolyn Mills, *QC Mgr*
Debbie Molenstra, *Human Res Dir*
Marc Fox, *Mktg Dir*
Marge Colbertson, *Manager*
EMP: 80
SQ FT: 53,000
SALES (est): 23.6MM  Privately Held
WEB: www.hqcinc.com
SIC: 3089  Injection molding of plastics

**(G-16930)**
**QUICK SIGNS INC**
424 Treasure Dr  (60543-7936)
PHONE................................630 554-7370
Fax: 630 554-7372
Kevin Hanna, *President*
Michael Nielsen, *Vice Pres*
Deborah Hanna, *Shareholder*
EMP: 6
SQ FT: 5,000
SALES (est): 886K  Privately Held
SIC: 3993  Signs & advertising specialties

**(G-16931)**
**RADIAC ABRASIVES INC**
101 Kendall Point Dr  (60543-8801)
PHONE................................630 898-0315
Fax: 630 898-1796
Bill Burke, *Purch Mgr*
John Mariani, *Engineer*
Marty Myers, *Controller*
Rob Knierim, *Sales Staff*
Gary Smith, *Sales Staff*
EMP: 47
SALES (corp-wide): 698.3MM  Privately Held
WEB: www.radiac.com
SIC: 3291  3541  Wheels, grinding: artificial; machine tools, metal cutting type
HQ: Radiac Abrasives, Inc.
    1015 S College St
    Salem IL 62881
    618 548-4200

**(G-16932)**
**SEALTEC**
Also Called: Dqm
120 Kendall Point Dr  (60543-8803)
PHONE................................630 692-0633
Charles Herrera, *President*
Carla Herrera, *Vice Pres*
EMP: 13
SQ FT: 12,000
SALES: 1MM  Privately Held
WEB: www.dqm.com
SIC: 3053  Gaskets & sealing devices

**(G-16933)**
**SEGINUS INC**
114 Kirkland Cir Ste B  (60543-8067)
PHONE................................630 800-2795
Erik Hatch, *President*
▼ EMP: 2
SQ FT: 3,500
SALES (est): 357.3K  Privately Held
SIC: 3728  Aircraft parts & equipment

**(G-16934)**
**SILENT W COMMUNICATIONS INC**
Also Called: Keystroke Graphics
2758 Us Highway 34  (60543-8301)
PHONE................................630 978-2050
Laura Wrasman, *President*
Mark Wrasman, *Vice Pres*
EMP: 8
SALES (est): 1.8MM  Privately Held
WEB: www.weddingguidechicago.com
SIC: 2721  Magazines: publishing & printing

**(G-16935)**
**SPARKLE EXPRESS**
1545 Us Highway 34  (60543-8524)
PHONE................................630 375-9801
Thomas Howard, *Managing Prtnr*
EMP: 4
SALES (est): 546.1K  Privately Held
SIC: 3589  Car washing machinery

**(G-16936)**
**TEMPLE DISPLAY LTD**
114 Kirkland Cir Ste C  (60543-8067)
P.O. Box 965  (60543-0965)
PHONE................................630 851-3331
Tyler Temple, *President*
Maggie Washburn, *Marketing Staff*
▲ EMP: 9
SALES (est): 2.3MM  Privately Held
SIC: 5199  3699  Christmas novelties; household electrical equipment

**(G-16937)**
**TKS CONTROL SYSTEMS INC**
88 Templeton Dr  (60543-7000)
PHONE................................630 554-3020
Timothy E Neal, *President*
Kimberly Neal, *Corp Secy*
EMP: 11
SQ FT: 12,000
SALES (est): 3.1MM  Privately Held
SIC: 3567  Industrial furnaces & ovens

**(G-16938)**
**VEAL TECH INC**
15 Stonehill Rd  (60543-9449)
PHONE................................630 554-0410
Fax: 630 554-0415
Richard Dennis, *President*
Connie Dennis, *Corp Secy*
Bernard Moe, *Vice Pres*
EMP: 7
SQ FT: 50,000
SALES (est): 733.8K  Privately Held
WEB: www.vealtech.com
SIC: 2048  Prepared feeds

**(G-16939)**
**WALK 4 LIFE INC**
1981c Wiesbrook Rd  (60543-8311)
PHONE................................815 439-2340
Fax: 815 439-2414
Ruthmarie Carver, *President*
Jeff Murrow, *Opers Staff*
Peggy Boris, *Finance*
Eric Carver, *Regl Sales Mgr*
EMP: 19
SQ FT: 11,000
SALES: 3MM  Privately Held
SIC: 3824  Pedometers

## GEOGRAPHIC SECTION

### Ottawa - Lasalle County (G-16964)

**(G-16940)**
**WIN SOON CHICAGO INC**
190 Kendall Point Dr (60543-8803)
PHONE..................................630 585-7090
EMP: 238 EST: 2014
SALES (est): 77.3MM Privately Held
SIC: 2086 Carbonated beverages, nonalcoholic: bottled & canned

**(G-16941)**
**WINDO WELL COVER CO**
2374 Wolf Rd (60543-8479)
P.O. Box 898 (60543-0898)
PHONE..................................630 554-0366
Deborah Wolski, Partner
Dave Wolski, Partner
EMP: 6
SALES: 200M Privately Held
SIC: 3272 Areaways, basement window: concrete

**(G-16942)**
**WISDOM MEDICAL TECHNOLOGY LLC**
19 Stonehill Rd (60543-9449)
PHONE..................................630 803-6383
Jack Furcht, Mng Member
Anthony Jakubowski,
EMP: 7 EST: 2015
SALES: 1MM Privately Held
SIC: 3841 Surgical & medical instruments;

**(G-16943)**
**ZING ENTERPRISES LLC**
83 Templeton Dr Ste G (60543-7026)
P.O. Box 789 (60543-0789)
PHONE..................................608 201-9490
Martha Kent, Accountant
Thomas R Prinzing,
EMP: 9
SALES: 1.7MM Privately Held
SIC: 3999 Identification plates

### Ottawa
*Lasalle County*

**(G-16944)**
**4L TECHNOLOGIES INC (PA)**
Also Called: Clover Global
4200 Columbus St (61350-9538)
PHONE..................................815 431-8100
Dan Ruhl, President
Brian Hines, Vice Pres
James Cerkleski, Admin Sec
EMP: 58
SALES (est): 627.3MM Privately Held
WEB: www.clovertechnologies.com
SIC: 3555 Printing trades machinery

**(G-16945)**
**A WILEY & ASSOCIATES**
Also Called: Awa
707 E Dayton Rd (61350-9545)
P.O. Box 1040 (61350-6040)
PHONE..................................815 343-7401
Nicholas Crisler, Owner
EMP: 6
SALES: 950K Privately Held
SIC: 3999 Manufacturing industries

**(G-16946)**
**AMERICAN FUEL ECONOMY INC**
1772 N 2753rd Rd (61350-9701)
PHONE..................................815 433-3226
Diania K Heiss, President
EMP: 4 EST: 1975
SQ FT: 12,000
SALES (est): 489.2K Privately Held
SIC: 3585 3634 3444 3433 Heating equipment, complete; electric housewares & fans; sheet metalwork; heating equipment, except electric

**(G-16947)**
**ANBEK INC (PA)**
Also Called: Designs & Signs By Anderson
104 W Madison St (61350-5006)
PHONE..................................815 434-7340
Toll Free:..................................888 -
Fax: 815 434-2542
Gene Anderson, President
Doug Beckman, Vice Pres
Kathy Hider, Purch Mgr

Sherlyn Beckman, Treasurer
Diane Anderson, Admin Sec
EMP: 4
SQ FT: 7,200
SALES (est): 1.2MM Privately Held
WEB: www.beansigns.com
SIC: 3993 5199 Electric signs; advertising specialties

**(G-16948)**
**B&BIMC LLC**
707 E Dayton Rd (61350-9545)
P.O. Box 1040 (61350-6040)
PHONE..................................815 433-5100
Beth Nettles, Controller
EMP: 55 EST: 2012
SALES (est): 4.3MM
SALES (corp-wide): 1.1B Privately Held
SIC: 3629 Electronic generation equipment
HQ: B+B Smartworx Inc.
707 E Dayton Rd
Ottawa IL 61350
815 433-5100

**(G-16949)**
**B+B SMARTWORX INC (HQ)**
Also Called: Advantech Bb Smartworx
707 E Dayton Rd (61350-9545)
P.O. Box 1040 (61350-6040)
PHONE..................................815 433-5100
Fax: 815 434-7094
Jerry O'Gorman, President
Mike Fahrion, Vice Pres
Andrew Ross, Project Mgr
Doug Zabel, Mfg Mgr
Michael Stridde, Purch Mgr
▲ EMP: 99
SQ FT: 36,000
SALES (est): 64.3MM
SALES (corp-wide): 1.1B Privately Held
WEB: www.bb-elec.com
SIC: 3674 3825 Semiconductors & related devices; instruments to measure electricity
PA: Advantech Co., Ltd.
1, Alley 20, Lane 26, Jui Kuang Rd.,
Taipei City TAP 11491
227 927-818

**(G-16950)**
**BR MACHINE INC**
3312 E 2153rd Rd (61350-9431)
P.O. Box 9, Wedron (60557-0009)
PHONE..................................815 434-0427
Bob Rogowski, President
Anthony Rogowski, Vice Pres
Nancy Rogowski, Vice Pres
EMP: 10 EST: 1974
SQ FT: 10,000
SALES (est): 1.5MM Privately Held
WEB: www.wedrongrills.com
SIC: 3599 3441 3631 3443 Machine shop, jobbing & repair; fabricated structural metal; household cooking equipment; fabricated plate work (boiler shop)

**(G-16951)**
**BURMAC MANUFACTURING INC**
4000 Burmac Rd (61350-9542)
P.O. Box 828 (61350-0828)
PHONE..................................815 434-1660
William E Burns Jr, President
John A Burns, Treasurer
Joan Lamb, Office Mgr
Gerald Dauck, Data Proc Mgr
Jan Cappellini, Admin Sec
EMP: 4
SQ FT: 28,000
SALES (est): 264.6K Privately Held
SIC: 3599 Machine shop, jobbing & repair
PA: Burns Machine Company
4000 Burmac Rd
Ottawa IL 61350

**(G-16952)**
**BURNS MACHINE COMPANY**
4000 Burmac Rd (61350-9542)
P.O. Box 828 (61350-0828)
PHONE..................................815 434-3131
Fax: 815 434-1755
William E Burns Jr, President
John A Burns, Treasurer
Jerry Dauck, Info Tech Mgr
Jan Cappellini, Admin Sec
EMP: 30 EST: 1917
SQ FT: 33,000

SALES: 3MM Privately Held
SIC: 3599 7692 3549 3544 Machine shop, jobbing & repair; welding repair; metalworking machinery; special dies, tools, jigs & fixtures
PA: Burns Machine Company
4000 Burmac Rd
Ottawa IL 61350

**(G-16953)**
**BURNS MACHINE COMPANY (PA)**
4000 Burmac Rd (61350-9542)
PHONE..................................815 434-1660
Fax: 815 434-1663
William E Burns Jr, President
John Burns, Shareholder
Jan Cappellina, Admin Sec
▲ EMP: 29
SQ FT: 33,000
SALES (est): 3.8MM Privately Held
SIC: 3599 3443 Machine shop, jobbing & repair; fabricated plate work (boiler shop)

**(G-16954)**
**CLEAR PRINT INC**
768 Adams St (61350-3806)
PHONE..................................815 795-6225
Jesse Fleming, President
Lean Gribbins, Manager
EMP: 7 EST: 1996
SALES (est): 700K Privately Held
SIC: 2752 Commercial printing, lithographic

**(G-16955)**
**CLIFFORD W ESTES CO INC**
1289 W Marquette St (61350-1755)
PHONE..................................815 433-0944
Fax: 815 433-2254
Mick Lawsha, Manager
Steve Stull, Manager
EMP: 16
SALES (corp-wide): 12.1MM Privately Held
WEB: www.estesco.com
SIC: 7389 1446 Personal service agents, brokers & bureaus; industrial sand
PA: Clifford W. Estes Co., Inc.
182 Fairfield Rd Ste 8
Fairfield NJ 07004
800 962-5128

**(G-16956)**
**CLOVER TECHNOLOGIES GROUP LLC (HQ)**
Also Called: Ces
4200 Columbus St (61350-9538)
PHONE..................................815 431-8100
Fax: 815 431-8121
George Milton, COO
Ino Landa, Exec VP
Julie Falconer, Vice Pres
Allen Witkowski, Transptn Dir
Roger Kaufman, Prdtn Mgr
◆ EMP: 765
SQ FT: 109,000
SALES (est): 587.7MM
SALES (corp-wide): 627.3MM Privately Held
SIC: 3861 Printing equipment, photographic
PA: 4l Technologies Inc.
4200 Columbus St
Ottawa IL 61350
815 431-8100

**(G-16957)**
**CLOVER TECHNOLOGIES GROUP LLC**
700 E Dayton Rd (61350-9062)
PHONE..................................815 431-8100
Chuck Schmidt, Marketing Staff
Brian McCandless, Director
EMP: 433
SALES (corp-wide): 627.3MM Privately Held
SIC: 3861 5943 Printing equipment, photographic; office forms & supplies
HQ: Clover Technologies Group, Llc
4200 Columbus St
Ottawa IL 61350

**(G-16958)**
**FAIRMOUNT SANTROL INC**
Also Called: Innovation Center
4115 Progress Dr (61350-9548)
P.O. Box 736 (61350-0736)
PHONE..................................815 433-2449
Janet Raber, Branch Mgr
EMP: 10
SALES (corp-wide): 535MM Publicly Held
SIC: 1446 Industrial sand
HQ: Fairmount Santrol Inc.
8834 Mayfield Rd Ste A
Chesterland OH 44026
440 214-3200

**(G-16959)**
**FAIRMOUNT SANTROL INC**
776 Centennial Dr (61350-1002)
PHONE..................................815 587-4410
Lynn Hiser, Vice Pres
Janet Raber, Purch Agent
John Edney, Engineer
EMP: 20 EST: 2015
SALES (est): 1.5MM Privately Held
SIC: 1442 Construction sand & gravel

**(G-16960)**
**FREQUENCY DEVICES INC**
1784 Chessie Ln Unit 1 (61350-9626)
PHONE..................................815 434-7800
William H Franklin III, President
Nancy Kelly, General Mgr
Bill Franklin, Vice Pres
William Franklin Jr, Vice Pres
Don Carolan, Engineer
▼ EMP: 12
SQ FT: 10,000
SALES (est): 1.3MM Privately Held
WEB: www.freqdev.com
SIC: 3825 3823 3564 Analog-digital converters, electronic instrumentation type; industrial instrmnts msrmnt display/control process variable; blowers & fans

**(G-16961)**
**HEISS WELDING INC**
Also Called: HWI
260 W Marquette St (61350-1914)
PHONE..................................815 434-1838
Fax: 815 434-1839
Robert Heiss, President
EMP: 10
SQ FT: 5,000
SALES (est): 1.7MM Privately Held
SIC: 7692 Welding repair

**(G-16962)**
**ILLINOIS OFFICE SUP ELECT PRTG**
1119 La Salle St (61350-2020)
PHONE..................................815 434-0186
Fax: 815 434-2665
Robert J Keeney, President
Peggy Keeney, Vice Pres
EMP: 20
SALES (est): 2.7MM Privately Held
WEB: www.electprint.com
SIC: 2752 2791 2789 2759 Commercial printing, offset; typesetting; bookbinding & related work; commercial printing

**(G-16963)**
**JAMESON BOOKS INC**
722 Columbus St (61350-5002)
P.O. Box 738 (61350-0738)
PHONE..................................815 434-7905
Caroline Campaigne, President
Jameson Campaigne, President
EMP: 3
SQ FT: 2,000
SALES (est): 236.6K Privately Held
WEB: www.jamesonbooks.com
SIC: 2731 Books: publishing only

**(G-16964)**
**JOHNSON PATTERN & MCH WORKS**
350 W Marquette St (61350-1916)
PHONE..................................815 433-2775
Fax: 815 433-1121
Esther Johnson, President
Mark Dale, Purch Mgr
Stan Dale, Treasurer
Diane Dale, Admin Sec

# Ottawa - Lasalle County (G-16965) — GEOGRAPHIC SECTION

**EMP:** 20
**SQ FT:** 32,000
**SALES (est):** 3.5MM **Privately Held**
**SIC:** 3599 3543 3545 Custom machinery; foundry cores; machine tool accessories

### (G-16965)
### L M K FABRICATION INC
1779 Chessie Ln (61350-9687)
**PHONE** .................................. 815 433-1530
Larry Kiest, *President*
Gina Fox, *Executive*
**EMP:** 14
**SALES (est):** 2.3MM **Privately Held**
**WEB:** www.lmkinteriorsltd.com
**SIC:** 3498 Fabricated pipe & fittings

### (G-16966)
### LA SALLE CO ESDA
711 E Etna Rd (61350-1040)
**PHONE** .................................. 815 433-5622
**EMP:** 3
**SALES (est):** 171.9K **Privately Held**
**SIC:** 3568 Joints & couplings

### (G-16967)
### LMK TECHNOLOGIES LLC
1779 Chessie Ln (61350-9687)
**PHONE** .................................. 815 433-1530
Michael J Reardon, *CEO*
Larry W Kiest Jr, *President*
Bruce Kamin, *General Mgr*
Shain Cheney, *Vice Pres*
James A Gordon, *Vice Pres*
**EMP:** 73
**SQ FT:** 20,000
**SALES (est):** 20.6MM **Privately Held**
**WEB:** www.performanceliner.com
**SIC:** 3552 Spindles, textile

### (G-16968)
### MARQUTTE STL SUP FBRCATION INC
800 W Marquette St (61350-1814)
**PHONE** .................................. 815 433-0178
**Fax:** 815 433-0451
James Sheridan Jr, *President*
William T Sheridan, *Vice Pres*
Charles Sheridan, *Admin Sec*
**EMP:** 12
**SQ FT:** 14,000
**SALES (est):** 2.1MM **Privately Held**
**SIC:** 3312 1791 3441 Structural shapes & pilings, steel; structural steel erection; fabricated structural metal

### (G-16969)
### MINIGRIP INC
Also Called: ITW Minigrip/Zip-Pak
1510 Warehouse Dr (61350-9003)
**PHONE** .................................. 845 680-2710
**Fax:** 815 431-0500
Jack Campbell, *President*
Vincent Zaccheo, *Controller*
▲ **EMP:** 95
**SQ FT:** 100,000
**SALES (est):** 15.5MM
**SALES (corp-wide):** 13.6B **Publicly Held**
**SIC:** 3081 3965 Unsupported plastics film & sheet; zipper
**PA:** Illinois Tool Works Inc.
 155 Harlem Ave
 Glenview IL 60025
 847 724-7500

### (G-16970)
### MUCCI KIRKPATRICK SHEET METAL
1908 Ottawa Ave (61350-3443)
**PHONE** .................................. 815 433-3350
**Fax:** 815 433-3375
Debbie Mucci, *President*
Gary Kirkpatrick, *Vice Pres*
**EMP:** 9
**SQ FT:** 1,200
**SALES (est):** 400K **Privately Held**
**SIC:** 5075 7623 3444 Warm air heating & air conditioning; refrigeration service & repair; sheet metalwork

### (G-16971)
### MUFFYS INC
423 W Madison St (61350-2832)
**PHONE** .................................. 815 433-6839
Gerena Muffler, *Owner*
**EMP:** 4
**SALES (est):** 396.8K **Privately Held**
**SIC:** 2599 Bar, restaurant & cafeteria furniture

### (G-16972)
### NORTHERN ILLINOIS GAS COMPANY
Also Called: Nicor Gas
1629 Champlain St (61350-1698)
**PHONE** .................................. 815 433-3850
**Fax:** 815 433-5644
Patricia McKibbon, *Branch Mgr*
**EMP:** 65
**SALES (corp-wide):** 19.9B **Publicly Held**
**WEB:** www.nicor.com
**SIC:** 4924 1382 4923 Natural gas distribution; oil & gas exploration services; gas transmission & distribution
**HQ:** Northern Illinois Gas Company
 1844 W Ferry Rd
 Naperville IL 60563
 630 983-8676

### (G-16973)
### OAKWOOD MEMORIAL PARK INC
Also Called: Brooke Burial Vault Co
2405 Champlain St (61350-1260)
**PHONE** .................................. 815 433-0313
Richard Brooke, *President*
James Brooke, *Corp Secy*
**EMP:** 4 **EST:** 1938
**SQ FT:** 3,600
**SALES (est):** 289.4K **Privately Held**
**SIC:** 6553 3272 Cemeteries, real estate operation; burial vaults, concrete or precast terrazzo

### (G-16974)
### ODL INC (PA)
1304 Starfire Dr (61350-1624)
**PHONE** .................................. 815 434-0655
**Fax:** 815 434-0760
Luke Caruso III, *President*
Jim Caruso, *President*
Joanie Bretag, *Vice Pres*
Sandy Erwin, *Vice Pres*
Joan Darif, *Production*
▲ **EMP:** 60
**SQ FT:** 15,000
**SALES (est):** 8.5MM **Privately Held**
**WEB:** www.ottawadentallab.com
**SIC:** 8072 3843 Artificial teeth production; crown & bridge production; denture production; orthodontic appliance production; dental equipment & supplies

### (G-16975)
### OTTAWA PUBLISHING CO INC (HQ)
Also Called: Daily Times, The
110 W Jefferson St (61350-5018)
**PHONE** .................................. 815 433-2000
**Fax:** 815 433-1639
Len R Small, *President*
James Malley, *General Mgr*
John A Newby, *Editor*
Allyson Risley, *Business Mgr*
Cindy Liptak, *Sls & Mktg Exec*
**EMP:** 106
**SQ FT:** 20,000
**SALES (est):** 8.8MM
**SALES (corp-wide):** 168.9MM **Privately Held**
**SIC:** 2711 2752 Commercial printing & newspaper publishing combined; commercial printing, lithographic
**PA:** Small Newspaper Group
 8 Dearborn Sq
 Kankakee IL 60901
 815 937-3300

### (G-16976)
### OTTAWA PUBLISHING CO INC
Also Called: Adventure Advertising
300 W Joliet St (61350-1925)
**PHONE** .................................. 815 434-3330
**Fax:** 815 431-1006
Harold Clemins, *Manager*
**EMP:** 13
**SALES (corp-wide):** 168.9MM **Privately Held**
**SIC:** 2711 2759 Commercial printing & newspaper publishing combined; commercial printing
**HQ:** Ottawa Publishing Co Inc
 110 W Jefferson St
 Ottawa IL 61350
 815 433-2000

### (G-16977)
### PATIO PLUS
1624 W Main St (61350-2525)
**PHONE** .................................. 815 433-2399
Andy Ruger, *Owner*
**EMP:** 7
**SQ FT:** 11,000
**SALES (est):** 240K **Privately Held**
**SIC:** 2519 2531 2511 Fiberglass & plastic furniture; public building & related furniture; wood household furniture

### (G-16978)
### PERSONALIZED THREADS
2655 E 1559th Rd (61350-9290)
**PHONE** .................................. 815 431-1815
Peggy Enquist, *President*
**EMP:** 4
**SALES (est):** 188.9K **Privately Held**
**WEB:** www.personalized-threads.com
**SIC:** 2395 Emblems, embroidered

### (G-16979)
### PILKINGTON NORTH AMERICA INC
300 Center 20th St (61350)
**PHONE** .................................. 815 433-0932
James Leng, *Managing Dir*
Bill Ebener, *Opers Staff*
Scott Kennedy, *Purch Agent*
Mark Christmann, *Electrical Engi*
R Okkerse, *Finance*
**EMP:** 238
**SALES (corp-wide):** 5.3B **Privately Held**
**WEB:** www.low-eglass.com
**SIC:** 3211 3231 Flat glass; products of purchased glass
**HQ:** Pilkington North America, Inc.
 811 Madison Ave Fl 1
 Toledo OH 43604
 419 247-4955

### (G-16980)
### POLANCICS MEATS & TENDERLOINS
412 W Norris Dr (61350-1435)
**PHONE** .................................. 815 433-0324
Jim Polancic, *President*
**EMP:** 7
**SQ FT:** 4,500
**SALES (est):** 806.6K **Privately Held**
**SIC:** 2013 5421 Prepared pork products from purchased pork; meat markets, including freezer provisioners

### (G-16981)
### R AND B DISTRIBUTORS INC
Also Called: Vitner Chips
1217 Saint Clair St (61350-2338)
**PHONE** .................................. 815 433-6843
Ronald E Chismarick, *President*
**EMP:** 2
**SQ FT:** 22,000
**SALES (est):** 475K **Privately Held**
**SIC:** 2096 Potato chips & similar snacks

### (G-16982)
### SABIC INNOVATIVE PLAS US LLC
2148 N 2753rd Rd (61350-9766)
P.O. Box 658 (61350-0658)
**PHONE** .................................. 815 434-7000
Brian Serby, *Human Resources*
Hugh Morton, *Branch Mgr*
Darren Mays, *Manager*
Allen Sather, *Manager*
Russ Prechtl, *Senior Mgr*
**EMP:** 450 **Privately Held**
**WEB:** www.sabic-ip.com
**SIC:** 2821 Plastics materials & resins
**HQ:** Sabic Innovative Plastics Us Llc
 2500 City W Blvd Ste 100
 Houston TX 77042
 713 430-2300

### (G-16983)
### SIGAN AMERICA LLC
1111 W Mckinley Rd (61350-4732)
**PHONE** .................................. 815 431-9830
Jaime Osejos, *Research*
Dean Gangbar, *Mng Member*
Greg Rubin,
Manjit Singh,
▲ **EMP:** 40
**SQ FT:** 190,000
**SALES (est):** 5.4MM **Privately Held**
**SIC:** 2844 Toilet preparations

### (G-16984)
### SIGMA GRAPHICS INC
4001 Baker Rd (61350-9536)
P.O. Box 260, Decatur (62525-0260)
**PHONE** .................................. 815 433-1000
**Fax:** 815 433-4747
Thomas W Kowa, *President*
Karen Mason, *Office Mgr*
**EMP:** 18
**SQ FT:** 24,000
**SALES (est):** 3MM **Privately Held**
**WEB:** www.sigmagraphics.net
**SIC:** 2752 Commercial printing, offset

### (G-16985)
### SIKA CORPORATION
1515 Titanium Dr (61350-8905)
**PHONE** .................................. 815 431-1080
Todd Stindler, *Branch Mgr*
**EMP:** 4
**SALES (corp-wide):** 5.6B **Privately Held**
**WEB:** www.sikacorp.com
**SIC:** 2891 2899 Epoxy adhesives; sealants; chemical preparations; concrete curing & hardening compounds
**HQ:** Sika Corporation
 201 Polito Ave
 Lyndhurst NJ 07071
 201 933-8800

### (G-16986)
### THE TIMES
110 W Jefferson St (61350-5010)
**PHONE** .................................. 815 433-2000
**Fax:** 815 795-3446
Mike Bertok, *Plant Mgr*
Charles Stanley, *Manager*
Betty Walsh, *Admin Sec*
**EMP:** 9
**SALES (est):** 584K **Privately Held**
**SIC:** 2711 Newspapers, publishing & printing

### (G-16987)
### TYSON FRESH MEATS INC
621 E Stevenson Rd (61350-9104)
**PHONE** .................................. 815 431-9501
Stefaine Kaecker, *Human Res Dir*
Chris Sparks, *Sales Executive*
Walter Kohler, *Branch Mgr*
**EMP:** 394
**SALES (corp-wide):** 36.8B **Publicly Held**
**SIC:** 2011 Boxed beef from meat slaughtered on site
**HQ:** Tyson Fresh Meats, Inc.
 800 Stevens Port Dr
 Dakota Dunes SD 57049
 605 235-2061

### (G-16988)
### U S SILICA COMPANY
701 Boyce Memorial Dr (61350-2561)
**PHONE** .................................. 815 434-0188
**Fax:** 815 434-7536
Jim Vaccari, *Div Sub Head*
Robert Morrow, *Vice Pres*
John Robinson, *Safety Mgr*
Darrell Fleming, *Engineer*
Aaron Piper, *Personnel*
**EMP:** 125
**SALES (corp-wide):** 559.6MM **Publicly Held**
**WEB:** www.u-s-silica.com
**SIC:** 1446 3291 Silica mining; abrasive products
**HQ:** U. S. Silica Company
 8490 Progress Dr Ste 300
 Frederick MD 21701
 301 682-0600

### (G-16989)
### UNIMIN CORPORATION
4000 Baker Rd (61350-9500)
**PHONE** .................................. 815 431-2200
**Fax:** 815 434-2658
Donald Higgins, *Engineer*
Dianne Gaines, *Branch Mgr*
**EMP:** 40

# GEOGRAPHIC SECTION

Palatine - Cook County (G-17016)

SALES (corp-wide): 117.6MM **Privately Held**
WEB: www.unimin.com
SIC: **1446** Industrial sand
HQ: Unimin Corporation
258 Elm St
New Canaan CT 06840
203 966-8880

*(G-16990)*
**UNIMIN CORPORATION**
4000 Baker Rd (61350-9500)
PHONE.................815 434-5363
Bill Bratey, *Principal*
EMP: 27
SALES (corp-wide): 117.6MM **Privately Held**
WEB: www.unimin.com
SIC: **1446** Industrial sand
HQ: Unimin Corporation
258 Elm St
New Canaan CT 06840
203 966-8880

*(G-16991)*
**WESTERN SAND & GRAVEL CO**
4220 Mbl Dr (61350-9352)
PHONE.................815 433-1600
Mike Sitterly, *Owner*
EMP: 10
SALES (est): 654.2K **Privately Held**
SIC: **5032** 3999 Brick, stone & related material; manufacturing industries

*(G-16992)*
**WOODHILL CABINETRY DESIGN INC**
3381 N State Route 23 (61350-9007)
PHONE.................815 431-0545
Fax: 815 431-0557
Craig H Sweeney, *President*
Mary J Sweeney, *Admin Sec*
EMP: 7
SALES (est): 798.1K **Privately Held**
SIC: **2434** 2541 2521 2517 Wood kitchen cabinets; wood partitions & fixtures; wood office furniture; wood television & radio cabinets

## Ozark
### Johnson County

*(G-16993)*
**CORNERSTONE POLISHING COMPANY**
85 Zach Ln (62972-1116)
PHONE.................618 777-2754
Mark Kelton, *Owner*
EMP: 3
SALES (est): 178.2K **Privately Held**
SIC: **3471** Polishing, metals or formed products

## Palatine
### Cook County

*(G-16994)*
**3 GOLDENSTAR INC**
545 E Dundee Rd (60074-2815)
PHONE.................847 963-0451
Abdul Zakir, *President*
EMP: 16
SALES: 687K **Privately Held**
SIC: **3999** Manufacturing industries

*(G-16995)*
**ACADEMY CORP**
219 Avondale Dr (60067-8638)
PHONE.................847 359-3000
Fax: 847 359-3199
Paul Petrillo, *Principal*
EMP: 2
SALES (est): 268.7K **Privately Held**
SIC: **3339** Precious metals

*(G-16996)*
**ACURA PHARMACEUTICALS INC (PA)**
616 N North Ct Ste 120 (60067-8121)
PHONE.................847 705-7709
Fax: 847 705-5399
Robert B Jones, *President*
James F Emigh, *Vice Pres*
James Emigh, *Vice Pres*
Peter A Clemens, *CFO*
Robert A Seiser, *Treasurer*
EMP: 15 EST: 1935
SQ FT: 1,600
SALES: 4.4MM **Publicly Held**
WEB: www.halseydrug.com
SIC: **2834** Pharmaceutical preparations; tablets, pharmaceutical

*(G-16997)*
**ADRIAN ORGAS GHEORGHE**
1010 N Apple Tree Ct (60067-3470)
PHONE.................773 355-1200
Diana Orgas, *Principal*
EMP: 3
SALES (est): 151.1K **Privately Held**
SIC: **4731** 3462 Freight transportation arrangement; iron & steel forgings

*(G-16998)*
**ADVANCED PROTOTYPE MOLDING**
263 N Woodwork Ln (60067-4930)
PHONE.................847 202-4200
Fax: 847 202-4270
Bruce Megleo, *President*
Mike Megleo, *Principal*
Henry Herman, *Office Mgr*
Laura Megleo, *Admin Sec*
▲ EMP: 6
SQ FT: 5,400
SALES: 600K **Privately Held**
WEB: www.advancedprototype.com
SIC: **3542** 3089 2821 2822 Machine tools, metal forming type; molding primary plastic; molding compounds, plastics; silicone rubbers

*(G-16999)*
**AIMTRON CORPORATION (PA)**
555 S Vermont St (60067-6947)
PHONE.................630 372-7500
Mukesh Vasani, *President*
Larry Whitis, *Mfg Staff*
Gulab Singh, *Purchasing*
Jason Duerr, *Engineer*
Bharat Sampat, *Controller*
▲ EMP: 85
SQ FT: 49,400
SALES (est): 23.5MM **Privately Held**
SIC: **3679** Electronic circuits

*(G-17000)*
**AMERICAN DATA CENTRE INC (PA)**
25 W Palatine Rd (60067-5199)
PHONE.................847 358-7111
Patrick Flavin, *Ch of Bd*
Ronald Blum, *Vice Pres*
Susan Flavin, *Vice Pres*
EMP: 4
SQ FT: 3,000
SALES (est): 731.1K **Privately Held**
WEB: www.adcnoc.com
SIC: **3663** 7361 8721 8741 Satellites, communications; employment agencies; accounting, auditing & bookkeeping; financial management for business

*(G-17001)*
**AMTECH INDUSTRIES LLC**
Also Called: Ai Technologies
666 S Vermont St (60067-6950)
PHONE.................847 202-3488
Betty Wirth, *Accounts Mgr*
Steve Pearlman,
Char Kovac, *Administration*
EMP: 55
SALES (est): 4.8MM **Privately Held**
SIC: **3089** Injection molding of plastics

*(G-17002)*
**AR CONCEPTS USA INC**
520 N Hicks Rd Ste 120 (60067-3607)
PHONE.................847 392-4608
John Conti, *CEO*
EMP: 2
SALES: 220K **Privately Held**
SIC: **3669** 1629 Railroad signaling devices, electric; railroad & subway construction

*(G-17003)*
**ARLINGTON PLATING COMPANY**
600 S Vermont St (60067-6999)
P.O. Box 974 (60078-0974)
PHONE.................847 359-1490
Fax: 847 359-1499
Marvin E Gollob, *Ch of Bd*
Rich Macary, *President*
Paul Duncan, *Human Res Dir*
Lisa A Finke, *Admin Sec*
David Gollob, *Admin Sec*
▲ EMP: 180
SQ FT: 60,000
SALES (est): 24.8MM **Privately Held**
WEB: www.arlingtonplating.com
SIC: **3471** Electroplating of metals or formed products; polishing, metals or formed products; buffing for the trade

*(G-17004)*
**AVASARALA INC**
1 E Northwest Hwy Ste 214 (60067-1700)
PHONE.................847 969-0630
TT Mani, *President*
Narayana Raju Kothapalli, *Vice Pres*
EMP: 2
SQ FT: 500
SALES: 805.5K
SALES (corp-wide): 15.6MM **Privately Held**
SIC: **3535** 5051 Conveyors & conveying equipment; rods, wire (not insulated)
PA: Avasarala Technologies Limited
No.47, 36th Main Road,
Bengaluru KAR 56006
802 843-5207

*(G-17005)*
**B N BLANCE ENRGY SOLUTIONS LLC**
2019 N Wainwright Ct (60074-1219)
PHONE.................847 287-7466
Brenda Neumann, *Manager*
Brenda S Neumann,
EMP: 2
SALES (est): 241.4K **Privately Held**
SIC: **3511** Turbines & turbine generator sets

*(G-17006)*
**BIAS POWER TECHNOLOGY INC**
414 S Vermont St (60067-6946)
PHONE.................847 991-2427
Dr Kenneth Kayser, *Ch of Bd*
Bharat Shah, *President*
EMP: 9
SQ FT: 5,000
SALES (est): 1MM **Privately Held**
SIC: **3677** Transformers power supply, electronic type

*(G-17007)*
**CAB COMMUNICATIONS INC**
Also Called: Recreation Management
50 N Brockway St Ste 4-11 (60067-5072)
PHONE.................847 963-8740
Fax: 847 963-8745
Chris Belbin, *President*
Deborah Vence, *Director*
Dale Dodson, *Assistant*
EMP: 5 EST: 1999
SQ FT: 1,500
SALES (est): 420K **Privately Held**
SIC: **2741** Business service newsletters: publishing & printing

*(G-17008)*
**CCI POWER SUPPLIES LLC**
616 N North Ct Ste 250 (60067-8170)
PHONE.................847 362-6500
William Trzyna, *Branch Mgr*
EMP: 155
SALES (corp-wide): 8MM **Privately Held**
SIC: **3613** Power switching equipment
PA: Cci Power Supplies, Llc
100 Industrial Dr
Pardeeville WI 53954
608 429-2144

*(G-17009)*
**CENTEC AUTOMATION INC**
420 S Vermont St (60067-6946)
PHONE.................847 791-9430
Fax: 847 776-5271
Thomas Vrenios, *President*
EMP: 8
SQ FT: 3,000
SALES (est): 1.3MM **Privately Held**
SIC: **3569** 5084 Assembly machines, non-metalworking; baling machines, for scrap metal, paper or similar material; conveyor systems

*(G-17010)*
**CGR TECHNOLOGIES INC**
350 W Colfax St (60067-2516)
PHONE.................847 934-7622
Fax: 847 934-7629
Gregory Muncer, *President*
Robert Muncer, *Admin Sec*
EMP: 20
SQ FT: 8,000
SALES (est): 4.4MM **Privately Held**
WEB: www.cgrtech.com
SIC: **3544** Die sets for metal stamping (presses)

*(G-17011)*
**CLIFFORDS PUB INC**
1503 N Rand Rd (60074-2931)
PHONE.................847 259-3000
Struckmon Carol, *Principal*
EMP: 5
SALES (est): 409.3K **Privately Held**
SIC: **2085** Cocktails, alcoholic

*(G-17012)*
**COAKLEY MFG & METROLOGY**
1141 N Doe Rd (60067-1812)
PHONE.................847 202-9331
Bryan W Coakley, *President*
Michael Coakley, *Vice Pres*
Olyai Griffin, *Manager*
EMP: 10
SQ FT: 5,200
SALES (est): 1.6MM **Privately Held**
WEB: www.cmmautomation.com
SIC: **3548** Welding & cutting apparatus & accessories

*(G-17013)*
**COLFAX WELDING & FABRICATING**
605 W Colfax St (60067-2374)
PHONE.................847 359-4433
Fax: 847 359-0254
Peter Altman, *President*
Lee Altman, *Corp Secy*
EMP: 4
SQ FT: 5,500
SALES (est): 260K **Privately Held**
SIC: **7692** 3444 3443 Welding repair; sheet metalwork; fabricated plate work (boiler shop)

*(G-17014)*
**COMPLETE LAWN AND SNOW SERVICE**
Also Called: Class
544 W Colfax St Ste 5 (60067-2523)
P.O. Box 1442 (60078-1442)
PHONE.................847 776-7287
Fax: 847 776-9552
Paul Munagian, *President*
Brenda Munagian, *Vice Pres*
EMP: 14 EST: 1986
SALES (est): 860K **Privately Held**
SIC: **0782** 4959 0783 3251 Lawn care services; snowplowing; removal services, bush & tree; paving brick, clay

*(G-17015)*
**CONNELLY & ASSOCIATES**
892 E Glencoe St (60074-6435)
PHONE.................847 372-5001
Thomas Connelly, *Owner*
EMP: 25
SALES (est): 1.3MM **Privately Held**
SIC: **7372** Prepackaged software

*(G-17016)*
**CONSOLIDATED MILL SUPPLY INC (PA)**
Also Called: Vestis Group
1530 E Dundee Rd Ste 200 (60074-8318)
PHONE.................847 706-6715
Kenneth J Pies, *CEO*
Mark Kaplan, *President*
Andy Mass, *Vice Pres*
Michelle Mendenhall, *Vice Pres*
Adam Barshefski, *CFO*

▲ EMP: 4
SQ FT: 2,000
SALES (est): 3.1MM Privately Held
WEB: www.consolidatedmillsupply.com
SIC: 3312 Blast furnaces & steel mills

**(G-17017)**
**CONSTRUCTION BUS MEDIA LLC**
579 N 1st Bank Dr Ste 220 (60067-8126)
PHONE.................................847 359-6493
Fax: 847 359-6754
Jim Crockett, *Editor*
Tim Shea,
Gary Redmond,
EMP: 6
SALES (est): 1MM Privately Held
WEB: www.arch-products.com
SIC: 2721 Magazines: publishing only, not printed on site

**(G-17018)**
**CONTOUR TOOL WORKS INC**
1712 N Lee Ct (60074-1117)
PHONE.................................847 947-4700
Darrin Knuth, *President*
Wayne Knuth, *President*
EMP: 8
SQ FT: 5,500
SALES (est): 830K Privately Held
WEB: www.contourtoolworks.com
SIC: 7389 3312 Grinding, precision: commercial or industrial; tool & die steel

**(G-17019)**
**DANIEL BRUCE LLC**
Also Called: Dibi Accessories
2365 N Irene Dr (60074-1036)
PHONE.................................917 583-1538
Daniel Wimer,
▲ EMP: 10
SALES (est): 1.4MM Privately Held
SIC: 2339 2389 Women's & misses' accessories; men's miscellaneous accessories

**(G-17020)**
**DARDA ENTERPRISES INC**
Also Called: Midwest Foundry Products
301 N Dean Dr (60074-5541)
P.O. Box 91865, Elk Grove Village (60009-1865)
PHONE.................................847 270-0410
Richard Darda, *President*
Robert L Carter, *Superintendent*
Roberta J Darda, *Vice Pres*
Linda Darda Smith, *Manager*
EMP: 15
SALES: 1MM Privately Held
SIC: 3369 3549 White metal castings (lead, tin, antimony), except die; metalworking machinery

**(G-17021)**
**DELANEY SHEET METAL CO**
Also Called: Delaney Sheetmetal
116 N Benton St (60067-5239)
PHONE.................................847 991-9579
John P Delaney, *President*
Joan Delaney, *Vice Pres*
EMP: 4
SQ FT: 1,600
SALES (est): 500K Privately Held
SIC: 3444 Sheet metalwork

**(G-17022)**
**DELTA PRESS INC**
756 W Kimball Ave (60067-6776)
PHONE.................................847 671-3200
Fax: 847 671-3298
Mark Masciola, *Ch of Bd*
Michael Naselli, *President*
John Masciola, *Vice Pres*
Meredith Neag, *Office Mgr*
Michael Selli, *Supervisor*
EMP: 27 EST: 1935
SQ FT: 15,000
SALES (est): 3.1MM Privately Held
SIC: 7336 2796 2675 Commercial art & graphic design; platemaking services; die-cut paper & board

**(G-17023)**
**DIX MCGUIRE COMMODITIES LLC**
Also Called: Inc., Dix McGuire Intl
201 E Dundee Rd Ste 2 (60074-2806)
PHONE.................................847 496-5320
Richard Feldman,
▼ EMP: 4
SALES (est): 354.7K Privately Held
SIC: 2041 Flour & other grain mill products

**(G-17024)**
**DOLCHE TRUCKLOAD CORP**
473 W Northwest Hwy 2e (60067-0209)
PHONE.................................800 719-4921
Desi Evans, *President*
EMP: 4
SQ FT: 1,300
SALES: 2.5MM Privately Held
SIC: 3715 Truck trailers

**(G-17025)**
**EMMETTS TAVERN & BREWING CO**
Also Called: Emmett's Ale House
110 N Brockway St (60067-5063)
PHONE.................................847 359-1533
Fax: 847 359-0961
EMP: 11
SALES (corp-wide): 3MM Privately Held
SIC: 5812 2082 5182 Chicken restaurant; beer (alcoholic beverage); wine & distilled beverages
PA: Emmett's Tavern & Brewing Co.
128 W Main St
West Dundee IL 60118
847 428-4500

**(G-17026)**
**ENCAP TECHNOLOGIES INC (PA)**
707 S Vermont St (60067-7138)
PHONE.................................510 337-2700
Griffith Neal, *President*
EMP: 11
SQ FT: 70,000
SALES: 20MM Privately Held
SIC: 3621 Electric motor & generator parts

**(G-17027)**
**ENCAP TECHNOLOGIES INC**
640 S Vermont St (60067-6950)
PHONE.................................510 337-2700
Griffith Neal, *President*
EMP: 314
SALES (corp-wide): 20MM Privately Held
SIC: 3621 Electric motor & generator parts
PA: Encap Technologies, Inc.
707 S Vermont St
Palatine IL 60067
510 337-2700

**(G-17028)**
**FHB LIGHTING INC**
800 E Northwest Hwy # 700 (60074-6519)
PHONE.................................888 364-8802
Okan Anter, *CEO*
EMP: 3
SALES (est): 311.3K Privately Held
SIC: 3449 Miscellaneous metalwork

**(G-17029)**
**FJW OPTICAL SYSTEMS INC**
322 N Woodwork Ln (60067-4933)
PHONE.................................847 358-2500
Frank J Warzak, *President*
Barry Durr, *General Mgr*
Felix Marin, *Vice Pres*
Barry F Warzak, *Vice Pres*
Saul Jameikis, *Senior Engr*
EMP: 10 EST: 1945
SQ FT: 8,000
SALES (est): 1.8MM Privately Held
WEB: www.fjwopticalsystems.com
SIC: 3823 Infrared instruments, industrial process type

**(G-17030)**
**GRACE AUTO BODY FRAME**
320 W Colfax St (60067-2516)
PHONE.................................847 963-1234
Gret Lee, *Owner*
EMP: 2
SALES (est): 207.9K Privately Held
SIC: 3465 7532 7513 Body parts, automobile: stamped metal; body shop, automotive; truck rental & leasing, no drivers

**(G-17031)**
**GREEN EARTH TECHNOLOGIES INC**
617 S Middleton Ave (60067-6642)
PHONE.................................847 991-0436
Mathew Zuckerman, *Ch of Bd*
Jeff Marshall, *President*
Lou Petrucci, *COO*
Greg D Adams, *CFO*
Louis Ball, *VP Sales*
EMP: 4
SALES (est): 20MM Privately Held
WEB: www.getg.com
SIC: 2875 Compost

**(G-17032)**
**H-O-H WATER TECHNOLOGY INC (PA)**
500 S Vermont St (60067-6948)
P.O. Box 487 (60078-0487)
PHONE.................................847 358-7400
Fax: 847 358-7082
Thomas F Hutchison, *President*
Wallace Hood, *Division Mgr*
Chris Lawson, *Division Mgr*
Nathan Rentschler, *Division Mgr*
Cory Reneau, *Area Mgr*
EMP: 47
SQ FT: 39,300
SALES (est): 38.3MM Privately Held
SIC: 3589 2899 Water treatment equipment, industrial; chemical preparations

**(G-17033)**
**HARRIER INTERIOR PRODUCTS**
319 W Colfax St (60067-2525)
PHONE.................................847 934-1310
EMP: 2
SQ FT: 1,800
SALES (est): 210K Privately Held
SIC: 2531 Manufactures Library Shelving

**(G-17034)**
**HAVOLINE XPRESS LUBE LLC**
1402 N Rand Rd (60067-2923)
PHONE.................................847 221-5724
EMP: 7
SALES (corp-wide): 9.1MM Privately Held
SIC: 2992 Mfg Lubricating Oils/Greases
PA: Havoline Xpress Lube Llc
810 Sunset Dr
Round Lake IL 60073
224 757-5628

**(G-17035)**
**HB FULLER CNSTR PDTS INC**
315 S Hicks Rd (60067-6940)
PHONE.................................847 776-4375
Steve Bratspies, *Chief Mktg Ofcr*
Jim Griffin, *Manager*
EMP: 13
SALES (corp-wide): 2B Publicly Held
WEB: www.fosterproducts.com
SIC: 2891 Adhesives
HQ: H.B. Fuller Construction Products Inc.
1105 S Frontenac St
Aurora IL 60504
630 978-7766

**(G-17036)**
**HIGH-LIFE PRODUCTS INC**
615 W Colfax St (60067-2340)
PHONE.................................847 991-9449
EMP: 4 EST: 2010
SALES (est): 250K Privately Held
SIC: 3493 Mfg Steel Springs-Nonwire

**(G-17037)**
**HONEYWELL INTERNATIONAL INC**
407 N Quentin Rd (60067-4832)
PHONE.................................847 701-3038
EMP: 699
SALES (corp-wide): 39.3B Publicly Held
SIC: 3724 Aircraft engines & engine parts
PA: Honeywell International Inc.
115 Tabor Rd
Morris Plains NJ 07950
973 455-2000

**(G-17038)**
**HP INC**
1935 S Plum Grove Rd # 199 (60067-7258)
PHONE.................................847 207-9118
Don Prest, *Manager*
EMP: 6
SALES (corp-wide): 48.2B Publicly Held
SIC: 3571 Personal computers (microcomputers)
PA: Hp Inc.
1501 Page Mill Rd
Palo Alto CA 94304
650 857-1501

**(G-17039)**
**IMPERIAL WOODWORKING COMPANY (PA)**
310 N Woodwork Ln (60067-4933)
PHONE.................................847 221-2107
Fax: 847 358-0905
Frank Huschitt Sr, *Ch of Bd*
Frank Huschitt III, *President*
Paul Garvin, *Vice Pres*
Marion Huschitt, *Vice Pres*
Richard Stiers, *Vice Pres*
▲ EMP: 100
SQ FT: 65,000
SALES (est): 43.9MM Privately Held
WEB: www.imperialwoodworking.com
SIC: 2541 Store fixtures, wood; store fronts, prefabricated: wood

**(G-17040)**
**IMPERIAL WOODWORKING ENTPS INC**
310 N Woodwork Ln (60067-4933)
PHONE.................................847 358-6920
Frank Huschitt Sr, *President*
Frank Huschitt III, *Exec VP*
Annette Huschitt, *Vice Pres*
▲ EMP: 20
SALES (est): 147.3K Privately Held
WEB: www.imperialwoodworkingenterprises.com
SIC: 2431 Millwork

**(G-17041)**
**INC 1105 MEDIA**
800 E Northwest Hwy # 306 (60074-6519)
PHONE.................................847 358-7272
Fax: 847 358-7433
Tom Creevy, *Manager*
EMP: 2
SALES: 1.5MM
SALES (corp-wide): 145MM Privately Held
SIC: 2721 Periodicals
PA: 1105 Media, Inc.
9201 Oakdale Ave Ste 101
Chatsworth CA 91311
818 814-5200

**(G-17042)**
**INSTY PRINTS PALATINE INC**
Also Called: Insty-Prints
453 S Vermont St Ste A (60067-6968)
PHONE.................................847 963-0000
Lorraine Walsh, *President*
Brian Walsh, *Vice Pres*
Pat Walsh, *Vice Pres*
EMP: 10
SQ FT: 6,000
SALES (est): 31.9K Privately Held
SIC: 2752 2791 2789 Lithographic Commercial Printing Typesetting Services Bookbinding/Related Work

**(G-17043)**
**INTEC-MEXICO LLC**
666 S Vermont St (60067-6950)
PHONE.................................847 358-0088
Steven Perlman, *Mng Member*
Daryl Dishong, *Mng Member*
Michael Greeby, *Mng Member*
Scott Perlman, *Mng Member*
Cheryl Kilgore, *Manager*
EMP: 360
SQ FT: 70,000
SALES (est): 76.3MM
SALES (corp-wide): 120.6MM Privately Held
WEB: www.intecgrp.com
SIC: 3089 Molding primary plastic

PA: The Intec Group Inc
666 S Vermont St
Palatine IL 60067
847 358-0088

### (G-17044)
### INTERIOR FASHIONS CONTRACT
Also Called: Window Fashion Unlimited
120 S Northwest Hwy (60074-6233)
**PHONE** ............................847 358-6050
**Fax:** 847 358-4969
Patricia McCormick, *President*
Randy McCormick, *Corp Secy*
Brian McCormick, *Vice Pres*
**EMP:** 3
**SQ FT:** 2,400
**SALES:** 500K **Privately Held**
**SIC:** 2391 2392 Curtains & draperies; household furnishings

### (G-17045)
### J P GOLDENNE INCORPORATED
Also Called: Digital Homes Technologies
346 N Northwest Hwy (60067-5329)
**PHONE** ............................847 776-5063
**Fax:** 847 776-1297
John P Goldenne, *President*
Richard Ault, *Vice Pres*
Chris Decker, *Office Mgr*
**EMP:** 10
**SQ FT:** 5,000
**SALES (est):** 1.8MM **Privately Held**
**SIC:** 3643 3651 Connectors & terminals for electrical devices; household audio & video equipment

### (G-17046)
### JAY PRINTING
553 N Hicks Rd (60067)
**PHONE** ............................847 934-6103
**EMP:** 3 **EST:** 1994
**SQ FT:** 4,000
**SALES:** 250K **Privately Held**
**SIC:** 2752 2791 2789 Lithographic Commercial Printing Typesetting Services Bookbinding/Related Work

### (G-17047)
### K D IRON WORKS
542 W Colfax St Ste 5 (60067-2524)
**PHONE** ............................847 991-3039
Karl Deutschmann, *President*
Michael Deutschmann, *Vice Pres*
**EMP:** 2
**SQ FT:** 1,400
**SALES (est):** 305.1K **Privately Held**
**SIC:** 3446 1799 Railings, bannisters, guards, etc.: made from metal pipe; ornamental metal work

### (G-17048)
### KSR SOFTWARE LLC
388 N Chalary Ct (60067-0920)
**PHONE** ............................847 705-0100
**EMP:** 5
**SALES (est):** 390K **Privately Held**
**SIC:** 7372 Prepackaged Software Services

### (G-17049)
### LEANOPTIMA LLC
1311 N Deer Ave (60067-1852)
P.O. Box 59209, Schaumburg (60159-0209)
**PHONE** ............................847 648-1592
Stephanie Christopher,
**EMP:** 50
**SALES (est):** 2.1MM **Privately Held**
**SIC:** 7372 Prepackaged software

### (G-17050)
### LIGHT MATRIX INC
339 S Valor Ct (60074-6829)
**PHONE** ............................847 590-0856
Xinliang Yang, *President*
▲ **EMP:** 2
**SALES (est):** 212.1K **Privately Held**
**SIC:** 3641 Electric lamps

### (G-17051)
### LORAES DRAPERY WORKROOM INC
1204 W Colfax St (60067-2282)
**PHONE** ............................847 358-7999
Sharon Gillett, *President*

**EMP:** 7 **EST:** 1959
**SQ FT:** 1,800
**SALES (est):** 634.3K **Privately Held**
**SIC:** 2391 Draperies, plastic & textile: from purchased materials

### (G-17052)
### M&M EMBROIDERY CORP
1188 E Cunningham Dr (60074-2908)
**PHONE** ............................847 209-1086
Maria Vargas, *Principal*
**EMP:** 3
**SALES (est):** 106.7K **Privately Held**
**SIC:** 2395 Embroidery & art needlework

### (G-17053)
### MANUFASTENERS HOUSE IQ INC
427 S Middleton Ave (60067-5966)
**PHONE** ............................847 705-6538
Tim Millar, *CEO*
▲ **EMP:** 3
**SALES (est):** 226.5K **Privately Held**
**SIC:** 3496 Clips & fasteners, made from purchased wire

### (G-17054)
### MAYFAIR METAL SPINNING CO INC
538 S Vermont St (60067-6948)
**PHONE** ............................847 358-7450
**Fax:** 847 358-4806
John Janowski, *President*
Josephine Janowski, *Admin Sec*
**EMP:** 4
**SQ FT:** 5,500
**SALES:** 500K **Privately Held**
**SIC:** 3469 Spinning metal for the trade; stamping metal for the trade; machine parts, stamped or pressed metal

### (G-17055)
### MICHAELS DAWG HOUSE LLC
809 N Quentin Rd (60067-2031)
**PHONE** ............................847 485-7600
Michael Marras, *Mng Member*
**EMP:** 8
**SALES (est):** 105.5K **Privately Held**
**SIC:** 5812 2013 2096 Pizza restaurants; spreads, sandwich: meat from purchased meat; onion fries

### (G-17056)
### MIDWEST FUEL INJCTION SVC CORP
543 S Vermont St Ste A (60067-6978)
**PHONE** ............................847 991-7867
**Fax:** 847 991-7880
Bryant Yonan, *Parts Mgr*
Dean Bismark, *Branch Mgr*
Paul Thons, *Manager*
**EMP:** 11
**SALES (corp-wide):** 5.4MM **Privately Held**
**WEB:** www.metrosvc.com
**SIC:** 5084 3724 3561 Engines & parts, diesel; aircraft engines & engine parts; pumps & pumping equipment
**PA:** Midwest Fuel Injection Service, Corp.
1 Seidel Ct
Bolingbrook IL
708 532-1102

### (G-17057)
### MORKES INC
Also Called: Morkes Chocolates
1890 N Rand Rd (60074-1130)
**PHONE** ............................847 359-3511
**Fax:** 847 359-3553
Rhonda Morkes, *President*
Steve Wilson, *Manager*
**EMP:** 15
**SQ FT:** 5,200
**SALES (est):** 3.3MM **Privately Held**
**WEB:** www.morkeschocolates.com
**SIC:** 2064 2066 5441 Chocolate candy, except solid chocolate; chocolate candy, solid; candy; confectionery

### (G-17058)
### NEWKO TOOL & ENGINEERING CO
Also Called: Newko Proto Type
720 S Vermont St (60067-7139)
**PHONE** ............................847 359-1670

**Fax:** 847 359-8730
Scott Riddell, *President*
Scott Vanpelt, *General Mgr*
Susan Broderick, *Manager*
Barbara Newburg, *Admin Sec*
**EMP:** 25 **EST:** 1958
**SQ FT:** 1,400
**SALES (est):** 5.1MM **Privately Held**
**WEB:** www.newkogroup.com
**SIC:** 3544 3469 8711 3678 Special dies, tools, jigs & fixtures; metal stampings; engineering services; electronic connectors

### (G-17059)
### NORTHWEST FRAME COMPANY INC
252 N Cady Dr (60074-5522)
**PHONE** ............................847 359-0987
**Fax:** 847 202-0054
Steven M Chessin, *President*
Robert W Battaglia, *Admin Sec*
**EMP:** 4
**SQ FT:** 5,000
**SALES (est):** 280K **Privately Held**
**WEB:** www.nwfonline.com
**SIC:** 2499 Picture frame molding, finished

### (G-17060)
### NUEVOS SEMANA NEWSPAPER
1180 E Dundee Rd (60074-8305)
**PHONE** ............................847 991-3939
**EMP:** 3 **EST:** 2010
**SALES (est):** 126.7K **Privately Held**
**SIC:** 2711 Newspapers

### (G-17061)
### ORION STAR CORP
Also Called: Orion Offset
236 E Northwest Hwy Ste A (60067-8183)
**PHONE** ............................847 776-2300
**Fax:** 847 776-2300
Joyce R Day, *President*
Kathleen Giardina, *Vice Pres*
**EMP:** 10
**SQ FT:** 3,600
**SALES (est):** 1.3MM **Privately Held**
**WEB:** www.orionoffset.com
**SIC:** 2752 Commercial printing, lithographic

### (G-17062)
### OVERHEAD DOOR SOLUTIONS INC
920 W Kenilworth Ave (60067-5931)
**PHONE** ............................847 359-3667
Richard Terzo, *President*
Michael Bauer, *Vice Pres*
**EMP:** 6
**SALES (est):** 846K **Privately Held**
**SIC:** 3442 Garage doors, overhead: metal

### (G-17063)
### PARALLEL MACHINE PRODUCTS INC
255 N Woodwork Ln (60074-4930)
**PHONE** ............................847 359-1012
**Fax:** 847 359-1039
John Blyth, *President*
Donna Blyth, *Admin Sec*
**EMP:** 10
**SQ FT:** 4,800
**SALES:** 800K **Privately Held**
**SIC:** 3599 Machine shop, jobbing & repair

### (G-17064)
### PRINTOVATE TECHNOLOGIES INC
1931 N Meryls Ter (60074-1049)
**PHONE** ............................847 962-3106
Daniel Gamota, *President*
**EMP:** 2
**SALES:** 300K **Privately Held**
**SIC:** 3674 Semiconductors & related devices

### (G-17065)
### R & R CUSTOM CABINET MAKING
515 S Vermont St Ste B (60067-6919)
**PHONE** ............................847 358-6188
Phil Rybarczyk, *Mng Member*
Steve Rybarczyk, *Mng Member*
**EMP:** 4
**SQ FT:** 2,000

**SALES (est):** 405.8K **Privately Held**
**SIC:** 2434 2541 3083 1799 Wood kitchen cabinets; table or counter tops, plastic laminated; laminated plastics plate & sheet; counter top installation

### (G-17066)
### READY PRESS
340 W Colfax St (60067-2516)
**PHONE** ............................847 358-8655
**Fax:** 847 358-8697
Shelby Mazursky, *Owner*
Judy Mazursky, *Manager*
**EMP:** 5
**SQ FT:** 5,000
**SALES (est):** 534.2K **Privately Held**
**SIC:** 2752 2789 Commercial printing, offset; bookbinding & related work

### (G-17067)
### REMET CORPORATION
1540 E Dundee Rd Ste 170 (60074-8316)
**PHONE** ............................480 766-3464
John Paraszczak, *President*
Joe Dryer, *Manager*
▲ **EMP:** 20 **EST:** 1933
**SQ FT:** 95,000
**SALES (est):** 2.5MM
**SALES (corp-wide):** 74.1MM **Privately Held**
**WEB:** www.remet.com
**SIC:** 2891 Sealing wax
**PA:** Remet Pic, Inc.
210 Commons Rd
Utica NY 13502
315 797-8700

### (G-17068)
### ROAD RUNNER SPORTS INC
20291 N Rand Rd Ste 105 (60074-2019)
**PHONE** ............................847 719-8941
**EMP:** 16
**SALES (corp-wide):** 84.6MM **Privately Held**
**SIC:** 5961 3949 5661 Mail order house; sporting & athletic goods; footwear, athletic
**PA:** Road Runner Sports, Inc.
5549 Copley Dr
San Diego CA 92111
858 974-4200

### (G-17069)
### ROSEWOOD SOFTWARE INC
1531 N Haven Dr (60074-2425)
**PHONE** ............................847 438-2185
Richard Lloyd, *President*
Laura Lloyd, *Admin Sec*
**EMP:** 8
**SALES (est):** 625.9K **Privately Held**
**WEB:** www.rosewoodsoftware.com
**SIC:** 7372 Prepackaged software

### (G-17070)
### S-P-D INCORPORATED
678 S Middleton Ave (60067-6678)
**PHONE** ............................847 882-9820
**Fax:** 847 882-9825
David M Whitfield, *President*
Nicholas Di Giovanni, *Vice Pres*
Betty Lauer, *Admin Sec*
**EMP:** 6
**SQ FT:** 3,000
**SALES:** 3MM **Privately Held**
**WEB:** www.spdinc.com
**SIC:** 7629 3561 5084 Electrical repair shops; pumps, domestic: water or sump; instruments & control equipment; controlling instruments & accessories

### (G-17071)
### SALT CREEK RURAL PARK DISTRICT
530 S Williams Ave (60074-6499)
**PHONE** ............................847 259-6890
**Fax:** 847 259-9975
Drew O Burbidge, *Commissioner*
Michael Reiss, *Commissioner*
Diane Hilgers, *Director*
**EMP:** 13
**SALES (est):** 1MM **Privately Held**
**SIC:** 3479 Recreation services

## Palatine - Cook County (G-17072)

**(G-17072)**
**SEAL TECH SERVICES**
510 S Bennett Ave (60067-6704)
P.O. Box 536 (60078-0536)
PHONE.................................847 776-0043
Jack Castella, *Principal*
**EMP:** 3
**SALES (est):** 307.6K **Privately Held**
**SIC:** 2295 Laminating of fabrics

**(G-17073)**
**SHADY CREEK VINEYARD INC**
1238 N Wellington Dr (60067-2455)
PHONE.................................847 275-7979
**EMP:** 3 **EST:** 2010
**SALES (est):** 128.8K **Privately Held**
**SIC:** 2037 Frozen fruits & vegetables

**(G-17074)**
**SIGNS TODAY INC**
342 W Colfax St (60067-2516)
PHONE.................................847 934-9777
Fax: 847 934-9965
John Theodore, *President*
**EMP:** 6
**SQ FT:** 2,700
**SALES (est):** 440K **Privately Held**
**SIC:** 7389 3993 2752 5999 Sign painting & lettering shop; signs & advertising specialties; commercial printing, lithographic; trophies & plaques

**(G-17075)**
**SMARTBYTE SOLUTIONS INC**
712 W Slippery Rock Dr (60067-2573)
PHONE.................................847 925-1870
Orlin Momchev, *President*
Tonya Momchev, *CFO*
**EMP:** 5
**SALES:** 250K **Privately Held**
**WEB:** www.smartbytesolutions.com
**SIC:** 7372 Prepackaged software

**(G-17076)**
**SPUNKY DUNKER DONUTS (PA)**
Also Called: Northwest Donut
20 S Northwest Hwy (60074-6231)
PHONE.................................847 358-7935
Jan Daczewitz, *General Mgr*
**EMP:** 6
**SALES (est):** 592.2K **Privately Held**
**SIC:** 2051 Doughnuts, except frozen

**(G-17077)**
**SYTEK AUDIO SYSTEMS CORP**
350 N Eric Dr Ste B (60067-2511)
PHONE.................................847 345-6971
Mike Stoica, *President*
**EMP:** 10
**SALES:** 700K **Privately Held**
**SIC:** 3651 Audio electronic systems

**(G-17078)**
**TANE CORPORATION**
1122 W Partridge Dr (60067-7047)
PHONE.................................847 705-7125
Robert T Finegan, *President*
**EMP:** 5
**SALES (est):** 446.9K **Privately Held**
**WEB:** www.tanecorp.com
**SIC:** 3599 1711 Air intake filters, internal combustion engine, except auto; plumbing contractors

**(G-17079)**
**TB CARDWORKS LLC**
344 S Whitehall Dr (60067-5840)
PHONE.................................847 229-9990
Thomas Breen,
**EMP:** 26 **EST:** 2001
**SALES (est):** 2.7MM **Privately Held**
**WEB:** www.tbcardworks.com
**SIC:** 3083 7374 Plastic finished products, laminated; computer graphics service

**(G-17080)**
**TECHLINE STUDIO**
Also Called: Dh2 Studio
1463 W Winnetka St (60067-9210)
PHONE.................................212 674-1813
Fax: 847 433-4897
Deborah Hill, *President*
**EMP:** 2
**SALES (est):** 260K **Privately Held**
**WEB:** www.techline-troy.com
**SIC:** 2522 Office furniture, except wood

**(G-17081)**
**THE INTEC GROUP INC (PA)**
666 S Vermont St (60067-6950)
PHONE.................................847 358-0088
Steven M Perlman, *President*
John Martin, *General Mgr*
Michael Gaines, *Vice Pres*
Tom Katchmar, *Opers Staff*
Robin Ostick, *Opers Staff*
▲ **EMP:** 175
**SQ FT:** 60,000
**SALES (est):** 120.6MM **Privately Held**
**WEB:** www.intecgrp.com
**SIC:** 3089 Molding primary plastic; injection molding of plastics

**(G-17082)**
**THOMSON REUTERS (MARKETS) LLC**
West Group
651 N Williams Dr (60074-7268)
PHONE.................................847 705-7929
Fax: 847 948-7099
Nick Svalina, *Editor*
Michael Coffey, *Project Mgr*
John Collins, *Technical Mgr*
Bob Bridier, *Engineer*
James Gagne, *VP Finance*
**EMP:** 350
**SALES (corp-wide):** 3.7B **Publicly Held**
**WEB:** www.tfn.com
**SIC:** 2731 Book publishing
**HQ:** Thomson Reuters (Markets) Llc
3 Times Sq
New York NY 10036
646 223-4000

**(G-17083)**
**TUFF SHED INC**
1408 E Northwest Hwy (60074-7608)
PHONE.................................847 704-1147
**EMP:** 13
**SALES (corp-wide):** 275.6MM **Privately Held**
**SIC:** 2452 Prefabricated wood buildings
**PA:** Tuff Shed, Inc.
1777 S Harrison St # 600
Denver CO 80210
303 753-8833

**(G-17084)**
**UPHOLSTERED WALLS BY ANNE MARI**
Also Called: Upholstred Walls By Anne Marie
419 S Rose St (60067-6855)
PHONE.................................847 202-0642
Anne Marie Scherlag, *President*
Bob Scherlag, *Admin Sec*
**EMP:** 7
**SALES:** 850K **Privately Held**
**SIC:** 2221 Upholstery, tapestry & wall covering fabrics

**(G-17085)**
**VIDEO GAMING TECHNOLOGIES INC**
963 N Carmel Dr (60074-3703)
PHONE.................................847 776-3516
Frank Fortunato, *Principal*
**EMP:** 3
**SALES (est):** 174.2K **Privately Held**
**SIC:** 3944 7359 Electronic game machines, except coin-operated; video cassette recorder & accessory rental

**(G-17086)**
**WAIST UP IMPRNTD SPRTSWEAR LLC**
422 S Vermont St (60067-6946)
PHONE.................................847 963-1400
Don Banks, *Webmaster*
Bill Banks,
**EMP:** 5 **EST:** 2009
**SALES:** 300K **Privately Held**
**WEB:** www.waistup.com
**SIC:** 2395 2759 Embroidery & art needlework; screen printing

**(G-17087)**
**WASOWSKI JACEK**
Also Called: Midnight Marble
9a E Dundee Quarter Dr A (60074-1657)
PHONE.................................847 693-1878
Jacek Wasowski, *Owner*
**EMP:** 1

**SALES:** 800K **Privately Held**
**SIC:** 3281 Granite, cut & shaped

**(G-17088)**
**WEBER-STEPHEN PRODUCTS LLC (PA)**
Also Called: Weber Grills
1415 S Roselle Rd (60067-7337)
PHONE.................................847 934-5700
Fax: 847 407-8900
Thomas D Koos, *CEO*
Tom Koos, *CEO*
James C Stephen Sr, *President*
Len Gryn, *Exec VP*
Michael J Kempster, *Exec VP*
◆ **EMP:** 277 **EST:** 2010
**SQ FT:** 300,000
**SALES (est):** 1.2B **Privately Held**
**SIC:** 3631 Barbecues, grills & braziers (outdoor cooking)

**(G-17089)**
**WEBER-STEPHEN PRODUCTS LLC**
Also Called: Weber Grills
306 E Helen Rd (60067-6939)
PHONE.................................224 836-8536
**EMP:** 9
**SALES (corp-wide):** 1.2B **Privately Held**
**SIC:** 3631 Barbecues, grills & braziers (outdoor cooking)
**PA:** Weber-Stephen Products Llc
1415 S Roselle Rd
Palatine IL 60067
847 934-5700

**(G-17090)**
**WINDY CITY PUBLISHERS LLC**
1051 S Hiddenbrook Trl (60067-9100)
PHONE.................................847 925-9434
Lise Marinelli, *President*
**EMP:** 3
**SALES:** 60K **Privately Held**
**SIC:** 2731 Book publishing

**(G-17091)**
**WOLF CABINETRY & GANITE**
1703 N Rand Rd (60074-2357)
PHONE.................................847 358-9922
Andy Huang, *Owner*
**EMP:** 4
**SALES (est):** 488.9K **Privately Held**
**SIC:** 2434 Wood kitchen cabinets

**(G-17092)**
**ZIPWHAA INC**
3191 Brockway St (60067-7431)
PHONE.................................630 898-4330
David A Cook, *President*
Donald L Moffett, *Vice Pres*
Tamara Cook, *Admin Sec*
Ray Keller, *Admin Sec*
**EMP:** 4
**SALES (est):** 330.9K **Privately Held**
**WEB:** www.zipwhaa.com
**SIC:** 2754 3944 Playing cards; gravure printing; games, toys & children's vehicles

### Palestine
*Crawford County*

**(G-17093)**
**ILLIANA CORES INC**
10156 N 1725th St (62451-2646)
P.O. Box 189 (62451-0189)
PHONE.................................618 586-9800
Fax: 618 586-9801
Randal L Burtch, *President*
Michael D Murray, *Vice Pres*
Michelle Hamilton, *Accountant*
Melissa Deamann, *Marketing Staff*
**EMP:** 25
**SQ FT:** 28,000
**SALES (est):** 6.2MM **Privately Held**
**SIC:** 2655 Tubes, fiber or paper: made from purchased material

**(G-17094)**
**LINCOLNLAND AGRI-ENERGY LLC**
10406 N 1725th St (62451-2652)
PHONE.................................618 586-2321
Fax: 618 586-2430

Eric Mosbey, *General Mgr*
Randy Schutte, *Chairman*
Neal Steffey, *Plant Mgr*
Nathan Kemp, *Prdtn Mgr*
Kurt Dillon, *Maint Spvr*
**EMP:** 41
**SQ FT:** 4,500
**SALES (est):** 15.6MM **Privately Held**
**WEB:** www.lincolnlandagrienergy.com
**SIC:** 2869 Ethyl alcohol, ethanol

**(G-17095)**
**S FLYING INC**
Also Called: Flying S
17583 E 500th Ave (62451-2051)
PHONE.................................618 586-9999
David Shaw, *Owner*
Peter Bowman, *Engineer*
Larry Zuber, *Engineer*
Penelope Shaw, *Manager*
**EMP:** 14
**SQ FT:** 16,000
**SALES (est):** 2.6MM **Privately Held**
**SIC:** 8711 3812 Engineering services; acceleration indicators & systems components, aerospace

**(G-17096)**
**TURNER SAND & GRAVEL INC**
15250 N 1720th St (62451-2845)
PHONE.................................618 586-2486
Fax: 618 586-5181
Bill R Turner, *President*
Moonyeen Turner, *Corp Secy*
Stacy Poke, *Vice Pres*
**EMP:** 8
**SALES (est):** 510K **Privately Held**
**SIC:** 1442 Construction sand mining

### Palmyra
*Macoupin County*

**(G-17097)**
**PALMYRA MODESTO WATER COMM**
9934 Water Plant Rd (62674-6324)
P.O. Box 104, Modesto (62667-0104)
PHONE.................................217 436-2519
James Launer, *President*
Larry Garst, *Superintendent*
**EMP:** 5
**SALES:** 139K **Privately Held**
**SIC:** 3589 Water treatment equipment, industrial

### Palos Heights
*Cook County*

**(G-17098)**
**ADDISON BUSINESS SYSTEMS INC**
12555 S Menard Ave (60463-2423)
PHONE.................................708 371-5454
Addison Ryan, *CEO*
**EMP:** 4 **EST:** 1977
**SQ FT:** 2,500
**SALES (est):** 300K **Privately Held**
**WEB:** www.addisonbusinessassociation.org
**SIC:** 3589 7699 Shredders, industrial & commercial; office equipment & accessory customizing

**(G-17099)**
**AUBURN IRON WORKS INC**
12924 S Forestview Rd (60463-2128)
PHONE.................................708 422-7330
Fax: 708 422-7336
Anthony J Pietro Sr, *President*
**EMP:** 15 **EST:** 1955
**SQ FT:** 18,000
**SALES (est):** 2.9MM **Privately Held**
**SIC:** 3441 Fabricated structural metal

**(G-17100)**
**BLEW CHEMICAL COMPANY**
12501 S Richard Ave (60463-1360)
P.O. Box 501 (60463-0501)
PHONE.................................708 448-5780
Fax: 708 448-5781

Betsy Ochoa, *President*
William R Brew Jr, *Treasurer*
Besty Blew, *Admin Sec*
**EMP:** 5
**SALES:** 1.2MM **Privately Held**
**SIC: 2841** Soap: granulated, liquid, cake, flaked or chip; detergents, synthetic organic or inorganic alkaline

**(G-17101)**
**CHASE CORPORATION**
12657 S Ridgeland Ave (60463-1871)
**PHONE** .................................. 708 385-4679
**Fax:** 708 824-9975
Andrew Lau, *Branch Mgr*
**EMP:** 11
**SALES (corp-wide):** 238MM **Publicly Held**
**SIC: 3644** Noncurrent-carrying wiring services
**PA:** Chase Corporation
   295 University Ave
   Westwood MA 02090
   508 819-4200

**(G-17102)**
**CONTINENTAL SUPPLY CO**
21 Carriage Trl (60463-1221)
**PHONE** .................................. 708 448-2728
Joyce Moone, *President*
**EMP:** 5
**SALES (est):** 407.6K **Privately Held**
**SIC: 2851** Lacquers, varnishes, enamels & other coatings

**(G-17103)**
**DENDICK ENGINEERING AND MCH CO**
Also Called: Dendick Wire EDM Specialist
6040 W 129th Pl (60463-2361)
**PHONE** .................................. 815 464-6100
Michael Hord, *President*
Gabe Hord, *Bookkeeper*
Kenneth Dickerson, *Admin Sec*
**EMP:** 5
**SQ FT:** 1,300
**SALES (est):** 523.3K **Privately Held**
**SIC: 3599** Machine shop, jobbing & repair

**(G-17104)**
**GALVANIZE LABS INC**
6728 W Highland Dr (60463-2219)
**PHONE** .................................. 630 258-1476
Moria Hardek, *President*
Neal Hardek, *Chairman*
**EMP:** 9
**SALES:** 800K **Privately Held**
**SIC: 3999** Education aids, devices & supplies

**(G-17105)**
**GOOD NEWS PRINTING**
5535 W 131st St (60463)
P.O. Box 626 (60463-0626)
**PHONE** .................................. 708 389-1127
Gerald Prosapio, *President*
**EMP:** 3
**SALES (est):** 292.2K **Privately Held**
**WEB:** www.goodnewsprinting.com
**SIC: 2759** Publication printing

**(G-17106)**
**GRAPHIC COMMUNICATORS INC**
Also Called: Family Record
12500 S Meade Ave (60463-1838)
**PHONE** .................................. 708 385-7550
Edward Zapalik, *President*
**EMP:** 3
**SALES (est):** 200K **Privately Held**
**SIC: 2741** Miscellaneous publishing

**(G-17107)**
**HOPPER GRAPHICS INC**
6106 W 127th St (60463-2370)
**PHONE** .................................. 708 489-0459
John Stefanik, *President*
**EMP:** 6
**SALES (est):** 258.4K **Privately Held**
**SIC: 7336** 2732 2759 Commercial art & graphic design; book printing; commercial printing

**(G-17108)**
**MACHINE CONTROL SYSTEMS INC (PA)**
12424 S Austin Ave (60463-1820)
**PHONE** .................................. 708 389-2160
Bernard A Plummer, *President*
Margaret Plummer, *Admin Sec*
**EMP:** 2
**SALES (est):** 680.6K **Privately Held**
**SIC: 3625** 3613 Control equipment, electric; control panels, electric

**(G-17109)**
**S I A INC (PA)**
11743 Southwest Hwy (60463-1058)
**PHONE** .................................. 708 361-3100
James M Regan, *President*
Joseph P Cairo, *Corp Secy*
Phillip G Regan, *Director*
Harry Clements, *Shareholder*
Thomas P Regan, *Shareholder*
**EMP:** 2
**SQ FT:** 2,000
**SALES (est):** 1.9MM **Privately Held**
**SIC: 3728** Aircraft assemblies, subassemblies & parts

**(G-17110)**
**SPACIL CONSTRUCTION CO**
6018 W 123rd St (60463-1803)
**PHONE** .................................. 708 448-3809
Frank Spacil, *President*
Paddy Spacial, *Office Mgr*
**EMP:** 5
**SALES:** 400K **Privately Held**
**SIC: 3272** Building materials, except block or brick: concrete

**(G-17111)**
**TERRAPIN XPRESS INC**
7801 W 123rd Pl (60463-1217)
P.O. Box 366 (60463-0366)
**PHONE** .................................. 866 823-7323
Priscilla Davis, *President*
**EMP:** 5
**SALES (est):** 249.4K **Privately Held**
**SIC: 2679** 5113 7389 Building, insulating & packaging paperboard; industrial & personal service paper; eating utensils, disposable plastic; bags, paper & disposable plastic; corrugated & solid fiber boxes;

**(G-17112)**
**TYPE CONCEPTS INC**
12216 S Harlem Ave Ste B (60463-2088)
**PHONE** .................................. 708 361-1005
Camille M Krecioch, *President*
Dolores A Krecioch, *Admin Sec*
**EMP:** 3
**SALES (est):** 377.2K **Privately Held**
**SIC: 2752** 2791 2759 2396 Commercial printing, lithographic; typesetting; commercial printing; automotive & apparel trimmings

**(G-17113)**
**WALTER & KATHY ANCZEREWICZ (PA)**
Also Called: Dunkin' Donuts
12807 S Harlem Ave (60463-2132)
**PHONE** .................................. 708 448-3676
**Fax:** 708 396-9705
Walter Anczerewicz, *Partner*
Kathy Anczerewicz, *Partner*
**EMP:** 2
**SALES (est):** 1.5MM **Privately Held**
**SIC: 5461** 2051 5812 Doughnuts; doughnuts, except frozen; ice cream stands or dairy bars

## Palos Hills
### Cook County

**(G-17114)**
**ASSOCIATED DESIGN INC**
Also Called: Associated Design Service
11160 Southwest Hwy Ste B (60465-2473)
**PHONE** .................................. 708 974-9100
**Fax:** 708 974-1949
Mary Noone, *President*
Mary C Kirby, *Corp Secy*
Thomas Noone, *Vice Pres*
**EMP:** 10
**SQ FT:** 7,800
**SALES (est):** 904.7K **Privately Held**
**WEB:** www.associated-design.com
**SIC: 8711** 7389 8249 3999 Designing: ship, boat, machine & product; drafting service, except temporary help; vocational schools; models, general, except toy; commercial printing

**(G-17115)**
**COUNTER-INTELLIGENCE**
8150 W 107th St (60465-1870)
**PHONE** .................................. 708 974-3326
Mark Drong, *Principal*
**EMP:** 3
**SALES (est):** 228.6K **Privately Held**
**SIC: 3131** Counters

**(G-17116)**
**D L SHEET METAL**
8717 W 98th Pl (60465-1137)
**PHONE** .................................. 708 599-5538
**Fax:** 708 599-2852
Mary Barbour, *Owner*
**EMP:** 5
**SALES (est):** 553.4K **Privately Held**
**SIC: 3444** Sheet metalwork

**(G-17117)**
**GAMMA PRODUCTS INC**
7730 W 114th Pl Ste 1 (60465-2748)
P.O. Box 190, Palos Park (60464-0190)
**PHONE** .................................. 708 974-4100
**Fax:** 708 974-0071
Nancy Meier, *CEO*
Walter Meier, *President*
Blake Meier, *Vice Pres*
Ellen Hismudy, *Bookkeeper*
**EMP:** 10 **EST:** 1965
**SQ FT:** 10,000
**SALES (est):** 1.9MM **Privately Held**
**WEB:** www.gammaproducts.com
**SIC: 3829** Nuclear radiation & testing apparatus

**(G-17118)**
**GRAPHICS & TECHNICAL SYSTEMS**
11137 Northwest Rd Apt E (60465-2154)
**PHONE** .................................. 708 974-3806
Robert McCrea, *President*
**EMP:** 2
**SALES (est):** 250K **Privately Held**
**SIC: 2752** Color lithography

**(G-17119)**
**MIDWEST LASER INCORPORATED**
10639 S 82nd Ct (60465-1848)
**PHONE** .................................. 708 974-0084
Josie Tokarski, *President*
Michael Tokarski, *Treasurer*
**EMP:** 3
**SQ FT:** 1,500
**SALES:** 200K **Privately Held**
**WEB:** www.ml-toner.com
**SIC: 3861** 7378 Toners, prepared photographic (not made in chemical plants); computer peripheral equipment repair & maintenance

**(G-17120)**
**PARK PRINTING INC (PA)**
9903 S Roberts Rd (60465-1532)
**PHONE** .................................. 708 430-4878
Carol Park, *President*
Tim Park, *Vice Pres*
▲ **EMP:** 5
**SQ FT:** 1,000
**SALES (est):** 520.9K **Privately Held**
**WEB:** www.parkprintcenters.com
**SIC: 2752** 2791 Commercial printing, offset; typesetting

**(G-17121)**
**PEEPS INC**
8945 W 103rd St (60465-1642)
**PHONE** .................................. 708 935-4201
Rimvydas Tveras, *President*
**EMP:** 2
**SALES (est):** 160.6K **Privately Held**
**SIC: 3089** Injection molded finished plastic products

**(G-17122)**
**QUICK BUILDING SYSTEMS INC**
9748 S Cambridge Ct (60465-1157)
**PHONE** .................................. 708 598-6733
Joost Zerwijs, *President*
Anne Schipper, *Admin Sec*
**EMP:** 4
**SALES:** 265K **Privately Held**
**SIC: 3272** Building materials, except block or brick: concrete

**(G-17123)**
**R J S SILK SCREENING CO**
Also Called: Rjs Silk Screening
10708 S Roberts Rd (60465-2314)
**PHONE** .................................. 708 974-3009
**Fax:** 708 974-3045
Bob Stramaglia, *Owner*
**EMP:** 5
**SQ FT:** 1,500
**SALES (est):** 377.6K **Privately Held**
**SIC: 7336** 2396 Silk screen design; automotive & apparel trimmings

**(G-17124)**
**SIGNS BY DESIGN**
10330 S Harlem Ave (60465-2036)
**PHONE** .................................. 708 599-9970
**Fax:** 708 599-9950
Mark King, *Principal*
**EMP:** 7
**SALES (est):** 510.9K **Privately Held**
**SIC: 3993** Signs & advertising specialties

**(G-17125)**
**SIGNTASTIC INC**
10352 S Aspen Dr (60465-1710)
**PHONE** .................................. 708 598-4749
Ronald Van Blaricom, *President*
Nanci Van Blaricom, *Vice Pres*
**EMP:** 2
**SQ FT:** 1,000
**SALES:** 200K **Privately Held**
**SIC: 3993** 7389 Signs, not made in custom sign painting shops; design services

## Palos Park
### Cook County

**(G-17126)**
**A CUT ABOVE ENGRAVING INC**
12741 S La Grange Rd (60464-1712)
**PHONE** .................................. 708 671-9800
**Fax:** 708 671-9808
David Kutz, *CEO*
Frank Romza, *Admin Sec*
**EMP:** 3
**SALES:** 205K **Privately Held**
**SIC: 5199** 7389 2754 Advertising specialties; engrossing: diplomas, resolutions, etc.; engraving service; calendar & card printing, except business: gravure

**(G-17127)**
**CARE EDUCATION GROUP INC**
126 Commons Dr (60464-3106)
P.O. Box 180 (60464-0180)
**PHONE** .................................. 708 361-4110
Eric D Joseph, *President*
Nancy E Webster, *Vice Pres*
**EMP:** 3
**SQ FT:** 2,000
**SALES:** 750K **Privately Held**
**SIC: 8299** 8742 2721 Educational services; hospital & health services consultant; periodicals

**(G-17128)**
**EXTOL HYDRO TECHNOLOGIES INC**
13020 Ridgewood Dr (60464-2513)
**PHONE** .................................. 708 717-4371
Ibrahim Taha, *Director*
**EMP:** 10
**SALES:** 500K **Privately Held**
**SIC: 3589** Sewage & water treatment equipment

**(G-17129)**
**JOHN DAGYS MEDIA LLC**
Also Called: Sportscar365
8011 W 125th St (60464-1924)
**PHONE** .................................. 708 373-0180

Jonathan Dagys, *President*
EMP: 4
SALES (est): 97.9K **Privately Held**
SIC: 2711 7389 Newspapers: publishing only, not printed on site;

### (G-17130)
### RESPIRONICS INC
12515 S 82nd Ave (60464-2011)
PHONE..................708 923-6200
Jim Orzech, *Marketing Mgr*
Leverda Wallace, *Surgery Dir*
EMP: 164
SALES (corp-wide): 25.9B **Privately Held**
SIC: 3842 Surgical appliances & supplies
HQ: Respironics, Inc.
1010 Murry Ridge Ln
Murrysville PA 15668
724 387-5200

### (G-17131)
### SIEMENS AG
12841 W Tanglewood Cir (60464-1688)
PHONE..................708 345-7290
EMP: 3
SALES (est): 205.5K **Privately Held**
SIC: 3661 Telephones & telephone apparatus

### (G-17132)
### SIMPLE CIRCUITS INC
12756 S 80th Ave (60464-2131)
P.O. Box 68 (60464-0068)
PHONE..................708 671-9600
EMP: 5
SALES (est): 608.4K **Privately Held**
SIC: 3679 Electronic circuits

### (G-17133)
### SIRIUS BUSINESS SOFTWARE
42 Birchwood Dr (60464-1573)
PHONE..................708 361-5538
John Beechen, *Principal*
EMP: 5
SALES (est): 260K **Privately Held**
SIC: 7372 Prepackaged software

### (G-17134)
### WATER & GAS TECHNOLOGIES
Also Called: Wgt
8046 W 128th Pl (60464-2147)
PHONE..................708 829-3254
Luis Simas, *Principal*
EMP: 4
SALES (est): 188.6K **Privately Held**
SIC: 1389 Impounding & storing salt water, oil & gas field

## Pana
### *Christian County*

### (G-17135)
### PANA LIMESTONE COMPANY
325 N 1600 East Rd (62557-6843)
PHONE..................217 562-4231
David Flatt, *President*
Regina Edmond, *Office Mgr*
EMP: 3
SALES (est): 160K **Privately Held**
SIC: 1411 Limestone, dimension-quarrying

### (G-17136)
### PANA MONUMENT CO (PA)
Also Called: Adams & Masterson Memorials
2 N Poplar St (62557-1102)
PHONE..................217 562-5121
Fax: 217 562-5121
Danny Adams, *Partner*
Richard Masterson, *Partner*
EMP: 4
SQ FT: 4,000
SALES (est): 499.1K **Privately Held**
SIC: 5999 3281 Monuments, finished to custom order; rock & stone specimens; monuments & tombstones; cut stone & stone products

### (G-17137)
### PANA NEWS INC (PA)
Also Called: Pana News Palladium
205 S Locust St (62557-1605)
P.O. Box 200 (62557-0200)
PHONE..................217 562-2111
Fax: 217 562-3729
Thomas J Phillips, *President*
Beth Bennett, *Principal*
Cynthia Lotinis, *Principal*
Patricia Spracklen, *Principal*
Doris Phillips, *Vice Pres*
EMP: 15 EST: 1933
SQ FT: 14,000
SALES (est): 1.8MM **Privately Held**
WEB: www.pananews.com
SIC: 2752 2711 2759 Commercial printing, offset; newspapers, publishing & printing; commercial printing

### (G-17138)
### PBI REDI MIX & TRUCKING
2 N Walnut St (62557-1186)
PHONE..................217 562-3717
Fax: 217 563-7771
James Randolph, *President*
EMP: 25
SALES (est): 2.5MM **Privately Held**
SIC: 3273 Ready-mixed concrete

## Paris
### *Edgar County*

### (G-17139)
### ABITEC CORPORATION
1800 S Main St (61944-2945)
P.O. Box 878 (61944-0878)
PHONE..................217 465-8577
Toby Wilson, *Opers Dir*
Robert Zulliger, *Opers Dir*
Mike Beesley, *QC Dir*
Peter Blagdon, *Manager*
Norma Pruiett, *Manager*
EMP: 21
SALES (corp-wide): 17.5B **Privately Held**
WEB: www.abiteccorp.com
SIC: 5149 5141 2077 2076 Shortening, vegetable; groceries, general line; animal & marine fats & oils; vegetable oil mills
HQ: Abitec Corporation
501 W 1st Ave
Columbus OH 43215

### (G-17140)
### ALUMINITE OF PARIS
2009 S Main St (61944-2961)
PHONE..................217 463-2233
▲ EMP: 3
SALES (est): 238.7K **Privately Held**
SIC: 3442 Screen & storm doors & windows

### (G-17141)
### AMERICAN BUFF INTL INC
219 W Court St (61944-1720)
P.O. Box 581 (61944-0581)
PHONE..................217 465-1411
Anthony Holloway, *President*
▲ EMP: 15
SQ FT: 14,000
SALES (est): 1.3MM **Privately Held**
WEB: www.americanbuff.com
SIC: 3291 Polishing wheels; buffing or polishing wheels, abrasive or nonabrasive

### (G-17142)
### CADILLAC PRODUCTS PACKAGING CO
Also Called: Cppc, Paris Plant
2005 S Main St (61944-2961)
PHONE..................217 463-1444
Fax: 217 463-1341
Michael Switzer, *Plant Mgr*
Jerome Kossak, *QC Dir*
Jaime Houlihan, *Human Res Mgr*
Debra Osborn, *Manager*
EMP: 110 **Privately Held**
SIC: 3081 Polyethylene film
PA: Cadillac Products Packaging Company
5800 Crooks Rd
Troy MI 48098

### (G-17143)
### CARGILL DRY CORN INGRDENTS INC (HQ)
616 S Jefferson St (61944-2000)
PHONE..................217 465-5331
Rex Winter, *President*
Chris Eldredge, *Vice Pres*
Edna Buntain, *Manager*
Tracie Hewitt, *Manager*
▼ EMP: 5 EST: 1934
SQ FT: 20,000
SALES (est): 13.5MM
SALES (corp-wide): 107.1B **Privately Held**
SIC: 2041 2048 5153 Corn meal; corn flour; corn grits & flakes, for brewers' use; grain mills (except rice); prepared feeds; grain elevators
PA: Cargill, Incorporated
15407 Mcginty Rd W
Wayzata MN 55391
952 742-7575

### (G-17144)
### CHRISMAN FUEL
102 Mcmillan St (61944-1302)
PHONE..................217 463-3400
Randy Moore, *Manager*
EMP: 3
SALES (est): 137K **Privately Held**
SIC: 2869 Fuels

### (G-17145)
### CUSTOM TOOL INC
926 N Central Ave (61944-1172)
P.O. Box 817 (61944-0817)
PHONE..................217 465-8538
Fax: 217 463-3061
Robert I Wilson, *President*
Carolyn Wilson, *Vice Pres*
Donita Thomas, *Office Mgr*
EMP: 10
SQ FT: 1,800
SALES (est): 1.6MM **Privately Held**
WEB: www.customtool.com
SIC: 3541 3699 3545 3544 Machine tools, metal cutting type; electrical equipment & supplies; machine tool accessories; special dies, tools, jigs & fixtures

### (G-17146)
### DONCASTERS INC
Also Called: Meco Doncasters
2121 S Main St (61944-2965)
PHONE..................217 465-6500
Tim Garrett, *Plant Mgr*
EMP: 125 **Privately Held**
SIC: 3511 3823 3724 Turbines & turbine generator sets & parts; industrial instrmnts msrmnt display/control process variable; aircraft engines & engine parts
HQ: Doncasters Inc.
36 Spring Ln
Farmington CT 06032
860 677-1376

### (G-17147)
### EDGAR COUNTY LOCKER SERVICE
116 E Steidl Rd (61944-5997)
PHONE..................217 466-5000
Jim Dunn, *President*
Elizabeth Humphrey, *General Mgr*
Bill Moss, *Admin Sec*
EMP: 5
SALES (est): 492.3K **Privately Held**
SIC: 2011 4222 2013 Meat packing plants; storage, frozen or refrigerated goods; sausages & other prepared meats

### (G-17148)
### GSI GROUP LLC
Also Called: Grain Systems
13217 Illinois Hwy 133 W (61944)
PHONE..................217 463-1612
Fax: 217 463-1029
John Vilk, *Purchasing*
David Weder, *Engineer*
Morgan Bland, *Accountant*
Chuck Smith, *Branch Mgr*
Kim Derek, *Manager*
EMP: 200
SALES (corp-wide): 7.4B **Publicly Held**
WEB: www.grainsystems.com
SIC: 5083 3535 3441 Livestock equipment; conveyors & conveying equipment; fabricated structural metal
HQ: The Gsi Group Llc
1004 E Illinois St
Assumption IL 62510
217 226-4421

### (G-17149)
### GSI GROUP LLC
13217 Il Highway 133 (61944-6701)
PHONE..................217 463-8016
Craig Sloan, *Manager*
EMP: 60
SALES (corp-wide): 7.4B **Publicly Held**
WEB: www.grainsystems.com
SIC: 2048 Prepared feeds
HQ: The Gsi Group Llc
1004 E Illinois St
Assumption IL 62510
217 226-4421

### (G-17150)
### IET-MECO
Also Called: Doncasters
2121 S Main St (61944-2965)
PHONE..................217 465-6575
Marvin Miller, *President*
Kyle Bare, *Engineer*
Alan Minnick, *Engineer*
Tim Jordan, *CFO*
EMP: 125
SALES: 35MM **Privately Held**
SIC: 3519 Internal combustion engines

### (G-17151)
### KARENS KRAFTS
8057 Il Hwy 16 (61944-7604)
PHONE..................217 466-8100
Karen Newhart, *Owner*
EMP: 3
SALES (est): 182.2K **Privately Held**
SIC: 2022 Processed cheese

### (G-17152)
### KEYS MANUFACTURING COMPANY INC
13338 N 1900th St (61944-8227)
PHONE..................217 465-4001
Joseph Keys, *President*
Sherrie Wilson, *Office Mgr*
Sheila Keys, *Admin Sec*
▲ EMP: 20
SQ FT: 30,000
SALES (est): 4.3MM **Privately Held**
SIC: 3999 Pet supplies

### (G-17153)
### M & B SERVICES LTD INC
213 E Union St (61944-1810)
P.O. Box 1058 (61944-5058)
PHONE..................217 463-2162
Michael J Bradley, *President*
EMP: 17
SALES (est): 970K **Privately Held**
SIC: 3471 Plating & polishing

### (G-17154)
### MORGAN ROBT INC
1914 S Central Ave (61944)
P.O. Box 877 (61944-0877)
PHONE..................217 466-4777
Fax: 217 463-4777
Robert Morgan, *President*
Floyd Rodrick, *General Mgr*
Cathy Morgan, *Corp Secy*
Karen Woods, *Manager*
▼ EMP: 40
SALES (est): 6.2MM **Privately Held**
WEB: www.robtmorganinc.com
SIC: 2048 Livestock feeds

### (G-17155)
### NORTH AMERICAN LIGHTING INC (HQ)
2275 S Main St (61944-2963)
PHONE..................217 465-6600
Takashi Ohtake, *CEO*
Jun Toyota, *President*
Jose Garcia, *General Mgr*
Jun Kobayashi, *General Mgr*
Deb Oberlee, *General Mgr*
▲ EMP: 1000
SQ FT: 400,000
SALES (est): 666.7MM
SALES (corp-wide): 7.4B **Privately Held**
WEB: www.nal.com
SIC: 3647 Automotive lighting fixtures
PA: Koito Manufacturing Co., Ltd.
4-8-3, Takanawa
Minato-Ku TKY 108-0
334 437-111

# GEOGRAPHIC SECTION

## (G-17156)
**PARIS BEACON NEWS**
218 N Main St  (61944-1738)
PHONE..................................217 465-6424
Fax: 217 463-1232
Ned Jenison, *President*
Kevin Jenison, *Vice Pres*
EMP: 26
SQ FT: 3,640
SALES (est): 1.6MM **Privately Held**
WEB: www.parisbeacon.com
SIC: 2711 Newspapers, publishing & printing

## (G-17157)
**PARIS METAL PRODUCTS LLC**
13571 Il Highway 133  (61944-6953)
PHONE..................................217 465-6321
Mary Wheeler, *CTO*
Corey Risden,
EMP: 76
SQ FT: 200,000
SALES (est): 12.5MM **Privately Held**
WEB: www.parismetal.com
SIC: 3469 Boxes: tool, lunch, mail, etc.: stamped metal

## (G-17158)
**PRINTERS INK OF PARIS INC**
Also Called: Printers The
124 W Court St  (61944-1735)
PHONE..................................217 463-2552
Fax: 217 465-7542
Carole Berl, *President*
EMP: 2
SALES (est): 247.6K **Privately Held**
SIC: 2752 5199 Commercial printing, lithographic; advertising specialties

## (G-17159)
**PVC CONTAINER CORPORATION**
Also Called: Novapack
2015 S Main St  (61944-2961)
PHONE..................................217 463-6600
Fax: 217 463-6601
Dojai Hill, *Manager*
Les Jamison, *Manager*
EMP: 150 **Privately Held**
WEB: www.airopak.com
SIC: 3085 Plastics bottles
HQ: Pvc Container Corporation
15450 South Outer 40 Rd # 120
Chesterfield MO 63017
732 542-0060

## (G-17160)
**QUANEX SCREENS LLC**
13323 Illinois Hwy 133  (61944)
PHONE..................................217 463-2233
Jeff Willaman, *Branch Mgr*
EMP: 6 **Publicly Held**
SIC: 3442 Screen doors, metal
HQ: Quanex Screens Llc
1800 West Loop S Ste 1500
Houston TX 77027
713 961-4600

## (G-17161)
**SECRETARY OF STATE ILLINOIS**
714 Grandview St  (61944-2039)
PHONE..................................217 466-5220
EMP: 3 **Privately Held**
SIC: 3469 Automobile license tags, stamped metal
HQ: Secretary Of State, Illinois
213 State House
Springfield IL 62706
217 782-2201

## (G-17162)
**SIMONTON BUILDING PRODUCTS INC**
Also Called: Simonton Windows
13263 Il Highway 133  (61944-6701)
PHONE..................................217 466-2851
Fax: 217 465-2854
EMP: 350
SALES (corp-wide): 64.4MM **Privately Held**
SIC: 3089 Manufactures Window Products
HQ: Simonton Building Products, Inc.
5300 Briscoe Rd
Parkersburg WV 26105
304 659-2851

## (G-17163)
**SIMONTON WINDOWS INC**
Also Called: Simonton Windows & Doors
13263 Il Highway 133  (61944-6701)
PHONE..................................217 466-2851
Fax: 217 465-2854
Sam Ross, *Principal*
EMP: 5
SALES (est): 455.9K
SALES (corp-wide): 1.9B **Publicly Held**
SIC: 3089 Window frames & sash, plastic
PA: Ply Gem Holdings, Inc.
5020 Weston Pkwy Ste 400
Cary NC 27513
919 677-3900

## (G-17164)
**WHITE SHEET METAL**
303 N Austin St  (61944-1315)
PHONE..................................217 465-3195
John White, *Owner*
Cheryl White, *Partner*
EMP: 3
SALES (est): 180.6K **Privately Held**
SIC: 1711 7623 3444 Boiler & furnace contractors; air conditioning repair; sheet metalwork

## (G-17165)
**YOTTA PET PRODUCTS INC**
1977 S Central Ave  (61944-2700)
P.O. Box 877  (61944-0877)
PHONE..................................217 466-4777
Robert Morgan, *President*
Bob Bridwell, *Sales Mgr*
EMP: 10
SALES (est): 646.8K **Privately Held**
SIC: 2047 Dog food

## Park City
### Lake County

## (G-17166)
**MARKET SQUARE FOOD COMPANY**
475 Keller Dr  (60085-4787)
PHONE..................................847 599-6070
Blair Lockhart, *President*
Andrew Winick, *Managing Dir*
David Lockhart, *Chairman*
EMP: 10
SQ FT: 8,500
SALES: 1MM **Privately Held**
SIC: 2052 Cookies & crackers

## (G-17167)
**WILSON RAILING & METAL FABG CO**
640 Wilson Ave  (60085-5741)
PHONE..................................847 662-1747
Fax: 847 662-6668
Steve Albert, *President*
Kurt Brueggemann, *Plant Mgr*
Lillian Albert, *Treasurer*
Gary Kratz, *Manager*
EMP: 8
SQ FT: 3,200
SALES (est): 1.3MM **Privately Held**
SIC: 3444 3446 Sheet metalwork; railings, bannisters, guards, etc.: made from metal pipe

## Park Forest
### Cook County

## (G-17168)
**AFRICAN AMERICAN CTR FOR HNB**
Also Called: Afrogen Tech & Centers
123 Indianwood Blvd # 1062  (60466-4515)
PHONE..................................618 549-3965
Catrina Johnson, *CEO*
Joyce Willis, *Exec Dir*
EMP: 99
SALES (est): 2.2MM **Privately Held**
SIC: 8733 8071 3841 8299 Research institute; medical laboratories; diagnostic apparatus, medical; educational services; snack foods

## (G-17169)
**CONTINENTAL/MIDLAND LLC (DH)**
Also Called: Cmg Contmid Group
24000 S Western Ave  (60466-3428)
PHONE..................................708 747-1200
Fax: 708 747-1290
Philip Johnson, *CEO*
Joe Ballarini, *Vice Pres*
Anderson Gene, *Opers Mgr*
Ken Breiner, *Warehouse Mgr*
Scott Crompton, *Purch Mgr*
EMP: 250
SALES (est): 225.1MM **Privately Held**
WEB: www.contmid.com
SIC: 3452 Bolts, nuts, rivets & washers
HQ: Contmid Holdings, Inc.
24000 S Western Ave
Park Forest IL 60466
704 747-1200

## (G-17170)
**CONTMID INC**
24000 S Western Ave  (60466-3428)
PHONE..................................708 747-1200
Phil Johnson, *President*
Mike Delfin, *Vice Pres*
Fred Rake, *Vice Pres*
Chuck Beto, *CFO*
Kym Gibson, *Human Resources*
EMP: 4
SALES (est): 204.8K **Privately Held**
SIC: 3965 Fasteners
HQ: Contmid Holdings, Inc.
24000 S Western Ave
Park Forest IL 60466
704 747-1200

## (G-17171)
**DYNAMIC IRON INC**
24001 S Western Ave  (60466-3427)
PHONE..................................708 672-7617
Brian Widstrom, *Owner*
EMP: 2
SALES (est): 291.2K **Privately Held**
SIC: 3446 Architectural metalwork

## (G-17172)
**IMAGEWORKS MANUFACTURING INC**
Also Called: Shipshapes Brands
49 Shell St  (60466-1241)
PHONE..................................708 503-1122
Fax: 708 503-1133
Thomas Becker, *President*
Tom Johnson, *Vice Pres*
Tiffany Narwick, *Vice Pres*
Mark Zickert, *Vice Pres*
Dave O'Neill, *Sales Dir*
EMP: 45 **EST:** 1966
SQ FT: 35,000
SALES (est): 16MM **Privately Held**
WEB: www.imageworksmfg.com
SIC: 3577 3993 3442 3354 Computer peripheral equipment; signs & advertising specialties; name plates: except engraved, etched, etc.: metal; metal doors, sash & trim; aluminum extruded products

## (G-17173)
**JAI-S RECORD LABEL**
22011 Central Park Ave  (60466-1504)
PHONE..................................708 351-4279
Jessica Hill, *Principal*
EMP: 4
SALES: 50K **Privately Held**
SIC: 3663 Studio equipment, radio & television broadcasting

## (G-17174)
**MARKHAM DIVISION 9 INC**
2213 W Wolpers Rd  (60466-3424)
PHONE..................................708 503-0657
Tammie Cerf, *President*
Vern Paul, *Vice Pres*
Marc Cerf, *Admin Sec*
EMP: 25
SALES: 1.5MM **Privately Held**
SIC: 3589 Commercial cleaning equipment

## (G-17175)
**RONALD J NIXON**
Also Called: Champion Silkscreen & EMB
56 South St  (60466-1206)
PHONE..................................708 748-8130
Sanford Nixon, *Manager*
EMP: 9
SALES (corp-wide): 867.2K **Privately Held**
SIC: 5136 2396 2395 Sportswear, men's & boys'; automotive & apparel trimmings; pleating & stitching
PA: Ronald J Nixon
2135 183rd St Ste 1
Homewood IL 60430
708 799-0240

## Park Forest
### Will County

## (G-17176)
**ALRO STEEL CORPORATION**
777 Industrial Dr  (60484-4101)
PHONE..................................708 534-5400
Fax: 708 534-5563
Tony Talarico, *Safety Mgr*
Jim Varnum, *Manager*
EMP: 7
SALES (corp-wide): 1.6B **Privately Held**
WEB: www.alro.com
SIC: 3441 Fabricated structural metal
PA: Alro Steel Corporation
3100 E High St
Jackson MI 49203
517 787-5500

## Park Ridge
### Cook County

## (G-17177)
**AANA PUBLISHING INC**
222 S Prospect Ave  (60068-4001)
PHONE..................................847 692-7050
Christopher Betton, *President*
William Yeo, *Treasurer*
Names Additional, *Director*
Luanne Irvin, *Director*
Jamie Hogan, *Education*
EMP: 2
SALES: 900K
SALES (corp-wide): 25.7MM **Privately Held**
WEB: www.aana.com
SIC: 2721 Trade journals: publishing only, not printed on site
PA: American Association Of Nurse Anesthetists
222 S Prospect Ave
Park Ridge IL 60068
847 692-7050

## (G-17178)
**ADVANCED TECHNOLOGIES INC**
Also Called: Tekvend
310 Busse Hwy Ste 241  (60068-3251)
PHONE..................................847 329-9875
Bob Mahoney, *President*
Vic Schlagman, *Vice Pres*
Dominick Szwarc, *Engineer*
R Stryker, *Marketing Staff*
Suzzie Kim, *Executive Asst*
EMP: 5
SQ FT: 1,500
SALES: 610K **Privately Held**
SIC: 3679 3581 3823 3625 Harness assemblies for electronic use: wire or cable; mechanisms for coin-operated machines; industrial instrmnts msrmnt display/control process variable; relays & industrial controls

## (G-17179)
**AIRES PRESS INC**
227 Murphy Lake Ln  (60068-2832)
PHONE..................................847 698-6813
Fax: 312 226-4607
William B Hameder, *President*
EMP: 5
SQ FT: 9,000

SALES (est): 410K  Privately Held
WEB: www.airespress.com
SIC: 2752  Commercial printing, offset

**(G-17180)**
**ALBERT WHITMAN & COMPANY**
250 S Northwest Hwy # 320  (60068-4237)
PHONE..................................847 232-2800
John Quattrocchi, *President*
Kristin Zelazko, *Editor*
Mike Spradlin, *Marketing Staff*
Denise Shanahgan, *Advt Staff*
Wendy McClure, *Senior Editor*
▲ **EMP:** 23  **EST:** 1919
**SQ FT:** 20,000
**SALES (est):** 2.5MM  Privately Held
WEB: www.awhitmanco.com
SIC: 2731  Books: publishing only

**(G-17181)**
**APOLINSKI  JOHN**
Also Called: Jca International
920 Brookline Ln  (60068-2612)
PHONE..................................847 696-3156
John C Apolinski, *Owner*
**EMP:** 2
**SALES:** 1.2MM  Privately Held
WEB: www.jcaintl.com
SIC: 5084  3648  Pumps & pumping equipment; lighting equipment

**(G-17182)**
**ARBOR PRODUCTS**
614 Wisner St  (60068-3429)
PHONE..................................847 653-6210
**EMP:** 4
**SALES (est):** 330.2K  Privately Held
SIC: 2899  Mfg Chemical Preparations

**(G-17183)**
**BELLISARIO HOLDINGS LLC**
117 Elmore St  (60068-3519)
PHONE..................................847 867-2960
Paul Bellisario,
Laura Bellisario,
**EMP:** 3
**SALES:** 300K  Privately Held
SIC: 2099  Food preparations; baking soda; sugar; rice, uncooked: packaged with other ingredients

**(G-17184)**
**BLACK SPECTACLES BLOG**
1105 S Vine Ave  (60068-4823)
PHONE..................................312 884-9091
Marc Teer, *Principal*
**EMP:** 3
**SALES (est):** 303.2K  Privately Held
SIC: 3851  Spectacles

**(G-17185)**
**BOUND + D TERMINED INC**
60 S Dee Rd Apt E  (60068-3731)
PHONE..................................847 696-1501
Fax: 847 696-1502
Janis M Boehm, *President*
▲ **EMP:** 3
**SALES (est):** 140K  Privately Held
WEB: www.bound-determined.com
SIC: 2782  Scrapbooks, albums & diaries

**(G-17186)**
**CANDY TECH LLC**
309 S Northwest Hwy # 2  (60068-4281)
PHONE..................................847 229-1011
Fax: 847 229-1211
David Babiarz,
▲ **EMP:** 18
**SALES (est):** 4.2MM  Privately Held
WEB: www.sterlingcandy.com
SIC: 2064  Candy & other confectionery products

**(G-17187)**
**CLEAR NDA  LLC**
Also Called: Clearnda
350 S Northwest Hwy # 300  (60068-4216)
PHONE..................................470 222-6320
Carl Gatenio, *CEO*
Greg Doerr, *Exec VP*
**EMP:** 11
**SQ FT:** 5,000
**SALES (est):** 468.8K  Privately Held
SIC: 7372  Prepackaged software; business oriented computer software

**(G-17188)**
**CONTINENTAL USA  INC**
Also Called: Continental Chicago
1100 N Cumberland Ave  (60068-2049)
PHONE..................................847 823-0958
Tatiana Boitchouk, *President*
Natalie Boitchouk, *Admin Sec*
**EMP:** 4
**SALES (est):** 355.1K  Privately Held
SIC: 8748  2599  4513  Business consulting; carts, restaurant equipment; package delivery, private air

**(G-17189)**
**DEMIS PRINTING INC**
1601 Oakton St  (60068-1946)
PHONE..................................773 282-9128
Bill Demitropoulos, *President*
George Demitropoulos, *Vice Pres*
Nicolette Demitropoulos, *Admin Sec*
**EMP:** 4
**SALES:** 300K  Privately Held
SIC: 2752  2791  2789  Commercial printing, offset; typesetting; bookbinding & related work

**(G-17190)**
**DLC INC**
3 S 080 Talbot Ave  (60068)
PHONE..................................224 567-8656
James D Cook, *Mng Member*
**EMP:** 15
**SALES (est):** 1.8MM  Privately Held
SIC: 3531  Aerial work platforms: hydraulic/elec. truck/carrier mounted

**(G-17191)**
**DRAPERY HOUSE  INC**
Also Called: Retail Window Treatments
1420 Oakton St  (60068-2069)
PHONE..................................847 318-1161
Urszula Lisiecki, *Owner*
**EMP:** 3  **EST:** 1949
**SALES (est):** 231.2K  Privately Held
WEB: www.draperyhousecanada.com
SIC: 5719  5714  2391  Window shades; bedding (sheets, blankets, spreads & pillows); draperies; curtains & draperies

**(G-17192)**
**FANBOYS GAMES & MOVIES LLC**
400 Ascot Dr  (60068-3684)
PHONE..................................847 894-6448
David M Schrempf, *Principal*
**EMP:** 3
**SALES (est):** 155.9K  Privately Held
SIC: 2711  Newspapers

**(G-17193)**
**FEDEX OFFICE & PRINT SVCS INC**
678 N Northwest Hwy  (60068-2540)
PHONE..................................847 823-9360
Seringe Jarjusey, *Manager*
**EMP:** 7
**SALES (corp-wide):** 50.3B  Publicly Held
WEB: www.kinkos.com
SIC: 7334  2791  2789  Photocopying & duplicating services; typesetting; bookbinding & related work
HQ: Fedex Office And Print Services, Inc.
7900 Legacy Dr
Plano TX 75024
214 550-7000

**(G-17194)**
**FEELSURE HEALTH CORPARATION**
120 Columbia Ave  (60068-4922)
PHONE..................................847 823-0137
William Bartlett, *President*
Jim Habschmidt, *President*
**EMP:** 3
**SALES (est):** 182.9K  Privately Held
SIC: 3841  Diagnostic apparatus, medical

**(G-17195)**
**FOOD SERVICE PUBLISHING CO**
1440 Renaissance Dr # 210  (60068-1356)
PHONE..................................847 699-3300
Valerie Miller, *President*
**EMP:** 7
**SALES (est):** 119.6K  Privately Held
SIC: 2741  Miscellaneous publishing

**(G-17196)**
**FULLING MOTOR USA INC**
1601 Park Ridge Pt  (60068-1309)
P.O. Box 1101  (60068-7101)
PHONE..................................847 894-6238
Brian Ranallo, *President*
Hanrong Zhang, *Treasurer*
Yufei Wang, *Admin Sec*
▲ **EMP:** 2
**SQ FT:** 1,000
**SALES (est):** 213.2K  Privately Held
SIC: 3621  Collector rings, for electric motors or generators

**(G-17197)**
**FUSION CHEMICAL CORPORATION**
350 S Northwest Hwy # 300  (60068-4262)
PHONE..................................847 656-5285
**EMP:** 3
**SALES (est):** 190.5K  Privately Held
SIC: 2819  Industrial inorganic chemicals

**(G-17198)**
**GENERAL BANDAGES INC**
717 N Washington Ave  (60068-2716)
PHONE..................................847 966-8383
Fax: 847 966-7733
John D Hinkamp, *President*
Philip Hinkamp, *Corp Secy*
Jim Hinkamp, *Vice Pres*
**EMP:** 19  **EST:** 1935
**SQ FT:** 20,000
**SALES (est):** 2.5MM  Privately Held
WEB: www.generalbandages.com
SIC: 3842  5047  Adhesive tape & plasters, medicated or non-medicated; gauze, surgical; tape, adhesive: medicated or non-medicated; medical equipment & supplies

**(G-17199)**
**GRAPHIC SCORE BOOK CO INC**
306 Busse Hwy  (60068-3251)
PHONE..................................847 823-7382
William Smyrthe, *President*
**EMP:** 4
**SALES (est):** 210K  Privately Held
SIC: 2731  5942  Books: publishing & printing; book stores

**(G-17200)**
**GREAT LAKES LUMBER AND PALLET**
2137 N Home Ave  (60068-1021)
PHONE..................................773 243-6839
**EMP:** 4  **EST:** 2015
**SALES (est):** 326.6K  Privately Held
SIC: 2448  Pallets, wood & wood with metal

**(G-17201)**
**GRIFFITH SOLUTIONS INC**
Also Called: Sullivan Press
529 Warren Ave  (60068-4355)
PHONE..................................847 384-1810
Richard Griffith, *President*
Ruth Griffith, *Treasurer*
Sean Griffith, *Manager*
**EMP:** 5
**SQ FT:** 4,200
**SALES (est):** 820K  Privately Held
WEB: www.griffithsolutions.com
SIC: 2752  2791  2789  2671  Commercial printing, lithographic; typesetting; bookbinding & related work; packaging paper & plastics film, coated & laminated

**(G-17202)**
**HOMECONTROLPLUS INCORPORATED**
1884 Fenton Ln  (60068-1502)
PHONE..................................847 823-8414
Jasna Ostojich, *President*
**EMP:** 2
**SALES (est):** 239.8K  Privately Held
WEB: www.homecontrolplus.net
SIC: 3822  Auto controls regulating residntl & coml environmt & applncs

**(G-17203)**
**HOORAY PUREE INC**
310 Busse Hwy Ste 322  (60068-3251)
PHONE..................................312 515-0266
Krista Ward, *CEO*
**EMP:** 5
**SQ FT:** 80,000
**SALES (est):** 445.3K  Privately Held
SIC: 2033  Vegetable purees: packaged in cans, jars, etc.

**(G-17204)**
**INTERRA GLOBAL CORPORATION**
800 Busse Hwy Ste 101  (60068-2300)
P.O. Box 101  (60068-0101)
PHONE..................................847 292-8600
William Wallace, *President*
Bill Wallace, *VP Sales*
Jason Skiersch, *Admin Sec*
▲ **EMP:** 11
**SQ FT:** 2,500
**SALES (est):** 9MM  Privately Held
WEB: www.interraglobal.com
SIC: 5169  2899  2819  Industrial chemicals; chemical preparations; water treating compounds; aluminum compounds; silica gel

**(G-17205)**
**JPMORGAN CHASE BANK NAT ASSN**
500 Busse Hwy  (60068-3144)
PHONE..................................847 685-0490
Allison Vara, *Branch Mgr*
**EMP:** 4
**SALES (corp-wide):** 105.4B  Publicly Held
SIC: 3644  Insulators & insulation materials, electrical
HQ: Jpmorgan Chase Bank, National Association
1111 Polaris Pkwy
Columbus OH 43240
614 436-3055

**(G-17206)**
**LEGACY INTERNATIONAL ASSOC LLC**
1420 Park Ridge Blvd  (60068-5042)
PHONE..................................847 823-1602
William Ristau, *President*
Pattie Risau, *Marketing Staff*
Mike Boychuck, *Manager*
Katie Ristau, *Analyst*
**EMP:** 6
**SALES (est):** 514.7K  Privately Held
SIC: 3317  Steel pipe & tubes

**(G-17207)**
**MAKI SUSHI & NOODLE SHOP**
12 S Northwest Hwy  (60068-4227)
PHONE..................................847 318-1920
Fax: 847 318-1924
Daniel Cummins, *Owner*
**EMP:** 8
**SALES (est):** 599.7K  Privately Held
SIC: 2098  Noodles (e.g. egg, plain & water), dry

**(G-17208)**
**MAR-DON CORPORATION**
115 Columbia Ave  (60068-4921)
P.O. Box 1024  (60068-7024)
PHONE..................................847 823-4958
Marilyn Goll, *President*
**EMP:** 2
**SALES (est):** 500K  Privately Held
WEB: www.mar-don-corp.com
SIC: 3661  Telephone & telegraph apparatus

**(G-17209)**
**MORNINGFIELDS**
800 Devon Ave Ste 7  (60068-4760)
PHONE..................................847 309-8460
Fax: 847 696-4958
Marilyn Schuman, *Principal*
**EMP:** 9
**SALES (est):** 733.1K  Privately Held
SIC: 2051  Cakes, bakery: except frozen

**(G-17210)**
**NANTSOUND  INC**
Also Called: Sound World Solutions
960 N Northwest Hwy  (60068-2358)
PHONE..................................847 939-6101
Stavros P Basseas, *President*
Wayne Bayever, *Vice Pres*
Michael Kilhefner, *Engineer*
Cindy Kaempfer, *CFO*
Cindy Kempfer, *CFO*

▲ **EMP:** 10
**SALES (est):** 1.1MM **Privately Held**
**SIC:** 3651 Amplifiers: radio, public address or musical instrument

**(G-17211)**
**NASHUA CORPORATION**
250 S Northwest Hwy # 203 (60068-4252)
**PHONE** .................................. 847 692-9130
Rosendo Sardinas, *Plant Mgr*
Charles Bonnier, *Engineer*
Diana Shultz, *Manager*
Susan Pestrak, *Director*
**EMP:** 68 **Publicly Held**
**WEB:** www.nashua.com
**SIC:** 2679 3955 2672 2671 Telegraph, teletype & adding machine paper; tags & labels, paper; carbon paper & inked ribbons; coated & laminated paper; packaging paper & plastics film, coated & laminated
**HQ:** Nashua Corporation
59 Daniel Webster Hwy A
Merrimack NH 03054
603 880-1100

**(G-17212)**
**NICE CARD COMPANY**
803 S Aldine Ave (60068-4416)
**PHONE** .................................. 773 467-8450
**Fax:** 773 467-8454
Christopher Kean, *President*
**EMP:** 5
**SQ FT:** 2,000
**SALES:** 200K **Privately Held**
**WEB:** www.nicepublishing.com
**SIC:** 2741 Miscellaneous publishing

**(G-17213)**
**NORTHWEST INSTRUMENTATION INC**
310 Busse Hwy 259 (60068-3251)
**PHONE** .................................. 847 825-0699
Michael Fallon, *CEO*
Mitch Alton, *President*
Hector Diaz, *Treasurer*
**EMP:** 32
**SALES (est):** 1.3MM **Privately Held**
**SIC:** 1731 3613 Electronic controls installation; control panels, electric

**(G-17214)**
**OSBON LITHOGRAPHERS**
1218 S Crescent Ave (60068-5317)
**PHONE** .................................. 847 825-7727
Oscar Gonzalez, *Owner*
**EMP:** 3
**SQ FT:** 1,200
**SALES:** 140K **Privately Held**
**SIC:** 2752 2789 Commercial printing, lithographic; bookbinding & related work

**(G-17215)**
**PALLETS PLUS INC**
1000 Cedar St (60068-3203)
**PHONE** .................................. 847 318-1853
Frank P Falzone, *Principal*
**EMP:** 4
**SALES (est):** 492.5K **Privately Held**
**SIC:** 2448 Wood pallets & skids

**(G-17216)**
**PILOT CORPORATION OF AMERICA**
1300 Higgins Rd Ste 214 (60068-5766)
**PHONE** .................................. 773 792-1111
Jim Matese, *Principal*
Tom Caulfield, *Natl Sales Mgr*
Mark Puppolo, *Manager*
Karina Farha, *Supervisor*
**EMP:** 3
**SALES (corp-wide):** 888.7MM **Privately Held**
**WEB:** www.pilotpen.com
**SIC:** 3951 Pens & mechanical pencils
**HQ:** Pilot Corporation Of America
3855 Regent Blvd
Jacksonville FL 32224
904 645-9999

**(G-17217)**
**PORCHE PHARMACEUTICAL STAFFING**
350 S Northwest Hwy # 300 (60068-4216)
**PHONE** .................................. 312 259-3982

**EMP:** 3
**SALES (est):** 158.3K **Privately Held**
**SIC:** 2834 Pharmaceutical preparations

**(G-17218)**
**QUINN PRINT INC**
508 Higgins Rd (60068-5732)
**PHONE** .................................. 847 823-9100
Eugene Walker, *President*
Mike Quinn, *Vice Pres*
**EMP:** 5
**SQ FT:** 1,600
**SALES (est):** 573.9K **Privately Held**
**SIC:** 2752 2791 2789 Commercial printing, offset; typesetting; bookbinding & related work

**(G-17219)**
**RAYALCO INC**
Also Called: Rayalco Software
712 S Fairview Ave (60068-4707)
**PHONE** .................................. 847 692-7422
**Fax:** 847 692-4511
Allan H Paschke, *President*
Joseph S Bianco, *Admin Sec*
**EMP:** 4
**SQ FT:** 750
**SALES (est):** 340K **Privately Held**
**WEB:** www.rayalco.com
**SIC:** 7372 Prepackaged software

**(G-17220)**
**ROYAL STAIRS CO**
98 East Ave (60068-3504)
**PHONE** .................................. 847 685-9448
Krystyna Hryszko, *Principal*
**EMP:** 3
**SALES (est):** 247.7K **Privately Held**
**SIC:** 3446 Stairs, staircases, stair treads: prefabricated metal

**(G-17221)**
**RUSSELL ENTERPRISES INC (PA)**
865 Busse Hwy (60068-2359)
**PHONE** .................................. 847 692-6050
Richard Mathes, *President*
Don Popernik, *Corp Secy*
**EMP:** 35
**SALES (est):** 32.1MM **Privately Held**
**WEB:** www.stdcar.com
**SIC:** 6141 8249 3743 3321 Personal finance licensed loan companies, small; trade school; freight cars & equipment; ductile iron castings; gray iron castings

**(G-17222)**
**SOLARI R MFG JEWELERS**
Also Called: Solari and Huntington
100 1/2 Main St (60068-4030)
**PHONE** .................................. 847 823-4354
Robert Solari, *Owner*
**EMP:** 6
**SQ FT:** 2,000
**SALES (est):** 616.6K **Privately Held**
**WEB:** www.solariandhuntington.com
**SIC:** 5944 3961 Jewelry, precious stones & precious metals; costume jewelry

**(G-17223)**
**STEVEN E WASKO & ASSOCIATES**
1580 N Northwest Hwy # 212 (60068-1444)
**PHONE** .................................. 773 693-2330
Steven Wasko, *Principal*
**EMP:** 3
**SALES (est):** 218.4K **Privately Held**
**SIC:** 3743 Dining cars & equipment

**(G-17224)**
**STRAUSS FACTER ASSOC INC**
Also Called: 4 Seasons Sales and Marketing
1440 Renaissance Dr (60068-1356)
**PHONE** .................................. 847 759-1100
George Curtis, *President*
▲ **EMP:** 4 **EST:** 1975
**SALES (est):** 299.5K **Privately Held**
**SIC:** 3721 Balloons, hot air (aircraft)

**(G-17225)**
**SUBURBAN FIX & INSTALLATION**
420 S Fairview Ave (60068-4753)
**PHONE** .................................. 847 823-4047

Robert Tamburrino, *President*
Martin K Sullivan, *Vice Pres*
Patricia G Tamburrino, *Vice Pres*
**EMP:** 2 **EST:** 1978
**SALES (est):** 1.5MM **Privately Held**
**WEB:** www.suburbanfixtures.com
**SIC:** 2541 1751 Store & office display cases & fixtures; store fixture installation

**(G-17226)**
**TANCHER CORP**
1493 Vernon Ave (60068-1593)
**PHONE** .................................. 847 668-8765
Mark Menarick, *CEO*
Joshua Barmey, *COO*
Anton Tyurin, *CFO*
Aleksey Voitovich, *Administration*
**EMP:** 15
**SALES (est):** 400K **Privately Held**
**SIC:** 3661 Telephones & telephone apparatus

**(G-17227)**
**UNION STREET TIN CO**
350 S Northwest Hwy (60068-4216)
**PHONE** .................................. 312 379-8200
John B Powers, *President*
James Magnano, *Accounts Exec*
▲ **EMP:** 8
**SALES (est):** 786K **Privately Held**
**SIC:** 3053 Packing, metallic

**(G-17228)**
**UNITED RAWHIDE MFG CO**
1315 Linden Ave (60068-5523)
**PHONE** .................................. 847 692-2791
Stefan F Palansky, *President*
Chester R Davis Jr, *Admin Sec*
**EMP:** 6 **EST:** 1950
**SQ FT:** 3,000
**SALES (est):** 510K **Privately Held**
**SIC:** 3111 Rawhide

**(G-17229)**
**WORKPLACE INK INC**
1712 Marguerite St (60068-1939)
**PHONE** .................................. 312 939-0296
Daniel Mix, *President*
**EMP:** 4
**SALES:** 2MM **Privately Held**
**WEB:** www.workplaceink.com
**SIC:** 2759 Commercial printing

## Patoka
### Marion County

**(G-17230)**
**ARCHER-DANIELS-MIDLAND COMPANY**
408 S Railroad St (62875)
**PHONE** .................................. 618 432-7194
**Fax:** 618 432-7194
Scott Sporleder, *Branch Mgr*
**EMP:** 3
**SALES (corp-wide):** 62.3B **Publicly Held**
**SIC:** 5191 2048 Animal feeds; prepared feeds
**PA:** Archer-Daniels-Midland Company
77 W Wacker Dr Ste 4600
Chicago IL 60601
312 634-8100

**(G-17231)**
**FOLTZ WELDING LTD**
501 E Clinton Ave (62875-1153)
**PHONE** .................................. 618 432-7777
**Fax:** 618 432-7717
Jeff Foltz, *President*
Ron Ruhler, *Accounts Mgr*
**EMP:** 150
**SQ FT:** 1,800
**SALES (est):** 42.5MM **Privately Held**
**WEB:** www.foltzwelding.com
**SIC:** 1389 1623 Pipe testing, oil field service; water, sewer & utility lines

**(G-17232)**
**JENKINS DISPLAYS CO**
Also Called: Jenkins Truck & Farm
107 S Railroad St (62875-1082)
**PHONE** .................................. 618 335-3874
**Fax:** 618 432-5541
Scott Jenkins, *President*

**EMP:** 5 **EST:** 1935
**SQ FT:** 30,000
**SALES:** 1MM **Privately Held**
**SIC:** 3993 5999 0762 Electric signs; farm equipment & supplies; farm management services

## Paw Paw
### Lee County

**(G-17233)**
**PAW PAW CO-OPERATIVE GRAIN**
243 Flagg St (61353-8909)
P.O. Box 10, Leland (60531-0010)
**PHONE** .................................. 815 627-2071
Jeff Svendsen, *Manager*
**EMP:** 4
**SQ FT:** 1,000
**SALES (est):** 270K **Privately Held**
**SIC:** 3523 Elevators, farm

## Pawnee
### Sangamon County

**(G-17234)**
**HARSCO CORPORATION**
226 E 1640 Rd (62558)
P.O. Box 652 (62558-0652)
**PHONE** .................................. 217 237-4335
Hary Marcorees, *Office Mgr*
**EMP:** 12
**SALES (corp-wide):** 1.4B **Publicly Held**
**WEB:** www.harsco.com
**SIC:** 3295 3291 2952 Minerals, ground or treated; abrasive products; asphalt felts & coatings
**PA:** Harsco Corporation
350 Poplar Church Rd
Camp Hill PA 17011
717 763-7064

**(G-17235)**
**PINS & NEEDLES CONSINGMENT**
7580 N Pawnee Rd (62558-4624)
**PHONE** .................................. 217 299-7365
Sally Neumann, *Partner*
**EMP:** 3 **EST:** 2006
**SALES (est):** 190.7K **Privately Held**
**SIC:** 3452 Pins

## Paxton
### Ford County

**(G-17236)**
**BEE BOAT CO INC**
209 E Green St (60957-1701)
**PHONE** .................................. 217 379-2605
**Fax:** 217 379-2605
Philip Raymond Diskin, *President*
Dorcas Diskin, *Admin Sec*
**EMP:** 2
**SQ FT:** 30,000
**SALES (est):** 258.8K **Privately Held**
**WEB:** www.beeboat.com
**SIC:** 3089 7699 Plastic boats & other marine equipment; boat repair

**(G-17237)**
**HTS HANCOCK TRANSCRIPTIONS SVC (PA)**
Also Called: Picket Fence Florist
136 S Market St (60957-1222)
**PHONE** .................................. 217 379-9241
**Fax:** 217 379-2591
Teri Hancock, *Owner*
**EMP:** 20
**SALES (est):** 1.5MM **Privately Held**
**WEB:** www.htsservice.com
**SIC:** 2752 5992 Commercial printing, lithographic; florists

# Paxton - Ford County (G-17238)

**(G-17238)**
**NEXSTEP COMMERCIAL PDTS LLC**
Also Called: Ncp Commercial
1450 W Ottawa Rd (60957-4205)
P.O. Box 71 (60957-0071)
PHONE..................217 379-2377
Todd Leventhal,
Stanley Koschnick,
◆ EMP: 8
SALES (est): 1.8MM **Privately Held**
SIC: 3991 Brooms & brushes

**(G-17239)**
**NEXSTEP COMMERCIAL PRODUCTS**
1450 W Ottawa Rd (60957-4205)
PHONE..................217 379-2377
Todd Leventhal, *Principal*
Teresa Stone, *Manager*
EMP: 4
SALES (est): 230K **Privately Held**
SIC: 3423 Hand & edge tools

**(G-17240)**
**O-CEDAR COMMERCIAL**
131 N Railroad Ave (60957-1358)
P.O. Box 71 (60957-0071)
PHONE..................217 379-3634
Frank Schossler, *Principal*
EMP: 2
SALES (est): 211.6K **Privately Held**
SIC: 3532 Cleaning machinery, mineral

**(G-17241)**
**PAXTON PACKING LLC**
Also Called: Big Frontire
145 W State Ave (60957-1143)
PHONE..................623 707-5604
Glen Kerby,
Tony Alford,
EMP: 11
SQ FT: 18,000
SALES: 1.1MM **Privately Held**
SIC: 2013 Snack sticks, including jerky: from purchased meat

**(G-17242)**
**PAXTON READY MIX INC**
745 N Market St (60957-1023)
P.O. Box 177 (60957-0177)
PHONE..................217 379-2303
Fax: 217 379-3634
Gregory Whitcomb, *President*
Carol Whitcomb, *Corp Secy*
Terry Whitcomb, *Vice Pres*
EMP: 8
SQ FT: 800
SALES (est): 1.3MM **Privately Held**
SIC: 3273 Ready-mixed concrete

**(G-17243)**
**PLASTIC DESIGNS INC**
Also Called: AG Solutions
1330 S Vermillion St (60957-1700)
PHONE..................217 379-9214
Fax: 217 379-2022
Steven G Glazik, *President*
Gary Glacik, *Vice Pres*
Amy Withest, *Human Res Dir*
Donna Bruns, *Human Res Mgr*
Debbi Faster, *Manager*
EMP: 35
SQ FT: 50,000
SALES: 5MM **Privately Held**
WEB: www.pdipaxton.com
SIC: 3089 Molding primary plastic; injection molding of plastics

**(G-17244)**
**PRO-TYPE PRINTING INC (PA)**
130 N Market St (60957-1220)
PHONE..................217 379-4715
Fax: 217 379-3153
Robin Niewold, *Principal*
Mark Johnson, *Manager*
Jenni Burgess, *Graphic Designe*
EMP: 8
SALES (est): 725.1K **Privately Held**
WEB: www.protypeonline.com
SIC: 2752 2791 2789 Commercial printing, offset; typesetting; bookbinding & related work

**(G-17245)**
**SOUTHFIELD CORPORATION**
100 N 2280e Rd (60957-4186)
PHONE..................217 379-3606
Eric Mills, *Manager*
EMP: 5
SALES (corp-wide): 273.9MM **Privately Held**
WEB: www.prairiegroup.com
SIC: 1442 Common sand mining; gravel mining
PA: Southfield Corporation
8995 W 95th St
Palos Hills IL 60465
708 344-1000

## Payson
### Adams County

**(G-17246)**
**PITTSFIELD MCH TL & WLDG CO**
306 W State St (62360-1188)
PHONE..................217 656-4000
Johnnie Leithoff, *President*
Darlene Leithoff, *Corp Secy*
EMP: 3
SQ FT: 10,500
SALES (est): 344.7K **Privately Held**
SIC: 3599 3441 3444 Machine shop, jobbing & repair; fabricated structural metal; sheet metalwork

## Pearl
### Pike County

**(G-17247)**
**MARTHA LACEY**
Also Called: Lacey-Bauer
47424 212th Ave (62361-2016)
PHONE..................217 723-4380
Martha Lacey, *Owner*
EMP: 3 EST: 1945
SQ FT: 600
SALES: 125K **Privately Held**
SIC: 1422 Crushed & broken limestone

## Pearl City
### Stephenson County

**(G-17248)**
**LOBERG EXCAVATING INC**
12268 W Sabin Church Rd (61062-9225)
PHONE..................815 443-2874
Fax: 815 443-2387
Richard Loberg, *President*
Connie Loberg, *Corp Secy*
Talena Wuebbels, *Administration*
EMP: 25
SQ FT: 4,450
SALES (est): 3.3MM **Privately Held**
WEB: www.lobergexcavating.com
SIC: 1794 1411 Excavation work; dimension stone

**(G-17249)**
**PEARL VALLEY ORGANIX INC**
968 S Kent Rd (61062-9170)
PHONE..................815 443-2170
David Thompson, *President*
Ben Thomson, *Sales Mgr*
Terry Sue Thompson, *Admin Sec*
Terry Thompson, *Admin Sec*
EMP: 10
SQ FT: 165,000
SALES (est): 2.2MM **Privately Held**
SIC: 2875 Compost

## Pecatonica
### Winnebago County

**(G-17250)**
**ANPEC INDUSTRIES INC**
216 Main St (61063-9196)
P.O. Box 539 (61063-0539)
PHONE..................815 239-2303
Fax: 815 239-1843
Douglas Allen, *President*
Brad Wagner, *Vice Pres*
EMP: 35 EST: 1968
SQ FT: 24,000
SALES (est): 7.9MM **Privately Held**
WEB: www.anpecindustries.com
SIC: 3451 Screw machine products

**(G-17251)**
**BAY VALLEY FOODS LLC**
215 W 3rd St (61063-7001)
P.O. Box 359 (61063-0359)
PHONE..................815 239-2631
Walt Mangus, *QC Dir*
John Bankson, *Personnel*
George Perez, *Branch Mgr*
John Van Liere, *Director*
EMP: 100
SALES (corp-wide): 6.1B **Publicly Held**
SIC: 2023 2026 Cream substitutes; fluid milk
HQ: Bay Valley Foods, Llc
3200 Riverside Dr Ste A
Green Bay WI 54301
800 558-4700

**(G-17252)**
**IPSEN INC**
Ipsen Ceramics Div
325 John St (61063-7735)
P.O. Box 420 (61063-0420)
PHONE..................815 239-2385
Fax: 815 239-2387
John Menne, *Finance Other*
Brenda Elliot, *Supervisor*
EMP: 20
SQ FT: 30,703
SALES (corp-wide): 105.9K **Privately Held**
WEB: www.ipsen-intl.com
SIC: 3269 3567 3297 3433 Laboratory & industrial pottery; industrial furnaces & ovens; nonclay refractories; heating equipment, except electric; nonferrous foundries
HQ: Ipsen, Inc.
984 Ipsen Rd
Cherry Valley IL 61016
815 332-4941

## Pekin
### Tazewell County

**(G-17253)**
**AMERICAN MILLING COMPANY**
1811 American St (61554-5419)
PHONE..................309 347-6888
Fax: 309 347-1256
Stan Walshman, *Manager*
EMP: 12
SALES (corp-wide): 32.7MM **Privately Held**
SIC: 5191 2041 Feed; flour & other grain mill products
PA: The American Milling Company
3 Cargill Rd
Cahokia IL 62206
618 337-8877

**(G-17254)**
**APEX PATTERN WORKS**
836 Brenkman Dr (61554-1523)
PHONE..................309 346-2905
Ken Peters, *Owner*
Kay Peters, *Manager*
EMP: 9
SQ FT: 6,000
SALES: 410K **Privately Held**
SIC: 3543 3544 Foundry patternmaking; special dies, tools, jigs & fixtures

**(G-17255)**
**AVENTINE RENEWABLE ENERGY (HQ)**
1300 S 2nd St (61554-5402)
PHONE..................309 347-9200
Fax: 309 347-8541
Mark Beemer, *CEO*
Brian Steenhard, *CFO*
EMP: 53
SALES (est): 93.5MM
SALES (corp-wide): 1.6B **Publicly Held**
SIC: 2869 Ethyl alcohol, ethanol
PA: Pacific Ethanol, Inc.
400 Capitol Mall Ste 2060
Sacramento CA 95814
916 403-2123

**(G-17256)**
**CITY OF PEKIN**
Also Called: Street Dept
1208 Koch St (61554-5936)
PHONE..................309 477-2325
Fax: 309 477-2322
David Pagliaro, *Branch Mgr*
Bob Shaw, *Manager*
EMP: 16 **Privately Held**
SIC: 3648 9111 Street lighting fixtures; mayors' offices
PA: City Of Pekin
111 S Capitol St Ste 200
Pekin IL 61554
309 477-2300

**(G-17257)**
**CONTINENTAL CARBONIC PDTS INC**
140 Distillery Rd (61554-4075)
PHONE..................309 346-7515
Fax: 309 346-9349
David Butts, *Vice Pres*
Jeff Johnston, *Vice Pres*
Jack Oriley, *Vice Pres*
Mark Gossick, *Prdtn Mgr*
Tim Pleasant, *Branch Mgr*
EMP: 38
SALES (corp-wide): 32.6B **Privately Held**
WEB: www.ccpidryice.com
SIC: 5169 2813 Dry ice; industrial gases
HQ: Continental Carbonic Products, Inc.
3985 E Harrison Ave
Decatur IL 62526
217 428-2068

**(G-17258)**
**DCX-CHOL ENTERPRISES INC**
Elecsys Division of Dcx-Chol
225 Enterprise Dr (61554-9311)
PHONE..................309 353-4455
Fax: 309 353-4445
Mike Jamison, *General Mgr*
EMP: 50
SALES (corp-wide): 150.6MM **Privately Held**
SIC: 3671 3643 Electron tubes; current-carrying wiring devices
PA: Dcx-Chol Enterprises, Inc.
12831 S Figueroa St
Los Angeles CA 90061
310 516-1692

**(G-17259)**
**DISTILLERY WINE & ALLIED**
300 Mclean St (61554-4414)
PHONE..................309 347-1444
Brian Camden, *President*
Wayne Hasty, *Vice Pres*
Bill Kortkamp, *Vice Pres*
Mark Meyer, *Manager*
EMP: 6
SALES (est): 205.1K **Privately Held**
SIC: 2084 Wines, brandy & brandy spirits

**(G-17260)**
**DJ ILLINOIS RIVER VALLEY CALLS**
7949 State Rte 78 (61554)
PHONE..................309 348-2112
David Jackson, *CEO*
Randy Ruskey, *Administration*
EMP: 5
SALES (est): 320.4K **Privately Held**
SIC: 3949 Game calls

# GEOGRAPHIC SECTION
## Pekin - Tazewell County (G-17285)

### (G-17261)
**ENVIRO-SAFE REFRIGERANTS INC**
400 Margaret St Ste 1  (61554-3260)
PHONE...............................309 346-1110
Fax: 309 346-1237
Julie C Price, *President*
Randy Price, *Vice Pres*
Meiilsa King, *Manager*
Juna Novoa, *Manager*
Melissa A King, *Admin Sec*
◆ **EMP:** 24
**SQ FT:** 10,000
**SALES (est):** 4.3MM  **Privately Held**
**WEB:** www.es-refrigerants.com
**SIC:** 3221  Bottles for packing, bottling & canning: glass

### (G-17262)
**FEDERAL PRISON INDUSTRIES**
Also Called: Unicor
2600 S 2nd St  (61554-8297)
P.O. Box 7000  (61555-7000)
PHONE...............................309 346-8588
Peter Spartz, *Manager*
**EMP:** 175  **Publicly Held**
**WEB:** www.unicor.gov
**SIC:** 2299  3621  3546  2353  Batting, wadding, padding & fillings; motors & generators; power-driven handtools; hats, caps & millinery; brooms & brushes; correctional institutions;
**HQ:** Federal Prison Industries, Inc
320 1st St Nw
Washington DC 20534
202 305-3500

### (G-17263)
**FLSMIDTH PEKIN LLC (DH)**
Also Called: FLS Pekin
14425 Wagonseller Rd  (61554-8831)
P.O. Box 188  (61555-0188)
PHONE...............................309 347-3031
Fax: 309 353-5591
Kim Hammond, *Accountant*
Carolyn Pierce, *Human Res Mgr*
Fred Gross, *Mng Member*
◆ **EMP:** 59
**SALES (est):** 12.4MM
**SALES (corp-wide):** 2.5B  **Privately Held**
**WEB:** www.ffeminerals.com
**SIC:** 3531  Rock crushing machinery, portable
**HQ:** Flsmidth Inc.
2040 Avenue C
Bethlehem PA 18017
610 264-6011

### (G-17264)
**FRYMAN ELECTRIC**
3801 Sheridan Rd  (61554-9706)
PHONE...............................309 387-6540
Josh Fryman, *Owner*
**EMP:** 4  **EST:** 2007
**SALES (est):** 368.5K  **Privately Held**
**SIC:** 3699  Electrical equipment & supplies

### (G-17265)
**HANNA STEEL CORPORATION**
Pekin Division
220 Hanna Dr  (61554-8793)
PHONE...............................309 478-3800
Fax: 309 478-3810
Sergio Becerra, *General Mgr*
Bob Steele, *Marketing Staff*
**EMP:** 110
**SALES (corp-wide):** 2MM  **Privately Held**
**WEB:** www.hannasteel.com
**SIC:** 3317  Welded pipe & tubes
**PA:** Hanna Steel Corporation
4527 Southlake Pkwy
Hoover AL 35244
205 820-5200

### (G-17266)
**HARSCO CORPORATION**
13090 E Manito Rd  (61554)
PHONE...............................309 347-1962
Jonathan Watt, *Manager*
**EMP:** 9
**SALES (corp-wide):** 1.4B  **Publicly Held**
**SIC:** 1481  Nonmetallic mineral services
**PA:** Harsco Corporation
350 Poplar Church Rd
Camp Hill PA 17011
717 763-7064

### (G-17267)
**HOME SCHOOL ENRICHMENT INC**
124 Thrush Ave  (61554-6462)
PHONE...............................309 347-1392
Frank Lewis, *CEO*
Jonathan Lewis, *Editor*
**EMP:** 3
**SALES:** 375K  **Privately Held**
**SIC:** 2721  Magazines: publishing & printing

### (G-17268)
**ILLINOIS CORN PROCESSING LLC**
1301 S Front St  (61554-4065)
P.O. Box 1069  (61555-1069)
PHONE...............................309 353-3990
Donald Oldham, *President*
Randy Schrick, *President*
Thomas Ray, *Purch Mgr*
Doug Leathers, *QC Mgr*
Donald L Shippy, *Controller*
**EMP:** 75
**SALES:** 200MM
**SALES (corp-wide):** 830.9MM  **Publicly Held**
**SIC:** 2085  Grain alcohol for beverage purposes
**PA:** Seacor Holdings Inc.
2200 Eller Dr
Fort Lauderdale FL 33316
954 523-2200

### (G-17269)
**ILLINOIS OIL MARKETING EQP INC (PA)**
850 Brenkman Dr  (61554-1523)
PHONE...............................309 347-1819
Fax: 309 347-1881
Kevin Lane, *President*
Mark McLaren, *Regional Mgr*
Joyce Hale, *Corp Secy*
Brad Rodgers, *Vice Pres*
John Schumaker, *Vice Pres*
**EMP:** 44  **EST:** 1954
**SQ FT:** 21,000
**SALES:** 22.5MM  **Privately Held**
**WEB:** www.iome.com
**SIC:** 3443  Tanks, standard or custom fabricated: metal plate

### (G-17270)
**INSULCO INC**
825 S 2nd St  (61554-4372)
PHONE...............................309 353-6145
Fax: 309 353-6146
Tom Justus, *Manager*
**EMP:** 10
**SALES (est):** 489.4K  **Privately Held**
**WEB:** www.insulco.biz
**SIC:** 3086  Insulation or cushioning material, foamed plastic

### (G-17271)
**K D L MACHINING INC**
1917 S 2nd St  (61554-5413)
PHONE...............................309 477-3036
Fax: 309 477-3063
Deborah Lutz, *President*
**EMP:** 9  **EST:** 1998
**SQ FT:** 14,000
**SALES:** 400K  **Privately Held**
**WEB:** www.kdlmachining.com
**SIC:** 3599  Machine shop, jobbing & repair

### (G-17272)
**KEGLEY MACHINE CO**
615 Main St  (61554-4305)
PHONE...............................309 346-8914
Chris Kegley, *Owner*
**EMP:** 2
**SALES (est):** 200K  **Privately Held**
**WEB:** www.kegleymachine.com
**SIC:** 3599  Machine shop, jobbing & repair

### (G-17273)
**LINDE NORTH AMERICA INC**
125 Distillery Rd  (61554-4082)
PHONE...............................309 353-9717
John Diller, *Branch Mgr*
**EMP:** 40
**SALES (corp-wide):** 17.9B  **Privately Held**
**WEB:** www.bocsureflow.com
**SIC:** 2813  Carbon dioxide
**HQ:** Linde North America, Inc.
200 Somerset Corporate Bl
Bridgewater NJ 08807
908 464-8100

### (G-17274)
**MGP INGREDIENTS ILLINOIS INC**
1301 S Front St  (61554-4065)
P.O. Box 130, Atchison KS  (66002-0130)
PHONE...............................309 353-3990
Cloud L Cray, *Ch of Bd*
Ladd Seaberg, *President*
Dave Wilbur, *Vice Pres*
Jerry Boo, *Purch Mgr*
Brian Cahill, *Admin Sec*
**EMP:** 190
**SALES:** 210.7K
**SALES (corp-wide):** 318.2MM  **Publicly Held**
**WEB:** www.midwestgrain.com
**SIC:** 2046  2869  2085  2048  Gluten feed; alcohols, industrial: denatured (non-beverage); gin (alcoholic beverage); vodka (alcoholic beverage); prepared feeds
**HQ:** Mgpi Processing, Inc.
100 Commercial St
Atchison KS 66002
913 367-1480

### (G-17275)
**MGPI PROCESSING INC**
Also Called: Midwest Grain Products
1301 S Front St  (61554-4065)
P.O. Box 130, Atchison KS  (66002-0130)
PHONE...............................309 353-3990
Fax: 309 353-4588
Dave Wilbur, *General Mgr*
A Petricol, *Manager*
**EMP:** 150
**SALES (corp-wide):** 318.2MM  **Publicly Held**
**WEB:** www.midwestgrain.com
**SIC:** 2869  2085  2046  Ethyl alcohol, ethanol; ethyl alcohol for beverage purposes; gluten feed; gluten meal
**HQ:** Mgpi Processing, Inc.
100 Commercial St
Atchison KS 66002
913 367-1480

### (G-17276)
**NIKLI FUELS INC**
801 S 2nd St  (61554-4309)
PHONE...............................309 363-2425
**EMP:** 4
**SALES (est):** 295.9K  **Privately Held**
**SIC:** 2869  Fuels

### (G-17277)
**OX PAPERBOARD LLC**
Also Called: Pekin Mill
1525 S 2nd St  (61554-5405)
PHONE...............................309 346-4118
Jeffrey Lyman, *General Mgr*
Steven Smith, *Production*
Katelyn Kegley, *Human Res Mgr*
Katelyn Tassart, *Human Res Mgr*
Kevin J Hayward, *Branch Mgr*
**EMP:** 64
**SALES (corp-wide):** 16.1MM  **Privately Held**
**SIC:** 2631  Paperboard mills; container board
**PA:** Ox Paperboard, Llc
331 Maple Ave
Hanover PA 17331
304 725-2076

### (G-17278)
**PACIFIC ETHANOL CANTON LLC**
1300 S 2nd St  (61554-5402)
P.O. Box 10  (61555-0010)
PHONE...............................309 347-9200
Neil Koehler, *President*
**EMP:** 4
**SALES (est):** 241.6K  **Privately Held**
**SIC:** 2869  Industrial organic chemicals

### (G-17279)
**PACIFIC ETHANOL PEKIN INC**
Also Called: Aventine Rnwble Energy Holdings
1300 S 2nd St  (61554-5402)
PHONE...............................309 347-9200
Fax: 309 346-0742
John Castle, *President*
Mark Beemer, *President*
Ronald H Miller, *President*
Daniel R Trunfio Jr, *COO*
Brian Steenhard, *Vice Pres*
**EMP:** 200
**SALES (est):** 83.3MM
**SALES (corp-wide):** 1.6B  **Publicly Held**
**SIC:** 2869  Alcohols, industrial: denatured (non-beverage)
**HQ:** Aventine Renewable Energy Holdings, Llc
1300 S 2nd St
Pekin IL 61554
309 347-9200

### (G-17280)
**PAL HEALTH TECHNOLOGIES INC (PA)**
Also Called: Podiatry Arts Lab
1805 Riverway Dr  (61554-9314)
PHONE...............................309 347-8785
Fax: 309 477-4456
Jeff Schoenfeld, *Ch of Bd*
Darcy Burke, *Opers Staff*
John Bouchey, *Purchasing*
Cara Sanders, *Manager*
Cynthia Chambers, *Consultant*
▲ **EMP:** 99
**SQ FT:** 40,000
**SALES (est):** 12.2MM  **Privately Held**
**WEB:** www.palhealth.com
**SIC:** 3842  8011  Braces, orthopedic; offices & clinics of medical doctors

### (G-17281)
**PEKIN PAPERBOARD COMPANY LP**
1525 S 2nd St  (61554-5405)
P.O. Box 520  (61555-0520)
PHONE...............................309 346-4118
Larry Fields, *Partner*
**EMP:** 50
**SALES (est):** 11.1MM  **Privately Held**
**SIC:** 2631  Paperboard mills

### (G-17282)
**PEKIN SAND AND GRAVEL LLC**
13018 E Manito Rd  (61554-8586)
PHONE...............................309 347-8917
Derrek Henry,
**EMP:** 7
**SALES (est):** 454.2K  **Privately Held**
**SIC:** 1442  Construction sand & gravel

### (G-17283)
**PRAIRE STATE FLOOR COVERING**
333 South St  (61554-5661)
PHONE...............................309 253-5982
Stephen L Collier, *Owner*
**EMP:** 3
**SALES (est):** 19K  **Privately Held**
**SIC:** 3069  Rubber floor coverings, mats & wallcoverings

### (G-17284)
**PRAXAIR DISTRIBUTION INC**
2100 N 8th St  (61554-1599)
PHONE...............................309 346-3164
Marty Pape, *Manager*
Daniel Barding, *Manager*
Steven C Nellis, *Admin Sec*
**EMP:** 3
**SALES (corp-wide):** 10.5B  **Publicly Held**
**SIC:** 3548  Welding apparatus
**HQ:** Praxair Distribution, Inc.
10 Riverview Dr
Danbury CT 06810
203 837-2000

### (G-17285)
**QUIKRETE COMPANIES INC**
Also Called: Quikrete of Peoria
11150 Garman Rd  (61554-8181)
PHONE...............................309 346-1184
John Trotter, *Prdtn Mgr*
Dean M Cornick, *Manager*
**EMP:** 12  **Privately Held**
**SIC:** 3271  3272  2951  Concrete block & brick; concrete products; asphalt paving mixtures & blocks

**Pekin - Tazewell County (G-17286)** — GEOGRAPHIC SECTION

HQ: The Quikrete Companies Llc
5 Concourse Pkwy Ste 1900
Atlanta GA 30328
404 634-9100

**(G-17286)**
**R L LEWIS INDUSTRIES INC (PA)**
14215 Towerline Rd (61554-8725)
PHONE..................................309 353-7670
Fax: 309 353-1056
Tracy Williams, *President*
Byron Young, *COO*
George Herald, *QA Dir*
Brad Funk, *Manager*
Shelly Nielsen, *Admin Sec*
EMP: 43
SQ FT: 22,000
SALES (est): 6.8MM **Privately Held**
WEB: www.rllewisind.com
SIC: 3599 Machine shop, jobbing & repair

**(G-17287)**
**RIVER CITY CUPCAKE LLC**
1900 Saint Clair Dr (61554-6335)
PHONE..................................309 613-1312
Green Roanna, *Principal*
EMP: 4 EST: 2013
SALES (est): 159.8K **Privately Held**
SIC: 2051 Bread, cake & related products

**(G-17288)**
**SCREEN GRAPHICS**
840 Kennedy Dr (61554-1534)
PHONE..................................309 699-8513
Fax: 309 699-2474
Daniel Jones, *President*
Patricia Jones, *Corp Secy*
Scott Ulrich, *Vice Pres*
Jeff Ulrich, *Manager*
EMP: 4
SQ FT: 3,660
SALES: 200K **Privately Held**
SIC: 2759 2752 2396 Screen printing; commercial printing, lithographic; automotive & apparel trimmings

**(G-17289)**
**SMB TOOLROOM INC**
206 Derby St (61554-5504)
P.O. Box 326 (61555-0326)
PHONE..................................309 353-7396
Fax: 309 353-7396
William Baird, *CEO*
Sherry Baird, *Corp Secy*
EMP: 5
SALES: 150K **Privately Held**
SIC: 3569 Filters

**(G-17290)**
**SUPERIOR INDUSTRIES INC**
14425 Wagonseller Rd (61554-8831)
PHONE..................................309 346-1742
Jarrod Adcock, *Design Engr*
EMP: 1202
SALES (corp-wide): 216.2MM **Privately Held**
SIC: 3535 Conveyors & conveying equipment
PA: Superior Industries, Inc.
315 State Highway 28
Morris MN 56267
320 589-2406

**(G-17291)**
**TAZEWELL MACHINE WORKS INC**
2015 S 2nd St (61554-5465)
P.O. Box 895 (61555-0895)
PHONE..................................309 347-3181
Fax: 309 347-4857
Mack V Cakora, *President*
Alice F Cakora, *Corp Secy*
Daniel J Rose, *Vice Pres*
Diane Reid, *Office Mgr*
Diane Bradley, *Shareholder*
EMP: 134
SQ FT: 104,000
SALES (est): 25.2MM **Privately Held**
WEB: www.tazewellmachine.com
SIC: 3365 3599 Aluminum & aluminum-based alloy castings; machine shop, jobbing & repair

**(G-17292)**
**VARSITY PUBLICATIONS INC**
Also Called: Athletic Fundraising.com
309 Railroad Ave (61554-2732)
PHONE..................................309 353-4570
EMP: 4
SALES (est): 310K **Privately Held**
SIC: 2741 Misc Publishing

**(G-17293)**
**WE-B-PRINT INC**
Also Called: American Speedy Printing
1107 N 8th St (61554-2817)
PHONE..................................309 353-8801
Fax: 309 353-2348
Marvin Eberle, *President*
Terri Hills, *Services*
EMP: 9
SQ FT: 2,000
SALES (est): 1.4MM **Privately Held**
SIC: 2752 7334 2789 Commercial printing, offset; photocopying & duplicating services; bookbinding & related work

**(G-17294)**
**WHEEL WORX NORTH LLC**
200 Hanna Dr (61554-8793)
P.O. Box 641 (61555-0641)
PHONE..................................309 346-3535
Gary Schoenfeldt, *President*
Justin Schoefeldt, *Vice Pres*
Jerry Solt, *Vice Pres*
EMP: 2
SALES (est): 359.5K **Privately Held**
SIC: 3312 Wheels

**(G-17295)**
**WINPAK HEAT SEAL CORP**
1821 Riverway Dr (61554-9309)
PHONE..................................309 477-6600
Bruce Hoerr, *Manager*
Gale Abernathy, *Manager*
EMP: 53
SALES (corp-wide): 822.5MM **Privately Held**
SIC: 3497 Metal foil & leaf
HQ: Emballages Winpak Heat Seal Inc, Les
21919 Ch Dumberry
Vaudreuil-Dorion QC J7V 8
450 424-0191

**(G-17296)**
**WOODWORKERS SHOP INC (PA)**
Also Called: Pekin Hardwood Lumber Co.
13587 E Manito Rd (61554-8593)
P.O. Box 277 (61555-0277)
PHONE..................................309 347-5111
Fax: 309 347-1471
Rick A Butler, *Principal*
Linda Foster, *Controller*
Scott Barbault, *Branch Mgr*
Jason Snyder, *Manager*
▲ EMP: 20 EST: 1935
SALES (est): 4.4MM **Privately Held**
WEB: www.pekinhardwood.com
SIC: 2426 5031 5211 Lumber, hardwood dimension; lumber: rough, dressed & finished; lumber products

---

## Peoria
### Peoria County

**(G-17297)**
**A LUCAS & SONS**
1328 Sw Washington St (61602-1798)
PHONE..................................309 673-8547
Fax: 309 673-7213
Margaret A Hanley, *President*
John P Hanley, *President*
Terry Machetti, *Admin Sec*
EMP: 20
SALES (est): 5.8MM **Privately Held**
SIC: 3441 Fabricated structural metal

**(G-17298)**
**A MILLER & CO**
Also Called: Allied Iron & Steel
Foot Of Clark St (61607)
PHONE..................................309 637-7756
Fax: 309 637-6502
John Miller, *Manager*
EMP: 15
SALES (corp-wide): 5.4MM **Privately Held**
SIC: 5093 3341 Scrap & waste materials; secondary nonferrous metals
PA: A. Miller & Co.
1612 Sw Adams St
Peoria IL 61602
309 674-1101

**(G-17299)**
**AAA GALVANIZING - PEORIA INC**
6718 W Plank Rd Ste 2 (61604-7218)
PHONE..................................309 697-4100
Fax: 309 697-8100
Sean Eogan, *President*
Mark Johnson, *Sales Mgr*
Sheila Buhl, *Manager*
▲ EMP: 40
SALES (est): 4.9MM
SALES (corp-wide): 858.9MM **Publicly Held**
WEB: www.aztecgalvanizing.com
SIC: 3479 Galvanizing of iron, steel or end-formed products
PA: Azz Inc.
3100 W 7th St Ste 500
Fort Worth TX 76107
817 810-0095

**(G-17300)**
**ACADEMY SCREENPRINTING AWARDS**
Also Called: Academy of Awards II
1316 E War Memorial Dr (61614-7725)
PHONE..................................309 686-0026
Fax: 309 686-0621
Dolores Hoop, *Owner*
Debbie Hallar, *Manager*
EMP: 6
SQ FT: 7,000
SALES (est): 615.3K **Privately Held**
SIC: 5999 5699 5947 3993 Trophies & plaques; T-shirts, custom printed; gift shop; signs, not made in custom sign painting shops

**(G-17301)**
**ACEVA LLC**
624 W Glen Ave (61614-4831)
PHONE..................................201 978-7928
Cristina Esposito, *Principal*
EMP: 5
SALES (est): 652.6K **Privately Held**
SIC: 2834 Pharmaceutical preparations

**(G-17302)**
**ADAMS OUTDOOR ADVG LTD PARTNR**
Also Called: Adams Outdoor Advg Peoria
911 Sw Adams St (61602-1608)
PHONE..................................309 692-2482
Fax: 309 692-8452
Mark Dunlap, *Controller*
Chris Koller, *Sales Mgr*
Amy McCaw, *Sales Staff*
Kortney Mueller, *Office Mgr*
Brad Mitchell, *Manager*
EMP: 20
SALES (corp-wide): 49.4MM **Privately Held**
WEB: www.adamsoutdoor.com
SIC: 7312 3993 Outdoor advertising services; signs & advertising specialties
PA: Adams Outdoor Advertising Limited Partnership
500 Colonial Center Pkwy
Roswell GA 30076
770 333-0399

**(G-17303)**
**AG-DEFENSE SYSTEMS INC**
Also Called: ADS
801 W Main St Ste A118 (61606-1877)
PHONE..................................309 495-7258
Ken Owen, *CEO*
Beth S Turnbull-Dyer, *President*
Rex Dyer, *Principal*
EMP: 2
SALES (est): 284.7K **Privately Held**
SIC: 3826 Analytical instruments

**(G-17304)**
**AGRISCIENCE INC**
5115 N Martha St (61614-4946)
PHONE..................................212 365-4214
Robert Littmann, *Principal*
Kevin Riley, *Principal*
EMP: 3 EST: 2015
SALES (est): 183.6K **Privately Held**
SIC: 2879 4953 8711 Agricultural chemicals; recycling, waste materials; chemical engineering

**(G-17305)**
**AIR VENT INC**
7700 N Harker Dr Ste B (61615-5807)
PHONE..................................309 692-6969
Fax: 309 689-6305
Shelly Doubet, *Branch Mgr*
EMP: 8
SALES (corp-wide): 1B **Publicly Held**
WEB: www.airvent.com
SIC: 3444 Ventilators, sheet metal
HQ: Air Vent Inc.
4117 Pinnacle Point Dr # 400
Dallas TX 75211
800 247-8368

**(G-17306)**
**ALCAST COMPANY (PA)**
8821 N University St (61615-1674)
PHONE..................................309 691-5513
Fax: 309 691-9031
Steve Wessels, *President*
Brian A Holt, *Vice Pres*
Viston Batey, *Plant Mgr*
Jayson Campbell, *Safety Mgr*
Andrew Melendy, *VP Sales*
▲ EMP: 79
SQ FT: 42,688
SALES: 25.6MM **Privately Held**
WEB: www.alcastcompany.com
SIC: 3365 Aluminum & aluminum-based alloy castings

**(G-17307)**
**ALCAST COMPANY**
8820 N Pioneer Rd (61615-1520)
PHONE..................................309 691-5513
Steve Wessels, *President*
Tim Sommer, *Engineer*
EMP: 71
SALES (corp-wide): 25.6MM **Privately Held**
SIC: 3365 Aluminum & aluminum-based alloy castings
PA: Alcast Company
8821 N University St
Peoria IL 61615
309 691-5513

**(G-17308)**
**APANA INC**
7201 N Drake Ct (61615-9291)
PHONE..................................309 303-4007
Diana Burritt, *Director*
EMP: 4
SALES (est): 204.9K **Privately Held**
SIC: 3845 Ultrasonic scanning devices, medical

**(G-17309)**
**ARCHER-DANIELS-MIDLAND COMPANY**
Also Called: ADM
1 Edmund St (61602-1775)
P.O. Box 99, Dunlap (61525-0099)
PHONE..................................309 673-7828
Fax: 309 673-7324
Gary Alsbury, *Plant Mgr*
Nick Lauer, *Mfg Staff*
Jana Thomas, *Purchasing*
Mark Resnik, *Manager*
Kim Bean, *Manager*
EMP: 225
SALES (corp-wide): 62.3B **Publicly Held**
WEB: www.admworld.com
SIC: 2869 2041 Alcohols, non-beverage; flour & other grain mill products
PA: Archer-Daniels-Midland Company
77 W Wacker Dr Ste 4600
Chicago IL 60601
312 634-8100

# GEOGRAPHIC SECTION

Peoria - Peoria County (G-17334)

**(G-17310)**
**ARMITAGE MACHINE CO INC**
6035 Washington St (61607-2501)
P.O. Box 1472 (61655-1472)
PHONE.................................309 697-9050
David A Armitage, *President*
Tom Hyde, *Superintendent*
Ted Ewald, *Purch Agent*
Rich Terrian, *Manager*
**EMP:** 10 **EST:** 1969
**SQ FT:** 22,000
**SALES (est):** 1.4MM **Privately Held**
**SIC: 3599** Machine shop, jobbing & repair

**(G-17311)**
**ARVENS TECHNOLOGY INC**
801 W Main St (61606-1877)
PHONE.................................650 776-5443
Sudhir Seth, *President*
**EMP:** 3
**SALES (est):** 202K **Privately Held**
**SIC: 2869** Industrial organic chemicals

**(G-17312)**
**B & M AUTOMOTIVE**
1811 S Oakwood Ave (61605-2649)
PHONE.................................309 637-4977
Marcia A Donahue, *Partner*
Bill Donahue, *Partner*
**EMP:** 3
**SALES (est):** 189K **Privately Held**
**SIC: 3519** Marine engines

**(G-17313)**
**BAKER DRAPERY CORPORATION**
Also Called: Snap-A-Pleat Drapery System
5516 N Big Hollow Rd (61615-1995)
PHONE.................................309 691-3295
Fax: 309 691-3296
Chad Baker Jr, *President*
Larry Vicary, *Prdtn Mgr*
**EMP:** 2
**SQ FT:** 16,000
**SALES (est):** 270K **Privately Held**
**SIC: 5023** 3429 2591 2391 Draperies; manufactured hardware (general); drapery hardware & blinds & shades; curtains & draperies

**(G-17314)**
**BARNES & NOBLE COLLEGE**
Also Called: Bradley University Bookstore
830 N Elmwood Ave (61606-1176)
PHONE.................................309 677-2320
Fax: 309 677-3709
Paul Kroenke, *Manager*
**EMP:** 20
**SQ FT:** 800
**SALES (corp-wide):** 1.8B **Publicly Held**
**WEB:** www.bkstore.com
**SIC: 5942** 2395 Book stores; embroidery & art needlework
**HQ:** Barnes & Noble College Booksellers, Llc
120 Mountainview Blvd A
Basking Ridge NJ 07920
908 991-2665

**(G-17315)**
**BELLA ELEVATOR LLC**
10000 N Galena Rd (61615-9452)
PHONE.................................410 685-0344
Richard A Crane, *Mng Member*
Richard Crane, *Mng Member*
Stefani Gries,
Kevin Heyungs,
Paul B Luber,
▲ **EMP:** 17
**SQ FT:** 10,000
**SALES (est):** 8.9MM **Privately Held**
**SIC: 3534** Elevators & moving stairways; elevators & equipment

**(G-17316)**
**BENCHMARK CABINETS & MLLWK INC**
5913 W Plank Rd (61604-5226)
PHONE.................................309 697-5855
Fax: 309 697-5857
Joseph R Hart, *President*
Deanna McMurtry, *Office Mgr*
**EMP:** 20
**SALES (est):** 2.8MM **Privately Held**
**SIC: 2434** 2431 5712 Wood kitchen cabinets; brackets, wood; cabinet work, custom

**(G-17317)**
**BETTER EARTH PREMIUM COMPOST**
1400 S Cameron Ln (61607-9331)
PHONE.................................309 697-0963
Paul Rosebohm, *Owner*
Paul Rosbohnm, *Principal*
**EMP:** 6
**SALES (est):** 594.7K **Privately Held**
**SIC: 2875** 2611 Compost; pulp manufactured from waste or recycled paper

**(G-17318)**
**BIDDISON AUTOBODY**
3100 W Farmington Rd A (61604-4887)
PHONE.................................309 673-6277
Harry Biddison, *Owner*
**EMP:** 4 **EST:** 2008
**SALES (est):** 216.4K **Privately Held**
**SIC: 7532** 3713 Paint shop, automotive; truck & bus bodies

**(G-17319)**
**BOX MANUFACTURING INC**
201 Spring St (61603-7002)
PHONE.................................309 637-6228
Fax: 309 637-1031
Don Allen, *Principal*
Tim Streit, *Principal*
**EMP:** 5
**SQ FT:** 10,000
**SALES (est):** 200K **Privately Held**
**SIC: 2653** Boxes, corrugated: made from purchased materials

**(G-17320)**
**BUILDERS WAREHOUSE INC**
812 Sw Washington St (61602-1627)
PHONE.................................309 672-1760
Fax: 309 672-1767
Dan Holbrock, *President*
John Coker, *Manager*
▲ **EMP:** 3
**SALES (est):** 645K **Privately Held**
**SIC: 2426** Hardwood dimension & flooring mills

**(G-17321)**
**CALIHAN PORK PROCESSORS INC**
1 South St (61602-1851)
P.O. Box 1155 (61653-1155)
PHONE.................................309 674-9175
Fax: 309 674-3003
Tom Landon, *CEO*
Louis M Landon, *President*
Al Schmid, *CFO*
Kathleen J Landon, *Treasurer*
**EMP:** 60
**SQ FT:** 26,000
**SALES (est):** 9.5MM **Privately Held**
**WEB:** www.calihanpork.com
**SIC: 2011** 5147 Meat packing plants; pork products from pork slaughtered on site; meats & meat products

**(G-17322)**
**CAPITOL IMPRESSIONS INC**
1622 W Moss Ave (61606-1641)
PHONE.................................309 633-1400
Mark Matuszak, *President*
Tracey Heine, *Vice Pres*
**EMP:** 23
**SQ FT:** 12,000
**SALES (est):** 2.7MM **Privately Held**
**WEB:** www.cimpress.com
**SIC: 2752** 2759 5943 2789 Commercial printing, offset; embossing on paper; office forms & supplies; bookbinding & related work

**(G-17323)**
**CAST TECHNOLOGIES INC (PA)**
1100 Sw Washington St (61602-1633)
P.O. Box 959 (61653-0959)
PHONE.................................309 676-1715
Mike McLaughlin, *President*
Clay D Canterbury, *President*
William J Carman, *CFO*
**EMP:** 128
**SQ FT:** 148,000
**SALES (est):** 18.4MM **Privately Held**
**WEB:** www.casttechnologies.net
**SIC: 3365** 3366 Aluminum foundries; brass foundry

**(G-17324)**
**CATERPILLAR BRAZIL LLC (HQ)**
100 Ne Adams St (61629-0002)
PHONE.................................309 675-1000
Luiz Carlos Calil, *Principal*
Douglas Vieira, *Buyer*
▼ **EMP:** 1
**SALES (est):** 287.2MM
**SALES (corp-wide):** 38.5B **Publicly Held**
**SIC: 3523** Farm machinery & equipment
**PA:** Caterpillar Inc.
100 Ne Adams St
Peoria IL 61629
309 675-1000

**(G-17325)**
**CATERPILLAR GB LLC**
100 Ne Adams St (61629-0002)
PHONE.................................309 675-1000
David Thomas, *CEO*
**EMP:** 5
**SALES (est):** 434.3K
**SALES (corp-wide):** 38.5B **Publicly Held**
**WEB:** www.cat.com
**SIC: 3519** Internal combustion engines
**PA:** Caterpillar Inc.
100 Ne Adams St
Peoria IL 61629
309 675-1000

**(G-17326)**
**CATERPILLAR INC (PA)**
100 Ne Adams St (61629-0002)
PHONE.................................309 675-1000
Fax: 309 675-1768
D James Umpleby III, *CEO*
Douglas R Oberhelman, *Ch of Bd*
Robert B Charter, *President*
Bob De Lange, *President*
Bradley M Halverson, *President*
◆ **EMP:** 1176
**SALES:** 38.5B **Publicly Held**
**WEB:** www.cat.com
**SIC: 3531** 3519 3511 6531 Construction machinery; engines, diesel & semi-diesel or dual-fuel; gasoline engines; gas turbine generator set units, complete; hydraulic turbine generator set units, complete; fiduciary, real estate; accident insurance carriers; fire, marine & casualty insurance: stock

**(G-17327)**
**CATERPILLAR INC**
7022 W Middle Rd (61607-8446)
PHONE.................................309 675-5681
Mike Quimerson, *Manager*
Al Miller, *Manager*
**EMP:** 20
**SALES (corp-wide):** 38.5B **Publicly Held**
**WEB:** www.cat.com
**SIC: 3531** Construction machinery
**PA:** Caterpillar Inc.
100 Ne Adams St
Peoria IL 61629
309 675-1000

**(G-17328)**
**CATERPILLAR INC**
501 Sw Jefferson Ave (61605-2500)
PHONE.................................888 614-4328
Evan Jacobson, *Engineer*
Parag Mehresh, *Senior Engr*
Sairam Thiagarajan, *Senior Engr*
Benjamin Holt, *Branch Mgr*
**EMP:** 360
**SALES (corp-wide):** 38.5B **Publicly Held**
**SIC: 3531** 3519 3511 6531 Construction machinery; engines, diesel & semi-diesel or dual-fuel; gasoline engines; gas turbine generator set units, complete; hydraulic turbine generator set units, complete; fiduciary, real estate; accident insurance carriers; fire, marine & casualty insurance: stock
**PA:** Caterpillar Inc.
100 Ne Adams St
Peoria IL 61629
309 675-1000

**(G-17329)**
**CATERPILLAR INC**
300 Hamilton Blvd Ste 300 (61602-1234)
PHONE.................................309 675-4408
Jorge Medina, *Accounting Mgr*
Chris Carseman, *Manager*
**EMP:** 5
**SALES (corp-wide):** 38.5B **Publicly Held**
**WEB:** www.cat.com
**SIC: 3462** Construction or mining equipment forgings, ferrous
**PA:** Caterpillar Inc.
100 Ne Adams St
Peoria IL 61629
309 675-1000

**(G-17330)**
**CATERPILLAR INC**
1335 Sw Washington St (61602-1705)
PHONE.................................309 675-1000
Fax: 309 675-5696
Bob Oliverius, *Manager*
**EMP:** 50
**SALES (corp-wide):** 38.5B **Publicly Held**
**WEB:** www.cat.com
**SIC: 3531** Construction machinery
**PA:** Caterpillar Inc.
100 Ne Adams St
Peoria IL 61629
309 675-1000

**(G-17331)**
**CATERPILLAR INC**
330 Sw Washington St (61602-1406)
PHONE.................................309 578-8250
**EMP:** 355
**SALES (corp-wide):** 38.5B **Publicly Held**
**WEB:** www.cat.com
**SIC: 3531** Construction machinery
**PA:** Caterpillar Inc.
100 Ne Adams St
Peoria IL 61629
309 675-1000

**(G-17332)**
**CATERPILLAR INC**
330 Sw Adams St (61602-1527)
PHONE.................................309 675-1000
Steve Monday, *Analyst*
**EMP:** 355
**SALES (corp-wide):** 38.5B **Publicly Held**
**WEB:** www.cat.com
**SIC: 3531** Construction machinery
**PA:** Caterpillar Inc.
100 Ne Adams St
Peoria IL 61629
309 675-1000

**(G-17333)**
**CATERPILLAR INC**
2400 Sw Washington St (61602-1846)
PHONE.................................309 675-6590
**EMP:** 355
**SALES (corp-wide):** 38.5B **Publicly Held**
**SIC: 3531** 3519 3511 6153 Construction machinery; tractors, crawler; tractors, construction; loaders, shovel: self-propelled; engines, diesel & semi-diesel or dual-fuel; gasoline engines; gas turbine generator set units, complete; hydraulic turbine generator set units, complete; mercantile financing; accident insurance carriers; fire, marine & casualty insurance: stock
**PA:** Caterpillar Inc.
100 Ne Adams St
Peoria IL 61629
309 675-1000

**(G-17334)**
**CATERPILLAR LUXEMBOURG LLC (HQ)**
100 Ne Adams St (61629-0002)
PHONE.................................309 675-1000
▲ **EMP:** 4 **EST:** 2011
**SALES (est):** 1.8MM
**SALES (corp-wide):** 38.5B **Publicly Held**
**SIC: 3531** Construction machinery
**PA:** Caterpillar Inc.
100 Ne Adams St
Peoria IL 61629
309 675-1000

## Peoria - Peoria County (G-17335) — GEOGRAPHIC SECTION

**(G-17335)**
**CATERPILLAR POWER SYSTEMS**
100 Ne Adams St (61629-0002)
PHONE .................. 309 675-1000
Ringo Siu Keung Chow, *President*
Jerome Vannitamby, *Business Mgr*
Sean P Leuba, *Admin Sec*
**EMP:** 9
**SALES (est):** 2.2MM
**SALES (corp-wide):** 38.5B **Publicly Held**
**WEB:** www.cat.com
**SIC:** 3531 Construction machinery
**PA:** Caterpillar Inc.
100 Ne Adams St
Peoria IL 61629
309 675-1000

**(G-17336)**
**CENTRAL ILLINOIS BUS PUBLS INC**
5005 N Glen Park Place Rd (61614-4677)
PHONE .................. 309 683-3060
Janet Wright, *CEO*
Michael Gudat, *VP Sales*
Jessica Moroz, *Manager*
Jan Benson Wright, *IT/INT Sup*
**EMP:** 5 **EST:** 1989
**SQ FT:** 2,000
**SALES (est):** 800K **Privately Held**
**WEB:** www.peoriamagazines.com
**SIC:** 2721 Magazines: publishing & printing

**(G-17337)**
**CENTRAL ILLINOIS HOMES GUIDE**
7307 N Willow Lake Ct (61614-8227)
PHONE .................. 309 688-6419
Nancy Koch, *President*
▲ **EMP:** 7
**SALES (est):** 420K **Privately Held**
**WEB:** www.centralillinoishomesguide.com
**SIC:** 2721 2741 Magazines: publishing only, not printed on site; miscellaneous publishing

**(G-17338)**
**CENTRAL ILLINOIS SCALE CO**
6000 Washington St Ste 2 (61607-2579)
P.O. Box 4189 (61607-0189)
PHONE .................. 309 697-0033
Howard Schuette, *President*
**EMP:** 3
**SALES (corp-wide):** 5.3MM **Privately Held**
**SIC:** 3545 Scales, measuring (machinists' precision tools)
**PA:** Central Illinois Scale Co.
2560 Parkway Ct
Decatur IL 62526
217 428-0923

**(G-17339)**
**CENTRAL RC HOBBIES**
Peoria Hts (61616)
PHONE .................. 309 686-8004
Rick Jacobson, *Owner*
**EMP:** 8
**SALES (est):** 687K **Privately Held**
**SIC:** 3944 5092 5945 Board games, puzzles & models, except electronic; hobby supplies; hobbies; toys & games

**(G-17340)**
**CERTIFIED HEAT TREATING CO**
8917 N University St (61615-1637)
P.O. Box 5609 (61601-5609)
PHONE .................. 309 693-7711
**Fax:** 309 693-0502
Joseph P O'Brien, *President*
Steven Matthew, *General Mgr*
Mary L Flanagan, *Corp Secy*
**EMP:** 18
**SQ FT:** 15,000
**SALES (est):** 3.6MM **Privately Held**
**SIC:** 3398 Metal heat treating

**(G-17341)**
**CHESTER WHITE SWINE RCORD ASSN**
6320 N Sheridan Rd Ste A (61614-3053)
P.O. Box 9758 (61612-9758)
PHONE .................. 309 691-0151
**Fax:** 309 691-0168
Jack Wall, *President*
**EMP:** 3
**SQ FT:** 100
**SALES (est):** 282K **Privately Held**
**SIC:** 0751 2721 8611 Pedigree record services, livestock; magazines: publishing only, not printed on site; business associations

**(G-17342)**
**CISCO HEATING & COOLING**
3304 W Linda Ln (61605-2639)
PHONE .................. 309 637-6809
Harry Cisco, *Owner*
Mary Cisco, *Co-Owner*
**EMP:** 4
**SALES (est):** 277K **Privately Held**
**SIC:** 3585 Refrigeration & heating equipment

**(G-17343)**
**CITYBLUE TECHNOLOGIES LLC (PA)**
404 Sw Adams St (61602-1520)
P.O. Box 1169 (61653-1169)
PHONE .................. 309 676-1701
**Fax:** 309 676-1701
Thomas Jacobson, *CFO*
Carolyn McWethy, *Accounts Mgr*
Nathan Peters, *Technology*
Michael McConnell,
**EMP:** 10
**SQ FT:** 13,000
**SALES (est):** 3.7MM **Privately Held**
**WEB:** www.citybluetechnologies.com
**SIC:** 2759 5734 Commercial printing; printers & plotters: computers

**(G-17344)**
**COBATCO INC**
1215 Ne Adams St (61603-4005)
PHONE .................. 309 676-2663
**Fax:** 309 676-2667
Donald O Stephens, *President*
Amy Stephens, *Corp Secy*
Brian Fiddes, *Natl Sales Mgr*
◆ **EMP:** 19
**SQ FT:** 11,000
**SALES (est):** 4.7MM **Privately Held**
**WEB:** www.cobatco.com
**SIC:** 3556 Food products machinery

**(G-17345)**
**COMPONENTA USA LLC**
8515 N University St (61615-1629)
PHONE .................. 309 691-7000
Heikki Lehtonen, *Principal*
**EMP:** 6
**SALES (est):** 791.2K **Privately Held**
**SIC:** 3325 Steel foundries

**(G-17346)**
**CONSOLIDATED PAVING INC**
6918 N Galena Rd (61614-3112)
PHONE .................. 309 693-3505
**EMP:** 4
**SALES:** 750K **Privately Held**
**WEB:** www.consolidatedpaving.com
**SIC:** 2951 Asphalt paving mixtures & blocks

**(G-17347)**
**CUB FOODS INC**
5001 N Big Hollow Rd # 5 (61615-3540)
PHONE .................. 309 689-0140
**Fax:** 309 689-0150
Scott Presuhn, *Manager*
**EMP:** 160
**SQ FT:** 40,000
**SALES (corp-wide):** 12.4B **Publicly Held**
**SIC:** 5411 5421 5921 5992 Supermarkets; meat markets, including freezer provisioners; liquor stores; florists; bread, cake & related products
**HQ:** Cub Foods, Inc
421 3rd St S
Stillwater MN 55082
651 439-7200

**(G-17348)**
**DENTAL SEALANTS & MORE**
214 W Wolf Rd (61614-2156)
PHONE .................. 309 692-6435
Clifford A Brown, *Principal*
**EMP:** 5
**SALES (est):** 489.6K **Privately Held**
**SIC:** 2891 Sealants

**(G-17349)**
**DESIGN PLUS INDUSTRIES INC (PA)**
6311 W Development Dr (61604-5283)
PHONE .................. 309 697-9778
**Fax:** 309 697-9686
Michael Seibert, *President*
Laurie Dean, *Vice Pres*
Kim Stull, *Controller*
Stacy Marcille, *Office Mgr*
▲ **EMP:** 7
**SALES (est):** 2.5MM **Privately Held**
**WEB:** www.designplusgranite.com
**SIC:** 3999 1799 Coin-operated amusement machines; counter top installation

**(G-17350)**
**DRUMHELLER BAG CORPORATION**
1114 Sw Adams St (61602-1613)
PHONE .................. 309 676-1006
David V Drumheller, *President*
Jackie Lampkin, *Treasurer*
Amy Pasdik, *Accounts Mgr*
**EMP:** 52
**SQ FT:** 4,500
**SALES (est):** 11.9MM **Privately Held**
**SIC:** 2673 Bags: plastic, laminated & coated

**(G-17351)**
**DUST PATROL INC**
Also Called: D.P. Filters
2706 Sw Washington St (61602-1956)
PHONE .................. 309 676-1161
**Fax:** 309 676-5211
Sean Donavan, *Opers Staff*
Jerry Swanson, *Branch Mgr*
**EMP:** 9
**SALES (corp-wide):** 5.2MM **Privately Held**
**WEB:** www.dpsystemsllc.com
**SIC:** 5075 3564 Dust collecting equipment; blowers & fans
**PA:** Dust Patrol, Inc.
1041 W Republic Dr
Addison IL 60101
630 543-5221

**(G-17352)**
**EG GROUP INC**
8703 N University St F (61615-1659)
PHONE .................. 309 692-0968
**Fax:** 309 689-0600
James E Thrush, *President*
**EMP:** 5
**SQ FT:** 2,000
**SALES (est):** 466.1K **Privately Held**
**SIC:** 3494 3822 3498 Valves & pipe fittings; auto controls regulating residntl & coml environmt & applncs; fabricated pipe & fittings

**(G-17353)**
**EHS SOLUTIONS LLC**
1530 W Altorfer Dr (61615-1921)
PHONE .................. 309 282-9121
Robert Herrmann, *Mng Member*
Miranda Gudeman, *Admin Sec*
Nathan Steffen,
**EMP:** 8
**SALES (est):** 2.4MM **Privately Held**
**SIC:** 2655 Fiber cans, drums & containers

**(G-17354)**
**ELISE S ALLEN**
Also Called: Traveler Printing
1600 Mrtn Lthr Kng Jr Dr (61605-1816)
PHONE .................. 309 673-2613
Elise S Allen, *Owner*
**EMP:** 3
**SALES (est):** 188.3K **Privately Held**
**SIC:** 2752 2711 Commercial printing, lithographic; newspapers

**(G-17355)**
**ELITE PUBLISHING AND DESIGN**
616 Abington St (61603-3522)
PHONE .................. 888 237-8119
Nicole Alksnis, *President*
**EMP:** 4
**SALES (est):** 249.3K **Privately Held**
**SIC:** 2741 Miscellaneous publishing

**(G-17356)**
**EM SMITH & CO**
826 W Detweiller Dr (61615-2183)
PHONE .................. 309 691-6812
**Fax:** 309 691-8883
Jack Cook, *President*
Dale Swearingen, *Exec VP*
Brian Davidson, *Treasurer*
Matt Chatwell, *Office Mgr*
Jamie Anderson, *Manager*
**EMP:** 26
**SQ FT:** 40,000
**SALES (est):** 4.2MM **Privately Held**
**SIC:** 3599 Machine shop, jobbing & repair

**(G-17357)**
**EMACK & BOLIOS**
4534 N Prospect Rd (61616-6500)
PHONE .................. 309 682-3530
**EMP:** 8
**SALES (est):** 508.1K **Privately Held**
**SIC:** 2051 Cakes, bakery: except frozen

**(G-17358)**
**EVERYTHING XCLUSIVE**
4010 N Brandywine Dr (61614-6866)
PHONE .................. 309 370-7450
La'tisha Hughes, *Owner*
**EMP:** 3
**SALES (est):** 101.9K **Privately Held**
**SIC:** 2791 Typesetting

**(G-17359)**
**FEDEX OFFICE & PRINT SVCS INC**
3465 N University St (61604-1322)
PHONE .................. 309 685-4093
Larry Richards, *Sales Executive*
Nabarun Dasgupta, *Manager*
Deep Dasgupta, *Manager*
**EMP:** 24
**SALES (corp-wide):** 50.3B **Publicly Held**
**WEB:** www.kinkos.com
**SIC:** 7334 3993 2789 2759 Photocopying & duplicating services; signs & advertising specialties; bookbinding & related work; commercial printing; coated & laminated paper; typesetting
**HQ:** Fedex Office And Print Services, Inc.
7900 Legacy Dr
Plano TX 75024
214 550-7000

**(G-17360)**
**FELDE TOOL & MACHINE CO INC**
2324 W Altorfer Dr (61615-1890)
PHONE .................. 309 692-5870
**Fax:** 309 692-9792
Heinrich Felde, *President*
Vicky Vanbruwaene, *Office Mgr*
**EMP:** 11
**SQ FT:** 6,250
**SALES (est):** 1.5MM **Privately Held**
**WEB:** www.hfeldemachining.com
**SIC:** 3599 7692 Machine shop, jobbing & repair; welding repair

**(G-17361)**
**FIREFLY INTERNATIONAL ENRGY CO (PA)**
6533 N Galena Rd (61614-3120)
PHONE .................. 781 937-0619
Rajendra Patel, *President*
Macduff Robert, *Manager*
Kurt Kelly, *CTO*
**EMP:** 1 **EST:** 2010
**SQ FT:** 54,000
**SALES:** 1MM **Privately Held**
**SIC:** 8731 3691 Commercial physical research; storage batteries

**(G-17362)**
**FISKARS BRANDS INC**
Nelson
1 Sprinkler Ln (61615-9544)
PHONE .................. 800 635-7668
**EMP:** 14
**SALES (corp-wide):** 1.2B **Privately Held**
**SIC:** 3432 Lawn hose nozzles & sprinklers
**HQ:** Fiskars Brands, Inc.
7800 Discovery Dr
Middleton WI 53562
608 259-1649

▲ = Import ▼ = Export
◆ = Import/Export

# GEOGRAPHIC SECTION

Peoria - Peoria County (G-17389)

**(G-17363)**
**FISKARS BRANDS INC**
Gilmour
1 Sprinkler Ln (61615-9544)
PHONE.................................309 690-2200
Charles L Beal, *Principal*
Brett Henry, *Principal*
Toby Burke, *Vice Pres*
Ron Kerger, *Vice Pres*
Linda Knox, *Vice Pres*
**EMP:** 375
**SALES (corp-wide):** 1.2B **Privately Held**
**WEB:** www.vacorp.com
**SIC:** 3425 3524 3432 Saw blades & handsaws; lawn & garden equipment; plumbing fixture fittings & trim
**HQ:** Fiskars Brands, Inc.
7800 Discovery Dr
Middleton WI 53562
608 259-1649

**(G-17364)**
**FOREMOST ELECTRIC & TRANSM INC (PA)**
Also Called: Foremost Industrial Tech
6518 W Plank Rd (61604-5239)
PHONE.................................309 699-2200
Fax: 309 699-2289
Michael C Moran, *President*
Jeff Dahnsen, *General Mgr*
April Bright, *CFO*
John Humphrey, *Treasurer*
Suzanne Schadgett, *Controller*
**EMP:** 20
**SQ FT:** 5,500
**SALES (est):** 8.5MM **Privately Held**
**WEB:** www.foremost-fit.com
**SIC:** 5063 7694 Motors, electric; power transmission equipment, electric; electric motor repair

**(G-17365)**
**FORMS DESIGN PLUS COLEMAN PRTG**
1105 E War Memorial Dr # 1 (61616-7772)
PHONE.................................309 685-6000
Fax: 309 685-2572
Lawrence J Dunn, *President*
Debra Dunn, *Corp Secy*
**EMP:** 4
**SQ FT:** 4,100
**SALES:** 980K **Privately Held**
**SIC:** 5112 2752 2789 Business forms; commercial printing, offset; bookbinding & related work

**(G-17366)**
**FREDMAN BROS FURNITURE CO INC**
Also Called: Glideaway Bed Carriage Mf
908 Sw Washington St (61602-1629)
PHONE.................................309 674-2011
Fax: 309 674-0407
Carmi Fredman, *President*
Herbert Fredman, *Project Mgr*
Zalman Stein, *Director*
**EMP:** 50
**SALES (corp-wide):** 55.1MM **Privately Held**
**WEB:** www.glideaway.com
**SIC:** 2515 2511 Sleep furniture; wood household furniture
**PA:** Fredman Bros. Furniture Company, Inc.
8226 Lackland Rd
Saint Louis MO 63114
314 426-3999

**(G-17367)**
**FREDRICK HOY**
5405 N Knoxville Ave Fl 1 (61614-5079)
PHONE.................................309 691-4410
Frederick Hoy, *Principal*
**EMP:** 3
**SALES (est):** 163.8K **Privately Held**
**SIC:** 3845 Surgical support systems: heart-lung machine, exc. iron lung

**(G-17368)**
**GATEHOUSE MEDIA ILL HOLDINGS**
Also Called: Money Stretcher
1 News Plz (61643-0001)
PHONE.................................585 598-0030
Fax: 618 268-4325
James Bond, *Principal*
Janette Bond, *Principal*
Garrett J Cummings,
**EMP:** 9
**SALES:** 1.2MM
**SALES (corp-wide):** 1.2B **Publicly Held**
**SIC:** 2711 2741 Newspapers: publishing only, not printed on site; miscellaneous publishing
**PA:** New Media Investment Group Inc.
1345 Avenue Of The Americ
New York NY 10105
212 479-3160

**(G-17369)**
**GEEBEES INC**
Also Called: Fastsigns
3024 N University St (61604-2614)
PHONE.................................309 682-5300
Fax: 309 682-5397
Frank Smith, *President*
Scott Turk, *Executive*
**EMP:** 5
**SQ FT:** 2,500
**SALES (est):** 499.6K **Privately Held**
**SIC:** 3993 5999 Signs & advertising specialties; banners, flags, decals & posters

**(G-17370)**
**GENACC LLC**
60 State St Ste 101 (61602-5153)
PHONE.................................309 253-9034
James H Richmond, *Mng Member*
Eric Samuel Delgado,
Jill Rene Donahue,
Scott Thomas Gall,
Zachary Vernon Lloyd Holcomb,
**EMP:** 8
**SALES (est):** 850K **Privately Held**
**SIC:** 3463 Engine or turbine forgings, nonferrous

**(G-17371)**
**GEO J ROTHAN CO**
1200 W Johnson St (61605-2080)
PHONE.................................309 674-5189
Fax: 309 674-9615
George J Rothan Jr, *President*
Jim McColloch, *Bookkeeper*
Christopher H Rothan, *Admin Sec*
**EMP:** 20 **EST:** 1873
**SQ FT:** 4,000
**SALES (est):** 3.9MM **Privately Held**
**SIC:** 2431 Millwork

**(G-17372)**
**GETZ FIRE EQUIPMENT CO**
Also Called: Getz Industrial
1440 Sw Jefferson Ave (61605-3878)
PHONE.................................309 637-1440
Jesse Getz, *Manager*
**EMP:** 25
**SALES (corp-wide):** 37.5MM **Privately Held**
**WEB:** www.getzfire.com
**SIC:** 3589 High pressure cleaning equipment
**PA:** Getz Fire Equipment Co.
1615 Sw Adams St
Peoria IL 61602
309 673-0761

**(G-17373)**
**GORMAN & ASSOCIATES**
7501 N University St # 122 (61614-1244)
PHONE.................................309 691-9087
Fax: 309 691-9668
Carol Gorman, *President*
**EMP:** 7
**SQ FT:** 2,000
**SALES:** 1MM **Privately Held**
**SIC:** 2791 2731 Typesetting; books: publishing & printing

**(G-17374)**
**GUILDHALL PUBLISHERS LTD**
931 W Loire Ct Apt 1306 (61614-1812)
PHONE.................................309 693-9232
Albina L Aspell, *President*
John J Dietzen, *Vice Pres*
**EMP:** 3
**SALES (est):** 130K **Privately Held**
**SIC:** 2731 Books: publishing only

**(G-17375)**
**GUNDERSON RAIL SERVICES LLC**
Also Called: Greenbrier Castings
15 Leland St (61602-1818)
PHONE.................................309 676-1597
Michael Marriot, *Branch Mgr*
Gocal Geri, *Office Admin*
**EMP:** 20
**SALES (corp-wide):** 2.6B **Publicly Held**
**SIC:** 3743 Railroad equipment
**HQ:** Gunderson Rail Services Llc
1 Centerpointe Dr Ste 200
Lake Oswego OR 97035
503 684-7000

**(G-17376)**
**GUTTER MASTERS**
2117 E Cornell St (61614-7921)
PHONE.................................309 686-1234
**EMP:** 4 **EST:** 2010
**SALES (est):** 455.9K **Privately Held**
**SIC:** 3569 Filters

**(G-17377)**
**H3 GROUP LLC**
900 Sw Adams St (61602-1609)
PHONE.................................309 222-6027
Lisa Kulavic, *Treasurer*
Jay Kulavic,
Frank Mendoza,
**EMP:** 10
**SQ FT:** 18,000
**SALES:** 1.8MM **Privately Held**
**SIC:** 3449 Bars, concrete reinforcing: fabricated steel

**(G-17378)**
**HANLEY DESIGN INC**
2519 N Rockwood Dr (61604-2215)
PHONE.................................309 682-9665
**EMP:** 9
**SQ FT:** 10,000
**SALES:** 275K **Privately Held**
**SIC:** 2541 5712 2531 2522 Mfg Wood Partitionsfixt Ret Furniture Mfg Public Building Furn Nonwood Office Furn & Wood Household Furn

**(G-17379)**
**HARDIN SIGNS INC**
3116 N Biltmore Ave (61604-1294)
PHONE.................................309 688-4111
Fax: 309 688-3217
William F Hardin, *President*
Jim Hardin, *Vice Pres*
**EMP:** 14
**SQ FT:** 12,000
**SALES (est):** 1.6MM **Privately Held**
**SIC:** 1799 3993 Sign installation & maintenance; signs & advertising specialties

**(G-17380)**
**HARRIS CLOTHING & UNIFORMS INC**
Also Called: S Harris Uniforms
1025 N Sheridan Rd (61606-1957)
PHONE.................................309 671-4543
Fax: 309 673-5966
Karla Dennhardt, *President*
Todd Denhart, *Manager*
**EMP:** 10
**SALES (est):** 1.1MM **Privately Held**
**SIC:** 2326 Men's & boys' work clothing

**(G-17381)**
**HEAVY METAL INDUSTRIES LLC**
6718 W Plank Rd Ste 4 (61604-7218)
PHONE.................................309 966-3007
Nancy E Gunther,
Nancy Gunther,
**EMP:** 10
**SALES (est):** 800K **Privately Held**
**SIC:** 7692 Welding repair

**(G-17382)**
**HERITAGE RSTORATION DESIGN INC**
207 Voris St (61603-7000)
PHONE.................................309 637-5404
Michael Berlinger, *President*
Eerika Walters, *Admin Sec*
▲ **EMP:** 7

**SALES (est):** 996.8K **Privately Held**
**WEB:** www.heritagerd.com
**SIC:** 2531 Church furniture

**(G-17383)**
**HOLLAND SPECIALTY CO**
Also Called: Holland Laboratories
4611 W Middle Rd (61605-1055)
PHONE.................................309 697-9262
Stephen W Swanson, *President*
Carol Ellis, *Vice Pres*
Eric Swanson, *Vice Pres*
**EMP:** 25
**SQ FT:** 2,688
**SALES:** 10MM **Privately Held**
**WEB:** www.hollandspecialtytours.com
**SIC:** 2844 3843 Denture cleaners; dental equipment & supplies

**(G-17384)**
**IDEAL TURF INC**
614 W Ravinwoods Rd (61615-1369)
PHONE.................................309 691-3362
Andy D Zeigler, *Principal*
Jeffrey D Stahl, *Admin Sec*
**EMP:** 2
**SALES (est):** 280.4K **Privately Held**
**SIC:** 3523 Turf equipment, commercial

**(G-17385)**
**ILLINI FOUNDRY CO INC**
6523 N Galena Rd (61614-3103)
PHONE.................................309 697-3142
Fax: 309 697-5442
William Bank, *President*
**EMP:** 5 **EST:** 1929
**SQ FT:** 10,000
**SALES (est):** 928.4K **Privately Held**
**WEB:** www.illinifoundry.com
**SIC:** 3365 3366 3321 3369 Aluminum foundries; brass foundry; gray iron castings; nonferrous foundries

**(G-17386)**
**ILLINOIS RETINA INSTITUTE SC**
4505 N Rockwood Dr 1 (61615-3803)
PHONE.................................309 589-1880
Lynn Tamborini, *Branch Mgr*
**EMP:** 10
**SALES (corp-wide):** 2.2MM **Privately Held**
**SIC:** 3851 Eyes, glass & plastic
**PA:** Illinois Retina Institute, S.C.
3602 Marquette Rd
Peru IL 61354
815 223-7400

**(G-17387)**
**ILLINOIS VALLEY GLASS & MIRROR**
3300 Ne Adams St Ste A (61603-2374)
PHONE.................................309 682-6603
Fax: 309 682-6744
Warren R Watkins, *President*
Matt Allen, *Vice Pres*
Mary A Watkins, *Vice Pres*
**EMP:** 13
**SQ FT:** 20,000
**SALES (est):** 2.4MM **Privately Held**
**SIC:** 1793 3231 7536 3444 Glass & glazing work; insulating glass: made from purchased glass; automotive glass replacement shops; sheet metalwork

**(G-17388)**
**ILLINOIS VALLEY PRINTING INC**
619 Spring St (61603-4132)
PHONE.................................309 674-4942
Loveta J Ogden, *President*
Molly Ogden, *Vice Pres*
Glenn E Ogden, *Admin Sec*
**EMP:** 4 **EST:** 1928
**SQ FT:** 8,000
**SALES:** 350K **Privately Held**
**WEB:** www.ivprinting.com
**SIC:** 2759 Embossing on paper

**(G-17389)**
**INDUSTRIAL TOOL AND REPAIR**
218 S Starr Ln Ste A (61604-7204)
PHONE.................................309 633-0939
Fax: 309 633-0954
Ben Hamilton, *President*
**EMP:** 5
**SQ FT:** 7,000

SALES (est): 508K  Privately Held
SIC: 3599  Machine shop, jobbing & repair

**(G-17390)**
**INDUSTRIAL WASTE ELIMINATION**
115 N Martha St  (61614)
PHONE..............................312 498-0880
Robert Littmann, *CEO*
EMP: 10
SQ FT: 2,500
SALES (est): 409.5K  Privately Held
SIC: 2899  Chemical preparations

**(G-17391)**
**ISATES INC**
Also Called: Signs Now
2251 W Altorfer Dr  (61615-1807)
PHONE..............................309 691-8822
Fax: 309 692-9778
Irv Hodel, *President*
Sharon Hodel, *Corp Secy*
EMP: 6
SQ FT: 3,000
SALES: 600K  Privately Held
SIC: 3993  Signs & advertising specialties

**(G-17392)**
**JIM MAUI INC**
1 Aloha Ln  (61615-1871)
PHONE..............................888 666-5905
Fax: 309 692-6719
Michael Dalton, *President*
Larry Mills, *Vice Pres*
Andy Erickson, *Maintenance Dir*
Donna Ansell, *Opers Mgr*
Axel Raschke, *Opers Mgr*
EMP: 4
SALES (est): 50.2K  Privately Held
SIC: 5099  3851  Sunglasses; glasses, sun or glare

**(G-17393)**
**JOANS TROPHY & PLAQUE CO**
508 Ne Jefferson Ave  (61603-3891)
P.O. Box 5939  (61601-5939)
PHONE..............................309 674-6500
Fax: 309 674-3290
Diana E Gustin, *CEO*
Donald R Gustin, *President*
Robert Hammermeister, *Manager*
Timothy Stubhar, *Manager*
▲ EMP: 21
SQ FT: 6,500
SALES (est): 3MM  Privately Held
WEB: www.awardsnow.com
SIC: 5999  5094  3993  Trophies & plaques; trophies; signs & advertising specialties

**(G-17394)**
**JOHNSON ROLAN CO INC**
718 Sw Adams St  (61602-1605)
PHONE..............................309 674-9671
Fred T Johnson, *President*
William Barr, *Vice Pres*
Pamela Barr, *Admin Sec*
EMP: 4
SQ FT: 4,800
SALES: 526K  Privately Held
SIC: 7319  2396  Display advertising services; automotive & apparel trimmings

**(G-17395)**
**KEMP MANUFACTURING COMPANY (PA)**
4310 N Voss St  (61616-6592)
PHONE..............................309 682-7292
Fax: 309 682-1847
Hylee F Kemp, *President*
Mary K Kemp, *Corp Secy*
Brian F Kemp, *Vice Pres*
Hylee M Kemp, *Vice Pres*
Tim Edwards, *QC Mgr*
EMP: 40  EST: 1946
SALES: 8.1MM  Privately Held
WEB: www.kempmfg.com
SIC: 3599  3999  Machine & other job shop work; custom pulverizing & grinding of plastic materials

**(G-17396)**
**KEYSTONE CONSOLIDATED INDS INC**
Keystone Energy
7000 S Adams St  (61641-0002)
PHONE..............................309 697-7020
Fax: 309 697-7120
Jim Riggenbach, *Purch Mgr*
Darold Hogue, *Purchasing*
Mark Martin, *Sales Mgr*
David Cheek, *Branch Mgr*
Jeff Klokkenga, *Manager*
EMP: 33
SALES (corp-wide): 1.8B  Publicly Held
WEB: www.keystonesteel.com
SIC: 3312  3496  Billets, steel; miscellaneous fabricated wire products
HQ: Keystone Consolidated Industries, Inc.
5430 Lyndon B Johnson Fwy # 1740
Dallas TX 75240
800 441-0308

**(G-17397)**
**KOMATSU AMERICA CORP**
2300 Ne Adams St  (61639-0001)
P.O. Box 240  (61650-0240)
PHONE..............................309 672-7000
Fax: 309 672-7353
Don Thrush, *Vice Pres*
Sam Wrigley, *Safety Dir*
Greta Copeland, *Purchasing*
J Favorita, *Purchasing*
Wiliam Hatfield, *Chief Engr*
EMP: 146
SALES (corp-wide): 15.8B  Privately Held
WEB: www.equipmentcentralexpo.com
SIC: 3532  Mining machinery
HQ: Komatsu America Corp.
1701 Golf Rd Ste 1-100
Rolling Meadows IL 60008
847 437-5800

**(G-17398)**
**KONICA MINOLTA BUSINESS SOLUTI**
401 Sw Water St  (61602-1571)
PHONE..............................309 671-1360
Dennis Merschbrock, *Sales Mgr*
Natalie Dewolfe, *Accounts Exec*
Marty Schopp, *Branch Mgr*
EMP: 46
SALES (corp-wide): 8.4B  Privately Held
SIC: 7629  5045  5044  3571  Business machine repair, electric; computers, peripherals & software; copying equipment; electronic computers
HQ: Konica Minolta Business Solutions U.S.A., Inc.
100 Williams Dr
Ramsey NJ 07446
201 825-4000

**(G-17399)**
**LANGSTON BAG OF PEORIA LLC**
1114 Sw Adams St  (61602-1613)
PHONE..............................309 676-1006
Fax: 309 676-1225
Robert E Langston Jr, *CEO*
Butch Conward, *General Mgr*
George T Parkey, *COO*
George Gardner, *Opers Staff*
EMP: 63
SALES (est): 13.6MM
SALES (corp-wide): 65.8MM  Privately Held
SIC: 2674  Shipping bags or sacks, including multiwall & heavy duty
PA: Langston Companies, Inc.
1760 S 3rd St
Memphis TN 38109
901 774-4440

**(G-17400)**
**LEONARD A UNES PRINTING CO**
619 Spring St  (61603-4132)
P.O. Box 9573  (61612-9573)
PHONE..............................309 674-4942
Fax: 309 674-4971
Leonard A Unes II, *Owner*
Glenn Ogden, *Purch Dir*
Joann Ogden, *Treasurer*
Molly Ogden, *VP Sales*
EMP: 5
SQ FT: 12,500
SALES (est): 410K  Privately Held
SIC: 2752  Commercial printing, offset

**(G-17401)**
**LIGHTS PROSTHETIC EYES INC**
1318 W Candletree Dr # 3  (61614-8509)
PHONE..............................309 676-3663
Fax: 309 676-0359
Randy Light, *President*
Gwen Light, *Corp Secy*
Benjamin Leroy Light, *Vice Pres*
EMP: 3
SQ FT: 1,000
SALES (est): 200K  Privately Held
WEB: www.waoetv.com
SIC: 3851  Ophthalmic goods

**(G-17402)**
**LOUISVILLE LADDER INC**
7921 N Hale Ave  (61615-2047)
PHONE..............................309 692-1895
Lumis Craig, *Branch Mgr*
EMP: 8
SALES (corp-wide): 172.4MM  Privately Held
SIC: 3499  Metal ladders
PA: Louisville Ladder Inc.
7765 National Tpke # 190
Louisville KY 40214
502 636-2811

**(G-17403)**
**LUMEC CONTROL PRODUCTS INC**
1711 W Detweiller Dr  (61615-1611)
P.O. Box 395, Dunlap  (61525-0395)
PHONE..............................309 691-4747
Paul Luebbers, *Ch of Bd*
Amanda Winkler, *Business Mgr*
Eric McMasters, *Vice Pres*
BJ Caragher, *VP Opers*
EMP: 7
SQ FT: 800
SALES (est): 1MM
SALES (corp-wide): 2.1MM  Privately Held
WEB: www.lumecllc.com
SIC: 3625  Industrial controls: push button, selector switches, pilot
PA: Lumec L.L.C.
8400 N Allen Rd Ste B
Peoria IL 61615
309 691-4747

**(G-17404)**
**MACHINE MEDICS LLC**
5726 W Plank Rd  (61604-5223)
PHONE..............................309 633-5454
Eric Bruce,
Harry Murphy,
EMP: 3
SALES (est): 450.8K  Privately Held
WEB: www.machinemedics.com
SIC: 3541  Machine tool replacement & repair parts, metal cutting types

**(G-17405)**
**MELTON ELECTRIC CO**
5900 Washington St  (61607-2046)
P.O. Box 4168  (61607-0168)
PHONE..............................309 697-1422
Fax: 309 697-0925
Robert J Adams, *President*
James W Spear, *Treasurer*
Jene Glen, *Manager*
Brenda Adams, *Admin Sec*
EMP: 9
SQ FT: 10,000
SALES (est): 3.7MM  Privately Held
WEB: www.meltonelectric.com
SIC: 5063  7694  Motors, electric; electric motor repair

**(G-17406)**
**MID-CENTRAL BUSINESS FORMS**
1413 W Sunnyview Dr  (61614-4620)
PHONE..............................309 692-9090
Andy Matarelli, *President*
Rene Matarelli, *Admin Sec*
EMP: 2
SALES: 450K  Privately Held
SIC: 5112  2752  5943  Business forms; commercial printing, lithographic; office forms & supplies

**(G-17407)**
**MIDWEST HYDRA-LINE INC**
Also Called: MFC
817 Ne Adams St  (61603-3901)
PHONE..............................309 674-6570
Fax: 309 677-6471
Jason Drake, *Branch Mgr*
EMP: 4
SALES (corp-wide): 31.3MM  Privately Held
SIC: 5085  3443  Hose, belting & packing; cylinders, pressure: metal plate
HQ: Midwest Hydra-Line, Inc.
698 Us Highway 150 E
Galesburg IL 61401
309 342-6171

**(G-17408)**
**MIDWEST MARKETING DISTRS INC (PA)**
Also Called: Sun Gard Window Fashions
2000 E War Memorial Dr # 2  (61614-7918)
PHONE..............................309 688-8858
Fax: 309 688-8894
Jim House, *President*
Darla House, *Corp Secy*
Dan Ohlemiller, *Controller*
Gillian Ziegler, *Controller*
Dawn Behrends, *Human Resources*
▲ EMP: 19  EST: 1973
SQ FT: 18,000
SALES: 5MM  Privately Held
WEB: www.sun-gard.com
SIC: 5719  3081  7549  Window shades; unsupported plastics film & sheet; automotive customizing services, non-factory basis

**(G-17409)**
**MIDWESTERN FAMILY MAGAZINE LLC**
3823 N Harmon Ave  (61614-6630)
PHONE..............................309 303-7309
Ms Jennifer Rudd, *Principal*
EMP: 3
SALES (est): 169.8K  Privately Held
SIC: 2721  Periodicals

**(G-17410)**
**MODERN METHODS CREATIVE INC**
2613 N Knoxville Ave  (61604-3623)
PHONE..............................309 263-4100
Dan Martin, *President*
EMP: 4
SALES (est): 477.9K  Privately Held
SIC: 7319  5949  5199  2759  Advertising; sewing, needlework & piece goods; nondurable goods; commercial printing

**(G-17411)**
**MODERN PATTERN WORKS INC**
1100 Sw Washington St  (61602-1633)
PHONE..............................309 676-2157
William B Mehlenbeck, *President*
James Collie, *Corp Secy*
Jack Harris, *Vice Pres*
Paul Markum, *Vice Pres*
EMP: 4
SQ FT: 80,000
SALES (est): 359.5K
SALES (corp-wide): 18.4MM  Privately Held
SIC: 3543  Industrial patterns
PA: Cast Technologies, Inc.
1100 Sw Washington St
Peoria IL 61602
309 676-1715

**(G-17412)**
**MONTEFUSCO HEATING & SHTMTL CO**
Also Called: Montefusco Htg Shtmtl & A Con
2200 W Altorfer Dr Ste D  (61615-1874)
P.O. Box 9755  (61612-9755)
PHONE..............................309 691-7400
Fax: 309 691-7402
Eric Guenther, *President*
Dave Legrande, *Vice Pres*
Kathy Ard, *Admin Sec*
EMP: 6
SQ FT: 15,000

# GEOGRAPHIC SECTION

Peoria - Peoria County (G-17437)

SALES (est): 1.3MM **Privately Held**
WEB: www.montefuscohvac.com
SIC: **1711** 3446 3444 3443 Warm air heating & air conditioning contractor; ventilation & duct work contractor; architectural metalwork; sheet metalwork; fabricated plate work (boiler shop); fabricated structural metal

### (G-17413)
**MUIR OMNI GRAPHICS INC (PA)**
908 W Main St (61606-1255)
PHONE...................309 673-7034
Andrew S Muir, *President*
Mike Harris, *Prdtn Dir*
Bryan Claude, *Production*
James Silver, *Manager*
Mary Sutton, *Admin Sec*
EMP: 46 EST: 1963
SQ FT: 30,000
SALES (est): 5.3MM **Privately Held**
WEB: www.muirgraphics.com
SIC: **2759** 7389 Screen printing; lettering & sign painting services

### (G-17414)
**NATURAL FIBER WELDING INC**
801 W Main St Lab B206 (61606)
PHONE...................309 685-3591
Luke Haverhals, *President*
Eric Pollitt, *Vice Pres*
EMP: 5
SALES (est): 228K **Privately Held**
SIC: **3552** Spinning machines, textile

### (G-17415)
**NEED TO KNOW INC**
Also Called: Key Source
1723 W Detweiller Dr (61615-1611)
PHONE...................309 691-3877
Fax: 309 691-8964
Jean Wyman, *President*
EMP: 5
SQ FT: 4,000
SALES (est): 556.6K **Privately Held**
WEB: www.buykappa.com
SIC: **5961** 2731 2752 2396 Catalog & mail-order houses; pamphlets: publishing only, not printed on site; commercial printing, lithographic; automotive & apparel trimmings; pleating & stitching

### (G-17416)
**NETWORK HARBOR INC**
5607 Washington St (61607-2075)
P.O. Box 4126 (61607-0126)
PHONE...................309 633-9118
David Daxenbichler, *President*
Mike Daxenbichler, *Vice Pres*
Al Juraco, *Admin Sec*
EMP: 8
SALES (est): 570K **Privately Held**
WEB: www.networkharbor.com
SIC: **7372** Prepackaged software

### (G-17417)
**NEW-INDY IVEX LLC**
1 Sloan St (61603)
P.O. Box 1820 (61656-1820)
PHONE...................309 686-3830
Fax: 309 686-0324
Daisy Kessler, *Vice Pres*
Katie Brenneky, *Controller*
Chuck Erwin, *Controller*
Mark Reardon, *Mng Member*
▼ EMP: 40
SQ FT: 5,000
SALES (corp-wide): 62.7MM **Privately Held**
SIC: **2679** Crepe paper or crepe paper products: purchased material
HQ: New-Indy Containerboard Llc
3500 Porsche Way Ste 150
Ontario CA 91764
909 296-3400

### (G-17418)
**NICKELS ELECTRIC**
1208 W Smith St (61605-2050)
PHONE...................309 676-1350
Albert Nickels, *Principal*
EMP: 3 EST: 2008
SALES (est): 179.2K **Privately Held**
SIC: **3356** Nickel

### (G-17419)
**ONEFIRE MEDIA GROUP INC**
214 Pecan St Ste 100 (61602-1640)
PHONE...................309 740-0345
Jason Parkinson, *President*
Kristie Sparling, *CFO*
Lyndon Perry, *Ch Credit Ofcr*
EMP: 24
SQ FT: 5,900
SALES (est): 495.8K **Privately Held**
SIC: **7372** Application computer software

### (G-17420)
**P & P PRESS INC**
6513 N Galena Rd (61614-3119)
PHONE...................309 691-8511
Fax: 309 691-1972
Arthur P Young, *President*
Linda Stewart, *Corp Secy*
Jim Rutz, *Prdtn Mgr*
David Garren, *Manager*
Michelle Young, *Director*
▼ EMP: 32
SQ FT: 30,000
SALES (est): 6.8MM **Privately Held**
WEB: www.pppress.com
SIC: **2752** Commercial printing, offset

### (G-17421)
**P & S COCHRAN PRINTERS INC (PA)**
Also Called: PIP Printing
8325 N Allen Rd (61615-2076)
PHONE...................309 691-6668
Paul L Cochran, *Ch of Bd*
Scott H Cochran, *President*
Chris Cochran, *Vice Pres*
Wendy Cochran, *Financial Exec*
Joanne Cochran, *Shareholder*
EMP: 20
SQ FT: 20,000
SALES: 2.5MM **Privately Held**
WEB: www.pippeoria.com
SIC: **2752** 2791 2789 Commercial printing, offset; typesetting; bookbinding & related work

### (G-17422)
**PACE FOUNDATION**
3528 W Chartwell Rd (61614-2326)
PHONE...................309 691-3553
Sue Patterson, *President*
Becky Cassidy, *Vice Pres*
Susan Stockman, *Treasurer*
Jodi Garger, *Admin Sec*
EMP: 31
SALES: 13K **Privately Held**
SIC: **2515** Foundations & platforms

### (G-17423)
**PEORIA JOURNAL STAR INC**
1 News Plz (61643-0001)
PHONE...................585 598-0030
Fax: 309 686-3205
Ken Mauser, *President*
Brian Kier, *Controller*
Jude Dunlap, *Credit Mgr*
Bev Gonzalez, *Human Res Mgr*
Clare Johnson, *Human Res Mgr*
▲ EMP: 217
SQ FT: 129,000
SALES (est): 32.5MM
SALES (corp-wide): 1.2B **Publicly Held**
SIC: **2711** Commercial printing & newspaper publishing combined
PA: New Media Investment Group Inc.
1345 Avenue Of The Americ
New York NY 10105
212 479-3160

### (G-17424)
**PEORIA NEUROINNOVATIONS LLC**
801 W Main St (61606-1877)
PHONE...................217 899-0443
Christopher Frank, *Co-Owner*
Joshua Bailey, *Co-Owner*
Julian Lin, *Co-Owner*
EMP: 4
SQ FT: 790
SALES (est): 210.8K **Privately Held**
SIC: **3842** Implants, surgical

### (G-17425)
**PEORIA OPEN M R I**
6708 N Knoxville Ave # 2 (61614-2863)
PHONE...................309 692-7674
Fax: 309 692-1209
Bob Gitomer, *President*
EMP: 4
SALES (est): 355.4K **Privately Held**
SIC: **3826** Magnetic resonance imaging apparatus

### (G-17426)
**PEORIA POST INC**
Also Called: Tradin Post Newspaper
834 E Glen Ave (61616-5206)
P.O. Box 1547 (61655-1547)
PHONE...................309 688-3628
Fax: 309 688-4285
Jack S Brisbin, *President*
Patricia Brisbin, *Admin Sec*
EMP: 15 EST: 1970
SQ FT: 800
SALES: 1.5MM **Privately Held**
SIC: **2741** 2711 Shopping news: publishing only, not printed on site; newspapers

### (G-17427)
**PERFORMANCE PATTERN & MCH INC**
Also Called: Ppm
2421 Sw Adams St (61602-1852)
PHONE...................309 676-0907
Fax: 309 676-8830
Tom Herman, *President*
Scott Herman, *Vice Pres*
Terry McCowan, *Foreman/Supr*
Wanda Shatzer, *Manager*
EMP: 24
SQ FT: 25,000
SALES (est): 4.5MM **Privately Held**
WEB: www.performancepattern.com
SIC: **3599** 8711 Machine shop, jobbing & repair; engineering services

### (G-17428)
**PIERCE PACKAGING CO**
2130 W Townline Rd (61615-1547)
PHONE...................815 636-5656
John McNabb, *Branch Mgr*
EMP: 5
SALES (corp-wide): 62.2MM **Privately Held**
SIC: **4783** 2441 Packing goods for shipping; crating goods for shipping; containerization of goods for shipping; boxes, wood
PA: Pierce Packaging Co.
2028 E Riverside Blvd
Loves Park IL 61111
815 636-5650

### (G-17429)
**PIERSONS MATTRESS INC**
Also Called: Piersons Mattress & Furn Co
1034 S Western Ave (61605-3353)
PHONE...................309 637-8455
Conrad G Pierson, *President*
EMP: 4
SQ FT: 12,500
SALES: 250K **Privately Held**
SIC: **2515** 5712 Mattresses, innerspring or box spring; furniture stores

### (G-17430)
**PMP FERMENTATION PRODUCTS INC**
900 Ne Adams St (61603-4200)
PHONE...................309 637-0400
Yuzo Kono, *President*
Randy Niedermeier, *Corp Secy*
Dennis Huff, *Vice Pres*
Steven Stenzel, *Engineer*
◆ EMP: 50 EST: 1985
SQ FT: 15,000
SALES (est): 16.1MM
SALES (corp-wide): 318.7MM **Privately Held**
WEB: www.pmpinc.com
SIC: **2869** 5169 Industrial organic chemicals; food additives & preservatives
PA: Fuso Chemical Co., Ltd.
4-3-10, Koraibashi, Chuo-Ku
Osaka OSK 541-0
662 034-771

### (G-17431)
**PORTABLE MVG STOR CNTL ILL INC**
10000 N Galena Rd (61615-9452)
PHONE...................309 693-7637
Richard Gunther, *President*
Jim Lamb, *General Mgr*
EMP: 7
SQ FT: 16,000
SALES: 500K **Privately Held**
SIC: **2631** Container, packaging & boxboard

### (G-17432)
**PPG ARCHITECTURAL FINISHES INC**
Also Called: Glidden Professional Paint Ctr
404 Sw Adams St (61602-1520)
PHONE...................309 673-3761
Fax: 309 673-2529
Tim Klise, *Branch Mgr*
EMP: 4
SALES (corp-wide): 14.7B **Publicly Held**
WEB: www.gliddenpaint.com
SIC: **5231** 5198 2851 Paint, glass & wallpaper; paints, varnishes & supplies; paints & allied products
HQ: Ppg Architectural Finishes, Inc.
1 Ppg Pl
Pittsburgh PA 15272
412 434-3131

### (G-17433)
**PRAGER ASSOCIATES**
4035 W Tangleoaks Ct (61615-8909)
PHONE...................309 691-1565
Steve Prager, *Owner*
EMP: 4
SALES (est): 200K **Privately Held**
SIC: **3651** 5064 Household video equipment; electrical entertainment equipment

### (G-17434)
**PRAIRIE FARMS DAIRY INC**
2004 N University St (61604-3103)
PHONE...................309 686-2400
Fax: 309 686-3788
Scott Deakin, *General Mgr*
James Rogers, *Div Sub Head*
Craig Bertrand, *Marketing Mgr*
Karen Frazier, *Manager*
Steve Hammond, *Manager*
EMP: 102
SQ FT: 30,000
SALES (corp-wide): 1.8B **Privately Held**
WEB: www.prairiefarms.com
SIC: **2026** Milk processing (pasteurizing, homogenizing, bottling)
PA: Prairie Farms Dairy, Inc.
1100 Broadway
Carlinville IL 62626
217 854-2547

### (G-17435)
**PREMIER SIGNS CREATIONS INC**
710 Fayette St (61603-3612)
PHONE...................309 637-6890
Fax: 309 637-6891
Adam Reiger, *Owner*
Adam Rieger, *Owner*
EMP: 4
SALES (est): 373K **Privately Held**
WEB: www.signsmatter.com
SIC: **3993** Signs & advertising specialties

### (G-17436)
**PROBOTIX**
8800b N Industrial Rd (61615)
PHONE...................309 691-2643
▲ EMP: 9
SALES (est): 1.3MM **Privately Held**
SIC: **3699** Electrical equipment & supplies

### (G-17437)
**PROFORM**
Also Called: Maco Business Forms
708 Fayette St (61603-3612)
PHONE...................309 676-2535
Fax: 309 676-5775
Tom James, *Manager*
EMP: 5
SALES (corp-wide): 1MM **Privately Held**
SIC: **2752** 2761 Fashion plates, lithographed; manifold business forms

# Peoria - Peoria County (G-17438)

**PA:** Proform
1315 E London Ave
Peoria IL 61603
309 685-5814

### (G-17438)
### QUALITY METAL PRODUCTS INC
7006 N Galena Rd (61614-2296)
**PHONE**.................................309 692-8014
**Fax:** 309 692-6679
Jo Ellen Dunbar, *President*
Lori Gaskins, *Vice Pres*
Derrick Brehm, *Prdtn Mgr*
Gina Begner, *Treasurer*
Shelly Keffeler, *Admin Sec*
**EMP:** 125
**SQ FT:** 62,000
**SALES:** 14.2MM **Privately Held**
**WEB:** www.qmpillinois.com
**SIC: 3599** Machine shop, jobbing & repair

### (G-17439)
### RABER PACKING COMPANY
1413 N Raber Rd (61604-4790)
**PHONE**.................................309 673-0721
**Fax:** 309 673-6308
Carroll Wetteraur, *President*
Allan Wetteraur, *Corp Secy*
**EMP:** 22 **EST:** 1954
**SQ FT:** 15,000
**SALES (est):** 1.5MM **Privately Held**
**SIC: 5421** 2011 Meat & fish markets; meat packing plants

### (G-17440)
### RAPID PRINT
934 N Bourland Ave (61606-1718)
**PHONE**.................................309 673-0826
**Fax:** 309 673-2612
Thomas Madigan, *Owner*
Cindy Madigan, *Co-Owner*
**EMP:** 3
**SQ FT:** 2,500
**SALES:** 200K **Privately Held**
**SIC: 2752** 7334 2789 Commercial printing, offset; photocopying & duplicating services; bookbinding & related work

### (G-17441)
### RELX INC
Lexisnexis
8512 N Allen Rd (61615-1527)
**PHONE**.................................309 689-1000
Chris Lemons, *Branch Mgr*
**EMP:** 49
**SALES (corp-wide):** 8.4B **Privately Held**
**SIC: 2721** Periodicals
**HQ:** Relx Inc.
230 Park Ave Ste 700
New York NY 10169
212 309-8100

### (G-17442)
### RIVER CITY OIL LLC
3310 W Chartwell Rd (61614-2322)
**PHONE**.................................309 693-2249
Chittaranjan Reddy, *Principal*
**EMP:** 3
**SALES (est):** 221.7K **Privately Held**
**SIC: 1311** Crude petroleum & natural gas

### (G-17443)
### RIVERSIDE TOOL & DIE CO
1616 W Chanute Rd Ste A (61615-1670)
**PHONE**.................................309 689-0104
**Fax:** 309 689-1923
Jeff Davis, *President*
Hunt Taylor, *Vice Pres*
Susan Myers, *Controller*
Mike Rodene, *Sales Mgr*
Maureen Pasker, *Office Mgr*
**EMP:** 14
**SQ FT:** 12,000
**SALES (est):** 1.7MM **Privately Held**
**SIC: 3544** Die sets for metal stamping (presses)

### (G-17444)
### RO-WEB INC
Also Called: Kwik Kopy Printing
4440 N Prospect Rd Ste C (61616-6580)
**PHONE**.................................309 688-2155
**Fax:** 309 688-8256
Roger G Weber, *President*
Judy Gullett, *Opers Mgr*
Carl Innis, *Data Proc Dir*
Leslie Strabley, *Data Proc Dir*
Beverly F Weber, *Admin Sec*
**EMP:** 4
**SQ FT:** 1,730
**SALES (est):** 330K **Privately Held**
**SIC: 2752** 7334 5943 2791 Commercial printing, lithographic; photocopying & duplicating services; office forms & supplies; typesetting; bookbinding & related work

### (G-17445)
### ROGER BURKE JEWELERS INC
Also Called: Burke, Roger G Jewelers
4700 N University St 6 (61614-5890)
**PHONE**.................................309 692-0210
Roger Burke, *President*
Kathy Burke, *Admin Sec*
**EMP:** 15
**SQ FT:** 1,800
**SALES:** 760K **Privately Held**
**SIC: 5944** 7631 3911 Jewelry, precious stones & precious metals; jewelry repair services; jewel settings & mountings, precious metal

### (G-17446)
### ROHN PRODUCTS LLC (PA)
1 Fairholm Ave (61603-2319)
P.O. Box 5999 (61601-5999)
**PHONE**.................................309 697-4400
**Fax:** 309 633-2694
Rollie Horton, *General Mgr*
Dan Ludolph, *CFO*
Daniel Ludolph, *CFO*
Joseph P O'Brien, *Mng Member*
Stephanie Tisdale, *Administration*
**EMP:** 80
**SQ FT:** 2,000
**SALES:** 30.2MM **Privately Held**
**SIC: 3441** Tower sections, radio & television transmission

### (G-17447)
### ROHN PRODUCTS LLC
6718 W Plank Rd Ste 2 (61604-7218)
**PHONE**.................................309 566-3000
Joseph P O'Brien, *Branch Mgr*
**EMP:** 41 **Privately Held**
**SIC: 3441** Tower sections, radio & television transmission
**PA:** Rohn Products, Llc
1 Fairholm Ave
Peoria IL 61603

### (G-17448)
### ROME INDUSTRIES INC (PA)
1703 W Detweiller Dr (61615-1688)
**PHONE**.................................309 691-7120
**Fax:** 309 691-2462
Rrichard O'Russa, *President*
Richard O'Russa, *President*
John Orussa, *Opers Mgr*
Mary O'Russa, *Treasurer*
Michael Orussa, *Sales Staff*
▲ **EMP:** 6 **EST:** 1964
**SQ FT:** 12,000
**SALES:** 3MM **Privately Held**
**WEB:** www.romeindustries.com
**SIC: 3999** 3365 Lawn ornaments; cooking/kitchen utensils, cast aluminum

### (G-17449)
### ROUTE 40 MEDIA LLC
4408 N Rockwood Dr # 240 (61615-3765)
**PHONE**.................................309 370-5809
Scott Leathers,
John Ingles,
Paul Johnson,
**EMP:** 3 **EST:** 2013
**SALES (est):** 124.4K **Privately Held**
**SIC: 7372** 8211 7389 Application computer software; specialty education;

### (G-17450)
### SENN ENTERPRISES INC (PA)
Also Called: University Sport Shop
1309 W Main St (61606-1148)
**PHONE**.................................309 637-1147
**Fax:** 309 677-6388
Carol Senn, *President*
**EMP:** 10
**SALES (est):** 932.3K **Privately Held**
**SIC: 5699** 2395 Sports apparel; embroidery & art needlework

### (G-17451)
### SENN ENTERPRISES INC
Also Called: Embroidery House
1829 W Main St (61606-1071)
**PHONE**.................................309 673-4384
Carol Senn, *President*
**EMP:** 3 **Privately Held**
**SIC: 2395** Embroidery & art needlework
**PA:** Senn Enterprises, Inc
1309 W Main St
Peoria IL 61606

### (G-17452)
### SEW WRIGHT EMBROIDERY INC
Also Called: Embroid ME
7810 N University St (61614-1206)
**PHONE**.................................309 691-5780
**Fax:** 309 691-5790
Patricia R Wright, *President*
Kim Goodwin, *Treasurer*
Toni D Waldschmidt, *Admin Sec*
**EMP:** 4
**SQ FT:** 1,700
**SALES (est):** 240K **Privately Held**
**SIC: 5949** 2759 Sewing, needlework & piece goods; screen printing; promotional printing

### (G-17453)
### SGS INTERNATIONAL LLC
Also Called: Multi-Ad Services
1720 W Detweiller Dr (61615-1612)
**PHONE**.................................309 690-5231
**Fax:** 309 692-8378
John F Kocher, *Branch Mgr*
Greg Potts, *Director*
**EMP:** 238
**SALES (corp-wide):** 303.8MM **Privately Held**
**SIC: 2741** 7374 3993 Miscellaneous publishing; computer graphics service; signs & advertising specialties
**HQ:** Sgs International, Llc
626 W Main St Ste 500
Louisville KY 40202
502 637-5443

### (G-17454)
### SHAMROCK PLASTICS INC
2615 Alta Ln (61615-9646)
P.O. Box 3530 (61612-3530)
**PHONE**.................................309 243-7723
**Fax:** 309 243-5852
Mary Cay Westphal, *President*
Michael Wilkinson, *General Mgr*
Gary Potter, *Prdtn Mgr*
Rhonda Jones, *Production*
Jack Hathaway, *Sales Mgr*
**EMP:** 30
**SQ FT:** 36,000
**SALES (est):** 4.1MM **Privately Held**
**WEB:** www.shamrockplastics.net
**SIC: 3089** Plastic processing

### (G-17455)
### SHERATON ROAD LUMBER
Also Called: Doubet Window & Door
6600 N Sheridan Rd (61614-2935)
**PHONE**.................................309 691-0858
Chuck Brown, *President*
Helen Unes, *President*
Robert Unes, *Corp Secy*
**EMP:** 15 **EST:** 1951
**SALES (est):** 1.7MM **Privately Held**
**SIC: 5211** 3442 Lumber products; doors, storm: wood or metal; windows, storm: wood or metal; prefabricated buildings; metal doors, sash & trim

### (G-17456)
### SIMFORMOTION LLC (PA)
316 Sw Washington St # 300 (61602-1406)
**PHONE**.................................309 263-7595
Renee Gorrell, *CEO*
Lara Aaron, *Vice Pres*
Brian Buss, *Project Mgr*
Calvin Quinn, *Purch Agent*
Brian McMahon, *Engineer*
▼ **EMP:** 19
**SALES (est):** 3.2MM **Privately Held**
**SIC: 3699** 8331 Automotive driving simulators (training aids), electronic; job training & vocational rehabilitation services

### (G-17457)
### SOLAZYME
910 Ne Adams St (61603-3904)
**PHONE**.................................309 258-5695
**EMP:** 4 **EST:** 2011
**SALES (est):** 320K **Privately Held**
**SIC: 2899** Mfg Chemical Preparations

### (G-17458)
### SOMMER PRODUCTS COMPANY INC
Also Called: Stryco Industries
6523 N Galena Rd (61614-3103)
**PHONE**.................................309 697-1216
William Banks, *President*
Dean Hainline, *Plant Mgr*
Mary A Lanane, *Purch Agent*
Martin Bray, *Engineer*
Jody Oltman, *Accountant*
▲ **EMP:** 54 **EST:** 1937
**SQ FT:** 20,000
**SALES (est):** 11.7MM **Privately Held**
**WEB:** www.sommerproducts.com
**SIC: 3548** Electric welding equipment

### (G-17459)
### SOUTHFIELD CORPORATION
Also Called: Prairie Construction Material
100 W Cass St (61602-1724)
**PHONE**.................................309 676-0576
Dave Minor, *Manager*
**EMP:** 30
**SALES (corp-wide):** 273.9MM **Privately Held**
**WEB:** www.prairiegroup.com
**SIC: 3273** 1442 Ready-mixed concrete; gravel mining
**PA:** Southfield Corporation
8995 W 95th St
Palos Hills IL 60465
708 344-1000

### (G-17460)
### STAFFCO INC
Also Called: River City Enterprises
3806 N Northwood Ave (61614-7342)
**PHONE**.................................309 688-3223
**Fax:** 309 686-3853
Stewart Boal Jr, *President*
S H Boal, *Vice Pres*
**EMP:** 4
**SALES (est):** 358K **Privately Held**
**WEB:** www.pistontech.com
**SIC: 2655** 3443 3412 3411 Fiber cans, drums & containers; fabricated plate work (boiler shop); metal barrels, drums & pails; metal cans; plastics plumbing fixtures

### (G-17461)
### STAINED GLASS OF PEORIA
512 Spring St (61603-4121)
**PHONE**.................................309 674-7929
Jerry McGowan, *President*
Rick Gowan, *Vice Pres*
Rick McGowan, *Vice Pres*
**EMP:** 4 **EST:** 1976
**SQ FT:** 4,000
**SALES (est):** 443.8K **Privately Held**
**WEB:** www.stainedglassofpeoria.com
**SIC: 5231** 5932 3231 Glass, leaded or stained; antiques; products of purchased glass

### (G-17462)
### STANDARD REGISTER INC
1100 W Glen Ave Ste 300 (61614-4823)
**PHONE**.................................309 693-3700
**Fax:** 309 693-7757
Brian Mahoney, *Sales/Mktg Mgr*
**EMP:** 8
**SALES (corp-wide):** 4.5B **Privately Held**
**WEB:** www.stdreg.com
**SIC: 2761** Manifold business forms
**HQ:** Standard Register, Inc.
600 Albany St
Dayton OH 45417
937 221-1000

### (G-17463)
### STANDARD SHEET METAL WORKS INC
220 N Commerce Pl (61604-5286)
**PHONE**.................................309 633-2300
**Fax:** 309 633-0961

# GEOGRAPHIC SECTION

Peotone - Will County (G-17491)

Jay C Harms, *Ch of Bd*
Nancy Harms, *Vice Pres*
Tom Hyde, *Sales Staff*
Brenda Van Atta, *Admin Sec*
Kent Higgins, *Maintence Staff*
**EMP:** 50 **EST:** 1939
**SALES (est):** 13.3MM Privately Held
**WEB:** www.standardsheet.com
**SIC:** 3441 Fabricated structural metal

**(G-17464)**
### SUPERIOR WATER SERVICES INC
Also Called: Superior Water Systems
5831 N Knoxville Ave (61614-4332)
**PHONE**.................................309 691-9287
Steven Warfield, *President*
**EMP:** 5
**SALES:** 700K Privately Held
**WEB:** www.superiorwaterservices.net
**SIC:** 3589 5078 5074 7389 Water purification equipment, household type; drinking water coolers, mechanical; water softeners; water softener service

**(G-17465)**
### T J P INVESTMENTS INC
Also Called: Kelch, Bob Floors
2522 W War Memorial Dr (61615-3506)
**PHONE**.................................309 673-8383
Ted Plotkin, *President*
**EMP:** 7
**SALES (est):** 1MM Privately Held
**SIC:** 2426 Flooring, hardwood

**(G-17466)**
### TAVERN ON PROSPECT LTD
5901 N Prospect Rd Ste 10 (61614-4336)
**PHONE**.................................309 693-8677
Jeff Stevenson, *Owner*
**EMP:** 6
**SALES (est):** 187K Privately Held
**SIC:** 5813 2084 Wine bar; wines, brandy & brandy spirits

**(G-17467)**
### TECHGRAPHIC SOLUTIONS INC
8824 N Industrial Rd (61615-1535)
**PHONE**.................................309 693-9400
**Fax:** 309 693-9700
Marc W Klass, *President*
Sheldon Katz, *Vice Pres*
▲ **EMP:** 10
**SQ FT:** 5,000
**SALES (est):** 1.6MM Privately Held
**WEB:** www.worldwidepens.com
**SIC:** 2759 3951 Business forms: printing; stylographic pens & parts

**(G-17468)**
### TECHNICRAFT SUPPLY CO (PA)
Also Called: Technicraft Display Graphics
419 Elm St (61605-3969)
**PHONE**.................................309 495-5245
Thomas J Whalen, *President*
Karen K Whalen, *Vice Pres*
Colleen Kimball, *Bus Dvlpt Dir*
Mary Ditch, *Manager*
**EMP:** 4
**SQ FT:** 6,000
**SALES (est):** 861.3K Privately Held
**SIC:** 5999 2759 3993 Picture frames, ready made; commercial printing; signs & advertising specialties

**(G-17469)**
### TIMKEN COMPANY
8415 N Allen Rd Ste 208 (61615-1892)
**PHONE**.................................309 692-8150
Blake Scanlon, *Manager*
**EMP:** 4
**SALES (corp-wide):** 2.6B Publicly Held
**SIC:** 3562 Ball & roller bearings
**PA:** The Timken Company
4500 Mount Pleasant St Nw
North Canton OH 44720
234 262-3000

**(G-17470)**
### TRANE US INC
8718 N University St (61615-1681)
**PHONE**.................................309 691-4224
David Hicke, *Controller*
Mike Hunzeker, *Manager*
**EMP:** 6 Privately Held
**SIC:** 3585 Refrigeration & heating equipment
**HQ:** Trane U.S. Inc.
1 Centennial Ave Ste 101
Piscataway NJ 08854
732 652-7100

**(G-17471)**
### TRUE ROYALTY SCENTS
2404 N Elmwood Ave (61604-3206)
**PHONE**.................................309 992-0688
**EMP:** 4
**SALES (est):** 332.4K Privately Held
**SIC:** 2844 Toilet preparations

**(G-17472)**
### UNION PACIFIC RAILROAD COMPANY
3918 Sw Adams St (61605-3161)
**PHONE**.................................309 637-9322
Kim Deyo, *Manager*
**EMP:** 5
**SALES (corp-wide):** 19.9B Publicly Held
**WEB:** www.uprr.com
**SIC:** 3743 Railway motor cars
**HQ:** Union Pacific Railroad Company Inc
1400 Douglas St
Omaha NE 68179
402 544-5000

**(G-17473)**
### UNITED READY MIX INC (PA)
1 Leland St (61602-1818)
**PHONE**.................................309 676-3287
**Fax:** 309 676-6063
Jack Hoffman, *President*
Lowell Hoffman, *Vice Pres*
Rick Duda, *Sales Mgr*
**EMP:** 26 **EST:** 1965
**SQ FT:** 15,000
**SALES (est):** 4.4MM Privately Held
**SIC:** 3273 Ready-mixed concrete

**(G-17474)**
### US SHREDDER CASTINGS GROUP INC
4408 N Rockwood Dr (61615-3765)
**PHONE**.................................309 359-3151
William Tigner, *President*
Bill Tigner, *President*
Troy Graves, *Manager*
▲ **EMP:** 2
**SALES (est):** 531.6K Privately Held
**SIC:** 3531 Construction machinery

**(G-17475)**
### USA EMBROIDERY
1605 W Candletree Dr # 102 (61614-1658)
**PHONE**.................................309 692-1391
Bill White, *Owner*
**EMP:** 3
**SALES (est):** 100K Privately Held
**SIC:** 2395 Embroidery products, except schiffli machine

**(G-17476)**
### USA TECHNOLOGIES INC
801 Sw Jefferson Ave (61605-3918)
**PHONE**.................................309 495-0829
Seiji Sakurada, *President*
Gary Eggerichs, *Exec VP*
Terry Cooper, *Plant Engr*
Julie Myers, *Manager*
▲ **EMP:** 120
**SQ FT:** 80,000
**SALES (est):** 21.2MM Privately Held
**SIC:** 3469 2679 Metal stampings; filter paper: made from purchased material

**(G-17477)**
### WALDOS SPORTS CORNER INC
Also Called: Sports Corner & Creations
1306 E Seiberling Ave (61616-6446)
**PHONE**.................................309 688-2425
Roger Waldo, *President*
Karen Waldo, *Admin Sec*
**EMP:** 3
**SQ FT:** 600
**SALES (est):** 230K Privately Held
**SIC:** 5699 5941 2396 2395 Uniforms; team sports equipment; automotive & apparel trimmings; pleating & stitching

**(G-17478)**
### WIRELESS EXPRESS INC CENTRAL
4732 N University St (61614-5831)
**PHONE**.................................309 689-9933
Gary Anderson, *Principal*
**EMP:** 4
**SALES (est):** 210K Privately Held
**SIC:** 2741 Miscellaneous publishing

**(G-17479)**
### YOUR TEAM SOCKS
8816 N Industrial Rd (61615-1553)
**PHONE**.................................309 713-1044
**EMP:** 3
**SALES (est):** 129.8K Privately Held
**SIC:** 2252 Socks

**(G-17480)**
### ZANFEL LABORATORIES INC (PA)
6901 N Knoxville Ave # 200 (61614-2816)
**PHONE**.................................309 683-3500
William M Yarbrough, *President*
Steve Sisler, *Vice Pres*
Robby Collier, *Opers Staff*
Linda Lillard, *Office Mgr*
Stacy Zepnak, *Office Mgr*
**EMP:** 5
**SQ FT:** 100,000
**SALES (est):** 1.6MM Privately Held
**WEB:** www.zanfel.com
**SIC:** 2844 Cosmetic preparations

**(G-17481)**
### ZANTECH INC
7501 N Harker Dr (61615-1848)
**PHONE**.................................309 692-8307
**Fax:** 309 692-8375
Marc Young, *CEO*
**EMP:** 4
**SALES (est):** 383.3K Privately Held
**WEB:** www.zantechinc.com
**SIC:** 3873 Watches, clocks, watchcases & parts

**(G-17482)**
### ZOE PUBLICATIONS LLC
5801 N Cypress Dr # 2905 (61615-3379)
**PHONE**.................................636 625-6622
Allan Wolf, *Principal*
**EMP:** 3
**SALES (est):** 214.3K Privately Held
**SIC:** 2759 Publication printing

---

## Peoria
### *Tazewell County*

**(G-17483)**
### ECOTHERMICS CORPORATION
3880 N Main St Ste D (61611-5555)
**PHONE**.................................217 621-2402
Daniel Sherman, *Engineer*
Thomas S Lewicki, *CFO*
**EMP:** 7
**SALES (est):** 1.3MM Privately Held
**SIC:** 3563 Air & gas compressors

---

## Peotone
### *Will County*

**(G-17484)**
### BC WELDING INC
Also Called: Bc Welding Service and Repair
308 E Crawford St (60468-9274)
**PHONE**.................................708 258-0076
Robert Cragin, *President*
**EMP:** 2
**SALES:** 200K Privately Held
**SIC:** 7692 Welding repair

**(G-17485)**
### CARLSON SCIENTIFIC INC
514 S Third St (60468-9208)
**PHONE**.................................708 258-6377
**Fax:** 708 258-6378
Jeffrey R Carlson, *President*
Dorothy Carlson, *Vice Pres*
**EMP:** 6
**SQ FT:** 8,000
**SALES (est):** 732.9K Privately Held
**WEB:** www.carlsonscientific.com
**SIC:** 3821 Laboratory equipment: fume hoods, distillation racks, etc.

**(G-17486)**
### CLEVELAND STEEL CONTAINER CORP
117 E Lincoln St (60468-8989)
**PHONE**.................................708 258-0700
**Fax:** 708 258-3328
Pat Luchessi, *Human Res Mgr*
Robert Harding, *Manager*
Dennis Puening, *Manager*
**EMP:** 50
**SALES (corp-wide):** 147.3MM Privately Held
**SIC:** 3412 Pails, shipping: metal
**PA:** Cleveland Steel Container Corporation
30310 Emerald Valley Pkwy
Solon OH 44139
440 349-8000

**(G-17487)**
### COUSINS PACKAGING INC
312 E Corning Ave (60468-8706)
P.O. Box 640 (60468-0640)
**PHONE**.................................708 258-0063
Neil Cousins, *Branch Mgr*
**EMP:** 3
**SALES (corp-wide):** 251.2K Privately Held
**SIC:** 2621 Wrapping & packaging papers
**PA:** Cousins Packaging Inc
6450 Northam Drive
Mississauga ON L4V 1
416 743-1341

**(G-17488)**
### DREIS AND KRUMP MFG CO
Also Called: Chicago Dreis & Krump
481 S Governors Hwy 2 (60468-9116)
**PHONE**.................................708 258-1200
**Fax:** 708 258-9684
Rudy Wolfer, *Ch of Bd*
Al Anderson, *Vice Pres*
Don Sedder, *Sales Mgr*
▲ **EMP:** 25
**SQ FT:** 180,000
**SALES (est):** 4.9MM Privately Held
**WEB:** www.dreis-krump.com
**SIC:** 3542 Metal deposit forming machines

**(G-17489)**
### HAWKINS INC
32040 S Route 45 (60468-9731)
**PHONE**.................................708 258-3797
Mike Carroll, *Branch Mgr*
**EMP:** 4
**SALES (corp-wide):** 483.5MM Publicly Held
**SIC:** 2899 Chemical preparations
**PA:** Hawkins, Inc.
2381 Rosegate
Roseville MN 55113
612 331-6910

**(G-17490)**
### KUSMIEREK INDUSTRIES INC
6434 W North Peotone Rd (60468-9390)
P.O. Box 415 (60468-0415)
**PHONE**.................................708 258-3100
James Kusmierek, *President*
**EMP:** 3
**SALES (est):** 400.7K Privately Held
**SIC:** 3312 Chemicals & other products derived from coking

**(G-17491)**
### NORTH AMERICA PACKAGING CORP
Also Called: Bennett Industries
515 N First St (60468-8975)
P.O. Box 519 (60468-0519)
**PHONE**.................................630 845-8726
James Engebretson, *Branch Mgr*
**EMP:** 113
**SALES (corp-wide):** 831.7MM Privately Held
**WEB:** www.nampac.com
**SIC:** 3089 Pails, plastic
**HQ:** North America Packaging Corp
1515 W 22nd St Ste 550
Oak Brook IL 60523
630 203-4100

## Peotone - Will County (G-17492)

**(G-17492)**
**RUSSELL PUBLICATIONS INC**
Also Called: Peotone Vidette
120 W North St (60468-9226)
P.O. Box 429 (60468-0429)
**PHONE**..................................708 258-3473
**Fax:** 708 258-6295
Christopher L Russell, *President*
Gilbert L Russell Jr, *President*
Mike Russell, *General Mgr*
Sharon Russell, *Corp Secy*
Chris Russell, *Vice Pres*
**EMP:** 20 **EST:** 1894
**SQ FT:** 1,500
**SALES (est):** 1.2MM **Privately Held**
**SIC:** 2711 Newspapers, publishing & printing

**(G-17493)**
**TERESA FOODS INC**
Also Called: Teresa Frozen Pizzas
116 Main St (60468-9265)
P.O. Box 1028 (60468-1028)
**PHONE**..................................708 258-6200
**Fax:** 708 258-9794
Robert T Nagel, *President*
Paul Nagel Jr, *Vice Pres*
Merllyne Nagel, *Office Mgr*
**EMP:** 15
**SQ FT:** 8,000
**SALES (est):** 2MM **Privately Held**
**SIC:** 2038 2099 Pizza, frozen; food preparations

**(G-17494)**
**YOUR LOGO HERE**
427 S Governors Hwy (60468-9116)
**PHONE**..................................708 258-6666
David Polhill, *Owner*
**EMP:** 2
**SALES (est):** 256.1K **Privately Held**
**SIC:** 2759 Screen printing

## Percy
### Randolph County

**(G-17495)**
**KNIGHT HAWK COAL LLC (PA)**
500 Cutler Trico Rd (62272-2716)
**PHONE**..................................618 426-3662
Keith Dailey, *General Mgr*
Dale Winter, *Plant Mgr*
Steve Carter, *Facilities Mgr*
Josh Norton, *Accounting Mgr*
Van Eaves, *Sales Staff*
**EMP:** 7
**SQ FT:** 6,000
**SALES (est):** 544.3MM **Privately Held**
**WEB:** www.knighthawkcoal.com
**SIC:** 1241 1222 Coal mining services; bituminous coal-underground mining

**(G-17496)**
**WILLIS PUBLISHING**
Also Called: County Journal
1101 E Pine St (62272-1333)
P.O. Box 369 (62272-0369)
**PHONE**..................................618 497-8272
**Fax:** 618 497-2607
Gerald Willis, *President*
Larry R Willis, *Vice Pres*
**EMP:** 19
**SQ FT:** 7,000
**SALES (est):** 1.1MM **Privately Held**
**WEB:** www.willispublishing.com
**SIC:** 2711 2752 Newspapers: publishing only, not printed on site; commercial printing, offset

## Perry
### Pike County

**(G-17497)**
**PIONEER EXPRESS**
404 W Highway St (62362-1045)
P.O. Box 158 (62362-0158)
**PHONE**..................................217 236-3022
Cheryl White, *Principal*
**EMP:** 5
**SALES (est):** 404K **Privately Held**
**SIC:** 3567 Industrial furnaces & ovens

## Peru
### Lasalle County

**(G-17498)**
**ACCUBOW LLC**
350 5th St Ste 266 (61354-2813)
**PHONE**..................................815 250-0607
Matthew Pell, *CEO*
Cody Grandadam, *COO*
Robert Pell, *Vice Pres*
Tim Turczyn, *CFO*
**EMP:** 4
**SALES (est):** 161.4K **Privately Held**
**SIC:** 3089 Injection molded finished plastic products

**(G-17499)**
**ANDREW C ARNOLD**
Also Called: Andys Pet Shop
2228 4th St (61354-3213)
**PHONE**..................................815 220-0282
Andrew C Arnold, *Owner*
**EMP:** 1
**SALES:** 200K **Privately Held**
**SIC:** 3999 3949 Pet supplies; sporting & athletic goods

**(G-17500)**
**APPLE PRESS INC**
329 N 25th Rd (61354-9496)
**PHONE**..................................815 224-1451
**Fax:** 815 224-1452
Greg Vaccaro, *Partner*
Chuck Allman, *Partner*
**EMP:** 4
**SQ FT:** 4,000
**SALES:** 210K **Privately Held**
**SIC:** 2759 2791 2789 2752 Commercial printing; typesetting; bookbinding & related work; commercial printing, lithographic

**(G-17501)**
**AUGUST HILL WINERY**
21 N 2551st Rd (61354-9411)
**PHONE**..................................815 224-8199
W August, *Principal*
▲ **EMP:** 7 **EST:** 2008
**SALES (est):** 688.8K **Privately Held**
**SIC:** 2084 Wines

**(G-17502)**
**CANAM STEEL CORPORATION**
9 Unytite Dr (61354-9710)
**PHONE**..................................815 224-9588
**EMP:** 128
**SALES (corp-wide):** 1.2B **Privately Held**
**SIC:** 3441 Building components, structural steel
**HQ:** Canam Steel Corporation
4010 Clay St
Point Of Rocks MD 21777
301 874-5141

**(G-17503)**
**CARUS CORPORATION (HQ)**
315 5th St (61354-2859)
P.O. Box 599 (61354-0599)
**PHONE**..................................815 223-1500
Inga Carus, *Ch of Bd*
David Kuzy, *President*
Bob Glaze, *Vice Pres*
Marie Marcenac, *Vice Pres*
Rick Deblois, *QC Mgr*
▲ **EMP:** 56 **EST:** 1915
**SQ FT:** 56,000
**SALES (est):** 79.2MM
**SALES (corp-wide):** 150.6MM **Privately Held**
**WEB:** www.caruscorporation.com
**SIC:** 2819 Industrial inorganic chemicals; potassium compounds or salts, except hydroxide or carbonate
**PA:** Carus Group Inc.
315 5th St
Peru IL 61354
815 223-1500

**(G-17504)**
**CARUS GROUP INC (PA)**
315 5th St (61354-2859)
**PHONE**..................................815 223-1500
Inga Carus, *Principal*
Gregory G Thiess, *Vice Pres*
Judy Wierman, *Vice Pres*
M Blouke Carus, *Chm Emeritus*
Mary Stachowicz, *Asst Sec*
**EMP:** 57
**SALES:** 150.6MM **Privately Held**
**SIC:** 2819 Industrial inorganic chemicals; potassium compounds or salts, except hydroxide or carbonate

**(G-17505)**
**COCACOLA BOTTLING CO**
3808 Progress Blvd (61354-1120)
**PHONE**..................................815 220-3100
Al Helton, *Plant Mgr*
**EMP:** 3
**SALES (est):** 153.4K **Privately Held**
**SIC:** 2086 Bottled & canned soft drinks

**(G-17506)**
**COUGAR INDUSTRIES INC**
3600 Cougar Dr (61354-9336)
**PHONE**..................................815 224-1200
**Fax:** 815 224-1241
Robert Ciulla, *President*
Dwight H Frick, *Vice Pres*
Don Papini, *Sales Engr*
Sue Griffith, *Marketing Staff*
Traci Ciulla, *Admin Sec*
▲ **EMP:** 23 **EST:** 1964
**SQ FT:** 10,000
**SALES (est):** 6.7MM
**SALES (corp-wide):** 175.3MM **Privately Held**
**WEB:** www.cougarindustries.com
**SIC:** 3531 Vibrators for concrete construction
**PA:** Martin Engineering Company
1 Martin Pl
Neponset IL 61345
309 852-2384

**(G-17507)**
**DRESBACH DISTRIBUTING CO**
102 Pike St (61354-3477)
**PHONE**..................................815 223-0116
Robert Dresbach, *President*
**EMP:** 7
**SQ FT:** 18,000
**SALES (est):** 1.6MM **Privately Held**
**SIC:** 5181 2671 Beer & other fermented malt liquors; packaging paper & plastics film, coated & laminated

**(G-17508)**
**EAKAS CORPORATION**
6251 State Route 251 (61354-9711)
**PHONE**..................................815 223-8811
**Fax:** 815 223-8898
Tomohisa Mori, *President*
Tom Shores, *General Mgr*
Cary Miller, *Plant Mgr*
Jeff Wagner, *Plant Mgr*
Anthony Mattizza, *Purch Dir*
▲ **EMP:** 275
**SQ FT:** 200,000
**SALES (est):** 90.1MM
**SALES (corp-wide):** 338.5MM **Privately Held**
**WEB:** www.eakas.com
**SIC:** 3089 Injection molding of plastics
**PA:** Sakae Riken Kogyo Co.,Ltd.
1-48, Nishibiwajimachomiyamae
Kiyosu 452-0
525 018-231

**(G-17509)**
**FLINT HILLS RESOURCES LP**
501 Brunner St (61354-3638)
**PHONE**..................................815 224-1525
Steven Emmett, *Opers Mgr*
Eric Michalski, *Safety Mgr*
Tim Toennis, *Production*
Leslie Goodwin, *Controller*
Brian Marcinkus, *Branch Mgr*
**EMP:** 85
**SALES (corp-wide):** 27.4B **Privately Held**
**WEB:** www.fhr.com
**SIC:** 1479 Ocher mining
**HQ:** Flint Hills Resources, Lp
4111 E 37th St N
Wichita KS 67220
800 292-3133

**(G-17510)**
**FLINT HLLS RSOURCES JOLIET LLC**
501 Brunner St (61354-3638)
**PHONE**..................................815 224-5232
**EMP:** 3
**SALES (corp-wide):** 27.4B **Privately Held**
**SIC:** 2821 Polystyrene resins
**HQ:** Flint Hills Resources Joliet, Llc
4111 E 37th St N
Wichita KS 67220

**(G-17511)**
**HARBISON CORPORATION**
Also Called: Pretium Packaging
4444 Hollerich Dr (61354-9334)
**PHONE**..................................815 224-2633
**Fax:** 815 224-2247
Robert Benton, *Plant Mgr*
Todd Lomack, *Plant Mgr*
John Kennedy, *Manager*
**EMP:** 80
**SALES (corp-wide):** 197.2MM **Privately Held**
**WEB:** www.pretiumpkg.com
**SIC:** 3089 3085 Molding primary plastic; plastics bottles
**PA:** Harbison Corporation
15450 South Outer 40 Rd # 120
Chesterfield MO 63017
314 727-8200

**(G-17512)**
**HUNTSMAN EXPNDABLE POLYMERS LC**
501 Brunner St (61354-3638)
**PHONE**..................................815 224-5463
Mark Tanner, *Accounts Mgr*
Mark Johnson, *Info Tech Dir*
Peter R Huntsman,
**EMP:** 111
**SALES (est):** 9.6MM
**SALES (corp-wide):** 9.6B **Publicly Held**
**SIC:** 3081 2821 Plastic film & sheet; plastics materials & resins; polyethylene resins; polypropylene resins; styrene resins
**HQ:** Huntsman-Cooper, L.L.C.
500 S Huntsman Way
Salt Lake City UT 84108
801 584-5700

**(G-17513)**
**ILLINOIS VALLEY CONTAINER INC**
2 Terminal Rd (61354-3700)
P.O. Box 49 (61354-0049)
**PHONE**..................................815 223-7200
**Fax:** 815 223-6003
Jay Alter, *President*
Julia Alter, *Corp Secy*
**EMP:** 20
**SQ FT:** 40,000
**SALES (est):** 6MM **Privately Held**
**SIC:** 2653 Boxes, corrugated: made from purchased materials

**(G-17514)**
**INK WELL PRINTING**
24 W Us Highway 6 (61354-2903)
**PHONE**..................................815 224-1366
**Fax:** 815 224-1374
Linda Sorrentino, *Partner*
James Sorrentino, *Partner*
**EMP:** 6
**SQ FT:** 1,800
**SALES (est):** 450K **Privately Held**
**SIC:** 2752 2791 2789 Commercial printing, lithographic; typesetting; bookbinding & related work

**(G-17515)**
**KAWNEER COMPANY INC**
2528 7th St (61354-2424)
**PHONE**..................................815 224-2708
**EMP:** 81
**SALES (corp-wide):** 23.9B **Publicly Held**
**SIC:** 3442 Mfg Metal Doors/Sash/Trim
**HQ:** Kawneer Company, Inc.
555 Guthridge Ct
Norcross GA 30092
770 449-5555

## GEOGRAPHIC SECTION

**(G-17516)**
**LANGHAM ENGINEERING**
1414 Shooting Park Rd (61354-1857)
**PHONE**.................................815 223-5250
J Michael Langham, *CEO*
Rob Pangicie, *Foreman/Supr*
Patricia Langham, *Purchasing*
**EMP:** 3
**SQ FT:** 4,000
**SALES (est):** 195.8K **Privately Held**
**SIC: 8711** 3825 3824 3663 Mechanical engineering; electrical or electronic engineering; instruments to measure electricity; fluid meters & counting devices; radio & TV communications equipment; switchgear & switchboard apparatus

**(G-17517)**
**LOUS SPRING AND WELDING SHOP**
Also Called: Lou's Spring & Welding
2850 May Rd (61354-9617)
**PHONE**.................................815 223-4282
Charles Pezanowski, *President*
Melvin Czanoski, *Admin Sec*
**EMP:** 4 **EST:** 1947
**SALES (est):** 453.2K **Privately Held**
**SIC: 7692** 7539 Welding repair; automotive repair shops

**(G-17518)**
**MERTEL GRAVEL COMPANY INC**
2400 Water St (61354-3494)
**PHONE**.................................815 223-0468
**Fax:** 815 223-0484
Susan J Happ, *President*
Terry Mertel, *Vice Pres*
Joe Liss, *Manager*
**EMP:** 10 **EST:** 1922
**SQ FT:** 800
**SALES (est):** 1.8MM **Privately Held**
**WEB:** www.mertelgravel.com
**SIC: 3273** 5032 1794 1442 Ready-mixed concrete; sand, construction; gravel; excavation work; construction sand & gravel

**(G-17519)**
**METOKOTE CORPORATION**
5750 State Route 251 (61354-9712)
**PHONE**.................................815 223-1190
**Fax:** 815 223-1191
James Kelly, *Manager*
**EMP:** 50
**SALES (corp-wide):** 14.7B **Publicly Held**
**WEB:** www.metokote.com
**SIC: 3479** 3471 Coating of metals & formed products; plating & polishing
**HQ:** Metokote Corporation
1340 Neubrecht Rd
Lima OH 45801
419 996-7800

**(G-17520)**
**MIDWEST TESTING SERVICES INC**
3705 Progress Blvd Ste 2 (61354-1185)
**PHONE**.................................815 223-6696
**Fax:** 815 223-6659
Joseph E Safranski, *President*
Randy Safranski, *Vice Pres*
Jeff Safranski, *Treasurer*
**EMP:** 8
**SALES (est):** 510K **Privately Held**
**SIC: 1481** Test boring for nonmetallic minerals

**(G-17521)**
**NANOCHEM SOLUTIONS INC**
5350 Donlar Ave (61354-9622)
**PHONE**.................................815 224-8480
Don Anderson, *Manager*
**EMP:** 6
**SALES (corp-wide):** 2.3MM **Privately Held**
**WEB:** www.nanochemsolutions.com
**SIC: 2819** Industrial inorganic chemicals
**PA:** Nanochem Solutions Inc.
1701 Quincy Ave Ste 10
Naperville IL 60540
708 563-9200

**(G-17522)**
**NEW CIE INC**
Motor Repair Division
3349 Becker Dr (61354-1161)
**PHONE**.................................815 224-1511
**Fax:** 815 223-4264
Harold Konieczki, *Manager*
Eric Eiseman, *Manager*
Erik Eiseman, *Manager*
**EMP:** 30
**SALES (corp-wide):** 11.4MM **Privately Held**
**SIC: 3537** 5063 7694 5999 Industrial trucks & tractors; electrical apparatus & equipment; armature rewinding shops; motors, electric; machine shop, jobbing & repair; machine moving & rigging
**PA:** New Cie, Inc.
1220 Wenzel Rd
Peru IL 61354
815 224-1510

**(G-17523)**
**NOVA CHEMICALS INC**
Also Called: Humpsman
501 Brunner St (61354-3638)
**PHONE**.................................815 224-1525
**Fax:** 815 224-5278
Jeff Moran, *Mfg Spvr*
Brian Marcinkus, *Manager*
**EMP:** 53 **Privately Held**
**SIC: 2821** Polystyrene resins
**HQ:** Nova Chemicals Inc.
400 Frankfort Rd
Monaca PA 15061
412 490-4560

**(G-17524)**
**PROMIER PRODUCTS INC**
350 5th St Ste 266 (61354-2813)
**PHONE**.................................815 223-3393
Cody Grandadam, *President*
Tim Turczyn, *CFO*
Phil Black, *Sales Executive*
**EMP:** 10
**SQ FT:** 1,500
**SALES:** 8MM **Privately Held**
**SIC: 3648** Flashlights

**(G-17525)**
**QUESSE MOVING & STORAGE INC**
Also Called: Wheaton Lines
4438 Hollerich Dr (61354-9334)
**PHONE**.................................815 223-0253
**Fax:** 815 223-4654
Gary Quesse, *President*
**EMP:** 4 **EST:** 1923
**SALES:** 360K **Privately Held**
**SIC: 2511** Storage chests, household: wood

**(G-17526)**
**ROYAL PUBLISHING INC**
4375 Venture Dr (61354-1014)
**PHONE**.................................815 220-0400
**Fax:** 815 220-0500
John Shurtleff, *Branch Mgr*
**EMP:** 9
**SALES (corp-wide):** 7MM **Privately Held**
**SIC: 2731** Pamphlets: publishing & printing
**PA:** Royal Publishing, Inc.
7620 N Harker Dr
Peoria IL
309 693-3171

**(G-17527)**
**SALES STRETCHER ENTERPRISES**
4920 E 103rd Rd (61354-9356)
P.O. Box 449 (61354-0449)
**PHONE**.................................815 223-9681
**Fax:** 815 223-4898
Rolif Loveland, *President*
▲ **EMP:** 18
**SALES (est):** 2.7MM **Privately Held**
**SIC: 2952** 5051 Coating compounds, tar; nails

**(G-17528)**
**T & T DISTRIBUTION INC**
Also Called: T&T Hydraulics
304 5th St (61354-2813)
**PHONE**.................................815 223-0715
Mike Turczyn, *President*
Tim Turczyn, *CFO*
Chester Turczyn, *Admin Sec*
**EMP:** 25
**SQ FT:** 18,000
**SALES (est):** 1.9MM **Privately Held**
**SIC: 3492** 5084 Hose & tube fittings & assemblies, hydraulic/pneumatic; drilling bits

**(G-17529)**
**UNYTITE INC**
1 Unytite Dr (61354-9710)
**PHONE**.................................815 224-2221
**Fax:** 815 224-3434
Jun Hashimoto, *President*
Yuji Ozeki, *Vice Pres*
Dan Savage, *Vice Pres*
Chris Facemire, *Plant Mgr*
Chuck Hundley, *Plant Mgr*
▲ **EMP:** 105
**SQ FT:** 125,000
**SALES (est):** 40.1MM
**SALES (corp-wide):** 83.4MM **Privately Held**
**WEB:** www.unytite.com
**SIC: 3452** Bolts, nuts, rivets & washers
**PA:** Unytite Corporation
3-1-12, Takatsukadai, Nishi-Ku
Kobe HYO 651-2
789 912-233

**(G-17530)**
**W H MAZE COMPANY (PA)**
Also Called: Maze Nails Div
1100 Water St (61354-3654)
P.O. Box 449 (61354-0449)
**PHONE**.................................815 223-1742
**Fax:** 815 223-1752
Roelif Loveland, *President*
Roger Vaccaro, *Vice Pres*
Joe Salz, *Sales Staff*
Kim Pohl, *Marketing Mgr*
Walt Kotecki, *Manager*
▲ **EMP:** 25
**SQ FT:** 15,700
**SALES (est):** 20.7MM **Privately Held**
**WEB:** www.mazelumber.com
**SIC: 3315** 5211 Nails, steel: wire or cut; lumber & other building materials

**(G-17531)**
**W H MAZE COMPANY**
Maze Nails Division
100 Church St (61354-3498)
P.O. Box 449 (61354-0449)
**PHONE**.................................815 223-8290
**Fax:** 815 223-7585
Len Kasperski, *Vice Pres*
George Maze, *Vice Pres*
James Kaszynski, *Purchasing*
Kimberald Pohl, *Marketing Staff*
Roelif Loveland, *Manager*
**EMP:** 99
**SALES (corp-wide):** 20.7MM **Privately Held**
**WEB:** www.mazelumber.com
**SIC: 3315** Nails, steel: wire or cut
**PA:** W. H. Maze Company
1100 Water St
Peru IL 61354
815 223-1742

**(G-17532)**
**WILLIAM N PASULKA**
Also Called: Home Water Products
15685 State Highway 71 (61354-5005)
**PHONE**.................................815 339-6300
William Pasulka, *Owner*
Nick Pasulka, *Co-Owner*
**EMP:** 1
**SQ FT:** 5,000
**SALES:** 5MM **Privately Held**
**SIC: 3589** 3651 Water purification equipment, household type; home entertainment equipment, electronic

### Pesotum
*Champaign County*

**(G-17533)**
**ROUTE 45 WAYSIDE**
101 S Chestnut St (61863-9500)
**PHONE**.................................217 867-2000
Christyn H Grassman, *Principal*
**EMP:** 4
**SALES (est):** 359.5K **Privately Held**
**SIC: 2599** Bar, restaurant & cafeteria furniture

### Petersburg
*Menard County*

**(G-17534)**
**CARLBERG DESIGN INC**
Also Called: Rugby America
1215 E Clary St (62675-1154)
**PHONE**.................................217 341-3291
**Fax:** 217 632-0124
James Carlberg, *President*
**EMP:** 5
**SALES (est):** 513.7K **Privately Held**
**SIC: 2741** 2759 7336 Miscellaneous publishing; commercial printing; graphic arts & related design

**(G-17535)**
**CURRY READY MIX OF PETERSBURG**
1106 N 7th St (62675-1178)
**PHONE**.................................217 632-2516
**Fax:** 217 632-4192
Dan Curry, *Owner*
Rick Boensel, *Manager*
**EMP:** 4
**SALES (est):** 349.1K **Privately Held**
**SIC: 3273** Ready-mixed concrete

**(G-17536)**
**INDESCO OVEN PRODUCTS INC**
15935 Whisper Ln (62675-7200)
**PHONE**.................................217 622-6345
Norman P Jones, *President*
**EMP:** 7
**SALES (est):** 750.6K **Privately Held**
**WEB:** www.indescoovenproducts.com
**SIC: 8742** 3822 Automation & robotics consultant; gas burner, automatic controls

**(G-17537)**
**PETERSBURG OBSERVER CO INC**
235 E Sangamon Ave (62675-1245)
P.O. Box 350 (62675-0350)
**PHONE**.................................217 632-2236
**Fax:** 217 632-2237
Harriett Shaw, *President*
Jane Cutright, *Corp Secy*
**EMP:** 7
**SQ FT:** 5,000
**SALES (est):** 350K **Privately Held**
**SIC: 2711** 2759 2752 Newspapers: publishing only, not printed on site; letterpress printing; commercial printing, lithographic

**(G-17538)**
**SNAGAMON VALLEY LOG BUILDERS**
21500 Old Farm Ave (62675-6072)
**PHONE**.................................217 632-7609
Jeff Fore, *Owner*
**EMP:** 3
**SALES (est):** 222.2K **Privately Held**
**SIC: 2452** Log cabins, prefabricated, wood

### Philo
*Champaign County*

**(G-17539)**
**JAMAICA PYROTECHNICS (PA)**
Also Called: Jpi
212 Franks Dr (61864-9676)
**PHONE**.................................217 649-2902
Todd Chew, *Partner*
**EMP:** 3
**SALES (est):** 321.9K **Privately Held**
**WEB:** www.jamaicapyro.com
**SIC: 2899** Fireworks

## Phoenix
### Cook County

**(G-17540)**
**CREAM TEAM LOGISTICS LLC**
15348 9th Ave (60426-2517)
Drawer 15348 9th, Harvey (60426)
PHONE.................................708 541-9128
Mario Beard, *Principal*
**EMP:** 10
**SALES (est):** 530.2K **Privately Held**
**SIC:** 3087 7389 Custom compound purchased resins;

**(G-17541)**
**JOHN J RICKHOFF SHTMTL CO INC**
320 E 152nd St (60426-2305)
PHONE.................................708 331-2970
Fax: 708 331-2531
John E Rickhoff, *President*
Judy Rickhoff, *Principal*
Anthony Rickhoff, *Vice Pres*
Donna Rickhoff, *Admin Sec*
**EMP:** 10 **EST:** 1937
**SQ FT:** 12,000
**SALES (est):** 1.1MM **Privately Held**
**SIC:** 1761 3542 3444 Sheet metalwork; machine tools, metal forming type; sheet metalwork

**(G-17542)**
**STERLING LUMBER COMPANY (PA)**
501 E 151st St (60426-2402)
PHONE.................................708 388-2223
Fax: 708 388-2224
John Sterling, *CEO*
Carter Sterling, *President*
Brad Zenner, *General Mgr*
Carson Sterling, *Vice Pres*
Christian Sterling, *Vice Pres*
◆ **EMP:** 127
**SQ FT:** 500,000
**SALES (est):** 100.1MM **Privately Held**
**WEB:** www.sterlinglumber.com
**SIC:** 5031 7389 2448 Lumber: rough, dressed & finished; log & lumber broker; pallets, wood; skids, wood

## Piasa
### Macoupin County

**(G-17543)**
**WAYMORE POWER CO INC**
8334 Piasa Rd (62079-2024)
PHONE.................................618 729-3876
Fax: 618 729-2100
Spencer Garrett, *President*
Julie Garrett, *Vice Pres*
John Lynch, *Manager*
**EMP:** 10
**SALES (est):** 1.2MM **Privately Held**
**WEB:** www.waymorepower.com
**SIC:** 7538 3519 Diesel engine repair: automotive; internal combustion engines

## Pinckneyville
### Perry County

**(G-17544)**
**BEELMAN READY-MIX INC**
5780 State Route 154 (62274-3420)
PHONE.................................618 357-6120
Kiah McCance, *Manager*
**EMP:** 7 **Privately Held**
**WEB:** www.beelmanrm.com
**SIC:** 3273 5211 Ready-mixed concrete; masonry materials & supplies
**PA:** Beelman Ready-Mix, Inc.
1 Racehorse Dr
East Saint Louis IL 62205

**(G-17545)**
**CONTEMPRI INDUSTRIES INC**
Also Called: Contempri Homes
1000 W Water St (62274-4163)
P.O. Box 69 (62274-0069)
PHONE.................................618 357-5361
Fax: 618 357-6629
John A Perry, *President*
Lawrence R Pericolosi, *Vice Pres*
Shawn Odun, *Accountant*
George Marifian, *Admin Sec*
**EMP:** 50 **EST:** 1978
**SQ FT:** 50,000
**SALES (est):** 7.5MM **Privately Held**
**WEB:** www.contemprihomes.com
**SIC:** 2452 Modular homes, prefabricated, wood

**(G-17546)**
**COOPER B-LINE INC**
Gs Metals
3764 Longspur Rd (62274-3103)
PHONE.................................618 357-5353
Kenneth Alessi, *Branch Mgr*
**EMP:** 170 **Privately Held**
**WEB:** www.cooperbline.com
**SIC:** 3446 Gratings, tread: fabricated metal
**HQ:** Cooper B-Line , Inc.
509 W Monroe St
Highland IL 62249
618 654-2184

**(G-17547)**
**DESIGNS UNLIMITED**
1242 S Main St (62274-3312)
PHONE.................................618 357-6728
Fax: 618 357-6728
Steve R Tanner, *Owner*
**EMP:** 4
**SALES (est):** 296.9K **Privately Held**
**SIC:** 3993 Signs & advertising specialties

**(G-17548)**
**FRESH FACS**
612 County Rd (62274-1512)
PHONE.................................618 357-9697
Ramona Hatch, *Owner*
**EMP:** 4
**SALES (est):** 297.4K **Privately Held**
**SIC:** 2741 Miscellaneous publishing

**(G-17549)**
**GRAFFS TOOLING CENTER INC**
801 S Main St (62274-1768)
PHONE.................................618 357-5005
Marvin Graff, *President*
**EMP:** 6
**SALES (est):** 756.6K **Privately Held**
**WEB:** www.grafftool.com
**SIC:** 3544 Special dies & tools

**(G-17550)**
**GS METALS CORP**
3764 Longspur Rd (62274-3103)
PHONE.................................618 357-3605
Fax: 618 357-3605
Kenneth W Coco, *President*
Ron Liefer, *Accountant*
Dennis J Gallitano, *Admin Sec*
▼ **EMP:** 170
**SALES (est):** 23.9MM **Privately Held**
**WEB:** www.gsmetals.com
**SIC:** 3446 Gratings, tread: fabricated metal

**(G-17551)**
**PHOENIX GRAPHIX**
4513 Swanwick Rice Rd (62274-2007)
PHONE.................................618 531-3664
Christopher Wright, *Owner*
**EMP:** 4
**SQ FT:** 2,000
**SALES:** 250K **Privately Held**
**SIC:** 2241 5131 7336 Apparel webbing; trimmings, apparel; creative services to advertisers, except writers

**(G-17552)**
**SIEMENS ENERGY INC**
4646 White Walnut Rd (62274-2726)
PHONE.................................618 357-6360
Tom Schrader, *Manager*
**EMP:** 209
**SALES (corp-wide):** 89.6B **Privately Held**
**SIC:** 3511 Turbines & turbine generator sets
**HQ:** Siemens Energy, Inc.
4400 N Alafaya Trl
Orlando FL 32826
407 736-2000

**(G-17553)**
**TREE-O LUMBER INC**
5492 Woodhaven Rd (62274-2616)
P.O. Box 366 (62274-0366)
PHONE.................................618 357-2576
Fred Kelly, *President*
Edreye Kelly, *Admin Sec*
**EMP:** 20
**SALES (est):** 1.7MM **Privately Held**
**SIC:** 2421 2431 2426 Sawmills & planing mills, general; millwork; hardwood dimension & flooring mills

**(G-17554)**
**WESTERN AUTO ASSOCIATE STR CO**
9 S Walnut St (62274-1313)
PHONE.................................618 357-5555
Charles Curt, *Owner*
**EMP:** 3
**SQ FT:** 5,000
**SALES (est):** 160K **Privately Held**
**SIC:** 3634 Personal electrical appliances

## Pingree Grove
### Kane County

**(G-17555)**
**ELGIN DIE MOLD CO**
14n002 Prairie St (60140-6314)
PHONE.................................847 464-0147
Fax: 847 464-0147
John Sapiente, *President*
Mike Quandt, *VP Mfg*
Brad Bishop, *Materials Mgr*
Jason Franklin, *Project Engr*
Valerie Moscato, *CFO*
**EMP:** 80 **EST:** 1967
**SALES (est):** 20.6MM **Privately Held**
**WEB:** www.elgindiemold.com
**SIC:** 3089 Molding primary plastic

**(G-17556)**
**MINUTEMAN INTERNATIONAL INC (DH)**
14n845 Us Highway 20 (60140-8893)
PHONE.................................630 627-6900
Steve Liew, *CEO*
Mario Schreiber, *President*
John Troy, *Division Mgr*
Stephen Boebel, *Vice Pres*
Ed Wasilick, *Purch Mgr*
◆ **EMP:** 120 **EST:** 1951
**SQ FT:** 112,230
**SALES (est):** 35.2MM **Privately Held**
**WEB:** www.multi-clean.com
**SIC:** 3589 2842 Commercial cleaning equipment; cleaning or polishing preparations
**HQ:** Hako Gmbh
Hamburger Str. 209-239
Bad Oldesloe 23843
453 180-60

**(G-17557)**
**TRIDENT MANUFACTURING INC**
14n2 Prairie St (60140)
PHONE.................................847 464-0140
Ronald Horney, *General Mgr*
John A Sapiente, *Chairman*
Britt O'Halloran, *Engineer*
▲ **EMP:** 20 **Privately Held**
**WEB:** www.triton-chemicals.com
**SIC:** 3089 Injection molding of plastics

## Piper City
### Ford County

**(G-17558)**
**ATS COMMERCIAL GROUP LLC**
Also Called: Ats Acoustics
15 W Main St (60959-6031)
P.O. Box 260 (60959-0260)
PHONE.................................815 686-2705
Adrienne Macz, *Sales Associate*
Mark Aardsma,
**EMP:** 11
**SQ FT:** 6,000
**SALES (est):** 1.4MM **Privately Held**
**WEB:** www.atsacoustics.com
**SIC:** 7379 3695 Computer related consulting services; computer software tape & disks: blank, rigid & floppy

## Pittsburg
### Williamson County

**(G-17559)**
**ANDERSON TRUSS COMPANY**
12418 Poordo Rd (62974-1802)
PHONE.................................618 982-9228
Boyd Anderson, *President*
**EMP:** 4
**SQ FT:** 3,840
**SALES (est):** 420K **Privately Held**
**SIC:** 2439 Trusses, wooden roof

## Pittsfield
### Pike County

**(G-17560)**
**5 STAR PUBLISHING INC**
1401 E Washington St (62363-9596)
PHONE.................................217 285-1355
Paul Ransom, *President*
**EMP:** 2
**SALES:** 300K **Privately Held**
**WEB:** www.ransoms.org
**SIC:** 2711 Newspapers: publishing only, not printed on site

**(G-17561)**
**B & B PRINTING COMPANY**
115 E Washington St A (62363-1436)
PHONE.................................217 285-6072
Fax: 217 285-2898
Christopher Metcalf, *Owner*
**EMP:** 4 **EST:** 1967
**SALES (est):** 220K **Privately Held**
**SIC:** 2752 2791 2789 2761 Commercial printing, offset; typesetting; bookbinding & related work; manifold business forms; commercial printing; packaging paper & plastics film, coated & laminated

**(G-17562)**
**BUCKLEY POWDER CO**
1353 W Washington St (62363-9549)
PHONE.................................217 285-5531
**EMP:** 17
**SALES (corp-wide):** 57MM **Privately Held**
**SIC:** 2892 Explosives
**PA:** Buckley Powder Co.
42 Inverness Dr E Ste 200
Englewood CO 80112
303 790-7007

**(G-17563)**
**CALLENDER CONSTRUCTION CO INC (PA)**
928 W Washington St (62363-1356)
PHONE.................................217 285-2161
Fax: 217 285-2053
Bruce Callender, *President*
**EMP:** 10
**SQ FT:** 5,000
**SALES (est):** 6.7MM **Privately Held**
**SIC:** 1422 4212 1794 Crushed & broken limestone; dump truck haulage; excavation & grading, building construction

**(G-17564)**
**CAMPBELL PUBLISHING CO INC**
Also Called: Pike Press
115 W Jefferson St (62363-1424)
P.O. Box 70 (62363-0070)
PHONE.................................217 285-2345
Fax: 217 285-5222
Nichole Liehr, *Editor*
Chuck Anthony, *Production*
Bruce Campbell, *Branch Mgr*
**EMP:** 18
**SALES (corp-wide):** 2MM **Privately Held**
**SIC:** 2711 Newspapers

PA: Campbell Publishing Co Inc
310 S County Rd
Hardin IL
618 576-2345

### (G-17565)
**CENTRAL STONE COMPANY**
26176 487th St (62363-2400)
PHONE..................................217 723-4410
Fax: 217 723-4126
Doug Brackett, *Manager*
EMP: 12
SALES (corp-wide): 3.9B **Privately Held**
SIC: 1422 Limestones, ground
HQ: Central Stone Company
1701 5th Ave
Moline IL 61265
309 757-8250

### (G-17566)
**COMMUNITY RADY MIX OF PTTSFELD**
Also Called: Community Ready Mix Pittsfield
1503 Kamar Dr (62363-2005)
PHONE..................................217 285-5548
Ray Curry, *President*
EMP: 5
SALES (est): 285.6K **Privately Held**
SIC: 3273 Ready-mixed concrete

### (G-17567)
**COMPLETE ASPHALT SERVICE CO**
Also Called: C A S C O
1601 Kaymar Dr (62363)
P.O. Box 457 (62363-0457)
PHONE..................................217 285-6099
Fax: 217 285-6094
Christopher Wingler, *President*
George Whitlock, *Vice Pres*
Karla Little, *Admin Sec*
EMP: 20
SALES (est): 3.6MM **Privately Held**
SIC: 2952 Asphalt felts & coatings

### (G-17568)
**GOD FAMILY COUNTRY LLC**
Also Called: Gfc
34273 210th Ave (62363-2716)
PHONE..................................217 285-6487
Fax: 217 285-6488
Owen Brown,
EMP: 13
SALES: 575K **Privately Held**
WEB: www.gfc.net
SIC: 2011 Beef products from beef slaughtered on site

### (G-17569)
**GOOD TIMES ROLL**
1241 W Washington St (62363-1656)
PHONE..................................217 285-4885
Lindel C Holp, *Owner*
Diana Holp, *Co-Owner*
EMP: 6
SALES (est): 137.7K **Privately Held**
SIC: 7999 3949 Skating rink operation services; skates & parts, roller

### (G-17570)
**JBS UNITED INC**
502 N Madison St (62363-1127)
P.O. Box 535 (62363-0535)
PHONE..................................217 285-2121
Thomas Hurd, *Manager*
EMP: 15
SALES (corp-wide): 136.8MM **Privately Held**
WEB: www.jbsunited.com
SIC: 2048 5153 5191 Prepared feeds; grains; animal feeds
PA: Jbs United, Inc.
4310 W State Road 38
Sheridan IN 46069
317 758-4495

### (G-17571)
**KCI SATELLITE**
101 N Industrial Park Dr (62363-2006)
PHONE..................................800 664-2602
Patrick Brian Shelton, *President*
EMP: 4
SALES (est): 519K **Privately Held**
SIC: 2599 Hospital beds

### (G-17572)
**OWEN WALKER**
Also Called: Walker's Repair Shop
837 W Adams St (62363-1311)
PHONE..................................217 285-4012
Fax: 217 285-4456
Owen Walker, *Owner*
Connie Walker, *Partner*
EMP: 3
SQ FT: 1,000
SALES: 100K **Privately Held**
SIC: 7699 5251 5261 5084 Knife, saw & tool sharpening & repair; lawn mower repair shop; chainsaws; lawnmowers & tractors; engines, gasoline; saws & sawing equipment

### (G-17573)
**PIKE COUNTY CONCRETE INC**
1503 Kamar Dr (62363-2005)
PHONE..................................217 285-5548
Steve Dunham, *President*
Dwight Dunham, *Vice Pres*
Scott Dunham, *Treasurer*
EMP: 6
SALES (est): 644.2K **Privately Held**
SIC: 3273 Ready-mixed concrete

### (G-17574)
**PIKE COUNTY EXPRESS**
Also Called: Coulson Publications
129 N Madison St (62363-1405)
P.O. Box 537 (62363-0537)
PHONE..................................217 285-5415
Fax: 217 285-9564
Warren Coulson, *Vice Pres*
Brian Shoemaker, *Manager*
EMP: 16
SALES (est): 801.2K **Privately Held**
SIC: 2711 Newspapers

## Plainfield
### Will County

### (G-17575)
**A AND J DEVELOPMENT PLUS LLC**
10101 S Mandel St Ste A (60585-6866)
PHONE..................................630 470-9539
Bill Shippy, *Owner*
EMP: 8
SALES: 160K **Privately Held**
SIC: 2431 Millwork

### (G-17576)
**AD DELUXE SIGN COMPANY INC**
Also Called: Ad-Deluxe Sign Co
23856 W Andrew Rd Ste 103 (60585-8771)
PHONE..................................815 556-8469
Fax: 773 378-4552
Ahmet Demir Sr, *President*
EMP: 3
SQ FT: 30,000
SALES: 480K **Privately Held**
SIC: 3993 7629 1799 Neon signs; signs, not made in custom sign painting shops; electrical repair shops; sign installation & maintenance

### (G-17577)
**AK STEEL CORPORATION**
24036 Nightingale Ct (60585-6170)
PHONE..................................815 267-3838
EMP: 298 **Publicly Held**
SIC: 3312 Blast furnaces & steel mills
HQ: Ak Steel Corporation
9227 Centre Pointe Dr
West Chester OH 45069
513 425-4200

### (G-17578)
**ALL FOR DOGS INC**
1707 Burshire Dr (60586-4136)
PHONE..................................708 744-4113
EMP: 3
SALES (est): 168.6K **Privately Held**
SIC: 3999 Pet supplies

### (G-17579)
**ALL TECH SYSTEMS & INSTALL**
11952 S Spaulding Schl Dr (60585-9535)
PHONE..................................815 609-0685
Paul Allen, *President*
William Allen, *Corp Secy*
Karen Allen, *Vice Pres*
EMP: 4
SQ FT: 7,000
SALES (est): 540K **Privately Held**
SIC: 3669 Burglar alarm apparatus, electric

### (G-17580)
**AMS SEALS INC**
12149 Rhea Dr (60585-9734)
PHONE..................................815 609-4977
Ernie Spiess, *President*
Ernest Steiss, *Manager*
EMP: 7
SQ FT: 5,500
SALES (est): 2.4MM **Privately Held**
SIC: 5085 3624 Seals, industrial; carbon & graphite products

### (G-17581)
**AUTHORITY SCREENPRINT & EMB**
10148 Clow Creek Rd Ste D (60585-6748)
PHONE..................................630 236-0289
Mandy Prendki, *President*
EMP: 2
SQ FT: 780
SALES (est): 244.3K **Privately Held**
WEB: www.authorityscreenprint.com
SIC: 2759 2396 Screen printing; automotive & apparel trimmings

### (G-17582)
**BEST TECHNOLOGY SYSTEMS INC**
12024 S Aero Dr (60585-9702)
PHONE..................................815 254-9554
Fax: 815 254-9558
Gary Chinn, *President*
Mona Lopez, *Office Mgr*
Barbra Crowder, *Administration*
EMP: 17
SQ FT: 2,800
SALES (est): 1MM **Privately Held**
WEB: www.technologysystemsinc.com
SIC: 7999 1799 3949 4959 Shooting range operation; decontamination services; sporting & athletic goods; shooting equipment & supplies, general; sanitary services

### (G-17583)
**CALLIES CUTIES INC**
24860 Madison St (60544-7444)
PHONE..................................815 566-6885
Laura Meehan, *President*
Thomas Meehan, *Admin Sec*
EMP: 4
SQ FT: 1,350
SALES (est): 275.7K **Privately Held**
SIC: 2051 5149 Cakes, bakery: except frozen; crackers, cookies & bakery products

### (G-17584)
**CAMBRIDGE SENSORS USA LLC**
Also Called: Cambridge Sensor Limited
23866 W Industrial Dr N (60585-8567)
PHONE..................................877 374-4062
Engimann Frederick, *Mng Member*
EMP: 3
SALES (est): 855K **Privately Held**
SIC: 3826 8099 Blood testing apparatus; childbirth preparation clinic

### (G-17585)
**CATHYS SWEET CREATIONS**
519 W Lockport Rd (60544-1831)
PHONE..................................815 886-6769
Catherine M Deavila, *President*
Cathy Deavila, *Owner*
EMP: 4
SALES (est): 366.6K **Privately Held**
SIC: 2051 Bakery products, partially cooked (except frozen)

### (G-17586)
**CHICAGO DSCOVERY SOLUTIONS LLC**
23561 W Main St (60544-7601)
PHONE..................................815 609-2071
Anita Mehta, *General Mgr*
Arvind Mehta,
Mukund S Chorghade,
EMP: 4
SQ FT: 700
SALES (est): 412.8K **Privately Held**
WEB: www.chicagodiscoverysolutions.com
SIC: 2834 8731 Pharmaceutical preparations; commercial physical research

### (G-17587)
**CITY UTILITY EQUIPMENT**
22414 W 143rd St (60544-7622)
PHONE..................................815 254-6673
Fax: 815 577-2476
John Jacobs, *Principal*
Louise John, *Admin Sec*
EMP: 10
SALES (est): 1.3MM **Privately Held**
SIC: 3713 Utility truck bodies

### (G-17588)
**CLEAR VIEW INDUSTRIES INC**
2429 Von Esch Rd Unit G (60586-9079)
PHONE..................................815 267-3593
Mike McWean, *President*
Richard Guerra, *Treasurer*
EMP: 3
SALES (est): 350.4K **Privately Held**
SIC: 3231 Doors, glass: made from purchased glass

### (G-17589)
**CNV ENTERPRISES INC**
8282 Old Ridge Rd (60544-9140)
PHONE..................................815 405-6762
Vance Cryder, *President*
EMP: 3 EST: 2006
SALES (est): 262.2K **Privately Held**
SIC: 2411 Stumps, wood

### (G-17590)
**DELUXE EXPRESS**
25026 Michele Dr (60544-7140)
PHONE..................................847 756-0429
Igoris Geguzinshas, *Principal*
EMP: 4 EST: 2010
SALES (est): 276.3K **Privately Held**
SIC: 2782 Checkbooks

### (G-17591)
**DIAGEO NORTH AMERICA INC**
24440 W 143rd St (60544-8704)
PHONE..................................815 267-4400
Matt Gilbreath, *Vice Pres*
Ron Sammeth, *Opers Mgr*
Richard Jacob, *Engineer*
Denise Anderson, *Manager*
Brandon Bowser, *Manager*
EMP: 42
SALES (corp-wide): 15.2B **Privately Held**
SIC: 2085 2084 Gin (alcoholic beverage); vodka (alcoholic beverage); wines, brandy & brandy spirits
HQ: Diageo North America Inc.
801 Main Ave
Norwalk CT 06851
203 229-2100

### (G-17592)
**DISPLAY WORLDWIDE LLC**
Also Called: Partner
2202 Portside Lakes Ct (60586-6252)
PHONE..................................815 439-2695
Jim Baranoski, *Principal*
▲ EMP: 2
SALES (est): 210K **Privately Held**
SIC: 2541 Display fixtures, wood

### (G-17593)
**E&D PRINTING SERVICES INC**
15857 Spanglers Farm Dr (60544-2160)
PHONE..................................815 609-8222
Evaristo Gallego, *President*
EMP: 3
SALES (est): 301.4K **Privately Held**
SIC: 2759 Commercial printing

# Plainfield - Will County (G-17594) — GEOGRAPHIC SECTION

**(G-17594)**
**ENDURE HOLDINGS INC**
Also Called: Polaris Technology Group
24317 W 143rd St Ste 103  (60544-8715)
PHONE..................224 558-1828
Norman Moore, *President*
**EMP:** 7
**SALES (est):** 164.3K  Privately Held
**SIC:** 7371  7372  Computer software development & applications; application computer software

**(G-17595)**
**ENGINEERING PRODUCTS COMPANY**
Also Called: Epco
15125 S Meadow Ln  (60544-1486)
PHONE..................815 436-9055
Sharon Fazio-Mammosser, *President*
Robert R Herman, *VP Sales*
Lyle W Hughart, *Admin Sec*
**EMP:** 3
**SQ FT:** 1,000
**SALES (est):** 800K  Privately Held
**SIC:** 5084  3545  3535  Conveyor systems; machine tool accessories; conveyors & conveying equipment

**(G-17596)**
**EURO-TECH CABINETRY RMDLG CORP**
12515 Rhea Dr  (60585-8507)
PHONE..................815 254-3876
Kim Moriarty, *President*
**EMP:** 8
**SALES (est):** 659K  Privately Held
**SIC:** 2434  Wood kitchen cabinets

**(G-17597)**
**F AND S ENTERPRISES PLAINFIELD**
2035 Havenhill Dr  (60586-6528)
P.O. Box 719  (60544-0719)
PHONE..................815 439-9655
Feda Haleem, *CEO*
**EMP:** 2
**SALES (est):** 201.3K  Privately Held
**SIC:** 3537  Forklift trucks

**(G-17598)**
**F-C ENTERPRISES INC**
12249 Rhea Dr Ste 3  (60585-8762)
PHONE..................815 254-7295
Debra Fagel, *President*
**EMP:** 4  EST: 1979
**SQ FT:** 2,200
**SALES (est):** 213K  Privately Held
**SIC:** 2759  Screen printing

**(G-17599)**
**FAST FORWARD WELDING INC**
23840 W Andrew Rd Ste 4  (60585-8769)
PHONE..................815 254-1901
Aaron Stapleton, *Principal*
**EMP:** 2
**SALES (est):** 203.1K  Privately Held
**SIC:** 7692  Welding repair

**(G-17600)**
**FLOLINE ARCHTCTRAL SYSTEMS LLC**
16108 S Rte 59 Ste 108  (60586-2932)
PHONE..................815 733-5044
Thomas Carron, *President*
John Carron, *Vice Pres*
**EMP:** 10
**SALES:** 1MM  Privately Held
**SIC:** 8712  3089  Architectural engineering; corrugated panels, plastic

**(G-17601)**
**FRESH CONCEPT ENTERPRISES INC**
12249 Rhea Dr  (60585-9586)
PHONE..................815 254-7295
Deborah Fagel, *President*
**EMP:** 3
**SQ FT:** 2,200
**SALES:** 300K  Privately Held
**SIC:** 2396  2759  Printing & embossing on plastics fabric articles; engraving

**(G-17602)**
**GLOBAL MEDICAL SERVICES LLC (PA)**
12904 Rockfish Ln  (60585-2544)
PHONE..................847 460-8086
Kelvin Udogu,
Shunjonna Udeogu,
**EMP:** 4
**SQ FT:** 1,200
**SALES (est):** 464.8K  Privately Held
**SIC:** 2834  Pharmaceutical preparations

**(G-17603)**
**GO JO PALLETS & SUPPLIES INC**
22538 Bass Lake Rd  (60544-7116)
PHONE..................815 254-1631
Josie Ortiz, *President*
Gelacio Ortiz, *Treasurer*
**EMP:** 10
**SALES (est):** 1.3MM  Privately Held
**SIC:** 2448  Wood pallets & skids

**(G-17604)**
**GRAPHIC PALLET & TRANSPORT**
10225 Bode St  (60585-6903)
PHONE..................630 904-4951
Fax: 630 904-6270
Christy Furmaniak, *President*
John Krawisz, *Admin Sec*
▲ **EMP:** 20
**SQ FT:** 30,000
**SALES:** 23MM  Privately Held
**SIC:** 2448  5085  Wood pallets & skids; industrial supplies

**(G-17605)**
**HEALTHDENTL LLC**
10052 Bode St Ste E  (60585-1973)
PHONE..................800 845-5172
Fax: 630 544-3301
Steve Bevilacqua, *Mng Member*
Amy Sullivan, *Manager*
Robert Bevilacqua,
**EMP:** 3
**SQ FT:** 1,996
**SALES:** 280.5K  Privately Held
**SIC:** 3843  Dental equipment & supplies

**(G-17606)**
**HPD LLC**
Also Called: HPD Evporation Crystallization
23563 W Main St  (60544-7660)
PHONE..................815 436-3013
Fax: 815 436-3010
Jim Brown, *President*
Ignacio Martinez, *Managing Dir*
Klaus Andersen, *COO*
Frank Benichou, *COO*
Mark Boone, *Vice Pres*
**EMP:** 165
**SALES (est):** 49.6K
**SALES (corp-wide):** 452.1MM  Privately Held
**WEB:** www.hpd.com
**SIC:** 3589  8711  Water treatment equipment, industrial; engineering services
**HQ:** Veolia Water Technologies
   250 Airside Dr
   Moon Township PA 15108
   412 809-6000

**(G-17607)**
**HUNTER-NUSPORT INC**
24317 W 143rd St  (60544-8714)
P.O. Box 321, Bloomingdale  (60108-0321)
PHONE..................815 254-7520
George Rogers, *General Mgr*
Karen Lawson,
▲ **EMP:** 5
**SALES (est):** 368.1K  Privately Held
**SIC:** 3949  2393  Bags, golf; duffle bags, canvas: made from purchased materials

**(G-17608)**
**I C DYNAMICS INC**
23716 Springs Ct Unit 111  (60585-2229)
PHONE..................708 922-0501
Jack R Saidel, *President*
Carol L Saidel, *Admin Sec*
▲ **EMP:** 8
**SALES (est):** 1.1MM  Privately Held
**WEB:** www.icdynamics.com
**SIC:** 3699  5521  Security devices; used car dealers

**(G-17609)**
**JEFFS SMALL ENGINE INC**
12438 S Route 59  (60585-4607)
PHONE..................630 904-6840
Jeff Witte, *CEO*
◆ **EMP:** 2
**SQ FT:** 2,000
**SALES:** 1.5MM  Privately Held
**SIC:** 3524  Lawn & garden equipment

**(G-17610)**
**JELINEK & SONS INC**
25400 W Hafenrichter Rd  (60585-9776)
PHONE..................630 355-3474
Robert F Kovac Jr, *President*
Gloria M Kovac, *Admin Sec*
**EMP:** 6  EST: 1995
**SALES (est):** 550K  Privately Held
**WEB:** www.jelinek.com
**SIC:** 1521  2431  2394  General remodeling, single-family houses; millwork; canvas & related products

**(G-17611)**
**JFB HART COATINGS INC**
10200 S Mandel St Ste C  (60585-5372)
PHONE..................949 724-9737
James F Beedie, *Manager*
**EMP:** 10  Privately Held
**SIC:** 2851  Shellac (protective coating)
**PA:** Jfb Hart Coatings, Inc.
   10200 S Mandel St Ste C
   Plainfield IL 60585

**(G-17612)**
**JFB HART COATINGS INC (PA)**
10200 S Mandel St Ste C  (60585-5372)
PHONE..................630 783-1917
James F Beedie, *President*
Bruce Duval, *Exec VP*
John Knox, *Exec VP*
Timothy Kingsbury, *CFO*
Bonnie Beedie, *Manager*
**EMP:** 10
**SQ FT:** 5,865
**SALES (est):** 3MM  Privately Held
**WEB:** www.jfbhartcoatings.com
**SIC:** 2851  Paints & allied products

**(G-17613)**
**JO GO PALLET & SUPPLIES**
22538 Bass Lake Rd  (60544-7116)
P.O. Box 821  (60544-0821)
PHONE..................815 254-1631
Josie Ortiz, *Owner*
**EMP:** 10
**SALES (est):** 550K  Privately Held
**SIC:** 2448  Wood pallets & skids

**(G-17614)**
**KARIMI SAIFUDDIN**
Also Called: Sunrise Hardware & Supplies
14017 S Lakeridge Dr  (60544-6994)
PHONE..................630 379-9344
Saifuddin Karimi, *Owner*
**EMP:** 5
**SQ FT:** 400
**SALES:** 1.1MM  Privately Held
**WEB:** www.sunrisehardware.com
**SIC:** 2841  7373  Soap & other detergents; computer system selling services

**(G-17615)**
**KASTELIC CANVAS INC**
15940 S Lincoln Hwy  (60586-5130)
PHONE..................815 436-8160
Mark Muehlfelt, *President*
Susan Kastelic, *Vice Pres*
**EMP:** 2
**SQ FT:** 14,500
**SALES (est):** 275.6K  Privately Held
**WEB:** www.kastelccanvas.com
**SIC:** 2394  Tents: made from purchased materials; tarpaulins, fabric: made from purchased materials; convertible tops, canvas or boat: from purchased materials

**(G-17616)**
**KUUSAKOSKI PHILADELPHIA LLC**
13543 S Route 30  (60544-1100)
PHONE..................215 533-8323
Timo Kuusakoski, *Mng Member*
Harri Pulli,
▼ **EMP:** 77
**SALES (est):** 13.3MM  Privately Held
**SIC:** 3559  Recycling machinery

**(G-17617)**
**LEGACY VULCAN LLC**
Midwest Division
Rr 126  (60544)
PHONE..................815 436-3535
Fax: 815 439-2891
Eric Steidl, *Manager*
Jake Bartels, *Manager*
**EMP:** 23
**SALES (corp-wide):** 3.5B  Publicly Held
**WEB:** www.vulcanmaterials.com
**SIC:** 1442  Construction sand & gravel
**HQ:** Legacy Vulcan, Llc
   1200 Urban Center Dr
   Vestavia AL 35242
   205 298-3000

**(G-17618)**
**LEGACY VULCAN LLC**
Also Called: Bolingbrook Quarry
22933 W Hassert Blvd  (60585-9596)
PHONE..................630 904-1110
Fax: 630 904-1112
Jon Carmack, *Plant Mgr*
Carol Carlini, *Opers Staff*
Craig Reynolds, *Sales Executive*
Phillip Hovis, *Manager*
**EMP:** 18
**SALES (corp-wide):** 3.5B  Publicly Held
**WEB:** www.vulcanmaterials.com
**SIC:** 1442  Construction sand & gravel
**HQ:** Legacy Vulcan, Llc
   1200 Urban Center Dr
   Vestavia AL 35242
   205 298-3000

**(G-17619)**
**LOGOPLASTE CHICAGO LLC**
14420 N Van Dyke Rd  (60544-5867)
PHONE..................815 230-6961
Rui Abelho, *General Mgr*
Lisa Ambrose, *Administration*
**EMP:** 1
**SALES (est):** 12.4MM  Privately Held
**SIC:** 3085  Plastics bottles
**HQ:** Logoplaste Usa, Inc.
   14420 N Van Dyke Rd
   Plainfield IL 60544
   815 230-6961

**(G-17620)**
**LOGOPLASTE FORT WORTH LLC**
14420 N Van Dyke Rd  (60544-5867)
PHONE..................815 230-6961
Filipe De Botton, *CEO*
**EMP:** 1
**SALES (est):** 1MM  Privately Held
**SIC:** 3085  Plastics bottles
**HQ:** Logoplaste Usa, Inc.
   14420 N Van Dyke Rd
   Plainfield IL 60544
   815 230-6961

**(G-17621)**
**LOGOPLASTE RACINE LLC**
14420 N Van Dyke Rd  (60544-5867)
PHONE..................815 230-6961
Filipe De Botton, *CEO*
**EMP:** 1
**SALES (est):** 1.8MM  Privately Held
**SIC:** 3085  Plastics bottles
**HQ:** Logoplaste Usa, Inc.
   14420 N Van Dyke Rd
   Plainfield IL 60544
   815 230-6961

**(G-17622)**
**LOGOPLASTE USA INC (DH)**
14420 N Van Dyke Rd  (60544-5867)
PHONE..................815 230-6961
Filipe De Botton, *CEO*
Michelle Bott, *Finance*
Rui Abelho, *Admin Sec*

## GEOGRAPHIC SECTION

### Plainfield - Will County (G-17650)

▲ EMP: 95
SALES: 100MM **Privately Held**
SIC: 3085 Plastics bottles
HQ: Logoplaste Portugal, Lda
Estrada Malveira Da Serra, 900
Cascais 2750-
214 858-500

**(G-17623)**
**LUBRICATION ENTERPRISES LLC**
12924 Tipperary Ln (60585-2835)
PHONE .................................. 800 537-7683
Vinod C Vasisth, *Principal*
Ben Weems, *Vice Pres*
Scott Leipprandt, *Technical Mgr*
Gary Salb, *Sales Staff*
Paul Grimes, *Marketing Mgr*
EMP: 8
SALES (est): 521.6K **Privately Held**
SIC: 2899 Corrosion preventive lubricant

**(G-17624)**
**MASTER FOG LLC**
23852 W Industrial Dr N (60585-8567)
PHONE .................................. 773 918-9080
Vincent Camerano, *Partner*
EMP: 3
SALES (est): 363K **Privately Held**
SIC: 2899 Chemical preparations

**(G-17625)**
**MIDWEST GROUND EFFECTS**
1713 Fox Ridge Dr (60586-5831)
PHONE .................................. 708 516-5874
EMP: 3
SALES (est): 309.7K **Privately Held**
SIC: 2851 Removers & cleaners

**(G-17626)**
**MIDWEST HOT RODS INC**
23533 W Main St (60544-7660)
PHONE .................................. 815 254-7637
Fax: 815 254-7640
Paul Quinn, *President*
Carol Thorne, *Corp Secy*
Dan Alrick, *Shareholder*
Randy Schwartz, *Shareholder*
EMP: 11
SALES (est): 1.8MM **Privately Held**
WEB: www.midwesthotrods.com
SIC: 3711 Automobile assembly, including specialty automobiles

**(G-17627)**
**MIDWEST SPORT TURF SYSTEMS LLC**
Also Called: Mwsts
10138 Bode St Ste E (60585-8779)
PHONE .................................. 630 923-8342
Jeffrey Nelson, *Mng Member*
Jody Factor,
EMP: 12
SQ FT: 4,000
SALES (est): 506K **Privately Held**
SIC: 3523 Greens mowing equipment

**(G-17628)**
**MIDWEST STONE SALES INC (PA)**
11926 S Aero Dr (60585-9559)
PHONE .................................. 815 254-6600
Fax: 630 978-2206
Christina Mercado, *President*
EMP: 11
SQ FT: 10,000
SALES (est): 1.5MM **Privately Held**
SIC: 3281 5032 Granite, cut & shaped; granite building stone

**(G-17629)**
**MOBILTY WORKS**
23855 W Andrew Rd Ste 3 (60585-8763)
PHONE .................................. 815 254-2000
Bill Kobelitz, *President*
EMP: 6
SQ FT: 7,000
SALES (est): 222.8K **Privately Held**
SIC: 7549 3716 3711 3999 Automotive customizing services, non-factory basis; motor homes; motor vehicles & car bodies; wheelchair lifts

**(G-17630)**
**NATURAL BEGINNINGS**
15904 S Selfridge Cir (60586-7212)
PHONE .................................. 773 457-0509
Phalice Benford, *Owner*
▲ EMP: 3
SQ FT: 2,500
SALES: 50K **Privately Held**
SIC: 2844 Hair preparations, including shampoos

**(G-17631)**
**NAVISTAR INC**
23815 W Lockport St (60544-2115)
PHONE .................................. 815 230-0060
EMP: 3
SALES (corp-wide): 8.1B **Publicly Held**
SIC: 3713 Truck & bus bodies
HQ: Navistar, Inc.
2701 Navistar Dr
Lisle IL 60532
331 332-5000

**(G-17632)**
**NEXT GENERATION INC**
13304 Skyline Dr (60585-1467)
PHONE .................................. 312 953-7514
Darrell Higueros, *President*
Heliza Higueros, *Admin Sec*
EMP: 4
SQ FT: 1,600
SALES (est): 1.2MM **Privately Held**
SIC: 7371 7372 Computer software development & applications; business oriented computer software

**(G-17633)**
**NNM MANUFACTURING LLC**
Also Called: Peterson Manufacturing Company
24133 W 143rd St (60544-8700)
PHONE .................................. 815 436-9201
Fax: 815 436-2863
Jerry Kusios, *General Mgr*
Randy Fugett, *Plant Mgr*
Dennis Vocu, *Human Res Mgr*
Marija Goich,
EMP: 40
SALES (est): 7.1MM **Privately Held**
SIC: 2296 Steel tire cords & tire cord fabrics

**(G-17634)**
**OFF THE PRESS**
16041 S Lincoln Hwy # 103 (60586-5180)
PHONE .................................. 815 436-9612
Fax: 815 436-6101
Paul Jackson, *Owner*
EMP: 6
SQ FT: 4,500
SALES (est): 776.7K **Privately Held**
SIC: 2752 2791 2789 2672 Commercial printing, offset; typesetting; bookbinding & related work; coated & laminated paper

**(G-17635)**
**PAPER BENDERS SUPPLY INC (PA)**
12024 S Aero Dr Ste 10 (60585-8796)
P.O. Box 960 (60544-0960)
PHONE .................................. 815 577-7583
James Hamilton, *President*
Randy Riley, *Vice Pres*
EMP: 5
SQ FT: 1,800
SALES (est): 450K **Privately Held**
SIC: 3555 Printing trades machinery

**(G-17636)**
**PENSTOCK CONSTRUCTION SERVICES**
2508 Ruth Fitzgerald Dr (60586-8244)
PHONE .................................. 630 816-2456
Mike Sobierajski, *Owner*
EMP: 1
SALES: 250K **Privately Held**
SIC: 1521 3448 7389 General remodeling, single-family houses; new construction, single-family houses; prefabricated metal buildings;

**(G-17637)**
**PERFORMANCE GEAR SYSTEMS INC**
14309 S Route 59 (60544-3889)
PHONE .................................. 630 739-6666
Fax: 630 739-6667
Patrick Odonnell, *President*
Ed Jedlicka, *Manager*
EMP: 35 EST: 1997
SALES: 15MM **Privately Held**
WEB: www.performance-gear.com
SIC: 3089 Blow molded finished plastic products

**(G-17638)**
**PERRYCO INC**
Enterprise Newspaper
15507 S Route 59 (60544-2723)
P.O. Box 1613 (60544-3613)
PHONE .................................. 815 436-2431
Fax: 815 436-2592
Wayne Perry, *Principal*
EMP: 16
SQ FT: 1,400
SALES (corp-wide): 3MM **Privately Held**
WEB: www.rushvilletimes.com
SIC: 2711 2752 2791 2789 Newspapers: publishing only, not printed on site; commercial printing, lithographic; typesetting; bookbinding & related work; commercial printing; packaging paper & plastics film, coated & laminated
PA: Perryco Inc
6920 Webster St
Downers Grove IL 60516
303 652-8282

**(G-17639)**
**PHOENIX LEATHER GOODS LLC**
Also Called: Beltoutlet.com
23824 W Andrew Rd Ste 102 (60585-8768)
PHONE .................................. 815 267-3926
Amy Monds, *Senior Buyer*
Gary Monds,
EMP: 8
SALES (est): 1.3MM **Privately Held**
WEB: www.beltoutlet.com
SIC: 5948 2295 Luggage & leather goods stores; leather, artificial or imitation

**(G-17640)**
**PLAINFIELD SIGNS INC**
219 W Main St (60544-1970)
PHONE .................................. 815 439-1063
Thomas Bowen, *President*
EMP: 3
SQ FT: 3,000
SALES (est): 268.3K **Privately Held**
SIC: 3993 Signs & advertising specialties; displays & cutouts, window & lobby; signs, not made in custom sign painting shops

**(G-17641)**
**POLYMER PLNFLD HLDINGS US INC (PA)**
24035 W Riverwalk Ct (60544-8145)
PHONE .................................. 815 436-5671
Robert Aldi, *President*
Jonathan Soucy, *President*
William Brian Kretzmer, *Chairman*
Rick Fogarty, *Vice Pres*
Elizabeth Ortiz, *Controller*
EMP: 153
SALES (est): 44.4MM **Privately Held**
SIC: 3089 3469 Injection molding of plastics; metal stampings

**(G-17642)**
**PRECISION ENGINE REBUILDERS**
Also Called: P E R
23807 W Andrew Rd Unit A (60585-4629)
PHONE .................................. 815 254-2333
Thomas R Crowley, *President*
EMP: 3
SALES (est): 490.1K **Privately Held**
SIC: 3519 Diesel engine rebuilding; gas engine rebuilding

**(G-17643)**
**PRECISION METAL CRAFTS INC**
12201 Rhea Dr (60585-9713)
PHONE .................................. 815 254-2306
Bozidar Skrlin, *President*
Daniel Skrlin, *Engineer*
EMP: 2
SQ FT: 1,800
SALES (est): 386.9K **Privately Held**
SIC: 3599 Machine shop, jobbing & repair

**(G-17644)**
**PREMIERE MOTORSPORTS LLC**
16300 S Lincoln Hwy 1 (60586-5152)
PHONE .................................. 708 634-0007
Czupta Christopher S, *Principal*
EMP: 2
SALES (est): 250.5K **Privately Held**
SIC: 3714 Motor vehicle engines & parts

**(G-17645)**
**PRO BUILT TOOL & MOLD INC**
23839 W Andrew Rd # 103 (60585-8764)
P.O. Box 829, Morris (60450-0829)
PHONE .................................. 815 436-9088
Steve Bergmann, *President*
Robert Green, *Exec VP*
EMP: 5
SQ FT: 3,200
SALES (est): 552.4K **Privately Held**
SIC: 3544 Industrial molds

**(G-17646)**
**ROCKDALE CONTROLS CO INC**
2419 Von Esch Rd (60586-9079)
PHONE .................................. 815 436-6181
Fax: 815 436-6277
Peter G Gavankar, *President*
Shande Mohra Gavankar, *Corp Secy*
Dwayne Kimak, *Design Engr*
Mary Lee Horvath, *Accountant*
EMP: 10
SQ FT: 8,000
SALES (est): 850K **Privately Held**
SIC: 3625 3556 Control equipment, electric; food products machinery

**(G-17647)**
**ROW WINDOW COMPANY**
13404 Wood Duck Dr (60585-7766)
PHONE .................................. 815 725-5491
Glen Brooks, *President*
William Gebhardt, *Vice Pres*
Patricia Malcom, *Purchasing*
Liz Riley, *Manager*
EMP: 1
SQ FT: 190,000
SALES (est): 210K **Privately Held**
WEB: www.rowwindow.com
SIC: 2431 Window frames, wood; window sashes, wood; doors & door parts & trim, wood

**(G-17648)**
**SIGNS BY TOMORROW**
16200 S Lincoln Hwy # 100 (60586-5167)
PHONE .................................. 815 436-0880
Jodi Murray, *Principal*
EMP: 3
SALES (est): 333.1K **Privately Held**
SIC: 3993 Signs & advertising specialties

**(G-17649)**
**SLICK SUGAR INC**
Also Called: Slicksugar.com
24935 Heritage Oaks Dr (60585-5773)
P.O. Box 154 (60544-0154)
PHONE .................................. 815 782-7101
Scott Mills, *President*
Jennifer Mills, *Vice Pres*
▼ EMP: 2
SALES (est): 204.5K **Privately Held**
WEB: www.slicksugar.com
SIC: 2369 5641 Girls' & children's outerwear; children's wear

**(G-17650)**
**SOUND DESIGN INC**
10104 S Mandel St Ste 1 (60585-8774)
PHONE .................................. 630 548-7000
Alfonso Marasco, *President*
Joseph Marasco, *President*
Jacqueline Mc Carthy, *Corp Secy*
Vince Marasco, *Vice Pres*
Frank Ditrolio, *Branch Mgr*
EMP: 5
SQ FT: 2,500
SALES (est): 730K **Privately Held**
SIC: 3699 5999 5731 Electric sound equipment; alarm signal systems; high fidelity stereo equipment

# Plainfield - Will County (G-17651) — GEOGRAPHIC SECTION

**(G-17651)**
**SPECIALTY PNTG SODA BLASTG INC**
24031 W Winners Circle Ct (60585-6124)
PHONE.................815 577-0006
Steven J Hackerson, *President*
Jane Hackerson, *Office Mgr*
**EMP:** 6
**SALES (est):** 690.1K  **Privately Held**
**WEB:** www.specialtypainting.com
**SIC:** 3479  3471  Painting of metal products; sand blasting of metal parts

**(G-17652)**
**STANDARD REGISTER INC**
24121 W Riverwalk Ct (60544-8146)
PHONE.................815 439-1050
Steve Makilo, *President*
**EMP:** 50
**SALES (corp-wide):** 4.5B  **Privately Held**
**WEB:** www.stdreg.com
**SIC:** 2761  Manifold business forms
**HQ:** Standard Register, Inc.
  600 Albany St
  Dayton OH 45417
  937 221-1000

**(G-17653)**
**STOLP GORE COMPANY**
10101 Bode St Ste A (60585-8731)
PHONE.................630 904-5180
Robert Sepper, *President*
Mary C Sepper, *Admin Sec*
**EMP:** 3  **EST:** 1922
**SQ FT:** 6,000
**SALES (est):** 500K  **Privately Held**
**SIC:** 3555  7699  Bookbinding machinery; industrial equipment services

**(G-17654)**
**STRITZEL AWNNG SVC/AURRA TENT**
Also Called: Aurora Tent & Awning Co
10206 Clow Creek Rd Ste A (60585-6891)
PHONE.................630 420-2000
Norman Dial, *Partner*
Sande K Dial, *Partner*
**EMP:** 35
**SQ FT:** 11,000
**SALES (est):** 3.4MM  **Privately Held**
**SIC:** 2394  7359  Awnings, fabric: made from purchased materials; tent & tarpaulin rental

**(G-17655)**
**STUHLMAN FAMILY LLC**
Also Called: Stuhlman Engrg Manfacturin Co
12435 S Industrial Dr E (60585-8578)
P.O. Box 236  (60544-0236)
PHONE.................815 436-2432
**Fax:** 815 436-6902
Tom Dravinski,
Pamela Dravinski,
**EMP:** 5
**SQ FT:** 8,000
**SALES:** 500K  **Privately Held**
**SIC:** 3599  7692  Machine shop, jobbing & repair; welding repair

**(G-17656)**
**SWS**
15720 S Route 59 (60544-2693)
PHONE.................815 267-7378
**EMP:** 3
**SALES (est):** 246.5K  **Privately Held**
**SIC:** 3272  Building materials, except block or brick: concrete

**(G-17657)**
**THERMA-KLEEN INC**
10212 S Mandel St Ste A (60585-5374)
PHONE.................630 718-0212
Andrew Heller, *President*
Linda Heller, *Vice Pres*
▲ **EMP:** 7
**SQ FT:** 4,000
**SALES (est):** 1.2MM  **Privately Held**
**WEB:** www.therma-kleen.com
**SIC:** 3559  5084  1799  Degreasing machines, automotive & industrial; cleaning equipment, high pressure, sand or steam steam cleaning of building exteriors

**(G-17658)**
**TMZ METAL FABRICATING INC**
23807 W Andrew Rd Unit C (60585-4629)
PHONE.................815 230-3071
Tim Putlak, *President*
**EMP:** 5  **EST:** 2010
**SQ FT:** 2,500
**SALES (est):** 665.5K  **Privately Held**
**SIC:** 3441  Fabricated structural metal

**(G-17659)**
**UDV NORTH AMERICA INC**
24440 W 143rd St (60544-8704)
PHONE.................815 267-4400
Jack Siljendahl, *Principal*
**EMP:** 3
**SALES (est):** 171.1K  **Privately Held**
**SIC:** 2085  Distillers' dried grains & solubles & alcohol

**(G-17660)**
**ULTIMATE MACHINING & ENGRG INC**
14015 S Van Dyke Rd (60544-3530)
PHONE.................815 439-8361
**Fax:** 815 439-8364
John Kulczuga, *President*
Aleksandra Kulczuga, *Manager*
Caroline Kulczuga, *Director*
**EMP:** 40
**SQ FT:** 30,000
**SALES (est):** 7.5MM  **Privately Held**
**WEB:** www.ultimateme.net
**SIC:** 3599  Machine shop, jobbing & repair

**(G-17661)**
**VOYAGER ENTERPRISE INC**
15507 S Route 59 (60544-2723)
PHONE.................815 436-2431
Richard Masterson, *President*
Laureen Crotteau, *Marketing Staff*
Andrea Earnest, *Assoc Editor*
**EMP:** 8
**SALES (est):** 1.1MM  **Privately Held**
**SIC:** 2621  Lithograph paper

---

## Plainville
### Adams County

**(G-17662)**
**ED KABRICK BEEF INC**
218 E Main St (62365-1016)
P.O. Box 158  (62365-0158)
PHONE.................217 656-3263
**Fax:** 217 656-3707
Daren Rex Kabrick, *President*
Vicki Kabrick, *Vice Pres*
**EMP:** 6
**SQ FT:** 2,500
**SALES (est):** 700K  **Privately Held**
**SIC:** 2011  5142  2013  Meat packing plants; packaged frozen goods; sausages & other prepared meats

---

## Plano
### Kendall County

**(G-17663)**
**DLT ELECTRIC LLC**
202 W Main St (60545-1433)
PHONE.................630 552-4115
David L Tremain,
▲ **EMP:** 12
**SQ FT:** 5,000
**SALES (est):** 910K  **Privately Held**
**SIC:** 3621  Motors, electric

**(G-17664)**
**FABTEK AERO LTD**
432 E South St (60545-9703)
PHONE.................630 552-3622
Michael A Chesnutt, *President*
Dave Tremain, *President*
Scott Chesnutt, *Principal*
Timothy Tremain, *Vice Pres*
Estela Martinez, *Executive Asst*
▲ **EMP:** 13
**SQ FT:** 10,000
**SALES:** 2.5MM  **Privately Held**
**WEB:** www.fabtekaero.com
**SIC:** 3443  Fabricated plate work (boiler shop)

**(G-17665)**
**FOX VALLEY MOLDING INC (PA)**
Also Called: F V M
113 S Center St (60545-1568)
PHONE.................630 552-3176
**Fax:** 630 552-8375
Don Haag, *CEO*
Donald L Haag, *President*
Alfonso Alvarado, *Warehouse Mgr*
Jeanne Case, *Manager*
Lydia Flores, *Manager*
▲ **EMP:** 110
**SQ FT:** 60,000
**SALES (est):** 22.2MM  **Privately Held**
**WEB:** www.foxvalleymolding.com
**SIC:** 3089  Injection molded finished plastic products; injection molding of plastics; molding primary plastic

**(G-17666)**
**MENARD INC**
2611 Eldamain Rd (60545-9723)
PHONE.................815 474-6767
**Fax:** 630 552-2322
Rene Hoffman, *Manager*
Kevin McCarty, *CIO*
Derek Liedl, *Technology*
**EMP:** 69
**SALES (corp-wide):** 15.2B  **Privately Held**
**SIC:** 2431  Millwork
**PA:** Menard, Inc.
  5101 Menard Dr
  Eau Claire WI 54703
  715 876-5911

**(G-17667)**
**MENARD INC**
2619 Eldamain Rd Bldg 220 (60545-9706)
PHONE.................715 876-5911
Marty Fischer, *Facilities Mgr*
Pat Berger, *Site Mgr*
Nicole Brandner, *Accountant*
Dennis T Anderson, *Security Mgr*
**EMP:** 68
**SALES (corp-wide):** 15.2B  **Privately Held**
**SIC:** 2431  Millwork
**PA:** Menard, Inc.
  5101 Menard Dr
  Eau Claire WI 54703
  715 876-5911

**(G-17668)**
**NATIONAL TRACTOR PARTS INC**
12127a Galena Rd (60545-9725)
P.O. Box 146  (60545-0146)
PHONE.................630 552-4235
**Fax:** 630 552-7699
Christopher J Gunier, *President*
Chuck Gunier, *Sales Staff*
Charles Gunier Jr, *Office Mgr*
Ed Endres, *Manager*
Matt Gunier, *Manager*
▲ **EMP:** 32
**SQ FT:** 28,000
**SALES (est):** 7MM  **Privately Held**
**SIC:** 3531  5083  Backhoes, tractors, cranes, plows & similar equipment; tractors, agricultural

**(G-17669)**
**OT SYSTEMS LIMITED**
18 W Main St (60545-1429)
PHONE.................630 554-9178
R J Frank, *Sales Dir*
Calvin Wong, *Manager*
Jeff Smith, *Info Tech Dir*
Joe Frank, *Director*
**EMP:** 1
**SALES:** 950K  **Privately Held**
**SIC:** 3679  Electronic components

**(G-17670)**
**OUTDOORS SYNERGY PRODUCTS TECH**
431 E South St (60545-1676)
PHONE.................630 552-3111
**EMP:** 57
**SALES (est):** 75.6K
**SALES (corp-wide):** 44MM  **Privately Held**
**SIC:** 2426  Hardwood dimension & flooring mills
**PA:** Plano Synergy Holding Inc.
  431 E South St
  Plano IL 60545
  630 552-3111

**(G-17671)**
**PAGEPATH TECHNOLOGIES INC**
13 E Main St (60545-1521)
PHONE.................630 689-4111
Gregory Witek, *President*
Michael Herz, *Sales Staff*
Lynn Witek, *Manager*
Adam Witek, *Technology*
Phil Grandsard, *Software Dev*
**EMP:** 11
**SQ FT:** 1,800
**SALES (est):** 1.4MM  **Privately Held**
**WEB:** www.pagepath.com
**SIC:** 7372  7379  7371  Business oriented computer software; computer related consulting services; custom computer programming services

**(G-17672)**
**PLANO METAL SPECIALTIES INC**
320 W State Rte 34 (60545)
P.O. Box 174  (60545-0174)
PHONE.................630 552-8510
**Fax:** 630 552-8524
Ralph Whitecotton, *Ch of Bd*
Rick Whitecotton, *Vice Pres*
Audrey Whitecotton, *Treasurer*
**EMP:** 10
**SQ FT:** 11,000
**SALES:** 800K  **Privately Held**
**WEB:** www.planoamerica.com
**SIC:** 3471  3089  Plating of metals or formed products; polishing, metals or formed products; finishing, metals or formed products; plastic processing

**(G-17673)**
**PLANO MOLDING COMPANY LLC (DH)**
431 E South St (60545-1676)
PHONE.................630 552-3111
**Fax:** 630 552-9898
Peter H Henning, *Ch of Bd*
Thomas Hurt, *President*
Paul Heller, *Vice Pres*
Jarrod Streng, *Vice Pres*
Robert Yarbrough, *Vice Pres*
◆ **EMP:** 1  **EST:** 1932
**SQ FT:** 190,000
**SALES:** 43.9MM
**SALES (corp-wide):** 44MM  **Privately Held**
**WEB:** www.planomolding.com
**SIC:** 3089  Boxes, plastic; molding primary plastic
**HQ:** Plano Holding Llc
  431 E South St
  Plano IL 60545
  630 552-3111

**(G-17674)**
**PLANO SYNERGY HOLDING INC (PA)**
431 E South St (60545-1676)
PHONE.................630 552-3111
Tom Hurt, *President*
Ben Harvey, *Exec VP*
Stephen Schwallie, *Vice Pres*
Jesse Simpkins, *Vice Pres*
Jackie Born, *Asst Controller*
**EMP:** 21
**SALES (est):** 44MM  **Privately Held**
**SIC:** 2426  5941  Gun stocks, wood; hunting equipment

**(G-17675)**
**PRYDE GRAPHICS PLUS**
306 Hubbard Cir (60545-1975)
PHONE.................630 882-5103
Richard Pryde, *Principal*
David Homyak, *Vice Pres*
**EMP:** 2

SALES (est): 222.6K **Privately Held**
SIC: 2759 Commercial printing

**(G-17676)**
**TALLWOOD**
15751 Burr Oak Rd (60545-9811)
PHONE.................................815 786-8186
Ben T Stevenson, *Owner*
EMP: 4
SALES (est): 227.9K **Privately Held**
SIC: 2411 Timber, cut at logging camp

**(G-17677)**
**TMF PLASTIC SOLUTIONS LLC**
12127b Galena Rd (60545-9725)
PHONE.................................630 552-7575
Kuppler Greg, *President*
Jackie Straub, *Accounts Mgr*
Heather Bigeck, *Manager*
Eldon Cunningham, *Manager*
Jeffrey Cunningham, *Manager*
▲ EMP: 75
SQ FT: 14,000
SALES (est): 22.4MM **Privately Held**
SIC: 3089 Casting of plastic

**(G-17678)**
**TMF POLYMER SOLUTIONS INC**
12127b Galena Rd (60545-9725)
PHONE.................................630 552-7575
Roy Lovell, *Manager*
EMP: 11
SALES (corp-wide): 5MM **Privately Held**
SIC: 3089 Automotive parts, plastic
PA: Tmf Polymer Solutions Inc.
    12127b Galena Rd
    Plano IL 60545
    541 479-7484

**(G-17679)**
**TMF POLYMER SOLUTIONS INC (PA)**
12127b Galena Rd (60545-9725)
PHONE.................................541 479-7484
Greg Kuppler, *President*
Tim Raymond, *Exec VP*
Jackie Straub, *Accounting Mgr*
Roy Lovell, *Manager*
▲ EMP: 2
SQ FT: 14,000
SALES (est): 5MM **Privately Held**
SIC: 3089 Automotive parts, plastic

### Pleasant Hill
*Pike County*

**(G-17680)**
**FRAME GAME**
119 E Quincy St (62366-2415)
P.O. Box 454 (62366-0454)
PHONE.................................573 754-2385
Kevin Willis, *President*
EMP: 3
SALES (est): 261.7K **Privately Held**
SIC: 2499 Wood products

### Pleasant Plains
*Sangamon County*

**(G-17681)**
**ALPHA AG INC (PA)**
8295 Bomke Rd (62677-3759)
PHONE.................................217 546-2724
Donald Trott, *President*
Robert Clark, *Manager*
Nanette Trott, *Manager*
◆ EMP: 3
SALES (est): 345.7K **Privately Held**
WEB: www.alphaag.com
SIC: 5999 2879 Farm machinery; agricultural chemicals

### Plymouth
*Hancock County*

**(G-17682)**
**R L ONEAL & SONS INC**
819 N County Road 3050 (62367-2220)
PHONE.................................309 458-3350
Fax: 309 458-3250
John C O'Neal, *President*
John C Jack O'Neal, *President*
Christen O'Neal, *Vice Pres*
Diane O'Neal, *Manager*
EMP: 11
SQ FT: 800
SALES (est): 2.3MM **Privately Held**
SIC: 1422 Crushed & broken limestone

### Pocahontas
*Bond County*

**(G-17683)**
**JOSEPH C RAKERS**
209 Pocahontas St (62275-1037)
P.O. Box 314 (62275-0314)
PHONE.................................618 670-6995
Joseph Rakers, *Owner*
EMP: 1
SALES: 300K **Privately Held**
SIC: 3679 Antennas, satellite: household use

**(G-17684)**
**JWT FARMS INC**
1072 Il Route 143 (62275-3811)
PHONE.................................618 664-3429
James W Tischhauser, *President*
Jeff Tischhauser, *Director*
EMP: 3
SALES: 50K **Privately Held**
SIC: 3523 Driers (farm): grain, hay & seed

**(G-17685)**
**SHAWS SHACK**
214 Main St (62275-1118)
P.O. Box 337 (62275-0337)
PHONE.................................618 669-2220
Steven Shaw, *Principal*
EMP: 4
SALES (est): 377.2K **Privately Held**
SIC: 3421 Table & food cutlery, including butchers'

**(G-17686)**
**STAINLESS SPECIALTIES INC**
329 Il Route 143 (62275-3649)
PHONE.................................618 654-7723
Victor Munie, *President*
Julius C Munie, *Vice Pres*
▲ EMP: 5
SQ FT: 7,200
SALES (est): 817.3K **Privately Held**
SIC: 1711 3444 Process piping contractor; restaurant sheet metalwork

### Polo
*Ogle County*

**(G-17687)**
**DESIGN ENHANCED MFG CO**
9796 W Il Route 64 (61064-8982)
PHONE.................................815 946-3562
Roger Groves, *President*
EMP: 2
SALES (est): 229.3K **Privately Held**
SIC: 3599 Machine shop, jobbing & repair

**(G-17688)**
**LEGACY PRINTS**
607 S Division Ave (61064-1834)
PHONE.................................815 946-9112
Marty Cox, *Owner*
Chrystal Bostian, *Marketing Staff*
EMP: 9
SALES (est): 520K **Privately Held**
SIC: 2759 Commercial printing

**(G-17689)**
**NATIONAL BUS TRADER INC**
Also Called: National Bus Trader Magazine
9698 W Judson Rd (61064-9015)
PHONE.................................815 946-2341
Larry J Plachno, *President*
Laura Wagenecht, *Editor*
Nancy Plachno, *Vice Pres*
Sherry Mekeel, *Manager*
EMP: 12
SQ FT: 2,500
SALES (est): 1.2MM **Privately Held**
WEB: www.busmag.com
SIC: 2721 2731 Magazines: publishing only, not printed on site; trade journals: publishing only, not printed on site; books: publishing only

**(G-17690)**
**PNC INC (PA)**
117 E Mason St (61064-1521)
PHONE.................................815 946-2328
Fax: 815 946-2483
C Keith Palmer, *President*
Scott Palmer, *QC Mgr*
John Kessinger, *Engineer*
Jim Weed, *VP Human Res*
Keith Palmer, *Marketing Staff*
EMP: 51
SQ FT: 22,000
SALES (est): 9.5MM **Privately Held**
SIC: 3677 3089 Coil windings, electronic; injection molding of plastics

**(G-17691)**
**XENA INTERNATIONAL INC**
910 S Division Ave (61064-1840)
PHONE.................................815 946-2626
Fax: 815 946-2752
Timothy Wharton, *Branch Mgr*
EMP: 46
SALES (corp-wide): 5.2MM **Privately Held**
WEB: www.xenainternational.com
SIC: 2819 5169 2869 Catalysts, chemical; chemicals & allied products; industrial organic chemicals
PA: Xena International, Inc.
    39w082 Foxwood Ln
    Saint Charles IL 60175
    630 587-2734

**(G-17692)**
**YORK INTERNATIONAL CORPORATION**
3820 S Il Route 26 (61064-9006)
PHONE.................................815 946-2351
Mark Stencel, *Branch Mgr*
EMP: 94
SALES (corp-wide): 36.8B **Privately Held**
SIC: 3585 Refrigeration & heating equipment; compressors for refrigeration & air conditioning equipment
HQ: York International Corporation
    631 S Richland Ave
    York PA 17403
    717 771-7890

### Pomona
*Jackson County*

**(G-17693)**
**LONNIE HICKAM**
2726 Sadler Rd (62975-2568)
PHONE.................................618 893-4223
Lonnie Hickam, *Executive*
EMP: 3
SALES (est): 240.7K **Privately Held**
SIC: 2411 Logging

**(G-17694)**
**POMONA WINERY**
2865 Hickory Ridge Rd (62975-2317)
PHONE.................................618 893-2623
Fax: 618 893-2623
Jayne Payne, *President*
George Majka, *Treasurer*
EMP: 7
SALES (est): 250K **Privately Held**
WEB: www.pomonawinery.com
SIC: 2084 Wines

**(G-17695)**
**VON JAKOB VINEYARD LIMITED**
Also Called: Van Jakob Vineyard
1309 Sadler Rd (62975-2554)
PHONE.................................618 893-4500
Rhoda Jacobs, *President*
Paul Jacobs, *Vice Pres*
EMP: 3
SALES (est): 338.2K **Privately Held**
WEB: www.vonjakobvineyard.com
SIC: 2084 Wines

### Pontiac
*Livingston County*

**(G-17696)**
**ANTHONY LIFTGATES INC**
1037 W Howard St (61764-1666)
P.O. Box 615 (61764-0615)
PHONE.................................815 842-3383
Fax: 815 844-3612
Thomas M Walker, *President*
Jeremy Walker, *Vice Pres*
Paul Walker, *Treasurer*
Carl Fleig, *Sales Associate*
Tracey Toews, *Manager*
◆ EMP: 200 EST: 1941
SQ FT: 100,000
SALES (est): 58.4MM
SALES (corp-wide): 80.6MM **Privately Held**
WEB: www.anthonyliftgates.com
SIC: 3537 3714 Lift trucks, industrial: fork, platform, straddle, etc.; motor vehicle parts & accessories
PA: Streator Industrial Handling, Inc.
    1705 N Shabbona St
    Streator IL 61364
    815 672-0551

**(G-17697)**
**CATERPILLAR INC**
1300 4h Park Rd (61764-9254)
P.O. Box 740 (61764-0740)
PHONE.................................815 842-6000
Fax: 815 842-6063
Bob Eckhoff, *Opers Mgr*
Larry D Gilmore, *Mfg Staff*
Merritt Henkel, *QC Mgr*
Doug Corrigan, *Engineer*
Scot Ward, *Engineer*
EMP: 334
SALES (corp-wide): 38.5B **Publicly Held**
WEB: www.cat.com
SIC: 3714 5084 Radiators & radiator shells & cores, motor vehicle; fuel injection systems
PA: Caterpillar Inc.
    100 Ne Adams St
    Peoria IL 61629
    309 675-1000

**(G-17698)**
**DONNELLS PRINTING & OFF PDTS**
708 W Howard St (61764-1602)
PHONE.................................815 842-6541
Fax: 815 842-4329
Joseph Mehrkens, *President*
Peggy Mehrkens, *Treasurer*
Brad Mehrkens, *Manager*
EMP: 4
SQ FT: 4,000
SALES: 300K **Privately Held**
WEB: www.donnellsonline.com
SIC: 2754 5943 2791 2789 Job printing, gravure; office forms & supplies; typesetting; bookbinding & related work; commercial printing; commercial printing, lithographic

**(G-17699)**
**DOW AGROSCIENCES LLC**
Also Called: Mycogen Seeds
18078 N 1500 East Rd (61764-2988)
PHONE.................................815 844-3128
Irene Moritz, *Branch Mgr*
EMP: 9
SALES (corp-wide): 48.1B **Publicly Held**
SIC: 2879 5191 0721 8731 Agricultural chemicals; fungicides; herbicides; insecticides & pesticides; seeds & bulbs; crop protecting services; agricultural research

# Pontiac - Livingston County (G-17700)

HQ: Dow Agrosciences Llc
9330 Zionsville Rd
Indianapolis IN 46268
317 337-3000

**(G-17700)**
**G P CONCRETE & IRON WORKS**
Rr 1 (61764-9801)
P.O. Box 495 (61764-0495)
PHONE..................................815 842-2270
Gary S Schulz, *Owner*
EMP: 3
SQ FT: 1,600
SALES (est): 378.6K  Privately Held
SIC: **3272**  3446  3442  Steps, prefabricated concrete; manhole covers or frames, concrete; septic tanks, concrete; railings, bannisters, guards, etc.: made from metal pipe; metal doors, sash & trim

**(G-17701)**
**GATEHOUSE MEDIA LLC**
Also Called: Daily Leader Newspaper
318 N Main St (61764-1930)
PHONE..................................815 842-1153
Linda Stlye, *Manager*
EMP: 25
SALES (corp-wide): 1.2B  Publicly Held
WEB: www.gatehousemedia.com
SIC: **2711**  Newspapers
HQ: Gatehouse Media, Llc
175 Sullys Trl Ste 300
Pittsford NY 14534
585 598-0030

**(G-17702)**
**GIOVANINI METALS CORP**
1320 N Main St (61764-1140)
P.O. Box 654 (61764-0654)
PHONE..................................815 842-0500
Frank Giovanini, *President*
John Giovanini, *Vice Pres*
EMP: 6 EST: 1939
SQ FT: 5,000
SALES: 700K  Privately Held
WEB: www.gmifab.com
SIC: **7692**  5251  3444  Welding repair; hardware; sheet metalwork

**(G-17703)**
**INTERLAKE MECALUX INC**
701 N Interlake Dr (61764-9033)
PHONE..................................815 844-7191
Ron Bakos, *Manager*
EMP: 246
SALES (corp-wide): 16.2K  Privately Held
SIC: **2542**  Partitions & fixtures, except wood
HQ: Interlake Mecalux, Inc.
1600 N 25th Ave
Melrose Park IL 60160
708 344-9999

**(G-17704)**
**JOHNSON PRESS AMERICA INC**
800 N Court St (61764-1046)
P.O. Box 592 (61764-0592)
PHONE..................................815 844-5161
Fax: 815 842-3000
Dale Flesburg, *President*
Jill Rambo, *Sales Staff*
Ann Adkins, *Manager*
Rick Bradbury, *Maintence Staff*
Bill Maston, *Maintence Staff*
EMP: 40 EST: 1945
SQ FT: 45,000
SALES (est): 7.7MM  Privately Held
WEB: www.jpapontiac.com
SIC: **2721**  2791  2789  2752  Trade journals: publishing & printing; bookbinding & related work; commercial printing, lithographic; book printing

**(G-17705)**
**LSC COMMUNICATIONS US LLC**
1600 N Main St (61764-1060)
PHONE..................................815 844-5181
Bruce Mustard, *Manager*
EMP: 750
SALES (corp-wide): 13B  Publicly Held
SIC: **2721**  Magazines: publishing & printing
HQ: Lsc Communications Us, Llc
191 N Wacker Dr Ste 1400
Chicago IL 60606
844 572-5720

**(G-17706)**
**MBI TOOLS  LLC**
Also Called: Mislich Bros
15116 E 2100 North Rd (61764-3261)
PHONE..................................815 844-0937
Rja D-Orazio, *CEO*
Justin Wolfe, *President*
EMP: 5
SQ FT: 18,000
SALES: 750K  Privately Held
SIC: **3449**  Miscellaneous metalwork

**(G-17707)**
**PONTIAC GRANITE COMPANY INC**
906 W North St (61764-1003)
P.O. Box 259 (61764-0259)
PHONE..................................815 842-1384
Fax: 815 844-6603
Mark Ifft, *President*
EMP: 10
SQ FT: 2,400
SALES (est): 710K  Privately Held
SIC: **3281**  5999  Cut stone & stone products; monuments & tombstones

**(G-17708)**
**PONTIAC RECYCLERS INC**
15355 E 1830 North Rd (61764-3634)
PHONE..................................815 844-6419
Michael Crouch, *President*
Michael Freeman, *Corp Secy*
David Egley, *Vice Pres*
EMP: 3
SALES (est): 320K  Privately Held
SIC: **3341**  3211  2621  4953  Aluminum smelting & refining (secondary); flat glass; paper mills; recycling, waste materials; metal scrap & waste materials

**(G-17709)**
**PRINTING CRAFTSMEN OF PONTIAC**
509 W Howard St (61764-1718)
P.O. Box 106 (61764-0106)
PHONE..................................815 844-7118
Fax: 815 844-4587
Dean Hamilton, *President*
Mary Hamilton, *Admin Sec*
EMP: 3 EST: 1959
SQ FT: 2,800
SALES (est): 371.3K  Privately Held
SIC: **2752**  2759  Commercial printing, offset; letterpress printing

**(G-17710)**
**R R DONNELLEY & SONS COMPANY**
Also Called: R R Donnelley
1600 N Main St (61764-1060)
PHONE..................................815 844-5181
Fax: 815 844-1432
Joe Keenan, *Director*
EMP: 700
SQ FT: 9,000
SALES (corp-wide): 6.9B  Publicly Held
WEB: www.rrdonnelley.com
SIC: **2752**  2789  2732  Commercial printing, lithographic; binding only: books, pamphlets, magazines, etc.; book printing
PA: R. R. Donnelley & Sons Company
35 W Wacker Dr Ste 3650
Chicago IL 60601
312 326-8000

**(G-17711)**
**SOUTHFIELD CORPORATION**
Also Called: Vcna Prairie
15887 E 1200 North Rd (61764-3652)
PHONE..................................815 842-2333
Chris Bashan, *Manager*
EMP: 25
SALES (corp-wide): 273.9MM  Privately Held
WEB: www.prairiegroup.com
SIC: **1422**  5032  Crushed & broken limestone; stone, crushed or broken
PA: Southfield Corporation
8995 W 95th St
Palos Hills IL 60465
708 344-1000

**(G-17712)**
**WJEZ THUNDER 93 7 WJBC WBNQ B1**
315 N Mill St (61764-1823)
PHONE..................................815 842-6515
Collins Miller, *Principal*
EMP: 3
SALES (est): 108.2K  Privately Held
SIC: **2711**  4832  Newspapers, publishing & printing; radio broadcasting stations

## Poplar Grove
### Boone County

**(G-17713)**
**JEWEL MACHINE INC**
302 Kingsbury Dr Se (61065-8791)
PHONE..................................815 765-3636
Jewel Kiefer, *Owner*
EMP: 2
SALES (est): 206.8K  Privately Held
SIC: **3599**  Machine shop, jobbing & repair

**(G-17714)**
**MIDWEST PUB SAFETY OUTFITTERS**
414 Redman Way Sw (61065-8964)
P.O. Box 391 (61065-0391)
PHONE..................................866 985-0013
Tom Kronas, *President*
Mike Farley, *Director*
EMP: 10 EST: 2013
SALES (est): 897.5K  Privately Held
SIC: **2389**  5941  5999  Uniforms & vestments; hunting equipment; safety supplies & equipment

**(G-17715)**
**NATURES BEST CHRISTMAS TREES**
13001 Il Route 76 (61065-8879)
PHONE..................................815 765-2960
Randy Kiene, *Principal*
EMP: 4 EST: 2008
SALES (est): 364.7K  Privately Held
SIC: **3699**  Christmas tree lighting sets, electric

**(G-17716)**
**POLYONICS RUBBER CO**
100 E Park St (61065-9789)
PHONE..................................815 765-2033
Fax: 815 765-1055
Bernard Hugus, *CEO*
Doug Stima, *President*
Christi Stima, *Vice Pres*
Darren Steen, *CFO*
EMP: 6
SQ FT: 10,000
SALES (est): 798.3K  Privately Held
WEB: www.polyonicsrubber.com
SIC: **3069**  Molded rubber products

**(G-17717)**
**STEVE FORREST**
Also Called: Forrest Pallet Service
290 E Park St (61065-9798)
PHONE..................................815 765-9040
Steve Forrest, *Owner*
EMP: 15
SQ FT: 4,000
SALES (est): 2.1MM  Privately Held
WEB: www.steveforrest.com
SIC: **2448**  Pallets, wood

## Port Barrington
### Lake County

**(G-17718)**
**BROKEN OAR INC**
614 Rawson Bridge Rd (60010-1011)
PHONE..................................847 639-9468
Fax: 847 639-6660
Michael E Haber, *President*
Bonnie Miske, *General Mgr*
Kathy Helman, *Accountant*
EMP: 3 EST: 1961
SQ FT: 3,000
SALES: 800K  Privately Held
WEB: www.brokenoar.com
SIC: **5813**  2731  Tavern (drinking places); book publishing

## Port Byron
### Rock Island County

**(G-17719)**
**CALVERT SYSTEMS**
Also Called: Sound Master & Calvert Systems
21114 94th Ave N (61275-9623)
PHONE..................................309 523-3262
Wade Calvert, *Owner*
EMP: 5
SALES (est): 307K  Privately Held
SIC: **8711**  2298  Electrical or electronic engineering; designing: ship, boat, machine & product; cable, fiber

**(G-17720)**
**J & C PREMIER CONCEPTS INC**
Also Called: Slayer Barbell
1506 N High St (61275-9124)
PHONE..................................309 523-2344
Jim Gehn, *Principal*
EMP: 4
SALES: 250K  Privately Held
SIC: **3949**  1721  3549  Exercise equipment; team sports equipment; industrial painting; wiredrawing & fabricating machinery & equipment, ex. die

**(G-17721)**
**MATERIAL CONTROL SYSTEMS INC (PA)**
Also Called: Matcon
201 N Main St (61275-9790)
P.O. Box 437 (61275-0437)
PHONE..................................309 523-3774
Fax: 309 523-3854
Donn R Larson, *President*
Judy Scott, *CFO*
Brad Palmer, *Manager*
Dave McClanihan, *CIO*
▲ EMP: 17
SALES (est): 26.8MM  Privately Held
WEB: www.matconusa.com
SIC: **5099**  2542  Containers: glass, metal or plastic; racks, merchandise display or storage: except wood

**(G-17722)**
**PORT BYRON MACHINE INC**
11420 228th St N (61275-9019)
PHONE..................................309 523-9111
Frederick Wassell, *President*
Kelly Wassell, *Corp Secy*
EMP: 2
SALES (est): 250.1K  Privately Held
SIC: **3599**  3545  3541  Machine shop, jobbing & repair; machine tool accessories; machine tools, metal cutting type

**(G-17723)**
**SANDSTROM PRODUCTS COMPANY (PA)**
224 S Main St (61275-9501)
P.O. Box 547 (61275-0547)
PHONE..................................309 523-2121
Fax: 309 523-3912
Brian Suhl, *President*
Rick Hartsock, *President*
Jeri Mead, *General Mgr*
Scott Jacobs, *Safety Dir*
Mark Lousberg, *Sales Dir*
▲ EMP: 24
SQ FT: 50,000
SALES (est): 4.1MM  Privately Held
WEB: www.sandstromproducts.com
SIC: **2851**  2891  2842  Paints & allied products; specialty cleaning, polishes & sanitation goods; adhesives

**(G-17724)**
**SANDSTROM PRODUCTS COMPANY**
224 S Main St (61275-9501)
P.O. Box 547 (61275-0547)
PHONE..................................309 523-2121
Rick Hartsock, *President*
James Morrison, *Vice Pres*
John Kemmis, *Purchasing*

EMP: 10
SALES (corp-wide): 4.1MM **Privately Held**
WEB: www.sandstromproducts.com
SIC: **2851** 2992 2891 2842 Paints & allied products; lubricating oils & greases; adhesives & sealants; specialty cleaning, polishes & sanitation goods
PA: Sandstrom Products Company
224 S Main St
Port Byron IL 61275
309 523-2121

**(G-17725)**
**SPARKS FIBERGLASS INC**
5415 227th Street Ct N (61275-9690)
PHONE.................................309 848-0077
Fax: 309 786-6497
Gary D Sparks, *President*
Janet Sparks, *Treasurer*
EMP: 15
SQ FT: 20,000
SALES (est): 1.8MM **Privately Held**
SIC: **3599** Machine shop, jobbing & repair

## Posen
### Cook County

**(G-17726)**
**A & A STEEL FABRICATING CO**
14100 S Harrison Ave (60469-1047)
PHONE.................................708 389-4499
Fax: 708 389-7552
Sharon Poe, *President*
Wayne Mc Cartney, *Vice Pres*
Allen Poe, *Vice Pres*
Denise McCartney, *Info Tech Mgr*
EMP: 10 EST: 1961
SQ FT: 28,800
SALES (est): 2.1MM **Privately Held**
WEB: www.aasteelfab.com
SIC: **3312** 3316 3444 3443 Blast furnaces & steel mills; bars, steel, cold finished, from purchased hot-rolled; sheet metalwork; fabricated plate work (boiler shop); fabricated structural metal

**(G-17727)**
**ACCURATE GRINDING CO INC**
14003 S Harrison Ave (60469-1022)
PHONE.................................708 371-1887
Fax: 708 371-1246
David M Niemeyer, *President*
Peter Niemeyer, *Vice Pres*
EMP: 8
SQ FT: 3,500
SALES (est): 1.2MM **Privately Held**
WEB: www.accurategrinding.com
SIC: **3544** Punches, forming & stamping

**(G-17728)**
**CONFAB SYSTEMS INC**
14831 S Mckinley Ave (60469-1524)
PHONE.................................708 388-4103
Fax: 708 388-4233
Daniel Rice, *President*
Michael Connor, *Admin Sec*
EMP: 10
SALES (est): 2MM **Privately Held**
SIC: **3535** Conveyors & conveying equipment

**(G-17729)**
**DANDURAND CUSTOM WOODWORKING**
2606 W Walter Zimny Dr (60469-1230)
PHONE.................................708 489-6440
Francis Dandurand, *Owner*
EMP: 2
SALES (est): 245.4K **Privately Held**
SIC: **2431** Millwork

**(G-17730)**
**G H MEISER & CO**
2407 W 140th Pl (60469-1054)
P.O. Box 315 (60469-0315)
PHONE.................................708 388-7867
Fax: 708 388-4053
Brian Parduhn, *President*
Bruce Parduhn, *Vice Pres*
Kim Quinski, *Director*
▲ EMP: 25 EST: 1906
SQ FT: 11,600
SALES (est): 4.9MM **Privately Held**
WEB: www.ghmeiser.com
SIC: **3824** 3563 Gauges for computing pressure temperature corrections; tire inflators, hand or compressor operated

**(G-17731)**
**GREMP STEEL CO**
14100 S Western Ave (60469-1059)
PHONE.................................708 389-7393
Fax: 708 489-1003
Rod Samardzija, *President*
Bronny Samardzija, *Vice Pres*
Greg Koscielski, *Purch Mgr*
Greg Kostielsky, *Purch Agent*
EMP: 25 EST: 1965
SQ FT: 55,000
SALES (est): 7.6MM **Privately Held**
WEB: www.gremp.com
SIC: **3441** Fabricated structural metal

**(G-17732)**
**MILK DESIGN COMPANY**
14150 S Western Ave (60469-1030)
PHONE.................................312 563-6455
Joseph A Colosi, *President*
Jessica Houston, *CFO*
Joslyn Paredes, *Office Mgr*
Jessica Colosi, *Admin Sec*
EMP: 5
SQ FT: 14,000
SALES (est): 1.1MM **Privately Held**
SIC: **3446** Architectural metalwork

**(G-17733)**
**NORTHSTAR CUSTOM CABINETRY**
14825 S Mckinley Ave (60469-1524)
PHONE.................................708 597-2099
Fax: 708 597-3581
Edward J McGunn, *Manager*
EMP: 2
SALES (est): 328.1K **Privately Held**
SIC: **2434** Wood kitchen cabinets

**(G-17734)**
**PARTS SPECIALISTS INC**
Also Called: Lincoln Land Enterprises
14639 S Short St (60469-1327)
PHONE.................................708 371-2444
Fax: 708 371-2477
Glenn Duncan, *President*
Sharon Duncan, *Corp Secy*
Mark Bajic, *Marketing Staff*
Chris Wiocio, *CTO*
◆ EMP: 7
SQ FT: 6,200
SALES (est): 1.1MM **Privately Held**
WEB: www.partsspecialistsinc.com
SIC: **5084** 3661 Elevators; industrial machine parts; telephones & telephone apparatus

**(G-17735)**
**REPLACEMENT ARTS INC**
14836 S Mckinley Ave (60469-1547)
PHONE.................................708 922-0580
Lee A Shirer, *President*
EMP: 2
SQ FT: 3,000
SALES (est): 375.4K **Privately Held**
SIC: **3842** Limbs, artificial

**(G-17736)**
**SOUTH SUBN WLDG & FABG CO INC**
14022 S Western Ave (60469-1029)
P.O. Box 346 (60469-0346)
PHONE.................................708 385-7160
Fax: 708 385-7133
George Bender, *President*
EMP: 9 EST: 1946
SQ FT: 10,000
SALES (est): 1.3MM **Privately Held**
SIC: **3444** 7692 3446 3443 Sheet metalwork; welding repair; architectural metalwork; fabricated plate work (boiler shop); fabricated structural metal

**(G-17737)**
**WOTKUN GROUP INC**
Also Called: Simko Grinding
14410 S Western Ave (60469-1330)
PHONE.................................708 396-2121
Richard Wotkun, *President*
EMP: 7
SALES (est): 500K **Privately Held**
SIC: **3999** Manufacturing industries

## Potomac
### Vermilion County

**(G-17738)**
**ILLINI FS INC**
Also Called: I F S
6637 E 3050 North Rd (61865-6506)
PHONE.................................217 442-4737
EMP: 4
SALES (corp-wide): 33MM **Privately Held**
SIC: **2869** 5191 5169 Mfg Industrial Organic Chemicals Whol Farm Supplies Whol Chemicals/Products
PA: Illini Fs Inc
1509 E University Ave
Urbana IL 61802
217 384-8300

## Prairie Du Rocher
### Randolph County

**(G-17739)**
**ELLNERS WELDING AND MACHINE SP**
8421 Nathan Ln (62277-2441)
PHONE.................................618 282-4302
Julie Ellner, *President*
EMP: 5
SALES (est): 80K **Privately Held**
SIC: **7692** Welding repair

## Princeton
### Bureau County

**(G-17740)**
**A & M PRODUCTS COMPANY**
575 Elm Pl (61356-1458)
P.O. Box 266 (61356-0266)
PHONE.................................815 875-2667
Fax: 815 879-0400
Mark Austin, *President*
Jeanne Austin, *Corp Secy*
John Austin, *Vice Pres*
▲ EMP: 9
SQ FT: 4,750
SALES (est): 1.3MM **Privately Held**
WEB: www.aandmproducts.com
SIC: **2499** 5947 Trophy bases, wood; gift, novelty & souvenir shop

**(G-17741)**
**ADVANCED ASPHALT CO (PA)**
308 W Railroad Ave (61356-1215)
P.O. Box 234 (61356-0234)
PHONE.................................815 872-9911
Fax: 815 872-0569
John Becker, *Superintendent*
Judith Nelson, *Vice Pres*
Rick Raabe, *Plant Mgr*
Brad Bruins, *Sls & Mktg Exec*
Wilbur Nelson, *Marketing Mgr*
EMP: 25 EST: 1961
SQ FT: 4,000
SALES (est): 10.2MM **Privately Held**
SIC: **1611** 2951 Highway & street construction; asphalt paving mixtures & blocks

**(G-17742)**
**ALLEGION S&S US HOLDING CO**
Also Called: Allegion Lcn & Falcon Closers
121 W Railroad Ave (61356-1201)
P.O. Box 100 (61356-0100)
PHONE.................................815 875-3311
Kristina Baldwin, *General Mgr*
Jason Krich, *Plant Mgr*
Tom Meadows, *Purch Agent*
Jonah Pattar, *Engineer*
Chris Casazza, *Sls & Mktg Exec*
EMP: 250
SQ FT: 200,000 **Privately Held**
WEB: www.ingersoll-rand.com
SIC: **3562** 3561 3429 3546 Ball & roller bearings; roller bearings & parts; ball bearings & parts; pumps & pumping equipment; furniture builders' & other household hardware; keys, locks & related hardware; power-driven handtools; air & gas compressors including vacuum pumps; winches
HQ: Allegion S&S Us Holding Company Inc
11819 N Pennsylvania St
Carmel IN 46032
317 810-3700

**(G-17743)**
**AMBASSADOR STEEL CORPORATION**
28 W Mechanic St (61356-1731)
PHONE.................................815 876-9089
Jim Hughes, *Manager*
EMP: 5
SALES (corp-wide): 16.2B **Publicly Held**
WEB: www.ambassadorsteel.com
SIC: **3441** Fabricated structural metal
HQ: Ambassador Steel Corporation
1340 S Grandstaff Dr
Auburn IN 46706
260 925-5440

**(G-17744)**
**B F SHAW PRINTING COMPANY**
Also Called: Bureau County Republican
800 Ace Rd (61356-9201)
P.O. Box 340 (61356-0340)
PHONE.................................815 875-4461
Sam R Fisher, *Publisher*
Kevin Hieronymus, *Editor*
Thomas Shaw, *COO*
Pam Pratt, *Sales Mgr*
Sandra Pistole, *Advt Staff*
EMP: 45
SQ FT: 11,250
SALES (corp-wide): 83.1MM **Privately Held**
WEB: www.bcrnews.com
SIC: **2711** 2796 2791 2789 Commercial printing & newspaper publishing combined; platemaking services; typesetting; bookbinding & related work; commercial printing; commercial printing, lithographic
PA: The B F Shaw Printing Company
444 Pine Hill Dr
Dixon IL
815 284-4000

**(G-17745)**
**COILCRAFT INCORPORATED**
1837 N Euclid Ave (61356-9676)
P.O. Box 68 (61356-0068)
PHONE.................................815 879-4408
Fax: 815 875-8407
Stan Balensiefin, *Manager*
EMP: 8
SALES (corp-wide): 476.5K **Privately Held**
SIC: **3677** Electronic coils, transformers & other inductors
PA: Coilcraft, Incorporated
1102 Silver Lake Rd
Cary IL 60013
847 639-2361

**(G-17746)**
**DENTAL CRAFTS LAB INC**
211 S 5th St (61356-1817)
P.O. Box 389 (61356-0389)
PHONE.................................815 872-3221
Kenneth Nordstrom, *President*
Barry Nordstrom, *Vice Pres*
Nancy Nordstrom, *Bookkeeper*
EMP: 5 EST: 1945
SALES (est): 413.7K **Privately Held**
SIC: **8072** 3843 Crown & bridge production; denture production; dental equipment & supplies

**(G-17747)**
**EMPIRE ACOUSTICAL SYSTEMS INC**
1111 Ace Rd (61356-9038)
PHONE.................................815 261-0072
Patrick McKeown, *President*
Dennis McKeown, *General Mgr*
EMP: 25
SALES (est): 70.4K **Privately Held**
SIC: **1442** Construction sand & gravel

# Princeton - Bureau County (G-17748)

**(G-17748)**
**ENNIS INC**
Also Called: GBS Document Solutions
200 W Railroad Ave (61356-1204)
PHONE..................815 875-2000
David Crysler, *Branch Mgr*
**EMP:** 30
**SALES (corp-wide):** 356.8MM **Publicly Held**
**WEB:** www.ennis.com
**SIC: 2752** 2761 2671 Business forms, lithographed; manifold business forms; packaging paper & plastics film, coated & laminated
**PA:** Ennis, Inc.
2441 Presidential Pkwy
Midlothian TX 76065
972 775-9801

**(G-17749)**
**GARDNER DENVER INC**
1301 N Euclid Ave (61356-9601)
PHONE..................209 823-0356
Christopher Bagatta, *Manager*
**EMP:** 10
**SQ FT:** 19,000
**SALES (corp-wide):** 1.9B **Publicly Held**
**WEB:** www.gardnerdenver.com
**SIC: 3563** Air & gas compressors including vacuum pumps
**HQ:** Gardner Denver, Inc.
222 E Erie St Ste 500
Milwaukee WI 53202

**(G-17750)**
**GARDNER DENVER INC**
Also Called: Champion A Gardner Denver Co
1301 N Euclid Ave (61356-9601)
PHONE..................815 875-3321
Brian Atwood, *Plant Mgr*
David Booth, *QC Dir*
Greg Ferrell, *QC Dir*
CAM Valle, *QC Dir*
Tim Hermeyer, *Engineer*
**EMP:** 100
**SALES (corp-wide):** 1.9B **Publicly Held**
**WEB:** www.gardnerdenver.com
**SIC: 3563** Air & gas compressors
**HQ:** Gardner Denver, Inc.
222 E Erie St Ste 500
Milwaukee WI 53202

**(G-17751)**
**ITALVIBRAS USA INC**
1940 Vans Way (61356-9037)
PHONE..................815 872-1350
Paolo Silingardi, *President*
Mike Kargl, *General Mgr*
Carlo Silingardi, *Principal*
Marc Kirschenbaum, *Sales Mgr*
Rob Beiersdorfer, *Accounts Mgr*
▲ **EMP:** 6
**SQ FT:** 2,000
**SALES (est):** 1.1MM **Privately Held**
**SIC: 3625** Industrial electrical relays & switches

**(G-17752)**
**L W SCHNEIDER INC**
1180 N 6th St (61356-9564)
PHONE..................815 875-3835
**Fax:** 815 875-1402
Lloyd W Schneider, *CEO*
Beverly Schneider, *President*
Lisa Kauski, *General Mgr*
Lisa Myers, *Vice Pres*
James Bender, *Mfg Dir*
▲ **EMP:** 50 **EST:** 1971
**SQ FT:** 13,000
**SALES (est):** 11.5MM **Privately Held**
**WEB:** www.lwschneider.com
**SIC: 3599** Machine shop, jobbing & repair

**(G-17753)**
**MC HENRY MACHINE CO INC**
1309 Il Highway 26 (61356-8341)
PHONE..................815 875-1953
**Fax:** 815 875-3701
John Williams, *President*
**EMP:** 4
**SQ FT:** 2,652
**SALES:** 900K **Privately Held**
**SIC: 3599** Machine shop, jobbing & repair

**(G-17754)**
**MISTIC METAL MOVER INC**
1160 N 6th St (61356-9564)
PHONE..................815 875-1371
**Fax:** 815 872-0915
Dwight K Thompson Jr, *President*
Hal Purky, *Vice Pres*
Brian Thompson, *Admin Sec*
Cynthia Thompson, *Admin Sec*
**EMP:** 4
**SQ FT:** 5,000
**SALES (est):** 591.8K **Privately Held**
**WEB:** www.misticmetal.com
**SIC: 2992** Cutting oils, blending: made from purchased materials

**(G-17755)**
**MONTEREY MUSHROOMS INC**
27268 Us Highway 6 (61356-8959)
PHONE..................815 875-4436
Timothy Crawford, *General Mgr*
Ramiro Madrigal, *Engineer*
Rod Wedekind, *Engineer*
James Howard, *Branch Mgr*
Patrick Guzzo, *Supervisor*
**EMP:** 4
**SALES (corp-wide):** 683.8MM **Privately Held**
**WEB:** www.montereymushrooms.com
**SIC: 0182** 2099 Mushrooms grown under cover; food preparations
**PA:** Monterey Mushrooms, Inc.
260 Westgate Dr
Watsonville CA 95076
831 763-5300

**(G-17756)**
**MTM JOSTENS INC**
615 S 6th St (61356-1873)
PHONE..................815 875-1111
**Fax:** 815 875-3593
Alm Dahms, *Principal*
**EMP:** 2
**SALES (est):** 314.2K **Privately Held**
**SIC: 3911** Jewelry, precious metal

**(G-17757)**
**MTM RECOGNITION CORPORATION**
615 S 6th St (61356-1873)
PHONE..................815 875-1111
Bev Eden, *Purch Agent*
Tom Tester, *Enginr/R&D Mgr*
E Dahms, *Controller*
Richard Unholz, *Controller*
Susan Fandel, *Executive*
**EMP:** 250
**SQ FT:** 50,000
**SALES (corp-wide):** 102.8MM **Privately Held**
**SIC: 3911** 3914 Jewelry, precious metal; trophies
**PA:** Mtm Recognition Corporation
3201 Se 29th St
Oklahoma City OK 73115
405 609-6900

**(G-17758)**
**PRINCETON FAST STOP**
720 N Main St (61356-1331)
PHONE..................815 872-0706
**Fax:** 815 875-1334
Mark Orr, *President*
**EMP:** 14
**SALES (est):** 1.5MM **Privately Held**
**SIC: 3589** Car washing machinery

**(G-17759)**
**PRINCETON READY-MIX INC**
533 E Railroad Ave (61356-1392)
P.O. Box 9 (61356-0009)
PHONE..................815 875-3359
**Fax:** 815 875-6007
Joan Perona, *President*
Keith Cain, *Plant Mgr*
Gwen Walsh, *Admin Sec*
**EMP:** 16
**SQ FT:** 1,200
**SALES (est):** 450K **Privately Held**
**SIC: 3273** Ready-mixed concrete

**(G-17760)**
**PRINCETON SEALING WAX CO**
106 W Long St (61356-1231)
PHONE..................815 875-1943
Caroline Tompson, *Partner*
Carolyn A Lokay, *Partner*
**EMP:** 3
**SQ FT:** 3,600
**SALES (est):** 434.7K **Privately Held**
**SIC: 2891** 2842 Sealing wax; adhesives; specialty cleaning, polishes & sanitation goods

**(G-17761)**
**QUALITY COATING CO**
2955 N Main St (61356-9044)
PHONE..................815 875-3228
**Fax:** 815 875-3236
Eldon Entwhistle, *President*
Marshann Entwhistle, *Vice Pres*
**EMP:** 18
**SQ FT:** 5,000
**SALES (est):** 1.8MM **Privately Held**
**WEB:** www.qualitycoatingco.com
**SIC: 3479** 3229 2851 Painting, coating & hot dipping; pressed & blown glass; paints & allied products

**(G-17762)**
**TRI-CON MATERIALS INC (PA)**
308 W Railroad Ave (61356-1215)
P.O. Box 304 (61356-0304)
PHONE..................815 872-3206
Richard L Nelson, *President*
Judith Nelson, *Vice Pres*
Steve Kelly, *Treasurer*
**EMP:** 2
**SQ FT:** 4,000
**SALES (est):** 6.4MM **Privately Held**
**SIC: 1442** Construction sand & gravel

## Princeville
### Peoria County

**(G-17763)**
**COKEL DJ WELDING BAY & MUFFLER**
Also Called: Cokel D J Wldg Stl Fabricators
224 E Evans St (61559-7531)
PHONE..................309 385-4567
Paul Cokel, *President*
**EMP:** 1
**SQ FT:** 4,500
**SALES (est):** 210.9K **Privately Held**
**SIC: 3441** 7692 Fabricated structural metal; welding repair

**(G-17764)**
**EC HARMS MET FABRICATORS INC**
1017 N Santa Fe Ave (61559-9279)
PHONE..................309 385-2132
**Fax:** 309 249-3203
Dennis L Stoecker, *President*
**EMP:** 13
**SQ FT:** 25,000
**SALES (est):** 3.4MM **Privately Held**
**WEB:** www.echarms.net
**SIC: 3443** Fabricated plate work (boiler shop)

**(G-17765)**
**FCA LLC**
610 S Walnut St (61559-9266)
PHONE..................309 385-2588
**Fax:** 309 385-2588
Joe Cave, *Branch Mgr*
**EMP:** 46 **Privately Held**
**WEB:** www.fcamfg.com
**SIC: 5085** 2448 2441 Industrial supplies; wood pallets & skids; nailed wood boxes & shook
**PA:** Fca, Llc
7601 John Deere Pkwy
Moline IL 61265

**(G-17766)**
**SENECA FOODS CORPORATION**
Also Called: Chiquita
606 S Tremont St (61559-9468)
PHONE..................309 385-4301
**Fax:** 309 385-2696
J Erck, *Vice Pres*
Eric Martin, *Opers Mgr*
Tim Prayne, *Purch Dir*
Tom L Davenport, *Purch Mgr*
Maryann Mercer, *CFO*
**EMP:** 36
**SQ FT:** 150,000
**SALES (corp-wide):** 1.2B **Publicly Held**
**SIC: 2033** Vegetables: packaged in cans, jars, etc.
**PA:** Seneca Foods Corporation
3736 S Main St
Marion NY 14505
315 926-8100

## Prophetstown
### Whiteside County

**(G-17767)**
**AMERICAN GEAR INC**
910 Swanson Dr (61277-9524)
P.O. Box 156 (61277-0156)
PHONE..................815 537-5111
**Fax:** 815 537-2871
Gregory W Scott, *President*
Pam Scott, *Treasurer*
**EMP:** 10
**SALES:** 1MM **Privately Held**
**WEB:** www.americangearinc.com
**SIC: 3714** Gears, motor vehicle

**(G-17768)**
**ECHO PROPHETSTOWN**
342 Washington St (61277-1115)
P.O. Box 7 (61277-0007)
PHONE..................815 537-5107
**Fax:** 815 537-2658
Neil Robinson, *Owner*
**EMP:** 4
**SALES (est):** 125.9K **Privately Held**
**SIC: 2711** Newspapers

**(G-17769)**
**GENESIS III INC**
5575 Lyndon Rd (61277-9588)
P.O. Box 186 (61277-0186)
PHONE..................815 537-7900
**Fax:** 815 537-7905
Roger Young, *Ch of Bd*
Jonathan Paul, *President*
Melissa Ott, *Office Mgr*
Dan Paul, *Technology*
Laurie Ferguson, *Exec Sec*
**EMP:** 26
**SQ FT:** 18,000
**SALES (est):** 6.6MM **Privately Held**
**SIC: 3531** Hammer mills (rock & ore crushing machines), portable

**(G-17770)**
**HERITAGE PRINTING (PA)**
219 Washington St (61277-1179)
P.O. Box 215 (61277-0215)
PHONE..................815 537-2372
**Fax:** 815 537-5799
Randy Jacobs, *Partner*
Mark Jacobs, *Partner*
**EMP:** 4 **EST:** 1969
**SQ FT:** 1,800
**SALES (est):** 343.2K **Privately Held**
**SIC: 2752** 2791 Commercial printing, offset; typesetting

**(G-17771)**
**PROPHET GEAR CO**
46 Grove St (61277-9375)
P.O. Box 3 (61277-0003)
PHONE..................815 537-2002
**Fax:** 815 537-2228
Kenneth Huizenga, *President*
Jackie Roman, *Manager*
**EMP:** 25
**SQ FT:** 17,000
**SALES (est):** 4.7MM **Privately Held**
**SIC: 3566** 3568 Gears, power transmission, except automotive; pulleys, power transmission

## Prospect Heights
### Cook County

**(G-17772)**
**ARCHITECTUAL WOODWORKING**
305 Brian Ln (60070-1609)
PHONE..................847 259-3331
Richard Kellerman, *Owner*

# GEOGRAPHIC SECTION

Quincy - Adams County (G-17797)

EMP: 3
SALES (est): 302.8K  Privately Held
SIC: 2431  Millwork

**(G-17773)**
**CAMERA READY COPIES INC**
740 Pinecrest Dr  (60070-1806)
P.O. Box 95585, Palatine  (60095-0585)
PHONE.................................847 215-8611
Fax: 847 215-2614
Brian Kowalski, *President*
Jim Heck, *Prdtn Mgr*
Kathy Popp, *Manager*
EMP: 25
SQ FT: 7,500
SALES (est): 2.6MM  Privately Held
WEB: www.crcprint.com
SIC: 2752  2789  Commercial printing, offset; bookbinding & related work

**(G-17774)**
**CONCRETE & MARBLE POLISHING &**
718 E Old Willow Rd  (60070-1914)
PHONE.................................773 968-6897
Russell Nakai, *President*
EMP: 5
SALES (est): 423.6K  Privately Held
SIC: 3272  Art marble, concrete

**(G-17775)**
**CREATIVE SCIENCE ACTIVITIES**
Also Called: Esd
2 E Clarendon St  (60070-1534)
PHONE.................................847 870-1746
Gerald T Anderson, *Owner*
EMP: 3
SALES: 300K  Privately Held
SIC: 3825  Digital test equipment, electronic & electrical circuits

**(G-17776)**
**DIRK VANDER NOOT**
811 Andover Ct  (60070-1169)
P.O. Box 438, Ingleside  (60041-0438)
PHONE.................................224 558-1878
Dirk Vander Noot, *Principal*
EMP: 3
SALES (est): 191K  Privately Held
SIC: 3089  Injection molding of plastics

**(G-17777)**
**EARLY BIRD ADVERTISING INC**
502 Grego Ct  (60070-1634)
PHONE.................................847 253-1423
Wayne Vipond, *President*
Dorothy Vipond, *Treasurer*
Wayne Ter Haar, *Personnel Exec*
EMP: 3  EST: 1959
SALES (est): 360K  Privately Held
SIC: 7311  7335  2791  Advertising agencies; commercial photography; typesetting, computer controlled

**(G-17778)**
**GEORGE WILSON**
477 Greystone Ln  (60070-2592)
PHONE.................................847 342-1111
Fax: 847 342-1112
George Wilson Jr, *Partner*
EMP: 2
SALES: 400K  Privately Held
SIC: 3861  Reproduction machines & equipment

**(G-17779)**
**GERALD R PAGE CORPORATION (PA)**
309 E Kenilworth Ave  (60070-1316)
PHONE.................................847 398-5575
Gerald R Page, *President*
Randy Randolph, *Principal*
Carol Winiarz, *Executive Asst*
Constance R Page, *Admin Sec*
EMP: 12
SQ FT: 10,000
SALES (est): 7.1MM  Privately Held
SIC: 3312  1542  1541  8712  Structural shapes & pilings, steel; pipes & tubes; commercial & office building, new construction; industrial buildings, new construction; architectural services

**(G-17780)**
**INSULATORS SUPPLY INC**
741 Pinecrest Dr  (60070-1807)
PHONE.................................847 394-2836
William Melton, *President*
Ronald Lemmon, *Vice Pres*
EMP: 3
SQ FT: 6,000
SALES (est): 460K  Privately Held
SIC: 5211  3442  5033  Insulation material, building; metal doors; insulation materials

**(G-17781)**
**JPMORGAN CHASE BANK NAT ASSN**
2 E Euclid Ave  (60070-2561)
PHONE.................................847 392-1600
William Taylor, *Manager*
EMP: 6
SALES (corp-wide): 105.4B  Publicly Held
SIC: 3578  Automatic teller machines (ATM)
HQ: Jpmorgan Chase Bank, National Association
    1111 Polaris Pkwy
    Columbus OH 43240
    614 436-3055

**(G-17782)**
**LEISURE TIME PRODUCTS INC**
Also Called: Detail Master
101 Patricia Ln  (60070-1645)
PHONE.................................847 287-2863
Robert E Boyer, *President*
Judy Boyer, *Vice Pres*
▲ EMP: 8
SQ FT: 6,500
SALES (est): 1MM  Privately Held
WEB: www.detailmasteronline.com
SIC: 3952  Artists' equipment; pyrography materials

**(G-17783)**
**LEXPRESS INC**
1176 Cove Dr  (60070-1905)
PHONE.................................773 517-7095
Eugeniu Dimbu, *Owner*
Carolina EMI, *Manager*
EMP: 5  EST: 2015
SALES (est): 159.6K  Privately Held
SIC: 4212  3537  7389  Delivery service, vehicular; trucks: freight, baggage, etc.: industrial, except mining;

**(G-17784)**
**STITCH BY STITCH INCORPORATED**
Also Called: Stitch Plus
65 E Palatine Rd Ste 217  (60070-1845)
PHONE.................................847 541-2543
Karen Locallo, *President*
Joanne Hansler, *Vice Pres*
EMP: 7
SALES (est): 618.6K  Privately Held
SIC: 2395  Pleating & stitching

**(G-17785)**
**SWISS E D M WIRECUT INC**
743 Pinecrest Dr  (60070-1807)
PHONE.................................847 459-4310
Fax: 847 459-9640
John E Strahammer, *President*
Josef V Strahammer, *Admin Sec*
EMP: 10
SQ FT: 6,000
SALES: 1MM  Privately Held
WEB: www.swissedm.com
SIC: 3599  Machine shop, jobbing & repair

**(G-17786)**
**WOOLENWEAR CO**
Also Called: Personalitee's
739 Pinecrest Dr  (60070-1807)
PHONE.................................847 520-9243
Fax: 847 520-9322
Jeffery Kroft, *President*
Gail Kroft, *Vice Pres*
Mary Harris, *Opers Mgr*
EMP: 10
SQ FT: 6,000

SALES: 710K  Privately Held
SIC: 2326  2339  2395  2759  Service apparel (baker, barber, lab, etc.), washable: men's; service apparel, washable: women's; embroidery products, except schiffli machine; screen printing

**(G-17787)**
**XD INDUSTRIES INC**
836 E Old Willow Rd  (60070-2163)
PHONE.................................847 293-0796
EMP: 3
SALES (est): 237.1K  Privately Held
SIC: 3999  Manufacturing industries

## Putnam
### Putnam County

**(G-17788)**
**RIVER VALLEY MECHANICAL INC**
1532 County Road 1500 E  (61560-9626)
PHONE.................................309 364-3776
Troy D Wilkerson, *President*
Troy D Wilkinson, *President*
Tom Wilkinson, *Vice Pres*
Sarah J Wilkinson, *Admin Sec*
EMP: 6
SALES (est): 921.3K  Privately Held
SIC: 2679  7692  Pipes & fittings, fiber: made from purchased material; welding repair

## Quincy
### Adams County

**(G-17789)**
**ADAMS TELEPHONE CO-OPERATIVE**
Also Called: Adams Network
301 Oak St  (62301-2516)
P.O. Box 247, Golden  (62339-0247)
PHONE.................................217 224-9566
David R Kelly, *Pastor*
Robert C Morwell, *Pastor*
Sheila M Pollard, *Pastor*
William S Renner, *Pastor*
Steven M Smith, *Pastor*
EMP: 30
SALES (corp-wide): 18.1MM  Privately Held
SIC: 7372  Prepackaged software
PA: Adams Telephone Co-Operative
    405 Emminga Rd
    Golden IL 62339
    217 696-4411

**(G-17790)**
**AGCO RECYCLING LLC**
4425 Gardner Expy  (62305-7525)
PHONE.................................217 224-9048
Fax: 217 224-9049
JD Albsmeyer, *Owner*
EMP: 17
SALES (est): 1MM  Privately Held
SIC: 2448  5031  Wood pallets & skids; molding, all materials

**(G-17791)**
**ALTER TRADING CORPORATION**
Also Called: Alter Scrap
2834 Gardner Expy  (62305-7529)
P.O. Box 766  (62306-0766)
PHONE.................................217 223-0156
Ron Stephenson, *General Mgr*
Chad Awbrey, *Manager*
EMP: 10
SALES (corp-wide): 850.2MM  Privately Held
WEB: www.altertrading.com
SIC: 5093  5051  4953  3341  Ferrous metal scrap & waste; metals service centers & offices; refuse systems; secondary nonferrous metals
HQ: Alter Trading Corporation
    700 Office Pkwy
    Saint Louis MO 63141
    314 872-2400

**(G-17792)**
**ANIMAL CENTER INTERNATIONAL**
4124 Kochs Ln  (62305-7684)
PHONE.................................217 214-0536
Flora Madey, *General Mgr*
▲ EMP: 8
SALES (est): 756.1K  Privately Held
SIC: 2833  Animal based products

**(G-17793)**
**ARCHER-DANIELS-MIDLAND COMPANY**
ADM Animal Nutrition
1000 N 30th St  (62301-3400)
PHONE.................................217 222-7100
Fax: 217 222-4069
Jenny Jenkins, *Human Res Mgr*
Steve Dale, *Branch Mgr*
Glen Brockmeier, *Manager*
Tracy Hildebrand, *Lab Dir*
EMP: 20
SALES (corp-wide): 62.3B  Publicly Held
WEB: www.admworld.com
SIC: 2048  Livestock feeds; feed supplements; mineral feed supplements
PA: Archer-Daniels-Midland Company
    77 W Wacker Dr Ste 4600
    Chicago IL 60601
    312 634-8100

**(G-17794)**
**ARCHER-DANIELS-MIDLAND COMPANY**
Also Called: ADM
2100 Gardner Expy  (62305-9376)
PHONE.................................217 224-1800
Fax: 217 221-0434
Larry Horn, *Principal*
Richard Ellerman, *Opers Mgr*
Lloyd Griggs, *Engineer*
Chad Howser, *Engineer*
Jonathan Kramer, *Engineer*
EMP: 20
SALES (corp-wide): 62.3B  Publicly Held
WEB: www.admworld.com
SIC: 4221  2079  2075  5153  Grain elevator, storage only; edible fats & oils; soybean oil mills; grain elevators
PA: Archer-Daniels-Midland Company
    77 W Wacker Dr Ste 4600
    Chicago IL 60601
    312 634-8100

**(G-17795)**
**ARCHER-DANIELS-MIDLAND COMPANY**
1900 Gardner Expy  (62301)
PHONE.................................217 224-1800
Todd Phillips, *Branch Mgr*
EMP: 58
SALES (corp-wide): 62.3B  Publicly Held
SIC: 2075  Soybean oil mills
PA: Archer-Daniels-Midland Company
    77 W Wacker Dr Ste 4600
    Chicago IL 60601
    312 634-8100

**(G-17796)**
**ARCHER-DANIELS-MIDLAND COMPANY**
Also Called: ADM
2701 Refinery Rd  (62305-8700)
P.O. Box 1045  (62306-1045)
PHONE.................................217 224-1875
Richard Ellerman, *Opers Mgr*
Rick Smith, *Research*
Mike Pulliam, *Manager*
Vance Higdon, *Maintence Staff*
EMP: 80
SALES (corp-wide): 62.3B  Publicly Held
WEB: www.admworld.com
SIC: 2079  5199  Vegetable refined oils (except corn oil); oils, animal or vegetable
PA: Archer-Daniels-Midland Company
    77 W Wacker Dr Ste 4600
    Chicago IL 60601
    312 634-8100

**(G-17797)**
**AWERKAMP MACHINE CO (PA)**
237 N 7th St  (62301-3093)
PHONE.................................217 222-3480
Toll Free:...............................888  -
Fax: 217 222-9408

# Quincy - Adams County (G-17798)  GEOGRAPHIC SECTION

William J Awerkamp, *President*
Kelvin Hufendick, *Office Mgr*
Donald T Awerkamp, *Admin Sec*
**EMP:** 35 **EST:** 1947
**SQ FT:** 45,000
**SALES:** 6.2MM **Privately Held**
**WEB:** www.awerkamp.com
**SIC:** 3599  7692  Machine shop, jobbing & repair; welding repair

### (G-17798)
### AWERKAMP MACHINE CO
Also Called: Awerkamp Steel
321 Broadway St  (62301-2722)
**PHONE** ................................. 217 222-3490
**Toll Free:** ................................ 888  -
**Fax:** 217 222-3577
Mark Terwelp, *Manager*
Rod Snodgrass, *Systems Mgr*
**EMP:** 10
**SALES (corp-wide):** 6.2MM **Privately Held**
**WEB:** www.awerkamp.com
**SIC:** 3599  5051  Machine shop, jobbing & repair; steel
**PA:** Awerkamp Machine Co.
   237 N 7th St
   Quincy IL 62301
   217 222-3480

### (G-17799)
### BAILEYS FUDGE & FINE GIFTS INC
307 N 36th St Ste 210  (62301-3760)
**PHONE** ................................. 217 231-3834
Melissa C Griswood, *President*
Rebecca Dorethy, *Vice Pres*
Ruth Phillips, *Admin Sec*
**EMP:** 7
**SQ FT:** 1,500
**SALES (est):** 717.5K **Privately Held**
**WEB:** www.baileysfudge.com
**SIC:** 2064  5441  5499  5947  Candy & other confectionery products; candy; coffee; gift shop

### (G-17800)
### BEANS PRINTING INC
3710 Broadway St  (62305-2822)
**PHONE** ................................. 217 223-5555
Justin Hurayt, *President*
**EMP:** 4
**SALES (est):** 300K **Privately Held**
**SIC:** 2752  Commercial printing, lithographic

### (G-17801)
### BEAUTICONTROL
1702 Locust St  (62301-1467)
**PHONE** ................................. 217 223-0382
Kimberly Caster, *Principal*
**EMP:** 3
**SALES (est):** 202.3K **Privately Held**
**SIC:** 3562  Casters

### (G-17802)
### BEI ELECTRONICS LLC (HQ)
Also Called: Broadcast Electronics
4100 N 24th St  (62305-7749)
**PHONE** ................................. 217 224-9600
Kameron Bridgeman, *Manager*
Elizabeth Keck,
**EMP:** 17
**SALES (est):** 27.9MM **Privately Held**
**SIC:** 3663  Transmitting apparatus, radio or television
**PA:** Iic Acquisitions Ii, Llc
   4100 N 24th St
   Quincy IL 62305
   217 224-9600

### (G-17803)
### BEI HOLDING CORPORATION
Also Called: Broadcast Electronics
4100 N 24th St  (62305-7749)
P.O. Box 3606  (62305-3606)
**PHONE** ................................. 217 224-9600
John Tedlow, *President*
Becky Keck, *CFO*
Elizabeth Keck, *CFO*
Ed Miller, *Clerk*
**EMP:** 2
**SQ FT:** 1,000
**SALES (est):** 255.2K **Privately Held**
**SIC:** 3663  Radio & TV communications equipment

### (G-17804)
### BICK BROADCASTING INC
Also Called: Sign Pro
408 N 24th St  (62301-3254)
**PHONE** ................................. 217 223-9693
Tim Gottman, *Manager*
Sandy Foster, *Manager*
**EMP:** 4
**SALES (corp-wide):** 2.2MM **Privately Held**
**SIC:** 3993  Signs & advertising specialties
**PA:** Bick Broadcasting Inc
   119 N 3rd St
   Hannibal MO 63401
   573 221-3450

### (G-17805)
### BLEIGH CONSTRUCTION COMPANY
Also Called: Quincy Ready Mix Co
3522 S 6th St  (62305-7557)
**PHONE** ................................. 217 222-5005
**Fax:** 217 222-5007
Mark E Tofall, *Branch Mgr*
**EMP:** 7
**SQ FT:** 1,000
**SALES (corp-wide):** 28.8MM **Privately Held**
**WEB:** www.bleigh.com
**SIC:** 3273  Ready-mixed concrete
**PA:** Bleigh Construction Company
   9037 Highway 168
   Palmyra MO 63461
   573 221-2247

### (G-17806)
### BOB ULRICHS PALLETS
5910 Dove Ln  (62305-6010)
**PHONE** ................................. 217 224-2568
**Fax:** 217 224-2577
Bob Ulrich, *Partner*
Phyllis Ulrich, *Partner*
**EMP:** 7
**SALES (est):** 530K **Privately Held**
**SIC:** 2448  Wood pallets & skids

### (G-17807)
### BOWTREE INC
720 E Tolton Dr  (62305-8379)
P.O. Box 3562  (62305-3562)
**PHONE** ................................. 217 430-8884
Michael A Ray, *President*
**EMP:** 3
**SALES:** 70K **Privately Held**
**WEB:** www.bowtree.com
**SIC:** 3949  Archery equipment, general

### (G-17808)
### BREWER UTILITY SYSTEMS INC
Also Called: Golfcar Utility Systems
1628 Madison St  (62301-5558)
**PHONE** ................................. 217 224-5975
Robert Brewer, *President*
Teresa Brewer, *Vice Pres*
**EMP:** 5
**SQ FT:** 14,000
**SALES (est):** 520K **Privately Held**
**SIC:** 5941  3799  Golf goods & equipment; golf carts, powered

### (G-17809)
### BROADCAST ELECTRONICS INC (DH)
Also Called: B E
4100 N 24th St  (62305-7749)
P.O. Box 3606  (62305-3606)
**PHONE** ................................. 217 224-9600
**Fax:** 217 224-9607
Tom Beck, *CEO*
Brian Lindemann, *President*
Dave Kroeger, *Engineer*
Don Backus, *Sales Mgr*
Janie Windmiller, *Mktg Coord*
◆ **EMP:** 120 **EST:** 1959
**SQ FT:** 70,000
**SALES:** 16.7MM
**SALES (corp-wide):** 27.9MM **Privately Held**
**WEB:** www.bdcast.com
**SIC:** 3663  8742  Radio broadcasting & communications equipment; industry specialist consultants

### (G-17810)
### CARROLL DISTRG & CNSTR SUP INC
2221 N 24th St  (62301-1207)
**PHONE** ................................. 217 223-8126
Steve Carroll, *President*
**EMP:** 3
**SALES (corp-wide):** 75.9MM **Privately Held**
**SIC:** 5082  3444  Contractors' materials; concrete forms, sheet metal
**PA:** Carroll Distributing & Construction Supply, Inc.
   205 S Iowa Ave
   Ottumwa IA 52501
   641 683-1888

### (G-17811)
### CENTRAL STONE COMPANY
Also Called: Crush Stone
8514 Rock Quarry Rd  (62305-8025)
**PHONE** ................................. 217 224-7330
Ray Barry, *Superintendent*
**EMP:** 11
**SALES (corp-wide):** 3.9B **Privately Held**
**SIC:** 1422  Limestones, ground
**HQ:** Central Stone Company
   1701 5th Ave
   Moline IL 61265
   309 757-8250

### (G-17812)
### CENTURY SIGNS INC
2704 N 30th St  (62305-1231)
**PHONE** ................................. 217 224-7419
**Fax:** 217 224-4002
Stanley Helkey, *President*
Lynn-Marie Walden, *Office Mgr*
Carol Helkey, *Officer*
**EMP:** 11
**SQ FT:** 14,000
**SALES:** 1MM **Privately Held**
**WEB:** www.centurysignsinc.com
**SIC:** 3993  7629  Electric signs; electrical repair shops

### (G-17813)
### CLASSIQUE SIGNS & ENGRV INC
1702 Harrison St  (62301-6712)
**PHONE** ................................. 217 228-7446
Rodney Moore, *President*
Steven Moore, *Vice Pres*
**EMP:** 6
**SQ FT:** 4,000
**SALES (est):** 900K **Privately Held**
**WEB:** www.classiqueast.com
**SIC:** 5094  5199  2759  3993  Trophies; advertising specialties; commercial printing; signs & advertising specialties; trophies & plaques; coated & laminated paper

### (G-17814)
### COCA-COLA BOTTLING CO CNSLD
3321 Cannonball Rd  (62305)
**PHONE** ................................. 217 223-5183
**Fax:** 217 223-9436
John Franklin Brock, *Principal*
Cory Jones, *Manager*
**EMP:** 32
**SALES (corp-wide):** 3.1B **Publicly Held**
**SIC:** 2086  Bottled & canned soft drinks
**PA:** Coca-Cola Bottling Co. Consolidated
   4100 Coca Cola Plz # 100
   Charlotte NC 28211
   704 557-4400

### (G-17815)
### COMCAST CORPORATION
2930 State St  (62301-5718)
**PHONE** ................................. 217 498-3274
Marci Musolino, *General Mgr*
Christopher Campbell, *Network Enginr*
**EMP:** 30
**SALES (corp-wide):** 80.4B **Publicly Held**
**SIC:** 3648  Spotlights
**PA:** Comcast Corporation
   1701 Jfk Blvd
   Philadelphia PA 19103
   215 286-1700

### (G-17816)
### CRAIG INDUSTRIES INC
Also Called: Enviro-Buildings
401 Delaware St  (62301-4877)
**PHONE** ................................. 217 228-2421
**Fax:** 217 228-2424
Ellis Craig, *President*
Luke Craig, *COO*
Allen Craig, *Vice Pres*
Brandy Hougland, *Plant Mgr*
Brandy Carr, *Purch Dir*
▼ **EMP:** 65
**SQ FT:** 40,000
**SALES (est):** 19.2MM **Privately Held**
**WEB:** www.communicationshelter.com
**SIC:** 3448  3632  Prefabricated metal buildings; household refrigerators & freezers

### (G-17817)
### DALE SCHAWITSCH
Also Called: Discount Battery Sales
234 N 4th St  (62301-2915)
**PHONE** ................................. 217 224-5161
**Fax:** 217 222-2129
Dale Schawitsch, *Owner*
**EMP:** 3
**SQ FT:** 80,000
**SALES:** 950K **Privately Held**
**SIC:** 5013  5531  3694  Automotive batteries; batteries, automotive & truck; generators, automotive & aircraft; motors, starting: automotive & aircraft

### (G-17818)
### DAVID SCHUTTE
1226 N 14th St  (62301-2037)
**PHONE** ................................. 217 223-5464
David Schutte, *President*
Mary Ruth Schutte, *Corp Secy*
**EMP:** 9
**SALES (est):** 365.5K **Privately Held**
**SIC:** 7699  7692  Industrial machinery & equipment repair; welding repair

### (G-17819)
### DAVID TAYLOR
Also Called: Selby Implement Company
2201 N 24th St  (62301-1207)
**PHONE** ................................. 217 222-6480
**Fax:** 217 222-6540
David Taylor, *President*
Dave Taylor, *Manager*
**EMP:** 20
**SALES (est):** 1.3MM **Privately Held**
**SIC:** 3523  3524  3751  Farm machinery & equipment; blowers & vacuums, lawn; gears, motorcycle & bicycle

### (G-17820)
### DE ASBURY INC
Also Called: Royal Printing Co
2615 Ellington Rd  (62305-8830)
P.O. Box 3857  (62305-3857)
**PHONE** ................................. 217 222-0617
**Fax:** 217 222-7426
Dan E Asbury, *President*
Patrice Higgins, *General Mgr*
Sharon Shouse, *General Mgr*
Andrew Asbury, *Vice Pres*
**EMP:** 33
**SQ FT:** 8,000
**SALES (est):** 5.6MM **Privately Held**
**SIC:** 2752  3993  2791  2789  Commercial printing, offset; signs & advertising specialties; typesetting; bookbinding & related work

### (G-17821)
### DOYLE EQUIPMENT MFG CO
4001 Broadway St  (62305-2808)
P.O. Box 3024  (62305-3024)
**PHONE** ................................. 217 222-1592
**Fax:** 217 223-3655
Monty Doyle, *President*
Doug Kopischke, *Vice Pres*
Reva Walker, *Accountant*
▼ **EMP:** 58
**SQ FT:** 36,000
**SALES (est):** 23.8MM **Privately Held**
**WEB:** www.doylemfg.com
**SIC:** 3523  5084  Spreaders, fertilizer; industrial machinery & equipment

## (G-17822)
### DRIESELMAN MANUFACTURING CO
2028 Quintron Way (62305-1207)
PHONE.................................217 222-1986
Fax: 217 222-2060
Thomas K Drieselman, *President*
Cindy Drieselman, *Vice Pres*
EMP: 20
SQ FT: 35,000
SALES (est): 3.4MM **Privately Held**
WEB: www.drieselmanmanufacturing.com
SIC: 2541 Store & office display cases & fixtures

## (G-17823)
### DYNEER CORPORATION
2701 Spruce St (62301-3473)
PHONE.................................217 228-6011
Maurice M Taylor Jr, *President*
EMP: 487
SQ FT: 1,000,000
SALES (est): 24.1MM
SALES (corp-wide): 1.2B **Publicly Held**
WEB: www.titan-intl.com
SIC: 3011 3069 3568 Tires, cushion or solid rubber; industrial tires, pneumatic; hard rubber & molded rubber products; hard rubber products; clutches, except vehicular
PA: Titan International, Inc.
 2701 Spruce St
 Quincy IL 62301
 217 228-6011

## (G-17824)
### E MC
906 Vermont St (62301-3050)
PHONE.................................217 228-1280
EMP: 3
SALES (est): 197.1K **Privately Held**
SIC: 3572 Computer storage devices

## (G-17825)
### EMCO WHEATON USA INC (DH)
1800 Gardner Expy (62305-9364)
PHONE.................................281 856-1300
Darren Sabino, *President*
◆ EMP: 40
SALES (est): 9.2MM
SALES (corp-wide): 1.9B **Publicly Held**
WEB: www.gardnerdenver.com
SIC: 3561 1799 Pumps & pumping equipment; service station equipment installation & maintenance

## (G-17826)
### EMERALD CITY JEWELRY INC
Also Called: Emerald City Jewelers
3236 Broadway St (62301-3712)
PHONE.................................217 222-8896
Sheri Busse, *President*
Denise C Feldkamp, *Manager*
EMP: 6
SALES: 750K **Privately Held**
WEB: www.emeraldcityjewelers.com
SIC: 3911 5944 7631 Jewelry, precious metal; jewelry stores; jewelry repair services

## (G-17827)
### EXPRESSIONS BY CHRISTINE INC
711 Maine St (62301-4012)
PHONE.................................217 223-2750
Fax: 217 223-9206
Christine Kaiser, *President*
EMP: 15
SQ FT: 3,000
SALES (est): 820K **Privately Held**
WEB: www.expbyc.com
SIC: 2395 Embroidery products, except schiffli machine

## (G-17828)
### GARDNER DENVER INC
1800 Gardner Expy (62305-9364)
PHONE.................................217 222-5400
Merton Porter, *Regional Mgr*
Edgar Rodriguez, *Area Mgr*
Karin Brunner, *Vice Pres*
Sam Wollard, *Production*
Monica Barreto, *Buyer*
EMP: 52
SALES (corp-wide): 1.9B **Publicly Held**
SIC: 3563 Air & gas compressors
HQ: Gardner Denver, Inc.
 222 E Erie St Ste 500
 Milwaukee WI 53202

## (G-17829)
### GAREN EATON FARMS LLC
630 Sunset Dr (62305-0480)
PHONE.................................217 228-0324
Eaton Gary W, *Principal*
EMP: 3
SALES (est): 250.3K **Privately Held**
SIC: 3625 Motor controls & accessories

## (G-17830)
### GATESAIR INC
3200 Wisman Ln (62301-1252)
PHONE.................................217 222-8200
Scott Armistead, *Engineer*
Bryant Burke, *Branch Mgr*
EMP: 200
SALES (corp-wide): 6.3B **Privately Held**
SIC: 1731 3663 7371 Communications specialization; radio & TV communications equipment; computer software development & applications
HQ: Gatesair, Inc.
 5300 Kings Island Dr
 Mason OH 45040
 513 459-3400

## (G-17831)
### GOLDEN HEALTH PRODUCTS INC
1701 Springmeier Dr (62305-1008)
PHONE.................................217 223-3209
Mary F Spence, *President*
EMP: 2
SALES (est): 220K **Privately Held**
WEB: www.goldenhealthproducts.com
SIC: 2834 5499 Vitamin, nutrient & hematinic preparations for human use; health & dietetic food stores

## (G-17832)
### GRIFFARD & ASSOCIATES LLC
Also Called: Rainmaker Brands
1022 Kochs Ln (62305-1336)
PHONE.................................217 316-1732
John Griffard, *Mng Member*
Gary Klingele,
Tom Ries,
▲ EMP: 3
SALES: 1MM **Privately Held**
SIC: 2421 7389 Outdoor wood structural products;

## (G-17833)
### H & B QUALITY TOOLING INC
924 Jersey St (62301-4031)
PHONE.................................217 223-2387
Fax: 217 223-5262
Roger Leenerts, *President*
Julie Leenerts, *Admin Sec*
EMP: 11
SQ FT: 14,000
SALES: 950K **Privately Held**
SIC: 3544 Dies & die holders for metal cutting, forming, die casting

## (G-17834)
### HARDY RADIATOR REPAIR
Also Called: Hardy's Auto Sales
1710 N 12th St (62301-1387)
PHONE.................................217 223-8320
Max Hardy, *Partner*
Rosemary Hardy, *Partner*
EMP: 11
SQ FT: 2,000
SALES (est): 650K **Privately Held**
SIC: 7539 3714 3433 Radiator repair shop, automotive; motor vehicle parts & accessories; heating equipment, except electric

## (G-17835)
### HERALD WHIG QUINCY
130 N 5th St (62301-2916)
P.O. Box 909 (62306-0909)
PHONE.................................217 222-7600
Tom Oakley, *CEO*
EMP: 2 **EST**: 2008
SALES (est): 207K **Privately Held**
SIC: 5994 2711 Newsstand; newspapers, publishing & printing

## (G-17836)
### HOLLISTER-WHITNEY ELEV CORP
2603 N 24th St (62305-1215)
P.O. Box 4025 (62305-4025)
PHONE.................................217 222-0466
Fax: 217 220-0493
Michael Gash, *General Mgr*
Herbert W Glaser, *Vice Pres*
Walter Glaser, *Vice Pres*
Frank H Musholt, *Vice Pres*
Angela Smith, *Production*
▲ EMP: 250 **EST**: 1900
SQ FT: 225,000
SALES (est): 110.3MM **Privately Held**
WEB: www.hollisterwhitney.com
SIC: 3534 Elevators & moving stairways

## (G-17837)
### HUBER CARBONATES LLC
3150 Gardner Expy (62305-9378)
PHONE.................................217 224-8737
Walter A Trott,
Douglas Grant,
David Riley,
EMP: 8
SALES (est): 597.8K
SALES (corp-wide): 901MM **Privately Held**
SIC: 1455 Kaolin mining
PA: J.M. Huber Corporation
 499 Thornall St Ste 8
 Edison NJ 08837
 732 603-3630

## (G-17838)
### IIC ACQUISITIONS II LLC (PA)
4100 N 24th St (62305-7749)
PHONE.................................217 224-9600
Elizabeth Keck, *Mng Member*
EMP: 3
SALES (est): 27.9MM **Privately Held**
SIC: 3663 Mobile communication equipment

## (G-17839)
### IN MIDWEST SERVICE ENTERPRISES
2221 N 24th St (62301-1207)
PHONE.................................217 224-1932
Chris Larson, *Owner*
Jeff Smith, *General Mgr*
EMP: 5
SALES: 500K **Privately Held**
SIC: 3429 Builders' hardware

## (G-17840)
### INTERSTATE ALL BATTERY CENTER
101 N 48th St (62305-0449)
PHONE.................................217 214-1069
Fax: 217 217-7979
Steve Leigh, *President*
EMP: 15 **EST**: 2011
SALES (est): 1.4MM **Privately Held**
SIC: 5531 5063 3691 Batteries, automotive & truck; batteries; storage batteries

## (G-17841)
### JM HUBER CORPORATION
Engineered Minerals Div
3150 Gardner Expy (62305-9378)
P.O. Box 4005 (62305-4005)
PHONE.................................217 224-1100
Fax: 217 224-7957
Anthony Lewis, *General Mgr*
Lois Campbell, *Safety Mgr*
Steve McQueen, *Opers Staff*
Michael Hughes, *Purch Agent*
Stacy Atteberry, *Human Res Mgr*
EMP: 32
SALES (corp-wide): 901MM **Privately Held**
WEB: www.huber.com
SIC: 2819 2899 Industrial inorganic chemicals; chemical preparations
PA: J.M. Huber Corporation
 499 Thornall St Ste 8
 Edison NJ 08837
 732 603-3630

## (G-17842)
### JOST & KIEFER PRINTING COMPANY
Also Called: J K Creative Printers
2029 Hllster Whitney Pkwy (62305-7601)
P.O. Box 2 (62306-0002)
PHONE.................................217 222-5145
Fax: 217 222-5549
Mike Nobis, *President*
Kevin Nobis, *Vice Pres*
Terri Brewer, *Treasurer*
Katherine Ridder, *Admin Sec*
Kathy Ridder, *Admin Sec*
EMP: 35
SQ FT: 35,000
SALES (est): 5.9MM **Privately Held**
WEB: www.jkcreative.com
SIC: 2752 Commercial printing, lithographic

## (G-17843)
### JP ORTHOTICS
9234 Broadway St (62305-8011)
PHONE.................................217 885-3047
Jonathan Horak, *Principal*
EMP: 3
SALES (est): 208.3K **Privately Held**
SIC: 3842 Orthopedic appliances

## (G-17844)
### KEVIN KEWNEY
Also Called: Laser Images
410 S 10th St (62301-4152)
PHONE.................................217 228-7444
Fax: 217 228-7458
Kevin Kewney, *Owner*
EMP: 3
SALES (est): 190K **Privately Held**
WEB: www.laser-images.com
SIC: 2759 2752 2791 2789 Commercial printing; commercial printing, lithographic; typesetting; bookbinding & related work

## (G-17845)
### KITCHEN & BATH GALLERY
615 Jersey St (62301-3905)
PHONE.................................217 214-0310
Kevin Bangert, *Owner*
EMP: 2
SQ FT: 2,000
SALES: 500K **Privately Held**
SIC: 5712 1711 3996 Cabinets, except custom made: kitchen; plumbing contractors; hard surface floor coverings

## (G-17846)
### KNAPHEIDE MANUFACTURING CO
436 S 6th St (62301-4118)
P.O. Box 7140 (62305-7140)
PHONE.................................217 222-7134
Fax: 800 654-8997
Jim Rubotton, *Owner*
Bob Garkie, *Production*
James R Mooney, *Treasurer*
James Mooney, *Treasurer*
Greg Schutte, *Manager*
EMP: 10
SALES (corp-wide): 54MM **Privately Held**
WEB: www.knapheide.com
SIC: 3713 Truck & bus bodies
PA: The Knapheide Manufacturing Company
 1848 Westphalia Strasse
 Quincy IL 62305
 217 222-7131

## (G-17847)
### KNAPHEIDE MANUFACTURING CO
1848 Westphalia Strasse (62305-7604)
P.O. Box 7140 (62305-7140)
PHONE.................................217 223-1848
Harold Knapheide, *President*
Tara Gilroy, *Vice Pres*
Robert F Overholser, *Vice Pres*
Ron Lehman, *Sales Mgr*
Jane Gardner, *Sales Staff*
EMP: 50

# Quincy - Adams County (G-17848)

SALES (corp-wide): 54MM **Privately Held**
WEB: www.knapheide.com
SIC: 3469 5084 1799 Boxes: tool, lunch, mail, etc.: stamped metal; industrial machinery & equipment; swimming pool construction
PA: The Knapheide Manufacturing Company
1848 Westphalia Strasse
Quincy IL 62305
217 222-7131

## (G-17848) KNAPHEIDE MFG CO
3109 N 30th St (62305)
PHONE..................................217 223-1848
H Knapheide, *Principal*
Steven Atchison, *Engineer*
John Kroeger, *Supervisor*
Ty Lopez, *Supervisor*
EMP: 23
SALES (est): 3MM **Privately Held**
SIC: 3999 Manufacturing industries

## (G-17849) KOENIG MACHINE & WELDING INC
2707 N 24th St (62305-1274)
PHONE..................................217 228-6538
Gary L Koening, *President*
EMP: 4 EST: 1998
SALES (est): 65K **Privately Held**
SIC: 3599 1799 Machine shop, jobbing & repair; welding on site

## (G-17850) KTM INDUSTRIES INC
2701 Weiss Ln (62305-1111)
PHONE..................................217 224-5861
Marian McKeon, *President*
Kathy Easterling, *Vice Pres*
EMP: 8
SQ FT: 22,000
SALES (est): 856.1K **Privately Held**
SIC: 2046 Starch

## (G-17851) KUESTER TOOL & DIE INC
1400 N 30th St (62301-3476)
P.O. Box 3583 (62305-3583)
PHONE..................................217 223-1955
Fax: 217 223-1967
Stanley C Musholt, *President*
Mary E Musholt, *Corp Secy*
EMP: 49
SQ FT: 80,000
SALES (est): 6.6MM **Privately Held**
WEB: www.kuestertool.com
SIC: 3469 3599 Stamping metal for the trade; machine shop, jobbing & repair

## (G-17852) LA QUINTA GAS PIPELINE COMPANY
1416 Donlee St (62305-1437)
PHONE..................................217 430-6781
Jerry McNay, *President*
Jeff Leenerts, *Admin Sec*
EMP: 2
SALES (est): 234.2K **Privately Held**
SIC: 1311 4924 Natural gas production; natural gas distribution

## (G-17853) LANDMARX SCREEN PRINTING
3902 Payson Rd (62305-6484)
PHONE..................................217 223-4601
Fax: 217 223-4671
Vincent Ed Moore, *President*
Jay Martin, *Principal*
EMP: 15
SQ FT: 8,000
SALES (est): 1.2MM **Privately Held**
WEB: www.landmarxinc.com
SIC: 2759 Commercial printing

## (G-17854) M J BURTON ENGRAVING CO
Also Called: Mj Burton Gifts & Engraving
300 N 12th St (62301-3025)
PHONE..................................217 223-7273
Fax: 217 223-7279
Michael A Jenkins, *Owner*
EMP: 5

SALES (est): 384.8K **Privately Held**
SIC: 7389 5947 3479 Engraving service; gift shop; engraving jewelry silverware, or metal

## (G-17855) MARLBORO WIRE LTD
2403 N 24th St (62305-1211)
P.O. Box 5058 (62305-5058)
PHONE..................................217 224-7989
Fax: 217 224-7990
Don Brown, *President*
Janeane S Reis, *Human Res Mgr*
EMP: 30
SQ FT: 34,000
SALES (est): 5.6MM **Privately Held**
WEB: www.marlborowire.com
SIC: 3496 7692 3469 Miscellaneous fabricated wire products; welding repair; metal stampings

## (G-17856) MASTER FOUNDRY INC
4808 Ellington Rd (62305-8671)
PHONE..................................217 223-7396
Fax: 217 223-7398
Paul H Mast, *President*
Joan Mast, *Vice Pres*
EMP: 15 EST: 1955
SALES (est): 790K **Privately Held**
SIC: 3365 3543 3369 Aluminum & aluminum-based alloy castings; industrial patterns; nonferrous foundries

## (G-17857) MICHELMANN STEEL CNSTR CO
Also Called: Mid-States Door and Hardware
137 N 2nd St (62301-2999)
P.O. Box 609 (62306-0609)
PHONE..................................217 222-0555
Fax: 217 222-0573
Laura Gerdes Ehrhart, *CEO*
John Esselman, *CFO*
EMP: 41 EST: 1865
SQ FT: 125,000
SALES (est): 26.7MM **Privately Held**
SIC: 5051 3441 3442 Structural shapes, iron or steel; fabricated structural metal; metal doors, sash & trim

## (G-17858) MID-AMERICA CARBONATES LLC
520 N 30th St (62301-3618)
PHONE..................................217 222-3500
Alex House, *President*
EMP: 7
SALES (est): 1MM
SALES (corp-wide): 1.9B **Publicly Held**
SIC: 1422 Crushed & broken limestone
HQ: White County Coal, Llc
1525 County Rd 1300 N
Carmi IL 62821
618 382-4651

## (G-17859) MIDWEST PATTERNS INC
4901 N 12th St (62305-8751)
PHONE..................................217 228-6900
Fax: 217 228-6906
Jeff Tushaus, *President*
Thomas Tushaus, *President*
Dennis Frericks, *Vice Pres*
Richard Tushaus, *Vice Pres*
Amy McGlaughlin, *Accounts Mgr*
EMP: 112 EST: 1956
SQ FT: 55,000
SALES (est): 20.9MM **Privately Held**
WEB: www.midwestpatterns.com
SIC: 3543 Industrial patterns

## (G-17860) MIDWEST TREASURE DETECTORS
2408 Cherry St Ste 1 (62301-3402)
PHONE..................................217 223-4769
Fax: 217 223-9353
Michael Zanger, *President*
EMP: 3 EST: 1975
SALES (est): 210K **Privately Held**
SIC: 3699 Security devices

## (G-17861) MODERN PRINTING OF QUINCY
2615 Ellington Rd (62305-8850)
PHONE..................................217 223-1063

Fax: 217 223-9642
Kevin Curran, *Partner*
David Rees, *Partner*
EMP: 10 EST: 1959
SQ FT: 8,000
SALES (est): 810K **Privately Held**
SIC: 2752 2759 2789 Commercial printing, offset; letterpress printing; bookbinding & related work

## (G-17862) NIEMANN FOODS FOUNDATION
Also Called: County Market
520 N 24th St (62301-3222)
PHONE..................................217 222-0190
Fax: 217 222-1243
Todd Musolino, *Manager*
EMP: 138
SALES (corp-wide): 121K **Privately Held**
SIC: 5411 5992 5812 2051 Grocery stores, chain; florists; eating places; bread, cake & related products
PA: Niemann Foods Foundation
923 N 12th St
Quincy IL 62301
217 221-5600

## (G-17863) ORTMAN FLUID POWER INC
1400 N 30th St Ste 20 (62301-3476)
PHONE..................................217 277-0321
Francis K McGonigle, *President*
EMP: 25
SALES (est): 987.6K
SALES (corp-wide): 3.5MM **Privately Held**
SIC: 3593 Fluid power cylinders, hydraulic or pneumatic
PA: Lehigh Fluid Power, Inc.
1413 Route 179
Lambertville NJ 08530
800 257-9515

## (G-17864) OTR WHEEL ENGINEERING INC (HQ)
4400 Kochs Ln (62305-7805)
P.O. Box 3743 (62305-3743)
PHONE..................................217 223-7705
Fax: 217 223-7805
Fred Taylor, *President*
Mary Ann Ogle, *Purch Mgr*
Bob Owens, *CFO*
Chad Taylor, *Admin Sec*
▲ EMP: 28
SQ FT: 20,000
SALES (est): 2.3MM
SALES (corp-wide): 77.9MM **Privately Held**
SIC: 3714 3011 5013 Wheels, motor vehicle; tires & inner tubes; wheels, motor vehicle
PA: Otr Wheel Engineering
6 Riverside Indus Park Ne
Rome GA 30161
706 235-9781

## (G-17865) OUTDOOR POWER INC
2703 Broadway St (62301-3638)
PHONE..................................217 228-9890
Fax: 217 228-9879
Jeff W Waterman, *President*
Sandy Waterman, *Vice Pres*
Dwight Hibbard, *Sales Staff*
EMP: 11
SQ FT: 5,800
SALES (est): 1.1MM **Privately Held**
WEB: www.outdoorpowerinc.com
SIC: 5261 5251 5571 7699 Lawnmowers & tractors; chainsaws; all-terrain vehicles; lawn mower repair shop; knife, saw & tool sharpening & repair; recreational vehicle repair services; contractors' materials; saws & sawing equipment

## (G-17866) PAM PRINTERS AND PUBLS INC (PA)
Also Called: Sunday Missal Service
1012 Vermont St (62305-3052)
PHONE..................................217 222-4030
Fax: 217 222-6808
Anaise Haubrich, *Ch of Bd*
Ronald T Haubrich, *President*
Timothy Haubrich, *Business Mgr*

Mike Haubrich, *Corp Secy*
EMP: 12 EST: 1935
SQ FT: 27,000
SALES: 1.1MM **Privately Held**
WEB: www.sundaymissalservice.com
SIC: 2721 Periodicals: publishing & printing

## (G-17867) PETERS BODY SHOP & TOWING INC
823 N 54th St (62305-7910)
PHONE..................................217 223-5250
Fax: 217 223-5260
Stan Peters, *Principal*
EMP: 3
SALES (est): 350.4K **Privately Held**
SIC: 3711 Motor vehicles & car bodies

## (G-17868) POWDER COAT PLUS
4126 Kochs Ln (62305-7684)
PHONE..................................217 228-0081
Dick Whicker, *CEO*
Laurie Whicker, *President*
EMP: 3
SALES (est): 434.3K **Privately Held**
SIC: 2851 Paints & allied products

## (G-17869) PRAIRIE FARMS DAIRY INC
415 N 24th St (62301-3253)
P.O. Box 1107 (62306-1107)
PHONE..................................217 223-5530
Fax: 217 223-8807
Kenneth Obert, *Plant Mgr*
Courtney Wright, *Human Res Mgr*
David Miller, *Branch Mgr*
EMP: 27
SALES (corp-wide): 1.8B **Privately Held**
WEB: www.prairiefarms.com
SIC: 2026 Milk processing (pasteurizing, homogenizing, bottling)
PA: Prairie Farms Dairy, Inc.
1100 Broadway
Carlinville IL 62626
217 854-2547

## (G-17870) PRECISION PLATING OF QUINCY
2611 Locust St (62301-3329)
PHONE..................................217 223-6590
William M Barnett, *President*
Eric Barnett, *Vice Pres*
Sandra Barnett, *Treasurer*
EMP: 8
SQ FT: 1,600
SALES (est): 430K **Privately Held**
SIC: 3471 Electroplating of metals or formed products

## (G-17871) PREMIUM WATERS INC
1811 N 30th St Stop 1 (62301-3313)
PHONE..................................217 222-0213
Fax: 217 222-0450
Wayne Glenn, *General Mgr*
Brent Bair, *Plant Mgr*
Tom Sheehan, *Mfg Staff*
EMP: 80
SALES (corp-wide): 357.4MM **Privately Held**
WEB: www.premiumwaters.com
SIC: 2086 Water, pasteurized: packaged in cans, bottles, etc.
HQ: Premium Waters, Inc.
2100 Summer St Ne Ste 200
Minneapolis MN 55413
612 379-4141

## (G-17872) PRINCE AGRI PRODUCTS INC
Also Called: Phibro Animal Health
229 Radio Rd (62305-7534)
PHONE..................................217 222-8854
Fax: 217 222-5098
Clayton Lamkin, *Vice Pres*
Breeana Deverger, *Mktg Coord*
Angie Norris, *Manager*
Troy Wistuba, *Manager*
Tim Costigan, *Director*
EMP: 50
SALES (corp-wide): 751.5MM **Publicly Held**
SIC: 2048 Feed supplements

# GEOGRAPHIC SECTION

## Quincy - Adams County (G-17898)

HQ: Prince Agri Products, Inc.
300 Frank W Burr Blvd
Teaneck NJ 07666
201 329-7300

### (G-17873)
**PRINCE MINERALS LLC**
223 Hampshire St (62301-2923)
P.O. Box 251 (62306-0251)
**PHONE**...................646 747-4222
Darryl Mayton, *General Mgr*
**EMP:** 3
**SALES (corp-wide):** 2B **Privately Held**
**SIC:** 2816 3313 Inorganic pigments; electrometallurgical products
HQ: Prince Minerals Llc
21 W 46th St Fl 14
New York NY 10036
646 747-4222

### (G-17874)
**PRINCE MINERALS LLC**
401 N Prince Plz (62305-0084)
P.O. Box 251 (62306-0251)
**PHONE**...................646 747-4200
Marcus T Shumaker, *Manager*
**EMP:** 3
**SALES (corp-wide):** 2B **Privately Held**
**SIC:** 2816 3313 Inorganic pigments; electrometallurgical products
HQ: Prince Minerals Llc
21 W 46th St Fl 14
New York NY 10036
646 747-4222

### (G-17875)
**QUINCY COMPRESSOR LLC**
3501 Wisman Ln (62301-1257)
**PHONE**...................217 222-7700
**Fax:** 217 222-8628
**EMP:** 150
**SALES (corp-wide):** 12.6B **Privately Held**
**SIC:** 3519 3563 3561 Mfg Internal Combustion Engines Mfg Air/Gas Compressors Mfg Pumps/Pumping Equipment
HQ: Quincy Compressor Llc
701 N Dobson Ave
Bay Minette AL 36507
251 937-5900

### (G-17876)
**QUINCY ELECTRIC & SIGN COMPANY**
1324 Spring Lake Cors (62305)
**PHONE**...................217 223-8404
James McEwen, *President*
**EMP:** 12
**SALES (est):** 1.8MM **Privately Held**
**SIC:** 3993 Signs & advertising specialties

### (G-17877)
**QUINCY FOUNDRY & PATTERN CO**
435 S Front St (62301-3867)
**PHONE**...................217 222-0718
**Fax:** 217 222-0718
John W Juette, *President*
Sharon Juette, *Admin Sec*
**EMP:** 5 **EST:** 1945
**SQ FT:** 2,500
**SALES (est):** 370K **Privately Held**
**SIC:** 3543 3369 3365 Industrial patterns; nonferrous foundries; aluminum foundries

### (G-17878)
**QUINCY HERALD-WHIG LLC**
130 S 5th St (62301-3916)
P.O. Box 909 (62306-0909)
**PHONE**...................217 223-5100
**Fax:** 217 223-5019
Deborah Husar, *Principal*
Jason Bailey, *Editor*
Phil Carlson, *Editor*
Don Obrien, *Editor*
Mary Richards, *Editor*
**EMP:** 19
**SALES (est):** 1.5MM **Privately Held**
**SIC:** 2711 Newspapers

### (G-17879)
**QUINCY MEDIA INC (PA)**
Also Called: Quincy Brdcast Print Intrctve
130 S 5th St (62301-3916)
P.O. Box 909 (62306-0909)
**PHONE**...................217 223-5100
**Fax:** 217 223-9757

Ralph M Oakley, *President*
Thomas A Oakley, *President*
Edward Husar, *Editor*
Bruce Briney, *Sales Staff*
Robby Warner, *Admin Mgr*
**EMP:** 150
**SQ FT:** 125,000
**SALES (est):** 221.7MM **Privately Held**
**WEB:** www.whig.com
**SIC:** 2711 4833 2752 2741 Newspapers, publishing & printing; television broadcasting stations; commercial printing, lithographic; miscellaneous publishing

### (G-17880)
**QUINCY SOCKS HOUSE**
112 N 6th St (62301-2904)
**PHONE**...................217 506-6106
**EMP:** 3
**SALES (est):** 212.4K **Privately Held**
**SIC:** 2252 Socks

### (G-17881)
**QUINCY SPECIALTIES COMPANY**
2828 Scotia Trl (62301-6251)
**PHONE**...................217 222-4057
**Fax:** 217 222-4065
Dwight Seeley, *President*
Doris Timpe, *Vice Pres*
**EMP:** 9 **EST:** 1935
**SQ FT:** 25,000
**SALES:** 850K **Privately Held**
**WEB:** www.quincyspecialtiesco.com
**SIC:** 2326 2339 Aprons, work, except rubberized & plastic: men's; medical & hospital uniforms, men's; aprons, except rubber or plastic: women's, misses', juniors'

### (G-17882)
**QUINCY TORQUE CONVERTER INC**
2220 Glenayre Way (62305-1270)
**PHONE**...................217 228-0852
**Fax:** 217 228-2155
Michael W Brandstatt, *President*
Teri Vollmer, *Manager*
**EMP:** 6
**SALES:** 500K **Privately Held**
**SIC:** 3714 3566 Motor vehicle parts & accessories; speed changers, drives & gears

### (G-17883)
**R L HOENER CO**
2923 Gardner Expy (62305-7528)
P.O. Box 1086 (62306-1086)
**PHONE**...................217 223-2190
**Fax:** 217 223-5804
Marty Jackson, *President*
Debbra Tritsch, *Vice Pres*
Lucky Tritch, *Sales Staff*
Laura Plunk, *Office Mgr*
Kelly Jackson, *Shareholder*
**EMP:** 20
**SQ FT:** 26,000
**SALES:** 3.4MM **Privately Held**
**SIC:** 1799 5172 3443 5084 Service station equipment installation, maintenance & repair; service station supplies, petroleum; tanks, standard or custom fabricated: metal plate; petroleum industry machinery

### (G-17884)
**RACK BUILDERS INC (PA)**
3809 Dye Rd (62305)
**PHONE**...................217 214-9482
Robert J Johannessen, *President*
**EMP:** 1
**SALES (est):** 313.4K **Privately Held**
**SIC:** 2542 Racks, merchandise display or storage: except wood

### (G-17885)
**RAH ENTERPRISES INC**
2630 S Commercial Dr (62305-8317)
**PHONE**...................217 223-1970
**Fax:** 217 223-2185
Robert Huseman, *President*
Tat Reinebach, *Office Mgr*
Dorothy Huseman, *Admin Sec*
**EMP:** 8
**SQ FT:** 4,400

**SALES:** 800K **Privately Held**
**SIC:** 3599 Machine & other job shop work

### (G-17886)
**REFRESHMENT SERVICES INC (PA)**
Also Called: Pepsico
1121 Locust St (62301-1919)
**PHONE**...................217 223-8600
**Fax:** 217 522-9580
Mike Bartel, *President*
Ronald J Vecchie, *Chairman*
Rodney Flowers, *Vice Pres*
Casey Hill, *Vice Pres*
Jack Taylor, *CFO*
**EMP:** 16
**SQ FT:** 3,000
**SALES (est):** 95.5MM **Privately Held**
**SIC:** 2086 Carbonated soft drinks, bottled & canned

### (G-17887)
**RICHARDS ELECTRIC MOTOR CO (PA)**
426 State St (62301-4197)
**PHONE**...................217 222-7154
**Fax:** 217 222-7018
Bill Dietrich, *President*
Jim Keller, *Corp Secy*
**EMP:** 40
**SQ FT:** 12,000
**SALES (est):** 13.7MM **Privately Held**
**WEB:** www.richardselectricmotor.com
**SIC:** 5063 7699 7694 1731 Motors, electric; industrial equipment services; armature rewinding shops; electrical work

### (G-17888)
**RIETSCHLE INC**
1800 Gardner Expy (62305-9364)
**PHONE**...................410 712-4100
Howard Barry, *Owner*
**EMP:** 3 **EST:** 2009
**SALES (est):** 255.2K **Privately Held**
**SIC:** 3563 Air & gas compressors

### (G-17889)
**ROBUSCHI USA INC**
1800 Gardner Expy (62305-9364)
**PHONE**...................704 424-1018
John Matela, *General Mgr*
Morceello Molesini, *Regional Mgr*
▲ **EMP:** 4
**SALES (est):** 853.8K **Privately Held**
**SIC:** 3564 Purification & dust collection equipment

### (G-17890)
**SEM MINERALS LP**
3806 Gardner Expy (62305-9343)
P.O. Box 1090, Bainbridge GA (39818-1090)
**PHONE**...................217 224-8766
Alec Poitevint, *President*
Keith Mizwicki, *Manager*
▲ **EMP:** 55
**SQ FT:** 20,000
**SALES (est):** 21.5MM **Privately Held**
**WEB:** www.mineralslp.com
**SIC:** 2048 3295 2879 Mineral feed supplements; minerals, ground or treated; trace elements (agricultural chemicals)

### (G-17891)
**SIGNATURE NAIL SYSTEMS LLC**
1304 S 30th St (62301-6206)
**PHONE**...................888 445-2786
Joe Nguyen,
▲ **EMP:** 4 **EST:** 2012
**SALES (est):** 37.2K **Privately Held**
**SIC:** 2844 Manicure preparations

### (G-17892)
**TEDS SHIRT SHACK INC**
2811 Bluff Ridge Dr (62305-1391)
**PHONE**...................217 224-9705
**Fax:** 217 224-8900
Marty Tappe, *President*
Nicholas Tappe, *President*
Martin Tappe, *Owner*
Ted M Tappe, *Owner*
Marty Tapp, *Manager*
**EMP:** 7
**SQ FT:** 5,000

**SALES:** 750K **Privately Held**
**WEB:** www.tedsshirtshack.com
**SIC:** 5651 2759 2396 3993 Family clothing stores; commercial printing; automotive & apparel trimmings; signs & advertising specialties; T-shirts, custom printed

### (G-17893)
**THOMAS GARDNER DENVER INC**
1800 Gardner Expy (62305-9364)
P.O. Box 4024 (62305-4024)
**PHONE**...................217 222-5400
Michael McGrath, *President*
David J Antoniuk, *Admin Sec*
**EMP:** 24 **EST:** 1984
**SALES (est):** 7.6MM **Privately Held**
**SIC:** 3563 Air & gas compressors including vacuum pumps; vacuum pumps, except laboratory

### (G-17894)
**TIMOTHY HELGOTH**
Also Called: Priority One Prtg & Mailing
839 Jersey St (62301-4010)
**PHONE**...................217 224-8008
Tim Helgoth, *Owner*
**EMP:** 6 **EST:** 1976
**SQ FT:** 1,300
**SALES (est):** 569.5K **Privately Held**
**SIC:** 2752 7334 Commercial printing, offset; photocopying & duplicating services

### (G-17895)
**TITAN INTERNATIONAL INC**
2701 Spruce St (62301-3473)
**PHONE**...................217 221-4498
Maurice Taylor, *President*
Pam Hunt, *Vice Pres*
William Sagar, *Vice Pres*
Todd Triplett, *Human Res Dir*
**EMP:** 700
**SALES (corp-wide):** 1.2B **Publicly Held**
**WEB:** www.titan-intl.com
**SIC:** 3312 Wheels
PA: Titan International, Inc.
2701 Spruce St
Quincy IL 62301
217 228-6011

### (G-17896)
**TITAN INTERNATIONAL INC (PA)**
2701 Spruce St (62301-3473)
**PHONE**...................217 228-6011
**Fax:** 217 228-3166
Maurice M Taylor Jr, *Ch of Bd*
Paul G Reitz, *President*
John R Hrudicka, *Senior VP*
Maureen Sredl, *Vice Pres*
Darrell Handy, *Opers Mgr*
◆ **EMP:** 277
**SQ FT:** 1,209,000
**SALES:** 1.2B **Publicly Held**
**WEB:** www.titan-intl.com
**SIC:** 3312 3714 3011 Blast furnaces & steel mills; wheels, motor vehicle; wheel rims, motor vehicle; motor vehicle brake systems & parts; differentials & parts, motor vehicle; agricultural tires, pneumatic; pneumatic tires, all types

### (G-17897)
**TITAN TIRE CORPORATION**
2701 Spruce St (62301-3473)
**PHONE**...................217 228-6011
Scott Jones, *General Mgr*
Zach Friedl, *Opers Staff*
Erin Smith, *Design Engr*
Greg Andrews, *Electrical Engi*
Justin Barnard, *Regl Sales Mgr*
**EMP:** 400
**SALES (corp-wide):** 1.2B **Publicly Held**
**SIC:** 3011 Tires & inner tubes
HQ: Titan Tire Corporation
2345 E Market St
Des Moines IA 50317

### (G-17898)
**TITAN WHEEL CORP ILLINOIS**
2701 Spruce St (62301-3477)
**PHONE**...................217 228-6023
P David Salen, *President*
Sheila Hester, *Purch Agent*
Lee Hall, *Engineer*
Mark Mickels, *Electrical Engi*

## Quincy - Adams County (G-17899)

James Reed, *Electrical Engi*
◆ **EMP:** 900
**SALES (est):** 182.7MM
**SALES (corp-wide):** 1.2B **Publicly Held**
**WEB:** www.titan-intl.com
**SIC: 3499** Wheels: wheelbarrow, stroller, etc.: disc, stamped metal
**PA:** Titan International, Inc.
2701 Spruce St
Quincy IL 62301
217 228-6011

### (G-17899)
### TRI-CITY SPORTS INC
4360 Broadway St (62305-9103)
**PHONE** .................................. 217 224-2489
**Fax:** 217 224-2497
Bruce Thomas, *President*
Kathy Thomas, *Corp Secy*
**EMP:** 5
**SQ FT:** 2,400
**SALES (est):** 390K **Privately Held**
**WEB:** www.tricitysports.com
**SIC: 5941** 5699 2759 Sporting goods & bicycle shops; sports apparel; screen printing

### (G-17900)
### TRI-STATE FOOD EQUIPMENT
1605 Chestnut St (62301-2115)
**PHONE** .................................. 217 228-1550
**Fax:** 217 221-1998
Kenny Miller, *Owner*
**EMP:** 1
**SQ FT:** 10,000
**SALES:** 225K **Privately Held**
**SIC: 5719** 5046 3632 3433 Kitchenware; commercial cooking & food service equipment; household refrigerators & freezers; heating equipment, except electric

### (G-17901)
### TWAIN MEDIA MARK PUBLISHING
617 Broadway St (62301-2706)
**PHONE** .................................. 217 223-7008
**Fax:** 217 223-6443
Harry Emrick, *President*
Sue Emrick, *Treasurer*
**EMP:** 7
**SALES (est):** 530K **Privately Held**
**SIC: 2731** Book publishing

### (G-17902)
### WALTER LOUIS CHEM & ASSOC INC
Also Called: Walter Louis Fluid Tech
530 S 5th St (62301-4808)
**PHONE** .................................. 217 223-2017
**Fax:** 217 223-7734
Walter L Giesing, *President*
Dianne Giesing, *Vice Pres*
Alex Clifford, *Materials Mgr*
Roger Smith, *Engineer*
Paula Kimball, *Administration*
**EMP:** 10
**SQ FT:** 15,000
**SALES (est):** 2.2MM **Privately Held**
**WEB:** www.walterlouis.com
**SIC: 3589** Water purification equipment, household type; water treatment equipment, industrial

### (G-17903)
### WEST ZWICK CORP
Also Called: Bauhaus Zwick Co
2132 Glenayre Way (62305-1258)
P.O. Box 527 (62306-0527)
**PHONE** .................................. 217 222-0228
**Fax:** 217 228-6305
James Vandiver, *President*
Ann Vandiver, *Corp Secy*
Joe Vandiver, *Foreman/Supr*
**EMP:** 4 **EST:** 1919
**SQ FT:** 11,000
**SALES:** 500K **Privately Held**
**SIC: 3993** 2431 2542 Signs, not made in custom sign painting shops; displays & cutouts, window & lobby; displays, paint process; millwork; partitions & fixtures, except wood

### (G-17904)
### WESTMIN CORPORATION
2733 Wild Horse (62305-0210)
**PHONE** .................................. 217 224-4570
**Fax:** 217 224-4551
Greg Jones, *President*
Robin Leonard, *Office Mgr*
**EMP:** 6 **EST:** 1973
**SQ FT:** 6,000
**SALES (est):** 678.3K **Privately Held**
**WEB:** www.westmincorp.com
**SIC: 2879** Agricultural chemicals

### (G-17905)
### WILBERT QUINCY VAULT CO
4128 Wisman Ln (62305-9554)
**PHONE** .................................. 217 224-8557
Steve Busch, *Owner*
**EMP:** 5
**SALES (est):** 260K **Privately Held**
**SIC: 3272** 5087 Burial vaults, concrete or precast terrazzo; concrete burial vaults & boxes

### (G-17906)
### WIRELESSUSA INC
Also Called: Wireless USA
2517 W Schneidman Dr E (62305-1237)
**PHONE** .................................. 217 222-4300
**Toll Free:** ........................... 866  -
George Brummell, *Branch Mgr*
**EMP:** 5
**SALES (corp-wide):** 24.5MM **Privately Held**
**SIC: 3651** 5065 FM & AM radio tuners; citizens band radios
**PA:** Wirelessusa, Inc.
148 Weldon Pkwy
Maryland Heights MO 63043
314 615-3100

### (G-17907)
### WIS - PAK INC
Also Called: Wis-Pak of Quincy
2400 N 30th St (62301-1278)
**PHONE** .................................. 217 224-6800
**Fax:** 217 224-0009
Jeff Nickell, *QC Mgr*
Jeff Lamm, *Branch Mgr*
Randy Gengenbacher, *Manager*
Bobbi Canavan, *Executive*
**EMP:** 91
**SALES (corp-wide):** 310.8MM **Privately Held**
**WEB:** www.wis-pak.com
**SIC: 3221** 2086 Bottles for packing, bottling & canning: glass; bottled & canned soft drinks
**PA:** Wis - Pak, Inc.
860 West St
Watertown WI 53094
920 262-6300

## Raleigh
### Saline County

### (G-17908)
### CENTRIFUGAL SERVICES INC
Also Called: C S I
5595 Highway 34 N (62977-1430)
**PHONE** .................................. 618 268-4850
**Fax:** 618 268-4573
Dale R Martin, *President*
Fred C Schulte, *Vice Pres*
Lusi Lukman, *Opers Staff*
Jack Miles, *Engineer*
Cindy Cook, *Personnel Exec*
◆ **EMP:** 51
**SQ FT:** 16,166
**SALES (est):** 15.7MM
**SALES (corp-wide):** 1.6B **Privately Held**
**WEB:** www.ohiorod.com
**SIC: 3532** Mineral beneficiation equipment
**HQ:** Elgin Equipment Group, Llc
2001 Bttrfeld Rd Ste 1020
Downers Grove IL 60515

### (G-17909)
### GARY & LARRY BROWN TRUCKING (PA)
Also Called: Raleigh Ready Mix
5525 Highway 34 N (62977-1430)
P.O. Box 218 (62977-0218)
**PHONE** .................................. 618 268-6377
Gary M Brown, *Partner*
Larry A Brown, *Partner*
**EMP:** 5
**SQ FT:** 7,200
**SALES:** 1.7MM **Privately Held**
**WEB:** www.raleighreadymix.com
**SIC: 3273** 5211 3272 1771 Ready-mixed concrete; masonry materials & supplies; concrete products, precast; concrete pumping; septic system construction

### (G-17910)
### PREVENTION HEALTH SCIENCES INC
5110 Highway 34 N (62977-1435)
P.O. Box 1916, Marion (62959-8124)
**PHONE** .................................. 618 252-6922
Dan Nicolosi, *President*
Wendy Sanders, *Vice Pres*
**EMP:** 3
**SALES:** 300.4K **Privately Held**
**SIC: 2844** Mouthwashes

### (G-17911)
### SF CONTRACTING LLC
1030 Hamburg Rd (62977-1214)
**PHONE** .................................. 618 926-1477
Shannon D Burnett,
Charles E Slykhuis,
**EMP:** 45
**SALES (est):** 3.8MM **Privately Held**
**SIC: 1081** 1629 Metal mining services; land reclamation

### (G-17912)
### WALLACE AUTO PARTS & SVCS INC
Also Called: Diesel Mining Equipment
5605 Highway 34 N (62977-1439)
P.O. Box 366, Harrisburg (62946-0366)
**PHONE** .................................. 618 268-4446
**Fax:** 618 268-4655
Dave Volkening, *Engineer*
Rod Wallace, *Admin Sec*
Jeff Clinton, *Representative*
▲ **EMP:** 45
**SQ FT:** 20,000
**SALES (est):** 9.4MM **Privately Held**
**SIC: 3532** 5531 7699 Mining machinery; automotive parts; aircraft & heavy equipment repair services

## Ramsey
### Fayette County

### (G-17913)
### G L BEAUMONT LUMBER COMPANY (PA)
Also Called: Main Office
Rr 51 Box S (62080)
**PHONE** .................................. 618 423-2323
Dana Beaumont, *President*
Debbie Beaumont, *Corp Secy*
**EMP:** 15
**SALES (est):** 1.9MM **Privately Held**
**WEB:** www.mainoffice.com
**SIC: 2421** 2426 Sawmills & planing mills, general; hardwood dimension & flooring mills

### (G-17914)
### MID-STATE TIMBER & VENEER CO
Rr Box 61 (62080)
**PHONE** .................................. 618 423-2619
Richard D Nash, *President*
**EMP:** 3
**SALES (est):** 217.8K **Privately Held**
**SIC: 2411** Logging

### (G-17915)
### RAMSEY NEWS JOURNAL
217 S Superior St (62080-2095)
P.O. Box 218 (62080-0218)
**PHONE** .................................. 618 423-2411
**Fax:** 618 423-2514
Robert J Mueller Jr, *Owner*
B J Mueller Jr, *Owner*
**EMP:** 3 **EST:** 1881
**SQ FT:** 2,400
**SALES (est):** 178.5K **Privately Held**
**SIC: 2711** Commercial printing & newspaper publishing combined

## Ransom
### Lasalle County

### (G-17916)
### ILLINOIS VALLEY MACHINE SP INC
108 N Lincoln St (60470-8501)
P.O. Box 188 (60470-0188)
**PHONE** .................................. 815 586-4511
Mark Coonan, *President*
Leah Coonan, *Vice Pres*
**EMP:** 10 **EST:** 1972
**SQ FT:** 5,000
**SALES (est):** 1.9MM **Privately Held**
**SIC: 3599** Machine shop, jobbing & repair

## Rantoul
### Champaign County

### (G-17917)
### ANALOG OUTFITTERS INC
701 Pacesetter Dr (61866-3659)
**PHONE** .................................. 217 202-6134
Ben B Juday, *President*
**EMP:** 6
**SALES (est):** 339.4K **Privately Held**
**SIC: 3931** Musical instruments

### (G-17918)
### ARROW EDM INC
Also Called: Hansvedt
1120 Veterans Pkwy (61866-3449)
**PHONE** .................................. 217 893-4277
**Fax:** 217 893-1887
Chris Baskis, *President*
Steve Early, *Opers Staff*
Kevin Vail, *Manager*
**EMP:** 10
**SALES (corp-wide):** 1.8MM **Privately Held**
**SIC: 5063** 3599 Electrical apparatus & equipment; flexible metal hose, tubing & bellows
**PA:** Arrow Edm, Inc.
7512 Dr Phillips Blvd
Orlando FL 32819
217 893-4277

### (G-17919)
### BELL SPORTS
909 Pacesetter Dr (61866-3444)
**PHONE** .................................. 309 693-2746
Tom Rettig, *Principal*
◆ **EMP:** 3 **EST:** 2013
**SALES (est):** 408.7K **Privately Held**
**SIC: 2329** 3949 Men's & boys' sportswear & athletic clothing; protective sporting equipment

### (G-17920)
### BELL SPORTS INC
1001 Innovation Rd (61866-4200)
P.O. Box 6001 (61866-6001)
**PHONE** .................................. 217 893-9300
**Fax:** 217 892-8727
Bill Oldham, *Branch Mgr*
**EMP:** 82 **Privately Held**
**SIC: 3949** Helmets, athletic
**HQ:** Bell Sports, Inc.
6333 N State Highway 161 # 300
Irving TX 75038
469 417-6600

### (G-17921)
### BRG SPORTS INC
1001 Innovation Rd (61866-4200)
P.O. Box 6005 (61866-6005)
**PHONE** .................................. 217 893-9300
**EMP:** 14 **Privately Held**
**SIC: 3949** 3751 Helmets, athletic; pads: football, basketball, soccer, lacrosse, etc.; protective sporting equipment; bicycles & related parts
**HQ:** Brg Sports, Inc.
9801 W Higgins Rd
Rosemont IL 60018
831 461-7500

▲ = Import ▼ = Export
◆ = Import/Export

# GEOGRAPHIC SECTION

**Red Bud - Randolph County (G-17946)**

*(G-17922)*
**CHARLES INDUSTRIES LTD**
201 Shellhouse Dr (61866-9711)
PHONE.................................217 893-8335
Joseph Charles, *President*
Steve Steele, *Plant Mgr*
Charles Todd, *Purchasing*
Tammy Ernst, *Personnel*
Bill Gray, *Manager*
**EMP:** 100
**SALES (corp-wide):** 131.6MM **Privately Held**
**WEB:** www.charlesmarine.com
**SIC:** 3661 3444 Toll switching equipment, telephone; sheet metalwork
**PA:** Charles Industries, Ltd.
5600 Apollo Dr
Rolling Meadows IL 60008
847 806-6300

*(G-17923)*
**COMBE LABORATORIES INC**
200 Shellhouse Dr (61866-9711)
PHONE.................................217 893-4490
**Fax:** 217 893-8804
Christopher B Combe, *Ch of Bd*
Douglas M McGraime, *President*
Daniel R Johnson, *Senior VP*
Peggy Stanley, *Opers Staff*
Amy Franklin, *Buyer*
▲ **EMP:** 110
**SALES (est):** 26.6MM
**SALES (corp-wide):** 150.9MM **Privately Held**
**WEB:** www.combe.com
**SIC:** 2841 2844 Soap & other detergents; cosmetic preparations; toilet preparations
**PA:** Combe Incorporated
1101 Westchester Ave
White Plains NY 10604
914 694-5454

*(G-17924)*
**CONAIR CORPORATION**
205 Shellhouse Dr (61866-9774)
PHONE.................................203 351-9000
**Fax:** 217 892-2479
Ronald T Diamond, *President*
Kathleen D Fong, *Admin Sec*
Richard Margules, *Admin Sec*
◆ **EMP:** 41 **EST:** 1972
**SALES (est):** 9.9MM **Privately Held**
**SIC:** 3634 3999 Irons, electric: household; hair dryers, electric; curling irons, electric; hair curlers, electric; barber & beauty shop equipment

*(G-17925)*
**EAGLE WINGS INDUSTRIES INC**
Also Called: E W I
400 Shellhouse Dr (61866-9700)
PHONE.................................217 892-4322
**Fax:** 217 892-2191
Tatsunori Shigeta, *President*
Hideki Hiraishi, *President*
Jim Schwartz, *Vice Pres*
Bob Ball, *Purchasing*
Kathy Graybill, *QC Mgr*
▲ **EMP:** 290
**SQ FT:** 314,200
**SALES:** 45MM **Privately Held**
**WEB:** www.ewiusa.com
**SIC:** 3714 Motor vehicle parts & accessories; motor vehicle body components & frame

*(G-17926)*
**EAST CENTRAL COMMUNICATIONS CO**
Also Called: Target
1332 Harmon Dr (61866-3310)
PHONE.................................217 892-9613
**Fax:** 217 892-9451
Dennis Kaster, *President*
Brendan Quealy, *Assistant*
**EMP:** 30
**SALES (est):** 3.9MM
**SALES (corp-wide):** 63.7MM **Privately Held**
**SIC:** 2759 2711 2752 Commercial printing; newspapers; commercial printing, lithographic
**PA:** The News-Gazette Inc
15 E Main St
Champaign IL 61820
217 351-5252

*(G-17927)*
**ENGINEERED PLASTIC COMPONENTS**
Also Called: EPC Rantoul
300 Shellhouse Dr (61866-9721)
PHONE.................................217 892-2026
**Fax:** 217 892-2251
Ed Predur, *Branch Mgr*
**EMP:** 120 **Privately Held**
**WEB:** www.epciowa.com
**SIC:** 3089 3086 Injection molding of plastics; carpet & rug cushions, foamed plastic
**PA:** Engineered Plastic Components, Inc
1408 Zimmerman Dr
Grinnell IA 50112

*(G-17928)*
**G&G MACHINE SHOP INC**
1580 E Grove Ave Ste 2 (61866-2777)
PHONE.................................217 892-9696
Peter Good, *President*
Nicholas Jankowski, *Manager*
Kirk Gosser, *Admin Sec*
**EMP:** 3
**SALES (est):** 272.6K **Privately Held**
**SIC:** 7539 7538 3599 Machine shop, automotive; general automotive repair shops; machine shop, jobbing & repair

*(G-17929)*
**JANCORP LLC (PA)**
Also Called: Criss Cross Express Illinois
608 Kopman St (61866-3716)
P.O. Box 227, Norwalk WI (54648-0227)
PHONE.................................217 892-4830
Frederick Stewart, *President*
Kristy Tormoen, *Manager*
**EMP:** 8
**SALES (est):** 1.2MM **Privately Held**
**SIC:** 2011 Meat packing plants

*(G-17930)*
**JELD-WEN INC**
Also Called: Jeld-Wen Windows
201 Evans Rd (61866-9778)
PHONE.................................217 893-4444
Alan Verploegh, *Div Sub Head*
Jody Wasser, *Vice Pres*
Ron Saxton, *Vice Pres*
Mike Hillmeyer, *VP Mfg*
Jim Lewis, *Purch Mgr*
**EMP:** 64
**SALES (corp-wide):** 22.5B **Publicly Held**
**WEB:** www.jeld-wen.com
**SIC:** 2431 Millwork
**HQ:** Jeld-Wen, Inc.
440 S Church St Ste 400
Charlotte NC 28202
800 535-3936

*(G-17931)*
**JOHN PARKER ADVERTISING CO**
520 E Grove Ave (61866-2429)
P.O. Box 918 (61866-0918)
PHONE.................................217 892-4118
Carol A Parker, *Owner*
**EMP:** 3 **EST:** 1954
**SALES:** 120K **Privately Held**
**SIC:** 5199 3993 Advertising specialties; signs & advertising specialties

*(G-17932)*
**KIM LABORATORIES INC**
601 S Century Blvd # 1203 (61866-2945)
PHONE.................................217 337-6666
Myung Kim, *President*
**EMP:** 6
**SQ FT:** 1,700
**SALES (est):** 752.3K **Privately Held**
**WEB:** www.kimlaboratories.com
**SIC:** 2835 Microbiology & virology diagnostic products

*(G-17933)*
**LASON INC**
1000 S Perimeter Rd (61866-3511)
PHONE.................................217 893-1515
Katy Carver, *Principal*
Jim Sackett, *Telecom Exec*
**EMP:** 3
**SALES (est):** 193.6K **Privately Held**
**SIC:** 3579 Office machines

*(G-17934)*
**MIDWEST SILKSCREENING INC**
104 N Century Blvd (61866-2305)
PHONE.................................217 892-9596
**Fax:** 217 893-0858
Mark Seaman, *CEO*
Leslie Seaman, *Admin Sec*
**EMP:** 4
**SALES:** 325K **Privately Held**
**SIC:** 7336 2759 Silk screen design; screen printing

*(G-17935)*
**POLYCONVERSIONS INC**
505 E Condit Dr (61866-3604)
PHONE.................................217 893-3330
**Fax:** 217 893-3003
Ronald Smith, *President*
Dennis B Smith, *Principal*
William B Smith, *Corp Secy*
Robert Smith, *Vice Pres*
Scott Carlson, *Sales Dir*
**EMP:** 50
**SQ FT:** 50,000
**SALES (est):** 12.3MM **Privately Held**
**SIC:** 2821 2835 3021 Plastics materials & resins; gowns, plastic: made from purchased materials; rubber & plastics footwear

*(G-17936)*
**RANTOUL FOODS LLC**
205 Turner Dr (61866-9787)
PHONE.................................217 892-4178
James Jendruczek, *President*
Alan Bressler, *Vice Pres*
David Bulgarelli, *Vice Pres*
Michael Lookingland, *Vice Pres*
David Piotrowski, *Vice Pres*
◆ **EMP:** 306
**SQ FT:** 300,000
**SALES (est):** 85.2MM **Privately Held**
**SIC:** 3556 0751 Meat processing machinery; slaughtering: custom livestock services

*(G-17937)*
**SPORT REDI-MIX LLC**
527 S Tanner St (61866-2923)
PHONE.................................217 892-4222
Ken Demarse, *Manager*
**EMP:** 21
**SALES (corp-wide):** 4.3MM **Privately Held**
**WEB:** www.sportredimix.com
**SIC:** 3241 Cement, hydraulic
**PA:** Sport Redi-Mix, L.L.C.
401 Wilbur Ave
Champaign IL 61822
217 355-4222

## Raymond
### Montgomery County

*(G-17938)*
**ED WEITEKAMP INC**
5046 N 23rd Ave (62560-5012)
PHONE.................................217 229-4239
Greg Weitekamp, *President*
**EMP:** 3
**SALES (est):** 271.1K **Privately Held**
**SIC:** 3599 Machine & other job shop work

*(G-17939)*
**POGGENPOHL LLC (PA)**
Also Called: Poggenpohl Construction & Mtls
31 Sparks St (62560)
P.O. Box 581 (62560-0581)
PHONE.................................217 229-3411
Russel Poggenpohl, *Mng Member*
Rhonda Scheiter, *Manager*
Bruce Poggenpohl,
**EMP:** 6
**SALES (est):** 2.3MM **Privately Held**
**SIC:** 1521 1542 3273 Single-family housing construction; commercial & office building contractors; ready-mixed concrete

## Red Bud
### Randolph County

*(G-17940)*
**EAGLE STONE AND BRICK INC**
450 N Main St (62278-1023)
P.O. Box 103 (62278-0103)
PHONE.................................618 282-6722
**Fax:** 618 282-3755
Glenn Gielow, *President*
**EMP:** 4
**SALES (est):** 1.3MM **Privately Held**
**WEB:** www.eagle-stone.com
**SIC:** 5032 3272 Brick, stone & related material; stone, cast concrete

*(G-17941)*
**FIRST STAGE FABRICATION INC**
340 Kennedy Dr (62278)
PHONE.................................618 282-8320
Scott Dilley, *President*
**EMP:** 3
**SALES:** 1MM **Privately Held**
**SIC:** 3441 Fabricated structural metal

*(G-17942)*
**HUMAN SVC CTR SOUTHERN METRO E (PA)**
10257 State Route 3 (62278-4418)
PHONE.................................618 282-6233
Gary Buatte, *Human Res Mgr*
Amy Bauer, *Manager*
Gary L Buatte, *Exec Dir*
Joni Chandler, *Director*
Kendra Kennedy, *Director*
**EMP:** 50
**SQ FT:** 7,200
**SALES:** 3.3MM **Privately Held**
**SIC:** 8322 3471 2511 2448 Individual & family services; plating & polishing; wood household furniture; wood pallets & skids

*(G-17943)*
**INTEGRATED MFG TECH LLC**
401 Randolph St (62278-1001)
PHONE.................................618 282-8306
Rudi Roeslein, *President*
Tom Reichardt, *Plant Mgr*
Joyce Fuhr, *Mng Member*
▲ **EMP:** 40
**SALES (est):** 6MM **Privately Held**
**SIC:** 3498 3999 3441 Coils, pipe: fabricated from purchased pipe; atomizers; toiletry; building components, structural steel

*(G-17944)*
**LAU NAE WINERY INC**
1522 State Route 3 (62278-1095)
PHONE.................................618 282-9463
Matt Mollet, *President*
Brett Sintzel, *Vice Pres*
**EMP:** 4
**SALES:** 400K **Privately Held**
**WEB:** www.lau-naewinery.com
**SIC:** 2084 5812 Wines; eating places

*(G-17945)*
**NORTH COUNTY NEWS INC**
124 S Main St (62278-1103)
P.O. Box 68 (62278-0068)
PHONE.................................618 282-3803
**Fax:** 618 282-6134
Victor L Mohr, *President*
Irma Birkner, *Sales Staff*
**EMP:** 6
**SQ FT:** 3,000
**SALES:** 400K **Privately Held**
**WEB:** www.northcountynews.com
**SIC:** 2711 2752 Newspapers: publishing only, not printed on site; commercial printing, lithographic

*(G-17946)*
**R & D MACHINE LLC**
126 Jackson St (62278-2104)
P.O. Box 182 (62278-0182)
PHONE.................................618 282-6262
**Fax:** 618 282-6898
Warren Snover,
**EMP:** 4
**SQ FT:** 4,500

# Red Bud - Randolph County (G-17947)

SALES (est): 572.6K **Privately Held**
WEB: www.rogerschmidt.com
SIC: **3599** Machine shop, jobbing & repair

**(G-17947)**
**RED BUD INDUSTRIES INC**
Also Called: Red Bud Industries
200 B And E Industrial Dr (62278-2198)
PHONE.....................................618 282-3801
Fax: 618 282-6718
Kalin N Kiefer, *President*
Dean Linders, *Vice Pres*
Don Morgan, *Vice Pres*
Jan Koudela, *Purch Dir*
John Hennekes, *Engineer*
▼ EMP: 131
SALES (est): 29.6MM **Privately Held**
WEB: www.redbudindustries.com
SIC: **3549** 5084 Metalworking machinery; industrial machinery & equipment

**(G-17948)**
**SECON RUBBER AND PLASTICS INC (PA)**
240 Kaskaskia Dr (62278-1386)
PHONE.....................................618 282-7700
Fax: 618 282-7702
Doug Siebenberger, *President*
Rob Ewen, *Corp Secy*
Cara Schmoll, *Office Mgr*
EMP: 40
SQ FT: 37,000
SALES (est): 8.3MM **Privately Held**
WEB: www.secon.com
SIC: **3069** Foam rubber

**(G-17949)**
**SOUTHERN IL CRANKSHAFT INC**
225 Kaskaskia Dr (62278-1387)
PHONE.....................................618 282-4100
Fax: 618 282-4144
Michael Schaefer, *President*
Jeannie Schaefer, *General Mgr*
Jeremy Schaefer, *Production*
EMP: 13
SQ FT: 30,000
SALES: 1MM **Privately Held**
SIC: **3599** Machine & other job shop work; crankshafts & camshafts, machining

**(G-17950)**
**TOTAL TITANIUM INC**
281 Kennedy Dr (62278-4217)
P.O. Box 10 (62278-0010)
PHONE.....................................618 473-2429
Brian Casey, *President*
Ron D Casey, *Senior VP*
EMP: 25
SQ FT: 11,000
SALES (est): 2.7MM **Privately Held**
WEB: www.totaltitanium.com
SIC: **3841** 3599 Surgical & medical instruments; machine & other job shop work

**(G-17951)**
**ULTRA PLAY SYSTEMS INC (DH)**
1675 Locust St (62278-1383)
PHONE.....................................618 282-8200
Fax: 618 282-8202
Robert A Farnsworth, *President*
Douglas R Korn, *President*
Michael Moll, *Vice Pres*
Nathan Schreder, *Production*
Jerry Walker, *Manager*
▲ EMP: 50 EST: 1999
SQ FT: 12,500
SALES: 20.5MM
SALES (corp-wide): 221.4MM **Privately Held**
WEB: www.ultraplay.com
SIC: **3949** Sporting & athletic goods; playground equipment; basketball equipment & supplies, general; soccer equipment & supplies
HQ: Playcore Wisconsin, Inc.
401 Chestnut St Ste 410
Chattanooga TN 37402
423 265-7529

## Reddick
### Kankakee County

**(G-17952)**
**PRO AG INC**
Also Called: Soil-Biotics
18500 W 3000s Rd (60961-8091)
PHONE.....................................815 365-2353
Richard Todd Zehr, *President*
Judith A Zehr, *Admin Sec*
EMP: 3
SALES (est): 118.3K **Privately Held**
SIC: **2873** Fertilizers: natural (organic), except compost

## Reynolds
### Rock Island County

**(G-17953)**
**RURSCH SPECIALTIES INC**
16420 132nd St W (61279-9760)
PHONE.....................................309 795-1502
Darrin Rursch, *President*
EMP: 2
SALES (est): 258.6K **Privately Held**
SIC: **3469** 5531 Machine parts, stamped or pressed metal; automobile & truck equipment & parts

## Richmond
### Mchenry County

**(G-17954)**
**815 PALLETS INC**
Also Called: Calco
11600 Sterling Pkwy (60071-7727)
P.O. Box 1922, Woodstock (60098-1922)
PHONE.....................................815 678-0012
Matthew Calhoun, *President*
Greg Calhoun, *Sales Staff*
EMP: 40
SALES (est): 8.6MM **Privately Held**
SIC: **2448** Pallets, wood & wood with metal

**(G-17955)**
**AARMEN TOOL & MANUFACTURING**
11475 Commercial St (60071-9109)
P.O. Box 697 (60071-0697)
PHONE.....................................815 678-4818
Fax: 815 678-4824
Richard B Smith, *President*
Margaret Smith, *Vice Pres*
EMP: 3 EST: 1954
SQ FT: 5,000
SALES (est): 260K **Privately Held**
SIC: **3599** Machine shop, jobbing & repair

**(G-17956)**
**ABLE AMERICAN PLASTICS INC**
9703 Us Highway 12 Frnt Unit (60071-9204)
PHONE.....................................815 678-4646
Fax: 815 678-4640
Tom Brown, *President*
Sheila Brown, *Vice Pres*
EMP: 10
SALES (est): 1.8MM **Privately Held**
SIC: **3089** Injection molded finished plastic products

**(G-17957)**
**ANDERSONS CANDY SHOP INC (PA)**
10301 N Main St (60071-7719)
PHONE.....................................815 678-6000
Fax: 815 678-3901
Lars Anderson, *President*
Leif Anderson, *Vice Pres*
Tracy Anderson, *Treasurer*
EMP: 15 EST: 1919
SQ FT: 2,000
SALES (est): 1.7MM **Privately Held**
WEB: www.andersonscandyshop.com
SIC: **2066** 2064 Chocolate & cocoa products; candy & other confectionery products

**(G-17958)**
**ATWOOD-HAMLIN MFG CO INC**
5614 Kenosha St (60071-7708)
P.O. Box 578 (60071-0578)
PHONE.....................................815 678-7291
Fax: 815 678-2130
Glen Hahnlein, *President*
Steven Hahnlein, *Plant Mgr*
Dave Cochron, *Accountant*
EMP: 13
SQ FT: 12,000
SALES (est): 1.6MM **Privately Held**
WEB: www.atwood-hamlin.com
SIC: **2531** Church furniture

**(G-17959)**
**CHARLES ATWATER ASSOC INC**
5705 George St (60071-9596)
P.O. Box 1188, Wheaton (60187-1188)
PHONE.....................................815 678-4813
Carson Atwater, *President*
Clark Atwater, *Vice Pres*
EMP: 8
SALES (est): 628.5K **Privately Held**
SIC: **3444** Awnings, sheet metal

**(G-17960)**
**CLAUD S GORDON COMPANY**
Also Called: Watlow Richmond
5710 Kenosha St (60071-9411)
PHONE.....................................815 678-2211
Fax: 815 678-3961
EMP: 300
SQ FT: 87,000
SALES (est): 64.1MM
SALES (corp-wide): 370MM **Privately Held**
WEB: www.watlow.com
SIC: **3823** Temperature measurement instruments, industrial; thermocouples, industrial process type
PA: Watlow Electric Manufacturing Company
12001 Lackland Rd
Saint Louis MO 63146
314 878-4600

**(G-17961)**
**EMS INDUSTRIAL AND SERVICE CO**
10800 N Main St (60071-9654)
P.O. Box 548 (60071-0548)
PHONE.....................................815 678-2700
Timothy Ellison, *President*
Cindy Marquart, *Business Mgr*
Judy Ellision, *Shareholder*
EMP: 20
SQ FT: 20,000
SALES: 5MM **Privately Held**
SIC: **3351** 3469 Copper pipe; metal stampings

**(G-17962)**
**EST LIGHTING INC**
10305 Covell St (60071-9594)
PHONE.....................................847 612-1705
Tim Tacheny, *Principal*
EMP: 2
SALES (est): 217.3K **Privately Held**
SIC: **3648** Lighting equipment

**(G-17963)**
**HANSEL WALTER J & ASSOC INC (PA)**
4311 Hill Rd (60071-9655)
PHONE.....................................815 678-6065
Walter J Hansel, *President*
EMP: 1
SALES (est): 432.9K **Privately Held**
SIC: **3549** Metalworking machinery

**(G-17964)**
**JAN-AIR INC**
10815 Commercial St (60071-7703)
P.O. Box J (60071-0909)
PHONE.....................................815 678-4516
Mark Sattersten, *President*
Kyle Pulvermacher, *Engineer*
Sandy Messick, *CFO*
Jared Heim, *Maintence Staff*
EMP: 30 EST: 1949
SQ FT: 19,600
SALES: 3.8MM **Privately Held**
WEB: www.jan-air.com
SIC: **3564** Blowers & fans

**(G-17965)**
**KEYSTONE PRINTING & PUBLISHING**
Also Called: Keystone Printing Service
5512 May Ave (60071-9541)
P.O. Box 467 (60071-0467)
PHONE.....................................815 678-2591
Fax: 815 678-2128
William L Finney III, *Owner*
EMP: 3 EST: 1961
SQ FT: 2,000
SALES (est): 260.6K **Privately Held**
SIC: **2752** 3993 2721 Commercial printing, offset; signs & advertising specialties; periodicals

**(G-17966)**
**M & N DENTAL**
9716 Ill Route 12 (60071)
PHONE.....................................815 678-0036
David Domenella, *Owner*
EMP: 3
SALES (est): 179.8K **Privately Held**
SIC: **3843** Dental hand instruments

**(G-17967)**
**MAGNUM MACHINING LLC**
11427 Coml Ave Unit 19 (60071)
PHONE.....................................815 678-6800
Lynn A Pertler, *Mng Member*
EMP: 5
SALES: 700K **Privately Held**
SIC: **3669** Emergency alarms

**(G-17968)**
**OLSUN ELECTRICS CORPORATION**
10901 Commercial St (60071-9642)
P.O. Box 1 (60071-0001)
PHONE.....................................815 678-2421
Fax: 815 678-4909
Cathleen Asta, *President*
Ed Trummer, *Purchasing*
Corey Keckel, *Controller*
Norman Walack, *Controller*
Bruce Morem, *Sales Mgr*
◆ EMP: 5 EST: 1965
SQ FT: 100,000
SALES (est): 2.6MM **Privately Held**
WEB: www.olsun.com
SIC: **3612** Specialty transformers; saturable reactors

**(G-17969)**
**R & S CUTTERHEAD MFG CO**
11401 Commercial St Ste A (60071-9527)
PHONE.....................................815 678-2611
Fax: 815 678-4226
Christian W Fischer, *President*
Margot A Fischer, *Corp Secy*
Sylvia Divoky, *Vice Pres*
Sylvia McClory, *Vice Pres*
Richard Fischer, *Manager*
EMP: 11
SQ FT: 16,000
SALES: 1.2MM **Privately Held**
SIC: **3425** 3546 Saw blades & handsaws; power-driven handtools

**(G-17970)**
**RODIFER ENTERPRISES INC**
Also Called: R E I
5700 Walnut St (60071-9201)
PHONE.....................................815 678-0100
EMP: 5
SALES (est): 450K **Privately Held**
SIC: **3541** Mfg Machine Tools-Cutting

**(G-17971)**
**SCHULHOF COMPANY**
5801 Ami Dr (60071-7704)
PHONE.....................................773 348-1123
Charlie Lienhard, *Principal*
EMP: 10
SALES (corp-wide): 23.4MM **Privately Held**
SIC: **3432** 5074 Plumbing fixture fittings & trim; plumbing & hydronic heating supplies
PA: Schulhof Company
4701 N Ravenwood
Manchester CT 06040
773 348-1123

# GEOGRAPHIC SECTION

**River Forest - Cook County (G-17998)**

**(G-17972)**
**STEEL CONSTRUCTION SVCS INC**
9618 Keystone Rd  (60071-9322)
PHONE...................................815 678-7509
Alvin Ruck Jr, *President*
Melissa Ruck, *Admin Sec*
**EMP:** 5
**SALES (est):** 410K  **Privately Held**
**SIC:** 3446  3441  Architectural metalwork; fabricated structural metal

**(G-17973)**
**STITCHIN IMAGE**
9203 Glacier Rdg  (60071-9006)
PHONE...................................815 578-9890
Kathleen S Rechisky, *Partner*
Russ Hoppe, *Partner*
**EMP:** 5
**SQ FT:** 1,500
**SALES (est):** 320K  **Privately Held**
**SIC:** 2395  Embroidery & art needlework

**(G-17974)**
**WOODEN WORLD OF RICHMOND INC**
7617 Il Route 31  (60071-9573)
PHONE...................................815 405-4503
David C Dubs, *President*
**EMP:** 4
**SQ FT:** 6,000
**SALES (est):** 328.9K  **Privately Held**
**WEB:** www.closetwalls.com
**SIC:** 2511  2431  Wood household furniture; millwork

## Richton Park
*Cook County*

**(G-17975)**
**AMELIO BROS MEATS**
4322 Whitehall Ln  (60471-1244)
PHONE...................................708 300-2920
Robert C Ryan, *Vice Pres*
**EMP:** 3
**SALES (est):** 244.7K  **Privately Held**
**SIC:** 2011  Meat packing plants

**(G-17976)**
**ANDREA AND ME AND ME TOO**
22401 Thomas Dr Apt 3n  (60471-1505)
PHONE...................................708 955-3850
Ann Finney, *Owner*
**EMP:** 5
**SALES (est):** 222.1K  **Privately Held**
**SIC:** 2389  Apparel & accessories

**(G-17977)**
**ILLINOIS TOOL WORKS INC**
Also Called: ITW Deltar Bdy Intr Richton Pk
22501 Bohlmann Pkwy  (60471-1200)
PHONE...................................708 720-7800
Doug Marciniak, *Manager*
**EMP:** 92
**SQ FT:** 62,000
**SALES (corp-wide):** 13.6B  **Publicly Held**
**SIC:** 3089  Plastic processing
**PA:** Illinois Tool Works Inc.
  155 Harlem Ave
  Glenview IL 60025
  847 724-7500

**(G-17978)**
**JOE ANTHONY & ASSOCIATES**
Also Called: Joe Chicken & Fish
5151 Sauk Trl  (60471-1023)
PHONE...................................708 935-0804
Joe Webber, *Owner*
**EMP:** 5
**SQ FT:** 10,200
**SALES:** 100K  **Privately Held**
**SIC:** 2599  5541  Bar, restaurant & cafeteria furniture; gasoline service stations

**(G-17979)**
**KISHKNOWS INC**
3831 Janis Dr  (60471-2701)
PHONE...................................708 252-3648
Kisia Coleman, *President*
**EMP:** 3 EST: 2012

**SALES (est):** 184.4K  **Privately Held**
**SIC:** 7379  8748  2731  Tape recertification service; business consulting; book publishing

**(G-17980)**
**TOBY SMALL ENGINE REPAIR**
22704 Millard Ave  (60471-2529)
PHONE...................................708 699-6021
Lloyd Smith, *Owner*
**EMP:** 3
**SALES (est):** 147.9K  **Privately Held**
**SIC:** 3423  Mechanics' hand tools

## Richview
*Washington County*

**(G-17981)**
**RAPCO LTD**
Also Called: Rapco Building Pdts & Sup Co
405 E 1st South St  (62877)
PHONE...................................618 249-6614
**Fax:** 618 249-8559
Roger A Pierjok, *Owner*
**EMP:** 6
**SQ FT:** 2,500
**SALES:** 500K  **Privately Held**
**SIC:** 3599  3273  7692  Machine shop, jobbing & repair; ready-mixed concrete; welding repair

**(G-17982)**
**TA OIL FIELD SERVICE INC**
27573 State Route 177  (62877-1015)
PHONE...................................618 249-9001
**EMP:** 5
**SALES (est):** 267.3K  **Privately Held**
**SIC:** 1389  1381  Oil & gas field services; drilling oil & gas wells

## Ridgway
*Gallatin County*

**(G-17983)**
**BOND BROTHERS HARDWOODS**
412 W Main St  (62979)
PHONE...................................618 272-4811
Cleve Bond, *Partner*
Cletus Bond, *Partner*
**EMP:** 5
**SQ FT:** 30,000
**SALES (est):** 780.4K  **Privately Held**
**SIC:** 5031  2431  2426  2421  Lumber, plywood & millwork; millwork; hardwood dimension & flooring mills; sawmills & planing mills, general

**(G-17984)**
**EXTREME WELDING & MACHINE SERV**
529 S Jarrell St  (62979-1436)
PHONE...................................618 272-7237
Smith Thomason, *Principal*
**EMP:** 5
**SALES (est):** 404K  **Privately Held**
**SIC:** 7692  Welding repair

**(G-17985)**
**GILSTER-MARY LEE CORPORATION**
606 W Main St  (62979-1004)
P.O. Box 358  (62979-0358)
PHONE...................................618 272-3261
**EMP:** 3
**SALES (corp-wide):** 1.1B  **Privately Held**
**SIC:** 2099  Food preparations
**HQ:** Gilster-Mary Lee Corporation
  1037 State St
  Chester IL 62233
  618 826-2361

## Ringwood
*Mchenry County*

**(G-17986)**
**A&W TOOL INC**
5309 Bus Pkwy Unit 101  (60072)
PHONE...................................815 653-1700
Gaylen Wester, *President*
Gabriel Garcia, *Purchasing*
Cathy Rausch, *Office Mgr*
**EMP:** 9
**SQ FT:** 5,000
**SALES (est):** 1MM  **Privately Held**
**SIC:** 3541  3545  7699  Machine tools, metal cutting type; machine tool accessories; industrial tool grinding

**(G-17987)**
**APEX MANUFACTURING INC**
5409 Craftwell Dr Ste A  (60072-9402)
PHONE...................................815 728-0108
**Fax:** 815 653-2166
David W Dowell, *President*
Kathy Dowell, *Admin Sec*
**EMP:** 4
**SALES (est):** 370K  **Privately Held**
**SIC:** 3599  Machine shop, jobbing & repair

**(G-17988)**
**BURNEX CORPORATION**
5418 Business Pkwy  (60072-9412)
PHONE...................................815 728-1317
**Fax:** 815 728-1217
Manfred Suhr, *CEO*
Scott Suhr, *President*
Joe Guercio, *Marketing Mgr*
Kerry Gibson, *Office Mgr*
**EMP:** 30
**SQ FT:** 11,000
**SALES (est):** 6.5MM  **Privately Held**
**WEB:** www.burnexcorp.com
**SIC:** 3469  3493  3496  3545  Stamping metal for the trade; steel springs, except wire; woven wire products; tools & accessories for machine tools

**(G-17989)**
**DOW CHEMICAL COMPANY**
5005 Barnard Mill Rd  (60072-9652)
P.O. Box 238  (60072-0238)
PHONE...................................815 653-2411
Ellen Bauman, *Personnel*
Sidney Martin, *Branch Mgr*
Divyesh Patel, *Network Mgr*
Herbert Cox, *Executive*
**EMP:** 210
**SALES (corp-wide):** 48.1B  **Publicly Held**
**SIC:** 2819  2821  Industrial inorganic chemicals; plastics materials & resins
**HQ:** The Dow Chemical Company
  25500 Whitesell St
  Hayward CA 94545
  510 786-0100

**(G-17990)**
**FOX VALLEY CHEMICAL COMPANY**
5201 Mann Dr  (60072-9664)
P.O. Box 129  (60072-0129)
PHONE...................................815 653-2660
**Fax:** 815 653-2509
Russell A Hopp, *President*
Matthew Hopp, *Vice Pres*
Cathy Niedert, *Manager*
Christopher Wirtz, *Manager*
▲ **EMP:** 8
**SQ FT:** 14,000
**SALES (est):** 1.2MM  **Privately Held**
**WEB:** www.foxvalleychemical.com
**SIC:** 2842  Wax removers; floor waxes

**(G-17991)**
**HUNTSMAN INTERNATIONAL LLC**
5015 Barnard Mill Rd  (60072-9652)
P.O. Box 220  (60072-0220)
PHONE...................................815 653-1500
**Fax:** 815 653-2218
Peter Devries, *Principal*
Mark Horner, *Engineer*
Maria Pedraza, *Manager*
Steve Rush, *Manager*
Peter D Vries, *Manager*

**EMP:** 70
**SALES (corp-wide):** 9.6B  **Publicly Held**
**SIC:** 2821  Polyurethane resins
**HQ:** Huntsman International Llc
  10003 Woodloch Forest Dr # 260
  The Woodlands TX 77380
  281 719-6000

**(G-17992)**
**MOONLIGHT WOODWORKING**
5409 Craftwell Dr  (60072-9402)
PHONE...................................815 728-9121
Carl Almoren, *Principal*
**EMP:** 4
**SALES (est):** 414.2K  **Privately Held**
**SIC:** 2431  Millwork

**(G-17993)**
**MORTON INTL INC ADHSVES SPCLTY**
5005 Barnard Mill Rd  (60072-9652)
PHONE...................................815 653-2042
Divyesh Patel, *Principal*
**EMP:** 3
**SALES (est):** 220.4K  **Privately Held**
**SIC:** 2891  Adhesives

**(G-17994)**
**OBERRY ENTERPRISES INC (PA)**
5306 Bsineil Pkwy Ste 110  (60072)
P.O. Box 130  (60072-0130)
PHONE...................................815 728-9480
Patrick O'Berry, *President*
Rita O'Berry, *Admin Sec*
▲ **EMP:** 3
**SQ FT:** 3,600
**SALES:** 1MM  **Privately Held**
**WEB:** www.oberry-enterprises.com
**SIC:** 3429  5072  Manufactured hardware (general); hardware

**(G-17995)**
**SURVYVN LTD**
4613 Glacial Trl  (60072-9503)
PHONE...................................847 977-8665
Gary Wiener, *President*
**EMP:** 2
**SALES:** 351K  **Privately Held**
**SIC:** 3089  Injection molding of plastics

## River Forest
*Cook County*

**(G-17996)**
**BARNES & NOBLE COLLEGE**
7400 Augusta St  (60305-1402)
PHONE...................................708 209-3173
**EMP:** 4
**SALES (corp-wide):** 1.8B  **Publicly Held**
**SIC:** 2731  Books: publishing & printing
**HQ:** Barnes & Noble College Booksellers, Llc
  120 Mountainview Blvd A
  Basking Ridge NJ 07920
  908 991-2665

**(G-17997)**
**DURABLE DESIGN PRODUCTS INC**
1520 Franklin Ave  (60305-1043)
PHONE...................................708 707-1147
Diane Herman, *President*
**EMP:** 1 EST: 2012
**SALES:** 1MM  **Privately Held**
**SIC:** 2514  2522  2541  Beds, including folding & cabinet, household: metal; kitchen cabinets: metal; tables, household: metal; filing boxes, cabinets & cases: except wood; cabinets, lockers & shelving

**(G-17998)**
**LEOS DANCEWEAR INC**
7601 North Ave  (60305-1133)
PHONE...................................773 889-7700
**Fax:** 773 889-7593
Edward Harris, *Ch of Bd*
Glenn Baruck, *President*
▲ **EMP:** 75 EST: 1923
**SQ FT:** 45,000

**River Forest - Cook County (G-17999)**

SALES (est): 15.2MM **Privately Held**
WEB: www.discountdancedirect.com
SIC: 5139 5137 3144 3143 Shoes; women's & children's clothing; women's footwear, except athletic; men's footwear, except athletic; rubber & plastics footwear

**(G-17999)**
**PROTACTIC GOLF ENTERPRISES**
504 River Oaks Dr (60305-1653)
PHONE .................. 708 209-1120
Lee Paul Rosasco, *President*
Dan Borcher, *Sales Mgr*
▲ EMP: 15
SQ FT: 35,000
SALES (est): 810K **Privately Held**
SIC: 3949 Shafts, golf club

**(G-18000)**
**SANTELLI CUSTOM CABINETRY**
1531 Forest Ave Apt 3 (60305-1072)
PHONE .................. 708 771-3884
Karen Diaferia Santelli, *Principal*
EMP: 4
SALES (est): 442.7K **Privately Held**
SIC: 2434 Wood kitchen cabinets

**(G-18001)**
**SCIENTIFIC CMPT ASSOC CORP (PA)**
Also Called: Sca
212 Lathrop Ave (60305-2121)
PHONE .................. 708 771-4567
Fax: 708 366-0849
Chin Te Liu, *President*
Lon-Mu Liu, *Principal*
Mervin Muller, *Principal*
George C Tiao, *Principal*
William Lattyak, *Vice Pres*
EMP: 5
SQ FT: 2,200
SALES (est): 761.9K **Privately Held**
WEB: www.scausa.com
SIC: 7372 5734 Business oriented computer software; software, business & non-game

**(G-18002)**
**T & T MACHINERY INC**
604 Ashland Ave (60305-1827)
PHONE .................. 708 366-8747
Eric Taubman, *President*
Karen Taubman, *Admin Sec*
EMP: 2
SALES (est): 385.8K **Privately Held**
SIC: 3565 Packaging machinery

**(G-18003)**
**TENEXCO INC**
414 Clinton Pl Ste 106 (60305-2286)
PHONE .................. 708 771-7870
Fax: 708 771-6616
Richard S Incandela, *President*
Richard Incandela II, *Vice Pres*
Sharon S Incandela, *Admin Sec*
EMP: 6
SQ FT: 1,700
SALES (est): 884.3K **Privately Held**
SIC: 1382 Oil & gas exploration services

## River Grove
### Cook County

**(G-18004)**
**A & J PLATING INC**
8058 Grand Ave (60171-1551)
PHONE .................. 708 453-9713
Fax: 708 453-9731
Abraham Delamora, *President*
EMP: 5
SQ FT: 3,700
SALES (est): 736K **Privately Held**
SIC: 3914 Silverware & plated ware

**(G-18005)**
**BANNER MOULDED PRODUCTS**
3050 River Rd (60171-1009)
PHONE .................. 708 452-0033
Fax: 708 625-6439
Michael R Randazzo, *President*
Tony Randazzo, *Vice Pres*
Dennis Casto, *Sales Mgr*
Bob McSherry, *Sales Staff*
Beverly Danna, *Office Mgr*
EMP: 35
SQ FT: 14,100
SALES (est): 5.8MM **Privately Held**
WEB: www.bannermp.com
SIC: 3555 3544 2796 Printing plates; special dies, tools, jigs & fixtures; platemaking services

**(G-18006)**
**BAZAAR INC**
1900 5th Ave (60171-1931)
PHONE .................. 708 583-1800
Fax: 708 583-9782
Robert Nardick, *President*
Gene Wisniewski, *Exec VP*
Arlene Nardick, *Vice Pres*
Tony Briganza, *Controller*
Gloria Dooley, *Manager*
▼ EMP: 100
SQ FT: 295,000
SALES (est): 15.9MM **Privately Held**
WEB: www.thebazaarinc.com
SIC: 7549 2389 Automotive maintenance services; men's miscellaneous accessories

**(G-18007)**
**BOWLMOR AMF CORP**
Also Called: Brunswick Zone River Grove
3111 River Rd (60171-1010)
PHONE .................. 708 456-4100
Mathew Fletchered, *Branch Mgr*
Doug Claine, *Manager*
EMP: 88
SALES (corp-wide): 292.7MM **Privately Held**
PA: Bowlmor Amf Corp.
222 W 44th St
New York NY 10036
212 777-2214

**(G-18008)**
**EXPERT METAL FINISHING INC**
2120 West St (60171-1904)
PHONE .................. 708 583-2550
Gus Garza, *Manager*
EMP: 14
SALES (est): 1.8MM **Privately Held**
SIC: 3471 Cleaning, polishing & finishing

**(G-18009)**
**FORDOC INCORPORATED**
2636 Haymond Ave (60171-1512)
P.O. Box 126, Rock Falls (61071-0126)
PHONE .................. 708 452-8400
Fax: 847 825-1912
EMP: 3
SQ FT: 8,000
SALES (est): 260K **Privately Held**
SIC: 3541 7389 Machine tools, metal cutting type; design services

**(G-18010)**
**LIBORIO BAKING CO INC**
8212 Grand Ave (60171-1518)
P.O. Box 328 (60171-0328)
PHONE .................. 708 452-7222
Fax: 708 452-8560
Andrea Letizia, *President*
Rita Letizia, *Treasurer*
EMP: 6
SQ FT: 50,000
SALES (est): 825K **Privately Held**
SIC: 2051 2099 Bakery: wholesale or wholesale/retail combined; food preparations

**(G-18011)**
**MATRIX MACHINE & TOOL MFG**
8044 Grand Ave (60171-1597)
PHONE .................. 708 452-8707
Fax: 708 452-9579
William Shekut, *President*
Roman Wojcik, *Vice Pres*
EMP: 5
SQ FT: 1,975
SALES (est): 596.5K **Privately Held**
SIC: 3599 7692 Machine shop, jobbing & repair; welding repair

**(G-18012)**
**PALDO SIGN AND DISPLAY COMPANY**
8110 Grand Ave (60171-1510)
PHONE .................. 708 456-1711
Fax: 708 456-3552
Madeline Paldo, *President*
John Paldo, *Vice Pres*
Joseph Paldo, *Vice Pres*
EMP: 7
SQ FT: 5,000
SALES (est): 900K **Privately Held**
WEB: www.paldosigns.com
SIC: 3993 7532 Electric signs; neon signs; truck painting & lettering

**(G-18013)**
**R N R PHOTOGRAPHERS INC**
Also Called: R & R Lithography
8115 Grand Ave (60171-1509)
P.O. Box 32 (60171-0032)
PHONE .................. 708 453-1868
Fax: 708 453-1878
Jan Ross, *President*
Jack Ross, *President*
Richard Ross, *Vice Pres*
Jaclynne Delarco, *Office Mgr*
Frank Noverini, *Admin Sec*
EMP: 7
SQ FT: 5,000
SALES (est): 1.2MM **Privately Held**
SIC: 2752 2759 2791 Commercial printing, offset; letterpress printing; typesetting

## Riverdale
### Cook County

**(G-18014)**
**ARCELORMITTAL RIVERDALE INC**
13500 S Perry Ave (60827-1148)
PHONE .................. 708 849-8803
Fax: 708 849-3340
Gary Norgren, *President*
David Pearson, *Division Mgr*
Terry Fedor, *General Mgr*
Mike Rippey, *Principal*
Robert Bertuca, *Project Mgr*
▲ EMP: 320
SALES (est): 119.9MM **Privately Held**
SIC: 3316 Strip steel, flat bright, cold-rolled: purchased hot-rolled
HQ: Arcelormittal Usa Llc
1 S Dearborn St Ste 1800
Chicago IL 60603
312 346-0300

**(G-18015)**
**ATHERTON FOUNDRY PRODUCTS INC**
13000 S Halsted St (60827-1119)
PHONE .................. 708 849-4615
Fax: 708 849-7225
Owen Smith, *President*
Virginia Smith, *Corp Secy*
Larry Smith, *Vice Pres*
Mark Smith, *Vice Pres*
EMP: 9 EST: 1956
SQ FT: 10,000
SALES (est): 710K **Privately Held**
SIC: 3365 3366 Aluminum & aluminum-based alloy castings; castings (except die): brass; castings (except die): bronze

**(G-18016)**
**BONELL MANUFACTURING COMPANY**
13521 S Halsted St Fl 1 (60827-1190)
PHONE .................. 708 849-1770
Fax: 708 849-3434
Thomas R Okleshen, *President*
Alex Okleshen, *Vice Pres*
James Franz, *Engng Exec*
Shannon Carroll, *Accountant*
Robert Drobick, *Director*
EMP: 40 EST: 1947
SQ FT: 64,500
SALES (est): 8.9MM **Privately Held**
WEB: www.bonellmfg.com
SIC: 3547 3398 3316 7699 Rolling mill machinery; metal heat treating; cold finishing of steel shapes; industrial machinery & equipment repair

**(G-18017)**
**CALUMET ARMATURE AND ELC LLC**
1050 W 134th St (60827-1097)
PHONE .................. 708 841-6880
Fax: 708 841-3465
Hugh Scott, *President*
William Wisniewski, *Vice Pres*
Mike Hicks, *Purch Agent*
Jerry Cak, *Human Resources*
▲ EMP: 40
SQ FT: 33,000
SALES (est): 6.8MM **Publicly Held**
WEB: www.calumetarmature.com
SIC: 7694 3621 5063 Electric motor repair; rebuilding motors, except automotive; coils, for electric motors or generators; electrical apparatus & equipment
HQ: Ies Subsidiary Holdings, Inc
5433 Westheimer Rd # 500
Houston TX 77056
713 860-1500

**(G-18018)**
**E & E MACHINE & ENGINEERING CO**
14016 S Indiana Ave (60827-2248)
PHONE .................. 708 841-5208
Fax: 708 841-4164
Erwin Eiduk, *Owner*
Bernie Eiduk, *Purchasing*
EMP: 4
SQ FT: 12,000
SALES: 400K **Privately Held**
SIC: 3599 7692 Machine shop, jobbing & repair; welding repair

**(G-18019)**
**ESSROC CEMENT CORP**
1400 W 134th St (60827-1005)
PHONE .................. 708 388-0797
Fax: 708 388-0798
Jim Bear, *Manager*
EMP: 3
SALES (corp-wide): 16B **Privately Held**
WEB: www.essroc.com
SIC: 3241 Cement, hydraulic
HQ: Essroc Cement Corp.
3251 Bath Pike
Nazareth PA 18064
610 837-6725

**(G-18020)**
**JM INDUSTRIES LLC**
Also Called: Standard Boiler Tank & Testing
1000 W 142nd St (60827-2343)
PHONE .................. 708 849-4700
Fax: 708 849-5343
Mara Goich, *Mng Member*
Mary Beth Palka, *Manager*
Jenee Rinearson, *Info Tech Mgr*
EMP: 20
SQ FT: 26,000
SALES (est): 5.6MM **Privately Held**
WEB: www.standardboiler.com
SIC: 3443 7699 1791 Tanks, standard or custom fabricated: metal plate; vessels, process or storage (from boiler shops): metal plate; tanks, lined: metal plate; boiler repair shop; storage tanks, metal: erection

**(G-18021)**
**MFI INDUSTRIES INC**
14000 S Stewart Ave (60827-2163)
PHONE .................. 708 841-0727
Christopher Matulajtys, *General Mgr*
EMP: 10
SALES (est): 1.5MM **Privately Held**
WEB: www.mfiindustries.com
SIC: 3433 Boilers, low-pressure heating: steam or hot water

**(G-18022)**
**PHOENIX SERVICES LLC**
13500 S Perry Ave (60827-1148)
P.O. Box 277999 (60827-7999)
PHONE .................. 708 849-3527

Vaughn Massey, *Branch Mgr*
Mike Hale, *Manager*
**EMP:** 6 **Privately Held**
**SIC:** 3295 Perlite, aggregate or expanded
**HQ:** Metal Services Llc
148 W State St Ste 301
Kennett Square PA 19348
610 347-0444

**(G-18023)**
**R & N MACHINE CO**
14020 S Stewart Ave (60827-2163)
P.O. Box 563, South Holland (60473-0563)
**PHONE**.................................708 841-5555
**Fax:** 708 841-6774
Randy Zart, *President*
Carol Zart, *Treasurer*
**EMP:** 12
**SQ FT:** 7,000
**SALES (est):** 1.4MM **Privately Held**
**SIC:** 3599 3452 3451 Machine shop, jobbing & repair; bolts, nuts, rivets & washers; screw machine products

**(G-18024)**
**RIVERDALE PLTG HEAT TRTING LLC**
680 W 134th St (60827-1194)
**PHONE**.................................708 849-2050
**Fax:** 708 849-6010
James See, *President*
Lisa McKinstry, *Treasurer*
Nick Brammer, *Manager*
Richard Kaeding,
Rico Mugnaini,
**EMP:** 50 **EST:** 1950
**SQ FT:** 110,000
**SALES (est):** 9.1MM **Privately Held**
**WEB:** www.rpht.com
**SIC:** 3471 3398 Plating of metals or formed products; annealing of metal

**(G-18025)**
**RT PROPERTIES & CNSTR CORP**
14227 S Parnell Ave (60827-2314)
**PHONE**.................................708 913-7607
Renie Thurman, *President*
Katrina Love, *Admin Sec*
**EMP:** 6
**SQ FT:** 8,000
**SALES (est):** 206.8K **Privately Held**
**SIC:** 2211 Awning stripes, cotton

**(G-18026)**
**WAGENATE ENTPS HOLDINGS LLC**
14331 S Clark St (60827-2741)
**PHONE**.................................773 503-1306
Nate Carson, *CEO*
Michael Striverson, *COO*
Sam McNabb, *Vice Pres*
Eddie Richards, *CFO*
**EMP:** 9
**SALES (est):** 352.6K **Privately Held**
**SIC:** 3621 8731 Power generators; energy research

**(G-18027)**
**WALTER PAYTON POWER EQP LLC (HQ)**
930 W 138th St (60827-1673)
**PHONE**.................................708 656-7700
**Fax:** 708 532-1273
Robert Johnson, *General Mgr*
Bob Johnson, *VP Sales*
Chuck Brobst, *Manager*
Brian Lynch, *Manager*
Dave Wisnieski, *Manager*
**EMP:** 30
**SALES (est):** 14.5MM
**SALES (corp-wide):** 24.9MM **Privately Held**
**SIC:** 3531 Crane carriers
**PA:** Lanigan Holdings Llc
3111 167th St
Hazel Crest IL 60429
708 596-5200

## Riverside
### Cook County

**(G-18028)**
**ANART INC**
440 Repton Rd (60546-1622)
**PHONE**.................................708 447-0225
Anna Maria Gallegos, *President*
**EMP:** 35
**SALES (est):** 2.8MM **Privately Held**
**SIC:** 2339 Women's & misses' outerwear

**(G-18029)**
**BIOCHEMICAL LAB**
247 Addison Rd (60546-2003)
**PHONE**.................................708 447-3923
Robert Novak, *Principal*
**EMP:** 3
**SALES (est):** 237.9K **Privately Held**
**SIC:** 3273 Ready-mixed concrete

**(G-18030)**
**ENGINEERING PROTOTYPE INC**
2537 S 6th Ave (60546-1243)
**PHONE**.................................708 447-3155
**Fax:** 847 671-0219
Edo S Cecic, *President*
Ophelia Cecic, *Vice Pres*
**EMP:** 10
**SQ FT:** 5,000
**SALES (est):** 768K **Privately Held**
**SIC:** 3728 Aircraft parts & equipment

**(G-18031)**
**HIGGINS GLASS STUDIO LLC**
Also Called: Higgins Handcrafted Glass
33 E Quincy St Ste A (60546-2289)
**PHONE**.................................708 447-2787
**Fax:** 708 447-2787
Louise Wimmer, *Owner*
Frances Higgins, *Owner*
**EMP:** 3
**SQ FT:** 3,125
**SALES (est):** 249.9K **Privately Held**
**WEB:** www.higginsglass.com
**SIC:** 5719 3211 Glassware; flat glass

**(G-18032)**
**OCULARIS PHARMA**
2436 S 6th Ave (60546-1242)
**PHONE**.................................708 712-6263
Alan R Meyer, *Principal*
Keith Terry, *Senior VP*
**EMP:** 6
**SALES (est):** 523.6K **Privately Held**
**SIC:** 2834 Pharmaceutical preparations

**(G-18033)**
**PELEGAN INC**
277 Northwood Rd (60546-1882)
**PHONE**.................................708 442-9797
Gayle J Egan, *President*
**EMP:** 3
**SALES:** 260K **Privately Held**
**SIC:** 2759 7336 Promotional printing; graphic arts & related design

## Riverton
### Sangamon County

**(G-18034)**
**REQUEST ELECTRIC**
8290 E State Route 54 # 1 (62561-8076)
P.O. Box 498 (62561-0498)
**PHONE**.................................217 629-7789
Adrian Burcham, *Executive Asst*
**EMP:** 4
**SALES (est):** 652.4K **Privately Held**
**SIC:** 3699 Electrical equipment & supplies

**(G-18035)**
**RIVERTON REGISTER**
Also Called: Rhodes Publications
100 N 6th St (62561-8168)
P.O. Box 17 (62561-0017)
**PHONE**.................................217 629-9247
Barbara Rhodes, *Owner*
**EMP:** 3
**SALES:** 73.4K **Privately Held**
**SIC:** 2711 Newspapers

**(G-18036)**
**ROADSAFE TRAFFIC SYSTEMS INC**
104 Douglas St (62561-6074)
**PHONE**.................................217 629-7139
**Fax:** 217 629-7148
Richard Ricca, *Manager*
**EMP:** 4
**SALES (corp-wide):** 679.1MM **Privately Held**
**SIC:** 3531 Construction machinery
**PA:** Roadsafe Traffic Systems, Inc.
8750 W Bryn Mawr Ave # 400
Chicago IL 60631
773 724-3300

## Riverwoods
### Lake County

**(G-18037)**
**CCH INCORPORATED (DH)**
2700 Lake Cook Rd (60015-3867)
**PHONE**.................................847 267-7000
**Fax:** 800 224-8299
Jason Marx, *CEO*
Christopher F Kane, *President*
Peter Berkery, *Publisher*
Susan Berry, *Publisher*
William Zale, *Principal*
▲ **EMP:** 600
**SQ FT:** 205,000
**SALES (est):** 1B
**SALES (corp-wide):** 4.5B **Privately Held**
**WEB:** www.cch.com
**SIC:** 2721 2731 7389 7338 Statistical reports (periodicals): publishing & printing; books: publishing & printing; pamphlets: publishing & printing; legal & tax services; secretarial & typing service; research services, except laboratory; computer software development
**HQ:** Wolters Kluwer United States Inc.
2700 Lake Cook Rd
Riverwoods IL 60015
847 580-5000

**(G-18038)**
**GUARDIAN ENERGY TECH INC**
Also Called: Spray Foam Direct
2033 Milwaukee Ave # 136 (60015-3581)
**PHONE**.................................800 516-0949
Janelle Munns, *President*
Mark Munns, *Principal*
**EMP:** 11 **EST:** 2007
**SALES (est):** 2MM **Privately Held**
**SIC:** 3644 5169 Insulators & insulation materials, electrical; polyurethane products

**(G-18039)**
**INDORAMA VENTURES OXIDE & GLYL (HQ)**
2610 Lake Cook Rd Ste 133 (60015-5710)
**PHONE**.................................800 365-0794
Satyanarayan Mohta, *President*
James A Bryan, *Partner*
J Thomas Hurvis, *Partner*
Richard Jago, *Partner*
Riaz H Waraich, *Partner*
▼ **EMP:** 24
**SALES (est):** 15.1MM
**SALES (corp-wide):** 7.3B **Privately Held**
**SIC:** 2869 Industrial organic chemicals
**PA:** Indorama Ventures Public Company Limited
75/102 Soi Sukhumvit 19 (Wattana),
Asok Road
Wattana 10110
266 166-61

**(G-18040)**
**KAN-DU MANUFACTURING CO INC**
1776 Clendenin Ln (60015-1722)
**PHONE**.................................708 681-0370
**Fax:** 708 681-0373
Michael Feldman, *President*
**EMP:** 7 **EST:** 1956
**SQ FT:** 12,800
**SALES:** 518.5K **Privately Held**
**SIC:** 3496 3495 Miscellaneous fabricated wire products; wire springs

**(G-18041)**
**ORIGINAL SYSTEMS**
2590 Chianti Trl (60015-3802)
**PHONE**.................................847 945-7660
**Fax:** 847 945-7662
Ronald Baranski, *Owner*
**EMP:** 4
**SALES:** 2MM **Privately Held**
**SIC:** 5084 3589 Industrial machinery & equipment; commercial cleaning equipment

**(G-18042)**
**ROEVOLUTION 226 LLC (PA)**
2610 Lake Cook Rd (60015-5711)
**PHONE**.................................773 658-4022
Ken Nowak, *CFO*
Bernard Donaldson,
David Feder,
Mark Knepper,
Brian Lemay,
**EMP:** 0
**SALES (est):** 10.3MM **Privately Held**
**SIC:** 6719 5021 2521 Investment holding companies, except banks; office furniture; wood office furniture

**(G-18043)**
**SANTAS BEST (PA)**
3750 Deerfield Rd # 1000 (60015-3541)
**PHONE**.................................847 459-3301
Edward H Ruff, *CEO*
Barry Hausauer, *COO*
Sally Djurdjevic, *Accountant*
**EMP:** 18
**SQ FT:** 9,600
**SALES (est):** 28.5MM **Privately Held**
**WEB:** www.santasbest.com
**SIC:** 3699 3641 Christmas tree lighting sets, electric; electric lamps & parts for specialized applications

**(G-18044)**
**STEVEN FISHER**
Also Called: Caribbean Adventures Magazine
610 Thornmeadow Rd (60015-3751)
**PHONE**.................................847 317-1128
Steve Fisher, *President*
Rick Perlman, *Corp Secy*
Sarah Tucker Fisher, *Vice Pres*
**EMP:** 3
**SALES (est):** 165K **Privately Held**
**SIC:** 2721 Magazines: publishing only, not printed on site

**(G-18045)**
**TORGO INC**
2033 Milwaukee Ave # 352 (60015-3581)
**PHONE**.................................800 360-5910
**EMP:** 4
**SALES (est):** 381.2K **Privately Held**
**SIC:** 7372 Prepackaged software

**(G-18046)**
**WOLTERS KLUWER US INC (DH)**
2700 Lake Cook Rd (60015-3867)
**PHONE**.................................847 580-5000
**Fax:** 847 580-5193
Richard Flynn, *CEO*
Deidra D Gold, *President*
Steven Hardy, *President*
Brian Kiernan, *President*
Nancy McKinstry, *President*
◆ **EMP:** 50
**SALES (est):** 3.7B
**SALES (corp-wide):** 4.5B **Privately Held**
**SIC:** 2731 2721 2741 2759 Books: publishing only; trade journals: publishing only, not printed on site; directories: publishing & printing; commercial printing
**HQ:** Wolters Kluwer International Holding B.V.
Zuidpoolsingel 2
Alphen Aan Den Rijn
172 641-400

## Roanoke
*Woodford County*

**(G-18047)**
**AMIGONI CONSTRUCTION**
800 N State St (61561-7545)
P.O. Box 491 (61561-0491)
PHONE..................................309 923-3701
Terry Monge, *Owner*
**EMP:** 3 **EST:** 1950
**SALES (est):** 214.4K **Privately Held**
**SIC: 1794** 1442 Excavation work; gravel mining

**(G-18048)**
**B J FEHR MACHINE CO**
209 N Main St (61561-7514)
P.O. Box 987 (61561-0987)
PHONE..................................309 923-8691
**Fax:** 309 923-7412
Walter Fehr, *Owner*
**EMP:** 4
**SQ FT:** 8,160
**SALES (est):** 202.1K **Privately Held**
**SIC: 7699** 7692 7629 3523 Blacksmith shop; welding repair; electrical repair shops; farm machinery & equipment; welding on site

**(G-18049)**
**CHARLES RIVER LABORATORIES INC**
117 W Husseman St (61561-7565)
P.O. Box 507 (61561-0507)
PHONE..................................309 923-7122
Dwate Schwake, *Opers-Prdtn-Mfg*
**EMP:** 63
**SALES (corp-wide):** 1.6B **Publicly Held**
**WEB:** www.criver.com
**SIC: 2836** Vaccines
**HQ:** Charles River Laboratories, Inc.
251 Ballardvale St
Wilmington MA 01887
978 658-6000

**(G-18050)**
**GINGRICH ENTERPRISES INC**
Also Called: G E I
1503 W Front St (61561-7431)
PHONE..................................309 923-7312
Ross Gingrich, *President*
Eric Sieben, *Opers Mgr*
Debra Hartman, *Admin Sec*
**EMP:** 37
**SALES (est):** 6.3MM **Privately Held**
**SIC: 5531** 5063 3469 Batteries, automotive & truck; batteries; machine parts, stamped or pressed metal

**(G-18051)**
**KEVS KANS INC**
1501 W Front St (61561-7431)
PHONE..................................309 303-3999
Kevin Wagner, *Principal*
**EMP:** 4
**SALES (est):** 405.3K **Privately Held**
**SIC: 3089** Garbage containers, plastic

**(G-18052)**
**LIFTS OF ILLINOIS INC**
415 W Front St (61561-7817)
P.O. Box 289 (61561-0289)
PHONE..................................309 923-7450
Jim Braker, *President*
**EMP:** 5
**SALES (est):** 700K **Privately Held**
**SIC: 3999** 3534 5084 1796 Wheelchair lifts; elevators & equipment; elevators; elevator installation & conversion

**(G-18053)**
**PARSONS COMPANY INC**
1386 State Route 117 (61561-7721)
PHONE..................................309 467-9100
Robert Parsons, *President*
Kevin Trantina, *COO*
Patrick Weber, *Treasurer*
Mike Hasty, *Supervisor*
**EMP:** 221
**SQ FT:** 225,000
**SALES (est):** 51.7MM **Privately Held**
**WEB:** www.parsonscompany.com
**SIC: 3599** Custom machinery

**(G-18054)**
**ROANOKE MILLING CO**
211 W Husseman St (61561-7648)
P.O. Box 379 (61561-0379)
PHONE..................................309 923-5731
Arthur Wilkey, *President*
Carolyn Wilkey, *Admin Sec*
**EMP:** 8
**SQ FT:** 10,000
**SALES:** 1MM **Privately Held**
**SIC: 2048** 2041 Prepared feeds; flour & other grain mill products

## Robinson
*Crawford County*

**(G-18055)**
**BELL BROTHERS**
201 N Jefferson St (62454-2720)
PHONE..................................618 544-2157
**Fax:** 618 544-8484
Christopher B Pappageorge, *Owner*
**EMP:** 5
**SQ FT:** 3,000
**SALES (est):** 380.8K **Privately Held**
**WEB:** www.bellbros.com
**SIC: 1382** 1311 Oil & gas exploration services; crude petroleum production

**(G-18056)**
**BERTRAM OIL CO**
604 W Locust Ln (62454-1305)
P.O. Box 411 (62454-0411)
PHONE..................................618 546-1122
Donald Bertram, *President*
Sue J Bertram, *Vice Pres*
**EMP:** 3
**SALES (est):** 240K **Privately Held**
**SIC: 1311** Crude petroleum production

**(G-18057)**
**BEST WAY CARPET & UPHL CLG**
1401 N Johnson St (62454-1025)
PHONE..................................618 544-8585
Michael Dunlap, *Partner*
Sue Dunlap, *Partner*
**EMP:** 3
**SALES:** 65K **Privately Held**
**SIC: 3589** 7359 Carpet sweepers, except household electric vacuum sweepers; carpet & upholstery cleaning equipment rental

**(G-18058)**
**CRAWFORD COUNTY OIL LLC**
7005 E 1050th Ave (62454-4727)
P.O. Box 229 (62454-0229)
PHONE..................................618 544-3493
Kay Williams, *Controller*
Larry Clark, *Mng Member*
**EMP:** 50
**SALES (est):** 9MM **Privately Held**
**SIC: 1382** Oil & gas exploration services

**(G-18059)**
**DAILY LAWRENCEVILLE RECORD (PA)**
Also Called: Daily News/Daily Record
302 S Cross St (62454-2137)
P.O. Box 639 (62454-0639)
PHONE..................................618 544-2101
Larry H Lewis, *President*
Kathy Lewis, *Admin Sec*
**EMP:** 2
**SALES (est):** 827.6K **Privately Held**
**SIC: 2711** Newspapers: publishing only, not printed on site

**(G-18060)**
**DAILY ROBINSON NEWS INC**
Also Called: Robinson Daily News
302 S Cross St (62454-2137)
P.O. Box 639 (62454-0639)
PHONE..................................618 544-2101
**Fax:** 618 544-9533
Larry H Lewis, *President*
Wally Dean, *Advt Staff*
Robert Fox, *Manager*
Kathy Lewis, *Admin Sec*
**EMP:** 30
**SQ FT:** 5,200
**SALES (est):** 1.9MM **Privately Held**
**SIC: 2711** Commercial printing & newspaper publishing combined

**(G-18061)**
**DANA SEALING MANUFACTURING LLC**
Also Called: Dana Corp Power Tech Group
1201 E Victor Dana Rd (62454-5853)
P.O. Box 599 (62454-0599)
PHONE..................................618 544-8651
**Fax:** 618 544-8651
Jeff Arnold, *COO*
Mark Burtch, *Purch Mgr*
Steve Orey, *Branch Mgr*
**EMP:** 300
**SALES (corp-wide):** 5.8B **Publicly Held**
**SIC: 3714** 3053 Motor vehicle parts & accessories; gaskets, packing & sealing devices
**HQ:** Dana Sealing Manufacturing, Llc
3939 Technology Dr
Maumee OH 43537
419 887-3000

**(G-18062)**
**E H BAARE CORPORATION**
500 S Heath Toffee Ave (62454-1699)
PHONE..................................618 546-1575
**Fax:** 618 546-0130
John Reynolds, *President*
Joel Owens, *Engineer*
Mike Uptmor, *Data Proc Exec*
Brad Murray, *Assistant*
**EMP:** 206
**SALES (corp-wide):** 23.2MM **Privately Held**
**WEB:** www.ehbaare.com
**SIC: 3315** 3496 3469 3443 Wire & fabricated wire products; miscellaneous fabricated wire products; metal stampings; fabricated plate work (boiler shop); steel foundries; gray & ductile iron foundries
**PA:** E. H. Baare Corporation
3620 W 73rd St
Anderson IN 46011
765 778-7895

**(G-18063)**
**GSG INDUSTRIES**
1708 W Main St (62454-4845)
P.O. Box 429 (62454-0429)
PHONE..................................618 544-7976
**Fax:** 618 544-7976
**EMP:** 10
**SALES (est):** 550K **Privately Held**
**SIC: 3677** 3612 Mfg Electronic Coils/Transformers Mfg Transformers

**(G-18064)**
**HERSHEY COMPANY**
1401 W Main St (62454-1263)
P.O. Box 800 (62454-0800)
PHONE..................................618 544-3111
Brian Lange, *Plant Mgr*
Todd Whitemore, *Opers Mgr*
Dennis Gilbey, *Prdtn Mgr*
Judy Kieth, *Safety Mgr*
Brad Redman, *Maint Spvr*
**EMP:** 750
**SALES (corp-wide):** 7.4B **Publicly Held**
**WEB:** www.hersheys.com
**SIC: 2064** 2066 Candy & other confectionery products; chocolate & cocoa products
**PA:** Hershey Company
100 Crystal A Dr
Hershey PA 17033
717 534-4200

**(G-18065)**
**L C NEELYDRILLING INC**
702 N Jackson St (62454-3357)
PHONE..................................618 544-2726
**Fax:** 618 547-7314
Larry C Neely, *President*
Sue M Neely, *Treasurer*
**EMP:** 8
**SQ FT:** 2,500
**SALES (est):** 1.5MM **Privately Held**
**SIC: 1381** Drilling oil & gas wells

**(G-18066)**
**MARATHON PETROLEUM COMPANY LP**
400 S Marathon Ave (62454-3400)
P.O. Box 1200 (62454-1200)
PHONE..................................618 544-2121
**Fax:** 618 544-9541
Jerry Welch, *Plant Mgr*
Mike Armbrester, *Manager*
**EMP:** 600 **Publicly Held**
**WEB:** www.mapllc.com
**SIC: 5172** 2992 Petroleum products; re-refining lubricating oils & greases
**HQ:** Marathon Petroleum Company Lp
539 S Main St
Findlay OH 45840

**(G-18067)**
**MORRIS CONSTRUCTION INC**
Marathon Ave (62454)
P.O. Box 377 (62454-0377)
PHONE..................................618 544-8504
Kenneth Mattsey, *President*
**EMP:** 20
**SALES (corp-wide):** 13.2MM **Privately Held**
**SIC: 1542** 3498 3441 Commercial & office building, new construction; fabricated pipe & fittings; fabricated structural metal
**PA:** Morris Construction, Inc.
1406 S Eaton St
Robinson IL 62454
618 544-9215

**(G-18068)**
**PIONEER LABELS INC**
Also Called: Datamax Oneil Printer Supplies
7656 E 700th Ave (62454-5124)
PHONE..................................618 546-5418
**Fax:** 618 546-1518
Paul Sindoni, *President*
Christian Lefort, *President*
Brat Dirk, *Plant Mgr*
Joe Tredway, *Controller*
Ted Quinain, *Manager*
▼**EMP:** 105
**SQ FT:** 65,000
**SALES (est):** 19.3MM
**SALES (corp-wide):** 39.3B **Publicly Held**
**WEB:** www.datamaxcorp.com
**SIC: 2754** 2672 2671 Labels: gravure printing; coated & laminated paper; packaging paper & plastics film, coated & laminated
**HQ:** Datamax-O'neil Corporation
4501 Pkwy Commerce Blvd
Orlando FL 32808

**(G-18069)**
**POOL & POOL OIL PRODUCTIONS**
1724 W Main St (62454-4845)
PHONE..................................618 544-7590
Stanley E Pool, *Owner*
**EMP:** 1 **EST:** 1982
**SQ FT:** 1,500
**SALES (est):** 450K **Privately Held**
**SIC: 1311** Crude petroleum production

**(G-18070)**
**R & L READY MIX INC**
602 N Steel St (62454-3342)
PHONE..................................618 544-7514
Chadd Murray, *President*
Linda Wilson, *Bookkeeper*
**EMP:** 11 **EST:** 1953
**SQ FT:** 3,000
**SALES:** 350K **Privately Held**
**SIC: 3273** Ready-mixed concrete

**(G-18071)**
**RAIN CII CARBON LLC**
12187 E 950th Ave (62454-5844)
PHONE..................................618 544-2193
Trudy Ferguson, *President*
Steve Rowland, *Vice Pres*
Dan Fearday, *Plant Mgr*
Randell Bergeron, *Opers Staff*
Rickey James, *Production*
**EMP:** 26 **EST:** 1958
**SALES (est):** 3.6MM **Privately Held**
**WEB:** www.ciicarbon.com
**SIC: 7389** 3312 Petroleum refinery inspection service; blast furnaces & steel mills

HQ: Rain Cii Carbon Llc
1330 Greengate Dr Ste 300
Covington LA 70433
281 318-2400

**(G-18072)**
**S D CUSTOM MACHINING**
9094 E 1050th Ave (62454-7400)
PHONE..................................618 544-7007
Glenn Wilson, *Owner*
EMP: 3
SQ FT: 3,800
SALES (est): 263.9K **Privately Held**
SIC: 3599 7692 3993 Machine & other job shop work; welding repair; signs & advertising specialties

**(G-18073)**
**SUPERIOR WELDING INC**
9172 E 1050th Ave (62454-4824)
PHONE..................................618 544-8822
Fax: 618 544-7095
Howard Bilyew, *President*
EMP: 12
SQ FT: 7,200
SALES (est): 1.6MM **Privately Held**
SIC: 7692 Welding repair

**(G-18074)**
**TEMPCO PRODUCTS CO**
301 E Tempco Ave (62454-2600)
P.O. Box 155 (62454-0155)
PHONE..................................618 544-3175
Fax: 618 544-2244
Steve Mc Gahey, *President*
Matt Johnson, *Plant Mgr*
John Spitz, *Sales Mgr*
Jerry Snider, *Admin Sec*
EMP: 90 EST: 1952
SQ FT: 60,000
SALES (est): 15.6MM **Privately Held**
WEB: www.tempcoproducts.com
SIC: 3089 3442 Window frames & sash, plastic; storm doors or windows, metal

**(G-18075)**
**WESTERN OIL & GAS DEV CO**
9234 E 1050th Ave (62454-4825)
P.O. Box 165 (62454-0165)
PHONE..................................618 544-8646
Fax: 618 544-2496
Gregory Leavell, *President*
EMP: 14
SALES (est): 1.8MM **Privately Held**
SIC: 1311 Crude petroleum production

## Rochelle
### Ogle County

**(G-18076)**
**A & G MANUFACTURING  INC**
Also Called: AG Manufacturing - Illinois
200 E Avenue G (61068-3502)
PHONE..................................815 562-2107
V C Edozien, *President*
Todd Brachat, *General Mgr*
Gae Schabacker, *Prdtn Mgr*
Tonya Barton, *Info Tech Dir*
Chuck Hacker, *Maintence Staff*
▲ EMP: 50
SALES (est): 950K **Privately Held**
SIC: 3714 Motor vehicle parts & accessories

**(G-18077)**
**AIRDRONIC TEST & BALANCE INC**
801 1st Ave (61068-1817)
PHONE..................................815 561-0339
Richard Eraas, *President*
Angela Eraas, *Vice Pres*
EMP: 6
SALES (est): 725.8K **Privately Held**
SIC: 3585 Heating equipment, complete

**(G-18078)**
**ALLOY ROD PRODUCTS  INC**
100 Quarry Rd (61068-3510)
PHONE..................................815 562-8200
Cristi A Hoffman, *President*
Jeff Thomas, *Manager*
EMP: 12

SALES (est): 1.6MM **Privately Held**
SIC: 3356 Silver & silver alloy bars, rods, sheets, etc.

**(G-18079)**
**BEST MANUFACTURING & WLDG INC**
231 Powers Rd 251n (61068-8925)
PHONE..................................815 562-4107
Fax: 815 562-4108
Patricia Best, *CEO*
▼ EMP: 20
SALES (est): 3.2MM **Privately Held**
SIC: 3441 Fabricated structural metal

**(G-18080)**
**C B & A  INC**
Also Called: Cardinal Forge
1040 S Main St (61068-2174)
P.O. Box 567, Dekalb (60115-0567)
PHONE..................................815 561-0255
Jon Rogers, *President*
Jeffrey T Jones, *Vice Pres*
Jon Roges, *Engineer*
Kent A Paul, *CFO*
Ken Deutsch, *Manager*
EMP: 15
SQ FT: 23,000
SALES (est): 2MM **Privately Held**
WEB: www.cardinalforge.com
SIC: 3366 3363 Castings (except die): brass; aluminum die-castings

**(G-18081)**
**C U PLASTIC LLC**
100 4th Ave (61068-1710)
PHONE..................................888 957-9993
Nandy Lin, *Accountant*
Ll Rong Lin, *Mng Member*
Yu Tan Zheng,
▲ EMP: 6 EST: 2010
SALES (est): 876.9K **Privately Held**
SIC: 2869 Ethylene

**(G-18082)**
**CAIN MILLWORK  INC**
1 Cain Pkwy (61068-3501)
PHONE..................................815 561-9700
Fax: 815 561-8404
Daniel Levin, *CEO*
Don Lupa, *President*
Roger Cain, *Vice Pres*
Mike Leali, *Vice Pres*
Joe Sebek, *Vice Pres*
EMP: 67 EST: 1979
SQ FT: 2,000
SALES: 15.2MM **Privately Held**
WEB: www.cainmillwork.com
SIC: 2431 Millwork

**(G-18083)**
**CLARKWESTERN DIETRICH BUILDING**
501 S Steward Rd (61068-9304)
PHONE..................................815 561-2360
Fax: 815 561-2370
Mike Garrett, *Branch Mgr*
EMP: 35
SALES (corp-wide): 8.1B **Privately Held**
WEB: www.clarksteel.com
SIC: 3441 Fabricated structural metal
HQ: Clarkwestern Dietrich Building Systems Llc
9100 Centre Pointe Dr # 210
West Chester OH 45069

**(G-18084)**
**DEL MONTE FOODS  INC**
600 N 15th St (61068-1255)
PHONE..................................815 562-1359
Paul Quitno, *Branch Mgr*
EMP: 15
SALES (corp-wide): 2.2B **Privately Held**
SIC: 2033 Vegetables & vegetable products in cans, jars, etc.
HQ: Del Monte Foods, Inc.
3003 Oak Rd Ste 600
Walnut Creek CA 94597
925 949-2772

**(G-18085)**
**DEL MONTE FOODS  INC**
451 Willis Ave (61068-8816)
PHONE..................................630 836-8131
Marv Berg, *Branch Mgr*
EMP: 14

SALES (corp-wide): 2.2B **Privately Held**
SIC: 2033 8741 Vegetables & vegetable products in cans, jars, etc.; management services
HQ: Del Monte Foods, Inc.
3003 Oak Rd Ste 600
Walnut Creek CA 94597
925 949-2772

**(G-18086)**
**E & D WEB INC**
1100a S Main St (61068-3509)
PHONE..................................815 562-5800
Fax: 708 656-4154
Christopher Love, *CEO*
Barton Love, *Ch of Bd*
Kenneth Love, *President*
Sofie Siek, *Treasurer*
Edward Berg, *Accountant*
EMP: 150
SQ FT: 145,000
SALES (est): 21.6MM **Privately Held**
WEB: www.eanddweb.com
SIC: 2752 2759 Lithographing on metal; commercial printing, offset; commercial printing

**(G-18087)**
**EATON CORPORATION**
Also Called: Eaton Cor Actuator & Sensor Di
200 E Avenue G (61068-3502)
PHONE..................................815 562-2107
Fax: 815 562-9174
Dave Ross, *Purch Mgr*
Brooke Rabold, *Human Res Mgr*
Todd Brachta, *Branch Mgr*
Todd Brachart, *Manager*
Donald Bullock, *CIO*
EMP: 250 **Privately Held**
WEB: www.eaton.com
SIC: 3714 3625 5012 Motor vehicle parts & accessories; relays & industrial controls; automobiles
HQ: Eaton Corporation
1000 Eaton Blvd
Cleveland OH 44122
216 523-5000

**(G-18088)**
**ERIE GROUP INTERNATIONAL INC**
1201 S Main St (61068-3515)
P.O. Box 30 (61068-0030)
PHONE..................................309 659-2233
Mark Delaney, *Vice Pres*
James Klein, *Vice Pres*
Carl Janudoo, *Enginr/R&D Mgr*
James Jacoby, *Branch Mgr*
Jim Jacoby, *Manager*
EMP: 60
SALES (corp-wide): 19.5MM **Privately Held**
WEB: www.eriefoods.com
SIC: 2023 2026 Dried milk preparations; fluid milk
PA: Erie Group International, Inc.
401 7th Ave
Erie IL 61250
309 659-2233

**(G-18089)**
**FBC INDUSTRIES  INC**
110 E Avenue H (61068-2193)
P.O. Box 173 (61068-0173)
PHONE..................................847 839-0880
Fax: 815 562-3018
Patrick Gabriele, *CFO*
Mike Pierce, *Manager*
Paul Roland, *Manager*
EMP: 9
SALES (corp-wide): 5.7MM **Privately Held**
WEB: www.fbcindustries.com
SIC: 2099 2087 2869 Emulsifiers, food; flavoring extracts & syrups; perfumes, flavorings & food additives
PA: F.B.C. Industries, Inc.
1933 N Meacham Rd Ste 550
Schaumburg IL 60173
847 241-6143

**(G-18090)**
**FIRE CHARIOT  LLC**
770 Wiscold Dr (61068-8502)
PHONE..................................815 561-3688
Jeffrey Brue, *Mng Member*

Allen Brue,
EMP: 2
SALES (est): 258.2K **Privately Held**
SIC: 3714 Motor vehicle engines & parts

**(G-18091)**
**GARDNER PRODUCTS  INC**
224 4th Ave (61068-1615)
PHONE..................................815 562-6011
Fax: 815 562-6193
Jack B Gardner, *President*
Sharon Gardner, *Corp Secy*
Tracy Gardner, *Manager*
EMP: 12
SQ FT: 15,000
SALES (est): 550K **Privately Held**
SIC: 3599 Machine shop, jobbing & repair

**(G-18092)**
**GRAPHIC ARTS BINDERY LLC**
1020 S Main St (61068-2174)
PHONE..................................708 416-4290
Christopher Love, *Owner*
EMP: 65
SALES (est): 586.5K **Privately Held**
SIC: 2789 Binding only: books, pamphlets, magazines, etc.

**(G-18093)**
**HILLSHIRE BRANDS COMPANY**
600 Wiscold Dr (61068-8519)
PHONE..................................800 727-2533
EMP: 255
SALES (corp-wide): 36.8B **Publicly Held**
SIC: 2013 Sausages & other prepared meats
HQ: The Hillshire Brands Company
400 S Jefferson St Fl 1
Chicago IL 60607
312 614-6000

**(G-18094)**
**HUB PRINTING COMPANY INC**
Also Called: Hub Printing & Office Supplies
101 Maple Ave (61068-8927)
PHONE..................................815 562-7057
Fax: 815 562-3811
Steve Haas, *President*
Brent Tracy, *Plant Mgr*
Catherine Haas, *Admin Sec*
EMP: 15
SALES (est): 3.6MM **Privately Held**
SIC: 2752 5943 2791 2789 Commercial printing, offset; office forms & supplies; typesetting; bookbinding & related work; commercial printing

**(G-18095)**
**ILLINOIS RIVER ENERGY  LLC**
Also Called: CHS Rochelle
4000 N Division (61068)
PHONE..................................815 561-0650
Michael O'Connor, *Controller*
Amir Saeed, *Mng Member*
Stanley R Blunier, *Mng Member*
Bradley A Riskedal, *Mng Member*
Richard Ruebe, *Mng Member*
▼ EMP: 60
SALES (est): 19.3MM
SALES (corp-wide): 30.3B **Publicly Held**
SIC: 2869 Ethyl alcohol, ethanol
PA: Chs Inc.
5500 Cenex Dr
Inver Grove Heights MN 55077
651 355-6000

**(G-18096)**
**MACKLIN INC (PA)**
6089 Dement Rd (61068-8501)
PHONE..................................815 562-4803
Fax: 815 562-7790
Maryann Macklin, *President*
Keith Harvey, *Manager*
EMP: 10
SQ FT: 1,200
SALES (est): 2MM **Privately Held**
WEB: www.macklin.com
SIC: 1422 Crushed & broken limestone; whiting mining, crushed & broken-quarrying

**(G-18097)**
**MAPLEHURST FARMS  INC (PA)**
936 S Moore Rd (61068-9789)
PHONE..................................815 562-8723
Carol Hayenga, *CEO*

# Rochelle - Ogle County (G-18098)

Lyn Carmichael, *President*
Dee Williams, *Opers Staff*
Barbara Koehnke, *CFO*
Barb Konhnke, *Controller*
**EMP:** 10
**SQ FT:** 3,000
**SALES (est):** 160.3MM **Privately Held**
**SIC: 5153** 2879 4212 Grain & field beans; agricultural chemicals; local trucking, without storage

### (G-18098)
### MASTER GRAPHICS LLC
1100 S Main St (61068-3509)
**PHONE**.................................815 562-5800
**Fax:** 815 562-6600
Sophie Siek, *Marketing Staff*
Jim Gaustad, *Manager*
Christopher Barton Love,
Kenneth Barton Love,
**EMP:** 99
**SQ FT:** 225,000
**SALES (est):** 36.1MM **Privately Held**
**SIC: 2752** Commercial printing, offset

### (G-18099)
### MOUNTAINEER NEWSPAPERS INC (DH)
211 E Il Route 38 (61068-2303)
P.O. Box 46 (61068-0046)
**PHONE**.................................815 562-2061
John C Tompkins, *President*
Michael R Tompkins, *Vice Pres*
R Michael Tompkins, *Vice Pres*
John Pearson, *Accounting Mgr*
Michael Rand, *Admin Sec*
**EMP:** 33
**SQ FT:** 20,000
**SALES (est):** 4.3MM **Privately Held**
**WEB:** www.mountainstatesman.com
**SIC: 2711** Newspapers
**HQ:** Rochelle Newspapers Inc
211 E Il Route 38
Rochelle IL 61068
815 562-2061

### (G-18100)
### NEWS MEDIA CORPORATION (PA)
211 E Il Route 38 (61068-2303)
P.O. Box 46 (61068-0046)
**PHONE**.................................815 562-2061
John C Tompkins, *President*
Bret Yager, *Vice Pres*
R Michael Tompkins, *Treasurer*
John Pearson, *Accounting Mgr*
Joni Spartz, *Accounting Mgr*
**EMP:** 30
**SQ FT:** 6,000
**SALES (est):** 90.9MM **Privately Held**
**WEB:** www.newsmediacorporation.com
**SIC: 2711** Newspapers

### (G-18101)
### NIPPON SHARYO MFG LLC
1600 Ritchie Ct (61068-9306)
**PHONE**.................................815 562-8600
Udit Dave, *Engineer*
▲ **EMP:** 1 **EST:** 2010
**SALES (est):** 527.5K
**SALES (corp-wide):** 15.4B **Privately Held**
**SIC: 3711** Motor vehicles & car bodies
**HQ:** Nippon Sharyo U.S.A., Inc.
2340 S Arlington Heights
Arlington Heights IL 60005
847 228-2700

### (G-18102)
### PRINTING ETC INC
1135 Lincoln Hwy (61068-1516)
**PHONE**.................................815 562-6151
**Fax:** 815 561-8089
Sherri Barber, *President*
Russ Barber, *Co-Owner*
**EMP:** 5
**SQ FT:** 2,000
**SALES:** 310K **Privately Held**
**SIC: 2752** 2791 2789 2672 Commercial printing, offset; typesetting; bookbinding & related work; coated & laminated paper

### (G-18103)
### QUICK START PDTS & SOLUTIONS
770 Wiscold Dr (61068-8502)
P.O. Box 665 (61068-0665)
**PHONE**.................................815 562-5414
Allen Brue, *President*
Jeff Brue, *Vice Pres*
Tammy Kemnitz, *MIS Mgr*
**EMP:** 15
**SQ FT:** 15,000
**SALES (est):** 2.4MM **Privately Held**
**WEB:** www.quickstart-ether.com
**SIC: 3694** Motors, starting: automotive & aircraft

### (G-18104)
### REGIONAL READY MIX LLC
15051 E Lind Rd (61068-9727)
**PHONE**.................................815 562-1901
**Fax:** 815 562-1953
Kevin Johnson, *Mng Member*
Brent Johnson,
Hugh McKiski,
Krista Watson,
**EMP:** 13
**SALES (est):** 2.1MM **Privately Held**
**SIC: 3273** Ready-mixed concrete

### (G-18105)
### ROCHELLE FOODS LLC
1001 S Main St (61068-2190)
**PHONE**.................................815 562-4141
Paul Hardcastel, *Safety Dir*
Eric Van Hise, *Materials Mgr*
Mark Montieth, *Plant Engr*
Jennifer Hilkin, *Controller*
Scott Morrison, *Human Res Dir*
**EMP:** 700
**SALES (est):** 93.4MM
**SALES (corp-wide):** 9.5B **Publicly Held**
**SIC: 2013** 2011 Sausages & other prepared meats; meat packing plants
**PA:** Hormel Foods Corporation
1 Hormel Pl
Austin MN 55912
507 437-5611

### (G-18106)
### ROCHELLE NEWSPAPERS INC (HQ)
Also Called: Rochelle News Leader
211 E Il Route 38 (61068-1183)
P.O. Box 46 (61068-0046)
**PHONE**.................................815 562-2061
John C Tompkins, *President*
Eric Chalus, *Editor*
Michael Tompkins, *Vice Pres*
Pat Duffy, *Sales Mgr*
Patrick Duffy, *Sales Mgr*
**EMP:** 50 **EST:** 1933
**SQ FT:** 7,500
**SALES (est):** 28.3MM **Privately Held**
**WEB:** www.rochellenewsleader.com
**SIC: 2711** 2721 Newspapers: publishing only, not printed on site; periodicals: publishing only

### (G-18107)
### ROCHELLE NEWSPAPERS INC
Also Called: Rochelle News Leader
211 E State Route 38 (61068-1183)
**PHONE**.................................815 562-4171
John Thompkins, *CEO*
**EMP:** 30 **Privately Held**
**WEB:** www.rochellenewsleader.com
**SIC: 2711** Newspapers, publishing & printing
**HQ:** Rochelle Newspapers Inc
211 E Il Route 38
Rochelle IL 61068
815 562-2061

### (G-18108)
### ROCHELLE VAULT CO
2119 S Il Route 251 (61068-9721)
P.O. Box 25 (61068-0025)
**PHONE**.................................815 562-6484
**Fax:** 815 562-8227
David Williams, *President*
David Wiliams, *President*
Margarite Allison, *Corp Secy*
Thomas Johnson, *Vice Pres*
Nancy Kranbuhl, *Admin Sec*
**EMP:** 5 **EST:** 1948
**SQ FT:** 5,000
**SALES (est):** 541.3K **Privately Held**
**SIC: 1711** 3272 Septic system construction; concrete products

### (G-18109)
### SILGAN CONTAINERS LLC
400 N 15th St (61068-1272)
**PHONE**.................................815 562-1250
**Fax:** 815 562-6218
Terry Cooper, *Plant Mgr*
**EMP:** 80
**SALES (corp-wide):** 3.6B **Publicly Held**
**SIC: 3411** Metal cans
**HQ:** Silgan Containers Llc
21800 Oxnard St Ste 600
Woodland Hills CA 91367
818 710-3700

### (G-18110)
### SOUTHEAST WOOD TREATING INC
Also Called: Idaho Timber
300 E Avenue G (61068-3517)
**PHONE**.................................815 562-5007
Belinda Seaton, *Manager*
**EMP:** 10
**SALES (corp-wide):** 115.9MM **Privately Held**
**WEB:** www.southeastwoodtreating.com
**SIC: 2421** 2491 5031 Lumber: rough, sawed or planed; structural lumber & timber, treated wood; lumber: rough, dressed & finished
**PA:** Southeast Wood Treating, Inc.
3077 Carter Hill Rd
Montgomery AL 36111
321 631-1003

### (G-18111)
### T M T INDUSTRIES INC
770 Wiscold Dr (61068-8502)
**PHONE**.................................815 562-0111
**Fax:** 815 562-8914
Thomas Takach, *President*
Marie Takach, *Corp Secy*
**EMP:** 30
**SQ FT:** 20,000
**SALES (est):** 1.4MM **Privately Held**
**WEB:** www.tmtind.com
**SIC: 3471** 3544 Polishing, metals or formed products; chromium plating of metals or formed products; special dies, tools, jigs & fixtures

### (G-18112)
### TRANSWORLD PLASTIC FILMS INC
150 N 15th St (61068-1218)
**PHONE**.................................815 561-7117
Ronald Mounts, *President*
Josephine Mounts, *President*
Joseph Burke, *Plant Mgr*
Kimberly McGee, *Manager*
Toribia Mounts, *Admin Mgr*
▼ **EMP:** 10
**SQ FT:** 29,500
**SALES (est):** 2.6MM **Privately Held**
**SIC: 3081** Unsupported plastics film & sheet

### (G-18113)
### U S SILICA COMPANY
Also Called: Coated Sand Solutions
1951 Steward Rd (61068-9508)
**PHONE**.................................815 562-7336
Sara Renner, *Branch Mgr*
**EMP:** 44
**SALES (corp-wide):** 559.6MM **Publicly Held**
**SIC: 1446** Silica sand mining
**HQ:** U. S. Silica Company
8490 Progress Dr Ste 300
Frederick MD 21701
301 682-0600

## Rochester
### *Sangamon County*

### (G-18114)
### ACM PUBLISHING
Also Called: Antiques & Crafts Monthly, The
5378 Possum Trot Rd (62563-8312)
**PHONE**.................................217 498-7500
Robert Ley, *Owner*
**EMP:** 5
**SALES (est):** 210K **Privately Held**
**SIC: 2721** 2711 Periodicals; newspapers

### (G-18115)
### APPLIANCE INFORMATION AND REPR
Also Called: A I R
10190 Buckhart Rd (62563)
P.O. Box 1150, Springfield (62705-1150)
**PHONE**.................................217 698-8858
Michael Smith, *President*
**EMP:** 3
**SALES (est):** 72K **Privately Held**
**WEB:** www.a-i-r-inc.com
**SIC: 3694** Battery cable wiring sets for internal combustion engines

### (G-18116)
### COE EQUIPMENT INC
5953 Cherry St (62563-8078)
**PHONE**.................................217 498-7200
Marty Coe, *President*
Debra Coe, *Corp Secy*
Scott Ostrowski, *Sales Mgr*
Brad Franklin, *Sales Staff*
Lenny Gall, *Marketing Staff*
**EMP:** 4
**SALES (est):** 750K **Privately Held**
**SIC: 5084** 7699 3589 Industrial machinery & equipment; sewer cleaning & rodding; sewer cleaning equipment, power

### (G-18117)
### EDWIN WALDMIRE & VIRGINIA
Also Called: Cardinal Hill Candles & Crafts
Hc 2 (62563)
**PHONE**.................................217 498-9375
**Fax:** 217 498-8275
Arlene S Waldmire, *Partner*
Edwin S Waldmire, *Partner*
Virginia Waldmire, *Partner*
**EMP:** 4
**SALES (est):** 422.4K **Privately Held**
**SIC: 3944** 5999 Craft & hobby kits & sets; candle shops

### (G-18118)
### ILL DEPT NATURAL RESOURCES
Also Called: Sangchris Lake State Park
9898 Cascade Rd (62563-6048)
**PHONE**.................................217 498-9208
**Fax:** 217 498-8476
Steven Kerry, *Manager*
**EMP:** 6 **Privately Held**
**WEB:** www.il.gov
**SIC: 9512** 2531 Land, mineral & wildlife conservation; ; picnic tables or benches, park
**HQ:** Illinois Department Of Natural Resources
1 Natural Resources Way # 100
Springfield IL 62702
217 782-6302

### (G-18119)
### LEGACY VULCAN LLC
Also Called: Rochester Sand & Gravel
1200 Jostes Rd (62563-8421)
**PHONE**.................................217 498-7263
Rob McMahan, *Principal*
Monica Colvin, *Sales Executive*
**EMP:** 22
**SALES (corp-wide):** 3.5B **Publicly Held**
**WEB:** www.vulcanmaterials.com
**SIC: 1442** Construction sand & gravel
**HQ:** Legacy Vulcan, Llc
1200 Urban Center Dr
Vestavia AL 35242
205 298-3000

# Rock Falls - Whiteside County (G-18146)

**(G-18120)**
**METRO CABINET REFINISHERS**
7032 Ramblewood Dr (62563-9768)
PHONE..............................217 498-7174
EMP: 3
SALES (est): 275K  Privately Held
SIC: 2434  Wood kitchen cabinets

**(G-18121)**
**SANGAMON VALLEY SAND & GRAVEL**
102 Maple Ln (62563-9527)
PHONE..............................217 498-7189
Fax: 217 498-9377
Dave Kilnard, *President*
EMP: 4 EST: 1973
SALES (est): 283.4K  Privately Held
SIC: 1442  Construction sand & gravel

**(G-18122)**
**TAILORED PRINTING  INC**
4855 Sage Rd (62563-9485)
PHONE..............................217 522-6287
Kevin J Slot, *President*
Evelyn Slot, *CFO*
EMP: 4
SALES (est): 533.8K  Privately Held
SIC: 2759  7389  Commercial printing; brokers' services

**(G-18123)**
**WALNUT ST WINERY PLUS SAUNAS**
309 S Walnut St (62563-9703)
PHONE..............................217 498-9800
Loren Shanle, *Owner*
EMP: 7
SALES (est): 572.6K  Privately Held
SIC: 2084  Wines, brandy & brandy spirits

## Rock City
### *Stephenson County*

**(G-18124)**
**BERNER FOOD & BEVERAGE LLC**
10010 N Rock City Rd (61070-9515)
PHONE..............................815 865-5136
EMP: 50
SALES (corp-wide): 121.9MM  Privately Held
WEB: www.bernerfoods.com
SIC: 2022  2026  Cheese, natural & processed; fluid milk
PA: Berner Food & Beverage, Llc
   2034 E Factory Rd
   Dakota IL 61018
   815 563-4222

**(G-18125)**
**DEVANSOY INC**
10010 N Rock City Rd (61070-9515)
PHONE..............................712 792-9665
Elmer Schettler, *President*
John Ranson, *CFO*
EMP: 5
SQ FT: 5,000
SALES (est): 670K  Privately Held
WEB: www.devansoy.com
SIC: 2075  Soybean powder

## Rock Falls
### *Whiteside County*

**(G-18126)**
**BELT-WAY SCALES  INC**
1 Beltway Rd (61071-3169)
PHONE..............................815 625-5573
Christopher McCoy, *President*
Colony Linville, *Opers Mgr*
Doran Dockstader, *Engineer*
Dockstader Doran, *Engineer*
Michael Murphy, *Sales Dir*
EMP: 50
SQ FT: 16,000
SALES (est): 9.5MM  Privately Held
WEB: www.beltwayscales.com
SIC: 3596  Industrial scales

**(G-18127)**
**BIMBO BAKERIES USA  INC**
1204 12th Ave (61071-2601)
PHONE..............................815 626-6797
Groups Bcelery, *Principal*
EMP: 76
SALES (corp-wide): 12.3B  Privately Held
SIC: 2051  Bread, cake & related products
HQ: Bimbo Bakeries Usa, Inc
   255 Business Center Dr # 200
   Horsham PA 19044
   215 347-5500

**(G-18128)**
**CHAMPION CHISEL WORKS  INC**
804 E 18th St (61071-2128)
PHONE..............................815 535-0647
Fax: 815 622-6023
Bradley J Schreiner, *President*
Joey Cogdell, *Regl Sales Mgr*
Dave Mammosser, *Regl Sales Mgr*
James Wike, *Regl Sales Mgr*
Sheila Schreiner, *Sales Staff*
▲ EMP: 11
SALES (est): 3.1MM  Privately Held
WEB: www.championchisel.com
SIC: 3545  3546  5072  Machine tool accessories; power-driven handtools; hardware

**(G-18129)**
**CHAS O LARSON CO**
Also Called: Larson Hardware Manufacturing
2602 E Rock Falls Rd (61071-3712)
PHONE..............................815 625-0503
Fax: 815 625-8786
Richard Larson, *President*
John Larson, *Vice Pres*
Charles Phillips, *Vice Pres*
EMP: 30
SQ FT: 69,000
SALES (est): 6MM  Privately Held
SIC: 3496  3452  3429  Miscellaneous fabricated wire products; bolts, nuts, rivets & washers; manufactured hardware (general)

**(G-18130)**
**CUSTOM MONOGRAMMING**
206 Dixon Ave Ste D (61071-1783)
PHONE..............................815 625-9044
Fax: 815 625-5193
Barbara J Gillen, *Owner*
EMP: 2
SQ FT: 1,000
SALES: 120K  Privately Held
SIC: 2395  2396  Pleating & stitching; automotive & apparel trimmings

**(G-18131)**
**DEKALB FEEDS  INC (PA)**
Also Called: Jones and Coontz
105 Dixon Ave (61071-1776)
P.O. Box 111 (61071-0111)
PHONE..............................815 625-4546
Kelly Keaschall, *President*
James E Kieschnick, *President*
Lawrence Acton, *Business Mgr*
Thomas Peters, *Vice Pres*
Carl Wade, *Opers Staff*
EMP: 53
SQ FT: 25,000
SALES (est): 22MM  Privately Held
WEB: www.dekalbfeeds.com
SIC: 2048  Livestock feeds

**(G-18132)**
**FOLSOMS BAKERY  INC**
319 1st Ave (61071-1241)
PHONE..............................815 622-7870
Fax: 815 622-0816
Gerald Folsom Jr, *President*
EMP: 13 EST: 2001
SALES (est): 1.5MM  Privately Held
SIC: 2051  Bakery: wholesale or wholesale/retail combined

**(G-18133)**
**FRAZER MANUFACTURING CORP**
903 Industrial Park Rd (61071-3158)
P.O. Box 576, Sterling (61081-0576)
PHONE..............................815 625-5411
Fax: 815 625-5508
Rick Chaffee, *President*
EMP: 2 EST: 1956
SQ FT: 15,000
SALES (est): 600K  Privately Held
SIC: 3312  Fence posts, iron & steel

**(G-18134)**
**HEAT SEAL TOOLING CORPORATION**
300 Avenue A (61071-5111)
PHONE..............................815 626-6009
Mike A Anderson, *President*
Karen L Anderson, *Admin Sec*
EMP: 3
SALES (est): 453K  Privately Held
SIC: 3544  7389  Special dies, tools, jigs & fixtures; design services

**(G-18135)**
**HILL HOLDINGS  INC**
Also Called: Tramec Hill Fastener
1602 Mcneil Rd (61071-3200)
PHONE..............................815 625-6600
Fax: 815 625-2407
Robert W Hill, *President*
Jerry Mammosser, *Purchasing*
Gary Blake, *Sales Staff*
David Gawlik, *Sales Staff*
Marv Needleman, *Marketing Staff*
EMP: 40
SQ FT: 48,000
SALES (est): 13.5MM
SALES (corp-wide): 60MM  Privately Held
WEB: www.hillfastener.com
SIC: 3452  Nuts, metal; bolts, metal
PA: Tramec, L.L.C.
   30 Davis St
   Iola KS 66749
   620 365-6977

**(G-18136)**
**HILLS ELECTRIC MOTOR SERVICE**
305 1st Ave (61071-1241)
P.O. Box 190 (61071-0190)
PHONE..............................815 625-0305
Fax: 815 625-0494
Robert A Sandusky, *Owner*
EMP: 4
SQ FT: 5,000
SALES (est): 362.7K  Privately Held
SIC: 7694  5063  5999  Electric motor repair; motors, electric; motors, electric

**(G-18137)**
**I FORGE COMPANY  LLC**
Also Called: Illinois Forge Company
2900 E Rock Falls Rd (61071-3718)
PHONE..............................815 535-0600
Fax: 815 535-0700
Kent Paul, *CFO*
Jeffrey T Jones, *Mng Member*
Randy Donoho, *Manager*
Virginia Nutt, *Manager*
Peter Harms, *Director*
EMP: 2
SALES (est): 342.8K  Privately Held
SIC: 3462  Iron & steel forgings

**(G-18138)**
**IFH GROUP  INC (PA)**
3300 E Rock Falls Rd (61071-3708)
P.O. Box 550 (61071-0550)
PHONE..............................800 435-7003
Fax: 815 626-1438
Keith D Ellefsen, *President*
John Pope, *Vice Pres*
Tom Welton, *Design Engr Mgr*
John Nagy, *Treasurer*
James L King Jr, *Admin Sec*
▼ EMP: 100 EST: 1998
SQ FT: 106,000
SALES (est): 23.3MM  Privately Held
WEB: www.ifhgroup.com
SIC: 3594  3443  Fluid power pumps; fuel tanks (oil, gas, etc.); metal plate

**(G-18139)**
**INDUSTRIAL WELDING  INC**
805 Antec Rd (61071-2301)
P.O. Box 506 (61071-0506)
PHONE..............................815 535-9300
Paul Heiss, *CEO*
Paul Prahl, *Corp Secy*
Kent Foster, *Office Mgr*
EMP: 15
SQ FT: 16,000
SALES (est): 1.2MM  Privately Held
SIC: 7692  Welding repair

**(G-18140)**
**L & M TOOL & DIE WORKS**
803 Avenue C (61071-1856)
PHONE..............................815 625-3256
Fax: 815 625-5229
Delmar C Mc Ninch, *Owner*
EMP: 3
SALES: 80K  Privately Held
SIC: 3544  Special dies, tools, jigs & fixtures

**(G-18141)**
**L M MACHINE SHOP  INC**
803 Avenue C (61071-1856)
PHONE..............................815 625-3256
Delmar Mc Ninch, *President*
EMP: 2
SQ FT: 2,500
SALES (est): 203.6K  Privately Held
SIC: 3599  7692  7629  Machine shop, jobbing & repair; welding repair; electrical repair shops

**(G-18142)**
**METAL SPINNERS  INC**
Also Called: Rock Falls Div
802 E 11th St (61071-3157)
PHONE..............................815 625-0390
Fax: 815 625-3878
James Baumgart, *Principal*
Tom Williams, *Production*
EMP: 48
SALES (corp-wide): 50MM  Privately Held
WEB: www.metalspinners.com
SIC: 3469  3444  Spinning metal for the trade; sheet metalwork
PA: Metal Spinners, Inc.
   800 Growth Pkwy
   Angola IN 46703
   260 665-2192

**(G-18143)**
**MICRO INDUSTRIES  INC**
200 W 2nd St (61071-1294)
P.O. Box 400 (61071-0400)
PHONE..............................815 625-8000
Fax: 815 625-2000
Lance Robinson, *President*
David Gagliano, *Vice Pres*
Gloria Anderson, *Office Mgr*
EMP: 50 EST: 1959
SQ FT: 45,000
SALES (est): 9.1MM  Privately Held
WEB: www.microdiecast.com
SIC: 3364  Zinc & zinc-base alloy die-castings

**(G-18144)**
**MID-CONTINENT FASTENER INC**
1104 E 17th St (61071-3156)
PHONE..............................815 625-1081
Fax: 815 625-2990
Greg Ahsmann, *President*
▲ EMP: 8
SQ FT: 70,000
SALES (est): 1MM  Privately Held
WEB: www.midcontinentfastener.com
SIC: 3452  Bolts, nuts, rivets & washers

**(G-18145)**
**MIDWEST HARDFACING  LLC**
2505 E 4th St (61071)
P.O. Box 506 (61071-0506)
PHONE..............................815 622-9420
Mike Young, *President*
Arnie Nusbaum, *Vice Pres*
Kent Foster, *Materials Mgr*
EMP: 12
SALES (est): 2MM  Privately Held
SIC: 3599  Machine shop, jobbing & repair

**(G-18146)**
**PRODUCTS IN MOTION  INC**
804 Industrial Park Rd (61071-3157)
PHONE..............................815 213-7251
Doug Krause, *President*
Jeff Frazer, *Principal*
EMP: 3
SALES (est): 381K  Privately Held
SIC: 3462  Iron & steel forgings

# Rock Falls - Whiteside County (G-18147)

## GEOGRAPHIC SECTION

**(G-18147)**
**R&R RF INC**
1104 E 17th St (61071-3156)
PHONE...................847 669-3720
Greg Ahsmann, *President*
**EMP:** 45 **EST:** 2008
**SQ FT:** 70,000
**SALES (est):** 7.6MM **Privately Held**
**SIC:** 3444 Sheet metalwork

**(G-18148)**
**RIVERVIEW MFG HOUSE SA**
901 Regan Rd (61071-2320)
PHONE...................815 625-1459
Frank De Haan, *Owner*
**EMP:** 3
**SALES (est):** 178K **Privately Held**
**SIC:** 3999 Manufacturing industries

**(G-18149)**
**ROCK RIVER READY MIX INC**
Also Called: Rock River Sand & Gravel
24261 Prophet Rd (61071-9638)
P.O. Box 384, Dixon (61021-0384)
PHONE...................815 438-2510
Adel Moborak, *Branch Mgr*
**EMP:** 4
**SALES (corp-wide):** 6.7MM **Privately Held**
**SIC:** 1442 Construction sand & gravel; gravel mining
**PA:** Rock River Ready Mix, Inc.
2320 S Galena Ave
Dixon IL 61021
815 288-2260

**(G-18150)**
**ROTARY AIRLOCK LLC**
707 E 17th St (61071-3163)
PHONE...................800 883-8955
Fax: 815 626-5366
Hilty Chester D, *Principal*
Cem Brinckley, *Sales Mgr*
Jill Near, *Office Mgr*
Glen McClure,
Chester Hilty,
**EMP:** 20
**SQ FT:** 2,500
**SALES (est):** 6.3MM **Privately Held**
**WEB:** www.rotaryairlock.com
**SIC:** 3443 Airlocks

**(G-18151)**
**SCUBA OPTICS INC**
Also Called: Discount Eyewear
1405 8th Ave (61071-2814)
PHONE...................815 625-7272
Fax: 815 625-9735
Robert Klomann, *President*
▲ **EMP:** 7
**SQ FT:** 1,800
**SALES (est):** 560K **Privately Held**
**SIC:** 3851 Lenses, ophthalmic

**(G-18152)**
**SCUVA OPTICS INC**
1405 8th Ave (61071-2814)
PHONE...................815 625-6195
Robert Klomann, *President*
Robert Clovan, *President*
**EMP:** 7
**SALES (est):** 452.7K **Privately Held**
**SIC:** 3827 Optical instruments & lenses

**(G-18153)**
**STERLING WIRE PRODUCTS INC**
804 E 10th St (61071-1868)
P.O. Box 110 (61071-0110)
PHONE...................815 625-3015
Fax: 815 625-3218
Wayne A Moore, *President*
Hope Moore, *Corp Secy*
Gary Smith, *Manager*
**EMP:** 8
**SQ FT:** 12,000
**SALES:** 1.4MM **Privately Held**
**SIC:** 3496 Miscellaneous fabricated wire products

**(G-18154)**
**TOMPKINS ALUMINUM FOUNDRY INC**
23876 Prophet Rd (61071-9635)
PHONE...................815 438-5578
David L Tompkins, *President*
Shirley Tompkins, *Treasurer*
Dale Tompkins, *Manager*
**EMP:** 3
**SQ FT:** 8,800
**SALES:** 100K **Privately Held**
**SIC:** 3363 3369 3365 Aluminum die-castings; nonferrous foundries; aluminum foundries

**(G-18155)**
**TONER TECH PLUS**
1304 Lincoln St (61071-1428)
PHONE...................815 625-7006
Gary Campbell, *Principal*
**EMP:** 2
**SALES (est):** 200.3K **Privately Held**
**SIC:** 3861 Toners, prepared photographic (not made in chemical plants)

**(G-18156)**
**TURNROTH SIGN COMPANY INC**
Also Called: Outdoor Advertising
1207 E Rock Falls Rd (61071-3115)
PHONE...................815 625-1155
Fax: 815 625-1158
Eric Turnroth, *President*
Richard Turnroth, *Vice Pres*
Barry Cox, *Sales Staff*
Kathy Wilhite, *Manager*
**EMP:** 10
**SQ FT:** 6,800
**SALES (est):** 890K **Privately Held**
**SIC:** 3993 7312 Signs & advertising specialties; outdoor advertising services

## Rock Island
### Rock Island County

**(G-18157)**
**AD HUESING CORPORATION**
Also Called: Pepsi Cola Btlg Co Rock Island
527 37th Ave (61201-5956)
P.O. Box 6880 (61204-6880)
PHONE...................309 788-5652
Fax: 309 788-7266
Esta Helpenstell, *President*
Jim Mills, *General Mgr*
Franz Helpenstell, *Chairman*
Corey Schultz, *Senior VP*
Denise Ormsby, *Controller*
**EMP:** 90 **EST:** 1939
**SQ FT:** 25,000
**SALES (est):** 14.8MM **Privately Held**
**WEB:** www.huesing.com
**SIC:** 2086 Carbonated soft drinks, bottled & canned

**(G-18158)**
**AFS CLASSICO LLC**
Also Called: Mama Bosso Pizza
507 34th Ave (61201-5948)
PHONE...................309 786-8833
Fax: 309 786-3328
Scott Florence, *President*
Doug Passini, *Sales Dir*
**EMP:** 50
**SALES (est):** 7MM **Privately Held**
**SIC:** 2038 Pizza, frozen

**(G-18159)**
**ALM POSITIONERS INC**
8080 Centennial Expy (61201-7316)
PHONE...................309 787-6200
Kevin Toft, *President*
Joshua Clare, *Principal*
Mark Ross, *Principal*
**EMP:** 5
**SALES (est):** 724K **Privately Held**
**SIC:** 3544 Welding positioners (jigs)

**(G-18160)**
**B & B MACHINE INC**
1221 2nd Ave (61201-8501)
PHONE...................309 786-3279
Chris Begyn, *President*
**EMP:** 8
**SALES (est):** 890K **Privately Held**
**WEB:** www.bandbmachine.com
**SIC:** 3541 Home workshop machine tools, metalworking

**(G-18161)**
**BEARDSLEY PRINTERY INC**
1103 51st Ave (61201-6858)
PHONE...................309 788-4041
Fax: 309 788-4057
Charles D Van Blair, *President*
Loretta Van Blair, *Admin Sec*
**EMP:** 4 **EST:** 1967
**SQ FT:** 3,600
**SALES (est):** 400K **Privately Held**
**SIC:** 2752 Commercial printing, offset; letters, circular or form: lithographed

**(G-18162)**
**BEDDING GROUP INC (PA)**
Also Called: Bedding Group, The
2350 5th St (61201-4021)
PHONE...................309 788-0401
Jeffrey Sherman, *President*
J R Rath, *Purchasing*
Darren Sodikoff, *VP Sales*
Jerry Reese, *Sales Executive*
Dave Horst, *Executive*
▲ **EMP:** 50 **EST:** 1989
**SQ FT:** 80,000
**SALES (est):** 17MM **Privately Held**
**WEB:** www.thebeddinggroup.com
**SIC:** 2515 Mattresses, innerspring or box spring

**(G-18163)**
**BERGE PLATING WORKS INC (PA)**
Also Called: Chrome Shop The
617 25th Ave (61201-5254)
PHONE...................309 788-2831
Fax: 309 794-2111
Douglas Matheson, *President*
Doug Mathason, *General Mgr*
Mike Penry, *Vice Pres*
Victor J Jackson, *Manager*
John P Matheson, *Shareholder*
**EMP:** 8
**SQ FT:** 10,600
**SALES (est):** 1.4MM **Privately Held**
**SIC:** 3471 Electroplating of metals or formed products

**(G-18164)**
**BEUTEL CORPORATION (PA)**
Also Called: Cambridge Monument Co
1800 11th Ave (61201-4310)
P.O. Box 4006 (61204-4006)
PHONE...................309 786-8134
Fax: 309 786-8400
Louis W Beutel, *President*
Mary Rita Beutel, *Vice Pres*
**EMP:** 5
**SALES (est):** 1MM **Privately Held**
**SIC:** 5999 3281 Monuments, finished to custom order; cut stone & stone products

**(G-18165)**
**BOETJE FOODS INC**
2736 12th St (61201-5330)
PHONE...................309 788-4352
Fax: 309 788-4365
Robert F Kropp, *President*
Dorothy Kropp, *Corp Secy*
Will Kropp, *Manager*
**EMP:** 5
**SQ FT:** 1,200
**SALES (est):** 260K **Privately Held**
**SIC:** 2035 Mustard, prepared (wet)

**(G-18166)**
**BRIAN KINNEY**
1529 28th St (61201-3724)
PHONE...................309 206-4219
Brian M Kinney, *Principal*
**EMP:** 3
**SALES (est):** 164.6K **Privately Held**
**SIC:** 2411 Logging

**(G-18167)**
**COCA-COLA REFRESHMENTS USA INC**
4415 85th Ave W (61201-7679)
PHONE...................309 787-1700
Tom Walker, *Manager*
**EMP:** 41
**SALES (corp-wide):** 41.8B **Publicly Held**
**WEB:** www.cokecce.com
**SIC:** 2086 Bottled & canned soft drinks
**HQ:** Coca-Cola Refreshments Usa, Inc.
2500 Windy Ridge Pkwy Se
Atlanta GA 30339
770 989-3000

**(G-18168)**
**COPE PLASTICS INC**
8110 42nd St W (61201-7325)
PHONE...................309 787-4465
Fax: 309 787-4466
Steve Riexinger, *Principal*
Diana Soliz, *Asst Mgr*
**EMP:** 6
**SQ FT:** 10,000
**SALES (corp-wide):** 239.4MM **Privately Held**
**WEB:** www.copeplastics.com
**SIC:** 5162 2821 Plastics materials; plastics materials & resins
**PA:** Cope Plastics, Inc.
4441 Indl Dr
Alton IL 62002
618 466-0221

**(G-18169)**
**CRAWFORD HEATING & COOLING CO**
Also Called: Crawford Company
1306 Mill St (61201-3266)
PHONE...................309 788-4573
Fax: 309 788-4691
Robert B Frink Jr, *President*
Ian A Frank, *Admin Sec*
**EMP:** 86 **EST:** 1962
**SALES (est):** 40.7MM **Privately Held**
**SIC:** 1711 1761 3444 Plumbing, heating, air-conditioning contractors; heating & air conditioning contractors; ventilation & duct work contractor; sheet metalwork; ducts, sheet metal

**(G-18170)**
**CUMMINS DIST HOLDCO INC**
Also Called: Cummins Great Plains Diesel
7820 42nd St W (61201-7319)
PHONE...................309 787-4300
Fax: 309 787-4397
Dick Dearborn, *Manager*
**EMP:** 22
**SALES (corp-wide):** 17.5B **Publicly Held**
**SIC:** 5084 7538 3519 Engines & parts, air-cooled; truck engine repair, except industrial; internal combustion engines
**HQ:** Cummins Distribution Holdco Inc.
500 Jackson St
Columbus IN 47201
812 377-5000

**(G-18171)**
**CUMMINS INC**
7820 42nd St W (61201-7319)
PHONE...................309 787-4300
Roy Magnuson, *General Mgr*
Rick Verkler, *General Mgr*
Richard Dearborn, *Branch Mgr*
**EMP:** 20
**SALES (corp-wide):** 17.5B **Publicly Held**
**WEB:** www.cummins.com
**SIC:** 3519 Internal combustion engines
**PA:** Cummins Inc.
500 Jackson St
Columbus IN 47201
812 377-5000

**(G-18172)**
**DEELONE DISTRIBUTING INC**
1419 9th St (61201-3431)
PHONE...................309 788-1444
Lc Dawson, *President*
**EMP:** 2
**SALES:** 405K **Privately Held**
**SIC:** 2299 Textile goods

**(G-18173)**
**DELS METAL CO**
1605 1st St (61201-3250)
PHONE...................309 788-1993
Fax: 309 788-9762
Wanda Schumacher, *President*
Amadeo Diaz, *Vice Pres*
Del Schumacher, *Sales Mgr*
**EMP:** 16
**SALES (est):** 3MM **Privately Held**
**SIC:** 3341 5093 4953 Secondary nonferrous metals; metal scrap & waste materials; recycling, waste materials

## Rock Island - Rock Island County (G-18199)

**(G-18174)**
**DEXTON ENTERPRISES**
1324 2nd St  (61201-3224)
PHONE..................................309 788-1881
Fax: 309 788-1902
Dave Thomas, *President*
June McKeag, *Controller*
**EMP:** 8
**SQ FT:** 168,000
**SALES (est):** 1.4MM  **Privately Held**
**SIC: 2448**  2653  2441  Pallets, wood & metal combination; skids, wood & metal combination; corrugated & solid fiber boxes; nailed wood boxes & shook

**(G-18175)**
**DIAMOND ICIC CORPORATION**
916 21st St  (61201-2765)
P.O. Box 4542  (61204-4542)
PHONE..................................309 269-8652
Angela Johnson, *President*
**EMP:** 50
**SALES (est):** 2.4MM  **Privately Held**
**SIC: 1499**  7011  7389  5094  Gemstone & industrial diamond mining; casino hotel; apparel designers, commercial; jewelry & precious stones

**(G-18176)**
**ESSILOR LABORATORIES AMER INC**
Also Called: Customeyes
4470 48th Avenue Ct  (61201-9213)
PHONE..................................309 787-2727
Robert Kane, *President*
**EMP:** 50
**SALES (corp-wide):** 938.9MM  **Privately Held**
**SIC: 3851**  Eyeglasses, lenses & frames
**HQ:** Essilor Laboratories Of America, Inc.
13515 N Stemmons Fwy
Dallas TX 75234
972 241-4141

**(G-18177)**
**GRAY MACHINE & WELDING INC**
710 30th Ave  (61201-5269)
PHONE..................................309 788-2501
Fax: 309 788-2563
Henry Gray, *President*
Lois Gray, *Corp Secy*
Martin Gray, *Vice Pres*
**EMP:** 10
**SQ FT:** 11,000
**SALES (est):** 1.9MM  **Privately Held**
**SIC: 3599**  3714  Machine shop, jobbing & repair; motor vehicle transmissions, drive assemblies & parts

**(G-18178)**
**HABEGGER CORPORATION**
520 2nd St  (61201-8212)
PHONE..................................309 793-7172
Fax: 309 793-7710
Brett Molfberry, *Branch Mgr*
**EMP:** 15
**SALES (corp-wide):** 92.8MM  **Privately Held**
**SIC: 5075**  3585  1711  Warm air heating equipment & supplies; heating equipment, complete; warm air heating & air conditioning contractor
**PA:** The Habegger Corporation
4995 Winton Rd
Cincinnati OH 45232
513 853-6644

**(G-18179)**
**HAGGERTY CORPORATION**
520 2nd St  (61201-8212)
PHONE..................................309 793-4328
Brett Molfberry, *Manager*
**EMP:** 5
**SALES (est):** 214.8K  **Privately Held**
**SIC: 3585**  5075  Heating equipment, complete; warm air heating equipment & supplies

**(G-18180)**
**HAYNES EXPRESS  INC**
Also Called: Haynes Motor Express
2000 5th St  (61201-4017)
PHONE..................................309 793-6080
Fax: 309 793-6090
Teresa Duffek, *Principal*
**EMP:** 2
**SALES (est):** 282.1K  **Privately Held**
**SIC: 3715**  Truck trailers

**(G-18181)**
**HERMANS  INC**
Also Called: Herman's World of Embroidery
2820 46th Ave  (61201-6948)
P.O. Box 4748  (61204-4748)
PHONE..................................309 206-4892
Fax: 309 786-8296
Gary S Segal, *President*
Judith T Stroud, *Vice Pres*
Donn Stroud, *CFO*
Teresa Devotour, *Manager*
▲ **EMP:** 24 **EST:** 1952
**SQ FT:** 43,000
**SALES (est):** 3MM  **Privately Held**
**WEB:** www.hhsink.com
**SIC: 2395**  5137  5136  Embroidery & art needlework; sportswear, women's & children's; underwear: women's, children's & infants'; hosiery: women's, children's & infants'; sportswear, men's & boys'; underwear, men's & boys'; hosiery, men's & boys'

**(G-18182)**
**HONEYWELL SAFETY PDTS USA INC**
101 13th Ave  (61201-3207)
PHONE..................................309 786-7741
Fax: 309 786-6923
Afshin Enshaie, *Vice Pres*
Glenn Smith, *Engineer*
Randy Peters, *Plant Engr*
Dale Pogar, *Controller*
Ban Hochstatter, *Human Res Dir*
**EMP:** 125
**SALES (corp-wide):** 39.3B  **Publicly Held**
**WEB:** www.nspusa.com
**SIC: 3021**  8748  Rubber & plastics footwear; business consulting
**HQ:** Honeywell Safety Products Usa, Inc.
900 Douglas Pike
Smithfield RI 02917
401 233-0333

**(G-18183)**
**ILLINOIS OIL PRODUCTS INC**
2715 36th St  (61201-5642)
PHONE..................................309 788-1896
Fax: 309 786-4472
Robert Jackson, *President*
Wayne Thompson, *Asst Treas*
**EMP:** 16 **EST:** 1945
**SQ FT:** 165,000
**SALES (est):** 2.8MM  **Privately Held**
**WEB:** www.illinoisoilproducts.com
**SIC: 2992**  2899  5084  Oils & greases, blending & compounding; antifreeze compounds; industrial machinery & equipment

**(G-18184)**
**INPRO/SEAL LLC**
4221 81st Ave W  (61201-7336)
PHONE..................................309 787-8940
Fax: 309 787-6114
David C Orlowski, *CEO*
Paul Christieson, *District Mgr*
Mark Lee, *Vice Pres*
Stacy Holland, *CFO*
Brandon Christiansen, *Controller*
**EMP:** 135 **EST:** 1966
**SALES (est):** 52.3MM
**SALES (corp-wide):** 6.7B  **Publicly Held**
**SIC: 5085**  3053  Bearings; gaskets, packing & sealing devices
**HQ:** Waukesha Bearings Corporation
W231n2811 Roundy Cir E
Pewaukee WI 53072
262 506-3000

**(G-18185)**
**JC AUTOMATION INC**
Also Called: Hawk Technology
8072 Centennial Expy  (61201-7316)
PHONE..................................309 270-7000
Joshua Clare, *President*
Robert Hurlburt, *Controller*
Liz Hartman, *Human Resources*
**EMP:** 25
**SALES (est):** 1MM  **Privately Held**
**SIC: 3544**  Special dies, tools, jigs & fixtures

**(G-18186)**
**LIBERTY DIVERSIFIED INTL INC**
Also Called: Miller Container
3402 78th Ave W  (61201-7331)
PHONE..................................309 787-6161
**EMP:** 250
**SALES (corp-wide):** 607.8MM  **Privately Held**
**SIC: 2653**  Boxes, corrugated: made from purchased materials
**PA:** Liberty Diversified International, Inc.
5600 Highway 169 N
New Hope MN 55428
763 536-6600

**(G-18187)**
**MANDUS GROUP LTD**
2408 4th Ave  (61201-9007)
PHONE..................................309 786-1507
Kevin M Jansen, *President*
Fred Jansen, *Principal*
Kyle Jensen, *Principal*
Jerry Dykes, *Program Mgr*
**EMP:** 15 **EST:** 1999
**SQ FT:** 2,500
**SALES (est):** 1.7MM  **Privately Held**
**WEB:** www.mandusgroup.com
**SIC: 8742**  3594  Foreign trade consultant; pumps, hydraulic power transfer

**(G-18188)**
**MENASHA PACKAGING COMPANY  LLC**
7800 14th St W  (61201-7402)
PHONE..................................309 787-1747
**EMP:** 300
**SALES (corp-wide):** 1.6B  **Privately Held**
**SIC: 2653**  Display items, corrugated: made from purchased materials
**HQ:** Menasha Packaging Company, Llc
1645 Bergstrom Rd
Neenah WI 54956
920 751-1000

**(G-18189)**
**METAL SALES MANUFACTURING CORP**
8111 29th St W  (61201-7674)
PHONE..................................309 787-1200
Fax: 309 787-1833
John Hoffman, *Prdtn Mgr*
Virgil Carol, *Manager*
**EMP:** 40
**SALES (corp-wide):** 336.9MM  **Privately Held**
**SIC: 3444**  Siding, sheet metal
**HQ:** Metal Sales Manufacturing Corporation
545 S 3rd St Ste 200
Louisville KY 40202
502 855-4300

**(G-18190)**
**MONOXIVENT SYSTEMS INC**
1306 Mill St  (61201-3225)
PHONE..................................309 764-9605
John A Sandberg, *Principal*
Drake Devore, *Principal*
**EMP:** 3
**SALES (est):** 104.2K  **Privately Held**
**SIC: 3564**  Blowers & fans

**(G-18191)**
**PAK SOURCE INC**
690 Mill St  (61201-8200)
P.O. Box 267, Moline  (61266-0267)
PHONE..................................309 786-7374
Brenda Gillman, *President*
Rob Gillman, *Vice Pres*
▲ **EMP:** 20
**SQ FT:** 170,000
**SALES (est):** 8.8MM  **Privately Held**
**WEB:** www.paksource.com
**SIC: 5199**  2441  2448  2653  Packaging materials; nailed wood boxes & shook; wood pallets & skids; corrugated & solid fiber boxes; bags: plastic, laminated & coated

**(G-18192)**
**PREMIUM MANUFACTURING INC**
Also Called: Evans Manufacturing
4608 78th Ave W  (61201-7309)
P.O. Box 978, Milan  (61264-0978)
PHONE..................................309 787-3882
Stephanie Acri, *President*
Deb Ryckeghem, *Marketing Mgr*
Mary Nokes, *Manager*
John Taravella, *Manager*
**EMP:** 40
**SQ FT:** 38,500
**SALES (est):** 6.7MM  **Privately Held**
**SIC: 3599**  Machine shop, jobbing & repair

**(G-18193)**
**PRINTERS MARK**
1512 4th Ave  (61201-8614)
PHONE..................................309 732-1174
Gary Weinstein, *CEO*
**EMP:** 4
**SALES (est):** 320.4K  **Privately Held**
**SIC: 2752**  Commercial printing, lithographic

**(G-18194)**
**QUAD CITY PROSTHETICS INC (PA)**
Also Called: Quad Cy Prsthetic-Orthotic Lab
4730 44th St Ste 1  (61201-7152)
PHONE..................................309 676-2276
Amit Bhanti, *CEO*
Tara Ferencik, *President*
Todd Nelson, *COO*
**EMP:** 10
**SALES (est):** 2.1MM  **Privately Held**
**SIC: 3842**  Limbs, artificial; orthopedic appliances

**(G-18195)**
**R & D CONCRETE PRODUCTS INC**
8002 31st St W  (61201-7408)
P.O. Box 1158, Milan  (61264-1158)
PHONE..................................309 787-0264
Ronald D Bjustrom, *President*
Ron Bjustrom, *President*
Angela Bjustrom, *Admin Sec*
**EMP:** 40
**SALES (est):** 17.7MM  **Privately Held**
**SIC: 3271**  Blocks, concrete: landscape or retaining wall

**(G-18196)**
**RABBIT TOOL USA INC (PA)**
105 9th St  (61201-8353)
PHONE..................................309 793-4375
O J Birkestrand, *President*
Scott Yates, *Prdtn Mgr*
**EMP:** 7
**SQ FT:** 13,000
**SALES:** 1MM  **Privately Held**
**WEB:** www.rabbittool.com
**SIC: 3541**  Machine tools, metal cutting type; pipe cutting & threading machines

**(G-18197)**
**RCM SMITH  INC**
507 34th Ave  (61201-5948)
PHONE..................................309 786-8833
Randy Smith, *President*
Chris Smith, *Vice Pres*
**EMP:** 10
**SQ FT:** 8,000
**SALES:** 690K  **Privately Held**
**SIC: 2038**  Pizza, frozen

**(G-18198)**
**RED HILL LAVA PRODUCTS  INC (PA)**
8002 31st St W  (61201-7404)
P.O. Box 925, Milan  (61264-0925)
PHONE..................................800 528-2765
Conner Bjustrom, *President*
**EMP:** 1
**SALES (est):** 232.8K  **Privately Held**
**SIC: 1411**  Volcanic rock, dimension-quarrying

**(G-18199)**
**REVIEW PRINTING CO INC**
1326 40th St  (61201-3116)
PHONE..................................309 788-7094
Fax: 309 786-6430
Michael Goodnight, *President*
**EMP:** 2 **EST:** 1955
**SALES:** 200K  **Privately Held**
**SIC: 2675**  2752  2791  2789  Die-cut paper & board; commercial printing, lithographic; typesetting; bookbinding & related work; commercial printing

# Rock Island - Rock Island County (G-18200)

**(G-18200)**
**RILCO FLUID CARE**
1320 1st St (61201-3218)
P.O. Box 5015 (61204-5015)
PHONE..................309 788-1854
Conrad Wagner, *President*
**EMP:** 50
**SALES (est):** 1.8MM  Privately Held
**SIC:** 2992  Lubricating oils & greases

**(G-18201)**
**RIVERSTONE GROUP  INC**
Also Called: General Sand & Gravel
Junction Of 280amp (61201)
PHONE..................309 787-1415
Larry Stone, *Branch Mgr*
**EMP:** 6
**SALES (corp-wide):** 3.9B  Privately Held
**WEB:** www.riverstonegrp.com
**SIC:** 1442  Sand mining
**PA:** Riverstone Group, Inc.
   1701 5th Ave
   Moline IL 61265
   309 757-8250

**(G-18202)**
**RIVERSTONE GROUP INC**
Also Called: Rock Island Ready Mixed
1603 Mill St (61201-3227)
PHONE..................309 788-9543
Richard Cox, *Superintendent*
**EMP:** 10
**SALES (corp-wide):** 4.3B  Privately Held
**WEB:** www.riverstonegrp.com
**SIC:** 3273  Ready-mixed concrete
**PA:** Riverstone Group, Inc.
   1701 5th Ave
   Moline IL 61265
   309 757-8250

**(G-18203)**
**ROCK ISLAND CANNON COMPANY**
2408 4th Ave (61201-9007)
PHONE..................309 786-1507
Kevin Jansen, *President*
Keith Jansen, *Vice Pres*
Kris Jansen, *Vice Pres*
Sam Kupresin, *Vice Pres*
**EMP:** 4
**SALES (est):** 125.1K  Privately Held
**SIC:** 3999  Models, except toy

**(G-18204)**
**STECKER GRAPHICS INC**
2215 4th Ave (61201-8903)
PHONE..................309 786-4973
Robert G Stecker, *President*
Peter Ruklic, *QC Dir*
Karla Stecker, *Office Mgr*
**EMP:** 8
**SQ FT:** 2,700
**SALES (est):** 790K  Privately Held
**SIC:** 2752  3993  Commercial printing, lithographic; signs & advertising specialties

**(G-18205)**
**STEEL WHSE QUAD CITIES LLC**
4305 81st Ave W (61201-7311)
PHONE..................309 756-1089
**Fax:** 309 756-0493
David Lerman, *CEO*
Mike Lerman, *President*
Chris Levington, *Plant Mgr*
Glen Dunteman, *Sales Mgr*
Joel Danley, *Sales Associate*
◆ **EMP:** 50
**SQ FT:** 84,000
**SALES (est):** 14.3MM
**SALES (corp-wide):** 555.8MM  Privately Held
**WEB:** www.steelwarehouse.net
**SIC:** 5051  3312  Metals service centers & offices; blast furnaces & steel mills
**PA:** Steel Warehouse Company Llc
   2722 Tucker Dr
   South Bend IN 46619
   574 236-5100

**(G-18206)**
**THER A PEDIC MIDWEST INC**
2350 5th St (61201-4088)
PHONE..................309 788-0401
**Fax:** 309 788-1252
Jeffrey Sherman, *Principal*
**EMP:** 3
**SALES (est):** 239.8K  Privately Held
**SIC:** 2515  Mattresses & bedsprings

**(G-18207)**
**TIBOR MACHINE PRODUCTS INC**
2832 5th St Ste 2 (61201-4027)
PHONE..................309 786-3052
**Fax:** 309 786-3054
Dewey Behrle, *Manager*
Doug Clark, *Manager*
Barb Vanselow, *Manager*
**EMP:** 27
**SALES (corp-wide):** 22.6MM  Privately Held
**SIC:** 3599  Machine shop, jobbing & repair
**PA:** Tibor Machine Products, Inc.
   7400 W 100th Pl
   Bridgeview IL 60455
   708 499-0017

**(G-18208)**
**TOFFEE TIME**
2510 22 1/2 Ave (61201-4634)
PHONE..................309 788-2466
Jody Schmitz, *Owner*
**EMP:** 3
**SALES:** 3K  Privately Held
**SIC:** 2064  Candy & other confectionery products

**(G-18209)**
**TRI-CITY HEAT TREAT CO  INC**
2020 5th St (61201-4090)
PHONE..................309 786-2689
**Fax:** 309 786-4352
Ronald Damewood Jr, *President*
Gary I Damewood, *Vice Pres*
Dale Phipps, *Purchasing*
Juan Escontrias, *Controller*
Scott Damewood, *Manager*
**EMP:** 56  **EST:** 1960
**SQ FT:** 52,000
**SALES (est):** 11.9MM  Privately Held
**SIC:** 3398  Metal heat treating

**(G-18210)**
**USAC AERONAUTICS RIA-JMTC**
1 Rock Islnd Arl Bldg 210 (61299-0001)
PHONE..................949 680-8167
Michael Sammon, *CEO*
▲ **EMP:** 25
**SALES (est):** 2.3MM  Privately Held
**SIC:** 3728  Aircraft parts & equipment

**(G-18211)**
**WEAR COTE INTERNATIONAL INC**
101 10th St (61201-8445)
P.O. Box 4177 (61204-4177)
PHONE..................309 793-1250
**Fax:** 309 786-6558
Jim Henry, *CEO*
Mark Henry, *COO*
Bonnie Henry, *Treasurer*
Laura Henry, *Office Mgr*
**EMP:** 25  **EST:** 1946
**SQ FT:** 38,000
**SALES (est):** 1.1MM  Privately Held
**WEB:** www.wear-cote.com
**SIC:** 3479  3471  Coating of metals & formed products; plating & polishing

## Rockbridge
### Greene County

**(G-18212)**
**ROCKBRIDGE CASTING INC**
25 State St (62081)
P.O. Box 266 (62081-0266)
PHONE..................618 753-3188
Mark C Petersen, *President*
Kurt Petersen, *Vice Pres*
Linda V Kienstra, *Admin Sec*
**EMP:** 6
**SQ FT:** 20,000
**SALES (est):** 1MM  Privately Held
**SIC:** 3363  3364  3543  3369  Aluminum die-castings; nonferrous die-castings except aluminum; industrial patterns; nonferrous foundries

## Rockdale
### Will County

**(G-18213)**
**ALLEGHENY COLOR CORPORATION**
1401 Mound Rd (60436-2859)
PHONE..................815 741-1391
**EMP:** 30
**SQ FT:** 2,000
**SALES (est):** 2.5MM
**SALES (corp-wide):** 50.7MM  Privately Held
**WEB:** www.apollocolors.com
**SIC:** 2865  2816  Color pigments, organic; inorganic pigments
**PA:** Scientific Colors, Inc.
   1401 Mound Rd
   Rockdale IL 60436
   815 741-1391

**(G-18214)**
**B M S ENTERPRISE**
1039 Railroad St Frnt (60436-8573)
PHONE..................815 730-3450
Sharon Pote, *President*
Michael Pote, *Admin Sec*
**EMP:** 4
**SALES (est):** 250K  Privately Held
**SIC:** 3599  Machine shop, jobbing & repair

**(G-18215)**
**CALGON CARBON CORPORATION**
303 Mound Rd Ste A1 (60436-2858)
PHONE..................815 741-5452
Fernando Villalphando, *Manager*
**EMP:** 5
**SALES (corp-wide):** 514.2MM  Publicly Held
**WEB:** www.calgoncarbon.com
**SIC:** 2819  Charcoal (carbon), activated
**PA:** Calgon Carbon Corporation
   3000 Gsk Dr
   Moon Township PA 15108
   412 787-6700

**(G-18216)**
**CATERPILLAR INC**
2200 Channahon Rd (60436-8562)
PHONE..................815 729-5511
Teresa Davis, *Purchasing*
Michael Enright, *Engineer*
Marek Golebiowski, *Engineer*
Mark Dethorne, *Design Engr*
Lawrence Lines, *Branch Mgr*
**EMP:** 5
**SALES (corp-wide):** 38.5B  Publicly Held
**SIC:** 3462  3519  3511  Construction or mining equipment forgings, ferrous; engines, diesel & semi-diesel or dual-fuel; gasoline engines; gas turbine generator set units, complete; hydraulic turbine generator set units, complete
**PA:** Caterpillar Inc.
   100 Ne Adams St
   Peoria IL 61629
   309 675-1000

**(G-18217)**
**CHILLIN PRODUCTS INC**
1039 Railroad St Frnt (60436-8573)
PHONE..................815 725-7253
Sharon Pote, *President*
Mike Pote, *Vice Pres*
◆ **EMP:** 3
**SALES (est):** 337.3K  Privately Held
**WEB:** www.chillinproducts.com
**SIC:** 2511  Console tables: wood

**(G-18218)**
**CONTAINER SERVICE GROUP INC**
2132 Gould Ct Unit A (60436-9545)
PHONE..................815 744-8693
John Driscoll, *President*
Tracy Driscoll, *Corp Secy*
Steven Sowski, *Vice Pres*
**EMP:** 15
**SQ FT:** 15,000
**SALES:** 3.3MM  Privately Held
**WEB:** www.containerservicegroup.com
**SIC:** 3535  Conveyors & conveying equipment

**(G-18219)**
**FERRO ASPHALT COMPANY**
2111 Moen Ave (60436-9335)
P.O. Box 156, Joliet (60434-0156)
PHONE..................815 744-6633
John Ferro, *President*
Richard Rahn, *Treasurer*
James Ferro, *Admin Sec*
**EMP:** 9
**SQ FT:** 10,000
**SALES (est):** 1.3MM  Privately Held
**SIC:** 2951  Asphalt paving mixtures & blocks

**(G-18220)**
**HOPE PALLET INC**
936 Moen Ave Ste 16 (60436-2509)
PHONE..................815 412-4606
**EMP:** 4
**SALES (est):** 377.7K  Privately Held
**SIC:** 2448  Pallets, wood & wood with metal

**(G-18221)**
**JOHNS MANVILLE CORPORATION**
2151 Channahon Rd (60436-8559)
PHONE..................815 744-1545
**Fax:** 815 741-6147
Joseph F Dionne Jr, *Principal*
John Dembowski, *Plant Mgr*
Randy Bascom, *Engineer*
Doug Kestel, *Personnel*
Randy Roth, *Sales Staff*
**EMP:** 192
**SALES (corp-wide):** 223.6B  Publicly Held
**WEB:** www.jm.com
**SIC:** 3296  Mineral wool
**HQ:** Johns Manville Corporation
   717 17th St Ste 800
   Denver CO 80202
   303 978-2000

**(G-18222)**
**JOLIET SAND AND GRAVEL COMPANY**
2509 Mound Rd (60436-9028)
PHONE..................815 741-2090
**Fax:** 815 741-1337
George L Comerford, *President*
Glen A Weeks, *Vice Pres*
Don Jickson, *Plant Mgr*
Cody Tucker, *Plant Mgr*
Mark Walsh, *Treasurer*
**EMP:** 70
**SQ FT:** 2,000
**SALES (est):** 5.5MM  Privately Held
**SIC:** 1411  1442  Limestone, dimension-quarrying; construction sand & gravel

**(G-18223)**
**KWM GUTTERMAN  INC**
795 S Larkin Ave (60436-2451)
PHONE..................815 725-9205
**Fax:** 815 725-4429
Lois Minor, *President*
Keith Minor Jr, *COO*
Kenneth W Minor Sr, *CFO*
▼ **EMP:** 48
**SQ FT:** 33,000
**SALES (est):** 12.7MM  Privately Held
**WEB:** www.kwmgutterman.com
**SIC:** 1761  3542  Sheet metalwork; machine tools, metal forming type

**(G-18224)**
**LAFARGE NORTH AMERICA INC**
2509 Mound Rd (60436-9028)
PHONE..................815 741-2090
Zachary Kistinger, *Engineer*
**EMP:** 27
**SALES (corp-wide):** 26.6B  Privately Held
**SIC:** 3241  Cement, hydraulic
**HQ:** Lafarge North America Inc.
   8700 W Bryn Mawr Ave Ll
   Chicago IL 60631
   703 480-3600

## Rockford - Winnebago County (G-18250)

### (G-18225)
**LEONARDS UNIT STEP CO**
1515 Channahon Rd (60436-9516)
PHONE..................815 744-1263
Fax: 815 744-1263
George H Buck, *President*
Thomas W Buck, *Vice Pres*
Tim Buck, *Treasurer*
Joan Buck, *Admin Sec*
EMP: 5
SQ FT: 11,000
SALES (est): 230K  Privately Held
SIC: 3272  3446  Concrete products, pre-cast; ornamental metalwork

### (G-18226)
**MC BRADY ENGINEERING INC**
Also Called: Mc Brady Exports
1251 S Larkin Ave (60436-9326)
P.O. Box 2549, Joliet (60434-2549)
PHONE..................815 744-8900
Fax: 815 744-8901
William Mc Brady, *President*
Patricia Mc Brady, *Treasurer*
Garrett W Mc Brady, *VP Sales*
Nathan Daugherty, *Office Mgr*
◆ EMP: 18
SQ FT: 19,000
SALES (est): 4.1MM  Privately Held
WEB: www.mcbradyengineering.com
SIC: 3556  Food products machinery

### (G-18227)
**MIDWEST RECYCLING CO**
2324 Mound Rd (60436-9026)
PHONE..................815 744-4922
David Kalumvy, *Vice Pres*
David Kaluzny, *Vice Pres*
EMP: 40
SALES (est): 3.4MM  Privately Held
SIC: 4953  2992  Recycling, waste materials; lubricating oils & greases

### (G-18228)
**QUATUM STRUCTURE AND DESIGN**
2145 Moen Ave Unit 2 (60436-9018)
PHONE..................815 741-0733
Dennis Tuggle, *President*
EMP: 15
SQ FT: 9,000
SALES (est): 1.1MM  Privately Held
SIC: 3993  1799  Signs & advertising specialties; sign installation & maintenance

### (G-18229)
**R & H PRODUCTS INC**
800 Moen Ave Unit 7 (60436-2698)
P.O. Box 3787, Joliet (60434-3787)
PHONE..................815 744-4110
Janice Rafac, *President*
John Hawkins, *Vice Pres*
Doug Shaughnessy, *Treasurer*
Robert Rambo, *Admin Sec*
EMP: 4
SALES (est): 430K  Privately Held
SIC: 2449  2448  2441  Rectangular boxes & crates, wood; wood pallets & skids; nailed wood boxes & shook

### (G-18230)
**REX RADIATOR AND WELDING CO**
14 Meadow Ave Unit 1 (60436-2694)
PHONE..................815 725-6655
Jerry Baker, *Manager*
EMP: 5
SALES (corp-wide): 3.4MM  Privately Held
SIC: 7539  7692  Automotive repair shops; welding repair
PA: Rex Radiator And Welding Co Inc
1440 W 38th St
Chicago IL 60609
312 421-1531

### (G-18231)
**SANDENO INC**
2115 Moen Ave (60436-9335)
PHONE..................815 730-9415
Todd Sandeno, *President*
Tamara L Hansen, *Admin Sec*
EMP: 3
SALES (est): 262.9K  Privately Held
SIC: 2951  Asphalt paving mixtures & blocks

### (G-18232)
**SCIENTIFIC COLORS  INC (PA)**
Also Called: Apollo Colors
1401 Mound Rd (60436-2859)
PHONE..................815 741-1391
Fax: 815 741-2599
David Klebine, *President*
Richard P Milord, *Corp Secy*
Michele Brant, *COO*
Larry Bykerk, *Vice Pres*
Matt McClure, *Vice Pres*
▲ EMP: 16
SQ FT: 7,000
SALES (est): 50.7MM  Privately Held
WEB: www.apollocolors.com
SIC: 2865  2816  Color pigments, organic; inorganic pigments

### (G-18233)
**SCIENTIFIC COLORS  INC**
Also Called: Apollo Colors Mfg Plant
1550 Mound Rd (60436-2800)
PHONE..................815 744-5650
Fax: 815 744-4564
Kimberly Apgar, *Purch Mgr*
Glenn Przybylski, *Engineer*
Glenn Przybhlski, *Plant Engr*
Larry Bykerk, *Sales Mgr*
Bruce Wright, *Branch Mgr*
EMP: 170
SALES (corp-wide): 50.7MM  Privately Held
WEB: www.apollocolors.com
SIC: 2893  2865  Lithographic ink; cyclic crudes & intermediates
PA: Scientific Colors, Inc.
1401 Mound Rd
Rockdale IL 60436
815 741-1391

### (G-18234)
**UIC  INC**
1225 Channahon Rd Ste 2 (60436-8570)
P.O. Box 3986, Joliet (60434-3986)
PHONE..................815 744-4477
Fax: 815 744-4696
Jerold L Armstrong, *Ch of Bd*
Waver Armstrong, *President*
Robert W Johnson, *Accounting Dir*
Stacy Chandler, *Info Tech Mgr*
Tom McClintock, *Technology*
EMP: 9
SQ FT: 28,000
SALES: 1.2MM  Privately Held
WEB: www.uicinc.com
SIC: 5049  3567  3823  Scientific instruments; distillation ovens, charcoal & coke; coulometric analyzers, industrial process type

---

### Rockford
*Winnebago County*

---

### (G-18235)
**11TH STREET EXPRESS PRTG INC**
2135 11th St (61104-7214)
PHONE..................815 968-0208
Fax: 815 968-0383
Gary Ehrhardt, *President*
EMP: 10
SQ FT: 5,000
SALES: 1.4MM  Privately Held
WEB: www.11thstreetexpress.com
SIC: 2752  2791  7334  2789  Commercial printing, offset; hand composition typesetting; photocopying & duplicating services; bookbinding & related work; die-cut paper & board

### (G-18236)
**425 MANUFACTURING**
5004 27th Ave (61109-1711)
PHONE..................815 873-7066
Tyler Thomason, *Facilities Mgr*
EMP: 3
SALES (est): 48K  Privately Held
SIC: 3999  Manufacturing industries

### (G-18237)
**A & B MACHINE SHOP**
1920 20th Ave (61104-7320)
PHONE..................815 397-0495
Fax: 815 397-5808
Roy E Baumgardt, *Partner*
Timothy F Baumgardt, *Partner*
EMP: 5
SQ FT: 3,600
SALES (est): 549.1K  Privately Held
SIC: 3599  3544  Machine shop, jobbing & repair; special dies, tools, jigs & fixtures

### (G-18238)
**A & L DRILLING INC**
1453 Hunting Woods Trl (61102-2348)
PHONE..................815 962-7538
Fax: 815 962-0340
Lewis Benjamin, *President*
Nora Benjamin, *Treasurer*
EMP: 13
SQ FT: 8,500
SALES: 500K  Privately Held
SIC: 3599  3471  Machine shop, jobbing & repair; plating & polishing

### (G-18239)
**A E ISKRA INC (PA)**
4814 American Rd (61109-2640)
PHONE..................815 874-4022
Richard Schwartz, *President*
Ivan Lisjak, *Vice Pres*
Joyce Schwartz, *Admin Sec*
▲ EMP: 3
SQ FT: 600
SALES (est): 626.5K  Privately Held
WEB: www.iskraae.com
SIC: 3621  3694  Starters, for motors; alternators, automotive

### (G-18240)
**A E ISKRA INC**
4814 American Rd (61109-2640)
PHONE..................815 874-4022
Ofelia Leal, *Manager*
EMP: 4  Privately Held
WEB: www.iskraae.com
SIC: 3694  Battery charging alternators & generators
PA: A E Iskra Inc
4814 American Rd
Rockford IL 61109

### (G-18241)
**A&B APPAREL**
1029 Broadway Frnt (61104-1433)
PHONE..................815 962-5070
EMP: 3 EST: 2010
SALES (est): 225.9K  Privately Held
SIC: 5621  5611  2844  2253  Ready-to-wear apparel, women's; men's & boys' clothing stores; perfumes & colognes; hats & headwear, knit; shoes

### (G-18242)
**A+ PRINTING CO**
Also Called: A Printing
920 2nd Ave (61104-2113)
PHONE..................815 968-8181
Richard Hein, *Partner*
Charles V Stull Jr, *Partner*
EMP: 2
SQ FT: 3,300
SALES: 250K  Privately Held
SIC: 7389  2791  2789  2752  Printers' services: folding, collating; typesetting; bookbinding & related work; commercial printing, lithographic

### (G-18243)
**A-1 LAPPING & MACHINE  INC**
539 Grable St (61109-2001)
PHONE..................815 398-1465
Fax: 815 398-1466
Gordon A Greenberg, *President*
Bruce Greenberg, *Vice Pres*
Joanne Greenberg, *Treasurer*
EMP: 12
SQ FT: 10,000
SALES (est): 1.3MM  Privately Held
SIC: 3599  Machine shop, jobbing & repair

### (G-18244)
**AARO ROLLER CORP**
4338 11th St (61109-3028)
PHONE..................815 398-7655
Fax: 815 398-7669
Ricky D Wilson, *President*
Jeffrey S Wilson, *Vice Pres*
Patricia Wilson, *Admin Sec*
EMP: 6
SQ FT: 10,000
SALES (est): 470K  Privately Held
WEB: www.aaroroller.com
SIC: 3471  Plating of metals or formed products

### (G-18245)
**ABACUS MANUFACTURING GROUP INC**
516 18th Ave (61104-5131)
PHONE..................815 654-7050
Robert Voigtlander, *President*
EMP: 4
SALES (est): 420.2K  Privately Held
SIC: 3599  Crankshafts & camshafts, machining

### (G-18246)
**ABBOTT PLASTICS & SUPPLY CO**
3302 Lonergan Dr (61109-2670)
PHONE..................815 874-8500
Fax: 815 874-6297
Robert C Nelson, *President*
Steve Forberg, *Sales Staff*
Rodney Wright, *Manager*
Cindy Wright, *Officer*
Jon Bengtson, *Administration*
EMP: 45
SQ FT: 25,000
SALES (est): 9.8MM  Privately Held
WEB: www.abbottplastics.com
SIC: 3081  3082  3089  Unsupported plastics film & sheet; unsupported plastics profile shapes; vulcanized fiber plates, sheets, rods or tubes

### (G-18247)
**ABG BAG  INC**
Also Called: Alpha Bag Group
1925 Elmwood Rd (61103-1205)
PHONE..................815 963-9525
Fax: 815 963-9585
William Bennett, *President*
Sandra Bennett, *Principal*
Dennis Sole, *Plant Mgr*
Jim Bennett, *Sales Mgr*
▲ EMP: 15
SQ FT: 20,000
SALES (est): 1.9MM  Privately Held
WEB: www.abgpackaging.com
SIC: 2393  2673  Bags & containers, except sleeping bags: textile; bags: plastic, laminated & coated

### (G-18248)
**ABLAZE WELDING & FABRICATING**
2003 Kishwaukee St (61104-5123)
PHONE..................815 965-0046
Fax: 815 965-0047
Charles Mc Clenthen, *President*
EMP: 7
SQ FT: 2,000
SALES: 303.5K  Privately Held
SIC: 7692  3443  3444  3441  Welding repair; weldments; sheet metalwork; fabricated structural metal

### (G-18249)
**ABS TOOL & MACHINE INC**
1202 20th Ave (61104-5355)
PHONE..................815 968-4630
Robert Renwick, *President*
Jacqueline Renwick, *Treasurer*
EMP: 2
SQ FT: 2,500
SALES (est): 309.5K  Privately Held
SIC: 3599  Machine shop, jobbing & repair

### (G-18250)
**ABSOLUTE GRINDING AND MFG**
2400 11th St (61104-7218)
PHONE..................815 964-1999
Fax: 815 964-9159
Gordon Rose, *President*
Vickie Blegen, *CFO*
Sue Rose, *Human Res Dir*
Roberto Delgado, *Manager*
EMP: 18

# Rockford - Winnebago County (G-18251)

SALES (est): 3.1MM **Privately Held**
WEB: www.absolute-grinding.com
SIC: 3599 Grinding castings for the trade

**(G-18251)**
**ACCELRTED MCH DESIGN ENGRG LLC**
3044 Eastrock Ct (61109-1760)
PHONE..................................815 316-6381
Mark C Tingley,
EMP: 14
SQ FT: 18,000
SALES (est): 2.1MM **Privately Held**
SIC: 8711 3569 3559 3541 Consulting engineer; robots, assembly line: industrial & commercial; pharmaceutical machinery; numerically controlled metal cutting machine tools; assembly machines, including robotic

**(G-18252)**
**ACCU CUT INC**
1617 Magnolia St (61104-5142)
PHONE..................................815 229-3525
Jason Bolen, *President*
EMP: 7
SALES (est): 1MM **Privately Held**
SIC: 3699 Linear accelerators

**(G-18253)**
**ACCUCAST INC**
5113 27th Ave (61109-1712)
P.O. Box 5232 (61125-0232)
PHONE..................................815 394-1875
Judy Cottrell, *President*
EMP: 7
SQ FT: 6,000
SALES (est): 1.2MM **Privately Held**
SIC: 3364 Zinc & zinc-base alloy die-castings

**(G-18254)**
**ACCURATE METALS ILLINOIS LLC**
2524 11th St (61104-7220)
PHONE..................................815 966-6320
William Alverson, *President*
Craig White, *General Mgr*
EMP: 18
SQ FT: 72,000
SALES (est): 3.4MM **Privately Held**
SIC: 7389 3312 Metal cutting services; structural shapes & pilings, steel

**(G-18255)**
**ACE MACHINING OF ROCKFORD INC**
3380 Forest View Rd (61109-1645)
PHONE..................................815 398-3200
Nancy Night, *President*
Richard Night, *Vice Pres*
EMP: 3
SALES (est): 356.4K **Privately Held**
SIC: 3599 Machine & other job shop work

**(G-18256)**
**ACTION TOOL & MFG INC**
5573 Sandy Hollow Rd (61109-2793)
PHONE..................................815 874-5775
Fax: 815 874-2233
Troy Gay, *President*
Merle Keller, *Corp Secy*
Eddy Kuball, *Sales Staff*
EMP: 20
SQ FT: 75,000
SALES (est): 5.8MM **Privately Held**
WEB: www.actiontool.com
SIC: 3469 3544 Metal stampings; special dies & tools

**(G-18257)**
**ADVANCED MACHINE & ENGRG CO**
2500 Latham St (61103-3972)
PHONE..................................815 962-6076
Willy J Goellner, *Ch of Bd*
Dietmar Goellner, *President*
Mike Mihajlovic, *Engineer*
David Leezer, *CFO*
Ken Davis, *Manager*
▼ EMP: 110 EST: 1966
SQ FT: 141,000
SALES (est): 18.6MM
SALES (corp-wide): 115.6MM **Privately Held**
WEB: www.goellner.com
SIC: 3599 3452 3429 3541 Machine shop, jobbing & repair; bolts, nuts, rivets & washers; manufactured hardware (general); drilling & boring machines
PA: Goellner, Inc.
    2500 Latham St
    Rockford IL 61103
    815 962-6076

**(G-18258)**
**AIM DISTRIBUTION INC**
510 18th Ave (61104-5131)
PHONE..................................815 986-2770
Fax: 815 986-2786
Mark T Kofron, *President*
Gordy Hall, *Principal*
Wendy R Morris, *Admin Sec*
EMP: 10
SQ FT: 4,800
SALES (est): 2.7MM **Privately Held**
SIC: 2621 5162 Towels, tissues & napkins: paper & stock; plastics products

**(G-18259)**
**ALLIED PRODUCTION DRILLING**
4004 Auburn St (61101-2505)
PHONE..................................815 969-0940
Donald Oldham, *President*
Terry Oldham, *Vice Pres*
Nicholas Selk, *Plant Supt*
Jennifer Eakins, *Admin Asst*
EMP: 10
SQ FT: 4,000
SALES: 620K **Privately Held**
WEB: www.apdrockford.com
SIC: 3469 Stamping metal for the trade

**(G-18260)**
**ALPHAGAGE**
5245 27th Ave (61109-1714)
PHONE..................................815 391-6400
Jack Nagus, *Ch of Bd*
James Hoard, *President*
EMP: 5
SQ FT: 12,000
SALES (est): 623.1K
SALES (corp-wide): 4.6MM **Privately Held**
WEB: www.alphagage.com
SIC: 3829 Gauges, motor vehicle: oil pressure, water temperature
PA: Janco Industrial, Inc
    5245 27th Ave
    Rockford IL
    815 399-0900

**(G-18261)**
**AMBI-DESIGN INCORPORATED**
4654 Crested Butte Trl (61114-7331)
PHONE..................................815 964-7568
Sivaraman S Sundaram, *President*
EMP: 4
SALES (est): 350K **Privately Held**
SIC: 3589 Water treatment equipment, industrial

**(G-18262)**
**AMERICAN FAS & COMPONENTS**
810 20th St (61104-3507)
PHONE..................................815 397-2698
Bob Lawlor, *Principal*
▲ EMP: 6
SALES (est): 741.6K **Privately Held**
SIC: 3965 5949 Fasteners; sewing & needlework

**(G-18263)**
**AMERICAN QUALITY MFG INC**
3519 Kishwaukee St Ste 1 (61109-2000)
PHONE..................................815 226-9301
Fax: 815 394-1016
Mark Dzurisin, *President*
Mike Moncur, *Corp Secy*
Jason Barrett, *Vice Pres*
EMP: 34
SQ FT: 11,500
SALES (est): 5.5MM **Privately Held**
WEB: www.aqmonline.com
SIC: 3599 Machine shop, jobbing & repair

**(G-18264)**
**AMJ INDUSTRIES INC**
4000 Auburn St Unit 104 (61101-2500)
P.O. Box 246, Huntley (60142-0246)
PHONE..................................815 654-9000
Arthur J Lietz, *President*
Jeffrey Lietz, *Vice Pres*
Frances L Lietz, *Admin Sec*
▲ EMP: 12
SQ FT: 100,000
SALES (est): 1.6MM **Privately Held**
WEB: www.amjimports.com
SIC: 7694 5084 Rebuilding motors, except automotive; industrial machinery & equipment

**(G-18265)**
**AMPHENOL ANTENNA SOLUTIONS INC (HQ)**
Also Called: Amphenol Antel
1300 Capital Dr (61109-3076)
PHONE..................................815 399-0001
Fax: 815 399-0156
R Adam Norwitt, *President*
Michael Willging, *General Mgr*
Elizabeth Coll, *Purch Mgr*
Huy Cao, *Engineer*
Jason Hayward, *Accountant*
◆ EMP: 130
SQ FT: 54,680
SALES (est): 33.1MM
SALES (corp-wide): 6.2B **Publicly Held**
WEB: www.antelinc.com
SIC: 3663 Antennas, transmitting & communications
PA: Amphenol Corporation
    358 Hall Ave
    Wallingford CT 06492
    203 265-8900

**(G-18266)**
**AMTECH INC**
Also Called: American Header Tool Tech
1819 9th St (61104-5324)
PHONE..................................815 962-0500
Fax: 815 962-0567
Douglas Johnson, *President*
EMP: 12
SQ FT: 7,000
SALES (est): 1.2MM **Privately Held**
SIC: 3544 Special dies, tools, jigs & fixtures

**(G-18267)**
**ANDERSON TAGE CO**
2316 7th Ave (61104-3441)
PHONE..................................815 397-3040
Fax: 815 397-3048
Glen Ekberg, *President*
Jeffery Lingel, *Opers Staff*
Jeff Lingel, *Manager*
EMP: 8 EST: 1949
SQ FT: 5,500
SALES (est): 600K **Privately Held**
SIC: 3599 Machine shop, jobbing & repair

**(G-18268)**
**ANDROCK HARDWARE CORPORATION**
711 19th St (61104-3434)
PHONE..................................815 229-1144
Fax: 815 229-1895
Mark Maffei, *President*
Julie Maffei, *Corp Secy*
Linda McHee, *Vice Pres*
EMP: 19
SQ FT: 30,000
SALES (est): 3.6MM **Privately Held**
SIC: 3496 Miscellaneous fabricated wire products

**(G-18269)**
**ARDEKIN PRECISION LLC**
1321 Capital Dr (61109-3067)
PHONE..................................815 397-1069
Ron Soave, *President*
EMP: 15 EST: 2008
SQ FT: 16,000
SALES (est): 2.2MM
SALES (corp-wide): 13.1MM **Privately Held**
WEB: www.rtma-usa.com
SIC: 3599 Machine shop, jobbing & repair
PA: Kaney Group, Llc
    1321 Capital Dr
    Rockford IL 61109
    815 986-4359

**(G-18270)**
**ARROW ENGINEERING INC**
5191 27th Ave (61109-1770)
P.O. Box 5035 (61125-0035)
PHONE..................................815 397-0862
Fax: 815 397-0868
Timothy O Hawley, *President*
Nicholas J Hawley, *Vice Pres*
Hawley Nicholas, *Opers Staff*
Steve Stroud, *Design Engr*
Bernie Simonson, *Manager*
EMP: 25
SQ FT: 8,000
SALES (est): 4.8MM **Privately Held**
WEB: www.arrow-eng.com
SIC: 3544 8711 3545 Special dies & tools; jigs & fixtures; designing: ship, boat, machine & product; machine tool accessories

**(G-18271)**
**ARTLINE SCREEN PRINTING INC**
1309 7th St (61104-4908)
PHONE..................................815 963-8125
Fax: 815 963-8126
Janet Hooker, *President*
Jason Smeltzer, *Vice Pres*
EMP: 3
SQ FT: 2,400
SALES: 150K **Privately Held**
WEB: www.artlineprinting.com
SIC: 2759 Screen printing

**(G-18272)**
**AUXITROL SA**
B V R Aero Precision
3358 N Publishers Dr (61109-6318)
PHONE..................................815 874-2471
Gary Frederick, *Manager*
EMP: 9
SALES (corp-wide): 1.9B **Publicly Held**
WEB: www.auxitrol.com
SIC: 3728 3812 Gears, aircraft power transmission; navigational systems & instruments
HQ: Auxitrol Sa
    Zac De L Echangeur
    Bourges 18000
    248 667-878

**(G-18273)**
**AWARD DESIGNS INC**
1947 N Lyford Rd Ste B (61107-2880)
PHONE..................................815 227-1264
Ken McBee, *President*
Joan Talmer, *Corp Secy*
EMP: 8
SALES (est): 930K **Privately Held**
WEB: www.awarddesigns.net
SIC: 3499 7336 Novelties & giftware, including trophies; commercial art & graphic design

**(G-18274)**
**AZIMUTH CNC INC**
5291 28th Ave (61109-1772)
PHONE..................................815 399-4433
Fax: 815 399-4491
James K Epperson, *President*
Brad Hollandsworth, *Engineer*
Andy Bergstrom, *Admin Sec*
EMP: 10
SALES (est): 1.6MM **Privately Held**
WEB: www.cadcamsystemsinc.com
SIC: 3544 3599 3728 3769 Special dies & tools; machine shop, jobbing & repair; research & dev by manuf., aircraft parts & auxiliary equip; guided missile & space vehicle parts & aux eqpt, rsch & dev

**(G-18275)**
**B & B TOOL CO**
5005 27th Ave (61109-1710)
PHONE..................................815 229-5792
Fax: 815 229-1239
Kent L Akerman, *President*
Victoria J Akerman, *Corp Secy*
Tom Heck, *Supervisor*
EMP: 20
SQ FT: 18,000

SALES (est): 3.2MM **Privately Held**
SIC: **3599** 3544 Machine & other job shop work; special dies, tools, jigs & fixtures

**(G-18276)**
**BARNES INTERNATIONAL INC (PA)**
814 Chestnut St (61102-2242)
P.O. Box 1203 (61105-1203)
PHONE..................................815 964-8661
Fax: 815 964-5074
David A Gollob, *Ch of Bd*
Marvin E Gollob, *Principal*
David K Dent, *Vice Pres*
Rick Lundy, *Vice Pres*
Dennis Donahue, *CFO*
EMP: 122 EST: 1907
SQ FT: 70,000
SALES: 35MM **Privately Held**
WEB: www.barnesintl.com
SIC: **3677** 5084 Filtration devices, electronic; metalworking machinery

**(G-18277)**
**BARRON METAL FINISHING LLC**
1350 Preston St (61102-2045)
PHONE..................................815 962-8053
Judy Barron,
Dennis Barron,
EMP: 12
SQ FT: 200
SALES: 700K **Privately Held**
SIC: **3471** Polishing, metals or formed products; buffing for the trade

**(G-18278)**
**BC MACHINE**
1704 16th Ave (61104-5451)
PHONE..................................815 962-7884
William E Coon, *Owner*
EMP: 3
SALES (est): 229.7K **Privately Held**
SIC: **3599** Machine & other job shop work

**(G-18279)**
**BEECHNER HEAT TREATING CO INC**
905 Brooke Rd (61109-1165)
PHONE..................................815 397-4314
Fax: 815 397-4426
Gary Bagwell, *President*
Barbara Bagwell, *Vice Pres*
Brian Bagwell, *Admin Sec*
EMP: 5
SQ FT: 11,250
SALES: 350K **Privately Held**
SIC: **3398** Metal heat treating

**(G-18280)**
**BERG INDUSTRIES INC**
3455 S Mulford Rd (61109-2703)
PHONE..................................815 874-1588
Fax: 815 874-1766
Michael Stroud, *President*
Mike Stroud, *Opers Mgr*
EMP: 10 EST: 1920
SQ FT: 14,000
SALES (est): 1.2MM **Privately Held**
SIC: **7359** 2394 2391 Tent & tarpaulin rental; furniture rental; awnings, fabric: made from purchased materials; tarpaulins, fabric: made from purchased materials; convertible tops, canvas or boat: from purchased materials; curtains & draperies

**(G-18281)**
**BERGSTROM CLIMATE SYSTEMS LLC (HQ)**
2390 Blackhawk Rd (61109-3605)
P.O. Box 6007 (61125-1007)
PHONE..................................815 874-7821
Jack Shaffer, *President*
David Rydell, *Mng Member*
▲ EMP: 337
SQ FT: 250,000
SALES: 277MM
SALES (corp-wide): 455.3MM **Privately Held**
SIC: **3585** Air conditioning units, complete: domestic or industrial
PA: Bergstrom Inc.
2390 Blackhawk Rd
Rockford IL 61109
815 874-7821

**(G-18282)**
**BERGSTROM ELECTRIFIED SYSTEMS**
2390 Blackhawk Rd (61109-3605)
PHONE..................................815 874-7821
J B Shaffer, *President*
EMP: 3 EST: 2015
SALES (est): 152.4K
SALES (corp-wide): 455.3MM **Privately Held**
SIC: **3531** Cabs, for construction machinery
PA: Bergstrom Inc.
2390 Blackhawk Rd
Rockford IL 61109
815 874-7821

**(G-18283)**
**BERGSTROM INC (PA)**
2390 Blackhawk Rd (61109-3605)
P.O. Box 6007 (61125-1007)
PHONE..................................815 874-7821
Fax: 815 874-2144
David Rydell, *Ch of Bd*
J B Shaffer, *President*
George Lammero, *General Mgr*
Patrick Bai, *Chairman*
Steven L Boyle, *Vice Pres*
▲ EMP: 500 EST: 1949
SQ FT: 250,000
SALES (est): 455.3MM **Privately Held**
WEB: www.bergstrominc.com
SIC: **3531** Cabs, for construction machinery

**(G-18284)**
**BERGSTROM PARTS LLC**
5910 Falcon Rd (61109-2916)
PHONE..................................815 874-7821
J B Shaffer, *President*
▲ EMP: 3 EST: 2014
SALES (est): 138.9K
SALES (corp-wide): 455.3MM **Privately Held**
SIC: **3531** Cabs, for construction machinery
PA: Bergstrom Inc.
2390 Blackhawk Rd
Rockford IL 61109
815 874-7821

**(G-18285)**
**BIOAFFINITY INC**
641 S Main St (61101-1410)
PHONE..................................815 988-5077
David Ayres, *President*
EMP: 1 EST: 2009
SQ FT: 20,000
SALES: 300K **Privately Held**
SIC: **2836** Biological products, except diagnostic

**(G-18286)**
**BLACK-JACK GROUT PUMPS INC**
4871 Hydraulic Rd (61109-7204)
PHONE..................................815 494-2904
Perry Hochkammer, *President*
EMP: 3
SQ FT: 5,000
SALES: 300K **Privately Held**
SIC: **3531** Concrete grouting equipment

**(G-18287)**
**BLAKE CO INC**
Also Called: Blake Awning
1135 Charles St (61104-1220)
PHONE..................................815 962-3852
Fax: 815 962-9558
David Blake, *President*
Jennifer Nelson, *Office Mgr*
EMP: 4
SQ FT: 10,000
SALES (est): 240K **Privately Held**
WEB: www.blakeflags.com
SIC: **2394** 5999 Awnings, fabric: made from purchased materials; awnings

**(G-18288)**
**BORING INDUSTRIES**
2219 N Central Ave (61101-2347)
PHONE..................................815 986-1172
Leanne Alwood, *President*
EMP: 16

SALES (est): 1.3MM **Privately Held**
SIC: **3599** Machine shop, jobbing & repair

**(G-18289)**
**BOURN & BOURN INC**
2500 Kishwaukee St (61104-7010)
PHONE..................................815 965-4013
Tim Helle, *President*
Brian Cluff, *Vice Pres*
Nancy Hendrick, *Purchasing*
Michael Malawski, *Project Engr*
Justin Barton, *Controller*
EMP: 130
SQ FT: 130,000
SALES (est): 10.8MM **Privately Held**
SIC: **3542** 3545 3541 Presses: forming, stamping, punching, sizing (machine tools); milling machine attachments (machine tool accessories); planers (metal cutting machine tools)

**(G-18290)**
**BOURN & KOCH INC (PA)**
2500 Kishwaukee St (61104-7010)
PHONE..................................815 965-4013
Terry Derrico, *President*
Hans Grass, *President*
Nancy Hendricks, *COO*
Brian Cluff, *Vice Pres*
Carl Eckberg, *Vice Pres*
▲ EMP: 65
SQ FT: 130,000
SALES (est): 35.8MM **Privately Held**
WEB: www.bourn-koch.com
SIC: **3541** 7699 Machine tools, metal cutting type; gear cutting & finishing machines; machine tool replacement & repair parts, metal cutting types; industrial machinery & equipment repair

**(G-18291)**
**BRYNOLF MANUFACTURING INC**
412 18th Ave (61104-5129)
PHONE..................................815 873-8878
Fax: 815 873-8898
Robert Brynolf, *CEO*
Daniel Brynolf, *President*
Carol Hall, *QC Mgr*
Ron Williams, *QC Mgr*
Chris Brynolf, *Manager*
▲ EMP: 24
SQ FT: 38,000
SALES: 6MM **Privately Held**
WEB: www.brynolfmanufacturing.com
SIC: **3452** Screws, metal

**(G-18292)**
**BUWW COVERINGS INCORPORATED (PA)**
4462 Boeing Dr (61109-2931)
PHONE..................................815 394-1985
Fax: 815 962-2897
Phil Zeilinger, *President*
Yvette Farias, *Accountant*
EMP: 26
SQ FT: 30,000
SALES (est): 5.2MM **Privately Held**
WEB: www.buww.com
SIC: **3444** Sheet metalwork

**(G-18293)**
**BWT LLC**
Also Called: Bluewater Thermal Solutions
5136 27th Ave (61109-1713)
PHONE..................................630 210-4577
Mike Lesiak, *Branch Mgr*
Larry Ford, *Manager*
Sean Gill, *Manager*
EMP: 25 **Privately Held**
SIC: **3398** Metal heat treating
HQ: Bwt Llc
201 Brookfield Pkwy
Greenville SC 29607
864 990-0050

**(G-18294)**
**C & E SPECIALTIES INC**
2530 Laude Dr (61109-1446)
PHONE..................................815 229-9230
Fax: 815 229-9231
Chad C Endsley, *President*
Jodi Hancock, *Finance*
EMP: 20
SQ FT: 18,000

SALES (est): 8.3MM **Privately Held**
SIC: **5199** 2759 Advertising specialties; screen printing

**(G-18295)**
**CAMPBELL SCIENCE CORP**
641 S Main St (61101-1410)
PHONE..................................815 962-7415
Fax: 815 966-0112
Dave Ayres, *President*
Dave Ayres, *President*
EMP: 10
SALES (est): 1.9MM **Privately Held**
SIC: **2819** Chemicals, reagent grade: refined from technical grade

**(G-18296)**
**CARLSON CAPITOL MFG CO**
Also Called: Carlson Capitol Mfg Co
2319 23rd Ave (61104-7336)
P.O. Box 6165 (61125-1165)
PHONE..................................815 398-3110
Fax: 815 398-1906
Roger W Kjellstrom, *President*
EMP: 11 EST: 1945
SQ FT: 11,900
SALES (est): 2.2MM **Privately Held**
SIC: **3469** Stamping metal for the trade

**(G-18297)**
**CARLYLE BREWING CO**
215 E State St (61104-1010)
PHONE..................................815 963-2739
Don Carlyle, *Owner*
EMP: 6
SALES (est): 396.3K **Privately Held**
WEB: www.carlylebrewing.com
SIC: **2082** Malt beverages

**(G-18298)**
**CARMONA GEAR CUTTING**
1707 Magnolia St (61104-5144)
PHONE..................................815 963-8236
Fax: 815 963-9203
Frank A Carmona, *Owner*
EMP: 5
SQ FT: 2,000
SALES: 250K **Privately Held**
SIC: **3599** 3462 Machine & other job shop work; iron & steel forgings

**(G-18299)**
**CASA DI CASTRONOVO INC**
Also Called: Castronovo's Bridal Shop
722 N Main St (61103-6904)
PHONE..................................815 962-4731
Frances Castronovo, *President*
Nino Castronovo, *Vice Pres*
EMP: 5
SQ FT: 2,500
SALES: 120K **Privately Held**
SIC: **5621** 2335 Women's specialty clothing stores; bridal shops; dress shops; ready-to-wear apparel, women's; wedding gowns & dresses

**(G-18300)**
**CDV CORP**
Also Called: Precise Punch Products Co
5085 27th Ave (61109-1710)
P.O. Box 5085 (61125-0085)
PHONE..................................815 397-3903
Fax: 815 397-3905
Gary Kiely, *President*
Horst Stuhr, *Exec VP*
EMP: 10
SQ FT: 12,800
SALES (est): 1.3MM **Privately Held**
WEB: www.cdvcorp.com
SIC: **3544** 3541 Special dies & tools; machine tools, metal cutting type

**(G-18301)**
**CELINCO INC (PA)**
Also Called: Ingram
2320 Kishwaukee St (61104-7006)
PHONE..................................815 964-2256
Celia Skrzypczak, *President*
Henry Skrzypczak, *Owner*
Henry Shrzypczak, *Vice Pres*
EMP: 8
SQ FT: 6,000

# Rockford - Winnebago County (G-18302)

SALES (est): 300K **Privately Held**
WEB: www.egd.com
SIC: **3821** 3599 3829 3471 Laboratory apparatus, except heating & measuring; machine shop, jobbing & repair; measuring & controlling devices; plating & polishing

### (G-18302)
### CELLUSUEDE PRODUCTS INC
1515 Elmwood Rd (61103-1213)
PHONE..................................815 964-8619
Fax: 815 964-7949
David Honkamp, *Principal*
Robert Yates, *Plant Mgr*
Steve Hoeppner, *CFO*
Steve Dorfman, *Controller*
Andy Honkamp, *Sales Mgr*
▲ EMP: 35 EST: 1938
SQ FT: 65,000
SALES (est): 6.8MM **Privately Held**
WEB: www.cellusuede.com
SIC: **2299** Flock (recovered textile fibers)

### (G-18303)
### CHAD MAZEIKA
Also Called: Rkfdcnc
3705 Burrmont Rd (61107-2167)
PHONE..................................815 298-8118
Chad Mazeika, *Owner*
EMP: 5
SALES (est): 302.2K **Privately Held**
SIC: **3541** 8742 Machine tools, metal cutting type; management consulting services

### (G-18304)
### CHARLES R FRONTCZAK
Also Called: E M F Y & Associates
4816 Mohawk Rd (61107-2333)
PHONE..................................224 392-4151
Charles Frontczek, *Owner*
Charles Frontczek, *Owner*
EMP: 3
SALES: 248K **Privately Held**
SIC: **3621** Motors, electric

### (G-18305)
### CHEM PROCESSING INC (PA)
Also Called: CPI
3910 Linden Oaks Dr (61109-5552)
PHONE..................................815 874-8118
Fax: 815 874-8234
Curtis E Cedarleaf, *President*
Matthew Smazik, *Director*
EMP: 65
SQ FT: 45,600
SALES (est): 12.1MM **Privately Held**
WEB: www.chemprocessing.com
SIC: **3471** 3479 Electroplating of metals or formed products; coating of metals & formed products

### (G-18306)
### CHEM PROCESSING INC
715 N Madison St (61107-3933)
PHONE..................................815 965-1037
Linda Hunt, *Branch Mgr*
EMP: 10
SALES (corp-wide): 12.1MM **Privately Held**
WEB: www.chemprocessing.com
SIC: **3471** 3479 Electroplating of metals or formed products; anodizing (plating) of metals or formed products; coating of metals & formed products
PA: Chem Processing, Inc.
3910 Linden Oaks Dr
Rockford IL 61109
815 874-8118

### (G-18307)
### CHOCOLAT BY DANIEL
211 E State St (61104-1010)
PHONE..................................815 969-7990
Daniel Nelson, *Principal*
EMP: 3
SALES (est): 176.2K **Privately Held**
SIC: **2066** Chocolate & cocoa products

### (G-18308)
### CIRCLE BORING & MACHINE CO (PA)
3161 Forest View Rd (61109-1694)
PHONE..................................815 398-4150
Fax: 815 387-0062
Kurt Ekberg, *President*
Gary French, *Principal*
John Ekberg, *Treasurer*
Roger Alfors, *Manager*
EMP: 1
SQ FT: 24,000
SALES (est): 3.8MM **Privately Held**
WEB: www.circleboring.com
SIC: **3599** Machine shop, jobbing & repair

### (G-18309)
### CIRCLE BORING & MACHINE CO
2316 7th Ave (61104-3441)
PHONE..................................815 397-3040
Glen Ekberg, *Branch Mgr*
EMP: 7
SALES (corp-wide): 3.8MM **Privately Held**
WEB: www.circleboring.com
SIC: **3599** Machine shop, jobbing & repair
PA: Circle Boring & Machine Co.
3161 Forest View Rd
Rockford IL 61109
815 398-4150

### (G-18310)
### CIRCLE CUTTING TOOLS INC
3161 Forest View Rd (61109-1641)
PHONE..................................815 398-4153
Glen Ekberg, *President*
Rich Rugg, *President*
Kurt Ekberg, *Corp Secy*
EMP: 7 EST: 1982
SQ FT: 3,600
SALES (est): 630K **Privately Held**
WEB: www.circlecuttingtools.com
SIC: **3545** 3541 Cutting tools for machine tools; machine tools, metal cutting type

### (G-18311)
### CLASS A GRINDING
3704 Samuelson Rd (61109-3238)
PHONE..................................815 874-2118
Fax: 815 931-6499
Thomas Lawson, *Owner*
EMP: 4
SQ FT: 3,000
SALES (est): 200K **Privately Held**
SIC: **3599** Grinding castings for the trade

### (G-18312)
### CLEO COMMUNICATIONS INC (PA)
Also Called: Streem & Cleo Communications
4949 Harrison Ave Ste 200 (61108-7947)
P.O. Box 15835, Loves Park (61132-5835)
PHONE..................................815 654-8110
Mahesh Rajasekharan, *CEO*
Sumit Garg, *President*
Jorge Rodriguez, *Senior VP*
Todd Enneking, *Vice Pres*
Ken Lyons, *Vice Pres*
EMP: 33
SQ FT: 11,870
SALES (est): 17.8MM **Privately Held**
SIC: **7373** 7372 Computer integrated systems design; prepackaged software

### (G-18313)
### CLINKENBEARD & ASSOCIATES INC
577 Grable St (61109-2086)
PHONE..................................815 226-0291
Fax: 815 226-1766
Ronald L Gustafson, *President*
Michael Barlow, *Vice Pres*
Karen Spencer, *QC Mgr*
Dave Hughes, *Engineer*
Kevin Knight, *Engineer*
EMP: 23 EST: 1966
SQ FT: 13,400
SALES (est): 4.8MM **Privately Held**
SIC: **3599** 3543 3369 Machine shop, jobbing & repair; industrial patterns; nonferrous foundries

### (G-18314)
### COLOR CORPORATION OF AMERICA
200 Sayre St (61104-4661)
PHONE..................................815 987-3700
Fax: 815 964-0559
Michael Brandt, *General Mgr*
Linda Coleman, *Admin Sec*
EMP: 76 EST: 1961
SQ FT: 50,000
SALES (est): 7.4MM
SALES (corp-wide): 11.8B **Publicly Held**
SIC: **2851** 2816 2821 Paints & allied products; inorganic pigments; plastics materials & resins
HQ: The Valspar Corporation
1101 S 3rd St
Minneapolis MN 55415
612 851-7000

### (G-18315)
### COLORLAB COSMETICS INC (PA)
1112 5th Ave (61104-3125)
PHONE..................................815 965-0026
Fax: 815 965-2007
Mary Swaab, *President*
Jason Buell, *Vice Pres*
Mary Olson, *Sales Dir*
Rhonda Schaffer, *Marketing Staff*
Jim Reuter, *Manager*
▲ EMP: 30
SQ FT: 18,000
SALES (est): 4MM **Privately Held**
WEB: www.colorlabcosmetics.com
SIC: **2844** Cosmetic preparations

### (G-18316)
### COMET FABRICATING & WELDING CO
5620 Falcon Rd (61109-2985)
PHONE..................................815 229-0468
Fax: 815 964-9226
Anthony J Capriola Jr, *President*
Joseph A Capriola Jr, *President*
EMP: 50 EST: 1973
SQ FT: 68,000
SALES (est): 9.1MM **Privately Held**
SIC: **7692** 3441 Welding repair; fabricated structural metal

### (G-18317)
### COMMERCIAL PRTG OF ROCKFORD
1120 2nd Ave (61104-2202)
PHONE..................................815 965-4759
Fax: 815 965-4762
Rebecca Hillburst, *President*
Darcie Powelson, *Manager*
EMP: 5 EST: 1951
SQ FT: 1,600
SALES (est): 489.7K **Privately Held**
SIC: **2752** Commercial printing, offset

### (G-18318)
### COMMUNITY CLLABRATION ACQUATIO
303 N Main St Ste 803 (61101-1049)
PHONE..................................815 316-6390
Allan Barsema, *Principal*
Dianna Hillers, *Office Mgr*
EMP: 9
SALES (est): 368.3K **Privately Held**
SIC: **7372** Prepackaged software

### (G-18319)
### COMMUNITY COLLABORATION INC
303 N Main St Ste 800 (61101-1050)
PHONE..................................815 316-4660
Steven H Burchett, *CEO*
Dianna Hillers, *Principal*
EMP: 7
SALES (est): 1.3MM **Privately Held**
SIC: **7372** Prepackaged software

### (G-18320)
### COMPAK INC
Also Called: Action Packaging
1139 Alton Ave (61109-1132)
PHONE..................................815 399-2699
Fax: 815 399-2738
Kyle Hultgren, *President*
Kathy Messink, *Treasurer*
Mark O'Neal, *Manager*
Stacey Maaske, *Info Tech Mgr*
Mary K Woollums, *Admin Sec*
EMP: 23
SQ FT: 22,000
SALES (est): 6.2MM **Privately Held**
WEB: www.compak-pkg.com
SIC: **2653** 3599 5113 Boxes, corrugated: made from purchased materials; machine shop, jobbing & repair; shipping supplies

### (G-18321)
### COMPETITION ELECTRONICS INC
3469 Precision Dr (61109-2771)
PHONE..................................815 874-8001
Fax: 815 874-8181
James Bailey, *President*
Paula Bailey, *Vice Pres*
EMP: 6
SQ FT: 4,800
SALES (est): 1MM **Privately Held**
WEB: www.competitionelectronics.com
SIC: **3625** 3823 Timing devices, electronic; industrial instrmnts msrmnt display/control process variable

### (G-18322)
### CONCENTRIC ROCKFORD INC
2222 15th St (61104-7313)
PHONE..................................815 398-4400
Andy Modzik, *Prdtn Mgr*
Ed Hebb, *Mfg Staff*
William Kivett, *Engineer*
Scott Paterson, *Engineer*
Shannon Bentley, *Sales Staff*
EMP: 130
SALES (corp-wide): 216.3MM **Privately Held**
SIC: **3594** Pumps, hydraulic power transfer
HQ: Rockford Concentric Inc
2222 15th St
Rockford IL 61104
815 398-4400

### (G-18323)
### CONTROL PANELS INC
1350 Harder Ct (61103-1118)
PHONE..................................815 654-6000
Fax: 815 654-3719
Jeanette L Thompson, *President*
James P Nance, *Corp Secy*
David L Adkins, *Vice Pres*
Michael Rehberg, *Vice Pres*
David Smith, *Vice Pres*
EMP: 13
SQ FT: 19,000
SALES: 1.9MM **Privately Held**
WEB: www.controlpanelsinc.net
SIC: **3613** 1731 8711 Control panels, electric; general electrical contractor; consulting engineer

### (G-18324)
### CORRIGAN MANUFACTURING CO (PA)
1818 Christina St (61104-5139)
PHONE..................................815 399-9326
Fax: 815 399-9510
Lyle Corrigan, *President*
Douglas Corrigan, *Vice Pres*
Joseph Corrigan, *Vice Pres*
Roger Corrigan, *Treasurer*
EMP: 12
SQ FT: 12,000
SALES (est): 1.5MM **Privately Held**
WEB: www.corriganmfg.com
SIC: **3599** Machine shop, jobbing & repair

### (G-18325)
### CROWN MACHINE INC
2707 N Main St (61103-3111)
PHONE..................................815 877-7700
Fax: 815 877-7763
Daniel J Glavin, *President*
John Peterson, *Vice Pres*
Patrick Cleaver, *Purch Mgr*
Dave Frederick, *QA Dir*
Randy Bontjes, *QC Mgr*
EMP: 30
SQ FT: 27,000
SALES (est): 5.1MM **Privately Held**
WEB: www.crownmachineinc.com
SIC: **3599** Custom machinery

### (G-18326)
### CUSTOM AP & PROMOTIONS INC
4602 E State St Ste 1 (61108-2153)
PHONE..................................815 398-9823
Michelle Phillips, *President*
EMP: 4
SQ FT: 1,000
SALES: 250K **Privately Held**
SIC: **2395** Embroidery & art needlework

# GEOGRAPHIC SECTION

Rockford - Winnebago County (G-18355)

**(G-18327)**
**CUSTOM DESIGN SERVICES & ASSOC**
220 E State St (61104-1035)
**PHONE**..........815 226-9747
Frank Dajka, *President*
**EMP:** 15
**SQ FT:** 3,400
**SALES (est):** 1MM **Privately Held**
**SIC:** 2741 8999 Technical manuals: publishing only, not printed on site; technical manual preparation

**(G-18328)**
**CUSTOM METAL PRODUCTS CORP**
Also Called: Custom Metal Products Div
1827 Broadway (61104-5409)
**PHONE**..........815 397-3306
**Fax:** 815 397-0324
Joseph P Klinck, *President*
Marilyn S Klinck, *Treasurer*
**EMP:** 30
**SQ FT:** 70,000
**SALES (est):** 5MM **Privately Held**
**WEB:** www.rockfordco.com
**SIC:** 3469 3452 Stamping metal for the trade; screws, metal

**(G-18329)**
**CYCLOPS INDUSTRIAL INC**
126 Monroe St (61101-5027)
**PHONE**..........815 962-1984
Matthew McGuire, *President*
Martha Kunz, *Treasurer*
Matt McGuyre, *Admin Sec*
**EMP:** 9
**SQ FT:** 12,000
**SALES (est):** 800K **Privately Held**
**WEB:** www.cyclops-industrial.com
**SIC:** 3648 Lighting equipment

**(G-18330)**
**D & R AUTOCHUCK INC**
5248 27th Ave (61109-1715)
**PHONE**..........815 398-9131
Tod Kreissler, *CEO*
Tammy Ward, *Office Admin*
**EMP:** 25
**SQ FT:** 10,000
**SALES (est):** 1MM **Privately Held**
**WEB:** www.drautochuck.com
**SIC:** 3599 Machine shop, jobbing & repair

**(G-18331)**
**D & R EKSTROM CARLSON CO**
5248 27th Ave (61109-1715)
**PHONE**..........815 394-1744
Todd Kreissler, *President*
**EMP:** 2 **EST:** 1997
**SALES (est):** 210K **Privately Held**
**SIC:** 3545 Machine tool accessories

**(G-18332)**
**D AND S MOLDING & DCTG INC**
2816 Kishwaukee St (61109-1019)
**PHONE**..........815 399-2734
**Fax:** 815 399-2872
Melvin Wilton, *President*
**EMP:** 5
**SQ FT:** 7,000
**SALES (est):** 764.3K **Privately Held**
**SIC:** 3089 1711 Injection molded finished plastic products; injection molding of plastics; heating & air conditioning contractors

**(G-18333)**
**DANS RUBBER STAMP & SIGNS**
1704 Burton St (61103-4515)
**PHONE**..........815 964-5603
Daniel J Madden, *President*
Raya Madden, *Corp Secy*
**EMP:** 2
**SALES (est):** 209.1K **Privately Held**
**SIC:** 3069 3993 3953 Stationers' rubber sundries; signs & advertising specialties; marking devices

**(G-18334)**
**DAR ENTERPRISES INC**
Also Called: J & J Fish
217 7th St (61104-1208)
**PHONE**..........815 961-8748
**Fax:** 815 969-7921
Darnel Watkins, *President*
**EMP:** 5
**SALES (est):** 333.8K **Privately Held**
**WEB:** www.darenterprises.com
**SIC:** 2092 Seafoods, fresh: prepared

**(G-18335)**
**DASCO PRO INC**
340 Blackhawk Park Ave (61104-5133)
**PHONE**..........815 962-3727
**Fax:** 815 962-8915
Donald D Dray, *President*
Brad Groves, *General Mgr*
Bob Rich, *General Mgr*
Bill Leber, *COO*
John R Bacher, *Vice Pres*
▲ **EMP:** 77
**SQ FT:** 220,000
**SALES (est):** 23MM **Privately Held**
**WEB:** www.dascopro.com
**SIC:** 3423 Carpenters' hand tools, except saws: levels, chisels, etc.; mechanics' hand tools

**(G-18336)**
**DATUM MACHINE WORKS INC**
2219 N Central Ave (61101-2347)
**PHONE**..........815 877-8502
Leon Wellwood, *President*
Kayleen Brown, *Office Mgr*
**EMP:** 12
**SALES (est):** 1.5MM **Privately Held**
**WEB:** www.datummw.com
**SIC:** 3599 Custom machinery

**(G-18337)**
**DAVISON CO LTD**
1812 Harlem Blvd (61103-6344)
**PHONE**..........815 966-2905
James R Davison, *Owner*
▲ **EMP:** 3
**SALES (est):** 276.5K **Privately Held**
**SIC:** 3792 Travel trailers & campers

**(G-18338)**
**DEAN FOODS COMPANY**
1126 Kilburn Ave (61101-5996)
**Fax:** 815 962-0684
George Muck, *Vice Pres*
Brett Johnson, *VP Opers*
Jim Persson, *Plant Supt*
Mary Thompson, *Foreman/Supr*
David Holcomb, *Opers-Prdtn-Mfg*
**EMP:** 100 **Publicly Held**
**WEB:** www.deanfoods.com
**SIC:** 2026 Fluid milk
**PA:** Dean Foods Company
2711 N Haskell Ave
Dallas TX 75204

**(G-18339)**
**DELTA POWER COMPANY (PA)**
4484 Boeing Dr (61109-2998)
P.O. Box 5906 (61125-0906)
**PHONE**..........815 397-6628
**Fax:** 815 397-2526
John Fulton, *President*
Gerald Lang, *Corp Secy*
Steve Ruhman, *Project Mgr*
Ed Uchno, *QC Mgr*
John Tackes, *Research*
▲ **EMP:** 75
**SQ FT:** 55,000
**SALES (est):** 15.2MM **Privately Held**
**WEB:** www.delta-power.com
**SIC:** 3492 Control valves, fluid power: hydraulic & pneumatic

**(G-18340)**
**DG DIGITAL PRINTING**
214 N Rockton Ave (61103-6645)
**PHONE**..........815 961-0000
Don Giacone, *Principal*
**EMP:** 2 **EST:** 2009
**SALES (est):** 292.3K **Privately Held**
**SIC:** 2759 Commercial printing

**(G-18341)**
**DIAL INDUSTRIES INC**
2902 Eastrock Dr (61109-1738)
P.O. Box 5246 (61125-0246)
**PHONE**..........815 397-7994
Eric Anderberg, *President*
Jeffrey M Anderberg, *Corp Secy*
Eric Anderverg, *Purchasing*
Bill Frye, *Engineer*
**EMP:** 15 **EST:** 1997
**SQ FT:** 45,000
**SALES (est):** 2.3MM **Privately Held**
**SIC:** 3599 Machine shop, jobbing & repair

**(G-18342)**
**DIAL MACHINE INC**
2902 Eastrock Dr (61109-1738)
P.O. Box 5246 (61125-0246)
**PHONE**..........815 397-6660
**Fax:** 815 397-0562
Malcolm C Anderberg, *CEO*
Jeffrey M Anderberg, *President*
Leah Anderberg, *Corp Secy*
Jeriene Gauthier, *Bookkeeper*
Eric R Anderberg, *Admin Sec*
**EMP:** 50 **EST:** 1966
**SQ FT:** 45,000
**SALES (est):** 9.6MM **Privately Held**
**WEB:** www.dialmachine.com
**SIC:** 3599 Machine shop, jobbing & repair

**(G-18343)**
**DIAMOND HEAT TREAT INC**
3691 Publishers Dr (61109-2773)
**PHONE**..........815 873-1348
**Fax:** 815 874-8764
Carl D Neiber, *President*
Bill Akre, *Vice Pres*
Bill Denning, *Vice Pres*
William Denning, *Vice Pres*
Rod Beverley, *Manager*
**EMP:** 35
**SQ FT:** 25,000
**SALES (est):** 8.9MM **Privately Held**
**SIC:** 3398 Metal heat treating

**(G-18344)**
**DIE WORLD STEEL RULE DIES**
2519 15th Ave (61108-5703)
**PHONE**..........815 399-8675
**Fax:** 815 399-8675
Lindsey Earnest, *Owner*
**EMP:** 1
**SALES (est):** 300K **Privately Held**
**SIC:** 3544 Dies, steel rule

**(G-18345)**
**DIP SEAL PLASTICS INC**
2311 23rd Ave (61104-7392)
**PHONE**..........815 398-3533
**Fax:** 815 398-0353
Jeffrey Holmgaard, *President*
Bob Remily, *Purchasing*
Becky Stein, *Manager*
**EMP:** 5
**SQ FT:** 10,000
**SALES (est):** 2MM **Privately Held**
**WEB:** www.dipseal.com
**SIC:** 2821 3443 2891 2851 Plastics materials & resins; fabricated plate work (boiler shop); adhesives & sealants; paints & allied products

**(G-18346)**
**DISPLAY LINK INC**
311 S Main St (61101-1309)
**PHONE**..........815 968-0778
**Fax:** 815 968-0781
Gary Severson, *CEO*
Fred H Ware, *Ch of Bd*
Jeffrey A Lindquist, *President*
**EMP:** 3 **EST:** 1949
**SQ FT:** 16,000
**SALES (est):** 221K **Privately Held**
**WEB:** www.displaylinkrkfd.com
**SIC:** 3993 2759 Displays & cutouts, window & lobby; screen printing

**(G-18347)**
**DIVERSIFIED MACHINING INC**
6151 Montague Rd (61102-3724)
**PHONE**..........815 316-8561
**EMP:** 3
**SALES (est):** 302.2K **Privately Held**
**SIC:** 3599 Machine shop, jobbing & repair

**(G-18348)**
**DLM MANUFACTURING INC**
919 Taylor St (61101-5859)
**PHONE**..........815 964-3800
Duntai Mathews, *President*
Steve Smith, *General Mgr*
**EMP:** 10
**SALES (est):** 1.4MM **Privately Held**
**WEB:** www.dlmmanufacturing.com
**SIC:** 2599 Restaurant furniture, wood or metal

**(G-18349)**
**DMTG NORTH AMERICA LLC**
1301 Eddy Ave (61103-3173)
**PHONE**..........815 637-8500
Kelvin Zhao, *General Mgr*
Rich Ellison, *Principal*
Mike Throgmartin, *Opers Mgr*
John Quan, *Sales Mgr*
Jack Holthaus, *Accounts Mgr*
▲ **EMP:** 4
**SALES (est):** 250K **Privately Held**
**SIC:** 3549 Metalworking machinery

**(G-18350)**
**DOLLAR EXPRESS**
4225 Charles St (61108-6230)
**PHONE**..........815 399-9719
Luann Baxter, *Principal*
**EMP:** 3
**SALES (est):** 165K **Privately Held**
**SIC:** 3643 Outlets, electric: convenience

**(G-18351)**
**DRAWING TECHNOLOGY INC**
Also Called: Dti
1550 Elmwood Rd (61103-1217)
**PHONE**..........815 877-5133
Charels Schooley, *President*
Michael Yankaitis, *Admin Sec*
▲ **EMP:** 8
**SALES (est):** 1.8MM **Privately Held**
**WEB:** www.drawingtechnology.com
**SIC:** 3549 Wiredrawing & fabricating machinery & equipment, ex. die

**(G-18352)**
**DS SERVICES OF AMERICA INC**
Also Called: Hinckley Spring
2425 Laude Dr (61109)
**PHONE**..........800 322-6272
**Fax:** 815 227-1891
Mario Pseifer, *Branch Mgr*
**EMP:** 15
**SALES (corp-wide):** 3.2B **Privately Held**
**WEB:** www.suntorywatergroup.com
**SIC:** 2086 5963 Mineral water, carbonated: packaged in cans, bottles, etc.; bottled water delivery
**HQ:** Ds Services Of America, Inc.
2300 Windy Ridge Pkwy Se 500n
Atlanta GA 30339
770 933-1400

**(G-18353)**
**DSPC COMPANY (PA)**
3939 S Central Ave (61102-4200)
**PHONE**..........815 997-1116
Christopher C De Muth, *Ch of Bd*
John Gazley, *President*
Paul Antonou, *Manager*
**EMP:** 20 **EST:** 1919
**SQ FT:** 33,000
**SALES (est):** 2.9MM **Privately Held**
**WEB:** www.demuth.com
**SIC:** 3523 3448 3535 Silo fillers & unloaders; cattle feeding, handling & watering equipment; silos, metal; conveyors & conveying equipment

**(G-18354)**
**EATON CORPORATION**
2477 Eastrock Dr Ste B (61108-8077)
**PHONE**..........815 398-6585
**Fax:** 815 398-2074
Teslik George, *Manager*
**EMP:** 217 **Privately Held**
**WEB:** www.eaton.com
**SIC:** 3625 Motor controls & accessories
**HQ:** Eaton Corporation
1000 Eaton Blvd
Cleveland OH 44122
216 523-5000

**(G-18355)**
**EATON TOOL & MACHINE INC**
4677 Stenstrom Rd (61109-2637)
P.O. Box 6850 (61125-1850)
**PHONE**..........815 874-6664
John Eaton, *President*
Danon Eaton, *Vice Pres*
**EMP:** 4

# Rockford - Winnebago County (G-18356) — GEOGRAPHIC SECTION

SQ FT: 1,100
SALES: 450K **Privately Held**
SIC: 3599 Machine shop, jobbing & repair

### (G-18356)
### ECLIPSE  INC (HQ)
Also Called: Elster Thermal Solutions
1665 Elmwood Rd  (61103-1299)
PHONE.................................815 877-3031
David M Cote, *Ch of Bd*
Timothy Lee, *General Mgr*
Katherine L Adams, *Senior VP*
Dan Mills, *VP Opers*
Thomas A Szlosek, *CFO*
◆ EMP: 64
SQ FT: 130,000
SALES: 125MM
SALES (corp-wide): 39.3B **Publicly Held**
WEB: www.eclipsenet.com
SIC: 3564  3433  3822  3823 Blowing fans; industrial or commercial; gas-oil burners, combination; gas burners, industrial; gas burner, automatic controls; flame safety controls for furnaces & boilers; temperature instruments: industrial process type; heat exchangers, condensers & components; valves & pipe fittings
PA: Honeywell International Inc.
   115 Tabor Rd
   Morris Plains NJ 07950
   973 455-2000

### (G-18357)
### ECLIPSE COMBUSTION  INC (DH)
1665 Elmwood Rd  (61103-1299)
PHONE.................................815 877-3031
Fax: 815 877-3212
Douglas Perks, *CEO*
Lachlan L Perks, *President*
Chet Allen, *Vice Pres*
Greg Bubp, *Vice Pres*
▲ EMP: 220
SQ FT: 140,000
SALES (est): 86.6MM
SALES (corp-wide): 39.3B **Publicly Held**
SIC: 3433 Gas burners, industrial; gas-oil burners, combination; oil burners, domestic or industrial
HQ: Eclipse, Inc.
   1665 Elmwood Rd
   Rockford IL 61103
   815 877-3031

### (G-18358)
### EDGEBROOK EYECARE
1603 N Alpine Rd Ste 121  (61107-1439)
PHONE.................................815 397-5959
Fax: 815 397-5540
David Nielsen, *Owner*
EMP: 10
SALES (est): 864.1K **Privately Held**
SIC: 5995  3851 Eyeglasses, prescription; lens grinding, except prescription: ophthalmic

### (G-18359)
### EGD MANUFACTURING INC
2320 Kishwaukee St  (61104-7006)
PHONE.................................815 964-2900
Fax: 815 964-2267
Henry Skrzypczak, *President*
Cecilia Skrzypczak, *Vice Pres*
EMP: 8
SQ FT: 2,200
SALES (est): 1.5MM **Privately Held**
WEB: www.egdmfg.com
SIC: 3569 Industrial shock absorbers

### (G-18360)
### EKSTROM CARLSON FABRICATING CO
Also Called: Eccofab
1204 Milford Ave  (61109-3692)
PHONE.................................815 226-1511
Fax: 815 226-9722
Gerald Bauer, *President*
John E Nelson, *Treasurer*
▲ EMP: 5
SQ FT: 10,000
SALES (est): 1MM **Privately Held**
SIC: 7692  3441  3444  3443 Welding repair; fabricated structural metal; sheet metalwork; fabricated plate work (boiler shop)

### (G-18361)
### ELAN EXPRESS  INC
3815 N Mulford Rd Ste 4  (61114-5622)
PHONE.................................815 713-1190
Gregory Denning, *President*
EMP: 30
SQ FT: 100
SALES (est): 1.8MM **Privately Held**
SIC: 3721 Aircraft

### (G-18362)
### ELECTION SYSTEMS & SFTWR LLC
Also Called: Election Services Division
929 S Alpine Rd Ste 301  (61108-3939)
PHONE.................................815 397-8144
Fax: 815 397-4299
Steve Pearson, *Vice Pres*
Gary Webber, *Manager*
Kathy Radant, *Programmer Anys*
Jason Fletcher, *Software Dev*
Fox Rhoda, *Software Dev*
EMP: 16
SQ FT: 5,500
SALES (corp-wide): 116.7MM **Privately Held**
SIC: 3571 Computers, digital, analog or hybrid
PA: Election Systems & Software Llc
   11208 John Galt Blvd
   Omaha NE 68137
   402 593-0101

### (G-18363)
### ELITE FASTENERS  INC
2005 15th St  (61104-5552)
PHONE.................................815 397-8848
Fax: 815 397-8335
John Lane, *President*
Mike Lane, *Foreman/Supr*
▲ EMP: 23
SQ FT: 20,000
SALES (est): 4.8MM **Privately Held**
SIC: 3452 Bolts, nuts, rivets & washers

### (G-18364)
### ENCHANTED SIGNS OF ROCKFORD (PA)
4626 Shropshire Dr  (61109-3224)
PHONE.................................815 874-5100
Ragina Tomzak, *Owner*
Curtis Tomzak, *Co-Owner*
Curtis Tomczak, *Technical Mgr*
EMP: 2
SALES (est): 384.7K **Privately Held**
SIC: 3993 Signs & advertising specialties

### (G-18365)
### ENGINE SOLUTIONS INC
1928 12th St  (61104-7308)
PHONE.................................815 979-2312
Greg Tucker, *President*
▲ EMP: 1
SALES (est): 282K **Privately Held**
SIC: 3714 Motor vehicle engines & parts

### (G-18366)
### ENGINERED POLYMR SOLUTIONS INC
1215 Nelson Blvd  (61104-4773)
PHONE.................................815 987-3700
Sandra Smith, *Purchasing*
James Moore, *QC Dir*
Pamela Powers, *Personnel*
Chuck Matlock, *Branch Mgr*
EMP: 50
SALES (corp-wide): 11.8B **Publicly Held**
SIC: 2295  2851 Resin or plastic coated fabrics; paints & paint additives
HQ: Engineered Polymer Solutions, Inc.
   1400 N State St
   Marengo IL 60152

### (G-18367)
### EQUILIBRIUM CONTACT CENTER INC
1410 Auburn St  (61103-4679)
PHONE.................................888 708-1405
David Levi, *President*
EMP: 3
SQ FT: 1,500
SALES (est): 71.1K **Privately Held**
SIC: 7372 Business oriented computer software

### (G-18368)
### EQUITY CONCEPTS CO INC (PA)
5758 Elaine Dr  (61108-3102)
PHONE.................................815 226-1300
Tony L Lamia, *President*
Gerald T Lamia, *Admin Sec*
EMP: 3
SQ FT: 1,550
SALES (est): 626.7K **Privately Held**
SIC: 6531  6211  7372  7349 Real estate brokers & agents; real estate managers; syndicate shares (real estate, entertainment, equip.) sales; prepackaged software; building maintenance, except repairs

### (G-18369)
### ERICKSON TOOL & MACHINE CO
1903 20th Ave  (61104-7319)
PHONE.................................815 397-2653
Fax: 815 397-2668
Chris Erickson, *President*
EMP: 5 EST: 1953
SQ FT: 6,000
SALES (est): 788.4K **Privately Held**
SIC: 3599  3544  3469 Machine shop, jobbing & repair; special dies, tools, jigs & fixtures; metal stampings

### (G-18370)
### ESTWING MANUFACTURING CO INC
2647 8th St  (61109-1190)
PHONE.................................815 397-9521
Fax: 815 397-8665
Robert H Youngren, *President*
John Ryan, *Vice Pres*
Mark Youngren, *Vice Pres*
Steve Flosi, *Foreman/Supr*
Timothy Feldmiller, *Plt & Fclts Mgr*
▲ EMP: 500
SQ FT: 110,200
SALES (est): 101.7MM **Privately Held**
WEB: www.estwing.com
SIC: 3423  3546  3545  3429 Hammers (hand tools); axes & hatchets; garden & farm tools, including shovels; power-driven handtools; machine tool accessories; manufactured hardware (general); cutlery; saw blades & handsaws

### (G-18371)
### EVER READY PIN & MANUFACTURING
5560 International Dr  (61109-2784)
PHONE.................................815 874-4949
Fax: 815 874-6080
Norma Whotton, *Corp Secy*
Ray King, *Executive*
Steve Liphart, *Admin Sec*
EMP: 80
SQ FT: 40,000
SALES (est): 12.3MM **Privately Held**
WEB: www.everreadypin.com
SIC: 3544  7389 Punches, forming & stamping; grinding, precision: commercial or industrial

### (G-18372)
### EVOQUA WATER TECHNOLOGIES LLC
4669 Shepherd Trl  (61103-1294)
PHONE.................................815 921-8325
Gary Cappeline, *Principal*
Danny Mann, *Plant Mgr*
Jeff Summers, *Opers Mgr*
EMP: 18
SALES (corp-wide): 1.2B **Publicly Held**
SIC: 3589 Sewage & water treatment equipment
HQ: Evoqua Water Technologies Llc
   181 Thorn Hill Rd
   Warrendale PA 15086
   724 772-0044

### (G-18373)
### EWIKON MOLDING TECH INC
Also Called: Emt
5652 International Dr  (61109-2778)
PHONE.................................815 874-7270
Fax: 847 844-9352
David Boxall, *President*
Tim Arnold, *Area Mgr*
Thomas Battefeld, *Area Mgr*
Falco Czeczatka, *Area Mgr*
Volker Kwyk, *Area Mgr*
▲ EMP: 5
SALES (est): 830.8K **Privately Held**
SIC: 3829  3544  3559 Thermometers & temperature sensors; industrial molds; plastics working machinery

### (G-18374)
### EXACT MACHINE COMPANY INC
2502 Preston St  (61102-1898)
PHONE.................................815 963-7905
Fax: 815 963-0236
Patricia Barnett, *President*
James W Barnett, *President*
EMP: 12
SQ FT: 20,000
SALES (est): 1MM **Privately Held**
WEB: www.exactmachineco.com
SIC: 3599 Machine shop, jobbing & repair

### (G-18375)
### EXCELSIOR  INC
4982 27th Ave  (61109-1709)
P.O. Box 970  (61105-0970)
PHONE.................................815 987-2900
Fax: 815 962-5466
Mike Abrahams, *President*
EMP: 25 EST: 1916
SALES: 4.2MM **Privately Held**
WEB: www.excelsiorinc.com
SIC: 3069  3053  3086  3061 Washers, rubber; gaskets, all materials; packing, leather; packing, metallic; plastics foam products; mechanical rubber goods; synthetic rubber; plastics materials & resins

### (G-18376)
### EXCELSIOR  INC
4982 27th Ave  (61109-1709)
PHONE.................................815 987-2900
EMP: 3
SALES (est): 167.8K **Privately Held**
SIC: 3053 Gaskets, all materials

### (G-18377)
### EXCLUSIVE PRO SPORTS LTD
5035 28th Ave  (61109-1718)
PHONE.................................815 877-8585
Fax: 815 226-5606
Terry D Taylor, *President*
Lynette Taylor, *Vice Pres*
Courtland Taylor, *Manager*
EMP: 30
SQ FT: 5,200
SALES (est): 1.8MM **Privately Held**
WEB: www.exclusivepro.com
SIC: 2339  2329 Uniforms, athletic: women's, misses' & juniors'; men's & boys' athletic uniforms

### (G-18378)
### F AND F SCREW PRODUCTS
2136 12th St  (61104-7365)
PHONE.................................815 968-7330
Francisco Rosales, *Owner*
EMP: 4 EST: 2014
SALES (est): 246.3K **Privately Held**
SIC: 3451 Screw machine products

### (G-18379)
### FAHRNER ASPHALT SEALERS LLC
129 Phelps Ave Ste 215  (61108-2446)
PHONE.................................815 986-1180
Tom Johndro, *Manager*
EMP: 7
SALES (corp-wide): 57.3MM **Privately Held**
SIC: 2951 Asphalt paving mixtures & blocks
PA: Fahrner Asphalt Sealers, L.L.C.
   2800 Mecca Dr
   Plover WI 54467
   715 341-2868

### (G-18380)
### FEDEX OFFICE & PRINT SVCS INC
6240 Mulford Village Dr  (61107-6615)
PHONE.................................815 229-0033
Kim Kistner, *Manager*
EMP: 15

# GEOGRAPHIC SECTION
## Rockford - Winnebago County (G-18403)

SALES (corp-wide): 50.3B **Publicly Held**
WEB: www.kinkos.com
SIC: **7334** 2791 2789 Photocopying & duplicating services; typesetting; bookbinding & related work
HQ: Fedex Office And Print Services, Inc.
7900 Legacy Dr
Plano TX 75024
214 550-7000

### (G-18381)
### FIBERGLASS INNOVATIONS LLC
2219 Kishwaukee St (61104-7008)
PHONE..................................815 962-9338
Fax: 815 962-9353
Brad Groves, *General Mgr*
Al Smith, *Plant Mgr*
Robert Reitsch, *CFO*
Donald D Dray,
Richard Provi,
**EMP:** 10
**SQ FT:** 44,000
**SALES (est):** 3.9MM **Privately Held**
WEB: www.fiberglassinnovations.com
SIC: **3089** Plastic hardware & building products

### (G-18382)
### FIBRO INC (DH)
Also Called: Fibromanta
139 Harrison Ave (61104-7044)
P.O. Box 5924 (61125-0924)
PHONE..................................815 229-1300
Fax: 815 229-1303
Jurgen Gurt Postfach, *President*
H Schoenau, *President*
Wilfried Dehne, *Vice Pres*
Lynndon Bried, *Engineer*
Jason Forde, *Sales Mgr*
▲ **EMP:** 12
**SQ FT:** 30,000
**SALES:** 12.4MM
**SALES (corp-wide):** 480.9MM **Privately Held**
WEB: www.fibroinc.com
SIC: **3532** 5084 5013 Loading machines, underground; mobile; machine tools & accessories; materials handling machinery; tools & equipment, automotive
HQ: F I B R O Gmbh
Weidachstr. 41-43
Weinsberg 74189
713 473-0

### (G-18383)
### FLOW-EZE COMPANY
Also Called: McCarren Group, The
3209 Auburn St (61101-3399)
PHONE..................................815 965-1062
Fax: 815 965-1329
Patrick D Mc Carren, *President*
Jeremy Rutherford, *Manager*
Shaun Patrick Carren, *Admin Sec*
▲ **EMP:** 18 EST: 1947
**SQ FT:** 43,000
**SALES (est):** 2.8MM **Privately Held**
WEB: www.flow-eze.com
SIC: **3993** 5199 3089 5162 Advertising novelties; advertising specialties; plastic containers, except foam; closures, plastic; plastics products; commercial printing, offset; screen printing

### (G-18384)
### FOCUS MFG
1833 Madron Rd (61107-1714)
PHONE..................................815 877-6043
Rick Pearce, *Owner*
**EMP:** 3
**SQ FT:** 2,400
**SALES:** 250K **Privately Held**
SIC: **3599** Machine shop, jobbing & repair

### (G-18385)
### FOLKERTS MANUFACTURING INC
2229 23rd Ave (61104-7334)
PHONE..................................815 968-7426
Fax: 815 968-7451
Ron Folkerts Jr, *President*
**EMP:** 7
**SQ FT:** 10,000
**SALES (est):** 1MM **Privately Held**
WEB: www.folkertsmfg.com
SIC: **3599** 3452 3541 Machine shop, jobbing & repair; nuts, metal; screw & thread machines

### (G-18386)
### FOREST CITY AUTO ELECTRIC CO
Also Called: Western Motor Service Div
1255 23rd Ave (61104-7160)
PHONE..................................815 963-4350
Fax: 815 963-3536
Richard Nicholls, *President*
Kim Venable, *Manager*
▲ **EMP:** 14
**SQ FT:** 10,000
**SALES:** 2.4MM **Privately Held**
SIC: **3621** Motors, electric

### (G-18387)
### FOREST CITY DIAGNOSTIC IMAGING
735 N Perryville Rd Ste 2 (61107-6236)
PHONE..................................815 398-1300
Vickie Lysord, *Principal*
Vickie Lyford, *Opers Mgr*
Lisa Gille, *Manager*
**EMP:** 20
**SALES (est):** 3.3MM **Privately Held**
SIC: **3826** Magnetic resonance imaging apparatus

### (G-18388)
### FOREST CITY GRINDING INC
Also Called: Nobleson and Associates
4844 Stenstrom Rd (61109-2628)
PHONE..................................815 874-2424
Fax: 815 874-2491
Noble D Shepherd, *President*
David P Johnson, *Corp Secy*
**EMP:** 3
**SQ FT:** 9,000
**SALES (est):** 468K **Privately Held**
SIC: **3599** Machine shop, jobbing & repair

### (G-18389)
### FOREST CITY TECHNOLOGIES INC
892 Southrock Dr (61102-4298)
PHONE..................................815 965-5880
John Cloud, *President*
Jeffrey Petras, *Vice Pres*
Dale Hillers, *Sales Mgr*
**EMP:** 20
**SALES (corp-wide):** 305.9MM **Privately Held**
WEB: www.foxrunbedandbreakfast.com
SIC: **3965** Fasteners
PA: Forest City Technologies, Inc.
299 Clay St
Wellington OH 44090
440 647-2115

### (G-18390)
### FORGINGS & STAMPINGS INC (PA)
1025 23rd Ave (61104-7148)
PHONE..................................815 962-5597
Fax: 815 962-5601
David Johnson, *President*
Pete Sireci, *Plant Mgr*
Diann Johnson, *Treasurer*
Pam Svatos, *Office Mgr*
Pam Fields, *Manager*
**EMP:** 24
**SQ FT:** 7,620
**SALES (est):** 6.7MM **Privately Held**
WEB: www.forgingsandstampings.com
SIC: **3462** Iron & steel forgings

### (G-18391)
### FORM WALERN GRINDING INC
Also Called: Walern Form Grinding
4717 Colt Rd (61109-2610)
PHONE..................................815 874-7000
Fax: 815 874-2888
Ernest Chisamore, *CEO*
James Chisamore, *President*
Hisako Chisamore, *Treasurer*
Carrie Harris, *Admin Sec*
**EMP:** 6 EST: 1970
**SQ FT:** 7,000

SALES (est): 600K **Privately Held**
SIC: **3599** 3544 Grinding castings for the trade; special dies, tools, jigs & fixtures

### (G-18392)
### FRED KENNERLY
1619 Arden Ave (61107-2027)
PHONE..................................815 398-6861
Fred Kennerly, *Owner*
**EMP:** 3
**SALES (est):** 248.7K **Privately Held**
SIC: **3663** 4841 5999 Cable television equipment; cable television services; audio-visual equipment & supplies

### (G-18393)
### FREEWAY-ROCKFORD INC
4701 Boeing Dr (61109-2995)
PHONE..................................815 397-6425
Fax: 815 397-8562
Raymond Scherler, *Ch of Bd*
Robb Scherler, *President*
Scott Sommers, *Vice Pres*
Michael Rosegger, *VP Finance*
Pam Rigotti, *Manager*
**EMP:** 32
**SQ FT:** 23,000
**SALES:** 5.7MM
**SALES (corp-wide):** 38.7MM **Privately Held**
WEB: www.freewaycorp.com
SIC: **3452** Washers, metal
PA: Freeway Corporation
9301 Allen Dr
Cleveland OH 44125
216 524-9700

### (G-18394)
### FUTURE TOOL INC
2029 23rd Ave (61104-7330)
PHONE..................................815 395-0012
Fax: 815 395-0013
Michael R Bloom, *President*
Raymond Hodyniak Jr, *Vice Pres*
Judy Shervon, *Office Mgr*
Judy Sherbon, *Manager*
**EMP:** 10
**SQ FT:** 8,000
**SALES (est):** 1.7MM **Privately Held**
SIC: **3599** 3544 Machine shop, jobbing & repair; special dies, tools, jigs & fixtures

### (G-18395)
### GALACTIC TOOL CO
1402 18th Ave (61104-5437)
P.O. Box 3396 (61106-3396)
PHONE..................................815 962-3420
Fax: 815 962-8807
Pat Healy, *Owner*
**EMP:** 6
**SQ FT:** 12,000
**SALES (est):** 622.9K **Privately Held**
SIC: **3599** Machine shop, jobbing & repair

### (G-18396)
### GBJ I LLC
Also Called: National Detroit
1590 Northrock Ct (61103-1234)
PHONE..................................815 877-4041
Bill Harrell, *President*
Gary Swanson, *Chairman*
William Lally, *CFO*
**EMP:** 13
**SQ FT:** 29,900
**SALES (est):** 1.4MM **Privately Held**
SIC: **3546** Sanders, hand: electric

### (G-18397)
### GENERAL FORGING DIE CO INC
4635 Hydraulic Rd (61109-2615)
PHONE..................................815 874-4224
Fax: 815 874-7904
Ralph A Morgan, *CEO*
Mark Morgan, *Purchasing*
**EMP:** 24
**SQ FT:** 13,700
**SALES (est):** 3.7MM **Privately Held**
SIC: **3544** 3462 Special dies, tools, jigs & fixtures; iron & steel forgings

### (G-18398)
### GKI INCORPORATED
Also Called: Gki Cutting Tools
1639 N Alpine Rd Ste 401 (61107-1481)
PHONE..................................815 459-2330

Fax: 815 459-2432
Olaf Klutke, *President*
Eric Klutke, *Vice Pres*
Jackie Jesse, *Manager*
Ilse Klutke, *Admin Sec*
**EMP:** 37
**SQ FT:** 12,000
**SALES (est):** 8.3MM **Privately Held**
WEB: www.gkitool.com
SIC: **3599** 3545 5085 Machine shop, jobbing & repair; machine tool accessories; industrial tools

### (G-18399)
### GLOBAL DISPLAY SOLUTIONS INC
5217 28th Ave (61109-1722)
PHONE..................................815 282-2328
Giovanni Cariolato, *President*
Robert Heise, *General Mgr*
Thomas Lentz, *Chairman*
Emmanuel Grodzinski, *Treasurer*
Simona Dobre, *Human Res Mgr*
▲ **EMP:** 45
**SALES (est):** 30K
**SALES (corp-wide):** 23.7K **Privately Held**
WEB: www.gds.com
SIC: **3679** Liquid crystal displays (LCD)
HQ: Global Display Solutions Spa
Via Tezze 20/A
Cornedo Vicentino VI 36073
044 542-8991

### (G-18400)
### GOELLNER INC (PA)
Also Called: Advanced Machine and Engrg
2500 Latham St (61103-3963)
PHONE..................................815 962-6076
Fax: 815 962-0483
Willy Goellner, *CEO*
Dietmiar Goellner, *President*
David Leezer, *CFO*
Marika Mertz, *Admin Sec*
**EMP:** 224
**SALES (est):** 115.6MM **Privately Held**
WEB: www.goellner.com
SIC: **3599** Machine & other job shop work

### (G-18401)
### GOLFERS FAMILY CORPORATION
Also Called: Gfi Metal Treating
1531 Preston St (61102-2047)
PHONE..................................815 968-0094
Richard G Francis, *President*
Denise J Francis, *Admin Sec*
**EMP:** 23
**SALES (est):** 5.5MM **Privately Held**
SIC: **3398** Metal heat treating

### (G-18402)
### GOODRICH CORPORATION
Also Called: UTC Aerospace Systems
4747 Harrison Ave (61108-7929)
PHONE..................................815 226-6000
Doug Hartman, *General Mgr*
Kevin U Cerny, *Business Mgr*
Randy U Voigt, *Project Mgr*
Susan Bartelli, *QC Mgr*
Jagadish Krishnan, *Engineer*
**EMP:** 73
**SALES (corp-wide):** 57.2B **Publicly Held**
SIC: **3823** Industrial instrmnts msrmnt display/control process variable
HQ: Goodrich Corporation
2730 W Tyvola Rd
Charlotte NC 28217
704 423-7000

### (G-18403)
### GOODRICH CORPORATION
Also Called: UTC Aerospace Systems
4747 Harrison Ave (61108-7929)
PHONE..................................815 226-6000
**EMP:** 99
**SALES (corp-wide):** 57.2B **Publicly Held**
WEB: www.hamilton-standard.com
SIC: **3823** Industrial instrmnts msrmnt display/control process variable
HQ: Goodrich Corporation
2730 W Tyvola Rd
Charlotte NC 28217
704 423-7000

## Rockford - Winnebago County (G-18404)

**(G-18404)**
**GRAFCOR PACKAGING INC (PA)**
121 Loomis St (61101-1408)
PHONE..................815 963-1300
Fax: 815 963-1635
William E Hall, *President*
Thomas Wieland, *CFO*
Barbara Brelsford, *Accounts Mgr*
Robert E Hall, *Shareholder*
EMP: 17
SQ FT: 60,000
SALES (est): 5.9MM **Privately Held**
SIC: 2631 3086 Container, packaging & boxboard; corrugating medium; folding boxboard; setup boxboard; packaging & shipping materials, foamed plastic

**(G-18405)**
**GREENLEE TEXTRON INC (HQ)**
4455 Boeing Dr (61109-2932)
PHONE..................815 397-7070
Fax: 815 397-2402
J Scott Hall, *President*
Dzura Mike, *Principal*
Klever Keltner, *Regional Mgr*
Amanda Mera, *Business Mgr*
Scott Fenton, *Vice Pres*
▲ EMP: 100
SQ FT: 60,000
SALES (est): 310.9MM
SALES (corp-wide): 13.7B **Publicly Held**
SIC: 3549 3541 3546 Metalworking machinery; machine tools, metal cutting type; power-driven handtools
PA: Textron Inc.
40 Westminster St
Providence RI 02903
401 421-2800

**(G-18406)**
**GREENSLADE FASTENER SVCS LLC**
129 Phelps Ave Ste 800 (61108-2421)
PHONE..................815 398-4073
John Bergstron, *Mng Member*
Berg Strom,
EMP: 3
SQ FT: 500
SALES (est): 360K **Privately Held**
SIC: 3965 Fasteners

**(G-18407)**
**GUNITE CORPORATION (DH)**
302 Peoples Ave (61104-7092)
PHONE..................815 490-6260
Fax: 815 965-9197
James Cirar, *CEO*
Richard Dauch, *President*
Omar Fakhoury, *Vice Pres*
Jeff Clark, *Opers Mgr*
Michael Huber, *Foreman/Supr*
▲ EMP: 259
SQ FT: 619,113
SALES (est): 309.1MM
SALES (corp-wide): 111.2MM **Privately Held**
SIC: 3714 Motor vehicle brake systems & parts; brake drums, motor vehicle; wheels, motor vehicle
HQ: Truck Components, Inc.
8819 N Brooks St
Tampa FL 33604
813 933-1166

**(G-18408)**
**GUNITE CORPORATION**
Also Called: Transportation Tech Industires
302 Peoples Ave (61104-7092)
PHONE..................815 964-3301
James Cirar, *President*
Robert L Wells, *Purch Mgr*
Paul Zeienjr, *Manager*
John Aldrich, *Info Tech Dir*
Coleman Derek, *IT/INT Sup*
EMP: 410
SALES (corp-wide): 111.2MM **Privately Held**
SIC: 3714 Motor vehicle parts & accessories
HQ: Gunite Corporation
302 Peoples Ave
Rockford IL 61104
815 490-6260

**(G-18409)**
**GUNITE EMI CORPORATION**
Also Called: EMI Division
302 Peoples Ave (61104-7035)
PHONE..................815 964-7124
James Sirar, *President*
▼ EMP: 285 EST: 1880
SQ FT: 432,000
SALES (est): 25.8MM
SALES (corp-wide): 111.2MM **Privately Held**
SIC: 3321 3714 Ductile iron castings; gray iron castings; brake drums, motor vehicle; motor vehicle wheels & parts
HQ: Gunite Corporation
302 Peoples Ave
Rockford IL 61104
815 490-6260

**(G-18410)**
**H&Z FUEL & FOOD INC**
3420 E State St (61108-1808)
PHONE..................815 399-9108
Aviz Choudry, *Regional Mgr*
EMP: 5
SALES (est): 596.6K **Privately Held**
SIC: 2869 Fuels

**(G-18411)**
**HAMILTON SUNDSTRAND CORP**
4747 Harrison Ave (61108-7900)
PHONE..................815 226-6000
Fax: 815 226-7278
Bill Deuerling, *General Mgr*
Philip Meseck, *General Mgr*
Robert Michaels, *General Mgr*
Mike Teagardin, *Business Mgr*
Lynn Bonnett, *Project Mgr*
EMP: 2300
SALES (corp-wide): 57.2B **Publicly Held**
SIC: 3728 Aircraft assemblies, subassemblies & parts
HQ: Hamilton Sundstrand Corporation
1 Hamilton Rd
Windsor Locks CT 06096
860 654-6000

**(G-18412)**
**HANSON AGGREGATES EAST LLC**
5011 E State St (61108-2310)
PHONE..................815 398-2300
Casey Singles, *Branch Mgr*
EMP: 30
SALES (corp-wide): 16B **Privately Held**
SIC: 3272 Concrete products
HQ: Hanson Aggregates East Llc
3131 Rdu Center Dr
Morrisville NC 27560
919 380-2500

**(G-18413)**
**HARDER SIGNS INC**
4695 Stenstrom Rd (61109-2637)
PHONE..................815 874-7777
Fax: 815 874-7711
John Harder, *President*
Donna D Harder, *Vice Pres*
EMP: 12
SQ FT: 6,800
SALES (est): 1.3MM **Privately Held**
WEB: www.hardersigns.com
SIC: 3993 7389 2542 Neon signs; signs, not made in custom sign painting shops; displays & cutouts, window & lobby; sign painting & lettering shop; partitions & fixtures, except wood

**(G-18414)**
**HEADER DIE AND TOOL INC**
3022 Eastrock Ct (61109-1760)
P.O. Box 5846 (61125-0846)
PHONE..................815 397-0123
Fax: 815 397-7672
Lucas Derry, *President*
Richard Bried, *Vice Pres*
Veronica Corey, *Purchasing*
EMP: 60 EST: 1954
SQ FT: 23,650
SALES (est): 11.1MM **Privately Held**
WEB: www.header.com
SIC: 3544 Special dies & tools

**(G-18415)**
**HEALING SCENTS**
1986 Will James Rd (61109-4851)
PHONE..................815 874-0924
Kathleen Hembree, *Principal*
EMP: 3
SALES (est): 264.5K **Privately Held**
SIC: 2844 Toilet preparations

**(G-18416)**
**HEIMAN SIGN STUDIO**
6909 Canter Ct (61108-4303)
PHONE..................815 397-6909
Jon W Heiman, *Owner*
EMP: 3
SALES (est): 157.9K **Privately Held**
SIC: 3993 2399 Signs & advertising specialties; fabricated textile products

**(G-18417)**
**HERITAGE MOLD INCORPORATED**
3170 Forest View Rd (61109-1642)
PHONE..................815 397-1117
Fax: 815 397-2511
Bennett Franzen, *President*
Tim Barkdoll, *Foreman/Supr*
Jaci Franzen, *Treasurer*
Shelley Gamon, *Marketing Staff*
Mark Fehler, *Manager*
EMP: 15
SQ FT: 6,400
SALES (est): 3MM **Privately Held**
WEB: www.heritagemold.com
SIC: 3544 Industrial molds

**(G-18418)**
**HG-FARLEY LASERLAB USA INC**
4635 Colt Rd (61109-2609)
PHONE..................815 874-1400
John Johnson, *President*
Jody Hickey, *Corp Secy*
▲ EMP: 9
SALES (est): 2.1MM **Privately Held**
SIC: 3545 5082 Machine tool accessories; construction & mining machinery
PA: Hg-Farley Holdings, L.L.C.
6833 Stalter Dr
Rockford IL 61108

**(G-18419)**
**HIGH STANDARD FABRICATING INC**
3336 Seward Ave (61108-7549)
PHONE..................815 965-6517
Fax: 815 965-7843
Rick Rubert, *President*
Elaine Rubert, *Corp Secy*
Charles Rubert, *Vice Pres*
Karen Rubert, *Treasurer*
Diana Lyman, *Office Mgr*
EMP: 20
SQ FT: 24,000
SALES (est): 3.3MM **Privately Held**
SIC: 3441 Fabricated structural metal

**(G-18420)**
**HOHLFLDER A H SHTMTL HTG COOLG**
Also Called: AG Hohlfelder Sheet Metal
2911 Prairie Rd (61102-3960)
PHONE..................815 965-9134
Theresa Hohlfelder, *President*
EMP: 4
SALES (est): 200K **Privately Held**
SIC: 1711 1761 3585 3444 Warm air heating & air conditioning contractor; ventilation & duct work contractor; sheet metalwork; refrigeration & heating equipment; sheet metalwork

**(G-18421)**
**HOME FIRES INC**
Also Called: Saffire Grill Co.
1100 11th St (61104-5061)
PHONE..................815 967-4100
Stephen Benson, *President*
Shawn Benson, *Manager*
▲ EMP: 2 EST: 2005
SALES (est): 220K **Privately Held**
SIC: 3556 Smokers, food processing equipment

**(G-18422)**
**HOMEFIRE HEARTH INC**
3815 Marsh Ave (61114-6039)
PHONE..................815 997-1123
Steve Benson, *President*
EMP: 7
SALES (est): 204.8K **Privately Held**
SIC: 3631 Barbecues, grills & braziers (outdoor cooking)

**(G-18423)**
**HOT SHOTS NM LLC**
Also Called: Pharmacy Services of Rockford
4330 Charles St (61108-6249)
PHONE..................815 484-0500
Fax: 815 484-6114
Don Kapolnek, *Branch Mgr*
EMP: 8
SALES (corp-wide): 7.9MM **Privately Held**
SIC: 2834 Pharmaceutical preparations
PA: Hot Shots Nm, Llc
2017 E Kimberly Rd
Davenport IA 52807
563 391-0404

**(G-18424)**
**HURST CHEMICAL COMPANY**
2020 Cunningham Rd (61102-2653)
PHONE..................815 964-0451
Fax: 815 964-0688
Linda Rager, *Manager*
Linda Ragar, *Director*
EMP: 4
SQ FT: 7,200
SALES (corp-wide): 4.1MM **Privately Held**
SIC: 2869 4226 5169 2893 Industrial organic chemicals; special warehousing & storage; chemicals & allied products; printing ink; specialty cleaning, polishes & sanitation goods; platemaking services
PA: Hurst Chemical Company
167 Lambert St Ste 123
Oxnard CA 93036
800 723-2004

**(G-18425)**
**IBANUM MANUFACTURING LLC**
5963 Cambridge Chase (61107-2500)
PHONE..................815 262-5373
Barlow Michael, *Mng Member*
Barlow Michael A, *Mng Member*
EMP: 1
SALES (est): 600K **Privately Held**
SIC: 3721 3541 3728 Aircraft; machine tools, metal cutting type; aircraft parts & equipment

**(G-18426)**
**IDEAL ADVERTISING & PRINTING (PA)**
Also Called: Vanco Printers Division
116 N Winnebago St (61101-1026)
PHONE..................815 965-1713
Fax: 815 965-8161
John G Schmit, *Owner*
Charles Fricke, *Manager*
EMP: 10
SQ FT: 6,000
SALES (est): 7.8MM **Privately Held**
WEB: www.idealad.com
SIC: 2752 2759 7311 2791 Commercial printing, offset; letterpress printing; advertising agencies; typesetting; bookbinding & related work

**(G-18427)**
**ILLINOIS SOC FOR RSPRTORY CARE**
6110 Thorncrest Dr (61109-4574)
PHONE..................815 742-9367
EMP: 3 EST: 2015
SALES: 129.7K **Privately Held**
SIC: 3842 Respirators

**(G-18428)**
**IMPERIAL PUNCH & MANUFACTURING**
2016 23rd Ave (61104-7372)
PHONE..................815 226-8200
Fax: 815 226-8208
Bruce A Keirn, *President*
Rosalynn M Keirn, *Vice Pres*
EMP: 18

# GEOGRAPHIC SECTION

Rockford - Winnebago County (G-18451)

SQ FT: 9,000
SALES: 1.8MM Privately Held
SIC: 3544 3366 Special dies & tools; copper foundries

**(G-18429)**
**INDEV GAUGING SYSTEMS INC**
5235 26th Ave (61109-1707)
PHONE..................................815 282-4463
Jim Wickert, *Manager*
▲ EMP: 29 EST: 1999
SALES (est): 6.5MM
SALES (corp-wide): 14.5MM Privately Held
SIC: 3823 Draft gauges, industrial process type
PA: Jasch Industries Limited
502, Block C, Jasch House,
New Delhi DEL 11003
112 872-3749

**(G-18430)**
**INDUSTRIAL MOLDS INC (PA)**
Also Called: True-Cut Wire EDM Div
5175 27th Ave (61109-1783)
PHONE..................................815 397-2971
Fax: 815 397-0474
Jack D Peterson, *President*
Mark Hill, *Business Mgr*
Joe Hansen, *Engineer*
Sue Denevew, *Accountant*
Jan Kuntz, *Finance*
▲ EMP: 60
SQ FT: 44,000
SALES (est): 19.1MM Privately Held
WEB: www.industrialmolds.com
SIC: 3544 Forms (molds), for foundry & plastics working machinery

**(G-18431)**
**INGENIUM AEROSPACE LLC**
5389 International Dr (61109-2775)
PHONE..................................815 525-2000
Allen White, *Design Engr*
Debbie Johnson, *Accountant*
Joann Cossey, *Manager*
Darrin Kopala,
Stephen Carter,
EMP: 10
SALES (est): 2.5MM Privately Held
SIC: 3728 Aircraft parts & equipment

**(G-18432)**
**INGERSOLL CUTTING TOOL COMPANY (HQ)**
845 S Lyford Rd (61108-2749)
PHONE..................................815 387-6600
Fax: 815 387-6337
Charles Elder, *President*
Richard Sollich, *Vice Pres*
Tom Taormina, *Purch Agent*
Ed Horsa, *Purchasing*
Eric Van Est, *Accounts Mgr*
▲ EMP: 320
SQ FT: 235,000
SALES (est): 74.4MM
SALES (corp-wide): 80.1MM Privately Held
WEB: www.ingersollcuttingtools.com
SIC: 3545 Machine tool accessories
PA: Imc Group Usa Holdings Inc
300 Westway Pl
Arlington TX 76018
817 258-3200

**(G-18433)**
**INGERSOLL MACHINE TOOLS INC (DH)**
707 Fulton Ave (61103-4069)
PHONE..................................815 987-6000
Tino Oldani, *President*
James W Keeling, *Vice Pres*
Brian McIntyre, *Vice Pres*
Gary Johnson, *Purch Agent*
Roberta Smith, *Buyer*
◆ EMP: 220
SALES: 55.4MM Privately Held
WEB: www.ingersoll.com
SIC: 3541 3545 Machine tools, metal cutting type; machine tool accessories
HQ: Camozzi Spa
Via Eritrea 20/I
Brescia BS 25126
030 379-21

**(G-18434)**
**INGERSOLL PROD SYSTEMS LLC (DH)**
Also Called: I P S
1301 Eddy Ave (61103-3173)
PHONE..................................815 637-8500
Fax: 815 637-8580
William Kalp, *Vice Pres*
Duff Singer, *Engineer*
Dave Ewaldz, *Project Engr*
Belinda Cronk, *Controller*
John Stonecliffe, *Sales Engr*
▲ EMP: 75
SQ FT: 100,000
SALES (est): 14.1MM Privately Held
WEB: www.ingersollprodsys.com
SIC: 3541 Machine tools, metal cutting type
HQ: Dalian Machine Tool Group Co., Ltd.
No.100, Liaohe East Road, Shuang D Harbor, Development Zone
Dalian 11662
411 875-8267

**(G-18435)**
**INNOVATIVE FIX SOLUTIONS LLC**
1122 Milford Ave (61109-3636)
PHONE..................................815 395-8500
EMP: 10 EST: 2014
SQ FT: 212,805
SALES (est): 590K Privately Held
SIC: 3496 Mfg Misc Fabricated Wire Products

**(G-18436)**
**INNOVATIVE FIX SOLUTIONS LLC**
1122 Milford Ave (61109-3636)
PHONE..................................815 395-8500
Shaun Starbuck, *CEO*
Carrie Conzolman, *Controller*
EMP: 100
SALES: 25MM Privately Held
SIC: 2511 Magazine racks: wood

**(G-18437)**
**INTEGRATED LABEL CORPORATION**
3407 Pyramid Dr (61109-2737)
PHONE..................................815 874-2500
Fax: 815 874-2556
Marty Chowanski, *CEO*
Barret Ewing, *President*
▲ EMP: 10
SQ FT: 10,000
SALES (est): 1.9MM Privately Held
WEB: www.integratedlabels.com
SIC: 2679 Cardboard products, except die-cut

**(G-18438)**
**INTER-STATE STUDIO & PUBG CO**
3446 Colony Bay Dr (61109-2560)
PHONE..................................815 874-0342
Matt Waldschmidt, *Branch Mgr*
EMP: 52
SALES (corp-wide): 38.3MM Privately Held
SIC: 2741 Miscellaneous publishing
PA: Inter-State Studio & Publishing Co.
3500 Snyder Ave
Sedalia MO 65301
660 826-1764

**(G-18439)**
**INTERNATIONAL PAPER COMPANY**
2100 23rd Ave (61104-7333)
P.O. Box 6227 (61125-1227)
PHONE..................................815 398-2100
Fax: 815 398-2120
Dave Kerch, *QC Dir*
Don Light, *Engineer*
John Liermann, *Controller*
Roxie Gordon, *Human Res Dir*
Joseph Domino, *Maintence Staff*
EMP: 130
SQ FT: 125,000
SALES (corp-wide): 21B Publicly Held
WEB: www.internationalpaper.com
SIC: 2653 Corrugated & solid fiber boxes

PA: International Paper Company
6400 Poplar Ave
Memphis TN 38197
901 419-9000

**(G-18440)**
**INTERSTATE POWER SYSTEMS INC**
3736 11th St (61109-3019)
PHONE..................................952 854-2044
Gordon Galarneau, *Ch of Bd*
Rochelle Protho, *Accounting Mgr*
Jack Kamin, *Manager*
EMP: 99 EST: 2015
SQ FT: 50,000
SALES (est): 3.2MM Privately Held
SIC: 3714 5084 Motor vehicle parts & accessories; industrial machinery & equipment

**(G-18441)**
**J & M PLATING INC**
4500 Kishwaukee St (61109-2924)
PHONE..................................815 964-4975
Fax: 815 961-7353
Mark Morris, *President*
Rick Morris, *Vice Pres*
Christy Hoffman, *Manager*
David Morris, *Admin Sec*
▲ EMP: 135
SQ FT: 185,000
SALES (est): 27.2MM Privately Held
WEB: www.jmplating.com
SIC: 3471 Electroplating of metals or formed products; finishing, metals or formed products; polishing, metals or formed products

**(G-18442)**
**JAEGER SAW AND CUTTER INC**
Also Called: Jaeger Saw & Cutter Works
81005 5th Ave (61104)
PHONE..................................815 963-0313
Fax: 815 963-0313
Randolph Ray, *President*
Rosanna Ray, *Admin Sec*
EMP: 3
SQ FT: 1,500
SALES (est): 178.8K Privately Held
SIC: 7699 3425 Knife, saw & tool sharpening & repair; saw blades & handsaws

**(G-18443)**
**JERHEN INDUSTRIES INC**
5052 28th Ave (61109-1719)
PHONE..................................815 397-0400
Fax: 815 397-0710
Roger Jerie, *President*
Tom Henderson, *Treasurer*
Judy Kruse, *Office Mgr*
▲ EMP: 60
SQ FT: 20,000
SALES (est): 10.8MM Privately Held
WEB: www.jerhen.com
SIC: 3545 3549 Hopper feed devices; assembly machines, including robotic

**(G-18444)**
**JGC UNITED PUBLISHING CORPS**
Also Called: John Gile
1710 N Main St Fl 1 (61103-4706)
PHONE..................................815 968-6601
Fax: 815 968-6600
John Gile, *Owner*
EMP: 3
SALES (est): 285.6K Privately Held
SIC: 2731 Book publishing

**(G-18445)**
**JIM STERNER MACHINES**
Also Called: Sterner Screw Machine
2500 N Main St Ste 25 (61103-4078)
PHONE..................................815 962-8983
Fax: 815 962-8955
James Sterner, *Owner*
Laura Mason, *Co-Owner*
EMP: 5
SQ FT: 4,000
SALES (est): 431.3K Privately Held
SIC: 3599 3451 Machine & other job shop work; screw machine products

**(G-18446)**
**JL CLARK LLC**
2300 S 6th St (61104-7199)
PHONE..................................815 961-5677
Ray Rowland, *Chairman*
Walter Pietruch, *Engineer*
EMP: 8
SALES (corp-wide): 1.4B Privately Held
SIC: 3089 Plastic containers, except foam
HQ: J.L. Clark Llc
923 23rd Ave
Rockford IL 61104
815 961-5609

**(G-18447)**
**JL CLARK LLC (DH)**
Also Called: J. L. Clark, Inc.
923 23rd Ave (61104-7173)
PHONE..................................815 961-5609
Fax: 815 966-5862
Phil Baerenwald, *President*
Susan Waskiewics, *Senior Buyer*
Susan Waskiewicz, *Senior Buyer*
Linda Guenther, *Buyer*
Dave Swenson, *QC Mgr*
▲ EMP: 219
SQ FT: 454,000
SALES: 80MM
SALES (corp-wide): 1.4B Privately Held
SIC: 3411 3499 2752 3089 Metal cans; magnetic shields, metal; lithographing on metal; plastic containers, except foam
HQ: Cc Industries Inc.
222 N La Salle St # 1000
Chicago IL 60601
312 855-4000

**(G-18448)**
**JOHNSON CONTROLS INC**
7316 Argus Dr 1 (61107-5864)
PHONE..................................815 397-5147
Fax: 815 874-5503
David Anderson, *Branch Mgr*
EMP: 30
SALES (corp-wide): 36.8B Privately Held
SIC: 3822 Building services monitoring controls, automatic
PA: Johnson Controls, Inc.
5757 N Green Bay Ave
Milwaukee WI 53209
414 524-1200

**(G-18449)**
**JOHNSON PUMPS AMERICA INC**
5885 11th St (61109-3650)
PHONE..................................847 671-7867
Marc Michael, *President*
David Kowalski, *President*
Gregg Pardus, *General Mgr*
Ribarchik Andy, *Vice Pres*
Bill Pack, *Purch Agent*
▲ EMP: 44
SQ FT: 2,000
SALES (est): 11.8MM
SALES (corp-wide): 2B Publicly Held
WEB: www.johnson-pump.com
SIC: 5084 3561 Pumps & pumping equipment; industrial pumps & parts; pumps, domestic: water or sump
PA: Spx Flow, Inc.
13320 Balntyn Corp Pl
Charlotte NC 28277
704 752-4400

**(G-18450)**
**JW FASTENERS INC**
1311 Preston St (61102-2044)
PHONE..................................815 963-2658
Fax: 815 963-2668
Jeff Weatherford, *President*
Bill Weatherford, *Vice Pres*
Scott Weatherford, *Vice Pres*
Bobbie Renner, *Office Mgr*
EMP: 6
SALES (est): 580K Privately Held
WEB: www.jwfasteners.com
SIC: 3452 Screws, metal

**(G-18451)**
**K&J FINISHING INC**
Also Called: Northern Illinois Metal Finshg
716 Cedar St (61102-2950)
PHONE..................................815 965-9655
Fax: 815 963-4644
Keith Beach, *President*

# Rockford - Winnebago County (G-18452)

EMP: 16
SQ FT: 41,000
SALES (est): 3.6MM **Privately Held**
SIC: 3559 Metal finishing equipment for plating, etc.

### (G-18452)
### KADON PRECISION MACHINING INC
3744 Publishers Dr (61109-6316)
PHONE..................................815 874-5850
Fax: 815 874-4956
Jeff Franklin, *Principal*
Cheryl L Spencer, *Corp Secy*
Justin Franklin, *Prdtn Mgr*
EMP: 100
SQ FT: 19,000
SALES (est): 21.5MM **Privately Held**
WEB: www.kadonprecision.com
SIC: 3451 Screw machine products

### (G-18453)
### KANEY GROUP LLC (PA)
1321 Capital Dr (61109-3067)
PHONE..................................815 986-4359
Jeffrey J Kaney Sr, *CEO*
Ronald J Soave, *President*
Susan Jones, *Marketing Staff*
EMP: 4 EST: 2009
SALES (est): 13.1MM **Privately Held**
SIC: 3812 Acceleration indicators & systems components, aerospace

### (G-18454)
### KENNAMETAL INC
21 Airport Dr (61109-2901)
PHONE..................................815 226-0650
Jim Kurtz, *Human Res Dir*
Lee Taylor, *Analyst*
EMP: 137
SALES (corp-wide): 2.1B **Publicly Held**
WEB: www.kennametal.com
SIC: 3545 3532 Machine tool accessories; mining machinery
PA: Kennametal Inc.
600 Grant St Ste 5100
Pittsburgh PA 15219
412 248-8200

### (G-18455)
### KENS STREET ROD REPAIR
5521 International Dr (61109-2783)
PHONE..................................815 874-1811
Ken Barnhart, *Owner*
EMP: 1
SALES: 375K **Privately Held**
SIC: 3711 Automobile assembly, including specialty automobiles

### (G-18456)
### KENT NUTRITION GROUP INC
1612 S Bend Rd (61109-4834)
PHONE..................................815 874-2411
Fax: 815 874-2410
Tom Smollen, *Branch Mgr*
EMP: 12
SALES (corp-wide): 613.2MM **Privately Held**
WEB: www.kentfeeds.com
SIC: 2048 Livestock feeds
HQ: Kent Nutrition Group, Inc.
1600 Oregon St
Muscatine IA 52761
866 647-1212

### (G-18457)
### KROGER CO
Also Called: Hilander 00805
2206 Barnes Blvd (61112-2000)
PHONE..................................815 332-7267
Fax: 815 332-7689
EMP: 116
SALES (corp-wide): 115.3B **Publicly Held**
WEB: www.kroger.com
SIC: 5411 7384 5992 5912 Grocery stores; photofinish laboratories; florists; drug stores & proprietary stores; cookies & crackers; bread, cake & related products
PA: The Kroger Co
1014 Vine St Ste 1000
Cincinnati OH 45202
513 762-4000

### (G-18458)
### L & T SERVICES INC
1004 Samuelson Rd (61109-3640)
PHONE..................................815 397-6260
Fax: 815 397-1266
Toni R Seagren, *President*
EMP: 2
SALES (est): 260K **Privately Held**
SIC: 5013 5531 3647 Automotive supplies & parts; automobile & truck equipment & parts; motor vehicle lighting equipment

### (G-18459)
### L T L CO
4801 American Rd (61109-2643)
PHONE..................................815 874-0913
Fax: 815 874-0614
James Landquist, *President*
James F Landquist, *President*
Ted M Myers, *Manager*
EMP: 13
SQ FT: 24,000
SALES: 1.5MM **Privately Held**
SIC: 3544 Special dies & tools; jigs: inspection, gauging & checking

### (G-18460)
### L/J FABRICATORS INC
Also Called: Lj Fabricators
944 Research Pkwy (61109-2942)
PHONE..................................815 397-9099
Gregory Johnson, *President*
Christopher Johnson, *Vice Pres*
Cesar Meza, *Engineer*
Kent Ogden, *VP Finance*
Ron Schooler, *Sales Staff*
EMP: 35
SQ FT: 54,000
SALES (est): 9.7MM **Privately Held**
WEB: www.ljfabricators.com
SIC: 3444 Sheet metalwork; sheet metal specialties, not stamped

### (G-18461)
### LAMSON OIL COMPANY (HQ)
2217 20th Ave (61104-7325)
P.O. Box 5303 (61125-0303)
PHONE..................................815 226-8090
Raymond La Mantia, *President*
Greg La Mantia, *Vice Pres*
Dan Thorn, *Engineer*
Angela Stahl, *Sales Staff*
Barbara La Mantia, *Admin Sec*
EMP: 2
SQ FT: 20,000
SALES: 2MM
SALES (corp-wide): 5.7MM **Privately Held**
WEB: www.lamsonoil.com
SIC: 2911 Oils, lubricating
PA: Lsp Industries, Inc.
5060 27th Ave
Rockford IL 61109
815 226-8090

### (G-18462)
### LARRYS GARAGE & MACHINE SHOP
101 Vista Ter (61102-1775)
PHONE..................................815 968-8416
Fax: 815 986-0137
Larry McCammond, *Partner*
Art McCammond, *Partner*
EMP: 3
SQ FT: 5,000
SALES: 35K **Privately Held**
SIC: 7538 7692 General automotive repair shops; automotive welding

### (G-18463)
### LBS MARKETING LTD
1525 Kilburn Ave (61101-3443)
PHONE..................................815 965-5234
Rodger Scheiddgger, *President*
EMP: 1
SQ FT: 2,600
SALES: 2MM **Privately Held**
SIC: 5085 3471 Industrial supplies; plating of metals or formed products

### (G-18464)
### LEADING EDGE GROUP INC (PA)
Also Called: Leading Edge Hydraulics
1800 16th Ave (61104-5453)
PHONE..................................815 316-3500
Fax: 815 316-0623
Russell Dennis Sr, *CEO*
Russell Dennis Jr, *President*
Willa Almond, *Production*
Becky Williams, *Purchasing*
Chuck Westholder, *QC Mgr*
▲ EMP: 120 EST: 1966
SQ FT: 45,000
SALES (est): 26.4MM **Privately Held**
WEB: www.lehydraulics.com
SIC: 3599 3498 3594 3547 Machine shop, jobbing & repair; tube fabricating (contract bending & shaping); fluid power pumps & motors; rolling mill machinery; steel pipe & tubes

### (G-18465)
### LEGACY PLASTICS INC
5040 27th Ave (61109-1711)
PHONE..................................815 226-3013
Fax: 815 399-3797
Bennett Franzen, *President*
Steve Wyler, *Manager*
EMP: 9
SQ FT: 2,500
SALES (est): 1.4MM **Privately Held**
SIC: 3089 Injection molding of plastics

### (G-18466)
### LEGGERO FOODS
2625 N Mulford Rd 134 (61114-5670)
PHONE..................................815 871-9640
Brian Leggero, *President*
EMP: 4
SALES (est): 149.8K **Privately Held**
SIC: 2038 Frozen specialties

### (G-18467)
### LEONARD ASSOCIATES INC
6733 Hedgewood Rd (61108-5633)
PHONE..................................815 226-9609
Jayme J Leonard, *Branch Mgr*
EMP: 41
SALES (corp-wide): 8.4MM **Privately Held**
SIC: 3559 Petroleum refinery equipment
PA: Leonard Associates, Inc.
1340 Kemper Meadow Dr
Cincinnati OH 45240
513 574-9500

### (G-18468)
### LESTER MANUFACTURING INC
2219 N Central Ave (61101-2347)
P.O. Box 1057 (61105-1057)
PHONE..................................815 986-1172
Dai Bui, *President*
EMP: 50
SALES (est): 6.3MM **Privately Held**
SIC: 3549 Marking machines, metalworking

### (G-18469)
### LETRAW MANUFACTURING CO
200 Quaker Rd Ste 2 (61104-7068)
PHONE..................................815 987-9670
Ralph Wartell,
▲ EMP: 5
SQ FT: 4,000
SALES: 250K **Privately Held**
WEB: www.letraw.com
SIC: 3496 Miscellaneous fabricated wire products

### (G-18470)
### LIND-REMSEN PRINTING CO INC
Also Called: Thrift-Remsen Printers
3918 S Central Ave (61102-4290)
PHONE..................................815 969-0610
Fax: 815 969-9813
Robert Remsen, *President*
Thomas Remsen, *Vice Pres*
Timothy Remsen, *Treasurer*
Kristy Provi, *Admin Sec*
EMP: 12 EST: 1931
SQ FT: 20,000
SALES (est): 1.3MM **Privately Held**
WEB: www.thriftremsen.com
SIC: 2752 2789 Commercial printing, lithographic; bookbinding & related work

### (G-18471)
### LITTLESON INC (PA)
Also Called: Winchester Estates-Div
124 N Water St Ste 204 (61107-3959)
PHONE..................................815 968-8349
Fax: 815 226-5645
Robert L Soehnlen, *President*
Joanne Sjostrom, *Corp Secy*
Roberta McConnel, *Vice Pres*
EMP: 5
SQ FT: 1,000
SALES (est): 609.3K **Privately Held**
SIC: 6515 3295 6512 Mobile home site operators; slag, crushed or ground; non-residential building operators

### (G-18472)
### LLOYD AMERICAN CORPORATION (PA)
Also Called: Lloyd Hearing Aid
4435 Manchester Dr (61109-1655)
P.O. Box 7355 (61126-7355)
PHONE..................................815 964-4191
Fax: 815 964-8378
Andrew Palmquist, *President*
Pat Longnecker, *Manager*
EMP: 18
SQ FT: 8,000
SALES (est): 2.2MM **Privately Held**
WEB: www.hearngo.com
SIC: 3842 Hearing aids

### (G-18473)
### LONNIES STONECRAFTERS INC
3291 S Alpine Rd (61109-2602)
PHONE..................................815 316-6565
Fax: 815 316-2295
Rick George, *President*
Mark Presson, *Vice Pres*
Mike Thomas, *Opers Mgr*
Tony Bubelis, *Manager*
▲ EMP: 26
SALES (est): 3.7MM **Privately Held**
WEB: www.lonniesstonecrafters.com
SIC: 3281 Cut stone & stone products

### (G-18474)
### LSP INDUSTRIES INC (PA)
5060 27th Ave (61109-1711)
P.O. Box 5303 (61125-0303)
PHONE..................................815 226-8090
Fax: 815 226-9250
Raymond La Mantia, *President*
Brad La Mantia, *Vice Pres*
Greg La Mantia, *Vice Pres*
Gregory Lamantia, *Vice Pres*
Mark Wessmann, *Purch Mgr*
EMP: 15
SQ FT: 12,000
SALES (est): 5.7MM **Privately Held**
WEB: www.lspind.com
SIC: 3569 2992 3423 Lubrication equipment, industrial; re-refining lubricating oils & greases; hammers (hand tools)

### (G-18475)
### LUNQUIST MANUFACTURING CORP
5681 11th St (61109-3654)
PHONE..................................815 874-2437
Fax: 815 874-2428
Johathan G Lunquist, *President*
Mark Dixon, *Vice Pres*
EMP: 28 EST: 1959
SQ FT: 20,000
SALES (est): 4.7MM **Privately Held**
SIC: 3599 Machine shop, jobbing & repair

### (G-18476)
### M & W GRINDING OF ROCKFORD
4697 Hydraulic Rd (61109-2615)
PHONE..................................815 874-9481
Scott R Monge, *President*
Maskey Heath, *Vice Pres*
EMP: 7
SQ FT: 4,800
SALES (est): 590K **Privately Held**
SIC: 3599 Machine shop, jobbing & repair; grinding castings for the trade

# GEOGRAPHIC SECTION
## Rockford - Winnebago County (G-18502)

**(G-18477)**
**M E F CORP**
Also Called: Penguin Foods
1614 Christina St (61104-5137)
PHONE.................................815 965-8604
Fax: 815 965-8669
Kathy Ciembronowicz, *President*
John Ciembronowicz, *Vice Pres*
**EMP:** 18
**SQ FT:** 4,615
**SALES (est):** 710K  Privately Held
**SIC:** 5812  5421  2013  Fast-food restaurant, chain; meat markets, including freezer provisioners; sausages & other prepared meats

**(G-18478)**
**MAASSCORP INC**
1400 Eddy Ave (61103-3171)
PHONE.................................763 383-1400
A Edward Maass, *President*
Ed Maass, *Personnel Exec*
John Maass, *Manager*
**EMP:** 6 EST: 1977
**SQ FT:** 3,500
**SALES (est):** 580K  Privately Held
**WEB:** www.magnecorp.com
**SIC:** 2542  Stands, merchandise display: except wood

**(G-18479)**
**MACO-SYS LLC**
4317 Maray Dr (61107-4967)
PHONE.................................779 888-3260
David Spahr, *Mng Member*
Emma Robbins, *Manager*
**EMP:** 14
**SALES (est):** 1.1MM  Privately Held
**SIC:** 3699  Security control equipment & systems

**(G-18480)**
**MAGNA-LOCK USA INC**
Also Called: Magna-Lock Acquisition
2730 Eastrock Dr (61109-1734)
P.O. Box 5045 (61125-0045)
PHONE.................................815 962-8700
Fax: 815 398-0285
David Nordman, *President*
▼ **EMP:** 11
**SQ FT:** 20,000
**SALES (est):** 2.1MM  Privately Held
**SIC:** 3545  3599  Machine tool accessories; rotary tables; machine shop, jobbing & repair

**(G-18481)**
**MAIN SOURCE MACHINING**
2411 Latham St (61103-3953)
PHONE.................................815 962-8770
Brian Heaslip, *President*
Polly Heaslip, *Vice Pres*
**EMP:** 4
**SALES (est):** 300K  Privately Held
**SIC:** 3599  Machine shop, jobbing & repair

**(G-18482)**
**MANUFACTURING TECH GROUP INC**
3520 N Main St (61103-2116)
P.O. Box 93 (61105-0093)
PHONE.................................815 966-2300
James Jackson, *President*
Randy Warkentien, *Partner*
Lisa Przytulski, *Associate*
**EMP:** 3
**SQ FT:** 1,500
**SALES (est):** 240K  Privately Held
**SIC:** 7372  7371  Prepackaged software; custom computer programming services

**(G-18483)**
**MARTIN AUTOMATIC INC**
1661 Northrock Ct (61103-1296)
PHONE.................................815 654-4800
Fax: 815 654-4810
Roger Cederholm, *President*
John R Martin, *Chairman*
Hope Hu, *Regional Mgr*
Gavin Rittmeyer, *Regional Mgr*
Brian Sager, *Regional Mgr*
◆ **EMP:** 180
**SQ FT:** 165,000
**SALES (est):** 59.8MM  Privately Held
**WEB:** www.martinautomatic.com
**SIC:** 3565  3625  3823  3555  Packaging machinery; relays & industrial controls; industrial instrmnts msrmnt display/control process variable; presses, gravure

**(G-18484)**
**MASTER MACHINE CRAFT INC**
6401 Falcon Rd (61109-4365)
PHONE.................................815 874-3078
Randy Loomis, *CEO*
**EMP:** 4
**SQ FT:** 21,000
**SALES (est):** 580.5K  Privately Held
**SIC:** 3549  Metalworking machinery

**(G-18485)**
**MASTERS PLATING CO INC**
2228 20th Ave (61104-7326)
PHONE.................................815 226-8846
Larry R Farr, *President*
Bonnie Farr, *Vice Pres*
**EMP:** 5
**SALES (est):** 475.7K  Privately Held
**SIC:** 3471  Plating of metals or formed products

**(G-18486)**
**MASTERS YATES INC**
Also Called: Masters & Yates Machine
2430 20th St (61104-7452)
PHONE.................................815 227-9585
Fax: 815 399-9397
Dave J Masters, *President*
**EMP:** 3 EST: 1979
**SQ FT:** 5,000
**SALES (est):** 750K  Privately Held
**SIC:** 3451  Screw machine products

**(G-18487)**
**MC CHEMICAL COMPANY (PA)**
Also Called: Lincoln State Steel Div
720 South St (61102-2126)
P.O. Box 1926 (61110-0426)
PHONE.................................815 964-7687
Fax: 815 964-3820
Kathleen Hurka, *President*
Kathy Hurka, *COO*
Tom Seipts, *Research*
Don Bailey, *Controller*
Bruce Gabel, *Natl Sales Mgr*
**EMP:** 24 EST: 1969
**SQ FT:** 40,000
**SALES (est):** 4.9MM  Privately Held
**SIC:** 2899  3312  Chemical preparations; blast furnaces & steel mills

**(G-18488)**
**MDM CONSTRUCTION SUPPLY LLC**
815 N Church St Ste 3 (61103-6983)
PHONE.................................815 847-7340
Michael Close, *Vice Pres*
Rosario Ocampo - Strategos,
**EMP:** 8
**SALES (est):** 719.5K  Privately Held
**SIC:** 1389  Construction, repair & dismantling services

**(G-18489)**
**MECHANICAL TOOL & ENGRG CO (PA)**
Also Called: Mte Hydraulics
4701 Kishwaukee St (61109-2926)
P.O. Box 5906 (61125-0906)
PHONE.................................815 397-4701
Fax: 815 399-5528
Richard D Nordlof, *President*
Gregory S Nordlof, *President*
John Fulton, *Principal*
Gerald Lang, *Corp Secy*
Rich Thurman, *Vice Pres*
▲ **EMP:** 160 EST: 1946
**SQ FT:** 150,000
**SALES (est):** 69.1MM  Privately Held
**SIC:** 3594  3542  Pumps, hydraulic power transfer; presses: forming, stamping, punching, sizing (machine tools)

**(G-18490)**
**MECHANICAL TOOL & ENGRG CO**
Also Called: M T E Hydraulics
4700 Boeing Dr (61109-2904)
P.O. Box 5906 (61125-0906)
PHONE.................................815 397-4701
Fax: 815 226-0026
Gerald Lang, *General Mgr*
Randy Welch, *Superintendent*
Richard Thurman, *Sales Mgr*
Kathy Ross, *Prgrmr*
**EMP:** 200
**SALES (corp-wide):** 69.1MM  Privately Held
**SIC:** 3594  3599  Pumps, hydraulic power transfer; machine shop, jobbing & repair
**PA:** Mechanical Tool & Engineering Co Inc
4701 Kishwaukee St
Rockford IL 61109
815 397-4701

**(G-18491)**
**MENCARINI ENTERPRISES INC**
Also Called: PIP Printing
4911 26th Ave (61109-1637)
P.O. Box 5403 (61125-0403)
PHONE.................................815 398-9565
Fax: 815 398-9568
Dominic Mencarini, *President*
Margaret Mencarini, *Treasurer*
Mike Badour, *Manager*
**EMP:** 10
**SQ FT:** 4,000
**SALES (est):** 1.5MM  Privately Held
**SIC:** 2752  2789  2791  Commercial printing, offset; bookbinding & related work; typesetting

**(G-18492)**
**MERIDIAN HEALTHCARE**
1718 Northrock Ct (61103-1201)
PHONE.................................815 633-5326
Sherri Reicher, *Principal*
**EMP:** 3
**SALES (est):** 238.8K  Privately Held
**SIC:** 2834  Pharmaceutical preparations

**(G-18493)**
**MERLIN TECHNOLOGIES INC**
Also Called: Para Tech Systems Company
2724 Country Club Ter (61103-3106)
PHONE.................................630 232-9223
William H Pope, *President*
Rudolph Allison, *Vice Pres*
▲ **EMP:** 5
**SALES (est):** 460K  Privately Held
**WEB:** www.merlindarts.com
**SIC:** 3944  Darts & dart games

**(G-18494)**
**MESSER MACHINE**
2327 20th Ave (61104-7327)
PHONE.................................815 398-6248
David R Messer, *President*
**EMP:** 6
**SQ FT:** 3,500
**SALES (est):** 750K  Privately Held
**WEB:** www.messermachine.com
**SIC:** 3599  Machine & other job shop work

**(G-18495)**
**METAL CUTTING TOOLS CORP**
Also Called: Metcut
21 Airport Dr (61109-2994)
PHONE.................................815 226-0650
Fax: 815 391-6253
Bruce Swanson, *QC Mgr*
Mike Wayman, *Director*
Gus Liepins, *Director*
▲ **EMP:** 130 EST: 1941
**SQ FT:** 35,000
**SALES (est):** 22.8MM
**SALES (corp-wide):** 1.5B  Privately Held
**WEB:** www.harbourgroup.com
**SIC:** 3541  Machine tools, metal cutting type
**PA:** Harbour Group Ltd.
7701 Forsyth Blvd Ste 600
Saint Louis MO 63105
314 727-5550

**(G-18496)**
**METAL PREP SERVICES INC**
5434 International Dr (61109-2776)
PHONE.................................815 874-7631
William R Wessel, *President*
**EMP:** 4
**SQ FT:** 5,000
**SALES (est):** 338.2K  Privately Held
**WEB:** www.metalprepservices.com
**SIC:** 1721  1799  3479  Industrial painting; sandblasting of building exteriors; painting, coating & hot dipping; coating of metals & formed products

**(G-18497)**
**METALS USA ROCKFORD**
4902 Hydraulic Rd (61109-2621)
PHONE.................................815 874-8536
Dennis Anderson, *Branch Mgr*
**EMP:** 13
**SALES (corp-wide):** 9.9MM  Privately Held
**SIC:** 3599  Amusement park equipment
**PA:** Metals Usa Rockford
305 Peoples Ave
Rockford IL 61104
815 874-8536

**(G-18498)**
**METROLOGY RESOURCE GROUP INC**
3503 20th St (61109-2337)
P.O. Box 6436 (61125-1436)
PHONE.................................815 703-3141
Patrick Murphy, *President*
**EMP:** 3
**SQ FT:** 3,200
**SALES (est):** 340K  Privately Held
**SIC:** 3823  Industrial process measurement equipment

**(G-18499)**
**MICRO MACHINES INTL LLC**
605 Fulton Ave (61103-4183)
PHONE.................................815 985-3652
Hollis A Hanson, *President*
**EMP:** 1
**SALES (est):** 500K  Privately Held
**SIC:** 3541  Machine tools, metal cutting type

**(G-18500)**
**MICRO PUNCH & DIE CO**
5536 International Dr (61109-2784)
P.O. Box 5252 (61125-0252)
PHONE.................................815 874-5544
Fax: 815 874-4560
Nordahl Kirking, *President*
Judith Kirking, *Corp Secy*
**EMP:** 15
**SQ FT:** 8,000
**SALES (est):** 2.2MM  Privately Held
**WEB:** www.micropunch.com
**SIC:** 3544  Dies & die holders for metal cutting, forming, die casting; punches, forming & stamping

**(G-18501)**
**MICRO SCREW MACHINE CO INC**
2115 15th St (61104-7310)
PHONE.................................815 397-2115
Fax: 815 397-0096
Ronald L Jacobson, *President*
Barbara L Jacobson, *Admin Sec*
**EMP:** 5
**SQ FT:** 3,000
**SALES:** 250K  Privately Held
**WEB:** www.microscrewmachine.com
**SIC:** 3451  Screw machine products

**(G-18502)**
**MID-STATES FORGING DIE-TOOL**
2844 Eastrock Dr (61109-1736)
P.O. Box 5025 (61125-0025)
PHONE.................................815 226-2313
Fax: 815 226-2370
Gregory P Heim, *President*
Richard Heim, *COO*
Joyce Young, *Office Mgr*
Virginia D Heim, *Admin Sec*
**EMP:** 6
**SQ FT:** 20,800
**SALES (est):** 87.1K
**SALES (corp-wide):** 8.8MM  Privately Held
**WEB:** www.modernforge.com
**SIC:** 3544  Special dies & tools

# Rockford - Winnebago County (G-18503)  GEOGRAPHIC SECTION

PA: Modern Drop Forge Company, Llc
8757 Colorado St
Merrillville IN 46410
708 489-4208

**(G-18503)**
**MID-STATES SCREW CORPORATION**
1817 18th Ave (61104-7399)
PHONE.................815 397-2440
Fax: 815 398-1047
Bruce E Horst, *President*
Michael Kranish, *General Mgr*
Patricia Horst, *Corp Secy*
Doug Walters, *Foreman/Supr*
Tom Felvey, *Controller*
▲ EMP: 40
SQ FT: 33,000
SALES (est): 9.7MM Privately Held
WEB: www.midstatesscrew.com
SIC: 3452 Screws, metal

**(G-18504)**
**MIDWEST CONVERTERS INC**
5112 28th Ave (61109-1721)
PHONE.................815 229-9808
Fax: 815 229-9874
Dennis G Sneath, *President*
Cathleen A Sneath, *Vice Pres*
EMP: 10
SQ FT: 20,000
SALES (est): 1.4MM Privately Held
WEB: www.raceconverters.com
SIC: 3714 3566 Motor vehicle transmissions, drive assemblies & parts; torque converters, except automotive

**(G-18505)**
**MIDWEST DISPLAY & MFG INC**
127 N Wyman St Apt 4 (61101-1114)
PHONE.................815 962-2199
Kyle Bevers, *President*
EMP: 2
SQ FT: 2,400
SALES (est): 210K Privately Held
SIC: 2541 Cabinets, except refrigerated: show, display, etc.: wood; table or counter tops, plastic laminated; display fixtures, wood

**(G-18506)**
**MIDWEST RAIL JUNCTION**
1907 Cumberland St (61103-4763)
PHONE.................815 963-0200
Fax: 815 963-0285
Scott Matejka, *Owner*
EMP: 2
SALES (est): 202.2K Privately Held
WEB: www.midwestrailjunction.com
SIC: 3944 5092 5945 Board games, puzzles & models, except electronic; model kits; children's toys & games, except dolls

**(G-18507)**
**MIDWEST STITCH**
Also Called: D Castris
6767 Charles St (61108-6832)
PHONE.................815 394-1516
Daniel De Castris, *Owner*
Danel Decastris, *Manager*
EMP: 7
SALES (est): 750K Privately Held
WEB: www.midweststitch.com
SIC: 2395 2396 Embroidery products, except schiffli machine; automotive & apparel trimmings

**(G-18508)**
**MIDWEST WIRE WORKS (PA)**
4657 Stenstrom Rd (61109-2637)
PHONE.................815 874-1701
Fax: 815 874-1702
Pete Dickerson, *Owner*
Kellee Dickerson, *Office Mgr*
Lauren Head, *Office Mgr*
Robin Kelley, *Office Mgr*
EMP: 10
SQ FT: 20,000
SALES (est): 1.8MM Privately Held
SIC: 3496 Miscellaneous fabricated wire products

**(G-18509)**
**MNP PRECISION PARTS LLC (HQ)**
1111 Samuelson Rd (61109-3620)
PHONE.................815 391-5256
Karen Leary, *Vice Pres*
Martin Schnurr, *Vice Pres*
Tom Peck, *Engineer*
Larry Berman,
EMP: 189
SQ FT: 650,000
SALES (est): 22.9MM
SALES (corp-wide): 203MM Privately Held
SIC: 3452 3465 3469 Bolts, metal; automotive stampings; electronic enclosures, stamped or pressed metal
PA: Mnp Corporation
44225 Utica Rd
Utica MI 48317
586 254-1320

**(G-18510)**
**MOBILITY CONNECTION INC**
4100 E State St (61108-2008)
PHONE.................815 965-8090
Fax: 815 965-8061
Roger Lichey, *President*
Christine Calvert, *Manager*
Becky Lichey, *Manager*
Paul Bertolini, *Director*
EMP: 5
SALES: 570.9K Privately Held
SIC: 3842 5047 Wheelchairs; medical equipment & supplies; therapy equipment

**(G-18511)**
**MRS FISHERS INC**
Also Called: Mrs. Fisher's Chips
1231 Fulton Ave (61103-4025)
PHONE.................815 964-9114
Fax: 815 964-3880
Roma Hailman, *President*
Mark Hailman, *Corp Secy*
EMP: 11 EST: 1932
SQ FT: 10,000
SALES (est): 1.7MM Privately Held
WEB: www.mrsfisherschips.com
SIC: 2096 Potato chips & other potato-based snacks

**(G-18512)**
**MULLER-PINEHURST DAIRY INC**
Also Called: Prairie Farms Dairy
2110 Ogilby Rd (61102-3400)
P.O. Box 299 (61105-0299)
PHONE.................815 968-0441
Fax: 815 961-1625
Neal L Rosinsky, *President*
Cox Winston, *Plant Mgr*
Scott Runyard, *Manager*
EMP: 150
SALES (corp-wide): 18.3MM Privately Held
SIC: 2026 2024 2097 Milk & cream, except fermented, cultured & flavored; milk processing (pasteurizing, homogenizing, bottling); ice cream & ice milk; manufactured ice
PA: Muller-Pinehurst Dairy, Inc.
1100 N Brdwy St
Carlinville IL 62626
217 854-2547

**(G-18513)**
**MYCO INC**
1122 Milford Ave (61109-3636)
PHONE.................815 395-8500
Robert Yedor, *President*
Jim Musick, *Plant Mgr*
Bill Schooley, *Manager*
EMP: 220
SALES (est): 32.2MM Privately Held
SIC: 3496 Miscellaneous fabricated wire products; shelving, made from purchased wire

**(G-18514)**
**N & S PATTERN CO**
4911 Hydraulic Rd (61109-2620)
PHONE.................815 874-6166
Fax: 815 874-6274
Lavern Neff, *President*
Blair Neff, *Treasurer*
Jane Neff, *Bookkeeper*
EMP: 12 EST: 1970
SQ FT: 9,000
SALES (est): 1.1MM Privately Held
SIC: 3543 Industrial patterns

**(G-18515)**
**NATIONAL DETROIT INC**
1590 Northrock Ct (61103-1234)
P.O. Box 2285, Loves Park (61131-0285)
PHONE.................815 877-4041
Fax: 815 877-4050
EMP: 33 EST: 1939
SQ FT: 32,000
SALES (est): 6.1MM Privately Held
SIC: 3546 Mfg Power-Driven Handtools

**(G-18516)**
**NATIONAL HEADER DIE CORP**
1190 Anvil Rd (61115-1483)
PHONE.................815 636-7201
Fax: 815 636-8017
Randal G Loomis, *CEO*
EMP: 19
SALES: 2MM Privately Held
WEB: www.nationalheaderdie.com
SIC: 3544 Special dies & tools

**(G-18517)**
**NATIONAL TECHNICAL SYSTEMS INC**
Also Called: NTS Technical Systems
3761 S Central Ave (61102-4294)
PHONE.................815 315-9250
Ellie Taylor, *General Mgr*
EMP: 15
SALES (corp-wide): 193.9MM Privately Held
SIC: 3825 Instruments to measure electricity
HQ: National Technical Systems, Inc.
24007 Ventura Blvd # 200
Calabasas CA 91302
818 591-0776

**(G-18518)**
**NATURAL CHOICE CORPORATION**
5677 Sockness Dr (61109-6331)
PHONE.................815 874-4444
Fax: 815 874-4445
George Knoll, *President*
Melissa Klenke, *Business Mgr*
Gerta Knoll, *Admin Sec*
Teresa Rodriquez, *Admin Asst*
▲ EMP: 18
SQ FT: 10,000
SALES (est): 4.4MM Privately Held
WEB: www.naturalchoicewater.com
SIC: 3589 3585 5078 Water purification equipment, household type; soda fountain & beverage dispensing equipment & parts; drinking water coolers, mechanical

**(G-18519)**
**NELSON MANUFACTURING CO INC**
2516 20th St (61104-7454)
PHONE.................815 229-0161
Fax: 815 229-7043
Gordon S Nelson, *President*
Doris Nelson, *Corp Secy*
Julie Way, *Bookkeeper*
EMP: 11
SQ FT: 10,000
SALES (est): 2.2MM Privately Held
SIC: 3469 3444 Stamping metal for the trade; sheet metalwork

**(G-18520)**
**NORTHERN ILL BLOOD BNK INC (PA)**
Also Called: ROCK RIVER VALLEY BLOOD CENTER
419 N 6th St (61107-4104)
P.O. Box 4305 (61110-0805)
PHONE.................815 965-8751
Fax: 815 965-8756
Linda Garber, *CEO*
Heidi Ognibene, *General Mgr*
Thomas Mulcahy, *Facilities Mgr*
Lisa Entrikin, *Opers Staff*
Lisa Munson, *Controller*
EMP: 65
SQ FT: 20,000
SALES: 9.5MM Privately Held
WEB: www.nibb.org
SIC: 2836 Blood derivatives; extracts; plasmas

**(G-18521)**
**NORTHERN ILLI ELECTRCL JNT APP**
619 Southrock Dr (61102-4600)
PHONE.................815 969-8484
Fax: 815 969-8400
Todd Kindred, *Administration*
Michael Tongue, *Administration*
EMP: 10
SALES: 773.9K Privately Held
SIC: 3699 Electronic training devices

**(G-18522)**
**NORTHERN PROSTHETICS**
2629 Charles St (61108-1608)
PHONE.................815 226-0444
Fax: 815 226-1819
Erich Schulze, *President*
Tina Hoeo, *Manager*
Herbert Schulze, *Orthopedist*
EMP: 8 EST: 1961
SQ FT: 5,738
SALES (est): 640K Privately Held
SIC: 3842 Orthopedic appliances; limbs, artificial

**(G-18523)**
**NYCLO SCREW MACHINE PDTS INC**
3610 Mansfield St (61109-2007)
PHONE.................815 229-7900
Fax: 815 229-7981
Timothy Clow, *President*
Peggy Clow, *Admin Sec*
EMP: 12
SQ FT: 14,000
SALES: 2MM Privately Held
WEB: www.nyclo.com
SIC: 3451 Screw machine products

**(G-18524)**
**O & L MACHINE INC**
1115 18th Ave (61104-5358)
PHONE.................815 963-6600
Dan Olivotti, *President*
Nicholas Lamarca, *Admin Sec*
EMP: 8
SQ FT: 7,000
SALES: 610K Privately Held
SIC: 3599 Machine shop, jobbing & repair

**(G-18525)**
**OLE SALTYS OF ROCKFORD INC**
3131 Summerdale Ave (61101-3422)
PHONE.................815 637-2447
Al Domico, *President*
EMP: 5
SALES (corp-wide): 1.1MM Privately Held
SIC: 2096 Potato chips & other potato-based snacks
PA: Ole Salty's Of Rockford, Inc.
1920 E Riverside Blvd
Loves Park IL 61111
815 637-2447

**(G-18526)**
**OLSON ALUMINUM CASTINGS LTD**
2135 15th St (61104-7310)
P.O. Box 6106 (61125-1106)
PHONE.................815 229-3292
Fax: 815 229-7082
Tad L Olson, *President*
Raylin J Olson, *Corp Secy*
Zac Utsinger, *Vice Pres*
Bill Cote, *QC Mgr*
Mike Stahl, *Sales Mgr*
EMP: 40
SQ FT: 39,000
SALES (est): 10.2MM Privately Held
WEB: www.olsonalum.com
SIC: 3365 3543 Aluminum & aluminum-based alloy castings; foundry patternmaking

# GEOGRAPHIC SECTION
## Rockford - Winnebago County (G-18552)

**(G-18527)**
**OWENS CORNING SALES LLC**
2710 Laude Dr (61109-1448)
PHONE..................................815 226-4627
Jill Nielson, *Human Resources*
Joe Hanna, *Manager*
EMP: 81
SQ FT: 90,000
SALES (corp-wide): 5.6B **Publicly Held**
WEB: www.owenscorning.com
SIC: 3275 3086 2821 Gypsum products; plastics foam products; plastics materials & resins
HQ: Owens Corning Sales, Llc
1 Owens Corning Pkwy
Toledo OH 43659
419 248-8000

**(G-18528)**
**PAL MIDWEST LTD (PA)**
1030 S Main St (61101-1418)
P.O. Box 624 (61105-0624)
PHONE..................................815 965-2981
Fax: 815 399-6201
Mary Lea Sagona Blum, *President*
David Blum, *Vice Pres*
EMP: 5
SQ FT: 20,000
SALES: 120K **Privately Held**
WEB: www.rashcream.com
SIC: 2834 2844 Pharmaceutical preparations; toilet preparations

**(G-18529)**
**PAMACHEYON PUBLISHING INC**
305 Saint Louis Ave (61104-1522)
PHONE..................................815 395-0101
EMP: 5
SALES (est): 380K **Privately Held**
SIC: 2731 Books-Publishing/Printing

**(G-18530)**
**PATKUS MACHINE CO**
2607 Marshall St (61109-1334)
PHONE..................................815 398-7818
Fax: 815 226-1626
Terry Lynn Patkus, *President*
EMP: 6
SQ FT: 11,000
SALES (est): 1.1MM **Privately Held**
SIC: 5084 3599 7692 Tool & die makers' equipment; machine shop, jobbing & repair; welding repair

**(G-18531)**
**PATRICK HOLDINGS INC (PA)**
Also Called: Area Rigging & Millwright Svcs
5894 Sandy Hollow Rd (61109-2767)
PHONE..................................815 874-5300
Fax: 815 874-0250
James E Patrick, *President*
Linda Patrick, *Corp Secy*
Kathleen Englin, *Manager*
EMP: 10
SQ FT: 18,000
SALES (est): 3.3MM **Privately Held**
SIC: 7699 3441 3446 7353 Industrial equipment services; fabricated structural metal; railings, prefabricated metal; heavy construction equipment rental; installing building equipment

**(G-18532)**
**PEARSON FASTENER CORPORATION**
1400 Samuelson Rd (61109-3607)
PHONE..................................815 397-4460
Fax: 815 398-3250
Brad Pearson, *Chairman*
Lisbeth J Pearson, *Corp Secy*
Scott Morris, *Marketing Mgr*
David Pearson, *Manager*
Paul Chandler, *Director*
EMP: 13 EST: 1971
SQ FT: 56,000
SALES (est): 3MM **Privately Held**
WEB: www.pearsonfastener.com
SIC: 3452 Bolts, metal; rivets, metal; screws, metal

**(G-18533)**
**PGI MFG LLC**
Also Called: Deephole Drilling Service
614 Grable St (61109-2004)
PHONE..................................815 398-0313
Fax: 815 398-4352
Gail Swanson, *Purchasing*
Don Marlin, *QA Dir*
John Razzano, *Mng Member*
EMP: 6
SALES (corp-wide): 41.7MM **Privately Held**
SIC: 3546 Drills & drilling tools
PA: Pgi Mfg., Llc
100 E Wayne St Ste 320
South Bend IN 46601
574 968-3222

**(G-18534)**
**PGI MFG LLC**
Also Called: La Salle Mfg & Mch Co
614 Grable St (61109-2004)
P.O. Box 625, Rochester IN (46975-0625)
PHONE..................................800 821-3475
Charles Chamberlain, *Engineer*
Tom Brown, *Manager*
EMP: 82
SALES (corp-wide): 41.7MM **Privately Held**
SIC: 3599 Custom machinery; machine shop, jobbing & repair
PA: Pgi Mfg., Llc
100 E Wayne St Ste 320
South Bend IN 46601
574 968-3222

**(G-18535)**
**PHELPS INDUSTRIES LLC**
5213 26th Ave (61109-1707)
PHONE..................................815 397-0236
Douglas Nelson, *Manager*
EMP: 30
SQ FT: 20,000
SALES (corp-wide): 52.8MM **Privately Held**
WEB: www.phelpsindustriesinc.com
SIC: 2047 Dog food
HQ: Phelps Industries Llc
599 North Ave Ste 9-4
Wakefield MA 01880
781 224-9666

**(G-18536)**
**PIEMONTE BAKERY COMPANY INC**
1122 Rock St (61101-1431)
PHONE..................................815 962-4833
Steve Mc Keever, *President*
William J Mc Keever, *Systems Mgr*
EMP: 25
SQ FT: 8,000
SALES (est): 3.3MM **Privately Held**
SIC: 5149 2051 Crackers, cookies & bakery products; bread, cake & related products

**(G-18537)**
**PRECISION GOVERNORS LLC**
1715 Northrock Ct (61103-1201)
PHONE..................................815 229-5300
Fax: 815 229-5342
Jeff Palzer, *Safety Mgr*
Leonardo Gonzalez, *Purchasing*
Chad Clendening, *Engineer*
George Kuczenski, *Engineer*
Ryan Satterlee, *Engineer*
▲ EMP: 20
SQ FT: 10,000
SALES (est): 4.5MM **Privately Held**
WEB: www.precisiongovernors.com
SIC: 3714 Governors, motor vehicle

**(G-18538)**
**PRECISION HEADER TOOLING INC**
3441 Precision Dr (61109-2771)
PHONE..................................815 874-9116
Fax: 815 874-9018
David Tollin, *President*
Dave Tollin, *President*
Charlotte Tollin, *Admin Sec*
EMP: 10 EST: 1971
SQ FT: 9,000
SALES (est): 1.3MM **Privately Held**
SIC: 3545 3542 3544 Reamers, machine tool; headers; dies & die holders for metal cutting, forming, die casting

**(G-18539)**
**PRECISION MASTERS**
2801 Eastrock Dr (61109-7502)
PHONE..................................815 397-3894
Fax: 815 397-9586
James Baker, *President*
John W Kozyra, *Vice Pres*
Pat Cleeland, *Treasurer*
Pam Kozyra, *Admin Sec*
EMP: 24
SQ FT: 9,000
SALES (est): 5.6MM **Privately Held**
SIC: 3545 3599 Machine tool accessories; precision measuring tools; precision tools, machinists'; scales, measuring (machinists' precision tools); machine shop, jobbing & repair

**(G-18540)**
**PREMIUM OIL COMPANY**
923 Fairview Ct (61101-5952)
PHONE..................................815 963-3800
Fax: 815 963-3805
Richard A Fedeli, *President*
Kevin Fedeli, *Vice Pres*
Helen Fedeli, *Admin Sec*
EMP: 10
SQ FT: 14,000
SALES (est): 2.3MM **Privately Held**
SIC: 2992 5171 2842 Oils & greases, blending & compounding; petroleum bulk stations; specialty cleaning, polishes & sanitation goods

**(G-18541)**
**PRINZINGS OF ROCKFORD**
2046 Schell Dr (61109-4832)
PHONE..................................815 874-9654
Richard T Prinzing, *Owner*
EMP: 3
SALES: 1K **Privately Held**
SIC: 3589 Service industry machinery

**(G-18542)**
**PROCESS GRAPHICS CORP**
Also Called: Pg Display
4801 Shepherd Trl (61103-1221)
PHONE..................................815 637-2500
Fax: 815 637-2600
Timothy Farrell, *President*
Judith Farrell, *Corp Secy*
Dan Farrell, *Vice Pres*
Stefanie Page, *Office Mgr*
EMP: 30
SQ FT: 82,240
SALES (est): 5.2MM **Privately Held**
WEB: www.pgdisplay.com
SIC: 2759 3993 Screen printing; displays & cutouts, window & lobby

**(G-18543)**
**PROTECH DESIGN & MANUFACTURING**
1848 18th Ave (61104-7318)
PHONE..................................815 398-7520
Fax: 815 398-7940
Ronald Sjedin, *President*
Matt Juric, *Principal*
EMP: 7
SQ FT: 4,500
SALES: 450K **Privately Held**
WEB: www.protech-dmfg.com
SIC: 3599 Machine shop, jobbing & repair

**(G-18544)**
**PURE FLO BOTTLING INC**
2430 N Main St (61103-4046)
PHONE..................................815 963-4797
Steve Souza, *President*
Carol Souza, *Vice Pres*
EMP: 3
SQ FT: 10,500
SALES: 250K **Privately Held**
SIC: 8748 2086 Business consulting; water, pasteurized: packaged in cans, bottles, etc.

**(G-18545)**
**PWF**
8123 Harrison Rd (61101-7309)
PHONE..................................815 967-0218
Michael Helwig, *Owner*
EMP: 2
SALES (est): 259.5K **Privately Held**
SIC: 3537 Forklift trucks

**(G-18546)**
**R-TECH FEEDERS INC**
5292 American Rd (61109-6311)
PHONE..................................815 874-2990
Fax: 815 874-4661
Jeffrey Richards, *President*
Tammy Richards, *Vice Pres*
EMP: 22
SQ FT: 11,500
SALES (est): 4.2MM **Privately Held**
WEB: www.rtechfeeders.com
SIC: 3523 Feed grinders, crushers & mixers

**(G-18547)**
**RAMSPLITTER LOG SPLITTERS INC**
1936 11th St (61104-5412)
PHONE..................................815 398-4726
Douglas Davidson, *President*
EMP: 6
SQ FT: 15,000
SALES (est): 23.7K **Privately Held**
SIC: 3531 5082 Log splitters; logging equipment & supplies

**(G-18548)**
**RAPID AIR**
2812 22nd St (61109-1445)
PHONE..................................815 397-2578
EMP: 4 EST: 2011
SALES (est): 468.5K **Privately Held**
SIC: 3542 Machine tools, metal forming type

**(G-18549)**
**RAYCAR GEAR & MACHINE COMPANY**
6125 11th St (61109-4342)
PHONE..................................815 874-3948
Fax: 815 874-3817
Dan Schwartz, *President*
Ron Hansen, *Site Mgr*
Joy Schwartz, *Financial Exec*
Kim Macc, *Clerk*
EMP: 21 EST: 1964
SQ FT: 10,000
SALES: 3MM **Privately Held**
WEB: www.raycargear.com
SIC: 3566 3568 3462 3599 Speed changers, drives & gears; power transmission equipment; gears, forged steel; machine shop, jobbing & repair

**(G-18550)**
**RDH INC OF ROCKFORD**
3445 Lonergan Dr (61109-2622)
P.O. Box 5744 (61125-0744)
PHONE..................................815 874-9421
Fax: 815 874-9425
Larry Bull, *President*
Charlie Enright, *Purch Mgr*
Cindy Mace, *Purchasing*
Dave McNamara, *Chief Engr*
Marshall Hurley, *Design Engr*
EMP: 18
SQ FT: 17,000
SALES (est): 3.7MM **Privately Held**
WEB: www.rockforddrillhead.com
SIC: 3541 3594 3546 3545 Drilling & boring machines; tapping machines; fluid power pumps & motors; power-driven handtools; machine tool accessories

**(G-18551)**
**RED MANGO ROCKFORD**
6876 Spring Creek Rd # 118 (61114-7405)
PHONE..................................815 282-1020
Paul Hornick, *Owner*
EMP: 3
SALES (est): 193.2K **Privately Held**
SIC: 2024 Ice cream & frozen desserts

**(G-18552)**
**RED WING BRANDS AMERICA INC**
Also Called: Red Wings Shoe Store 276
845 S Perryvil Rd Unit 1 (61108)
PHONE..................................815 394-1328
Amy Stenlund, *Accountant*
Nick Diaz, *Manager*
EMP: 5
SALES (corp-wide): 599.7MM **Privately Held**
SIC: 3149 Children's footwear, except athletic

# Rockford - Winnebago County (G-18553)

HQ: Red Wing Brands Of America, Inc.
314 Main St
Red Wing MN 55066
844 314-6246

### (G-18553)
### REDIN PARTS INC
Also Called: Redin Production Machine
1922 7th St Ste 4d  (61104-5391)
PHONE.................................815 398-1010
Fax: 815 398-1055
John Konopa, *President*
Terry Arterberry, *Purchasing*
Andrew Lineberry, *Project Engr*
EMP: 5
SQ FT: 20,000
SALES (est): 889.9K  **Privately Held**
WEB: www.redinmachine.com
SIC: 3541  Deburring machines

### (G-18554)
### RELIABLE MACHINE COMPANY
1327 10th Ave  (61104-5095)
PHONE.................................815 968-8803
Fax: 815 968-5902
Gloria Stuhr-Pernacciaro, *President*
David Weber, *Vice Pres*
Nancy Tomlin, *Executive Asst*
EMP: 45 EST: 1921
SQ FT: 150,000
SALES (est): 9.9MM  **Privately Held**
WEB: www.reliablemachine.com
SIC: 3469  3429  Stamping metal for the trade; keys, locks & related hardware

### (G-18555)
### RING CONTAINER TECH LLC
Also Called: Ring Can of Illinois
4689 Assembly Dr  (61109-3083)
PHONE.................................815 229-9110
Fax: 815 229-9145
Joe Ricks, *Prdtn Mgr*
Tim Redler, *Opers Staff*
Steve Davis, *Manager*
Cindy Utley, *Manager*
Matt Galli, *Info Tech Mgr*
EMP: 30
SALES (corp-wide): 291.7MM  **Privately Held**
WEB: www.ringcontainer.com
SIC: 3085  Plastics bottles
PA: Ring Container Technologies, Llc.
1 Industrial Park
Oakland TN 38060
800 280-7464

### (G-18556)
### RIVER CITY MILLWORK INC
200 Quaker Rd Ste 3  (61104-7068)
PHONE.................................800 892-9297
Fax: 815 965-2678
William Sarbaugh, *President*
Tim Zumbro, *Purch Agent*
Janet Sarbaugh, *Admin Sec*
▲ EMP: 53
SQ FT: 95,000
SALES (est): 27.8MM  **Privately Held**
WEB: www.rivercitymillwork.com
SIC: 5031  3442  3231  2431  Millwork; building materials, exterior; building materials, interior; metal doors, sash & trim; products of purchased glass; millwork

### (G-18557)
### RIVERSIDE SPRING COMPANY
2136 12th St Ste 121  (61104-7374)
PHONE.................................815 963-3334
Fax: 815 963-9321
Charles A Davis Jr, *President*
Jerry Davis, *Vice Pres*
Charlotte Vincer, *Manager*
Charles A Davis Sr, *Admin Sec*
EMP: 6
SQ FT: 6,800
SALES (est): 700K  **Privately Held**
WEB: www.riversidespring.com
SIC: 3495  3496  Wire springs; miscellaneous fabricated wire products

### (G-18558)
### RIVERVIEW PRINTING INC
99 E State St  (61104-1009)
PHONE.................................815 987-1425
Fax: 815 961-5839
Steve Walker, *Manager*
EMP: 8
SALES: 400K  **Privately Held**
WEB: www.riverviewprinting.com
SIC: 2752  Commercial printing, lithographic

### (G-18559)
### RJ LINK INTERNATIONAL INC
Also Called: Rj Link
3741 Publishers Dr  (61109-6316)
PHONE.................................815 874-8110
Fax: 815 874-8833
Rodney J Link, *President*
Greg Farris, *Manager*
Moana Pena, *Manager*
Anne D Link, *Admin Sec*
▼ EMP: 16
SQ FT: 14,600
SALES (est): 3.2MM  **Privately Held**
WEB: www.rjlink.com
SIC: 3599  3566  3462  3321  Custom machinery; speed changers, drives & gears; iron & steel forgings; gray & ductile iron foundries

### (G-18560)
### RMC IMAGING INC
780 Creek Bluff Ln  (61114-6872)
PHONE.................................815 885-4521
Robert Czechowicz, *President*
EMP: 1
SALES: 300K  **Privately Held**
SIC: 3571  Electronic computers

### (G-18561)
### RO PAL GRINDING INC
1916 20th Ave  (61104-7320)
PHONE.................................815 964-5894
Fax: 815 964-5896
Ronald Nauschwander, *Vice Pres*
Ronald Neuschwander, *Vice Pres*
EMP: 10 EST: 1964
SQ FT: 5,200
SALES: 800K  **Privately Held**
SIC: 7389  3479  Grinding, precision: commercial or industrial; coating of metals & formed products

### (G-18562)
### ROCK RIVER BLENDING
1515 Cunningham St  (61102-2601)
PHONE.................................815 968-7860
Daniel McLoraine, *Owner*
EMP: 6
SQ FT: 24,000
SALES (est): 702.9K  **Privately Held**
SIC: 2841  Soap & other detergents

### (G-18563)
### ROCK RIVER TIMES
128 N Church St  (61101-1002)
PHONE.................................815 964-9767
Fax: 815 964-9825
Susan Johnson, *Editor*
Sally Alberts, *Bookkeeper*
Marilyn Lamar, *Office Mgr*
Frank Schier, *Manager*
Dick Hynes, *Manager*
EMP: 13
SALES (est): 730K  **Privately Held**
WEB: www.rockrivertimes.com
SIC: 2711  Newspapers

### (G-18564)
### ROCK ROAD COMPANIES INC
801 Beale Ct  (61109-4308)
PHONE.................................815 874-2441
Fax: 815 874-2774
Mike Greenan, *Branch Mgr*
EMP: 10
SALES (corp-wide): 33.9MM  **Privately Held**
WEB: www.rockroads.com
SIC: 1611  2951  1771  Highway & street paving contractor; asphalt paving mixtures & blocks; concrete work
PA: Rock Road Companies, Inc.
Us Hwy 51 &Townline Rd
Janesville WI 53545
608 752-8944

### (G-18565)
### ROCK VALLEY DIE SINKING INC
2457 Baxter Rd  (61109-5079)
PHONE.................................815 874-5511
Fax: 815 874-6603
Joseph Livingston, *President*

Timothy A Poshka, *Vice Pres*
Connie Tait, *Office Mgr*
EMP: 10
SQ FT: 3,200
SALES (est): 1.4MM  **Privately Held**
SIC: 3544  3542  Special dies, tools, jigs & fixtures; machine tools, metal forming type

### (G-18566)
### ROCKFORD BALL SCREW COMPANY
940 Southrock Dr  (61102-4299)
PHONE.................................815 961-7700
Fax: 815 961-7701
Linda McGary, *President*
Linda Mc Gary, *President*
Randy M Bain, *Vice Pres*
Randy Mc Bain, *Vice Pres*
Denis Bermingham, *Opers Mgr*
EMP: 60
SQ FT: 56,000
SALES (est): 12.5MM  **Privately Held**
WEB: www.rockfordballscrew.com
SIC: 3451  Screw machine products

### (G-18567)
### ROCKFORD BOLT & STEEL CO
126 Mill St  (61101-1491)
PHONE.................................815 968-0514
Fax: 815 968-3111
Michael G Rosman, *President*
John Moore, *Vice Pres*
John Petty, *Plant Mgr*
James Buchanan, *Engineer*
Bill Higbee, *Manager*
EMP: 48
SQ FT: 90,000
SALES (est): 12.2MM  **Privately Held**
SIC: 3452  Bolts, metal; screws, metal

### (G-18568)
### ROCKFORD BROACH INC
4993 27th Ave  (61109-1708)
PHONE.................................815 484-0409
Fax: 815 484-0413
Harold Hackworth, *President*
Janet Hackworth, *Vice Pres*
EMP: 12
SQ FT: 14,500
SALES (est): 990K  **Privately Held**
WEB: www.rockfordbroach.com
SIC: 3541  Broaching machines

### (G-18569)
### ROCKFORD BURRALL MCH CO INC
4520 Shepherd Trl  (61103-1238)
PHONE.................................815 877-7428
Fax: 815 877-7420
Raymond J Smith, *President*
Edmund P Freberg, *Vice Pres*
Tom Smith, *Foreman/Supr*
EMP: 28
SQ FT: 12,000
SALES (est): 5.2MM  **Privately Held**
SIC: 3599  Machine shop, jobbing & repair

### (G-18570)
### ROCKFORD CARBIDE DIE & TOOL
1920 20th Ave  (61104-7320)
PHONE.................................815 394-0645
Fax: 815 965-0564
Tim Baumgardt, *Partner*
Roy Baumgardt, *Partner*
Doug Johnson, *Partner*
EMP: 5
SQ FT: 2,000
SALES (est): 586.1K  **Privately Held**
SIC: 3544  Dies & die holders for metal cutting, forming, die casting

### (G-18571)
### ROCKFORD CEMENT PRODUCTS CO
315 Peoples Ave  (61104-7034)
PHONE.................................815 965-0537
Robert C Beale, *President*
Rock Yachasz, *Corp Secy*
Jeremy Beale, *Vice Pres*
EMP: 14 EST: 1911
SQ FT: 10,000

SALES (est): 3MM  **Privately Held**
SIC: 3272  3271  Covers, catch basin: concrete; manhole covers or frames, concrete; septic tanks, concrete; architectural concrete: block, split, fluted, screen, etc.; blocks, concrete or cinder: standard; brick, concrete; paving blocks, concrete

### (G-18572)
### ROCKFORD DROP FORGE COMPANY
2011 10th St  (61104-5390)
P.O. Box 567, Dekalb  (60115-0567)
PHONE.................................815 963-9611
Fax: 815 963-7950
Donald G Jones, *President*
Kent A Paul, *CFO*
Jeffrey T Jones, *Admin Sec*
Crystal Klinefelter, *Administration*
EMP: 70
SQ FT: 200,000
SALES (est): 11.2MM  **Privately Held**
WEB: www.rockforddropforge.com
SIC: 3462  Iron & steel forgings

### (G-18573)
### ROCKFORD ELECTRIC EQUIPMENT CO
2010 Harrison Ave  (61104-7343)
PHONE.................................815 398-4096
Fax: 815 398-4173
Bernard R Beishir, *President*
Stephan J Beishir, *Vice Pres*
EMP: 8
SQ FT: 10,000
SALES (est): 600K  **Privately Held**
SIC: 7694  7629  5063  Electric motor repair; electronic equipment repair; electrical apparatus & equipment; motors, electric

### (G-18574)
### ROCKFORD FOUNDRIES INC
212 Mill St  (61101-1490)
PHONE.................................815 965-7243
Fax: 815 965-0455
Peter Rundquist, *President*
Linda Graham, *Office Mgr*
John Rundquist, *Admin Sec*
EMP: 12
SQ FT: 20,000
SALES (est): 1.8MM  **Privately Held**
WEB: www.rockfordfoundries.com
SIC: 3365  3366  3369  Aluminum & aluminum-based alloy castings; castings (except die): brass; nonferrous foundries

### (G-18575)
### ROCKFORD HEAT TREATERS INC
4704 American Rd  (61109-2629)
PHONE.................................815 874-0089
Bob Deutsch, *President*
Ted Deutsch, *Vice Pres*
Tom Deutsch, *Vice Pres*
Doug Colson, *QC Mgr*
Don Shriver, *Admin Sec*
EMP: 24
SQ FT: 36,600
SALES (est): 5.6MM  **Privately Held**
SIC: 3398  Metal heat treating; annealing of metal; brazing (hardening) of metal; tempering of metal

### (G-18576)
### ROCKFORD JOBBING SERVICE INC
4955 28th Ave  (61109-1716)
PHONE.................................815 398-8661
Fax: 815 226-4314
Brian D Hornbeck, *President*
EMP: 7 EST: 1964
SQ FT: 10,000
SALES (est): 825K  **Privately Held**
WEB: www.rjsgears.com
SIC: 3599  3568  3566  3545  Machine shop, jobbing & repair; power transmission equipment; speed changers, drives & gears; machine tool accessories; iron & steel forgings

### (G-18577)
### ROCKFORD LINEAR ACTUATION
2111 23rd Ave  (61104-7332)
PHONE.................................815 986-4400

## GEOGRAPHIC SECTION
## Rockford - Winnebago County (G-18602)

Robert Trogan, *CEO*
Dave Morris, *Purch Agent*
**EMP:** 7
**SALES (est):** 1MM **Privately Held**
**WEB:** www.rockfordlinear.com
**SIC:** 3599 Custom machinery

**(G-18579)**
### ROCKFORD LINEAR MOTION LLC
940 Southrock Dr (61102-4299)
**PHONE**..................815 961-7900
Rick Sonneson, *Vice Pres*
Andy O'Connell, *Engineer*
Amy Hendrickson, *Accounting Mgr*
**EMP:** 3
**SALES (est):** 234.1K **Privately Held**
**SIC:** 3699 Linear accelerators

**(G-18580)**
### ROCKFORD MAP PUBLISHERS INC
124 N Water St Ste 10 (61107-3970)
P.O. Box 6126 (61125-1126)
**PHONE**..................815 708-6324
**Fax:** 815 544-7441
Suzanne Young, *President*
Donna Thompson, *Controller*
Susan Meyer, *Human Resources*
Susan Snyder, *Sales Mgr*
Donna Werle, *Office Mgr*
**EMP:** 18 **EST:** 1944
**SQ FT:** 4,500
**SALES (est):** 1.7MM **Privately Held**
**WEB:** www.rockfordmap.com
**SIC:** 2741 Globe covers (maps); publishing only, not printed on site

**(G-18580)**
### ROCKFORD NEWSPAPERS INC
Also Called: Rockford Register Star
99 E State St (61104-1009)
P.O. Box 679 (61105-0679)
**PHONE**..................815 987-1200
**Fax:** 815 961-5308
Fredrick Jacobi, *President*
Jack Burke, *Rsch/Dvlpt Dir*
Lori Laye, *Controller*
**EMP:** 420 **EST:** 1855
**SQ FT:** 10,000
**SALES (est):** 40MM
**SALES (corp-wide):** 1.2B **Publicly Held**
**SIC:** 2711 2752 Newspapers; commercial printing, lithographic
**HQ:** Gatehouse Media, Llc
175 Sullys Trl Ste 300
Pittsford NY 14534
585 598-0030

**(G-18581)**
### ROCKFORD ORNAMENTAL IRON INC
1817 Michigan Ave (61102-3053)
**PHONE**..................815 633-1162
Rob Kapala, *President*
Fred Kapala, *Principal*
Vicki Kapala, *Admin Sec*
**EMP:** 11 **EST:** 1951
**SALES (est):** 126.9K **Privately Held**
**SIC:** 3446 3441 Mfg Architectural Mtlwrk Structural Metal Fabrctn

**(G-18582)**
### ROCKFORD PRECISION MACHINE
4729 Hydraulic Rd (61109-2617)
**PHONE**..................815 873-1018
**Fax:** 815 873-1020
John D Casarotto Sr, *President*
John Casarotto Jr, *Vice Pres*
Theresa Casarotto, *Treasurer*
**EMP:** 10
**SQ FT:** 33,000
**SALES (est):** 1.6MM **Privately Held**
**SIC:** 3599 7692 Machine shop, jobbing & repair; welding repair

**(G-18583)**
### ROCKFORD PROCESS CONTROL INC (PA)
2020 7th St (61104-5353)
**PHONE**..................815 966-2000
**Fax:** 815 966-2026
Patrick Derry, *President*
Dennis Swick, *President*
Mike Jones, *VP Opers*
Mark Priewe, *Purch Mgr*
Mike Sheridan, *Engineer*
▲ **EMP:** 125
**SQ FT:** 170,000
**SALES (est):** 33.5MM **Privately Held**
**WEB:** www.rockfordprocess.com
**SIC:** 3429 Manufactured hardware (general); door opening & closing devices, except electrical

**(G-18584)**
### ROCKFORD QUALITY GRINDING INC
3160 Forest View Rd (61109-1642)
**PHONE**..................815 227-9001
Todd Henning, *President*
Ann Henning, *Vice Pres*
**EMP:** 10
**SALES:** 500K **Privately Held**
**SIC:** 3999 Custom pulverizing & grinding of plastic materials

**(G-18585)**
### ROCKFORD RAMS PRODUCTS INC
2902 Eastrock Dr (61109-1738)
P.O. Box 5246 (61125-0246)
**PHONE**..................815 226-0016
Malcolm Anderberg, *President*
Leah Anderberg, *Vice Pres*
Eric Anderverg, *Purchasing*
Ed Krull, *Controller*
Jeffrey Anderberg, *Admin Sec*
**EMP:** 6
**SQ FT:** 3,000
**SALES:** 200K **Privately Held**
**SIC:** 3829 Hardness testing equipment

**(G-18586)**
### ROCKFORD SECONDARY CO
2424 Laude Dr (61109-1450)
**PHONE**..................815 398-0401
**Fax:** 815 398-0406
Jimmie Clark, *Owner*
John Clark, *General Mgr*
**EMP:** 9
**SQ FT:** 20,000
**SALES (est):** 500K **Privately Held**
**SIC:** 3599 3316 Machine shop, jobbing & repair; cold finishing of steel shapes

**(G-18587)**
### ROCKFORD SYSTEMS LLC
4620 Hydraulic Rd (61109-2695)
**PHONE**..................815 874-7891
Frederick Eck,
**EMP:** 52
**SALES (est):** 10.6MM **Privately Held**
**SIC:** 3549 Wiredrawing & fabricating machinery & equipment, ex. die
**PA:** The Randolph Group Inc
211 W Wacker Dr
Chicago IL
312 263-4900

**(G-18588)**
### ROCKFORD TOOL AND MFG CO
3023 Eastrock Ct (61109-1761)
**PHONE**..................815 398-5876
**Fax:** 815 398-5673
Gary McGregor, *President*
**EMP:** 10
**SQ FT:** 16,000
**SALES:** 1MM **Privately Held**
**SIC:** 3544 3599 Special dies & tools; machine shop, jobbing & repair

**(G-18589)**
### ROCKFORD TOOLCRAFT INC (PA)
766 Research Pkwy (61109-2938)
**PHONE**..................815 398-5507
**Fax:** 815 398-0132
Jerry Busse, *CEO*
Gerald A Busse, *President*
Thomas A Busse, *President*
Jim Whale, *Plant Mgr*
Jose Pina, *Foreman/Supr*
**EMP:** 150 **EST:** 1973
**SQ FT:** 200,000
**SALES (est):** 46.5MM **Privately Held**
**WEB:** www.rockfordtoolcraft.com
**SIC:** 3469 3544 Metal stampings; special dies & tools; jigs & fixtures

**(G-18590)**
### ROCKFORD WELLNESS & DIAGNOSTIC
223 W State St (61101)
**PHONE**..................815 708-0125
Kim Osborne, *Owner*
**EMP:** 3
**SALES (est):** 195.3K **Privately Held**
**SIC:** 3841 Diagnostic apparatus, medical

**(G-18591)**
### ROCKFORM TOOLING & MACHINERY (PA)
2974 Eastrock Dr (61109-1738)
P.O. Box 4487, Canton GA (30114-0018)
**PHONE**..................770 345-4624
Richard D Smith, *CEO*
James Erickson, *Vice Pres*
Phil Priebel, *Project Engr*
Sonia C Smith, *Treasurer*
▲ **EMP:** 30
**SALES (est):** 4.2MM **Privately Held**
**SIC:** 2819 Carbides

**(G-18592)**
### ROCKFORM TOOLING & MACHINERY
Also Called: Gator Die Supplies
2974 Eastrock Dr (61109-1738)
**PHONE**..................815 398-7650
James Erickson, *Manager*
**EMP:** 4
**SALES (corp-wide):** 4.2MM **Privately Held**
**SIC:** 3545 5084 Cutting tools for machine tools; machine tools & accessories
**PA:** Rockform Tooling & Machinery, Inc
2974 Eastrock Dr
Rockford IL 61109
770 345-4624

**(G-18593)**
### ROCKWIND VENTURE PARTNERS LLC (PA)
8500 E State St (61108-2736)
**PHONE**..................630 881-6664
Richard Johnson, *Mng Member*
Chet Kolodziej,
**EMP:** 2
**SALES (est):** 351.9K **Privately Held**
**SIC:** 3511 Turbines & turbine generator sets & parts

**(G-18594)**
### ROGERS BROTHERS CO
Also Called: Rogers Brothers Galvanizing
1925 Kishwaukee St (61104-5121)
**PHONE**..................815 965-5132
**Fax:** 815 965-3765
Raymond McKinnon, *Ch of Bd*
Michael R McKinnon, *President*
Judith A Ferolie, *Corp Secy*
Lorraine Shelburne, *Vice Pres*
**EMP:** 70 **EST:** 1898
**SQ FT:** 13,000
**SALES (est):** 10.1MM **Privately Held**
**WEB:** www.rogersbrothers.com
**SIC:** 3479 Hot dip coating of metals or formed products

**(G-18595)**
### ROGERS READY MIX & MTLS INC
5510 S Mulford Rd (61109-4156)
**PHONE**..................815 874-6626
**Fax:** 815 874-8874
Toby Rogers, *Manager*
**EMP:** 25
**SALES (corp-wide):** 14.3MM **Privately Held**
**SIC:** 3273 Ready-mixed concrete
**PA:** Rogers Ready Mix & Materials, Inc.
8128 N Walnut St
Byron IL 61010
815 234-8212

**(G-18596)**
### ROMA BAKERIES INC
523 Marchesano Dr (61102-3518)
**PHONE**..................815 964-6737
**Fax:** 815 964-6057
John Bowler, *President*
**EMP:** 14
**SQ FT:** 2,000
**SALES:** 1MM **Privately Held**
**SIC:** 5461 5149 2099 2051 Bread; bakery products; food preparations; bread, cake & related products; cookies & crackers

**(G-18597)**
### RONDEX PRODUCTS INCORPORATED
324 N Gardiner Ave (61107-4337)
**PHONE**..................815 226-0452
**Fax:** 815 226-0457
Gene Russell Baldwin, *President*
Marit Baldwin, *Admin Sec*
▲ **EMP:** 12
**SALES (est):** 1.7MM **Privately Held**
**WEB:** www.rondex.com
**SIC:** 3842 Respiratory protection equipment, personal

**(G-18598)**
### ROTHENBERGER USA LLC
4455 Boeing Dr (61109-2932)
**PHONE**..................815 397-7617
**Fax:** 815 397-6174
Ed Certisimol, *CEO*
David Shumaker, *Manager*
◆ **EMP:** 52
**SALES (est):** 6.5MM **Privately Held**
**SIC:** 5074 3423 Plumbing fittings & supplies; plumbers' hand tools
**HQ:** Dr. Helmut Rothenberger Holding Gmbh.
Niederalm 96/WalterstraBe 1
Anif
624 672-0914

**(G-18599)**
### ROWALD REFRIGERATION SYSTEMS
515 Grable St (61109-2001)
**PHONE**..................815 397-7733
**Fax:** 815 397-5936
Robert W Rowald, *President*
Debra S Rowald, *Vice Pres*
**EMP:** 7
**SQ FT:** 15,000
**SALES (est):** 1.2MM **Privately Held**
**WEB:** www.rowald.com
**SIC:** 3585 Refrigeration equipment, complete

**(G-18600)**
### RUST-OLEUM CORPORATION
440 Blackhawk Park Ave (61104-5140)
**PHONE**..................815 967-4258
John Bito, *General Mgr*
Mona Mustafa, *Exec VP*
Kristin Schiro, *Purch Dir*
Jenny Brasfield, *Purch Mgr*
Carol Stumpf, *Purch Mgr*
**EMP:** 60
**SALES (corp-wide):** 4.8B **Publicly Held**
**SIC:** 2851 2891 3089 3944 Enamels; lacquer: bases, dopes, thinner; adhesives; cement, except linoleum & tile; kits, plastic; games, toys & children's vehicles; brushes, air, artists'
**HQ:** Rust-Oleum Corporation
11 E Hawthorn Pkwy
Vernon Hills IL 60061
847 367-7700

**(G-18601)**
### S & J WOODPRODUCTS
5305 Forest Hills Rd (61114-5209)
**PHONE**..................815 973-1970
Joyce Weiss, *Owner*
**EMP:** 3
**SALES:** 50K **Privately Held**
**SIC:** 2521 Wood office furniture

**(G-18602)**
### S & K BORING INC
3360 Forest View Rd (61109-1645)
**PHONE**..................815 227-4394
**Fax:** 815 227-5824
Mike Stupka, *President*
**EMP:** 2
**SQ FT:** 2,800
**SALES (est):** 330.4K **Privately Held**
**SIC:** 3599 Machine shop, jobbing & repair

# Rockford - Winnebago County (G-18603)

**(G-18603)**
**S R DOOR INC**
Also Called: Seal-Rite Door
5960 Falcon Rd (61109-2916)
PHONE...............................815 227-1148
Fax: 815 873-1524
Jeff Rogers, *Branch Mgr*
EMP: 35
SALES (corp-wide): 12.6MM **Privately Held**
WEB: www.seal-ritedoor.com
SIC: 2431 3442 3211 Doors, wood; metal doors; construction glass
PA: S R Door, Inc.
1120 O Neill Dr
Hebron OH 43025
740 927-3558

**(G-18604)**
**SA INDUSTRIES 2 INC**
999 Sandy Hollow Rd (61109-2114)
P.O. Box 5, Lake Orion MI (48361-0005)
PHONE...............................815 381-6200
Stan Aldridge, *CEO*
Boyd S Aldridge, *President*
Laura Wiggs, *Accountant*
A Joseph Garafalo, *Admin Sec*
EMP: 3
SALES (est): 338.4K **Privately Held**
SIC: 3451 Screw machine products

**(G-18605)**
**SACO USA (IL)INC**
3391 Sage Dr (61114-5391)
PHONE...............................815 877-8832
Ming Zhang, *Manager*
▲ EMP: 7 EST: 2010
SALES (est): 496.2K **Privately Held**
SIC: 3621 Motors & generators

**(G-18606)**
**SAFEWAY PRODUCTS INC**
1810 15th Ave (61104-5431)
PHONE...............................815 226-8322
Phil Fillweber, *President*
Renee Barker, *Officer*
EMP: 19 EST: 2000
SQ FT: 32,000
SALES: 1.8MM **Privately Held**
WEB: www.safewayproductsinc.com
SIC: 3089 Plastic containers, except foam

**(G-18607)**
**SAFEWAY SERVICES ROCKFORD INC**
1310 Samuelson Rd (61109-3646)
PHONE...............................815 986-1504
Fax: 815 986-1507
Thomas Lynde, *President*
Jamie Hanson, *Manager*
EMP: 22
SQ FT: 54,000
SALES: 950K **Privately Held**
WEB: www.safewayservicesinc.com
SIC: 3479 Etching & engraving

**(G-18608)**
**SCHNEIDER ELC BUILDINGS LLC (DH)**
Also Called: Invensys Environmental Contrls
839 N Perryville Rd (61107-6202)
PHONE...............................815 381-5000
Jean-Pascal Tricoire, *CEO*
Barry Coflan, *Principal*
Aurelie Richard, *Principal*
Derek Hook, *Business Mgr*
Clemens Blum, *Exec VP*
▲ EMP: 500 EST: 1836
SQ FT: 500,000
SALES (est): 329.3MM
SALES (corp-wide): 241K **Privately Held**
WEB: www.tac.com
SIC: 3822 1711 3625 3823 Building services monitoring controls, automatic; mechanical contractor; relays & industrial controls; motor control accessories, including overload relays; motor controls, electric; actuators, industrial; industrial process control instruments; motors, electric

**(G-18609)**
**SCHNEIDER ELC BUILDINGS LLC**
Invensys Environmental Contrls
4104 Charles St (61108-6229)
PHONE...............................815 227-4000
L C Peterson, *Manager*
EMP: 50
SALES (corp-wide): 241K **Privately Held**
SIC: 3822 1711 Building services monitoring controls, automatic; mechanical contractor
HQ: Schneider Electric Buildings, Llc
839 N Perryville Rd
Rockford IL 61107
815 381-5000

**(G-18610)**
**SENDELE WIRELESS SOLUTIONS**
1475 Temple Cir (61108-4448)
PHONE...............................815 227-4212
Steve Sendele, *President*
EMP: 2
SALES: 1MM **Privately Held**
SIC: 3823 Computer interface equipment for industrial process control

**(G-18611)**
**SEOCO INC**
3384 N Publs Dr Ste F (61109)
PHONE...............................815 874-9565
Ed Schmidt, *President*
David King, *President*
EMP: 3 EST: 1999
SALES (est): 988.7K
SALES (corp-wide): 2.9MM **Privately Held**
WEB: www.seoco.com
SIC: 3851 Lenses, ophthalmic
PA: Seoco, Inc.
901 Parkland Ct
Champaign IL
217 352-7865

**(G-18612)**
**SEREEN LLC**
Also Called: Sereen Boats
4543 Sable Ln (61109-4036)
PHONE...............................386 527-4876
Earl Eggert,
Logan Schnake,
EMP: 4
SALES (est): 247.3K **Privately Held**
SIC: 5551 3732 Outboard boats; outboard motors; motorboats, inboard or outboard: building & repairing

**(G-18613)**
**SERVICE MACHINE JOBS**
1308 Barnes St (61104-4721)
PHONE...............................815 986-3033
Bounnam Khempaseuth, *Owner*
EMP: 3
SQ FT: 4,000
SALES (est): 185.3K **Privately Held**
SIC: 3541 3544 3599 3542 Machine tools, metal cutting type; special dies, tools, jigs & fixtures; custom machinery; machine shop, jobbing & repair; die casting & extruding machines

**(G-18614)**
**SHAARS INTERNATIONAL INC**
129 Phelps Ave Ste 901a (61108-2484)
PHONE...............................815 315-0717
Shahid Naseer, *CEO*
EMP: 1
SALES (est): 317.3K **Privately Held**
SIC: 5099 5191 2834 8734 Firearms & ammunition, except sporting; animal feeds; veterinary pharmaceutical preparations; veterinary testing

**(G-18615)**
**SHEET METAL CONNECTORS INC**
5601 Sandy Hollow Rd (61109-2780)
PHONE...............................815 874-4600
Fax: 815 874-9979
Eric Lyzhoft, *CFO*
EMP: 17
SALES (corp-wide): 15.8MM **Privately Held**
SIC: 3444 Sheet metalwork

PA: Sheet Metal Connectors, Inc.
5850 Main St Ne
Minneapolis MN 55432
763 572-0000

**(G-18616)**
**SIEMENS INDUSTRY INC**
4669 Shepherd Trl (61103-1294)
PHONE...............................815 877-3041
Roger Rockwell, *Vice Pres*
Gerg Bachman, *Branch Mgr*
EMP: 80
SALES (corp-wide): 89.6B **Privately Held**
SIC: 3589 Water treatment equipment, industrial
HQ: Siemens Industry, Inc.
1000 Deerfield Pkwy
Buffalo Grove IL 60089
847 215-1000

**(G-18617)**
**SIGMA TOOL & MACHINING**
2324 23rd Ave (61104-7337)
PHONE...............................815 874-0500
Jon Leid, *Principal*
EMP: 7
SALES (est): 1.3MM **Privately Held**
SIC: 3599 Machine shop, jobbing & repair

**(G-18618)**
**SIMPLY COMPUTER SOFTWARE INC**
6085 Strathmoor Dr Ste 2b (61107-6636)
PHONE...............................815 231-0063
Duane Tinsley, *Owner*
EMP: 5
SALES (est): 426K **Privately Held**
SIC: 7372 Prepackaged software

**(G-18619)**
**SKYWARD PROMOTIONS INC**
1140 Charles St (61104-1219)
PHONE...............................815 969-0909
Fax: 815 969-0808
Timothy Dingus, *President*
Sandy Dingus, *Marketing Staff*
EMP: 7
SQ FT: 6,600
SALES (est): 1.2MM **Privately Held**
WEB: www.skywardpromotions.com
SIC: 5199 3993 Advertising specialties; signs & advertising specialties

**(G-18620)**
**SLIDEMATIC INDUSTRIES INC**
1303 Samuelson Rd (61109-3645)
PHONE...............................815 986-0500
Randy Baker, *President*
Laura Duncan, *General Mgr*
Brad Baker, *Plant Mgr*
Diane Belsan, *Accountant*
Randee Hansen, *Accountant*
▲ EMP: 125 EST: 1983
SALES (est): 65.6MM **Privately Held**
WEB: www.slidematic.com
SIC: 3452 Bolts, nuts, rivets & washers; nuts, metal; bolts, metal

**(G-18621)**
**SLIDEMTIC PRCSION CMPNENTS INC**
1303 Samuelson Rd (61109-3645)
PHONE...............................815 986-0500
Jamie Higgins, *Engineer*
Mark Woodbury, *Info Tech Mgr*
Janet Kingsbury, *Executive*
▲ EMP: 4
SALES (est): 174.7K **Privately Held**
SIC: 3452 Bolts, nuts, rivets & washers

**(G-18622)**
**SMITH INDUSTRIAL RUBBER & PLAS**
5463 International Dr (61109-2777)
P.O. Box 5486 (61125-0486)
PHONE...............................815 874-5364
Fax: 815 874-5390
Scott Greenfield, *President*
Thomas Rubnicki, *General Mgr*
Thomas Rudnicki, *Vice Pres*
Robynn Yost, *Manager*
EMP: 12
SQ FT: 10,000

SALES: 1.6MM **Privately Held**
WEB: www.smithindustrial.com
SIC: 3069 3999 Bags, rubber or rubberized fabric; atomizers, toiletry

**(G-18623)**
**SOUTHERN IMPERIAL INC (PA)**
Also Called: Sunbelt Plastic Extrusions
1400 Eddy Ave (61103-3198)
PHONE...............................815 877-7041
Fax: 815 877-8138
Stanley Valiulis, *President*
Steven Vandemore, *President*
Gary Rothmeyer, *District Mgr*
Paul Quinn, *VP Opers*
Jimmie Helmick, *Plant Mgr*
▲ EMP: 320 EST: 1956
SQ FT: 320,000
SALES (est): 132.8MM **Privately Held**
WEB: www.southernimperial.com
SIC: 5046 2542 Store fixtures & display equipment; fixtures: display, office or store: except wood; racks, merchandise display or storage: except wood

**(G-18624)**
**SPARE PART SOLUTIONS INC**
Also Called: Ward C N C Machining
3374 Precision Dr (61109-2768)
PHONE...............................815 637-1490
Fax: 815 637-1496
Doug Sosnowski, *President*
Dan Scott, *IT/INT Sup*
Barb Huber, *Administration*
▲ EMP: 15
SQ FT: 1,500
SALES (est): 3.8MM **Privately Held**
WEB: www.sparepartsolutions.com
SIC: 3469 Machine parts, stamped or pressed metal

**(G-18625)**
**SPECIALIZED SEPARATORS INC**
1800 16th Ave (61104-5453)
PHONE...............................815 316-0626
Russell Dennis, *President*
Richard Spades, *General Mgr*
EMP: 10
SALES (est): 851.9K **Privately Held**
WEB: www.lorine.com
SIC: 3569 3443 2992 2077 Gas producers, generators & other gas related equipment; fabricated plate work (boiler shop); lubricating oils & greases; animal & marine fats & oils

**(G-18626)**
**SPECIALTY SCREW CORPORATION**
2801 Huffman Blvd (61103-3997)
PHONE...............................815 969-4100
Fax: 815 964-2300
Russell W Johansson, *President*
Syd Nolan, *Mfg Dir*
Bill Tiburg, *Production*
Dave Marales, *Purch Agent*
Beth Halfman, *QC Mgr*
▲ EMP: 90
SQ FT: 79,000
SALES: 20.1MM **Privately Held**
WEB: www.specialtyscrew.com
SIC: 3452 Screws, metal

**(G-18627)**
**SPENCER AND KRAHN MCH TL SLS (PA)**
Also Called: S&K Machine
2621 Springdale Dr (61114-6451)
PHONE...............................815 282-3300
William Spencer, *President*
Ronald Krahn, *Corp Secy*
EMP: 2
SALES: 5MM **Privately Held**
SIC: 5084 3541 Machine tools & accessories; grinding machines, metalworking

**(G-18628)**
**SPIDER COMPANY INC (PA)**
Also Called: SCI
2340 11th St (61104-7246)
PHONE...............................815 961-8200
Fax: 815 961-8243
Thomas Diehl, *President*
Jack West, *Engineer*
Jeff Johnson, *Manager*
Adam Wiemers, *Technology*

# GEOGRAPHIC SECTION
## Rockford - Winnebago County (G-18653)

Marvis R Trosper, *Director*
**EMP:** 75
**SQ FT:** 72,000
**SALES (est):** 21.9MM **Privately Held**
**WEB:** www.spiderswebsite.com
**SIC: 3441** Fabricated structural metal

### (G-18629)
### SPIDER COMPANY INC
2340 11th St (61104-7246)
**PHONE**................................815 961-8200
Tim Troster, *Manager*
**EMP:** 100
**SALES (corp-wide):** 21.9MM **Privately Held**
**WEB:** www.spiderswebsite.com
**SIC: 3471** Finishing, metals or formed products
**PA:** Spider Company, Inc.
  2340 11th St
  Rockford IL 61104
  815 961-8200

### (G-18630)
### SPX COOLING TECHNOLOGIES INC
Also Called: SPX Haydraulic Technologies
5885 11th St (61109-3650)
**PHONE**................................815 873-3767
Jeffrey N Darbut, *Branch Mgr*
**EMP:** 68
**SALES (corp-wide):** 1.4B **Publicly Held**
**SIC: 3443** Cooling towers, metal plate; heat exchangers: coolers (after, inter), condensers, etc.
**HQ:** Spx Cooling Technologies, Inc.
  7401 W 129th St
  Overland Park KS 66213
  913 664-7400

### (G-18631)
### SPX CORPORATION
5885 11th St (61109-3650)
**PHONE**................................815 874-5556
Tom Farrell, *Principal*
Nick Hobson, *Sr Corp Ofcr*
Rich Haffey, *Engineer*
Gary Nieroff, *VP Finance*
Jim Corbett, *Personnel Exec*
**EMP:** 450
**SALES (corp-wide):** 1.4B **Publicly Held**
**WEB:** www.spx.com
**SIC: 3443** Cooling towers, metal plate
**PA:** Spx Corporation
  13320a Balntyn Corp Pl
  Charlotte NC 28277
  980 474-3700

### (G-18632)
### SPX FLOW US LLC
5885 11th St (61109-3650)
**PHONE**................................815 874-5556
Chris Kearney, *President*
Robert B Foreman, *Exec VP*
Megan Stelzer, *Engineer*
Jeremy Smeltser, *CFO*
**EMP:** 5
**SALES (est):** 185.8K **Privately Held**
**SIC: 3494** Valves & pipe fittings

### (G-18633)
### STEEL FABRICATING INC
2806 22nd St (61109-1445)
P.O. Box 1057 (61105-1057)
**PHONE**................................815 977-5355
Dai Bui, *President*
Jan Burgess, *General Mgr*
**EMP:** 12
**SALES (est):** 2.2MM **Privately Held**
**SIC: 3449** Bars, concrete reinforcing: fabricated steel

### (G-18634)
### STEPHEN PAOLI MFG CORP
Also Called: Paoli, Stephen International
2531 11th St (61104-7219)
**PHONE**................................815 965-0621
**Fax:** 815 965-5393
Louis Paoli, *President*
Shawn Lee, *General Mgr*
Neal Ryan, *Sales Staff*
Sarah Terrazino, *Office Mgr*
**EMP:** 5
**SQ FT:** 193,000
**SALES (est):** 920K **Privately Held**
**WEB:** www.stephenpaoli.com
**SIC: 3556** Meat processing machinery; poultry processing machinery

### (G-18635)
### STRICTLY DENTURES
3920 E State St Ste 2 (61108-2051)
**PHONE**................................815 969-0531
Michael Peterson, *Owner*
Melissa Peterson, *Owner*
**EMP:** 5
**SALES (est):** 561.1K **Privately Held**
**SIC: 3843** Dental laboratory equipment

### (G-18636)
### STUHR MANUFACTURING CO
Also Called: Cdv
5085 27th Ave (61109-1701)
P.O. Box 6246 (61125-1246)
**PHONE**................................815 398-2460
**Fax:** 815 398-2469
Gary Kiely, *President*
Bernie Hanson, *Office Mgr*
**EMP:** 10
**SQ FT:** 20,000
**SALES (est):** 1.3MM **Privately Held**
**SIC: 3541 3423** Balancing machines (machine tool accessories); centering machines; hand & edge tools

### (G-18637)
### SUB SOURCE INC
600 18th Ave (61104-5159)
**PHONE**................................815 968-7800
**Fax:** 815 968-7850
Kristen Reinhardt, *President*
Kim Reinhardt, *Manager*
Michael Reinhardt, *Admin Sec*
**EMP:** 40
**SQ FT:** 15,000
**SALES (est):** 5.2MM **Privately Held**
**WEB:** www.subsourceinc.com
**SIC: 7389 3479** Inspection & testing services; coating of metals & formed products

### (G-18638)
### SWATH INTERNATIONAL LIMITED
1661 Northrock Ct (61103-1202)
**PHONE**................................815 654-4800
Ronald Gieseke, *Corp Secy*
John Martin, *Director*
**EMP:** 2
**SQ FT:** 165,000
**SALES (est):** 260.2K **Privately Held**
**SIC: 3731 7389** Shipbuilding & repairing; design services

### (G-18639)
### T D C INC
Also Called: Tra-Doc Communications
2517 Pelham Rd (61107-1860)
**PHONE**................................815 229-7064
Larry Runestad, *President*
Melanie Anderson, *Graphic Designe*
**EMP:** 16
**SQ FT:** 500
**SALES:** 200K **Privately Held**
**WEB:** www.tra-doc.com
**SIC: 2741** Technical manuals: publishing only, not printed on site

### (G-18640)
### T J KELLOGG INC
4949 Safford Rd (61101-2331)
**PHONE**................................815 969-0524
Peter P Gwizdala, *President*
Tim Gwizdala, *Corp Secy*
**EMP:** 3
**SALES (est):** 60K **Privately Held**
**SIC: 2511 3083 2541** Whatnot shelves: wood; laminated plastics plate & sheet; wood partitions & fixtures

### (G-18641)
### TARGET LASER & MACHINING INC
2433 Fremont St (61103-4071)
**PHONE**................................815 963-6706
**Fax:** 815 963-0382
Stephen B Reiter, *President*
Brent M Reiter, *Vice Pres*
**EMP:** 25
**SQ FT:** 50,000
**SALES (est):** 4.8MM **Privately Held**
**WEB:** www.targetlaser.com
**SIC: 3599** Machine shop, jobbing & repair

### (G-18642)
### TAURUS DIE CASTING LLC
5196 27th Ave (61109-1713)
P.O. Box 7391 (61126-7391)
**PHONE**................................815 316-6160
Kelly Geishert, *Plant Mgr*
Patty Russ, *Office Mgr*
Francesco Ledonne, *Supervisor*
Roberto Marselli,
**EMP:** 15 **EST:** 2015
**SALES (est):** 608.5K **Privately Held**
**SIC: 3364 3465** Zinc & zinc-base alloy die-castings; body parts, automobile: stamped metal

### (G-18643)
### TEMPERATURE EQUIPMENT CORP
1818 18th Ave (61104-7318)
**PHONE**................................815 229-2935
**EMP:** 4
**SALES (corp-wide):** 106.1MM **Privately Held**
**SIC: 3585** Mfg Refrigeration/Heating Equipment
**HQ:** Temperature Equipment Corporation
  17725 Volbrecht Rd Ste 1
  Lansing IL 60438
  708 418-0900

### (G-18644)
### TESTOR CORPORATION
615 Buckbee St (61104-4834)
**PHONE**................................815 962-6654
**Fax:** 815 962-7401
Charles Leichtweis, *President*
Jack Horner, *Buyer*
Jenny Brasfield, *Natl Sales Mgr*
Rick Hoffman, *Natl Sales Mgr*
Kathy Jolly, *Natl Sales Mgr*
▲ **EMP:** 60 **EST:** 1983
**SALES (est):** 14.9MM
**SALES (corp-wide):** 4.8B **Publicly Held**
**WEB:** www.testors.com
**SIC: 2851 2891 3089 3952** Enamels; lacquer: bases, dopes, thinner; adhesives; cement, except linoleum & tile; kits, plastic; brushes, air, artists'; games, toys & children's vehicles
**HQ:** Rpm Consumer Holding Company
  2628 Pearl Rd
  Medina OH 44256

### (G-18645)
### TETRA PAK INC
5691 International Dr (61109-2779)
**PHONE**................................815 873-1222
Mark Hale, *Manager*
Mary Sharlow, *Manager*
**EMP:** 82
**SALES (corp-wide):** 6.4B **Privately Held**
**SIC: 2671** Paper coated or laminated for packaging
**HQ:** Tetra Pak Inc.
  3300 Airport Rd
  Denton TX 76207
  940 565-8800

### (G-18646)
### TEXTRON INC
510 18th Ave (61104-5131)
**PHONE**................................815 961-5293
Thomas Sullivan, *Branch Mgr*
**EMP:** 64
**SALES (corp-wide):** 13.7B **Publicly Held**
**SIC: 3721** Aircraft
**PA:** Textron Inc.
  40 Westminster St
  Providence RI 02903
  401 421-2800

### (G-18647)
### THERMOPLASTEC INC
4755 Colt Rd (61109-2610)
**PHONE**................................815 873-9288
**Fax:** 815 873-9285
Shyam Singh, *President*
Sheela Singh, *Corp Secy*
**EMP:** 10
**SALES (est):** 1.7MM **Privately Held**
**WEB:** www.thermoplastec.com
**SIC: 3545** Tools & accessories for machine tools

### (G-18648)
### THOMAS ENGINEERING INC
Also Called: Triangle Metals Division
2500 Harrison Ave (61108-7458)
**PHONE**................................815 398-0280
**Fax:** 815 398-6988
Milo Waterhouse, *Prdtn Mgr*
Peter Frost, *Engineer*
Carl Spangler, *Engineer*
Doug Kanne, *Branch Mgr*
**EMP:** 20
**SALES (corp-wide):** 24.7MM **Privately Held**
**WEB:** www.thomaseng.com
**SIC: 3444 3559** Sheet metal specialties, not stamped; pharmaceutical machinery
**PA:** Thomas Engineering Inc.
  575 W Central Rd
  Hoffman Estates IL 60192
  847 358-5800

### (G-18649)
### THOMASON MACHINE WORKS INC (PA)
5459 11th St (61109-3656)
**PHONE**................................815 874-8217
**Fax:** 815 874-5044
James F Thomason, *President*
Dave Thomason, *Vice Pres*
Mike Thomason, *Office Mgr*
Marge Thomason, *Admin Sec*
**EMP:** 9
**SQ FT:** 13,000
**SALES (est):** 1.8MM **Privately Held**
**WEB:** www.thomasonmachine.com
**SIC: 3599** Machine shop, jobbing & repair

### (G-18650)
### THORWORKS INDUSTRIES INC
Also Called: Sealmaster
904 7th St (61104-4654)
**PHONE**................................815 969-0664
Kenneth Horton, *Branch Mgr*
**EMP:** 5
**SALES (corp-wide):** 92.9MM **Privately Held**
**SIC: 2951** Asphalt paving mixtures & blocks
**PA:** Thorworks Industries, Inc.
  2520 Campbell St
  Sandusky OH 44870
  419 626-4375

### (G-18651)
### TIMOTHY ANDERSON CORPORATION
Also Called: Signs Now
700 20th St (61104-3505)
**PHONE**................................815 398-8371
**Fax:** 815 398-1127
Tim Anderson, *President*
**EMP:** 12
**SQ FT:** 17,000
**SALES:** 1.5MM **Privately Held**
**SIC: 3993** Signs & advertising specialties

### (G-18652)
### TOLEDO SCREW MACHINE PRODUCTS
5257 Northrock Dr (61103-1235)
**PHONE**................................815 877-8213
**Fax:** 815 877-8423
William Bjork, *President*
Alan Bjork, *Vice Pres*
Dorothy Bjork, *Admin Sec*
**EMP:** 9
**SQ FT:** 18,000
**SALES (est):** 1.5MM **Privately Held**
**WEB:** www.toledoscrew.com
**SIC: 3451** Screw machine products

### (G-18653)
### TOMERMO INC
Also Called: Rockford Separators
5127 28th Ave (61109-1720)
P.O. Box 5963 (61125-0963)
**PHONE**................................815 229-5077
**Fax:** 815 229-5108
Merritt Mott, *President*
Jim Griffin, *VP Mfg*

# Rockford - Winnebago County (G-18654)

## GEOGRAPHIC SECTION

Judy Johnson, *Manager*
▲ **EMP:** 35 **EST:** 1963
**SQ FT:** 35,000
**SALES (est):** 7.5MM **Privately Held**
**WEB:** www.rkfdseparators.com
**SIC: 3569** Separators for steam, gas, vapor or air (machinery)

### (G-18654)
### TOOL ENGRG CONSULTING MFG LLC
2932 Eastrock Dr (61109-1738)
**PHONE**.................................815 316-2304
Joel Zehrung, *Vice Pres*
**EMP:** 8 **EST:** 2006
**SQ FT:** 3,000
**SALES:** 700K **Privately Held**
**SIC: 3545** Cutting tools for machine tools

### (G-18655)
### TOOLMASTERS LLC (PA)
1204 Milford Ave (61109-3638)
**PHONE**.................................815 968-0961
John Nelson, *CEO*
Roger Dawson, *Purchasing*
**EMP:** 25 **EST:** 1996
**SQ FT:** 2,000
**SALES (est):** 2.7MM **Privately Held**
**WEB:** www.toolmastersllc.com
**SIC: 3545** Cutting tools for machine tools

### (G-18656)
### TRI-CAM INC
Also Called: Magnalock
2730 Eastrock Dr (61109-1734)
**PHONE**.................................815 226-9200
Danny Pearse, *President*
David Nordman, *Vice Pres*
Laura Pellegrim, *Executive Asst*
◆ **EMP:** 13
**SQ FT:** 44,000
**SALES (est):** 1.9MM **Privately Held**
**WEB:** www.tricaminc.com
**SIC: 3541 3537** Drilling machine tools (metal cutting); grinding machines, metalworking; sawing & cutoff machines (metalworking machinery); stacking machines, automatic

### (G-18657)
### TRIDENT MACHINE CO
3491 N Meridian Rd (61101-9322)
**PHONE**.................................815 968-1585
**Fax:** 815 986-0141
Lyle Sheley, *Partner*
Lylia Pierce, *Partner*
Mary Sheley, *Partner*
**EMP:** 8 **EST:** 1964
**SQ FT:** 5,000
**SALES (est):** 625.9K **Privately Held**
**SIC: 3599 3812 3728** Machine shop, jobbing & repair; search & navigation equipment; aircraft parts & equipment

### (G-18658)
### TY PRECISION AUTOMATICS INC
2606 Falund St (61109-1042)
**PHONE**.................................815 963-9668
**Fax:** 815 963-0701
John W Tallman, *President*
Todd T Tallman, *Vice Pres*
**EMP:** 16
**SQ FT:** 26,000
**SALES:** 150K **Privately Held**
**WEB:** www.typrecision.com
**SIC: 3451** Screw machine products

### (G-18659)
### UHLAR INC
Also Called: J & L Engineering
1626 Magnolia St (61104-5143)
**PHONE**.................................815 961-0970
John Uhlar, *President*
Loretta Uhlar, *Admin Sec*
**EMP:** 4
**SQ FT:** 4,100
**SALES (est):** 220K **Privately Held**
**SIC: 3599 7692** Machine shop, jobbing & repair; welding repair

### (G-18660)
### ULTRA STAMPING & ASSEMBLY INC
4590 Hydraulic Rd (61109-2614)
**PHONE**.................................815 874-9888
**Fax:** 815 874-5588
Charles Cushman, *President*
Tracy Cushman, *Vice Pres*
Gary Kuhls, *Accountant*
Gordon Cushman, *Sales Executive*
Jon Legge, *Manager*
**EMP:** 21
**SQ FT:** 25,000
**SALES (est):** 5MM **Privately Held**
**WEB:** www.ultrastamping.com
**SIC: 3441 3469** Fabricated structural metal; stamping metal for the trade

### (G-18661)
### UNITED SKILLED INC
3412 Precision Dr (61109-2770)
**PHONE**.................................815 874-9696
**Fax:** 815 874-3962
Norman Tangerose, *President*
Jeremy Tangerose, *President*
**EMP:** 4
**SQ FT:** 6,000
**SALES (est):** 165K **Privately Held**
**SIC: 3544** Special dies, tools, jigs & fixtures

### (G-18662)
### UNITED STATES FILTER/IWT
4669 Shepherd Trl (61103-1294)
**PHONE**.................................815 877-3041
**Fax:** 815 633-5906
Marvin Deam, *Principal*
**EMP:** 8
**SALES (est):** 1.1MM **Privately Held**
**SIC: 3569** Filters

### (G-18663)
### UNITED TECHNOLOGIES CORP
4747 Harrison Ave (61108-7929)
**PHONE**.................................815 226-6000
Alan Nelson, *Principal*
Patrick Doan, *Engineer*
David Hill, *Engineer*
Joseph Voss, *Master*
**EMP:** 268
**SALES (corp-wide):** 57.2B **Publicly Held**
**SIC: 3585 3721 3534 3724** Refrigeration & heating equipment; helicopters; research & development on aircraft by the manufacturer; elevators & equipment; escalators, passenger & freight; aircraft engines & engine parts; research & development on aircraft engines & parts; high-energy particle physics equipment
**PA:** United Technologies Corporation
10 Farm Springs Rd
Farmington CT 06032
860 728-7000

### (G-18664)
### UNIVERSAL HOVERCRAFT AMER INC
1218 Buchanan St (61101-1404)
**PHONE**.................................815 963-1200
**Fax:** 815 943-1800
William Zang, *President*
**EMP:** 12
**SQ FT:** 12,000
**SALES (est):** 1.1MM **Privately Held**
**WEB:** www.hovercraft.com
**SIC: 3089** Kits, plastic

### (G-18665)
### USA TODAY INC
Also Called: Rockford Register Star
99 E State St (61104-1009)
**PHONE**.................................815 987-1400
Fritz Jacob, *President*
Paula Buckner, *Editor*
Eloisa Oceguera, *Editor*
Matt Torman, *Editor*
Barry Wood, *Editor*
**EMP:** 6
**SALES (est):** 328.2K **Privately Held**
**SIC: 2711 8611** Newspapers; business associations

### (G-18666)
### VALSPAR
200 Sayre St (61104-4661)
**PHONE**.................................815 962-9969
David Samuelsen, *Principal*
▲ **EMP:** 3 **EST:** 2010
**SALES (est):** 422.4K **Privately Held**
**SIC: 2851** Varnishes

### (G-18667)
### VALSPAR CORPORATION
1215 Nelson Blvd (61104-4773)
**PHONE**.................................815 962-9986
**Fax:** 815 987-9828
Rob Vanvleet, *Maint Spvr*
Michael Brandt, *Branch Mgr*
David Knego, *Manager*
**EMP:** 15
**SALES (corp-wide):** 11.8B **Publicly Held**
**SIC: 2816** Inorganic pigments
**HQ:** The Valspar Corporation
1101 S 3rd St
Minneapolis MN 55415
612 851-7000

### (G-18668)
### VALSPAR CORPORATION
1215 Nelson Blvd (61104-4773)
**PHONE**.................................815 987-3701
Will Anderson, *Principal*
**EMP:** 3
**SALES (corp-wide):** 11.8B **Publicly Held**
**SIC: 2821** Plastics materials & resins
**HQ:** The Valspar Corporation
1101 S 3rd St
Minneapolis MN 55415
612 851-7000

### (G-18669)
### VALSPAR CORPORATION
1215 Nelson Blvd (61104-4773)
**PHONE**.................................815 962-9986
Ken Carter, *Principal*
David Knego, *Mfg Mgr*
**EMP:** 87
**SALES (corp-wide):** 11.8B **Publicly Held**
**SIC: 2851** Varnishes
**HQ:** The Valspar Corporation
1101 S 3rd St
Minneapolis MN 55415
612 851-7000

### (G-18670)
### VIETNOW NATIONAL HEADQUARTERS
1835 Broadway (61104-5409)
**PHONE**.................................815 395-8484
**Fax:** 815 227-5127
Rich Sanders, *President*
Terry Buscher, *Treasurer*
Jill Boskie, *Executive Asst*
**EMP:** 5
**SQ FT:** 2,000
**SALES (est):** 1.9MM **Privately Held**
**WEB:** www.vietnow.com
**SIC: 8641 2721** Veterans' organization; periodicals

### (G-18671)
### W A WHITNEY CO (HQ)
650 Race St (61101-1486)
P.O. Box 1206 (61105-1206)
**PHONE**.................................815 964-6771
**Fax:** 815 964-3175
Robert L Green, *President*
Robert Green, *General Mgr*
Lee Kindgren, *General Mgr*
Gary Vosberg, *Principal*
Dean Dick, *Natl Sales Mgr*
▲ **EMP:** 238
**SQ FT:** 225,000
**SALES (est):** 38.6MM
**SALES (corp-wide):** 1.9B **Publicly Held**
**WEB:** www.wawhitney.com
**SIC: 3544 3542 3549 3545** Special dies & tools; machine tools, metal forming type; metalworking machinery; machine tool accessories; sheet metalwork; cutlery
**PA:** Esterline Technologies Corp
500 108th Ave Ne Ste 1500
Bellevue WA 98004
425 453-9400

### (G-18672)
### WANXIANG NEW ENERGY LLC
5985 Logistics Pkwy (61109-3606)
**PHONE**.................................815 226-0884
Pin Ni,
▲ **EMP:** 15
**SQ FT:** 60,000
**SALES (est):** 1.6MM
**SALES (corp-wide):** 2.9B **Privately Held**
**SIC: 3674** Photovoltaic devices, solid state
**HQ:** Wanxiang America Corporation
88 Airport Rd
Elgin IL 60123

### (G-18673)
### WARTHOG INC
2615 Yonge St (61101-4265)
**PHONE**.................................815 540-7197
**Fax:** 815 964-5830
Michael Clayton, *President*
**EMP:** 4
**SALES (est):** 307.5K **Privately Held**
**SIC: 3949** Sporting & athletic goods

### (G-18674)
### WATT PUBLISHING CO (PA)
303 N Main St Ste 500 (61101-1025)
**PHONE**.................................815 966-5400
**Fax:** 815 966-6416
James W Watt, *Ch of Bd*
Gregory A Watt, *President*
Debbie P Donaldson, *Editor*
Roy Leidahl, *Vice Pres*
Bruce Plantz, *Vice Pres*
**EMP:** 50 **EST:** 1917
**SQ FT:** 32,000
**SALES (est):** 11.5MM **Privately Held**
**WEB:** www.wattnet.com
**SIC: 2721** Periodicals

### (G-18675)
### WATT PUBLISHING CO
303 N Main St Ste 500 (61101-1025)
**PHONE**.................................815 966-5400
Bruce Plantz, *Branch Mgr*
**EMP:** 27
**SALES (corp-wide):** 11.5MM **Privately Held**
**WEB:** www.wattnet.com
**SIC: 2721** Periodicals
**PA:** Watt Publishing Co.
303 N Main St Ste 500
Rockford IL 61101
815 966-5400

### (G-18676)
### WELLIVER & SONS INC
1540 New Milford Schl Rd (61109-4399)
**PHONE**.................................815 874-2400
**Fax:** 815 874-7787
Barry Welliver, *President*
John Shoults, *CFO*
**EMP:** 25 **EST:** 1945
**SQ FT:** 18,000
**SALES (est):** 2.8MM **Privately Held**
**SIC: 3546** Power-driven handtools

### (G-18677)
### WEMA VOGTLAND AMERICA LLC
4793 Colt Rd (61109-2610)
**PHONE**.................................815 544-0526
Andreas Quak, *President*
Matt Diwo, *Purch Mgr*
**EMP:** 15
**SQ FT:** 9,000
**SALES:** 10MM
**SALES (corp-wide):** 44.6MM **Privately Held**
**SIC: 3545** Machine tool accessories
**HQ:** Wema Vogtland Technology Gmbh
Schenkendorfstr. 14
Plauen 08525
374 159-20

### (G-18678)
### WEST SIDE TRACTOR SALES CO
Also Called: John Deere Authorized Dealer
3110 Prairie Rd (61102-3948)
**PHONE**.................................815 961-3160
**Fax:** 815 965-1810
Kip Bancroft, *Sales Mgr*
Roger Svartoien, *Manager*
**EMP:** 20

# GEOGRAPHIC SECTION
## Rockton - Winnebago County (G-18700)

SALES (corp-wide): 223.9MM **Privately Held**
WEB: www.westsidetractorsales.com
SIC: 3531 5261 5082 Construction machinery; lawnmowers & tractors; construction & mining machinery
PA: West Side Tractor Sales Co.
1400 W Ogden Ave
Naperville IL 60563
630 355-7150

### (G-18679)
### WESTERN MOTOR MFG CO
1211 23rd Ave (61104-7160)
PHONE..................................815 986-2214
Marianne Anderson, *President*
Janet Champlin, *Regional Mgr*
Greg Sundeen, *Vice Pres*
Marty Anderson, *Manager*
▲ EMP: 3
SQ FT: 30,000
SALES (est): 405.1K **Privately Held**
SIC: 3621 Motors & generators

### (G-18680)
### WEYERHAEUSER COMPANY
1753 23rd Ave (61104-7356)
PHONE..................................815 987-0395
Robert Schultz, *Branch Mgr*
EMP: 6
SALES (corp-wide): 6.3B **Publicly Held**
SIC: 4783 2621 Containerization of goods for shipping; paper mills
PA: Weyerhaeuser Company
220 Occidental Ave S
Seattle WA 98104
206 539-3000

### (G-18681)
### WHITNEY ROPER LLC
Also Called: Roper Whitney
2833 Huffman Blvd (61103-3906)
PHONE..................................815 962-3011
Fax: 815 962-2227
Mark Smith, *President*
Brad Smith, *Vice Pres*
Mike Smith, *Vice Pres*
▲ EMP: 56
SQ FT: 125,000
SALES: 15.8MM **Privately Held**
SIC: 3542 3546 3544 3423 Metal deposit forming machines; power-driven handtools; special dies, tools, jigs & fixtures; hand & edge tools; cutlery

### (G-18682)
### WHITNEY ROPER ROCKFORD INC
Also Called: Rw Acquisition
2833 Huffman Blvd (61103-3906)
PHONE..................................815 962-3011
Mark Smith, *President*
Brad Smith, *Vice Pres*
Mike Smith, *Vice Pres*
Chris Gyorkos, *Opers Staff*
Les Johnson, *Purchasing*
▲ EMP: 56
SQ FT: 125,000
SALES (est): 47.6K **Privately Held**
WEB: www.roperwhitney.com
SIC: 3542 3546 3544 3423 Sheet metalworking machines; power-driven handtools; special dies, tools, jigs & fixtures; hand & edge tools; cutlery

### (G-18683)
### WILLIAM DACH
Also Called: Dach Fence Co
4901 W State St (61102-1242)
PHONE..................................815 962-3455
Fax: 815 962-3366
William Dach, *Owner*
Robert Clay, *Vice Pres*
Sandy Dunnavan, *Office Mgr*
EMP: 10
SALES (est): 925K **Privately Held**
SIC: 1799 5211 3496 3354 Fence construction; fencing; miscellaneous fabricated wire products; aluminum extruded products; steel wire & related products

### (G-18684)
### WILSON MFG SCREW MCH PDTS
2500 N Main St Ste 10 (61103-4074)
PHONE..................................815 964-8724
Fax: 815 964-7033
Michael Wilson Sr, *President*
Sharon Wilson, *Corp Secy*
EMP: 10
SALES: 750K **Privately Held**
SIC: 3451 Screw machine products

### (G-18685)
### WILSON TOOL CORPORATION
2401 20th St (61104-7451)
PHONE..................................815 226-0147
Fax: 815 226-0763
Virginia A Wilson, *President*
Kimberly Bradford, *General Mgr*
Frank Lasala, *Vice Pres*
Brad Wilson, *Purchasing*
John Smyth, *Sales Staff*
EMP: 25
SQ FT: 25,000
SALES (est): 5.4MM **Privately Held**
WEB: www.wilsontoolcorp.com
SIC: 3599 3769 Machine shop, jobbing & repair; guided missile & space vehicle parts & aux eqpt, rsch & dev

### (G-18686)
### WIRETECH INC
521 18th Ave (61104-5130)
PHONE..................................815 986-9614
Mark Nelson, *Branch Mgr*
EMP: 8
SALES (corp-wide): 43.7MM **Privately Held**
SIC: 3315 Steel wire & related products
PA: Wiretech, Inc.
6440 Canning St
Commerce CA 90040
212 239-1010

### (G-18687)
### WNTA STUDIO LINE
830 Sandy Hollow Rd (61109-2027)
PHONE..................................815 874-7861
Bob Rhey, *Principal*
Timothy Crull, *Purch Agent*
EMP: 3
SALES (est): 143.2K **Privately Held**
SIC: 2711 4832 Newspapers, publishing & printing; radio broadcasting stations

### (G-18688)
### WOODS EQUIPMENT COMPANY
Also Called: Tisco Parts
1818 Elmwood Rd Ste 2 (61103-1210)
PHONE..................................815 732-2141
Robert Mudloff, *Manager*
Randy Carey, *Info Tech Mgr*
EMP: 56
SALES (corp-wide): 828.5MM **Privately Held**
WEB: www.woodsequipment.com
SIC: 3523 Farm machinery & equipment; turf & grounds equipment
HQ: Woods Equipment Company
2606 S Il Route 2
Oregon IL 61061
815 732-2141

### (G-18689)
### WORLD CLASS TOOL & MACHINE
2422 N Main St (61103-4046)
PHONE..................................815 962-2081
David Loveland, *President*
Shawn Sweeney, *Treasurer*
EMP: 8
SQ FT: 6,000
SALES (est): 1.1MM **Privately Held**
SIC: 3599 Machine shop, jobbing & repair

### (G-18690)
### X-TECH INNOVATIONS INC
424 18th Ave (61104-5129)
PHONE..................................815 962-4127
Fax: 815 962-4121
Jordan Kingsbury, *President*
EMP: 5
SALES (est): 500K **Privately Held**
WEB: www.xtechinnovations.com
SIC: 3599 7389 Custom machinery; industrial & commercial equipment inspection service

---

## Rockton
### Winnebago County

### (G-18691)
### BALSLEY PRINTING INC
119 E Main St (61072-2519)
PHONE..................................815 637-8787
John Balsley, *Manager*
EMP: 5
SALES (corp-wide): 1.9MM **Privately Held**
WEB: www.balsleyprinting.com
SIC: 5943 2752 Office forms & supplies; commercial printing, lithographic
PA: Balsley Printing, Inc.
119 E Main St
Rockton IL 61072
815 624-7515

### (G-18692)
### BALSLEY PRINTING INC (PA)
Also Called: Balsley Fast Printing
119 E Main St (61072-2519)
PHONE..................................815 624-7515
Fax: 815 624-2203
James E Balsley, *President*
Denise Balsley, *Treasurer*
Katherine Cook, *Sales Staff*
Billie Balsley, *Manager*
Coleen Chiodini, *Manager*
EMP: 13 EST: 1979
SQ FT: 8,500
SALES (est): 1.9MM **Privately Held**
WEB: www.balsleyprinting.com
SIC: 2752 Commercial printing, offset

### (G-18693)
### CARRIER COMMERCIAL RFRGN INC
Taylor Company
750 N Blackhawk Blvd (61072-2104)
P.O. Box 410 (61072-0410)
PHONE..................................815 624-8333
Fax: 815 624-8000
Clark Wangaard, *President*
Jacky Wang, *Vice Chairman*
Tom Franken, *Vice Pres*
Dobrowolski Jeremy, *Vice Pres*
Dave Marchant, *Vice Pres*
EMP: 627
SQ FT: 100,000
SALES (corp-wide): 57.2B **Publicly Held**
WEB: www.ccr.carrier.com
SIC: 3556 Ice cream manufacturing machinery
HQ: Carrier Commercial Refrigeration, Inc.
3 Farm Glen Blvd Ste 301
Farmington CT 06032
336 245-6400

### (G-18694)
### CHEMTOOL INCORPORATED (DH)
Also Called: Metalcote
801 W Rockton Rd (61072-1647)
PHONE..................................815 957-4140
Fax: 815 624-0381
Tom Rajewski, *President*
Deborah Mahnke, *Purchasing*
Chuck Kleeberger, *Controller*
Mike Sirchio, *VP Human Res*
Steve Deal, *Sales Engr*
◆ EMP: 125 EST: 1963
SQ FT: 100,000
SALES (est): 151.2MM
SALES (corp-wide): 223.6B **Publicly Held**
WEB: www.chemtool.com
SIC: 2992 2899 2842 2841 Lubricating oils & greases; cutting oils, blending: made from purchased materials; rust arresting compounds, animal or vegetable oil base; rust resisting compounds; water treating compounds; specialty cleaning, polishes & sanitation goods; soap & other detergents
HQ: The Lubrizol Corporation
29400 Lakeland Blvd
Wickliffe OH 44092
440 943-4200

### (G-18695)
### CREATIVE CONTROLS SYSTEMS INC
15929 Hauley Rd (61072-9769)
PHONE..................................815 629-2358
Fax: 815 629-2228
Allen R Holecek, *President*
Doris Holecek, *Corp Secy*
Dan Ebneter, *Vice Pres*
EMP: 6 EST: 1972
SQ FT: 3,100
SALES: 500K **Privately Held**
SIC: 3823 7371 3822 3625 Computer interface equipment for industrial process control; custom computer programming services; auto controls regulating residntl & coml environmt & applncs; relays & industrial controls

### (G-18696)
### EXPANDABLE HABITATS
11022 N Main St (61072-9458)
PHONE..................................815 624-6784
Tricia David, *Owner*
Gregory David, *Co-Owner*
EMP: 5
SQ FT: 3,600
SALES (est): 330K **Privately Held**
WEB: www.expandablehabitats.com
SIC: 3496 3316 Miscellaneous fabricated wire products; cold finishing of steel shapes

### (G-18697)
### KENENT SCREW MACHINE PRODUCTS
4843 Yale Bridge Rd (61072-9503)
PHONE..................................815 624-7216
Mary Linda Kennedy, *Owner*
Tony Kennedy, *Co-Owner*
EMP: 10
SQ FT: 5,000
SALES: 500K **Privately Held**
SIC: 3451 Screw machine products

### (G-18698)
### LEADER ACCESSORIES LLC
14225 Hansberry Rd (61072-9752)
PHONE..................................877 662-9808
Richard Chin, *President*
Wayne Chin, *Manager*
EMP: 3
SQ FT: 30,000
SALES: 3MM **Privately Held**
SIC: 2399 Automotive covers, except seat & tire covers

### (G-18699)
### NOVEL PRODUCTS INC
3266 Yale Bridge Rd (61072-9635)
P.O. Box 408 (61072-0408)
PHONE..................................815 624-4888
Fax: 815 624-4866
Carol Muehlenbein, *President*
James A Muehlenbein, *Shareholder*
EMP: 3 EST: 1975
SALES: 600K **Privately Held**
WEB: www.novelproducts.com
SIC: 3821 Calibration tapes for physical testing machines

### (G-18700)
### PAPERCHINE INC (HQ)
1155 Prairie Hill Rd (61072-1545)
PHONE..................................815 389-8200
Fax: 815 389-8171
Laurie Wicks, *President*
Jean-Pierre Bouchard, *Vice Pres*
James Ewald, *Vice Pres*
Daniel Morris, *Vice Pres*
Dave Brandt, *Project Mgr*
▲ EMP: 130
SQ FT: 120,000
SALES (est): 20.8MM
SALES (corp-wide): 609.3MM **Privately Held**
WEB: www.paperchine.com
SIC: 3554 7699 5084 Paper industries machinery; industrial machinery & equipment repair; paper manufacturing machinery
PA: Astenjohnson, Inc.
4399 Corporate Rd
North Charleston SC 29405
843 747-7800

## Rockton - Winnebago County (G-18701)

**(G-18701)**
**PHELPS FARMS**
4639 W Rockton Rd (61072-9648)
PHONE..................815 624-7263
Stanton Phelps, *Partner*
Robert Phelps, *Partner*
EMP: 2
SALES: 400K **Privately Held**
SIC: 3523 0291 Driers (farm): grain, hay & seed; livestock farm, general

**(G-18702)**
**SENTRO PRINTING EQUIP N MOVERS**
332 Harwich Pl (61072-2989)
PHONE..................779 423-0255
Keith Sessler, *Principal*
EMP: 3
SALES (est): 226.2K **Privately Held**
SIC: 2759 Commercial printing

**(G-18703)**
**WOODWARD INC**
12533 Wagon Wheel Rd (61072-3335)
PHONE..................815 877-7441
EMP: 5
SALES (corp-wide): 2B **Publicly Held**
SIC: 3625 Electric controls & control accessories, industrial
PA: Woodward, Inc.
1081 Woodward Way
Fort Collins CO 80524
970 482-5811

## Rockwood
### Randolph County

**(G-18704)**
**JONES WOOD PRODUCTS**
11801 Ebenezer Rd (62280-1219)
PHONE..................618 826-2682
Harry M Jones, *Owner*
EMP: 4
SALES (est): 232.7K **Privately Held**
SIC: 2499 Wood products

## Rolling Meadows
### Cook County

**(G-18705)**
**4200 KIRCHOFF CORP**
Also Called: Marathon Gas
4200 Kirchoff Rd (60008-2006)
PHONE..................773 551-1541
Jose Mathew, *President*
EMP: 5
SALES (est): 220.3K **Privately Held**
SIC: 2911 Petroleum refining

**(G-18706)**
**A M TOOL & DIE**
1000 Carnegie St (60008-1007)
PHONE..................847 398-7530
Fax: 847 392-6298
Alan Mortenson, *Owner*
EMP: 30
SQ FT: 6,000
SALES: 5MM **Privately Held**
SIC: 3544 Special dies & tools

**(G-18707)**
**ADAPTIVE INSIGHTS INC**
1600 Golf Rd (60008-4263)
PHONE..................800 303-6346
EMP: 40
SALES (corp-wide): 143.6MM **Privately Held**
SIC: 7372 Business oriented computer software
PA: Adaptive Insights, Inc.
3350 W Byshore Rd Ste 200
Palo Alto CA 94303
800 303-6346

**(G-18708)**
**ADESSO SOLUTIONS LLC**
3701 Algonquin Rd Ste 270 (60008-3188)
PHONE..................847 342-1095
Fax: 847 342-1099
Ron Reed, *CEO*
Fred Schroeder, *President*
Tom Utgard, *Principal*
Rich Jones, *Exec VP*
Jim Charles, *Vice Pres*
EMP: 13
SALES (est): 2.5MM **Privately Held**
WEB: www.adessosolutions.com
SIC: 7372 Business oriented computer software

**(G-18709)**
**AMERICAN ASSN NUROSURGEONS INC (PA)**
Also Called: A A N S
5550 Meadowbrook Dr (60008)
PHONE..................847 378-0500
Fax: 847 378-0661
Fyeta Keo, *General Mgr*
William T John, *Accounts Mgr*
Jon N Mau, *Marketing Mgr*
M R Bullock, *Corp Counsel*
Bill John, *Manager*
EMP: 40 EST: 1931
SQ FT: 33,000
SALES: 21.1MM **Privately Held**
SIC: 8621 2721 Medical field-related associations; periodicals

**(G-18710)**
**APEX TOOL WORKS INC**
Also Called: Wangren Machine
3200 Tollview Dr (60008-3706)
PHONE..................847 394-5810
Fax: 847 394-2739
Michael C Collins, *President*
Phillip Whittenhall, *Vice Pres*
Inge Ohnona, *Purchasing*
Diane Ericson, *Engineer*
Jim Whittenhal, *Engineer*
▲ EMP: 46 EST: 1919
SQ FT: 48,364
SALES (est): 9.6MM **Privately Held**
WEB: www.apextool.com
SIC: 3544 Special dies, tools, jigs & fixtures

**(G-18711)**
**ATS SORTIMAT USA LLC**
Also Called: Sortimat Techonology
5655 Meadowbrook Indus Ct (60008-3833)
PHONE..................847 925-1234
Fax: 847 925-1234
Hans Dieter Baumtrog, *CEO*
Mike Gondhi, *Engineer*
James Marlega, *Comptroller*
David Oshoa, *Marketing Staff*
Gipget Cruse, *Admin Mgr*
◆ EMP: 60
SQ FT: 35,000
SALES (est): 22.6MM **Privately Held**
WEB: www.sortimat.com
SIC: 3569 3549 3599 7692 Assembly machines, non-metalworking; assembly machines, including robotic; custom machinery; welding repair; packaging machinery

**(G-18712)**
**AUTOMATIC BUILDING CONTRLS LLC**
3315 Algonquin Rd Ste 550 (60008-3240)
PHONE..................847 296-4000
Mark Bevill, *CEO*
Grant Bevill, *President*
Carey Lee, *Vice Pres*
Brian Wheeland, *Vice Pres*
Patrick McKinney, *Engineer*
EMP: 50 EST: 1988
SQ FT: 8,000
SALES (est): 11.6MM **Privately Held**
WEB: www.fixconsulting.com
SIC: 3822 Temperature controls, automatic

**(G-18713)**
**AUTOTYPE AMERICAS INCORPORATED**
1675 Winnetka Cir (60008-1372)
PHONE..................847 818-8262
Frank Monteiro, *Principal*
David Moore, *Manager*
EMP: 3
SALES (est): 240K **Privately Held**
SIC: 2796 5084 Lithographic plates, positives or negatives; printing trades machinery, equipment & supplies

**(G-18714)**
**AWESOME HAND SERVICES LLC**
1151 Rohlwing Rd (60008-1030)
PHONE..................630 445-8695
Donald James Hesch,
Chris Donald Hesch,
Craig Anthony Hesch,
Joel Chris McSwain,
EMP: 7
SALES (est): 916.7K **Privately Held**
SIC: 3999 Slot machines

**(G-18715)**
**BANDJWET ENTERPRISES INC**
Also Called: B & J Wet Enterprises
3603 Edison Pl (60008-1012)
PHONE..................847 797-9250
Robert Wettermann, *President*
Christine Kraner, *CFO*
Daniel Sanchez, *IT/INT Sup*
EMP: 30
SQ FT: 24,000
SALES (est): 4.8MM **Privately Held**
WEB: www.solder.net
SIC: 8249 3672 Vocational apprentice training; circuit boards, television & radio printed

**(G-18716)**
**BAPS INVESTORS GROUP LLC**
Also Called: Midwest Insert Composite Mold
3940 Industrial Ave (60008-1024)
PHONE..................847 818-8444
Fax: 847 818-8368
Ripan Sheth, *President*
Kanti Patel,
▲ EMP: 25
SQ FT: 35,000
SALES (est): 5.1MM **Privately Held**
WEB: www.micmolding.com
SIC: 3089 Injection molding of plastics

**(G-18717)**
**BESTPROTO INC**
3603 Edison Pl (60008-1012)
PHONE..................224 387-3280
Gary Lynch, *President*
Robert Wettermann, *Chairman*
Christine Kraner, *CFO*
Garths Cates, *Treasurer*
Brandon Ischar, *Cust Mgr*
EMP: 10
SALES: 1.5MM **Privately Held**
SIC: 3672 Circuit boards, television & radio printed

**(G-18718)**
**BINGAMAN-PRECISION METAL SPINI**
Also Called: Bingaman Metal Spinning
1000 Carnegie St (60008-1007)
PHONE..................847 392-5620
Dorothy L Doumakes, *President*
EMP: 40
SQ FT: 35,000
SALES (est): 6.6MM **Privately Held**
SIC: 3469 Spinning metal for the trade

**(G-18719)**
**CHARLES INDUSTRIES LTD (PA)**
5600 Apollo Dr (60008-4049)
PHONE..................847 806-6300
Fax: 847 806-6231
Joseph T Charles, *President*
Robert Novak, *President*
Roger McCaslin, *General Mgr*
G Wes Kimes, *Vice Pres*
Mark Rahmel, *Vice Pres*
◆ EMP: 60
SQ FT: 72,000
SALES (est): 131.6MM **Privately Held**
WEB: www.charlesmarine.com
SIC: 3661 3629 3677 Telephones & telephone apparatus; electronic generation equipment; electronic transformers

**(G-18720)**
**CHICAGO KILN SERVICE**
2312 Wing St (60008-1633)
PHONE..................847 436-0919
Carl Mankert, *Principal*
EMP: 1
SALES (est): 214.2K **Privately Held**
WEB: www.chicagokilnservice.com
SIC: 3559 Kilns

**(G-18721)**
**CIC NORTH AMERICA INC**
5410 Newport Dr Ste 40 (60008-3722)
PHONE..................847 873-0860
Jason Lim, *Principal*
▲ EMP: 3
SALES (est): 471.3K **Privately Held**
SIC: 3559 Electronic component making machinery

**(G-18722)**
**CKD USA CORPORATION (HQ)**
4080 Winnetka Ave (60008-1374)
PHONE..................847 368-0539
Fax: 847 788-0575
Atsumi Nonoda, *President*
Tim Cochrane, *Corp Secy*
Tim Cochran, *Human Res Dir*
Troy Manley, *Natl Sales Mgr*
Mark Preissig, *Natl Sales Mgr*
▲ EMP: 28
SQ FT: 13,000
SALES (est): 4.6MM
SALES (corp-wide): 827.2MM **Privately Held**
WEB: www.ckdusa.com
SIC: 3492 3572 Control valves, aircraft: hydraulic & pneumatic; control valves, fluid power: hydraulic & pneumatic; disk drives, computer
PA: Ckd Corporation
2-250, Oji
Komaki AIC 485-0
568 771-111

**(G-18723)**
**CLICK-BLOCK CORPORATION**
Also Called: Click Block
1100 Hicks Rd (60008-1016)
PHONE..................847 749-1651
Byung Whang, *President*
Sungwhan Kim, *Principal*
▲ EMP: 36
SALES: 500K **Privately Held**
SIC: 3944 Blocks, toy

**(G-18724)**
**CRYSTAL DIE AND MOLD INC**
5521 Meadowbrook Indus Ct (60008-3818)
PHONE..................847 658-6535
Mike Biangardi, *President*
Maria Sanmiguel, *Controller*
Nancy Krahn, *Manager*
▲ EMP: 50 EST: 1966
SQ FT: 24,000
SALES (est): 7.8MM **Privately Held**
WEB: www.cdmsolutions.com
SIC: 3089 3544 Injection molding of plastics; industrial molds

**(G-18725)**
**DIGITAL OPTICS TECH INC**
1645 Hicks Rd Ste H (60008-1222)
PHONE..................847 358-2592
Selim Shahriar, *President*
Juanita Riccobono, *Exec VP*
Nicholas Condon, *Vice Pres*
EMP: 4
SALES (est): 400K **Privately Held**
SIC: 3674 8731 Microprocessors; computer (hardware) development

**(G-18726)**
**DYTEC MIDWEST INC (PA)**
1855 Rohlwing Rd Ste C (60008-1474)
PHONE..................847 255-3200
James D Okon, *President*
Armando Prado, *Sales Engr*
Margo Halpern, *Office Mgr*
EMP: 6
SQ FT: 3,000
SALES (est): 1.3MM **Privately Held**
WEB: www.dytecmw.com
SIC: 5065 5045 3825 Electronic parts & equipment; computers, peripherals & software; test equipment for electronic & electric measurement

# GEOGRAPHIC SECTION
## Rolling Meadows - Cook County (G-18751)

**(G-18727)**
**ELIM PDTRIC PHRMACEUTICALS INC**
Eppi and Consulting
Corp Ctr 1600 Glf Rd 12 (60008)
**PHONE** .................. 412 266-5968
Dr Moji Adeyeye, *Branch Mgr*
**EMP:** 3
**SALES (corp-wide):** 450.9K **Privately Held**
**SIC: 2834** Pharmaceutical preparations
**PA:** Elim Pediatric Pharmaceuticals Inc.
Corp Ctr 1600
Rolling Meadows IL 60008
412 266-5968

**(G-18728)**
**FELIX PARTNERS LLC**
1845 Hicks Rd Ste C (60008-1269)
**PHONE** .................. 847 648-8449
Michael Lichter,
Felicia Shelfo,
**EMP:** 2 **EST:** 2007
**SALES (est):** 229.4K **Privately Held**
**SIC: 3559** Electronic component making machinery

**(G-18729)**
**FOUR STAR TOOL INC**
5521 Meadowbrook Ct (60008)
**PHONE** .................. 224 735-2419
**Fax:** 847 228-0999
Helmut Hoppe, *CEO*
Mike Biangardi, *President*
Matthias Biangardi, *Vice Pres*
John Sariadek, *Purchasing*
▲ **EMP:** 100 **EST:** 1966
**SQ FT:** 36,000
**SALES (est):** 13.1MM **Privately Held**
**WEB:** www.inject-it.com
**SIC: 3679** 3469 3089 Electronic circuits; metal stampings; injection molded finished plastic products

**(G-18730)**
**FUJIFILM HUNT CHEM USA INC**
Also Called: Fuji Hunt
900 Carnegie St (60008-1006)
**PHONE** .................. 847 259-8800
**Fax:** 847 259-7682
Dan Larkin, *Vice Pres*
Kathy Srednicki, *Foreman/Supr*
Malcolm Penman, *Mfg Staff*
Bruce Gray, *Opers-Prdtn-Mfg*
Todd Sander, *Purch Mgr*
**EMP:** 130
**SALES (corp-wide):** 21.2B **Privately Held**
**WEB:** www.fujihuntusa.com
**SIC: 3861** 4225 5169 Photographic processing chemicals; general warehousing; industrial chemicals
**HQ:** Fujifilm Hunt Chemicals U.S.A., Inc.
40 Boroline Rd
Allendale NJ 07401
201 995-2200

**(G-18731)**
**FUSECO**
2255 Lois Dr (60008-4134)
**PHONE** .................. 847 749-4158
Jeff Tabak, *Manager*
**EMP:** 3
**SALES (est):** 335.9K **Privately Held**
**SIC: 3613** Fuses, electric

**(G-18732)**
**GLOBAL TECH & RESOURCES INC**
Also Called: Db Professionals
3601 Algonquin Rd Ste 650 (60008-3184)
**PHONE** .................. 630 364-4260
Velu Palani, *President*
**EMP:** 2
**SALES:** 1.2MM **Privately Held**
**SIC: 7372** 8748 Prepackaged software; systems analysis & engineering consulting services

**(G-18733)**
**HEICO OHMITE LLC**
1600 Golf Rd Ste 850 (60008-4204)
**PHONE** .................. 847 258-0300
**EMP:** 15
**SALES (est):** 1.8MM **Privately Held**
**SIC: 3629** Electronic generation equipment

**(G-18734)**
**INSIGNIA DESIGN LTD**
2118 Plum Grove Rd 191 (60008-1932)
**PHONE** .................. 301 254-9221
Pamela Roark, *President*
James M Roark, *Principal*
**EMP:** 2
**SALES:** 250K **Privately Held**
**SIC: 3993** 2262 Signs & advertising specialties; printing: manmade fiber & silk broadwoven fabrics

**(G-18735)**
**JAMES COLEMAN COMPANY**
1500 Hicks Rd (60008-1200)
**PHONE** .................. 847 963-8100
**Fax:** 847 963-8200
Chris Wade, *President*
Matthew Wade, *Vice Pres*
Nancy Perryman, *Sales Staff*
◆ **EMP:** 14 **EST:** 1972
**SQ FT:** 5,000
**SALES (est):** 2MM **Privately Held**
**WEB:** www.jimcolemanltd.com
**SIC: 3999** Advertising display products

**(G-18736)**
**JQL ELECTRONICS INC (PA)**
3501 Algonquin Rd Ste 230 (60008-3103)
**PHONE** .................. 630 873-2020
Jack Zhu, *President*
Christina Huan, *Vice Pres*
**EMP:** 16
**SALES (est):** 2.6MM **Privately Held**
**SIC: 3822** 3674 Hydronic circulator control, automatic; optical isolators

**(G-18737)**
**KOMATSU AMERICA CORP (HQ)**
1701 Golf Rd Ste 1-100 (60008-4234)
**PHONE** .................. 847 437-5800
**Fax:** 847 437-1016
Rod Schrader, *Ch of Bd*
Max Masayuki Moriyama, *President*
Tom Gill, *General Mgr*
Jim Mathis, *General Mgr*
Masao Murayama, *General Mgr*
◆ **EMP:** 300
**SQ FT:** 102,000
**SALES (est):** 2.9B
**SALES (corp-wide):** 15.8B **Privately Held**
**WEB:** www.equipmentcentralexpo.com
**SIC: 5082** 3532 3531 Mining machinery & equipment, except petroleum; mining machinery; construction machinery
**PA:** Komatsu Ltd.
2-3-6, Akasaka
Minato-Ku TKY 107-0
355 612-616

**(G-18738)**
**KOMATSU FORKLIFT USA LLC (HQ)**
Also Called: Kfi
1701 Golf Rd Ste 1 (60008-4234)
**PHONE** .................. 847 437-5800
Robert Colarullo, *Engineer*
Jeff Victor, *Manager*
Akira Yamakawa,
▲ **EMP:** 30
**SALES (est):** 20.1MM
**SALES (corp-wide):** 15.8B **Privately Held**
**SIC: 3537** 5084 Forklift trucks; lift trucks & parts
**PA:** Komatsu Ltd.
2-3-6, Akasaka
Minato-Ku TKY 107-0
355 612-616

**(G-18739)**
**KOMORI AMERICA CORPORATION (HQ)**
5520 Meadowbrook Indus Ct (60008-3898)
**PHONE** .................. 847 806-9038
**Fax:** 847 806-9038
Kazuyoshi Miyao, *President*
Hiro Hoshino, *Exec VP*
Robert J Rath, *Exec VP*
Jacki Hudmon, *Senior VP*
Andrew Katz, *Info Tech Mgr*
▲ **EMP:** 65
**SQ FT:** 48,000
**SALES (est):** 39.8MM
**SALES (corp-wide):** 814.6MM **Privately Held**
**SIC: 5044** 3542 3555 Office equipment; machine tools, metal forming type; printing trades machinery
**PA:** Komori Corporation
3-11-1, Azumabashi
Sumida-Ku TKY 130-0
356 087-811

**(G-18740)**
**L C MOLD INC**
3640 Edison Pl (60008-1013)
**PHONE** .................. 847 593-5004
Leonid Danushevsky, *President*
John Linder, *Business Dir*
Margaret Danushevsky, *Admin Sec*
**EMP:** 36
**SQ FT:** 15,000
**SALES (est):** 5.4MM **Privately Held**
**WEB:** www.lcmold.com
**SIC: 3089** 3544 8742 Injection molding of plastics; special dies, tools, jigs & fixtures; training & development consultant

**(G-18741)**
**L3 TECHNOLOGIES INC**
1200 Hicks Rd (60008-1017)
**PHONE** .................. 212 697-1111
Joseph Valin, *Mfg Mgr*
Kai Liu, *Electrical Engi*
James J Stillwell, *Business Dir*
**EMP:** 13
**SALES (corp-wide):** 10.5B **Publicly Held**
**SIC: 3663** Radio & TV communications equipment
**PA:** L3 Technologies, Inc.
600 3rd Ave Fl 34
New York NY 10016
212 697-1111

**(G-18742)**
**M & R PRINTING INC**
Also Called: Allegra Print & Imaging
5100 Newport Dr Ste 4 (60008-3825)
**PHONE** .................. 847 398-2500
Michael E Tarpinian, *President*
**EMP:** 6
**SQ FT:** 2,800
**SALES (est):** 894.6K **Privately Held**
**WEB:** www.allegrausa.com
**SIC: 2752** 7389 2791 Commercial printing, offset; design, commercial & industrial; typesetting

**(G-18743)**
**METAMATION INC (PA)**
3501 Algonquin Rd Ste 680 (60008-3160)
**PHONE** .................. 775 826-1717
Kartik Vaidyanathan, *President*
Anupam Chakraborty, *Vice Pres*
Alex Lopez, *Info Tech Mgr*
**EMP:** 10
**SALES (est):** 1.7MM **Privately Held**
**WEB:** www.metamation-us.com
**SIC: 7372** Prepackaged software

**(G-18744)**
**METHODE ELECTRONICS INC**
Power Solutions Group
1700 Hicks Rd (60008-1229)
**PHONE** .................. 847 577-9545
**Fax:** 847 392-9404
Andrew Urda, *General Mgr*
Jim Quillen, *Vice Pres*
Chris Ogden, *Engrg Mgr*
Denis M Lindsey, *Engineer*
Joe August, *Senior Engr*
**EMP:** 158
**SQ FT:** 1,145
**SALES (corp-wide):** 809.1MM **Publicly Held**
**WEB:** www.methode.com
**SIC: 3678** 3643 Electronic connectors; current-carrying wiring devices
**PA:** Methode Electronics, Inc
7401 W Wilson Ave
Chicago IL 60706
708 867-6777

**(G-18745)**
**MITSUTOYO-KIKO USA INC**
1600 Golf Rd Ste 1200 (60008-4229)
**PHONE** .................. 847 981-5200
Tamotsu Ozaki, *President*
**EMP:** 4
**SALES:** 600K
**SALES (corp-wide):** 30.1MM **Privately Held**
**SIC: 3462** Machinery forgings, ferrous
**PA:** Mitsutoyo-Kiko Co.,Ltd.
1-4-12, Higashinoshinmachi
Kasugai AIC 486-0
568 814-111

**(G-18746)**
**MODAGRAFICS INC**
5300 Newport Dr (60008-3702)
**PHONE** .................. 800 860-3169
**Fax:** 847 392-3989
Paul Pirkle, *President*
Michael Antongiovanni, *CFO*
C Scott Marple, *VP Sales*
Bob Traut, *Manager*
Carlson Leonnard, *Admin Sec*
**EMP:** 80
**SQ FT:** 75,000
**SALES (est):** 21.5MM **Privately Held**
**WEB:** www.modagrafics.com
**SIC: 2759** 3993 7389 Screen printing; signs, not made in custom sign painting shops; interior decorating

**(G-18747)**
**NANTPHARMA LLC**
1701 Golf Rd Ste 3-1007 (60008-4270)
**PHONE** .................. 847 243-1200
Ralph Yamamoto, *Vice Pres*
Kevin Forney, *Director*
Chris Anaya, *Director*
Bob Pahl, *Director*
Marie Thompson, *Director*
**EMP:** 1
**SALES (est):** 11.2MM
**SALES (corp-wide):** 112.8MM **Publicly Held**
**SIC: 2834** Adrenal pharmaceutical preparations
**PA:** Nantworks, Llc
9920 Jefferson Blvd
Culver City CA 90232
310 405-7539

**(G-18748)**
**NARIMA INC**
3350 Kirchoff Rd (60008-1824)
**PHONE** .................. 847 818-9620
Ramzal Ali, *President*
**EMP:** 4 **EST:** 2000
**SALES (est):** 242.1K **Privately Held**
**WEB:** www.narima-lanta.com
**SIC: 2051** Doughnuts, except frozen

**(G-18749)**
**NATIONAL TECHNOLOGY INC**
1101 Carnegie St (60008-1008)
**PHONE** .................. 847 506-1300
**Fax:** 847 506-1340
Roger Patel, *CEO*
Robert Keisler, *President*
Carl Schlemmer, *QC Dir*
Vijay Patel, *Treasurer*
Jeff Phillips, *Controller*
◆ **EMP:** 40
**SQ FT:** 55,000
**SALES (est):** 8.7MM **Privately Held**
**WEB:** www.nationaltech.com
**SIC: 3672** Printed circuit boards

**(G-18750)**
**NISSHIN HOLDING INC**
Also Called: Nisshin Steel USA
1701 Golf Rd Ste 3-1004 (60008-4270)
**PHONE** .................. 847 290-5100
Craig Stoll, *Branch Mgr*
Y Fukami, *Exec Dir*
**EMP:** 4
**SALES (corp-wide):** 4.6B **Privately Held**
**SIC: 3325** Steel foundries
**HQ:** Nisshin Holding, Inc.
1701 Golf Rd
Rolling Meadows IL 60008

**(G-18751)**
**NITEK INTERNATIONAL LLC**
5410 Newport Dr Ste 24 (60008-3722)
**PHONE** .................. 847 259-8900
Lisa Austerlade, *Production*
Jim Hertrich, *Engineer*
Chad Szekeres, *Natl Sales Mgr*
Ed Planek,

▲ EMP: 4
SALES (est): 740.9K  Privately Held
WEB: www.nitek.net
SIC: 3699  Security control equipment & systems

### (G-18752)
### NORTHERN INFORMATION TECH
Also Called: I Tech
5410 Newport Dr Ste 24  (60008-3722)
PHONE............................800 528-4343
Fax: 847 259-1300
Edward Polanek, President
EMP: 16 EST: 1984
SQ FT: 6,400
SALES (est): 1.7MM  Privately Held
SIC: 3663  Television closed circuit equipment

### (G-18753)
### NORTHROP GRUMMAN SYSTEMS CORP
600 Hicks Rd  (60008-1015)
PHONE............................847 259-9600
Fax: 847 870-5705
James Stephenson, Counsel
Dean Vanek, Counsel
Tom Hopkins, Purchasing
David Cherry, Engineer
Robert Delboca, Branch Mgr
EMP: 637
SQ FT: 400,000  Publicly Held
WEB: www.sperry.ngc.com
SIC: 3663  3679  3671  3651  Radio broadcasting & communications equipment; electronic circuits; electron tubes; household audio & video equipment; motors & generators; electronic computers
HQ: Northrop Grumman Systems Corporation
    2980 Fairview Park Dr
    Falls Church VA 22042
    703 280-2900

### (G-18754)
### NORTHROP GRUMMAN TECHNICAL
600 Hicks Rd  (60008-1015)
PHONE............................847 259-2396
Fax: 847 870-5712
Murray Nance, Business Mgr
Jim Guzak, Project Mgr
George Cala, Opers Mgr
Tom Norris, Opers Staff
Gary Wildman, Purch Agent
EMP: 143  Publicly Held
WEB: www.afqrc.com
SIC: 3812  Acceleration indicators & systems components, aerospace
HQ: Northrop Grumman Technical Services, Inc.
    2340 Dulles Corner Blvd
    Herndon VA 20171
    703 713-4096

### (G-18755)
### OBERWEIS DAIRY INC
1735 Algonquin Rd  (60008-4112)
PHONE............................847 290-9222
Fax: 847 290-9223
Dave Hassler, Marketing Mgr
Jen Shabec, Manager
Scott Thrasher, Manager
EMP: 10
SALES (corp-wide): 202.6MM  Privately Held
WEB: www.webfc.net
SIC: 2026  5963  5451  Milk processing (pasteurizing, homogenizing, bottling); milk delivery; milk; ice cream (packaged)
PA: Oberweis Dairy, Inc.
    951 Ice Cream Dr
    North Aurora IL 60542
    630 801-6100

### (G-18756)
### P K NEUSES INCORPORATED
Also Called: Neuses Tools
1401 Rohlwing Rd  (60008-1398)
P.O. Box 100, Arlington Heights  (60006-0100)
PHONE............................847 253-6555
Fax: 847 253-6652
Gary B Neuses, President
Guy Neuses, Vice Pres
Kathy Neuses, Admin Sec
EMP: 6 EST: 1944
SQ FT: 8,000
SALES (est): 710K  Privately Held
WEB: www.pkneuses.com
SIC: 3825  3678  3545  3423  Measuring instruments & meters, electric; electronic connectors; machine tool accessories; hand & edge tools

### (G-18757)
### PALATINE WELDING COMPANY
3848 Berdnick St  (60008-1003)
PHONE............................847 358-1075
Dana Piacenza, President
Robin Piacenza, Manager
Carl S Piacenza, Admin Sec
EMP: 26 EST: 1973
SQ FT: 40,000
SALES (est): 6.8MM  Privately Held
WEB: www.palatinewelding.com
SIC: 3441  Fabricated structural metal

### (G-18758)
### PARTH CONSULTANTS INC
Also Called: Brijen Electronics
5005 Newport Dr Ste 204  (60008-3838)
P.O. Box 331, Mount Prospect  (60056-0331)
PHONE............................847 758-1400
Fax: 847 758-1410
Maya Patel, President
Sam Patel, Vice Pres
EMP: 21
SQ FT: 5,000
SALES (est): 1.7MM  Privately Held
SIC: 8742  3672  Management consulting services; circuit boards, television & radio printed

### (G-18759)
### PEARSON INDUSTRIES INC
5420 Newport Dr Ste 56  (60008-3723)
PHONE............................847 963-9633
Todd H Pearson, President
EMP: 3
SQ FT: 3,900
SALES (est): 150K  Privately Held
SIC: 3444  Metal ventilating equipment

### (G-18760)
### PEI/GENESIS INC
3701 Algonquin Rd Ste 710  (60008-3165)
PHONE............................215 673-0400
Eileen Shapiro, Branch Mgr
EMP: 7
SALES (corp-wide): 340.1MM  Privately Held
WEB: www.suresealconnections.com
SIC: 3675  3676  Electronic capacitors; electronic resistors
PA: Pei/Genesis, Inc.
    2180 Hornig Rd Ste 2
    Philadelphia PA 19116
    215 464-1410

### (G-18761)
### PEPSI COLA GEN BTTLERS OF LIMA (DH)
Also Called: Pepsico
3501 Algonquin Rd Ste 700  (60008-3133)
PHONE............................847 253-1000
EMP: 6
SQ FT: 55,000
SALES (est): 49.5MM
SALES (corp-wide): 63B  Publicly Held
SIC: 2086  5149  Mfg Bottled/Canned Soft Drinks Whol Groceries
HQ: Pepsi-Cola General Bottlers, Inc.
    1475 E Wdfeld Rd Ste 1300
    Schaumburg IL 60173
    847 598-3000

### (G-18762)
### PEPSI-COLA GENERAL BOTTLERS VA
3501 Algonquin Rd  (60008-3103)
PHONE............................847 253-1000
Robert Pohlad, President
John Jarvis, Business Mgr
Julie Janik, Manager
Charles Pace, Analyst
EMP: 300
SALES (est): 20.7MM
SALES (corp-wide): 62.8B  Publicly Held
SIC: 2086  Carbonated soft drinks, bottled & canned
HQ: Pepsi-Cola General Bottlers, Inc.
    1475 E Wdfeld Rd Ste 1300
    Schaumburg IL 60173
    847 598-3000

### (G-18763)
### PLIANT LLC
Also Called: Roll-O-Sheets
1701 Golf Rd Ste 2-900  (60008-4255)
PHONE............................812 424-2904
Harold Davis, President
Len Azzaro, President
Ian Rayner, General Mgr
Rich Wierman, Regional Mgr
R David Corey, COO
▼ EMP: 2800
SALES (est): 224.1MM
SALES (corp-wide): 6.4B  Publicly Held
WEB: www.pliantcorp.com
SIC: 3081  2673  3089  Plastic film & sheet; bags: plastic, laminated & coated; food storage & frozen food bags, plastic; air mattresses, plastic
HQ: Berry Global, Inc.
    101 Oakley St
    Evansville IN 47710
    812 424-2904

### (G-18764)
### PLIANT CORP INTERNATIONAL
1701 Golf Rd Ste 2-900  (60008-4255)
PHONE............................847 969-3300
Harold C Bevis, President
Michelle Wilson, President
Jim Harder, Exec VP
Lori C Roberts, Senior VP
Stephen T Auburn, Vice Pres
EMP: 3
SALES (est): 340K  Privately Held
SIC: 3081  Plastic film & sheet

### (G-18765)
### POSITIVE PACKAGING INC
Also Called: Positive Packaging & Graphics
1100 Hicks Rd  (60008-1016)
PHONE............................847 392-4405
Todd Beidler, President
▲ EMP: 3
SALES (est): 579.1K  Privately Held
WEB: www.positivepackaging.com
SIC: 3086  Packaging & shipping materials, foamed plastic

### (G-18766)
### PPG INDUSTRIES INC
Also Called: PPG 5532
2180 Plum Grove Rd  (60008-1932)
PHONE............................847 991-0620
Steve Miller, Manager
Fred Schrber, Manager
EMP: 24
SALES (corp-wide): 14.7B  Publicly Held
WEB: www.ppg.com
SIC: 2851  Paints & allied products
PA: Ppg Industries, Inc.
    1 Ppg Pl
    Pittsburgh PA 15272
    412 434-3131

### (G-18767)
### PRECISION METAL SPINNING CORP
Also Called: A M Tool
1000 Carnegie St  (60008-1007)
PHONE............................847 392-5672
Dorothy L Doumakes, President
Al Doumakes, Vice Pres
EMP: 38 EST: 1974
SALES (est): 4.1MM  Privately Held
SIC: 3469  Spinning metal for the trade

### (G-18768)
### PRECISION METAL TECHNOLOGIES
2255 Lois Dr Ste 2  (60008-4100)
PHONE............................847 228-6630
Timothy Perry, President
Donna Palmer, Admin Sec
EMP: 10
SQ FT: 5,000
SALES: 1MM  Privately Held
SIC: 3469  8711  3398  Metal stampings; engineering services; metal heat treating

### (G-18769)
### PREMIER PRINTING AND PACKAGING
1881 Hicks Rd Ste B  (60008-1214)
PHONE............................847 970-9434
P Nuzzo, Vice Pres
EMP: 2
SALES (est): 267.5K  Privately Held
SIC: 2759  Commercial printing

### (G-18770)
### PROBLEND-EUROGERM LLC
1801 Hicks Rd Ste H  (60008-1226)
PHONE............................847 221-5004
Sebastien Jollet, CEO
EMP: 5
SALES (est): 202.2K  Privately Held
SIC: 2041  Flour & other grain mill products

### (G-18771)
### QCIRCUITS INC (PA)
2775 Algonquin Rd Ste 300  (60008-3835)
PHONE............................847 797-6678
Jeffery Cosman, President
Ed Waytula, Vice Pres
▲ EMP: 25
SQ FT: 12,000
SALES (est): 8.7MM  Privately Held
WEB: www.bel-tronicscorp.com
SIC: 3677  3672  3679  Coil windings, electronic; printed circuit boards; electronic circuits

### (G-18772)
### RATIONAL COOKING SYSTEMS INC
1701 Golf Rd Ste C-LI  (60008-4236)
PHONE............................224 366-3500
Gunter Blaschke, CEO
Chris Koehler, President
Bjoern Rowland, President
Juliet Hope, Area Mgr
Bradley Morris, Area Mgr
▲ EMP: 73
SQ FT: 2,000
SALES (est): 11.6MM
SALES (corp-wide): 648.2MM  Privately Held
WEB: www.rationalusa.com
SIC: 3556  Ovens, bakery
PA: Rational Ag
    Iglinger Str. 62
    Landsberg Am Lech  86899
    819 132-70

### (G-18773)
### RAYTHEON COMPANY
4110 Winnetka Ave  (60008-1375)
PHONE............................630 295-6394
EMP: 450
SALES (corp-wide): 24B  Publicly Held
SIC: 3812  Defense systems & equipment
PA: Raytheon Company
    870 Winter St
    Waltham MA 02451
    781 522-3000

### (G-18774)
### RF IDEAS INC (HQ)
4020 Winnetka Ave  (60008-1374)
PHONE............................847 870-1723
David Cottingham, President
Rosabel Ramos, Area Mgr
Jim Dahlin, Opers Mgr
Harvey Kuehn, Controller
Terry Morrissey, Marketing Staff
▲ EMP: 54
SQ FT: 8,000
SALES (est): 18.7MM
SALES (corp-wide): 3.7B  Publicly Held
WEB: www.rfideas.com
SIC: 3699  5734  Security devices; personal computers
PA: Roper Technologies, Inc.
    6901 Prof Pkwy E Ste 200
    Sarasota FL 34240
    941 556-2601

# GEOGRAPHIC SECTION

Romeoville - Will County (G-18797)

**(G-18775)**
**RTC INDUSTRIES INC (PA)**
Also Called: RTC USA World Headquarters
2800 Golf Rd (60008-4023)
PHONE.....................847 640-2400
Fax: 847 640-5175
Walter Nathan, *Ch of Bd*
Richard Nathan, *President*
Kevin Green, *Managing Dir*
Howard Topping, *Exec VP*
Gary Cohen, *Senior VP*
▲ **EMP**: 350 **EST**: 1951
**SQ FT**: 140,000
**SALES** (est): 257.9MM **Privately Held**
**WEB**: www.rtc.com
**SIC**: 2599 5211 Boards: planning, display, notice; closets, interiors & accessories

**(G-18776)**
**SAFEMOBILE INC**
3601 Algonquin Rd Ste 320 (60008-3107)
PHONE.....................847 818-1649
Dorel Nasui, *CEO*
Leslie Wick, *Opers Mgr*
Cristi Ene, *Software Engr*
**EMP**: 12
**SALES** (est): 5MM **Privately Held**
**SIC**: 3679 3663 Electronic circuits;

**(G-18777)**
**SCREEN NORTH AMER HOLDINGS INC (HQ)**
5110 Tollview Dr (60008-3715)
PHONE.....................847 870-7400
Hiroshi Hara, *President*
**EMP**: 11 **EST**: 1996
**SALES** (est): 77.6MM
**SALES** (corp-wide): 2.6B **Privately Held**
**SIC**: 7371 3861 7699 8742 Computer software development; graphic arts plates, sensitized; photographic & optical goods equipment repair services; management consulting services; survey service: marketing, location, etc.
**PA**: Screen Holdings Co., Ltd.
Horikawadori-Teranouchi, Kamigyo-Ku
Kyoto KYO 602-0
754 147-155

**(G-18778)**
**SECURITY LIGHTING SYSTEMS INC**
2100 Golf Rd Ste 460 (60008-4704)
PHONE.....................800 544-4848
Fax: 847 279-0642
Timothy Powers, *President*
Dave Levinson, *Vice Pres*
Mark Werth, *Engineer*
Laurie Dinse, *Credit Mgr*
Darryl Lathrop, *Natl Sales Mgr*
▲ **EMP**: 40
**SALES** (est): 4.9MM
**SALES** (corp-wide): 3.5B **Publicly Held**
**WEB**: www.securitylighting.com
**SIC**: 3646 Commercial indusl & institutional electric lighting fixtures
**PA**: Hubbell Incorporated
40 Waterview Dr
Shelton CT 06484
475 882-4000

**(G-18779)**
**SOLIDYNE CORPORATION**
4731 Woodland Ct (60008-2243)
PHONE.....................847 394-3333
Fax: 847 394-8083
Baha Erturk, *CEO*
Joann Golbeck, *Opers Mgr*
Adem Erturk, *Technical Mgr*
Adam Erturk, *Engineer*
Matt Gardner, *Engineer*
▲ **EMP**: 15
**SQ FT**: 6,000
**SALES** (est): 1.5MM **Privately Held**
**SIC**: 3822 Auto controls regulating residntl & coml environmt & applncs

**(G-18780)**
**SORTIMAT TECHNOLOGY LP**
5655 Meadowbrook Indus Ct (60008-3833)
PHONE.....................847 925-1234
Fax: 847 640-2851
Eric Pasman, *President*
Tom Kramer, *Partner*
Hans-Dieter Baumtrog, *Partner*
Ulrich Kloepfer, *Partner*
Paul Nordin, *Project Dir*
▼ **EMP**: 61
**SALES** (est): 10.6MM **Privately Held**
**SIC**: 3549 Assembly machines, including robotic

**(G-18781)**
**SPARTANICS LTD**
3605 Edison Pl (60008-1077)
PHONE.....................847 394-5700
Fax: 847 394-0409
Thomas Kleeman, *CEO*
Thomas O'Hara, *President*
David Birch, *Business Mgr*
Jim Matts, *Business Mgr*
William Gillen, *COO*
▲ **EMP**: 38
**SQ FT**: 25,000
**SALES** (est): 11.7MM **Privately Held**
**WEB**: www.spartanics.com
**SIC**: 3577 3824 3699 Optical scanning devices; mechanical & electromechanical counters & devices; teaching machines & aids, electronic

**(G-18782)**
**THOMAS PACKAGING LLC**
Also Called: Service Industries, LLC
3885 Industrial Ave (60008-1038)
PHONE.....................847 392-1652
Fax: 847 392-0276
Wesley Mancoff, *President*
Lindsay Carpenter, *Accountant*
Joel Gray, *Manager*
▲ **EMP**: 13
**SALES** (est): 2.8MM
**SALES** (corp-wide): 25.2MM **Privately Held**
**WEB**: www.serviceindustries.biz
**SIC**: 3545 Machine tool accessories
**PA**: Thomas Engineering Inc.
575 W Central Rd
Hoffman Estates IL 60192
847 358-5800

**(G-18783)**
**TKK USA INC (DH)**
2550 Golf Rd Ste 800 (60008-4026)
PHONE.....................847 439-7821
Brad Niwa, *Corp Secy*
Austin Wu, *MIS Mgr*
◆ **EMP**: 3
**SQ FT**: 15,000
**SALES** (est): 32MM
**SALES** (corp-wide): 32.6B **Privately Held**
**SIC**: 3429 3086 Vacuum bottles or jugs; ice chests or coolers (portable), foamed plastic
**HQ**: Thermos K.K.
4-1-23, Shiba
Minato-Ku TKY 108-0
357 300-130

**(G-18784)**
**TRANSLOGIC CORPORATION**
Also Called: Swisslog Consulting
1951 Rohlwing Rd Ste C (60008-1300)
PHONE.....................847 392-3700
Fax: 847 392-3738
**EMP**: 15
**SALES** (corp-wide): 2.6B **Privately Held**
**SIC**: 3535 Mfg Conveyors/Equipment
**HQ**: Translogic Corporation
10825 E 47th Ave
Denver CO 80239
303 371-7770

**(G-18785)**
**TRI-TOWER PRINTING INC**
Also Called: Printing/Typesetting
1701 Golf Rd Ste L01 (60008-4233)
PHONE.....................847 640-6633
Fax: 847 640-6988
Joseph Mulae, *President*
**EMP**: 4
**SQ FT**: 2,500
**SALES**: 600K **Privately Held**
**SIC**: 2752 7334 2791 2789 Commercial printing, offset; multilithing; mimeographing; typesetting, computer controlled; bookbinding & related work; commercial printing

**(G-18786)**
**UNITED CHEMI-CON INC (HQ)**
1701 Golf Rd Ste 1-1200 (60008-4245)
PHONE.....................847 696-2000
Fax: 847 696-9278
Masatoshi Boi, *President*
Tsuneo Ohta, *President*
Steve Watlock, *General Mgr*
John Kolbow, *Financial Exec*
Sandy Calhoun, *Human Res Mgr*
▲ **EMP**: 40
**SQ FT**: 10,692
**SALES** (est): 62.4MM
**SALES** (corp-wide): 1B **Privately Held**
**SIC**: 3675 Electronic capacitors
**PA**: Nippon Chemi-Con Corporation
5-6-4, Osaki
Shinagawa-Ku TKY 141-0
354 367-711

**(G-18787)**
**VALUE ENGINEERED PRODUCTS**
Also Called: Vep
1700 Hicks Rd (60008-1229)
PHONE.....................708 867-6777
Fax: 630 416-9028
Ed Luzader, *President*
Ms Tracy Shemwell, *Opers Mgr*
Rick Overstreet, *Engineer*
**EMP**: 30
**SQ FT**: 30,000
**SALES** (est): 3.4MM **Privately Held**
**SIC**: 3429 3674 Clamps, metal; semiconductors & related devices

**(G-18788)**
**VONBERG VALVE INC**
3800 Industrial Ave (60008-1085)
PHONE.....................847 259-3800
Fax: 847 259-3997
Joseph M Levon, *CEO*
Michael D Levon, *President*
Randall Hess, *Plant Mgr*
Carl Patterson, *Mfg Engineer*
James Carucio, *Chief Engr*
**EMP**: 30
**SQ FT**: 20,000
**SALES** (est): 7MM **Privately Held**
**WEB**: www.vonberg.com
**SIC**: 3492 3728 3494 3491 Control valves, aircraft: hydraulic & pneumatic; aircraft parts & equipment; valves & pipe fittings; industrial valves

**(G-18789)**
**ZIV USA INC (HQ)**
5410 Newport Dr Ste 38 (60008-3722)
PHONE.....................224 735-3961
Norberto Santiago, *President*
Juan Dorado, *Vice Pres*
Erich Keller, *Engineer*
Oscare Bol, *Manager*
Oscar Bolado, *Manager*
▲ **EMP**: 5
**SQ FT**: 2,000
**SALES** (est): 1.9MM
**SALES** (corp-wide): 10.6MM **Privately Held**
**WEB**: www.zivusa.com
**SIC**: 3575 Computer terminals, monitors & components
**PA**: Ziv Aplicaciones Y Tecnologia Sociedad Limitada
Poligono Teknologi Elkartegia 210
Zamudio 48170
944 522-003

---
**Romeoville**
**Will County**
---

**(G-18790)**
**ADEL WOODWORKS (PA)**
15523 Weber Rd Ste 104 (60446-3502)
PHONE.....................815 886-9006
Gerimangas Saputis, *President*
**EMP**: 2
**SALES** (est): 356.9K **Privately Held**
**SIC**: 2499 Decorative wood & woodwork

**(G-18791)**
**ADVANCED DIAMOND TECH INC**
48 E Belmont Dr (60446-1764)
PHONE.....................815 293-0900
John D Yerger III, *President*
Linda Pickering, *Manager*
**EMP**: 21
**SQ FT**: 12,000
**SALES** (est): 6.8MM **Privately Held**
**SIC**: 2819 Industrial inorganic chemicals

**(G-18792)**
**AEROPULSE LLC**
1336 Enterprise Dr (60446-1016)
PHONE.....................215 245-7600
Joe Tafilowski, *Engineer*
Francis Shields, *Branch Mgr*
**EMP**: 3
**SALES** (corp-wide): 1.1MM **Privately Held**
**SIC**: 3564 Filters, air: furnaces, air conditioning equipment, etc.
**PA**: Aeropulse, Llc
1746 Winchester Rd Fl 2
Bensalem PA 19020
215 245-7554

**(G-18793)**
**ALL STONE INC**
1525 Azalea Cir (60446-4987)
PHONE.....................815 529-1754
Gerald Jagodzinski, *Principal*
**EMP**: 2
**SALES** (est): 257.5K **Privately Held**
**SIC**: 2541 Counter & sink tops

**(G-18794)**
**ALLEGRA PRINT & IMAGING**
576 W Taylor Rd (60446-4611)
PHONE.....................815 524-3902
Thomas J Wilhelm, *Owner*
**EMP**: 6
**SALES** (est): 614.9K **Privately Held**
**SIC**: 2752 Commercial printing, offset

**(G-18795)**
**AMERICAN INKS AND COATINGS CO**
1225 Lakeside Dr 1 (60446-3971)
PHONE.....................630 226-0994
Jerry Mosley, *President*
Robert Raeke, *Admin Sec*
**EMP**: 6 **EST**: 2012
**SALES** (est): 833.9K **Privately Held**
**SIC**: 2752 Lithographing on metal

**(G-18796)**
**AMERICAN STAIR CORPORATION INC**
642 Forestwood Dr (60446-1354)
PHONE.....................815 886-9600
Fax: 815 372-3683
Gordon Fitzsimmons, *President*
Ross Johnson, *Vice Pres*
John Munoz, *Mfg Staff*
Zeljko Novakovich, *Engineer*
Rocco Maggio, *Accounts Mgr*
**EMP**: 90 **EST**: 1956
**SQ FT**: 66,000
**SALES** (est): 30.1MM **Privately Held**
**WEB**: www.americanstair.com
**SIC**: 3446 Architectural metalwork; railings, bannisters, guards, etc.: made from metal pipe; stairs, staircases, stair treads: prefabricated metal

**(G-18797)**
**AMERISOURCEBERGEN CORPORATION**
1001 Taylor Rd (60446-4265)
PHONE.....................815 221-3600
Carol Sherk, *Principal*
**EMP**: 29
**SALES** (corp-wide): 146.8B **Publicly Held**
**WEB**: www.amerisourcebergen.net
**SIC**: 2834 Pills, pharmaceutical
**PA**: Amerisourcebergen Corporation
1300 Morris Dr Ste 100
Chesterbrook PA 19087
610 727-7000

# Romeoville - Will County (G-18798)

**(G-18798)**
**AMSYSCO INC**
1200 Windham Pkwy (60446-1673)
PHONE..................................630 296-8383
Fax: 630 296-8380
Rattan L Khosa, *President*
Neel Khosa, *Treasurer*
EMP: 23
SQ FT: 55,000
SALES (est): 6.9MM **Privately Held**
WEB: www.amsyscoinc.com
SIC: 3496 Cable, uninsulated wire: made from purchased wire

**(G-18799)**
**APPLIED THERMAL COATINGS**
221 Rocbaar Dr (60446-1163)
PHONE..................................815 372-4305
EMP: 18
SALES: 950K **Privately Held**
SIC: 3479 Coating of metals & formed products

**(G-18800)**
**ARYZTA LLC**
Also Called: Aryzta Great Kitchens
300 Innovation Dr (60446-4612)
PHONE..................................815 306-7171
Barb Parks, *Project Mgr*
John Yamin, *Manager*
Nancy Cecil, *Manager*
EMP: 130
SALES (corp-wide): 4.3B **Privately Held**
SIC: 2038 Frozen specialties
HQ: Aryzta Llc
  6080 Center Dr Ste 900
  Los Angeles CA 90045
  310 417-4700

**(G-18801)**
**AUTOMATED DESIGN CORP**
Also Called: ADC 360
1404 Joliet Rd Ste B (60446-4410)
PHONE..................................630 783-1150
Thomas C Bitsky, *President*
Joseph Bitsky, *Vice Pres*
Lisa Bitsky, *Vice Pres*
EMP: 9
SQ FT: 5,500
SALES: 1.5MM **Privately Held**
WEB: www.automatedesign.com
SIC: 7699 5063 3599 Recreational sporting equipment repair services; electrical apparatus & equipment; custom machinery

**(G-18802)**
**BARRY-WHMLLER CONT SYSTEMS INC (DH)**
Also Called: Bw Container Systems
1305 Lakeview Dr (60446-3900)
PHONE..................................630 759-6800
Fax: 630 759-2299
Pete Carlson, *CEO*
Phillip G Ostapowicz, *President*
Robert H Chapman, *Chairman*
Eric Collier, *Vice Pres*
David M Gianini, *Vice Pres*
▼ EMP: 165
SQ FT: 121,000
SALES (est): 142.8MM
SALES (corp-wide): 1.9B **Privately Held**
WEB: www.fleetinc.com
SIC: 3535 Conveyors & conveying equipment
HQ: Barry-Wehmiller Companies, Inc.
  8020 Forsyth Blvd
  Saint Louis MO 63105
  314 862-8000

**(G-18803)**
**BOSCH AUTO SVC SOLUTIONS INC**
1385 N Weber Rd (60446-4307)
PHONE..................................815 407-3900
Mike Tuttle, *Manager*
Jackie McRaw, *Manager*
EMP: 16
SALES (corp-wide): 236.4MM **Privately Held**
SIC: 3465 Body parts, automobile: stamped metal
HQ: Bosch Automotive Service Solutions Inc.
  28635 Mound Rd
  Warren MI 48092
  586 574-2332

**(G-18804)**
**C K NORTH AMERICA INC**
1243 Naperville Dr (60446-1041)
PHONE..................................815 524-4246
EMP: 10
SALES (est): 740K **Privately Held**
SIC: 3423 Mfg Hand/Edge Tools

**(G-18805)**
**C P ENVIRONMENTAL INC**
Also Called: Micronics Engineered Filtrtion
1336 Enterprise Dr Ste 2 (60446-1062)
P.O. Box 7096 (60446-0996)
PHONE..................................630 759-8866
Fax: 630 759-7065
Thomas J Carr, *President*
Mike Schmidt, *Vice Pres*
Carol Marshall, *Mfg Staff*
Kim Sugars, *Sales Staff*
Terri Schackle, *Manager*
EMP: 10
SALES (est): 3.4MM **Privately Held**
SIC: 7699 5084 8711 3564 Industrial equipment services; pollution control equipment, air (environmental); pollution control engineering; blowers & fans
HQ: Micronics, Inc.
  200 West Rd
  Portsmouth NH 03801
  603 433-1299

**(G-18806)**
**CARD DYNAMIX LLC**
1120 Windham Pkwy (60446-1692)
PHONE..................................630 685-4060
Connie Sanfilippo, *CEO*
Ray Brian, *Controller*
Cyze James, *Mng Member*
Doherty Thomas B, *Mng Member*
Duncan Joe, *Mng Member*
▲ EMP: 105
SALES (est): 15.6MM **Privately Held**
SIC: 3083 8999 Laminated plastics plate & sheet; greeting card painting by hand
PA: Psa Equity, Llc
  485 E Half Day Rd Ste 500
  Buffalo Grove IL 60089

**(G-18807)**
**CENTRAL GRAPHICS CORP**
1302 Enterprise Dr (60446-1016)
PHONE..................................630 759-1696
Fax: 630 759-1792
James Crivellone, *President*
▲ EMP: 12
SQ FT: 10,000
SALES (est): 2.7MM **Privately Held**
SIC: 3555 Printing trades machinery

**(G-18808)**
**CGI AUTOMATED MFG INC**
275 Innovation Dr (60446-4613)
PHONE..................................815 221-5300
Janice M Nieman, *President*
Dorothy Bell, *Manager*
Stephanie Panninger, *Manager*
Gary Gurzynski, *Admin Sec*
EMP: 45
SQ FT: 62,500
SALES: 8MM **Privately Held**
WEB: www.cgimfg.com
SIC: 3444 Sheet metalwork

**(G-18809)**
**CHECKPOINT SYSTEMS INC**
1140 Windham Pkwy (60446-1692)
PHONE..................................630 771-4240
Pamela Rollo, *Mktg Dir*
Cliff Denzy, *Manager*
EMP: 80
SALES (corp-wide): 188.4K **Privately Held**
WEB: www.checkpointsystems.com
SIC: 3699 3812 3663 Security control equipment & systems; detection apparatus: electronic/magnetic field, light/heat; television closed circuit equipment
HQ: Checkpoint Systems, Inc.
  101 Wolf Dr
  West Deptford NJ 08086
  856 848-1800

**(G-18810)**
**CHICAGO TUBE AND IRON COMPANY**
Also Called: Boiler Tube & Fabrication Div
1 Chicago Tube Dr (60446-2402)
PHONE..................................815 834-2500
Bruce Butterfield, *General Mgr*
Susan Hamilton, *VP Admin*
Ronald Romanski, *Project Mgr*
Wally Walstrom, *Marketing Staff*
Susan O DEA, *Admin Sec*
EMP: 25
SALES (corp-wide): 1B **Publicly Held**
WEB: www.chicagotube.com
SIC: 3498 7692 5051 3317 Tube fabricating (contract bending & shaping); welding repair; metals service centers & offices; steel pipe & tubes
HQ: Chicago Tube And Iron Company
  1 Chicago Tube Dr
  Romeoville IL 60446
  815 834-2500

**(G-18811)**
**CICERO PLASTIC PRODUCTS INC**
121 Anton Dr (60446-4074)
PHONE..................................815 886-9522
Fax: 815 886-9277
George Driggers, *President*
Dave Driggers, *Vice Pres*
EMP: 21 EST: 1943
SQ FT: 12,000
SALES: 2.5MM **Privately Held**
WEB: www.ciceroplastics.com
SIC: 3469 3089 Machine parts, stamped or pressed metal; plastic processing

**(G-18812)**
**CIRCUITRON INC**
Also Called: Progressive Model Design
211 Rocbaar Dr (60446-1163)
PHONE..................................815 886-9010
Fax: 815 886-9076
Steve Worack, *President*
Katherine Yendrek, *Admin Sec*
EMP: 9
SQ FT: 11,000
SALES (est): 500K **Privately Held**
WEB: www.circuitron.com
SIC: 3944 Electronic toys

**(G-18813)**
**CMG PRECISION MACHINING CO INC**
1342 Enterprise Dr (60446-1016)
PHONE..................................630 759-8080
Craig Grinolds, *President*
Valarie Grinolds, *Vice Pres*
EMP: 9
SQ FT: 8,000
SALES (est): 1.2MM **Privately Held**
SIC: 3599 Machine & other job shop work

**(G-18814)**
**COLLAPSIBLE CORE INC**
631 Superior Dr (60446-1287)
PHONE..................................630 408-1693
Garry Zydron, *Principal*
Shaun Zydron, *Sales Mgr*
EMP: 3 EST: 2011
SALES (est): 207.8K **Privately Held**
SIC: 3089 Injection molding of plastics

**(G-18815)**
**CUSTOMWOOD STAIRS INC**
1424 Sherman Rd (60446-4046)
PHONE..................................630 739-5252
Gary R Waters, *President*
EMP: 40
SQ FT: 20,000
SALES (est): 6MM **Privately Held**
WEB: www.customwoodstairs.com
SIC: 2431 5031 Millwork; building materials, interior

**(G-18816)**
**DATA CABLE TECHNOLOGIES INC**
1306 Enterprise Dr Ste E (60446-4408)
PHONE..................................630 226-5600
Fax: 630 226-5602
Lionel Hawkins, *President*
Joe Mika, *Treasurer*
EMP: 18 EST: 1996
SQ FT: 4,000
SALES: 2MM **Privately Held**
WEB: www.datacabletech.com
SIC: 3643 Current-carrying wiring devices

**(G-18817)**
**DSS RAPAK INC**
1201 Windham Pkwy Ste D (60446-1699)
PHONE..................................630 296-2000
EMP: 5
SALES (est): 489K **Privately Held**
SIC: 3089 Plastic processing

**(G-18818)**
**ECO-PUR SOLUTIONS LLC**
1245 Naperville Dr (60446-1041)
PHONE..................................630 226-2300
David Frank, *Mng Member*
EMP: 9 EST: 2012
SALES (est): 1.4MM **Privately Held**
SIC: 8748 2891 Business consulting; adhesives & sealants

**(G-18819)**
**EMECOLE INC**
50 Montrose (60446-1475)
P.O. Box 7486 (60446-0486)
PHONE..................................815 372-2493
Fax: 815 372-3893
Louis F Cole, *President*
Patrick Buchmiller, *Mktg Dir*
Lucy Barthelme, *Manager*
Walter Seliga, *Manager*
Samme Cuthbertson, *Director*
▲ EMP: 12
SQ FT: 10,000
SALES (est): 3.8MM **Privately Held**
WEB: www.emecole.com
SIC: 2891 Adhesives & sealants

**(G-18820)**
**ESSEN NUTRITION CORPORATION**
1414 Sherman Rd (60446-4046)
PHONE..................................630 739-6700
Fax: 630 739-6464
Madhavan Anirudhan, *President*
Arun Aniruhan, *Vice Pres*
Augustine Jeremy, *Production*
Shirley Peterson, *Office Mgr*
John Brown, *Maintence Staff*
◆ EMP: 22
SQ FT: 38,000
SALES: 6.4MM **Privately Held**
WEB: www.essen-nutrition.com
SIC: 2099 2032 2035 2086 Desserts, ready-to-mix; soups & broths: canned, jarred, etc.; pickles, sauces & salad dressings; bottled & canned soft drinks; food additives & preservatives

**(G-18821)**
**EXCLUSIVELY EXPO (PA)**
1225 Naperville Dr (60446-1041)
PHONE..................................630 378-4600
Fax: 630 378-4617
James F Buehner, *President*
Gerald L Czaban,
Kim E Stevenson,
▲ EMP: 25
SQ FT: 34,900
SALES (est): 20.3MM **Privately Held**
WEB: www.bonesafety.com
SIC: 5046 3081 5131 Display equipment, except refrigerated; unsupported plastics film & sheet; drapery material, woven

**(G-18822)**
**EXCLUSIVELY EXPO**
Bone Safety Signs
1201 Naperville Dr (60446-1041)
PHONE..................................630 378-4600
Herman Brown, *Division Mgr*
EMP: 15

## GEOGRAPHIC SECTION
### Romeoville - Will County (G-18847)

SALES (corp-wide): 20.3MM **Privately Held**
WEB: www.bonesafety.com
SIC: 3993 Signs & advertising specialties
PA: Exclusively Expo
1225 Naperville Dr
Romeoville IL 60446
630 378-4600

**(G-18823)**
**EXEX HOLDING CORPORATION**
Also Called: Online Eei
1201 Naperville Dr (60446-1041)
PHONE.................................815 703-7295
James F Buehner, *President*
Kevin Kriebs, *CFO*
EMP: 2
SALES (est): 239.3K **Privately Held**
SIC: 3993 Signs & advertising specialties

**(G-18824)**
**FABRICATED METAL SYSTEMS INC**
646 Forestwood Dr Ste C (60446-1379)
PHONE.................................815 886-6200
Brian Filipiak, *President*
Kristin Frodin, *Office Mgr*
EMP: 6
SALES: 1MM **Privately Held**
SIC: 3441 Fabricated structural metal

**(G-18825)**
**FLOOR-CHEM INC**
1313 Enterprise Dr Ste D (60446-1183)
PHONE.................................630 789-2152
Ike Basir, *President*
EMP: 3
SQ FT: 3,000
SALES: 250K **Privately Held**
SIC: 3471 2841 2842 Cleaning, polishing & finishing; soap & other detergents; cleaning or polishing preparations

**(G-18826)**
**G K L CORPORATION**
Also Called: National Bathing Products
5 Greenwood Ave (60446-1340)
PHONE.................................815 886-5900
Kenneth J Salach, *President*
Diane Salach, *Treasurer*
Kitty Matusak, *Accounts Mgr*
EMP: 80
SQ FT: 30,000
SALES (est): 15.3MM **Privately Held**
WEB: www.nationalbath.com
SIC: 3088 Tubs (bath, shower & laundry), plastic; shower stalls, fiberglass & plastic

**(G-18827)**
**GARY GALASSI AND SONS INC**
Also Called: Gary Galassi Stone & Steel
44 Devonwood Ave (60446-1349)
PHONE.................................815 886-3906
Fax: 815 886-4461
Gary Galassi, *President*
Dave Downey, *Vice Pres*
Adam Pleszka, *Safety Mgr*
EMP: 32
SALES (est): 6.3MM **Privately Held**
WEB: www.ggsas.com
SIC: 1411 Dimension stone

**(G-18828)**
**GEA FARM TECHNOLOGIES INC**
Chemical Division
1354 Enterprise Dr (60446-1069)
PHONE.................................630 759-1063
Paul Becker, *Opers Mgr*
Carl Hoffman, *Opers-Prdtn-Mfg*
M Pawlak, *Marketing Staff*
EMP: 50
SALES (corp-wide): 4.7B **Privately Held**
WEB: www.westfaliasurge.com
SIC: 2841 2842 Soap & other detergents; specialty cleaning, polishes & sanitation goods
HQ: Gea Farm Technologies, Inc.
1880 Country Farm Dr
Naperville IL 60563
630 548-8200

**(G-18829)**
**GREEN PRODUCTS LLC**
221 Rocbaar Dr (60446-1163)
PHONE.................................815 407-0900
Jim Hoselton,
EMP: 15
SALES: 1,000K **Privately Held**
WEB: www.greenproducts.net
SIC: 2891 Adhesives & sealants

**(G-18830)**
**HARRIS BMO BANK NATIONAL ASSN**
630 N Independence Blvd (60446-1374)
PHONE.................................815 886-1900
Albert D Ottavio, *CEO*
David Glasscock, *Manager*
EMP: 50
SALES (corp-wide): 16.2B **Privately Held**
SIC: 6022 2782 State commercial banks; passbooks: bank, etc.
HQ: Harris Bmo Bank National Association
111 W Monroe St Ste 1200
Chicago IL 60603
312 461-2323

**(G-18831)**
**ISOVAC PRODUCTS LLC**
1306 Enterprise Dr Ste A (60446-4408)
PHONE.................................630 679-1740
Peter Jenkner, *General Mgr*
Joseph Petrovic, *COO*
James Gauger, *Vice Pres*
Pete Jenkner, *Mng Member*
Chris Schultz, *Info Tech Mgr*
EMP: 6
SALES: 10K **Privately Held**
WEB: www.isovacproducts.com
SIC: 3089 3085 8731 3845 Plastic containers, except foam; plastics bottles; biological research; electromedical apparatus

**(G-18832)**
**JIGSAW SOLUTIONS INC**
1296 Lakeview Dr (60446-3901)
PHONE.................................630 926-1948
▲ EMP: 7
SALES (est): 835.1K **Privately Held**
SIC: 3089 Bottle caps, molded plastic

**(G-18833)**
**JOHN HARLAND COMPANY**
1003 Birch Ln (60446-3949)
PHONE.................................815 293-4350
John Harland, *Principal*
EMP: 3
SALES (est): 233.3K **Privately Held**
SIC: 3577 Printers & plotters

**(G-18834)**
**KENEAL INDUSTRIES INC**
Also Called: Keneal Graphic Solutions
679 Parkwood Ave (60446-1348)
PHONE.................................815 886-1300
Fax: 815 886-1344
Wayne R Cassells, *President*
Kent Cassells, *Vice Pres*
Bernice Ambrose, *Office Mgr*
Neal Cassells, *Director*
Claudia Cassells, *Admin Sec*
EMP: 12
SQ FT: 15,000
SALES (est): 1.8MM **Privately Held**
WEB: www.keneal.com
SIC: 2759 2752 3953 2761 Letterpress printing; flexographic printing; lithographing on metal; marking devices; manifold business forms; coated & laminated paper; pleating & stitching

**(G-18835)**
**KIMBERLY-CLARK CORPORATION**
740 Pro Logis Pkwy (60446-4502)
PHONE.................................815 886-7872
EMP: 213
SALES (corp-wide): 18.2B **Publicly Held**
WEB: www.kimberly-clark.com
SIC: 2621 3841 3842 Paper mills; facial tissue stock; toilet tissue stock; sanitary tissue paper; surgical & medical instruments; surgical instruments & apparatus; surgical appliances & supplies
PA: Kimberly-Clark Corporation
351 Phelps Dr
Irving TX 75038
972 281-1200

**(G-18836)**
**LASER PRODUCTS INDUSTRIES INC**
1344 Enterprise Dr (60446-1016)
PHONE.................................877 679-1300
Fax: 630 679-1356
Daniel Louis, *President*
Jim Hoffman, *Regl Sales Mgr*
Jeff Larson, *Regl Sales Mgr*
Matt Thomson, *Regl Sales Mgr*
Joe Allen, *Manager*
EMP: 8
SQ FT: 3,000
SALES (est): 3MM **Privately Held**
WEB: www.lasersquare.com
SIC: 3826 Laser scientific & engineering instruments

**(G-18837)**
**LASERSKETCH LTD**
1319 Enterprise Dr (60446-1050)
PHONE.................................630 243-6360
Judy Mc Creary, *Owner*
◆ EMP: 16
SALES (est): 2.3MM **Privately Held**
WEB: www.lasersketch.com
SIC: 2759 5999 Embossing on paper; miscellaneous retail stores

**(G-18838)**
**LEGACY VULCAN LLC**
Midwest Division
1361 Joliet Rd (60446-4053)
PHONE.................................630 739-0182
Fax: 630 739-0470
Mark Tomkins, *Vice Pres*
Corey Fries, *Director*
EMP: 17
SALES (corp-wide): 3.5B **Publicly Held**
WEB: www.vulcanmaterials.com
SIC: 1442 Construction sand & gravel
HQ: Legacy Vulcan, Llc
1200 Urban Center Dr
Vestavia AL 35242
205 298-3000

**(G-18839)**
**LENNOX INDUSTRIES INC**
860 W Crossroads Pkwy (60446-4332)
PHONE.................................630 378-7054
Nate Slynn, *Branch Mgr*
EMP: 68
SALES (corp-wide): 3.6B **Publicly Held**
SIC: 5075 3585 Warm air heating & air conditioning; air conditioning units, complete: domestic or industrial; furnaces, warm air: electric
HQ: Lennox Industries Inc.
2100 Lake Park Blvd
Richardson TX 75080
972 497-5000

**(G-18840)**
**LI GEAR INC**
1292 Lakeview Dr (60446-3901)
PHONE.................................630 226-1688
Yumin Li, *President*
▲ EMP: 2
SALES (est): 328K **Privately Held**
SIC: 3566 Gears, power transmission, except automotive

**(G-18841)**
**MAGID GLOVE SAFETY MFG CO LLC (PA)**
1300 Naperville Dr (60446-1043)
PHONE.................................773 384-2070
Lisa Boeding, *President*
Marc Grubert, *President*
Susan Salcines, *President*
Carol Anthony, *District Mgr*
Lark Billick, *District Mgr*
▲ EMP: 377 EST: 1946
SQ FT: 500,000
SALES (est): 105.3MM **Privately Held**
WEB: www.magidglove.com
SIC: 3151 2381 5699 3842 Gloves, leather: work; gloves, work: woven or knit, made from purchased materials; work clothing; surgical appliances & supplies; men's & boys' work clothing

**(G-18842)**
**MATERIAL SERVICE CORPORATION**
Also Called: Hanson Material Service
681 S Material Rd (60446-2203)
PHONE.................................815 838-2400
Jim Vallera, *Principal*
EMP: 20
SALES (corp-wide): 16B **Privately Held**
WEB: www.materialservice.com
SIC: 3272 3273 5032 1442 Concrete products; ready-mixed concrete; concrete mixtures; concrete building products; sand, construction; gravel; construction sand & gravel
HQ: Material Service Corporation
2235 Entp Dr Ste 3504
Westchester IL 60154
708 731-2600

**(G-18843)**
**MATERIAL SERVICE CORPORATION**
125 N Independence Blvd (60446-1834)
PHONE.................................815 942-1830
Fax: 815 942-1714
John C Halloran, *Superintendent*
Elaine Rohde, *Admin Sec*
EMP: 20
SALES (corp-wide): 16B **Privately Held**
WEB: www.materialservice.com
SIC: 1442 Common sand mining; gravel mining
HQ: Material Service Corporation
2235 Entp Dr Ste 3504
Westchester IL 60154
708 731-2600

**(G-18844)**
**MATERIAL SERVICE CORPORATION**
Also Called: Material Svc Yard 67
125 N Independence Blvd (60446-1834)
PHONE.................................815 838-3420
Fax: 815 838-8166
Ed Senn, *Manager*
EMP: 50
SALES (corp-wide): 16B **Privately Held**
WEB: www.materialservice.com
SIC: 1442 Construction sand & gravel
HQ: Material Service Corporation
2235 Entp Dr Ste 3504
Westchester IL 60154
708 731-2600

**(G-18845)**
**METROPOLITAN INDUSTRIES INC**
Also Called: Metropolitan Pump Company
37 Forestwood Dr (60446-1343)
PHONE.................................815 886-9200
Fax: 815 886-4573
John R Kochan Jr, *President*
Carole S Kochan, *Admin Sec*
▲ EMP: 130
SQ FT: 100,000
SALES (est): 66.7MM **Privately Held**
WEB: www.metropolitanind.com
SIC: 3561 5064 7699 Pump jacks & other pumping equipment; water heaters, electric; pumps & pumping equipment repair

**(G-18846)**
**MICROPRINT INC**
1294 Lakeview Dr (60446-3901)
PHONE.................................630 969-1710
Arvin Bhargava, *President*
Neelam Bhargava, *Director*
EMP: 4
SQ FT: 5,000
SALES (est): 625.1K **Privately Held**
WEB: www.microprint.com
SIC: 2752 Commercial printing, offset

**(G-18847)**
**MID-WEST SPRING & STAMPING INC (HQ)**
1404 Joliet Rd Ste C (60446-4407)
PHONE.................................630 739-3800
Fax: 630 353-7388
Jeffrey Ellison, *President*
Tom Vanmunster, *Engineer*
Michael Curran, *CFO*
Linda Vandenberg, *Human Res Mgr*
EMP: 5 EST: 1928

# Romeoville - Will County (G-18848)

SQ FT: 3,000
SALES (est): 11MM
SALES (corp-wide): 17.6MM Privately Held
WEB: www.mwspring.com
SIC: 3495 3493 3469 Wire springs; torsion bar springs; metal stampings
PA: Spring Mid-West Manufacturing Company
1404 Joliet Rd Ste C
Romeoville IL 60446
630 739-3800

### (G-18848)
### MID-WEST SPRING & STAMPING INC
Also Called: Mid-West Spring Mfg Co
1404 Joliet Rd Ste C (60446-4407)
PHONE.................................630 739-3800
John Tennessen, Office Mgr
Henry Orlawski, Branch Mgr
EMP: 8
SALES (corp-wide): 17.6MM Privately Held
WEB: www.mwspring.com
SIC: 3493 3495 5085 Steel springs, except wire; wire springs; springs
HQ: Spring Mid-West And Stamping Inc
1404 Joliet Rd Ste C
Romeoville IL 60446
630 739-3800

### (G-18849)
### MID-WEST SPRING MFG CO (PA)
Also Called: Mid-West Spring and Stamping
1404 Joliet Rd Ste C (60446-4407)
PHONE.................................630 739-3800
Fax: 630 739-3890
Jeffery Ellison, President
CJ Overmyer, VP Mfg
Nancy Carder, QC Mgr
Michael Curran, CFO
EMP: 4
SQ FT: 2,000
SALES: 17.6MM Privately Held
SIC: 3493 3495 Torsion bar springs; automobile coiled flat springs; wire springs

### (G-18850)
### MONDI ROMEOVILLE INC
1140 Arbor Dr (60446-1188)
PHONE.................................630 378-9886
Rick Jones, Opers Mgr
David Gonzalez, Controller
Steve Sutton, Finance Mgr
Peter Windeit, Director
◆ EMP: 67 EST: 2003
SQ FT: 125,000
SALES (est): 35.2MM Privately Held
SIC: 2674 Bags: uncoated paper & multi-wall
PA: Mondi Plc
Building 1 1st Floor Aviator Park
Addlestone KT15

### (G-18851)
### NAFISCO INC
Also Called: Flexible Safety Zoning Co
808 Forestwood Dr (60446-1165)
PHONE.................................815 372-3300
Fax: 708 544-0660
John G Knox Sr, President
EMP: 10
SQ FT: 2,400
SALES: 1.4MM Privately Held
WEB: www.nafisco.com
SIC: 5063 3669 3499 3993 Signaling equipment, electrical; signaling apparatus, electric; barricades, metal; signs & advertising specialties

### (G-18852)
### NANOPHASE TECHNOLOGIES CORP (PA)
1319 Marquette Dr (60446-4011)
PHONE.................................630 771-6708
Fax: 630 771-0825
James A Henderson, Ch of Bd
Jess Jankowski, President
Glenn Judd, Vice Pres
Frank Cesario, CFO
Nancy Baldwin, VP Human Res
EMP: 40
SQ FT: 36,000
SALES: 10.7MM Publicly Held
WEB: www.nanophase.com
SIC: 3399 3299 Powder, metal; ceramic fiber

### (G-18853)
### NEW AGE SURFACES LLC
1237 Naperville Dr (60446-1041)
PHONE.................................630 226-0011
Fax: 630 226-0077
Matt Domanico, Mng Member
Joanne Domanico,
▲ EMP: 5
SALES: 700K Privately Held
SIC: 2541 Counter & sink tops

### (G-18854)
### NEW TECH MARKETING INC
1312 Marquette Dr Ste H (60446-1180)
PHONE.................................630 378-4300
Fax: 630 378-0343
Jaff Butt, President
Steve Sperry, Vice Pres
EMP: 10
SALES (est): 1.4MM Privately Held
SIC: 3491 Industrial valves

### (G-18855)
### NORTHSTAR TRADING LLC
1411 Enterprise Dr (60446-1092)
PHONE.................................224 422-6050
Sunjay M Kantharia, Mng Member
EMP: 13
SQ FT: 14,000
SALES: 1MM Privately Held
SIC: 3089 Plastic processing

### (G-18856)
### ORANGE CRUSH LLC
1001 N Independence Blvd (60446-4054)
PHONE.................................630 739-5560
Ed Lebau, Branch Mgr
EMP: 4
SALES (corp-wide): 47.3MM Privately Held
SIC: 2951 1795 Asphalt paving mixtures & blocks; concrete breaking for streets & highways
PA: Orange Crush, L.L.C.
321 Center St
Hillside IL 60162
708 544-9440

### (G-18857)
### PLASTIC FILM CORP AMERICA INC (PA)
Also Called: PFC
1287 Naperville Dr Ste A (60446-1187)
PHONE.................................630 887-0800
Joel M Bittner, President
Chris Justice, Warehouse Mgr
Felix Lanier, Purchasing
Joel Bittner, Controller
Jim Drake, Manager
▲ EMP: 15 EST: 1982
SQ FT: 110,000
SALES (est): 6MM Privately Held
WEB: www.plasticfilmcorporation.com
SIC: 3089 5162 Plastic processing; plastics sheets & rods

### (G-18858)
### POLLMANN NORTH AMERICA INC
950 Chicago Tube Dr (60446-2202)
PHONE.................................815 834-1122
Fax: 815 293-3265
Marcos Cielak, CEO
Peter Eleuteri, Engineer
Andreas Miloczki, Human Res Mgr
Melodie Luk, Sales Associate
Michaela Kellner, CTO
▲ EMP: 41
SQ FT: 34,000
SALES (est): 13.9MM
SALES (corp-wide): 145MM Privately Held
WEB: www.pollmann-na.com
SIC: 3559 Automotive related machinery
PA: Pollmann International Gmbh
Raabser StraBe 1
Karlstein An Der Thaya 3822
284 422-30

### (G-18859)
### POLYONE CORPORATION
Polyone Distribution
1275 Windham Pkwy (60446-1763)
PHONE.................................630 972-0505
Melissa Marin, Human Res Mgr
George Ramming, Marketing Staff
John Rubinic, Branch Mgr
Jennifer Scott, Manager
EMP: 75 Publicly Held
WEB: www.polyone.com
SIC: 3087 5162 2865 2851 Custom compound purchased resins; plastics resins; cyclic crudes & intermediates; paints & allied products; plastics materials & resins
PA: Polyone Corporation
33587 Walker Rd
Avon Lake OH 44012

### (G-18860)
### PRECISION MCHNED CMPONENTS INC
Also Called: P M C
1348 Enterprise Dr (60446-1016)
PHONE.................................630 759-5555
Fax: 847 808-8180
Steven Wunar, President
Robert Wunar, President
▲ EMP: 25 EST: 1945
SQ FT: 15,500
SALES (est): 4.9MM Privately Held
WEB: www.precisionmachinedcomponents.com
SIC: 3451 3541 Screw machine products; machine tools, metal cutting type

### (G-18861)
### PRINT & MAILING SOLUTIONS LLC (PA)
1053 N Schmidt Rd (60446-1181)
PHONE.................................708 544-9400
James Hezinger,
Patrick Delmonico III,
EMP: 4 EST: 2006
SALES (est): 518.4K Privately Held
SIC: 2752 Commercial printing, lithographic

### (G-18862)
### RAPAK LLC (HQ)
Also Called: Packaging Systems
1201 Windham Pkwy Ste D (60446-1699)
PHONE.................................630 296-2000
Fax: 630 296-2195
Karen Deleon, Controller
Kevin Grogan, Mng Member
Richard Garrett, Manager
Noe Liera, Manager
◆ EMP: 140
SQ FT: 121,000
SALES (est): 66.4MM
SALES (corp-wide): 5.7B Privately Held
WEB: www.rapak.com
SIC: 2671 Plastic film, coated or laminated for packaging
PA: Ds Smith Plc
7th Floor 350 Euston Road
London NW1 3
207 756-1800

### (G-18863)
### REYNOLDS HOLDINGS INC
Also Called: Signarama Bolingbrook
684 S Phillips Unit 2 (60446)
PHONE.................................630 739-0110
John Reynolds, CEO
EMP: 2
SALES: 300K Privately Held
SIC: 2499 Signboards, wood

### (G-18864)
### ROLL MCHNING TECH SLUTIONS INC
Also Called: Rmts
641 Forestwood Dr (60446-1392)
PHONE.................................815 372-9100
Joseph Olson, CEO
Rick Olson, President
▲ EMP: 30
SQ FT: 20,000
SALES (est): 7.5MM Privately Held
SIC: 3317 3545 Steel pipe & tubes; machine tool accessories

### (G-18865)
### ROTATION DYNAMICS CORPORATION
Also Called: Rotadyne-Roll Group
1101 Windham Pkwy (60446-1790)
PHONE.................................630 679-7053
John Fredrick, Marketing Staff
Kirby Savage, Branch Mgr
EMP: 36
SALES (corp-wide): 128.8MM Privately Held
SIC: 3069 Printers' rolls & blankets: rubber or rubberized fabric
PA: Rotation Dynamics Corporation
8140 Cass Ave
Darien IL 60561
630 769-9255

### (G-18866)
### SATO LBLING SOLUTIONS AMER INC (PA)
1140 Windham Pkwy (60446-1692)
PHONE.................................630 771-4200
Fax: 630 771-4300
Joseph Podsedly, President
Jean Ampen, General Mgr
James Gibson, Vice Pres
Duane Hunt, Mfg Dir
Chris Brooks, Prdtn Mgr
▲ EMP: 76
SQ FT: 200,000
SALES (est): 20.3MM Privately Held
WEB: www.satolabeling.com
SIC: 2759 2269 Labels & seals: printing; labels, cotton: printed

### (G-18867)
### SCHWAB PAPER PRODUCTS COMPANY
636 Schwab Cir (60446-1144)
PHONE.................................815 372-2233
Fax: 815 372-1701
Katherine S Obrien, President
Michael Schwab, Owner
Mary Rebellato, Corp Secy
Tom Schwab, CFO
Kathy Obrien, Manager
EMP: 32
SQ FT: 55,000
SALES (est): 9.3MM Privately Held
WEB: www.schwabpaper.com
SIC: 2679 Paperboard products, converted

### (G-18868)
### SHERWIN-WILLIAMS COMPANY
664 S Weber Rd (60446-4999)
PHONE.................................815 254-3559
EMP: 3
SALES (corp-wide): 11.8B Publicly Held
SIC: 5231 5198 2851 Paint & painting supplies; paints, varnishes & supplies; wood fillers or sealers
PA: The Sherwin-Williams Company
101 W Prospect Ave # 1020
Cleveland OH 44115
216 566-2000

### (G-18869)
### SPX CORPORATION
1385 N Weber Rd (60446-4307)
PHONE.................................815 407-3915
Jackie McRaw, Branch Mgr
EMP: 16
SALES (corp-wide): 1.4B Publicly Held
SIC: 3465 Body parts, automobile: stamped metal
PA: Spx Corporation
13320a Balntyn Corp Pl
Charlotte NC 28277
980 474-3700

### (G-18870)
### STEPAC USA CORPORATION (HQ)
1201 Windham Pkwy (60446-1698)
PHONE.................................630 296-2000
Don Stidham, President
Karen De Leon, Controller
◆ EMP: 4
SQ FT: 121,000

# GEOGRAPHIC SECTION

Roscoe - Winnebago County (G-18897)

SALES (est): 678.9K
SALES (corp-wide): 5.7B **Privately Held**
SIC: 0723 2671 Fruit (fresh) packing services; vegetable packing services; packaging paper & plastics film, coated & laminated
PA: Ds Smith Plc
7th Floor 350 Euston Road
London NW1 3
207 756-1800

**(G-18871)**
**STUCCHI USA INC**
1105 Windham Pkwy (60446-1790)
PHONE...................847 956-9720
Fax: 847 956-9723
Scott Rolston, *President*
Lucas Stucchi, *Vice Pres*
Denzil Dsouza, *CFO*
Lorenzo Zaffaroni, *Admin Sec*
▲ EMP: 19
SQ FT: 15,000
SALES (est): 4.4MM **Privately Held**
WEB: www.stucchiusa.com
SIC: 3429 Clamps, couplings, nozzles & other metal hose fittings

**(G-18872)**
**SUPREME SCREW INC**
Also Called: S S I
1224 N Independence Blvd (60446-1057)
PHONE...................630 226-9000
Debbie Wood, *President*
Tommy Wood, *Sales Mgr*
▲ EMP: 8
SALES (est): 1.3MM **Privately Held**
SIC: 5943 3965 5072 Office forms & supplies; fasteners; bolts, nuts & screws; washers (hardware)

**(G-18873)**
**TDW SERVICES INC**
Also Called: Great Lakes Service Center
565 Anderson Dr Ste A (60446-1762)
PHONE...................815 407-0675
Gary Buckles, *Branch Mgr*
EMP: 12
SALES (corp-wide): 539.5MM **Privately Held**
WEB: www.tdwilliamson.com
SIC: 1389 Oil field services
HQ: Tdw Services, Inc.
6801 S 65th West Ave
Tulsa OK 74131
918 447-5000

**(G-18874)**
**US HOSE CORP (PA)**
815 Forestwood Dr (60446-1167)
PHONE...................815 886-1140
John Devine, *President*
Carol Wissmiller, *President*
Ken Hovorka, *Purch Mgr*
◆ EMP: 79
SQ FT: 75,000
SALES (est): 26.1MM **Privately Held**
WEB: www.flexonics.com
SIC: 3599 Flexible metal hose, tubing & bellows; hose, flexible metallic

**(G-18875)**
**V & N CONCRETE PRODUCTS INC**
35 Forestwood Dr (60446-1343)
PHONE...................815 293-0315
Fax: 815 293-0317
Charles Voss, *President*
Don Sykora, *Manager*
EMP: 12
SQ FT: 38,000
SALES (est): 1.8MM **Privately Held**
SIC: 3272 Concrete products; covers, catch basin: concrete; chimney caps, concrete

**(G-18876)**
**VLASICI HARDWOOD FLOORS CO**
1959 Somerset Dr (60446-3987)
PHONE...................815 505-4308
Svetlana Vlasici, *Owner*
EMP: 5
SALES (est): 347.3K **Privately Held**
SIC: 2426 Flooring, hardwood

**(G-18877)**
**WALCO TOOL & ENGINEERING CORP**
18954 Airport Rd (60446-3531)
PHONE...................815 834-0225
Fax: 815 838-6046
Dave Walsh, *CEO*
Bill Bucciarelli, *President*
Mike Abbott, *Project Engr*
Dawn Washburn, *CFO*
Dennis Rothermel, *Controller*
▲ EMP: 100
SQ FT: 65,000
SALES (est): 24.5MM **Privately Held**
WEB: www.walcotool.com
SIC: 3599 7692 Machine & other job shop work; welding repair

**(G-18878)**
**WESTFALIA-SURGE INC**
1354 Enterprise Dr (60446-1069)
PHONE...................630 759-7346
Bob Lewis, *President*
EMP: 2
SALES (est): 218.8K **Privately Held**
SIC: 2841 Soap & other detergents

**(G-18879)**
**WILTON INDUSTRIES INC**
1125 Taylor Rd (60446-4215)
PHONE...................815 834-9390
Fax: 815 834-9399
Seteria Bain, *Manager*
Stephanie Goode, *Manager*
EMP: 10 **Privately Held**
SIC: 5023 2731 2721 7812 Kitchenware; kitchen tools & utensils; frames & framing, picture & mirror; books: publishing only; periodicals: publishing only; video tape production; water purification equipment; candy making goods & supplies
HQ: Wilton Industries, Inc.
2240 75th St
Woodridge IL 60517
630 963-7100

**(G-18880)**
**WM WRIGLEY JR COMPANY**
Also Called: Wrigley Midwest
825 Bluff Rd (60446-4007)
PHONE...................312 644-2121
EMP: 214
SALES (corp-wide): 35B **Privately Held**
SIC: 2067 Chewing gum base
HQ: Wm. Wrigley Jr. Company
930 W Evergreen Ave
Chicago IL 60642
312 280-4710

**(G-18881)**
**ZAINAB ENTERPRISES INC**
Also Called: Sign-A-Rama
684 Phelps Ave (60446-1533)
PHONE...................630 739-0110
Fax: 630 739-0120
Qusai Tyebjee, *President*
EMP: 3
SALES: 300K **Privately Held**
SIC: 3993 Signs & advertising specialties

## Roodhouse
*Greene County*

**(G-18882)**
**CLOVERLEAF FEED CO INC**
Rr 267 Box S (62082)
Rural Route 3 Box 27 (62082-9538)
PHONE...................217 589-5010
Fax: 217 589-5010
Martin Rhodes, *Partner*
Nancy Rhodes, *Partner*
Tony Rhodes, *Partner*
EMP: 4 EST: 1948
SALES (est): 480K **Privately Held**
SIC: 2048 5191 Prepared feeds; farm supplies

**(G-18883)**
**MILLER PALLET**
Rr 1 Box 34a (62082-9506)
PHONE...................217 589-4411
Norman Miller, *Owner*
EMP: 10

SALES (est): 724.8K **Privately Held**
SIC: 3952 Palettes, artists'

**(G-18884)**
**ROODHOUSE ENVELOPE CO**
Also Called: Reco
414 S State St (62082-1544)
PHONE...................217 589-4321
Fax: 217 589-4425
Gary Randall, *President*
Charles Strain, *Vice Pres*
John Strain, *Vice Pres*
Thomas A Martin, *Treasurer*
EMP: 70 EST: 1911
SQ FT: 26,200
SALES (est): 9.7MM **Privately Held**
SIC: 2677 Envelopes

**(G-18885)**
**ROODHOUSE FIRE PROTECTION DST**
1140 S State St (62082-1669)
P.O. Box 112 (62082-0112)
PHONE...................217 589-5134
Bob Hart, *Principal*
Terry Hawkins, *Chief*
Thomas Meehan, *Corp Secy*
EMP: 25
SQ FT: 2,000
SALES (est): 2.7MM **Privately Held**
SIC: 3569 Firefighting apparatus & related equipment

**(G-18886)**
**STIX ENVELOPE & MFG CO**
1086 S Morse St (62082-1670)
PHONE...................217 589-5122
Fax: 217 589-5228
James Stickelmaier, *Owner*
EMP: 9
SALES (est): 440K **Privately Held**
SIC: 2752 Commercial printing, offset

## Roscoe
*Winnebago County*

**(G-18887)**
**3DP UNLIMITED**
6402 E Rockton Rd (61073-8812)
PHONE...................815 389-5667
Kecheng Lu, *Principal*
EMP: 2
SALES (est): 215.7K **Privately Held**
SIC: 5045 7389 3999 Printers, computer; printers' services: folding, collating; atomizers, toiletry

**(G-18888)**
**ACCURATE CNC MACHINING INC**
Also Called: Accurate Cnc Machine
5365 Edith Ln (61073-9573)
PHONE...................815 623-6516
Fax: 815 637-2051
Richard Fluegel, *President*
Amanda Fluegel, *Sales Staff*
Daniel Fluegel, *Shareholder*
Phillip Fluegel, *Shareholder*
EMP: 9
SQ FT: 12,000
SALES (est): 1MM **Privately Held**
WEB: www.accuratecnc.net
SIC: 3469 Machine parts, stamped or pressed metal

**(G-18889)**
**AMERICAN ALUM EXTRUSION CO LLC**
Also Called: Aaec
5253 Mccurry Rd (61073-9552)
PHONE...................877 896-2236
Mark Johnson, *Opers Mgr*
Lou Leggero, *CFO*
Mike Zintak, *Sales Mgr*
Rich Grenfell, *Accounts Mgr*
Sam Popa, *Mng Member*
EMP: 6
SALES (est): 408K **Privately Held**
SIC: 3354 3355 3999 Aluminum extruded products; aluminum rolling & drawing; atomizers, toiletry

**(G-18890)**
**AMERICAN BELL SCREEN PRTG CO**
11447 2nd St Ste 1 (61073-9522)
PHONE...................815 623-5522
Fax: 815 633-1521
Vanessa Knipp, *President*
Tamara Shoevlin, *Corp Secy*
EMP: 4
SQ FT: 4,000
SALES (est): 479.2K **Privately Held**
SIC: 2759 Screen printing

**(G-18891)**
**CABINETS BY CUSTOM CRAFT INC**
5261 Swanson Rd (61073-9457)
PHONE...................815 637-4001
Fax: 815 637-1519
Steve Levins, *President*
Glenn Hammock, *Vice Pres*
Merle Hammock, *Admin Sec*
EMP: 4
SQ FT: 3,600
SALES (est): 445.7K **Privately Held**
SIC: 2541 2517 2434 Cabinets, lockers & shelving; wood television & radio cabinets; wood kitchen cabinets

**(G-18892)**
**DECISION SYSTEMS COMPANY**
8937 Sheringham Dr (61073-8040)
PHONE...................815 885-3000
Laverne Ohlwine, *Owner*
EMP: 3
SALES (est): 197.5K **Privately Held**
SIC: 7372 5045 Operating systems computer software; computers

**(G-18893)**
**DELLS RACEWAY PARK INC**
13750 Metric Rd (61073-7638)
PHONE...................815 494-0074
Matt Panure, *Principal*
EMP: 4 EST: 2012
SALES (est): 321.3K **Privately Held**
SIC: 3644 Raceways

**(G-18894)**
**DGM ELECTRONICS INC**
13654 Metric Rd (61073-7636)
PHONE...................815 389-2040
Dennis Makovec, *President*
Connie Makovec, *Corp Secy*
EMP: 6
SQ FT: 3,000
SALES (est): 850.1K **Privately Held**
WEB: www.dgmelectronics.com
SIC: 3825 3625 Time code generators; relays & industrial controls

**(G-18895)**
**ECOLAB INC**
5151 E Rockton Rd (61073-7649)
PHONE...................815 389-8132
Robert Roth, *Vice Pres*
Dan Modica, *Warehouse Mgr*
Joseph D Radlinger, *Controller*
Robert Zoeller, *Branch Mgr*
EMP: 38
SALES (corp-wide): 13.1B **Publicly Held**
WEB: www.ecolab.com
SIC: 2842 Sanitation preparations, disinfectants & deodorants
PA: Ecolab Inc.
1 Ecolab Pl
Saint Paul MN 55102
800 232-6522

**(G-18896)**
**ESSENTIAL ELMNTS THERAPEUTIC M**
5516 Clayton Cir (61073-9533)
PHONE...................815 623-6810
EMP: 3
SALES (est): 206.6K **Privately Held**
SIC: 2819 Mfg Industrial Inorganic Chemicals

**(G-18897)**
**EXCEL GEAR INC**
11865 Main St (61073-8276)
PHONE...................815 623-3414
Fax: 815 623-3414
N K Chinnusamy, *President*

# Roscoe - Winnebago County (G-18898)

William Bill, *Marketing Mgr*
Willy Goellner, *Admin Sec*
▲ **EMP:** 25
**SQ FT:** 35,000
**SALES (est):** 5.1MM **Privately Held**
**WEB:** www.excelgear.com
**SIC:** 3462 Gears, forged steel

### (G-18898)
### G & M FABRICATING INC
9014 Swanson Dr (61073-9415)
P.O. Box 399 (61073-0399)
**PHONE** ................................ 815 282-1744
**Fax:** 815 282-9659
George Owen, *President*
**EMP:** 5
**SQ FT:** 13,000
**SALES:** 800K **Privately Held**
**SIC:** 3499 3567 3446 3444 Machine bases, metal; industrial furnaces & ovens; architectural metalwork; sheet metalwork; fabricated plate work (boiler shop); fabricated structural metal

### (G-18899)
### GT FLOW TECHNOLOGY INC
5364 Mainsail Dr (61073-7212)
**PHONE** ................................ 815 636-9982
**Fax:** 815 636-9983
Thomas Rogers, *President*
**EMP:** 4
**SQ FT:** 4,000
**SALES:** 1.4MM **Privately Held**
**WEB:** www.gtflowtech.com
**SIC:** 3554 Pulp mill machinery

### (G-18900)
### ILLINOIS PNEUMATIC INC
9325 Starboard Dr Ste B (61073-6908)
**PHONE** ................................ 815 654-9301
**Fax:** 815 654-9426
Kurt Eversole, *President*
Sheila Eversole, *Corp Secy*
Steve Ow, *Manager*
Steve Pissow, *Manager*
**EMP:** 6
**SQ FT:** 5,400
**SALES (est):** 630K **Privately Held**
**WEB:** www.illpneumatics.com
**SIC:** 3593 Fluid power cylinders, hydraulic or pneumatic

### (G-18901)
### ILLINOIS WATER TECH INC
5443 Swanson Ct (61073-7174)
P.O. Box 19 (61073-0019)
**PHONE** ................................ 815 636-8884
Scott Lipke, *Principal*
Bill Helman, *Principal*
Scott J Lipke, *CFO*
Paul Byrd, *Human Res Mgr*
Pete Hosa, *Cust Mgr*
▲ **EMP:** 31
**SQ FT:** 21,000
**SALES:** 7.1MM **Privately Held**
**WEB:** www.illinoiswatertech.com
**SIC:** 3589 Water treatment equipment, industrial

### (G-18902)
### LIBCO INDUSTRIES INC
Also Called: Liberty Engineering Company
10567 Main St (61073-8830)
P.O. Box 470 (61073-0470)
**PHONE** ................................ 815 623-7677
Brian Belardi, *President*
Rob Klein, *General Mgr*
David Belardi, *Vice Pres*
John Akelaitis, *Plant Mgr*
Lori Wincapaw, *Manager*
**EMP:** 12 **EST:** 1942
**SQ FT:** 23,000
**SALES (est):** 2.9MM **Privately Held**
**WEB:** www.libertyengineering.com
**SIC:** 3829 3544 3565 3369 Testing equipment: abrasion, shearing strength, etc.; industrial molds; packaging machinery; nonferrous foundries

### (G-18903)
### LIGHTNING GRAPHIC
10444 Rock Ln (61073-9422)
**PHONE** ................................ 815 623-1937
Jeff Boelkes, *Owner*
**EMP:** 2
**SALES (est):** 210K **Privately Held**
**SIC:** 3993 Signs & advertising specialties

### (G-18904)
### MAGNA-FLUX INTERNATIONAL
11898 Burnside Ln (61073-8632)
**PHONE** ................................ 815 623-7634
Bruce Handy, *Owner*
**EMP:** 2
**SALES:** 200K **Privately Held**
**SIC:** 3695 Magnetic & optical recording media; magnetic disks & drums

### (G-18905)
### MAIN STREET MARKET ROSCOE INC
Also Called: Main Street Meat Co
9515 N 2nd St (61073-7205)
**PHONE** ................................ 815 623-6328
James A King, *President*
Amy J King, *Admin Sec*
**EMP:** 2
**SALES (est):** 246.6K **Privately Held**
**SIC:** 2011 2084 Beef products from beef slaughtered on site; bacon, slab & sliced from meat slaughtered on site; wines

### (G-18906)
### MAKERITE MFG CO INC
13571 Metric Rd (61073-9712)
P.O. Box 700 (61073-0700)
**PHONE** ................................ 815 389-3902
**Fax:** 815 389-1648
Paul Burke Sr, *President*
Paul Burke Jr, *Vice Pres*
Beverly Burke, *Treasurer*
Paul Burkes, *Human Res Dir*
Roger Smith, *Sales Executive*
**EMP:** 31
**SQ FT:** 14,000
**SALES:** 6.5MM **Privately Held**
**WEB:** www.makerite.com
**SIC:** 3451 3714 3728 Screw machine products; motor vehicle parts & accessories; aircraft parts & equipment

### (G-18907)
### MEISTER INDUSTRIES INC
6608 Saladino Dr (61073-9258)
P.O. Box 535 (61073-0535)
**PHONE** ................................ 815 623-8919
William Dickson, *President*
**EMP:** 3
**SALES (est):** 267K **Privately Held**
**SIC:** 3625 Electric controls & control accessories, industrial

### (G-18908)
### MOLDWORKS INC
11052 Jasmine Dr (61073-9414)
P.O. Box 802 (61073-0802)
**PHONE** ................................ 815 520-8819
**EMP:** 3
**SALES (est):** 202.1K **Privately Held**
**SIC:** 3952 Lead pencils & art goods

### (G-18909)
### MZM MANUFACTURING INC
5409 Swanson Ct (61073-7174)
**PHONE** ................................ 815 624-8666
**Fax:** 815 639-0618
Jeffrey Marotta, *President*
**EMP:** 7 **EST:** 1997
**SQ FT:** 6,500
**SALES:** 1.5MM **Privately Held**
**SIC:** 3542 Machine tools, metal forming type

### (G-18910)
### NELSON ENTERPRISES INC
5447 Mainsail Dr (61073-9460)
**PHONE** ................................ 815 633-1100
**Fax:** 815 633-2163
Allen Nelson, *President*
**EMP:** 5
**SALES (est):** 488.1K **Privately Held**
**SIC:** 5531 3519 2395 Speed shops, including race car supplies; parts & accessories, internal combustion engines; embroidery & art needlework

### (G-18911)
### PACIFIC BEARING CORP (PA)
Also Called: Pbc Linear
6402 E Rockton Rd (61073-8812)
P.O. Box 6980, Rockford (61125-1980)
**PHONE** ................................ 815 389-5600
**Fax:** 815 389-5790
Robert Schroeder, *President*
Bob Schmidt, *Controller*
Ron Wonzer, *Manager*
▲ **EMP:** 130
**SQ FT:** 100,000
**SALES:** 23MM **Privately Held**
**WEB:** www.pacific-bearing.com
**SIC:** 3562 3599 Ball bearings & parts; custom machinery

### (G-18912)
### REGAL CUTTING TOOLS INC
5330 E Rockton Rd (61073-7652)
**PHONE** ................................ 815 389-3461
Ho K Song, *President*
Richard Hartnett, *General Mgr*
Jim Dhom, *Vice Pres*
Dennis Weiland, *Plant Mgr*
Randy Algrim, *Purchasing*
▲ **EMP:** 200
**SALES (est):** 32.8MM
**SALES (corp-wide):** 254.1MM **Privately Held**
**WEB:** www.regalcuttingtools.com
**SIC:** 3545 Cutting tools for machine tools
**PA:** Yg-1 Co., Ltd.
  Chungchun-Dong
  Incheon 21300
  325 260-909

### (G-18913)
### REVIEW GRAPHICS INC
10760 Main St (61073-8337)
P.O. Box 116 (61073-0116)
**PHONE** ................................ 815 623-2570
**Fax:** 815 623-2570
Bill Johnson, *CEO*
**EMP:** 3
**SQ FT:** 2,400
**SALES (est):** 438.4K **Privately Held**
**SIC:** 2752 2791 Commercial printing, offset; typesetting

### (G-18914)
### ROCKFORD RIGGING INC (PA)
5401 Mainsail Dr (61073-8669)
**PHONE** ................................ 309 263-0566
**Fax:** 815 877-0064
John Malcotte, *President*
Phil Herra, *Vice Pres*
Sherry Blakeflee, *Controller*
James Alexander, *Admin Sec*
▲ **EMP:** 15
**SQ FT:** 35,000
**SALES (est):** 9.4MM **Privately Held**
**SIC:** 3643 3496 3339 3315 Current-carrying wiring devices; miscellaneous fabricated wire products; primary nonferrous metals; steel wire & related products

### (G-18915)
### ROGERS READY MIX & MTLS INC
14615 N 2nd St (61073)
P.O. Box 703 (61073-0703)
**PHONE** ................................ 815 389-2223
Gary Bronkema, *Manager*
**EMP:** 16
**SALES (corp-wide):** 14.3MM **Privately Held**
**SIC:** 3273 1442 5032 Ready-mixed concrete; construction sand & gravel; stone, crushed or broken
**PA:** Rogers Ready Mix & Materials, Inc.
  8128 N Walnut St
  Byron IL 61010
  815 234-8212

### (G-18916)
### ROSCOE GLASS CO
11212 Main St (61073-8854)
**PHONE** ................................ 815 623-6268
Michael Flowers, *President*
Duane Flowers, *Vice Pres*
**EMP:** 3
**SQ FT:** 3,600
**SALES:** 100K **Privately Held**
**WEB:** www.roscoeglass.com/index.html
**SIC:** 3231 7536 Products of purchased glass; automotive glass replacement shops

### (G-18917)
### ROSCOE READY-MIX INC
4896 Mccurry Rd (61073-8636)
P.O. Box 425 (61073-0425)
**PHONE** ................................ 815 389-0888
**Fax:** 815 389-1143
Stephen Bauch, *President*
Margaret Bauch, *Corp Secy*
Bill Bauch, *Vice Pres*
**EMP:** 3
**SALES (est):** 563.6K **Privately Held**
**SIC:** 3273 1771 Ready-mixed concrete; concrete pumping

### (G-18918)
### ROSCOE TOOL & MANUFACTURING
5339 Stern Dr (61073-8341)
**PHONE** ................................ 815 633-8808
**Fax:** 815 877-7670
Edward W Forsling, *President*
Irvin Hammack, *Vice Pres*
Glenn Hammack, *Treasurer*
Becky Garton, *Bookkeeper*
Merle Hammack, *Admin Sec*
**EMP:** 20
**SQ FT:** 6,000
**SALES (est):** 2.1MM **Privately Held**
**SIC:** 3544 3545 3599 Jigs & fixtures; precision measuring tools; machine shop, jobbing & repair

### (G-18919)
### RWS DESIGN AND CONTROLS INC
13979 Willowbrook Rd (61073-9700)
**PHONE** ................................ 815 654-6000
**Fax:** 815 316-2873
Edison S Wirth Jr, *President*
Michael Rehberg, *Vice Pres*
David Smith, *Vice Pres*
Scott Lindvall, *Opers Mgr*
Clarke Hughbanks, *Engineer*
**EMP:** 40
**SQ FT:** 6,000
**SALES:** 16MM **Privately Held**
**WEB:** www.rwscontrols.com
**SIC:** 8711 3613 Electrical or electronic engineering; control panels, electric

### (G-18920)
### SCHAFER GEAR WORKS ROSCOE LLC
Also Called: Schafer Gear Wrks Rockford LLC
5466 E Rockton Rd (61073-7606)
**PHONE** ................................ 815 874-4327
Bepin Doshi, *President*
Christopher Boudreau, *General Mgr*
Stan Blenke, *Vice Pres*
Greg Parnin, *Controller*
Stanley Blenke, *Mng Member*
▲ **EMP:** 110
**SQ FT:** 42,000
**SALES (est):** 17MM
**SALES (corp-wide):** 30.1MM **Privately Held**
**WEB:** www.schafergear.com
**SIC:** 3462 Gears, forged steel
**PA:** Schafer Industries, Inc.
  4701 Nimtz Pkwy
  South Bend IN 46628
  574 234-4116

### (G-18921)
### SHADE AIRE COMPANY
Also Called: Shade Aire Decorating
7511 Grace Dr (61073-8163)
**PHONE** ................................ 815 623-7597
Roger H Stoeckel, *Partner*
Gail Stoeckel, *Partner*
Roger Stoeckel, *Partner*
**EMP:** 2
**SALES:** 300K **Privately Held**
**SIC:** 7389 2591 2391 Interior designer; drapery hardware & blinds & shades; curtains & draperies

# GEOGRAPHIC SECTION

Roselle - Dupage County (G-18948)

**(G-18922)**
**STATE LINE FOUNDRIES INC**
13227 N 2nd St (61073-7729)
P.O. Box 530 (61073-0530)
**PHONE** ..............................815 389-3921
**Fax:** 815 389-1249
Steve Holdeman, *President*
Yvonne M Holdeman, *Admin Sec*
**EMP:** 54
**SQ FT:** 67,000
**SALES (est):** 11.3MM **Privately Held**
**WEB:** www.slfcastings.com
**SIC: 3321** Gray iron castings; ductile iron castings

**(G-18923)**
**T MAC CYLINDERS INC**
9014 Swanson Dr (61073-9415)
**PHONE** ..............................815 877-7090
Tom McMahon, *President*
Joan L Mc Mahon, *Vice Pres*
**EMP:** 5
**SQ FT:** 3,000
**SALES (est):** 510K **Privately Held**
**SIC: 3593** Fluid power cylinders & actuators

**(G-18924)**
**TAYLOR DESIGN INC**
5375 E Rockton Rd (61073-7651)
**PHONE** ..............................815 389-3991
**Fax:** 815 389-3993
John G Taylor, *President*
**EMP:** 7 **EST:** 1959
**SQ FT:** 10,000
**SALES (est):** 1.1MM **Privately Held**
**SIC: 3544** 3599 8711 7692 Special dies, tools, jigs & fixtures; custom machinery; designing; ship, boat, machine & product; welding repair

**(G-18925)**
**UWD INC**
9135 N 2nd St Ste 100 (61073-8517)
**PHONE** ..............................815 316-3080
Daniel Keller, *President*
Steven Keller, *Admin Sec*
**EMP:** 12
**SALES (est):** 1.9MM **Privately Held**
**SIC: 3089** Injection molding of plastics

## Roselle
### *Dupage County*

**(G-18926)**
**AQUION INC (PA)**
101 S Gary Ave Unit A (60172-1672)
**PHONE** ..............................847 725-3000
Michael Madsen, *President*
Andrew Palframan, *Senior VP*
Edward Meil, *Vice Pres*
Steven Widerski, *Vice Pres*
Andrew Kajpust, *Engineer*
◆ **EMP:** 75
**SQ FT:** 90,000
**SALES:** 56MM **Privately Held**
**WEB:** www.awtp.com
**SIC: 3589** Water filters & softeners, household type; water purification equipment, household type; water treatment equipment, industrial

**(G-18927)**
**ARO METAL STAMPING COMPANY INC**
78 Congress Cir W (60172-3911)
**PHONE** ..............................630 351-7676
**Fax:** 630 351-9958
Tony Dupasquier, *President*
Anthony Dupasquier, *President*
Connie Thomas, *Accounts Mgr*
**EMP:** 25
**SQ FT:** 40,000
**SALES (est):** 9.3MM **Privately Held**
**WEB:** www.arometal.com
**SIC: 3599** 3469 Machine shop, jobbing & repair; stamping metal for the trade

**(G-18928)**
**BELLA SIGN CO**
9 Presidential Dr (60172-3914)
**PHONE** ..............................630 539-0343
Lou Porcaro, *Owner*
**EMP:** 3
**SALES (est):** 290.5K **Privately Held**
**SIC: 3993** 1799 Signs & advertising specialties; sign installation & maintenance

**(G-18929)**
**BRISCOE SIGNS LLC**
119 N Bokelman St (60172-1543)
**PHONE** ..............................630 529-1616
**Fax:** 630 529-7881
Tim Briscoe,
**EMP:** 3
**SQ FT:** 1,600
**SALES (est):** 231.8K **Privately Held**
**SIC: 3993** Signs, not made in custom sign painting shops

**(G-18930)**
**CATER CHEMICAL CO**
30 Monaco Dr (60172-1955)
**PHONE** ..............................630 980-2300
Vinod M Patel, *President*
Jack Patel, *Treasurer*
Abhi Patel, *Sales Associate*
▲ **EMP:** 6
**SQ FT:** 5,000
**SALES (est):** 1MM **Privately Held**
**WEB:** www.caterchem.com
**SIC: 2841** 5169 2899 2842 Soap & other detergents; chemicals & allied products; chemical preparations; specialty cleaning, polishes & sanitation goods; industrial inorganic chemicals

**(G-18931)**
**CD MAGIC INC**
116 S Prospect St (60172-2049)
P.O. Box 126, Bloomingdale (60108-0126)
**PHONE** ..............................708 582-3496
Tom Price, *President*
Edward V Edens, *Shareholder*
Lawrence M Taggart, *Shareholder*
**EMP:** 5
**SQ FT:** 1,500
**SALES (est):** 200K **Privately Held**
**SIC: 2899** Chemical preparations

**(G-18932)**
**CIGTECHS (PA)**
173 W Irving Park Rd (60172-1119)
**PHONE** ..............................630 855-6513
Chris Ray, *Owner*
**EMP:** 7
**SALES (est):** 665.3K **Privately Held**
**SIC: 2111** Cigarettes

**(G-18933)**
**COMPOSITION ONE INC**
Also Called: Document Centre
400 Lake St Ste 110b (60172-3571)
**PHONE** ..............................630 588-1900
**Fax:** 630 588-1960
David R Rohe, *President*
Robin A Rohe, *Admin Sec*
**EMP:** 20
**SALES (est):** 2.3MM **Privately Held**
**WEB:** www.rheemteamliterature.com
**SIC: 2791** Photocomposition, for the printing trade

**(G-18934)**
**COOK MERRITT**
Also Called: Cook's Sports
800 Lake St Ste 118 (60172-2890)
**PHONE** ..............................630 980-3070
**Fax:** 630 980-3540
Merritt Cook Jr, *Owner*
Carol Cook, *Co-Owner*
**EMP:** 2
**SQ FT:** 3,000
**SALES (est):** 250K **Privately Held**
**WEB:** www.cooksport.com
**SIC: 2396** 5699 5999 7389 Screen printing on fabric articles; sports apparel; trophies & plaques; engraving service

**(G-18935)**
**COORDINATE MACHINE COMPANY**
59 Congress Cir W (60172-3912)
**PHONE** ..............................630 894-9880
Shirley Luschen, *President*
Michael Gaffney, *Director*
Scott Luschen, *Admin Sec*
**EMP:** 25
**SALES (est):** 4.3MM **Privately Held**
**SIC: 3545** Tools & accessories for machine tools

**(G-18936)**
**CORPORATE SIGN SYSTEMS INC**
920 Central Ave (60172-1742)
**PHONE** ..............................847 882-6100
Erik Olsen, *President*
**EMP:** 10
**SQ FT:** 5,000
**SALES:** 10MM **Privately Held**
**SIC: 3993** Signs & advertising specialties

**(G-18937)**
**CROWN COVERINGS INC**
814 Central Ave (60172-1849)
**PHONE** ..............................630 546-2959
Rocco Molfese, *President*
Cheryl Molfese, *Admin Sec*
**EMP:** 20
**SALES (est):** 3.4MM **Privately Held**
**SIC: 2434** 2541 Vanities, bathroom: wood; counter & sink tops

**(G-18938)**
**CUSTOM DIRECT INC**
715 E Irving Park Rd (60172-4332)
**PHONE** ..............................630 529-1936
**Fax:** 630 529-6072
John Georgas, *President*
Colleen Senn, *Marketing Staff*
Dorine Dorn, *Manager*
**EMP:** 11
**SQ FT:** 6,000
**SALES (est):** 1.5MM **Privately Held**
**SIC: 8742** 7336 7335 2791 Marketing consulting services; commercial art & graphic design; commercial photography; typesetting

**(G-18939)**
**DANA PLASTIC CONTAINER CORP**
200 W Central Rd (60172)
P.O. Box 545, Arlington Heights (60006-0545)
**PHONE** ..............................630 529-7878
**Fax:** 630 529-7165
Daniel Hiddings, *Manager*
**EMP:** 21
**SALES (corp-wide):** 11.7MM **Privately Held**
**WEB:** www.danaplastic.com
**SIC: 3085** 3083 Plastics bottles; laminated plastics plate & sheet
**HQ:** Dana Plastic Container Corp
6 N Hickory Ave
Arlington Heights IL 60004
847 670-0650

**(G-18940)**
**EKLUNDS TYPESETTING & PRTG LLC**
11 W Irving Park Rd (60172-1117)
**PHONE** ..............................630 924-0057
Denise Romano, *Mng Member*
Vince Romano,
**EMP:** 3
**SALES (est):** 210K **Privately Held**
**SIC: 2791** 2761 Typesetting; manifold business forms

**(G-18941)**
**ELECTRI-FLEX COMPANY (DEL)**
222 Central Ave (60172-1902)
P.O. Box 72260 (60172-0260)
**PHONE** ..............................630 307-1095
Jason Kinander, *CEO*
Edward Marinelli, *President*
Alexandria Kinander Kelly, *Vice Pres*
Dan Coolidge, *Engrg Dir*
H Kinander Jr, *Treasurer*
▲ **EMP:** 95
**SQ FT:** 115,000
**SALES (est):** 35.7MM **Privately Held**
**SIC: 3644** 3599 3699 Electric conduits & fittings; hose, flexible metallic; electrical equipment & supplies

**(G-18942)**
**GEMINI DIGITAL INC**
860 Lake St Ste 606 (60172-2891)
**PHONE** ..............................630 894-9430
Edward Baran, *President*
Cynthia Baran, *Corp Secy*
**EMP:** 3
**SQ FT:** 1,500
**SALES (est):** 372.4K **Privately Held**
**WEB:** www.getgemini.com
**SIC: 2752** Commercial printing, offset

**(G-18943)**
**GENESIS INC (PA)**
980 Central Ave (60172-1742)
**PHONE** ..............................630 351-4400
**Fax:** 630 894-6669
Tom Stringfellow, *General Mgr*
Thomas M Stringfellow, *Principal*
Scott Stringfellow, *Vice Pres*
Patrick Moloney, *Purch Agent*
▲ **EMP:** 90 **EST:** 1977
**SQ FT:** 60,000
**SALES (est):** 25.7MM **Privately Held**
**SIC: 3444** Sheet metal specialties, not stamped

**(G-18944)**
**GROHE AMERICA INC (DH)**
200 N Gary Ave Ste G (60172-1681)
**PHONE** ..............................630 582-7711
Jim Griffin, *CEO*
Frank Profiti, *General Mgr*
John P Shannon, *Vice Pres*
Vinod Kumar, *Project Mgr*
Dave Morgan, *Prdtn Mgr*
▲ **EMP:** 66
**SQ FT:** 87,000
**SALES:** 150MM **Privately Held**
**SIC: 2499** Kitchen, bathroom & household ware: wood
**HQ:** Grohe North America Gmbh
Feldmuhleplatz 15
Dusseldorf
237 293-0

**(G-18945)**
**I C T W INK (PA)**
968 Lake St Ste A (60172-3305)
**PHONE** ..............................630 893-4658
Dee Leonard, *COO*
▲ **EMP:** 3
**SALES (est):** 650.7K **Privately Held**
**SIC: 2893** Printing ink

**(G-18946)**
**ILLINOIS TOOL WORKS INC**
Also Called: ITW Buildex
86 Chancellor Dr (60172-3903)
**PHONE** ..............................630 595-3500
Mark Fontana, *Manager*
**EMP:** 275
**SALES (corp-wide):** 13.6B **Publicly Held**
**SIC: 5072** 3089 Screws; security devices, locks; injection molded finished plastic products
**PA:** Illinois Tool Works Inc.
155 Harlem Ave
Glenview IL 60025
847 724-7500

**(G-18947)**
**INSTRMNTATION CTRL SYSTEMS INC**
Also Called: I C S
360 Heritage Dr (60172-2978)
**PHONE** ..............................630 543-6200
**Fax:** 630 543-6244
Marion L Servos, *President*
Doug Miller, *Prdtn Mgr*
Gunter Sengel, *Engineer*
Alan Servos, *Treasurer*
MEI Wang, *Finance*
**EMP:** 10 **EST:** 1964
**SQ FT:** 20,000
**SALES:** 1MM **Privately Held**
**WEB:** www.ics-timers.com
**SIC: 3625** Relays & industrial controls

**(G-18948)**
**IPS & LUGGAGE CO INC**
685 Washington Ct (60172-5034)
**PHONE** ..............................630 894-2414
Paul Park, *President*
**EMP:** 2
**SALES (est):** 260K **Privately Held**
**SIC: 3161** Luggage

## Roselle - Dupage County (G-18949) — GEOGRAPHIC SECTION

**(G-18949)**
**JIMINEES INC**
Also Called: Jiminee's Doll Clothes
359 W Irving Park Rd D  (60172-1124)
PHONE .................................. 630 295-8002
Eunice Debuhr, *President*
Eunice De Buhr, *President*
James De Buhr, *Treasurer*
James Debuhr, *Treasurer*
▲ **EMP:** 8
**SALES (est):** 750K  **Privately Held**
**WEB:** www.jiminees.com
**SIC:** 3942  5945  Clothing, doll; dolls & accessories

**(G-18950)**
**KONICA MINOLTA**
1000 Stevenson Ct Ste 109  (60172-4314)
PHONE .................................. 630 893-8238
Eva Branch, *Owner*
Russ Niles, *Info Tech Mgr*
**EMP:** 5
**SALES (est):** 428.5K  **Privately Held**
**SIC:** 7629  5045  5044  3571  Business machine repair, electric; computers, peripherals & software; copying equipment; electronic computers

**(G-18951)**
**LARSON-JUHL US LLC**
550 Congress Cir N  (60172-3905)
PHONE .................................. 630 307-9700
**Fax:** 630 307-9678
Sheldon Schur, *General Mgr*
**EMP:** 80
**SALES (corp-wide):** 223.6B  **Publicly Held**
**SIC:** 2499  5023  Picture frame molding, finished; home furnishings
**HQ:** Larson-Juhl Us Llc
3900 Steve Reynolds Blvd
Norcross GA 30093
770 279-5200

**(G-18952)**
**LEGNA IRON WORKS INC**
80 Central Ave  (60172-1904)
PHONE .................................. 630 894-8056
**Fax:** 630 894-8061
Mike Gonzalez, *President*
Leticia Gonzalez, *Corp Secy*
Robert Garcia, *Finance Mgr*
Dawn Sanchez, *Office Mgr*
**EMP:** 25
**SQ FT:** 11,000
**SALES (est):** 5.4MM  **Privately Held**
**WEB:** www.legnairon.com
**SIC:** 3446  1521  7692  1799  Architectural metalwork; general remodeling, single-family houses; welding repair; ornamental metal work

**(G-18953)**
**LYNFRED WINERY INC (PA)**
15 S Roselle Rd  (60172-2043)
PHONE .................................. 630 529-9463
**Fax:** 630 529-4971
Fred E Koehler, *President*
Diane Schramer, *Corp Secy*
Matt Phillips, *Store Mgr*
Diane Koehler, *Manager*
Gregory Hayes, *Consultant*
▲ **EMP:** 45
**SQ FT:** 28,800
**SALES (est):** 6MM  **Privately Held**
**WEB:** www.lynfredwinery.com
**SIC:** 2084  5812  2033  2032  Wines; eating places; canned fruits & specialties; canned specialties

**(G-18954)**
**M & R PRINTING EQUIPMENT INC (HQ)**
Also Called: M & R Sales and Service
440 Medinah Rd  (60172-2329)
PHONE .................................. 800 736-6431
**Fax:** 630 858-6134
Richard Hoffman, *CEO*
Ronnie Riggs, *President*
Rick Bach, *Regional Mgr*
John Carroll, *Regional Mgr*
Tyler Kimball, *Regional Mgr*
▲ **EMP:** 375
**SALES (est):** 174MM  **Privately Held**
**SIC:** 3555  3552  5084  Printing trades machinery; printing machinery, textile; printing trades machinery, equipment & supplies

**(G-18955)**
**M&R HOLDINGS INC (PA)**
Also Called: M&R Printing
440 Medinah Rd  (60172-2329)
PHONE .................................. 630 858-6101
**Fax:** 630 858-4783
Richard Hoffman, *President*
Howard Bloom, *Vice Pres*
Richard Nesladek, *Vice Pres*
Michael Downs, *Accounts Mgr*
Jojo Jaballa, *Sales Staff*
▲ **EMP:** 200
**SQ FT:** 120,000
**SALES (est):** 174MM  **Privately Held**
**SIC:** 3552  Printing machinery, textile

**(G-18956)**
**MARKS CUSTOM SEATING**
Also Called: MCS Booths
816 Central Ave  (60172-1849)
PHONE .................................. 630 980-8270
Mark Ehlers, *Owner*
**EMP:** 5
**SALES (est):** 376K  **Privately Held**
**SIC:** 7641  2599  Furniture upholstery repair; bar, restaurant & cafeteria furniture

**(G-18957)**
**METAL TECH INC**
80 Monaco Dr  (60172-1955)
PHONE .................................. 630 529-7400
**Fax:** 630 529-5999
Lohtar Schick, *President*
Tony Castrovillari, *Vice Pres*
Dana Cobos, *Manager*
Carlene Schick, *Admin Sec*
**EMP:** 22
**SQ FT:** 15,000
**SALES (est):** 4.3MM  **Privately Held**
**SIC:** 3441  Sheet metalwork

**(G-18958)**
**MIDLAND PLASTICS INC**
295 W Walnut St  (60172-3801)
PHONE .................................. 262 938-7000
**Fax:** 773 539-4474
Joseph B Tremback, *President*
Joseph S Tremback, *Vice Pres*
Alan Aleksandrowicz, *Controller*
**EMP:** 32  **EST:** 1962
**SQ FT:** 24,000
**SALES (est):** 4.7MM  **Privately Held**
**WEB:** www.midlandplasticsinc.com
**SIC:** 3089  Blow molded finished plastic products

**(G-18959)**
**NETWORK MERCHANTS LLC**
201 Main St  (60172-2009)
PHONE .................................. 847 352-4850
Jeff Rooney, *Engineer*
Kyle Pexton, *CFO*
**EMP:** 8
**SALES (est):** 250.7K  **Privately Held**
**SIC:** 3625  Switches, electronic applications

**(G-18960)**
**NUARC COMPANY INC (DH)**
440 Medinah Rd  (60172-2329)
PHONE .................................. 847 967-4400
**Fax:** 847 967-0417
Ronnie Riggs, *President*
Lisa Olson, *Executive Asst*
**EMP:** 1
**SQ FT:** 200,000
**SALES (est):** 645.4K  **Privately Held**
**SIC:** 3861  Photographic equipment & supplies; printing equipment, photographic
**HQ:** M & R Printing Equipment, Inc.
440 Medinah Rd
Roselle IL 60172
800 736-6431

**(G-18961)**
**NYPRO HANOVER PARK**
401 S Gary Ave  (60172-1654)
PHONE .................................. 630 868-3517
**EMP:** 3  **EST:** 2011
**SALES (est):** 176.8K  **Privately Held**
**SIC:** 3083  Plastic finished products, laminated

**(G-18962)**
**PHILIPS LIGHTING N AMER CORP**
440 Medinah Rd  (60172-2329)
PHONE .................................. 708 307-3000
Ed Shamsabad, *Principal*
Leverda Wallace, *Surgery Dir*
**EMP:** 32  **Privately Held**
**WEB:** www.usa.philips.com
**SIC:** 3651  5063  Household audio & video equipment; transformers, electric
**HQ:** Philips Lighting North America Corporation
3 Burlington Woods Dr # 4
Burlington MA 01803
617 423-9999

**(G-18963)**
**PRINTING PLUS OF ROSELLE INC**
205 E Irving Park Rd  (60172-2057)
PHONE .................................. 630 893-0410
**Fax:** 630 893-1782
Mark Borough, *President*
Cara Steetz, *Sales Dir*
**EMP:** 9
**SQ FT:** 3,000
**SALES (est):** 1.4MM  **Privately Held**
**WEB:** www.printingplusroselle.com
**SIC:** 5199  7334  2752  3993  Advertising specialties; photocopying & duplicating services; commercial printing, offset; signs & advertising specialties; typesetting; bookbinding & related work

**(G-18964)**
**PRO-MOLD INCORPORATED**
Also Called: Pro Mold & Die
55 Chancellor Dr  (60172-3900)
PHONE .................................. 630 893-3594
**Fax:** 847 893-4773
Walter Schaub, *President*
Roger Reiner, *Vice Pres*
Don Donnelly, *Engineer*
David Long, *CFO*
Leanne Delia, *Manager*
**EMP:** 56
**SQ FT:** 35,000
**SALES (est):** 10.9MM  **Privately Held**
**WEB:** www.promolddie.com
**SIC:** 3544  Industrial molds; dies, plastics forming

**(G-18965)**
**RASOI RESTURAUNT**
15 Clair Ct  (60172-4517)
PHONE .................................. 847 455-8888
**Fax:** 847 455-8889
Sam Lakhia, *Owner*
**EMP:** 4
**SALES (est):** 293.4K  **Privately Held**
**SIC:** 3949  Indian clubs

**(G-18966)**
**REDI-STRIP COMPANY**
100 Central Ave  (60172-1950)
P.O. Box 72199  (60172-0199)
PHONE .................................. 630 529-2442
**Fax:** 630 529-3626
John Carlisle, *President*
Robert Kernan, *Vice Pres*
Barbara A Carlisle, *Admin Sec*
**EMP:** 9  **EST:** 1995
**SQ FT:** 44,000
**SALES (est):** 850K  **Privately Held**
**SIC:** 3471  Cleaning & descaling metal products

**(G-18967)**
**RHT INC**
Also Called: Liners Direct
401 S Gary Ave Unit A  (60172-1655)
PHONE .................................. 630 227-1737
Jeffrey B Conner, *President*
**EMP:** 40
**SQ FT:** 56,000
**SALES (est):** 13.6MM  **Privately Held**
**WEB:** www.linersdirectinc.com
**SIC:** 3088  Tubs (bath, shower & laundry), plastic; bathroom fixtures, plastic

**(G-18968)**
**ROMUS INCORPORATED**
932 Central Ave  (60172-1742)
PHONE .................................. 414 350-6233
Jay Schabelski, *President*
Kathleen Schabelski, *Treasurer*
**EMP:** 2  **EST:** 2000
**SALES (est):** 300K  **Privately Held**
**WEB:** www.romusinc.com
**SIC:** 3829  Hardness testing equipment

**(G-18969)**
**ROSELLE CUSTOM WOODWORK LLC**
57 N Garden Ave  (60172-1733)
PHONE .................................. 630 980-5655
Keith Zawrazkyrazky", *Vice Pres*
Lisa Tyrell, *Info Tech Mgr*
Steve Wright,
John Valentine,
**EMP:** 3
**SQ FT:** 4,500
**SALES (est):** 310K  **Privately Held**
**SIC:** 2499  Decorative wood & woodwork

**(G-18970)**
**RR DONNELLEY LOGISTICS SE**
Also Called: D L S
200 N Gary Ave  (60172-1681)
PHONE .................................. 630 672-2500
**EMP:** 7
**SALES (corp-wide):** 6.9B  **Publicly Held**
**SIC:** 2759  2741  Commercial printing; miscellaneous publishing
**HQ:** Rr Donnelley Logistics Services Worldwide, Inc.
1000 Windham Pkwy
Bolingbrook IL 60490

**(G-18971)**
**SAACHI INC**
Also Called: Www.vltg-Cnvrtr-Transformer-com
364 Jennifer Ln  (60172-4927)
PHONE .................................. 630 775-1700
Khushjiwan Kaur, *CEO*
▲ **EMP:** 7
**SQ FT:** 8,000
**SALES (est):** 4MM  **Privately Held**
**SIC:** 3612  7389  Transformers, except electric

**(G-18972)**
**SANDMANCOM INC**
219 E Irving Park Rd  (60172-2004)
PHONE .................................. 630 980-7710
Charles Hall, *President*
Ronald Bailey, *Manager*
William Widmann, *Manager*
Andrew Tuszynski, *Admin Sec*
**EMP:** 7
**SQ FT:** 5,000
**SALES (est):** 346K  **Privately Held**
**SIC:** 3661  Telephone station equipment & parts, wire

**(G-18973)**
**SATURN ELECTRICAL SERVICES INC**
380 Monaco Dr  (60172-1954)
PHONE .................................. 630 980-0300
George Schembari, *President*
Nicky Thorson, *Admin Asst*
**EMP:** 5
**SALES (est):** 580.3K  **Privately Held**
**WEB:** www.saturn-es.com
**SIC:** 1731  3612  Electrical work; generator voltage regulators

**(G-18974)**
**SCHOLASTIC INC**
301 S Gary Ave  (60172-1657)
PHONE .................................. 630 671-0601
Marvin Parrott, *Opers Mgr*
Greg Carter, *Branch Mgr*
Christy Lavine, *Consultant*
Andrea Peters, *Admin Asst*
**EMP:** 28
**SALES (corp-wide):** 1.6B  **Publicly Held**
**WEB:** www.scholasticdealer.com
**SIC:** 2731  Textbooks: publishing only, not printed on site

# GEOGRAPHIC SECTION
## Rosemont - Cook County (G-18998)

HQ: Scholastic Inc.
557 Broadway Lbby 1
New York NY 10012
800 724-6527

**(G-18975)**
**SCIENTIFIC METAL TREATING CO**
106 Chancellor Dr (60172-3903)
PHONE.................................630 582-0071
Fax: 630 582-0081
Wayne Harelson, *CEO*
Kevin Harelson, *President*
Kevin Haraldson, *Engineer*
Mickey Mullins, *Manager*
EMP: 28
SALES (est): 6.5MM  Privately Held
SIC: 3398  Metal heat treating

**(G-18976)**
**SELECT TOOL & DIE INC**
324 Pinecroft Dr (60172-2469)
PHONE.................................630 980-8458
Robert Siemers, *President*
EMP: 3
SALES: 550K  Privately Held
SIC: 3544  Special dies, tools, jigs & fixtures

**(G-18977)**
**SERVICE STAMPINGS OF IL INC**
251 Central Ave (60172-1901)
P.O. Box 72157 (60172-0157)
PHONE.................................630 894-7880
Fax: 630 894-4866
Michael Grant, *President*
Timothy Grant, *Vice Pres*
Jim Zay, *Treasurer*
Jaunita Grant, *Bookkeeper*
James Christensen, *Admin Sec*
EMP: 20  EST: 1963
SQ FT: 30,000
SALES (est): 3.8MM  Privately Held
WEB: www.servicestampingsil.com
SIC: 3469  Stamping metal for the trade

**(G-18978)**
**SNEGDE DEEP**
Also Called: Allegra Print & Imaging
994 Woodside Dr (60172-2728)
PHONE.................................630 351-7111
Ramesh Gandhi, *President*
EMP: 5
SQ FT: 1,900
SALES: 299K  Privately Held
SIC: 2752  7334  2759  Commercial printing, offset; photocopying & duplicating services; commercial printing

**(G-18979)**
**SPORT CONNECTION**
741 E Nerge Rd (60172-1061)
PHONE.................................630 980-1787
Fax: 630 980-5839
Sharon M Mattioda, *President*
Barbara Butt, *Vice Pres*
Jody Butt, *Vice Pres*
EMP: 4  EST: 1978
SQ FT: 2,000
SALES (est): 198K  Privately Held
SIC: 5699  2396  Sports apparel; uniforms; T-shirts, custom printed; automotive & apparel trimmings

**(G-18980)**
**STERNBERG LANTERNS INC (PA)**
Also Called: Sternberg Lighting
555 Lawrence Ave (60172-1568)
PHONE.................................847 588-3400
Joseph Waldau, *President*
Mark Dean, *Vice Pres*
Dan Radochonski, *Vice Pres*
John Seidel, *Mfg Mgr*
Michael Fortman, *Purchasing*
▲ EMP: 106  EST: 1923
SQ FT: 130,000
SALES (est): 36.6MM  Privately Held
WEB: www.sternberglighting.com
SIC: 3646  3648  3645  3354  Ornamental lighting fixtures, commercial; lighting equipment; residential lighting fixtures; aluminum extruded products

**(G-18981)**
**TERACO-IL INC**
Also Called: Innovative Plastic A Teraco Co
910 Lake St Ste 116 (60172-3384)
PHONE.................................630 539-4400
Raymond McDowell, *President*
Craig McCune, *CFO*
Mike Beck, *Regl Sales Mgr*
EMP: 30
SALES (est): 7.7MM
SALES (corp-wide): 52.8MM  Privately Held
WEB: www.teraco.com
SIC: 3089  3993  Identification cards, plastic; advertising novelties
HQ: Teraco, Inc.
2080 Commerce Dr
Midland TX 79703
800 687-3999

**(G-18982)**
**THRICE PUBLISHING NFP**
734 Berwick Pl (60172-2734)
PHONE.................................630 776-0478
Robert Spryszak, *President*
EMP: 3
SALES (est): 81.1K  Privately Held
SIC: 2731  Book publishing

**(G-18983)**
**TKT ENTERPRISES INC (PA)**
Also Called: Dealers Transmission Exchange
95 Chancellor Dr (60172-3901)
PHONE.................................630 307-9355
Fax: 630 307-9355
David F Horvath Sr, *President*
Daniel Horvath, *Vice Pres*
Timothy J Horvath, *Vice Pres*
Karen Rurka, *Admin Sec*
▲ EMP: 30
SQ FT: 30,000
SALES (est): 7.9MM  Privately Held
WEB: www.dealerstrans.com
SIC: 5013  3714  Automotive engines & engine parts; rebuilding engines & transmissions, factory basis

**(G-18984)**
**TRIM SUITS BY SHOW-OFF INC**
Also Called: Show Off
48 Congress Cir W (60172-3911)
PHONE.................................630 894-0100
Fax: 630 894-0300
Ena Fenn, *President*
EMP: 9
SALES (est): 1.1MM  Privately Held
WEB: www.showoffinc.com
SIC: 2339  2369  5961  Athletic clothing: women's, misses' & juniors'; warm-up, jogging & sweat suits: girls' & children's; women's apparel, mail order; clothing, mail order (except women's)

**(G-18985)**
**WINGS OF ROSELLE LLC**
840 Lake St Ste 414 (60172-2894)
PHONE.................................630 529-5700
Denise Romano, *Principal*
EMP: 8
SALES (est): 812.2K  Privately Held
SIC: 3421  Table & food cutlery, including butchers'

**(G-18986)**
**WRITTEN WORD INC**
986 Lake St Ste 108 (60172-3390)
PHONE.................................630 671-9803
Albert Chin-A-Young, *Owner*
Mitzi Pierce-Morton, *Editor*
EMP: 2
SQ FT: 700
SALES (est): 214.7K  Privately Held
SIC: 7372  Prepackaged software

**(G-18987)**
**XPRESS PRINTING & COPYING CO**
147 W Irving Park Rd (60172-1119)
PHONE.................................630 980-9600
Byron Myrhe, *President*
EMP: 3  EST: 1999
SQ FT: 2,400
SALES (est): 500K  Privately Held
SIC: 2754  Commercial printing, gravure

**(G-18988)**
**YKK AP AMERICA INC**
1000 Stevenson Ct Ste 101 (60172-4314)
PHONE.................................630 582-9616
Fax: 630 582-9602
Max Mazoto, *Branch Mgr*
Michael Bourassa, *Branch Mgr*
Bryce Hanson, *Manager*
EMP: 15
SALES (corp-wide): 750.5MM  Privately Held
SIC: 3442  Sash, door or window: metal
HQ: Ykk Ap America Inc.
270 Riverside Pkwy Sw A
Austell GA 30168
678 838-6000

## Rosemont
### Cook County

**(G-18989)**
**APPLETON GRP LLC (DH)**
Also Called: Appleton Group
9377 W Higgins Rd (60018-4973)
PHONE.................................847 268-6000
Ross Kerseter, *President*
Scott Anderson, *President*
Jerry Mc Quade, *Vice Pres*
Harley M Smith, *Vice Pres*
Ray Dubiel, *Engineer*
▲ EMP: 120  EST: 1903
SQ FT: 750,000
SALES (est): 810.8MM
SALES (corp-wide): 14.5B  Publicly Held
WEB: www.egseg.com
SIC: 3644  3643  3613  3646  Junction boxes, electric; electric conduits & fittings; plugs, electric; electric switches; starting switches, fluorescent; switchgear & switchgear accessories; power circuit breakers; panelboards & distribution boards, electric; commercial indusl & institutional electric lighting fixtures; extension cords
HQ: Apple Jv Holding Corp.
8000 West Florissant Ave
Saint Louis MO 63136
314 553-2000

**(G-18990)**
**BRG SPORTS INC (HQ)**
9801 W Higgins Rd (60018-4704)
PHONE.................................831 461-7500
Dan Arment, *CEO*
Timothy P Mayhew, *President*
Chris Zimmerman, *President*
Tony Donofrio, *COO*
Daniel J Arment, *Exec VP*
▲ EMP: 234
SQ FT: 56,647
SALES (est): 796.1MM  Privately Held
SIC: 3949  3751  Helmets, athletic; pads: football, basketball, soccer, lacrosse, etc.; protective sporting equipment; bicycles & related parts

**(G-18991)**
**BUILDERS CHICAGO CORPORATION**
9820 W Foster Ave (60018-5306)
PHONE.................................224 654-2122
Richard C Crandall Jr, *President*
Michael Kerley, *General Mgr*
Frank Kutschke, *Vice Pres*
Mike Kilbridge, *Controller*
John O'Brien, *Controller*
EMP: 60  EST: 1927
SQ FT: 15,000
SALES (est): 8MM  Privately Held
WEB: www.builderschicago.com
SIC: 7699  1791  3442  1751  Garage door repair; structural steel erection; garage doors, overhead: metal; garage door, installation or erection; window & door (prefabricated) installation; barricades, metal; dock equipment installation, industrial

**(G-18992)**
**CELERITY PHARMACEUTICALS LLC**
9450 Bryn Mawr Ave # 640 (60018-5276)
PHONE.................................847 999-0131
Julie Lavoie, *Business Mgr*
Dan Robins, *Mng Member*
Alan Heller,
Peter Strothman,
EMP: 9  EST: 2013
SQ FT: 3,000
SALES (est): 1.7MM  Privately Held
SIC: 2834  Pharmaceutical preparations

**(G-18993)**
**CHEMALLOY COMPANY LLC**
Also Called: Metal Briquetters
9700 W Higgins Rd # 1000 (60018-4743)
Jim Davis, *Manager*
EMP: 25
SALES (corp-wide): 618.6MM  Privately Held
WEB: www.chemalloy.com
SIC: 2999  Fuel briquettes or boulets: made with petroleum binder
HQ: Chemalloy Company Llc
1301 Conshohocken Rd
Conshohocken PA 19428
610 527-2130

**(G-18994)**
**CULLIGAN INTERNATIONAL COMPANY (HQ)**
9399 W Higgins Rd # 1100 (60018-4940)
PHONE.................................847 430-2800
Scott G Clawson, *CEO*
David Rich, *President*
Janet Shawcross, *General Mgr*
Jeff Owens, *Business Mgr*
Marty Armstrong, *Senior VP*
◆ EMP: 150  EST: 1986
SALES (est): 741.7MM  Privately Held
WEB: www.culligan.com
SIC: 3589  Sewage & water treatment equipment; water treatment equipment, industrial; water filters & softeners, household type

**(G-18995)**
**CURLEE MFG**
9377 W Higgins Rd (60018-4973)
PHONE.................................847 268-6517
EMP: 8  EST: 2009
SALES (est): 540K  Privately Held
SIC: 3999  Mfg Misc Products

**(G-18996)**
**CUSTOM HARD CHROME SERVICE CO**
7083 Barry St (60018-3401)
P.O. Box 1234, Oak Park (60304-0234)
PHONE.................................847 759-1420
Philip Bolas, *President*
Craig Bolas, *Vice Pres*
EMP: 5
SQ FT: 11,500
SALES (est): 594.7K  Privately Held
SIC: 3471  Electroplating of metals or formed products; chromium plating of metals or formed products; finishing, metals or formed products

**(G-18997)**
**CUSTOM SUPERFINISHING GRINDING**
Also Called: Horizon Sperfinishing Grinding
7083 Barry St (60018-3401)
PHONE.................................847 699-9710
Fax: 847 699-9326
EMP: 4
SQ FT: 5,000
SALES (est): 260K  Privately Held
SIC: 3599  Grinding And Superfinishing Job Shop

**(G-18998)**
**DIGITAL MINDS INC**
Also Called: Touch Quest
9501 W Devon Ave Ste 603 (60018-4818)
PHONE.................................847 430-3390
Joseph P Fiduccia, *President*
Andy Gomez, *Vice Pres*
Roderick Jadczak, *CTO*
EMP: 4
SQ FT: 1,700
SALES: 1MM  Privately Held
WEB: www.touchquest.com
SIC: 3993  7372  Signs & advertising specialties; prepackaged software

# Rosemont - Cook County (G-18999)

## GEOGRAPHIC SECTION

**(G-18999)**
**DIRECT SELLING STRATEGIES**
5600 N River Rd Ste 800 (60018-5166)
PHONE.................................847 993-3188
**EMP:** 3 **EST:** 2010
**SALES (est):** 150K **Privately Held**
**SIC: 3399** Mfg Primary Metal Products

**(G-19000)**
**EASY HEAT INC**
9377 W Higgins Rd (60018-4973)
PHONE.................................847 268-6000
Michael O'Toole, *President*
Doug Henderson, *Purchasing*
Ben Arnold, *Controller*
Ben Shoemaker, *Sales Staff*
▲ **EMP:** 40
**SALES (est):** 4.6MM
**SALES (corp-wide):** 14.5B **Publicly Held**
**SIC: 3433** Heating equipment, except electric
**HQ:** Appleton Grp Llc
9377 W Higgins Rd
Rosemont IL 60018
847 268-6000

**(G-19001)**
**FEDEX OFFICE & PRINT SVCS INC**
Also Called: Fedex Office Print & Ship Ctr
9300 Bryn Mawr Ave (60018-5202)
PHONE.................................847 292-7176
Fax: 847 292-1465
Dustin Burgness, *Manager*
Bob Wojnicki, *Exec Dir*
**EMP:** 4
**SALES (corp-wide):** 50.3B **Publicly Held**
**SIC: 2752** Commercial printing, lithographic
**HQ:** Fedex Office And Print Services, Inc.
7900 Legacy Dr
Plano TX 75024
214 550-7000

**(G-19002)**
**FONTERRA (USA) INC (HQ)**
9525 Bryn Mawr Ave # 700 (60018-5250)
PHONE.................................847 928-1600
Emma Blott, *General Mgr*
Wendy Burton, *General Mgr*
Joe Coote, *General Mgr*
Simon Hughes, *General Mgr*
Miles Hurrell, *General Mgr*
◆ **EMP:** 63 **EST:** 1971
**SALES (est):** 33MM
**SALES (corp-wide):** 12B **Privately Held**
**WEB:** www.fonterra.com
**SIC: 2023** Dried milk; powdered whey
**PA:** Fonterra Co-Operative Group Limited
109 Fanshawe Street
Auckland, 1010
800 656-568

**(G-19003)**
**GRASS VALLEY USA LLC**
10600 W Higgins Rd (60018-3706)
PHONE.................................847 803-8060
Michael Moakley, *Principal*
Neil Silber, *Accounts Exec*
**EMP:** 35
**SALES (corp-wide):** 2.3B **Publicly Held**
**SIC: 3663** Radio & TV communications equipment
**HQ:** Grass Valley Usa, Llc
125 Crown Point Ct
Grass Valley CA 95945

**(G-19004)**
**GREAT LAKES COCA-COLA DIST LLC**
6250 N River Rd Ste 9000 (60018-4241)
PHONE.................................847 227-6500
David Reyes, *Mng Member*
**EMP:** 121
**SALES (est):** 23.5MM **Privately Held**
**SIC: 2086** 5142 5149 Bottled & canned soft drinks; packaged frozen goods; soft drinks
**PA:** Reyes Holdings, L.L.C.
6250 N River Rd Ste 9000
Rosemont IL 60018

**(G-19005)**
**HW HOLDCO LLC**
Also Called: Aberdeen Group
5600 N River Rd Ste 250 (60018-5118)
PHONE.................................773 824-2400
Fax: 630 543-3112
Amara Rozgus, *General Mgr*
Mandy Owens, *Human Res Mgr*
Mary Skelnik, *Manager*
Glenn Stevens, *Manager*
Jess Guzy, *IT/INT Sup*
**EMP:** 100
**SALES (corp-wide):** 198.7MM **Privately Held**
**WEB:** www.toolsofthetrade.org
**SIC: 2721** Trade journals: publishing only, not printed on site
**PA:** Hw Holdco, Llc
1 Thomas Cir Nw Ste 600
Washington DC 20005
202 452-0800

**(G-19006)**
**INDUSTRIAL MODERN PATTERN**
7115 Barry St (60018-3403)
PHONE.................................847 296-4930
Fax: 847 296-7395
Jared Megleo, *President*
Branden James, *Pub Rel Mgr*
Natalia Guzman, *Sales Engr*
Tony Bastek, *Sales Staff*
Jaimee Kinsman, *Office Mgr*
**EMP:** 9
**SQ FT:** 7,500
**SALES (est):** 1.1MM **Privately Held**
**WEB:** www.industrialmodern.com
**SIC: 3544** Forms (molds), for foundry & plastics working machinery

**(G-19007)**
**JING MEI INDUSTRIAL USA INC (PA)**
10275 W Higgins Rd # 470 (60018-3886)
PHONE.................................847 671-0800
Raymond C Wai, *President*
Steve Edwards, *General Mgr*
▲ **EMP:** 22
**SQ FT:** 50,000
**SALES (est):** 3.5MM **Privately Held**
**SIC: 3999** Coins & tokens, non-currency

**(G-19008)**
**KAAS INDUSTRIES INC**
7035 Barry St (60018-3401)
PHONE.................................847 298-9106
Fax: 847 298-9109
Jakub Koeller-Kmicikiewicz, *President*
Jan Malarz, *Vice Pres*
▲ **EMP:** 7
**SQ FT:** 7,000
**SALES (est):** 1MM **Privately Held**
**SIC: 3599** Machine shop, jobbing & repair

**(G-19009)**
**LEXMARK INTERNATIONAL INC**
9700 W Higgins Rd Ste 930 (60018-4713)
PHONE.................................847 318-5700
Fax: 847 318-5757
Maureen Mitchell, *Marketing Staff*
Dennis Valadez, *Manager*
Willie Howard, *Manager*
Shehla Zafar, *Applctn Conslt*
**EMP:** 40
**SALES (corp-wide):** 3.5B **Privately Held**
**WEB:** www.lexmark.com
**SIC: 3577** Computer peripheral equipment
**PA:** Lexmark International, Inc.
740 W New Circle Rd
Lexington KY 40511
859 438-2468

**(G-19010)**
**LIFE FITNESS INC (HQ)**
9525 Bryn Mawr Ave Fl 6 (60018-5249)
PHONE.................................847 288-3300
Chris E Clawson, *President*
Chris Connor, *General Mgr*
Scot Stermitz, *Regional Mgr*
Jay Megna, *Exec VP*
Tom Zentefis, *Senior VP*
▼ **EMP:** 253 **EST:** 1999
**SALES (est):** 175MM
**SALES (corp-wide):** 4.4B **Publicly Held**
**SIC: 3949** Exercise equipment
**PA:** Brunswick Corporation
1 N Field Ct
Lake Forest IL 60045
847 735-4700

**(G-19011)**
**LIFE FITNESS INC**
Life Fitness A Div Brunswick
9525 Bryn Mawr Ave (60018-5249)
PHONE.................................800 494-6344
Chris E Clawson, *President*
Chris Clawson, *President*
Pat O'Dell, *Surgery Dir*
Minerva Babilonia, *Administration*
**EMP:** 128
**SALES (corp-wide):** 4.4B **Publicly Held**
**WEB:** www.lifefitness.com
**SIC: 3949** Exercise equipment
**HQ:** Life Fitness, Inc.
9525 Bryn Mawr Ave Fl 6
Rosemont IL 60018
847 288-3300

**(G-19012)**
**LIFEWATCH CORP (HQ)**
10255 W Higgins Rd # 100 (60018-5608)
PHONE.................................847 720-2100
George Michelson, *President*
Brent Cohen, *Principal*
Jason Centers, *Area Mgr*
Jake Mendelsohn, *Exec VP*
Dan Pawlik, *Vice Pres*
**EMP:** 4
**SQ FT:** 32,000
**SALES (est):** 191.2MM **Privately Held**
**SIC: 8099** 5047 3845 Physical examination & testing services; patient monitoring equipment; electro-medical equipment; electrocardiographs
**PA:** Lifewatch Ag
Baarerstrasse 139
Zug ZG
417 286-777

**(G-19013)**
**LIFEWATCH SERVICES INC (DH)**
10255 W Higgins Rd # 100 (60018-5608)
PHONE.................................847 720-2100
Fax: 847 720-2111
Stephan Rietiker, *CEO*
Roger K Richardson, *President*
Yacov Geva, *Principal*
Dan Eliasoff, *Project Mgr*
Kobi Ben Efraim, *CFO*
**EMP:** 370
**SQ FT:** 56,000
**SALES (est):** 180.2MM **Privately Held**
**WEB:** www.lifewatchinc.com
**SIC: 5047** 8099 3845 8071 Patient monitoring equipment; electro-medical equipment; physical examination service, insurance; health screening service; physical examination & testing services; electrocardiographs; testing laboratories
**HQ:** Lifewatch Corp
10255 W Higgins Rd # 100
Rosemont IL 60018
847 720-2100

**(G-19014)**
**LIFEWATCH TECHNOLOGIES INC**
Also Called: Instrumentics
10255 W Higgins Rd # 100 (60018-5606)
PHONE.................................800 633-3361
Frederick Mindermann, *President*
Roger K Richardson, *COO*
Meg McGilley, *Vice Pres*
Francis Leonard, *CFO*
John M Tumblin, *Officer*
▲ **EMP:** 95 **EST:** 2000
**SALES (est):** 10.9MM **Privately Held**
**WEB:** www.instromedix.com
**SIC: 3845** 5047 Electromedical equipment; electro-medical equipment
**HQ:** Lifewatch Corp
10255 W Higgins Rd # 100
Rosemont IL 60018
847 720-2100

**(G-19015)**
**MATTHEW WARREN INC (DH)**
Also Called: Mw Industries
9501 Tech Blvd Ste 401 (60018)
PHONE.................................847 349-5760
William Marcum, *CEO*
Chris Thomas, *President*
John Everette, *General Mgr*
Chester Kwasniak, *CFO*
John Anderson, *Manager*
**EMP:** 30
**SALES (est):** 385.5MM
**SALES (corp-wide):** 115.4MM **Privately Held**
**SIC: 3493** Coiled flat springs; cold formed springs; helical springs, hot wound: railroad equipment etc.; hot wound springs, except wire
**HQ:** Mw Industries, Inc.
9501 Tech Blvd Ste 401
Rosemont IL 60018
847 349-5760

**(G-19016)**
**MILK PRODUCTS HOLDINGS N AMER (HQ)**
9525 Bryn Mawr Ave (60018-5249)
PHONE.................................847 928-1600
Martin Bates, *President*
Teresa Smart, *Assistant*
◆ **EMP:** 48
**SQ FT:** 30,000
**SALES (est):** 29.5MM
**SALES (corp-wide):** 12B **Privately Held**
**WEB:** www.fonterra.com
**SIC: 5143** 2023 Dairy products, except dried or canned; dry, condensed, evaporated dairy products
**PA:** Fonterra Co-Operative Group Limited
109 Fanshawe Street
Auckland, 1010
800 656-568

**(G-19017)**
**MILLER AND COMPANY LLC (DH)**
9700 W Higgins Rd # 1000 (60018-4743)
PHONE.................................847 696-2400
John A Adcock, *President*
James LI, *Opers Mgr*
Dimitra Kotsinonos, *CFO*
Ryan Lacoursiere, *VP Sales*
Sudhir Gupta, *Marketing Mgr*
▲ **EMP:** 35 **EST:** 1919
**SQ FT:** 10,500
**SALES (est):** 60.3MM
**SALES (corp-wide):** 618.6MM **Privately Held**
**WEB:** www.millerandco.com
**SIC: 5051** 3313 Pig iron; ferroalloys; alloys, additive, except copper: not made in blast furnaces
**HQ:** Nizi International Sa
Rue Pafebruch 89e
Luxembourg 8308
442 222-

**(G-19018)**
**NICHOLAS MACHINE & TOOL INC**
7027 Barry St (60018-3401)
PHONE.................................847 298-2035
Eugene Bereza, *President*
Josephine Bereza, *Vice Pres*
Diane Bereza, *Admin Sec*
▲ **EMP:** 6
**SALES (est):** 530K **Privately Held**
**WEB:** www.nicholasmachine.com
**SIC: 3599** 3544 3541 Machine shop, jobbing & repair; special dies, tools, jigs & fixtures; machine tools, metal cutting type

**(G-19019)**
**NUESTRO QUESO LLC (PA)**
9500 Bryn Mawr Ave (60018-5211)
PHONE.................................224 366-4320
Dan Brown, *QC Mgr*
Jorge Machado, *VP Finance*
Anthony Andrate, *Mng Member*
Mark Braun, *Mng Member*
**EMP:** 25
**SQ FT:** 33,000
**SALES:** 48.3MM **Privately Held**
**SIC: 2022** 5143 Cheese, natural & processed; cheese

**(G-19020)**
**PERQ/HCI LLC (DH)**
Also Called: Srds
5600 N River Rd Ste 900 (60018-5167)
PHONE.................................847 375-5000
Fax: 847 375-5002

▲ = Import ▼=Export
◆ =Import/Export

# GEOGRAPHIC SECTION

**Rosemont - Cook County (G-19044)**

Tom Drouillard, *CEO*
Dave Emery, *Publisher*
Bernadette Cognac, *Vice Pres*
Trish Delaurier, *Vice Pres*
Dave Kostolansky, *Vice Pres*
**EMP:** 150 **EST:** 1919
**SALES (est):** 30.6MM
**SALES (corp-wide):** 17.7B **Privately Held**
**WEB:** www.srds.com
**SIC: 2741** Directories: publishing only, not printed on site
**HQ:** Young & Rubicam Inc.
  3 Columbus Cir Fl 8
  New York NY 10019
  212 210-3000

**(G-19021)**
**PERRY JOHNSON INC**
Also Called: Perry Johnson Consulting
10255 W Higgins Rd # 140 (60018-5606)
**PHONE**.................847 635-0010
**Fax:** 847 635-0021
Jeff Goldsher, *Manager*
**EMP:** 13
**SALES (corp-wide):** 31.4MM **Privately Held**
**WEB:** www.pji.com
**SIC: 7389** 2731 8748 7812 Speakers' bureau; inspection & testing services; textbooks: publishing & printing; books: publishing & printing; business consulting; video tape production; business oriented computer software
**PA:** Perry Johnson, Inc.
  755 W Big Beaver Rd # 1300
  Troy MI 48084
  248 356-4410

**(G-19022)**
**PHILIPS LIGHTING N AMER CORP**
Also Called: Forecast
10275 W Higgins Rd # 800 (60018-5625)
**PHONE**.................800 825-5844
**Fax:** 847 622-2542
Brian Hart, *Branch Mgr*
Lindsay Johnson, *Director*
Leverda Wallace, *Surgery Dir*
Lyn McDonald, *Assistant*
**EMP:** 190 **Privately Held**
**WEB:** www.lightguard.com
**SIC: 3646** 5063 Commercial indusl & institutional electric lighting fixtures; electrical apparatus & equipment
**HQ:** Philips Lighting North America Corporation
  3 Burlington Woods Dr # 4
  Burlington MA 01803
  617 423-9999

**(G-19023)**
**PICIS CLINICAL SOLUTIONS INC**
9500 W Higgins Rd # 1100 (60018-4963)
**PHONE**.................847 993-2200
**EMP:** 10
**SALES (corp-wide):** 60.1MM **Privately Held**
**SIC: 7372** 7371 Prepackaged Software Services Custom Computer Programing
**PA:** Picis Clinical Solutions, Inc.
  100 Quannapowitt Pkwy # 405
  Wakefield MA 01880
  336 397-5336

**(G-19024)**
**POLAR CONTAINER CORP INC**
7123 Barry St (60018-3403)
**PHONE**.................847 299-5030
**Fax:** 847 299-5032
Robert OHM, *President*
Linda OHM, *Vice Pres*
**EMP:** 3 **EST:** 1958
**SQ FT:** 3,500
**SALES (est):** 275K **Privately Held**
**SIC: 7699** 3364 3561 3523 Pumps & pumping equipment repair; copper & copper alloy die-castings; pumps & pumping equipment; farm machinery & equipment

**(G-19025)**
**PROSPAN MANUFACTURING**
10013 Norwood St (60018-4326)
**PHONE**.................847 815-0191
Jim Sullivan, *President*
**EMP:** 4
**SALES (est):** 308.6K **Privately Held**
**SIC: 3999** Manufacturing industries

**(G-19026)**
**RANDA ACCESSORIES LEA GDS LLC (PA)**
5600 N River Rd Ste 500 (60018-5188)
**PHONE**.................847 292-8300
Jeffrey O Spiegel, *CEO*
John Hastings, *Exec VP*
Mary Rice, *Senior VP*
Edward Turner, *Senior VP*
Daniel Gallery, *Purchasing*
◆ **EMP:** 90
**SQ FT:** 26,000
**SALES (est):** 423.5MM **Privately Held**
**SIC: 5136** 5948 3172 Apparel belts, men's & boys'; luggage & leather goods stores; personal leather goods

**(G-19027)**
**RIDDELL INC (DH)**
Also Called: Riddell Sports
9801 W Higgins Rd Ste 800 (60018-4706)
**PHONE**.................847 292-1472
William Sherman, *President*
Paul E Harrigton, *President*
Robert Brasser, *Senior VP*
Mike Devel, *Vice Pres*
Thad Ide, *Vice Pres*
▲ **EMP:** 140 **EST:** 1929
**SQ FT:** 95,000
**SALES (est):** 91.1MM **Privately Held**
**WEB:** www.riddellsports.com
**SIC: 5091** 3949 Athletic goods; helmets, athletic
**HQ:** Brg Sports, Inc.
  9801 W Higgins Rd
  Rosemont IL 60018
  831 461-7500

**(G-19028)**
**RNW MACHINING CO INC**
7101 Barry St (60018-3403)
**PHONE**.................847 635-6560
Wayne Kelly, *President*
Ivan Mandaric, *Admin Sec*
**EMP:** 7
**SQ FT:** 7,200
**SALES:** 600K **Privately Held**
**SIC: 3599** Machine shop, jobbing & repair

**(G-19029)**
**SALZGITTER INTERNATIONAL**
9701 W Higgins Rd Ste 380 (60018-4716)
**PHONE**.................847 692-6312
**Fax:** 847 692-6313
Mike Salterelli, *Plant Mgr*
**EMP:** 2
**SALES (est):** 210.2K **Privately Held**
**SIC: 3315** Steel wire & related products

**(G-19030)**
**SAPA EXTRUSIONS INC**
6250 N River Rd Ste 5000 (60018-4214)
**PHONE**.................847 233-9105
Patrick Lawlor, *CEO*
Stephen Jackson, *Business Mgr*
Susanne Rothstein, *Vice Pres*
Pat Meyer, *Plant Mgr*
Srinivas Kolli, *Manager*
**EMP:** 50
**SALES (corp-wide):** 6.3B **Privately Held**
**SIC: 3354** Aluminum extruded products
**HQ:** Sapa Extrusions, Inc.
  6250 N River Rd Ste 5000
  Rosemont IL 60018

**(G-19031)**
**SAPA EXTRUSIONS INC (DH)**
6250 N River Rd Ste 5000 (60018-4214)
**PHONE**.................877 710-7272
**Fax:** 847 233-9105
Charlie Straface, *President*
Charles Straface, *President*
Jacques Podszun, *Managing Dir*
Belcastro Jacquelyne, *Principal*
Kavanaugh Robert, *Principal*
▲ **EMP:** 154
**SALES (est):** 1.2B
**SALES (corp-wide):** 6.3B **Privately Held**
**WEB:** www.sapagroup.com
**SIC: 3354** Aluminum extruded products
**HQ:** Sapa Profiler Ab
  Metallvagen
  Vetlanda 574 3
  383 941-00

**(G-19032)**
**SAPA EXTRUSIONS NORTH AMER LLC**
6250 N River Rd Ste 5000 (60018-4214)
**PHONE**.................877 922-7272
Andrea Bauer-Kuczma, *Principal*
**EMP:** 7
**SALES (est):** 591.1K **Privately Held**
**SIC: 3354** Aluminum extruded products

**(G-19033)**
**STANDARD CAR TRUCK COMPANY (DH)**
6400 Shafer Ct Ste 450 (60018-4948)
**PHONE**.................847 692-6050
**Fax:** 847 692-6299
Richard A Mathes, *President*
Donald Popernik, *Corp Secy*
Daniel Schroeder, *Vice Pres*
David Watson, *Vice Pres*
Dave Bode, *Opers Staff*
◆ **EMP:** 40
**SQ FT:** 12,000
**SALES (est):** 114.8MM
**SALES (corp-wide):** 2.9B **Publicly Held**
**SIC: 3743** 3321 Freight cars & equipment; ductile iron castings; gray iron castings

**(G-19034)**
**SUGAR FACTORY ROSEMONT LLC**
5445 Park Pl (60018-3732)
**PHONE**.................847 349-9161
Vincent Rizzo, *Mng Member*
Kevin Killerman, *Mng Member*
**EMP:** 10
**SALES (est):** 1.5MM **Privately Held**
**SIC: 2099** Sugar grinding; sugar, industrial maple

**(G-19035)**
**SUMMIT STINLESS STL HOLDG CORP**
6133 N River Rd Ste 700 (60018-5174)
**PHONE**.................732 297-9500
Frank Tairaku, *President*
Kenneth Elkin, *Admin Sec*
**EMP:** 11
**SALES (est):** 1.4MM
**SALES (corp-wide):** 35.1B **Privately Held**
**WEB:** www.sumitomocorp.co.jp
**SIC: 3312** Stainless steel
**PA:** Sumitomo Corporation
  1-8-11, Harumi
  Chuo-Ku TKY 104-0
  351 665-000

**(G-19036)**
**TERRELL MATERIALS CORPORATION**
10600 W Higgins Rd # 300 (60018-3716)
**PHONE**.................312 376-0105
**Fax:** 773 894-4623
Patrick C Terrell, *President*
Carla Kieffer, *Vice Pres*
Troufelda Lagrone, *QC Mgr*
Myesha Maloy, *Manager*
**EMP:** 20
**SALES (est):** 5MM **Privately Held**
**WEB:** www.terrellmaterials.com
**SIC: 3271** Concrete block & brick

**(G-19037)**
**TRANSPORTATION EQP ADVISORS**
6250 N River Rd Ste 5000 (60018-4214)
**PHONE**.................847 318-7575
Jack Thomas, *President*
Mary Gonzalez, *Asst Director*
**EMP:** 80
**SALES (est):** 4.2MM
**SALES (corp-wide):** 94.1B **Publicly Held**
**WEB:** www.firstunionrail.com
**SIC: 2721** Trade journals: publishing only, not printed on site
**HQ:** Wells Fargo Rail Corporation
  1 Ohare Center 625
  Rosemont IL 60018

**(G-19038)**
**TWH WATER TREATMENT INDUSTRIES**
5600 N River Rd Ste 800 (60018-5166)
**PHONE**.................847 457-1813
Larry Quick, *CEO*
**EMP:** 99
**SALES (est):** 2.9MM **Privately Held**
**SIC: 3589** Mfg Service Industry Machinery

**(G-19039)**
**US FOODS CULINARY EQP SUPS LLC (PA)**
9399 W Higgins Rd Ste 500 (60018-4992)
**PHONE**.................847 720-8000
James Pyle, *Principal*
**EMP:** 6 **EST:** 2000
**SALES (est):** 1.6MM **Privately Held**
**SIC: 5719** 2514 Kitchenware; metal kitchen & dining room furniture

**(G-19040)**
**VELSICOL CHEMICAL LLC**
10400 W Higgins Rd # 600 (60018-3705)
**PHONE**.................847 813-7888
**Fax:** 847 298-9015
Walter Bullock, *Vice Pres*
Robert Loving, *Vice Pres*
Paul Bakunos, *Purchasing*
Pat Schellinger, *CFO*
James D Groszek, *Controller*
▲ **EMP:** 68 **EST:** 1931
**SALES (est):** 17.7MM
**SALES (corp-wide):** 689.7MM **Privately Held**
**WEB:** www.velsicol.com
**SIC: 2819** Industrial inorganic chemicals
**PA:** Arsenal Capital Partners Lp
  100 Park Ave Fl 31
  New York NY 10017
  212 771-1717

**(G-19041)**
**WKI HOLDING COMPANY INC (PA)**
9525 Bryn Mawr Ave # 300 (60018-5249)
**PHONE**.................847 233-8600
Joseph T Mallot, *President*
Ralph Denisco, *President*
James A Sharman, *President*
Raymond J Kulla, *Vice Pres*
Jeff MEI, *Vice Pres*
◆ **EMP:** 65
**SALES (est):** 559.3MM **Privately Held**
**SIC: 3229** 3469 Pressed & blown glass; household cooking & kitchen utensils, metal

**(G-19042)**
**WORLD KITCHEN LLC (PA)**
9525 Bryn Mawr Ave (60018-5249)
**PHONE**.................847 233-8600
Carl Warschausky, *CEO*
Kris Malkoski, *President*
Branka Zivanovic, *District Mgr*
Luisa Giardina, *Business Mgr*
Jim Carney, *Counsel*
◆ **EMP:** 200
**SQ FT:** 22,661
**SALES (est):** 1.3B **Privately Held**
**WEB:** www.worldkitchen.com
**SIC: 3229** 3469 3365 3421 Pressed & blown glass; household cooking & kitchen utensils, metal; cooking/kitchen utensils, cast aluminum; cutlery; kitchenware

**(G-19043)**
**XEROX CORPORATION**
5500 Pearl St Ste 100 (60018-5303)
**PHONE**.................847 928-5500
Jan Evans, *Program Mgr*
**EMP:** 400
**SALES (corp-wide):** 10.7B **Publicly Held**
**WEB:** www.xerox.com
**SIC: 3861** Photographic equipment & supplies
**PA:** Xerox Corporation
  201 Merritt 7
  Norwalk CT 06851
  203 968-3000

**(G-19044)**
**ZOTOS INTERNATIONAL INC**
10600 W Higgins Rd # 415 (60018-3706)
**PHONE**.................847 390-0984

**Fax:** 847 390-6701
Bruce Selan, *Branch Mgr*
**EMP:** 107
**SALES (corp-wide):** 7.6B  **Privately Held**
**WEB:** www.zotos.com
**SIC: 2844** Hair preparations, including shampoos
**HQ:** Zotos International, Inc.
100 Tokeneke Rd
Darien CT 06820
203 655-8911

## Roseville
### Warren County

**(G-19045)**
**FUSION TECH INTEGRATED INC (PA)**
218 20th Ave  (61473-9144)
**PHONE**..............................309 774-4275
Kathryn Bentz, *President*
Bryan Ahee, *Vice Pres*
Brandon Bentz, *Vice Pres*
Dan Bentz, *Vice Pres*
Jon Williams, *Purch Agent*
**EMP:** 53
**SQ FT:** 25,000
**SALES (est):** 13.6MM  **Privately Held**
**WEB:** www.ftiinc.org
**SIC: 3914** Plated ware (all metals)

**(G-19046)**
**MICROWEB**
550 N Main St  (61473-9692)
**PHONE**..............................309 426-2385
Linda Carlberg, *President*
**EMP:** 6
**SALES (est):** 681.9K  **Privately Held**
**SIC: 2676** Toilet paper: made from purchased paper

## Rosiclare
### Hardin County

**(G-19047)**
**C-E MINERALS INC**
Ferrell Rd  (62982)
Rural Route 1 Box 47  (62982-9701)
**PHONE**..............................618 285-6558
Fred Bressel, *Opers-Prdtn-Mfg*
Janice Dutton, *Office Mgr*
**EMP:** 25
**SALES (corp-wide):** 1.2MM  **Privately Held**
**WEB:** www.ceminerals.com
**SIC: 3295** Minerals, ground or treated
**HQ:** C-E Minerals, Inc.
100 Mansell Ct E Ste 615
Roswell GA 30076
770 225-7900

**(G-19048)**
**HASTIE MINING & TRUCKING**
68 Bohn St  (62982)
**PHONE**..............................618 285-3600
Donnie Oxford, *Branch Mgr*
**EMP:** 9
**SALES (corp-wide):** 19.2MM  **Privately Held**
**SIC: 1481** Nonmetallic mineral services
**PA:** Hastie Mining & Trucking
Hwy 146
Cave In Rock IL 62919
618 289-4536

**(G-19049)**
**PRINCE MINERALS INC**
Ferrell St  (62982)
**PHONE**..............................618 285-6558
**Fax:** 618 285-6241
J Willson Ropp, *President*
Charles Belt, *Principal*
▼ **EMP:** 17
**SALES (est):** 2MM  **Privately Held**
**SIC: 3295** Minerals, ground or otherwise treated

## Rossville
### Vermilion County

**(G-19050)**
**NORTON MACHINE CO**
711 S Chicago St  (60963-9704)
P.O. Box 204  (60963-0204)
**PHONE**..............................217 748-6115
Mark Norton, *Owner*
▲ **EMP:** 4
**SQ FT:** 1,500
**SALES:** 160K  **Privately Held**
**SIC: 3599** 7692 Machine shop, jobbing & repair; welding repair

## Round Lake
### Lake County

**(G-19051)**
**AIR MITE DEVICES INC**
Also Called: Airmite Devices Inc Cylndrs
606 Long Lake Dr  (60073-2812)
**PHONE**..............................224 338-0071
**Fax:** 773 286-4703
Bert Stryker, *President*
Peter Striker, *Manager*
Rose Wrobel, *Admin Sec*
Gabby Jones, *Admin Asst*
**EMP:** 25 **EST:** 1945
**SQ FT:** 15,000
**SALES (est):** 4.4MM  **Privately Held**
**WEB:** www.airmite.com
**SIC: 3541** 5084 Home workshop machine tools, metalworking; industrial machinery & equipment

**(G-19052)**
**BAXALTA US INC**
25212 W Il Route 120  (60073-9610)
**PHONE**..............................847 948-2000
**Fax:** 847 473-6938
Sue Scott, *President*
Tahua Yang, *President*
Michael Gatling, *Vice Pres*
Cliff Holmes, *Vice Pres*
Tom Progar, *Vice Pres*
**EMP:** 92
**SALES (corp-wide):** 6.4B  **Privately Held**
**SIC: 2835** Blood derivative diagnostic agents
**HQ:** Baxalta Us Inc.
1 Baxter Pkwy
Deerfield IL 60015
224 948-2000

**(G-19053)**
**BAXTER HEALTHCARE CORPORATION**
32360 N Wilson Rd  (60073-9401)
**PHONE**..............................224 270-6300
Dee Miranda, *Engineer*
Gary Hnline, *Branch Mgr*
Ken Lynn, *Director*
**EMP:** 900
**SALES (corp-wide):** 10.1B  **Publicly Held**
**SIC: 3841** Surgical & medical instruments
**HQ:** Baxter Healthcare Corporation
1 Baxter Pkwy
Deerfield IL 60015
224 948-2000

**(G-19054)**
**BAXTER HEALTHCARE CORPORATION**
25212 W Illinois Rte 120  (60073)
**PHONE**..............................847 940-6599
David Drohan, *President*
Norbert G Riedel, *Vice Pres*
WEI Xie, *Research*
Keith Anderson, *Engineer*
Christopher Bishof, *Engineer*
**EMP:** 300
**SALES (corp-wide):** 10.1B  **Publicly Held**
**SIC: 2834** Pharmaceutical preparations
**HQ:** Baxter Healthcare Corporation
1 Baxter Pkwy
Deerfield IL 60015
224 948-2000

**(G-19055)**
**EXTREME WOODWORKING INC**
24650 W Luther Ave Apt B  (60073-1409)
**PHONE**..............................224 338-8179
**Fax:** 847 223-7050
Mike Spychal, *President*
**EMP:** 3
**SQ FT:** 2,000
**SALES:** 250K  **Privately Held**
**SIC: 2431** Woodwork, interior & ornamental

**(G-19056)**
**G M SIGN INC**
704 Sunset Dr  (60073-2826)
**PHONE**..............................847 546-0424
**Fax:** 847 546-0447
George Matiasek Jr, *President*
Beverly Kelly, *Corp Secy*
Richard Shaw, *Sales Mgr*
**EMP:** 51
**SQ FT:** 30,000
**SALES (est):** 5.5MM  **Privately Held**
**SIC: 3993** Signs & advertising specialties; neon signs

**(G-19057)**
**GENERAL MOTOR SIGN**
704 Sunset Dr  (60073-2826)
**PHONE**..............................847 546-0424
**EMP:** 3
**SALES (est):** 374.4K  **Privately Held**
**SIC: 3993** Signs & advertising specialties

**(G-19058)**
**GOODRICH SENSOR SYSTEMS**
34232 N Bluestem Rd  (60073-5245)
**PHONE**..............................847 546-5749
Tyler Reid, *Principal*
**EMP:** 2
**SALES (est):** 226.9K  **Privately Held**
**SIC: 3822** Built-in thermostats, filled system & bimetal types

**(G-19059)**
**GRIEVE CORPORATION**
500 Hart Rd  (60073-2898)
**PHONE**..............................847 546-8225
**Fax:** 847 546-9210
D V Grieve, *CEO*
Pat J Calabrese, *President*
Tom Hammonds, *Mfg Staff*
Betty Hunt, *Purchasing*
Judi Becker, *Controller*
▼ **EMP:** 90 **EST:** 1949
**SQ FT:** 110,000
**SALES (est):** 27.4MM  **Privately Held**
**WEB:** www.grievecorp.com
**SIC: 3567** 3821 3433 Industrial furnaces & ovens; ovens, laboratory; furnaces, laboratory; heating equipment, except electric

**(G-19060)**
**HAVOLINE XPRESS LUBE LLC (PA)**
810 Sunset Dr  (60073-2828)
**PHONE**..............................224 757-5628
Pena Anthony, *Mng Member*
**EMP:** 17
**SALES (est):** 9.1MM  **Privately Held**
**SIC: 2992** Lubricating oils & greases

**(G-19061)**
**LA LUC BAKERY INC**
246 N Cedar Lake Rd Frnt  (60073-3284)
**PHONE**..............................847 740-0303
Montes Veoca, *President*
**EMP:** 6
**SALES (est):** 497.8K  **Privately Held**
**SIC: 2051** Bakery: wholesale or wholesale/retail combined

**(G-19062)**
**LAKEVIEW EQUIPMENT CO**
1327 W Wash Blvf U 5f  (60073)
**PHONE**..............................847 548-7705
**Fax:** 847 223-5317
Irv Epstein, *President*
Tony Murawski, *Vice Pres*
**EMP:** 7
**SQ FT:** 2,500
**SALES:** 1.2MM  **Privately Held**
**SIC: 3841** Surgical & medical instruments

**(G-19063)**
**MVS MOLDING INC**
701 Long Lake Dr  (60073-2813)
**PHONE**..............................847 740-7700
**Fax:** 815 740-7104
Miroslav Smid, *President*
Marie Smid, *Corp Secy*
**EMP:** 9
**SQ FT:** 14,200
**SALES (est):** 980K  **Privately Held**
**SIC: 3089** Injection molding of plastics

**(G-19064)**
**NUSOURCE INC**
26575 W Cmmrc Dr 505  (60073)
P.O. Box 2131  (60073-0624)
**PHONE**..............................847 201-8934
**Fax:** 847 201-8937
John Spina, *President*
Gary Clauss, *General Mgr*
Rita Habel, *Vice Pres*
Sue Spina, *Treasurer*
Dan Habel, *Admin Sec*
**EMP:** 16
**SQ FT:** 5,000
**SALES:** 1.1MM  **Privately Held**
**SIC: 3679** 5063 Electronic circuits; motor controls, starters & relays: electric

**(G-19065)**
**ROUND LAKE PALLETS INC**
740 Sunset Dr  (60073-2826)
**PHONE**..............................847 637-6162
Juvenal Garcia, *President*
**EMP:** 3
**SALES (est):** 169.9K  **Privately Held**
**SIC: 2448** 7699 Pallets, wood; pallet repair

**(G-19066)**
**SAE CUSTOMS INC**
27764 Volo Village Rd F  (60073-9681)
**PHONE**..............................855 723-2878
Eric Schildkraut, *President*
**EMP:** 6
**SALES (est):** 856K  **Privately Held**
**SIC: 3711** Services

**(G-19067)**
**SIGN CENTRAL**
34039 N Hainesville Rd  (60073-9711)
**PHONE**..............................847 543-7600
Rita Buttacavola, *Owner*
**EMP:** 4 **EST:** 1998
**SQ FT:** 1,012
**SALES (est):** 320K  **Privately Held**
**WEB:** www.signcentral.com
**SIC: 3993** 7532 Signs & advertising specialties; truck painting & lettering

**(G-19068)**
**STARK PRINTING COMPANY**
208 W Olmsted Ln  (60073-5670)
**PHONE**..............................847 234-8430
**Fax:** 847 234-8437
Larry Stark, *President*
Marie Stark, *Vice Pres*
**EMP:** 8 **EST:** 1996
**SQ FT:** 3,800
**SALES (est):** 800K  **Privately Held**
**WEB:** www.starkprinting.com
**SIC: 2752** 7336 2791 2789 Commercial printing, offset; commercial art & graphic design; typesetting; bookbinding & related work

**(G-19069)**
**UNITED SKYS LLC**
702 Magna Dr  (60073-2817)
**PHONE**..............................847 546-7776
**Fax:** 847 546-7785
Charles McCartney, *President*
**EMP:** 15
**SQ FT:** 14,000
**SALES (est):** 4.7MM  **Privately Held**
**WEB:** www.unitedskys.com
**SIC: 1761** 3444 Skylight installation; skylights, sheet metal

**(G-19070)**
**WEST MACHINE PRODUCTS INC**
606 Long Lake Dr  (60073-2812)
**PHONE**..............................847 740-2404
**Fax:** 847 740-3480

Robert Szwaya, *President*
Amy Szwaya, *Vice Pres*
**EMP:** 20
**SQ FT:** 2,300
**SALES (est):** 3.1MM **Privately Held**
**SIC:** 3599 Machine shop, jobbing & repair

**(G-19071)**
**WHITSON BINDERY SERVICES**
25527 W Brooks Farm Rd (60073-5249)
**PHONE** ................................ 847 515-8371
**Fax:** 312 282-1441
Thomas Whitson, *President*
Arlene Whitson, *Corp Secy*
Brian Whitson, *Manager*
**EMP:** 10
**SQ FT:** 10,000
**SALES (est):** 640K **Privately Held**
**SIC:** 2789 Binding only: books, pamphlets, magazines, etc.; paper cutting

## Round Lake Beach
### Lake County

**(G-19072)**
**AXIOS MEDTECH INC**
2167 N Camden Ln (60073-4892)
**PHONE** ................................ 312 224-7856
Tamas Ban, *President*
**EMP:** 3
**SALES:** 100K **Privately Held**
**SIC:** 3845 Electromedical equipment

**(G-19073)**
**BLUE BROTHERS COATINGS**
2415 N Quaker Hollow Ln (60073-4854)
**PHONE** ................................ 847 265-5400
John Blue, *Owner*
**EMP:** 4
**SALES (est):** 284K **Privately Held**
**SIC:** 3479 Painting, coating & hot dipping

**(G-19074)**
**CLEARCHOICE MOBILITY INC**
839 E Rollins Rd (60073-2244)
**PHONE** ................................ 847 986-6313
Leo Zeltser, *Manager*
**EMP:** 4 **Privately Held**
**WEB:** www.clearchoice-wireless.com
**SIC:** 3663 Cellular radio telephone
**PA:** Clearchoice Mobility Inc.
1435 W Lake St
Addison IL 60101

**(G-19075)**
**DRG MOLDING & PAD PRINTING INC**
1631 Wood St D (60073-2250)
**PHONE** ................................ 847 223-3398
Dave Geborek, *President*
**EMP:** 5
**SQ FT:** 10,000
**SALES (est):** 698.5K **Privately Held**
**SIC:** 3089 Injection molding of plastics

**(G-19076)**
**IVES-WAY PRODUCTS INC**
2030 N Nicole Ln (60073-2288)
P.O. Box 70, Round Lake (60073-0070)
**PHONE** ................................ 847 740-0658
Glenn R Ours, *President*
Laura Ours, *Vice Pres*
**EMP:** 2
**SQ FT:** 2,000
**SALES (est):** 210K **Privately Held**
**SIC:** 3542 Metal container making machines: cans, etc.

**(G-19077)**
**M & P TALKING TEES INC**
960 W Rollins Rd (60073-1229)
**PHONE** ................................ 262 495-4000
**Fax:** 847 546-8877
Linda Parker, *President*
Carla Mc Graw, *Vice Pres*
Greg Parker, *Vice Pres*
Mark Mc Graw, *Treasurer*
**EMP:** 12
**SQ FT:** 6,800
**SALES (est):** 1MM **Privately Held**
**SIC:** 5699 2261 T-shirts, custom printed; uniforms; finishing plants, cotton

**(G-19078)**
**PC CONCEPTS**
2388 N Fox Chase Dr (60073-4187)
**PHONE** ................................ 847 223-6490
**Fax:** 847 886-2735
Rich Neumuller, *President*
Susan Neumuller, *Corp Secy*
**EMP:** 3
**SALES (est):** 50K **Privately Held**
**WEB:** www.pcconcepts-inc.com
**SIC:** 7372 Business oriented computer software

**(G-19079)**
**RADIO CONTROLLED MODELS INC**
Also Called: Ram R-C Models
229 E Rollins Rd (60073-1329)
**PHONE** ................................ 847 740-8726
Ralph P Warner, *President*
Elizabeth Warner, *Treasurer*
**EMP:** 8
**SQ FT:** 5,000
**SALES (est):** 1MM **Privately Held**
**WEB:** www.ramrcandramtrack.com
**SIC:** 3825 Oscillators, audio & radio frequency (instrument types); radio frequency measuring equipment

**(G-19080)**
**VELASQUEZ & SONS MUFFLER SHOP**
507 W Rollins Rd (60073-1220)
**PHONE** ................................ 847 740-6990
Juan Velasquez, *Principal*
**EMP:** 2
**SALES (est):** 216.5K **Privately Held**
**WEB:** www.velasquez.com
**SIC:** 7533 3714 5015 Auto exhaust system repair shops; mufflers (exhaust), motor vehicle; automotive parts & supplies, used

## Round Lake Heights
### Lake County

**(G-19081)**
**M MARTINEZ INC**
828 Warrior St (60073-1145)
**PHONE** ................................ 847 740-6364
Munuel Martinez, *President*
**EMP:** 2
**SALES (est):** 208.7K **Privately Held**
**SIC:** 3524 Grass catchers, lawn mower

**(G-19082)**
**NORTH SHORE PAVING INC**
24752 W Orchard Pl (60073-1067)
**PHONE** ................................ 847 201-1710
**EMP:** 4
**SALES (est):** 119.3K **Privately Held**
**SIC:** 3271 Brick, concrete

## Round Lake Park
### Lake County

**(G-19083)**
**B RADTKE AND SONS INC**
101 W Main St Ste 2 (60073-3510)
**PHONE** ................................ 847 546-3999
**Fax:** 847 546-4008
John A Radtke, *President*
Hope Dreyer, *Manager*
**EMP:** 6
**SQ FT:** 7,500
**SALES (est):** 835K **Privately Held**
**SIC:** 3544 3469 3451 3599 Special dies & tools; metal stampings; screw machine products; machine shop, jobbing & repair

## Roxana
### Madison County

**(G-19084)**
**GEMINI INDUSTRIES INC**
1 Gemini Industrial Dr (62084-2747)
**PHONE** ................................ 618 251-3352
**Fax:** 618 251-4740
Pam Schaeffer, *Marketing Staff*
Christopher Schaeffer, *Admin Sec*
▲ **EMP:** 75
**SQ FT:** 150,000
**SALES (est):** 10.1MM **Privately Held**
**SIC:** 3993 Advertising novelties

**(G-19085)**
**RS USED OIL SERVICES INC**
4559 Wagon Wheel Rd (62084-2715)
**PHONE** ................................ 618 781-1717
**EMP:** 4
**SALES (corp-wide):** 2.7B **Publicly Held**
**SIC:** 2992 Lubricating oils & greases
**HQ:** Rs Used Oil Services, Inc.
2932 N Ohio St
Wichita KS 67219
866 778-7336

**(G-19086)**
**SPECIALTY PRINTING MIDWEST**
1 Gemini Industrial Dr (62084-2747)
**PHONE** ................................ 618 799-8472
**EMP:** 2
**SALES (est):** 229.4K **Privately Held**
**SIC:** 2752 Commercial printing, lithographic

**(G-19087)**
**W R B REFINERY LLC**
900 S Central Ave (62084-1337)
**PHONE** ................................ 618 255-2345
Jerry Knoyle, *Plant Mgr*
▲ **EMP:** 38
**SALES (est):** 16.7MM **Privately Held**
**SIC:** 2911 Petroleum refining

## Ruma
### Randolph County

**(G-19088)**
**ROGERS REDI-MIX INC (PA)**
55 E Mill St (62278-2715)
**PHONE** ................................ 618 282-3844
**Fax:** 618 282-3847
Roger Koester, *President*
Barbara A Koester, *Corp Secy*
**EMP:** 18 **EST:** 1965
**SALES (est):** 2.5MM **Privately Held**
**SIC:** 3273 1442 Ready-mixed concrete; construction sand & gravel

**(G-19089)**
**SOUTHERN ILLINOIS CRANKSHAFTS**
225 Kaskaskia St (62278)
**PHONE** ................................ 618 282-4100
Michael Schaefer, *President*
Jeremy Schaefer, *Prgrmr*
**EMP:** 10 **EST:** 2009
**SALES (est):** 1.1MM **Privately Held**
**SIC:** 3599 Crankshafts & camshafts, machining

## Rushville
### Schuyler County

**(G-19090)**
**B T TECHNOLOGY INC**
Also Called: BT Tech
320 N Railroad St (62681-1284)
P.O. Box 49 (62681-0049)
**PHONE** ................................ 217 322-3768
**Fax:** 217 322-3767
Brian D Tomlinson, *President*
Mackenzie E Malcomson, *Vice Pres*
Michael Tomlinson, *Opers Mgr*
**EMP:** 3
**SQ FT:** 500
**SALES (est):** 497.3K **Privately Held**
**WEB:** www.bttechnology.com
**SIC:** 3825 3821 Test equipment for electronic & electric measurement; laboratory apparatus & furniture

**(G-19091)**
**HALL FABRICATION INC**
429 W Clinton St (62681-1359)
**PHONE** ................................ 217 322-2212
Jamie Lane, *Manager*
**EMP:** 2
**SALES (est):** 225K **Privately Held**
**SIC:** 3399 Primary metal products

**(G-19092)**
**HOUSER MEATS**
14320 Scotts Mill Rd (62681-4246)
Rural Route Box 180b (62681-9656)
**PHONE** ................................ 217 322-4994
Doug Houser, *Partner*
Terri Houser, *General Ptnr*
**EMP:** 7
**SQ FT:** 1,000
**SALES:** 350K **Privately Held**
**WEB:** www.housermeats.com
**SIC:** 0751 2013 Slaughtering: custom livestock services; sausages & other prepared meats

**(G-19093)**
**INNOVATIVE DESIGN AND RES INC**
Also Called: Idrc
338 W Lafayette St (62681-1324)
**PHONE** ................................ 217 322-3907
Daniel J Meyer, *President*
**EMP:** 3
**SALES:** 100K **Privately Held**
**SIC:** 3724 Research & development on aircraft engines & parts

**(G-19094)**
**PERRYCO INC**
Also Called: Rushville Times
110 E Lafayette St (62681-1412)
P.O. Box 226 (62681-0226)
**PHONE** ................................ 217 322-3321
**Fax:** 217 322-2138
Alan Icenogle, *General Mgr*
Teresa Haines, *Adv Mgr*
**EMP:** 9
**SALES (corp-wide):** 3MM **Privately Held**
**WEB:** www.rushvilletimes.com
**SIC:** 2711 Job printing & newspaper publishing combined
**PA:** Perryco Inc
6920 Webster St
Downers Grove IL 60516
303 652-8282

**(G-19095)**
**SOUTH SIDE HM KIT EMPORIUM INC**
110 W Lafayette St (62681-1415)
**PHONE** ................................ 217 322-3708
Steve Maxwell, *President*
Elizabeth Maxwell, *Treasurer*
Carol Burke, *Admin Sec*
**EMP:** 3
**SALES (est):** 286.7K **Privately Held**
**SIC:** 2511 Kitchen & dining room furniture

**(G-19096)**
**STITCHABLES EMBROIDERY**
Also Called: J Gayleen Hammond
416 Silverleaf St (62681-1231)
P.O. Box 406 (62681-0406)
**PHONE** ................................ 217 322-3000
**Fax:** 217 322-3000
Janet Gayleen Hammond, *Partner*
Janet Gayleenhammond, *Partner*
Julie Zorn, *Partner*
**EMP:** 3
**SALES:** 81K **Privately Held**
**SIC:** 2395 Emblems, embroidered

## Russell
### Lake County

**(G-19097)**
**I94 RV LLC** ✪
16125 Russel Rd (60075)
P.O. Box 332 (60075-0332)
**PHONE** ................................ 847 395-9500
Ed Collier, *Principal*
**EMP:** 17 **EST:** 2016
**SALES (est):** 94.6K **Privately Held**
**SIC:** 3792 7032 Mfg Travel Trailers/Campers Sport/Recreation Camp

# S Chicago Hts
## Cook County

**(G-19098)**
**ACME AUTO ELECTRIC CO**
2626 Chicago Rd (60411-4760)
PHONE.................................708 754-5420
Fax: 708 756-2359
Kenneth Eatinger, *President*
Garrett Eatinger, *Plant Mgr*
**EMP:** 9
**SQ FT:** 3,600
**SALES:** 500K **Privately Held**
**WEB:** www.acmeautoelectric.com
**SIC:** 3714 7539 Motor vehicle engines & parts; automotive repair shops

**(G-19099)**
**ALLOYS TECH INC**
3305 Butler St (60411-5506)
PHONE.................................708 248-5041
Surendra Daga, *Principal*
**EMP:** 3
**SALES (est):** 208.8K **Privately Held**
**SIC:** 3325 Alloy steel castings, except investment

**(G-19100)**
**ARROW PIN AND PRODUCTS INC**
51 E 34th St (60411-5501)
PHONE.................................708 755-7575
Fax: 708 755-7975
Charles R Prucha Jr, *President*
Laura J Prucha, *Treasurer*
Kim Bridges, *Administration*
**EMP:** 11
**SQ FT:** 10,000
**SALES (est):** 2.3MM **Privately Held**
**SIC:** 3452 Pins

**(G-19101)**
**COATING SPECIALTY INC**
3311 Holeman Ave Ste 7 (60411-5559)
PHONE.................................708 754-3311
Robert Buckley, *President*
**EMP:** 9
**SQ FT:** 5,500
**SALES (est):** 600K **Privately Held**
**SIC:** 3471 5531 Cleaning, polishing & finishing; automotive & home supply stores

**(G-19102)**
**COSMOS MANUFACTURING INC**
111 E 34th St (60411-5502)
PHONE.................................708 756-1400
Fax: 708 756-1404
John Michelon, *President*
Gabriella Michelon, *Corp Secy*
Pam Vasquez, *Credit Mgr*
Jim Knetl, *Manager*
Jerry Scherwin, *Manager*
▲ **EMP:** 135
**SQ FT:** 60,000
**SALES (est):** 40.7MM **Privately Held**
**SIC:** 3714 Motor vehicle parts & accessories

**(G-19103)**
**DO-RITE DIE & ENGINEERING CO**
3344 Butler St (60411-5507)
PHONE.................................708 754-4355
Fax: 708 754-8695
Alan R Szymanski, *President*
Edward B Szymanski, *Vice Pres*
Paul Symanski, *Engineer*
Cynthia S Szymanski, *Admin Sec*
**EMP:** 12
**SQ FT:** 10,000
**SALES:** 2MM **Privately Held**
**SIC:** 3544 Forms (molds), for foundry & plastics working machinery; dies & die holders for metal cutting, forming, die casting

**(G-19104)**
**HENNESSY SHEET METAL**
3256 Butler St (60411-5505)
PHONE.................................708 754-6342
Pat Hennessey, *President*
**EMP:** 7
**SQ FT:** 6,000
**SALES (est):** 680K **Privately Held**
**SIC:** 3444 Sheet metalwork

**(G-19105)**
**INDUSTRIAL PARK MACHINE & TOOL**
3326 Butler St (60411-5507)
PHONE.................................708 754-7080
Fax: 708 754-7083
Sergio Zorzi, *President*
Paul Dressler, *Vice Pres*
Todd Schutte, *Vice Pres*
**EMP:** 10
**SQ FT:** 12,000
**SALES (est):** 500K **Privately Held**
**WEB:** www.fishingbuckets.com
**SIC:** 3544 3469 Special dies & tools; stamping metal for the trade

**(G-19106)**
**MASON WELDING INC**
3321 Holeman Ave (60411-5517)
PHONE.................................708 755-0621
Fax: 708 755-8956
Bret Mason, *President*
Kathy Mason, *Admin Sec*
**EMP:** 3
**SALES (est):** 452.9K **Privately Held**
**SIC:** 7692 Welding repair

**(G-19107)**
**MAX MILLER**
Also Called: Miller's Ready Mix
3000 State St (60411-4844)
PHONE.................................708 758-7760
Fax: 708 758-7762
Max Miller, *Owner*
**EMP:** 12 **EST:** 1974
**SQ FT:** 3,500
**SALES:** 2MM **Privately Held**
**SIC:** 3273 Ready-mixed concrete

**(G-19108)**
**METAL EDGE INC**
47 E 34th St (60411-5501)
PHONE.................................708 756-4696
Thomas Brueck, *President*
**EMP:** 17
**SALES (est):** 4.7MM **Privately Held**
**SIC:** 3446 Architectural metalwork

**(G-19109)**
**MID STATES CORPORATION**
3245 Holeman Ave (60411-5599)
PHONE.................................708 754-1760
Fax: 708 754-6985
Donald Bartolini, *President*
Robert Bartolini, *Vice Pres*
Barb Cundari, *Human Resources*
Donna Burk, *Executive*
Peter Bartolini, *Admin Sec*
**EMP:** 30 **EST:** 1978
**SQ FT:** 18,000
**SALES (est):** 7.6MM **Privately Held**
**WEB:** www.midstatescorp.com
**SIC:** 3535 Conveyors & conveying equipment

**(G-19110)**
**PHOENIX FABRICATION & SUP INC**
3215 Butler St (60411-5504)
PHONE.................................708 754-5901
Steve Anderson, *President*
Carolyn Walden, *Admin Sec*
**EMP:** 8
**SQ FT:** 55,000
**SALES (est):** 1.8MM **Privately Held**
**SIC:** 3441 Fabricated structural metal

**(G-19111)**
**PRODUCTION FABG & STAMPING INC**
3311 Butler St (60411-5588)
PHONE.................................708 755-5468
Fax: 708 755-4603
Paul Gilliam, *President*
**EMP:** 15 **EST:** 1971
**SQ FT:** 26,000
**SALES (est):** 3.6MM **Privately Held**
**SIC:** 3469 3444 3544 7692 Stamping metal for the trade; sheet metalwork; special dies & tools; welding repair; metal cutting services

**(G-19112)**
**R W G MANUFACTURING INC**
3309 Holeman Ave Ste 7 (60411-5558)
PHONE.................................708 755-8035
Ron Giannantonia, *President*
**EMP:** 5
**SQ FT:** 5,000
**SALES (est):** 250K **Privately Held**
**SIC:** 3842 2431 Technical aids for the handicapped; millwork

**(G-19113)**
**TANKO BROS SCREW MCH PDTS CORP**
3361 Holeman Ave (60411-5517)
PHONE.................................708 755-8823
Kenneth Tanko, *President*
Linda A Tanko, *Corp Secy*
**EMP:** 15 **EST:** 2001
**SQ FT:** 7,000
**SALES (est):** 1.2MM **Privately Held**
**SIC:** 3599 Machine shop, jobbing & repair

**(G-19114)**
**UNIVERSIAL CAT LLC**
111 E 34th St (60411-5502)
PHONE.................................708 753-8070
John Michelon, *President*
Sandra Casey, *Manager*
◆ **EMP:** 49
**SALES (est):** 4.1MM **Privately Held**
**WEB:** www.cosmosmfg.com
**SIC:** 2819 Catalysts, chemical

**(G-19115)**
**WAXSTAR INC**
3224 Butler St (60411-5505)
PHONE.................................708 755-3530
Lawrence J Czaszwicz Jr, *President*
Noreen Czaszwicz, *Admin Sec*
**EMP:** 1 **EST:** 1970
**SQ FT:** 49,000
**SALES (est):** 270.6K **Privately Held**
**WEB:** www.waxstar.com
**SIC:** 2673 2671 2674 Bags: plastic, laminated & coated; waxed paper: made from purchased material; bags: uncoated paper & multiwall

**(G-19116)**
**WOODMAC INDUSTRIES INC**
3233 Holeman Ave (60411-5515)
PHONE.................................708 755-3545
Fax: 708 755-3563
James T McLaughlin, *President*
Guy Giasson, *Opers-Prdtn-Mfg*
**EMP:** 16
**SQ FT:** 26,000
**SALES (est):** 1.8MM **Privately Held**
**WEB:** www.woodmacind.com
**SIC:** 2499 2426 Picture frame molding, finished; stepladders, wood; hardwood dimension & flooring mills

# Sadorus
## Champaign County

**(G-19117)**
**DEEDRICK MACHINE INC**
105 E Market St (61872-7505)
PHONE.................................217 598-2366
Fax: 217 598-2503
Donald Deedrick, *President*
John Deedrick, *Vice Pres*
Robin Scanull-Sonner, *Vice Pres*
Robin Fonner, *Marketing Staff*
**EMP:** 20
**SQ FT:** 20,000
**SALES (est):** 3.5MM **Privately Held**
**WEB:** www.deedrick.com
**SIC:** 3599 Machine shop, jobbing & repair

# Saint Anne
## Kankakee County

**(G-19118)**
**BERENS INC**
1269 E 5000s Rd (60964-4231)
PHONE.................................815 935-3237
Mark A Berens, *President*
**EMP:** 7 **EST:** 1988
**SALES (est):** 591.2K **Privately Held**
**WEB:** www.berens.net
**SIC:** 3315 Steel wire & related products

**(G-19119)**
**DOUGLAS NET COMPANY**
Also Called: Ericson Textile Co
200 Eastern Illinois Rd (60964-7323)
P.O. Box 320 (60964-0320)
PHONE.................................815 427-6350
Fax: 815 427-6355
Kelly Douglas, *President*
Karen J Douglas, *Admin Sec*
**EMP:** 10
**SQ FT:** 5,000
**SALES (est):** 550K **Privately Held**
**SIC:** 2298 Fishing lines, nets, seines: made in cordage or twine mills

**(G-19120)**
**EASTERN ILLINOIS CLAY COMPANY (PA)**
Also Called: Dom Plastic Div
460 S Elm Ave (60964-7245)
P.O. Box 657 (60964-0657)
PHONE.................................815 427-8144
Ronald Meier, *President*
Dennis Meier, *Corp Secy*
Duane Meier, *Vice Pres*
Chad Nicholson, *Sales Mgr*
**EMP:** 10
**SQ FT:** 19,500
**SALES:** 3.6MM **Privately Held**
**WEB:** www.domcoplastics.com
**SIC:** 3084 Plastics pipe

**(G-19121)**
**EASTERN ILLINOIS CLAY COMPANY**
Also Called: Dom Plastics
498 S Oak St (60964)
P.O. Box 657 (60964-0657)
PHONE.................................815 427-8106
Fax: 815 427-8150
Duane Meier, *Manager*
**EMP:** 15
**SALES (corp-wide):** 3.6MM **Privately Held**
**WEB:** www.domcoplastics.com
**SIC:** 3084 Plastics pipe
**PA:** Eastern Illinois Clay Company Inc
460 S Elm Ave
Saint Anne IL 60964
815 427-8144

**(G-19122)**
**F & L DRAPERY INC**
6279 Warren St (60964-5306)
PHONE.................................815 932-8997
Lynn Wagner, *President*
**EMP:** 3
**SALES (est):** 213K **Privately Held**
**SIC:** 2211 5714 Draperies & drapery fabrics, cotton; drapery & upholstery stores

**(G-19123)**
**MCGOWEN RIFLE BARRELS**
Also Called: Mc Gowen Rifle Barrels
5961 Spruce Ln (60964-5332)
PHONE.................................815 937-9816
Fax: 815 937-4024
Harry McGowen, *Owner*
**EMP:** 6 **EST:** 1959
**SALES:** 1MM **Privately Held**
**SIC:** 3484 7699 Rifles or rifle parts, 30 mm. & below; gunsmith shop

**(G-19124)**
**MIDWEST MACHINE TOOL INC**
485 S Oak St (60964-7292)
P.O. Box 457 (60964-0457)
PHONE.................................815 427-8665
Fax: 815 427-6425
Myron D Wendt, *President*
Alyssa Wendt, *Corp Secy*
**EMP:** 5
**SALES (est):** 631.8K **Privately Held**
**SIC:** 3544 3545 3532 3599 Special dies & tools; vises, machine (machine tool accessories); drills & drilling equipment, mining (except oil & gas); machine shop, jobbing & repair; farm machinery repair; industrial machinery & equipment repair; drill presses

# GEOGRAPHIC SECTION

## Saint Charles - Kane County (G-19151)

**(G-19125)**
**RDA INC**
400 N 3rd Ave (60964-7326)
P.O. Box 229 (60964-0229)
PHONE.................................815 427-8444
Fax: 815 427-8440
Raymond Hubert, *President*
Regina Hubert, *Admin Sec*
**EMP:** 18
**SALES (est):** 2.5MM **Privately Held**
**SIC: 2899** Patching plaster, household

**(G-19126)**
**THERMOPOL INC**
150 W Grant St (60964-7278)
P.O. Box 105 (60964-0105)
PHONE.................................815 422-0400
Shlomo Beitner, *President*
Alon Beitner, *Vice Pres*
Irene Beitner, *Admin Sec*
**EMP:** 4
**SQ FT:** 4,300
**SALES (est):** 2MM **Privately Held**
**WEB:** www.thermopol.com
**SIC: 3841 3845** Medical instruments & equipment, blood & bone work; electromedical equipment

**(G-19127)**
**TRU-CUT MACHINE INCORPORATED**
480 S Oak St (60964-5357)
P.O. Box 497 (60964-0497)
PHONE.................................815 422-5047
Jim Butler, *President*
**EMP:** 5
**SQ FT:** 9,500
**SALES (est):** 400K **Privately Held**
**SIC: 3599** Machine shop, jobbing & repair

## Saint Augustine
### Knox County

**(G-19128)**
**VALLEY QUARRY**
772 175th St (61474-9744)
PHONE.................................309 462-3003
Harry Flessner, *Superintendent*
**EMP:** 7
**SALES (est):** 334.9K **Privately Held**
**SIC: 1422** Cement rock, crushed & broken-quarrying

## Saint Charles
### Kane County

**(G-19129)**
**8 ELECTRONIC CIGARETTE INC**
Also Called: 8 Electronic Cigarettes
1830 Wallace Ave Ste 201 (60174-3417)
PHONE.................................630 708-6803
Michael Goduco, *CEO*
**EMP:** 4
**SALES (est):** 307.4K **Privately Held**
**SIC: 2111 7389 5194** Cigarettes; ; tobacco & tobacco products

**(G-19130)**
**A & C MOLD COMPANY INC**
Also Called: AC Mold
3870 Swenson Ave (60174-3438)
PHONE.................................630 587-0177
Fax: 630 587-0173
Andrew Mendala, *President*
Christine Mendala, *Admin Sec*
▲ **EMP:** 45
**SQ FT:** 20,000
**SALES (est):** 9.1MM **Privately Held**
**WEB:** www.acmold.com
**SIC: 3544** Industrial molds

**(G-19131)**
**AC PRECISION TOOL INC**
6n553 Crestwood Dr (60175-8423)
PHONE.................................630 797-5161
Fax: 630 761-0014
Kenneth Chmelar, *President*
Shirley Chmelar, *Corp Secy*
**EMP:** 5
**SQ FT:** 10,000
**SALES:** 500K **Privately Held**
**SIC: 3541 3544** Machine tool replacement & repair parts, metal cutting types; special dies & tools

**(G-19132)**
**AJR ENTERPRISES INC**
1200 Rukel Way (60174-3427)
PHONE.................................630 377-8886
Fax: 630 377-8887
Jacob Rukel, *CEO*
Angelo Rukel, *President*
John Rukel, *COO*
Diana Butler, *Human Res Mgr*
Eric Kilinski, *Sales Associate*
**EMP:** 250 **EST:** 1997
**SQ FT:** 450,000
**SALES (est):** 27.9MM **Privately Held**
**SIC: 2393** Textile bags

**(G-19133)**
**ALLCARE INC (PA)**
2580 Foxfield Rd Ste 101 (60174-1403)
PHONE.................................630 830-7486
Jj Zhang, *Admin Sec*
**EMP:** 6
**SALES (est):** 950.8K **Privately Held**
**WEB:** www.allcaredirect.com
**SIC: 3841** Surgical & medical instruments

**(G-19134)**
**AMERICAN CHURCH SUPPLY**
Also Called: C Rockelmann Co
41w699 Foxtail Cir (60175-8466)
PHONE.................................847 464-4140
Steve Zanis, *Owner*
Beth Zanis, *Co-Owner*
Deth Zanis, *Co-Owner*
▲ **EMP:** 3
**SALES:** 200K **Privately Held**
**SIC: 2389 5049** Clergymen's vestments; religious supplies

**(G-19135)**
**AMERICAN POWDER COATINGS INC**
420 38th Ave (60174-5426)
PHONE.................................630 762-0100
Fax: 630 762-0111
Brett Suvagia, *Principal*
Dave Suvagia, *Vice Pres*
Joe Alisia, *Manager*
▲ **EMP:** 50
**SQ FT:** 40,000
**SALES (est):** 13.4MM **Privately Held**
**WEB:** www.americanpowder.com
**SIC: 2851** Enamels

**(G-19136)**
**AMERICAN TRISTAR INC (DH)**
525 Dunham Rd (60174-1458)
PHONE.................................920 872-2181
Gordon Gruszka, *President*
Ernest Shepard, *Vice Pres*
Chuck Woods, *Exec Dir*
Gary Gross, *Director*
Dave Jensen, *Director*
**EMP:** 40
**SALES (est):** 355.1MM
**SALES (corp-wide):** 60.6B **Privately Held**
**WEB:** www.exel.com/exel/pp_home.jsp
**SIC: 2099** Food preparations
**HQ:** Exel Inc.
570 Polaris Pkwy
Westerville OH 43082
614 865-8500

**(G-19137)**
**ARCTURUS PERFORMANCE PDTS LLC**
3955 Commerce Dr (60174-5321)
P.O. Box 268 (60174-0268)
PHONE.................................630 204-0211
John R Palmer, *Principal*
Hugh V Palmer, *Mng Member*
**EMP:** 4
**SALES (est):** 286.7K **Privately Held**
**SIC: 2819** Catalysts, chemical

**(G-19138)**
**ARK TECHNOLOGIES INC (PA)**
Also Called: A R K
3655 Ohio Ave (60174-5445)
PHONE.................................630 377-8855
Fax: 630 377-0660
Al Kabeshita, *CEO*
Minoru Kabeshita, *President*
Yutaka Kabeshita, *Vice Pres*
Jorge Reta, *Opers Spvr*
Eric Takeda, *Purch Mgr*
▲ **EMP:** 105
**SALES (est):** 18MM **Privately Held**
**WEB:** www.arktechno.com
**SIC: 3495 3694 3469** Instrument springs, precision; engine electrical equipment; metal stampings

**(G-19139)**
**ASSURANCE CLG RESTORATION LLC**
3740 Stern Ave (60174-5404)
PHONE.................................630 444-3600
Fax: 630 444-3530
Mary Bruno, *Marketing Staff*
Shawn Campbell, *Marketing Staff*
Thomas Kollar, *Mng Member*
Lee Godinez,
**EMP:** 18
**SQ FT:** 24,000
**SALES:** 1.5MM **Privately Held**
**WEB:** www.assurancecleaning.com
**SIC: 3544** Industrial molds

**(G-19140)**
**AVID OF ILLINOIS INC**
Also Called: AlphaGraphics
2740 E Main St (60174-2445)
PHONE.................................847 698-2775
Fax: 630 513-7761
Mari Connelly, *President*
**EMP:** 10
**SQ FT:** 4,300
**SALES:** 1.5MM **Privately Held**
**SIC: 2752 2791 2789** Commercial printing, lithographic; typesetting; bookbinding & related work

**(G-19141)**
**AWARD CONCEPTS INC**
Also Called: Award Concepts Mfg Co
110 S 11th Ave (60174-2226)
P.O. Box 4305 (60174-9075)
PHONE.................................630 513-7801
Fax: 630 513-7809
Gordon L Campbell, *President*
Joanie Asendorf, *President*
Robert Lafrenier, *Vice Pres*
Donald H Martens, *Vice Pres*
Rick Greinke, *Plant Mgr*
▲ **EMP:** 50
**SQ FT:** 20,000
**SALES (est):** 9.3MM **Privately Held**
**WEB:** www.awardconceptsinc.com
**SIC: 3911 5199** Jewelry, precious metal; gifts & novelties

**(G-19142)**
**BESTAR TECHNOLOGIES INC**
4n53 Old Lafox Rd B (60175-7845)
PHONE.................................520 439-9204
Paul Gillespie, *President*
Dirk W Deyoung, *President*
Helene De Young, *Manager*
▲ **EMP:** 7
**SQ FT:** 4,800
**SALES:** 3MM **Privately Held**
**SIC: 3679** Electronic circuits

**(G-19143)**
**BISON GEAR & ENGINEERING CORP (PA)**
3850 Ohio Ave (60174-5462)
PHONE.................................630 377-0153
Fax: 630 377-6777
Martin Swarbrick, *President*
Ronald D Bullock, *Chairman*
Doug Quinn, *Business Mgr*
George E Thomas, *Exec VP*
Andrew Burnette, *Senior VP*
▲ **EMP:** 175
**SQ FT:** 114,200
**SALES (est):** 50.1MM **Privately Held**
**WEB:** www.bisongear.com
**SIC: 3621 3714 4789** Motors & generators; air conditioner parts, motor vehicle; cargo loading & unloading services

**(G-19144)**
**BLACK START LABS INC**
1500 Foundry St Ste 8 (60174-1555)
P.O. Box 1308 (60174-7308)
PHONE.................................630 444-1800
**EMP:** 3
**SALES (est):** 184.4K **Privately Held**
**SIC: 2834** Pills, pharmaceutical

**(G-19145)**
**BRADLEY ADHSIVE APPLCTIONS INC (PA)**
Also Called: Bradley Group, The
410 38th Ave (60174-5426)
PHONE.................................630 443-8424
Fax: 630 443-8421
Bradley Stefan, *President*
Bruce Stefan, *Treasurer*
Melissa Gonzalez, *Manager*
**EMP:** 120
**SQ FT:** 25,000
**SALES (est):** 12.7MM **Privately Held**
**SIC: 2891** Adhesives & sealants

**(G-19146)**
**BUTTON MAN PRINTING INC**
7 E Main St (60174-1925)
PHONE.................................630 549-0438
Jacob Martens, *President*
Mark Burger, *Admin Sec*
**EMP:** 3 **EST:** 2013
**SALES (est):** 92.3K **Privately Held**
**SIC: 2752** Commercial printing, lithographic

**(G-19147)**
**C M C INDUSTRIES INC**
Also Called: Cutco Abrasive Co
2525 Production Dr (60174-3349)
PHONE.................................630 377-0530
William C Mc Cormick, *President*
Glenn Yerges, *Manager*
Suzanne Mc Cormick, *Admin Sec*
**EMP:** 12
**SQ FT:** 10,000
**SALES (est):** 935.6K **Privately Held**
**SIC: 3291** Grindstones, artificial

**(G-19148)**
**C-STORM ELECTRONIC LLC**
441 Horizon Dr W (60175-6551)
PHONE.................................630 406-1353
Jean Cole,
Brandon Cole,
**EMP:** 10
**SALES:** 637K **Privately Held**
**SIC: 3625** Timing devices, electronic

**(G-19149)**
**CAIN TUBULAR PRODUCTS INC**
310 Kirk Rd (60174-3430)
PHONE.................................630 584-5330
Fax: 630 584-0201
John Cain, *President*
Michael Cain, *Treasurer*
Robert Cain, *Admin Sec*
Kimberly Bauer, *Administration*
Kara Armstrong, *Assistant*
**EMP:** 9 **EST:** 1966
**SQ FT:** 16,000
**SALES (est):** 2MM **Privately Held**
**WEB:** www.caintubular.com
**SIC: 3498** Tube fabricating (contract bending & shaping)

**(G-19150)**
**CARBCO MANUFACTURING INC**
2525 Production Dr (60174-3349)
P.O. Box 135, Geneva (60134-0135)
PHONE.................................630 377-1410
Fax: 630 377-1411
William C Mc Cormick, *President*
**EMP:** 19
**SALES (est):** 2.9MM **Privately Held**
**WEB:** www.carbco.com
**SIC: 3291 3545** Tungsten carbide abrasive; machine tool accessories

**(G-19151)**
**CARTONCRAFT INC**
2900 Dukane Dr Ste 2 (60174-3348)
PHONE.................................630 377-1230
Fax: 630 377-1240
Felipe A Reyes, *President*
Lee A Haggas, *CFO*
Joann Hansen, *Sales Executive*
Jen Whiteley, *Marketing Staff*
Barb Aleman, *Manager*
▼ **EMP:** 80
**SQ FT:** 125,000

# Saint Charles - Kane County (G-19152)   GEOGRAPHIC SECTION

SALES (est): 31.8MM **Privately Held**
WEB: www.cartoncraftinc.com
SIC: **2657** Folding paperboard boxes

**(G-19152)**
**CHICAGO MOLD ENGRG CO INC**
615 Stetson Ave (60174-3458)
PHONE..................................630 584-1311
Fax: 630 584-8695
Ralph Oswald, *CEO*
Richard Laverty, *President*
Jeffrey Oswald, *President*
Thomas E Heindl, *Corp Secy*
Roger Kent, *Prdtn Mgr*
EMP: 58
SQ FT: 39,000
SALES (est): 14MM **Privately Held**
WEB: www.chicagomold.com
SIC: **3544** 7699 Forms (molds), for foundry & plastics working machinery; plastics products repair

**(G-19153)**
**CINO INCORPORATED**
3n264 Loretta Dr (60175-7608)
PHONE..................................630 377-7242
Thomas A Sparacino, *President*
Jodi Sparacino, *Vice Pres*
EMP: 2
SQ FT: 400
SALES (est): 494.8K **Privately Held**
WEB: www.cino.net
SIC: **5047** 3944 Medical equipment & supplies; games, toys & children's vehicles

**(G-19154)**
**CLARKE AQUATIC SERVICES INC**
675 Sidwell Ct (60174-3492)
PHONE..................................630 894-2000
J Lyell Clarke III, *CEO*
Kevin Magro, *Exec VP*
Joel Fruendt, *Vice Pres*
Terry Phillips, *Vice Pres*
Julie Reiter, *Vice Pres*
EMP: 99
SALES (est): 12.7MM **Privately Held**
SIC: **2879** Agricultural chemicals

**(G-19155)**
**CLARKE GROUP INC**
675 Sidwell Ct (60174-3492)
PHONE..................................630 894-2000
J Lyell Clarke III, *President*
Stephanie Rodriguez, *Vice Pres*
EMP: 160
SALES (est): 15.5MM **Privately Held**
SIC: **2879** Insecticides & pesticides

**(G-19156)**
**CLARKE MOSQUITO CTRL PDTS INC (PA)**
675 Sidwell Ct (60174-3492)
P.O. Box 72197, Roselle (60172-0197)
PHONE..................................630 894-2000
J Lyell Clarke III, *President*
Kevin Magro, *Exec VP*
Joel Fruendt, *Vice Pres*
Karen Larson, *Vice Pres*
Terry Phillips, *Vice Pres*
◆ EMP: 116
SQ FT: 27,000
SALES (est): 45.9MM **Privately Held**
SIC: **2879** Insecticides & pesticides

**(G-19157)**
**CLASSIC FASTENERS LLC**
3540 Stern Ave (60174-5409)
PHONE..................................630 605-0195
Fax: 630 444-1901
Bennett Jordan, *President*
Cheryl Jordan,
▲ EMP: 9
SQ FT: 2,000
SALES (est): 1.2MM **Privately Held**
SIC: **3965** 3089 3569 5085 Fasteners, buttons, needles & pins; billfold inserts, plastic; sifting & screening machines; fasteners, industrial: nuts, bolts, screws, etc.; bolts, nuts, rivets & washers; washers; bolts, nuts & screws

**(G-19158)**
**COCA-COLA REFRESHMENTS USA INC**
105 Industrial Dr (60174-2428)
PHONE..................................630 513-5247
Fax: 630 584-3642
Jeff Scarb, *Manager*
Matt Gallagher, *Manager*
Mark Lee, *Director*
EMP: 250
SALES (corp-wide): 41.8B **Publicly Held**
WEB: www.cokecce.com
SIC: **2086** 5149 Soft drinks: packaged in cans, bottles, etc.; groceries & related products
HQ: Coca-Cola Refreshments Usa, Inc.
2500 Windy Ridge Pkwy Se
Atlanta GA 30339
770 989-3000

**(G-19159)**
**CODING SOLUTIONS INC**
394 38th Ave (60174-5424)
PHONE..................................630 377-5825
Denis Wienhoff, *President*
Robert Wienhoff, *Shareholder*
Donna Wienhoff, *Admin Sec*
EMP: 13
SQ FT: 5,000
SALES (est): 2.4MM **Privately Held**
WEB: www.chicagocoding.com
SIC: **2672** 5085 Labels (unprinted), gummed: made from purchased materials; industrial supplies

**(G-19160)**
**CODING SOLUTIONS INC**
394 38th Ave (60174-5424)
PHONE..................................630 443-9602
Denis E Wienhoff, *President*
EMP: 15
SALES (est): 2MM **Privately Held**
SIC: **2679** Tags & labels, paper; labels, paper: made from purchased material; gift wrap & novelties, paper; novelties, paper: made from purchased material

**(G-19161)**
**COMET ROLL & MACHINE COMPANY**
405 Stone Dr (60174-3301)
PHONE..................................630 268-1407
Pasek Gregory, *President*
Dan Mennecke, *Vice Pres*
Juan Rios, *Vice Pres*
Kolleen Monahan, *Manager*
Skiba Robert, *Admin Sec*
EMP: 20
SQ FT: 32,000
SALES (est): 4MM **Privately Held**
WEB: www.cometroll.com
SIC: **3444** 3599 3353 Forming machine work, sheet metal; machine shop, jobbing & repair; aluminum sheet, plate & foil

**(G-19162)**
**CONTINENTAL AUTOMATION INC**
303 N 4th St (60174-1823)
P.O. Box 205 (60174-0205)
PHONE..................................630 584-5100
Fax: 630 584-5100
Harry Kinscheck, *President*
Ron Denk, *Manager*
EMP: 25
SQ FT: 20,000
SALES (est): 2.8MM **Privately Held**
SIC: **3451** 3542 3549 3678 Screw machine products; machine tools, metal forming type; die casting machines; assembly machines, including robotic; electronic connectors; nonferrous die-castings except aluminum; aluminum die-castings

**(G-19163)**
**CONTROL WORKS INC**
2701 Dukane Dr Ste B (60174-3343)
PHONE..................................630 444-1942
David Cossey, *President*
David Locke, *Vice Pres*
EMP: 6
SQ FT: 2,000
SALES (est): 1MM **Privately Held**
SIC: **3613** 8711 7699 Control panels, electric; electrical or electronic engineering; industrial machinery & equipment repair

**(G-19164)**
**CORPORATE GRAPHICS INC**
3710 Illinois Ave (60174-2421)
PHONE..................................630 762-9000
Jerry R Penick, *President*
Scott Penick, *Vice Pres*
Norma K Penick, *Admin Sec*
EMP: 4
SQ FT: 10,000
SALES (est): 320K **Privately Held**
SIC: **3577** 7336 Graphic displays, except graphic terminals; graphic arts & related design

**(G-19165)**
**CREATIVE CONCEPTS FABRICATION**
3725 Stern Ave (60174-5403)
PHONE..................................630 940-0500
Fax: 630 940-0101
Brian Koestner, *President*
EMP: 10
SALES (est): 2.3MM **Privately Held**
WEB: www.creativeconceptsfab.net
SIC: **3089** Plastic processing

**(G-19166)**
**CUSTOM WOODWORKING INC**
125 N 11th Ave (60174-2285)
PHONE..................................630 584-7106
Maurice Mc Nalley, *President*
Maurice McNalley, *President*
Kathleen Mc Nalley, *Vice Pres*
EMP: 5
SALES (est): 550K **Privately Held**
SIC: **2431** Millwork

**(G-19167)**
**DASHER DEPENDABLE REINDEER LLC**
3010 Royal Queens Ct (60174-8713)
PHONE..................................630 513-7737
Alan Jania, *Mng Member*
Patrcik Henning, *Mng Member*
Carmelita Linden, *Mng Member*
EMP: 3
SQ FT: 180
SALES (est): 101.6K **Privately Held**
SIC: **2731** Book publishing

**(G-19168)**
**DAVID JESKEY**
Also Called: Rj45s.com
1523 Banbury Ave (60174-4453)
PHONE..................................630 659-6337
David Jeskey, *Owner*
EMP: 6
SALES (est): 6MM **Privately Held**
SIC: **5065** 3613 3643 3678 Communication equipment; connectors, electronic; power connectors, electric; connectors & terminals for electrical devices; solderless connectors (electric wiring devices); electronic connectors

**(G-19169)**
**DEC TOOL CORP**
2651 Dukane Dr (60174-3341)
PHONE..................................630 513-9883
Fax: 630 513-9887
Jeff Decore, *President*
Jeffery A Decore, *Principal*
Buffy Hisaw, *Manager*
EMP: 25
SQ FT: 3,000
SALES (est): 5.4MM **Privately Held**
WEB: www.dectool.com
SIC: **3544** Special dies, tools, jigs & fixtures

**(G-19170)**
**DIAGER USA INC**
1820 Wallace Ave Ste 122 (60174-3413)
PHONE..................................630 762-8443
Francois Defougeres, *CEO*
Patti Lemke, *Treasurer*
Mark Lemke, *Director*
◆ EMP: 6
SQ FT: 3,500

SALES (est): 585.1K **Privately Held**
SIC: **3532** Drills, bits & similar equipment

**(G-19171)**
**DIAMOND SPRAY PAINTING INC**
1840 Production Dr (60174-2473)
PHONE..................................630 513-5600
Fax: 630 513-5640
Stephanie Schmidt, *President*
Ted Schnidt, *President*
▲ EMP: 8
SQ FT: 21,000
SALES: 750K **Privately Held**
SIC: **3479** 3471 Coating of metals & formed products; plating & polishing

**(G-19172)**
**DIAMONDAIRE CORP**
117 W Main St Ste 110 (60174-1860)
PHONE..................................630 355-7464
Lauren Stallings, *President*
▲ EMP: 6 EST: 2011
SALES (est): 479.9K **Privately Held**
SIC: **5094** 7631 3961 Jewelry; jewelry repair services; costume jewelry

**(G-19173)**
**DOMINICKS FINER FOODS INC**
2063 Lincoln Hwy (60174-1580)
PHONE..................................630 584-1750
EMP: 70
SALES (corp-wide): 44.2B **Publicly Held**
SIC: **5411** 5912 2051 Ret Groceries Ret Drugs/Sundries Mfg Bread/Related Prdts
HQ: Dominick's Finer Foods Inc
711 Jorie Blvd Ste 1
Oak Brook IL 60523
630 891-5000

**(G-19174)**
**DTC PRODUCTS INC**
2651 Dukane Dr (60174-3341)
PHONE..................................630 513-3323
Jeffrey Decore, *President*
EMP: 3
SALES: 60K **Privately Held**
SIC: **3569** General industrial machinery

**(G-19175)**
**DUKANE CORPORATION (PA)**
2900 Dukane Dr (60174-3395)
PHONE..................................630 797-4900
Fax: 630 797-4949
Michael W Ritschdorff, *President*
Mark Iannantuoni, *Regional Mgr*
Jeremiah Lenert, *Business Mgr*
Ian Wallace, *Business Mgr*
Terry Goldman, *Vice Pres*
▲ EMP: 215 EST: 1922
SQ FT: 298,000
SALES (est): 50.7MM **Privately Held**
WEB: www.dukane-store.com
SIC: **3861** 3699 Projectors, still or motion picture, silent or sound; welding machines & equipment, ultrasonic

**(G-19176)**
**DUKANE IAS LLC**
2900 Dukane Dr (60174-3348)
PHONE..................................630 797-4900
Michael Johnston,
Andrew W Byrd,
Kenneth W Weaver,
EMP: 99
SALES (est): 4.8MM **Privately Held**
SIC: **3089** Plastic hardware & building products

**(G-19177)**
**EAGLESTONE INC**
3705 Swenson Ave (60174-3439)
PHONE..................................630 587-1115
Carmen Sammauro, *President*
Richard Payne, *Engineer*
Gerry Ness, *Supervisor*
David Summers, *Admin Sec*
EMP: 15
SQ FT: 10,000
SALES (est): 6.7MM **Privately Held**
WEB: www.eaglestone.net
SIC: **3535** 3599 Conveyors & conveying equipment; machine shop, jobbing & repair

# GEOGRAPHIC SECTION
## Saint Charles - Kane County (G-19201)

**(G-19178)**
**EIFELER COATINGS TECH INC**
Also Called: Eifeler-Lafer Inc.
3800 Commerce Dr (60174-5323)
PHONE..............................630 587-1220
Fax: 630 587-1230
Hanz Eifeler, *CEO*
Luigi Parenti, *President*
Wibke Eifeler, *Vice Pres*
Dave Schwab, *Vice Pres*
Wiebke Yovanovic, *VP Finance*
▲ EMP: 25 EST: 2001
SALES (est): 4.3MM
SALES (corp-wide): 12.3B **Privately Held**
WEB: www.eifeler-lafer.com
SIC: 3479 Painting, coating & hot dipping
HQ: Bohler-Uddeholm Corporation
     2505 Millennium Dr
     Elgin IL 60124
     877 992-8764

**(G-19179)**
**ELFRING FONTS INC**
2020 Dean St Ste N (60174-1665)
PHONE..............................630 377-3520
Gary Elfring, *President*
Art Miller, *Vice Pres*
EMP: 4
SQ FT: 2,000
SALES (est): 649.1K **Privately Held**
WEB: www.micrfont.com
SIC: 3577 5045 7371 Computer peripheral equipment; computer software; computer software systems analysis & design, custom

**(G-19180)**
**ELITE EXTRUSION TECHNOLOGY INC**
3620 Ohio Ave (60174-5446)
PHONE..............................630 485-2020
Glen Galloway, *President*
Fred Gross, *General Mgr*
Eric Kainer, *Prdtn Mgr*
Eva Mayer, *Office Mgr*
Juan Valdivia, *Supervisor*
EMP: 1
SALES (est): 1.4MM
SALES (corp-wide): 18.9MM **Privately Held**
SIC: 7819 2671 Film processing, editing & titling: motion picture; plastic film, coated or laminated for packaging
PA: Galloway Consolidated Holdings, Inc.
     744 N Oaklawn Ave
     Elmhurst IL 60126
     630 279-7800

**(G-19181)**
**ENDEAVOR TECHNOLOGIES INC**
417 Stone Dr (60174-3301)
PHONE..............................630 562-0300
Fax: 630 562-0303
Charles Nichols, *President*
Scott Applehoff, *Vice Pres*
Jeffrey Mackey, *Shareholder*
Browne Nichlos, *Executive Asst*
Thomas Mayer, *Admin Sec*
EMP: 20
SQ FT: 15,685
SALES (est): 5.2MM **Privately Held**
WEB: www.endtec.com
SIC: 7694 Rebuilding motors, except automotive

**(G-19182)**
**ENGINUITY COMMUNICATIONS CORP**
3545 Stern Ave (60174-5407)
PHONE..............................630 444-0778
Sean Iwasaki, *President*
Stephen Todd, *General Mgr*
Steve Todd, *General Mgr*
EMP: 40
SQ FT: 25,000
SALES (est): 8.4MM **Privately Held**
WEB: www.enginuitycom.com
SIC: 3699 Electrical equipment & supplies

**(G-19183)**
**FARM PROGRESS COMPANIES INC (DH)**
Also Called: Feedstffs Intrnet Subscription
255 38th Ave Ste P (60174-5410)
PHONE..............................630 690-5600
David Kieselstein, *President*
Jeff Lapin, *Principal*
Frank Holdmeyer, *Editor*
Cory Huseby, *COO*
Katheryn Kirk, *COO*
EMP: 150
SALES (est): 26.3MM
SALES (corp-wide): 1.3B **Privately Held**
WEB: www.farmprogress.com
SIC: 7389 2721 Promoters of shows & exhibitions; periodicals: publishing only; magazines: publishing only, not printed on site
HQ: Rural Press Pty Limited
     159 Bells Line Of Rd
     North Richmond NSW 2754
     245 704-444

**(G-19184)**
**FIRST & MAIN INC**
2400 E Main St (60174-2436)
PHONE..............................630 587-1000
Fax: 630 587-1001
Brad Holes, *President*
Nancy Buckles, *Vice Pres*
▲ EMP: 25
SQ FT: 60,000
SALES (est): 7.1MM **Privately Held**
WEB: www.eplush.com
SIC: 5092 3942 Toys & hobby goods & supplies; stuffed toys, including animals

**(G-19185)**
**FONA INTERNATIONAL INC**
Also Called: Fona Distribution Center
3940 Swenson Ave (60174-3446)
PHONE..............................630 578-8600
Stephanie Paredes, *Branch Mgr*
EMP: 3
SALES (corp-wide): 87.5MM **Privately Held**
SIC: 2087 Extracts, flavoring; syrups, flavoring (except drink)
PA: Fona International Inc.
     1900 Averill Rd
     Geneva IL 60134
     630 578-8600

**(G-19186)**
**FOREMAN TOOL & MOLD CORP (PA)**
3850 Swenson Ave (60174-3438)
PHONE..............................630 377-6389
Fax: 630 377-5364
Richard W Foreman, *President*
Kathleen C Foreman, *Corp Secy*
Piotr Kedzierski, *Vice Pres*
Michelle Shaw, *Human Res Mgr*
Nancy Sikich, *Analyst*
EMP: 50
SQ FT: 33,000
SALES (est): 7.7MM **Privately Held**
WEB: www.foremantool.com
SIC: 3089 Injection molding of plastics

**(G-19187)**
**FORM PLASTICS COMPANY**
Also Called: Pappas & Pappas Enterprises
3825 Stern Ave (60174-5457)
PHONE..............................630 443-1400
Fax: 630 443-1491
James D Pappas, *Principal*
John Gross, *Engineer*
Dawn Vitale, *Accountant*
Jennifer Ruffolo, *Human Res Dir*
Jim Adams, *Sales Dir*
▲ EMP: 100
SQ FT: 120,000
SALES (est): 22.8MM **Privately Held**
WEB: www.formplastics.com
SIC: 3086 Packaging & shipping materials, foamed plastic

**(G-19188)**
**FOX ENTERPRISES INC**
50 N 17th St (60174-1622)
P.O. Box 1126 (60174-7126)
PHONE..............................630 513-9010
Gary Fox, *President*
Jeff Fox, *Vice Pres*
EMP: 2
SQ FT: 2,500
SALES (est): 1MM **Privately Held**
SIC: 3714 3081 Motor vehicle parts & accessories; unsupported plastics film & sheet

**(G-19189)**
**GIG KARASEK LLC**
3955 Commerce Dr (60174-5321)
P.O. Box 268 (60174-0268)
PHONE..............................630 549-0394
Hugh Palmer,
Andreas Karasek,
John Palmer,
EMP: 10
SALES (est): 1.8MM **Privately Held**
SIC: 8711 1629 2824 Chemical engineering; waste water & sewage treatment plant construction; organic fibers, noncellulosic

**(G-19190)**
**HCI CABINETRY AND DESIGN INC**
3755 E Main St (60174-2463)
PHONE..............................630 584-0266
Kris Blaesing, *President*
EMP: 8
SQ FT: 5,000
SALES: 1.7MM **Privately Held**
SIC: 5031 2434 1799 Kitchen cabinets; wood kitchen cabinets; kitchen cabinet installation

**(G-19191)**
**HEAVY EQUIPMENT PRODUCTS**
11 S 2nd Ave Ste 3 (60174-1941)
PHONE..............................630 377-3005
Les Hepler, *Owner*
EMP: 2
SALES (est): 340K **Privately Held**
SIC: 3743 Mining locomotives & parts, electric or nonelectric

**(G-19192)**
**HI TECH COLORANTS**
5n634 Lostview Ln (60175-8218)
PHONE..............................630 762-0368
George Scarpelli, *Owner*
EMP: 2 EST: 1989
SALES: 300K **Privately Held**
SIC: 2865 Color pigments, organic

**(G-19193)**
**HONEYWELL INTERNATIONAL INC**
3825 Ohio Ave (60174-5467)
PHONE..............................630 377-6580
Mike Masters, *Purch Agent*
Eduardo Vazquez, *Engineer*
Cindy Edwards, *Controller*
Richard Braun, *Persnl Mgr*
Mark Nelson, *Sales Staff*
EMP: 500
SALES (corp-wide): 39.3B **Publicly Held**
WEB: www.honeywell.com
SIC: 3724 Aircraft engines & engine parts
PA: Honeywell International Inc.
     115 Tabor Rd
     Morris Plains NJ 07950
     973 455-2000

**(G-19194)**
**HOWARD PET PRODUCTS INC**
425 38th Ave (60174-5425)
PHONE..............................973 398-3038
▲ EMP: 21
SALES: 1MM **Privately Held**
SIC: 5199 2048 7389 Pets & pet supplies; prepared feeds;

**(G-19195)**
**HRB AMERICA CORPORATION**
3485 Swenson Ave (60174-3449)
PHONE..............................630 513-1800
Xiangyang LI, *President*
Clayton Chang, *Vice Pres*
▲ EMP: 4
SQ FT: 10,000
SALES (est): 440K **Privately Held**
SIC: 3562 Ball & roller bearings

**(G-19196)**
**INCON INDUSTRIES INC**
3955 Commerce Dr (60174-5321)
P.O. Box 268 (60174-0268)
PHONE..............................630 728-4014
Fax: 630 761-1190
Hugh Palmer, *President*
Hugh Palmesr, *President*
John Palmer III, *Vice Pres*
EMP: 5
SQ FT: 6,000
SALES (est): 1.2MM **Privately Held**
SIC: 2819 Chemicals, high purity: refined from technical grade

**(G-19197)**
**INNOVATE TECHNOLOGIES INC**
761 N 17th St (60174-1664)
PHONE..............................630 587-4220
Fax: 630 587-4219
Joseph Talarczyk, *President*
Dee Sparling, *Manager*
EMP: 4 EST: 1998
SQ FT: 3,000
SALES (est): 1.1MM **Privately Held**
SIC: 3542 High energy rate metal forming machines

**(G-19198)**
**INNOVATION PLUS POWER SYSTEMS**
3960 Commerce Dr (60174-5319)
PHONE..............................630 457-1105
Afshin Montazeri, *President*
Amy Majewski, *Accounts Mgr*
EMP: 13
SALES (est): 2.3MM
SALES (corp-wide): 802.5K **Privately Held**
SIC: 3629 Capacitors, a.c., for motors or fluorescent lamp ballasts; capacitors, fixed or variable
PA: Innovation Plus Power Systems Inc
     1220 Corporate Dr
     Burlington ON L7L 5
     905 331-1839

**(G-19199)**
**INTERNATIONAL GRAPHICS & ASSOC**
38w598 Clubhouse Dr (60175-6179)
PHONE..............................630 584-2248
Curt Burson, *Owner*
Kyle Burson, *Sales Mgr*
EMP: 12
SQ FT: 5,000
SALES: 1.5MM **Privately Held**
SIC: 2752 2754 2791 2789 Commercial printing, lithographic; business form & card printing, lithographic; commercial printing, gravure; envelopes: gravure printing; typesetting; bookbinding & related work

**(G-19200)**
**ITASCA PLASTICS INC**
3750 Ohio Ave (60174-5438)
PHONE..............................630 443-4446
Fax: 630 443-8930
Alan Field, *President*
Duncan Mathieson, *Vice Pres*
Fred Morris, *Vice Pres*
Emmy Field, *Admin Sec*
Susan Field, *Admin Sec*
▲ EMP: 29
SQ FT: 81,000
SALES (est): 11.7MM **Privately Held**
SIC: 2821 Plastics materials & resins

**(G-19201)**
**J STILLING ENTERPRISES INC**
Also Called: Rice Chem
330 S 2nd St Ste A (60174-2868)
P.O. Box 310 (60174-0310)
PHONE..............................630 584-5050
Fax: 630 584-9935
Jim Stilling, *President*
Barbara Stilling, *Treasurer*
EMP: 3
SQ FT: 2,600
SALES (est): 349.9K **Privately Held**
SIC: 2819 Industrial inorganic chemicals

# Saint Charles - Kane County (G-19202) — GEOGRAPHIC SECTION

### (G-19202)
**JEWEL OSCO INC**
Also Called: Jewel-Osco 3331
2073 Prairie St (60174-3594)
PHONE .................................. 630 584-4594
Jim Mc Kay, *General Mgr*
John Partyski, *Director*
EMP: 175
SALES (corp-wide): 58.8B  Privately Held
WEB: www.jewelosco.com
SIC: 5411  5149  2051  Supermarkets, chain; groceries & related products; bread, cake & related products
HQ: Jewel Osco, Inc.
150 E Pierce Rd Ste 200
Itasca IL 60143
630 948-6000

### (G-19203)
**KANELAND PUBLICATIONS INC**
Also Called: Elburn Herald
333 N Randall Rd Ste 111 (60174-1500)
PHONE .................................. 630 365-6446
Fax: 630 365-2251
Stephen Cooper, *President*
Richard Cooper, *Vice Pres*
Carly Brown, *Financial Exec*
Bo Smith, *Sales Staff*
Benjamin Draper, *Assoc Editor*
EMP: 10  EST: 1908
SALES (est): 853.2K  Privately Held
WEB: www.elburnherald.com
SIC: 2711  Job printing & newspaper publishing combined

### (G-19204)
**KOHLERT MANUFACTURING CORP**
2851 Dukane Dr (60174-3345)
PHONE .................................. 630 584-0013
Fax: 630 584-7140
John Kohlert, *President*
EMP: 4
SQ FT: 3,000
SALES (est): 440K  Privately Held
SIC: 3599  Machine & other job shop work

### (G-19205)
**KRISTEL LIMITED PARTNERSHIP**
Also Called: Kristel Displays
555 Kirk Rd (60174-3406)
PHONE .................................. 630 443-1290
Fax: 630 443-1390
Chris Petri, *President*
George Kinney, *Partner*
Bruce Gordon, *Purchasing*
Matt Margaras, *Engineer*
▲ EMP: 100
SQ FT: 100,000
SALES (est): 36.6MM  Privately Held
WEB: www.kristel.com
SIC: 3575  Cathode ray tube (CRT), computer terminal

### (G-19206)
**LA BOOST INC**
3n555 17th St (60174-1683)
PHONE .................................. 630 444-1755
Mahammad Choudhry, *President*
Yasmeen Choudhry, *Admin Sec*
▲ EMP: 2
SALES (est): 314.5K  Privately Held
SIC: 2869  2087  Perfumes, flavorings & food additives; extracts, flavoring

### (G-19207)
**LAMP CO OF AMERICA INC**
214 S 13th Ave (60174-3119)
PHONE .................................. 630 584-4001
Fax: 630 513-1145
Lawrence Denna, *President*
EMP: 3
SALES (est): 395.5K  Privately Held
SIC: 3646  3645  Commercial indusl & institutional electric lighting fixtures; residential lighting fixtures

### (G-19208)
**LECHLER INC**
445 Kautz Rd (60174-5301)
PHONE .................................. 630 377-6611
Fax: 630 377-6657
Adolf Pfeiffer, *President*
Dennis Theesfeld, *Plant Mgr*
Manish Mittal, *Project Mgr*
Dinesh Patel, *Opers Mgr*
Tim Lovings, *QA Dir*
▲ EMP: 69  EST: 1912
SQ FT: 45,000
SALES: 18MM
SALES (corp-wide): 111.7MM  Privately Held
WEB: www.lechlerusa.com
SIC: 3499  Nozzles, spray: aerosol, paint or insecticide
HQ: Lechler International Gesellschaft Mit Beschrankter Haftung
Ulmer Str. 128
Metzingen 72555
712 396-20

### (G-19209)
**LEVITON MANUFACTURING CO INC**
3837 E Main St Ste 331 (60174-2424)
PHONE .................................. 630 443-0500
Julie Jensen, *Business Mgr*
Robert Kiehl, *Business Mgr*
Mark Michael, *Business Mgr*
Maurice Zetena, *Business Mgr*
Jennifer Crumrine, *Engineer*
EMP: 150
SALES (corp-wide): 1.5B  Privately Held
WEB: www.leviton.com
SIC: 3643  Current-carrying wiring devices
PA: Leviton Manufacturing Co., Inc.
201 N Service Rd
Melville NY 11747
631 812-6000

### (G-19210)
**LFA INDUSTRIES INC**
1820 Wallace Ave Ste 122 (60174-3413)
PHONE .................................. 630 762-7391
Mark Lemke, *President*
Patti Jo Lemke, *Vice Pres*
Carol Lemke, *Treasurer*
Patty Lemke, *Director*
▲ EMP: 6
SQ FT: 3,500
SALES (est): 805.4K  Privately Held
WEB: www.lfausa.com
SIC: 3545  Chucks: drill, lathe or magnetic (machine tool accessories)

### (G-19211)
**LIGHTING INNOVATIONS INC**
Also Called: Fc Lighting
3609 Swenson Ave (60174-3441)
PHONE .................................. 630 889-8100
Bruce Bukas, *President*
Maria San-Roman, *Purch Mgr*
Mark Macauley, *CFO*
Hayden Bukas, *Sales Dir*
▲ EMP: 30
SQ FT: 58,000
SALES: 6.3MM  Privately Held
WEB: www.fclighting.com
SIC: 3648  Lighting equipment

### (G-19212)
**MAKO MOLD CORPORATION**
3820 Ohio Ave Ste 7 (60174-5461)
PHONE .................................. 630 377-9010
Fax: 630 377-9055
Philip Denemark, *President*
Michael Armbrust, *Manager*
EMP: 4
SQ FT: 3,000
SALES (est): 600K  Privately Held
SIC: 3089  Injection molded finished plastic products

### (G-19213)
**MANUFACTURED SPECIALTIES INC**
Also Called: MSI
3575 Stern Ave (60174-5412)
PHONE .................................. 630 444-1992
Fax: 630 444-1993
Cynthia J Jagmin, *CEO*
Michael A Jagmin, *President*
Donald Palomaki, *Admin Sec*
▲ EMP: 14
SQ FT: 25,000
SALES (est): 1.8MM  Privately Held
WEB: www.msi-products.com
SIC: 3498  Fabricated pipe & fittings

### (G-19214)
**MAR-FRE MANUFACTURING CO**
2541 Dukane Dr (60174-3396)
PHONE .................................. 630 377-1022
Fax: 630 377-1574
Bruce H Johnson, *President*
Diane Y Johnson, *Vice Pres*
EMP: 18  EST: 1950
SQ FT: 14,000
SALES (est): 2.2MM  Privately Held
SIC: 3599  7692  Machine shop, jobbing & repair; welding repair

### (G-19215)
**MARINE CANADA ACQUISITION**
Also Called: Bluskies International
3491 Swenson Ave (60174-3449)
PHONE .................................. 630 513-5809
EMP: 3
SALES (corp-wide): 54MM  Privately Held
SIC: 3531  3822  Marine related equipment; auto controls regulating residntl & coml environmt & applncs
PA: Marine Canada Acquisition Limited Partnership
3831 No. 6 Rd
Richmond BC V6V 1
604 270-6899

### (G-19216)
**MCC TECHNOLOGY INC**
2422 W Main St Unit 4d (60175-1010)
PHONE .................................. 630 377-7200
James J Kunzer, *President*
John Kunzer, *Vice Pres*
EMP: 10
SQ FT: 4,000
SALES: 1.4MM  Privately Held
WEB: www.varstar.com
SIC: 5045  5063  3669  Computers, peripherals & software; transformers & transmission equipment; intercommunication systems, electric

### (G-19217)
**MELT DESIGN INC**
3803 Illinois Ave (60174-2422)
PHONE .................................. 630 443-4000
Fax: 630 443-4140
Panos Trakas, *President*
Joanna Accetta, *Director*
Emmy Trakas, *Admin Sec*
EMP: 11
SQ FT: 12,100
SALES (est): 1.1MM  Privately Held
WEB: www.meltdesign.com
SIC: 3829  Thermometers & temperature sensors

### (G-19218)
**MET CO INDUSTRIES INC**
303 N 4th St (60174-1823)
PHONE .................................. 630 584-5100
Fax: 630 584-7740
Harry Kinscheck, *President*
EMP: 20
SQ FT: 3,000
SALES (est): 2MM  Privately Held
SIC: 3398  Brazing (hardening) of metal

### (G-19219)
**METAL TECHNOLOGY SOLUTIONS**
Also Called: M T S
36w797 Red Gate Ct (60175-6295)
PHONE .................................. 630 587-1450
Fax: 630 587-1451
William Kowal, *President*
EMP: 2
SALES (est): 267.1K  Privately Held
WEB: www.mtsmfg.com
SIC: 3469  Metal stampings

### (G-19220)
**MICHAEL CLESEN**
Also Called: L & M Greenhouses
4n932 Clesen Dr (60175-4903)
PHONE .................................. 630 377-3075
Michael Clesen, *Owner*
EMP: 3
SQ FT: 30,000
SALES (est): 265.1K  Privately Held
SIC: 3089  Synthetic resin finished products

### (G-19221)
**MIDWEST DRIVESHAFT INC**
3712 Illinois Ave (60174-2421)
PHONE .................................. 630 513-9292
Fax: 630 513-9387
Joseph M Viereckl, *President*
Karen Viereckl, *Admin Sec*
EMP: 7
SQ FT: 2,100
SALES (est): 926.5K  Privately Held
WEB: www.mdsdriveshaft.com
SIC: 3714  5013  Drive shafts, motor vehicle; automotive supplies & parts

### (G-19222)
**MIDWEST POWDER COATINGS INC**
3865 Swenson Ave (60174-3437)
PHONE .................................. 630 587-2918
Larry McNeely, *President*
Andreas Gass, *COO*
▲ EMP: 25
SQ FT: 20,000
SALES (est): 8.2MM  Privately Held
SIC: 2851  Paints & allied products

### (G-19223)
**MINUTEMAN PRESS**
1574 E Main St (60174-2327)
PHONE .................................. 630 584-7383
Fax: 630 584-8956
Joe Tomsa, *President*
Jerry Prasse, *Vice Pres*
EMP: 8
SQ FT: 3,000
SALES (est): 1.1MM  Privately Held
WEB: www.minuteman2000.com
SIC: 2752  5112  2791  2759  Commercial printing, lithographic; business forms, lithographed; business forms; typesetting; commercial printing

### (G-19224)
**MSYSTEMS GROUP LLC**
38w426 Mallard Lake Rd (60175-5445)
PHONE .................................. 630 567-3930
Calvin Moy, *Owner*
EMP: 3
SALES (est): 73.7K  Privately Held
SIC: 3355  Aluminum rolling & drawing

### (G-19225)
**OAKLAND ENTERPRISES INC**
Also Called: Oei Products
310 N 5th St (60174-1831)
P.O. Box 528 (60174-0528)
PHONE .................................. 630 377-1121
Jim Geraghty, *President*
Vanessa Geraghty, *Manager*
EMP: 5
SQ FT: 1,000
SALES: 450K  Privately Held
SIC: 5999  2679  Safety supplies & equipment; tags & labels, paper

### (G-19226)
**OAS SOFTWARE CORP**
2801 Majestic Oaks Ln (60174-7969)
PHONE .................................. 630 513-2990
Fax: 630 513-2995
Anthony Shaneen, *President*
Andy R Ro, *Mktg Dir*
EMP: 15
SQ FT: 6,000
SALES (est): 1.5MM  Privately Held
WEB: www.oasvas.com
SIC: 7371  7372  Computer software development; computer software systems analysis & design, custom; prepackaged software

### (G-19227)
**ODORITE INTERNATIONAL INC**
Also Called: Fragrance Master
320 37th Ave (60174-5414)
PHONE .................................. 816 920-5000
Dan Bunch, *Ch of Bd*
Mark Algaier, *Vice Pres*
Carrie Lesan, *Accounts Mgr*
▲ EMP: 16  EST: 1934
SQ FT: 45,000
SALES (est): 1.8MM  Privately Held
SIC: 2842  Specialty cleaning, polishes & sanitation goods; deodorants, nonpersonal

## Saint Charles - Kane County (G-19253)

### (G-19228)
**OLCOTT PLASTICS INC**
95 N 17th St (60174-1636)
**PHONE**...................630 584-0555
**Fax:** 630 584-5655
Joseph M Brodner, *President*
John R Brodner, *Vice Pres*
Andre Greene, *Opers Mgr*
Ken Johnston, *Prdtn Mgr*
Mark Herzog, *Controller*
**EMP:** 95
**SQ FT:** 60,000
**SALES (est):** 34.1MM **Privately Held**
**WEB:** www.olcottplastics.com
**SIC:** 3089 Plastic containers, except foam

### (G-19229)
**OMRON AUTOMOTIVE ELEC INC (DH)**
Also Called: Omron Global
3709 Ohio Ave (60174-5437)
**PHONE**...................630 443-6800
**Fax:** 630 443-6898
Yoshihito Yamada, *CEO*
Fumio Tateishi, *Ch of Bd*
Yoshinobu Morishita, *President*
Katsuhiro Wada, *President*
Yoshinori Suzuki, *Chairman*
▲ **EMP:** 565
**SQ FT:** 100,000
**SALES (est):** 497.7MM
**SALES (corp-wide):** 7.1B **Privately Held**
**SIC:** 5065 3625 3714 8742 Electronic parts; relays & industrial controls; motor vehicle parts & accessories; real estate consultant
**HQ:** Omron Management Center Of America, Inc.
2895 Greenspoint Pkwy # 100
Hoffman Estates IL 60169
224 520-7650

### (G-19230)
**ORAT INC**
761 N 17th St Ste 4 (60174-1664)
P.O. Box 417 (60174-0417)
**PHONE**...................630 567-6728
Doug Turner, *President*
**EMP:** 4
**SALES (est):** 413.9K **Privately Held**
**WEB:** www.orat.net
**SIC:** 3599 Custom machinery

### (G-19231)
**OUTBACK USA INC**
5n825 Prairie Springs Dr (60175-6944)
**PHONE**...................863 699-2220
Kay Johnston, *President*
Darrel Johnston, *Vice Pres*
**EMP:** 7 **EST:** 1996
**SQ FT:** 1,800
**SALES (est):** 1.2MM **Privately Held**
**WEB:** www.outbackusa.com
**SIC:** 3732 4499 5199 5091 Pontoons, except aircraft & inflatable; motorboats, inboard or outboard: building & repairing; boat & ship rental & leasing, except pleasure; bait, fishing; fishing tackle; propane gas, bottled

### (G-19232)
**PACKAGING PRTG SPECIALISTS INC**
Also Called: P P S
3915 Stern Ave (60174-5441)
**PHONE**...................630 513-8060
**Fax:** 630 513-8062
Ken Russo, *President*
Jennifer Russo, *Treasurer*
Joy Weiss, *Manager*
**EMP:** 15
**SQ FT:** 25,000
**SALES (est):** 4MM **Privately Held**
**WEB:** www.ppsofil.com
**SIC:** 2759 2671 Flexographic printing; packaging paper & plastics film, coated & laminated

### (G-19233)
**PACTIV LLC**
315 Kirk Rd (60174-3429)
**PHONE**...................630 262-6335
**Fax:** 630 377-5991
Norman Sterns, *COO*
Robert Reschke, *Plant Mgr*
Lee Richardson, *Purchasing*
Norma Rapp, *QC Dir*
Dave Ovenshire, *Plant Engr*
**EMP:** 200 **Privately Held**
**WEB:** www.depaco.com
**SIC:** 2657 2656 Food containers, folding: made from purchased material; sanitary food containers
**HQ:** Pactiv Llc
1900 W Field Ct
Lake Forest IL 60045
847 482-2000

### (G-19234)
**PERFECT PLASTIC PRINTING CORP**
311 Kautz Rd Ste 1 (60174-5304)
**PHONE**...................630 584-1600
**Fax:** 630 584-0648
Chris Smoczynski, *President*
Dave Moser, *Vice Pres*
Matt Smoczynski, *Vice Pres*
Bob Stram, *Vice Pres*
Robert M Stram, *Vice Pres*
▲ **EMP:** 170
**SQ FT:** 47,000
**SALES (est):** 34MM **Privately Held**
**WEB:** www.perfectplastic.com
**SIC:** 2752 3089 Commercial printing, lithographic; identification cards, plastic

### (G-19235)
**PETROCHEM INC**
6n999 Whispering Trl (60175-6363)
**PHONE**...................630 513-6350
Carole J Sluski, *President*
Jill E Dohner, *Vice Pres*
**EMP:** 5
**SALES (est):** 2.8MM **Privately Held**
**SIC:** 5172 2851 Lubricating oils & greases; removers & cleaners

### (G-19236)
**POLYTEC PLASTICS INC**
3730 Stern Ave (60174-5404)
**PHONE**...................630 584-8282
**Fax:** 630 584-8294
Karl R Blum, *President*
Paul Medrano, *Vice Pres*
**EMP:** 40
**SQ FT:** 16,000
**SALES (est):** 6.4MM **Privately Held**
**WEB:** www.polytecplastics.com
**SIC:** 3082 Unsupported plastics profile shapes

### (G-19237)
**POLYTECH INDUSTRIES INC**
1755 Wallace Ave (60174-3402)
P.O. Box 551, Geneva (60134-0551)
**PHONE**...................630 443-6030
**Fax:** 630 443-6035
Richard J Walls, *President*
Timothy S Walls, *Vice Pres*
Kevin Payne, *QC Mgr*
Carmon Taylor, *Design Engr*
Wilma Walls, *Treasurer*
**EMP:** 25
**SQ FT:** 20,000
**SALES (est):** 4.2MM **Privately Held**
**WEB:** www.polytch-ind.com
**SIC:** 3089 Plastic processing

### (G-19238)
**POWER INDUSTRIES INC**
3102 Greenwood Ln (60175-5623)
**PHONE**...................630 443-0671
Stephen A Power, *President*
Linda Power, *Vice Pres*
▲ **EMP:** 6
**SALES (est):** 250K **Privately Held**
**WEB:** www.vaporeze.com
**SIC:** 3634 Vaporizers, electric: household

### (G-19239)
**POWERONE CORP**
Also Called: Powerone Environmental
2325 Dean St Ste 200 (60175-4810)
**PHONE**...................630 443-6500
James Chaggaris, *President*
**EMP:** 3
**SALES (est):** 375.8K **Privately Held**
**WEB:** www.pwrone.com
**SIC:** 3629 5199 3443 Electrical industrial apparatus; ice, manufactured or natural; reactor containment vessels, metal plate

### (G-19240)
**PRECISION COMPONENTS INC**
1020 Cedar Ave Ste 215 (60174-2279)
**PHONE**...................630 462-9110
William J Gray Jr, *President*
Lou Battistoni, *Exec VP*
**EMP:** 90
**SQ FT:** 900
**SALES:** 5MM **Privately Held**
**SIC:** 3661 3612 Telephones & telephone apparatus; transformers, except electric

### (G-19241)
**PRECISION SCREEN SPECIALTIES**
3905 Commerce Dr (60174-5321)
**PHONE**...................630 762-9548
**Fax:** 630 762-9543
**EMP:** 8 **EST:** 1957
**SQ FT:** 8,000
**SALES:** 850K **Privately Held**
**SIC:** 2759 3555 3231 2396 Commercial Printing Mfg Printing Trades Mach Mfg Prdt-Purchased Glass Mfg Auto/Apparel Trim

### (G-19242)
**PROELL INC**
2751 Dukane Dr (60174-3343)
**PHONE**...................630 587-2300
**Fax:** 630 587-2666
Werner Port, *President*
Reinhard Port, *Exec VP*
Edwin Brooks, *Asst Treas*
Jane Scott, *Sales Mgr*
**EMP:** 8
**SQ FT:** 13,500
**SALES (est):** 1MM **Privately Held**
**SIC:** 2759 2261 Screen printing; screen printing of cotton broadwoven fabrics

### (G-19243)
**PROTEK INC**
Also Called: Pro-Tek
209 S 3rd St (60174-2839)
**PHONE**...................888 536-5466
Pamela Hendricks, *President*
**EMP:** 4
**SQ FT:** 10,500
**SALES (est):** 220K **Privately Held**
**WEB:** www.pro-tekinc.com
**SIC:** 2782 Looseleaf binders & devices

### (G-19244)
**PULS LP**
2560 Foxfield Rd Ste 260 (60174-1478)
**PHONE**...................630 587-9780
**Fax:** 630 587-9735
Bernard Erdl, *President*
Bernhard Erdl, *President*
Ed Merkle, *Engineer*
Sandra Doneske, *Finance Mgr*
Tanja Friederichs, *VP Human Res*
▲ **EMP:** 30
**SALES (est):** 4.2MM **Privately Held**
**SIC:** 3679 Power supplies, all types: static

### (G-19245)
**PURE ESSENTIAL SUPPLY INC**
1835 Wallace Ave (60174-3403)
Pam Ernst, *President*
Philip Ernst, *Treasurer*
**EMP:** 3
**SALES:** 100K **Privately Held**
**SIC:** 2844 Toilet preparations

### (G-19246)
**PYRAMID MANUFACTURING CORP**
3815 Illinois Ave (60174-2422)
**PHONE**...................630 443-0141
**Fax:** 630 584-8437
Paul Hernandez, *President*
John Hernandez, *Vice Pres*
Tim Casson, *Office Mgr*
▲ **EMP:** 100
**SQ FT:** 50,000
**SALES (est):** 17.5MM **Privately Held**
**WEB:** www.4pyramidmfg.com
**SIC:** 3444 Sheet metalwork

### (G-19247)
**QUALITY BAKERIES LLC**
Also Called: Burry Foodservice
1750 E Main St Ste 260 (60174-4729)
**PHONE**...................630 553-7377
Steve Spoerl, *President*
Robert Pim, *Exec VP*
Jeanne Markus, *Vice Pres*
Pat Uli, *Vice Pres*
Dave Phillips, *CFO*
**EMP:** 17
**SALES:** 144MM **Privately Held**
**WEB:** www.burryfoods.com
**SIC:** 2053 Frozen bakery products, except bread

### (G-19248)
**QUALITY SPRAYING SCREEN PRTG**
3815 Illinois Ave (60174-2422)
**PHONE**...................630 584-8324
Paul Hernandez, *Partner*
John Hernandez, *Partner*
**EMP:** 40
**SQ FT:** 50,000
**SALES (est):** 1.2MM **Privately Held**
**SIC:** 7532 2396 Lettering & painting services; automotive & apparel trimmings

### (G-19249)
**R W WILSON PRINTING COMPANY**
220 N 4th St (60174-1822)
P.O. Box 989 (60174-0989)
**PHONE**...................630 584-4100
**Fax:** 630 584-4236
Doug Wilson, *President*
Sherry Vickery, *Treasurer*
**EMP:** 8 **EST:** 1955
**SQ FT:** 9,000
**SALES:** 500K **Privately Held**
**SIC:** 2752 2759 Commercial printing, lithographic; commercial printing

### (G-19250)
**RAVENSCROFT INC**
473 Dunham Rd Ste 209 (60174-1427)
**PHONE**...................630 513-9911
Peter Biagioni, *President*
▲ **EMP:** 5
**SALES (est):** 496.7K **Privately Held**
**SIC:** 3089 Extruded finished plastic products

### (G-19251)
**RAY TOOL & ENGINEERING INC**
Also Called: Rte
2440 Production Dr (60174-2455)
**PHONE**...................630 587-0000
**Fax:** 630 587-0100
Michael Almgren, *President*
Mike Selmer, *Vice Pres*
Pat Kooima, *Project Mgr*
Gail Dewitt, *Marketing Mgr*
Jess Forester, *Info Tech Dir*
**EMP:** 24
**SQ FT:** 10,000
**SALES (est):** 4.1MM **Privately Held**
**SIC:** 3544 Special dies & tools

### (G-19252)
**REICHEL HARDWARE COMPANY INC**
1820 Wallace Ave Ste 122 (60174-3413)
**PHONE**...................630 762-7394
**Fax:** 630 762-7393
Patti Jo Lemke, *President*
▲ **EMP:** 4
**SALES (est):** 426.9K **Privately Held**
**WEB:** www.diagerusa.com
**SIC:** 3429 3545 Manufactured hardware (general); chucks: drill, lathe or magnetic (machine tool accessories)

### (G-19253)
**ROCKTENN CP LLC**
417 37th Ave (60174-5415)
**PHONE**...................630 587-9429
Dan Kurtz, *General Mgr*
**EMP:** 30
**SALES (corp-wide):** 14.1B **Publicly Held**
**WEB:** www.smurfit-stone.com
**SIC:** 2631 Paperboard mills

# Saint Charles - Kane County (G-19254)

HQ: Westrock Cp, Llc
504 Thrasher St
Norcross GA 30071

### (G-19254)
### RR DONNELLEY & SONS COMPANY
Also Called: W C S
1750 Wallace Ave (60174-3401)
PHONE..................................630 377-2586
Fax: 800 233-2016
Keith Gonnerman, *VP Mfg*
John Sladek, *Research*
Diane Schriener, *Merchandise Mgr*
Michael Kappel, *Software Dev*
EMP: 175
SALES (corp-wide): 6.9B **Publicly Held**
WEB: www.rrdonnelley.com
SIC: 2761 Manifold business forms
PA: R. R. Donnelley & Sons Company
35 W Wacker Dr Ste 3650
Chicago IL 60601
312 326-8000

### (G-19255)
### RR DONNELLEY & SONS COMPANY
Also Called: Banta Book Group
609 Kirk Rd (60174-3433)
PHONE..................................630 513-4681
Dave Bull, *Manager*
EMP: 100
SALES (corp-wide): 6.9B **Publicly Held**
WEB: www.rrdonnelley.com
SIC: 2732 Books: printing & binding
PA: R. R. Donnelley & Sons Company
35 W Wacker Dr Ste 3650
Chicago IL 60601
312 326-8000

### (G-19256)
### RR DONNELLEY & SONS COMPANY
Also Called: RR Donnelley
609 Kirk Rd (60174-3433)
PHONE..................................630 762-7600
Troy Lancor, *Plant Mgr*
EMP: 60
SALES (corp-wide): 6.9B **Publicly Held**
WEB: www.moore.com
SIC: 2752 2671 2396 Commercial printing, lithographic; packaging paper & plastics film, coated & laminated; automotive & apparel trimmings
PA: R. R. Donnelley & Sons Company
35 W Wacker Dr Ste 3650
Chicago IL 60601
312 326-8000

### (G-19257)
### RUTHERFORD & ASSOCIATES
42w465 Foxfield Dr (60175-7932)
PHONE..................................630 365-5263
Hal Rutherford, *Owner*
Sean Berens, *Manager*
EMP: 2
SALES (est): 210.5K **Privately Held**
SIC: 8711 3599 7389 Designing: ship, boat, machine & product; machine & other job shop work; design services

### (G-19258)
### SAASOOM LLC
7n063 Plymouth Ct (60175-5801)
PHONE..................................630 561-7300
Maung Aung Khin, *Principal*
Maung Khin,
EMP: 3
SALES (est): 100.5K **Privately Held**
SIC: 2023 Dietary supplements, dairy & non-dairy based

### (G-19259)
### SC AVIATION INC
1433 Lancaster Ave (60174-3321)
PHONE..................................800 416-4176
Fax: 630 443-0491
John Bullock, *Manager*
EMP: 3
SALES (est): 220K **Privately Held**
SIC: 3721 Aircraft

### (G-19260)
### SCANLAB AMERICA INC
100 Illinois St Ste 200 (60174-1867)
PHONE..................................630 797-2044
Georg Hofner, *CEO*
Dale Sabo, *Vice Pres*
Dirk Thomas, *Admin Sec*
EMP: 4
SQ FT: 1,200
SALES: 10MM
SALES (corp-wide): 96.8MM **Privately Held**
WEB: www.scanlab-america.com
SIC: 3821 Laser beam alignment devices
HQ: Scanlab Gmbh
Siemensstr. 2a
Puchheim 82178
898 007-460

### (G-19261)
### SCHOLASTIC INC
2315 Dean St Ste 600 (60175-4823)
PHONE..................................630 443-8197
Gaye Masnjak, *VP Sales*
Gaye Masanjak, *Manager*
Michelle Clark, *Manager*
Joyce Temple, *Manager*
Russell Danna, *Consultant*
EMP: 28
SALES (corp-wide): 1.6B **Publicly Held**
WEB: www.scholasticdealer.com
SIC: 2731 8742 Books: publishing only; sales (including sales management) consultant
HQ: Scholastic Inc.
557 Broadway Lbby 1
New York NY 10012
800 724-6527

### (G-19262)
### SEK CORPORATION (PA)
Also Called: Snap Edge
3925 Stern Ave (60174-5441)
PHONE..................................630 762-0606
Fred Strobl, *President*
Brad Le Gare, *Vice Pres*
Bradley Legare, *Vice Pres*
Keith Ogrady, *Vice Pres*
Laura Anderson, *Manager*
▲ EMP: 37
SQ FT: 1,500
SALES (est): 8.3MM **Privately Held**
WEB: www.snapedgeusa.com
SIC: 3089 Flat panels, plastic

### (G-19263)
### SKYJACK EQUIPMENT INC (HQ)
3451 Swenson Ave (60174-3449)
PHONE..................................630 797-3299
Linda Hasenfratz, *President*
Dan Boivin, *Purch Mgr*
Linda Moritz, *Accountant*
George Kidwell, *Sales Mgr*
Chuck Berls, *Director*
▼ EMP: 38
SQ FT: 25,000
SALES: 26.6MM
SALES (corp-wide): 4.4B **Privately Held**
SIC: 3531 3441 Aerial work platforms: hydraulic/elec. truck/carrier mounted; fabricated structural metal
PA: Linamar Corporation
287 Speedvale Ave W
Guelph ON N1H 1
519 836-7550

### (G-19264)
### SKYJACK INC
Also Called: Skyjack Parts & Svc Skyjack
3451 Swenson Ave (60174-3449)
PHONE..................................630 262-0005
Fax: 630 262-0006
Chuck Burls, *General Mgr*
Dick Pomponio, *Regl Sales Mgr*
Chuck Berls, *Manager*
Dan Woodruff, *Manager*
Robert Klein, *Admin Asst*
EMP: 7
SALES (corp-wide): 4.4B **Privately Held**
SIC: 3531 Aerial work platforms: hydraulic/elec. truck/carrier mounted
HQ: Skyjack Inc
55 Campbell Rd Suite 1
Guelph ON N1H 1
519 837-0888

### (G-19265)
### SOFTWARE SUPPORT SYSTEMS INC
803 S 5th Ave (60174-2933)
PHONE..................................630 587-2999
Lynn Brueswitz, *President*
EMP: 2
SQ FT: 1,200
SALES (est): 206.5K **Privately Held**
SIC: 7372 Prepackaged software

### (G-19266)
### SOLID STATE LUMINAIRES LLC
3609 Swenson Ave (60174-3441)
PHONE..................................877 775-4733
Bruce J Bukas, *Mng Member*
▲ EMP: 5
SALES (est): 648.5K **Privately Held**
SIC: 3674 Light emitting diodes

### (G-19267)
### SPECIALTY GRAPHICS SUPPLY INC
3875 Commerce Dr (60174-5325)
PHONE..................................630 584-8202
David Lawrence, *President*
Pamela Lawrence, *Admin Sec*
EMP: 5
SALES (est): 320K **Privately Held**
WEB: www.specialty-graphics.com
SIC: 3993 Signs & advertising specialties

### (G-19268)
### ST CHARLES MEMORIAL WORKS INC (PA)
Also Called: Elgin Granite Works
1640 W Main St (60174-1630)
PHONE..................................630 584-0183
Fax: 630 584-0189
Terry Carlson, *President*
Susan Carlson, *Corp Secy*
Christian Carlson, *Vice Pres*
Jean Downing, *Office Mgr*
EMP: 4
SQ FT: 3,000
SALES (est): 856.6K **Privately Held**
SIC: 5999 7261 1542 3281 Monuments, finished to custom order; funeral service & crematories; mausoleum construction; cut stone & stone products

### (G-19269)
### ST CHARLES STAMPING INC
318 N 4th St (60174-1824)
P.O. Box 1029 (60174-7029)
PHONE..................................630 584-2029
Fax: 630 584-1091
Bernie W Klein, *President*
Dave Blankenship, *President*
Gunter L Steves, *Corp Secy*
Sharon Russell, *Vice Pres*
EMP: 19
SQ FT: 25,000
SALES (est): 3.9MM **Privately Held**
WEB: www.scstamping.com
SIC: 3469 Stamping metal for the trade

### (G-19270)
### STELLAR PLASTICS CORPORATION
3627 Stern Ave (60174-5405)
PHONE..................................630 443-1200
Greg Freimuth, *President*
Daniel Scioli, *Vice Pres*
Michael Tobolt, *Plant Mgr*
Rose Freund, *Controller*
Jeff Frasher, *Manager*
EMP: 70
SQ FT: 30,000
SALES: 6MM **Privately Held**
SIC: 3089 Injection molding of plastics

### (G-19271)
### STERLING SYSTEMS SALES CORP
3745 Stern Ave (60174-5403)
PHONE..................................630 584-3580
Jerome D Schultz, *President*
Ruth Schultz, *Admin Sec*
▲ EMP: 6
SQ FT: 20,000
SALES: 1.4MM **Privately Held**
WEB: www.sterlingsystems.com
SIC: 3559 Electroplating machinery & equipment

### (G-19272)
### STRATA-TAC INC
3980 Swenson Ave (60174-3446)
PHONE..................................630 879-9388
Charles L Casagrande, *President*
Andrew Schwarzbauer, *Vice Pres*
Thomas Yeager, *Vice Pres*
Kari Necas, *Accountant*
Jeff Graham, *Marketing Staff*
▲ EMP: 17
SQ FT: 12,750
SALES (est): 5.8MM **Privately Held**
WEB: www.stratatac.cc
SIC: 2672 5085 5113 5131 Adhesive papers, labels or tapes: from purchased material; tape, pressure sensitive: made from purchased materials; adhesives, tape & plasters; pressure sensitive tape; synthetic fabrics

### (G-19273)
### STRATHMORE PRESS
Also Called: C N F
2400 E Main St (60174-2436)
PHONE..................................513 483-3600
Steven Sigewald, *CEO*
Jean Harmeyer, *Accountant*
Dan Carter, *Manager*
EMP: 29
SQ FT: 25,000
SALES (est): 4.8MM
SALES (corp-wide): 8.7MM **Privately Held**
WEB: www.strathmorepress.com
SIC: 2759 Publication printing
PA: Cns Inc
3716 Montgomery Rd
Cincinnati OH 45207
513 631-7073

### (G-19274)
### SUN CHEMICAL CORPORATION
Also Called: Coates Screen
2445 Production Dr (60174-2454)
PHONE..................................630 513-5348
Fax: 630 587-5226
Dennis Haiman, *Opers Mgr*
Mike Kellen, *Mktg Dir*
Tim Tesmer, *Marketing Mgr*
Brian Breidigan, *Branch Mgr*
John Goles, *Manager*
EMP: 160
SALES (corp-wide): 6.7B **Privately Held**
WEB: www.sunchemical.com
SIC: 2899 5085 Ink or writing fluids; ink, printers'
HQ: Sun Chemical Corporation
35 Waterview Blvd Ste 100
Parsippany NJ 07054
973 404-6000

### (G-19275)
### SUREBOND INC
3925 Stern Ave (60174-5441)
PHONE..................................630 762-0606
Todd Asmuth, *President*
Leslie Gallagher, *Manager*
EMP: 26
SQ FT: 2,000
SALES (est): 5.3MM
SALES (corp-wide): 8.3MM **Privately Held**
WEB: www.surebond.com
SIC: 2891 Adhesives; glue; caulking compounds; sealing compounds, synthetic rubber or plastic
PA: Sek Corporation
3925 Stern Ave
Saint Charles IL 60174
630 762-0606

### (G-19276)
### SWIFTY PRINT
210 W Main St (60174-1880)
P.O. Box 281 (60174-0281)
PHONE..................................630 584-9063
Fax: 630 584-9075
Gordon Brown, *President*
Anne C Brown, *Admin Sec*
EMP: 5
SQ FT: 1,200

# GEOGRAPHIC SECTION

**Saint Elmo - Fayette County (G-19303)**

**SALES (est):** 649.2K  **Privately Held**
**SIC:** 2752 2791 2789 2759 Commercial printing, offset; typesetting; bookbinding & related work; commercial printing

**(G-19277)**
### T F N W INC
Also Called: Minuteman Press
1574 E Main St (60174-2327)
**PHONE** .................................. 630 584-7383
Jerry Prasse, *President*
**EMP:** 4
**SQ FT:** 1,300
**SALES (est):** 429.1K  **Privately Held**
**SIC:** 2752 2759 2791 2789 Commercial printing, lithographic; ready prints; typesetting; bookbinding & related work

**(G-19278)**
### T P R RESOURCES INC
3604 Greenwood Ln (60175-5638)
**PHONE** .................................. 630 443-9060
**EMP:** 4 **EST:** 1996
**SALES (est):** 230K  **Privately Held**
**SIC:** 3999 Mfg Misc Products

**(G-19279)**
### TANDEM INDUSTRIES INC
3820 Ohio Ave Ste 16 (60174-5463)
**PHONE** .................................. 630 761-6615
**Fax:** 630 293-4417
James Burian, *President*
Lois Burian, *Officer*
**EMP:** 6
**SQ FT:** 4,250
**SALES:** 600K  **Privately Held**
**SIC:** 3448 3444 Ramps; prefabricated metal; sheet metalwork

**(G-19280)**
### TEAM CNC INC
761 N 17th St Ste 22 (60174-1667)
**PHONE** .................................. 630 377-2723
Gary Carpenter, *President*
**EMP:** 5 **EST:** 2006
**SALES (est):** 645K  **Privately Held**
**SIC:** 3545 Precision tools, machinists'

**(G-19281)**
### THE ATHLETIC EQUIPMENT SOURCE
1820 Wallace Ave Ste 124 (60174-3413)
**PHONE** .................................. 630 587-9333
Michael Fontana, *President*
**EMP:** 20
**SALES (est):** 2.4MM  **Privately Held**
**SIC:** 3949 Sporting & athletic goods

**(G-19282)**
### THOMAS & BETTS CORP
2580 Foxfield Rd Ste 306 (60174-1412)
**PHONE** .................................. 630 444-2151
David Kapfhamer, *Manager*
**EMP:** 4
**SALES (est):** 330K  **Privately Held**
**SIC:** 3699 Electrical equipment & supplies

**(G-19283)**
### THUROW TOOL WORKS INC
41 W 523 Rr 64 (60175)
**PHONE** .................................. 630 377-6403
Mark Thurow, *President*
**EMP:** 3 **EST:** 1989
**SQ FT:** 1,500
**SALES:** 370K  **Privately Held**
**SIC:** 3089 Injection molding of plastics

**(G-19284)**
### TOMS SIGNS
Also Called: Acclaim Sign Company
6n592 Il Route 25 (60174-5630)
**PHONE** .................................. 630 377-8525
**Fax:** 630 485-5164
Tom Deppe, *Owner*
**EMP:** 2
**SALES (est):** 384.5K  **Privately Held**
**WEB:** www.acclaimsignco.com
**SIC:** 3993 2759 Signs & advertising specialties; screen printing

**(G-19285)**
### TOOLS AVIATION LLC
Also Called: Personal Battery Caddy
3850 Swenson Ave (60174-3438)
**PHONE** .................................. 630 377-7260
Shawnta Mateja,
Kathy Foreman,
Richard Foreman,
**EMP:** 3
**SALES:** 410K  **Privately Held**
**SIC:** 3069 Battery boxes, jars or parts; hard rubber

**(G-19286)**
### TRIAD CONTROLS INC (PA)
3715 Swenson Ave (60174-3439)
**PHONE** .................................. 630 443-9343
Kenneth L Barron Jr, *President*
F Gary Kovac, *Vice Pres*
**EMP:** 50
**SALES (est):** 4.4MM  **Privately Held**
**WEB:** www.triadcontrols.com
**SIC:** 3842 Personal safety equipment

**(G-19287)**
### TRYAD SPECIALTIES INC (PA)
2015 Dean St Ste 6 (60174-1577)
**PHONE** .................................. 630 549-0079
**Fax:** 630 365-5446
Randy Norris, *President*
Jody Harness, *Vice Pres*
**EMP:** 11
**SQ FT:** 2,250
**SALES (est):** 5.5MM  **Privately Held**
**SIC:** 5199 2395 7371 Advertising specialties; emblems, embroidered; embroidery products, except schiffli machine; computer software systems analysis & design, custom

**(G-19288)**
### UNIPHASE INC
425 38th Ave (60174-5425)
**PHONE** .................................. 630 584-4747
**Fax:** 630 584-9295
William Morici, *President*
Perry Norsworthy, *Engineer*
Helen Morrissey, *Persnl Dir*
**EMP:** 38
**SQ FT:** 35,000
**SALES (est):** 9.6MM  **Privately Held**
**SIC:** 3089 Injection molded finished plastic products

**(G-19289)**
### UNITED LABORATORIES INC (PA)
320 37th Ave (60174-5464)
P.O. Box 410 (60174-0410)
**PHONE** .................................. 630 377-0900
**Fax:** 630 433-2087
Daniel Young, *Ch of Bd*
Eric Frazier, *President*
Julie Benson, *Vice Pres*
Michael Cusumano, *Vice Pres*
Timothy Dalrymple, *Vice Pres*
◆ **EMP:** 65 **EST:** 1964
**SQ FT:** 80,000
**SALES (est):** 45.6MM  **Privately Held**
**WEB:** www.beearthsmart.com
**SIC:** 2842 5169 Specialty cleaning preparations; specialty cleaning & sanitation preparations

**(G-19290)**
### UP NORTH PRINTING INC
1519 E Main St Ste 600 (60174-2392)
**PHONE** .................................. 630 584-8675
William Pickford, *President*
Evette Montoya, *Office Mgr*
Paula Labash, *Manager*
**EMP:** 6
**SALES (est):** 694.6K  **Privately Held**
**SIC:** 2752 Commercial printing, lithographic

**(G-19291)**
### WARWICK PUBLISHING COMPANY
2601 E Main St (60174-4289)
**PHONE** .................................. 630 584-3871
Robert H Paschal, *CEO*
James P Paschal, *Principal*
Don F Paschal, *Principal*
Nancy Irmiter, *Vice Pres*
Sandy Peterman, *Purch Mgr*
▲ **EMP:** 100 **EST:** 1881
**SQ FT:** 115,000
**SALES (est):** 19.3MM  **Privately Held**
**SIC:** 2752 2675 Calendars, lithographed; folders, filing, die-cut; made from purchased materials

**(G-19292)**
### WATER DYNAMICS INC (PA)
Also Called: Leasing Dynamics
1553 Allen Ln (60174-2319)
**PHONE** .................................. 630 584-8475
**Fax:** 630 377-7404
William E Bergmann Jr, *President*
Mary Collin, *Vice Pres*
Mary E Collins, *Vice Pres*
James L Collins, *Treasurer*
Mary M Bergmann, *Admin Sec*
**EMP:** 6
**SQ FT:** 3,500
**SALES:** 920K  **Privately Held**
**WEB:** www.waterdynamics.com
**SIC:** 3589 7389 Water treatment equipment, industrial; water softener service

**(G-19293)**
### WEST VLY GRAPHICS & PRINT INC
Also Called: Kwik Kopy Printing
201 S 3rd St (60174-2839)
**PHONE** .................................. 630 377-7575
William R Ledvora, *President*
Margaret M Ledvora, *Admin Sec*
**EMP:** 9
**SQ FT:** 2,500
**SALES (est):** 1.6MM  **Privately Held**
**SIC:** 2752 2796 2789 Commercial printing, lithographic; platemaking services; bookbinding & related work

**(G-19294)**
### WESTROCK CP LLC
415 37th Ave (60174-5415)
**PHONE** .................................. 630 443-3538
**Fax:** 630 443-0215
Robert Curran, *Branch Mgr*
**EMP:** 60
**SALES (corp-wide):** 14.1B  **Publicly Held**
**WEB:** www.smurfit-stone.com
**SIC:** 2631 Paperboard mills
**HQ:** Westrock Cp, Llc
504 Thrasher St
Norcross GA 30071

**(G-19295)**
### WHITE INTERNATIONAL INC
2560 Foxfield Rd Ste 200 (60174-1492)
P.O. Box 3670 (60174-9088)
**PHONE** .................................. 630 377-9966
Bob M White, *President*
Lita K Jimenez, *Exec VP*
Julie Holdsworth, *Opers Mgr*
Phillip Noffke, *Director*
Kathy Kregul, *Executive Asst*
**EMP:** 20
**SQ FT:** 7,500
**SALES (est):** 4.4MM  **Privately Held**
**SIC:** 5153 4741 2048 4011 Grains; rental of railroad cars; feed supplements; railroads, line-haul operating; marine towing services; tugboat service

**(G-19296)**
### WILDLIFE COOKIE COMPANY
1815 Wallace Ave Ste 305 (60174-3421)
P.O. Box 1158 (60174-7158)
**PHONE** .................................. 630 377-6196
Kenneth Smith, *President*
**EMP:** 4
**SQ FT:** 2,000
**SALES (est):** 350.2K  **Privately Held**
**SIC:** 2052 Cookies

**(G-19297)**
### WINFIELD TECHNOLOGY INC
53 Stirrup Cup Ct (60174-1432)
**PHONE** .................................. 630 584-0475
James E Spitzer, *President*
Roberta L Spitzer, *Corp Secy*
**EMP:** 13
**SQ FT:** 11,000
**SALES (est):** 960K  **Privately Held**
**SIC:** 3069 Tape, pressure sensitive; rubber

**(G-19298)**
### WISE PLASTICS TECHNOLOGIES INC (PA)
Also Called: Wise Hamlin Plastics
3810 Stern Ave (60174-5402)
**PHONE** .................................. 630 584-2307
**Fax:** 847 697-2011
Fred W Wise, *President*
Mike Cusack, *Vice Pres*
Dave Laboda, *Vice Pres*
Joe Shad, *Vice Pres*
Lenore J Tocki, *Vice Pres*
▲ **EMP:** 125
**SQ FT:** 100,000
**SALES (est):** 36.7MM  **Privately Held**
**WEB:** www.wiseplastics.com
**SIC:** 3089 Injection molding of plastics

**(G-19299)**
### WORK AREA PROTECTION CORP
2500 Production Dr (60174-3350)
P.O. Box 4087 (60174-9081)
**PHONE** .................................. 630 377-9100
**Fax:** 630 377-9270
Joseph B Ford, *President*
James W Van Buren, *Principal*
Douglas S Comstock, *Vice Pres*
Donald L Detwiler, *Vice Pres*
Steven B Detwiler, *Vice Pres*
▼ **EMP:** 55
**SQ FT:** 50,000
**SALES (est):** 23.1MM
**SALES (corp-wide):** 651.9MM  **Privately Held**
**WEB:** www.workareaprotection.com
**SIC:** 3089 Stock shapes, plastic
**PA:** New Enterprise Stone & Lime Co., Inc.
3912 Brumbaugh Rd
New Enterprise PA 16664
814 224-6883

**(G-19300)**
### WRITE STUFF
5n465 Hazelwood Ct (60175-8168)
**PHONE** .................................. 630 365-4425
Michele Dannewitz, *Sales Mgr*
**EMP:** 3
**SALES (est):** 73K  **Privately Held**
**SIC:** 5943 5112 3999 Stationery stores; stationery & office supplies; manufacturing industries

**(G-19301)**
### XENA INTERNATIONAL INC (PA)
39w082 Foxwood Ln (60175-6187)
**PHONE** .................................. 630 587-2734
Richard Sikorski, *President*
Judith Sikorski, *Chairman*
Salvatore Ziccarelli, *Vice Pres*
Amanda Clark, *Manager*
▲ **EMP:** 2
**SQ FT:** 23,000
**SALES (est):** 5.2MM  **Privately Held**
**WEB:** www.xenainternational.com
**SIC:** 2099 Food preparations

**(G-19302)**
### ZELLER + GMELIN CORPORATION
3820 Ohio Ave Ste 1 (60174-5461)
**PHONE** .................................. 630 443-8800
Katrina Herrera, *Branch Mgr*
Dan Watson, *Manager*
**EMP:** 5
**SALES (corp-wide):** 246.3MM  **Privately Held**
**WEB:** www.zeller-gmelin.com
**SIC:** 5085 2899 Ink, printers'; ink or writing fluids
**HQ:** Zeller + Gmelin Corporation
4801 Audubon Dr
Richmond VA 23231
804 275-8486

---

## Saint Elmo
### *Fayette County*

**(G-19303)**
### BASIN TRANSPORTS
112 E 4th St (62458-1609)
**PHONE** .................................. 618 829-3323
**EMP:** 4

# Saint Elmo - Fayette County (G-19304)

SQ FT: 1,000
SALES (est): 347.7K **Privately Held**
SIC: 1311 Crude Oil Producer

**(G-19304)**
**BELDEN ENTERPRISES LP**
801 N Elm St (62458-1362)
P.O. Box 159 (62458-0159)
PHONE.................................618 829-3274
Fax: 618 829-5510
David Belden, *Partner*
Susan Belden, *Partner*
EMP: 10
SQ FT: 1,800
SALES (est): 1.1MM **Privately Held**
SIC: 1311 Crude petroleum production

**(G-19305)**
**D & Z EXPLORATION INC**
901 N Elm St (62458-1361)
P.O. Box 159 (62458-0159)
PHONE.................................618 829-3274
Zane Belden, *Treasurer*
EMP: 3
SALES: 950K **Privately Held**
SIC: 1311 Crude petroleum & natural gas

**(G-19306)**
**ECOLAB FF APERION CARE ST**
221 E Cumberland Rd (62458-1662)
PHONE.................................618 829-5581
EMP: 6
SALES (est): 506.1K **Privately Held**
SIC: 2841 Soap & other detergents

**(G-19307)**
**FELLER OILFIELD SERVICE INC**
Hwy 40 W (62458)
P.O. Box 67 (62458-0067)
PHONE.................................618 267-5650
Kirk V Feller, *President*
EMP: 10
SQ FT: 7,200
SALES: 3.4MM **Privately Held**
SIC: 1389 Oil field services

**(G-19308)**
**MARATHON PETROLEUM COMPANY LP**
200 E 4th St (62458-1611)
P.O. Box 35 (62458-0035)
PHONE.................................618 829-3288
Jeremy Dilley, *Branch Mgr*
EMP: 6 **Publicly Held**
WEB: www.mapllc.com
SIC: 5172 5032 2951 Petroleum products; asphalt mixture; asphalt paving mixtures & blocks
HQ: Marathon Petroleum Company Lp
   539 S Main St
   Findlay OH 45840

**(G-19309)**
**NATURAL GAS PIPELINE AMER LLC**
6 Miles N On Elm St (62458)
Rr # 2 Box 142b (62458-4079)
PHONE.................................618 829-3224
Fax: 618 829-3317
Gary Buchler, *Principal*
EMP: 23
SALES (corp-wide): 13B **Publicly Held**
SIC: 4922 1311 Natural gas transmission; crude petroleum & natural gas
HQ: Natural Gas Pipeline Company Of America Llc
   1001 Louisiana St
   Houston TX 77002
   713 369-9000

**(G-19310)**
**PINNACLE FOODS GROUP LLC**
1000 Brewbaker Dr (62458-1234)
PHONE.................................618 829-3275
Ryan Durbin, *Engineer*
Mark Hansen, *Plant Engr*
Laura Wharton, *Branch Mgr*
Kent Trick, *Technical Staff*
EMP: 300
SALES (corp-wide): 2.5B **Publicly Held**
WEB: www.aurorafoods.com
SIC: 2038 4225 Frozen specialties; breakfasts, frozen & packaged; pizza, frozen; waffles, frozen; general warehousing & storage

HQ: Pinnacle Foods Group Llc
   399 Jefferson Rd
   Parsippany NJ 07054

**(G-19311)**
**SMITH WELDING LLC**
2238 N 2225 St (62458-4054)
P.O. Box 2 (62458-0002)
PHONE.................................618 829-5414
Terry Smith, *Principal*
EMP: 3 EST: 1976
SQ FT: 4,400
SALES (est): 309.9K **Privately Held**
SIC: 7692 Welding repair

## Saint Francisville
### Lawrence County

**(G-19312)**
**D LITTLE DRILLING**
4734 Country Club Rd (62460-3042)
PHONE.................................618 943-3721
David Hulfachor, *Owner*
Denise Hulfachor, *Co-Owner*
EMP: 3
SALES (est): 278.7K **Privately Held**
SIC: 1311 Crude petroleum production

**(G-19313)**
**GRAYS CABINET CO**
Rr 1 (62460-9801)
P.O. Box 310 (62460-0310)
PHONE.................................618 948-2211
Shane Gray, *President*
Helen Gray, *Admin Sec*
EMP: 1 EST: 1945
SQ FT: 1,200
SALES (est): 202.9K **Privately Held**
SIC: 2521 2431 2517 2434 Cabinets, office: wood; millwork; wood television & radio cabinets; wood kitchen cabinets

**(G-19314)**
**TUSSEY G K OIL EXPLRTN & PRDC**
4th & Main St (62460)
P.O. Box 69 (62460-0069)
PHONE.................................618 948-2871
Gary K Tussey, *Owner*
Cindy Hasler, *Manager*
EMP: 3
SALES (est): 180K **Privately Held**
SIC: 1311 1381 Crude petroleum production; drilling oil & gas wells

## Saint Jacob
### Madison County

**(G-19315)**
**FIFTH QUARTER**
1770 Triad Rd (62281-1108)
PHONE.................................618 346-6659
EMP: 3
SALES (est): 339.9K **Privately Held**
SIC: 3131 Mfg Footwear Cut Stock

## Saint Joseph
### Champaign County

**(G-19316)**
**LEADER**
429 E Warren St (61873-9203)
PHONE.................................217 469-0045
Scott Hunter, *President*
Nora Maberry, *Publisher*
EMP: 3
SALES (est): 131.3K **Privately Held**
SIC: 2711 Newspapers, publishing & printing

**(G-19317)**
**RIVER BEND WILD GAME & SAUSAGE**
1161 County Road 2400 E (61873-9726)
PHONE.................................217 688-3337
Mary Ellen Stites, *Owner*
EMP: 4

SALES (est): 340.4K **Privately Held**
SIC: 3421 Table & food cutlery, including butchers'

**(G-19318)**
**SHAPE MASTER INC**
704 E Lincoln St (61873-9028)
PHONE.................................217 469-7027
Kenneth Cooley Jr, *Principal*
EMP: 4
SALES (est): 247.7K **Privately Held**
SIC: 3082 Unsupported plastics profile shapes

**(G-19319)**
**WYLDEWOOD CELLARS 2 LLC**
218 E Lincoln St (61873)
PHONE.................................217 469-9463
Tracie Trotter,
EMP: 3 EST: 2010
SALES (est): 262.4K **Privately Held**
SIC: 2084 Wines

## Saint Peter
### Fayette County

**(G-19320)**
**AUTHENTIC STREET SIGNS INC**
183 Main St (62880)
PHONE.................................618 349-8878
Mark Wollin, *CEO*
◆ EMP: 4
SQ FT: 35,000
SALES (est): 495.1K **Privately Held**
WEB: www.authenticstreetsigns.com
SIC: 3993 Signs & advertising specialties

**(G-19321)**
**COURSONS CORING & DRILLING**
Nr Hwy 185 (62880)
Rr # 1 Box 38a (62880-0222)
PHONE.................................618 349-8765
Richard Courson, *President*
Doris Courson, *Admin Sec*
EMP: 3
SALES (est): 220K **Privately Held**
SIC: 1381 1781 Directional drilling oil & gas wells; water well drilling

**(G-19322)**
**FLINT GROUP US LLC**
619 N 2200 St (62880-0222)
PHONE.................................618 349-8384
David Frescon, *Principal*
Johnny Perret, *Safety Mgr*
Michael Hackett, *Manager*
EMP: 19
SALES (corp-wide): 3.8B **Privately Held**
WEB: www.flintink.com
SIC: 2893 Printing ink
PA: Flint Group Us Llc
   14909 N Beck Rd
   Plymouth MI 48170
   734 781-4600

## Sainte Marie
### Jasper County

**(G-19323)**
**D M MANUFACTURING 2 INC**
490 S Main St (62459)
P.O. Box 8 (62459-0008)
PHONE.................................618 455-3550
Fax: 618 455-3083
Don E Geltz, *President*
Barbara Geltz, *Admin Sec*
EMP: 8
SQ FT: 18,000
SALES (est): 1.7MM **Privately Held**
SIC: 3523 7692 Hog feeding, handling & watering equipment; welding repair

**(G-19324)**
**HARTRICH MEATS INC**
326 W Embarras St (62459-1003)
P.O. Box 27 (62459-0027)
PHONE.................................618 455-3172
Mark Hartrich, *President*
Lucy Hartrich, *Treasurer*

Tony Hartrich, *Admin Sec*
EMP: 9
SQ FT: 6,000
SALES: 500K **Privately Held**
SIC: 2011 5421 5411 2013 Meat packing plants; meat & fish markets; grocery stores; sausages & other prepared meats

**(G-19325)**
**MONT EAGLE PRODUCTS INC (PA)**
219 S Main St (62459)
P.O. Box 176 (62459-0176)
PHONE.................................618 455-3344
Fax: 618 455-3346
Rick Seamon, *President*
Kent Deisher, *Admin Sec*
EMP: 5
SQ FT: 7,200
SALES (est): 598.7K **Privately Held**
SIC: 2048 5191 Feed premixes; farm supplies

## Salem
### Marion County

**(G-19326)**
**AMERICANA BUILDING PDTS INC (PA)**
2 Industrial Dr (62881-5865)
P.O. Box 1290 (62881-6290)
PHONE.................................618 548-2800
Gerald G Purcell, *President*
David Allen, *Vice Pres*
Melanie Johnson, *Treasurer*
Melissa Ortiz, *Credit Mgr*
Nancy Clark, *Human Res Mgr*
◆ EMP: 75 EST: 1949
SQ FT: 117,000
SALES (est): 3.2MM **Privately Held**
SIC: 3448 2394 3444 Prefabricated metal buildings; carports: prefabricated metal; ramps: prefabricated metal; awnings, fabric: made from purchased materials; awnings, sheet metal

**(G-19327)**
**BAILEY BUSINESS GROUP**
3089 State Route 37 (62881-3667)
PHONE.................................618 548-3566
Keith Bailey, *Owner*
Rachel Bailey, *Co-Owner*
EMP: 2
SALES (est): 203K **Privately Held**
WEB: www.baileybusinessgroup.com
SIC: 8741 2421 7389 3559 Business management; sawmills & planing mills, general; music recording producer; kilns

**(G-19328)**
**BOATMAN SIGNS**
1700 E Main St (62881-3535)
PHONE.................................618 548-6567
Dale Boatman, *Owner*
EMP: 3
SALES (est): 255.8K **Privately Held**
SIC: 3993 Signs & advertising specialties

**(G-19329)**
**DEEP ROCK ENERGY CORPORATION**
631 S Broadway Ave (62881-2210)
P.O. Box 160, Kinmundy (62854-0160)
PHONE.................................618 548-2779
Ben Webster, *President*
EMP: 15
SQ FT: 1,500
SALES (est): 1.6MM **Privately Held**
SIC: 1311 Crude petroleum & natural gas production

**(G-19330)**
**DUNCAN OIL COMPANY INC**
Also Called: Precision Pump & Valve Service
300 S Washington St (62881-3027)
P.O. Box 218 (62881-0218)
PHONE.................................618 548-2923
Gene L Duncan, *President*
Mary Duncan, *Vice Pres*
EMP: 8
SQ FT: 1,800

# GEOGRAPHIC SECTION
## Salem - Marion County (G-19354)

SALES (est): 800K **Privately Held**
SIC: **1311** 1389 Crude petroleum production; oil field services

### (G-19331)
### ESI STEEL & FABRICATION
Also Called: E S I Steel Fabrication
1645 N Broadway Ave (62881-4234)
PHONE..................618 548-3017
**Fax:** 618 548-3062
Marshall C Smith, *President*
Kerry Smith, *Vice Pres*
Vivian Petrea, *Office Mgr*
Billie Smith, *Admin Sec*
**EMP:** 12
**SQ FT:** 37,000
**SALES (est):** 2MM **Privately Held**
SIC: **3441** 3448 3444 Fabricated structural metal; prefabricated metal buildings; sheet metalwork

### (G-19332)
### FIBER WINDERS INC
1111 S Broadway Ave (62881-2431)
P.O. Box 40 (62881-0040)
PHONE..................618 548-6388
**Fax:** 618 548-6388
**EMP:** 4
**SQ FT:** 14,000
**SALES (est):** 34.2K **Privately Held**
SIC: **3089** 3088 Plastic & fiberglass tanks; plastics plumbing fixtures

### (G-19333)
### FINKS OIL CO INC
519 W Boone St (62881-1222)
PHONE..................618 548-5757
**EMP:** 3 **EST:** 1974
**SQ FT:** 2,000
**SALES (est):** 270K **Privately Held**
SIC: **1311** Crude Oil Producer

### (G-19334)
### GEMTAR INC
138 Woodland Dr (62881-2635)
PHONE..................618 548-1353
**Fax:** 618 548-9853
Jim Rainwater, *President*
Betty Rainwater, *Admin Sec*
**EMP:** 4
**SALES (est):** 350K **Privately Held**
SIC: **3533** 3536 3531 Oil field machinery & equipment; drilling tools for gas, oil or water wells; hoists, cranes & monorails; construction machinery

### (G-19335)
### GOSSETT PRINTING INC
2100 Old Texas Ln (62881-5835)
P.O. Box 631 (62881-0631)
PHONE..................618 548-2583
**Fax:** 618 548-2597
Jayson Gossett, *President*
**EMP:** 3
**SQ FT:** 2,400
**SALES (est):** 302.7K **Privately Held**
**WEB:** www.gossettprinting.com
SIC: **2752** 2791 2789 Commercial printing, lithographic; typesetting; bookbinding & related work

### (G-19336)
### HAROLD PREFINISHED WOOD INC
5318 State Route 37 (62881-4754)
PHONE..................618 548-1414
**Fax:** 618 548-1427
Harold Smith, *Owner*
Kay Smith, *Corp Secy*
Tony Boyles, *Vice Pres*
**EMP:** 15
**SQ FT:** 30,000
**SALES (est):** 880K **Privately Held**
SIC: **2431** Doors, wood

### (G-19337)
### JERRY D GRAHAM OIL
Also Called: Indian Point Oil & Gas
1213 S Broadway Ave (62881-2406)
P.O. Box 1118 (62881-6118)
PHONE..................618 548-5540
Jerry Graham, *Owner*
**EMP:** 3
**SALES (est):** 186.7K **Privately Held**
SIC: **1381** Drilling oil & gas wells

### (G-19338)
### MERZ VAULT COMPANY INC
2918 State Route 37 (62881-3664)
P.O. Box 382 (62881-0382)
PHONE..................618 548-2859
**Fax:** 618 548-2878
William Randy Vogt, *President*
Jan Vogt, *Admin Sec*
**EMP:** 23 **EST:** 1947
**SQ FT:** 28,000
**SALES (est):** 3.3MM **Privately Held**
SIC: **3272** 7261 Burial vaults, concrete or precast terrazzo; funeral service & crematories

### (G-19339)
### MINOR LEAGUE INC
905 E Main St (62881-2940)
PHONE..................618 548-8040
**Fax:** 618 548-8051
Jeff Morgan, *President*
Michael Bolton, *Corp Secy*
**EMP:** 3
**SQ FT:** 3,400
**SALES (est):** 410K **Privately Held**
**WEB:** www.minorleague.com
SIC: **5941** 2395 5999 Team sports equipment; embroidery & art needlework; trophies & plaques

### (G-19340)
### NORTH AMERICAN LIGHTING INC
Also Called: Signal Lighting Operations
1875 W Main St (62881-5839)
PHONE..................618 548-6249
**Fax:** 618 548-6256
Mike Page, *QA Dir*
Mike Blackburn, *Engineer*
Gregory Goodnight, *Engineer*
Wayne Howard, *Engineer*
Shannon Iffert, *Engineer*
**EMP:** 900
**SALES (corp-wide):** 7.4B **Privately Held**
**WEB:** www.nal.com
SIC: **3647** 3641 Automotive lighting fixtures; electric lamps
**HQ:** North American Lighting, Inc.
2275 S Main St
Paris IL 61944
217 465-6600

### (G-19341)
### P J REPAIR SERVICE INC
108 S Missouri Ave (62881)
P.O. Box 426 (62881-0426)
PHONE..................618 548-5690
**Fax:** 618 548-5691
Phill Dial, *President*
Kim Dial, *Vice Pres*
**EMP:** 13
**SQ FT:** 8,885
**SALES:** 1MM **Privately Held**
SIC: **7699** 1389 Aircraft & heavy equipment repair services; oil field services

### (G-19342)
### PARK VIEW MANUFACTURING CORP
2510 S Broadway Ave (62881-3650)
PHONE..................618 548-9054
**Fax:** 618 548-9439
Juliette I Nimmons, *Ch of Bd*
John Mansfield, *President*
James Walker, *Vice Pres*
Ron Scharf, *Admin Sec*
▲ **EMP:** 100
**SQ FT:** 106,000
**SALES (est):** 5.8MM **Privately Held**
SIC: **3949** 8732 Helmets, athletic; pads: football, basketball, soccer, lacrosse, etc.; research services, except laboratory

### (G-19343)
### POLAR CORPORATION
Also Called: Jarco
1414 S Broadway Ave (62881-2437)
P.O. Box 56 (62881-0056)
PHONE..................618 548-3660
**Fax:** 618 548-9824
Don Haiker, *QC Dir*
Bernie Bjorndahl, *Sales Staff*
William Soulon, *Manager*
**EMP:** 25

**SALES (corp-wide):** 572.7MM **Privately Held**
SIC: **3715** 7538 5531 5084 Truck trailers; general automotive repair shops; automotive & home supply stores; industrial machinery & equipment; truck & bus bodies
**HQ:** Polar Corporation
1015 W St Germain St 42 Ste 420
Hopkins MN 55305
612 430-6401

### (G-19344)
### PRECISION CONTAINER INC
1370 W Main St (62881-3802)
PHONE..................618 548-2830
Daniel Ackman, *President*
Angie Tolliver, *Officer*
**EMP:** 9
**SALES (est):** 770K **Privately Held**
**WEB:** www.precisioncontainer.com
SIC: **3089** Plastic containers, except foam

### (G-19345)
### PRECISION TRUCK PRODUCTS INC
2625 S Broadway Ave (62881-3601)
P.O. Box 1224 (62881-6224)
PHONE..................618 548-9011
**Fax:** 618 548-9016
Dave Burdin, *CEO*
Bert Kingsley, *COO*
David McIntosh, *VP Sales*
Adam Ansberry, *Agent*
Taylor Burdin, *Agent*
**EMP:** 40
**SALES:** 5.6MM **Privately Held**
SIC: **3714** Trailer hitches, motor vehicle

### (G-19346)
### QUAD-COUNTY READY MIX CORP
3782 Hotze Rd (62881-2443)
PHONE..................618 548-2477
Jan Hubbell, *Manager*
**EMP:** 7
**SALES (corp-wide):** 18.9MM **Privately Held**
SIC: **3273** Ready-mixed concrete
**PA:** Quad-County Ready Mix Corp.
300 W 12th St
Okawville IL 62271
618 243-6430

### (G-19347)
### RADIAC ABRASIVES INC (HQ)
Also Called: National Grinding Wheel
1015 S College St (62881-2499)
P.O. Box 1410 (62881-7410)
PHONE..................618 548-4200
Chris Dashiell, *Plant Mgr*
James Fell, *Prdtn Mgr*
Aaron Degler, *Production*
Kelvin Thompson, *Purchasing*
Byron Weigler, *Purchasing*
◆ **EMP:** 196
**SQ FT:** 150,000
**SALES (est):** 140MM
**SALES (corp-wide):** 698.3MM **Privately Held**
**WEB:** www.radiac.com
SIC: **3291** Grindstones, artificial; wheels, abrasive
**PA:** Tyrolit - Schleifmittelwerke Swarovski K.G.
SwarovskistraBe 33
Schwaz 6130
524 260-60

### (G-19348)
### RONNIE JOE GRAHAM
Also Called: R J Graham Oil Company
420 W Schwartz St (62881-1552)
P.O. Box 474 (62881-0474)
PHONE..................618 548-5544
**Fax:** 618 548-3736
Ronnie Joe Graham, *Owner*
**EMP:** 2
**SQ FT:** 1,800
**SALES (est):** 288.7K **Privately Held**
SIC: **1311** Crude petroleum production

### (G-19349)
### SALEM TIMES-COMMONER PUBG CO (HQ)
Also Called: Tc Printers
120 S Broadway Ave (62881-1610)
PHONE..................618 548-3330
John Perrine, *President*
Dan Nichols, *General Mgr*
William Perrine, *Admin Sec*
**EMP:** 25 **EST:** 1946
**SQ FT:** 70,000
**SALES (est):** 6.2MM
**SALES (corp-wide):** 10.9MM **Privately Held**
SIC: **2711** 2791 2789 2752 Newspapers, publishing & printing; typesetting; bookbinding & related work; commercial printing, lithographic
**PA:** Centralia Press, Ltd
232 E Broadway
Centralia IL 62801
618 532-5604

### (G-19350)
### SHAWNEE STONE LLC (PA)
202 W Main St (62881-1519)
PHONE..................618 548-1585
Bryan Temple Hood,
Doug Alberson,
Rebecca S Weber,
**EMP:** 15
**SQ FT:** 15,600
**SALES:** 2MM **Privately Held**
SIC: **1422** Crushed & broken limestone

### (G-19351)
### SHETLEY MANAGEMENT INC
Also Called: Salem Business Center
112 W Main St (62881-1518)
PHONE..................618 548-1556
**Fax:** 618 548-6893
Marilyn Shetley, *President*
**EMP:** 4
**SALES (est):** 469.3K **Privately Held**
SIC: **2759** Business forms: printing

### (G-19352)
### SQUIBB TANK COMPANY
1001 S Broadway Ave (62881-2402)
P.O. Box 40 (62881-0040)
PHONE..................618 548-0141
Stephen M Squibb, *President*
Wayne T Puricelli, *Vice Pres*
**EMP:** 10
**SQ FT:** 19,000
**SALES (est):** 1.4MM **Privately Held**
SIC: **3533** 3443 Oil field machinery & equipment; fabricated plate work (boiler shop)

### (G-19353)
### STANFORD BETTENDORF INC
Also Called: Bettendorf Stanford
1370 W Main St (62881-3802)
P.O. Box 790 (62881-0790)
PHONE..................618 548-3555
**Fax:** 618 548-3557
John Stanford, *President*
Tim McCalip, *Vice Pres*
Don Hahn, *Controller*
Matt Stanford, *Sales Mgr*
Linny Bookhout, *Marketing Staff*
▲ **EMP:** 52
**SQ FT:** 15,000
**SALES (est):** 15.8MM **Privately Held**
**WEB:** www.bettendorfstanford.com
SIC: **3556** 3535 Food products machinery; conveyors & conveying equipment

### (G-19354)
### STANFORD PRODUCTS LLC (HQ)
1139 S Broadway Ave (62881-2404)
PHONE..................618 548-2600
Ron Simpson, *Engineer*
Chuck C Voss, *Controller*
Cindy Webster, *Marketing Staff*
Shamus Lafferty,
◆ **EMP:** 8
**SQ FT:** 12,000
**SALES (est):** 1.7MM **Privately Held**
**WEB:** www.stanfordproductsllc.com
SIC: **2679** Paperboard products, converted

# Sandoval
## Marion County

**(G-19355)**
**BEELMAN READY-MIX INC**
100 Cemetery Rd (62882-1429)
PHONE..................................618 247-3866
Kirk Becker, *Manager*
**EMP:** 8 **Privately Held**
**WEB:** www.beelmanrm.com
**SIC:** 3273 3271 Ready-mixed concrete; concrete block & brick
**PA:** Beelman Ready-Mix, Inc.
    1 Racehorse Dr
    East Saint Louis IL 62205

**(G-19356)**
**EVERGREEN POOL & SPA LLC**
Also Called: Evergreen Pool & Spa Center
Us Hwys 50 & 51 (62882)
P.O. Box 70 (62882-0070)
PHONE..................................618 247-3555
**Fax:** 618 247-3344
Michael Stock, *Owner*
Geralyn Dock, *COO*
Chris Stock, *Office Mgr*
**EMP:** 4
**SQ FT:** 15,000
**SALES (est):** 250K **Privately Held**
**SIC:** 3949 5999 5091 Swimming pools, except plastic; swimming pools, above ground; sauna equipment & supplies; swimming pools, equipment & supplies; spa equipment & supplies

**(G-19357)**
**GENERAL CONTRACTOR INC**
190 Industrial Park Dr (62882)
PHONE..................................618 533-5213
Darryl Souger, *Manager*
**EMP:** 5
**SALES (corp-wide):** 1.4MM **Privately Held**
**SIC:** 2951 Asphalt paving mixtures & blocks
**PA:** General Contractor Inc
    1 Industrial Dr
    Salem IL

**(G-19358)**
**SANDOVAL MACHINE WORKS INC**
4379 Pope Rd (62882-2437)
PHONE..................................618 247-3588
**Fax:** 618 247-3310
George Dalton, *President*
Lucille Dulton, *Admin Sec*
**EMP:** 3
**SALES:** 150K **Privately Held**
**SIC:** 3599 Machine shop, jobbing & repair

**(G-19359)**
**SYNERGY POWER GROUP LLC**
Also Called: Team Fenex
610 E Illinois Ave (62882-1430)
PHONE..................................618 247-3200
**Fax:** 618 247-3203
Luciano Rapa, *Sales Dir*
Blake Hyde, *Cust Mgr*
Kristy Ramey, *Sales Associate*
James M Cleary,
Lenny Mackie,
**EMP:** 35
**SALES:** 13MM **Privately Held**
**SIC:** 3537 3621 Industrial trucks & tractors; motors & generators

# Sandwich
## Dekalb County

**(G-19360)**
**BLACK MAGIC CUSTOMS INC**
4686 E 29th Rd (60548-9104)
PHONE..................................815 786-1977
Phil Hoffman, *President*
Tom Wade, *Vice Pres*
**EMP:** 4
**SALES:** 125K **Privately Held**
**WEB:** www.blackmagiccustoms.com
**SIC:** 3751 Motorcycles & related parts

**(G-19361)**
**DESIGNED STAIRS INC (PA)**
Also Called: Heartland Bench and Pew
1480 E 6th St (60548-7021)
PHONE..................................815 786-2021
**Fax:** 815 786-6500
Robert S Ducharme, *Ch of Bd*
Michelle Ducharme, *President*
Angela Douell, *Accounts Mgr*
Brent Peterson, *Marketing Staff*
Kim Jansen, *Technology*
**EMP:** 28
**SQ FT:** 50,000
**SALES (est):** 5.6MM **Privately Held**
**WEB:** www.designstairs.com
**SIC:** 2431 Staircases, stairs & railings

**(G-19362)**
**ELGINEX CORPORATION**
1002 E 3rd St (60548-1873)
PHONE..................................815 786-8406
Randy Holver, *Manager*
**EMP:** 8
**SALES (corp-wide):** 1.5MM **Privately Held**
**WEB:** www.tartangroup.com
**SIC:** 3842 Surgical appliances & supplies
**PA:** Elginex Corporation
    480 Quail Ridge Dr
    Westmont IL 60559
    630 268-1000

**(G-19363)**
**FORTUNE METAL MIDWEST LLC**
1212 E 6th St (60548-1864)
PHONE..................................630 778-7776
**Fax:** 630 778-7077
Victor Ng, *Mng Member*
Mark Matza,
John Ng,
**EMP:** 50
**SQ FT:** 53,000
**SALES (est):** 7.5MM **Privately Held**
**SIC:** 3559 Recycling machinery

**(G-19364)**
**G & L COUNTER TOPS CORPORATION**
1010 E 3rd St Ste C (60548-1991)
PHONE..................................815 786-2244
George L Perez, *President*
**EMP:** 15
**SALES (est):** 1.6MM **Privately Held**
**SIC:** 3281 Cut stone & stone products

**(G-19365)**
**GAVIN WOODWORKING INC**
Also Called: Gavin Machine & Manufacturing
16119 Chicago Rd (60548-4017)
P.O. Box 46 (60548-0046)
PHONE..................................815 786-2242
**Fax:** 815 786-2296
Elizabeth Gavin, *President*
Gregory Gavin, *Vice Pres*
**EMP:** 4
**SALES:** 638.1K **Privately Held**
**SIC:** 7641 3599 2499 2511 Office furniture repair & maintenance; reupholstery; machine shop, jobbing & repair; spools, wood; wood household furniture; millwork

**(G-19366)**
**GORD INDUSTRIAL PLASTICS INC**
1310 E 6th St (60548-7018)
PHONE..................................815 786-9494
**Fax:** 815 786-6045
James F Gord, *President*
Wendy S Gord, *Corp Secy*
▲ **EMP:** 15
**SQ FT:** 31,000
**SALES (est):** 7.6MM **Privately Held**
**SIC:** 3089 Molding primary plastic

**(G-19367)**
**HADDOCK TOOL & MANUFACTURING**
917 E Railroad St (60548-1823)
P.O. Box 67 (60548-0067)
PHONE..................................815 786-2739
**Fax:** 815 786-7808
John Haddock, *President*
**EMP:** 3 **EST:** 1965
**SQ FT:** 6,640
**SALES (est):** 200K **Privately Held**
**WEB:** www.chicagocustomwasher.com
**SIC:** 3429 3469 3452 Furniture hardware; metal stampings; bolts, nuts, rivets & washers

**(G-19368)**
**HENDERSON ENGINEERING CO INC (PA)**
Also Called: Sahara Air Dryers
95 N Main St (60548-1597)
PHONE..................................815 786-9471
**Fax:** 815 786-6117
Terry D Henderson, *President*
Dean Krause, *Engineer*
Charles A Henderson, *Treasurer*
Bill Aeppli, *Executive*
**EMP:** 1 **EST:** 1956
**SQ FT:** 157,000
**SALES (est):** 18MM **Privately Held**
**WEB:** www.saharahenderson.com
**SIC:** 3564 3567 3845 Filters, air: furnaces, air conditioning equipment, etc.; driers & redriers, industrial process; electromedical equipment

**(G-19369)**
**J-MARCS CORPORATION**
1074 W Church St (60548-2059)
P.O. Box 509 (60548-0509)
PHONE..................................815 786-2293
**Fax:** 815 786-6922
Bill Jerris, *President*
**EMP:** 10
**SQ FT:** 4,000
**SALES:** 1.1MM **Privately Held**
**WEB:** www.jmarcs.com
**SIC:** 3599 Machine shop, jobbing & repair

**(G-19370)**
**JK AUDIO INC**
Also Called: Telecom Audio
1311 E 6th St (60548-7022)
PHONE..................................815 786-2929
**Fax:** 815 786-8502
Joseph Klinger, *President*
Alberto Colin, *Technical Staff*
Eric Klinger, *Art Dir*
Linda M Klinger, *Admin Sec*
**EMP:** 17
**SQ FT:** 12,500
**SALES (est):** 3.6MM **Privately Held**
**WEB:** www.jkaudio.com
**SIC:** 3699 Sound signaling devices, electrical

**(G-19371)**
**KING & SONS MONUMENTS**
131 E Center St Ste 1 (60548-1689)
PHONE..................................815 786-6321
**Fax:** 815 786-2910
William R King, *Owner*
Linda King, *Co-Owner*
**EMP:** 4
**SQ FT:** 6,500
**SALES (est):** 280K **Privately Held**
**SIC:** 3281 Monuments, cut stone (not finishing or lettering only)

**(G-19372)**
**OFFWORLD DESIGNS**
624 W Center St (60548-1429)
PHONE..................................815 786-7080
Barbara Van Tilburg, *President*
Raymond Van Tilburg, *Vice Pres*
Krysta Olson, *Manager*
**EMP:** 6
**SALES:** 600K **Privately Held**
**WEB:** www.offworlddesigns.com
**SIC:** 2759 2396 Commercial printing; automotive & apparel trimmings

**(G-19373)**
**PLANO MOLDING COMPANY LLC**
510 Duvick Ave (60548-7032)
PHONE..................................630 552-9557
Dean Boatman, *Manager*
George Hamill, *Manager*
**EMP:** 124
**SALES (corp-wide):** 44MM **Privately Held**
**SIC:** 3089 Plastic containers, except foam
**HQ:** Plano Molding Company, Llc
    431 E South St
    Plano IL 60545
    630 552-3111

**(G-19374)**
**PLANO MOLDING COMPANY LLC**
500 Duvick Ave (60548-7032)
PHONE..................................815 786-3331
**Fax:** 815 786-6121
Jeff Covert, *Sales Dir*
Dean Boatman, *Manager*
John Coldway, *Manager*
Sonia Darteaga, *Manager*
Mike Franklin, *Maintence Staff*
**EMP:** 200
**SALES (corp-wide):** 44MM **Privately Held**
**WEB:** www.planomolding.com
**SIC:** 3089 3161 Plastic containers, except foam; luggage
**HQ:** Plano Molding Company, Llc
    431 E South St
    Plano IL 60545
    630 552-3111

**(G-19375)**
**PRINT SHOP**
17 E Center St (60548-1562)
PHONE..................................815 786-8278
Maury Killui, *Owner*
**EMP:** 3
**SALES (est):** 252K **Privately Held**
**SIC:** 2752 Commercial printing, lithographic

**(G-19376)**
**QUICK NIC JUICE LLC**
122 Indian Springs Dr # 5 (60548-1987)
PHONE..................................815 315-8523
Richard M Schure,
Adele Schure,
**EMP:** 11
**SQ FT:** 6,000
**SALES (est):** 1.1MM **Privately Held**
**SIC:** 3634 Vaporizers, electric: household

**(G-19377)**
**SANDWICH MILLWORKS INC**
700 W Center St (60548-1442)
PHONE..................................815 786-2700
John G Knur, *President*
Thomas Freiders, *Shareholder*
**EMP:** 6
**SQ FT:** 7,500
**SALES:** 360K **Privately Held**
**SIC:** 2431 Moldings, wood: unfinished & prefinished

**(G-19378)**
**TRI-COUNTY CONCRETE INC**
331 W Church St (60548-2007)
P.O. Box 26 (60548-0026)
PHONE..................................815 786-2179
**Fax:** 815 786-8319
Michael Zerby, *President*
Craig Chapman, *Vice Pres*
**EMP:** 8 **EST:** 1973
**SQ FT:** 2,400
**SALES:** 1MM **Privately Held**
**SIC:** 3273 Ready-mixed concrete

**(G-19379)**
**TRIO FOUNDRY INC**
Also Called: Sandwich Casting & Machine
924 W Church St (60548-2058)
PHONE..................................815 786-6616
**Fax:** 815 786-7263
Gary Streff, *Manager*
**EMP:** 24
**SALES (corp-wide):** 6.9MM **Privately Held**
**SIC:** 3365 3369 Aluminum foundries; non-ferrous foundries
**PA:** Trio Foundry, Inc.
    1985 Aucutt Rd
    Montgomery IL 60538
    630 892-1676

**(G-19380)**
**WEEKLY JAMES**
1305 Vale St (60548-2330)
PHONE..................................815 786-8203
**EMP:** 3

**GEOGRAPHIC SECTION**     Savanna - Carroll County (G-19402)

SALES (est): 151.9K **Privately Held**
SIC: 2711 Newspapers

## Sauget
### St. Clair County

**(G-19381)**
**AFFTON FABG & WLDG CO INC**
1635 Sauget Business Blvd (62206-1455)
PHONE.................................314 781-4100
Fax: 618 337-5470
Matt Tucker, *President*
Robert D Pfeil, *President*
Larry Henson, *Principal*
Charles Pfeil, *Principal*
Robert Pfeil, *Principal*
EMP: 19 EST: 1956
SQ FT: 46,500
SALES (est): 5.2MM **Privately Held**
WEB: www.afwc.com
SIC: 3441 7692 Fabricated structural metal; welding repair

**(G-19382)**
**BIG RIVER ZINC CORPORATION**
2401 Mississippi Ave (62201-1085)
PHONE.................................618 274-5000
Fax: 618 274-6280
George M Obeldobel, *President*
John Likarish, *Vice Pres*
Lawrence S Thaier, *CFO*
▼ EMP: 7
SQ FT: 200,000
SALES (est): 1.7MM
SALES (corp-wide): 597K **Privately Held**
WEB: www.bigriverzinc.com
SIC: 3356 3369 3341 3339 Lead & zinc; lead, zinc & white metal; secondary nonferrous metals; primary nonferrous metals; industrial inorganic chemicals; lead & zinc ores
PA: Zincox Resources Plc
Crown House High Street
Hook HANTS RG27
127 645-0100

**(G-19383)**
**BRANDING IRON HOLDINGS INC (PA)**
1682 Sauget Business Blvd (62206-1454)
PHONE.................................618 337-8400
R Scott Hudspeth, *CEO*
Michael H Holten, *President*
Craig Allen, *CFO*
EMP: 3
SALES (est): 89.5MM **Privately Held**
SIC: 2013 5147 Sausages & other prepared meats; meats & meat products

**(G-19384)**
**CENTER ETHANOL COMPANY LLC**
231 Monsanto Ave (62201-1010)
PHONE.................................618 875-3008
Barry W Frazier, *President*
David Baugh, *Controller*
Gary Barker, *Mng Member*
James Banks, *Manager*
Denny Crown, *Manager*
EMP: 47
SQ FT: 25,000
SALES (est): 12.8MM **Privately Held**
WEB: www.centerethanol.com
SIC: 2869 Ethyl alcohol, ethanol

**(G-19385)**
**CERRO FLOW PRODUCTS LLC (DH)**
3000 Mississippi Ave (62206-1057)
P.O. Box 66800, Saint Louis MO (63166-6800)
PHONE.................................618 337-6000
Fax: 618 337-7273
Gary Ewing, *President*
Michael Duggan, *President*
John Gerfen, *General Mgr*
John Sundstrom, *General Mgr*
Nick Bogen, *Regional Mgr*
◆ EMP: 200 EST: 1977
SALES (est): 221.1MM
SALES (corp-wide): 223.6B **Publicly Held**
SIC: 3351 3331 3498 3585 Tubing, copper & copper alloy; primary copper; fabricated pipe & fittings; refrigeration & heating equipment; metals service centers & offices; copper sheets, plates, bars, rods, pipes, etc.; tubing, metal
HQ: Marmon Holdings, Inc.
181 W Madison St Ste 2600
Chicago IL 60602
312 372-9500

**(G-19386)**
**HOLTEN MEAT INC**
1682 Sauget Business Blvd (62206-1454)
PHONE.................................618 337-8400
Fax: 618 337-3292
Michael Holten, *President*
Earl Lavelle, *Regional Mgr*
Robert S Hudspeth, *COO*
Jeff Schempp, *Opers Staff*
Craig Allen, *CFO*
EMP: 90
SQ FT: 82,000
SALES (est): 22MM
SALES (corp-wide): 89.5MM **Privately Held**
WEB: www.holtenmeat.com
SIC: 2013 Frozen meats from purchased meat
PA: Branding Iron Holdings, Inc.
1682 Sauget Business Blvd
Sauget IL 62206
618 337-8400

**(G-19387)**
**MIDWEST NONWOVENS LLC**
1642 Sauget Business Blvd (62206-1454)
PHONE.................................618 337-9662
Christopher Look, *COO*
Bryan Speight,
▲ EMP: 25
SQ FT: 80,000
SALES (est): 7.2MM **Privately Held**
SIC: 2297 Nonwoven fabrics

**(G-19388)**
**OCCIDENTAL CHEMICAL CORP**
Also Called: OXY Chem
520 Monsanto Ave (62206)
PHONE.................................618 482-6346
Rick Rauler, *Manager*
EMP: 12
SALES (corp-wide): 10.4B **Publicly Held**
WEB: www.oxychem.com
SIC: 2812 Alkalies & chlorine
HQ: Occidental Chemical Corporation
5005 Lyndon B Johnson Fwy # 2200
Dallas TX 75244
972 404-3800

**(G-19389)**
**SCF SERVICES LLC**
8 Pitzman Ave (62201-1066)
PHONE.................................314 436-7559
Tim Power,
Kenneth Gillum,
Myron McDonough,
EMP: 30 EST: 2010
SALES (est): 4.6MM **Privately Held**
SIC: 3732 Boat building & repairing

**(G-19390)**
**SOLUTIA INC**
500 Monsanto Ave (62201-1137)
PHONE.................................618 482-6536
Tim Jackson, *Accounts Mgr*
Bill Lashley, *Branch Mgr*
EMP: 560
SALES (corp-wide): 9B **Publicly Held**
SIC: 2899 Chemical preparations
HQ: Solutia Inc.
575 Maryville Centre Dr
Saint Louis MO 63141
423 229-2000

## Sauk Village
### Cook County

**(G-19391)**
**C & J INDUSTRIES**
21850 Sunset Ln (60411-5224)
PHONE.................................708 757-4495
Chuck Moek, *Owner*
EMP: 3
SALES (est): 291.6K **Privately Held**
SIC: 3999 Manufacturing industries

**(G-19392)**
**PRATT INDUSTRIES** ✪
21700 Mark Collins Dr (60411-4988)
PHONE.................................630 254-0271
Anthony Pratt, *CEO*
EMP: 99 EST: 2016
SALES (est): 2MM **Privately Held**
SIC: 3999 Manufacturing industries

**(G-19393)**
**SET ENTERPRISES OF MI INC**
21905 Cottage Grove Ave (60411-4331)
PHONE.................................708 758-1111
Ken Pachla, *President*
EMP: 10
SALES (corp-wide): 94.4MM **Privately Held**
WEB: www.michsteel.com
SIC: 3325 Steel foundries
HQ: Set Enterprises Of Mi, Inc.
30500 Van Dyke Ave # 701
Warren MI 48093
586 573-3600

**(G-19394)**
**WINPAK PORTION PACKAGING INC**
1111 Winpak Way (60411-6111)
PHONE.................................708 753-5700
Bob Calcanas, *Branch Mgr*
EMP: 14
SALES (corp-wide): 822.5MM **Privately Held**
SIC: 3565 Packaging machinery
HQ: Winpak Portion Packaging, Inc.
828a Newtown Yardley Rd # 101
Newtown PA 18940
267 685-8200

## Saunemin
### Livingston County

**(G-19395)**
**QUAD COUNTY FIRE EQUIPMENT**
37 Main St (61769-6110)
P.O. Box 155 (61769-0155)
PHONE.................................815 832-4475
Denist Moore, *Owner*
EMP: 5
SALES (est): 639.4K **Privately Held**
SIC: 3713 Specialty motor vehicle bodies

## Savanna
### Carroll County

**(G-19396)**
**EAST SAVANNA WELDING**
Also Called: East Savanna Welding & Repairs
525 3rd St Apt 215 (61074-1568)
PHONE.................................815 273-7371
Fax: 815 273-7371
Jim Mills, *Owner*
Sharon Mills, *Co-Owner*
EMP: 4
SALES: 250K **Privately Held**
SIC: 7692 Welding repair

**(G-19397)**
**ELKAY MANUFACTURING COMPANY**
Corly Tempright
6400 Penn Ave (61074-2923)
PHONE.................................815 273-7001
Fax: 815 273-3916
Ed Perz, *Opers-Prdtn-Mfg*
Angela Determan, *Purch Mgr*
Merle B Oberbroekling, *Purch Mgr*
Doug Hawbecker, *Finance Mgr*
Phyllis G Roth, *Human Res Mgr*
EMP: 300
SALES (corp-wide): 1.1B **Privately Held**
WEB: www.elkayusa.com
SIC: 3443 3431 3585 Air coolers, metal plate; drinking fountains, metal; refrigeration & heating equipment
PA: Elkay Manufacturing Company Inc
2222 Camden Ct
Oak Brook IL 60523
630 574-8484

**(G-19398)**
**FACEMAKERS INC (PA)**
140 N 5th St (61074-1902)
PHONE.................................815 273-3944
Fax: 815 273-3966
Alan St George, *President*
Adrianne St George, *Vice Pres*
Doris Judge, *Administration*
EMP: 12
SQ FT: 9,000
SALES (est): 2.6MM **Privately Held**
WEB: www.facemakersincorporated.com
SIC: 2389 Theatrical costumes

**(G-19399)**
**FACEMAKERS INC**
800 Chicago Ave (61074-2208)
PHONE.................................815 273-3944
Fax: 815 273-3993
Nancy Willis, *Manager*
Suzanne Silvestri, *Manager*
EMP: 42
SALES (est): 2.6MM **Privately Held**
WEB: www.facemakersincorporated.com
SIC: 2389 Theatrical costumes
PA: Facemakers, Inc
140 N 5th St
Savanna IL 61074
815 273-3944

**(G-19400)**
**METFORM LLC**
Also Called: Extrusion Science
2551 Wacker Rd (61074-2898)
PHONE.................................815 273-2201
Fax: 815 273-2528
Dennis Keesey, *Vice Pres*
Ted Hofman, *Plant Mgr*
Steve Whiting, *Plant Mgr*
Roman Dombrowski, *QC Dir*
Danielle Lippens, *Engineer*
EMP: 190
SALES (corp-wide): 1.4B **Privately Held**
SIC: 3462 3452 Iron & steel forgings; bolts, nuts, rivets & washers
HQ: Metform, L.L.C.
1000 Allanson Rd
Mundelein IL 60060
847 566-0010

**(G-19401)**
**METFORM LLC**
7034 Rte 84 S (61074)
PHONE.................................815 273-0230
Matthias Praus, *Vice Pres*
Steve Whiting, *Plant Mgr*
Nick Bird, *Engineer*
EMP: 32
SALES (corp-wide): 1.4B **Privately Held**
SIC: 3398 3462 3452 Metal heat treating; iron & steel forgings; bolts, nuts, rivets & washers
HQ: Metform, L.L.C.
1000 Allanson Rd
Mundelein IL 60060
847 566-0010

**(G-19402)**
**MIDWEST WOOD INC**
2727 Wacker Rd (61074-2909)
P.O. Box 204 (61074-0204)
PHONE.................................815 273-3333
Todd Puckett, *President*
EMP: 12
SQ FT: 5,000
SALES (est): 1MM **Privately Held**
SIC: 2448 2421 Pallets, wood; sawmills & planing mills, general

## Savanna - Carroll County

**(G-19403)**
**MILLS MACHINE INC**
Also Called: Savanna Gas and Welding Sups
2416 Jackson St (61074-2836)
PHONE...................................815 273-4707
Fax: 815 273-7074
Andrew Mills, *President*
Phillip Mills, *General Mgr*
Jill Holtman, *Manager*
Rob Wienhoff, *Technical Staff*
EMP: 8
SQ FT: 13,500
SALES: 1.1MM **Privately Held**
WEB: www.labelmill.com
SIC: 3599 5984 Machine shop, jobbing & repair; liquefied petroleum gas dealers

**(G-19404)**
**POWERLAB INC**
9741 Powerlab Rd (61074)
P.O. Box 308 (61074-0308)
PHONE...................................815 273-7718
Fax: 815 273-2145
Don Rabon, *Engineer*
Robert Themas, *Manager*
EMP: 14
SALES (corp-wide): 13.7MM **Privately Held**
WEB: www.powerlabinc.com
SIC: 2819 3339 Lead compounds or salts, inorganic, not used in pigments; primary nonferrous metals
PA: Powerlab, Inc.
1145 Highway 34 S
Terrell TX 75160
972 563-1477

**(G-19405)**
**SAVANNA QUARRY INC**
9859 Scenic Bluff Rd (61074-8416)
PHONE...................................815 273-4208
Charles Brandt, *President*
Kelly Bisby, *CFO*
Rick Burkemper, *Controller*
Terence Brandt, *Admin Sec*
EMP: 3
SQ FT: 2,800
SALES (est): 307.7K **Privately Held**
SIC: 1422 2951 Crushed & broken limestone; asphalt & asphaltic paving mixtures (not from refineries)

**(G-19406)**
**SAVANNA TIMES JOURNAL**
121 Main St (61074-1931)
PHONE...................................815 273-2277
Fax: 815 273-2715
Bob Watson, *Owner*
EMP: 6
SALES (est): 210.7K **Privately Held**
SIC: 2711 Newspapers

**(G-19407)**
**WILKOS INDUSTRIES**
3199 School Dr (61074-8671)
PHONE...................................563 249-6691
Quinn Wilkin, *Vice Pres*
EMP: 3
SALES (est): 200K **Privately Held**
SIC: 3443 Fabricated plate work (boiler shop)

### Savoy
#### Champaign County

**(G-19408)**
**ACOUSTIC MEDSYSTEMS INC**
Also Called: Acoustx
208 Burwash Ave (61874-9510)
PHONE...................................217 355-8888
Fax: 217 239-0905
Everette C Burdette, *Ch of Bd*
Jennifer Williams, *General Mgr*
EMP: 3
SALES (est): 529.7K **Privately Held**
SIC: 3845 Electromedical equipment

**(G-19409)**
**GCOM INC**
1201 Fieldstone Dr (61874-7454)
PHONE...................................217 351-4241
Fax: 217 351-4240
David M Grothe, *President*
Donald Elmore, *COO*
Jacquie Berkman, *Manager*
Chuck Bennett, *Webmaster*
EMP: 14
SQ FT: 6,000
SALES (est): 1.5MM **Privately Held**
WEB: www.gcom.com
SIC: 7372 5045 Business oriented computer software; computers, peripherals & software

**(G-19410)**
**INNOVATIVE SEC SYSTEMS INC**
Also Called: Argus Systems Group
1809 Woodfield Dr (61874-9505)
P.O. Box 187, Effingham (62401-0187)
PHONE...................................217 355-6308
Fax: 217 355-1433
Andrew Jones, *President*
Mac N Macgregor, *Vice Pres*
N E Macgregor, *Vice Pres*
Keith Fults, *VP Sales*
Steve Ortegenn, *Sales Mgr*
EMP: 16
SALES (est): 1.5MM **Privately Held**
WEB: www.argus-systems.com
SIC: 7372 Prepackaged software

**(G-19411)**
**LUON ENERGY LLC**
605 Buttercup Dr (61874-9465)
PHONE...................................217 419-2678
Fax: 217 333-2906
Nie Luo,
Lizhang Yang,
◆ EMP: 4
SALES (est): 247.5K **Privately Held**
SIC: 3621 7389 Storage battery chargers, motor & engine generator type;

**(G-19412)**
**THERMAL SOLUTIONS INC**
1706 Lyndhurst Dr (61874-9522)
PHONE...................................217 352-7019
EMP: 2 EST: 2001
SALES (est): 210K **Privately Held**
SIC: 3567 Mfg Industrial Furnaces/Ovens

### Saybrook
#### Mclean County

**(G-19413)**
**AGRO-CHEM INC**
Also Called: Agro Chem West
127 S Center St (61770-9664)
P.O. Box 289 (61770-0289)
PHONE...................................309 475-8311
Jim Dunham, *Manager*
EMP: 10
SALES (corp-wide): 20.7MM **Privately Held**
WEB: www.agrochem.net
SIC: 0782 3563 Fertilizing services, lawn; air & gas compressors
PA: Agro-Chem Inc
2045 S Wabash St
Wabash IN 46992
800 686-5680

**(G-19414)**
**PRO TECH ENGINEERING**
129 W Lincoln St (61770-7558)
P.O. Box 50 (61770-0050)
PHONE...................................309 475-2502
Jim Gravitt, *President*
EMP: 2
SALES (est): 260.6K **Privately Held**
SIC: 3484 Machine guns or machine gun parts, 30 mm. & below

### Scales Mound
#### Jo Daviess County

**(G-19415)**
**GUIDE LINE INDUSTRIES INC**
1453 W Schapville Rd (61075-9551)
PHONE...................................815 777-3722
Fax: 815 777-3723
Dave Pingel, *President*
Hans A Pingel, *Principal*
Hella Pingel, *Admin Sec*
EMP: 18
SQ FT: 4,000
SALES (est): 3MM **Privately Held**
WEB: www.guidelineindustries.com
SIC: 3496 3545 Miscellaneous fabricated wire products; machine tool accessories

**(G-19416)**
**WEEKLY VISITOR**
101 E Burrall Ave (61075-9567)
PHONE...................................815 845-2328
EMP: 3
SALES (est): 149.2K **Privately Held**
SIC: 2711 Newspapers

### Schaumburg
#### Cook County

**(G-19417)**
**A & J FINISHERS**
623 Lunt Ave (60193-4410)
PHONE...................................847 352-5408
Fax: 847 352-5409
Charlie Kalaria, *Owner*
EMP: 7
SQ FT: 8,200
SALES (est): 340K **Privately Held**
WEB: www.ajfinishers.com
SIC: 3471 Polishing, metals or formed products

**(G-19418)**
**A A SWIFT PRINT INC**
30 Standish Ln (60193-1263)
PHONE...................................847 301-1122
Fax: 847 301-1093
EMP: 5
SALES (est): 240K **Privately Held**
SIC: 2752 7334 2789 Lithographic Commercial Printing Photocopying Services Bookbinding/Related Work

**(G-19419)**
**A J SMOY CO INC**
163 Chatsworth Cir (60194-5152)
PHONE...................................773 775-8282
Fax: 773 775-8283
Ronald Smoy Sr, *President*
Ronald Smoy Jr, *Vice Pres*
Charlene Smoy, *Admin Sec*
EMP: 20
SQ FT: 4,000
SALES (est): 660K **Privately Held**
WEB: www.ajsmoy.com
SIC: 3677 3612 Coil windings, electronic; electronic transformers; transformers, except electric

**(G-19420)**
**ACCESS MEDICAL SUPPLY INC**
1672 Wright Blvd (60193-4512)
PHONE...................................847 891-6210
John Hamparian, *President*
EMP: 3
SALES (est): 418.6K **Privately Held**
WEB: www.accessmedicalsupply.com
SIC: 2834 3841 Medicines, capsuled or ampuled; surgical & medical instruments

**(G-19421)**
**ACRESSO SOFTWARE INC**
1000 E Wdfield Rd Ste 400 (60173)
PHONE...................................408 642-3865
Sridevi Ravuri, *Principal*
Trish Reilly, *Manager*
Shawn Blond, *Analyst*
EMP: 3
SALES (est): 121K **Privately Held**
SIC: 7372 Prepackaged software

**(G-19422)**
**ACTION CARBIDE GRINDING CO**
Also Called: Action Prcsion Crbide Grinding
1118 Lunt Ave Ste B (60193-4441)
PHONE...................................847 891-9026
Fax: 847 891-9464
Louis Pacini, *President*
Jean Pacini, *Corp Secy*
Terry Pacini, *Vice Pres*
EMP: 3
SQ FT: 1,200
SALES: 130K **Privately Held**
SIC: 3599 Grinding castings for the trade

**(G-19423)**
**ADVANCED MICRODERM INC**
904 S Roselle Rd 302 (60193-3963)
PHONE...................................630 980-3300
Andrew Goodwin, *Exec VP*
EMP: 21
SALES (est): 2.7MM **Privately Held**
WEB: www.advancedmicroderm.com
SIC: 3841 Surgical instruments & apparatus

**(G-19424)**
**AERO PRODUCTS HOLDINGS INC**
Also Called: Aero Products International
1834 Walden Office Sq # 300 (60173-4292)
P.O. Box 2931, Wichita KS (67201-2931)
PHONE...................................847 485-3200
Tim Horne, *President*
Mike Seno, *Controller*
Rochelle Helgeland, *Administration*
▲ EMP: 45
SALES (est): 4.1MM **Privately Held**
SIC: 2599 5712 Inflatable beds; furniture stores

**(G-19425)**
**AERO-TECH LIGHT BULB CO (PA)**
534 Pratt Ave N (60193-4555)
PHONE...................................847 534-6580
Fax: 847 351-4999
Raymond M Schlosser, *President*
Kathy M Schlosser, *Vice Pres*
Harold Linskey, *Engineer*
Tom Locascio, *Sales Mgr*
▲ EMP: 16
SQ FT: 15,000
SALES (est): 6.3MM **Privately Held**
WEB: www.aerolights.com
SIC: 3641 5063 Lamps, incandescent filament, electric; light bulbs & related supplies

**(G-19426)**
**AGRIBASE INTERNATIONAL INC**
1901 N Roselle Rd Ste 800 (60195-3186)
PHONE...................................847 810-0167
Gene Liu, *President*
▼ EMP: 2
SALES: 18MM **Privately Held**
SIC: 2048 Livestock feeds

**(G-19427)**
**ALARM PRESS**
1325 Remington Rd Ste H (60173-4815)
PHONE...................................312 341-1290
Chris Force, *Owner*
Miranda Myers, *Accounts Exec*
▲ EMP: 4
SALES (est): 193.9K **Privately Held**
SIC: 2721 Periodicals: publishing only

**(G-19428)**
**ALDEA TECHNOLOGIES INC**
904 S Roselle Rd 394 (60193-3963)
PHONE...................................800 804-0635
Jeffrey Rayner, *President*
David A Reiche Jr, *Vice Pres*
▲ EMP: 21
SALES (est): 1.6MM **Privately Held**
WEB: www.aldeatech.com
SIC: 7372 7379 Prepackaged software; computer related consulting services

**(G-19429)**
**ALERT TUBING FABRICATORS INC**
8019 Commercial Ave (60193)
PHONE...................................847 253-7237
Fax: 847 524-5816
John Coffey, *President*
EMP: 8
SQ FT: 5,000
SALES (est): 1MM **Privately Held**
SIC: 3498 3446 3444 3441 Tube fabricating (contract bending & shaping); architectural metalwork; sheet metalwork; fabricated structural metal

▲ = Import  ▼=Export
◆ =Import/Export

# GEOGRAPHIC SECTION
## Schaumburg - Cook County (G-19456)

### (G-19430)
**ALLEGRA MARKETING PRINT MAIL**
1945 Wright Blvd (60193-4567)
**PHONE**.................................630 790-0444
Gary Blaski, *Owner*
Cindy Blaski, *Owner*
Katie Schulte, *Accounts Mgr*
Larry Naselli, *Marketing Staff*
**EMP:** 8
**SALES (est):** 41.9K **Privately Held**
**SIC: 8742** 2759 Marketing consulting services; commercial printing

### (G-19431)
**ALLIANCE CREATIVE GROUP INC (PA)**
Also Called: St. Louis Packaging
1066 National Pkwy (60173-4519)
**PHONE**.................................847 885-1800
Fax: 773 496-6671
Steven M St Louis, *CEO*
Paul Sorkin, *COO*
Greg Kardasz, *Vice Pres*
Kevin Piemonte, *Vice Pres*
Paul Sorkan, *Admin Sec*
**EMP:** 22
**SQ FT:** 13,000
**SALES:** 10MM **Publicly Held**
**SIC: 5199** 2752 8742 Packaging materials; commercial printing, lithographic; marketing consulting services

### (G-19432)
**ALLPRINT GRAPHICS INC**
Also Called: Class Printing
1034 National Pkwy (60173-4519)
**PHONE**.................................847 519-9898
Walter Nagel Jr, *President*
Walter Nagle Sr, *Vice Pres*
Gary Parker, *Manager*
Carl Nagle, *Admin Sec*
**EMP:** 3
**SQ FT:** 2,500
**SALES (est):** 550K **Privately Held**
**WEB:** www.classprinting.net
**SIC: 2759** 2752 Commercial printing; commercial printing, lithographic

### (G-19433)
**ALLTECH PLASTICS INC**
821 Thornton Ct Apt 2b (60193-4854)
**PHONE**.................................847 352-2309
Ingemar Alexander, *President*
**EMP:** 4
**SALES (est):** 285.8K **Privately Held**
**SIC: 3089** Plastics products

### (G-19434)
**ALTERA CORPORATION**
425 N Martingale Rd # 1320 (60173-2297)
**PHONE**.................................847 240-0313
Fax: 847 240-0266
Richard Catizone, *Business Mgr*
Joe Ward, *Manager*
**EMP:** 4
**SALES (corp-wide):** 59.3B **Publicly Held**
**WEB:** www.altera.com
**SIC: 3823** Industrial instrmnts msrmnt display/control process variable
HQ: Altera Corporation
   101 Innovation Dr
   San Jose CA 95134
   408 544-7000

### (G-19435)
**ALTERNATIVE BEARINGS CORP**
870 E Higgins Rd Ste 135 (60173-4787)
**PHONE**.................................847 240-9630
Tom Malloy, *President*
Maia Tihista, *Treasurer*
Malia Berg, *Office Mgr*
▲ **EMP:** 5
**SQ FT:** 2,500
**SALES (est):** 1.6MM **Privately Held**
**SIC: 5085** 3562 Bearings; ball & roller bearings

### (G-19436)
**AMERICAN CIRCUIT SERVICES INC**
801 Albion Ave Ste B (60193-4500)
**PHONE**.................................847 895-0500
Nick Chaudhai, *President*
**EMP:** 6 **EST:** 2000
**SQ FT:** 2,500
**SALES:** 400K **Privately Held**
**WEB:** www.testpcb.net
**SIC: 3672** Printed circuit boards

### (G-19437)
**AMERICAN INDUSTRIAL WERKS INC**
904 S Roselle Rd Ste 208 (60193-3963)
**PHONE**.................................847 477-2648
Craig A Knickerbocker, *President*
**EMP:** 10
**SQ FT:** 12,000
**SALES:** 61.1K **Privately Held**
**SIC: 1796** 1795 1711 4213 Machine moving & rigging; millwright; wrecking & demolition work; mechanical contractor; heavy machinery transport; fabricated structural metal; general warehousing & storage

### (G-19438)
**AMERICAN LABEL COMPANY**
1678 Wright Blvd Ste D (60193-4512)
**PHONE**.................................630 830-4444
Mohammed Saleem, *Vice Pres*
**EMP:** 3
**SALES (est):** 98.2K **Privately Held**
**SIC: 2759** Labels & seals: printing

### (G-19439)
**AMERICAN LIGHT BULB MFG INC**
534 Pratt Ave N (60193-4555)
**PHONE**.................................843 464-0755
Fax: 843 464-0155
Ray Schlosser, *President*
Kathy Schlosser, *Vice Pres*
▲ **EMP:** 58
**SQ FT:** 82,000
**SALES (est):** 3.3MM **Privately Held**
**SIC: 3641** Electric lamps

### (G-19440)
**AMERICAN PHRM PARTNERS INC**
1501 E Woodfield Rd (60173-6052)
**PHONE**.................................847 969-2700
Jeffrey Yordon, *President*
Linda Hejmanowski, *Senior Mgr*
**EMP:** 23
**SALES (est):** 4.7MM **Privately Held**
**SIC: 2834** Pharmaceutical preparations

### (G-19441)
**ANALOG DEVICES INC**
1901 N Roselle Rd Ste 100 (60195-3178)
**PHONE**.................................847 519-3669
Bill Wilson, *Sales Staff*
Bill Wison, *Branch Mgr*
**EMP:** 8
**SALES (corp-wide):** 3.4B **Publicly Held**
**WEB:** www.analog.com
**SIC: 3674** Integrated circuits, semiconductor networks, etc.
PA: Analog Devices, Inc.
   1 Technology Way
   Norwood MA 02062
   781 329-4700

### (G-19442)
**ANOTHER VISION**
2133 Hitching Post Ln (60194-3809)
**PHONE**.................................847 884-7325
**EMP:** 3
**SALES (est):** 237.6K **Privately Held**
**SIC: 2721** Periodicals: publishing only

### (G-19443)
**ANSELMO DIE AND INDEX CO INC**
Also Called: Anselmo Index
2235 Hammond Dr Ste F (60173-3848)
**PHONE**.................................847 397-1200
Fax: 847 397-1249
John Anselmo, *President*
**EMP:** 12
**SQ FT:** 10,000
**SALES (est):** 2.4MM **Privately Held**
**SIC: 2675** Index cards, die-cut: made from purchased materials

### (G-19444)
**ANTENEX INC**
1751 Wilkening Ct (60173-5310)
**PHONE**.................................847 839-6910
Don Cislo, *President*
Robert Moist, *Purchasing*
Bruce Juhl, *Sales Staff*
Andrea Casebeer, *Admin Sec*
▲ **EMP:** 85
**SQ FT:** 25,000
**SALES (est):** 12MM
**SALES (corp-wide):** 986.8MM **Privately Held**
**WEB:** www.antenex.com
**SIC: 3663** Antennas, transmitting & communications
HQ: Laird Technologies, Inc.
   3481 Rider Trl S
   Earth City MO 63045
   636 898-6000

### (G-19445)
**APPLIED POLYMER SYSTEM INC**
507 Estes Ave (60193-4428)
**PHONE**.................................847 301-1712
Kevin Murray, *President*
**EMP:** 3
**SALES (est):** 335.3K **Privately Held**
**WEB:** www.applied-polymer-solutions.com
**SIC: 3089** Injection molded finished plastic products

### (G-19446)
**ARC INDUSTRIES INC**
2020 Hammond Dr (60173-3810)
**PHONE**.................................847 303-5005
Fax: 847 303-5010
Dennis A Sjodin, *President*
Carolyn Sjodin, *Admin Sec*
**EMP:** 35
**SQ FT:** 58,000
**SALES (est):** 5.6MM **Privately Held**
**SIC: 3544** Industrial molds; dies & die holders for metal cutting, forming, die casting

### (G-19447)
**ASPEN SHUTTERS INC**
2235 Hammond Dr Ste F (60173-3848)
**PHONE**.................................847 979-0166
Douglas Plager, *President*
**EMP:** 5 **EST:** 2008
**SQ FT:** 3,500
**SALES (est):** 398.3K **Privately Held**
**SIC: 2431** Blinds (shutters), wood

### (G-19448)
**ASSOCIATED EQUIPMENT DISTRS (PA)**
Also Called: Non-For Profit Nat Trade Assn
650 E Algonquin Rd # 305 (60173-3853)
**PHONE**.................................630 574-0650
Fax: 630 574-0132
Jonathan Mack, *President*
Jason Blake, *Vice Pres*
Joan Burton, *Accounting Dir*
Sara Smith, *Marketing Staff*
Heather Jarmusz, *Manager*
**EMP:** 23 **EST:** 1919
**SQ FT:** 12,000
**SALES:** 127.3K **Privately Held**
**WEB:** www.machinemart.com
**SIC: 8611** 2721 7389 8621 Trade associations; trade journals: publishing only, not printed on site; trade show arrangement; professional membership organizations

### (G-19449)
**ATHENEX PHARMACEUTICAL DIV LLC**
10 N Martingale Rd # 230 (60173-2099)
**PHONE**.................................847 922-8041
Tom Moutvic, *Principal*
James Bennett, *Consultant*
**EMP:** 30
**SQ FT:** 13,500
**SALES (est):** 1.3MM **Privately Held**
**SIC: 2834** Powders, pharmaceutical; solutions, pharmaceutical

### (G-19450)
**AUTOMATIC FEEDER COMPANY INC**
921 Albion Ave (60193-4550)
**PHONE**.................................847 534-2300
Fax: 847 534-2354
Jack Verhasselt, *CEO*
Ken Eversole, *President*
Kirk Verhasselt, *Vice Pres*
Jerry Kuntz, *Opers Staff*
Maureen Maniates, *Accounts Mgr*
**EMP:** 15
**SQ FT:** 24,000
**SALES:** 2.4MM **Privately Held**
**WEB:** www.automaticfeeder.com
**SIC: 3569** 3535 Assembly machines, non-metalworking; conveyors & conveying equipment

### (G-19451)
**AUTROL CORPORATION OF AMERICA**
Also Called: Autrol America
10 N Martingale Rd # 470 (60173-2099)
**PHONE**.................................847 779-5000
Hermant Narayan, *President*
Unni Ken, *Principal*
Ken Unni, *Natl Sales Mgr*
▲ **EMP:** 8
**SALES (est):** 1.2MM **Privately Held**
**SIC: 3823** Transmitters of process variables, stand. signal conversion

### (G-19452)
**AVAYA INC**
2500 W Higgins Rd (60195)
**PHONE**.................................847 885-3598
Becky Runes, *Branch Mgr*
**EMP:** 11
**SALES (corp-wide):** 4B **Privately Held**
**WEB:** www.avaya.com
**SIC: 7372** Prepackaged software
HQ: Avaya Inc.
   4655 Great America Pkwy
   Santa Clara CA 95054
   908 953-6000

### (G-19453)
**AVEDA CORPORATION**
L325 Woodfield Mall (60173-5808)
**PHONE**.................................847 413-0438
Fax: 847 413-0449
Emily Hayes, *Manager*
**EMP:** 4
**SALES (corp-wide):** 11.2B **Publicly Held**
**WEB:** www.aveda.com
**SIC: 2844** Shampoos, rinses, conditioners: hair
HQ: Aveda Corporation
   4000 Pheasant Ridge Dr Ne
   Blaine MN 55449
   763 783-4250

### (G-19454)
**AVI-SPL EMPLOYEE**
2266 Palmer Dr (60173-3822)
**PHONE**.................................847 437-7712
**EMP:** 350
**SALES (corp-wide):** 596.9MM **Privately Held**
**SIC: 3669** 3861 3663 3651 Mfg Communications Equip Mfg Photo Equip/Supplies Mfg Radio/Tv Comm Equip Mfg Home Audio/Video Eqp Whol Photo Equip/Supply
HQ: Avi-Spl Employee Emergency Relief Fund, Inc.
   6301 Benjamin Rd Ste 101
   Tampa FL 33634
   813 884-7168

### (G-19455)
**AZILSA INC**
1425 W Schaumburg Rd (60194-4051)
**PHONE**.................................312 919-1741
Pierre Schimper, *President*
**EMP:** 23
**SALES (est):** 839.2K **Privately Held**
**SIC: 3699** Security control equipment & systems

### (G-19456)
**B M I INC**
Also Called: Boldt Metronics International
1751 Wilkening Ct (60173-5310)
**PHONE**.................................847 839-6000
Melvin W Boldt, *Ch of Bd*
Robert Martin, *President*
Jon Anderson, *Vice Pres*
Lance Wroblewski, *Buyer*
Brett Gleixner, *Engineer*

# Schaumburg - Cook County (G-19457)

**EMP:** 200
**SQ FT:** 161,000
**SALES (est):** 18.7MM **Privately Held**
**SIC:** 3678 3672 3496 3469 Electronic connectors; printed circuit boards; miscellaneous fabricated wire products; metal stampings; sheet metalwork

### (G-19457)
### BDC CAPITAL ENTERPRISES LLC
Also Called: Office & Commercial RE Mag
1515 E Wdfield Rd Ste 110 (60173)
 **PHONE** .................................. 847 908-0650
 Byron Collins, *COO*
 **EMP:** 2
 **SQ FT:** 5,000
 **SALES (est):** 220K **Privately Held**
 **SIC:** 2759 Publication printing

### (G-19458)
### BEE CLEAN SPECIALTIES LLC
550 Albion Ave (60193-4546)
 **PHONE** .................................. 847 451-0844
 Jim McCabery,
 Scott McAbery, *Technician*
 **EMP:** 4
 **SALES (est):** 645.7K **Privately Held**
 **SIC:** 5075 3564 Air pollution control equipment & supplies; air filters; air purification equipment; air cleaning systems

### (G-19459)
### BELMONTE PRINTING CO
525 W Wise Rd Ste D (60193-3882)
 **PHONE** .................................. 847 352-8841
 **Fax:** 847 352-8878
 Anthony J Belmonte, *Partner*
 Linda Belmonte, *Partner*
 **EMP:** 5
 **SQ FT:** 1,800
 **SALES (est):** 420K **Privately Held**
 **SIC:** 2759 2791 2752 Commercial printing; typesetting; commercial printing, lithographic

### (G-19460)
### BEM MOLD INC
Also Called: Bem Cnc
410 Remington Rd (60173-4540)
 **PHONE** .................................. 847 805-9750
 Eugene Bozek, *President*
 Mark Bozek, *Vice Pres*
 Bogdan Falat, *Vice Pres*
 **EMP:** 45
 **SQ FT:** 20,000
 **SALES (est):** 11.5MM **Privately Held**
 **WEB:** www.bemcnc.com
 **SIC:** 3599 Machine shop, jobbing & repair

### (G-19461)
### BERRY GLOBAL INC
Also Called: Smurfit - Stone Flexible Packg
1228 Tower Rd (60173-4308)
 **PHONE** .................................. 847 884-1200
 Chuck Amenta, *Vice Pres*
 James Cutter, *Vice Pres*
 Ronald Hackney, *Vice Pres*
 John Knudsen, *Vice Pres*
 Joe Marinacci, *Vice Pres*
 **EMP:** 125
 **SALES (corp-wide):** 6.4B **Publicly Held**
 **SIC:** 2631 Folding boxboard
 **HQ:** Berry Global, Inc.
  101 Oakley St
  Evansville IN 47710
  812 424-2904

### (G-19462)
### BIRCHER AMERICA INC
870 Pratt Ave N (60193-4561)
 **PHONE** .................................. 847 952-3730
 Barac Bieri, *President*
 Roland Shibli, *President*
 ▲ **EMP:** 6
 **SQ FT:** 5,000
 **SALES (est):** 2.2MM **Privately Held**
 **WEB:** www.bircheramerica.com
 **SIC:** 5063 3679 Safety switches; switches, stepping
 **HQ:** Bircher Reglomat Ag
  Wiesengasse 20
  Beringen SH 8222
  526 871-111

### (G-19463)
### BISCO ENTERPRISE INC
550 Albion Ave Ste 40 (60193-4547)
 **PHONE** .................................. 630 628-1831
 Martin Diener, *President*
 Cheryl Diener, *Manager*
 Gregory Diener, *Admin Sec*
 **EMP:** 10
 **SQ FT:** 10,000
 **SALES (est):** 3.7MM **Privately Held**
 **WEB:** www.biscoenterprise.com
 **SIC:** 5085 5075 5039 3564 Filters, industrial; air filters; air ducts, sheet metal; purification & dust collection equipment

### (G-19464)
### BISCO INC
1100 W Irving Park Rd (60193-3569)
 **PHONE** .................................. 847 534-6000
 **Fax:** 847 534-6111
 Byoung I Suh, *President*
 Chris Chung, *General Mgr*
 Julie Suh, *VP Opers*
 Larry Cohen, *Purch Agent*
 Brian Suh, *Purchasing*
 ▲ **EMP:** 100
 **SQ FT:** 90,000
 **SALES (est):** 18.2MM **Privately Held**
 **SIC:** 3843 8021 Dental materials; cement, dental; compounds, dental; offices & clinics of dentists

### (G-19465)
### BOEING COMPANY
1515 E Wdfield Rd Ste 320 (60173)
 **PHONE** .................................. 847 240-0767
 **Fax:** 847 240-0747
 Dave Bayless, *Manager*
 **EMP:** 6
 **SALES (corp-wide):** 94.5B **Publicly Held**
 **SIC:** 3721 3812 3761 Airplanes, fixed or rotary wing; search & navigation equipment; defense systems & equipment; aircraft control systems, electronic; navigational systems & instruments; guided missiles, complete; guided missiles & space vehicles, research & development
 **PA:** The Boeing Company
  100 N Riverside Plz
  Chicago IL 60606
  312 544-2000

### (G-19466)
### BROCADE CMMNCTIONS SYSTEMS INC
20 N Martingale Rd # 290 (60173-2412)
 **PHONE** .................................. 630 273-5530
 Armando Pena, *Manager*
 **EMP:** 15 **Publicly Held**
 **WEB:** www.foundrynet.com
 **SIC:** 3661 Telephones & telephone apparatus
 **PA:** Brocade Communications Systems, Inc.
  130 Holger Way
  San Jose CA 95134

### (G-19467)
### CACINI INC
Also Called: Sign-A-Rama
711 E Golf Rd (60173-4511)
 **PHONE** .................................. 847 884-1162
 **Fax:** 847 884-1186
 Kim Brancamp, *President*
 Vern Brancamp, *Vice Pres*
 **EMP:** 8
 **SQ FT:** 2,000
 **SALES (est):** 788.3K **Privately Held**
 **SIC:** 3993 5199 Signs & advertising specialties; advertising specialties

### (G-19468)
### CAPITOL COIL INC
821 Albion Ave Ste B (60193-4522)
 **PHONE** .................................. 847 891-1390
 **Fax:** 847 891-3177
 Edwin Jablonski, *President*
 Michael Jablonski, *Treasurer*
 Carrie Tobias, *Office Mgr*
 David Jablonski, *Admin Sec*
 ▲ **EMP:** 15 **EST:** 1932
 **SQ FT:** 6,500

 **SALES:** 1.3MM **Privately Held**
 **WEB:** www.capitalcoil.com
 **SIC:** 3495 3496 3493 3316 Mechanical springs, precision; miscellaneous fabricated wire products; steel springs, except wire; cold finishing of steel shapes

### (G-19469)
### CATAPULT COMMUNICATIONS CORP
1821 Walden Office Sq # 120 (60173-4295)
 **PHONE** .................................. 847 884-0048
 **Fax:** 847 884-0162
 Steve Kurtz, *Sales Mgr*
 Lisa Carey, *Office Mgr*
 Toni Biesterfeld, *Manager*
 **EMP:** 7
 **SALES (corp-wide):** 2.9B **Publicly Held**
 **WEB:** www.catapult.com
 **SIC:** 7372 7371 Prepackaged software; computer software development
 **HQ:** Catapult Communications Corporation
  26601 Agoura Rd
  Calabasas CA 91302
  818 871-1800

### (G-19470)
### CERVONES WELDING SERVICE INC
1104 Lunt Ave (60193-4421)
 **PHONE** .................................. 847 985-6865
 **Fax:** 847 985-6937
 Michael Cervone, *President*
 **EMP:** 5
 **SQ FT:** 3,500
 **SALES (est):** 466.6K **Privately Held**
 **SIC:** 7692 3441 Welding repair; fabricated structural metal

### (G-19471)
### CHICAGO FREIGHT CAR LEASING CO (PA)
Also Called: Cfcl
425 N Martingale Rd Fl 6 (60173-2301)
P.O. Box 75129, Chicago (60675-5129)
 **PHONE** .................................. 847 318-8000
 **Fax:** 847 318-8045
 Fred Sasser, *CEO*
 Paul Deasy, *President*
 Shad Peterson, *COO*
 John Cooney, *Vice Pres*
 Todd Kahnm, *Vice Pres*
 **EMP:** 66 **EST:** 1947
 **SQ FT:** 9,500
 **SALES (est):** 77.8MM **Privately Held**
 **WEB:** www.crdx.com
 **SIC:** 4741 3643 Rental of railroad cars; electric switches

### (G-19472)
### CIFUENTES LUIS & NICOLE INC
Also Called: AlphaGraphics
636 Remington Rd Ste D (60193-5612)
 **PHONE** .................................. 847 490-3660
 **Fax:** 847 490-3778
 Luis Cifuentes, *President*
 Catherine Cifuntes, *General Mgr*
 Rodrigo Abreu, *Vice Pres*
 Art Coley, *Vice Pres*
 Doug Baker, *Manager*
 **EMP:** 9
 **SALES (est):** 1.1MM **Privately Held**
 **SIC:** 2752 2791 2789 2759 Commercial printing, lithographic; typesetting; bookbinding & related work; commercial printing

### (G-19473)
### CLEAN AND SCIENCE USA CO LTD
475 N Martingale Rd (60173-2405)
 **PHONE** .................................. 847 461-9292
 **EMP:** 4 **EST:** 2010
 **SALES (est):** 470K **Privately Held**
 **SIC:** 5075 3564 3599 Whol Heat/Air Cond Equipment/Supplies Mfg Blowers/Fans Mfg Industrial Machinery

### (G-19474)
### CLOOS ROBOTIC WELDING INC (DH)
Also Called: Cloos Robotics De Mexico
911 Albion Ave (60193-4550)
 **PHONE** .................................. 847 923-9988

 **Fax:** 847 923-9989
 Hartmut Boegel, *President*
 Virgil Payne, *Controller*
 ▲ **EMP:** 16
 **SQ FT:** 14,000
 **SALES:** 12MM
 **SALES (corp-wide):** 114MM **Privately Held**
 **WEB:** www.cloos-robot.com
 **SIC:** 3542 7699 Robots for metal forming: pressing, extruding, etc.; industrial machinery & equipment repair
 **HQ:** Carl Cloos Schweißtechnik Gesellschaft Mit Beschränkter Haftung
  Industriestr. 22-36
  Haiger 35708
  277 385-0

### (G-19475)
### CNE INC
Also Called: Sign Max
1018 Lunt Ave (60193-4419)
 **PHONE** .................................. 847 534-7135
 **Fax:** 847 534-5594
 Gokan Oner, *President*
 **EMP:** 4
 **SQ FT:** 5,000
 **SALES (est):** 330K **Privately Held**
 **SIC:** 3993 Electric signs; neon signs

### (G-19476)
### COMMAX INC
1171 Tower Rd (60173-4305)
 **PHONE** .................................. 847 995-0994
 Ning Yang, *President*
 Judy Bielinski, *Assistant*
 **EMP:** 6
 **SQ FT:** 700
 **SALES (est):** 1.3MM **Privately Held**
 **SIC:** 2911 Fuel additives

### (G-19477)
### COMPONENT PRODUCTS INC
Also Called: Tucker Company Division
521 Morse Ave (60193-4529)
 **PHONE** .................................. 847 301-1000
 **Fax:** 847 301-0100
 Douglas Savage, *President*
 James Guertler, *Principal*
 Linda Guertler, *Principal*
 Jay Mullen, *Vice Pres*
 Rodrigo Rodriguez, *Opers Mgr*
 ▲ **EMP:** 20
 **SQ FT:** 12,000
 **SALES (est):** 13.9MM **Privately Held**
 **WEB:** www.componentproducts.com
 **SIC:** 5085 3569 3599 Signmaker equipment & supplies; liquid automation machinery & equipment; machine shop, jobbing & repair

### (G-19478)
### COMPSOFT TECH SLTONS GROUP INC
1701 E Wdfield Rd Ste 211 (60173)
 **PHONE** .................................. 847 517-9608
 Joseph Amirthaseelan, *Corp Secy*
 Shanthi Varadharajan, *Director*
 **EMP:** 18
 **SQ FT:** 2,000
 **SALES:** 1.7MM **Privately Held**
 **SIC:** 7379 7372 ; application computer software

### (G-19479)
### CONFORM INDUSTRIES INC
561 Estes Ave (60193-4428)
 **PHONE** .................................. 630 285-0272
 **Fax:** 630 285-0282
 Marty Walker, *President*
 David Selenis, *Opers Mgr*
 **EMP:** 10
 **SQ FT:** 7,500
 **SALES:** 2MM **Privately Held**
 **SIC:** 3599 3544 Grinding castings for the trade; special dies, tools, jigs & fixtures

### (G-19480)
### CONNOR ELECTRIC SERVICES INC
Also Called: Connor Voice and Data Tech
649 Estes Ave (60193-4402)
 **PHONE** .................................. 630 823-8230
 Lisa Szlenk, *President*
 John Szlenk Jr, *Principal*
 **EMP:** 24

SALES (est): 6.7MM **Privately Held**
**SIC: 3699** 1731 Electrical equipment & supplies; electrical work

**(G-19481)**
**CONTAINER GRAPHICS CORP**
492 Lunt Ave (60193-4408)
**PHONE**.................................847 584-0299
**Fax:** 847 584-9226
Don Moore, *Vice Pres*
Wayne Wisinski, *Branch Mgr*
**EMP:** 25
**SALES (corp-wide):** 75.1MM **Privately Held**
**WEB:** www.containergraphics.com
**SIC: 3555** Printing trades machinery
**PA:** Container Graphics Corp.
114 Ednbrgh S Dr Ste 104
Cary NC 27511
919 481-4200

**(G-19482)**
**CONTROL EQUIPMENT COMPANY INC**
1115 Morse Ave (60193-4505)
**PHONE**.................................847 891-7500
**Fax:** 847 891-7548
James M Pish, *President*
Jerry J Pish, *Admin Sec*
**EMP:** 10
**SQ FT:** 19,000
**SALES (est):** 1.2MM **Privately Held**
**WEB:** www.cedampers.com
**SIC: 3822** 3494 3444 Damper operators: pneumatic, thermostatic, electric; valves & pipe fittings; sheet metalwork

**(G-19483)**
**CONTROL RESEARCH INC**
908 Albion Ave (60193-4551)
P.O. Box 4103, Redondo Beach CA (90277-1745)
**PHONE**.................................847 352-4920
**Fax:** 847 392-4853
Lars Malmberg, *President*
**EMP:** 4
**SQ FT:** 6,000
**SALES (est):** 380K **Privately Held**
**WEB:** www.controlresearchinc.com
**SIC: 3625** Electric controls & control accessories, industrial

**(G-19484)**
**CONVERTING SYSTEMS INC**
1045 Remington Rd (60173-4517)
**PHONE**.................................847 519-0232
William Englehardt, *President*
Bonnie Engelhardt, *Director*
Marty Nixon, *Admin Sec*
**EMP:** 4
**SALES (est):** 897.4K **Privately Held**
**SIC: 7373** 3829 Systems engineering, computer related; measuring & controlling devices

**(G-19485)**
**CORPORATE ELECTRIC INC**
926 Estes Ct (60193-4426)
**PHONE**.................................847 963-2800
Michael Kohls, *Principal*
**EMP:** 2
**SALES (est):** 229.5K **Privately Held**
**SIC: 3699** Electrical equipment & supplies

**(G-19486)**
**CORUS AMERICA INC**
475 N Martingale Rd # 400 (60173-2257)
**PHONE**.................................847 585-2599
Dean Blakeney, *General Mgr*
◆ **EMP:** 24
**SQ FT:** 800
**SALES (est):** 1.5MM **Privately Held**
**SIC: 3355** Aluminum rolling & drawing

**(G-19487)**
**CREATIVE HI-TECH LTD**
710 Cooper Ct (60173-4537)
**PHONE**.................................224 653-4000
**Fax:** 847 718-0656
Popatlal Radadia, *President*
Mukesh Vasani, *Vice Pres*
Gopal Radadia, *Opers Mgr*
Mitali Shah, *Project Engr*
EDS Sloan, *Sales Mgr*
**EMP:** 50
**SQ FT:** 30,000
**SALES (est):** 7.9MM **Privately Held**
**WEB:** www.creativehitech.com
**SIC: 3672** Printed circuit boards

**(G-19488)**
**CREATIVE LITHOCRAFT INC (PA)**
1730 Wright Blvd (60193-4514)
**PHONE**.................................847 352-7002
**Fax:** 847 351-6767
Charles Horist, *President*
Carol Horist, *Corp Secy*
**EMP:** 14 **EST:** 1981
**SALES (est):** 1MM **Privately Held**
**WEB:** www.creativelithocraft.com
**SIC: 2759** 2752 Embossing on paper; commercial printing, offset

**(G-19489)**
**CREATIVE LITHOCRAFT INC**
Also Called: Gift Chech Graphics
1730 Wright Blvd (60193-4514)
P.O. Box 72847, Roselle (60172-0847)
**PHONE**.................................847 352-7002
Charles Horist, *President*
Carol Horist, *Vice Pres*
**EMP:** 8
**SALES (corp-wide):** 1MM **Privately Held**
**WEB:** www.creativelithocraft.com
**SIC: 2759** 2752 2796 2789 Embossing on paper; commercial printing, offset; platemaking services; bookbinding & related work; die-cut paper & board
**PA:** Creative Lithocraft Inc
1730 Wright Blvd
Schaumburg IL 60193
847 352-7002

**(G-19490)**
**CRESCEND TECHNOLOGIES LLC (PA)**
140 E State Pkwy (60173-5335)
**PHONE**.................................847 908-5400
**Fax:** 847 908-5408
Jim Hougo, *President*
Mark Obermann, *President*
David Pedersen, *President*
Jeff Kendell, *Vice Pres*
Lawrence Fitzgerald, *VP Opers*
▲ **EMP:** 21
**SQ FT:** 15,000
**SALES (est):** 10MM **Privately Held**
**WEB:** www.crescendtech.com
**SIC: 3663** Amplifiers, RF power & IF

**(G-19491)**
**CRONUS TECHNOLOGIES INC**
424 E State Pkwy (60173-6405)
**PHONE**.................................847 839-0088
**EMP:** 93 **EST:** 1994
**SALES (est):** 9.8MM **Privately Held**
**SIC: 7373** 3661 Computer Systems Design Mfg Telephone/Telegraph Apparatus

**(G-19492)**
**CROWN EQUIPMENT CORPORATION**
Also Called: Crown Lift Trucks
2055 Hammond Dr (60173-3809)
**PHONE**.................................847 397-1900
**Fax:** 847 397-1918
Kevin Miller, *Manager*
**EMP:** 110
**SALES (corp-wide):** 5.5B **Privately Held**
**SIC: 3537** Lift trucks, industrial: fork, platform, straddle, etc.
**PA:** Crown Equipment Corporation
44 S Washington St
New Bremen OH 45869
419 629-2311

**(G-19493)**
**CRYSTAL PARTNERS INC**
838 Prince Charles Ct (60195-2933)
**PHONE**.................................847 882-0467
William Russell, *President*
Robert Wagner, *Relations*
**EMP:** 1 **EST:** 1992
**SQ FT:** 2,400
**SALES:** 250K **Privately Held**
**WEB:** www.parabs.com
**SIC: 3651** Household audio & video equipment; household audio equipment; household video equipment

**(G-19494)**
**CUBE TOMATO INC**
636 Remington Rd Ste B (60173-5612)
**PHONE**.................................224 653-2655
Byung Lee, *Publisher*
**EMP:** 3
**SALES (est):** 240K **Privately Held**
**SIC: 2721** Periodicals: publishing only

**(G-19495)**
**CUSTOM ASSEMBLY SOLUTIONS INC**
Also Called: Nortech
101 E State Pkwy (60173-5336)
**PHONE**.................................847 224-5800
Bojan Jovanovic, *President*
Sarah Taylor, *Vice Pres*
▲ **EMP:** 12
**SQ FT:** 2,500
**SALES (est):** 3MM **Privately Held**
**SIC: 3549** Assembly machines, including robotic

**(G-19496)**
**D & J PLASTICS INC**
735 Morse Ave (60193-4533)
**PHONE**.................................847 534-0601
Dianne Wiseman, *President*
▲ **EMP:** 8
**SQ FT:** 10,000
**SALES (est):** 880.4K **Privately Held**
**SIC: 3089** Thermoformed finished plastic products

**(G-19497)**
**D AND R TECH**
1118 Lunt Ave Ste F (60193-4441)
**PHONE**.................................224 353-6693
John Traple, *Principal*
**EMP:** 3
**SALES (est):** 269.4K **Privately Held**
**SIC: 2851** Paints & allied products

**(G-19498)**
**D G PRINTING INC**
2246 Palmer Dr Ste 106 (60173-3852)
**PHONE**.................................847 397-7779
Mark Gagliano, *President*
**EMP:** 20
**SQ FT:** 40,000
**SALES (est):** 3MM **Privately Held**
**WEB:** www.dgprinting.com
**SIC: 7331** 2759 Mailing service; commercial printing

**(G-19499)**
**DART TECHNOLOGY INC**
801 Lunt Ave (60193-4414)
**PHONE**.................................847 534-0357
**Fax:** 847 321-7126
Leon Dodin, *President*
Rodney Kruse, *CFO*
Maria Shilov, *Admin Sec*
**EMP:** 9
**SQ FT:** 2,500
**SALES (est):** 1.1MM **Privately Held**
**WEB:** www.darttech.com
**SIC: 3469** 3599 Machine parts, stamped or pressed metal; machine shop, jobbing & repair

**(G-19500)**
**DE LUCA VISUAL SOLUTIONS INC**
Also Called: Fastsigns 100201
1084 National Pkwy (60173-4519)
**PHONE**.................................847 884-6300
Anthony De Luca, *President*
Donna De Luca, *Vice Pres*
**EMP:** 4
**SALES (est):** 142K **Privately Held**
**SIC: 3993** Signs & advertising specialties

**(G-19501)**
**DEMPSEY TOOL INC**
735 Lunt Ave (60193-4412)
**PHONE**.................................815 210-4896
**Fax:** 847 891-4121
James R Dempsey, *President*
Michael Dempsey, *Vice Pres*
Muriel Dempsey, *Treasurer*
**EMP:** 3
**SQ FT:** 5,000
**SALES (est):** 120K **Privately Held**
**WEB:** www.dempseytool.com
**SIC: 3599** Machine shop, jobbing & repair

**(G-19502)**
**DEPT 28 INC**
1169 Tower Rd (60173-4305)
**PHONE**.................................847 285-1343
Andrzej Ciesielski, *Principal*
▲ **EMP:** 4
**SALES (est):** 237.4K **Privately Held**
**SIC: 2082** Malt liquors

**(G-19503)**
**DEZURIK INC**
Also Called: Dezurik Apco Hilton
1420 Wright Blvd (60193-4508)
**PHONE**.................................847 985-5580
Bill Van Sant, *Branch Mgr*
**EMP:** 10
**SALES (corp-wide):** 149.9MM **Privately Held**
**SIC: 3491** Water works valves
**PA:** Dezurik, Inc.
250 Riverside Ave N
Sartell MN 56377
320 259-2000

**(G-19504)**
**DIEBOLD INCORPORATED**
900 National Pkwy Ste 420 (60173-5168)
**PHONE**.................................847 598-3300
**Fax:** 847 598-3275
Brad Browder, *General Mgr*
Jim Domke, *Project Mgr*
**EMP:** 60
**SALES (corp-wide):** 3.3B **Publicly Held**
**WEB:** www.diebold.com
**SIC: 3578** 5044 Automatic teller machines (ATM); vaults & safes
**PA:** Diebold Nixdorf, Incorporated
5995 Mayfair Rd
North Canton OH 44720
330 490-4000

**(G-19505)**
**DIMENSION DATA NORTH AMER INC**
1700 E Golf Rd Ste 1100 (60173-5864)
**PHONE**.................................847 278-6413
Jason Szerlong, *Vice Pres*
John Freres, *Branch Mgr*
Ernie Demers, *Manager*
Mark James, *Consultant*
Harford Daryll, *Info Tech Dir*
**EMP:** 10
**SALES (corp-wide):** 98.6B **Privately Held**
**WEB:** www.dimensiondata.com
**SIC: 7373** 7372 Computer integrated systems design; systems integration services; application computer software
**HQ:** Dimension Data North America, Inc.
110 Penn Plz Fl 16
New York NY 10119
212 613-1220

**(G-19506)**
**DK PRECISION INC**
614 Lunt Ave (60193-4411)
**PHONE**.................................847 985-8008
**Fax:** 847 980-8019
Donald F Knapp Sr, *President*
Donald E Knapp Jr, *Vice Pres*
Barb Knapp, *Purchasing*
**EMP:** 6
**SQ FT:** 4,400
**SALES (est):** 975.9K **Privately Held**
**WEB:** www.dkprecision.com
**SIC: 3599** Machine shop, jobbing & repair

**(G-19507)**
**DML DISTRIBUTION INC**
Also Called: D M L
1814 W Weathersfield Way (60193-2338)
**PHONE**.................................630 839-9041
Dan Long, *President*
▲ **EMP:** 16 **EST:** 2007
**SALES (est):** 1.4MM **Privately Held**
**SIC: 3452** Screws, metal

**(G-19508)**
**DREAMLAND**
1415 W Schaumburg Rd (60194-4051)
**PHONE**.................................847 524-6060
Rich Biedrzycki, *President*
**EMP:** 4

# Schaumburg - Cook County (G-19509)

## GEOGRAPHIC SECTION

SQ FT: 2,500
SALES (est): 407.3K **Privately Held**
WEB: www.comixxpress.com
SIC: **2721** Comic books: publishing & printing

**(G-19509)**
**DUAL VOLTAGE DISTRIBUTORS**
Also Called: Dvd Overseas Electronics
1252 Remington Rd Ste A (60173-4843)
PHONE ................................ 847 519-1201
Tushar Patel, *President*
Bufhar Patel, *President*
Sanjay Patel, *Vice Pres*
Fanjay Patel, *Admin Sec*
EMP: 6
SALES (est): 666.3K **Privately Held**
WEB: www.dvdoverseas.com
SIC: **3612** Transformers, except electric

**(G-19510)**
**E+E ELEKTRONIK CORPORATION**
333 E State Pkwy (60173-5337)
PHONE ................................ 508 530-3068
Rick Korte, *President*
Martin Bussert, *CFO*
Gregg Leighton, *Manager*
EMP: 5
SALES (est): 473.4K **Privately Held**
SIC: **3822** Thermostats & other environmental sensors

**(G-19511)**
**EAGLE ELECTRONICS INC**
1735 Mitchell Blvd (60193-4565)
PHONE ................................ 847 891-5800
Fax: 847 891-5874
Mike Kalaria, *President*
Madhukar S Kalaria, *Principal*
Brett McCoy, *Vice Pres*
Nori Luciano, *Opers Mgr*
Darius Shahreza, *Opers Mgr*
EMP: 90
SQ FT: 45,000
SALES (est): 15.2MM **Privately Held**
WEB: www.eagle-elec.com
SIC: **3672** Printed circuit boards

**(G-19512)**
**EBOOKS2GO**
1111 N Plaza Dr Ste 652 (60173-4951)
PHONE ................................ 847 598-1145
Ramana Abbaraju, *Principal*
John Bean, *Mktg Coord*
EMP: 3 EST: 2011
SALES (est): 146.6K **Privately Held**
SIC: **2731** Book publishing

**(G-19513)**
**EDUCATIONAL DIRECTORIES INC**
1025 W Wise Rd Ste 101 (60193-3746)
P.O. Box 68097 (60168-0097)
PHONE ................................ 847 891-1250
Douglas Moody, *President*
Doug Moody, *President*
Jim Burns, *MIS Mgr*
Lloyd Moody, *MIS Mgr*
EMP: 8
SQ FT: 1,800
SALES: 1MM **Privately Held**
WEB: www.ediusa.com
SIC: **2741** Directories: publishing only, not printed on site

**(G-19514)**
**EFFICI INC** ◆
939 N Plum Grove Rd (60173-5183)
PHONE ................................ 401 584-2266
Michael Stolarz, *CEO*
EMP: 6 EST: 2017
SALES (est): 135.3K **Privately Held**
SIC: **7372** Application computer software

**(G-19515)**
**ELECTRO-CIRCUITS INC**
1651 Mitchell Blvd (60193-4526)
PHONE ................................ 630 339-3389
Fax: 847 351-5073
Dal Vaghasiya, *President*
Nilesh Shah, *Controller*
Dennis Holtane, *Sales Mgr*
Bhagu Patel, *Marketing Staff*
EMP: 35 EST: 1981
SQ FT: 50,000
SALES (est): 4.9MM **Privately Held**
WEB: www.electrocircuits.com
SIC: **3672** Printed circuit boards

**(G-19516)**
**ENERGY PARTS SOLUTIONS INC**
820 Estes Ave (60193-4407)
PHONE ................................ 224 653-9412
Marek Przepiorka, *President*
Bob Beal, *Opers Mgr*
Dan McCarthy, *Admin Sec*
EMP: 12 EST: 2005
SQ FT: 18,500
SALES (est): 3.4MM **Privately Held**
SIC: **3511** Steam turbines

**(G-19517)**
**EPLAN SOFTWARE & SVCS N AMERI**
425 N Martingale Rd # 470 (60173-2406)
PHONE ................................ 517 762-5800
Thomas Martin, *Principal*
EMP: 5
SALES (est): 374K **Privately Held**
SIC: **7372** Prepackaged software

**(G-19518)**
**EQUUS POWER I LP**
1900 E Golf Rd Ste 1030 (60173-5076)
PHONE ................................ 847 908-2878
Tk Komiyama, *Principal*
Equus GP Holdco LLC, *General Ptnr*
EMP: 10
SALES (est): 1.1MM **Privately Held**
SIC: **3612** Transformers, except electric

**(G-19519)**
**ESPEE**
1701 E Wdfeld Rd Ste 636 (60173)
PHONE ................................ 224 256-9570
Dru West, *Principal*
EMP: 4
SALES (est): 259.6K **Privately Held**
SIC: **2834** Druggists' preparations (pharmaceuticals)

**(G-19520)**
**ESPEE BIOPHARMA & FINECHEM LLC**
1701 E Woodfield Rd # 636 (60173-5905)
PHONE ................................ 888 851-6667
Drew West, *Accounts Mgr*
Swapnil Shah, *Director*
Ravi Patel,
Alka Shah,
▲ EMP: 4
SALES (est): 1.9MM **Privately Held**
SIC: **5122** 2834 Pharmaceuticals; pharmaceutical preparations

**(G-19521)**
**ESSEX ELECTRO ENGINEERS INC**
2015 Mitchell Blvd (60193-4563)
PHONE ................................ 847 891-4444
Fax: 847 891-9111
Frank Pawlowski, *CEO*
Glenn F Pawlowski, *President*
Mark Pichla, *General Mgr*
Abdul Gilani, *QC Dir*
George Duresa, *QC Mgr*
▲ EMP: 30 EST: 1964
SQ FT: 50,000
SALES (est): 14MM **Privately Held**
WEB: www.essexelectro.com
SIC: **3679** 3724 3625 7389 Power supplies, all types: static; nonelectric starters, aircraft; control circuit relays, industrial; control equipment, electric; interior designer

**(G-19522)**
**ESTES LASER & MFG INC**
930 Lunt Ave (60193-4417)
PHONE ................................ 847 301-8231
Fax: 847 301-8240
Peter Tararo, *President*
EMP: 13
SQ FT: 7,500
SALES (est): 2.1MM **Privately Held**
WEB: www.esteslaser.com
SIC: **3444** Sheet metalwork

**(G-19523)**
**ETEL INC**
333 E State Pkwy (60173-5337)
PHONE ................................ 847 519-3380
Fax: 847 490-0151
Rick Korte, *President*
Alan Ehlers, *Area Mgr*
Arthur Holvknecht, *Vice Pres*
Dave Bugarewicz, *Engineer*
Rick Glos, *VP Sales*
▲ EMP: 6
SQ FT: 1,000
SALES: 3MM **Privately Held**
WEB: www.etelmotors.com
SIC: **3559** Electronic component making machinery
HQ: Heidenhain Corporation
333 E State Pkwy
Schaumburg IL 60173
847 490-1191

**(G-19524)**
**FASTWAY PRINTING INC**
Also Called: Fastway Printing Service
14 E Schaumburg Rd Ste 3 (60194-3555)
PHONE ................................ 847 882-0950
Fax: 847 882-7846
Chirag N Patel, *President*
Shilpa C Patel, *Admin Sec*
EMP: 3
SALES (est): 134.9K **Privately Held**
SIC: **2752** 2789 Commercial printing, offset; bookbinding & related work

**(G-19525)**
**FBC INDUSTRIES INC (PA)**
1933 N Meacham Rd Ste 550 (60173-4342)
PHONE ................................ 847 241-6143
Robert W Bloom, *President*
Felicia S Bloom, *Corp Secy*
Glen Hyden, *Controller*
▲ EMP: 6
SQ FT: 3,500
SALES (est): 5.7MM **Privately Held**
WEB: www.fbcindustries.com
SIC: **2099** Emulsifiers, food

**(G-19526)**
**FETZER SURGICAL LLC**
1019 W Wise Rd Ste 201 (60193-3754)
PHONE ................................ 630 635-2520
Chad Fetzer,
Max Fetzer,
EMP: 5
SALES (est): 218.2K **Privately Held**
SIC: **3841** Surgical & medical instruments

**(G-19527)**
**FINER LINE INC**
Also Called: Finer Line Engraving
1306 N Plum Grove Rd (60173-4546)
PHONE ................................ 847 884-1611
Fax: 847 884-1611
Mark C Case, *President*
Ryan Wyzinski, *Prdtn Mgr*
Bonnie Domino, *Accounts Mgr*
Andi Hull, *Accounts Mgr*
Kimberly A Case, *Admin Sec*
EMP: 11
SQ FT: 7,800
SALES (est): 990K **Privately Held**
WEB: www.finerline.com
SIC: **7389** 5999 5199 3479 Engraving service; trophies & plaques; badges; engraving jewelry silverware, or metal; glassware, art or decorative; engraving equipment & supplies

**(G-19528)**
**FINISHING GROUP**
1300 Basswood Rd Ste 200r (60173-4522)
PHONE ................................ 847 884-4890
Terry Reed, *Owner*
EMP: 7 EST: 2011
SALES (est): 360K **Privately Held**
SIC: **2732** Books: printing & binding

**(G-19529)**
**FIREFLY MOBILE INC**
1325 Remington Rd Ste H (60173-4815)
PHONE ................................ 305 538-2777
Patrick Marry, *President*
Don Deubler, *Vice Pres*
Donald Deubler Jr, *Vice Pres*
James Heagney, *CFO*

▲ EMP: 25
SQ FT: 3,000
SALES (est): 1.9MM **Privately Held**
WEB: www.fireflymobile.com
SIC: **5999** 3661 Mobile telephones & equipment; telephone sets, all types except cellular radio

**(G-19530)**
**FKAVPC INC**
Also Called: Apco Valve & Primer
1420 Wright Blvd (60193-4508)
PHONE ................................ 847 524-9000
Fax: 847 524-9007
George Christofidis, *President*
Ken King, *Vice Pres*
Bud Bartosch, *Adv Mgr*
Robert Mauriello, *Marketing Staff*
EMP: 85
SALES (corp-wide): 6.5MM **Privately Held**
WEB: www.apcovalves.com
SIC: **3491** Industrial valves
PA: Fkavpc, Inc.
1100 Via Callejon
San Clemente CA
949 361-9900

**(G-19531)**
**FLUID-AIRE DYNAMICS INC**
Also Called: Pneutech Products
530 Albion Ave (60193-4594)
PHONE ................................ 847 678-8388
Garth Taylor, *President*
Kevin Taylor, *General Mgr*
Derrick Taylor, *Vice Pres*
Ed Diener, *Manager*
Joan Taylor, *Manager*
▲ EMP: 28
SQ FT: 15,000
SALES: 7.4MM **Privately Held**
SIC: **3563** 7699 3053 Air & gas compressors; compressor repair; packing: steam engines, pipe joints, air compressors, etc.

**(G-19532)**
**FOSTER ELECTRIC (USA) INC (HQ)**
Also Called: Foster Electric America
1000 E State Pkwy Ste G (60173-4592)
PHONE ................................ 847 310-8200
Fax: 847 310-8212
Roy Chen, *President*
Michael McGowan, *Exec VP*
Eugene Fraczkowski, *CFO*
Lynda Teal, *Supervisor*
Yoichi Takahashi, *Director*
▲ EMP: 11
SQ FT: 7,000
SALES: 18.2MM
SALES (corp-wide): 1.4B **Privately Held**
SIC: **3651** 5065 Audio electronic systems; speaker systems; sound equipment, electronic
PA: Foster Electric Company, Limited
1-1-109, Tsutsujigaoka
Akishima TKY 196-0
425 462-311

**(G-19533)**
**FREEDOM FASTENER INC (PA)**
869 E Schaumburg Rd # 149 (60194-3654)
PHONE ................................ 847 891-3686
Vicki Scharringhausen, *President*
Michael Scharringhausen, *General Mgr*
EMP: 2
SALES (est): 378.9K **Privately Held**
SIC: **3452** Bolts, nuts, rivets & washers

**(G-19534)**
**FUTABA CORPORATION OF AMERICA (HQ)**
711 E State Pkwy (60173-4530)
PHONE ................................ 847 884-1444
Fax: 847 884-1635
Masaharu Tomita, *President*
Yuze Daimon, *Vice Pres*
Shin Takahashi, *Vice Pres*
Craig Henry, *CFO*
Jim Gulland, *Manager*
▲ EMP: 22
SQ FT: 27,000

# GEOGRAPHIC SECTION
## Schaumburg - Cook County (G-19557)

SALES (est): 31.6MM
SALES (corp-wide): 564.5MM **Privately Held**
WEB: www.futaba.com
SIC: 3679 Antennas, receiving
PA: Futaba Corporation
629, Oshiba
Mobara CHI 297-0
475 241-111

**(G-19535)**
**GANNON GRAPHICS**
1015 Morse Ave (60193-4503)
PHONE.................847 895-1043
Fax: 847 895-1108
Gannon Marty, *Principal*
Lori Corso, *Assistant*
EMP: 2 EST: 2012
SALES (est): 255.5K **Privately Held**
SIC: 2752 Commercial printing, lithographic

**(G-19536)**
**GERMAIN SAINT PRESS INC**
1120 Stonehedge Dr (60194-1323)
PHONE.................847 882-7400
Fax: 847 882-1117
Arnold Perris, *Vice Pres*
Sydney Lanier, *Treasurer*
Elizabeth Redman, *Admin Sec*
EMP: 7
SQ FT: 7,500
SALES (est): 692.5K
SALES (corp-wide): 1.7MM **Privately Held**
WEB: www.saintgermainpress.com
SIC: 2721 2731 Magazines: publishing only, not printed on site; books: publishing only
PA: Saint Germain Foundation
1120 Stonehedge Dr
Dunsmuir CA 96025
530 235-2994

**(G-19537)**
**GLOBAL BRASS COP HOLDINGS INC (PA)**
475 N Marti Rd (60173)
PHONE.................847 240-4700
John H Walker, *Ch of Bd*
John J Wasz, *President*
Kevin W Bense, *President*
Devin K Denner, *President*
William G Toler, *President*
EMP: 25
SALES: 1.3B **Publicly Held**
SIC: 3351 3341 3469 Copper rolling & drawing; brass rolling & drawing; copper smelting & refining (secondary); metal stampings

**(G-19538)**
**GM PARTNERS**
219 Lundy Ln (60193-1709)
PHONE.................847 895-7627
Steve Gorfsmin, *Partner*
Steve Grossman, *Partner*
Jeff Kuhn, *Partner*
EMP: 3
SALES: 150K **Privately Held**
WEB: www.gmpartners.com
SIC: 4226 3999 Household goods, warehousing; pet supplies

**(G-19539)**
**GONNELLA BAKING CO (PA)**
1117 Wiley Rd (60173-4337)
PHONE.................312 733-2020
Fax: 847 884-8829
Nick Marcucci, *President*
Steve Hanrahan, *General Mgr*
Larry Klasen, *District Mgr*
Bob Gonnella, *Vice Pres*
Robert Gonnella Jr, *Vice Pres*
▲ EMP: 60
SQ FT: 35,000
SALES (est): 140.2MM **Privately Held**
SIC: 2051 5812 2099 2038 Bread, all types (white, wheat, rye, etc): fresh or frozen; eating places; food preparations; frozen specialties

**(G-19540)**
**GONNELLA BAKING CO**
Gonnella Frozen Products Div
1117 Wiley Rd (60173-4337)
PHONE.................312 733-2020
Kenneth Gonnella, *Manager*
EMP: 90
SALES (corp-wide): 140.2MM **Privately Held**
SIC: 2051 Bread, all types (white, wheat, rye, etc): fresh or frozen; pastries, e.g. danish: except frozen
PA: Gonnella Baking Co.
1117 Wiley Rd
Schaumburg IL 60173
312 733-2020

**(G-19541)**
**GONNELLA BAKING CO**
2361 Palmer Dr (60173-3812)
PHONE.................847 884-8829
Bob Gonnella Jr, *Owner*
Dan Herzog, *Vice Pres*
David Marcucci, *Info Tech Dir*
EMP: 90
SALES (corp-wide): 140.2MM **Privately Held**
SIC: 2051 Bread, all types (white, wheat, rye, etc): fresh or frozen
PA: Gonnella Baking Co.
1117 Wiley Rd
Schaumburg IL 60173
312 733-2020

**(G-19542)**
**GONNELLA FROZEN PRODUCTS LLC (HQ)**
1117 Wiley Rd (60173-4337)
PHONE.................847 884-8829
Fax: 847 884-9469
Nicholas Marcucci, *President*
Kent Beernink, *Plant Mgr*
Ken Gonnella, *Engineer*
Jennifer Smolzer, *Accountant*
Roy Zoller, *Sales Staff*
EMP: 154 EST: 1886
SALES (est): 77.5MM
SALES (corp-wide): 140.2MM **Privately Held**
SIC: 2051 Bread, all types (white, wheat, rye, etc): fresh or frozen; rolls, bread type: fresh or frozen
PA: Gonnella Baking Co.
1117 Wiley Rd
Schaumburg IL 60173
312 733-2020

**(G-19543)**
**GREEN BOX AMERICA INC**
1900 E Golf Rd Ste 950 (60173-5034)
PHONE.................630 616-5400
Sasha Logan, *President*
Michael Teysar, *Sales Staff*
Matt Smith, *VP Mktg*
Michael Peyser, *Director*
Maria Bianchini, *Representative*
▲ EMP: 3 EST: 2009
SALES: 1MM **Privately Held**
SIC: 3585 Parts for heating, cooling & refrigerating equipment

**(G-19544)**
**GRIFFITH COMPANY**
1102 Helene Ln (60193-1331)
P.O. Box 68023 (60168-0023)
PHONE.................847 524-4173
Gordon Mac Millan, *Owner*
EMP: 3
SALES (est): 160K **Privately Held**
SIC: 3841 7699 Surgical & medical instruments; medical equipment repair, non-electric

**(G-19545)**
**GUNTNER US (DH)**
110 W Hillcrest Blvd # 105 (60195-3110)
PHONE.................847 781-0900
EMP: 2
SQ FT: 2,700
SALES (est): 306.4K
SALES (corp-wide): 366.3MM **Privately Held**
SIC: 3433 Heating equipment, except electric
HQ: Basetec Products & Solutions Gmbh
Hans-Guntner-Str. 2-6
Furstenfeldbruck 82256
814 124-2490

**(G-19546)**
**HALLMARK INDUSTRIES INC**
624 Estes Ave (60193-4403)
PHONE.................847 301-8050
Henry Huang, *President*
Jackie Wu, *Vice Pres*
▲ EMP: 10
SALES: 2MM **Privately Held**
WEB: www.hallmarkind.com
SIC: 3621 5063 3545 Motors, electric; electrical apparatus & equipment; machine tool accessories

**(G-19547)**
**HAMALOT INC (PA)**
Also Called: Electrowire
933 Remington Rd (60173-4515)
PHONE.................847 944-1500
Mickey M Hamano, *President*
Dave Lange, *General Mgr*
Paul Gray, *Business Mgr*
Kevin Mc Namara, *Vice Pres*
Nichole Peters, *Production*
▲ EMP: 25
SQ FT: 116,000
SALES (est): 72.6MM **Privately Held**
WEB: www.electrowire.com
SIC: 5063 3496 3315 Wire & cable; electronic wire & cable; miscellaneous fabricated wire products; steel wire & related products

**(G-19548)**
**HARTZ MOUNTAIN CORPORATION**
1100 E Woodfield Rd (60173-5116)
PHONE.................847 517-2596
Bob Cowhey, *Manager*
William Tobin, *Manager*
EMP: 44
SALES (corp-wide): 6.4B **Privately Held**
SIC: 2047 Dog & cat food
HQ: The Hartz Mountain Corporation
400 Plaza Dr Ste 400
Secaucus NJ 07094
800 275-1414

**(G-19549)**
**HAVING A GOOD TIME**
1710 E Woodfield Rd (60173-5153)
PHONE.................847 330-8460
EMP: 3
SALES (est): 294.7K **Privately Held**
SIC: 2131 Smoking tobacco

**(G-19550)**
**HEALTHLIGHT LLC**
920 E State Pkwy Unit B (60173-4527)
PHONE.................224 231-0342
Warren Graber, *President*
Donald Baldwin, *CFO*
Chris Johl, *Director*
EMP: 11 EST: 2015
SALES: 2MM **Privately Held**
SIC: 3845 Electromedical apparatus

**(G-19551)**
**HEIDENHAIN CORPORATION (DH)**
333 E State Pkwy (60173-5337)
PHONE.................847 490-1191
Ludwig Wagatha, *Ch of Bd*
Rick J Korte, *President*
Scott Warner, *Regional Mgr*
Randy Booth, *Area Mgr*
Robert Gee, *Area Mgr*
▲ EMP: 68
SQ FT: 110,000
SALES (est): 35.6MM **Privately Held**
WEB: www.heidenhain.com
SIC: 5084 3825 Measuring & testing equipment, electrical; instruments to measure electricity
HQ: Heidenhain Holding Inc
333 E State Pkwy
Schaumburg IL 60173
716 661-1700

**(G-19552)**
**HEIDENHAIN HOLDING INC (DH)**
333 E State Pkwy (60173-5337)
PHONE.................716 661-1700
Rainer Burkhard, *Ch of Bd*
Dr Thomas Sesselmann, *Systems Staff*
Sally Overend, *Admin Sec*
▲ EMP: 2
SQ FT: 118,000
SALES (est): 66.2MM **Privately Held**
SIC: 3545 5084 Machine tool accessories; measuring & testing equipment, electrical
HQ: Dr. Johannes Heidenhain Gesellschaft Mit Beschrankter Haftung
Dr.-Johannes-Heidenhain-Str. 5
Traunreut 83301
866 931-0

**(G-19553)**
**HI-GRADE WELDING AND MFG LLC**
Also Called: Hi-Grade Welding & Mfg
140 Commerce Dr (60173-5328)
PHONE.................847 640-8172
Fax: 847 981-7839
William Downey, *General Mgr*
Jon Frejd, *Vice Pres*
Dan Melcher, *Prdtn Mgr*
Don Ullrich, *QC Mgr*
Christine Juretzko, *VP Sales*
▼ EMP: 44
SQ FT: 48,000
SALES (est): 11.9MM
SALES (corp-wide): 1.1B **Publicly Held**
WEB: www.higradeinc.com
SIC: 3444 Sheet metalwork
HQ: Capital For Business, Inc.
11 S Meramec Ave Ste 1330
Saint Louis MO 63105
314 746-7427

**(G-19554)**
**HILDEBRANT J BOYD & CO INC**
1305 Remington Rd (60173-4833)
P.O. Box 68487 (60168-0487)
PHONE.................847 839-0850
Fax: 847 925-0897
J Boyd Hildebrant, *President*
Jim Hildebrant, *VP Engrg*
EMP: 9 EST: 1983
SALES (est): 734.7K **Privately Held**
SIC: 7372 Prepackaged software

**(G-19555)**
**HILLSHIRE BRANDS COMPANY**
Bil Mar Foods
1355 Remington Rd Ste U (60173-4818)
PHONE.................847 310-9400
Denis Raptata, *Branch Mgr*
EMP: 8
SALES (corp-wide): 36.8B **Publicly Held**
SIC: 2013 Sausages & other prepared meats; sausages from purchased meat; frankfurters from purchased meat; prepared pork products from purchased pork
HQ: The Hillshire Brands Company
400 S Jefferson St Fl 1
Chicago IL 60607
312 614-6000

**(G-19556)**
**HIS COMPANY INC**
Also Called: Hisco
1601 Wilkening Rd (60173-5323)
PHONE.................847 885-2922
Fax: 847 885-3527
Ted Kalata, *Marketing Staff*
Jim Caprile, *Branch Mgr*
Troy Reed, *Director*
EMP: 8
SALES (corp-wide): 177.4MM **Privately Held**
WEB: www.hiscoinc.com
SIC: 3679 Electronic circuits
PA: His Company, Inc
6650 Concord Park Dr
Houston TX 77040
713 934-1600

**(G-19557)**
**HMK MATTRESS HOLDINGS LLC**
180 Barrington Rd (60194-4800)
PHONE.................847 798-8023
EMP: 3
SALES (corp-wide): 1.6B **Privately Held**
SIC: 2515 Mattresses & foundations

Schaumburg - Cook County (G-19558)  GEOGRAPHIC SECTION

HQ: Hmk Mattress Holdings Llc
1000 S Oyster Bay Rd
Hicksville NY 11801
800 934-6848

### (G-19558)
### HOME DESIGN ALTERNATIVES INC (PA)
1325 Remington Rd Ste H (60173-4815)
PHONE..................314 731-1427
Robert F Ketterer, President
Michael Kirchwehm, Senior VP
Rick Hanson, Vice Pres
Joe O'Hanlon, Vice Pres
Jane Victor, Vice Pres
EMP: 50
SQ FT: 10,000
SALES (est): 10.2MM Privately Held
WEB: www.hdainc.com
SIC: 8712 2731 5192 House designer; pamphlets: publishing only, not printed on site; books: publishing only; books, periodicals & newspapers; books

### (G-19559)
### HUGO BOSS USA INC
5 Woodfield Mall (60173-5012)
PHONE..................847 517-1461
EMP: 19
SALES (corp-wide): 2.8B Privately Held
SIC: 5611 2299 Clothing accessories: men's & boys'; broadwoven fabrics: linen, jute, hemp & ramie
HQ: Hugo Boss Usa, Inc.
55 Water St Fl 48
New York NY 10041
212 940-0600

### (G-19560)
### HUNTER FOUNDRY MACHINERY CORP
2222 Hammond Dr (60196-3814)
PHONE..................847 397-5110
Fax: 847 397-8254
William G Hunter, President
Linda Jones, Vice Pres
Kevin Purdy, Vice Pres
Amy Heinzl, Senior Buyer
Dean Pfau, Controller
◆ EMP: 53 EST: 1964
SQ FT: 120,000
SALES (est): 15.2MM Privately Held
WEB: www.hunterauto.com
SIC: 3559 Foundry machinery & equipment

### (G-19561)
### HY TECH CNC MACHINING INC
600 Morse Ave Ste D (60193-4582)
David Weinmann, President
Christine Weinmann, Admin Sec
EMP: 2
SQ FT: 3,500
SALES: 200K Privately Held
SIC: 3089 3599 Injection molding of plastics; machine shop, jobbing & repair

### (G-19562)
### IDENTITI RESOURCES LTD
1201 Wiley Rd Ste 150 (60173-4387)
PHONE..................847 301-0510
Lawrence Sicher, President
Bryan Brotonel, Project Mgr
Douglas Franklin, Project Mgr
Mindy Michalak, Project Mgr
Lauren Zook, Project Mgr
EMP: 42
SQ FT: 42,000
SALES: 3.7MM Privately Held
WEB: www.identiti.net
SIC: 3993 8742 Signs & advertising specialties; management consulting services

### (G-19563)
### IDOT NORTH SIDE SIGN SHOP
201 Center Ct (60196-1096)
PHONE..................847 705-4033
EMP: 5
SALES (est): 353.1K Privately Held
SIC: 3993 Signs & advertising specialties

### (G-19564)
### INC MIDWEST DIE MOLD
624 Lunt Ave (60193-4411)
PHONE..................224 353-6417
Gary Little, Principal

EMP: 5
SALES (est): 454.7K Privately Held
SIC: 3544 Industrial molds

### (G-19565)
### INFORMATION BUILDERS INC
20 N Martingale Rd # 430 (60173-2438)
PHONE..................630 971-6700
Ron Dickson, Accounts Exec
Tom McKenzie, Manager
George Brown, Info Tech Mgr
EMP: 40
SQ FT: 1,600
SALES (corp-wide): 430.5MM Privately Held
WEB: www.informationbuilders.com
SIC: 7377 5734 7372 7371 Computer rental & leasing; computer software & accessories; prepackaged software; custom computer programming services
PA: Information Builders, Inc.
2 Penn Plz Fl 28
New York NY 10121
212 736-4433

### (G-19566)
### INK WELL PRINTING & DESIGN LTD
604 Albion Ave (60193-4519)
PHONE..................847 923-8060
Fax: 847 924-9409
Pete Costanza, President
Laurine Johnson, Corp Secy
EMP: 5
SQ FT: 10,000
SALES (est): 560K Privately Held
WEB: www.tiwprinting.com
SIC: 2752 2791 2789 Commercial printing, lithographic; commercial printing, offset; typesetting; bookbinding & related work

### (G-19567)
### INNOVATIVE COMPONENTS INC
1050 National Pkwy (60173-4519)
PHONE..................847 885-9050
Fax: 847 885-9005
Mike O Connor, President
Brent Bodine, Opers Staff
Jerry Campos, QC Mgr
Christine Motschull, Controller
Bob Fashingbauer, Finance Dir
◆ EMP: 50
SQ FT: 30,326
SALES (est): 12MM Privately Held
WEB: www.knobsource.com
SIC: 3089 3429 5072 Injection molding of plastics; furniture hardware; furniture hardware

### (G-19568)
### INNOVATIVE MKTG SOLUTIONS INC
1320 N Plum Grove Rd (60173-4546)
PHONE..................630 227-4300
Fax: 630 227-4310
Benjamin E Van Amerongen, President
John Sotos, Admin Sec
EMP: 12
SQ FT: 13,000
SALES (est): 3.1MM Privately Held
SIC: 2542 2511 Office & store showcases & display fixtures; wood household furniture

### (G-19569)
### INNOVATIVE PROJECTS LAB INC
150 N Martingale Rd # 838 (60173-2408)
PHONE..................847 605-2125
Christopher Galassi, President
EMP: 2
SALES (est): 225.6K Privately Held
WEB: www.ipli.com
SIC: 3821 Laboratory apparatus, except heating & measuring

### (G-19570)
### INTEL AMERICAS INC
425 N Matingale 1500 (60173)
PHONE..................847 706-5779
Greg Baur, District Mgr
Rick Lisa, Sales Dir
Kim Carlton, Sales Staff
Marni Anderson, Manager

Greg Reiff, Manager
EMP: 40
SALES (corp-wide): 59.3B Publicly Held
SIC: 3674 Semiconductors & related devices
HQ: Intel Americas, Inc
2200 Mission College Blvd
Santa Clara CA 95054
408 765-8080

### (G-19571)
### INTERMET METALS SERVICES INC
1375 E Wdfield Rd Ste 520 (60173)
PHONE..................847 605-1300
Timothy R Jaster, President
Timothy R Jaster, Finance Mgr
▲ EMP: 20
SALES (est): 6.4MM Privately Held
WEB: www.intermetmetals.com
SIC: 5051 3366 Metals service centers & offices; bronze foundry

### (G-19572)
### INTERNATIONAL BUS MCHS CORP
Also Called: IBM
425 N Martingale Rd (60173-2406)
PHONE..................847 706-3461
Edward Deane, Principal
Keith Clayton, Engineer
Patrick Kerin, Treasurer
EMP: 923
SALES (corp-wide): 79.9B Publicly Held
WEB: www.ibm.com
SIC: 3571 Minicomputers
PA: International Business Machines Corporation
1 New Orchard Rd Ste 1
Armonk NY 10504
914 499-1900

### (G-19573)
### INTERNATIONAL TECHNOLOGIES INC
627 Estes Ave (60193-4402)
PHONE..................847 301-9005
Al Gildemeister, President
▲ EMP: 2
SALES (est): 380.1K Privately Held
SIC: 3549 Wiredrawing & fabricating machinery & equipment, ex. die

### (G-19574)
### INTERNTONAL HAIR SOLUTIONS LLC
120 W Golf Rd (60195-5179)
PHONE..................404 474-3547
Karthik Ramasamy,
EMP: 3
SALES (est): 130.9K Privately Held
SIC: 3999 7299 Hair & hair-based products; hair weaving or replacement

### (G-19575)
### INTEX LIGHTING LLC
1300 E Wdfield Rd Ste 400 (60173)
PHONE..................847 380-2027
Charles Gavzer, Principal
EMP: 4
SALES (est): 244.3K Privately Held
SIC: 3648 Lighting equipment

### (G-19576)
### INX DIGITAL INTERNATIONAL CO
150 N Martingale Rd # 700 (60173-2009)
PHONE..................630 382-1800
◆ EMP: 14
SQ FT: 6,500
SALES (corp-wide): 1.3B Privately Held
SIC: 2893 Printing ink
HQ: The Inx Group Ltd
150 N Martingale Rd # 700
Schaumburg IL 60173
630 382-1800

### (G-19577)
### INX GROUP LTD (HQ)
150 N Martingale Rd # 700 (60173-2408)
PHONE..................630 382-1800
Hiroshi Ota, Ch of Bd
Kotaro Morita, President
Richard Clendenning, President
Greg Polasik, COO

Akio Miyata, Treasurer
◆ EMP: 3
SQ FT: 21,000
SALES (est): 361.6MM
SALES (est): 1.3B Privately Held
WEB: www.inxinternational.com
SIC: 2893 Printing ink
PA: Sakata Inx Corporation
1-23-37, Edobori, Nishi-Ku
Osaka OSK 550-0
664 475-811

### (G-19578)
### INX INTERNATIONAL INK CO (DH)
150 N Martingale Rd # 700 (60173-2009)
PHONE..................630 382-1800
Fax: 847 969-9758
Kotaro Morita, Ch of Bd
Rick Clendenning, President
Michael J Tennis, Senior VP
Matthew Mason, Vice Pres
Joe Finan, Engineer
◆ EMP: 100
SQ FT: 21,000
SALES (est): 361.6MM
SALES (corp-wide): 1.3B Privately Held
SIC: 2893 Printing ink
HQ: The Inx Group Ltd
150 N Martingale Rd # 700
Schaumburg IL 60173
630 382-1800

### (G-19579)
### INX INTERNATIONAL INK CO
150 N Martingale Rd # 700 (60173-2009)
PHONE..................800 233-4657
Rick Clendenning, President
EMP: 21
SALES (corp-wide): 1.3B Privately Held
SIC: 2893 Printing ink
HQ: Inx International Ink Co
150 N Martingale Rd # 700
Schaumburg IL 60173
630 382-1800

### (G-19580)
### INX INTERNATIONAL INK CO
150 N Martingale Rd # 700 (60173-2009)
PHONE..................630 382-1800
Scott Strachota, Manager
EMP: 22
SALES (corp-wide): 1.3B Privately Held
SIC: 2893 Printing ink
HQ: Inx International Ink Co
150 N Martingale Rd # 700
Schaumburg IL 60173
630 382-1800

### (G-19581)
### INX INTERNATIONAL INK CO
150 N Martingale Rd # 700 (60173-2009)
PHONE..................630 382-1800
Fax: 630 981-0443
Doug Duffert, Div Sub Head
Greg Hazen, Manager
EMP: 18
SALES (corp-wide): 1.3B Privately Held
SIC: 2893 2899 Printing ink; ink or writing fluids
HQ: Inx International Ink Co
150 N Martingale Rd # 700
Schaumburg IL 60173
630 382-1800

### (G-19582)
### ISCO INTERNATIONAL INC (PA)
444 E State Pkwy Ste 123 (60173-6416)
PHONE..................630 283-3100
Gordon Reichard Jr, CEO
Ralph Pini, Ch of Bd
George Calhoun, Principal
Torbjorn Folkebrant, Principal
Stephen McCarthy, Principal
EMP: 4
SQ FT: 15,000
SALES (est): 12.1MM Privately Held
WEB: www.iscointl.com
SIC: 3663 Radio receiver networks

### (G-19583)
### ISCO INTERNATIONAL LLC
444 E State Pkwy Ste 123 (60173-6416)
PHONE..................847 391-9400
Fax: 224 222-1691
Gordon Reichard Jr, CEO

Sanjay Huprikar, *Vice Pres*
Evi Sukandi, *Controller*
Wardell Redman, *Sales Dir*
Dr Amir Abdelmonem, *CTO*
▲ **EMP:** 35
**SALES (est):** 8.9MM **Privately Held**
**SIC:** 3661 Telephone & telegraph apparatus

**(G-19584)**
### ISEWAN USA INC
10 N Martingale Rd # 400 (60173-2099)
**PHONE**.................................630 561-2807
**EMP:** 3
**SALES (corp-wide):** 378MM **Privately Held**
**SIC:** 3541 7371 Machine tools, metal cutting type; custom computer programming services
**HQ:** Isewan U.S.A., Inc.
9101 Southrn Pne Blvd350 Ste 350
Charlotte NC 28273
704 521-2825

**(G-19585)**
### ITALIA FOODS INC
2127 Hammond Dr (60173-3811)
**PHONE**.................................847 397-4479
**Fax:** 847 397-6817
Arsenio Carabetta, *Ch of Bd*
Filippo Carabetta, *President*
Micolina Carabetta, *Corp Secy*
Maria Arjmand, *Vice Pres*
Maria Carabetta, *Vice Pres*
▲ **EMP:** 26
**SQ FT:** 6,000
**SALES (est):** 6MM **Privately Held**
**WEB:** www.impasti.com
**SIC:** 2038 5812 2099 Ethnic foods, frozen; eating places; food preparations

**(G-19586)**
### J R FINISHERS INC
616 Albion Ave (60193-4519)
**PHONE**.................................847 301-2556
**Fax:** 847 301-2559
Joe Rocco, *President*
Len Isbella, *Vice Pres*
Joe Rocco, *CFO*
**EMP:** 75
**SQ FT:** 23,000
**SALES:** 2MM **Privately Held**
**WEB:** www.jrfinishers.com
**SIC:** 2789 Binding only: books, pamphlets, magazines, etc.

**(G-19587)**
### JEFFREY ELEVATOR CO INC
Also Called: Jeco Equipment Company
570 Estes Ave (60193-4446)
**PHONE**.................................847 524-2400
**Fax:** 630 671-2985
Nickey T Budmats, *President*
Theresa R Budmats, *Admin Sec*
▲ **EMP:** 16
**SQ FT:** 8,000
**SALES:** 3MM **Privately Held**
**SIC:** 1796 3537 Elevator installation & conversion; industrial trucks & tractors

**(G-19588)**
### JEWERLY AND BEYOND
608 Newbury Ln B (60173-4746)
**PHONE**.................................312 833-6785
Marlo Gardner, *Owner*
**EMP:** 4 **EST:** 2013
**SALES (est):** 91K **Privately Held**
**SIC:** 3961 7389 Costume jewelry;

**(G-19589)**
### JJS GLOBAL VENTURES INC
1900 E Golf Rd Ste 950 (60173-5034)
**PHONE**.................................847 999-4313
Joe Spratley, *Principal*
**EMP:** 4 **EST:** 2000
**SALES (est):** 669.1K **Privately Held**
**SIC:** 3823 Industrial instrmnts msrmnt display/control process variable

**(G-19590)**
### JOSHI BROTHERS INC
Also Called: Country Donut
1218 S Roselle Rd (60193-4633)
**PHONE**.................................847 895-0200
**Fax:** 847 895-0746
Indrani Joshi, *President*
Manan Joshi, *Admin Sec*
▲ **EMP:** 23
**SQ FT:** 2,600
**SALES:** 1MM **Privately Held**
**SIC:** 2045 5812 Doughnut mixes, prepared: from purchased flour; coffee shop

**(G-19591)**
### JOURNEY CIRCUITS INC
830 E Higgins Rd Ste 111h (60173-4792)
**PHONE**.................................630 283-0604
Sarah Fatima, *President*
**EMP:** 3
**SALES (est):** 391.4K **Privately Held**
**SIC:** 3679 3672 Electronic circuits; printed circuit boards

**(G-19592)**
### JUPITER INDUSTRIES INC (PA)
1821 Walden Office Sq # 400 (60173-4295)
**PHONE**.................................847 925-5120
George E Murphy, *President*
Beverly Welling, *Controller*
Edna Forman, *Clerk*
**EMP:** 1
**SALES (est):** 1.9MM **Privately Held**
**WEB:** www.jupiterindustries.com
**SIC:** 1711 3452 Plumbing contractors; fire sprinkler system installation; mechanical contractor; warm air heating & air conditioning contractor; bolts, nuts, rivets & washers

**(G-19593)**
### JVC ADVANCED MEDIA USA INC
10 N Martingale Rd # 575 (60173-2298)
**PHONE**.................................630 237-2439
◆ **EMP:** 3
**SALES (est):** 196.5K
**SALES (corp-wide):** 1.9B **Privately Held**
**SIC:** 3695 Mfg Magnetic/Optical Recording Media
**HQ:** Victor Advanced Media Co.,Ltd.
2-26-5, Nihombashiningyocho
Chuo-Ku TKY
368 927-879

**(G-19594)**
### JX NIPPON OIL & ENERGY LUBRICA
20 N Martingale Rd # 300 (60173-2412)
**PHONE**.................................847 413-2188
Sunami Motoshi, *President*
Takahashi Tomohiro, *Treasurer*
Sonya Reynolds, *Manager*
Yamaguchi Kenji, *Admin Sec*
Tomo Carson, *Administration*
▲ **EMP:** 16
**SALES (est):** 3.6MM
**SALES (corp-wide):** 47.4MM **Privately Held**
**SIC:** 2992 Lubricating oils & greases
**PA:** Jx Group Kenko Hoken Kumiai
2-6-3, Otemachi
Chiyoda-Ku TKY
362 755-028

**(G-19595)**
### K & M PRINTING COMPANY INC
Also Called: Spotlight Graphics
1410 N Meacham Rd Frnt (60173-4845)
**PHONE**.................................847 884-1100
**Fax:** 847 884-1286
Ken J Stobart, *President*
Michael Stobart, *Vice Pres*
Chris Kelly, *Prdtn Mgr*
Bruce Frentz, *Sales Staff*
Mike Grunewald, *Sales Staff*
**EMP:** 95
**SQ FT:** 36,000
**SALES (est):** 25.9MM **Privately Held**
**WEB:** www.kmprinting.com
**SIC:** 2752 2791 2789 Commercial printing, offset; typesetting; bookbinding & related work

**(G-19596)**
### KAMAN AUTOMATION INC
1261 Wiley Rd Ste A (60173-4353)
**PHONE**.................................847 273-9050
Den Lucas, *Branch Mgr*
**EMP:** 11

**SALES (corp-wide):** 1.8B **Publicly Held**
**WEB:** www.minarikdrives.com
**SIC:** 5063 3621 Motors, electric; electric motor & generator auxillary parts
**HQ:** Kaman Automation, Inc.
1 Vision Way
Bloomfield CT 06002
860 687-5000

**(G-19597)**
### KILT OF SCHAUMBURG
1140 E Higgins Rd (60173-4709)
**PHONE**.................................847 413-2000
Harry Voulgaris, *Principal*
Dave Abraham, *Site Mgr*
**EMP:** 6
**SALES (est):** 571.2K **Privately Held**
**SIC:** 3421 Table & food cutlery, including butchers'

**(G-19598)**
### KING CIRCUIT
1651 Mitchell Blvd (60193-4526)
**PHONE**.................................630 629-7300
Bhagvan Patel, *President*
Arvind Patel, *Principal*
Kanti Patel, *Principal*
Suresh Patel, *Principal*
Tulshi Patel, *Principal*
**EMP:** 35
**SQ FT:** 10,500
**SALES:** 2.1MM **Privately Held**
**WEB:** www.kingcircuit.com
**SIC:** 3672 Printed circuit boards

**(G-19599)**
### KITAGAWA USA INC
301 Commerce Dr (60173-5305)
**PHONE**.................................847 310-8198
**Fax:** 847 310-9791
Kazuya Kitagawa, *President*
Frank Fujikawa, *Vice Pres*
Spencer Hastert, *VP Sales*
▲ **EMP:** 21
**SQ FT:** 30,000
**SALES:** 3.5MM
**SALES (corp-wide):** 450.6MM **Privately Held**
**SIC:** 3545 3593 Chucks: drill, lathe or magnetic (machine tool accessories); fluid power cylinders & actuators
**PA:** Kitagawa Iron Works Co., Ltd.
77-1, Motomachi
Fuchu HIR 726-0
847 454-560

**(G-19600)**
### KITAGAWA-NORTHTECH INC
Also Called: Northtech Work Holding
301 Commerce Dr (60173-5305)
**PHONE**.................................847 310-8787
Mike Mizumoto, *President*
Yochiharu Shimizu, *President*
Yusuf Ali, *Business Mgr*
Tim Winard, *COO*
Kenichiro Shichi, *Treasurer*
▲ **EMP:** 30
**SQ FT:** 30,000
**SALES (est):** 3.5MM
**SALES (corp-wide):** 16.5B **Privately Held**
**WEB:** www.ntwhi.com
**SIC:** 3545 Chucks: drill, lathe or magnetic (machine tool accessories)
**HQ:** Nippon Steel & Sumikin Bussan Americas, Inc.
200 N Martingale Rd # 801
Schaumburg IL 60173
847 882-6700

**(G-19601)**
### KOKOKU RUBBER INC (HQ)
1375 E Wdfield Rd Ste 560 (60173)
**PHONE**.................................847 517-6770
**Fax:** 847 517-6775
Shinichiro Eno, *CEO*
Tomoki Eno, *President*
Nick Kawahara, *Engineer*
Toba Takashi, *Treasurer*
Peter Cepican, *Accounts Mgr*
▲ **EMP:** 7
**SQ FT:** 1,500

**SALES (est):** 16.6MM
**SALES (corp-wide):** 191.3MM **Privately Held**
**WEB:** www.kokokuruuber.com
**SIC:** 3061 Automotive rubber goods (mechanical)
**PA:** Kokoku Intech Co., Ltd.
2-7, Kojimachi
Chiyoda-Ku TKY 102-0
332 304-661

**(G-19602)**
### KOMET AMERICA HOLDING INC (DH)
2050 Mitchell Blvd (60193-4544)
**PHONE**.................................847 923-8400
**Fax:** 847 924-8463
Dietmar Bolkhart, *President*
F Hans Grandin, *Principal*
Tom Brand, *Vice Pres*
James Gulzinski, *Sales Engr*
Pat Maigatter, *Sales Engr*
**EMP:** 7
**SQ FT:** 67,000
**SALES (est):** 36.8MM **Privately Held**
**SIC:** 3541 3365 Machine tools, metal cutting type; aerospace castings, aluminum
**HQ:** Komet Group Gmbh
Zeppelinstr. 3
Besigheim 74354
714 337-30

**(G-19603)**
### KOMET OF AMERICA INC
2050 Mitchell Blvd (60193-4544)
**PHONE**.................................847 923-8400
Jan Pflugfelder, *President*
Dietmar Bolkhart, *Vice Pres*
Thomas Brand, *Vice Pres*
Kevin McCoy, *Vice Pres*
John Catanzaro, *Design Engr*
▲ **EMP:** 180 **EST:** 1982
**SQ FT:** 90,000
**SALES (est):** 34.8MM **Privately Held**
**WEB:** www.komet.com
**SIC:** 3541 Machine tools, metal cutting type
**HQ:** Komet Of America Holding, Inc.
2050 Mitchell Blvd
Schaumburg IL 60193
847 923-8400

**(G-19604)**
### KORHUMEL INC
Also Called: Kory Farm Equipment Division
230 Parktrail Ct (60173-2150)
**PHONE**.................................847 330-0335
Irene Korhumel, *President*
Larry Lauritzen, *General Mgr*
Charlotte Whetstone, *Vice Pres*
**EMP:** 2
**SQ FT:** 6,200
**SALES (est):** 365.5K **Privately Held**
**SIC:** 3523 3312 Farm machinery & equipment; tubes, steel & iron

**(G-19605)**
### KORNICK ENTERPRISES LLC
711 E Golf Rd (60173-4511)
**PHONE**.................................847 884-1162
Philip Kornick,
Helen Kornick,
**EMP:** 5
**SALES (est):** 379.4K **Privately Held**
**SIC:** 3993 Signs & advertising specialties

**(G-19606)**
### KRONOS INCORPORATED
475 N Martingale Rd # 870 (60173-2227)
**PHONE**.................................847 969-6501
Brian Gosselin, *President*
Jami Howland, *Project Mgr*
Donna Huntsman, *Project Mgr*
Fred Miller, *Project Mgr*
Carol Anderson, *Finance Mgr*
**EMP:** 15
**SALES (corp-wide):** 1.2B **Privately Held**
**WEB:** www.kronos.com
**SIC:** 7372 Prepackaged software
**HQ:** Kronos Incorporated
297 Billerica Rd
Chelmsford MA 01824
978 250-9800

Schaumburg - Cook County (G-19607)

**(G-19607)**
**KTM LAB SERVICE CO INC**
716 Morse Ave (60193-4534)
P.O. Box 68219 (60168-0219)
PHONE..................708 351-6780
Scott Kegarise, *President*
Art Mann, *Vice Pres*
Tom Turner, *Vice Pres*
**EMP:** 2
**SQ FT:** 1,000
**SALES:** 325K **Privately Held**
**SIC:** 1389 Testing, measuring, surveying & analysis services

**(G-19608)**
**KURIYAMA OF AMERICA INC (HQ)**
360 E State Pkwy (60173-5335)
PHONE..................847 755-0360
Fax: 847 885-0996
Lester A Kraska, *President*
Brian Dutton, *General Mgr*
Hassan Salim, *General Mgr*
Motohiro Majikina, *Vice Pres*
Motohiro Majikina, *Vice Pres*
▲ **EMP:** 80 **EST:** 1968
**SQ FT:** 170,000
**SALES (est):** 86.1MM
**SALES (corp-wide):** 405.1MM **Privately Held**
**WEB:** www.kuriyama.thomasnet.com
**SIC:** 5085 3052 Hose, belting & packing; rubber & plastics hose & beltings
**PA:** Kuriyama Holdings Corporation
 1-12-4, Nishinakajima, Yodogawa-Ku
 Osaka OSK 532-0
 663 052-871

**(G-19609)**
**L K BEUTEL MACHINING CO INC**
536 Morse Ave (60193-4530)
PHONE..................847 895-5310
Ludwig K Beutel, *President*
**EMP:** 3
**SQ FT:** 2,500
**SALES (est):** 417.4K **Privately Held**
**SIC:** 3599 Machine shop, jobbing & repair

**(G-19610)**
**LAIRD TECHNOLOGIES INC**
1751 Wilkening Ct (60173-5310)
PHONE..................847 839-6900
Fax: 847 519-9682
John Sturm, *General Mgr*
Kim Kornacki, *Opers Mgr*
Lori Toro, *Accountant*
Glen Page, *Manager*
George Panackal, *Technology*
**EMP:** 140
**SALES (corp-wide):** 986.8MM **Privately Held**
**WEB:** www.lairdtechnologies.com
**SIC:** 3499 Magnetic shields, metal
**HQ:** Laird Technologies, Inc.
 3481 Rider Trl S
 Earth City MO 63045
 636 898-6000

**(G-19611)**
**LAMINARP**
1670 Basswood Rd (60173-5307)
PHONE..................847 884-9298
Donald Krog, *Owner*
**EMP:** 48
**SALES (est):** 3MM **Privately Held**
**WEB:** www.laminart.com
**SIC:** 3089 Plastics products

**(G-19612)**
**LAMINART INC**
1670 Basswood Rd (60173-5307)
PHONE..................800 323-7624
Donald Krog, *President*
Georgy Olivieri, *Vice Pres*
Kevin Geijer, *Site Mgr*
Paul Micek, *CFO*
Matthew Krog, *Treasurer*
◆ **EMP:** 48
**SALES (est):** 19.7MM **Privately Held**
**SIC:** 5085 5162 3083 Industrial supplies; plastics materials & basic shapes; thermoplastic laminates: rods, tubes, plates & sheet; thermosetting laminates: rods, tubes, plates & sheet

**(G-19613)**
**LARSEN & TOUBRO INFOTECH LTD**
1821 Walden Office Sq # 400 (60173-4273)
PHONE..................847 303-3900
A M Nik, *CEO*
Mahesh D Kulkarni, *Program Mgr*
Atul Rane, *Manager*
Uma Shetty, *Asst Mgr*
**EMP:** 5
**SALES (est):** 516.3K **Privately Held**
**SIC:** 7372 Prepackaged software

**(G-19614)**
**LEGEND RACING ENTERPRISES INC**
Also Called: Lre
616 Morse Ave (60193-4532)
PHONE..................847 923-8979
Doug Roden, *President*
**EMP:** 3
**SQ FT:** 5,000
**SALES (est):** 210K **Privately Held**
**SIC:** 7538 7549 3711 General automotive repair shops; high performance auto repair & service; automobile assembly, including specialty automobiles

**(G-19615)**
**LETTERS UNLIMITED INC**
1010 Morse Ave Ste E (60193-4584)
PHONE..................847 891-7811
Steve Koestler, *Principal*
**EMP:** 4
**SALES (est):** 452.4K **Privately Held**
**WEB:** www.lettersunlimited.com
**SIC:** 3081 3953 3993 Vinyl film & sheet; marking devices; signs & advertising specialties

**(G-19616)**
**LEVI STRAUSS & CO**
5 Woodfeld Shopg Ctr 11 # 114 (60173)
PHONE..................847 619-0655
**EMP:** 94
**SALES (corp-wide):** 4.5B **Privately Held**
**WEB:** www.levistrauss.com
**SIC:** 2325 Jeans: men's, youths' & boys'
**PA:** Levi Strauss & Co.
 1155 Battery St
 San Francisco CA 94111
 415 501-6000

**(G-19617)**
**LIFTING & COMPONENTS PARTS LLC** ✪
1900 E Golf Rd Ste 950a (60173-5034)
PHONE..................224 315-5294
Elizabeth Czajkowski, *Principal*
Kara Smith, *Manager*
**EMP:** 4 **EST:** 2016
**SALES (est):** 174K **Privately Held**
**SIC:** 2298 Slings, rope

**(G-19618)**
**LINKHOUSE LLC**
274 Northbury Ct Unit B1 (60193-1978)
PHONE..................312 671-2225
Shamaila Janjua, *Ch of Bd*
Rauf Choudhry, *President*
**EMP:** 5
**SALES (est):** 278.7K **Privately Held**
**SIC:** 7372 7389 Business oriented computer software;

**(G-19619)**
**LINTEC OF AMERICA INC**
935 National Pkwy # 93553 (60173-5334)
PHONE..................847 229-0547
Chooka Kaoru, *President*
Kazuyshio Node, *President*
Junpei Odaka, *Managing Dir*
▲ **EMP:** 7
**SALES (est):** 1.3MM **Privately Held**
**SIC:** 2891 Adhesives

**(G-19620)**
**LITTELL LLC**
1211 Tower Rd (60173-4307)
PHONE..................630 916-6662
Cory Smith, *Engineer*
Heather Milos, *Controller*
Kevin Roberts,
▲ **EMP:** 40

**SQ FT:** 37,000
**SALES (est):** 8.9MM **Privately Held**
**SIC:** 3547 3549 3599 3537 Rolling mill machinery; metalworking machinery; machine & other job shop work; industrial trucks & tractors

**(G-19621)**
**LITTELL INTERNATIONAL INC**
1211 Tower Rd (60173-4307)
PHONE..................630 622-4950
Fax: 630 622-4747
Sterling Stevenson, *President*
Paul Raimondi, *Vice Pres*
Cindy Lwin, *Purchasing*
Jason Lynch, *Engineer*
Heather Milos, *Controller*
▲ **EMP:** 45 **EST:** 1918
**SALES (est):** 6.2MM **Privately Held**
**WEB:** www.littell.com
**SIC:** 3542 3441 3549 3548 Machine tools, metal forming type; fabricated structural metal; metalworking machinery; welding apparatus

**(G-19622)**
**LOGAN SQUARE ALUMINUM SUP INC**
Also Called: Studio 41
1450 Mitchell Blvd (60193-4542)
PHONE..................847 985-1700
Bill Schmitt, *Branch Mgr*
**EMP:** 67
**SALES (corp-wide):** 101.1MM **Privately Held**
**WEB:** www.remodelerssupply.com
**SIC:** 3442 3444 5031 Window & door frames; awnings, sheet metal; building materials, exterior
**PA:** Logan Square Aluminum Supply, Inc.
 2500 N Pulaski Rd
 Chicago IL 60639
 773 235-2500

**(G-19623)**
**LORBERN MFG INC**
708 Morse Ave (60193-4534)
PHONE..................847 301-9441
Fax: 847 301-9441
Bernard Treffy, *President*
Lorraine Treffy, *Corp Secy*
Laura Treffy, *Vice Pres*
Robert Treffy, *Vice Pres*
**EMP:** 21
**SQ FT:** 10,000
**SALES (est):** 4MM **Privately Held**
**WEB:** www.lorbern.com
**SIC:** 3469 3599 Machine parts, stamped or pressed metal; machine shop, jobbing & repair

**(G-19624)**
**LUREN PRECISION CHICAGO CO LTD**
707 Remington Rd Ste 1 (60173-4572)
PHONE..................847 882-1388
Chihew Kuo, *President*
Jaime Fischer, *Accounts Mgr*
**EMP:** 3
**SALES (est):** 449.6K **Privately Held**
**SIC:** 3449 Miscellaneous metalwork

**(G-19625)**
**LUVO USA LLC (PA)**
2095 Hammond Dr (60173-3809)
PHONE..................847 485-8595
David Negus, *President*
Jenna Beveridge, *Controller*
**EMP:** 60
**SALES (est):** 8.8MM **Privately Held**
**SIC:** 2038 Lunches, frozen & packaged

**(G-19626)**
**LUVO USA LLC**
2095 Hammond Dr (60173-3809)
PHONE..................847 485-8595
**EMP:** 10
**SALES (corp-wide):** 8.8MM **Privately Held**
**SIC:** 2038 Lunches, frozen & packaged
**PA:** Luvo Usa, Llc
 2095 Hammond Dr
 Schaumburg IL 60173
 847 485-8595

**(G-19627)**
**LYNDA HERVAS**
Also Called: Tri Star Manufacturing
800 Morse Ave (60193-4583)
PHONE..................847 985-1690
Lynda Hervas, *Owner*
**EMP:** 4
**SQ FT:** 3,000
**SALES (est):** 183.5K **Privately Held**
**SIC:** 3499 Novelties & specialties, metal

**(G-19628)**
**M & R MEDIA INC**
Also Called: Fastsigns
1084 National Pkwy (60173-4519)
PHONE..................847 884-6300
Merle Silverstein, *President*
**EMP:** 5
**SALES (est):** 340K **Privately Held**
**SIC:** 3993 Signs & advertising specialties

**(G-19629)**
**M13 INC**
Also Called: M13 Graphics
1300 Basswood Rd Ste 100 (60173-4522)
PHONE..................847 310-1913
Fax: 847 781-5206
Daniel Banakis, *President*
Jessica Banakis, *CFO*
Rene Sanchez, *Cust Mgr*
**EMP:** 43
**SQ FT:** 50,000
**SALES (est):** 11MM **Privately Held**
**WEB:** www.m13graphics.com
**SIC:** 7373 2752 Computer integrated systems design; commercial printing, lithographic

**(G-19630)**
**MANU INDUSTRIES INC**
977 Lunt Ave (60193-4416)
PHONE..................847 891-6412
Manu Jayswal, *President*
Vipul Jayswal, *Sales Engr*
**EMP:** 10
**SQ FT:** 8,000
**SALES (est):** 1.2MM **Privately Held**
**WEB:** www.manuind.com
**SIC:** 3672 5063 Printed circuit boards; wire & cable

**(G-19631)**
**MARTIN TOOL WORKS INC**
Also Called: Komet
2050 Mitchell Blvd (60193-4544)
PHONE..................847 923-8400
Fax: 630 924-8463
F Hans Grandin, *President*
**EMP:** 14 **EST:** 1956
**SQ FT:** 67,000
**SALES (est):** 2MM **Privately Held**
**SIC:** 3365 Aerospace castings, aluminum
**HQ:** Komet Of America Holding, Inc.
 2050 Mitchell Blvd
 Schaumburg IL 60193
 847 923-8400

**(G-19632)**
**MARTY GANNON**
Also Called: Gannon Graphics
1025 Morse Ave (60193-4503)
PHONE..................847 895-1059
Marty Gannon, *CEO*
**EMP:** 25 **EST:** 2001
**SALES (est):** 3MM **Privately Held**
**SIC:** 2732 2752 Book printing; commercial printing, lithographic

**(G-19633)**
**MASCO CORPORATION**
1821 Walden Office Sq # 400 (60173-4273)
PHONE..................847 303-3088
Jimmy Hsu, *Branch Mgr*
**EMP:** 94
**SALES (corp-wide):** 7.3B **Publicly Held**
**WEB:** www.masco.com
**SIC:** 2434 Wood kitchen cabinets
**PA:** Masco Corporation
 21001 Van Born Rd
 Taylor MI 48180
 313 274-7400

## (G-19634)
### MASTER CUT E D M INC
1025 Lunt Ave Ste C (60193-4472)
PHONE..................847 534-0343
Scott Phillips, *President*
Harold Bartman, *Vice Pres*
**EMP:** 5
**SQ FT:** 2,500
**SALES (est):** 728.2K **Privately Held**
**SIC:** 3599 Electrical discharge machining (EDM)

## (G-19635)
### MASTER HYDRAULICS & MACHINING
540 Morse Ave (60193-4530)
PHONE..................847 895-5578
Fax: 847 894-5585
Harold J Schafer, *President*
Diana Schaefer, *Vice Pres*
Diana Schafer, *Vice Pres*
Micheal Schaefer, *Office Mgr*
**EMP:** 11
**SQ FT:** 5,000
**SALES (est):** 1MM **Privately Held**
**WEB:** www.mastershydraulics.com
**SIC:** 7699 3599 3593 Hydraulic equipment repair; machine shop, jobbing & repair; fluid power cylinders & actuators

## (G-19636)
### MATERIAL HAULERS INC
Also Called: Crete Rod, The
655 Lunt Ave (60193-4410)
PHONE..................815 857-4336
Jim Deetjen, *President*
▼ **EMP:** 2
**SALES:** 350K **Privately Held**
**SIC:** 3272 7359 Concrete products; tool rental

## (G-19637)
### MATRIX PRESS
1258 Remington Rd Ste A (60173-4841)
PHONE..................847 885-7076
Sal Farhan, *President*
Tracy Farhan, *Principal*
**EMP:** 2
**SQ FT:** 4,500
**SALES:** 500K **Privately Held**
**WEB:** www.matrix-press.com
**SIC:** 2759 Commercial printing

## (G-19638)
### MEADOWORKS LLC
935 National Pkwy # 93510 (60173-5150)
PHONE..................847 640-8580
Brian Walsh,
**EMP:** 15 **EST:** 2008
**SALES (est):** 2MM **Privately Held**
**SIC:** 3086 Mfg Plastic Foam Products

## (G-19639)
### MEDIEVAL BUILDERS LLC
508 Lunt Ave (60193-4408)
PHONE..................331 245-7791
**EMP:** 6
**SALES (est):** 245.2K **Privately Held**
**SIC:** 3448 Prefabricated metal buildings

## (G-19640)
### MEGA CORPORATION
516 Morse Ave (60193-4530)
P.O. Box 3036, Barrington (60011-3036)
PHONE..................847 985-1900
Fax: 847 985-3581
A William Van Meter, *President*
Robert E Shropshire, *Vice Pres*
Patti A Rein, *Director*
Beth Fleury Van Meter, *Admin Sec*
▲ **EMP:** 20 **EST:** 1980
**SQ FT:** 5,000
**SALES (est):** 3.1MM **Privately Held**
**WEB:** www.megacorporation.com
**SIC:** 3089 Injection molding of plastics

## (G-19641)
### MERCURY PRODUCTS CORP (PA)
1201 Mercury Dr (60193-3513)
PHONE..................847 524-4400
Fax: 847 524-8225
Bruce C Hael, *President*
Bruce Havel, *President*
Jack Ehlinger, *Managing Dir*
Maria Jimenez, *Buyer*
Ron Anderson, *QC Mgr*
▲ **EMP:** 200 **EST:** 1946
**SQ FT:** 93,280
**SALES (est):** 90MM **Privately Held**
**WEB:** www.pressedcorp.com
**SIC:** 3465 3469 3714 Automotive stampings; machine parts, stamped or pressed metal; motor vehicle engines & parts; exhaust systems & parts, motor vehicle

## (G-19642)
### MERCURY PRODUCTS CORP
1201 Mercury Dr (60193-3513)
PHONE..................847 524-4400
Vincent A Wrzos, *Branch Mgr*
**EMP:** 170
**SALES (corp-wide):** 90MM **Privately Held**
**WEB:** www.pressedcorp.com
**SIC:** 3465 3469 3714 Automotive stampings; machine parts, stamped or pressed metal; motor vehicle engines & parts; exhaust systems & parts, motor vehicle
**PA:** Mercury Products Corp.
1201 Mercury Dr
Schaumburg IL 60193
847 524-4400

## (G-19643)
### MERICHEM CHEM RFINERY SVCS LLC
650 E Algonquin Rd (60173-3846)
PHONE..................847 285-3850
Dayong Dong, *General Mgr*
Sohail Khan, *QC Mgr*
Laura Thrasher, *Accountant*
Edward Nelson, *Sr Project Mgr*
Jaffer Syed, *Manager*
**EMP:** 17
**SALES (est):** 285.8K **Privately Held**
**SIC:** 2819 Catalysts, chemical

## (G-19644)
### MICROSTRATEGY INCORPORATED
475 N Martingale Rd # 770 (60173-2255)
PHONE..................703 589-0734
**EMP:** 4
**SALES (corp-wide):** 512.1MM **Publicly Held**
**SIC:** 7372 Prepackaged software
**PA:** Microstrategy Incorporated
1850 Towers Crescent Plz # 700
Tysons Corner VA 22182
703 848-8600

## (G-19645)
### MID AMERICA EMS INDUSTRIES
818 Dighton Ln (60173-4736)
PHONE..................630 916-8203
Fax: 630 627-7414
**EMP:** 6
**SQ FT:** 6,000
**SALES (est):** 500K **Privately Held**
**SIC:** 3565 Packaging machinery

## (G-19646)
### MIDDLETONS MOULDINGS INC
1325 Remington Rd Ste H (60173-4815)
PHONE..................517 278-6610
Jim Brock, *President*
▲ **EMP:** 53
**SQ FT:** 19,800
**SALES (est):** 10.2MM **Privately Held**
**WEB:** www.middletonsmouldings.com
**SIC:** 2431 3442 2542 2434 Stair railings, wood; moldings & baseboards, ornamental & trim; metal doors, sash & trim; partitions & fixtures, except wood; wood kitchen cabinets

## (G-19647)
### MIDWEST CAD DESIGN INC
2385 Hammond Dr Ste 14 (60173-3844)
PHONE..................847 397-0220
Fax: 847 397-0028
Jim Saltouros, *President*
Larry Palesh, *Treasurer*
**EMP:** 5
**SQ FT:** 2,800
**SALES:** 1.1MM **Privately Held**
**WEB:** www.midwestcad.com
**SIC:** 3672 5065 8711 Printed circuit boards; electronic parts & equipment; engineering services

## (G-19648)
### MIDWEST SKYLITE SERVICE INC
907 Lunt Ave (60193-4416)
PHONE..................847 214-9505
Fax: 847 351-9684
John Harris, *President*
**EMP:** 4
**SQ FT:** 11,000
**SALES (est):** 340.8K **Privately Held**
**SIC:** 3444 Sheet metalwork

## (G-19649)
### MITSUBISHI MATERIALS USA CORP
1314 N Plum Grove Rd (60173-4546)
PHONE..................847 519-1601
Fax: 847 519-1732
Y Murakami, *Manager*
**EMP:** 10
**SALES (corp-wide):** 11.4B **Privately Held**
**SIC:** 5084 3545 Machine tools & accessories; cutting tools for machine tools
**HQ:** Mitsubishi Materials Usa Corp
11250 Slater Ave
Fountain Valley CA 92708
714 352-6100

## (G-19650)
### MOSSAN INC
28 Ashburn Ct Unit Z1 (60193-5757)
PHONE..................857 247-4122
Gustavo Frederico Mosquero, *CEO*
Gustavo Jesuf Mosquero, *CFO*
Gustavo Armando Mosquero, *Marketing Staff*
**EMP:** 3
**SALES:** 90K **Privately Held**
**SIC:** 2821 Molding compounds, plastics

## (G-19651)
### MOTOROLA INTERNATIONAL CAPITAL
1303 E Algonquin Rd (60196-1079)
PHONE..................847 576-5000
Mike Zevirovski, *President*
**EMP:** 1
**SALES (est):** 383.9K
**SALES (corp-wide):** 6B **Publicly Held**
**WEB:** www.motorola.com
**SIC:** 3674 Semiconductors & related devices
**PA:** Motorola Solutions, Inc.
500 W Monroe St Ste 4400
Chicago IL 60661
847 576-5000

## (G-19652)
### MOTOROLA SOLUTIONS INC
1295 E Algonquin Rd (60196-1097)
PHONE..................847 576-8600
Fax: 847 576-8691
Ginger Knowles, *Branch Mgr*
**EMP:** 142
**SALES (corp-wide):** 6B **Publicly Held**
**WEB:** www.motorola.com
**SIC:** 3663 3674 3571 3812 Radio & TV communications equipment; mobile communication equipment; pagers (one-way); cellular radio telephone; semiconductors & related devices; metal oxide silicon (MOS) devices; random access memory (RAM); microprocessors; personal computers (microcomputers); radar systems & equipment; position indicators for aircraft equipment; navigational systems & instruments; warfare counter-measure equipment; modems; multiplex equipment; telephone & telegraph; ignition apparatus, internal combustion engines
**PA:** Motorola Solutions, Inc.
500 W Monroe St Ste 4400
Chicago IL 60661
847 576-5000

## (G-19653)
### MOTOROLA SOLUTIONS INC
1100 E Woodfield Rd # 535 (60173-5116)
PHONE..................708 476-8226
Kirk Guy, *Principal*
Gerry Mita, *Branch Mgr*
**EMP:** 142
**SALES (corp-wide):** 6B **Publicly Held**
**WEB:** www.motorola.com
**SIC:** 3663 Radio & TV communications equipment
**PA:** Motorola Solutions, Inc.
500 W Monroe St Ste 4400
Chicago IL 60661
847 576-5000

## (G-19654)
### MOTOROLA SOLUTIONS INC
1303 E Algonquin Rd (60196-1079)
P.O. Box 804358, Chicago (60680-4105)
PHONE..................800 331-6456
**EMP:** 142
**SALES (corp-wide):** 6B **Publicly Held**
**SIC:** 3663 Radio & TV communications equipment
**PA:** Motorola Solutions, Inc.
500 W Monroe St Ste 4400
Chicago IL 60661
847 576-5000

## (G-19655)
### MT TOOL AND MANUFACTURING INC
1118 Lunt Ave Ste E (60193-4441)
PHONE..................847 985-6211
Thomas J Lechner, *President*
Margaret H Lechner, *Admin Sec*
**EMP:** 2
**SQ FT:** 1,000
**SALES (est):** 294.2K **Privately Held**
**SIC:** 3312 Tool & die steel

## (G-19656)
### MTA USA CORP
710 E State Pkwy Ste B (60173-4534)
PHONE..................847 847-5503
Antonio Falchetti, *President*
Bob Socha, *Sales Mgr*
▲ **EMP:** 5
**SQ FT:** 7,000
**SALES:** 3MM
**SALES (corp-wide):** 164.1MM **Privately Held**
**SIC:** 3694 Engine electrical equipment
**PA:** Mta Spa
Viale Dell' Industria 12
Codogno LO 26845
052 218-2720

## (G-19657)
### MURATA ELECTRONICS N AMER INC
425 N Martingale Rd # 1540 (60173-2213)
PHONE..................847 330-9200
Greg Taylor, *Accounts Mgr*
Chris Borwski, *Manager*
Randall Michaels, *Senior Mgr*
**EMP:** 8
**SALES (corp-wide):** 9.9B **Privately Held**
**WEB:** www.murata.com
**SIC:** 3675 3679 7629 Electronic capacitors; electronic circuits; electronic equipment repair
**HQ:** Murata Electronics North America, Inc.
2200 Lake Park Dr Se
Smyrna GA 30080
770 436-1300

## (G-19658)
### MURRAY PRINTING SERVICE INC
635 Remington Rd Ste F (60173-4578)
PHONE..................847 310-8959
David Koltonuk, *President*
**EMP:** 5 **EST:** 1963
**SALES:** 750K **Privately Held**
**SIC:** 2759 Letterpress printing

## (G-19659)
### MURRAYS DISC AUTO STORES INC
38 E Golf Rd Ste C (60173-3708)
PHONE..................847 882-4384
Ed Pavon, *Branch Mgr*
**EMP:** 4 **Publicly Held**
**WEB:** www.murraysdiscount.com
**SIC:** 7699 7694 7538 5531 Engine repair & replacement, non-automotive; rebuilding motors, except automotive; engine repair; automotive parts

## Schaumburg - Cook County (G-19660)

HQ: Murray's Discount Auto Stores, Inc.
8080 Haggerty Rd
Belleville MI 48111
734 957-8080

**(G-19660)**
**N BUJARSKI INC**
Also Called: Quiet Graphics
725 E Golf Rd (60173-4511)
PHONE..................847 884-1600
Fax: 847 884-9907
Norvell Bujarski, *President*
EMP: 6
SQ FT: 2,100
SALES (est): 570K **Privately Held**
WEB: www.quietgraphicsprinting.com
SIC: 2752 3993 2796 2791 Commercial printing, offset; signs & advertising specialties; platemaking services; typesetting; bookbinding & related work; manifold business forms

**(G-19661)**
**NATION PIZZA PRODUCTS LP**
Also Called: Nation Pizza and Foods
601 E Algonquin Rd (60173-3803)
PHONE..................847 397-3320
Fax: 847 397-9456
Richard Auskalnis, *President*
Marshall Bauer, *Co-CEO*
Jay Bauer, *Co-CEO*
Joseph Giglio, *Exec VP*
Mike Alagna, *Vice Pres*
EMP: 700
SQ FT: 200,000
SALES (est): 176.8MM **Privately Held**
SIC: 2038 2045 2033 Pizza, frozen; pizza doughs, prepared: from purchased flour; pizza sauce: packaged in cans, jars, etc.

**(G-19662)**
**NAVATEK RESOURCES INC**
1505 Wright Blvd (60193-4509)
PHONE..................847 301-0174
Giuseppe Paelmo, *President*
Gary Paelmo, *Admin Sec*
EMP: 3
SALES: 1MM **Privately Held**
WEB: www.navatekresources.com
SIC: 3679 Electronic circuits

**(G-19663)**
**NEPTUNE USA INC**
1022 Howard Dr (60193-4138)
PHONE..................847 987-3804
Jay Shah, *President*
▲ EMP: 1
SALES: 7MM **Privately Held**
SIC: 2221 3081 Polypropylene broadwoven fabrics; polypropylene film & sheet

**(G-19664)**
**NEWPORT PRINTING SERVICES INC**
1250 Remington Rd (60173-4812)
PHONE..................847 632-1000
Michael Parla, *CEO*
EMP: 2
SALES: 500K **Privately Held**
SIC: 2759 3993 Commercial printing; signs & advertising specialties

**(G-19665)**
**NIPPON ELECTRIC GLASS AMER INC (HQ)**
Also Called: Nega
1515 E Wdfield Rd Ste 720 (60173)
PHONE..................630 285-8323
Tsuyoshi, *President*
Cheryl Stevens, *Controller*
Makoto Nishimura, *Admin Sec*
▲ EMP: 8
SQ FT: 3,000
SALES (est): 2.3MM
SALES (corp-wide): 2.1B **Privately Held**
WEB: www.neg.co.jp
SIC: 3229 Glassware, industrial
PA: Nippon Electric Glass Co., Ltd.
2-7-1, Seiran
Otsu SGA 520-0
775 371-700

**(G-19666)**
**NISSHA USA INC (HQ)**
1051 Perimeter Dr Ste 600 (60173-5853)
PHONE..................847 413-2665
Fax: 847 413-4085
Junya Suzuki, *President*
Wataru Watanabe, *General Mgr*
Rocky Tsuruta, *CFO*
Yoshio Nakano, *Director*
Ayumu Takashiba, *Admin Sec*
▲ EMP: 20
SQ FT: 3,000
SALES (est): 33.3MM
SALES (corp-wide): 1B **Privately Held**
WEB: www.nisshausa.com
SIC: 2759 2752 Commercial printing; commercial printing, lithographic
PA: Nissha Printing Co.,Ltd.
3, Hanaicho, Mibu, Nakagyo-Ku
Kyoto KYO 604-8
758 118-111

**(G-19667)**
**NOBU NUTRITIONAL BAKING CO INC**
13 Quindel Ave (60193-1633)
PHONE..................847 344-7336
Kurt Schmitt, *President*
EMP: 3
SQ FT: 6,000
SALES (est): 270K **Privately Held**
SIC: 2047 Dog & cat food

**(G-19668)**
**NORTECH PACKAGING LLC**
Also Called: Tishma Technologies
101 E State Pkwy (60173-5336)
PHONE..................847 884-1805
David Showman, *Mng Member*
Jody Lambargo, *Mangr*
EMP: 7
SALES (est): 730.2K **Privately Held**
SIC: 3565 Packaging machinery

**(G-19669)**
**NORTHFIELD HOLDINGS LLC**
700 Wiley Farm Ct (60173-5342)
PHONE..................847 755-0700
Fax: 847 755-9900
Charles J Vogle,
▲ EMP: 26
SQ FT: 30,000
SALES (est): 5.9MM **Privately Held**
WEB: www.northfieldind.com
SIC: 3469 Machine parts, stamped or pressed metal

**(G-19670)**
**NOVASPECT INC (PA)**
1124 Tower Rd (60173-4306)
PHONE..................847 956-8020
Fax: 847 885-8200
Terry Voigt, *President*
Timothy Holcer, *President*
Angela Musial, *General Mgr*
David Schneider, *Business Mgr*
Kurt Detloff, *Project Mgr*
EMP: 140
SQ FT: 19,000
SALES (est): 70MM **Privately Held**
WEB: www.novaspect.com
SIC: 7372 5084 Prepackaged software; controlling instruments & accessories

**(G-19671)**
**O E M MARKETING INC (PA)**
1015 Lunt Ave (60193-4418)
P.O. Box 8444, Bartlett (60103-8444)
PHONE..................847 985-9490
Fax: 847 985-9443
Scott Sutter, *President*
Claudia Sutter, *Treasurer*
Shirley Kaminski, *Office Mgr*
▲ EMP: 10
SQ FT: 10,000
SALES (est): 1.5MM **Privately Held**
WEB: www.oemincorporated.com
SIC: 3824 5084 Odometers; measuring & testing equipment, electrical

**(G-19672)**
**OERLIKON**
1475 E Wdfield Rd Ste 201 (60173)
PHONE..................847 619-5541
Loc Cheynet, *President*
Manisha K Sinha, *General Mgr*
Jim Criscuolo, *VP Opers*
Patrick Vermeylen, *Controller*
Brian Stocks, *Accounts Mgr*
EMP: 17
SALES (est): 1.6MM **Privately Held**
SIC: 3479 Etching & engraving

**(G-19673)**
**OERLIKON BLZERS CATING USA INC (DH)**
1475 E Wdfield Rd Ste 201 (60173)
PHONE..................847 619-5541
Fax: 847 619-5653
Christian Kunz, *CEO*
Kent Connell, *President*
Vivek Prakash, *COO*
Mario Vitale, *Vice Pres*
Michael Kruse, *Opers Mgr*
▲ EMP: 12
SALES (est): 117.6MM
SALES (corp-wide): 2.3B **Privately Held**
WEB: www.balzers.com
SIC: 3479 3471 Coating of metals & formed products; finishing, metals or formed products
HQ: Oerlikon Balzers Coating Ag
Iramali 18
Balzers
388 570-1

**(G-19674)**
**OLYMPIC PETROLEUM CORPORATION**
1171 Tower Rd (60173-4305)
PHONE..................847 995-0996
Wendy Pierson, *Manager*
EMP: 75
SALES (corp-wide): 38.6MM **Privately Held**
SIC: 2992 Lubricating oils & greases
PA: Olympic Petroleum Corporation
5000 W 41st St
Cicero IL 60804
708 876-7900

**(G-19675)**
**OLYMPIC STEEL INC**
1901 Mitchell Blvd (60193-4538)
PHONE..................847 584-4000
Fax: 847 584-4003
Brad Clifford, *General Mgr*
Jason Redden, *Manager*
EMP: 20
SALES (corp-wide): 1B **Publicly Held**
WEB: www.olysteel.com
SIC: 5051 3441 3312 Metals service centers & offices; fabricated structural metal; blast furnaces & steel mills
PA: Olympic Steel, Inc.
22901 Millcreek Blvd # 650
Cleveland OH 44122
216 292-3800

**(G-19676)**
**OZKO SIGN & LIGHTING COMPANY**
1119 Lunt Ave (60193-4420)
PHONE..................224 653-8531
Engin Komu, *Partner*
Volkan Ovdemir, *Partner*
EMP: 8 EST: 2010
SQ FT: 6,000
SALES: 900K **Privately Held**
SIC: 1799 3993 Sign installation & maintenance; electric signs

**(G-19677)**
**P & J TECHNOLOGIES**
1356 Saint Claire Pl (60173-6186)
PHONE..................847 995-1108
David Ballotto, *Owner*
EMP: 4
SALES: 200K **Privately Held**
SIC: 3699 Security control equipment & systems

**(G-19678)**
**P M MOLD COMPANY (PA)**
800 Estes Ave (60193-4407)
PHONE..................847 923-5400
Fax: 847 923-5494
Lawrence Hauck, *President*
Larry Hauck, *General Mgr*
John O'Kelly, *Engineer*
David Bradley, *Treasurer*
David Erbach, *Program Mgr*
▲ EMP: 23
SQ FT: 45,000
SALES (est): 13.5MM **Privately Held**
WEB: www.pmmold.com
SIC: 3544 Forms (molds), for foundry & plastics working machinery; industrial molds

**(G-19679)**
**P M MOLD COMPANY**
800 Estes Ave (60193-4407)
PHONE..................847 923-5400
Larry Hauch, *General Mgr*
Larry Hauck, *Manager*
EMP: 23
SALES (corp-wide): 13.5MM **Privately Held**
WEB: www.pmmold.com
SIC: 3544 Forms (molds), for foundry & plastics working machinery; industrial molds
PA: P. M. Mold Company
800 Estes Ave
Schaumburg IL 60193
847 923-5400

**(G-19680)**
**PADDOCK PUBLICATIONS INC**
Also Called: Daily Herald
1000 Albion Ave (60193-4549)
P.O. Box 280, Arlington Heights (60006-0280)
PHONE..................847 427-5545
Jerry Schur, *Manager*
Karen Nelson, *Executive Asst*
EMP: 250
SALES (corp-wide): 122.6MM **Privately Held**
WEB: www.dailyherald.com
SIC: 2711 Newspapers, publishing & printing
PA: Paddock Publications, Inc.
155 E Algonquin Rd
Arlington Heights IL 60005
847 427-4300

**(G-19681)**
**PAR GOLF SUPPLY INC**
550 Pratt Ave N (60193-4555)
PHONE..................847 891-1222
Fax: 847 891-1286
Mike Gallichio, *President*
Lauren Urbanek, *Sales Mgr*
Dave Moy, *Sales Staff*
Amy Daughert, *Manager*
▼ EMP: 28
SQ FT: 8,000
SALES (est): 6.2MM **Privately Held**
WEB: www.pargolf.com
SIC: 5091 3949 Golf equipment; golf equipment

**(G-19682)**
**PARAGON INTERNATIONAL INC**
Also Called: Paragon Valuation Group
1901 N Roselle Rd Ste 711 (60195-5711)
PHONE..................847 240-2981
Fax: 847 519-0904
Richard R Swarts, *President*
Kathi James, *Vice Pres*
Scott R Swarts, *Vice Pres*
Diana Martin, *Office Mgr*
Keith Danek, *Executive*
EMP: 16
SQ FT: 3,600
SALES (est): 2MM **Privately Held**
WEB: www.paragoninternational.com
SIC: 7372 7373 8721 8748 Business oriented computer software; value-added resellers, computer systems; accounting services, except auditing; business consulting; inventory computing service

**(G-19683)**
**PARALLEL SOLUTIONS LLC**
1251 N Plum Grove Rd # 160 (60173-5603)
PHONE..................847 708-9227
Vince Panico, *Principal*
EMP: 2
SALES (est): 332.8K **Privately Held**
SIC: 7372 Prepackaged software

**(G-19684)**
**PARKING SYSTEMS INC**
911 Estes Ct (60193-4427)
P.O. Box 72031, Roselle (60172-0031)
PHONE..................847 891-3819

## GEOGRAPHIC SECTION
## Schaumburg - Cook County (G-19710)

Fax: 847 895-0816
Larry A Landis, *President*
Faye Landis, *Vice Pres*
**EMP:** 3
**SQ FT:** 5,000
**SALES (est):** 300K **Privately Held**
**WEB:** www.parking-systems.com
**SIC:** 3625 3559 3829 Control equipment, electric; parking facility equipment & supplies; measuring & controlling devices

### (G-19685)
### PARTNERS MANUFACTURING INC
625 Lunt Ave (60193-4410)
**PHONE**..........847 352-1080
Michael Lagioia, *President*
**EMP:** 28
**SALES:** 2MM **Privately Held**
**SIC:** 3544 Special dies, tools, jigs & fixtures

### (G-19686)
### PECORA TOOL & DIE CO INC
520 Morse Ave (60193-4530)
**PHONE**..........847 524-1275
Fax: 847 524-8127
Mario Pecora, *President*
Mary Pecora, *Admin Sec*
**EMP:** 4
**SQ FT:** 5,000
**SALES (est):** 482.6K **Privately Held**
**SIC:** 3544 Die sets for metal stamping (presses); jigs & fixtures

### (G-19687)
### PECORA TOOL SERVICE INC
520 Morse Ave (60193-4530)
**PHONE**..........847 524-1275
Mario Pecora, *President*
**EMP:** 4
**SALES (est):** 430K **Privately Held**
**SIC:** 3469 Metal stampings

### (G-19688)
### PEPSI-COLA GEN BOTTLERS INC (DH)
Also Called: Pepsico
1475 E Wdfeld Rd Ste 1300 (60173)
**PHONE**..........847 598-3000
Kenneth E Keiser, *President*
Jay Hulbert, *Vice Pres*
Lisa Schmittle, *Opers Spvr*
Maribeth Casey, *Opers Staff*
Keith Melaragno, *Engng Exec*
▼ **EMP:** 450 **EST:** 1939
**SQ FT:** 100,000
**SALES (est):** 1.7B
**SALES (corp-wide):** 62.8B **Publicly Held**
**WEB:** www.pepsiamericas.com
**SIC:** 2086 5149 Soft drinks: packaged in cans, bottles, etc.; carbonated beverages, nonalcoholic: bottled & canned; soft drinks
**HQ:** Pepsi Americas, Inc.
   60 S 6th St
   Minneapolis MN 55402
   612 661-4000

### (G-19689)
### PHILIP MORRIS USA INC
300 N Martingale Rd # 700 (60173-2091)
**PHONE**..........847 605-9595
Andy Macray, *Vice Pres*
Marcia Sullivan, *Director*
**EMP:** 100
**SALES (corp-wide):** 25.7B **Publicly Held**
**WEB:** www.philipmorrisusa.com
**SIC:** 2111 Cigarettes
**HQ:** Philip Morris Usa Inc.
   6601 W Brd St
   Richmond VA 23230
   804 274-2000

### (G-19690)
### PHILLY FASTENERS CORP
224 W Beech Dr (60193-1549)
P.O. Box 681038 (60168-1038)
**PHONE**..........847 584-9408
Gale Vodicka, *President*
**EMP:** 5
**SALES (est):** 350.2K **Privately Held**
**SIC:** 3452 Bolts, nuts, rivets & washers

### (G-19691)
### PITNEY BOWES INC
2330 Hammond Dr Ste G (60173-3869)
**PHONE**..........312 209-2216
Steve Pace, *Manager*
**EMP:** 20
**SALES (corp-wide):** 3.4B **Publicly Held**
**SIC:** 3579 7359 Postage meters; business machine & electronic equipment rental services
**PA:** Pitney Bowes Inc.
   3001 Summer St Ste 3
   Stamford CT 06905
   203 356-5000

### (G-19692)
### PLASTIC PRODUCTS INC
1515 E Wdfield Rd Ste 860 (60173)
**PHONE**..........847 874-3440
William A Degironemo, *President*
Scott Mackey, *Vice Pres*
**EMP:** 25
**SALES (est):** 1.8MM **Privately Held**
**WEB:** www.plasticpalletsinc.com
**SIC:** 3089 Pallets, plastic

### (G-19693)
### PLASTIC SPECIALTIES & TECH INC
Also Called: American Gasket & Rubber
119 Commerce Dr (60173-5311)
**PHONE**..........847 781-2414
Sam Maged, *General Mgr*
Tim Killinger, *Vice Pres*
Stan Kroll, *Vice Pres*
Jim Pearse, *Vice Pres*
Sam Majeed, *Manager*
**EMP:** 30
**SQ FT:** 60,000
**SALES (corp-wide):** 1.1B **Privately Held**
**SIC:** 3053 5085 2822 Gaskets, packing & sealing devices; gaskets; synthetic rubber
**HQ:** Plastic Specialties And Technologies Inc.
   101 Railroad Ave
   Ridgefield NJ 07657
   201 941-2900

### (G-19694)
### PLATE AND PRE-PRESS MANAGEMENT
431 Westover Ln (60193-2428)
**PHONE**..........847 352-0462
Joe Babich, *President*
Barbara Babich, *Admin Sec*
**EMP:** 5
**SQ FT:** 2,300
**SALES:** 214.3K **Privately Held**
**SIC:** 3861 3555 Photographic film, plate & paper holders; printing plates

### (G-19695)
### PLIANT CORPORATION OF CANADA
Also Called: Roll-O-Sheets
1475 E Woodfield Rd # 700 (60173-4980)
**PHONE**..........847 969-3300
**EMP:** 5
**SALES (est):** 323.9K **Privately Held**
**SIC:** 3081 Plastic film & sheet

### (G-19696)
### PLIANT INVESTMENT INC
1475 E Wdfield Rd Ste 600 (60173)
**PHONE**..........847 969-3300
**EMP:** 3
**SALES:** 194.5K **Privately Held**
**SIC:** 3081 Plastic film & sheet

### (G-19697)
### PLIANT SOLUTIONS CORPORATION
1475 E Wdfield Rd Ste 600 (60173)
**PHONE**..........847 969-3300
Fax: 847 969-3339
Craig Miller, *President*
Michelle Wilson, *President*
Gary Penna, *Owner*
Paul Frantz, *Senior VP*
Greg E Gard, *Senior VP*
**EMP:** 33
**SALES (est):** 6.6MM **Privately Held**
**SIC:** 3081 Plastic film & sheet

### (G-19698)
### PLUSTECH INC
735 Remington Rd (60173-4552)
**PHONE**..........847 490-8130
Fax: 847 490-3192
Koji Yamauchi, *President*
R Scott Fernandez, *Admin Sec*
▲ **EMP:** 7
**SQ FT:** 3,500
**SALES:** 10MM
**SALES (corp-wide):** 3.9B **Privately Held**
**WEB:** www.plustech.com
**SIC:** 3089 Injection molding of plastics
**PA:** Yamazen Corporation
   2-3-16, Itachibori, Nishi-Ku
   Osaka OSK 550-0
   665 343-021

### (G-19699)
### PRACTICAL COMMUNICATIONS INC
Also Called: Outside Plant Magazine
1320 Tower Rd (60173-4309)
**PHONE**..........773 754-3250
Fax: 847 934-3346
Sharon Vollman, *President*
Janice Oliva, *Senior VP*
Carrie Naber, *Vice Pres*
Tim Yount, *Vice Pres*
Tammy Snyder, *Opers Staff*
**EMP:** 29
**SQ FT:** 10,000
**SALES (est):** 4.3MM **Privately Held**
**WEB:** www.ospmag.com
**SIC:** 2721 7331 Trade journals: publishing only, not printed on site; mailing service

### (G-19700)
### PRECISION LANGUAGE & GRAPHICS
Also Called: Digitone
800 E Woodfield Rd # 107 (60173-4739)
**PHONE**..........847 413-1688
Fax: 847 413-1690
Hongxian Helen Shi, *President*
Eric Zhang, *Vice Pres*
Lesley Wong, *Manager*
**EMP:** 7
**SQ FT:** 1,200
**SALES (est):** 927.6K **Privately Held**
**SIC:** 2791 Typesetting

### (G-19701)
### PROMOFRAMES LLC
1113 Tower Rd (60173-4305)
**PHONE**..........866 566-7224
Steve Lim,
▼ **EMP:** 5
**SQ FT:** 5,100
**SALES:** 500K **Privately Held**
**WEB:** www.proax.com
**SIC:** 5043 7389 3953 2752 Cameras & photographic equipment; advertising, promotional & trade show services; stationery embossers, personal; offset & photolithographic printing

### (G-19702)
### PROTEC EQUIPMENT RESOURCES INC
1501 Wright Blvd (60193-4509)
**PHONE**..........847 434-5808
Dan Allison, *Branch Mgr*
**EMP:** 3
**SALES (corp-wide):** 6MM **Privately Held**
**SIC:** 3825 Engine electrical test equipment
**PA:** Protec Equipment Resources, Inc.
   1517 W North Carrier 11
   Grand Prairie TX 75050
   972 352-5550

### (G-19703)
### PRU DENT MFG INC
1929 Wright Blvd (60193-4567)
**PHONE**..........847 301-1170
Tim Prusaitis, *President*
**EMP:** 8
**SALES (est):** 985.7K **Privately Held**
**SIC:** 3999 Manufacturing industries

### (G-19704)
### PULLR HOLDING COMPANY LLC
Also Called: Maasdam Pow'r-Pull
415 E State Pkwy (60173-4539)
**PHONE**..........224 366-2500
Fax: 847 228-6021
Jason Liu, *CFO*
Tony Ranallo, *Financial Exec*
Sharon Lin, *Manager*
Vincent Lin,
Anthony Ranallo,
▲ **EMP:** 35
**SALES (est):** 7.1MM **Privately Held**
**SIC:** 3423 Hand & edge tools

### (G-19705)
### PUTMAN MEDIA INC (PA)
Also Called: Food Processing Magazine
1501 E Wdfield Rd Ste 400n (60173)
**PHONE**..........630 467-1301
Fax: 630 467-0157
John Cappelletti, *CEO*
Steve Diogo, *Publisher*
Mike Bacidore, *Editor*
Dave Fusaro, *Editor*
Christine L Grace, *Editor*
▼ **EMP:** 51 **EST:** 1938
**SQ FT:** 16,000
**SALES:** 13MM **Privately Held**
**WEB:** www.putmanpublishing.com
**SIC:** 2721 2731 Trade journals: publishing only, not printed on site; book publishing

### (G-19706)
### QUADRANT 4 SYSTEM CORPORATION (PA)
Also Called: Q4
1501 E Woodfield Rd 250s (60173-4961)
**PHONE**..........855 995-7367
Robert Steele, *CEO*
Shekhar Iyer, *COO*
**EMP:** 350
**SALES:** 52MM **Publicly Held**
**WEB:** www.aventura-holdings.com
**SIC:** 7379 7372 Computer related consulting services; prepackaged software; business oriented computer software

### (G-19707)
### QUADRANT TOOL AND MFG CO
1720 W Irving Park Rd (60193-5477)
**PHONE**..........847 352-6977
Fax: 847 352-6939
Kenneth G Kraemer, *President*
Lillian Kraemer, *Vice Pres*
Mike Fregeau, *Engineer*
Helayne Przeslicke, *Treasurer*
Kathryn Good, *Admin Sec*
**EMP:** 25
**SQ FT:** 18,500
**SALES:** 4.5MM **Privately Held**
**WEB:** www.quadranttool.com
**SIC:** 3599 Machine shop, jobbing & repair

### (G-19708)
### QUALITY MACHINE TOOL SERVICES
2385 Hammond Dr Ste 12 (60173-3844)
**PHONE**..........847 776-0073
Dave Polido, *Owner*
**EMP:** 2 **EST:** 2011
**SALES (est):** 238.5K **Privately Held**
**SIC:** 7699 3599 Industrial equipment services; machine shop, jobbing & repair

### (G-19709)
### QUALITY SERVICE & INSTALLATION
923 Sharon Ln (60193-1348)
**PHONE**..........847 352-4000
Jeff Ficarrotta, *President*
**EMP:** 3
**SALES:** 100K **Privately Held**
**SIC:** 3669 Communications equipment

### (G-19710)
### QUINTUM TECHNOLOGIES INC
1821 Walden Office Sq # 200 (60173-4271)
**PHONE**..........847 348-7730
Melissa Rohring, *Manager*
**EMP:** 15

Schaumburg - Cook County (G-19711)

SALES (corp-wide): 252.5MM **Publicly Held**
WEB: www.quintumtechnologies.com
SIC: 3661 Telephone & telegraph apparatus
HQ: Quintum Technologies, Inc.
71 James Way
Eatontown NJ 07724
732 460-9000

**(G-19711)**
**RAAJRTNA STINLESS WIRE USA INC**
1015 W Wise Rd Ste 201 (60193-3777)
PHONE..........................847 923-8000
Gene Stall, *Principal*
▲ EMP: 13
SALES (est): 2.8MM **Privately Held**
SIC: 3315 Steel wire & related products
PA: Raajratan Metal Industries
Mittal Court, No 126, Nariman Point
Mumbai MH

**(G-19712)**
**RITTAL CORP (DH)**
425 N Martingale Rd # 400 (60173-2202)
PHONE..........................847 240-4600
Douglas E Peterson, *President*
John Boudreaux, *Senior VP*
James Wiest, *Senior VP*
Jim Nichols, *Vice Pres*
Tony Varga, *Vice Pres*
◆ EMP: 635
SQ FT: 25,000
SALES (est): 177MM **Privately Held**
WEB: www.ripac.com
SIC: 3469 5065 Electronic enclosures, stamped or pressed metal; electronic parts & equipment
HQ: Rittal Gmbh & Co. Kg
Auf Dem Stutzelberg
Herborn 35745
277 250-50

**(G-19713)**
**ROBERT MCCORMICK TRIBUNE LBRRY**
1400 N Roosevelt Blvd (60173-4377)
PHONE..........................847 619-7980
Francie Bauer, *Director*
EMP: 3
SALES (est): 109.7K **Privately Held**
SIC: 2711 Newspapers, publishing & printing

**(G-19714)**
**RSF ELECTRONICS INC (DH)**
333 E State Pkwy (60173-5337)
PHONE..........................847 490-0351
John Thormodsgard, *President*
EMP: 17
SQ FT: 10,000
SALES (est): 1.1MM **Privately Held**
WEB: www.rsf.net
SIC: 3621 Phase or rotary converters (electrical equipment)
HQ: Heidenhain Corporation
333 E State Pkwy
Schaumburg IL 60173
847 490-1191

**(G-19715)**
**S & S TOOL COMPANY**
1107 Lunt Ave Ste 1 (60193-4442)
PHONE..........................847 891-0780
Fax: 847 352-1086
Karl Stein, *Partner*
Michael Lagioia, *Partner*
EMP: 3
SALES (est): 399.3K **Privately Held**
SIC: 3544 3541 7389 Special dies & tools; numerically controlled metal cutting machine tools; grinding, precision: commercial or industrial

**(G-19716)**
**SAGENT LOGISTICS LP**
1901 N Roselle Rd Ste 450 (60195-3181)
PHONE..........................847 908-1600
Peter Kaemmerer, *CEO*
Sean Brynjelsen, *Exec VP*
Donald Bullock, *Exec VP*
Frank Harmon, *Exec VP*
Jeffrey Greve, *Controller*
EMP: 10

SALES (est): 409.5K **Privately Held**
SIC: 2834 Pharmaceutical preparations

**(G-19717)**
**SAGENT PHARMACEUTICALS INC (HQ)**
1901 N Roselle Rd Ste 700 (60195-3194)
PHONE..........................847 908-1600
Peter Kaemmerer, *CEO*
Bruce Levins, *President*
Ken Chaney, *Business Mgr*
Jodi Evenson, *Business Mgr*
Brynn Jackson, *Business Mgr*
▲ EMP: 100
SQ FT: 23,500
SALES: 318.3MM
SALES (corp-wide): 1.2B **Privately Held**
SIC: 2834 5122 Pharmaceutical preparations; pharmaceuticals
PA: Nichi-Iko Pharmaceutical Co.,Ltd.
1-6-21, Sogawa
Toyama TYM 930-0
764 322-121

**(G-19718)**
**SANDVIK INC**
Also Called: Sandvik Crmant Prductivity Ctr
1665 N Penny Ln (60173-4593)
PHONE..........................847 519-1737
Jim Gondeck, *President*
Martin Hitra, *Marketing Staff*
EMP: 100
SALES (corp-wide): 8.8B **Privately Held**
SIC: 3316 Strip steel, cold-rolled: from purchased hot-rolled; wire, flat, cold-rolled strip: not made in hot-rolled mills
HQ: Sandvik, Inc.
17-02 Nevins Rd
Fair Lawn NJ 07410
201 794-5000

**(G-19719)**
**SBIC AMERICA INC**
205 Travis Ct Apt 304 (60195-5116)
PHONE..........................847 303-5430
Samuel Kim, *Principal*
Helen Chung, *Manager*
Hyung Jung, *Relations*
EMP: 5 EST: 2007
SALES (est): 490K **Privately Held**
SIC: 3462 Iron & steel forgings

**(G-19720)**
**SC LIGHTING**
607 W Wise Rd (60193-3865)
PHONE..........................630 849-3384
EMP: 4
SALES (est): 349.5K **Privately Held**
SIC: 3648 Lighting equipment

**(G-19721)**
**SCHAUMBURG SPECIALTIES CO**
550 Albion Ave Ste 30 (60193-4547)
PHONE..........................847 451-0070
Charles Schaumburg, *President*
Steven Schaumburg, *Business Mgr*
Joel Bidmead, *Vice Pres*
Eric Schaumburg, *Vice Pres*
Jeff Schaumburg, *Sales Staff*
▼ EMP: 7
SQ FT: 5,000
SALES (est): 1.2MM **Privately Held**
SIC: 5084 2542 Materials handling machinery; office & store showcases & display fixtures

**(G-19722)**
**SCHNEIDER ELC HOLDINGS INC (HQ)**
200 N Martingale Rd # 100 (60173-2033)
PHONE..........................717 944-5460
Jean-Pascal Tricoire, *CEO*
Martin Hanna, *President*
Bobby Rogers, *President*
Stephen Litchfield, *Counsel*
Laurent Vernerey, *Exec VP*
▲ EMP: 4619

SALES (est): 7B
SALES (corp-wide): 241K **Privately Held**
SIC: 3822 1711 3625 3823 Building services monitoring controls, automatic; mechanical contractor; relays & industrial controls; motor control accessories, including overload relays; motor controls, electric; industrial process control instruments; motors, electric
PA: Schneider Electric Se
35 Rue Joseph Monier
Rueil Malmaison
141 297-000

**(G-19723)**
**SCHNEIDER ELECTRIC USA INC**
200 N Martingale Rd # 100 (60173-2026)
PHONE..........................847 441-2526
Terry Harvey, *Project Mgr*
Matthew Okane, *Branch Mgr*
EMP: 25
SALES (corp-wide): 241K **Privately Held**
SIC: 3643 3613 Bus bars (electrical conductors); switchgear & switchboard apparatus
HQ: Schneider Electric Usa, Inc.
800 Federal St
Andover MA 01810
978 975-9600

**(G-19724)**
**SE RELAYS LLC (DH)**
Also Called: Magnecraft
200 N Martingale Rd # 100 (60173-2033)
PHONE..........................847 827-9880
Bill Lafabve, *Treasurer*
Doug Cunningham, *Controller*
James Steinback, *Mng Member*
Kevin Aumuller, *Manager*
▲ EMP: 6
SQ FT: 4,200
SALES: 15MM
SALES (corp-wide): 241K **Privately Held**
WEB: www.squared.com
SIC: 3625 Relays & industrial controls
HQ: Schneider Electric Usa, Inc.
800 Federal St
Andover MA 01810
978 975-9600

**(G-19725)**
**SENARIO LLC**
1325 Remington Rd Ste H (60173-4815)
PHONE..........................847 882-0677
T R Turner, *CFO*
Mike Nakamura,
Martha Goode, *Admin Sec*
Karin Gabany, *Assistant*
▲ EMP: 18
SQ FT: 17,600
SALES (est): 15.7MM **Privately Held**
WEB: www.senario.com
SIC: 3651 5942 Home entertainment equipment, electronic; children's books

**(G-19726)**
**SHINWA MEASURING TOOLS CORP**
1320 Tower Rd (60173-4309)
PHONE..........................847 598-3701
Toru Watanabe, *President*
Yugo Takahashi, *Vice Pres*
▲ EMP: 2
SALES (est): 212.3K **Privately Held**
SIC: 3545 Scales, measuring (machinists' precision tools)

**(G-19727)**
**SIEMENS MED SOLUTIONS USA INC**
Also Called: Dosimetry Medicine Group
2501 N Barrington Rd (60195)
PHONE..........................847 304-7700
Fax: 847 304-7707
Steve Wille, *Manager*
EMP: 70
SALES (corp-wide): 89.6B **Privately Held**
WEB: www.siemensmedical.com
SIC: 3841 Diagnostic apparatus, medical
HQ: Siemens Medical Solutions Usa, Inc.
40 Liberty Blvd
Malvern PA 19355
610 219-6300

**(G-19728)**
**SIR SPEEDY PRINTING CTR 6080**
525 W Wise Rd Ste D (60193-3882)
PHONE..........................708 351-8841
Fax: 630 351-8878
Anthony J Belmonte, *Partner*
Linda Belmonte, *Partner*
EMP: 8
SQ FT: 1,800
SALES (est): 530K **Privately Held**
SIC: 2752 Commercial printing, lithographic

**(G-19729)**
**SK HYNIX AMERICA INC**
Also Called: Hsa Chicago Office
1920 Thoreau Dr N (60173-4176)
PHONE..........................847 925-0196
Mike Peterson, *Branch Mgr*
EMP: 4
SALES (corp-wide): 16.4B **Privately Held**
SIC: 3825 Semiconductor test equipment
HQ: Sk Hynix America Inc.
3101 N 1st St
San Jose CA 95134
408 232-8000

**(G-19730)**
**SOFT O SOFT INC**
1701 E Wdfield Rd Ste 215 (60173)
PHONE..........................630 741-4414
Syam C Thotakura, *President*
Geta Thotakura, *Manager*
EMP: 20
SALES (est): 1.6MM **Privately Held**
WEB: www.softosoft.com
SIC: 7372 Prepackaged software

**(G-19731)**
**SOLEIL SYSTEMS INC**
1325 Remington Rd Ste H (60173-4815)
PHONE..........................847 427-0428
Fred Rieble, *President*
Raymond Bellan, *Vice Pres*
▲ EMP: 40
SQ FT: 25,000
SALES (est): 3.4MM **Privately Held**
SIC: 3648 Sun tanning equipment, incl. tanning beds

**(G-19732)**
**SPARTON AUBREY LLC**
425 N Martingale Rd Ste 2 (60173-2406)
PHONE..........................386 740-5381
Delana McGuire, *Asst Controller*
Maricela Posada, *Credit Staff*
EMP: 30
SALES (est): 1.4MM
SALES (corp-wide): 419.3MM **Publicly Held**
SIC: 3674 Microprocessors
PA: Sparton Corporation
425 N Martingale Rd
Schaumburg IL 60173
847 762-5800

**(G-19733)**
**SPARTON AYDIN LLC**
Also Called: Aydin Displays
425 N Martingale Rd (60173-2406)
PHONE..........................800 772-7866
Delana McGuire, *Asst Controller*
Maricela Posada, *Credit Staff*
EMP: 4
SALES (est): 350.1K
SALES (corp-wide): 419.3MM **Publicly Held**
SIC: 3577 3625 Computer peripheral equipment; control equipment, electric
PA: Sparton Corporation
425 N Martingale Rd
Schaumburg IL 60173
847 762-5800

**(G-19734)**
**SPARTON CORPORATION (PA)**
425 N Martingale Rd (60173-2406)
PHONE..........................847 762-5800
Joseph J Hartnet, *CEO*
James R Swartwout, *Ch of Bd*
Steven M Korwin, *Senior VP*
Gordon B Madlock, *Senior VP*
Michael A Gaul, *Vice Pres*
▲ EMP: 277 EST: 1900
SQ FT: 22,000

**SALES:** 419.3MM **Publicly Held**
**WEB:** www.sparton.com
**SIC:** 3674 3672 Microprocessors; printed circuit boards

**(G-19735)**
## SPARTON DESIGN SERVICES LLC (HQ)
425 N Martingale Rd # 2050 (60173-2406)
**PHONE**..................847 762-5800
**EMP:** 5 **EST:** 2015
**SALES (est):** 2.8MM
**SALES (corp-wide):** 419.3MM **Publicly Held**
**SIC:** 3674 3672 Microprocessors; printed circuit boards
**PA:** Sparton Corporation
425 N Martingale Rd
Schaumburg IL 60173
847 762-5800

**(G-19736)**
## SPARTON EMT LLC (HQ)
425 N Martingale Rd Ste 2 (60173-2406)
**PHONE**..................800 772-7866
**EMP:** 4
**SALES (est):** 75.9MM
**SALES (corp-wide):** 419.3MM **Publicly Held**
**SIC:** 3674 Microprocessors
**PA:** Sparton Corporation
425 N Martingale Rd
Schaumburg IL 60173
847 762-5800

**(G-19737)**
## SPARTON IED LLC
425 N Martingale Rd (60173-2406)
**PHONE**..................847 762-5800
James R Swartwout, *Ch of Bd*
Steven M Korwin, *Senior VP*
Gordon B Madlock, *Senior VP*
Michael W Osborne, *Senior VP*
Donald Pearson, *CFO*
**EMP:** 66 **EST:** 2014
**SALES (est):** 3.6MM
**SALES (corp-wide):** 419.3MM **Publicly Held**
**SIC:** 3674 3672 Microprocessors; printed circuit boards
**PA:** Sparton Corporation
425 N Martingale Rd
Schaumburg IL 60173
847 762-5800

**(G-19738)**
## SPIE TOOL CO
1350 Wright Blvd (60193-4456)
**PHONE**..................847 891-6556
**Fax:** 847 891-6896
Mabel Khoshaba, *President*
David Khoshaba, *Vice Pres*
Dorothy Loughlin, *Vice Pres*
Amy Khoshaba, *Human Res Dir*
Angelic Wechet, *Office Mgr*
◆ **EMP:** 45 **EST:** 1976
**SQ FT:** 10,000
**SALES (est):** 7MM **Privately Held**
**WEB:** www.spietool.com
**SIC:** 3545 Cutting tools for machine tools

**(G-19739)**
## SRV PROFESSIONAL PUBLICATIONS
235 Monson Ct (60173-2113)
**PHONE**..................847 330-1260
S RAO Vallabhaneni, *President*
**EMP:** 2
**SALES:** 500K **Privately Held**
**SIC:** 7372 8742 Publishers' computer software; marketing consulting services

**(G-19740)**
## STERLING PRODUCTS INC (DH)
Also Called: ACS Group
1100 E Woodfield Rd # 550 (60173-5135)
**PHONE**..................847 273-7700
James E Holbrook, *President*
Jim Cook, *Sr Corp Ofcr*
Barbara Otoole, *Sr Corp Ofcr*
Randy Smith, *Sr Corp Ofcr*
Larry Bowman, *Vice Pres*
◆ **EMP:** 65

**SALES (est):** 179.6MM
**SALES (corp-wide):** 1.5B **Privately Held**
**SIC:** 3559 3823 3542 Plastics working machinery; industrial process control instruments; presses: hydraulic & pneumatic, mechanical & manual
**HQ:** Acs Auxiliaries Group, Inc.
1100 E Woodfield Rd # 550
Schaumburg IL 60173
847 273-7700

**(G-19741)**
## STREAMWOOD PLASTICS LTD
979 Lunt Ave (60193-4416)
P.O. Box 427, Streamwood (60107-0427)
**PHONE**..................847 895-9190
**Fax:** 847 895-9025
Richard L Monson, *President*
Robert Monson, *Corp Secy*
Larry Maty, *Vice Pres*
Linda Matysiewski, *Office Mgr*
**EMP:** 5 **EST:** 1976
**SALES (est):** 1MM **Privately Held**
**SIC:** 5162 3082 Plastics materials; unsupported plastics profile shapes

**(G-19742)**
## SUMIDA AMERICA COMPONENTS INC (HQ)
1251 N Plum Grove Rd # 150 (60173-5603)
**PHONE**..................847 545-6700
**Fax:** 847 545-6720
Shigeyuki Yawata, *CEO*
Ken Hori, *General Mgr*
Franz Friedl, *Vice Pres*
Peter Rutkowski, *Engineer*
Barbara Rowlen, *Director*
▲ **EMP:** 17
**SALES (est):** 3.2MM
**SALES (corp-wide):** 732.4MM **Privately Held**
**SIC:** 3679 Electronic circuits
**PA:** Sumida Corporation
1-8-10, Harumi
Chuo-Ku TKY 104-0
367 582-470

**(G-19743)**
## SUMIDA AMERICA INC
1251 N Plum Grove Rd # 150 (60173-5603)
**PHONE**..................847 545-6700
Dan Chiu, *President*
Hans-Joachim Dittloff, *COO*
Franz Friedl, *Vice Pres*
Douglas Malcolm, *Vice Pres*
William Ng, *Treasurer*
**EMP:** 25
**SQ FT:** 4,000
**SALES (est):** 24.8K
**SALES (corp-wide):** 732.4MM **Privately Held**
**SIC:** 3679 5065 Electronic loads & power supplies; electronic parts & equipment
**PA:** Sumida Corporation
1-8-10, Harumi
Chuo-Ku TKY 104-0
367 582-470

**(G-19744)**
## SUNSTAR AMERICAS INC (HQ)
301 E Central Rd (60195-1901)
**PHONE**..................773 777-4000
Daniel Descary, *President*
Hiroki Nakanishi, *Exec VP*
Eduardo Vargas, *Exec VP*
Yoshihiro Kaneda, *Vice Pres*
Mike Mercurio, *Vice Pres*
◆ **EMP:** 460 **EST:** 1923
**SALES (est):** 155MM
**SALES (corp-wide):** 557MM **Privately Held**
**WEB:** www.sunstaramericas.com
**SIC:** 3843 Dental equipment & supplies
**PA:** Sunstar Inc.
3-1, Asahimachi
Takatsuki OSK 569-1
726 825-541

**(G-19745)**
## SUPERIOR BIOLOGICS IL INC
2050 E Algonquin Rd # 606 (60173-4161)
**PHONE**..................847 469-2400
Kamyar Ghazvini, *President*
**EMP:** 8

**SALES (est):** 1.2MM **Privately Held**
**SIC:** 2834 Pharmaceutical preparations

**(G-19746)**
## SURTREAT CONSTRUCTION SVCS LLC
854 E Algonquin Rd # 110 (60173-3864)
**PHONE**..................630 986-0780
Guido Pisani,
**EMP:** 2
**SALES (est):** 263.7K **Privately Held**
**SIC:** 1521 3272 5039 Single-family housing construction; pressure pipe, reinforced concrete; metal buildings

**(G-19747)**
## SURUGA USA CORP
1717 N Penny Ln Ste 200 (60173-5627)
**PHONE**..................630 628-0989
Masayuki Takaya, *President*
Hiroto Ito, *Vice Pres*
Wally Campbell, *Plant Mgr*
Atsu Takamura, *Accountant*
Patrick Barger, *Supervisor*
▲ **EMP:** 35
**SQ FT:** 10,200
**SALES:** 3.1MM
**SALES (corp-wide):** 2.2B **Privately Held**
**WEB:** www.surugausa.com
**SIC:** 3544 Special dies & tools; punches, forming & stamping
**HQ:** Suruga Production Platform Co.,Ltd.
505, Nanatsushin-Ya, Shimizu-Ku
Shizuoka SZO 424-0
543 440-311

**(G-19748)**
## SWEET ENDEAVORS INC
Also Called: 1101 Flavors
1101 Tower Rd (60173-4305)
**PHONE**..................224 653-2700
Rieko T Wada, *President*
Rieko Wada, *President*
**EMP:** 4
**SALES (est):** 283K **Privately Held**
**SIC:** 2066 Chocolate & cocoa products

**(G-19749)**
## SYNOPSYS INC
475 N Martingale Rd # 250 (60173-2220)
**PHONE**..................847 706-2000
**Fax:** 847 706-2020
John Kapinos, *Branch Mgr*
**EMP:** 12
**SALES (corp-wide):** 2.4B **Publicly Held**
**WEB:** www.synopsys.com
**SIC:** 7372 Prepackaged software
**PA:** Synopsys, Inc.
690 E Middlefield Rd
Mountain View CA 94043
650 584-5000

**(G-19750)**
## T H K HOLDINGS OF AMERICA LLC (HQ)
200 Commerce Dr (60173-5340)
**PHONE**..................847 310-1111
Mikio Matsui, *President*
Takeki Shirai, *Director*
Toshihiro Teramachi, *Director*
Takao Yamada, *Director*
Akihiro Teahachi,
◆ **EMP:** 6
**SALES (est):** 47.6MM
**SALES (corp-wide):** 2.4B **Privately Held**
**SIC:** 6712 3469 Bank holding companies; metal stampings
**PA:** Thk Co., Ltd.
3-11-6, Nishigotanda
Shinagawa-Ku TKY 141-0
354 340-300

**(G-19751)**
## TACMINA USA CORPORATION
105 W Central Rd (60195-1945)
**PHONE**..................312 810-8128
Joseph S Parisi, *Principal*
**EMP:** 3
**SALES (est):** 325.7K **Privately Held**
**SIC:** 3561 Pumps, domestic: water or sump

**(G-19752)**
## TANAKA KIKINZOKU INTL AMER INC
475 N Martingale Rd # 150 (60173-2405)
**PHONE**..................224 653-8309
Atfushi Nozawa, *Director*
**EMP:** 4
**SALES (est):** 564.2K **Privately Held**
**SIC:** 3339 Precious metals

**(G-19753)**
## TANAKA KKNZOKU INTRNATIONAL KK
Also Called: Tanaka Kikinzoku International
475 N Martingale Rd # 150 (60173-2405)
**PHONE**..................224 653-8309
Andrew Farry, *Branch Mgr*
**EMP:** 3
**SALES (corp-wide):** 98.2MM **Privately Held**
**SIC:** 3339 Precious metals
**PA:** Tanaka Holdings Co., Ltd.
2-7-3, Marunouchi
Chiyoda-Ku TKY 100-0
363 115-511

**(G-19754)**
## TBW MACHINING INC
1030 Morse Ave (60193-4504)
**PHONE**..................847 524-1501
Bernard Panski, *Owner*
**EMP:** 12
**SALES (est):** 1.7MM **Privately Held**
**SIC:** 3599 Industrial machinery

**(G-19755)**
## TC ELECTRIC CONTROLS LLC
1320 Tower Rd (60173-4309)
**PHONE**..................847 598-3508
Amer Jaber,
**EMP:** 5
**SQ FT:** 144
**SALES (est):** 284K **Privately Held**
**SIC:** 3625 Relays & industrial controls

**(G-19756)**
## TDM SYSTEMS INC
1901 N Roselle Rd Ste 800 (60195-3186)
**PHONE**..................847 605-1269
Harald Kaiser, *Vice Pres*
Maxim Fleitling, *Technology*
Dan Speidel, *Director*
**EMP:** 4
**SALES:** 500K
**SALES (corp-wide):** 8.8B **Privately Held**
**WEB:** www.tdmsystems.com
**SIC:** 3695 Computer software tape & disks: blank, rigid & floppy
**PA:** Sandvik Ab
Stationsgatan 22
Sandviken 811 3
262 600-00

**(G-19757)**
## TEGRATECS DEVELOPMENT CORP
1320 Tower Rd (60173-4309)
**PHONE**..................847 397-0088
F Rexford Smith II, *President*
Paul Wampach, *Vice Pres*
**EMP:** 8
**SALES (est):** 1MM **Privately Held**
**WEB:** www.financialportrait.com
**SIC:** 5734 7372 7379 Computer software & accessories; prepackaged software; computer related consulting services

**(G-19758)**
## TELEMEDICINE SOLUTIONS LLC
Also Called: Wound Rounds
425 N Martingale Rd # 1250 (60173-2406)
**PHONE**..................847 519-3500
John Croghan MD, *Chairman*
David Loveland, *COO*
David R Devereaux, *Exec VP*
Rhett Gustafson, *Exec VP*
Cory Fosco, *Vice Pres*
**EMP:** 16
**SQ FT:** 4,592
**SALES (est):** 1MM **Privately Held**
**SIC:** 7372 Prepackaged software

## Schaumburg - Cook County (G-19759)

**(G-19759)**
**TENDER LOVING CARE INDS INC**
Also Called: TLC Industries
815 Lunt Ave (60193-4414)
PHONE..................847 891-0230
Fax: 847 891-2515
Edward Bender, *President*
Bob Goodman, *Vice Pres*
Jenifer Baier, *Accounts Mgr*
Hank Parker, *Data Proc Staff*
Valerie Gisel, *Director*
EMP: 70
SQ FT: 20,000
SALES (est): 8MM  Privately Held
WEB: www.tlcind.com
SIC: 2511  2499  Juvenile furniture: wood; decorative wood & woodwork

**(G-19760)**
**THERMOS LLC (PA)**
475 N Martingale Rd # 1100 (60173-2051)
PHONE..................847 439-7821
Fax: 847 593-5570
Alex Huang, *CEO*
Rick Dias, *President*
Gene Parker, *Partner*
Gregory Aubert, *General Mgr*
Ken Burns, *Top Exec*
◆ EMP: 50
SALES (est): 41.2MM  Privately Held
WEB: www.thermos.com
SIC: 3429  3086  Manufactured hardware (general); plastics foam products

**(G-19761)**
**THIESSEN COMMUNICATIONS INC**
Also Called: T C
1300 Basswood Rd (60173-4522)
PHONE..................847 884-0980
Allen Steinberg, *President*
William Drew Whitaker, *Admin Sec*
EMP: 27  EST: 2008
SALES (est): 4.8MM  Privately Held
SIC: 2752  Commercial printing, lithographic

**(G-19762)**
**THK AMERICA  INC (DH)**
200 Commerce Dr (60173-5340)
PHONE..................847 310-1111
Fax: 847 310-1271
Masaki Sugita, *President*
Ed Johnson, *General Mgr*
Koki Shirai, *General Mgr*
James Sama, *Regional Mgr*
Tom Lewis, *District Mgr*
▲ EMP: 125
SQ FT: 105,000
SALES (est): 70.1MM
SALES (corp-wide): 2.4B  Privately Held
WEB: www.thkamerica.com
SIC: 3568  Bearings, bushings & blocks; joints & couplings
HQ: T H K Holdings Of America Llc
200 Commerce Dr
Schaumburg IL 60173
847 310-1111

**(G-19763)**
**TI SQUARED TECHNOLOGIES INC**
1019 W Wise Rd Ste 101 (60193-3754)
PHONE..................541 367-2929
Ronald E Shadle, *President*
Jim Dippel, *Vice Pres*
EMP: 12
SALES (est): 1.8MM  Privately Held
SIC: 3364  Titanium die-castings

**(G-19764)**
**TNT PLASTICS INC**
1425 Wright Blvd (60193-4537)
PHONE..................847 895-6921
Fax: 847 895-0058
Michael A Tracey, *President*
Peter J Turza, *Admin Sec*
EMP: 18
SQ FT: 4,700
SALES (est): 2.3MM  Privately Held
SIC: 3089  Injection molding of plastics

**(G-19765)**
**TOUCHTUNES MUSIC CORPORATION**
450 Remington Rd (60173-4540)
PHONE..................847 253-8708
Christine Pereira, *Branch Mgr*
EMP: 23
SALES (corp-wide): 7.8MM  Privately Held
SIC: 3651  Household audio & video equipment
HQ: Touchtunes Music Corporation
850 3rd Ave Ste 15c
New York NY 10022
847 419-3300

**(G-19766)**
**TOWERLEAF  LLC**
1680 Wright Blvd (60193-4512)
PHONE..................847 985-1937
Christine Thornblad, *Mng Member*
Al Thornblad, *Manager*
▲ EMP: 9
SALES (est): 1.3MM  Privately Held
SIC: 2421  Sawmills & planing mills, general

**(G-19767)**
**TPR AMERICA  INC**
10 N Martingale Rd (60173-2099)
PHONE..................847 446-5336
Fax: 847 446-5344
Kazuhiro Haneishi, *President*
Shinichiro Kondo, *Vice Pres*
Toru Takahashi, *Vice Pres*
Masakazu Katsumaru, *Manager*
▲ EMP: 9
SQ FT: 3,500
SALES: 70MM
SALES (corp-wide): 1.4B  Privately Held
SIC: 3519  5013  Parts & accessories, internal combustion engines; automotive engines & engine parts
PA: Tpr Co., Ltd.
1-6-2, Marunouchi
Chiyoda-Ku TKY 100-0
352 932-811

**(G-19768)**
**TRANSPAC USA**
1515 E Wdfield Rd Ste 340 (60173)
PHONE..................847 605-1616
Karim Klat, *President*
Jeff Wiley, *General Mgr*
Gregory Handrahan, *Vice Pres*
Lucas Kunk, *Opers Mgr*
▲ EMP: 8
SALES (est): 1.5MM  Privately Held
WEB: www.transpacusa.com
SIC: 2621  Book paper
PA: Codefine S.A.
Avenue Du Leman 21
Lausanne VD
213 458-211

**(G-19769)**
**TRELLBORG SLING SLTIONS US INC**
Also Called: Lutz Sales Company
20 N Martingale Rd # 210 (60173-2412)
PHONE..................630 539-5500
Fax: 630 437-3691
Richard Banks, *Principal*
EMP: 14
SALES (est): 2.9B  Privately Held
WEB: www.dowtyauto.com
SIC: 3089  Plastic processing; bearings, plastic
HQ: Trelleborg Sealing Solutions Us, Inc.
2531 Bremer Rd
Fort Wayne IN 46803
260 749-9631

**(G-19770)**
**TRI SECT CORPORATION**
717 Morse Ave (60193-4533)
PHONE..................847 524-1119
Fax: 847 524-5581
Joseph Barna, *President*
Jim Tobin, *Vice Pres*
Jim Arnold, *Manager*
Joyce Barna, *Manager*
EMP: 10
SQ FT: 13,000
SALES (est): 2.1MM  Privately Held
WEB: www.trisectcorp.com
SIC: 2842  2841  Specialty cleaning, polishes & sanitation goods; cleaning or polishing preparations; disinfectants, household or industrial plant; degreasing solvent; soap & other detergents

**(G-19771)**
**TRI STAR PLOWING**
876 Asbury Ln (60193-4101)
PHONE..................847 584-5070
Linda Johnson, *Principal*
EMP: 5
SALES (est): 259.5K  Privately Held
SIC: 4959  2759  Snowplowing; screen printing

**(G-19772)**
**TRIAD CUTTING TOOLS SVC & MFG**
1025 Lunt Ave Ste E (60193-4472)
PHONE..................847 352-0459
Fax: 847 352-0501
Mark Morris, *President*
Visilis Papateodoru, *Vice Pres*
EMP: 8
SQ FT: 2,000
SALES (est): 1.2MM  Privately Held
SIC: 3545  Cutting tools for machine tools

**(G-19773)**
**TRIDENT INDUSTRIES**
1900 E Golf Rd Ste L100 (60173-5157)
PHONE..................847 285-1316
EMP: 10
SALES (est): 2.2MM  Privately Held
SIC: 3999  Barber & beauty shop equipment

**(G-19774)**
**TRIPLEX SALES COMPANY INC**
1143 Tower Rd (60173-4305)
PHONE..................847 839-8442
Brian Quint, *President*
Jack Quint, *Admin Sec*
EMP: 4  EST: 1960
SQ FT: 1,750
SALES: 3MM  Privately Held
WEB: www.triplexsales.com
SIC: 3589  Cooking equipment, commercial

**(G-19775)**
**TRUFAB GROUP USA LLC**
550 Albion Ave Ste 90 (60193-4547)
PHONE..................630 994-3286
Gareth Trewarn, *Vice Pres*
Stuart Trewarn, *Mng Member*
Phil Diener, *Info Tech Mgr*
Charles Schaumburg, *In Trewarn*,
▲ EMP: 20
SQ FT: 30,000
SALES (est): 8MM  Privately Held
SIC: 3599  Machine & other job shop work

**(G-19776)**
**TWR SERVICE CORPORATION**
940 Lunt Ave (60193-4417)
PHONE..................847 923-0692
Fax: 847 923-0977
Daniel Moore, *President*
Scott Hiestand, *Corp Secy*
EMP: 14
SQ FT: 10,000
SALES (est): 1.9MM  Privately Held
WEB: www.twrservice.com
SIC: 3471  Finishing, metals or formed products; electroplating of metals or formed products; plating of metals or formed products

**(G-19777)**
**ULTRA POLISHING INC**
640 Pratt Ave N (60193-4557)
PHONE..................630 635-2926
Fax: 847 352-4052
Casey Gwozdz, *President*
Lester Doniec, *Vice Pres*
Sheri Richards, *Manager*
EMP: 40
SQ FT: 9,000
SALES (est): 7.7MM  Privately Held
WEB: www.ultrapolishing.com
SIC: 3544  3471  Special dies & tools; plating & polishing

**(G-19778)**
**UMW  INC**
601 Lunt Ave (60193-4410)
PHONE..................847 352-5252
Arina Muradyan, *CEO*
Boris Muradyan, *President*
EMP: 15
SQ FT: 20,000
SALES (est): 3.8MM  Privately Held
SIC: 3599  Machine shop, jobbing & repair

**(G-19779)**
**UNIFLEX OF AMERICA LTD**
1088 National Pkwy (60173-4519)
PHONE..................847 519-1100
Garry Kreuz, *General Mgr*
Dr Friedrich Von Waitz, *Mng Member*
▲ EMP: 6  EST: 1999
SQ FT: 8,000
SALES (est): 600K  Privately Held
SIC: 3542  Crimping machinery, metal

**(G-19780)**
**UNITED ENGRAVERS  INC**
618 Pratt Ave N (60193-4557)
PHONE..................847 301-3740
Fax: 847 301-3750
Peter P Cappas, *President*
Peter Cappas, *President*
EMP: 50
SALES (est): 7.7MM  Privately Held
WEB: www.unitedengravers.com
SIC: 2754  Job printing, gravure

**(G-19781)**
**UNITED MACHINE WORKS  INC**
601 Lunt Ave (60193-4410)
PHONE..................847 352-5252
Boris Muradyan, *President*
Arina Muradyan, *Manager*
EMP: 3
SQ FT: 6,000
SALES (est): 600K  Privately Held
SIC: 3599  7692  Machine shop, jobbing & repair; welding repair

**(G-19782)**
**UNITED WOODWORKING INC**
729 Lunt Ave (60193-4412)
PHONE..................847 352-3066
Fax: 847 352-3575
Stanley Chraca, *President*
Angie Chraca, *Vice Pres*
Mark Bobson, *Project Mgr*
William Ignatowski, *Sales Staff*
EMP: 30
SQ FT: 16,000
SALES (est): 4.1MM  Privately Held
SIC: 2511  Wood household furniture

**(G-19783)**
**URBAN SERVICES OF AMERICA (PA)**
1901 N Roselle Rd Ste 740 (60195-3194)
PHONE..................847 278-3210
Douglas Ritter, *President*
Gordon Mc Tavish, *Treasurer*
EMP: 8
SALES (est): 4.1MM  Privately Held
SIC: 3089  Toilets, portable chemical: plastic

**(G-19784)**
**V & S TOOL CO**
129 Dunlap Pl (60194-3928)
PHONE..................847 891-0780
Sean B Soelter, *President*
EMP: 2
SQ FT: 2,400
SALES: 400K  Privately Held
SIC: 3544  Special dies, tools, jigs & fixtures

**(G-19785)**
**VENUS PRINTING INC**
549 Morse Ave (60193-4529)
PHONE..................847 985-7510
Fax: 847 985-7510
Phillip Touzios, *President*
Pat Touzios, *Principal*
EMP: 3
SQ FT: 3,000
SALES: 350K  Privately Held
SIC: 2752  Commercial printing, offset

# GEOGRAPHIC SECTION

Schiller Park - Cook County (G-19811)

**(G-19786)**
**VERTEX CONSULTING SERVICES INC**
935 N Plum Grove Rd Ste D (60173-4770)
**PHONE**.................313 492-5154
Abdul Mohammad, *President*
Abdul Mannan Khan, *Vice Pres*
**EMP:** 10 **EST:** 2011
**SALES (est):** 282.3K **Privately Held**
**SIC: 7371** 7372 7373 7374 Custom computer programming services; computer software development; prepackaged software; computer integrated systems design; data processing & preparation

**(G-19787)**
**WELLMARK INT FARNAM CO**
1501 E Wdfeld Rd Ste 200w (60173)
**PHONE**.................925 948-4000
Kay Schwichtenberg, *President*
Richard Tanguay, *Controller*
Nancy Stratinsky, *Manager*
**EMP:** 350
**SALES (est):** 48.9MM **Privately Held**
**SIC: 2833** 2879 Animal based products; insecticides & pesticides

**(G-19788)**
**WESTROCK DSPENSING SYSTEMS INC**
1325 Remington Rd Ste H (60173-4815)
**PHONE**.................847 310-3073
**Fax:** 847 490-1043
Ed Baumann, *Branch Mgr*
**EMP:** 6
**SALES (corp-wide):** 14.1B **Publicly Held**
**WEB:** www.calmar.com
**SIC: 3089** Plastic containers, except foam
**HQ:** Westrock Dispensing Systems, Inc.
11901 Grandview Rd
Grandview MO 64030
816 986-6000

**(G-19789)**
**WIDE IMAGE INCORPORATED**
Also Called: Chicago Printing Center
1187 Tower Rd (60173-4305)
**PHONE**.................773 279-9183
Tudor Fartaes, *President*
**EMP:** 3
**SALES (est):** 220.1K **Privately Held**
**SIC: 2759** Commercial printing

**(G-19790)**
**WISE EQUIPMENT & RENTALS INC**
1475 Rodenburg Rd (60193-3532)
**PHONE**.................847 895-5555
**Fax:** 847 895-5006
Edward J Zawilla, *President*
Dorothy Wright, *Manager*
◆ **EMP:** 11
**SALES (est):** 3.7MM **Privately Held**
**SIC: 5261** 7699 7359 5999 Lawn & garden equipment; lawn mower repair shop; party supplies rental services; tents; trailers & trailer equipment

**(G-19791)**
**WJ DIE MOLD INC**
Also Called: Unique Plastics
915 Estes Ct (60193-4427)
**PHONE**.................847 895-6561
**Fax:** 847 895-3688
Wayne Johnson, *President*
James Goddyn, *Vice Pres*
Steve Goddyn, *Manager*
**EMP:** 10
**SQ FT:** 6,000
**SALES (est):** 900K **Privately Held**
**WEB:** www.wjdiemold.com
**SIC: 3089** Injection molding of plastics

**(G-19792)**
**XTREMEDATA INC**
999 N Plaza Dr Ste 570 (60173-5407)
**PHONE**.................847 871-0379
Ravi Chandran, *President*
Jay Desai, *Senior VP*
Susan Clarke, *Vice Pres*
Geno Valente, *VP Sales*
Arianne Clarke, *Manager*
**EMP:** 20
**SQ FT:** 6,062
**SALES (est):** 3.5MM **Privately Held**
**WEB:** www.xtremedatainc.com
**SIC: 3674** Integrated circuits, semiconductor networks, etc.

**(G-19793)**
**YOUNG SHIN USA LIMITED**
1320 Tower Rd Ste 111 (60173-4309)
**PHONE**.................847 598-3611
Richard Lee, *President*
Phillip Mack, *Admin Sec*
▲ **EMP:** 3
**SALES (est):** 390.7K **Privately Held**
**SIC: 2675** Die-cut paper & board

**(G-19794)**
**YOUR IMAGES GROUP INC**
1300 Basswood Rd Ste 200 (60173-4522)
**PHONE**.................847 437-6688
Bryan Tillmanns, *President*
**EMP:** 4
**SALES:** 900K **Privately Held**
**SIC: 2759** 7331 Commercial Printing Direct Mail Advertising Services

**(G-19795)**
**ZACROS AMERICA INC (HQ)**
1821 Walden Office Sq # 400 (60173-4295)
**PHONE**.................847 397-6191
Richard Broo, *CEO*
Kazuhiko Maeda, *President*
Maurice Lecompte, *COO*
Taku Shimoda, *Vice Pres*
Joseph Wolfson, *Vice Pres*
▲ **EMP:** 2 **EST:** 2012
**SALES:** 1MM
**SALES (corp-wide):** 866MM **Privately Held**
**SIC: 2671** Plastic film, coated or laminated for packaging
**PA:** Fujimori Kogyo Co., Ltd.
1-23-7, Nishishinjuku
Shinjuku-Ku TKY 160-0
363 814-211

## Schiller Park
### Cook County

**(G-19796)**
**A J EXPRESS POWER TOOLS**
4918 River Rd (60176-1120)
**PHONE**.................847 678-8200
John Jacnick, *Principal*
**EMP:** 4
**SALES (est):** 321.1K **Privately Held**
**SIC: 2741** Miscellaneous publishing

**(G-19797)**
**ABLE DIE CASTING CORPORATION**
3907 Wesley Ter (60176-2131)
**PHONE**.................847 678-1991
**Fax:** 847 678-9649
Nestor Hernandez, *President*
Robert Stout, *Vice Pres*
Nes Hernandez, *Vice Pres*
Fred Aguilar, *Mfg Mgr*
Scott Richter, *Purch Mgr*
**EMP:** 54 **EST:** 1920
**SQ FT:** 14,000
**SALES (est):** 13.3MM **Privately Held**
**WEB:** www.abledie.com
**SIC: 3369** 3363 3365 Zinc & zinc-base alloy castings, except die-castings; aluminum die-castings; aluminum foundries

**(G-19798)**
**ACCENT METAL FINISHING INC**
9331 Byron St (60176-2303)
**PHONE**.................847 678-7420
**Fax:** 847 678-7450
Douglas Mangino, *President*
Kelly Aylward, *Office Mgr*
**EMP:** 10
**SQ FT:** 9,500
**SALES:** 1MM **Privately Held**
**WEB:** www.accentmetal.com
**SIC: 3479** 3471 Coating of metals & formed products; anodizing (plating) of metals or formed products

**(G-19799)**
**ACRA ELECTRIC CORPORATION**
3801 25th Ave (60176-2116)
**PHONE**.................847 678-8870
Robert G Browne, *President*
Janet Mc Laughlin, *Vice Pres*
Jim Ambrosia, *Controller*
Steven Malato, *Admin Sec*
**EMP:** 85 **EST:** 1928
**SQ FT:** 40,000
**SALES:** 4.3MM **Privately Held**
**SIC: 3567** Heating units & devices, industrial: electric

**(G-19800)**
**ALLOY CHROME INC**
9328 Bernice Ave (60176-2302)
**PHONE**.................847 678-2880
**Fax:** 847 678-8646
Richard Feign, *President*
**EMP:** 9
**SQ FT:** 5,000
**SALES (est):** 1.2MM **Privately Held**
**SIC: 3471** 2899 Chromium plating of metals or formed products; chemical preparations

**(G-19801)**
**AMERICAN NTN BEARING MFG CORP**
9515 Winona Ave (60176-1083)
**PHONE**.................847 671-5450
**Fax:** 847 671-0963
John Welch, *General Mgr*
Steven Fletcher, *Purchasing*
John Rudisel, *QC Mgr*
Darlene Myles, *Human Res Dir*
Marqy Fukuda, *Manager*
**EMP:** 40
**SALES (corp-wide):** 6B **Privately Held**
**SIC: 3562** Ball bearings & parts
**HQ:** American Ntn Bearing Manufacturing Corporation
1525 Holmes Rd
Elgin IL 60123
847 741-4545

**(G-19802)**
**AMERLINE ENTERPRISES CO INC**
9509 Winona Ave (60176-1024)
**PHONE**.................847 671-6554
**Fax:** 847 671-6542
Thomas A Krepelka, *President*
Mike Urosev, *Purch Dir*
Lydia Friyz, *Admin Sec*
Patricia Krepelka, *Admin Sec*
▲ **EMP:** 42
**SQ FT:** 30,000
**SALES (est):** 8.8MM **Privately Held**
**WEB:** www.amerline.com
**SIC: 3643** 3694 3357 Connectors & terminals for electrical devices; engine electrical equipment; nonferrous wiredrawing & insulating

**(G-19803)**
**ANDERSON - SNOW CORP**
Also Called: Anscor
9225 Ivanhoe St (60176-2352)
P.O. Box 2126 (60176-0126)
**PHONE**.................847 678-2084
**Fax:** 847 678-0413
Ted R Campbell, *President*
Donald W Ruback Jr, *Vice Pres*
Deanna Larson, *Marketing Staff*
Ildefonso Solis, *Admin Sec*
**EMP:** 20 **EST:** 1958
**SQ FT:** 36,000
**SALES:** 1.7MM **Privately Held**
**WEB:** www.anscorcoils.com
**SIC: 3585** Parts for heating and refrigerating equipment

**(G-19804)**
**APV CONSOLIDATED INC**
5100 River Rd Fl 3 (60176-1058)
**PHONE**.................847 678-4300
Michael Francis, *President*
A Paul Lewis, *Vice Pres*
Joe Sierawski, *Purch Mgr*
Andy Hoy, *Controller*
Mike Drennan, *VP Finance*
**EMP:** 11
**SQ FT:** 30,000
**SALES (est):** 1.9MM
**SALES (corp-wide):** 1.4B **Publicly Held**
**SIC: 3556** Food products machinery
**PA:** Spx Corporation
13320a Balntyn Corp Pl
Charlotte NC 28277
980 474-3700

**(G-19805)**
**ARPAC LLC (PA)**
9555 Irving Park Rd (60176-1960)
**PHONE**.................847 678-9034
**Fax:** 847 671-7006
Richard Allegretti, *President*
Howard Dittmer, *President*
Gary Ehmka, *Vice Pres*
John Wolf, *Vice Pres*
Behzad Jafari, *Project Mgr*
◆ **EMP:** 240
**SQ FT:** 250,000
**SALES (est):** 61.6MM **Privately Held**
**WEB:** www.arpac.com
**SIC: 3565** Wrapping machines

**(G-19806)**
**ASSURED WELDING SERVICE INC**
9301 Byron St (60176-2303)
**PHONE**.................847 671-1414
**Fax:** 847 671-1475
Dean Schwabe, *President*
Gina Schwabe, *Purchasing*
**EMP:** 5
**SALES (est):** 440K **Privately Held**
**SIC: 7692** Welding repair

**(G-19807)**
**AVERS MACHINE & MFG INC**
3999 25th Ave (60176-2175)
**PHONE**.................847 447-3430
**Fax:** 708 867-3553
Chris Wellman, *President*
Margie Sliz, *Office Mgr*
**EMP:** 22
**SQ FT:** 12,000
**SALES (est):** 1.8MM **Privately Held**
**SIC: 3599** Machine & other job shop work

**(G-19808)**
**BARRON 2M INC**
3745 Ruby St Apt 5 (60176-2555)
**PHONE**.................847 219-3650
Stanislava N Dimitrova, *President*
Petko Dimitrov, *Vice Pres*
**EMP:** 3
**SALES:** 550K **Privately Held**
**SIC: 3715** Truck trailers

**(G-19809)**
**BRANER USA INC (PA)**
9301 W Bernice St (60176)
**PHONE**.................847 671-6210
**Fax:** 847 671-0537
Douglas Matsunaga, *President*
Charles Damore, *President*
Rosemarie Gervais, *Exec VP*
Mike De Young, *Engineer*
Zbigniew Winnicki, *Project Engr*
▲ **EMP:** 40
**SQ FT:** 60,000
**SALES (est):** 17.4MM **Privately Held**
**WEB:** www.braner.com
**SIC: 3549** Rotary slitters (metalworking machines)

**(G-19810)**
**BURDZY TOOL & DIE CO**
9355 Byron St (60176-2303)
**PHONE**.................847 671-6666
**Fax:** 847 671-2660
Boytek Burdzy, *President*
**EMP:** 12
**SALES:** 1.2MM **Privately Held**
**SIC: 3599** Machine shop, jobbing & repair

**(G-19811)**
**CASTLE METAL FINISHING CORP**
4631 25th Ave (60176-1302)
**PHONE**.................847 678-6041
Phillip Meier, *President*
Dale Weter, *Vice Pres*
Betty Meier, *Admin Sec*
**EMP:** 17 **EST:** 1960
**SQ FT:** 22,000

# Schiller Park - Cook County (G-19812)  GEOGRAPHIC SECTION

SALES (est): 1.8MM  Privately Held
WEB: www.castlemetalfinishing.com
SIC: 3471  Finishing, metals or formed products

### (G-19812)
### CELCO TOOL & ENGINEERING INC
9300 Bernice Ave  (60176-2302)
PHONE..............................847 671-2520
Fax: 847 671-2598
John Cielak, President
Stanley Cielak, Corp Secy
Adam Cielak, Vice Pres
EMP: 19 EST: 1965
SQ FT: 10,000
SALES (est): 2.9MM  Privately Held
SIC: 3544  Special dies, tools, jigs & fixtures

### (G-19813)
### CHICAGO POWDERED METAL PDTS CO
Also Called: Camet
9700 Waveland Ave  (60131-1773)
P.O. Box 2128  (60176-0128)
PHONE..............................847 678-2836
Fax: 847 678-0125
Thomas J Miller, President
Bill Sider, Opers Staff
David Gardner, QC Mgr
Sandra Peterson, QC Mgr
Michael F Miller, Treasurer
▼ EMP: 89 EST: 1948
SQ FT: 200,000
SALES (est): 19.6MM  Privately Held
WEB: www.chipm.com
SIC: 3599  Machine shop, jobbing & repair

### (G-19814)
### CLASSIC MOLDING CO INC
3800 Wesley Ter  (60176-2130)
PHONE..............................847 671-7888
Thomas E Gebhardt, President
Robert Caldrone, Vice Pres
Avadis Muradian, QC Dir
Jim Caldrone, Sales Mgr
James Caldrone, Sales Executive
EMP: 80
SQ FT: 35,000
SALES (est): 30.1MM
SALES (corp-wide): 101.4MM  Privately Held
SIC: 3089  Injection molded finished plastic products
PA: Corporate Group, Inc.
7123 W Calumet Rd
Milwaukee WI 53223
414 355-7740

### (G-19815)
### COMMUNICATION COIL INC
9601 Soreng Ave  (60176-2104)
P.O. Box 111, Gowanda NY  (14070-0111)
PHONE..............................847 671-1333
Elliot Goldman, President
John Quintanar, Plant Mgr
EMP: 65
SQ FT: 20,000
SALES (est): 9.9MM  Privately Held
WEB: www.communicationcoil.com
SIC: 3677  5065  3621  3612  Electronic coils, transformers & other inductors; inductors, electronic; filtration devices, electronic; transformers power supply, electronic type; electronic parts & equipment; motors & generators; transformers, except electric; blowers & fans

### (G-19816)
### COOLEY WIRE PRODUCTS MFG CO
5025 River Rd  (60176-1016)
PHONE..............................847 678-8585
Fax: 847 678-8612
Duane Halleck, President
Harold Young, Vice Pres
Jim Hauser, Design Engr
Debbie Bergman, Office Mgr
▲ EMP: 25 EST: 1893
SQ FT: 21,000
SALES (est): 5.9MM  Privately Held
WEB: www.cooleywire.com
SIC: 3496  3471  3398  Woven wire products; plating & polishing; metal heat treating

### (G-19817)
### CRAFTSMAN CUSTOM METALS LLC
3838 River Rd  (60176-2300)
PHONE..............................847 655-0040
Fax: 847 678-4469
Evelio Amanza, Opers Staff
Eric Siegal, VP Sales
Julio Gesklin, Mng Member
Evelio Almanza, Director
▼ EMP: 56
SQ FT: 65,000
SALES: 10.5MM  Privately Held
SIC: 3444  3469  3312  Sheet metalwork; metal stampings; tool & die steel

### (G-19818)
### CUSTOM MACHINERY INC
3910 Wesley Ter  (60176-2184)
PHONE..............................847 678-3033
Fax: 847 678-4051
Owen R Deike, President
EMP: 5 EST: 1963
SQ FT: 2,600
SALES: 500K  Privately Held
WEB: www.cmcwash.com
SIC: 3599  3469  7692  3549  Custom machinery; machine parts, stamped or pressed metal; welding repair; metalworking machinery; conveyors & conveying equipment

### (G-19819)
### DAMY CORP
Also Called: Atlas Screen Supply Co.
9353 Seymour Ave  (60176-2206)
PHONE..............................847 233-0515
David Gayton, President
EMP: 11
SQ FT: 11,000
SALES (est): 2.1MM  Privately Held
WEB: www.atlasscreensupply.com
SIC: 2759  Screen printing

### (G-19820)
### DAVID V MICHALS
9505 Winona Ave  (60176-1024)
PHONE..............................847 671-6767
David V Michals, President
Carl Smigiel, General Mgr
Kathy Michals, Vice Pres
EMP: 80 EST: 2001
SALES (est): 4.9MM  Privately Held
SIC: 3495  Wire springs

### (G-19821)
### E J BASLER CO
9511 Ainslie St  (60176-1115)
P.O. Box 87618, Chicago  (60680-0618)
PHONE..............................847 678-8880
Fax: 847 678-8896
Edwin J Basler, CEO
Dennis E Basler, President
Larry Florey, COO
Brian Basler, Vice Pres
Elias Serruya, Prdtn Mgr
▲ EMP: 87 EST: 1940
SQ FT: 55,000
SALES (est): 32.9MM  Privately Held
WEB: www.ejbasler.com
SIC: 3451  Screw machine products

### (G-19822)
### EARTH STONE PRODUCTS ILL INC
4535 25th Ave  (60176-1455)
PHONE..............................847 671-3000
Dorota Rajch, President
EMP: 3
SQ FT: 1,000
SALES (est): 500K  Privately Held
SIC: 3281  Granite, cut & shaped

### (G-19823)
### ECLIPSE LIGHTING INC (PA)
9245 Ivanhoe St  (60176-2305)
P.O. Box 2351  (60176-0351)
PHONE..............................847 260-0333
Fax: 847 260-0344
Robert Fiermuga, President
Crystal Fiermuga, VP Admin
Rudolph Nunkovich, Engineer
▲ EMP: 34
SQ FT: 20,000
SALES (est): 4.8MM  Privately Held
WEB: www.eclipselightinginc.com
SIC: 3646  3645  Commercial indusl & institutional electric lighting fixtures; residential lighting fixtures

### (G-19824)
### ENCLOSURES INC (HQ)
9200 Ivanhoe St  (60176-2306)
PHONE..............................847 678-2020
Lee Simeone, CEO
Thomas J Simeone, President
Kenneth M Galeno, Vice Pres
Linda Galeno, Director
Milton Ross, Director
EMP: 2
SQ FT: 32,050
SALES (est): 4.5MM
SALES (corp-wide): 10MM  Privately Held
WEB: www.enclosures.com
SIC: 2542  Telephone booths: except wood
PA: Manor Tool And Manufacturing Co. Inc
9200 Ivanhoe St
Schiller Park IL 60176
847 678-2020

### (G-19825)
### ENROLLMENT RX  LLC
9511 River St Ste 100  (60176-1019)
PHONE..............................847 233-0088
Marc Satin, Vice Pres
Karmel Kifarkis, Accounting Mgr
Tim Bailey, Sales Dir
Sean Gottlieb, Accounts Exec
Xian Zhang, Sales Staff
EMP: 16
SALES (est): 2.6MM  Privately Held
SIC: 7372  Application computer software

### (G-19826)
### ESPE MANUFACTURING CO
9220 Ivanhoe St  (60176-2474)
PHONE..............................847 678-8950
Fax: 847 678-0253
Robert Pethes Jr, President
Pat Pethes, Vice Pres
EMP: 12 EST: 1948
SQ FT: 30,000
SALES (est): 2.3MM  Privately Held
WEB: www.espemfg.com
SIC: 3299  Non-metallic mineral statuary & other decorative products

### (G-19827)
### EURO MARBLE & GRANITE INC
4552 Ruby St  (60176-1443)
PHONE..............................847 233-0700
Fax: 847 233-0727
Wojtek Rajch, President
Nicolae Iepan, President
▲ EMP: 19
SALES: 1MM  Privately Held
WEB: www.euromarbles.com
SIC: 3281  Granite, cut & shaped

### (G-19828)
### EURO MARBLE SUPPLY  LTD
4552 Ruby St  (60176-1443)
PHONE..............................847 233-0700
Wojciech Rajch, President
EMP: 3
SALES (est): 110.5K  Privately Held
SIC: 3272  Floor slabs & tiles, precast concrete

### (G-19829)
### EXCEL GLASS  INC
10507 Delta Pkwy  (60176-1721)
PHONE..............................847 801-5200
Enrique Badani, CEO
Leon Johnson, CEO
George Cutro, Accountant
EMP: 1
SQ FT: 12,200
SALES: 1.6MM  Privately Held
SIC: 2759  Imprinting

### (G-19830)
### EXCEL SCREEN PRTG & EMB INC
10507 Delta Pkwy  (60176-1721)
PHONE..............................847 801-5200
Fax: 847 801-5205
Leon Johnson, President
Agnes Odono, Sales Mgr
Judy Kosmoski, Marketing Staff
Chris Stefo, Manager
Geret Arguelles, Supervisor
▲ EMP: 88
SQ FT: 49,150
SALES (est): 10MM  Privately Held
WEB: www.excelscreenprinting.com
SIC: 2396  Screen printing on fabric articles

### (G-19831)
### FRACAR SHEET METAL MFG CO INC
9521 Ainslie St  (60176-1115)
PHONE..............................847 678-1600
Fax: 847 678-9569
John Dombek, President
EMP: 20 EST: 1970
SQ FT: 30,000
SALES: 1.2MM  Privately Held
WEB: www.wistool.com
SIC: 3444  Sheet metal specialties, not stamped

### (G-19832)
### FRATELLI COFFEE COMPANY
4936 River Rd  (60176-1120)
PHONE..............................847 671-7300
Fax: 847 671-6300
Sam Zarcone, President
Zarcone Sam, Sales Mgr
Sue Row, Manager
▲ EMP: 7
SQ FT: 3,000
SALES: 900K  Privately Held
WEB: www.fratellicoffee.com
SIC: 2095  Roasted coffee

### (G-19833)
### GAYTON GROUP  INC
Also Called: Ameribest Fasteners
9353 Seymour Ave  (60176-2206)
PHONE..............................847 233-0509
Dan Gayton, President
Melanie Gayton, Vice Pres
EMP: 5
SALES (est): 663.6K  Privately Held
WEB: www.ameribestfasteners.com
SIC: 3089  Injection molding of plastics

### (G-19834)
### GGC CORP
4300 United Pkwy  (60176-1712)
PHONE..............................847 671-6500
Warren Hanssen, Ch of Bd
Catherine Moritz, President
Dan Caithamer, CFO
Chris Allen, VP Sales
Barbara Petraglia, Sales Staff
▲ EMP: 100
SQ FT: 125,000
SALES (est): 11.2MM  Privately Held
WEB: www.gallantgreetings.com
SIC: 2771  Greeting cards

### (G-19835)
### GLO-MOLD INC
3800 Wesley Ter  (60176-2130)
PHONE..............................847 671-1762
Larry Caldrone, President
Gloria Caldrone, Vice Pres
EMP: 14
SQ FT: 35,500
SALES (est): 2.1MM
SALES (corp-wide): 101.4MM  Privately Held
SIC: 3544  Forms (molds), for foundry & plastics working machinery
PA: Corporate Group, Inc.
7123 W Calumet Rd
Milwaukee WI 53223
414 355-7740

### (G-19836)
### HI-TECH MANUFACTURING  LLC (PA)
Also Called: Gcm Chicago
9815 Leland Ave  (60176-1328)
PHONE..............................847 678-1616
Fax: 847 678-1617
Michael Halfpenny, Engineer
Barton Vanberburg, Mng Member
Todd Arcari, Manager
Darrell Schuyler, Manager
Simon Sorsher, Manager
EMP: 130
SQ FT: 47,000

SALES (est): 30.9MM  Privately Held
SIC: 3541  Machine tools, metal cutting: exotic (explosive, etc.)

**(G-19837)**
**HMSHOST CORPORATION**
10201 Belle Plaine Ave  (60176-1875)
PHONE..............................847 678-2098
Tom Meol, *Branch Mgr*
EMP: 20
SALES (corp-wide): 9.4MM  Privately Held
SIC: 2095  Roasted coffee
HQ: Hmshost Corporation
    6905 Rockledge Dr Fl 1
    Bethesda MD 20817

**(G-19838)**
**HOFFMAN J&M FARM HOLDINGS INC**
3999 25th Ave  (60176-2175)
P.O. Box 2093  (60176-0093)
PHONE..............................847 671-6280
Francine F Hoffman, *President*
Maida E Hoffman, *Corp Secy*
Alan Blitstein, *Vice Pres*
Thomas McKenna, *Research*
Dan Follis, *Controller*
▲ EMP: 85
SQ FT: 60,000
SALES (est): 19MM  Privately Held
WEB: www.hpcworld.com
SIC: 3541  3577  5087  Keysetting machines; computer peripheral equipment; locksmith equipment & supplies

**(G-19839)**
**HOUSE GRANITE & MARBLE CORP**
5136 Pearl St  (60176-1051)
PHONE..............................847 928-1111
Henryk Zajkowski, *President*
Piotr Topolewicz, *Admin Sec*
▲ EMP: 3
SALES (est): 260K  Privately Held
SIC: 3281  5032  Granite, cut & shaped; marble building stone

**(G-19840)**
**ILLINOIS BROACHING CO (PA)**
4200 Grace St  (60176-1981)
PHONE..............................847 678-3080
Fax: 847 678-5445
Thomas Kelly, *President*
Gregory Crabtree, *Corp Secy*
Jack Crabtree, *Vice Pres*
Patrick Kelly, *Treasurer*
Judy Fain, *Office Mgr*
EMP: 5 EST: 1945
SQ FT: 16,600
SALES (est): 2.1MM  Privately Held
WEB: www.ilbroach.com
SIC: 3541  3544  3545  Broaching machines; special dies, tools, jigs & fixtures; machine tool accessories

**(G-19841)**
**JOSEPH WOODWORKING CORPORATION**
4226 Grace St  (60176-1912)
PHONE..............................847 233-9766
Fax: 847 233-9767
James P Helm, *President*
Terry N Lee, *Vice Pres*
EMP: 18
SQ FT: 11,000
SALES: 1.8MM  Privately Held
SIC: 2499  Decorative wood & woodwork

**(G-19842)**
**KAYLEN INDUSTRIES INC**
9505 Winona Ave  (60176-1024)
PHONE..............................847 671-6767
Fax: 847 671-6784
David V Michals, *President*
Carl Smigiel, *General Mgr*
James Strok, *Vice Pres*
Kathleen Michals, *Admin Sec*
EMP: 55 EST: 1960
SQ FT: 40,000
SALES (est): 12.4MM  Privately Held
WEB: www.mohawkspring.com
SIC: 3495  Mechanical springs, precision

**(G-19843)**
**M J CELCO INC (PA)**
3900 Wesley Ter  (60176-2132)
PHONE..............................847 671-1900
Michael Cielak, *President*
Steve Mikalakis, *General Mgr*
Tom Sikorski, *General Mgr*
Stanley Cielak, *Corp Secy*
Marcel Ciungan, *Project Mgr*
▲ EMP: 80
SQ FT: 100,000
SALES: 50MM  Privately Held
SIC: 3469  Metal stampings

**(G-19844)**
**MAKRAY MANUFACTURING COMPANY**
9515 Seymour Ave  (60176-2125)
PHONE..............................847 260-5408
EMP: 36
SALES (corp-wide): 19.4MM  Privately Held
SIC: 3999  Atomizers, toiletry
PA: Makray Manufacturing Company Inc
    4400 N Harlem Ave
    Norridge IL 60706
    708 456-7100

**(G-19845)**
**MANOR TOOL AND MFG CO (PA)**
9200 Ivanhoe St  (60176-2306)
PHONE..............................847 678-2020
Fax: 847 678-6937
Thomas Simeone, *President*
Tom Simeone, *President*
Kenneth Galeno, *Vice Pres*
Jackie Sorgani, *Cust Svc Mgr*
Marilyn Hoppe, *Office Mgr*
EMP: 45
SQ FT: 47,000
SALES: 10MM  Privately Held
WEB: www.manortool.com
SIC: 3469  3544  Stamping metal for the trade; special dies & tools

**(G-19846)**
**MARVEL ELECTRIC CORPORATION**
Also Called: Magnetic Components
9520 Ainslie St  (60176-1116)
PHONE..............................847 671-0632
Fax: 847 671-9419
Dave Carr, *Purchasing*
Joseph Williams, *Branch Mgr*
EMP: 25
SALES (corp-wide): 10.5MM  Privately Held
SIC: 3677  3612  3548  Inductors, electronic; electronic transformers; transformers, except electric; welding apparatus
PA: Marvel Electric Corporation
    3425 N Ashland Ave
    Chicago IL 60657
    773 327-2644

**(G-19847)**
**MATTHEW WARREN INC**
Also Called: Mohawk Spring
9505 Winona Ave  (60176-1024)
PHONE..............................847 671-6767
EMP: 4
SALES (corp-wide): 115.4MM  Privately Held
SIC: 3495  Mechanical springs, precision
HQ: Matthew Warren, Inc.
    9501 Tech Blvd Ste 401
    Rosemont IL 60018
    847 349-5760

**(G-19848)**
**MBR TOOL INC**
5118 Pearl St  (60176-1051)
PHONE..............................847 671-4491
Raymond Stanis, *President*
EMP: 6
SQ FT: 4,000
SALES (est): 708.3K  Privately Held
WEB: www.mbr.nlm.nih.gov
SIC: 3599  Machine shop, jobbing & repair

**(G-19849)**
**MENNON RUBBER & SAFETY PDTS**
4932 River Rd  (60176-1120)
PHONE..............................847 678-8250
Fax: 847 678-8264
Mary A Cibulka, *President*
James F Cibulka, *Vice Pres*
EMP: 5
SQ FT: 3,000
SALES: 2MM  Privately Held
WEB: www.mennonsafety.com
SIC: 5139  5136  5661  5699  Shoes; men's & boys' clothing; men's shoes; work clothing; men's & boys' work clothing

**(G-19850)**
**MIDLAND STAMPING AND**
9521 Ainslie St  (60176-1115)
PHONE..............................847 678-7573
Alan Blankshain, *President*
EMP: 2
SALES (est): 224.5K  Privately Held
SIC: 3469  Metal stampings

**(G-19851)**
**MIDLAND STAMPING AND FABG CORP (PA)**
9521 Ainslie St  (60176-1115)
PHONE..............................847 678-7573
Alan Blankshain, *President*
EMP: 70
SALES (est): 23.7MM  Privately Held
SIC: 3469  3499  Metal stampings; novelties & specialties, metal

**(G-19852)**
**MJ CELCO INTERNATIONAL LLC**
3900 Wesley Ter  (60176-2132)
PHONE..............................847 671-1900
Lorie Gawlik, *Manager*
Michael Cielak,
Patrick Cielak,
▲ EMP: 25
SALES (est): 2.5MM  Privately Held
SIC: 3444  3469  Sheet metalwork; ornamental metal stampings

**(G-19853)**
**MOFFITT CO**
9347 Seymour Ave  (60176-2206)
PHONE..............................847 678-5450
Fax: 847 678-5463
EMP: 4
SALES (est): 397K  Privately Held
SIC: 3567  Mfg Industrial Furnaces/Ovens

**(G-19854)**
**NOSKO MANUFACTURING INC**
3901 25th Ave  (60176-2117)
PHONE..............................847 678-0813
Grace Nosko, *President*
Anthony Derosa, *Vice Pres*
Beverly Bowling, *Admin Asst*
EMP: 13
SQ FT: 30,000
SALES (est): 2.2MM  Privately Held
WEB: www.noskomfg.com
SIC: 3543  Industrial patterns

**(G-19855)**
**OHARE SHELL PARTNERS INC**
4111 Mannheim Rd  (60176-1840)
PHONE..............................847 678-1900
Ashanti Tippins, *Principal*
EMP: 5
SALES (est): 950.8K  Privately Held
SIC: 3578  Automatic teller machines (ATM)

**(G-19856)**
**ORBIT MACHINING COMPANY**
9440 Ainslie St  (60176-1140)
PHONE..............................847 678-1050
George Zarytsky, *President*
Brian Kowal, *Plant Mgr*
Susan Marino, *Manager*
EMP: 20 EST: 1967
SALES (est): 4.5MM  Privately Held
WEB: www.orbitmachining.com
SIC: 3599  Machine shop, jobbing & repair

**(G-19857)**
**PANATECH COMPUTER MANAGEMENT**
9950 Lawrence Ave Ste 318  (60176-1216)
PHONE..............................847 678-8848
Fax: 847 678-8891
Henry G Fiorentini, *President*
EMP: 3
SQ FT: 1,500
SALES (est): 582.8K  Privately Held
SIC: 5045  7379  7372  Computers; computer related consulting services; business oriented computer software

**(G-19858)**
**PEOPLE & PLACES NEWSPAPER**
4303 Atlantic Ave  (60176-1950)
PHONE..............................847 804-6985
Barbara Piltaver, *Publisher*
EMP: 4
SALES (est): 152.3K  Privately Held
SIC: 2711  Newspapers

**(G-19859)**
**PLASTIC POWER EXTRUSIONS CORP**
3860 River Rd  (60176-2307)
PHONE..............................847 233-9901
Peter Cackowski, *President*
Luke Wodgick, *Manager*
EMP: 20
SQ FT: 42,000
SALES: 5MM  Privately Held
SIC: 3355  Extrusion ingot, aluminum: made in rolling mills

**(G-19860)**
**POINT FIVE PACKAGING LLC**
9555 Irving Park Rd  (60176-1960)
PHONE..............................847 678-5016
Bogdan Kumala, *Engineer*
Andre Versocki, *Engineer*
Paul Kincaid, *Sales Mgr*
Audrey Gulbinas, *Marketing Staff*
Greg Levy, *Mng Member*
▲ EMP: 6
SQ FT: 10,000
SALES (est): 2.2MM  Privately Held
SIC: 3565  Packing & wrapping machinery

**(G-19861)**
**PRECISE ROTARY DIE INC**
9250 Ivanhoe St  (60176-2306)
PHONE..............................847 678-0001
Fax: 847 678-0082
Ray Barak, *President*
EMP: 40
SQ FT: 19,024
SALES (est): 6.9MM  Privately Held
WEB: www.preciserotarydie.com
SIC: 3544  Special dies & tools

**(G-19862)**
**PRECISION STAMPING PDTS INC**
4848 River Rd  (60176-1119)
PHONE..............................847 678-0800
John J Sharkey, *President*
Mike Smyrn, *Regl Sales Mgr*
Mike Smyrniotis, *Regl Sales Mgr*
Lu Lopresto, *Marketing Staff*
Marvin Adams, *Manager*
▲ EMP: 30 EST: 1919
SQ FT: 75,000
SALES (est): 10.2MM  Privately Held
WEB: www.precisionstamp.com
SIC: 3469  Stamping metal for the trade

**(G-19863)**
**PRIME STAINLESS PRODUCTS LLC**
4848 River Rd  (60176-1119)
PHONE..............................847 678-0800
Dean Sharkey,
Michael Sharkey,
◆ EMP: 2
SALES (est): 820.2K  Privately Held
SIC: 5051  3462  Iron & steel (ferrous) products; armor plate, forged iron or steel

**(G-19864)**
**R B HAYWARD COMPANY**
9556 River St  (60176-1020)
PHONE..............................847 671-0400
Fax: 847 671-1689
Robert Kuechenberg, *CEO*
Donald R Malzahn, *President*
Jeff Laskey, *Vice Pres*
Randal Novak, *Vice Pres*
Scott Simantz, *Project Mgr*
EMP: 50 EST: 1915
SQ FT: 35,000

# Schiller Park - Cook County (G-19865)

SALES (est): 9.4MM **Privately Held**
WEB: www.haywardhvac.com
SIC: 1711 3444 Mechanical contractor; metal ventilating equipment; ducts, sheet metal

### (G-19865)
### RAO DESIGN INTERNATIONAL INC
Also Called: American Plastics Technologies
9451 Ainslie St (60176-1139)
PHONE.................847 671-6182
RAO K Murukurthy, *President*
Nadh Murukurthy, *Vice Pres*
Davy P Murukurthy, *Admin Sec*
▲ EMP: 2
SQ FT: 62,000
SALES (est): 454.3K **Privately Held**
SIC: 3559 3544 Plastics working machinery; forms (molds), for foundry & plastics working machinery

### (G-19866)
### RAYMOND BROTHERS INC
Also Called: Sweet Baby Ray's
3919 Wesley Ter (60176-2119)
PHONE.................847 928-9300
Fax: 847 928-9341
David Raymond, *President*
Larry Raymond, *Vice Pres*
Nancy Brian, *Finance Mgr*
Mike O'Brien, *VP Sales*
EMP: 13
SQ FT: 10,000
SALES: 22MM **Privately Held**
WEB: www.sweetbabyrays.com
SIC: 2033 5812 Barbecue sauce: packaged in cans, jars, etc.; eating places

### (G-19867)
### REX MORIOKA
Also Called: Railroad Electronics
4257 Wesley Ter (60176-1925)
PHONE.................847 651-9400
Rex Morioka, *Owner*
EMP: 1
SALES: 500K **Privately Held**
SIC: 3559 Electronic component making machinery

### (G-19868)
### ROENTGEN USA LLC
3725 25th Ave (60176-2147)
PHONE.................847 787-0135
Fax: 847 787-0138
Sandy Bach, *Opers-Prdtn-Mfg*
Egon Arntz,
▲ EMP: 5
SQ FT: 5,200
SALES (est): 2MM
SALES (corp-wide): 48.2MM **Privately Held**
WEB: www.roentgen-usa.com
SIC: 3425 Saw blades for hand or power saws
PA: Robert Rontgen Gmbh & Co. Kg.
    Auf Dem Knapp 44
    Remscheid 42855
    219 137-301

### (G-19869)
### RT WHOLESALE (PA)
Also Called: Food Evolution
4260 Old River Rd (60176-1630)
PHONE.................847 678-3663
Bret Schultz, *Mng Member*
Jeronimo Maldonado, *Mng Member*
Judd Rosenberg, *Mng Member*
Susan Waarich,
EMP: 100
SALES (est): 11.7MM **Privately Held**
WEB: www.foodevolution.com
SIC: 5812 2099 Caterers; food preparations

### (G-19870)
### RUSH IMPRESSIONS INC
3941 25th Ave (60176-2117)
PHONE.................847 671-0622
Russell Dolhun, *President*
EMP: 4
SALES (est): 424.6K **Privately Held**
SIC: 2759 Advertising literature: printing

### (G-19871)
### SCHNEIDER ELECTRIC USA INC
9522 Winona Ave (60176-1025)
PHONE.................630 428-3849
Mary Scholin, *Purchasing*
Richard Goeden, *Branch Mgr*
EMP: 125
SALES (corp-wide): 241K **Privately Held**
WEB: www.squared.com
SIC: 3613 Panel & distribution boards & other related apparatus
HQ: Schneider Electric Usa, Inc.
    800 Federal St
    Andover MA 01810
    978 975-9600

### (G-19872)
### SCIS AIR SECURITY CORPORATION
4321 United Pkwy (60176-1711)
PHONE.................847 671-9502
Fax: 847 671-9504
Steve Skogland, *President*
EMP: 3
SALES (corp-wide): 33.4B **Privately Held**
WEB: www.scisairsecurity.com
SIC: 3699 Electrical equipment & supplies
HQ: Scis Air Security Corporation
    1521 N Cooper St Ste 300
    Arlington TX 76011
    817 792-4500

### (G-19873)
### SMITHCO FABRICATORS INC
9555 Ainslie St (60176-1115)
PHONE.................847 678-1619
John Dumbuk, *President*
Enza Denora, *Manager*
EMP: 15 EST: 1963
SALES (est): 2MM **Privately Held**
SIC: 3469 3544 3479 Stamping metal for the trade; special dies, tools, jigs & fixtures; painting of metal products

### (G-19874)
### SOFIFLEX LLC
4432 Grace St (60176-1613)
PHONE.................847 261-4849
Stoyanka Tsaneva, *Mng Member*
EMP: 10 EST: 2009
SALES (est): 1.1MM **Privately Held**
WEB: www.sofiflex.com
SIC: 3081 Film base, cellulose acetate or nitrocellulose plastic

### (G-19875)
### SOLDY MANUFACTURING INC
Also Called: Aluminum and Zinc Die
9370 Byron St (60176-2304)
PHONE.................847 671-3396
Alex Gemignani, *President*
Alexander Gemignani, *President*
Ryan O'Leary, *VP Sales*
Gabor Puska, *Manager*
Sandra Steiner, *Admin Sec*
EMP: 80 EST: 1982
SQ FT: 22,000
SALES (est): 13.2MM **Privately Held**
WEB: www.soldy.com
SIC: 3544 3364 3363 Industrial molds; zinc & zinc-base alloy die-castings; aluminum die-castings

### (G-19876)
### SPECO INC
3946 Willow St (60176-2311)
PHONE.................847 678-4240
Fax: 847 678-8037
Craig W Hess, *President*
Ron Schulmeister, *Vice Pres*
Dan Dowling, *Opers Mgr*
Orlando Abalde, *Production*
Jaclyn M Hess, *Purch Agent*
▲ EMP: 49 EST: 1924
SQ FT: 25,000
SALES (est): 10.3MM **Privately Held**
WEB: www.speco.com
SIC: 3421 3544 3556 Knives: butchers', hunting, pocket, etc.; special dies, tools, jigs & fixtures; food products machinery

### (G-19877)
### SUNRISE PRINTING INC
9701 Cary Ave (60176-2436)
PHONE.................847 928-1800
Fax: 847 928-0808

Michael Martin, *President*
Anna Martin, *Corp Secy*
Jennifer Kuleck, *Manager*
EMP: 16
SQ FT: 8,000
SALES (est): 3MM **Privately Held**
WEB: www.sunriseprintinginc.com
SIC: 2752 Commercial printing, offset

### (G-19878)
### UNIFIED TOOL DIE & MFG CO INC
9331 Seymour Ave (60176-2292)
PHONE.................847 678-3773
Fax: 847 678-3774
Steve Sciurba, *President*
Jon Schebur, *Manager*
EMP: 15
SQ FT: 8,700
SALES (est): 2.7MM **Privately Held**
WEB: www.unifiedtool.com
SIC: 3544 3469 3699 Special dies, tools, jigs & fixtures; stamping metal for the trade; electrical equipment & supplies

### (G-19879)
### UNITED CARBURETOR INC (PA)
Also Called: United Carburator
9550 Soreng Ave (60176-2128)
PHONE.................773 777-1223
Fax: 773 777-0814
Robert Portman, *CEO*
Alan Portman, *Vice Pres*
David Portman, *Vice Pres*
EMP: 40
SQ FT: 20,000
SALES (est): 7.1MM **Privately Held**
WEB: www.unitedautocarecenter.com
SIC: 3592 3714 Carburetors; motor vehicle steering systems & parts; fuel systems & parts, motor vehicle

### (G-19880)
### UNITED REMANUFACTURING CO INC (HQ)
Also Called: UNITED CARBURATOR
9550 Soreng Ave (60176-2128)
PHONE.................773 777-1223
Fax: 847 678-2373
David Portman, *Vice Pres*
Alan Portman, *Vice Pres*
Scott Portman, *VP Sales*
▲ EMP: 6
SQ FT: 20,000
SALES: 2.8MM
SALES (corp-wide): 7.1MM **Privately Held**
SIC: 3592 3714 5085 5013 Carburetors; motor vehicle steering systems & parts; fuel systems & parts, motor vehicle; industrial supplies; automotive supplies & parts
PA: United Carburetor Inc
    9550 Soreng Ave
    Schiller Park IL 60176
    773 777-1223

### (G-19881)
### UNITED REMANUFACTURING CO INC
Also Called: United Carborator
9550 Soreng Ave (60176-2128)
PHONE.................847 678-2233
Jerry Portman, *President*
Alan Portman, *General Mgr*
J Rasinski, *Purchasing*
Danny Portman, *Chief Engr*
Fred Wolf, *Sales Staff*
EMP: 30
SQ FT: 20,000
SALES (est): 7.1MM **Privately Held**
SIC: 3592 3714 Carburetors; steering mechanisms, motor vehicle
HQ: United Remanufacturing Co Inc
    9550 Soreng Ave
    Schiller Park IL 60176
    773 777-1223

### (G-19882)
### W D MOLD FINISHING INC
3923 Wesley Ter (60176-2131)
PHONE.................847 678-8449
Fax: 847 678-8449
Thomas Dinkel, *President*
Walter J Dinkel, *Consultant*

Agnes Dinkel, *Admin Sec*
EMP: 3
SQ FT: 7,200
SALES (est): 373.6K **Privately Held**
SIC: 3471 Plating & polishing

### (G-19883)
### WESTERN PRINTING MACHINERY CO (PA)
Also Called: Wpm
9229 Ivanhoe St (60176-2305)
PHONE.................847 678-1740
Fax: 847 678-6176
Paul G Kapolnek, *CEO*
Paul Kaponek, *CEO*
Elmer Piper, *Engineer*
Kalvin O'Meora, *CFO*
Frank Piper, *Sales Dir*
▲ EMP: 30 EST: 1933
SALES (est): 11MM **Privately Held**
SIC: 3555 7371 Printing trades machinery; computer software writing services

### (G-19884)
### WESTERN PRINTING MACHINERY CO
9228 Ivanhoe St (60176-2306)
PHONE.................847 678-1740
Michael K Musgrave, *President*
EMP: 25
SALES (corp-wide): 11MM **Privately Held**
SIC: 3555 7371 Printing trades machinery; computer software writing services
PA: Western Printing Machinery Company
    9229 Ivanhoe St
    Schiller Park IL 60176
    847 678-1740

## Scott Air Force Base
*St. Clair County*

### (G-19885)
### DLA DOCUMENT SERVICES
901 South Dr Bldg 700e (62225-5103)
PHONE.................618 256-4686
Lenny Exavier, *Director*
EMP: 10 **Publicly Held**
SIC: 2752 9711 Commercial printing, lithographic; national security;
HQ: Dla Document Services
    5450 Carlisle Pike Bldg 9
    Mechanicsburg PA 17050
    717 605-2362

## Seneca
*Lasalle County*

### (G-19886)
### GRIFFIN INDUSTRIES LLC
Also Called: Bakery Feeds
410 Shipyard Rd (61360-9305)
PHONE.................815 357-8200
David Grassl, *Branch Mgr*
EMP: 5
SALES (corp-wide): 3.4B **Publicly Held**
WEB: www.griffinind.com
SIC: 2843 2053 2052 Oils & greases; frozen bakery products, except bread; bakery products, dry
HQ: Griffin Industries Llc
    4221 Alexandria Pike
    Cold Spring KY 41076
    859 781-2010

### (G-19887)
### JOHN A BIEWER LUMBER COMPANY
Also Called: Biewer John A Co of Seneca
524 E Union St (61360-9493)
PHONE.................815 357-6792
Fax: 815 357-8663
Richard Hales, *Manager*
Cheryl Husted, *Administration*
EMP: 15
SALES (corp-wide): 102.2MM **Privately Held**
SIC: 2491 Structural lumber & timber, treated wood

# GEOGRAPHIC SECTION

**Shelbyville - Shelby County (G-19908)**

PA: John A. Biewer Lumber Company
812 S Riverside Ave
Saint Clair MI 48079
810 329-4789

**(G-19888)**
**MID-STATES INDUSTRIAL INC**
519 Shipyard Rd (61360-9203)
P.O. Box 559 (61360-0559)
PHONE.................................815 357-1663
Fax: 815 357-1665
James Christian Basso, *President*
David Both, *Vice Pres*
Todd Evans, *Foreman/Supr*
Jennifer Crouse, *Manager*
Brian Wheeler, *Admin Sec*
▲ EMP: 15
SQ FT: 5,000
SALES (est): 3.4MM **Privately Held**
WEB: www.midstatesindustrial.com
SIC: 3795 Tanks & tank components

**(G-19889)**
**REG SENECA LLC**
614 Shipyard Rd (61360-9469)
P.O. Box 888, Ames IA (50010-0888)
PHONE.................................888 734-8686
Daniel J OH, *President*
Natalie Lischer, *Corp Secy*
Brad Albin, *Vice Pres*
EMP: 35
SALES (est): 11.9MM
SALES (corp-wide): 2B **Publicly Held**
SIC: 2869 Industrial organic chemicals
PA: Renewable Energy Group, Inc.
416 S Bell Ave
Ames IA 50010
515 239-8000

**(G-19890)**
**SENECA CUSTOM CABINETRY**
2957 Us Highway 6 (61360-9520)
PHONE.................................815 357-1322
Ken Bertrand, *Owner*
EMP: 7
SALES: 300K **Privately Held**
SIC: 2434 Wood kitchen cabinets

**(G-19891)**
**SENECA SAND & GRAVEL LLC**
2962 N 2553rd Rd (61360)
P.O. Box 828 (61360-0828)
PHONE.................................630 746-9183
Brandon S Boughton, *Partner*
EMP: 4 EST: 2009
SALES (est): 618K **Privately Held**
SIC: 1442 Construction sand & gravel

## Serena
### Lasalle County

**(G-19892)**
**KONA BLACKBIRD INC**
Also Called: Wedron Flux Div
3624 E 2351st Rd (60549-9730)
P.O. Box 236, Wedron (60557-0236)
PHONE.................................815 792-8750
Dave Caskey, *QA Dir*
Jeff Merritt, *Sales Staff*
Doug Gerner, *Branch Mgr*
Tony Sinning, *Manager*
Burnette Smith, *Manager*
EMP: 15
SALES (corp-wide): 4.2MM **Privately Held**
WEB: www.blacklabcorp.com
SIC: 5032 3291 1446 3241 Brick, stone & related material; abrasive products; industrial sand; masonry cement; fluxes: brazing, soldering, galvanizing & welding; flooring brick, clay
PA: Kona Blackbird, Inc.
11730 Ravenna Rd
Chardon OH 44024
440 285-3189

**(G-19893)**
**MIDAMERICAN TECHNOLOGY INC**
3708 E 25th Rd (60549-9734)
PHONE.................................815 496-2400
Kevin E Bailey, *President*
Scott Warner, *Regional Mgr*
EMP: 4
SQ FT: 4,200
SALES: 700K **Privately Held**
SIC: 3812 Search & detection systems & instruments

## Sesser
### Franklin County

**(G-19894)**
**C AND H PUBLISHING CO (PA)**
Also Called: American Cooner
114 E Franklin St (62884-1844)
P.O. Box 777 (62884-0777)
PHONE.................................618 625-2711
Fax: 618 625-6221
Terry Walker, *Owner*
EMP: 8
SQ FT: 12,500
SALES (est): 559K **Privately Held**
WEB: www.americancooner.com
SIC: 2721 Magazines: publishing & printing

**(G-19895)**
**SESSER CONCRETE PRODUCTS CO**
910 S Cockrum St (62884-2028)
P.O. Box 100 (62884-0100)
PHONE.................................618 625-2811
Fax: 618 625-6906
Michael K Thompson, *President*
Juanita Cook, *Vice Pres*
Susie Doty, *Administration*
EMP: 14 EST: 1948
SALES: 1.8MM **Privately Held**
WEB: www.sesserconcrete.com
SIC: 3271 5032 Blocks, concrete or cinder: standard; brick, except refractory

## Seward
### Winnebago County

**(G-19896)**
**EICKMANS PROCESSING CO INC**
3226 S Pecatonica Rd (61077)
P.O. Box 118 (61077-0118)
PHONE.................................815 247-8451
Fax: 815 247-8463
Michael P Eickman, *President*
Lori Eickman, *Corp Secy*
EMP: 27
SQ FT: 15,000
SALES (est): 3.4MM **Privately Held**
SIC: 2011 5421 5147 5812 Beef products from beef slaughtered on site; pork products from pork slaughtered on site; sausages from meat slaughtered on site; meat markets, including freezer provisioners; meats, fresh; caterers; storage, frozen or refrigerated goods; sausages & other prepared meats

## Seymour
### Champaign County

**(G-19897)**
**FIRST-LIGHT USA LLC**
205 S Main St (61875-4806)
PHONE.................................217 687-4048
Leslie Kirby, *Sales Mgr*
Jeremy Ross,
Chris Kutsor,
Jason Logsdon,
EMP: 10
SALES (est): 1.7MM **Privately Held**
SIC: 3648 Flashlights

**(G-19898)**
**SAVIND INC**
Also Called: E Pharm Nutrition
205 S Main St Ste B (61875-4807)
PHONE.................................217 687-2710
India Boodram, *President*
EMP: 7
SALES (est): 888.4K **Privately Held**
SIC: 2834 Vitamin, nutrient & hematinic preparations for human use

## Shannon
### Carroll County

**(G-19899)**
**L & J INDUSTRIAL STAPLES INC**
15 W Market St (61078-9005)
P.O. Box 104 (61078-0104)
PHONE.................................815 864-3337
Fax: 815 864-3307
Luther Revels, *President*
Lana Baker, *General Mgr*
Sue Revels, *Vice Pres*
▲ EMP: 8
SQ FT: 65,000
SALES (est): 1.2MM **Privately Held**
WEB: www.ljindustrialstaplesinc.net
SIC: 3399 3315 Staples, nonferrous metal or wire; nails, steel: wire or cut

**(G-19900)**
**MB MACHINE INC**
10214 N Mount Vernon Rd (61078-9404)
PHONE.................................815 864-3555
Michael Baker, *President*
EMP: 11
SQ FT: 10,000
SALES (est): 730K **Privately Held**
SIC: 3599 7692 3444 Machine shop, jobbing & repair; welding repair; sheet metalwork

**(G-19901)**
**PROCESS SCREW PRODUCTS INC**
10 N Shannon Rte (61078-9361)
P.O. Box 545 (61078-0545)
PHONE.................................815 864-2220
Fax: 815 864-2254
Marilyn A Hammer, *President*
Marilyn Hammer, *President*
Joseph Hammer, *Vice Pres*
EMP: 25 EST: 1963
SQ FT: 20,000
SALES (est): 4MM **Privately Held**
WEB: www.processscrew.com
SIC: 3451 3462 3643 3568 Screw machine products; gears, forged steel; current-carrying wiring devices; power transmission equipment; machine tools, metal cutting type; valves & pipe fittings

**(G-19902)**
**SAINT TECHNOLOGIES INC**
10 N Locust St (61078-9009)
P.O. Box 66 (61078-0066)
PHONE.................................815 864-3035
James F L Blair, *President*
Marilyn K Blair, *Corp Secy*
EMP: 4
SQ FT: 7,500
SALES (est): 472.3K **Privately Held**
WEB: www.sainttechnologies.net
SIC: 3452 Lock washers

**(G-19903)**
**TEE LEE POPCORN INC**
101 W Badger St (61078-9020)
P.O. Box 108 (61078-0108)
PHONE.................................815 864-2363
Fax: 815 864-2388
James D Weaver, *President*
Gary Armstrong, *General Mgr*
Carolyn L Weaver, *Vice Pres*
Ken Weaver, *Vice Pres*
Diane Weaver, *Human Res Mgr*
▼ EMP: 20
SQ FT: 25,000
SALES (est): 8.2MM **Privately Held**
SIC: 2099 5145 5046 2096 Popcorn, packaged: except already popped; popcorn & supplies; commercial equipment; potato chips & similar snacks

## Shawneetown
### Gallatin County

**(G-19904)**
**JADER FUEL CO INC**
Also Called: Downen Enterprises
117 S Edison St (62984-3138)
P.O. Box 520 (62984-0520)
PHONE.................................618 269-3101
Fax: 618 269-3341
Robert Downen, *President*
Philip Downen, *Vice Pres*
William Downen, *Vice Pres*
Edward Downen, *Admin Sec*
C Donald Downen, *Asst Sec*
EMP: 8
SQ FT: 1,500
SALES: 1.2MM **Privately Held**
SIC: 1221 Strip mining, bituminous

## Shelbyville
### Shelby County

**(G-19905)**
**BARNES MACHINE SHOP LLC**
209 N Pine St (62565-1266)
PHONE.................................217 774-5308
Fax: 217 774-5310
Paul Barnes, *President*
EMP: 7
SALES (est): 916.5K **Privately Held**
SIC: 3599 Machine shop, jobbing & repair

**(G-19906)**
**COMMUNITY NEWSPPR HOLDINGS INC**
Also Called: Shelbyville Daily Union
100 W Main St (62565-1652)
PHONE.................................217 774-2161
Shannon Allen, *Sls & Mktg Exec*
Bob Dennis, *Manager*
Sue Grant, *Manager*
EMP: 13 **Privately Held**
WEB: www.clintonnc.com
SIC: 2711 Commercial printing & newspaper publishing combined
PA: Community Newspaper Holdings, Inc.
445 Dexter Ave Ste 7000
Montgomery AL 36104

**(G-19907)**
**FOX REDI-MIX INC**
1300 W South 5th St (62565-1724)
P.O. Box 558 (62565-0558)
PHONE.................................217 774-2110
Shane Fox, *President*
Douglas Fox, *President*
Stephen Fox, *Corp Secy*
Stuart Fox, *Vice Pres*
Vickie Rudman, *Admin Sec*
EMP: 8
SQ FT: 6,500
SALES (est): 700K **Privately Held**
SIC: 3273 Ready-mixed concrete

**(G-19908)**
**IHI TURBO AMERICA CO (HQ)**
1598 State Highway 16 (62565-4470)
Rural Route 36 (62565)
PHONE.................................217 774-9571
Fax: 217 774-3834
Hiromu Furukawa, *President*
Bruce Renton, *General Mgr*
Michael Price, *Corp Secy*
Kevin Kowalis, *Engineer*
Michael Sinclair, *Sales Mgr*
▲ EMP: 75
SQ FT: 56,000
SALES (est): 25.4MM
SALES (corp-wide): 13B **Privately Held**
WEB: www.ihi-turbo.com
SIC: 3724 3999 Turbo-superchargers, aircraft; atomizers, toiletry
PA: Ihi Corporation
3-1-1, Toyosu
Koto-Ku TKY 135-0
362 047-800

# Shelbyville - Shelby County (G-19909)

**(G-19909)**
**INTERNATIONAL PAPER COMPANY**
500 W Dacey Dr (62565-9118)
PHONE.....................217 774-2176
Robert Eades, *Plant Mgr*
John McCloud, *Purchasing*
Vicki Bender, *Human Res Mgr*
Joanne Kendall, *Human Res Mgr*
Paul Glenney, *Manager*
**EMP:** 800
**SQ FT:** 350,000
**SALES (corp-wide):** 21B **Publicly Held**
**WEB:** www.internationalpaper.com
**SIC:** 2631 Paperboard mills
**PA:** International Paper Company
6400 Poplar Ave
Memphis TN 38197
901 419-9000

**(G-19910)**
**MACARI SERVICE CENTER INC (PA)**
Also Called: Macari Appliance Center
N Rte 128 (62565)
P.O. Box 64 (62565-0064)
PHONE.....................217 774-4214
Fax: 217 774-4214
Joe Beck, *President*
Ron Saddoris, *Vice Pres*
Lisa Allen, *Manager*
**EMP:** 3
**SQ FT:** 12,000
**SALES:** 2MM **Privately Held**
**SIC:** 1711 3444 5722 Heating & air conditioning contractors; ducts, sheet metal; electric household appliances; electric household appliances, major; gas household appliances

**(G-19911)**
**P & H MANUFACTURING CO**
604 S Lodge St (62565-1929)
P.O. Box 349 (62565-0349)
PHONE.....................217 774-2123
Fax: 217 774-5341
Earl D Peifer, *President*
Earl A Holland, *Principal*
Charles D Peifer, *Principal*
Dave Russell, *Traffic Mgr*
Mark Montgomery, *QC Mgr*
◆ **EMP:** 100 **EST:** 1943
**SQ FT:** 250,000
**SALES (est):** 23MM **Privately Held**
**WEB:** www.phmfg.com
**SIC:** 3599 3523 Machine & other job shop work; farm machinery & equipment

**(G-19912)**
**PRAIRIE PURE BOTTLED WATER**
603 W North 4th St (62565-1424)
PHONE.....................217 774-7873
Toll Free:............................877 -
Tom Phinks, *President*
Jim Phinks, *Principal*
Mason Phinks, *Principal*
Connie Rooney, *Principal*
**EMP:** 3 **EST:** 1998
**SALES (est):** 312.2K **Privately Held**
**SIC:** 2086 Pasteurized & mineral waters, bottled & canned

**(G-19913)**
**PROSSER CONSTRUCTION CO**
1410 N 1500 East Rd (62565-4423)
PHONE.....................217 774-5032
Fax: 217 774-3402
David Cruitt, *President*
Charlie Adams, *Vice Pres*
Troy Wade, *Safety Mgr*
Ken Ozier, *Treasurer*
Vicky Redman, *Admin Sec*
**EMP:** 15
**SQ FT:** 3,500
**SALES (est):** 1MM **Privately Held**
**SIC:** 1611 1442 3272 2951 Highway & street paving contractor; gravel mining; concrete products; asphalt paving mixtures & blocks; concrete work

**(G-19914)**
**REBER WELDING SERVICE**
142 S Washington St (62565-2330)
PHONE.....................217 774-3441
Fax: 217 774-3441
Rick D Reber, *Owner*
**EMP:** 3 **EST:** 1943
**SQ FT:** 5,000
**SALES:** 150K **Privately Held**
**SIC:** 7692 3548 3492 3441 Welding repair; welding apparatus; fluid power valves & hose fittings; fabricated structural metal

**(G-19915)**
**SHELBY TOOL & DIE INC**
1804 W South 2nd St (62565-9577)
P.O. Box 376 (62565-0376)
PHONE.....................217 774-2189
Fax: 217 774-3133
Howard Ray Tull, *President*
Todd Furr, *Vice Pres*
**EMP:** 8 **EST:** 1960
**SQ FT:** 5,800
**SALES:** 400K **Privately Held**
**SIC:** 3544 3545 Special dies & tools; machine tool accessories

**(G-19916)**
**STA-RITE GINNIE LOU INC**
245 E South 1st St (62565-2332)
P.O. Box 435 (62565-0435)
PHONE.....................217 774-3921
Noel Bolinger, *President*
▲ **EMP:** 10 **EST:** 1917
**SQ FT:** 18,000
**SALES:** 610K **Privately Held**
**WEB:** www.sta-riteginnielou.com
**SIC:** 3965 Hairpins, except rubber; hair curlers

**(G-19917)**
**TONY WEISHAAR**
Also Called: Tony's Welding & Repair Svc
Hwy 16 One 16th Mile E (62565)
Rr # 4 Box 1 (62565-4630)
PHONE.....................217 774-2774
Tony Weishaar, *Owner*
**EMP:** 3
**SALES (est):** 229.5K **Privately Held**
**SIC:** 7692 Welding repair

## Sheridan
### Lasalle County

**(G-19918)**
**HANSELS CUSTOM TECH INC**
405 E Si Johnson Ave (60551)
P.O. Box 555 (60551-0555)
PHONE.....................815 496-2345
Kevin Hansel, *President*
**EMP:** 6 **EST:** 1993
**SALES:** 635K **Privately Held**
**SIC:** 3544 Special dies, tools, jigs & fixtures

**(G-19919)**
**TACOM HQ INC**
3908 E 2599th Rd (60551-9762)
P.O. Box 268 (60551-0268)
PHONE.....................630 251-8919
John Baker, *President*
Mike Thompson, *Corp Secy*
Jacob Baker, *Vice Pres*
**EMP:** 4 **EST:** 2014
**SALES:** 100K **Privately Held**
**SIC:** 3229 Optical glass

## Shirley
### Mclean County

**(G-19920)**
**STARK MATERIALS INC**
9359 E 1000 North Rd (61772-9594)
PHONE.....................309 828-8520
Dave Stark, *President*
**EMP:** 20
**SALES (est):** 708.6K **Privately Held**
**SIC:** 1442 Construction sand & gravel

## Shobonier
### Fayette County

**(G-19921)**
**DUTCH PRAIRIE CONVEYORS**
844 N 1625 St (62885-4147)
PHONE.....................618 349-6177
Harlan Weaver, *Owner*
**EMP:** 2
**SALES:** 600K **Privately Held**
**SIC:** 3523 Planting machines, agricultural

**(G-19922)**
**NEDRAS PRINTING INC**
897 E 900 Ave (62885-4062)
PHONE.....................618 846-3853
Fax: 618 283-2599
Nedra Haynes, *President*
Carrol Haynes, *Vice Pres*
**EMP:** 2
**SALES (est):** 209.2K **Privately Held**
**SIC:** 2752 Commercial printing, lithographic

## Shorewood
### Will County

**(G-19923)**
**BRAKUR CUSTOM CABINETRY INC**
18656 S State Route 59 (60404-8625)
PHONE.....................630 355-2244
Fax: 815 436-1813
Chad T Kurtz, *President*
Joe Spreitzer, *General Mgr*
Joe Kuban, *Accountant*
Jim Sinadinos, *Human Res Mgr*
Dave Lynn, *Sales Mgr*
**EMP:** 130
**SQ FT:** 50,000
**SALES (est):** 20.6MM **Privately Held**
**WEB:** www.brakur.com
**SIC:** 2541 2434 Wood partitions & fixtures; wood kitchen cabinets

**(G-19924)**
**BUTLER BROS STEEL RULE DIE CO**
303 Amendodge Dr (60404-8200)
PHONE.....................815 630-4629
John Small, *Branch Mgr*
**EMP:** 3
**SALES (corp-wide):** 3.4MM **Privately Held**
**SIC:** 2675 Die-cut paper & board
**PA:** Butler Bros Steel Rule Die Co Inc
730 N 18th St
Saint Louis MO 63103
314 241-1540

**(G-19925)**
**ETHAN COMPANY INCORPORATED**
306 Harvard Ct (60404-9136)
PHONE.....................815 715-2283
William Long, *Principal*
**EMP:** 3
**SALES (est):** 329.2K **Privately Held**
**SIC:** 2759 Commercial printing

**(G-19926)**
**EXPRESS SIGNS & LIGHTING MAINT**
212 Amendodge Dr (60404-9362)
PHONE.....................815 725-9080
Fax: 815 725-7543
Mary T Hartsell, *President*
Eddie B Hartsell, *Vice Pres*
Lisa Taylor, *Administration*
Ken Laas, *Teacher*
**EMP:** 12
**SQ FT:** 5,400
**SALES (est):** 1.6MM **Privately Held**
**SIC:** 3993 1799 Electric signs; cable splicing service

**(G-19927)**
**GAMMON GROUP INC**
1009 Geneva St (60404-9409)
PHONE.....................815 722-6400
Fax: 815 722-6404
Dan Stefanish, *President*
**EMP:** 5
**SALES (est):** 565.6K **Privately Held**
**WEB:** www.gammongroup.com
**SIC:** 7336 7311 8742 2752 Graphic arts & related design; advertising agencies; marketing consulting services; commercial printing, lithographic

**(G-19928)**
**GRAPHIC PROMOTIONS INC**
405 Earl Rd (60404-9402)
PHONE.....................815 726-3288
Stacey Sladek, *President*
Daryl Sladek, *Vice Pres*
**EMP:** 15
**SQ FT:** 20,000
**SALES:** 1MM **Privately Held**
**SIC:** 2752 Commercial printing, lithographic

**(G-19929)**
**LANE CONSTRUCTION CORPORATION**
611 W Jefferson St 201aa (60404-7306)
PHONE.....................815 846-4466
Fax: 815 651-2145
John Roddy, *Branch Mgr*
**EMP:** 15
**SALES (corp-wide):** 4.8K **Privately Held**
**SIC:** 1622 1611 1629 3272 Highway construction, elevated; bridge construction; airport runway construction; dam construction; subway construction; power plant construction; building materials, except block or brick; concrete; paving materials
**HQ:** The Lane Construction Corporation
90 Fieldstone Ct
Cheshire CT 06410
203 235-3351

**(G-19930)**
**PRAIRIE MATERIALS GROUP**
19515 Ne Frontage Rd (60404-3567)
PHONE.....................815 207-6750
**EMP:** 3
**SALES (est):** 39.1K **Privately Held**
**SIC:** 3273 Ready-mixed concrete

**(G-19931)**
**RAPID FOODS INC**
Also Called: Standard Provision Co
1007 Geneva St (60404-9409)
P.O. Box 307, Forest Park (60130-0307)
PHONE.....................708 366-0321
Fax: 708 366-7636
Joseph Stone, *Ch of Bd*
Michael Stone, *President*
Faith Stone, *Corp Secy*
**EMP:** 7
**SQ FT:** 1,300
**SALES (est):** 4.1MM **Privately Held**
**SIC:** 5147 2013 Meats, fresh; sausages & other prepared meats

## Shumway
### Effingham County

**(G-19932)**
**KREMER PRECISION MACHINE INC**
10748 E 1850th Ave (62461-2217)
PHONE.....................217 868-2627
Fax: 217 868-5832
Eugene J Kremer, *President*
Douglas Kremer, *Vice Pres*
Phyllis Kremer, *Vice Pres*
Charles Willenborg, *Engineer*
Pamela Kiefer, *Treasurer*
**EMP:** 17
**SQ FT:** 7,600
**SALES (est):** 2.5MM **Privately Held**
**SIC:** 3599 Machine shop, jobbing & repair

## GEOGRAPHIC SECTION
**Skokie - Cook County (G-19958)**

**(G-19933)**
**MANUFCTRNG-RESOURCING INTL INC**
5265 E 1800th Ave (62461-2018)
**PHONE**.................................217 821-3733
Sandy Cornett, *President*
▲ **EMP:** 10
**SQ FT:** 25,000
**SALES:** 2MM **Privately Held**
**SIC: 3581** Mechanisms & parts for automatic vending machines

**(G-19934)**
**METAL WORKS MACHINE INC**
11100 E 1850th Ave (62461-2244)
**PHONE**.................................217 868-5111
Carol Levitt, *President*
Ed Levitt, *Admin Sec*
**EMP:** 4
**SALES (est):** 379.9K **Privately Held**
**SIC: 3599** Machine & other job shop work

**(G-19935)**
**SOUTHERN ILLINOIS MCHY CO INC**
Also Called: Sim Products
6903 E 1600th Ave (62461-2343)
**PHONE**.................................217 868-5431
**Fax:** 217 868-5446
John A Newsome, *President*
Howard Stuemke, *Vice Pres*
Angie Newsome, *Purchasing*
Roger Bonham, *Engineer*
Jeff Petrowich, *Engineer*
▲ **EMP:** 80
**SQ FT:** 50,000
**SALES (est):** 17MM **Privately Held**
**WEB:** www.simproducts.com
**SIC: 3555** Bookbinding machinery

### Sidney
*Champaign County*

**(G-19936)**
**FRITO-LAY NORTH AMERICA INC**
1050 County Road 2300 E (61877)
**PHONE**.................................217 776-2320
**Fax:** 217 688-2746
Chuck Schmitz, *Site Mgr*
Lance Knutson, *Opers-Prdtn-Mfg*
**EMP:** 21
**SALES (corp-wide):** 62.8B **Publicly Held**
**WEB:** www.fritolay.com
**SIC: 2096** Potato chips & other potato-based snacks
**HQ:** Frito-Lay North America, Inc.
7701 Legacy Dr
Plano TX 75024

**(G-19937)**
**MITCHELL OPTICS INC**
2072 County Road 1100 N (61877-9602)
**PHONE**.................................217 688-2219
George Mitchell, *Owner*
**EMP:** 3
**SALES (est):** 247.1K **Privately Held**
**SIC: 3827** Telescopes: elbow, panoramic, sighting, fire control, etc.

### Sigel
*Shelby County*

**(G-19938)**
**SIGEL WELDING**
103 S Main St (62462-1014)
**PHONE**.................................217 844-2412
Eric McWhorter, *Owner*
Kent Jansen, *Co-Owner*
**EMP:** 1
**SALES (est):** 250K **Privately Held**
**SIC: 7692** Welding repair

### Silvis
*Rock Island County*

**(G-19939)**
**NATIONAL RAILWAY EQUIPMENT CO**
300 9th St N (61282-1075)
**PHONE**.................................309 755-6800
Willie Bremermann, *Assistant VP*
Bryan Mohus, *Plant Mgr*
Bernie Fedorchek, *QC Dir*
Rob Riley, *Controller*
Lorrie Winters, *Manager*
**EMP:** 150
**SALES (corp-wide):** 324.9MM **Privately Held**
**WEB:** www.nationalrailway.com
**SIC: 3743** 5088 Locomotives & parts; railroad equipment & supplies
**PA:** National Railway Equipment Co.
1100 Shawnee St
Mount Vernon IL 62864
618 242-6590

**(G-19940)**
**RIVER CITY SIGN COMPANY INC**
Also Called: Carol Douglas Company
915 1st Ave (61282-1046)
**PHONE**.................................309 796-3606
Carol Small, *President*
Douglas Small, *Vice Pres*
▲ **EMP:** 3
**SQ FT:** 4,000
**SALES:** 100K **Privately Held**
**SIC: 3999** Wind chimes

### Sims
*Wayne County*

**(G-19941)**
**ROBERTSON REPAIR**
Hwy 15 (62886)
**PHONE**.................................618 895-2593
Bill Robertson, *Owner*
**EMP:** 4
**SALES (est):** 120K **Privately Held**
**SIC: 7692** Automotive welding

### Skokie
*Cook County*

**(G-19942)**
**A J CARBIDE GRINDING**
8509 E Prairie Rd (60076-2322)
**PHONE**.................................847 675-5112
Arthur J Sala, *Owner*
**EMP:** 2
**SALES:** 500K **Privately Held**
**SIC: 7389** 3542 3544 Grinding, precision: commercial or industrial; machine tools, metal forming type; special dies, tools, jigs & fixtures

**(G-19943)**
**A TO Z OFFSET PRTG & PUBG INC**
9115 Terminal Ave (60077-1570)
**PHONE**.................................847 966-3016
**Fax:** 847 966-3099
Joseph Zetouny, *President*
Leah Zetouny, *Vice Pres*
Sigalit Zetouny, *Vice Pres*
**EMP:** 8
**SQ FT:** 12,000
**SALES (est):** 2.5MM **Privately Held**
**SIC: 2752** 2731 2789 2721 Commercial printing, offset; books: publishing & printing; bookbinding & related work; periodicals

**(G-19944)**
**ABBAS FOODS CORP**
8111 Saint Louis Ave (60076-2968)
**PHONE**.................................847 213-0093
Abdulkader A Abbas, *Principal*
**EMP:** 6 **EST:** 2013
**SALES (est):** 704.3K **Privately Held**
**SIC: 2099** Ready-to-eat meals, salads & sandwiches

**(G-19945)**
**ABLE ENGRAVERS INC**
9521 Kedvale Ave (60076-1499)
**PHONE**.................................847 676-3737
**Fax:** 847 676-3135
Eric Cooper, *President*
**EMP:** 2 **EST:** 1973
**SALES:** 780K **Privately Held**
**WEB:** www.able-engravers.com
**SIC: 3555** Engraving machinery & equipment, except plates

**(G-19946)**
**ACE PCB DESIGN INC**
5138 Conrad St (60077-2114)
**PHONE**.................................847 674-8745
**Fax:** 847 647-8110
John Callas, *President*
**EMP:** 3
**SALES (est):** 222.1K **Privately Held**
**SIC: 3571** Electronic computers

**(G-19947)**
**ALL CNC SOLUTIONS INC**
7617 Parkside Ave (60077-2633)
**PHONE**.................................847 972-1139
Miroslav Kainovic, *Principal*
**EMP:** 5 **EST:** 2008
**SALES:** 658K **Privately Held**
**SIC: 8711** 3599 Machine tool design; machine & other job shop work

**(G-19948)**
**ALL-VAC INDUSTRIES INC**
7350 Central Park Ave (60076-4003)
**PHONE**.................................847 675-2290
Mitchell Stern, *President*
Harriet R Stern, *Treasurer*
Maureen Rottinger, *Office Mgr*
▲ **EMP:** 10
**SQ FT:** 5,000
**SALES (est):** 1.2MM **Privately Held**
**WEB:** www.allvacindustries.com
**SIC: 3565** 3086 3537 3444 Vacuum packaging machinery; cups & plates, foamed plastic; industrial trucks & tractors; sheet metalwork

**(G-19949)**
**ALLIANCE INVESTMENT CORP**
Also Called: Midland Printing
9150 Kenneth Ave (60076-1647)
**PHONE**.................................847 933-0400
**Fax:** 847 933-0075
Hossein Birjandi, *President*
**EMP:** 11
**SQ FT:** 3,000
**SALES:** 1MM **Privately Held**
**SIC: 2752** Menus, lithographed

**(G-19950)**
**AMERICAN LOUVER COMPANY (PA)**
Also Called: American Store Fixtures
7700 Austin Ave (60076-2603)
P.O. Box 206 (60076-0206)
**PHONE**.................................847 470-0400
**Fax:** 847 581-0046
Geoffrey M Glass Jr, *President*
Kevin Harley, *Regional Mgr*
Glen Swazey, *Regional Mgr*
David Foy, *Vice Pres*
Craig Dzierwa, *Opers Mgr*
▲ **EMP:** 108
**SQ FT:** 55,000
**SALES (est):** 34.2MM **Privately Held**
**WEB:** www.americanlouver.com
**SIC: 3083** Plastic finished products, laminated

**(G-19951)**
**AMERICAN VACUUM CO**
Also Called: A R C O
7301 Monticello Ave (60076-4024)
**PHONE**.................................847 674-8383
**Fax:** 847 674-0214
Jack Person, *President*
Tim Person, *Project Mgr*
Anthony Tripicchio, *Purchasing*
▲ **EMP:** 5 **EST:** 1939
**SQ FT:** 7,000
**SALES:** 3.5MM **Privately Held**
**WEB:** www.americanvacuum.com
**SIC: 3589** 3548 Vacuum cleaners & sweepers, electric: industrial; electric welding equipment

**(G-19952)**
**AMERICUT WIRE EDM INC**
8045 Ridgeway Ave (60076-3408)
**PHONE**.................................847 675-1754
Nicola Babatchev, *President*
Nick Babatchev, *President*
**EMP:** 13
**SALES:** 950K **Privately Held**
**WEB:** www.americutedm.com
**SIC: 3679** Electronic components

**(G-19953)**
**AMMERAAL BELTECH INC (DH)**
7501 Saint Louis Ave (60076-4033)
**PHONE**.................................847 673-6720
Mercy Virly, *Principal*
Angel Cancel, *Plant Mgr*
Gary Williamson, *Opers Mgr*
Jeff Crum, *Traffic Mgr*
Richard Ruiz, *Senior Buyer*
◆ **EMP:** 100 **EST:** 1913
**SQ FT:** 105,000
**SALES (est):** 58.1MM **Privately Held**
**WEB:** www.ammeraalbeltechusa.com
**SIC: 3052** Rubber & plastics hose & beltings
**HQ:** Ammeraal Beltech Holding B.V.
Comeniusstraat 8
Alkmaar 1817
725 751-212

**(G-19954)**
**AMMERAAL BELTECH INC**
7501 Saint Louis Ave (60076-4033)
**PHONE**.................................847 673-1736
Ted Roper, *Branch Mgr*
**EMP:** 5 **Privately Held**
**WEB:** www.ammeraalbeltechusa.com
**SIC: 2399** Belting & belt products
**HQ:** Ammeraal Beltech, Inc.
7501 Saint Louis Ave
Skokie IL 60076
847 673-6720

**(G-19955)**
**AMMERAAL BELTECH INC**
7455 Saint Louis Ave (60076-4031)
**PHONE**.................................847 673-6720
Terry Roche, *President*
**EMP:** 80 **Privately Held**
**SIC: 3496** Conveyor belts
**HQ:** Ammeraal Beltech, Inc.
7501 Saint Louis Ave
Skokie IL 60076
847 673-6720

**(G-19956)**
**APOLLO MACHINE & MANUFACTURING**
7617 Parkside Ave (60077-2633)
**PHONE**.................................847 677-6444
**Fax:** 847 677-3040
Danicia Kaninovic, *President*
Danica Kaninovic, *President*
Danny Kainovic, *Treasurer*
**EMP:** 1
**SQ FT:** 5,000
**SALES:** 400K **Privately Held**
**SIC: 3599** 7692 3544 Machine shop, jobbing & repair; welding repair; special dies, tools, jigs & fixtures

**(G-19957)**
**APR GRAPHICS INC**
4825 Main St (60077-2508)
**PHONE**.................................847 329-7800
Wayne Romano, *President*
Mark Billman, *Manager*
Christine Romano, *Admin Sec*
**EMP:** 3
**SQ FT:** 1,200
**SALES (est):** 388.9K **Privately Held**
**SIC: 2791** 2796 Typesetting; platemaking services

**(G-19958)**
**AR-EN PARTY PRINTERS INC**
3416 Oakton St (60076-2951)
**PHONE**.................................847 673-7390
Gary Morrison, *President*

## Skokie - Cook County (G-19959)

▲ EMP: 28 EST: 1978
SQ FT: 9,500
SALES (est): 6.9MM Privately Held
SIC: 2679 5199 Paper products, converted; party favors, balloons, hats, etc.

**(G-19959)**
**ART OF SHAVING - FL LLC**
4999 Old Orchard Ctr M14 (60077-1467)
PHONE..................................(847) 568-0881
Paul Weinkauf, Branch Mgr
EMP: 3
SALES (corp-wide): 65.3B Publicly Held
SIC: 2844 Toilet preparations
HQ: The Art Of Shaving - Fl Llc
  6100 Blue Lagoon Dr # 150
  Miami FL 33126

**(G-19960)**
**ATA FINISHING CORP**
8225 Kimball Ave (60076-2990)
PHONE..................................847 677-8560
Fax: 847 677-8791
Ronald Anderson, President
Brian Anderson, Vice Pres
Goldie Anderson, Admin Sec
EMP: 9
SQ FT: 5,000
SALES (est): 660K Privately Held
SIC: 3471 2851 Finishing, metals or formed products; plating of metals or formed products; polishing, metals or formed products; paints & allied products

**(G-19961)**
**AUDIO VIDEO ELECTRONICS LLC**
Also Called: Bombay Electronics
7440 Long Ave (60077-3214)
PHONE..................................847 983-4761
Shethwala Fuzail, Mng Member
Mubashir Shethwala,
EMP: 2
SQ FT: 10,000
SALES: 3.1MM Privately Held
SIC: 3651 3612 Household audio & video equipment; power transformers, electric

**(G-19962)**
**BC INTERNATIONAL**
4909 Old Orchard Ctr (60077-1439)
PHONE..................................847 674-7384
Denny Hosch, Principal
EMP: 3
SALES (est): 153.4K Privately Held
SIC: 3221 5084 Bottles for packing, bottling & canning: glass; food industry machinery

**(G-19963)**
**BEST CUTTING DIE CO (PA)**
8080 Mccormick Blvd (60076-2919)
PHONE..................................847 675-5522
Fax: 847 675-5617
Edward J Porento Sr, President
Gary Porento, Principal
Marion Porento, Principal
Robert Porento, Principal
Valentina Vecerdea, Accounting Mgr
▲ EMP: 110 EST: 1966
SQ FT: 60,000
SALES (est): 23.7MM Privately Held
WEB: www.bestcuttingdie.com
SIC: 3544 Paper cutting dies

**(G-19964)**
**BIRNBERG MACHINERY INC**
4828 Main St (60077-2512)
PHONE..................................847 673-5242
Fax: 847 679-6600
Robert W Birnberg, President
Cynthia Haskins, Treasurer
▼ EMP: 4
SQ FT: 1,500
SALES (est): 1.1MM Privately Held
WEB: www.bagsealers.com
SIC: 5084 3565 3554 3552 Packaging machinery & equipment; packaging machinery; paper industries machinery; textile machinery; conveyors & conveying equipment

**(G-19965)**
**BLOCK STEEL CORP**
Samson Roll Formed Pdts Div
6101 Oakton St Ste 2 (60077-2678)
PHONE..................................847 965-6700
Darlene Brennan, Marketing Staff
Terry Felus, Branch Mgr
EMP: 20
SALES (corp-wide): 34.3MM Privately Held
WEB: www.blocksteel.com
SIC: 3312 Blast furnaces & steel mills; hot-rolled iron & steel products; tool & die steel
HQ: Block Steel Corp
  6101 Oakton St Ste 2
  Skokie IL 60077
  847 966-3000

**(G-19966)**
**BLUE RIBBON FASTENER COMPANY**
8220 Kimball Ave Frnt (60076-2976)
PHONE..................................847 673-1248
Walter Nathan, President
Wendy Nathan, Vice Pres
▲ EMP: 10
SQ FT: 13,000
SALES (est): 1.9MM Privately Held
WEB: www.blueribbonfastener.com
SIC: 3965 Fasteners

**(G-19967)**
**BP ELC MTRS PUMP & SVC INC**
8135 Ridgeway Ave (60076-3352)
PHONE..................................773 539-4343
Hasmij Papazion, President
Berg J Papazion, Vice Pres
EMP: 5
SQ FT: 4,200
SALES: 500K Privately Held
SIC: 7694 5999 5063 Electric motor repair; motors, electric; motors, electric

**(G-19968)**
**BR CONCEPTS INTERNATIONAL INC**
Also Called: BRC Manufacturing Co
7436 Kildare Ave (60076-3822)
PHONE..................................847 674-9481
Naum Ligum, President
EMP: 5
SALES: 5MM Privately Held
SIC: 3443 Metal parts

**(G-19969)**
**BRANDON MTDBA OKAERI NOODLE SP**
5432 Main St (60077-2030)
PHONE..................................847 966-0991
Robert Mita, Principal
EMP: 3
SALES (est): 154K Privately Held
SIC: 2098 Noodles (e.g. egg, plain & water), dry

**(G-19970)**
**BRIAN ROBERT AWNING CO**
8152 Lawndale Ave (60076-3322)
PHONE..................................847 679-1140
Fax: 847 679-1165
Robert Lucius, President
Joan Lucius, Admin Sec
EMP: 4
SQ FT: 5,000
SALES: 369.9K Privately Held
WEB: www.rbawning.com
SIC: 2394 Awnings, fabric: made from purchased materials

**(G-19971)**
**BRIGHTON COLLECTIBLES LLC**
4999 Old Orchard Ctr M17 (60077-1467)
PHONE..................................847 674-6719
Jerry Kohl, Branch Mgr
EMP: 45
SALES (corp-wide): 378.3MM Privately Held
SIC: 3111 Accessory products, leather
PA: Brighton Collectibles, Llc
  14022 Nelson Ave
  City Of Industry CA 91746
  626 961-9381

**(G-19972)**
**C D T MANUFACTURING INC**
8020 Monticello Ave (60076-3438)
PHONE..................................847 679-2361
Fax: 847 679-1829
Dieter Tantius, President
EMP: 4
SQ FT: 2,200
SALES (est): 468.6K Privately Held
SIC: 3541 3678 Machine tools, metal cutting type; electronic connectors

**(G-19973)**
**CAPITAL TOURS & TRAVEL INC**
Also Called: Capital Computer Consultants
8820 Skokie Blvd 105 (60077-2224)
PHONE..................................847 274-1138
Fax: 847 677-6130
Irina Finkler, Principal
EMP: 2 EST: 2010
SALES (est): 211.8K Privately Held
SIC: 4724 4725 7372 8748 Travel agencies; sightseeing tour companies; application computer software; business oriented computer software; systems engineering consultant, ex. computer or professional

**(G-19974)**
**CASTWELL PRODUCTS LLC**
7800 Austin Ave (60077-2641)
PHONE..................................847 966-9552
Charlie Hoffman, President
Michael Jacobs, Purch Agent
Ray Flynn, QC Mgr
Alfred Hembd, Manager
Anthony M Morrongiello, Manager
EMP: 250
SALES (est): 72.9MM Privately Held
WEB: www.castwell.com
SIC: 3321 Gray & ductile iron foundries

**(G-19975)**
**CELL-SAFE LIFE SCIENCES LLC**
7350 Ridgeway Ave (60076-4027)
PHONE..................................847 674-7075
Michael Dalton, CEO
EMP: 4
SALES (est): 149.2K Privately Held
SIC: 3841 Surgical & medical instruments

**(G-19976)**
**CENTRAL SHEET METAL PDTS INC**
7251 Linder Ave (60077-3216)
PHONE..................................773 583-2424
Fax: 847 676-9677
Sheldon Silverstein, President
Joel Silverstein, Vice Pres
Peter Silverstein, Vice Pres
Ronald Silver, Engineer
Claire Silverstein, Admin Sec
EMP: 25 EST: 1912
SQ FT: 18,000
SALES (est): 4.9MM Privately Held
WEB: www.centralsheet.com
SIC: 3444 2542 Sheet metalwork; casings, sheet metal; cabinets: show, display or storage: except wood

**(G-19977)**
**CENTURY FASTENERS & MCH CO INC**
Also Called: Gail Glasser Brickman
4901 Fairview Ln Ste 1 (60077-3523)
P.O. Box 681 (60076-0681)
PHONE..................................773 463-3900
Fax: 773 463-7474
Gail Brickman, CEO
Randy Gibbs, Sales Associate
Bernice Brickman, Administration
EMP: 12 EST: 1955
SQ FT: 10,000
SALES: 900K Privately Held
WEB: www.centuryfastener.com
SIC: 3452 3561 Nuts, metal; bolts, metal; screws, metal; pumps & pumping equipment

**(G-19978)**
**CHEM TRADE GLOBAL**
3832 Dobson St (60076-3717)
PHONE..................................847 675-2682
Ellen Jesse, President
▲ EMP: 3

SALES: 1MM Privately Held
SIC: 2899 Chemical supplies for foundries

**(G-19979)**
**CHICAGO JEWISH NEWS**
5301 Dempster St Ste 100 (60077-1800)
PHONE..................................847 966-0606
Fax: 847 966-1656
Joseph Aaron, Owner
Ann Yellon, Manager
EMP: 10
SQ FT: 1,900
SALES: 929K Privately Held
WEB: www.chicagojewishnews.com
SIC: 2711 8661 Newspapers, publishing & printing; religious organizations

**(G-19980)**
**CHICAGO PROTECTIVE APPAREL INC**
3425 Cleveland St (60076-2915)
PHONE..................................847 674-7900
Fax: 847 674-7906
Scott Sherman, President
John Merikoski, Vice Pres
Myrna Sherman, Vice Pres
Delfa Sanchez, Purchasing
Andrew Shalla, Comptroller
▲ EMP: 60 EST: 1913
SQ FT: 40,000
SALES (est): 10MM Privately Held
WEB: www.chicagoprotective.com
SIC: 2389 Men's miscellaneous accessories

**(G-19981)**
**CHICAGO SPORTS MEDIA INC**
Also Called: The Amateur Athlete Magazine
7842 Lincoln Ave (60077-3644)
PHONE..................................847 676-1900
Fax: 847 675-2903
Jerry Solomon, Marketing Mgr
Elliot Wineberg, Manager
EMP: 6
SQ FT: 1,000
SALES: 50K Privately Held
SIC: 2721 2741 Magazines: publishing only, not printed on site; miscellaneous publishing

**(G-19982)**
**CHOICE FURNISHINGS INC**
7518 Saint Louis Ave # 1053 (60076-4002)
PHONE..................................847 329-0004
Fax: 847 329-0050
Maurice Freedman, President
Judice Freedman, Admin Sec
▲ EMP: 10
SQ FT: 4,000
SALES (est): 1.1MM Privately Held
SIC: 2511 5021 Chairs, household, except upholstered: wood; chairs

**(G-19983)**
**CLOZ COMPANIES INC (PA)**
Also Called: Adco Amrcn Day Camp Outfitters
5550 Touhy Ave Ste 202 (60077-3254)
PHONE..................................773 247-8879
Fax: 773 247-7445
Michael Cohen, President
Randall Siegel, Senior VP
Janice Burke, Manager
EMP: 43
SQ FT: 22,000
SALES (est): 10.3MM Privately Held
WEB: www.cloz.com
SIC: 2329 2339 2369 2395 Men's & boys' sportswear & athletic clothing; women's & misses' outerwear; girls' & children's outerwear; embroidery & art needlework; screen printing; advertising specialties

**(G-19984)**
**CO-FAIR CORPORATION**
7301 Saint Louis Ave (60076-4029)
PHONE..................................847 626-1500
Fax: 847 626-4900
Robert Kaplan, President
EMP: 20
SQ FT: 25,000
SALES (est): 5.5MM Privately Held
SIC: 5033 2952 5211 Roofing, siding & insulation; roofing materials; lumber products

## GEOGRAPHIC SECTION
### Skokie - Cook County (G-20012)

**(G-19985)**
**COFAIR PRODUCTS INC**
7301 Saint Louis Ave (60076-4029)
PHONE..................847 626-1500
Robert Kaplan, *President*
Sheli Kaplan, *Manager*
**EMP:** 3
**SALES (est):** 2.1MM **Privately Held**
**SIC:** 5033 2952 1761 1751 Roofing & siding materials; roofing materials; roofing & gutter work; window & door installation & erection

**(G-19986)**
**CORALITE DENTAL PRODUCTS INC**
7227 Hamlin Ave (60076-3901)
PHONE..................847 679-3400
Mildred Goldstein, *President*
Herbert Pozen, *Vice Pres*
Don R Schlitz, *Sales Staff*
**EMP:** 3 **EST:** 1958
**SQ FT:** 65,000
**SALES (est):** 181K
**SALES (corp-wide):** 6.4MM **Privately Held**
**WEB:** www.bosworth.com
**SIC:** 3843 Dental equipment & supplies
**PA:** Harry J. Bosworth Company
   820 Davis St Ste 216
   Evanston IL 60201
   847 679-3400

**(G-19987)**
**COYLE PRINT GROUP INC**
5115 Suffield Ter (60077-1511)
P.O. Box 1045, Northbrook (60065-1045)
PHONE..................847 784-1080
Fax: 847 400-0797
Sean Coyle, *President*
Ed Coyle, *Vice Pres*
Pat Coyle, *Vice Pres*
**EMP:** 4 **EST:** 1999
**SQ FT:** 700
**SALES (est):** 244.9K **Privately Held**
**WEB:** www.coyleprint.com
**SIC:** 7389 2752 Printing broker; commercial printing, lithographic

**(G-19988)**
**CP MOYEN CO**
8157 Monticello Ave (60076-3325)
PHONE..................847 673-6866
Fax: 847 673-2812
Robert E Foss, *President*
Linda Wiesneth, *Vice Pres*
John Wiesneth, *Vice Pres*
**EMP:** 7 **EST:** 1930
**SQ FT:** 6,500
**SALES (est):** 3MM **Privately Held**
**WEB:** www.cpmoyen.com
**SIC:** 2891 Adhesives; epoxy adhesives

**(G-19989)**
**CUSTOM CUT EDM INC**
5423 Fargo Ave (60077-3211)
PHONE..................847 647-9500
**EMP:** 4
**SQ FT:** 4,500
**SALES:** 702K **Privately Held**
**SIC:** 3599 Custom Machine Shop Edm

**(G-19990)**
**DENOYER - GEPPERT SCIENCE CO**
7514 Saint Louis Ave (60076-4034)
P.O. Box 1727 (60076-8727)
PHONE..................800 621-1014
Mary Andros, *President*
Mark Gilbert, *Vice Pres*
Yongjoon Lee, *Vice Pres*
Robert Ortegon, *Purch Mgr*
John Duval, *Engineer*
▲ **EMP:** 30
**SQ FT:** 17,000
**SALES (est):** 3.8MM **Privately Held**
**WEB:** www.denoyer.com
**SIC:** 3999 Models, general, except toy

**(G-19991)**
**EDEN FUELS LLC**
Also Called: Eden's and Old Orchard's Shell
5025 Old Orchard Rd (60077-1019)
PHONE..................847 676-9470
Sherri L Maddox, *Principal*
**EMP:** 6
**SALES (est):** 724.5K **Privately Held**
**SIC:** 2869 7538 Fuels; general automotive repair shops

**(G-19992)**
**ELECTRIC VEHICLE TECHNOLOGIES**
7320 Linder Ave (60077-3217)
PHONE..................847 673-8330
Vincent V Roberti, *President*
Dave Haskell, *Vice Pres*
Joseph Roberti, *Admin Sec*
▲ **EMP:** 20
**SALES (est):** 1.3MM **Privately Held**
**WEB:** www.evtronics.com
**SIC:** 3625 3621 Motor starters & controllers, electric; motors, electric

**(G-19993)**
**ENGERT CO INC**
8103 Monticello Ave (60076-3325)
PHONE..................847 673-1633
Fax: 847 673-1881
Mark Heller, *President*
Gary Heller, *Vice Pres*
▼ **EMP:** 25 **EST:** 1934
**SALES (est):** 3.3MM **Privately Held**
**WEB:** www.handlelatch.com
**SIC:** 5072 3429 Hardware; manufactured hardware (general)

**(G-19994)**
**ENGILITY CORPORATION**
5600 Old Orchard Rd Bsmt (60077-1051)
PHONE..................847 583-1216
Anna Kakotariti, *Branch Mgr*
**EMP:** 5
**SALES (corp-wide):** 2B **Publicly Held**
**SIC:** 3812 Inertial guidance systems; navigational systems & instruments
**HQ:** Engility Corporation
   35 New Engld Busctr Dr200
   Andover MA 01810
   978 749-2100

**(G-19995)**
**ENVIROCOAT INC**
7440 Saint Louis Ave (60076-4032)
PHONE..................847 673-3649
Igor Murokh, *Owner*
**EMP:** 5
**SALES (est):** 456.8K **Privately Held**
**SIC:** 3471 3479 Finishing, metals or formed products; painting, coating & hot dipping

**(G-19996)**
**EVERLIGHTS INC**
8027 Lawndale Ave (60076-3435)
PHONE..................773 734-9873
Kelly Gallagher, *President*
Nancy Golding, *Manager*
Joann Maniquis, *Manager*
Mike Withkowski, *Manager*
**EMP:** 17 **EST:** 1995
**SQ FT:** 10,000
**SALES:** 5.9MM **Privately Held**
**WEB:** www.everlights.com
**SIC:** 3646 Fluorescent lighting fixtures, commercial

**(G-19997)**
**EXPERCOLOR INC**
Also Called: Triangle
3737 Chase Ave (60076-4008)
P.O. Box 1141, Northbrook (60065-1141)
PHONE..................773 465-3400
Harvey Saltzman, *President*
David Saltzman, *Vice Pres*
Robert Toton, *Plant Mgr*
Mike Mueller, *Prdtn Mgr*
Benjamin Schneider, *Design Engr*
**EMP:** 50 **EST:** 1954
**SQ FT:** 50,000
**SALES (est):** 3.9MM **Privately Held**
**SIC:** 2796 7336 Color separations for printing; commercial art & graphic design

**(G-19998)**
**EXPRESS PRINTING CTR OF LIBERT**
5125 Sherwin Ave (60077-3473)
PHONE..................847 675-0659
Fax: 847 675-0659
Roger Fischoff, *Mng Member*
**EMP:** 2
**SALES (est):** 204.3K **Privately Held**
**SIC:** 2752 Commercial printing, offset

**(G-19999)**
**FEDERAL-MOGUL CORPORATION**
7450 Mccormick Blvd (60076-4046)
PHONE..................847 674-7700
Fax: 847 568-1901
Peter Mlynarski, *Engineer*
Edgar Nunez, *Engineer*
Dave Ohlson, *Engineer*
Hoover Oliver, *Engineer*
Derek Data, *Manager*
**EMP:** 1500
**SALES (corp-wide):** 16.3B **Publicly Held**
**SIC:** 3053 Gaskets, packing & sealing devices
**HQ:** Federal-Mogul Llc
   27300 W 11 Mile Rd
   Southfield MI 48034

**(G-20000)**
**FLAHERTY INCORPORATED**
9047 Terminal Ave (60077-1570)
PHONE..................773 472-8456
Fax: 847 966-1072
Catherine Flaherty, *President*
**EMP:** 3
**SQ FT:** 15,000
**SALES (est):** 440.1K **Privately Held**
**SIC:** 2035 2099 Mustard, prepared (wet); food preparations

**(G-20001)**
**FORMULATIONS INC**
Also Called: Natural Formulations
8050 Ridgeway Ave (60076-3409)
PHONE..................847 674-9141
William Schwaber, *President*
**EMP:** 5
**SQ FT:** 10,000
**SALES:** 1MM **Privately Held**
**SIC:** 2841 2842 3471 2844 Soap & other detergents; ammonia, household; plating & polishing; toilet preparations

**(G-20002)**
**FRESENIUS KABI USA LLC**
The Illinois Scienc (60077)
PHONE..................847 983-7100
Michael Awe, *QC Mgr*
Brian Hoffman, *QC Mgr*
Nazario Odeste, *Research*
Chris Bryant, *Branch Mgr*
Bahadir Cakmak, *Manager*
**EMP:** 35
**SALES (corp-wide):** 31.1B **Privately Held**
**SIC:** 2834 Pharmaceutical preparations
**HQ:** Fresenius Kabi Usa, Llc
   3 Corporate Dr Ste 300
   Lake Zurich IL 60047
   847 550-2300

**(G-20003)**
**GAERTNER SCIENTIFIC CORP**
3650 Jarvis Ave (60076-4018)
PHONE..................847 673-5006
Fax: 847 673-5009
Rusty Kutko, *President*
Sharlene Kutko, *General Mgr*
Lucilla Abad, *Treasurer*
Chris Grajek, *Office Mgr*
Wsewolod A Popov, *Admin Sec*
**EMP:** 22 **EST:** 1896
**SQ FT:** 20,000
**SALES (est):** 3.7MM **Privately Held**
**WEB:** www.gartnerscientific.com
**SIC:** 3827 3826 Optical test & inspection equipment; analytical instruments

**(G-20004)**
**GODIVA CHOCOLATIER INC**
27 Old Orchard Rd Ste D25 (60077)
PHONE..................847 329-8620
Lissa Kiefer, *Manager*
**EMP:** 10 **Privately Held**
**WEB:** www.godiva.com
**SIC:** 2066 Chocolate
**HQ:** Godiva Chocolatier, Inc.
   333 W 34th St Fl 6
   New York NY 10001
   212 984-5900

**(G-20005)**
**GRACE PRINTING AND MAILING**
8130 Saint Louis Ave (60076-2925)
PHONE..................847 423-2100
**EMP:** 16 **EST:** 2010
**SALES (est):** 2.4MM **Privately Held**
**SIC:** 2759 Commercial printing

**(G-20006)**
**GREAT LAKES ART FOUNDRY INC**
Also Called: Great Lakes Metal Works
7336 Ridgeway Ave (60076-4027)
PHONE..................847 213-0800
**EMP:** 4
**SALES (est):** 360K **Privately Held**
**WEB:** www.greatlakesmetalworks.com
**SIC:** 2491 3411 3443 Wood preserving; metal cans; fabricated plate work (boiler shop)

**(G-20007)**
**GROVER WELDING COMPANY**
9120 Terminal Ave (60077-1514)
PHONE..................847 966-3119
Fax: 847 966-3164
Lawrence Grover, *President*
Linda Grover, *CFO*
**EMP:** 5 **EST:** 1934
**SQ FT:** 3,000
**SALES (est):** 643.1K **Privately Held**
**SIC:** 7692 5082 3441 Welding repair; general construction machinery & equipment; fabricated structural metal

**(G-20008)**
**H L CLAUSING INC**
8038 Monticello Ave (60076-3438)
PHONE..................847 676-0330
Fax: 847 676-2930
HI Clausing, *President*
Patricia Clausing, *Manager*
**EMP:** 7 **EST:** 1927
**SQ FT:** 5,500
**SALES:** 900K **Privately Held**
**WEB:** www.clausing.com
**SIC:** 3827 Mirrors, optical

**(G-20009)**
**HADCO TOOL CO LLC**
8105 Monticello Ave (60076-3325)
PHONE..................847 677-6263
Fax: 847 677-8510
Steve Salbeck, *President*
**EMP:** 4 **EST:** 1955
**SQ FT:** 3,500
**SALES (est):** 370K **Privately Held**
**SIC:** 3599 Machine shop, jobbing & repair

**(G-20010)**
**HANGABLES INC**
7237 Saint Louis Ave (60076-4047)
P.O. Box 4572 (60076-4572)
PHONE..................847 673-9770
Roberta Schnepper, *Partner*
Alan Schnepper, *Partner*
**EMP:** 11
**SQ FT:** 4,200
**SALES (est):** 1MM **Privately Held**
**WEB:** www.hangables.net
**SIC:** 3999 3315 3089 2396 Novelties, bric-a-brac & hobby kits; hangers (garment), wire; plastic processing; automotive & apparel trimmings

**(G-20011)**
**HARIG MANUFACTURING CORP**
5423 Fargo Ave (60077-3211)
PHONE..................847 647-9500
Fax: 847 647-8351
Theodore H Eckert, *Ch of Bd*
Theodore M Eckert, *Vice Pres*
Alice Edlbauer, *Manager*
▲ **EMP:** 26 **EST:** 1937
**SQ FT:** 55,000
**SALES (est):** 5.7MM **Privately Held**
**SIC:** 3545 3544 3469 Tools & accessories for machine tools; die sets for metal stamping (presses); jigs & fixtures; stamping metal for the trade

**(G-20012)**
**HARRIS SKOKIE**
9731 Skokie Blvd (60077-1383)
PHONE..................847 675-6300

# Skokie - Cook County (G-20013)

David Langebach, *Principal*
John Woo, *Manager*
**EMP:** 3
**SALES (est):** 196.6K  **Privately Held**
**SIC: 3944**  Banks, toy

**(G-20013)**
### HY SPRECKMAN & SONS INC
9725 Woods Dr Unit 1302  (60077-4455)
**PHONE**.................................312 236-2173
**Fax:** 312 236-5675
Hyman Spreckman, *President*
Jeffrey Spreckman, *Vice Pres*
Steven Spreckman, *Vice Pres*
Shabbir Poonawalla, *Accountant*
Sakina Khambati, *Bookkeeper*
▼ **EMP:** 10
**SQ FT:** 2,500
**SALES (est):** 1.2MM  **Privately Held**
**SIC: 3911** 5094  Jewel settings & mountings, precious metal; diamonds (gems)

**(G-20014)**
### HYDRO INK CORP
7331 Monticello Ave  (60076-4024)
**PHONE**.................................847 674-0057
**EMP:** 5 **EST:** 1988
**SQ FT:** 5,000
**SALES:** 610K  **Privately Held**
**SIC: 3952** 2893  Mfg Lead Pencils/Art Goods Mfg Printing Ink

**(G-20015)**
### INDUSTRIAL MARKET PLACE
Also Called: Imp
7842 Lincoln Ave Ste 100  (60077-3644)
**PHONE**.................................847 676-1900
Joel Wineberg, *President*
Adrienne Gallender, *Vice Pres*
Harvey Wineberg, *Treasurer*
Eliot Wineberg, *Finance Mgr*
Kathy Hebel, *Bookkeeper*
**EMP:** 25 **EST:** 1951
**SQ FT:** 6,000
**SALES (est):** 2.3MM  **Privately Held**
**WEB:** www.industrialmktpl.com
**SIC: 2721**  Trade journals: publishing only, not printed on site

**(G-20016)**
### INTEGRATED DNA TECH MODEM
8930 Gross Point Rd  (60077-1854)
**PHONE**.................................847 745-1700
Sweet Jeffrey, *Principal*
Nathaniel Bailey, *Admin Asst*
**EMP:** 12 **EST:** 2010
**SALES (est):** 1.6MM  **Privately Held**
**SIC: 3661**  Modems

**(G-20017)**
### INTERTECH DEVELOPMENT COMPANY
7401 Linder Ave  (60077-3220)
**PHONE**.................................847 679-3377
**Fax:** 847 679-3391
Jacques E Hoffmann, *President*
David Balke, *Engineer*
Andrzej Jakubek, *Engineer*
Gerald Sim, *Engineer*
Alan Wojciechowski, *Project Engr*
**EMP:** 52
**SQ FT:** 25,000
**SALES:** 10.1MM  **Privately Held**
**WEB:** www.intertechdevelopment.com
**SIC: 3569**  Assembly machines, non-metal-working

**(G-20018)**
### INVENTIVE MFG INC
5423 Fargo Ave  (60077-3211)
**PHONE**.................................847 647-9500
**Fax:** 847 677-9755
Theodore H Eckert Sr, *President*
Kevork Narinian, *Manager*
Theodore H Eckert Jr, *Admin Sec*
**EMP:** 10 **EST:** 1945
**SQ FT:** 10,000
**SALES (est):** 1.3MM  **Privately Held**
**SIC: 3599** 3544  Electrical discharge machining (EDM); machine shop, jobbing & repair; special dies, tools, jigs & fixtures

**(G-20019)**
### JEWEL OSCO INC
Also Called: Jewel-Osco 3465
9449 Skokie Blvd  (60077-1317)
**PHONE**.................................847 677-3331
**Fax:** 847 673-1721
John Colton, *Manager*
**EMP:** 152
**SALES (corp-wide):** 58.8B  **Privately Held**
**WEB:** www.jewelosco.com
**SIC: 5411** 2052 2051  Supermarkets, chain; cookies & crackers; bread, cake & related products
**HQ:** Jewel Osco, Inc.
150 E Pierce Rd Ste 200
Itasca IL 60143
630 948-6000

**(G-20020)**
### K-B-K TOOL AND MFG INC
7309 Monticello Ave  (60076-4024)
**PHONE**.................................847 674-3636
**Fax:** 847 674-4003
Kenneth L Hedeen, *Owner*
▲ **EMP:** 15
**SQ FT:** 6,000
**SALES (est):** 2.8MM  **Privately Held**
**WEB:** www.kbktool.com
**SIC: 3599** 3544  Machine shop, jobbing & repair; special dies, tools, jigs & fixtures

**(G-20021)**
### KAFKO INTERNATIONAL LTD
3555 Howard St  (60076-4052)
**PHONE**.................................847 763-0333
Nicholas Kafkis, *Chairman*
Bob Kafkis, *Vice Pres*
George Kafkis, *Vice Pres*
Rick Morgando, *Sales Executive*
Beth Raebel, *Office Mgr*
◆ **EMP:** 35
**SALES (est):** 10.1MM  **Privately Held**
**WEB:** www.kafkointl.com
**SIC: 2819** 2842 4783  Industrial inorganic chemicals; specialty cleaning, polishes & sanitation goods; packing goods for shipping

**(G-20022)**
### KECKLEY MANUFACTURING COMPANY
3400 Cleveland St  (60076-2916)
**PHONE**.................................847 674-8422
Philip K Miller, *President*
Donald S Miller, *Corp Secy*
**EMP:** 50 **EST:** 1914
**SQ FT:** 40,000
**SALES (est):** 7.7MM  **Privately Held**
**SIC: 3491** 3494  Pressure valves & regulators, industrial; valves & pipe fittings
**PA:** O. C. Keckley Company
3400 Cleveland St
Skokie IL 60076
847 674-8422

**(G-20023)**
### L L BEAN INC
4999 Old Orchard Ctr F18  (60077-1455)
**PHONE**.................................847 568-3600
**EMP:** 4
**SALES (corp-wide):** 1.1B  **Privately Held**
**SIC: 3949**  Sporting & athletic goods
**PA:** L. L. Bean, Inc.
15 Casco St
Freeport ME 04033
207 552-2000

**(G-20024)**
### LAKE SHORE PRINTING
Also Called: Sir Speedy
4124 Oakton St Apt C  (60076-3267)
**PHONE**.................................847 679-4110
**Fax:** 847 679-0483
Don Defrain Jr, *President*
Deena Defrain, *Admin Sec*
**EMP:** 5
**SQ FT:** 1,250
**SALES (est):** 300K  **Privately Held**
**WEB:** www.lakeshoreprinting.com
**SIC: 2752** 2791 2789  Commercial printing, lithographic; typesetting; bookbinding & related work

**(G-20025)**
### LANZATECH INC (HQ)
Also Called: Freedom Pines
8045 Lamon Ave Ste 400  (60077-5318)
**PHONE**.................................630 439-3050
Jennifer Holmgren, *CEO*
Carl Wolf, *Business Mgr*
Jean Paul Michel, *Exec VP*
Mark Burton, *Vice Pres*
Ken C Lai, *Vice Pres*
▲ **EMP:** 80
**SQ FT:** 1,500
**SALES (est):** 24.4MM
**SALES (corp-wide):** 4.1MM  **Privately Held**
**WEB:** www.lanzatech.com
**SIC: 2869**  Industrial organic chemicals
**PA:** Lanzatech New Zealand Limited
24 Balfour Rd
Auckland 1052
930 421-10

**(G-20026)**
### LASER REPRODUCTIONS INC
Also Called: Care Creations
8228 Mccormick Blvd  (60076-2921)
**PHONE**.................................847 410-0397
**Fax:** 847 933-3496
Cary Green, *President*
◆ **EMP:** 20
**SQ FT:** 30,000
**SALES (est):** 6.2MM  **Privately Held**
**WEB:** www.laserreproductions.com
**SIC: 5084** 3555  Printing trades machinery, equipment & supplies; printing trades machinery

**(G-20027)**
### LAUREL METAL PRODUCTS INC
3500 W Touhy Ave  (60076-6218)
P.O. Box 14, Glenview  (60025-0014)
**PHONE**.................................847 674-0064
**Fax:** 847 674-0094
Patrick Kent, *President*
Chip Kent, *Vice Pres*
**EMP:** 20 **EST:** 1960
**SQ FT:** 17,500
**SALES (est):** 4.1MM  **Privately Held**
**WEB:** www.laurelmetal.com
**SIC: 3581**  Automatic vending machines; mechanisms for coin-operated machines

**(G-20028)**
### LBL LIGHTING LLC (PA)
7400 Linder Ave  (60077-3219)
**PHONE**.................................708 755-2100
**Fax:** 708 755-3443
Joan M Stone, *Corp Secy*
Tom Sargeant, *Vice Pres*
Steve Sorenso, *Vice Pres*
Don Clark, *Mfg Staff*
Jeremy Friedman, *Regl Sales Mgr*
▲ **EMP:** 12 **EST:** 1971
**SQ FT:** 7,000
**SALES (est):** 3.1MM  **Privately Held**
**SIC: 3648** 5063  Lighting fixtures, except electric: residential; lighting fixtures

**(G-20029)**
### LETTERING SPECIALISTS INC
8020 Lawndale Ave  (60076-3436)
**PHONE**.................................847 674-3414
**Fax:** 847 674-9571
Robert L Narens, *President*
Frank D Billeck, *Corp Secy*
David Narens, *Controller*
**EMP:** 10
**SQ FT:** 5,000
**SALES (est):** 830K  **Privately Held**
**WEB:** www.asigncompany.com
**SIC: 3993**  Signs & advertising specialties

**(G-20030)**
### LITTLE JOURNEYS LIMITED
7914 Kildare Ave  (60076-3518)
**PHONE**.................................847 677-0350
David S Lee, *President*
Davids Lee, *President*
Ronanna Berk, *Vice Pres*
**EMP:** 2

**SALES (est):** 230K  **Privately Held**
**SIC: 2339** 2369 5023  Women's & misses' outerwear; women's & misses' jackets & coats, except sportswear; girls' & children's outerwear; coats: girls', children's & infants'; decorative home furnishings & supplies

**(G-20031)**
### LOVATT & RADCLIFFE LTD
9635 Keystone Ave  (60076-1134)
**PHONE**.................................815 568-9797
Jeanette Peterlin, *President*
**EMP:** 2
**SALES:** 400K  **Privately Held**
**SIC: 3429** 5087 5251 7699  Locks or lock sets; locksmith equipment & supplies; door locks & lock sets; locksmith shop

**(G-20032)**
### LUTAMAR ELECTRICAL ASSEMBLIES
8030 Ridgeway Ave  (60076-3409)
**PHONE**.................................847 679-5400
**Fax:** 847 679-0452
Ida Wilk, *President*
Carl J Wilk, *Vice Pres*
Karen Kotsovetis, *Office Mgr*
▲ **EMP:** 30
**SQ FT:** 10,000
**SALES (est):** 2.9MM  **Privately Held**
**SIC: 3644** 3699 3643  Terminal boards; electrical equipment & supplies; current-carrying wiring devices

**(G-20033)**
### MARK COLLINS
Also Called: Sign-A-Rama
4443 Oakton St  (60076-3222)
**PHONE**.................................847 324-5500
**Fax:** 847 324-5502
Mark Collins, *President*
**EMP:** 3
**SQ FT:** 1,200
**SALES (est):** 240K  **Privately Held**
**SIC: 3993**  Signs & advertising specialties

**(G-20034)**
### MAYA ROMANOFF CORPORATION (PA)
3435 Madison St  (60076-2928)
**PHONE**.................................773 465-6909
Maya Romanoff, *President*
Joyce Romanoff, *President*
Sara Lamoureux, *Editor*
Monica Bauman, *Controller*
Carl Blando, *Sales Dir*
▲ **EMP:** 41
**SQ FT:** 18,000
**SALES (est):** 6.6MM  **Privately Held**
**SIC: 2221** 2211  Wall covering fabrics, manmade fiber & silk; upholstery, tapestry & wall coverings: cotton

**(G-20035)**
### MAYFAIR GAMES INC (PA)
8060 Saint Louis Ave  (60076-2923)
**PHONE**.................................847 677-6655
**Fax:** 847 677-6253
Pete Fenlon, *CEO*
Larry Roznai, *President*
Bridget Roznai, *Office Mgr*
Robert Carty, *Director*
Moren Roznai, *Executive Asst*
▲ **EMP:** 22
**SQ FT:** 18,000
**SALES:** 5MM  **Privately Held**
**WEB:** www.mayfairgames.com
**SIC: 3944**  Games, toys & children's vehicles

**(G-20036)**
### MDM COMMUNICATIONS INC
8737 Central Park Ave  (60076-2304)
**PHONE**.................................708 582-9667
Rick Arons, *Principal*
**EMP:** 3
**SALES (est):** 207.5K  **Privately Held**
**SIC: 2721**  Trade journals: publishing only, not printed on site

**(G-20037)**
### METRO TOOL COMPANY
3650 Oakton St  (60076-3494)
**PHONE**.................................847 673-6790
**Fax:** 847 673-0247

# GEOGRAPHIC SECTION
## Skokie - Cook County (G-20064)

Ramandahi Patel, *President*
Nigel Groves, *Vice Pres*
Fred Metzger, *Vice Pres*
Mildred Sachs, *Bookkeeper*
**EMP:** 3 **EST:** 1965
**SQ FT:** 3,600
**SALES (est):** 472.5K **Privately Held**
**SIC:** 3544 3542 Industrial molds; machine tools, metal forming type

**(G-20038)**
**MICRO CRAFT MANUFACTURING CO**
7248 Saint Louis Ave (60076-4028)
**PHONE**.................................847 679-2022
**Fax:** 847 679-2025
Jewel Mc Wherter, *President*
Debra Mc Wherter, *Vice Pres*
Debra McWherter, *Vice Pres*
**EMP:** 10
**SQ FT:** 5,000
**SALES (est):** 1.4MM **Privately Held**
**SIC:** 3599 Machine shop, jobbing & repair

**(G-20039)**
**MIDLAND MANUFACTURING CORP**
7733 Gross Point Rd (60077-2615)
**PHONE**.................................847 677-0333
**Fax:** 847 677-0138
Thomas Zant, *President*
Kevin Cook, *Vice Pres*
Tom Noonan, *CFO*
▲ **EMP:** 120 **EST:** 1994
**SQ FT:** 100,000
**SALES (est):** 39.2MM
**SALES (corp-wide):** 6.7B **Publicly Held**
**WEB:** www.midlandmfg.net
**SIC:** 3494 3715 3731 3545 Valves & pipe fittings; truck trailers; barges, building & repairing; machine tool accessories; industrial valves
**HQ:** Dover Artificial Lift International, Llc
3005 Highland Pkwy
Downers Grove IL 60515
630 743-2563

**(G-20040)**
**MIDWEST TROPICAL ENTPS INC**
3420 W Touhy Ave (60076-6217)
**PHONE**.................................847 679-6666
**Fax:** 847 679-6669
Ken Burnett, *President*
Mike Burnett, *Vice Pres*
Susan Burnett, *Vice Pres*
Gerson Garcia, *Engineer*
Michael Burnett, *Sales Staff*
**EMP:** 20
**SQ FT:** 20,000
**SALES (est):** 3.5MM **Privately Held**
**WEB:** www.midwest-tropical.com
**SIC:** 3231 3089 Aquariums & reflectors, glass; aquarium accessories, plastic

**(G-20041)**
**MODERN TRADE COMMUNICATIONS (PA)**
Also Called: Metal Construction News
8833 Gross Point Rd # 308 (60077-1859)
**PHONE**.................................847 674-2200
**Fax:** 847 674-3676
John S Lawrence, *CEO*
John Lawrence, *President*
Blanca Arteaga, *Opers Mgr*
Quentin Brown, *Prdtn Mgr*
Tina Lawrence, *Treasurer*
**EMP:** 10
**SQ FT:** 3,200
**SALES (est):** 1.5MM **Privately Held**
**WEB:** www.metalarchitecture.com
**SIC:** 2721 2741 2752 Trade journals: publishing only, not printed on site; directories: publishing only, not printed on site; cards, lithographed

**(G-20042)**
**MULLEN CIRCLE BRAND INC**
3514 W Touhy Ave (60076-6218)
P.O. Box 8487, Northfield (60093-8487)
**PHONE**.................................847 676-1880
Kenneth Reed, *President*
Shirley R Reed, *Vice Pres*
**EMP:** 10
**SQ FT:** 40,000
**SALES (est):** 1.9MM **Privately Held**
**WEB:** www.circlecut.com
**SIC:** 2992 Oils & greases, blending & compounding; rust arresting compounds, animal or vegetable oil base

**(G-20043)**
**MULTIPLE METAL PRODUCTION**
8030 Lawndale Ave (60076-3436)
**PHONE**.................................847 679-1510
Joe Clouser, *Owner*
**EMP:** 4
**SALES (est):** 400K **Privately Held**
**SIC:** 3312 Tool & die steel

**(G-20044)**
**NATIONWIDE NEWS MONITOR**
9239 Kilpatrick Ave (60076-1530)
**PHONE**.................................312 424-4224
**EMP:** 3
**SALES (est):** 127.1K **Privately Held**
**SIC:** 2711 Newspapers, publishing & printing

**(G-20045)**
**NOBILITY CORPORATION**
5404 Touhy Ave (60077-3232)
**PHONE**.................................847 677-3204
Bruce E Creger, *Ch of Bd*
Richard F Wharton, *President*
▲ **EMP:** 30
**SQ FT:** 30,000
**SALES (est):** 3MM **Privately Held**
**WEB:** www.safcol.com
**SIC:** 3678 Electronic connectors

**(G-20046)**
**NORFOLK MEDICAL PRODUCTS INC**
Also Called: Access Technologies
7350 Ridgeway Ave (60076-4027)
**PHONE**.................................847 674-7075
**Fax:** 847 674-7066
Michael J Dalton, *President*
Jordan Dalton, *COO*
Jordan M Dalton, *COO*
Martin Christian, *Engineer*
Natan Pheil, *Development*
**EMP:** 15 **EST:** 1981
**SQ FT:** 11,000
**SALES (est):** 2.5MM **Privately Held**
**WEB:** www.norfolkaccess.com
**SIC:** 3842 8731 Implants, surgical; commercial physical research

**(G-20047)**
**NUMAT TECHNOLOGIES INC**
8025 Lamon Ave Ste 43 (60077-5319)
**PHONE**.................................301 233-5329
Benjamin Hernandez, *CEO*
**EMP:** 4 **EST:** 2012
**SALES (est):** 675.1K **Privately Held**
**SIC:** 2869 Laboratory chemicals, organic

**(G-20048)**
**O C KECKLEY COMPANY (PA)**
3400 Cleveland St (60076-2900)
P.O. Box 67 (60076-0067)
**PHONE**.................................847 674-8422
**Fax:** 847 674-2106
Ross Miller, *President*
Donald S Miller, *Corp Secy*
Keith Lankton, *Vice Pres*
Debbie Cook, *Office Mgr*
▲ **EMP:** 50 **EST:** 1914
**SQ FT:** 45,000
**SALES (est):** 7.7MM **Privately Held**
**SIC:** 3625 5085 3491 3494 Relays & industrial controls; valves & fittings; pressure valves & regulators, industrial; valves & pipe fittings

**(G-20049)**
**OCTURA MODELS INC**
7351 Hamlin Ave (60076-3998)
**PHONE**.................................847 674-7351
**Fax:** 847 674-7363
Thomas Perzentka, *President*
Ruth Perzentka, *Corp Secy*
**EMP:** 3 **EST:** 1954
**SQ FT:** 2,400
**SALES (est):** 325.8K **Privately Held**
**SIC:** 3944 Boat & ship models, toy & hobby

**(G-20050)**
**ONEIMS PRINTING LLC**
8833 Groil Pt Rd Ste 202 (60077)
**PHONE**.................................773 297-2050
Solomon Thimothy, *Principal*
**EMP:** 2
**SALES (est):** 291.2K **Privately Held**
**SIC:** 2752 Commercial printing, lithographic

**(G-20051)**
**OPEN WATERS SEAFOOD COMPANY**
5010 Howard St (60077-2829)
**PHONE**.................................847 329-8585
Leo Dy, *President*
**EMP:** 5
**SALES (est):** 318.7K **Privately Held**
**SIC:** 2092 Seafoods, frozen: prepared

**(G-20052)**
**P S GREETINGS INC**
4901 Main St (60077-2515)
**PHONE**.................................847 673-7255
Mark McCracken, *Branch Mgr*
**EMP:** 15
**SALES (corp-wide):** 44.7MM **Privately Held**
**WEB:** www.psgreetings.com
**SIC:** 2771 Greeting cards
**PA:** P. S. Greetings, Inc.
5730 N Tripp Ave
Chicago IL 60646
708 831-5340

**(G-20053)**
**PATRIN PHARMA INC**
7817 Babb Ave (60077-3636)
P.O. Box 1481 (60076-8481)
**PHONE**.................................800 936-3088
Jay Trivedi, *President*
Smita Quinn, *Admin Sec*
**EMP:** 25
**SALES (est):** 4.1MM **Privately Held**
**SIC:** 2834 Pharmaceutical preparations

**(G-20054)**
**PERMOBIL INC**
Also Called: Prairie Seating
7515 Linder Ave (60077-3223)
**PHONE**.................................847 568-0001
**Fax:** 847 568-0002
**EMP:** 10
**SALES (corp-wide):** 6.7B **Privately Held**
**SIC:** 3842 Orthopedic appliances; wheelchairs
**HQ:** Permobil, Inc.
300 Duke Dr
Lebanon TN 37090
615 547-1889

**(G-20055)**
**PINOY MONTHLY**
5323 Wright Ter (60077-2073)
**PHONE**.................................847 329-1073
Mariano Santos, *Owner*
**EMP:** 3
**SALES (est):** 175.6K **Privately Held**
**SIC:** 2711 Newspapers, publishing & printing

**(G-20056)**
**POLYERA CORPORATION**
8025 Lamon Ave Ste 43 (60077-5319)
**PHONE**.................................847 677-7517
Ed Zschau, *Ch of Bd*
Philippe Inagaki, *President*
Brenden Florez, *General Mgr*
Chung Chin Hsiao, *Senior VP*
Prakash Ramachandran, *Admin Sec*
**EMP:** 25
**SQ FT:** 10,000
**SALES (est):** 5.4MM **Privately Held**
**SIC:** 3679 Electronic circuits

**(G-20057)**
**POWER GRAPHICS & PRINT INC**
7345 Monticello Ave (60076-4024)
**PHONE**.................................847 568-1808
Phat Chung, *President*
**EMP:** 5
**SQ FT:** 2,600
**SALES (est):** 557.2K **Privately Held**
**SIC:** 2752 Commercial printing, lithographic

**(G-20058)**
**PRECISION MACHINING & TOOL CO**
7341 Monticello Ave (60076-4024)
**PHONE**.................................847 674-7111
**Fax:** 847 674-7161
Alex Pagakis, *President*
**EMP:** 3
**SALES (est):** 140K **Privately Held**
**SIC:** 3599 Machine shop, jobbing & repair

**(G-20059)**
**PRIKOS & BECKER LLC**
8109 Lawndale Ave (60076-3321)
**PHONE**.................................847 675-3910
Max Wakeman, *President*
William R Becker, *Vice Pres*
Michael L George, *Vice Pres*
**EMP:** 55
**SQ FT:** 20,000
**SALES (est):** 10.4MM **Privately Held**
**SIC:** 3469 Metal stampings
**PA:** Blackland Group, Llc
2351 W Northwest Hwy # 1130
Dallas TX 75220
972 980-5970

**(G-20060)**
**PRINCESS FOODS INC**
Also Called: Sangam
8100 Central Park Ave (60076-2907)
**PHONE**.................................847 933-1820
Babu Dalal, *President*
Kamlesh Shah, *Vice Pres*
Varsha Dalal, *Treasurer*
Ketki Shah, *Admin Sec*
▲ **EMP:** 10
**SQ FT:** 2,500
**SALES (est):** 1MM **Privately Held**
**WEB:** www.sangamam.com
**SIC:** 2064 2099 Candy & other confectionery products; food preparations

**(G-20061)**
**PRINT XPRESS**
8058 Lincoln Ave (60077-3613)
**PHONE**.................................847 677-5555
**Fax:** 847 677-5757
Sam Eckerling, *President*
Samuel Eckerling, *President*
**EMP:** 4
**SQ FT:** 2,000
**SALES (est):** 636.2K **Privately Held**
**SIC:** 2752 2791 Commercial printing, offset; typesetting, computer controlled

**(G-20062)**
**PROCRAFT ENGRAVING INC**
8241 Christiana Ave (60076-2910)
**PHONE**.................................847 673-1500
**Fax:** 847 673-1505
Milan Milojevic, *President*
Kenneth Schutz, *Vice Pres*
**EMP:** 4
**SQ FT:** 2,100
**SALES (est):** 290K **Privately Held**
**SIC:** 3544 7389 Special dies & tools; engraving service

**(G-20063)**
**PROFILE NETWORK INC**
Also Called: Sports Profiles Plus
4709 Golf Rd Ste 807 (60076-1258)
**PHONE**.................................847 673-0592
**Fax:** 847 673-0633
Lisa Levine, *President*
Paula Blaine, *Vice Pres*
**EMP:** 25
**SQ FT:** 3,000
**SALES (est):** 1.6MM **Privately Held**
**WEB:** www.sportsprofilesplus.com
**SIC:** 7941 2721 Professional & semi-professional sports clubs; magazines: publishing only, not printed on site

**(G-20064)**
**PROMARK ASSOCIATES INC**
3856 Oakton St Ste 250 (60076-3454)
**PHONE**.................................847 676-1894
Jeffrey L Roseberry, *President*
Bernice Valantinas, *Corp Secy*
Carolyn Wangelyn, *Manager*

## Skokie - Cook County (G-20065)

EMP: 5
SQ FT: 33,300
SALES: 800K **Privately Held**
WEB: www.promarkassociates.com
SIC: **3564** 8748 Air purification equipment; business consulting

### (G-20065)
### PROMPT MOTOR REWINDING SERVICE
7509 Keystone Ave (60076-3928)
PHONE..................................847 675-7155
Rick Joseph, *CEO*
EMP: 5
SALES (est): 257.6K **Privately Held**
SIC: **7694** Rewinding stators

### (G-20066)
### PROTECTION CONTROLS INC
Also Called: Protectofire
7317 Lawndale Ave (60076-4055)
P.O. Box 287 (60076-0287)
PHONE..................................773 763-3110
Fax: 847 674-7009
Bruce G Yates, *President*
Douglas H Yates, *Corp Secy*
Ray Ostrowski, *Director*
EMP: 30
SQ FT: 27,000
SALES (est): 5.4MM **Privately Held**
WEB: www.protectioncontrolsinc.com
SIC: **3613** 3823 3699 3625 Control panels, electric; industrial instrmnts msrmnt display/control process variable; electrical equipment & supplies; relays & industrial controls

### (G-20067)
### PUBLISHERS ROW
Also Called: Varda Graphics
9001 Keating Ave (60076-1505)
PHONE..................................847 568-0593
Alexander Gendler, *Owner*
EMP: 11
SALES (est): 711.1K **Privately Held**
WEB: www.publishersrow.com
SIC: **7372** Publishers' computer software

### (G-20068)
### R E BURKE ROOFING CO INC
Also Called: Burke R E Roofing & Shtmtl Co
7667 Gross Point Rd (60077-2629)
PHONE..................................847 675-5010
Fax: 847 675-6990
Robert E Burke Jr, *President*
EMP: 15 EST: 1965
SQ FT: 12,000
SALES (est): 2MM **Privately Held**
SIC: **1761** 3444 2952 Roofing contractor; sheet metalwork; sheet metalwork; asphalt felts & coatings

### (G-20069)
### RAND MCNALLY & COMPANY
9855 Woods Dr (60077-1127)
PHONE..................................847 329-8100
Peter Nolan, *Ch of Bd*
Robert S Apatoff, *President*
Sharon Kohn, *Counsel*
Jim Rodi, *Senior VP*
Robert P Denaro, *Vice Pres*
▲ EMP: 262 EST: 1856
SALES (est): 29.4MM
SALES (corp-wide): 3.9B **Privately Held**
WEB: www.randmcally.com
SIC: **2741** 5045 Maps: publishing only, not printed on site; atlases: publishing only, not printed on site; globe covers (maps): publishing only, not printed on site; computer software
PA: Patriarch Partners, Llc
  1 Liberty Plz Rm 3500
  New York NY 10006
  212 825-0550

### (G-20070)
### RAND MCNALLY INTERNATIONAL CO
9855 Woods Dr (60077-1127)
PHONE..................................847 329-8100
Andrzej Wrobel, *President*
EMP: 200

SALES (est): 6.4MM **Privately Held**
SIC: **2741** Maps: publishing only, not printed on site; atlases: publishing only, not printed on site; globe covers (maps): publishing only, not printed on site

### (G-20071)
### RAW THRILLS INC
5441 Fargo Ave (60077-3211)
PHONE..................................847 679-8373
Eugene Jarvis, *Principal*
Bob Yoest, *Engineer*
Matt Davis, *Design Engr*
Joshua Sharpe, *CFO*
Jeff Tash, *Marketing Staff*
◆ EMP: 60
SQ FT: 22,000
SALES: 58.8MM **Privately Held**
WEB: www.rawthrills.com
SIC: **3944** Video game machines, except coin-operated

### (G-20072)
### RAYES BOILER & WELDING LTD
8252 Christiana Ave (60076-2911)
PHONE..................................847 675-6655
Raman Rayes, *Owner*
EMP: 5
SALES (est): 611.1K **Privately Held**
SIC: **3443** 7699 Fabricated plate work (boiler shop); boiler repair shop

### (G-20073)
### RELIABLE MAIL SERVICES INC
5116 Grove St (60077-1541)
PHONE..................................847 677-6245
Fax: 847 967-9676
Mark Conton, *President*
EMP: 15
SQ FT: 32,000
SALES (est): 2.5MM **Privately Held**
WEB: www.rmsmail.com
SIC: **7331** 2752 Mailing service; commercial printing, lithographic

### (G-20074)
### REMCO TECHNOLOGY INC
7441 Channel Rd (60076-4042)
PHONE..................................847 329-8090
Ben Boris Schwartz, *President*
Eugeane Rapoporg, *Vice Pres*
Tuman Tseren, *Manager*
EMP: 12
SQ FT: 8,000
SALES (est): 1MM **Privately Held**
WEB: www.remco-tech.com
SIC: **3086** Insulation or cushioning material, foamed plastic

### (G-20075)
### REZNIK INSTRUMENT CO
7337 Lawndale Ave (60076-4021)
PHONE..................................847 673-3444
Fax: 847 673-3447
Ben Reznik, *President*
Edith Reznik, *Admin Sec*
EMP: 4
SQ FT: 5,600
SALES (est): 521.1K **Privately Held**
SIC: **3841** Surgical & medical instruments

### (G-20076)
### RIKEN CORPORATION OF AMERICA
4709 Golf Rd Ste 807 (60076-1258)
PHONE..................................847 673-1400
Takuma Suzuki, *President*
Rick Okano, *President*
Tetsuya Okumura, *Corp Secy*
Paul Takeda, *Agent*
▲ EMP: 103
SALES (est): 10.9MM
SALES (corp-wide): 626.3MM **Privately Held**
WEB: www.riken.co.jp
SIC: **3089** 5013 3592 Molding primary plastic; injection molding of plastics; motor vehicle supplies & new parts; carburetors, pistons, rings, valves
PA: Riken Corporation
  8-1, Sambancho
  Chiyoda-Ku TKY 102-0
  332 303-911

### (G-20077)
### RM ACQUISITION LLC (PA)
Also Called: Rand McNally
9855 Woods Dr (60077-1127)
P.O. Box 7600, Chicago (60680-7600)
PHONE..................................847 329-8100
Fax: 847 673-0534
Paul Leib, *Vice Pres*
Gene Kogan, *Engineer*
Rebecca Boykin, *Pub Rel Mgr*
Norman Smagley, *CFO*
Christopher Dean, *Controller*
▲ EMP: 140 EST: 2006
SQ FT: 85,000
SALES (est): 46.3MM **Privately Held**
SIC: **2741** Miscellaneous publishing

### (G-20078)
### ROGERS METAL SERVICES INC (PA)
7330 Monticello Ave (60076-4025)
PHONE..................................847 679-4642
Fax: 847 679-4645
Jonathan Zimmerman, *President*
EMP: 30
SQ FT: 5,600
SALES (est): 3.8MM **Privately Held**
SIC: **3398** Brazing (hardening) of metal

### (G-20079)
### ROGERS METAL SERVICES INC
7330 Monticello Ave (60076-4025)
PHONE..................................847 679-4642
Jonathan Zimmerman, *President*
Terry Piazza, *Vice Pres*
EMP: 30
SQ FT: 5,600
SALES (est): 2.4MM
SALES (corp-wide): 3.8MM **Privately Held**
SIC: **3398** 7692 Brazing (hardening) of metal; welding repair
PA: Rogers Metal Services, Inc.
  7330 Monticello Ave
  Skokie IL 60076
  847 679-4642

### (G-20080)
### RT ENTERPRISES INC
7540 Linder Ave (60077-3222)
PHONE..................................847 675-1444
Fax: 847 675-8889
William P Ryan, *President*
▲ EMP: 13
SQ FT: 12,500
SALES (est): 1.6MM **Privately Held**
SIC: **5085** 3061 3053 Seals, industrial; mechanical rubber goods; gaskets, packing & sealing devices

### (G-20081)
### SAFCO LLC
7631 Austin Ave (60077-2602)
PHONE..................................847 677-3204
Fax: 847 677-4970
Ula Jewusiak, *Plant Mgr*
Mike Kehr, *Facilities Mgr*
Brenda Bailey, *Buyer*
Allan C Ryan, *Engineer*
Grace Labrador, *Design Engr*
▲ EMP: 23
SALES (est): 5.4MM **Privately Held**
SIC: **3643** Current-carrying wiring devices

### (G-20082)
### SCIENTIFIC INSTRUMENTS INC
8236 Mccormick Blvd (60076-2921)
PHONE..................................847 679-1242
Fax: 847 679-7916
Jean Falk, *President*
EMP: 7 EST: 1962
SALES (est): 550K **Privately Held**
WEB: www.sciinst.com
SIC: **7389** 3826 3829 3822 Design, commercial & industrial; analytical instruments; measuring & controlling devices; auto controls regulating residntl & coml environmt & applncs; laboratory apparatus & furniture; relays & industrial controls

### (G-20083)
### SETHNESS PRODUCTS COMPANY (PA)
Also Called: Sethness Caramel Color
3422 W Touhy Ave Ste 1 (60076-6207)
P.O. Box 1014, Rahway NJ (07065-1014)
PHONE..................................847 329-2080
Fax: 847 329-2090
Henry B Sethness, *President*
Jeffrey Morrison, *Business Mgr*
Brian Sethness, *Exec VP*
Willard M Grimes, *Research*
Robert Derdak, *CFO*
◆ EMP: 12 EST: 1880
SQ FT: 15,000
SALES (est): 14.9MM **Privately Held**
SIC: **2087** Food colorings

### (G-20084)
### SG2
5250 Old Orchard Rd # 700 (60077-4463)
PHONE..................................847 779-5500
Shelley Myers, *Owner*
Eric Louie, *Officer*
EMP: 2
SALES (est): 287.7K **Privately Held**
SIC: **5085** 3577 Textile printers' supplies; printers, computer

### (G-20085)
### SHARP GRAPHICS INC
9144 Terminal Ave Unit B (60077-1516)
PHONE..................................847 966-7000
Fax: 847 966-8224
Larry E Plotzker, *President*
EMP: 3
SQ FT: 3,100
SALES (est): 354.4K **Privately Held**
WEB: www.sharpergfx.com
SIC: **2752** 2791 7336 Commercial printing, lithographic; typesetting; graphic arts & related design

### (G-20086)
### SKOKIE HOUSE
7887 Lincoln Ave (60077-3641)
PHONE..................................847 679-4570
Danny Thomas, *Owner*
EMP: 2
SALES (est): 269.8K **Privately Held**
SIC: **2599** Bar, restaurant & cafeteria furniture

### (G-20087)
### SKOKIE MILLWORK INC
8108 Lawndale Ave (60076-3322)
PHONE..................................847 673-7868
Fax: 847 673-7870
Herman Grosse Jr, *President*
Jim Grosse, *Vice Pres*
James Grosse, *Treasurer*
Paul Grosse, *Admin Sec*
EMP: 6 EST: 1950
SQ FT: 5,500
SALES: 1.3MM **Privately Held**
WEB: www.skokiemillwork.com
SIC: **2431** 5211 Millwork; lumber products

### (G-20088)
### SONS ENTERPRISES
4826 Main St (60077-2512)
PHONE..................................847 677-4444
Fax: 847 677-4450
Chuck Kmieciak, *President*
EMP: 12
SQ FT: 2,900
SALES (est): 1.2MM **Privately Held**
SIC: **2791** 2752 Typesetting; commercial printing, lithographic

### (G-20089)
### SPEEDPRO NORTH SHORE
8246 Kimball Ave (60076-2918)
PHONE..................................847 983-0095
EMP: 4
SALES (est): 178.5K **Privately Held**
SIC: **2752** Commercial printing, lithographic

### (G-20090)
### STANLEY HARTCO CO
7707 Austin Ave (60077-2604)
PHONE..................................847 967-1122
Fax: 847 967-9808
John Lundgren, *Chairman*

▲ = Import ▼=Export
◆ =Import/Export

Clarence Johnson, *Manager*
▲ **EMP:** 47
**SQ FT:** 42,000
**SALES (est):** 3.6MM
**SALES (corp-wide):** 11.4B **Publicly Held**
**WEB:** www.stanleyworks.com
**SIC: 3429** 3423 3544 3496 Clamps, metal; hand & edge tools; special dies, tools, jigs & fixtures; miscellaneous fabricated wire products; iron & steel forgings; bolts, nuts, rivets & washers
**PA:** Stanley Black & Decker, Inc.
1000 Stanley Dr
New Britain CT 06053
860 225-5111

**(G-20091)**
## STAR MEDIA GROUP
Also Called: Chicago Jewish Star
8200 Niles Center Rd (60077)
**PHONE**...................847 674-7827
**Fax:** 847 674-0014
Douglas Wertheimer, *President*
**EMP:** 4
**SALES (est):** 285.4K **Privately Held**
**SIC: 2711** Newspapers

**(G-20092)**
## STRUCTUREPOINT LLC
5420 Old Orchard Rd (60077-1053)
**PHONE**...................847 966-4357
Iyad M Alsamsam, *Mng Member*
**EMP:** 12
**SALES (est):** 1.2MM **Privately Held**
**WEB:** www.structurepoint.org
**SIC: 7372** 7371 8711 Prepackaged software; publishers' computer software; computer software development; civil engineering; structural engineering

**(G-20093)**
## STUDIO TECHNOLOGIES INC
7440 Frontage Rd (60077-3212)
**PHONE**...................847 676-9177
Gordon Kapes, *President*
Frank Cavoto, *Purch Agent*
Bob Deville, *Controller*
Joe Urbanczyk, *Sales Executive*
Carrie Gage, *Comms Mgr*
**EMP:** 15
**SQ FT:** 10,000
**SALES (est):** 2.4MM **Privately Held**
**WEB:** www.studio-tech.com
**SIC: 3651** 3663 Audio electronic systems; radio & TV communications equipment

**(G-20094)**
## SUB-SURFACE SIGN CO LTD
Also Called: ACS Susico
7410 Niles Center Rd (60077-3230)
**PHONE**...................847 675-6530
**Fax:** 847 675-6559
Harry Kreiter, *President*
Daniel Shulman, *Sales Mgr*
Julia Kligman, *Manager*
Dan Rould, *MIS Mgr*
▲ **EMP:** 20 **EST:** 1981
**SQ FT:** 4,000
**SALES (est):** 1.5MM **Privately Held**
**SIC: 3993** Signs & advertising specialties; signs, not made in custom sign painting shops

**(G-20095)**
## SUPERIOR KNIFE INC
8120 Central Park Ave (60076-2907)
**PHONE**...................847 982-2280
**Fax:** 847 982-6573
Claudio Cozzini, *President*
Marco Cozzini, *Vice Pres*
Silvano Cozzini, *Vice Pres*
Robert Cozzini, *Treasurer*
Cherie Larson, *Office Mgr*
▲ **EMP:** 40
**SQ FT:** 12,000
**SALES (est):** 7.9MM **Privately Held**
**WEB:** www.superiorknife.com
**SIC: 5023** 3421 Kitchen tools & utensils; cutlery

**(G-20096)**
## SUPPORT CENTRAL INC
8820 Skokie Blvd Ste 320 (60077-2224)
**PHONE**...................702 202-3500
Ronald Korrub, *President*
**EMP:** 6

**SALES:** 750K **Privately Held**
**SIC: 3585** 1711 Parts for heating, cooling & refrigerating equipment; heating & air conditioning contractors

**(G-20097)**
## SWAROVSKI US HOLDING LIMITED
4999 Old Orchard Ctr B22 (60077-1450)
**PHONE**...................847 679-8670
Jonathan Generous, *Branch Mgr*
**EMP:** 5
**SALES (corp-wide):** 4.2B **Privately Held**
**SIC: 3961** Costume jewelry
**HQ:** Swarovski U.S. Holding Limited
1 Kenney Dr
Cranston RI 02920
401 463-6400

**(G-20098)**
## SYMBOL TOOL INC
8106 Ridgeway Ave (60076-3318)
**PHONE**...................847 674-1080
**Fax:** 847 674-2722
Alex Kogan, *President*
Elizabeth Kogan, *Vice Pres*
**EMP:** 8
**SQ FT:** 3,000
**SALES (est):** 1.2MM **Privately Held**
**SIC: 3599** 3714 Machine shop, jobbing & repair; motor vehicle parts & accessories

**(G-20099)**
## TANAKA DENTAL ENTERPRISES INC
Also Called: Tanaka Dental Products Div
8001 Lincoln Ave Ste 201 (60077-3678)
**PHONE**...................847 679-1610
**Fax:** 847 674-5761
Asami Tanaka, *President*
Benita Zarling, *Vice Pres*
Debbie Williams, *Purchasing*
Asako Tanaka, *Admin Sec*
**EMP:** 14
**SQ FT:** 5,000
**SALES (est):** 1.3MM **Privately Held**
**SIC: 8072** 3843 8249 8221 Dental laboratories; dental equipment & supplies; dental tools; medical training services; colleges universities & professional schools

**(G-20100)**
## TEMPRO INTERNATIONAL CORP
8343 Niles Center Rd (60077-2626)
P.O. Box 242 (60076-0242)
**PHONE**...................847 677-5370
**Fax:** 847 677-5383
Kevin C Wade, *President*
Debbie Wade, *Admin Sec*
▲ **EMP:** 8 **EST:** 1973
**SQ FT:** 5,000
**SALES:** 590K **Privately Held**
**SIC: 3823** 3567 3829 3822 Thermocouples, industrial process type; heating units & devices, industrial; electric; measuring & controlling devices; auto controls regulating residntl & coml environmt & applncs; semiconductors & related devices; electric housewares & fans

**(G-20101)**
## TOTAL GRAPHICS SERVICES INC
8343 Niles Center Rd (60077-2626)
P.O. Box 554 (60076-0554)
**PHONE**...................847 675-0800
Mark Greenfield, *President*
**EMP:** 5
**SALES (est):** 420K **Privately Held**
**SIC: 2752** Commercial printing, offset

**(G-20102)**
## TRAVEL HAMMOCK INC
Also Called: Grand Trunk
8136 Monticello Ave (60076-3326)
**PHONE**...................847 486-0005
Kevin M Kaiser, *President*
Douglas R Kaiser, *CFO*
▲ **EMP:** 5
**SALES (est):** 680.6K **Privately Held**
**WEB:** www.thetravelhammock.com
**SIC: 2399** Hammocks, fabric: made from purchased materials

**(G-20103)**
## TRIANGLE PRINTERS INC
3737 Chase Ave (60076-4008)
P.O. Box 1141, Northbrook (60065-1141)
**PHONE**...................847 675-3700
**Fax:** 847 674-1230
Harvey Saltzman, *President*
David Saltzman, *Vice Pres*
Gordon Davies, *Project Mgr*
Ted Yusen, *Project Mgr*
**EMP:** 47 **EST:** 1955
**SQ FT:** 50,000
**SALES (est):** 6MM **Privately Held**
**SIC: 2752** Color lithography

**(G-20104)**
## UMF CORPORATION (PA)
Also Called: Perfectclean
4709 Golf Rd Ste 300a (60076-1233)
**PHONE**...................847 920-0370
George Clarke, *CEO*
B I Slezak, *Vice Pres*
Red Degala, *Vice Pres*
William Slezak, *Vice Pres*
Donna Craig, *Manager*
▲ **EMP:** 14
**SQ FT:** 4,700
**SALES:** 5MM **Privately Held**
**SIC: 2842** 3589 5047 Specialty cleaning, polishes & sanitation goods; commercial cleaning equipment; hospital equipment & furniture

**(G-20105)**
## URESIL LLC
5418 Touhy Ave (60077-3232)
**PHONE**...................847 982-0200
**Fax:** 847 982-0106
Brenten Kinnison, *Regional Mgr*
Jake Boerger, *Vice Pres*
Matthew Mahon, *QA Dir*
John Morrissey, *CFO*
Marlena Zelazowska, *Sales Staff*
**EMP:** 39
**SQ FT:** 35,000
**SALES (est):** 8.8MM **Privately Held**
**WEB:** www.uresil.com
**SIC: 3841** Surgical instruments & apparatus

**(G-20106)**
## URWAY DESIGN AND MANUFACTURING
8101 Monticello Ave (60076-3325)
**PHONE**...................847 674-7464
Mark Bogdan, *President*
**EMP:** 3
**SQ FT:** 2,800
**SALES (est):** 300K **Privately Held**
**SIC: 3544** Special dies, tools, jigs & fixtures

**(G-20107)**
## VAC SERVE INC
4240 Oakton St (60076-3263)
**PHONE**...................224 766-6445
Vanio Ivanov, *Manager*
**EMP:** 3
**SALES (est):** 140.9K **Privately Held**
**SIC: 3821** Vacuum pumps, laboratory

**(G-20108)**
## VANS INC
4999 Old Orchard Ctr K13 (60077-1493)
**PHONE**...................847 673-0628
**EMP:** 3
**SALES (corp-wide):** 12B **Publicly Held**
**SIC: 3021** Rubber & plastics footwear
**HQ:** Vans, Inc.
6550 Katella Ave
Cypress CA 90630
714 889-6100

**(G-20109)**
## WAG INDUSTRIES INC
4117 Grove St (60076-1713)
**PHONE**...................847 329-8932
Gail Gilbert, *President*
Doris Gilbert, *Admin Sec*
**EMP:** 10
**SQ FT:** 35,000

**SALES (est):** 663.8K **Privately Held**
**WEB:** www.cateringtrucks.com
**SIC: 2599** 5046 3713 3556 Bar furniture; commercial cooking & food service equipment; truck & bus bodies; food products machinery

**(G-20110)**
## WAYNE ENGINEERING (PA)
8242 Christiana Ave (60076-2911)
**PHONE**...................847 674-7166
Harry Wayne, *Owner*
Elaine Wayne, *Owner*
**EMP:** 1
**SQ FT:** 3,000
**SALES (est):** 250K **Privately Held**
**SIC: 3827** Optical instruments & lenses

**(G-20111)**
## WM W NUGENT & CO INC
3440 Cleveland St (60076-2916)
P.O. Box 948 (60076-0948)
**PHONE**...................847 673-8109
**Fax:** 847 674-0379
Brian Sabin, *President*
David Covelli, *Plt & Fclts Mgr*
Dale Clark, *Purchasing*
Abnash Narula, *Engineer*
**EMP:** 35 **EST:** 1897
**SQ FT:** 40,000
**SALES (est):** 10.6MM **Privately Held**
**WEB:** www.wnugent.com
**SIC: 3569** Lubricating systems, centralized

**(G-20112)**
## WOODS MFG AND MACHINING CO
8055 Ridgeway Ave (60076-3408)
**PHONE**...................847 982-9585
**Fax:** 847 982-9699
William Wlodarczyk, *President*
Jim Wallgren, *Admin Sec*
Charlie Baker, *Administration*
**EMP:** 14
**SQ FT:** 5,000
**SALES (est):** 1.9MM **Privately Held**
**SIC: 3599** 3444 Machine shop, jobbing & repair; sheet metalwork

**(G-20113)**
## WOODWARD INC
7320 Linder Ave (60077-3217)
**PHONE**...................847 673-8300
Larry Guther, *Purch Agent*
Richmond Baffour, *QC Mgr*
Joseph Gondek, *Engineer*
Senad Jakupovic, *Engineer*
Kevin Nowobilski, *Engineer*
**EMP:** 17
**SALES (corp-wide):** 2B **Publicly Held**
**SIC: 3625** 3824 Industrial controls: push button, selector switches, pilot; mechanical & electromechanical counters & devices
**PA:** Woodward, Inc.
1081 Woodward Way
Fort Collins CO 80524
970 482-5811

**(G-20114)**
## WOODWARD CONTROLS INC (HQ)
7320 Linder Ave (60077-3217)
**PHONE**...................847 673-8300
Thomas A Gendron, *CEO*
Robert F Weber Jr, *CFO*
▲ **EMP:** 200 **EST:** 1935
**SQ FT:** 70,000
**SALES (est):** 17.5MM
**SALES (corp-wide):** 2B **Publicly Held**
**SIC: 3625** 3643 3613 Industrial electrical relays & switches; switches, electric power; switches, electronic applications; solenoid switches (industrial controls); current-carrying wiring devices; switchgear & switchboard apparatus
**PA:** Woodward, Inc.
1081 Woodward Way
Fort Collins CO 80524
970 482-5811

**(G-20115)**
## WRAP & SEND SERVICES
Also Called: Gift Wrapping Center
4909 Old Orchard Ctr (60077-1439)
**PHONE**...................847 329-2559

## Skokie - Cook County (G-20116)

EMP: 16
SALES (est): 1.1MM  Privately Held
SIC: 3086  Mfg Plastic Foam Products

**(G-20116)**
**ZELDACO LTD (PA)**
Also Called: Zelda's Sweet Shoppe
4113 Main St (60076-2753)
PHONE..................847 679-0033
Linda Neiman, President
Daniel Neiman, Opers Mgr
Sandra Brooker, Opers Staff
Leah Neiman, Manager
Elliott Neiman, Systems Mgr
EMP: 11
SQ FT: 14,000
SALES (est): 2MM  Privately Held
WEB: www.zeldas.net
SIC: 2064  2051  Chocolate candy, except solid chocolate; popcorn balls or other treated popcorn products; bread, cake & related products

### Sleepy Hollow
### Kane County

**(G-20117)**
**AMERICAN WOODWORKS**
718 Hillcrest Dr (60118-1905)
PHONE..................630 279-1629
Bob Mucha, Owner
EMP: 2
SALES: 450K  Privately Held
SIC: 2431  Millwork

**(G-20118)**
**SCIENTIFIC MANUFACTURING INC**
209 Hilltop Ln (60118-1843)
PHONE..................847 414-5658
Michael Harris, Principal
EMP: 3
SALES (est): 201.6K  Privately Held
SIC: 3999  Manufacturing industries

### Smithfield
### Fulton County

**(G-20119)**
**CORSAW HARDWOOD LUMBER INC**
26015 N County Highway 2 (61477-9433)
PHONE..................309 293-2055
Fax: 309 293-4991
Lyndell Corsaw, President
Marie Corsaw, Corp Secy
EMP: 14
SQ FT: 15,000
SALES (est): 2.2MM  Privately Held
SIC: 2448  2421  2431  5211  Pallets, wood; sawmills & planing mills, general; millwork; lumber products; landscaping equipment; floor coverings

### Smithton
### St. Clair County

**(G-20120)**
**HYDAC RUBBER MANUFACTURING**
Also Called: Hy-Dac Rubber Mfg Co
301 S Main St (62285-1801)
P.O. Box 326 (62285-0326)
PHONE..................618 233-2129
Fax: 618 233-2361
Jeanne E Brown, President
Richard Sexton, General Mgr
Pat Carr, Vice Pres
David Stellhorn, Plant Mgr
Julie Lentz, Admin Sec
EMP: 25
SQ FT: 20,000
SALES (est): 5MM  Privately Held
WEB: www.hy-dac.com
SIC: 3069  Rolls, solid or covered rubber

**(G-20121)**
**INDUSTRIAL ROLLER CO (PA)**
218 N Main St (62285-1512)
P.O. Box 329 (62285-0329)
PHONE..................618 234-0740
Fax: 618 234-0237
George Linne, President
E A Karandjeff Jr, Chairman
Eric Adlersfluegel, Plant Mgr
Vicki Wanaki, Manager
Richard Klaber, Admin Sec
EMP: 18
SQ FT: 20,000
SALES (est): 2.8MM  Privately Held
WEB: www.industrialroller.com
SIC: 3069  3061  Roll coverings, rubber; mechanical rubber goods

**(G-20122)**
**INDUSTRIAL ROLLER CO**
211 N Smith St (62285-1523)
P.O. Box 329 (62285-0329)
PHONE..................618 234-0740
EMP: 18
SALES (corp-wide): 2.6MM  Privately Held
SIC: 3069  Mfg Fabricated Rubber Products
PA: Industrial Roller Co.
218 N Main St
Smithton IL 62285
618 234-0740

**(G-20123)**
**PADDOCK INDUSTRIES INC**
306 N Main St (62285-1514)
P.O. Box 906 (62285-0906)
PHONE..................618 277-1580
Fax: 618 277-1580
Philip S Boekers, President
Julie M Boekers, Vice Pres
Virginia Collins, Marketing Staff
EMP: 16
SQ FT: 12,000
SALES (est): 400K
SALES (corp-wide): 1MM  Privately Held
WEB: www.paddock-inc.com
SIC: 3993  8661  3469  2396  Signs & advertising specialties; religious organizations; metal stampings; automotive & apparel trimmings
PA: Pantech Industries Inc
306 N Main St
Smithton IL
618 277-1680

### Somonauk
### Dekalb County

**(G-20124)**
**AMERICAN MACHINING INC**
405 E Lafayette St Ste 1 (60552-9128)
PHONE..................815 498-1593
Rich Lindhout, President
Kent L Clevnger, Admin Sec
Joe Alla, Admin Asst
EMP: 7
SALES (est): 949.8K  Privately Held
SIC: 3599  Machine shop, jobbing & repair

**(G-20125)**
**DURO CAST INC**
145 E Market St (60552-3225)
PHONE..................815 498-2317
James C Schrader Jr, President
William Schrader, Vice Pres
Maggie Kaminky, Controller
EMP: 1
SALES (est): 6.1MM
SALES (corp-wide): 6.3MM  Privately Held
SIC: 3363  Aluminum die-castings
PA: Precision Enterprises Foundry & Machine Inc.
1000 E Precision Dr
Somonauk IL 60552
815 797-1000

**(G-20126)**
**IMPERIAL MARBLE CORP**
327 E Lasalle St (60552-9561)
PHONE..................815 498-2303
Fax: 815 498-3732
Richard Williams, President
Barbara Abbott, Safety Dir
Kim Williams, CFO
Kim William, Controller
Leann Hatcher, Human Res Mgr
EMP: 170
SQ FT: 100,000
SALES (est): 37.1MM  Privately Held
WEB: www.imperialmarblecorp.com
SIC: 3281  2542  Bathroom fixtures, cut stone; cabinets: show, display or storage: except wood

**(G-20127)**
**PRAIRIE MANUFACTURING INC**
405 E Lafayette St Ste 1 (60552-9128)
P.O. Box 356 (60552-0356)
PHONE..................815 498-1593
Darwin Classon, Owner
EMP: 4
SALES (est): 280K  Privately Held
SIC: 3599  Machine & other job shop work

**(G-20128)**
**PRECISION ENTPS FNDRY MCH INC (PA)**
1000 E Precision Dr (60552)
PHONE..................815 797-1000
Fax: 630 393-3847
James C Schrader Jr, President
Jeff Schrader, Vice Pres
William Schrader, Vice Pres
Mike Schrader, VP Sales
Jeff Smith, Sales Dir
EMP: 5
SALES (est): 6.3MM  Privately Held
SIC: 3363  3542  3543  Aluminum die-castings; die casting machines; industrial patterns

**(G-20129)**
**PRECISION ENTPS FNDRY MCH INC**
Also Called: Amco Machines Division
900 E Precision Dr (60552)
P.O. Box 307 (60552-0307)
PHONE..................815 498-2317
Bill Schrader, Branch Mgr
EMP: 30
SALES (corp-wide): 6.3MM  Privately Held
SIC: 3363  3365  Aluminum die-castings; aluminum & aluminum-based alloy castings
PA: Precision Enterprises Foundry & Machine Inc.
1000 E Precision Dr
Somonauk IL 60552
815 797-1000

**(G-20130)**
**WEAKLEY ENTERPRISES INC**
Also Called: Creative Design
119 W Market St (60552-9846)
P.O. Box 339 (60552-0339)
PHONE..................815 498-3429
Tonya Weakley, President
EMP: 4
SQ FT: 1,000
SALES: 165K  Privately Held
WEB: www.peddlersden.com
SIC: 2759  Commercial printing

### South Barrington
### Lake County

**(G-20131)**
**BINDERY & DISTRIBUTION SERVICE**
9 Overbrook Rd (60010-9568)
PHONE..................847 550-7000
Fax: 847 842-8800
Dennis D Uchimoto, President
EMP: 2
SALES (est): 223.7K  Privately Held
SIC: 2789  7336  Bookbinding & repairing: trade, edition, library, etc.; graphic arts & related design

**(G-20132)**
**SMALLCAKES CUPCAKERY OF SOUTH**
100 W Higgins Rd Unit H65 (60010-9413)
PHONE..................773 433-0059
Aponte Christian, Principal
EMP: 4
SALES (est): 227.4K  Privately Held
SIC: 2051  Bread, cake & related products

**(G-20133)**
**TEENFITNATION LLC**
12 Westlake Dr (60010-5341)
PHONE..................847 322-2953
SRI Ranjitha Yammanuru, CEO
Lalitha Gundlapalli, President
Rama Gundlapalli, Vice Pres
Rama Yammanuru, Vice Pres
Prafulla Srinivasan, CFO
EMP: 6
SALES (est): 264.5K  Privately Held
SIC: 7372  Educational computer software; application computer software

**(G-20134)**
**TEMCO JAPAN CO LTD**
Also Called: Temco Communications
13 Chipping Campden Dr (60010-6121)
PHONE..................847 359-3277
Sidric Nakajo, Manager
EMP: 3
SALES (corp-wide): 11.8MM  Privately Held
SIC: 4899  3663  Communication signal enhancement network system; radio broadcasting & communications equipment
PA: Temco Japan Co.,Ltd.
2-21-4, Honan
Suginami-Ku TKY 168-0
333 148-001

### South Beloit
### Winnebago County

**(G-20135)**
**ADVANCED ENGNEERED SYSTEMS INC**
Also Called: AES
14328 Commercial Pkwy (61080-2623)
PHONE..................815 624-7797
John H Stewart, CEO
George P Messina, COO
Brandon Bedward, Natl Sales Mgr
Tim Moran, Marketing Mgr
Glenn Isensee, CTO
◆ EMP: 26
SQ FT: 30,000
SALES (est): 7.6MM  Privately Held
WEB: www.advengsys.com
SIC: 3569  3625  Assembly machines, non-metalworking; relays & industrial controls

**(G-20136)**
**ALL METAL MACHINE**
14305 Dorr Rd (61080-2571)
PHONE..................815 389-0168
Lavern C Bumeister, Owner
EMP: 2
SALES: 200K  Privately Held
SIC: 7692  Welding repair

**(G-20137)**
**AMERICAN CONTROL ELEC LLC**
Also Called: Minarik Drives
14300 De La Tour Dr (61080-3006)
P.O. Box 275 (61080-0275)
PHONE..................815 624-6950
Dan Schnabel, President
Chris Fordell, Opers Staff
Debra McGinniss, Accounting Mgr
Darcy Wilson, Human Res Mgr
Brandon Jones, Technical Staff
EMP: 1
SQ FT: 35,000
SALES: 8MM
SALES (corp-wide): 19.1MM  Privately Held
SIC: 3625  Electric controls & control accessories, industrial
PA: Hti Technology And Industries, Inc.
315 Tech Park Dr Ste 100
La Vergne TN 37086
615 793-0495

## South Beloit - Winnebago County (G-20162)

**(G-20138)**
**AMERICAN EXTRUSION INTL CORP (PA)**
498 Prairie Hill Rd (61080-2563)
PHONE................815 624-6616
Fax: 815 624-6628
Richard J Warner, *President*
Mauriem Warner, *Corp Secy*
Rick Warner, *Director*
◆ EMP: 35
SQ FT: 64,000
SALES (est): 8.6MM **Privately Held**
WEB: www.americanextrusion.com
SIC: 3556 Food products machinery

**(G-20139)**
**ASPHALT MAINT SYSTEMS INC (PA)**
238 Charles St (61080-1920)
PHONE................815 986-6977
Nick Yoss, *President*
Vanessa Voss, *Vice Pres*
EMP: 18
SQ FT: 6,000
SALES: 1.3MM **Privately Held**
SIC: 2952 Asphalt felts & coatings

**(G-20140)**
**BELOIT PATTERN WORKS**
819 Ingersoll Pl (61080-1336)
P.O. Box 333, Beloit WI (53512-0333)
PHONE................815 389-2578
Fax: 815 389-4757
Kenneth Hanson, *Partner*
Darleen Hanson, *Partner*
David Hanson, *General Mgr*
Robert Sherwood, *Engineer*
EMP: 15
SQ FT: 7,500
SALES (est): 2.4MM **Privately Held**
SIC: 3543 2431 Industrial patterns; millwork

**(G-20141)**
**BESLY CUTTING TOOLS INC**
16200 Woodmint Ln (61080-9588)
PHONE................815 389-2231
Ho Keun Song, *President*
Richard Bugbee, *Prdtn Mgr*
Andy Brocklan, *Facilities Mgr*
John Kocik, *Purch Mgr*
Linda Cunningham, *Human Res Dir*
EMP: 17
SALES (est): 2.5MM **Privately Held**
SIC: 3545 Machine tool accessories

**(G-20142)**
**CHALLENGER FABRICATORS INC**
4095 Prairie Hill Rd (61080-2518)
PHONE................815 704-0077
Robert Rasmussen, *President*
Debbie Rasmussen, *Vice Pres*
EMP: 8
SALES: 400K **Privately Held**
SIC: 3441 Fabricated structural metal

**(G-20143)**
**D C ESTATE WINERY**
8925 Stateline Rd (61080-9574)
PHONE................815 218-0573
Heidi Wirth, *Owner*
EMP: 4 EST: 2014
SALES (est): 408.2K **Privately Held**
SIC: 2084 Wines

**(G-20144)**
**ECOLAB INC**
5151 E Rockton Rd (61080)
P.O. Box 1018, Beloit WI (53512-1018)
PHONE................815 389-4063
Fax: 815 389-0699
Laurie Beyer, *Opers Staff*
John Rimstidt, *Engineer*
Mike Smith, *Branch Mgr*
Karen Torkelson, *Manager*
EMP: 38
SALES (corp-wide): 13.1B **Publicly Held**
WEB: www.ecolab.com
SIC: 2842 Sanitation preparations, disinfectants & deodorants
PA: Ecolab Inc.
   1 Ecolab Pl
   Saint Paul MN 55102
   800 232-6522

**(G-20145)**
**FIRST AMRCN PLSTIC MLDING ENTP**
810 Progressive Ln (61080-2625)
P.O. Box 6342, Choctaw MS (39350-6342)
PHONE................815 624-8538
Bill Bartlett, *Partner*
Robert Deperro, *Partner*
Paul Petriekis, *Partner*
John Schwan, *Partner*
William Bartlett, *General Ptnr*
▲ EMP: 67
SQ FT: 39,000
SALES (est): 11.1MM **Privately Held**
SIC: 3089 Injection molding of plastics

**(G-20146)**
**FIVES LANDIS CORP**
Also Called: Gardner Abrasive Products
481 Gardner St (61080-1326)
PHONE................815 389-2251
Fax: 815 389-5024
Bill Kirchner, *Opers Mgr*
Andy Rovelstad, *Chief Engr*
Bill Holliday, *Controller*
Teresa Monehan, *Human Res Mgr*
John Kane, *Indl Rel Mgr*
EMP: 100
SALES (corp-wide): 5.8MM **Privately Held**
SIC: 3541 Grinding machines, metalworking
HQ: Fives Landis Corp.
   16778 Halfway Blvd
   Hagerstown MD 21740
   301 797-3400

**(G-20147)**
**FORTERRA PRESSURE PIPE INC (PA)**
4416 Prairie Hill Rd (61080-2545)
P.O. Box 569470, Dallas TX (75356-9470)
PHONE................815 389-4800
Mark Carpenter, *President*
Sam Arnaut, *Senior VP*
Ken Primavera, *Senior VP*
Leslie D Pape, *Vice Pres*
Steven M Paul, *CFO*
▲ EMP: 46 EST: 2000
SQ FT: 20,000
SALES (est): 101.5MM **Privately Held**
SIC: 3272 3317 Pressure pipe, reinforced concrete; steel pipe & tubes

**(G-20148)**
**FORTERRA PRESSURE PIPE INC**
4416 Prairie Hill Rd (61080-2545)
PHONE................815 389-4800
Bruce Weiser, *Branch Mgr*
EMP: 150
SALES (corp-wide): 101.5MM **Privately Held**
SIC: 3272 Prestressed concrete products
PA: Forterra Pressure Pipe, Inc.
   4416 Prairie Hill Rd
   South Beloit IL 61080
   815 389-4800

**(G-20149)**
**GLOBE PRECISION MACHINING INC**
1317 Railtree Ave (61080-2180)
PHONE................815 389-4586
Mark Defendi, *President*
Judi Defendi, *Admin Sec*
EMP: 7
SQ FT: 7,500
SALES (est): 1MM **Privately Held**
SIC: 3451 Screw machine products

**(G-20150)**
**GREENBERG CASEWORK COMPANY INC**
592 Quality Ln (61080-2628)
PHONE................815 624-0288
Fax: 815 624-0290
Troy Greenberg, *President*
Von Ortiz, *General Mgr*
Josh Kinney, *Warehouse Mgr*
Dave Hubbard, *Asst Mgr*
Darius Evans, *Director*
EMP: 20
SQ FT: 18,000
SALES (est): 3.4MM **Privately Held**
WEB: www.greenbergcustomcabinets.com
SIC: 2541 1751 Store & office display cases & fixtures; cabinet & finish carpentry

**(G-20151)**
**J & L THREAD GRINDING INC**
816 Dearborn Ave (61080-2096)
PHONE................815 389-4644
Fax: 815 389-4648
Larry Williams, *President*
Nancy Williams, *Corp Secy*
Kim Thorpe, *Office Mgr*
EMP: 5
SQ FT: 10,000
SALES (est): 330.6K **Privately Held**
SIC: 3599 Machine shop, jobbing & repair

**(G-20152)**
**JAMCO PRODUCTS INC (HQ)**
1 Jamco Ct (61080-2600)
PHONE................815 624-0400
Fax: 815 624-0600
James Alexander, *CEO*
Dan Johnson, *President*
Dave Tanner, *Vice Pres*
EMP: 74
SQ FT: 50,000
SALES (est): 28.3MM **Privately Held**
SALES (corp-wide): 558MM **Publicly Held**
WEB: www.jamcoproducts.com
SIC: 3312 5084 Blast furnaces & steel mills; industrial machinery & equipment
PA: Myers Industries, Inc.
   1293 S Main St
   Akron OH 44301
   330 253-5592

**(G-20153)**
**JJJ BRASS AND ALUMINUM FOUNDRY**
413 Clark St (61080-1315)
PHONE................608 363-9225
Hosze Moran, *Principal*
EMP: 4
SALES: 50K **Privately Held**
SIC: 3399 Brads: aluminum, brass or other nonferrous metal or wire

**(G-20154)**
**KEENE TECHNOLOGY INC**
698 Quality Ln (61080-2608)
PHONE................815 624-8988
Mike Wolfe, *Purch Agent*
Mark Sweet, *Manager*
EMP: 13
SALES (corp-wide): 15.8MM **Privately Held**
WEB: www.keenetech.com
SIC: 3599 Machine shop, jobbing & repair
PA: Keene Technology, Inc.
   14357 Commercial Pkwy
   South Beloit IL 61080
   815 624-8989

**(G-20155)**
**KEENE TECHNOLOGY INC (PA)**
14357 Commercial Pkwy (61080-2621)
PHONE................815 624-8989
Fax: 815 624-4223
Danny Pearse, *President*
Scott Wallace, *General Mgr*
Dave Culvey, *Vice Pres*
Bill Carpenter, *Opers Mgr*
Eric Lynch, *Prdtn Mgr*
◆ EMP: 79
SQ FT: 75,000
SALES (est): 15.8MM **Privately Held**
WEB: www.keenetech.com
SIC: 3554 Paper industries machinery

**(G-20156)**
**KJK CORP**
7306 Barngate Dr (61080-8025)
PHONE................815 389-0566
Phillis Burgess, *Principal*
EMP: 5
SALES (est): 461.4K **Privately Held**
SIC: 2631 Paperboard mills

**(G-20157)**
**MARLAND CLUTCH**
449 Gardner St (61080-1326)
PHONE................800 216-3515
Fax: 630 455-1794
Myron Angel, *Principal*
Lorrie Sculpner, *Accountant*
EMP: 3
SALES (est): 202.6K **Privately Held**
SALES (corp-wide): 708.9MM **Publicly Held**
WEB: www.altramotion.com
SIC: 3568 Clutches, except vehicular
PA: Altra Industrial Motion Corp.
   300 Granite St Ste 201
   Braintree MA 02184
   781 917-0600

**(G-20158)**
**MATRIX INTERNATIONAL LTD**
449 Gardner St (61080-1326)
PHONE................815 389-3771
R Burnett, *President*
EMP: 4
SALES (est): 303K **Privately Held**
SALES (corp-wide): 708.9MM **Publicly Held**
SIC: 3714 Clutches, motor vehicle
PA: Altra Industrial Motion Corp.
   300 Granite St Ste 201
   Braintree MA 02184
   781 917-0600

**(G-20159)**
**MC CLEARY EQUIPMENT INC**
239 Oak Grove Ave (61080-1936)
P.O. Box 187 (61080-0187)
PHONE................815 389-3053
Charles P Mc Cleary, *President*
EMP: 2
SQ FT: 36,000
SALES: 571.8K **Privately Held**
SIC: 3556 Food products machinery

**(G-20160)**
**MCCLEARY INC (PA)**
Also Called: Trans-Astro
239 Oak Grove Ave (61080-1936)
P.O. Box 187 (61080-0187)
PHONE................815 389-3053
Fax: 815 389-9842
Pat McCleary, *CEO*
Jerry Stokely, *President*
Jerry L Stokely, *President*
Leon Schwitters, *Prdtn Mgr*
Natalie Latino, *Controller*
EMP: 145
SQ FT: 80,000
SALES (est): 32.6MM **Privately Held**
WEB: www.mcclearys.com
SIC: 2096 2064 Tortilla chips; popcorn balls or other treated popcorn products

**(G-20161)**
**MEADOWELD MACHINE INC**
530 Eastern Ave (61080-1924)
PHONE................815 623-3939
Fax: 815 623-3813
Casey Meadows, *President*
Terri Meadows, *Corp Secy*
Cassidy Meadows, *Vice Pres*
Jaime Wallace, *Treasurer*
EMP: 5
SQ FT: 10,600
SALES (est): 825K **Privately Held**
WEB: www.meadoweld.com
SIC: 5084 3541 7692 3743 Industrial machine parts; saws & sawing machines; welding repair; railroad equipment; metalworking machinery

**(G-20162)**
**MID-STATES CONCRETE INDS LLC**
500 S Park Ave 550 (61080-2099)
P.O. Box 58, Beloit WI (53512-0058)
PHONE................815 389-2277
Fax: 815 389-2339
Charles H Harker, *CEO*
Hagen Harker, *President*
Joel Purdy, *Plant Mgr*
Kevin Wald, *Opers Mgr*
Mike Wolff, *Safety Mgr*
▲ EMP: 55 EST: 1946
SQ FT: 80,000
SALES (est): 23.7MM **Privately Held**
SIC: 3272 8711 Concrete products, precast; engineering services

## South Beloit - Winnebago County

**(G-20163)**
**PAPER MACHINE SERVICES INC**
7283 Barngate Dr (61080-8027)
PHONE..................608 365-8095
Duane Steinert, *President*
Cindy Steinert, *Vice Pres*
EMP: 5
SALES (est): 518.8K **Privately Held**
SIC: 2621 Paper mills

**(G-20164)**
**PRECISION QUINCY OVENS LLC**
483 Gardner St (61080-1326)
P.O. Box 483 (61080-0483)
PHONE..................302 602-8738
Matthew Zakaras, *President*
EMP: 30
SALES (est): 4MM **Privately Held**
SIC: 3567 Industrial furnaces & ovens

**(G-20165)**
**PRICE BROTHERS CO**
4416 Prairie Hill Rd (61080-2545)
P.O. Box 67 (61080-0067)
PHONE..................815 389-4800
James S Clift, *Ch of Bd*
Harold Gibson, *Manager*
Bruce Wiser, *Maintence Staff*
EMP: 75
SALES (est): 4.6MM **Privately Held**
WEB: www.cretexinc.com
SIC: 3272 Prestressed concrete products

**(G-20166)**
**QUAD INC (PA)**
810 Progressive Ln (61080-2625)
PHONE..................815 624-8538
William Bartlett, *President*
Robert Deperro, *President*
Robin White, *Controller*
Linda Bartlett, *Human Res Mgr*
John H Schwan, *Admin Sec*
▲ EMP: 49 EST: 1993
SQ FT: 39,000
SALES (est): 14.9MM **Privately Held**
SIC: 3089 Injection molding of plastics

**(G-20167)**
**RT BLACKHAWK MCH PDTS INC**
956 Gardner St (61080-1402)
P.O. Box 55 (61080-0055)
PHONE..................815 389-3632
Fax: 815 389-4684
Russell Tiritilli, *President*
Kay Tiritilli, *Corp Secy*
Gina Rand, *Manager*
EMP: 7
SQ FT: 6,400
SALES (est): 550K **Privately Held**
WEB: www.callblackhawk.com
SIC: 3599 3462 Machine shop, jobbing & repair; iron & steel forgings

**(G-20168)**
**S G ACQUISITION INC**
14392 De La Tour Dr (61080-3006)
P.O. Box 894, Roscoe (61073-0894)
PHONE..................815 624-6501
Bob Sealy, *President*
Tom Grossner, *Vice Pres*
EMP: 14
SQ FT: 4,500
SALES (est): 1.3MM **Privately Held**
SIC: 3556 3565 7699 Food products machinery; packaging machinery; industrial machinery & equipment repair

**(G-20169)**
**SUGAR RIVER MACHINE SHOP**
667 Progressive Ln (61080-2615)
PHONE..................815 624-0214
Fax: 815 624-0603
David J Klingenmeyer, *Owner*
Heath Alberts, *Opers Mgr*
James Christie, *Finance Mgr*
Heath Albert, *Manager*
Becky Brunner, *Manager*
EMP: 20
SALES (est): 2.2MM **Privately Held**
WEB: www.sugarrivermachine.com
SIC: 3599 3444 Machine shop, jobbing & repair; sheet metalwork

**(G-20170)**
**TREEHOUSE PRIVATE BRANDS INC**
1450 Pate Plaza Dr (61080-1430)
PHONE..................815 389-2745
Keith Simpson, *Finance Mgr*
Carol Amundson, *Executive*
EMP: 200
SALES (corp-wide): 6.1B **Publicly Held**
SIC: 2052 Cookies
HQ: Treehouse Private Brands, Inc.
  800 Market St Ste 2600
  Saint Louis MO 63101

**(G-20171)**
**UNITED TOOL AND ENGINEERING CO**
4095 Prairie Hill Rd (61080-2518)
PHONE..................815 389-3021
Fax: 815 389-1968
Glen Leasure, *President*
Rodney Meade, *President*
Connie Meade, *Admin Sec*
EMP: 65 EST: 1956
SQ FT: 60,000
SALES (est): 13.1MM **Privately Held**
WEB: www.unitedtooleng.com
SIC: 3544 3469 3541 7692 Special dies, tools, jigs & fixtures; metal stampings; milling machines; welding repair

**(G-20172)**
**WALLACE INDUSTRIES INC**
530 Eastern Ave (61080-1924)
PHONE..................815 389-8999
Douglas Wallace, *President*
EMP: 5
SQ FT: 11,000
SALES (est): 360.3K **Privately Held**
SIC: 3743 Railroad equipment

**(G-20173)**
**WALNUT CREEK HARDWOOD**
Also Called: Laser Creations
851 Doner Dr (61080-2199)
PHONE..................815 389-3317
Fax: 815 389-3305
Frank Long, *President*
Julie Long, *Vice Pres*
Lynn Fofler, *Admin Sec*
EMP: 7
SQ FT: 5,000
SALES (est): 630K **Privately Held**
WEB: www.walnutcreekhardwood.com
SIC: 2435 3993 7389 5999 Panels, hardwood plywood; signs & advertising specialties; engraving service; trophies & plaques; taxidermist tools & equipment

**(G-20174)**
**WARNER ELECTRIC LLC (HQ)**
Also Called: Warner Electric Indus Pdts
449 Gardner St (61080-1397)
PHONE..................815 389-4300
Fax: 815 389-2582
Carl Brehm, *Business Mgr*
Richard Czeslawski, *Sr Corp Ofcr*
Kevin Powell, *Vice Pres*
Bruce Becker, *Engineer*
Scott Fuller, *Engineer*
▲ EMP: 230
SALES (est): 132.7MM
SALES (corp-wide): 708.9MM **Publicly Held**
WEB: www.warnerelectric.com
SIC: 3714 Clutches, motor vehicle
PA: Altra Industrial Motion Corp.
  300 Granite St Ste 201
  Braintree MA 02184
  781 917-0600

**(G-20175)**
**WESTRAN THERMAL PROCESSING LLC**
483 Gardner St (61080-1326)
P.O. Box 483 (61080-0483)
PHONE..................815 634-1001
William Diemel,
EMP: 28
SQ FT: 45,000
SALES (est): 1.3MM **Privately Held**
SIC: 3567 Industrial furnaces & ovens

**(G-20176)**
**WINNEBAGO FOUNDRY INC**
132 Blackhawk Blvd (61080-1366)
P.O. Box 5 (61080-0005)
PHONE..................815 389-3533
Fax: 815 389-1624
Gary Anderson, *President*
Dennis Basham, *General Mgr*
Jed Weldon, *Vice Pres*
Arlinda Benn, *Prdtn Mgr*
Kelli Rebman, *Office Mgr*
EMP: 74
SQ FT: 30,000
SALES (est): 15.6MM **Privately Held**
WEB: www.winnfoundry.com
SIC: 3321 Gray iron castings; ductile iron castings

**(G-20177)**
**WORLD CONTRACT PACKAGERS INC**
14392 De La Tour Dr (61080-3006)
PHONE..................815 624-6501
Bob Seay, *President*
EMP: 6
SALES (est): 661.6K **Privately Held**
SIC: 2671 Plastic film, coated or laminated for packaging

**(G-20178)**
**WORLD CUP PACKAGING INC**
14392 De La Tour Dr (61080-3006)
P.O. Box 894, Roscoe (61073-0894)
PHONE..................815 624-6501
Bob R Seay, *President*
Tom Grossner, *Vice Pres*
Mel Jahn, *Sales Staff*
Belinda Smith, *Manager*
EMP: 8
SQ FT: 11,600
SALES (est): 1.6MM **Privately Held**
WEB: www.worldcuppack.com
SIC: 3556 3565 7699 Food products machinery; packaging machinery; industrial machinery & equipment repair

## South Elgin
### Kane County

**(G-20179)**
**ADVANCE PALLET INCORPORATED**
600 Woodbury St (60177-1359)
PHONE..................847 697-5700
Fax: 847 697-5770
Jerry Anderson, *President*
George Hanson, *Vice Pres*
Lori Schefler, *Manager*
EMP: 35
SQ FT: 22,000
SALES (est): 5.7MM **Privately Held**
WEB: www.advancepalletinc.com
SIC: 2448 Wood pallets & skids

**(G-20180)**
**ALLCOM PRODUCTS ILLINOIS LLC**
695 Sundown Rd (60177-1145)
PHONE..................847 468-8830
Sallie Furmanksi, *General Mgr*
Cathy Parsons, *Office Mgr*
William R Kohl III,
EMP: 22
SQ FT: 9,000
SALES (est): 4.2MM **Privately Held**
WEB: www.allcompc.com
SIC: 3663 Radio & TV communications equipment

**(G-20181)**
**AM SWISS SCREW MCH PDTS INC**
345 Industrial Dr (60177-1198)
PHONE..................847 468-9300
Fax: 847 468-9319
Jim Brewer, *President*
Bill Leod, *Vice Pres*
Bill Mac Leod, *Vice Pres*
EMP: 15
SQ FT: 16,500
SALES (est): 1MM **Privately Held**
WEB: www.amswisssouthelgin.com
SIC: 3451 Screw machine products

**(G-20182)**
**ARMIN MOLDING CORP**
Also Called: Armin Industries
1500 N La Fox St (60177-1240)
Rural Route 1500 N Lafox St (60177)
PHONE..................847 742-1864
Fax: 847 742-9446
Paul Stoll, *President*
Arthur C Stoll, *Chairman*
Robert Forschler, *Sales Executive*
Kathy S Stoll, *Admin Sec*
EMP: 45
SQ FT: 72,000
SALES (est): 9.6MM **Privately Held**
SIC: 3089 Injection molding of plastics

**(G-20183)**
**ARMIN TOOL AND MFG CO (PA)**
1500 N Lafox St (60177)
PHONE..................847 742-1864
Fax: 847 742-1864
Arthur C Stoll, *Ch of Bd*
Paul R Stoll, *President*
EMP: 82 EST: 1951
SQ FT: 102,000
SALES (est): 13.8MM **Privately Held**
WEB: www.armin-ind.com
SIC: 3544 Special dies, tools, jigs & fixtures

**(G-20184)**
**BABBITTING SERVICE INC**
1617 Louise Dr (60177-2242)
P.O. Box 1051, Belvidere (61008-1051)
PHONE..................847 841-8008
Fax: 847 841-8004
Kristoffer S Farrar, *President*
Heather Kromer, *Corp Secy*
Dave Farrar, *Vice Pres*
James Morgan, *Sales Staff*
Ashley Lange,
▲ EMP: 80 EST: 1961
SQ FT: 14,500
SALES: 15.5MM **Privately Held**
WEB: www.babbitting.com
SIC: 3568 Bearings, plain

**(G-20185)**
**BAUM HOLDINGS INC**
506 Sundown Rd (60177-1146)
PHONE..................847 488-0650
Simon Nussbaum,
EMP: 7
SALES (est): 499.8K **Privately Held**
SIC: 3993 7336 Electric signs; graphic arts & related design

**(G-20186)**
**BECSIS LLC**
2197 Brookwood Dr (60177-3235)
PHONE..................630 400-6454
Michael Boruta, *Managing Prtnr*
Nicholas Boruta, *Managing Prtnr*
Jerome Nalywajko, *Managing Prtnr*
EMP: 4 EST: 2014
SALES (est): 246.3K **Privately Held**
SIC: 3621 Power generators

**(G-20187)**
**BERNY METAL PRODUCTS INC**
655 Sundown Rd (60177-1145)
PHONE..................847 742-8500
Fax: 847 622-0065
Harold Reich, *President*
Lucille Reich, *Corp Secy*
Bill Reich, *Vice Pres*
Julie Lundborg, *Manager*
EMP: 9
SQ FT: 20,000
SALES (est): 770K **Privately Held**
WEB: www.bernymetalproducts.com
SIC: 3469 Metal stampings

**(G-20188)**
**CAT I MANUFACTURING INC**
Also Called: Cat-I Glass Manufacturing
865 Commerce Dr (60177-2633)
P.O. Box 208 (60177-0208)
PHONE..................847 931-1200
Fax: 847 931-0394
Robert Jaynes, *President*
Travis Jaynes, *General Mgr*

# GEOGRAPHIC SECTION
## South Elgin - Kane County (G-20215)

Ruth Smith, *General Mgr*
Cary Ostdick, *COO*
Robert Russell, *Engineer*
▲ **EMP:** 170
**SQ FT:** 70,000
**SALES (est):** 20.7MM **Privately Held**
**WEB:** www.catiglass.com
**SIC:** 3211 Flat glass

### (G-20189)
### CHICAGO INDUSTRIAL PUMP CO
822 Schneider Dr (60177-2641)
**PHONE** ............................ 847 214-8988
Matthew R Vetter, *President*
**EMP:** 6
**SQ FT:** 5,000
**SALES (est):** 1.4MM **Privately Held**
**WEB:** www.pitbullpumps.com
**SIC:** 3561 Industrial pumps & parts

### (G-20190)
### COLD STONE CREAMERY 488
324 Randall Rd (60177-2261)
Sam Ayyash, *Principal*
**EMP:** 4
**SALES (est):** 339.6K **Privately Held**
**SIC:** 2024 Ice cream & ice milk

### (G-20191)
### CUSTOM ALUMINUM PRODUCTS INC (PA)
Also Called: Winco Finishing Div
414 Division St (60177-1196)
**PHONE** ............................ 847 717-5000
**Fax:** 847 741-2266
John Castoro, *CEO*
James J Castoro, *Ch of Bd*
Steve Dillett, *President*
Kyle Wille, *Prdtn Mgr*
Anthony Glynn, *Production*
▲ **EMP:** 310 **EST:** 1960
**SQ FT:** 380,000
**SALES (est):** 77.1MM **Privately Held**
**WEB:** www.custom-aluminum.com
**SIC:** 3354 3442 Aluminum extruded products; sash, door or window: metal; metal doors

### (G-20192)
### CUSTOM COUNTERTOP CREATIONS
330 Randall Rd (60177-2261)
**PHONE** ............................ 847 695-8800
**EMP:** 14
**SALES (est):** 2.1MM **Privately Held**
**SIC:** 2541 Counter & sink tops

### (G-20193)
### DATUM TOOL AND MFG INC
200 Kane St (60177-1516)
**PHONE** ............................ 847 742-4092
**Fax:** 847 742-1333
Michael Long, *President*
Georgeann Long, *Vice Pres*
**EMP:** 18
**SQ FT:** 11,000
**SALES (est):** 2MM **Privately Held**
**SIC:** 3599 Custom machinery

### (G-20194)
### ELGIN SHEET METAL CO
695 Schneider Dr Ste 1 (60177-1103)
P.O. Box 509 (60177-0509)
**PHONE** ............................ 847 742-3486
**Fax:** 847 742-9037
Jon P Hudgens, *President*
Mark J Hardie, *Treasurer*
Paula Redmont, *Manager*
**EMP:** 27
**SQ FT:** 14,000
**SALES (est):** 4.3MM **Privately Held**
**WEB:** www.elginsheetmetalco.com
**SIC:** 1711 3444 Mechanical contractor; ducts, sheet metal; elbows, for air ducts, stovepipes, etc.: sheet metal; flues & pipes, stove or furnace: sheet metal

### (G-20195)
### ELITE IMPRESSIONS & GRAPHICS
645 Stevenson Rd (60177-1134)
**PHONE** ............................ 847 695-3730
Barbara Mozina, *President*
Victor Meuraskas, *Manager*
**EMP:** 4
**SQ FT:** 50,000
**SALES (est):** 200K **Privately Held**
**WEB:** www.eliteimpressions-az.com
**SIC:** 2759 Imprinting

### (G-20196)
### EXTRACTOR CORPORATION
685 Martin Dr (60177-1171)
**PHONE** ............................ 847 742-3532
**Fax:** 847 742-3552
H Jon Hoffman, *President*
**EMP:** 16
**SQ FT:** 13,000
**SALES (est):** 3.8MM **Privately Held**
**WEB:** www.suitmate.com
**SIC:** 3582 3634 Extractors, commercial laundry; electric housewares & fans

### (G-20197)
### FOX VALLEY PREGNANCY CENTER (PA)
101 E State St (60177-2048)
**PHONE** ............................ 847 697-0200
Christopher Hahn, *Principal*
**EMP:** 8
**SALES (est):** 289.6K **Privately Held**
**SIC:** 2835 Pregnancy test kits

### (G-20198)
### FOX VALLEY STAMPING COMPANY
385 Production Dr (60177-2636)
**PHONE** ............................ 847 741-2277
**Fax:** 847 741-0251
Doug Morrison, *President*
Cindy Morrison, *Treasurer*
Constantine Constance, *Admin Sec*
**EMP:** 17 **EST:** 1965
**SQ FT:** 81,000
**SALES (est):** 3.2MM **Privately Held**
**WEB:** www.foxvalleystamping.com
**SIC:** 3469 Stamping metal for the trade

### (G-20199)
### GENEVA MANUFACTURING CO
900 Schneider Dr (60177-2642)
P.O. Box 620 (60177-0620)
**PHONE** ............................ 847 697-1161
**Fax:** 847 697-1185
Marshall Lance, *President*
Christine White, *Manager*
▲ **EMP:** 18
**SQ FT:** 40,000
**SALES (est):** 4.3MM **Privately Held**
**WEB:** www.genevamfg.com
**SIC:** 2542 Partitions & fixtures, except wood; stands, merchandise display: except wood

### (G-20200)
### GLOBETEC MIDWEST PARTNERS LLC
403 Joseph Dr (60177-2268)
**PHONE** ............................ 847 608-9300
Richard Nemeth,
Thomas M Hazelhurst,
Mark Sokniewicz,
**EMP:** 5
**SALES (est):** 540.6K **Privately Held**
**SIC:** 3523 Farm machinery & equipment

### (G-20201)
### GRAPHIC INDUSTRIES INC
645 Stevenson Rd (60177-1134)
**PHONE** ............................ 847 357-9870
**Fax:** 847 357-9924
S Joseph Kukla III, *President*
Doug Leonard, *Vice Pres*
Stephanie Rodgers, *Accountant*
Bill Abraham, *Manager*
**EMP:** 24 **EST:** 2000
**SQ FT:** 25,000
**SALES (est):** 4.1MM **Privately Held**
**WEB:** www.graphicindustries.com
**SIC:** 2754 2677 Commercial printing, gravure; envelopes

### (G-20202)
### GREAT LAKES FINISHING EQP INC
842 Schneider Dr (60177-2641)
**PHONE** ............................ 708 345-5300
Tom Milo, *President*
Rick Nowak, *Corp Secy*
**EMP:** 6
**SQ FT:** 6,000
**SALES:** 1.4MM **Privately Held**
**WEB:** www.greatfinishing.com
**SIC:** 3471 Cleaning & descaling metal products; cleaning, polishing & finishing; finishing, metals or formed products; sand blasting of metal parts

### (G-20203)
### HOFFER PLASTICS CORPORATION
500 N Collins St (60177-1195)
**PHONE** ............................ 847 741-5740
**Fax:** 847 741-3086
William A Hoffer, *President*
Jay Grizzle, *Business Mgr*
Charlotte Hoffer, *Vice Pres*
Jack Shedd, *Vice Pres*
Alan Bixby, *Foreman/Supr*
◆ **EMP:** 375 **EST:** 1953
**SQ FT:** 360,000
**SALES (est):** 114MM **Privately Held**
**WEB:** www.hofferplastics.com
**SIC:** 3089 Injection molding of plastics

### (G-20204)
### I F & G METAL CRAFT CO
405 Industrial Dr (60177-1188)
**PHONE** ............................ 847 488-0630
Ignacio Fernadez, *Owner*
**EMP:** 6
**SALES:** 750K **Privately Held**
**SIC:** 3444 Sheet metalwork

### (G-20205)
### IF WALLS COULD TALK
323 W Harvard Cir (60177-2735)
**PHONE** ............................ 847 219-5527
Victoria Kozlowski, *Owner*
**EMP:** 4
**SALES (est):** 197K **Privately Held**
**SIC:** 2851 Paints & allied products

### (G-20206)
### INTEGRATED PRINT GRAPHICS INC (PA)
Also Called: I P G
645 Stevenson Rd (60177-1134)
**PHONE** ............................ 847 695-6777
Gary Mozina, *President*
John Brahm, *Exec VP*
John Petruso, *Plant Mgr*
Chris Mastny, *Purchasing*
Denise Hansen, *Sales Mgr*
**EMP:** 77
**SQ FT:** 62,000
**SALES (est):** 31.2MM **Privately Held**
**WEB:** www.ipandginc.com
**SIC:** 2752 7331 2761 Business forms, lithographed; direct mail advertising services; manifold business forms

### (G-20207)
### INTEGRATED PRINT GRAPHICS INC
J. B. Vision Graphics
635 Stevenson Rd (60177-1134)
**PHONE** ............................ 847 888-2880
**Fax:** 847 888-3285
**EMP:** 130
**SALES (corp-wide):** 31.2MM **Privately Held**
**SIC:** 2752 Business forms, lithographed
**PA:** Integrated Print & Graphics, Inc.
  645 Stevenson Rd
  South Elgin IL 60177
  847 695-6777

### (G-20208)
### INTERACTIVE INKS COATINGS CORP
1610 Shanahan Dr (60177-2277)
P.O. Box 158 (60177-0158)
**PHONE** ............................ 847 289-8710
**Fax:** 847 289-8762
Thomas Tinerella, *President*
Felicia Tinerella, *Corp Secy*
Bob Giancarlo, *Purchasing*
Tom Brennan, *Cust Mgr*
Mark Vandenbosch, *Sales Staff*
**EMP:** 15
**SQ FT:** 10,000
**SALES (est):** 3MM **Privately Held**
**WEB:** www.interactiveinks.com
**SIC:** 2899 Ink or writing fluids

### (G-20209)
### J & J EXPRESS ENVELOPES INC
645 Stevenson Rd (60177-1134)
**PHONE** ............................ 847 253-7146
**Fax:** 847 717-8271
Jimmy Popovtschak, *President*
**EMP:** 8
**SQ FT:** 6,500
**SALES (est):** 760K **Privately Held**
**SIC:** 2759 Envelopes: printing

### (G-20210)
### KINETIC BEI LLC
2197 Brookwood Dr (60177-3235)
**PHONE** ............................ 847 888-8060
M Boruta J Jerovek, *Principal*
**EMP:** 10
**SALES (est):** 571K **Privately Held**
**SIC:** 3861 Developing machines & equipment, still or motion picture

### (G-20211)
### KRIS DEE AND ASSOCIATES INC
Also Called: Krisdee
755 Schneider Dr (60177-1161)
**PHONE** ............................ 630 503-4093
**Fax:** 847 608-8400
Russell P Majewski, *President*
Mark Lau, *Vice Pres*
Sal Pernice, *Sales Mgr*
Terri Minnaect, *Executive*
Jeffrey Majewski, *Admin Sec*
▲ **EMP:** 70
**SQ FT:** 40,000
**SALES (est):** 17.5MM **Privately Held**
**WEB:** www.krisdee.com
**SIC:** 3599 Machine shop, jobbing & repair

### (G-20212)
### LAFARGE AGGREGATES ILL INC (DH)
7n394 S Mclean Blvd (60177)
**PHONE** ............................ 847 742-6060
Nathan Creech, *General Mgr*
**EMP:** 6
**SQ FT:** 2,000
**SALES (est):** 10.1MM
**SALES (corp-wide):** 26.6B **Privately Held**
**SIC:** 1411 1442 Limestone, dimension-quarrying; common sand mining; gravel mining
**HQ:** Lafarge North America Inc.
  8700 W Bryn Mawr Ave Ll
  Chicago IL 60631
  703 480-3600

### (G-20213)
### LAFARGE NORTH AMERICA INC
1310 Rt 31 (60177)
**PHONE** ............................ 847 742-6060
Nathan Creech, *Branch Mgr*
**EMP:** 27
**SALES (corp-wide):** 26.6B **Privately Held**
**SIC:** 3241 Cement, hydraulic
**HQ:** Lafarge North America Inc.
  8700 W Bryn Mawr Ave Ll
  Chicago IL 60631
  703 480-3600

### (G-20214)
### LAFOX SCREW PRODUCTS INC
440 N Gilbert St (60177-1397)
**PHONE** ............................ 847 695-1732
**Fax:** 847 695-0721
Samuel Joy, *President*
Walter Kiel, *Vice Pres*
Kathy Joy, *Admin Sec*
**EMP:** 5
**SQ FT:** 7,500
**SALES (est):** 975K **Privately Held**
**SIC:** 3451 Screw machine products

### (G-20215)
### LAKEVIEW PRCSION MACHINING INC
751 Schneider Dr (60177-1161)
**PHONE** ............................ 847 742-7170
**Fax:** 847 742-8088
Debra Sommers, *President*
**EMP:** 15 **EST:** 1951

## South Elgin - Kane County (G-20216)

**SQ FT:** 18,000
**SALES:** 3.4MM Privately Held
**WEB:** www.lakeviewprecision.com
**SIC:** 3451 Screw machine products

**(G-20216)**
**LANE TOOL & MFG CO INC**
655 Sundown Rd (60177-1145)
**PHONE** .................... 847 622-1506
**Fax:** 847 622-1576
Edward Arnieri, *Principal*
John Gallagher, *Supervisor*
**EMP:** 30
**SQ FT:** 20,000
**SALES (est):** 4.8MM Privately Held
**WEB:** www.lanetool.com
**SIC:** 3599 3544 3549 Machine shop, jobbing & repair; special dies, tools, jigs & fixtures; metalworking machinery

**(G-20217)**
**MATRIX DESIGN LLC**
Also Called: Matrix Design Automation
1627 Louise Dr (60177-2242)
**PHONE** .................... 847 841-8260
Patrick Bertsche, *President*
**EMP:** 70
**SQ FT:** 50,000
**SALES (est):** 24.2MM Privately Held
**SIC:** 3535 Robotic conveyors

**(G-20218)**
**MB CORP & ASSOCIATES**
Also Called: Mbc-Aerosol
860 Commerce Dr (60177-2632)
**PHONE** .................... 847 214-8843
Jim McBride, *President*
Pete Burt, *Vice Pres*
**EMP:** 13
**SQ FT:** 14,000
**SALES (est):** 3MM Privately Held
**SIC:** 3542 3565 Crimping machinery, metal; bottling machinery: filling, capping, labeling; bag opening, filling & closing machines

**(G-20219)**
**MIDWEST SKYLITE COMPANY INC**
1505 Gilpen Ave (60177-1211)
**PHONE** .................... 847 214-9505
John F Harris, *President*
**EMP:** 20
**SALES (est):** 194.8K Privately Held
**SIC:** 3444 1761 Skylights, sheet metal; skylight installation

**(G-20220)**
**MOLDING SERVICES GROUP INC**
2051 N La Fox St Lowr 1 (60177-1205)
**PHONE** .................... 847 931-1491
Vincent Occhipinti, *President*
**EMP:** 30
**SQ FT:** 45,000
**SALES (est):** 5.9MM Privately Held
**SIC:** 3089 Molding primary plastic

**(G-20221)**
**NEW IMAGE UPHOLSTERY**
21 Cedar Ct (60177-2823)
**PHONE** .................... 630 542-5560
Robert J Stahulak, *Principal*
**EMP:** 10
**SALES (est):** 612K Privately Held
**SIC:** 2512 Upholstered household furniture

**(G-20222)**
**OPTIMUM GRANITE & MARBLE INC**
735 Schneider Dr Ste 4 (60177-2645)
**PHONE** .................... 800 920-6033
Denis Bahic, *President*
Ajit Choudhary, *Vice Pres*
Salih Bahic, *Shareholder*
Safet Basha, *Shareholder*
▲ **EMP:** 4 **EST:** 2006
**SQ FT:** 4,000
**SALES (est):** 1.5MM Privately Held
**SIC:** 3281 Curbing, granite or stone

**(G-20223)**
**RESIDNTIAL STL FABRICATORS INC**
1555 Gilpen Ave (60177-1211)
**PHONE** .................... 847 695-3400
**Fax:** 847 695-3438
James Czechowski, *President*
Michael Russell, *Controller*
**EMP:** 42
**SQ FT:** 20,000
**SALES (est):** 8.1MM Privately Held
**SIC:** 3312 Blast furnaces & steel mills

**(G-20224)**
**RICHARDS FINE JEWELRY & DESIGN**
Also Called: Richars's
321 Randall Rd (60177-2248)
**PHONE** .................... 847 697-4053
Richard C Zimmerman, *President*
Richard Zimmerman, *President*
Renette Zimmerman, *Vice Pres*
**EMP:** 2
**SALES (est):** 257.3K Privately Held
**SIC:** 5944 3911 Jewelry, precious stones & precious metals; jewelry, precious metal

**(G-20225)**
**SAKAMOTO KANAGATA USA INC**
433 Joseph Dr (60177-2268)
**PHONE** .................... 224 856-2008
Seiji Tanigaki, *President*
Sachiko Peter, *Manager*
Gerhard Kelter Jr, *Admin Sec*
▲ **EMP:** 5
**SALES (est):** 704.6K
**SALES (corp-wide):** 20.9MM Privately Held
**SIC:** 3089 Injection molding of plastics
**PA:** Sakamoto Kanagata Co.,Ltd.
3-30, Ikagamidorimachi
Hirakata OSK 573-0
728 441-121

**(G-20226)**
**SOFRITO FOODS LLC**
Also Called: Fillo's Frijoles
771 Reserve Ct (60177-3306)
**PHONE** .................... 630 302-8615
Daniel Caballero, *Mng Member*
**EMP:** 1 **EST:** 2015
**SQ FT:** 100
**SALES:** 300K Privately Held
**SIC:** 2032 Canned specialties

**(G-20227)**
**T & C GRAPHICS INC**
Also Called: Singles Plus Printing
645 Stevenson Rd (60177-1134)
P.O. Box 249, Addison (60101-0249)
**PHONE** .................... 630 532-5050
**Fax:** 630 932-1036
Chris Mueller, *Principal*
**EMP:** 38
**SQ FT:** 12,800
**SALES (est):** 5.4MM Privately Held
**SIC:** 2752 Business forms, lithographed

**(G-20228)**
**T-MOBILE USA INC**
416 Randall Rd (60177-3325)
**PHONE** .................... 847 289-9988
Dan Georgen, *Owner*
**EMP:** 11
**SALES (corp-wide):** 77.2B Publicly Held
**SIC:** 4812 3663 Cellular telephone services; mobile communication equipment
**HQ:** T-Mobile Usa, Inc.
12920 Se 38th St
Bellevue WA 98006
425 378-4000

**(G-20229)**
**TRI-PAR DIE AND MOLD CORP**
670 Sundown Rd (60177-1144)
**PHONE** .................... 630 232-8800
**Fax:** 630 232-8805
William Plocinski, *Manager*
Mary Hereford, *Manager*
Shirley Plocinski, *Admin Sec*
**EMP:** 26
**SALES (corp-wide):** 3MM Privately Held
**SIC:** 3544 3089 Special dies, tools, jigs & fixtures; molding primary plastic

**PA:** Tri-Par Die And Mold Corporation
143 Roma Jean Pkwy
Streamwood IL

**(G-20230)**
**TRIPLE EDGE MANUFACTURING INC**
320 Production Dr (60177-2637)
**PHONE** .................... 847 468-9156
**Fax:** 847 468-9158
Kirk Johnson, *CEO*
Ann-Marie Johnson, *President*
Ewa Gubernat, *Vice Pres*
Krzysztof Gubernat, *Admin Sec*
**EMP:** 8 **EST:** 1999
**SQ FT:** 7,500
**SALES:** 1.2MM Privately Held
**SIC:** 3599 Custom machinery

**(G-20231)**
**UCA GROUP INC**
Also Called: Head Manaufacturing
201 N Center St (60177-1715)
**PHONE** .................... 847 742-7151
David Head, *Branch Mgr*
**EMP:** 24
**SALES (corp-wide):** 32.6MM Privately Held
**SIC:** 3451 Screw machine products
**PA:** Uca Group, Inc
412 N State St
Elgin IL 60123
847 742-8870

**(G-20232)**
**WAMPACH WOODWORK INC**
1650 Shanahan Dr (60177-2277)
**PHONE** .................... 847 742-1900
**Fax:** 847 742-1919
William F Wampach, *President*
Betty Wampach, *Vice Pres*
Sue Dale, *Office Mgr*
Dale Benson, *Manager*
Scott Degenova, *Manager*
**EMP:** 15
**SQ FT:** 13,000
**SALES (est):** 1.7MM Privately Held
**WEB:** www.wampachwoodwork.com
**SIC:** 2431 Woodwork, interior & ornamental

**(G-20233)**
**WARNER OFFSET INC**
640 Stevenson Rd (60177-1133)
**PHONE** .................... 847 695-9400
**Fax:** 847 695-3999
Mark J Warner, *President*
Richard W Doyle, *Vice Pres*
**EMP:** 32
**SQ FT:** 12,100
**SALES (est):** 4.2MM Privately Held
**SIC:** 2752 Commercial printing, offset

**(G-20234)**
**WHITE JIG GRINDING**
625 Martin Dr (60177-1171)
**PHONE** .................... 847 888-2260
**Fax:** 847 888-2260
William R White Jr, *President*
**EMP:** 2
**SQ FT:** 1,000
**SALES (est):** 225.3K Privately Held
**SIC:** 3544 Jigs & fixtures

**(G-20235)**
**WIENMAR INC**
Also Called: Marble Works
1601 N La Fox St (60177-1247)
**PHONE** .................... 847 742-9222
Thomas J Wienckowski Jr, *President*
**EMP:** 125
**SQ FT:** 45,000
**SALES (est):** 16.4MM Privately Held
**WEB:** www.marble-works.com
**SIC:** 3281 1799 Household articles, except furniture: cut stone; counter top installation

**(G-20236)**
**YORK SPRING CO**
1551 N La Fox St (60177-1209)
P.O. Box 36 (60177-0036)
**PHONE** .................... 847 695-5978
**Fax:** 847 695-0384
James R York, *CEO*
Zelma York, *President*

Betty L York, *Exec VP*
Michael York, *Vice Pres*
**EMP:** 45 **EST:** 1956
**SQ FT:** 16,000
**SALES (est):** 7.6MM Privately Held
**WEB:** www.yorkspring.com
**SIC:** 3493 Steel springs, except wire

## South Holland
### Cook County

**(G-20237)**
**3V PALLET**
133 W 154th St (60473-1020)
**PHONE** .................... 708 620-7790
**EMP:** 4 **EST:** 2013
**SALES (est):** 489.1K Privately Held
**SIC:** 2448 Pallets, wood & wood with metal

**(G-20238)**
**A J ADHESIVES INC**
15461 La Salle St (60473-1220)
**PHONE** .................... 708 210-1111
Andy Schwartz, *CEO*
**EMP:** 4
**SALES (corp-wide):** 1.9MM Privately Held
**SIC:** 2891 Adhesives
**PA:** A. J. Adhesives, Inc.
4800 Miami St
Saint Louis MO 63116
314 652-4583

**(G-20239)**
**ABBOTTS MINUTE PRINTING INC**
611 E 170th St (60473-3408)
**PHONE** .................... 708 339-6010
**Fax:** 708 339-6022
Linda Abbott, *President*
Michael Abbott, *Vice Pres*
**EMP:** 5
**SQ FT:** 2,000
**SALES:** 350K Privately Held
**WEB:** www.abbottprint.net
**SIC:** 2752 Commercial printing, offset

**(G-20240)**
**AE2009 TECHNOLOGIES INC**
Also Called: Ability Engineering
16140 Vincennes Ave (60473-1256)
**PHONE** .................... 708 331-0025
Eugene Botsoe, *President*
Joseph A Zawistowski, *Exec VP*
Sandra Morgan, *Treasurer*
Patricia D Zawistowski, *Admin Sec*
▲ **EMP:** 25
**SQ FT:** 40,000
**SALES (est):** 6.5MM Privately Held
**WEB:** www.abilityengineering.com
**SIC:** 3441 3443 Fabricated structural metal; fabricated plate work (boiler shop); reactor containment vessels, metal plate

**(G-20241)**
**ALL-STEEL STRUCTURES INC**
16301 Vincennes Ave (60473-2017)
**PHONE** .................... 708 210-1313
**Fax:** 708 210-9669
Theodore Bratsos, *President*
Jeff Strolle, *Accounts Mgr*
Jan Sarek, *Manager*
▲ **EMP:** 24
**SQ FT:** 22,500
**SALES:** 6MM Privately Held
**WEB:** www.allsteelinc.com
**SIC:** 3993 3446 3449 1799 Signs, not made in custom sign painting shops; stairs, staircases, stair treads: prefabricated metal; miscellaneous metalwork; sign installation & maintenance; ornamental metal work

**(G-20242)**
**AMERICAN CATHOLIC PRESS INC**
Also Called: ACP PUBLICATIONS
16565 State St (60473-2025)
**PHONE** .................... 708 331-5485
Joseph Russo, *Treasurer*
Michael Gilligan, *Exec Dir*
Connor Loesch, *Admin Sec*
**EMP:** 10

## GEOGRAPHIC SECTION

**South Holland - Cook County (G-20267)**

SQ FT: 4,400
SALES: 227.5K **Privately Held**
WEB: www.americancatholicpress.org
SIC: 2721 2731 Magazines: publishing only, not printed on site; periodicals: publishing only; books: publishing only; book music: publishing only, not printed on site

### (G-20243)
### AMERICAN CLASSIC REBAR CORP
15810 Suntone Dr (60473-1238)
PHONE.................................708 225-1010
Pete Pidrak, *Vice Pres*
EMP: 4
SALES: 400K **Privately Held**
SIC: 3449 Bars, concrete reinforcing: fabricated steel

### (G-20244)
### AMERICAN PIPING PRODUCTS INC
15801 Van Drunen Rd (60473-1245)
PHONE.................................708 339-1753
Alfred Rheinnecker, *Branch Mgr*
EMP: 32 **Privately Held**
SIC: 3498 Fabricated pipe & fittings
PA: American Piping Products, Inc.
  825 Maryville Centre Dr
  Chesterfield MO 63017

### (G-20245)
### ANIMATED MANUFACTURING COMPANY
106 W 154th St (60473-1015)
P.O. Box 448 (60473-0448)
PHONE.................................708 333-6688
Fax: 708 333-6692
Allen White, *CEO*
Randy R Schafer, *President*
Pauline White, *Vice Pres*
EMP: 18 EST: 1953
SQ FT: 30,000
SALES: 3MM **Privately Held**
WEB: www.animatedmfgco.com
SIC: 3469 Stamping metal for the trade

### (G-20246)
### ARMACELL LLC
16800 S Canal St (60473-2729)
PHONE.................................708 596-9501
Denny Costello, *Plant Mgr*
John Kieras, *Plant Engr*
Denny Castello, *Manager*
EMP: 100
SALES (corp-wide): 75.4MM **Privately Held**
WEB: www.armacell.com
SIC: 3086 Insulation or cushioning material, foamed plastic
HQ: Armacell, Llc
  55 Vilcom Center Dr # 200
  Chapel Hill NC 27514

### (G-20247)
### ARMIL/CFS INC
15660 La Salle St (60473-1273)
P.O. Box 114 (60473-0114)
PHONE.................................708 339-6810
Walter Parduhn, *President*
Andrea Odom, *Finance*
Tom Krowl, *Sales Staff*
◆ EMP: 30 EST: 1968
SQ FT: 20,000
SALES (est): 11.6MM **Privately Held**
WEB: www.armilcfs.com
SIC: 3567 5085 Industrial furnaces & ovens; refractory material

### (G-20248)
### ASKO INC
15600 Vincennes Ave (60473-1249)
PHONE.................................773 785-4515
Fax: 708 339-3757
Frank Raupach, *Sales Engr*
Robert O'Malley, *Branch Mgr*
EMP: 25
SQ FT: 10,000
SALES (corp-wide): 22.1MM **Privately Held**
WEB: www.askobv.com
SIC: 3545 Machine tool accessories

PA: Asko, Inc.
  501 W 7th Ave
  Homestead PA 15120
  412 461-4110

### (G-20249)
### BEDFORD RAKIM
17125 Evans Dr (60473-3475)
PHONE.................................773 759-3947
Rakim Bedford, *Owner*
EMP: 4
SALES (est): 159.5K **Privately Held**
SIC: 3714 Transmissions, motor vehicle

### (G-20250)
### BENNU GROUP INC
Also Called: Ability Engineering Technology
16140 Vincennes Ave (60473-1256)
PHONE.................................708 331-0025
Fax: 708 331-5090
Eugene Botsoe, *President*
Tim Niehof, *Accountant*
Fred Dion, *Mktg Dir*
Michael Morgan, *Office Mgr*
Miguel Salazar, *Info Tech Mgr*
EMP: 19
SALES: 10MM **Privately Held**
SIC: 3443 Industrial vessels, tanks & containers; boilers: industrial, power, or marine

### (G-20251)
### BESSCO TUBE BENDING PIPE FABG
16000 Van Drunen Rd (60473-1242)
PHONE.................................708 339-3977
EMP: 4 EST: 2009
SALES (est): 28.2K **Privately Held**
SIC: 3498 Tube fabricating (contract bending & shaping)

### (G-20252)
### BROOK CROMPTON USA INC
Also Called: Brook Crompton Americas
350 W Armory Dr (60473-2820)
PHONE.................................708 893-0690
EMP: 5
SALES (est): 514.2K **Privately Held**
SIC: 3621 Electric motor & generator parts

### (G-20253)
### BROWN PACKING COMPANY INC (PA)
Also Called: Dutch Valley Veal
1 Dutch Valley Dr (60473-1967)
P.O. Box 703 (60473-0703)
PHONE.................................708 849-7990
Fax: 708 849-8094
John A Oedzes, *President*
Bryan Scott, *COO*
Brian Oedzes, *Vice Pres*
Joe Faron, *Executive*
EMP: 40 EST: 1944
SQ FT: 50,000
SALES (est): 6.9MM **Privately Held**
WEB: www.dutchvalleyveal.com
SIC: 2011 2013 Veal from meat slaughtered on site; sausages & other prepared meats

### (G-20254)
### BUDDING POLISHING & MET FINSHG
130 E 168th St (60473-2836)
PHONE.................................708 396-1166
Fax: 708 396-9965
Todd Kuipers, *Owner*
Warren Kuipers, *Co-Owner*
EMP: 3
SQ FT: 3,300
SALES: 499K **Privately Held**
SIC: 3471 Finishing, metals or formed products; polishing, metals or formed products

### (G-20255)
### CARPENTERS MILLWORK CO
16046 Vandustrial Ln (60473-1255)
PHONE.................................708 339-7707
Fax: 708 339-0711
Gary Smits, *President*
EMP: 10

SALES (corp-wide): 2.1MM **Privately Held**
SIC: 5031 2434 2431 2421 Lumber, plywood & millwork; doors & windows; wood kitchen cabinets; millwork; sawmills & planing mills, general
PA: Carpenters Millwork Co (Inc)
  224 W Stone Rd
  Villa Park IL 60181
  708 339-7707

### (G-20256)
### CHESTERFIELD AWNING CO INC (PA)
Also Called: Independent Awning Co
16999 Van Dam Rd (60473-2660)
PHONE.................................708 596-4434
Fax: 708 596-9469
Howard B Ausema, *President*
David Ausema, *Vice Pres*
Ed Ritzema, *Sales Associate*
Steve Agonis, *Manager*
EMP: 18
SQ FT: 10,000
SALES (est): 3.4MM **Privately Held**
WEB: www.chesterfieldawning.com
SIC: 2394 5999 3444 Canvas awnings & canopies; awnings; sheet metalwork

### (G-20257)
### CHICAGO-WILCOX MFG CO (PA)
16928 State St (60473-2841)
P.O. Box 126 (60473-0126)
PHONE.................................708 339-5000
Fax: 312 339-9876
Ed Gardiner, *VP Admin*
Michael Sullivan, *VP Opers*
Mona Stelter, *Purch Mgr*
Michael Winland, *QA Dir*
David Soliday, *Engineer*
▲ EMP: 38 EST: 1906
SQ FT: 40,000
SALES: 9MM **Privately Held**
WEB: www.chicagowilcox.com
SIC: 3053 3499 3452 Gaskets, all materials; shims, metal; washers, metal

### (G-20258)
### DALEC CONTROLS INC
16140 Vincennes Ave (60473-1256)
PHONE.................................847 671-7676
Susan Lewers, *President*
EMP: 5 EST: 2014
SQ FT: 1,200
SALES (est): 712.3K **Privately Held**
SIC: 3823 Industrial instrmnts msrmnt display/control process variable

### (G-20259)
### DALEC ELECTRONICS INC
16140 Vincennes Ave (60473-1256)
PHONE.................................847 671-7676
Ted Knapczyk, *President*
Tom Lewers, *Vice Pres*
EMP: 5
SQ FT: 6,000
SALES (est): 480K **Privately Held**
WEB: www.dalec.com
SIC: 3629 Electronic generation equipment

### (G-20260)
### DAVID H VANDER PLOEG
Also Called: Rapid Printing Service
534 W 162nd St (60473-2011)
PHONE.................................708 331-7700
Fax: 708 331-7171
David H Vander Ploeg, *Owner*
EMP: 6 EST: 1970
SQ FT: 5,000
SALES (est): 630.9K **Privately Held**
SIC: 2752 2791 2789 Commercial printing, offset; typesetting; bookbinding & related work

### (G-20261)
### DEBCOR INC
513 W Taft Dr (60473-2030)
PHONE.................................708 333-2191
Fax: 708 333-2245
Doris Wilson, *President*
Larry Oswald, *Office Mgr*
Howard Wilson, *Director*
EMP: 3
SQ FT: 1,100

SALES (est): 420.8K **Privately Held**
WEB: www.debcor.net
SIC: 5049 3443 2522 2521 School supplies; fabricated plate work (boiler shop); office furniture, except wood; wood office furniture; wood household furniture

### (G-20262)
### DOCTORS INTERIOR PLANTSCAPING
255 W Taft Dr (60473-2052)
PHONE.................................708 333-3323
Cynthia Dorn, *President*
EMP: 5
SALES: 225K **Privately Held**
WEB: www.docterinteriorplants.com
SIC: 2431 0782 Interior & ornamental woodwork & trim; lawn & garden services

### (G-20263)
### EAGLE PLASTICS & SUPPLY INC
15446 Wentworth Ave (60473-1251)
PHONE.................................708 331-6232
Jack Panek, *President*
EMP: 7
SALES: 400K **Privately Held**
SIC: 3089 Plastic & fiberglass tanks

### (G-20264)
### EBSCO INDUSTRIES INC
Vitronic Promotional Group
555 W Taft Dr (60473-2065)
PHONE.................................800 245-7224
Fax: 800 245-8224
J Stephens, *Division Mgr*
Andrew Tess, *General Mgr*
Kathy Reynolds, *Opers Mgr*
Sharon Fredette, *Credit Mgr*
Nancy White, *Sales Mgr*
EMP: 12
SALES (corp-wide): 1.8B **Privately Held**
WEB: www.ebscoind.com
SIC: 2741 Magazines
PA: Ebsco Industries, Inc.
  5724 Highway 280 E
  Birmingham AL 35242
  205 991-6600

### (G-20265)
### ELITE DIE & FINISHING INC
358 W Armory Dr (60473-2820)
PHONE.................................708 389-4848
Fax: 708 389-4807
Steve Stanek, *President*
Eileen Slagle, *Manager*
EMP: 9
SQ FT: 7,000
SALES: 500K **Privately Held**
WEB: www.elitedie.com
SIC: 7383 3544 2759 Press service; special dies, tools, jigs & fixtures; commercial printing

### (G-20266)
### ENGINEERED FOAM SOLUTIONS INC
16000 Van Drunen Rd # 600 (60473-1242)
P.O. Box 699, Flossmoor (60422-0699)
PHONE.................................708 769-4130
Keith Hasty, *President*
Aqui Hasty, *Vice Pres*
EMP: 5
SQ FT: 10,000
SALES (est): 389.7K **Privately Held**
SIC: 3086 Plastics foam products

### (G-20267)
### ESMA INC
450 Taft Dr Ste 101 (60473-2056)
P.O. Box 734 (60473-0734)
PHONE.................................708 331-0456
Fax: 708 331-8919
Tim Beezhold, *President*
Paul Beezhold, *Vice Pres*
◆ EMP: 8
SQ FT: 5,000
SALES (est): 1.5MM **Privately Held**
WEB: www.esmainc.com
SIC: 2819 3841 5169 Industrial inorganic chemicals; ultrasonic medical cleaning equipment; chemicals & allied products

## South Holland - Cook County (G-20268)

**(G-20268)**
**EUNICE LARRY**
Also Called: Allocator Logistics
22 W 154th St (60473-1013)
PHONE.....................708 339-5678
Eunice Larry, *Owner*
Kizzy Larry, *Accountant*
**EMP:** 3
**SALES (est):** 168.9K **Privately Held**
**SIC:** 3613 Power circuit breakers; power switching equipment; control panels, electric

**(G-20269)**
**G F LTD**
Also Called: Standard Wire & Steel Works
16255 Vincennes Ave (60473-1268)
P.O. Box 710 (60473-0710)
PHONE.....................708 333-8300
Jess Sehgal, *President*
Jagdish S Sehgal, *President*
Ken Czaja, *Vice Pres*
▲ **EMP:** 25 **EST:** 1895
**SQ FT:** 30,000
**SALES (est):** 5.5MM **Privately Held**
**WEB:** www.standardwiresteel.com
**SIC:** 3496 Mesh, made from purchased wire

**(G-20270)**
**GIBRALTAR CHEMICAL WORKS INC**
114 E 168th St (60473-2836)
PHONE.....................708 333-0600
Fax: 708 333-0631
James R Fencil, *President*
Joe Wolak, *Plant Engr*
Rebecca Mason, *Manager*
Joan Fencil, *Admin Sec*
▲ **EMP:** 19
**SQ FT:** 100,000
**SALES (est):** 6.1MM **Privately Held**
**WEB:** www.gibraltarchemical.com
**SIC:** 2851 Paints & allied products

**(G-20271)**
**GRIER ABRASIVE CO INC**
123 W Taft Dr (60473-2034)
PHONE.....................708 333-6445
Fax: 708 333-6554
Chris Price, *General Mgr*
David Yaksic, *COO*
Virginia Yaksic, *Vice Pres*
Roberta Dubuc, *Vice Pres*
William Humphrey, *Vice Pres*
▲ **EMP:** 120
**SALES (est):** 19.3MM **Privately Held**
**WEB:** www.grierabrasive.com
**SIC:** 3291 7389 Wheels, abrasive;

**(G-20272)**
**GRISWOLD MACHINE CO (PA)**
241 W Taft Dr (60473-2036)
PHONE.....................708 333-4258
Larry Griswold, *President*
**EMP:** 2
**SALES (est):** 302.2K **Privately Held**
**SIC:** 3599 Machine shop, jobbing & repair

**(G-20273)**
**GURTLER CHEMICALS INC (PA)**
Also Called: Gurtler Industries
15475 La Salle St (60473-1277)
PHONE.....................708 331-2550
Fax: 708 331-9087
Gregory B Gurtler, *President*
Jake Gurtler, *Vice Pres*
Thomas Yohn, *VP Opers*
Gary Shaw, *Purchasing*
Michael Jacobs, *Engineer*
▼ **EMP:** 30
**SQ FT:** 36,000
**SALES (est):** 14.6MM **Privately Held**
**WEB:** www.gurtler.com
**SIC:** 2841 Detergents, synthetic organic or inorganic alkaline

**(G-20274)**
**HADADY CORPORATION (PA)**
510 W 172nd St (60473-2717)
PHONE.....................219 322-7417
Fax: 708 596-7563
Jane Sullivan, *President*
Tom Casper, *Vice Pres*
William Sweeney, *Vice Pres*
Mike Mustradi, *Production*

Joe Huss, *Engineer*
▲ **EMP:** 30
**SALES (est):** 27.6MM **Privately Held**
**WEB:** www.hadadycorp.com
**SIC:** 3499 3743 3452 Machine bases, metal; locomotives & parts; pins

**(G-20275)**
**HEMINGWAY CHIMNEY INC**
16940 Vincennes Ave (60473-2807)
PHONE.....................708 333-0355
Scott Sievert, *President*
**EMP:** 7 **EST:** 2015
**SQ FT:** 12,000
**SALES (est):** 299.4K **Privately Held**
**SIC:** 1761 3444 Architectural sheet metal work; elbows, for air ducts, stovepipes, etc.: sheet metal; restaurant sheet metalwork

**(G-20276)**
**HERSHEY CREAMERY COMPANY**
601 W 167th St (60473-2703)
PHONE.....................708 339-4656
Fax: 708 339-5481
Matt Kramer, *Manager*
**EMP:** 10
**SALES (corp-wide):** 160.2MM **Privately Held**
**SIC:** 2024 Ice cream & frozen desserts
**PA:** Hershey Creamery Company
301 S Cameron St
Harrisburg PA 17101
717 238-8134

**(G-20277)**
**HI TECH MACHINING & WELDING**
16120 Vincennes Ave (60473-1256)
PHONE.....................708 331-3608
Joe Olson, *Principal*
**EMP:** 7
**SALES (est):** 560K **Privately Held**
**SIC:** 3599 Machine shop, jobbing & repair

**(G-20278)**
**HOLLAND PRINTING INC**
922 E 162nd St (60473-2442)
PHONE.....................708 596-9000
Fax: 708 596-0999
Wesley Potts, *President*
Mark La Reau, *Sales Mgr*
Mark Lareau, *Director*
**EMP:** 11
**SQ FT:** 4,364
**SALES:** 988K **Privately Held**
**WEB:** www.hollandprinting.com
**SIC:** 2752 Commercial printing, lithographic

**(G-20279)**
**HYSPAN PRECISION PRODUCTS INC**
Also Called: Universal Metal Hose
17111 Wallace St (60473-2735)
PHONE.....................773 277-0700
Fax: 773 277-0727
S Powell, *Vice Pres*
Frank Goodwin, *Purch Mgr*
Rich Snyder, *Purch Agent*
Mark Jennings, *QC Dir*
F Szot, *Treasurer*
**EMP:** 32
**SALES (corp-wide):** 95.4MM **Privately Held**
**WEB:** www.hyspan.com
**SIC:** 3568 3498 3429 3441 Ball joints, except aircraft & automotive; fabricated pipe & fittings; manufactured hardware (general); fabricated structural metal
**PA:** Hyspan Precision Products, Inc.
1685 Brandywine Ave
Chula Vista CA 91911
619 421-1355

**(G-20280)**
**INDUSTRIAL SPECIALTY CHEM INC (DH)**
Also Called: ISC Water Solutions
410 W 169th St (60473-2713)
PHONE.....................708 339-1313
Fax: 708 339-6430
Christopher Dooley, *President*
Debie Lebine, *Bookkeeper*

Mary Joe, *Manager*
**EMP:** 30
**SQ FT:** 24,000
**SALES (est):** 4.9MM **Privately Held**
**WEB:** www.industrialspecialtychemicals.com
**SIC:** 2899 3589 Chemical preparations; sewage & water treatment equipment
**HQ:** Industrial Water Treatment Solutions Corporation
16880 Lathrop Ave
Harvey IL 60426
708 339-1313

**(G-20281)**
**INPHARMCO INC**
1028 E 168th St (60473-3028)
PHONE.....................708 596-9262
Marion Smith, *President*
**EMP:** 3
**SALES (est):** 296.2K **Privately Held**
**SIC:** 2834 Pharmaceutical preparations

**(G-20282)**
**KB PUBLISHING INC (PA)**
Also Called: Park Press
924 E 162nd St (60473-2442)
PHONE.....................708 331-6352
Fax: 708 596-9688
Daniell Kallemeyn, *President*
David Kallemeyn, *Vice Pres*
Arlo Kallemeyn, *Admin Sec*
**EMP:** 75
**SQ FT:** 6,000
**SALES (est):** 9.1MM **Privately Held**
**SIC:** 2752 Commercial printing, offset

**(G-20283)**
**KB PUBLISHING INC**
930 E 162nd St (60473-2442)
PHONE.....................708 331-6352
Arlo Kallemeyn, *Partner*
Alonzo Kallemeyn, *Branch Mgr*
Daniell Kallemeyn, *Manager*
**EMP:** 25
**SALES (corp-wide):** 9.1MM **Privately Held**
**SIC:** 2752 Commercial printing, offset
**PA:** K.B. Publishing Inc.
924 E 162nd St
South Holland IL 60473
708 331-6352

**(G-20284)**
**KRYGIER MACHINE COMPANY INC**
15938 Suntone Dr (60473-1239)
PHONE.....................708 331-5255
Fax: 708 331-9274
Larry Krygier, *President*
Tom Haskins, *General Mgr*
Debbie Johannes, *Finance Other*
Linda Lou Waterson, *Shareholder*
**EMP:** 7
**SQ FT:** 3,306
**SALES (est):** 902.5K **Privately Held**
**WEB:** www.krygiermachine.com
**SIC:** 3599 Machine shop, jobbing & repair

**(G-20285)**
**KUNZ INDUSTRIES INC**
15800 Suntone Dr (60473-1238)
PHONE.....................708 596-7717
Fax: 708 596-7725
Gordon Kunz Sr, *President*
Gordon Kunz Jr, *Treasurer*
Yvonne Kunz, *Bookkeeper*
**EMP:** 6
**SQ FT:** 5,500
**SALES (est):** 679.4K **Privately Held**
**WEB:** www.kunzind.com
**SIC:** 2821 7699 Plastics materials & resins; polyurethane resins; wheel & caster repair

**(G-20286)**
**LITTLE DOLORAS**
Also Called: Fancher Printers
130 W 168th St (60473-2839)
PHONE.....................708 331-1330
Fax: 708 331-9225
Dolores Little, *Owner*
Ken Little, *General Mgr*
Fran Bialobrzeski, *Finance Other*
**EMP:** 3 **EST:** 1931
**SQ FT:** 4,750

**SALES:** 426K **Privately Held**
**SIC:** 2752 2759 2761 7331 Commercial printing, offset; letterpress printing; manifold business forms; mailing service

**(G-20287)**
**MAREN ENGINEERING CORPORATION**
111 W Taft Dr (60473-2049)
PHONE.....................708 333-6250
Fax: 708 333-7507
Derek Simons, *President*
Ryan Barnhart, *Engineer*
Alan Davis, *Design Engr*
Tamara Caanon, *Bookkeeper*
Aaron Krueger, *Sales Dir*
**EMP:** 35
**SQ FT:** 42,000
**SALES (est):** 14.9MM **Privately Held**
**WEB:** www.marenengineering.com
**SIC:** 3559 Recycling machinery

**(G-20288)**
**MCKERNIN EXHIBITS INC**
570 W Armory Dr (60473-2824)
PHONE.....................708 333-4500
Fax: 708 333-4585
Dan Mc Kernin, *President*
James McKernin, *Vice Pres*
Tim Mc Kernin, *Treasurer*
Jim Mc Kernin, *Admin Sec*
**EMP:** 18
**SQ FT:** 40,000
**SALES (est):** 3MM **Privately Held**
**WEB:** www.mckerninexhibits.com
**SIC:** 3993 Displays & cutouts, window & lobby

**(G-20289)**
**MFW SERVICES INC**
215 W 155th St (60473-1208)
P.O. Box 429, Worth (60482-0429)
PHONE.....................708 522-5879
David Clark, *President*
**EMP:** 3
**SALES (est):** 366.3K **Privately Held**
**SIC:** 3549 7692 Metalworking machinery; welding repair

**(G-20290)**
**MH/1993/FOODS INC**
Also Called: Michele Foods
16117 La Salle St (60473-2064)
PHONE.....................708 331-7453
Fax: 708 862-5347
Michele Hoskins, *President*
Christal Gray, *Vice Pres*
**EMP:** 12
**SQ FT:** 5,000
**SALES:** 3MM **Privately Held**
**WEB:** www.michelefoods.com
**SIC:** 2087 Flavoring extracts & syrups

**(G-20291)**
**MID COUNTRY MALT SUPPLY**
330 W Armory Dr (60473-2820)
PHONE.....................708 339-7005
Bryan Bechard, *General Mgr*
Gregory Burke, *Sales Mgr*
Glenn Gallagher, *Asst Mgr*
▲ **EMP:** 7
**SALES (est):** 255.9K **Privately Held**
**SIC:** 2083 Malt

**(G-20292)**
**MSEED GROUP LLC**
535 W Taft Dr (60473-2030)
PHONE.....................847 226-1147
Erica Douglas, *CEO*
Barry W Williams, *COO*
**EMP:** 5
**SQ FT:** 6,000
**SALES (est):** 341.5K **Privately Held**
**SIC:** 2844 Cosmetic preparations

**(G-20293)**
**NIAGARA LASALLE CORPORATION**
16655 S Canal St (60473-2726)
PHONE.....................708 596-2700
Fax: 708 596-7262
Mark Ruder, *Branch Mgr*
**EMP:** 150

SALES (corp-wide): 584.6MM **Privately Held**
SIC: 3316 Bars, steel, cold finished, from purchased hot-rolled
HQ: Niagara Lasalle Corporation
1412 150th St
Hammond IN 46327
219 853-6000

**(G-20294)**
**PALLETS INTERNATIONAL HOLDING**
500 W Armory Dr (60473-2851)
PHONE.................................773 391-7223
Norman H Gordon, *Manager*
EMP: 4
SALES (est): 396K **Privately Held**
SIC: 2448 Pallets, wood & wood with metal

**(G-20295)**
**PARK PRESS INC**
930 E 162nd St (60473-2442)
PHONE.................................708 331-6352
Dam Kallemeyn, *President*
Dan Kallemeyn, *Human Res Dir*
Don Woo, *Manager*
EMP: 15
SALES (est): 1.3MM **Privately Held**
SIC: 2759 Newspapers: printing

**(G-20296)**
**PASSION FRUIT DRINK INC**
17335 Sterling Ct (60473-3779)
PHONE.................................708 769-4749
Grover Calvert, *President*
EMP: 4
SALES (est): 330K **Privately Held**
WEB: www.passionfruitdrink.com
SIC: 2087 Beverage bases, concentrates, syrups, powders & mixes

**(G-20297)**
**PEERLESS CHAIN COMPANY**
Also Called: Letellier Material Hdlg Eqp
16650 State St (60473-2826)
PHONE.................................708 339-0545
Bob Dwyer, *Branch Mgr*
EMP: 35
SALES (corp-wide): 87MM **Privately Held**
SIC: 3536 Hoists
HQ: Peerless Chain Company
1416 E Sanborn St
Winona MN 55987
507 457-9100

**(G-20298)**
**PERKINS ENTERPRISE INC**
15518 S Park Ave (60473-1303)
PHONE.................................708 560-3837
Wayne Perkins, *President*
EMP: 5
SALES: 100K **Privately Held**
SIC: 3571 Electronic computers

**(G-20299)**
**R & C PATTERN WORKS INC**
Also Called: R & C Castings
146 W 154th St (60473-1015)
PHONE.................................708 331-1882
Shirl Paw, *President*
Michael Bost, *Superintendent*
Kevin Paw, *Vice Pres*
EMP: 7 EST: 1968
SQ FT: 5,100
SALES (est): 1.2MM **Privately Held**
WEB: www.rcpatterns.com
SIC: 3543 Industrial patterns

**(G-20300)**
**R C CASTINGS INC**
146 W 154th St (60473-1015)
PHONE.................................708 331-1882
Fax: 708 331-1896
Shirl Paw, *President*
Kevin Paw, *Vice Pres*
EMP: 7
SQ FT: 5,000
SALES (est): 1.4MM **Privately Held**
SIC: 5051 3543 Castings, rough: iron or steel; industrial patterns

**(G-20301)**
**ROBERTS COLONIAL HOUSE INC**
Also Called: Roberts Displays
15960 Suntone Dr (60473-1239)
PHONE.................................708 331-6233
Fax: 708 331-0538
Floyd Hurley, *President*
Dolores Hurley, *Corp Secy*
Rita Barett, *Manager*
▲ EMP: 15 EST: 1941
SQ FT: 8,000
SALES (est): 1.8MM **Privately Held**
SIC: 3999 Advertising display products

**(G-20302)**
**ROEDA SIGNS INC**
Also Called: Screentech
16931 State St (60473-2832)
PHONE.................................708 333-3021
Randy Roeda, *President*
Robert Roeda, *Corp Secy*
Debbie Warn, *Sales Staff*
Scott Graefen, *Manager*
▲ EMP: 27
SQ FT: 20,000
SALES (est): 4.8MM **Privately Held**
WEB: www.screentech.com
SIC: 3993 2759 Signs & advertising specialties; screen printing

**(G-20303)**
**S & J INDUSTRIAL SUPPLY CORP**
16060 Suntone Dr (60473-1240)
PHONE.................................708 339-1708
Fax: 708 339-7039
Robert C Stuart, *President*
John Johnson, *Manager*
Cathy Popjevach, *Manager*
EMP: 17
SQ FT: 10,000
SALES (est): 6.5MM **Privately Held**
WEB: www.s-jindustrial.com
SIC: 5085 3545 3546 3425 Industrial supplies; machine tool accessories; power-driven handtools; saw blades & handsaws; abrasive products

**(G-20304)**
**SHAMROCK MANUFACTURING CO INC**
15920 Suntone Dr (60473-1239)
PHONE.................................708 331-7776
Fax: 708 331-3337
Robert Bacon, *President*
Laura Bacon, *Office Mgr*
EMP: 5
SQ FT: 4,000
SALES: 320K **Privately Held**
SIC: 3441 3444 Fabricated structural metal; sheet metalwork

**(G-20305)**
**SOUTH CHICAGO PACKING LLC (PA)**
16250 Vincennes Ave (60473-1260)
PHONE.................................708 589-2400
Ron Miniat, *Ch of Bd*
David J Miniat, *President*
Tim Meyer, *Vice Pres*
Charles Nalon, *Vice Pres*
Curt Hizy, *Controller*
▼ EMP: 99
SQ FT: 92,000
SALES (est): 101.5MM **Privately Held**
SIC: 2079 Compound shortenings

**(G-20306)**
**STEEL-GUARD SAFETY CORP**
16520 Vincennes Ave (60473-2020)
PHONE.................................708 589-4588
Greg J Pretsch, *President*
▼ EMP: 8
SALES (est): 1.5MM **Privately Held**
WEB: www.steelguardsafety.com
SIC: 3625 3842 3442 5085 Noise control equipment; personal safety equipment; rolling doors for industrial buildings or warehouses, metal; industrial supplies; welding supplies; welding supplies

**(G-20307)**
**SURGE CLUTCH & DRIVE LINE CO**
16145 Thornton Blue Is (60473)
P.O. Box 100 (60473-0100)
PHONE.................................708 331-1352
Rhonda Jesernik, *President*
George Polmen, *Corp Secy*
EMP: 9
SQ FT: 11,000
SALES: 900K **Privately Held**
WEB: www.surgeclutch.com
SIC: 3714 5013 3568 3566 Drive shafts, motor vehicle; clutches, motor vehicle; clutches; power transmission equipment; speed changers, drives & gears

**(G-20308)**
**TECHNO - GRPHICS TRNSLTONS INC**
Also Called: Electronic Technology Group
1451 E 168th St (60473-2641)
PHONE.................................708 331-3333
Fax: 708 331-0003
David L Bond, *President*
Dan McFalls, *Manager*
Mary W Bond, *Admin Sec*
EMP: 25
SQ FT: 5,000
SALES (est): 2.6MM **Privately Held**
WEB: www.wetrans4u.com
SIC: 2741 7389 7373 Technical manuals: publishing only, not printed on site; translation services; value-added resellers, computer systems

**(G-20309)**
**TERRE HAUTE TENT & AWNING INC**
Also Called: Steel Guard Safety
16520 Vincennes Ave (60473-2020)
PHONE.................................812 235-6068
Carole Pretsch, *President*
Greg Pretsch, *Vice Pres*
Cheryl Drake, *Manager*
EMP: 10 EST: 1913
SQ FT: 8,000
SALES: 700K **Privately Held**
SIC: 2211 2394 7359 3949 Filter cloth, cotton; tents: made from purchased materials; awnings, fabric: made from purchased materials; tent & tarpaulin rental; sporting & athletic goods; blowers & fans; textile bags

**(G-20310)**
**THE CALUMET CARTON COMPANY (PA)**
16920 State St (60473-2841)
P.O. Box 405 (60473-0405)
PHONE.................................708 331-7910
Fax: 708 333-8540
Albert Inwood, *Ch of Bd*
John A Inwood, *President*
Kenneth J Roush, *President*
Kris Schmaling, *General Mgr*
John Inwood, *Vice Pres*
▲ EMP: 90 EST: 1930
SQ FT: 110,000
SALES (est): 19.6MM **Privately Held**
WEB: www.calumetcarton.com
SIC: 2653 2677 2657 2631 Boxes, solid fiber: made from purchased materials; envelopes; folding paperboard boxes; paperboard mills

## South Jacksonville
### Morgan County

**(G-20311)**
**OUTBREAK DESIGNS ✪**
1458 S Main St (62650-3440)
PHONE.................................217 370-5418
Rick Rolson, *Owner*
EMP: 5 EST: 2017
SALES: 400K **Privately Held**
SIC: 2759 Screen printing

## South Roxana
### Madison County

**(G-20312)**
**CORRECTIVE ASPHALT MTLS LLC**
300 Daniel Boone Trl (62087)
P.O. Box 87129 (62087-7129)
PHONE.................................618 254-3855
Tony Witte, *CEO*
Marc Taillon, *Vice Pres*
Mike McPherson, *Opers Mgr*
Russ Wheat, *Opers Mgr*
Jack Witte, *Project Engr*
EMP: 9
SQ FT: 5,000
SALES: 1.5MM **Privately Held**
SIC: 1611 2951 Highway & street paving contractor; asphalt & asphaltic paving mixtures (not from refineries)

**(G-20313)**
**MIDWEST BIODIESEL PRODUCTS LLC**
7350 State Route 111 (62087-1788)
PHONE.................................618 254-2920
Terry Zintel, *Mng Member*
Dawn Shaver, *Executive Asst*
EMP: 10
SALES (est): 3.5MM **Privately Held**
SIC: 2869 Industrial organic chemicals

**(G-20314)**
**MIKES INC (PA)**
Also Called: John Deere Authorized Dealer
109 Velma Ave (62087-1528)
P.O. Box 87069 (62087-7069)
PHONE.................................618 254-4491
Fax: 618 254-2958
Mike Marko Sr, *President*
Jane Shea, *Manager*
Sharon Kessler, *Admin Sec*
▲ EMP: 51
SQ FT: 20,000
SALES (est): 10.8MM **Privately Held**
WEB: www.mikesinc.com
SIC: 3731 7538 5082 Shipbuilding & repairing; general automotive repair shops; construction & mining machinery

## Sparland
### Marshall County

**(G-20315)**
**STEUBEN TOWNSHIP**
374 County Road 850 E (61565-9393)
PHONE.................................309 208-7073
Josh Crobyn, *Commissioner*
EMP: 12
SALES (est): 840K **Privately Held**
SIC: 3531 Drags, road (construction & road maintenance equipment)

## Sparta
### Randolph County

**(G-20316)**
**CWI**
8384 Valley Steel Rd (62286-3675)
PHONE.................................618 443-2030
Jeff Quivey, *Principal*
EMP: 3
SALES (est): 211.3K **Privately Held**
SIC: 3089 Garbage containers, plastic

**(G-20317)**
**JMS METALS INC**
1255 W Broadway St (62286-1659)
PHONE.................................618 443-1000
Joan Stork, *President*
Ron Stork, *Treasurer*
EMP: 5
SALES (est): 566.9K **Privately Held**
WEB: www.jmsmetals.com
SIC: 3499 Machine bases, metal

# Sparta - Randolph County (G-20318) — GEOGRAPHIC SECTION

**(G-20318)**
**LEE GILSTER-MARY CORPORATION**
403 E 4th St (62286-1886)
PHONE..............................618 443-5676
Steve Armstrong, *Manager*
**EMP:** 45
**SALES (corp-wide):** 1.1B **Privately Held**
**WEB:** www.gilstermarylee.com
**SIC:** 2098 2043 2099 2045 Macaroni products (e.g. alphabets, rings & shells), dry; cereal breakfast foods; popcorn, packaged: except already popped; blended flour: from purchased flour; plastic containers, except foam
**HQ:** Gilster-Mary Lee Corporation
1037 State St
Chester IL 62233
618 826-2361

**(G-20319)**
**NORVIDA USA INC**
Also Called: Big T Graphics
310 S Vine St (62286-1832)
PHONE..............................618 282-2992
**Fax:** 618 443-3437
Joe Tanner, *President*
**EMP:** 2
**SALES (est):** 200K **Privately Held**
**WEB:** www.jerron.com
**SIC:** 3861 Graphic arts plates, sensitized

**(G-20320)**
**SIGN SOLUTIONS**
1255 W Broadway St (62286-1659)
P.O. Box 271 (62286-0271)
PHONE..............................618 443-6565
**EMP:** 2
**SALES (est):** 286K **Privately Held**
**SIC:** 3993 Mfg Signs/Advertising Specialties

**(G-20321)**
**SPARTAN LIGHT METAL PDTS INC (PA)**
510 E Mcclurken Ave (62286-1850)
PHONE..............................618 443-4346
Donald A Jubel, *President*
Jeremy Long, *General Mgr*
Mike Sparks, *Exec VP*
Mike Dierks, *Vice Pres*
Scott Homan, *Vice Pres*
◆ **EMP:** 25 **EST:** 1961
**SQ FT:** 132,000
**SALES:** 137MM **Privately Held**
**SIC:** 3363 3364 3369 3365 Aluminum die-castings; magnesium & magnesium-base alloy die-castings; nonferrous foundries; aluminum foundries

**(G-20322)**
**SPARTAN LIGHT METAL PDTS INC**
405 E 4th St (62286)
PHONE..............................618 443-4346
Ed Bean, *CFO*
**EMP:** 600
**SALES (corp-wide):** 137MM **Privately Held**
**SIC:** 3363 3364 Aluminum die-castings; magnesium & magnesium-base alloy die-castings
**PA:** Spartan Light Metal Products, Inc.
510 E Mcclurken Ave
Sparta IL 62286
618 443-4346

## Spring Grove
### Mchenry County

**(G-20323)**
**A PLUS APPAREL**
9902 Fox Bluff Ln (60081-8829)
P.O. Box 205 (60081-0205)
PHONE..............................815 675-2117
Cheryl Ready, *Principal*
**EMP:** 1
**SALES:** 200K **Privately Held**
**WEB:** www.aplusapparel.com
**SIC:** 2395 Embroidery & art needlework

**(G-20324)**
**ACTOWN-ELECTROCOIL INC**
2414 Highview St (60081-9609)
P.O. Box 248 (60081-0248)
Grooms-Herr Scher, *Principal*
Al Zimmerman, *Engng Exec*
**EMP:** 3
**SALES (est):** 99K **Privately Held**
**SIC:** 3677 3612 Electronic coils, transformers & other inductors; transformers, except electric

**(G-20325)**
**ALL-RITE SPRING CO**
2200 Spring Ridge Dr (60081)
PHONE..............................815 675-1350
**Fax:** 815 675-9730
John S Bilik, *President*
Shaun Semler, *Vice Pres*
Chris Tix, *Prdtn Mgr*
Mike Steel, *Engineer*
Oliver Pluckett, *CFO*
▲ **EMP:** 46 **EST:** 1947
**SQ FT:** 32,000
**SALES:** 15.2MM **Privately Held**
**WEB:** www.allrite.com
**SIC:** 3493 3495 Steel springs, except wire; wire springs

**(G-20326)**
**ASTRO-CRAFT INC**
7509 Spring Grove Rd (60081-8916)
PHONE..............................815 675-1500
**Fax:** 815 675-1600
Richard Dschida, *President*
Richard F Dschida, *President*
Linda Dshida, *Manager*
Edward Dschida, *Admin Sec*
**EMP:** 24 **EST:** 1966
**SQ FT:** 15,000
**SALES:** 2.9MM **Privately Held**
**WEB:** www.astrocraft.com
**SIC:** 3599 3451 Machine shop, jobbing & repair; screw machine products

**(G-20327)**
**AUTONAMIC CORPORATION**
7806 Industrial Dr (60081-8251)
P.O. Box 43 (60081-0043)
PHONE..............................815 675-6300
**Fax:** 815 675-6358
Roger Dumke, *President*
Inga Norden, *Finance*
Aaron Stieg, *Manager*
**EMP:** 6 **EST:** 1965
**SQ FT:** 14,000
**SALES (est):** 1.1MM **Privately Held**
**SIC:** 3451 Screw machine products

**(G-20328)**
**BAXTER HEALTHCARE CORPORATION**
1606 Beech St (60081-8080)
PHONE..............................847 948-3206
Martha Olson, *Principal*
**EMP:** 105
**SALES (corp-wide):** 10.1B **Publicly Held**
**SIC:** 2835 Blood derivative diagnostic agents
**HQ:** Baxter Healthcare Corporation
1 Baxter Pkwy
Deerfield IL 60015
224 948-2000

**(G-20329)**
**C R V ELECTRONICS CORP**
2249 Pierce Dr (60081-9703)
PHONE..............................815 675-6500
**Fax:** 815 675-6503
James Vyduna, *President*
Matthew W Krueger, *Vice Pres*
Jeanette Vyduna, *Treasurer*
**EMP:** 60
**SQ FT:** 16,000
**SALES (est):** 16.2MM **Privately Held**
**WEB:** www.crvelectronics.com
**SIC:** 3679 3496 3357 5063 Electronic circuits; miscellaneous fabricated wire products; nonferrous wiredrawing & insulating; electrical apparatus & equipment

**(G-20330)**
**CLEAN HARBORS WICHITA LLC**
2500 Westward Dr (60081-8828)
PHONE..............................815 675-1272
**EMP:** 3
**SALES (corp-wide):** 142.1MM **Privately Held**
**SIC:** 2992 Oils & greases, blending & compounding
**HQ:** Clean Harbors Wichita, Llc
2824 N Ohio St
Wichita KS 67219
316 832-0151

**(G-20331)**
**COILTECHNIC INC**
2402 Spring Ridge Dr C (60081-8693)
PHONE..............................815 675-9260
**Fax:** 847 675-3118
Rick Scott, *President*
Tim Scott, *Vice Pres*
**EMP:** 12
**SQ FT:** 5,400
**SALES:** 956K **Privately Held**
**SIC:** 3612 Transformers, except electric

**(G-20332)**
**D & G WELDING SUPPLY COMPANY**
7705 Industrial Dr Ste E (60081-8359)
PHONE..............................815 675-9890
George Van Liere, *President*
**EMP:** 2
**SALES (est):** 247K **Privately Held**
**SIC:** 3548 Welding apparatus

**(G-20333)**
**DIRECT AUTOMATION INC**
7800 Winn Rd (60081-7801)
PHONE..............................815 675-0588
**Fax:** 847 487-9566
Keith Oehlsen, *President*
Sandra Oehlsen, *Admin Sec*
**EMP:** 10
**SQ FT:** 12,400
**SALES (est):** 1.2MM **Privately Held**
**WEB:** www.directautomation.com
**SIC:** 3599 Machine shop, jobbing & repair

**(G-20334)**
**DYNAMIC MACHINING INC**
2304 Spring Ridge Dr C (60081-8646)
P.O. Box 467 (60081-0467)
PHONE..............................815 675-3330
Leo Navoichick, *President*
**EMP:** 5
**SALES (est):** 1MM **Privately Held**
**SIC:** 3599 Machine & other job shop work

**(G-20335)**
**ELAS TEK MOLDING INC**
Also Called: Elastek Molding
7517 Meyer Rd Ste 1 (60081-7805)
PHONE..............................815 675-9012
**Fax:** 815 675-9123
Jayne Davis, *President*
**EMP:** 22
**SQ FT:** 9,000
**SALES:** 1MM **Privately Held**
**SIC:** 3089 3841 2822 Injection molded finished plastic products; surgical & medical instruments; synthetic rubber

**(G-20336)**
**HAWTHORNE PRESS INC**
208 Chateau Dr (60081-8928)
PHONE..............................847 587-0582
Raymond W Freitag, *President*
Elizabeth Freitag, *Corp Secy*
**EMP:** 4
**SALES (est):** 270K **Privately Held**
**SIC:** 2752 2791 2789 Commercial printing, offset; typesetting; bookbinding & related work

**(G-20337)**
**INTERMATIC INCORPORATED (PA)**
7777 Winn Rd (60081-9698)
PHONE..............................815 675-2321
**Fax:** 815 675-7105
Douglas M Kinney Sr, *Ch of Bd*
David Schroeder, *President*
Victor Quiroz, *General Mgr*
Rick Boutilier, *Principal*
Patti Hamilton, *District Mgr*
▲ **EMP:** 769
**SQ FT:** 357,000
**SALES (est):** 228.7MM **Privately Held**
**WEB:** www.intermatic.com
**SIC:** 3612 3645 Line voltage regulators; residential lighting fixtures

**(G-20338)**
**INTERNATIONAL TRAFFIC CORP**
2402 Spring Ridge Dr E (60081-8693)
PHONE..............................815 675-1430
Jack Scott, *President*
Mark Fayta, *Sales Staff*
▲ **EMP:** 6
**SQ FT:** 3,500
**SALES (est):** 430K **Privately Held**
**WEB:** www.coiltechcorp.com
**SIC:** 3824 Fluid meters & counting devices

**(G-20339)**
**JOHNSON CUSTOM CABINETS**
7609 Blivin St (60081-9689)
PHONE..............................815 675-9690
Edward Johnson, *Owner*
**EMP:** 2
**SALES (est):** 236.8K **Privately Held**
**SIC:** 2434 Wood kitchen cabinets

**(G-20340)**
**K K GOURMET LLC**
9817 N Hunters Ln (60081-8677)
PHONE..............................847 727-5858
Kathleen M Schramm Smith, *Principal*
**EMP:** 3 **EST:** 2011
**SALES (est):** 160.7K **Privately Held**
**SIC:** 2099 Sauces: gravy, dressing & dip mixes

**(G-20341)**
**KITCHEN KRAFTERS INC**
7801 Industrial Dr Ste D (60081-8298)
PHONE..............................815 675-6061
**Fax:** 815 675-2638
Jeff Johnson, *President*
Moira Johnson, *Admin Sec*
**EMP:** 6
**SQ FT:** 2,560
**SALES:** 460K **Privately Held**
**SIC:** 2541 1799 2434 Counter & sink tops; counter top installation; wood kitchen cabinets

**(G-20342)**
**KNOLL STEEL INC**
2851 N Us Highway 12 (60081-7808)
PHONE..............................815 675-9400
**Fax:** 815 675-6297
Kenneth R Knoll, *President*
**EMP:** 16
**SALES (est):** 1MM **Privately Held**
**SIC:** 3441 Fabricated structural metal

**(G-20343)**
**KOSMOS TOOL INC**
2727 Rt 12 (60081)
P.O. Box 279 (60081-0279)
PHONE..............................815 675-2200
**Fax:** 815 675-2994
John Ferguson, *President*
Larry Pedley, *General Mgr*
Larry Tedlay, *General Mgr*
Rick Sadowski, *Admin Sec*
**EMP:** 14
**SQ FT:** 18,000
**SALES (est):** 2.2MM **Privately Held**
**WEB:** www.kosmostool.com
**SIC:** 3613 3544 3469 Distribution boards, electric; special dies, tools, jigs & fixtures; stamping metal for the trade

**(G-20344)**
**KUNA CORP**
Also Called: Netnotes
1512 Spring Ct (60081-7811)
PHONE..............................815 675-0140
Barbara Johnson, *President*
Mary Kay Martin, *President*
**EMP:** 6
**SALES (est):** 338.8K **Privately Held**
**SIC:** 3661 Telephone central office equipment, dial or manual

**(G-20345)**
**LED INDUSTRIES INC**
3001 N Us Highway 12 (60081-9668)
PHONE..............................888 700-7815
J Brian Henrie, *CEO*
Robert Ripley, *President*

Thomas Hoffelder, *Production*
Douglas A Van Camp, *CFO*
▲ **EMP:** 35
**SQ FT:** 25,500
**SALES (est):** 5MM **Privately Held**
**SIC:** 3674 Light emitting diodes

*(G-20346)*
**MIDWEST KEYLESS INC**
2414 Highview St (60081-9609)
**PHONE**.................................815 675-0404
Richard Lehecka, *Principal*
▲ **EMP:** 2
**SALES (est):** 408.8K **Privately Held**
**SIC:** 3429 Keys, locks & related hardware

*(G-20347)*
**MIKE MEIER & SONS FENCE MFG**
7501 Meyer Rd Ste 1 (60081-8600)
**PHONE**.................................847 587-1111
**Fax:** 847 675-1113
Debbie Meier, *President*
Mike Meier, *Vice Pres*
Mary Smith, *Manager*
**EMP:** 20
**SQ FT:** 6,000
**SALES (est):** 2.7MM **Privately Held**
**SIC:** 2499 3446 5211 Fencing, wood; fences or posts, ornamental iron or steel; fencing

*(G-20348)*
**MINIC PRECISION INC**
7706 Industrial Dr Ste K (60081-8278)
**PHONE**.................................815 675-0451
**Fax:** 815 675-0452
Michael K Gajewski, *President*
**EMP:** 10
**SQ FT:** 3,000
**SALES (est):** 750K **Privately Held**
**WEB:** www.minicprecision.com
**SIC:** 3451 Screw machine products

*(G-20349)*
**MODERN ABRASIVE CORP**
2855 N Us Highway 12 (60081-7808)
P.O. Box 219 (60081-0219)
**PHONE**.................................815 675-2352
**Fax:** 815 675-2822
Edward Prebe, *Ch of Bd*
Harvey B Nudelman, *President*
Harvey Nudelman, *President*
Mark Salmon, *Vice Pres*
Jerry Turner, *Vice Pres*
▲ **EMP:** 75 **EST:** 1959
**SQ FT:** 45,000
**SALES (est):** 13.3MM **Privately Held**
**WEB:** www.modernabrasive.com
**SIC:** 3291 Wheels, abrasive

*(G-20350)*
**NATIONAL CAP AND SET SCREW CO**
2991 N Us Highway 12 (60081-7809)
P.O. Box 280 (60081-0280)
**PHONE**.................................815 675-2363
**Fax:** 815 675-2211
Peter C May, *President*
Teresa Twardy, *Corp Secy*
Timothy May, *Shareholder*
**EMP:** 14 **EST:** 1941
**SQ FT:** 15,588
**SALES:** 1MM **Privately Held**
**SIC:** 3451 3452 5072 Screw machine products; screws, metal; bolts, nuts & screws

*(G-20351)*
**NATIONAL EMERGENCY MED ID INC**
100 Lincolnwood Ct (60081-8726)
**PHONE**.................................847 366-1267
Melissa Wilhelm, *President*
**EMP:** 3
**SQ FT:** 1,100
**SALES (est):** 647.3K **Privately Held**
**SIC:** 5099 3089 7363 Safety equipment & supplies; identification cards, plastic; help supply services

*(G-20352)*
**NORTHERN ORDINANCE CORPORATION**
Also Called: Nordco
7806 Industrial Dr (60081-8251)
P.O. Box 194 (60081-0194)
**PHONE**.................................815 675-6400
Roger N Dumke, *President*
Pat Browning, *Corp Secy*
**EMP:** 3
**SQ FT:** 300
**SALES (est):** 334.8K **Privately Held**
**SIC:** 3423 3484 Mechanics' hand tools; guns (firearms) or gun parts, 30 mm. & below

*(G-20353)*
**NOWFAB**
6413 Johnsburg Rd (60081-9686)
**PHONE**.................................815 675-2916
Steven Nowaczek, *President*
**EMP:** 2
**SALES (est):** 200K **Privately Held**
**SIC:** 3441 Fabricated structural metal

*(G-20354)*
**OLSON MACHINING INC**
1804 Holian Dr (60081-7904)
**PHONE**.................................815 675-2900
**Fax:** 815 675-2901
John R Olson, *President*
Frank William Olson III, *Vice Pres*
Sherri Ring, *Manager*
Deborah G Olson, *Admin Sec*
**EMP:** 27
**SQ FT:** 13,000
**SALES (est):** 6.8MM **Privately Held**
**WEB:** www.olsonmachining.com
**SIC:** 3599 Machine shop, jobbing & repair

*(G-20355)*
**PATLIN ENTERPRISES INC**
2907 N Us Highway 12 (60081-7809)
P.O. Box 98 (60081-0098)
**PHONE**.................................815 675-6606
**Fax:** 815 675-6535
Thomas Fry, *President*
Patricia Fry, *Corp Secy*
**EMP:** 10
**SQ FT:** 18,000
**SALES (est):** 1.6MM **Privately Held**
**SIC:** 3599 Custom machinery

*(G-20356)*
**PIMCO PLASTICS INC**
7517 Meyer Rd (60081-7805)
P.O. Box 40 (60081-0040)
**PHONE**.................................815 675-6464
Robert Schuehle, *President*
**EMP:** 4
**SALES (est):** 577.8K **Privately Held**
**SIC:** 3089 Injection molded finished plastic products

*(G-20357)*
**PRECISION CUSTOM MOLDERS INC**
1802 Holian Dr (60081-7904)
P.O. Box 190 (60081-0190)
**PHONE**.................................815 675-1370
Ed Krajecki, *President*
Sandy Krajecki, *Vice Pres*
Ed Crucyzky, *Human Res Mgr*
**EMP:** 20
**SQ FT:** 12,000
**SALES (est):** 2.7MM **Privately Held**
**WEB:** www.precisioncustommolders.com
**SIC:** 3089 Injection molding of plastics

*(G-20358)*
**PRECISION MOLDED CONCEPTS**
Also Called: P M C
2402 Spring Ridge Dr C (60081-8693)
**PHONE**.................................815 675-0060
**Fax:** 815 675-3118
Tim Scott, *President*
Richard Scott, *Vice Pres*
**EMP:** 12
**SQ FT:** 6,000
**SALES:** 1.2MM **Privately Held**
**WEB:** www.precisionmolded.com
**SIC:** 3089 Injection molding of plastics

*(G-20359)*
**PRO CIRCLE GOLF CENTERS INC**
Also Called: Pro Circle Golf Driving Range
1810 N Us Highway 12 (60081-5700)
**PHONE**.................................815 675-2747
**Fax:** 815 675-9527
Clarence W Shastal, *President*
Gary Shastal, *President*
Mildred C Shastal, *Corp Secy*
Gary W Shastal, *Vice Pres*
**EMP:** 3 **EST:** 1965
**SQ FT:** 2,800
**SALES (est):** 408.2K **Privately Held**
**WEB:** www.procirclegolf.com
**SIC:** 5941 7999 3949 Golf goods & equipment; golf driving range; miniature golf course operation; golf equipment

*(G-20360)*
**QUICKER ENGINEERING**
7516 Buena Vis (60081-8925)
**PHONE**.................................815 675-6516
Richard Derosa, *Owner*
**EMP:** 3
**SALES (est):** 166.3K **Privately Held**
**SIC:** 3944 Cars, play (children's vehicles)

*(G-20361)*
**RAINBOW SIGNS**
2404 Spring Ridge Dr A (60081-8692)
**PHONE**.................................815 675-6750
**Fax:** 815 675-6832
Ronald Ottinger, *President*
**EMP:** 14
**SQ FT:** 6,000
**SALES (est):** 1.5MM **Privately Held**
**SIC:** 3993 Signs & advertising specialties; neon signs

*(G-20362)*
**RINGMASTER MFG**
8001 Winn Rd (60081-9687)
P.O. Box 8 (60081-0008)
**PHONE**.................................815 675-4230
**EMP:** 5
**SALES (est):** 536K **Privately Held**
**SIC:** 3999 Manufacturing industries

*(G-20363)*
**RIVER NORTH INDUSTRIES INC**
1905 Spring Ct (60081-8644)
**PHONE**.................................773 600-4960
**EMP:** 3
**SALES (est):** 272.7K **Privately Held**
**SIC:** 3999 Manufacturing industries

*(G-20364)*
**SCOT FORGE COMPANY (PA)**
8001 Winn Rd (60081-9687)
P.O. Box 8 (60081-0008)
**PHONE**.................................815 675-1000
**Fax:** 815 587-2007
John L Cain, *President*
Michelle Riedel, *President*
Matt Nowakowski, *General Mgr*
Ronald E Hahn, *COO*
Mike Peglow, *Prdtn Mgr*
▲ **EMP:** 325 **EST:** 1893
**SQ FT:** 375,000
**SALES (est):** 145.7MM **Privately Held**
**WEB:** www.scotforge.com
**SIC:** 3462 Aircraft forgings, ferrous

*(G-20365)*
**SPORTDECALS SPORT & SPIRIT PRO**
Also Called: Absolutely Custom
2504 Spring Ridge Dr (60081-8698)
P.O. Box 860 (60081-0860)
**PHONE**.................................800 435-6110
Don Metivier, *Ch of Bd*
Christopher Gagnon, *President*
Terri Pagels, *Purch Mgr*
Heidi Hackler, *Buyer*
Curt Rodgers, *CFO*
**EMP:** 90
**SQ FT:** 40,000
**SALES (est):** 25.7MM **Privately Held**
**WEB:** www.sdind.com
**SIC:** 2759 Decals: printing

*(G-20366)*
**SUNNYWOOD INCORPORATED**
2503 Spring Ridge Dr H (60081-7807)
**PHONE**.................................815 675-9777
**Fax:** 815 675-9788
William Woo, *President*
Suzanne Reuss, *General Mgr*
▲ **EMP:** 4
**SQ FT:** 5,000
**SALES (est):** 1.2MM **Privately Held**
**WEB:** www.sunnywood.net
**SIC:** 3944 2389 3961 Games, toys & children's vehicles; costumes; costume jewelry

*(G-20367)*
**THREAD & GAGE CO INC**
3000 N Us Highway 12 (60081-9362)
P.O. Box 6 (60081-0006)
**PHONE**.................................815 675-2305
**Fax:** 815 675-2229
Deno A Buralli Jr, *President*
Joseph Buralli, *Vice Pres*
**EMP:** 2 **EST:** 1956
**SQ FT:** 28,000
**SALES:** 400K **Privately Held**
**WEB:** www.threadgageco.com
**SIC:** 3452 3545 3823 3541 Screws, metal; gauges (machine tool accessories); industrial instrmnts msrmnt display/control process variable; machine tools, metal cutting type; hand & edge tools

*(G-20368)*
**THREE R PLASTICS INC**
1801 Holian Dr (60081-7930)
**PHONE**.................................815 675-0844
Michael Gore, *President*
Raymond Gore, *Vice Pres*
Theresa Gore, *Manager*
**EMP:** 15
**SQ FT:** 5,000
**SALES (est):** 3.3MM **Privately Held**
**WEB:** www.threerplastics.com
**SIC:** 3089 Injection molding of plastics

*(G-20369)*
**TONERHEAD INC**
Also Called: Laser Tek Industries
3106 N Us Highway 12 (60081-9362)
**PHONE**.................................815 331-3200
**Fax:** 815 675-0028
Harold E Nicodem, *President*
Allen Jenner, *Controller*
▼ **EMP:** 46
**SALES (est):** 7.4MM **Privately Held**
**SIC:** 3955 Print cartridges for laser & other computer printers

*(G-20370)*
**TRACK MASTER INC**
7451 Spring Grove Rd (60081-8860)
**PHONE**.................................815 675-6603
Daniel Smith, *President*
**EMP:** 6
**SALES (est):** 455.7K **Privately Held**
**SIC:** 3648 Lighting equipment

*(G-20371)*
**TRACO INDUSTRIES INC**
7451 Spring Grove Rd A (60081-8860)
**PHONE**.................................815 675-6603
**Fax:** 815 675-6919
Carol Smith, *President*
Jerry Odwair, *Manager*
**EMP:** 6
**SQ FT:** 10,000
**SALES (est):** 640K **Privately Held**
**SIC:** 3599 3498 3444 3443 Machine shop, jobbing & repair; fabricated pipe & fittings; sheet metalwork; fabricated plate work (boiler shop)

*(G-20372)*
**TRU-MACHINE CO INC**
7502 Mayo Ct Unit 3 (60081-7905)
**PHONE**.................................815 675-6735
Lou Sikora, *President*
Daintri Sikora, *Vice Pres*
**EMP:** 3
**SQ FT:** 10,000
**SALES:** 500K **Privately Held**
**SIC:** 3469 Machine parts, stamped or pressed metal

# Spring Grove - Mchenry County (G-20373) — GEOGRAPHIC SECTION

**(G-20373)**
**US POST CO INC**
2701 N Us Highway 12 A (60081-7815)
PHONE..............................815 675-9313
Richard A Parent, *President*
Michele Kasper, *Manager*
**EMP:** 5
**SQ FT:** 500
**SALES:** 550K **Privately Held**
**WEB:** www.cleanpc.com
**SIC: 3444** Mail (post office) collection or storage boxes, sheet metal

## Spring Valley
### Bureau County

**(G-20374)**
**AQUA CONTROL INC**
Also Called: Aci
6a Wolfer Industrial Park (61362-9504)
PHONE..............................815 664-4900
Fax: 815 664-4901
Willis Dane, *President*
Reanna Pelszynski, *General Mgr*
Adam Pacholski, *Electrical Engi*
Joellen Nienaber, *Accountant*
Maryjo Credi, *Cust Mgr*
▲ **EMP:** 30
**SQ FT:** 35,000
**SALES (est):** 7.9MM **Privately Held**
**WEB:** www.aquacontrol.com
**SIC: 3561** 3272 3523 Pumps & pumping equipment; fountains, concrete; farm machinery & equipment

**(G-20375)**
**M BUCKMAN & SON CO**
200 S Greenwood St (61362)
PHONE..............................815 663-9411
George Buckman, *President*
**EMP:** 3 **EST:** 1913
**SQ FT:** 1,500
**SALES (est):** 410K **Privately Held**
**SIC: 5093** 3341 Scrap & waste materials; secondary nonferrous metals

**(G-20376)**
**MAUTINO DISTRIBUTING CO INC**
501 W 1st St (61362-1204)
P.O. Box 190 (61362-0190)
PHONE..............................815 664-4311
Fax: 815 664-2224
Mark Mautino, *President*
Anton F Mautino, *Admin Sec*
▲ **EMP:** 50 **EST:** 1905
**SQ FT:** 36,000
**SALES (est):** 5.3MM **Privately Held**
**SIC: 5963** 2037 Bottled water delivery; fruit juices

**(G-20377)**
**OLD COLONY BAKING COMPANY INC**
29699 Il Highway 29 (61362-9209)
P.O. Box 1111, Northbrook (60065-1111)
PHONE..............................847 498-5434
Anne Kaufman, *CEO*
Jeff Kaufman, *President*
**EMP:** 4 **EST:** 1997
**SALES (est):** 415.1K **Privately Held**
**WEB:** www.ocolony.com
**SIC: 2052** Cookies

**(G-20378)**
**REGENEX CORP**
1 Wolfer Industrial Park (61362-9601)
P.O. Box 169 (61362-0169)
PHONE..............................815 663-2003
Fax: 815 663-3004
Daniel J Berent, *President*
Doug Woerner, *Plant Mgr*
**EMP:** 11
**SALES (est):** 1.1MM **Privately Held**
**SIC: 2611** Pulp manufactured from waste or recycled paper

**(G-20379)**
**RIVERFRONT MACHINE INC**
6 Wolfer Industrial Park (61362-9702)
PHONE..............................815 663-5000
Fax: 815 663-5001
John O Zurliene, *President*
**EMP:** 75
**SQ FT:** 90,000
**SALES (est):** 14.3MM **Privately Held**
**SIC: 3469** Metal stampings

**(G-20380)**
**RONKEN INDUSTRIES INC**
9 Wolfer Industrial Park (61362-9601)
PHONE..............................815 664-5306
Fax: 815 664-5308
Donald E Plochocki Sr, *President*
Sandy Milota, *Controller*
Luanne M Plochocki, *Admin Sec*
John Dzierzynski, *Maintence Staff*
**EMP:** 48 **EST:** 1980
**SQ FT:** 15,000
**SALES (est):** 7.3MM **Privately Held**
**WEB:** www.ronkenind.com
**SIC: 3629** Capacitors & condensers

**(G-20381)**
**SHEET WISE PRINTING**
208 E Saint Paul St (61362-2140)
PHONE..............................815 664-3025
Christina Heller, *Owner*
**EMP:** 3
**SALES:** 95K **Privately Held**
**SIC: 2752** Commercial printing, lithographic

## Springerton
### White County

**(G-20382)**
**DON POORE SAW MILL INC**
Also Called: Universal Saw Mill
15694 Blairsville Rd (62887-2166)
PHONE..............................618 757-2240
Don Poore, *President*
Judy Poore, *Vice Pres*
**EMP:** 3
**SALES (est):** 247.3K **Privately Held**
**SIC: 2421** Sawmills & planing mills, general

## Springfield
### Sangamon County

**(G-20383)**
**A & B PRINTING SERVICE INC**
2122 N Republic St (62702-1851)
PHONE..............................217 789-9034
Randy Bruso, *President*
Elmer Bruso, *Vice Pres*
Kelsey Miller, *Office Mgr*
**EMP:** 5
**SQ FT:** 2,000
**SALES (est):** 16.9K **Privately Held**
**SIC: 2752** Lithographic Commercial Printing

**(G-20384)**
**ACE SIGN CO**
2540 S 1st St (62704-4700)
PHONE..............................217 522-8417
Fax: 217 522-6842
Dennis Bringuet, *President*
Jo E Higgins, *General Mgr*
Matt Larison, *Project Mgr*
Tyson Horacek, *Production*
Scott Bringuet, *Sales Mgr*
**EMP:** 23 **EST:** 1940
**SALES (est):** 3.5MM **Privately Held**
**WEB:** www.acesignco.com
**SIC: 3993** Signs & advertising specialties

**(G-20385)**
**ACOUSTIC AVENUE INC**
Also Called: Legacy Audio
3023 E Sangamon Ave (62702-1422)
PHONE..............................217 544-9810
Fax: 217 744-1483
William Dudleston, *President*
Chris Daniels, *Engineer*
Doug Brown, *VP Sales*
Victoria Dudleston, *Marketing Mgr*
Kathy Schappaugh, *Manager*
◆ **EMP:** 12
**SALES (est):** 2.2MM **Privately Held**
**SIC: 3651** 5064 5731 7622 Speaker systems; high fidelity equipment; radio, television & electronic stores; home entertainment repair services

**(G-20386)**
**AFAR IMPORTS & INTERIORS INC (PA)**
Also Called: Tuxhorn Drapery
3125 S Douglas Ave (62704-5813)
PHONE..............................217 744-3262
Tara McVary, *President*
**EMP:** 3
**SQ FT:** 1,200
**SALES (est):** 799K **Privately Held**
**SIC: 5714** 3499 5231 5713 Draperies; trophies, metal, except silver; ladders, portable: metal; wallpaper; floor covering stores; gifts & novelties; interior design services

**(G-20387)**
**APPLE LUBE CENTER**
3316 Robbins Rd Ste A (62704-7403)
PHONE..............................217 787-7035
Bob Appleton, *Owner*
**EMP:** 2
**SALES (est):** 216.1K **Privately Held**
**SIC: 2911** Oils, lubricating

**(G-20388)**
**ARNOLD MONUMENT CO INC (PA)**
1621 Wabash Ave (62704-5310)
PHONE..............................217 546-2102
Thomas A Green Jr, *President*
Mary Green, *Corp Secy*
**EMP:** 5
**SALES (est):** 641.5K **Privately Held**
**SIC: 5999** 3471 3281 Monuments & tombstones; plating & polishing; cut stone & stone products

**(G-20389)**
**ASSOCIATES ENGRAVING COMPANY**
Also Called: Metal Decor
2601 Colt Rd (62707-9782)
P.O. Box 19452 (62794-9452)
PHONE..............................217 523-4565
Fax: 217 753-3068
Stephen Wells, *President*
Gary Hills, *Regional Mgr*
Dan Tennant, *Business Mgr*
Mark Pierce, *Opers Staff*
Diane Dolenc, *Treasurer*
▲ **EMP:** 80 **EST:** 1961
**SQ FT:** 48,000
**SALES (est):** 10.7MM **Privately Held**
**WEB:** www.metaldecor.com
**SIC: 2796** Engraving on copper, steel, wood or rubber: printing plates

**(G-20390)**
**ATLAS CONCRETE PRODUCTS CO**
2500 Peerless Mine Rd (62702-1417)
PHONE..............................217 528-7368
Fax: 217 528-7383
Janet Kalb, *Manager*
**EMP:** 12
**SQ FT:** 13,000
**SALES (est):** 1.4MM **Privately Held**
**SIC: 3271** 5032 3272 Blocks, concrete or cinder: standard; brick, except refractory; concrete building products; concrete products

**(G-20391)**
**AUDIBEL HEARING CENTER**
2347 W Monroe St (62704-1452)
PHONE..............................217 670-1183
Fax: 217 793-3515
Doug Haws, *Partner*
Devonna Haws, *Partner*
**EMP:** 3 **EST:** 1983
**SALES (est):** 194.6K **Privately Held**
**SIC: 3842** Hearing aids

**(G-20392)**
**AWEM CORPORATION**
1 W Old State Capitol Plz # 703 (62701-1378)
PHONE..............................217 670-1451
Andreas Knauer, *CEO*
**EMP:** 3
**SALES (est):** 215.2K **Privately Held**
**SIC: 3621** Windmills, electric generating

**(G-20393)**
**AZTEC PRODUCTS**
3321 Blueberry Ln (62711-8253)
PHONE..............................217 726-8631
Robert Lee Smith, *President*
Linda Mae Smith, *Admin Sec*
**EMP:** 6
**SQ FT:** 10,000
**SALES (est):** 74.6K **Privately Held**
**SIC: 3069** 3061 Molded rubber products; mechanical rubber goods

**(G-20394)**
**BAILEY HARDWOODS INC**
628 Kimble Ct (62703-4760)
PHONE..............................217 529-6800
Fax: 217 529-6880
Jennifer J Desart, *President*
Jennifer Bailey, *Treasurer*
**EMP:** 6
**SQ FT:** 6,500
**SALES:** 498.2K **Privately Held**
**WEB:** www.baileyhardwoods.com
**SIC: 5211** 2431 3446 Millwork & lumber; staircases & stairs, wood; moldings, wood: unfinished & prefinished; architectural metalwork

**(G-20395)**
**BEMCO MATTRESS INC**
Also Called: Bemco Matress
4952 Industrial Ave (62703-5346)
PHONE..............................217 529-0777
Fax: 217 529-1421
Michele Buyan, *President*
Sean Patridge, *Vice Pres*
Joshua Patridge, *Admin Sec*
**EMP:** 30
**SQ FT:** 45,000
**SALES (est):** 4.9MM **Privately Held**
**WEB:** www.bemco.com
**SIC: 2515** Mattresses, innerspring or box spring; bedsprings, assembled

**(G-20396)**
**BI-PETRO INC (PA)**
3150 Executive Park Dr (62703-4509)
P.O. Box 19246 (62794-9246)
PHONE..............................217 535-0181
Fax: 217 535-2774
Lawrence A Sweat, *CEO*
John F Homeier, *Ch of Bd*
Skippy G Homeier, *President*
Charlie Woods, *Corp Secy*
Seanna Malek, *Senior VP*
**EMP:** 20
**SQ FT:** 10,000
**SALES (est):** 27.5MM **Privately Held**
**WEB:** www.bipetro.com
**SIC: 5171** 1311 Petroleum terminals; crude petroleum production

**(G-20397)**
**BILL WEEKS INC**
Also Called: Weeks Seatcovers
229 N Grand Ave W (62702-2550)
PHONE..............................217 523-8735
Fax: 217 523-8727
Dorathy Weeks, *CEO*
Dorthory Weeks, *President*
Rodney Weeks, *President*
Delilah Weeks, *Admin Sec*
**EMP:** 4 **EST:** 1938
**SQ FT:** 9,600
**SALES (est):** 352.7K **Privately Held**
**SIC: 7641** 2399 2511 7532 Reupholstery; seat covers, automobile; wood household furniture; tops (canvas or plastic), installation or repair: automotive; motor vehicle parts & accessories

**(G-20398)**
**BOB FOLDER LURES CO**
2071 Hazlett Rd (62707-2600)
PHONE..............................217 787-1116
Robert L Folder, *Owner*
Mary Folder, *Treasurer*
**EMP:** 10
**SALES (est):** 579.4K **Privately Held**
**SIC: 3949** 5091 Fishing tackle, general; flies, fishing: artificial; fishing tackle

▲ = Import ▼ = Export ◆ = Import/Export

# GEOGRAPHIC SECTION
## Springfield - Sangamon County (G-20423)

**(G-20399)**
**BRANDT CONSOLIDATED INC (PA)**
Also Called: Agvision
2935 S Koke Mill Rd (62711-9651)
PHONE..................217 547-5800
Fax: 217 547-5801
Glen A Brandt, *Ch of Bd*
Rick C Brandt, *President*
Gregory Jackson, *Regional Mgr*
Glen Kitson, *Regional Mgr*
Chris Bassaber, *Business Mgr*
▲ **EMP:** 45
**SQ FT:** 25,000
**SALES (est):** 180MM **Privately Held**
**WEB:** www.indresgroup.com
**SIC: 2875** 5191 Fertilizers, mixing only; farm supplies

**(G-20400)**
**BSN SPORTS LLC**
510 E Apple Orchard Rd # 100 (62703-4017)
PHONE..................217 788-0914
Fax: 217 788-0915
**EMP:** 4
**SALES (corp-wide):** 1.1B **Privately Held**
**WEB:** www.haydens.com
**SIC: 3949** Sporting & athletic goods
**HQ:** Bsn Sports, Llc
1901 Diplomat Dr
Farmers Branch TX 75234
972 484-9484

**(G-20401)**
**BUNN-O-MATIC CORPORATION**
825 S Airport Dr (62707-8486)
PHONE..................217 528-8739
Matthew Algie, *Managing Dir*
David Williamson, *Managing Dir*
Jim H Anson, *Senior VP*
Scott Ball, *Vice Pres*
Frank Houmiel, *Vice Pres*
**EMP:** 9
**SALES (corp-wide):** 215.3MM **Privately Held**
**SIC: 3589** Coffee brewing equipment
**PA:** Bunn-O-Matic Corporation
5020 Ash Grove Dr
Springfield IL 62711
217 529-6601

**(G-20402)**
**BUNN-O-MATIC CORPORATION**
1500 Stevenson Dr (62703-4229)
PHONE..................217 529-6601
**EMP:** 3
**SALES (corp-wide):** 215.3MM **Privately Held**
**SIC: 3589** Asbestos removal equipment
**PA:** Bunn-O-Matic Corporation
5020 Ash Grove Dr
Springfield IL 62711
217 529-6601

**(G-20403)**
**CANE PLUS**
2225 S Whittier Ave (62704-4651)
P.O. Box 9409 (62791-9409)
PHONE..................217 522-4035
Ronald Earley, *President*
Maureen Earley, *Vice Pres*
Chris Redcliff, *Manager*
**EMP:** 4
**SALES (est):** 276.3K **Privately Held**
**SIC: 3999** Canes & cane trimmings, except precious metal

**(G-20404)**
**CANHAM GRAPHICS**
4524 Industrial Ave (62703-5316)
P.O. Box 435, Pawnee (62558-0435)
PHONE..................217 585-5085
Fax: 217 585-5083
Bill Canham, *Owner*
**EMP:** 3
**SQ FT:** 3,600
**SALES (est):** 180K **Privately Held**
**SIC: 7532** 3993 Truck painting & lettering; signs & advertising specialties

**(G-20405)**
**CAPITOL CITY MACHINE**
2840 Adlai Stevenson Dr (62703-4482)
PHONE..................217 529-0293
Tim Wilkerson, *Principal*
**EMP:** 2 **EST:** 2001
**SALES (est):** 245.2K **Privately Held**
**SIC: 3599** Machine shop, jobbing & repair

**(G-20406)**
**CAPITOL CITY TOOL & DESIGN**
1330 Taylor Ave (62703-5638)
PHONE..................217 544-9250
Fax: 217 544-9250
Michael Moe, *President*
**EMP:** 2 **EST:** 1951
**SQ FT:** 5,000
**SALES:** 250K **Privately Held**
**SIC: 3544** Die sets for metal stamping (presses)

**(G-20407)**
**CAPITOL READY-MIX INC (PA)**
1900 E Mason St (62702-5812)
PHONE..................217 528-1100
Fax: 217 528-0204
Lou Marcy, *President*
Jamie Maley, *General Mgr*
Mike Young, *Sales Executive*
**EMP:** 25
**SQ FT:** 1,200
**SALES (est):** 5.2MM **Privately Held**
**SIC: 3273** Ready-mixed concrete

**(G-20408)**
**CAPITOL WOOD WORKS LLC**
Also Called: Kwik-Wall Company
1010 E Edwards St (62703-1327)
PHONE..................217 522-5553
Mark Jennings, *Purchasing*
Jordan Frank, *Bookkeeper*
Chris Hand, *Human Res Mgr*
Andy Marr, *Sales Mgr*
Robert Mazzier, *Marketing Staff*
▲ **EMP:** 75 **EST:** 1929
**SQ FT:** 75,000
**SALES (est):** 18.6MM **Privately Held**
**WEB:** www.kwik-wall.com
**SIC: 2542** 3446 2541 Partitions & fixtures, except wood; architectural metalwork; wood partitions & fixtures

**(G-20409)**
**CAST INDUSTRIES INC**
580 North St (62704-5801)
PHONE..................217 522-8292
Fax: 217 522-8378
James Stevens, *President*
Ron Stevens, *Vice Pres*
Sharon Stevens, *Treasurer*
Steve Hedges, *Executive*
**EMP:** 28
**SQ FT:** 4,500
**SALES (est):** 3.3MM **Privately Held**
**WEB:** www.castind.com
**SIC: 3949** Lures, fishing: artificial

**(G-20410)**
**CDS OFFICE SYSTEMS INC (PA)**
Also Called: Cds Office Technologies
612 S Dirksen Pkwy (62703-2183)
P.O. Box 3566 (62708-3566)
PHONE..................800 367-1508
Fax: 217 753-6536
Jerome L Watson, *President*
Markham F Watson, *President*
Dave Raman, *General Mgr*
Russell Taylor, *Regional Mgr*
John Bolser, *Vice Pres*
**EMP:** 83
**SQ FT:** 23,000
**SALES (est):** 132.4MM **Privately Held**
**SIC: 5044** 5999 7629 7378 Office equipment; copying equipment; business machines & equipment; facsimile equipment; business machine repair, electric; computer maintenance & repair; photographic equipment & supplies; computer peripheral equipment

**(G-20411)**
**CDS OFFICE SYSTEMS INC**
Also Called: C D S Office Technologies
612 S Dirksen Pkwy (62703-2183)
PHONE..................630 305-9034
Fax: 630 305-9876
Richard Eden, *Manager*
**EMP:** 14

**SALES (corp-wide):** 132.4MM **Privately Held**
**SIC: 5044** 7629 5999 5943 Office equipment; business machine repair, electric; business machines & equipment; stationery stores; commercial printing, lithographic
**PA:** C.D.S. Office Systems Incorporated
612 S Dirksen Pkwy
Springfield IL 62703
800 367-1508

**(G-20412)**
**CENTRAL CONCRETE PRODUCTS (PA)**
3241 Terminal Ave (62707-4503)
P.O. Box 3705 (62708-3705)
PHONE..................217 523-7964
Fax: 217 522-4216
Tom Luka, *President*
**EMP:** 10
**SQ FT:** 15,000
**SALES (est):** 2.1MM **Privately Held**
**SIC: 3272** 1711 Septic tanks, concrete; burial vaults, concrete or precast terrazzo; septic system construction

**(G-20413)**
**CENTRAL ILL COMMUNICATIONS LLC**
Also Called: Illinois Times
1240 S 6th St (62703-2408)
P.O. Box 5256 (62705-5256)
PHONE..................217 753-2226
Fax: 217 753-2281
Fletcher F Farrar Jr, *President*
Beth Irwin, *Manager*
**EMP:** 12
**SALES (est):** 530K **Privately Held**
**SIC: 7383** 8661 2711 News reporting services for newspapers & periodicals; religious organizations; commercial printing & newspaper publishing combined

**(G-20414)**
**CENTRAL ILLINOIS SIGN COMPANY**
3040 E Linden Ave (62702-6018)
Drawer 1417 N Stephens (62702)
PHONE..................217 523-4740
Fax: 217 523-4740
Elloise Conaway, *President*
Fred Conaway, *Vice Pres*
Phil Watson, *Office Mgr*
**EMP:** 4
**SQ FT:** 5,000
**SALES (est):** 316.9K **Privately Held**
**SIC: 3993** 1721 7389 Electric signs; neon signs; letters for signs, metal; commercial painting; lettering & sign painting services

**(G-20415)**
**CERTIFIED TANK & MFG LLC**
3520 Norman St (62702-1100)
PHONE..................217 525-1433
William D Rohr, *President*
Sally Craft, *Manager*
Kc White, *Manager*
Brent Brandvold,
**EMP:** 40
**SQ FT:** 50,000
**SALES:** 6MM **Privately Held**
**WEB:** www.certified-tank-equip.com
**SIC: 3795** 3411 Tanks & tank components; metal cans

**(G-20416)**
**CHARLES C THOMAS PUBLISHER**
2600 S 1st St (62704-4730)
P.O. Box 19265 (62794-9265)
PHONE..................217 789-8980
Fax: 217 789-9130
Michael Thomas, *President*
Jo Turner, *Purchasing*
Darleen McCarty, *Admin Sec*
**EMP:** 19 **EST:** 1927
**SQ FT:** 50,000
**SALES:** 2MM **Privately Held**
**WEB:** www.ccthomas.com
**SIC: 2731** 2752 2732 Book publishing; commercial printing, lithographic; book printing

**(G-20417)**
**CHGO DAILY LAW BULLETIN**
401 S 2nd St (62701-1727)
PHONE..................217 525-6735
Lanning Macfarland, *Principal*
**EMP:** 3
**SALES (est):** 123.3K **Privately Held**
**SIC: 2711** Newspapers, publishing & printing

**(G-20418)**
**CHRISTIAN SPECIALIZED SERVICES**
2312 S Wiggins Ave (62704-4373)
PHONE..................217 546-7338
Judy Noll, *Partner*
**EMP:** 3
**SALES (est):** 150K **Privately Held**
**SIC: 8661** 2741 Religious organizations; miscellaneous publishing

**(G-20419)**
**CLEAR LAKE SAND & GRAVEL CO**
2500 Shadow Chaser Dr (62711-7225)
PHONE..................217 725-6999
Ronald Drennan, *President*
David Drennan, *Vice Pres*
**EMP:** 10
**SQ FT:** 1,500
**SALES:** 900K **Privately Held**
**SIC: 1442** Construction sand mining; gravel mining

**(G-20420)**
**COCA-COLA REFRESHMENTS USA INC**
3495 E Sangamon Ave (62707-9731)
PHONE..................217 544-4892
Fax: 217 544-8749
Ken White, *Area Mgr*
Erica Jizmejian, *Business Mgr*
Tom Harrington, *Division VP*
David Ethridge, *Vice Pres*
Norman George, *Vice Pres*
**EMP:** 50
**SALES (corp-wide):** 41.8B **Publicly Held**
**WEB:** www.cokecce.com
**SIC: 2086** 5182 Bottled & canned soft drinks; neutral spirits
**HQ:** Coca-Cola Refreshments Usa, Inc.
2500 Windy Ridge Pkwy Se
Atlanta GA 30339
770 989-3000

**(G-20421)**
**CONTECH ENGNERED SOLUTIONS LLC**
1110 Stevenson Dr (62703-4222)
PHONE..................217 529-5461
Fax: 217 529-7054
Mike Heer, *Sales Staff*
Doug Bower, *Branch Mgr*
**EMP:** 50
**SQ FT:** 55,000 **Privately Held**
**SIC: 3443** Fabricated plate work (boiler shop)
**HQ:** Contech Engineered Solutions Llc
9025 Ctr Pinte Dr Ste 400
West Chester OH 45069
513 645-7000

**(G-20422)**
**COUNTY MATERIALS CORP**
2917 N Dirksen Pkwy (62702-1409)
PHONE..................217 544-4607
Thomas Anderson, *Branch Mgr*
**EMP:** 33
**SALES (corp-wide):** 422.4MM **Privately Held**
**WEB:** www.ctymaterials.com
**SIC: 3271** 3273 5211 Blocks, concrete or cinder: standard; ready-mixed concrete; lumber & other building materials; masonry materials & supplies
**PA:** County Materials Corp.
205 North St
Marathon WI 54448
715 443-2434

**(G-20423)**
**CRAZY HORSE CONCRETE INC**
1600 E Clear Lake Ave (62703-1172)
PHONE..................217 523-4420
Jan Melley, *General Mgr*

# Springfield - Sangamon County (G-20424)

Jack Davis, *Principal*
Ron Anderson, *CFO*
**EMP:** 30
**SQ FT:** 4,000
**SALES (est):** 3.8MM **Privately Held**
**SIC:** 3273 Ready-mixed concrete

### (G-20424)
### CREASEY CONSTRUCTION ILL INC
3540 S Park Ave (62704)
P.O. Box 9286 (62791-9286)
**PHONE**...................................217 546-1277
Jan W Creasey, *President*
Dee Lemasters, *Owner*
Lisa Creasey, *Admin Sec*
**EMP:** 10
**SALES (est):** 1.1MM **Privately Held**
**SIC:** 3564 Filters, air: furnaces, air conditioning equipment, etc.

### (G-20425)
### CREASEY PRINTING SERVICES INC
1905 Morning Sun Ln (62711-5635)
**PHONE**...................................217 787-1055
William Creasey, *CEO*
Kelli Lynch, *President*
Greg Lynch, *Corp Secy*
Suzy Creasey, *Exec VP*
Tracey Irsik, *Manager*
**EMP:** 7
**SALES (est):** 919K **Privately Held**
**WEB:** www.creaseyprinting.com
**SIC:** 2741 2752 2732 Catalogs: publishing & printing; commercial printing, lithographic; book printing

### (G-20426)
### CUSTOM CHEMICAL INC
Also Called: Custom Chemical Engineering
4524 Industrial Ave (62703-5316)
**PHONE**...................................217 529-0878
Jack D Fair, *President*
Virgene Fair, *Corp Secy*
Scott Fair, *Vice Pres*
**EMP:** 4
**SQ FT:** 7,000
**SALES (est):** 500K **Privately Held**
**WEB:** www.customchemicalengineering.com
**SIC:** 2899 2851 2841 2869 Water treating compounds; paint removers; soap: granulated, liquid, cake, flaked or chip; industrial organic chemicals

### (G-20427)
### CUSTOM WOODWORK & INTERIORS (PA)
Also Called: Gary Bryan Kitchens & Bath
3208 S Douglas Ave (62704-5816)
**PHONE**...................................217 546-0006
**Fax:** 217 787-0055
Michael P Bedolli, *President*
Doris Pierce, *Vice Pres*
Sharon Bedolli, *Treasurer*
Pat Dippel, *Office Mgr*
**EMP:** 22 **EST:** 1976
**SQ FT:** 30,000
**SALES (est):** 1.8MM **Privately Held**
**WEB:** www.garybryankitchens.com
**SIC:** 2434 5211 2541 Wood kitchen cabinets; vanities, bathroom: wood; lumber & other building materials; wood partitions & fixtures

### (G-20428)
### DAL ACRES WEST KENNEL
2508 W Jefferson St (62702-3405)
**PHONE**...................................217 793-3647
**Fax:** 217 793-2864
Patricia Hudspeth, *President*
Kathy Knoles, *Owner*
**EMP:** 6
**SALES (est):** 452.1K **Privately Held**
**SIC:** 3999 Pet supplies

### (G-20429)
### DONATH AIRCRAFT SERVICE
1733 S Glenwood Ave (62704-4005)
**PHONE**...................................217 528-6667
Bob Donath, *Owner*
**EMP:** 4

**SALES (est):** 190K **Privately Held**
**WEB:** www.donathaircraft.com
**SIC:** 3721 Aircraft

### (G-20430)
### DR PEPPER/7 UP BOTTLING GROUP
4600 Industrial Ave (62703-5318)
**PHONE**...................................217 585-1496
**Fax:** 217 585-2094
Jamil Saba, *Principal*
Jamil Abusaba, *Sales Executive*
**EMP:** 7
**SALES (est):** 510K **Privately Held**
**SIC:** 2086 Bottled & canned soft drinks

### (G-20431)
### EAGLE CHASSIS INC
2877 N Dirksen Pkwy (62702-1408)
**PHONE**...................................217 525-1941
**Fax:** 217 525-1884
Jerry Russell, *President*
**EMP:** 3
**SALES (est):** 236.5K **Privately Held**
**SIC:** 3399 Powder, metal

### (G-20432)
### EDDIES COUSIN INC
1951 W Monroe St (62704-1530)
**PHONE**...................................217 679-5777
Will Hoeberk, *Owner*
**EMP:** 4
**SALES (est):** 348K **Privately Held**
**SIC:** 2599 Bar, restaurant & cafeteria furniture

### (G-20433)
### ELASTOCON TPE TECHNOLOGIES INC
3105 E Dotmar Dr (62703)
P.O. Box 463, Rochester (62563-0463)
**PHONE**...................................217 498-8500
**Fax:** 217 498-8558
David Barkus, *President*
**EMP:** 25
**SQ FT:** 35,000
**SALES (est):** 1.2MM **Privately Held**
**WEB:** www.elastocon.net
**SIC:** 3087 Custom compound purchased resins

### (G-20434)
### ELLIOT INSTITUTE FOR SOCIAL SC
Also Called: ACORN BOOK
524 E Lawrence Ave (62703-2319)
P.O. Box 7348 (62791-7348)
**PHONE**...................................217 525-8202
**Fax:** 217 525-8202
Loretta Durbin, *Vice Pres*
David C Reardon, *Exec Dir*
Ann Liston, *Admin Sec*
**EMP:** 3
**SALES:** 105.1K **Privately Held**
**SIC:** 2731 2741 8733 Book publishing; pamphlets: publishing only, not printed on site; newsletter publishing; noncommercial research organizations

### (G-20435)
### ENVIRNMNTAL CTRL SOLUTIONS INC (PA)
Also Called: Ecsi
2020 Timberbrook Dr (62702-4627)
**PHONE**...................................217 793-8966
**Fax:** 217 793-1716
Steven Foster, *President*
Tom Bee, *General Mgr*
Chris Benson, *Vice Pres*
Jarrod Bergman, *Project Mgr*
Steven Sours, *Foreman/Supr*
**EMP:** 7
**SQ FT:** 5,000
**SALES (est):** 942.8K **Privately Held**
**SIC:** 3625 5063 Relays & industrial controls; motor controls, starters & relays: electric

### (G-20436)
### EXCITINGWINDOWS BY SUSAN DAY
47 Fairview Ln (62711-9455)
**PHONE**...................................217 652-2821
Scott Day, *Owner*
**EMP:** 3

**SALES (est):** 431.2K **Privately Held**
**SIC:** 2591 Window blinds

### (G-20437)
### F J MURPHY & SON INC
1800 Factory St (62702-2820)
**PHONE**...................................217 787-3477
**Fax:** 217 528-4147
Robert L Murphy, *Ch of Bd*
John M Pasko, *President*
Roger Marmor, *Senior VP*
Brian Sickinger, *Vice Pres*
Don Wisnasky, *Sales Staff*
**EMP:** 60 **EST:** 1956
**SQ FT:** 23,000
**SALES (est):** 8.9MM **Privately Held**
**WEB:** www.fjmurphy.com
**SIC:** 1711 3321 Plumbing contractors; warm air heating & air conditioning contractor; fire sprinkler system installation; gray & ductile iron foundries

### (G-20438)
### FARMER BROS CO
Also Called: Farmers Brothers Coffee
3430c Constitution Dr (62711)
**PHONE**...................................217 787-7565
**Fax:** 217 793-0135
Frank Carol, *Manager*
**EMP:** 8
**SALES (corp-wide):** 544.3MM **Publicly Held**
**WEB:** www.farmerbros.com
**SIC:** 2095 5149 Coffee roasting (except by wholesale grocers); coffee & tea
**PA:** Farmer Bros. Co.
1912 Farmer Brothers Dr
Northlake TX 76262
888 998-2468

### (G-20439)
### FINANCIAL AND PROFESSIONAL REG
Also Called: State Comptroller Print Shop
325 W Adams St Lbby (62704-7306)
**PHONE**...................................217 782-2127
Daniel W Hynes, *Comptroller*
Rhonda Rathbone, *Branch Mgr*
**EMP:** 5 **Privately Held**
**WEB:** www.idfpr.com
**SIC:** 2752 9311 Commercial printing, lithographic; finance, taxation & monetary policy;
**HQ:** State Of Illinois
320 W Washington St Fl 3
Springfield IL 62701
217 785-0820

### (G-20440)
### FIRST ELECTRIC MOTOR SHOP INC
1130 W Reynolds St (62702-2311)
**PHONE**...................................217 698-0672
**Fax:** 217 698-0674
Jack Burris Jr, *President*
Dave Burris, *Vice Pres*
**EMP:** 4 **EST:** 1949
**SQ FT:** 4,600
**SALES (est):** 531K **Privately Held**
**SIC:** 7694 5999 Electric motor repair; motors, electric

### (G-20441)
### FIRST STEP WOMENS CENTER
104 E North Grand Ave A (62702-3880)
**PHONE**...................................217 523-0100
Gregory Brewer, *Principal*
Debbie Shultz, *Principal*
**EMP:** 4
**SALES (est):** 181.5K **Privately Held**
**SIC:** 8011 2899 Primary care medical clinic

### (G-20442)
### FREEMAN ENERGY CORPORATION (DH)
3008 Happy Landing Dr (62711-6259)
**PHONE**...................................217 698-3949
Walter A Gregory, *President*
**EMP:** 10
**SALES (est):** 94.7MM
**SALES (corp-wide):** 31.3B **Publicly Held**
**SIC:** 1241 Coal mining services

**HQ:** Material Service Resources Corp
222 N La Salle St # 1200
Chicago IL 60601
630 325-7736

### (G-20443)
### FREEMAN UNITED COAL MINING CO (DH)
4440 Ash Grove Dr Ste A (62711-6423)
**PHONE**...................................217 698-3300
**Fax:** 217 698-3381
Walter Gregory, *President*
Victor Vencill, *Corp Secy*
Michael Caldwell, *Vice Pres*
Neal Merrifield, *Vice Pres*
Ernie Overton, *Purch Agent*
**EMP:** 33
**SQ FT:** 10,000
**SALES (est):** 45.3MM
**SALES (corp-wide):** 31.3B **Publicly Held**
**SIC:** 1241 Coal mining exploration & test boring
**HQ:** Freeman Energy Corporation
3008 Happy Landing Dr
Springfield IL 62711
217 698-3949

### (G-20444)
### FRYE-WILLIAMSON PRESS INC
901 N Macarthur Blvd (62702-2307)
P.O. Box 1057 (62705-1057)
**PHONE**...................................217 522-7744
**Fax:** 217 522-7785
Richard Lee Serena, *President*
Lynn Serena, *Vice Pres*
Emil Rose, *Sales Staff*
AMI Teegarden, *Marketing Staff*
Steve Kesegi, *Manager*
**EMP:** 29
**SQ FT:** 12,000
**SALES (est):** 5.6MM **Privately Held**
**WEB:** www.fryewilliamson.com
**SIC:** 2759 2752 Commercial printing; commercial printing, offset

### (G-20445)
### GATEHOUSE MEDIA LLC
State Journal-Register, The
1 Copley Plz (62701-1927)
**PHONE**...................................217 788-1300
Patrick Coburn, *Principal*
Thomas Lynn, *Foreman/Supr*
William Deemer, *Controller*
James Myers, *Controller*
Gary R Kreppert, *Adv Mgr*
**EMP:** 375
**SQ FT:** 80,000
**SALES (corp-wide):** 1.2B **Publicly Held**
**WEB:** www.copleynewspapers.com
**SIC:** 2711 2791 2752 Newspapers, publishing & printing; typesetting; commercial printing, lithographic
**HQ:** Gatehouse Media, Llc
175 Sullys Trl Ste 300
Pittsford NY 14534
585 598-0030

### (G-20446)
### GATEHOUSE MEDIA ILLINOIS HO
Also Called: State Journal Register, The
1 Copley Plz (62701-1927)
**PHONE**...................................217 788-1300
**Fax:** 217 788-1372
Patrick Coburn, *Principal*
Gary Schieffer, *Editor*
William Deemer, *Controller*
Jim Myers, *Controller*
Suzanne Lair, *Asst Controller*
**EMP:** 375
**SALES (est):** 56.2MM
**SALES (corp-wide):** 1.2B **Publicly Held**
**SIC:** 2711 Commercial printing & newspaper publishing combined
**PA:** New Media Investment Group Inc.
1345 Avenue Of The Americ
New York NY 10105
212 479-3160

### (G-20447)
### GONE FOR GOOD
1411 E Jefferson St (62703-1042)
**PHONE**...................................217 753-0414
Char Fanning, *Principal*
**EMP:** 3

# GEOGRAPHIC SECTION

Springfield - Sangamon County (G-20474)

SALES (est): 306.6K  Privately Held
SIC: 3559  Tire shredding machinery

**(G-20448)**
**HART - CLAYTON INC**
2000 E Cornell Ave Ste 2 (62703-3396)
PHONE..................217 525-1610
George Hart, *President*
Lorraine Hart, *Corp Secy*
EMP: 14
SQ FT: 17,000
SALES (est): 2.2MM  Privately Held
WEB: www.hartclayton.com
SIC: 2449  Rectangular boxes & crates, wood

**(G-20449)**
**HEART 4 HEART INC (PA)**
2924 N Dirksen Pkwy (62702-1434)
PHONE..................217 544-2699
Gerald Davis, *President*
Luann Davis, *Vice Pres*
Richard May, *Manager*
EMP: 7
SQ FT: 4,000
SALES (est): 1.2MM  Privately Held
WEB: www.heart4heart.com
SIC: 3842  Wheelchairs

**(G-20450)**
**HEARTLAND PUBLICATIONS INC**
7900 Olde Carriage Way (62712-6829)
PHONE..................217 529-9506
Lynell Loftus, *Principal*
EMP: 3
SALES (est): 275.4K  Privately Held
SIC: 2741  Miscellaneous publishing

**(G-20451)**
**HENDERSON EYE CENTER**
3330 Ginger Creek Dr C (62711-9625)
PHONE..................217 698-9477
Fax: 217 698-9474
Wade Henderson, *President*
EMP: 14
SALES (est): 1.7MM  Privately Held
SIC: 3851  Eyes, glass & plastic

**(G-20452)**
**HORSE CREEK OUTFITTERS**
600 S Dirksen Pkwy 600a (62702-2111)
PHONE..................217 544-2740
Mandy McCormick, *Owner*
EMP: 9
SQ FT: 4,000
SALES: 300K  Privately Held
WEB: www.horsecreekoutfitters.com
SIC: 5699  3144  Western apparel; boots, canvas or leather: women's

**(G-20453)**
**ILL DEPT NATURAL RESOURCES**
Land Reclamation Div
1 Natural Resources Way # 100 (62702-1290)
PHONE..................217 782-4970
Don Pflederer, *Branch Mgr*
EMP: 16  Privately Held
WEB: www.il.gov
SIC: 9512  1411  Land, mineral & wildlife conservation; ; dimension stone
HQ: Illinois Department Of Natural Resources
1 Natural Resources Way # 100
Springfield IL 62702
217 782-6302

**(G-20454)**
**ILLINOIS INST CNTNG LEGL ED**
Also Called: Iicle
2395 W Jefferson St (62702-2209)
PHONE..................217 787-2080
Fax: 217 787-9757
Valerie Merrihew, *Business Mgr*
Nora Crandall, *Exec Dir*
Chris Hull, *Tech/Comp Coord*
EMP: 49
SQ FT: 11,000
SALES: 4MM  Privately Held
WEB: www.iicle.com
SIC: 8244  2731  Business & secretarial schools; book publishing

**(G-20455)**
**ILLINOIS NEWSPAPER IN EDUCATN**
1 Copley Plz (62701-1927)
P.O. Box 280, Arlington Heights (60006-0280)
PHONE..................847 427-4388
Susan Groves, *President*
Edith Weaver, *President*
EMP: 10
SALES (est): 380.2K  Privately Held
SIC: 2711  Newspapers, publishing & printing

**(G-20456)**
**INFO CORNER MATERIALS INC**
4300 Bachmann Dr (62707-7607)
P.O. Box 258, Sherman (62684-0258)
PHONE..................217 566-3561
Fax: 217 522-7388
Delmar Donley, *President*
Todd Donely, *Vice Pres*
EMP: 10
SALES (est): 1MM  Privately Held
SIC: 3273  4213  Ready-mixed concrete; heavy hauling

**(G-20457)**
**INFORMATIVE SYSTEMS INC**
Also Called: ISI Printing
5119 Old Route 36 (62707-3124)
P.O. Box 13347 (62791-3347)
PHONE..................217 523-8422
Fax: 217 523-2484
James A Palazzolo, *President*
Maryann Palazzolo, *Vice Pres*
Christy Wells, *Admin Sec*
Eric Wells, *Services*
EMP: 10
SQ FT: 12,000
SALES (est): 1.7MM  Privately Held
SIC: 5112  2752  2791  Business forms; commercial printing, offset; typesetting

**(G-20458)**
**ITG BRANDS LLC**
900 Christopher Ln Ste 7 (62712-8707)
PHONE..................217 529-5746
Mary Kessler, *CEO*
EMP: 4
SALES (corp-wide): 35.8B  Privately Held
SIC: 5194  2111  Tobacco & tobacco products; cigarettes
HQ: Itg Brands, Llc
714 Green Valley Rd
Greensboro NC 27408
336 335-7000

**(G-20459)**
**J & J ELECTRIC MOTOR REPAIR SP**
2800 S 11th St (62703-4170)
PHONE..................217 529-0015
Fax: 217 529-0297
James W Riba, *President*
Sandra Riba, *Corp Secy*
Robin Riba, *Vice Pres*
EMP: 5
SQ FT: 2,880
SALES (est): 973.2K  Privately Held
SIC: 7694  Electric motor repair

**(G-20460)**
**J & W COUNTER TOPS INC (PA)**
600 North St (62704-5897)
PHONE..................217 544-0876
Fax: 217 527-1315
Walter Justison, *President*
Hilda Justison, *Treasurer*
EMP: 21
SALES (est): 3.2MM  Privately Held
SIC: 5031  2541  5169  5074  Wallboard; counters or counter display cases, wood; chemicals & allied products; plumbing & hydronic heating supplies; hardware

**(G-20461)**
**J GOOCH & ASSOCIATES INC**
Also Called: Gooch & Associates Printing
140 W Lenox Ave (62704-4713)
PHONE..................217 522-7575
Fax: 217 787-4251
James Feagans, *President*
Sherry Feagans, *Vice Pres*
EMP: 7

SQ FT: 5,800
SALES (est): 760K  Privately Held
SIC: 2752  2761  Commercial printing, offset; manifold business forms

**(G-20462)**
**JAVA EXPRESS**
1827 N Peoria Rd (62702-2756)
PHONE..................217 525-2430
EMP: 9
SALES (est): 340K  Privately Held
SIC: 2741  Misc Publishing

**(G-20463)**
**JEFFERIES ORCHARD SAWMILL**
1016 Jefferies Rd (62707-8578)
PHONE..................217 487-7582
Dale Jefferies, *Principal*
EMP: 6
SALES (est): 763.9K  Privately Held
SIC: 2421  Sawmills & planing mills, general

**(G-20464)**
**JOHNSON CONTROLS INC**
4231 Westgate Dr (62711-7059)
PHONE..................217 793-8858
Fax: 217 793-8759
Rich Kern, *Manager*
EMP: 18
SALES (corp-wide): 36.8B  Privately Held
SIC: 3822  1731  7629  Building services monitoring controls, automatic; environmental system control installation; computerized controls installation; electrical equipment repair services; electronic equipment repair
PA: Johnson Controls, Inc.
5757 N Green Bay Ave
Milwaukee WI 53209
414 524-1200

**(G-20465)**
**L P S EXPRESS INC**
1620 S 5th St Ste A (62703-3174)
PHONE..................217 636-7683
Roger Krick, *President*
Roger Kreck, *President*
Karen Kollmann, *Finance*
Debbie Kreck, *Manager*
EMP: 5
SALES (est): 861.1K  Privately Held
WEB: www.lpsexpress.com
SIC: 2893  7378  Printing ink; computer peripheral equipment repair & maintenance

**(G-20466)**
**LAKE AREA DISPOSAL SERVICE INC**
Also Called: Lake Area Recycling Services
2742 S 6th St (62703-4070)
PHONE..................217 522-9271
Fax: 217 522-9352
Donny Crenshaw, *Manager*
EMP: 20
SALES (corp-wide): 3.8MM  Privately Held
WEB: www.lakeareadisposal.com
SIC: 4953  5093  3341  2611  Recycling, waste materials; metal scrap & waste materials; secondary nonferrous metals; pulp mills
PA: Lake Area Disposal Service, Inc.
2106 E Cornell Ave
Springfield IL 62703
217 522-9317

**(G-20467)**
**LASER INNOVATIONS INC**
2276 North Grand Ave E (62702-4300)
PHONE..................217 522-8580
Fax: 217 522-8587
Ricky L Smith, *President*
Charlotte Watkinsons, *General Mgr*
Richard Shull, *Manager*
EMP: 11
SQ FT: 5,000
SALES: 1MM  Privately Held
SIC: 3955  7699  Print cartridges for laser & other computer printers; office equipment & accessory customizing

**(G-20468)**
**LEGAL FILES SOFTWARE INC**
801 S Durkin Dr Ste A (62704-6028)
PHONE..................217 726-6000

Fax: 217 726-7777
John Kanoski, *CEO*
Eric Hoadley, *Project Mgr*
Gordon Hack, *Sales Dir*
Teresa Gathard, *Manager*
Jon Stearns, *CIO*
EMP: 30  EST: 1990
SQ FT: 8,000
SALES (est): 3.6MM  Privately Held
WEB: www.legalfiles.com
SIC: 7372  Prepackaged software

**(G-20469)**
**LEGISLATIVE PRINTING**
401 S Spring St (62706-4600)
PHONE..................217 782-7312
Fax: 217 524-1388
Mark Wenda, *Principal*
EMP: 2
SALES (est): 532.4K  Privately Held
SIC: 2752  Commercial printing, lithographic

**(G-20470)**
**LINCOLN GREEN MAZDA INC**
3760 6th Street Frontage (62703-4788)
P.O. Box 13315 (62791-3315)
PHONE..................217 391-2400
Fax: 217 391-2401
Todd Green, *General Mgr*
Melanie Sharp, *Admin Sec*
EMP: 17  EST: 2011
SALES (est): 3.2MM  Privately Held
SIC: 5511  5521  3999  Automobiles, new & used; used car dealers; atomizers, toiletry

**(G-20471)**
**LOCAL 46 TRAINING PROGRAM TR**
2888 E Cook St (62703-2167)
PHONE..................217 528-4041
George Stezz, *Principal*
EMP: 7
SALES: 185K  Privately Held
SIC: 1389  8631  Construction, repair & dismantling services; labor unions & similar labor organizations

**(G-20472)**
**LONG ELEVATOR AND MCH CO INC (DH)**
2908 Old Rochester Rd (62703-5659)
PHONE..................217 629-9648
Fax: 217 629-8432
Patrick Long, *President*
Warren Long Jr, *Treasurer*
Peggy Savorgino, *Credit Mgr*
Michael Long, *Admin Sec*
EMP: 60  EST: 1929
SQ FT: 48,000
SALES: 7.1MM
SALES (corp-wide): 650.6MM  Privately Held
SIC: 3534  7699  Elevators & equipment; elevators: inspection, service & repair
HQ: Kone Inc.
4225 Naperville Rd # 400
Lisle IL 60532
630 577-1650

**(G-20473)**
**MAGROS PROCESSING**
3150 Stanton St (62703-4318)
PHONE..................217 438-2880
Tony Magro, *Principal*
EMP: 4
SALES (est): 398.6K  Privately Held
SIC: 2011  Meat packing plants

**(G-20474)**
**MARUCCO STDDARD FRENBACH WALSH**
Also Called: MSF&w
3445 Liberty Dr (62704-6521)
PHONE..................217 698-3535
John Marucco, *President*
Bob Ferenbach, *Treasurer*
Darrel Stoddard, *Admin Sec*
EMP: 39
SQ FT: 8,000
SALES: 4MM  Privately Held
WEB: www.msfw.com
SIC: 7371  7372  Computer software systems analysis & design, custom; prepackaged software

## Springfield - Sangamon County (G-20475)

**(G-20475)**
**MAXIM INC**
2709 E Ash St (62703-5606)
PHONE .................................... 217 544-7015
Fax: 217 544-7068
Charles T Merrill, *President*
Marilyn Gutierrez, *Office Mgr*
EMP: 13
SALES (est): 1.8MM **Privately Held**
SIC: 3711 3714 Motor vehicles & car bodies; motor vehicle parts & accessories

**(G-20476)**
**MEL-O-CREAM DONUTS (PA)**
Also Called: Stevenson's Mel-O-Cream Donuts
217 E Laurel St (62704-3990)
PHONE .................................... 217 544-4644
Fax: 217 544-4818
Jeff Stauffer, *President*
Robbi Greger, *Sales Staff*
EMP: 12 EST: 1970
SALES (est): 3MM **Privately Held**
SIC: 5461 2051 Doughnuts; bread, cake & related products

**(G-20477)**
**MEL-O-CREAM DONUTS**
Also Called: Stevensons Mel-O-Cream Donuts
525 North Grand Ave E (62702-3926)
PHONE .................................... 217 528-2303
Ralf Stevenson, *Branch Mgr*
EMP: 4
SALES (corp-wide): 3MM **Privately Held**
SIC: 2051 5461 Doughnuts, except frozen; doughnuts
PA: Mel-O-Cream Donuts
    217 E Laurel St
    Springfield IL 62704
    217 544-4644

**(G-20478)**
**MEL-O-CREAM DONUTS INTL INC**
5456 International Pkwy (62711-7086)
PHONE .................................... 217 483-1825
Fax: 217 483-7744
David W Waltrip, *President*
Dan Alewelt, *Prdtn Mgr*
Evan Durako, *Facilities Mgr*
Jeff Alexander, *Opers Staff*
Adam Booher, *Engineer*
EMP: 80 EST: 1932
SQ FT: 73,000
SALES (est): 22.9MM **Privately Held**
SIC: 2053 Doughnuts, frozen

**(G-20479)**
**MEMORIAL BREAST DIAGNSTC SVCS**
747 N Rutledge St (62702-6700)
PHONE .................................... 217 788-4042
Stephanie Lowers, *Branch Mgr*
EMP: 3
SALES (est): 202.5K **Privately Held**
SIC: 3845 Electromedical equipment

**(G-20480)**
**MERVIS INDUSTRIES INC**
Also Called: Mervis Recycling
1100 S 9th St (62703-2523)
PHONE .................................... 217 753-1492
Fax: 217 753-0017
David Sample, *Branch Mgr*
EMP: 6
SALES (corp-wide): 140.2MM **Privately Held**
SIC: 4953 3341 5093 5051 Recycling, waste materials; secondary nonferrous metals; metal scrap & waste materials; steel
PA: Mervis Industries, Inc.
    3295 E Main St Ste C
    Danville IL 61834
    217 442-5300

**(G-20481)**
**MICHAEL P JONES**
Also Called: Jones Watch and Jewelry Repair
3124 Montvale Dr Ste C (62704-6938)
PHONE .................................... 217 787-7457
Michael P Jones, *Owner*
EMP: 4
SQ FT: 1,100
SALES (est): 140K **Privately Held**
SIC: 7631 3911 Jewelry repair services; watch repair; jewel settings & mountings, precious metal

**(G-20482)**
**MID-ILLINOIS CALIPER CO INC**
2803 N Dirksen Pkwy (62702-1408)
P.O. Box 9316 (62791-9316)
Fax: 217 528-6422
Kevin R Lehmann, *President*
Darrell Donley, *Vice Pres*
Terri Marbold, *Finance Other*
Dennis Ferguson, *Regl Sales Mgr*
Linda Denny, *Data Proc Staff*
EMP: 14 EST: 1975
SQ FT: 15,000
SALES (est): 970K **Privately Held**
WEB: www.midilcaliper.com
SIC: 3714 Motor vehicle brake systems & parts

**(G-20483)**
**MIDWEST FABRICATION-COUNTERTOP**
2863 Singer Ave (62703-2132)
PHONE .................................... 217 528-0571
Fax: 217 787-2518
Wayne Shephard, *Principal*
EMP: 2 EST: 1993
SALES (est): 267.8K **Privately Held**
SIC: 2541 Counter & sink tops

**(G-20484)**
**MIDWEST FIBER SOLUTIONS**
1600 Hunter Ridge Dr (62704-6580)
PHONE .................................... 217 971-7400
Robert Patterson, *Principal*
EMP: 3
SALES (est): 500.7K **Privately Held**
SIC: 3643 Current-carrying wiring devices

**(G-20485)**
**MR AUTO ELECTRIC**
2649 E Cook St (62703-1901)
PHONE .................................... 217 523-3659
Michael Atterberry, *Owner*
EMP: 4
SQ FT: 2,200
SALES (est): 250K **Privately Held**
SIC: 3714 7539 Motor vehicle electrical equipment; electrical services

**(G-20486)**
**NAPIER MACHINE & WELDING INC**
2519 South Grand Ave E (62703-5614)
PHONE .................................... 217 525-8740
Fax: 217 525-5059
Keith Napier, *President*
EMP: 2 EST: 1946
SQ FT: 6,000
SALES (est): 274.8K **Privately Held**
SIC: 3599 7692 7629 Machine shop, jobbing & repair; welding repair; electrical repair shops

**(G-20487)**
**NIEMANN FOODS FOUNDATION**
Also Called: Cub Foods 83
3001 S Veterans Pkwy (62704-6405)
PHONE .................................... 217 793-4091
Fax: 217 793-8687
Rick Gardner, *Manager*
Meta-Jo Floyd, *Manager*
EMP: 250
SQ FT: 62,000
SALES (corp-wide): 121K **Privately Held**
SIC: 5411 5992 5812 2051 Supermarkets; florists; eating places; bread, cake & related products
PA: Niemann Foods Foundation
    923 N 12th St
    Quincy IL 62301
    217 221-5600

**(G-20488)**
**NPI HOLDING CORP (DH)**
1500 Taylor Ave (62703-5663)
PHONE .................................... 217 391-1229
Darryl Rosser, *President*
EMP: 5

SALES (est): 73.9MM
SALES (corp-wide): 532.5MM **Privately Held**
SIC: 3083 3089 5033 3444 Plastic finished products, laminated; extruded finished plastic products; fiberglass building materials; awnings, sheet metal; investment holding companies, except banks
HQ: Stabilit America, Inc.
    285 Industrial Dr
    Moscow TN 38057
    901 877-3010

**(G-20489)**
**NUDO PRODUCTS INC**
2508 South Grand Ave E (62703-5613)
PHONE .................................... 217 528-5636
Fax: 217 528-8722
Patrick Eudo, *Vice Pres*
EMP: 125
SALES (corp-wide): 532.5MM **Privately Held**
WEB: www.nudo.com
SIC: 3083 Plastic finished products, laminated
HQ: Nudo Products, Inc.
    1500 Taylor Ave
    Springfield IL 62703
    217 528-5636

**(G-20490)**
**NUDO PRODUCTS INC (DH)**
1500 Taylor Ave (62703-5663)
PHONE .................................... 217 528-5636
Darryl Rosser, *President*
Charles Pineau, *COO*
Mark Jutte, *Vice Pres*
Eric McMillan, *Purch Agent*
Len Farrell, *CFO*
▲ EMP: 200
SQ FT: 250,000
SALES (est): 73.9MM
SALES (corp-wide): 532.5MM **Privately Held**
WEB: www.nudo.com
SIC: 3083 3089 5033 3444 Plastic finished products, laminated; extruded finished plastic products; fiberglass building materials; awnings, sheet metal
HQ: Npi Holding Corp.
    1500 Taylor Ave
    Springfield IL 62703
    217 391-1229

**(G-20491)**
**OCTAPHARMA PLASMA INC**
1770 Wabash Ave (62704-5302)
PHONE .................................... 217 546-8605
Dallas York, *Branch Mgr*
Craig Devore, *Director*
EMP: 3
SALES (corp-wide): 1.4B **Privately Held**
SIC: 2836 Plasmas
PA: Octapharma Nordic Ab
    Elersvagen 40
    Stockholm 112 5
    856 643-000

**(G-20492)**
**OGLESBY & OGLESBY GUNMAKERS**
744 W Andrew Rd (62707-4626)
PHONE .................................... 217 487-7100
Fax: 217 487-7980
William D Oglesby, *President*
EMP: 7
SALES (est): 3MM **Privately Held**
SIC: 3484 7699 5941 Guns (firearms) or gun parts, 30 mm. & below; gun parts made to individual order; firearms

**(G-20493)**
**ORATECH INC**
4777 Alex Blvd (62711-6346)
P.O. Box 13486 (62791-3486)
PHONE .................................... 217 793-2735
Fax: 217 793-3195
Norman Ross, *President*
Denise Dineen, *HR Admin*
Lisa Barker, *Office Mgr*
EMP: 30
SQ FT: 2,000
SALES (est): 2MM **Privately Held**
SIC: 8072 3843 Dental laboratories; dental equipment & supplies

**(G-20494)**
**ORGANIZED HOME**
2601 Chuckwagon Dr (62711-7127)
PHONE .................................... 217 698-6460
Fax: 217 698-6462
George Poontz, *President*
EMP: 3
SALES (est): 600K **Privately Held**
SIC: 2542 Cabinets: show, display or storage: except wood

**(G-20495)**
**ORTHOTIC & PROSTHETIC ASSOC**
355 W Carpenter St Ste B (62702-4945)
PHONE .................................... 217 789-1450
Fax: 217 789-1454
Daryl Barth, *Owner*
EMP: 3
SALES (est): 241.7K **Privately Held**
SIC: 3842 Orthopedic appliances

**(G-20496)**
**PACK 2000 INC**
Also Called: Midas Muffler
2109 Stevenson Dr (62703-4307)
PHONE .................................... 217 529-4408
Fax: 217 529-4410
Kent Childs, *Vice Pres*
EMP: 7
SALES (corp-wide): 9.6MM **Privately Held**
SIC: 3714 Motor vehicle parts & accessories
PA: Pack 2000 Inc
    12 Park Pl
    Evansville IN 47713
    812 421-0123

**(G-20497)**
**PALLETS SHOP**
5312 Deerwood Lk (62703-5366)
PHONE .................................... 618 920-6875
Lorandus Stone, *Principal*
EMP: 7 EST: 2010
SALES (est): 652.5K **Privately Held**
SIC: 2448 Pallets, wood & wood with metal

**(G-20498)**
**PANHANDLE EASTRN PIPE LINE LP**
1801 Business Park Dr (62703-5626)
PHONE .................................... 217 753-1108
Tom Walker, *Purch Agent*
Paul Degenhart, *Branch Mgr*
EMP: 34
SALES (corp-wide): 37.5B **Publicly Held**
SIC: 1389 Pipe testing, oil field service
HQ: Panhandle Eastern Pipe Line Company, Lp
    8111 Westchester Dr # 600
    Dallas TX 75225
    214 981-0700

**(G-20499)**
**PARKWAY PRINTERS**
3755 N Dirksen Pkwy (62707-7612)
PHONE .................................... 217 525-2485
Fax: 217 753-9260
Charles Martin, *Owner*
EMP: 2
SALES (est): 226.4K **Privately Held**
SIC: 2752 Commercial printing, lithographic

**(G-20500)**
**PAWNEE OIL CORPORATION**
1204 N 5th St (62702-3818)
P.O. Box 1425 (62705-1425)
PHONE .................................... 217 522-5440
Fax: 217 522-8785
Frank Vala, *President*
Rosalie Mc Dermott, *Corp Secy*
EMP: 10
SQ FT: 2,400
SALES (est): 1.1MM **Privately Held**
SIC: 1311 Crude petroleum production

**(G-20501)**
**PEASES INC (PA)**
Also Called: Pease's Candy Shops
1701 S State St (62704-4011)
PHONE .................................... 217 523-3721
Robert M Flesher, *President*
Douglas Anderson, *Vice Pres*

# GEOGRAPHIC SECTION

## Springfield - Sangamon County (G-20528)

EMP: 12 EST: 1930
SQ FT: 1,200
SALES (est) 2.5MM **Privately Held**
WEB: www.peasescandy.com
SIC: 5441 2064 Candy; nuts; candy & other confectionery products

### (G-20502)
### PEASES INC
4753 Jeffory St (62703-5377)
PHONE..................217 529-2912
Fax: 217 391-0168
EMP: 15
SALES (corp-wide): 2.4MM **Privately Held**
SIC: 5441 2068 2066 2064 Ret Candy/Confectionery Mfg Roasted Nuts/Seeds Mfg Chocolate/Cocoa Prdt Mfg Candy/Confectionery
PA: Pease's, Inc.
  1701 S State St
  Springfield IL 62704
  217 523-3721

### (G-20503)
### PERTEN INSTRUMENTS INC
6444 6th Street Frontage A (62712-6882)
P.O. Box 13424 (62791-3424)
PHONE..................217 585-9440
Fax: 217 585-9441
Gavin O'Reilly, *President*
Larry Black, *Opers Mgr*
▲ EMP: 35
SQ FT: 10,000
SALES (est): 5.8MM **Privately Held**
WEB: www.perten.com
SIC: 8734 3821 Testing laboratories; laboratory measuring apparatus
HQ: Perten Instruments Ab
  Instrumentvagen 31
  Hagersten 126 5
  888 099-0

### (G-20504)
### PETERSBURG POWER WASHING INC
Also Called: Petersburg Painting & Pwr Wshg
829 S 11th St (62703-1716)
PHONE..................217 415-9013
Donna Hillyer, *President*
EMP: 6
SALES: 100K **Privately Held**
SIC: 3479 Metal coating & allied service

### (G-20505)
### POOL CENTER INC
3740 Wabash Ave Ste C (62711-9622)
PHONE..................217 698-7665
Fax: 217 698-7865
Edward Osman, *President*
Diane Osman, *Admin Sec*
EMP: 2
SALES: 1MM **Privately Held**
SIC: 8748 1389 7389 Business consulting; construction, repair & dismantling services; swimming pool & hot tub service & maintenance

### (G-20506)
### PPG INDUSTRIES INC
Also Called: PPG 4612
3040 S 6th St (62703-5923)
PHONE..................217 757-9080
Ron Herbstrith, *Branch Mgr*
Todd Chastain, *Manager*
EMP: 24
SALES (corp-wide): 14.7B **Publicly Held**
WEB: www.ppg.com
SIC: 2851 Paints & allied products
PA: Ppg Industries, Inc.
  1 Ppg Pl
  Pittsburgh PA 15272
  412 434-3131

### (G-20507)
### PREMIUM PALLETS
2877 N Dirksen Pkwy (62702-1408)
PHONE..................217 974-0155
EMP: 4
SALES (est): 259.2K **Privately Held**
SIC: 2448 Pallets, wood & wood with metal

### (G-20508)
### PT HOLDINGS INC (PA)
2 White Oak Rd (62711-9206)
PHONE..................217 691-1793
William Patrick Riters, *President*
Timothy M Lyons, *Admin Sec*
EMP: 8
SALES (est): 5.9MM **Privately Held**
SIC: 6719 3469 Personal holding companies, except banks; kitchen fixtures & equipment; porcelain enameled; kitchen fixtures & equipment: metal, except cast aluminum

### (G-20509)
### PURE SKIN LLC
4000 Westgate Dr (62711-7066)
PHONE..................217 679-6267
Marivic Lohse, *Principal*
EMP: 5
SALES (est): 533.9K **Privately Held**
SIC: 2657 1799 Paperboard backs for blister or skin packages; spa or hot tub installation or construction

### (G-20510)
### R W BRADLEY SUPPLY COMPANY
Also Called: R W Bradley Supply
403 N 4th St (62702-5293)
PHONE..................217 528-8438
Roger J Reese, *President*
Becky Reese, *Vice Pres*
EMP: 5
SQ FT: 30,000
SALES (est): 1.7MM **Privately Held**
SIC: 5082 7699 5051 3449 General construction machinery & equipment; contractors' materials; construction equipment repair; metals service centers & offices; miscellaneous metalwork; fabricated structural metal
PA: Chapin Reese Corporation
  403 N 4th St 405
  Springfield IL 62702
  217 528-8438

### (G-20511)
### REFRESHMENT SERVICES INC
Also Called: Pepsico
1337 E Cook St (62703)
PHONE..................217 522-8841
Keith Creceoious, *Manager*
EMP: 50
SALES (corp-wide): 95.5MM **Privately Held**
SIC: 2086 Carbonated soft drinks, bottled & canned
PA: Refreshment Services, Inc.
  1121 Locust St
  Quincy IL 62301
  217 223-8600

### (G-20512)
### RICHARDS STHMAN RBR STAMPS LLC
317 E Monroe St (62701-1408)
PHONE..................217 522-6801
Jeff Burton,
EMP: 3 EST: 1954
SQ FT: 1,500
SALES (est): 240K **Privately Held**
SIC: 3953 Marking devices

### (G-20513)
### RICHARDSON MANUFACTURING CO
2209 Old Jacksonville Rd (62704-2299)
PHONE..................217 546-2249
Fax: 217 546-9433
William L Richardson Jr, *President*
W L Richardson Jr, *Corp Secy*
Jeff Richardson, *Vice Pres*
Gary Russell, *Opers Staff*
Bill Coonan, *Engineer*
EMP: 100
SQ FT: 125,000
SALES (est): 23.4MM **Privately Held**
WEB: www.rmc-bigcnc.com
SIC: 3599 Machine shop, jobbing & repair

### (G-20514)
### ROLLING MEADOWS BREWERY LLC
1660 W Leland Ave (62704-3388)
PHONE..................217 725-2492
Caren C Trudeau, *Mng Member*
EMP: 3
SALES (est): 280K **Privately Held**
SIC: 2082 Brewers' grain

### (G-20515)
### RUDIN PRINTING COMPANY INC
927 E Jackson St (62701-1914)
PHONE..................217 528-5111
Fax: 217 528-7699
Carl P Rudin, *President*
EMP: 12
SQ FT: 4,000
SALES (est): 1.2MM **Privately Held**
SIC: 2752 7334 2791 2789 Commercial printing, offset; photocopying & duplicating services; typesetting; bookbinding & related work

### (G-20516)
### RUYLE INCORPORATED
1325 Ne Bond St (62703)
PHONE..................309 674-6644
Fax: 309 974-9060
Chris Benson, *Vice Pres*
EMP: 50 EST: 2007
SALES (est): 3.2MM **Privately Held**
SIC: 1711 5075 3585 Warm air heating & air conditioning contractor; air conditioning & ventilation equipment & supplies; refrigeration & heating equipment

### (G-20517)
### SAGA COMMUNICATIONS INC
Also Called: Illinois Radio Network
3501 E Sangamon Ave (62707-9777)
PHONE..................248 631-8099
Fax: 312 943-2620
Chris Krug, *General Mgr*
Sharon Johnson, *Principal*
Dale Barnes, *Marketing Staff*
Dennis Mellott, *Branch Mgr*
EMP: 7
SALES (corp-wide): 142.5MM **Publicly Held**
WEB: www.rock102.com
SIC: 3663 Radio receiver networks
PA: Saga Communications, Inc.
  73 Kercheval Ave
  Grosse Pointe Farms MI 48236
  313 886-7070

### (G-20518)
### SARA LEE BAKING GROUP
6100 S 2nd St (62711-7405)
PHONE..................217 585-3462
Don Anthony, *Principal*
EMP: 4
SALES (est): 219.9K **Privately Held**
SIC: 2051 Bakery: wholesale or wholesale/retail combined

### (G-20519)
### SCUBA SPORTS INC
1609 S Macarthur Blvd (62704-3622)
PHONE..................217 787-3483
Jeff Unland, *President*
EMP: 4 EST: 1976
SQ FT: 500
SALES (est): 411.1K **Privately Held**
WEB: www.scubasports.net
SIC: 5941 7999 3949 5091 Skin diving, scuba equipment & supplies; scuba & skin diving instruction; sporting & athletic goods; diving equipment & supplies

### (G-20520)
### SECRETARY OF STATE ILLINOIS
316 N Klein St (62702-5149)
PHONE..................217 782-4850
Fax: 217 557-8238
Dave Bertetto, *General Mgr*
EMP: 9 **Privately Held**
SIC: 3469 Automobile license tags, stamped metal
HQ: Secretary Of State, Illinois
  213 State House
  Springfield IL 62706
  217 782-2201

### (G-20521)
### SELVAGGIO ORNA & STRL STL INC
1119 W Dorlan Ave (62702-2302)
PHONE..................217 528-4077
Fax: 217 528-7677
Mark Selvaggio, *President*
Tony Selvaggio, *Vice Pres*
Cathy Murphy, *Office Mgr*
EMP: 24
SQ FT: 18,000
SALES (est): 6.1MM **Privately Held**
WEB: www.selvaggiosteel.com
SIC: 3441 3446 Fabricated structural metal; architectural metalwork

### (G-20522)
### SENATE DEMOCRAT LEADER OFFICE
301 S 2nd St (62706-1720)
PHONE..................708 687-9696
Emil Jones, *Principal*
EMP: 4
SALES (est): 230.6K **Privately Held**
SIC: 2711 Newspapers, publishing & printing

### (G-20523)
### SHINN ENTERPRISES
Also Called: Bad Boys Neons
3310 W Jefferson St (62707-9623)
PHONE..................217 698-3344
Rossetta Shinn, *President*
EMP: 8
SALES (est): 714.8K **Privately Held**
SIC: 2813 3993 Neon; neon signs

### (G-20524)
### SIGNKRAFT CO
1215 W Miller St (62702-3627)
PHONE..................217 787-7105
Fax: 217 787-7105
Cecil Hill, *Owner*
EMP: 3
SQ FT: 1,600
SALES (est): 220.8K **Privately Held**
WEB: www.signkraftsigns.com
SIC: 3993 5999 Signs & advertising specialties; banners, flags, decals & posters

### (G-20525)
### SIGNWORX SIGN & LIGHTING CO
1048 Francella Ct (62702-2331)
PHONE..................217 413-2532
Michael Gay, *President*
EMP: 4 EST: 2014
SALES (est): 125.8K **Privately Held**
SIC: 3993 Electric signs

### (G-20526)
### SIMPLEX INC
5300 Rising Moon Rd (62711-6228)
P.O. Box 7388 (62791-7388)
PHONE..................217 483-1600
Thomas Debrey, *President*
Jill Debrey, *COO*
Juan Zurita, *Project Engr*
Stephen Cappellin, *CFO*
John Hartman, *Sales Staff*
▼ EMP: 190 EST: 1931
SQ FT: 100,000
SALES (est): 52.6MM **Privately Held**
WEB: www.simplexdirect.com
SIC: 3613 3643 3625 3612 Generator control & metering panels; current-carrying wiring devices; relays & industrial controls; transformers, except electric; fabricated plate work (boiler shop)

### (G-20527)
### SOLOMON COLORS INC (PA)
4050 Color Plant Rd (62702-1060)
P.O. Box 8288 (62791-8288)
PHONE..................217 522-3112
Fax: 217 522-3145
Richard R Solomon, *President*
Charles Kreutzer, *Vice Pres*
John Boxman, *Treasurer*
Kait Shanks, *Accounts Mgr*
Gina Solomon, *Admin Sec*
▲ EMP: 80
SQ FT: 150,000
SALES (est): 31.4MM **Privately Held**
WEB: www.solomoncolors.com
SIC: 2816 Inorganic pigments

### (G-20528)
### SOLUTION PRINTING INC
Also Called: Solution Printing & Signs
3135 S 14th St (62703-4128)
PHONE..................217 529-9700
Steve Shelton, *President*

# Springfield - Sangamon County (G-20529)

Mike Shelton, *VP Human Res*
Greg Shelton, *Manager*
Nick Gentry, *Graphic Designe*
**EMP:** 2
**SALES (est):** 529.2K **Privately Held**
**WEB:** www.solutionprint.com
**SIC:** 2752 Commercial printing, lithographic

### (G-20529)
### SPRINGFIELD IRON & METAL CO
930 N Wolfe St (62702-4335)
**PHONE**..........................217 544-7131
Russell Weller, *President*
**EMP:** 6 **EST:** 1956
**SQ FT:** 1,200
**SALES (est):** 720.2K **Privately Held**
**SIC:** 5093 3341 Automotive wrecking for scrap; secondary nonferrous metals

### (G-20530)
### SPRINGFIELD PEPSI COLA BTLG CO (PA)
Also Called: Pepsico
2900 Singer Ave (62703-2135)
P.O. Box 4146 (62708-4146)
**PHONE**..........................217 522-8841
**Fax:** 217 522-6361
John Faloon, *President*
Shawn Vecchie, *Vice Pres*
Jack Taylor, *Controller*
Eileen White, *Info Tech Mgr*
**EMP:** 50
**SQ FT:** 4,000
**SALES (est):** 13.4MM **Privately Held**
**WEB:** www.springfield.il.us
**SIC:** 2086 Carbonated soft drinks, bottled & canned

### (G-20531)
### SPRINGFIELD PRINTING INC
Also Called: Byers Printing Company
3500 Constitution Dr (62711-7192)
P.O. Box 548 (62705-0548)
**PHONE**..........................217 787-3500
**Fax:** 217 787-4319
Victor Krumm, *President*
**EMP:** 7
**SALES (est):** 1.2MM **Privately Held**
**SIC:** 2761 2789 2731 2752 Manifold business forms; bookbinding & related work; books: publishing & printing; commercial printing, lithographic

### (G-20532)
### SPRINGFIELD PUBLISHERS INC
Also Called: Springfield Business Journal
1118 W Laurel St (62704-3562)
**PHONE**..........................217 726-6600
**Fax:** 217 492-5525
Brant W Mackey, *President*
Beth Parkes-Irwin, *Advt Staff*
John Schilsky, *Admin Sec*
Scott Faingold, *Correspondent*
**EMP:** 5
**SQ FT:** 4,000
**SALES (est):** 353.4K **Privately Held**
**SIC:** 2711 Newspapers: publishing only, not printed on site

### (G-20533)
### SPRINGFIELD SALES ASSOC INC
3513 Tamarak Dr (62712-9102)
**PHONE**..........................217 529-6987
Jack Milbourn, *President*
Howard Sutker, *President*
**EMP:** 4
**SALES (est):** 422.5K **Privately Held**
**SIC:** 3143 3144 5661 Orthopedic shoes, men's; orthopedic shoes, women's; custom & orthopedic shoes

### (G-20534)
### SPRINGFIELD WELDING & AUTO BDY
Also Called: Springfield Auto Ctr Stor Pool
2720 Holmes Ave (62704-5110)
**PHONE**..........................217 523-5365
**Fax:** 217 544-1407
James Paoli, *President*
Ronald Paoli, *President*
**EMP:** 22
**SQ FT:** 12,800
**SALES:** 1.2MM **Privately Held**
**SIC:** 7532 7539 7521 7692 Body shop, automotive; machine shop, automotive; automobile storage garage; automotive welding; general automotive repair shops

### (G-20535)
### STANDARD REGISTER INC
450 S Durkin Dr Ste C (62704-7211)
P.O. Box 7319 (62791-7319)
**PHONE**..........................217 793-1900
Mike Jastram, *Branch Mgr*
**EMP:** 4
**SALES (corp-wide):** 4.5B **Privately Held**
**WEB:** www.stdreg.com
**SIC:** 2761 Manifold business forms
**HQ:** Standard Register, Inc.
600 Albany St
Dayton OH 45417
937 221-1000

### (G-20536)
### STATE ATTORNEY APPELLATE
Also Called: Iepa Printing
1021 E North Grand Ave (62702-4059)
P.O. Box 19276 (62794-9276)
**PHONE**..........................217 782-3397
Michael J Boland, *Vice Chairman*
Jay Carlson, *Business Mgr*
Jason Musgrave, *Business Mgr*
Brad Dales, *Purch Agent*
Cathy Visintin, *Purch Agent*
**EMP:** 7 **Privately Held**
**SIC:** 2752 9222 Commercial printing, lithographic; Attorney General's office;
**HQ:** The State's Attorneys Appellate Prosecutor Illinois Office Of
725 S 2nd St
Springfield IL 62704

### (G-20537)
### STEPPING STONES GPS LLC
2860 Stanton St (62703-4347)
**PHONE**..........................217 529-6697
Kari Allen, *Office Mgr*
Sean Watts, *Mng Member*
**EMP:** 5
**SALES (est):** 253.2K **Privately Held**
**SIC:** 3575 Computer terminals, monitors & components

### (G-20538)
### STEVIE S ITALIAN FOODS INC (PA)
1909 Grist Mill Dr (62711-6611)
**PHONE**..........................217 793-9693
Joseph J Crifasi, *CEO*
Derek Crifasi, *President*
Nino Crifasi, *Principal*
Stephen D Crifasi, *Vice Pres*
Cari Crifasi, *CFO*
**EMP:** 4
**SQ FT:** 110,000
**SALES (est):** 5.7MM **Privately Held**
**SIC:** 2098 2032 2079 Macaroni & spaghetti; Italian foods: packaged in cans, jars, etc.; olive oil

### (G-20539)
### STUDIO MOULDING
2650 Colt Rd (62707-8862)
**PHONE**..........................217 523-2101
Karl Kienitz, *Branch Mgr*
**EMP:** 3
**SALES (corp-wide):** 243.8K **Privately Held**
**SIC:** 3089 Molding primary plastic
**PA:** Studio Moulding
918 Avenue N
Grand Prairie TX 75050
972 602-6883

### (G-20540)
### SUPERIOR HOME PRODUCTS INC
3000 Great Northern (62711-6097)
**PHONE**..........................217 726-9300
**Fax:** 217 726-9322
Dan Ulrich, *Branch Mgr*
**EMP:** 7
**SALES (corp-wide):** 9MM **Privately Held**
**SIC:** 3281 7389 Cut stone & stone products: marble, building: cut & shaped; advertising, promotional & trade show services
**PA:** Superior Home Products, Inc.
211 Edinger Rd
Wentzville MO
636 332-9040

### (G-20541)
### TAFT STREET COMPANY INC
2300 N 16th St (62702-1228)
**PHONE**..........................217 544-3471
David F Flatt, *President*
Anthony Stanley, *Corp Secy*
Truman L Flatt Jr, *Vice Pres*
**EMP:** 3
**SQ FT:** 1,000
**SALES (est):** 300K **Privately Held**
**SIC:** 2951 Asphalt paving mixtures & blocks

### (G-20542)
### TEEJET TECHNOLOGIES LLC (HQ)
1801 Business Park Dr (62703-5626)
**PHONE**..........................630 665-5002
Duane Stewart, *President*
Pam Yasinski, *Purch Agent*
Duston Traylor, *Design Engr*
Margaret Robertson, *Accountant*
Marty Wagner, *Sales Mgr*
◆ **EMP:** 53
**SQ FT:** 21,000
**SALES (est):** 15.4MM
**SALES (corp-wide):** 384.3MM **Privately Held**
**WEB:** www.teejet.com
**SIC:** 3679 Electronic circuits
**PA:** Spraying Systems Co.
200 W North Ave
Glendale Heights IL 60139
630 665-5000

### (G-20543)
### TEMPLEGATE PUBLISHERS
302 E Adams St (62701-1403)
P.O. Box 5152 (62705-5152)
**PHONE**..........................217 522-3353
**Fax:** 217 522-3362
Thomas Garvey, *Owner*
Nancy Wu, *Sales Staff*
**EMP:** 4 **EST:** 1947
**SQ FT:** 4,800
**SALES:** 500K **Privately Held**
**WEB:** www.templegate.com
**SIC:** 2731 8661 Books: publishing only; religious organizations

### (G-20544)
### THERMIONICS CORP (PA)
1214 Bunn Ave Ste 5 (62703-5339)
P.O. Box 2526, Sioux Falls SD (57101-2526)
**PHONE**..........................800 800-5728
Gregg Harwood, *President*
Rob Newbold, *QC Mgr*
Nell Renfro, *Natl Sales Mgr*
▲ **EMP:** 14
**SQ FT:** 4,800
**SALES:** 2.5MM **Privately Held**
**WEB:** www.thermipaq.com
**SIC:** 3299 Ceramic fiber

### (G-20545)
### TODD SCANLAN
Also Called: Woodhaven Woodworks
3112 Normandy Rd (62703-5875)
**PHONE**..........................217 585-1717
Todd Scanlan, *Owner*
Kaleigh Bartlett, *Office Mgr*
**EMP:** 7
**SQ FT:** 7,500
**SALES:** 400K **Privately Held**
**SIC:** 2499 Decorative wood & woodwork

### (G-20546)
### TRANSPORTATION ILLINOIS DEPT
Dist 6 Traffic Sign Shop
701 N Macarthur Blvd (62702-2303)
**PHONE**..........................217 785-0288
Mike Bull, *Principal*
**EMP:** 11 **Privately Held**
**WEB:** www.illinoistollway.com
**SIC:** 3993 9621 Signs & advertising specialties; regulation, administration of transportation
**HQ:** Illinois Department Of Transportation
2300 S Dirksen Pkwy
Springfield IL 62764
217 782-7820

### (G-20547)
### UPPER LIMITS MIDWEST INC
1205 S 2nd St Ste B (62704-3067)
**PHONE**..........................217 679-4315
Matt Fortin, *President*
**EMP:** 5
**SALES:** 100K **Privately Held**
**SIC:** 5251 3634 Hardware; vaporizers, electric: household

### (G-20548)
### WYZZ INC
Also Called: W I C S
2680 E Cook St (62703-1902)
P.O. Box 3920 (62708-3920)
**PHONE**..........................217 753-5620
**Fax:** 217 753-8177
Jack Connors, *President*
**EMP:** 60
**SALES (corp-wide):** 2.7B **Publicly Held**
**WEB:** www.wyzztv.com
**SIC:** 4833 2711 Television broadcasting stations; newspapers
**HQ:** Wyzz Inc
2714 E Lincoln St
Bloomington IL 61704
309 661-4343

### (G-20549)
### XTREM GRAPHIX SOLUTIONS INC
1810 W Jefferson St Ste C (62702-3675)
**PHONE**..........................217 698-6424
Jeryn Meister, *President*
**EMP:** 5 **EST:** 2012
**SALES (est):** 488.8K **Privately Held**
**SIC:** 7336 3993 Commercial art & graphic design; signs & advertising specialties

### (G-20550)
### Y T PACKING CO
Also Called: Turasky Meats
1129 Taintor Rd (62702-1760)
P.O. Box 57 (62705-0057)
**PHONE**..........................217 522-3345
**Fax:** 217 522-6395
Joseph Turasky, *President*
**EMP:** 10 **EST:** 1949
**SQ FT:** 13,000
**SALES:** 2MM **Privately Held**
**WEB:** www.turaskymeats.com
**SIC:** 5147 5421 2013 2011 Meats, fresh; meat markets, including freezer provisioners; sausages & other prepared meats; meat packing plants

## Stanford
### Mclean County

### (G-20551)
### D N D COATING
313 W Main St (61774-7541)
P.O. Box 209 (61774-0209)
**PHONE**..........................309 379-3021
**Fax:** 309 379-2401
Gerry Doehrmann, *Partner*
**EMP:** 8
**SALES (est):** 489.7K **Privately Held**
**SIC:** 3479 5014 Coating of metals with silicon; truck tires & tubes

### (G-20552)
### QUALITY METAL WORKS INC
Also Called: Speidel Applicators
200 School St (61774-7577)
P.O. Box 358 (61774-0358)
**PHONE**..........................309 379-5311
Ronald Lubke, *President*
Linda Lubke, *Vice Pres*
Debby Martin, *Bookkeeper*
**EMP:** 3
**SQ FT:** 14,000

SALES: 300K **Privately Held**
WEB: www.qualitymetalworks.com
SIC: **3523** 3599 7692 3444 Farm machinery & equipment; weeding machines, agricultural; plows, agricultural: disc, moldboard, chisel, listers, etc.; machine shop, jobbing & repair; welding repair; sheet metalwork

## Staunton
### Macoupin County

**(G-20553)**
BOFA AMERICAS INC
303 S Madison St (62088-1929)
P.O. Box 235 (62088-0235)
PHONE..........................618 205-5007
John Podwojski, *President*
Annie Podwojski, *Accountant*
▲ EMP: 7 **EST:** 2008
SQ FT: 7,500
SALES (est): 1.7MM **Privately Held**
WEB: www.bofaamericas.com
SIC: **3564** Air purification equipment
HQ: Bofa International Ltd.
   21-22 Balena Close
   Poole BH17
   120 269-9444

**(G-20554)**
BRIAN BEQUETTE CABINETRY
18630 White City Rd (62088-4012)
PHONE..........................618 670-5427
Brian Bequette, *Principal*
EMP: 2
SALES (est): 221.6K **Privately Held**
SIC: **2434** Wood kitchen cabinets

**(G-20555)**
C I F INDUSTRIES INC
20988 Old Route 66 (62088-4312)
PHONE..........................618 635-2010
Fax: 618 362-9001
Rick C Clark, *President*
EMP: 14
SALES (est): 1.6MM **Privately Held**
SIC: **7692** 5521 3713 Welding repair; trucks, tractors & trailers: used; dump truck bodies

**(G-20556)**
CIF INDUSTRIES INC
20988 Old Route 66 (62088-4312)
PHONE..........................618 635-2010
Richard C Clark Jr, *President*
Noel Malone, *Manager*
EMP: 12
SALES: 3.2MM **Privately Held**
SIC: **3537** Truck trailers, used in plants, docks, terminals, etc.

**(G-20557)**
SANKS MACHINING INC
22991 Ruschaupt Rd (62088-4410)
PHONE..........................618 635-8279
William Sanks, *President*
Janie Sanks, *Admin Sec*
EMP: 5
SQ FT: 2,400
SALES (est): 200K **Privately Held**
SIC: **3599** Machine shop, jobbing & repair

**(G-20558)**
SHALE LAKE LLC
Also Called: Winery At Shale Lake The
1499 Washington Ave (62088-3047)
PHONE..........................618 637-2470
David Wesa, *Principal*
EMP: 4
SALES (est): 319K **Privately Held**
SIC: **2084** 7032 0721 0752 Wine cellars, bonded: engaged in blending wines; recreational camps; orchard tree & vine services; animal boarding services; boarding services, horses: racing & non-racing

**(G-20559)**
STAR-TIMES PUBLISHING CO INC
Also Called: Staunton Star Times
108 W Main St (62088-1453)
P.O. Box 180 (62088-0180)
PHONE..........................618 635-2000
Fax: 618 635-5281
Walter F Haase Jr, *President*
EMP: 8 **EST:** 1933
SQ FT: 3,000
SALES (est): 721.8K **Privately Held**
SIC: **2711** 2759 Newspapers; commercial printing

## Steeleville
### Randolph County

**(G-20560)**
DORMA USA INC
Also Called: Dorma Architectural Hardware
1003 W Broadway (62288-1311)
P.O. Box 8 (62288-0008)
PHONE..........................717 336-3881
Gary Seiwell, *Manager*
Seiwell Gary, *Manager*
EMP: 70 **Privately Held**
SIC: **3231** 3429 Products of purchased glass; builders' hardware
HQ: Dorma Usa, Inc.
   100 Dorma Dr
   Reamstown PA 17567
   717 336-3881

**(G-20561)**
LEE GILSTER-MARY CORPORATION
705 N Sparta St (62288-1547)
PHONE..........................618 965-3426
Fax: 618 965-9238
Louis Oulvey, *Opers-Prdtn-Mfg*
Becky Brockmeyer, *Purch Agent*
Richard Tretter, *Sales Executive*
Lloyd Stern, *Manager*
EMP: 100
SALES (corp-wide): 1.1B **Privately Held**
WEB: www.gilstermarylee.com
SIC: **2045** 2099 2098 2087 Prepared flour mixes & doughs; food preparations; macaroni & spaghetti; flavoring extracts & syrups; canned specialties
HQ: Gilster-Mary Lee Corporation
   1037 State St
   Chester IL 62233
   618 826-2361

**(G-20562)**
LEE GILSTER-MARY CORPORATION
10 Industrial Park (62288-1246)
PHONE..........................618 965-3449
Fax: 618 965-9679
Louis Oulvey, *Superintendent*
Gary Stull, *QC Mgr*
Rob Welge, *Personnel*
EMP: 500
SALES (corp-wide): 1.1B **Privately Held**
WEB: www.gilstermarylee.com
SIC: **7389** 2098 2063 2062 Packaging & labeling services; macaroni & spaghetti; beet sugar; cane sugar refining
HQ: Gilster-Mary Lee Corporation
   1037 State St
   Chester IL 62233
   618 826-2361

**(G-20563)**
MC CHEMICAL COMPANY
1208 N Cherry St (62288-1255)
P.O. Box 52 (62288-0052)
PHONE..........................618 965-3668
Fax: 618 965-9590
Denny Fulkrod, *Branch Mgr*
EMP: 4
SALES (corp-wide): 4.9MM **Privately Held**
SIC: **2899** 2296 Chemical preparations; tire cord & fabrics
PA: Mc Chemical Company
   720 South St
   Rockford IL 61102
   815 964-7687

**(G-20564)**
VISION MACHINE & FABRICATION
1102 N Cherry St (62288-1254)
P.O. Box 66 (62288-0066)
PHONE..........................618 965-3199
Fax: 618 965-3088
Ronald P Scherby, *President*
Wayne Heincke, *Vice Pres*
Steppinie Heineche, *Admin Asst*
EMP: 7
SQ FT: 12,000
SALES: 1.3MM **Privately Held**
SIC: **3556** Food products machinery

## Steger
### Cook County

**(G-20565)**
1 FEDERAL SUPPLY SOURCE INC
30 E 34th St (60475-1759)
PHONE..........................708 964-2222
Darnell Muhammad, *President*
EMP: 5
SALES (est): 124.6K **Privately Held**
SIC: **5047** 3841 3842 3821 Whol Med/Hospital Equip Mfg Surgical/Med Instr Mfg Surgical Appliances Mfg Lab Apparatus/Furn Whol Drugs/Sundries

**(G-20566)**
ALL PRO PAVING INC
27 E 36th St (60475-1780)
P.O. Box 1297, Frankfort (60423-7297)
PHONE..........................815 806-2222
Fax: 815 806-2224
Vincent J Falaschetti, *President*
Joan Falaschetti, *Vice Pres*
EMP: 12
SALES: 1MM **Privately Held**
WEB: www.allpropaving.com
SIC: **2951** Asphalt paving blocks (not from refineries)

**(G-20567)**
ALL-RIGHT SIGN INC
3628 Union Ave (60475-1748)
PHONE..........................708 754-6366
Fax: 708 754-6066
Teresa Bowen, *President*
James M Bowen, *Vice Pres*
Michelle Hiland, *Office Mgr*
EMP: 12
SQ FT: 2,500
SALES (est): 500K **Privately Held**
SIC: **3993** 1799 Signs & advertising specialties; sign installation & maintenance

**(G-20568)**
ARCHER GENERAL CONTG & FABG
22498 Miller Rd (60475-5560)
P.O. Box 264 (60475-0264)
PHONE..........................708 757-7902
Fax: 708 757-7976
Roger Buchler, *President*
Judy Buchler, *Treasurer*
Douglas R Buchler, *Admin Sec*
EMP: 6
SQ FT: 6,000
SALES: 390K **Privately Held**
SIC: **1731** 3441 Electrical work; fabricated structural metal

**(G-20569)**
BUILDERS IRONWORKS INC
3242 Louis Sherman Dr (60475-1184)
PHONE..........................708 754-4092
Richard Wories, *Manager*
EMP: 6
SALES (corp-wide): 578.5K **Privately Held**
SIC: **3423** Ironworkers' hand tools
PA: Builders Ironworks Inc
   20659 Bensley Ave
   Lynwood IL

**(G-20570)**
BYTTOW ENTERPRISES INC
3205 Loverock Ave (60475-1231)
PHONE..........................708 754-4995
Norman Byttow, *President*
Mark Byttow, *Treasurer*
EMP: 4
SQ FT: 8,000
SALES (est): 380K **Privately Held**
SIC: **2434** 2431 Wood kitchen cabinets; millwork

**(G-20571)**
CYLINDER MAINTENANCE & SUP INC
3305 Butler Ave (60475-1113)
PHONE..........................708 754-5040
Ken Carpenter, *President*
Stan Wiater, *Corp Secy*
EMP: 14
SQ FT: 20,000
SALES (est): 1.5MM **Privately Held**
SIC: **3569** Generators: steam, liquid oxygen or nitrogen

**(G-20572)**
FRAMARX CORPORATION
Also Called: Framarx Waxstar
3224 Butler Ave (60475-1143)
PHONE..........................708 755-3530
Fax: 708 755-3617
Lawrence Czaszwicz Jr, *President*
Noreen Czaszwicz, *Chairman*
Cynthia Cofran, *CFO*
Bethel Tapia, *Legal Staff*
▲ EMP: 40
SQ FT: 49,000
SALES (est): 10.1MM **Privately Held**
WEB: www.framarx.com
SIC: **2671** Packaging paper & plastics film, coated & laminated

**(G-20573)**
HERR DISPLAY VANS INC
3328 Louis Sherman Dr (60475-1187)
PHONE..........................708 755-7926
Timothy Herr, *President*
James Herr, *Vice Pres*
Carol Herr, *Treasurer*
Steve Herr, *Admin Sec*
EMP: 6
SQ FT: 6,000
SALES (est): 1MM **Privately Held**
WEB: www.herrdisplayvans.com
SIC: **3713** Truck bodies & parts

**(G-20574)**
J D M COATINGS INC
3300 Louis Sherman Dr (60475-1187)
PHONE..........................708 755-6300
Fax: 708 755-6312
Donald F Schultz, *President*
Janice Schultz, *Corp Secy*
Kenneth Latzky, *Vice Pres*
EMP: 6
SQ FT: 7,400
SALES (est): 363K **Privately Held**
SIC: **3399** Metal powders, pastes & flakes

**(G-20575)**
P & L TOOL & MANUFACTURING CO
3624 Union Ave (60475-1748)
PHONE..........................708 754-4777
Louis Lucente, *President*
Paolo Pizzoferrato, *Vice Pres*
EMP: 4
SQ FT: 2,600
SALES: 350K **Privately Held**
SIC: **3544** Special dies, tools, jigs & fixtures

**(G-20576)**
SPECIALTY CRATE FACTORY (PA)
3320 Louis Sherman Dr (60475-1187)
PHONE..........................708 756-2100
K Michael Bless, *Owner*
EMP: 2
SQ FT: 1,800
SALES (est): 406.1K **Privately Held**
SIC: **2449** 5031 Rectangular boxes & crates, wood; doors & windows

**(G-20577)**
STONECRAFT CAST STONE LLC
3025 Louis Sherman Dr (60475-1190)
P.O. Box 45 (60475-0045)
PHONE..........................708 653-1477

EMP: 3
SALES (est): 320K  Privately Held
SIC: 3272  Concrete products

*(G-20578)*
**TROPHIES AND AWARDS PLUS**
3344 Chicago Rd Ste 3  (60475-1233)
PHONE...................................708 754-7127
Fax: 708 754-7137
Priscilla Kidd, *Owner*
EMP: 3
SQ FT: 3,000
SALES: 150K  Privately Held
SIC: 5999  3479  Trophies & plaques; engraving jewelry silverware, or metal

*(G-20579)*
**TTS GRANITE  INC (PA)**
3225 Louis Sherman Dr  (60475-1185)
PHONE...................................708 755-5200
Joseph Nicolazzi, *President*
Aldo Nicolazzi Jr, *Vice Pres*
Scott Smith, *Accountant*
Joan Nicolazzi, *Admin Sec*
▲ EMP: 30
SQ FT: 24,000
SALES (est): 9.1MM  Privately Held
WEB: www.ttsgranite.com
SIC: 2542  Cabinets: show, display or storage: except wood

*(G-20580)*
**UNION AVE AUTO INC**
3236 Union Ave  (60475-1121)
PHONE...................................708 754-3899
Fax: 708 755-5564
Dennis Delisio, *President*
Marlene Delisio, *Vice Pres*
EMP: 5
SQ FT: 12,800
SALES (est): 390K  Privately Held
SIC: 7538  7532  5511  3732  Engine repair; body shop, automotive; automobiles, new & used; boat building & repairing

*(G-20581)*
**UNIVERSAL COATINGS INC**
3001 Louis Sherman Dr  (60475-1190)
PHONE...................................708 756-7000
Sandra Casey, *President*
Pam Vasquez, *Admin Asst*
EMP: 2
SALES (est): 246K  Privately Held
SIC: 3471  Finishing, metals or formed products

## Sterling
### Whiteside County

*(G-20582)*
**ASTEC MOBILE SCREENS  INC**
2704 W Le Fevre Rd  (61081-7703)
PHONE...................................815 626-6374
Timothy Gonigam, *President*
Mike Shell, *Purch Mgr*
Larry Landuit, *Engineer*
Christophe Schumacher, *Engineer*
David Osterhaus, *Controller*
▲ EMP: 116
SQ FT: 60,000
SALES: 47.1MM
SALES (corp-wide): 1.1B  Publicly Held
WEB: www.astecmobilescreens.com
SIC: 3535  Conveyors & conveying equipment
PA: Astec Industries, Inc.
    1725 Shepherd Rd
    Chattanooga TN 37421
    423 899-5898

*(G-20583)*
**AZCON INC**
101 Avenue K  (61081-3229)
PHONE...................................815 548-7000
Fax: 815 548-9240
Lance Caldwell, *Branch Mgr*
EMP: 16

SALES (corp-wide): 77.9MM  Privately Held
SIC: 3533  3715  3823  3589  Water well drilling equipment; semitrailers for truck tractors; water quality monitoring & control systems; garbage disposers & compactors, commercial; ferrous metal scrap & waste; structural shapes, iron or steel
PA: Azcon, Inc.
    820 W Jackson Blvd # 425
    Chicago IL 60607
    312 559-3100

*(G-20584)*
**B F SHAW PRINTING COMPANY**
Also Called: Sauk Valley Newspaper
3200 E Lincolnway  (61081-1773)
P.O. Box 498  (61081-0498)
PHONE...................................815 625-3600
Thomas Shaw, *President*
Terri Swegle, *CFO*
Kathleen Schultz, *Manager*
EMP: 145
SALES: 1,000K
SALES (corp-wide): 83.1MM  Privately Held
WEB: www.saukvalley.com
SIC: 2711  2752  Newspapers; commercial printing, lithographic
PA: The B F Shaw Printing Company
    444 Pine Hill Dr
    Dixon IL
    815 284-4000

*(G-20585)*
**BOSTON LEATHER INC**
1801 Eastwood Dr  (61081-9234)
P.O. Box 1213  (61081-8213)
PHONE...................................815 622-1635
Fax: 815 622-3014
Geri Valentino, *President*
Anthony E Valentino, *Vice Pres*
Katie Valentino, *Manager*
▲ EMP: 25 EST: 1938
SQ FT: 15,000
SALES (est): 3.8MM  Privately Held
WEB: www.bostonleather.com
SIC: 3199  Leather garments; holsters, leather

*(G-20586)*
**C W PUBLICATIONS  INC**
1705 37th Ave  (61081-4231)
P.O. Box 744  (61081-0744)
PHONE...................................800 554-5537
Fax: 815 626-3043
Charles Wilkinson, *President*
Maryellen Wilkinson, *Consultant*
EMP: 1
SALES: 500K  Privately Held
WEB: www.cwpub.com
SIC: 5961  7372  7812  2741  Educational supplies & equipment, mail order; educational computer software; video tape production; miscellaneous publishing; book publishing

*(G-20587)*
**CARTRIDGE WORLD STERLING**
3307 E Lincolnway Ste 1  (61081-9752)
PHONE...................................815 625-2345
Douglas Watson, *Manager*
EMP: 5
SALES: 300K  Privately Held
SIC: 3861  Photographic equipment & supplies

*(G-20588)*
**DANA DRIVESHAFT MFG LLC**
Also Called: Dana Driveshaft Products
2001 Eastwood Dr  (61081-9234)
PHONE...................................815 626-6700
Fax: 815 626-6747
Kevin Gladhill, *Opers Staff*
Kelvin Wright, *Manager*
EMP: 48
SQ FT: 30,000
SALES (corp-wide): 5.8B  Publicly Held
SIC: 3714  Drive shafts, motor vehicle
HQ: Dana Driveshaft Manufacturing, Llc
    3939 Technology Dr
    Maumee OH 43537
    419 887-3000

*(G-20589)*
**DK KNUTSEN**
609 W 3rd St  (61081-3358)
PHONE...................................815 626-4388
Fax: 815 626-4388
Kraig Knutsen, *Owner*
EMP: 4
SALES (est): 319K  Privately Held
SIC: 2541  Counter & sink tops

*(G-20590)*
**EIKENBERRY SHEET METAL WORKS**
412 E 3rd St  (61081-3702)
PHONE...................................815 626-0955
Fax: 815 625-0251
Norden Scalan, *President*
Ann Scalan, *Admin Sec*
EMP: 6
SQ FT: 1,500
SALES (est): 750K  Privately Held
SIC: 1711  3444  Warm air heating & air conditioning contractor; ventilation & duct work contractor; sheet metalwork

*(G-20591)*
**FRANTZ MANUFACTURING COMPANY (PA)**
Also Called: Frantz Bearing Division
3201 W Lefevre Rd  (61081)
P.O. Box 497  (61081-0497)
PHONE...................................815 625-3333
Fax: 815 626-8866
El Froeliger, *Ch of Bd*
J M Gvozdjak, *President*
Deborah Combs, *Purch Mgr*
Colleen McCarter, *QC Mgr*
Ken Stewart, *Project Engr*
▲ EMP: 5
SQ FT: 6,900
SALES (est): 53.8MM  Privately Held
WEB: www.sterlingsteelball.com
SIC: 3562  Roller bearings & parts; ball bearings & parts

*(G-20592)*
**FRANTZ MANUFACTURING COMPANY**
Also Called: Sterling Steel Ball
3809 W Lincoln Hwy  (61081)
P.O. Box 497  (61081-0497)
PHONE...................................815 625-7063
Fax: 815 625-1162
Kyle Dir, *Branch Mgr*
EMP: 54
SALES (corp-wide): 53.8MM  Privately Held
WEB: www.sterlingsteelball.com
SIC: 3562  5084  3624  Ball bearings & parts; industrial machinery & equipment; carbon & graphite products
PA: Frantz Manufacturing Company Inc
    3201 W Lefevre Rd
    Sterling IL 61081
    815 625-3333

*(G-20593)*
**FRANTZ MANUFACTURING COMPANY**
Also Called: Bearing Division
3201 W Le Fevre Rd  (61081-9230)
P.O. Box 497  (61081-0497)
PHONE...................................815 564-0991
Rod Temple, *Purchasing*
Larry Anderson, *Engineer*
Kyle Dir, *Engineer*
Craig Hagel, *Sales Staff*
Carl Boehm, *Branch Mgr*
EMP: 95
SALES (corp-wide): 53.8MM  Privately Held
WEB: www.sterlingsteelball.com
SIC: 3535  3714  3568  Conveyors & conveying equipment; motor vehicle parts & accessories; power transmission equipment
PA: Frantz Manufacturing Company Inc
    3201 W Lefevre Rd
    Sterling IL 61081
    815 625-3333

*(G-20594)*
**GALLOWAY COMO PROCESSING**
Also Called: Galloway Meats & Poultry
24578 Stone St  (61081-8898)
P.O. Box 70, Galt  (61037-0070)
PHONE...................................815 626-0305
Darin Galloway, *Owner*
EMP: 2
SALES (est): 209.1K  Privately Held
SIC: 2011  2015  Meat packing plants; poultry slaughtering & processing

*(G-20595)*
**JJM PRINTING  INC**
311 1st Ave  (61081-3601)
PHONE...................................815 499-3067
EMP: 3
SALES (est): 228.1K  Privately Held
SIC: 2752  Commercial printing, lithographic

*(G-20596)*
**MALLARD HANDLING SOLUTIONS LLC (PA)**
Also Called: Mallard Manufacturing
101 Mallard Rd  (61081-1217)
PHONE...................................815 625-9491
Fax: 815 625-9498
Mike Gunderson, *Principal*
Randy Miller, *Opers Mgr*
Scott Mascho, *Warehouse Mgr*
Scott Garriott, *Engineer*
Sue Wahl, *Treasurer*
▲ EMP: 34
SQ FT: 45,000
SALES (est): 6.2MM  Privately Held
SIC: 3535  Conveyors & conveying equipment

*(G-20597)*
**MARVIN SCHUMAKER PLBG INC**
25457 Front St  (61081-8966)
PHONE...................................815 626-8130
Caroline Schumaker, *President*
Dennis Schumaker, *Vice Pres*
David Schumaker, *Admin Sec*
EMP: 3 EST: 1945
SALES (est): 223.5K  Privately Held
SIC: 1711  3585  Plumbing contractors; warm air heating & air conditioning contractor; refrigeration & heating equipment

*(G-20598)*
**MENK USA  LLC**
2207 Enterprise Dr  (61081-8930)
PHONE...................................815 626-9730
Fax: 815 626-9740
Kathleen Knack, *Controller*
Karl Gross,
▲ EMP: 40
SQ FT: 52,000
SALES (est): 9.4MM
SALES (corp-wide): 39.3MM  Privately Held
WEB: www.menk-usa.com
SIC: 3634  Radiators, electric
PA: Menk Apparatebau Gmbh
    Fritz-Von-Opel-Str. 20
    Bad Marienberg (Westerwald)  56470
    266 162-10

*(G-20599)*
**MICRON INDUSTRIES CORPORATION**
Also Called: Micron Power
1801 Westwood Dr Ste 2  (61081-9221)
PHONE...................................815 380-2222
Vincent Lamparelli, *VP Sales*
Allen Wade, *Manager*
Raquel Martinez, *Prgrmr*
EMP: 89
SALES (corp-wide): 23.4MM  Privately Held
SIC: 3612  Control transformers
PA: Micron Industries Corporation
    1211 W 22nd St Ste 200
    Oak Brook IL 60523
    630 516-1222

*(G-20600)*
**MOORE MACHINE WORKS**
706 Gregden Shores Dr  (61081-9602)
PHONE...................................815 625-0536
Fax: 815 626-5999

# GEOGRAPHIC SECTION

Stickney - Cook County (G-20624)

Evan Moore, *President*
John Moore, *Vice Pres*
Judy Moore, *Treasurer*
**EMP:** 5 **EST:** 1942
**SQ FT:** 15,000
**SALES:** 500K **Privately Held**
**SIC:** 3599 Machine shop, jobbing & repair

**(G-20601)**
**NEW MILLENIUM DIRECTORIES (PA)**
324 1st Ave (61081-3602)
**PHONE**................815 626-5737
**Fax:** 815 626-5717
Terry Brininger, *President*
Chris Fudala, *Graphic Designe*
**EMP:** 22
**SQ FT:** 1,200
**SALES:** 1.5MM **Privately Held**
**WEB:** www.bigprintphonebook.com
**SIC:** 2741 Miscellaneous publishing

**(G-20602)**
**P & P INDUSTRIES INC (PA)**
2100 Enterprise Dr (61081-8929)
**PHONE**................815 623-3297
Warren Pruis, *President*
Marsha Pruis, *Vice Pres*
Tom Slater, *Safety Dir*
Larry Garlough, *Opers Mgr*
Dick Adams, *Safety Mgr*
**EMP:** 51
**SQ FT:** 50,000
**SALES (est):** 12.5MM **Privately Held**
**WEB:** www.ppind.com
**SIC:** 3089 Injection molding of plastics

**(G-20603)**
**PINNEY PRINTING COMPANY (PA)**
1991 Industrial Dr (61081-9064)
**PHONE**................815 626-2727
Charles Arp, *President*
**EMP:** 5 **EST:** 1909
**SQ FT:** 15,000
**SALES:** 2.2MM **Privately Held**
**WEB:** www.pinney.com
**SIC:** 2752 2789 Commercial printing, offset; bookbinding & related work

**(G-20604)**
**PINNEY PRINTING COMPANY**
1991 Industrial Dr (61081-9064)
**PHONE**................815 626-2727
Tim Determan, *Manager*
**EMP:** 20
**SQ FT:** 5,000
**SALES (corp-wide):** 2.2MM **Privately Held**
**WEB:** www.pinney.com
**SIC:** 2752 2791 2752 2759 Commercial printing, offset; typesetting; bookbinding & related work; commercial printing
**PA:** Pinney Printing Company
1991 Industrial Dr
Sterling IL 61081
815 626-2727

**(G-20605)**
**PRESCOTTS INC**
Also Called: Prescott's TV & Appliance
3610 E Lincolnway (61081-9756)
**PHONE**................815 626-2996
James L Prescott, *President*
Rick Renner, *Vice Pres*
**EMP:** 5
**SQ FT:** 28,000
**SALES (est):** 580K **Privately Held**
**SIC:** 3651 Audio electronic systems

**(G-20606)**
**PRINCE RACE CAR ENGINEERING**
1880 Eastwood Dr (61081-9293)
**PHONE**................815 625-8116
Patrick Prince, *President*
**EMP:** 4
**SQ FT:** 7,200
**SALES:** 280K **Privately Held**
**SIC:** 3711 7538 5531 Chassis, motor vehicle; general automotive repair shops; automotive parts; automotive accessories; speed shops, including race car supplies

**(G-20607)**
**QUALITY PLATING**
406 Oak Ave (61081-1860)
**PHONE**................815 626-5223
**Fax:** 815 626-5244
Gary Schultz, *Owner*
**EMP:** 3
**SALES (est):** 213.2K **Privately Held**
**SIC:** 3471 3751 Plating of metals or formed products; motorcycles, bicycles & parts

**(G-20608)**
**QUALITY READY MIX CONCRETE CO**
13134 Galt Rd (61081-8913)
**PHONE**................815 625-0750
**Fax:** 815 625-0751
Roger Dykema, *Manager*
**EMP:** 8
**SALES (corp-wide):** 2.9MM **Privately Held**
**SIC:** 3273 Ready-mixed concrete
**PA:** Quality Ready Mix Concrete Co.
14849 Lyndon Rd
Morrison IL 61270
815 772-7181

**(G-20609)**
**R & C AUTO SUPPLY CORP**
Also Called: Ron's Automotive Machine Shop
2526 E Lincolnway (61081-3052)
**PHONE**................815 625-4414
**Fax:** 815 625-4478
Ronald George, *President*
Carol George, *Treasurer*
**EMP:** 3
**SQ FT:** 4,000
**SALES (est):** 395.7K **Privately Held**
**SIC:** 7538 5531 3519 General automotive repair shops; automotive parts; internal combustion engines

**(G-20610)**
**RONNIE P FABER**
Also Called: Faber Builders Discount
2901 Polo Rd (61081-9724)
**PHONE**................815 626-4561
Ronnie P Faber, *Owner*
**EMP:** 2
**SALES:** 200K **Privately Held**
**WEB:** www.buildersdiscountmart.com
**SIC:** 5211 2434 Lumber & other building materials; wood kitchen cabinets

**(G-20611)**
**SAUK VALLEY CONTAINER CORP**
1980 Eastwood Dr (61081-9233)
**PHONE**................815 626-9657
**Fax:** 815 626-9662
Jake Amsbaugh, *President*
Lynn Hammer, *Vice Pres*
John Eyre, *Sales Mgr*
**EMP:** 15
**SQ FT:** 8,000
**SALES (est):** 3MM **Privately Held**
**WEB:** www.saukvalleycontainer.com
**SIC:** 2653 Boxes, corrugated: made from purchased materials

**(G-20612)**
**SAUK VALLEY SHOPPER INC**
Also Called: Sauk Valley Newspaper
3200 E Lincolnway (61081-1773)
P.O. Box 498 (61081-0498)
**PHONE**................815 625-6700
Tom Shaw, *President*
David Hand, *General Mgr*
Travis Mayfield, *General Mgr*
**EMP:** 130
**SALES (est):** 550K **Privately Held**
**WEB:** www.saukvalleyshopper.com
**SIC:** 2711 2741 Newspapers; miscellaneous publishing

**(G-20613)**
**STEIN INC**
Also Called: Stein Steel Mini Services
610 Wallace St (61081-3300)
P.O. Box 1206 (61081-8206)
**PHONE**................815 626-9355
**Fax:** 815 626-9358
Gary Grantham, *Branch Mgr*
**EMP:** 11

**SALES (corp-wide):** 83.3MM **Privately Held**
**WEB:** www.stein.com
**SIC:** 3312 Blast furnaces & steel mills
**PA:** Stein, Inc.
1929 E Royalton Rd Ste C
Cleveland OH 44147
440 526-9301

**(G-20614)**
**STERLING STEEL COMPANY LLC**
Also Called: Sterling Steel 0530
101 Avenue K (61081-3229)
**PHONE**................815 548-7000
Andy Moore, *General Mgr*
Tobin Kirk, *Safety Dir*
Coldy Snyder, *Safety Mgr*
Patrick Eden, *Engineer*
Tom Vercillo, *Controller*
▲ **EMP:** 260
**SALES (est):** 114.6MM
**SALES (corp-wide):** 3.7B **Publicly Held**
**WEB:** www.sscllc.com
**SIC:** 3312 Rods, iron & steel: made in steel mills
**PA:** Leggett & Platt, Incorporated
1 Leggett Rd
Carthage MO 64836
417 358-8131

**(G-20615)**
**STERLING SYSTEMS & CONTROLS**
Also Called: Prater-Sterling
24711 Emerson Rd (61081-9171)
P.O. Box 418 (61081-0418)
**PHONE**................815 625-0852
**Fax:** 815 625-3103
Robert S Prater, *Chairman*
Don Goshert, *Vice Pres*
**EMP:** 18 **EST:** 1973
**SQ FT:** 12,000
**SALES (est):** 4.2MM
**SALES (corp-wide):** 25.1MM **Privately Held**
**SIC:** 3625 Relays & industrial controls
**HQ:** Prater Industries, Inc.
2 Sammons Ct
Bolingbrook IL 60440
630 679-3200

**(G-20616)**
**STERLING VAULT COMPANY**
Also Called: Wilbert Vault
2411 W Lincolnway (61081-8981)
**PHONE**................815 625-0077
**Fax:** 815 625-0070
Michael Banks, *President*
Kathy Banks, *Corp Secy*
Jeanne Crane, *Office Mgr*
**EMP:** 11
**SQ FT:** 13,500
**SALES:** 2MM **Privately Held**
**SIC:** 3272 7261 Burial vaults, concrete or precast terrazzo; crematory

**(G-20617)**
**TORQUE-TRACTION INTEGRATION**
2001 Eastwood Dr (61081-9234)
**PHONE**................815 759-7388
**EMP:** 2
**SALES (est):** 208.4K **Privately Held**
**SIC:** 3714 Motor vehicle parts & accessories

**(G-20618)**
**UNITED CRAFTSMEN LTD**
1500 W 4th St (61081-3121)
**PHONE**................815 626-7802
**Fax:** 815 626-7803
Mark Sedig, *President*
Charles Sedig, *Corp Secy*
Glen Leland, *Vice Pres*
Glenn V Sedig, *Treasurer*
Kathy Sedig, *Bookkeeper*
**EMP:** 10
**SQ FT:** 13,000
**SALES:** 1.1MM **Privately Held**
**WEB:** www.unitedcraftsmenltd.com
**SIC:** 3599 3544 Machine shop, jobbing & repair; special dies, tools, jigs & fixtures

**(G-20619)**
**WAHL CLIPPER CORPORATION (PA)**
2900 Locust St (61081-9500)
P.O. Box 578 (61081-0578)
**PHONE**................815 625-6525
**Fax:** 815 625-6745
John Wahl, *CEO*
Gregory S Wahl, *President*
James O Wahl, *Exec VP*
Don Ouellette, *Vice Pres*
Scott Hamilton, *CFO*
◆ **EMP:** 720 **EST:** 1911
**SQ FT:** 380,000
**SALES:** 424MM **Privately Held**
**WEB:** www.iso-tip.com
**SIC:** 3999 Hair clippers for human use, hand & electric

**(G-20620)**
**WAHL CLIPPER CORPORATION**
2902 Locust St (61081)
**PHONE**................815 625-6525
**Fax:** 815 625-0091
Jerold I Horn, *Branch Mgr*
**EMP:** 12
**SALES (corp-wide):** 424MM **Privately Held**
**SIC:** 3999 Hair clippers for human use, hand & electric
**PA:** Wahl Clipper Corporation
2900 Locust St
Sterling IL 61081
815 625-6525

**(G-20621)**
**WATER INC**
2404 Locust St (61081-1222)
**PHONE**................815 626-8844
Robert Stouffer, *President*
**EMP:** 5
**SALES (est):** 433.1K **Privately Held**
**SIC:** 3589 Water treatment equipment, industrial

**(G-20622)**
**WESTWOOD MACHINE & TOOL CO**
Also Called: M SM
1703 Westwood Dr (61081-9296)
**PHONE**................815 626-5090
**Fax:** 815 626-3719
David Hurless, *President*
Jerry Crenshaw, *Treasurer*
Ellen Beck, *Manager*
Joseph Schneiderbauer, *Admin Sec*
**EMP:** 19
**SQ FT:** 15,000
**SALES:** 2MM **Privately Held**
**WEB:** www.wmtool.com
**SIC:** 3544 Special dies, tools, jigs & fixtures

## Steward
### Lee County

**(G-20623)**
**DAVID HAYES**
Also Called: Hayes Cabinets
1935 Locust Rd (60553-9753)
P.O. Box 86 (60553-0086)
**PHONE**................815 238-7690
Dave Hayes, *Owner*
**EMP:** 2
**SALES (est):** 221K **Privately Held**
**SIC:** 2434 Wood kitchen cabinets

## Stickney
### Cook County

**(G-20624)**
**M & A GROCERY**
6719 Pershing Rd (60402-4069)
**PHONE**................708 749-9786
**EMP:** 3
**SALES (est):** 180K **Privately Held**
**SIC:** 3999 Mfg Misc Products

## Stillman Valley
### Ogle County

**(G-20625)**
**DESIGNOVATIONS INC**
7339 E Wildwood Rd (61084-9411)
P.O. Box 8945, Rockford (61126-8945)
PHONE.................................815 645-8598
Fax: 815 645-2389
Janis E Anderson, *President*
Jennifer Schiess, *General Mgr*
**EMP:** 3
**SQ FT:** 5,000
**SALES (est):** 550K **Privately Held**
WEB: www.designovations.com
**SIC: 3993** Signs & advertising specialties

**(G-20626)**
**R C SALES & MANUFACTURING INC**
5999 N Cox Rd (61084-9358)
PHONE.................................815 645-8898
Roger Carlson, *President*
Yvonne Raymond, *Corp Secy*
Brad Cain, *Vice Pres*
Natalie Haugse, *Office Mgr*
**EMP:** 8
**SQ FT:** 9,000
**SALES (est):** 466.4K **Privately Held**
WEB: www.rcsalesandmanufacturing.com
**SIC: 3089** 3599 Plastic processing; machine shop, jobbing & repair

**(G-20627)**
**ROCK VALLEY ANTIQUE AUTO PARTS**
5800 N Rothwell (61084)
P.O. Box 352 (61084-0352)
PHONE.................................815 645-2272
Scott McCullough, *President*
Dale Mathison, *Treasurer*
**EMP:** 7
**SQ FT:** 10,000
**SALES (est):** 839.6K **Privately Held**
**SIC: 3714** Motor vehicle parts & accessories

**(G-20628)**
**STRAIT-O-FLEX**
7372 Kishwaukee Rd (61084-9529)
PHONE.................................815 965-2625
Vicki Walker, *Principal*
**EMP:** 3
**SALES (est):** 187.1K **Privately Held**
**SIC: 3498** Tube fabricating (contract bending & shaping)

**(G-20629)**
**TOOLMASTERS LLC**
Also Called: Small Tools Div
206 S Walnut St (61084-8917)
P.O. Box 115 (61084-0115)
PHONE.................................815 645-2224
**EMP:** 13
**SALES (corp-wide):** 2.5MM **Privately Held**
**SIC: 3545** 3546 Mfg Machine Tool Accessories Mfg Power-Driven Handtools
PA: Toolmasters Llc
1439 Railroad Ave Ste 1
Rockford IL 61109
815 968-0961

## Stockton
### Jo Daviess County

**(G-20630)**
**BREWSTER CHEESE COMPANY**
300 W Railroad Ave (61085-1545)
PHONE.................................815 947-3361
John Scott, *Principal*
Teresa Wulff, *Purchasing*
Ronda Dower, *Manager*
**EMP:** 90
**SALES (corp-wide):** 122.8MM **Privately Held**
**SIC: 2022** Cheese, natural & processed
PA: Brewster Cheese Company
800 Wabash Ave S
Brewster OH 44613
330 767-3492

**(G-20631)**
**DURA OPERATING LLC**
301 S Simmons St (61085-1513)
PHONE.................................815 947-3333
Karl F Storrie, *President*
**EMP:** 125
**SALES (corp-wide):** 3.9B **Privately Held**
WEB: www.heywoodwilliamsusa.com
**SIC: 3089** 3429 Injection molded finished plastic products; manufactured hardware (general)
HQ: Dura Operating, Llc
1780 Pond Run
Auburn Hills MI 48326
248 299-7500

## Stone Park
### Cook County

**(G-20632)**
**AMERICAN WELDING & GAS INC**
3900 W North Ave (60165-1036)
PHONE.................................630 527-2550
Ray Petty, *President*
Mark Stears, *Vice Pres*
Kimberly Jodrdan, *Purchasing*
Scott Spears, *Manager*
Andreas Boone, *Director*
**EMP:** 39
**SALES (corp-wide):** 128.3MM **Privately Held**
**SIC: 7692** 5999 5169 5084 Welding repair; welding supplies; industrial gases; petroleum industry machinery
PA: American Welding & Gas, Inc.
4900 Falls Of Neuse Rd # 150
Raleigh NC 27609
800 231-8462

**(G-20633)**
**EES INC**
4300 W North Ave (60165-1038)
PHONE.................................708 343-1800
Jacek Helenowski, *President*
Tim Green, *Info Tech Mgr*
**EMP:** 6 **EST:** 2012
**SALES (est):** 626.1K **Privately Held**
**SIC: 5063** 3621 3629 Generators; power transmission equipment, electric; generating apparatus & parts, electrical; electronic generation equipment

**(G-20634)**
**ENGINE REBUILDERS & SUPPLY**
4010 W North Ave (60165-1037)
PHONE.................................708 338-1113
Andy Frontzak, *President*
**EMP:** 4 **EST:** 1940
**SQ FT:** 5,000
**SALES (est):** 542K **Privately Held**
**SIC: 7699** 7538 3714 3621 Engine repair & replacement, non-automotive; engine rebuilding: automotive; motor vehicle parts & accessories; motors & generators

**(G-20635)**
**FRA NO 3800 W DIVISION**
3800 Division St (60165-1115)
PHONE.................................708 338-0690
Fax: 708 338-0699
Paul Basile, *Publisher*
Fred L Gardaphe, *Assoc Editor*
**EMP:** 5
**SALES (est):** 268.8K **Privately Held**
**SIC: 2711** Newspapers

**(G-20636)**
**PPG INDUSTRIES INC**
Also Called: PPG 5526
3500 W North Ave (60165-1042)
PHONE.................................708 345-1515
E Contreras, *Branch Mgr*
**EMP:** 3
**SALES (corp-wide):** 14.7B **Publicly Held**
WEB: www.ppg.com
**SIC: 2851** Paints & allied products
PA: Ppg Industries, Inc.
1 Ppg Pl
Pittsburgh PA 15272
412 434-3131

## Stonefort
### Saline County

**(G-20637)**
**CARDINAL ENTERPRISES**
562 Ferrel Rd (62987-1205)
PHONE.................................618 994-4454
Steve Borntrater, *Partner*
**EMP:** 2
**SALES (est):** 200.7K **Privately Held**
**SIC: 3448** Prefabricated metal buildings

## Streamwood
### Cook County

**(G-20638)**
**A 1 TROPHIES AWARDS & ENGRV**
Also Called: Allen Awards
1534 Brandy Pkwy (60107-1810)
PHONE.................................630 837-6000
Fax: 630 837-5657
Ray Begy, *President*
Susan Begy, *Vice Pres*
**EMP:** 4
**SALES:** 520K **Privately Held**
**SIC: 5094** 5999 3993 Trophies; trophies & plaques; signs & advertising specialties

**(G-20639)**
**ADVANCED ASSEMBLY**
703 Blue Ridge Dr (60107-4503)
PHONE.................................630 379-6158
Manu Patel, *Manager*
Ravi Patel, *Director*
**EMP:** 2
**SALES:** 300K **Privately Held**
**SIC: 3449** Bars, concrete reinforcing: fabricated steel

**(G-20640)**
**AKINSUN HEAT CO INC**
1538 Brandy Pkwy (60107-1810)
PHONE.................................630 289-9506
Fax: 630 289-9506
Syed Musevi, *CEO*
Zak Karmali, *Vice Pres*
Sandra Kunzandorf, *Plant Mgr*
Syed Masavi, *Engineer*
▲ **EMP:** 19
**SQ FT:** 7,000
**SALES (est):** 3.3MM **Privately Held**
WEB: www.akinsun.com
**SIC: 3567** 3634 Heating units & devices, industrial: electric; electric housewares & fans

**(G-20641)**
**ALUMINUM COIL ANODIZING CORP (PA)**
Also Called: A C A
501 E Lake St (60107-4100)
PHONE.................................630 837-4000
Fax: 630 837-0814
Michael Venie, *President*
Gary Rusch, *General Mgr*
Ronald L Rusch, *Treasurer*
Elaine Hurtzeck, *Human Res Dir*
Mike Moomey, *VP Sales*
▲ **EMP:** 135 **EST:** 1960
**SQ FT:** 105,000
**SALES (est):** 38.7MM **Privately Held**
WEB: www.acacorp.com
**SIC: 3471** 5051 Anodizing (plating) of metals or formed products; aluminum bars, rods, ingots, sheets, pipes, plates, etc.

**(G-20642)**
**AMERICAN CONCORDE SYSTEMS**
1548 Burgundy Pkwy (60107-1812)
P.O. Box 1011, Northbrook (60065-1011)
PHONE.................................773 342-9951
Fax: 773 342-9960
Paul Hansfield, *President*
Ron Kaplan, *General Mgr*
**EMP:** 15
**SQ FT:** 12,500
**SALES:** 1.5MM **Privately Held**
**SIC: 3728** Aircraft parts & equipment

**(G-20643)**
**ANDERSON ENGRG NEW PRAGUE INC**
312 Roma Jean Pkwy (60107-2933)
PHONE.................................630 736-0900
Peter Sochacki, *Branch Mgr*
Paula Mills, *Manager*
**EMP:** 3
**SALES (corp-wide):** 2MM **Privately Held**
WEB: www.andeng.net
**SIC: 3612** 8711 Voltage regulating transformers, electric power; electrical or electronic engineering
PA: Anderson Engineering Of New Prague, Inc.
20526 330th St
New Prague MN 56071
507 364-7373

**(G-20644)**
**ATHLETIC & SPORTS SEATING**
676 Bonded Pkwy Ste L (60107-1815)
PHONE.................................630 837-5566
Daisy Gonzalez, *Principal*
**EMP:** 3
**SALES (est):** 220.8K **Privately Held**
**SIC: 5712** 5021 2511 Furniture stores; household furniture; chairs, household, except upholstered: wood

**(G-20645)**
**BARNES INDUSTRIAL EQUIPMENT**
155 Sangra Ct (60107-2913)
PHONE.................................630 213-9240
James Barnes, *CEO*
**EMP:** 3
**SALES (est):** 346.1K **Privately Held**
**SIC: 3537** Industrial trucks & tractors

**(G-20646)**
**BROLITE PRODUCTS INCORPORATED**
1900 S Park Ave (60107-2944)
PHONE.................................630 830-0340
Fax: 630 830-0356
David Del Ghingaro, *President*
Ken Skrzypiec, *Vice Pres*
Sheila Ghingaro, *Manager*
Sheila K Spinner, *Admin Asst*
**EMP:** 49
**SQ FT:** 30,000
**SALES:** 14MM **Privately Held**
WEB: www.bakewithbrolite.com
**SIC: 2045** Prepared flour mixes & doughs

**(G-20647)**
**CAFFERO TOOL & MFG**
Also Called: Jim's Plumbing
1537 Brandy Pkwy (60107-1809)
P.O. Box 288, Gilberts (60136-0288)
PHONE.................................224 293-2600
Paul Caffero, *CEO*
Lisa Caffero, *Manager*
**EMP:** 75
**SALES:** 505K **Privately Held**
**SIC: 3599** Machine & other job shop work

**(G-20648)**
**CENTURION NON DESTRUCTIVE TSTG**
Also Called: Centurion N D T
1400 Yorkshire Dr (60107-2272)
PHONE.................................630 736-5500
Fax: 630 736-5700
Kenneth F Strass Jr, *President*
Norma Strass, *Corp Secy*
**EMP:** 10
**SQ FT:** 5,000
**SALES (est):** 920K **Privately Held**
WEB: www.centurionndt.com
**SIC: 3825** 8734 3829 Test equipment for electronic & electrical circuits; testing laboratories; measuring & controlling devices

## Streamwood - Cook County (G-20677)

**(G-20649)**
**CONSOLIDATED CARQUEVILLE PRTG**
1536 Bourbon Pkwy (60107-1808)
PHONE..................630 246-6451
Fax: 630 837-7691
Philip Wicklander, *President*
Tom Simunek, *President*
Chuck McDermott, *Vice Pres*
John Nowicki, *Vice Pres*
June Anderson, *Human Res Dir*
**EMP:** 110
**SQ FT:** 78,000
**SALES (est):** 26.5MM
**SALES (corp-wide):** 6.9B **Publicly Held**
**WEB:** www.consolidatedgraphics.com
**SIC:** 2752 Commercial printing, lithographic
**HQ:** Consolidated Graphics, Inc.
  5858 Westheimer Rd # 200
  Houston TX 77057
  713 787-0977

**(G-20650)**
**CONTROLLED THERMAL PROCESSING (PA)**
1521 Bourbon Pkwy (60107-1836)
PHONE..................847 651-5511
Frederick Diekman, *President*
**EMP:** 3
**SQ FT:** 2,400
**SALES:** 500K **Privately Held**
**SIC:** 3823 3399 Thermal conductivity instruments, industrial process type; cryogenic treatment of metal

**(G-20651)**
**DONE RITE SEALCOATING INC**
412 E North Ave (60107-2524)
P.O. Box 8410, Bartlett (60103-8410)
PHONE..................630 830-5310
Anthony Ducato, *President*
Tricia Ducato, *Admin Sec*
**EMP:** 6
**SALES:** 550K **Privately Held**
**SIC:** 2951 Asphalt & asphaltic paving mixtures (not from refineries)

**(G-20652)**
**DSR SCREENPRINTING**
676 Bonded Pkwy Ste L (60107-1815)
PHONE..................630 855-2790
Wayne Sommers, *Owner*
**EMP:** 6
**SALES (est):** 861.9K **Privately Held**
**SIC:** 2752 Commercial printing, lithographic

**(G-20653)**
**ELITE MANUFACTURER LLC**
1402 Laurel Oaks Dr (60107-3314)
PHONE..................779 777-3857
Farhan Farooqui,
**EMP:** 3
**SALES (est):** 121.7K **Privately Held**
**SIC:** 3199 Leather goods

**(G-20654)**
**EMBEDDEDKITS**
1025 Oakland Dr (60107-2106)
PHONE..................847 401-7488
Silvano Romeo, *Owner*
**EMP:** 5
**SALES (est):** 497.3K **Privately Held**
**WEB:** www.embeddedkits.com
**SIC:** 3544 Special dies & tools

**(G-20655)**
**ENVELOPES ONLY INC**
2000 S Park Ave (60107-2945)
PHONE..................630 213-2500
Fax: 630 213-7455
Deborah L Craig, *President*
Anthony Natalizio, *Marketing Mgr*
Fran Kowal, *Office Mgr*
**EMP:** 23
**SQ FT:** 20,000
**SALES (est):** 4.6MM **Privately Held**
**SIC:** 2752 5112 Commercial printing, lithographic; envelopes

**(G-20656)**
**FRESH EXPRESS INCORPORATED**
1109 E Lake St (60107-4332)
PHONE..................630 736-3900
Stuart Wilcox, *Principal*
Silvija Lackajs, *Human Res Mgr*
Olga Soto, *Manager*
**EMP:** 41
**SALES (corp-wide):** 2.8B **Privately Held**
**SIC:** 0723 2099 Vegetable packing services; food preparations
**HQ:** Fresh Express Incorporated
  4757 The Grove Dr Ste 260
  Windermere FL 34786
  407 612-5000

**(G-20657)**
**FRICKE DENTAL MANUFACTURING CO**
165 Roma Jean Pkwy (60107-2962)
PHONE..................630 540-1900
Lawrence R Fricke Jr, *President*
Ronald Schumann, *Sales Mgr*
Nancy Fricke, *Admin Sec*
Rose Tekstar, *Admin Asst*
**EMP:** 6 **EST:** 1939
**SQ FT:** 7,500
**SALES (est):** 779.3K **Privately Held**
**SIC:** 3843 8021 Dental equipment & supplies; offices & clinics of dentists

**(G-20658)**
**J R MOLD INC**
65 Sangra Ct (60107-2908)
PHONE..................630 289-2192
Joseph M Raia, *President*
Patirica J Raia, *Corp Secy*
**EMP:** 5 **EST:** 1980
**SQ FT:** 1,500
**SALES:** 500K **Privately Held**
**SIC:** 3544 Forms (molds), for foundry & plastics working machinery

**(G-20659)**
**JAMESONS ASPHALT SERVICE**
123 W Green Meadows Blvd (60107-1181)
PHONE..................630 830-7266
Jameson R White, *Owner*
**EMP:** 2
**SALES (est):** 259K **Privately Held**
**SIC:** 3531 Asphalt plant, including gravel-mix type

**(G-20660)**
**JB ENTERPRISES II INC (PA)**
Also Called: Sealmaster Industries
375 Roma Jean Pkwy (60107-2932)
PHONE..................630 372-8300
Michael J Bashir, *President*
Jonathan Bashir, *Vice Pres*
Irene Bashir, *Admin Sec*
**EMP:** 20
**SQ FT:** 4,250
**SALES (est):** 2.2MM **Privately Held**
**SIC:** 2891 Asphalt paving mixtures & blocks

**(G-20661)**
**JC TOOL AND MOLD INC**
1529 Burgundy Pkwy (60107-1811)
PHONE..................630 483-2203
Jack J Coldsetti, *President*
**EMP:** 3
**SALES (est):** 311.8K **Privately Held**
**SIC:** 3544 Industrial molds

**(G-20662)**
**KOOL TECHNOLOGIES INC**
Also Called: Alpine Refrigeration
714 Bonded Pkwy Ste A (60107-1803)
PHONE..................630 483-2256
Kristine Schmitz, *President*
**EMP:** 4
**SALES:** 2MM **Privately Held**
**WEB:** www.kooltechnologies.com
**SIC:** 3585 1711 7623 Refrigeration & heating equipment; heating & air conditioning contractors; refrigeration service & repair

**(G-20663)**
**KSO METALFAB INC**
250 Roma Jean Pkwy (60107-2963)
PHONE..................630 372-1200
Fax: 630 372-1251
Dora Kuzelka, *President*
Kenneth Kuzelka, *General Mgr*
Jeff T Nguyen, *Project Mgr*
Jeff Nguyen, *Project Mgr*
Jack Cook, *Engineer*
**EMP:** 39
**SQ FT:** 34,000
**SALES (est):** 14MM **Privately Held**
**WEB:** www.kso.com
**SIC:** 3441 Fabricated structural metal

**(G-20664)**
**KUT-RITE TOOL COMPANY**
1539 Brandy Pkwy (60107-1809)
PHONE..................630 837-8130
Mark Retondo, *President*
**EMP:** 12
**SQ FT:** 6,000
**SALES:** 500K **Privately Held**
**SIC:** 3545 Machine tool attachments & accessories

**(G-20665)**
**L I K INC**
304 Roma Jean Pkwy (60107-2933)
PHONE..................630 213-1282
Fax: 630 213-1297
Lisa Jurgens Carso, *President*
◆ **EMP:** 15
**SQ FT:** 14,000
**SALES (est):** 3.4MM **Privately Held**
**WEB:** www.kli-inc.com
**SIC:** 3679 Electronic circuits; harness assemblies for electronic use: wire or cable

**(G-20666)**
**MENUS TO GO**
676 Bonded Pkwy Ste A (60107-1815)
PHONE..................630 483-0848
**EMP:** 3
**SALES (est):** 288.6K **Privately Held**
**SIC:** 2752 Commercial printing, lithographic

**(G-20667)**
**NATIONAL PUBLISHING COMPANY**
Also Called: National Locksmith Magazine
1533 Burgundy Pkwy (60107-1811)
PHONE..................630 837-2044
Fax: 630 837-1210
Marc Goldberg, *President*
Eric Zimmerman, *Publisher*
Jeff Adair, *Advt Staff*
**EMP:** 10
**SALES (est):** 1.2MM **Privately Held**
**WEB:** www.thenationallocksmith.com
**SIC:** 2721 Magazines: publishing only, not printed on site

**(G-20668)**
**OMNITRONIX CORPORATION**
349 Roma Jean Pkwy (60107-2932)
PHONE..................630 837-1400
Fax: 630 837-1660
Allen M Ernst, *President*
Jason Ernst, *Vice Pres*
**EMP:** 18
**SQ FT:** 15,950
**SALES (est):** 3.4MM **Privately Held**
**WEB:** www.omnitronixcorp.com
**SIC:** 3679 5065 Harness assemblies for electronic use: wire or cable; connectors, electronic

**(G-20669)**
**PALLET SOLUTION**
205 S Bartlett Rd (60107-1304)
PHONE..................773 837-8677
Roberto De Lara, *Principal*
**EMP:** 4
**SALES (est):** 273.6K **Privately Held**
**SIC:** 2448 Pallets, wood & wood with metal

**(G-20670)**
**RANDOLPH PACKING CO**
Also Called: Imperial Pizza
275 Roma Jean Pkwy (60107-2964)
PHONE..................630 830-3100
Fax: 630 830-1872
A W Carmignani, *President*
Angelo B Carmignani, *Vice Pres*
Brooks Carmignani, *Vice Pres*
**EMP:** 100 **EST:** 1960
**SQ FT:** 50,000
**SALES (est):** 20.8MM **Privately Held**
**WEB:** www.randolphpacking.com
**SIC:** 2013 5143 5149 7389 Sausages & other prepared meats; cheese; pizza supplies; packaging & labeling services; meat, frozen: packaged

**(G-20671)**
**RETONDO ENTERPRISES INC**
Also Called: Kut-Rite Tool Co.
1539 Brandy Pkwy (60107-1809)
PHONE..................630 837-8130
Mark E Retondo, *President*
**EMP:** 4
**SALES (est):** 291.2K **Privately Held**
**SIC:** 3545 Machine tool attachments & accessories

**(G-20672)**
**SCIMITAR PROTOTYPING INC**
1529 Bourbon Pkwy (60107-1836)
PHONE..................630 483-3875
Stuart Garner, *President*
Jeffrey Garner, *Manager*
**EMP:** 3
**SQ FT:** 2,400
**SALES (est):** 648K **Privately Held**
**WEB:** www.sci-proto.com
**SIC:** 3089 Molding primary plastic

**(G-20673)**
**SJS PACKAGING INC**
46 Mckinley Ln (60107-2316)
PHONE..................630 855-4755
Joachim Saldanha, *President*
Steven Saldanha, *Admin Sec*
▲ **EMP:** 4
**SALES (est):** 304.7K **Privately Held**
**WEB:** www.sjspackaging.com
**SIC:** 2671 Plastic film, coated or laminated for packaging

**(G-20674)**
**SPARX EDM INC**
65 Sangra Ct (60107-2908)
PHONE..................847 722-7577
Joseph Raia, *President*
Laura Raia, *Admin Sec*
**EMP:** 7
**SQ FT:** 3,500
**SALES:** 600K **Privately Held**
**SIC:** 3089 5084 Injection molding of plastics; machinists' precision measuring tools

**(G-20675)**
**STREAMWOOD PLATING CO**
1545 Brandy Pkwy (60107-1809)
P.O. Box 569 (60107-0569)
PHONE..................630 830-6363
Fax: 630 830-6364
Andy Patel, *President*
Nancy Rupp, *Bookkeeper*
**EMP:** 9
**SQ FT:** 5,800
**SALES (est):** 1.1MM **Privately Held**
**SIC:** 3471 Plating of metals or formed products

**(G-20676)**
**THREE CASTLE PRESS INC**
213 Mayfield Dr (60107-1724)
PHONE..................630 540-0120
**EMP:** 3 **EST:** 1969
**SQ FT:** 2,000
**SALES (est):** 220K **Privately Held**
**SIC:** 2759 2752 Commercial Printing Lithographic Commercial Printing

**(G-20677)**
**TRELLBORG SLING SLTIONS US INC**
Also Called: Trelleborg Slng Slns Strmwd
901 Phoenix Lake Ave (60107-2362)
PHONE..................630 289-1500
Tom Zobitz, *General Mgr*
Phill McDaniels, *Project Mgr*
Tom McClintock, *Facilities Mgr*
Michael Bender, *Design Engr*
Ken Edl, *Cust Mgr*
**EMP:** 99
**SALES (corp-wide):** 2.9B **Privately Held**
**WEB:** www.dowtyauto.com
**SIC:** 3492 3053 Fluid power valves & hose fittings; gaskets, packing & sealing devices

# Streamwood - Cook County (G-20678)

HQ: Trelleborg Sealing Solutions Us, Inc.
2531 Bremer Rd
Fort Wayne IN 46803
260 749-9631

**(G-20678)**
**TRIANGLE TECHNOLOGIES INC**
687 Bonded Pkwy (60107-1840)
P.O. Box 8180, Bartlett (60103-8180)
PHONE..................630 736-3318
Roger Mauer, *President*
Roger Maurer, *General Mgr*
John C Schramm, *Manager*
▲ **EMP:** 5
**SALES:** 1MM **Privately Held**
**WEB:** www.triangletechnologies.com
**SIC:** 3565  8711  Packaging machinery; consulting engineer

**(G-20679)**
**TVP COLOR GRAPHICS INC**
230 Roma Jean Pkwy (60107-2963)
PHONE..................630 837-3600
Uma Ravi, *President*
Bhaskar Ravi, *Vice Pres*
Chris Scheffki, *Prdtn Mgr*
Sudhir Ravi, *VP Mktg*
▲ **EMP:** 6
**SALES:** 930K **Privately Held**
**SIC:** 2752  7334  2732  Commercial printing, offset; photocopying & duplicating services; books: printing & binding

**(G-20680)**
**VISOS MACHINE SHOP & MFG**
686 Bonded Pkwy (60107-1839)
PHONE..................630 372-3925
Darlene Viso, *President*
Nino Viso, *Vice Pres*
**EMP:** 2
**SQ FT:** 2,500
**SALES (est):** 200K **Privately Held**
**SIC:** 3599  Amusement park equipment

**(G-20681)**
**WOODWORK APTS LLC**
124 Linden Ave (60107-3161)
PHONE..................224 595-9691
**EMP:** 4
**SALES (est):** 200K **Privately Held**
**SIC:** 2431  Millwork

## Streator
### Lasalle County

**(G-20682)**
**ALM MATERIALS HANDLING LLC**
200 Benchmark Indus Dr (61364-9400)
PHONE..................815 673-5546
Douglas Grunnet, *President*
Patricia Galick, *Admin Sec*
**EMP:** 30
**SQ FT:** 30,000
**SALES:** 7MM **Privately Held**
**SIC:** 3544  5084  Welding positioners (jigs); lift trucks & parts

**(G-20683)**
**ANCHOR GLASS CONTAINER CORP**
1901 N Shabbona St (61364-1381)
PHONE..................815 672-7761
Jack Porter, *Purch Mgr*
Pat Daly, *Engineer*
Jo Sirriani, *Manager*
**EMP:** 43
**SALES (corp-wide):** 2.3B **Privately Held**
**WEB:** www.anchorglass.com
**SIC:** 3221  Glass containers
HQ: Anchor Glass Container Corporation
401 E Jackson St Ste 1100
Tampa FL 33602

**(G-20684)**
**BRAVE PRODUCTS INC**
1705 N Shabbona St (61364-1301)
PHONE..................815 672-0551
Paul Walker, *President*
Wayne Bihler, *CIO*
**EMP:** 6 **EST:** 2001
**SALES (est):** 650K **Privately Held**
**WEB:** www.braveproducts.com
**SIC:** 3531  Log splitters

**(G-20685)**
**COMMERCIAL FAST PRINT**
318 E Main St (61364-2962)
PHONE..................815 673-1196
Fax: 815 673-1191
Mary Yurko, *Owner*
**EMP:** 2
**SALES (est):** 260.2K **Privately Held**
**SIC:** 2752  2791  Commercial printing, lithographic; typesetting

**(G-20686)**
**CORAS WELDING SHOP INC**
Also Called: Coras Trailer Manufacturing
410 W Broadway St (61364-2112)
P.O. Box 566 (61364-0566)
PHONE..................815 672-7950
Luis Castaneda, *President*
Carlos Castaneda, *President*
Michelle Fowler, *Office Mgr*
▲ **EMP:** 8
**SALES (est):** 2.1MM **Privately Held**
**SIC:** 3715  Truck trailers

**(G-20687)**
**DOVIN MACHINE SHOP**
521 Lundy St (61364-3013)
PHONE..................815 672-5247
William Dovin Jr, *Owner*
**EMP:** 2
**SALES (est):** 271.6K **Privately Held**
**SIC:** 3599  Machine shop, jobbing & repair

**(G-20688)**
**FLINK COMPANY (PA)**
502 N Vermillion St (61364-2245)
PHONE..................815 673-4321
Fax: 815 672-2678
Mike Supergan, *President*
Duane Kruger, *Opers Staff*
Eddy Hunter, *Mfg Staff*
Dan Flavel, *Purchasing*
Randy Hart, *Purchasing*
**EMP:** 49 **EST:** 1929
**SQ FT:** 24,000
**SALES (est):** 10.7MM **Privately Held**
**SIC:** 3531  Snow plow attachments; aggregate spreaders

**(G-20689)**
**GUARDIAN ANGEL OUTREACH**
405 S Illinois St (61364-3044)
PHONE..................815 672-4567
Joyce Redfern, *Director*
**EMP:** 3
**SALES (est):** 193.2K **Privately Held**
**SIC:** 2835  Pregnancy test kits

**(G-20690)**
**GUZZLER MANUFACTURING INC**
1621 S Illinois St (61364-3945)
P.O. Box 66, Birmingham AL (35201-0066)
PHONE..................815 672-3171
Bill Gass, *President*
Phil Walker, *Project Mgr*
Greg Grant, *Opers Staff*
Doug Johnson, *QC Mgr*
Kevin Kimes, *Engineer*
**EMP:** 170
**SALES (est):** 27.4MM **Privately Held**
**SIC:** 3559  3561  Automotive related machinery; industrial pumps & parts

**(G-20691)**
**IMAGE PRINT INC (PA)**
810 W Bridge St (61364-2714)
PHONE..................815 672-1068
Fax: 815 672-1699
David C Fitzsimmons, *President*
Thomas Fitzsimmons, *Vice Pres*
**EMP:** 5
**SQ FT:** 5,000
**SALES (est):** 456.5K **Privately Held**
**WEB:** www.gojrc.com
**SIC:** 2752  2791  2789  Commercial printing, offset; typesetting; bookbinding & related work

**(G-20692)**
**JOE HATZER & SON INC (PA)**
Also Called: Hatzer Ready Mix
602 Lundy St (61364-3051)
PHONE..................815 673-5571
Dennis Hatzer, *President*
Sandra Hatzer, *Corp Secy*
Jeff Hatzer, *Vice Pres*
**EMP:** 5
**SQ FT:** 7,500
**SALES (est):** 2.4MM **Privately Held**
**SIC:** 3273  1794  7353  Ready-mixed concrete; excavation work; cranes & aerial lift equipment, rental or leasing

**(G-20693)**
**JOE HATZER & SON INC**
Also Called: Hatzer Ready Mix
2515 1/2 N Bloomington St (61364)
PHONE..................815 672-2161
Fax: 815 673-1545
Dennis Hatzer, *President*
**EMP:** 5
**SALES (corp-wide):** 2.4MM **Privately Held**
**SIC:** 3273  Ready-mixed concrete
PA: Joe Hatzer & Son Inc
602 Lundy St
Streator IL 61364
815 673-5571

**(G-20694)**
**MID-AMERICA TRUCK CORPORATION**
Also Called: U S Truck Body-Midwest
1807 N Bloomington St (61364-1317)
PHONE..................815 672-3211
Fax: 815 672-1490
Paul Walker, *President*
James L Walker, *Vice Pres*
Leann Liptak, *Manager*
Chris Walker, *Admin Sec*
Thomas Walker, *Admin Sec*
**EMP:** 70
**SQ FT:** 48,000
**SALES (est):** 13.2MM
**SALES (corp-wide):** 80.6MM **Privately Held**
**WEB:** www.ustruckbody.com
**SIC:** 3713  Van bodies
PA: Streator Industrial Handling, Inc.
1705 N Shabbona St
Streator IL 61364
815 672-0551

**(G-20695)**
**MORTON BUILDINGS INC**
1519 N Il Route 23 (61364-9393)
PHONE..................630 904-1122
Fax: 630 904-1161
**EMP:** 13
**SALES (corp-wide):** 418.2MM **Privately Held**
**SIC:** 3448  1542  Mfg Prefabricated Metal Buildings Nonresidential Construction
PA: Morton Buildings, Inc.
252 W Adams St
Morton IL 61550
309 263-7474

**(G-20696)**
**MURRAY CABINETRY & TOPS INC**
Also Called: Luxury Bath Systems
407 N Bloomington St (61364-2201)
PHONE..................815 672-6992
Fax: 815 672-6821
Doug J Murray, *Owner*
Pauline Murray, *Principal*
**EMP:** 6
**SQ FT:** 20,000
**SALES (est):** 1MM **Privately Held**
**SIC:** 2541  2542  2434  Counters or counter display cases, wood; office & store showcases & display fixtures; wood kitchen cabinets

**(G-20697)**
**MUSHRO MACHINE & TOOL CO**
819 E Bridge St (61364-3034)
PHONE..................815 672-5848
Fax: 815 672-0682
Chris Walker, *President*
Paul Walker, *Vice Pres*
Mike Mushro, *Plant Mgr*
Dan Kusch, *Treasurer*
Shirley Hammer, *Office Mgr*
**EMP:** 10 **EST:** 1975
**SQ FT:** 5,300
**SALES:** 750K
**SALES (corp-wide):** 80.6MM **Privately Held**
**WEB:** www.mushro.com
**SIC:** 3599  7692  3544  Machine shop, jobbing & repair; welding repair; special dies, tools, jigs & fixtures
PA: Streator Industrial Handling, Inc.
1705 N Shabbona St
Streator IL 61364
815 672-0551

**(G-20698)**
**OI GLASS CONTAINERS OI G9**
901 N Shabbona St (61364-2058)
PHONE..................815 673-1548
Ken Sokol, *Plant Mgr*
Thomas Hearons, *Manager*
Cathy Gresham, *Maintence Staff*
▲ **EMP:** 2
**SALES (est):** 925.7K **Privately Held**
**SIC:** 3231  Products of purchased glass

**(G-20699)**
**OWENS-BROCKWAY GLASS CONT INC**
901 N Shabbona St (61364-2096)
PHONE..................815 673-3141
Fax: 815 673-5194
Tom Wagner, *Plant Engr*
Ken Sokol, *Systems Mgr*
**EMP:** 210
**SALES (corp-wide):** 6.7B **Publicly Held**
**SIC:** 3221  Packers' ware (containers), glass
HQ: Owens-Brockway Glass Container Inc.
1 Michael Owens Way
Perrysburg OH 43551
567 336-8449

**(G-20700)**
**PHOTO GRAPHIC DESIGN SERVICE**
124 N Bloomington St (61364-2208)
PHONE..................815 672-4417
Fax: 815 672-4417
James C Olmsted, *President*
Barbara Olmsted, *Vice Pres*
**EMP:** 4
**SQ FT:** 2,000
**SALES (est):** 240K **Privately Held**
**SIC:** 2752  2791  Commercial printing, offset; typesetting

**(G-20701)**
**SHREDDERHOTLINECOM COMPANY**
Also Called: Global Development
1215 N Bloomington St (61364-1581)
P.O. Box 399 (61364-0399)
PHONE..................815 674-5802
Dan Burda, *President*
Andres Salazar, *Partner*
Ian Weston, *Partner*
▲ **EMP:** 125
**SQ FT:** 40,000
**SALES:** 31MM **Privately Held**
**WEB:** www.shredderhotline.com
**SIC:** 3599  Machine & other job shop work

**(G-20702)**
**SIEMENS INDUSTRY INC**
810 W Grant St (61364-1912)
PHONE..................815 672-2653
Greg Garbs, *Manager*
**EMP:** 5
**SALES (corp-wide):** 89.6B **Privately Held**
**SIC:** 3589  Sewage & water treatment equipment
HQ: Siemens Industry, Inc.
1000 Deerfield Pkwy
Buffalo Grove IL 60089
847 215-1000

**(G-20703)**
**STREATOR ASPHALT INC**
1019 E Livingston Rd (61364-3928)
PHONE..................815 672-8683
Norman C Riordan, *President*
**EMP:** 8

**SALES (corp-wide):** 2.8MM  **Privately Held**
**SIC: 3531** 2951 Asphalt plant, including gravel-mix type; asphalt paving mixtures & blocks
**HQ:** Streator Asphalt, Inc
104 S Park Rd
Herscher IL 60941
815 426-2164

**(G-20704)**
**STREATOR INDUSTRIAL HDLG INC (PA)**
Also Called: Streator Dependable Mfg
1705 N Shabbona St (61364-1301)
**PHONE** ............................ 815 672-0551
**Fax:** 815 672-7631
Paul Walker, *President*
Chris G Walker, *Exec VP*
Mark Lamboley, *Vice Pres*
James Walker, *Vice Pres*
Jeremy Walker, *Vice Pres*
◆ **EMP:** 60 **EST:** 1945
**SQ FT:** 80,000
**SALES (est):** 80.6MM  **Privately Held**
**WEB:** www.streatordependable.com
**SIC: 3443** Industrial vessels, tanks & containers; bins, prefabricated metal plate

**(G-20705)**
**STREATOR MACHINE COMPANY**
Also Called: Streator Machine Mfg Co
504 E Larue St (61364-2040)
**PHONE** ............................ 815 672-2436
**Fax:** 815 672-2397
Rody J Hays, *President*
Donna Hays, *Corp Secy*
Patricia Hays, *Vice Pres*
Arthur Hays, *Director*
**EMP:** 5
**SQ FT:** 5,000
**SALES (est):** 590.2K  **Privately Held**
**SIC: 3599** Machine shop, jobbing & repair

**(G-20706)**
**SUN TIMES NEWS AGENCY**
56 Sunset Dr (61364-2623)
**PHONE** ............................ 815 672-1260
Michael Renner, *Principal*
**EMP:** 5
**SALES (est):** 149.1K  **Privately Held**
**SIC: 2711** 7383 Newspapers, publishing & printing; news syndicates

**(G-20707)**
**TELEWELD INC**
502 N Vermillion St (61364-2256)
**PHONE** ............................ 815 672-4561
**Fax:** 815 672-5763
Mike Suergan, *President*
Joseph Sobin, *Plant Mgr*
Duane Kruger, *Opers Staff*
John Plese, *Sales Mgr*
Chad Wissen, *Sales Staff*
**EMP:** 10
**SQ FT:** 11,000
**SALES (est):** 2.3MM  **Privately Held**
**WEB:** www.teleweld.net
**SIC: 3743** 3531 Railroad equipment, except locomotives; railway track equipment

**(G-20708)**
**TIMES-PRESS PUBLISHING CO**
115 Oak St (61364-2805)
**PHONE** ............................ 815 673-3771
**Fax:** 815 672-9332
Jean Alice Small, *Ch of Bd*
James Malley, *President*
**EMP:** 35
**SQ FT:** 10,000
**SALES (est):** 1.6MM
**SALES (corp-wide):** 168.9MM  **Privately Held**
**SIC: 2711** Newspapers: publishing only, not printed on site
**HQ:** Ottawa Publishing Co Inc
110 W Jefferson St
Ottawa IL 61350
815 433-2000

**(G-20709)**
**TRANSCO PRODUCTS INC**
1215 E 12th St (61364-3967)
**PHONE** ............................ 815 672-2197
**Fax:** 815 673-2432
Russell Artman, *Principal*

Tim Ruppert, *Plant Mgr*
Gary Sharisky, *Site Mgr*
Billy Hester, *Engineer*
Steve Lawless, *Manager*
**EMP:** 30
**SQ FT:** 5,000
**SALES (corp-wide):** 109.8MM  **Privately Held**
**WEB:** www.transcoinc.com
**SIC: 3053** 3648 3444 3354 Gaskets, packing & sealing devices; lighting equipment; sheet metalwork; aluminum extruded products; aluminum sheet, plate & foil
**HQ:** Transco Products Inc.
200 N La Salle St # 1550
Chicago IL 60601
312 427-2818

**(G-20710)**
**VACTOR MANUFACTURING INC**
1621 S Illinois St (61364-3945)
**PHONE** ............................ 815 672-3171
Samuel Miceli, *President*
Dan Schueller, *President*
Tammy Luckey, *General Mgr*
Kathy Kudrick, *COO*
Phil Rankin, *Vice Pres*
◆ **EMP:** 1500 **EST:** 1911
**SQ FT:** 109,488
**SALES (est):** 228.8MM
**SALES (corp-wide):** 707.9MM  **Publicly Held**
**WEB:** www.federalsignal.com
**SIC: 3537** Industrial trucks & tractors
**PA:** Federal Signal Corporation
1415 W 22nd St Ste 1100
Oak Brook IL 60523
630 954-2000

**(G-20711)**
**WILBERT SHULTZ VAULT CO INC**
Also Called: Schultz Crematories
115 S Shabbona St (61364-3060)
P.O. Box 376 (61364-0376)
**PHONE** ............................ 815 672-2049
George J Schultz, *President*
Charles Schultz, *Vice Pres*
**EMP:** 10
**SQ FT:** 2,500
**SALES (est):** 980K  **Privately Held**
**SIC: 3272** 7261 Burial vaults, concrete or precast terrazzo; crematory

## Stronghurst
### Henderson County

**(G-20712)**
**D C COOPER CORPORATION**
Junction 116 & 94 (61480)
**PHONE** ............................ 309 924-1941
**Fax:** 309 924-1945
Kim R Gullberg, *President*
Shirley Gullberg, *Personnel*
**EMP:** 9
**SQ FT:** 12,500
**SALES (est):** 1.8MM  **Privately Held**
**WEB:** www.dccoopertanks.com
**SIC: 3443** Industrial vessels, tanks & containers; metal parts

**(G-20713)**
**HENDERSON HANCOCK QUILL INC**
Also Called: Henderson County Quill
102 N Broadway St (61480-5023)
P.O. Box 149 (61480-0149)
**PHONE** ............................ 309 924-1871
**Fax:** 309 924-1212
Dessa Roddeffer, *President*
Shirley Linder, *Editor*
**EMP:** 5
**SALES (est):** 209.7K  **Privately Held**
**WEB:** www.quillnewspaper.com
**SIC: 2711** Newspapers

## Sublette
### Lee County

**(G-20714)**
**COUNTRY VILLAGE MEATS**
401 N Pennsylvania St (61367-9400)
**PHONE** ............................ 815 849-5532
Edward L Morrissey, *President*
**EMP:** 5
**SALES (est):** 427.2K  **Privately Held**
**SIC: 5421** 2013 2011 Meat markets, including freezer provisioners; sausages & other prepared meats; meat packing plants

**(G-20715)**
**ERBES ELECTRIC**
409 W Main St (61367-9443)
P.O. Box 92 (61367-0092)
**PHONE** ............................ 815 849-5508
Douglas Erbes, *Owner*
**EMP:** 2
**SALES (est):** 250K  **Privately Held**
**SIC: 7694** 1731 Electric motor repair; electrical work

## Sugar Grove
### Kane County

**(G-20716)**
**ACE WOOD PRODUCTS LLC**
3s854 Finley Rd (60554-9662)
**PHONE** ............................ 630 557-2115
Linda Brinkman,
David Brinkman,
**EMP:** 4
**SQ FT:** 82,000
**SALES (est):** 210K  **Privately Held**
**SIC: 3999** Pet supplies

**(G-20717)**
**AXIS DESIGN ARCHITECTUAL MLLWK**
239 State Route 47 (60554-9423)
P.O. Box 154 (60554-0154)
**PHONE** ............................ 630 466-4549
Bear Wegener, *President*
Dina Amato, *Project Mgr*
Edward Wegener, *Treasurer*
Jeanine Butler, *Manager*
Casey Shatters, *Manager*
**EMP:** 10
**SQ FT:** 3,300
**SALES (est):** 400K  **Privately Held**
**WEB:** www.axisdesigns.net
**SIC: 2499** 1751 Food handling & processing products, wood; cabinet & finish carpentry

**(G-20718)**
**BETA PAK INC**
1600 Beta Dr (60554-7901)
**PHONE** ............................ 708 466-7844
**Fax:** 312 466-1284
John Bensen, *President*
**EMP:** 10
**SALES (est):** 453.7K  **Privately Held**
**SIC: 2782** Looseleaf binders & devices

**(G-20719)**
**CHICAGO JET GROUP LLC (PA)**
43 W 522 Rr 30 (60554)
**PHONE** ............................ 630 466-3600
Michael J Mitera, *Mng Member*
Bicki Rencosik, *Manager*
Kim Copeland, *Administration*
**EMP:** 20
**SALES (est):** 5.4MM  **Privately Held**
**WEB:** www.chicagojetgroup.com
**SIC: 3519** Jet propulsion engines

**(G-20720)**
**CMC ELECTRONICS AURORA LLC**
84 N Dugan Rd (60554-9417)
**PHONE** ............................ 630 556-9619
Beth Lecuyer, *Human Res Dir*
Don Hohn, *Info Tech Mgr*
Joseph Biel, *Software Engr*
Greg Yeldon,

**EMP:** 100
**SQ FT:** 6,000
**SALES (est):** 17.3MM
**SALES (corp-wide):** 1.9B  **Publicly Held**
**WEB:** www.cmcelectronics.us
**SIC: 3728** Aircraft parts & equipment
**PA:** Esterline Technologies Corp
500 108th Ave Ne Ste 1500
Bellevue WA 98004
425 453-9400

**(G-20721)**
**CYLINDER SERVICES INC**
629 N Heartland Dr (60554-9594)
**PHONE** ............................ 630 466-9820
Art Gehrs, *President*
Michael Gehrs, *Vice Pres*
Holly Gehrs, *Admin Sec*
**EMP:** 5
**SQ FT:** 5,000
**SALES (est):** 636.9K  **Privately Held**
**WEB:** www.cylinderservices.net
**SIC: 7699** 7692 Hydraulic equipment repair; welding repair

**(G-20722)**
**DEEP COAT LLC**
550 N Heartland Dr (60554-9586)
P.O. Box 468 (60554-0468)
**PHONE** ............................ 630 466-1505
**Fax:** 630 466-1602
Rick Fellabaum, *Mfg Dir*
Kim Thorson, *Engineer*
Kim M Thorson, *Mng Member*
**EMP:** 25 **EST:** 2008
**SQ FT:** 30,000
**SALES (est):** 2.4MM  **Privately Held**
**SIC: 3471** Plating of metals or formed products

**(G-20723)**
**FALEX CORPORATION**
Also Called: F L C
1020 Airpark Dr (60554-9452)
**PHONE** ............................ 630 556-3679
**Fax:** 630 556-3679
Leslie R Heerdt, *Ch of Bd*
Todd Turnquist, *Engineer*
Gary Beraga, *Accounts Mgr*
Andrew M Faville, *Admin Sec*
**EMP:** 47 **EST:** 1929
**SQ FT:** 15,000
**SALES (est):** 8.3MM  **Privately Held**
**WEB:** www.falex.com
**SIC: 8742** 3829 3825 Management consulting services; physical property testing equipment; instruments to measure electricity

**(G-20724)**
**FINISHES UNLIMITED INC**
Also Called: C C I
482 Wheeler Rd (60554-9749)
P.O. Box 69 (60554-0069)
**PHONE** ............................ 630 466-4881
**Fax:** 630 466-1064
Kenneth W Burton, *President*
Peter Smelyansky, *Vice Pres*
John R Schwartz, *VP Mfg*
Francis Stama, *Engineer*
Jill Olson, *Treasurer*
**EMP:** 17
**SQ FT:** 20,000
**SALES (est):** 6.5MM  **Privately Held**
**WEB:** www.finishesunlimited.com
**SIC: 2851** Paints & paint additives; lacquers, varnishes, enamels & other coatings

**(G-20725)**
**FRANKLIN AUTOMATION INC**
1981 Bucktail Ln (60554-9609)
**PHONE** ............................ 630 466-1900
**Fax:** 630 466-1902
Frank Kigyos Jr, *President*
Kevin Kigyos, *Vice Pres*
Susan J Kigyos, *Vice Pres*
Jason Plohr, *Plant Mgr*
John Amery, *Sales Staff*
▲ **EMP:** 15
**SQ FT:** 10,000
**SALES (est):** 9MM  **Privately Held**
**WEB:** www.franklinautomation.com
**SIC: 5084** 3599 Conveyor systems; custom machinery

# Sugar Grove - Kane County (G-20726)

**(G-20726)**
**GLANCER MAGAZINE**
248 Belle Vue Ln (60554-9476)
PHONE..................................630 428-4387
Lindy Kleivo, *Principal*
EMP: 5
SALES (est): 480.1K **Privately Held**
SIC: 2721 Periodicals

**(G-20727)**
**HFR PRECISION MACHINING INC**
1015 Airpark Dr (60554-9585)
PHONE..................................630 556-4325
Fax: 630 556-4326
Leslie R Heerdt, *Ch of Bd*
Richard Tarbaz, *President*
Andrew R Faville, *COO*
▲ EMP: 50
SQ FT: 50,000
SALES (est): 10.1MM **Privately Held**
WEB: www.hfrprecision.com
SIC: 3599 7692 Machine shop, jobbing & repair; grinding castings for the trade; welding repair

**(G-20728)**
**HY-TEK MANUFACTURING CO INC**
Also Called: HMC
1998 Bucktail Ln (60554-9609)
PHONE..................................630 466-7664
Fax: 630 466-7678
John Bastian, *President*
Chris Bastian, *President*
Lonnie Parrish, *Project Mgr*
John Jude, *Engineer*
Bob Danner, *Manager*
▲ EMP: 46
SQ FT: 45,000
SALES (est): 8.3MM **Privately Held**
WEB: www.hytekmfg.com
SIC: 3599 Machine shop, jobbing & repair

**(G-20729)**
**MET-L-FLO INC**
720 N Heartland Dr Ste S (60554-9864)
PHONE..................................630 409-9860
Fax: 630 409-9869
Carlton Dekker, *President*
Brian McNamara, *Prdtn Mgr*
Brenda Marcinkus, *Office Mgr*
Tony Pronenko, *Manager*
EMP: 15
SQ FT: 11,000
SALES (est): 2.7MM **Privately Held**
WEB: www.met-l-flo.com
SIC: 8742 8731 8748 3089 Industry specialist consultants; commercial physical research; testing services; plastic processing; design services

**(G-20730)**
**PLASTAK INC**
44w40 Scott Rd (60554)
PHONE..................................630 466-4100
Susan Slamans, *President*
Bruce Slamans, *General Mgr*
EMP: 8
SALES (est): 667.3K **Privately Held**
SIC: 3599 Machine & other job shop work

**(G-20731)**
**PRODUCERS CHEMICAL COMPANY**
1960 Bucktail Ln (60554-9609)
PHONE..................................630 466-4584
Fax: 630 879-2734
Peter Whinfrey, *President*
Roger T Harris, *President*
Brian Shannon, *Vice Pres*
David Sweigert, *Vice Pres*
Jeff Szklarek, *CFO*
EMP: 23
SQ FT: 45,000
SALES (est): 19.3MM **Privately Held**
WEB: www.producerschemical.com
SIC: 5169 2899 Industrial chemicals; chemical preparations

**(G-20732)**
**QUALIFIED INNOVATION INC**
1016 Airpark Dr Ste B (60554-9847)
PHONE..................................630 556-4136
Fax: 630 556-4136

Gary L Fuller, *President*
Sue Fuller, *Manager*
EMP: 10
SQ FT: 37,000
SALES (est): 2.5MM **Privately Held**
WEB: www.qualifiedinnovation.com
SIC: 2672 5113 Coated & laminated paper; industrial & personal service paper

**(G-20733)**
**QUANTUM SIGN CORPORATION**
693 N Heartland Dr (60554-9594)
PHONE..................................630 466-0372
Fax: 630 466-0564
David Stover, *President*
Roger Perotti, *Vice Pres*
Jen Glock, *Manager*
▲ EMP: 19
SQ FT: 12,000
SALES (est): 10.2MM **Privately Held**
WEB: www.quantumsigncorp.com
SIC: 5046 3993 Signs, electrical; signs & advertising specialties

**(G-20734)**
**SCOT INDUSTRIES INC**
1961 W Us Highway 30 (60554-9615)
P.O. Box 309 (60554-0309)
PHONE..................................630 466-7591
Fax: 630 466-7226
Kevin Smaps, *Principal*
Steve Zimmerman, *Plant Mgr*
Jake Hanson, *Prdtn Mgr*
Michael Bunkleman, *Opers Spvr*
Paul Taylor, *Opers Staff*
EMP: 58
SALES (corp-wide): 193.3MM **Privately Held**
WEB: www.scotindustries.com
SIC: 3589 5051 3498 3471 Machine shop, jobbing & repair; metals service centers & offices; fabricated pipe & fittings; plating & polishing
PA: Scot Industries, Inc.
    3756 Fm 250 N
    Lone Star TX 75668
    903 639-2551

**(G-20735)**
**SELECTIVE LABEL & TABS INC**
1962 Us Rte 30 (60554)
PHONE..................................630 466-0091
Fax: 630 466-0095
Tom Kennedy, *President*
Ralph Chneider, *President*
Helen Hornung, *Principal*
Dale Klungland, *Vice Pres*
Diane Dissell, *Manager*
EMP: 10
SQ FT: 10,000
SALES (est): 1.4MM **Privately Held**
WEB: www.selectivelabel.com
SIC: 2759 Labels & seals: printing

**(G-20736)**
**SELECTIVE LABEL & TABS INC**
1962 W Us Highway 30 (60554-9621)
PHONE..................................630 466-0091
Tom Kennedy, *President*
EMP: 7
SQ FT: 6,000
SALES (est): 630K **Privately Held**
SIC: 2759 Labels & seals: printing

**(G-20737)**
**SUPERIOR METAL PRODUCTS INC**
1993 Bucktail Ln (60554-9609)
PHONE..................................630 466-1150
Fax: 630 466-1158
Brian Warren, *President*
Beth Warren, *Corp Secy*
Darrell Warren, *Vice Pres*
EMP: 14
SQ FT: 13,000
SALES (est): 2.2MM **Privately Held**
SIC: 3469 Stamping metal for the trade

**(G-20738)**
**TUSKIN EQUIPMENT CORPORATION**
483 N Heartland Dr Ste F (60554-8206)
PHONE..................................630 466-5590
Kristine O'Dwyer, *President*
Jeffrey O'Dwyer, *Admin Sec*
EMP: 5

SQ FT: 7,000
SALES: 750K **Privately Held**
WEB: www.tuskin.com
SIC: 3561 3559 Industrial pumps & parts; plastics working machinery

## Sullivan
*Moultrie County*

**(G-20739)**
**B & B FABRICATIONS LLC**
901 W Jefferson St (61951-1753)
PHONE..................................217 620-3210
Michael Bernius, *President*
Joshua Bernius, *Vice Pres*
EMP: 2
SQ FT: 12,000
SALES (est): 972K **Privately Held**
SIC: 3317 3441 Steel pipe & tubes; fabricated structural metal

**(G-20740)**
**BEST NEWSPAPERS IN ILLINOIS**
Also Called: News Progress
100 W Monroe St (61951-1427)
P.O. Box 290 (61951-0290)
PHONE..................................217 728-7381
Fax: 217 728-2020
Robert Best, *President*
Bob Best, *General Mgr*
Dan Hagen, *Editor*
Dallas Weston, *Editor*
Ruth Suddarth, *Business Mgr*
EMP: 8 EST: 1961
SQ FT: 4,800
SALES (est): 350K **Privately Held**
SIC: 2711 Newspapers, publishing & printing; job printing & newspaper publishing combined

**(G-20741)**
**CARROLLS WELDING & FABRICATION**
819 N Market St (61951-8802)
PHONE..................................217 728-8720
John Carroll, *Owner*
Al Euygabroad, *Office Mgr*
EMP: 4
SQ FT: 5,500
SALES (est): 254.2K **Privately Held**
SIC: 7692 Welding repair

**(G-20742)**
**CENTRAL WOOD PRODUCTS INC**
1819 Cr 1300e (61951)
PHONE..................................217 728-4412
Fax: 217 543-3505
Kenny Bontraaer, *President*
EMP: 20
SQ FT: 18,000
SALES (est): 3.6MM **Privately Held**
WEB: www.centralwoodproducts.com
SIC: 2448 2449 2441 Pallets, wood; wood containers; nailed wood boxes & shook

**(G-20743)**
**CHIPS MARINE**
1068 Cr 1025n (61951-6515)
PHONE..................................217 728-2610
Martin Christensen, *Principal*
EMP: 2
SALES (est): 241.9K **Privately Held**
SIC: 3731 Lighters, marine: building & repairing

**(G-20744)**
**CIRCLE T MFG**
1801a Cr 1300e (61951-6535)
PHONE..................................217 728-4834
Clarence Otto, *Owner*
EMP: 8
SALES (est): 952.6K **Privately Held**
SIC: 3999 Manufacturing industries

**(G-20745)**
**EVERLAST PORTABLE BUILDINGS**
1565 Cr 1800n (61951-6576)
PHONE..................................217 543-4080
Eldon Miller, *Owner*
Vernon Miller, *Accounting Mgr*

EMP: 5
SQ FT: 3,200
SALES (est): 1MM **Privately Held**
SIC: 2452 Prefabricated wood buildings

**(G-20746)**
**FAZE CHANGE PRODUX**
Also Called: Econodome Kits
1331 Cr 1470e (61951-6862)
PHONE..................................217 728-2184
Wil Fidroeff, *Owner*
EMP: 30
SQ FT: 3,000
SALES (est): 1.9MM **Privately Held**
WEB: www.decahome.com
SIC: 2452 Prefabricated wood buildings

**(G-20747)**
**HEALTHCOM INC**
1600 W Jackson St (61951-1066)
PHONE..................................217 728-8331
Fax: 217 728-8333
Ralph Kirk, *President*
Aaron Kirk, *President*
Derek Carter, *Vice Pres*
Sean Harshman, *QC Mgr*
Brian Schultz, *VP Sales*
EMP: 26
SQ FT: 15,000
SALES (est): 5MM **Privately Held**
WEB: www.carelink1.com
SIC: 3663 Radio & TV communications equipment

**(G-20748)**
**HYDRO-GEAR INC (HQ)**
1411 S Hamilton St (61951-2264)
PHONE..................................217 728-2581
Fax: 217 728-7665
Ray Hauser, *President*
Agri Fab, *Partner*
Ronald D Harshman, *Partner*
Gary Harvey, *Partner*
Jack Obiala, *Partner*
▲ EMP: 244
SQ FT: 80,000
SALES (est): 77MM
SALES (corp-wide): 5.5B **Privately Held**
SIC: 3594 Hydrostatic drives (transmissions)
PA: Danfoss A/S
    Nordborgvej 81
    Nordborg 6430
    748 822-22

**(G-20749)**
**ILLINOIS PRINTING SERVICES INC**
800 S Patterson Rd (61951-8403)
P.O. Box 106 (61951-0106)
PHONE..................................217 728-2786
Thomas M Bunfill, *President*
Chris Eckel, *Production*
EMP: 6
SALES (est): 697.3K **Privately Held**
WEB: www.illinoisprintingservices.com
SIC: 2759 Commercial printing

**(G-20750)**
**KITE WOODWORKING CO**
1124 W Harrison St (61951-1060)
P.O. Box 556 (61951-0556)
PHONE..................................217 728-4346
Fax: 217 728-2012
Donald E Jesse, *President*
Eric Barnard, *Production*
EMP: 20 EST: 1951
SQ FT: 28,120
SALES (est): 1.1MM **Privately Held**
WEB: www.monarchcabinetry.com
SIC: 2431 Doors & door parts & trim, wood

**(G-20751)**
**MID-STATE TANK CO INC**
1357 Johnson Creek Rd (61951)
P.O. Box 317 (61951-0317)
PHONE..................................217 728-8383
Fax: 217 728-8384
Gery V Conlin, *President*
Elmer Gingrich, *Vice Pres*
Gene Good, *Vice Pres*
Scott Marlow, *Materials Mgr*
Jason Fleming, *QC Mgr*
EMP: 88
SQ FT: 33,000

# GEOGRAPHIC SECTION

Swansea - St. Clair County (G-20777)

SALES (est): 36.6MM **Privately Held**
WEB: www.midstatetank.com
SIC: **3443** Tanks, standard or custom fabricated: metal plate

**(G-20752)**
**MIDSTATE INDUSTRIES**
809 S Hamilton St (61951-2209)
PHONE..................217 268-3900
EMP: 3 EST: 2013
SALES (est): 260.7K **Privately Held**
SIC: **3999** Manufacturing industries

**(G-20753)**
**MONARCH MFG CORP AMER**
Hc 32 Box S (61951)
P.O. Box 653 (61951-0653)
PHONE..................217 728-2552
Fax: 217 728-8712
Donald Jesse, *President*
Pam Jesse, *Vice Pres*
Kim Voegel, *Purchasing*
Amy Graven, *Controller*
Cathrine Craig, *Finance*
EMP: 32
SQ FT: 16,000
SALES (est): 5.1MM **Privately Held**
SIC: **2434** Wood kitchen cabinets

**(G-20754)**
**MOULTRI CNTY HSTRCL/GNLGCL SCT**
Also Called: Historcl Genealogical Soc Mou
117 E Harrison St (61951-2001)
P.O. Box 588 (61951-0588)
PHONE..................217 728-4085
Jenny Sutton, *President*
Mary L Storm, *Director*
EMP: 10
SALES (est): 243.3K **Privately Held**
SIC: **7299** 7532 1711 3599 Genealogical investigation service; exterior repair services; boiler & furnace contractors; machine shop, jobbing & repair

**(G-20755)**
**MOULTRIE COUNTY REDI-MIX CO**
622 S Worth St (61951-2199)
PHONE..................217 728-2334
Fax: 217 728-2335
Roger Daily, *Owner*
Barb Daily, *Corp Secy*
David Daily, *Vice Pres*
EMP: 7
SALES (est): 1.4MM **Privately Held**
WEB: www.moultrieonline.com
SIC: **3273** Ready-mixed concrete

**(G-20756)**
**O K JOBBERS INC**
Also Called: O.k Jobbers
215 S Hamilton St (61951-1951)
PHONE..................217 728-7378
Fax: 217 728-4016
Chad Dust, *CEO*
Ron Jenkins, *Manager*
EMP: 5 EST: 1946
SQ FT: 12,000
SALES (est): 723.6K **Privately Held**
SIC: **5013** 5531 3599 Automotive supplies & parts; automotive parts; automotive accessories; machine shop, jobbing & repair

**(G-20757)**
**PALLETT WILSON**
1858 Cr 1300e (61951-6533)
PHONE..................217 543-3555
Wilson Pallett, *Owner*
▲ EMP: 7
SQ FT: 18,000
SALES: 1.5MM **Privately Held**
SIC: **2449** 2448 Rectangular boxes & crates, wood; pallets, wood

**(G-20758)**
**QUALITY NETWORK SOLUTIONS INC**
Also Called: Q N S
111 E Jefferson St (61951-2025)
PHONE..................217 728-3155
Mel Workman, *President*
Lisa Shuman, *Bookkeeper*
Debbie Suha, *Office Mgr*

Tim Caraway, *Manager*
Toby Scott, *Network Tech*
EMP: 40 EST: 1998
SQ FT: 7,200
SALES (est): 8MM **Privately Held**
WEB: www.qnsk12.com
SIC: **7372** Prepackaged software

## Summit Argo
### Cook County

**(G-20759)**
**ACH FOOD COMPANIES INC**
Also Called: Best Foods Baking Group
6400 S Archer Rd (60501-1935)
P.O. Box 448 (60501-0448)
PHONE..................708 458-8690
Fax: 708 458-8787
Kevin Katajamaki, *Plant Mgr*
John Darmstandt, *Prdtn Mgr*
Gary Senter, *Mktg Dir*
Ronald Kuehn, *Branch Mgr*
Mary Kelly, *Manager*
EMP: 200
SALES (corp-wide): 17.3B **Privately Held**
WEB: www.achfood.com
SIC: **5149** 2079 Groceries & related products; edible fats & oils
HQ: Ach Food Companies, Inc.
7171 Goodlett Farms Pkwy
Cordova TN 38016
901 381-3000

**(G-20760)**
**ACTION TURBINE REPAIR SVC INC**
5120 W Lawndale Ave (60501-1075)
PHONE..................708 924-9601
Jozef Krezel, *President*
Charles Siebert, *Sales Staff*
EMP: 10 EST: 2008
SALES (est): 2MM **Privately Held**
SIC: **3511** 7699 Turbines & turbine generator sets; industrial machinery & equipment repair

**(G-20761)**
**COMPU-TAP INC**
Also Called: Scottish Modern Enterprises
6257 S Archer Rd Ste A (60501-1743)
PHONE..................708 594-5773
Jack A Thompson, *President*
Helen Thompson, *Vice Pres*
EMP: 3 EST: 1974
SQ FT: 7,000
SALES (est): 255.5K **Privately Held**
WEB: www.thescottishshop.com
SIC: **2311** 5136 5947 2326 Men's & boys' uniforms; jackets, tailored suit-type: men's & boys'; uniforms, men's & boys'; novelties; men's & boys' work clothing

**(G-20762)**
**DYERS MACHINE SERVICE INC**
Also Called: Dyer's Superchargers
7665 W 63rd St (60501-1811)
PHONE..................708 496-8100
Fax: 708 496-8113
Gary Dyer, *President*
Bill Dyer, *Vice Pres*
EMP: 6
SQ FT: 6,000
SALES: 260K **Privately Held**
SIC: **3599** 7692 Machine shop, jobbing & repair; welding repair

**(G-20763)**
**HERITAGE MEDIA SVCS CO OF ILL**
Also Called: Des Plaines Valley News
7676 W 63rd St (60501-1812)
P.O. Box 348 (60501-0348)
PHONE..................708 594-9340
Fax: 708 594-9494
Bob Bong, *Principal*
Jeff Boryardt, *Manager*
EMP: 6
SQ FT: 3,000
SALES (est): 205K **Privately Held**
WEB: www.desplainesvalleynews.com
SIC: **2711** 2791 Newspapers: publishing only, not printed on site; typesetting

**(G-20764)**
**INGREDION INCORPORATED**
6400 S Archer Rd (60501-1935)
PHONE..................708 728-3535
Ilene S Gordon, *Branch Mgr*
EMP: 152
SALES (corp-wide): 5.7B **Publicly Held**
SIC: **2046** Wet corn milling
PA: Ingredion Incorporated
5 Westbrook Corporate Ctr # 500
Westchester IL 60154
708 551-2600

**(G-20765)**
**SAM SOLUTIONS INC**
5120 S Lawndale Ave (60501)
PHONE..................708 594-0480
Renata Malecki, *President*
Joseph Malecki, *Admin Sec*
EMP: 5
SALES (est): 961.9K **Privately Held**
WEB: www.samsolutions.com
SIC: **3537** Industrial trucks & tractors

**(G-20766)**
**SUMMIT SHEET METAL SPECIALISTS**
7325 W 59th St (60501-1419)
PHONE..................708 458-8622
Katheleen M Pavloski, *President*
EMP: 17
SQ FT: 3,600
SALES: 2MM **Privately Held**
SIC: **3444** Sheet metal specialties, not stamped

**(G-20767)**
**SUMMIT WINDOW CO INC**
7719 W 60th Pl Ste 6 (60501-1591)
PHONE..................708 594-3200
Fax: 708 594-3242
Alex Nitchoff, *President*
EMP: 6
SALES (est): 720K **Privately Held**
SIC: **3442** Window & door frames

**(G-20768)**
**VONDRAK PUBLISHING CO INC**
Also Called: Southwest Senior
7676 W 63rd St (60501-1812)
PHONE..................773 476-4800
Fax: 773 476-7811
James Von Drak, *President*
Rob Gusanders, *Vice Pres*
Naheda Jablonski, *Purchasing*
EMP: 35
SQ FT: 9,500
SALES (est): 2.2MM **Privately Held**
WEB: www.swnewsherald.com
SIC: **2711** 7313 2741 Newspapers: publishing only, not printed on site; radio, television, publisher representatives; miscellaneous publishing

**(G-20769)**
**WILLIMS-HYWARD INTL CTINGS INC (PA)**
Also Called: Williams-Hayward Protective Co
7425 W 59th St (60501-1417)
PHONE..................708 563-5182
Fax: 708 563-6266
Wayne E Kurcz, *CEO*
Joseph F Kurcz, *President*
Jacqueline Kurcz, *Vice Pres*
Ashley Kurcz, *Research*
Edward J Kurcz, *CFO*
◆ EMP: 28 EST: 1920
SQ FT: 1,200
SALES (est): 10.8MM **Privately Held**
SIC: **2851** Paints & allied products

## Sumner
### Lawrence County

**(G-20770)**
**FRANK E GALLOWAY**
Also Called: Galloway Logging
4808 Moffett Ln (62466-4716)
PHONE..................618 948-2578
Frank Galloway, *Principal*
EMP: 3
SALES (est): 274.9K **Privately Held**
SIC: **2411** Logging

**(G-20771)**
**J B OIL FIELD CNSTR & SUP**
218 E Sycamore St (62466-1076)
PHONE..................618 936-2350
Jerry Brian, *President*
Pamela K Brian, *Corp Secy*
EMP: 4
SALES (est): 270K **Privately Held**
SIC: **1389** Lease tanks, oil field: erecting, cleaning & repairing; oil & gas wells: building, repairing & dismantling

**(G-20772)**
**SUMNER PRESS**
216 S Christy Ave (62466-1142)
P.O. Box 126 (62466-0126)
PHONE..................618 936-2212
Fax: 618 936-2858
J C Cunningham, *President*
Jo Ann Dowty, *Editor*
Linda Mason, *Sales Staff*
Roscoe D Cunningham, *Admin Sec*
EMP: 4 EST: 1947
SALES (est): 217K **Privately Held**
WEB: www.sumnerpress.com
SIC: **2711** Newspapers

**(G-20773)**
**YODERS PORTABLE BUILDINGS LLC (PA)**
5425 Larkspur Rd (62466-4756)
PHONE..................618 936-2419
Wilhelm Marten, *Mng Member*
Joseph Marten,
EMP: 2
SQ FT: 280
SALES (est): 1.2MM **Privately Held**
SIC: **2452** Farm buildings, prefabricated or portable: wood

## Swansea
### St. Clair County

**(G-20774)**
**ARROW ASPHALT PAVING (PA)**
910 N 2nd St (62226-4314)
PHONE..................618 277-3009
Jim Wells, *Owner*
EMP: 3
SALES (est): 280.3K **Privately Held**
SIC: **2951** Asphalt paving mixtures & blocks

**(G-20775)**
**CALSER CORP**
302 N Belt E (62226-2419)
PHONE..................618 277-0329
Fax: 618 277-0196
Thomas R Gagen, *President*
EMP: 6
SALES (est): 1.1MM **Privately Held**
SIC: **3559** Concrete products machinery; zipper making machinery

**(G-20776)**
**CHARLES E MAHONEY COMPANY**
Also Called: Mahoney Asphalt
209 Service St (62226-3944)
PHONE..................618 235-3355
Fax: 618 235-3356
Charles K Mahoney, *President*
Michael P Mahoney, *Treasurer*
EMP: 20
SQ FT: 5,000
SALES (est): 4.5MM **Privately Held**
SIC: **2951** 1611 1771 Asphalt paving mixtures & blocks; highway & street paving contractor; concrete work

**(G-20777)**
**CROWDSOURCE SOLUTIONS INC (PA)**
33 Bronze Pointe Blvd (62226-8305)
PHONE..................855 276-9376
Stephanie Leffler, *CEO*
Ryan Noble, *President*
Sean Cook, *Sales Dir*
Audra Arendt, *Accounts Mgr*
Amanda Wobbe, *Accounts Mgr*
EMP: 14

Swansea - St. Clair County (G-20778)

**(G-20778)**
**METRO EAST MANUFACTURING**
1120 N Illinois St (62226-4378)
P.O. Box 348, Belleville (62222-0348)
PHONE ............................. 618 233-0182
Jeffrey R Lutz, *President*
**EMP:** 12
**SALES (corp-wide):** 1.1MM **Privately Held**
**WEB:** www.century-brass.com
**SIC:** 3599 Grinding castings for the trade
**PA:** Metro East Manufacturing
1150 N Illinois St
Swansea IL
618 233-0182

**(G-20779)**
**QUAD COUNTY READY MIX SWANSEA**
300 Old Fullerton Rd (62226-2906)
PHONE ............................. 618 257-9530
Kant Hustedde, *Manager*
**EMP:** 7
**SALES (est):** 480.2K **Privately Held**
**SIC:** 3273 Ready-mixed concrete

**(G-20780)**
**QUANTUM VISION CENTERS**
3990 N Illinois St (62226-1919)
PHONE ............................. 618 656-7774
**EMP:** 3
**SALES (est):** 215.3K **Privately Held**
**SIC:** 3572 Computer storage devices

**(G-20781)**
**RAUCKMAN HIGH VOLTAGE SALES**
37 Ednick Dr (62226-1914)
PHONE ............................. 618 239-0399
James Rauckman, *Owner*
Shirley Rauckman, *Manager*
**EMP:** 5
**SALES (est):** 457.8K **Privately Held**
**WEB:** www.rauckman.com
**SIC:** 3613 Distribution boards, electric

**(G-20782)**
**SAMTEK INTERNATIONAL INC**
10 Emerald Ter Ste C (62226-2310)
PHONE ............................. 314 954-4005
Ameem Eajwa, *Manager*
**EMP:** 1 **EST:** 2009
**SQ FT:** 12,000
**SALES:** 500K **Privately Held**
**SIC:** 1389 Oil & gas wells: building, repairing & dismantling

**(G-20783)**
**STEIBEL LICENSE SERVICE**
2704 N Illinois St Ste D (62226-2313)
PHONE ............................. 618 233-7555
Susan Steibel, *Owner*
**EMP:** 4
**SALES (est):** 296.9K **Privately Held**
**SIC:** 3469 Automobile license tags, stamped metal

## Sycamore
### Dekalb County

**(G-20784)**
**3-D RESOURCE**
Also Called: 3d Resource
1005 Brickville Rd (60178-1267)
P.O. Box 407 (60178-0407)
PHONE ............................. 815 899-8600
Fax: 815 895-4858
Marvin Wildenradt, *Partner*
Edward Richter, *Partner*
**EMP:** 2
**SQ FT:** 10,000
**SALES (est):** 222.7K **Privately Held**
**SIC:** 3993 Signs & advertising specialties

**(G-20785)**
**ADIENT US LLC**
Also Called: Automotive Systems Group
1701 Bethany Rd (60178-3104)
PHONE ............................. 815 895-2095
Fax: 815 895-2459

SALES (est): 4.2MM **Privately Held**
**SIC:** 7372 Prepackaged software
Victor Reister, *QC Dir*
Andre Ware, *Manager*
Dan Hamilton, *Manager*
Scott Ringonan, *Manager*
Randy Huffhines, *Technical Staff*
**EMP:** 175
**SQ FT:** 75,000 **Privately Held**
**SIC:** 2531 Seats, automobile
**HQ:** Adient Us Llc
49200 Halyard Dr
Plymouth MI 48170
734 254-5000

**(G-20786)**
**AMPLE SUPPLY COMPANY**
Also Called: ASC Fasteners
1401 S Prairie Dr (60178-3225)
PHONE ............................. 815 895-3500
Michael J Larocco, *President*
Marilyn Bruno, *Credit Mgr*
Mary E Larocco, *Admin Sec*
▲ **EMP:** 20
**SALES (est):** 12MM **Privately Held**
**WEB:** www.amplesupply.com
**SIC:** 5085 3965 Staplers & tackers; fasteners

**(G-20787)**
**AQUAVIVA WINERY (PA)**
219 W State St (60178-1418)
PHONE ............................. 815 899-4444
**EMP:** 5
**SALES (est):** 510.9K **Privately Held**
**SIC:** 2084 Wines, brandy & brandy spirits

**(G-20788)**
**AUTO METER PRODUCTS INC**
413 W Elm St (60178-1796)
PHONE ............................. 815 991-2292
Fax: 815 895-3859
Jeff King, *President*
John Thorn, *General Mgr*
Dean Panettieri, *Vice Pres*
Rocko McCombs, *Project Mgr*
Tim Chapman, *Safety Mgr*
▲ **EMP:** 195 **EST:** 1957
**SQ FT:** 5,000
**SALES (est):** 34MM **Privately Held**
**WEB:** www.autometer.com
**SIC:** 3824 3825 3829 3823 Tachometer, centrifugal; speedometers; gauges for computing pressure temperature corrections; battery testers, electrical; measuring & controlling devices; industrial instrmnts msrmnt display/control process variable; motor vehicle parts & accessories; machine tool accessories
**PA:** Promus Equity Partners, Llc
30 S Wacker Dr Ste 1600
Chicago IL 60606
312 784-3990

**(G-20789)**
**BARNABY INC**
Also Called: Barnaby Complete Printing Svcs
1620 Dekalb Ave (60178-2706)
PHONE ............................. 815 895-6555
Fax: 815 895-3617
Paul Barnaby Sr, *Ch of Bd*
Paul Barnaby Jr, *President*
Betty Barnaby, *Corp Secy*
Steve Barnaby, *Vice Pres*
**EMP:** 10 **EST:** 1915
**SQ FT:** 22,500
**SALES (est):** 1.8MM **Privately Held**
**WEB:** www.barnaby.com
**SIC:** 2752 2791 2789 2759 Commercial printing, offset; typesetting; bookbinding & related work; commercial printing

**(G-20790)**
**D & D SUKACH INC**
Also Called: D & D Jewelers
303 W State St (60178-1420)
PHONE ............................. 815 895-3377
Clyde Cooper, *President*
**EMP:** 4
**SALES (est):** 549.2K **Privately Held**
**SIC:** 3961 7631 Costume jewelry; watch, clock & jewelry repair

**(G-20791)**
**DAWN EQUIPMENT COMPANY INC**
370 N Cross St (60178-1230)
P.O. Box 497 (60178-0497)
PHONE ............................. 815 899-8000
Fax: 815 899-3663
James H Bassett, *President*
Joseph D Bassett, *President*
Margarett Bassett, *Corp Secy*
James Kolterman, *Prdtn Mgr*
Josh Richards, *Manager*
**EMP:** 17
**SQ FT:** 30,000
**SALES (est):** 6.3MM **Privately Held**
**WEB:** www.dawnequipment.com
**SIC:** 3523 Farm machinery & equipment

**(G-20792)**
**DER HOLTZMACHER LTD**
Also Called: Der-Holtzmacher
1649 Afton Rd (60178-3253)
PHONE ............................. 815 895-4887
Fax: 815 899-3077
Michael Holtz, *President*
Barbara Holtz, *Admin Sec*
**EMP:** 6
**SQ FT:** 12,300
**SALES (est):** 790.7K **Privately Held**
**WEB:** www.holtzmacher.com
**SIC:** 2431 2541 2517 2434 Interior & ornamental woodwork & trim; wood partitions & fixtures; home entertainment unit cabinets, wood; vanities, bathroom: wood

**(G-20793)**
**DOTY & SONS CONCRETE PRODUCTS**
1275 E State St (60178-9578)
PHONE ............................. 815 895-2884
Calvin L Doty, *President*
Thomas C Doty, *Vice Pres*
Samuel J Doty, *Treasurer*
Paula Doty, *Office Mgr*
Helen C Doty, *Admin Sec*
**EMP:** 13
**SQ FT:** 17,000
**SALES (est):** 2.5MM **Privately Held**
**WEB:** www.dotyconcrete.com
**SIC:** 3272 Concrete products, precast

**(G-20794)**
**DRIV-LOK INC (PA)**
1140 Park Ave (60178-2999)
PHONE ............................. 815 895-8161
Fax: 815 895-4265
Gary Seegers, *President*
Joanne Devick, *General Mgr*
Tim Gasparich, *Vice Pres*
Jim Atwell, *Mfg Spvr*
Divya Behl, *Opers Staff*
**EMP:** 5
**SQ FT:** 70,000
**SALES (est):** 18.2MM **Privately Held**
**WEB:** www.driv-lok.com
**SIC:** 3429 Metal fasteners

**(G-20795)**
**E K KUHN INC**
Also Called: Banner Up Signs
1170 E State St (60178-9576)
PHONE ............................. 815 899-9211
Fax: 630 208-1217
Ed Kuhn, *President*
Karen Kuhn, *Corp Secy*
Jon Kuhn, *Vice Pres*
**EMP:** 4
**SQ FT:** 3,000
**SALES:** 600K **Privately Held**
**SIC:** 3993 2759 7532 Signs & advertising specialties; screen printing; truck painting & lettering

**(G-20796)**
**EFFICIENT ENERGY LIGHTING INC**
530 Hopkins Ln (60178-9559)
P.O. Box 111 (60178-0111)
PHONE ............................. 630 272-9388
**EMP:** 2
**SALES (est):** 208.2K **Privately Held**
**SIC:** 3648 Lighting equipment

**(G-20797)**
**ELMER L LARSON L C (PA)**
21218 Airport Rd (60178-8215)
PHONE ............................. 815 895-4837
Fax: 815 895-4237
Chris Alessia, *Treasurer*
Gary Lee, *Manager*
John S Larson,
Dan Larson, *Admin Sec*
Michael D Larson,
**EMP:** 14 **EST:** 1933
**SQ FT:** 1,600
**SALES (est):** 3.8MM **Privately Held**
**SIC:** 1442 1422 6552 Construction sand & gravel; crushed & broken limestone; subdividers & developers

**(G-20798)**
**GENOA BUSINESS FORMS INC**
445 Park Ave (60178-2100)
P.O. Box 450 (60178-0450)
PHONE ............................. 815 895-2800
Fax: 815 895-8206
David Paulson, *President*
Ernest Westlund, *Finance*
**EMP:** 49
**SQ FT:** 38,000
**SALES (est):** 9.7MM **Privately Held**
**WEB:** www.genoabusforms.com
**SIC:** 2752 2761 Commercial printing, offset; business form & card printing, lithographic; manifold business forms

**(G-20799)**
**HEARTLAND INSPECTION COMPANY**
Also Called: Play It Again Sports 11417
510 Nathan Lattin Ln (60178-8755)
PHONE ............................. 630 788-3607
Edward Saunders, *President*
Susan Saunders, *Manager*
**EMP:** 6
**SQ FT:** 3,612
**SALES (est):** 380K **Privately Held**
**SIC:** 3949 Sporting & athletic goods

**(G-20800)**
**IDEAL INDUSTRIES INC (PA)**
1375 Park Ave (60178-2429)
PHONE ............................. 815 895-5181
Fax: 815 895-5269
David W Juday, *Ch of Bd*
Jim James, *President*
Nick Shkordoff, *General Mgr*
Joe Saganowich, *Vice Pres*
Vicki Slomka, *Vice Pres*
▲ **EMP:** 250 **EST:** 1916
**SQ FT:** 60,000
**SALES (est):** 366.2MM **Privately Held**
**WEB:** www.idealindustries.com
**SIC:** 3825 3643 Electrical power measuring equipment; current-carrying wiring devices

**(G-20801)**
**IDEAL INDUSTRIES INC**
434 Borden Ave Dock14 (60178-2428)
PHONE ............................. 815 895-1108
Randy Thomson, *Branch Mgr*
**EMP:** 200
**SALES (corp-wide):** 366.2MM **Privately Held**
**WEB:** www.idealindustries.com
**SIC:** 3643 3825 3625 3545 Current-carrying wiring devices; electrical power measuring equipment; relays & industrial controls; machine tool accessories; abrasive products; hand & edge tools
**PA:** Ideal Industries, Inc.
1375 Park Ave
Sycamore IL 60178
815 895-5181

**(G-20802)**
**IDEAL INDUSTRIES INC**
1000 Park Ave (60178-2420)
PHONE ............................. 815 895-5181
David W Juday, *CEO*
Deanna Glass, *Vice Pres*
Casey Allen, *Buyer*
Patrick Holtz, *Engineer*
Tim Clark, *Manager*
**EMP:** 200
**SQ FT:** 87,000

SALES (corp-wide): 366.2MM **Privately Held**
WEB: www.idealindustries.com
SIC: 3643 Current-carrying wiring devices
PA: Ideal Industries, Inc.
 1375 Park Ave
 Sycamore IL 60178
 815 895-5181

*(G-20803)*
**JENSEN AND SON INC**
353 N Maple St (60178-1436)
PHONE................................815 895-3855
Fax: 815 895-8908
Daniel Jensen, *President*
Toni Jensen, *Corp Secy*
EMP: 7 EST: 1943
SQ FT: 5,000
SALES (est): 846.4K **Privately Held**
SIC: 3544 Special dies & tools

*(G-20804)*
**K & S PRINTING SERVICES**
510 N Main St Ste 1 (60178-1236)
PHONE................................815 899-2923
Steve Caldwell, *Owner*
EMP: 1
SALES: 300K **Privately Held**
SIC: 2759 Commercial printing

*(G-20805)*
**KANE COUNTY CRONICLE**
Also Called: Genoa Kingston Kirkland News
513 W State St (60178-1327)
PHONE................................815 895-7033
Fax: 815 899-4329
Kim Kubiank, *Principal*
Kim Kubiank, *Principal*
EMP: 6
SALES (est): 164.4K **Privately Held**
SIC: 2711 Newspapers

*(G-20806)*
**KRESSER PRECISION INDS INC**
433 N California St # 2 (60178-1297)
PHONE................................815 899-2202
John Kresser, *President*
Lisa Kresser, *Admin Sec*
EMP: 5
SQ FT: 5,000
SALES: 250K **Privately Held**
SIC: 3599 Machine shop, jobbing & repair

*(G-20807)*
**LEGACY VULCAN LLC**
Midwest Division
12502 Lloyd Rd (60178-8118)
PHONE................................815 895-6501
Dan Larson, *Manager*
EMP: 15
SALES (corp-wide): 3.5B **Publicly Held**
WEB: www.vulcanmaterials.com
SIC: 1442 Gravel mining
HQ: Legacy Vulcan, Llc
 1200 Urban Center Dr
 Vestavia AL 35242
 205 298-3000

*(G-20808)*
**M & M WELDING INC**
410 N Main St (60178-1216)
PHONE................................815 895-3955
Greg Mathey, *President*
EMP: 2
SALES (est): 327K **Privately Held**
SIC: 7692 Welding repair

*(G-20809)*
**MARK S MACHINE SHOP INC**
416 N Main St (60178-1216)
PHONE................................815 895-3955
Fax: 815 895-5173
Francis Mathey, *President*
EMP: 7
SQ FT: 4,800
SALES (est): 1.1MM **Privately Held**
SIC: 5012 7539 7692 Truck bodies; automotive repair shops; automotive welding

*(G-20810)*
**NEWBY OIL COMPANY INC**
Also Called: Newby, Wayne Nsp
2270 Oakland Dr (60178-3112)
PHONE................................815 756-7688
Fax: 815 756-3050
Viola Newby, *President*
Wayne Newby, *President*
Dave Newby, *Vice Pres*
EMP: 8
SQ FT: 5,625
SALES (est): 2.6MM **Privately Held**
SIC: 5171 2842 5999 5091 Petroleum bulk stations; window cleaning preparations; swimming pool chemicals, equipment & supplies; swimming pools, equipment & supplies

*(G-20811)*
**ODOM TOOL AND TECHNOLOGY INC**
216 W Page St (60178-1439)
PHONE................................815 895-8545
Fax: 815 895-8557
Jim W Odom, *President*
Ronda Odom, *Vice Pres*
EMP: 7
SQ FT: 10,000
SALES (est): 847.9K **Privately Held**
SIC: 3544 7692 Special dies & tools; welding repair

*(G-20812)*
**ORORA PACKAGING SOLUTIONS**
Also Called: Mpp Sycamore Div 6063
215 Fair St (60178-1644)
PHONE................................815 895-2343
Matthew Seidner, *Senior VP*
Patricia Huff, *Sales Staff*
Larry Kendzora, *Manager*
EMP: 54
SALES (corp-wide): 2.8B **Privately Held**
SIC: 5113 2653 Paper & products, wrapping or coarse; boxes, corrugated: made from purchased materials
HQ: Orora Packaging Solutions
 6600 Valley View St
 Buena Park CA 90620
 714 562-6000

*(G-20813)*
**PRATT-READ TOOLS LLC**
1375 Park Ave (60178-2429)
PHONE................................815 895-1121
Jerry Leasseur, *Treasurer*
Joyce Myers, *Accountant*
Erin Walker, *Manager*
Robin Lawrence, *Info Tech Mgr*
James Pfotenhauer,
▲ EMP: 4
SALES (est): 571.3K **Privately Held**
SIC: 3423 Screw drivers, pliers, chisels, etc. (hand tools)

*(G-20814)*
**RICHARD A ANDERSON**
Also Called: Anderson, Richard Shop
1653 W Motel Rd (60178)
PHONE................................815 895-5627
Richard A Anderson, *Owner*
EMP: 7 EST: 1981
SALES (est): 572K **Privately Held**
SIC: 3599 Machine shop, jobbing & repair

*(G-20815)*
**SEYMOUR OF SYCAMORE INC (PA)**
917 Crosby Ave (60178-1394)
PHONE................................815 895-9101
Fax: 815 895-8475
Nancy Seymour Heatley, *CEO*
Steve Olshever, *Division Mgr*
Christopher Heatley, *Vice Pres*
Don Jankowski, *Plant Mgr*
Debra Burris, *Research*
◆ EMP: 135 EST: 1949
SQ FT: 80,000
SALES (est): 34.4MM **Privately Held**
WEB: www.seymourpaint.com
SIC: 2851 2899 Paints: oil or alkyd vehicle or water thinned; enamels; lacquer: bases, dopes, thinner; coating, air curing; chemical preparations

*(G-20816)*
**SK HAND TOOL LLC**
1600 S Prairie Dr (60178-3203)
PHONE................................815 895-7701
Claude Fuger, *CEO*
Cliff Rusnak, *Chairman*
Shiela Johnsen, *Vice Pres*
James Pfotenhauer, *Vice Pres*
Joe Saganowich, *Vice Pres*
EMP: 15
SALES (est): 4.5MM
SALES (corp-wide): 366.2MM **Privately Held**
SIC: 3423 Wrenches, hand tools; screw drivers, pliers, chisels, etc. (hand tools)
PA: Ideal Industries, Inc.
 1375 Park Ave
 Sycamore IL 60178
 815 895-5181

*(G-20817)*
**SMART MOTION ROBOTICS INC**
805 Thornwood Dr (60178-8881)
PHONE................................815 895-8550
Scott Gilmore, *President*
Douglas Jones, *President*
Donald A Vincent, *Exec VP*
Victoria L Gilmore, *CFO*
Vickie Gilmore, *Administration*
▼ EMP: 20
SQ FT: 35,000
SALES (est): 5.4MM **Privately Held**
SIC: 3535 4783 5084 Robotic conveyors; packing & crating; industrial machinery & equipment

*(G-20818)*
**SYCAMORE CONTAINERS INC**
Also Called: Kent H Landsberg Co
215 Fair St (60178-1600)
PHONE................................815 895-2343
Fax: 815 895-5555
Gene Shelton, *President*
Larry Kendoza, *Division Mgr*
Brent Norman, *Vice Pres*
Bruce Hippler, *Opers Mgr*
Bob Krueger, *Sales Mgr*
EMP: 60
SQ FT: 62,000
SALES (est): 11.2MM
SALES (corp-wide): 2.8B **Privately Held**
WEB: www.syccontainers.com
SIC: 2653 Boxes, corrugated: made from purchased materials
HQ: Orora Packaging Solutions
 6600 Valley View St
 Buena Park CA 90620
 714 562-6000

*(G-20819)*
**THOMPSON INDUSTRIES INC**
1018 Crosby Ave (60178-1348)
P.O. Box 127 (60178-0127)
PHONE................................815 899-6670
Fax: 815 899-1918
Tim Siegmeier, *Prdtn Mgr*
Karen Swanson, *Office Mgr*
Edward Thompson Sr, *Shareholder*
EMP: 26
SQ FT: 22,000
SALES (est): 4.9MM **Privately Held**
WEB: www.thompsoncnc.com
SIC: 3599 Machine & other job shop work

*(G-20820)*
**TRAFFICGUARD DIRECT LLC**
1730 Afton Rd (60178-3224)
P.O. Box 201, Geneva (60134-0201)
PHONE................................815 899-8471
Michael D Schram,
Jon Schram,
▼ EMP: 5
SALES (est): 570K **Privately Held**
WEB: www.trafficguard.net
SIC: 3699 Security devices

*(G-20821)*
**TRENDY SCREENPRINTING**
155 E Maplewood Dr (60178-1142)
PHONE................................815 895-0081
Jerry Breiling, *Owner*
EMP: 3
SALES (est): 299.3K **Privately Held**
SIC: 2759 Screen printing

*(G-20822)*
**UPSTAGING INC (PA)**
821 Park Ave (60178-2419)
PHONE................................815 899-9888
Fax: 815 899-1080
Robert Carone, *President*
Shawn Haynes, *General Mgr*
Robin Shaw, *Vice Pres*
Matt McGregor, *Production*
Chuck Spector, *Purch Agent*
▼ EMP: 168 EST: 1972
SQ FT: 124,000
SALES (est): 23.5MM **Privately Held**
SIC: 7922 3537 Lighting, theatrical; trucks, tractors, loaders, carriers & similar equipment

*(G-20823)*
**VISUAL PERSUASION INC**
Also Called: Priority Promotions
337 E State St (60178-1513)
PHONE................................815 899-6609
Patrick Marsden, *President*
Cindy Carlson, *Treasurer*
Josephine Kingsbury, *Marketing Mgr*
EMP: 10
SQ FT: 2,500
SALES (est): 763.6K **Privately Held**
SIC: 7389 2395 Embroidering of advertising on shirts, etc.; embroidery products, except schiffli machine

*(G-20824)*
**VULCAN MATERIALS COMPANY**
12502 Lloyd Rd (60178-8118)
PHONE................................815 899-7204
Fax: 815 895-3883
EMP: 20
SALES (corp-wide): 3.4B **Publicly Held**
SIC: 1422 Crushed/Broken Limestone
PA: Vulcan Materials Company
 1200 Urban Center Dr
 Vestavia AL 35242
 205 298-3000

*(G-20825)*
**WEHRLI CUSTOM FABRICATION**
417 Borden Ave (60178-2446)
PHONE................................630 277-8239
Jason Wehrli, *Owner*
EMP: 17
SALES (est): 3.3MM **Privately Held**
SIC: 3499 Novelties & giftware, including trophies

## Tamms
### Alexander County

*(G-20826)*
**UNIMIN CORPORATION**
Also Called: Unimin Specialty Minerals
32079 State Highway 127 (62988-3011)
PHONE................................618 747-2338
Fax: 618 747-2459
Al Jonier, *Branch Mgr*
EMP: 25
SQ FT: 25,000
SALES (corp-wide): 117.6MM **Privately Held**
WEB: www.unimin.com
SIC: 1446 Silica mining
HQ: Unimin Corporation
 258 Elm St
 New Canaan CT 06840
 203 966-8880

*(G-20827)*
**UNIMIN CORPORATION**
Also Called: Unimin Specialty Minerals
32079 State Highway 127 (62988-3011)
P.O. Box 340 (62988-0340)
PHONE................................618 747-2311
Seibert Cowley, *Corp Secy*
EMP: 59
SALES (corp-wide): 117.6MM **Privately Held**
WEB: www.unimin.com
SIC: 1446 Silica mining
HQ: Unimin Corporation
 258 Elm St
 New Canaan CT 06840
 203 966-8880

## Tampico
### Whiteside County

**(G-20828)**
**MIDWEST BIO MANUFACTURING DIV**
310 2650 N Ave (61283-9017)
PHONE.................................815 542-6417
Edwin Blosser, *President*
Carey Richardson, *Principal*
Ernest Blosser, *Vice Pres*
**EMP:** 12
**SALES (est):** 1.1MM **Privately Held**
**SIC:** 2836 Biological products, except diagnostic

**(G-20829)**
**MIDWEST BIO-SYSTEMS INC**
28933 35 E St (61283-9003)
PHONE.................................815 438-7200
**Fax:** 815 438-7028
Edwin Blosser, *President*
Ernest Blosser, *Vice Pres*
Kelly Young, *Consultant*
Karla J Blosser, *Admin Sec*
◆ **EMP:** 11
**SQ FT:** 2,000
**SALES:** 3.5MM **Privately Held**
**WEB:** www.midwestbiosystems.com
**SIC:** 3523 0711 Farm machinery & equipment; soil testing services

## Taylor Ridge
### Rock Island County

**(G-20830)**
**QUAD CITY HOSE**
9707 86th Street Ct W (61284-9248)
PHONE.................................563 386-8936
J Gary Zespy, *President*
Jim Zarlatane, *General Mgr*
Renee Lofgren, *Office Mgr*
**EMP:** 25
**SQ FT:** 21,500
**SALES (est):** 6.9MM **Privately Held**
**WEB:** www.qchose.com
**SIC:** 3492 3052 Hose & tube fittings & assemblies, hydraulic/pneumatic; rubber & plastics hose & beltings

## Taylorville
### Christian County

**(G-20831)**
**AHLSTROM FILTRATION LLC**
1200 E Elm St (62568-1642)
P.O. Box 680 (62568-0680)
PHONE.................................217 824-9611
**Fax:** 217 824-9514
Rosetta Alaria, *QA Dir*
Terry Dolenc, *Human Res Dir*
J R Burdick, *Sales Mgr*
Susan M Reardon, *Sales Mgr*
John Flahive, *Manager*
**EMP:** 60
**SALES (corp-wide):** 401.1MM **Privately Held**
**SIC:** 2621 Filter paper
**HQ:** Ahlstrom Filtration Llc
215 Nebo Rd
Madisonville KY 42431
270 821-0140

**(G-20832)**
**AQUA GOLF INC (PA)**
6 Manor Ct (62568-8926)
PHONE.................................217 824-2097
Deane Peabody, *President*
Pamela Peabody, *Corp Secy*
**EMP:** 2 **EST:** 1997
**SQ FT:** 5,000
**SALES:** 1.5MM **Privately Held**
**SIC:** 3944 Games, toys & children's vehicles

**(G-20833)**
**BIG M MANUFACTURING LLC**
928 E 1090 North Rd (62568-8341)
PHONE.................................217 824-9372
Mel Repscher,
**EMP:** 5
**SALES:** 300K **Privately Held**
**SIC:** 3585 Heating equipment, complete

**(G-20834)**
**BOTKIN LUMBER COMPANY INC**
Also Called: Illinois Box & Pallet
201 S Baughman Rd (62568-9387)
PHONE.................................217 287-2127
**Fax:** 217 287-1323
Phil Kelmel, *Plant Mgr*
Philip Kelmel, *Branch Mgr*
**EMP:** 20
**SQ FT:** 54,500
**SALES (corp-wide):** 18.7MM **Privately Held**
**SIC:** 2421 2448 2441 Lumber: rough, sawed or planed; pallets, wood; packing cases, wood: nailed or lock corner; shipping cases, wood: nailed or lock corner
**PA:** Botkin Lumber Company, Inc.
1901 Progress Dr
Farmington MO 63640
573 756-2400

**(G-20835)**
**BREEZE PRINTING CO (PA)**
Also Called: Breeze-Courier
212 S Main St (62568-2219)
P.O. Box 440 (62568-0440)
PHONE.................................217 824-2233
**Fax:** 217 824-2026
Mary Lee Rasar, *President*
Mary Lee Lasswell, *President*
Wilda Cooper, *Vice Pres*
Owen Lasswels, *CFO*
J Robert Cooper, *Admin Sec*
**EMP:** 18
**SQ FT:** 20,000
**SALES (est):** 1.7MM **Privately Held**
**WEB:** www.breezecourier.com
**SIC:** 2711 7359 Job printing & newspaper publishing combined; equipment rental & leasing

**(G-20836)**
**CHRISTIAN CNTY MNTAL HLTH ASSN (PA)**
Also Called: CCMHA
707 Mcadam Dr (62568-2300)
P.O. Box 438 (62568-0438)
PHONE.................................217 824-9675
**Fax:** 217 824-3070
Brent De Michael, *President*
Joe Brookens, *Production*
**EMP:** 90
**SALES:** 7.3MM **Privately Held**
**WEB:** www.ccmha.net
**SIC:** 2499 8621 Spools, wood; health association

**(G-20837)**
**DESIGN MANUFACTURING & EQP CO**
400 S Baughman Rd (62568-9378)
PHONE.................................217 824-9219
**Fax:** 217 824-9532
Tony Elinger, *Manager*
**EMP:** 15
**SALES (corp-wide):** 1.9MM **Privately Held**
**SIC:** 3523 3316 Planting, haying, harvesting & processing machinery; cold finishing of steel shapes
**PA:** Design Manufacturing & Equipment Co Inc
5215 Northrup Ave
Saint Louis MO 63110
314 771-0503

**(G-20838)**
**DOMINO ENGINEERING CORP**
208 S Spresser St (62568-9282)
P.O. Box 376 (62568-0376)
PHONE.................................217 824-9441
**Fax:** 217 824-3349
Lawrence Peterson, *President*
Alan J Peterson, *Treasurer*
**EMP:** 10
**SALES:** 500K **Privately Held**
**WEB:** www.dominoengineering.com
**SIC:** 3625 Relays & industrial controls

**(G-20839)**
**GSI GROUP LLC**
2400 S Spresser St (62568-9227)
PHONE.................................217 287-6244
Trula Stalets, *Buyer*
Waylon Jesse, *Engineer*
Gary Parkinson, *Human Resources*
Brian Atwood, *Manager*
**EMP:** 120
**SALES (corp-wide):** 7.4B **Publicly Held**
**WEB:** www.grainsystems.com
**SIC:** 3523 Crop storage bins; driers (farm): grain, hay & seed; poultry brooders, feeders & waterers; hog feeding, handling & watering equipment
**HQ:** The Gsi Group Llc
1004 E Illinois St
Assumption IL 62510
217 226-4421

**(G-20840)**
**HEARWELL**
1221 W Spresser St (62568-1714)
PHONE.................................217 824-5210
Donald Bettis, *Principal*
**EMP:** 2 **EST:** 2011
**SALES (est):** 221.4K **Privately Held**
**SIC:** 3842 Hearing aids

**(G-20841)**
**LLA EXPLORATION INC**
1747 N 800 East Rd (62568-7843)
PHONE.................................217 623-4096
Clifford Mansfield, *President*
**EMP:** 1
**SALES:** 700K **Privately Held**
**SIC:** 1382 Oil & gas exploration services

**(G-20842)**
**MACON METAL PRODUCTS CO**
Also Called: Mmp Company
803 W Calvert St (62568-9222)
P.O. Box 200 (62568-0200)
PHONE.................................217 824-7205
**Fax:** 217 824-3460
Stanley J Bogaczyk, *CEO*
Mark Bogaczyk, *President*
Ellis Marlena, *Opers Mgr*
Thomas Kotal, *Manager*
Claire Bogaczyk, *Admin Sec*
**EMP:** 30 **EST:** 1948
**SQ FT:** 84,000
**SALES (est):** 7MM **Privately Held**
**SIC:** 3469 3444 2542 2599 Stamping metal for the trade; sheet metalwork; racks, merchandise display or storage: except wood; work benches, factory; coating of metals & formed products

**(G-20843)**
**MIDSTATE SALVAGE CORP**
Also Called: Midstate Iron & Metals
1402 W South St (62568-9385)
PHONE.................................217 824-6047
**Fax:** 217 824-8522
William Neal Lebeter, *President*
Robin Vancil, *Admin Sec*
**EMP:** 7
**SQ FT:** 1,000
**SALES (est):** 905.6K **Privately Held**
**SIC:** 5093 3341 Ferrous metal scrap & waste; secondary nonferrous metals

**(G-20844)**
**POGGENPOHL LLC**
105 N Baughman Rd (62568-9304)
PHONE.................................217 824-2020
Russell Poggenpohl, *Partner*
**EMP:** 3
**SALES (corp-wide):** 2.3MM **Privately Held**
**SIC:** 1521 1542 3273 Single-family housing construction; commercial & office building contractors; ready-mixed concrete
**PA:** Poggenpohl, L.L.C.
31 Sparks St
Raymond IL 62560
217 229-3411

**(G-20845)**
**RAMSEYS MACHINE CO**
1333 N Webster St (62568-2729)
PHONE.................................217 824-2320
John Harris, *Owner*
**EMP:** 3
**SALES (est):** 259.4K **Privately Held**
**SIC:** 3536 7692 Hoists; welding repair

**(G-20846)**
**WATSON INC**
1900 S Spresser St (62568-9383)
PHONE.................................217 824-4440
**Fax:** 217 824-4284
Miles Feller, *Manager*
**EMP:** 25
**SALES (corp-wide):** 74.5MM **Privately Held**
**SIC:** 2045 2087 Prepared flour mixes & doughs; flavoring extracts & syrups
**PA:** Watson Inc.
301 Heffernan Dr
West Haven CT 06516
203 932-3000

## Teutopolis
### Effingham County

**(G-20847)**
**BRUMLEVE INDUSTRIES INC**
Also Called: Brumleve Canvas Products
1317 W Main St (62467-1215)
P.O. Box 279 (62467-0279)
PHONE.................................217 857-3777
**Fax:** 217 857-3514
Donald J Brumleve, *President*
Joan Brumleve, *Vice Pres*
Linda Pruemer, *Office Mgr*
**EMP:** 15
**SALES (est):** 5.6MM **Privately Held**
**WEB:** www.brumleveind.com
**SIC:** 5199 3792 2394 Canvas products; travel trailers & campers; canvas & related products

**(G-20848)**
**C & H GRAVEL C INC**
Also Called: C and H Gravel
14046 N 1600th St (62467-3427)
PHONE.................................217 857-3425
**Fax:** 217 849-2323
Paul Harmon, *Manager*
**EMP:** 6
**SALES (corp-wide):** 3.8MM **Privately Held**
**SIC:** 1442 4212 Gravel mining; local trucking, without storage
**PA:** C & H Gravel C Inc
1406 E Fayette Ave
Teutopolis IL
217 857-3425

**(G-20849)**
**CASEY STONE CO**
14046 N 1600th St (62467-3427)
PHONE.................................217 857-3425
Janice Heuerman, *President*
Rod Harman, *Manager*
Becky Landers, *Admin Sec*
**EMP:** 8
**SALES (est):** 1.2MM **Privately Held**
**WEB:** www.caseystone.com
**SIC:** 3272 Cast stone, concrete

**(G-20850)**
**COMMUNITY SUPPORT SYSTEMS (PA)**
618 W Main St (62467-1210)
PHONE.................................217 705-4300
**Fax:** 217 857-6343
Debra Parmenter, *Business Mgr*
Linda Bruner, *Manager*
Carter Kim, *Manager*
Tim Woodall, *MIS Dir*
Andy Kistler, *Technology*
**EMP:** 75
**SQ FT:** 13,000
**SALES:** 6.5MM **Privately Held**
**SIC:** 8331 8361 2448 2441 Sheltered workshop; home for the mentally retarded; wood pallets & skids; nailed wood boxes & shook

**(G-20851)**
**D D SALES INC**
Also Called: Dale's Diesel Service
1608 W Main St (62467-1283)
**PHONE**.................................217 857-3196
Dale Ruholl, *President*
Neil Ruholl, *Manager*
**EMP:** 21 **EST:** 1986
**SALES (est):** 2.5MM **Privately Held**
**SIC: 7538** 3715 7532 General truck repair; truck trailers; top & body repair & paint shops

**(G-20852)**
**FARMWELD INC**
18413 E Us Highway 40 (62467-3502)
**PHONE**.................................217 857-6423
Frank A Brummer, *President*
Aaron Niebrugge, *Sales Mgr*
Lori Runde, *Manager*
Lora K Runde, *Admin Sec*
▲ **EMP:** 30
**SALES (est):** 8.3MM **Privately Held**
**WEB:** www.farmweld.com
**SIC: 3523** 7692 3444 Farm machinery & equipment; welding repair; sheet metalwork

**(G-20853)**
**K & W AUTO ELECTRIC**
103 N Automotive Dr (62467-1285)
**PHONE**.................................217 857-1717
**Fax:** 217 857-1919
Rick Kreke, *Partner*
Karl Wendt, *Partner*
**EMP:** 10
**SQ FT:** 7,200
**SALES (est):** 750K **Privately Held**
**SIC: 3714** 3694 3625 Motor vehicle engines & parts; engine electrical equipment; relays & industrial controls

**(G-20854)**
**PERFORMANCE LAWN & POWER**
1311 W Main St (62467-1215)
**PHONE**.................................217 857-3717
**Fax:** 217 857-3717
Thomas Mette, *Owner*
**EMP:** 2
**SALES (est):** 220K **Privately Held**
**SIC: 2431** 5251 Millwork; tools, power

**(G-20855)**
**SIEMER ENTERPRISES INC (PA)**
Also Called: Mangelsdorf Seed Co
515 W Main St (62467-1209)
P.O. Box 580 (62467-0580)
**PHONE**.................................217 857-3171
**Fax:** 217 857-3226
Gwenn S Croft, *Corp Secy*
Dave Bohnenstiehl, *VP Sales*
Connie Barr, *Sales Executive*
Alan Waggoner, *Info Tech Mgr*
Sunil Maheshwari, *Director*
▲ **EMP:** 50
**SQ FT:** 105,000
**SALES (est):** 33.9MM **Privately Held**
**WEB:** www.siemerent.com
**SIC: 5191** 2048 5083 Feed; bird food, prepared; lawn machinery & equipment; garden machinery & equipment

**(G-20856)**
**STEVENS CABINETS INC (PA)**
Also Called: Stevens Tot-Mate
704 W Main St (62467-1212)
**PHONE**.................................217 857-7100
**Fax:** 217 540-3101
Tom Wegman, *President*
Todd Wegman, *President*
James Buhnerkempe, *Corp Secy*
Dylan Bartels, *Project Mgr*
Ryan Lee, *Safety Mgr*
◆ **EMP:** 400 **EST:** 1967
**SQ FT:** 480,000
**SALES (est):** 123.3MM **Privately Held**
**WEB:** www.stevensind.com
**SIC: 2531** 2679 2511 Public building & related furniture; wallboard, decorated: made from purchased material; juvenile furniture: wood

**(G-20857)**
**THREE-Z PRINTING CO (PA)**
Also Called: Three Z Printing
902 W Main St (62467-1329)
P.O. Box 550 (62467-0550)
**PHONE**.................................217 857-3153
**Fax:** 217 857-3010
Dan Zerrusen, *President*
William Zerrusen, *Assistant VP*
Bill Zerrusen, *Vice Pres*
Bill Zerrusenis, *Vice Pres*
Lorraine Zerrusen, *Treasurer*
**EMP:** 375
**SQ FT:** 450,000
**SALES (est):** 139.1MM **Privately Held**
**WEB:** www.threez.com
**SIC: 2752** Commercial printing, offset

## Third Lake
### Lake County

**(G-20858)**
**ROBBI JOY EKLOW**
4 Galleon Ct (60030-2633)
**PHONE**.................................847 223-0460
Robbi Eklow, *Principal*
**EMP:** 4 **EST:** 2010
**SALES (est):** 293K **Privately Held**
**SIC: 3052** Cotton fabric, rubber lined hose

## Thomasboro
### Champaign County

**(G-20859)**
**ALTAMONT CO**
901 N Church St (61878-9700)
P.O. Box 309 (61878-0309)
**PHONE**.................................800 626-5774
Kenneth Enright, *President*
Jennifer Wendling, *Research*
Denise Enright, *Admin Sec*
▲ **EMP:** 90
**SQ FT:** 45,000
**SALES (est):** 19.4MM **Privately Held**
**WEB:** www.altamontco.com
**SIC: 3089** 3949 Handles, brush or tool: plastic; sporting & athletic goods

**(G-20860)**
**MASTERS SHOP**
Also Called: The Master's Shop
1621 County Road 2500 N (61878-9663)
**PHONE**.................................217 643-7826
John L Powell, *President*
**EMP:** 1
**SALES:** 300K **Privately Held**
**WEB:** www.wrightlight.com
**SIC: 1751** 2434 Finish & trim carpentry; wood kitchen cabinets

## Thompsonville
### Franklin County

**(G-20861)**
**3ABN**
6020 Green Meadow Rd (62890-2410)
P.O. Box 220, West Frankfort (62896-0220)
**PHONE**.................................618 627-4651
**EMP:** 3 **EST:** 2008
**SALES (est):** 150K **Privately Held**
**SIC: 2836** Biological Products, Except Diagnostic

**(G-20862)**
**KEYROCK ENERGY LLC**
20227 Thorn Rd (62890-4408)
**PHONE**.................................618 982-9710
**EMP:** 40
**SALES (corp-wide):** 8MM **Privately Held**
**SIC: 1241** Coal mining exploration & test boring
**PA:** Keyrock Energy Llc
106 Ferrell Ave Ste 5
Kingsport TN 37663
423 726-2070

**(G-20863)**
**MCFARLAND WELDING AND MACHINE**
4066 N Thompsonville Rd (62890-2601)
**PHONE**.................................618 627-2838
Jerome McFarland, *Owner*
**EMP:** 3
**SQ FT:** 4,000
**SALES:** 50K **Privately Held**
**SIC: 7692** Welding repair

## Thomson
### Carroll County

**(G-20864)**
**CARROLL COUNTY REVIEW**
809 W Main St (61285-7776)
P.O. Box 369 (61285-0369)
**PHONE**.................................815 259-2131
**Fax:** 815 259-3226
Jonathan Whitney, *Owner*
William Gengenbach, *Advt Staff*
Nancy Whitney, *Advt Staff*
**EMP:** 5
**SQ FT:** 4,200
**SALES (est):** 170K **Privately Held**
**SIC: 2711** Commercial printing & newspaper publishing combined

**(G-20865)**
**E I DU PONT DE NEMOURS & CO**
Also Called: Danisco Sweeteners
10994 Three Mile Rd (61285-7633)
**PHONE**.................................815 259-3311
Diane Burke, *Purch Mgr*
Peter Biedenharn, *Engineer*
Craig Myers, *Branch Mgr*
**EMP:** 70
**SALES (corp-wide):** 24.5B **Publicly Held**
**SIC: 2099** Food preparations; emulsifiers, food; pectin
**PA:** E. I. Du Pont De Nemours And Company
974 Centre Rd
Wilmington DE 19805
302 774-1000

## Thornton
### Cook County

**(G-20866)**
**A B C BLIND INC**
108 S Julian St (60476-1230)
**PHONE**.................................708 877-7100
Katherine Snell, *President*
Harry Snells, *Vice Pres*
Audra Coniglio, *Admin Sec*
**EMP:** 3
**SQ FT:** 4,000
**SALES:** 250K **Privately Held**
**SIC: 2591** 2211 Window blinds; draperies & drapery fabrics, cotton

**(G-20867)**
**AMERICAN SHTMTL FBRICATORS INC**
525 N Williams St (60476-1018)
**PHONE**.................................708 877-7200
Dennis Debartolo, *President*
**EMP:** 11 **EST:** 2011
**SALES:** 2MM **Privately Held**
**SIC: 3444** Sheet metalwork

**(G-20868)**
**BOEKELOO HEATING & SHEET METAL**
601 N Williams St (60476-1097)
**PHONE**.................................708 877-6560
**Fax:** 708 877-6570
David Boekeloo, *President*
Dolores Boekeloo, *Corp Secy*
**EMP:** 6
**SQ FT:** 1,200
**SALES (est):** 750K **Privately Held**
**SIC: 1711** 1761 3444 Warm air heating & air conditioning contractor; siding contractor; sheet metalwork

**(G-20869)**
**FREE-FLOW PACKAGING INTL INC**
Also Called: FP International
16850 Canal St (60476-1072)
**PHONE**.................................708 589-6500
**Fax:** 708 589-0183
Tom Anzur, *Plant Mgr*
Jay Lumkes, *Sales Mgr*
Michael Neal, *Sales Staff*
Donna Johnson, *Marketing Mgr*
Barbara Bukwa, *Manager*
**EMP:** 75
**SALES (corp-wide):** 139MM **Privately Held**
**WEB:** www.fpintl.com
**SIC: 3086** Plastics foam products; insulation or cushioning material, foamed plastic; packaging & shipping materials, foamed plastic
**PA:** Free-Flow Packaging International, Inc.
34175 Ardenwood Blvd
Fremont CA 94555
650 261-5300

**(G-20870)**
**GPL INDUSTRIES INCORPORATED**
395 Armory Dr (60476-1046)
**PHONE**.................................708 877-8200
**Fax:** 708 877-8980
Leo Piekosz, *Principal*
Mary Peksa, *Office Mgr*
**EMP:** 52
**SQ FT:** 60,000
**SALES (est):** 9.1MM **Privately Held**
**SIC: 3599** Machine shop, jobbing & repair

**(G-20871)**
**GROUP INDUSTRIES INC**
Drum Parts Midwest Div
459 N Williams St (60476-1059)
**PHONE**.................................708 877-6200
**Fax:** 708 877-6202
Lane Zamin, *President*
Steven Zamin, *Vice Pres*
Dale Zelesnick, *Finance Mgr*
Dale Zeleznik, *Finance*
Judy Vana, *Sales Associate*
**EMP:** 25
**SQ FT:** 26,000
**SALES (corp-wide):** 10.5MM **Privately Held**
**WEB:** www.drumpartsinc.com
**SIC: 3442** 3499 3443 3444 Moldings & trim, except automobile: metal; fire- or burglary-resistive products; iron & steel forgings; sheet metalwork; gray & ductile iron foundries
**PA:** Group Industries, Inc.
7580 Garfield Blvd
Cleveland OH 44125
216 271-0702

**(G-20872)**
**HARCROS CHEMICALS INC**
17031 Canal St (60476-1064)
**PHONE**.................................815 740-9971
Sandra Clifton, *Purch Mgr*
Peter Osten, *Sales Mgr*
Steve Weigel, *Accounts Mgr*
Tom Worth, *Manager*
Park McCalley, *Manager*
**EMP:** 5
**SALES (corp-wide):** 639.4MM **Privately Held**
**WEB:** www.harcroschem.com
**SIC: 2899** Chemical supplies for foundries
**PA:** Harcros Chemicals Inc.
5200 Speaker Rd
Kansas City KS 66106
913 321-3131

**(G-20873)**
**INDUSTRA SHARP INC**
107 E Juliette St Ste 1 (60476-1366)
**PHONE**.................................708 877-1200
Adam Wojcik, *CEO*
**EMP:** 5
**SALES (est):** 642.2K **Privately Held**
**WEB:** www.industrasharp.com
**SIC: 3599** Machine shop, jobbing & repair

# Thornton - Cook County (G-20874)

**(G-20874)**
**INTEGRATED POWER SERVICES LLC**
17001 Vincennes Rd  (60476-1066)
**PHONE**..................708 877-5310
Jon Radde, *Sales Engr*
Rich Harris, *Manager*
Tim Thorne, *Manager*
**EMP**: 50
**SALES (corp-wide)**: 1.3B  **Privately Held**
**WEB**: www.integratedps.com
**SIC**: 7629  7694  3621  Electrical repair shops; armature rewinding shops; motors & generators
**HQ**: Integrated Power Services Llc
3 Independence Pt Ste 100
Greenville SC 29615
864 451-5600

**(G-20875)**
**MATERIAL SERVICE CORPORATION**
620 W 183rd St  (60476-1026)
**PHONE**..................708 877-6540
**Fax**: 708 877-5724
David Stanccak, *Sales Staff*
Toby Breedlove, *Branch Mgr*
**EMP**: 80
**SALES (corp-wide)**: 16B  **Privately Held**
**WEB**: www.materialservice.com
**SIC**: 3295  1422  Minerals, ground or treated; crushed & broken limestone
**HQ**: Material Service Corporation
2235 Entp Dr Ste 3504
Westchester IL 60154
708 731-2600

**(G-20876)**
**VENTURA FOODS LLC**
Also Called: Marie's Salad Dressings
201 Armory Dr  (60476-1044)
**PHONE**..................708 877-5150
**Fax**: 708 877-1312
Brian Peyton, *Purchasing*
Keith Luchon, *Plant Engr*
Ray McCoy, *Branch Mgr*
**EMP**: 40  **Privately Held**
**WEB**: www.venturafoods.com
**SIC**: 2079  Salad oils, except corn: vegetable refined
**PA**: Ventura Foods, Llc
40 Pointe Dr
Brea CA 92821

## Tilden
### Randolph County

**(G-20877)**
**SOUTHERN ILL AUTO ELEC INC**
Also Called: S I A Electronics
730 N Minnie Ave  (62292-1101)
**PHONE**..................618 587-3308
**Fax**: 618 587-6408
Scott A Bement, *President*
Charles Welch, *General Mgr*
Linda K Baker, *Accountant*
**EMP**: 12
**SQ FT**: 7,200
**SALES (est)**: 1.8MM  **Privately Held**
**WEB**: www.siaelec.com
**SIC**: 3694  Automotive electrical equipment

## Tilton
### Vermilion County

**(G-20878)**
**CARNAGHI TOWING & REPAIR INC**
2000 Georgetown Rd  (61833-8121)
**PHONE**..................217 446-0333
**Fax**: 217 442-0094
Brian Carnaghi, *President*
Carole Carnaghi, *Vice Pres*
Stephanie Carnaghi, *Vice Pres*
**EMP**: 12  **EST**: 1924
**SQ FT**: 3,500
**SALES (est)**: 1.4MM  **Privately Held**
**SIC**: 7549  5541  2097  7538  Towing service, automotive; filling stations, gasoline; manufactured ice; general automotive repair shops

**(G-20879)**
**CITY OF DANVILLE**
5 Southgate Ct  (61833-8132)
**PHONE**..................217 442-1564
**Fax**: 217 442-1295
Brenda Bostic, *Branch Mgr*
**EMP**: 3  **Privately Held**
**SIC**: 3469  Automobile license tags, stamped metal
**PA**: City Of Danville
17 W Main St
Danville IL 61832
217 431-2200

**(G-20880)**
**CUSTOM SIGNS ON METAL LLC**
Also Called: Photosteel
301 Mayfield St  (61833-7460)
**PHONE**..................217 443-5347
Don Davis, *Mng Member*
Donnie L Davis, *Manager*
Jeff Davis, *Manager*
Joe Davis,
**EMP**: 10
**SQ FT**: 14,000
**SALES**: 500K  **Privately Held**
**WEB**: www.photosteel.com
**SIC**: 3993  Signs & advertising specialties

**(G-20881)**
**FAMACO CORP**
110 Atwood St  (61833-7599)
**PHONE**..................217 442-4412
**Fax**: 217 442-0217
S Gale Edwards, *President*
Janice Edwards, *Vice Pres*
**EMP**: 20
**SQ FT**: 20,000
**SALES (est)**: 2.9MM  **Privately Held**
**SIC**: 3599  3544  3444  3441  Machine shop, jobbing & repair; special dies, tools, jigs & fixtures; sheet metalwork; fabricated structural metal

**(G-20882)**
**RUMSHINE DISTILLING LLC**
8 Hodge St  (61832-7609)
**PHONE**..................217 446-6960
Ernie L Trinkle II, *Mng Member*
Tyler Langston, *Mng Member*
**EMP**: 3  **EST**: 2014
**SALES (est)**: 172.7K  **Privately Held**
**SIC**: 2085  5813  Distilled & blended liquors; cocktail lounge

**(G-20883)**
**TROXEL INDUSTRIES INC**
580 N J St  (61833-7404)
**PHONE**..................217 431-8674
**Fax**: 217 431-8679
Bonnie Troxel, *President*
Tammy Latoz, *Vice Pres*
Sandy Ray, *Accounts Mgr*
**EMP**: 30
**SQ FT**: 22,000
**SALES**: 3MM  **Privately Held**
**SIC**: 3444  3531  Sheet metalwork; construction machinery

## Timewell
### Brown County

**(G-20884)**
**C & L TILING INC (PA)**
Also Called: Timewell Tile
196 Us24 1075n Ave  (62375)
**PHONE**..................217 773-3357
**Fax**: 217 773-2008
Donald Colclasure, *President*
Susan Colclasure, *Admin Sec*
**EMP**: 80
**SALES (est)**: 65.6MM  **Privately Held**
**WEB**: www.timewelltile.com
**SIC**: 1629  3259  Irrigation system construction; clay sewer & drainage pipe & tile

**(G-20885)**
**C & L TILING INC**
Timewell Drainage Products
196 Us24 1075n Ave  (62375)
**PHONE**..................217 773-3357
Don Colclasure, *President*
**EMP**: 100
**SALES (corp-wide)**: 65.6MM  **Privately Held**
**SIC**: 3272  Concrete products used to facilitate drainage
**PA**: C & L Tiling, Inc.
196 Us24 1075n Ave
Timewell IL 62375
217 773-3357

## Tinley Park
### Cook County

**(G-20886)**
**AERO RUBBER COMPANY INC**
8100 185th St  (60487-9201)
**PHONE**..................800 662-1009
John A Kasman, *President*
John Kuhn, *Marketing Staff*
Judy Kovicki, *Manager*
▲ **EMP**: 45
**SALES (est)**: 16.3MM  **Privately Held**
**WEB**: www.aerorubber.com
**SIC**: 3069  Molded rubber products; sheets, hard rubber; tubing, rubber

**(G-20887)**
**ALL-STYLE CUSTOM TOPS**
5555 175th St  (60477-3007)
**PHONE**..................708 532-6606
Tom Manzke, *Partner*
Ed Manzke, *Partner*
**EMP**: 3
**SQ FT**: 2,600
**SALES (est)**: 393.2K  **Privately Held**
**SIC**: 2541  Table or counter tops, plastic laminated

**(G-20888)**
**ALLSTATES RUBBER & TOOL CORP**
8201 183rd St Ste M  (60487-9752)
**PHONE**..................708 342-1030
**Fax**: 708 342-1033
Mike Burke, *President*
Bill Burke, *Vice Pres*
Harold Bleck, *Director*
William Burke, *Admin Sec*
▲ **EMP**: 10
**SQ FT**: 5,400
**SALES**: 1.9MM  **Privately Held**
**WEB**: www.allstatesrubber.com
**SIC**: 5085  5084  2822  Rubber goods, mechanical; materials handling machinery; synthetic rubber

**(G-20889)**
**ALLTEC GATES INC (PA)**
15941 Harlem Ave Ste 325  (60477-1609)
**PHONE**..................708 301-9361
**EMP**: 3  **EST**: 2011
**SALES (est)**: 384.7K  **Privately Held**
**SIC**: 3452  Gate hooks

**(G-20890)**
**AMERICAN GRAPHIC SYSTEMS INC**
7650 185th St Ste A  (60477-6290)
**PHONE**..................708 614-7007
**Fax**: 708 614-7272
Timothy Vernon, *President*
Larry Baker, *VP Opers*
Nelson Patrick, *Sales Mgr*
Rosemary Kuhns, *Office Mgr*
Mike Graphics, *Manager*
▲ **EMP**: 35
**SQ FT**: 50,000
**SALES (est)**: 4.4MM  **Privately Held**
**WEB**: www.americangraphicsystems.com
**SIC**: 2396  2759  Printing & embossing on plastics fabric articles; letterpress & screen printing; decals: printing

**(G-20891)**
**AMERICAS FOOD TECHNOLOGIES INC**
Also Called: Amfotek
7700 185th St  (60477-6770)
**PHONE**..................708 532-1222
**Fax**: 708 532-1221
Ellen Jordan Reidy, *President*
Wayne Kuhl, *Vice Pres*
Sheila Graphy, *Manager*
Sheila Graffy, *Teacher*
**EMP**: 42
**SALES (est)**: 14.8MM  **Privately Held**
**WEB**: www.amfotek.com
**SIC**: 2034  Fruit juices, dehydrated

**(G-20892)**
**AMEX NOOTER LLC (DH)**
18501 Maple Creek Dr  (60477-5122)
**PHONE**..................708 429-8300
**Fax**: 708 429-8320
Bernie Wicklein, *President*
Greg Harper, *Senior VP*
Jim Stalley, *Safety Dir*
Pat Vanier, *Project Mgr*
Dan Pullen, *Purch Mgr*
**EMP**: 1
**SALES (est)**: 4.8MM
**SALES (corp-wide)**: 754.1MM  **Privately Held**
**SIC**: 1541  3443  3479  Industrial buildings & warehouses; tanks, standard or custom fabricated: metal plate; etching & engraving
**HQ**: Nooter Construction Company
1500 S 2nd St
Saint Louis MO 63104
314 621-6000

**(G-20893)**
**ANCHOR ABRASIVES COMPANY**
7651 185th St  (60477-6267)
**PHONE**..................708 444-4300
**Fax**: 708 444-1300
John C Shoemaker, *President*
Frank Shoemaker, *Vice Pres*
Carl Manchester, *Sales Staff*
Scott Clegg, *Marketing Staff*
Susan Doyle, *Manager*
**EMP**: 45
**SALES (est)**: 12.5MM  **Privately Held**
**WEB**: www.anchorabrasives.com
**SIC**: 3291  Abrasive products

**(G-20894)**
**ANVIL INTERNATIONAL LLC**
7979 183rd St Ste D  (60477-5391)
**PHONE**..................708 534-1414
**Fax**: 708 535-5534
Hugh Brennan, *Vice Pres*
Dean Taylor, *Vice Pres*
James Glowacki, *Controller*
Kaytrina Henderson, *Accounting Mgr*
William Hertneky, *Human Resources*
**EMP**: 100
**SALES (corp-wide)**: 1.5B  **Privately Held**
**WEB**: www.anvilint.com
**SIC**: 3498  Fabricated pipe & fittings
**HQ**: Anvil International, Llc
2 Holland Way
Exeter NH 03833
603 418-2800

**(G-20895)**
**ATLAS PUTTY PRODUCTS CO**
8351 185th St  (60487-9282)
**PHONE**..................708 429-5858
**Fax**: 708 429-4280
David Payton, *President*
Jackie Bueschel, *COO*
Jack Payton, *Vice Pres*
Nancy Payton, *Vice Pres*
Tom Michalak, *Plant Mgr*
▲ **EMP**: 55  **EST**: 1947
**SQ FT**: 100,000
**SALES (est)**: 22.6MM  **Privately Held**
**WEB**: www.putty.com
**SIC**: 2851  4783  Putty, wood fillers & sealers; putty; wood fillers or sealers; packing & crating

# GEOGRAPHIC SECTION

**Tinley Park - Cook County (G-20923)**

**(G-20896)**
**BELLMAN-MELCOR HOLDINGS INC**
7575 183rd St (60477-6208)
PHONE.................................708 532-5000
Steven Campbell, *President*
Joy Ausec, *Agent*
▲ **EMP:** 14
**SALES (est):** 2.2MM **Privately Held**
**SIC:** 2819 Alkali metals: lithium, cesium, francium, rubidium

**(G-20897)**
**BENNETT TECHNOLOGIES INC**
6732 173rd St Ste 9 (60477-3498)
PHONE.................................708 389-9501
Fax: 708 389-9510
William J Bennett, *CEO*
Paul Bennett, *President*
Lynn Bennett, *Admin Sec*
**EMP:** 10
**SALES (est):** 870.9K **Privately Held**
**SIC:** 8072 3843 Crown & bridge production; dental equipment & supplies

**(G-20898)**
**BEST-TRONICS MFG INC**
18500 Graphic Ct (60477-6265)
PHONE.................................708 802-9677
Fax: 708 802-9676
Stanley F Bartosz, *President*
Kip Bartosz, *Vice Pres*
Terri Loekle, *Office Mgr*
Janet Vecchi, *Admin Sec*
▲ **EMP:** 150
**SQ FT:** 21,000
**SALES (est):** 27.9MM **Privately Held**
**WEB:** www.best-tronics.com
**SIC:** 3661 Telephones & telephone apparatus; data sets, telephone or telegraph

**(G-20899)**
**BLACK BOX CORPORATION**
9365 Windsor Pkwy (60487-7361)
PHONE.................................312 656-8807
John Toops, *Branch Mgr*
**EMP:** 11
**SALES (corp-wide):** 855.7MM **Publicly Held**
**WEB:** www.blackbox.com
**SIC:** 3577 Computer peripheral equipment
**PA:** Black Box Corporation
1000 Park Dr
Lawrence PA 15055
724 746-5500

**(G-20900)**
**BROKERS PRINT MAIL RSOURCE INC**
17732 Oak Park Ave (60477-3934)
PHONE.................................708 532-9900
Thomas Lewis, *President*
**EMP:** 3 **EST:** 2010
**SQ FT:** 1,000
**SALES:** 2.5MM **Privately Held**
**SIC:** 2752 Commercial printing, lithographic

**(G-20901)**
**BRYCO MACHINE INC**
8059 185th St (60487-9200)
PHONE.................................708 614-1900
Fax: 708 444-0102
Bryon Bettinardi, *President*
Dennis Gilhooley Jr, *Vice Pres*
Ed Rade, *QC Mgr*
Angela Zehner, *Human Resources*
Dan Schultz, *Manager*
▲ **EMP:** 38
**SQ FT:** 25,000
**SALES (est):** 6.8MM **Privately Held*
**WEB:** www.brycocnc.com
**SIC:** 3599 Machine shop, jobbing & repair

**(G-20902)**
**CONDOR LABELS INC**
7613 185th St (60477-6267)
PHONE.................................708 429-0707
Robert Biel, *President*
**EMP:** 2
**SQ FT:** 4,500
**SALES:** 275K **Privately Held**
**SIC:** 2759 2672 Flexographic printing; labels & seals: printing; coated & laminated paper

**(G-20903)**
**CORTUBE PRODUCTS CO**
18500 Spring Creek Dr (60477-6237)
PHONE.................................708 429-6700
Fax: 708 429-6747
Albert J Roth, *President*
Tom Roth, *Vice Pres*
▲ **EMP:** 8
**SQ FT:** 15,000
**SALES (est):** 760K **Privately Held**
**WEB:** www.cornhole-game.org
**SIC:** 3498 5074 3083 Tube fabricating (contract bending & shaping); plumbing & hydronic heating supplies; laminated plastics plate & sheet

**(G-20904)**
**CREATIVE CAKES LLC**
16649 Oak Park Ave Ste F (60477-1843)
PHONE.................................708 614-9755
Elizabeth Fahey,
Rebecca Palermo,
**EMP:** 22
**SQ FT:** 3,050
**SALES (est):** 1.2MM **Privately Held**
**SIC:** 2051 5812 Cakes, pies & pastries; caterers

**(G-20905)**
**CREATIVE PERKY CUISINE LLC**
6601 Martin France Cir (60477-6447)
PHONE.................................312 870-0282
Shay Atkins, *Principal*
**EMP:** 5
**SALES (est):** 363.9K **Privately Held**
**SIC:** 3275 Gypsum products

**(G-20906)**
**CROSSMARK PRINTING INC (PA)**
18400 76th Ave Ste A (60477-6222)
PHONE.................................708 532-8263
Martin F Ward, *President*
Andrea Sommer, *Manager*
Nancy R Ward, *Admin Sec*
**EMP:** 14
**SQ FT:** 2,400
**SALES (est):** 1.9MM **Privately Held**
**WEB:** www.ecrossmark.com
**SIC:** 2752 2796 2791 2789 Commercial printing, offset; platemaking services; typesetting; bookbinding & related work

**(G-20907)**
**CYPRESS MULTIGRAPHICS LLC (PA)**
Also Called: CM Associates
8500 185th St Ste A (60487-9346)
PHONE.................................708 633-1166
Fax: 708 633-1168
Raymond Gray, *General Mgr*
Roger Szafranski,
**EMP:** 20
**SQ FT:** 13,000
**SALES (est):** 6.6MM **Privately Held**
**SIC:** 3993 2672 2752 Name plates: except engraved, etched, etc.: metal; signs, not made in custom sign painting shops; labels (unprinted), gummed: made from purchased materials; decals, lithographed

**(G-20908)**
**D W RAM MANUFACTURING CO**
18530 Spring Creek Dr # 1 (60477-6244)
PHONE.................................708 633-7900
Fax: 708 633-7904
Douglas Murdaugh, *CEO*
Michael Kehrenbacher, *President*
Ken Pieper, *Manager*
**EMP:** 20
**SQ FT:** 30,000
**SALES (est):** 3.8MM **Privately Held**
**SIC:** 3663 3556 Radio & TV communications equipment; food products machinery

**(G-20909)**
**ED CO**
8304 Lilac Ln (60477-6574)
PHONE.................................708 614-0695
Ed Slechter, *Owner*
**EMP:** 20
**SALES (est):** 1.3MM **Privately Held**
**SIC:** 3663 Cable television equipment

**(G-20910)**
**EVEREADY WELDING SERVICE INC**
18111 Harlem Ave (60477-3608)
PHONE.................................708 532-2432
Robert Haavig Jr, *President*
Janet Haavig, *Vice Pres*
Robert Haavig Sr, *Treasurer*
**EMP:** 5
**SALES (est):** 670K **Privately Held**
**SIC:** 7692 Welding repair

**(G-20911)**
**EYELATION LLC**
18501 Maple Creek Dr # 400 (60477-5122)
PHONE.................................888 308-4703
Stephanie Guldan, *Opers Mgr*
Bradley Kirschner,
**EMP:** 12
**SALES (est):** 1.6MM
**SALES (corp-wide):** 1.9MM **Privately Held**
**SIC:** 5995 7372 Optical goods stores; prepackaged software
**PA:** Kirschner Optometric Assoc
2156 183rd St
Homewood IL 60430
708 957-7700

**(G-20912)**
**FAMILY EYE CARE**
17730 Oak Park Ave Ste B (60477-2065)
PHONE.................................708 614-2311
Dennis Gaeta, *Principal*
**EMP:** 3
**SALES (est):** 249.2K **Privately Held**
**SIC:** 3851 Eyeglasses, lenses & frames

**(G-20913)**
**FIRST STRING ENTERPRISES INC (PA)**
Also Called: Force Enterprises
18650 Graphic Ct (60477-6254)
PHONE.................................708 614-1200
Fax: 708 612-0200
Ronald A Strenge, *President*
Bruce A Nelson, *Vice Pres*
Joyce Strenge, *Admin Sec*
**EMP:** 20
**SQ FT:** 27,200
**SALES (est):** 3.2MM **Privately Held**
**WEB:** www.forcecent.com
**SIC:** 2759 2789 7331 Thermography; binding only: books, pamphlets, magazines, etc.; mailing service

**(G-20914)**
**FL WEST CORPORATION**
7610 162nd Pl (60477-1427)
PHONE.................................708 342-0500
Tom Sundling, *CEO*
**EMP:** 4
**SALES (est):** 280K **Privately Held**
**SIC:** 3799 Transportation equipment

**(G-20915)**
**FOUR-TECH INDUSTRIES CO**
18545 West Creek Dr (60477-6246)
PHONE.................................708 444-8230
Dariusz Fudala, *President*
**EMP:** 6
**SQ FT:** 3,000
**SALES (est):** 1.2MM **Privately Held**
**SIC:** 3599 Machine shop, jobbing & repair

**(G-20916)**
**FREDDIE BEAR SPORTS**
Also Called: Freddie Bear Sports.com
17250 Oak Park Ave (60477-3402)
PHONE.................................708 532-4133
Fax: 708 532-1141
Theodore Lutger, *Owner*
**EMP:** 12 **EST:** 1978
**SQ FT:** 4,000
**SALES (est):** 800K **Privately Held**
**WEB:** www.freddiebearsports.com
**SIC:** 5941 5961 2759 Sporting goods & bicycle shops; hunting equipment; fishing equipment; clothing, mail order (except women's); advertising literature: printing

**(G-20917)**
**GIRLYGIRL**
17037 Odell Ave (60477-2623)
PHONE.................................708 633-7290
Annette Paravich, *Owner*
**EMP:** 3
**SALES (est):** 117.5K **Privately Held**
**SIC:** 2399 Fabricated textile products

**(G-20918)**
**GLOBAL GENERAL CONTRACTORS LLC**
9018 Walnut Ln (60487-5250)
PHONE.................................708 663-0476
Bill Asmar,
Jose Morales,
**EMP:** 3
**SALES (est):** 166.8K **Privately Held**
**SIC:** 1521 1522 1542 1389 Single-family housing construction; condominium construction; commercial & office building, new construction; construction, repair & dismantling services; building construction consultant

**(G-20919)**
**GOODHEART-WILLCOX COMPANY INC (PA)**
Also Called: Goodheart Wilcox Publisher
18604 West Creek Dr (60477-6243)
PHONE.................................708 687-0315
Fax: 708 687-0315
John F Flanagan, *Ch of Bd*
Bob Cassel, *Editor*
Scott Gauthier, *Editor*
Paul Schreiner, *Editor*
Faith Zosky, *Editor*
**EMP:** 92 **EST:** 1972
**SQ FT:** 122,000
**SALES (est):** 14.1MM **Publicly Held**
**WEB:** www.g-w.com
**SIC:** 2731 Textbooks: publishing only, not printed on site

**(G-20920)**
**HARBOR MANUFACTURING INC**
8300 185th St (60487-9275)
PHONE.................................708 614-6400
John E Stratta, *President*
John G Stratta Sr, *Corp Secy*
Arnold Lorenzini, *Opers-Prdtn-Mfg*
**EMP:** 75
**SQ FT:** 85,000
**SALES (est):** 14.6MM **Privately Held**
**SIC:** 3599 7692 3544 Machine shop, jobbing & repair; welding repair; special dies, tools, jigs & fixtures

**(G-20921)**
**ILLIANA ORTHOPEDICS INC**
17378 Overhill Ave (60477-3269)
PHONE.................................708 532-0061
John Seibt Jr, *President*
Catherine Seibt, *Corp Secy*
**EMP:** 2
**SQ FT:** 1,200
**SALES:** 200K **Privately Held**
**SIC:** 3842 Limbs, artificial; braces, orthopedic

**(G-20922)**
**ILLINOIS TOOL WORKS INC**
Also Called: ITW
8402 183rd St Ste D (60487-9285)
PHONE.................................708 479-7200
Franco Cisternino, *Branch Mgr*
**EMP:** 5
**SALES (corp-wide):** 13.6B **Publicly Held**
**SIC:** 3089 3714 3544 Plastic hardware & building products; motor vehicle parts & accessories; special dies, tools, jigs & fixtures
**PA:** Illinois Tool Works Inc.
155 Harlem Ave
Glenview IL 60025
847 724-7500

**(G-20923)**
**IMAGE PACT PRINTING**
18650 Graphic Ct (60477-6254)
PHONE.................................708 460-6070
Bruce Nelson, *President*
Ronald S A Strenge, *Owner*
**EMP:** 20
**SALES (est):** 1.5MM **Privately Held**
**SIC:** 2752 Commercial printing, lithographic

# Tinley Park - Cook County (G-20924)    GEOGRAPHIC SECTION

### (G-20924)
**ITT WATER & WASTEWATER USA INC**
8402 W 183 Th Ste A (60477)
PHONE..............................708 342-0484
Michael Retter, *Branch Mgr*
**EMP**: 11 **Publicly Held**
WEB: www.flygtus.com
**SIC**: 5084 3561 3511 Industrial machinery & equipment; pumps & pumping equipment; turbines & turbine generator sets
HQ: Itt Water & Wastewater U.S.A., Inc.
   1 Greenwich Pl Ste 2
   Shelton CT 06484
   203 712-8999

### (G-20925)
**J&E STORM SERVICES INC**
17807 65th Ct (60477-4376)
PHONE..............................630 401-3793
Anthony Jones, *President*
Dina Humbert, *Vice Pres*
**EMP**: 2
**SQ FT**: 1,000
**SALES**: 350K **Privately Held**
**SIC**: 2431 Storm windows, wood

### (G-20926)
**JR LIGHTING DESIGN INC**
18464 West Creek Dr (60477-6273)
PHONE..............................708 460-6319
Jason Reberski, *President*
Denise Koziel, *CFO*
Justin Litterio, *Manager*
Kevin Rosenhagen, *Director*
Denise Reberski, *Admin Sec*
**EMP**: 2
**SALES (est)**: 300.1K **Privately Held**
**SIC**: 3648 Lighting fixtures, except electric: residential

### (G-20927)
**KVH INDUSTRIES INC**
8412 185th St (60487-9237)
PHONE..............................708 444-2800
**Fax**: 708 444-2801
Sid Bennett, *Vice Pres*
Jay Napoli, *Vice Pres*
Al Nobis, *Opers Mgr*
Jerry Lavery, *Senior Buyer*
John Bello, *Engineer*
**EMP**: 50
**SALES (corp-wide)**: 176.1MM **Publicly Held**
WEB: www.kvh.com
**SIC**: 3812 3663 Navigational systems & instruments; mobile communication equipment
PA: Kvh Industries, Inc.
   50 Enterprise Ctr
   Middletown RI 02842
   401 847-3327

### (G-20928)
**LAKE SARA PROPERTIES LLC**
8100 163rd St (60477-8215)
PHONE..............................708 267-1187
James Fernandes,
**EMP**: 2
**SALES (est)**: 203.3K **Privately Held**
**SIC**: 3599 Machine shop, jobbing & repair

### (G-20929)
**LAST MINUTE PRTG & COPY CTR**
Also Called: Last Minute Copy Shop
8201 183rd St Ste C (60487-9208)
PHONE..............................888 788-2965
Michiel D Burnett, *Principal*
**EMP**: 3
**SALES (est)**: 419.2K **Privately Held**
**SIC**: 7334 2759 Photocopying & duplicating services; commercial printing

### (G-20930)
**LEESONS CAKES INC**
6713 163rd Pl (60477-1717)
PHONE..............................708 429-1330
**Fax**: 708 429-1368
Scott Leeson, *President*
Nancy Leeson, *Vice Pres*
**EMP**: 3
**SALES (est)**: 50K **Privately Held**
WEB: www.leesonscakes.net
**SIC**: 5149 5461 2051 Bakery products; cakes; bread, cake & related products

### (G-20931)
**LIBERTY LITHOGRAPHERS INC**
Also Called: Liberty Graphics
18625 West Creek Dr (60477-6247)
PHONE..............................708 633-7450
**Fax**: 708 633-7449
Angela L Hipelius, *President*
Pauliano Pe, *Controller*
John Hipelius, *Sales Mgr*
Jake Egner, *Cust Mgr*
William Oconnell, *Marketing Mgr*
**EMP**: 108 **EST**: 1964
**SQ FT**: 13,000
**SALES (est)**: 32.7MM **Privately Held**
**SIC**: 2752 Commercial printing, offset

### (G-20932)
**MIDLAND PRODUCT LLC**
Also Called: Tilestar
18600 Graphic Ct (60477-6230)
PHONE..............................708 444-8200
Nancy Klinker, *Sales Associate*
John Roth, *Mng Member*
Phil Gariboldi,
**EMP**: 14
**SQ FT**: 23,000
**SALES**: 3.5MM **Privately Held**
**SIC**: 3999 Soap dispensers

### (G-20933)
**MIDWEST SUBURBAN PUBLISHING (DH)**
Also Called: News Marketer
6901 159th St Unit 2 (60477-1789)
PHONE..............................708 633-6880
**Fax**: 708 802-8021
Larry Kelly, *President*
Michael Waters, *Publisher*
John P Kern, *Vice Pres*
Julie Barrett, *Sales Mgr*
Rena Watson, *Info Tech Mgr*
▲ **EMP**: 520
**SALES (est)**: 22.8MM
**SALES (corp-wide)**: 304.8MM **Privately Held**
**SIC**: 2711 2752 2741 Commercial printing & newspaper publishing combined; publication printing, lithographic; miscellaneous publishing
HQ: Sun-Times Media Group, Inc.
   350 N Orleans St Fl 10
   Chicago IL 60654
   312 321-2299

### (G-20934)
**NELSON STUD WELDING INC**
18601 Graphic Ct (60477-6262)
PHONE..............................708 430-3770
**Fax**: 708 430-3975
Jake Fogle, *Sales Associate*
Don Sues, *Manager*
Bernie Durkin, *Physician Asst*
**EMP**: 6 **Privately Held**
**SIC**: 3452 Bolts, nuts, rivets & washers
HQ: Nelson Stud Welding, Inc.
   7900 W Ridge Rd
   Elyria OH 44035
   440 329-0400

### (G-20935)
**NUEVA VIDA PRODUCTIONS INC**
Also Called: Music Evolution
17531 70th Ct (60477-3809)
PHONE..............................708 444-8474
Antonio Delgado, *President*
**EMP**: 2
**SALES (est)**: 223.1K **Privately Held**
**SIC**: 3651 Household audio & video equipment

### (G-20936)
**P W C SPORTS**
Also Called: Kayacht
8200 185th St (60487-9232)
PHONE..............................708 516-6183
Paul Howey, *Owner*
Karen Howey, *Owner*
**EMP**: 5
**SALES (est)**: 332.7K **Privately Held**
**SIC**: 3732 5091 Kayaks, building & repairing; boats, canoes, watercrafts & equipment

### (G-20937)
**PANDUIT CORP (PA)**
18900 Panduit Dr (60487-3600)
PHONE..............................708 532-1800
**Fax**: 708 532-1811
Thomas C Donovan, *President*
Terry Lavigne, *General Mgr*
Mike Berg, *Business Mgr*
McConnell Chris, *Business Mgr*
Mark Acklin, *Vice Pres*
◆ **EMP**: 1100 **EST**: 1953
**SALES (est)**: 1B **Privately Held**
WEB: www.panduit.com
**SIC**: 3699 3644 5063 Electrical equipment & supplies; electric conduits & fittings; electrical apparatus & equipment

### (G-20938)
**PEORIA MANUFACTURING CO INC**
17620 Duvan Dr (60477-3698)
P.O. Box 338 (60477-0338)
PHONE..............................708 429-4200
**Fax**: 708 429-2124
Raymond Glassmeyer Jr, *President*
Matt Glassmeyer, *General Mgr*
Robert Glassmeyer, *Vice Pres*
Anne Keefe, *Vice Pres*
Barbara Glassmeyer, *Persnl Mgr*
**EMP**: 5 **EST**: 1952
**SQ FT**: 20,000
**SALES (est)**: 805.4K **Privately Held**
WEB: www.peoriamfg.com
**SIC**: 3599 Machine shop, jobbing & repair

### (G-20939)
**PROCESS PIPING INC**
18005 Semmler Dr (60487-8617)
PHONE..............................708 717-0513
Jenny Leblanc, *President*
**EMP**: 4
**SALES (est)**: 530.3K **Privately Held**
**SIC**: 3494 Pipe fittings

### (G-20940)
**PYRAMID**
9013 178th St (60487-6170)
PHONE..............................708 468-8140
**EMP**: 3
**SALES (est)**: 91K **Privately Held**
**SIC**: 2082 Malt beverages

### (G-20941)
**Q B F GRAPHIC GROUP**
18650 Graphic Ct (60477-6254)
PHONE..............................708 781-9580
**Fax**: 708 781-9733
Kenneth Larney Jr, *President*
Steve Scahill, *Sales Mgr*
Mary Lou Larney, *Admin Sec*
**EMP**: 9
**SQ FT**: 20,000
**SALES**: 1.7MM **Privately Held**
**SIC**: 2759 Advertising literature: printing

### (G-20942)
**QUALITY INTGRTED SOLUTIONS INC**
18521 Spring Creek Dr (60477-6202)
PHONE..............................815 464-4772
Ted Kowalczyk, *President*
Mike Montvidas, *Opers Mgr*
**EMP**: 8
**SALES (est)**: 1.1MM **Privately Held**
**SIC**: 1731 3699 5099 Closed circuit television installation; security devices; fire extinguishers

### (G-20943)
**ROBS AQUATICS**
17135 Harlem Ave (60477-3369)
PHONE..............................708 444-7627
**EMP**: 3
**SALES (est)**: 229.7K **Privately Held**
**SIC**: 3999 Pet supplies

### (G-20944)
**SIGNS TO YOU**
17121 Olcott Ave (60477-2635)
PHONE..............................708 429-6783
Jeremy Siegers, *Principal*
**EMP**: 2
**SALES (est)**: 205.9K **Privately Held**
**SIC**: 3993 Signs & advertising specialties

### (G-20945)
**SILK SCREEN EXPRESS INC**
7611 185th St (60477-6267)
PHONE..............................708 845-5600
Dawn Coleman, *President*
Corrinne Kosek, *Sls & Mktg Exec*
Julia Novak, *Manager*
**EMP**: 15
**SQ FT**: 15,000
**SALES (est)**: 4.3MM **Privately Held**
WEB: www.silkscreenx.com
**SIC**: 2321 Uniform shirts: made from purchased materials

### (G-20946)
**SOUTHTOWN STAR NEWSPAPERS**
18312 West Creek Dr (60477-6240)
PHONE..............................708 633-4800
**EMP**: 3 **EST**: 2014
**SALES (est)**: 17.1K **Privately Held**
**SIC**: 2711 Newspapers

### (G-20947)
**STROMBERG ALLEN AND COMPANY**
18504 West Creek Dr (60477-6242)
PHONE..............................773 847-7131
G William Kruchko, *President*
Peter Kruchko, *CFO*
Nicole Kelly, *Controller*
Gloria Olbera, *Info Tech Mgr*
Mary K Skoning, *Admin Sec*
▲ **EMP**: 43
**SQ FT**: 80,000
**SALES (est)**: 7.1MM **Privately Held**
WEB: www.strombergallen.com
**SIC**: 2752 2759 7389 Commercial printing, lithographic; letterpress printing; printers' services: folding, collating

### (G-20948)
**TIMKENSTEEL CORPORATION**
Also Called: Timkensteel Chicago Sales Off
18660 Graphic Dr Ste 202 (60477-6260)
PHONE..............................708 263-6868
Eric L Simms, *Senior Mgr*
**EMP**: 3
**SALES (corp-wide)**: 869.5MM **Publicly Held**
**SIC**: 3321 Gray & ductile iron foundries
PA: Timkensteel Corporation
   1835 Dueber Ave Sw
   Canton OH 44706
   330 471-7000

### (G-20949)
**TIN HLA HEALTH SVCS**
7809 Joliet Dr S (60477-4572)
PHONE..............................708 633-0426
Tin HLA, *Principal*
**EMP**: 4
**SALES (est)**: 307.6K **Privately Held**
**SIC**: 3356 Tin

### (G-20950)
**TOMANTRON INC**
17942 66th Ave (60477-4133)
PHONE..............................708 532-2456
Jiri Toman, *President*
**EMP**: 10
**SALES**: 840K **Privately Held**
WEB: www.tomantron.com
**SIC**: 3823 3625 3577 Digital displays of process variables; relays & industrial controls; computer peripheral equipment

### (G-20951)
**TRANE US INC**
18452 West Creek Dr (60477-6273)
PHONE..............................708 532-8004
Manny Guerrero, *Branch Mgr*
**EMP**: 3 **Privately Held**
**SIC**: 3585 Refrigeration & heating equipment
HQ: Trane U.S. Inc.
   1 Centennial Ave Ste 101
   Piscataway NJ 08854
   732 652-7100

▲ = Import ▼=Export
◆ =Import/Export

**(G-20952)**
**U S RAILWAY SERVICES**
8201 183rd St Ste C  (60487-9208)
P.O. Box 1125  (60477-7925)
**PHONE**.................................708 468-8343
James J Provencher, *Principal*
**EMP:** 6 **EST:** 2012
**SALES (est):** 970.9K  **Privately Held**
**SIC:** 4011  3531  Interurban railways; railway track equipment

**(G-20953)**
**UGN  INC (HQ)**
18410 Crossing Dr Ste C  (60487-6209)
**PHONE**.................................773 437-2400
Peter Anthony, *President*
Randy Khalaf, *COO*
Darrell Cook, *Vice Pres*
Esther Jones, *Vice Pres*
Nicolas Leclercq, *Vice Pres*
▲ **EMP:** 91
**SQ FT:** 28,000
**SALES (est):** 401.9MM
**SALES (corp-wide):** 2.1B  **Privately Held**
**WEB:** www.ugn.com
**SIC:** 3714  Motor vehicle parts & accessories
**PA:** Autoneum Holding Ag
    Schlosstalstrasse 43
    Winterthur ZH
    522 448-282

**(G-20954)**
**US MINERALS  INC (PA)**
18635 West Creek Dr Ste 2  (60477-6224)
P.O. Box 547, Anaconda MT  (59711-0547)
**PHONE**.................................219 864-0909
Fred Vukas, *President*
Dale Yogan, *Corp Secy*
Jason Vukas, *Vice Pres*
Snezana Novakovic, *Manager*
Jean McMullin, *Admin Asst*
▲ **EMP:** 10
**SALES (est):** 34.6MM  **Privately Held**
**SIC:** 3291  Abrasive products

**(G-20955)**
**V2 FLOW CONTROLS  LLC**
8608 Tullamore Dr  (60487-4499)
**PHONE**.................................708 945-9331
Sheri Reiplinger, *Vice Pres*
Cory Drews, *VP Sales*
**EMP:** 5
**SALES (est):** 420K  **Privately Held**
**WEB:** www.v2environmentalservices.com
**SIC:** 3823  Primary elements for process flow measurement

**(G-20956)**
**WYMAN AND COMPANY**
17324 Oak Park Ave  (60477-3404)
**PHONE**.................................708 532-9064
Kathy Wyman, *Owner*
**EMP:** 3
**SALES (est):** 130K  **Privately Held**
**SIC:** 2499  Picture frame molding, finished

**(G-20957)**
**X-CEL TECHNOLOGIES  INC**
7800 Graphic Dr  (60477-6266)
**PHONE**.................................708 802-7400
**Fax:** 708 802-7401
Robert J Bettinardi, *President*
Mike Crockett, *Sales Staff*
John Geimer, *Sales Staff*
Stacy Scherer, *Office Mgr*
Terese Mueller, *Manager*
▲ **EMP:** 30
**SQ FT:** 30,000
**SALES (est):** 6.7MM  **Privately Held**
**WEB:** www.bettinardi.com
**SIC:** 3599  Custom machinery; machine shop, jobbing & repair

### Tiskilwa
*Bureau County*

**(G-20958)**
**BUREAU VALLEY CHIEF**
108 W Main St  (61368-9652)
P.O. Box 476  (61368-0476)
**PHONE**.................................815 646-4731
**Fax:** 815 646-4376
John Murphy, *Owner*
Ginger Murphy, *Co-Owner*
**EMP:** 3
**SQ FT:** 1,790
**SALES:** 100K  **Privately Held**
**SIC:** 2711  2752  5994  Newspapers: publishing only, not printed on site; commercial printing, offset; news dealers & newsstands

**(G-20959)**
**HYDROTEC SYSTEMS COMPANY INC (PA)**
Also Called: H2o Mobil
145 E Main St  (61368-9659)
P.O. Box 61  (61368-0061)
**PHONE**.................................815 624-6644
**Fax:** 815 624-6644
Warren Searles, *President*
Doreen Searles, *Treasurer*
**EMP:** 3
**SQ FT:** 15,000
**SALES:** 500K  **Privately Held**
**SIC:** 3589  8742  Water treatment equipment, industrial; automation & robotics consultant

**(G-20960)**
**VESTAS-AMERICAN WIND TECH INC**
Also Called: Nestus American Wind Tech
6250 Rte 1475  (61368)
**PHONE**.................................815 646-4280
Dean Waldinger, *Manager*
**EMP:** 8
**SALES (corp-wide):** 10.8B  **Privately Held**
**SIC:** 3621  Windmills, electric generating
**HQ:** Vestas-American Wind Technology, Inc.
    1417 Nw Everett St
    Portland OR 97209
    503 327-2000

### Toledo
*Cumberland County*

**(G-20961)**
**BAG AND BARRIER CORPORATION**
505 E Rte 121  (62468)
P.O. Box 129  (62468-0129)
**PHONE**.................................217 849-3271
**Fax:** 217 849-3281
Timothy Olmstead, *President*
Sandy Olmstead, *Corp Secy*
**EMP:** 4 **EST:** 1951
**SQ FT:** 10,000
**SALES (est):** 349.9K  **Privately Held**
**WEB:** www.bagbarriercorp.com
**SIC:** 5632  2674  2673  Handbags; paper bags: made from purchased materials; bags: plastic, laminated & coated

**(G-20962)**
**ERVIN EQUIPMENTS (HQ)**
608 N Ohio St  (62468-1127)
P.O. Box 306  (62468-0306)
**PHONE**.................................217 849-3125
Greg Ervin, *CEO*
**EMP:** 2
**SALES (est):** 323K
**SALES (corp-wide):** 50.4MM  **Privately Held**
**SIC:** 3799  Trailers & trailer equipment
**PA:** Ervin Equipment Inc.
    608 N Ohio St
    Toledo IL 62468
    217 849-5262

**(G-20963)**
**GENTRY SMALL ENGINE REPAIR**
124 Court House Sq  (62468)
P.O. Box 269  (62468-0269)
**PHONE**.................................217 849-3378
**Fax:** 217 849-2587
Mike Gentry, *Partner*
Julie Gentry, *Partner*
**EMP:** 3
**SALES:** 250K  **Privately Held**
**SIC:** 7699  5261  3546  Engine repair & replacement, non-automotive; lawn & garden equipment; saws & sawing equipment

**(G-20964)**
**HIGH POINT RECOVERY COMPANY**
603 County Road 500 E  (62468-4042)
**PHONE**.................................217 821-7777
Irvin Figgins Jr, *President*
**EMP:** 4
**SALES (est):** 295.1K  **Privately Held**
**SIC:** 3531  Automobile wrecker hoists

**(G-20965)**
**SCHROCK CUSTOM WOODWORKING**
705 Industrial Dr  (62468-4236)
P.O. Box 249  (62468-0249)
**PHONE**.................................217 849-3375
**Fax:** 217 849-3089
Jeffrey Schrock, *President*
**EMP:** 6
**SALES (est):** 760.4K  **Privately Held**
**SIC:** 2434  2541  Wood kitchen cabinets; store fixtures, wood

**(G-20966)**
**SOUTH CENTRAL FS  INC**
403 E Madison St  (62468-1113)
**PHONE**.................................217 849-2242
**Fax:** 217 849-2241
Jim Meinhart, *Sales Staff*
Bellmark Markwell, *Manager*
**EMP:** 10
**SALES (corp-wide):** 118.3MM  **Privately Held**
**SIC:** 2875  5191  5172  5153  Fertilizers, mixing only; fertilizer & fertilizer materials; feed; seeds: field, garden & flower; petroleum brokers; grain elevators
**PA:** South Central Fs, Inc.
    405 S Banker St
    Effingham IL 62401
    217 342-9231

**(G-20967)**
**TOLEDO DEMOCRAT**
116 Court House Sq  (62468)
**PHONE**.................................217 849-2000
Billie Chambers, *Partner*
Wes Chambers, *Partner*
**EMP:** 3 **EST:** 1926
**SALES (est):** 254.9K  **Privately Held**
**SIC:** 2711  2791  2759  2752  Job printing & newspaper publishing combined; commercial printing & newspaper publishing combined; typesetting; commercial printing; commercial printing, lithographic

**(G-20968)**
**TOLEDO MACHINE & WELDING INC**
607 E Illinois Rt 121  (62468)
P.O. Box 84  (62468-0084)
**PHONE**.................................217 849-2251
Chuck Pruemer, *President*
**EMP:** 3
**SALES (est):** 390.4K  **Privately Held**
**SIC:** 7692  Welding repair

**(G-20969)**
**TSC PYROFERRIC INTERNATIONAL (PA)**
Also Called: TSC Ferrite International
507 E Madison  (62468)
**PHONE**.................................217 849-2230
Tim Smith, *President*
Tempel Smith, *Chairman*
▲ **EMP:** 110
**SQ FT:** 30,000
**SALES (est):** 11.1MM  **Privately Held**
**WEB:** www.tscinternational.com
**SIC:** 3264  3356  Ferrite & ferrite parts; nickel & nickel alloy: rolling, drawing or extruding

**(G-20970)**
**WARNER  HARVEY LEE FARM INC**
Also Called: Warner Farms
556 County Road 800 E  (62468-4031)
**PHONE**.................................217 849-2548
Harvey Lee Warner, *Owner*
**EMP:** 3
**SALES (est):** 109.1K  **Privately Held**
**SIC:** 2083  0191  Corn malt; general farms, primarily crop

### Tolono
*Champaign County*

**(G-20971)**
**ILLINOIS FOUNDATION SEEDS INC**
1178 County Road 900 N  (61880-9624)
**PHONE**.................................217 485-6420
**Fax:** 217 485-3867
Dave Deutscher, *Branch Mgr*
Lowell Behrens, *Manager*
Kory Maughan, *Manager*
**EMP:** 14
**SALES (corp-wide):** 20MM  **Privately Held**
**WEB:** www.ifsi.com
**SIC:** 2068  5191  8731  0723  Seeds: dried, dehydrated, salted or roasted; seeds: field, garden & flower; commercial physical research; crop preparation services for market
**PA:** Illinois Foundation Seeds Inc
    1083 County Road 900 N
    Tolono IL
    217 485-6260

### Toluca
*Marshall County*

**(G-20972)**
**AJINOMOTO WINDSOR  INC**
301 W 3rd St  (61369-9686)
**PHONE**.................................815 452-2361
**EMP:** 216
**SALES (corp-wide):** 270.8MM  **Privately Held**
**SIC:** 2038  Frozen specialties
**HQ:** Windsor Ajinomoto Inc
    4200 Concours Ste 100
    Ontario CA 91764
    909 477-4700

### Tonica
*Lasalle County*

**(G-20973)**
**DAUBER COMPANY  INC**
577 N 18tth Rd Tth  (61370)
**PHONE**.................................815 442-3569
**Fax:** 815 442-3669
Eric Dauber, *President*
William Dauber, *President*
Gayle Dauber, *Vice Pres*
Ken Miller, *Safety Dir*
Cindy Dauber, *Manager*
▲ **EMP:** 23
**SQ FT:** 1,800
**SALES (est):** 10.7MM  **Privately Held**
**WEB:** www.daubercompany.com
**SIC:** 3674  2819  3295  Silicon wafers, chemically doped; industrial inorganic chemicals; minerals, ground or treated

**(G-20974)**
**ILLINOIS VALLEY MINERALS LLC**
575 N 18th Rd  (61370-9423)
P.O. Box 376, Hennepin  (61327-0376)
**PHONE**.................................815 442-8402
Eric E Dauber, *CEO*
Bill Johnson,
John Redshaw,
**EMP:** 7
**SQ FT:** 30,000
**SALES (est):** 621.2K  **Privately Held**
**SIC:** 1481  Nonmetallic mineral services

**(G-20975)**
**TONICA NEWS**
Also Called: Putnam Co Records
242 S Lasalle St  (61370)
**PHONE**.................................815 442-8419

Elin Arnold, *CEO*
EMP: 8
SALES (est): 424K
SALES (corp-wide): 559K **Privately Held**
SIC: 2711 Newspapers
PA: Putnam County Record
325 S Mccoy St
Granville IL

## Toulon
### Stark County

**(G-20976)**
**BRYTON TECHNOLOGY INC (PA)**
3134 State Route 78 (61483-9150)
P.O. Box 300 (61483-0300)
PHONE...................309 995-3379
Rebecca Ptashnik, *President*
David Heinz, *President*
Rick McGhee, *Exec VP*
Wynne Johnson, *Sales Dir*
EMP: 40
SQ FT: 21,000
SALES (est): 7.5MM **Privately Held**
WEB: www.brytoninc.com
SIC: 3679 Harness assemblies for electronic use: wire or cable

**(G-20977)**
**STARK COUNTY COMMUNICATIONS**
101 W Main St (61483-5229)
P.O. Box 240 (61483-0240)
PHONE...................309 286-4444
Jim Nowlan, *President*
EMP: 6
SALES (est): 440K **Privately Held**
WEB: www.countyenews.com
SIC: 2711 Newspapers, publishing & printing

## Towanda
### Mclean County

**(G-20978)**
**ALEXANDER MANUFACTURING CO**
500 Lincoln St (61776)
PHONE...................309 728-2224
Fax: 309 728-2227
Shelley Bryant, *Prdtn Mgr*
Marilyn Beard, *Human Res Dir*
Jeff Wilkerson, *Branch Mgr*
Paul Nitzke, *Manager*
EMP: 75
SALES (corp-wide): 12MM **Privately Held**
WEB: www.alexandermc.com
SIC: 3993 3952 3951 Signs & advertising specialties; lead pencils & art goods; pens & mechanical pencils
PA: Alexander Manufacturing Company
1283 Research Blvd
Saint Louis MO 63132
314 692-7030

**(G-20979)**
**WINDY HILL WOODWORKING INC**
4 Candle Ridge Rd (61776-7514)
PHONE...................309 275-2415
Jayson Hines, *President*
Barbara Welch, *Vice Pres*
EMP: 3
SALES: 150K **Privately Held**
SIC: 2541 Cabinets, except refrigerated: show, display, etc.: wood

## Tower Hill
### Shelby County

**(G-20980)**
**REALT IMAGES INC**
Also Called: R I Plastics
172 Williamsburg Hl A (62571)
PHONE...................217 567-3487
Fax: 217 567-3212
Alan L Thompson, *President*
Barry Thompson, *Vice Pres*
EMP: 9
SQ FT: 6,000
SALES: 300K **Privately Held**
WEB: www.riplastics.com
SIC: 3081 3993 Plastic film & sheet; signs & advertising specialties

## Tremont
### Tazewell County

**(G-20981)**
**CULLINAN & SONS INC (PA)**
Also Called: Rowe Construction Div
121 W Park St (61568-7520)
P.O. Box 166 (61568-0166)
PHONE...................309 925-2711
Fax: 309 925-7131
Michael N Cullinan, *Ch of Bd*
Stephen Cullinan, *Principal*
Elizabeth Mathers, *Principal*
Ronald L Olson, *Treasurer*
John G Moser, *Admin Sec*
EMP: 40 EST: 1914
SQ FT: 3,500
SALES (est): 16.3MM **Privately Held**
WEB: www.rivercitysupply.biz
SIC: 1611 2951 1752 1731 Highway & street construction; asphalt paving mixtures & blocks; floor laying & floor work; electrical work; water, sewer & utility lines; construction sand & gravel

**(G-20982)**
**G T SERVICES OF ILLIONOIS INC**
Also Called: Gt Business Services
22387 State Route 9 (61568-9102)
PHONE...................309 925-5111
Greg Mills, *President*
Tammy Mills, *Vice Pres*
EMP: 6
SQ FT: 4,000
SALES (est): 220K **Privately Held**
WEB: www.gtbs.net
SIC: 2752 7336 Commercial printing, lithographic; commercial art & graphic design

**(G-20983)**
**K R J INC**
Also Called: Litwiller Machine and Supply
101 S West St (61568-7518)
P.O. Box 1404 (61568-1404)
PHONE...................309 925-5123
Kenneth Ropp, *President*
Joyce Ropp, *Corp Secy*
EMP: 3
SALES (est): 250K **Privately Held**
SIC: 3599 1731 Machine shop, jobbing & repair; general electrical contractor

**(G-20984)**
**MATHIS ENERGY LLC**
701 E Pearl St (61568-7507)
P.O. Box 102 (61568-0102)
PHONE...................309 925-3177
Danivan L Mathis,
EMP: 2
SALES (est): 227.8K **Privately Held**
SIC: 3568 Couplings, shaft: rigid, flexible, universal joint, etc.

**(G-20985)**
**RED NOSE INC**
Also Called: Adventure Sports Outdoors
1408 Downing Ct (61568-9768)
PHONE...................309 925-7313
Harry Canterbury, *President*
EMP: 2
SALES: 275K **Privately Held**
SIC: 2711 Newspapers

**(G-20986)**
**TREKON COMPANY INC**
115 E South St (61568-7919)
P.O. Box 1126 (61568-1126)
PHONE...................309 925-7942
Fax: 309 925-5227
Steve Gunter, *President*
Greg Gunter, *Vice Pres*
Jim Lonergan, *Production*
Denny Wresinski, *Marketing Mgr*
Cynthia Springer, *Admin Sec*
EMP: 8
SQ FT: 30,000
SALES (est): 1.6MM **Privately Held**
SIC: 2677 Envelopes

**(G-20987)**
**TREMONT KITCHEN TOPS INC**
100 N West St (61568-7982)
P.O. Box 1402 (61568-1402)
PHONE...................309 925-5736
Sheila Robbins, *President*
Jeff Graves, *Vice Pres*
EMP: 5
SALES (est): 200K **Privately Held**
SIC: 2541 Counter & sink tops

**(G-20988)**
**TREND SETTERS LTD**
22500 State Route 9 (61568-9156)
PHONE...................309 929-7012
Joellyn Jablonski, *President*
EMP: 15 EST: 1989
SQ FT: 16,000
SALES (est): 1.2MM **Privately Held**
SIC: 3861 7384 Printing frames, photographic; photofinishing laboratory

## Trenton
### Clinton County

**(G-20989)**
**BAER HEATING & COOLING INC**
11974 Old Us Highway 50 (62293-2046)
P.O. Box 21 (62293-0021)
PHONE...................618 224-7344
Randall S Baer, *President*
Laura Tomerlin, *Manager*
EMP: 8
SQ FT: 2,000
SALES (est): 2.1MM **Privately Held**
SIC: 3585 Parts for heating, cooling & refrigerating equipment

**(G-20990)**
**COUNTY ASPHALT INC**
427 S Madison St (62293-1143)
PHONE...................618 224-9033
Dawn Gruender, *President*
Bart Gruender, *Treasurer*
EMP: 3
SALES (est): 234K **Privately Held**
SIC: 2951 Asphalt paving mixtures & blocks

**(G-20991)**
**EAST WISCONSIN LLC**
Also Called: Art Classics Ltd
11 E Wisconsin St (62293-1403)
PHONE...................618 224-9133
Patricia R Schmidt, *Mng Member*
John Schmidt, *Administration*
John E Schmidt,
Ryan P Schmidt,
▲ EMP: 25
SQ FT: 40,000
SALES: 3MM **Privately Held**
WEB: www.artclassicsltd.com
SIC: 2741 Art copy & poster publishing

**(G-20992)**
**K & D COUNTER TOPS INC (PA)**
102 N Lincoln St (62293-1082)
P.O. Box 1007 (62293-0207)
PHONE...................618 224-9630
Fax: 618 224-9632
John Daiber, *President*
David Kapp, *Vice Pres*
Troy Kapp, *Business Dir*
EMP: 44
SQ FT: 10,000
SALES (est): 6.6MM **Privately Held**
WEB: www.kdtops.com
SIC: 2541 Counter & sink tops

**(G-20993)**
**KMK METAL FABRICATORS INC**
Also Called: K M K
408 E Broadway (62293-1608)
PHONE...................618 224-2000
Kirk Kassel, *President*
Kraig Kassel, *Vice Pres*
David Mollett, *Vice Pres*
Kim Jackson, *Purch Agent*
Mike Wetzell, *Engineer*
EMP: 32
SQ FT: 100,000
SALES (est): 10.1MM **Privately Held**
SIC: 3441 Fabricated structural metal

**(G-20994)**
**KUNZ CARPENTRY (PA)**
16 E Broadway (62293-1302)
PHONE...................618 224-7892
Fax: 618 224-9887
Frank Kunz, *Owner*
Doris Hortsmann, *Manager*
Cara Schuette, *Manager*
EMP: 8
SQ FT: 700
SALES (est): 1MM **Privately Held**
WEB: www.kunzcarpentry.com
SIC: 5712 2511 2434 Furniture stores; wood household furniture; vanities, bathroom: wood

**(G-20995)**
**PACKAGING CORPORATION AMERICA**
11620 Old Us Highway 50 (62293-2047)
PHONE...................618 934-3100
EMP: 3
SALES (corp-wide): 5.7B **Publicly Held**
SIC: 2653 Corrugated & solid fiber boxes
PA: Packaging Corporation Of America
1955 W Field Ct
Lake Forest IL 60045
847 482-3000

**(G-20996)**
**PACTIV LLC**
11620 Hwy 50 (62293)
P.O. Box 126 (62293-0126)
PHONE...................618 934-4311
James J Siegel, *Opers-Prdtn-Mfg*
Rick Langhauser, *Purchasing*
EMP: 80 **Privately Held**
WEB: www.pactiv.com
SIC: 2679 Honeycomb core & board: made from purchased material
HQ: Pactiv Llc
1900 W Field Ct
Lake Forest IL 60045
847 482-2000

**(G-20997)**
**PREGIS LLC**
11620 Old Us Highway 50 (62293-2047)
PHONE...................618 934-4311
Michael McDonnell, *Principal*
Jim Siegel, *Manager*
EMP: 65
SALES (corp-wide): 5.6B **Privately Held**
SIC: 2671 Paper coated or laminated for packaging
HQ: Pregis Llc
1650 Lake Cook Rd Ste 400
Deerfield IL 60015
847 597-9330

**(G-20998)**
**TRENTON SUN**
15 W Broadway (62293-1303)
P.O. Box 118 (62293-0118)
PHONE...................618 224-9422
Fax: 618 224-9422
Michael Conley, *Owner*
Sybil Conley, *Co-Owner*
EMP: 4 EST: 1880
SQ FT: 3,000
SALES: 75K **Privately Held**
WEB: www.trentonsun.com
SIC: 2711 2791 2752 Commercial printing & newspaper publishing combined; typesetting; commercial printing, lithographic

## Trivoli
### Peoria County

**(G-20999)**
**FRAME MATERIAL SUPPLY INC**
Also Called: Fms
520 N Trivoli Rd (61569-9701)
P.O. Box 133 (61569-0133)
PHONE...................309 362-2323

Fax: 309 362-2343
Bradley Stevens, *President*
Mary Stevens, *Admin Sec*
**EMP:** 2
**SQ FT:** 17,500
**SALES (est):** 356.5K **Privately Held**
**SIC:** 3547 Steel rolling machinery

**(G-21000)**
**MIDLAND COAL COMPANY**
2203 N Trivoli Rd (61569-9542)
**PHONE** .................. 309 362-2795
Philip Christy, *Manager*
**EMP:** 1
**SALES:** 250K **Privately Held**
**SIC:** 0191 1031 0115 0116 General farms, primarily crop; lead & zinc ores; corn; soybeans

## Trout Valley
### Mchenry County

**(G-21001)**
**POLITECH INC**
108 Turkey Run Rd (60013-2455)
**PHONE** .................. 847 516-2717
Peter Politeki, *President*
**EMP:** 5
**SALES (est):** 430K **Privately Held**
**WEB:** www.politech.com
**SIC:** 7372 Prepackaged software

## Troy
### Madison County

**(G-21002)**
**ADVANTEX INC**
326 Bargraves Blvd (62294-2304)
**PHONE** .................. 618 505-0701
**Fax:** 618 288-6431
Gregory Byers, *Owner*
**EMP:** 5
**SALES (est):** 569.5K **Privately Held**
**SIC:** 2299 Textile goods

**(G-21003)**
**CCO HOLDINGS LLC**
523 Troy Plz (62294-1349)
**PHONE** .................. 618 505-3505
**EMP:** 3
**SALES (corp-wide):** 29B **Publicly Held**
**SIC:** 5064 4841 3663 3651 Electrical appliances, television & radio; cable & other pay television services; radio & TV communications equipment; household audio & video equipment
**HQ:** Cco Holdings, Llc
400 Atlantic St
Stamford CT 06901
203 905-7801

**(G-21004)**
**COOPER B-LINE INC**
816 Lions Dr (62294-2440)
**PHONE** .................. 618 667-6779
**Fax:** 618 667-7896
Sarah Kalmer, *QC Mgr*
Erik Hanson, *Branch Mgr*
Chuck Nellis, *Maintence Staff*
**EMP:** 14 **Privately Held**
**WEB:** www.cooperbline.com
**SIC:** 3643 Current-carrying wiring devices
**HQ:** Cooper B-Line , Inc.
509 W Monroe St
Highland IL 62249
618 654-2184

**(G-21005)**
**CUSTOM FOAM WORKS INC**
31 Sequoia Dr (62294-3226)
**PHONE** .................. 618 920-2810
Dane Tippett, *President*
**EMP:** 8
**SALES (est):** 740K **Privately Held**
**WEB:** www.customfoamworks.com
**SIC:** 3086 Plastics foam products

**(G-21006)**
**EATON HYDRAULICS LLC**
816 Lions Dr (62294-2440)
**PHONE** .................. 618 667-2553

**EMP:** 4 **Privately Held**
**SIC:** 3625 Motor controls & accessories
**HQ:** Eaton Hydraulics Llc
14615 Lone Oak Rd
Eden Prairie MN 55344
952 937-9800

**(G-21007)**
**HICKORY STREET CABINETS**
208 S Hickory St (62294-1626)
**PHONE** .................. 618 667-9676
Jon Dillard, *Owner*
Steve Hein, *Manager*
**EMP:** 2
**SQ FT:** 3,800
**SALES:** 350K **Privately Held**
**SIC:** 5712 2541 5211 2434 Cabinet work, custom; wood partitions & fixtures; cabinets, kitchen; wood kitchen cabinets

**(G-21008)**
**HILLING SERVICES INC**
Also Called: Blind Quest
546 Troy Ofallon Rd (62294-2930)
**PHONE** .................. 618 667-2005
Lindell Hilling, *President*
**EMP:** 4
**SALES:** 750K **Privately Held**
**WEB:** www.hillingdonhomes.ltd.uk
**SIC:** 2431 Blinds (shutters), wood

**(G-21009)**
**JUST ANOTHER BUTTON**
116 W Market St (62294-1412)
**PHONE** .................. 618 667-8531
**Fax:** 618 667-8504
Cecile McPeak, *Partner*
Patti Connor, *Partner*
**EMP:** 13 **EST:** 1996
**SALES (est):** 1.6MM **Privately Held**
**WEB:** www.justanotherbuttoncompany.com
**SIC:** 3965 Buttons & parts

**(G-21010)**
**NEWSPRINT INK INC**
Also Called: Times-Tribune
201 E Market St Stop 6 (62294-1518)
P.O. Box 68 (62294-0068)
**PHONE** .................. 618 667-3111
**Fax:** 618 667-3128
Leonard Suess, *President*
Paul Ping, *Corp Secy*
Ewald Hoffman, *Vice Pres*
**EMP:** 10
**SQ FT:** 2,000
**SALES (est):** 573.7K **Privately Held**
**SIC:** 2711 Newspapers: publishing only, not printed on site

**(G-21011)**
**R L ALLEN INDUSTRIES**
Also Called: National Peace Officers' Press
120 Collinsville Rd Ofc (62294-1396)
**PHONE** .................. 618 667-2544
Terry Allen, *President*
Eva Allen, *Vice Pres*
**EMP:** 2
**SQ FT:** 8,000
**SALES (est):** 252.8K **Privately Held**
**SIC:** 2759 8399 3999 2741 Promotional printing; fund raising organization, non-fee basis; identification plates; miscellaneous publishing

## Troy Grove
### Lasalle County

**(G-21012)**
**FAIRMOUNT SANTROL INC**
Also Called: Technisand
300 Vermillion St (61372)
P.O. Box 50 (61372-0050)
**PHONE** .................. 815 538-2645
**Fax:** 815 539-6159
George Oak, *Branch Mgr*
Mary Kibilka, *Manager*
**EMP:** 26
**SALES (corp-wide):** 535MM **Publicly Held**
**WEB:** www.fairmountminerals.com
**SIC:** 1442 Construction sand & gravel

**HQ:** Fairmount Santrol Inc.
8834 Mayfield Rd Ste A
Chesterland OH 44026
440 214-3200

**(G-21013)**
**UNIMIN CORPORATION**
S Peru St (61372)
P.O. Box 110 (61372-0110)
**PHONE** .................. 815 539-6734
**Fax:** 815 538-4186
Scott Atkins, *Opers-Prdtn-Mfg*
**EMP:** 5
**SALES (corp-wide):** 117.6MM **Privately Held**
**WEB:** www.unimin.com
**SIC:** 1446 Silica sand mining
**HQ:** Unimin Corporation
258 Elm St
New Canaan CT 06840
203 966-8880

## Tuscola
### Douglas County

**(G-21014)**
**ALLOY TECH**
608 E Pinzon St (61953-1952)
**PHONE** .................. 217 253-3939
Ron D Clapp, *Owner*
**EMP:** 3
**SQ FT:** 1,000
**SALES:** 200K **Privately Held**
**SIC:** 3714 Motor vehicle engines & parts

**(G-21015)**
**AMISH COUNTRY HEIRLOOMS LLC**
1304 Tuscola Blvd Unit 14 (61953-2078)
P.O. Box 51, Arthur (61911-0051)
**PHONE** .................. 217 253-9200
Karen K Gingerich,
Karen Gingerich, *Admin Sec*
**EMP:** 2
**SALES (est):** 228K **Privately Held**
**SIC:** 2511 Wood household furniture

**(G-21016)**
**BEAR CREEK TRUSS INC**
615 N County Road 250 E (61953-7037)
**PHONE** .................. 217 543-3329
**Fax:** 217 543-3124
Dave Rocke, *President*
Andrew Gingerich, *Vice Pres*
**EMP:** 40
**SQ FT:** 8,640
**SALES (est):** 6.2MM **Privately Held**
**WEB:** www.bearcreektruss.com
**SIC:** 2439 Trusses, wooden roof

**(G-21017)**
**CABOT CORPORATION**
700 E Us Highway 36 (61953-7520)
**PHONE** .................. 217 253-3370
Daniel Gilliland, *Marketing Staff*
Georgia Wilkinson, *Marketing Staff*
David Kaul, *Branch Mgr*
Ken Koehler, *Director*
**EMP:** 180
**SALES (corp-wide):** 2.4B **Publicly Held**
**WEB:** www.cabot-corp.com
**SIC:** 2819 Industrial inorganic chemicals
**PA:** Cabot Corporation
2 Seaport Ln Ste 1300
Boston MA 02210
617 345-0100

**(G-21018)**
**CABOT CORPORATION**
700 E Us Highway 36 (61953-7520)
P.O. Box 307, Waverly WV (26184)
**PHONE** .................. 217 253-5752
Raj Ahuja, *Manager*
James Rowe, *Director*
**EMP:** 53
**SALES (corp-wide):** 2.4B **Publicly Held**
**WEB:** www.cabot-corp.com
**SIC:** 2895 3624 2899 Carbon black; carbon & graphite products; chemical preparations

**PA:** Cabot Corporation
2 Seaport Ln Ste 1300
Boston MA 02210
617 345-0100

**(G-21019)**
**EQUISTAR CHEMICALS LP**
625 E Us Highway 36 (61953-7507)
**PHONE** .................. 217 253-3311
Leo Wiessing, *QC Dir*
Steven Brunner, *Plant Engr*
Larry Noonan, *Personnel*
Bill Foot, *Manager*
**EMP:** 34
**SALES (corp-wide):** 29.2B **Privately Held**
**WEB:** www.lyondell.com
**SIC:** 2869 Butadiene (industrial organic chemical)
**HQ:** Equistar Chemicals, Lp
1221 Mckinney St Ste 700
Houston TX 77010

**(G-21020)**
**HASTINGS PRINTING**
111 Sale St (61953)
**PHONE** .................. 217 253-5086
Randy Hastings, *President*
Greg Hasting, *Owner*
**EMP:** 3
**SALES (est):** 269.8K **Privately Held**
**SIC:** 2759 Commercial printing

**(G-21021)**
**HERSCHBERGER WINDOW MFG**
623 N County Road 250 E (61953-7037)
**PHONE** .................. 217 543-2106
Darrell L Herschberger, *Owner*
**EMP:** 3
**SQ FT:** 2,500
**SALES:** 400K **Privately Held**
**SIC:** 3089 5031 Windows, plastic; metal doors, sash & trim

**(G-21022)**
**PVH CORP**
Also Called: Van Heusen
1011 E Southline Rd (61953)
**PHONE** .................. 217 253-3398
Crystal Schrock, *Manager*
**EMP:** 10
**SALES (corp-wide):** 8.2B **Publicly Held**
**WEB:** www.pvh.com
**SIC:** 2321 Men's & boys' dress shirts
**PA:** Pvh Corp.
200 Madison Ave Bsmt 1
New York NY 10016
212 381-3500

**(G-21023)**
**R & N COMPONENTS CO**
261 E County Road 600 N (61953-7039)
**PHONE** .................. 217 543-3495
Ruben Gingerich, *Owner*
**EMP:** 9
**SALES (est):** 1.5MM **Privately Held**
**SIC:** 2452 Panels & sections, prefabricated, wood

**(G-21024)**
**SYNGENTA SEEDS INC**
1200 E Southline Rd (61953-2063)
P.O. Box 377 (61953-0377)
**PHONE** .................. 217 253-5646
Lou Rhodes, *Manager*
**EMP:** 16
**SALES (corp-wide):** 12.1B **Privately Held**
**SIC:** 2076 Vegetable oil mills
**HQ:** Syngenta Seeds, Inc.
11055 Wayzata Blvd
Hopkins MN 55305
612 656-8600

**(G-21025)**
**TEWELL BROS MACHINE INC**
300 N Parke St (61953-1408)
**PHONE** .................. 217 253-6303
Thomas A Tewell, *President*
John Tewell, *Treasurer*
John P Tewell, *Admin Sec*
**EMP:** 11 **EST:** 2000
**SALES (est):** 5MM **Privately Held**
**SIC:** 5084 7692 3537 3444 Metalworking tools (such as drills, taps, dies, files); welding repair; industrial trucks & tractors; sheet metalwork

# Tuscola - Douglas County (G-21026)

## GEOGRAPHIC SECTION

**(G-21026)**
**TUSCOLA JOURNAL INCORPORATED**
Also Called: Tri County Journal
115 W Sale St (61953-1443)
P.O. Box 170 (61953-0170)
PHONE...................217 253-5086
Fax: 217 253-5460
Beverly Hastings, *President*
EMP: 5
SALES: 170K **Privately Held**
SIC: 2711 Newspapers, publishing & printing

**(G-21027)**
**TUSCOLA PACKAGING GROUP LLC** ◆
211 E Buckner St (61953-1039)
PHONE...................734 268-2877
Zena Onstott, *President*
EMP: 9 EST: 2016
SALES (est): 450.8K **Privately Held**
SIC: 2653 3089 5084 Boxes, corrugated: made from purchased materials; pads, corrugated: made from purchased materials; pallets, corrugated: made from purchased materials; picnic jugs, plastic; engines & parts, diesel

**(G-21028)**
**TUSCOLA STONE COMPANY**
1199 E Us Highway 36 (61953-8043)
P.O. Box 318 (61953-0318)
PHONE...................217 253-4705
Fax: 217 253-4699
Randy Reed, *Superintendent*
Alan Shoemaker, *Manager*
EMP: 15
SALES (corp-wide): 7.7MM **Privately Held**
SIC: 1422 5032 Agricultural limestone, ground; stone, crushed or broken
PA: Tuscola Stone Company
1250 Larkin Ave Ste 10
Elgin IL

**(G-21029)**
**VAULT ARTS COLLECTIVE**
100 N Main St (61953-1420)
PHONE...................217 599-1215
EMP: 3
SALES (est): 245.7K **Privately Held**
SIC: 3272 Burial vaults, concrete or precast terrazzo

**(G-21030)**
**WENGER WOODCRAFT**
676 N County Road 250 E (61953-7037)
PHONE...................217 578-3440
Fax: 217 578-3440
Steve Wenger, *Partner*
Keith Schmidt, *Partner*
Gregory Wenger, *Partner*
EMP: 4
SALES: 140K **Privately Held**
SIC: 2431 5211 1799 1751 Doors & door parts & trim, wood; cabinets, kitchen; kitchen & bathroom remodeling; cabinet & finish carpentry

## Ullin
### Pulaski County

**(G-21031)**
**JACK SHEPARD LOGGING**
14225 Shepard Ln (62992-3007)
PHONE...................618 845-3496
Jack Shepard, *Owner*
EMP: 5
SALES (est): 382K **Privately Held**
SIC: 2411 Logging camps & contractors

**(G-21032)**
**RODNEY TITE WELDING**
391 N Locust St (62992-1024)
PHONE...................618 845-9072
Rodney Tite, *Owner*
Lori Tite, *Co-Owner*
EMP: 5
SALES (est): 205.7K **Privately Held**
SIC: 7692 Welding repair

## Union
### Mchenry County

**(G-21033)**
**BAGMAKERS INC**
6606 S Union Rd (60180-9535)
PHONE...................815 923-2247
Fax: 815 458-9023
Maribeth Sandford, *CEO*
Jeremy Bayness, *President*
Chuck Sandford, *President*
Stephanie Fleming, *Business Mgr*
D'Anna Zimmer, *Business Mgr*
◆ EMP: 400
SQ FT: 40,000
SALES (est): 119.3MM **Privately Held**
WEB: www.bagmakersinc.com
SIC: 2673 2674 Plastic bags: made from purchased materials; paper bags: made from purchased materials

**(G-21034)**
**CENTRAL WIRE INC (HQ)**
6509 Olson Rd (60180-9730)
P.O. Box 423 (60180-0423)
PHONE...................815 923-2131
Paul From, *CEO*
H Lopes, *President*
John Zaharek, *President*
Jerry Roupp, *Controller*
Richard Gustasson, *Product Mgr*
▲ EMP: 102
SALES (est): 26.4MM
SALES (corp-wide): 27.4MM **Privately Held**
SIC: 3315 3312 Wire & fabricated wire products; wire products, steel or iron
PA: Central Wire Industries Ltd
1 North St
Perth ON K7H 2
613 267-3752

**(G-21035)**
**JAS EXPRESS INC**
8307 Seeman Rd (60180-9531)
PHONE...................847 836-7984
Jaime Velazquez, *Principal*
EMP: 4
SALES (est): 362.4K **Privately Held**
SIC: 2741 Miscellaneous publishing

**(G-21036)**
**ND MANIFOLD**
6614 S Union Rd (60180-9514)
PHONE...................815 923-4305
Nancy Halwix, *Principal*
EMP: 2
SALES (est): 229.2K **Privately Held**
SIC: 3599 Industrial machinery

**(G-21037)**
**NEW DIMENSIONS PRECISION MAC**
6614 S Union Rd (60180-9514)
PHONE...................815 923-8300
Fax: 815 923-8304
Martin Halwix III, *CEO*
Nancy Ann Halwix, *President*
Marco Alejandre, *Plant Mgr*
Vicki Fleix, *Purch Dir*
Jeff Doud, *Engineer*
EMP: 98
SQ FT: 117,000
SALES (est): 24.8MM **Privately Held**
WEB: www.newdims.com
SIC: 3594 Fluid power pumps & motors

**(G-21038)**
**PRO FORM INDUSTRIES INC**
17714 Jefferson St (60180-9536)
P.O. Box 24 (60180-0024)
PHONE...................815 923-2555
Michael Szczesny, *President*
EMP: 5
SALES: 500K **Privately Held**
SIC: 3069 Fabricated rubber products

## Union Hill
### Kankakee County

**(G-21039)**
**VAN VOORST LUMBER COMPANY INC**
1 Center St (60969-9800)
P.O. Box 35 (60969-0035)
PHONE...................815 426-2544
Fax: 815 426-2548
Hugh E Van Voorst, *President*
Grant Voorst, *Manager*
Leann R Anderson, *Admin Sec*
EMP: 36
SQ FT: 2,000
SALES (est): 6.6MM **Privately Held**
SIC: 2449 5211 Wood containers; lumber & other building materials

**(G-21040)**
**VANFAB INC**
1 Center St (60969-9800)
P.O. Box 15 (60969-0015)
PHONE...................815 426-2544
Hugh E Van Voorst, *President*
Grant Van Voorst, *Vice Pres*
EMP: 20 EST: 1976
SQ FT: 20,000
SALES (est): 6.9MM **Privately Held**
SIC: 3444 Casings, sheet metal

## University Park
### Will County

**(G-21041)**
**APPLIED SYSTEMS INC (PA)**
Also Called: Ivans Insurance Solutions
200 Applied Pkwy (60484-4131)
PHONE...................708 534-5575
Fax: 708 534-5682
Reid French Jr, *CEO*
Mark Layden, *COO*
Mark P Layden, *COO*
James R White, *Exec VP*
Kristin Hackney, *Senior VP*
EMP: 600
SQ FT: 160,723
SALES: 248MM **Privately Held**
WEB: www.appliedsystems.com
SIC: 7371 7372 Computer software development; business oriented computer software

**(G-21042)**
**AVATAR CORPORATION**
500 Central Ave (60484-3147)
PHONE...................708 534-5511
Fax: 708 430-4240
Michael L Shamie, *President*
Bill Kersey, *Exec VP*
Steve Rosati, *VP Opers*
Vaccarro Lewis, *Opers Staff*
Giovanna Blaylock, *Buyer*
▲ EMP: 65
SQ FT: 125
SALES (est): 28.9MM **Privately Held**
SIC: 2843 2841 2079 2869 Surface active agents; edible fats & oils; lubricating oils & greases; industrial organic chemicals; soap & other detergents

**(G-21043)**
**BC ASI CAPITAL II INC**
200 Applied Pkwy (60484-4110)
PHONE...................708 534-5575
Bruce Cox, *Principal*
Christine Prescher, *Marketing Staff*
EMP: 622
SALES (est): 13.6MM **Privately Held**
SIC: 7371 5045 7378 8711 Computer software development; computers, peripherals & software; computer maintenance & repair; engineering services; prepackaged software

**(G-21044)**
**BIMBA MANUFACTURING COMPANY (PA)**
25150 S Governors Hwy (60484-8895)
P.O. Box 68, Monee (60449-0068)
PHONE...................708 534-8544
Fax: 708 534-5767
Charles W Bimba Jr, *Ch of Bd*
Patrick J Ormsby, *President*
Adam Schrank, *Regional Mgr*
Kent Sowatzke, *COO*
Mary Fote, *Vice Pres*
▲ EMP: 325 EST: 1969
SQ FT: 150,000
SALES (est): 128.7MM **Privately Held**
WEB: www.bimba.com
SIC: 3593 Fluid power cylinders, hydraulic or pneumatic

**(G-21045)**
**BLUE LINX CORPORATION**
2101 Dralle Rd (60484-4122)
PHONE...................708 235-4200
Tim M Cubbin, *Principal*
EMP: 13
SALES (est): 2MM **Privately Held**
SIC: 3272 Building materials, except block or brick: concrete

**(G-21046)**
**BRENNAN EQUIPMENT AND MFG INC**
Also Called: Little Giant
730 Central Ave (60484-3138)
PHONE...................708 534-5500
Fax: 708 534-5520
Terry D Thomason, *President*
John Brennan, *President*
Peter Sullivan, *Plant Mgr*
Jim Reschke, *VP Sales*
Jim Rescke, *Sales Mgr*
▲ EMP: 75 EST: 1954
SQ FT: 48,000
SALES (est): 23.1MM **Privately Held**
SIC: 3537 Industrial trucks & tractors

**(G-21047)**
**ELCO LABORATORIES INC (PA)**
Also Called: Fresh Solutions For Your Home
2450 W Horner Ave (60484-3114)
PHONE...................708 534-3000
Fax: 708 534-0445
Norman L Elliott, *President*
Robert Hettinger, *President*
William G Elliott, *Vice Pres*
Bhupen Trivedi, *Vice Pres*
Anthony Rogganbuck, *QA Dir*
▲ EMP: 55
SQ FT: 57,500
SALES (est): 10.8MM **Privately Held**
WEB: www.elcolabs.com
SIC: 2842 Rug, upholstery, or dry cleaning detergents or spotters; specialty cleaning preparations

**(G-21048)**
**FEDERAL SIGNAL CORPORATION**
Also Called: Federal Signal-Codespear
2645 Federal Signal Dr (60484-3195)
PHONE...................708 534-4756
Fax: 708 534-4852
Connie Froida, *Prdtn Mgr*
Jim Schmidt, *Finance Mgr*
Mark Reid, *Branch Mgr*
Ed Babush, *Manager*
Linda Fragale, *Manager*
EMP: 20
SALES (corp-wide): 707.9MM **Publicly Held**
WEB: www.federalsignal.com
SIC: 3711 Chassis, motor vehicle
PA: Federal Signal Corporation
1415 W 22nd St Ste 1100
Oak Brook IL 60523
630 954-2000

**(G-21049)**
**FEDERAL SIGNAL CORPORATION**
2645 Federal Signal Dr (60484-3195)
PHONE...................708 534-3400
Scott Cassidy, *Engineer*
EMP: 86

# GEOGRAPHIC SECTION

Urbana - Champaign County (G-21073)

SALES (corp-wide): 707.9MM **Publicly Held**
SIC: 3993 Signs & advertising specialties
PA: Federal Signal Corporation
1415 W 22nd St Ste 1100
Oak Brook IL 60523
630 954-2000

**(G-21050)**
**FEDERAL SIGNAL CORPORATION**
Also Called: Security Systems Group
2645 Federal Signal Dr (60484-3195)
PHONE....................708 534-3400
Ron Featherly, *Branch Mgr*
EMP: 25
SALES (corp-wide): 707.9MM **Publicly Held**
WEB: www.federalsignal.com
SIC: 3711 Chassis, motor vehicle
PA: Federal Signal Corporation
1415 W 22nd St Ste 1100
Oak Brook IL 60523
630 954-2000

**(G-21051)**
**FS DEPOT INC**
2645 Federal Signal Dr (60484-3167)
PHONE....................847 468-2350
Fax: 847 622-7077
Daniel Schueller, *President*
Jennifer L Sherman, *Admin Sec*
◆ EMP: 3
SALES (est): 727.5K
SALES (corp-wide): 707.9MM **Publicly Held**
SIC: 3711 Motor vehicles & car bodies
PA: Federal Signal Corporation
1415 W 22nd St Ste 1100
Oak Brook IL 60523
630 954-2000

**(G-21052)**
**HIGH IMPACT FABRICATING LLC**
1149 Central Ave (60484-3166)
PHONE....................708 235-8912
Elijah Kragulj,
EMP: 6
SALES (est): 512.8K **Privately Held**
SIC: 3714 Bumpers & bumperettes, motor vehicle

**(G-21053)**
**KENNAMTAL TRICON MTLS SVCS INC**
2605 Federal Signal Dr (60484-4104)
PHONE....................708 235-0563
Fax: 708 235-8117
Dean Aring, *Manager*
Mike Grohe, *Manager*
EMP: 23
SALES (corp-wide): 191.6MM **Privately Held**
SIC: 5051 3443 Steel; fabricated plate work (boiler shop)
HQ: Tricon Wear Solutions Llc
2700 5th Ave S
Irondale AL 35210
205 956-2567

**(G-21054)**
**M & R GRAPHICS INC**
2401 Bond St (60484-3101)
PHONE....................708 534-6621
Fax: 708 534-6756
Ruth Moore, *President*
Keith Reimel, *Vice Pres*
Keith Reimeo, *Vice Pres*
Chris Moore, *Prdtn Mgr*
EMP: 16
SQ FT: 11,800
SALES (est): 2.7MM **Privately Held**
WEB: www.mrgraphic.com
SIC: 2759 2672 Labels & seals: printing; coated & laminated paper

**(G-21055)**
**M LIZEN MANUFACTURING CO**
Also Called: A A Coil Products
2625 Federal Signal Dr (60484-4104)
PHONE....................708 755-7213
Bradley K Lizen, *President*
EMP: 24 EST: 1933
SQ FT: 30,000

SALES (est): 5.6MM **Privately Held**
SIC: 3469 3495 Metal stampings; wire springs

**(G-21056)**
**METALTEK FABRICATING INC**
Also Called: Chicago Bullet Proof System
2595 Bond St (60484-3103)
PHONE....................708 534-9102
Fax: 708 534-9132
Peter Stohr, *CEO*
Benedict Stohr, *President*
Alex Ktenas, *Vice Pres*
Pam Litko, *Office Mgr*
Max Stohr, *Manager*
EMP: 17
SQ FT: 22,000
SALES: 2.5MM **Privately Held**
SIC: 3441 1799 Fabricated structural metal; screening contractor: window, door, etc.

**(G-21057)**
**MIDWEST CUSTOM CASE INC (PA)**
Also Called: Midwest Store Fixtures
425 Crossing Dr Unit A (60484-4133)
PHONE....................708 672-2900
Karen A Papiese, *President*
Paul Murawski, *Project Mgr*
Jim Conley, *Purch Mgr*
Bob Murawski, *Purch Agent*
Richard J Papiese, *CFO*
◆ EMP: 103
SQ FT: 500,000
SALES: 53.1MM **Privately Held**
WEB: www.midwestcustomcase.com
SIC: 2541 Store fixtures, wood

**(G-21058)**
**MILLER PRODUCTS INC**
Also Called: M P I Labels Systems
825 Central Ave (60484-3141)
PHONE....................708 534-5111
John Holley, *Branch Mgr*
Mary Davey, *Executive*
EMP: 25
SALES (corp-wide): 32.3MM **Privately Held**
SIC: 2672 2759 2671 Labels (unprinted), gummed: made from purchased materials; commercial printing; packaging paper & plastics film, coated & laminated
PA: Miller Products, Inc.
450 Courtney Rd
Sebring OH 44672
330 938-2134

**(G-21059)**
**PACTIV LLC**
1175 Central Ave Ste 1 (60484-3185)
PHONE....................708 534-6595
Ken Derry, *Manager*
EMP: 150 **Privately Held**
WEB: www.pactiv.com
SIC: 2631 Paperboard mills
HQ: Pactiv Llc
1900 W Field Ct
Lake Forest IL 60045
847 482-2000

**(G-21060)**
**QH INC**
Also Called: Supreme Hinge
2412 Bond St (60484-3102)
PHONE....................708 534-7801
Fax: 708 534-7882
Greg Grimler, *President*
George Boss, *Vice Pres*
Allie Grimler, *Manager*
Susan Zureawski, *Office Admin*
EMP: 25
SQ FT: 15,000
SALES (est): 5.9MM **Privately Held**
WEB: www.qualityhinges.com
SIC: 3442 Metal doors, sash & trim
PA: Supreme Hinge, Inc.
2412 Bond St
University Park IL 60484

**(G-21061)**
**QUALITY HNGE A DIV SPREME HNGE**
2412 Bond St (60484-3102)
PHONE....................708 534-7801
Greg Grimler, *President*

EMP: 28
SALES (est): 987K **Privately Held**
SIC: 3429 Manufactured hardware (general)

**(G-21062)**
**SOLVAY USA INC**
24601 Governors Hwy (60484-4127)
PHONE....................708 235-7200
Dave Hardin, *Branch Mgr*
EMP: 22
SALES (corp-wide): 11.4MM **Privately Held**
SIC: 2899 2869 2821 Chemical preparations; fluorinated hydrocarbon gases; silicones; plastics materials & resins
HQ: Solvay Usa Inc.
504 Carnegie Ctr
Princeton NJ 08540
609 860-4000

**(G-21063)**
**SUPREME HINGE INC (PA)**
2412 Bond St (60484-3102)
PHONE....................708 534-7801
Greg Grimler, *President*
George Boss, *Admin Sec*
EMP: 2
SALES (est): 5.9MM **Privately Held**
SIC: 3442 Metal doors, sash & trim

**(G-21064)**
**TINLEY ICE COMPANY**
Also Called: Three Penguin Ice
450 Central Ave Ste A (60484-3160)
PHONE....................708 532-8777
Fax: 708 532-8856
Timothy Teehan, *President*
EMP: 38
SQ FT: 19,000
SALES: 3MM **Privately Held**
SIC: 2097 Manufactured ice

**(G-21065)**
**U S NAVAL INSTITUTE**
2427 Bond St (60484-3177)
PHONE....................800 233-8764
Thomas Wilkerson, *Branch Mgr*
EMP: 4
SALES (corp-wide): 10.3MM **Privately Held**
SIC: 2731 Book publishing
PA: U S Naval Institute
291 Wood Rd Fl 2
Annapolis MD 21402
410 268-6110

**(G-21066)**
**WELDSTAR COMPANY**
1100 Hamilton Ave (60484-3134)
PHONE....................708 534-6419
Fax: 708 534-7819
Tim Shanahan, *Manager*
EMP: 9
SALES (corp-wide): 27.3MM **Privately Held**
WEB: www.weldstar.com
SIC: 3548 5084 Welding apparatus; industrial machinery & equipment
PA: Weldstar Company
1750 Mitchell Rd
Aurora IL 60505
630 859-3100

**(G-21067)**
**YOSHINO AMERICA CORPORATION**
2500 Palmer Ave (60484-3164)
PHONE....................708 534-1141
Fax: 708 891-4075
Keiji Shimamoto, *President*
Yataro Yoshino, *Principal*
Robert Stuart, *Human Resources*
Joann Burklow, *Accounts Mgr*
Shigeru Nakayama, *Admin Sec*
◆ EMP: 50
SQ FT: 200,000
SALES (est): 14.2MM
SALES (corp-wide): 1.8B **Privately Held**
WEB: www.yoshinoamerica.com
SIC: 3089 Plastic containers, except foam
PA: Yoshino Kogyosho Co., Ltd.
3-2-6, Ojima
Koto-Ku TKY 136-0
336 821-141

## Urbana
### Champaign County

**(G-21068)**
**AF ANTRONICS INC**
1906 N Federal Dr (61801-1049)
PHONE....................217 328-0800
Fred Ore Jr, *President*
Alice Ore, *Admin Sec*
EMP: 3
SQ FT: 3,000
SALES (est): 368.2K **Privately Held**
SIC: 3663 Antennas, transmitting & communications

**(G-21069)**
**AMNET SYSTEMS LLC**
110 W Main St (61801-2715)
PHONE....................217 954-0130
Theodore Young, *Mng Member*
Jamie Armstrong, *Manager*
Joshua Evans, *Manager*
Pete Feely, *Manager*
Aashish Agarwaal,
EMP: 12
SQ FT: 3,000
SALES (est): 838.1K **Privately Held**
SIC: 2741 Miscellaneous publishing
PA: Amnet Systems Private Limited
1st Floor Jvl Plaza
Chennai TN 60001

**(G-21070)**
**APL ENGINEERED MATERIALS INC**
2401 Willow Rd (61802-7332)
PHONE....................217 367-1340
Fax: 217 367-9084
Wayne Hellman, *Ch of Bd*
James Schoolenberg, *President*
Dianne Szydel, *President*
Amanda Foust, *Regional Mgr*
Sharon Fotzler, *Corp Secy*
▲ EMP: 50
SQ FT: 120,000
SALES (est): 12.3MM
SALES (corp-wide): 209.5MM **Privately Held**
SIC: 3648 Lighting equipment
HQ: Advanced Lighting Technologies, Inc.
7905 Cochran Rd Ste 300
Solon OH 44139

**(G-21071)**
**BENDER MAT FCTRY FTON SLEPSHOP (PA)**
Also Called: Benders Mat Fctry Sleep Shoppe
1206 N Cunningham Ave A (61802-1812)
PHONE....................217 328-1700
Thomas Bender, *President*
Dale Habeck, *Manager*
EMP: 8
SQ FT: 8,000
SALES (est): 971.5K **Privately Held**
SIC: 2515 2511 Mattresses, innerspring or box spring; wood household furniture

**(G-21072)**
**BIG R CAR WASH INC (PA)**
501 E University Ave (61802-2059)
PHONE....................217 367-4958
Ivan Richardson, *President*
EMP: 2
SQ FT: 3,200
SALES (est): 329.7K **Privately Held**
SIC: 3589 Car washing machinery

**(G-21073)**
**BIRKEYS FARM STORE INC**
Also Called: Birkeys Construction Equipment
2202 S High Cross Rd (61802-9598)
P.O. Box 17130 (61803-7130)
PHONE....................217 337-1772
Fax: 217 337-1775
Jeffrey Hedge, *Branch Mgr*
Wayne Coffin, *Agent*
EMP: 40

# Urbana - Champaign County (G-21074) — GEOGRAPHIC SECTION

SALES (corp-wide): 210.2MM **Privately Held**
WEB: www.birkeys.com
SIC: **5083** 7699 5511 5082 Farm implements; agricultural equipment repair services; automobiles, new & used; excavating machinery & equipment; farm supplies; farm machinery & equipment
PA: Birkey's Farm Store, Inc.
2102 W Park Ct
Champaign IL 61821
217 693-7200

### (G-21074)
**BROWNFIELD SPORTS INC**
300 S Broadway Ave (61801-3449)
PHONE..................217 367-8321
Kristi Brownfield, *President*
Mark Brownfield, *Vice Pres*
EMP: 8
SQ FT: 3,000
SALES (est): 570K **Privately Held**
SIC: **2759** 3993 2396 2395 Screen printing; signs & advertising specialties; automotive & apparel trimmings; pleating & stitching

### (G-21075)
**CAVITON INC**
3401 S Deer Ridge Dr (61802-7000)
PHONE..................217 621-5746
David Kellner, *CEO*
Cy Herring, *President*
EMP: 4
SALES (est): 272.1K **Privately Held**
WEB: www.caviton.com
SIC: **3822** Auto controls regulating residntl & coml environmt & applncs

### (G-21076)
**CENTRAL ILL FBRCATION WHSE INC**
Also Called: Kurland Steel Company
510 E Main St (61802-2747)
P.O. Box 442 (61803-0442)
PHONE..................217 367-2323
Fax: 217 328-6758
Jeffry M Ping, *President*
Cathy Mitchell, *Principal*
Keith Wolfe, *Principal*
Albert L Mitchell, *CFO*
Kim Lewis, *Mktg Dir*
EMP: 17
SQ FT: 13,000
SALES (est): 5.5MM **Privately Held**
WEB: www.kurlandsteel.com
SIC: **3441** 5051 Building components, structural steel; metals service centers & offices

### (G-21077)
**CHAMPAIGN CNTY TENT & AWNG CO**
Also Called: Twin City Tent & Awning Co
308 E Anthony Dr (61802-7345)
P.O. Box 638 (61803-0638)
PHONE..................217 328-5749
Fax: 217 328-5759
Kevin Yonce, *CEO*
Byron Yonce, *President*
Wayne M Yonce, *President*
Rick Shoop, *Vice Pres*
Wanda K Yonce, *Vice Pres*
EMP: 25 EST: 1929
SQ FT: 32,600
SALES (est): 4.1MM **Privately Held**
WEB: www.awning-tent.com
SIC: **2394** 7359 Canvas & related products; equipment rental & leasing; tent & tarpaulin rental

### (G-21078)
**COCA-COLA REFRESHMENTS USA INC**
2809 N Lincoln Ave (61802-7298)
PHONE..................217 367-1761
Fax: 217 328-2972
Brian Dodd, *General Mgr*
Tina Withers, *Office Mgr*
EMP: 28
SALES (corp-wide): 41.8B **Publicly Held**
WEB: www.cokecce.com
SIC: **2086** Bottled & canned soft drinks
HQ: Coca-Cola Refreshments Usa, Inc.
2500 Windy Ridge Pkwy Se
Atlanta GA 30339
770 989-3000

### (G-21079)
**CONCRETE SUPPLY TOLONO INC**
Also Called: Csi of Tolono
1466 County Road 1100 N (61802-7135)
PHONE..................217 485-3100
Kerrelton D Grove, *President*
Becky Grove, *Admin Sec*
EMP: 4
SALES (est): 514.7K **Privately Held**
SIC: **3273** Ready-mixed concrete

### (G-21080)
**COX ELECTRIC MOTOR SERVICE**
1409 Triumph Dr (61802-9767)
PHONE..................217 344-2458
Fax: 217 344-2464
Melissa Brown, *President*
EMP: 6
SQ FT: 3,600
SALES (est): 761K **Privately Held**
SIC: **7629** 5063 7694 Electrical repair shops; motors, electric; armature rewinding shops

### (G-21081)
**EMULSICOAT INC**
705 E University Ave (61802-2031)
PHONE..................217 344-7775
Fax: 217 344-4174
Fred M Fehsenfeld Jr, *President*
Lewis L Davis, *Corp Secy*
Rick Beyers, *Vice Pres*
Evelyn Matthews, *Office Mgr*
EMP: 11
SQ FT: 3,000
SALES (est): 2MM
SALES (corp-wide): 323.2MM **Privately Held**
SIC: **2952** 2891 2951 Asphalt felts & coatings; coating compounds, tar; adhesives; asphalt paving mixtures & blocks
PA: Asphalt Materials, Inc.
5400 W 86th St
Indianapolis IN 46268
317 872-6010

### (G-21082)
**ENTIENCE**
305 W Michigan Ave (61801-4945)
PHONE..................217 649-2590
Rhanor Gillette, *CEO*
Ekaterina Gribkova, *Co-Venturer*
Mikhail Voloshin, *Co-Venturer*
EMP: 3
SALES (est): 71.1K **Privately Held**
SIC: **7372** Application computer software

### (G-21083)
**EXPRESS PRINT CHAMPAIGN LLC**
510 N Cunningham Ave # 10 (61802-1715)
PHONE..................217 693-7079
James Craig, *Mng Member*
Teresa Craig, *President*
EMP: 2
SALES (est): 313.6K **Privately Held**
SIC: **2752** Commercial printing, lithographic

### (G-21084)
**FLEX-N-GATE CHICAGO LLC** ◆
502 E Anthony Dr (61802-7347)
PHONE..................217 255-5098
David Ekblad, *CFO*
EMP: 2 EST: 2016
SALES: 30MM
SALES (corp-wide): 3.3B **Privately Held**
SIC: **3089** Automotive parts, plastic
PA: Flex-N-Gate Corporation
1306 E University Ave
Urbana IL 61802
217 384-6600

### (G-21085)
**FLEX-N-GATE CORPORATION (PA)**
1306 E University Ave (61802-2093)
P.O. Box 727 (61803-0727)
PHONE..................217 384-6600
Fax: 217 278-2616
Shahid Khan, *President*
Chris Demerah, *General Mgr*
Andy Scheele, *General Mgr*
Dawn Robbins, *Exec VP*
Bill Beistline, *Vice Pres*
▲ EMP: 340
SQ FT: 75,000
SALES (corp-wide): 3.3B **Privately Held**
WEB: www.flex-n-gate.com
SIC: **3714** Bumpers & bumperettes, motor vehicle

### (G-21086)
**FLEX-N-GATE CORPORATION**
Also Called: Flex-N-Gate Plant
1306 E University Ave (61802-2093)
PHONE..................217 384-6600
Brad Annis, *Business Mgr*
Kathy Lecik, *Empl Rel Mgr*
Robb Springfield, *Corp Comm Staff*
Bill Beistline, *Branch Mgr*
Sherrie Griffith, *Director*
EMP: 300
SALES (corp-wide): 3.3B **Privately Held**
WEB: www.flex-n-gate.com
SIC: **3714** Bumpers & bumperettes, motor vehicle
PA: Flex-N-Gate Corporation
1306 E University Ave
Urbana IL 61802
217 384-6600

### (G-21087)
**FLEX-N-GATE CORPORATION**
502 E Anthony Dr (61802-7347)
PHONE..................217 255-5025
Suzi Puckett, *Manager*
Bill B Beistline, *Manager*
Nathan Hughes, *Manager*
Nick Wiegand, *Manager*
Joel Cody, *Director*
EMP: 504
SALES (corp-wide): 3.3B **Privately Held**
WEB: www.flex-n-gate.com
SIC: **3714** Motor vehicle parts & accessories
PA: Flex-N-Gate Corporation
1306 E University Ave
Urbana IL 61802
217 384-6600

### (G-21088)
**FLEX-N-GATE CORPORATION**
Also Called: Guardian West
601 Guardian Way (61802-2880)
PHONE..................217 278-2400
Fax: 217 278-2570
Jack Antonini, *Branch Mgr*
Jeannie Deck, *Manager*
Dave Kittell, *Maintence Staff*
EMP: 504
SALES (corp-wide): 3.3B **Privately Held**
WEB: www.flex-n-gate.com
SIC: **3714** Motor vehicle parts & accessories
PA: Flex-N-Gate Corporation
1306 E University Ave
Urbana IL 61802
217 384-6600

### (G-21089)
**FRASCA INTERNATIONAL INC (PA)**
Also Called: Frasca Air Services
906 Airport Rd (61802-7375)
PHONE..................217 344-9200
Fax: 217 344-9207
Rudolf Frasca, *Ch of Bd*
John Frasca, *President*
Craig Zysk, *President*
Tony Haley, *Business Mgr*
Debby Flick, *Corp Secy*
▲ EMP: 160
SQ FT: 93,000
SALES (est): 24.5MM **Privately Held**
WEB: www.frasca.com
SIC: **3728** Aircraft training equipment

### (G-21090)
**GREAT PLANES MODEL MFG INC**
706 W Bradley Ave (61801-1002)
P.O. Box 788 (61803-0788)
PHONE..................217 367-2707
Wayne J Hemming, *President*
Steven Ellison, *Vice Pres*
Richard Sumner, *Opers Staff*
Willard K Muirheid, *Admin Sec*
EMP: 38
SQ FT: 17,500
SALES (est): 4.6MM **Privately Held**
SIC: **3944** Airplane models, toy & hobby

### (G-21091)
**HOBBICO INC**
Also Called: Great Plains Model Maufacturing
706 W Bradley Ave (61801-1002)
P.O. Box 788 (61803-0788)
PHONE..................217 367-2707
Fax: 217 367-2239
Hans Olsen, *Engineer*
Dick Sumner, *Manager*
Rod Clinton, *MIS Dir*
EMP: 40
SALES (corp-wide): 129.8MM **Privately Held**
WEB: www.hobbyservices.com
SIC: **5941** 3952 3944 Fishing equipment; lead pencils & art goods; games, toys & children's vehicles
PA: Hobbico, Inc.
1608 Interstate Dr
Champaign IL 61822
217 398-3630

### (G-21092)
**JMK COMPUTERIZED TDIS INC**
703 S Glover Ave (61802-4426)
PHONE..................217 384-8891
Fax: 217 384-8099
James Krakower, *President*
EMP: 5
SALES (est): 530K **Privately Held**
WEB: www.jmktdis.com
SIC: **7372** Prepackaged software

### (G-21093)
**LUMBER SPECIALISTS INC**
Also Called: News Gazette
300 W Main St (61801-2624)
P.O. Box 6677 (61801)
PHONE..................217 351-5311
Fax: 217 351-5259
Jeff D'Alessio, *Editor*
Betty Raat, *Human Resources*
Amy Eckard, *Manager*
EMP: 10
SALES (corp-wide): 63.7MM **Privately Held**
SIC: **2711** Newspapers
PA: The News-Gazette Inc
15 E Main St
Champaign IL 61820
217 351-5252

### (G-21094)
**MID-AMERICA SAND & GRAVEL**
Also Called: Billing Office
2906 N Oak St (61802-7203)
PHONE..................217 355-1307
Bill Booker, *Manager*
EMP: 9
SALES (corp-wide): 2MM **Privately Held**
SIC: **1442** Construction sand & gravel
PA: Mid-America Sand & Gravel
250 County Rd 2050 N
Mahomet IL 61853
217 586-4536

### (G-21095)
**MUFFLER**
Also Called: Red's Muffler Shop
102 W University Ave (61801-1739)
PHONE..................217 344-1676
Wayne Shaw, *President*
EMP: 4
SQ FT: 3,000
SALES (est): 180K **Privately Held**
SIC: **3564** Exhaust fans: industrial or commercial

# GEOGRAPHIC SECTION

## Vandalia - Fayette County (G-21120)

**(G-21096)**
**OSO TECHNOLOGIES INC**
Also Called: Plantlink
722 W Killarney St (61801-1015)
PHONE..................................844 777-2575
Mercedes Mane, *President*
EMP: 5
SALES (est): 196.6K
SALES (corp-wide): 2.8B **Publicly Held**
SIC: 3494 3825 Valves & pipe fittings; analog-digital converters, electronic instrumentation type
PA: The Scotts Miracle-Gro Company
14111 Scottslawn Rd
Marysville OH 43040
937 644-0011

**(G-21097)**
**PERSONIFY**
Also Called: Nuvixa
208a W Main St (61801)
PHONE..................................217 840-2638
Sanjay Patel, *CEO*
EMP: 15
SALES (est): 1.1MM **Privately Held**
WEB: www.nuvixa.com
SIC: 7372 7819 Prepackaged software; services allied to motion pictures

**(G-21098)**
**PLASTIC CONTAINER CORPORATION (PA)**
Also Called: PCC
2508 N Oak St (61802-7207)
P.O. Box 438, Champaign (61824-0438)
PHONE..................................217 352-2722
Fax: 217 352-2822
Ronald E Rhoades, *President*
Bob Turpin, *Plant Mgr*
Penick Brett, *CFO*
Brett Penick, *CFO*
Shannon Wingler, *Human Res Dir*
▲ EMP: 100
SQ FT: 102,000
SALES (est): 32.4MM **Privately Held**
WEB: www.netpcc.com
SIC: 3085 3089 3999 Plastics bottles; plastic containers, except foam; atomizers, toiletry

**(G-21099)**
**PRIVATE STUDIOS**
705 Western Ave (61801-3114)
PHONE..................................217 367-3530
Jonathan Pines, *Owner*
EMP: 7
SQ FT: 6,500
SALES: 150K **Privately Held**
SIC: 3652 8742 Pre-recorded records & tapes; industrial & labor consulting services

**(G-21100)**
**PROJECT TE INC**
Also Called: Project T C
2209 E University Ave B (61802-2811)
PHONE..................................217 344-9833
Fax: 217 344-9835
Maurice Mehling, *President*
EMP: 4
SQ FT: 1,400
SALES: 120K **Privately Held**
SIC: 2759 Screen printing

**(G-21101)**
**ROBERT HIGGINS**
Also Called: Super Phone Store
405 E Pennsylvania Ave (61801-5130)
PHONE..................................217 337-0734
Fax: 217 337-0586
Robert Higgins, *CEO*
EMP: 90
SALES (est): 7.3MM **Privately Held**
WEB: www.robhiggins.com
SIC: 3625 Switches, electronic applications

**(G-21102)**
**SAGAMORE PUBLISHING LLC**
1807 N Federal Dr (61801-1051)
PHONE..................................217 359-5940
Fax: 217 359-5975
Joseph Bannon, *Ch of Bd*
Peter Bannon, *President*
EMP: 12
SQ FT: 36,000
SALES (est): 1.2MM **Privately Held**
SIC: 2731 2721 Books: publishing only; trade journals: publishing only, not printed on site

**(G-21103)**
**TOM MCCOWAN ENTERPRISES INC**
Also Called: Wood-N-Ware
1004 E Pennsylvania Ave (61801-5241)
P.O. Box 213, Bondville (61815-0213)
PHONE..................................217 369-9352
Thomas Mc Cowan, *President*
EMP: 3
SALES: 40K **Privately Held**
WEB: www.wood-n-ware.com
SIC: 3087 Custom compound purchased resins

**(G-21104)**
**VENTURE PUBLISHING INC**
1807 N Federal Dr (61801-1051)
PHONE..................................217 359-5940
Frank Guadagnolo, *President*
Geoff Godbey, *Editor*
Richard Yocum, *Mfg Staff*
Kay Whiteside, *Manager*
EMP: 6
SALES (est): 540K **Privately Held**
WEB: www.venturepublish.com
SIC: 2731 Book publishing; textbooks: publishing only, not printed on site

## Ursa
### Adams County

**(G-21105)**
**KAYSER LURE CORP**
107 Junction St (62376-1040)
P.O. Box 68 (62376-0068)
PHONE..................................217 964-2110
Terry Kayser, *President*
Carol Virginia Kayser, *Vice Pres*
EMP: 6
SALES (est): 469.2K **Privately Held**
SIC: 3949 Fishing equipment; fishing tackle, general

## Utica
### Lasalle County

**(G-21106)**
**AUGUSTHILL WINERY CO**
106 Mill St (61373-9450)
PHONE..................................815 667-5211
Susanne Bullock, *Marketing Staff*
Nojo Sawin, *Manager*
Teri Venzel, *Executive*
EMP: 4
SALES (est): 323.4K **Privately Held**
SIC: 2084 Wines

**(G-21107)**
**PQ CORPORATION**
340 E Grove St (61373-9001)
P.O. Box 410 (61373-0410)
PHONE..................................815 667-4241
Fax: 815 667-5230
Stan Slusser, *Plant Mgr*
Craig R Powers, *Opers-Prdtn-Mfg*
Pete Bray, *Purchasing*
EMP: 45
SALES (corp-wide): 1B **Privately Held**
WEB: www.pqcorp.com
SIC: 2819 2899 Industrial inorganic chemicals; chemical preparations
HQ: Pq Corporation
300 Lindenwood Dr
Malvern PA 19355
610 651-4429

**(G-21108)**
**U S SILICA COMPANY**
727 N 3029th Rd (61373-9740)
PHONE..................................800 635-7263
EMP: 5
SALES (corp-wide): 559.6MM **Publicly Held**
SIC: 1446 Silica sand mining
HQ: U. S. Silica Company
8490 Progress Dr Ste 300
Frederick MD 21701
301 682-0600

**(G-21109)**
**UNIMIN CORPORATION**
402 Mill St (61373-9323)
P.O. Box 409 (61373-0409)
PHONE..................................815 667-5102
Fax: 815 667-5280
Scott Atkins, *Manager*
EMP: 50
SALES (corp-wide): 117.6MM **Privately Held**
WEB: www.unimin.com
SIC: 1446 3295 Silica sand mining; minerals, ground or treated
HQ: Unimin Corporation
258 Elm St
New Canaan CT 06840
203 966-8880

**(G-21110)**
**UTICA STONE CO INC**
773 N 27th Rd (61373)
PHONE..................................815 667-4690
Fax: 815 667-4635
Toni Biagioni, *Manager*
EMP: 4
SALES (est): 167.3K **Privately Held**
SIC: 1422 Crushed & broken limestone

**(G-21111)**
**UTICA TERMINAL INC**
715 N 27th Rd (61373)
PHONE..................................815 667-5131
Fax: 815 667-5241
Devon Davidsmyer, *CEO*
Jeff Davidsmeyer, *President*
Greg Pennel, *Manager*
Tom Atkins, *Manager*
Thomas Slayback, *Admin Sec*
EMP: 7
SQ FT: 3,000
SALES (est): 1.4MM
SALES (corp-wide): 36.8MM **Privately Held**
SIC: 3531 Asphalt plant, including gravel-mix type
PA: Illinois Road Contractors, Inc.
520 N Webster Ave
Jacksonville IL 62650
217 245-6181

## Valmeyer
### Monroe County

**(G-21112)**
**MAR GRAPHICS**
523 S Meyer Ave (62295-3120)
PHONE..................................618 935-2111
Richard D Roever, *President*
Audrey A Roever, *Corp Secy*
Bobbie Klinkhardt, *Vice Pres*
Scott Roever, *Vice Pres*
Al Linnemann, *Plant Mgr*
EMP: 90 EST: 1961
SALES (est): 30.3MM **Privately Held**
WEB: www.margraphics.com
SIC: 2752 Commercial printing, offset

## Vandalia
### Fayette County

**(G-21113)**
**FAYCO ENTERPRISES INC (PA)**
1313 Sunset Dr (62471-3212)
P.O. Box 277 (62471-0277)
PHONE..................................618 283-0638
Fax: 217 532-9244
Robert Lindberg, *General Mgr*
Kim Stone, *Business Mgr*
Paula Green, *CPA*
Kim Taylor, *Finance*
Dede Koher, *Manager*
EMP: 40
SQ FT: 25,000
SALES: 5.4MM **Privately Held**
SIC: 3951 Ball point pens & parts

**(G-21114)**
**FOUR WINDS MUSIC PUBG LLC**
1226 N 5th St (62471-1229)
PHONE..................................618 699-1356
Jourdan Clifford, *Principal*
EMP: 3
SALES (est): 127.3K **Privately Held**
SIC: 2711 Newspapers

**(G-21115)**
**GSI GROUP LLC**
Also Called: Grain Systems
110 S Coles St (62471-2520)
PHONE..................................618 283-9792
EMP: 60
SALES (corp-wide): 10.7B **Publicly Held**
SIC: 5083 3556 Whol Farm/Garden Machinery Mfg Food Products Machinery
HQ: The Gsi Group Llc
1004 E Illinois St
Assumption IL 62510
217 226-4421

**(G-21116)**
**MID-ILLINOIS CONCRETE INC**
Also Called: Vandalia Ready-Mix
1021 Janette Dr (62471-3530)
PHONE..................................618 283-1600
Fax: 618 283-1602
Glenn Gelsinger, *Manager*
Glenn Gelstnger, *Manager*
Matt Meyer, *Manager*
EMP: 14
SALES (corp-wide): 17.2MM **Privately Held**
WEB: www.mid-illinoisconcrete.com
SIC: 3272 3273 Concrete products, precast; ready-mixed concrete
PA: Mid-Illinois Concrete, Inc.
1805 S 4th St
Effingham IL
217 342-2115

**(G-21117)**
**MIDWEST BLOW MOLDING LLC**
1111 Imco Dr (62471-3522)
PHONE..................................618 283-9223
John F Romano, *CEO*
EMP: 1 EST: 2015
SALES (est): 219K
SALES (corp-wide): 34.9MM **Privately Held**
SIC: 3089 Molding primary plastic
PA: The Fountainhead Group Inc
23 Garden St
New York Mills NY 13417
315 736-0037

**(G-21118)**
**OLD CAPITOL MONUMENT WORKS INC (PA)**
627 S 6th St (62471-3016)
P.O. Box 27 (62471-0027)
PHONE..................................217 324-5673
Fax: 618 283-0292
Roy G Nichols, *President*
John Cocagne, *Vice Pres*
Lavonda L Nichols, *Vice Pres*
Arthur Perry, *Vice Pres*
Rochelle Carpenter, *Treasurer*
EMP: 5
SALES (est): 683.4K **Privately Held**
SIC: 3281 5999 Monuments, cut stone (not finishing or lettering only); monuments, finished to custom order

**(G-21119)**
**P & G MACHINE & TOOL INC**
Also Called: P & G Machine Shop
1910 Illini Ave (62471-3421)
PHONE..................................618 283-0273
Fax: 618 283-0805
Charles Philpot, *President*
Ramona Philpot, *Admin Sec*
EMP: 5 EST: 1963
SQ FT: 2,400
SALES (est): 699K **Privately Held**
SIC: 3599 7692 Machine shop, jobbing & repair; welding repair

**(G-21120)**
**PRAIRIE PROFILE**
1437 E 1050 Ave (62471-4110)
PHONE..................................618 846-2116
Jason Weaver, *Partner*
Marian Weaver, *Partner*

# Vandalia - Fayette County (G-21121)

**EMP:** 4
**SQ FT:** 7,000
**SALES:** 213.1K **Privately Held**
**SIC:** 5191 3312 5999 Beekeeping supplies (non-durable); beehive coke oven products; alcoholic beverage making equipment & supplies

### (G-21121)
### PRO-FAB METALS INC
10949 Us Hwy 40 (62471)
**PHONE**.................................618 283-2986
**Fax:** 618 283-2945
Charles E Wagoner, *Owner*
Marilyn Welch, *Office Mgr*
**EMP:** 3 **EST:** 1996
**SQ FT:** 3,000
**SALES (est):** 366.5K **Privately Held**
**SIC:** 7692 3441 Welding repair; building components, structural steel

### (G-21122)
### PURINA MILLS LLC
1500 Veterans Ave (62471-3315)
**PHONE**.................................618 283-2291
**Fax:** 618 283-1653
Tom Murfin, *QC Dir*
Calvin Scott, *Branch Mgr*
**EMP:** 26
**SALES (corp-wide):** 14.9B **Privately Held**
**WEB:** www.purina-mills.com
**SIC:** 2048 Prepared feeds
**HQ:** Purina Mills, Llc
 555 Maryvle Univ Dr 200
 Saint Louis MO 63141
 877 454-7094

### (G-21123)
### SHRINE MEMORIAL MAUSOLEUM CO
Also Called: Shrine Memorial Vault Co
627 S 6th St (62471-3016)
P.O. Box 27 (62471-0027)
**PHONE**.................................618 283-0153
**Fax:** 618 283-9692
Roy Nichols, *President*
Donald W Carpenter, *President*
Rochelle K Carpenter, *Corp Secy*
Arthur N Perry, *Vice Pres*
**EMP:** 4 **EST:** 1920
**SQ FT:** 6,300
**SALES:** 283.3K **Privately Held**
**SIC:** 3272 Tombstones, precast terrazzo or concrete

### (G-21124)
### SHULMAN BROTHERS INC
101 S 4th St (62471-2809)
P.O. Box 99 (62471-0099)
**PHONE**.................................618 283-3253
Maurice Shulman, *CEO*
Todd Shulman, *Vice Pres*
**EMP:** 8 **EST:** 1938
**SQ FT:** 250
**SALES (est):** 871.7K **Privately Held**
**SIC:** 1311 Crude petroleum production

### (G-21125)
### SIGNATURE LABEL OF ILLINOIS
2025 N 8th St (62471-4003)
**PHONE**.................................618 283-5145
Jay Viery, *President*
Angelique Bohannon, *Purch Mgr*
**EMP:** 4
**SALES (est):** 744.3K **Privately Held**
**WEB:** www.signature-label.com
**SIC:** 3552 2671 2396 2672 Silk screens for textile industry; packaging paper & plastics film, coated & laminated; automotive & apparel trimmings; coated & laminated paper

### (G-21126)
### SOUTH CENTRAL FS INC
10 Interstate Dr (62471-3432)
**PHONE**.................................618 283-1557
John Wait, *Branch Mgr*
**EMP:** 27
**SALES (corp-wide):** 118.3MM **Privately Held**
**SIC:** 5171 5191 2875 Petroleum bulk stations; farm supplies; fertilizers, mixing only
**PA:** South Central Fs, Inc.
 405 S Banker St
 Effingham IL 62401
 217 342-9231

### (G-21127)
### T C4 INC
1207 N Carlisle Rd (62471)
**PHONE**.................................618 335-3486
Tina Cook, *President*
Joseph Cook, *Vice Pres*
**EMP:** 15
**SALES:** 1MM **Privately Held**
**SIC:** 2048 Cereal-, grain-, & seed-based feeds

### (G-21128)
### VANDALIA ELECTRIC MTR SVC INC
561 Il 185 (62471-3449)
**PHONE**.................................618 283-0068
Kurt Kroll, *President*
Katrina Kroll, *Manager*
**EMP:** 5
**SQ FT:** 4,800
**SALES (est):** 1MM **Privately Held**
**SIC:** 7694 5063 Electric motor repair; motors, electric

### (G-21129)
### VANDALIA SAND & GRAVEL INC
Rr 2 (62471-9802)
P.O. Box 391 (62471-0391)
**PHONE**.................................618 283-4029
Michael Themig, *President*
Debbie Themig, *Admin Sec*
**EMP:** 10
**SALES (est):** 745.3K **Privately Held**
**SIC:** 1442 Construction sand & gravel

### (G-21130)
### VANSEAL CORPORATION
815 Payne Dr (62471-4006)
**PHONE**.................................618 283-4700
Thomas E Gebhardt, *President*
Glen Hobbie, *General Mgr*
Kathy Kidd, *Plant Mgr*
Ken Land, *Engrg Mgr*
Darrell Virden, *Engineer*
**EMP:** 100
**SQ FT:** 125,000
**SALES:** 11.5MM **Privately Held**
**WEB:** www.polymersealing.com
**SIC:** 3053 Gaskets, packing & sealing devices

### (G-21131)
### WEHRLE LUMBER CO INC
820 E 1900 Ave (62471-4555)
**PHONE**.................................618 283-4859
**Fax:** 618 283-4854
Ruth Duggins, *President*
Eric Wehrle, *Admin Sec*
**EMP:** 15
**SQ FT:** 18,000
**SALES (est):** 2.7MM **Privately Held**
**SIC:** 2653 Pallets, solid fiber: made from purchased materials

## Varna
### Marshall County

### (G-21132)
### ADAPT SEALS CO
Also Called: Lake Country Storage
565 Lake Wildwood Dr (61375-9546)
P.O. Box 21 (61375-0021)
**PHONE**.................................309 463-2482
James Jamour, *Owner*
**EMP:** 7
**SALES (est):** 330K **Privately Held**
**SIC:** 3069 Sponge rubber & sponge rubber products

### (G-21133)
### BRIAN LINDSTROM
Also Called: Lindstrom Farm
2412 Wenona Rd (61375-9469)
**PHONE**.................................309 463-2388
Brian Lindstrom, *Owner*
**EMP:** 4
**SALES (est):** 133.7K **Privately Held**
**SIC:** 3523 Driers (farm): grain, hay & seed

### (G-21134)
### KOHNS ELECTRIC
1555 Key Ct S (61375-9405)
**PHONE**.................................309 463-2331
Jeffrey Akohn, *Principal*
**EMP:** 4
**SALES (est):** 417.6K **Privately Held**
**SIC:** 3699 1731 Electrical equipment & supplies; electrical work

### (G-21135)
### MYERS INC
99999 Route 1 S (61375)
P.O. Box 197, Cooksville (61730-0197)
**PHONE**.................................309 725-3710
**Fax:** 309 725-3361
**EMP:** 3
**SALES (est):** 110K **Privately Held**
**SIC:** 2875 Mfg Fertilizers-Mix Only

## Venedy
### Washington County

### (G-21136)
### GATEWAY FS INC
18 N Mill Rd (62214-1222)
P.O. Box 525, Addieville (62214)
**PHONE**.................................618 824-6631
Ken Lintker, *Branch Mgr*
**EMP:** 6
**SALES (corp-wide):** 57.9MM **Privately Held**
**SIC:** 4221 2873 2874 Grain elevator, storage only; nitrogenous fertilizers; phosphatic fertilizers
**PA:** Gateway Fs, Inc.
 221 E Pine St
 Red Bud IL 62278
 618 282-4000

## Venice
### Madison County

### (G-21137)
### SHO PAK LLC
Also Called: Ics Saint Louis
1226 Bissell St (62090-1183)
**PHONE**.................................618 876-1597
Chris Johnson, *Mng Member*
**EMP:** 4
**SALES:** 1MM **Privately Held**
**SIC:** 2631 Container, packaging & boxboard

## Vermont
### Fulton County

### (G-21138)
### MAHONEY FOUNDRIES INC
Vermont Foundry Co
29 N Main St (61484)
P.O. Box 290 (61484-0290)
**PHONE**.................................309 784-2311
**Fax:** 309 784-6331
Steven Shutter, *Purch Mgr*
Steve Mahoney, *Purchasing*
Joan Mahoney, *Finance*
John Mahoney Jr, *Branch Mgr*
**EMP:** 40
**SQ FT:** 39,681
**SALES (corp-wide):** 15.1MM **Privately Held**
**SIC:** 3364 3363 3369 3366 Brass & bronze die-castings; aluminum die-castings; nonferrous foundries; copper foundries; secondary nonferrous metals; primary copper
**PA:** Mahoney Foundries Inc
 209 W Ohio St
 Kendallville IN 46755
 260 347-1768

## Vernon
### Marion County

### (G-21139)
### BURKS SAWMILL
Also Called: Burks Hardwood Lumber
9411 Us Highway 51 (62892-1236)
P.O. Box 4 (62892-0004)
**PHONE**.................................618 432-5451
**Fax:** 618 432-5568
Jim Burks, *Owner*
**EMP:** 12
**SQ FT:** 900
**SALES (est):** 1.3MM **Privately Held**
**SIC:** 2421 Sawmills & planing mills, general

### (G-21140)
### CHICAP PIPELINE
1505 Dickey Pond Rd (62892-1711)
**PHONE**.................................618 432-5311
Jim Eagleton, *Principal*
**EMP:** 8
**SALES (est):** 1MM **Privately Held**
**SIC:** 2911 Petroleum refining

## Vernon Hills
### Lake County

### (G-21141)
### ABBVIE INC
75 N Fairway Dr (60061-1845)
**PHONE**.................................847 367-7621
**EMP:** 6
**SALES (corp-wide):** 25.6B **Publicly Held**
**SIC:** 2834 Pharmaceutical preparations
**PA:** Abbvie Inc.
 1 N Waukegan Rd
 North Chicago IL 60064
 847 932-7900

### (G-21142)
### AGAVE LOCO LLC
1175 Corporate Woods Pkwy # 218 (60061-4169)
P.O. Box 323, Deerfield (60015-0323)
**PHONE**.................................847 383-6052
Tom Maas,
**EMP:** 13
**SALES (est):** 2MM **Privately Held**
**SIC:** 2085 5182 Distilled & blended liquors; wine & distilled beverages

### (G-21143)
### AKORN INC
50 Lake Pkwy Ste 110 (60061)
**PHONE**.................................847 279-6166
Biswajit Pati, *Branch Mgr*
**EMP:** 7
**SALES (corp-wide):** 1.1B **Publicly Held**
**SIC:** 2834 Pharmaceutical preparations
**PA:** Akorn, Inc.
 1925 W Field Ct Ste 300
 Lake Forest IL 60045
 847 279-6100

### (G-21144)
### ALI GROUP NORTH AMERICA CORP (DH)
101 Corporate Woods Pkwy (60061-3109)
**PHONE**.................................847 215-6565
Filipo Berti, *President*
Bradford Willis, *CFO*
Ashley Bentley, *Manager*
**EMP:** 26
**SALES (est):** 543.9MM **Privately Held**
**SIC:** 3589 Cooking equipment, commercial
**HQ:** Ali Spa
 Via Piero Gobetti 2/A
 Cernusco Sul Naviglio MI 20063
 029 219-91

### (G-21145)
### ALLSTAR DENTAL INC
204 Us Highway 45 (60061-2347)
**PHONE**.................................847 325-5134
Eric Strohmeier, *President*
Nate Langlois, *Marketing Mgr*
**EMP:** 5
**SQ FT:** 2,500

# GEOGRAPHIC SECTION
## Vernon Hills - Lake County (G-21173)

**SALES (est):** 1MM **Privately Held**
**SIC: 3843** Dental equipment

**(G-21146)**
**BAUERMEISTER INC**
601 Corporate Woods Pkwy (60061-3111)
**PHONE** ............................. 901 363-0921
E L G Hermann Bauermeister, *Principal*
▲ **EMP:** 8 **EST:** 2012
**SALES (est):** 1.3MM **Privately Held**
**SIC: 3556** Grinders, commercial, food

**(G-21147)**
**BAXTER HEALTHCARE CORPORATION**
400 Lakeview Pkwy (60061-1843)
**PHONE** ............................. 847 522-8600
Marcey Guralnick, *Principal*
Lloyd Love, *Vice Pres*
Scott Kaya, *Purch Dir*
E J Donaghey, *Sls & Mktg Exec*
Blair Olexa, *Finance*
**EMP:** 260
**SALES (corp-wide):** 10.1B **Publicly Held**
**SIC: 2834** Pharmaceutical preparations
**HQ:** Baxter Healthcare Corporation
1 Baxter Pkwy
Deerfield IL 60015
224 948-2000

**(G-21148)**
**BAXTER HEALTHCARE CORPORATION**
440 N Fairway Dr (60061-1836)
**PHONE** ............................. 847 367-2544
Robert L Parkinson, *CEO*
Dhiresh Pant, *Project Mgr*
Sriharsha Kalle, *Project Engr*
Lisa Williams, *HR Admin*
Vicky Lando, *Manager*
**EMP:** 250
**SALES (corp-wide):** 10.1B **Publicly Held**
**SIC: 3841** Surgical & medical instruments
**HQ:** Baxter Healthcare Corporation
1 Baxter Pkwy
Deerfield IL 60015
224 948-2000

**(G-21149)**
**BENCHMARC DISPLAY INCORPORATED (PA)**
1001 Woodlands Pkwy (60061-3181)
**PHONE** ............................. 847 541-2828
**Fax:** 847 541-4742
Robert Osmond, *President*
Lou Fanning, *President*
Nicole Rafferty, *General Mgr*
Isaac Callejas, *Prdtn Mgr*
Jordan Swartzentruber, *Draft/Design*
◆ **EMP:** 30 **EST:** 1974
**SQ FT:** 32,000
**SALES (est):** 5.7MM **Privately Held**
**WEB:** www.benchmarc.com
**SIC: 3993** Displays & cutouts, window & lobby

**(G-21150)**
**BENDE INC**
925 Corporate Woods Pkwy (60061-3159)
**PHONE** ............................. 847 913-0304
Eniko B Suto, *President*
**EMP:** 8 **EST:** 1996
**SALES (est):** 1MM **Privately Held**
**WEB:** www.bende.com
**SIC: 2013** Sausages & related products, from purchased meat

**(G-21151)**
**BLAST ZONE**
645 Lakeview Pkwy (60061-1829)
**PHONE** ............................. 847 996-0100
Carlos Rodriguez, *General Mgr*
**EMP:** 19
**SALES (est):** 1.1MM **Privately Held**
**SIC: 3999** Coin-operated amusement machines

**(G-21152)**
**BOWLMOR AMF CORP**
316 Center Dr (60061-1532)
**PHONE** ............................. 847 367-1600
Bill Spigner, *Branch Mgr*
**EMP:** 72
**SALES (corp-wide):** 292.7MM **Privately Held**
**SIC: 3949** Sporting & athletic goods
**PA:** Bowlmor Amf Corp.
222 W 44th St
New York NY 10036
212 777-2214

**(G-21153)**
**CAREFUSION CORPORATION**
75 N Fairway Dr (60061-1845)
**PHONE** ............................. 858 617-2000
Andreas Lex, *Vice Pres*
Steve Murkin, *Branch Mgr*
Richard Cisneroz, *Manager*
Brent McInnis, *Consultant*
Amy Montalbano, *Consultant*
**EMP:** 51
**SALES (corp-wide):** 12.4B **Publicly Held**
**SIC: 3841** Surgical & medical instruments
**HQ:** Carefusion Corporation
3750 Torrey View Ct
San Diego CA 92130

**(G-21154)**
**CHICAGO SIGN GROUP**
305 Albert Dr (60061-1613)
**PHONE** ............................. 847 899-9021
David E Bromley, *Principal*
▲ **EMP:** 9
**SALES (est):** 1MM **Privately Held**
**SIC: 3993** Signs & advertising specialties

**(G-21155)**
**DAIGGER SCIENTIFIC INC**
620 Lakeview Pkwy (60061-1828)
**PHONE** ............................. 800 621-7193
James Woldenberg, *President*
Kathy Madaj, *Sales Mgr*
**EMP:** 46 **EST:** 2014
**SQ FT:** 5,000
**SALES (est):** 6.2MM **Privately Held**
**SIC: 3821** Autoclaves, laboratory

**(G-21156)**
**DENNIS WRIGHT**
229 Augusta Dr (60061-2033)
**PHONE** ............................. 847 816-6110
Dennis Wright, *Principal*
**EMP:** 3
**SALES (est):** 254.4K **Privately Held**
**SIC: 3577** Optical scanning devices

**(G-21157)**
**DERINGER-NEY INC (PA)**
616 Atrium Dr Ste 100 (60061-1713)
**PHONE** ............................. 847 566-4100
Rod Lamm, *President*
John L Wallace, *President*
Robert Deringer, *Vice Pres*
Lee Trimble, *Vice Pres*
Richard Rzeszotarski, *Plant Mgr*
▲ **EMP:** 20 **EST:** 1950
**SQ FT:** 36,000
**SALES (est):** 110.6MM **Privately Held**
**WEB:** www.deringerney.com
**SIC: 3643** 3542 3469 3452 Contacts, electrical; machine tools, metal forming type; metal stampings; bolts, nuts, rivets & washers; cold finishing of steel shapes

**(G-21158)**
**EDUCATIONAL INSIGHTS INC**
380 N Fairway Dr (60061-1836)
**PHONE** ............................. 847 573-8400
Scott McCabe, *President*
Kelly Cole, *Vice Pres*
Jennifer Neuman, *Vice Pres*
**EMP:** 20
**SALES (corp-wide):** 34.6MM **Privately Held**
**WEB:** www.edin.com
**SIC: 3999** 3944 Education aids, devices & supplies; games, toys & children's vehicles
**HQ:** Educational Insights, Inc.
152 W Walnut St Ste 201
Gardena CA 90248
800 995-4536

**(G-21159)**
**ELORAC INC (PA)**
100 N Fairway Dr Ste 134 (60061-1859)
**PHONE** ............................. 847 362-8200
Joel E Bernstein, *President*
Scott B Phillips, *Senior VP*
John E Kallal PHD, *Vice Pres*
David Henninger, *VP Opers*
Barry Hollingsworth, *CFO*
**EMP:** 10
**SALES (est):** 891.4K **Privately Held**
**SIC: 2834** Pharmaceutical preparations

**(G-21160)**
**EMBROIDERY EXPERTS INC**
595 Lakeview Pkwy (60061-1827)
**PHONE** ............................. 847 403-0200
Michael Schrimmer, *President*
Gary David, *Vice Pres*
**EMP:** 50
**SALES:** 1MM **Privately Held**
**SIC: 2395** Embroidery products, except schiffli machine

**(G-21161)**
**ENVIRO-CHEM INC**
228 Alexandria Dr (60061-2048)
**PHONE** ............................. 847 549-7797
Tom Conway, *Manager*
**EMP:** 3
**SALES (corp-wide):** 3.9MM **Privately Held**
**SIC: 3341** Secondary precious metals
**PA:** Enviro-Chem, Inc.
21821 Industrial Blvd
Rogers MN 55374
763 428-4002

**(G-21162)**
**ETI SOLID STATE LIGHTING INC**
720 Corporate Woods Pkwy (60061-3153)
**PHONE** ............................. 855 384-7754
Eva Kim Yung Chan, *CEO*
Gary Van Winkle, *Vice Pres*
Suk Yee Leung, *CFO*
Kyle Webb, *Sales Dir*
▲ **EMP:** 20
**SQ FT:** 15,000
**SALES:** 18MM **Privately Held**
**WEB:** www.etiled.us
**SIC: 3646** 5719 Commercial indusl & institutional electric lighting fixtures; lighting, lamps & accessories

**(G-21163)**
**FEDEX CORPORATION**
281 W Townline Rd Ste 100 (60061-4334)
**PHONE** ............................. 847 918-7730
**Fax:** 847 918-7247
**EMP:** 11
**SALES (corp-wide):** 47.4B **Publicly Held**
**SIC: 7389** 5099 2752 Business Services Whol Durable Goods Lithographic Commercial Printing
**PA:** Fedex Corporation
942 Shady Grove Rd S
Memphis TN 38120
901 818-7500

**(G-21164)**
**GB MARKETING INC**
200 N Fairway Dr Ste 202 (60061-1861)
**PHONE** ............................. 847 367-0101
**Fax:** 847 367-9305
Thomas Gust, *President*
Gerard Gust, *Vice Pres*
Graham Yemm, *Associate*
**EMP:** 16
**SQ FT:** 4,000
**SALES (est):** 2.8MM **Privately Held**
**WEB:** www.gbmarketing.com
**SIC: 3577** 5064 Computer peripheral equipment; electrical entertainment equipment

**(G-21165)**
**GHETZLER AERO-POWER CORP**
26 Manchester Ln (60061-2312)
**PHONE** ............................. 224 513-5636
Richard Ghetzler, *President*
Michael Mast, *Vice Pres*
**EMP:** 8
**SQ FT:** 12,200
**SALES (est):** 950K **Privately Held**
**WEB:** www.ghetzleraeropower.com
**SIC: 3621** 8711 5049 Power generators; engineering services; engineers' equipment & supplies

**(G-21166)**
**GO CALENDARS**
106 Hawthorn Ctr (60061-1502)
**PHONE** ............................. 847 816-1563
**EMP:** 4
**SALES (est):** 119.3K **Privately Held**
**SIC: 5943** 5112 2752 Office forms & supplies; stationery & office supplies; calendar & card printing, lithographic

**(G-21167)**
**GODIVA CHOCOLATIER INC**
116 Hawthorn Ctr Ste 116 (60061-1502)
**PHONE** ............................. 847 918-0124
Lisa Kalenbach, *Manager*
**EMP:** 24 **Privately Held**
**WEB:** www.godiva.com
**SIC: 2066** Chocolate
**HQ:** Godiva Chocolatier, Inc.
333 W 34th St Fl 6
New York NY 10001
212 984-5900

**(G-21168)**
**GREEN PLANET BOTTLING LLC**
105 W Townline Rd Ste 125 (60061-1424)
**PHONE** ............................. 312 962-4444
Brad Schulamn,
Gary Radville,
Danny Rubenstein,
Brad Schulman,
**EMP:** 10 **EST:** 2008
**SALES (est):** 782.6K **Privately Held**
**SIC: 2086** Pasteurized & mineral waters, bottled & canned; water, pasteurized: packaged in cans, bottles, etc.

**(G-21169)**
**GREENLEES FILTER LLC**
350 Corporate Woods Pkwy (60061-3107)
**PHONE** ............................. 708 366-3256
Roy Greenlees, *Mng Member*
Jerry Plitt, *Manager*
**EMP:** 53
**SQ FT:** 50,000
**SALES (est):** 7.8MM **Privately Held**
**WEB:** www.greenleesfilter.com
**SIC: 3564** Filters, air: furnaces, air conditioning equipment, etc.

**(G-21170)**
**H & H GRAPHICS ILLINOIS INC**
450 Corporate Woods Pkwy (60061-4117)
**PHONE** ............................. 847 383-6285
**Fax:** 847 933-9472
Michelle Leissner, *President*
Dariusz D Celewicz, *VP Opers*
John Lipkowski, *VP Sales*
Todd Perry, *Accounts Exec*
Cathy Nilson, *Office Mgr*
**EMP:** 25
**SQ FT:** 50,000
**SALES (est):** 4.4MM **Privately Held**
**WEB:** www.hhgraphics.net
**SIC: 2759** Screen printing

**(G-21171)**
**HEATHROW SCIENTIFIC LLC**
620 Lakeview Pkwy (60061-1828)
**PHONE** ............................. 847 816-5070
**Fax:** 847 816-5072
Douglas C Reed, *President*
Barbara Hester, *Purch Mgr*
Erin Hankforth, *Mktg Dir*
Carolyn Cadandan, *Manager*
Rainer Wohlgemuth, *Manager*
▲ **EMP:** 15 **EST:** 1998
**SALES:** 3.4MM **Privately Held**
**WEB:** www.heathrowscientific.com
**SIC: 3089** Plastic processing

**(G-21172)**
**ILEESH PRODUCTS LLC**
100 N Fairway Dr Ste 114 (60061-1859)
**PHONE** ............................. 847 383-6695
Oleg Lee, *President*
▲ **EMP:** 6
**SQ FT:** 10,000
**SALES (est):** 749.9K **Privately Held**
**SIC: 2392** Cushions & pillows

**(G-21173)**
**ILLINI/ALTCO INC**
450 Bunker Ct (60061-1831)
**PHONE** ............................. 847 549-0321
**Fax:** 847 549-0352

# Vernon Hills - Lake County (G-21174)    GEOGRAPHIC SECTION

Neil Fine, *President*
Lois Fine, *Vice Pres*
Crissy Ocheltree, *Natl Sales Mgr*
Sabrina Wilt, *Marketing Mgr*
Patricia Hones, *Office Mgr*
◆ **EMP:** 65 **EST:** 1951
**SQ FT:** 63,000
**SALES (est):** 8.9MM
**SALES (corp-wide):** 17.9MM **Privately Held**
**WEB:** www.illiniline.com
**SIC:** 3993 5013 2759 Signs & advertising specialties; motor vehicle supplies & new parts; commercial printing
**PA:** Neil International, Inc.
  450 Bunker Ct
  Vernon Hills IL 60061
  847 549-7627

### (G-21174)
### ILLINOIS TOOL WORKS INC
ITW AMP
888 Forest Edge Dr (60061-3105)
**PHONE** .................... 847 821-2170
Tom Southall, *General Mgr*
Robert McGrath, *Vice Pres*
Harry Andrews, *Purch Mgr*
Johnny Holloway, *Purch Agent*
Pam Foster, *Controller*
**EMP:** 7
**SALES (corp-wide):** 13.6B **Publicly Held**
**SIC:** 3423 3315 3496 Hand & edge tools; nails, steel: wire or cut; staples, made from purchased wire
**PA:** Illinois Tool Works Inc.
  155 Harlem Ave
  Glenview IL 60025
  847 724-7500

### (G-21175)
### INDEPENDENT EYEWEAR MFG LLC
Also Called: IEM
255 Corp Woods Pkwy (60061-3109)
**PHONE** .................... 847 537-0008
Jerry Wolowicz,
Jason Stanley,
**EMP:** 54
**SQ FT:** 50,000
**SALES (est):** 1.6MM **Privately Held**
**SIC:** 3851 Protective eyeware

### (G-21176)
### IO LIGHTING LLC
370 Corporate Woods Pkwy (60061-3107)
**PHONE** .................... 847 735-7000
Ann REO, *CEO*
Trisha Elsbuay, *Administration*
▲ **EMP:** 29
**SQ FT:** 2,100
**SALES (est):** 3.9MM **Privately Held**
**WEB:** www.iolighting.com
**SIC:** 3645 Residential lighting fixtures
**HQ:** Cooper Industries Unlimited Company
  41 A B Drury Street
  Dublin

### (G-21177)
### KANAFLEX CORPORATION ILLINOIS (DH)
800 Woodlands Pkwy (60061-3170)
**PHONE** .................... 847 634-6100
**Fax:** 847 634-6249
Shigeki Kanao, *President*
Tokiyoshi Kosaka, *Vice Pres*
Ken Miyazaki, *Engrg Mgr*
Alla Nudelman, *Accountant*
Tetsunhi Myoda, *Sales Mgr*
▲ **EMP:** 5
**SQ FT:** 100,000
**SALES (est):** 1.6MM
**SALES (corp-wide):** 109.5MM **Privately Held**
**WEB:** www.kanaflexspa.com
**SIC:** 3052 Heater hose, plastic; heater hose, rubber

### (G-21178)
### L S STARRETT CO
50 Lakeview Pkwy Ste 107 (60061-1578)
**PHONE** .................... 847 816-9999
Doug Starrett, *President*
**EMP:** 4
**SALES (est):** 230K **Privately Held**
**SIC:** 3545 Precision measuring tools

### (G-21179)
### LA FORCE INC
280 Corporate Woods Pkwy (60061-3171)
**PHONE** .................... 847 415-5107
**Fax:** 847 634-2727
Andrew Roznowski, *Production*
Donna Kyler, *Sales Staff*
Andrew Lien, *Sales Staff*
Tom Van Ess, *Sales Staff*
John Knier, *Branch Mgr*
**EMP:** 25
**SALES (corp-wide):** 153.6MM **Privately Held**
**WEB:** www.laforceinc.com
**SIC:** 3442 Metal doors, sash & trim
**PA:** La Force, Inc.
  1060 W Mason St
  Green Bay WI 54303
  920 497-7100

### (G-21180)
### LAKE CONSUMER PRODUCTS
730 Corporate Woods Pkwy (60061-3153)
P.O. Box 198, Jackson WI (53037-0198)
**PHONE** .................... 847 793-0230
Gary Burns, *President*
**EMP:** 3
**SALES (est):** 316.6K **Privately Held**
**SIC:** 2834 Pharmaceutical preparations

### (G-21181)
### LEARNING RESOURCES INC (PA)
380 N Fairway Dr (60061-1836)
**PHONE** .................... 847 573-9471
**Fax:** 847 573-8425
Richard M Woldenberg, *President*
Scott McCabe, *Vice Pres*
Barb Plain, *Vice Pres*
Brian Schmidt, *Project Mgr*
Kim Radke, *Prdtn Mgr*
◆ **EMP:** 100
**SQ FT:** 216,000
**SALES (est):** 34.6MM **Privately Held**
**SIC:** 3999 5092 Education aids, devices & supplies; educational toys

### (G-21182)
### LOOMCRAFT TEXTILE & SUPPLY CO
647 Lakeview Pkwy (60061-1829)
**PHONE** .................... 847 680-0000
**Fax:** 847 680-0611
Bob Meroney, *Manager*
**EMP:** 50
**SQ FT:** 728,000
**SALES (corp-wide):** 55.7MM **Privately Held**
**WEB:** www.loomcraft.com
**SIC:** 5131 5714 5719 2221 Upholstery fabrics, woven; drapery & upholstery stores; upholstery materials; window furnishings; broadwoven fabric mills, man-made
**PA:** Loomcraft Textile & Supply Company
  2801 Lawndale Dr
  Greensboro NC 27408
  336 222-0515

### (G-21183)
### MITSUBISHI ELC AUTOMTN INC (DH)
Also Called: Meau
500 Corporate Woods Pkwy (60061-3108)
P.O. Box 52778 Eagle Way, Chicago (60678-0001)
**PHONE** .................... 847 478-2100
**Fax:** 847 478-0327
Toshio Kawai, *President*
Dwayne Gray, *General Mgr*
Matthew Lopinski, *Vice Pres*
Tony Verissimo, *Vice Pres*
Ellen Yang, *Vice Pres*
▲ **EMP:** 200
**SQ FT:** 228,000
**SALES (est):** 61.3MM
**SALES (corp-wide):** 37.3B **Privately Held**
**WEB:** www.meau.com
**SIC:** 3625 3566 3612 3613 Relays & industrial controls; speed changers, drives & gears; transformers, except electric; switchgear & switchboard apparatus; auto controls regulating residntl & coml environmt & applncs; measuring & controlling devices
**HQ:** Mitsubishi Electric Us Holdings, Inc.
  5900 Katella Ave Ste A
  Cypress CA 90630
  714 220-2500

### (G-21184)
### NEIL ENTERPRISES INC
450 Bunker Ct (60061-1831)
**PHONE** .................... 847 549-0321
Jerry Fine, *Ch of Bd*
Neil Fine, *President*
Lois Fine, *Corp Secy*
Carol Jacobson, *Vice Pres*
Brian Garbutt, *Warehouse Mgr*
▲ **EMP:** 40
**SQ FT:** 63,000
**SALES (est):** 8.9MM
**SALES (corp-wide):** 17.9MM **Privately Held**
**WEB:** www.neilenterprises.com
**SIC:** 3089 Injection molded finished plastic products
**PA:** Neil International, Inc.
  450 Bunker Ct
  Vernon Hills IL 60061
  847 549-7627

### (G-21185)
### NEIL INTERNATIONAL INC (PA)
450 Bunker Ct (60061-1831)
**PHONE** .................... 847 549-7627
Jerry Fine, *Ch of Bd*
Neil Fine, *President*
Lois Fine, *Admin Sec*
▲ **EMP:** 6
**SQ FT:** 63,000
**SALES (est):** 17.9MM **Privately Held**
**SIC:** 3089 3993 Injection molded finished plastic products; signs & advertising specialties

### (G-21186)
### P H C ENTERPRISES INC
Also Called: AlphaGraphics
222 Hawthorn Vlg Cmns (60061-1519)
**PHONE** .................... 847 816-7373
**Fax:** 847 816-7376
Patrick Canary, *President*
Barbara Canary, *Vice Pres*
Michael Zelmar, *Admin Sec*
**EMP:** 8
**SQ FT:** 2,000
**SALES (est):** 950K **Privately Held**
**SIC:** 2752 2791 2789 2759 Commercial printing, offset; typesetting; bookbinding & related work; commercial printing

### (G-21187)
### PACTRA CORP
2112 Beaver Creek Dr (60061-3813)
**PHONE** .................... 847 281-0308
Robert J Cheon, *Principal*
**EMP:** 5
**SALES (est):** 640.9K **Privately Held**
**SIC:** 3612 5065 Transformers, except electric; electronic parts & equipment

### (G-21188)
### PARKER INTERNATIONAL PDTS INC
Also Called: Parker Metal
650 Forest Edge Dr (60061-4115)
**PHONE** .................... 815 524-5831
Jordan Levy, *President*
Dennis Foley, *Vice Pres*
Richard Noonan, *Treasurer*
▲ **EMP:** 96 **EST:** 1969
**SQ FT:** 170,000
**SALES (est):** 8.4MM **Privately Held**
**WEB:** www.parkercarts.com
**SIC:** 3452 6512 8741 Screws, metal; bolts, metal; washers, metal; commercial & industrial building operation; hotel or motel management

### (G-21189)
### PARKSON CORPORATION
562 Bunker Ct (60061-1831)
**PHONE** .................... 847 816-3700
Tai Nguyen, *Engineer*
Pradeep Vibhuti, *Design Engr*
Joseph Ramirez, *Accounting Mgr*
Fernando Esquivel, *Regl Sales Mgr*
Chuck Meier, *Branch Mgr*
**EMP:** 9

**SALES (corp-wide):** 467.2MM **Privately Held**
**SIC:** 3559 Refinery, chemical processing & similar machinery
**HQ:** Parkson Corporation
  1401 W Cypress Creek Rd # 100
  Fort Lauderdale FL 33309
  954 974-6610

### (G-21190)
### PRECISION RESOURCE INC
Also Called: Precision Resource III Div
700 Hickory Hill Dr (60061-3104)
**PHONE** .................... 847 383-1300
Vito Grimaldi, *Accounting Dir*
Curt Krueger, *Branch Mgr*
**EMP:** 120
**SALES (corp-wide):** 204.7MM **Privately Held**
**WEB:** www.precisionresource.com
**SIC:** 3469 3544 Metal stampings; special dies, tools, jigs & fixtures
**PA:** Precision Resource, Inc.
  25 Forest Pkwy
  Shelton CT 06484
  203 925-0012

### (G-21191)
### RAINBOW MIDWEST INC
Also Called: Rainbow Play Systems Illinois
300 Corporate Woods Pkwy (60061-3107)
**PHONE** .................... 847 955-9300
**Fax:** 847 955-9493
Joanie Barrus, *Manager*
**EMP:** 4 **Privately Held**
**SIC:** 3949 5941 Playground equipment; playground equipment
**PA:** Rainbow Midwest Inc
  900 W 80th St
  Minneapolis MN 55420

### (G-21192)
### REVISS SERVICES INC
175 E Hawthorn Pkwy # 142 (60061-1493)
**PHONE** .................... 847 680-4522
Ian Latham, *President*
John Schrader, *Vice Pres*
◆ **EMP:** 3
**SQ FT:** 1,500
**SALES:** 3MM
**SALES (est):** 445K **Privately Held**
**WEB:** www.reviss.com
**SIC:** 3821 Sterilizers
**PA:** Reviss Services (Uk) Limited
  Unit N
  Bourne End BUCKS

### (G-21193)
### RICHARD WOLF MED INSTRS CORP
353 Corporate Woods Pkwy (60061-3110)
**PHONE** .................... 847 913-1113
**Fax:** 847 913-1488
Juergen Pfab, *President*
Alfons Notheis, *President*
Siegfried Karst, *COO*
Bert Gaide, *Prdtn Mgr*
Klaus Schilde, *Mfg Staff*
▼ **EMP:** 193
**SQ FT:** 165,000
**SALES (est):** 114.2MM **Privately Held**
**WEB:** www.richardwolfusa.com
**SIC:** 5047 3841 Medical equipment & supplies; surgical & medical instruments
**HQ:** Richard Wolf Gmbh
  Pforzheimer Str. 32
  Knittlingen 75438
  704 335-0

### (G-21194)
### RUST-OLEUM (CANADA) LTD
11 E Hawthorn Pkwy (60061-1402)
**PHONE** .................... 847 367-7700
Tom Reed, *CEO*
Wilbert Bartelt Sr, *Vice Pres*
Charlie Leichtweis, *Controller*
**EMP:** 350 **EST:** 1970
**SQ FT:** 50,000
**SALES (est):** 14.9K
**SALES (corp-wide):** 4.8B **Publicly Held**
**SIC:** 2899 Rust resisting compounds
**HQ:** Rust-Oleum Corporation
  11 E Hawthorn Pkwy
  Vernon Hills IL 60061
  847 367-7700

# GEOGRAPHIC SECTION
## Vernon Hills - Lake County (G-21219)

### (G-21195)
**RUST-OLEUM CORPORATION (HQ)**
11 E Hawthorn Pkwy  (60061-1499)
PHONE..................................847 367-7700
Fax: 847 816-2330
Thomas E Reed, *President*
Tom Schweiger, *Principal*
Oscar Rubio, *Regional Mgr*
Dave Steckel, *Regional Mgr*
Jim Doody, *Area Mgr*
◆ **EMP:** 150 EST: 1932
**SQ FT:** 100,000
**SALES (est):** 671.4MM
**SALES (corp-wide):** 4.8B  Publicly Held
WEB: www.rust-oleum.com
**SIC: 2891**  2899 2816 2842 Adhesives & sealants; chemical preparations; inorganic pigments; specialty cleaning, polishes & sanitation goods; paints, waterproof
PA: Rpm International Inc.
   2628 Pearl Rd
   Medina OH 44256
   330 273-5090

### (G-21196)
**SAB TOOL SUPPLY CO (PA)**
Also Called: Yg-1 Tool USA
730 Corporate Woods Pkwy  (60061-3153)
PHONE..................................847 634-3700
Fax: 847 634-3755
Heather Lee, *President*
Nancy Han, *Admin Sec*
▲ **EMP:** 2
**SALES (est):** 510.1K  Privately Held
**SIC: 5251**  3423 Tools; hand & edge tools

### (G-21197)
**SCOTSMAN GROUP INC (DH)**
Also Called: Scotsman Ice Systems Division
101 Corporate Woods Pkwy  (60061-3109)
PHONE..................................847 215-4500
Fax: 847 541-1759
Mark McClanahan, *President*
**EMP:** 100
**SQ FT:** 36,000
**SALES (est):** 51.5MM  Privately Held
**SIC: 3585**  Ice making machinery
HQ: Scotsman Industries, Inc.
   101 Corporate Woods Pkwy
   Vernon Hills IL 60061
   847 215-4501

### (G-21198)
**SCOTSMAN ICE SYSTEMS**
101 Corporate Woods Pkwy  (60061-3151)
PHONE..................................847 215-4500
Kevin Clark, *President*
**EMP:** 50
**SALES (est):** 1.8MM  Privately Held
**SIC: 3585**  Ice making machinery

### (G-21199)
**SCOTSMAN INDUSTRIES INC (DH)**
Also Called: Scotsman of Los Angeles
101 Corporate Woods Pkwy  (60061-3109)
PHONE..................................847 215-4501
Fax: 847 913-9844
Jeff Biel, *Manager*
David McCulloch,
Kenneth Batko,
David Wrech,
▲ **EMP:** 65
**SALES (est):** 263.1MM  Privately Held
WEB: www.scotsman-ice.com
**SIC: 3585**  3632 Refrigeration equipment, complete; ice making machinery; ice boxes, industrial; cold drink dispensing equipment (not coin-operated); ice boxes, household: metal or wood; refrigerators, mechanical & absorption: household
HQ: Ali Spa
   Via Piero Gobetti 2/A
   Cernusco Sul Naviglio MI 20063
   029 219-91

### (G-21200)
**SECURITY LOCKNUT LLC**
999 Forest Edge Dr  (60061-3106)
PHONE..................................847 970-4050
Ray Wiltgen, *Mng Member*
David May,
▲ **EMP:** 22
**SALES:** 3.4MM  Privately Held
WEB: www.securitylocknut.com
**SIC: 3452**  3451 Nuts, metal; bolts, metal; screw machine products

### (G-21201)
**SENNA DESIGN LLC**
100 Corporate Woods Pkwy  (60061-4127)
PHONE..................................847 821-7877
**EMP:** 8
**SQ FT:** 20,000
**SALES (est):** 80.6K  Privately Held
**SIC: 3469**  3264 Mfg Metal Stampings Mfg Porcelain Electrical Suppplies

### (G-21202)
**SENSOR SYNERGY**
200 N Fairway Dr Ste 198  (60061-1861)
P.O. Box 5019, Buffalo Grove  (60089-5019)
PHONE..................................847 353-8200
Fax: 847 353-8232
James Wiczer, *President*
Michael Wiczer, *Engineer*
**EMP:** 6
**SALES (est):** 540K  Privately Held
WEB: www.sensorsynergy.com
**SIC: 3823**  Computer interface equipment for industrial process control

### (G-21203)
**SOLUTION DESIGNS INC**
2042 Laurel Valley Dr  (60061-4556)
PHONE..................................847 680-7788
Patrick Marsek, *President*
Tracy Rieke, *Admin Sec*
**EMP:** 5
**SALES (est):** 604.5K  Privately Held
**SIC: 2873**  Nitrogenous fertilizers

### (G-21204)
**STEAMGARD LLC**
Also Called: Engineering Resources
730 Forest Edge Dr  (60061-3172)
PHONE..................................847 913-8400
Fax: 847 913-8488
Philip Stavropoulos, *General Mgr*
C Stavropoulos, *Principal*
REA S Lorence, *Principal*
Nicholas Stavropoulos, *Principal*
Peter Kopsaftis, *Business Mgr*
**EMP:** 30 EST: 2002
**SQ FT:** 11,000
**SALES (est):** 6.8MM  Privately Held
WEB: www.steamgard.com
**SIC: 3494**  8711 Steam fittings & specialties; designing: ship, boat, machine & product

### (G-21205)
**SWAGGER FOODS CORPORATION**
900 Corporate Woods Pkwy  (60061-3155)
PHONE..................................847 913-1200
Fax: 847 913-1263
Tai Ryang Shin, *President*
Jerry Hedlin, *Plant Mgr*
Maria Whelen, *Finance Mgr*
Catherine Ahn, *Human Res Mgr*
Erica Shin, *Marketing Staff*
**EMP:** 20
**SQ FT:** 41,500
**SALES (est):** 5.1MM  Privately Held
WEB: www.swaggerfoods.com
**SIC: 2099**  Sauces: dry mixes; gravy mixes, dry; seasonings: dry mixes

### (G-21206)
**SWAROVSKI NORTH AMERICA LTD**
116 Hawthorne Shopg Ctr  (60061)
PHONE..................................847 680-5150
Luz Osequera, *Branch Mgr*
Brian Willing, *Manager*
**EMP:** 7
**SALES (corp-wide):** 4.2B  Privately Held
**SIC: 3961**  Costume jewelry
HQ: Swarovski North America Limited
   1 Kenney Dr
   Cranston RI 02920
   401 463-6400

### (G-21207)
**TELEGRAPH HILL INC**
100 N Fairway Dr Ste 106  (60061-1859)
PHONE..................................415 252-9097
Maria Spurlock, *CEO*
Robert Spurlock, *President*
▲ **EMP:** 3
**SALES:** 1.2MM  Privately Held
WEB: www.telegraphhill.com
**SIC: 2384**  Bathrobes, men's & women's: made from purchased materials

### (G-21208)
**TETRA PAK INC**
600 Bunker Ct  (60061-1847)
PHONE..................................847 955-6000
Jason Pelz, *Vice Pres*
John Ward, *Research*
Matthew Michlin, *Engineer*
Brent Williams, *Engineer*
Perry Naylor, *Data Proc Staff*
**EMP:** 75
**SALES (corp-wide):** 6.4B  Privately Held
**SIC: 2671**  3565 5084 Paper coated or laminated for packaging; packaging machinery; hydraulic systems equipment & supplies
HQ: Tetra Pak Inc.
   3300 Airport Rd
   Denton TX 76207
   940 565-8800

### (G-21209)
**TETRA PAK MATERIALS LP (DH)**
101 Corporate Woods Pkwy  (60061-3109)
PHONE..................................847 955-6000
Uno Kjellberg, *President*
◆ **EMP:** 100
**SQ FT:** 2,000
**SALES (est):** 162.4MM
**SALES (corp-wide):** 6.4B  Privately Held
**SIC: 2671**  Paper coated or laminated for packaging
HQ: Tetra Pak Inc.
   3300 Airport Rd
   Denton TX 76207
   940 565-8800

### (G-21210)
**TETRA PAK US HOLDINGS INC (DH)**
101 Corporate Woods Pkwy  (60061-3109)
PHONE..................................940 565-8800
Fax: 847 955-6500
Dennis Jonsson, *CEO*
Ruben Lopez, *President*
Todd Hutson, *Managing Dir*
Per Lauritzen, *Managing Dir*
Muhammad Azhar, *Business Mgr*
◆ **EMP:** 150
**SQ FT:** 90,000
**SALES (est):** 421.8MM
**SALES (corp-wide):** 6.4B  Privately Held
**SIC: 2656**  Food containers (liquid tight), including milk cartons
HQ: Tetra Laval International Sa
   Avenue General-Guisan 70
   Pully VD 1009
   217 292-211

### (G-21211)
**THERMOSOFT INTERNATIONAL CORP**
701 Corporate Woods Pkwy  (60061-3112)
PHONE..................................847 279-3800
Eric Kochman, *President*
Mike Lavit, *Vice Pres*
Dmitry Kochman, *Project Mgr*
Eugene Pavloutine, *Opers Mgr*
Vera Terpay, *Accountant*
▲ **EMP:** 47
**SQ FT:** 15,000
**SALES (est):** 9.1MM  Privately Held
WEB: www.thermosoftinternational.com
**SIC: 3634**  Heaters, tape; heating pads, electric

### (G-21212)
**THREE HANDS TECHNOLOGIES**
462 Harrison Ct  (60061-1369)
PHONE..................................847 680-5358
Tom McGuigan, *President*
**EMP:** 3
**SALES:** 100K  Privately Held
**SIC: 3699**  Electronic training devices

### (G-21213)
**TRI INDUSTRIES NFP**
Also Called: Tri Industies
780 Corporate Woods Pkwy  (60061-3153)
PHONE..................................773 754-3100
Ann Curley, *Business Mgr*
Ken Bell, *Exec Dir*
▲ **EMP:** 30
**SQ FT:** 15,000
**SALES:** 5.5MM  Privately Held
WEB: www.tri-industries.org
**SIC: 3861**  Toners, prepared photographic (not made in chemical plants)

### (G-21214)
**US VISION INC**
Also Called: JC Penney Optical
4 Hawthorn Ctr  (60061-1520)
PHONE..................................847 367-0420
Jerri Shupe, *Branch Mgr*
**EMP:** 3
**SALES (corp-wide):** 367.5MM  Privately Held
WEB: www.usvision.com
**SIC: 3851**  Ophthalmic goods
HQ: U.S. Vision, Inc.
   1 Harmon Dr
   Glendora NJ 08029
   856 227-8339

### (G-21215)
**VMA GROUP INC**
13 Saint Clair Ln  (60061-3225)
PHONE..................................847 877-7039
Vadim Klugman, *Principal*
▲ **EMP:** 4
**SALES (est):** 320K  Privately Held
**SIC: 2084**  Wines, brandy & brandy spirits

### (G-21216)
**WAGNER INTERNATIONAL LLC**
Also Called: My Sports Warehouse
105 W Townline Rd Ste 160  (60061-1424)
PHONE..................................224 619-9247
Jim Wagner, *Mng Member*
**EMP:** 1
**SALES:** 400K  Privately Held
WEB: www.mysportswarehouse.com
**SIC: 7389**  3949 2759 Embroidering of advertising on shirts, etc.; sporting & athletic goods; screen printing

### (G-21217)
**WINSTON PHARMACEUTICALS INC (HQ)**
100 N Fairway Dr Ste 134  (60061-1859)
PHONE..................................847 362-8200
Joel E Bernstein MD, *President*
Neal S Penneys MD, *Principal*
Robert A Yolles, *Principal*
Scott B Phillips MD, *Senior VP*
David Starr, *CFO*
**EMP:** 9
**SQ FT:** 7,300
**SALES (est):** 2.4MM  Privately Held
**SIC: 2834**  Pharmaceutical preparations

### (G-21218)
**WONDERLIC INC**
400 Lakeview Pkwy Ste 200  (60061-1850)
PHONE..................................847 680-4900
Charles F Wonderlic Jr, *CEO*
David Hammond, *President*
David Arnold, *Vice Pres*
Richard E Wonderlic, *CFO*
Sally Garrett, *Asst Controller*
**EMP:** 83
**SQ FT:** 24,193
**SALES:** 14.3MM
**SALES (corp-wide):** 12.8MM  Privately Held
WEB: www.phonapp.com
**SIC: 2741**  Miscellaneous publishing
PA: Wonderlic Holdings, Inc.
   400 Lakeview Pkwy Ste 200
   Vernon Hills IL 60061
   877 605-9496

### (G-21219)
**WORLD WIDE FITTINGS INC (PA)**
600 Corporate Woods Pkwy  (60061-3113)
PHONE..................................847 588-2200
Fax: 847 588-1212
Joseph McCarthy, *President*

Michael Schwocher, *General Mgr*
Jay McBride, *COO*
Sean McCarthy, *Exec VP*
Casey Michael, *Senior VP*
▲ **EMP:** 191
**SQ FT:** 52,000
**SALES (est):** 70.7MM **Privately Held**
**WEB:** www.worldwidefittings.com
**SIC: 3494** Valves & pipe fittings

*(G-21220)*
**XOMI INSTRUMENTS CO LTD**
1463 Pinehurst Dr (60061-1230)
**PHONE**..............................847 660-4614
Jie Xie, *President*
**EMP:** 3
**SALES (est):** 53.2K **Privately Held**
**SIC: 3669** Communications equipment

*(G-21221)*
**ZF SERVICES LLC**
777 Hickory Hill Dr (60061-3182)
**PHONE**..............................734 416-6200
Stefan Sommer, *CEO*
Ron Davis, *Plant Mgr*
Jan Okal, *Purch Mgr*
Marty Abernathy, *Purchasing*
Bonnie Kendrick, *Human Res Mgr*
**EMP:** 7 **Privately Held**
**SIC: 3714** Motor vehicle parts & accessories
**HQ:** Zf Services, Llc
   15811 Centennial Dr
   Northville MI 48168

## Vienna
### *Johnson County*

*(G-21222)*
**DRY SYSTEMS TECHNOLOGIES LLC**
1430 Us Highway 45 N (62995-2675)
**PHONE**..............................618 658-3000
Terry McDonald, *Branch Mgr*
**EMP:** 11
**SALES (corp-wide):** 9MM **Privately Held**
**SIC: 3532** Mining machinery
**HQ:** Dry Systems Technologies Llc
   10420 Rising Ct
   Woodridge IL 60517
   630 427-2051

*(G-21223)*
**MATT SNELL AND SONS**
4530 Mount Shelter Rd (62995-3119)
**PHONE**..............................618 695-3555
Matt Snell, *Owner*
**EMP:** 4
**SALES (est):** 193K **Privately Held**
**SIC: 0191** 3715 General farms, primarily crop; truck trailers

*(G-21224)*
**REYNOLDS ROCK OF AGES (PA)**
Also Called: Reynolds J W Rock Ages Mmrials
103 S 5th St (62995-1746)
P.O. Box 665 (62995-0665)
**PHONE**..............................618 658-2911
**Fax:** 618 658-5097
Rhonda Webb, *Manager*
**EMP:** 13 **EST:** 1888
**SALES (est):** 1.6MM **Privately Held**
**SIC: 3281** Monuments, cut stone (not finishing or lettering only)

*(G-21225)*
**SHAWNEE WINERY**
200 Commercial St (62995-1689)
**PHONE**..............................618 658-8400
**EMP:** 5
**SQ FT:** 6,000
**SALES (est):** 340K **Privately Held**
**SIC: 2084** Wine Manufacture

*(G-21226)*
**W BOZARTH LOGGING**
540 Hillside Ln (62995-2325)
**PHONE**..............................618 658-4016
Wayne Bozart, *Owner*
**EMP:** 2
**SALES (est):** 288.5K **Privately Held**
**SIC: 2411** Logging camps & contractors

## Villa Grove
### *Douglas County*

*(G-21227)*
**DEEM WOODWORKS**
22 N Deer Lk (61956-9622)
**PHONE**..............................217 832-9614
Charles Deem, *Owner*
**EMP:** 2
**SALES:** 250K **Privately Held**
**SIC: 2431** Millwork

*(G-21228)*
**HERMAN BADE & SONS**
Also Called: Bade Herman & Son Trucking
608 N Henson Rd (61956-1643)
**PHONE**..............................217 832-9444
Everett Bade, *Partner*
Phillip Bade, *Partner*
Stanley Bade, *Partner*
**EMP:** 3 **EST:** 1936
**SALES (est):** 210K **Privately Held**
**SIC: 1771** 5039 3273 Concrete work; mobile homes; ready-mixed concrete

*(G-21229)*
**LAKE FABRICATION INC**
4 S Sycamore St (61956-1533)
P.O. Box 136 (61956-0136)
**PHONE**..............................217 832-2761
Pete Lake, *Owner*
Randy Lake, *Co-Owner*
**EMP:** 2
**SQ FT:** 20,000
**SALES (est):** 380.9K **Privately Held**
**SIC: 3535** 7699 7692 Belt conveyor systems, general industrial use; farm machinery repair; welding repair

*(G-21230)*
**PAULS MACHINE & WELDING CORP (PA)**
Also Called: Mordern Flow Equipment
650 N Sycamore St (61956-9772)
**PHONE**..............................217 832-2541
**Fax:** 217 832-3311
Edward Cler, *President*
Keith Cler, *Corp Secy*
Thomas D Cler, *Vice Pres*
Charles Rohlfing, *Controller*
Ahmed Seclair, *Sales Staff*
▲ **EMP:** 70
**SQ FT:** 40,000
**SALES (est):** 14.8MM **Privately Held**
**WEB:** www.paulsmachine.com
**SIC: 3599** Machine shop, jobbing & repair

## Villa Park
### *Dupage County*

*(G-21231)*
**A TO Z TOOL INC**
400 W Saint Charles Rd # 1 (60181-2442)
**PHONE**..............................630 787-0478
**Fax:** 630 279-4134
**EMP:** 9
**SQ FT:** 12,400
**SALES:** 600K **Privately Held**
**SIC: 3423** Mfg Hand Tools

*(G-21232)*
**ADDISON ENGRAVING INC**
204 W Ridge Rd (60181-1515)
**PHONE**..............................630 833-9123
Gerald D Dobey, *President*
Steven E Dobey, *Vice Pres*
Alice Dobey, *Administration*
**EMP:** 2 **EST:** 1960
**SQ FT:** 1,800
**SALES (est):** 201.9K **Privately Held**
**WEB:** www.addisonengraving.com
**SIC: 3479** 3993 Engraving jewelry silverware, or metal; name plates: engraved, etched, etc.; signs & advertising specialties

*(G-21233)*
**ADVANCE PRESS SIGN INC**
719 N Addison Rd (60181-1493)
**PHONE**..............................630 833-1600
**Fax:** 630 833-1435
Geary Mallek, *President*
Mildred Mallek, *Vice Pres*
**EMP:** 4
**SQ FT:** 2,500
**SALES:** 250K **Privately Held**
**SIC: 2759** 3993 Screen printing; signs & advertising specialties

*(G-21234)*
**AIR LAND AND SEA INTERIORS**
Also Called: Riggs Brothers Auto Interiors
220 E Saint Charles Rd (60181-2433)
**PHONE**..............................630 834-1717
**Fax:** 630 834-1795
William Keifer, *President*
Linda Keifer, *Admin Sec*
**EMP:** 3
**SQ FT:** 2,800
**SALES (est):** 160K **Privately Held**
**SIC: 7641** 3732 3728 3714 Reupholstery; boat building & repairing; aircraft parts & equipment; motor vehicle parts & accessories; canvas & related products

*(G-21235)*
**ALL METAL RECYCLING COMPANY**
409 N Addison Rd (60181-1950)
**PHONE**..............................847 530-4825
Tom Mitchell, *Owner*
**EMP:** 4 **EST:** 2014
**SALES (est):** 196.6K **Privately Held**
**SIC: 3559** 3569 Recycling machinery; baling machines, for scrap metal, paper or similar material

*(G-21236)*
**AMERICAN METAL INSTALLERS & FA**
55 W Home Ave (60181-2566)
**PHONE**..............................630 993-0812
**Fax:** 630 993-0890
Roy Splingaire, *President*
**EMP:** 2
**SQ FT:** 9,200
**SALES:** 499K **Privately Held**
**SIC: 1711** 7692 3556 3444 Ventilation & duct work contractor; welding repair; food products machinery; sheet metalwork

*(G-21237)*
**BATTERIES PLUS 287**
240 E Roosevelt Rd (60181-3500)
**PHONE**..............................630 279-3478
**Fax:** 630 279-3589
Paul Bessey, *Principal*
**EMP:** 3
**SALES (est):** 299.8K **Privately Held**
**SIC: 3691** 5063 5531 Storage batteries; batteries; batteries, automotive & truck

*(G-21238)*
**BIEWER FABRICATING INC**
208 W Stone Rd (60181-1518)
**PHONE**..............................630 530-8922
**Fax:** 630 530-8947
Joe Biewer, *President*
Judy Biewer, *Vice Pres*
**EMP:** 7
**SQ FT:** 2,500
**SALES:** 1.1MM **Privately Held**
**SIC: 3441** Fabricated structural metal

*(G-21239)*
**BURDETT BURNER MFG INC**
335 S Ardmore Ave (60181-2943)
**PHONE**..............................630 617-5060
Thomas L Monick, *President*
**EMP:** 4
**SALES (est):** 450K **Privately Held**
**WEB:** www.burdettburner.com
**SIC: 3567** Fuel-fired furnaces & ovens

*(G-21240)*
**C KELLER MANUFACTURING INC**
925 N Ellsworth Ave (60181-1107)
**PHONE**..............................630 833-5593
**Fax:** 630 832-7012
Fred Keller, *CEO*
John Jacobi, *President*
Tony Marzovilla, *Vice Pres*
Ron Rigwood, *QC Mgr*
Dan Piorek, *Engineer*
**EMP:** 40
**SQ FT:** 15,000
**SALES (est):** 8.3MM **Privately Held**
**WEB:** www.ckellermfg.com
**SIC: 3441** 3469 7692 3444 Fabricated structural metal; stamping metal for the trade; welding repair; sheet metalwork

*(G-21241)*
**CARPENTERS MILLWORK CO (PA)**
224 W Stone Rd (60181-1518)
**PHONE**..............................708 339-7707
**Fax:** 630 941-8011
Gary Smits, *President*
Deborah J Smits, *Corp Secy*
**EMP:** 9
**SQ FT:** 10,000
**SALES (est):** 2.1MM **Privately Held**
**SIC: 5031** 2434 2431 2421 Lumber, plywood & millwork; doors & windows; wood kitchen cabinets; millwork; sawmills & planing mills, general

*(G-21242)*
**CASTLE CRAFT PRODUCTS INC**
1133 N Ellsworth Ave (60181-1040)
**PHONE**..............................630 279-7494
Gregory Venchus, *President*
Maryland Venchus, *CFO*
**EMP:** 12
**SALES (est):** 2.5MM **Privately Held**
**SIC: 2541** 2521 Store fixtures, wood; cabinets, office: wood

*(G-21243)*
**COBALT TOOL & MANUFACTURING**
131 W Home Ave (60181-2568)
**PHONE**..............................630 530-8898
Fred J Hoyne Jr, *President*
Barbara Jeanne Hoyne, *Vice Pres*
**EMP:** 4
**SQ FT:** 1,200
**SALES (est):** 320K **Privately Held**
**SIC: 3599** 3825 Machine shop, jobbing & repair; instruments to measure electricity

*(G-21244)*
**CONSTRUCTION SOLUTIONS LLC**
222 W Stone Rd (60181-1518)
**PHONE**..............................630 834-1929
Frank Sullivan,
Meg Sullivan,
**EMP:** 8
**SALES (est):** 1MM **Privately Held**
**SIC: 3479** Painting, coating & hot dipping

*(G-21245)*
**CONXALL CORPORATION**
601 E Wildwood Ave (60181-2762)
**PHONE**..............................630 834-7504
**Fax:** 630 834-8540
Keith A Bandolik, *President*
Robert Macnamara, *Purch Mgr*
James Collado, *Engineer*
Chuck Smaczny, *Engineer*
Jerome J Vorel, *Engineer*
**EMP:** 150
**SQ FT:** 33,500
**SALES (est):** 28.3MM
**SALES (corp-wide):** 1.3B **Publicly Held**
**WEB:** www.conxall.com
**SIC: 3678** Electronic connectors
**HQ:** Switchcraft, Inc.
   5555 N Elston Ave
   Chicago IL 60630
   773 792-2700

*(G-21246)*
**COURTESY METAL POLISHING**
735 N Addison Rd Ste B (60181-1469)
**PHONE**..............................630 832-1862
Juventino Dorado, *Owner*
**EMP:** 3
**SQ FT:** 2,500
**SALES (est):** 190K **Privately Held**
**SIC: 3471** Buffing for the trade; polishing, metals or formed products

## Villa Park - Dupage County (G-21273)

**(G-21247)**
**CROWN BATTERY MANUFACTURING CO**
1199 N Ellsworth Ave (60181-1040)
PHONE................630 530-8060
Fax: 630 530-8071
Peter Chavez, *Branch Mgr*
EMP: 6
SALES (corp-wide): 222.1MM Privately Held
WEB: www.crownbattery.com
SIC: 3691 Storage batteries
PA: Crown Battery Manufacturing Company
1445 Majestic Dr
Fremont OH 43420
419 332-0563

**(G-21248)**
**DELTA ERECTORS INC**
18w178 Buckingham Ln (60181-3820)
PHONE................708 267-9721
Thomas R Chambers, *President*
EMP: 10
SALES (est): 520K Privately Held
SIC: 1791 3441 3449 7389 Building front installation metal; building components, structural steel; curtain walls for buildings, steel;

**(G-21249)**
**E A A ENTERPRISES INC**
Also Called: Sir Speedy Print Signs Mktg
250 E Saint Charles Rd (60181-2472)
PHONE................630 279-0150
Fax: 630 279-0153
Bill Schaub, *President*
Ann Schaub, *Vice Pres*
EMP: 6
SQ FT: 2,500
SALES (est): 996.3K Privately Held
SIC: 2752 3993 Commercial printing, lithographic; signs & advertising specialties

**(G-21250)**
**EMERSON INDUSTRIES LLC (PA)**
721 N Yale Ave (60181-1607)
PHONE................630 279-0920
Fax: 630 279-0379
Walter A Emerson, *Mng Member*
Judith Emerson,
EMP: 10 EST: 1969
SQ FT: 27,000
SALES (est): 1.9MM Privately Held
WEB: www.emersonplasticmold.com
SIC: 3544 Industrial molds

**(G-21251)**
**EMPIRE SCREW MANUFACTURING CO**
747 N Yale Ave (60181-1679)
PHONE................630 833-7060
Fax: 630 833-7094
Peter Sparacio, *President*
Toni Sparacio, *Corp Secy*
Antoinette Sparacio, *Vice Pres*
EMP: 18 EST: 1944
SQ FT: 5,000
SALES (est): 750K Privately Held
SIC: 3451 Screw machine products

**(G-21252)**
**FLORIDA METROLOGY LLC**
Also Called: Acme Scale Systems
1100 N Villa Ave (60181-1054)
PHONE................630 833-3800
Fax: 630 833-0044
Ron Kupper, *Mng Member*
EMP: 15
SALES (corp-wide): 4.9MM Privately Held
SIC: 5046 7699 7359 3821 Scales, except laboratory; scale repair service; equipment rental & leasing; calibration tapes for physical testing machines
HQ: Florida Metrology, Llc
645 Nw Entp Dr Ste 106
Port Saint Lucie FL 34986
772 212-7158

**(G-21253)**
**FRICKE INTERNATIONAL INC**
208 W Ridge Rd (60181-1515)
PHONE................630 833-2627
Fax: 630 833-3148
Lawrence R Fricke Jr, *President*
▲ EMP: 12
SQ FT: 7,500
SALES (est): 1.3MM Privately Held
SIC: 3843 Dental equipment & supplies

**(G-21254)**
**GALAXY SOURCING INC**
744 N Michigan Ave (60181-1503)
PHONE................630 532-5003
Shakil Merchant, *President*
▲ EMP: 3
SQ FT: 5,000
SALES (est): 1.9MM Privately Held
WEB: www.forcetorque.com
SIC: 3545 3568 Machine tool accessories; sprockets (power transmission equipment); pulleys, power transmission

**(G-21255)**
**GLENDALE INCORPORATED**
Also Called: Glendale Pharma
322 Ste B W St Charles Rd (60181)
PHONE................630 770-1965
Mariam Murtaza, *President*
EMP: 10
SALES (est): 430K Privately Held
SIC: 2834 Syrups, pharmaceutical

**(G-21256)**
**GRAPHIC ARTS SERVICES INC (PA)**
333 W Saint Charles Rd (60181-2451)
PHONE................630 629-7770
Fax: 630 832-2141
George Hoganson, *Ch of Bd*
Thomas Hoganson, *President*
Mary Hoganson, *Admin Sec*
EMP: 25
SQ FT: 8,500
SALES (est): 4.1MM Privately Held
WEB: www.g-a-s-inc.com
SIC: 2759 Commercial printing

**(G-21257)**
**GRAPHIC CHEMICAL & INK CO**
728 N Yale Ave (60181-1683)
P.O. Box 7027 (60181-7027)
PHONE................630 832-6004
Dean Clark, *Principal*
Susan Clark, *Vice Pres*
Sarah C Canniff, *Treasurer*
Elizabeth A Clark, *Admin Sec*
▲ EMP: 18 EST: 1920
SQ FT: 10,000
SALES (est): 3.2MM Privately Held
WEB: www.graphicchemical.com
SIC: 3952 2893 5111 Artists' materials, except pencils & leads; gravure ink; letterpress or offset ink; lithographic ink; fine paper

**(G-21258)**
**HAIMER USA LLC**
134 E Hill St (60181-1805)
PHONE................630 833-1500
Fax: 630 833-1507
Claudia Haimer, *CEO*
Brendt Holden, *President*
Jordan Tetzlaff, *Regional Mgr*
Craig Schepers, *Regl Sales Mgr*
Francisco Martinez, *Sales Staff*
▲ EMP: 5
SALES (est): 1.2MM
SALES (corp-wide): 31.3MM Privately Held
SIC: 3545 Tool holders
PA: Haimer Gmbh
Weiherstr. 21
Hollenbach 86568
825 799-880

**(G-21259)**
**J & L GEAR INCORPORATED**
726 N Princeton Ave Ste C (60181-1657)
PHONE................630 832-1880
Fax: 630 941-8889
Joseph Lovecchio Jr, *President*
Tom Lovecchio, *Plant Mgr*
EMP: 10
SQ FT: 4,000
SALES (est): 920K Privately Held
SIC: 3462 3541 Gears, forged steel; machine tools, metal cutting type

**(G-21260)**
**JOHN TOBIN MILLWORK CO (PA)**
231 W North Ave (60181-1160)
PHONE................630 832-3780
Fax: 630 832-3784
John B Tobin Jr, *President*
Patrick Tobin, *Managing Dir*
Julianne Driscoll, *Treasurer*
EMP: 8 EST: 1960
SQ FT: 3,400
SALES (est): 2.5MM Privately Held
SIC: 5211 2431 Millwork & lumber; door & window products; millwork; doors & door parts & trim, wood

**(G-21261)**
**JOMAR ELECTRIC COIL MFG INC**
218 W Stone Rd (60181-1518)
PHONE................630 279-1499
Fax: 630 279-1494
Joseph Petitto, *President*
Mary Petitto, *Admin Sec*
EMP: 4
SALES (est): 250K Privately Held
SIC: 3621 Motors & generators

**(G-21262)**
**KABERT INDUSTRIES INC (PA)**
321 W Saint Charles Rd (60181-2493)
P.O. Box 6270 (60181-5317)
PHONE................630 833-2115
Fax: 630 833-9298
Robert A Peacock, *President*
Elizabeth Peacock, *Corp Secy*
Karen Hartman, *Vice Pres*
Karl Hatman, *VP Sales*
Karl Hartman, *Sales Mgr*
▲ EMP: 2
SQ FT: 15,000
SALES (est): 11.3MM Privately Held
WEB: www.kabert.com
SIC: 2221 3369 Fiberglass fabrics; nonferrous foundries

**(G-21263)**
**KENCOR STAIRS & WOODWORKING**
311 W Stone Rd (60181-1521)
PHONE................630 279-8980
Fax: 630 279-3382
Tom Kennedy, *President*
EMP: 9 EST: 1962
SQ FT: 6,000
SALES (est): 1.6MM Privately Held
SIC: 2431 3446 Staircases & stairs, wood; stair railings, wood; architectural metalwork

**(G-21264)**
**KEPNER PRODUCTS COMPANY**
995 N Ellsworth Ave (60181-1192)
PHONE................630 279-1550
Fax: 630 279-9669
Hugh G Kepner, *President*
Janet Engstrom, *Vice Pres*
Janet Kepner, *Vice Pres*
Steve Suhajda, *Materials Mgr*
Robert Reese, *Purch Mgr*
EMP: 65 EST: 1948
SQ FT: 31,500
SALES (est): 13.9MM Privately Held
WEB: www.kepner.com
SIC: 3494 3492 Valves & pipe fittings; fluid power valves & hose fittings

**(G-21265)**
**KKJ INDUSTRIES LLC**
49 E Van Buren St (60181-3260)
PHONE................630 202-9160
Kyle Resuali, *Principal*
EMP: 3
SALES (est): 97.7K Privately Held
SIC: 3999 Manufacturing industries

**(G-21266)**
**M F K ENTERPRISES INC**
717 N Yale Ave (60181-1607)
PHONE................630 516-1230
Fax: 630 516-1232
Mark Keller, *President*
Beth Keller, *Treasurer*
EMP: 15
SQ FT: 18,000
SALES (est): 1.9MM Privately Held
SIC: 3089 Injection molding of plastics

**(G-21267)**
**MAJOR-PRIME PLASTICS INC**
649 N Ardmore Ave (60181-1699)
P.O. Box 6240 (60181-5316)
PHONE................630 834-9400
John E Hadley, *President*
Dan Schoepke, *Plant Mgr*
Matt Land, *Prdtn Mgr*
Brandon W Kearns, *MIS Mgr*
◆ EMP: 30
SQ FT: 100,000
SALES (est): 7MM Privately Held
WEB: www.majorprime.com
SIC: 3087 7389 4226 5162 Custom compound purchased resins; packaging & labeling services; special warehousing & storage; resins, synthetic

**(G-21268)**
**MANUFACTURERS ALLIANCE CORP**
Also Called: Productionpro
320 W Saint Charles Rd (60181-2403)
PHONE................847 696-1600
Fax: 847 696-1696
P Douglas Tello, *Principal*
Christopher Smith, *Info Tech Dir*
EMP: 10
SALES (est): 2MM Privately Held
SIC: 3552 Creels, textile machinery

**(G-21269)**
**MASTER MANUFACTURING CO**
747 N Yale Ave (60181-1679)
PHONE................630 833-7060
Peter Sparacio, *President*
Salvatore Sparacio, *Vice Pres*
Antoinette Sparacio, *Treasurer*
Toni Sparacio, *Bookkeeper*
EMP: 10 EST: 1932
SQ FT: 5,000
SALES (est): 1.1MM Privately Held
SIC: 3563 3564 3549 Spraying outfits: metals, paints & chemicals (compressor); blowers & fans; metalworking machinery

**(G-21270)**
**MOBIL TRAILER TRANSPORT INC**
223 E Adele Ct (60181-1208)
PHONE................630 993-1200
Fax: 630 993-1207
Lois Pivar, *President*
EMP: 20
SALES (est): 25K Privately Held
SIC: 4213 2451 Mobile homes transport; mobile homes

**(G-21271)**
**MOLD SHIELDS INC**
230 N 2nd Ave (60181-2028)
PHONE................708 983-5931
Reginald Phillips, *President*
EMP: 4
SALES: 39K Privately Held
WEB: www.moldshields.com
SIC: 3441 8299 Fabricated structural metal; educational services

**(G-21272)**
**MORTGAGE MARKET INFO SVCS**
53 E Saint Charles Rd (60181-2465)
PHONE................630 834-7555
Jay Galvin, *Manager*
Kathy Baker, *Manager*
EMP: 40
SQ FT: 2,500
SALES (est): 3.1MM Privately Held
WEB: www.mmis.com
SIC: 2759 Advertising literature: printing

**(G-21273)**
**NIKRO INDUSTRIES INC**
1115 N Ellsworth Ave (60181-1040)
PHONE................630 530-0558
Fax: 630 530-0740
James Nicholson, *President*
Jim Nicholson, *General Mgr*
Jim Milloy, *Sales Mgr*
Amanda Janousek, *Manager*
Kate Sweeney, *Manager*

# Villa Park - Dupage County (G-21274)

◆ EMP: 15
SQ FT: 7,000
SALES (est): 4.1MM **Privately Held**
WEB: www.nikro.com
SIC: 3589 Vacuum cleaners & sweepers, electric; industrial

**(G-21274)**
**OLY OLA EDGING INC**
Also Called: Olyola Etching
124 E Saint Charles Rd (60181-2414)
PHONE.............................630 833-3033
Fax: 630 833-0816
Sandra Hechler, *President*
Sandra Olson, *Treasurer*
Carol Mueller, *Office Mgr*
EMP: 10 EST: 1978
SQ FT: 3,500
SALES (est): 3.8MM **Privately Held**
WEB: www.olyola.com
SIC: 5083 2821 Landscaping equipment; plastics materials & resins

**(G-21275)**
**PARK TOOL & MACHINE CO INC**
111 W Home Ave (60181-2568)
PHONE.............................630 530-5110
Roger Porter, *President*
Vince Zaccardi, *Office Mgr*
EMP: 7 EST: 1973
SQ FT: 3,500
SALES (est): 975.1K **Privately Held**
SIC: 3599 7692 3549 3544 Machine shop, jobbing & repair; welding repair; metalworking machinery; special dies, tools, jigs & fixtures

**(G-21276)**
**PEP INDUSTRIES INC**
725 N Wisconsin Ave (60181-1506)
PHONE.............................630 833-0404
Fax: 630 833-7709
Phil Greco, *President*
Bruce Campbell, *General Mgr*
Phyllis Greco, *Corp Secy*
EMP: 12 EST: 1950
SQ FT: 13,000
SALES (est): 970K **Privately Held**
SIC: 2531 3446 3281 3444 Church furniture; ornamental metalwork; church furniture, cut stone; sheet metalwork

**(G-21277)**
**PHOENIX PRESS INC**
140 E Hill St (60181-1805)
PHONE.............................630 833-2381
Patricia L Danda, *President*
David Conn, *Admin Sec*
EMP: 2
SALES (est): 223.5K **Privately Held**
SIC: 2752 5963 2741 Commercial printing, lithographic; newspapers, home delivery, not by printers or publishers; patterns, paper: publishing & printing

**(G-21278)**
**PRECISION ENGINEERING & DEV CO**
Also Called: Pedco
701 N Iowa Ave (60181-1592)
PHONE.............................630 834-5956
Fax: 630 834-2039
Dan Wagner, *President*
Carolyn Wagner, *Vice Pres*
Henry Zalewski, *Research*
EMP: 20 EST: 1949
SQ FT: 5,500
SALES (est): 1.5MM **Privately Held**
WEB: www.pedco-inc.com
SIC: 3544 3599 Jigs & fixtures; machine shop, jobbing & repair

**(G-21279)**
**PRINTED IMPRESSIONS INC**
Also Called: Commercial Prtg Graphics Arts
1640 S Ardmore Ave (60181-3742)
PHONE.............................773 604-8585
Fax: 773 604-8777
Manish Patel, *President*
Anjana Patel, *Vice Pres*
EMP: 2
SQ FT: 6,500
SALES: 300K **Privately Held**
SIC: 2752 2791 Commercial printing, offset; typesetting

**(G-21280)**
**PROGRAF LLC**
119 W Home Ave (60181-2568)
P.O. Box 398, Oregon (61061-0398)
PHONE.............................815 234-4848
Doug Calabro,
EMP: 3
SQ FT: 3,000
SALES (est): 205.2K **Privately Held**
WEB: www.prograf.com
SIC: 3728 5084 Blades, aircraft propeller: metal or wood; printing trades machinery, equipment & supplies

**(G-21281)**
**QC POWDER INC**
226 E Sidney Ct (60181-1138)
PHONE.............................630 832-0606
Fax: 630 832-0791
Charles Stitzel, *President*
Paul Podedworny, *Admin Sec*
EMP: 45
SQ FT: 26,000
SALES (est): 4.9MM **Privately Held**
SIC: 3479 Painting, coating & hot dipping

**(G-21282)**
**SAICOR INC**
708 N Princeton Ave (60181-1604)
PHONE.............................630 530-0350
Idris Atcha, *President*
EMP: 7 EST: 1979
SQ FT: 3,000
SALES (est): 1.1MM **Privately Held**
WEB: www.saicorinc.com
SIC: 3569 Baling machines, for scrap metal, paper or similar material

**(G-21283)**
**SCHMID TOOL & ENGINEERING CORP**
930 N Villa Ave (60181-1140)
PHONE.............................630 333-1733
Fax: 847 455-0432
Nancy Schmid, *President*
Heidi Leahy, *Vice Pres*
Eric Schmid, *Vice Pres*
EMP: 25
SQ FT: 11,600
SALES (est): 5.7MM **Privately Held**
WEB: www.schmidtool.com
SIC: 3599 3549 3462 3452 Machine shop, jobbing & repair; metalworking machinery; iron & steel forgings; bolts, nuts, rivets & washers

**(G-21284)**
**SIGN A RAMA INC**
Also Called: Sign-A-Rama
100 E Roosevelt Rd Ste 34 (60181-3529)
PHONE.............................630 359-5125
Steve Peterson, *Branch Mgr*
EMP: 5
SALES (corp-wide): 88.5MM **Privately Held**
SIC: 3993 Signs & advertising specialties
HQ: Sign A Rama Inc.
2121 Vista Pkwy
West Palm Beach FL 33411
561 640-5570

**(G-21285)**
**SIR COOPER INC**
203 W Saint Charles Rd (60181-2402)
PHONE.............................630 279-0162
EMP: 6
SALES (est): 500K **Privately Held**
SIC: 2759 Commercial Printing

**(G-21286)**
**SUBURBAN DRIVELINE INC**
Also Called: Suburban Drive Line
747 W North Ave (60181-1322)
PHONE.............................630 941-7101
Fax: 630 941-8458
Phil Floral, *President*
Rosemarie Floral, *Corp Secy*
EMP: 8
SQ FT: 3,000
SALES (est): 1.3MM **Privately Held**
SIC: 3714 5013 Drive shafts, motor vehicle; automotive supplies & parts

**(G-21287)**
**SUPERTEK SCIENTIFIC LLC**
744 N Michigan Ave (60181-1503)
PHONE.............................630 345-3450
Shayan Merchant,
Shakil Merchant,
EMP: 5
SALES (est): 239.7K **Privately Held**
SIC: 3821 3231 3841 3826 Laboratory measuring apparatus; laboratory glassware; surgical & medical instruments; analytical instruments

**(G-21288)**
**UXM STUDIO INC**
707 N Iowa Ave (60181-1510)
PHONE.............................773 359-1333
Marc Cain, *President*
Scott Goldberg, *Treasurer*
Christopher Anderson, *Admin Sec*
EMP: 7 EST: 2015
SALES (est): 279K **Privately Held**
SIC: 7372 7371 Application computer software; custom computer programming services

**(G-21289)**
**VALUE LINK 1 ENTERPRISES**
240 N Michigan Ave (60181-2073)
PHONE.............................630 833-6243
Dennis Chesney, *Principal*
EMP: 2
SALES (est): 210.6K **Privately Held**
WEB: www.valuelink1.com
SIC: 5251 3679 Hardware; electronic components

## Village of Lakewood
### Mchenry County

**(G-21290)**
**DVA MAYDAY CORPORATION**
8108 Redtail Dr (60014-3324)
PHONE.............................847 848-7555
Michael May, *President*
EMP: 1 EST: 2012
SQ FT: 1,500
SALES: 2MM **Privately Held**
SIC: 3646 3433 Commercial indusl & institutional electric lighting fixtures; solar heaters & collectors

**(G-21291)**
**PERSPECTO MAP COMPANY INC**
367 Cumberland Ln (60014-5507)
P.O. Box 1288, Crystal Lake (60039-1288)
PHONE.............................815 356-1288
Fax: 815 356-6356
Teresa Conrad, *President*
EMP: 5
SQ FT: 500
SALES: 150K **Privately Held**
WEB: www.perspectomap.com
SIC: 2741 Atlas, map & guide publishing

## Viola
### Mercer County

**(G-21292)**
**MIDWEST FIBRE PRODUCTS INC**
2819 95th Ave (61486-9527)
P.O. Box 397 (61486-0397)
PHONE.............................309 596-2955
Fax: 309 596-2901
Joseph Di Iulio, *President*
Joseph Di Iulio, *President*
Elizabeth Joan Di Iulio, *Corp Secy*
Pete Di Iulio, *Vice Pres*
Elizabeth Di Iulio, *Treasurer*
EMP: 35 EST: 1962
SQ FT: 44,000
SALES (est): 7.7MM **Privately Held**
SIC: 2653 3161 2657 Boxes, corrugated: made from purchased materials; boxes, solid fiber: made from purchased materials; luggage; folding paperboard boxes

**(G-21293)**
**P R MANUFACTURING CO**
2650 85th Ave (61486-9585)
P.O. Box 308 (61486-0308)
PHONE.............................309 596-2986
Fax: 309 596-2990
Ron Mayne, *Owner*
Paul Tompkins, *VP Opers*
Dale Thomas, *Plant Supt*
Marco Mayne, *VP Sales*
Bill Polillo, *Office Mgr*
EMP: 8 EST: 2011
SALES (est): 1.1MM **Privately Held**
SIC: 3441 Fabricated structural metal

**(G-21294)**
**PAUL & RON MANUFACTURING INC**
2650 85th Ave (61486-9585)
P.O. Box 308 (61486-0308)
PHONE.............................309 596-2986
Ronald E Mayne, *President*
Paul Tompkins, *Vice Pres*
Marco Mayne, *Manager*
Sherri Crow, *Admin Sec*
EMP: 13
SALES (est): 1.2MM **Privately Held**
SIC: 3544 Special dies, tools, jigs & fixtures

**(G-21295)**
**VIOLA ICE CREAM SHOPPE**
Also Called: Milkhouse Diner
1003 13th St (61486-9437)
PHONE.............................309 596-2131
Cheryl Naynard, *President*
EMP: 9
SALES (est): 312.9K **Privately Held**
SIC: 2024 Ice cream & frozen desserts

## Virden
### Macoupin County

**(G-21296)**
**FIVE STAR PRINTING INC**
Also Called: Gold Market Publications
169 W Jackson St (62690-1269)
P.O. Box 440 (62690-0440)
PHONE.............................217 965-3355
Martin Jones, *President*
Nathan Jones, *Vice Pres*
Norris Jones, *Vice Pres*
Chris Schmitt, *Treasurer*
Joe Michlich, *Admin Sec*
EMP: 9
SQ FT: 2,500
SALES: 680K **Privately Held**
WEB: www.fivestarprinting.com
SIC: 2752 Commercial printing, offset

**(G-21297)**
**GOLD NUGGET PUBLICATIONS INC (PA)**
Also Called: Virden Recorder
169 W Jackson St (62690-1269)
P.O. Box 440 (62690-0440)
PHONE.............................217 965-3355
Fax: 217 965-4512
Norris Jones, *Vice Pres*
Martin Jones, *Vice Pres*
Nathan Jones, *Vice Pres*
Julie Westenhausen, *Manager*
EMP: 30 EST: 1866
SQ FT: 4,000
SALES (est): 1.9MM **Privately Held**
SIC: 2711 5943 Newspapers: publishing only, not printed on site; office forms & supplies

**(G-21298)**
**LUMBERYARD SUPPLIERS INC**
Also Called: Truss Slater
700 S Springfield St (62690-1600)
P.O. Box 20 (62690-0020)
PHONE.............................217 965-4911
Fax: 217 965-4914
Douglas Slater, *Manager*
EMP: 40

SALES (corp-wide): 44MM **Privately Held**
SIC: **2439** 5211 2435 Trusses, except roof: laminated lumber; trusses, wooden roof; planing mill products & lumber; hardwood veneer & plywood
PA: Lumberyard Suppliers, Inc.
300 Pinecrest Dr
East Peoria IL 61611
309 694-4356

**(G-21299)**
**MASTER ENGRAVING**
246 E Dean St (62690-1402)
PHONE..................................217 965-5885
Rick Roberts, *Owner*
EMP: 3 EST: 2000
SALES (est): 257.3K **Privately Held**
WEB: www.engravingmasterseries.com
SIC: **2789** 2759 Bookbinding & related work; invitation & stationery printing & engraving

**(G-21300)**
**MILLER TILING CO INC**
17951 Nine Mile Rd (62690-4549)
PHONE..................................217 971-4709
Anthony Miller, *President*
Lois J Miller, *Admin Sec*
EMP: 3 EST: 1995
SALES (est): 252.9K **Privately Held**
SIC: **3251** Brick & structural clay tile

**(G-21301)**
**ROYER SYSTEMS INC**
Also Called: Royell Communications
427 W Dean St (62690-1335)
PHONE..................................217 965-3699
Joseph Royer, *President*
Debra Royer, *Vice Pres*
EMP: 6
SALES (est): 724.7K **Privately Held**
SIC: **3571** 4813 Electronic computers;

## Virgil
### Kane County

**(G-21302)**
**C S O CORP (PA)**
Also Called: Sauber Mfg. Co.
10 N Sauber Rd (60151-1001)
PHONE..................................630 365-6600
Fax: 630 365-6610
Charles J Sauber, *CEO*
Doris Reynolds, *CFO*
Mike Blaser, *Sales Mgr*
George Delask, *Project Leader*
▲ EMP: 44
SQ FT: 90,000
SALES (est): 27.3MM **Privately Held**
WEB: www.csocorp.com
SIC: **5082** 3531 3713 Construction & mining machinery; construction machinery attachments; truck bodies (motor vehicles)

**(G-21303)**
**SAUBER MANUFACTURING COMPANY**
10 N Sauber Rd (60151-1001)
PHONE..................................630 365-6600
Charles J Sauber, *CEO*
Jim Sauber, *President*
Jeannie Petesch, *Human Res Mgr*
Ken Aurand, *Manager*
Doris Reynolds, *Admin Sec*
EMP: 85
SQ FT: 90,000
SALES (est): 13.5MM
SALES (corp-wide): 27.3MM **Privately Held**
WEB: www.saubermanufacturing.com
SIC: **3531** 3713 5082 Construction machinery attachments; truck bodies (motor vehicles); construction & mining machinery
PA: C S O, Corp.
10 N Sauber Rd
Virgil IL 60151
630 365-6600

## Virginia
### Cass County

**(G-21304)**
**BPS FUELS INC**
352 N Morgan St (62691-1373)
P.O. Box 1263, Bloomington (61702-1263)
PHONE..................................217 452-7608
Lois Dotzert, *Manager*
EMP: 4
SALES (est): 388.1K **Privately Held**
SIC: **2869** Fuels

**(G-21305)**
**CASS MEATS**
5815 Il Route 78 (62691-1398)
PHONE..................................217 452-3072
Frank Bell, *Owner*
EMP: 4
SQ FT: 2,000
SALES (est): 140K **Privately Held**
SIC: **0751** 2011 5421 2013 Slaughtering: custom livestock services; meat packing plants; meat markets, including freezer provisioners; sausages & other prepared meats

**(G-21306)**
**DARYL KEYLOR**
Also Called: Kathy's Kitchen
201 N Pitt St (62691-1000)
PHONE..................................217 452-3035
Daryl Keylor, *Owner*
Kathy Keylor, *Co-Owner*
EMP: 4
SALES: 105K **Privately Held**
SIC: **2035** Pickles, sauces & salad dressings

**(G-21307)**
**PRECISION TANK & EQUIPMENT CO (PA)**
3503 Conover Rd (62691-8013)
P.O. Box 20 (62691-0020)
PHONE..................................217 452-7228
Fax: 217 452-3956
David Hemmimg, *CEO*
Ron Swearingen, *Vice Pres*
Vernon E Ames, *Project Mgr*
Greg Blakeman, *Purchasing*
Brent Hicks, *CFO*
EMP: 22
SQ FT: 25,000
SALES (est): 11MM **Privately Held**
WEB: www.precisiontank.com
SIC: **3523** Fertilizing machinery, farm

## Volo
### Lake County

**(G-21308)**
**BIO GREEN INC**
30937 N Gilmer Rd (60073-9525)
PHONE..................................847 740-9637
Fax: 847 740-3615
Jim Keith, *President*
Carol Keith, *Treasurer*
Stacie Brandt, *Marketing Mgr*
EMP: 5
SALES (est): 772K **Privately Held**
WEB: www.biogreeninc.com
SIC: **2875** 0782 2873 Fertilizers, mixing only; lawn care services; nitrogenous fertilizers

**(G-21309)**
**C N C HI-TECH INC**
26575 W Commerce Dr # 611 (60073-9662)
PHONE..................................847 201-8151
James J Liles Jr, *President*
Annette M Liles, *Admin Sec*
EMP: 5
SQ FT: 2,000
SALES (est): 500K **Privately Held**
SIC: **3469** Machine parts, stamped or pressed metal

**(G-21310)**
**CHICAGO SEA RAY INC**
31535 N Us Highway 12 (60073-9773)
PHONE..................................815 385-2720
Fax: 815 385-7105
Mike Pretasky Sr, *President*
Dennis Ellerbrock, *VP Opers*
Bob Lusardi, *Manager*
▼ EMP: 33
SQ FT: 66,000
SALES (est): 5.4MM **Privately Held**
SIC: **5551** 5941 5699 3732 Motor boat dealers; outboard motors; marine supplies; skiing equipment; sports apparel; boat building & repairing

**(G-21311)**
**COMPOSITE CUTTER TECH INC**
Also Called: C C T
31632 N Ellis Dr Unit 210 (60073-9673)
PHONE..................................847 740-6875
Fax: 847 740-6871
Glenn Isaacson, *President*
EMP: 4
SALES (est): 1.2MM **Privately Held**
SIC: **3541** Machine tools, metal cutting: exotic (explosive, etc.)

**(G-21312)**
**GLOBAL FASTENER ENGRG INC**
31632 N Ellis Dr Unit 302 (60073-9673)
PHONE..................................847 929-9563
Dasheng Jiang, *President*
EMP: 10
SALES (est): 1.8MM
SALES (corp-wide): 13.4MM **Privately Held**
SIC: **3452** Bolts, nuts, rivets & washers
PA: Hubei Boshlong Technology Corp.
No.269 Chutian Road, Dongqiao Town
Zhongxiang 43190
724 439-5359

**(G-21313)**
**GOLDIES BAKING INC**
31632 N Ellis Dr Unit 306 (60073-9673)
PHONE..................................224 757-0820
Deanna Nassar, *General Mgr*
Victor Nassar, *Principal*
EMP: 11 EST: 2013
SQ FT: 5,000
SALES (est): 1.5MM **Privately Held**
SIC: **2053** Frozen bakery products, except bread

**(G-21314)**
**J AND K MOLDING**
31632 N Ellis Dr Unit 201 (60073-9672)
PHONE..................................224 276-3355
EMP: 3
SALES (est): 295.8K **Privately Held**
SIC: **3089** Molding primary plastic

**(G-21315)**
**KENNETH W TEMPLEMAN**
382 Minuet Cir (60073-5917)
PHONE..................................847 912-2740
Kenneth Templeman, *Principal*
EMP: 2
SALES (est): 217.1K **Privately Held**
SIC: **3499** 7692 7389 Fabricated metal products; welding repair;

**(G-21316)**
**KOENEMANN SAUSAGE CO**
27090 Volo Village Rd (60073-9669)
PHONE..................................815 385-6260
Fax: 815 385-6269
William F Koenemann, *President*
Hilde M Koenemann, *Vice Pres*
Gerlinde M Koenemann, *Admin Sec*
EMP: 9
SQ FT: 20,000
SALES (est): 3MM **Privately Held**
WEB: www.koenemannsausage.com
SIC: **5141** 5411 2013 Groceries, general line; grocery stores, independent; sausages & other prepared meats

**(G-21317)**
**LAKE ELECTRONICS INC**
31632 N Ellis Dr Unit 203 (60073-9672)
PHONE..................................847 201-1270
Fax: 847 201-1273
Pat Sahay, *President*
Jeff Wisniewski, *Vice Pres*
EMP: 15
SQ FT: 6,000
SALES (est): 3MM **Privately Held**
SIC: **3823** Computer interface equipment for industrial process control

**(G-21318)**
**MARINE TECHNOLOGIES INC**
Also Called: M T I Industries
31632 N Ellis Dr Unit 301 (60073-9673)
PHONE..................................847 546-9001
Thomas Wisniewski, *President*
Sandra Wisniewski, *Corp Secy*
Bob Wisniewski, *Marketing Staff*
▲ EMP: 20
SQ FT: 8,000
SALES (est): 4.3MM **Privately Held**
WEB: www.mtiindustries.com
SIC: **3669** 3812 Emergency alarms; burglar alarm apparatus, electric; smoke detectors; search & detection systems & instruments; detection apparatus: electronic/magnetic field, light/heat

**(G-21319)**
**MIKUS ELC & GENERATORS INC**
31632 N Ellis Dr Unit 109 (60073-9672)
PHONE..................................224 757-5534
Michael Belleno, *President*
EMP: 4
SALES (est): 286.9K **Privately Held**
SIC: **3699** Electrical equipment & supplies

**(G-21320)**
**WOLD PRINTING SERVICES LTD**
26639 W Commerce Dr # 402 (60073-9639)
PHONE..................................847 546-3110
Fax: 847 546-3112
Terrill Wold, *President*
Cris Wold, *Vice Pres*
Scott Wold, *Manager*
Ester Wold, *Admin Sec*
EMP: 8
SQ FT: 1,000
SALES: 1MM **Privately Held**
WEB: www.woldprinting.com
SIC: **2752** 2759 2732 Commercial printing, lithographic; commercial printing; book printing

## Wadsworth
### Lake County

**(G-21321)**
**15679 WADSWORTH INC**
15679 W Wadsworth Rd (60083-9125)
PHONE..................................847 662-4561
EMP: 5 EST: 2004
SALES (est): 460K **Privately Held**
SIC: **1321** Natural Gas Liquids Production

**(G-21322)**
**FERRITE INTERNATIONAL COMPANY**
Also Called: TSC Ferrite International
39105 Magnetics Blvd (60083-8914)
PHONE..................................847 249-4900
Tempel Smith Jr, *President*
Brian Biklek, *Purch Mgr*
Roger Swope, *Engineer*
John Hankey, *Finance*
Scott Fraser, *Manager*
▲ EMP: 47
SALES (est): 10.1MM **Privately Held**
SIC: **3612** Specialty transformers

**(G-21323)**
**JSQ INC**
13950 W Adams Rd (60083-9241)
P.O. Box 51, Winthrop Harbor (60096-0051)
PHONE..................................847 731-8800
Eugene Mauser, *President*
EMP: 4
SALES: 400K **Privately Held**
WEB: www.jsqsolutions.com
SIC: **1389** Construction, repair & dismantling services

# Wadsworth - Lake County (G-21324)           GEOGRAPHIC SECTION

### (G-21324)
**LAKE COUNTY TOOL WORKS NORTH**
15986 Hwy 173  (60083)
P.O. Box 280  (60083-0280)
PHONE.................................847 662-4542
Peter Dodich, *President*
**EMP:** 4
**SALES (est):** 374.5K  **Privately Held**
**SIC: 8711** 3599 3544 Engineering services; machine shop, jobbing & repair; special dies, tools, jigs & fixtures

### (G-21325)
**PERSONALIZED PILLOWS CO**
16783 W Old Orchard Dr  (60083-9608)
PHONE.................................847 226-7393
Ann-Marie Burke, *Owner*
**EMP:** 3
**SALES (est):** 100K  **Privately Held**
**SIC: 2392** Pillowcases: made from purchased materials

### (G-21326)
**R & L TRUCK SERVICE  INC**
39935 N Prairie View Dr  (60083-9609)
PHONE.................................847 489-7135
Ron Kelver, *President*
Laurie Kelver, *Manager*
**EMP:** 10
**SALES (est):** 1.5MM  **Privately Held**
**SIC: 3713** Truck & bus bodies

### (G-21327)
**ROYAL FABRICATORS INC**
38360 N Cashmore Rd  (60083-9718)
PHONE.................................847 775-7466
Royal Rockow, *President*
Judy Rockow, *Corp Secy*
Bart Rockow, *Marketing Staff*
**EMP:** 17
**SQ FT:** 7,200
**SALES (est):** 2.1MM  **Privately Held**
**SIC: 2541** 2434 2542 2511 Counter & sink tops; cabinets, except refrigerated: show, display, etc.: wood; wood kitchen cabinets; partitions & fixtures, except wood; wood household furniture

### (G-21328)
**TSC INTERNATIONAL  INC**
Also Called: TSC Ferrite International
39105 Magnetics Blvd  (60083-8914)
P.O. Box 399  (60083-0399)
PHONE.................................847 249-4900
Tempel Smith, *President*
Scott Fraser, *Admin Mgr*
Tim Olrick, *Admin Sec*
**EMP:** 12
**SALES (est):** 2MM  **Privately Held**
**SIC: 3499** Magnetic shields, metal

## Walnut
### Bureau County

### (G-21329)
**AVANTI FOODS COMPANY**
Also Called: Gino's Pizza
109 Depot St  (61376)
P.O. Box 457  (61376-0457)
PHONE.................................815 379-2155
Fax: 815 379-9357
Anthony Zueger, *President*
Robert Linley, *Corp Secy*
**EMP:** 45 **EST:** 1955
**SQ FT:** 100,000
**SALES (est):** 8.1MM  **Privately Held**
**WEB:** www.avantifoods.com
**SIC: 2022** 2038 5149 Cheese, natural & processed; pizza, frozen; pizza supplies

### (G-21330)
**EBE INDUSTRIAL  LLC**
507 N North St  (61376-9495)
P.O. Box 160  (61376-0160)
PHONE.................................815 379-2400
Fax: 815 379-2449
Tom Schuler, *CFO*
Mark Ebersole, *Accountant*
**EMP:** 15
**SALES (est):** 2.6MM  **Privately Held**
**WEB:** www.ebeindustrial.com
**SIC: 3542** Riveting machines

### (G-21331)
**TRICON INDS MFG & EQP SLS**
Also Called: TCI Manufacturing & Eqp Sls
28524 1250 E St  (61376)
P.O. Box 306  (61376-0306)
PHONE.................................815 379-2090
Michael Maynard, *President*
Carolyn Thompson, *Admin Sec*
◆ **EMP:** 40 **EST:** 2001
**SQ FT:** 26,000
**SALES (est):** 21.7MM  **Privately Held**
**WEB:** www.tcimfg.com
**SIC: 3535** Conveyors & conveying equipment

### (G-21332)
**WALNUT CUSTOM HOMES  INC (PA)**
300 Wyanet Rd  (61376)
P.O. Box 605  (61376-0605)
PHONE.................................815 379-2151
Fax: 815 379-2011
Charles Gonigam, *President*
Charles Gonigan, *Exec VP*
Gary L Erickson, *Vice Pres*
Charlie Gonigam, *Vice Pres*
Ron Skaggs, *Opers Staff*
**EMP:** 30
**SALES (est):** 10.7MM  **Privately Held**
**SIC: 2452** Prefabricated wood buildings

### (G-21333)
**WALNUT CUSTOM HOMES  INC**
300 Wyanet Rd  (61376)
P.O. Box 605  (61376-0605)
PHONE.................................815 379-2151
Gary Erickson, *VP Prdtn*
Sharon L Free, *Nurse*
**EMP:** 40
**SALES (corp-wide):** 10.7MM  **Privately Held**
**SIC: 3441** Building components, structural steel
**PA:** Walnut Custom Homes, Inc.
300 Wyanet Rd
Walnut IL 61376
815 379-2151

## Walnut Hill
### Marion County

### (G-21334)
**SCHWARTZ OILFIELD SERVICES (PA)**
501 Schwartz Rd  (62893-1039)
P.O. Box Ac, Centralia,  (62801-9163)
PHONE.................................618 532-0232
Fax: 618 532-0241
Tony Schwartz, *President*
**EMP:** 30
**SQ FT:** 8,000
**SALES:** 2MM  **Privately Held**
**SIC: 1389** Cementing oil & gas well casings

## Warren
### Jo Daviess County

### (G-21335)
**HIXSTERS UPPER DECK**
162 E Main St  (61087-9367)
PHONE.................................815 745-2700
Aaron Hicks, *Owner*
**EMP:** 4
**SALES (est):** 439.4K  **Privately Held**
**SIC: 2599** Bar, restaurant & cafeteria furniture

### (G-21336)
**SFC OF ILLINOIS  INC**
400 S Railroad St  (61087-9428)
PHONE.................................815 745-2100
**EMP:** 50 **EST:** 1932
**SQ FT:** 32,000
**SALES (est):** 7.9MM  **Privately Held**
**SIC: 3621** 3825 3566 Mfg Motors/Generators Mfg Elec Measuring Instr Mfg Speed Changer/Drives

### (G-21337)
**STABLE BEGINNING CORPORATION**
Also Called: Carter Motor Company
400 S Railroad St  (61087-9428)
PHONE.................................815 745-2100
Fax: 815 745-2135
Keith Geisler, *President*
Roxanne Geisler, *Vice Pres*
**EMP:** 25
**SQ FT:** 30,000
**SALES (est):** 1.1MM  **Privately Held**
**SIC: 3621** Electric motor & generator parts

## Warrensburg
### Macon County

### (G-21338)
**CROWN CORK & SEAL USA INC**
970 W North St  (62573-9700)
PHONE.................................217 672-3533
Fax: 217 672-3545
Nick Tucker, *Maint Spvr*
Larry Casey, *Human Resources*
Jerry Nelson, *Manager*
Tim Carpenter, *Manager*
**EMP:** 59
**SALES (corp-wide):** 8.2B  **Publicly Held**
**WEB:** www.crowncork.com
**SIC: 3411** Metal cans
**HQ:** Crown Cork & Seal Usa, Inc.
1 Crown Way
Philadelphia PA 19154
215 698-5100

### (G-21339)
**PROGRESSIVE ELECTRONICS**
266 Hwy 121 Ste 3  (62573)
PHONE.................................217 672-8434
Ronald G Timmons, *Owner*
**EMP:** 2
**SQ FT:** 3,000
**SALES:** 360K  **Privately Held**
**SIC: 3812** Radar systems & equipment

## Warrenville
### Dupage County

### (G-21340)
**ACTION SCREEN PRINT  INC**
30 W 260 Butterfield  (60555)
P.O. Box 827  (60555-0827)
PHONE.................................630 393-1990
Fax: 630 393-1820
Alan Arrighi, *President*
Dana Arrighi, *Vice Pres*
**EMP:** 11 **EST:** 1978
**SQ FT:** 5,000
**SALES (est):** 1MM  **Privately Held**
**SIC: 2395** 2396 Embroidery & art needlework; fabric printing & stamping

### (G-21341)
**AMOS INDUSTRIES  INC**
30w102 Butterfield Rd  (60555-1563)
PHONE.................................630 393-0606
Fax: 630 393-0707
William Y Tein, *President*
Jack Chen, *Vice Pres*
Michael Corbett, *Sales Mgr*
Derald Leufzler, *Sales Staff*
Linda Delvescovo, *Office Mgr*
▲ **EMP:** 12
**SQ FT:** 5,800
**SALES (est):** 3.6MM
**SALES (corp-wide):** 99.1MM  **Privately Held**
**WEB:** www.amosmarinehardware.com
**SIC: 3429** Builders' hardware
**PA:** Shengrui Transmission Corporation Limited
No.518, Shengrui St., High-Tech Industrial Development Zone
Weifang  26120
536 560-5031

### (G-21342)
**ARROWHEAD BRICK PAVERS INC**
30w218 Bttrfield Rd Unit A  (60555)
PHONE.................................630 393-1584
Michael Borsuk, *President*
Mark Dalki, *Vice Pres*
Jamie Mayorga, *Vice Pres*
Beth Keenan, *Manager*
**EMP:** 32
**SQ FT:** 5,000
**SALES (est):** 2.7MM  **Privately Held**
**WEB:** www.arrowheadbp.com
**SIC: 3251** Paving brick, clay

### (G-21343)
**ASCO POWER TECHNOLOGIES LP**
3s701 West Ave Ste 300  (60555-3267)
PHONE.................................630 505-4050
Joe La Martina, *Manager*
**EMP:** 5  **Privately Held**
**SIC: 3699** Electrical equipment & supplies
**HQ:** Asco Power Technologies, L.P.
160 Park Ave
Florham Park NJ 07932

### (G-21344)
**BP AMERICA INC (HQ)**
4101 Winfield Rd Ste 200  (60555-3523)
PHONE.................................630 420-5111
Fax: 630 821-3099
H Lamar McKay, *Ch of Bd*
Orlando Alvarez, *Counsel*
Graham Dudley, *Exec VP*
Jennifer Johnson, *Exec VP*
David Newey, *Exec VP*
▲ **EMP:** 2000
**SALES:** 12B
**SALES (corp-wide):** 183B  **Privately Held**
**SIC: 2911** 5171 4612 4613 Petroleum refining; petroleum bulk stations & terminals; crude petroleum pipelines; refined petroleum pipelines; deep sea domestic transportation of freight

### (G-21345)
**DRAGON DIE MOLD INC**
30w250 Butterfield Rd # 311  (60555-1568)
PHONE.................................630 836-0699
Joe Kotvan, *President*
**EMP:** 4 **EST:** 1995
**SALES (est):** 310K  **Privately Held**
**SIC: 3544** Industrial molds

### (G-21346)
**ESP T-SHIRT CO INC**
2s130 Roxbury Ct  (60555-1262)
PHONE.................................630 393-1033
Fax: 630 393-0299
Steven Pyszka, *President*
Elva Pyszka, *Corp Secy*
**EMP:** 4
**SALES (est):** 425.8K  **Privately Held**
**SIC: 2759** 2396 Screen printing; automotive & apparel trimmings

### (G-21347)
**FROMM AIRPAD  INC**
3s320 Rockwell St  (60555-2919)
PHONE.................................630 393-9790
Eugene Gerhardstein, *President*
Olga K Gerhardstein, *Corp Secy*
Tom Gerhardstein, *Vice Pres*
Sandra Harris, *Accountant*
▲ **EMP:** 10
**SQ FT:** 6,000
**SALES (est):** 2.5MM  **Privately Held**
**SIC: 5084** 5199 3565 Packaging machinery & equipment; packaging materials; packaging machinery

### (G-21348)
**FUEL TECH  INC (PA)**
27601 Bella Vista Pkwy  (60555-1617)
PHONE.................................630 845-4500
Fax: 630 845-4502
Douglas G Bailey, *Ch of Bd*
Vincent J Arnone, *President*
Albert G Grigonis, *Senior VP*
Robert E Puissant, *Senior VP*
Michael Grady, *Project Mgr*
◆ **EMP:** 182
**SQ FT:** 40,000

# GEOGRAPHIC SECTION

Warsaw - Hancock County (G-21370)

**SALES:** 55.1MM  **Publicly Held**
**WEB:** www.ftek.com
**SIC: 3564** 3823  Blowers & fans; boiler controls: industrial, power & marine type

*(G-21349)*
### KLEEN CUT TOOL INC
30w250 Butterfield Rd # 309 (60555-1564)
**PHONE** ................................ 630 447-7020
**Fax:** 630 543-8467
Mark E Wujciga, *President*
**EMP:** 6
**SQ FT:** 4,000
**SALES:** 800K  **Privately Held**
**WEB:** www.kleencuttool.com
**SIC: 3544** 3469  Special dies, tools, jigs & fixtures; metal stampings

*(G-21350)*
### M H ELECTRIC MOTOR & CTRL CORP
30w250 Calumet Ave W (60555-1516)
**PHONE** ................................ 630 393-3736
Michael Holz, *President*
Michael H Holz, *Vice Pres*
**EMP:** 6
**SQ FT:** 10,000
**SALES (est):** 1MM  **Privately Held**
**WEB:** www.mhelectricmotors.com
**SIC: 7694** 5999  Electric motor repair; motors, electric

*(G-21351)*
### NORTHERN TECHNOLOGIES INC
4350 Weaver Pkwy (60555-3925)
**PHONE** ................................ 440 246-6999
▲ **EMP:** 8
**SQ FT:** 24,000
**SALES (est):** 233.2K
**SALES (corp-wide):** 14.5B  **Publicly Held**
**WEB:** www.northern-tech.com
**SIC: 3823** 5065  Controllers for process variables, all types; electronic parts & equipment
**HQ:** Jtp Industries, Inc.
6084 Via Hermosa Ct
El Paso TX 79912

*(G-21352)*
### OHMITE HOLDING LLC (HQ)
Also Called: Ohmite Manufacturing
27501 Bella Vista Pkwy (60555-1609)
**PHONE** ................................ 847 258-0300
**Fax:** 847 574-7522
Greg Pace, *President*
Donald Kennedy, *Mfg Spvr*
Rick Lange, *Finance*
Sandra Novack, *Manager*
▲ **EMP:** 30
**SQ FT:** 250,000
**SALES (est):** 89.8MM
**SALES (corp-wide):** 1.7B  **Privately Held**
**WEB:** www.ohmite.com
**SIC: 3625** 5065  Resistors & resistor units; rheostats; industrial electrical relays & switches; resistors, electronic; electronic parts
**PA:** The Heico Companies L L C
70 W Madison St Ste 5600
Chicago IL 60602
312 419-8220

*(G-21353)*
### PATTERSON MEDICAL PRODUCTS INC (HQ)
Also Called: Sammons Preston
28100 Torch Pkwy (60555-3938)
**PHONE** ................................ 630 393-6671
**Fax:** 630 378-6310
Edward Donnelly, *President*
Edwin Hinton, *Accounts Exec*
▲ **EMP:** 200
**SALES (est):** 168.7MM
**SALES (corp-wide):** 5.3B  **Publicly Held**
**SIC: 3841**  Medical instruments & equipment, blood & bone work
**PA:** Patterson Companies, Inc.
1031 Mendota Heights Rd
Saint Paul MN 55120
651 686-1600

*(G-21354)*
### PHONAK LLC (DH)
4520 Weaver Pkwy Ste 1 (60555-4027)
**PHONE** ................................ 630 821-5000
**Fax:** 630 393-7400
Mark A Sanger, *President*
Dipak Aher, *General Mgr*
William Lesiecki, *General Mgr*
Claude Diversi, *Managing Dir*
Vincent Lefevre, *Managing Dir*
▲ **EMP:** 600
**SALES (est):** 179.1MM
**SALES (corp-wide):** 2.3B  **Privately Held**
**WEB:** www.phonak-us.com
**SIC: 3842** 5999  Hearing aids; hearing aids
**HQ:** Sonova Ag
Laubisrutistrasse 28
StAfa ZH 8712
589 280-101

*(G-21355)*
### PLYMOUTH TUBE COMPANY (PA)
Also Called: None
29w 150 Warrenville Rd (60555)
**PHONE** ................................ 630 393-3550
**Fax:** 630 393-3551
Donald C Van Pelt Sr, *Ch of Bd*
Donald C Van Pelt Jr, *President*
David Crouch, *General Mgr*
Marvin Dunham, *General Mgr*
Gavin Ford, *General Mgr*
◆ **EMP:** 50  **EST:** 1924
**SQ FT:** 10,000
**SALES (est):** 278.9MM  **Privately Held**
**WEB:** www.plymouth.com
**SIC: 3317** 3354  Tubes, seamless steel; tubes, wrought: welded or lock joint; shapes, extruded aluminum; tube, extruded or drawn, aluminum

*(G-21356)*
### PLYMOUTH TUBE COMPANY
29w150 Warrenville Rd (60555-3528)
**PHONE** ................................ 262 642-8201
Bill Hennricks, *General Mgr*
Robert Jones, *Manager*
**EMP:** 90
**SALES (corp-wide):** 278.9MM  **Privately Held**
**WEB:** www.plymouth.com
**SIC: 3317** 3354  Tubes, seamless steel; tubes, wrought: welded or lock joint; shapes, extruded aluminum; tube, extruded or drawn, aluminum
**PA:** Plymouth Tube Company
29w 150 Warrenville Rd
Warrenville IL 60555
630 393-3550

*(G-21357)*
### PRECISE PRODUCTS INC
3s286 Talbot Ave (60555-1544)
P.O. Box 310 (60555-0310)
**PHONE** ................................ 630 393-9698
**Fax:** 630 393-6819
Ernest Tucker, *President*
Michael Cummings, *General Mgr*
Jeff Spiewak, *General Mgr*
Robert Goblet, *Vice Pres*
Jill Suhs, *Marketing Mgr*
▲ **EMP:** 40
**SQ FT:** 10,000
**SALES (est):** 8.5MM  **Privately Held**
**WEB:** www.preciseproductsinc.com
**SIC: 3451**  Screw machine products

*(G-21358)*
### PREMIUM TEST EQUIPMENT CORP
30 W 270 Butterfield (60555)
P.O. Box 577 (60555-0577)
**PHONE** ................................ 630 400-2681
**Fax:** 630 393-2725
Jeffrey Newman, *President*
**EMP:** 3  **EST:** 2012
**SALES (est):** 321.9K  **Privately Held**
**SIC: 3825**  Test equipment for electronic & electric measurement

*(G-21359)*
### PREZIOSIO LTD
Also Called: East Side Cafe
30 W 270 Butterfield Rd D (60555)
**PHONE** ................................ 630 393-0920

**Fax:** 630 393-0921
Anthony Preziosio, *President*
Julie Preziosio, *Vice Pres*
Peggy Preziosio, *Treasurer*
Fred J Preziosio, *Admin Sec*
**EMP:** 11
**SALES (est):** 1.5MM  **Privately Held**
**SIC: 2038**  Pizza, frozen

*(G-21360)*
### PROCESS TECHNOLOGIES GROUP
Also Called: PTG Impax
30w106 Butterfield Rd (60555-1563)
**PHONE** ................................ 630 393-4777
Jerrold McCabe, *President*
Jerrold Mc Cabe, *President*
Ed Evensen, *Vice Pres*
Jaime Smith, *Office Mgr*
Brian Flowers, *Systems Mgr*
**EMP:** 8
**SQ FT:** 5,000
**SALES:** 300K  **Privately Held**
**WEB:** www.impaxptg.com
**SIC: 3625** 5084 3823  Relays & industrial controls; instruments & control equipment; industrial instrmnts msrmnt display/control process variable

*(G-21361)*
### ROBAL COMPANY INC
Also Called: B & H Industries
30 W 250th Butterfield304 (60555)
**PHONE** ................................ 630 393-0777
**Fax:** 630 393-0888
Jim Hurckes, *Partner*
**EMP:** 10
**SALES (corp-wide):** 15MM  **Privately Held**
**WEB:** www.bhindustries.com
**SIC: 7334** 2789 2759  Blueprinting service; bookbinding & related work; commercial printing
**PA:** Robal Company, Inc.
80 W Seegers Rd
Arlington Heights IL 60005
847 593-3161

*(G-21362)*
### STANDARD OIL COMPANY (DH)
Also Called: BP
4101 Winfield Rd Ste 100 (60555-3522)
**PHONE** ................................ 630 836-5000
Brian Gilvary, *Principal*
Samuel Andrews, *Principal*
Henry M Flagler, *Principal*
John D Rockefeller, *Principal*
Kelly Taylor, *Manager*
◆ **EMP:** 40  **EST:** 1870
**SQ FT:** 877,000
**SALES (est):** 873.8MM
**SALES (corp-wide):** 183B  **Privately Held**
**WEB:** www.crystal-enterprise.com
**SIC: 2911**  Petroleum refining; gasoline; intermediate distillates; jet fuels
**HQ:** Bp America Inc
4101 Winfield Rd Ste 200
Warrenville IL 60555
630 420-5111

*(G-21363)*
### TEXAS INSTRUMENTS INCORPORATED
27715 Diehl Rd (60555-3998)
**PHONE** ................................ 630 836-2827
**Fax:** 630 393-6530
John Bonfitto, *Design Engr*
Vince Paku, *Design Engr*
Steve Anderson, *Branch Mgr*
Charles Devries, *Manager*
Miles Sumar, *MIS Staff*
**EMP:** 100
**SALES (corp-wide):** 13.3B  **Publicly Held**
**WEB:** www.ti.com
**SIC: 3613**  Switches, electric power except snap, push button, etc.; regulators, power
**PA:** Texas Instruments Incorporated
12500 Ti Blvd
Dallas TX 75243
214 479-3773

*(G-21364)*
### TITUS ENTERPRISES LLC
2s766 Winchester Cir W (60555-2477)
**PHONE** ................................ 773 441-7222
Lawrence Daughrity, *Principal*

Laverne Daughrity, *Vice Pres*
**EMP:** 3  **EST:** 2012
**SALES (est):** 230K  **Privately Held**
**SIC: 3728** 5047 1711  Research & dev by manuf., aircraft parts & auxiliary equip; medical & hospital equipment; solar energy contractor

*(G-21365)*
### TOX- PRESSOTECHNIK LLC
4250 Weaver Pkwy (60555-3924)
**PHONE** ................................ 630 447-4600
**EMP:** 7
**SALES (corp-wide):** 30MM  **Privately Held**
**SIC: 7699** 3542 3545  Repair Services Mfg Machine Tools- Forming Mfg Machine Tool Accessories
**PA:** Tox- Pressotechnik L.L.C.
4250 Weaver Pkwy
Warrenville IL 60555
630 447-4600

*(G-21366)*
### TRU-COLOUR PRODUCTS LLC
27575 Ferry Rd Fl 2 (60555-3862)
**PHONE** ................................ 630 447-0559
Toby Meisenheimer, *CEO*
**EMP:** 5
**SQ FT:** 4,000
**SALES (est):** 276.6K  **Privately Held**
**SIC: 2211**  Bandage cloths, cotton

*(G-21367)*
### TWO BROTHERS BREWING COMPANY
30w315 Calumet Ave W (60555-1565)
**PHONE** ................................ 630 393-2337
**Fax:** 630 393-2323
Jason Ebel, *President*
James V Ebel II, *Vice Pres*
Brian Martin, *Marketing Staff*
▲ **EMP:** 7
**SQ FT:** 10,000
**SALES (est):** 2.6MM  **Privately Held**
**WEB:** www.twobrosbrew.com
**SIC: 5921** 2095 5812  Wine & beer; roasted coffee; family restaurants

*(G-21368)*
### WEIMER DESIGN & PRINT LTD INC
Also Called: Minuteman Press
3s25 State Route 59 (60555)
**PHONE** ................................ 630 393-3334
**Fax:** 630 393-3354
Gregory M Weimer, *President*
Lauren Palmer, *Mfg Dir*
**EMP:** 4
**SQ FT:** 1,400
**SALES (est):** 401.2K  **Privately Held**
**SIC: 7389** 7334 2791 2789  Printing broker; photocopying & duplicating services; typesetting; bookbinding & related work; commercial printing, lithographic; office forms & supplies

*(G-21369)*
### WOODLAND FENCE FOREST PDTS INC
3 S 264 Hc 59 (60555)
**PHONE** ................................ 630 393-2220
**Fax:** 630 393-2236
Stewart Aschauer, *President*
Stuart Aschauer, *President*
**EMP:** 4
**SQ FT:** 1,200
**SALES (est):** 516K  **Privately Held**
**SIC: 5941** 5211 1799 3949  Playground equipment; fencing; fence construction; sporting & athletic goods; miscellaneous fabricated wire products

---
### Warsaw
*Hancock County*
---

*(G-21370)*
### MIDWEST MKTG/PDCTN MFG CO
Also Called: Realty World
521 Main St (62379-1248)
**PHONE** ................................ 217 256-3414

**Warsaw - Hancock County (G-21371)** — GEOGRAPHIC SECTION

Fax: 217 256-3346
Steven C Siegrist, *Owner*
James S Clinton, *Principal*
EMP: 1
SQ FT: 25,000
SALES (est): 206K **Privately Held**
SIC: **6531** 2449 Real estate agent, residential; containers, plywood & veneer wood

*(G-21371)*
**PRODUCTION MANUFACTURING**
Also Called: Production Engineering
305 Main St (62379-1244)
PHONE..................................217 256-4211
Kenneth Jones, *Owner*
EMP: 3
SQ FT: 15,000
SALES: 200K **Privately Held**
SIC: **3599** 2449 7692 3444 Machine shop, jobbing & repair; containers, plywood & veneer wood; welding repair; sheet metalwork; metal barrels, drums & pails

## Wasco
### Kane County

*(G-21372)*
**ARGO MANUFACTURING CO**
4n944 Old Lafox Rd (60183-8000)
P.O. Box 359 (60183-0359)
PHONE..................................630 377-1750
Ken Mitson, *President*
Darlene Mitson, *Corp Secy*
▲ EMP: 17
SQ FT: 17,000
SALES (est): 2.7MM **Privately Held**
SIC: **3599** Custom machinery; machine shop, jobbing & repair

*(G-21373)*
**PACE MACHINERY GROUP INC**
4n944 Old Lafox Rd (60183-8000)
P.O. Box 359 (60183-0359)
PHONE..................................630 377-1750
Ken Mitson, *President*
Darlene Mitson, *Corp Secy*
James Jenkins, *Sales Staff*
▲ EMP: 15
SQ FT: 20,000
SALES (est): 3.3MM **Privately Held**
WEB: www.pace-asp.com
SIC: **3545** Tools & accessories for machine tools

## Washburn
### Marshall County

*(G-21374)*
**ALVAR INC**
112 State Route 89 (61570-9767)
PHONE..................................309 248-7523
Fax: 309 248-7526
Arthur F Lersch, *President*
Martha Kyle Allen, *Admin Sec*
▲ EMP: 15
SQ FT: 21,000
SALES (est): 5.1MM **Privately Held**
SIC: **2851** Varnishes; intaglio ink vehicle

*(G-21375)*
**GREBNER MACHINE & TOOL INC**
1866 County Road 00 N (61570-9792)
PHONE..................................309 248-7768
Alvin A Grebner, *President*
Mike Grebner, *Treasurer*
Beth Grebner, *Admin Sec*
EMP: 4
SQ FT: 4,000
SALES: 200K **Privately Held**
SIC: **3599** Machine & other job shop work

*(G-21376)*
**K B METAL COMPANY**
1172 County Road 2100 N (61570-9366)
PHONE..................................309 248-7355
Don Kennell, *Managing Prtnr*
Bill Kennell, *Partner*
Lawrence Kennell, *Partner*
Nancy Kennell, *Partner*
EMP: 4
SALES (est): 406.6K **Privately Held**
SIC: **3444** Housings for business machines, sheet metal

## Washington
### Tazewell County

*(G-21377)*
**ALLIANCE WHEEL SERVICES LLC**
302 W Holland St (61571-2515)
PHONE..................................309 444-4334
Kevin Deany,
Robert Coup,
EMP: 4
SALES (est): 1.1MM **Privately Held**
SIC: **3743** Railroad equipment

*(G-21378)*
**BAKER AVENUE INVESTMENTS INC (PA)**
Also Called: Lincoln Office
205 Eastgate Dr (61571-9238)
PHONE..................................309 427-2500
William E Pape, *President*
Jerry Sweet, *CFO*
EMP: 3 EST: 2005
SALES (est): 49.3MM **Privately Held**
SIC: **1799** 7389 5021 2273 Home/office interiors finishing, furnishing & remodeling; office furniture installation; interior design services; office & public building furniture; carpets & rugs; office furniture, except wood; tables, office: except wood; panel systems & partitions, office: except wood; office cabinets & filing drawers: except wood; personal holding companies, except banks

*(G-21379)*
**BTD MANUFACTURING INC**
118 Muller Rd (61571-2343)
PHONE..................................309 444-1268
Paul Gintner, *President*
EMP: 24 **Publicly Held**
SIC: **3441** Fabricated structural metal
HQ: Btd Manufacturing, Inc.
1111 13th Ave Se
Detroit Lakes MN 56501
218 847-4446

*(G-21380)*
**CATERPILLAR INC**
28194 Caterpillar Ln (61571-9600)
P.O. Box 1895, Peoria (61656-1895)
PHONE..................................309 578-2086
EMP: 355
SALES (corp-wide): 38.5B **Publicly Held**
SIC: **3531** Construction machinery
PA: Caterpillar Inc.
100 Ne Adams St
Peoria IL 61629
309 675-1000

*(G-21381)*
**COMET SUPPLY INC**
312 Muller Rd (61571-2347)
P.O. Box 98 (61571-0098)
PHONE..................................309 444-2712
Fax: 309 444-9213
Wayne Pruss, *President*
Betty Pruss, *Manager*
EMP: 6
SQ FT: 20,000
SALES (est): 1.4MM **Privately Held**
WEB: www.cometsupply.com
SIC: **2992** Lubricating oils & greases

*(G-21382)*
**FUGATE INC**
204 Loren St (61571-1732)
PHONE..................................309 472-6830
Brett Fugate, *CEO*
EMP: 4
SALES (est): 153.8K **Privately Held**
SIC: **3931** Percussion instruments & parts; drums, parts & accessories (musical instruments); marimbas; vibraphones

*(G-21383)*
**IPLASTICS LLC (PA)**
Also Called: Illinois Valley Plastics
300 N Cummings Ln (61571-2198)
PHONE..................................309 444-8884
Daryl R Lindemann, *CEO*
Tom Williams, *Vice Pres*
Kim Diaz, *Director*
▲ EMP: 90 EST: 1953
SQ FT: 52,000
SALES (est): 22.6MM **Privately Held**
WEB: www.ivplastics.com
SIC: **3089** 3544 Injection molding of plastics; industrial molds

*(G-21384)*
**JAMES RANDALL**
201 Monroe St (61571-1465)
PHONE..................................309 444-8765
James Randall, *Owner*
Rebecca Randall, *Co-Owner*
EMP: 7
SALES (est): 499K **Privately Held**
SIC: **2395** 4212 Tucking, for the trade; local trucking, without storage

*(G-21385)*
**LINCOLN OFFICE LLC (HQ)**
205 Eastgate Dr (61571-9238)
PHONE..................................309 427-2500
William E Pape, *President*
Joyce Anderson, *Opers Staff*
Jerry Sweet, *CFO*
Jim Morrison, *Sales Associate*
Kathy Shishalla, *Marketing Staff*
EMP: 52
SQ FT: 35,000
SALES (est): 54.8MM **Privately Held**
WEB: www.lincolnoffice.com
SIC: **5021** 7389 1799 2522 Office & public building furniture; interior design services; home/office interiors finishing, furnishing & remodeling; office furniture installation; office furniture, except wood; tables, office: except wood; panel systems & partitions, office: except wood; office cabinets & filing drawers: except wood
PA: Baker Avenue Investments, Inc
205 Eastgate Dr
Washington IL 61571
309 427-2500

*(G-21386)*
**MAXHEIMER CONSTRUCTION INC**
Also Called: Maxco Ready Mix
25130 Schuck Rd (61571-9789)
PHONE..................................309 444-4200
Fax: 309 444-8500
Steven Maxheimer, *President*
EMP: 4
SQ FT: 3,000
SALES (est): 529.9K **Privately Held**
SIC: **3273** Ready-mixed concrete

*(G-21387)*
**PRAIRIELAND PRINTING**
Also Called: Prarieland Printing Spp
1237 Peoria St (61571-2352)
PHONE..................................309 647-5425
Carol A Reed, *Owner*
David Reed, *Co-Owner*
EMP: 5
SALES (est): 436K **Privately Held**
SIC: **7334** 2789 2752 Photocopying & duplicating services; bookbinding & related work; commercial printing, lithographic

*(G-21388)*
**PRO-LINE WINNING WAYS & PENLAN**
2095 Washington Rd (61571-2059)
PHONE..................................309 745-8530
Paige Hirstein, *Owner*
EMP: 2
SALES (est): 237.3K **Privately Held**
SIC: **2844** 3944 Shampoos, rinses, conditioners: hair; games, toys & children's vehicles

*(G-21389)*
**PUBPAL LLC**
25130 Schuck Rd (61571-9789)
PHONE..................................309 222-5062
Michael Maxheimer,
Josh Jacob,
EMP: 4
SALES: 1K **Privately Held**
SIC: **7372** Prepackaged software

*(G-21390)*
**RICH PRODUCTS CORPORATION**
1902 Cobblestone (61571-3429)
PHONE..................................309 886-2465
Todd High, *Branch Mgr*
EMP: 750
SALES (corp-wide): 3.2B **Privately Held**
SIC: **2053** Frozen bakery products, except bread
PA: Rich Products Corporation
1 Robert Rich Way
Buffalo NY 14213
716 878-8000

*(G-21391)*
**SALZMAN PRINTING**
Also Called: Any Color
105 Grant St (61571-1921)
PHONE..................................309 745-3016
Stanley Salzman, *President*
EMP: 4
SQ FT: 6,000
SALES (est): 230K **Privately Held**
SIC: **2759** Commercial printing

*(G-21392)*
**SERVICE AUTO SUPPLY**
Also Called: U-Haul
101 N Wood St (61571-2577)
PHONE..................................309 444-9704
Fax: 309 444-3079
Bill Donnager, *President*
EMP: 12
SQ FT: 6,500
SALES (est): 1.3MM **Privately Held**
SIC: **7538** 5531 3599 5261 General automotive repair shops; automotive & home supply stores; machine shop, jobbing & repair; garden tractors & tillers; truck rental & leasing, no drivers

*(G-21393)*
**TEAM WORKS BY HOLZHAUER INC**
2168 Washington Rd (61571-1954)
PHONE..................................309 745-9924
Kathleen Holzhauer, *President*
Roger Holzhauer, *Vice Pres*
EMP: 5
SALES: 550K **Privately Held**
SIC: **2396** Screen printing on fabric articles

*(G-21394)*
**WASHINGTON COURIER**
Also Called: Courier Publishing Co
100 Ford Ln (61571-2668)
P.O. Box 349 (61571-0349)
PHONE..................................309 444-3139
Fax: 309 444-8505
Roger Lyle Hagel, *President*
EMP: 15 EST: 1958
SQ FT: 4,000
SALES (est): 955.4K **Privately Held**
SIC: **2711** 2759 Newspapers: publishing only, not printed on site; letterpress printing

*(G-21395)*
**WASHINGTON WOODWORKING**
1514 Willow Dr (61571-9345)
PHONE..................................309 339-0913
Thomas Stefani, *Principal*
EMP: 2 EST: 2011
SALES (est): 224.8K **Privately Held**
SIC: **2431** Millwork

*(G-21396)*
**WICC LTD**
119 Muller Rd (61571-2357)
P.O. Box 252 (61571-0252)
PHONE..................................309 444-4125
Fax: 309 444-3313
Terry Bierrie, *President*
Dennis Russman, *Engineer*
Chris Siebert, *Sales Executive*
EMP: 61
SQ FT: 16,000

SALES (est): 11.3MM  Privately Held
WEB: www.wiccltd.com
SIC: 3612  Power transformers, electric

**(G-21397)**
**ZG3 SYSTEMS  LLC**
25232 Spring Creek Rd  (61571-9724)
PHONE..................................309 745-3398
Richard E Brummett, *President*
Douglas A Rasmussen, *Vice Pres*
EMP: 3 EST: 2014
SQ FT: 1,920
SALES: 2.3MM  Privately Held
SIC: 3536  Hoists, cranes & monorails

## Wataga
### Knox County

**(G-21398)**
**H & S PUBLICATIONS INC**
2310 Us Highway 150 N  (61488-9520)
PHONE..................................309 344-1333
Fax: 309 344-1165
Robert T Self Sr, *President*
EMP: 7 EST: 1970
SALES: 825K  Privately Held
SIC: 2721  Magazines: publishing only, not printed on site

**(G-21399)**
**WEST CENTRAL FS INC**
Also Called: Spoon River F S
686 N Depot Rd  (61488-9614)
PHONE..................................309 375-6904
Fax: 309 375-6729
Doug Long, *Manager*
EMP: 6
SALES (corp-wide): 81.2MM  Privately Held
WEB: www.riverlandfs.com
SIC: 2875  5261  1542  Fertilizers, mixing only; nurseries & garden centers; agricultural building contractors
PA: West Central Fs Inc
    1445 Monmouth Blvd
    Galesburg IL 61401
    309 343-1600

## Waterloo
### Monroe County

**(G-21400)**
**COLUMBIA QUARRY COMPANY**
5440 Quarry Dr  (62298-2838)
P.O. Box 58  (62298-0058)
PHONE..................................618 939-8833
Fax: 618 939-8691
Bill Groh, *Branch Mgr*
EMP: 22
SALES (corp-wide): 14.7MM  Privately Held
SIC: 1422  Crushed & broken limestone
PA: Columbia Quarry Company
    210 State Route 158
    Columbia IL 62236
    618 281-7631

**(G-21401)**
**D E SIGNS & STORAGE LLC**
Also Called: Dealers Edge
6167 State Route 3  (62298-3063)
PHONE..................................618 939-8050
Fax: 618 939-9619
Melinda L Sale, *EMP*
EMP: 3
SQ FT: 24,000
SALES (est): 245.4K  Privately Held
WEB: www.dealersedge.com
SIC: 4225  2752  3993  General warehousing & storage; business form & card printing, lithographic; signs & advertising specialties

**(G-21402)**
**LOHRBERG LUMBER**
5662 L Rd  (62298-5022)
PHONE..................................618 473-2061
Fax: 618 473-2083
Thor Lohrberg, *President*
EMP: 10
SQ FT: 2,275

SALES (est): 3.9MM  Privately Held
SIC: 2421  0211  4213  2426  Sawmills & planing mills, general; beef cattle feedlots; trucking, except local; hardwood dimension & flooring mills

**(G-21403)**
**OMEGA PRODUCTS INC**
502 Walnut St  (62298-1467)
P.O. Box 122  (62298-0122)
PHONE..................................618 939-3445
Fax: 618 939-3299
William Ebeler, *President*
Theresa Ebeler, *General Mgr*
Jeanne Ebeler, *Admin Sec*
EMP: 7
SQ FT: 5,000
SALES (est): 1.1MM  Privately Held
WEB: www.omegaproducts.com
SIC: 3312  3444  Stainless steel; sheet metalwork; ventilators, sheet metal; hoods, range: sheet metal

**(G-21404)**
**R & L BUSINESS FORMS INC**
8603 Gilmore Lake Rd  (62298)
P.O. Box 47  (62298-0047)
PHONE..................................618 939-6535
Fax: 618 939-8899
Larry E Menke, *President*
Robert W Menke, *Vice Pres*
EMP: 12
SQ FT: 10,860
SALES (est): 750K  Privately Held
SIC: 2761  Unit sets (manifold business forms); continuous forms, office & business

**(G-21405)**
**RAYS POWER WSHG SVC PEGGY RAY**
318 Bradford Ln  (62298-3250)
PHONE..................................618 939-6306
Ray Power, *Owner*
Peggy Power, *Co-Owner*
EMP: 5
SALES: 50K  Privately Held
SIC: 7542  3589  7389  Carwashes; floor washing & polishing machines, commercial;

**(G-21406)**
**REPUBLIC TIMES LLC**
205 W Mill St  (62298-1235)
P.O. Box 147  (62298-0147)
PHONE..................................618 939-3814
Fax: 618 939-3815
Kermit Constantine, *Mng Member*
Lynn Venhaus, *Manager*
EMP: 8
SALES (est): 369.8K  Privately Held
WEB: www.republictimes.net
SIC: 2711  Newspapers: publishing only, not printed on site

## Waterman
### Dekalb County

**(G-21407)**
**KAUFFMAN POULTRY FARMS INC**
Also Called: HO-KA TURKEY FARM
8519 Leland Rd  (60556-7069)
P.O. Box 205  (60556-0205)
PHONE..................................815 264-3470
Fax: 815 264-7820
Robert Kauffman, *President*
Jean L Clowers, *Corp Secy*
EMP: 13 EST: 1933
SQ FT: 6,000
SALES (est): 2.1MM  Privately Held
WEB: www.hokaturkeys.com
SIC: 2015  0115  Turkey processing & slaughtering; corn

**(G-21408)**
**MONSANTO COMPANY**
460 E Adams St  (60556-5000)
PHONE..................................815 264-8153
Daniel Luers, *CEO*
Shawn Etherton, *Manager*
EMP: 62

SALES (corp-wide): 13.5B  Publicly Held
SIC: 2879  Agricultural chemicals
PA: Monsanto Company
    800 N Lindbergh Blvd
    Saint Louis MO 63167
    314 694-1000

**(G-21409)**
**PRODUCTION CUTTING SERVICES**
9341 State Route 23  (60556-7163)
PHONE..................................815 264-3505
EMP: 52
SALES (corp-wide): 20MM  Privately Held
SIC: 3312  Blast furnaces & steel mills
PA: Production Cutting Services, Inc
    1201 7th St
    East Moline IL 61244
    309 755-4601

**(G-21410)**
**VISION PICKLING AND PROC INC**
Also Called: Pickling Steel
9341 State Route 23  (60556-7163)
PHONE..................................815 264-7755
Fax: 815 264-7778
Steven F Whitney, *President*
Elwood Gustafson, *Principal*
Jeremy Schoemaker, *Manager*
William J Dowsett, *Shareholder*
EMP: 13
SQ FT: 240,000
SALES (est): 2.2MM  Privately Held
WEB: www.visionpickling.com
SIC: 3547  3471  Picklers & pickling lines (rolling mill equipment); plating & polishing

**(G-21411)**
**WATERMAN WINERY & VINEYARDS**
11582 Waterman Rd  (60556-7194)
PHONE..................................815 264-3268
Terrie Tuntland, *President*
EMP: 4
SALES (est): 214.1K  Privately Held
SIC: 2084  5921  Wines; wine

**(G-21412)**
**WILLIAM BADAL**
Also Called: 5 B'S Catering Service
190 W Lincoln Hwy  (60556-9730)
P.O. Box 365  (60556-0365)
PHONE..................................815 264-7752
Fax: 815 264-7752
William Badal, *Owner*
EMP: 3
SQ FT: 4,000
SALES (est): 50K  Privately Held
SIC: 5812  2013  Caterers; sausages & other prepared meats

## Watseka
### Iroquois County

**(G-21413)**
**ALL AMERICAN ATHLETICS LTD**
100 Laird Ln  (60970-7561)
PHONE..................................815 432-8326
EMP: 3 EST: 2004
SALES (est): 170K  Privately Held
SIC: 3949  Sporting Goods

**(G-21414)**
**AUSTIN GRAPHIC**
105 N Jefferson St  (60970-1199)
PHONE..................................815 432-4983
Fax: 815 432-5188
Brandon Barragre, *President*
Nancy Barragre, *Office Mgr*
EMP: 5 EST: 1950
SQ FT: 3,000
SALES: 121.6K  Privately Held
SIC: 2752  Commercial printing, offset

**(G-21415)**
**B & M SCREW MACHINE INC**
Also Called: B & M Machine Shop
900 E Cherry St  (60970-1811)
P.O. Box 70  (60970-0070)
PHONE..................................815 432-5892

Fax: 815 432-4808
Richard Martin, *President*
Dave Sullivan, *General Mgr*
John W Grant, *Vice Pres*
Donald D Kelly, *Vice Pres*
William F Lewis, *Vice Pres*
EMP: 4 EST: 1965
SQ FT: 6,000
SALES: 400K  Privately Held
SIC: 3451  Screw machine products

**(G-21416)**
**BJS ENTERPRISES INC**
834 S Hanson Dr  (60970-1799)
PHONE..................................815 432-5176
Joanne Sherry, *President*
Robert Sherry, *Corp Secy*
EMP: 2
SQ FT: 2,800
SALES (est): 250K  Privately Held
SIC: 5084  3569  Paint spray equipment, industrial; baling machines, for scrap metal, paper or similar material

**(G-21417)**
**GRISWOLD FEED INC**
890 E Walnut St  (60970-1486)
PHONE..................................815 432-2811
Gary Griswold, *President*
Margaret Griswold, *Treasurer*
EMP: 5
SQ FT: 2,000
SALES (est): 387.3K  Privately Held
SIC: 2048  Livestock feeds

**(G-21418)**
**HIPRO MANUFACTURING INC**
1909 E 1800 N Rd  (60970)
PHONE..................................815 432-5271
Fax: 815 432-2600
Clifford Stan, *President*
Jerry McClain, *Plant Mgr*
Jody Harper, *Bookkeeper*
EMP: 20
SALES (est): 2.3MM  Privately Held
WEB: www.hipromfg.com
SIC: 3523  3524  Farm machinery & equipment; lawn & garden equipment

**(G-21419)**
**I D TOOL SPECIALTY COMPANY**
819 N Jefferson St  (60970)
P.O. Box 131  (60970-0131)
PHONE..................................815 432-2007
Larry Parks, *President*
Mary Parks, *Manager*
EMP: 8
SQ FT: 6,000
SALES (est): 818.1K  Privately Held
SIC: 1389  Well plugging & abandoning, oil & gas; servicing oil & gas wells

**(G-21420)**
**JAY A MORRIS (PA)**
Also Called: Jay Morris Trucking
2238 E Township Road 165  (60970-8731)
PHONE..................................815 432-6440
Jay Morris, *Owner*
Renee Morris, *Administration*
EMP: 2
SALES: 4MM  Privately Held
SIC: 2431  4212  1794  Millwork; local trucking, without storage; excavation work

**(G-21421)**
**LYON  LLC**
Also Called: Pride Metal
475 N Veterans Pkwy  (60970-1839)
PHONE..................................815 432-4595
George McGeorge, *Manager*
EMP: 125
SALES (corp-wide): 110.6MM  Privately Held
SIC: 3469  Metal stampings
HQ: Lyon, Llc
    420 N Main St
    Montgomery IL 60538
    630 892-8941

**(G-21422)**
**MASSEY GRAFIX**
1637 E 1900 North Rd  (60970-7901)
PHONE..................................815 644-4620
Craig Massey, *Owner*
Graig Massey, *Manager*
EMP: 4

# Watseka - Iroquois County (G-21423)

SALES: 120K **Privately Held**
SIC: 3993 Signs & advertising specialties

**(G-21423)**
**METAL MFG LLC**
Also Called: Pride Metal Products
475 N Veterans Pkwy (60970-1839)
PHONE.................................815 432-4595
Fax: 815 432-6324
Darren Crook, *Opers Mgr*
Tim Rieken, *Opers Mgr*
EMP: 150
SALES (est): 7.6MM **Privately Held**
WEB: www.pridemetal.com
SIC: 3429 Metal fasteners

**(G-21424)**
**PALLET RECYCLERS INC**
106 E Jefferson Ave (60970-1648)
PHONE.................................815 432-4022
Ernest Minor, *Principal*
EMP: 3
SALES (est): 159.2K **Privately Held**
SIC: 2448 Pallets, wood & wood with metal

**(G-21425)**
**PEOPLES COAL AND LUMBER CO (PA)**
Also Called: Peoples Cmplete Buiding Centre
121 S 3rd St (60970-1665)
P.O. Box 70 (60970-0070)
PHONE.................................815 432-2456
Fax: 815 432-2470
Richard A Martin, *Ch of Bd*
Daniel Martin, *President*
Samuel Martin II, *Vice Pres*
Kirk McTaggart, *Manager*
EMP: 14
SQ FT: 8,000
SALES (est): 2.7MM **Privately Held**
SIC: 5251 3273 5211 Hardware; ready-mixed concrete; lumber & other building materials

**(G-21426)**
**QSE INC (PA)**
316 W Hickory St (60970-1236)
P.O. Box 360 (60970-0360)
PHONE.................................815 432-5281
Fax: 815 432-6179
Anthony J Imburgia, *President*
▲ EMP: 20
SQ FT: 28,000
SALES (est): 10MM **Privately Held**
WEB: www.qse.com
SIC: 3677 Electronic coils, transformers & other inductors

**(G-21427)**
**STANDARD REGISTER INC**
Also Called: Uarco
112 E Walnut St Ste B (60970-1381)
PHONE.................................815 432-4203
Fax: 815 432-5106
EMP: 16
SQ FT: 236,000
SALES (corp-wide): 3.8B **Privately Held**
SIC: 2761 Mfg Manifold Business Forms
HQ: Standard Register, Inc.
600 Albany St
Dayton OH 45417
937 221-1000

**(G-21428)**
**STEEL SOLUTIONS USA**
602 E Walnut St (60970-1459)
PHONE.................................815 432-4938
Steve Huggins, *Principal*
Tonjia May, *Manager*
EMP: 9
SALES: 356.4K
SALES (corp-wide): 25.8MM **Privately Held**
SIC: 2522 Office furniture, except wood
PA: T And D Metal Products, L.L.C.
602 E Walnut St
Watseka IL 60970
815 432-4938

**(G-21429)**
**T & S BUSINESS GROUP LLC**
Also Called: Petersen/Tru-Cut Automotive
602 E Walnut St (60970-1459)
PHONE.................................815 432-7084
Roger Pj Dittrich,
EMP: 10

SQ FT: 70,000
SALES: 4MM **Privately Held**
SIC: 3559 Automotive related machinery

**(G-21430)**
**T AND D METAL PRODUCTS LLC (PA)**
Also Called: T&D Trucking
602 E Walnut St (60970-1459)
PHONE.................................815 432-4938
Fax: 815 432-6271
Melinda McKay, *Controller*
Jennifer Kibbons, *Human Res Mgr*
Roger P J Dittrich, *Mng Member*
Diana Dittrich, *Mng Member*
Troy Krumwiede, *Director*
EMP: 9
SQ FT: 140,000
SALES (est): 25.8MM **Privately Held**
WEB: www.tdmetal.com
SIC: 2542 3469 3799 Cabinets: show, display or storage: except wood; boxes: tool, lunch, mail, etc.: stamped metal; go-carts, except children's

**(G-21431)**
**TIMES REPUBLIC (HQ)**
Also Called: Twin States Publishing Co
1492 E Walnut St (60970-1806)
PHONE.................................815 432-5227
Fax: 815 432-6779
Larry Perrotto, *President*
Joan Williams, *Vice Pres*
Carol Christy, *Advt Staff*
EMP: 50
SQ FT: 2,500
SALES (est): 9.1MM **Privately Held**
WEB: www.communitymediagroup.com
SIC: 2711 2791 2759 2752 Newspapers: publishing only, not printed on site; type-setting; commercial printing; commercial printing, lithographic

**(G-21432)**
**UNITED VALIDATION & COM**
1728 E 1700 North Rd (60970-7636)
PHONE.................................815 953-6068
Raymond White, *President*
EMP: 1
SQ FT: 2,200
SALES: 500K **Privately Held**
SIC: 3559 Pharmaceutical machinery

## Watson
### Effingham County

**(G-21433)**
**K & P WELDING**
12374 E 550th Ave (62473-2238)
P.O. Box 38 (62473-0038)
PHONE.................................217 536-5245
Kenny Bergfeld, *Owner*
EMP: 2
SQ FT: 3,000
SALES: 250K **Privately Held**
SIC: 7692 Welding repair

## Wauconda
### Lake County

**(G-21434)**
**A J WAGNER & SON**
1120 N Rand Rd Frnt 1 (60084-1174)
PHONE.................................773 935-1414
Daniel A Wagner, *Vice Pres*
Albert J Wagner III, *Admin Sec*
EMP: 12
SQ FT: 8,000
SALES: 1MM **Privately Held**
WEB: www.albertwagnerandson.com
SIC: 1761 3444 Sheet metalwork; sheet metalwork

**(G-21435)**
**A TO Z ENGRAVING CO INC**
Also Called: A To Z Engrvg
1150 Brown St Ste G (60084-1154)
PHONE.................................847 526-7396
Fax: 847 526-7399
Joan Nelson, *President*
Gary Nelson, *Vice Pres*

EMP: 5 EST: 1954
SQ FT: 4,000
SALES (est): 620.3K **Privately Held**
SIC: 3089 3993 3953 2789 Engraving of plastic; signs & advertising specialties; marking devices; bookbinding & related work

**(G-21436)**
**ABOUT LEARNING INC**
441 W Bonner Rd (60084-1101)
PHONE.................................847 487-1800
Fax: 847 487-1811
Michael Mc Carthy, *CEO*
Bernice Mc Carthy, *President*
Dennis McCarthy, *Director*
EMP: 14
SQ FT: 5,000
SALES (est): 1.4MM **Privately Held**
WEB: www.aboutlearning.com
SIC: 2741 8733 Miscellaneous publishing; educational research agency

**(G-21437)**
**ACCU-GRIND MANUFACTURING INC**
386 Hollow Hill Rd (60084-9762)
PHONE.................................847 526-2700
Fax: 847 526-2719
Henry Sauer Sr, *President*
EMP: 11
SQ FT: 4,300
SALES: 800K **Privately Held**
SIC: 3545 7389 Gauges (machine tool accessories); grinding, precision: commercial or industrial

**(G-21438)**
**ALLIANCE LASER SALES INC (PA)**
275 Industrial Dr (60084-1078)
PHONE.................................847 487-1945
John P Demakis, *President*
Vincent G Sabella, *Vice Pres*
Jerry Garcia, *Bookkeeper*
▲ EMP: 21
SALES (est): 3.1MM **Privately Held**
SIC: 3699 Laser welding, drilling & cutting equipment

**(G-21439)**
**ALLIANCE SPECIALTIES CORP**
275 Industrial Dr (60084-1078)
PHONE.................................847 487-1945
Fax: 847 487-2945
Vincent G Sabella, *President*
John P De Makis, *Vice Pres*
Lynn McCutcheon, *Accounting Mgr*
Karen Demakis, *Manager*
EMP: 12
SQ FT: 20,000
SALES (est): 1.8MM **Privately Held**
SIC: 3471 Finishing, metals or formed products; polishing, metals or formed products

**(G-21440)**
**AMERICAN CUSTOM WOODWORKING**
1247 Karl Ct (60084-1098)
PHONE.................................847 526-5900
Thomas Peters, *President*
Pam Peters, *Corp Secy*
Curt Fiedler, *Project Mgr*
EMP: 10
SQ FT: 20,000
SALES: 1.5MM **Privately Held**
SIC: 2431 2434 Millwork; wood kitchen cabinets

**(G-21441)**
**AMERICAN QUICK PRINT INC**
Also Called: American Quickprint
1000 Brown St Ste 212 (60084-3110)
PHONE.................................847 253-2700
Fax: 847 253-2767
Joe Presz, *President*
EMP: 3
SQ FT: 1,000
SALES (est): 489.6K **Privately Held**
SIC: 2752 2791 2789 Commercial printing, offset; typesetting; bookbinding & related work

**(G-21442)**
**AMKINE INC**
Also Called: Regency Crystal
230 Industrial Dr (60084-1077)
PHONE.................................847 526-7088
Harshad Amin, *President*
Rita Amin, *Corp Secy*
EMP: 10
SQ FT: 8,000
SALES (est): 811.2K **Privately Held**
WEB: www.regencycrystal.com
SIC: 7389 3229 Engraving service; glassware, art or decorative

**(G-21443)**
**ART & SON SIGN INC**
Also Called: Art & Son Design
1090 Brown St (60084-1106)
PHONE.................................847 526-7205
Fax: 847 526-8945
Thomas Holland, *President*
Douglas Holland, *Vice Pres*
Arthur T Holland, *Director*
Madeline Holland, *Director*
EMP: 10
SQ FT: 10,000
SALES (est): 724K **Privately Held**
SIC: 3993 Signs, not made in custom sign painting shops

**(G-21444)**
**ATHLETIC SPECIALTIES INC**
240 Industrial Dr (60084-1077)
PHONE.................................847 487-7880
Fax: 847 487-6770
Carey Brunelli, *President*
Marla Felvey, *CFO*
Sallye Worthington, *Accountant*
Ann Gran, *Sales Executive*
▲ EMP: 9
SQ FT: 11,000
SALES: 10MM **Privately Held**
WEB: www.asisports.com
SIC: 5091 3949 Athletic goods; sporting & athletic goods

**(G-21445)**
**BECKER JULES D WOOD PRODUCTS**
25250 W Old Rand Rd (60084-2475)
PHONE.................................847 526-8002
Fax: 847 526-8002
EMP: 3 EST: 1960
SQ FT: 2,000
SALES (est): 210K **Privately Held**
SIC: 2434 2431 Cabinet Maker And Specialty Woodwork

**(G-21446)**
**BIKAST GRAPHICS INC**
1000 Brown St Ste 214 (60084-3110)
PHONE.................................847 487-8822
Greg Melankowski, *President*
EMP: 3
SQ FT: 2,000
SALES: 550K **Privately Held**
SIC: 2759 2791 2789 2752 Commercial printing; typesetting; bookbinding & related work; commercial printing, lithographic; automotive & apparel trimmings

**(G-21447)**
**BK PRODUCTION SPECIALTIES**
387 Hollow Hill Rd (60084-9794)
PHONE.................................847 526-5150
Fax: 847 526-5636
Boleslaw Kowaliszyn, *President*
Janina Kowaliszyn, *Admin Sec*
EMP: 8
SQ FT: 6,000
SALES: 1,000K **Privately Held**
SIC: 3599 Machine shop, jobbing & repair

**(G-21448)**
**BLANKE INDUSTRIES INCORPORATED**
1099 Brown St Ste 103 (60084-3106)
PHONE.................................847 487-2780
Fax: 847 487-2799
John Blanke, *President*
Dave Blanke, *Accounts Mgr*
EMP: 8
SQ FT: 1,000

SALES: 500K **Privately Held**
WEB: www.blankeindustries.com
SIC: **3826** 5531 Environmental testing equipment; automobile & truck equipment & parts

*(G-21449)*
**C D NELSON CONSULTING INC**
Also Called: Nelson C D Mfg & Sup Co
27421 N Darrell Rd (60084-9792)
PHONE....................847 487-4870
Clinton D Nelson, *President*
▲ **EMP:** 4
SALES: 312.7K **Privately Held**
SIC: **3915** 8742 Jewelers' materials & lapidary work; management consulting services

*(G-21450)*
**C M F ENTERPRISES INC**
Also Called: Cover Connection
950 N Rand Rd Ste 113 (60084-1108)
PHONE....................847 526-9499
Fax: 847 526-7495
Mary L Fisher, *President*
**EMP:** 10
SQ FT: 6,600
SALES (est): 2MM **Privately Held**
SIC: **3081** 5045 7389 7336 Vinyl film & sheet; computer peripheral equipment; embroidering of advertising on shirts, etc.; silk screen design; advertising novelties

*(G-21451)*
**C M SELL WOODWORK**
28116 W Maple Ave (60084-2222)
PHONE....................847 526-3627
Fax: 847 526-3627
Chuck Sell, *Owner*
**EMP:** 4
SALES: 500K **Privately Held**
SIC: **2434** 2517 Wood kitchen cabinets; wood television & radio cabinets

*(G-21452)*
**CAMPBELL INTERNATIONAL INC**
Also Called: Campbell Cab
120 Kent Ave (60084-2441)
P.O. Box 875 (60084-0875)
PHONE....................408 661-0794
Fax: 847 526-7447
James M Campbell III, *President*
Marcy Berglind, *Purch Agent*
Sandra Bradley, *Human Res Mgr*
Marilyn Lever, *Accounts Mgr*
Charlene Schriver, *Office Mgr*
**EMP:** 40 **EST:** 1946
SQ FT: 40,000
SALES (est): 474.3K **Privately Held**
WEB: www.campbellcab.com
SIC: **3713** 3567 Truck cabs for motor vehicles; industrial furnaces & ovens

*(G-21453)*
**CORTEK ENDOSCOPY INC**
206 Jamie Ln (60084)
PHONE....................847 526-2266
Cornel Topala, *President*
**EMP:** 4
SALES (est): 435.8K **Privately Held**
WEB: www.cortek-endoscopy.com
SIC: **7699** 3845 Optical instrument repair; endoscopic equipment, electromedical

*(G-21454)*
**DOMENY TOOL & STAMPING COMPANY**
354 Hollow Hill Rd (60084-3300)
PHONE....................847 526-5700
Fax: 847 526-5701
Marge Domeny, *President*
Kristin Ormes, *Plant Mgr*
Marilyn Ruiz, *Prdtn Mgr*
Anthony Ruiz, *Accounts Mgr*
Tony Ruiz, *Accounts Mgr*
▲ **EMP:** 19
SQ FT: 24,000
SALES: 2.5MM **Privately Held**
WEB: www.domenytool.com
SIC: **3469** 3544 Machine parts, stamped or pressed metal; special dies & tools

*(G-21455)*
**DONS WELDING**
552 S Rand Rd (60084-2321)
PHONE....................847 526-1177
Fax: 847 526-1767
Don Schaal, *President*
Stan Schaal, *President*
**EMP:** 8
SQ FT: 6,400
SALES (est): 825K **Privately Held**
SIC: **7692** Welding repair

*(G-21456)*
**DU BRO PRODUCTS INC**
Also Called: Pine Ridge Archery
480 W Bonner Rd (60084-1198)
P.O. Box 815 (60084-0815)
PHONE....................847 526-2136
Fax: 847 526-1604
Jim Broberg, *President*
Terry Weiland, *Purch Agent*
Gayle Lundgren, *Treasurer*
Brian Bychowski, *Sales Staff*
Jerry Tepps, *Sales Staff*
▲ **EMP:** 30
SQ FT: 40,000
SALES (est): 5.6MM **Privately Held**
SIC: **3944** 3452 3429 Board games, puzzles & models, except electronic; craft & hobby kits & sets; airplane models, toy & hobby; railroad models: toy & hobby; bolts, nuts, rivets & washers; manufactured hardware (general)

*(G-21457)*
**DURO-CHROME INDUSTRIES INC**
275 Indl Dr (60084)
PHONE....................847 487-2900
Margoreto Garcia, *President*
Vince Sabella, *Corp Secy*
John Demakis, *Vice Pres*
Jim Grantland, *Project Mgr*
Don McCloskey, *QC Mgr*
**EMP:** 23
SQ FT: 10,000
SALES (est): 3.5MM **Privately Held**
WEB: www.duro-chrome.com
SIC: **3471** Chromium plating of metals or formed products

*(G-21458)*
**DYNAMIC PRECISION PRODUCTS**
1280 Kyle Ct (60084-1076)
PHONE....................847 526-2054
Fax: 847 526-8531
Eric B Rasmussen, *President*
Mark Rasmussen, *Treasurer*
Janet L Hanchon, *Manager*
**EMP:** 13
SQ FT: 7,200
SALES (est): 2.1MM **Privately Held**
WEB: www.dynamicprecisionproducts.com
SIC: **3599** Machine shop, jobbing & repair

*(G-21459)*
**EMERGE TECHNOLOGY GROUP LLC**
1000 N Rand Rd Ste 111 (60084-3103)
P.O. Box 866, Antioch (60002-0866)
PHONE....................800 613-1501
Ross Curran, *Manager*
Ramsey Matarieh,
▲ **EMP:** 7
SQ FT: 2,200
SALES (est): 728.3K **Privately Held**
SIC: **3672** Printed circuit boards

*(G-21460)*
**ENZYMES INCORPORATED**
1099 Brown St Ste 102 (60084-3106)
PHONE....................847 487-5401
Edward G Brandau, *CEO*
Scott Thompson, *General Mgr*
Susan Brandau, *CFO*
▼ **EMP:** 4
SQ FT: 2,300
SALES (est): 556.7K **Privately Held**
SIC: **2869** Enzymes

*(G-21461)*
**EXTRUSION TOOLING TECHNOLOGY**
Also Called: Etti
1000 N Rand Rd Ste 210 (60084-3104)
PHONE....................847 526-1606
Fax: 847 526-7443
Wesley Scott, *President*
**EMP:** 7
SQ FT: 3,600
SALES (est): 1MM **Privately Held**
WEB: www.ettinc.com
SIC: **3544** Special dies & tools; extrusion dies

*(G-21462)*
**F & Y ENTERPRISES INC**
Also Called: Texas Brand
1205 Karl Ct Ste 115 (60084-1090)
PHONE....................847 526-0620
Frank J Vitek, *President*
**EMP:** 40
SQ FT: 6,000
SALES (est): 2MM **Privately Held**
SIC: **5147** 2013 Meat brokers; meats, cured or smoked; beef, dried: from purchased meat; smoked meats from purchased meat

*(G-21463)*
**FISH OVEN AND EQUIPMENT CORP**
120 Kent Ave (60084-2441)
P.O. Box 875 (60084-0875)
PHONE....................847 526-8686
James M Campbell III, *President*
Janice Campbell, *Vice Pres*
Sandra Bradley, *Human Resources*
**EMP:** 40
SQ FT: 40,000
SALES (est): 7.8MM **Privately Held**
WEB: www.campbellcab.com
SIC: **3567** Industrial furnaces & ovens

*(G-21464)*
**GEHRKE TECHNOLOGY GROUP INC (PA)**
1050 N Rand Rd (60084-1165)
PHONE....................847 498-7320
Fax: 847 487-9026
Greg Gehrke, *President*
Elizabeth Gehrke, *Admin Sec*
▲ **EMP:** 11
SALES (est): 5.6MM **Privately Held**
WEB: www.gehrketech.com
SIC: **4941** 5074 3589 Water supply; water purification equipment; water treatment equipment, industrial

*(G-21465)*
**GOLDMAN PRODUCTS INC**
Also Called: Goldman Dental
379 Hollow Hill Rd (60084-9794)
PHONE....................847 526-1166
Fax: 847 526-1363
Edward Kwan Rim, *President*
Marchin Krolonske, *Finance Mgr*
Elizabeth Gaffney, *Marketing Staff*
Juliet Rim, *Admin Sec*
**EMP:** 29
SQ FT: 10,000
SALES: 3MM **Privately Held**
WEB: www.goldmandental.com
SIC: **3843** Dental equipment

*(G-21466)*
**HELIVALUES**
Also Called: Offical Helicopter Blue Book
1001 N Old Rand Rd # 101 (60084-1288)
PHONE....................847 487-8258
Barry D Desfor, *Ch of Bd*
Sharon Desfor, *President*
Lindsay Higgins, *General Mgr*
Carol Busch, *Editor*
Sue Kandefer, *Vice Pres*
**EMP:** 8
SQ FT: 5,200
SALES (est): 800K **Privately Held**
WEB: www.helivalues.com
SIC: **2731** 3721 Book publishing; helicopters

*(G-21467)*
**HENDRIX INDUSTRIAL GASTRUX INC**
1301 N Old Rand Rd (60084-9764)
P.O. Box 638 (60084-0638)
PHONE....................847 526-1700
Fax: 847 526-1705
Todd Hendrix, *President*
**EMP:** 6
SQ FT: 7,000
SALES (est): 2MM **Privately Held**
WEB: www.hendrixsystems.com
SIC: **5013** 3714 Automotive engines & engine parts; exhaust systems (mufflers, tail pipes, etc.); exhaust systems & parts, motor vehicle

*(G-21468)*
**HI-TECH BUILIDNG SYSTEMS**
28613 N Jackson Ave (60084-1053)
P.O. Box 787 (60084-0787)
PHONE....................847 526-5310
Robert Tomczak, *Owner*
Bill Schmitz, *Chief Engr*
**EMP:** 3
SALES: 950K **Privately Held**
SIC: **3999** Manufacturing industries

*(G-21469)*
**HM MANUFACTURING INC**
1200 Henri Dr (60084-1000)
PHONE....................847 487-8700
Fax: 847 487-8707
Kenneth W Wolter, *President*
Mary Devlin, *Bookkeeper*
Mary E Devlin, *Admin Sec*
**EMP:** 10 **EST:** 1975
SQ FT: 10,000
SALES (est): 1.7MM **Privately Held**
WEB: www.hmmanufacturing.com
SIC: **3429** 3714 3462 Pulleys metal; power transmission equipment, motor vehicle; iron & steel forgings

*(G-21470)*
**HOLLAND DESIGN GROUP INC**
1090 Brown St (60084-1106)
PHONE....................847 526-8848
Thomas Holland, *President*
Douglas Holland, *Corp Secy*
**EMP:** 10
SQ FT: 10,000
SALES (est): 820K **Privately Held**
SIC: **3993** 1799 Signs & advertising specialties; sign installation & maintenance

*(G-21471)*
**ILLINOIS MOLD BUILDERS INC**
Also Called: Dynasty Mold Builders
250 Jamie Ln (60084-1079)
PHONE....................847 526-0400
Fax: 847 526-0543
Paul Makray, *President*
Mark Niggemann, *General Mgr*
Tom McDonald, *Engineer*
Don Nowack, *Manager*
Nancy Harney, *Admin Sec*
**EMP:** 12
SQ FT: 12,500
SALES (est): 2.2MM **Privately Held**
WEB: www.dynastymold.com
SIC: **3544** Industrial molds

*(G-21472)*
**ILLINOIS STERLING LTD**
540 S Rand Rd (60084-2375)
PHONE....................847 526-5151
Fax: 847 487-4340
Barbara Herrmann, *President*
**EMP:** 4
SQ FT: 22,000
SALES (est): 280K **Privately Held**
SIC: **3711** Motor vehicles & car bodies

*(G-21473)*
**INTECH INDUSTRIES INC**
Also Called: Midwest Control
1101 Brown St (60084-1105)
P.O. Box 100 (60084-0100)
PHONE....................847 487-5599
Fax: 847 487-0909
Terrence Connolly, *President*
Veda Connolly, *Vice Pres*
Kristen Drexler, *Vice Pres*
Judy Searles, *Purchasing*
Lureen Newquist, *Sales Associate*

## Wauconda - Lake County (G-21474)

▲ EMP: 11
SQ FT: 8,000
SALES: 3.5MM Privately Held
SIC: 3569 3822 3545 3494 Filters; gradual switches, pneumatic; machine tool accessories; valves & pipe fittings; gaskets, packing & sealing devices; fasteners, industrial: nuts, bolts, screws, etc.

### (G-21474)
**INTREPID MOLDING INC**
285 Industrial Dr (60084-1078)
PHONE..................847 526-9477
Fax: 847 526-9544
Mike Durkin, *President*
John Webb, *Treasurer*
Lindze Durkin, *Office Mgr*
Shirley Durkin, *Admin Sec*
▲ EMP: 30
SQ FT: 15,000
SALES (est): 5.9MM Privately Held
WEB: www.intrepidmolding.com
SIC: 3089 Injection molding of plastics

### (G-21475)
**JANCO PROCESS CONTROLS INC**
368 W Liberty St (60084-2493)
PHONE..................847 526-0800
James T Cheslock, *President*
EMP: 21
SALES (est): 4.5MM Privately Held
SIC: 3823 Industrial process control instruments

### (G-21476)
**KELLERMANN MANUFACTURING INC**
Also Called: Kellermann Manufacturing Co
1000 N Rand Rd Ste 224 (60084-3100)
PHONE..................847 526-7266
Robert M Kellermann, *President*
Robert Kellermann Jr, *Corp Secy*
EMP: 5
SALES: 400K Privately Held
WEB:
www.kellermannmanufacturingco.com
SIC: 3365 Aluminum & aluminum-based alloy castings

### (G-21477)
**KIPP MANUFACTURING COMPANY INC**
375 Hollow Hill Rd (60084-9794)
P.O. Box 2603, Glenview (60025-6603)
PHONE..................630 768-9051
Fax: 847 491-9440
Ron Kinder, *President*
Mike Ravesloot, *Vice Pres*
Kristine J Christ, *Admin Sec*
▲ EMP: 10 EST: 1944
SQ FT: 15,000
SALES: 900K Privately Held
SIC: 3465 3542 3444 3089 Moldings or trim, automobile: stamped metal; brakes, metal forming; spouts, sheet metal; spouting, plastic & glass fiber reinforced; metal stampings; crowns & closures

### (G-21478)
**KOSTO FOOD PRODUCTS COMPANY**
1325 N Old Rand Rd (60084-3302)
PHONE..................847 487-2600
Fax: 847 487-2654
Donald F Colby, *President*
Steve Colby, *General Mgr*
Richard Gray, *General Mgr*
Marleen Madigan, *Safety Mgr*
EMP: 10
SQ FT: 12,000
SALES (est): 1.3MM Privately Held
WEB: www.kostofoods.com
SIC: 2087 2099 2035 Food colorings; emulsifiers, food; packaged combination products: pasta, rice & potato; pickles, sauces & salad dressings

### (G-21479)
**LOGAN GRAPHIC PRODUCTS INC**
1100 Brown St (60084-1192)
PHONE..................847 526-5515
Fax: 847 526-5155
Malcolm Logan, *CEO*
Curt Logan, *President*
Lisa Schleehauf, *Materials Mgr*
Carlos Salvador, *Safety Mgr*
Bob Honeyman, *Research*
▲ EMP: 60 EST: 1971
SQ FT: 20,000
SALES (est): 11.3MM Privately Held
WEB: www.logangraphic.com
SIC: 3545 3496 3541 2631 Machine tool accessories; mats & matting; machine tools, metal cutting type; paperboard mills

### (G-21480)
**MARK INDUSTRIES**
535 N Legion Ct (60084)
PHONE..................847 487-8670
Mark Schneider, *Owner*
EMP: 4
SALES (est): 359.1K Privately Held
WEB: www.mark-solutions.com
SIC: 3844 5047 X-ray apparatus & tubes; hospital equipment & furniture

### (G-21481)
**MECHANICAL POWER INC**
135 Kerry Ln (60084-1134)
PHONE..................847 487-0070
Fax: 847 487-0080
Douglas Zwiener, *President*
James Dorn, *Chairman*
▲ EMP: 20
SQ FT: 20,000
SALES: 5MM Privately Held
WEB: www.mechanicalpower.net
SIC: 3562 Ball bearings & parts

### (G-21482)
**MENGES ROLLER CO INC**
Also Called: Prairieland Inv Property
260 Industrial Dr (60084-3215)
PHONE..................847 487-8877
Fax: 847 487-8897
Matthew Menges, *President*
Louis Menges, *Principal*
Armando Sandoval, *Plant Mgr*
Veronica Singh, *Purch Mgr*
Garrett Rausch, *Engineer*
EMP: 27
SQ FT: 20,000
SALES (est): 6.6MM Privately Held
WEB: www.mengesroller.com
SIC: 3069 5084 Roll coverings, rubber; printing trades machinery, equipment & supplies

### (G-21483)
**MIDWEST ASSEMBLY & PACKG INC**
1000 Brown St Ste 209 (60084-3110)
Tim Mehaffey, *President*
Bill Barber Jr, *Vice Pres*
EMP: 6
SQ FT: 8,800
SALES: 500K Privately Held
SIC: 3699 Electronic training devices

### (G-21484)
**MIK TOOL & DIE CO INC**
1000 Brown St Ste 304 (60084-3111)
PHONE..................847 487-4311
Fax: 847 487-4312
Nick Vadina, *President*
Jelena Vadina, *Admin Sec*
EMP: 4
SQ FT: 2,800
SALES (est): 632.2K Privately Held
SIC: 3544 Special dies & tools; jigs & fixtures

### (G-21485)
**ML CONTENT**
25566 W Ivanhoe Rd (60084-2407)
PHONE..................847 212-8824
EMP: 4
SALES (est): 171.4K Privately Held
SIC: 2711 Newspapers, publishing & printing

### (G-21486)
**MORRIS MAGNETICS INC**
1220 N Old Rand Rd (60084-1160)
PHONE..................847 487-0829
Elizabeth Morris, *President*
Michael Morris, *Vice Pres*
EMP: 30
SQ FT: 14,000
SALES (est): 3.3MM Privately Held
SIC: 3499 Magnets, permanent: metallic

### (G-21487)
**MUELLER DOOR COMPANY**
27100 N Darrell Rd (60084-9756)
P.O. Box 69 (60084-0069)
PHONE..................815 385-8550
Fax: 847 487-7040
Duer L Miller, *Ch of Bd*
Suzanne Miller, *President*
Peter Miller, *CFO*
EMP: 48
SQ FT: 90,000
SALES (est): 6.7MM Privately Held
SIC: 3089 3442 Doors, folding: plastic or plastic coated fabric; metal doors, sash & trim

### (G-21488)
**MURPHYS PUB**
110 Slocum Lake Rd (60084-1883)
PHONE..................847 526-1431
EMP: 4 EST: 1977
SQ FT: 2,000
SALES (est): 180K Privately Held
SIC: 5813 2261 Edrinking Place Cotton Finishing Plant

### (G-21489)
**NEX GEN MANUFACTURING INC**
1055 N Old Rand Rd (60084-1239)
PHONE..................847 487-7077
John Fyock, *President*
Chai Fyock, *Vice Pres*
EMP: 7
SQ FT: 9,000
SALES (est): 825K Privately Held
SIC: 3545 Precision measuring tools

### (G-21490)
**OCM INC**
1215 Henri Dr (60084-1075)
PHONE..................847 462-4258
EMP: 5
SALES (est): 522K Privately Held
SIC: 3542 Machine tools, metal forming type

### (G-21491)
**PARAGON GROUP INC**
Also Called: Premiere America
274 Jamie Ln (60084-1079)
PHONE..................847 526-1800
Fax: 847 526-1828
Brad Danielson, *Regional Mgr*
Greg Ricci, *Branch Mgr*
EMP: 4 Privately Held
WEB: www.paragongroup.com
SIC: 3695 5065 Video recording tape, blank; magnetic recording tape
PA: The Paragon Group Inc
55 S Atlantic St Ste 200
Seattle WA 98134

### (G-21492)
**PHP RACENGINES INC**
950 N Rand Rd Ste 107 (60084-1179)
PHONE..................847 526-9393
Fax: 847 526-4050
Barry Sale, *President*
Elizabeth Sale, *Admin Sec*
EMP: 3
SQ FT: 1,900
SALES: 200K Privately Held
SIC: 3714 Motor vehicle engines & parts

### (G-21493)
**PROFESSIONAL SALES ASSOCIATES**
Also Called: P S A
1000 Brown St Ste 303 (60084-3111)
PHONE..................847 487-1900
Fax: 847 487-1944
Bill Barber Jr, *President*
EMP: 4
SQ FT: 1,800
SALES (est): 340K Privately Held
SIC: 3953 5084 Marking devices; printing trades machinery, equipment & supplies

### (G-21494)
**PROGRSSIVE CMPONENTS INTL CORP (PA)**
235 Industrial Dr (60084-1078)
PHONE..................847 487-1000
Glenn Starkey, *President*
Holly Gregory, *Opers Mgr*
Deann Springer, *Engineer*
Michael Bolton, *CFO*
Jose Flores, *Manager*
▲ EMP: 55 EST: 1970
SQ FT: 15,000
SALES (est): 36.3MM Privately Held
SIC: 5084 3545 Tool & die makers' equipment; cutting tools for machine tools

### (G-21495)
**PROTECTIVE PRODUCTS INTL**
140 Kerry Ln (60084-1116)
PHONE..................847 526-1180
Alan Nishiguchi, *President*
Nancy Nishguchi, *Vice Pres*
Joanne Chapman, *Marketing Staff*
◆ EMP: 6
SALES (est): 1MM Privately Held
SIC: 3081 5162 2891 3069 Plastic film & sheet; plastics film; adhesives & sealants; specialty cleaning, polishes & sanitation goods

### (G-21496)
**PROTOTEK TOOL & MOLD INC**
375 Hollow Hill Rd (60084-9794)
PHONE..................847 487-2708
Fax: 847 487-2710
Michael Phipps, *President*
EMP: 5
SALES: 400K Privately Held
SIC: 3089 3544 Molding primary plastic; special dies, tools, jigs & fixtures

### (G-21497)
**PURDY PRODUCTS COMPANY**
Also Called: Stera-Sheen
1255 Karl Ct (60084-1098)
P.O. Box 456 (60084-0456)
PHONE..................847 526-5505
Fax: 847 526-5271
Robert D Husemoller, *President*
Carolyn Husemoller, *Corp Secy*
Paul Huesmoller, *Exec VP*
Keith Harrison, *Vice Pres*
Holly Marasco, *VP Finance*
▲ EMP: 12 EST: 1950
SALES (est): 3.2MM Privately Held
WEB: www.purdyproducts.com
SIC: 2842 Sanitation preparations

### (G-21498)
**R/K INDUSTRIES INC**
375 Hollow Hill Rd (60084-9794)
PHONE..................847 526-2222
Fax: 847 816-8307
Ronald Kinder, *President*
Sue Cross, *Office Mgr*
Karen Kinder, *Admin Sec*
EMP: 10
SQ FT: 5,000
SALES (est): 2.4MM Privately Held
WEB: www.rasaki.com
SIC: 5023 5192 3599 Kitchen tools & utensils; books, periodicals & newspapers; amusement park equipment

### (G-21499)
**RAM SYSTEMS & COMMUNICATION**
950 N Rand Rd Ste 202 (60084-1171)
P.O. Box 277 (60084-0277)
PHONE..................847 487-7575
Ronald Mitchell, *President*
Julie Mitchell, *Admin Sec*
EMP: 4 EST: 1983
SALES (est): 393.8K Privately Held
SIC: 3663 Radio & TV communications equipment

### (G-21500)
**ROBERT KELLERMAN & CO**
1000 N Rand Rd Ste 224 (60084-3100)
PHONE..................847 526-7266
Fax: 847 526-0646
Robert Kellerman, *Owner*
EMP: 3
SQ FT: 5,000

▲ = Import ▼=Export
◆ =Import/Export

**GEOGRAPHIC SECTION** — Waukegan - Lake County (G-21524)

SALES (est): 75K **Privately Held**
SIC: 8721 3369 3365 Accounting, auditing & bookkeeping; nonferrous foundries; aluminum foundries

**(G-21501)**
**SCHUBERT CONTROLS CORPORATION**
1099 Brown St Ste 109 (60084-3106)
PHONE................847 526-8200
Fax: 847 526-8490
Gabor L Solymossy, *President*
Mary F Solymossy, *Admin Sec*
EMP: 6
SQ FT: 4,600
SALES (est): 810K **Privately Held**
SIC: 3613 Control panels, electric

**(G-21502)**
**STACK-ON PRODUCTS CO (PA)**
Also Called: Stack On Products Company
1360 N Old Rand Rd (60084-9763)
P.O. Box 489 (60084-0489)
PHONE................847 526-1611
Fax: 847 526-6599
John W Lynn, *President*
William E Hallam, *Vice Pres*
Peter Wozniczka, *Vice Pres*
Chris Strauss, *Senior Buyer*
Paul Hunt, *Project Engr*
▲ EMP: 200
SQ FT: 210,000
SALES (est): 54.7MM **Privately Held**
WEB: www.stack-on.com
SIC: 3469 3444 5085 Boxes: tool, lunch, mail, etc.: stamped metal; metal housings, enclosures, casings & other containers; bins & containers, storage

**(G-21503)**
**STANDING WATER SOLUTIONS INC**
Also Called: Turtle Drain
950 N Rand Rd Ste 121 (60084-1197)
PHONE................847 469-8876
Matthew Kozem, *President*
Zane Robbins, *Vice Pres*
EMP: 4
SALES (est): 323.2K **Privately Held**
SIC: 3585 3444 Siphons, soda water; metal roofing & roof drainage equipment

**(G-21504)**
**STONECASTERS LLC**
1250 Henri Dr (60084-1000)
PHONE................847 526-5200
Frank Honold, *Mng Member*
Ken Krupa,
Mario Prosperi,
Frank Schnitzler,
John Semmelhack,
▲ EMP: 57 EST: 2012
SQ FT: 145,000
SALES (est): 8.8MM **Privately Held**
SIC: 3281 Cut stone & stone products

**(G-21505)**
**SUREBONDER ADHESIVES INC**
355 Hollow Hill Rd (60084-9794)
PHONE................847 487-4583
Michael Kamins, *President*
EMP: 5
SALES (est): 509.4K **Privately Held**
SIC: 2891 Adhesives

**(G-21506)**
**SYNERGY FLAVORS INC (HQ)**
1500 Synergy Dr (60084-1073)
PHONE................847 487-1011
Roderick Sowders, *President*
Amy Loomis, *Business Mgr*
Jim Abraham, *Vice Pres*
Robert Salisbury, *Vice Pres*
Jeremy Macht, *Plant Mgr*
▲ EMP: 58
SQ FT: 40,000
SALES (est): 25.8MM **Privately Held**
WEB: www.synergytaste.com
SIC: 2087 Flavoring extracts & syrups

**(G-21507)**
**SYNERGY FLAVORS NY COMPANY LLC (DH)**
Also Called: Vanlab
1500 Synergy Dr (60084-1073)
PHONE................585 232-6648
Robert Blassick,
Roderick Sowders,
▲ EMP: 30
SQ FT: 25,000
SALES (est): 3.5MM **Privately Held**
SIC: 2087 Extracts, flavoring; syrups, flavoring (except drink)
HQ: Synergy Flavors Inc
1500 Synergy Dr
Wauconda IL 60084
847 487-1011

**(G-21508)**
**TAMARACK PRODUCTS INC**
1071 N Old Rand Rd (60084-1239)
PHONE................847 526-9333
Fax: 847 526-9353
David Steidinger, *President*
Jayne Stork, *Corp Secy*
Mark Steidinger, *Vice Pres*
Greg D'Antonio, *Plant Mgr*
Tom Slager, *Sales Staff*
EMP: 22
SQ FT: 11,000
SALES: 3.1MM **Privately Held**
WEB: www.tamarackproducts.com
SIC: 3555 Printing trades machinery

**(G-21509)**
**TENT MAKER INDUSTRIAL SUP INC**
Also Called: T M I S
531 Brown St (60084-1261)
P.O. Box 151 (60084-0151)
PHONE................847 469-6070
David F Macphail, *President*
Virginia Macphail, *Vice Pres*
EMP: 4
SQ FT: 825
SALES (est): 1MM **Privately Held**
SIC: 5063 3599 Electrical apparatus & equipment; machine shop, jobbing & repair

**(G-21510)**
**THREE STAR MFG CO INC**
375 Hollow Hill Rd (60084-9794)
PHONE................847 526-2222
Fax: 708 345-6024
Ron Kinder, *President*
Renee Jensen, *Manager*
EMP: 9 EST: 1945
SQ FT: 26,800
SALES (est): 1.5MM **Privately Held**
WEB: www.threestarmfg.com
SIC: 3544 3469 Special dies, tools, jigs & fixtures; stamping metal for the trade

**(G-21511)**
**UNITED INDUSTRIES ILLINOIS LTD**
270 Jamie Ln (60084-1079)
PHONE................847 526-9485
Joel Aronson, *President*
EMP: 5
SALES (est): 855K **Privately Held**
SIC: 3441 Fabricated structural metal

**(G-21512)**
**WAGNER PUMP & SUPPLY CO INC**
809 Lake Shore Dr (60084-1529)
PHONE................847 526-8573
Fax: 847 526-7485
Bill Wagner, *Owner*
EMP: 4
SALES (est): 230.9K **Privately Held**
SIC: 5251 5084 5074 3561 Pumps & pumping equipment; pumps & pumping equipment; plumbing & hydronic heating supplies; pumps & pumping equipment

**(G-21513)**
**WEDDING BRAND INVESTORS LLC**
Also Called: Beverly Clark Collections
1225 Karl Ct (60084-1098)
PHONE................847 887-0071
Fax: 847 887-0072
Mike Heuer, *VP Opers*
Steven Kahn, *Manager*
James Kirsch,
Beverly Clark,
Nelson Clark,
▲ EMP: 35
SQ FT: 33,000
SALES (est): 3.1MM **Privately Held**
SIC: 2389 2731 Garters; book publishing

**(G-21514)**
**WEEB ENTERPRISES LLC**
770 Peninsula Dr (60084-1058)
P.O. Box 121 (60084-0121)
PHONE................815 861-2625
Chris Smith,
▼ EMP: 2
SALES (est): 209.1K **Privately Held**
SIC: 8748 3842 Business consulting; personal safety equipment

**(G-21515)**
**WIKOFF COLOR CORPORATION**
240 Jamie Ln (60084-1079)
PHONE................847 487-2704
Fax: 847 487-2844
Bowman Shaw, *Manager*
EMP: 8
SALES (corp-wide): 152.7MM **Privately Held**
WEB: www.wikoff.com
SIC: 2893 5084 Printing ink; printing trades machinery, equipment & supplies
PA: Wikoff Color Corporation
1886 Merritt Rd
Fort Mill SC 29715
803 548-2210

**Waukegan**
**Lake County**

**(G-21516)**
**AB SPECIALTY SILICONES LLC (PA)**
Also Called: A B
3790 Sunset Ave (60087-3212)
PHONE................908 273-8015
Mac Penman, *Principal*
Jane Cymansky, *Accounting Mgr*
Stephanie Penman, *Manager*
Jane Tymansky, *Manager*
Ellen Johnson, *Director*
▲ EMP: 48
SALES (est): 20MM **Privately Held**
SIC: 2869 Silicones

**(G-21517)**
**ABBVIE INC**
1150 S Northpoint Blvd (60085-6757)
PHONE................847 473-4787
Robert Zimmer, *Manager*
Janet Weeks, *Technology*
EMP: 47
SALES (corp-wide): 25.6B **Publicly Held**
SIC: 2834 Pharmaceutical preparations
PA: Abbvie Inc.
1 N Waukegan Rd
North Chicago IL 60064
847 932-7900

**(G-21518)**
**ADVANCE BINDERY CO**
3811 Hawthorne Ct (60087-3221)
P.O. Box 112, Evanston (60204-0112)
PHONE................847 662-2418
Fax: 847 283-2888
Todd Nickow, *President*
Charles Wagenberg, *Principal*
Ross Nickow, *Vice Pres*
Temma Wagenberg, *Admin Sec*
EMP: 10
SALES (est): 805.4K **Privately Held**
WEB: www.bindersandmore.com
SIC: 2782 Looseleaf binders & devices

**(G-21519)**
**AFX INC (PA)**
Also Called: Afco Lite American Fluorescent
2345 Ernie Krueger Cir (60087-3225)
PHONE................847 249-5970
Fax: 847 249-2788
William R Solomon, *CEO*
James Serra, *President*
Tim Tevyaw, *President*
Karin Koniarski, *Senior Buyer*
Steve Milewski, *Purchasing*
◆ EMP: 150 EST: 1938
SQ FT: 95,000
SALES: 80MM **Privately Held**
WEB: www.americanfluorescent.com
SIC: 3645 3646 Residential lighting fixtures; commercial indusl & institutional electric lighting fixtures

**(G-21520)**
**AKZO NOBEL COATINGS INC**
Also Called: Akzo Nobel Aerospace Coatings
E Water St (60085)
PHONE................847 623-4200
Davey Arnold, *Research*
Rob Walker, *Marketing Staff*
Rod McQueen, *Branch Mgr*
Trish Lewis, *Manager*
David Satzger, *Manager*
EMP: 15
SALES (corp-wide): 15B **Privately Held**
WEB: www.nam.sikkens.com
SIC: 2851 Paints: oil or alkyd vehicle or water thinned
HQ: Akzo Nobel Coatings Inc.
8220 Mohawk Dr
Strongsville OH 44136
440 297-5100

**(G-21521)**
**ALDON CO**
3410 Sunset Ave (60087-3295)
P.O. Box 66973, Chicago (60666-0973)
PHONE................847 623-8800
Fax: 847 623-6139
Ralph V Switzer, *Ch of Bd*
Joseph R Ornig, *President*
▲ EMP: 19
SQ FT: 13,000
SALES (est): 4.1MM **Privately Held**
WEB: www.aldonco.com
SIC: 3743 3536 3429 3423 Railroad equipment; hoists, cranes & monorails; manufactured hardware (general); hand & edge tools; blast furnaces & steel mills; wood pallets & skids

**(G-21522)**
**ALLIE WOODWORKING**
3035 Sunset Ave (60087-3437)
PHONE................847 244-1919
Fax: 847 623-7199
William Allie, *Owner*
EMP: 4
SALES (est): 238.7K **Privately Held**
SIC: 1751 2541 2511 2434 Carpentry work; wood partitions & fixtures; wood household furniture; wood kitchen cabinets; millwork

**(G-21523)**
**AMERICAN BLENDING & FILLING CO**
3505 Birchwood Dr (60085-8335)
PHONE................847 689-1000
Clayton B Bolke, *President*
David Waldron, *Vice Pres*
John Burquest, *Controller*
Karl Pepevnik, *Manager*
David L Waldon, *Admin Sec*
▲ EMP: 100
SALES (est): 45.6MM
SALES (corp-wide): 194.4MM **Privately Held**
SIC: 2844 Hair preparations, including shampoos
PA: Visual Pak Company
1909 S Waukegan Rd
Waukegan IL 60085
847 689-1000

**(G-21524)**
**AMERICAN OUTFITTERS LTD**
3700 Sunset Ave (60087-3212)
PHONE................847 623-3959
Fax: 847 623-0053
Lawrence A Rettig, *President*
Gary N Rettig, *Corp Secy*
Rick Larson, *Vice Pres*
Wendy Paulsen, *Buyer*
Mary Roegner, *Sales Staff*
EMP: 35
SQ FT: 30,000

# Waukegan - Lake County (G-21525)

**SALES (est):** 5.7MM  Privately Held
**WEB:** www.americanoutfitters.com
**SIC:** 7336  5699  5136  5137  Silk screen design; customized clothing & apparel; sportswear, men's & boys'; sportswear, women's & children's; screen printing

### (G-21525)
**AMERICAN PALLET CO INC**
1105 Greenfield Ave  (60085-7629)
**PHONE**.................................847 662-5525
Tammy Ash, *President*
**EMP:** 70
**SQ FT:** 10,000
**SALES (est):** 8.6MM  Privately Held
**WEB:** www.americanpallets.com
**SIC:** 2448  Pallets, wood & wood with metal

### (G-21526)
**AMETEK  INC**
Also Called: Ametek Powervar
1450 S Lakeside Dr  (60085-8301)
**PHONE**.................................847 596-7000
Chris Walsh, *Mktg Dir*
**EMP:** 143
**SALES (corp-wide):** 3.8B  Publicly Held
**SIC:** 3629  Electronic generation equipment
**PA:** Ametek, Inc.
  1100 Cassatt Rd
  Berwyn PA 19312
  610 647-2121

### (G-21527)
**ARCOA GROUP INC (PA)**
Also Called: Arcoa USA
3300 Washington St  (60085-4716)
**PHONE**.................................847 693-7519
Cari Clark, *Business Mgr*
Jeff Datkuliak, *Vice Pres*
Terry Levy, *Vice Pres*
Zack McGuire, *Accounts Exec*
Brad Schmidt, *Manager*
**EMP:** 30
**SALES (est):** 17MM  Privately Held
**SIC:** 3559  Recycling machinery

### (G-21528)
**B W M GLOBAL**
3740 Hawthorne Ct  (60087-3222)
**PHONE**.................................847 785-1355
Brad Fish, *Owner*
Bradford Fish, *Partner*
▲ **EMP:** 8
**SALES (est):** 1.1MM  Privately Held
**SIC:** 3993  Advertising novelties

### (G-21529)
**BAXTER HEALTHCARE CORPORATION**
2105 S Waukegan Rd  (60085-6737)
**PHONE**.................................847 578-4671
Chris Cooper, *Manager*
**EMP:** 30
**SALES (corp-wide):** 10.1B  Publicly Held
**SIC:** 3841  2835  2389  3842  Surgical & medical instruments; catheters; medical instruments & equipment, blood & bone work; surgical instruments & apparatus; blood derivative diagnostic agents; hospital gowns; surgical appliances & supplies; medical laboratory equipment
**HQ:** Baxter Healthcare Corporation
  1 Baxter Pkwy
  Deerfield IL 60015
  224 948-2000

### (G-21530)
**BOTTOMS UP INC**
Also Called: Bottoms Up Dy-Dee Wash Dpr Svc
201 N Green Bay Rd  (60085-4410)
**PHONE**.................................847 336-0040
Fax: 847 336-0155
Tonya Conde, *President*
Amy Gale, *Manager*
**EMP:** 7
**SQ FT:** 3,000
**SALES (est):** 400K  Privately Held
**SIC:** 2676  7219  Diapers, paper (disposable): made from purchased paper; diaper service

### (G-21531)
**BRADS PRINTING  INC**
925 W Glen Flora Ave  (60085-1840)
P.O. Box 8669  (60079-8669)
**PHONE**.................................847 662-0447
Fax: 847 662-0530
Jack A Bradbury, *Owner*
Sandy Bradbury, *Co-Owner*
**EMP:** 4
**SQ FT:** 8,000
**SALES:** 450K  Privately Held
**SIC:** 2752  2791  2789  2759  Commercial printing, lithographic; commercial printing, offset; typesetting; bookbinding & related work; commercial printing

### (G-21532)
**CARDINAL HEALTH  INC**
Also Called: Cardinal Medical Services
1500 S Waukegan Rd  (60085-6775)
**PHONE**.................................847 578-4443
Fax: 847 785-6055
Debra Schotz, *Senior VP*
Tatiana Downer, *Vice Pres*
David Hanlon, *Vice Pres*
Margot McGonigal, *Plant Mgr*
Rob Weinberg, *Engineer*
**EMP:** 400
**SALES (corp-wide):** 121.5B  Publicly Held
**SIC:** 3841  5047  Surgical & medical instruments; medical & hospital equipment
**PA:** Cardinal Health, Inc.
  7000 Cardinal Pl
  Dublin OH 43017
  614 757-5000

### (G-21533)
**CARDINAL HEALTH 200  LLC**
1300 S Waukegan Rd 124  (60085-6724)
**PHONE**.................................847 473-3200
Bryan Darrell, *Purch Agent*
Dennis Burke, *Manager*
**EMP:** 150
**SALES (corp-wide):** 121.5B  Publicly Held
**WEB:** www.allegiancehealth.com
**SIC:** 3841  Surgical & medical instruments
**HQ:** Cardinal Health 200, Llc
  3651 Birchwood Dr
  Waukegan IL 60085

### (G-21534)
**CARDINAL HEALTH 200  LLC**
1430 S Waukegan Rd  (60085-6787)
**PHONE**.................................847 689-8410
Rick Epstein, *Vice Pres*
Tryon Copeland, *Vice Pres*
Scott Donnelly, *VP Mktg*
**EMP:** 44
**SALES (corp-wide):** 121.5B  Publicly Held
**WEB:** www.allegiancehealth.com
**SIC:** 3841  Surgical & medical instruments
**HQ:** Cardinal Health 200, Llc
  3651 Birchwood Dr
  Waukegan IL 60085

### (G-21535)
**CASSINI CABINETRY**
701 Belvidere Rd  (60085-6309)
P.O. Box 9013  (60079-9013)
**PHONE**.................................847 244-9755
**EMP:** 3  **EST:** 2005
**SALES (est):** 180K  Privately Held
**SIC:** 2434  Mfg Wood Kitchen Cabinets

### (G-21536)
**CHASSIS SERVICE UNLIMITED**
2984 W Wadsworth Rd  (60087-1253)
**PHONE**.................................847 336-2305
Fax: 847 336-2366
Jim Quinn, *Owner*
▼ **EMP:** 4
**SQ FT:** 5,000
**SALES (est):** 327.6K  Privately Held
**SIC:** 3711  Automobile assembly, including specialty automobiles

### (G-21537)
**CHIMNEY KING LLC**
57 Noll St  (60085-3030)
P.O. Box 8, Gurnee  (60031-0008)
**PHONE**.................................847 244-8860
Derek Lidstrom, *Mng Member*
**EMP:** 6

**SALES:** 2.5MM  Privately Held
**WEB:** www.chimneyking.com
**SIC:** 3272  Chimney caps, concrete

### (G-21538)
**CIRCUIT WORKS CORPORATION (PA)**
3135 N Oak Grove Ave  (60087-1800)
**PHONE**.................................847 283-8600
Fax: 847 283-0299
Thomas D Thompson, *President*
Fred Wacker III, *Chairman*
Muhammad Saiduzzaman, *Vice Pres*
Lisa Edwards, *Purch Mgr*
Melissa Godsey, *Purchasing*
▲ **EMP:** 65
**SQ FT:** 57,000
**SALES (est):** 27.2MM  Privately Held
**SIC:** 3672  Printed circuit boards

### (G-21539)
**CNH INDUSTRIAL AMERICA LLC**
2450 W Air Ln  (60087-1480)
**PHONE**.................................847 263-5793
Matthew Cooth, *Manager*
Dick Delfrate, *Manager*
**EMP:** 9
**SALES (corp-wide):** 26.3B  Privately Held
**SIC:** 3523  Farm machinery & equipment
**HQ:** Cnh Industrial America Llc
  700 St St
  Racine WI 53404
  262 636-6011

### (G-21540)
**COLEMAN CABLE  LLC**
1530 S Shields Dr  (60085-8317)
**PHONE**.................................847 672-2508
G Gary Yetman, *CEO*
**EMP:** 54
**SALES (corp-wide):** 3.2B  Privately Held
**SIC:** 3643  Power line cable
**HQ:** Coleman Cable, Llc
  1530 S Shields Dr
  Waukegan IL 60085
  847 672-2300

### (G-21541)
**COLEMAN CABLE  LLC**
1530 S Shields Dr  (60085-8317)
**PHONE**.................................847 672-2300
Marvin Slater, *Mfg Staff*
Paul Young, *Purch Agent*
Paula Moreau, *Human Res Dir*
Gary McDonald, *Branch Mgr*
Ivonne Soto, *Manager*
**EMP:** 5
**SALES (corp-wide):** 3.2B  Privately Held
**SIC:** 3357  Nonferrous wiredrawing & insulating
**HQ:** Coleman Cable, Llc
  1530 S Shields Dr
  Waukegan IL 60085
  847 672-2300

### (G-21542)
**COLEMAN CABLE  LLC (HQ)**
Also Called: Southwire
1530 S Shields Dr  (60085-8317)
**PHONE**.................................847 672-2300
G Gary Yetman, *President*
Richard Burger, *Exec VP*
Richard Carr, *Exec VP*
Michael A Frigo, *Exec VP*
Kathy Jo Van, *Exec VP*
◆ **EMP:** 66
**SQ FT:** 30,175
**SALES:** 808.3MM
**SALES (corp-wide):** 3.2B  Privately Held
**WEB:** www.copperfieldllc.com
**SIC:** 3661  3357  3643  Telephone cords, jacks, adapters, etc.; nonferrous wiredrawing & insulating; power line cable
**PA:** Southwire Company, Llc
  1 Southwire Dr
  Carrollton GA 30119
  770 832-4242

### (G-21543)
**COLEMAN CABLE  LLC**
1530 S Shields Dr  (60085-8317)
**PHONE**.................................847 672-2300
Damien Dimaggio, *Engineer*
Mike Kendrick, *Engineer*
Scott Callaghan, *Branch Mgr*
**EMP:** 75

**SALES (corp-wide):** 3.2B  Privately Held
**WEB:** www.copperfieldllc.com
**SIC:** 3357  3661  3663  Communication wire; telephone & telegraph apparatus; radio & TV communications equipment
**HQ:** Coleman Cable, Llc
  1530 S Shields Dr
  Waukegan IL 60085
  847 672-2300

### (G-21544)
**CORNFIELDS  LLC**
3830 Sunset Ave  (60087-3258)
**PHONE**.................................847 263-7000
Claire Cretors, *President*
Ignacio Davila, *Plant Mgr*
Jeff Bilotti, *Purch Dir*
Jeffrey M McMahon, *CFO*
Monica Zuliek, *Accountant*
◆ **EMP:** 120
**SQ FT:** 208,000
**SALES (est):** 45.8MM
**SALES (corp-wide):** 200MM  Privately Held
**WEB:** www.cornfieldsinc.com
**SIC:** 2099  Popcorn, packaged: except already popped
**PA:** Eagle Family Foods Group Llc
  4020 Kinross Lakes Pkwy
  Richfield OH 44286
  330 382-3725

### (G-21545)
**COUNTER CRAFT INC**
2113 Northwestern Ave  (60087-4144)
**PHONE**.................................847 336-8205
Fax: 847 336-8249
Gregory Meyers, *President*
Scott Meyers, *Vice Pres*
**EMP:** 6
**SQ FT:** 1,800
**SALES:** 800K  Privately Held
**SIC:** 2541  5712  2434  Counter & sink tops; custom made furniture, except cabinets; cabinet work, custom; wood kitchen cabinets

### (G-21546)
**D N WELDING & FABRICATING INC**
3627 Washington St Bldg 5  (60085-4767)
**PHONE**.................................847 244-6410
Fax: 847 244-6469
Danny Darnell, *President*
Scott Nelson, *Vice Pres*
**EMP:** 4
**SQ FT:** 6,000
**SALES (est):** 410.4K  Privately Held
**SIC:** 7692  Welding repair

### (G-21547)
**D-M-S HOLDINGS  INC (HQ)**
Also Called: Healthsmart International
1931 Norman Dr  (60085-6715)
**PHONE**.................................847 680-6811
Merwyn Dan, *CEO*
Bruce Dan, *President*
Brad Mueller, *COO*
Vidya Vasudevan, *Electrical Engi*
Thomas Young, *CFO*
▲ **EMP:** 110  **EST:** 1972
**SQ FT:** 148,000
**SALES (est):** 37.2MM
**SALES (corp-wide):** 150MM  Privately Held
**SIC:** 3841  5047  Surgical & medical instruments; medical & hospital equipment
**PA:** Briggs Medical Service Company
  7300 Westown Pkwy Ste 100
  West Des Moines IA 50266
  515 327-6400

### (G-21548)
**DAVID LINDERHOLM**
Also Called: Edgetool Industrial Supplies
2210 Grand Ave Unit 2  (60085-3311)
**PHONE**.................................847 336-3755
Fax: 847 336-3791
David R Linderholm, *Owner*
**EMP:** 4
**SQ FT:** 1,500
**SALES (est):** 413.6K  Privately Held
**SIC:** 5085  7699  3545  Industrial supplies; industrial tools; knife, saw & tool sharpening & repair; machine tool accessories

# GEOGRAPHIC SECTION
## Waukegan - Lake County (G-21575)

**(G-21549)**
**DERSE INC**
3696 Bur Wood Dr (60085-8399)
PHONE.....................847 473-2149
Fax: 847 473-2556
Ken Aden-Buie, *General Mgr*
Mary Vanhook, *Manager*
EMP: 85
SALES (corp-wide): 122.4MM **Privately Held**
WEB: www.derse.com
SIC: 3993 Signs & advertising specialties
PA: Derse, Inc.
3800 W Canal St
Milwaukee WI 53208
414 257-2000

**(G-21550)**
**DESIGN PHASE INC**
1771 S Lakeside Dr (60085-8313)
PHONE.....................847 473-0077
Michael P Eckert, *President*
Lorna Wolter, *Principal*
Richard Alcala, *VP Prdtn*
Stephanie Wroblewski, *Opers Mgr*
Alex Kvasnicka, *Engineer*
▲ EMP: 22
SQ FT: 65,000
SALES (est): 4.8MM **Privately Held**
WEB: www.dphase.com
SIC: 3993 7319 Displays & cutouts, window & lobby; display advertising service

**(G-21551)**
**DEUBLIN COMPANY (PA)**
2050 Norman Dr (60085-8270)
PHONE.....................847 689-8600
Donald Deubler, *Ch of Bd*
Ronald Kelner, *President*
Matt Bell, *District Mgr*
Dave Short, *Plant Mgr*
Wesley Broszczak, *Materials Mgr*
◆ EMP: 200 EST: 1945
SQ FT: 110,000
SALES (est): 139MM **Privately Held**
WEB: www.deublin.com
SIC: 3498 3492 3568 3494 Fabricated pipe & fittings; fluid power valves & hose fittings; power transmission equipment; valves & pipe fittings

**(G-21552)**
**DIE CAST MACHINERY LLC**
3246 W Monroe St (60085-3029)
PHONE.....................847 360-9170
Kaufman David, *Principal*
Cochran Steven, *Principal*
Steve Cochran, *Sales Mgr*
Serene Weidner, *Marketing Staff*
David Kaufman, *Mng Member*
EMP: 10
SALES (est): 456.4K **Privately Held**
SIC: 3542 Die casting machines

**(G-21553)**
**DORIS COMPANY** ✪
1541 S Shields Dr (60085-8304)
PHONE.....................224 302-5605
Mike Sawant, *Admin Sec*
EMP: 5 EST: 2016
SALES (est): 252.7K **Privately Held**
SIC: 2842 Specialty cleaning preparations

**(G-21554)**
**E2 MANUFACTURING GROUP LLC**
3776 Hawthorne Ct (60087-3222)
PHONE.....................224 399-9608
James Martin,
EMP: 3
SALES (est): 294.1K **Privately Held**
SIC: 3999 Barber & beauty shop equipment

**(G-21555)**
**EAGLE HIGH MAST LTG CO INC**
1070a S Northpoint Blvd (60085-8213)
PHONE.....................847 473-3800
Fax: 847 473-3870
EMP: 7
SQ FT: 12,000
SALES (est): 680K **Privately Held**
SIC: 3648 5063 Mfg Lighting Equipment Whol Electrical Equip

**(G-21556)**
**EBSCO INDUSTRIES INC**
Luxor
2245 N Delany Rd (60087-1837)
PHONE.....................847 244-1800
Fax: 847 244-1818
Mary Zedler, *HR Admin*
Mike Whaley, *Accounts Exec*
Kim Fox, *Sales Associate*
Jessica Henry, *Sales Associate*
Robert Raw, *Branch Mgr*
EMP: 48
SALES (corp-wide): 1.8B **Privately Held**
WEB: www.ebscoind.com
SIC: 2741 Magazines
PA: Ebsco Industries, Inc.
5724 Highway 280 E
Birmingham AL 35242
205 991-6600

**(G-21557)**
**ELM PRODUCTS CORP**
2233 Northwestern Ave F (60087-4150)
P.O. Box 656, Antioch (60002-0656)
PHONE.....................847 336-0020
Fax: 847 336-1882
Edward L Magiera, *President*
L Magiera, *Admin Sec*
EMP: 25
SALES (est): 3.7MM **Privately Held**
SIC: 3625 3621 3613 Switches, electric power; motors & generators; switchgear & switchboard apparatus

**(G-21558)**
**F & R PLASTICS INC**
642 Westmoreland Ave (60085-3447)
PHONE.....................847 336-1330
Fax: 847 336-7381
Frank Mlinar, *President*
Rosalie Mlinar, *Vice Pres*
EMP: 3
SQ FT: 3,000
SALES: 200K **Privately Held**
SIC: 3089 3544 Injection molding of plastics; special dies, tools, jigs & fixtures

**(G-21559)**
**FERRO CORPORATION**
1219 Glen Rock Ave (60085-6230)
PHONE.....................847 623-0370
Tracy Stahlkopf, *Manager*
EMP: 250
SALES (corp-wide): 1.1B **Publicly Held**
WEB: www.ferro.com
SIC: 3264 Porcelain electrical supplies
PA: Ferro Corporation
6060 Parkland Blvd # 250
Mayfield Heights OH 44124
216 875-5600

**(G-21560)**
**FIRST MATE YACHT DETAILING**
35 E Madison St (60085-5623)
P.O. Box 572, Zion (60099-0572)
PHONE.....................847 249-7654
Gus Phillips, *President*
Jenifer Phillips, *Admin Sec*
EMP: 4
SQ FT: 1,700
SALES (est): 200K **Privately Held**
WEB: www.firstmatedetailing.com
SIC: 2842 Specialty cleaning preparations

**(G-21561)**
**G-P MANUFACTURING CO INC**
1535 S Lakeside Dr (60085-8312)
PHONE.....................847 473-9001
Robert Price, *CEO*
Harold Price, *President*
Frances Price, *Admin Sec*
EMP: 40 EST: 1938
SQ FT: 50,000
SALES (est): 6.6MM **Privately Held**
WEB: www.thermoflexcorp.com
SIC: 3081 3082 Packing materials, plastic sheet; rods, unsupported plastic; tubes, unsupported plastic

**(G-21562)**
**GENERAL LOOSE LEAF BINDERY INC**
3811 Hawthorne Ct (60087-3221)
PHONE.....................847 244-9700
Fax: 773 244-9741
Glenn Nickow, *President*
Ed Nickow, *Chairman*
Ross Nickow, *Vice Pres*
Todd Nickow, *Vice Pres*
Marcia Nickow, *Psychologist*
EMP: 35
SQ FT: 50,000
SALES (est): 4.7MM **Privately Held**
WEB: www.looseleaf.com
SIC: 2782 Looseleaf binders & devices

**(G-21563)**
**GGB NORTH AMERICA LLC**
Also Called: Ggb Chicago
2300 Norman Dr (60085-8279)
PHONE.....................847 775-1859
Pat Grasser, *Sales Staff*
Rich Farbaniac, *Branch Mgr*
EMP: 25
SALES (corp-wide): 1.1B **Publicly Held**
SIC: 3714 Bearings, motor vehicle
HQ: Ggb North America Llc
700 Mid Atlantic Pkwy
Thorofare NJ 08086
856 848-3200

**(G-21564)**
**GOLOSINAS EL CANTO**
1115 Washington St (60085-5301)
PHONE.....................847 625-5103
Mark Amirez, *Owner*
EMP: 8
SALES (est): 714.4K **Privately Held**
SIC: 2051 Bread, cake & related products

**(G-21565)**
**GREAT MIDWEST PACKAGING LLC**
Also Called: Innovative Swab Technologies
3828 Hawthorne Ct (60087-3220)
PHONE.....................847 395-4500
Thomas Jervis, *CFO*
Darrell Van Dyke,
EMP: 13
SALES (est): 1.2MM **Privately Held**
SIC: 3089 2671 Plastic containers, except foam; packaging paper & plastics film, coated & laminated

**(G-21566)**
**GRIFFIN MACHINING INC**
2233 Northwestern Ave D (60087-4150)
PHONE.....................847 360-0098
Fax: 847 360-0124
Elvin Griffin, *President*
Rebecca Griffin, *Admin Sec*
EMP: 7
SQ FT: 2,000
SALES (est): 550K **Privately Held**
SIC: 3599 Machine shop, jobbing & repair

**(G-21567)**
**HD ELECTRIC COMPANY**
1475 S Lakeside Dr (60085-8314)
PHONE.....................847 473-4980
Fax: 847 473-4981
Jim Fox, *COO*
Lori Ocepek, *Purch Mgr*
Chris Mecker, *Engineer*
Marc Bouthillier, *Sales Mgr*
Chris Norris, *Sales Mgr*
◆ EMP: 29 EST: 1933
SQ FT: 17,000
SALES (est): 7.9MM **Privately Held**
WEB: www.hdelectriccompany.com
SIC: 3825 Meters: electric, pocket, portable, panelboard, etc.; test equipment for electronic & electrical circuits

**(G-21568)**
**HFD MANUFACTURING INC**
Also Called: Hfd Graphics Equipment
1813 W Glen Flora Ave (60085-1724)
PHONE.....................847 263-5050
William E Dziallo, *President*
Debbie Roisland, *Office Mgr*
EMP: 3
SALES (est): 280K **Privately Held**
SIC: 3554 3541 Paper industries machinery; machine tools, metal cutting type

**(G-21569)**
**ILLINOIS CARBIDE TOOL CO INC (PA)**
Also Called: Brake Drum Tool Co America Div
1322 Belvidere Rd (60085-6206)
PHONE.....................847 244-1110
Fax: 847 249-0693
John Mini, *President*
A G Mini, *Chairman*
Michael Mini, *Vice Pres*
EMP: 17 EST: 1959
SQ FT: 20,000
SALES (est): 4.6MM **Privately Held**
SIC: 3545 Cutting tools for machine tools

**(G-21570)**
**INKN TEES**
2901 N Delany Rd Ste 105 (60087-1886)
PHONE.....................847 244-2266
Steven Stams, *Principal*
EMP: 3
SALES (est): 430.6K **Privately Held**
SIC: 2254 Shirts & t-shirts (underwear), knit

**(G-21571)**
**INSTYPRINTS OF WAUKEGAN INC**
Also Called: Insty-Prints
1711 Grand Ave Ste 1 (60085-3594)
PHONE.....................847 336-5599
James Bush, *President*
Lora Bush, *Vice Pres*
EMP: 4
SQ FT: 2,000
SALES (est): 525.8K **Privately Held**
SIC: 2752 2796 2791 2789 Commercial printing, offset; platemaking services; typesetting; bookbinding & related work

**(G-21572)**
**INTERNATIONAL PAINT LLC**
Akzo Nobel Aerospace Coatings
1 E Water St (60085-5635)
PHONE.....................847 623-4200
Fax: 847 625-3200
Dave Betti, *VP Finance*
Kevin Fleetwood, *Branch Mgr*
Robert Mather, *Representative*
EMP: 18
SALES (corp-wide): 15B **Privately Held**
WEB: www.epiglass.com
SIC: 2851 Paints & allied products; polyurethane coatings
HQ: International Paint Llc
6001 Antoine Dr
Houston TX 77091
713 682-1711

**(G-21573)**
**J D PLATING WORKS INC**
1424 12th St (60085-7693)
PHONE.....................847 662-6484
Fax: 847 662-6486
John Dobnikar, *CEO*
Jose A Gonzales, *Vice Pres*
EMP: 2 EST: 1938
SQ FT: 4,000
SALES (est): 271K **Privately Held**
SIC: 3471 Plating of metals or formed products; polishing, metals or formed products

**(G-21574)**
**JACOBSON ACQSTION HOLDINGS LLC**
Also Called: S. I. Jacobson Mfg. Company
1414 Jacobson Dr (60085-7601)
PHONE.....................847 623-1414
Fax: 847 623-2556
Charles Gonzalez, *CEO*
Patricia Stemp, *Principal*
Paul G Bryant, *Vice Pres*
Bobbi Douglas, *Purchasing*
Derek Crenshaw, *Design Engr*
▲ EMP: 225 EST: 1934
SQ FT: 87,500
SALES (est): 29MM **Privately Held**
WEB: www.sij.com
SIC: 2211 2673 3161 2782 Bags & bagging, cotton; plastic bags: made from purchased materials; briefcases; looseleaf binders & devices; signs & advertising specialties

**(G-21575)**
**K 9 TAG COMPANY INC (PA)**
Also Called: Kennedy's Creative Awards
2116 Grand Ave (60085-3416)
PHONE.....................847 304-8247
Fax: 847 304-8332
Dan Sherry, *President*

# Waukegan - Lake County (G-21576)

Marcia Sherry, *Vice Pres*
**EMP:** 5
**SQ FT:** 5,000
**SALES (est):** 1.7MM **Privately Held**
**SIC:** 5999 5941 5091 3993 Trophies & plaques; bowling equipment & supplies; bowling equipment; signs & advertising specialties

### (G-21576)
### K O G MFG & BINDERY CORP
1813 W Glen Flora Ave (60085-1724)
**PHONE** .................... 847 263-5050
Timothy W Arnold, *President*
**EMP:** 15
**SQ FT:** 20,000
**SALES:** 2MM **Privately Held**
**SIC:** 2789 Bookbinding & related work

### (G-21577)
### KAUFMAN-WORTHEN MACHINERY INC
2326 W Wadsworth Rd (60087-1244)
P.O. Box 7921, Gurnee (60031-7007)
**PHONE** .................... 847 360-9170
David Kaufman, *President*
Rick Worthen, *Vice Pres*
Steve Cochran, *Sales Mgr*
**EMP:** 6
**SALES (est):** 490K **Privately Held**
**WEB:** www.diecastkw.com
**SIC:** 3542 Die casting machines

### (G-21578)
### LA CONCHITA BAKERY
1703 Washington St (60085-5133)
P.O. Box 9148 (60079-9148)
**PHONE** .................... 847 623-4094
Hector Leal, *Partner*
Aurelia Leal, *Partner*
**EMP:** 7
**SALES (est):** 547.1K **Privately Held**
**SIC:** 2051 Bakery: wholesale or wholesale/retail combined

### (G-21579)
### LAFARGE NORTH AMERICA INC
315 E Sea Horse Dr (60085-2144)
**PHONE** .................... 847 599-0391
Larry Brewer, *Branch Mgr*
**EMP:** 11
**SALES (corp-wide):** 26.6B **Privately Held**
**WEB:** www.lafargenorthamerica.com
**SIC:** 3241 Cement, hydraulic
**HQ:** Lafarge North America Inc.
8700 W Bryn Mawr Ave Ll
Chicago IL 60631
703 480-3600

### (G-21580)
### LAKE COUNTY PRESS INC (PA)
98 Noll St (60085-3031)
P.O. Box 9209 (60079-9209)
**PHONE** .................... 847 336-4333
**Fax:** 847 336-5846
Ralph L Johnson, *President*
Dan Smith, *President*
Ned Steck, *President*
Donald Hyatt, *Business Mgr*
Peter Douglas, *Senior VP*
**EMP:** 223
**SQ FT:** 79,500
**SALES (est):** 87MM **Privately Held**
**WEB:** www.lakecountypress.com
**SIC:** 2791 7334 Typesetting; blueprinting service

### (G-21581)
### LIVINGSTON PRODUCTS INC
3242 W Monroe St (60085-3029)
**PHONE** .................... 847 808-0900
**Fax:** 847 808-0904
Troy W Livingston, *President*
Seren Livingston, *Vice Pres*
Megan Millman, *Purchasing*
Vladimir Rosenbaum, *CPA*
Carol Strub, *Director*
**EMP:** 18
**SQ FT:** 15,000
**SALES (est):** 3.1MM **Privately Held**
**WEB:** www.livingstonproducts.com
**SIC:** 3599 8711 Custom machinery; mechanical engineering

### (G-21582)
### LMT ONSRUD LP
Also Called: Onsrud Cutter LP
1081 S Northpoint Blvd (60085-8215)
**PHONE** .................... 847 362-1560
**Fax:** 847 473-1934
Robert Ostroga, *President*
Leslie Banduch, *Vice Pres*
Robert Wallwin, *Vice Pres*
Kurt Starovich, *VP Finance*
Julie Ostroga, *Accounting Mgr*
▲ **EMP:** 107
**SQ FT:** 60,000
**SALES:** 28.6MM
**SALES (corp-wide):** 402.9MM **Privately Held**
**SIC:** 3423 3545 Hand & edge tools; machine tool accessories
**HQ:** Lmt Tool Systems Gmbh
Heidenheimer Str. 84
Oberkochen 73447
736 495-790

### (G-21583)
### LMT USA INC
1081 S Northpoint Blvd (60085-8215)
**PHONE** .................... 630 969-5412
**EMP:** 6
**SALES (corp-wide):** 402.9MM **Privately Held**
**SIC:** 5084 3545 3544 3444 Whol Industrial Machinery Mfg Machine Tool Accessories Special Dies Tools Die Sets Sheet Metalwork & Steel Foundaries
**HQ:** Lmt Usa, Inc.
1081 S Northpoint Blvd
Waukegan IL 60085
630 969-5412

### (G-21584)
### LORDAHL MANUFACTURING CO (PA)
Also Called: Lordahl Engineering Co
1001 S Lewis Ave (60085-7665)
P.O. Box 5769, Buffalo Grove (60089-5769)
**PHONE** .................... 847 244-0448
**Fax:** 847 244-0136
Var E Lordahl Sr, *President*
Frank O'Sullivan, *Vice Pres*
Tatyama Rivtis, *Controller*
Carol Lordahl, *Admin Sec*
▲ **EMP:** 30
**SQ FT:** 30,000
**SALES (est):** 7.8MM **Privately Held**
**SIC:** 3088 Plastics plumbing fixtures

### (G-21585)
### LTC HOLDINGS INC (HQ)
Also Called: Laserage
3021 N Delany Rd (60087-1826)
**PHONE** .................... 847 249-5900
**Fax:** 847 336-1103
Stephen L Capp, *CEO*
Dan Capp, *Vice Pres*
Joseph S Coel, *Vice Pres*
Michael W Wimmer, *CFO*
**EMP:** 125
**SQ FT:** 34,000
**SALES:** 25MM
**SALES (corp-wide):** 3.8B **Publicly Held**
**WEB:** www.laserage.com
**SIC:** 3449 3841 Curtain wall, metal; inhalation therapy equipment
**PA:** Ametek, Inc.
1100 Cassatt Rd
Berwyn PA 19312
610 647-2121

### (G-21586)
### MARKET READY INC
3505 Birchwood Dr (60085-8335)
**PHONE** .................... 847 689-1000
Michael Sawant, *President*
Clayton Bolke, *Treasurer*
Paula Tennant, *Manager*
**EMP:** 4
**SALES (est):** 1.3MM **Privately Held**
**SIC:** 2844 Hair preparations, including shampoos

### (G-21587)
### MARQUETTE ENTERPRISES LLC
3505 Birchwood Dr (60085-8335)
**PHONE** .................... 877 689-0001
David L Waldron, *Principal*
**EMP:** 4 **EST:** 2008
**SALES (est):** 314.6K **Privately Held**
**SIC:** 3565 Packaging machinery

### (G-21588)
### MEDICAL RECORDS CO
Also Called: Computaforms
317 Stewart Ave (60085-2061)
**PHONE** .................... 847 662-6373
Thomas J Streit, *Owner*
Helen S Streit, *Co-Owner*
**EMP:** 5
**SALES (est):** 310K **Privately Held**
**SIC:** 5112 2752 Business forms; commercial printing, lithographic

### (G-21589)
### MEDLINE INDUSTRIES INC
1170 S Northpoint Blvd (60085-6757)
**PHONE** .................... 847 949-5500
Bill Sanders, *President*
Jim O'Brian, *General Mgr*
Matt Foster, *Mfg Mgr*
Terry Alwin, *QC Dir*
Maureen Reyes, *QC Mgr*
**EMP:** 400
**SALES (corp-wide):** 5.6B **Privately Held**
**WEB:** www.medline.com
**SIC:** 3842 3841 Surgical appliances & supplies; surgical & medical instruments
**PA:** Medline Industries, Inc.
3 Lakes Dr
Northfield IL 60093
847 949-5500

### (G-21590)
### MERCHANTS METALS LLC
2800 Northwestern Ave (60087-5333)
**PHONE** .................... 847 249-4086
**EMP:** 6
**SALES (corp-wide):** 1.7B **Privately Held**
**SIC:** 3446 Mfg Architectural Metalwork
**HQ:** Merchants Metals Llc
900 Ashwood Pkwy Ste 600
Atlanta GA 30346
770 741-0300

### (G-21591)
### MIDWEST ELECTRONICS RECYCLING
3300 Washington St (60085-4716)
**PHONE** .................... 847 249-7011
George Hinkle, *Manager*
**EMP:** 3
**SALES (est):** 189.4K **Privately Held**
**SIC:** 3559 Recycling machinery

### (G-21592)
### NEW NGC INC
515 E Sea Horse Dr (60085-2165)
**PHONE** .................... 847 623-8100
Gene Kropfelder, *Manager*
Marty Schenk, *Maintence Staff*
**EMP:** 92
**SALES (corp-wide):** 672.8MM **Privately Held**
**WEB:** www.natgyp.com
**SIC:** 3275 Gypsum products
**HQ:** New Ngc, Inc.
2001 Rexford Rd
Charlotte NC 28211
704 365-7300

### (G-21593)
### NORTH SHORE PRINTERS INC
535 S Sheridan Rd (60085-7553)
**PHONE** .................... 847 623-0037
**Fax:** 847 623-0290
Charlotte Wozniak, *President*
Amy Callahan, *Treasurer*
Victoria Drinka, *Branch Mgr*
Debbie Hall, *Manager*
Michael Galbraith, *Admin Sec*
**EMP:** 13
**SQ FT:** 30,000
**SALES:** 1.7MM **Privately Held**
**WEB:** www.nsprinters.com
**SIC:** 2752 Commercial printing, offset

### (G-21594)
### NORTH SHORE WTR RCLAMATION DST
Dahringer Rd (60085)
**PHONE** .................... 847 623-6060
Eugene Lukasik, *Branch Mgr*
**EMP:** 30
**SALES (corp-wide):** 13.6MM **Privately Held**
**WEB:** www.nssdist.org
**SIC:** 3589 Sewage treatment equipment
**PA:** North Shore Water Reclamation District
14770 W Wlliam Koepsel Dr
Gurnee IL 60031
847 623-6060

### (G-21595)
### NOSCO INC (HQ)
651 S Ml King Jr Ave (60085-7500)
**PHONE** .................... 847 336-4200
**Fax:** 847 360-4924
Russell S Haraf, *President*
Joseph S Haas, *Vice Pres*
Rick Potochnik, *Prdtn Mgr*
Scott Domkamp, *Facilities Mgr*
Dick Petkus, *Facilities Mgr*
▲ **EMP:** 333 **EST:** 1980
**SALES (est):** 130.3MM
**SALES (corp-wide):** 286.1MM **Privately Held**
**WEB:** www.nosco.com
**SIC:** 2752 2657 Commercial printing, lithographic; folding paperboard boxes
**PA:** Holden Industries, Inc.
500 Lake Cook Rd Ste 400
Deerfield IL 60015
847 940-1500

### (G-21596)
### OAK CREEK DISTRIBUTION LLC (PA)
Also Called: Home Owners Bargain Outlet
2650 Belvidere Rd (60085-6006)
**PHONE** .................... 800 244-5263
Scott Warner, *Mng Member*
**EMP:** 25
**SALES (est):** 4.2MM **Privately Held**
**SIC:** 2522 Cabinets, office: except wood

### (G-21597)
### OBROTHERS BAKERY INC
2820 Belvidere Rd (60085-6040)
**PHONE** .................... 847 249-0091
Ramiro Ortega, *President*
**EMP:** 7
**SALES (est):** 522.8K **Privately Held**
**SIC:** 2051 5461 Bakery: wholesale or wholesale/retail combined; bakeries

### (G-21598)
### OCTANE MOTORSPORTS LLC
3056 Washington St 2b (60085-4844)
**PHONE** .................... 224 419-5460
Renee Goodwin, *Principal*
Nick Christodoulou, *Mfg Mgr*
**EMP:** 4
**SALES (est):** 233K **Privately Held**
**SIC:** 3599 8711 7373 Machine & other job shop work; engineering services; computer-aided design (CAD) systems service; computer-aided manufacturing (CAM) systems service; computer-aided engineering (CAE) systems service

### (G-21599)
### OREILLYS AUTO PARTS STORE
2507 Grand Ave (60085-3316)
**PHONE** .................... 847 360-0012
Ted Weiss, *Branch Mgr*
**EMP:** 3
**SALES (corp-wide):** 1.1MM **Privately Held**
**SIC:** 7699 7694 7538 5531 Engine repair & replacement, non-automotive; rebuilding motors, except automotive; engine repair; automotive parts
**PA:** Oreilly's Auto Parts Store
316 Sw Marsh Wren St
Lees Summit MO 64082
816 525-0681

### (G-21600)
### PEER BEARING COMPANY (DH)
2200 Norman Dr (60085-8206)
**PHONE** .................... 877 600-7337

# GEOGRAPHIC SECTION
## Waukegan - Lake County (G-21623)

Fax: 847 578-1200
Patrick Tong, *President*
Sam Sung, *President*
John Hirst, *General Mgr*
Keith Hospodarsky, *Business Mgr*
Brian Cohen, *Vice Pres*
▲ **EMP:** 200 **EST:** 1961
**SALES (est):** 66.6MM
**SALES (corp-wide):** 546.3MM **Privately Held**
**WEB:** www.peerbearing.com
**SIC:** 3562 Ball & roller bearings
**HQ:** Skf Usa Inc.
890 Forty Foot Rd
Lansdale PA 19446
267 436-6000

### (G-21601)
### PFANSTIEHL INC
1219 Glen Rock Ave (60085-6230)
**PHONE** .................. 847 623-0370
Cindy Kerker, *President*
Sallie B Bailey, *Vice Pres*
V J Comanita, *Vice Pres*
Mark H Duesenberg, *Vice Pres*
Ann E Killian, *Vice Pres*
▲ **EMP:** 1 **EST:** 1997
**SQ FT:** 7,500
**SALES (est):** 40.5MM **Privately Held**
**WEB:** www.chembuyersguide.com
**SIC:** 2834 Pharmaceutical preparations
**PA:** Med Opportunity Partners, Llc
75 Holly Hill Ln Ste 100
Greenwich CT 06830
203 622-1333

### (G-21602)
### POLYMAX THERMOPLASTIC
Also Called: Polymax Tpe
3210 N Oak Grove Ave (60087-1887)
**PHONE** .................. 847 316-9900
Tom Castile, *VP Sales*
Yun Martin Lu,
Ron Sheu,
**EMP:** 25 **EST:** 2013
**SQ FT:** 41,108
**SALES (est):** 541.4K **Privately Held**
**SIC:** 2822 2821 Synthetic rubber; thermoplastic materials; elastomers, nonvulcanizable (plastics)

### (G-21603)
### POLYMER NATION LLC (PA)
405 N Oakwood Ave (60085-3006)
**PHONE** .................. 847 972-2157
Christopher O'Brien, *President*
Don Kessler, *CFO*
**EMP:** 1
**SALES (est):** 8MM **Privately Held**
**SIC:** 2851 1791 1752 1761 Paints & allied products; exterior wall system installation; access flooring system installation; ceilings, metal: erection & repair

### (G-21604)
### POWERVAR INC (HQ)
1450 S Lakeside Dr (60085-8301)
**PHONE** .................. 847 596-7000
Fax: 847 596-7100
George Z Lannert, *CEO*
Drew Raymond, *Principal*
Thomas Gornick, *Vice Pres*
Scott Moeller, *Vice Pres*
Gary Kriz, *Opers Staff*
◆ **EMP:** 120
**SQ FT:** 50,000
**SALES (est):** 29.4MM
**SALES (corp-wide):** 3.8B **Publicly Held**
**WEB:** www.powervar.com
**SIC:** 3629 Electronic generation equipment
**PA:** Ametek, Inc.
1100 Cassatt Rd
Berwyn PA 19312
610 647-2121

### (G-21605)
### POWERVAR HOLDINGS LLC
1450 S Lakeside Dr (60085-8301)
**PHONE** .................. 800 369-7179
**EMP:** 135
**SALES (est):** 5.2MM
**SALES (corp-wide):** 3.8B **Publicly Held**
**SIC:** 3629 Electronic generation equipment
**PA:** Ametek, Inc.
1100 Cassatt Rd
Berwyn PA 19312
610 647-2121

### (G-21606)
### PRECISION LABORATORIES LLC
1429 S Shields Dr (60085-8310)
**PHONE** .................. 800 323-6280
Fax: 847 596-3017
Richard L Wohlner, *President*
Chip Houmes, *District Mgr*
Erick Koskinen, *District Mgr*
Terry Culp, *COO*
Joe Jozaitis, *COO*
▲ **EMP:** 35
**SQ FT:** 40,000
**SALES (est):** 19.2MM **Privately Held**
**SIC:** 2879 Agricultural chemicals

### (G-21607)
### PRISTINE WATER SOLUTIONS INC
1570 S Lakeside Dr (60085-8309)
P.O. Box 599, Peru (61354-0599)
**PHONE** .................. 847 689-1100
Vince Verdone, *Vice Pres*
Scott Farman, *Controller*
Joe Schmidt, *Regl Sales Mgr*
**EMP:** 11
**SALES (est):** 2MM
**SALES (corp-wide):** 417MM **Publicly Held**
**WEB:** www.pristinewatersolutions.com
**SIC:** 3589 Water treatment equipment, industrial
**HQ:** Met-Pro Technologies Llc
460 E Swedesford Rd # 2030
Wayne PA 19087
215 717-7909

### (G-21608)
### PRONTO SIGNS AND ENGRAVING
2114 Grand Ave (60085-3416)
**PHONE** .................. 847 249-7874
Fax: 847 249-1043
Jim Cogan, *President*
**EMP:** 3 **EST:** 1999
**SALES (est):** 254.2K **Privately Held**
**SIC:** 3993 Signs & advertising specialties

### (G-21609)
### PROTOTYPE EQUIPMENT CORP
Also Called: Goodman Packaging Equipment
1081 S Northpoint Blvd (60085-8215)
**PHONE** .................. 847 596-9000
James A Goodman, *President*
Ann D Goodman, *Corp Secy*
William H Goodman, *Vice Pres*
Rick Daily, *VP Opers*
Tony Francsis, *Plant Mgr*
**EMP:** 70
**SQ FT:** 67,500
**SALES (est):** 13.5MM **Privately Held**
**WEB:** www.goodmanpkg.com
**SIC:** 3565 Packaging machinery

### (G-21610)
### ROCK-TRED 2 LLC (PA)
Also Called: Ora Holdings
405 N Oakwood Ave (60085-3006)
**PHONE** .................. 888 762-5873
Chris O'Brien, *CEO*
Mark Moran, *President*
Manuel Macias, *Plant Mgr*
Rosie Galler, *Controller*
Ben Bradley, *Marketing Mgr*
**EMP:** 29 **EST:** 1939
**SQ FT:** 120,000
**SALES (est):** 3.7MM **Privately Held**
**WEB:** www.rocktred.com
**SIC:** 2851 2842 Paints & allied products; polyurethane coatings; epoxy coatings; specialty cleaning, polishes & sanitation goods

### (G-21611)
### SALUD NATURAL ENTREPRENEUR INC
Also Called: Salud Natural Entrepreneurs
1120 Glen Rock Ave (60085-5458)
**PHONE** .................. 224 789-7400
Monica Velasquez, *General Mgr*
**EMP:** 26
**SQ FT:** 42,000 **Privately Held**
**SIC:** 2023 Dietary supplements, dairy & non-dairy based
**PA:** Salud Natural Entrepreneur, Inc.
1120 Glen Rock Ave
Waukegan IL 60085

### (G-21612)
### SALUD NATURAL ENTREPRENEUR INC (PA)
Also Called: Nopalina
1120 Glen Rock Ave (60085-5458)
**PHONE** .................. 224 789-7400
Hector Olivaa, *President*
Monica Oliva, *General Mgr*
Monica Velasquez, *General Mgr*
Sergio Oliva, *VP Sales*
Ricardo Caceres, *Asst Mgr*
▲ **EMP:** 26
**SQ FT:** 50,000
**SALES (est):** 12.3MM **Privately Held**
**SIC:** 2023 2041 Dietary supplements, dairy & non-dairy based; bran & middlings (except rice)

### (G-21613)
### SEASONAL DESIGNS INC (PA)
Also Called: Liberty Flags
1595 S Shields Dr (60085-8304)
**PHONE** .................. 847 688-0280
Fax: 847 688-0281
John Cutler, *President*
Bob Ahern, *Sales Mgr*
Karina Gutierrec, *Manager*
▲ **EMP:** 45
**SQ FT:** 40,000
**SALES (est):** 32.9MM **Privately Held**
**WEB:** www.seasonaldesigns.com
**SIC:** 5131 2399 Flags & banners; flags, fabric

### (G-21614)
### SELECTED CHEMICAL PRODUCTS CO
Also Called: Selected Beauty Products
2649 N Delany Rd (60087-1824)
**PHONE** .................. 847 623-2224
Fax: 847 623-2492
Esther Brutzkus, *Ch of Bd*
Sharon E Stein, *President*
Esther F Brutzkus, *Chairman*
Allen Brutzkus, *Vice Pres*
Joel Stein, *VP Sales*
▼ **EMP:** 25 **EST:** 1975
**SQ FT:** 48,000
**SALES (est):** 5.1MM **Privately Held**
**WEB:** www.selectedbeautyproducts.com
**SIC:** 2844 Hair preparations, including shampoos

### (G-21615)
### SHATTUC CORD SPECIALTIES INC
2340 Ernie Krueger Cir (60087-3224)
**PHONE** .................. 847 360-9500
John Runzel, *President*
Russel Novak, *President*
John S Runzel, *President*
David Chapa, *Sales Mgr*
**EMP:** 14
**SQ FT:** 3,500
**SALES (est):** 3.4MM **Privately Held**
**WEB:** www.cordof3strands.com
**SIC:** 3643 Connectors, electric cord

### (G-21616)
### SILGAN CONTAINERS MFG CORP
1301 W Dugdale Rd (60085-7225)
**PHONE** .................. 847 336-0552
Danile M Carson, *Vice Pres*
D Guzlas, *Mfg Staff*
Rick Warmbold, *Purchasing*
Joe Heaney, *CFO*
Bill Callale, *Manager*
**EMP:** 43
**SALES (corp-wide):** 3.6B **Publicly Held**
**WEB:** www.silgancontainers.com
**SIC:** 3411 Metal cans
**HQ:** Silgan Containers Manufacturing Corporation
21800 Oxnard St Ste 600
Woodland Hills CA 91367

### (G-21617)
### SILGAN EQUIPMENT COMPANY
1301 W Dugdale Rd (60085-7225)
**PHONE** .................. 847 336-0552
Arun Lamba, *General Mgr*
Dean Gzelyes, *Manager*
Frank W Hogan III, *Director*
▲ **EMP:** 44
**SALES (est):** 8.4MM
**SALES (corp-wide):** 3.6B **Publicly Held**
**WEB:** www.silgancontainers.com
**SIC:** 3411 3086 Metal cans; packaging & shipping materials, foamed plastic
**HQ:** Silgan Containers Llc
21800 Oxnard Rd Ste 600
Woodland Hills CA 91367
818 710-3700

### (G-21618)
### SIX COLOR PRINT LLC (PA)
3786 Hawthorne Ct (60087-3222)
**PHONE** .................. 847 336-3287
Zatz Steven G,
**EMP:** 14
**SALES (est):** 1.2MM **Privately Held**
**SIC:** 2752 Commercial printing, lithographic

### (G-21619)
### STEVE GREEN
Also Called: Lake County Machining
2233 Northwestern Ave B (60087-4150)
**PHONE** .................. 847 623-6327
Fax: 847 662-5625
Steve Green, *Owner*
**EMP:** 3
**SALES (est):** 326.8K **Privately Held**
**SIC:** 3599 Machine shop, jobbing & repair

### (G-21620)
### STEVENS INSTRUMENT COMPANY
111 W Greenwood Ave (60087-5134)
P.O. Box 193 (60079-0193)
**PHONE** .................. 847 336-9375
Sharon Kordt, *President*
Jon Kordt, *Corp Secy*
**EMP:** 6 **EST:** 1971
**SQ FT:** 6,000
**SALES (est):** 638.1K **Privately Held**
**WEB:** www.stevensinstrument.com
**SIC:** 3825 3829 Engine electrical test equipment; measuring & controlling devices

### (G-21621)
### TECHNIQUE ENG INC
968 S Northpoint Blvd (60085-8212)
**PHONE** .................. 847 816-1870
Rudy Avramovich, *President*
Julie Avramovich, *Finance*
Dejan Avramovich, *Office Mgr*
**EMP:** 12
**SALES (est):** 1.6MM **Privately Held**
**SIC:** 2821 Plastics materials & resins

### (G-21622)
### TECHNIQUE ENGINEERING INC
968 S Northpoint Blvd (60085-8212)
**PHONE** .................. 847 816-1870
Rudy Avramovich, *President*
Lucia Mazzocchetti, *Office Mgr*
**EMP:** 12
**SQ FT:** 20,000
**SALES (est):** 2.1MM **Privately Held**
**WEB:** www.techniqueng.com
**SIC:** 3544 8711 Special dies, tools, jigs & fixtures; mechanical engineering

### (G-21623)
### TECNOVA ELECTRONICS INC
2383 N Delany Rd (60087-1836)
**PHONE** .................. 847 336-6160
Fax: 847 336-6779
Terry Coleman Sr, *President*
Terry Coleman Jr, *Corp Secy*
▲ **EMP:** 90
**SQ FT:** 50,000
**SALES (est):** 26.5MM **Privately Held**
**WEB:** www.logicalproducts.com
**SIC:** 3672 7389 3823 Printed circuit boards; design services; industrial process control instruments

# Waukegan - Lake County (G-21624)

**(G-21624)**
**TELEFONIX INCORPORATED**
2340 Ernie Krueger Cir (60087-3224)
PHONE..................847 244-4500
Paul C Burke, *CEO*
Gloria J B Bruke, *Principal*
Allison Burke, *Exec VP*
Robert Brooks, *Opers Mgr*
Robert Bellei, *Prdtn Mgr*
▲ EMP: 60
SQ FT: 8,600
SALES (est): 24.8MM  **Privately Held**
WEB: www.telefonixinc.com
SIC: 3661  Telephone cords, jacks, adapters, etc.

**(G-21625)**
**THELEN SAND & GRAVEL INC**
Also Called: Waukegan Ready Mix
1020 Elizabeth St (60085-7626)
P.O. Box 730, Spring Grove (60081-0730)
PHONE..................847 662-0760
Mark Holtcamp, *Controller*
Frank Roznik, *Manager*
EMP: 12
SALES (corp-wide): 31.4MM  **Privately Held**
WEB: www.thelensg.com
SIC: 3273  Ready-mixed concrete
PA: Thelen Sand & Gravel, Inc.
 28955 W Il Route 173 # 1
 Antioch IL 60002
 847 838-8800

**(G-21626)**
**THERMOFLEX CORP (PA)**
1535 S Lakeside Dr (60085-8312)
PHONE..................847 473-9001
Robert Price, *President*
Rick Niesen, *Plant Mgr*
Mike Negus, *Project Mgr*
Anthony Rivera, *QC Mgr*
David Reband, *Engineer*
▼ EMP: 52
SALES: 15.7MM  **Privately Held**
SIC: 2821  Plastics materials & resins

**(G-21627)**
**THERMOFLEX CORP**
1817-1855 S Waukegan Rd (60085)
PHONE..................847 473-9001
Eric Weitz, *CFO*
EMP: 3
SALES (corp-wide): 15.7MM  **Privately Held**
SIC: 2821  Plastics materials & resins
PA: Thermoflex Corp.
 1535 S Lakeside Dr
 Waukegan IL 60085
 847 473-9001

**(G-21628)**
**TKG SWEEPING & SERVICES LLC**
345 N Lakewood Ave (60085-3049)
PHONE..................847 505-1400
Brett Katz, *Mng Member*
Daniel Katz, *Mng Member*
Richard Katz, *Mng Member*
EMP: 3
SALES (est): 551.6K  **Privately Held**
SIC: 4959  3589  Sweeping service: road, airport, parking lot, etc.; dirt sweeping units, industrial; carpet sweepers, except household electric vacuum sweepers

**(G-21629)**
**TOLERANCE MANUFACTURING INC**
1435 10th St (60085-7605)
PHONE..................847 244-8836
Fax: 847 244-8910
Barbara Furlan, *President*
Kenneth Furlan, *President*
Patti Tappa, *General Mgr*
Dryce Bohr, *Purchasing*
Megghan Ruiz, *Director*
EMP: 14
SQ FT: 7,200
SALES (est): 1.8MM  **Privately Held**
SIC: 3599  3429  Machine shop, jobbing & repair; furniture hardware

**(G-21630)**
**TONYS BAKERY**
1117 Washington St (60085-5301)
PHONE..................847 599-1590
Antonio Aricmedi, *Owner*
▼ EMP: 4
SALES (est): 231.6K  **Privately Held**
SIC: 2051  Bread, cake & related products

**(G-21631)**
**TORTILLERIA LAF MARIAS LLC**
922 Washington St (60085-5427)
PHONE..................224 399-9902
EMP: 3
SALES (est): 124.3K  **Privately Held**
SIC: 2099  Tortillas, fresh or refrigerated

**(G-21632)**
**TRIAD CIRCUITS INC**
3135 N Oak Grove Ave (60087-1800)
PHONE..................847 283-8600
Fax: 847 546-0902
Shawn Bixler, *President*
Kraig Knipp, *Prdtn Mgr*
Rob Uhwat, *Purchasing*
EMP: 30
SQ FT: 25,900
SALES: 3.5MM  **Privately Held**
WEB: www.triadc.com
SIC: 3672  Printed circuit boards

**(G-21633)**
**TRUMANS BRANDS LLC ◯**
1541 S Shields Dr (60085-8304)
PHONE..................224 302-5605
Michael Sawant,
John Esposito,
EMP: 10 EST: 2016
SALES (est): 409.5K  **Privately Held**
SIC: 2844  Toilet preparations

**(G-21634)**
**UCC HOLDINGS CORPORATION (HQ)**
2100 Norman Dr (60085-6752)
PHONE..................847 473-5900
Andrew Warrington, *President*
Fred Schroeder, *Controller*
Frederick K Schroeder, *Admin Sec*
EMP: 17
SALES (est): 143.5MM
SALES (corp-wide): 162.4MM  **Privately Held**
SIC: 3443  8711  Fabricated plate work (boiler shop); designing: ship, boat, machine & product

**(G-21635)**
**UNITED CONVEYOR CORPORATION (DH)**
Also Called: Chicago Conveyor
2100 Norman Dr (60085-6753)
PHONE..................847 473-5900
Fax: 847 473-5959
Douglas S Basler, *President*
Victor Mora, *Editor*
Michael Kipnis, *Senior VP*
Mark Burns, *Vice Pres*
Mark A Burns, *Vice Pres*
▲ EMP: 250 EST: 1920
SQ FT: 100,000
SALES (est): 119.3MM
SALES (corp-wide): 162.4MM  **Privately Held**
WEB: www.unitedconveyorsupply.com
SIC: 3535  Conveyors & conveying equipment

**(G-21636)**
**UNITED CONVEYOR SUPPLY COMPANY (DH)**
2100 Norman Dr (60085-6752)
PHONE..................847 672-5100
Douglas S Basler, *President*
Mark Springer, *CFO*
Fred Schroeder, *Controller*
Patty Berman, *VP Human Res*
▲ EMP: 56
SQ FT: 100,000
SALES (est): 24.2MM
SALES (corp-wide): 162.4MM  **Privately Held**
SIC: 3443  Fabricated plate work (boiler shop)

**(G-21637)**
**VARI-OP COMPANY**
1209 Pine St Apt 6 (60085-2777)
PHONE..................847 623-7667
Fax: 847 623-6699
William Hollen, *Owner*
Bill Hollen, *Owner*
EMP: 3
SQ FT: 4,000
SALES (est): 288.6K  **Privately Held**
SIC: 3599  Machine shop, jobbing & repair

**(G-21638)**
**VP PLASTICS AND ENGRG INC**
1270 S Waukegan Rd (60085-6722)
PHONE..................847 689-8900
Clayton Bolke, *President*
Kevin Fardoux, *Vice Pres*
Esmeralda Flores, *Manager*
David L Waldron, *Admin Sec*
EMP: 20
SQ FT: 40,000
SALES (est): 4.1MM
SALES (corp-wide): 194.4MM  **Privately Held**
WEB: www.blistersinc.com
SIC: 3089  Blister or bubble formed packaging, plastic
PA: Visual Pak Company
 1909 S Waukegan Rd
 Waukegan IL 60085
 847 689-1000

**(G-21639)**
**WAUKEGAN STEEL LLC**
1201 Belvidere Rd (60085-6203)
PHONE..................847 662-2810
Fax: 847 662-2818
Wayne Griesbaum, *President*
Marie G Kropp, *Chairman*
Lee T Simmons, *Corp Secy*
Bradley Vallem, *Controller*
James Centella, *Executive*
EMP: 40
SQ FT: 67,000
SALES (est): 19.4MM
SALES (corp-wide): 649.5MM  **Privately Held**
WEB: www.waukegansteel.com
SIC: 3441  3446  Fabricated structural metal; ornamental metalwork
PA: National Material L.P.
 1965 Pratt Blvd
 Elk Grove Village IL 60007
 847 806-7200

**(G-21640)**
**WESTERN RAILWAY DEVICES CORP**
Also Called: Western Railway Equipment
1214 14th St Ste A (60085-7815)
PHONE..................847 625-8500
Lockhart S Burnett, *President*
▲ EMP: 4
SQ FT: 10,000
SALES (est): 23.6K  **Privately Held**
SIC: 3743  5088  Railroad equipment; railroad equipment & supplies

**(G-21641)**
**WESTROCK CP LLC**
3145 Central Ave (60085-4865)
PHONE..................847 625-8284
Isaac Lopez, *Manager*
EMP: 3
SALES (corp-wide): 14.1B  **Publicly Held**
WEB: www.smurfit-stone.com
SIC: 2621  2631  Paper mills; paperboard mills
HQ: Westrock Cp, Llc
 504 Thrasher St
 Norcross GA 30071

**(G-21642)**
**YASKAWA AMERICA INC (HQ)**
Also Called: Drives & Motion Division
2121 Norman Dr (60085-6751)
PHONE..................847 887-7000
Gen Kudo, *CEO*
Steve Barhorst, *President*
Michael Knapek, *President*
Nory Takada, *President*
Robert Richard, *Area Mgr*
◆ EMP: 200
SQ FT: 112,530
SALES: 529.2MM
SALES (corp-wide): 3.4B  **Privately Held**
WEB: www.methodsmachine.com
SIC: 3621  7694  5063  3566  Motors, electric; electric motor repair; motors, electric; speed changers, drives & gears; industrial instrmnts msrmnt display/control process variable; relays & industrial controls
PA: Yaskawa Electric Corporation
 2-1, Kurosakishiroishi, Yahatanishi-Ku
 Kitakyushu FUK 806-0
 936 458-801

**(G-21643)**
**Z & L MACHINING INC (PA)**
3140 Central Ave (60085-4864)
PHONE..................847 623-9500
Fax: 847 623-9519
John E Lemm Jr, *President*
Paul Benz, *Vice Pres*
Amber Akers, *Purchasing*
John Lemm, *Controller*
Tom Hallam, *Sales Mgr*
▼ EMP: 42
SQ FT: 50,000
SALES: 8MM  **Privately Held**
WEB: www.zlmachfab.com
SIC: 3599  Machine shop, jobbing & repair

**(G-21644)**
**ZERO GROUND LLC**
2340 Ernie Krueger Cir (60087-3224)
PHONE..................847 360-9500
Mark Panko,
EMP: 11
SQ FT: 100,000
SALES: 5MM  **Privately Held**
SIC: 3679  3317  Harness assemblies for electronic use: wire or cable; conduit: welded, lock joint or heavy riveted

## Waverly
*Morgan County*

**(G-21645)**
**WAVERLY JOURNAL**
130 S Pearl St (62692-1166)
P.O. Box 78 (62692-0078)
PHONE..................217 435-9221
Fax: 217 435-4511
Nancy Copelin, *President*
Julie Springer, *Vice Pres*
EMP: 3
SQ FT: 1,400
SALES (est): 238K  **Privately Held**
SIC: 2711  Newspapers: publishing only, not printed on site

## Wedron
*Lasalle County*

**(G-21646)**
**WEDRON SILICA COMPANY**
3450 E 2056 Rd (60557)
P.O. Box 119 (60557-0119)
PHONE..................815 433-2449
Fax: 815 433-9393
Jenniffer Deckard, *President*
Charles Fowler, *President*
William Conway, *Chairman*
Joseph Fodo, *Vice Pres*
Steve King, *Vice Pres*
EMP: 90
SQ FT: 4,500
SALES: 44.1MM
SALES (corp-wide): 535MM  **Publicly Held**
SIC: 1446  Industrial sand
HQ: Fairmount Santrol Inc.
 8834 Mayfield Rd Ste A
 Chesterland OH 44026
 440 214-3200

GEOGRAPHIC SECTION                                    West Chicago - Dupage County (G-21671)

## Wenona
*Marshall County*

**(G-21647)**
**CROP PRODUCTION SERVICES INC**
795 County Road 3100 E (61377-7575)
P.O. Box 387 (61377-0387)
PHONE................815 853-4078
Don Miller, *Manager*
EMP: 9
SALES (corp-wide): 13.6B **Privately Held**
WEB: www.cropproductionservices.com
SIC: 2873 Nitrogenous fertilizers
HQ: Crop Production Services, Inc.
    3005 Rocky Mountain Ave
    Loveland CO 80538
    970 685-3300

**(G-21648)**
**HEARTHSIDE FOOD SOLUTIONS LLC**
Also Called: Oak State
775 State Route 251 (61377-7587)
PHONE................815 853-4348
EMP: 350 **Privately Held**
SIC: 2051 Bread, cake & related products
PA: Hearthside Food Solutions, Llc
    3250 Lacey Rd Ste 200
    Downers Grove IL 60515

**(G-21649)**
**WENONA FOOD & FUEL**
3075 Il Route 17 (61377-9662)
PHONE................815 853-4141
Rose Laus, *Principal*
EMP: 4
SALES (est): 364.5K **Privately Held**
SIC: 2869 Fuels

## West Chicago
*Dupage County*

**(G-21650)**
**2M CONTROL SYSTEMS INC**
245 W Roosevelt Rd Ste 86 (60185-4838)
PHONE................630 709-6225
Mariusz Smialek, *President*
▲ EMP: 5
SALES (est): 599.2K **Privately Held**
SIC: 3555 Printing trades machinery

**(G-21651)**
**A J HORNE INC**
893 Industrial Dr (60185-1833)
PHONE................630 231-8686
Fax: 630 231-8696
Paul Loomis, *President*
Rosemary Horne, *Vice Pres*
Deborah A Horne, *Treasurer*
Patrice Annerino, *Admin Sec*
EMP: 5 EST: 1946
SQ FT: 2,500
SALES: 260K **Privately Held**
WEB: www.ajhorneinc.com
SIC: 3599 3546 3452 Machine shop, jobbing & repair; power-driven handtools; bolts, nuts, rivets & washers

**(G-21652)**
**ADVANCED ELECTRONICS INC**
721 Winston St (60185-5121)
PHONE................630 293-3300
Fax: 630 293-3380
Prem Chaudhari, *President*
Nipul Patel, *Project Mgr*
Vickie Marshall, *Office Mgr*
Linda Skultety, *Manager*
Ramsi Chaudhari, *Admin Sec*
▲ EMP: 55
SQ FT: 25,000
SALES (est): 8.6MM **Privately Held**
WEB: www.advel.com
SIC: 3672 Printed circuit boards

**(G-21653)**
**AIRGAS USA LLC**
1250 W Washington St (60185-2653)
PHONE................630 231-9260
Fax: 630 231-7768
Amy Huff, *President*
Doug Fish, *Principal*
Jeff Allen, *Vice Pres*
Steve Franz, *Vice Pres*
William Poppenger, *Opers Mgr*
EMP: 24
SALES (corp-wide): 163.9MM **Privately Held**
SIC: 2813 3548 5084 5169 Industrial gases; welding apparatus; welding machinery & equipment; chemicals & allied products
HQ: Airgas Usa, Llc
    259 N Radnor Chester Rd # 100
    Radnor PA 19087
    610 687-5253

**(G-21654)**
**ALL RIGHT SALES INC**
28w240 Trieste Ln (60185-1481)
PHONE................773 558-4800
Fax: 773 588-7583
Amratlal S Patel, *President*
Shalies Patel, *Vice Pres*
▲ EMP: 7
SQ FT: 25,000
SALES (est): 740K **Privately Held**
WEB: www.allrightsales.com
SIC: 3499 5199 Picture frames, metal; variety store merchandise

**(G-21655)**
**AMERICAN CONTROLS & AUTOMATION**
897 Industrial Dr (60185-1833)
PHONE................630 293-8841
Paul Hoskins, *President*
Sang Cho, *Vice Pres*
Nikki Deuplack, *Manager*
EMP: 3
SQ FT: 2,500
SALES (est): 1.2MM **Privately Held**
WEB: www.ac-a.com
SIC: 3625 3672 7373 Industrial electrical relays & switches; circuit boards, television & radio printed; systems software development services

**(G-21656)**
**AMERICAN PARTSMITH INC**
901 Atlantic Dr (60185-5100)
PHONE................630 520-0432
Bonita Schroeder, *CEO*
EMP: 3
SALES (est): 283K **Privately Held**
SIC: 3469 3429 3499 Metal stampings; manufactured hardware (general); magnetic shields, metal

**(G-21657)**
**AMERICAN STANDARD CIRCUITS INC**
475 Industrial Dr (60185-1891)
PHONE................630 639-5444
Fax: 630 293-1240
Anaya Vardya, *CEO*
Francis Chackanad, *President*
Gira Vora, *General Mgr*
Gordhan Patel, *Chairman*
Jay Hirpara, *Exec VP*
▲ EMP: 115
SQ FT: 52,000
SALES: 16.3MM **Privately Held**
SIC: 3672 Printed circuit boards

**(G-21658)**
**AMETEK INC**
Also Called: Ametek Power Instruments
1725 Western Dr (60185-1880)
PHONE................630 621-3121
Fax: 630 621-3154
Tony Ciampitti, *President*
Frank Kay, *Opers Mgr*
Diana Rogers, *Buyer*
Sanjay Jivani, *QC Mgr*
Beverly Olson, *QC Mgr*
EMP: 50
SALES: 2MM **Privately Held**
SIC: 3669 Burglar alarm apparatus, electric

**(G-21659)**
**AN ENVIRONMENTAL INKS**
Also Called: Environmental Inks & Coatings
450 Wegner Dr (60185-2674)
PHONE................800 728-8200
Mark Denboer, *Manager*
EMP: 12
SALES (corp-wide): 940.5K **Privately Held**
SIC: 2899 Ink or writing fluids
HQ: Environmental Inks And Coatings Canada Ltd.
    1 Quality Products Rd
    Morganton NC 28655
    828 433-1922

**(G-21660)**
**ANCHOR BRAKE SHOE COMPANY LLC (DH)**
1920 Downs Dr (60185-1808)
PHONE................630 293-1110
Richard A Mathes, *President*
Michael Hawthorne, *President*
Daniel Gosselin, *General Mgr*
Donald Popernick, *Corp Secy*
Sam Laxman, *Facilities Mgr*
EMP: 8
SALES: 20MM **Privately Held**
WEB: www.anchorbrake.com
SIC: 3321 3743 5088 Railroad car wheels & brake shoes, cast iron; railroad equipment; railroad equipment & supplies

**(G-21661)**
**ARCHITECTURAL CAST STON**
2775 Norton Creek Dr (60185-6411)
PHONE................630 377-4800
Fax: 630 584-1774
Todd W Surta, *President*
Maybeth Graening, *Human Resources*
Sophie Kus, *Accounts Mgr*
Jean Bartlett, *Marketing Staff*
Paul Dianis, *Manager*
EMP: 50
SALES (est): 11.1MM **Privately Held**
SIC: 3272 5211 Concrete products, precast; masonry materials & supplies

**(G-21662)**
**ASSEMTECH INC**
245 W Roosevelt Rd Ste 8 (60185-4804)
PHONE................630 876-4990
Fax: 630 876-4991
Chuck Hall, *President*
Steve Murray, *Engineer*
Lauren Brooks, *Sales Dir*
EMP: 35
SQ FT: 10,000
SALES (est): 15.1MM **Privately Held**
WEB: www.assemtech-inc.com
SIC: 3569 Assembly machines, non-metalworking

**(G-21663)**
**ASTRO TOOL CO INC**
1200 Atlantic Dr (60185-5171)
PHONE................630 876-3402
William Kleiner, *President*
Robert Klehr, *Vice Pres*
Mary Ann Smith, *Office Mgr*
Leslie Kleiner, *Admin Sec*
EMP: 9
SQ FT: 12,000
SALES (est): 730K **Privately Held**
SIC: 3544 Special dies & tools

**(G-21664)**
**B N K INC**
Also Called: Dunkin' Donuts
330 S Neltnor Blvd (60185-2928)
PHONE................630 231-5640
Fax: 630 231-3943
Danny Patel, *President*
EMP: 8
SALES (est): 410.2K **Privately Held**
SIC: 5461 2051 5812 Doughnuts, except frozen; ice cream stands or dairy bars

**(G-21665)**
**BALL PUBLISHING**
622 Town Rd (60185-2614)
P.O. Box 1660 (60186-1660)
PHONE................630 208-9080
Fax: 630 231-5254
Engler Marilyn, *Principal*
◆ EMP: 14
SALES: 2.2MM **Privately Held**
SIC: 2741 Miscellaneous publishing

**(G-21666)**
**BARCO STAMPING CO (PA)**
1095 Carolina Dr (60185-1799)
PHONE................630 293-5155
Fax: 630 293-5159
Thomas Mullally, *President*
Brad Weber, *Vice Pres*
Manuel Velasquez, *Plant Mgr*
Ronald Tampa, *Treasurer*
Steve Stechman, *Manager*
▲ EMP: 45
SQ FT: 3,500
SALES (est): 19MM **Privately Held**
SIC: 3469 3544 Metal stampings; die sets for metal stamping (presses)

**(G-21667)**
**BARCODESOURCE INC (PA)**
Also Called: Barcodesupplies.com
245 W Roosevelt Rd # 109 (60185-3739)
PHONE................630 545-9590
Michael Galiga, *President*
EMP: 7 EST: 1998
SQ FT: 1,500
SALES (est): 1.4MM **Privately Held**
SIC: 7372 3577 3578 Prepackaged software; bar code (magnetic ink) printers; point-of-sale devices

**(G-21668)**
**BATAVIA INSTANT PRINT**
33w480 Fabyan Pkwy # 104 (60185-9611)
PHONE................630 262-0370
Fax: 630 262-0371
Brian R Pacetti, *President*
Bonny Pacetti, *Corp Secy*
Scot Brockner, *Vice Pres*
EMP: 8
SQ FT: 1,800
SALES: 800K **Privately Held**
SIC: 2759 2752 Ready prints; commercial printing, lithographic

**(G-21669)**
**BERRIDGE MANUFACTURING COMPANY**
1175 Carolina Dr (60185-1713)
PHONE................630 231-7495
Becky Wynne, *Human Res Dir*
Brandon Wynn, *Sales Associate*
Dan Mohs, *Manager*
Dana Bang, *Executive*
EMP: 3
SALES (corp-wide): 53.2MM **Privately Held**
SIC: 3444 5033 Metal roofing & roof drainage equipment; roofing, siding & insulation
PA: Berridge Manufacturing Company, Inc
    6515 Fratt Rd
    San Antonio TX 78218
    210 650-3050

**(G-21670)**
**BLACHFORD ENTERPRISES INC (HQ)**
1400 Nuclear Dr (60185-1636)
PHONE................630 231-8300
John L Blachford, *President*
Joseph Borean, *Vice Pres*
Greg Steuck, *VP Mfg*
Terry Hodges, *QC Dir*
Kendall Bush, *Engineer*
◆ EMP: 40
SQ FT: 45,000
SALES (est): 30.9MM
SALES (corp-wide): 51.6MM **Privately Held**
SIC: 3549 Wiredrawing & fabricating machinery & equipment, ex. die
PA: H.L. Blachford, Ltd
    2323 Royal Windsor Dr
    Mississauga ON L5J 1
    905 823-3200

**(G-21671)**
**BLACHFORD INVESTMENTS INC**
1400 Nuclear Dr (60185-1636)
PHONE................630 231-8300
Fax: 630 231-8321
M C Long, *President*
Joe Borean, *Vice Pres*
Steve Erickson, *Vice Pres*
Jean V Reid, *Vice Pres*

# West Chicago - Dupage County (G-21672)

Mark Funkhouser, *Purchasing*
◆ **EMP:** 107
**SQ FT:** 76,000
**SALES (est):** 24.4MM
**SALES (corp-wide):** 51.6MM **Privately Held**
**SIC: 3625** 3086 2273 Noise control equipment; plastics foam products; carpets & rugs
**HQ:** Blachford Enterprises, Inc.
1400 Nuclear Dr
West Chicago IL 60185
630 231-8300

### (G-21672)
**BLACK MARKET PARTS INC**
776 W Hawthorne Ln (60185-1968)
**PHONE** .................................. 630 562-9400
Dave Bauer, *President*
**EMP:** 4
**SALES (est):** 450K **Privately Held**
**SIC: 3559** Ammunition & explosives, loading machinery

### (G-21673)
**BORNS PICTURE FRAMES**
540 Bellview Ave (60185-2156)
**PHONE** .................................. 630 876-1709
Howard W Born, *President*
Erlaine Born, *Corp Secy*
**EMP:** 3
**SALES:** 400K **Privately Held**
**SIC: 2499** Picture & mirror frames, wood

### (G-21674)
**BRUCHER MACHINING INC**
1030 Atlantic Dr (60185-5101)
**PHONE** .................................. 630 876-1661
Scott E Kuhar, *President*
Peter Contos, *Engineer*
Melanie A Kuhar, *Admin Sec*
**EMP:** 12
**SQ FT:** 7,300
**SALES (est):** 2.2MM **Privately Held**
**WEB:** www.bruchermachining.com
**SIC: 3599** Machine shop, jobbing & repair

### (G-21675)
**BULK MOLDING COMPOUNDS INC (DH)**
1600 Powis Ct (60185-1016)
**PHONE** .................................. 630 377-1065
Mike Huff, *CEO*
Christopher Vaisvil, *President*
Mark Bieberstein, *General Mgr*
Gregory Knipp, *Vice Pres*
Francis Zappitelli, *Vice Pres*
▲ **EMP:** 71
**SQ FT:** 80,000
**SALES (est):** 143.2MM
**SALES (corp-wide):** 2.5B **Publicly Held**
**WEB:** www.bulkmolding.com
**SIC: 3087** Custom compound purchased resins
**HQ:** Citadel Plastics Holdings Inc
3637 Ridgewood Rd
Fairlawn OH 44333
330 666-3751

### (G-21676)
**CAMEO MOLD CORP**
Also Called: Cameo Mold & Duplicating
1125 Carolina Dr (60185-1713)
**PHONE** .................................. 630 876-1340
**Fax:** 630 876-1342
David Salvesen, *President*
**EMP:** 15
**SQ FT:** 7,500
**SALES (est):** 2.7MM **Privately Held**
**WEB:** www.cameomold.com
**SIC: 3544** Industrial molds

### (G-21677)
**CAMERON PRINTING INC**
1275 W Roosevelt Rd # 119 (60185-4815)
**PHONE** .................................. 630 231-3301
Martin J Finlayson, *President*
**EMP:** 3
**SQ FT:** 2,500
**SALES:** 600K **Privately Held**
**SIC: 2752** 2791 2789 Commercial printing, lithographic; business form & card printing, lithographic; typesetting; bookbinding & related work

### (G-21678)
**CAREY COLOR INC**
2500 Enterprise Cir (60185-9610)
**PHONE** .................................. 630 761-2605
Roger Dalberg, *General Mgr*
**EMP:** 3
**SALES (est):** 213.7K **Privately Held**
**SIC: 2752** Commercial printing, lithographic

### (G-21679)
**CENTRAL INK CORPORATION (PA)**
Also Called: Central Ink of Wisconsin Div
1100 Harvester Rd (60185-1608)
**PHONE** .................................. 630 231-6500
**Fax:** 630 231-6585
Richard E Breen, *CEO*
Gregg Dahleen, *President*
Jeff Ryder, *Corp Secy*
Daren Dabrowski, *Prdtn Mgr*
Jim Donnelly, *Prdtn Mgr*
▲ **EMP:** 88
**SQ FT:** 108,000
**SALES (est):** 42.5MM **Privately Held**
**WEB:** www.cicink.com
**SIC: 2893** Letterpress or offset ink

### (G-21680)
**CHICAGO MOTORCARS**
27w 110 North Ave (60185)
**PHONE** .................................. 630 221-1800
**Fax:** 630 221-1801
Phil Davero, *Sales Mgr*
Zoran Milovanovic, *Sales Associate*
Sam Salameh, *Director*
**EMP:** 22
**SALES (est):** 3.7MM **Privately Held**
**SIC: 3711** Motor vehicles & car bodies

### (G-21681)
**CHIPS MANUFACTURING INC**
741 Winston St (60185-5121)
**PHONE** .................................. 630 682-4477
**Fax:** 630 682-0772
James J Jett, *President*
Edward Stedman, *Corp Secy*
Michael Stern, *Opers Mgr*
Roberto Piga, *Facilities Mgr*
Edward Jedlicka, *QC Mgr*
**EMP:** 65
**SQ FT:** 45,000
**SALES (est):** 16.1MM **Privately Held**
**SIC: 3443** Metal parts

### (G-21682)
**CLARIANT PLAS COATINGS USA INC**
625 Wegner Dr (60185-6011)
**PHONE** .................................. 630 562-9700
Bob Anderson, *Business Mgr*
Chris Spencer, *Design Engr Mgr*
Maranda Barnard, *Engineer*
Kathy Lemaire, *Cust Mgr*
Ashley Bob Anderson, *Manager*
**EMP:** 100
**SALES (corp-wide):** 5.7B **Privately Held**
**WEB:** www.myclariant.com
**SIC: 2865** 2851 Dyes & pigments; paints & allied products
**HQ:** Clariant Plastics & Coatings Usa Inc.
4000 Monroe Rd
Charlotte NC 28205
704 331-7000

### (G-21683)
**CLOVER PLASTICS LLC**
1145 Howard Dr (60185-1621)
**PHONE** .................................. 630 473-6488
Kevin McNulty,
**EMP:** 6
**SQ FT:** 29,000
**SALES (est):** 670K **Privately Held**
**SIC: 3089** Air mattresses, plastic

### (G-21684)
**COBRA COAL INC**
3n060 Powis Rd (60185-1017)
**PHONE** .................................. 630 560-1050
David Hansen, *President*
Kenneth Phlamm, *Vice Pres*
Chris Vargas, *CFO*
▼ **EMP:** 30
**SALES (est):** 2MM **Privately Held**
**SIC: 1241** Coal mining services

### (G-21685)
**COMPONENT PRECAST SUPPLY INC**
4n325 Powis Rd (60185-1002)
**PHONE** .................................. 630 483-2900
**Fax:** 630 513-8926
John C Perritt, *President*
**EMP:** 6
**SALES (est):** 995.6K **Privately Held**
**SIC: 3272** Precast terrazo or concrete products

### (G-21686)
**CONSOLIDATED CONTAINER CO LLC**
1300 Northwest Ave (60185-1628)
**PHONE** .................................. 630 231-7150
Ed Sweeney, *Plant Mgr*
Mary Sniegowski, *Controller*
Sean Guinan, *Branch Mgr*
**EMP:** 115
**SQ FT:** 105,000
**SALES (corp-wide):** 13.1B **Publicly Held**
**SIC: 3085** Plastics bottles
**HQ:** Consolidated Container Company, Llc
3101 Towercreek Pkwy Se
Atlanta GA 30339
678 742-4600

### (G-21687)
**CONWED PLASTICS**
390 Wegner Dr Ste B (60185-2617)
P.O. Box 520 (60186-0520)
**PHONE** .................................. 630 293-3737
Mark Lewry, *President*
Kim Jarodsky, *Manager*
**EMP:** 75
**SALES (est):** 9.2MM **Privately Held**
**SIC: 3089** Plastics products

### (G-21688)
**CTC MACHINE SERVICE INC**
756 W Hawthorne Ln (60185-1968)
**PHONE** .................................. 630 876-5120
Robert A Berg, *President*
**EMP:** 7
**SALES (est):** 1MM **Privately Held**
**SIC: 3541** Machine tool replacement & repair parts, metal cutting types

### (G-21689)
**D/C INDUSTRIES LLC**
1215 Atlantic Dr (60185-5165)
**PHONE** .................................. 630 876-1100
Debbie Cottone, *Mng Member*
Mark Cottone,
Dan Ferguson,
**EMP:** 5
**SQ FT:** 28,000
**SALES (est):** 520K **Privately Held**
**SIC: 3613** 1761 Distribution boards, electric; sheet metalwork

### (G-21690)
**DELTA CIRCUITS INC**
730 W Hawthorne Ln (60185-1968)
**PHONE** .................................. 630 876-0691
**Fax:** 630 876-5300
Mike Chaudhari, *President*
Mukesh Chaudhari, *President*
Kieren Mike, *Vice Pres*
Rakesh Chaudhari, *Plant Mgr*
Kiran Chaudhari, *Engineer*
**EMP:** 25
**SQ FT:** 46,000
**SALES (est):** 4.7MM **Privately Held**
**SIC: 3672** 3679 Printed circuit boards; electronic circuits

### (G-21691)
**DEPENDABLE GRAPHICS & SERVICES**
911 Industrial Dr (60185-1835)
**PHONE** .................................. 630 231-2746
Asta Fico, *President*
**EMP:** 2
**SQ FT:** 1,550
**SALES (est):** 299.5K **Privately Held**
**SIC: 2752** Commercial printing, offset

### (G-21692)
**DF FAN SERVICES INC**
495 Wegner Dr (60185-2675)
**PHONE** .................................. 630 876-1495
**Fax:** 630 876-1497

Douglas Gifford Jr, *President*
Jay Rutz, *Purch Mgr*
Manus Sweetman, *Sales Mgr*
**EMP:** 10
**SQ FT:** 10,000
**SALES:** 900K **Privately Held**
**SIC: 3564** 5064 Blowers & fans; fans, household; electric

### (G-21693)
**DIPPIT INC**
Also Called: Prolong Tool
1879 N Neltnor Blvd 326 (60185-5932)
**PHONE** .................................. 630 762-6500
Steve Joyaux, *President*
**EMP:** 2
**SALES:** 400K **Privately Held**
**SIC: 3399** Cryogenic treatment of metal

### (G-21694)
**DML LLC**
419 Colford Ave (60185-2818)
**PHONE** .................................. 630 231-8873
Micheal Jankovic, *Partner*
**EMP:** 3
**SALES (est):** 181.4K **Privately Held**
**WEB:** www.rootripper.com
**SIC: 3589** Sewer cleaning equipment, power

### (G-21695)
**ENGINEERED SECURITY & SOUND**
1275 W Roosevelt Rd # 110 (60185-4815)
**PHONE** .................................. 630 876-8853
Jack Oulicky, *President*
Robert Stevenson, *Vice Pres*
Patrick Corso, *Treasurer*
Ronald Rocco, *Admin Sec*
**EMP:** 8
**SALES:** 1.2MM **Privately Held**
**WEB:** www.engineered-security.com
**SIC: 3699** Security control equipment & systems

### (G-21696)
**ENVIRONMENTAL INKS & CODING (PA)**
450 Wegner Dr (60185-2674)
**PHONE** .................................. 630 231-7313
**EMP:** 15
**SALES (est):** 1.1MM **Privately Held**
**SIC: 2893** Mfg Printing Ink

### (G-21697)
**EVO EXHIBITS LLC**
399 Wegner Dr (60185-2673)
**PHONE** .................................. 630 520-0710
Michael McCord, *General Mgr*
Kent Jean, *Principal*
Alyson Miller, *Project Mgr*
Krystal Dubovik, *Opers Mgr*
Jeff Blaisdell, *VP Sales*
**EMP:** 5
**SALES (est):** 1MM **Privately Held**
**SIC: 5999** 5963 3999 8742 Banners; direct sales, telemarketing; preparation of slides & exhibits; marketing consulting services

### (G-21698)
**EVOLUTION SORBENT PRODUCTS LLC**
1270 Nuclear Dr (60185-1632)
**PHONE** .................................. 630 293-8055
Bryan Sims,
**EMP:** 5 **Privately Held**
**SIC: 2621** Absorbent paper
**PA:** Evolution Sorbent Products, Llc
1149 Howard Dr
West Chicago IL 60185

### (G-21699)
**EVOLUTION SORBENT PRODUCTS LLC (PA)**
1149 Howard Dr (60185-1621)
**PHONE** .................................. 630 293-8055
Ron Bielski, *General Mgr*
Brian Albers, *Opers Staff*
Larry Wolf, *CFO*
Israel Ramirez, *Sales Staff*
Roxana Gomez, *Manager*
◆ **EMP:** 15
**SQ FT:** 40,000

# GEOGRAPHIC SECTION

**West Chicago - Dupage County (G-21725)**

**SALES:** 16.1MM **Privately Held**
**SIC: 2621** Absorbent paper

### (G-21700)
**EZTECH MANUFACTURING INC**
1200 Howard Dr (60185-1661)
**PHONE** ................................630 293-0010
**Fax:** 630 293-0463
Edwin T Smiling, *CEO*
Danny Gill, *General Mgr*
John Kramer, *Plant Mgr*
**EMP:** 16
**SQ FT:** 20,000
**SALES (est):** 3.4MM **Privately Held**
**SIC: 3699** 3444 Electrical equipment & supplies; sheet metalwork

### (G-21701)
**FIRST LIGHT INC**
Also Called: Fli Products
245 W Roosevelt Rd Ste 3 (60185-4838)
**PHONE** ................................630 520-0017
Kevin Cody, *President*
**EMP:** 5 **EST:** 2003
**SALES (est):** 1.5MM **Privately Held**
**SIC: 5063** 3646 Lighting fixtures, commercial & industrial; commercial indusl & institutional electric lighting fixtures

### (G-21702)
**FLI PRODUCTS LLC**
245 W Roosevelt Rd Ste 20 (60185-4805)
**PHONE** ................................630 520-0017
Kevin Cody,
**EMP:** 6 **EST:** 2013
**SQ FT:** 3,500
**SALES (est):** 604.4K **Privately Held**
**SIC: 3645** 3646 Residential lighting fixtures; desk lamps; wall lamps; commercial indusl & institutional electric lighting fixtures; desk lamps, commercial

### (G-21703)
**FLOLO CORPORATION (PA)**
1400 Harvester Rd (60185-1614)
**PHONE** ................................630 595-1010
**Fax:** 847 595-1327
George Flolo, *President*
Norman Flolo, *Vice Pres*
**EMP:** 41 **EST:** 1945
**SQ FT:** 42,000
**SALES:** 15MM **Privately Held**
**WEB:** www.flolo.com
**SIC: 7694** 5063 Electric motor repair; motors, electric

### (G-21704)
**FLOWSERVE CORPORATION**
1400 Powis Ct (60185-6413)
**PHONE** ................................630 762-4100
**Fax:** 630 762-8995
Doug Hendershot, *Plant Engr*
Mashall Heller, *Manager*
**EMP:** 30
**SALES (corp-wide):** 3.9B **Publicly Held**
**SIC: 3561** Pumps & pumping equipment
**PA:** Flowserve Corporation
5215 N Oconnor Blvd Connor
Irving TX 75039
972 443-6500

### (G-21705)
**FLOWSERVE CORPORATION**
1400 Powis Ct (60185-6413)
**PHONE** ................................630 762-4100
Harry Weber, *Branch Mgr*
**EMP:** 36
**SQ FT:** 12,000
**SALES (corp-wide):** 3.9B **Publicly Held**
**SIC: 3561** Pumps & pumping equipment
**PA:** Flowserve Corporation
5215 N Oconnor Blvd Connor
Irving TX 75039
972 443-6500

### (G-21706)
**FORMING AMERICA LTD (PA)**
1200 N Prince Crossing Rd (60185-1712)
**PHONE** ................................888 993-1304
James Langkamp, *President*
Natalie Yono, *Accounts Mgr*
Michael Start, *Sales Staff*
Joshua Jones, *Manager*
**EMP:** 30
**SALES (est):** 9.2MM **Privately Held**
**WEB:** www.formingamerica.com
**SIC: 5051** 3444 Forms, concrete construction (steel); concrete forms, sheet metal

### (G-21707)
**FRIGID COIL/FRICK INC**
1800 W Hawthorne Ln E2 (60185-1860)
**PHONE** ................................630 562-4602
Jim Spade, *Manager*
**EMP:** 4
**SALES (corp-wide):** 36.8B **Privately Held**
**SIC: 3556** Meat, poultry & seafood processing machinery
**HQ:** Frigid Coil/Frick, Inc.
1590 Dutch Rd
Dixon IL

### (G-21708)
**GLOBAL TURNINGS INC**
1092 Carolina Dr Ste 4 (60185-5191)
**PHONE** ................................630 562-0946
Robert Tirabasso, *Principal*
Glen Shannon, *Principal*
**EMP:** 5
**SQ FT:** 5,000
**SALES (est):** 594K **Privately Held**
**SIC: 3451** Screw machine products

### (G-21709)
**GO STEADY LLC**
505 Wegner Dr (60185-2626)
**PHONE** ................................630 293-3243
Leslie Doyle, *Opers Mgr*
Louanne Heinisch, *Treasurer*
Robert E Hendricks, *Mng Member*
**EMP:** 6
**SQ FT:** 600
**SALES:** 22.4K **Privately Held**
**SIC: 3842** 3069 Crutches & walkers; canes, orthopedic; grips or handles, rubber

### (G-21710)
**GRAHAM PACKAGING CO EUROPE LLC**
1760 W Hawthorne Ln (60185-1841)
**PHONE** ................................630 293-8616
Mario Escobar, *Plant Supt*
Dan Cyphers, *Plant Mgr*
Carlos Valdez, *Plant Mgr*
Mark Grant, *VP Sales*
Russell Killion, *VP Sales*
**EMP:** 1000 **Privately Held**
**SIC: 3089** Plastic containers, except foam
**HQ:** Graham Packaging Company Europe Llc
2401 Pleasant Valley Rd # 2
York PA 17402

### (G-21711)
**GRAHAM PACKAGING CO EUROPE LLC**
Also Called: Plant 4
1445 Northwest Ave (60185-1629)
**PHONE** ................................630 562-5912
**Fax:** 630 231-4373
Billy Williams, *President*
Dave Randall, *Vice Pres*
Gene Harned, *Prdtn Mgr*
Bill Wheeler, *Purchasing*
Dave Quinn, *Controller*
**EMP:** 150 **Privately Held**
**WEB:** www.liquidcontainer.com
**SIC: 3085** Plastics bottles
**HQ:** Graham Packaging Company Europe Llc
2401 Pleasant Valley Rd # 2
York PA 17402

### (G-21712)
**GRAHAM PACKAGING CO EUROPE LLC**
1275 Nuclear Dr (60185-1631)
**PHONE** ................................630 231-0850
David Randall, *Chief*
Russell Killion, *Vice Pres*
Francisco Gonzalez, *VP Mfg*
Craig Peterson, *Opers Mgr*
Steven Larrison, *Warehouse Mgr*
**EMP:** 400 **Privately Held**
**SIC: 3085** Plastics bottles
**HQ:** Graham Packaging Company Europe Llc
2401 Pleasant Valley Rd # 2
York PA 17402

### (G-21713)
**GRINDING SPECIALTY CO INC**
1879 N Neltnor Blvd (60185-5932)
**PHONE** ................................847 724-6493
Rhuia Smith, *President*
Dale Elkins, *Vice Pres*
Pat McNally, *Purchasing*
Patricia Derner, *Admin Sec*
**EMP:** 20
**SALES (est):** 2MM **Privately Held**
**SIC: 3544** Special dies, tools, jigs & fixtures

### (G-21714)
**HEALTHFUL HABITS LLC**
245 W Roosevelt Rd (60185-3739)
**PHONE** ................................224 489-4256
David Phoi, *Mng Member*
Jeff Adezcko,
Gloria Athanis,
**EMP:** 3
**SQ FT:** 5,000
**SALES:** 100K **Privately Held**
**SIC: 2064** Candy bars, including chocolate covered bars

### (G-21715)
**HOLLYWOOD TOOLS LLC**
Also Called: Snap-On Tools
1455 Marshview Ct Ste 8 (60185-5156)
**PHONE** ................................773 793-3119
George Hamilton,
**EMP:** 2
**SALES:** 900K **Privately Held**
**SIC: 3423** 7389 Ironworkers' hand tools;

### (G-21716)
**HOWLER FABRICATION & WLDG INC**
Also Called: H F I
1100 Carolina Dr (60185-5126)
**PHONE** ................................630 293-9300
**Fax:** 630 293-9413
Walter L Howler, *CEO*
Greg Enzenbacher, *Plant Mgr*
Hoa Tran, *Sales Staff*
Ray Hussman, *Director*
▼ **EMP:** 30 **EST:** 1967
**SQ FT:** 48,000
**SALES:** 10.6MM **Privately Held**
**WEB:** www.howler.net
**SIC: 3444** Sheet metalwork

### (G-21717)
**ILLINOIS LIFT EQUIPMENT INC**
1201 W Hawthorne Ln (60185-1815)
**PHONE** ................................888 745-0577
Michael Lopez, *President*
Matt Reif, *Sales Mgr*
◆ **EMP:** 21 **EST:** 2010
**SALES (est):** 15.7MM **Privately Held**
**SIC: 5084** 3537 Industrial machinery & equipment; industrial trucks & tractors

### (G-21718)
**INFINITI GOLF**
245 W Roosevelt Rd Ste 9 (60185-4804)
**PHONE** ................................630 520-0626
Eric Yeh, *President*
Tom Michalowski, *Vice Pres*
▲ **EMP:** 2
**SALES (est):** 245.7K **Privately Held**
**WEB:** www.infinitigolf.com
**SIC: 3949** Golf equipment

### (G-21719)
**INHANCE TECHNOLOGIES LLC**
829 W Hawthorne Ln (60185-1965)
**PHONE** ................................630 231-7515
**Fax:** 630 231-7616
Ginny Poole, *Plant Mgr*
Jinny Pool, *Branch Mgr*
**EMP:** 22
**SALES (corp-wide):** 8.9MM **Privately Held**
**WEB:** www.fluoroseal.com
**SIC: 3085** 2851 Plastics bottles; paints & allied products

**PA:** Inhance Technologies Llc
16223 Park Row Ste 100
Houston TX 77084
800 929-1743

### (G-21720)
**INLAND FASTENER INC**
770 W Hawthorne Ln (60185-1968)
**PHONE** ................................630 293-3800
**Fax:** 630 293-4916
James J Ricke, *President*
Tim Gardner, *Vice Pres*
Tracy Leonhard, *Vice Pres*
Carol Ricke, *Vice Pres*
Peggy Jones, *Opers Staff*
▲ **EMP:** 11 **EST:** 1959
**SQ FT:** 32,000
**SALES:** 3.5MM **Privately Held**
**WEB:** www.rickeco.com
**SIC: 3452** 3965 3429 Screws, metal; fasteners; manufactured hardware (general)

### (G-21721)
**INNOCOR INC**
Also Called: Advance Ureathane
1700 Downs Dr Ste 200 (60185-1834)
**PHONE** ................................630 231-0622
Cristine Rush, *Branch Mgr*
**EMP:** 417
**SALES (corp-wide):** 1B **Privately Held**
**SIC: 2515** Mattresses & foundations
**PA:** Innocor, Inc.
200 Schulz Dr Ste 2
Red Bank NJ 07701
844 824-9348

### (G-21722)
**INNOCOR FOAM TECH W CHCAGO LLC**
1750 Downs Dr (60185-1804)
**PHONE** ................................732 945-6222
Carol S Eicher, *CEO*
▲ **EMP:** 50
**SALES (est):** 5.8MM
**SALES (corp-wide):** 1B **Privately Held**
**SIC: 3495** 2392 2821 Wire springs; mattress pads; plastics materials & resins
**HQ:** Innocor Foam Technologies, Llc
200 Schulz Dr Ste 2
Red Bank NJ 07701
732 263-0800

### (G-21723)
**INNOCOR FOAM TECHNOLOGIES LLC**
1750 Downs Dr (60185-1804)
**PHONE** ................................630 293-0780
Michael C Thompson, *Branch Mgr*
**EMP:** 14
**SALES (corp-wide):** 1B **Privately Held**
**SIC: 3085** Plastics products
**HQ:** Innocor Foam Technologies, Llc
200 Schulz Dr Ste 2
Red Bank NJ 07701
732 263-0800

### (G-21724)
**INX INTERNATIONAL INK CO**
1860 Western Dr (60185-1881)
**PHONE** ................................630 681-7200
**Fax:** 630 293-4375
Tom Jasinski, *Manager*
Kevin Facklam, *Director*
Mike Glidwell, *Maintence Staff*
**EMP:** 35
**SALES (corp-wide):** 1.3B **Privately Held**
**SIC: 2893** 2899 Printing ink; ink or writing fluids
**HQ:** Inx International Ink Co
150 N Martingale Rd # 700
Schaumburg IL 60173
630 382-1800

### (G-21725)
**INX INTERNATIONAL INK CO**
1760 Western Dr (60185-1864)
**PHONE** ................................630 681-7100
Kotaro Moita, *Branch Mgr*
Byron Bright, *Manager*
Dennis Magdziak, *CTO*
**EMP:** 50
**SALES (corp-wide):** 1.3B **Privately Held**
**SIC: 8731** 2893 2899 Commercial physical research; printing ink; ink or writing fluids

# West Chicago - Dupage County (G-21726)

## GEOGRAPHIC SECTION

HQ: Inx International Ink Co
150 N Martingale Rd # 700
Schaumburg IL 60173
630 382-1800

**(G-21726)**
**J H H OF ILLINOIS INC**
Also Called: Jamar Packaging
1331 Howard Dr (60185-1625)
PHONE..................630 293-0739
Fax: 630 293-1041
Jeff H Heise, *President*
Dave Mayday, *Vice Pres*
**EMP:** 15 **EST:** 1979
**SQ FT:** 10,000
**SALES (est):** 4.3MM **Privately Held**
**SIC:** 2653 Corrugated & solid fiber boxes; boxes, corrugated: made from purchased materials

**(G-21727)**
**JEL SERT CO**
Also Called: J S
Conde St Rr 59 (60185)
PHONE..................630 231-7590
Fax: 630 231-3993
Gary Ricco, *CEO*
Charles T Wegner IV, *Ch of Bd*
Kenneth E Wegner, *President*
Bob Clements, *Vice Pres*
Yovani Valdivia, *Safety Dir*
◆ **EMP:** 277 **EST:** 1929
**SQ FT:** 400,000
**SALES (est):** 162.8MM **Privately Held**
**WEB:** www.jelsertpharmaceuticals.com
**SIC:** 2087 2024 2099 5499 Concentrates, flavoring (except drink); fruit pops, frozen; desserts, ready-to-mix; beverage stores; ice cream & ices

**(G-21728)**
**JJC EPOXY INC**
Also Called: Polygem
1105 Carolina Dr (60185-1713)
PHONE..................630 231-5600
Anton J Schmid, *President*
Catherine Lay, *Corp Secy*
Juan Alvarado, *Vice Pres*
**EMP:** 5
**SALES (est):** 1.2MM **Privately Held**
**SIC:** 2891 Adhesives & sealants

**(G-21729)**
**JUNKER INC**
391 Wegner Dr Ste A (60185-2695)
PHONE..................630 231-3770
Fax: 630 978-4051
Jason Drury, *CEO*
**EMP:** 9
**SALES (est):** 73.2K **Privately Held**
**SIC:** 3549 Metalworking machinery
HQ: Otto Junker Gesellschaft Mit Beschrankter Haftung
Jagerhausstr. 22
Simmerath 52152
247 360-10

**(G-21730)**
**KOALA CABINETS**
333 Charles Ct (60185-2604)
PHONE..................630 818-1289
**EMP:** 4 **EST:** 2010
**SALES (est):** 442.6K **Privately Held**
**SIC:** 2434 Wood kitchen cabinets

**(G-21731)**
**LIBBEY INC**
1850 Blackhawk Dr (60185-1666)
PHONE..................630 818-3400
Chris Fuentes, *Branch Mgr*
**EMP:** 128
**SALES (corp-wide):** 796.2MM **Publicly Held**
**SIC:** 3229 Pressed & blown glass
PA: Libbey Inc.
300 Madison Ave
Toledo OH 43604
419 325-2100

**(G-21732)**
**LIPSCOMB ENGINEERING INC**
1215 W Washington St (60185-2652)
PHONE..................630 231-3833
Fax: 630 231-0177
Robert J Lipscomb, *President*
Mary Ellen Lipscomb, *Admin Sec*
**EMP:** 9 **EST:** 1978
**SQ FT:** 10,000
**SALES (est):** 1.5MM **Privately Held**
**WEB:** www.rjlipscomb.com
**SIC:** 7699 3549 Industrial machinery & equipment repair; metalworking machinery

**(G-21733)**
**LIQUID CONTAINER INC**
1760 W Hawthorne Ln (60185-1841)
PHONE..................630 562-5812
Bill Williams, *Principal*
**EMP:** 24
**SALES (est):** 4.4MM **Privately Held**
**SIC:** 3085 Plastics bottles

**(G-21734)**
**LUXON PRINTING INC**
375 Wegner Dr (60185-2673)
PHONE..................630 293-7710
Fax: 630 293-7713
John W Luxon, *President*
Philip Rajski, *Sales Staff*
Fran Todd, *Office Mgr*
**EMP:** 15
**SQ FT:** 10,000
**SALES:** 900K **Privately Held**
**SIC:** 2752 Commercial printing, offset

**(G-21735)**
**M S TOOL & ENGINEERING**
Also Called: Ms Astral Tool
1200 Atlantic Dr (60185-5171)
PHONE..................630 876-3437
Daniel Kruger, *President*
**EMP:** 11
**SALES (est):** 1.1MM **Privately Held**
**WEB:** www.msastro.com
**SIC:** 3544 Special dies, tools, jigs & fixtures

**(G-21736)**
**MANUFCTURE DSIGN INNVATION INC**
Also Called: Mdi-Co
1760 Metoyer Ct Unit F (60185-6410)
PHONE..................773 526-7773
Drew Johnson, *President*
Arne Toman, *Treasurer*
Marcin Musial, *Admin Sec*
**EMP:** 5 **EST:** 2014
**SALES:** 400K **Privately Held**
**SIC:** 7389 3544 Design services; industrial molds

**(G-21737)**
**MAPEI CORPORATION**
Also Called: North American Adhesives
530 Industrial Dr (60185-1828)
PHONE..................630 293-5800
Jose Granillo, *Manager*
Janet Boggs, *Manager*
Curtis Yocum, *Manager*
Steven Cameron, *Director*
**EMP:** 100 **Privately Held**
**SIC:** 2891 2899 2821 Adhesives & sealants; chemical preparations; plastics materials & resins
HQ: Mapei Corporation
1144 E Newport Center Dr
Deerfield Beach FL 33442
954 246-8888

**(G-21738)**
**MARCY LABORATORIES INC**
4n215 Powis Rd (60185-1002)
PHONE..................630 377-6655
Fax: 630 377-1262
Larry Murison Sr, *President*
Merrily Murison, *Exec VP*
Larry Murison Jr, *Vice Pres*
▲ **EMP:** 35
**SQ FT:** 30,000
**SALES (est):** 6.7MM **Privately Held**
**WEB:** www.marcylaboratories.com
**SIC:** 2844 Perfumes, natural or synthetic; cosmetic preparations

**(G-21739)**
**MARINE ENGINE AND DRIVE S**
1330 W Washington St (60185-2655)
PHONE..................630 606-6124
Dan Cerling, *Owner*
**EMP:** 2
**SALES (est):** 204.1K **Privately Held**
**SIC:** 3519 Marine engines

**(G-21740)**
**MASONITE CORPORATION**
1955 Powis Rd (60185-1002)
PHONE..................630 584-6330
Michael McDonald, *Manager*
Mark Reynolds, *Manager*
John Bott, *Director*
**EMP:** 96
**SALES (corp-wide):** 1.9B **Publicly Held**
**SIC:** 2431 3469 Doors, wood; door parts & trim, wood; stamping metal for the trade
HQ: Masonite Corporation
1 Tampa City Center 20
Tampa FL 33602
813 877-2726

**(G-21741)**
**MASTER-HALCO INC**
1261 Atlantic Dr (60185-5165)
PHONE..................630 293-5560
Ray George, *Marketing Mgr*
Eric Goodman, *Branch Mgr*
**EMP:** 8
**SALES (corp-wide):** 42.5B **Privately Held**
**WEB:** www.fenceonline.com
**SIC:** 3315 Chain link fencing
HQ: Master-Halco, Inc.
3010 Lbj Fwy Ste 800
Dallas TX 75234
972 714-7300

**(G-21742)**
**MICROLITE CORPORATION (DH)**
Also Called: Lighting Control Systems
1150 Powis Rd Ste 8 (60185-1664)
PHONE..................630 876-0500
Fax: 630 876-0580
Darrell Chelcun, *Vice Pres*
**EMP:** 8
**SALES (est):** 1.3MM
**SALES (corp-wide):** 162.5MM **Privately Held**
**WEB:** www.microlite.net
**SIC:** 3648 5063 Lighting equipment; lighting fixtures
HQ: Musco Sports Lighting, Llc
100 1st Ave W
Oskaloosa IA 52577
641 673-0411

**(G-21743)**
**MIDWEST SAW INC**
850 Meadowview Xing Ste 4 (60185-2577)
PHONE..................630 293-4252
Joseph Denicolo, *President*
**EMP:** 7
**SQ FT:** 4,000
**SALES (est):** 1.1MM **Privately Held**
**WEB:** www.tiletools.com
**SIC:** 3425 7699 Saw blades for hand or power saws; knife, saw & tool sharpening & repair

**(G-21744)**
**MINERAL MASTERS CORPORATION**
130 W Grand Lake Blvd (60185-1937)
PHONE..................630 293-7727
Fax: 630 293-7765
Andrew Bassi, *President*
Pamela Bassi, *Admin Sec*
▲ **EMP:** 15
**SALES:** 5MM **Privately Held**
**SIC:** 2899 5169 Chemical preparations; chemicals, industrial & heavy

**(G-21745)**
**MOBILE PALLET SERVICE INC**
1300 W Roosevelt Rd (60185-4828)
PHONE..................630 231-6597
Nick Perez, *Manager*
Nathan Kant, *Admin Sec*
**EMP:** 15
**SALES (corp-wide):** 8.6MM **Privately Held**
**WEB:** www.mobilepalletservice.com
**SIC:** 2448 Wood pallets & skids
PA: Mobile Pallet Service, Inc.
858 S Main St
Wayland MI 49348
269 792-4200

**(G-21746)**
**MONCO FABRICATORS INC**
645 Joliet St (60185-3354)
PHONE..................630 293-0063
Peter Verive, *President*
Dawn Verive, *Corp Secy*
Steve Verive, *Vice Pres*
**EMP:** 3
**SQ FT:** 1,500
**SALES:** 400K **Privately Held**
**SIC:** 3498 Fabricated pipe & fittings

**(G-21747)**
**MOTOROLA SOLUTIONS INC**
2700 International Dr (60185-1670)
PHONE..................847 541-1014
Jim Myers, *Manager*
Frank Mountford, *IT/INT Sup*
Robert Bruhn, *Maintence Staff*
**EMP:** 40
**SALES (corp-wide):** 6B **Publicly Held**
**WEB:** www.motorola.com
**SIC:** 3663 Radio & TV communications equipment
PA: Motorola Solutions, Inc.
500 W Monroe St Ste 4400
Chicago IL 60661
847 576-5000

**(G-21748)**
**NATIONAL CONTROL HOLDINGS**
Also Called: Ametek-Ncc Holding
1725 Western Dr (60185-1880)
PHONE..................630 231-5900
Fax: 630 231-1377
Lawrence Froman, *Principal*
Don Buttle, *Engineer*
Phil Lockhart, *Sales Mgr*
John Kuschewski, *Data Proc Staff*
▲ **EMP:** 260
**SQ FT:** 78,000
**SALES (est):** 54.5MM
**SALES (corp-wide):** 3.8B **Publicly Held**
**SIC:** 3625 Electric controls & control accessories, industrial
PA: Ametek, Inc.
1100 Cassatt Rd
Berwyn PA 19312
610 647-2121

**(G-21749)**
**NATURAL POLYMERS LLC**
4n325 Powis Rd (60185-1002)
PHONE..................888 563-3111
Benjamin Brown, *President*
**EMP:** 5
**SALES (est):** 1.3MM **Privately Held**
**SIC:** 2821 Polyurethane resins

**(G-21750)**
**NEUERO CORPORATION**
1201 W Hawthorne Ln (60185-1815)
P.O. Box 1149, Batavia (60510-6149)
PHONE..................630 231-9020
Fax: 630 231-6120
Scott Neidigh, *President*
Jack Fox, *Director*
Gerald Gallagher, *Admin Sec*
▲ **EMP:** 14
**SQ FT:** 30,240
**SALES (est):** 3MM **Privately Held**
**WEB:** www.neuero.com
**SIC:** 3535 3537 3523 Pneumatic tube conveyor systems; industrial trucks & tractors; farm machinery & equipment
PA: Ecica Ag
C/O Lic.lur. Peter Georg Studer
Zug ZG
417 101-577

**(G-21751)**
**NORIX GROUP INC**
1800 W Hawthorne Ln Ste N (60185-1863)
PHONE..................630 231-1331
Fax: 630 231-4343
Richard B Karl, *CEO*
Scott C Karl, *President*
Heather L Karl, *Senior VP*
Willie Camarillo, *Project Mgr*
Sandy Heitman, *Project Mgr*
▲ **EMP:** 25
**SQ FT:** 45,000
**SALES (est):** 22.9MM **Privately Held**
**SIC:** 5021 2599 Furniture; office & public building furniture; cafeteria furniture

# GEOGRAPHIC SECTION

## West Chicago - Dupage County (G-21777)

**(G-21752)**
**NORTHWESTERN FLAVORS LLC**
120 N Aurora St (60185-1957)
PHONE .................... 630 231-6111
R V Clark, *Engineer*
Judy Piszczek, *Controller*
Steve Sharer, *Sales Mgr*
R J Simmons, *Manager*
Don Balster, *Director*
◆ **EMP:** 35
**SQ FT:** 79,000
**SALES (est):** 6.5MM
**SALES (corp-wide):** 35B **Privately Held**
**WEB:** www.wrigley.com
**SIC:** 2087 Extracts, flavoring
**HQ:** Wm. Wrigley Jr. Company
  930 W Evergreen Ave
  Chicago IL 60642
  312 280-4710

**(G-21753)**
**OPTI-SAND INCORPORATED**
31 W 037 North Ave (60185)
P.O. Box 565, Geneva (60134-0565)
PHONE .................... 630 293-1245
Robert Kohnke, *President*
Bob Kohnke, *Marketing Mgr*
**EMP:** 6
**SALES:** 410K **Privately Held**
**WEB:** www.opti-sand.com
**SIC:** 1442 Sand mining

**(G-21754)**
**OSI INDUSTRIES LLC**
Also Called: OSI Group
711 Industrial Dr (60185-1831)
P.O. Box 338 (60186-0338)
PHONE .................... 630 231-9090
Phyllis Antonacci, *Vice Pres*
Phil Hondlik, *Purchasing*
Lisa Niemann, *Hum Res Coord*
Joseph Rodgiuez, *Personnel*
Darren Lange, *Manager*
**EMP:** 220
**SALES (corp-wide):** 2.9B **Privately Held**
**SIC:** 5147 2013 Meats & meat products; sausages & other prepared meats
**HQ:** Osi Industries, Llc
  1225 Corp Blvd Ste 105
  Aurora IL 60505
  630 851-6600

**(G-21755)**
**PERFORMANCE BATTERY GROUP INC**
870 W Hawthorne Ln A (60185-1998)
P.O. Box 88803, Carol Stream (60188-0803)
PHONE .................... 630 293-5505
**Fax:** 630 407-0402
Gordon Close, *President*
Arron Smith, *General Ptnr*
Robert Hawco, *Business Mgr*
William Isett, *Sales Mgr*
**EMP:** 9
**SALES (est):** 1.1MM **Privately Held**
**SIC:** 3621 3691 Generators for storage battery chargers; storage batteries; lead acid batteries (storage batteries)

**(G-21756)**
**PERFORMANCE MANUFACTURING**
782 W Hawthorne Ln (60185-1968)
PHONE .................... 630 231-8099
Francis Winslow, *Principal*
**EMP:** 3
**SALES (est):** 209.7K **Privately Held**
**SIC:** 5013 3999 3714 Automotive brakes; manufacturing industries; motor vehicle brake systems & parts

**(G-21757)**
**PLASTIPAK PACKAGING INC**
1700 Western Dr (60185-1864)
PHONE .................... 630 231-7650
Joe Urban, *Maintence Staff*
**EMP:** 127
**SALES (corp-wide):** 36.3MM **Privately Held**
**SIC:** 3089 Blow molded finished plastic products

**HQ:** Plastipak Packaging, Inc.
  41605 Ann Arbor Rd E
  Plymouth MI 48170
  734 455-3600

**(G-21758)**
**POLARIS LASER LAMINATIONS LLC**
2725 Norton Creek Dr B2 (60185-6441)
PHONE .................... 630 444-0760
Lynn Girard,
Jozef Fela,
Toan Truong,
**EMP:** 5
**SALES (est):** 1.2MM **Privately Held**
**SIC:** 3399 7389 3479 Laminating steel; metal cutting services; coating of metals & formed products

**(G-21759)**
**POWERMASTER**
Also Called: Powermaster Motorsports
1833 Downs Dr (60185-1805)
PHONE .................... 630 957-4019
John Babcock, *President*
Betty Baldwin, *Controller*
**EMP:** 3
**SALES (est):** 244.5K **Privately Held**
**SIC:** 3694 Alternators, automotive

**(G-21760)**
**PRESS A LIGHT CORPORATION**
300 Industrial Dr (60185-1890)
PHONE .................... 630 231-6566
**Fax:** 630 231-6673
Paul R Chabria, *President*
Meena G Chabria, *Vice Pres*
▲ **EMP:** 15 **EST:** 1977
**SQ FT:** 20,000
**SALES (est):** 2.3MM **Privately Held**
**WEB:** www.pressalite.com
**SIC:** 3648 Flashlights

**(G-21761)**
**PRO-PAK INDUSTRIES INC**
Also Called: Pro-Line Safety Products
1099 Atlantic Dr Ste 1 (60185-5173)
PHONE .................... 630 876-1050
**Fax:** 630 876-1038
Darrell G Holmes, *President*
Dan Mehrodt, *Vice Pres*
Diane Chapman, *Accounting Mgr*
Bryan Holmes, *VP Sales*
Dan Mehrbrodt, *VP Sales*
▲ **EMP:** 15
**SQ FT:** 17,000
**SALES (est):** 3.4MM **Privately Held**
**WEB:** www.prolinesafety.com
**SIC:** 3953 2671 5063 2311 Marking devices; plastic film, coated or laminated for packaging; power wire & cable; coats, overcoats & vests

**(G-21762)**
**QUANTUM PRECISION INC**
385 Wegner Dr (60185-2673)
PHONE .................... 630 692-1545
Zygmunt Soszko Jr, *President*
**EMP:** 25
**SQ FT:** 10,000
**SALES (est):** 4.6MM **Privately Held**
**WEB:** www.quantumprecision.com
**SIC:** 3639 Buttonhole & eyelet machines & attachments, domestic

**(G-21763)**
**READY ACCESS INC**
1815 Arthur Dr (60185-1601)
PHONE .................... 800 621-5045
**Fax:** 630 876-7767
John R Radek Jr, *President*
James Orluck, *Plant Mgr*
Bob Mc Keever, *CFO*
Robert J McKeever, *Admin Sec*
▼ **EMP:** 32
**SQ FT:** 65,000
**SALES (est):** 7.1MM **Privately Held**
**WEB:** www.ready-access.com
**SIC:** 3444 Restaurant sheet metalwork

**(G-21764)**
**RICON COLORS INC**
675 Wegner Dr (60185-6011)
PHONE .................... 630 562-9000
**Fax:** 630 562-0700
Gerald P McDonald, *President*

Pete Patel, *Vice Pres*
Mary McGee, *Manager*
Mehndra Patel, *Manager*
**EMP:** 10
**SALES (est):** 1.4MM
**SALES (corp-wide):** 5.7B **Privately Held**
**WEB:** www.riconcolors.com
**SIC:** 3089 5169 Thermoformed finished plastic products; synthetic resins, rubber & plastic materials
**PA:** Clariant Ag
  Rothausstrasse 61
  Muttenz BL 4132
  614 695-111

**(G-21765)**
**RITE SYSTEMS EAST INC (DH)**
625 Wegner Dr (60185-6011)
PHONE .................... 630 293-9174
**Fax:** 630 562-9900
Manu Jogani, *President*
Drew Babcock, *Vice Pres*
Mary Beth McGee, *Opers Mgr*
Sue Schulz, *QC Dir*
Sue Wilson, *Manager*
▲ **EMP:** 40
**SQ FT:** 50,000
**SALES (est):** 4.2MM
**SALES (corp-wide):** 5.7B **Privately Held**
**WEB:** www.ritesystems.com
**SIC:** 2865 5169 Color pigments, organic; synthetic resins, rubber & plastic materials
**HQ:** Clariant Corporation
  4000 Monroe Rd
  Charlotte NC 28205
  704 331-7000

**(G-21766)**
**ROOSEVELT MOBILE**
60 W Roosevelt Rd (60185-3928)
PHONE .................... 630 293-7630
**EMP:** 3
**SALES (est):** 170K **Privately Held**
**SIC:** 1311 Crude Petroleum/Natural Gas Production

**(G-21767)**
**ROYAL CORINTHIAN INC**
603 Fenton Ln (60185-2671)
PHONE .................... 630 876-8899
**Fax:** 630 510-7241
Paul Savenok, *President*
Andy Savenok, *General Mgr*
Peter Savenok, *Vice Pres*
**EMP:** 25
**SALES (est):** 4MM **Privately Held**
**WEB:** www.royalcorinthian.com
**SIC:** 3272 Concrete stuctural support & building material

**(G-21768)**
**SANYO SEIKI AMERICA CORP**
333 Charles Ct Ste 105 (60185-2604)
PHONE .................... 630 876-8270
Koji Yamamae, *Branch Mgr*
**EMP:** 15
**SALES (corp-wide):** 11.4MM **Privately Held**
**SIC:** 3061 Mechanical rubber goods
**PA:** Sanyo Seiki Corporation
  125, Kaide
  Maniwa OKA 719-3
  867 524-936

**(G-21769)**
**SCHAFFER TOOL & DESIGN INC**
1320 W Washington St (60185-2655)
PHONE .................... 630 876-3800
Steven Schaffer, *President*
Michael Schaffer, *Mfg Dir*
**EMP:** 7
**SQ FT:** 12,000
**SALES:** 1.6MM **Privately Held**
**WEB:** www.schaffertool.com
**SIC:** 3549 Assembly machines, including robotic

**(G-21770)**
**SELROK INC**
1151 Atlantic Dr Ste 2 (60185-5166)
P.O. Box 48 (60186-0048)
PHONE .................... 630 876-8322
Stephanie Barkley, *Owner*
Charles Barkley, *Vice Pres*
**EMP:** 5

**SALES (est):** 688.7K **Privately Held**
**WEB:** www.selrok.com
**SIC:** 3589 Floor washing & polishing machines, commercial

**(G-21771)**
**SIEMENS INDUSTRY INC**
Engineered Products Division
1500 Harvester Rd (60185-1616)
John Carey, *Purchasing*
Karen Sporny, *Human Res Mgr*
John Deeter, *Marketing Mgr*
Karen Sanchez, *Marketing Mgr*
Terry Royer, *Branch Mgr*
**EMP:** 106
**SQ FT:** 35,000
**SALES (corp-wide):** 89.6B **Privately Held**
**WEB:** www.sea.siemens.com
**SIC:** 3625 3566 Motor control centers; speed changers, drives & gears
**HQ:** Siemens Industry, Inc.
  1000 Deerfield Pkwy
  Buffalo Grove IL 60089
  847 215-1000

**(G-21772)**
**SIGN A RAMA**
Also Called: Sign-A-Rama
946 N Neltnor Blvd # 114 (60185-5959)
PHONE .................... 630 293-7300
Don Infusino, *Owner*
**EMP:** 5
**SALES (est):** 409.2K **Privately Held**
**SIC:** 3993 5999 5099 Signs & advertising specialties; banners, flags, decals & posters; signs, except electric

**(G-21773)**
**SIMPSON STRONG-TIE COMPANY INC**
2505 Enterprise Cir (60185-9605)
PHONE .................... 630 293-2800
Alex Iniguez, *Branch Mgr*
**EMP:** 40
**SALES (corp-wide):** 860.6MM **Publicly Held**
**SIC:** 2891 Adhesives
**HQ:** Simpson Strong-Tie Company Inc.
  5956 W Las Positas Blvd
  Pleasanton CA 94588
  925 560-9000

**(G-21774)**
**SJ CONVERTING LLC**
1000 Atlantic Dr (60185-5101)
PHONE .................... 630 262-6640
Andres E Viloria, *Mng Member*
**EMP:** 4
**SALES (est):** 130K **Privately Held**
**SIC:** 3565 2621 Packaging machinery; paper mills

**(G-21775)**
**SONOCO PRODUCTS COMPANY**
1500 Powis Rd (60185-1646)
PHONE .................... 630 231-1489
**Fax:** 630 231-1168
John Lyon, *Materials Mgr*
Mark Whittingtonsteve Lutes, *Manager*
Andrew Suski, *Technology*
**EMP:** 80
**SALES (corp-wide):** 4.7B **Publicly Held**
**WEB:** www.sonoco.com
**SIC:** 2655 2653 2631 Fiber cans, drums & similar products; corrugated & solid fiber boxes; paperboard mills
**PA:** Sonoco Products Company
  1 N 2nd St
  Hartsville SC 29550
  843 383-7000

**(G-21776)**
**SPECTRUM MACHINING CO**
776 W Hawthorne Ln (60185-1968)
PHONE .................... 630 562-9400
Dave Bauer, *President*
Ken Jackson, *Manager*
**EMP:** 40
**SALES (est):** 3.5MM **Privately Held**
**SIC:** 3599 Machine shop, jobbing & repair

**(G-21777)**
**SUN PATTERN & MODEL INC**
505 Wegner Dr (60185-2626)
PHONE .................... 630 293-3366
**Fax:** 630 293-3365

## West Chicago - Dupage County (G-21778)

Dennis J Lee, *President*
Mary Lee, *Admin Sec*
**EMP:** 20
**SQ FT:** 25,000
**SALES (est):** 3MM **Privately Held**
**WEB:** www.sun-pattern.com
**SIC:** 3543 3999 3089 Industrial patterns; models, general, except toy; injection molded finished plastic products; injection molding of plastics

### (G-21778)
### TEMPRITE COMPANY
1555 W Hawthorne Ln 1e (60185-1809)
**PHONE** .................................. 630 293-5910
**Fax:** 630 293-9594
George Schmidt, *CEO*
Thomas Schmidt, *President*
John Canning, *Plant Mgr*
Fred Gerleve, *Opers Mgr*
Bill Degraf, *Engineer*
▲ **EMP:** 30
**SQ FT:** 12,000
**SALES (est):** 8MM **Privately Held**
**SIC:** 3822 3443 Air conditioning & refrigeration controls; fabricated plate work (boiler shop)

### (G-21779)
### TEXTRON AVIATION INC
2700 Intl Dr Ste 304 (60185-1658)
**PHONE** .................................. 630 443-5080
Ellen Stewart, *Branch Mgr*
**EMP:** 5
**SALES (corp-wide):** 13.7B **Publicly Held**
**SIC:** 3728 3721 5599 Aircraft parts & equipment; airplanes, fixed or rotary wing; research & development on aircraft by the manufacturer; aircraft dealers
**HQ:** Textron Aviation Inc.
1 Cessna Blvd
Wichita KS 67215
316 517-6000

### (G-21780)
### THERMAL-TECH SYSTEMS INC
1215 Atlantic Dr (60185-5165)
**PHONE** .................................. 630 639-5115
Monika Frary, *President*
Marian E Harmon, *Admin Sec*
**EMP:** 28
**SQ FT:** 25,000
**SALES (est):** 5.6MM **Privately Held**
**WEB:** www.thermal-tech.com
**SIC:** 3089 3545 Injection molding of plastics; machine tool accessories

### (G-21781)
### TNI PACKAGING INC
333 Charles Ct Ste 101 (60185-2604)
P.O. Box 577 (60186-0577)
**PHONE** .................................. 630 293-3030
Jerry J Marchese, *President*
▲ **EMP:** 6
**SQ FT:** 7,500
**SALES (est):** 375.7K **Privately Held**
**SIC:** 3089 3441 5199 Bands, plastic; fabricated structural metal; packaging materials

### (G-21782)
### TOMENSON MACHINE WORKS INC
1150 Powis Rd (60185-1664)
**PHONE** .................................. 630 377-7670
**Fax:** 630 377-7673
Scott T Roake, *President*
Ashley Piraino, *Purch Mgr*
Ted Kowalczyk, *Info Tech Mgr*
Jerry Blake, *Admin Sec*
**EMP:** 60 **EST:** 1976
**SALES (est):** 9.9MM **Privately Held**
**WEB:** www.tomenson.com
**SIC:** 3599 3594 Machine shop, jobbing & repair; fluid power pumps & motors

### (G-21783)
### TORNADO INDUSTRIES LLC
333 Charles Ct Ste 109 (60185-2604)
**PHONE** .................................. 817 551-6507
Michael D Schaffer, *President*
Gary V Cirone, *Admin Sec*
John Henry, *Representative*
▲ **EMP:** 53 **EST:** 1927
**SQ FT:** 88,000

**SALES (est):** 10MM
**SALES (corp-wide):** 183.7MM **Privately Held**
**WEB:** www.tacony.com
**SIC:** 3589 Vacuum cleaners & sweepers, electric: industrial; floor washing & polishing machines, commercial; carpet sweepers, except household electric vacuum sweepers
**PA:** Tacony Corporation
1760 Gilsinn Ln
Fenton MO 63026
636 349-3000

### (G-21784)
### TRAFFIC CONTROL & PROTECTION
31w 351 N Ave (60185)
**PHONE** .................................. 630 293-0026
**Fax:** 630 293-0029
Robert Chicoine, *President*
Paul M Chicoine, *President*
Marguerite Chicoine, *Vice Pres*
Denise Chicoine, *Sales Executive*
**EMP:** 32
**SQ FT:** 34,000
**SALES:** 25.3MM **Privately Held**
**SIC:** 3993 1611 7359 Signs & advertising specialties; highway & street sign installation; work zone traffic equipment (flags, cones, barrels, etc.)

### (G-21785)
### TREUDT CORPORATION
Also Called: West Chicago Printing Company
131 Fremont St (60185-1924)
**PHONE** .................................. 630 293-0500
**Fax:** 630 293-0588
W Bruce Treudt, *President*
Steve Treudt, *Vice Pres*
**EMP:** 9
**SQ FT:** 7,300
**SALES (est):** 1.2MM **Privately Held**
**SIC:** 2752 Lithographing on metal

### (G-21786)
### TURNER JCT PRTG & LITHO SVC
850 Meadowview Xing Ste 2 (60185-2576)
**PHONE** .................................. 630 293-1377
**Fax:** 630 293-1545
Craig A Bublitz, *President*
Scott Bublitz, *Vice Pres*
William S Bublitz, *Vice Pres*
Penny B Campbell, *Vice Pres*
Bonnie Bublitz, *Admin Sec*
**EMP:** 4
**SQ FT:** 2,500
**SALES:** 400K **Privately Held**
**SIC:** 2752 Lithographing on metal

### (G-21787)
### U S CONCEPTS INC
31w21 North Ave (60185)
**PHONE** .................................. 630 876-3110
Maria Niedbala, *President*
▲ **EMP:** 12
**SQ FT:** 10,000
**SALES:** 2MM **Privately Held**
**SIC:** 3549 5084 Metalworking machinery; woodworking machinery

### (G-21788)
### VATOR ACCESSORIES INC
1090 Atlantic Dr (60185-5101)
**PHONE** .................................. 630 876-8370
Lisa Grimes, *Principal*
Dave Davis, *Sales Staff*
◆ **EMP:** 2
**SALES (est):** 404.7K **Privately Held**
**SIC:** 3534 Elevators & equipment

### (G-21789)
### VEGA WAVE SYSTEMS INC
1275 W Roosevelt Rd # 104 (60185-4815)
**PHONE** .................................. 630 562-9433
Alan Sugg, *President*
Alan R Sugg, *President*
**EMP:** 4
**SALES (est):** 642K **Privately Held**
**WEB:** www.vegawave.com
**SIC:** 3674 Semiconductors & related devices

### (G-21790)
### VISCO ELECTRIC LLC
3n75 Woodcreek Ln (60185)
**PHONE** .................................. 630 336-7824
Albert M Viscogliosi, *Principal*
**EMP:** 4
**SALES (est):** 478.8K **Privately Held**
**SIC:** 3699 Electrical equipment & supplies

### (G-21791)
### VORIS COMMUNICATION CO INC
399 Wegner Dr (60185-2673)
**PHONE** .................................. 630 231-2425
Henry Tews Jr, *President*
**EMP:** 80
**SALES (corp-wide):** 26.3MM **Privately Held**
**SIC:** 2759 5199 2752 7379 Flexographic printing; advertising specialties; commercial printing, offset; ; mailing service
**PA:** The Voris Communication Company Inc
5656 Mcdermott Dr
Berkeley IL 60163
630 898-4268

### (G-21792)
### WES TECH PRINTING GRAPHIC
1555 W Hawthorne Ln (60185-1809)
**PHONE** .................................. 630 520-9041
Barbara Doyle, *Owner*
**EMP:** 4
**SALES (est):** 200K **Privately Held**
**SIC:** 2759 Commercial printing

### (G-21793)
### WISE PLASTICS TECHNOLOGIES INC
1601 W Hawthorne Ln (60185-1823)
**PHONE** .................................. 847 697-2840
**EMP:** 4 **EST:** 2015
**SALES (est):** 146.9K **Privately Held**
**SIC:** 3089 Plastics products

---

## West Dundee
### *Kane County*

### (G-21794)
### 144 INTERNATIONAL INC
740 S 8th St (60118-2102)
P.O. Box 178, Elgin (60121-0178)
**PHONE** .................................. 847 426-8881
David Perlman, *President*
Sandra Perlman, *Vice Pres*
**EMP:** 12
**SQ FT:** 1,200
**SALES (est):** 1.1MM **Privately Held**
**SIC:** 3915 Diamond cutting & polishing

### (G-21795)
### D&M PERLMAN FINE JWLY GIFT LLC
740 S 8th St (60118-2102)
**PHONE** .................................. 847 426-8881
**Fax:** 847 428-8465
David Perlman,
**EMP:** 5
**SQ FT:** 7,500
**SALES (est):** 440K **Privately Held**
**SIC:** 5944 3911 Jewelry, precious stones & precious metals; jewelry, precious metal

### (G-21796)
### EMMETTS TAVERN & BREWING CO (PA)
128 W Main St (60118-2017)
**PHONE** .................................. 847 428-4500
**Fax:** 847 428-4545
Andrew Burns, *President*
Timothy Burns, *Vice Pres*
Rob Kwiatek, *Executive*
**EMP:** 48
**SQ FT:** 16,000
**SALES (est):** 3MM **Privately Held**
**WEB:** www.emmettstavern.com
**SIC:** 5812 2082 5182 Chicken restaurant; beer (alcoholic beverage); wine & distilled beverages

### (G-21797)
### HAEGER INDUSTRIES INC (PA)
Also Called: Haeger Potteries Div
510 Market Loop Ste 104 (60118-2139)
**PHONE** .................................. 847 426-3441
**Fax:** 847 426-8108
Alexandra Haeger Estes, *CEO*
Craig S Zachrich, *COO*
Terry Rosborough, *VP Mfg*
Robert B Snyder, *CFO*
Diane Otteman, *Accountant*
▲ **EMP:** 62 **EST:** 1871
**SQ FT:** 220,000
**SALES (est):** 19.5MM **Privately Held**
**WEB:** www.haegerpotteries.com
**SIC:** 3269 Pottery household articles, except kitchen articles; pottery florists' articles

### (G-21798)
### JEWEL OSCO INC
1250 W Main St (60118-1902)
**PHONE** .................................. 847 428-3547
**Fax:** 847 428-0227
Glenn Paulson, *Manager*
**EMP:** 125
**SALES (corp-wide):** 58.8B **Privately Held**
**WEB:** www.jewelosco.com
**SIC:** 5411 5421 2051 Supermarkets, chain; meat & fish markets; bread, cake & related products
**HQ:** Jewel Osco, Inc.
150 E Pierce Rd Ste 200
Itasca IL 60143
630 948-6000

### (G-21799)
### KEY ONE GRAPHICS SERVICES INC
89 W Main St Ste 102 (60118-2053)
P.O. Box 59438, Schaumburg (60159-0438)
**PHONE**
Beverly Witcher, *President*
Vernon Witcher, *Vice Pres*
**EMP:** 7
**SQ FT:** 1,500
**SALES (est):** 500K **Privately Held**
**WEB:** www.keyonegraphics.com
**SIC:** 2791 7336 2741 2721 Typesetting; commercial art & graphic design; miscellaneous publishing; periodicals

### (G-21800)
### MANGOLD NETWORKS
514 S 1st St (60118-2904)
**PHONE** .................................. 224 402-0068
Joshua Mangold, *Principal*
**EMP:** 3
**SALES (est):** 110K **Privately Held**
**SIC:** 2011 Meat packing plants

### (G-21801)
### POLY-RESYN INC
518 Market Loop Ste A (60118-2182)
**PHONE** .................................. 847 428-4031
**Fax:** 847 428-0305
Robert Schreurs, *President*
Sharen J Schreurs, *Admin Sec*
Jeff Schreurs, *Administration*
Karen Schaden,
**EMP:** 10
**SALES (est):** 2MM **Privately Held**
**WEB:** www.polyresyn.com
**SIC:** 2821 Plastics materials & resins

### (G-21802)
### STITCH MAGIC USA INC
785 S 8th St (60118-2108)
**PHONE** .................................. 847 836-5000
**Fax:** 847 836-5500
Dan Denk, *Treasurer*
Larry Zenger, *Admin Sec*
**EMP:** 20
**SQ FT:** 2,800
**SALES (est):** 1.7MM **Privately Held**
**WEB:** www.stitch-magic.com
**SIC:** 2395 Emblems, embroidered; embroidery products, except schiffli machine

### (G-21803)
### WATERS INDUSTRIES INC
Also Called: Panthervision
213 W Main St (60118-2018)
**PHONE** .................................. 847 783-5900
Michael A Waters, *President*
Betsy Grutzmacher, *Sales Staff*

# GEOGRAPHIC SECTION

Augie Hinnenkamp, *Sales Staff*
Stacie Woltman, *Sales Staff*
Chris Sourwine, *Sales Associate*
▲ **EMP:** 30
**SQ FT:** 2,000
**SALES (est)**: 6.5MM **Privately Held**
**SIC:** 3851 3229 Ophthalmic goods; pressed & blown glass

## West Frankfort
### Franklin County

**(G-21804)**
**BIT BROKERS INTERNATIONAL LTD**
5568 Logan Rd (62896-4317)
P.O. Box 100, Logan (62856-0100)
**PHONE**..................618 435-5811
Fax: 618 435-2388
Tim Thomas, *President*
Annette Borgra, *Sales Staff*
Zach Peebels, *VP Mktg*
▲ **EMP:** 7
**SQ FT:** 7,500
**SALES:** 2MM **Privately Held**
**WEB:** www.bitbrokers.com
**SIC:** 5084 3423 Drilling bits; hammers (hand tools)

**(G-21805)**
**BUDMARK OIL COMPANY INC**
106 E Oak St (62896-2741)
**PHONE**..................618 937-2495
Fax: 618 937-2496
Jim Dunston, *President*
Judy Dunston, *Corp Secy*
**EMP:** 9
**SQ FT:** 4,000
**SALES:** 500K **Privately Held**
**SIC:** 1311 Crude petroleum production

**(G-21806)**
**DIXIE CREAM DONUT SHOP**
510 W Main St (62896-2231)
**PHONE**..................618 937-4866
Eugene Forgatch, *Owner*
Kimberly Fitzwater, *Manager*
**EMP:** 20
**SQ FT:** 2,000
**SALES (est):** 711.3K **Privately Held**
**SIC:** 5461 2051 Doughnuts; charlotte russe, bakery product: except frozen

**(G-21807)**
**FIELDERS CHOICE**
708 S Logan St (62896-2636)
**PHONE**..................618 937-2294
Fax: 618 932-8054
Carl Harris, *Owner*
Ann Harris, *Partner*
Max Lude, *Partner*
Sharon Lude, *Partner*
◆ **EMP:** 6
**SQ FT:** 1,800
**SALES:** 200K **Privately Held**
**SIC:** 5611 5947 5999 5699 Clothing, sportswear, men's & boys'; hats, men's & boys'; trading cards: baseball or other sports, entertainment, etc.; trophies & plaques; sports apparel; embroidery & art needlework

**(G-21808)**
**FREEDOM MATERIAL RESOURCES INC**
1186 State Highway 37 (62896-5005)
P.O. Box 248 (62896-0248)
**PHONE**..................618 937-6415
Robert Orr, *President*
Paul Farkas, *Sales Mgr*
**EMP:** 60
**SALES (est):** 10.6MM **Privately Held**
**SIC:** 3532 Mining machinery

**(G-21809)**
**GATEHOUSE MEDIA LLC**
Also Called: Daily American, The
111 S Emma St (62896-2729)
P.O. Box 617 (62896-0617)
**PHONE**..................618 937-2850
Fax: 618 932-2277
Scott Carr, *General Mgr*
**EMP:** 40

**SALES (corp-wide):** 1.2B **Publicly Held**
**WEB:** www.gatehousemedia.com
**SIC:** 2711 Newspapers, publishing & printing
**HQ:** Gatehouse Media, Llc
175 Sullys Trl Ste 300
Pittsford NY 14534
585 598-0030

**(G-21810)**
**KINSMAN ENTERPRISES INC**
10804 Mark Twain Rd (62896-4105)
**PHONE**..................618 932-3838
Fax: 618 932-8851
Ernest M Hanners, *President*
Judy Hanners, *Vice Pres*
Rick Hanners, *Vice Pres*
▲ **EMP:** 8
**SQ FT:** 4,000
**SALES (est):** 1.2MM **Privately Held**
**WEB:** www.kinsmanenterprises.com
**SIC:** 2599 3842 2531 Hospital furniture, except beds; surgical appliances & supplies; public building & related furniture

**(G-21811)**
**LEISURE PROPERTIES LLC**
Also Called: Crownline Boats
11884 Country Club Rd (62896-5064)
**PHONE**..................618 937-6426
Fax: 618 932-3426
Scott Lahrman, *President*
Larry Carter, *Purchasing*
Guy Coons, *CFO*
Celeste Higgins, *Human Resources*
Anthony Zielinski, *Mng Member*
▼ **EMP:** 550
**SQ FT:** 250,000
**SALES (est):** 163.6MM **Privately Held**
**WEB:** www.teamcrownline.com
**SIC:** 3732 Boats, fiberglass: building & repairing

**(G-21812)**
**LIBERTY GROUP PUBLISHING**
111 S Emma St (62896-2729)
P.O. Box 617 (62896-0617)
**PHONE**..................618 937-2850
Mary Mocaby, *Bookkeeper*
**EMP:** 5
**SALES (corp-wide):** 1.6MM **Privately Held**
**WEB:** www.geneseorepublic.com
**SIC:** 2711 Newspapers
**PA:** Liberty Group Publishing
108 W 1st St
Geneseo IL 61254
309 944-1779

**(G-21813)**
**LITTLE EGYPT GAS A & WLDG SUPS**
Also Called: A A A Cylinder
10603 Bencie Ln (62896-4716)
**PHONE**..................618 937-2271
Susan Collins, *President*
Bill Collins, *Vice Pres*
George Collins, *Vice Pres*
**EMP:** 3
**SALES:** 1MM **Privately Held**
**SIC:** 3714 5169 Cylinder heads, motor vehicle; oxygen

**(G-21814)**
**MILES BROS**
1000 S Jefferson St (62896-3313)
**PHONE**..................618 937-4115
Lisa King, *Principal*
**EMP:** 3
**SALES (est):** 335.2K **Privately Held**
**SIC:** 3556 Meat processing machinery

**(G-21815)**
**R&R RACING OF PALM BEACH INC**
15942 Mine 25 Rd Ste 28 (62896-5327)
**PHONE**..................618 937-6767
Brett Ray, *President*
Patty Ray, *Corp Secy*
**EMP:** 2
**SALES (est):** 238.2K **Privately Held**
**WEB:** www.r-r-racing.com
**SIC:** 3365 Aluminum foundries

**(G-21816)**
**RAYTECH MACHINING FABRICATION**
10925 Mainline Rd (62896-4293)
**PHONE**..................618 932-2511
Fax: 618 932-2759
Ray Measimer, *President*
Tim Liefer, *Engineer*
**EMP:** 20
**SQ FT:** 19,000
**SALES (est):** 2.5MM **Privately Held**
**SIC:** 2821 Plasticizer/additive based plastic materials

**(G-21817)**
**ROE MACHINE INC**
12725 Union Rd (62896)
P.O. Box 531 (62896-0531)
**PHONE**..................618 983-5524
Fax: 618 983-8390
Willard Strain, *CEO*
Jeff Kirby, *Principal*
Darla Strain, *Admin Sec*
**EMP:** 27
**SQ FT:** 8,000
**SALES (est):** 4.4MM **Privately Held**
**SIC:** 3599 3532 Machine shop, jobbing & repair; mining machinery

**(G-21818)**
**SANDNER ELECTRIC CO INC**
903 E Saint Louis St (62896-1448)
P.O. Box 158 (62896-0158)
**PHONE**..................618 932-2179
Harold Chase, *President*
Charles Lintner Sr, *Vice Pres*
**EMP:** 5 EST: 1934
**SQ FT:** 13,250
**SALES (est):** 330K **Privately Held**
**SIC:** 7694 5063 Electric motor repair; motors, electric

**(G-21819)**
**SIMPLE SOLUTIONS**
110 E Main St (62896-2430)
**PHONE**..................618 932-6177
Fax: 618 932-6177
Tim Grigsby, *Owner*
**EMP:** 3
**SQ FT:** 2,000
**SALES (est):** 253.9K **Privately Held**
**SIC:** 2741 2752 Miscellaneous publishing; commercial printing, offset

**(G-21820)**
**SPECIAL MINE SERVICES INC (PA)**
11782 Country Club Rd (62896-5037)
P.O. Box 188 (62896-0188)
**PHONE**..................618 937-2715
Fax: 618 932-2715
Dwayne Coffey, *President*
Steve Kissinger, *President*
**EMP:** 55
**SQ FT:** 33,000
**SALES:** 11MM **Privately Held**
**WEB:** www.smsconnectors.com
**SIC:** 3643 5063 Connectors & terminals for electrical devices; electrical apparatus & equipment

**(G-21821)**
**TWIN MILLS TIMBER & TIE CO INC**
3268 State Highway 37 (62896-4291)
P.O. Box 34 (62896-0034)
**PHONE**..................618 932-3662
Fax: 618 932-3662
Fred Wilson, *President*
Keith Wilson, *Admin Sec*
**EMP:** 22
**SALES (est):** 4.4MM **Privately Held**
**SIC:** 3537 Platforms, stands, tables, pallets & similar equipment

## West Peoria
### Peoria County

**(G-21822)**
**H&H CRUSHING INC**
2401 W Rhodora Ave (61604-3826)
**PHONE**..................309 275-0643

**EMP:** 3
**SALES (est):** 183.8K **Privately Held**
**SIC:** 1422 Crushed & broken limestone

**(G-21823)**
**KOENIG BODY & EQUIPMENT INC**
2428 W Farmington Rd (61604-5099)
**PHONE**..................309 673-7435
Fax: 309 673-6836
Mark Koenig, *President*
Richard Picton, *Accounts Mgr*
Cristy Scell, *Manager*
**EMP:** 22
**SQ FT:** 2,800
**SALES:** 5MM **Privately Held**
**WEB:** www.koenigbody.com
**SIC:** 3711 5012 Snow plows (motor vehicles), assembly of; truck bodies

## West Salem
### Edwards County

**(G-21824)**
**RODGERS BILL OIL MIN BITS SVC**
Also Called: Bill Rodgers Drlg & Producing
20226 Wabash 20 Ave (62476-3012)
**PHONE**..................618 299-7771
Bill Rodgers, *Owner*
Jenny Rodgers, *Manager*
**EMP:** 4
**SALES:** 300K **Privately Held**
**SIC:** 5084 1381 1311 Drilling bits; drilling oil & gas wells; crude petroleum & natural gas

**(G-21825)**
**WEST SALEM KNOX COUNTY HTCHY**
Also Called: George's Farm Supply
615 W Church St (62476-1258)
**PHONE**..................618 456-3601
Dince Goodwin, *President*
**EMP:** 5 EST: 1957
**SALES (est):** 50K **Privately Held**
**SIC:** 5999 2452 Farm equipment & supplies; artists' supplies & materials; fire extinguishers; farm & agricultural buildings, prefabricated wood

## West Union
### Clark County

**(G-21826)**
**FORESTECH WOOD PRODUCTS**
204 W Washington St (62477-1025)
**PHONE**..................217 279-3659
Steve Shawler, *Owner*
Corolyn Shawler, *Manager*
**EMP:** 4 EST: 1971
**SALES:** 250K **Privately Held**
**SIC:** 2421 Sawmills & planing mills, general

## Westchester
### Cook County

**(G-21827)**
**AABLE LICENSE CONSULTANTS**
1938 S Mannheim Rd (60154-4323)
P.O. Box 7460 (60154-7460)
**PHONE**..................708 836-1235
Fax: 708 836-1242
Gary F Leiss, *President*
Sharon Leiss, *Corp Secy*
**EMP:** 9
**SQ FT:** 1,300
**SALES:** 1.2MM **Privately Held**
**SIC:** 3469 Automobile license tags, stamped metal

# Westchester - Cook County (G-21828)

## (G-21828)
**AIRBUS DS COMMUNICATIONS INC**
10330 W Roosevelt Rd # 205 (60154-2571)
**PHONE**..................708 450-1911
**EMP:** 4
**SALES (corp-wide):** 69.2B **Privately Held**
**WEB:** www.peinc.com
**SIC:** 3661 Telephone & telegraph apparatus
**HQ:** Airbus Ds Communications, Inc.
42505 Rio Nedo
Temecula CA 92590
951 719-2100

## (G-21829)
**AMERICAN IMAGING MGT INC**
2 Westbrook Ct Ste 800 (60154)
**PHONE**..................708 236-8500
Brandon W Cady, *President*
**EMP:** 20
**SALES (corp-wide):** 84.8B **Publicly Held**
**SIC:** 3841 Diagnostic apparatus, medical
**HQ:** American Imaging Management, Inc.
8600 W Bryn Mawr Ave 800s
Chicago IL 60631
773 864-4600

## (G-21830)
**BDI ENTERPRISES**
9825 W Roosevelt Rd (60154-2747)
**PHONE**..................773 354-6433
Melichisa Boss, *Co-Owner*
**EMP:** 3
**SQ FT:** 1,000
**SALES (est):** 274.8K **Privately Held**
**SIC:** 2844 Shampoos, rinses, conditioners: hair; tonics, hair

## (G-21831)
**BRAINLAB INC**
5 Westbrook Corp Ctr (60154-5749)
**PHONE**..................800 784-7700
**Fax:** 708 409-1619
Stefan Vilsmeier, *CEO*
Sean Clark, *President*
Isabelle Doll, *General Mgr*
Chris Kemp, *Regional Mgr*
Matt Sardo, *Regional Mgr*
▲ **EMP:** 227
**SALES (est):** 180.4MM
**SALES (corp-wide):** 303.5MM **Privately Held**
**WEB:** www.brainlab.com
**SIC:** 5047 3841 Medical equipment & supplies; surgical & medical instruments
**PA:** Brainlab Ag
Olof-Palme-Str. 9
Munchen 81829
899 915-680

## (G-21832)
**CHIPITA AMERICA INC (HQ)**
1 Westbrook Corporate Ctr (60154-5701)
**PHONE**..................708 731-2434
George Chalkias, *CEO*
Antonios Pouftis, *CFO*
Tina Holden, *Manager*
▲ **EMP:** 20
**SQ FT:** 3,000
**SALES (est):** 43MM
**SALES (corp-wide):** 111.1MM **Privately Held**
**SIC:** 5461 2052 2096 5145 Bakeries; cookies & crackers; cookies; biscuits, dry; potato chips & similar snacks; confectionery; snack foods; groceries & related products; crackers, cookies & bakery products; cookies
**PA:** Chipita S.A.
Athinon - Lamias National Rd (12th Km)
Metamorfosi 14452
210 288-5000

## (G-21833)
**CLARICH MOLD CORP**
10119 W Roosevelt Rd (60154-2643)
**PHONE**..................708 865-8120
**Fax:** 708 865-8277
John M Buenger, *President*
Mike Province, *Vice Pres*
Liz Wilson, *Office Mgr*
**EMP:** 15
**SQ FT:** 9,500
**SALES (est):** 3.2MM **Privately Held**
**WEB:** www.clarich.com
**SIC:** 2821 Molding compounds, plastics; polyimides (skybond, kaplon)

## (G-21834)
**CML TECHNOLOGIES INC**
10330 W Roosevelt Rd # 205 (60154-2564)
**PHONE**..................708 450-1911
**Fax:** 708 540-1975
Marty Deleonardis, *President*
Robert Palm, *Vice Pres*
**EMP:** 3 **EST:** 1990
**SALES (est):** 331.9K **Privately Held**
**SIC:** 3661 Telephone & telegraph apparatus

## (G-21835)
**COMMSCOPE TECHNOLOGIES LLC (DH)**
4 Westbrook Corporate Ctr (60154-5752)
**PHONE**..................708 236-6600
**Fax:** 708 492-3898
Eddie Edwards, *President*
Tom Gravely, *President*
Frank B Wyatt II, *Principal*
Patrick Andrew, *COO*
Justin C Choi, *Senior VP*
◆ **EMP:** 1200
**SALES (est):** 2.2B **Publicly Held**
**WEB:** www.andrew.com
**SIC:** 3663 3357 3679 3812 Microwave communication equipment; antennas, transmitting & communications; television antennas (transmitting) & ground equipment; receiver-transmitter units (transceiver); communication wire; coaxial cable, nonferrous; waveguides & fittings; search & navigation equipment; radar systems & equipment; electrical equipment & supplies
**HQ:** Commscope, Inc. Of North Carolina
1100 Commscope Pl Se
Hickory NC 28602
828 324-2200

## (G-21836)
**COMPRESSED AIR ADVISORS INC**
11038 Martindale Dr (60154-4918)
**PHONE**..................877 247-2381
Craig Parmele, *CEO*
Lindsay Parmele, *Admin Sec*
**EMP:** 3
**SALES:** 75K **Privately Held**
**SIC:** 5084 7699 3563 Compressors, except air conditioning; compressor repair; air & gas compressors including vacuum pumps

## (G-21837)
**CROWN KANDY ENTERPRISE LTD**
Also Called: Crown Kandy Publishing
1127 S Mannheim Rd # 313 (60154-2570)
**PHONE**..................708 580-6494
Latoya M White, *CEO*
Antonio Ward, *Business Mgr*
Shyreeta Benbow, *Vice Pres*
Tammarah Silmon, *CFO*
**EMP:** 10
**SALES (est):** 321.4K **Privately Held**
**SIC:** 2731 Books: publishing & printing

## (G-21838)
**DRUG SOURCE COMPANY LLC**
1 Westbrook Corporate Ctr (60154-5701)
**PHONE**..................708 236-1768
Gary Doten, *Director*
Helen Anderson, *Director*
Catherine Qian, *Director*
**EMP:** 7
**SALES (est):** 955.3K **Privately Held**
**WEB:** www.drugsourceco.com
**SIC:** 2834 Pharmaceutical preparations

## (G-21839)
**ELPAC ELECTRONICS INC**
Also Called: Elpac Components
4 Westbrook Corporate Ctr # 900 (60154-5724)
**PHONE**..................708 316-4407
Marshall Wright, *COO*
▲ **EMP:** 189
**SQ FT:** 62,000
**SALES (est):** 11.5MM **Privately Held**
**WEB:** www.elpac.com
**SIC:** 3629 3679 3675 Capacitors, a.c., for motors or fluorescent lamp ballasts; power supplies, all types: static; electronic capacitors
**PA:** Inventus Power, Inc.
1200 Internationale Pkwy
Woodridge IL 60517

## (G-21840)
**ESSENTRA INTERNATIONAL LLC (HQ)**
2 Westbrook Corp Ctr # 200 (60154-5718)
**PHONE**..................866 800-0775
Scott Baum, *Manager*
Warren Bell, *Manager*
Brett York, *Manager*
**EMP:** 7
**SALES (est):** 176.1MM
**SALES (corp-wide):** 1.2B **Privately Held**
**SIC:** 2891 Adhesives & sealants
**PA:** Essentra Plc
201-249 Avebury Boulevard
Milton Keynes BUCKS MK9 1
190 835-9100

## (G-21841)
**ESSENTRA PACKAGING US INC (DH)**
2 Westbrook Corp Ctr (60154-5702)
**PHONE**..................704 418-8692
Brett J York, *President*
Kevin Friel, *Accountant*
◆ **EMP:** 5
**SALES (est):** 176.5MM
**SALES (corp-wide):** 1.2B **Privately Held**
**SIC:** 2673 2621 2752 8741 Plastic bags: made from purchased materials; business form paper; commercial printing, lithographic; management services
**HQ:** Essentra International Llc
2 Westbrook Corp Ctr # 200
Westchester IL 60154
866 800-0775

## (G-21842)
**H3 LIFE SCIENCE CORPORATION**
1 Westbrook Corporate Ctr (60154-5701)
**PHONE**..................708 705-1299
Gary R Doten, *COO*
**EMP:** 15
**SALES (est):** 1.1MM **Privately Held**
**SIC:** 2834 Pharmaceutical preparations

## (G-21843)
**IFPRA INC**
1127 S Mannheim Rd # 203 (60154-2562)
**PHONE**..................708 410-0100
Kimberly Raslison, *President*
**EMP:** 6
**SALES (est):** 470K **Privately Held**
**SIC:** 2731 Pamphlets: publishing & printing

## (G-21844)
**ILLINI PRECAST LLC**
2255 Entp Dr Ste 5501 (60154)
**PHONE**..................708 562-7700
Craig Wagenbach, *Principal*
Deb Messa, *Manager*
Ming King, *Manager*
**EMP:** 14
**SALES (est):** 3.1MM **Privately Held**
**SIC:** 3272 Precast terrazo or concrete products

## (G-21845)
**INGREDION INCORPORATED (PA)**
5 Westbrook Corporate Ctr # 500 (60154-5795)
**PHONE**..................708 551-2600
**Fax:** 708 551-2700
Ilene S Gordon, *Ch of Bd*
Anthony P Delio, *Senior VP*
Robert Stefansic, *Senior VP*
Robert Kee, *Vice Pres*
Stephen K Latreille, *Vice Pres*
◆ **EMP:** 800 **EST:** 1906
**SALES:** 5.7B **Publicly Held**
**WEB:** www.cornproducts.com
**SIC:** 2046 Wet corn milling; corn starch; corn oil products; corn sugars & syrups

## (G-21846)
**KW PRECAST LLC**
2255 Entp Dr Ste 1510 (60154)
**PHONE**..................708 562-7700
Debra Massa, *Accounting Mgr*
Raig R Wagenbach, *President*
**EMP:** 12
**SALES (est):** 2.3MM **Privately Held**
**SIC:** 3272 4789 Precast terrazo or concrete products; pipeline terminal facilities, independently operated

## (G-21847)
**LITT ALUMINIUM & SHTMTL CO**
9825 W Roosevelt Rd (60154-2747)
**PHONE**..................708 366-4720
Erich W Little, *President*
**EMP:** 7
**SQ FT:** 1,800
**SALES:** 600K **Privately Held**
**SIC:** 3444 Siding, sheet metal

## (G-21848)
**LORENZO FROZEN FOODS LTD**
Also Called: Fifth Ave Provision
9940 W Roosevelt Rd (60154-2760)
P.O. Box 7397 (60154-7397)
**PHONE**..................708 343-7670
Anthony Carmignani, *President*
Jorge Ayala, *Director*
Bill Gioia, *Director*
Terry Richardson, *Director*
Ellen Carmignani, *Admin Sec*
**EMP:** 9 **EST:** 1936
**SQ FT:** 6,000
**SALES (est):** 1MM **Privately Held**
**SIC:** 2013 2038 5142 Beef stew from purchased meat; pizza, frozen; packaged frozen goods

## (G-21849)
**MATERIAL SERVICE CORPORATION**
2235 Entp Dr Ste 3504 (60154)
**PHONE**..................708 447-1100
**Fax:** 708 442-0294
Don Stewart, *Principal*
**EMP:** 35
**SALES (corp-wide):** 16B **Privately Held**
**WEB:** www.materialservice.com
**SIC:** 3281 1442 Stone, quarrying & processing of own stone products; construction sand & gravel
**HQ:** Material Service Corporation
2235 Entp Dr Ste 3504
Westchester IL 60154
708 731-2600

## (G-21850)
**MATERIAL SERVICE CORPORATION (DH)**
Also Called: Hanson Material Service
2235 Entp Dr Ste 3504 (60154)
**PHONE**..................708 731-2600
Gerald Nagel, *President*
Dennis Dolan, *President*
Michael Stanczak, *President*
David Ruben, *Counsel*
Walter Serwa, *CFO*
**EMP:** 200
**SQ FT:** 80,000
**SALES (est):** 151.1MM
**SALES (corp-wide):** 16B **Privately Held**
**WEB:** www.materialservice.com
**SIC:** 1422 1442 Crushed & broken limestone; construction sand mining; gravel mining
**HQ:** Hanson Aggregates Llc
8505 Freport Pkwy Ste 500
Irving TX 75063
469 417-1200

## (G-21851)
**NEXERGY TAUBER LLC**
4 Westbrook Corp Ctr 90 (60154-5752)
**PHONE**..................708 316-4407
Stephen McClure, *President*
Joseph Italiano, *CFO*
**EMP:** 837
**SALES (est):** 33.3MM **Privately Held**
**SIC:** 3629 Battery chargers, rectifying or nonrotating
**PA:** Inventus Power, Inc.
1200 Internationale Pkwy
Woodridge IL 60517

# GEOGRAPHIC SECTION

**(G-21852)**
**P P GRAPHICS INC**
Also Called: Minuteman Press
1939 S Mannheim Rd  (60154-4322)
PHONE.................................708 343-2530
Fax: 708 343-2382
Paul Gangi, *President*
Michele Caron, *Engineer*
EMP: 3
SQ FT: 1,200
SALES (est): 451.2K  **Privately Held**
SIC: 2752  2791  2789  Commercial printing, lithographic; typesetting; bookbinding & related work

**(G-21853)**
**RUTKE SIGNS INC**
Also Called: Rutke Signs and Safety
1 Westbrook Corporate Ctr # 300 (60154-5701)
PHONE.................................708 841-6464
Julia Rutke, *President*
Robert Rutke Sr, *Vice Pres*
EMP: 3
SQ FT: 1,500
SALES: 500K  **Privately Held**
WEB: www.rutkesigns.com
SIC: 7389  3993  5999  Sign painting & lettering shop; signs & advertising specialties; safety supplies & equipment

**(G-21854)**
**SHERWIN-WILLIAMS COMPANY**
10551 W Cermak Rd  (60154-5222)
PHONE.................................708 409-4728
EMP: 3
SALES (corp-wide): 11.8B  **Publicly Held**
SIC: 5231  5198  2851  Paint & painting supplies; paints, varnishes & supplies; wood fillers or sealers
PA: The Sherwin-Williams Company
101 W Prospect Ave # 1020
Cleveland OH 44115
216 566-2000

**(G-21855)**
**SPARROW COFFEE ROASTERY**
10330 W Roosevelt Rd # 200 (60154-2571)
PHONE.................................321 648-6415
EMP: 5
SALES (corp-wide): 1.5MM  **Privately Held**
SIC: 2095  2099  Mfg Roasted Coffee Mfg Food Preparations
PA: Sparrow Coffee Roastery
1201 W Lake St Ste 2
Chicago IL

**(G-21856)**
**SUPERIOR ONE ELECTRIC INC**
1212 Gardner Rd  (60154-3716)
PHONE.................................630 655-3300
Gina Spata, *President*
EMP: 2
SALES (est): 375.1K  **Privately Held**
SIC: 1731  3699  General electrical contractor; electrical equipment & supplies

**(G-21857)**
**SYNERGY MECHANICAL INC**
9835 Derby Ln  (60154-3707)
P.O. Box 765, Hillside  (60162-0765)
PHONE.................................708 410-1004
Mike Descourouez, *President*
EMP: 5
SQ FT: 1,500
SALES (est): 437.5K  **Privately Held**
SIC: 1711  3444  Heating & air conditioning contractors; ducts, sheet metal

**(G-21858)**
**TNP MACHINERY CO INC**
9860 Derby Ln  (60154-3746)
PHONE.................................708 344-7750
Nick Belcin, *President*
Dennis A Parker, *Finance Other*
EMP: 6
SQ FT: 3,000
SALES: 750K  **Privately Held**
WEB: www.tnpmachine.com
SIC: 3599  Machine shop, jobbing & repair

**(G-21859)**
**TROTTIE PUBLISHING GROUP INC**
Also Called: West Suburban Journal News
9930 Derby Ln Ste 102  (60154-3770)
PHONE.................................708 344-5975
L Nicole Trottie, *Publisher*
EMP: 3  EST: 2011
SALES (est): 130.9K  **Privately Held**
SIC: 2741  Miscellaneous publishing

**(G-21860)**
**TY MILES INCORPORATED**
9855 Derby Ln  (60154-3792)
PHONE.................................708 344-5480
Fax: 708 344-0437
Steve Mueller, *President*
Raymond A Mueller, *Corp Secy*
Joseph McClearn, *Manager*
Phil Klos, *Data Proc Dir*
Rick Shea, *Technology*
EMP: 25
SQ FT: 18,000
SALES (est): 5.8MM  **Privately Held**
WEB: www.tymiles.com
SIC: 3541  3549  Machine tools, metal cutting type; metalworking machinery

**(G-21861)**
**USMSS INC**
2428 Pinecrest Ln  (60154-5944)
PHONE.................................708 409-9010
George Fleming, *Manager*
Bill Dow, *Exec Dir*
EMP: 2
SALES (est): 229.6K  **Privately Held**
SIC: 2759  Screen printing

## Western Springs
### Cook County

**(G-21862)**
**AALBORG COMPANY**
4521 Harvey Ave  (60558-1648)
PHONE.................................708 246-8858
James Larsen, *President*
Mary Larsen, *Admin Sec*
EMP: 3
SALES (est): 353.5K  **Privately Held**
SIC: 3821  Ovens, laboratory

**(G-21863)**
**ARC MOBILE LLC**
3944 Johnson Ave  (60558-1139)
PHONE.................................201 838-3410
Tyler Mendoza, *CEO*
Jimmy Dagher, *COO*
Joe Wroblewski, *Chief Engr*
EMP: 10  EST: 2012
SALES (est): 542.7K  **Privately Held**
SIC: 7372  7389  Application computer software;

**(G-21864)**
**ATLAS MATCH LLC**
5009 Lawn Ave  (60558-1821)
PHONE.................................815 469-2314
Jonathan Bradley, *Branch Mgr*
EMP: 59
SALES (corp-wide): 14.6MM  **Privately Held**
SIC: 3999  Matches & match books
PA: Atlas Match, L.L.C.
1801 S Airport Cir
Euless TX 76040
817 267-1500

**(G-21865)**
**CERTIFIED POLYMERS INC**
4479 Lawn Ave  (60558-2431)
P.O. Box 102  (60558-0102)
PHONE.................................630 515-0007
Gary C Kompare, *President*
EMP: 7
SALES (est): 1.7MM  **Privately Held**
SIC: 5162  3089  Plastics materials & basic shapes; synthetic resin finished products

**(G-21866)**
**DADO LIGHTING LLC**
4700 Gilbert Ave 47-217  (60558-1753)
PHONE.................................877 323-6584
EMP: 6  EST: 2015
SQ FT: 5,000
SALES: 700K  **Privately Held**
SIC: 3646  5063  Mfg Commercial Lighting Fixtures Whol Electrical Equipment

**(G-21867)**
**IMPACT TECHNOLOGIES INC**
Also Called: Intermodal Live
4521 Grand Ave  (60558-1546)
PHONE.................................708 246-5041
EMP: 4
SQ FT: 900
SALES: 1MM  **Privately Held**
SIC: 8741  7371  7372  Administrative management; computer software development; business oriented computer software

**(G-21868)**
**INITIALLY EWE**
1058 Hillgrove Ave  (60558-1420)
PHONE.................................708 246-7777
EMP: 3
SALES (est): 410.3K  **Privately Held**
SIC: 3552  Knitting machines

**(G-21869)**
**KINETIC ORTHOTIC INC**
3958 Rose Ave  (60558-1032)
PHONE.................................708 246-9266
Joe Skertich, *Owner*
EMP: 3
SALES (est): 426.4K  **Privately Held**
SIC: 3842  Orthopedic appliances

**(G-21870)**
**NORTHEAST ILLINOIS REGIONAL**
914 Burlington Ave  (60558-1569)
PHONE.................................708 246-0304
EMP: 1004
SALES (corp-wide): 379.7MM  **Privately Held**
SIC: 3462  Railroad, construction & mining forgings
PA: Northeast Illinois Regional Commuter Railroad Corporation
547 W Jackson Blvd Ste 1
Chicago IL 60661
312 322-6900

**(G-21871)**
**PROPELLER HR SOLUTIONS INC**
5350 Wolf Rd  (60558-1858)
PHONE.................................312 342-7355
Bill Blouin, *President*
EMP: 2
SALES (est): 200.7K  **Privately Held**
SIC: 3366  Propellers

**(G-21872)**
**REEL LIFE DVD LLC**
Also Called: Fodeo
5233 Clausen Ave  (60558-2026)
PHONE.................................708 579-1360
Valarie Moody, *Mng Member*
Tom Moody,
EMP: 3
SQ FT: 3,000
SALES: 200K  **Privately Held**
WEB: www.fodeo.net
SIC: 5023  5199  5085  5112  Mirrors & pictures, framed & unframed; gifts & novelties; industrial supplies; stationery & office supplies; games, toys & children's vehicles; commercial printing

**(G-21873)**
**RYLIN MEDIA LLC**
5028 Lawn Ave  (60558-1820)
PHONE.................................708 246-7599
Philip Saran, *Mng Member*
Roger D Herrin,
EMP: 5
SALES: 3MM  **Privately Held**
SIC: 2721  Magazines: publishing & printing

**(G-21874)**
**TAKE YOUR MARK SPORTS LLC**
1010 Longmeadow Ln  (60558-2108)
PHONE.................................708 655-0525
Robert Craig, *Mng Member*
Therese Craig,
EMP: 2
SALES: 500K  **Privately Held**
SIC: 3953  7389  Cancelling stamps, hand; rubber or metal;

## Westmont
### Dupage County

**(G-21875)**
**AMERICAN COUPLINGS CO**
40 Chestnut Ave  (60559-1128)
PHONE.................................630 323-4442
Fax: 630 323-4120
Jim Jablonsky, *Manager*
▲ EMP: 2
SALES (est): 202.2K  **Privately Held**
SIC: 3429  Clamps & couplings, hose

**(G-21876)**
**ASICO LLC**
26 Plaza Dr  (60559-1130)
PHONE.................................630 986-8032
Volha Dziadyk, *Accountant*
Srini Ram, *Accountant*
Kai Zhang, *Accountant*
Ravi Nallakrishnan,
Meenakshi Nallakrishnan,
EMP: 15
SQ FT: 7,000
SALES (est): 3MM  **Privately Held**
WEB: www.asico.com
SIC: 3851  5048  Ophthalmic goods; ophthalmic goods

**(G-21877)**
**BROAD OCEAN MOTORS LLC**
910 Pasquinelli Dr  (60559-5526)
PHONE.................................630 908-4720
Terry Zhang,
Chuping Lu,
Haiming Xu,
EMP: 20
SQ FT: 25,000
SALES (est): 3.5MM
SALES (corp-wide): 257MM  **Privately Held**
SIC: 3621  Motors, electric
HQ: Broad-Ocean Motor Ev Co., Ltd.
No.5, Yongfeng Road, Haidian District Beijing
105 871-1730

**(G-21878)**
**BURR RIDGE LIGHTING INC**
40 S Cass Ave  (60559-1864)
PHONE.................................630 323-4850
Walter Ejsmont, *Owner*
Juliana Ejsmont, *Manager*
EMP: 7
SALES (est): 1.1MM  **Privately Held**
SIC: 3699  Electrical equipment & supplies

**(G-21879)**
**CAMBRIDGE BUSINESS**
777 Oakmont Ln Ste 1800  (60559-5524)
PHONE.................................800 619-6473
EMP: 4
SALES (est): 205.5K  **Privately Held**
SIC: 2741  Miscellaneous publishing

**(G-21880)**
**CLEAR SIGHT INC**
220 Rosewood Ct  (60559-1577)
P.O. Box 918  (60559-0918)
PHONE.................................630 323-3590
Paul Osenkarski, *President*
EMP: 3
SALES (est): 211.6K  **Privately Held**
SIC: 3851  Ophthalmic goods

**(G-21881)**
**DATAIR EMPLOYEE BENEFT SYSTEMS**
735 N Cass Ave  (60559-1100)
PHONE.................................630 325-2600
Fax: 630 325-2660
Aaron Venouziou, *President*
Andrew Hoskins, *Senior VP*
Kathie Driscoll, *VP Admin*
William E Lilliquist, *Vice Pres*
Gary Saake, *Vice Pres*
EMP: 45
SQ FT: 15,600

# Westmont - Dupage County (G-21882)

## GEOGRAPHIC SECTION

SALES (est): 4.8MM Privately Held
WEB: www.datair.com
SIC: 7372  8742  Business oriented computer software; management consulting services

### (G-21882)
**DENBUR INC (PA)**
650 Blackhawk Dr (60559-9504)
P.O. Box 3473, Oak Brook (60522-3473)
PHONE..................................630 986-9667
Fax: 630 986-9688
Fariborz Maissami, *President*
Monica Maissami, *Vice Pres*
Sean Maissami, *Opers Staff*
Gloria Drzewiecki, *Accounts Mgr*
EMP: 8
SQ FT: 4,500
SALES (est): 4.8MM Privately Held
WEB: www.denbur.com
SIC: 3843  Dental equipment & supplies

### (G-21883)
**DESIGN TECHNOLOGY INC**
768 Burr Oak Dr (60559-1122)
PHONE..................................630 920-1300
Fax: 630 920-0011
Stephen O Myers, *President*
Edward Yelke, *Chairman*
Marjorie K Newpher, *Vice Pres*
Jeff Yelke, *Vice Pres*
▲ EMP: 21
SQ FT: 10,000
SALES (est): 3.6MM Privately Held
WEB: www.designtechnologyinc.com
SIC: 3825  8711  Measuring instruments & meters, electric; mechanical engineering

### (G-21884)
**DESIGNA ACCESS CORPORATION**
777 Oakmont Ln Ste 2000 (60559-5580)
PHONE..................................630 891-3105
Robert J Kane, *President*
Hans Michael Kraus, *Admin Sec*
EMP: 3
SALES (est): 170.6K Privately Held
SIC: 7372  Operating systems computer software

### (G-21885)
**DIXON BRASS**
40 Chestnut Ave (60559-1128)
PHONE..................................630 323-3716
Richard L Goodall, *Owner*
James Jablonsky, *General Mgr*
▲ EMP: 25
SALES (est): 3.3MM
SALES (corp-wide): 270.1MM Privately Held
WEB: www.americancouplings.com
SIC: 3494  5085  Pipe fittings; industrial supplies
PA: Dvcc, Inc.
    800 High St
    Chestertown MD 21620
    410 778-2000

### (G-21886)
**DVCC INC**
40 Chestnut Ave (60559-1128)
PHONE..................................630 323-3105
Richard L Goodall, *President*
EMP: 37
SALES (corp-wide): 270.1MM Privately Held
SIC: 3494  5085  Pipe fittings; industrial supplies
PA: Dvcc, Inc.
    800 High St
    Chestertown MD 21620
    410 778-2000

### (G-21887)
**EMT INTERNATIONAL INC**
760 Pasquinelli Dr # 300 (60559-1290)
PHONE..................................630 655-4145
Jim Driscoll, *Manager*
EMP: 3
SALES (corp-wide): 24MM Privately Held
WEB: www.emtinternational.com
SIC: 3555  3554  3544  5084  Printing trades machinery; paper industries machinery; punches, forming & stamping; printing trades machinery, equipment & supplies
PA: Emt International, Inc.
    780 Centerline Dr
    Hobart WI 54155
    920 468-5475

### (G-21888)
**HA-INTERNATIONAL LLC (DH)**
Also Called: Ha International
630 Oakmont Ln (60559-5548)
PHONE..................................630 575-5700
Fax: 630 575-5800
Douglas Sanford, *President*
Michael Feehan, *Vice Pres*
Joe Ebens, *Plant Mgr*
Robert Laitar, *Research*
Grady Collins, *CFO*
▲ EMP: 40
SQ FT: 22,000
SALES: 160.8MM Privately Held
SIC: 2869  Industrial organic chemicals
HQ: Ha-Usa, Inc.
    630 Oakmont Ln
    Westmont IL 60559
    630 575-5700

### (G-21889)
**HA-USA INC (DH)**
Also Called: Delta-Ha, Inc.
630 Oakmont Ln (60559-5548)
PHONE..................................630 575-5700
Donald W Hansen, *Ch of Bd*
Richard Smith, *President*
Peter J Puccio, *CFO*
EMP: 6 EST: 1933
SQ FT: 45,000
SALES (est): 160.8MM Privately Held
SIC: 2869  Industrial organic chemicals
HQ: HUttenes-Albertus Chemische Werke Gesellschaft Mit Beschrankter Haftung
    Wiesenstr. 23
    Dusseldorf  40549
    211 508-70

### (G-21890)
**HANTEMP CORPORATION**
Also Called: Hantemp Controls
33 Chestnut Ave (60559-1127)
PHONE..................................630 537-1049
Charles C Hansen, *Owner*
Ronald Johnson, *Project Mgr*
EMP: 6
SQ FT: 8,000
SALES: 400K Privately Held
SIC: 3592  Valves

### (G-21891)
**HIGH SPEED WELDING INC**
728 Vandustrial Dr Ste 5 (60559-2499)
PHONE..................................630 971-8929
Dennis Spal, *President*
EMP: 1
SQ FT: 1,350
SALES (est): 238K Privately Held
SIC: 7692  3711  Welding repair; automobile assembly, including specialty automobiles

### (G-21892)
**I HARDWARE DIRECT INC**
642 Blackhawk Dr (60559-1116)
PHONE..................................708 325-0000
Tim Scalf, *President*
EMP: 3
SQ FT: 8,000
SALES: 700K Privately Held
SIC: 3429  Manufactured hardware (general)

### (G-21893)
**INTERVRSITY CHRSTN FLLWSHP/USA**
Also Called: Intervarsity Press
430 Plaza Dr Frnt (60559-1247)
P.O. Box 1400, Downers Grove (60515-1426)
PHONE..................................630 734-4000
Fax: 630 734-4200
Belinda Collins, *Publisher*
Bob Fryling, *Principal*
Doug Secker, *Opers Staff*
Anne Gerth, *Opers Staff*
Mike Zeeman, *Opers Staff*
EMP: 90
SALES (corp-wide): 105.7MM Privately Held
WEB: www.ivpress.com
SIC: 2731  Book publishing
PA: Intervarsity Christian Fellowship/Usa
    635 Science Dr
    Madison WI 53711
    608 274-9001

### (G-21894)
**JJM PRODUCTS LLC**
1052 Zygmunt Cir (60559-2692)
PHONE..................................630 319-9325
Jeffery A Rozell, *Principal*
EMP: 4
SALES (est): 530.8K Privately Held
SIC: 2448  Pallets, wood

### (G-21895)
**JULIAN ELEC SVC & ENGRG INC**
701 Blackhawk Dr (60559-1159)
PHONE..................................630 920-8950
Jay Green, *Branch Mgr*
EMP: 40
SALES (corp-wide): 30.3MM Privately Held
SIC: 3679  3625  3694  3714  Mfg Relay/Indstl Control Mfg Elec Components Mfg Motor Vehicle Parts Mfg Engine Elec Equip Mfg Switchgear/Boards
PA: Julian Electrical Service And Engineering, Inc.
    15706 W 147th St
    Lockport IL 60491
    630 920-8951

### (G-21896)
**KAYBEE ENGINEERING COMPANY INC**
Also Called: Kaybee Engnrng
100 E Quincy St (60559-1823)
P.O. Box 316 (60559-0316)
PHONE..................................630 968-7100
Robert N Britz, *President*
Juliene Britz, *Administration*
EMP: 34
SQ FT: 4,400
SALES (est): 5.6MM Privately Held
SIC: 3699  3621  Electrical equipment & supplies; motors & generators

### (G-21897)
**KD STEEL INC**
4243 Chicago Ave (60559)
PHONE..................................630 201-1619
David Wilson, *President*
EMP: 9
SALES: 1.1MM Privately Held
SIC: 1791  3462  Structural steel erection; iron & steel forgings

### (G-21898)
**KELEEN LEATHERS INC**
1010 Executive Dr Ste 400 (60559-6156)
PHONE..................................630 590-5300
Rick Mullen, *President*
Linda Mullen, *VP Sales*
Frank Mullen, *Manager*
EMP: 17
SALES (est): 1.6MM Privately Held
SIC: 5948  5199  2386  Luggage & leather goods stores; leather goods, except footwear, gloves, luggage, belting; leather & sheep-lined clothing

### (G-21899)
**KMP PRODUCTS LLC**
Also Called: Safe Pet Products
1060 Zygmunt Cir (60559-2692)
PHONE..................................630 956-0438
Heather L Hester, *Owner*
John L Hester,
▲ EMP: 2 EST: 2007
SQ FT: 1,600
SALES: 1MM Privately Held
SIC: 3999  Pet supplies

### (G-21900)
**LITHOPRINT INC**
Also Called: Lithographics Services
111 E Chicago Ave (60559-1722)
PHONE..................................630 964-9200
Anton L Sekera, *President*
Tony Sekera, *President*
EMP: 6
SQ FT: 12,000
SALES (est): 335.3K Privately Held
SIC: 2752  Commercial printing, lithographic

### (G-21901)
**MAGNET-SCHULTZ AMER HOLDG LLC (PA)**
401 Plaza Dr (60559-1233)
PHONE..................................630 789-0600
David Stockwell, *President*
Wolfgang E Schultz, *Chairman*
Theodore D Gault, *CFO*
David L Stockwell,
EMP: 8
SALES (est): 20.1MM Privately Held
SIC: 3451  3625  3599  Screw machine products; solenoid switches (industrial controls); brakes, electromagnetic; machine & other job shop work

### (G-21902)
**MAGNET-SCHULTZ AMERICA INC**
Also Called: MSA
401 Plaza Dr (60559-1233)
PHONE..................................630 789-0600
David L Stockwell, *President*
Albert Schultz, *Vice Pres*
Tom Gates, *Purch Mgr*
Tom Corcoran, *QC Mgr*
Geoffrey Hogle, *Research*
▲ EMP: 85
SQ FT: 42,000
SALES (est): 20.1MM Privately Held
WEB: www.magnet-schultzamerica.com
SIC: 3451  3625  3599  Screw machine products; solenoid switches (industrial controls); brakes, electromagnetic; machine & other job shop work
PA: Magnet-Schultz America Holding, Llc
    401 Plaza Dr
    Westmont IL 60559

### (G-21903)
**MANROLAND INC (DH)**
Also Called: Manroland Websystems
800 E Oakhill Dr (60559-5587)
PHONE..................................630 920-2000
Fax: 630 920-1351
Michael Mugavero, *CEO*
Franz Von Frstenberg, *Managing Dir*
Chris Howes, *Assistant VP*
Jerry Burgoni, *Purch Agent*
Brian Gott, *CFO*
▲ EMP: 40
SQ FT: 120,000
SALES (est): 29.1MM
SALES (corp-wide): 949.8MM Privately Held
SIC: 3555  5084  Printing trades machinery; printing trades machinery, equipment & supplies
HQ: Manroland Sheetfed Gmbh
    Muhlheimer Str. 341
    Offenbach Am Main  63075
    698 305-0

### (G-21904)
**MCCRONE ASSOCIATES INC**
McCrone Microscopes & ACC
850 Pasquinelli Dr (60559-5594)
PHONE..................................630 887-7100
Jeffrey D McGinn, *President*
David Wiley, *President*
Charles Zona, *Principal*
EMP: 8
SALES (corp-wide): 7.6MM Privately Held
WEB: www.mccrone.com
SIC: 3826  3827  Analytical instruments; microscopes, except electron, proton & corneal
HQ: Mccrone Associates, Inc.
    850 Pasquinelli Dr
    Westmont IL 60559
    630 887-7100

## GEOGRAPHIC SECTION

**(G-21905)**
**MIDCO EXPLORATION INC**
414 Plaza Dr Ste 204  (60559-3507)
P.O. Box 1278  (60559-3878)
PHONE....................................630 655-2198
Kent Weltmer, *President*
Earl Joyce, *Vice Pres*
**EMP:** 3
**SALES (est):** 286.7K
**SALES (corp-wide):** 749.8K **Privately Held**
**SIC:** 1382  Oil & gas exploration services
**PA:** Midco Production Co Inc
  414 Plaza Dr Ste 204
  Westmont IL 60559
  630 655-2198

**(G-21906)**
**MIDCO PETROLEUM INC**
336 S Cass Ave  (60559-1932)
P.O. Box 1278  (60559-3878)
PHONE....................................630 655-2198
**Fax:** 630 655-2260
Kent H Weltmer, *President*
**EMP:** 3
**SALES (est):** 290K **Privately Held**
**WEB:** www.midcopetroleum.com
**SIC:** 1311  Crude petroleum & natural gas

**(G-21907)**
**MIDCO PRODUCTION CO INC (PA)**
414 Plaza Dr Ste 204  (60559-3507)
P.O. Box 1278  (60559-3878)
PHONE....................................630 655-2198
Kent H Weltmer, *President*
**EMP:** 4 **EST:** 1979
**SALES (est):** 749.8K **Privately Held**
**SIC:** 1311  Natural gas production

**(G-21908)**
**MODERNFOLD DOORS OF CHICAGO**
648 Blackhawk Dr  (60559-1116)
PHONE....................................630 654-4560
**Fax:** 630 654-4575
Danny Watson, *Principal*
**EMP:** 6 **EST:** 2010
**SALES (est):** 699.5K **Privately Held**
**SIC:** 3821  Laboratory apparatus & furniture

**(G-21909)**
**OOSTMAN FABRICATING & WLDG INC**
45 E Chicago Ave  (60559-1726)
PHONE....................................630 241-1315
Norman J Oostman, *President*
Roseann J Oostman, *Admin Sec*
**EMP:** 11
**SQ FT:** 12,000
**SALES (est):** 1.7MM **Privately Held**
**SIC:** 3599  7692 3441 3544 Machine shop, jobbing & repair; welding repair; fabricated structural metal; special dies, tools, jigs & fixtures

**(G-21910)**
**PERFORMANCE PRO PLUMBING INC**
3915 Liberty Blvd  (60559-1107)
PHONE....................................630 566-5207
Annmarie Cook, *Principal*
**EMP:** 5
**SALES (est):** 452.4K **Privately Held**
**SIC:** 3432  Plumbing fixture fittings & trim

**(G-21911)**
**PET KING BRANDS  INC**
Also Called: P K B
710 Vandustrial Dr  (60559-2499)
PHONE....................................630 241-3905
Pamela K Bosco, *President*
Deborah Brown, *Vice Pres*
**EMP:** 4
**SQ FT:** 5,000
**SALES (est):** 601.5K **Privately Held**
**WEB:** www.petkingbrands.com
**SIC:** 3999  5122 Pet supplies; animal medicines

**(G-21912)**
**POSITRON CORPORATION (PA)**
550 Oakmont Ln  (60559-3700)
PHONE....................................317 576-0183
Joseph G Oliverio, *Ch of Bd*

Michele Moore, *Project Mgr*
Corey N Conn, *CFO*
Ron Mojica, *Manager*
**EMP:** 22
**SQ FT:** 2,000
**SALES (est):** 1.4MM **Publicly Held**
**SIC:** 3845  Electromedical equipment; position emission tomography (PET scanner)

**(G-21913)**
**PPG INDUSTRIES  INC**
Also Called: PPG 9449
6136 S Cass Ave  (60559-2623)
PHONE....................................630 960-3600
Kevin Price, *Manager*
**EMP:** 3
**SALES (corp-wide):** 14.7B **Publicly Held**
**WEB:** www.ppg.com
**SIC:** 2851  Paints & allied products
**PA:** Ppg Industries, Inc.
  1 Ppg Pl
  Pittsburgh PA 15272
  412 434-3131

**(G-21914)**
**PROCURA LLC**
900 Oakmont Ln Ste 308  (60559-5571)
PHONE....................................801 265-4571
Scott Overhill, *CEO*
**EMP:** 3
**SALES (est):** 328.8K
**SALES (corp-wide):** 10.7MM **Privately Held**
**SIC:** 7372  Prepackaged software
**PA:** Develus Systems Inc
  1112 Fort St Suite 600
  Victoria BC
  250 388-0880

**(G-21915)**
**QUICK TABS  INC**
81 W 61st St  (60559-2615)
PHONE....................................630 969-7737
Terry R Rempert, *President*
Mary C Rempert, *Vice Pres*
**EMP:** 5
**SQ FT:** 5,000
**SALES (est):** 70.6K **Privately Held**
**WEB:** www.quicktabs.net
**SIC:** 2675  Index cards, die-cut: made from purchased materials

**(G-21916)**
**RAINBOW CLEANERS**
836 E Ogden Ave  (60559-1246)
PHONE....................................630 789-6989
**EMP:** 3
**SALES (est):** 75K **Privately Held**
**SIC:** 2842  Dry Cleaning & Laundry

**(G-21917)**
**REBCO MACHINE SPECIALTIES INC**
138 E Quincy St  (60559-1823)
PHONE....................................630 852-3419
Audrey Busse, *CEO*
James E Bresnahan, *President*
Ron Antos, *Opers Spvr*
**EMP:** 10
**SQ FT:** 12,000
**SALES (est):** 1.8MM **Privately Held**
**SIC:** 3599  Machine shop, jobbing & repair

**(G-21918)**
**SAFEGUARD 201 CORP**
Also Called: Safeguard Print & Promo
1129 Fairview Ave  (60559-2709)
PHONE....................................630 241-0370
Patrick Ryan, *President*
**EMP:** 6
**SALES:** 1MM **Privately Held**
**SIC:** 2752  Commercial printing, lithographic

**(G-21919)**
**SANDLOCK SANDBOX  LLC**
1069 Zygmunt Cir  (60559-2678)
PHONE....................................630 963-9422
Chris Freres, *Principal*
▲ **EMP:** 4 **EST:** 2005
**SQ FT:** 2,000
**SALES (est):** 500K **Privately Held**
**SIC:** 5941  2531 Playground equipment; school furniture

**(G-21920)**
**SHEER GRAPHICS INC**
47 Chestnut Ave  (60559-1127)
PHONE....................................630 654-4422
Nancy Sheers, *President*
Simon Sheers, *Treasurer*
**EMP:** 7 **EST:** 1972
**SALES (est):** 874.3K **Privately Held**
**WEB:** www.sheergraphics.com
**SIC:** 7334  2759 2752 2791 Photocopying & duplicating services; commercial printing; commercial printing, lithographic; typesetting; coated & laminated paper

**(G-21921)**
**SIEMENS CORPORATION**
601 Oakmont Ln Ste 180  (60559-5570)
PHONE....................................630 850-6973
Ben Gralla, *Manager*
**EMP:** 20
**SALES (corp-wide):** 89.6B **Privately Held**
**SIC:** 3661  Telephones & telephone apparatus
**HQ:** Siemens Corporation
  300 New Jersey Ave Nw # 10
  Washington DC 20001
  202 434-4800

**(G-21922)**
**SONOCO DISPLAY & PACKAGING LLC**
1111 Pasquinelli Dr # 600  (60559-1241)
PHONE....................................630 789-1111
Jim Ghere, *Branch Mgr*
**EMP:** 11
**SALES (corp-wide):** 4.7B **Publicly Held**
**SIC:** 2653  Display items, corrugated: made from purchased materials
**HQ:** Sonoco Display & Packaging, Llc
  555 Aureole St
  Winston Salem NC 27107
  336 784-0445

**(G-21923)**
**SPINECRAFT  LLC**
777 Oakmont Ln Ste 200  (60559-5589)
PHONE....................................630 920-7300
Wagdy W Asaad, *CEO*
Steven E Mather, *Ch of Bd*
AMI Akallal-Asaad, *Vice Pres*
Steven Mardjetko, *Bd of Directors*
**EMP:** 18
**SQ FT:** 8,000
**SALES (est):** 2.8MM **Privately Held**
**SIC:** 3841  Surgical & medical instruments

**(G-21924)**
**SURE-WAY DIE DESIGNS  INC (PA)**
Also Called: Sure-Way Products
407 Plaza Dr  (60559-1233)
PHONE....................................630 323-0370
**Fax:** 630 323-9812
Russell De Cicco, *President*
Debra Winkleman, *President*
Bruce McDaniel, *Opers Mgr*
Randy Stravel, *QC Dir*
Kenneth Sioup, *Finance*
**EMP:** 18 **EST:** 1967
**SQ FT:** 22,000
**SALES (est):** 2.4MM **Privately Held**
**WEB:** www.surewayproducts.com
**SIC:** 3469  3544 3542 Stamping metal for the trade; special dies, tools, jigs & fixtures; machine tools, metal forming type

**(G-21925)**
**TRADING SQUARE COMPANY INC**
6434 S Cass Ave  (60559-3209)
PHONE....................................630 960-0606
**Fax:** 630 960-0677
May Tsui, *President*
▲ **EMP:** 4
**SALES (est):** 190K **Privately Held**
**SIC:** 2395  Emblems, embroidered; embroidery products, except schiffli machine

**(G-21926)**
**TUBULAR STEEL  INC**
519 N Cass Ave Ste 202  (60559-1593)
PHONE....................................630 515-5000
**Fax:** 630 515-5005
Theresa Campbell, *Accounting Mgr*
Michael Birch, *Branch Mgr*

Dean Conners, *Manager*
**EMP:** 6
**SALES (corp-wide):** 8.6B **Publicly Held**
**WEB:** www.tubularsteel.com
**SIC:** 5051  3498 Tubing, metal; tube fabricating (contract bending & shaping)
**HQ:** Tubular Steel, Inc.
  1031 Executive Parkway Dr
  Saint Louis MO 63141
  314 851-9200

**(G-21927)**
**WESTMONT MRI CENTER**
Also Called: Hinsdale Hospital
6311 S Cass Ave  (60559-3206)
PHONE....................................630 856-4060
**Fax:** 630 856-4067
Chung J Wey MD, *Med Doctor*
Carrie Shiomonis, *Manager*
**EMP:** 2
**SQ FT:** 4,000
**SALES (est):** 260.8K **Privately Held**
**WEB:** www.hinsdalehospital.com
**SIC:** 3826  Magnetic resonance imaging apparatus

## Westville
### Vermilion County

**(G-21928)**
**BETTER BUILT BUILDINGS**
604 E Kelly Ave  (61883-1026)
PHONE....................................217 267-7824
Mark Lete, *Owner*
**EMP:** 6
**SALES (est):** 358.4K **Privately Held**
**SIC:** 2499  1542 Poles, wood; agricultural building contractors

**(G-21929)**
**DYNACHEM  INC**
15662 E 980 North Rd  (61883-6138)
P.O. Box 19, Georgetown  (61846-0019)
PHONE....................................217 662-2136
Keith Rife, *President*
Jason Wyatt, *QC Mgr*
Steve Kingsley, *Research*
Craig McCall, *CFO*
Jerry Smith, *CFO*
◆ **EMP:** 60
**SQ FT:** 25,000
**SALES (est):** 29.7MM **Privately Held**
**WEB:** www.dynacheminc.com
**SIC:** 2821  2869 Plastics materials & resins; industrial organic chemicals

**(G-21930)**
**LUBE RITE**
802 S State St  (61883-1744)
PHONE....................................217 267-7766
**EMP:** 5
**SALES:** 90K **Privately Held**
**SIC:** 2992  Mfg Lubricating Oils/Greases

**(G-21931)**
**WESTVILLE READY MIX INC**
1409 English St  (61883-1821)
PHONE....................................217 267-2082
Jenny Wiese, *President*
Keith Wiese, *Vice Pres*
**EMP:** 5 **EST:** 1946
**SALES (est):** 800K **Privately Held**
**SIC:** 3273  Ready-mixed concrete

## Wheaton
### Dupage County

**(G-21932)**
**A AND T LABS INCORPORATED**
1926 Berkshire Pl  (60189-8150)
P.O. Box 4884  (60189-4884)
PHONE....................................630 668-8562
Reinhard Metz, *President*
Isola Metz, *Vice Pres*
**EMP:** 2
**SALES (est):** 213.1K **Privately Held**
**SIC:** 3651  5961 Electronic kits for home assembly: radio, TV, phonograph; electronic kits & parts, mail order

# Wheaton - Dupage County (G-21933)

**(G-21933)**
**ACME SCREW CO (PA)**
1201 W Union Ave  (60187-4869)
P.O. Box 906  (60187-0906)
PHONE .................................. 630 665-2200
Fax: 630 665-9630
William J Roche, *Ch of Bd*
Christine M Roche, *President*
Steve Murray, *VP Admin*
Cliff Hauger, *Vice Pres*
George Kalebich, *Vice Pres*
▲ **EMP:** 100
**SQ FT:** 100,000
**SALES (est):** 20.8MM  **Privately Held**
**WEB:** www.acmecompanies.com
**SIC:** 3452  Bolts, nuts, rivets & washers; screws, metal; rivets, metal

**(G-21934)**
**ADM IMAGING  INC**
100 W Roosevelt Rd A1-200  (60187-5260)
PHONE .................................. 630 834-7100
Sam Kancherlapalli, *President*
Arnand Kancherlapalli, *Vice Pres*
**EMP:** 7
**SALES (est):** 702.9K  **Privately Held**
**SIC:** 3845  Position emission tomography (PET scanner)

**(G-21935)**
**AIXACCT SYSTEMS  INC**
715 N Wheaton Ave  (60187-4134)
PHONE .................................. 952 303-4077
Andreas Roelofs, *President*
**EMP:** 2
**SALES:** 500K  **Privately Held**
**SIC:** 3829  Measuring & controlling devices

**(G-21936)**
**ARID TECHNOLOGIES INC**
323 S Hale St  (60187-5219)
PHONE .................................. 630 681-8500
Tedmund Tiberi, *President*
Michael Heffernan, *Vice Pres*
Luke Howard, *Vice Pres*
Mary Tiberi, *Admin Sec*
**EMP:** 20
**SALES (est):** 3.9MM  **Privately Held**
**SIC:** 3533  Oil & gas field machinery

**(G-21937)**
**AUTUMN WOODS LTD**
112 N Main St  (60187-5327)
PHONE .................................. 630 868-3535
**EMP:** 9
**SALES (corp-wide):** 2.5MM  **Privately Held**
**SIC:** 2434  Wood kitchen cabinets
**PA:** Autumn Woods Ltd
  375 Gundersen Dr
  Carol Stream IL 60188
  630 668-2080

**(G-21938)**
**CALDWELL PLUMBING CO**
821 Childs St  (60187-4810)
PHONE .................................. 630 588-8900
Fax: 630 588-8953
Nick Tenerelli, *President*
Mike Tenerelli, *Vice Pres*
Carol Stratton, *Manager*
**EMP:** 12
**SQ FT:** 5,000
**SALES:** 13MM  **Privately Held**
**SIC:** 3432  4961  Plumbing fixture fittings & trim; air conditioning supply services

**(G-21939)**
**CARTERS  INC**
132 Danada Sq W  (60189-2041)
PHONE .................................. 630 690-6182
**EMP:** 11
**SALES (corp-wide):** 3.2B  **Publicly Held**
**SIC:** 2361  Dresses: girls', children's & infants'
**PA:** Carter's, Inc.
  3438 Peachtree Rd Ne # 1800
  Atlanta GA 30326
  678 791-1000

**(G-21940)**
**CHASE CORPORATION**
1800 S Naperville Rd  (60189-8130)
PHONE .................................. 630 752-3622
Sosilia Reddy, *Office Mgr*
Brad Karkula, *Branch Mgr*
**EMP:** 11
**SALES (corp-wide):** 238MM  **Publicly Held**
**SIC:** 3644  Noncurrent-carrying wiring services
**PA:** Chase Corporation
  295 University Ave
  Westwood MA 02090
  508 819-4200

**(G-21941)**
**CIRCUITRONICS**
201 N Gables Blvd  (60187-4818)
PHONE .................................. 630 668-5407
Job Varghese, *Mng Member*
Maria Casrejon, *Manager*
Manohar L Sharma,
**EMP:** 40
**SQ FT:** 46,000
**SALES (est):** 7.6MM  **Privately Held**
**WEB:** www.circuitronicsllc.com
**SIC:** 3672  Printed circuit boards

**(G-21942)**
**CROSSCOM  INC**
528 W Roosevelt Rd L1a  (60187-5092)
PHONE .................................. 630 871-5500
Daniel B Lites, *President*
Oscar Bonilla, *Manager*
**EMP:** 14 EST: 2010
**SQ FT:** 1,800
**SALES:** 6.5MM  **Privately Held**
**SIC:** 7389  7299  2952  Telephone services; home improvement & renovation contractor agency; roofing materials

**(G-21943)**
**DARK SPEED WORKS**
122 N Wheaton Ave # 551  (60187-6557)
P.O. Box 551  (60187-0551)
PHONE .................................. 312 772-3275
Greg Grunner, *Owner*
**EMP:** 5
**SALES (est):** 140K  **Privately Held**
**SIC:** 3949  Sporting & athletic goods

**(G-21944)**
**DIGITALDRIVE TECH**
1601 E Prairie Ave  (60187-3758)
PHONE .................................. 630 510-1580
Robert Anderson, *Owner*
Darcy Evon, *Co-Owner*
**EMP:** 4
**SALES (est):** 201K  **Privately Held**
**SIC:** 3621  Motors, electric

**(G-21945)**
**EMMETTS TAVERN & BREWING CO**
Also Called: Emmett's Ale House
121 W Front St  (60187-5108)
PHONE .................................. 630 480-7181
Allyssa Anderson, *Manager*
**EMP:** 4
**SALES (corp-wide):** 3MM  **Privately Held**
**SIC:** 5812  2082  5182  Chicken restaurant; beer (alcoholic beverage); wine & distilled beverages
**PA:** Emmett's Tavern & Brewing Co.
  128 W Main St
  West Dundee IL 60118
  847 428-4500

**(G-21946)**
**EVANGELICAL MISSIONS INFO SVC**
Also Called: Evangelical Missions Quarterly
500 College Ave  (60187-1909)
P.O. Box 794  (60187-0794)
PHONE .................................. 630 752-7158
Fax: 630 752-7155
Ken Gill, *Director*
Lonna Dickerson, *Director*
Eileen Dudich, *Assistant*
**EMP:** 6
**SALES (est):** 399.9K  **Privately Held**
**SIC:** 2721  Magazines: publishing only, not printed on site; periodicals: publishing only

**(G-21947)**
**EXPRESS DONUTS ENTERPRISE INC**
Also Called: Dunkin' Donuts
15 Danada Sq E  (60189-8484)
PHONE .................................. 630 510-9310
Fax: 630 510-0078
Manu Patel, *President*
**EMP:** 10
**SALES (est):** 354.4K  **Privately Held**
**SIC:** 5461  5812  2051  Doughnuts; eating places; doughnuts, except frozen

**(G-21948)**
**FLEMING MUSIC TECHNOLOGY CTR**
Also Called: Jeremiah Fleming Music Sites
408 W Elm St  (60189-6341)
PHONE .................................. 708 316-8662
Jeremiah Fleming, *President*
**EMP:** 6
**SALES (est):** 1.1K  **Privately Held**
**SIC:** 2741  7929  7389  Music books: publishing & printing; musical entertainers;

**(G-21949)**
**FLOWSERVE CORPORATION**
1311 Santa Rosa Ave  (60187-3630)
PHONE .................................. 630 260-1310
Herb Hillabrand, *Branch Mgr*
**EMP:** 46
**SALES (corp-wide):** 3.9B  **Publicly Held**
**SIC:** 3561  Pumps & pumping equipment
**PA:** Flowserve Corporation
  5215 N Oconnor Blvd Connor
  Irving TX 75039
  972 443-6500

**(G-21950)**
**GILBERTS CRAFT SAUSAGES LLC**
207a W Front St  (60187)
PHONE .................................. 630 923-8969
**EMP:** 2
**SALES (est):** 6.6MM  **Privately Held**
**SIC:** 3556  Sausage stuffers

**(G-21951)**
**GOOD NEWS PUBLISHERS (PA)**
Also Called: Crossway Bibles, Nfp
1300 Crescent St  (60187-5883)
PHONE .................................. 630 868-6025
Fax: 630 682-4785
Lane T Dennis, *President*
Baptist Church, *Pastor*
Paul Thomas, *Vice Pres*
Jeoffrey L Dennis, *Manager*
Greg Bailey, *Director*
◆ **EMP:** 50 EST: 1938
**SQ FT:** 43,000
**SALES:** 17.8MM  **Privately Held**
**WEB:** www.gnpcb.org
**SIC:** 2731  2732  Pamphlets: publishing only, not printed on site; textbooks: publishing only, not printed on site

**(G-21952)**
**HOLSTEIN GARAGE INC**
309 W Front St  (60187-5082)
PHONE .................................. 630 668-0328
Jeff Holstein, *President*
Mark Holstein, *Vice Pres*
**EMP:** 4 EST: 1906
**SQ FT:** 12,342
**SALES (est):** 460K  **Privately Held**
**WEB:** www.holsteinsgarage.com
**SIC:** 7538  7692  General automotive repair shops; automotive welding

**(G-21953)**
**HOUSE ON THE HILL INC**
2206 N Main St  (60187-9140)
PHONE .................................. 630 279-4455
Constance Meisinger, *President*
Stephen Meisinger, *Vice Pres*
**EMP:** 3
**SALES (est):** 269.7K  **Privately Held**
**SIC:** 2499  Bakers' equipment, wood

**(G-21954)**
**HTS CHICAGO  INC**
107 W Willow Ave  (60187-5236)
PHONE .................................. 630 352-3690
Derek Gordon, *President*
David Warner, *Vice Pres*
Jeff Smith, *Engrg Mgr*
David Kviring, *CFO*
Choudhry Raza, *Controller*
**EMP:** 7
**SQ FT:** 800
**SALES (est):** 5MM
**SALES (corp-wide):** 79.3MM  **Privately Held**
**SIC:** 3567  Heating units & devices, industrial: electric
**PA:** Hts Engineering Ltd
  115 Norfinch Dr
  North York ON M3N 1
  416 645-2275

**(G-21955)**
**IINDIGENOUS RAILROAD SVCS LLC**
205 S Lorraine Rd  (60187-5865)
PHONE .................................. 630 517-8207
Fred Barker, *Managing Prtnr*
Peter Probst, *Mng Member*
Jessica Bradish, *Manager*
**EMP:** 7
**SQ FT:** 1,000,000
**SALES (est):** 1.2MM  **Privately Held**
**SIC:** 3569  Baling machines, for scrap metal, paper or similar material

**(G-21956)**
**IMPRESS PRINTING**
210 N Hale St  (60187-5115)
PHONE .................................. 630 933-8966
Mike Hansen, *Owner*
**EMP:** 6
**SALES (est):** 434.4K  **Privately Held**
**WEB:** www.b-online.com
**SIC:** 2759  Commercial printing

**(G-21957)**
**INTELLIGENT DESIGNS LLC**
1640 Raleigh Ct  (60189-7466)
PHONE .................................. 630 235-7965
David Beering, *Mng Member*
Donna Beering,
**EMP:** 3
**SALES (est):** 226.2K  **Privately Held**
**SIC:** 3663  Space satellite communications equipment

**(G-21958)**
**INTERNTNAL AWKENING MINISTRIES**
123 N Washington St  (60187-5312)
P.O. Box 232  (60187-0232)
PHONE .................................. 630 653-8616
Fax: 630 653-8616
Richard Roberts, *President*
James Crain, *Treasurer*
Dave Bird, *Finance*
Lowell Yoder, *Admin Sec*
**EMP:** 3
**SALES:** 69.6K  **Privately Held**
**SIC:** 8661  2732  Religious organizations; book printing

**(G-21959)**
**JIMMY DIESEL  INC**
2s401 Burning Trl  (60189-5905)
PHONE .................................. 708 482-4500
Jerry W Weller, *President*
Donna L Weller, *Admin Sec*
**EMP:** 2
**SQ FT:** 25,000
**SALES (est):** 363.2K  **Privately Held**
**WEB:** www.jimmydiesel.com
**SIC:** 3714  3519  5013  7538  Transmissions, motor vehicle; diesel engine rebuilding; truck parts & accessories; general automotive repair shops

**(G-21960)**
**KJELLBERG PRINTING**
805 W Liberty Dr  (60187-4844)
P.O. Box 725  (60187-0725)
PHONE .................................. 630 653-2244
William S Kjellberg Jr, *President*
Doris J Kjellberg, *Corp Secy*
Kevin J Kjellberg, *Vice Pres*
G Kjellberg, *Production*
**EMP:** 12 EST: 1956
**SALES (est):** 1.2MM  **Privately Held*
**WEB:** www.kjellbergprinting.com
**SIC:** 2759  2752  2732  Letterpress printing; commercial printing, lithographic; book printing

## (G-21961)
**KMF ENTERPRISES INC**
Also Called: Towntees
20 Danada Sq W (60189-2000)
**PHONE**..................630 858-2210
Kevin Fahey, *President*
**EMP:** 4
**SALES (est):** 478.6K **Privately Held**
**WEB:** www.towntees.com
**SIC:** 2759 Screen printing

## (G-21962)
**KNOWLEDGESHIFT INC**
26w245 Grand Ave Ste 200 (60187-2967)
**PHONE**..................630 221-8759
Nancy Monroe, *President*
Kimberly C Colby, *Mktg Dir*
Dennis Monroe, *Admin Sec*
**EMP:** 3
**SQ FT:** 300
**SALES (est):** 226K **Privately Held**
**SIC:** 7372 8742 Publishers' computer software; management consulting services

## (G-21963)
**LAKESHORE LACROSSE LLC**
20 Danada Sq W Ste 289 (60189-2000)
**PHONE**..................773 350-4356
Bridget Olp, *Owner*
Michelle Sebastian, *Co-Owner*
**EMP:** 6
**SALES (est):** 363.7K **Privately Held**
**SIC:** 7032 3792 Sporting camps; travel trailers & campers

## (G-21964)
**LATTICE INCORPORATED**
1751 S Nprvlle Rd Ste 100 (60189)
**PHONE**..................630 949-3250
**Fax:** 630 949-3299
Peter Muzzy, *President*
Brian Schwarz, *Senior VP*
Patrick Heiniff, *Vice Pres*
Gail Davis, *Office Mgr*
Gregory Bungo, *Software Engr*
**EMP:** 47
**SALES (est):** 4.2MM **Privately Held**
**WEB:** www.lattice.com
**SIC:** 7372 7371 Prepackaged software; custom computer programming services

## (G-21965)
**LAWRENCE PACKAGING INTL**
1761 S Nprvlle Rd Ste 201 (60189)
**PHONE**..................630 682-2600
Lawrence Moravek, *President*
Kenneth Hubbard, *Manager*
▲ **EMP:** 4
**SQ FT:** 1,000
**SALES:** 1.7MM **Privately Held**
**SIC:** 2673 Pliofilm bags: made from purchased materials

## (G-21966)
**LEE-WEL PRINTING CORPORATION**
1554 S County Farm Rd (60189-7121)
**PHONE**..................630 682-0935
**Fax:** 630 279-1093
Thomas A Welter, *President*
Gail Welter, *Vice Pres*
Rosemary Welter, *Treasurer*
**EMP:** 6
**SQ FT:** 15,000
**SALES (est):** 450K **Privately Held**
**SIC:** 2752 5199 2789 2759 Commercial printing, offset; advertising specialties; bookbinding & related work; commercial printing; die-cut paper & board; automotive & apparel trimmings

## (G-21967)
**LIVINGSTONE CORPORATION**
205 N Washington St (60187-5314)
**PHONE**..................630 871-1212
**Fax:** 630 871-1651
Bruce Barton, *Principal*
Andy Culbertson, *Project Mgr*
Ashley Taylor, *Project Mgr*
Tom Freking, *Mktg Dir*
Larry Taylor, *Creative Dir*
**EMP:** 12
**SALES (est):** 1.1MM **Privately Held**
**WEB:** www.livingstonecorp.com
**SIC:** 2721 Periodicals

## (G-21968)
**MARS INCORPORATED**
418 N Washington St (60187-4231)
**PHONE**..................630 878-8877
**EMP:** 65
**SALES (corp-wide):** 35B **Privately Held**
**SIC:** 2047 Dog & cat food
**PA:** Mars, Incorporated
6885 Elm St
Mc Lean VA 22101
703 821-4900

## (G-21969)
**MASTERITE TOOL & MFG**
825 James Ct (60189-6344)
**PHONE**..................630 653-2028
**Fax:** 630 595-1541
George Tomek, *President*
David Tomek, *Vice Pres*
Bernadine Tomek, *Treasurer*
**EMP:** 7
**SQ FT:** 4,000
**SALES:** 400K **Privately Held**
**SIC:** 3544 Special dies, tools, jigs & fixtures

## (G-21970)
**NANO TECHNOLOGIES INC**
Also Called: I T Audit Search
1765 Mustang Ct (60189-8483)
**PHONE**..................630 517-8824
Ralph Dahm, *Principal*
**EMP:** 2
**SALES (est):** 262.7K **Privately Held**
**WEB:** www.nanotechinc.com
**SIC:** 3571 Computers, digital, analog or hybrid

## (G-21971)
**ORINOCO SYSTEMS LLC (PA)**
300 S Carlton Ave Ste 100 (60187-4830)
P.O. Box 1458 (60187-1458)
**PHONE**..................630 510-0775
Diego Ferrer, *Mng Member*
**EMP:** 2
**SQ FT:** 596
**SALES:** 1.5MM **Privately Held**
**SIC:** 7371 7372 7373 Computer software systems analysis & design, custom; computer software development & applications; application computer software; educational computer software; systems software development services

## (G-21972)
**PRINTWISE INC**
1670 Monticello Ct Unit E (60189-8235)
**PHONE**..................630 833-2845
Darrell Davis, *President*
Marilyn Davis, *Vice Pres*
**EMP:** 3
**SALES (est):** 288.4K **Privately Held**
**WEB:** www.printwise-inc.com
**SIC:** 2759 Commercial printing

## (G-21973)
**PRO-TEK PRODUCTS INC**
1755 S Nprvlle Rd Ste 100 (60189)
**PHONE**..................630 293-5100
Paul Zalantis, *President*
Wayne Niemie, *Vice Pres*
**EMP:** 4
**SQ FT:** 700
**SALES (est):** 493.4K **Privately Held**
**SIC:** 2879 Agricultural chemicals

## (G-21974)
**R H JOHNSON OIL CO INC (PA)**
Also Called: Johnson Oil Company
1017 Delles Rd (60189-6320)
P.O. Box 169 (60187-0169)
**PHONE**..................630 668-3649
Herbert Johnson, *President*
Reynold Johnson, *Admin Sec*
**EMP:** 5
**SALES:** 1.5MM **Privately Held**
**SIC:** 5172 1311 Fuel oil; crude petroleum & natural gas production

## (G-21975)
**REGUNATHAN & ASSOC INC**
1490 Jasper Dr (60189-8985)
**PHONE**..................630 653-0387
**Fax:** 630 653-0387
Perialwar Regunathan, *President*
**EMP:** 3 **EST:** 1999

## (G-21976)
**RMH ENTERPRISES**
611 Cadillac Dr (60187-3601)
**PHONE**..................630 525-5552
Roger Herforth, *Owner*
**EMP:** 1
**SALES:** 650K **Privately Held**
**SIC:** 3599 Industrial machinery

## (G-21977)
**ROBIS ELECTIONS INC**
1751 S Nprvlle Rd Ste 104 (60189)
P.O. Box 39 (60187-0039)
**PHONE**..................630 752-0220
David M Davoust, *President*
Lisa Davoust, *Vice Pres*
Timothy Herman, *Vice Pres*
Daryl Lucas, *Vice Pres*
**EMP:** 18
**SQ FT:** 5,500
**SALES (est):** 566.2K **Privately Held**
**SIC:** 7372 Business oriented computer software

## (G-21978)
**RV6 PERFORMANCE**
26w148 Waterbury Ct (60187-1306)
**PHONE**..................630 346-7998
Richard Wong, *Owner*
▲ **EMP:** 2
**SALES (est):** 201.2K **Privately Held**
**SIC:** 3448 Prefabricated metal buildings

## (G-21979)
**S G NELSON & CO**
209 N Hale St Ste 1 (60187-5100)
P.O. Box 121 (60187-0121)
**PHONE**..................630 668-7900
Stephen G Nelson, *Owner*
**EMP:** 4
**SQ FT:** 4,000
**SALES:** 500K **Privately Held**
**SIC:** 3911 5094 3915 Jewel settings & mountings, precious metal; jewelry & precious stones; diamond cutting & polishing

## (G-21980)
**SERVETECH WATER SOLUTIONS INC**
112 W Liberty Dr (60187-5123)
**PHONE**..................630 784-9050
**Fax:** 630 784-9040
Bryan Block, *President*
**EMP:** 5
**SALES (est):** 748.1K **Privately Held**
**SIC:** 3589 5074 Sewage & water treatment equipment; water purification equipment

## (G-21981)
**SIGN AUTHORITY**
901 W Liberty Dr A (60187-4846)
**PHONE**..................630 462-9850
Richard Tampier, *President*
Leanne Tampier, *Vice Pres*
Tracy Baran, *Prdtn Mgr*
Chris Wagoner, *Prdtn Mgr*
**EMP:** 3
**SALES (est):** 360.7K **Privately Held**
**SIC:** 3993 Signs & advertising specialties

## (G-21982)
**SWEET POPS BY CINDY**
120 Bridge St Ste 100 (60187-4845)
**PHONE**..................630 294-0640
**EMP:** 3
**SALES (est):** 109K **Privately Held**
**SIC:** 2024 Ice cream & frozen desserts

## (G-21983)
**TAGOBI LLC**
303 S Main St (60187-5233)
**PHONE**..................331 444-2951
Mohamad Khatib, *Business Mgr*
Jaspal Singh, *Engineer*
**EMP:** 8
**SALES (est):** 250.9K **Privately Held**
**SIC:** 7372 Application computer software; business oriented computer software

## (G-21984)
**THEOSOPHICAL SOCIETY IN AMER (PA)**
Also Called: THEOSOPHICAL PUBLISHING HOUSE
1926 N Main St (60187-3136)
P.O. Box 270 (60187-0270)
**PHONE**..................630 665-0130
**Fax:** 630 668-4976
Betty Bland, *President*
Tim Boyd, *President*
Rod Smoley, *Editor*
Ed Abdul, *Vice Pres*
Mark Roemmich, *Maintenance Dir*
**EMP:** 8
**SQ FT:** 200,000
**SALES:** 2.8MM **Privately Held**
**WEB:** www.theosophical.org
**SIC:** 8641 2721 2731 8661 Educator's association; periodicals; book publishing; non-church religious organizations

## (G-21985)
**THEOSOPHICAL SOCIETY IN AMER**
Also Called: Theosphcal Pubg Hs/Quest Bk Sp
306 W Geneva Rd (60187-2421)
P.O. Box 270 (60187-0270)
**PHONE**..................630 665-0123
Angel Fragassi, *Finance*
Angelique Boyd, *Sales Associate*
Jessica Salasek, *Mktg Dir*
David Bland, *Branch Mgr*
Christopher Dixon, *Manager*
**EMP:** 15
**SALES (corp-wide):** 2.8MM **Privately Held**
**WEB:** www.theosophical.org
**SIC:** 8641 2731 2721 8699 Educator's association; book publishing; periodicals; reading rooms & other cultural organizations
**PA:** Theosophical Society In America Inc
1926 N Main St
Wheaton IL 60187
630 665-0130

## (G-21986)
**THIA & CO**
519 W Front St (60187-4933)
**PHONE**..................630 510-9770
**EMP:** 3
**SALES (est):** 160K **Privately Held**
**SIC:** 5947 2759 Ret Gifts/Novelties Commercial Printing

## (G-21987)
**TOUCHSENSOR TECHNOLOGIES LLC**
203 N Gables Blvd (60187-4818)
**PHONE**..................630 221-9000
**Fax:** 630 221-0737
Thomas Schreiber, *CEO*
Andrew Livingston, *Engineer*
Dave Gradl, *Senior Engr*
Robert Arazmas, *CFO*
Lynne Burmeister, *Cust Mgr*
▲ **EMP:** 300
**SQ FT:** 25,000
**SALES (est):** 182.6MM
**SALES (corp-wide):** 809.1MM **Publicly Held**
**WEB:** www.touchsensor.com
**SIC:** 5065 3674 Electronic parts & equipment; modules, solid state
**PA:** Methode Electronics, Inc
7401 W Wilson Ave
Chicago IL 60706
708 867-6777

## (G-21988)
**WALL-FILL COMPANY -**
649 Childs St Ste 3 (60187-4886)
**PHONE**..................630 668-3400
**Fax:** 630 871-8740
Matt Lasiowski, *Principal*
**EMP:** 4
**SALES (est):** 592.4K **Privately Held**
**SIC:** 3442 Window & door frames

## Wheaton - Dupage County (G-21989)

**(G-21989)**
**WHEATON TROPHY & ENGRAVERS**
107 W Front St Ste 3 (60187-5148)
PHONE..................630 682-4200
Fax: 630 682-0247
EMP: 2
SQ FT: 2,200
SALES: 280K Privately Held
SIC: 5999 3479 Ret Misc Merchandise Coating/Engraving Service

**(G-21990)**
**WYCKOFF ADVERTISING INC**
Also Called: Equipmentbag.com
1024 College Ave (60187-5720)
PHONE..................630 260-2525
Thomas Wyckoff, President
Ellen G Wyckoff, Shareholder
EMP: 2
SQ FT: 2,400
SALES: 300K Privately Held
WEB: www.wyckoff.com
SIC: 7311 7335 7336 2752 Advertising agencies; photographic studio, commercial; graphic arts & related design; commercial printing, lithographic

### Wheeling
#### Cook County

**(G-21991)**
**10X MICROSTRUCTURES LLC**
420 Harvester Ct (60090-4735)
PHONE..................847 215-7448
Scott Thielman, President
EMP: 3
SALES (est): 286.5K Privately Held
SIC: 3542 Electroforming machines

**(G-21992)**
**3-D MOLD & TOOL INC**
2078 Foster Ave (60090-6521)
PHONE..................847 870-7150
Fax: 847 870-6006
Gottfried Winter, President
James A Puetz, Corp Secy
Marion Calvino, Office Mgr
EMP: 4
SQ FT: 3,000
SALES: 100K Privately Held
SIC: 3544 Forms (molds), for foundry & plastics working machinery

**(G-21993)**
**A & M TOOL CO INC**
5 W Waltz Dr (60090-6052)
PHONE..................847 215-8140
Fax: 847 215-8143
Dieter Ade, President
Reiner Mayer, Corp Secy
Alexander Mosenkis, Plant Mgr
Hanna Hopp, Admin Sec
EMP: 30
SQ FT: 20,270
SALES: 5.6MM Privately Held
SIC: 3469 Machine parts, stamped or pressed metal

**(G-21994)**
**AARGUS INDUSTRIES INC**
540 Allendale Dr Ste 100a (60090-2603)
PHONE..................847 325-4444
Fax: 847 325-4260
Jerome Starr, President
EMP: 7
SALES (est): 769.1K Privately Held
SIC: 2673 Plastic & pliofilm bags

**(G-21995)**
**AARGUS PLASTICS INC**
Also Called: Aargus Industries
540 Allendale Dr Ste 100a (60090-2603)
PHONE..................847 325-4444
Fax: 847 325-4260
Jerome Starr, President
Alfred Teo, Chairman
Scott Starr, Vice Pres
Bill Lavelle, CFO
Bob Schlink, Treasurer
▲ EMP: 110
SQ FT: 125,000
SALES (est): 46.3MM Privately Held
WEB: www.aargusplastics.com
SIC: 2673 3081 Plastic & pliofilm bags; polyethylene film

**(G-21996)**
**ABBOTT-INTERFAST CORPORATION**
190 Abbott Dr (60090-5872)
PHONE..................847 459-6200
Fax: 847 459-4076
James Calabrese, President
Bob Baer, Vice Pres
Robert Baer, Vice Pres
Phillip Davis, Purchasing
Joe Podgorski, Controller
▲ EMP: 75
SQ FT: 100,000
SALES (est): 18.4MM Privately Held
WEB: www.abbott-interfast.com
SIC: 3451 3452 Screw machine products; bolts, nuts, rivets & washers

**(G-21997)**
**ABSOLUTE TURN INC**
1704 S Wolf Rd (60090-6517)
PHONE..................847 459-4629
Fax: 847 459-4645
Roy H Urban, President
Ron R Urban, Vice Pres
Marie Urban, Admin Sec
EMP: 25
SQ FT: 8,000
SALES: 40MM Privately Held
WEB: www.absoluteturn.com
SIC: 3599 Machine & other job shop work

**(G-21998)**
**ACCU-FAB INCORPORATED**
1550 Abbott Dr (60090-5820)
PHONE..................847 541-4230
Fax: 847 541-4319
Patrick M Erickson, President
Michael Altieri, General Mgr
Joleen Licari, Purch Mgr
Brian Irvin, QC Mgr
Ken Larsen, Engineer
▲ EMP: 40
SQ FT: 60,000
SALES (est): 10.6MM Privately Held
WEB: www.accu-fabinc.com
SIC: 3613 Control panels, electric

**(G-21999)**
**AGSCO CORPORATION (PA)**
160 W Hintz Rd (60090-5755)
PHONE..................847 520-4455
Fax: 847 520-4970
Harvey R Plonsker, President
Michael D Michaelis, Vice Pres
Lucas Williams, Opers Staff
Jim Connelly, Purch Mgr
Denise Woodward, QC Mgr
◆ EMP: 33 EST: 1888
SQ FT: 60,000
SALES (est): 28.9MM Privately Held
SIC: 5085 3291 Abrasives; rouge, polishing: abrasive

**(G-22000)**
**ALEXETER TECHNOLOGIES LLC (PA)**
830 Seton Ct Ste 6 (60090-5772)
PHONE..................847 419-1507
Fax: 847 419-1648
James P Whelan PHD, General Mgr
James Whalen, General Mgr
Tom Myers, Controller
Tom Fryzel, Sales Mgr
EMP: 11
SQ FT: 5,000
SALES: 1.5MM Privately Held
WEB: www.alexeter.com
SIC: 3826 8111 Environmental testing equipment; legal services

**(G-22001)**
**ALFA CONTROLS INC**
311 Egidi Dr (60090-2653)
P.O. Box 100, Bloomington (61702)
PHONE..................847 978-9245
Felix Gorfin, President
Ana Koreshkov, Controller
Alexandre Kolobaw, Admin Sec
◆ EMP: 5
SQ FT: 12,000
SALES (est): 945.8K Privately Held
SIC: 3621 5084 Electric motor & generator parts; industrial machinery & equipment

**(G-22002)**
**AMERICA PRINTING INC**
716 Gregor Ln (60090-7302)
PHONE..................847 229-8358
William Schmitt, President
Linda Schmitt, Vice Pres
EMP: 5 EST: 1975
SQ FT: 2,000
SALES: 500K Privately Held
SIC: 2752 Commercial printing, offset

**(G-22003)**
**AMERICAN DRILLING INC**
625 Glenn Ave (60090-6017)
PHONE..................847 850-5090
Fax: 847 850-5095
Jim Shanahan Sr, President
Jim Shanahan Jr, Vice Pres
Tom Shanahan, Treasurer
EMP: 45
SQ FT: 19,200
SALES (est): 8.1MM Privately Held
SIC: 3599 Machine & other job shop work

**(G-22004)**
**AMERIFLON LTD (PA)**
930 Seton Ct (60090-5705)
PHONE..................847 541-6000
Alex Provenzano, President
George Bingham, Treasurer
EMP: 6
SQ FT: 12,000
SALES (est): 971.7K Privately Held
WEB: www.nafco.net
SIC: 3087 2992 2821 Custom compound purchased resins; lubricating oils & greases; plastics materials & resins

**(G-22005)**
**AMES METAL PRODUCTS COMPANY**
2211 Foster Ave (60090-6508)
PHONE..................773 523-3230
Fax: 773 523-3854
Lewis Edelstein, President
Jerome Kirsch, Treasurer
Dan Dudzik, Sales Staff
EMP: 10 EST: 1940
SQ FT: 40,000
SALES: 1.9MM Privately Held
SIC: 3356 3452 3369 3363 Tin; lead & lead alloy bars, pipe, plates, shapes, etc.; lead & lead alloy: rolling, drawing or extruding; bolts, nuts, rivets & washers; nonferrous foundries; aluminum die-castings; secondary nonferrous metals; primary nonferrous metals

**(G-22006)**
**ANDREW TECHNOLOGIES INC**
305 Alderman Ave (60090-6505)
PHONE..................847 520-5770
Fax: 847 520-5370
Kathleen A Michals, President
David Michals, Vice Pres
Laverle Franzen, Manager
Tim Kostelancik, Manager
EMP: 30
SQ FT: 15,000
SALES (est): 6.1MM Privately Held
WEB: www.andrewtechnologies.com
SIC: 3679 Electronic circuits

**(G-22007)**
**ARTISTIC FRAMING INC (PA)**
860 Chaddick Dr Ste F (60090-6462)
PHONE..................847 808-0200
Fax: 847 808-0205
Thomas M Wolk, CEO
Larry Thomas, President
Minda Smythe, Vice Pres
Cokkie West, Vice Pres
EMP: 200
SQ FT: 80,000
SALES (est): 29.4MM Privately Held
SIC: 2499 3499 Picture frame molding, finished; picture frames, metal

**(G-22008)**
**ARTTIG ART**
140 Shepard Ave Ste H (60090-6072)
PHONE..................847 804-8001
EMP: 3
SALES (est): 216.1K Privately Held
SIC: 3229 Art, decorative & novelty glassware

**(G-22009)**
**AVAILABLE SPRING AND MFG CO**
350 Holbrook Dr (60090-5812)
P.O. Box 526 (60090-0526)
PHONE..................847 520-4854
J Matthew Eggemeyer, President
Glenn Keats, General Mgr
Wade S Keats, Corp Secy
Matthew M Keats, Vice Pres
Donna Brand, Controller
EMP: 5 EST: 1971
SQ FT: 12,000
SALES (est): 437.8K Privately Held
SIC: 3495 3496 3469 Wire springs; miscellaneous fabricated wire products; metal stampings

**(G-22010)**
**B A I PUBLISHERS**
190 Abbott Dr Ste A (60090-5800)
PHONE..................847 537-1300
Richard Binder, President
EMP: 6
SALES: 320K Privately Held
SIC: 2741 Directories: publishing only, not printed on site

**(G-22011)**
**BADGER MOLDING INC**
2041 Foster Ave (60090-6520)
PHONE..................847 483-9005
Randy Huntress, President
Ed Poelster, Vice Pres
EMP: 15 EST: 2008
SQ FT: 50,000
SALES (est): 2.5MM Privately Held
SIC: 3089 Molding primary plastic

**(G-22012)**
**BAHR TOOL & DIE CO**
2201 Foster Ave (60090-6508)
PHONE..................847 392-4447
Heinz Bahr, Owner
EMP: 5 EST: 1977
SQ FT: 2,000
SALES: 380K Privately Held
SIC: 3544 Special dies & tools

**(G-22013)**
**BEACON FAS & COMPONENTS INC**
Also Called: Beacon Terminal Pin
198 Carpenter Ave (60090-6008)
PHONE..................847 541-0404
Robert Wegner, President
Gary Pavlik, Vice Pres
Joe Peplinski, Vice Pres
Jeff Ryan, Plant Mgr
Kathy Krueger, Purch Mgr
▲ EMP: 35
SQ FT: 35,000
SALES (est): 18.8MM Privately Held
SIC: 5072 3644 Bolts; nuts (hardware); rivets; screws; electric conduits & fittings

**(G-22014)**
**BIO INDUSTRIES INC**
540 Allendale Dr Ste B (60090-2603)
PHONE..................847 215-8999
Fax: 847 459-1303
Judy Hale, Ch of Bd
Gene Wisniewski, President
David Hale, Corp Secy
William Lavelle, CFO
Melany Henkets, Manager
EMP: 56
SQ FT: 35,000
SALES (est): 13MM Privately Held
WEB: www.newplastics.com
SIC: 2673 4953 Plastic bags: made from purchased materials; recycling, waste materials

**(G-22015)**
**BLOCK AND COMPANY INC**
Also Called: Mmf Pos
1111 Wheeling Rd (60090-5795)
PHONE..................847 537-7200
Fax: 800 435-5707
John Lanman III, President

Philip Robins, *General Mgr*
Gus Difiore, *Business Mgr*
Margie Porcello, *Vice Pres*
Thomas Coughlin, *Mfg Mgr*
▲ **EMP:** 190 **EST:** 1934
**SQ FT:** 130,000
**SALES (est):** 69.4MM **Privately Held**
**WEB:** www.mmfcashdrawer.com
**SIC: 3469** 2761 2393 5049 Cash & stamp boxes, stamped metal; manifold business forms; textile bags; bank equipment & supplies; stationery & office supplies

**(G-22016)**
**BOB C BEVERAGES LLC**
Also Called: Bob Chinn's Premium Beverages
419 Harvester Ct (60090-4734)
**PHONE** .................................. 847 520-7582
**EMP:** 3
**SQ FT:** 800
**SALES (est):** 1MM **Privately Held**
**SIC: 2082** Mfg Malt Beverages

**(G-22017)**
**BONA FIDE CORP**
100 Shepard Ave (60090-6022)
**PHONE** .................................. 847 970-8693
Marcin Cartek, *President*
Gabriela Chrapek, *Admin Sec*
**EMP:** 5
**SALES (est):** 953.3K **Privately Held**
**SIC: 3553** Cabinet makers' machinery

**(G-22018)**
**BOOM COMPANY INC**
Also Called: Slam Door Co
161 Wheeling Rd (60090-4807)
**PHONE** .................................. 847 459-6199
John Posch, *President*
**EMP:** 3
**SQ FT:** 2,700
**SALES (est):** 400.4K **Privately Held**
**SIC: 2431** 7699 3442 3231 Windows & window parts & trim, wood; door & window repair; metal doors, sash & trim; products of purchased glass; screens, door & window

**(G-22019)**
**BOWE BELL + HWELL HOLDINGS INC**
Also Called: Bowebellhowell
760 S Wolf Rd (60090-6232)
**PHONE** .................................. 312 541-9300
**Fax:** 847 568-6711
Leslie F Stern, *CEO*
Sheila Taylor, *President*
Woodall Beth, *Vice Pres*
Hendrik Fischer, *Vice Pres*
Hank Martin, *Vice Pres*
▲ **EMP:** 1710
**SQ FT:** 50,000
**SALES (est):** 225.5MM **Privately Held**
**SIC: 3579** Mailing, letter handling & addressing machines; address labeling machines

**(G-22020)**
**BOWE BELL + HWELL SCANNERS LLC**
760 S Wolf Rd (60090-6232)
**PHONE** .................................. 847 675-7600
Russell Hunt, *General Mgr*
Jeff Gruber, *Vice Pres*
David Stein, *Accounts Exec*
Joseph Taylor, *General Counsel*
**EMP:** 50
**SALES (est):** 3.7MM
**SALES (corp-wide):** 1.8B **Publicly Held**
**SIC: 3577** Optical scanning devices
**PA:** Eastman Kodak Company
343 State St
Rochester NY 14650
585 724-4000

**(G-22021)**
**C R PLASTICS INC**
851 Seton Ct Ste 1c (60090-5764)
**PHONE** .................................. 847 541-3601
**Fax:** 847 541-3934
Chester P Frychel, *President*
Ron Nystrom, *Vice Pres*
▲ **EMP:** 8
**SQ FT:** 10,000

**SALES (est):** 1.8MM **Privately Held**
**SIC: 3089** Plastic processing

**(G-22022)**
**C&R SCRAP IRON & METAL**
251 E Dundee Rd (60090-3072)
**PHONE** .................................. 847 459-9815
Ronald Misson, *Owner*
**EMP:** 3
**SALES (est):** 200K **Privately Held**
**SIC: 5093** 3341 Metal scrap & waste materials; secondary nonferrous metals

**(G-22023)**
**CADICAM INC**
2200 Foster Ave (60090-6509)
**PHONE** .................................. 847 394-3610
**Fax:** 847 394-3962
Egon R Jaeggin, *President*
Jim Waters, *General Mgr*
Karl Dahlstrom, *Vice Pres*
Curt Snyder, *Vice Pres*
Dave Lennartz, *Mfg Dir*
**EMP:** 28
**SQ FT:** 20,000
**SALES (est):** 26.2MM **Privately Held**
**WEB:** www.numericalprecision.com
**SIC: 3812** Acceleration indicators & systems components, aerospace

**(G-22024)**
**CAST FILMS INC**
401 Chaddick Dr (60090-6066)
**PHONE** .................................. 847 808-0363
**Fax:** 847 808-0665
Richard Witcraft, *President*
Becky Parr, *Manager*
Tedd Woods, *Manager*
**EMP:** 19
**SQ FT:** 34,200
**SALES (est):** 4.1MM **Privately Held**
**SIC: 3081** Plastic film & sheet

**(G-22025)**
**CHEF SOLUTIONS INC**
Also Called: Lafrancaise Bakery
120 W Palatine Rd (60090-5823)
**PHONE** .................................. 800 877-1157
**Fax:** 847 325-7596
Steven Silk, *CEO*
Robert Wotzak, *President*
Mike Cashula, *COO*
Kent Kring, *COO*
Craig Dergstrom, *Sr Corp Ofcr*
**EMP:** 150
**SQ FT:** 60,000
**SALES (est):** 23.4MM **Privately Held**
**SIC: 2099** Ready-to-eat meals, salads & sandwiches
**PA:** Mistral Equity Partners, Lp
650 5th Ave Fl 31
New York NY 10019

**(G-22026)**
**CITGO PETROLEUM CORPORATION**
775 W Dundee Rd (60090-2605)
**PHONE** .................................. 847 229-1159
Mike Poulos, *Branch Mgr*
**EMP:** 3 **Privately Held**
**WEB:** www.citgo.com
**SIC: 2911** Petroleum refining
**HQ:** Citgo Petroleum Corporation
1293 Eldridge Pkwy
Houston TX 77077
832 486-4000

**(G-22027)**
**CLOROX HIDDEN VALLEY MFG**
1197 Willis Ave (60090-5816)
**PHONE** .................................. 847 229-5500
**Fax:** 847 229-5501
James Zawacki, *Executive*
**EMP:** 15
**SALES (est):** 2.8MM **Privately Held**
**SIC: 5149** 2842 Condiments; bleaches, household: dry or liquid

**(G-22028)**
**CLOROX PRODUCTS MFG CO**
1197 Willis Ave (60090-5816)
**PHONE** .................................. 847 229-5500
Paul Unitas, *Manager*
**EMP:** 150
**SQ FT:** 68,000

**SALES (corp-wide):** 5.7B **Publicly Held**
**SIC: 2842** 2812 Specialty cleaning, polishes & sanitation goods; alkalies & chlorine
**HQ:** Clorox Products Manufacturing Company
1221 Broadway
Oakland CA 94612

**(G-22029)**
**COIN MACKE LAUNDRY**
124b Messner Dr (60090-6434)
**PHONE** .................................. 847 459-1109
**Fax:** 847 537-7405
Danny Thomas, *Manager*
**EMP:** 2
**SALES (est):** 226.4K **Privately Held**
**SIC: 3633** Household laundry equipment

**(G-22030)**
**CONTINENTAL SCREWS MCH PDTS**
160 Abbott Dr (60090-5802)
**PHONE** .................................. 847 459-7766
Martin Binder, *Ch of Bd*
Richard Binder, *President*
Jim Bubis, *Plant Mgr*
**EMP:** 45 **EST:** 1948
**SQ FT:** 12,000
**SALES (est):** 6MM **Privately Held**
**SIC: 3451** Screw machine products

**(G-22031)**
**CREDIT CARD SYSTEMS INC**
180 Shepard Ave (60090-6071)
**PHONE** .................................. 847 459-8320
**Fax:** 847 459-1296
Peter A Lazzari, *President*
Rita Lazzari, *Vice Pres*
**EMP:** 15
**SQ FT:** 12,000
**SALES (est):** 1.5MM **Privately Held**
**WEB:** www.ccsplastech.com
**SIC: 3083** 3559 Plastic finished products, laminated; plastics working machinery

**(G-22032)**
**CRESCENT CARDBOARD COMPANY LLC**
100 W Willow Rd (60090-6587)
**PHONE** .................................. 888 293-3956
C S Ozmun, *President*
Steven Kosmalski, *President*
Kevin McCarthy, *Vice Pres*
Wally Surmenkow, *Mfg Mgr*
Kathleen Carlson, *Opers Staff*
▲ **EMP:** 195
**SALES (est):** 51.2MM **Privately Held**
**WEB:** www.crescentcardboard.com
**SIC: 2679** Paperboard products, converted
**PA:** Potomac Corporation
2063 Foster Ave
Wheeling IL 60090
847 259-0546

**(G-22033)**
**CUSTOM LINEAR GRILLE INC**
Also Called: Custom Enclsrs Div Cstm Lnear
500 Harvester Ct Ste 3 (60090-4755)
P.O. Box 8560, Northfield (60093-8560)
**PHONE** .................................. 847 520-5511
**Fax:** 708 520-5588
Harris Jackson, *President*
**EMP:** 5
**SALES (est):** 390K **Privately Held**
**SIC: 3446** 3444 3433 Architectural metalwork; sheet metalwork; heating equipment, except electric

**(G-22034)**
**DIAMOND DIE & BEVEL CUTNG LLC**
2087 Foster Ave (60090-6520)
**PHONE** .................................. 224 387-3200
C S Ozmun, *President*
Chris Hosey, *General Mgr*
Matthew Ozmun, *Vice Pres*
Terry Boffeli, *Admin Sec*
▲ **EMP:** 25
**SALES (est):** 3.8MM **Privately Held**
**SIC: 3915** Diamond cutting & polishing

**(G-22035)**
**DIGI CELL COMMUNICATIONS**
98 E Dundee Rd (60090-3060)
**PHONE** .................................. 847 808-7900
Sandro Sanchez, *Partner*
Vicki Sanchez, *Partner*
Lupe Garcia, *Admin Asst*
**EMP:** 3
**SALES (est):** 378.2K **Privately Held**
**SIC: 3357** Communication wire

**(G-22036)**
**DISTINCTIVE FOODS LLC (PA)**
Also Called: Pie Piper Products
654 Wheeling Rd (60090-5707)
**PHONE** .................................. 847 459-3600
**Fax:** 847 459-3660
Mike Vovk, *Engineer*
Ron Buck, *CFO*
Lori Sproat, *Finance Mgr*
Stephanie Jacob, *Sales Mgr*
Andrew Holzman, *Sales Staff*
▼ **EMP:** 15
**SQ FT:** 15,000
**SALES (est):** 19.5MM **Privately Held**
**SIC: 2038** Frozen specialties

**(G-22037)**
**DTK CONSTRUCTION INC**
Also Called: Dtk Stone Works
200 Sumac Rd Ste A (60090-6429)
P.O. Box 241, Morton Grove (60053-0241)
**PHONE** .................................. 312 296-2762
Dimitre Koldanov, *President*
▲ **EMP:** 6
**SQ FT:** 10,000
**SALES:** 1.5MM **Privately Held**
**SIC: 3281** Cut stone & stone products

**(G-22038)**
**DUPAGE MECHANICAL**
270 Larkin Dr Ste D (60090-6472)
**PHONE** .................................. 630 620-1122
Debbie Squires, *Principal*
**EMP:** 3
**SALES (est):** 303.7K **Privately Held**
**SIC: 5075** 3585 Air conditioning equipment, except room units; air conditioning equipment, complete

**(G-22039)**
**DURABLE INC (PA)**
Also Called: Durable Packaging Intl
750 Northgate Pkwy (60090-2660)
**PHONE** .................................. 847 541-4400
**Fax:** 847 541-8360
Scott Anders, *President*
Michael Rabin, *CFO*
Brad Ravin, *Manager*
Darren Anders, *Admin Sec*
▲ **EMP:** 750 **EST:** 1943
**SQ FT:** 400,000
**SALES (est):** 111.3MM **Privately Held**
**WEB:** www.durablepackaging.com
**SIC: 3497** 3354 Foil containers for bakery goods & frozen foods; aluminum extruded products

**(G-22040)**
**DYNOMAX INC (PA)**
1535 Abbott Dr (60090-5821)
**PHONE** .................................. 847 680-8833
Richard Zic, *President*
Maura Zic, *Corp Secy*
Marc Zic, *Vice Pres*
Walter Zic, *Vice Pres*
Jean Werner, *Controller*
▲ **EMP:** 85
**SQ FT:** 20,000
**SALES (est):** 33.9MM **Privately Held**
**WEB:** www.dynospindles.com
**SIC: 3679** 3566 Electronic circuits; speed changers, drives & gears

**(G-22041)**
**EASTERN COMPANY**
Illinois Lock Company
301 W Hintz Rd (60090-5754)
P.O. Box 9068 (60090-9068)
**PHONE** .................................. 847 537-1800
**Fax:** 847 537-1881
Fred Tierhold, *Project Mgr*
Arlene Zajdel, *Production*
Michael Misner, *Design Engr*
Mark Pekovitch, *Design Engr*
Brian D Reed, *Sales/Mktg Mgr*

## Wheeling - Cook County (G-22042)

**EMP:** 120
**SQ FT:** 45,000
**SALES (corp-wide):** 137.6MM **Publicly Held**
**WEB:** www.easterncompany.com
**SIC:** 3429 5099 Locks or lock sets; locks & lock sets
**PA:** The Eastern Company
  112 Bridge St
  Naugatuck CT 06770
  203 729-2255

### (G-22042)
### EBERLE MANUFACTURING COMPANY
230 Larkin Dr (60090-6456)
**PHONE** ................................ 847 215-0100
**Fax:** 847 215-7881
Robert Eberle, *President*
Anna Eberle, *Corp Secy*
Wayne Kline, *Plant Mgr*
Dan Leisner, *Opers Mgr*
Oleg Berger, *Chief Engr*
**EMP:** 12 **EST:** 1953
**SQ FT:** 16,500
**SALES (est):** 830K **Privately Held**
**WEB:** www.eberlemfg.com
**SIC:** 3544 3569 Special dies, tools, jigs & fixtures; assembly machines, non-metalworking

### (G-22043)
### EDGAR A WEBER & COMPANY
Also Called: Weber Flavors
549 Palwaukee Dr (60090-6049)
P.O. Box 546 (60090-0546)
**PHONE** ................................ 847 215-1980
William Igou, *President*
Andrew G Plennert, *President*
Mike Sciore, *Plant Mgr*
David Samuels, *Opers Staff*
Carol Meyers, *Purch Mgr*
▲ **EMP:** 20
**SQ FT:** 5,000
**SALES (est):** 6.7MM **Privately Held**
**WEB:** www.weberflavors.com
**SIC:** 2087 Extracts, flavoring

### (G-22044)
### EDGAR A WEBER & COMPANY
Also Called: Weber Flavors
549 Palwaukee Dr (60090-6049)
P.O. Box 546 (60090-0546)
**PHONE** ................................ 847 215-1980
**EMP:** 20 **EST:** 1995
**SALES (est):** 2.8MM **Privately Held**
**SIC:** 2087 Mfg Flavor Extracts/Syrup

### (G-22045)
### EJ CADY & COMPANY
Also Called: Caddy
135 Wheeling Rd (60090-4807)
**PHONE** ................................ 847 537-2239
**Fax:** 847 537-1766
Thomas D Chatterton, *President*
Bonnie Chatterton, *Corp Secy*
Carlos Zamora, *Purch Agent*
**EMP:** 4 **EST:** 1895
**SQ FT:** 3,000
**SALES (est):** 675.4K **Privately Held**
**WEB:** www.ejcady.com
**SIC:** 3829 5084 3596 Testing equipment: abrasion, shearing strength, etc.; industrial machinery & equipment; analytical instruments; scales & balances, except laboratory; machine tool accessories

### (G-22046)
### ELENCO ELECTRONICS INC
150 Carpenter Ave (60090-6062)
**PHONE** ................................ 847 541-3800
James T Cecchin, *President*
David Jonesi, *General Mgr*
Linda Kramer, *Corp Secy*
Tony Agostinelli, *COO*
Gerald J Cecchin, *Vice Pres*
◆ **EMP:** 39
**SQ FT:** 56,000
**SALES (est):** 13.1MM **Privately Held**
**WEB:** www.elenco.com
**SIC:** 3825 5945 3699 3625 Oscillographs & oscilloscopes; power measuring equipment, electrical; hobby, toy & game shops; electrical equipment & supplies; relays & industrial controls; motors & generators; switchgear & switchboard apparatus

### (G-22047)
### ENGIS CORPORATION (PA)
105 W Hintz Rd (60090-5769)
**PHONE** ................................ 847 808-9400
**Fax:** 847 808-9430
Stephen Griffin, *President*
Siobhan Campos, *Principal*
Martin Steindler, *Chairman*
Sean Gilmore, *Vice Pres*
Kenneth Werner, *Vice Pres*
▲ **EMP:** 135 **EST:** 1938
**SQ FT:** 121,125
**SALES (est):** 38.1MM **Privately Held**
**SIC:** 3541 3291 3545 3471 Machine tools, metal cutting type; diamond powder; machine tool accessories; plating & polishing

### (G-22048)
### EPAZZ INC (PA)
325 N Milwaukee Ave Ste G (60090-3071)
**PHONE** ................................ 312 955-8161
**Fax:** 312 873-4283
Shaun Passley, *Ch of Bd*
Craig Passley, *Admin Sec*
**EMP:** 8
**SQ FT:** 2,522
**SALES (est):** 1.5MM **Publicly Held**
**SIC:** 7372 Prepackaged software; application computer software; business oriented computer software

### (G-22049)
### ETHNIC MEDIA LLC
704 S Milwaukee Ave (60090-6202)
**PHONE** ................................ 224 676-0778
Alexander Khodos,
**EMP:** 4
**SALES (est):** 384.7K **Privately Held**
**SIC:** 2711 Newspapers

### (G-22050)
### EVANGERS DOG AND CAT FD CO INC
221 Wheeling Rd (60090-4809)
**PHONE** ................................ 847 537-0102
**Fax:** 847 537-0179
Holly Sher, *President*
Joel Sher, *Vice Pres*
Cynthia Stoner, *Manager*
◆ **EMP:** 45
**SQ FT:** 15,000
**SALES (est):** 13.4MM **Privately Held**
**WEB:** www.evangersdogfood.com
**SIC:** 2047 Dog & cat food

### (G-22051)
### EXACT TOOL COMPANY INC
2123 Foster Ave (60090-6506)
**PHONE** ................................ 847 632-1140
**Fax:** 847 632-1148
Renate Drost, *President*
Chris Drost, *Vice Pres*
Ray Drost, *Vice Pres*
**EMP:** 8
**SQ FT:** 21,000
**SALES (est):** 1.2MM **Privately Held**
**SIC:** 3544 Dies & die holders for metal cutting, forming, die casting; punches, forming & stamping

### (G-22052)
### EXCELITAS TECHNOLOGIES CORP
160 E Marquardt Dr (60090-6428)
**PHONE** ................................ 847 537-4277
Sinisa Stojanovic, *Opers Staff*
Stefan Bedetti, *Senior Buyer*
Craig Fields, *Engineer*
Chris Hoffman, *Engineer*
Chris Schenkenfelder, *Engineer*
**EMP:** 45 **Privately Held**
**SIC:** 3679 Electronic circuits
**HQ:** Excelitas Technologies Corp.
  200 West St
  Waltham MA 02451

### (G-22053)
### FACTORY DIRECT WORLDWIDE LLC
230 Messner Dr (60090-6436)
**PHONE** ................................ 847 272-6464
Chris L Anetsberger,
▲ **EMP:** 13
**SALES (est):** 3.1MM **Privately Held**
**SIC:** 3523 Farm machinery & equipment

### (G-22054)
### FLP INDUSTRIES LLC
500 Harvester Ct Ste 2 (60090-4755)
**PHONE** ................................ 847 215-8650
**Fax:** 847 215-8675
Hajime Furukawa,
**EMP:** 11
**SALES (est):** 1.3MM **Privately Held**
**SIC:** 3679 Harness assemblies for electronic use: wire or cable

### (G-22055)
### FLUID MANAGEMENT INC (HQ)
Also Called: FM
1023 Wheeling Rd (60090-5776)
**PHONE** ................................ 847 537-0880
**Fax:** 847 537-0880
Dennis Williams, *Ch of Bd*
Suzanne Burns, *President*
Jerry N Derck, *Vice Pres*
Douglas C Lennox, *Vice Pres*
Wayne P Sayatovic, *Vice Pres*
◆ **EMP:** 290
**SQ FT:** 147,000
**SALES (est):** 83.7MM
**SALES (corp-wide):** 2.1B **Publicly Held**
**WEB:** www.fluidman.com
**SIC:** 3559 Paint making machinery
**PA:** Idex Corporation
  1925 W Field Ct Ste 200
  Lake Forest IL 60045
  847 498-7070

### (G-22056)
### FLUID MNAGEMENT OPERATIONS LLC (HQ)
1023 Wheeling Rd (60090-5768)
**PHONE** ................................ 847 537-0880
Lawrence D Kingsley, *Ch of Bd*
Eric McKinley, *Finance Mgr*
Kathleen Anderson, *Credit Mgr*
▲ **EMP:** 6
**SALES (est):** 8.1MM
**SALES (corp-wide):** 2.1B **Publicly Held**
**SIC:** 3531 Mixers: ore, plaster, slag, sand, mortar, etc.
**PA:** Idex Corporation
  1925 W Field Ct Ste 200
  Lake Forest IL 60045
  847 498-7070

### (G-22057)
### FOUNTAIN TECHNOLOGIES LTD
423 Denniston Ct (60090-4730)
**PHONE** ................................ 847 537-3677
Robert Watson, *President*
Mark Saulka, *Principal*
Pat Saulka, *Vice Pres*
Patricia Saulka, *Admin Sec*
**EMP:** 30
**SALES:** 4MM **Privately Held**
**WEB:** www.fountaintechnologies.com
**SIC:** 1799 3272 5145 Fountain installation; fountains, concrete; fountain supplies

### (G-22058)
### FRANKENSTITCH PROMOTIONS LLC
460 W Hintz Rd (60090-5757)
**PHONE** ................................ 847 459-4840
Adam Frank, *Mng Member*
Howard N Frank,
**EMP:** 6 **EST:** 1998
**SQ FT:** 5,200
**SALES (est):** 560K **Privately Held**
**SIC:** 5099 2261 5046 Signs, except electric; roller printing of cotton broadwoven fabrics; signs, electrical

### (G-22059)
### FUN INCORPORATED
333 Alice St (60090-5805)
**PHONE** ................................ 773 745-3837
Graham R Putnam, *President*

Steve Kirshenbaum, *General Mgr*
Kathryn Andersen-Putnam, *Vice Pres*
Tomas Medina, *Sales Staff*
▲ **EMP:** 20 **EST:** 1941
**SQ FT:** 42,500
**SALES (est):** 3.6MM **Privately Held**
**WEB:** www.funinc.com
**SIC:** 3944 3993 Games, toys & children's vehicles; advertising novelties

### (G-22060)
### FURNITURE SERVICES INC
410 Mercantile Ct (60090-4738)
**PHONE** ................................ 847 520-9490
Frank Lakes, *Owner*
▲ **EMP:** 3
**SALES (est):** 281.8K **Privately Held**
**SIC:** 5712 2431 1751 Furniture stores; millwork; carpentry work

### (G-22061)
### G & Z INDUSTRIES INC
541 Chaddick Dr (60090-6053)
**PHONE** ................................ 847 215-2300
**Fax:** 847 215-2579
David Gill, *President*
Wayne Schott, *Corp Secy*
Jesse Siwiec, *Vice Pres*
Dennis Monzel, *Opers Staff*
Lucy Vargas, *Purch Agent*
**EMP:** 48 **EST:** 1958
**SQ FT:** 19,000
**SALES (est):** 11.2MM **Privately Held**
**WEB:** www.gzind.com
**SIC:** 3469 Machine parts, stamped or pressed metal

### (G-22062)
### GENNCO INTERNATIONAL INC
200 Larkin Dr Ste F (60090-6498)
**PHONE** ................................ 847 541-3333
**Fax:** 847 541-4444
Kenneth Genender, *President*
Jerry Kushnir, *CFO*
Amy Genender, *Mktg Dir*
▲ **EMP:** 15
**SALES:** 5.5MM **Privately Held**
**SIC:** 2339 2389 5094 Women's & misses' outerwear; men's miscellaneous accessories; watches & parts

### (G-22063)
### H V MANUFACTURING VANGUAR
1197 Willis Ave (60090-5816)
**PHONE** ................................ 847 229-5502
Gerald Johnston, *CEO*
**EMP:** 3 **EST:** 2010
**SALES (est):** 285K **Privately Held**
**SIC:** 3999 Manufacturing industries

### (G-22064)
### HAGEN MANUFACTURING INC
318 Holbrook Dr (60090-5812)
**PHONE** ................................ 224 735-2099
Mark Hagen, *President*
**EMP:** 3 **EST:** 2011
**SALES (est):** 376K **Privately Held**
**SIC:** 3999 Chairs, hydraulic, barber & beauty shop

### (G-22065)
### HANDI-FOIL CORP (PA)
135 E Hintz Rd (60090-6059)
**PHONE** ................................ 847 520-1000
Norton Sarnoff, *President*
Brad Sarnoff, *Vice Pres*
Rich Kendzior, *Plant Mgr*
Peter Perkins, *CFO*
Patricia Rotondi, *Accounts Mgr*
▲ **EMP:** 700
**SQ FT:** 650,000
**SALES (est):** 91.6MM **Privately Held**
**SIC:** 3497 Foil containers for bakery goods & frozen foods

### (G-22066)
### HANDI-FOIL CORP
1234 Peterson Dr (60090-6454)
**PHONE** ................................ 847 520-5742
Scott Salzstein, *Branch Mgr*
**EMP:** 50
**SALES (corp-wide):** 91.6MM **Privately Held**
**SIC:** 3497 Foil containers for bakery goods & frozen foods

# GEOGRAPHIC SECTION
## Wheeling - Cook County (G-22091)

PA: Handi-Foil Corp.
135 E Hintz Rd
Wheeling IL 60090
847 520-1000

### (G-22067)
**HANDY BUTTON MACHINE CO (PA)**
Also Called: Handy Kenlin Group, The
29 E Hintz Rd (60090-6043)
PHONE...................847 459-0900
Michael Baritz, *CEO*
Kenneth Shonfeld, *President*
Allan Mendel, *Buyer*
Byron Paz, *Buyer*
Dawn Graese, *Controller*
▲ **EMP:** 40
**SQ FT:** 16,000
**SALES (est):** 6MM **Privately Held**
**WEB:** www.handykenlin.com
**SIC:** 3965 3552 Button backs & parts; button blanks & molds; textile machinery

### (G-22068)
**HANSON METAL FINISHING INC**
1057 Kenilworth Dr (60090-3964)
PHONE...................847 520-1463
Robert Shaffer, *Principal*
**EMP:** 3
**SALES (est):** 135K **Privately Held**
**SIC:** 3471 Cleaning, polishing & finishing

### (G-22069)
**HFA INC**
135 E Hintz Rd (60090-6035)
PHONE...................847 520-1000
Norton Sarnoff, *President*
Brad Sarnoff, *Vice Pres*
David Sarnoff, *Vice Pres*
Peter Perkins, *CFO*
Alex Wong, *Controller*
◆ **EMP:** 700
**SQ FT:** 500,000
**SALES (est):** 228.8MM **Privately Held**
**SIC:** 3497 Foil containers for bakery goods & frozen foods

### (G-22070)
**HI-TECH PLASTICS INC**
2074 Foster Ave 78 (60090-6521)
PHONE...................847 577-1805
Fax: 847 577-1826
James A Puetz, *President*
Gottfried Winter, *Corp Secy*
Marion Calvino, *Manager*
**EMP:** 10
**SQ FT:** 6,000
**SALES:** 1.1MM **Privately Held**
**WEB:** www.hi-techplastics.com
**SIC:** 3089 Injection molded finished plastic products

### (G-22071)
**HK WOODWORK**
925 Seton Ct Ste 7 (60090-5771)
PHONE...................773 964-2468
Jakub S Kosik, *Principal*
**EMP:** 2
**SALES (est):** 204.7K **Privately Held**
**SIC:** 2431 Millwork

### (G-22072)
**HOLBROOK MFG INC**
288 Holbrook Dr (60090-5810)
PHONE...................847 229-1999
Fax: 847 229-0996
Don Kuhns, *CEO*
Gary Vanderpoel, *President*
William Collopy, *Exec VP*
Bradley Yerkes, *Vice Pres*
Paul Graf, *Opers Staff*
▲ **EMP:** 85
**SQ FT:** 80,000
**SALES (est):** 17.7MM **Privately Held**
**WEB:** www.holbrookinc.com
**SIC:** 3452 Screws, metal

### (G-22073)
**IAM ACQUISITION LLC**
Also Called: Coregistics
230 W Palatine Rd (60090-5825)
PHONE...................847 259-7800
Erin Hunt, *Branch Mgr*
**EMP:** 35 **Privately Held**
**SIC:** 2671 Plastic film, coated or laminated for packaging

PA: Iam Acquisition, Llc
240 Northpoint Pkwy
Acworth GA 30102

### (G-22074)
**ILMACHINE COMPANY INC**
421 Harvester Ct (60090-4734)
PHONE...................847 243-9900
Fax: 847 243-9902
Igor Levin, *President*
Demitrius Sokolsky, *Vice Pres*
**EMP:** 13
**SQ FT:** 11,000
**SALES (est):** 2.6MM **Privately Held**
**SIC:** 3444 7692 Sheet metalwork; welding repair

### (G-22075)
**IMPERIAL GLASS STRUCTURES CO**
2120 Foster Ave (60090-6578)
PHONE...................847 253-6150
Fax: 847 253-6154
Dieter Jankowski, *President*
Mike Malicki, *Vice Pres*
**EMP:** 15
**SQ FT:** 16,000
**SALES:** 3.5MM **Privately Held**
**WEB:** www.imperialskylights.com
**SIC:** 3444 Skylights, sheet metal

### (G-22076)
**INDUSTRIAL MOTION CONTROL LLC (DH)**
Also Called: De-Sta-Co Camco Products
1444 S Wolf Rd (60090-6514)
PHONE...................847 459-5200
Fax: 847 459-3064
Ian Nilson, *CFO*
Cristie Panke, *Accountant*
Thomas Berner, *Manager*
Mitch Miller, *Manager*
Ryan Pagels, *Manager*
▲ **EMP:** 125
**SQ FT:** 100,000
**SALES:** 40MM
**SALES (corp-wide):** 6.7B **Publicly Held**
**SIC:** 3568 3535 3625 3566 Power transmission equipment; conveyors & conveying equipment; relays & industrial controls; speed changers, drives & gears
HQ: Dover Energy, Inc.
15 Corporate Dr
Auburn Hills MI 48326
248 836-6700

### (G-22077)
**INTERNATIONAL ELECTRO MAGNETIC**
Also Called: Instrument Laboratories Div
1033 Noel Ave (60090-5813)
PHONE...................847 358-4622
Fax: 847 947-8239
Anthony M Pretto, *President*
Dan Kantorski, *Engineer*
**EMP:** 5 **EST:** 1961
**SQ FT:** 5,000
**SALES (est):** 490K **Privately Held**
**WEB:** www.iemmag.com
**SIC:** 3825 Test equipment for electronic & electrical circuits

### (G-22078)
**IP MEDIA HOLDINGS**
55 E Hintz Rd (60090-6043)
PHONE...................847 714-1177
William Polich, *CEO*
Russell Chatskis, *President*
Elliot Portney, *Manager*
▲ **EMP:** 25
**SALES (est):** 4.5MM **Privately Held**
**WEB:** www.ipmedia.net
**SIC:** 3678 Electronic connectors

### (G-22079)
**JAB DISTRIBUTORS LLC**
Also Called: Protect-A-Bed
1500 S Wolf Rd (60090-6515)
PHONE...................847 998-6901
Fax: 847 998-6919
Jennifer Hillman, *Vice Pres*
Anneke Charny, *CFO*
James Bel, *Mng Member*
Clive Goldin, *Mng Member*
Miguel Marrero, *Info Tech Mgr*

▲ **EMP:** 50
**SQ FT:** 35,000
**SALES (est):** 9.2MM **Privately Held**
**WEB:** www.jabdistributors.com
**SIC:** 2392 5023 Mattress pads; mattress protectors, except rubber; floor cushion & padding

### (G-22080)
**JACOB HAY CO**
509 N Wolf Rd (60090-3027)
PHONE...................847 215-8880
Fax: 847 215-7066
Dennis H Gardino, *President*
Christopher Gardino, *Treasurer*
**EMP:** 7 **EST:** 1935
**SQ FT:** 3,000
**SALES (est):** 2.1MM **Privately Held**
**SIC:** 5085 5169 2842 Industrial supplies; polishes; specialty cleaning, polishes & sanitation goods

### (G-22081)
**JEFFREY JAE INC**
1125 Wheeling Rd (60090-5716)
PHONE...................847 808-2002
Fax: 847 537-1538
Jeffery-Jae Bersch, *CEO*
**EMP:** 40
**SQ FT:** 25,000
**SALES (corp-wide):** 11MM **Privately Held**
**SIC:** 3452 Bolts, nuts, rivets & washers
PA: Jae Jeffrey Inc
907 E Brookwood Dr
Arlington Heights IL 60004
847 394-1313

### (G-22082)
**JELCO INC**
450 Wheeling Rd (60090-4742)
PHONE...................847 459-5207
Fax: 847 459-5262
Edwin Elliott, *President*
Linda Elliott, *Treasurer*
Andy Kraus, *Accounting Mgr*
▲ **EMP:** 13
**SQ FT:** 21,000
**SALES (est):** 1.1MM **Privately Held**
**WEB:** www.jelcoinc.com
**SIC:** 3161 Attache cases; briefcases; camera carrying bags; cases, carrying

### (G-22083)
**KEATS MANUFACTURING CO**
350 Holbrook Dr (60090-5812)
P.O. Box 526 (60090-0526)
PHONE...................847 520-1133
Fax: 847 520-0114
Wade Keats, *CEO*
Matt Eggemeyer, *COO*
Matthew Keats, *Vice Pres*
Herb Fink, *Plant Mgr*
David Fink, *Materials Mgr*
▲ **EMP:** 100
**SQ FT:** 20,000
**SALES (est):** 27.8MM **Privately Held**
**WEB:** www.keatsmfg.com
**SIC:** 3496 3312 Clips & fasteners, made from purchased wire; tool & die steel

### (G-22084)
**KITAMURA MACHINERY USA INC (HQ)**
78 Century Dr (60090-6050)
PHONE...................847 520-7755
Fax: 847 520-7763
Koichiro Kitamura, *Ch of Bd*
Akihiro Aki Kitamura, *President*
Mike Umeno, *Vice Pres*
Shozo Kitamura, *Treasurer*
Minoru Umeno, *Admin Sec*
▲ **EMP:** 13
**SQ FT:** 20,000
**SALES:** 3.5MM
**SALES (corp-wide):** 91.2MM **Privately Held**
**SIC:** 3545 Cutting tools for machine tools
PA: Kitamura Machinery Co.,Ltd.
1870, Toidekomyoji
Takaoka TYM 939-1
766 631-100

### (G-22085)
**KIWI CODERS CORP**
265 Messner Dr (60090-6495)
PHONE...................847 541-4511

Fax: 847 541-6332
Allen Mc Kay, *President*
Brent Mc Kay, *Vice Pres*
Peter Zamora, *Manager*
Brent E Mc Kay, *Admin Sec*
**EMP:** 42
**SQ FT:** 55,000
**SALES (est):** 7.2MM **Privately Held**
**WEB:** www.kiwicoders.com
**SIC:** 3953 3555 Marking devices; printing trades machinery

### (G-22086)
**KLH PRINTING CORP**
664 Wheeling Rd (60090-5707)
PHONE...................847 459-0115
Fax: 847 459-0345
Kenneth Meyer, *President*
Jeannie Prohny, *Accountant*
**EMP:** 4
**SQ FT:** 2,800
**SALES (est):** 445.3K **Privately Held**
**SIC:** 2759 2752 2791 2789 Commercial printing; letterpress printing; color lithography; typesetting; bookbinding & related work

### (G-22087)
**KYOWA INDUSTRIAL CO LTD USA**
711 Glenn Ave (60090-6019)
PHONE...................847 459-3500
Fax: 847 459-7470
Tsuneo Matsui, *President*
Takatoshi Tanaka, *General Mgr*
Hideki Sakamoto, *Vice Pres*
Mutsimi Saito, *Bookkeeper*
▲ **EMP:** 15
**SQ FT:** 15,000
**SALES (est):** 2.8MM
**SALES (corp-wide):** 3.4MM **Privately Held**
**SIC:** 3544 Industrial molds
PA: Kyowa Industrial Co.,Ltd.
29-1, Kamisugoro
Sanjo NIG 955-0
256 344-440

### (G-22088)
**LAKE COUNTY C V JOINTS INC**
Also Called: Lake Cook C V
133 Wheeling Rd (60090-4807)
PHONE...................847 537-7588
Jerry Bullock, *President*
John Hudrick Jr, *Admin Sec*
**EMP:** 3
**SALES:** 250K **Privately Held**
**SIC:** 3944 Trains & equipment, toy: electric & mechanical

### (G-22089)
**LANG DENTAL MFG CO INC**
175 Messner Dr (60090-6433)
P.O. Box 969 (60090-0969)
PHONE...................847 215-6622
Fax: 847 215-6678
David J Lang, *President*
Daniel Beck, *Exec VP*
Joanne Lang, *Director*
◆ **EMP:** 18
**SQ FT:** 21,000
**SALES (est):** 4.8MM **Privately Held**
**WEB:** www.langdental.com
**SIC:** 3843 Dental equipment & supplies; compounds, dental

### (G-22090)
**LEAD N GLASS TM**
2039 Foster Ave Ste A (60090-6513)
PHONE...................847 255-2074
James La Caeyse, *President*
Jarett La Caeyse, *President*
Todd La Caeyse, *Vice Pres*
Sharon La Caeyse, *Treasurer*
**EMP:** 11
**SQ FT:** 5,500
**SALES (est):** 970K **Privately Held**
**SIC:** 3231 5031 Decorated glassware: chipped, engraved, etched, etc.; kitchen cabinets

### (G-22091)
**LECTRO GRAPHICS INC**
851 Seton Ct Ste 1b (60090-5764)
PHONE...................847 537-3592
Fax: 847 459-1861

# Wheeling - Cook County (G-22092) — GEOGRAPHIC SECTION

Michael Schaefges, *President*
**EMP:** 1
**SQ FT:** 500
**SALES:** 250K **Privately Held**
**WEB:** www.lectrographicsinc.com
**SIC:** 8711 3672 Electrical or electronic engineering; printed circuit boards

**(G-22092)**
**LEROYS WELDING & FABG INC**
363 Alice St (60090-5805)
**PHONE** ................................ 847 215-6151
**Fax:** 847 215-6154
Neil Rubly, *President*
Vince Centineo, *Vice Pres*
Tina Centineo, *Treasurer*
**EMP:** 10
**SQ FT:** 8,500
**SALES (est):** 1.7MM **Privately Held**
**SIC:** 7692 3441 Welding repair; fabricated structural metal

**(G-22093)**
**LEWIS PAPER PLACE INC**
220 E Marquardt Dr (60090-6430)
**PHONE** ................................ 847 808-1343
**EMP:** 2
**SALES (est):** 222K **Privately Held**
**SIC:** 5084 2679 5112 Industrial machinery & equipment; paper products, converted; office supplies

**(G-22094)**
**LINK-LETTERS LTD**
Also Called: Express Printing
309 N Wolf Rd (60090-2923)
**PHONE** ................................ 847 459-1199
**Fax:** 847 459-0854
Eric G Matye, *President*
Rich Schroeter, *Plant Mgr*
Chris Loveless, *Sls & Mktg Exec*
**EMP:** 10
**SQ FT:** 2,500
**SALES (est):** 1.4MM **Privately Held**
**WEB:** www.expressprintingctr.com
**SIC:** 2752 2791 2789 Commercial printing, offset; typesetting; bookbinding & related work

**(G-22095)**
**LISTS & LETTERS**
480 W Hintz Rd (60090-5765)
**PHONE** ................................ 847 520-5207
**Fax:** 847 520-5228
Joe Garza, *Owner*
**EMP:** 17
**SALES (est):** 2.5MM **Privately Held**
**WEB:** www.lucire.com
**SIC:** 7331 2791 2789 2752 Direct mail advertising services; mailing service; typesetting; bookbinding & related work; commercial printing, lithographic

**(G-22096)**
**LIVING ROYAL**
500 Quail Hollow Dr (60090-2651)
**PHONE** ................................ 312 906-7600
**EMP:** 16
**SALES (est):** 1.1MM **Privately Held**
**SIC:** 2252 Mfg Hosiery

**(G-22097)**
**MAILBOX INTERNATIONAL INC**
220 Messner Dr (60090-6436)
**PHONE** ................................ 847 541-8466
John Nugent, *Ch of Bd*
Graham R Wood, *President*
Mark Hayes, *Vice Pres*
**EMP:** 4
**SQ FT:** 9,900
**SALES:** 127.4K
**SALES (corp-wide):** 17.3MM **Privately Held**
**SIC:** 5084 3537 3444 3443 Materials handling machinery; industrial trucks & tractors; sheet metalwork; fabricated plate work (boiler shop); partitions & fixtures, except wood; carpets & rugs
**HQ:** Stamford Group Limited(The)
Stamford Mill
Stalybridge SK15
161 330-6511

**(G-22098)**
**MANAGED MARKETING INC**
Also Called: Direct Envelope
2232 Foster Ave (60090-6509)
**PHONE** ................................ 847 279-8260
Suzan Edwards, *President*
Dirk Edwards, *Admin Sec*
**EMP:** 9 **EST:** 1997
**SQ FT:** 15,000
**SALES:** 1.8MM **Privately Held**
**WEB:** www.directenv.com
**SIC:** 2677 2759 Envelopes; invitation & stationery printing & engraving

**(G-22099)**
**MANAN MEDICAL PRODUCTS INC (DH)**
Also Called: Argon Medical
241 W Palatine Rd (60090-5824)
**PHONE** ................................ 847 637-3333
**Fax:** 847 637-3334
Michael J Hudson, *President*
George Leondis, *General Mgr*
Sharon McNally, *Vice Pres*
Manfred Mittermeier, *Vice Pres*
John Pavelt, *Vice Pres*
▲ **EMP:** 69
**SALES (est):** 34.1MM
**SALES (corp-wide):** 304.8MM **Privately Held**
**SIC:** 3842 3841 Surgical appliances & supplies; surgical & medical instruments
**HQ:** Argon Medical Devices, Inc.
5151 Hdqtr Dr Ste 210
Plano TX 75024
903 675-9321

**(G-22100)**
**MANAN TOOL & MANUFACTURING**
241 W Palatine Rd (60090-5824)
**PHONE** ................................ 847 637-3333
Werner Mittermeier, *Principal*
Manfred Mittermeier, *Principal*
**EMP:** 1112
**SQ FT:** 82,000
**SALES (est):** 109.3MM **Privately Held**
**SIC:** 3541 3841 Machine tools, metal cutting type; needles, suture

**(G-22101)**
**MARATHON CUTTING DIE INC**
2340 Foster Ave (60090-6511)
**PHONE** ................................ 847 398-5165
**Fax:** 847 398-5195
Michael Bauer, *President*
Avis Davis, *Manager*
**EMP:** 22
**SALES (est):** 4.3MM **Privately Held**
**SIC:** 3544 Special dies & tools

**(G-22102)**
**MATERIAL TESTING TECH INC**
420 Harvester Ct (60090-4735)
**PHONE** ................................ 847 215-1211
**Fax:** 847 215-7449
W Scott Thielman, *President*
Nancy Kamka, *Manager*
Rose Brown, *Admin Asst*
**EMP:** 12
**SALES (est):** 1.2MM **Privately Held**
**WEB:** www.mttusa.net
**SIC:** 3829 Measuring & controlling devices

**(G-22103)**
**MATTS COOKIE COMPANY**
482 N Milwaukee Ave (60090-3067)
**PHONE** ................................ 847 537-3888
Mike Halverson, *CEO*
**EMP:** 5
**SALES (est):** 145.4K **Privately Held**
**SIC:** 2052 Cookies

**(G-22104)**
**MICROTECH MACHINE INC**
222 Camp Mcdonald Rd (60090-6533)
**PHONE** ................................ 847 870-0707
**Fax:** 847 870-1177
Elizabeth Iwanicki, *President*
Bob Buy, *Purchasing*
**EMP:** 20
**SQ FT:** 18,200
**SALES (est):** 3.8MM **Privately Held**
**SIC:** 3599 Machine shop, jobbing & repair

**(G-22105)**
**NATIONAL TOOL & MFG CO**
Also Called: Ntm
581 Wheeling Rd (60090-4743)
**PHONE** ................................ 847 806-9800
Jim Soderquist, *President*
Mitch Predki, *Vice Pres*
David Niedbalec, *Prdtn Mgr*
Michael Murtha, *Site Mgr*
Mike Murtha, *Purch Mgr*
**EMP:** 100
**SQ FT:** 38,000
**SALES (est):** 22.6MM **Privately Held**
**SIC:** 3599 Ties, form: metal

**(G-22106)**
**NETCOM INC**
599 Wheeling Rd (60090-4743)
**PHONE** ................................ 847 537-6300
**Fax:** 847 537-2700
Bob Cantarutti, *CEO*
Evangelos Argoudelis, *Ch of Bd*
Soren Pihlman, *President*
Steven Watts, *Vice Pres*
Don Arrington, *General Mgr*
◆ **EMP:** 121 **EST:** 1977
**SALES (est):** 35.3MM **Privately Held**
**WEB:** www.netcominc.com
**SIC:** 3679 3677 Electronic crystals; oscillators; power supplies, all types: static; filtration devices, electronic

**(G-22107)**
**NEWSPAPER 7 DAYS (PA)**
704 S Milwaukee Ave (60090-6205)
**PHONE** ................................ 847 272-2212
Roman Polinoski, *Principal*
**EMP:** 4
**SALES (est):** 475.6K **Privately Held**
**SIC:** 2711 Newspapers

**(G-22108)**
**NORTH AMERICAN SIGNAL CO**
605 Wheeling Rd (60090-5736)
**PHONE** ................................ 847 537-8888
**Fax:** 847 537-8895
William Neiman, *President*
Mary Hook, *Safety Dir*
Scott Tennant, *Sales Executive*
▲ **EMP:** 50 **EST:** 1959
**SQ FT:** 45,000
**SALES (est):** 12.3MM **Privately Held**
**WEB:** www.nasig.com
**SIC:** 3648 3669 Lighting equipment; sirens, electric: vehicle, marine, industrial & air raid

**(G-22109)**
**NPN360**
1400 S Wolf Rd (60090-6573)
**PHONE** ................................ 847 215-7300
**Fax:** 847 215-7314
Arthur B Collins Jr, *Exec VP*
Karl Johnson, *VP Sales*
Rick Drucker, *Accounts Exec*
Ron Gion, *Accounts Exec*
Lon Johnson, *Accounts Exec*
**EMP:** 30
**SQ FT:** 6,500
**SALES (est):** 9.4MM **Privately Held**
**WEB:** www.northernprint.com
**SIC:** 2752 Commercial printing, lithographic

**(G-22110)**
**NU-WAY SIGNS INC**
2320 Foster Ave (60090-6511)
**PHONE** ................................ 847 243-0164
Meir Dubinsky, *President*
▲ **EMP:** 10
**SQ FT:** 10,500
**SALES (est):** 1.1MM **Privately Held**
**SIC:** 3993 Signs & advertising specialties

**(G-22111)**
**NUMERIDEX INCORPORATED**
632 Wheeling Rd (60090-5707)
**PHONE** ................................ 847 541-8840
Alberto Hoyos, *President*
Rita Hoyos, *Marketing Mgr*
Stephen Ryd, *Admin Sec*
**EMP:** 10
**SQ FT:** 9,000
**SALES (est):** 2.4MM **Privately Held**
**WEB:** www.numeridex.com
**SIC:** 5049 5063 3572 Drafting supplies; electrical apparatus & equipment; tape storage units, computer

**(G-22112)**
**OMEX TECHNOLOGIES INC**
300 E Marquardt Dr # 107 (60090-6425)
**PHONE** ................................ 847 850-5858
Alexander Zaltz, *President*
Jenny Zaltz, *Vice Pres*
**EMP:** 5
**SQ FT:** 2,000
**SALES:** 750K **Privately Held**
**WEB:** www.omextech.com
**SIC:** 3826 3845 3827 3577 Spectroscopic & other optical properties measuring equipment; electromedical equipment; optical instruments & lenses; computer peripheral equipment

**(G-22113)**
**OMNI PUBLISHING CO**
45 Versailles Ct (60090-6756)
**PHONE** ................................ 847 483-9668
Zenja Glass, *President*
**EMP:** 4
**SALES (est):** 246.9K **Privately Held**
**SIC:** 2741 Miscellaneous publishing

**(G-22114)**
**ONLY FOR ONE PRINTERS**
540 Allendale Dr Ste K (60090-2603)
**PHONE** ................................ 847 947-4119
Gen Young Kim, *Principal*
▲ **EMP:** 11
**SALES (est):** 1.4MM **Privately Held**
**SIC:** 2752 Commercial printing, lithographic

**(G-22115)**
**ORANGE CRUSH LLC**
231 Wheeling Rd (60090-4809)
**PHONE** ................................ 847 537-7900
Ray Pagnozvi, *Branch Mgr*
**EMP:** 5
**SALES (corp-wide):** 47.3MM **Privately Held**
**SIC:** 1795 2951 Concrete breaking for streets & highways; asphalt paving mixtures & blocks
**PA:** Orange Crush, L.L.C.
321 Center St
Hillside IL 60162
708 544-9440

**(G-22116)**
**PACTIV LLC**
777 Wheeling Rd (60090-5708)
**PHONE** ................................ 847 459-8049
H M Weil, *Owner*
Wesley Reins, *Project Mgr*
John Lindquist, *QC Dir*
Bill Halford, *Engineer*
Bob Milwee, *Manager*
**EMP:** 350 **Privately Held**
**WEB:** www.pactiv.com
**SIC:** 3089 Thermoformed finished plastic products
**HQ:** Pactiv Llc
1900 W Field Ct
Lake Forest IL 60045
847 482-2000

**(G-22117)**
**PALWAUKEE PRINTING COMPANY**
1684 S Wolf Rd (60090-6516)
**PHONE** ................................ 847 459-0240
Joe Ropski, *President*
**EMP:** 4
**SQ FT:** 4,200
**SALES (est):** 380K **Privately Held**
**WEB:** www.palwaukeeprinting.com
**SIC:** 2752 Commercial printing, offset

**(G-22118)**
**PAMARCO GLOBAL GRAPHICS INC**
171 E Marquardt Dr (60090-6427)
**PHONE** ................................ 847 459-6000
Jim Nicpon, *Branch Mgr*
**EMP:** 15 **Privately Held**

▲ = Import ▼ = Export
◆ = Import/Export

## GEOGRAPHIC SECTION

**Wheeling - Cook County (G-22143)**

SIC: **3069** 3555 2796 Rubber rolls & roll coverings; printing trades machinery; platemaking services
HQ: Pamarco Global Graphics, Inc.
235 E 11th Ave
Roselle NJ 07203
908 241-1200

**(G-22119)**
**PAPER TUBE LLC** ○
971 N Milwaukee Ave # 22 (60090-1893)
PHONE.................................847 477-0563
Agrawal Parag, *Principal*
EMP: 4 EST: 2016
SALES (est): 329.8K **Privately Held**
SIC: **2655** Fiber cans, drums & similar products

**(G-22120)**
**PENRAY COMPANIES INC (PA)**
440 Denniston Ct (60090-4797)
PHONE.................................800 323-6329
Fax: 847 459-5043
Rodney H McKenzie, *President*
Ernest Breakenridge, *Warehouse Mgr*
Dave Campbell, *Purchasing*
Bill Dolatowski, *CFO*
Gwendolyn Watson, *Human Resources*
▼ EMP: 83 EST: 1916
SQ FT: 88,000
SALES (est): 30.6MM **Privately Held**
WEB: www.penray.com
SIC: **2899** 2842 2851 2869 Chemical preparations; oil treating compounds; fuel tank or engine cleaning chemicals; cleaning or polishing preparations; degreasing solvent; paints & allied products; undercoatings, paint; industrial organic chemicals

**(G-22121)**
**PETERSON INTL ENTP LTD**
504 Glenn Ave (60090-6016)
PHONE.................................847 541-3700
Fax: 847 541-3790
William Pfeifer, *President*
EMP: 12
SALES (est): 2.4MM **Privately Held**
WEB: www.petersoninternational.com
SIC: **3651** Household audio & video equipment

**(G-22122)**
**PHOENIX ART WOODWORKS**
500 Harvester Ct Ste 7 (60090-4755)
PHONE.................................847 279-1576
Ilya Ustr, *Owner*
EMP: 2
SALES (est): 231.3K **Privately Held**
SIC: **2431** Millwork

**(G-22123)**
**PLASTECH MOLDING INC**
2222 Foster Ave (60090-6509)
PHONE.................................847 398-0355
Stephan Memmem, *Principal*
EMP: 6
SALES (est): 704.8K **Privately Held**
SIC: **3089** Injection molding of plastics

**(G-22124)**
**PLATINUM AQUATECH LTD**
300 Industrial Ln (60090-6340)
PHONE.................................847 537-3800
James D Atlas, *President*
Terrence Smith, *Vice Pres*
EMP: 10
SQ FT: 30,000
SALES (est): 780K **Privately Held**
SIC: **1799** 3949 Swimming pool construction; swimming pools, except plastic

**(G-22125)**
**PLAZA TOOL & MOLD CO**
53 Century Dr (60090-6051)
PHONE.................................847 537-2320
Mark Plaza, *President*
Mike Plaza, *Vice Pres*
Ann Plaza, *Admin Sec*
EMP: 3
SQ FT: 5,500
SALES (est): 250K **Privately Held**
SIC: **3544** Industrial molds; special dies & tools

**(G-22126)**
**POTOMAC CORPORATION (PA)**
Also Called: Crescent Cardboard Co
2063 Foster Ave (60090-6520)
PHONE.................................847 259-0546
Fax: 847 537-7153
C S Ozmun, *President*
Dave Collin, *Senior VP*
Gary Szmurlo, *Purch Mgr*
Margie Sundstrom, *Finance*
Julie Wiseman, *Human Res Mgr*
◆ EMP: 200
SQ FT: 300,000
SALES (est): 51.2MM **Privately Held**
SIC: **2679** 0212 2675 Paperboard products, converted; beef cattle except feedlots; die-cut paper & board

**(G-22127)**
**PRECISION FINISHING SYSTEMS IN**
682 Chaddick Dr (60090-6057)
PHONE.................................847 907-4266
EMP: 12 EST: 2014
SALES (est): 1.6MM **Privately Held**
SIC: **3471** Cleaning, polishing & finishing

**(G-22128)**
**PRECISION PAPER TUBE COMPANY (PA)**
1033 Noel Ave (60090-5899)
PHONE.................................847 537-4250
Fax: 847 537-5777
Rick L Hatton, *President*
T Blakeslee, *Advt Staff*
Susan Hatton, *Admin Sec*
Janet Zack, *Admin Asst*
EMP: 45 EST: 1934
SQ FT: 100,000
SALES (est): 21.5MM **Privately Held**
WEB: www.pptube.com
SIC: **2655** Tubes, for chemical or electrical uses: paper or fiber

**(G-22129)**
**PROSPECT GRINDING INCORPORATED**
925 Seton Ct Ste 11 (60090-5771)
PHONE.................................847 229-9240
Carol Dyrkacz, *President*
Ralph Dyrkacz, *Vice Pres*
EMP: 4
SQ FT: 2,500
SALES: 400K **Privately Held**
SIC: **3599** 7389 Machine shop, jobbing & repair; grinding, precision: commercial or industrial

**(G-22130)**
**PROTOTYPE & PRODUCTION CO**
546 Quail Hollow Dr (60090-2651)
PHONE.................................847 419-1553
Fax: 847 419-1603
Sam Bakaturski, *President*
Michael Bakaturski, *Opers Mgr*
EMP: 20
SQ FT: 15,000
SALES (est): 2.2MM **Privately Held**
WEB: www.ppc2000.com
SIC: **3541** 3549 3545 3544 Machine tool replacement & repair parts, metal cutting types; sawing & cutoff machines (metalworking machinery); metalworking machinery; machine tool accessories; special dies, tools, jigs & fixtures

**(G-22131)**
**RAJNER QUALITY MACHINE WORKS**
2092 Foster Ave (60090-6521)
PHONE.................................847 394-8999
Fax: 847 394-4123
Richard Rajner, *President*
Lucy Rajner, *Corp Secy*
Edward Rajner, *Vice Pres*
Mark Rajner, *Vice Pres*
EMP: 2 EST: 1963
SALES (est): 288.8K **Privately Held**
SIC: **3599** 3544 Machine shop, jobbing & repair; special dies, tools, jigs & fixtures

**(G-22132)**
**RAND MANUFACTURING NETWORK INC**
840 Tanglewood Dr (60090-5775)
P.O. Box 414, Prospect Heights (60070-0414)
PHONE.................................847 299-8884
Neal E Katz, *President*
EMP: 3
SQ FT: 700
SALES (est): 472K **Privately Held**
SIC: **3089** Hardware, plastic

**(G-22133)**
**RCM INDUSTRIES INC**
Also Called: Northern Prints
161 Carpenter Ave (60090-6007)
PHONE.................................847 455-1950
Fax: 847 541-7461
Robert Marconi, *Owner*
Mike Armeni, *Vice Pres*
Samir Yousif, *Plant Mgr*
Richard Betcher, *Mfg Staff*
Jimmy Scatchell, *Purch Mgr*
EMP: 170
SALES (corp-wide): 170.7MM **Privately Held**
WEB: www.imperialdiecasting.com
SIC: **3363** 3365 Aluminum die-castings; aluminum foundries
PA: R.C.M. Industries, Inc.
3021 Cullerton St
Franklin Park IL 60131
847 455-1950

**(G-22134)**
**RED DEVIL MANUFACTURING CO**
422 Mercantile Ct (60090-4738)
PHONE.................................847 215-1377
Fax: 847 541-1780
Thomas Morgan, *President*
Frank Bellgrau, *Treasurer*
EMP: 8 EST: 1945
SQ FT: 15,000
SALES (est): 910K **Privately Held**
SIC: **3451** 3452 3356 Screw machine products; bolts, nuts, rivets & washers; nonferrous rolling & drawing

**(G-22135)**
**REMKE INDUSTRIES INC (PA)**
310 Chaddick Dr (60090-6039)
PHONE.................................847 541-3780
Fax: 847 541-7245
Thomas O'Gara, *CEO*
Mark Sweeney, *President*
Michael Zeddies, *Chairman*
Michael B Zeddies Jr, *Vice Pres*
Julie Savastio, *Controller*
▲ EMP: 65
SQ FT: 22,000
SALES: 14.9MM **Privately Held**
WEB: www.remke.com
SIC: **3643** Connectors & terminals for electrical devices

**(G-22136)**
**REMKE INDUSTRIES INC**
310 Chaddick Dr (60090-6039)
PHONE.................................847 325-7835
Julie Savastio, *Controller*
EMP: 65
SALES (corp-wide): 14.9MM **Privately Held**
SIC: **3643** Connectors & terminals for electrical devices
PA: Remke Industries, Inc.
310 Chaddick Dr
Wheeling IL 60090
847 541-3780

**(G-22137)**
**REMKE PRINTING INC**
1678 S Wolf Rd (60090-6516)
PHONE.................................847 520-7300
Fax: 847 255-0393
Karen Coli, *President*
Jim Coli, *Vice Pres*
EMP: 4
SALES (est): 450K **Privately Held**
SIC: **2752** 2791 2789 2759 Commercial printing, offset; typesetting; bookbinding & related work; commercial printing

**(G-22138)**
**RESINITE CORPORATION**
1033 Noel Ave (60090-5813)
PHONE.................................847 537-4250
Rick L Hatton, *President*
W A Bowers, *President*
R L Hatton, *President*
P Hatton, *Treasurer*
W Browning, *Admin Sec*
EMP: 150 EST: 1948
SQ FT: 100,000
SALES (est): 16MM
SALES (corp-wide): 21.5MM **Privately Held**
WEB: www.pptube.com
SIC: **3644** 3555 3544 3082 Insulators & insulation materials, electrical; printing trades machinery; special dies, tools, jigs & fixtures; unsupported plastics profile shapes; fiber cans, drums & similar products
PA: Precision Paper Tube Company Inc
1033 Noel Ave
Wheeling IL 60090
847 537-4250

**(G-22139)**
**RESOLUTE INDUSTRIAL LLC**
298 Messner Dr (60090-6436)
PHONE.................................800 537-9675
Robert Russel, *CEO*
EMP: 40
SALES: 30MM **Privately Held**
SIC: **3563** 1711 Air & gas compressors including vacuum pumps; boiler & furnace contractors

**(G-22140)**
**RICH PRODUCTS CORPORATION**
624 Wheeling Rd (60090-5707)
PHONE.................................847 459-5400
Bob Farmer, *Manager*
EMP: 120
SALES (corp-wide): 3.2B **Privately Held**
WEB: www.richs.com
SIC: **2023** Dry, condensed, evaporated dairy products
PA: Rich Products Corporation
1 Robert Rich Way
Buffalo NY 14213
716 878-8000

**(G-22141)**
**ROADEX CARRIERS INC**
446 Irvine Ct (60090-5127)
PHONE.................................773 454-8772
Oksana Lopatkin, *President*
William Lopatkin, *Vice Pres*
EMP: 4
SALES (est): 467.2K **Privately Held**
SIC: **3715** Truck trailers

**(G-22142)**
**RODIN ENTERPRISES INC**
Also Called: Minuteman Press
544b W Dundee Rd (60090-2675)
PHONE.................................847 412-1370
Fax: 847 537-9276
Allan Rodin, *President*
Aviva Rodin, *Admin Sec*
EMP: 3
SQ FT: 2,000
SALES (est): 333.6K **Privately Held**
SIC: **2752** 2791 2789 2759 Commercial printing, lithographic; typesetting; bookbinding & related work; commercial printing

**(G-22143)**
**RT ASSOCIATES INC**
385 Gilman Ave (60090-5807)
PHONE.................................847 577-0700
Fax: 847 577-0770
Robert Radzis, *President*
John Piumbroeck, *Sales Associate*
EMP: 63
SQ FT: 28,000
SALES (est): 10.3MM **Privately Held**
WEB: www.rtcolor.com
SIC: **2752** 2791 2759 Commercial printing, lithographic; typesetting; commercial printing

**(G-22144)**
**SATURN SIGN**
240 Industrial Ln Ste 1  (60090-6388)
PHONE.................................847 520-9009
Fax: 847 520-9019
Michael Williams, *Owner*
Fred Gawrick, *Accountant*
EMP: 2
SALES: 200K  **Privately Held**
SIC: 3993  Signs, not made in custom sign painting shops

**(G-22145)**
**SEAL OPERATION S L**
634 Glenn Ave  (60090-6018)
PHONE.................................847 537-8100
Judy Hicks, *Vice Pres*
EMP: 5
SALES (est): 516.7K  **Privately Held**
SIC: 3624  Carbon & graphite products

**(G-22146)**
**SEGERDAHL CORP (PA)**
Also Called: Sg360
1351 Wheeling Rd  (60090-5997)
PHONE.................................847 541-1080
Fax: 847 541-1056
Richard D Joutras, *President*
Mary Lee Schneider, *President*
Jeff Reimers, *Exec VP*
Paul White, *Exec VP*
Hans Kollinger, *Senior VP*
EMP: 190  EST: 1956
SQ FT: 246,000
SALES (est): 298MM  **Privately Held**
WEB: www.segerdahlgraphics.com
SIC: 2752  Commercial printing, offset

**(G-22147)**
**SEGERDAHL CORP**
Also Called: Sg360
385 Gilman Ave  (60090-5807)
PHONE.................................847 850-8811
Kirby Ashby, *General Mgr*
Paul White, *Accounts Exec*
EMP: 100
SALES (corp-wide): 298MM  **Privately Held**
WEB: www.segerdahlgraphics.com
SIC: 2752  Commercial printing, offset
PA: The Segerdahl Corp
    1351 Wheeling Rd
    Wheeling IL 60090
    847 541-1080

**(G-22148)**
**SEGERDAHL GRAPHICS INC**
1351 Wheeling Rd  (60090-5913)
PHONE.................................847 541-1080
Fax: 847 850-8801
Richard D Joutras, *President*
Terry McLaughlin, *Senior VP*
Gary Gardner, *Vice Pres*
Paul White, *Vice Pres*
John Annel, *VP Sls/Mktg*
▲ EMP: 350
SQ FT: 108,000
SALES (est): 127.2MM
SALES (corp-wide): 298MM  **Privately Held**
WEB: www.segerdahlgraphics.com
SIC: 2752  8742  Commercial printing, offset; marketing consulting services
PA: The Segerdahl Corp
    1351 Wheeling Rd
    Wheeling IL 60090
    847 541-1080

**(G-22149)**
**SHAPCO INC**
Also Called: R V Designer Collections
602 Wheeling Rd  (60090-5707)
PHONE.................................847 229-1439
Fax: 847 229-1843
David Shapiro, *President*
Catherine Huart, *Vice Pres*
Shanawaz M Khan, *Marketing Staff*
EMP: 8
SALES (est): 660K  **Privately Held**
SIC: 3429  5023  Manufactured hardware (general); window furnishings

**(G-22150)**
**SHURE INCORPORATED**
Also Called: Shure Elec of Ill Div Shure
995 Chaddick Dr  (60090-6449)
PHONE.................................847 520-4404
Fax: 847 419-4909
Anita Tucker, *Manager*
Bruce Mizuno, *Manager*
EMP: 11
SALES (corp-wide): 293MM  **Privately Held**
WEB: www.sm57.com
SIC: 3651  5099  Microphones; video & audio equipment
PA: Shure Incorporated
    5800 W Touhy Ave
    Niles IL 60714
    847 600-2000

**(G-22151)**
**SIGMA COACHAIR GROUP (US) INC**
Also Called: Sigma Coachair Group N.A.
1019 Ferndale Ct  (60090-2542)
PHONE.................................847 541-4446
Mark Parow, *President*
Richard Moss, *Admin Sec*
▲ EMP: 8  EST: 2007
SALES (est): 1MM  **Privately Held**
SIC: 3585  Air conditioning, motor vehicle
HQ: Sigma Air Conditioning Pty Ltd
    23-29 Factory St
    Granville NSW
    288 636-500

**(G-22152)**
**SIGNS OF DISTINCTION INC**
149 Wheeling Rd  (60090-4807)
PHONE.................................847 520-0787
Fax: 847 520-4589
William McDonald, *President*
EMP: 7
SQ FT: 4,000
SALES (est): 863.7K  **Privately Held**
WEB: www.floridahorse.com
SIC: 3993  Signs & advertising specialties

**(G-22153)**
**SLIDE PRODUCTS INC**
430 Wheeling Rd  (60090-4742)
P.O. Box 156  (60090-0156)
PHONE.................................847 541-7220
Fax: 847 541-7986
James Harms, *President*
Erica Young, *Vice Pres*
EMP: 18  EST: 1953
SQ FT: 17,000
SALES (est): 2.3MM  **Privately Held**
WEB: www.slideproducts.com
SIC: 2813  Aerosols

**(G-22154)**
**SNAP DIAGNOSTICS LLC**
5210 Capitol Dr  (60090-7901)
PHONE.................................847 777-0000
Robert Rose, *General Mgr*
Debbie Mainquist, *Vice Pres*
Laura Martis, *Sales Dir*
Rosemarie Brady, *Sales Mgr*
Loni Fagan, *Sales Mgr*
EMP: 10
SQ FT: 5,000
SALES (est): 1.8MM  **Privately Held**
SIC: 3845  Electromedical equipment

**(G-22155)**
**STELOC FASTENER CO**
160 Abbott Dr  (60090-5802)
PHONE.................................847 459-6200
Fax: 847 459-8241
Richard M Binder, *President*
Al Sherrill, *Plant Mgr*
James Calabrese, *Office Mgr*
Martin R Binder, *Admin Sec*
EMP: 15  EST: 1962
SQ FT: 12,000
SALES (est): 1.7MM  **Privately Held**
SIC: 3452  Bolts, nuts, rivets & washers

**(G-22156)**
**STERLING BRANDS LLC**
555 Allendale Dr  (60090-2638)
PHONE.................................847 229-1600
Rick Renjilian, *President*
Tom Grimm, *Senior VP*
Jerusha Bennett, *Vice Pres*

Albert Cheris,
Paul Moniuszko,
EMP: 22
SALES (est): 5.4MM  **Privately Held**
SIC: 3357  Building wire & cable, nonferrous

**(G-22157)**
**STIGLMEIER SAUSAGE CO INC**
619 Chaddick Dr  (60090-6053)
PHONE.................................847 537-9988
Fax: 847 537-1367
Gertrude Stiglmeier, *President*
Anton Stiglmeier, *Shareholder*
EMP: 12
SQ FT: 13,000
SALES: 2MM  **Privately Held**
WEB: www.stiglmeier.com
SIC: 2013  5812  2011  Sausages from purchased meat; eating places; meat packing plants

**(G-22158)**
**SUBURBAN MACHINE CORPORATION**
512 Northgate Pkwy  (60090-2664)
PHONE.................................847 808-9095
Fax: 847 808-9098
Dennis Salinas, *President*
Debi Salinas, *Office Mgr*
Daniel Salinas Jr, *Officer*
Baron Buehring, *Admin Sec*
EMP: 31
SQ FT: 20,000
SALES (est): 6.4MM  **Privately Held**
SIC: 3599  3565  Machine shop, jobbing & repair; packaging machinery

**(G-22159)**
**SUBURBAN SURGICAL CO**
275 12th St Ste A  (60090-2798)
PHONE.................................847 537-9320
Fax: 847 537-9061
James M Pinkerman, *President*
Steve Dephillips, *Sales Staff*
Bill Lemieux, *Data Proc Staff*
Karen Pinkerman, *Admin Sec*
▼ EMP: 200  EST: 1943
SQ FT: 200,000
SALES (est): 49.1MM  **Privately Held**
WEB: www.suburbansurgical.com
SIC: 3821  3914  Worktables, laboratory; trays, stainless steel

**(G-22160)**
**SUPREME SAW & SERVICE CO**
1480 S Wolf Rd  (60090-6514)
PHONE.................................708 396-1125
Gregory A Muntean, *President*
Dana W Dugan, *Vice Pres*
EMP: 2
SALES: 250K  **Privately Held**
WEB: www.supremesaw.com
SIC: 3425  Saw blades & handsaws

**(G-22161)**
**SWAN ANALYTICAL USA INC**
225 Larkin Dr Ste 4  (60090-7209)
PHONE.................................847 229-1290
Jeff Parke, *President*
Jason Posmer, *Warehouse Mgr*
Shaun Sharrett, *Research*
Steve Devilleneuve, *Regl Sales Mgr*
Nick Powers, *Regl Sales Mgr*
▲ EMP: 12
SQ FT: 6,000
SALES: 3MM  **Privately Held**
SIC: 3826  Water testing apparatus
PA: Swan Analytische Instrumente Ag
    Studbachstrasse 13
    Hinwil ZH
    449 436-300

**(G-22162)**
**SWISS PRECISION MACHINING INC**
Also Called: S P M
634 Glenn Ave  (60090-6018)
PHONE.................................847 647-7111
Fax: 847 647-7110
Michael W Haupers, *President*
Tim Sonnenberg, *General Mgr*
Kathy H Haupers, *Corp Secy*
Tatiana Pavel, *Engineer*
Daniel Malandrino, *Asst Controller*
▲ EMP: 90

SQ FT: 35,000
SALES (est): 21.4MM  **Privately Held**
SIC: 3451  Screw machine products

**(G-22163)**
**TAAP CORP**
300 Holbrook Dr  (60090-5812)
PHONE.................................224 676-0653
Seymour Ivice, *CEO*
Gary Ivice, *President*
Julie Miller, *Manager*
Abe Freeman, *Shareholder*
Jerome Ivice, *Shareholder*
▲ EMP: 15
SQ FT: 11,200
SALES (est): 3.1MM  **Privately Held**
WEB: www.taapcorp.com
SIC: 3714  Windshield wiper systems, motor vehicle

**(G-22164)**
**TAUBENSEE STEEL & WIRE COMPANY (PA)**
600 Diens Dr  (60090-2686)
PHONE.................................847 459-5100
Fax: 847 459-5187
Casey Bouton, *President*
Vern Abel, *President*
Kent T Taubensee, *President*
Robert Morrison, *COO*
Bruce Taubensee, *Senior VP*
▲ EMP: 110
SQ FT: 16,000
SALES (est): 61.3MM  **Privately Held**
WEB: www.taubensee.com
SIC: 3315  3316  Wire, steel: insulated or armored; bars, steel, cold finished, from purchased hot-rolled

**(G-22165)**
**TECHNATOOL INC**
2222 Foster Ave  (60090-6509)
PHONE.................................847 398-0355
Frank Hauptmann, *President*
Karen Kokinis, *Manager*
EMP: 8
SQ FT: 1,500
SALES: 1MM  **Privately Held**
SIC: 3089  Injection molding of plastics

**(G-22166)**
**TEX TREND INC**
767 Kristy Ln  (60090-5595)
PHONE.................................847 215-6796
Frank Dime, *Vice Pres*
Gina Belcastro, *Manager*
Richard A Rosen, *Admin Sec*
EMP: 35
SQ FT: 38,000
SALES (est): 3.5MM  **Privately Held**
SIC: 3089  2399  3296  Plastic processing; hand woven & crocheted products; mineral wool

**(G-22167)**
**THERM-O-WEB INC**
770 Glenn Ave  (60090-6020)
PHONE.................................847 520-5200
Fax: 847 520-0025
Bob Kirschner, *Purchasing*
Karen L Grandt, *Controller*
Sharon Contreras, *Accounts Mgr*
Sue Doherty, *Marketing Staff*
Julia Sandvoss, *Director*
▲ EMP: 35
SQ FT: 35,000
SALES (est): 9MM  **Privately Held**
WEB: www.thermoweb.com
SIC: 2891  Adhesives & sealants

**(G-22168)**
**TRES JOLI DESIGNS LTD**
634 Wheeling Rd  (60090-5707)
PHONE.................................847 520-3903
Mary Conlon, *President*
Martin Conlon, *Manager*
EMP: 8
SALES (est): 885.9K  **Privately Held**
SIC: 2391  5714  Curtains & draperies; draperies

**(G-22169)**
**TRU-CUT TOOL & SUPPLY CO**
1480 S Wolf Rd  (60090-6514)
PHONE.................................708 396-1122
Fax: 708 396-0902

Greg Muntean, *President*
**EMP:** 18
**SQ FT:** 15,000
**SALES (est):** 1.3MM  **Privately Held**
**SIC:** 3425  5084  Saw blades for hand or power saws; industrial machinery & equipment

**(G-22170)**
**UNILEVER MANUFACTURING US INC**
385 Sumac Rd  (60090-6338)
**PHONE**..............................847 541-8868
Bob Fash, *Manager*
**EMP:** 5
**SALES (corp-wide):** 55.5B  **Privately Held**
**SIC:** 2844  Toilet preparations
**HQ:** Unilever Manufacturing (Us), Inc.
800 Sylvan Ave
Englewood Cliffs NJ 07632
800 298-5018

**(G-22171)**
**UNITED AUTOMATION INC**
280 Camp Mcdonald Rd A  (60090-6502)
**PHONE**..............................847 394-7903
**Fax:** 847 394-7903
Mark Bidus, *President*
Jeff Runge, *Vice Pres*
April Agostini, *Office Mgr*
◆ **EMP:** 9 EST: 1999
**SQ FT:** 14,000
**SALES (est):** 1.1MM  **Privately Held**
**SIC:** 3549  Assembly machines, including robotic

**(G-22172)**
**US TSUBAKI HOLDINGS  INC  (HQ)**
Also Called: U.S.T.H.
301 E Marquardt Dr  (60090-6497)
**PHONE**..............................847 459-9500
**Fax:** 847 459-8508
Tetsuya Yamamoto, *President*
Dan Butterfield, *President*
Thomas Barton, *Senior VP*
Robert Engelmann, *Vice Pres*
Richard Renk, *Vice Pres*
▲ **EMP:** 150
**SQ FT:** 115,000
**SALES (est):** 287.2MM
**SALES (corp-wide):** 1.7B  **Privately Held**
**SIC:** 5085  3568  Power transmission equipment & apparatus; drives, chains & sprockets; sprockets (power transmission equipment)
**PA:** Tsubakimoto Chain Co.
3-3-3, Nakanoshima, Kita-Ku
Osaka OSK 530-0
664 410-011

**(G-22173)**
**US TSUBAKI POWER TRANSM LLC (DH)**
301 E Marquardt Dr  (60090-6497)
**PHONE**..............................847 459-9500
Kevin Powers, *Mng Member*
Tom Barton, *Mng Member*
Tadashi Ichikawa, *Mng Member*
**EMP:** 216
**SALES (est):** 134.4MM
**SALES (corp-wide):** 1.7B  **Privately Held**
**SIC:** 3568  5085  5063  3714  Drives, chains & sprockets; chain, power transmission; power transmission equipment & apparatus; chains, power transmission; power transmission equipment, electric; motor vehicle parts & accessories; iron & steel forgings; rolling mill rolls, cast steel
**HQ:** U.S. Tsubaki Holdings, Inc.
301 E Marquardt Dr
Wheeling IL 60090
847 459-9500

**(G-22174)**
**V & L ENTERPRISES INC**
422 Mercantile Ct  (60090-4738)
**PHONE**..............................847 541-1760
John Rozylowicz, *President*
Jim Bazdor, *Vice Pres*
Frank Bellgrav, *Treasurer*
**EMP:** 10 EST: 1951
**SQ FT:** 6,000
**SALES (est):** 1.5MM  **Privately Held**
**SIC:** 3599  Machine shop, jobbing & repair

**(G-22175)**
**VALSPAR CORPORATION**
Also Called: Valspar Coatings
1191 Wheeling Rd  (60090-5716)
**PHONE**..............................847 541-9000
**Fax:** 847 541-2752
Stuart Graff, *President*
Mike Wells, *COO*
Ed Daraskevich, *Research*
Sue Pfeiffer, *Engineer*
Laura Funteas, *Human Resources*
**EMP:** 99
**SALES (corp-wide):** 11.8B  **Publicly Held**
**SIC:** 2851  Paints & allied products; lacquers, varnishes, enamels & other coatings; stains: varnish, oil or wax; putty, wood fillers & sealers
**HQ:** The Valspar Corporation
1101 S 3rd St
Minneapolis MN 55415
612 851-7000

**(G-22176)**
**VALSPAR CORPORATION**
300 Gilman Ave  (60090-5808)
**PHONE**..............................847 541-9000
William Fotis, *Technical Mgr*
Mark Kubiak, *Research*
David Lee, *Manager*
Scott Eirich, *Director*
**EMP:** 87
**SALES (corp-wide):** 11.8B  **Publicly Held**
**SIC:** 2851  Paints & allied products
**HQ:** The Valspar Corporation
1101 S 3rd St
Minneapolis MN 55415
612 851-7000

**(G-22177)**
**VAN METER GRAPHX INC**
Also Called: Van Meter Mail
970 Seton Ct  (60090-5705)
**PHONE**..............................847 465-0600
**Fax:** 847 465-0665
Bruce Van Meter, *President*
**EMP:** 4
**SQ FT:** 3,500
**SALES (est):** 483.5K  **Privately Held**
**WEB:** www.vmmailing.com
**SIC:** 2741  7336  2752  7331  Catalogs: publishing only, not printed on site; graphic arts & related design; commercial printing, offset; mailing service

**(G-22178)**
**VICMA TOOL CO**
505 Harvester Ct Ste J  (60090-4754)
**PHONE**..............................847 541-0177
**Fax:** 847 541-3091
David Choma, *Owner*
**EMP:** 3
**SQ FT:** 3,600
**SALES (est):** 220K  **Privately Held**
**SIC:** 3544  Industrial molds

**(G-22179)**
**WACHS TECHNICAL SERVICES INC**
100 Shepard Ave  (60090-6022)
**PHONE**..............................847 537-8800
Edward H Wachs, *CEO*
John Novak, *Vice Pres*
Rodger Soeldner, *CFO*
Scott Weldan, *Controller*
Scott Ferrar, *Manager*
**EMP:** 20
**SQ FT:** 2,000
**SALES (est):** 143.4K
**SALES (corp-wide):** 13.6B  **Publicly Held**
**SIC:** 3599  7692  Machine & other job shop work; welding repair
**HQ:** 1883 Properties, Inc.
600 Knightsbridge Pkwy
Lincolnshire IL 60069
847 537-8800

**(G-22180)**
**WALDMANN LIGHTING COMPANY**
9 Century Dr  (60090-6051)
**PHONE**..............................847 520-1060
**Fax:** 847 520-1730
Gerhard Waldmann, *CEO*
Jan Schaefer, *President*
Gary Cardoza, *President*
Jason Dour, *Plant Mgr*
Les Kaminski, *Sales Mgr*
▲ **EMP:** 28
**SQ FT:** 30,000
**SALES:** 6.5MM
**SALES (est):** 57.1MM  **Privately Held**
**WEB:** www.waldmannlighting.com
**SIC:** 3646  Commercial indusl & institutional electric lighting fixtures
**PA:** Waldmann Beteiligungen Gmbh & Co. Kg
Peter-Henlein-Str. 5
Villingen-Schwenningen 78056
772 060-1100

**(G-22181)**
**WALTZ BROTHERS  INC**
10 W Waltz Dr  (60090-6052)
**PHONE**..............................847 520-1122
**Fax:** 847 520-1870
Larry Waltz, *President*
Larry D Waltz Jr, *Vice Pres*
▲ **EMP:** 47
**SQ FT:** 50,000
**SALES (est):** 10.8MM  **Privately Held**
**WEB:** www.waltzbros.com
**SIC:** 3812  3714  Acceleration indicators & systems components, aerospace; motor vehicle body components & frame

**(G-22182)**
**WIELAND METALS  INC (DH)**
567 Northgate Pkwy  (60090-2663)
**PHONE**..............................847 537-3990
**Fax:** 847 537-4085
Werner Traa, *President*
Jorg Nubling, *Managing Dir*
Marcus Schuler, *Exec VP*
Jim Meistad, *Project Mgr*
Ken Gauger, *Prdtn Mgr*
▲ **EMP:** 115
**SQ FT:** 130,000
**SALES (est):** 18.7MM
**SALES (corp-wide):** 504.7K  **Privately Held**
**WEB:** www.wielandus.com
**SIC:** 3351  Strip, copper & copper alloy
**HQ:** Wieland-Werke Ag
Graf-Arco-Str. 36
Ulm 89079
731 944-0

## White Hall
### Greene County

**(G-22183)**
**BALLARD BROS  INC**
Also Called: Ballard Bros Con Pdts & Excav
420 E Lincoln St  (62092-1344)
P.O. Box 341  (62092-0341)
**PHONE**..............................217 374-2137
**Fax:** 217 374-2075
James H Ballard, *President*
Dan Ballard, *Vice Pres*
Tony Bell, *Office Mgr*
**EMP:** 10 EST: 1960
**SQ FT:** 2,400
**SALES (est):** 689.3K  **Privately Held**
**SIC:** 1794  3273  Excavation & grading, building construction; ready-mixed concrete

**(G-22184)**
**DRAKE ENVELOPE PRINTING CO**
207 White St  (62092-1263)
P.O. Box 219  (62092-0219)
**PHONE**..............................217 374-2772
**Fax:** 217 374-6165
James Evans, *President*
Beverly Evans, *Corp Secy*
**EMP:** 9
**SQ FT:** 4,000
**SALES (est):** 1.6MM  **Privately Held**
**SIC:** 2759  2752  Commercial printing; commercial printing, lithographic

**(G-22185)**
**JAGJITA CORP**
654 N Main St  (62092-1153)
**PHONE**..............................217 374-6016
Archita Patel, *Vice Pres*
**EMP:** 3
**SALES (est):** 235.1K  **Privately Held**
**SIC:** 2869  Fuels

## Whittington
### Franklin County

**(G-22186)**
**GESELLS PUMP SALES & SERVICE**
Hwy 37 S  (62897)
P.O. Box 34  (62897-0034)
**PHONE**..............................618 439-7354
**Fax:** 618 435-3335
Brad Gesell, *President*
Mark Gesell, *Vice Pres*
Brenda Grimes, *Admin Sec*
**EMP:** 7
**SALES (est):** 1.3MM  **Privately Held**
**SIC:** 1389  Construction, repair & dismantling services

**(G-22187)**
**KNIFFEN BROTHERS SAWMILL**
16794 Buxton Rd  (62897-1102)
**PHONE**..............................618 629-2437
Terald Kniffen, *Owner*
**EMP:** 4
**SALES (est):** 200K  **Privately Held**
**SIC:** 2421  Sawmills & planing mills, general

**(G-22188)**
**PHEASANT HOLLOW WINERY INC**
14931 State Highway 37  (62897-1208)
**PHONE**..............................618 629-2302
**Fax:** 618 629-1822
Bruce Morgenstern, *President*
**EMP:** 8
**SALES (est):** 744.1K  **Privately Held**
**WEB:** www.pheasanthollowinery.com
**SIC:** 2084  Wines

## Williamsfield
### Knox County

**(G-22189)**
**HOMETOWN HANGOUT LLC**
106 S State Route 180  (61489-5485)
**PHONE**..............................309 639-2108
David H Doubet, *EMP:* 7
**SALES (est):** 87.2K  **Privately Held**
**SIC:** 5812  2599  5813  Eating places; food wagons, restaurant; drinking places

## Williamsville
### Sangamon County

**(G-22190)**
**CALDWELL WOODWORKS**
501 S Old Route 66  (62693-9057)
P.O. Box 109  (62693-0109)
**PHONE**..............................217 566-2434
Jack E Caldwell, *Owner*
**EMP:** 2
**SQ FT:** 1,600
**SALES (est):** 219.1K  **Privately Held**
**SIC:** 2431  2499  Millwork; decorative wood & woodwork

**(G-22191)**
**ICG ILLINOIS  LLC (DH)**
5945 Lester Rd  (62693-9205)
**PHONE**..............................217 566-3000
Paul Lang, *Principal*
Kayla Trimm, *Manager*
**EMP:** 10
**SALES (est):** 39.7MM
**SALES (corp-wide):** 2.9B  **Publicly Held**
**SIC:** 1241  Coal mining services
**HQ:** International Coal Group, Inc.
114 Smiley Dr
Saint Albans WV 25177
304 760-2400

## Willow Hill
*Jasper County*

**(G-22192)**
**KELLER GRAIN & LIVESTOCK INC**
7031 N 1900th St (62480-2307)
PHONE..................................618 455-3634
Robert Keller, *President*
EMP: 4
SALES: 1.2MM **Privately Held**
SIC: 3523 Driers (farm): grain, hay & seed

## Willow Springs
*Cook County*

**(G-22193)**
**C M S PUBLISHING INC**
Also Called: R & R Newkirk
8695 Archer Ave Ste 10 (60480-1295)
PHONE..................................708 839-9201
Fax: 708 839-9207
Mark Carmichael, *President*
Nicole Ferguson, *Chief Mktg Ofcr*
Karl Theimer, *Graphic Designe*
EMP: 9
SQ FT: 2,000
SALES (est): 1MM **Privately Held**
WEB: www.rrnewkirk.com
SIC: 2731 8111 Pamphlets: publishing & printing; legal services

**(G-22194)**
**CROSS TREAD INDUSTRIES INC**
12021 91st St (60480-1299)
PHONE..................................630 850-7100
Fax: 630 654-4114
David Hickey, *President*
Mark Hickey, *Vice Pres*
▲ EMP: 12
SQ FT: 35,000
SALES (est): 1.3MM **Privately Held**
WEB: www.crosstread.com
SIC: 3714 Motor vehicle parts & accessories

**(G-22195)**
**DATA COM PLD INC**
153 Santa Fe Ln (60480-1624)
PHONE..................................708 839-9620
James McLamore, *President*
EMP: 2
SALES: 500K **Privately Held**
WEB: www.datacompld.com
SIC: 2759 Business forms: printing

**(G-22196)**
**GEMCOM INC**
200 N Pearl St (60480-1348)
PHONE..................................800 871-6840
Fax: 708 839-0324
James J Mc Sweeney, *President*
Cynthia Mc Sweeney, *Corp Secy*
EMP: 4
SALES (est): 230K **Privately Held**
SIC: 3993 5099 Signs & advertising specialties; safety equipment & supplies

**(G-22197)**
**ILLINOIS PALLETS INC**
8075 Tec Air Ave (60480-1525)
PHONE..................................773 640-9228
Ranulfo Cardina, *President*
Silvia Salazar, *Administration*
EMP: 8
SALES (est): 863.2K **Privately Held**
SIC: 2448 Pallets, wood & wood with metal

**(G-22198)**
**PRIME DEVICES CORPORATION**
11450 German Church Rd (60480-1069)
PHONE..................................847 729-2550
Charles Cohon, *President*
Robert Shirley, *Sales Mgr*
EMP: 12
SALES (est): 980K **Privately Held**
WEB: www.primedevicescorporation.com
SIC: 3699 5084 Electrical equipment & supplies; industrial machinery & equipment

## Willowbrook
*Dupage County*

**(G-22199)**
**APPLIED TECH PUBLICATIONS INC**
Also Called: Maintenance Tech Training
535 Plainfield Rd Ste A (60527-7608)
PHONE..................................847 382-8100
Fax: 847 304-8603
Arthur L Rice, *CEO*
Rick Carter, *Editor*
Philip Saran, *Vice Pres*
Marolyn Hoggins, *Finance Mgr*
Donald Berry, *Manager*
EMP: 15
SQ FT: 4,553
SALES (est): 3.3MM **Privately Held**
WEB: www.mt-online.com
SIC: 2721 Magazines: publishing only, not printed on site

**(G-22200)**
**B & H BIOTECHNOLOGIES LLC**
6520 Chaucer Rd (60527-5405)
PHONE..................................630 915-3227
Jane Wang, *Owner*
EMP: 5
SALES (est): 393.2K **Privately Held**
SIC: 2834 Pharmaceutical preparations

**(G-22201)**
**BORSE INDUSTRIES INC**
7409 S Quincy St (60527-5521)
PHONE..................................630 325-1210
Fax: 630 325-1393
Brian Beth, *Principal*
EMP: 8 EST: 2013
SALES (est): 803.2K **Privately Held**
SIC: 3999 Manufacturing industries

**(G-22202)**
**BRIGHTER ELECTRIC INC**
5945 Bentley Ave (60527-1913)
PHONE..................................630 325-4915
EMP: 4
SALES (est): 462.8K **Privately Held**
SIC: 3699 Electrical equipment & supplies

**(G-22203)**
**CHICAGO DATA SOLUTIONS INC**
146 Somerset Rd (60527-5429)
PHONE..................................847 370-4609
Xiaohua Ning, *Chief Engr*
EMP: 3 EST: 2013
SALES (est): 74.9K **Privately Held**
SIC: 7372 7371 Application computer software; business oriented computer software; educational computer software; computer software development

**(G-22204)**
**CLOROX COMPANY**
7201 S Adams St (60527-5570)
PHONE..................................510 271-7000
Bob Dorsey, *Systems Staff*
Staci M Ball, *Director*
EMP: 36
SALES (corp-wide): 5.7B **Publicly Held**
WEB: www.clorox.com
SIC: 2842 3081 Laundry cleaning preparations; plastic film & sheet
PA: The Clorox Company
1221 Broadway Ste 1300
Oakland CA 94612
510 271-7000

**(G-22205)**
**COMVIGO INC**
410 Woodgate Ct (60527-5444)
PHONE..................................240 255-4093
James P Tanner, *President*
EMP: 4
SALES (est): 290K **Privately Held**
WEB: www.comvigo.com
SIC: 7379 7372 Computer related consulting services; application computer software

**(G-22206)**
**CONSOURCE LLC**
535 Plainfield Rd Ste A (60527-7608)
PHONE..................................847 382-8100
Arthur Rice,
EMP: 8
SALES (est): 975.2K **Privately Held**
SIC: 2721 Magazines: publishing only, not printed on site

**(G-22207)**
**CORRECTIONAL TECHNOLOGIES INC**
Also Called: Cortech USA
7530 Plaza Ct (60527-5611)
PHONE..................................630 455-0811
Joseph R Claffy, *President*
Edward Claffy, *Vice Pres*
Jesse Kolar, *Warehouse Mgr*
Patricia Miller, *CFO*
Paul Novak, *VP Sales*
EMP: 11
SQ FT: 10,000
SALES (est): 2.2MM **Privately Held**
WEB: www.cortechusa.com
SIC: 2531 Public building & related furniture

**(G-22208)**
**CZECH AMERICAN TV HERALD**
124 Sunset Ridge Rd (60527-8401)
P.O. Box 100001, Cape Coral FL (33910-0001)
PHONE..................................708 813-0028
Jan Honner, *Principal*
EMP: 3
SALES (est): 139.1K **Privately Held**
SIC: 2711 Newspapers, publishing & printing

**(G-22209)**
**D & D BUSINESS INC**
Also Called: Ddi Printing
10s428 Carrington Cir (60527-6945)
PHONE..................................630 935-3522
Darmi Parikh, *President*
P C Parikh, *Manager*
EMP: 5 EST: 1994
SQ FT: 3,000
SALES: 490K **Privately Held**
WEB: www.ddimage.com
SIC: 2752 Commercial printing, lithographic

**(G-22210)**
**EJL CUSTOM GOLF CLUBS INC (PA)**
825 75th St Ste F (60527-8428)
PHONE..................................630 654-8887
Everett J Lockenvitz, *President*
Josephine Lockenvitz, *Vice Pres*
EMP: 5
SALES: 950K **Privately Held**
WEB: www.ejlcustomgolf.com
SIC: 3949 5941 Golf equipment; shafts, golf club; golf goods & equipment

**(G-22211)**
**FEDERAL HEATH SIGN COMPANY LLC**
Also Called: Federal Sign
7501 S Quincy St Ste 175 (60527-8507)
PHONE..................................630 887-6800
Fax: 630 887-6975
Saul Stankus, *Accounts Exec*
James G Schmidt, *Manager*
Greg Katsaros, *Info Tech Mgr*
Penny Wier, *Administration*
Richard J Pankiewicz, *Analyst*
EMP: 10 **Privately Held**
WEB: www.zimsign.com
SIC: 3993 Signs & advertising specialties
PA: Federal Heath Sign Company, Llc
4602 North Ave
Oceanside CA 92056

**(G-22212)**
**FLEETPRIDE INC**
7630 S Madison St (60527-7545)
PHONE..................................630 455-6881
David Blitz, *President*
EMP: 10
SALES (corp-wide): 1.3B **Privately Held**
SIC: 7549 7694 Automotive maintenance services; motor repair services
PA: Fleetpride, Inc.
600 Las Colinas Blvd E # 400
Irving TX 75039
469 249-7500

**(G-22213)**
**GLOBAL MANUFACTURING**
324 Central Ave (60527-6156)
PHONE..................................630 908-7633
Eugene Miron, *Owner*
EMP: 3
SALES: 500K **Privately Held**
WEB: www.impex5.com
SIC: 3699 Electrical equipment & supplies

**(G-22214)**
**HERRIS GROUP LLC**
7780 S Quincy St (60527-5532)
PHONE..................................630 908-7393
Paul Michaels, *Mng Member*
▲ EMP: 5
SALES (est): 250.9K **Privately Held**
SIC: 2048 Feed premixes; feed supplements

**(G-22215)**
**ILF TECHNOLOGIES LLC**
7001 S Adams St (60527-7592)
PHONE..................................630 789-9770
Milan Pechavich, *Principal*
EMP: 6
SALES (est): 583.2K **Privately Held**
SIC: 2843 Finishing agents

**(G-22216)**
**ILLINOIS RIVER WINERY INC**
16w420 Timberlake Dr (60527-6159)
PHONE..................................815 691-8031
Gregory Kane, *President*
Heather Kane, *Admin Sec*
EMP: 2
SALES (est): 260K **Privately Held**
WEB: www.illinoisriverwinery.com
SIC: 2084 Wines

**(G-22217)**
**IMPERIAL PACKAGING CORPORATION**
640 Executive Dr (60527-5610)
PHONE..................................847 486-0800
EMP: 3
SALES (est): 156.8K **Privately Held**
SIC: 2631 Container, packaging & boxboard

**(G-22218)**
**LA FORCE INC**
7501 S Quincy St (60527-5574)
PHONE..................................630 325-1950
David Pink, *Project Mgr*
Donna Kyler, *Sales Staff*
Daryl Linnert, *Branch Mgr*
Larry Coenen, *Manager*
EMP: 7
SALES (corp-wide): 169MM **Privately Held**
WEB: www.laforceinc.com
SIC: 3442 5031 5072 Builders' hardware; window & door frames; doors
PA: La Force, Inc.
1060 W Mason St
Green Bay WI 54303
920 497-7100

**(G-22219)**
**LANXESS CORPORATION**
Wolff Walsrode
7330 S Madison St (60527-5588)
PHONE..................................630 789-8440
Timothy M McDivit, *General Mgr*
Tim McDivit, *Principal*
Mike Kazaitis, *Rsch/Dvlpt Dir*
Jim Westberg, *Sales Staff*
EMP: 32
SALES (corp-wide): 8.1B **Privately Held**
SIC: 5169 3861 2823 Chemicals & allied products; photographic equipment & supplies; cellulosic manmade fibers
HQ: Lanxess Corporation
111 Parkwest Dr
Pittsburgh PA 15275
800 526-9377

## GEOGRAPHIC SECTION

### (G-22220)
**MARQUARDT PRINTING COMPANY**
7530 S Madison St Ste 3 (60527-7573)
PHONE..................................630 887-8500
Fax: 630 887-9272
Barton J Marquardt Jr, *President*
Steve Marquardt, *Opers Mgr*
Jerri Remes, *Office Mgr*
Fredrick Marquardt, *Admin Sec*
EMP: 20
SQ FT: 15,000
SALES (est): 4.5MM  Privately Held
SIC: 2752  2789  Commercial printing, offset; bookbinding & related work

### (G-22221)
**MICHAEL WILTON CSTM HOMES INC**
Also Called: All Suburban Generator
6458 Cambridge Rd (60527-5402)
PHONE..................................630 508-1200
Michael Wilton, *President*
EMP: 2
SALES (est): 202.7K  Privately Held
SIC: 3511  Turbo-generators

### (G-22222)
**MIDTRONICS  INC (PA)**
7000 Monroe St (60527-5655)
PHONE..................................630 323-2800
Fax: 630 323-2844
Stephen J McShane, *President*
Randy Byrne, *QC Mgr*
Eric Fusinetti, *Engineer*
Laura Gong, *Engineer*
Jay Kotrba, *Engineer*
▲ EMP: 100
SQ FT: 60,000
SALES (est): 31.3MM  Privately Held
WEB: www.midtronics.com
SIC: 3825  7622  3694  Battery testers, electrical; meters: electric, pocket, portable, panelboard, etc.; radio repair shop; automotive electrical equipment

### (G-22223)
**MIDWEST TUNGSTEN SERVICE INC**
540 Executive Dr (60527-8449)
PHONE..................................630 325-1001
Fax: 630 325-3571
Joel R Stava, *President*
Sean Murray, *Project Mgr*
Jordan Anetsberger, *Manager*
Kevin M Anetsberger, *Admin Sec*
▲ EMP: 30
SALES (est): 7MM  Privately Held
WEB: www.tungsten.com
SIC: 3496  Miscellaneous fabricated wire products

### (G-22224)
**MIWON NA**
669 Executive Dr (60527-5603)
PHONE..................................630 568-5850
EMP: 3
SALES (est): 158.8K  Privately Held
SIC: 2869  Industrial organic chemicals

### (G-22225)
**MK ENVIRONMENTAL  INC (PA)**
7150 S Madison St Ste 2 (60527-7994)
PHONE..................................630 848-0585
Edward Tung, *President*
Nicholas Marnach, *Engineer*
James Reedy, *Manager*
EMP: 2
SALES (est): 663.3K  Privately Held
WEB: www.mkenv.com
SIC: 3826  Environmental testing equipment

### (G-22226)
**NATIONAL TEMP-TROL PRODUCTS**
Also Called: National Window Shade Co
667 Executive Dr (60527-5603)
PHONE..................................630 920-1919
Berislav Dujlovich, *President*
EMP: 4 EST: 1973
SALES (est): 390K  Privately Held
WEB: www.nationalwindowshade.com
SIC: 2591  Window shades

### (G-22227)
**OEC GRAPHICS-CHICAGO  LLC**
7630 S Quincy St (60527-5526)
PHONE..................................630 455-6700
Mark Jensen,
▲ EMP: 40
SQ FT: 18,000
SALES (est): 7.3MM
SALES (corp-wide): 68.5MM  Privately Held
WEB: www.seamex.com
SIC: 3555  2796  2759  Printing plates; platemaking services; commercial printing
PA: O E C Graphics, Inc.
555 W Waukau Ave
Oshkosh WI 54902
920 235-7770

### (G-22228)
**PREMIER TRAVEL MEDIA**
621 Plainfield Rd Ste 406 (60527-5391)
PHONE..................................630 794-0696
Jeff Gayduk, *President*
John Kloster, *Principal*
Cheryl Rash, *Regional Mgr*
Jim McCurdy, *Business Mgr*
Linda Ragusin, *Business Mgr*
EMP: 4
SALES (est): 314.2K  Privately Held
WEB: www.leisuretraveldirectory.com
SIC: 2741  Miscellaneous publishing

### (G-22229)
**REACT COMPUTER SERVICES INC**
7654 Plaza Ct (60527-5607)
PHONE..................................630 323-6200
John Edwards, *President*
Joe Bruzdzinsk, *Vice Pres*
EMP: 60
SALES (est): 6.5MM  Privately Held
SIC: 7372  7378  7371  Prepackaged software; computer maintenance & repair; custom computer programming services

### (G-22230)
**SCROLLEX CORPORATION**
7888 S Quincy St (60527-5534)
PHONE..................................630 887-8817
Jeff Jankiewicz, *President*
EMP: 5
SQ FT: 6,000
SALES (est): 156.9K  Privately Held
SIC: 3563  Air & gas compressors

### (G-22231)
**SHADOWTECH LABS  INC**
760 N Frontage Rd Ste 102 (60527-5656)
PHONE..................................630 413-4478
Michael Collins, *President*
Brian King, *Vice Pres*
David Nahlik, *Vice Pres*
Casey Walsh, *Vice Pres*
EMP: 4
SALES (est): 794K  Privately Held
SIC: 3728  Military aircraft equipment & armament

### (G-22232)
**SPLASH GRAPHICS  INC**
7001 S Adams St (60527-7592)
PHONE..................................630 230-5775
Valji Patel, *Principal*
Bhavesh Vanani, *Treasurer*
Dhiren Sanghani, *Admin Sec*
EMP: 10
SALES (est): 1.1MM  Privately Held
SIC: 2796  Color separations for printing

### (G-22233)
**STERIGENICS US  LLC**
7775 S Quincy St (60527-5531)
Sandra Haissig, *Manager*
EMP: 21
SALES (corp-wide): 616.3MM  Privately Held
SIC: 7342  7389  3821  Disinfecting services; product sterilization service; sterilizers
HQ: Sterigenics U.S., Llc
3 Parkway N Ste 100n
Deerfield IL 60015
847 607-6060

### (G-22234)
**TPC METALS  LLC (PA)**
7000 S Adams St (60527-7564)
PHONE..................................330 479-9510
Marty Mezydlo, *General Mgr*
Mike Crisan, *Vice Pres*
Sandy Cledanor, *Buyer*
EMP: 7
SALES (est): 2.5MM  Privately Held
SIC: 3339  5094  Precious metals; precious stones & metals

### (G-22235)
**TRU FRAGRANCE & BEAUTY LLC**
7725 S Quincy St (60527-5531)
PHONE..................................630 563-4110
Monte Henige, *CEO*
Melody Dworin, *President*
Mark Magliaro, *President*
Monique Maher, *Business Mgr*
Eric Bilenko, *COO*
▲ EMP: 36 EST: 1969
SQ FT: 31,000
SALES (est): 9.8MM  Privately Held
SIC: 2844  Perfumes & colognes

### (G-22236)
**UBIPASS INC**
5931 Stewart Dr Apt 1021 (60527-3158)
PHONE..................................312 626-4624
Nasser Ghazi, *President*
Saarah Ghazi, *Principal*
Zoya Ghazi, *Principal*
EMP: 3 EST: 2015
SALES (est): 127.8K  Privately Held
SIC: 7372  Application computer software

### (G-22237)
**VISCOSITY OIL COMPANY (DH)**
600 Joliet Rd Ste H (60527-5698)
PHONE..................................630 850-4000
Fax: 630 850-4020
Jeffrey Hoch, *President*
Domenico Ciaglia, *General Mgr*
Michael Lawitts, *Opers Mgr*
Brad Nevin, *CFO*
▲ EMP: 31 EST: 1892
SQ FT: 13,000
SALES (est): 10MM  Privately Held
WEB: www.viscosityoil.com
SIC: 2992  Oils & greases, blending & compounding
HQ: Petronas Lubricants Italy Spa
Via Santena 1
Villastellone TO 10029
029 243-61

### (G-22238)
**WALTER BARR  INC**
655 Executive Dr (60527-5603)
PHONE..................................630 325-7265
Walter Barr, *President*
Patricia Barr, *Vice Pres*
Greg Parenty, *Vice Pres*
EMP: 6
SQ FT: 2,700
SALES (est): 800K  Privately Held
SIC: 2759  2672  Flexographic printing; coated & laminated paper

### (G-22239)
**WEDCO MOLDED PRODUCTS**
7409 S Quincy St (60527-5521)
PHONE..................................630 455-6711
Fax: 630 455-9606
Brian Beth, *Principal*
EMP: 4
SALES (est): 308.8K  Privately Held
SIC: 3089  Injection molded finished plastic products

### (G-22240)
**ZONE INC**
Also Called: Alpha Printing
66 63rd St (60527-2982)
PHONE..................................630 887-8585
Fax: 630 887-0380
Abraham Thodemvelil, *President*
Kurt Elliott, *Sales Staff*
EMP: 4
SQ FT: 1,400
SALES (est): 500K  Privately Held
SIC: 2752  Commercial printing, offset

## Wilmette
### *Cook County*

### (G-22241)
**AL BAR LABORATORIES INC**
Also Called: Al Bar-Wilmette Platers
127 Green Bay Rd (60091-3398)
PHONE..................................847 251-1218
Fax: 847 251-0281
Robert M Mintz, *President*
Loraine Everett, *Project Mgr*
Greg Bettenhausen, *Chief Mktg Ofcr*
EMP: 10 EST: 1937
SQ FT: 3,000
SALES (est): 1.5MM  Privately Held
WEB: www.albarwilmette.com
SIC: 3471  5719  5944  Plating & polishing; housewares; silverware

### (G-22242)
**BAKED BY BETSY  INC**
707 Greenleaf Ave (60091-1917)
PHONE..................................847 292-1434
Betsy D'Attomo, *President*
EMP: 7
SALES (est): 631.6K  Privately Held
SIC: 2052  Bakery products, dry

### (G-22243)
**BELCO INTERNATIONAL TOY CO**
806 Lawler Ave (60091-2034)
PHONE..................................847 256-6818
Gabe Jacobson, *CEO*
Anna Bell Jacobson, *President*
Lynne Arons, *Vice Pres*
EMP: 4
SALES: 500K  Privately Held
SIC: 3944  5092  Games, toys & children's vehicles; toys

### (G-22244)
**BIERDEMAN BOX LLC**
3445 Riverside Dr (60091-1061)
PHONE..................................847 256-0302
Herb Goldstein, *President*
Herbert Goldstein, *Vice Pres*
Sarell Albert, *Treasurer*
EMP: 45 EST: 1932
SQ FT: 58,000
SALES (est): 4.4MM  Privately Held
WEB: www.bierdeman.com
SIC: 2652  Setup paperboard boxes

### (G-22245)
**BRANCH LINES LTD**
1200 N Branch Rd (60091-1035)
PHONE..................................847 256-4294
EMP: 3
SALES (est): 160.9K  Privately Held
SIC: 3944  Mfg Games/Toys

### (G-22246)
**BRANDT INTERIORS**
803 Ridge Rd (60091-2445)
PHONE..................................847 251-3543
Linda Runnfeldt, *Partner*
Frank Runnfeldt, *Partner*
EMP: 3 EST: 1936
SQ FT: 1,000
SALES (est): 180K  Privately Held
WEB: www.brandtinteriors.com
SIC: 7641  3842  Reupholstery; drapes, surgical (cotton)

### (G-22247)
**BREAKFAST FUEL LLC**
1222 Washington Ct (60091-2615)
PHONE..................................847 251-3835
Genevieve Lennon, *Principal*
EMP: 4
SALES (est): 479.4K  Privately Held
SIC: 2869  Fuels

### (G-22248)
**C2 PREMIUM PAINT**
101 Green Bay Rd (60091-3303)
PHONE..................................847 251-6906
Bruce Ekstrand, *Principal*
EMP: 3 EST: 2007
SALES (est): 189.5K  Privately Held
SIC: 2851  5231  Lacquer: bases, dopes, thinner; paint

## Wilmette - Cook County (G-22249)

**(G-22249)**
**CDJ TECHNOLOGIES INC**
2737 Blackhawk Rd (60091-1258)
PHONE...................................321 277-7807
James Hedrick, *Principal*
Chad Mirkin, *Principal*
David Walker, *COO*
**EMP:** 3
**SALES (est):** 102.3K **Privately Held**
**SIC:** 5162 3087 3555 Plastics products; custom compound purchased resins; printing trades machinery

**(G-22250)**
**CHALLINOR WOOD PRODUCTS INC**
1213 Wilmette Ave Ste 208 (60091-2566)
PHONE...................................847 256-8828
Mark A Challinor, *President*
Alice Challinor, *Treasurer*
Sania Buie, *Manager*
▲ **EMP:** 3 **EST:** 1978
**SQ FT:** 600
**SALES (est):** 526.7K **Privately Held**
**WEB:** www.challinorwood.com
**SIC:** 2435 7389 Hardwood veneer & plywood; log & lumber broker

**(G-22251)**
**DESIGN SCIENTIFIC INC**
1189 Wilmette Ave (60091-2719)
PHONE...................................616 582-5225
Dean Ball, *President*
Joanne Ball, *Treasurer*
**EMP:** 5
**SQ FT:** 1,800
**SALES (est):** 700K **Privately Held**
**WEB:** www.designscientific.com
**SIC:** 3826 8734 Analytical instruments; testing laboratories

**(G-22252)**
**FLYNN GUITARS INC**
Also Called: Flynn Guitars & Music
165 Green Bay Rd Ste B (60091-3361)
PHONE...................................800 585-9555
Michael Flynn, *President*
Peter Flynn, *Admin Sec*
**EMP:** 3
**SQ FT:** 3,000
**SALES (est):** 232.6K **Privately Held**
**WEB:** www.flynnguitars.com
**SIC:** 5736 3931 8299 Musical instrument stores; guitars & parts, electric & nonelectric; music school

**(G-22253)**
**HANIGS FOOTWEAR INC**
1515 Sheridan Rd Ste 2 (60091-1825)
PHONE...................................773 248-1977
**EMP:** 4
**SALES (est):** 113K **Privately Held**
**SIC:** 5661 3131 Shoe stores; boot & shoe accessories

**(G-22254)**
**HOMERS ICE CREAM INC**
Also Called: Homers Rest & Ice Cream Parlor
1237 Green Bay Rd (60091-1699)
PHONE...................................847 251-0477
Fax: 847 251-0495
Stephen G Poulos, *President*
JM Rowe, *Publisher*
Nick Poulos, *General Mgr*
John Poulos, *Corp Secy*
Dean Poulos, *Vice Pres*
**EMP:** 28 **EST:** 1925
**SQ FT:** 7,500
**SALES (est):** 3.7MM **Privately Held**
**WEB:** www.homersicecream.com
**SIC:** 2024 5812 Ice cream, bulk; eating places

**(G-22255)**
**INTERNATIONAL SOURCE SOLUTIONS**
3229 Wilmette Ave (60091-2956)
PHONE...................................847 251-8265
Yvette Stinehart, *Owner*
**EMP:** 2
**SALES (est):** 221.3K **Privately Held**
**SIC:** 3444 Sheet metal specialties, not stamped

**(G-22256)**
**KENILWORTH PRESS INCORPORATED**
1223 Green Bay Rd (60091-1643)
PHONE...................................847 256-5210
Fax: 847 256-5279
**EMP:** 5
**SQ FT:** 3,000
**SALES:** 300K **Privately Held**
**SIC:** 2752 2791 Lithographic Commercial Printing Typesetting Services

**(G-22257)**
**KERRIGAN CORPORATION INC**
811 Ridge Rd (60091-2445)
P.O. Box 314 (60091-0314)
PHONE...................................847 251-8994
Fax: 847 251-9433
Jerome Kerrigan, *President*
Mike Kerrigan, *Vice Pres*
Pat Kerrigen, *Admin Sec*
**EMP:** 4
**SALES:** 500K **Privately Held**
**SIC:** 3543 Industrial patterns

**(G-22258)**
**KILLEEN CONFECTIONERY LLC (PA)**
600 20th St (60091-2391)
PHONE...................................312 804-0009
Liam Killeen,
**EMP:** 1
**SALES (est):** 15MM **Privately Held**
**SIC:** 2064 Candy & other confectionery products

**(G-22259)**
**LIGHT WAVES LLC**
1000 Skokie Blvd (60091-1161)
PHONE...................................847 251-1622
Robert Russell,
**EMP:** 11
**SQ FT:** 2,800
**SALES (est):** 458.9K **Privately Held**
**SIC:** 3993 7389 Signs & advertising specialties; engraving service

**(G-22260)**
**LORTON GROUP LLC**
419 Vine St (60091-3131)
PHONE...................................844 352-5089
Stephen Hatton,
Marc Hatton,
**EMP:** 5
**SALES:** 500K **Privately Held**
**SIC:** 2299 Textile goods

**(G-22261)**
**MAKE IT BETTER LLC**
Also Called: Make It Better.net
1150 Wilmette Ave Ste I (60091-2642)
PHONE...................................847 256-4642
Julie Carter, *Accounts Exec*
Susan B Noyes, *Mng Member*
**EMP:** 6
**SALES (est):** 445.6K **Privately Held**
**SIC:** 2741 Telephone & other directory publishing

**(G-22262)**
**MID CENTRAL PRINTING & MAILING**
1211 Wilmette Ave (60091-2557)
PHONE...................................847 251-4040
Fax: 847 251-8703
John Korzak Jr, *President*
Carrie Korzak, *Vice Pres*
Gretchen Korzak, *Vice Pres*
**EMP:** 11 **EST:** 1953
**SQ FT:** 4,500
**SALES:** 740K **Privately Held**
**WEB:** www.mcpm.com
**SIC:** 7331 2752 2789 Mailing service; commercial printing, offset; bookbinding & related work

**(G-22263)**
**PLASTIC LETTER & SIGNS INC**
3223 Lake Ave Ste 15c (60091-1069)
PHONE...................................847 251-3719
James Kaspari, *President*
Demetra Kaspari, *Vice Pres*
Peter Pantos, *Manager*
**EMP:** 2
**SQ FT:** 4,000
**SALES:** 200K **Privately Held**
**SIC:** 3993 Signs & advertising specialties

**(G-22264)**
**REBEL BRANDS LLC**
600 20th St (60091-2391)
PHONE...................................312 804-0009
William Killeen, *CEO*
**EMP:** 1
**SALES:** 15MM **Privately Held**
**SIC:** 2064 7389 Candy & other confectionery products;
**PA:** Killeen Confectionery, Llc
600 20th St
Wilmette IL 60091
312 804-0009

**(G-22265)**
**RESOLUTION SYSTEMS INC**
1189 Wilmette Ave (60091-2719)
PHONE...................................616 392-8001
Mark Elliot, *President*
Julie Decook, *Corp Comm Staff*
**EMP:** 7
**SQ FT:** 8,000
**SALES (est):** 1.6MM **Privately Held**
**SIC:** 2833 Drugs & herbs: grading, grinding & milling

**(G-22266)**
**SOURCENNEX INTERNATIONAL CO**
825 Green Bay Rd Ste 240 (60091-2500)
PHONE...................................847 251-5500
Dennis S Xie, *President*
▲ **EMP:** 3
**SALES (est):** 240K **Privately Held**
**SIC:** 3842 Welders' hoods

**(G-22267)**
**TOP HAT COMPANY INC (PA)**
2407 Birchwood Ln (60091-2349)
P.O. Box 66 (60091-0066)
PHONE...................................847 256-6565
Fax: 847 256-6579
Marla Murray, *President*
**EMP:** 2
**SALES (est):** 1.9MM **Privately Held**
**WEB:** www.tophatcompany.com
**SIC:** 2099 Sauces: gravy, dressing & dip mixes

## Wilmington
### Will County

**(G-22268)**
**A & J SIGNS**
2104 Woodview Dr (60481-1756)
PHONE...................................815 476-0128
Jasson Robards, *Owner*
**EMP:** 10
**SALES (est):** 757.6K **Privately Held**
**WEB:** www.ajsigns.com
**SIC:** 3993 Signs & advertising specialties

**(G-22269)**
**ALLKUT TOOL INCORPORATED**
601 Davy Ln (60481-9236)
P.O. Box 217 (60481-0217)
PHONE...................................815 476-9656
Charles Nicholson, *President*
Diana Nicholson, *Treasurer*
**EMP:** 6
**SALES (est):** 990.1K **Privately Held**
**SIC:** 3545 7699 3425 Machine tool accessories; tool repair services; saw blades & handsaws

**(G-22270)**
**DOW CHEMICAL COMPANY**
901 E Kankakee River Dr # 1 (60481-7699)
PHONE...................................815 476-9688
Anthony Carbone, *Branch Mgr*
Bert Peters, *Manager*
Kevin Schmide, *Manager*
Chris Marlette, *Project Leader*
Joseph Halper, *Technician*
**EMP:** 100
**SALES (corp-wide):** 48.1B **Publicly Held**
**WEB:** www.dow.com
**SIC:** 2821 Thermoplastic materials
**PA:** The Dow Chemical Company
2030 Dow Ctr
Midland MI 48674
989 636-1000

**(G-22271)**
**ED HILL S CUSTOM CANVAS**
8655 E Mallard Ln (60481-9222)
PHONE...................................815 476-5042
Edward Hill, *Principal*
**EMP:** 4
**SALES (est):** 275.6K **Privately Held**
**SIC:** 2394 Canvas & related products

**(G-22272)**
**FREE PRESS NEWSPAPERS**
Also Called: Free Press Advocate
111 S Water St (60481-1373)
P.O. Box 327 (60481-0327)
PHONE...................................815 476-7966
Fax: 815 476-7002
Eric Fisher, *President*
Greg Fisher, *Systs Prg Mgr*
**EMP:** 30 **EST:** 1975
**SALES:** 1,000K **Privately Held**
**WEB:** www.gxcommunications.com
**SIC:** 2711 Newspapers: publishing only, not printed on site

**(G-22273)**
**G-W COMMUNICATIONS INC**
Also Called: Wilmington Free Press
111 S Water St (60481-1373)
P.O. Box 327 (60481-0327)
PHONE...................................815 476-7966
George Fisher, *President*
Janet A Fisher, *Treasurer*
**EMP:** 9
**SQ FT:** 3,000
**SALES (est):** 602.8K **Privately Held**
**SIC:** 2711 Newspapers: publishing only, not printed on site

**(G-22274)**
**HAYNES-BENT INC**
35179 S Old Chicago Rd (60481-9650)
PHONE...................................630 845-3316
Ronald D Kollman, *President*
**EMP:** 12
**SQ FT:** 150
**SALES (est):** 1.1MM **Privately Held**
**WEB:** www.haynesbent.com
**SIC:** 3825 Radio frequency measuring equipment

**(G-22275)**
**RS WOODWORKING**
119 N Water St (60481-1229)
PHONE...................................815 476-1818
Sam Madia, *President*
**EMP:** 3 **EST:** 2014
**SALES (est):** 206.9K **Privately Held**
**SIC:** 2431 Millwork

**(G-22276)**
**RWAY PLASTICS LTD**
30650 S State Route 53 (60481-9010)
P.O. Box 215 (60481-0215)
PHONE...................................815 476-5252
Fax: 815 476-5299
Larry Atkinson, *President*
Mike Szyamanski, *Admin Sec*
**EMP:** 15
**SQ FT:** 14,500
**SALES:** 1.5MM **Privately Held**
**SIC:** 3089 Injection molding of plastics

**(G-22277)**
**S & S MAINTENANCE**
1305 Widows Rd (60481-9389)
PHONE...................................815 725-9263
Stacey Wolcott, *President*
**EMP:** 2
**SALES (est):** 200K **Privately Held**
**SIC:** 3531 Road construction & maintenance machinery

## Winchester
*Scott County*

**(G-22278)**
**CAMPBELL PUBLISHING INC (PA)**
Also Called: Scott County Times
4 S Hill St (62694-1212)
P.O. Box 64 (62694-0064)
PHONE..................217 742-3313
Fax: 630 206-0367
James Bruce Campbell, *President*
Ray Johnson, *Treasurer*
Jessie Bugg, *Manager*
**EMP:** 3 **EST:** 1962
**SQ FT:** 3,500
**SALES (est):** 3MM **Privately Held**
**SIC:** 2711 2759 2752 Newspapers: publishing only, not printed on site; commercial printing; commercial printing, lithographic

**(G-22279)**
**FOURELL CORP**
410 E Jefferson St (62694-8034)
PHONE..................217 742-3186
John A Lashmett, *President*
**EMP:** 5
**SALES (corp-wide):** 1MM **Privately Held**
**SIC:** 2299 Felts & felt products; yarns & thread, made from non-fabric materials
**PA:** Fourell Corp
4645 N Magnolia Ave
Chicago IL
773 271-4776

**(G-22280)**
**IMCO PRECAST LLC**
730 State Route 106 (62694-3641)
PHONE..................217 742-5300
Dan Sheley, *Principal*
Patricia Sheley, *Mng Member*
**EMP:** 3
**SALES:** 130K **Privately Held**
**SIC:** 3272 Precast terrazo or concrete products

**(G-22281)**
**LASHCON INC**
Also Called: 4l Waterjet
540 Coultas Rd (62694-9796)
P.O. Box 226 (62694-0226)
PHONE..................217 742-3186
Fax: 217 742-9503
Dorothy Lashmett, *President*
**EMP:** 8
**SALES (est):** 1.7MM **Privately Held**
**WEB:** www.lashcon.com
**SIC:** 3532 Mining machinery

## Windsor
*Shelby County*

**(G-22282)**
**QUALITY PALLETS INC**
601 Kentucky Ave (61957-1655)
PHONE..................217 459-2655
Fax: 217 459-2343
Cinda M Smith, *President*
Greg Smith, *Vice Pres*
Joy Shumard, *Office Mgr*
**EMP:** 20
**SQ FT:** 9,500
**SALES (est):** 3.5MM **Privately Held**
**SIC:** 2448 3086 Pallets, wood; plastics foam products

## Winfield
*Dupage County*

**(G-22283)**
**BW INDUSTRIES**
27w230 Beecher Ave Ste 1 (60190-1220)
PHONE..................630 784-1020
Fax: 630 784-1022
Ken Le Beau, *Principal*
**EMP:** 8
**SALES (est):** 823.1K **Privately Held**
**SIC:** 3999 Manufacturing industries

**(G-22284)**
**CLEAVENGER ASSOCIATES INC**
27w474 Jewell Rd Ste 2w (60190-1225)
PHONE..................630 221-0007
Timothy Cleavenger, *President*
Barbara Keyes, *Admin Sec*
**EMP:** 2
**SQ FT:** 1,000
**SALES (est):** 250K **Privately Held**
**SIC:** 3569 5085 3229 7389 Gas producers, generators & other gas related equipment; valves & fittings; tubing, glass; interior decorating

**(G-22285)**
**EDISON PALLET & WOOD PRODUCTS**
371 County Farm Rd (60190)
P.O. Box 195 (60190-0195)
PHONE..................630 653-3416
Fax: 630 668-9298
Chester L Edison, *Owner*
Keith Edison, *Bookkeeper*
**EMP:** 2
**SALES (est):** 206.3K **Privately Held**
**WEB:** www.edisonpallet.com
**SIC:** 2448 Wood pallets & skids

**(G-22286)**
**JONES DESIGN GROUP LTD**
27w230 Beecher Ave Ste 1 (60190-1220)
PHONE..................630 462-9340
Ed Jones, *President*
**EMP:** 4
**SALES (est):** 470K **Privately Held**
**SIC:** 2434 1721 Wood kitchen cabinets; painting & paper hanging

**(G-22287)**
**LOCALFIX SOLUTIONS LLC**
26w194 Prestwick Ln (60190-2310)
PHONE..................312 569-0619
Matthew Ruesch, *CEO*
**EMP:** 3
**SALES (est):** 144.1K **Privately Held**
**SIC:** 7372 7371 Business oriented computer software; computer software writing services; computer software development

**(G-22288)**
**OSTROM & CO INC**
Also Called: Ostrom Glass & Metal Works
28w600 Roosevelt Rd (60190-1515)
PHONE..................503 281-6469
Chuck Toombs, *President*
▲ **EMP:** 13
**SQ FT:** 17,000
**SALES (est):** 1.2MM **Privately Held**
**WEB:** www.ostrom.us
**SIC:** 3231 3479 Ornamental glass: cut, engraved or otherwise decorated; etching on metals

**(G-22289)**
**PARADIGM DEVELOPMENT GROUP INC**
27 W 230 Becher Ave Ste 2 (60190)
PHONE..................847 545-9600
Fax: 847 545-9604
Steven Hund, *President*
Ken Zamecnik, *Vice Pres*
**EMP:** 18
**SQ FT:** 9,000
**SALES:** 1.5MM **Privately Held**
**WEB:** www.pardev.com
**SIC:** 3999 Models, general, except toy

**(G-22290)**
**PINEHURST BUS SOLUTIONS CORP**
26w362 Pinehurst Dr (60190-2329)
PHONE..................630 842-6155
Peter Arnolds, *President*
Pete Sandrabethea, *Sls & Mktg Exec*
**EMP:** 4
**SALES (est):** 100K **Privately Held**
**SIC:** 3571 3572 7373 7377 Electronic computers; computer storage devices; computer integrated systems design; computer rental & leasing; computer maintenance & repair; computer related maintenance services;

**(G-22291)**
**QUILT MERCHANT**
27w209 Geneva Rd (60190-2031)
PHONE..................630 480-3000
Docia Fuller, *Owner*
James Fuller, *Co-Owner*
**EMP:** 10
**SALES (est):** 185K **Privately Held**
**SIC:** 2395 Quilting & quilting supplies

**(G-22292)**
**S & R MONOGRAMMING INC**
28w600 Roosevelt Rd (60190-1515)
PHONE..................630 369-5468
Susan C Hallbauer, *President*
Richard D Hallbauer, *Admin Sec*
**EMP:** 2
**SALES:** 400K **Privately Held**
**SIC:** 5199 2395 Advertising specialties; pleating & stitching

**(G-22293)**
**SAGE CLOVER**
26w400 Torrey Pines Ct (60190-2354)
P.O. Box 288 (60190-0288)
PHONE..................630 220-9600
Krishna Narsimhan, *Principal*
**EMP:** 2
**SALES (est):** 314.7K **Privately Held**
**SIC:** 5092 2531 Educational toys; school furniture

## Winnebago
*Winnebago County*

**(G-22294)**
**A BURST OF SUN INC**
817 N Elida St (61088-8617)
PHONE..................815 335-2331
Tiffany Whitehead, *President*
**EMP:** 3 **EST:** 1999
**SQ FT:** 2,100
**SALES (est):** 311.1K **Privately Held**
**SIC:** 3648 Sun tanning equipment, incl. tanning beds

**(G-22295)**
**EQUISOFT INC**
8176 W Oliver Rd (61088-8843)
PHONE..................815 629-2789
Delvin Insko, *President*
Jaquline Santoro, *Corp Secy*
Kathryn Insko, *Admin Sec*
**EMP:** 3
**SALES (est):** 200K **Privately Held**
**WEB:** www.equisoftusa.com
**SIC:** 7372 Prepackaged software

**(G-22296)**
**FLOCK IT LTD**
13142 Murphy Rd (61088-9344)
PHONE..................815 247-8775
Jill Goldman, *Owner*
**EMP:** 2
**SALES (est):** 221.1K **Privately Held**
**SIC:** 2261 Flocking of cotton broadwoven fabrics

**(G-22297)**
**I D ROCKFORD SHOP INC**
105 N Pecatonica St (61088-9099)
PHONE..................815 335-1150
Fax: 815 335-1149
Robert D Dowdakin, *President*
William J Dowdakin, *Treasurer*
Pete N Gustavson, *Sales Mgr*
Savannah Liston, *Consultant*
Tammi Cunningham, *Admin Sec*
**EMP:** 8
**SQ FT:** 10,500
**SALES (est):** 1.2MM **Privately Held**
**WEB:** www.rockford-id.com
**SIC:** 3599 3451 3423 3724 Machine shop, jobbing & repair; screw machine products; hand & edge tools; aircraft engines & engine parts

**(G-22298)**
**TRU-CUT PRODUCTION INC**
211 W Main St (61088-7722)
P.O. Box 631 (61088-0631)
PHONE..................815 335-2215
Fax: 815 335-1015
Phil Whitehead, *President*
Wendell Whitehead, *Vice Pres*
**EMP:** 8
**SQ FT:** 100,000
**SALES (est):** 750K **Privately Held**
**SIC:** 3599 Machine shop, jobbing & repair

**(G-22299)**
**Z-TECH INC**
1958 S Winnebago Rd (61088-9162)
PHONE..................815 335-7395
Fax: 815 335-7323
Rebecca A Oakley, *President*
Myron Oakley, *Vice Pres*
**EMP:** 3
**SQ FT:** 3,000
**SALES (est):** 470.6K **Privately Held**
**WEB:** www.panelpunches.com
**SIC:** 3599 8711 3625 3549 Custom machinery; mechanical engineering; electrical or electronic engineering; relays & industrial controls; metalworking machinery; special dies, tools, jigs & fixtures

## Winnetka
*Cook County*

**(G-22300)**
**AL3 INC**
170 Linden St (60093-3862)
PHONE..................847 441-7888
James H Williamson, *President*
Janet Williamson, *Treasurer*
**EMP:** 5
**SALES (est):** 76.5K **Privately Held**
**SIC:** 3354 Aluminum extruded products

**(G-22301)**
**ALLIANCE ENVELOPE & PRINT LLC**
854 Prospect Ave (60093-1945)
PHONE..................847 446-4079
Joseph Reinert, *Manager*
**EMP:** 2
**SALES (est):** 2MM **Privately Held**
**SIC:** 2759 Commercial printing

**(G-22302)**
**APPSANITY ADVISORY LLC**
335 Auburn Ave (60093-3603)
PHONE..................847 638-1172
John S Ivers, *Mng Member*
**EMP:** 1
**SALES (est):** 400K **Privately Held**
**SIC:** 7372 Application computer software

**(G-22303)**
**BELLOWS SHOPPE**
1048 Gage St Ste 301 (60093-1703)
PHONE..................847 446-5533
Fax: 847 446-8376
Steven Schmid, *Owner*
**EMP:** 6
**SQ FT:** 1,200
**SALES (est):** 400K **Privately Held**
**WEB:** www.chicagolightingantiques.com
**SIC:** 5719 7629 7699 3471 Lamps & lamp shades; lamp repair & mounting; metal reshaping & replating services; plating & polishing

**(G-22304)**
**BLISS RING COMPANY INC**
Also Called: Ring-O-Bliss
1095 Willow Rd (60093-3642)
PHONE..................847 446-3440
Charles R Drucker II, *President*
Paul M Drucker, *Vice Pres*
Robert J Drucker, *Vice Pres*
Jean Drucker, *Admin Sec*
**EMP:** 17 **EST:** 1934
**SALES (est):** 1.2MM **Privately Held**
**SIC:** 3911 Rings, finger: precious metal

**(G-22305)**
**ELN GROUP LLC**
39 Longmeadow Rd (60093-3524)
PHONE..................847 477-1496
Lenore McCarthy,
Nina Krasikoff,
Eric Ladewig,
Laurine Sargent,
**EMP:** 4

# Winnetka - Cook County (G-22306)

SALES (est): 272.5K **Privately Held**
SIC: 3842 Surgical appliances & supplies; bandages & dressings

### (G-22306)
### FEELSURE HEALTH CORPORATION
503 Orchard Ln (60093-4114)
PHONE .............................. 847 446-7881
William Bartlett, *CEO*
EMP: 4
SALES (est): 295.9K **Privately Held**
SIC: 3841 Surgical & medical instruments

### (G-22307)
### HL METALS LLC
910 Spruce St (60093-2219)
PHONE .............................. 312 590-3360
Hui Lin Lim,
EMP: 1
SALES (est): 369.2K **Privately Held**
SIC: 3449 7389 Miscellaneous metalwork;

### (G-22308)
### KASKEY KIDS INC
1485 Scott Ave (60093-1448)
PHONE .............................. 847 441-3092
Cristy Kaskey, *President*
Fj Fee, *VP Sales*
Bruce Kaskey, *Admin Sec*
▲ EMP: 3
SALES (est): 250K **Privately Held**
SIC: 3944 Games, toys & children's vehicles

### (G-22309)
### LANTERNA MEDICAL TECH USA
821 Foxdale Ave (60093-1909)
PHONE .............................. 847 446-9995
Lyle Banks, *CEO*
EMP: 3
SALES (est): 129.1K **Privately Held**
SIC: 3842 Surgical appliances & supplies

### (G-22310)
### LOSANGELES FEATURES SYNDICATE
650 Winnetka Mews Apt 110 (60093-1955)
PHONE .............................. 847 446-4082
Fax: 847 446-4804
Alice Licht, *Owner*
EMP: 5
SALES (est): 158.4K **Privately Held**
SIC: 2711 Commercial printing & newspaper publishing combined

### (G-22311)
### MANCILLAS INTERNATIONAL LTD (PA)
Also Called: Mancillas Intl
47 Longmeadow Rd (60093-3524)
PHONE .............................. 847 441-7748
Marcial R Mancillas, *President*
Gerald Domanus, *Controller*
Mary Louise Mancillas, *Admin Sec*
EMP: 15 EST: 1970
SQ FT: 20,000
SALES (est): 1.5MM **Privately Held**
SIC: 2311 Suits, men's & boys': made from purchased materials

### (G-22312)
### MEDICAL ADHERENCE TECH INC
825 Heather Ln (60093-1316)
PHONE .............................. 847 525-6300
Sanjay Mehrotra, *President*
EMP: 3
SALES (est): 117.4K **Privately Held**
SIC: 3841 Surgical & medical instruments

### (G-22313)
### NANEX LLC
818 Elm St Uppr 2 (60093-2224)
PHONE .............................. 847 501-4787
Eric S Hunsader, *Mng Member*
Jeffrey Donovan, *Sr Software Eng*
EMP: 3
SALES (est): 247.5K **Privately Held**
WEB: www.nanex.net
SIC: 7372 Prepackaged software

### (G-22314)
### PHOEBE & FRANCES
566 Chestnut St (60093-2228)
PHONE .............................. 847 446-5480
Nina Busemi, *Partner*
Sarah Torenef, *Partner*
EMP: 10
SALES (est): 893.1K **Privately Held**
SIC: 2389 Apparel & accessories

### (G-22315)
### WILLIAMSON J HUNTER & COMPANY
170 Linden St (60093-3862)
PHONE .............................. 847 441-7888
Fax: 312 441-7560
James Williamson, *President*
EMP: 3
SALES (est): 300K **Privately Held**
SIC: 3731 Shipbuilding & repairing

### (G-22316)
### WINNETKA MEWS CONDOMINIUM ASSN
640 Winnetka Mews (60093-1966)
PHONE .............................. 847 501-2770
Marlyn Strauss, *Principal*
EMP: 3
SALES (est): 208.3K **Privately Held**
SIC: 8641 3273 Condominium association; ready-mixed concrete

## Winslow
### *Stephenson County*

### (G-22317)
### MITEK CORPORATION
Also Called: Mtx/Oaktron
1 Mitek Plz (61089-9700)
PHONE .............................. 608 328-5560
Loyd Ivey, *Div Sub Head*
Teresa Lobdell, *VP Opers*
George Cromwell, *Engineer*
Linda Haines, *VP Sales*
David Smythe, *Manager*
EMP: 110
SALES (corp-wide): 78.6MM **Privately Held**
WEB: www.mitekcorp.com
SIC: 3651 Speaker systems
PA: Mitek Corporation
4545 E Baseline Rd
Phoenix AZ 85042
602 438-4545

### (G-22318)
### MITEK CORPORATION
Also Called: Mtx
1 Mitek Plz (61089-9700)
P.O. Box 38 (61089-0038)
PHONE .............................. 815 367-3000
Fax: 815 367-3851
Rod Boyer, *Vice Pres*
Christine Patterson, *Safety Dir*
Teresa Lobdell, *Purchasing*
Ric Joranlien, *QC Mgr*
Nick Leiendecker, *Engineer*
EMP: 130
SALES (corp-wide): 78.6MM **Privately Held**
WEB: www.mitekcorp.com
SIC: 3651 Household audio equipment
PA: Mitek Corporation
4545 E Baseline Rd
Phoenix AZ 85042
602 438-4545

## Winthrop Harbor
### *Lake County*

### (G-22319)
### MEYER ENGINEERING CO
1139 Lewis Ave (60096-1428)
PHONE .............................. 847 746-1500
Fax: 847 746-1513
Martin H Meyer, *President*
Ernest McClannahan, *Prdtn Mgr*
Sandra L Meyer, *Admin Sec*
EMP: 7
SQ FT: 13,000
SALES (est): 2.1MM **Privately Held**
WEB: www.meyerengineering.com
SIC: 3429 Marine hardware

### (G-22320)
### RD DAILY ENTERPRISES
Also Called: Daily Highway Express
911 Fulton Ave (60096-1725)
P.O. Box 146 (60096-0146)
PHONE .............................. 847 872-7632
Roger Daily, *President*
EMP: 2
SALES (est): 266.8K **Privately Held**
SIC: 4212 2711 Local trucking, without storage; newspapers, publishing & printing

## Wonder Lake
### *Mchenry County*

### (G-22321)
### BAXTER HEALTHCARE CORPORATION
7621 Center Dr (60097-9261)
PHONE .............................. 847 270-4757
Peter Simpson, *Engrg Dir*
EMP: 5
SALES (corp-wide): 10.1B **Publicly Held**
SIC: 2834 Pharmaceutical preparations
HQ: Baxter Healthcare Corporation
1 Baxter Pkwy
Deerfield IL 60015
224 948-2000

### (G-22322)
### D & H PRECISION TOOLING CO
7522 Barnard Mill Rd (60097-8132)
PHONE .............................. 815 653-9611
Fax: 815 653-9611
David V Jones, *President*
EMP: 4 EST: 1968
SQ FT: 2,400
SALES (est): 200K **Privately Held**
SIC: 3599 7692 3544 Machine shop, jobbing & repair; welding repair; special dies, tools, jigs & fixtures

### (G-22323)
### FLIPTABS INC
7213 Loras Ln (60097-9736)
PHONE .............................. 815 701-2584
Homas Jones, *President*
EMP: 5
SQ FT: 2,700
SALES: 7.2K **Privately Held**
SIC: 3089 Caps, plastic

### (G-22324)
### MAY SAND AND GRAVEL INC
3013 Thompson Rd (60097-9494)
PHONE .............................. 815 338-4761
Roger May, *Owner*
EMP: 3
SALES (est): 188.8K **Privately Held**
SIC: 1442 Construction sand & gravel

### (G-22325)
### SPINCO TOOL & FABE
2518 Walnut Dr (60097-8581)
PHONE .............................. 815 578-8600
Lori Spindler, *President*
EMP: 2
SALES (est): 252.3K **Privately Held**
SIC: 3549 Metalworking machinery

## Wood Dale
### *Dupage County*

### (G-22326)
### AAR AIRCRAFT SERVICES INC (HQ)
Also Called: AAR Aircraft Svcs - Miami Inc
1100 N Wood Dale Rd (60191-1060)
PHONE .............................. 630 227-2000
Timothy J Romenesko, *President*
Timothy Romenesko, *President*
Brian Loomer, *General Mgr*
Mike Sedgwick, *General Mgr*
Sergio Fraile, *Project Mgr*
EMP: 23
SALES (est): 6.3MM
SALES (corp-wide): 1.6B **Publicly Held**
SIC: 3724 Aircraft engines & engine parts
PA: Aar Corp.
1100 N Wood Dale Rd
Wood Dale IL 60191
630 227-2000

### (G-22327)
### AAR ALLEN SERVICES INC (HQ)
1100 N Wood Dale Rd (60191-1060)
PHONE .............................. 630 227-2410
David Storch, *CEO*
Timothy J Romenesko, *President*
Jack M Arehart, *Vice Pres*
Russell Stehn, *Human Res Dir*
Robert Regan, *Admin Sec*
EMP: 95
SALES (est): 37.3MM
SALES (corp-wide): 1.6B **Publicly Held**
SIC: 3728 Aircraft parts & equipment
PA: Aar Corp.
1100 N Wood Dale Rd
Wood Dale IL 60191
630 227-2000

### (G-22328)
### AAR CORP (PA)
1100 N Wood Dale Rd (60191-1094)
PHONE .............................. 630 227-2000
Fax: 630 227-2039
David P Storch, *Ch of Bd*
Timothy J Romenesko, *Vice Chairman*
Jennifer Griffin, *Counsel*
Kathleen Cantillon, *Vice Pres*
Douglas Hara, *Vice Pres*
▲ EMP: 60 EST: 1951
SALES: 1.6B **Publicly Held**
WEB: www.aarcorp.com
SIC: 3724 4581 3537 5599 Aircraft engines & engine parts; aircraft maintenance & repair services; aircraft servicing & repairing; containers (metal), air cargo; aircraft, self-propelled; aircraft rental

### (G-22329)
### AAR SUPPLY CHAIN INC (HQ)
Also Called: AAR Defense Systems Logistics
1100 N Wood Dale Rd (60191-1060)
PHONE .............................. 630 227-2000
Fax: 630 227-2948
David Storch, *President*
Timothy J Romenesko, *President*
Amy Wood, *President*
Christopher Gross, *General Mgr*
Dave Cann, *Vice Pres*
▲ EMP: 200
SQ FT: 250,000
SALES (est): 175.8MM
SALES (corp-wide): 1.6B **Publicly Held**
SIC: 5088 3728 Aircraft & parts; aircraft parts & equipment
PA: Aar Corp.
1100 N Wood Dale Rd
Wood Dale IL 60191
630 227-2000

### (G-22330)
### ACCURATE RIVET MANUFACTURING
343 Beinoris Dr (60191-1222)
P.O. Box 7050 (60191-7050)
PHONE .............................. 630 766-3401
Fax: 630 766-3405
Joseph Losacco, *President*
Maria Losacco, *Corp Secy*
Joseph Losacco Jr, *Vice Pres*
EMP: 9 EST: 1958
SQ FT: 7,000
SALES: 1.2MM **Privately Held**
SIC: 3452 Rivets, metal

### (G-22331)
### ADVANCE THERMAL CORP
226 Gerry Dr (60191-1139)
PHONE .............................. 630 595-5150
Joseph Pirogovsky, *Branch Mgr*
EMP: 30
SALES (corp-wide): 109.8MM **Privately Held**
SIC: 3296 Mineral wool insulation products
HQ: Advance Thermal Corp.
226 Gerry Dr
Wood Dale IL 60191
630 595-5150

# GEOGRAPHIC SECTION

## Wood Dale - Dupage County (G-22358)

**(G-22332)**
**ADVANCE THERMAL CORP (HQ)**
226 Gerry Dr (60191-1139)
PHONE.................................630 595-5150
Fax: 630 595-5174
Joseph Pirogovsky, *President*
Arkady Feldman, *Assistant VP*
James Hargrove, *Vice Pres*
Ellen M Smith, *Vice Pres*
Alex Spivak, *Vice Pres*
▲ **EMP:** 75
**SQ FT:** 25,000
**SALES:** 18.3MM
**SALES (corp-wide):** 109.8MM **Privately Held**
**WEB:** www.advancethermalcorp.com
**SIC:** 3296 Mineral wool insulation products
**PA:** Transco Inc.
  200 N La Salle St # 1550
  Chicago IL 60601
  312 896-8527

**(G-22333)**
**AFFRI INC**
850 Dillon Dr (60191-1269)
PHONE.................................224 374-0931
Roberto Affri, *President*
John Lecoche, *General Mgr*
**EMP:** 3
**SQ FT:** 1,000
**SALES:** 500K **Privately Held**
**SIC:** 3599 5013 Amusement park equipment; testing equipment, engine

**(G-22334)**
**ALFA LAVAL INC**
321 Foster Ave (60191-1432)
PHONE.................................630 354-6090
Richard R Levin, *Branch Mgr*
**EMP:** 115
**SALES (corp-wide):** 3.8B **Privately Held**
**SIC:** 3585 3443 Parts for heating, cooling & refrigerating equipment; condensers, refrigeration; coolers, milk & water; electric; heat exchangers: coolers (after, inter), condensers, etc.
**HQ:** Alfa Laval Inc.
  5400 Intl Trade Dr
  Richmond VA 23231
  804 222-5300

**(G-22335)**
**ALLMETAL INC**
377 Balm Ct (60191-1253)
PHONE.................................630 350-2524
Fax: 630 350-0278
Mark Tatom, *Plant Mgr*
Roderic Cabrera, *Engineer*
John Glas, *Design Engr*
Randy King, *Manager*
Michael Lagdan, *Manager*
**EMP:** 40
**SALES (corp-wide):** 92.9MM **Privately Held**
**WEB:** www.allmetalinc.com
**SIC:** 3442 3444 Metal doors, sash & trim; sheet metalwork
**PA:** Allmetal, Inc.
  1 Pierce Pl Ste 900
  Itasca IL 60143
  630 250-8090

**(G-22336)**
**ALLSTATE METAL FABRICATORS INC**
365 Beinoris Dr (60191-1222)
PHONE.................................630 860-1500
Fax: 630 860-2420
Mike Mc Namara, *President*
Mike McNamara, *President*
Pat McNamara, *Vice Pres*
Luara McNamara, *Manager*
David McNamara, *Shareholder*
▼ **EMP:** 7
**SQ FT:** 10,600
**SALES (est):** 1.3MM **Privately Held**
**WEB:** www.allstatemetalfab.com
**SIC:** 3444 Sheet metalwork

**(G-22337)**
**ALTHEA CRUTEX INC**
Also Called: Minuteman Press
148 E Irving Park Rd (60191-2024)
PHONE.................................630 595-7200
Fax: 630 595-7279
Ray Brzezinski, *President*
Linda Dixon, *Office Mgr*
**EMP:** 2
**SQ FT:** 1,200
**SALES (est):** 271.6K **Privately Held**
**SIC:** 2752 Commercial printing, lithographic

**(G-22338)**
**AMAITIS AND ASSOCIATES INC (PA)**
810 Lively Blvd (60191-1202)
PHONE.................................847 428-1269
Fax: 630 595-8618
Edward J Amaitis Jr, *President*
Edward J Amaitis Sr, *Vice Pres*
Laurie Carberry, *Controller*
Jerry Amaitis, *Admin Sec*
**EMP:** 11
**SQ FT:** 10,000
**SALES (est):** 2.4MM **Privately Held**
**WEB:** www.amaitis.com
**SIC:** 7379 3572 Computer related consulting services; computer tape drives & components

**(G-22339)**
**AMBIR TECHNOLOGY INC**
Also Called: Document Capture Technologies
820 Sivert Dr (60191-2610)
PHONE.................................630 530-5400
Michael O'Leary, *President*
Rolf Schmoldt, *Partner*
Jeff Hargens, *Business Mgr*
Brian Blacher, *Sales Dir*
Rob Krums, *Manager*
▲ **EMP:** 8
**SALES (est):** 1.9MM **Privately Held**
**WEB:** www.ambirtechnology.com
**SIC:** 3577 Computer peripheral equipment

**(G-22340)**
**AMERICAN BULLNOSE CO MIDW**
373 Balm Ct (60191-1253)
PHONE.................................630 238-1300
Lou Harting, *Manager*
Joshua Jenkins, *Manager*
**EMP:** 6
**SALES:** 300K **Privately Held**
**SIC:** 3253 5032 Ceramic wall & floor tile; ceramic wall & floor tile

**(G-22341)**
**AMERICAN DIE SUPPLIES ACQUISIT**
618 N Edgewood Ave (60191-2604)
PHONE.................................630 766-6226
Robert Jarka, *Manager*
▲ **EMP:** 2
**SALES (est):** 223.2K **Privately Held**
**SIC:** 3544 Special dies & tools

**(G-22342)**
**AMERIKEN DIE SUPPLY INC**
618 N Edgewood Ave (60191-2604)
PHONE.................................630 766-6226
Dale Kengott, *President*
Pat Kennedy, *Administration*
▲ **EMP:** 50 **EST:** 1953
**SALES (est):** 8.2MM **Privately Held**
**WEB:** www.ameriken.com
**SIC:** 3544 Dies & die holders for metal cutting, forming, die casting

**(G-22343)**
**BECKMAN COULTER INC**
1500 N Mittel Blvd (60191-1072)
PHONE.................................800 526-3821
Paul Hodnick, *Manager*
**EMP:** 3
**SALES (corp-wide):** 16.8B **Publicly Held**
**WEB:** www.beckman.com
**SIC:** 3826 Analytical instruments
**HQ:** Beckman Coulter, Inc.
  250 S Kraemer Blvd
  Brea CA 92821
  714 993-5321

**(G-22344)**
**BI-PHASE TECHNOLOGIES LLC**
201 Mittel Dr (60191-1116)
PHONE.................................952 886-6450
Bryan White, *General Mgr*
Victor Van Dyke, *General Mgr*
Denise Flack, *Manager*
▲ **EMP:** 13
**SALES (est):** 3.5MM **Publicly Held**
**SIC:** 3714 7538 Fuel systems & parts, motor vehicle; general automotive repair shops
**PA:** Power Solutions International, Inc.
  201 Mittel Dr
  Wood Dale IL 60191

**(G-22345)**
**BITFORMS INC**
Also Called: AlphaGraphics 468
360 Georgetown Sq (60191-1832)
PHONE.................................630 595-6800
Jeff Bittner, *President*
Nicola Bittner, *Vice Pres*
Ronald Bittner, *Treasurer*
Bonnie Bittner, *Admin Sec*
**EMP:** 6
**SQ FT:** 3,100
**SALES (est):** 618.6K **Privately Held**
**SIC:** 2752 Commercial printing, lithographic

**(G-22346)**
**BJ MOLD & DIE INC**
780 Creel Dr Ste 1 (60191-2619)
PHONE.................................630 595-1797
Bogdan Janiszewski, *President*
**EMP:** 3
**SALES (est):** 505.5K **Privately Held**
**SIC:** 3089 Molding primary plastic

**(G-22347)**
**BRUNET SNOW SERVICE COMPANY**
174 Hawthorne Ave (60191-1455)
PHONE.................................847 846-0037
Bobby Brunet, *President*
**EMP:** 4
**SALES:** 100K **Privately Held**
**SIC:** 3585 7389 Snowmaking machinery;

**(G-22348)**
**C CRETORS & CO (PA)**
176 Mittel Dr (60191-1119)
PHONE.................................847 616-6900
Fax: 773 588-2171
Charles D Cretors, *CEO*
Andrew Cretors, *President*
John Concannon, *Vice Pres*
Bud Cretors, *Project Mgr*
Kevin Gorman, *Warehouse Mgr*
◆ **EMP:** 54 **EST:** 1885
**SQ FT:** 53,000
**SALES:** 30MM **Privately Held**
**WEB:** www.cretors.com
**SIC:** 3589 Popcorn machines, commercial

**(G-22349)**
**CACIQUE USA**
1371 N Wood Dale Rd (60191-1061)
PHONE.................................630 766-0059
**EMP:** 3
**SALES (est):** 309.9K **Privately Held**
**SIC:** 5143 2022 Dairy products, except dried or canned; cheese, natural & processed

**(G-22350)**
**CAL-TRONICS SYSTEMS INC**
729 Creel Dr (60191-2609)
PHONE.................................630 350-0044
Fax: 630 350-2409
Salvatore J Caldrone, *President*
Mary Koonce, *General Mgr*
Dean Duley, *Engineer*
Joe Scianna, *Engineer*
Tom Sampson, *Project Engr*
**EMP:** 36
**SALES (est):** 8.5MM **Privately Held**
**WEB:** www.cal-tronics.com
**SIC:** 3679 Electronic circuits

**(G-22351)**
**CHEM-IMPEX INTERNATIONAL INC**
935 Dillon Dr (60191-1274)
PHONE.................................630 350-5015
Nitin Shah, *President*
**EMP:** 20
**SALES (corp-wide):** 13.4MM **Privately Held**
**WEB:** www.chemimpex.com
**SIC:** 5122 2835 Biologicals & allied products; in vitro diagnostics; in vivo diagnostics
**PA:** Chem-Impex International, Inc.
  935 Dillon Dr
  Wood Dale IL 60191
  630 766-2112

**(G-22352)**
**CLASSIC PRTG THERMOGRAPHY INC**
735 N Edgewood Ave Ste F (60191-1261)
PHONE.................................630 595-7765
Christopher Wilk, *President*
Adrian Wilk, *Vice Pres*
**EMP:** 4
**SQ FT:** 2,000
**SALES (est):** 420K **Privately Held**
**SIC:** 2752 Commercial printing, offset

**(G-22353)**
**CMETRIX INC**
165 Mittel Dr (60191-1116)
PHONE.................................630 595-9800
Robert Mielcarski, *President*
Paul Machala, *Vice Pres*
**EMP:** 4
**SALES (est):** 2MM **Privately Held**
**SIC:** 3679 Electronic circuits

**(G-22354)**
**COMPOSITE BEARINGS MFG**
Also Called: MBC Cmpsite Bring Mnfactioring
720 N Edgewood Ave (60191-1249)
PHONE.................................630 595-8334
Luigi Mongodi, *President*
Matteo Rossi, *Plant Mgr*
▲ **EMP:** 12
**SQ FT:** 5,000
**SALES (est):** 2.1MM **Privately Held**
**WEB:** www.mbcbearings.com
**SIC:** 5085 3568 Bearings; bearings, plain

**(G-22355)**
**COSMOS GRANITE & MARBLE CORP**
Also Called: Cosmos Chicago
811 Lively Blvd (60191-1201)
PHONE.................................630 595-8025
Srinivas C Nallapati, *President*
▲ **EMP:** 6
**SALES (est):** 1.3MM **Privately Held**
**WEB:** www.cosmosgranite.com
**SIC:** 3281 Granite, cut & shaped

**(G-22356)**
**CUSTOM ASSEMBLY LLC**
Also Called: Milcon
555 Pond Dr (60191-1131)
PHONE.................................630 595-4855
Fax: 630 616-2299
Mike Machura, *President*
Bernard Machura, *President*
Doris Machura, *Treasurer*
Irina Garbar, *Human Res Mgr*
▲ **EMP:** 200
**SALES (est):** 12.7MM **Privately Held**
**WEB:** www.customassembly.net
**SIC:** 3678 Electronic connectors

**(G-22357)**
**DAMEN CARBIDE TOOL COMPANY INC**
344 Beinoris Dr (60191-1223)
PHONE.................................630 766-7875
Fax: 630 766-7880
John Bachmeier, *President*
Rita Olvera, *Vice Pres*
Jakob Bachmeier, *Treasurer*
Jeff Walters, *Manager*
▲ **EMP:** 25
**SQ FT:** 22,000
**SALES (est):** 9.3MM **Privately Held**
**WEB:** www.damencarbide.com
**SIC:** 3545 3546 Cutting tools for machine tools; power-driven handtools

**(G-22358)**
**DECO LABELS & TAGS LTD**
500 E Thorndale Ave Ste H (60191-1267)
PHONE.................................847 472-2100
Douglas Robert Ford, *President*

# Wood Dale - Dupage County (G-22359)

Theresa Catlin, *Accounts Mgr*
Cathy Demarco, *Manager*
**EMP:** 58
**SQ FT:** 25,000
**SALES (est):** 20.8MM
**SALES (corp-wide):** 3.6MM **Privately Held**
**WEB:** www.decolabels.com
**SIC:** 2679 Tags & labels, paper
**PA:** Deco Adhesive Products (1985) Limited
28 Greensboro Dr
Etobicoke ON M9W 1
416 247-7878

### (G-22359)
### DEIF INC
Also Called: Sub of Deif A/S, Denmark
185 Hansen Ct Ste 125 (60191-1105)
**PHONE** ................................. 970 530-2261
Mogens Garder, *CEO*
Jeff Custer, *President*
Cenk Eryigit, *General Mgr*
C Nielsen, *Managing Dir*
Inwoong Kang, *Business Mgr*
**EMP:** 7
**SQ FT:** 3,400
**SALES (est):** 1.8MM **Privately Held**
**SIC:** 5063 3613 3825 Power transmission equipment, electric; switchgear & switchboard apparatus; analog-digital converters, electronic instrumentation type

### (G-22360)
### DRAPERYLAND INC
368 Georgetown Sq (60191-1832)
**PHONE** ................................. 630 521-1000
Tony Altabello, *President*
William Schachner, *President*
**EMP:** 10
**SQ FT:** 2,000
**SALES (est):** 660K **Privately Held**
**SIC:** 5714 7389 2591 2391 Draperies; interior designer; drapery hardware & blinds & shades; curtains & draperies

### (G-22361)
### EARTHWISE ENVIRONMENTAL INC
777 N Edgewood Ave (60191-1254)
**PHONE** ................................. 630 475-3070
**Fax:** 630 475-3074
Robert Miller, *President*
**EMP:** 9
**SQ FT:** 4,000
**SALES (est):** 2.2MM **Privately Held**
**WEB:** www.earthwiseenvironmental.com
**SIC:** 3589 Water treatment equipment, industrial

### (G-22362)
### EMR MANUFACTURING INC
Also Called: J. P. Bell Fabricating, Inc.
617 N Central Ave (60191-1452)
**PHONE** ................................. 630 766-3366
**Fax:** 630 766-3569
Nate Rupczynski, *President*
Tim Dempsey, *Manager*
Heather Sender, *Administration*
**EMP:** 23
**SQ FT:** 16,500
**SALES (est):** 4.9MM **Privately Held**
**SIC:** 3444 Sheet metal specialties, not stamped

### (G-22363)
### ETS-LINDGREN INC (HQ)
Also Called: Ets Lindgren
1360 N Wood Dale Rd Ste G (60191-1075)
**PHONE** ................................. 630 307-7200
**Fax:** 630 307-7571
B E Butler, *President*
Kurt Wegener, *General Mgr*
William E Curran, *Vice Pres*
Luann Smit, *Project Mgr*
Michael Christopher, *Research*
◆ **EMP:** 150
**SQ FT:** 80,000

**SALES (est):** 27.2MM
**SALES (corp-wide):** 571.4MM **Publicly Held**
**WEB:** www.ets-lindgren.com
**SIC:** 3569 3677 3469 3444 Testing chambers for altitude, temperature, ordnance, power; electronic coils, transformers & other inductors; metal stampings; sheet metalwork; partitions & fixtures, except wood
**PA:** Esco Technologies Inc.
9900 Clayton Rd Ste A
Saint Louis MO 63124
314 213-7200

### (G-22364)
### EXTREME MANUFACTURING INC
735 N Edgewood Ave (60191-1212)
**PHONE** ................................. 630 350-8566
Steve Vermilyer, *President*
**EMP:** 8
**SALES (est):** 1.1MM **Privately Held**
**SIC:** 3444 Sheet metalwork

### (G-22365)
### FABMAX INC
501 N Edgewood Ave (60191-2621)
**PHONE** ................................. 630 766-0370
Chris Bigosinski, *President*
**EMP:** 12
**SQ FT:** 10,500
**SALES (est):** 2.2MM **Privately Held**
**WEB:** www.semiconductorfabtech.com
**SIC:** 3441 Fabricated structural metal

### (G-22366)
### FABRICATING MACHINERY SALES
Also Called: Fabricating Machinery & Eqp
640 Pond Dr Ste A (60191-1167)
**PHONE** ................................. 630 350-2266
**Fax:** 630 350-0238
John Joseph Rinaldo, *President*
Donna Rinaldo, *Admin Sec*
**EMP:** 20
**SQ FT:** 10,000
**SALES (est):** 2.2MM **Privately Held**
**SIC:** 3444 3312 3544 3469 Sheet metalwork; tool & die steel; special dies, tools, jigs & fixtures; metal stampings

### (G-22367)
### FINISH LINE TRANSMISSION INC
Also Called: F L T
801 N Central Ave (60191-1219)
**PHONE** ................................. 630 350-7776
**Fax:** 630 350-7736
Chuck Johnson, *President*
**EMP:** 3
**SALES (est):** 348K **Privately Held**
**SIC:** 3714 Transmissions, motor vehicle

### (G-22368)
### FIRST CHOICE BUILDING PDTS INC
740 N Edgewood Ave (60191-1249)
P.O. Box 958155, Hoffman Estates (60195-8155)
**PHONE** ................................. 630 350-2770
Michael Murray, *President*
▲ **EMP:** 12 **EST:** 2001
**SQ FT:** 2,500
**SALES (est):** 2.4MM **Privately Held**
**WEB:** www.firstchoicebuildingproducts.com
**SIC:** 3429 Manufactured hardware (general)

### (G-22369)
### FLOYD STEEL ERECTORS INC
310 Richert Rd (60191-1207)
**PHONE** ................................. 630 238-8383
**Fax:** 630 238-8395
Tim Flloyd, *President*
Tim Floyd, *President*
Kent Floyd, *Treasurer*
**EMP:** 17 **EST:** 1947
**SQ FT:** 13,500
**SALES:** 8.6MM **Privately Held**
**SIC:** 3441 7353 Fabricated structural metal; cranes & aerial lift equipment, rental or leasing

### (G-22370)
### FORBO SIEGLING LLC
Also Called: Siegling America
918 N Central Ave (60191-1216)
**PHONE** ................................. 630 595-4031
**Fax:** 630 595-9646
Nicholas Casali, *Marketing Staff*
Susan Durango, *Branch Mgr*
**EMP:** 11
**SALES (corp-wide):** 1.1B **Privately Held**
**SIC:** 3535 3568 Belt conveyor systems, general industrial use; power transmission equipment
**HQ:** Forbo Siegling, Llc
12201 Vanstory Dr
Huntersville NC 28078
704 948-0800

### (G-22371)
### FOREST AWARDS & ENGRAVING
336 E Irving Park Rd (60191-1647)
**PHONE** ................................. 630 595-2242
**Fax:** 630 595-2317
Gib F Beane, *President*
Barbara Beane, *Treasurer*
**EMP:** 3
**SQ FT:** 3,000
**SALES (est):** 346K **Privately Held**
**WEB:** www.forestawards.com
**SIC:** 3479 2499 3993 Name plates: engraved, etched, etc.; decorative wood & woodwork; signs & advertising specialties

### (G-22372)
### FORMCO METAL PRODUCTS INC
556 Clayton Ct (60191-1115)
**PHONE** ................................. 630 766-4441
**Fax:** 630 766-4517
Peter J Weiss, *President*
Jennifer Trage, *Prdtn Mgr*
Marile Sairbanks, *Office Mgr*
Dennis Henley, *Manager*
**EMP:** 25
**SQ FT:** 20,000
**SALES (est):** 5.8MM **Privately Held**
**WEB:** www.formcometal.com
**SIC:** 3469 Stamping metal for the trade

### (G-22373)
### FREY WISS PRCSION MCHINING INC
384 Beinoris Dr (60191-1223)
**PHONE** ................................. 630 595-9073
**Fax:** 630 595-0736
Adolf Frey, *Ch of Bd*
Ernie Pabon, *President*
Susan Ralph, *Vice Pres*
Ray Bonilla, *Manager*
**EMP:** 30
**SQ FT:** 10,046
**SALES (est):** 5.5MM **Privately Held**
**WEB:** www.freywiss.com
**SIC:** 3599 Machine shop, jobbing & repair

### (G-22374)
### G & M DIE CASTING COMPANY INC
284 Richert Rd (60191-1206)
**PHONE** ................................. 630 595-2340
**Fax:** 630 595-3746
Mark Hirsh, *President*
Erwin Fleps, *Manager*
Sandy Pennington, *Manager*
Clarissa M Fleps, *Admin Sec*
**EMP:** 80
**SQ FT:** 64,000
**SALES (est):** 16.2MM **Privately Held**
**WEB:** www.gmdiecasting.com
**SIC:** 3363 3544 Aluminum die-castings; special dies & tools

### (G-22375)
### G&G KRAFT BUILD
218 Fishing Ln (60191-1824)
**PHONE** ................................. 773 744-6522
Grzegorz Lewinski, *Principal*
**EMP:** 3 **EST:** 2011
**SALES (est):** 136.1K **Privately Held**
**SIC:** 2022 Processed cheese

### (G-22376)
### GE HEALTHCARE INC
945 N Edgewood Ave Ste A1 (60191-1252)
**PHONE** ................................. 630 595-6642
Otha Bright, *Manager*
**EMP:** 20 **Privately Held**
**SIC:** 2833 Medicinals & botanicals
**HQ:** Ge Healthcare Inc.
100 Results Way
Marlborough MA 01752
800 292-8514

### (G-22377)
### GLUETECH INC
701 Creel Dr (60191-2609)
**PHONE** ................................. 847 455-2707
**Fax:** 847 455-2869
James Nierodzik, *President*
**EMP:** 10
**SQ FT:** 11,000
**SALES (est):** 1.5MM **Privately Held**
**WEB:** www.gluetech.com
**SIC:** 2677 Envelopes

### (G-22378)
### GREG SCREW MACHINE PRODUCTS
647 N Central Ave Ste 103 (60191-1475)
**PHONE** ................................. 630 694-8875
**Fax:** 630 694-8876
Greg Rapacz, *President*
Miroslaw Reusicki, *Vice Pres*
Leslie Serowka, *Executive*
**EMP:** 2
**SQ FT:** 2,500
**SALES (est):** 319.2K **Privately Held**
**WEB:** www.gregscrewmachine.com
**SIC:** 3451 Screw machine products

### (G-22379)
### HOSPITAL THERAPY PRODUCTS INC
757 N Central Ave (60191-1240)
**PHONE** ................................. 630 766-7101
**Fax:** 630 766-1882
Thomas J Roberts Sr, *President*
Timothy Roberts, *Vice Pres*
Dan Stout, *Prdtn Mgr*
▲ **EMP:** 18 **EST:** 1975
**SQ FT:** 5,000
**SALES (est):** 2.6MM **Privately Held**
**SIC:** 3841 Surgical & medical instruments

### (G-22380)
### I S C AMERICA INC (PA)
750 Creel Dr (60191-2608)
**PHONE** ................................. 630 616-1331
**Fax:** 630 616-1339
Woo Chul, *CEO*
Suengyoon Han, *President*
▲ **EMP:** 5
**SQ FT:** 10,000
**SALES (est):** 1.5MM **Privately Held**
**SIC:** 2899 3555 2893 Ink or writing fluids; printing trades machinery; printing ink

### (G-22381)
### ICON METALCRAFT INC
940 Dillon Dr (60191-1233)
**PHONE** ................................. 630 766-5600
**Fax:** 630 766-5625
Silvia McLain, *CEO*
Saul Soto, *Vice Pres*
Sebastiano Fioccola, *Manager*
Thomas Harman, *Manager*
Lorena Garcia, *Admin Sec*
**EMP:** 105
**SQ FT:** 50,000
**SALES (est):** 24.3MM **Privately Held**
**WEB:** www.iconmetalcraft.com
**SIC:** 3444 3544 Sheet metal specialties, not stamped; special dies & tools

### (G-22382)
### INNOVATIVE RACK & GEAR COMPANY
365 Balm Ct (60191-1253)
**PHONE** ................................. 630 766-2652
**Fax:** 630 766-3245
Zenon Cichon, *President*
Jerry Cichon, *Vice Pres*
**EMP:** 14
**SQ FT:** 6,500

SALES (est): 3.3MM Privately Held
WEB: www.gearacks.com
SIC: 3462 Gear & chain forgings

**(G-22383)**
**K B K TRUCK AND TRLR REPR CO**
810 N Central Ave (60191-1217)
PHONE..................630 422-7265
Nick Byankov, Owner
EMP: 6 EST: 2012
SALES (est): 733.6K Privately Held
SIC: 3715 Truck trailers

**(G-22384)**
**K R KOMAREK INC (PA)**
548 Clayton Ct (60191-1115)
PHONE..................847 956-0060
Richard Komarek, President
Charles C Syperski, Corp Secy
Edward R Chapman, Vice Pres
Barney Dalton, Vice Pres
▲ EMP: 35
SQ FT: 20,000
SALES (est): 12.8MM Privately Held
WEB: www.komarek.com
SIC: 3559 3549 3547 3531 Chemical machinery & equipment; metalworking machinery; rolling mill machinery; construction machinery

**(G-22385)**
**KAMAN INDUSTRIAL TECH CORP**
827 N Central Ave (60191-1219)
PHONE..................317 248-8355
Tim Sulikowski, Branch Mgr
EMP: 20
SALES (corp-wide): 1.8B Publicly Held
SIC: 3721 Helicopters
HQ: Kaman Industrial Technologies Corporation
1 Vision Way
Bloomfield CT 06002
860 687-5000

**(G-22386)**
**KRAFT HEINZ FOODS COMPANY**
367 Haynes Dr (60191-2614)
PHONE..................630 227-1474
Fax: 630 350-9216
Greg Roman, Principal
EMP: 11
SALES (corp-wide): 26.4B Publicly Held
WEB: www.kraftfoods.com
SIC: 2141 Tobacco stemming & redrying
HQ: Kraft Heinz Foods Company
1 Ppg Pl Ste 3200
Pittsburgh PA 15222
412 456-5700

**(G-22387)**
**KRYGIER DESIGN INC**
635 Wheat Ln (60191-1128)
PHONE..................620 766-1001
Fax: 630 766-1002
Margaret Krygier, President
Kris Krygier, Vice Pres
Lukasse Kyeltyka, Manager
EMP: 10
SQ FT: 5,000
SALES (est): 1.3MM Privately Held
WEB: www.krygierdesign.com
SIC: 3535 Unit handling conveying systems

**(G-22388)**
**L A M INC DE**
620 Wheat Ln Ste B (60191-1164)
PHONE..................630 860-9700
Lavern A Miller, Ch of Bd
Malinda Cochran, President
Henry Farzaneh, Engineer
Michelle Pochay, Accounting Mgr
Yiping Wang, Info Tech Dir
EMP: 8
SQ FT: 27,000
SALES (est): 821.8K Privately Held
WEB: www.stoeltingco.com
SIC: 3826 3829 3821 3812 Analytical instruments; measuring & controlling devices; laboratory apparatus & furniture; search & navigation equipment; miscellaneous publishing

**(G-22389)**
**LANCER MANUFACTURING INC (PA)**
301 Beinoris Dr (60191-1222)
PHONE..................630 595-1150
Fax: 630 595-1387
Bill Harty, President
Wayne K Harty, President
Virginia Harty, Corp Secy
EMP: 12
SQ FT: 11,000
SALES (est): 1MM Privately Held
SIC: 3599 Machine shop, jobbing & repair

**(G-22390)**
**LEAFFILTER NORTH LLC**
587 N Edgewood Ave (60191-2600)
PHONE..................630 595-9605
Armando Garza, Principal
EMP: 26
SALES (corp-wide): 35.2MM Privately Held
SIC: 3569 Filters
PA: Leaffilter North Llc
1595 Georgetown Rd Ste G
Hudson OH 44236
330 655-7950

**(G-22391)**
**LTB GRAPHICS INC**
749 N Edgewood Ave (60191-1254)
PHONE..................630 238-1754
Fax: 630 238-9067
Kenneth Kent, President
EMP: 3
SQ FT: 1,760
SALES: 140K Privately Held
SIC: 2759 Screen printing

**(G-22392)**
**M & M TOOLING INC**
395 E Potter St (60191-2133)
PHONE..................630 595-8834
Michael Mirante, President
EMP: 3
SALES (est): 427.7K Privately Held
SIC: 3541 Machine tool replacement & repair parts, metal cutting types

**(G-22393)**
**MACLEAN SENIOR INDUSTRIES LLC**
610 Pond Dr (60191-1111)
PHONE..................630 350-1600
Fax: 630 350-1654
Matt Widtmann, Design Engr
John Bobrytzke, Sales Mgr
Mike Estes,
Joe Francaviglia,
Tom Smith,
◆ EMP: 28
SALES (est): 4.8MM
SALES (corp-wide): 1.4B Privately Held
SIC: 3643 3644 Ground clamps (electric wiring devices); pole line hardware
HQ: Maclean Power, L.L.C.
481 Munn Rd E Ste 300
Fort Mill SC 29715
847 455-0014

**(G-22394)**
**MADDEN COMMUNICATIONS INC (PA)**
901 Mittel Dr (60191-1118)
PHONE..................630 787-2200
Fax: 630 787-2215
James P Donahugh, Ch of Bd
Sean Madden, President
John McMahon, COO
Larry Gundrum, Senior VP
Kevin Heniff, Vice Pres
◆ EMP: 185
SQ FT: 251,000
SALES: 173.8MM Privately Held
SIC: 2752 Commercial printing, offset

**(G-22395)**
**MAGNETIC COIL MANUFACTURING CO**
325 Beinoris Dr Ste A (60191-2616)
PHONE..................630 787-1948
Joseph T Sommer Jr, President
Denna Myrda, Office Mgr
EMP: 25 EST: 1945
SQ FT: 12,500

SALES (est): 1.5MM Privately Held
WEB: www.magcoil.com
SIC: 3677 3621 3612 Coil windings, electronic; transformers power supply, electronic type; motors & generators; transformers, except electric

**(G-22396)**
**MASTERS CO INC**
890 Lively Blvd (60191-1202)
PHONE..................630 238-9292
Garret Garcia, President
Janet Garcia, Vice Pres
Bradley Dobryden, Research
Sue Gould, Accounting Dir
EMP: 30
SALES (est): 7MM Privately Held
WEB: www.marsh-mcbirney.com
SIC: 2819 Industrial inorganic chemicals

**(G-22397)**
**MATRIX TOOLING INC**
Also Called: Matrix Plastic Products
949 Aec Dr (60191-1143)
PHONE..................630 595-6144
Fax: 630 595-6276
Paul Ziegenhorn, President
Mark Ziegenhorn, Corp Secy
John Sauber, Vice Pres
Jim Ziegenhorn, Vice Pres
Tony Roman, Purch Mgr
EMP: 75
SQ FT: 28,000
SALES (est): 15.3MM Privately Held
WEB: www.matrixplasticproducts.com
SIC: 3544 3089 Industrial molds; injection molding of plastics

**(G-22398)**
**MET-PRO TECHNOLOGIES LLC**
Flex Kleen Division of Met Pro
905 Sivert Dr (60191-1210)
PHONE..................630 775-0707
Fax: 630 295-9019
Thomas F Walker, General Mgr
Thomas Edwards, Vice Pres
Donna Lehman, Safety Dir
Marsha Votava, Purch Agent
Pratt Melanie, Purchasing
EMP: 35
SALES (corp-wide): 417MM Publicly Held
WEB: www.met-pro.com
SIC: 3564 Air purification equipment
HQ: Met-Pro Technologies Llc
460 E Swedesford Rd # 2030
Wayne PA 19087
215 717-7909

**(G-22399)**
**MICH ENTERPRISES INC**
Also Called: Earl Mich
720 Creel Dr (60191-2608)
PHONE..................630 616-9000
Fax: 630 521-1588
Ben Mich, President
Greg McKay, Vice Pres
Brian Bogacz, Sales Staff
Corey Hennings, Info Tech Dir
Tiffany Bibby, Graphic Designe
EMP: 15
SQ FT: 10,000
SALES (est): 4MM Privately Held
WEB: www.earlmich.com
SIC: 2675 5085 3993 3953 Letters, cardboard, die-cut: from purchased materials; signmaker equipment & supplies; signs & advertising specialties; marking devices; commercial printing, lithographic; coated & laminated paper

**(G-22400)**
**MIDI MUSIC CENTER INC**
Also Called: Lowrey Organ Company
989 Aec Dr (60191-1143)
PHONE..................708 352-3388
Fax: 708 352-3464
Naoki Mori, President
Seijiro Imamura, Vice Pres
Tom Love, Vice Pres
George Hess, Buyer
Dennis Raffaelli, Controller
▲ EMP: 25
SQ FT: 41,000

SALES (est): 5.3MM
SALES (corp-wide): 585.5MM Privately Held
WEB: www.lowrey.com
SIC: 3931 Organs, all types: pipe, reed, hand, electronic, etc.
HQ: Kawai America Corporation
2055 E University Dr
Compton CA 90220
310 631-1771

**(G-22401)**
**MOTOR CAPACITORS INC**
335 Beinoris Dr (60191-1222)
PHONE..................773 774-6666
Fax: 773 774-6690
Liam Doherty, President
Terry Noon, President
Jim Olson, Vice Pres
Anthony Totolo, Manager
Carolyn Noone, Info Tech Mgr
▲ EMP: 17
SQ FT: 15,000
SALES (est): 2.2MM Privately Held
WEB: www.nantongcapacitors.com
SIC: 3629 3675 Capacitors & condensers; electronic capacitors

**(G-22402)**
**MT CASE COMPANY**
569 N Edgewood Ave (60191-2600)
PHONE..................630 227-1019
Fax: 630 690-9842
Mario Educate, President
Tom Heslin, General Mgr
Vickie Lenhart, Vice Pres
EMP: 17
SQ FT: 280
SALES: 850K Privately Held
SIC: 2522 Filing boxes, cabinets & cases: except wood

**(G-22403)**
**NATURAL DISTRIBUTION COMPANY**
550 Clayton Ct (60191-1115)
PHONE..................630 350-1700
Fax: 630 350-2050
Dennis P Ryan, President
EMP: 1
SALES (est): 534.1K Privately Held
SIC: 5149 2037 Groceries & related products; fruit juices

**(G-22404)**
**NEMETH TOOL INC (PA)**
143 Murray Dr (60191-2238)
PHONE..................630 595-0409
John F Nemeth, President
Mary Ann Nemeth, Admin Sec
EMP: 1 EST: 1979
SALES (est): 476.5K Privately Held
SIC: 3544 Industrial molds

**(G-22405)**
**NEP ELECTRONICS INC (PA)**
805 Mittel Dr (60191-1118)
PHONE..................630 595-8500
Fax: 630 595-8706
Thomas Lotus, President
William Federighi, Vice Pres
James Neff, Prdtn Mgr
Sean Fisher, Safety Mgr
Chris Corbett, Warehouse Mgr
▲ EMP: 106
SQ FT: 35,000
SALES (est): 61.2MM Privately Held
SIC: 5065 3679 3824 Electronic parts; harness assemblies for electronic use: wire or cable; electromechanical counters

**(G-22406)**
**NGK SPARK PLUGS (USA) INC**
Also Called: N G K Spark Plugs
850 Aec Dr (60191-1122)
PHONE..................630 595-7894
Fax: 630 595-5422
Andre Zangara, Sales/Mktg Mgr
Itaruy Yoshinga, Director
EMP: 26
SALES (corp-wide): 3.2B Privately Held
WEB: www.ngksparkplugs.com
SIC: 3694 Spark plugs for internal combustion engines

# Wood Dale - Dupage County (G-22407)

HQ: Ngk Spark Plugs (U.S.A.), Inc.
46929 Magellan
Wixom MI 48393
248 926-6900

**(G-22407)**
**NOVATRONIX INC**
600 Wheat Ln (60191-1109)
PHONE..................................630 860-4300
Fax: 630 860-2899
Anthony Kenevan, *President*
Edward Kenevan, *Vice Pres*
Curtis Swanson, *Mfg Spvr*
Donna Ellinger, *Purch Mgr*
Brook Canivan, *Accountant*
▲ **EMP:** 45
**SALES (est):** 13MM **Privately Held**
**SIC:** 3672 7629 Printed circuit boards; circuit board repair

**(G-22408)**
**O ADJUST MATIC PUMP COMPANY**
Also Called: Wood Dale Pipe & Supply Co
429 E Potter St (60191-2117)
P.O. Box 424 (60191-0424)
PHONE..................................630 766-1490
Fax: 630 766-0501
Joe Peters, *President*
Diane Peters, *Admin Sec*
**EMP:** 2
**SQ FT:** 10,000
**SALES (est):** 300K **Privately Held**
**SIC:** 3561 5084 Pumps & pumping equipment; industrial machinery & equipment

**(G-22409)**
**OCS AMERICA INC**
945 Dillon Dr (60191-1274)
PHONE..................................630 595-0111
Kazuki Ishikawa, *Manager*
Takahiro Abe, *Director*
**EMP:** 25
**SALES (corp-wide):** 15.5B **Privately Held**
**SIC:** 7389 5192 2711 5994 Courier or messenger service; newspapers; newspapers: publishing only, not printed on site; newsstand; magazine stand
HQ: Ocs America Inc.
11100 Hindry Ave
Los Angeles CA 90045
310 417-0650

**(G-22410)**
**P & P ARTEC INC (HQ)**
Also Called: P & P Artec Handrail Div
700 Creel Dr (60191-2608)
PHONE..................................630 860-2990
Fax: 630 860-5913
Christian Potthoff-Sewing, *President*
Rick A Fritz, *Natl Sales Mgr*
Beata Ferenczi, *Sales Mgr*
Patric Truyen, *Sales Mgr*
Martina Engler, *Marketing Mgr*
▲ **EMP:** 19
**SQ FT:** 15,000
**SALES (est):** 3.1MM
**SALES (corp-wide):** 182.6MM **Privately Held**
**WEB:** www.artec-rail.com
**SIC:** 3446 Ornamental metalwork
PA: Poppe + Potthoff Gmbh
Dammstr. 17
Werther (Westf.) 33824
520 391-660

**(G-22411)**
**PARAMOUNT LAMINATES INC**
907 N Central Ave (60191-1218)
PHONE..................................630 594-1840
Paul Lee, *President*
Dick Golden, *Manager*
Cindy L Wong, *Admin Sec*
Bryan Wong, *Relations*
▲ **EMP:** 2
**SALES (est):** 408.7K **Privately Held**
**WEB:** www.paramountlaminates.net
**SIC:** 3672 Printed circuit boards; circuit boards, television & radio printed

**(G-22412)**
**PRECISION INDUSTRIAL KNIFE**
850 Dillon Dr (60191-1269)
PHONE..................................630 350-7898
Kenneth Machynia, *President*
**EMP:** 5
**SQ FT:** 8,000
**SALES:** 1.2MM **Privately Held**
**SIC:** 3423 Knives, agricultural or industrial

**(G-22413)**
**PRECISION MACHINE PRODUCTS**
655 N Central Ave Ste G (60191-1467)
PHONE..................................630 860-0861
Fax: 630 860-7990
Jan Glabus, *President*
**EMP:** 3
**SQ FT:** 2,300
**SALES:** 190K **Privately Held**
**SIC:** 3599 Machine shop, jobbing & repair

**(G-22414)**
**PRIME LABEL & PACKAGING LLC**
501 N Central Ave (60191-1473)
PHONE..................................630 227-1300
Kollman Kevin J,
Patsy Mousel, *Administration*
**EMP:** 65
**SQ FT:** 57,600
**SALES (est):** 10MM **Privately Held**
**WEB:** www.primegraphicsinc.com
**SIC:** 2759 2671 Flexographic printing; packaging paper & plastics film, coated & laminated
PA: Prime Packaging, Llc
1000 Garey Dr
Yardley PA 19067

**(G-22415)**
**QUALITY SURFACE MOUNT INC**
965 Dillon Dr (60191-1274)
PHONE..................................630 350-8556
Fax: 630 350-9868
Steve Zielinski, *President*
Jack Kopis, *Vice Pres*
Alice Kopis, *Office Mgr*
**EMP:** 20
**SQ FT:** 12,000
**SALES (est):** 5.2MM **Privately Held**
**WEB:** www.qsmt.com
**SIC:** 3672 Circuit boards, television & radio printed

**(G-22416)**
**REBA MACHINE CORP**
767 N Edgewood Ave (60191-1254)
PHONE..................................630 595-1272
Mario Lew, *CEO*
**EMP:** 6 **EST:** 1998
**SALES (est):** 927.1K **Privately Held**
**SIC:** 3599 Custom machinery

**(G-22417)**
**RUCO USA INC**
915 N Central Ave (60191-1218)
PHONE..................................866 373-7912
▲ **EMP:** 24
**SALES (est):** 2.5MM **Privately Held**
**SIC:** 2759 Commercial printing

**(G-22418)**
**S & M GROUP INC**
Also Called: Flextron Circuit Assembly
300 Bauman Ct (60191-1141)
PHONE..................................630 766-1000
Fax: 630 766-1006
Sanjay Vora, *President*
Cary Wolf, *Buyer*
Praful Khunt, *Engineer*
Steve Lieber, *Sales Mgr*
**EMP:** 15
**SQ FT:** 16,000
**SALES (est):** 4MM **Privately Held**
**WEB:** www.flextronassembly.com
**SIC:** 8711 3672 Electrical or electronic engineering; printed circuit boards; circuit boards, television & radio printed; wiring boards

**(G-22419)**
**SCARZONE PRINTING SERVICES**
601 W Montrose Ave (60191-1718)
PHONE..................................630 595-2690
Fax: 708 718-1023
John Scarzone, *President*
Barbara Lukowski, *Admin Sec*
**EMP:** 2
**SQ FT:** 1,000
**SALES:** 600K **Privately Held**
**SIC:** 2752 Commercial printing, offset

**(G-22420)**
**SEA CONVERTING INC**
895 Sivert Dr (60191-1208)
PHONE..................................630 694-9178
Paula Johnson, *President*
Sue Moy, *General Mgr*
Jim Johnson, *Vice Pres*
**EMP:** 15
**SQ FT:** 17,000
**SALES:** 1MM **Privately Held**
**WEB:** www.seaconverting.com
**SIC:** 3353 Coils, sheet aluminum

**(G-22421)**
**SEABEE SUPPLY CO**
390 E Irving Park Rd (60191-1645)
PHONE..................................630 860-1293
Grace Jamrozik, *Owner*
**EMP:** 4
**SALES:** 75K **Privately Held**
**SIC:** 2679 Paper products, converted

**(G-22422)**
**SIMU LTD (PA)**
201 Mittel Dr (60191-1116)
PHONE..................................630 350-1060
Fax: 630 350-1089
Michael L Simon, *President*
Ira Epstein, *Vice Pres*
Craig Simon, *Vice Pres*
Daniel J Simon, *Vice Pres*
Ernest Simon, *Vice Pres*
◆ **EMP:** 14
**SQ FT:** 256,000
**SALES (est):** 412MM **Privately Held**
**WEB:** www.simu.com
**SIC:** 5113 5141 5142 2782 Industrial & personal service paper; groceries, general line; packaged frozen goods; loose-leaf binders & devices; menus: printing; packaging paper

**(G-22423)**
**SLOAN INDUSTRIES INC**
1550 N Michael Dr (60191-1003)
PHONE..................................630 350-1614
Fax: 630 350-1094
Henry Slowinski, *President*
Adam Niedospial, *Vice Pres*
Sherry Steiner, *Manager*
▲ **EMP:** 30
**SQ FT:** 24,000
**SALES (est):** 4.9MM **Privately Held**
**WEB:** www.sloan-industries.com
**SIC:** 7699 8711 3542 Industrial equipment services; machine tool design; machine tools, metal forming type

**(G-22424)**
**STAR LITE MFG**
735 N Edgewood Ave Ste C (60191-1261)
PHONE..................................630 595-8338
Chris Zinkiewicz, *Owner*
**EMP:** 8
**SALES (est):** 838.7K **Privately Held**
**SIC:** 3999 Manufacturing industries

**(G-22425)**
**SUMA AMERICA INC**
855 N Wood Dale Rd Unit A (60191-1138)
PHONE..................................847 427-7880
Suma Kpandhi, *Principal*
◆ **EMP:** 3
**SALES (est):** 329.3K **Privately Held**
**SIC:** 2911 Gases & liquefied petroleum gases

**(G-22426)**
**T T T INC**
387 Crestwood Rd (60191-2551)
P.O. Box 7080 (60191-7080)
PHONE..................................630 860-7499
Dennis F Sowa, *President*
**EMP:** 2
**SALES:** 5MM **Privately Held**
**SIC:** 3823 Industrial process measurement equipment

**(G-22427)**
**TARGIN SIGN SYSTEMS INC**
160 W Irving Park Rd (60191-1340)
PHONE..................................630 766-7667
Fax: 630 766-7798
Steve A Gruber, *President*
**EMP:** 7
**SQ FT:** 7,000
**SALES (est):** 648.4K **Privately Held**
**WEB:** www.targinsigns.com
**SIC:** 3993 7336 Signs & advertising specialties; electric signs; art design services; graphic arts & related design

**(G-22428)**
**TECHNYMON TECHNOLOGY USA INC**
730 N Edgewood Ave (60191-1249)
PHONE..................................630 787-0501
Luigi Mongodi, *President*
Tiffanya Belussi, *Manager*
▲ **EMP:** 9
**SQ FT:** 10,000
**SALES:** 1.4MM **Privately Held**
**SIC:** 3568 Bearings, plain

**(G-22429)**
**TEMPCO ELECTRIC HEATER CORP (PA)**
607 N Central Ave (60191-1452)
PHONE..................................630 350-2252
Fax: 630 350-0232
Fermin Adames, *President*
Richard Sachs, *Senior VP*
Tom Hittie, *Prdtn Mgr*
Earnest Diosdado, *Purch Mgr*
Bo Heinman, *Purch Mgr*
▲ **EMP:** 330
**SQ FT:** 130,000
**SALES (est):** 77.8MM **Privately Held**
**WEB:** www.tempco.com
**SIC:** 3567 3369 3829 Heating units & devices, industrial: electric; castings, except die-castings, precision; thermocouples

**(G-22430)**
**THERMAL INDUSTRIES INC**
830 Sivert Dr (60191-2610)
PHONE..................................800 237-0560
Fax: 630 238-6993
Linda Cade, *Manager*
Pete Hoster, *Manager*
Bob McGillivray, *Manager*
**EMP:** 20
**SALES (corp-wide):** 1.2B **Privately Held**
**WEB:** www.thermalindustries.com
**SIC:** 3442 3081 Screens, window, metal; vinyl film & sheet
HQ: Thermal Industries, Inc.
3700 Haney Ct
Murrysville PA 15668
724 325-6100

**(G-22431)**
**THERMO-PAK CO**
360 Balm Ct (60191-1253)
PHONE..................................630 860-1303
Fax: 630 860-1649
Daniel Simpson, *President*
Doug Schaaf, *QC Dir*
Cynthia Hernandez, *Human Resources*
Lauren Simpson, *Manager*
Bill Shappee, *Director*
**EMP:** 25
**SQ FT:** 100,000
**SALES (est):** 3.9MM **Privately Held**
**SIC:** 3089 Blister or bubble formed packaging, plastic

**(G-22432)**
**TOYO INK INTERNATIONAL CORP (HQ)**
1225 N Michael Dr (60191-1019)
PHONE..................................866 969-8696
Fusao Ito, *President*
John Higgins, *CFO*
Jane Krasmer, *Treasurer*
Eric Avilef, *Accounts Mgr*
Nancy Ikehara, *Relations*
◆ **EMP:** 15
**SALES (est):** 101.2MM
**SALES (corp-wide):** 2.3B **Privately Held**
**WEB:** www.toyoink.com
**SIC:** 2893 5112 Printing ink; writing ink
PA: Toyo Ink Sc Holdings Co., Ltd.
2-2-1, Kyobashi
Chuo-Ku TKY 104-0
332 725-731

# GEOGRAPHIC SECTION

**Woodridge - Dupage County (G-22457)**

**(G-22433)**
**TROPAR TROPHY MANUFACTURING CO**
839 N Central Ave (60191-1219)
PHONE...................................630 787-1900
Peter Ilaria, *Principal*
**EMP:** 20
**SALES (corp-wide):** 9.9MM **Privately Held**
**SIC:** 8742 3999 Industrial & labor consulting services; atomizers, toiletry
**PA:** Tropar Trophy Manufacturing Co. Inc
5 Vreeland Rd
Florham Park NJ 07932
973 822-2400

**(G-22434)**
**TRUSTY WARNS INC (PA)**
229 N Central Ave (60191-1603)
PHONE...................................630 766-9015
Fax: 630 766-0483
Karl O Niedermeyer, *President*
Mary Calssner, *Vice Pres*
Amy R Niedermeyer, *Vice Pres*
Pamela McDonald, *CFO*
**EMP:** 20
**SQ FT:** 8,600
**SALES (est):** 3.1MM **Privately Held**
**WEB:** www.trustywarns.com
**SIC:** 3561 3533 3523 Pumps & pumping equipment; oil & gas field machinery; farm machinery & equipment

**(G-22435)**
**TWINPLEX MANUFACTURING CO**
Also Called: Twinplex Stamping Company
840 Lively Blvd (60191-1202)
PHONE...................................630 595-2040
Fax: 630 595-4068
Kenneth O Floyd, *President*
Steve Floyd, *Vice Pres*
Christine Shanahan, *Accountant*
**EMP:** 17 **EST:** 1941
**SQ FT:** 60,000
**SALES (est):** 4.4MM **Privately Held**
**SIC:** 3469 Stamping metal for the trade

**(G-22436)**
**VIDEOJET TECHNOLOGIES INC (HQ)**
Also Called: Videojet Systems
1500 N Mittel Blvd (60191-1072)
PHONE...................................630 860-7300
Fax: 630 616-3623
Christopher Riley, *President*
Ian Watson, *Managing Dir*
Ranjana Bhagwakar, *Vice Pres*
Fred H Hagedorn, *Vice Pres*
Rick Hoffmann, *Vice Pres*
◆ **EMP:** 650
**SQ FT:** 250,000
**SALES:** 380MM
**SALES (corp-wide):** 16.8B **Publicly Held**
**WEB:** www.videojet.com
**SIC:** 3579 Addressing machines, plates & plate embossers
**PA:** Danaher Corporation
2200 Penn Ave Nw Ste 800w
Washington DC 20037
202 828-0850

**(G-22437)**
**WATERS TECHNOLOGIES CORP**
Also Called: Waters Associates
1360 N Wood Dale Rd Ste C (60191-1075)
PHONE...................................630 766-6249
Tim Willamson, *Branch Mgr*
**EMP:** 12 **Publicly Held**
**SIC:** 3826 Chromatographic equipment, laboratory type
**HQ:** Waters Technologies Corporation,
34 Maple St
Milford MA 01757
508 478-2000

**(G-22438)**
**WOODS MANUFACTURING CO INC**
735 N Edgewood Ave Ste J (60191-1261)
PHONE...................................630 595-6620
Fax: 630 595-3209
Michael Woods, *President*
Deborah Woods, *Admin Sec*
**EMP:** 4 **EST:** 1978

**SQ FT:** 3,000
**SALES (est):** 592.7K **Privately Held**
**WEB:** www.woodsmfg.com
**SIC:** 3053 3492 Gaskets, packing & sealing devices; fluid power valves & hose fittings

**(G-22439)**
**XISYNC LLC**
Also Called: Mastertrak
655 Wheat Ln (60191-1128)
PHONE...................................630 350-9400
Kim Londono, *Finance Dir*
Gary Winemaster,
Tom Somodi,
Ken Winemaster,
**EMP:** 150
**SALES (est):** 11MM **Privately Held**
**WEB:** www.mastertrak.com
**SIC:** 3823 Industrial process measurement equipment

## Wood River
### Madison County

**(G-22440)**
**AMERICLEAN INC**
23 E Ferguson Ave (62095-1903)
P.O. Box 557 (62095-0557)
PHONE...................................314 741-8901
George R Adams, *President*
Carolyn Drake, *Corp Secy*
Robert D Drake Sr, *Vice Pres*
**EMP:** 12
**SQ FT:** 5,000
**SALES (est):** 2.2MM **Privately Held**
**WEB:** www.americlean.com
**SIC:** 2899 3559 Chemical preparations; recycling machinery

**(G-22441)**
**BUDGET SIGNS**
Also Called: Budget Signs Trophies Plaques
333 E Edwardsville Rd (62095-1647)
PHONE...................................618 259-4460
Fax: 618 259-8107
Dan Jones, *Owner*
**EMP:** 10
**SALES (est):** 844.2K **Privately Held**
**SIC:** 3993 3914 3299 5099 Signs & advertising specialties; advertising novelties; trophies; plaques: clay, plaster or papier mache; signs, except electric; trophies & plaques; novelties

**(G-22442)**
**ELK HEATING & SHEET METAL INC**
473 N Wood River Ave (62095-1529)
P.O. Box 559 (62095-0559)
PHONE...................................618 251-4747
Fax: 618 251-5183
Sondra Rohr, *President*
Robert H McPherson, *Vice Pres*
Robert J Rohr, *Treasurer*
Beverly Wade, *Office Mgr*
**EMP:** 12
**SQ FT:** 11,000
**SALES:** 1.8MM **Privately Held**
**WEB:** www.elkheating.com
**SIC:** 1711 3444 Warm air heating & air conditioning contractor; sheet metalwork

**(G-22443)**
**GAMESTOP CORP**
662 Wesley Dr (62095-1894)
PHONE...................................618 258-8611
Wendy Thurig, *Branch Mgr*
**EMP:** 4
**SALES (corp-wide):** 8.6B **Publicly Held**
**SIC:** 5945 3944 Hobby, toy & game shops; video game machines, except coin-operated
**PA:** Gamestop Corp.
625 Westport Pkwy
Grapevine TX 76051
817 424-2000

**(G-22444)**
**PUMP HOUSE**
1523 E Edwardsville Rd (62095-2295)
PHONE...................................618 216-2404
Gary Vollmer, *Owner*

**EMP:** 3
**SALES (est):** 363.1K **Privately Held**
**SIC:** 5084 3561 Pumps & pumping equipment; pumps & pumping equipment

**(G-22445)**
**SHELL OIL COMPANY**
200 E Lorena Ave (62095-2020)
P.O. Box 76, Roxana (62084-0068)
PHONE...................................618 254-7371
Fax: 618 255-2003
E G Johnson, *Branch Mgr*
Andy Macias, *Assistant*
**EMP:** 140
**SALES (corp-wide):** 233.5B **Privately Held**
**SIC:** 2911 Gasoline
**HQ:** Shell Oil Company
910 Louisiana St Ste 1500
Houston TX 77002
713 241-6161

**(G-22446)**
**WOOD RIVER PRINTING & PUBG CO**
22 N 1st St (62095-2039)
P.O. Box 101 (62095-0101)
PHONE...................................618 254-3134
Fax: 618 254-3127
Bradney Racey, *President*
Tony Hall, *CFO*
W Joseph Racey, *Admin Sec*
**EMP:** 13 **EST:** 1917
**SQ FT:** 10,000
**SALES (est):** 1.4MM **Privately Held**
**WEB:** www.woodriverprinting.com
**SIC:** 2752 2789 2759 Commercial printing, offset; bookbinding & related work; commercial printing

## Woodridge
### Dupage County

**(G-22447)**
**A CORPORATE PRINTING SERVICE**
7705 Dalewood Pkwy (60517-2903)
PHONE...................................630 515-0432
James Rennie, *Principal*
**EMP:** 10
**SALES (est):** 939.4K **Privately Held**
**SIC:** 2759 Commercial printing

**(G-22448)**
**A-CREATIONS INC**
8102 Lemont Rd Ste 1500 (60517-7776)
PHONE...................................630 541-5801
Jim Earl, *President*
**EMP:** 9
**SALES (est):** 1.1MM **Privately Held**
**SIC:** 2759 Screen printing

**(G-22449)**
**ACTION FLAG CO**
1900 Egerton Ct (60517-4600)
PHONE...................................800 669-9639
George D Mara, *Vice Pres*
**EMP:** 2
**SALES:** 450K **Privately Held**
**SIC:** 2399 Banners, pennants & flags

**(G-22450)**
**AH TENSOR INTERNATIONAL LLC**
10304 Argonne Woods Dr # 300 (60517-5088)
PHONE...................................630 739-9600
Mattias Andersson, *CEO*
Michael Pavone, *COO*
◆ **EMP:** 40 **EST:** 2012
**SALES (est):** 5.9MM
**SALES (corp-wide):** 6.5MM **Privately Held**
**SIC:** 2752 Offset & photolithographic printing; commercial printing, offset
**PA:** Automation House Sweden Ab
Haggastrandsvagen 5
Kinna 511 4

**(G-22451)**
**AMERICAN HOLIDAY LIGHTS INC**
6813 Hobson Valley Dr # 102 (60517-1451)
PHONE...................................630 769-9999
Jeff Krall, *President*
**EMP:** 2
**SALES (est):** 215.5K **Privately Held**
**SIC:** 3699 5063 Christmas tree lighting sets, electric; lighting fixtures

**(G-22452)**
**ANJU SOFTWARE INC**
Also Called: Online Bus Applications
9018 Heritage Pkwy # 600 (60517-5041)
PHONE...................................630 243-9810
**EMP:** 46
**SALES (corp-wide):** 1.7MM **Privately Held**
**SIC:** 7372 Business oriented computer software
**PA:** Anju Software, Inc
251 W 19th St
New York NY

**(G-22453)**
**APL LOGISTICS AMERICAS LTD**
2649 Internationale Pkwy (60517-4803)
PHONE...................................630 783-0200
Fax: 630 783-1793
Crystal Stram, *President*
▲ **EMP:** 21
**SALES (est):** 134.5MM
**SALES (corp-wide):** 4.1B **Privately Held**
**SIC:** 3531 Construction machinery
**HQ:** Apl Logistics Americas, Ltd.
16220 N Scottsdale Rd
Scottsdale AZ 85254
602 586-4800

**(G-22454)**
**AUTOMAX CORPORATION**
1940 Internationale Pkwy # 550 (60517-3186)
PHONE...................................630 972-1919
Frank L Gronowski, *President*
Raymond S Gronowski, *Vice Pres*
**EMP:** 8
**SQ FT:** 3,800
**SALES:** 580K **Privately Held**
**WEB:** www.automaxonline.com
**SIC:** 5084 3822 3561 Controlling instruments & accessories; materials handling machinery; auto controls regulating residntl & coml environmt & applncs; pumps & pumping equipment

**(G-22455)**
**BARK PROJECT MANAGEMENT INC**
7017 Roberts Dr (60517-1904)
PHONE...................................630 964-5876
Robert S Kennard Sr, *President*
**EMP:** 3
**SALES (est):** 441.2K **Privately Held**
**WEB:** www.barkpm.com
**SIC:** 2542 Office & store showcases & display fixtures

**(G-22456)**
**BEST MACHINE & WELDING CO INC**
2729 Meadowdale Ln (60517-3755)
PHONE...................................708 343-4455
Fax: 708 343-1154
Edmund Paprocki Sr, *President*
Laddie Svoboda, *Corp Secy*
**EMP:** 20 **EST:** 1974
**SQ FT:** 16,000
**SALES (est):** 2.2MM **Privately Held**
**WEB:** www.bestmachineracing.com
**SIC:** 3599 3441 7692 2796 Machine shop, jobbing & repair; fabricated structural metal; welding repair; platemaking services

**(G-22457)**
**BOLER COMPANY**
Also Called: Hendrickson
800 S Frontage Rd (60517-4900)
PHONE...................................630 910-2800
Paul Lamantia, *Purch Dir*
Keith Gelinas, *Persnl Mgr*
John Boler, *Branch Mgr*

## Woodridge - Dupage County (G-22458) — GEOGRAPHIC SECTION

Jerome Cortez, *Info Tech Mgr*
Bob Tomy, *MIS Mgr*
**EMP:** 133
**SALES (corp-wide):** 1B **Privately Held**
**SIC:** 3714 Motor vehicle parts & accessories
**PA:** The Boler Company
  500 Park Blvd Ste 1010
  Itasca IL 60143
  630 773-9111

### (G-22458)
### CARGILL MEAT SOLUTIONS CORP
Also Called: Cargill Food Distribution
10420 Woodward Ave (60517-4934)
**PHONE** ............................. 630 739-1746
**EMP:** 182
**SALES (corp-wide):** 107.1B **Privately Held**
**SIC:** 2011 Meat packing plants
**HQ:** Cargill Meat Solutions Corp
  151 N Main St Ste 900
  Wichita KS 67202
  316 291-2500

### (G-22459)
### CFPG LTD (DH)
Also Called: Gerber Plumbing Fixtures
2500 Intrntonale Pkwy (60517-4979)
**PHONE** ............................. 630 679-1420
Frank Feraco, *President*
Ila J Lewis, *President*
Brian Sheehy, *Business Mgr*
Ronald Grabski, *Vice Pres*
James Schwartz, *Controller*
▲ **EMP:** 129 **EST:** 1932
**SQ FT:** 20,000
**SALES (est):** 31.9MM
**SALES (corp-wide):** 613.9MM **Privately Held**
**WEB:** www.gerberonline.com
**SIC:** 3261 3432 Plumbing fixtures, vitreous china; plumbers' brass goods: drain cocks, faucets, spigots, etc.
**HQ:** Globe Union Group Inc.
  2500 Internationale Pkwy
  Woodridge IL 60517
  630 679-1420

### (G-22460)
### CHAMPION PACKAGING & DIST INC
1840 Internationale Pkwy (60517-4944)
**PHONE** ............................. 630 755-4220
Thomas J Pecora, *CEO*
Steve Cahill, *Prdtn Mgr*
Jon Lemire, *Prdtn Mgr*
Chad Pecora, *Facilities Mgr*
Chuck Hughes, *Manager*
**EMP:** 160
**SQ FT:** 160,000
**SALES (est):** 85.2MM **Privately Held**
**WEB:** www.champakinc.com
**SIC:** 2842 2812 Ammonia, household; chlorine, compressed or liquefied

### (G-22461)
### CLARKE EQUIPMENT COMPANY
2649 Internationale Pkwy (60517-4803)
**PHONE** ............................. 701 241-8700
**EMP:** 3
**SALES (corp-wide):** 3.1B **Privately Held**
**SIC:** 3531 Backhoes, tractors, cranes, plows & similar equipment
**HQ:** Clark Equipment Company
  250 E Beaton Dr
  West Fargo ND 58078
  701 241-8700

### (G-22462)
### COLUMBUS MCKINNON CORPORATION
Ces Material Handling
2143 Internationale Pkwy (60517-4825)
**PHONE** ............................. 630 783-2188
**EMP:** 8
**SALES (corp-wide):** 637.1MM **Publicly Held**
**SIC:** 3536 Hoists, cranes & monorails
**PA:** Columbus Mckinnon Corporation
  205 Crosspoint Pkwy
  Getzville NY 14068
  716 689-5400

### (G-22463)
### COLUMBUS MCKINNON CORPORATION
Also Called: Abel Howe Crane
10321 Werch Dr Ste 100 (60517-4812)
**PHONE** ............................. 630 783-1195
**Fax:** 630 226-5229
Eric Bach, *Manager*
**EMP:** 40
**SALES (corp-wide):** 637.1MM **Publicly Held**
**WEB:** www.cmworks.com
**SIC:** 3536 Hoists
**PA:** Columbus Mckinnon Corporation
  205 Crosspoint Pkwy
  Getzville NY 14068
  716 689-5400

### (G-22464)
### COMPONENTS EXPRESS INC
10330 Argonne Woods Dr # 100 (60517-5047)
**PHONE** ............................. 630 257-0605
John M Berst, *President*
Clarice Flynn, *General Mgr*
Frances P Berst, *Vice Pres*
John R Berst, *Vice Pres*
Steve Mott, *VP Opers*
▲ **EMP:** 40
**SQ FT:** 28,000
**SALES (est):** 7.4MM **Privately Held**
**WEB:** www.networkcable.com
**SIC:** 3674 Computer logic modules

### (G-22465)
### COMTEC INDUSTRIES LTD
10210 Werch Dr Ste 204 (60517-4816)
**PHONE** ............................. 630 759-9000
James Reilly, *President*
Dolores T Reilly, *Corp Secy*
Arthur J Reilly, *Shareholder*
**EMP:** 8 **EST:** 1964
**SQ FT:** 3,000
**SALES (est):** 1.3MM **Privately Held**
**WEB:** www.comtecindustriesltd.com
**SIC:** 3556 3544 Food products machinery; special dies, tools, jigs & fixtures

### (G-22466)
### CUPCAKE HOLDINGS LLC
2240 75th St (60517-2333)
**PHONE** ............................. 800 794-5866
Rob Begala, *Finance*
Jerry W Levin, *Mng Member*
**EMP:** 200
**SALES (est):** 17.2MM **Privately Held**
**SIC:** 5023 2731 2721 7812 Kitchenware; kitchen tools & utensils; frames & framing, picture & mirror; books: publishing only; periodicals: publishing only; video tape production; candy making goods & supplies

### (G-22467)
### DANZE INC
2500 Internationale Pkwy (60517-4073)
**PHONE** ............................. 630 754-0277
Michael Werner, *President*
Noreen Buczkowski, *Finance*
Faith Walker, *Sales Mgr*
Ron Cox, *Regl Sales Mgr*
Alyson Angotti, *Marketing Mgr*
◆ **EMP:** 100 **EST:** 2002
**SQ FT:** 300,000
**SALES (est):** 25.8MM
**SALES (corp-wide):** 613.9MM **Privately Held**
**WEB:** www.danze.com
**SIC:** 3088 Plastics plumbing fixtures
**HQ:** Globe Union Group Inc.
  2500 Internationale Pkwy
  Woodridge IL 60517
  630 679-1420

### (G-22468)
### DARBE PRODUCTS COMPANY INC
2936 Two Paths Dr (60517-4511)
**PHONE** ............................. 630 985-0769
**Fax:** 630 985-0777
**EMP:** 4
**SALES:** 150K **Privately Held**
**SIC:** 3496 5085 Mfg Miscellaneous Fabricated Wire Products & Whol Industrial Supplies

### (G-22469)
### DAVID MICHAEL PRODUCTIONS
1340 Internationale Pkwy # 100 (60517-5115)
**PHONE** ............................. 630 972-9640
David Pollock, *President*
Ray Braasch, *Project Mgr*
Dave Feczko, *Project Mgr*
Ollivette Scott, *Producer*
Corrine Updegraff, *Director*
**EMP:** 10
**SALES (est):** 2.5MM **Privately Held**
**WEB:** www.davidmichaelproductions.com
**SIC:** 3648 Lighting equipment

### (G-22470)
### DIETER CONSTRUCTION INC
Also Called: Tops By Dieter
6817 Hobson Valley Dr # 120 (60517-1452)
**PHONE** ............................. 630 960-9662
**Fax:** 630 960-0202
Randall Dieter, *President*
Susan L Dieter, *Treasurer*
Steve Steciak, *Manager*
**EMP:** 5
**SQ FT:** 4,000
**SALES (est):** 796.5K **Privately Held**
**SIC:** 1799 2541 Counter top installation; counter & sink tops

### (G-22471)
### DOBER CHEMICAL CORP (PA)
Also Called: Dober Group
11230 Katherines Crossin Ste 100 (60517)
**PHONE** ............................. 630 410-7300
**Fax:** 708 388-9344
John G Dobrez, *President*
Simon Allen, *Senior VP*
Scott Smith, *Senior VP*
Scott Dobrez, *Vice Pres*
Jeff Gorney, *Vice Pres*
◆ **EMP:** 140 **EST:** 1957
**SALES (est):** 33.5MM **Privately Held**
**WEB:** www.dobergroup.com
**SIC:** 2842 2899 Specialty cleaning, polishes & sanitation goods; water treating compounds

### (G-22472)
### DOMINOS PIZZA LLC
10410 Woodward Ave # 100 (60517-4934)
**PHONE** ............................. 630 783-0738
**Fax:** 630 783-1854
Jim Bail, *Rsch/Dvlpt Dir*
Lisa Walker, *Accounting Dir*
Greg Higgins, *Manager*
**EMP:** 40
**SALES (corp-wide):** 2.4B **Publicly Held**
**WEB:** www.dominos.com
**SIC:** 5812 2045 Pizzeria, chain; prepared flour mixes & doughs
**HQ:** Domino's Pizza Llc
  30 Frank Lloyd Wright Dr
  Ann Arbor MI 48105
  734 930-3030

### (G-22473)
### DRY SYSTEMS TECHNOLOGIES LLC (HQ)
10420 Rising Ct (60517-7789)
**PHONE** ............................. 630 427-2051
Phil Reid, *Accountant*
Ronald D Eberhart, *Mng Member*
◆ **EMP:** 47
**SALES (est):** 4.7MM
**SALES (corp-wide):** 9MM **Privately Held**
**SIC:** 3532 Mining machinery
**PA:** Yorkshire Equity Llc
  100 Fillmore St Ste 500
  Denver CO 80206
  303 385-8434

### (G-22474)
### ECP INCORPORATED
Also Called: Protector, The
11210 Katherines Xing # 100 (60517-4043)
P.O. Box 1098, Oak Brook (60522-1098)
**PHONE** ............................. 630 754-4200
Larry Bettendorf, *President*
Peter Miehl, *Vice Pres*
Christopher Pieroni, *Vice Pres*
Gregoary Weizeorick, *Treasurer*
Don Bishop, *Sales Mgr*
**EMP:** 54
**SQ FT:** 136,000
**SALES (est):** 19.1MM **Privately Held**
**WEB:** www.ecpinc.net
**SIC:** 2842 2899 2841 5169 Specialty cleaning preparations; automobile polish; waxes for wood, leather & other materials; rust resisting compounds; soap & other detergents; rustproofing chemicals

### (G-22475)
### EGAN WAGNER CORPORATION
2929 Two Paths Dr (60517-4512)
**PHONE** ............................. 630 985-8007
**Fax:** 630 910-8254
Richard Wagner, *President*
Bonnie Egan, *Chairman*
**EMP:** 4
**SALES:** 450K **Privately Held**
**SIC:** 3694 Engine electrical equipment

### (G-22476)
### ELEVANCE RNEWABLE SCIENCES INC (PA)
2501 Davey Rd (60517-4957)
**PHONE** ............................. 630 296-8880
K'Lynne Johnson, *CEO*
Geoffrey Duyk, *Partner*
John Lim, *General Mgr*
Mel Luetkens, *COO*
Del Craig, *Exec VP*
◆ **EMP:** 139
**SALES (est):** 55.4MM **Privately Held**
**WEB:** www.elevance.com
**SIC:** 2869 Industrial organic chemicals

### (G-22477)
### ELGALABWATER LLC
5 Earl Ct Ste 100 (60517-7622)
**PHONE** ............................. 630 343-5251
Miguel Soto, *Accountant*
Klaus Andersen, *Mng Member*
Sandra Purcell, *Administration*
▲ **EMP:** 6
**SALES (est):** 570K **Privately Held**
**SIC:** 3542 Machine tools, metal forming type

### (G-22478)
### ENDOTRONIX INC
1005 Intrnle Pkwy Ste 104 (60517-4985)
**PHONE** ............................. 630 504-2861
Harry Rowland, *CEO*
Anthony Nunez, *President*
Mike Dilworth, *Vice Pres*
Michael Nagy, *Vice Pres*
Olivia Nichols, *Opers Mgr*
**EMP:** 8
**SALES (est):** 1.7MM **Privately Held**
**SIC:** 3841 Blood pressure apparatus

### (G-22479)
### FLOWSERVE FSD CORPORATION
1020 Davey Rd Ste 100 (60517-5108)
**PHONE** ............................. 630 783-1468
Vince Vorreyer, *Office Spvr*
John Stillane, *Manager*
Paul Bender, *Manager*
Mark Heuchert, *Manager*
**EMP:** 55
**SALES (corp-wide):** 3.9B **Publicly Held**
**SIC:** 3053 Gaskets, packing & sealing devices
**HQ:** Flowserve Fsd Corporation
  2100 Factory St
  Kalamazoo MI 49001
  269 226-3954

### (G-22480)
### FRI JADO INC
1401 Davey Rd Ste 100 (60517-4964)
**PHONE** ............................. 630 633-7944
Erik J Bos, *President*
Ernst Goettsch, *Managing Dir*
Edwin Van Sprundel, *CFO*
Martin Pb Wawrzyniak, *Admin Sec*
▲ **EMP:** 8
**SALES (est):** 1.1MM **Privately Held**
**SIC:** 3221 Food containers, glass
**HQ:** Fri-Jado B.V.
  Oude Kerkstraat 2
  Etten-Leur 4878
  765 085-200

# GEOGRAPHIC SECTION
## Woodridge - Dupage County (G-22501)

**(G-22481)**
**GENERAL FAS ACQUISITION CO**
Also Called: Casey Products
11230 Katherines Xing (60517-5127)
PHONE .................. 630 960-3360
Brian Wojokowski, *CEO*
**EMP:** 28 **EST:** 1999
**SALES (est):** 1.5MM **Privately Held**
**SIC:** 3451 Screw machine products

**(G-22482)**
**GERBER PLUMBING FIXTURES LLC**
2500 Intrntonale Pkwy (60517-4073)
PHONE .................. 630 679-1420
Keith Yurco, *President*
James Schwartz, *Controller*
Bryan Fiala, *Admin Sec*
▲ **EMP:** 53
**SALES:** 165MM
**SALES (corp-wide):** 613.9MM **Privately Held**
**SIC:** 3261 Plumbing fixtures, vitreous china
**HQ:** Globe Union Group Inc.
2500 Internationale Pkwy
Woodridge IL 60517
630 679-1420

**(G-22483)**
**GKN AMERICA CORP (DH)**
2715 Davey Rd Ste 300 (60517-5064)
PHONE .................. 630 972-9300
Grey Denham, *President*
John A Giannangeli, *Vice Pres*
Hugo Perez, *Treasurer*
Paul Westman, *Asst Treas*
Barbara Gustafson, *Asst Sec*
◆ **EMP:** 15
**SALES (est):** 808.3MM
**SALES (corp-wide):** 10.8B **Privately Held**
**SIC:** 3714 Universal joints, motor vehicle; drive shafts, motor vehicle
**HQ:** G.K.N. Industries Limited
Ipsley House
Redditch WORCS
152 751-7715

**(G-22484)**
**GKN NORTH AMERICA SERVICES INC (HQ)**
2715 Davey Rd Ste 300 (60517-5064)
PHONE .................. 630 972-9300
Fax: 630 719-7242
Hans Buthker, *CEO*
Kevin Cummings, *CEO*
Mike Grunza, *CEO*
Mike McCann, *CEO*
Daniele Cagnatel, *Senior VP*
◆ **EMP:** 15
**SQ FT:** 110,000
**SALES (est):** 192.7MM
**SALES (corp-wide):** 10.8B **Privately Held**
**SIC:** 3714 5013 Motor vehicle transmissions, drive assemblies & parts; transmissions, motor vehicle; motor vehicle supplies & new parts
**PA:** Gkn Plc
Ipsley House
Redditch WORCS B98 0
152 751-7715

**(G-22485)**
**GKN STROMAG INC**
2715 Davey Rd Ste 100 (60517-5064)
PHONE .................. 937 433-3882
James Albrecht, *President*
Sharol Albrecht, *Opers Mgr*
Melinda Dahle, *Purch Agent*
Natalie Chandler, *Sales Mgr*
Gary Stout, *Executive*
▲ **EMP:** 25
**SQ FT:** 24,000
**SALES (est):** 6.8MM
**SALES (corp-wide):** 10.8B **Privately Held**
**WEB:** www.stromaginc.com
**SIC:** 3568 3714 3643 3621 Power transmission equipment; clutches, except vehicular; couplings, shaft: rigid, flexible, universal joint, etc.; drives: belt, cable or rope; motor vehicle parts & accessories; current-carrying wiring devices; motors & generators; speed changers, drives & gears

**PA:** Gkn Plc
Ipsley House
Redditch WORCS B98 0
152 751-7715

**(G-22486)**
**GKN WALTERSCHEID INC**
2715 Davey Rd (60517-5064)
PHONE .................. 630 972-9300
Fax: 630 972-9392
Peter Roettgen, *President*
Phil Brown, *Managing Dir*
Ernie Balogh, *CFO*
Christina Villafuerte, *Bookkeeper*
Kathy Mayer, *Persnl Mgr*
▲ **EMP:** 139
**SQ FT:** 75,000
**SALES:** 39MM
**SALES (corp-wide):** 10.8B **Privately Held**
**WEB:** www.gkn-walterscheid.com
**SIC:** 5083 3568 Agricultural machinery & equipment; power transmission equipment
**HQ:** Gkn Walterscheid Gmbh
Hauptstr. 150
Lohmar 53797
224 612-0

**(G-22487)**
**GLOBE UNION GROUP INC (HQ)**
2500 Internationale Pkwy (60517-5090)
PHONE .................. 630 679-1420
Dennis Dugas, *Principal*
Keith Yurko, *Vice Pres*
Craig Holthus, *Opers Staff*
Bridget Palmer, *Research*
Robert Perry, *VP Sls/Mktg*
◆ **EMP:** 100
**SALES (est):** 222.7MM
**SALES (corp-wide):** 613.9MM **Privately Held**
**SIC:** 3261 3432 7699 Plumbing fixtures, vitreous china; plumbers' brass goods: drain cocks, faucets, spigots, etc.; general household repair services
**PA:** Globe Union Industrial Corp.
22, Chien Kuo Rd.,
Taichung City 42760
425 349-676

**(G-22488)**
**GOSS INTERNATIONAL LLC (HQ)**
Also Called: Goss International Corporation
9018 Heritage Pkwy # 1200 (60517-5136)
PHONE .................. 630 796-7560
Fax: 630 755-9301
Richard Nichols, *CEO*
Jochen Meissner, *President*
Matt Sharkady, *General Mgr*
Richard F Schultz, *Senior VP*
Jacques C Navarre, *Vice Pres*
◆ **EMP:** 21
**SALES (est):** 226.9MM
**SALES (corp-wide):** 9.1MM **Privately Held**
**SIC:** 3555 5084 Printing presses; printing trades machinery, equipment & supplies
**PA:** Shanghai Electric Corp.
No.110, Sichuan Middle Road
Shanghai 20000
216 321-5530

**(G-22489)**
**GOVQA INC**
900 S Frontage Rd Ste 110 (60517-4902)
PHONE .................. 630 985-1300
John Dilenschneider, *CEO*
Gregory Pengiel, *CTO*
Jennifer Snyder, *Security Dir*
William Repole,
**EMP:** 18 **EST:** 2002
**SALES (est):** 108.2K **Privately Held**
**SIC:** 7372 Prepackaged software
**PA:** Webqa Incorporated
900 S Frontage Rd Ste 110
Woodridge IL 60517

**(G-22490)**
**GRAHAM PACKAGING COMPANY LP**
2400 Internationale Pkwy # 1 (60517-4977)
PHONE .................. 630 739-9150
Fax: 630 739-9156
Paul Wu, *General Mgr*
Mick Lawson, *Plant Mgr*
Juan Saucedo, *QC Mgr*
Bob Seeger, *QC Mgr*
Tom Krieger, *Engineer*
**EMP:** 50 **Privately Held**
**WEB:** www.grahampackaging.com
**SIC:** 3089 3085 Plastic containers, except foam; plastics bottles
**HQ:** Graham Packaging Company, L.P.
700 Indian Springs Dr # 100
Lancaster PA 17601
717 849-8500

**(G-22491)**
**GREAT LAKES TOOL & MOLD INC**
6817 Hobson Valley Dr # 116 (60517-1452)
PHONE .................. 630 964-7121
Steve Creagan, *Owner*
**EMP:** 2
**SQ FT:** 2,100
**SALES (est):** 232.3K **Privately Held**
**WEB:** www.greatlakestoolsupply.com
**SIC:** 3544 Special dies, tools, jigs & fixtures

**(G-22492)**
**GYCOR INTERNATIONAL LTD**
10216 Werch Dr Ste 108 (60517-5124)
PHONE .................. 630 754-8070
Fax: 630 323-2751
David J Rogers, *President*
John Gyann, *President*
Stephen Allison, *COO*
Dave Rogers, *VP Opers*
Karen Decaro, *Bookkeeper*
**EMP:** 14
**SQ FT:** 12,000
**SALES (est):** 3.4MM **Privately Held**
**SIC:** 2819 2099 2087 Industrial inorganic chemicals; food preparations; flavoring extracts & syrups

**(G-22493)**
**H C SCHAU & SON INC**
10350 Argonne Dr Ste 400 (60517-4999)
PHONE .................. 630 783-1000
Fax: 630 783-9619
Charles H Schau, *CEO*
Randall C Schau, *Vice Pres*
Jim Bush, *Controller*
Claire Fondren, *Manager*
Fay Schau, *Admin Sec*
**EMP:** 200
**SALES (est):** 143.9MM **Privately Held**
**WEB:** www.hcschau.com
**SIC:** 5147 2099 Meats, fresh; food preparations
**HQ:** Greencore Us Holdings
222 Rosewood Dr Ste 240
Danvers MA 01923
508 586-8418

**(G-22494)**
**HOME RUN INN FROZEN FOODS CORP**
1300 Internationale Pkwy (60517-4928)
PHONE .................. 630 783-9696
Fax: 630 783-0069
Joseph Perrino, *President*
Marilyn Carlson, *President*
Lucretia Costello, *President*
Nick Perrino, *Business Mgr*
Tom Dangelo, *Vice Pres*
**EMP:** 100
**SQ FT:** 44,000
**SALES (est):** 27MM **Privately Held**
**SIC:** 2038 Pizza, frozen

**(G-22495)**
**INTELLIGRATED SYSTEMS INC**
9014 Heritage Pkwy # 308 (60517-5078)
PHONE .................. 630 985-4350
Jeffrey Cortez, *Opers Staff*
Paula Steffensmeier, *Manager*
**EMP:** 264
**SALES (corp-wide):** 39.3B **Publicly Held**
**SIC:** 3535 5084 7371 Conveyors & conveying equipment; industrial machinery & equipment; computer software development
**HQ:** Intelligrated Systems, Inc.
7901 Innovation Way
Mason OH 45040
866 936-7300

**(G-22496)**
**INVENTUS POWER INC (PA)**
1200 Internationale Pkwy (60517-4975)
PHONE .................. 630 410-7900
Patrick Trippel, *CEO*
Stephen McClure, *President*
John Gatti, *Exec VP*
Anson Martin, *Vice Pres*
Chris Turner, *Vice Pres*
▲ **EMP:** 200
**SALES (est):** 509.3MM **Privately Held**
**SIC:** 3629 Battery chargers, rectifying or nonrotating

**(G-22497)**
**INVENTUS POWER (ILLINOIS) LLC**
1200 Internationale Pkwy (60517-4975)
PHONE .................. 630 410-7900
Fax: 630 968-5050
John Gatti, *President*
Thomas Golab, *Vice Pres*
Anson Martin, *Vice Pres*
Chris Turner, *Vice Pres*
Like Xie, *Vice Pres*
▲ **EMP:** 140
**SQ FT:** 17,000
**SALES (est):** 43.3MM **Privately Held**
**WEB:** www.microsuntech.com
**SIC:** 3699 Electrical equipment & supplies
**HQ:** Palladium Energy Group, Inc.
1200 Internationale Pkwy # 101
Woodridge IL 60517

**(G-22498)**
**INVENTUS POWER HOLDINGS INC**
Also Called: Iccn Holdings
1200 Internationale Pkwy (60517-4975)
PHONE .................. 630 410-7900
Patrick Trippel, *CEO*
Michael Foy, *CFO*
Kelly Dobson, *Accountant*
**EMP:** 99
**SALES (est):** 2.8MM **Privately Held**
**SIC:** 3691 Storage batteries

**(G-22499)**
**J J COLLINS SONS INC (PA)**
Also Called: J. J. Collins Printers
7125 Janes Ave Ste 200 (60517-2347)
PHONE .................. 630 960-2525
Fax: 630 960-7487
James F Collins Sr, *Ch of Bd*
James F Collins Jr, *President*
Kevin Rankin, *President*
Thomas M Collins, *Exec VP*
Bev Fouliard, *Buyer*
▲ **EMP:** 30
**SQ FT:** 140,000
**SALES (est):** 32.2MM **Privately Held**
**WEB:** www.jjcollins.com
**SIC:** 2752 Business forms, lithographed

**(G-22500)**
**KARA GRAPHICS INC**
6823 Hobson Valley Dr # 201 (60517-5454)
PHONE .................. 630 964-8122
Fax: 630 964-8102
Teri Reuter, *President*
Ken Reuter, *Vice Pres*
**EMP:** 7
**SQ FT:** 600
**SALES (est):** 1.3MM **Privately Held**
**SIC:** 2759 Commercial printing; business forms: printing

**(G-22501)**
**MAGNUSON GROUP INC**
1400 Internationale Pkwy (60517-4942)
PHONE .................. 630 783-8100
Fax: 630 783-8181
Kelly Quackbush, *President*
Peter Magnuson, *Chairman*
Jan Warnecke, *Manager*
◆ **EMP:** 15
**SQ FT:** 25,000
**SALES (est):** 2.6MM **Privately Held**
**WEB:** www.magnusongroup.com
**SIC:** 2521 Wood office furniture

# Woodridge - Dupage County (G-22502)

**(G-22502)**
**MICROSUN ELECTRONICS CORP**
1200 Internationale Pkwy # 101
(60517-4976)
PHONE..................630 410-7900
Nancie Elshafei, *CEO*
Mandi Kostroski, *Accountant*
EMP: 11 EST: 2011
SALES (est): 1.2MM **Privately Held**
SIC: 3672 Circuit boards, television & radio printed

**(G-22503)**
**MONOLITHIC INDUSTRIES INC**
7613 Woodridge Dr (60517-2813)
PHONE..................630 985-6009
Fax: 630 985-4405
Ken Earle, *President*
EMP: 3
SALES (est): 367.1K **Privately Held**
SIC: 3825 8748 Test equipment for electronic & electrical circuits; business consulting

**(G-22504)**
**NAVITAS ELECTRONICS CORP**
1200 Internationale Pkwy # 125
(60517-5042)
PHONE..................702 293-4670
Alan Elshafei, *President*
Mark Aramli, *President*
Ralph Kuprewicz, *General Mgr*
Thomas Golab, *Vice Pres*
Chad Allison, *Opers Mgr*
EMP: 35
SQ FT: 22,000
SALES (est): 5MM **Privately Held**
WEB: www.microsunelectronics.com
SIC: 3679 Electronic circuits

**(G-22505)**
**NESTLE WATERS NORTH AMER INC**
10335 Argonne Woods Dr (60517-5130)
PHONE..................630 271-7300
Greg Swinicki, *Manager*
EMP: 98
SALES (corp-wide): 88.4B **Publicly Held**
WEB: www.zephyronline.com
SIC: 2086 Water, pasteurized; packaged in cans, bottles, etc.
HQ: Nestle Waters North America Inc.
900 Long Ridge Rd Bldg 2
Stamford CT 06902

**(G-22506)**
**ORBUS LLC (PA)**
Also Called: Orbus Exhibit & Display Group
9033 Murphy Rd (60517-1100)
PHONE..................630 226-1155
Fax: 773 486-5131
Giles Douglas, *President*
Kate Kincaid, *Regional Mgr*
Aaron Kozar, *Vice Pres*
Charles Rummel, *Purch Mgr*
Dave Fugiel, *Design Engr*
▲ EMP: 185 EST: 2005
SQ FT: 128,000
SALES (est): 76.5MM **Privately Held**
SIC: 3999 Advertising display products

**(G-22507)**
**PALLADIUM ENERGY GROUP INC (HQ)**
1200 Internationale Pkwy # 101
(60517-4976)
PHONE..................630 410-7900
John J Gatti, *CEO*
Ken Tarbell, *President*
Melissa Davis, *Vice Pres*
Dr Like Xie, *Vice Pres*
Amer Alshafei, *Opers Staff*
EMP: 55
SALES (est): 43.3MM **Privately Held**
SIC: 3691 Batteries, rechargeable

**(G-22508)**
**PARKER-HANNIFIN CORPORATION**
Integrated Elastomeric Sys
10625 Beaudin Blvd (60517-4993)
PHONE..................630 427-2020
Rick Assad, *Materials Mgr*
Godwin Sarpey, *Engineer*
Paul Reeves, *Design Engr*
Jill Nelson, *Human Res Dir*
Doug Vanlue, *Branch Mgr*
EMP: 160
SALES (corp-wide): 11.3B **Publicly Held**
WEB: www.parker.com
SIC: 2822 Synthetic rubber
PA: Parker-Hannifin Corporation
6035 Parkland Blvd
Cleveland OH 44124
216 896-3000

**(G-22509)**
**POWERS WOODWORKING**
6804 Hobson Valley Dr # 117 (60517-1448)
PHONE..................630 663-9644
Fax: 630 663-9926
Michael Powers, *Principal*
EMP: 8
SALES (est): 814.1K **Privately Held**
SIC: 2499 Decorative wood & woodwork

**(G-22510)**
**PRINTSMART PRINTING & GRAPHICS**
3024 Hobson Rd (60517-1510)
PHONE..................630 434-2000
Fax: 630 434-2107
Michael Burke, *President*
Constance Burke, *Treasurer*
EMP: 4
SQ FT: 1,600
SALES (est): 458K **Privately Held**
SIC: 2752 Commercial printing, lithographic

**(G-22511)**
**PRISMIER LLC**
10216 Werch Dr Ste 118 (60517-5096)
PHONE..................630 592-4515
David Tummillo, *Project Mgr*
Jennifer Nelson, *Controller*
Alex Cosmas, *Marketing Staff*
David Low, *Mng Member*
Lynn Low, *Info Tech Mgr*
▲ EMP: 20
SQ FT: 10,000
SALES: 12MM **Privately Held**
SIC: 3089 3444 3469 3363 Injection molding of plastics; housings for business machines, sheet metal; forming machine work, sheet metal; metal stampings; aluminum die-castings

**(G-22512)**
**PRODUCEPRO INC (PA)**
9014 Heritage Pkwy # 304 (60517-5078)
PHONE..................630 395-9700
David R Donat, *President*
Rick Hurst, *Business Mgr*
Nick Campanile, *Treasurer*
Marc Hatfield, *Natl Sales Mgr*
Tom Boyle, *Sales Mgr*
EMP: 3
SQ FT: 6,500
SALES (est): 7.3MM **Privately Held**
SIC: 7372 Application computer software

**(G-22513)**
**RANCILIO NORTH AMERICA INC**
1340 Internationale Pkwy (60517-4954)
PHONE..................630 427-1703
Glenn Surlet, *Admin Sec*
◆ EMP: 26
SALES (est): 6.1MM **Privately Held**
WEB: www.rancilio-na.com
SIC: 3556 Roasting machinery: coffee, peanut, etc.

**(G-22514)**
**ROBINSPORT LLC**
2613 York Ct (60517-1609)
PHONE..................630 724-9280
Kreig Robinson,
EMP: 5
SALES (est): 419.4K **Privately Held**
SIC: 4212 3713 4789 Local trucking, without storage; truck cabs for motor vehicles; cargo loading & unloading services

**(G-22515)**
**SAMUEL STRAPPING SYSTEMS INC (HQ)**
Also Called: Steel Fab
1401 Davey Rd Ste 300 (60517-4991)
PHONE..................630 783-8900
Fax: 630 783-8901
Robert Hickey, *President*
Bobby Gosschalk, *General Mgr*
Victoria Peat, *General Mgr*
Roy Wilkinson, *General Mgr*
Mark Menning, *Vice Pres*
◆ EMP: 60
SQ FT: 30,000
SALES (est): 128.9MM
SALES (corp-wide): 1.9B **Publicly Held**
WEB: www.samuelstrapping.com
SIC: 3499 5085 Strapping, metal; industrial supplies
PA: Samuel, Son & Co., Limited
2360 Dixie Rd
Mississauga ON L4Y 1
905 279-5460

**(G-22516)**
**SCHAU SOUTHEAST SUSHI INC**
10350 Argonne Dr Ste 400 (60517-5114)
PHONE..................630 783-1000
Charles H Schau, *CEO*
Randall C Schau, *President*
Faye L Schau, *Treasurer*
Jim Bush, *Controller*
EMP: 30
SALES (est): 800K **Privately Held**
SIC: 5147 5812 2099 Meats & meat products; eating places; food preparations

**(G-22517)**
**SCOTTS COMPANY LLC**
1030 Internationale Pkwy (60517-4924)
PHONE..................630 343-4070
Fax: 630 739-1196
James Hagedorn, *Branch Mgr*
EMP: 24
SALES (corp-wide): 2.8B **Publicly Held**
SIC: 2873 Fertilizers: natural (organic), except compost
HQ: The Scotts Company Llc
14111 Scottslawn Rd
Marysville OH 43040
937 644-3729

**(G-22518)**
**SPECTRUM TECHNOLOGIES INTL LTD**
6368 Greene Rd (60517-1497)
PHONE..................630 961-5244
Kirk Kreutzig, *President*
EMP: 3
SALES (est): 336.2K **Privately Held**
WEB: www.spectrumfilters.com
SIC: 3443 Nuclear reactors, military or industrial

**(G-22519)**
**SUNNY DIRECT LLC (PA)**
3540 Seven Bridges Dr # 160
(60517-1271)
PHONE..................630 795-0800
Tom Kinsella, *General Mgr*
Lori Plese, *Production*
Bob O'Brien, *Sales Staff*
Jerry Variola, *Sales Staff*
Dawn Hastings, *Marketing Staff*
EMP: 8
SALES (est): 2.1MM **Privately Held**
WEB: www.sunnydirect.com
SIC: 2759 Commercial printing

**(G-22520)**
**SYMBRIA RX SERVICES LLC**
Also Called: Friendly Remedies
7125 Janes Ave Ste 300 (60517-2304)
PHONE..................630 981-8000
Jill Krueger, *CEO*
Thomas Noesen Jr, *CFO*
Jay Mandra, *Director*
Dawn Gratzke, *Admin Asst*
EMP: 34 EST: 1997
SALES (est): 7.3MM **Privately Held**
SIC: 2834 5122 Pharmaceutical preparations; pharmaceuticals

**(G-22521)**
**TACKNOLOGIES**
10720 Beaudin Blvd Ste A (60517-5121)
PHONE..................630 729-9900
Robert Listello, *Principal*
EMP: 3
SALES (est): 699.7K **Privately Held**
SIC: 3443 Liners/lining

**(G-22522)**
**TELEDYNE REYNOLDS INC**
Also Called: Teledyne Storm Microwave
10221 Werch Dr (60517-4973)
PHONE..................630 754-3300
Ian Brown, *General Mgr*
Alex Villarreal, *Business Mgr*
Mark Kotilinek, *Opers Staff*
Ken Bugarewicz, *Purchasing*
Pat McGee, *Purchasing*
EMP: 117
SALES (corp-wide): 2.1B **Publicly Held**
WEB: www.stormproducts.com
SIC: 3357 Nonferrous wiredrawing & insulating; coaxial cable, nonferrous
HQ: Teledyne Reynolds, Inc.
5005 Mcconnell Ave
Los Angeles CA 90066
310 823-5491

**(G-22523)**
**WEBQA INCORPORATED (PA)**
900 S Frontage Rd Ste 110 (60517-4807)
PHONE..................630 985-1300
John Dilenschneider, *CEO*
Kim Sullivan, *Business Mgr*
David Bernhard, *Opers Mgr*
Kent Hartsfield, *Sales Mgr*
Rocco Barbanente, *Accounts Mgr*
EMP: 32
SALES (est): 6.8MM **Privately Held**
SIC: 7372 Application computer software

**(G-22524)**
**WESTERN REMAC INC (PA)**
Also Called: Wri
1740 Internationale Pkwy (60517-4994)
PHONE..................630 972-7770
Fax: 630 972-9680
Michael Conoscenti, *President*
Vicki Fiegl, *Vice Pres*
Jimmy Domschke, *Production*
Jill Longoria, *CFO*
Greg Longoria, *Manager*
EMP: 42
SQ FT: 44,000
SALES (est): 9.4MM **Privately Held**
WEB: www.westernremac.com
SIC: 3993 3669 Signs & advertising specialties; visual communication systems

**(G-22525)**
**WILLOW RIDGE GLASS INC (PA)**
8102 Lemont Rd Ste 100 (60517-7760)
PHONE..................630 910-8300
Fax: 630 910-3600
Glenn O James, *President*
Millicent James, *Corp Secy*
Mark Olin, *Vice Pres*
EMP: 12
SALES (est): 1.3MM **Privately Held**
SIC: 1793 3211 Glass & glazing work; tempered glass

**(G-22526)**
**WILTON BRANDS LLC (HQ)**
Also Called: Ek Success Brands
2240 75th St (60517-2333)
PHONE..................630 963-7100
Fax: 630 810-2712
Sue Buchta, *CEO*
Christopher Skinner, *CEO*
Kevin Fick, *President*
Dave Ferreira, *General Mgr*
Patricia Desimone, *Counsel*
◆ EMP: 430
SQ FT: 38,000
SALES (est): 649MM **Privately Held**
SIC: 5023 2731 2721 7812 Kitchenware; books; publishing only; periodicals: publishing only; video tape production; candy making goods & candy

**(G-22527)**
**WILTON HOLDINGS INC (PA)**
Also Called: Wilton Industries
2240 75th St (60517-2333)
PHONE..................630 963-7100
Steven Fraser, *CEO*
Deborah Bennett, *President*
Dan Kochenash, *COO*
Rodney Poole, *Senior VP*
▼ EMP: 6

## GEOGRAPHIC SECTION

**Woodstock - Mchenry County (G-22550)**

SALES (est): 649MM  **Privately Held**
SIC: 5023  2731  2721  7812  Kitchenware; books: publishing only; periodicals: publishing only; video tape production; candy making goods & supplies

**(G-22528)**
**WILTON INDUSTRIES  INC (DH)**
Also Called: Wilton Enterprises
2240 75th St  (60517-2333)
PHONE..................................630 963-7100
Fax: 630 963-7299
Daniel Butler, *President*
Steve Frazer, *COO*
Mary Merfield, *CFO*
Thomas Delonay, *Credit Staff*
Rob Begala, *Finance*
◆ EMP: 450
SQ FT: 38,000
SALES (est): 417.5MM  **Privately Held**
WEB: www.swiftaviationgroup.com
SIC: 5023  2731  2721  7812  Kitchenware; kitchen tools & utensils; frames & framing; picture & mirror; books: publishing only; periodicals: publishing only; video tape production; candy making goods & supplies

**(G-22529)**
**YCL INTERNATIONAL  INC**
3118 Whispering Oaks Ln  (60517-3757)
PHONE..................................630 873-0768
Chung LI, *President*
Yong Jiu Yang, *Admin Sec*
EMP: 50
SALES (est): 5.7MM  **Privately Held**
SIC: 3714  8742  Motor vehicle parts & accessories; management consulting services

### Woodson
*Morgan County*

**(G-22530)**
**CENTRAL CONCRETE PRODUCTS**
Perfection Vault Company
403 N Ladue Rd  (62695)
PHONE..................................217 673-6111
EMP: 14
SALES (corp-wide): 2.1MM  **Privately Held**
SIC: 3272  Burial vaults, concrete or precast terrazzo
PA: Central Concrete Products, Inc
3241 Terminal Ave
Springfield IL 62707
217 523-7964

**(G-22531)**
**PERFECTION VAULT CO INC**
403 N Ladue Rd  (62695)
P.O. Box 155  (62695-0155)
PHONE..................................217 673-6111
EMP: 14
SALES: 1.3MM  **Privately Held**
SIC: 3272  Mfg Burial Vaults & Septic Tanks

### Woodstock
*Mchenry County*

**(G-22532)**
**A & A MAGNETICS  INC**
520 Magnet Way  (60098-9432)
P.O. Box 1427  (60098-1427)
PHONE..................................815 338-6054
Fax: 815 338-8590
Jeffrey Arnold, *President*
Mike Learman, *General Mgr*
Gail Arnold, *Vice Pres*
EMP: 14
SQ FT: 20,000
SALES: 1.5MM  **Privately Held**
WEB: www.motojack.com
SIC: 3542  Magnetic forming machines

**(G-22533)**
**A HARTLETT & SONS INC**
406 N Eastwood Dr  (60098-3533)
PHONE..................................815 338-0109
Tom Hartlett, *President*

EMP: 2
SALES (est): 232.1K  **Privately Held**
SIC: 3444  1711  Sheet metalwork; plumbing, heating, air-conditioning contractors

**(G-22534)**
**ADVANCE DESIGN INC**
10915 Pheasant Ln  (60098-8576)
PHONE..................................815 338-0843
Fax: 815 943-7968
Earl Vosburgh, *President*
Rosalie Vosburgh, *Corp Secy*
Dean A Vosburgh, *Vice Pres*
EMP: 4
SQ FT: 16,300
SALES: 190K  **Privately Held**
SIC: 3089  3544  Molding primary plastic; special dies, tools, jigs & fixtures

**(G-22535)**
**ADVANCED MOLDING TECH INC**
1425 Lake Ave  (60098-7419)
PHONE..................................815 334-3600
Fax: 815 337-0377
Kevin Kelly, *President*
Mohamad Agha, *General Mgr*
Michael J Kelly, *Chairman*
Kevin Holsteen, *Controller*
Chuck Shortridge, *Sales Staff*
EMP: 80 EST: 1977
SQ FT: 60,000
SALES (est): 13.6MM
SALES (corp-wide): 90.8MM  **Privately Held**
WEB: www.advancedmoldingtechnologies.com
SIC: 3544  3089  Special dies, tools, jigs & fixtures; injection molded finished plastic products
HQ: Guardian Electric Manufacturing Co.
1425 Lake Ave
Woodstock IL 60098
815 334-3600

**(G-22536)**
**ADVANTECH PLASTICS LLC**
2500 S Eastwood Dr  (60098-9112)
PHONE..................................815 338-8383
Fax: 815 338-8763
Albert Zoller, *CEO*
Tracey Purvey, *Purchasing*
Don Moline, *QA Dir*
Pat Terrault, *Office Mgr*
Dan Rosado, *Manager*
▲ EMP: 62
SQ FT: 26,000
SALES (est): 16.8MM  **Privately Held**
WEB: www.advantechplastics.com
SIC: 3089  Injection molding of plastics
PA: Advan-Tech Industries, Inc.
100 N Waukegan Rd Ste 200
Lake Bluff IL 60044
847 295-1867

**(G-22537)**
**ADVOCATIONS INC**
17709 Collins Rd  (60098-9241)
PHONE..................................815 568-7505
Dinnes Obraits, *Owner*
EMP: 4
SALES (est): 299.8K  **Privately Held**
SIC: 3732  Boats, fiberglass: building & repairing

**(G-22538)**
**AMERICAN AD BAG COMPANY INC**
1510 Lamb Rd  (60098-9688)
PHONE..................................815 338-0300
Fax: 815 338-0397
Virginia Semrow, *President*
Gary Semrow, *Vice Pres*
Danielle Schultz, *Manager*
▲ EMP: 120
SALES (est): 16.7MM  **Privately Held**
WEB: www.adbag.com
SIC: 2759  Bag, wrapper & seal printing & engraving; bags, plastic: printing

**(G-22539)**
**AMERICAN PACKAGING MCHY INC**
Also Called: A P M
2550 S Eastwood Dr  (60098-9112)
PHONE..................................815 337-8580
Fax: 815 337-8583

Tadija Peric, *President*
Mary Anna, *Manager*
Mato Zovkic, *Manager*
John A Cook, *Admin Sec*
EMP: 25
SQ FT: 10,000
SALES (est): 7.2MM  **Privately Held**
WEB: www.apm-machinery.com
SIC: 3565  Packaging machinery

**(G-22540)**
**APT TOOL INC**
1301 Cobblestone Way  (60098-5202)
PHONE..................................815 337-0051
Fax: 815 337-0219
Guy Thompson, *President*
Anita Thompson, *Vice Pres*
EMP: 7
SQ FT: 3,600
SALES (est): 860.2K  **Privately Held**
WEB: www.online.magadan.su
SIC: 3544  Forms (molds), for foundry & plastics working machinery

**(G-22541)**
**ARNTZEN CORPORATION**
14600 Washington St  (60098-9308)
PHONE..................................815 334-0788
Fax: 815 334-0778
John Arntzen, *Branch Mgr*
EMP: 20
SALES (corp-wide): 14.8MM  **Privately Held**
WEB: www.arntzenrolling.com
SIC: 3317  5051  3498  3444  Steel pipe & tubes; steel; fabricated pipe & fittings; sheet metalwork; blast furnaces & steel mills
PA: Arntzen Corporation
1025 School St
Rockford IL 61101
815 964-9413

**(G-22542)**
**ARROW ALUMINUM CASTINGS INC**
2617 S Il Route 47  (60098-7557)
P.O. Box 648  (60098-0648)
PHONE..................................815 338-4480
Denis J Moeller, *President*
Virginia Moeller, *Corp Secy*
EMP: 8 EST: 1946
SQ FT: 7,000
SALES (est): 530K  **Privately Held**
SIC: 3363  3365  Aluminum die-castings; aluminum foundries

**(G-22543)**
**B T M INDUSTRIES  INC**
604 Washington St  (60098-2251)
PHONE..................................815 338-6464
Fax: 815 338-3556
Timothy Porter, *President*
Julie Wyatt, *Office Mgr*
▲ EMP: 9 EST: 1976
SQ FT: 14,000
SALES (est): 1.2MM  **Privately Held**
WEB: www.btmindustries.com
SIC: 3599  Machine shop, jobbing & repair

**(G-22544)**
**BERRY GLOBAL  INC**
1008 Courtaulds Dr  (60098-7390)
PHONE..................................815 334-5225
David Gentry, *Vice Pres*
Pam Saathoff, *Vice Pres*
David Harden, *Plant Mgr*
Chris Luscavich, *Engineer*
Olga Camacho, *Human Res Dir*
EMP: 127
SALES (corp-wide): 6.4B  **Publicly Held**
WEB: www.6sens.com
SIC: 3089  Bottle caps, molded plastic
HQ: Berry Global, Inc.
101 Oakley St
Evansville IN 47710
812 424-2904

**(G-22545)**
**BEST METAL CORPORATION**
925 Dieckman St  (60098-9262)
PHONE..................................815 337-0420
Fax: 815 337-8803
Craig Paul, *President*
Shawn Kenny, *General Mgr*
Susan Paullin, *Admin Sec*

EMP: 29
SQ FT: 15,000
SALES: 5.9MM
SALES (corp-wide): 38.6MM  **Privately Held**
WEB: www.bestmetal.com
SIC: 3411  Oil cans, metal
PA: Psm Industries, Inc.
14000 Avalon Blvd
Los Angeles CA 90061
888 663-8256

**(G-22546)**
**BOTTS WELDING AND TRCK SVC INC (PA)**
335 N Eastwood Dr  (60098-3504)
P.O. Box 430  (60098-0430)
PHONE..................................815 338-0594
Gordon R Botts, *President*
EMP: 20
SQ FT: 22,500
SALES (est): 8MM  **Privately Held**
WEB: www.bottswelding.com
SIC: 5013  7539  7538  7692  Truck parts & accessories; frame repair shops, automotive; general truck repair; automotive welding

**(G-22547)**
**BROCK EQUIPMENT COMPANY (PA)**
455 Borden St  (60098-2132)
P.O. Box 218, Crystal Lake  (60039-0218)
PHONE..................................815 459-4210
Fax: 815 455-0025
Marvin H Richer, *President*
Gail L Richer, *Corp Secy*
Ray Opal, *Purchasing*
Susan Morris, *Controller*
Donald P Phillips, *Sales Mgr*
EMP: 20 EST: 1945
SQ FT: 90,000
SALES (est): 1.3MM  **Privately Held**
SIC: 3594  3563  3566  Pumps, hydraulic power transfer; air & gas compressors including vacuum pumps; speed changers, drives & gears

**(G-22548)**
**BULL VALLEY HARDWOOD (PA)**
18014 Collins Rd  (60098-9243)
PHONE..................................815 701-9400
Daniel Deserto, *President*
Silvio Deserto, *Vice Pres*
EMP: 3 EST: 2015
SQ FT: 14,150
SALES: 1MM  **Privately Held**
SIC: 2421  5031  5211  Sawmills & planing mills, general; lumber, plywood & millwork; millwork & lumber

**(G-22549)**
**CARL GORR PRINTING CO (PA)**
Also Called: Gorr Communication Products
1002 Mchenry Ave  (60098-3036)
P.O. Box 105, Cary  (60013-0105)
PHONE..................................815 338-3191
Fax: 847 639-8089
Fred Gorr, *President*
David W Gorr, *Vice Pres*
John Urban, *Sales Staff*
Fredrica Brown, *Admin Sec*
EMP: 7
SQ FT: 15,000
SALES (est): 1.2MM  **Privately Held**
WEB: www.carlgorrprinting.com
SIC: 2759  3083  2396  Screen printing; laminated plastics plate & sheet; automotive & apparel trimmings

**(G-22550)**
**CATALENT PHARMA SOLUTIONS INC**
2210 Lake Shore Dr  (60098-6919)
PHONE..................................815 338-9500
Fax: 815 206-1335
Gary Lemaire, *Senior Buyer*
Mike Hitchingham, *Manager*
Monica Smith, *Manager*
Alexandre Alves, *Info Tech Mgr*
Kay Zhang, *Director*
EMP: 200  **Publicly Held**
SIC: 2834  Pharmaceutical preparations

# Woodstock - Mchenry County (G-22551)

HQ: Catalent Pharma Solutions, Inc.
14 Schoolhouse Rd
Somerset NJ 08873
732 537-6200

### (G-22551)
**CHARTER DURA-BAR INC (HQ)**
Also Called: Dura-Bar Div
2100 W Lake Shore Dr
PHONE...................815 338-3900
Fax: 815 338-3950
Thomas W Wells, *President*
Frank Abruzzo, *Vice Pres*
Arthur Berman, *Vice Pres*
Michael Hackworthy, *Vice Pres*
Timothy Heagney, *Vice Pres*
▲ EMP: 25 EST: 1946
SQ FT: 380,000
SALES (est): 78.6MM
SALES (corp-wide): 762.9MM **Privately Held**
WEB: www.wellsmanufacturing.com
SIC: 3321  5051  Gray iron castings; ductile iron castings; bars, metal
PA: Charter Manufacturing Company, Inc.
1212 W Glen Oaks Ln
Mequon WI 53092
262 243-4700

### (G-22552)
**CHARTER DURA-BAR INC**
Also Called: Dura Bar Division
1800 W Lake Shore Dr (60098-7426)
PHONE...................815 338-7800
Fax: 815 338-1549
Brian Schlump, *General Mgr*
Anthony Guitterez, *Vice Pres*
Martin Busching, *Safety Dir*
Robert Paladino, *Foreman/Supr*
Mariusz Bronkowski, *Opers Staff*
EMP: 225
SQ FT: 325,000
SALES (corp-wide): 762.9MM **Privately Held**
WEB: www.wellsmanufacturing.com
SIC: 3321  8711  3441  3369  Gray & ductile iron foundries; engineering services; fabricated structural metal; nonferrous foundries
HQ: Charter Dura-Bar, Inc.
2100 W Lake Shore Dr
Woodstock IL 60098
815 338-3900

### (G-22553)
**CONTEMPO INDUSTRIES INC**
Also Called: Woodstock Gardens
455 Borden St (60098-2132)
P.O. Box 1206 (60098-1206)
PHONE...................815 337-6267
Ken Pawela, *President*
Richard Szyzska, *Vice Pres*
EMP: 82
SQ FT: 42,000
SALES (est): 14.1MM **Privately Held**
SIC: 3524  Lawn & garden equipment

### (G-22554)
**COOL FLUIDICS INC**
123 S Eastwood Dr Ste 145 (60098-3519)
PHONE...................815 861-4063
Christina Coalson, *CEO*
EMP: 3
SALES (est): 229.2K **Privately Held**
SIC: 3561  Pumps & pumping equipment

### (G-22555)
**COPY EXPRESS INC**
301 E Calhoun St Ste 2 (60098-4290)
PHONE...................815 338-7161
James A O'Leary, *President*
Vicki O'Leary, *Vice Pres*
Kate Emricson, *Graphic Designe*
EMP: 10
SQ FT: 7,000
SALES (est): 970K **Privately Held**
WEB: www.copyexpressyes.com
SIC: 2752  7334  2791  Photo-offset printing; photocopying & duplicating services; typesetting

### (G-22556)
**CRESWELL WOODWORKING CA**
911 Rail Dr Unit C (60098-9435)
PHONE...................847 381-9222
Fax: 847 381-9226
Mike Creswell, *Owner*
EMP: 4
SALES (est): 349.9K **Privately Held**
SIC: 2431  Millwork

### (G-22557)
**CUSTOM TELEPHONE PRINTING INC**
1002 Mchenry Ave (60098-3036)
PHONE...................815 338-0000
Fax: 815 338-0009
John Farella, *President*
Rick Houda, *Corp Secy*
Mark Demarest, *COO*
Ed Kaplon, *Sales Mgr*
Jon Balthazar, *Systems Admin*
EMP: 10
SALES (est): 1.2MM **Privately Held**
WEB: www.customtel.com
SIC: 2752  3993  2396  Commercial printing, offset; signs & advertising specialties; automotive & apparel trimmings

### (G-22558)
**DALE K BROWN**
Also Called: Schmidt Printing
130 Wshngton St Unit Rear (60098)
PHONE...................815 338-0222
Fax: 815 338-0258
Dale K Brown, *Owner*
EMP: 3
SALES (est): 170K **Privately Held**
SIC: 2752  2759  2791  2789  Commercial printing, offset; letterpress printing; typesetting; bookbinding & related work

### (G-22559)
**DEAGOSTINI PUBLISHING USA INC**
121 E Calhoun St Ste E (60098-3284)
PHONE...................212 432-4070
Vince Murray, *President*
Darren Deguire, *General Mgr*
EMP: 4 EST: 2012
SALES (est): 307.5K **Privately Held**
SIC: 2731  Book publishing

### (G-22560)
**DILARS EMBROIDERY & MONOGRAMS**
1320 Zimmerman Rd (60098-7786)
PHONE...................815 338-6066
Larry Monaghan, *Owner*
Marlene Monaghan, *Bookkeeper*
EMP: 5
SALES: 160K **Privately Held**
WEB: www.dilars.com
SIC: 2395  Embroidery & art needlework

### (G-22561)
**DMR INTERNATIONAL INC**
720 S Eastwood Dr Ste 243 (60098-4635)
PHONE...................815 704-5678
Rick Latella, *President*
EMP: 3 EST: 2011
SALES (est): 123.2K **Privately Held**
SIC: 2821  Mfg Plastic Materials/Resins

### (G-22562)
**DORDAN MANUFACTURING COMPANY**
2025 Castle Rd (60098-9271)
PHONE...................815 334-0087
Fax: 815 334-0089
Daniel J Slavin, *CEO*
Alice Whatley, *Vice Pres*
John R Kreider, *Admin Sec*
EMP: 50
SALES (est): 13.7MM **Privately Held**
WEB: www.dordan.com
SIC: 3089  Blister or bubble formed packaging, plastic

### (G-22563)
**DRAMATIC PUBLISHING COMPANY**
311 Washington St (60098-3308)
P.O. Box 129 (60098-0129)
PHONE...................815 338-7170
Fax: 815 338-7212
Christopher Sergel Jr, *President*
Gayle Sergel, *Vice Pres*
Susan Sergel, *Vice Pres*
Linda Habjan, *Manager*
Maureen Sergel, *Information Mgr*
EMP: 19
SQ FT: 10,000
SALES (est): 1.7MM **Privately Held**
WEB: www.dpcplays.com
SIC: 2741  7922  Miscellaneous publishing; theatrical producers & services

### (G-22564)
**E3 ARTISAN INC**
Also Called: Ethereal Confections
113 S Benton St (60098-3205)
PHONE...................815 575-9315
Ervin Sara, *President*
EMP: 19
SALES (est): 2.8MM **Privately Held**
SIC: 2099  Pasta, uncooked: packaged with other ingredients

### (G-22565)
**EMTECH MACHINING & GRINDING**
911 Rail Dr (60098-9435)
P.O. Box 1810 (60098-1810)
PHONE...................815 338-1580
Fax: 815 338-9339
Charlotte Emricson, *President*
Shelly Eslick, *Office Mgr*
EMP: 7 EST: 1957
SQ FT: 38,000
SALES (est): 820K **Privately Held**
WEB: www.emtechinc.com
SIC: 3599  3545  Machine shop, jobbing & repair; machine tool accessories

### (G-22566)
**EPS SOLUTIONS INCORPORATED**
1525 W Lake Shore Dr (60098-6917)
PHONE...................815 206-0868
David H Hoffmann, *CEO*
Mark C Coleman, *President*
Jeffrey A Richardson, *President*
Christopher P Massey, *Principal*
Erik R Watts, *Principal*
EMP: 606
SQ FT: 9,000
SALES (est): 141.5MM **Privately Held**
SIC: 2676  Towels, napkins & tissue paper products

### (G-22567)
**FLEX-WELD INC**
Also Called: Keflex
1425 Lake Ave (60098-7419)
PHONE...................815 334-3662
Fax: 815 334-3689
Kevin G Kelly, *CEO*
Michael J Kelly, *Ch of Bd*
Stephanie Babineau, *Accountant*
Tom Leith, *Manager*
Jan Sims, *Manager*
▲ EMP: 58
SQ FT: 100,000
SALES (est): 10.1MM **Privately Held**
WEB: www.flex-weld.com
SIC: 3599  3568  3643  3498  Bellows, industrial: metal; hose, flexible metallic; joints, swivel & universal, except aircraft & automotive; current-carrying wiring devices; fabricated pipe & fittings; fabricated structural metal

### (G-22568)
**FOX TOOL & MANUFACTURING INC (PA)**
900 Dieckman St (60098-9286)
P.O. Box 855 (60098-0855)
PHONE...................815 338-4580
Fax: 815 338-4589
Barry Glass, *President*
Bruce D Glass, *Vice Pres*
EMP: 16
SQ FT: 12,000
SALES (est): 3MM **Privately Held**
SIC: 3599  Machine shop, jobbing & repair

### (G-22569)
**GAMA ELECTRONICS INC**
1240 Cobblestone Way (60098-5205)
PHONE...................815 356-9600
Carl Gerken, *Owner*
Tom Golbeck, *COO*
Sharon Oswald, *Technology*
Steve Golbeck, *Officer*
▲ EMP: 13
SQ FT: 6,000
SALES (est): 3MM **Privately Held**
WEB: www.steri-sealer.com
SIC: 3565  8711  3844  Packaging machinery; engineering services; X-ray apparatus & tubes

### (G-22570)
**GRO PRODUCTS INC**
1010 Trakk Ln Ste D (60098-9415)
PHONE...................815 308-5423
Cheryl Scordato, *President*
Charles Scordato, *Vice Pres*
EMP: 5
SQ FT: 4,000
SALES: 174K **Privately Held**
SIC: 2511  Cedar chests

### (G-22571)
**GUARDIAN CONSOLIDATED TECH INC (HQ)**
1425 Lake Ave (60098-7419)
PHONE...................815 334-3600
Kevin Kelly, *President*
Michael J Kelly, *Chairman*
Heather Swanson, *Admin Sec*
EMP: 4
SQ FT: 100,000
SALES (est): 72.8MM
SALES (corp-wide): 90.8MM **Privately Held**
SIC: 3625  Relays & industrial controls
PA: Kelco Industries, Inc.
1425 Lake Ave
Woodstock IL 60098
815 334-3600

### (G-22572)
**GUARDIAN ELECTRIC MFG CO (DH)**
1425 Lake Ave (60098-7419)
PHONE...................815 334-3600
Fax: 815 337-0377
Kevin Kelly, *President*
Michael Kelly, *Chairman*
Heather Thurman, *Cust Mgr*
Don Grandt, *Manager*
Cacilia Rakiewicz, *Info Tech Mgr*
▲ EMP: 80 EST: 1931
SQ FT: 100,000
SALES (est): 31.1MM
SALES (corp-wide): 90.8MM **Privately Held**
WEB: www.guardian-electric.com
SIC: 3679  3625  Solenoids for electronic applications; relays & industrial controls; relays, electric power; switches, electric power; solenoid switches (industrial controls)

### (G-22573)
**HAL MATHER & SONS INCORPORATED**
Also Called: Mather Dataforms
11803 Highway 120 (60098-8516)
PHONE...................815 338-4000
Fax: 815 338-3003
Douglas L Mather, *President*
Dave Diverde, *General Mgr*
James R Mather, *Vice Pres*
EMP: 32 EST: 1934
SQ FT: 33,850
SALES (est): 4MM **Privately Held**
SIC: 2759  2752  Commercial printing; letterpress printing; coupons: printing; commercial printing, offset

### (G-22574)
**INDE ENTERPRISES INC**
Also Called: Indepth Graphics & Printing
671 E Calhoun St (60098-4262)
PHONE...................815 338-8844
Cheryl Wormley, *President*
Denise Graff Ponstein, *President*
Kathie Comella, *Manager*
Margie Moore, *Manager*
Richard Rostron, *Manager*
EMP: 20
SQ FT: 1,200
SALES (est): 1.3MM **Privately Held**
SIC: 2711  7336  Newspapers: publishing only, not printed on site; graphic arts & related design

## Woodstock - Mchenry County (G-22601)

### (G-22575)
**INNOQUEST INC**
910 Hobe Rd (60098-9010)
PHONE...............................815 337-8555
William Hughes, *President*
Jason Pilman, *Engineer*
▲ EMP: 6
SQ FT: 4,000
SALES: 700K **Privately Held**
WEB: www.innoquestinc.com
SIC: 3829 Rain gauges

### (G-22576)
**KAM TOOL AND MOLD**
1300 Cobblestone Way (60098-5201)
PHONE...............................815 338-8360
Kurt W Johnson, *Owner*
EMP: 5 EST: 1978
SQ FT: 3,750
SALES (est): 250K **Privately Held**
SIC: 3544 Special dies, tools, jigs & fixtures

### (G-22577)
**KELCO INDUSTRIES INC (PA)**
1425 Lake Ave (60098-7419)
PHONE...............................815 334-3600
Fax: 815 338-6558
Michael J Kelly, *Ch of Bd*
Kevin G Kelly, *President*
Marietta Kelly, *Vice Pres*
▲ EMP: 6
SQ FT: 2,000
SALES (est): 90.8MM **Privately Held**
SIC: 3599 3069 3494 3585 Flexible metal hose, tubing & bellows; molded rubber products; valves & pipe fittings; expansion joints pipe; heating equipment, complete; air conditioning units, complete; domestic or industrial; industrial molds; relays, for electronic use; switches, electronic applications

### (G-22578)
**KHC CORPORATION**
333 E Judd St (60098-3417)
PHONE...............................815 337-7630
Fax: 815 337-7636
Sota Katahira, *CEO*
Shuichi Katahira, *President*
Pete Hostetler, *Vice Pres*
Michael Mitchell, *Plant Mgr*
Sandra Rupert, *Manager*
▲ EMP: 25
SQ FT: 10,000
SALES (est): 4.4MM
SALES (corp-wide): 14.1MM **Privately Held**
SIC: 3493 Steel springs, except wire
PA: Keihin Hatsujyo Co., Ltd.
5-2931, Uragocho
Yokosuka KNG 237-0
468 658-391

### (G-22579)
**KNIGHT PLASTICS LLC**
1008 Courtaulds Dr (60098-7390)
PHONE...............................815 334-1240
Fax: 815 334-1244
Ira Boots, *President*
Jimi White, *Info Tech Mgr*
▲ EMP: 160
SALES (est): 16.9MM
SALES (corp-wide): 6.4B **Publicly Held**
WEB: www.knightengr.com
SIC: 3089 Plastic processing
HQ: Berry Global, Inc.
101 Oakley St
Evansville IN 47710
812 424-2904

### (G-22580)
**KRAFT HEINZ FOODS COMPANY**
1300 Claussen Dr (60098-2155)
PHONE...............................815 338-7000
Fax: 815 338-9244
John Lillie, *Vice Pres*
Glenda O'Brien, *Plant Mgr*
Kevin Ripley, *Plant Mgr*
Gary Mader, *Materials Mgr*
Ernesto Gonzalez, *Maint Spvr*
EMP: 400
SQ FT: 132,000
SALES (corp-wide): 26.4B **Publicly Held**
WEB: www.kraftfoods.com
SIC: 2035 2033 Pickles, vinegar; canned fruits & specialties
HQ: Kraft Heinz Foods Company
1 Ppg Pl Ste 3200
Pittsburgh PA 15222
412 456-5700

### (G-22581)
**LANDAIRSEA SYSTEMS INC**
2040 Dillard Ct (60098-6600)
PHONE...............................847 462-8100
Robert Wagner, *President*
Todd Eisenbarth, *Sales Mgr*
Vincent Lee, *Director*
▲ EMP: 15
SALES (est): 2.2MM **Privately Held**
SIC: 3823 Transmitters of process variables, stand. signal conversion

### (G-22582)
**LAS SYSTEMS INC**
2040 Dillard Ct (60098-6600)
PHONE...............................847 462-8100
Robert Wagner, *President*
Lin Xu, *Shareholder*
▲ EMP: 25
SQ FT: 3,000
SALES (est): 3.6MM **Privately Held**
WEB: www.landairsea.com
SIC: 3663 3625 Transmitter-receivers, radio; timing devices, electronic

### (G-22583)
**LEADING ENERGY DESIGNS LTD**
440 Lawndale Ave (60098-4029)
PHONE...............................815 382-8852
Anne Maidment, *President*
Thomas Frawley, *Vice Pres*
EMP: 2
SALES (est): 234.2K **Privately Held**
SIC: 3646 Commercial indusl & institutional electric lighting fixtures

### (G-22584)
**LEMKE MACHINE PRODUCTS INC**
629 W Kimball Ave (60098-3637)
PHONE...............................815 338-1560
Fax: 815 338-1591
Eugene Lemke, *President*
Rosemary Lemke, *Admin Sec*
EMP: 12
SQ FT: 8,000
SALES (est): 2MM **Privately Held**
WEB: www.lemkemachine.com
SIC: 3599 Machine shop, jobbing & repair

### (G-22585)
**LESTER L BROSSARD CO**
930 Dieckman St (60098-9286)
P.O. Box 708 (60098-0708)
PHONE...............................815 338-7825
Fax: 815 338-7954
George L Brossard, *President*
Bob Wise, *Accountant*
George Clifford, *Manager*
Patricia Brossard, *Director*
▲ EMP: 10
SQ FT: 10,000
SALES (est): 1.3MM **Privately Held**
WEB: www.brossardmirrors.com
SIC: 3231 3842 Mirrored glass; surgical appliances & supplies

### (G-22586)
**LUSTER LEAF PRODUCTS INC (PA)**
2220 Tech Ct (60098-9200)
PHONE...............................815 337-5560
Fax: 815 337-5567
Larry Holbein, *President*
Margaret Godfrey, *Admin Sec*
▲ EMP: 9
SQ FT: 9,400
SALES (est): 1.5MM **Privately Held**
WEB: www.lusterleaf.com
SIC: 2899 3829 3423 Soil testing kits; measuring & controlling devices; hand & edge tools

### (G-22587)
**MARKHAM INDUSTRY INC**
Also Called: Sno-Belt Industries
1013 E Kimball Ave (60098-4235)
PHONE...............................815 338-0116
R W Markham, *President*
Mary E Markham, *Admin Sec*
EMP: 7
SQ FT: 6,000
SALES: 750K **Privately Held**
SIC: 3471 Finishing, metals or formed products; polishing, metals or formed products; buffing for the trade

### (G-22588)
**MATRIX IV INC**
610 E Judd St (60098-3424)
PHONE...............................815 338-4500
Fax: 815 338-2909
Patricia Miller, *President*
▲ EMP: 50
SQ FT: 76,000
SALES (est): 12.5MM **Privately Held**
WEB: www.matrixiv.com
SIC: 3089 8711 Molding primary plastic; engineering services

### (G-22589)
**MICHAEL CHRISTOPHER LTD**
1007 Trakk Ln (60098-9488)
PHONE...............................815 308-5018
Michael Amster, *President*
EMP: 8
SALES: 750K **Privately Held**
SIC: 2844 Perfumes & colognes

### (G-22590)
**MIGATRON CORPORATION**
935 Dieckman St Ste A (60098-9203)
P.O. Box 1229 (60098-1229)
PHONE...............................815 338-5800
Fax: 815 338-5803
Frank C Wroga Jr, *President*
William Richard Wroga, *Vice Pres*
Elizabeth A Wroga, *CFO*
Dave Sheets, *Sales Executive*
Oscar Villalva, *Associate*
EMP: 20 EST: 1979
SQ FT: 9,000
SALES (est): 3.8MM **Privately Held**
WEB: www.migatron.com
SIC: 3829 Ultrasonic testing equipment; electrical equipment & supplies

### (G-22591)
**MILLER MIDWESTERN DIE CO**
1076 Lake Ave (60098-7408)
PHONE...............................815 338-6686
Fax: 815 338-0941
Thomas L Miller, *President*
Charles Ruth, *Admin Sec*
EMP: 6
SQ FT: 9,000
SALES: 900K **Privately Held**
WEB: www.millermidwestern.com
SIC: 3544 Dies & die holders for metal cutting, forming, die casting

### (G-22592)
**MIX N MINGLE**
124 Cass St Ste 2 (60098-3296)
PHONE...............................815 308-5170
Nat Grindeland, *Principal*
EMP: 3
SALES (est): 425.4K **Privately Held**
SIC: 3273 Ready-mixed concrete

### (G-22593)
**MP MANUFACTURING INC**
13802 Washington St Ste B (60098-9489)
PHONE...............................815 334-1112
Dale Hildebrand, *Principal*
EMP: 9
SALES (est): 921.1K **Privately Held**
SIC: 3999 Atomizers, toiletry

### (G-22594)
**MULTITECH INDUSTRIES**
10603 Arabian Trl (60098-8494)
PHONE...............................815 206-0015
Jeffery Mossman, *Principal*
Tony Papa, *Accounts Mgr*
EMP: 2
SALES (est): 236.3K **Privately Held**
SIC: 3312 3316 Primary finished or semi-finished shapes; cold finishing of steel shapes

### (G-22595)
**MURPHY USA INC**
1265 Lake Ave (60098-7415)
PHONE...............................815 337-2440
EMP: 43 **Publicly Held**
SIC: 5541 1311 Gasoline service stations; crude petroleum & natural gas production
PA: Murphy Usa Inc.
200 E Peach St
El Dorado AR 71730

### (G-22596)
**ORTHO MOLECULAR PRODUCTS INC (PA)**
1991 Duncan Pl (60098-7394)
PHONE...............................815 337-0089
Gary Powers, *President*
William Borrmann, *Vice Pres*
Sara Hubner, *Design Engr*
Nathan Albertson, *Human Res Dir*
Kristen Brokaw, *Sales Staff*
▲ EMP: 25
SALES (est): 13MM **Privately Held**
WEB: www.orthomolecularproducts.com
SIC: 2834 Antiseptics, medicinal

### (G-22597)
**P B R W ENTERPRISES INC**
Also Called: Software Maniacs
12201 Baker Ter (60098-8721)
P.O. Box 64, Sharpsburg MD (21782-0064)
PHONE...............................815 337-5519
Wendy Powers, *President*
EMP: 4
SALES (est): 265.4K **Privately Held**
SIC: 7372 Prepackaged software

### (G-22598)
**PACIFIC ELECTRONICS CORP**
Also Called: Pacific Industries Intl
10200 Us Highway 14 (60098-7365)
PHONE...............................815 206-5450
Fax: 815 206-5460
Jim Gorman, *President*
Terry Neeley, *Exec VP*
Julie Duran, *Controller*
▲ EMP: 15
SQ FT: 50,000
SALES (est): 3.4MM **Privately Held**
WEB: www.pacificelectronicscorp.com
SIC: 3669 Emergency alarms; intercommunication systems, electric

### (G-22599)
**PHOENIX WOODWORKING CORP**
2000 Duncan Pl (60098-7311)
PHONE...............................815 338-9338
Fax: 815 338-9383
Sandra Pierce, *President*
Brett Pierce, *Vice Pres*
Frank Lefever, *Opers Mgr*
EMP: 20
SQ FT: 21,450
SALES (est): 3.5MM **Privately Held**
SIC: 2599 Cabinets, factory

### (G-22600)
**POWERS PAINT SHOP INC**
1065 Dieckman St (60098-9262)
PHONE...............................815 338-3619
Fax: 815 338-4011
Daniel F Powers, *President*
Cindy Powers, *Corp Secy*
Cindy Given, *Office Mgr*
EMP: 4
SQ FT: 8,000
SALES (est): 360K **Privately Held**
SIC: 3479 3471 Painting, coating & hot dipping; painting of metal products; plating & polishing

### (G-22601)
**PRECISION VISION INC**
1725 Kilkenny Ct (60098-7437)
PHONE...............................815 223-2022
Fax: 815 223-2224
Ed Kopidlansky, *President*
Chris Greening, *Vice Pres*
EMP: 7
SQ FT: 22,000

# Woodstock - Mchenry County (G-22602)

SALES (est): 1.2MM **Privately Held**
**SIC:** 3841 3827 Eye examining instruments & apparatus; optical instruments & lenses

### (G-22602)
### PSM INDUSTRIES INC
Also Called: Bestmetal, A Division of PSM
925 Dieckman St (60098-9262)
**PHONE**.................................815 337-8800
Sean Kenney, *Principal*
**EMP:** 29
**SALES (corp-wide):** 38.6MM **Privately Held**
**WEB:** www.pacificsintered.com
**SIC:** 3499 Friction material, made from powdered metal
**PA:** Psm Industries, Inc.
14000 Avalon Blvd
Los Angeles CA 90061
888 663-8256

### (G-22603)
### R & B METAL PRODUCTS INC
801 Mchenry Ave (60098-3031)
**PHONE**.................................815 338-1890
**Fax:** 815 338-7945
John Kise, *CEO*
Joseph Kelter, *Vice Pres*
**EMP:** 22 **EST:** 1945
**SQ FT:** 23,000
**SALES (est):** 4MM **Privately Held**
**WEB:** www.rbmetalproducts.com
**SIC:** 3599 3446 3444 3443 Machine shop, jobbing & repair; architectural metalwork; sheet metalwork; fabricated plate work (boiler shop); fabricated structural metal

### (G-22604)
### R & S SCREEN PRINTING INC
739 Mchenry Ave (60098-3058)
**PHONE**.................................815 337-3935
Tim Redden, *President*
Ryan Redden, *Vice Pres*
Nancy Redden, *Admin Sec*
**EMP:** 3
**SALES:** 250K **Privately Held**
**SIC:** 2752 Commercial printing, lithographic

### (G-22605)
### RANGER REDI-MIX & MTLS INC
1100 Borden Ln (60098-2320)
**PHONE**.................................815 337-2662
Steve Gavers, *President*
Dan Gavers, *Vice Pres*
**EMP:** 4
**SALES (est):** 445.4K **Privately Held**
**SIC:** 3273 Ready-mixed concrete

### (G-22606)
### S & S MOLD CORPORATION
14431 Trinity Ct (60098-7007)
**PHONE**.................................815 385-0818
Gary Schleicher, *President*
Susan Schleicher, *Vice Pres*
**EMP:** 4
**SQ FT:** 1,800
**SALES (est):** 613.5K **Privately Held**
**WEB:** www.fabrikind.com
**SIC:** 3089 Injection molding of plastics

### (G-22607)
### SAND SCULPTURE CO
327 S Jefferson St (60098-3909)
**PHONE**.................................815 334-9101
Theodore Siebert, *Partner*
Laura Siebert, *Partner*
**EMP:** 4
**SALES:** 350K **Privately Held**
**WEB:** www.sandsculpting.com
**SIC:** 3299 8412 Architectural sculptures: gypsum, clay, papier mache, etc.; museums & art galleries

### (G-22608)
### SERIEN MANUFACTURING INC
Also Called: L M J Tooling & Manufacturing
900 S Eastwood Dr (60098-4639)
P.O. Box 215 (60098-0215)
**PHONE**.................................815 337-1447
**Fax:** 815 337-1427
Tracey A Odishoo, *President*
**EMP:** 5
**SQ FT:** 7,000

**SALES (est):** 400K **Privately Held**
**SIC:** 3541 Machine tools, metal cutting type

### (G-22609)
### SHANNON INDUSTRIAL CORPORATION (PA)
2041 Dillard Ct (60098-6600)
**PHONE**.................................815 337-2349
**Fax:** 815 337-2715
Gerald W Grossi, *President*
Nick Antonelli, *Plant Mgr*
Steve Margolis, *Accounts Mgr*
▲ **EMP:** 10
**SQ FT:** 65,000
**SALES (est):** 22.9MM **Privately Held**
**SIC:** 5162 3087 Plastics materials; custom compound purchased resins

### (G-22610)
### SHANNON INDUSTRIES INC
Also Called: Jones Products Co
114 S Shannon Dr (60098-9475)
**PHONE**.................................815 338-8960
Paul Fitzpatrick, *President*
**EMP:** 7
**SQ FT:** 5,000
**SALES (est):** 640K **Privately Held**
**WEB:** www.theshannongroup.com
**SIC:** 3089 Netting, plastic

### (G-22611)
### SHERWIN-WILLIAMS COMPANY
631 S Eastwood Dr (60098-4632)
**PHONE**.................................815 337-0942
**Fax:** 815 337-0961
**EMP:** 4
**SALES (corp-wide):** 11.8B **Publicly Held**
**SIC:** 5231 5198 2851 Paint & painting supplies; paints, varnishes & supplies; wood fillers or sealers
**PA:** The Sherwin-Williams Company
101 W Prospect Ave # 1020
Cleveland OH 44115
216 566-2000

### (G-22612)
### SILGAN PLASTICS LLC
1005 Courtaulds Dr (60098-7390)
**PHONE**.................................815 334-1200
Leroy Crooks, *Plant Mgr*
James Hill, *Branch Mgr*
**EMP:** 230
**SALES (corp-wide):** 3.6B **Publicly Held**
**WEB:** www.silganplastics.com
**SIC:** 3089 Plastic containers, except foam
**HQ:** Silgan Plastics Llc
14515 North Outer 40 Rd # 210
Chesterfield MO 63017
800 274-5426

### (G-22613)
### SOTOS PALLETS INC
1150 N Rose Farm Rd (60098-9504)
**PHONE**.................................815 338-7750
Raul Soto, *Principal*
**EMP:** 8
**SALES (est):** 1MM **Privately Held**
**SIC:** 2448 Pallets, wood & wood with metal

### (G-22614)
### SUBURBAN SCREW MACHINE PDTS
16210 Us Highway 14 (60098-9477)
**PHONE**.................................815 337-0434
**Fax:** 815 337-0105
Russell Evertsen, *CEO*
Ella Evertsen, *Corp Secy*
Herbert Evertsen, *Vice Pres*
**EMP:** 6
**SQ FT:** 5,000
**SALES (est):** 250K **Privately Held**
**SIC:** 3451 Screw machine products

### (G-22615)
### SUPERIOR X RAY TUBE COMPANY
1220 Claussen Dr (60098-2139)
**PHONE**.................................815 338-4424
**Fax:** 815 338-9452
Mark McDonnell, *President*
Todd Carlson, *Engineer*
**EMP:** 9
**SQ FT:** 9,000

**SALES (est):** 1.2MM **Privately Held**
**WEB:** www.superiorxraytube.com
**SIC:** 3844 X-ray apparatus & tubes

### (G-22616)
### SWS INDUSTRIES INC
Also Called: McGill
280 Prairie Ridge Dr (60098-4183)
**PHONE**.................................904 482-0091
Wayne Schwartzman, *President*
Becki McDaniel, *Exec VP*
▲ **EMP:** 40
**SQ FT:** 57,000
**SALES (est):** 6.1MM **Privately Held**
**WEB:** www.mcgillinc.com
**SIC:** 3579 5044 5199 3544 Binding machines, plastic & adhesive; paper cutters, trimmers & punches; office equipment; art goods & supplies; special dies, tools, jigs & fixtures; heating equipment, except electric; hand & edge tools

### (G-22617)
### T & K TOOL & MANUFACTURING CO
2250 S Eastwood Dr (60098-4608)
P.O. Box 47 (60098-0047)
**PHONE**.................................815 338-0954
**Fax:** 815 338-0233
Robert Thurow, *President*
Erich Thurow, *Admin Sec*
**EMP:** 4 **EST:** 1944
**SQ FT:** 4,800
**SALES (est):** 275K **Privately Held**
**SIC:** 3599 3544 3549 Machine shop, jobbing & repair; special dies, tools, jigs & fixtures; metalworking machinery

### (G-22618)
### T K O WATERPROOF COATING LLP
427 E Judd St (60098-3419)
**PHONE**.................................815 338-2006
Britt Isham, *Managing Prtnr*
**EMP:** 6
**SALES (est):** 884.8K **Privately Held**
**SIC:** 2899 Waterproofing compounds

### (G-22619)
### TU-STAR MANUFACTURING CO INC
1200 Cobblestone Way (60098-5205)
**PHONE**.................................815 338-5760
Doyle E Green, *Owner*
**EMP:** 5
**SQ FT:** 3,000
**SALES (est):** 343.3K **Privately Held**
**SIC:** 3499 3469 3444 Machine bases, metal; metal stampings; sheet metalwork

### (G-22620)
### USA PRINTWORKS LLC
1525 W Lake Shore Dr (60098-6917)
**PHONE**.................................815 206-0854
Jeffrey Richardson, *CEO*
Tania Boon-Richardson, *Manager*
**EMP:** 40
**SALES (est):** 1.1MM **Privately Held**
**SIC:** 2759 Promotional printing

### (G-22621)
### VETERANS PARKING LOT MAINT
240 Mchenry Ave (60098-3452)
**PHONE**.................................815 245-7584
Mark Finn, *Principal*
**EMP:** 2
**SALES:** 100K **Privately Held**
**SIC:** 2951 Asphalt paving mixtures & blocks

### (G-22622)
### WARNER MACHINE PRODUCTS INC
2705 S Il Route 47 (60098-7557)
**PHONE**.................................815 338-2100
**Fax:** 815 338-4949
Stephen L Warner, *President*
Kimberly J Warner, *Admin Sec*
**EMP:** 4
**SQ FT:** 4,000
**SALES (est):** 408.7K **Privately Held**
**WEB:** www.warnermachineproducts.com
**SIC:** 3599 Machine shop, jobbing & repair

### (G-22623)
### WESTERN CONSOLIDATED TECH INC
1425 Lake Ave (60098-7419)
**PHONE**.................................815 334-3684
Kim Kelly, *Opers Staff*
**EMP:** 9
**SALES (est):** 1.7MM **Privately Held**
**SIC:** 3052 Rubber & plastics hose & beltings

### (G-22624)
### WHEELING SERVICE & SUPPLY
Also Called: P V S Manufacturing Div
15920 Nelson Rd (60098-9526)
P.O. Box 189 (60098-0189)
**PHONE**.................................815 338-6410
**Fax:** 815 338-4738
Lawrence J Larson, *President*
Brenda Walter, *Manager*
Lois A Larson, *Admin Sec*
**EMP:** 13
**SQ FT:** 36,000
**SALES (est):** 3.4MM **Privately Held**
**SIC:** 3479 Coating, rust preventive

### (G-22625)
### WILLIAM J KLINE & CO INC
425 Borden St (60098-2132)
**PHONE**.................................815 338-2055
**Fax:** 815 338-2128
Mark Emricson, *President*
Marilyn Kline, *Vice Pres*
Tami Emricson, *Treasurer*
Bev Hodges, *Treasurer*
**EMP:** 12
**SQ FT:** 5,500
**SALES:** 1.2MM **Privately Held**
**SIC:** 3544 Industrial molds

### (G-22626)
### WONDER TUCKY DISTILLERY & BTLG
315 E South St (60098-4219)
**PHONE**.................................224 678-4396
**EMP:** 4
**SALES (est):** 288.1K **Privately Held**
**SIC:** 2086 Bottled & canned soft drinks

### (G-22627)
### WOODSTOCK POWERSPORTS
2055 S Eastwood Dr (60098-4602)
**PHONE**.................................815 308-5705
Karen Randazzo, *Owner*
**EMP:** 2
**SALES (est):** 265.4K **Privately Held**
**SIC:** 3799 All terrain vehicles (ATV)

### (G-22628)
### WOODSTOCK SPECIAL MACHINING
1019 Rail Dr Ste B (60098-9465)
**PHONE**.................................815 338-7383
**Fax:** 815 338-7425
William Awe, *President*
Revene Awe, *Vice Pres*
Thelma R Awe, *Vice Pres*
**EMP:** 2
**SQ FT:** 3,500
**SALES:** 300K **Privately Held**
**SIC:** 3542 Electroforming machines

### (G-22629)
### ZOIA MONUMENT COMPANY
222 Washington St (60098-3307)
**PHONE**.................................815 338-0358
**Fax:** 815 338-0375
James Zoia, *President*
Shirley Zoia, *Corp Secy*
Anthony Zoia, *Manager*
**EMP:** 5
**SQ FT:** 5,000
**SALES (est):** 535.5K **Privately Held**
**SIC:** 5999 3281 Monuments, finished to custom order; cut stone & stone products

## Woosung
### Ogle County

**(G-22630)**
**MIDWEST CEMENT PRODUCTS INC**
809 Central St (61091)
PHONE...............................815 284-2342
**Fax:** 815 284-9372
Douglas Nielsen, *President*
Clarence D Nielsen, *Vice Pres*
**EMP:** 4 **EST:** 1922
**SQ FT:** 2,800
**SALES (est):** 542.2K **Privately Held**
**WEB:** www.midwestcement.com
**SIC:** 3272 3271 Concrete products; concrete block & brick

## Worth
### Cook County

**(G-22631)**
**ACCURATE ELC MTR & PUMP CO**
6955 W 111th St (60482-1824)
PHONE...............................708 448-2792
**Fax:** 708 448-9520
Patrick Macias, *President*
Mark Stabosz, *Vice Pres*
Sue Stabosz, *Manager*
**EMP:** 3
**SQ FT:** 5,000
**SALES:** 2MM **Privately Held**
**SIC:** 5999 7694 7699 5063 Motors, electric; electric motor repair; pumps & pumping equipment repair; motors, electric
**PA:** All Electric Motor Repair & Service, Inc.
6726 S Ashland Ave
Chicago IL 60636
773 925-2404

**(G-22632)**
**AUTO HEAD AND ENGINE EXCHANGE**
Also Called: Worth Auto Parts
6603 W 111th St (60482-1909)
PHONE...............................708 448-8762
Anthony Uzzardo, *President*
Alfred Uzzardo, *Corp Secy*
Theresa Uzzardo, *Manager*
**EMP:** 3
**SQ FT:** 6,500
**SALES:** 300K **Privately Held**
**WEB:** www.autohead.com
**SIC:** 3599 Machine & other job shop work

**(G-22633)**
**BEST ADVERTISING SPC & PRTG**
11437 S Natoma Ave (60482-2131)
PHONE...............................708 448-1110
**Fax:** 708 636-4247
Jerry Janicki, *Owner*
**EMP:** 4
**SQ FT:** 1,000
**SALES:** 80K **Privately Held**
**SIC:** 2752 5947 3993 Offset & photolithographic printing; gift, novelty & souvenir shop; signs & advertising specialties

**(G-22634)**
**MR DVR LLC**
6723 W 111th St (60482-1911)
PHONE...............................708 827-5030
Ayman A Sallouha, *Principal*
**EMP:** 4
**SALES (est):** 455.1K **Privately Held**
**SIC:** 3663 Satellites, communications

**(G-22635)**
**TIMES ENERGY**
11241 S Natoma Ave (60482-1903)
PHONE...............................773 444-9282
Aamer Alobaidi, *Business Mgr*
**EMP:** 3
**SALES (est):** 157K **Privately Held**
**SIC:** 1382 5983 Oil & gas exploration services; fuel oil dealers

## Wyoming
### Stark County

**(G-22636)**
**ALDRICO INC**
Also Called: Aldrich Company
341 E Williams St (61491-1505)
P.O. Box 97 (61491-0097)
PHONE...............................309 695-2311
**Fax:** 309 695-5779
Susan Howard, *President*
Amy Hillan, *Vice Pres*
**EMP:** 22
**SQ FT:** 65,000
**SALES:** 3.7MM **Privately Held**
**WEB:** www.aldrichco.com
**SIC:** 3433 Heating equipment, except electric

**(G-22637)**
**CARDINAL CATTLE**
9736 Modena Rd (61491-9025)
PHONE...............................309 479-1302
Jack Riley, *Owner*
**EMP:** 3
**SALES (est):** 96K **Privately Held**
**SIC:** 0212 3523 Beef cattle except feedlots; cattle feeding, handling & watering equipment

**(G-22638)**
**FMC CORPORATION**
Hwy 17 E (61491)
P.O. Box 180 (61491-0180)
PHONE...............................309 695-2571
**Fax:** 309 695-2407
Bryan Westerby, *Manager*
**EMP:** 20
**SALES (corp-wide):** 3.2B **Publicly Held**
**WEB:** www.fmc.com
**SIC:** 2879 Insecticides, agricultural or household
**PA:** Fmc Corporation
2929 Walnut St
Philadelphia PA 19104
215 299-6668

**(G-22639)**
**QUALITY CABLE & COMPONENTS INC**
109 N Madison Ave (61491-1425)
P.O. Box 88 (61491-0088)
PHONE...............................309 695-3435
**Fax:** 309 695-6006
Cindy M Brittingham, *Owner*
**EMP:** 35
**SQ FT:** 10,000
**SALES (est):** 6.3MM **Privately Held**
**SIC:** 3679 5063 Harness assemblies for electronic use: wire or cable; wire & cable

**(G-22640)**
**STAHL LUMBER COMPANY (PA)**
Also Called: Stahl Ready Mix Concrete
11719 S Galena Ave (61491)
PHONE...............................309 695-4331
**Fax:** 309 695-4332
James I Stahl, *Ch of Bd*
Joanne K Holman, *Corp Secy*
**EMP:** 13 **EST:** 1933
**SQ FT:** 3,000
**SALES (est):** 1.4MM **Privately Held**
**SIC:** 3273 1521 5211 Ready-mixed concrete; single-family housing construction; lumber & other building materials

**(G-22641)**
**STAHL LUMBER COMPANY**
Also Called: Stahl Ready Concrete
117 S Galena Ave (61491-1407)
PHONE...............................309 385-2552
James Stahl, *Manager*
**EMP:** 10
**SALES (corp-wide):** 1.7MM **Privately Held**
**SIC:** 3273 Ready-mixed concrete
**PA:** Stahl Lumber Company
11719 S Galena Ave
Wyoming IL 61491
309 695-4331

**(G-22642)**
**YER KILN ME LLC**
108 N 7th St (61491-4406)
PHONE...............................309 606-9007
Cox Nicole, *Principal*
**EMP:** 3 **EST:** 2015
**SALES (est):** 155.2K **Privately Held**
**SIC:** 3559 Kilns

## Xenia
### Clay County

**(G-22643)**
**BRENDA MILLER**
Also Called: M & W Curios
130 Old Highway 50 (62899-2291)
PHONE...............................618 678-2639
**Fax:** 618 678-2640
Brenda Miller, *Owner*
**EMP:** 6 **EST:** 1996
**SALES (est):** 467.9K **Privately Held**
**WEB:** www.brendamiller.com
**SIC:** 3231 Glass sheet, bent: made from purchased glass

**(G-22644)**
**M D HARMON INC (PA)**
752 Jupiter Dr (62899)
P.O. Box 196 (62899-0196)
PHONE...............................618 662-8925
Martin Harmon, *President*
Ryan Harmon, *Admin Sec*
**EMP:** 11
**SQ FT:** 22,000
**SALES:** 800K **Privately Held**
**SIC:** 2421 0212 Sawmills & planing mills, general; beef cattle except feedlots

**(G-22645)**
**XENIA MFG INC (PA)**
1507 Church St (62899-1283)
P.O. Box 237 (62899-0237)
PHONE...............................618 678-2218
Paul Andrew Knapp, *President*
Rick L Forth, *Corp Secy*
Charles Knapp, *Vice Pres*
Ed Knapp, *Vice Pres*
Bob Pieplow, *Purch Mgr*
**EMP:** 140
**SQ FT:** 40,000
**SALES:** 22MM **Privately Held**
**WEB:** www.xmiharness.com
**SIC:** 3694 Harness wiring sets, internal combustion engines

## Yates City
### Knox County

**(G-22646)**
**BURT COYOTE CO**
104 N Union St (61572-7521)
P.O. Box 165 (61572-0165)
PHONE...............................309 358-1602
Curtis Price, *President*
Eric Price, *Vice Pres*
Ivan Price, *Vice Pres*
**EMP:** 14
**SQ FT:** 1,232
**SALES (est):** 1.7MM **Privately Held**
**WEB:** www.burtcoyote.com
**SIC:** 3949 Archery equipment, general

## Yorkville
### Kendall County

**(G-22647)**
**ABBA PLASTICS INC**
207 Beaver St (60560-1706)
PHONE...............................630 385-2156
Michael Corum, *President*
Doug Downing, *Manager*
**EMP:** 5
**SQ FT:** 4,800
**SALES (est):** 526K **Privately Held**
**SIC:** 3089 Injection molding of plastics

**(G-22648)**
**ALPHA PRECISION INC**
9750 Rte 126 (60560)
PHONE...............................630 553-7331
Kevin W Brolsma, *President*
Jake Brolsma, *Business Mgr*
Tom Schiffer, *Plant Mgr*
**EMP:** 19
**SQ FT:** 10,000
**SALES (est):** 2.3MM **Privately Held**
**WEB:** www.alphaprecision.com
**SIC:** 3229 Pressed & blown glass

**(G-22649)**
**ANDREW TOSCHAK**
1025 Mchugh Rd (60560-1228)
PHONE...............................630 553-3434
Andrew Toschak, *President*
**EMP:** 3
**SALES (est):** 212K **Privately Held**
**SIC:** 3599 Machine shop, jobbing & repair

**(G-22650)**
**AURORA SPCLTY TXTLES GROUP INC**
2705 N Bridge St (60560-9256)
P.O. Box 70, Aurora (60507-0070)
PHONE...............................800 864-0303
**Fax:** 630 892-1706
Robert P Matz, *President*
Marcia Ayala, *Vice Pres*
Kathy Murphy, *Vice Pres*
Daniel Laturno, *VP Opers*
Alexis Vonesh, *Purch Mgr*
▼ **EMP:** 78
**SALES (est):** 27.1MM
**SALES (corp-wide):** 374.1MM **Privately Held**
**SIC:** 2261 2231 Finishing plants, cotton; broadwoven fabric mills, wool
**PA:** Meridian Industries, Inc.
735 N Water St Ste 630
Milwaukee WI 53202
414 224-0610

**(G-22651)**
**CHARTNET TECHNOLOGIES INC**
220 Garden St (60560-8921)
P.O. Box 285, Hudson OH (44236-0285)
PHONE...............................630 385-4100
Lee Tkachuk, *CEO*
Tom Trainor, *CFO*
**EMP:** 11
**SALES:** 300K **Privately Held**
**WEB:** www.chartnettech.com
**SIC:** 7372 Prepackaged software

**(G-22652)**
**CIVILIAN FORCE ARMS INC**
1208b Badger St (60560-1701)
PHONE...............................630 926-6982
Yonas Hagos, *CEO*
Ernest Johnson, *Marketing Staff*
Armando Velasquez, *Shareholder*
**EMP:** 3 **EST:** 2014
**SALES (est):** 324.8K **Privately Held**
**SIC:** 3484 3482 5091 5099 Guns (firearms) or gun parts, 30 mm. & below; small arms ammunition; firearms, sporting; firearms, except sporting; firearms

**(G-22653)**
**D AND K PLASTICS**
2127 State Route 47 (60560-4521)
P.O. Box 668 (60560-0668)
PHONE...............................712 723-5372
**Fax:** 630 553-9268
Cheri Little, *Owner*
**EMP:** 4
**SQ FT:** 3,800
**SALES (est):** 338.3K **Privately Held**
**SIC:** 3599 5162 Machine shop, jobbing & repair; plastics sheets & rods

**(G-22654)**
**DANKO INDUSTRIES**
181 Wolf St Unit C (60560-1955)
PHONE...............................630 882-6070
Ernest Brain, *Owner*
**EMP:** 5
**SALES (est):** 569.3K **Privately Held**
**SIC:** 3999 Manufacturing industries

# Yorkville - Kendall County (G-22655)

## GEOGRAPHIC SECTION

**(G-22655)**
**DEVICE TECHNOLOGIES INC**
1211 Badger St Ste H  (60560-1785)
PHONE .................................. 630 553-7178
Richard Kunzelman, *President*
Susan Kunzelman, *Treasurer*
EMP: 3
SQ FT: 4,000
SALES (est): 500K **Privately Held**
SIC: 7389  3599  7692  Design, commercial & industrial; machine shop, jobbing & repair; welding repair

**(G-22656)**
**DEYCO INC**
Also Called: Meryll 200000 Mile Check
102 Beaver St  (60560-1703)
PHONE .................................. 630 553-5666
Terry Young, *President*
EMP: 8
SALES (est): 309.9K **Privately Held**
SIC: 7539  3535  8711  2399  Automotive repair shops; unit handling conveying systems; engineering services; seat belts, automobile & aircraft

**(G-22657)**
**EDWARD J WARREN JR**
Also Called: Tdr Transport
2921 Alden Ave  (60560-4698)
PHONE .................................. 630 882-8817
Edward J Warren Jr, *Principal*
EMP: 4
SALES (est): 365.9K **Privately Held**
SIC: 3537  7389  Trucks: freight, baggage, etc.; industrial, except mining;

**(G-22658)**
**FLURRY INDUSTRIES INC**
2002 Prairie Rose Ln  (60560-1912)
PHONE .................................. 630 882-8361
Christopher Maury, *President*
EMP: 5
SALES (est): 405.7K **Privately Held**
SIC: 3999  Manufacturing industries

**(G-22659)**
**FOX VALLEY SANDBLASTING INC**
1211 Badger St  (60560-1783)
P.O. Box 63  (60560-0063)
PHONE .................................. 630 553-6050
James Schwebke, *President*
Andrea Schwebke, *Admin Sec*
EMP: 2
SALES (est): 484.7K **Privately Held**
SIC: 1799  3471  Exterior cleaning, including sandblasting; plating & polishing

**(G-22660)**
**FREEMANS SPORTS INC**
129 E Hydraulic St  (60560-1529)
PHONE .................................. 630 553-0515
Fax: 630 553-7151
Bonnie Freeman, *President*
Eric Freeman, *Vice Pres*
Greg Freeman, *Vice Pres*
EMP: 4
SQ FT: 2,025
SALES (est): 492.8K **Privately Held**
WEB: www.freemansports.com
SIC: 3949  5941  Fishing tackle, general; ice skates, parts & accessories; bobsleds; bait & tackle

**(G-22661)**
**H E ASSOCIATES INC**
201 Beaver St  (60560-1706)
PHONE .................................. 630 553-6382
Fax: 630 553-7648
Harvey A Knell, *President*
Margaret Knell, *Corp Secy*
EMP: 15
SALES (est): 2.2MM **Privately Held**
SIC: 3089  3645  3423  Planters, plastic; residential lighting fixtures; hand & edge tools

**(G-22662)**
**KENDALL COUNTY RECORD (PA)**
109 W Veterans Pkwy  (60560-1905)
PHONE .................................. 630 553-7034
Fax: 630 553-7085
Jeff Farren, *President*
Kathleen Farren, *Principal*
Roger Matile, *Advt Staff*
EMP: 22 EST: 1864
SQ FT: 5,000
SALES (est): 1.3MM **Privately Held**
WEB: www.kcrecord.com
SIC: 2711  Newspapers

**(G-22663)**
**KENDALL PRINTING CO**
948 N Bridge St  (60560-1109)
PHONE .................................. 630 553-9200
Fax: 630 553-9201
Annette Powell, *Owner*
EMP: 3
SQ FT: 1,000
SALES (est): 324.7K **Privately Held**
SIC: 2752  2791  2789  Commercial printing, offset; typesetting; bookbinding & related work

**(G-22664)**
**MCKILLIP INDUSTRIES INC (PA)**
Also Called: Usa/Docufinish
207 Beaver St  (60560-1706)
PHONE .................................. 815 439-1050
John McKillip MBA, *CEO*
Jason Lambert, *Vice Pres*
Greg Gryzlak, *CFO*
Robert Szablewski, *Admin Sec*
EMP: 45
SQ FT: 50,000
SALES (est): 7.8MM **Privately Held**
WEB: www.usadocufinish.com
SIC: 2759  Commercial printing

**(G-22665)**
**MEADOWVALE INC**
109 Beaver St  (60560-1797)
PHONE .................................. 630 553-0202
Fax: 630 553-0262
Steve Steinwart, *President*
Marl Kloster, *Plant Mgr*
Mark Newport, *QC Mgr*
Jason Leslie, *VP Sales*
Eduardo Cajina, *Marketing Staff*
EMP: 20 EST: 1967
SQ FT: 15,000
SALES (est): 5.5MM **Privately Held**
WEB: www.meadowvale-inc.com
SIC: 2023  Ice cream mix, unfrozen: liquid or dry; milkshake mix

**(G-22666)**
**OLIVE LECLAIRE OIL CO**
1524 Coral Dr  (60560-3060)
PHONE .................................. 888 255-1867
EMP: 3
SALES (est): 110.5K **Privately Held**
SIC: 2079  Olive oil

**(G-22667)**
**OMALLEY WELDING AND FABG**
1209 Badger St  (60560-1702)
PHONE .................................. 630 553-1604
Fax: 630 553-1605
Mark O'Malley, *President*
EMP: 3
SQ FT: 6,500
SALES (est): 750K **Privately Held**
SIC: 3449  Bars, concrete reinforcing: fabricated steel

**(G-22668)**
**P M MFG SERVICES INC**
9626 Lisbon Rd  (60560-9338)
PHONE .................................. 630 553-6924
Dawn E Mulligan, *President*
Paul Mulligan, *Vice Pres*
EMP: 3
SQ FT: 2,400
SALES: 200K **Privately Held**
WEB: www.fiberfin.com
SIC: 3599  3357  Machine shop, jobbing & repair; nonferrous wiredrawing & insulating

**(G-22669)**
**PREMIUM PRODUCTS INC**
207 Wolf St  (60560-1739)
P.O. Box 9335, Naperville  (60567-0335)
PHONE .................................. 630 553-6160
Fax: 630 553-6118
D G Dhake, *President*
EMP: 12
SQ FT: 25,000
SALES: 7MM **Privately Held**
WEB: www.premiumproductsinc.com
SIC: 2851  Paints & allied products

**(G-22670)**
**PRIMEDIA SOURCE LLC**
627 White Oak Way  (60560-9581)
PHONE .................................. 630 553-8451
Jennifer Cherney, *President*
EMP: 1
SALES (est): 238.5K **Privately Held**
WEB: www.primediasource.com
SIC: 5112  2672  5085  5113  Stationery & office supplies; adhesive papers, labels or tapes: from purchased material; industrial supplies; shipping supplies; labels & seals: printing; flexographic printing

**(G-22671)**
**STRAUSBERGER ASSOC SLS & MKTG**
Also Called: Jns Glass Coating
621 White Oak Way  (60560-9244)
PHONE .................................. 630 553-3447
Joseph Strausberger, *President*
EMP: 6 EST: 1995
SQ FT: 3,000
SALES: 2MM **Privately Held**
WEB: www.strausberger.com
SIC: 3827  Optical instruments & lenses

**(G-22672)**
**TIEM ENGINEERING CORPORATION**
202 Beaver St  (60560-1705)
P.O. Box 790  (60560-0790)
PHONE .................................. 630 553-7484
Fax: 630 553-6097
John Lovetere, *President*
Philip D Lovetere, *Corp Secy*
David Lovetere, *Vice Pres*
Lori Eallonardo, *Info Tech Mgr*
Marianne Linebaugh, *Shareholder*
EMP: 10
SQ FT: 20,000
SALES: 934.5K **Privately Held**
WEB: www.tiemengineering.com
SIC: 4783  2759  Packing goods for shipping; labels & seals: printing

**(G-22673)**
**TITAN INJECTION PARTS & SVC**
Also Called: Tips
204 Beaver St Ste A  (60560-1995)
P.O. Box 547  (60560-0547)
PHONE .................................. 630 882-8455
Jaime Torres, *President*
Ricardo Valle, *Vice Pres*
EMP: 5
SALES (est): 1MM **Privately Held**
WEB: www.tipsinc.us
SIC: 3556  Smokers, food processing equipment

**(G-22674)**
**VALLEY RUN STONE INC**
6369 Whitetail Ridge Ct  (60560-3239)
PHONE .................................. 630 553-7974
Maryl Betzwiser, *President*
Grant Avery, *Owner*
David Avery, *Vice Pres*
Mike Avery, *Vice Pres*
EMP: 20 EST: 1946
SALES (est): 1.7MM **Privately Held**
SIC: 1442  Gravel & pebble mining

**(G-22675)**
**WATER PRODUCTS COMPANY ILL INC**
Cascade Water Works
1213 Badger St  (60560-1702)
PHONE .................................. 630 553-0840
Fax: 630 553-0181
Sam Eskew, *Branch Mgr*
EMP: 20
SALES (corp-wide): 20.5MM **Privately Held**
SIC: 3569  Filters & strainers, pipeline
PA: Water Products Company Of Illinois, Inc.
3255 E New York St
Aurora IL 60504
630 898-6100

**(G-22676)**
**WISE CONSTRUCTION SERVICES**
1107 S Bridge St Ste E  (60560-1747)
PHONE .................................. 630 553-6350
Joseph Wisniewski, *President*
Beverly Weeks, *Manager*
EMP: 3
SALES (est): 308.1K **Privately Held**
WEB: www.wiseconstruction.net
SIC: 5719  3292  Wicker, rattan or reed home furnishings; wick, asbestos

**(G-22677)**
**WRIGLEY MANUFACTURING CO LLC**
Also Called: Wrigley's
2800 State Route 47  (60560-9441)
PHONE .................................. 630 553-4800
William Walsh, *Vice Pres*
Tim Gydan, *Engineer*
Bill Moskites, *Engineer*
Rita White, *Marketing Mgr*
Lupe Alvarez, *Manager*
EMP: 400
SALES (corp-wide): 35B **Privately Held**
WEB: www.wrigleys.com
SIC: 2067  2064  Chewing gum; candy & other confectionery products
HQ: Wrigley Manufacturing Company Llc
410 N Michigan Ave
Chicago IL 60611
312 644-2121

## Zion
*Lake County*

**(G-22678)**
**ANDERSSON TOOL & DIE LLP**
1717 Kenosha Rd  (60099-9342)
PHONE .................................. 847 746-8866
Fax: 847 746-8871
Rolf A Andersson, *Partner*
George Andersson, *Partner*
Carol Andersson, *Office Mgr*
EMP: 12
SQ FT: 6,000
SALES (est): 60K **Privately Held**
SIC: 3599  3544  Machine shop, jobbing & repair; special dies, tools, jigs & fixtures

**(G-22679)**
**ATLANTIC ENGINEERING**
42008 N Delany Rd  (60099-9661)
PHONE .................................. 847 782-1762
Fax: 847 878-3009
Henry Scheffner, *Owner*
EMP: 2
SQ FT: 3,500
SALES: 200K **Privately Held**
SIC: 3469  3544  Stamping metal for the trade; special dies, tools, jigs & fixtures

**(G-22680)**
**CORAL CHEMICAL COMPANY**
1915 Industrial Ave  (60099-1435)
PHONE .................................. 847 246-6666
Joseph D Pemberton, *Principal*
EMP: 40
SALES (corp-wide): 20.5MM **Privately Held**
WEB: www.coral.com
SIC: 2842  2812  Cleaning or polishing preparations; alkalies & chlorine
PA: Coral Chemical Company
1915 Indusrial Ave
Zion IL 60099
847 246-6666

**(G-22681)**
**D & M TOOL LLC**
2013 Horizon Ct  (60099-1488)
PHONE .................................. 847 731-3600
Fax: 847 731-3800
Dave Velcover, *Owner*
EMP: 4
SQ FT: 3,750
SALES: 400K **Privately Held**
SIC: 3599  3544  Machine shop, jobbing & repair; special dies, tools, jigs & fixtures

## GEOGRAPHIC SECTION
### Zion - Lake County (G-22701)

**(G-22682)**
**DILL BROTHERS INC**
3401 20th St (60099-1492)
PHONE..................................847 746-8323
Fax: 847 746-0163
William E Dill, *President*
Evelyn Dill, *Corp Secy*
David Morgan, *Engineer*
**EMP:** 18 **EST:** 1957
**SQ FT:** 42,000
**SALES (est):** 3.2MM **Privately Held**
**WEB:** www.dill-bros.com
**SIC:** 3599 3443 3441 Machine shop; jobbing & repair; custom machinery; fabricated plate work (boiler shop); fabricated structural metal

**(G-22683)**
**DYNACOIL INC**
2000 Lewis Ave (60099-1546)
PHONE..................................847 731-3300
Tony Devito, *President*
Henry Demeyer, *General Mgr*
Peter Dosedla, *Vice Pres*
Mike Burns, *Project Mgr*
Bill Steinhoff, *Project Mgr*
**EMP:** 45
**SQ FT:** 35,000
**SALES (est):** 13.2MM **Privately Held**
**WEB:** www.dynacoil.com
**SIC:** 3444 Sheet metalwork

**(G-22684)**
**ERA TOOL AND MANUFACTURING CO**
3200 16th St (60099-1416)
PHONE..................................847 298-6333
Fax: 847 298-6355
Rosa Molina, *Ch of Bd*
Robert J Lonze, *President*
Howard Jack, *Vice Pres*
Pat Carter, *Manager*
Fredeick Schutter, *Manager*
**EMP:** 40 **EST:** 1937
**SQ FT:** 20,000
**SALES (est):** 7.2MM **Privately Held**
**SIC:** 3469 3544 Stamping metal for the trade; die sets for metal stamping (presses)

**(G-22685)**
**FEDERAL EQUIPMENT & SVCS INC**
3200 16th St (60099-1416)
PHONE..................................847 731-9002
Rosa Molina, *President*
Abades Duluata, *General Mgr*
▲ **EMP:** 10
**SQ FT:** 10,000
**SALES (est):** 1.2MM **Privately Held**
**SIC:** 5198 3363 Paints, varnishes & supplies; aluminum die-castings

**(G-22686)**
**GRAPHIC PARTNERS INC**
Also Called: GP
4300 Il Route 173 (60099-4089)
PHONE..................................847 872-9445
Fax: 847 746-7651
Arthur Larsen, *President*
Judy Burgess, *Vice Pres*
Kirk Larsen, *Vice Pres*
Keith Love, *Vice Pres*
Daniel Sikora, *Admin Sec*
**EMP:** 50
**SQ FT:** 26,000
**SALES (est):** 1.1MM **Privately Held**
**WEB:** www.graphicpartners.com
**SIC:** 2752 Commercial printing, lithographic; advertising posters, lithographed; post cards, picture: lithographed

**(G-22687)**
**H A FRIEND & COMPANY INC (PA)**
1535 Lewis Ave (60099-1493)
PHONE..................................847 746-1248
Fax: 847 746-4962
Richard W Friend Sr, *Ch of Bd*
William F Friend, *President*
Randy Friend, *Corp Secy*
Richard Friend Jr, *Vice Pres*
**EMP:** 37
**SQ FT:** 40,000
**SALES (est):** 3.4MM **Privately Held**
**SIC:** 2759 5112 5021 5044 Embossing on paper; office supplies; office furniture; office equipment

**(G-22688)**
**IVANHOE INDUSTRIES INC**
3333 20th St (60099-1486)
PHONE..................................847 872-3311
Fax: 847 872-3328
Hung Tran, *General Mgr*
Heather Klausch, *Purch Agent*
Teri Popp, *Bookkeeper*
Faye Blanton, *Cust Mgr*
Dan Hamlet, *Manager*
**EMP:** 20
**SQ FT:** 16,000
**SALES (corp-wide):** 11.1MM **Privately Held**
**WEB:** www.ivanhoeind.com
**SIC:** 5169 2869 2842 Chemicals & allied products; industrial organic chemicals; specialty cleaning, polishes & sanitation goods
**PA:** Ivanhoe Industries Inc.
26267 N Hickory Rd
Mundelein IL 60060
847 566-7170

**(G-22689)**
**JOSEPH KRISTAN**
Also Called: J & J Powder Coating
2805 Ebenezer Ave (60099-2753)
PHONE..................................847 731-3131
Joseph Kristan, *Owner*
**EMP:** 3
**SALES (est):** 204.4K **Privately Held**
**SIC:** 3479 Coating of metals & formed products

**(G-22690)**
**K-LOG INC**
Also Called: Vast Market
1224 27th St Zion (60099)
P.O. Box 5 (60099-0005)
PHONE..................................847 872-6611
Fax: 847 872-3728
Timothy C Klebe, *President*
John Murphy, *COO*
Linda Lester, *Vice Pres*
Lisa Johnson, *Accounting Mgr*
Gary Klebe, *Marketing Mgr*
▼ **EMP:** 30
**SQ FT:** 6,000
**SALES (est):** 9.6MM **Privately Held**
**WEB:** www.k-log.com
**SIC:** 2621 5021 2522 2531 Catalog, magazine & newsprint papers; office & public building furniture; office furniture, except wood; school furniture; wood office furniture

**(G-22691)**
**MC KINNEY STEEL & SALES INC**
813 29th St (60099-3263)
PHONE..................................847 746-3344
Fax: 847 746-6516
Ryan Rodbro, *President*
Ron Gossman, *Project Mgr*
Juliana Calbruner, *Accounting Mgr*
Debra Rodbro, *Admin Sec*
**EMP:** 20
**SQ FT:** 20,000
**SALES (est):** 5.4MM **Privately Held**
**WEB:** www.mckinneysteel.com
**SIC:** 3441 Fabricated structural metal

**(G-22692)**
**NORTHPOINT HEATING & AIR COND**
1101 Shiloh Blvd Rear 2 (60099-2602)
P.O. Box 303, Winthrop Harbor (60096-0303)
PHONE..................................847 731-1067
Paul Sheppard, *Owner*
**EMP:** 4
**SALES (est):** 258.8K **Privately Held**
**SIC:** 3567 Industrial furnaces & ovens

**(G-22693)**
**OLIVE TREE FOODS INC**
2439 Galilee Ave (60099-2908)
PHONE..................................847 872-2762
Craig Peterson, *Principal*
**EMP:** 4
**SALES (est):** 325K **Privately Held**
**SIC:** 3421 Table & food cutlery, including butchers'

**(G-22694)**
**ONCQUEST**
Also Called: Oncquest Pharma
43323 N Oak Crest Ln (60099-9413)
PHONE..................................847 682-4703
Richard J Pariza, *Principal*
Kathryn Pariza, *Principal*
**EMP:** 5
**SALES (est):** 310.5K **Privately Held**
**SIC:** 2834 Pharmaceutical preparations

**(G-22695)**
**PARAMOUNT SINTERED PDTS LLP**
1717 Kenosha Rd (60099-9342)
PHONE..................................847 746-8866
George Anderson, *Partner*
Rolf Andersson, *Partner*
David Johnson, *Partner*
**EMP:** 5
**SQ FT:** 7,000
**SALES (est):** 474.9K **Privately Held**
**SIC:** 3599 Machine shop, jobbing & repair

**(G-22696)**
**S & D DEVELOPMENT & PROTOTYPE**
Also Called: Pit Pal Product
2009 Horizon Ct (60099-1488)
PHONE..................................847 872-7257
Fax: 847 872-7258
David De Vito, *President*
Jody Schmeisser, *Vice Pres*
Chris Burden, *Sales Mgr*
Steve Smith, *Sales Mgr*
Jennifer Langer, *Sales Associate*
**EMP:** 18
**SALES (est):** 2.9MM **Privately Held**
**WEB:** www.pitpal.com
**SIC:** 3599 Machine shop, jobbing & repair

**(G-22697)**
**S & G IRON WORKS**
2173 Galilee Ave (60099-2226)
Fax: 847 395-6325
Stephan Sarver, *Owner*
**EMP:** 4
**SQ FT:** 3,200
**SALES (est):** 442.5K **Privately Held**
**SIC:** 3446 Stairs, staircases, stair treads: prefabricated metal

**(G-22698)**
**UNITED COMMUNICATIONS CORP**
2711 Sheridan Rd Ste 202 (60099-2650)
PHONE..................................847 746-1515
**EMP:** 118
**SALES (corp-wide):** 64.2MM **Privately Held**
**SIC:** 2711 Newspapers-Publishing/Printing
**PA:** United Communications Corporation
5800 7th Ave
Kenosha WI 53140
262 657-1000

**(G-22699)**
**UNITED COMMUNICATIONS CORP**
Bargineer
2711 Shrridon Rd Unit 202 (60099)
P.O. Box 111 (60099-0111)
PHONE..................................847 746-4700
Frank Misureli, *Manager*
**EMP:** 20
**SALES (corp-wide):** 73.4MM **Privately Held**
**WEB:** www.kenoshanews.com
**SIC:** 2711 Newspapers
**PA:** United Communications Corporation
5800 7th Ave
Kenosha WI 53140
262 657-1000

**(G-22700)**
**WAUKEGAN ARCHITECTURAL INC**
3505 16th St (60099-1421)
PHONE..................................847 746-9077
Fax: 847 746-9080
Michael Maglio, *President*
▲ **EMP:** 8
**SQ FT:** 8,000
**SALES (est):** 1.2MM **Privately Held**
**SIC:** 3446 3444 3442 3341 Ornamental metalwork; sheet metalwork; metal doors, sash & trim; secondary nonferrous metals

**(G-22701)**
**WHITESIDE DRAPERY FABRICATORS**
2701 Deborah Ave Ste A (60099-2793)
PHONE..................................847 746-5300
Fax: 847 746-5300
Bryan Mueller, *President*
Jon Whiteside, *Corp Secy*
**EMP:** 17
**SQ FT:** 15,000
**SALES (est):** 1.5MM **Privately Held**
**SIC:** 2391 Draperies, plastic & textile: from purchased materials

# SIC INDEX

*Standard Industrial Classification Alphabetical Index*

| SIC NO | PRODUCT |
|---|---|

## A

3291 Abrasive Prdts
2891 Adhesives & Sealants
3563 Air & Gas Compressors
3585 Air Conditioning & Heating Eqpt
3721 Aircraft
3724 Aircraft Engines & Engine Parts
3728 Aircraft Parts & Eqpt, NEC
2812 Alkalies & Chlorine
3363 Aluminum Die Castings
3354 Aluminum Extruded Prdts
3365 Aluminum Foundries
3355 Aluminum Rolling & Drawing, NEC
3353 Aluminum Sheet, Plate & Foil
3483 Ammunition, Large
3826 Analytical Instruments
2077 Animal, Marine Fats & Oils
1231 Anthracite Mining
2389 Apparel & Accessories, NEC
2387 Apparel Belts
3446 Architectural & Ornamental Metal Work
7694 Armature Rewinding Shops
3292 Asbestos products
2952 Asphalt Felts & Coatings
3822 Automatic Temperature Controls
3581 Automatic Vending Machines
3465 Automotive Stampings
2396 Automotive Trimmings, Apparel Findings, Related Prdts

## B

2673 Bags: Plastics, Laminated & Coated
2674 Bags: Uncoated Paper & Multiwall
3562 Ball & Roller Bearings
2836 Biological Prdts, Exc Diagnostic Substances
1221 Bituminous Coal & Lignite: Surface Mining
1222 Bituminous Coal: Underground Mining
2782 Blankbooks & Looseleaf Binders
3312 Blast Furnaces, Coke Ovens, Steel & Rolling Mills
3564 Blowers & Fans
3732 Boat Building & Repairing
3452 Bolts, Nuts, Screws, Rivets & Washers
2732 Book Printing, Not Publishing
2789 Bookbinding
2731 Books: Publishing & Printing
3131 Boot & Shoe Cut Stock & Findings
2342 Brassieres, Girdles & Garments
2051 Bread, Bakery Prdts Exc Cookies & Crackers
3251 Brick & Structural Clay Tile
3991 Brooms & Brushes
3995 Burial Caskets
2021 Butter

## C

3578 Calculating & Accounting Eqpt
2064 Candy & Confectionery Prdts
2033 Canned Fruits, Vegetables & Preserves
2032 Canned Specialties
2394 Canvas Prdts
3624 Carbon & Graphite Prdts
2895 Carbon Black
3955 Carbon Paper & Inked Ribbons
3592 Carburetors, Pistons, Rings & Valves
2273 Carpets & Rugs
2823 Cellulosic Man-Made Fibers
3241 Cement, Hydraulic
3253 Ceramic Tile
2043 Cereal Breakfast Foods
2022 Cheese
1479 Chemical & Fertilizer Mining
2899 Chemical Preparations, NEC
2067 Chewing Gum
2361 Children's & Infants' Dresses & Blouses
3261 China Plumbing Fixtures & Fittings
3262 China, Table & Kitchen Articles
2066 Chocolate & Cocoa Prdts
2111 Cigarettes
2121 Cigars
2257 Circular Knit Fabric Mills
3255 Clay Refractories
1459 Clay, Ceramic & Refractory Minerals, NEC
1241 Coal Mining Svcs
3479 Coating & Engraving, NEC
2095 Coffee
3316 Cold Rolled Steel Sheet, Strip & Bars
3582 Commercial Laundry, Dry Clean & Pressing Mchs
2759 Commercial Printing
2754 Commercial Printing: Gravure
2752 Commercial Printing: Lithographic
3646 Commercial, Indl & Institutional Lighting Fixtures
3669 Communications Eqpt, NEC
3577 Computer Peripheral Eqpt, NEC
3572 Computer Storage Devices
3575 Computer Terminals
3271 Concrete Block & Brick
3272 Concrete Prdts
3531 Construction Machinery & Eqpt
1442 Construction Sand & Gravel
2679 Converted Paper Prdts, NEC
3535 Conveyors & Eqpt
2052 Cookies & Crackers
3366 Copper Foundries
1021 Copper Ores
2298 Cordage & Twine
2653 Corrugated & Solid Fiber Boxes
3961 Costume Jewelry & Novelties
2261 Cotton Fabric Finishers
2211 Cotton, Woven Fabric
2074 Cottonseed Oil Mills
3466 Crowns & Closures
1311 Crude Petroleum & Natural Gas
1423 Crushed & Broken Granite
1422 Crushed & Broken Limestone
1429 Crushed & Broken Stone, NEC
3643 Current-Carrying Wiring Devices
2391 Curtains & Draperies
3087 Custom Compounding Of Purchased Plastic Resins
3281 Cut Stone Prdts
3421 Cutlery
2865 Cyclic-Crudes, Intermediates, Dyes & Org Pigments

## D

3843 Dental Eqpt & Splys
2835 Diagnostic Substances
2675 Die-Cut Paper & Board
3544 Dies, Tools, Jigs, Fixtures & Indl Molds
1411 Dimension Stone
2047 Dog & Cat Food
3942 Dolls & Stuffed Toys
2591 Drapery Hardware, Window Blinds & Shades
2381 Dress & Work Gloves
2034 Dried Fruits, Vegetables & Soup
1381 Drilling Oil & Gas Wells

## E

3263 Earthenware, Whiteware, Table & Kitchen Articles
3634 Electric Household Appliances
3641 Electric Lamps
3694 Electrical Eqpt For Internal Combustion Engines
3629 Electrical Indl Apparatus, NEC
3699 Electrical Machinery, Eqpt & Splys, NEC
3845 Electromedical & Electrotherapeutic Apparatus
3313 Electrometallurgical Prdts
3675 Electronic Capacitors
3677 Electronic Coils & Transformers
3679 Electronic Components, NEC
3571 Electronic Computers
3678 Electronic Connectors
3676 Electronic Resistors
3471 Electroplating, Plating, Polishing, Anodizing & Coloring
3534 Elevators & Moving Stairways
3431 Enameled Iron & Metal Sanitary Ware
2677 Envelopes
2892 Explosives

## F

2241 Fabric Mills, Cotton, Wool, Silk & Man-Made
3499 Fabricated Metal Prdts, NEC
3498 Fabricated Pipe & Pipe Fittings
3443 Fabricated Plate Work
3069 Fabricated Rubber Prdts, NEC
3441 Fabricated Structural Steel
2399 Fabricated Textile Prdts, NEC
2295 Fabrics Coated Not Rubberized
2297 Fabrics, Nonwoven
3523 Farm Machinery & Eqpt
3965 Fasteners, Buttons, Needles & Pins
2875 Fertilizers, Mixing Only
2655 Fiber Cans, Tubes & Drums
2091 Fish & Seafoods, Canned & Cured
2092 Fish & Seafoods, Fresh & Frozen
3211 Flat Glass
2087 Flavoring Extracts & Syrups
2045 Flour, Blended & Prepared
2041 Flour, Grain Milling
3824 Fluid Meters & Counters
3593 Fluid Power Cylinders & Actuators
3594 Fluid Power Pumps & Motors
3492 Fluid Power Valves & Hose Fittings
2657 Folding Paperboard Boxes
3556 Food Prdts Machinery
2099 Food Preparations, NEC
3149 Footwear, NEC
2053 Frozen Bakery Prdts
2037 Frozen Fruits, Juices & Vegetables
2038 Frozen Specialties
2371 Fur Goods
2599 Furniture & Fixtures, NEC

## G

3944 Games, Toys & Children's Vehicles
3524 Garden, Lawn Tractors & Eqpt
3053 Gaskets, Packing & Sealing Devices
2369 Girls' & Infants' Outerwear, NEC
3221 Glass Containers
3231 Glass Prdts Made Of Purchased Glass
1041 Gold Ores
3321 Gray Iron Foundries
2771 Greeting Card Publishing
3769 Guided Missile/Space Vehicle Parts & Eqpt, NEC
3764 Guided Missile/Space Vehicle Propulsion Units & parts
3761 Guided Missiles & Space Vehicles
2861 Gum & Wood Chemicals
3275 Gypsum Prdts

## H

3423 Hand & Edge Tools
3425 Hand Saws & Saw Blades
3171 Handbags & Purses
3429 Hardware, NEC
2426 Hardwood Dimension & Flooring Mills
2435 Hardwood Veneer & Plywood
2353 Hats, Caps & Millinery
3433 Heating Eqpt
3536 Hoists, Cranes & Monorails
2252 Hosiery, Except Women's
2251 Hosiery, Women's Full & Knee Length
2392 House furnishings: Textile
3639 Household Appliances, NEC
3651 Household Audio & Video Eqpt
3631 Household Cooking Eqpt
2519 Household Furniture, NEC
3633 Household Laundry Eqpt
3632 Household Refrigerators & Freezers
3635 Household Vacuum Cleaners

## I

2097 Ice
2024 Ice Cream
2819 Indl Inorganic Chemicals, NEC
3823 Indl Instruments For Meas, Display & Control
3569 Indl Machinery & Eqpt, NEC
3567 Indl Process Furnaces & Ovens
3537 Indl Trucks, Tractors, Trailers & Stackers
2813 Industrial Gases
2869 Industrial Organic Chemicals, NEC
3543 Industrial Patterns
1446 Industrial Sand
3491 Industrial Valves
2816 Inorganic Pigments
3825 Instrs For Measuring & Testing Electricity
3519 Internal Combustion Engines, NEC
3462 Iron & Steel Forgings
1011 Iron Ores

## J

3915 Jewelers Findings & Lapidary Work
3911 Jewelry: Precious Metal

## K

1455 Kaolin & Ball Clay
2253 Knit Outerwear Mills

# SIC INDEX

| SIC NO | PRODUCT |
|---|---|
| 2254 | Knit Underwear Mills |
| 2259 | Knitting Mills, NEC |

## L

| SIC NO | PRODUCT |
|---|---|
| 3821 | Laboratory Apparatus & Furniture |
| 1031 | Lead & Zinc Ores |
| 3952 | Lead Pencils, Crayons & Artist's Mtrls |
| 2386 | Leather & Sheep Lined Clothing |
| 3151 | Leather Gloves & Mittens |
| 3199 | Leather Goods, NEC |
| 3111 | Leather Tanning & Finishing |
| 3648 | Lighting Eqpt, NEC |
| 3274 | Lime |
| 3996 | Linoleum & Hard Surface Floor Coverings, NEC |
| 2085 | Liquors, Distilled, Rectified & Blended |
| 2411 | Logging |
| 2992 | Lubricating Oils & Greases |
| 3161 | Luggage |

## M

| SIC NO | PRODUCT |
|---|---|
| 2098 | Macaroni, Spaghetti & Noodles |
| 3545 | Machine Tool Access |
| 3541 | Machine Tools: Cutting |
| 3542 | Machine Tools: Forming |
| 3599 | Machinery & Eqpt, Indl & Commercial, NEC |
| 3322 | Malleable Iron Foundries |
| 2083 | Malt |
| 2082 | Malt Beverages |
| 2761 | Manifold Business Forms |
| 3999 | Manufacturing Industries, NEC |
| 3953 | Marking Devices |
| 2515 | Mattresses & Bedsprings |
| 3829 | Measuring & Controlling Devices, NEC |
| 3586 | Measuring & Dispensing Pumps |
| 2011 | Meat Packing Plants |
| 3568 | Mechanical Power Transmission Eqpt, NEC |
| 2833 | Medicinal Chemicals & Botanical Prdts |
| 2329 | Men's & Boys' Clothing, NEC |
| 2323 | Men's & Boys' Neckwear |
| 2325 | Men's & Boys' Separate Trousers & Casual Slacks |
| 2321 | Men's & Boys' Shirts |
| 2311 | Men's & Boys' Suits, Coats & Overcoats |
| 2326 | Men's & Boys' Work Clothing |
| 3143 | Men's Footwear, Exc Athletic |
| 3412 | Metal Barrels, Drums, Kegs & Pails |
| 3411 | Metal Cans |
| 3442 | Metal Doors, Sash, Frames, Molding & Trim |
| 3497 | Metal Foil & Leaf |
| 3398 | Metal Heat Treating |
| 2514 | Metal Household Furniture |
| 1081 | Metal Mining Svcs |
| 1099 | Metal Ores, NEC |
| 3469 | Metal Stampings, NEC |
| 3549 | Metalworking Machinery, NEC |
| 2026 | Milk |
| 2023 | Milk, Condensed & Evaporated |
| 2431 | Millwork |
| 3296 | Mineral Wool |
| 3295 | Minerals & Earths: Ground Or Treated |
| 3532 | Mining Machinery & Eqpt |
| 3496 | Misc Fabricated Wire Prdts |
| 2741 | Misc Publishing |
| 3449 | Misc Structural Metal Work |
| 1499 | Miscellaneous Nonmetallic Mining |
| 2451 | Mobile Homes |
| 3061 | Molded, Extruded & Lathe-Cut Rubber Mechanical Goods |
| 3716 | Motor Homes |
| 3714 | Motor Vehicle Parts & Access |
| 3711 | Motor Vehicles & Car Bodies |
| 3751 | Motorcycles, Bicycles & Parts |
| 3621 | Motors & Generators |
| 3931 | Musical Instruments |

## N

| SIC NO | PRODUCT |
|---|---|
| 1321 | Natural Gas Liquids |
| 2711 | Newspapers: Publishing & Printing |
| 2873 | Nitrogenous Fertilizers |
| 3297 | Nonclay Refractories |
| 3644 | Noncurrent-Carrying Wiring Devices |
| 3364 | Nonferrous Die Castings, Exc Aluminum |
| 3463 | Nonferrous Forgings |
| 3369 | Nonferrous Foundries: Castings, NEC |
| 3357 | Nonferrous Wire Drawing |
| 3299 | Nonmetallic Mineral Prdts, NEC |
| 1481 | Nonmetallic Minerals Svcs, Except Fuels |

## O

| SIC NO | PRODUCT |
|---|---|
| 2522 | Office Furniture, Except Wood |
| 3579 | Office Machines, NEC |
| 1382 | Oil & Gas Field Exploration Svcs |
| 1389 | Oil & Gas Field Svcs, NEC |
| 3533 | Oil Field Machinery & Eqpt |
| 3851 | Ophthalmic Goods |
| 3827 | Optical Instruments |
| 3489 | Ordnance & Access, NEC |
| 3842 | Orthopedic, Prosthetic & Surgical Appliances/Splys |

## P

| SIC NO | PRODUCT |
|---|---|
| 3565 | Packaging Machinery |
| 2851 | Paints, Varnishes, Lacquers, Enamels |
| 2671 | Paper Coating & Laminating for Packaging |
| 2672 | Paper Coating & Laminating, Exc for Packaging |
| 3554 | Paper Inds Machinery |
| 2621 | Paper Mills |
| 2631 | Paperboard Mills |
| 2542 | Partitions & Fixtures, Except Wood |
| 2951 | Paving Mixtures & Blocks |
| 3951 | Pens & Mechanical Pencils |
| 2844 | Perfumes, Cosmetics & Toilet Preparations |
| 2721 | Periodicals: Publishing & Printing |
| 3172 | Personal Leather Goods |
| 2879 | Pesticides & Agricultural Chemicals, NEC |
| 2911 | Petroleum Refining |
| 2834 | Pharmaceuticals |
| 3652 | Phonograph Records & Magnetic Tape |
| 1475 | Phosphate Rock |
| 2874 | Phosphatic Fertilizers |
| 3861 | Photographic Eqpt & Splys |
| 2035 | Pickled Fruits, Vegetables, Sauces & Dressings |
| 3085 | Plastic Bottles |
| 3086 | Plastic Foam Prdts |
| 3083 | Plastic Laminated Plate & Sheet |
| 3084 | Plastic Pipe |
| 3088 | Plastic Plumbing Fixtures |
| 3089 | Plastic Prdts |
| 3082 | Plastic Unsupported Profile Shapes |
| 3081 | Plastic Unsupported Sheet & Film |
| 2821 | Plastics, Mtrls & Nonvulcanizable Elastomers |
| 2796 | Platemaking & Related Svcs |
| 2395 | Pleating & Stitching For The Trade |
| 3432 | Plumbing Fixture Fittings & Trim, Brass |
| 3264 | Porcelain Electrical Splys |
| 1474 | Potash, Soda & Borate Minerals |
| 2096 | Potato Chips & Similar Prdts |
| 3269 | Pottery Prdts, NEC |
| 2015 | Poultry Slaughtering, Dressing & Processing |
| 3546 | Power Hand Tools |
| 3612 | Power, Distribution & Specialty Transformers |
| 3448 | Prefabricated Metal Buildings & Cmpnts |
| 2452 | Prefabricated Wood Buildings & Cmpnts |
| 7372 | Prepackaged Software |
| 2048 | Prepared Feeds For Animals & Fowls |
| 3229 | Pressed & Blown Glassware, NEC |
| 3692 | Primary Batteries: Dry & Wet |
| 3399 | Primary Metal Prdts, NEC |
| 3339 | Primary Nonferrous Metals, NEC |
| 3334 | Primary Production Of Aluminum |
| 3331 | Primary Smelting & Refining Of Copper |
| 3672 | Printed Circuit Boards |
| 2893 | Printing Ink |
| 3555 | Printing Trades Machinery & Eqpt |
| 2999 | Products Of Petroleum & Coal, NEC |
| 2531 | Public Building & Related Furniture |
| 2611 | Pulp Mills |
| 3561 | Pumps & Pumping Eqpt |

## R

| SIC NO | PRODUCT |
|---|---|
| 3663 | Radio & T V Communications, Systs & Eqpt, Broadcast/Studio |
| 3671 | Radio & T V Receiving Electron Tubes |
| 3743 | Railroad Eqpt |
| 3273 | Ready-Mixed Concrete |
| 2493 | Reconstituted Wood Prdts |
| 3695 | Recording Media |
| 3625 | Relays & Indl Controls |
| 3645 | Residential Lighting Fixtures |
| 2044 | Rice Milling |
| 2384 | Robes & Dressing Gowns |
| 3547 | Rolling Mill Machinery & Eqpt |
| 3351 | Rolling, Drawing & Extruding Of Copper |
| 3356 | Rolling, Drawing-Extruding Of Nonferrous Metals |
| 3021 | Rubber & Plastic Footwear |
| 3052 | Rubber & Plastic Hose & Belting |

## S

| SIC NO | PRODUCT |
|---|---|
| 2068 | Salted & Roasted Nuts & Seeds |
| 2656 | Sanitary Food Containers |
| 2676 | Sanitary Paper Prdts |
| 2013 | Sausages & Meat Prdts |
| 2421 | Saw & Planing Mills |
| 3596 | Scales & Balances, Exc Laboratory |
| 2397 | Schiffli Machine Embroideries |
| 3451 | Screw Machine Prdts |
| 3812 | Search, Detection, Navigation & Guidance Systs & Instrs |
| 3341 | Secondary Smelting & Refining Of Nonferrous Metals |
| 3674 | Semiconductors |
| 3589 | Service Ind Machines, NEC |
| 2652 | Set-Up Paperboard Boxes |
| 3444 | Sheet Metal Work |
| 3731 | Shipbuilding & Repairing |
| 2079 | Shortening, Oils & Margarine |
| 3993 | Signs & Advertising Displays |
| 2262 | Silk & Man-Made Fabric Finishers |
| 2221 | Silk & Man-Made Fiber |
| 1044 | Silver Ores |
| 3914 | Silverware, Plated & Stainless Steel Ware |
| 3484 | Small Arms |
| 3482 | Small Arms Ammunition |
| 2841 | Soap & Detergents |
| 2086 | Soft Drinks |
| 2436 | Softwood Veneer & Plywood |
| 2075 | Soybean Oil Mills |
| 2842 | Spec Cleaning, Polishing & Sanitation Preparations |
| 3559 | Special Ind Machinery, NEC |
| 2429 | Special Prdt Sawmills, NEC |
| 3566 | Speed Changers, Drives & Gears |
| 3949 | Sporting & Athletic Goods, NEC |
| 2678 | Stationery Prdts |
| 3511 | Steam, Gas & Hydraulic Turbines & Engines |
| 3325 | Steel Foundries, NEC |
| 3324 | Steel Investment Foundries |
| 3317 | Steel Pipe & Tubes |
| 3493 | Steel Springs, Except Wire |
| 3315 | Steel Wire Drawing & Nails & Spikes |
| 3691 | Storage Batteries |
| 3259 | Structural Clay Prdts, NEC |
| 2439 | Structural Wood Members, NEC |
| 2063 | Sugar, Beet |
| 2061 | Sugar, Cane |
| 2062 | Sugar, Cane Refining |
| 2843 | Surface Active & Finishing Agents, Sulfonated Oils |
| 3841 | Surgical & Medical Instrs & Apparatus |
| 3613 | Switchgear & Switchboard Apparatus |
| 2824 | Synthetic Organic Fibers, Exc Cellulosic |
| 2822 | Synthetic Rubber (Vulcanizable Elastomers) |

## T

| SIC NO | PRODUCT |
|---|---|
| 3795 | Tanks & Tank Components |
| 3661 | Telephone & Telegraph Apparatus |
| 2393 | Textile Bags |
| 2269 | Textile Finishers, NEC |
| 2299 | Textile Goods, NEC |
| 3552 | Textile Machinery |
| 2284 | Thread Mills |
| 2296 | Tire Cord & Fabric |
| 3011 | Tires & Inner Tubes |
| 2141 | Tobacco Stemming & Redrying |
| 2131 | Tobacco, Chewing & Snuff |
| 3799 | Transportation Eqpt, NEC |
| 3792 | Travel Trailers & Campers |
| 3713 | Truck & Bus Bodies |
| 3715 | Truck Trailers |
| 2791 | Typesetting |

## U

| SIC NO | PRODUCT |
|---|---|
| 1094 | Uranium, Radium & Vanadium Ores |

## V

| SIC NO | PRODUCT |
|---|---|
| 3494 | Valves & Pipe Fittings, NEC |
| 2076 | Vegetable Oil Mills |
| 3647 | Vehicular Lighting Eqpt |

## W

| SIC NO | PRODUCT |
|---|---|
| 3873 | Watch & Clock Devices & Parts |
| 2385 | Waterproof Outerwear |
| 3548 | Welding Apparatus |
| 7692 | Welding Repair |
| 2046 | Wet Corn Milling |
| 2084 | Wine & Brandy |
| 3495 | Wire Springs |
| 2331 | Women's & Misses' Blouses |
| 2335 | Women's & Misses' Dresses |
| 2339 | Women's & Misses' Outerwear, NEC |
| 2337 | Women's & Misses' Suits, Coats & Skirts |
| 3144 | Women's Footwear, Exc Athletic |
| 2341 | Women's, Misses' & Children's Underwear & Nightwear |
| 2441 | Wood Boxes |
| 2449 | Wood Containers, NEC |
| 2511 | Wood Household Furniture |

## SIC INDEX

| SIC NO | PRODUCT |
|---|---|
| 2512 | Wood Household Furniture, Upholstered |
| 2434 | Wood Kitchen Cabinets |
| 2521 | Wood Office Furniture |
| 2448 | Wood Pallets & Skids |
| 2499 | Wood Prdts, NEC |
| 2491 | Wood Preserving |
| 2517 | Wood T V, Radio, Phono & Sewing Cabinets |
| 2541 | Wood, Office & Store Fixtures |
| 3553 | Woodworking Machinery |
| 2231 | Wool, Woven Fabric |

### X

| SIC NO | PRODUCT |
|---|---|
| 3844 | X-ray Apparatus & Tubes |

# SIC INDEX

**Standard Industrial Classification Numerical Index**

| SIC NO | PRODUCT |
|---|---|

### 10 METAL MINING
1011 Iron Ores
1021 Copper Ores
1031 Lead & Zinc Ores
1041 Gold Ores
1044 Silver Ores
1081 Metal Mining Svcs
1094 Uranium, Radium & Vanadium Ores
1099 Metal Ores, NEC

### 12 COAL MINING
1221 Bituminous Coal & Lignite: Surface Mining
1222 Bituminous Coal: Underground Mining
1231 Anthracite Mining
1241 Coal Mining Svcs

### 13 OIL AND GAS EXTRACTION
1311 Crude Petroleum & Natural Gas
1321 Natural Gas Liquids
1381 Drilling Oil & Gas Wells
1382 Oil & Gas Field Exploration Svcs
1389 Oil & Gas Field Svcs, NEC

### 14 MINING AND QUARRYING OF NONMETALLIC MINERALS, EXCEPT FUELS
1411 Dimension Stone
1422 Crushed & Broken Limestone
1423 Crushed & Broken Granite
1429 Crushed & Broken Stone, NEC
1442 Construction Sand & Gravel
1446 Industrial Sand
1455 Kaolin & Ball Clay
1459 Clay, Ceramic & Refractory Minerals, NEC
1474 Potash, Soda & Borate Minerals
1475 Phosphate Rock
1479 Chemical & Fertilizer Mining
1481 Nonmetallic Minerals Svcs, Except Fuels
1499 Miscellaneous Nonmetallic Mining

### 20 FOOD AND KINDRED PRODUCTS
2011 Meat Packing Plants
2013 Sausages & Meat Prdts
2015 Poultry Slaughtering, Dressing & Processing
2021 Butter
2022 Cheese
2023 Milk, Condensed & Evaporated
2024 Ice Cream
2026 Milk
2032 Canned Specialties
2033 Canned Fruits, Vegetables & Preserves
2034 Dried Fruits, Vegetables & Soup
2035 Pickled Fruits, Vegetables, Sauces & Dressings
2037 Frozen Fruits, Juices & Vegetables
2038 Frozen Specialties
2041 Flour, Grain Milling
2043 Cereal Breakfast Foods
2044 Rice Milling
2045 Flour, Blended & Prepared
2046 Wet Corn Milling
2047 Dog & Cat Food
2048 Prepared Feeds For Animals & Fowls
2051 Bread, Bakery Prdts Exc Cookies & Crackers
2052 Cookies & Crackers
2053 Frozen Bakery Prdts
2061 Sugar, Cane
2062 Sugar, Cane Refining
2063 Sugar, Beet
2064 Candy & Confectionery Prdts
2066 Chocolate & Cocoa Prdts
2067 Chewing Gum
2068 Salted & Roasted Nuts & Seeds
2074 Cottonseed Oil Mills
2075 Soybean Oil Mills
2076 Vegetable Oil Mills
2077 Animal, Marine Fats & Oils
2079 Shortening, Oils & Margarine
2082 Malt Beverages
2083 Malt
2084 Wine & Brandy
2085 Liquors, Distilled, Rectified & Blended
2086 Soft Drinks
2087 Flavoring Extracts & Syrups
2091 Fish & Seafoods, Canned & Cured
2092 Fish & Seafoods, Fresh & Frozen
2095 Coffee
2096 Potato Chips & Similar Prdts
2097 Ice
2098 Macaroni, Spaghetti & Noodles
2099 Food Preparations, NEC

### 21 TOBACCO PRODUCTS
2111 Cigarettes
2121 Cigars
2131 Tobacco, Chewing & Snuff
2141 Tobacco Stemming & Redrying

### 22 TEXTILE MILL PRODUCTS
2211 Cotton, Woven Fabric
2221 Silk & Man-Made Fiber
2231 Wool, Woven Fabric
2241 Fabric Mills, Cotton, Wool, Silk & Man-Made
2251 Hosiery, Women's Full & Knee Length
2252 Hosiery, Except Women's
2253 Knit Outerwear Mills
2254 Knit Underwear Mills
2257 Circular Knit Fabric Mills
2259 Knitting Mills, NEC
2261 Cotton Fabric Finishers
2262 Silk & Man-Made Fabric Finishers
2269 Textile Finishers, NEC
2273 Carpets & Rugs
2284 Thread Mills
2295 Fabrics Coated Not Rubberized
2296 Tire Cord & Fabric
2297 Fabrics, Nonwoven
2298 Cordage & Twine
2299 Textile Goods, NEC

### 23 APPAREL AND OTHER FINISHED PRODUCTS MADE FROM FABRICS AND SIMILAR MATERIAL
2311 Men's & Boys' Suits, Coats & Overcoats
2321 Men's & Boys' Shirts
2323 Men's & Boys' Neckwear
2325 Men's & Boys' Separate Trousers & Casual Slacks
2326 Men's & Boys' Work Clothing
2329 Men's & Boys' Clothing, NEC
2331 Women's & Misses' Blouses
2335 Women's & Misses' Dresses
2337 Women's & Misses' Suits, Coats & Skirts
2339 Women's & Misses' Outerwear, NEC
2341 Women's, Misses' & Children's Underwear & Nightwear
2342 Brassieres, Girdles & Garments
2353 Hats, Caps & Millinery
2361 Children's & Infants' Dresses & Blouses
2369 Girls' & Infants' Outerwear, NEC
2371 Fur Goods
2381 Dress & Work Gloves
2384 Robes & Dressing Gowns
2385 Waterproof Outerwear
2386 Leather & Sheep Lined Clothing
2387 Apparel Belts
2389 Apparel & Accessories, NEC
2391 Curtains & Draperies
2392 House furnishings: Textile
2393 Textile Bags
2394 Canvas Prdts
2395 Pleating & Stitching For The Trade
2396 Automotive Trimmings, Apparel Findings, Related Prdts
2397 Schiffli Machine Embroideries
2399 Fabricated Textile Prdts, NEC

### 24 LUMBER AND WOOD PRODUCTS, EXCEPT FURNITURE
2411 Logging
2421 Saw & Planing Mills
2426 Hardwood Dimension & Flooring Mills
2429 Special Prdt Sawmills, NEC
2431 Millwork
2434 Wood Kitchen Cabinets
2435 Hardwood Veneer & Plywood
2436 Softwood Veneer & Plywood
2439 Structural Wood Members, NEC
2441 Wood Boxes
2448 Wood Pallets & Skids
2449 Wood Containers, NEC
2451 Mobile Homes
2452 Prefabricated Wood Buildings & Cmpnts
2491 Wood Preserving
2493 Reconstituted Wood Prdts
2499 Wood Prdts, NEC

### 25 FURNITURE AND FIXTURES
2511 Wood Household Furniture
2512 Wood Household Furniture, Upholstered
2514 Metal Household Furniture
2515 Mattresses & Bedsprings
2517 Wood T V, Radio, Phono & Sewing Cabinets
2519 Household Furniture, NEC
2521 Wood Office Furniture
2522 Office Furniture, Except Wood
2531 Public Building & Related Furniture
2541 Wood, Office & Store Fixtures
2542 Partitions & Fixtures, Except Wood
2591 Drapery Hardware, Window Blinds & Shades
2599 Furniture & Fixtures, NEC

### 26 PAPER AND ALLIED PRODUCTS
2611 Pulp Mills
2621 Paper Mills
2631 Paperboard Mills
2652 Set-Up Paperboard Boxes
2653 Corrugated & Solid Fiber Boxes
2655 Fiber Cans, Tubes & Drums
2656 Sanitary Food Containers
2657 Folding Paperboard Boxes
2671 Paper Coating & Laminating for Packaging
2672 Paper Coating & Laminating, Exc for Packaging
2673 Bags: Plastics, Laminated & Coated
2674 Bags: Uncoated Paper & Multiwall
2675 Die-Cut Paper & Board
2676 Sanitary Paper Prdts
2677 Envelopes
2678 Stationery Prdts
2679 Converted Paper Prdts, NEC

### 27 PRINTING, PUBLISHING, AND ALLIED INDUSTRIES
2711 Newspapers: Publishing & Printing
2721 Periodicals: Publishing & Printing
2731 Books: Publishing & Printing
2732 Book Printing, Not Publishing
2741 Misc Publishing
2752 Commercial Printing: Lithographic
2754 Commercial Printing: Gravure
2759 Commercial Printing
2761 Manifold Business Forms
2771 Greeting Card Publishing
2782 Blankbooks & Looseleaf Binders
2789 Bookbinding
2791 Typesetting
2796 Platemaking & Related Svcs

### 28 CHEMICALS AND ALLIED PRODUCTS
2812 Alkalies & Chlorine
2813 Industrial Gases
2816 Inorganic Pigments
2819 Indl Inorganic Chemicals, NEC
2821 Plastics, Mtrls & Nonvulcanizable Elastomers
2822 Synthetic Rubber (Vulcanizable Elastomers)
2823 Cellulosic Man-Made Fibers
2824 Synthetic Organic Fibers, Exc Cellulosic
2833 Medicinal Chemicals & Botanical Prdts
2834 Pharmaceuticals
2835 Diagnostic Substances
2836 Biological Prdts, Exc Diagnostic Substances
2841 Soap & Detergents
2842 Spec Cleaning, Polishing & Sanitation Preparations
2843 Surface Active & Finishing Agents, Sulfonated Oils
2844 Perfumes, Cosmetics & Toilet Preparations
2851 Paints, Varnishes, Lacquers, Enamels
2861 Gum & Wood Chemicals
2865 Cyclic-Crudes, Intermediates, Dyes & Org Pigments
2869 Industrial Organic Chemicals, NEC
2873 Nitrogenous Fertilizers
2874 Phosphatic Fertilizers
2875 Fertilizers, Mixing Only
2879 Pesticides & Agricultural Chemicals, NEC
2891 Adhesives & Sealants
2892 Explosives
2893 Printing Ink
2895 Carbon Black

# SIC INDEX

| SIC NO | PRODUCT |
|---|---|
| 2899 | Chemical Preparations, NEC |

## 29 PETROLEUM REFINING AND RELATED INDUSTRIES

- 2911 Petroleum Refining
- 2951 Paving Mixtures & Blocks
- 2952 Asphalt Felts & Coatings
- 2992 Lubricating Oils & Greases
- 2999 Products Of Petroleum & Coal, NEC

## 30 RUBBER AND MISCELLANEOUS PLASTICS PRODUCTS

- 3011 Tires & Inner Tubes
- 3021 Rubber & Plastic Footwear
- 3052 Rubber & Plastic Hose & Belting
- 3053 Gaskets, Packing & Sealing Devices
- 3061 Molded, Extruded & Lathe-Cut Rubber Mechanical Goods
- 3069 Fabricated Rubber Prdts, NEC
- 3081 Plastic Unsupported Sheet & Film
- 3082 Plastic Unsupported Profile Shapes
- 3083 Plastic Laminated Plate & Sheet
- 3084 Plastic Pipe
- 3085 Plastic Bottles
- 3086 Plastic Foam Prdts
- 3087 Custom Compounding Of Purchased Plastic Resins
- 3088 Plastic Plumbing Fixtures
- 3089 Plastic Prdts

## 31 LEATHER AND LEATHER PRODUCTS

- 3111 Leather Tanning & Finishing
- 3131 Boot & Shoe Cut Stock & Findings
- 3143 Men's Footwear, Exc Athletic
- 3144 Women's Footwear, Exc Athletic
- 3149 Footwear, NEC
- 3151 Leather Gloves & Mittens
- 3161 Luggage
- 3171 Handbags & Purses
- 3172 Personal Leather Goods
- 3199 Leather Goods, NEC

## 32 STONE, CLAY, GLASS, AND CONCRETE PRODUCTS

- 3211 Flat Glass
- 3221 Glass Containers
- 3229 Pressed & Blown Glassware, NEC
- 3231 Glass Prdts Made Of Purchased Glass
- 3241 Cement, Hydraulic
- 3251 Brick & Structural Clay Tile
- 3253 Ceramic Tile
- 3255 Clay Refractories
- 3259 Structural Clay Prdts, NEC
- 3261 China Plumbing Fixtures & Fittings
- 3262 China, Table & Kitchen Articles
- 3263 Earthenware, Whiteware, Table & Kitchen Articles
- 3264 Porcelain Electrical Splys
- 3269 Pottery Prdts, NEC
- 3271 Concrete Block & Brick
- 3272 Concrete Prdts
- 3273 Ready-Mixed Concrete
- 3274 Lime
- 3275 Gypsum Prdts
- 3281 Cut Stone Prdts
- 3291 Abrasive Prdts
- 3292 Asbestos products
- 3295 Minerals & Earths: Ground Or Treated
- 3296 Mineral Wool
- 3297 Nonclay Refractories
- 3299 Nonmetallic Mineral Prdts, NEC

## 33 PRIMARY METAL INDUSTRIES

- 3312 Blast Furnaces, Coke Ovens, Steel & Rolling Mills
- 3313 Electrometallurgical Prdts
- 3315 Steel Wire Drawing & Nails & Spikes
- 3316 Cold Rolled Steel Sheet, Strip & Bars
- 3317 Steel Pipe & Tubes
- 3321 Gray Iron Foundries
- 3322 Malleable Iron Foundries
- 3324 Steel Investment Foundries
- 3325 Steel Foundries, NEC
- 3331 Primary Smelting & Refining Of Copper
- 3334 Primary Production Of Aluminum
- 3339 Primary Nonferrous Metals, NEC
- 3341 Secondary Smelting & Refining Of Nonferrous Metals
- 3351 Rolling, Drawing & Extruding Of Copper
- 3353 Aluminum Sheet, Plate & Foil
- 3354 Aluminum Extruded Prdts
- 3355 Aluminum Rolling & Drawing, NEC
- 3356 Rolling, Drawing-Extruding Of Nonferrous Metals
- 3357 Nonferrous Wire Drawing
- 3363 Aluminum Die Castings
- 3364 Nonferrous Die Castings, Exc Aluminum
- 3365 Aluminum Foundries
- 3366 Copper Foundries
- 3369 Nonferrous Foundries: Castings, NEC
- 3398 Metal Heat Treating
- 3399 Primary Metal Prdts, NEC

## 34 FABRICATED METAL PRODUCTS, EXCEPT MACHINERY AND TRANSPORTATION EQUIPMENT

- 3411 Metal Cans
- 3412 Metal Barrels, Drums, Kegs & Pails
- 3421 Cutlery
- 3423 Hand & Edge Tools
- 3425 Hand Saws & Saw Blades
- 3429 Hardware, NEC
- 3431 Enameled Iron & Metal Sanitary Ware
- 3432 Plumbing Fixture Fittings & Trim, Brass
- 3433 Heating Eqpt
- 3441 Fabricated Structural Steel
- 3442 Metal Doors, Sash, Frames, Molding & Trim
- 3443 Fabricated Plate Work
- 3444 Sheet Metal Work
- 3446 Architectural & Ornamental Metal Work
- 3448 Prefabricated Metal Buildings & Cmpnts
- 3449 Misc Structural Metal Work
- 3451 Screw Machine Prdts
- 3452 Bolts, Nuts, Screws, Rivets & Washers
- 3462 Iron & Steel Forgings
- 3463 Nonferrous Forgings
- 3465 Automotive Stampings
- 3466 Crowns & Closures
- 3469 Metal Stampings, NEC
- 3471 Electroplating, Plating, Polishing, Anodizing & Coloring
- 3479 Coating & Engraving, NEC
- 3482 Small Arms Ammunition
- 3483 Ammunition, Large
- 3484 Small Arms
- 3489 Ordnance & Access, NEC
- 3491 Industrial Valves
- 3492 Fluid Power Valves & Hose Fittings
- 3493 Steel Springs, Except Wire
- 3494 Valves & Pipe Fittings, NEC
- 3495 Wire Springs
- 3496 Misc Fabricated Wire Prdts
- 3497 Metal Foil & Leaf
- 3498 Fabricated Pipe & Pipe Fittings
- 3499 Fabricated Metal Prdts, NEC

## 35 INDUSTRIAL AND COMMERCIAL MACHINERY AND COMPUTER EQUIPMENT

- 3511 Steam, Gas & Hydraulic Turbines & Engines
- 3519 Internal Combustion Engines, NEC
- 3523 Farm Machinery & Eqpt
- 3524 Garden, Lawn Tractors & Eqpt
- 3531 Construction Machinery & Eqpt
- 3532 Mining Machinery & Eqpt
- 3533 Oil Field Machinery & Eqpt
- 3534 Elevators & Moving Stairways
- 3535 Conveyors & Eqpt
- 3536 Hoists, Cranes & Monorails
- 3537 Indl Trucks, Tractors, Trailers & Stackers
- 3541 Machine Tools: Cutting
- 3542 Machine Tools: Forming
- 3543 Industrial Patterns
- 3544 Dies, Tools, Jigs, Fixtures & Indl Molds
- 3545 Machine Tool Access
- 3546 Power Hand Tools
- 3547 Rolling Mill Machinery & Eqpt
- 3548 Welding Apparatus
- 3549 Metalworking Machinery, NEC
- 3552 Textile Machinery
- 3553 Woodworking Machinery
- 3554 Paper Inds Machinery
- 3555 Printing Trades Machinery & Eqpt
- 3556 Food Prdts Machinery
- 3559 Special Ind Machinery, NEC
- 3561 Pumps & Pumping Eqpt
- 3562 Ball & Roller Bearings
- 3563 Air & Gas Compressors
- 3564 Blowers & Fans
- 3565 Packaging Machinery
- 3566 Speed Changers, Drives & Gears
- 3567 Indl Process Furnaces & Ovens
- 3568 Mechanical Power Transmission Eqpt, NEC
- 3569 Indl Machinery & Eqpt, NEC
- 3571 Electronic Computers
- 3572 Computer Storage Devices
- 3575 Computer Terminals
- 3577 Computer Peripheral Eqpt, NEC
- 3578 Calculating & Accounting Eqpt
- 3579 Office Machines, NEC
- 3581 Automatic Vending Machines
- 3582 Commercial Laundry, Dry Clean & Pressing Mchs
- 3585 Air Conditioning & Heating Eqpt
- 3586 Measuring & Dispensing Pumps
- 3589 Service Ind Machines, NEC
- 3592 Carburetors, Pistons, Rings & Valves
- 3593 Fluid Power Cylinders & Actuators
- 3594 Fluid Power Pumps & Motors
- 3596 Scales & Balances, Exc Laboratory
- 3599 Machinery & Eqpt, Indl & Commercial, NEC

## 36 ELECTRONIC AND OTHER ELECTRICAL EQUIPMENT AND COMPONENTS, EXCEPT COMPUTER

- 3612 Power, Distribution & Specialty Transformers
- 3613 Switchgear & Switchboard Apparatus
- 3621 Motors & Generators
- 3624 Carbon & Graphite Prdts
- 3625 Relays & Indl Controls
- 3629 Electrical Indl Apparatus, NEC
- 3631 Household Cooking Eqpt
- 3632 Household Refrigerators & Freezers
- 3633 Household Laundry Eqpt
- 3634 Electric Household Appliances
- 3635 Household Vacuum Cleaners
- 3639 Household Appliances, NEC
- 3641 Electric Lamps
- 3643 Current-Carrying Wiring Devices
- 3644 Noncurrent-Carrying Wiring Devices
- 3645 Residential Lighting Fixtures
- 3646 Commercial, Indl & Institutional Lighting Fixtures
- 3647 Vehicular Lighting Eqpt
- 3648 Lighting Eqpt, NEC
- 3651 Household Audio & Video Eqpt
- 3652 Phonograph Records & Magnetic Tape
- 3661 Telephone & Telegraph Apparatus
- 3663 Radio & T V Communications, Systs & Eqpt, Broadcast/Studio
- 3669 Communications Eqpt, NEC
- 3671 Radio & T V Receiving Electron Tubes
- 3672 Printed Circuit Boards
- 3674 Semiconductors
- 3675 Electronic Capacitors
- 3676 Electronic Resistors
- 3677 Electronic Coils & Transformers
- 3678 Electronic Connectors
- 3679 Electronic Components, NEC
- 3691 Storage Batteries
- 3692 Primary Batteries: Dry & Wet
- 3694 Electrical Eqpt For Internal Combustion Engines
- 3695 Recording Media
- 3699 Electrical Machinery, Eqpt & Splys, NEC

## 37 TRANSPORTATION EQUIPMENT

- 3711 Motor Vehicles & Car Bodies
- 3713 Truck & Bus Bodies
- 3714 Motor Vehicle Parts & Access
- 3715 Truck Trailers
- 3716 Motor Homes
- 3721 Aircraft
- 3724 Aircraft Engines & Engine Parts
- 3728 Aircraft Parts & Eqpt, NEC
- 3731 Shipbuilding & Repairing
- 3732 Boat Building & Repairing
- 3743 Railroad Eqpt
- 3751 Motorcycles, Bicycles & Parts
- 3761 Guided Missiles & Space Vehicles
- 3764 Guided Missile/Space Vehicle Propulsion Units & parts
- 3769 Guided Missile/Space Vehicle Parts & Eqpt, NEC
- 3792 Travel Trailers & Campers
- 3795 Tanks & Tank Components
- 3799 Transportation Eqpt, NEC

## 38 MEASURING, ANALYZING AND CONTROLLING INSTRUMENTS; PHOTOGRAPHIC, MEDICAL AN

- 3812 Search, Detection, Navigation & Guidance Systs & Instrs
- 3821 Laboratory Apparatus & Furniture
- 3822 Automatic Temperature Controls
- 3823 Indl Instruments For Meas, Display & Control
- 3824 Fluid Meters & Counters
- 3825 Instrs For Measuring & Testing Electricity
- 3826 Analytical Instruments
- 3827 Optical Instruments
- 3829 Measuring & Controlling Devices, NEC
- 3841 Surgical & Medical Instrs & Apparatus
- 3842 Orthopedic, Prosthetic & Surgical Appliances/Splys
- 3843 Dental Eqpt & Splys
- 3844 X-ray Apparatus & Tubes
- 3845 Electromedical & Electrotherapeutic Apparatus
- 3851 Ophthalmic Goods
- 3861 Photographic Eqpt & Splys
- 3873 Watch & Clock Devices & Parts

# SIC INDEX

| SIC NO | PRODUCT |
|---|---|
| **39 MISCELLANEOUS MANUFACTURING INDUSTRIES** | |
| 3911 | Jewelry: Precious Metal |
| 3914 | Silverware, Plated & Stainless Steel Ware |
| 3915 | Jewelers Findings & Lapidary Work |
| 3931 | Musical Instruments |
| 3942 | Dolls & Stuffed Toys |
| 3944 | Games, Toys & Children's Vehicles |
| 3949 | Sporting & Athletic Goods, NEC |
| 3951 | Pens & Mechanical Pencils |
| 3952 | Lead Pencils, Crayons & Artist's Mtrls |
| 3953 | Marking Devices |
| 3955 | Carbon Paper & Inked Ribbons |
| 3961 | Costume Jewelry & Novelties |
| 3965 | Fasteners, Buttons, Needles & Pins |
| 3991 | Brooms & Brushes |
| 3993 | Signs & Advertising Displays |
| 3995 | Burial Caskets |
| 3996 | Linoleum & Hard Surface Floor Coverings, NEC |
| 3999 | Manufacturing Industries, NEC |
| **73 BUSINESS SERVICES** | |
| 7372 | Prepackaged Software |
| **76 MISCELLANEOUS REPAIR SERVICES** | |
| 7692 | Welding Repair |
| 7694 | Armature Rewinding Shops |

# SIC SECTION

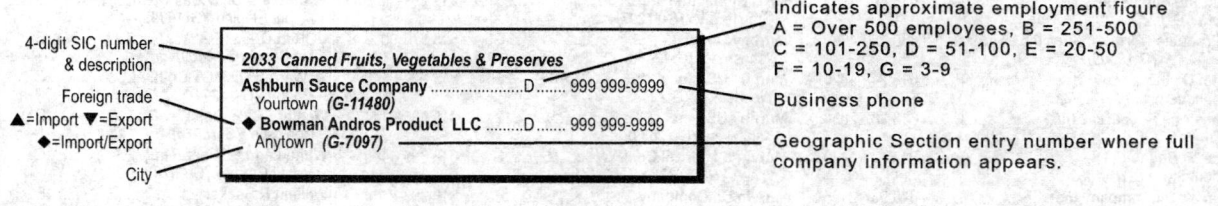

- 4-digit SIC number & description
- Foreign trade
- ▲=Import ▼=Export
- ◆=Import/Export
- City

2033 Canned Fruits, Vegetables & Preserves
Ashburn Sauce Company .................... D ...... 999 999-9999
  Yourtown (G-11480)
◆ Bowman Andros Product LLC ........ D ...... 999 999-9999
  Anytown (G-7097)

Indicates approximate employment figure
A = Over 500 employees, B = 251-500
C = 101-250, D = 51-100, E = 20-50
F = 10-19, G = 3-9

Business phone

Geographic Section entry number where full company information appears.

*See footnotes for symbols and codes identification.*

- The SIC codes in this section are from the latest Standard Industrial Classification manual published by the U.S. Government's Office of Management and Budget. For more information regarding SICs, see the Explanatory Notes.
- Companies may be listed under multiple classifications.

## 10 METAL MINING

### 1011 Iron Ores
Global Technologies I LLC ................. D ...... 312 255-8350
  Chicago (G-4960)
Q Lotus Holdings Inc ......................... G ...... 312 379-1800
  Chicago (G-6234)
▲ Regal Converting Co Inc ................. F ...... 630 257-3581
  Lockport (G-13742)

### 1021 Copper Ores
▲ Ventec USA LLC ............................. G ...... 847 621-2261
  Elk Grove Village (G-9805)

### 1031 Lead & Zinc Ores
▼ Big River Zinc Corporation ............. G ...... 618 274-5000
  Sauget (G-19382)
Ebers Drilling Co ............................... G ...... 618 826-5398
  Chester (G-3655)
Midland Coal Company ..................... G ...... 309 362-2795
  Trivoli (G-21000)

### 1041 Gold Ores
Billy Cash For Gold Inc ...................... G ...... 773 905-2447
  Melrose Park (G-14600)
Coeur Mining Inc ............................... D ...... 312 489-5800
  Chicago (G-4419)
Global Technologies I LLC ................. D ...... 312 255-8350
  Chicago (G-4960)

### 1044 Silver Ores
▼ Callahan Mining Corporation .......... D ...... 312 489-5800
  Chicago (G-4216)
Coeur Mining Inc ............................... D ...... 312 489-5800
  Chicago (G-4419)
Coeur Rochester Inc ......................... G ...... 312 661-2436
  Chicago (G-4420)

### 1081 Metal Mining Svcs
Able Electropolishing Co Inc ............. E ...... 773 277-1600
  Chicago (G-3710)
Ave Inc ............................................. G ...... 815 727-0153
  Joliet (G-12457)
Caterpillar Inc ................................... A ...... 309 675-6223
  Mossville (G-15251)
Caterpillar Inc ................................... B ...... 309 494-0858
  Aurora (G-1126)
Coeur Capital Inc .............................. G ...... 312 489-5800
  Chicago (G-4418)
Ingersoll-Rand Company ................... E ...... 630 530-3800
  Elmhurst (G-9886)
Metal Sprmarkets Chicago Niles ........ G ...... 847 647-2423
  Niles (G-16003)
Regal Johnson Co ............................. G ...... 630 885-0688
  Bolingbrook (G-2364)
SF Contracting LLC ........................... E ...... 618 926-1477
  Raleigh (G-17911)
T Cat Enterprise Inc .......................... G ...... 630 330-6800
  Franklin Park (G-10602)
Ultron Inc .......................................... F ...... 618 244-3303
  Mount Vernon (G-15447)

### 1094 Uranium, Radium & Vanadium Ores
Phosphate Resource Ptrs .................. A ...... 847 739-1200
  Lake Forest (G-12945)

### 1099 Metal Ores, NEC
Alro Steel Corporation ...................... E ...... 708 202-3200
  Melrose Park (G-14591)
Staging By Tish ................................. G ...... 630 852-9595
  Downers Grove (G-8527)

## 12 COAL MINING

### 1221 Bituminous Coal & Lignite: Surface Mining
Alpha Natural Resources Inc ............. C ...... 618 298-2394
  Keensburg (G-12660)
Blue Blaze Coal Cpitl Resource .......... E ...... 309 647-2000
  Canton (G-2982)
Hickman Williams & Company .......... F ...... 708 656-8818
  Cicero (G-7202)
▲ Hillsboro Energy LLC ...................... G ...... 217 532-3983
  Hillsboro (G-11894)
Hnrc Dissolution Co .......................... C ...... 618 758-4501
  Coulterville (G-7400)
Illinois Fuel Company LLC ................. D ...... 618 275-4486
  Herod (G-11747)
▲ Interminal Services ......................... E ...... 773 978-8129
  Chicago (G-5218)
Jader Fuel Co Inc .............................. G ...... 618 269-3101
  Shawneetown (G-19904)
Keller Group Inc ............................... B ...... 847 446-7550
  Northfield (G-16405)
Material Service Resources ............... D ...... 630 325-7736
  Chicago (G-5651)
Peabody Midwest Mining LLC .......... C ...... 618 276-5006
  Equality (G-9990)
Power Planter Inc ............................. G ...... 217 379-2614
  Loda (G-13754)
Standard Laboratories Inc ................. E ...... 618 539-5836
  Freeburg (G-10642)
▲ Sun Coke International Inc ............. D ...... 630 824-1000
  Lisle (G-13665)
▲ White County Coal LLC .................. C ...... 618 382-4651
  Carmi (G-3084)

### 1222 Bituminous Coal: Underground Mining
Alpha Natural Resources Inc ............. C ...... 618 298-2394
  Keensburg (G-12660)
▲ American Coal Company ................ G ...... 618 268-6311
  Galatia (G-10711)
Blue Blaze Coal Cpitl Resource .......... E ...... 309 647-2000
  Canton (G-2982)
Exxon Mobil Corporation .................. B ...... 217 854-3291
  Carlinville (G-3038)
Illinois Fuel Company LLC ................. D ...... 618 275-4486
  Herod (G-11747)
Jewell Resources Corporation ........... G ...... 276 935-8810
  Lisle (G-13610)
Keller Group Inc ............................... B ...... 847 446-7550
  Northfield (G-16405)
Knight Hawk Coal LLC ..................... G ...... 618 426-3662
  Percy (G-17495)
Peabody Coal Company .................... C ...... 618 758-2395
  Coulterville (G-7402)
▲ Sun Coke International Inc ............. D ...... 630 824-1000
  Lisle (G-13665)

### 1231 Anthracite Mining
Fabick Mining LLC ............................ F ...... 618 982-9000
  Norris City (G-16114)
Jii Holdings LLC ................................ G ...... 847 945-5591
  Deerfield (G-8018)

### 1241 Coal Mining Svcs
Coal Field Development Co ............... G ...... 630 653-3700
  Carol Stream (G-3131)
▼ Cobra Coal Inc ............................... E ...... 630 560-1050
  West Chicago (G-21684)
Exxon Mobil Corporation .................. B ...... 217 854-3291
  Carlinville (G-3038)
Fjcj LLC ............................................ F ...... 618 785-2217
  Baldwin (G-1250)
Fred Hutson Mineral Products ........... G ...... 618 994-4383
  Harrisburg (G-11599)
Freeman Energy Corporation ............. F ...... 217 698-3949
  Springfield (G-20442)
Freeman United Coal Mining Co ....... 217 627-2161
  Girard (G-10945)
Freeman United Coal Mining Co ....... 217 698-3300
  Springfield (G-20443)
Hamilton County Coal LLC ............... B ...... 618 648-2603
  Dahlgren (G-7690)
Icg Illinois ......................................... G ...... 217 947-2332
  Elkhart (G-9825)
Icg Illinois LLC .................................. F ...... 217 566-3000
  Williamsville (G-22191)
Keyrock Energy LLC ......................... G ...... 618 982-9710
  Thompsonville (G-20862)
Knight Hawk Coal LLC ..................... G ...... 618 426-3662
  Percy (G-17495)
Knight Hawk Coal LLC ..................... C ...... 618 497-2768
  Cutler (G-7687)
Mach Mining LLC ............................. G ...... 618 983-3020
  Marion (G-14271)
Macoupin Energy LLC ....................... F ...... 217 854-3291
  Carlinville (G-3043)
Macoupin Energy LLC ....................... G ...... 217 854-3291
  Carlinville (G-3044)
Peabody Arclar Mining LLC .............. G ...... 618 273-4314
  Equality (G-9989)
Seneca Rebuild LLC .......................... F ...... 618 435-9445
  Macedonia (G-14047)
Suncoke Energy Inc .......................... B ...... 630 824-1000
  Lisle (G-13666)
Surface Mining Reclamation Off ........ E ...... 618 463-6460
  Alton (G-591)
▲ White Oak Resources LLC .............. A ...... 618 643-5500
  Dahlgren (G-7693)
Wildcat Hills ..................................... G ...... 618 273-8600
  Eldorado (G-8926)
Williamson Energy LLC ..................... G ...... 618 983-3020
  Marion (G-14295)

## 13 OIL AND GAS EXTRACTION

### 1311 Crude Petroleum & Natural Gas
Ashley Oil Co .................................... G ...... 217 932-2112
  Casey (G-3380)
B Quad Oil Inc .................................. G ...... 618 656-4419
  Edwardsville (G-8790)
Basin Transports .............................. G ...... 618 829-3323
  Saint Elmo (G-19303)
Basnetts Investments ....................... G ...... 618 842-4040
  Fairfield (G-10136)
Belden Enterprises LP ....................... F ...... 618 829-3274
  Saint Elmo (G-19304)
Bell Brothers .................................... G ...... 618 544-2157
  Robinson (G-18055)
Bertram Oil Co .................................. G ...... 618 546-1122
  Robinson (G-18056)
Bi-Petro Inc ...................................... E ...... 217 535-0181
  Springfield (G-20396)

Booth Oil Co Inc G 618 662-7696
Flora (G-10200)
Booth Resources Inc G 618 662-4955
Flora (G-10201)
BP Products North America Inc G 630 420-4300
Naperville (G-15609)
Brehm Oil Inc F 618 242-4620
Mount Vernon (G-15402)
Brookstone Resources Inc G 618 382-2893
Carmi (G-3062)
Bruce McCullough G 217 773-3130
Mount Sterling (G-15390)
Budmark Oil Company Inc G 618 937-2495
West Frankfort (G-21805)
Carter Anna Brooks LLC G 618 382-3939
Carmi (G-3065)
Chicap Pipe Line Company F 708 479-1219
Mokena (G-14858)
Citation Oil & Gas Corp E 618 966-2101
Crossville (G-7521)
Collins Brothers Oil Corp G 618 244-1093
Mount Vernon (G-15404)
Concord Well Service Inc G 618 395-4405
Olney (G-16765)
▲ Continental Resources Ill Inc E 618 242-1717
Mount Vernon (G-15405)
D & Z Exploration Inc G 618 829-3274
Saint Elmo (G-19305)
D Little Drilling G 618 943-3721
Saint Francisville (G-19312)
Dedica Energy Corporation G 217 235-9191
Mattoon (G-14388)
Deep Rock Energy Corporation F 618 548-2779
Salem (G-19329)
Duncan Oil Company Inc G 618 548-2923
Salem (G-19330)
Ensource Inc G 312 912-1048
Chicago (G-4758)
ES Investments Inc G 618 345-6151
Collinsville (G-7323)
Evans Talaiha G 618 327-8200
Nashville (G-15835)
Finks Oil Co Inc G 618 548-5757
Salem (G-19333)
Friend Oil Co G 618 842-9161
Fairfield (G-10142)
Glover Oil Field Service Inc F 618 395-3624
Olney (G-16770)
Gulf Coast Exploration Inc G 847 226-4654
Highland Park (G-11838)
Gulf Petroleum LLC G 312 803-0373
Chicago (G-5012)
Herman L Loeb LLC E 618 943-2227
Lawrenceville (G-13202)
Hocking Oil Company Inc G 618 263-3258
Mount Carmel (G-15267)
Horizontal Systems Inc G 217 932-6218
Casey (G-3385)
Howard Energy Corporation G 618 263-3000
Mount Carmel (G-15268)
J R G Oil Co Inc G 618 842-9131
Fairfield (G-10144)
J W Rudy Co Inc F 618 676-1616
Clay City (G-7265)
Jarvis Bros & Marcell Inc G 217 422-3120
Decatur (G-7899)
Jarvis Drilling Co G 217 422-3120
Decatur (G-7900)
Jbl - Alton G 618 466-0411
Alton (G-580)
Jim Haley Oil Production Co F 618 382-7338
Carmi (G-3070)
Kerogen Resources Inc G 618 382-3114
Carmi (G-3071)
L & J Producers Inc G 217 932-5639
Casey (G-3387)
La Quinta Gas Pipeline Company G 217 430-6781
Quincy (G-17852)
Lampley Oil Inc G 618 439-6288
Benton (G-2034)
Lawrence Oil Company Inc G 618 262-4138
Mount Carmel (G-15272)
Midco Petroleum Inc G 630 655-2198
Westmont (G-21906)
Midco Production Co Inc G 630 655-2198
Westmont (G-21907)
Midwest Oil LLC G 309 456-3663
Good Hope (G-11243)
Midwest Radiant Oil and Gas G 618 476-1303
Millstadt (G-14830)
Mitchco Farms LLC F 618 382-5032
Carmi (G-3075)
MRC Global (us) Inc F 314 231-3400
Granite City (G-11297)
Murphy USA G 815 578-9053
Johnsburg (G-12438)
Murphy USA Inc E 815 337-2440
Woodstock (G-22595)
Murphy USA Inc D 815 936-6144
Kankakee (G-12639)
Murvin & Meir Oil Co G 618 395-4405
Olney (G-16783)
Murvin Oil Company E 618 393-2124
Olney (G-16784)
Natural Gas Pipeline Amer LLC E 618 495-2211
Centralia (G-3423)
Natural Gas Pipeline Amer LLC F 815 426-2151
Herscher (G-11760)
Natural Gas Pipeline Amer LLC E 618 829-3224
Saint Elmo (G-19309)
New Triangle Oil Company G 618 262-4131
Mount Carmel (G-15278)
Oelze Equipment Company LLC E 618 327-9111
Nashville (G-15845)
Orion Petro Corporation G 618 244-2370
Mount Vernon (G-15436)
Pawnee Oil Corporation F 217 522-5440
Springfield (G-20500)
Petco Petroleum Corporation D 618 242-8718
Mount Vernon (G-15440)
Petron Oil Production Inc G 618 783-4486
Newton (G-15946)
Phosphate Resource Ptrs A 847 739-1200
Lake Forest (G-12945)
Pool & Pool Oil Productions G 618 544-7590
Robinson (G-18069)
R & D Oil Producers G 217 773-9299
Mount Sterling (G-15393)
R & W Oil Company G 618 686-3084
Louisville (G-13909)
R H Johnson Oil Co Inc G 630 668-3649
Wheaton (G-21974)
Republic Oil Co Inc G 618 842-7591
Fairfield (G-10153)
Revelle Resources Inc G 217 875-7336
Forsyth (G-10271)
Rex Energy Corporation E 618 943-8700
Bridgeport (G-2454)
River City Oil LLC G 309 693-2249
Peoria (G-17442)
Robinson Production Inc G 618 842-6111
Fairfield (G-10154)
Rodgers Bill Oil Min Bits Svc G 618 299-7771
West Salem (G-21824)
Ron Absher G 618 382-4646
Carmi (G-3079)
Ronnie Joe Graham G 618 548-5544
Salem (G-19348)
Roosevelt Mobile G 630 293-7630
West Chicago (G-21766)
Ross Oil Co Inc G 618 592-3808
Oblong (G-16733)
Shawnee Exploration Partners G 618 382-3223
Carmi (G-3080)
Shulman Brothers Inc G 618 283-3253
Vandalia (G-21124)
Smoco Inc G 618 662-6458
Flora (G-10218)
Southern Triangle Oil Company F 618 262-4131
Mount Carmel (G-15282)
Spartan Petroleum Company G 618 262-4197
Mount Carmel (G-15283)
St Pierre Oil Company Inc G 618 783-4441
Newton (G-15949)
Star Energy Corp Inc G 618 584-3631
Flat Rock (G-10197)
Steven A Zanetis G 618 393-2176
Olney (G-16797)
Stewart Producers Inc G 618 244-3754
Mount Vernon (G-15446)
Team Energy LLC G 618 943-1010
Bridgeport (G-2456)
Tipps Casing Pulling Company G 618 847-7986
Fairfield (G-10156)
Tri Family Oil Co G 618 654-1137
Highland (G-11813)
Tri-State Producing Developing G 618 393-2176
Olney (G-16798)
Trojan Oil Inc G 618 754-3474
Newton (G-15951)
Tussey G K Oil Explrtn & Prdc G 618 948-2871
Saint Francisville (G-19314)
Two Rivers Oil & Gas Co Inc G 217 773-3356
Mount Sterling (G-15395)
UOP LLC D 708 442-7400
Mc Cook (G-14460)
▲ Warren Oil MGT Co IL LLC G 618 997-5951
Marion (G-14294)
Western Oil & Gas Dev Co F 618 544-8646
Robinson (G-18075)
White Land & Mineral Inc G 618 262-5102
Mount Carmel (G-15288)
William R Becker F 618 378-3337
Norris City (G-16116)
Wood Energy Inc G 618 244-1590
Mount Vernon (G-15449)
Yockey Oil Incorporated G 618 393-6236
Olney (G-16802)
Zanetis Oil Company G 618 262-4593
Mount Carmel (G-15289)

## 1321 Natural Gas Liquids

15679 Wadsworth Inc G 847 662-4561
Wadsworth (G-21321)
Alliance Pipeline Inc G 815 941-5874
Morris (G-15092)
▲ Aux Sable Liquid Products LP E 815 941-5800
Morris (G-15095)
Aux Sable Midstream LLC E 815 941-5800
Morris (G-15096)
Enterprise Products Company G 708 534-6266
Monee (G-14993)
Ferrellgas LP G 815 599-8967
Machesney Park (G-14074)
Ferrellgas LP G 815 877-7333
Machesney Park (G-14073)
FMC Technologies Inc G 312 803-4321
Chicago (G-4865)

## 1381 Drilling Oil & Gas Wells

Baker Hghes Olfld Oprtions Inc F 618 393-2919
Olney (G-16761)
Black Bison Water Services LLC G 630 272-5935
Chicago (G-4119)
Booth Resources Inc G 618 662-4955
Flora (G-10201)
C&R Directional Boring G 630 458-0055
Addison (G-66)
Coursons Coring & Drilling G 618 349-8765
Saint Peter (G-19321)
Coy Oil Inc G 618 966-2126
Crossville (G-7522)
Crystal Precision Drilling G 815 633-5460
Loves Park (G-13930)
Dee Drilling Co E 618 262-4136
Mount Carmel (G-15264)
Ebers Drilling Co G 618 826-5398
Chester (G-3655)
Evergreen Energy LLC G 618 384-9295
Carmi (G-3067)
F L Beard Service Corp E 618 262-5193
Mount Carmel (G-15265)
Five P Drilling Inc E 618 943-9771
Bridgeport (G-2452)
G&E Transportation Inc E 404 350-6497
Chicago (G-4903)
Geo N Mitchell Drlg Co Inc G 618 382-2343
Carmi (G-3068)
Glover Oil Field Service Inc F 618 395-3624
Olney (G-16770)
Grosch Irrigation Company F 217 482-5479
Mason City (G-14364)
J H Robison & Associates Ltd G 847 559-9662
Northbrook (G-16281)
Jackson Oil Corporation G 618 263-6521
Mount Carmel (G-15270)
Jerry D Graham Oil G 618 548-5540
Salem (G-19337)
Kapp Company LLC G 618 676-1000
Olney (G-16776)
Kinoco Inc G 618 378-3802
Norris City (G-16115)
L C Neelydrilling Inc G 618 544-2726
Robinson (G-18065)
Les Wilson Inc C 618 382-4667
Carmi (G-3073)
Marion Oelze G 618 327-9224
Nashville (G-15839)
Mashburn Well Drilling G 217 794-3728
Maroa (G-14306)

**Mid-America Underground LLC** E 630 443-9999
Aurora *(G-1188)*
**Murvin & Meier Oil Co** G 847 277-8380
Barrington *(G-1293)*
**Pep Drilling Co** G 618 242-2205
Mount Vernon *(G-15438)*
**Quad Cities Directional Boring** G 309 792-3070
Colona *(G-7346)*
**Quality Drilling Service LLP** G 937 663-4715
Alton *(G-587)*
**Raimonde Drilling Corp** F 630 458-0590
Addison *(G-268)*
**Rays Electrical Service LLC** F 847 214-2944
Elgin *(G-9161)*
**Reef Development Inc** F 618 842-7711
Fairfield *(G-10152)*
**Rodgers Bill Oil Min Bits Svc** G 618 299-7771
West Salem *(G-21824)*
**Royal Drilling & Producing** G 618 966-2221
Crossville *(G-7523)*
**Runyon Oil Production Inc** G 618 395-8510
Olney *(G-16794)*
**Southern Triangle Oil Company** F 618 262-4131
Mount Carmel *(G-15282)*
**Spartan Petroleum Company** G 618 262-4197
Mount Carmel *(G-15283)*
**Ta Oil Field Service Inc** G 618 249-9001
Richview *(G-17982)*
**Tussey G K Oil Explrtn & Prdc** G 618 948-2871
Saint Francisville *(G-19314)*
▲ **Universal Hrzntal Drctnal Drlg** G 847 847-3300
Lake Zurich *(G-13140)*

## 1382 Oil & Gas Field Exploration Svcs

**Angel Rose Energy LLC** G 618 392-3700
Olney *(G-16760)*
**Baker Hghes Olfld Oprtions Inc** F 618 393-2919
Olney *(G-16761)*
**Bell Brothers** G 618 544-2157
Robinson *(G-18055)*
**Benchmark Properties Ltd** G 618 395-7023
Olney *(G-16762)*
**Crawford County Oil LLC** E 618 544-3493
Robinson *(G-18058)*
**Digital H2o Inc** F 847 456-8424
Chicago *(G-4601)*
**East End Express Lube Inc** G 618 257-1049
Belleville *(G-1629)*
**Energy Group Inc** E 847 836-2000
Dundee *(G-8561)*
**Howard Energy Corporation** G 618 263-3000
Mount Carmel *(G-15268)*
**J H Robison & Associates Ltd** G 847 559-9662
Northbrook *(G-16281)*
**Laron Oil Corporation** G 847 836-2000
Dundee *(G-8563)*
**Lla Exploration Inc** G 217 623-4096
Taylorville *(G-20841)*
**Martin Exploration Mgt Co** G 708 385-6500
Alsip *(G-488)*
**Mid States Salvage** G 618 842-6741
Fairfield *(G-10150)*
**Midco Exploration Inc** G 630 655-2198
Westmont *(G-21905)*
**Mohican Petroleum Inc** G 312 782-6385
Chicago *(G-5788)*
**Moran Properties Inc** G 312 440-1962
Chicago *(G-5804)*
**Murphy USA Inc** E 630 801-4950
Montgomery *(G-15063)*
**Northern Illinois Gas Company** E 630 983-8676
Kankakee *(G-12640)*
**Northern Illinois Gas Company** F 217 357-3105
Carthage *(G-3318)*
**Northern Illinois Gas Company** C 630 983-8676
Crystal Lake *(G-7620)*
**Northern Illinois Gas Company** D 815 433-3850
Ottawa *(G-16972)*
**Northern Illinois Gas Company** C 815 693-3907
Joliet *(G-12546)*
**Northern Illinois Gas Company** F 815 223-8097
Mendota *(G-14729)*
**Ofgd Inc** G 708 283-7101
Olympia Fields *(G-16804)*
**Strata Exploration Inc** G 618 842-2610
Fairfield *(G-10155)*
**Tenexco Inc** G 708 771-7870
River Forest *(G-18003)*
**Third Day Oil & Gas LLC** G 618 553-5538
Oblong *(G-16736)*
**Times Energy** G 773 444-9282
Worth *(G-22635)*
**Woodrow Todd** G 618 838-9105
Flora *(G-10222)*

## 1389 Oil & Gas Field Svcs, NEC

**1 Heavy Equipment Loading Inc** F 773 581-7374
Bedford Park *(G-1528)*
**Abner Trucking Co Inc** G 618 676-1301
Clay City *(G-7261)*
**Abundance House Treasure Nfp** G 312 788-4316
Chicago *(G-3711)*
**Advanced Lubrication Inc** G 815 932-3288
Kankakee *(G-12602)*
**ANR Pipeline Company** G 309 667-2158
New Windsor *(G-15929)*
**B & B Equipment** F 217 562-2511
Assumption *(G-930)*
**B & B Tank Truck Construction** F 618 378-3337
Norris City *(G-16111)*
**Baker Hghes Olfld Oprtions Inc** F 618 393-2919
Olney *(G-16761)*
**Bangert Casing Pulling Corp** G 618 676-1411
Clay City *(G-7262)*
**Buckeye Terminals LLC** G 217 342-2336
Effingham *(G-8828)*
**Campbell Energy LLC** G 618 382-3939
Carmi *(G-3063)*
**Citation Oil & Gas Corp** F 618 548-2331
Odin *(G-16739)*
**Clinton Oil Corp** G 815 356-1124
Crystal Lake *(G-7555)*
**Concord Oil & Gas Corporation** E 618 393-2124
Olney *(G-16764)*
**Craftwood Inc** F 630 758-1740
Elmhurst *(G-9858)*
**Cross Oil & Well Service Inc** F 618 592-4609
Oblong *(G-16731)*
▲ **Crystatech Inc** F 847 768-0500
Des Plaines *(G-8178)*
**D Kersey Construction Co** G 847 919-4980
Northbrook *(G-16237)*
**De Vries International Inc** E 773 248-6695
Chicago *(G-4568)*
**Deep Rock Energy Corporation** E 618 548-2779
Kinmundy *(G-12709)*
**Dontrell Percy** F 773 418-4900
Chicago *(G-4631)*
**Duncan Oil Company Inc** G 618 548-2923
Salem *(G-19330)*
**East St Louis Trml & Stor Co** E 618 271-2185
East Saint Louis *(G-8749)*
**Evergreen Marathon** G 708 636-5700
Evergreen Park *(G-10114)*
**F L Beard Service Corp** E 618 262-5193
Mount Carmel *(G-15265)*
**Fairfield Acid and Frac Co** F 618 842-9186
Fairfield *(G-10140)*
**Feller Oilfield Service Inc** F 618 267-5650
Saint Elmo *(G-19307)*
**Finite Resources Ltd** G 618 252-3733
Harrisburg *(G-11598)*
**Foltz Welding Ltd** C 618 432-7777
Patoka *(G-17231)*
**Franklin Well Services Inc** D 812 494-2800
Lawrenceville *(G-13200)*
**Gesell Oil Well Service LLC** G 618 547-7114
Kinmundy *(G-12710)*
**Gesells Pump Sales & Service** G 618 439-7354
Whittington *(G-22186)*
**Gholson Pump & Repairs Co** G 618 382-4730
Carmi *(G-3069)*
**Global General Contractors LLC** G 708 663-0476
Tinley Park *(G-20918)*
**Glover Oil Field Service Inc** F 618 395-3624
Olney *(G-16770)*
**Haggard Well Services Inc** G 618 262-5060
Mount Carmel *(G-15266)*
**Harold L Ray Truck & Trctr Svc** G 618 673-2701
Cisne *(G-7252)*
**Heafner Contracting Inc** F 618 466-3678
Godfrey *(G-11225)*
**Howard Energy Corporation** G 618 263-3000
Mount Carmel *(G-15268)*
**I D Tool Specialty Company** G 815 432-2007
Watseka *(G-21419)*
**J B Oil Field Cnstr & Sup** G 618 936-2350
Sumner *(G-20771)*
**Jsq Inc** G 847 731-8800
Wadsworth *(G-21323)*
**Koontz Services** G 618 375-7613
Carmi *(G-3072)*
**Ktm Lab Service Co Inc** G 708 351-6780
Schaumburg *(G-19607)*
**Local 46 Training Program Tr** G 217 528-4041
Springfield *(G-20471)*
**M & I Acid Company Inc** G 618 676-1638
Clay City *(G-7266)*
**M & L Well Service Inc** E 618 393-7144
Olney *(G-16778)*
**M & L Well Service Inc** G 618 395-4538
Olney *(G-16779)*
**M & S Oil Well Cementing Co** G 618 262-7962
Mount Carmel *(G-15273)*
**Map Oil Co Inc** G 618 375-7616
Grayville *(G-11374)*
**Marlow Hill Drilling Inc** F 618 867-2978
Murphysboro *(G-15578)*
**Mason Well Servicing Inc** G 618 375-4411
Grayville *(G-11375)*
**Matrix North Amercn Cnstr Inc** G 312 754-6605
Chicago *(G-5654)*
**McLean Subsurface Utility** G 336 988-2520
Decatur *(G-7911)*
**McNdt Pipeline Ltd** G 815 467-5200
Channahon *(G-3579)*
**Mdm Construction Supply LLC** G 815 847-7340
Rockford *(G-18488)*
**Mid-States Services LLC** F 618 842-4726
Fairfield *(G-10151)*
**Miller Testing Service** E 618 262-5911
Mount Carmel *(G-15274)*
**Mitchco Farms LLC** F 618 382-5032
Carmi *(G-3075)*
**Oelze Equipment Company LLC** E 618 327-9111
Nashville *(G-15845)*
**Ordner Well Service Inc** G 618 676-1950
Clay City *(G-7267)*
**P J Repair Service Inc** F 618 548-5690
Salem *(G-19341)*
**Panhandle Eastrn Pipe Line LP** E 217 753-1108
Springfield *(G-20498)*
**Patriot Home Improvement Inc** F 630 800-1901
Aurora *(G-1203)*
**Petco Petroleum Corporation** G 630 654-1740
Hinsdale *(G-11956)*
**Pinnacle Exploration Corp** G 618 395-8100
Olney *(G-16790)*
**Platt G Mostardi** F 630 993-2100
Hoffman Estates *(G-12034)*
**Pool Center Inc** G 217 698-7665
Springfield *(G-20505)*
**Precision Plugging and Sls Inc** F 618 395-8510
Olney *(G-16792)*
**Protus Construction** G 773 405-9999
Chicago *(G-6218)*
**Purified Lubricants Inc** E 708 478-3500
Mokena *(G-14899)*
**Pyrophase Inc** G 773 324-8645
Chicago *(G-6233)*
**R Energy LLC** G 618 382-7313
Carmi *(G-3077)*
**Roark Oil Field Services Inc** G 618 382-4703
Carmi *(G-3078)*
**Runyon Oil Tools Inc** G 618 395-5045
Olney *(G-16795)*
**Samtek International Inc** G 314 954-4005
Swansea *(G-20782)*
**Schwartz Oilfield Services** E 618 532-0232
Walnut Hill *(G-21334)*
**Seip Service & Supply Inc** F 618 532-1923
Centralia *(G-3432)*
**Sids Well Service** G 618 375-5411
Grayville *(G-11377)*
**Sims Company Inc** G 618 665-3901
Louisville *(G-13910)*
**Stages Construction Inc** G 773 619-2977
Chicago *(G-6568)*
**Stewart Producers Inc** G 618 244-3754
Mount Vernon *(G-15446)*
**T-Rex Excavating Inc** G 815 547-9955
Belvidere *(G-1787)*
**Ta Oil Field Service Inc** G 618 249-9001
Richview *(G-17982)*
**Tdw Services Inc** F 815 407-0675
Romeoville *(G-18873)*
**Team Energy LLC** G 618 943-1010
Bridgeport *(G-2456)*
**Toppert Jetting Service Inc** G 309 755-2240
Hillsdale *(G-11904)*

**Tri Kote Inc** ....G.... 618 262-4156
Mount Carmel *(G-15285)*
**Tri State Acid Co Inc** ....G.... 618 676-1111
Clay City *(G-7268)*
**Tri-Zee Services Inc** ....G.... 630 543-8677
Addison *(G-324)*
**United Oil Co** ....G.... 309 378-3049
Downs *(G-8549)*
**Wabash Production & Dev** ....G.... 618 847-7401
Fairfield *(G-10158)*
**Warren Service Company** ....G.... 618 384-2117
Carmi *(G-3083)*
**Water & Gas Technologies** ....G.... 708 829-3254
Palos Park *(G-17134)*
**Wayne County Well Surveys Inc** ....F.... 618 842-9116
Fairfield *(G-10160)*
**Wilpro** ....G.... 618 382-4667
Carmi *(G-3085)*

## 14 MINING AND QUARRYING OF NONMETALLIC MINERALS, EXCEPT FUELS

### *1411 Dimension Stone*

**Anna Quarries Inc** ....E.... 618 833-5121
Anna *(G-600)*
**Blue Pearl Stone Tech LLC** ....G.... 708 698-5700
La Grange *(G-12726)*
**C & V Granite Inc** ....G.... 847 966-0275
Morton Grove *(G-15191)*
▲ **Eastern Kitchen & Bath** ....G.... 312 492-7248
Chicago *(G-4684)*
**F Lee Charles & Sons Inc** ....G.... 815 547-7141
Kirkland *(G-12712)*
**Gary Galassi and Sons Inc** ....E.... 815 886-3906
Romeoville *(G-18827)*
**Ill Dept Natural Resources** ....F.... 217 782-4970
Springfield *(G-20453)*
**JKS Ventures Inc** ....G.... 708 345-9344
Melrose Park *(G-14662)*
**Joliet Sand and Gravel Company** ....D.... 815 741-2090
Rockdale *(G-18222)*
**Lafarge Aggregates Ill Inc** ....G.... 847 742-6060
South Elgin *(G-20212)*
**Loberg Excavating Inc** ....E.... 815 443-2874
Pearl City *(G-17248)*
**Material Service Corporation** ....D.... 708 485-8211
Mc Cook *(G-14451)*
**Nokomis Quarry Company** ....F.... 217 563-2011
Nokomis *(G-16059)*
**Pana Limestone Company** ....G.... 217 562-4231
Pana *(G-17135)*
**PC Marble Inc** ....E.... 708 385-3360
Alsip *(G-505)*
**Picture Stone Inc** ....G.... 773 875-5021
Mount Prospect *(G-15365)*
**Red Hill Lava Products Inc** ....G.... 800 528-2765
Rock Island *(G-18198)*
**Stolle Casper Quar & Contg Co** ....E.... 618 337-5212
Dupo *(G-8579)*
▲ **Stone Usa Inc** ....G.... 312 356-0988
Chicago *(G-6598)*
**Tri-State Cut Stone Co** ....E.... 815 469-7550
Frankfort *(G-10371)*
▲ **Wendell Adams** ....E.... 217 345-9587
Charleston *(G-3615)*

### *1422 Crushed & Broken Limestone*

**Anna Quarries Inc** ....E.... 618 833-5121
Anna *(G-600)*
**Argyle Cut Stone Co** ....E.... 847 456-6210
Des Plaines *(G-8151)*
**Calhoun Quarry Incorporated** ....F.... 618 396-2229
Batchtown *(G-1517)*
**Calhoun Quarry Incorporated** ....G.... 618 576-9223
Hardin *(G-11593)*
**Callender Construction Co Inc** ....F.... 217 285-2161
Pittsfield *(G-17563)*
**Central Limestone Company Inc** ....F.... 815 736-6341
Morris *(G-15101)*
**Central Stone Company** ....D.... 309 757-8250
Moline *(G-14921)*
**Central Stone Company** ....F.... 309 776-3900
Colchester *(G-7307)*
**Central Stone Company** ....G.... 217 327-4300
Chambersburg *(G-3443)*
**Central Stone Company** ....F.... 217 723-4410
Pittsfield *(G-17565)*
**Central Stone Company** ....F.... 217 224-7330
Quincy *(G-17811)*
**Charleston Stone Company** ....E.... 217 345-6292
Ashmore *(G-928)*
**Civil Constructors Inc** ....G.... 815 858-2691
Elizabeth *(G-9241)*
**Collinson Stone Co** ....F.... 309 787-7983
Milan *(G-14780)*
**Columbia Quarry Company** ....E.... 618 281-7631
Columbia *(G-7354)*
**Columbia Quarry Company** ....E.... 618 939-8833
Waterloo *(G-21400)*
**Conmat Inc** ....E.... 815 235-2200
Freeport *(G-10651)*
**Elmer L Larson L C** ....F.... 815 895-4837
Sycamore *(G-20797)*
**Elmhurst-Chicago Stone Company** ....E.... 630 983-6410
Bolingbrook *(G-2305)*
**Gray Quarries Inc** ....F.... 217 847-2712
Hamilton *(G-11534)*
**H&H Crushing Inc** ....G.... 309 275-0643
West Peoria *(G-21822)*
**Hastie Mining & Trucking** ....E.... 618 289-4536
Cave In Rock *(G-3402)*
**Heisler Stone Co Inc** ....G.... 815 244-2685
Mount Carroll *(G-15291)*
**Huyear Trucking Inc** ....G.... 217 854-3551
Carlinville *(G-3039)*
**Iola Quarry Inc** ....F.... 217 682-3865
Mode *(G-14849)*
**Kimmaterials Inc** ....G.... 618 466-0352
Godfrey *(G-11227)*
**Le Claire Investment Inc** ....G.... 309 757-8250
Moline *(G-14953)*
**Legacy Vulcan LLC** ....E.... 815 468-8141
Manteno *(G-14186)*
**Macklin Inc** ....F.... 815 562-4803
Rochelle *(G-18096)*
**Martha Lacey** ....G.... 217 723-4380
Pearl *(G-17247)*
**Material Service Corporation** ....C.... 708 731-2600
Westchester *(G-21850)*
**Material Service Corporation** ....E.... 217 563-2531
Nokomis *(G-16058)*
**Material Service Corporation** ....E.... 217 732-2117
Athens *(G-939)*
**Material Service Corporation** ....D.... 708 877-6540
Thornton *(G-20875)*
**Meyer Material Co Merger Corp** ....D.... 815 943-2605
Harvard *(G-11641)*
**Mid-America Carbonates LLC** ....G.... 217 222-3500
Quincy *(G-17858)*
**Mill Creek Mining Inc** ....G.... 309 787-1414
Milan *(G-14794)*
**Mining International LLC** ....F.... 630 232-4246
Geneva *(G-10850)*
**Mining International LLC** ....E.... 815 722-0900
Joliet *(G-12543)*
**Nokomis Quarry Company** ....F.... 217 563-2011
Nokomis *(G-16059)*
**Omni Materials Inc** ....E.... 618 262-5118
Mount Carmel *(G-15279)*
**Quality Lime Company** ....F.... 217 826-2343
Marshall *(G-14328)*
**R L ONeal & Sons Inc** ....F.... 309 458-3350
Plymouth *(G-17682)*
**Renner Quarries Ltd** ....G.... 815 288-6699
Dixon *(G-8343)*
**Riverstone Group Inc** ....F.... 309 523-3159
Hillsdale *(G-11903)*
**Riverstone Group Inc** ....F.... 309 933-1123
Cleveland *(G-7271)*
**Riverstone Group Inc** ....E.... 309 787-3141
Milan *(G-14804)*
**Savanna Quarry Inc** ....G.... 815 273-4208
Savanna *(G-19405)*
**Shawnee Stone LLC** ....F.... 618 548-1585
Salem *(G-19350)*
**Southern Illinois Stone Co** ....E.... 618 995-2392
Buncombe *(G-2801)*
**Southern Illinois Stone Co** ....F.... 573 334-5261
Buncombe *(G-2800)*
**Southfield Corporation** ....E.... 815 842-2333
Pontiac *(G-17711)*
**Southfield Corporation** ....F.... 815 468-8700
Manteno *(G-14194)*
**St Marys Cement** ....G.... 773 995-5100
Chicago *(G-6567)*
**Stolle Casper Quar & Contg Co** ....E.... 618 337-5212
Dupo *(G-8579)*
**Tower Rock Stone Company** ....F.... 618 281-4106
Columbia *(G-7364)*
**Tri-State Cut Stone Co** ....E.... 815 469-7550
Frankfort *(G-10371)*
**Tuscola Stone Company** ....F.... 217 253-4705
Tuscola *(G-21028)*
**Utica Stone Co Inc** ....G.... 815 667-4690
Utica *(G-21110)*
**Valley Quarry** ....G.... 309 462-3003
Saint Augustine *(G-19128)*
**Valley View Industries Inc** ....E.... 815 358-2236
Cornell *(G-7382)*
**Vulcan Construction Mtls LLC** ....E.... 630 955-8500
Naperville *(G-15779)*
**Vulcan Materials Company** ....F.... 262 639-2803
Naperville *(G-15780)*
**Vulcan Materials Company** ....E.... 815 899-7204
Sycamore *(G-20824)*
**William Charles Cnstr Co LLC** ....G.... 815 654-4720
Belvidere *(G-1797)*

### *1423 Crushed & Broken Granite*

**Martin Marietta Materials Inc** ....F.... 618 285-6267
Golconda *(G-11241)*
**Pacific Granites Inc** ....G.... 312 835-7777
Chicago *(G-6052)*

### *1429 Crushed & Broken Stone, NEC*

**Gateway Crushing & Screening** ....E.... 618 337-1954
East Saint Louis *(G-8753)*
**Mid Illinois Quarry Company** ....G.... 217 932-2611
Casey *(G-3389)*
**Monmouth Stone Co** ....F.... 309 734-7951
Monmouth *(G-15022)*

### *1442 Construction Sand & Gravel*

**A E Frasz Inc** ....F.... 630 232-6223
Elburn *(G-8872)*
**Aggregate Materials Company** ....G.... 815 747-2430
East Dubuque *(G-8616)*
**Allendale Gravel Co Inc** ....G.... 618 263-3521
Allendale *(G-420)*
**Amigoni Construction** ....G.... 309 923-3701
Roanoke *(G-18047)*
**Beverly Materials LLC** ....G.... 847 695-9300
Hoffman Estates *(G-11994)*
**Bluemastiff Group LLC** ....G.... 708 704-3529
Chicago *(G-4129)*
**Buckner Sand Co** ....G.... 630 653-3700
Carol Stream *(G-3120)*
**C & H Gravel C Inc** ....G.... 217 857-3425
Teutopolis *(G-20848)*
**Carlyle Sand & Gravel Ltd** ....G.... 618 594-8263
Carlyle *(G-3053)*
**Clear Lake Sand & Gravel Co** ....F.... 217 725-6999
Springfield *(G-20419)*
**Consolidated Materials Inc** ....G.... 815 568-1538
Marengo *(G-14222)*
**Contractors Ready-Mix Inc** ....G.... 217 482-5530
Mason City *(G-14362)*
**County Materials Corp** ....E.... 217 352-4181
Champaign *(G-3470)*
**Cullinan & Sons Inc** ....E.... 309 925-2711
Tremont *(G-20981)*
**Dans Dirt and Gravel** ....G.... 630 479-6622
Aurora *(G-1138)*
**Edk Construction Inc** ....G.... 630 853-3484
Darien *(G-7793)*
**Elmer L Larson L C** ....F.... 815 895-4837
Sycamore *(G-20797)*
**Elmhurst-Chicago Stone Company** ....E.... 630 832-4000
Elmhurst *(G-9865)*
**Elmhurst-Chicago Stone Company** ....F.... 630 557-2446
Kaneville *(G-12599)*
**Elmhurst-Chicago Stone Company** ....E.... 630 983-6410
Bolingbrook *(G-2305)*
**Empire Acoustical Systems Inc** ....E.... 815 261-0072
Princeton *(G-17747)*
**Fairmount Santrol Inc** ....E.... 815 587-4410
Ottawa *(G-16959)*
**Fairmount Santrol Inc** ....E.... 815 538-2645
Troy Grove *(G-21012)*
**Fox Ridge Stone Co** ....G.... 630 554-9101
Oswego *(G-16918)*
**Galena Road Gravel Inc** ....E.... 309 274-6388
Chillicothe *(G-7166)*
**GBS Liquidating Corp** ....G.... 309 342-4155
Galesburg *(G-10753)*
**H & H Services Inc** ....F.... 618 633-2837
Hamel *(G-11528)*

**Hastie Mining & Trucking** ........E ....... 618 289-4536
Cave In Rock *(G-3402)*
**Jackson County Sand & Grav Co** ........G ....... 618 763-4711
Gorham *(G-11254)*
**Joliet Sand and Gravel Company** ........D ....... 815 741-2090
Rockdale *(G-18222)*
**Lafarge Aggregates III Inc** ........G ....... 847 742-6060
South Elgin *(G-20212)*
**Lafarge Aux Sable LLC** ........G ....... 815 941-1423
Morris *(G-15112)*
▲ **Lafarge North America Inc** ........C ....... 703 480-3600
Chicago *(G-5435)*
**Lake County Grading Co LLC** ........E ....... 847 362-2590
Libertyville *(G-13341)*
**Le Claire Investment Inc** ........G ....... 309 757-8250
Moline *(G-14953)*
**Legacy Vulcan LLC** ........D ....... 630 955-8500
Naperville *(G-15687)*
**Legacy Vulcan LLC** ........E ....... 815 468-8141
Manteno *(G-14186)*
**Legacy Vulcan LLC** ........E ....... 847 437-4181
Elk Grove Village *(G-9593)*
**Legacy Vulcan LLC** ........F ....... 217 932-2611
Casey *(G-3388)*
**Legacy Vulcan LLC** ........F ....... 815 726-6900
Joliet *(G-12533)*
**Legacy Vulcan LLC** ........F ....... 630 739-0182
Romeoville *(G-18838)*
**Legacy Vulcan LLC** ........E ....... 217 498-7263
Rochester *(G-18119)*
**Legacy Vulcan LLC** ........D ....... 708 485-6602
Mc Cook *(G-14450)*
**Legacy Vulcan LLC** ........F ....... 815 895-6501
Sycamore *(G-20807)*
**Legacy Vulcan LLC** ........G ....... 217 963-2196
Harristown *(G-11607)*
**Legacy Vulcan LLC** ........E ....... 815 436-3535
Plainfield *(G-17617)*
**Legacy Vulcan LLC** ........G ....... 847 578-9622
Lake Bluff *(G-12853)*
**Legacy Vulcan LLC** ........G ....... 847 548-4623
Grayslake *(G-11350)*
**Legacy Vulcan LLC** ........F ....... 630 904-1110
Plainfield *(G-17618)*
**Legacy Vulcan Corp** ........E ....... 815 937-7928
Kankakee *(G-12637)*
**Material Service Corporation** ........E ....... 815 942-1830
Romeoville *(G-18843)*
**Material Service Corporation** ........E ....... 815 838-3420
Romeoville *(G-18844)*
**Material Service Corporation** ........E ....... 847 658-4559
Algonquin *(G-400)*
**Material Service Corporation** ........E ....... 708 447-1100
Westchester *(G-21849)*
**Material Service Corporation** ........C ....... 708 731-2600
Westchester *(G-21850)*
**Material Service Corporation** ........E ....... 815 838-2400
Romeoville *(G-18842)*
**Material Service Resources** ........D ....... 630 325-7736
Chicago *(G-5651)*
**May Sand and Gravel Inc** ........G ....... 815 338-4761
Wonder Lake *(G-22324)*
**Mel Price Company Inc** ........F ....... 217 442-9092
Danville *(G-7754)*
**Menoni & Mocogni Inc** ........F ....... 847 432-0850
Highland Park *(G-11854)*
**Mertel Gravel Company Inc** ........F ....... 815 223-0468
Peru *(G-17518)*
**Meyer Material Co Merger Corp** ........F ....... 847 658-7811
Elburn *(G-8891)*
**Meyer Material Co Merger Corp** ........E ....... 815 568-6119
Elburn *(G-8893)*
**Mid-America Sand & Gravel** ........G ....... 217 586-4536
Mahomet *(G-14161)*
**Mid-America Sand & Gravel** ........G ....... 217 355-1307
Urbana *(G-21094)*
**Newton Ready Mix Inc** ........F ....... 618 783-8611
Newton *(G-15944)*
**Opti-Sand Incorporated** ........G ....... 630 293-1245
West Chicago *(G-21753)*
**Otter Creek Sand & Gravel** ........F ....... 309 759-4293
Havana *(G-11700)*
**Parkview Sand & Gravel Inc** ........G ....... 262 534-4347
Lake In The Hills *(G-13003)*
**Pdss Construction** ........F ....... 847 980-6090
Morton Grove *(G-15226)*
**Pekin Sand and Gravel LLC** ........G ....... 309 347-8917
Pekin *(G-17282)*
**Petersen Sand & Gravel Inc** ........F ....... 815 344-1060
Lakemoor *(G-13145)*
**Plote Construction Inc** ........E ....... 847 695-0422
Hoffman Estates *(G-12035)*
**Plote Construction Inc** ........D ....... 847 695-9300
Hoffman Estates *(G-12036)*
**Plote Inc** ........D ....... 847 695-9467
Hoffman Estates *(G-12037)*
**Prosser Construction Co** ........F ....... 217 774-5032
Shelbyville *(G-19913)*
**Quality Sand Company Inc** ........G ....... 618 346-1070
Collinsville *(G-7339)*
**Randy Wright & Son Cnstr** ........G ....... 217 478-4171
Alexander *(G-374)*
**Reliable Sand and Gravel Co** ........G ....... 815 385-5020
McHenry *(G-14551)*
**Riverstone Group Inc** ........G ....... 309 787-1415
Rock Island *(G-18201)*
**Rock River Ready Mix Inc** ........G ....... 815 288-2260
Dixon *(G-8344)*
**Rock River Ready Mix Inc** ........G ....... 815 438-2510
Rock Falls *(G-18149)*
**Rockford Sand & Gravel Co** ........E ....... 815 654-4700
Loves Park *(G-13986)*
**Rogers Ready Mix & Mtls Inc** ........F ....... 815 389-2223
Roscoe *(G-18915)*
**Rogers Ready Mix & Mtls Inc** ........D ....... 815 234-8212
Byron *(G-2920)*
**Rogers Redi-Mix Inc** ........F ....... 618 282-3844
Ruma *(G-19088)*
**Sand & Gravel Service** ........G ....... 309 648-4585
Metamora *(G-14749)*
**Sand Valley Sand & Gravel Inc** ........F ....... 217 446-4210
Danville *(G-7765)*
**Sangamon Valley Sand & Gravel** ........G ....... 217 498-7189
Rochester *(G-18121)*
**Seneca Sand & Gravel LLC** ........G ....... 630 746-9183
Seneca *(G-19891)*
**Southfield Corporation** ........G ....... 217 379-3606
Paxton *(G-17245)*
**Southfield Corporation** ........E ....... 309 676-0576
Peoria *(G-17459)*
**Stark Materials Inc** ........E ....... 309 828-8520
Shirley *(G-19920)*
**Stokes Sand & Gravel Inc** ........G ....... 815 489-0680
Batavia *(G-1499)*
**Super Aggregates Inc** ........G ....... 815 385-8000
McHenry *(G-14560)*
**Thelen Sand & Gravel Inc** ........D ....... 847 838-8800
Antioch *(G-656)*
**Tri-Con Materials Inc** ........G ....... 815 872-3206
Princeton *(G-17762)*
**Turner Sand & Gravel Inc** ........G ....... 618 586-2486
Palestine *(G-17096)*
**Valley Run Stone Inc** ........E ....... 630 553-7974
Yorkville *(G-22674)*
**Vandalia Sand & Gravel Inc** ........F ....... 618 283-4029
Vandalia *(G-21129)*
**Wayland Ready Mix Concrete Svc** ........F ....... 309 833-2064
Macomb *(G-14134)*
**William Charles Cnstr Co LLC** ........D ....... 815 654-4700
Loves Park *(G-14007)*

## 1446 Industrial Sand

**Clifford W Estes Co Inc** ........F ....... 815 433-0944
Ottawa *(G-16955)*
**Fairmount Santrol Inc** ........F ....... 815 433-2449
Ottawa *(G-16958)*
**Fjcj LLC** ........F ....... 618 785-2217
Baldwin *(G-1250)*
**Kona Blackbird Inc** ........F ....... 815 792-8750
Serena *(G-19892)*
**Snyder Industries Inc** ........D ....... 630 773-9510
Bensenville *(G-1993)*
**Spectron Manufacturing** ........G ....... 720 879-7605
Bloomingdale *(G-2138)*
**U S Silica Company** ........E ....... 815 562-7336
Rochelle *(G-18113)*
**U S Silica Company** ........G ....... 800 635-7263
Utica *(G-21108)*
**U S Silica Company** ........C ....... 815 434-0188
Ottawa *(G-16988)*
**Unimin Corporation** ........E ....... 815 667-5102
Utica *(G-21109)*
**Unimin Corporation** ........E ....... 815 732-2121
Oregon *(G-16833)*
**Unimin Corporation** ........G ....... 815 539-6734
Troy Grove *(G-21013)*
**Unimin Corporation** ........E ....... 618 747-2338
Tamms *(G-20826)*
**Unimin Corporation** ........D ....... 618 747-2311
Tamms *(G-20827)*
**Unimin Corporation** ........E ....... 815 431-2200
Ottawa *(G-16989)*
**Unimin Corporation** ........E ....... 815 434-5363
Ottawa *(G-16990)*
**Wedron Silica Company** ........D ....... 815 433-2449
Wedron *(G-21646)*

## 1455 Kaolin & Ball Clay

**Huber Carbonates LLC** ........G ....... 217 224-8737
Quincy *(G-17837)*

## 1459 Clay, Ceramic & Refractory Minerals, NEC

◆ **Amcol International Corp** ........E ....... 847 851-1500
Hoffman Estates *(G-11991)*
**American Colloid Company** ........E ....... 618 452-8143
Granite City *(G-11263)*
**American Colloid Company** ........F ....... 304 882-2123
Elgin *(G-8947)*
◆ **American Colloid Company** ........E ....... 847 851-1700
Hoffman Estates *(G-11992)*
▼ **American Colloid Minerals Co** ........E ....... 800 527-9948
Arlington Heights *(G-709)*
**Carpentersville Quarry Inc** ........F ....... 847 836-1550
Carpentersville *(G-3278)*
**Oil-Dri Corporation America** ........D ....... 618 745-6881
Mounds *(G-15259)*
**Oil-Dri Corporation America** ........B ....... 312 321-1516
Chicago *(G-5976)*
◆ **Profile Products LLC** ........E ....... 847 215-1144
Buffalo Grove *(G-2756)*

## 1474 Potash, Soda & Borate Minerals

◆ **Pcs Phosphate Company Inc** ........D ....... 847 849-4200
Northbrook *(G-16336)*
**Potash Corp Ssktchewan Fla Inc** ........C ....... 847 849-4200
Northbrook *(G-16340)*

## 1475 Phosphate Rock

◆ **Pcs Phosphate Company Inc** ........D ....... 847 849-4200
Northbrook *(G-16336)*
**Phosphate Resource Ptrs** ........A ....... 847 739-1200
Lake Forest *(G-12945)*
**Potash Corp Ssktchewan Fla Inc** ........C ....... 847 849-4200
Northbrook *(G-16340)*

## 1479 Chemical & Fertilizer Mining

**Flint Hills Resources LP** ........D ....... 815 224-1525
Peru *(G-17509)*
**Hastie Mining & Trucking** ........E ....... 618 289-4536
Cave In Rock *(G-3402)*
**Morton International LLC** ........F ....... 773 235-2341
Chicago *(G-5808)*
▲ **Morton International LLC** ........C ....... 312 807-2696
Chicago *(G-5807)*
◆ **Morton Salt Inc** ........C ....... 312 807-2000
Chicago *(G-5809)*

## 1481 Nonmetallic Minerals Svcs, Except Fuels

**Harsco Corporation** ........G ....... 309 347-1962
Pekin *(G-17266)*
**Hastie Mining & Trucking** ........G ....... 618 285-3600
Rosiclare *(G-19048)*
**Illinois Valley Minerals LLC** ........G ....... 815 442-8402
Tonica *(G-20974)*
**Midwest Testing Services Inc** ........G ....... 815 223-6696
Peru *(G-17520)*
**Montana Minerals Dev Co** ........G ....... 800 426-5564
Arlington Heights *(G-804)*
**Natural Resources Ill Dept** ........E ....... 618 439-4320
Benton *(G-2036)*
**Raimonde Drilling Corp** ........F ....... 630 458-0590
Addison *(G-268)*
**Vigo Coal Operating Co Inc** ........C ....... 618 262-7022
Mount Carmel *(G-15286)*

## 1499 Miscellaneous Nonmetallic Mining

**Diamond Icic Corporation** ........E ....... 309 269-8652
Rock Island *(G-18175)*
**Markman Peat Corp** ........E ....... 815 772-4014
Morrison *(G-15146)*
**Mulch It Inc** ........G ....... 847 566-9372
Mundelein *(G-15533)*
**Professional Gem Sciences Inc** ........G ....... 312 920-1541
Chicago *(G-6209)*

SIC

Employee Codes: A=Over 500 employees, B=251-500
C=101-250, D=51-100, E=20-50, F=10-19, G=3-9

2017 Harris Illinois
Industrial Directory

911

# 20 FOOD AND KINDRED PRODUCTS

## 2011 Meat Packing Plants

Allens Farm Quality Meats .................. G ...... 217 896-2532
  Homer *(G-12073)*
Amelio Bros Meats ............................ G ...... 708 300-2920
  Richton Park *(G-17975)*
American Food Distrs Corp .................. F ...... 708 331-1982
  Harvey *(G-11655)*
▼ Amity Packing Company Inc .............. D ...... 312 942-0270
  Chicago *(G-3889)*
Antioch Packing House ...................... G ...... 847 838-6800
  Antioch *(G-618)*
Aurora Packing Company Inc .............. C ...... 630 897-0551
  North Aurora *(G-16119)*
Bar-B-Que Industries Inc ..................... F ...... 773 227-5400
  Chicago *(G-4040)*
▲ Belmont Sausage Company .............. E ...... 847 357-1515
  Elk Grove Village *(G-9340)*
Best Chicago Meat Company LLC ........ F ...... 773 523-8161
  Chicago *(G-4090)*
Brown Packing Company Inc .............. E ...... 708 849-7990
  South Holland *(G-20253)*
▲ Bruss Company ............................. C ...... 773 282-2900
  Chicago *(G-4179)*
Bushnell Locker Service ..................... G ...... 309 772-2783
  Bushnell *(G-2899)*
Butterball LLC .................................. B ...... 800 575-3365
  Montgomery *(G-15035)*
Calihan Pork Processors Inc .............. D ...... 309 674-9175
  Peoria *(G-17321)*
Cargill Meat Solutions Corp ................ C ...... 630 739-1746
  Woodridge *(G-22458)*
Cass Meats ..................................... G ...... 217 452-3072
  Virginia *(G-21305)*
Chenoa Locker Inc ........................... G ...... 815 945-7323
  Chenoa *(G-3633)*
Cherry Meat Packers Inc ................... E ...... 773 927-1200
  Chicago *(G-4297)*
Chicago Meat Authority Inc ................ B ...... 773 254-3811
  Chicago *(G-4331)*
▼ City Foods Inc .............................. C ...... 773 523-1566
  Chicago *(G-4382)*
Consumers Packing Co Inc ................ D ...... 708 344-0047
  Melrose Park *(G-14611)*
Country Village Meats ....................... G ...... 815 849-5532
  Sublette *(G-20714)*
Dawn Food Products Inc ................... G ...... 815 933-0600
  Bradley *(G-2419)*
Deer Processing ............................... F ...... 309 799-5994
  Coal Valley *(G-7295)*
Dutch Valley Meats Inc ...................... G ...... 217 543-3354
  Arthur *(G-897)*
Earlville Cold Stor Lckr LLC ............... G ...... 815 246-9469
  Earlville *(G-8593)*
Ed Kabrick Beef Inc .......................... G ...... 217 656-3263
  Plainville *(G-17662)*
Edgar County Locker Service ............ G ...... 217 466-5000
  Paris *(G-17147)*
Eickmans Processing Co Inc .............. E ...... 815 247-8451
  Seward *(G-19896)*
Eureka Locker Inc ............................ F ...... 309 467-2731
  Eureka *(G-9998)*
Fabbri Sausage Manufacturing ........... E ...... 312 829-6363
  Chicago *(G-4808)*
Farina Locker Service ....................... G ...... 618 245-6491
  Farina *(G-10175)*
Farmers Packing Inc ......................... F ...... 618 445-3822
  Albion *(G-363)*
Farmington Locker/Ice Plant Co ......... G ...... 309 245-4621
  Farmington *(G-10185)*
Fema L & L Food Services Inc ........... G ...... 217 835-2018
  Benld *(G-1805)*
Galloway Como Processing ............... G ...... 815 626-0305
  Sterling *(G-20594)*
God Family Country LLC .................. F ...... 217 285-6487
  Pittsfield *(G-17568)*
Golden Locker Inc ............................ G ...... 217 696-4456
  Camp Point *(G-2973)*
Grant Park Packing Company Inc ....... E ...... 312 421-4096
  Franklin Park *(G-10482)*
▼ Great Lakes Packing Co Intl ............ G ...... 773 927-6660
  Chicago *(G-4998)*
◆ Grecian Delight Foods Inc ............... C ...... 847 364-1010
  Elk Grove Village *(G-9511)*
Gridley Meats Inc ............................. G ...... 309 747-2120
  Gridley *(G-11405)*
H A Gartenberg & Company ............... F ...... 847 821-7590
  Buffalo Grove *(G-2700)*

Halsted Packing House Co ................ G ...... 312 421-5147
  Chicago *(G-5038)*
Hansen Packing Co ........................... G ...... 618 498-3714
  Jerseyville *(G-12423)*
Hartrich Meats Inc ............................ G ...... 618 455-3172
  Sainte Marie *(G-19324)*
Heinkels Packing Company Inc ........... E ...... 217 428-4401
  Decatur *(G-7888)*
Honey Foods Inc .............................. G ...... 847 928-9300
  Franklin Park *(G-10488)*
J Brodie Meat Products Inc ................ F ...... 309 342-1500
  Galesburg *(G-10761)*
Jancorp LLC .................................... G ...... 217 892-4830
  Rantoul *(G-17929)*
Jbs Usa LLC .................................... E ...... 217 323-3774
  Beardstown *(G-1522)*
▼ John Hofmeister & Son Inc ............. D ...... 773 847-0700
  Chicago *(G-5314)*
Johnsons Processing Plant ................ G ...... 815 684-5183
  Chadwick *(G-3442)*
Jones Packing Co ............................. G ...... 815 943-4488
  Harvard *(G-11639)*
▼ Kelly Corned Beef Co Chicago ......... E ...... 773 588-2882
  Chicago *(G-5372)*
Korte Meat Processing Inc ................. G ...... 618 654-3813
  Highland *(G-11801)*
Lake Pacific Partners LLC .................. B ...... 312 578-1110
  Chicago *(G-5440)*
Lena AJS Maid Meats ........................ F ...... 815 369-4522
  Lena *(G-13277)*
Magros Processing ........................... G ...... 217 438-2880
  Springfield *(G-20473)*
Main Street Market Roscoe Inc ........... G ...... 815 623-6328
  Roscoe *(G-18905)*
Mangold Networks ............................ G ...... 224 402-0068
  West Dundee *(G-21800)*
▼ Meats By Linz Inc ......................... E ...... 708 862-0830
  Calumet City *(G-2946)*
Momence Packing Co ........................ B ...... 815 472-6485
  Momence *(G-14984)*
Morris Meat Packing Co Inc ............... G ...... 708 865-8566
  Maywood *(G-14429)*
Moweaqua Packing Plant ................... G ...... 217 768-4714
  Moweaqua *(G-15458)*
National Beef Packing Co LLC ............ G ...... 312 332-6166
  Chicago *(G-5859)*
Nea Agora Packing Co ....................... G ...... 312 421-5130
  Chicago *(G-5878)*
Olympia Meat Packers Inc ................. G ...... 312 666-2222
  Chicago *(G-5986)*
Oriental Kitchen Corporation .............. G ...... 312 738-2850
  Chicago *(G-6007)*
Paris Frozen Foods Inc ..................... G ...... 217 532-3822
  Hillsboro *(G-11897)*
Park Packing Company Inc ................ E ...... 773 254-0100
  Chicago *(G-6083)*
Peer Foods Inc ................................. G ...... 773 927-1440
  Chicago *(G-6095)*
Peoria Packing Ltd ........................... F ...... 312 226-2600
  Chicago *(G-6104)*
Peoria Packing Ltd ........................... F ...... 815 465-9824
  Grant Park *(G-11313)*
Pluesters Quality Meat Co ................. E ...... 618 396-2224
  Hardin *(G-11594)*
▲ Plumrose Usa Inc ......................... E ...... 732 257-6600
  Downers Grove *(G-8504)*
Pork King Packing Inc ....................... C ...... 815 568-8024
  Marengo *(G-14239)*
Prince Meat Co ................................ F ...... 815 729-2333
  Darien *(G-7801)*
Raber Packing Company .................... E ...... 309 673-0721
  Peoria *(G-17439)*
Reasons Inc .................................... G ...... 309 537-3424
  Buffalo Prairie *(G-2797)*
Rochelle Foods LLC .......................... A ...... 815 562-4141
  Rochelle *(G-18105)*
Rose Packing Company Inc ............... A ...... 708 458-9300
  Chicago *(G-6395)*
Ryan Meat Company ......................... G ...... 773 783-3840
  Chicago *(G-6416)*
Smithfield Farmland Corp .................. G ...... 815 747-8809
  East Dubuque *(G-8623)*
Smithfield Farmland Corp .................. A ...... 309 734-5353
  Monmouth *(G-15023)*
Smithfield Foods Inc ......................... F ...... 312 577-5650
  Chicago *(G-6536)*
▲ Smithfield Global Products Inc ........ G ...... 630 281-5000
  Lisle *(G-13659)*
Sommers Fare LLC ........................... E ...... 877 377-9797
  Mundelein *(G-15558)*

Specialty Foods Holdings Inc ............. G ...... 630 599-5900
  Lombard *(G-13855)*
Spectrum Preferred Meats Inc ............ D ...... 815 946-3816
  Mount Morris *(G-15300)*
Steinbach Provision Company ............ G ...... 773 538-1511
  Chicago *(G-6583)*
Stewart Brothers Packing Co .............. G ...... 217 422-7741
  Decatur *(G-7944)*
Stiglmeier Sausage Co Inc ................. F ...... 847 537-9988
  Wheeling *(G-22157)*
T & J Meatpacking Inc ....................... D ...... 708 757-6930
  Chicago Heights *(G-7129)*
◆ Teys (usa) Inc ............................... G ...... 312 492-7163
  Chicago *(G-6707)*
Thrushwood Frms Qlty Meats Inc ....... F ...... 309 343-5193
  Galesburg *(G-10778)*
▼ Togo Packing Co Inc ..................... B ...... 800 575-3365
  Montgomery *(G-15067)*
Tomcyndi Inc ................................... E ...... 773 847-5400
  Chicago *(G-6737)*
Tyson Fresh Meats Inc ...................... B ...... 815 431-9501
  Ottawa *(G-16987)*
Tyson Fresh Meats Inc ...................... G ...... 847 836-5550
  Elgin *(G-9218)*
Tyson Fresh Meats Inc ...................... C ...... 309 658-2291
  Hillsdale *(G-11905)*
Tyson Fresh Meats Inc ...................... C ...... 309 658-3377
  Hillsdale *(G-11906)*
Tyson Fresh Meats Inc ...................... E ...... 309 965-2565
  Goodfield *(G-11249)*
Valley Meats LLC .............................. E ...... 309 799-7341
  Coal Valley *(G-7299)*
Victor Food Products ........................ G ...... 773 478-9529
  Chicago *(G-6893)*
Weber Meat Inc ................................ G ...... 217 357-2130
  Carthage *(G-3319)*
Y T Packing Co ................................ F ...... 217 522-3345
  Springfield *(G-20550)*
Zabiha Halal Meat Processors ............ G ...... 630 620-5000
  Addison *(G-349)*

## 2013 Sausages & Meat Prdts

A New Dairy Company ....................... E ...... 312 421-1234
  Chicago *(G-3690)*
A P Deli IV Inc .................................. F ...... 708 335-4462
  Hazel Crest *(G-11706)*
Alef Sausage Inc .............................. F ...... 847 968-2533
  Mundelein *(G-15467)*
Allens Farm Quality Meats ................. G ...... 217 896-2532
  Homer *(G-12073)*
▲ Andys Deli and Mikolajczyk ............ E ...... 773 722-1000
  Chicago *(G-3905)*
Another Chance Community Dev ........ E ...... 773 998-1641
  Chicago *(G-3913)*
Arts Tamales ................................... G ...... 309 367-2850
  Metamora *(G-14739)*
Atk Foods Inc .................................. E ...... 312 829-2250
  Chicago *(G-3976)*
Atlantic Beverage Company Inc .......... G ...... 847 412-6200
  Northbrook *(G-16207)*
B B M Packing Co Inc ....................... G ...... 312 243-1061
  Chicago *(G-4019)*
Ba Le Meat Processing & Whl Co ....... F ...... 773 506-2499
  Chicago *(G-4023)*
Bar-B-Que Industries Inc ................... F ...... 773 227-5400
  Chicago *(G-4040)*
Beatrice Companies Inc .................... E ...... 602 225-2000
  Chicago *(G-4069)*
▲ Belmont Sausage Company ............ E ...... 847 357-1515
  Elk Grove Village *(G-9340)*
Bende Inc ....................................... G ...... 847 913-0304
  Vernon Hills *(G-21150)*
Bert Packing Co Inc .......................... E ...... 312 733-0346
  Chicago *(G-4087)*
Bob Evans Farms Inc ........................ D ...... 309 932-2194
  Galva *(G-10785)*
Branding Iron Holdings Inc ................ G ...... 618 337-8400
  Sauget *(G-19383)*
▲ Bridgford Foods Corporation .......... B ...... 312 733-0300
  Chicago *(G-4168)*
Brown Packing Company Inc ............. E ...... 708 849-7990
  South Holland *(G-20253)*
▲ Bruss Company ............................ C ...... 773 282-2900
  Chicago *(G-4179)*
C & F Packing Co Inc ........................ E ...... 847 245-2000
  Lake Villa *(G-13012)*
▲ Capitol Wholesale Meats Inc .......... B ...... 708 485-4800
  Mc Cook *(G-14446)*
Carl Buddig and Company ................. E ...... 708 798-0900
  Homewood *(G-12093)*

Carroll County Locker .................G....... 815 493-2370
  Lanark (G-13151)
Cass Meats .................................G....... 217 452-3072
  Virginia (G-21305)
Charles Autin Limited ..................D....... 312 432-0888
  Chicago (G-4289)
Charwat Food Group Ltd ...........G....... 630 847-3473
  Hinsdale (G-11944)
Cherry Meat Packers Inc ............E....... 773 927-1200
  Chicago (G-4297)
Chicago Local Foods LLC .........G....... 312 432-6575
  Chicago (G-4329)
Columbus Meats Inc ...................G....... 312 829-2480
  Chicago (G-4433)
◆ Conagra Brands Inc .................C....... 312 549-5000
  Chicago (G-4444)
Conagra Brands Inc ....................C....... 630 857-1000
  Naperville (G-15633)
Consumers Packing Co Inc ........D....... 708 344-0047
  Melrose Park (G-14611)
Country Village Meats ................G....... 815 849-5532
  Sublette (G-20714)
Crawford Sausage Co Inc ..........E....... 773 277-3095
  Chicago (G-4495)
Creta Farms Usa LLC .................G....... 630 282-5964
  Bolingbrook (G-2291)
Dabecca Natural Foods Inc .......C....... 773 291-1428
  Chicago (G-4540)
Danielson Food Products Inc .....E....... 773 285-2111
  Chicago (G-4555)
Dawn Food Products Inc ............G....... 815 933-0600
  Bradley (G-2419)
Direct Marketing 1 Corporation ..E....... 773 234-9122
  Chicago (G-4608)
Dons Meat Market .......................G....... 309 968-6026
  Manito (G-14174)
Dreymiller & Kray Inc ...................G....... 847 683-2271
  Hampshire (G-11547)
Earlville Cold Stor Lckr LLC .........G....... 815 246-9469
  Earlville (G-8593)
Ed Kabrick Beef Inc .....................G....... 217 656-3263
  Plainville (G-17662)
Edgar County Locker Service .....G....... 217 466-5000
  Paris (G-17147)
Eickmans Processing Co Inc ......E....... 815 247-8451
  Seward (G-19896)
Elburn Market Inc .........................E....... 630 365-6461
  Elburn (G-8884)
Emmel Inc ....................................G....... 847 254-5178
  Lake In The Hills (G-12992)
▼ Equitrade Group .........................G....... 312 499-9500
  Chicago (G-4770)
Eureka Locker Inc ........................F....... 309 467-2731
  Eureka (G-9998)
F & Y Enterprises Inc ..................E....... 847 526-0620
  Wauconda (G-21462)
Fabbri Sausage Manufacturing ...E....... 312 829-6363
  Chicago (G-4808)
Farina Locker Service .................G....... 618 245-6491
  Farina (G-10175)
▼ Farmington Foods Inc ................C....... 708 771-3600
  Forest Park (G-10243)
Farmington Locker/Ice Plant Co .G....... 309 245-4621
  Farmington (G-10185)
Fema L & L Food Services Inc ...G....... 217 835-2018
  Benld (G-1805)
Food Purveyors Logistics ............F....... 630 229-6168
  Naperville (G-15659)
Freda Custom Foods Inc ............C....... 847 412-5900
  Northbrook (G-16261)
Freedom Sausage Inc .................F....... 815 792-8276
  Earlville (G-8594)
George Nottoli & Sons Inc ..........G....... 773 589-1010
  Chicago (G-4944)
Givaudan Flavors Corporation ....C....... 630 682-5600
  Carol Stream (G-3158)
Glenmark Industries Ltd ..............G....... 773 927-4800
  Chicago (G-4955)
Golden Locker Inc ........................G....... 217 696-4456
  Camp Point (G-2973)
▲ Grante Foods International LLC .F....... 773 751-9551
  Elk Grove Village (G-9507)
◆ Grecian Delight Foods Inc .........C....... 847 364-1010
  Elk Grove Village (G-9511)
▲ Greenridge Farm Inc ..................E....... 847 434-1803
  Elk Grove Village (G-9513)
Gridley Meats Inc ........................G....... 309 747-2120
  Gridley (G-11405)
Gurman Food Co ..........................F....... 847 837-1100
  Mundelein (G-15505)

H & B Hams .................................G....... 618 372-8690
  Brighton (G-2541)
Halsted Packing House Co .........G....... 312 421-5147
  Chicago (G-5038)
Hansen Packing Co .....................G....... 618 498-3714
  Jerseyville (G-12423)
Hartrich Meats Inc .......................G....... 618 455-3172
  Sainte Marie (G-19324)
▼ Hillshire Brands Company ..........B....... 312 614-6000
  Chicago (G-5089)
Hillshire Brands Company ...........B....... 800 727-2533
  Rochelle (G-18093)
Hillshire Brands Company ...........E....... 312 614-6000
  Chicago (G-5090)
Hillshire Brands Company ...........G....... 847 310-9400
  Schaumburg (G-19555)
Holten Meat Inc ............................D....... 618 337-8400
  Sauget (G-19386)
Honey Bear Ham ..........................E....... 312 942-1160
  Chicago (G-5105)
Houser Meats ...............................G....... 217 322-4994
  Rushville (G-19092)
▲ Ifa International Inc .....................F....... 847 566-0008
  Mundelein (G-15508)
▼ Interntional Casings Group Inc ...D....... 773 376-9200
  Chicago (G-5225)
J Brodie Meat Products Inc ........F....... 309 342-1500
  Galesburg (G-10761)
John J Moesle Wholesale Meats F....... 773 847-4900
  Chicago (G-5315)
Johnsons Processing Plant .........G....... 815 684-5183
  Chadwick (G-3442)
Jones Packing Co ........................G....... 815 943-4488
  Harvard (G-11639)
Koenemann Sausage Co ............G....... 815 385-6260
  Volo (G-21316)
Korte Meat Processing Inc .........G....... 618 654-3813
  Highland (G-11801)
Kraft Foods Asia PCF Svcs LLC G....... 847 943-4000
  Deerfield (G-8026)
Kronos Foods Corp .....................B....... 773 847-2250
  Glendale Heights (G-11039)
Lake Pacific Partners LLC ..........B....... 312 578-1110
  Chicago (G-5440)
▲ Land OFrost Inc .........................C....... 708 474-7100
  Lansing (G-13169)
Lena AJS Maid Meats ..................F....... 815 369-4522
  Lena (G-13277)
Lodolce Meat Co Inc ....................G....... 708 863-4655
  Cicero (G-7216)
Lorenzo Frozen Foods Ltd ..........G....... 708 343-7670
  Westchester (G-21848)
M E F Corp ...................................F....... 815 965-8604
  Rockford (G-18477)
Makowskis Real Sausage Co .....E....... 312 842-5330
  Chicago (G-5605)
▼ Meats By Linz Inc ......................E....... 708 862-0830
  Calumet City (G-2946)
Michaels Dawg House LLC ........G....... 847 485-7600
  Palatine (G-17055)
Momence Packing Co ..................B....... 815 472-6485
  Momence (G-14984)
◆ Mondelez International Inc .........A....... 847 943-4000
  Deerfield (G-8038)
Morris Meat Packing Co Inc .......G....... 708 865-8566
  Maywood (G-14429)
Moweaqua Packing Plant ............G....... 217 768-4714
  Moweaqua (G-15458)
Nationwide Foods Inc ..................B....... 773 787-4900
  Chicago (G-5869)
Nea Agora Packing Co ...............G....... 312 421-5130
  Chicago (G-5878)
New Packing Company ................F....... 312 666-1314
  Chicago (G-5892)
New Specialty Products Inc ........E....... 773 847-0230
  Chicago (G-5894)
O Chilli Frozen Foods Inc ............F....... 847 562-1991
  Northbrook (G-16321)
Ogden Foods LLC .......................E....... 773 277-8207
  Chicago (G-5970)
Ogden Foods LLC .......................G....... 773 801-0125
  Chicago (G-5971)
Old Fashioned Meat Co Inc ........G....... 312 421-4555
  Chicago (G-5978)
On-Cor Frozen Foods LLC .........D....... 630 692-2283
  Aurora (G-1200)
▲ On-Cor Frozen Foods LLC .........E....... 630 692-2283
  Aurora (G-1199)
Oriental Kitchen Corporation ......G....... 312 738-2850
  Chicago (G-6007)

Oriental Kitchen Corporation ......G....... 312 738-2850
  Chicago (G-6008)
Original Greek Specialties ..........E....... 773 735-2250
  Chicago (G-6012)
Oscars Foods Inc .........................G....... 773 622-6822
  Chicago (G-6020)
OSI Industries LLC .....................C....... 630 231-9090
  West Chicago (G-21754)
OSI Industries LLC .....................B....... 773 847-2000
  Chicago (G-6021)
▲ OSI International Foods Ltd .......D....... 630 851-6600
  Aurora (G-1060)
Papa Charlies Inc .........................E....... 773 522-7900
  Chicago (G-6071)
Park Packing Company Inc ........G....... 773 254-0100
  Chicago (G-6083)
▲ Parker House Sausage Company E....... 773 538-1112
  Chicago (G-6086)
Paxton Packing LLC ....................F....... 623 707-5604
  Paxton (G-17241)
▲ Plumrose Usa Inc ........................E....... 732 257-6600
  Downers Grove (G-8504)
Polancics Meats & Tenderloins ...G....... 815 433-0324
  Ottawa (G-16980)
Portillos Food Service Inc ...........G....... 630 620-0460
  Addison (G-248)
Powers John ................................G....... 309 742-8929
  Elmwood (G-9965)
Preferred Foods Products Inc .....F....... 773 847-0230
  Chicago (G-6173)
Prince Meat Co ............................F....... 815 729-2333
  Darien (G-7801)
R&R Meat Co ...............................G....... 270 898-6296
  Metropolis (G-14761)
Randolph Packing Co ..................D....... 630 830-3100
  Streamwood (G-20670)
Rapid Foods Inc ............................G....... 708 366-0321
  Shorewood (G-19931)
Rochelle Foods LLC ...................A....... 815 562-4141
  Rochelle (G-18105)
Roma Packing Co .........................G....... 773 927-7371
  Chicago (G-6386)
Rose Packing Company Inc .......A....... 708 458-9300
  Chicago (G-6395)
Russo Wholesale Meat Inc .........G....... 708 385-0500
  Alsip (G-525)
Ryan Meat Company ...................G....... 773 783-3840
  Chicago (G-6416)
Seifferts Locker & Meat Proc ......F....... 618 594-3921
  Carlyle (G-3058)
Smithfield Farmland Corp ...........A....... 309 734-5353
  Monmouth (G-15023)
Smolich Bros .................................G....... 815 727-2144
  Joliet (G-12576)
Sparrer Sausage Company Inc ..C....... 773 762-3334
  Chicago (G-6551)
Specialty Foods Holdings Inc .....G....... 630 599-5900
  Lombard (G-13855)
▲ Stampede Meat Inc .....................A....... 773 376-4300
  Bridgeview (G-2531)
Steinbach Provision Company ....G....... 773 538-1511
  Chicago (G-6583)
Stiglmeier Sausage Co Inc .........F....... 847 537-9988
  Wheeling (G-22157)
T & J Meatpacking Inc .................D....... 708 757-6930
  Chicago Heights (G-7129)
Tomcyndi Inc .................................G....... 773 847-5400
  Chicago (G-6737)
Tyson Fresh Meats Inc ................F....... 847 836-5550
  Elgin (G-9218)
V A M D Inc ...................................G....... 773 631-8400
  Chicago (G-6865)
▼ Vienna Beef Ltd ..........................E....... 773 278-7800
  Chicago (G-6896)
Viscofan Usa Inc ..........................D....... 217 444-8000
  Danville (G-7779)
William Badal ................................G....... 815 264-7752
  Waterman (G-21412)
Wurst Kitchen Inc .........................G....... 630 898-9242
  Aurora (G-1235)
Y T Packing Co .............................F....... 217 522-3345
  Springfield (G-20550)

## 2015 Poultry Slaughtering, Dressing & Processing

2000plus Groups Inc ...................G....... 630 528-3220
  Oak Brook (G-16483)
2000plus Groups Inc ...................C....... 800 939-6268
  Chicago (G-3663)

Employee Codes: A=Over 500 employees, B=251-500
C=101-250, D=51-100, E=20-50, F=10-19, G=3-9

# 20 FOOD AND KINDRED PRODUCTS

Aspen Foods Inc .................................. C  312 829-7282
  Chicago *(G-3964)*
Central Illinois Poultry Proc ................ F  217 543-2937
  Arthur *(G-886)*
Charles Autin Limited ......................... D  312 432-0888
  Chicago *(G-4289)*
Galloway Como Processing ................. G  815 626-0305
  Sterling *(G-20594)*
Gift Check Program 2013 Inc ............. G  630 986-5081
  Downers Grove *(G-8450)*
Grant Park Packing Company Inc ....... E  312 421-4096
  Franklin Park *(G-10482)*
Handcut Foods LLC ............................ D  312 239-0381
  Chicago *(G-5040)*
Hillshire Brands Company ................... E  312 614-6000
  Chicago *(G-5090)*
Jcg Industries Inc ............................... C  312 829-7282
  Chicago *(G-5286)*
Kauffman Poultry Farms Inc .............. F  815 264-3470
  Waterman *(G-21407)*
Kelly Flour Company .......................... G  312 933-3104
  Chicago *(G-5373)*
Koch Meat Co Inc .............................. B  847 384-5940
  Chicago *(G-5396)*
Lean Protein Team LLC ...................... G  440 525-1532
  Chicago *(G-5479)*
Love ME Tenders LLC ........................ G  847 564-2533
  Northbrook *(G-16298)*
Midway Food LLC ............................... G  773 294-0730
  Chicago *(G-5738)*
Midwest Poultry Services LP ............. D  217 386-2313
  Loda *(G-13753)*
Nduja Artisans Co .............................. G  312 550-6991
  Chicago *(G-5877)*
New Specialty Products Inc ............... E  773 847-0230
  Chicago *(G-5894)*
▲ Pelbo Americas Inc ........................ G  630 395-7788
  Naperville *(G-15723)*
Tru-Native Enterprises ........................ G  630 409-3258
  Addison *(G-325)*
Tru-Native Enterprises ........................ G  630 409-3258
  Addison *(G-326)*
West Liberty Foods LLC .................... B  603 679-2300
  Bolingbrook *(G-2382)*

## 2021 Butter

Danish Maid Butter Company ............. F  773 731-8787
  Chicago *(G-4556)*
▼ Hoogwegt US Inc .......................... D  847 918-8787
  Lake Forest *(G-12905)*
Madison Farms Butter Company ........ F  217 854-2547
  Carlinville *(G-3045)*
Old Heritage Creamery LLC ............... G  217 268-4355
  Arcola *(G-680)*
Prairie Farms Dairy Inc ..................... G  618 451-5600
  Granite City *(G-11299)*

## 2022 Cheese

Avanti Foods Company ...................... E  815 379-2155
  Walnut *(G-21329)*
▲ Bel Brands Usa Inc ....................... C  312 462-1500
  Chicago *(G-4072)*
Berner Food & Beverage LLC ............ B  815 563-4222
  Dakota *(G-7694)*
Berner Food & Beverage LLC ............ E  815 865-5136
  Rock City *(G-18124)*
Bn Delfi USA Inc ................................ G  847 280-0447
  Elgin *(G-8968)*
Brewster Cheese Company ................ D  815 947-3361
  Stockton *(G-20630)*
Cacique USA ..................................... G  630 766-0059
  Wood Dale *(G-22349)*
Carl Buddig and Company ................. E  708 798-0900
  Homewood *(G-12093)*
Charwat Food Group Ltd ................... G  630 847-3473
  Hinsdale *(G-11944)*
◆ Cheese Merchants America LLC ... B  630 221-0580
  Bartlett *(G-1338)*
▲ Churny Company Inc .................... B  847 646-5500
  Chicago *(G-4375)*
◆ Conagra Dairy Foods Company .... B  630 848-0975
  Chicago *(G-4445)*
El Encanto Products Inc .................... F  773 940-1807
  Chicago *(G-4707)*
G&G Kraft Build ................................. G  773 744-6522
  Wood Dale *(G-22375)*
GF Parent LLC ................................... G  312 255-4800
  Chicago *(G-4949)*
Handcut Foods LLC ............................ D  312 239-0381
  Chicago *(G-5040)*

▼ Hoogwegt US Inc .......................... D  847 918-8787
  Lake Forest *(G-12905)*
Karens Krafts .................................... 217 466-8100
  Paris *(G-17151)*
▲ Kolb-Lena Inc ................................ D  815 369-4577
  Lena *(G-13275)*
Kraft Fods Ltin Amer Holdg LLC ........ F  847 646-2000
  Northfield *(G-16406)*
Kraft Foods Asia PCF Svcs LLC ........ G  847 943-4000
  Deerfield *(G-8026)*
Kraft Heinz Company .......................... C  847 646-2000
  Glenview *(G-11160)*
Kraft Heinz Foods Company ............... C  847 646-3690
  Glenview *(G-11161)*
Kraft Heinz Foods Company ............... C  847 646-2000
  Northfield *(G-16407)*
Kraft Heinz Foods Company ............... C  217 378-1900
  Champaign *(G-3507)*
Kraft Services ................................... 309 662-6178
  Bloomington *(G-2191)*
La Hispamex Food Products Inc ........ G  708 780-1808
  Cicero *(G-7213)*
▲ Ludwig Dairy Products Inc ............ G  847 860-8646
  Elk Grove Village *(G-9599)*
Mancuso Cheese Company ................ F  815 722-2475
  Joliet *(G-12536)*
Marcoot Jersey Creamery LLC .......... G  618 664-1110
  Greenville *(G-11398)*
▲ Mondelez Global LLC ................... G  847 943-4000
  Deerfield *(G-8037)*
◆ Mondelez International Inc .......... A  847 943-4000
  Deerfield *(G-8038)*
Nuestro Queso LLC ........................... C  815 443-2100
  Kent *(G-12666)*
Nuestro Queso LLC ........................... E  224 366-4320
  Rosemont *(G-19019)*
Prairie Farms Dairy Inc ..................... G  618 451-5600
  Granite City *(G-11299)*
Prairie Pure Cheese ........................... G  815 568-5000
  Marengo *(G-14240)*
Saputo Cheese USA Inc .................... C  847 267-1100
  Lincolnshire *(G-13475)*
▲ Saputo Cheese USA Inc ............... D  847 267-1100
  Lincolnshire *(G-13476)*
Savencia Cheese USA LLC ................ G  815 369-4577
  Lena *(G-13283)*
Sheri Lyn Kraft ................................... 847 724-4718
  Glenview *(G-11196)*
Topz Dairy Products Co .................... 815 726-5700
  Joliet *(G-12583)*
Two Tribes LLC ................................. G  847 272-7711
  Glenview *(G-11211)*
V & V Supremo Foods Inc ................. C  312 733-5652
  Chicago *(G-6864)*
▲ V Formusa Co ................................ F  224 938-9360
  Des Plaines *(G-8296)*
We Love Soy Inc ............................... G  630 629-9667
  Lombard *(G-13881)*
Wengers Springbrook Cheese Inc ..... F  815 865-5855
  Davis *(G-7809)*
Wiscon Corp ...................................... E  708 450-0074
  Melrose Park *(G-14711)*
◆ Wiscon Corp .................................. E  708 450-0074
  Melrose Park *(G-14710)*

## 2023 Milk, Condensed & Evaporated

Abbott Laboratories ........................... A  847 938-8717
  North Chicago *(G-16163)*
Armada Nutrition LLC ........................ G  931 451-7808
  Carol Stream *(G-3105)*
Bay Valley Foods LLC ........................ D  815 239-2631
  Pecatonica *(G-17251)*
Corefx Ingredients LLC ...................... G  773 271-2663
  Chicago *(G-4468)*
Corefx Ingredients LLC ...................... F  773 271-2663
  Orangeville *(G-16814)*
Deja Investments Inc ......................... D  630 408-9222
  Bolingbrook *(G-2301)*
▲ Emsur USA LLC ............................. E  847 274-9450
  Elk Grove Village *(G-9456)*
Erie Group International Inc .............. G  309 659-2233
  Rochelle *(G-18088)*
◆ Fonterra (usa) Inc ........................ E  847 928-1600
  Rosemont *(G-19002)*
Glazers Stoller Distrg LLC ................. G  847 350-3200
  Franklin Park *(G-10479)*
◆ Health King Enterprise Inc .......... C  312 567-9978
  Chicago *(G-5059)*
▼ Hoogwegt US Inc .......................... D  847 918-8787
  Lake Forest *(G-12905)*

Kelly Flour Company .......................... G  312 933-3104
  Chicago *(G-5373)*
▲ Lifeway Foods Inc ......................... B  847 967-1010
  Morton Grove *(G-15213)*
Liqua Fit Inc ...................................... G  630 965-8067
  Grayslake *(G-11351)*
Mead Johnson Nutrition Company ..... E  312 466-5800
  Chicago *(G-5671)*
Meadowvale Inc .................................. G  630 553-0202
  Yorkville *(G-22665)*
◆ Milk Products Holdings N Amer ... E  847 928-1600
  Rosemont *(G-19016)*
MSI Green Inc .................................... C  312 421-6550
  Chicago *(G-5826)*
▲ Muller Quaker Dairy LLC .............. C  312 821-1000
  Chicago *(G-5830)*
Nestle Usa Inc ................................... C  309 263-2651
  Morton *(G-15172)*
Nestle Usa Inc ................................... C  217 243-9175
  Jacksonville *(G-12403)*
Nestle Usa Inc ................................... C  630 773-2090
  Itasca *(G-12330)*
Nestle Usa Inc ................................... E  630 505-5387
  Naperville *(G-15711)*
Nestle Usa Inc ................................... C  309 829-1031
  Bloomington *(G-2206)*
Nestle Usa Inc ................................... C  847 808-5300
  Buffalo Grove *(G-2748)*
Rich Products Corporation ................. F  847 581-1749
  Niles *(G-16027)*
Rich Products Corporation ................. C  847 459-5400
  Wheeling *(G-22140)*
Saasoom LLC ..................................... G  630 561-7300
  Saint Charles *(G-19258)*
Salud Natural Entrepreneur Inc ......... E  224 789-7400
  Waukegan *(G-21611)*
▲ Salud Natural Entrepreneur Inc .... E  224 789-7400
  Waukegan *(G-21612)*
Treehouse Foods Inc ......................... B  708 483-1300
  Oak Brook *(G-16565)*
Vital Proteins LLC .............................. E  224 544-9110
  Chicago *(G-6907)*
Vital Proteins LLC .............................. E  224 544-9110
  Elk Grove Village *(G-9809)*

## 2024 Ice Cream

Al Gelato Chicago LLC ...................... G  847 455-5355
  Franklin Park *(G-10388)*
Amani Froyo LLC ............................... G  941 744-1111
  Oakbrook Terrace *(G-16695)*
Annies Frozen Custard ...................... E  618 656-0289
  Edwardsville *(G-8787)*
Baked ................................................. G  773 384-7655
  Chicago *(G-4028)*
Baldwin Richardson Foods Co ........... G  815 464-9994
  Oakbrook Terrace *(G-16698)*
Cold Stone Creamery 488 ................. G
  South Elgin *(G-20190)*
Conopco Inc ....................................... G  847 520-8002
  Buffalo Grove *(G-2677)*
Deja Investments Inc ......................... G  630 408-9222
  Bolingbrook *(G-2301)*
Five Star Desserts and Foods ........... G  773 375-5100
  Chicago *(G-4853)*
Flamingos Icecream ........................... G  708 749-4287
  Berwyn *(G-2066)*
Gayety Candy Co Inc ......................... E  708 418-0062
  Lansing *(G-13163)*
Gelato Enterprises LLC ...................... F  847 432-2233
  Highland Park *(G-11835)*
Gelato Enterprises LLC ...................... G  630 210-8457
  Naperville *(G-15663)*
Gregs Frozen Custard Company ........ G  847 837-4175
  Mundelein *(G-15504)*
Gyood ................................................ G  773 360-8810
  Chicago *(G-5014)*
Hershey Creamery Company .............. F  708 339-4656
  South Holland *(G-20276)*
Homers Ice Cream Inc ....................... F  847 251-0477
  Wilmette *(G-22254)*
Huddlestun Creamery Inc .................. F  815 609-1893
  Joliet *(G-12512)*
Icream Group LLC ............................. G  773 342-2834
  Chicago *(G-5137)*
Instantwhip-Chicago Inc ..................... F  773 235-5588
  Chicago *(G-5206)*
◆ Jel Sert Co ................................... B  630 231-7590
  West Chicago *(G-21727)*
Joint Asia Dev Group LLC ................. E  847 223-1804
  Grayslake *(G-11349)*

SIC SECTION 20 FOOD AND KINDRED PRODUCTS

**Kent Precision Foods Group Inc** ........... E ....... 630 226-0071
Bolingbrook *(G-2331)*
**La Nueva Michoacana** ........... G ....... 815 722-3720
Joliet *(G-12531)*
**Lezza Spumoni and Desserts Inc** ........... E ....... 708 547-5969
Bellwood *(G-1712)*
**Lorenzos Delectable LLC** ........... G ....... 773 791-3327
Chicago *(G-5542)*
**Los Mangos** ........... G ....... 773 542-1522
Chicago *(G-5544)*
**ME and Gia Inc** ........... G ....... 708 583-1111
Elmwood Park *(G-9972)*
**Mitchlls Cndies Ice Creams Inc** ........... F ....... 708 799-3835
Homewood *(G-12104)*
**Muller-Pinehurst Dairy Inc** ........... C ....... 815 968-0441
Rockford *(G-18512)*
**Neveria Michoacana LLC** ........... G ....... 630 783-3518
Bolingbrook *(G-2351)*
▲ **Paleteria Azteca Inc** ........... G ....... 773 277-1423
Chicago *(G-6060)*
**Paleteria El Sabor** ........... G ....... 312 243-2308
Chicago *(G-6061)*
**Paleteria El Sabor De Michoacn** ........... G ....... 773 376-3880
Chicago *(G-6062)*
**Panchos Ice Cream** ........... G ....... 773 254-3141
Chicago *(G-6067)*
**Prairie Farms Dairy Inc** ........... G ....... 618 451-5600
Granite City *(G-11299)*
**Prairie Farms Dairy Inc** ........... E ....... 618 632-3632
O Fallon *(G-16476)*
**Prairie Farms Dairy Inc** ........... D ....... 217 423-3459
Decatur *(G-7929)*
**Red Mango Rockford** ........... G ....... 815 282-1020
Rockford *(G-18551)*
**Roesers Bakery** ........... E ....... 773 489-6900
Chicago *(G-6379)*
**Sisler Dairy Products Company** ........... G ....... 815 376-2913
Ohio *(G-16753)*
**Smooches Ice Cream** ........... G ....... 708 370-0282
Chicago *(G-6537)*
**Suzys Swirl LLC** ........... G ....... 847 855-9987
Gurnee *(G-11510)*
**Sweet Pops By Cindy** ........... G ....... 630 294-0640
Wheaton *(G-21982)*
**Union Foods Inc** ........... G ....... 201 327-2828
Chicago *(G-6814)*
**Viola Ice Cream Shoppe** ........... G ....... 309 596-2131
Viola *(G-21295)*
**We Love Soy Inc** ........... G ....... 630 629-9667
Lombard *(G-13881)*

## *2026 Milk*

**Bay Valley Foods LLC** ........... D ....... 815 239-2631
Pecatonica *(G-17251)*
**Berner Food & Beverage LLC** ........... B ....... 815 563-4222
Dakota *(G-7694)*
**Berner Food & Beverage LLC** ........... E ....... 815 865-5136
Rock City *(G-18124)*
**Chester Dairy Company Inc** ........... F ....... 618 826-2394
Chester *(G-3653)*
**Chester Dairy Company Inc** ........... G ....... 618 826-2395
Chester *(G-3654)*
**Dean Foods Company** ........... D .....
Rockford *(G-18338)*
**Dean Foods Company** ........... C ....... 847 669-5123
Huntley *(G-12137)*
**Dean Foods Company** ........... C ....... 815 943-7375
Harvard *(G-11630)*
**Dean Foods Company** ........... D ....... 217 428-6726
Decatur *(G-7867)*
**Deja Investments Inc** ........... D ....... 630 408-9222
Bolingbrook *(G-2301)*
**Douglas Graybill** ........... G ....... 815 218-1749
Freeport *(G-10653)*
**East Side Jersey Dairy Inc** ........... E ....... 217 854-2547
Carlinville *(G-3036)*
**Erie Group International Inc** ........... D ....... 309 659-2233
Rochelle *(G-18088)*
**Instantwhip-Chicago Inc** ........... F ....... 773 235-5588
Chicago *(G-5206)*
**Kilgus Farmstead Inc** ........... G ....... 815 692-6080
Fairbury *(G-10129)*
**Kraft Heinz Foods Company** ........... D ....... 217 378-1900
Champaign *(G-3507)*
▲ **Lifeway Foods Inc** ........... B ....... 847 967-1010
Morton Grove *(G-15213)*
**Lulus Real Froyo** ........... G ....... 630 299-3854
Aurora *(G-1049)*
**Midwest Ice Cream Company LLC** ........... G ....... 630 879-0800
Batavia *(G-1470)*
**Midwest Ice Cream Company LLC** ........... F ....... 815 544-2105
Belvidere *(G-1772)*
**Muller-Pinehurst Dairy Inc** ........... C ....... 815 968-0441
Rockford *(G-18512)*
**Oberweis Dairy Inc** ........... F ....... 847 368-9060
Arlington Heights *(G-810)*
**Oberweis Dairy Inc** ........... E ....... 630 906-6455
Oswego *(G-16928)*
**Oberweis Dairy Inc** ........... E ....... 708 660-1350
Oak Park *(G-16678)*
**Oberweis Dairy Inc** ........... F ....... 630 782-0141
Elmhurst *(G-9917)*
**Oberweis Dairy Inc** ........... F ....... 847 290-9222
Rolling Meadows *(G-18755)*
**Oberweis Dairy Inc** ........... E ....... 630 474-0284
Glen Ellyn *(G-10983)*
**Pet OFallon LLC** ........... D ....... 618 628-3300
O Fallon *(G-16473)*
**Prairie Farms Dairy Inc** ........... E ....... 217 223-5530
Quincy *(G-17869)*
**Prairie Farms Dairy Inc** ........... D ....... 618 393-2128
Olney *(G-16791)*
**Prairie Farms Dairy Inc** ........... C ....... 217 854-2547
Carlinville *(G-3047)*
**Prairie Farms Dairy Inc** ........... E ....... 618 632-3632
O Fallon *(G-16476)*
**Prairie Farms Dairy Inc** ........... E ....... 618 457-4167
Carbondale *(G-3018)*
**Prairie Farms Dairy Inc** ........... C ....... 309 686-2400
Peoria *(G-17434)*
**Prairie Farms Dairy Inc** ........... D ....... 217 423-3459
Decatur *(G-7929)*
**Prairie Farms Dairy Inc** ........... F ....... 217 245-4413
Jacksonville *(G-12408)*
**Prairie Farms Dairy Inc** ........... G ....... 618 451-5600
Granite City *(G-11299)*
**Rich Products Corporation** ........... D ....... 847 581-1749
Niles *(G-16027)*
▲ **Socius Ingredients LLC** ........... F ....... 847 440-0156
Evanston *(G-10094)*
**Starfruit LLC** ........... G ....... 312 527-3674
Chicago *(G-6576)*

## *2032 Canned Specialties*

**AA Superb Food Corporation** ........... E ....... 773 927-3233
Chicago *(G-3698)*
▲ **Alm Distributors LLC** ........... G ....... 708 865-8000
Melrose Park *(G-14589)*
**Archer-Daniels-Midland Company** ........... E ....... 309 772-2141
Bushnell *(G-2897)*
**Avoco International LLC** ........... G ....... 847 795-0200
Elk Grove Village *(G-9325)*
**Beatrice Companies Inc** ........... E ....... 602 225-2000
Chicago *(G-4069)*
**Castro Foods Wholesale Inc** ........... E ....... 773 869-0641
Chicago *(G-4253)*
**Ciprianis Pasta & Sauce Inc** ........... E ....... 630 851-3086
Aurora *(G-1131)*
**Dial Corporation** ........... C ....... 630 892-4381
Montgomery *(G-15041)*
**Earthgrains** ........... G ....... 630 859-8782
North Aurora *(G-16128)*
▼ **Ebro Foods Inc** ........... D ....... 773 696-0150
Chicago *(G-4690)*
◆ **Essen Nutrition Corporation** ........... E ....... 630 739-6700
Romeoville *(G-18820)*
**Hong Kong Market Chicago Inc** ........... G ....... 312 791-9111
Chicago *(G-5108)*
▲ **Hop Kee Incorporated** ........... E ....... 312 791-9111
Chicago *(G-5109)*
**Jaali Bean Inc** ........... G ....... 312 730-5095
Chicago *(G-5265)*
**Kraft Heinz Company** ........... B ....... 412 456-5700
Chicago *(G-5410)*
**Kraft Heinz Foods Company** ........... C ....... 847 291-3900
Northbrook *(G-16290)*
**Lee Gilster-Mary Corporation** ........... D ....... 618 965-3426
Steeleville *(G-20561)*
**Lpz Inc** ........... G ....... 773 579-6120
Chicago *(G-5551)*
▲ **Lynfred Winery Inc** ........... E ....... 630 529-9463
Roselle *(G-18953)*
**McShares Inc** ........... E ....... 217 762-2561
Monticello *(G-15079)*
**Mead Johnson & Company LLC** ........... F ....... 847 832-2420
Chicago *(G-5670)*
**Mexico Enterprise Corporation** ........... G ....... 920 568-8900
Chicago *(G-5710)*
**Mexifeast Foods Inc** ........... G ....... 773 356-6386
Chicago *(G-5711)*
**Michaelangelo Foods LLC** ........... G ....... 773 425-3498
Chicago *(G-5720)*
**Nara Dips Inc** ........... G ....... 773 837-0601
Dekalb *(G-8108)*
**Nestle Usa Inc** ........... D ....... 847 808-5404
Buffalo Grove *(G-2747)*
**Nestle Usa Inc** ........... C ....... 847 808-5300
Buffalo Grove *(G-2748)*
**Nogi Brands LLC** ........... G ....... 312 371-7974
Chicago *(G-5922)*
**Ole Mexican Foods Inc** ........... E ....... 708 458-3296
Bedford Park *(G-1568)*
**Pastorelli Food Products Inc** ........... G ....... 312 455-1006
Chicago *(G-6089)*
▲ **Quay Corporation Inc** ........... F ....... 847 676-4233
Lincolnwood *(G-13531)*
**Sofrito Foods LLC** ........... G ....... 630 302-8615
South Elgin *(G-20226)*
**Stevie S Italian Foods Inc** ........... G ....... 217 793-9693
Springfield *(G-20538)*
**Supreme Tamale Co** ........... G ....... 773 622-3777
Elk Grove Village *(G-9763)*
**Teasdale Foods Inc** ........... D ....... 217 283-7771
Hoopeston *(G-12118)*
**Tom Tom Tamales Mfg Co Inc** ........... F ....... 773 523-5675
Chicago *(G-6736)*
**Treehouse Foods Inc** ........... B ....... 708 483-1300
Oak Brook *(G-16565)*
▲ **Vanee Foods Company** ........... D ....... 708 449-7300
Berkeley *(G-2050)*
**Windy Acquisition LLC** ........... E ....... 630 595-5744
Bensenville *(G-2015)*

## *2033 Canned Fruits, Vegetables & Preserves*

▲ **78 Brand Co** ........... G ....... 312 344-1602
Chicago *(G-3676)*
**Andrias Food Group Inc** ........... G ....... 618 632-3118
O Fallon *(G-16462)*
**Andrias Food Group Inc** ........... E ....... 618 632-4866
O Fallon *(G-16461)*
**Bay Valley Foods LLC** ........... D ....... 773 927-7700
Chicago *(G-4058)*
**Bear-Stewart Corporation** ........... E ....... 773 276-0400
Chicago *(G-4065)*
**Beatrice Companies Inc** ........... E ....... 602 225-2000
Chicago *(G-4069)*
**Berner Food & Beverage LLC** ........... B ....... 815 563-4222
Dakota *(G-7694)*
**Captain Curts Food Products** ........... E ....... 773 783-8400
Chicago *(G-4233)*
**Cider Gould & Apple** ........... G ....... 630 365-2233
Elburn *(G-8880)*
**Del Monte Foods Inc** ........... G ....... 309 968-7033
Manito *(G-14173)*
**Del Monte Foods Inc** ........... F ....... 815 562-1359
Rochelle *(G-18084)*
**Del Monte Foods Inc** ........... F ....... 630 836-8131
Rochelle *(G-18085)*
**Dingo Inc** ........... G ....... 217 868-5615
Effingham *(G-8832)*
**Florida Fruit Juices Inc** ........... E ....... 773 586-6200
Chicago *(G-4863)*
**General Mills Inc** ........... E ....... 815 544-7399
Belvidere *(G-1754)*
**H J M P Corp** ........... C ....... 708 345-5370
Melrose Park *(G-14650)*
**Hooray Puree Inc** ........... G ....... 312 515-0266
Park Ridge *(G-17203)*
**Iya Foods LLC** ........... G ....... 630 854-7107
North Aurora *(G-16135)*
◆ **Juice Tyme Inc** ........... F ....... 773 579-1291
Chicago *(G-5335)*
**Key Colony Inc** ........... G ....... 630 783-8572
Lemont *(G-13237)*
**Korinek & Co Inc** ........... G ....... 708 652-2870
Cicero *(G-7210)*
**Kraft Heinz Company** ........... B ....... 412 456-5700
Chicago *(G-5410)*
**Kraft Heinz Foods Company** ........... C ....... 847 291-3900
Northbrook *(G-16290)*
**Kraft Heinz Foods Company** ........... E ....... 630 505-0170
Lisle *(G-13615)*
**Kraft Heinz Foods Company** ........... B ....... 618 512-9100
Granite City *(G-11290)*
**Kraft Heinz Foods Company** ........... B ....... 815 338-7000
Woodstock *(G-22580)*
**Kuntry Kettle** ........... G ....... 618 426-1600
Ava *(G-1238)*
▼ **Lawrence Foods Inc** ........... C ....... 847 437-2400
Elk Grove Village *(G-9588)*

S I C

Employee Codes: A=Over 500 employees, B=251-500
C=101-250, D=51-100, E=20-50, F=10-19, G=3-9
2017 Harris Illinois
Industrial Directory
915

**Legacy Foods Mfg LLC** F 847 595-9106
Elk Grove Village *(G-9592)*
**▲ Lynfred Winery Inc** E 630 529-9463
Roselle *(G-18953)*
**Mancuso Cheese Company** F 815 722-2475
Joliet *(G-12536)*
**Margies Brands Inc** E 773 643-1417
Chicago *(G-5615)*
**Millers Country Crafts Inc** G 618 426-3108
Ava *(G-1240)*
**MSI Green Inc** G 312 421-6550
Chicago *(G-5826)*
**Mullen Foods LLC** G 773 716-9001
Chicago *(G-5829)*
**Mullins Food Products Inc** B 708 344-3224
Broadview *(G-2599)*
**Nation Pizza Products LP** A 847 397-3320
Schaumburg *(G-19661)*
**Nestle Usa Inc** C 847 808-5300
Buffalo Grove *(G-2748)*
**Odwalla Inc** E 773 687-8667
Chicago *(G-5968)*
**Pappone Inc** G 630 234-4738
Chicago *(G-6073)*
**Pastorelli Food Products Inc** G 312 455-1006
Chicago *(G-6089)*
**Planks Apple Butter** G 217 268-4933
Arcola *(G-681)*
**▼ R&B Foods Inc** E 847 590-0059
Mount Prospect *(G-15367)*
**Rana Meal Solutions LLC** F 630 581-4100
Bartlett *(G-1367)*
**▲ Rana Meal Solutions LLC** C 630 581-4100
Oak Brook *(G-16558)*
**Raymond Brothers Inc** F 847 928-9300
Schiller Park *(G-19866)*
**Russo Wholesale Meat Inc** G 708 385-0500
Alsip *(G-525)*
**Seneca Foods Corporation** E 309 385-4301
Princeville *(G-17766)*
**Simply Salsa LLC** G 815 514-3993
Homer Glen *(G-12087)*
**◆ Sokol and Company** D 708 482-8250
Countryside *(G-7443)*
**Stewart Ingrdients Systems Inc** F 312 254-3539
Chicago *(G-6596)*
**Treehouse Foods Inc** B 708 483-1300
Oak Brook *(G-16565)*
**▲ V Formusa Co** F 224 938-9360
Des Plaines *(G-8296)*
**▲ Vegetable Juices Inc** D 708 924-9500
Bedford Park *(G-1589)*
**Vins Bbq LLC** G 847 302-3259
Glenview *(G-11214)*
**Wisconsin Wilderness Food Pdts** G 847 735-8661
Lake Bluff *(G-12872)*

## *2034 Dried Fruits, Vegetables & Soup*

**Americas Food Technologies Inc** E 708 532-1222
Tinley Park *(G-20891)*
**Bernard Food Industries Inc** D 847 869-5222
Evanston *(G-10015)*
**Bran-Zan Holdings LLC** F 847 342-0000
Arlington Heights *(G-728)*
**Custom Culinary Inc** D 630 928-4898
Lombard *(G-13787)*
**Goodhome Foods Inc** G 847 816-6832
Lake Forest *(G-12903)*
**Griffith Laboratories USA Inc** E 773 523-7509
Chicago *(G-5004)*
**H A Gartenberg & Company** F 847 821-7590
Buffalo Grove *(G-2700)*
**Handcut Foods LLC** D 312 239-0381
Chicago *(G-5040)*
**◆ Hot Mexican Peppers Inc** G 773 843-9774
Chicago *(G-5118)*
**K M J Enterprises Inc** E 847 688-1200
Gurnee *(G-11465)*
**▼ Karlin Foods Corp** F 847 441-8330
Northfield *(G-16404)*
**Kent Precision Foods Group Inc** E 630 226-0071
Bolingbrook *(G-2331)*
**Kent Precision Foods Group Inc** E 630 226-0498
Bolingbrook *(G-2332)*
**Noon Hour Food Products Inc** E 312 382-1177
Chicago *(G-5924)*
**◆ R J Van Drunen & Sons Inc** D 815 472-3100
Momence *(G-14987)*
**R J Van Drunen & Sons Inc** E 830 422-2167
Momence *(G-14988)*
**R J Van Drunen & Sons Inc** D 815 472-3211
Momence *(G-14989)*
**Sono Italiano Corporation** G 817 472-8903
Manteno *(G-14193)*
**Swiss Products LP** E 773 394-6480
Chicago *(G-6651)*
**TEC Foods Inc** E 800 315-8002
Chicago *(G-6683)*
**▼ Terri Lynn Inc** C 847 741-1900
Elgin *(G-9210)*
**Turtle Island Inc** F 815 759-9000
Johnsburg *(G-12443)*
**▲ Vanee Foods Company** D 708 449-7300
Berkeley *(G-2050)*

## *2035 Pickled Fruits, Vegetables, Sauces & Dressings*

**Andrias Food Group Inc** G 618 632-3118
O Fallon *(G-16462)*
**Andrias Food Group Inc** E 618 632-4866
O Fallon *(G-16461)*
**Arts Tamales** G 309 367-2850
Metamora *(G-14739)*
**Boetje Foods Inc** G 309 788-4352
Rock Island *(G-18165)*
**Daryl Keylor** G 217 452-3035
Virginia *(G-21306)*
**▲ E Formella & Sons Inc** E 708 598-0909
Countryside *(G-7422)*
**▼ Earthgrains Refrigertd Dough P** A 630 455-5200
Downers Grove *(G-8438)*
**◆ Essen Nutrition Corporation** E 630 739-6700
Romeoville *(G-18820)*
**Fgfi LLC** E 708 598-0909
Countryside *(G-7424)*
**Flaherty Incorporated** G 773 472-8456
Skokie *(G-20000)*
**Foods & Things Inc** G 618 526-4478
Breese *(G-2444)*
**Fournie Farms Inc** E 618 344-8527
Collinsville *(G-7325)*
**▲ Hop Kee Incorporated** E 312 791-9111
Chicago *(G-5109)*
**Kosto Food Products Company** F 847 487-2600
Wauconda *(G-21478)*
**Kraft Foods Asia PCF Svcs LLC** G 847 943-4000
Deerfield *(G-8026)*
**Kraft Heinz Company** C 847 646-2000
Glenview *(G-11160)*
**Kraft Heinz Foods Company** B 815 338-7000
Woodstock *(G-22580)*
**Kraft Heinz Foods Company** C 847 646-2000
Glenview *(G-11162)*
**Kraft Heinz Foods Company** D 217 378-1900
Champaign *(G-3507)*
**Legacy Foods Mfg LLC** F 847 595-9106
Elk Grove Village *(G-9592)*
**◆ Mizkan America Inc** E 847 590-0059
Mount Prospect *(G-15347)*
**◆ Mondelez International Inc** A 847 943-4000
Deerfield *(G-8038)*
**Mullins Food Products Inc** B 708 344-3224
Broadview *(G-2599)*
**New Specialty Products Inc** E 773 847-0230
Chicago *(G-5894)*
**North Star Pickle LLC** F 847 970-5555
Lake Zurich *(G-13109)*
**▲ Pastafresh Co** G 773 745-5888
Chicago *(G-6088)*
**Pickles Sorrel Inc** F 773 379-4748
Chicago *(G-6121)*
**Plochman Inc** E 815 468-3434
Manteno *(G-14190)*
**Simply Salsa LLC** G 815 514-3993
Homer Glen *(G-12087)*
**Treehouse Foods Inc** B 708 483-1300
Oak Brook *(G-16565)*
**Treehouse Private Brands Inc** F 630 455-5265
Downers Grove *(G-8534)*
**▲ V Formusa Co** F 224 938-9360
Des Plaines *(G-8296)*
**▼ Vienna Beef Ltd** E 773 278-7800
Chicago *(G-6896)*
**Wisconsin Wilderness Food Pdts** G 847 735-8661
Lake Bluff *(G-12872)*

## *2037 Frozen Fruits, Juices & Vegetables*

**Dulce Vida Juice Bar LLC** G 224 236-5045
Hanover Park *(G-11579)*
**General Mills Inc** E 815 544-7399
Belvidere *(G-1754)*
**▲ Greenwood Associates Inc** F 847 579-5500
Niles *(G-15985)*
**H J M P Corp** C 708 345-5370
Melrose Park *(G-14650)*
**Harvest Food Group Inc** F 773 847-3313
Chicago *(G-5052)*
**J J Mata Inc** G 773 750-0643
Chicago *(G-5260)*
**◆ Juice Tyme Inc** F 773 579-1291
Chicago *(G-5335)*
**Key Colony Inc** G 630 783-8572
Lemont *(G-13237)*
**Kraft Heinz Foods Company** B 618 512-9100
Granite City *(G-11290)*
**Kraft Heinz Foods Company** C 847 291-3900
Northbrook *(G-16290)*
**Lawlor Marketing** G 847 357-1080
Arlington Heights *(G-791)*
**Maaldar Pukhtoon Group LLC** G 630 696-1723
Glendale Heights *(G-11044)*
**▲ Mautino Distributing Co Inc** E 815 664-4311
Spring Valley *(G-20376)*
**◆ McCain Foods Usa Inc** B 630 955-0400
Lisle *(G-13620)*
**▼ McCain Usa Inc** C 800 938-7799
Lisle *(G-13621)*
**Midway Food LLC** G 773 294-0730
Chicago *(G-5738)*
**Natural Distribution Company** G 630 350-1700
Wood Dale *(G-22403)*
**Premier Beverage Solutions LLC** G 309 369-7117
East Peoria *(G-8728)*
**R J Van Drunen & Sons Inc** D 815 472-3211
Momence *(G-14989)*
**◆ R J Van Drunen & Sons Inc** D 815 472-3100
Momence *(G-14987)*
**R J Van Drunen & Sons Inc** E 830 422-2167
Momence *(G-14988)*
**Shady Creek Vineyard Inc** G 847 275-7979
Palatine *(G-17073)*

## *2038 Frozen Specialties*

**A New Dairy Company** E 312 421-1234
Chicago *(G-3690)*
**Afs Classico LLC** E 309 786-8833
Rock Island *(G-18158)*
**Ajinomoto Windsor Inc** C 815 452-2361
Toluca *(G-20972)*
**Aryzta LLC** C 815 306-7171
Romeoville *(G-18800)*
**Avanti Foods Company** E 815 379-2155
Walnut *(G-21329)*
**Beatrice Companies Inc** E 602 225-2000
Chicago *(G-4069)*
**BF Manufacturing LLC** D 312 446-1163
Chicago *(G-4100)*
**▲ Biagios Gourmet Foods Inc** E 708 867-4641
Chicago *(G-4103)*
**Champion Foods LLC** G 815 648-2725
Hebron *(G-11716)*
**Chateau Food Products Inc** F 708 863-4207
Chicago *(G-4296)*
**◆ Conagra Brands Inc** C 312 549-5000
Chicago *(G-4444)*
**Conagra Brands Inc** C 630 857-1000
Naperville *(G-15633)*
**▲ Creapan USA Corp** G 312 836-3704
Chicago *(G-4496)*
**▲ Danziger Kosher Catering Inc** E 847 982-1818
Lincolnwood *(G-13506)*
**Dfg Confectionary LLC** B 847 412-1961
Northbrook *(G-16241)*
**Dianas Bananas Inc** F 773 638-6800
Chicago *(G-4594)*
**▼ Distinctive Foods LLC** F 847 459-3600
Wheeling *(G-22036)*
**Distinctive Foods LLC** E 847 459-3600
Bensenville *(G-1880)*
**Doreens Pizza Inc** F 708 862-7499
Calumet City *(G-2937)*
**Fema L & L Food Services Inc** G 217 835-2018
Benld *(G-1805)*
**General Mills Inc** E 815 544-7399
Belvidere *(G-1754)*
**General Mills Green Giant** G 815 547-5311
Belvidere *(G-1755)*
**Givaudan Flavors Corporation** C 630 682-5600
Carol Stream *(G-3158)*

SIC SECTION
20 FOOD AND KINDRED PRODUCTS

**Globus Food Products LLC** G 847 378-8221
Elk Grove Village *(G-9505)*
▲ **Gonnella Baking Co** D 312 733-2020
Schaumburg *(G-19539)*
**Greg El- Inc** F 773 478-9050
Chicago *(G-5001)*
▼ **Hearthside Food Solutions LLC** E 630 967-3600
Downers Grove *(G-8456)*
▲ **Heartland Harvest Inc** G 815 932-2100
Kankakee *(G-12621)*
**Herman Seekamp Inc** C 630 628-6555
Addison *(G-145)*
**Home Run Inn Frozen Foods Corp** D 630 783-9696
Woodridge *(G-22494)*
▲ **Italia Foods Inc** E 847 397-4479
Schaumburg *(G-19585)*
**Jo MO Enterprises Inc** F 708 599-8098
Bridgeview *(G-2503)*
▲ **Kasias Deli Inc** F 312 666-2900
Chicago *(G-5363)*
**Kraft Heinz Company** B 412 456-5700
Chicago *(G-5410)*
**Kraft Heinz Foods Company** C 847 291-3900
Northbrook *(G-16290)*
▼ **Kraft Pizza Company Inc** E 847 646-2000
Glenview *(G-11163)*
**Leggero Foods** G 815 871-9640
Rockford *(G-18466)*
**Lezza Spumoni and Desserts Inc** E 708 547-5969
Bellwood *(G-1712)*
**Little Lady Foods Inc** C 847 806-1440
Elk Grove Village *(G-9597)*
**Lorenzo Frozen Foods Ltd** G 708 343-7670
Westchester *(G-21848)*
**Luvo Usa LLC** D 847 485-8595
Schaumburg *(G-19625)*
**Luvo Usa LLC** F 847 485-8595
Schaumburg *(G-19626)*
▼ **McCain Usa Inc** C 800 938-7799
Lisle *(G-13621)*
▲ **Mjs-Cn LLC** F 630 580-7200
Carol Stream *(G-3200)*
**Mondelez Intl Holdings LLC** G 800 572-3847
Deerfield *(G-8039)*
**Moon Guy Hong Food Inc** F 773 927-3233
Chicago *(G-5801)*
**Nation Pizza Products LP** A 847 397-3320
Schaumburg *(G-19661)*
**Nestle Prepared Foods Company** B 630 671-3721
Glendale Heights *(G-11051)*
**O Chilli Frozen Foods Inc** E 847 562-1991
Northbrook *(G-16321)*
▲ **On-Cor Frozen Foods LLC** E 630 692-2283
Aurora *(G-1199)*
**On-Cor Frozen Foods LLC** D 630 692-2283
Aurora *(G-1200)*
**Open Kitchens Inc** E 312 666-5334
Chicago *(G-5995)*
◆ **Paani Foods Inc** F 312 420-4624
Chicago *(G-6047)*
**Pinnacle Foods Group LLC** B 618 829-3275
Saint Elmo *(G-19310)*
**Pinnacle Foods Group LLC** C 731 343-4995
Centralia *(G-3426)*
**Preziosio Ltd** F 630 393-0920
Warrenville *(G-21359)*
**RCM Smith Inc** F 309 786-8833
Rock Island *(G-18197)*
**Reggios Pizza Inc** D 773 488-1411
Chicago *(G-6325)*
**Rollys Convenient Foods Inc** G 630 766-4070
Bensenville *(G-1979)*
**Supreme Tamale Co** G 773 622-3777
Elk Grove Village *(G-9763)*
**Teresa Foods Inc** F 708 258-6200
Peotone *(G-17493)*
**WEI-Chuan USA Inc** F 708 352-8886
Hodgkins *(G-11987)*

## 2041 Flour, Grain Milling

**ADM Grain Company** E 217 424-5200
Decatur *(G-7820)*
**ADM Milling Co** E 312 666-2465
Chicago *(G-3753)*
▲ **Agritech Worldwide Inc** F 847 549-6002
Mundelein *(G-15466)*
**American Milling Company** F 309 347-6888
Pekin *(G-17253)*
**Archer-Daniels-Midland Company** G 217 424-5236
Decatur *(G-7834)*
**Archer-Daniels-Midland Company** E 217 424-5200
Decatur *(G-7838)*
◆ **Archer-Daniels-Midland Company** A 312 634-8100
Chicago *(G-3941)*
**Archer-Daniels-Midland Company** C 309 673-7828
Peoria *(G-17309)*
**Archer-Daniels-Midland Company** E 217 424-5413
Decatur *(G-7835)*
**Ardent Mills LLC** C 618 463-4411
Alton *(G-561)*
**Ardent Mills LLC** E 618 826-2371
Chester *(G-3650)*
**Bay Foods Inc** E 312 346-5757
Chicago *(G-4057)*
**Bio Fuels By American Farmers** F 561 859-6251
Benton *(G-2023)*
**Bunge Milling Inc** C 217 442-1801
Danville *(G-7708)*
▼ **Cargill Dry Corn Ingrdents Inc** G 217 465-5331
Paris *(G-17143)*
▼ **Dix McGuire Commodities LLC** G 847 496-5320
Palatine *(G-17023)*
▼ **Earthgrains Refrigertd Dough P** A 630 455-5200
Downers Grove *(G-8438)*
**Farmers Mill Inc** G 618 445-2114
Albion *(G-362)*
**General Mills Inc** E 309 342-9165
Galesburg *(G-10754)*
**General Mills Inc** F 630 577-3800
Lisle *(G-13594)*
**Hayden Mills Inc** E 618 962-3136
Omaha *(G-16807)*
▲ **Hodgson Mill Inc** C 217 347-0105
Effingham *(G-8839)*
▲ **J R Short Milling Company** G 815 937-2635
Kankakee *(G-12627)*
**J R Short Milling Company** C 815 937-2633
Kankakee *(G-12628)*
**Kws Cereals Usa LLC** G 815 200-2666
Champaign *(G-3508)*
**Lacertus Branding LLC** F 224 523-5100
Buffalo Grove *(G-2720)*
▲ **LLC Urban Farmer** F 815 468-7200
Manteno *(G-14187)*
**McShares Inc** E 217 762-2561
Monticello *(G-15079)*
◆ **McShares Inc** E 217 762-2561
Monticello *(G-15080)*
**Mennel Milling Co** F 217 999-2161
Mount Olive *(G-15305)*
**Natures American Co** G 630 246-4274
Chicago *(G-5870)*
**Nauvoo Mill & Bakery** G 217 453-6734
Nauvoo *(G-15854)*
▼ **New Alliance Production LLC** E 309 928-3123
Farmer City *(G-10180)*
▼ **Nu-World Amaranth Inc** G 630 369-6819
Naperville *(G-15717)*
**Pillsbury Company LLC** G 847 541-8888
Buffalo Grove *(G-2753)*
**Problend-Eurogerm LLC** G 847 221-5004
Rolling Meadows *(G-18770)*
**Quaker Oats Company** A 217 443-4995
Danville *(G-7761)*
**Roanoke Milling Co** G 309 923-5731
Roanoke *(G-18054)*
**Ron & Pats Pizza Shack** G 847 395-5005
Antioch *(G-653)*
**Roquette America Inc** G 630 232-2157
Geneva *(G-10864)*
▲ **Salud Natural Entrepreneur Inc** E 224 789-7400
Waukegan *(G-21612)*
▲ **Sunrise Distributors Inc** G 630 400-8786
Elk Grove Village *(G-9761)*
**Tasty Breads International Inc** D 847 451-4000
Franklin Park *(G-10604)*
**TEC Foods Inc** E 800 315-8002
Chicago *(G-6683)*
**Temperance Beer Company LLC** G 847 864-1000
Evanston *(G-10101)*
▼ **U S Soy LLC** F 217 235-1020
Mattoon *(G-14411)*

## 2043 Cereal Breakfast Foods

**BF Foods Inc** E 773 252-6113
Chicago *(G-4099)*
**Care Child Companies** G 630 295-6770
Bloomingdale *(G-2099)*
**General Mills Inc** D 630 844-1125
Montgomery *(G-15045)*
**General Mills Inc** B 630 231-1140
Calumet City *(G-2939)*
**General Mills Inc** F 630 577-3800
Lisle *(G-13594)*
▼ **Gilster-Mary Lee Corporation** A 618 826-2361
Chester *(G-3657)*
▼ **Hearthside Food Solutions LLC** E 630 967-3600
Downers Grove *(G-8456)*
**Kellogg Company** B 773 254-0900
Chicago *(G-5370)*
**Kellogg Company** F 217 258-3251
Mattoon *(G-14397)*
**Kellogg Company** E 630 820-9457
Oak Brook *(G-16531)*
**Kellogg Company** A 773 995-7200
Chicago *(G-5371)*
**Kraft Foods Asia PCF Svcs LLC** G 847 943-4000
Deerfield *(G-8026)*
**Kraft Heinz Company** C 847 646-2000
Glenview *(G-11160)*
**Kws Cereals Usa LLC** G 815 200-2666
Champaign *(G-3508)*
**Lee Gilster-Mary Corporation** G 618 826-2361
Chester *(G-3658)*
**Lee Gilster-Mary Corporation** E 618 443-5676
Sparta *(G-20318)*
◆ **Mary Lee Packaging Corporation** E 618 826-2361
Chester *(G-3659)*
**Mondelez Global LLC** B 630 369-1909
Naperville *(G-15699)*
◆ **Mondelez International Inc** A 847 943-4000
Deerfield *(G-8038)*
**Quaker Manufacturing LLC** F 312 222-7111
Chicago *(G-6241)*
◆ **Quaker Oats Company** A 312 821-1000
Chicago *(G-6242)*
**Quaker Oats Company** A 217 443-4995
Danville *(G-7761)*
**Quaker Oats Europe Inc** G 312 821-1000
Chicago *(G-6243)*
**Treehouse Private Brands Inc** F 630 455-5265
Downers Grove *(G-8534)*

## 2044 Rice Milling

▲ **International Golden Foods Inc** F 630 860-5552
Bensenville *(G-1921)*

## 2045 Flour, Blended & Prepared

▲ **Arlington Specialties Inc** G 847 545-9500
Elk Grove Village *(G-9313)*
**Arro Corporation** E 708 352-7412
Hodgkins *(G-11971)*
**Arro Corporation** C 708 352-8200
Hodgkins *(G-11970)*
**Arro Corporation** G 773 978-1251
Chicago *(G-3947)*
▲ **Barilla America Inc** D 515 956-4400
Northbrook *(G-16211)*
**Bear-Stewart Corporation** E 773 276-0400
Chicago *(G-4065)*
**Brolite Products Incorporated** E 630 830-0340
Streamwood *(G-20646)*
**Continental Mills Inc** C 217 540-4000
Effingham *(G-8830)*
**Diversfied Ill Green Works LLC** D 773 544-7777
Chicago *(G-4613)*
**Dominos Pizza LLC** E 630 783-0738
Woodridge *(G-22472)*
**Fleetchem LLC** G 708 957-5311
Flossmoor *(G-10224)*
▼ **Gilster-Mary Lee Corporation** A 618 826-2361
Chester *(G-3657)*
**Glen Lake Inc** F 630 668-3492
Carol Stream *(G-3159)*
**Gust-John Foods & Pdts Corp** G 630 879-8700
Batavia *(G-1453)*
▲ **Hodgson Mill Inc** C 217 347-0105
Effingham *(G-8839)*
**Inside Beverages** C 847 438-1338
Lake Zurich *(G-13088)*
▲ **Joshi Brothers Inc** E 847 895-0200
Schaumburg *(G-19590)*
**Kerry Inc** D 708 450-3260
Melrose Park *(G-14666)*
**Lee Gilster-Mary Corporation** D 618 965-3426
Steeleville *(G-20561)*
**Lee Gilster-Mary Corporation** G 618 826-2361
Chester *(G-3658)*
**Lee Gilster-Mary Corporation** E 618 443-5676
Sparta *(G-20318)*

SIC

20 FOOD AND KINDRED PRODUCTS SIC SECTION

Lee Gilster-Mary Corporation ....D .... 815 472-6456
Momence (G-14983)
Loders Croklaan BV ....C .... 815 730-5200
Channahon (G-3577)
Nation Pizza Products LP ....A .... 847 397-3320
Schaumburg (G-19661)
Parke & Son Inc ....G .... 217 875-0572
Decatur (G-7925)
◆ Quaker Oats Company ....A .... 312 821-1000
Chicago (G-6242)
Quaker Oats Europe Inc ....G .... 312 821-1000
Chicago (G-6243)
Russo Wholesale Meat Inc ....G .... 708 385-0500
Alsip (G-525)
Simple Mills LLC ....G .... 312 600-6196
Chicago (G-6514)
Watson Foods Co Inc ....D .... 847 245-8404
Lindenhurst (G-13550)
Watson Inc ....E .... 217 824-4440
Taylorville (G-20846)

## 2046 Wet Corn Milling

ADM Holdings LLC ....G .... 217 422-7281
Decatur (G-7821)
ADM Holdings LLC ....G .... 312 634-8100
Chicago (G-3752)
▼ ADM Holdings LLC ....G .... 217 424-5200
Decatur (G-7822)
ADM Trucking Inc ....G .... 217 451-4288
Decatur (G-7823)
◆ Archer-Daniels-Midland Company ....A .... 312 634-8100
Chicago (G-3941)
Archer-Daniels-Midland Company ....C .... 217 935-3620
Clinton (G-7277)
Archer-Daniels-Midland Company ....E .... 217 424-5413
Decatur (G-7835)
Archer-Daniels-Midland Company ....C .... 217 424-5200
Decatur (G-7841)
Bio Fuels By American Farmers ....F .... 561 859-6251
Benton (G-2023)
Cargill Incorporated ....E .... 630 505-7788
Naperville (G-15616)
Enjoy Life Natural Brands LLC ....E .... 773 632-2163
Chicago (G-4756)
Gro Alliance LLC ....E .... 217 792-3355
Mount Pulaski (G-15388)
◆ Ingredion Incorporated ....A .... 708 551-2600
Westchester (G-21845)
Ingredion Incorporated ....D .... 309 550-9136
Mapleton (G-14210)
Ingredion Incorporated ....G .... 708 551-2600
Chicago (G-5193)
Ingredion Incorporated ....C .... 708 728-3535
Summit Argo (G-20764)
Ingredion Incorporated ....C .... 708 563-2400
Argo (G-693)
Ktm Industries Inc ....G .... 217 224-5861
Quincy (G-17850)
Lee Gilster-Mary Corporation ....D .... 815 472-6456
Momence (G-14983)
Mgp Ingredients Illinois Inc ....C .... 309 353-3990
Pekin (G-17274)
Mgpi Processing Inc ....C .... 309 353-3990
Pekin (G-17275)
PPG Architectural Finishes Inc ....D .... 773 523-6333
Chicago (G-6161)
Tate & Lyle Americas LLC ....E .... 847 396-7500
Hoffman Estates (G-12063)
◆ Tate & Lyle Americas LLC ....C .... 217 421-2964
Decatur (G-7949)
◆ Tate Lyle Ingrdnts Amricas LLC ....A .... 217 423-4411
Decatur (G-7950)
Tate Lyle Ingrdnts Amricas LLC ....G .... 309 473-2721
Heyworth (G-11766)

## 2047 Dog & Cat Food

Diddy Dogs Inc ....G .... 815 517-0451
Dekalb (G-8088)
◆ Evangers Dog and Cat Fd Co Inc ....E .... 847 537-0102
Wheeling (G-22050)
Hartz Mountain Corporation ....E .... 847 517-2596
Schaumburg (G-19548)
Kraft Heinz Foods Company ....C .... 847 291-3900
Northbrook (G-16290)
Lincoln Bark LLC ....G .... 800 428-4027
Chicago (G-5506)
Mars Incorporated ....D .... 630 878-8877
Wheaton (G-21968)
Midwestern Pet Foods Inc ....E .... 309 734-3121
Monmouth (G-15019)
Nestle Usa Inc ....C .... 847 808-5300
Buffalo Grove (G-2748)
Nobu Nutritional Baking Co Inc ....G .... 847 344-7336
Schaumburg (G-19667)
Papmpered Pups ....G .... 815 782-8383
Joliet (G-12549)
▲ Pedigree Ovens Inc ....E .... 815 943-8144
Harvard (G-11643)
Pet Celebrations Inc ....G .... 630 832-6549
Elmhurst (G-9921)
▲ Pet Factory Inc ....C .... 847 281-8054
Mundelein (G-15544)
◆ Pet-Ag Inc ....E .... 847 683-2288
Hampshire (G-11558)
Phelps Industries LLC ....E .... 815 397-0236
Rockford (G-18535)
Yotta Pet Products Inc ....F .... 217 466-4777
Paris (G-17165)

## 2048 Prepared Feeds For Animals & Fowls

▲ Agresearch Inc ....F .... 815 726-0410
Joliet (G-12451)
▼ Agribase International Inc ....G .... 847 810-0167
Schaumburg (G-19426)
▲ All-Feed Proc & Packg Inc ....F .... 309 629-0001
Alpha (G-425)
All-Feed Proc & Packg Inc ....G .... 309 932-3119
Galva (G-10782)
Altair Corporation (del) ....E .... 847 634-9540
Lincolnshire (G-13426)
Aqua-Tech Co ....G .... 847 383-7075
Elgin (G-8956)
Archer-Daniels-Midland Company ....E .... 217 222-7100
Quincy (G-17793)
Archer-Daniels-Midland Company ....E .... 217 342-3986
Effingham (G-8824)
Archer-Daniels-Midland Company ....E .... 217 424-5858
Decatur (G-7837)
Archer-Daniels-Midland Company ....F .... 217 732-6678
Lincoln (G-13404)
Archer-Daniels-Midland Company ....D .... 217 424-5785
Decatur (G-7839)
Archer-Daniels-Midland Company ....F .... 815 362-2180
German Valley (G-10890)
Archer-Daniels-Midland Company ....G .... 618 432-7194
Patoka (G-17230)
Ardent Mills LLC ....E .... 618 826-2371
Chester (G-3650)
B B Milling Co Inc ....G .... 217 376-3131
Emden (G-9983)
B&A Livestock Feed Company LLC ....G .... 618 245-6422
Farina (G-10173)
Bill Chandler Farms ....G .... 618 752-7551
Noble (G-16049)
Blackwing For Pets Inc ....G .... 203 762-8620
Antioch (G-624)
Cargill Incorporated ....F .... 618 662-8070
Flora (G-10202)
▼ Cargill Dry Corn Ingrdents Inc ....G .... 217 465-5331
Paris (G-17143)
Chatham Corporation ....F .... 847 634-5506
Lincolnshire (G-13436)
Cherry Valley Feed Supplies ....G .... 815 332-7665
Cherry Valley (G-3640)
Cloverleaf Feed Co Inc ....G .... 217 589-5010
Roodhouse (G-18882)
Darling Ingredients Inc ....E .... 309 476-8111
Lynn Center (G-14016)
Darling International Inc ....E .... 708 388-3223
Blue Island (G-2245)
▼ Dawes LLC ....F .... 847 577-2020
Arlington Heights (G-745)
Dekalb Feeds Inc ....D .... 815 625-4546
Rock Falls (G-18131)
Effingham Equity Inc ....F .... 217 268-5128
Arcola (G-668)
Fish King Inc ....G .... 773 736-4974
Chicago (G-4850)
◆ Furst-Mcness Company ....D .... 800 435-5100
Freeport (G-10659)
Garver Feeds ....E .... 217 422-2201
Decatur (G-7884)
Griswold Feed Inc ....G .... 815 432-2811
Watseka (G-21417)
Gsi Group LLC ....D .... 217 463-8016
Paris (G-17149)
Helfter Enterprises Inc ....F .... 309 522-5505
Osco (G-16899)
▲ Herris Group LLC ....G .... 630 908-7393
Willowbrook (G-22214)
▲ Howard Pet Products Inc ....E .... 973 398-3038
Saint Charles (G-19194)
Hueber LLC ....F .... 815 393-4879
Creston (G-7472)
Jbs United Inc ....F .... 217 285-2121
Pittsfield (G-17570)
Jbs United Inc ....E .... 309 747-2196
Gridley (G-11407)
Kent Nutrition Group Inc ....F .... 815 874-2411
Rockford (G-18456)
Kent Nutrition Group Inc ....F .... 217 323-1216
Beardstown (G-1523)
Lebanon Seaboard Corporation ....E .... 217 446-0983
Danville (G-7746)
Liberty Feed Mill ....F .... 217 645-3441
Liberty (G-13296)
Lockport Fish Pantry ....G .... 815 588-3543
Lockport (G-13727)
Lokman Enterprises Inc ....G .... 773 654-0525
Chicago (G-5534)
M & W Feed Service ....G .... 815 858-2412
Elizabeth (G-9243)
Mendota Agri-Products Inc ....E .... 815 539-5633
Mendota (G-14724)
Mgp Ingredients Illinois Inc ....C .... 309 353-3990
Pekin (G-17274)
Mont Eagle Products Inc ....G .... 618 455-3344
Sainte Marie (G-19325)
▼ Morgan Robt Inc ....E .... 217 466-4777
Paris (G-17154)
◆ Nutriad Inc ....E .... 847 214-4860
Hampshire (G-11556)
Oceanic Food Express Inc ....G .... 847 480-7217
Northbrook (G-16322)
Packers By Products Inc ....F .... 618 271-0660
National Stock Yards (G-15851)
Pcs Phosphate Company Inc ....E .... 815 795-5111
Marseilles (G-14316)
◆ Pet-Ag Inc ....E .... 847 683-2288
Hampshire (G-11558)
Prince Agri Products Inc ....E .... 217 222-8854
Quincy (G-17872)
Purina Mills LLC ....E .... 618 283-2291
Vandalia (G-21122)
Quality Liquid Feeds Inc ....F .... 815 224-1553
La Salle (G-12782)
Rare Birds Inc ....G .... 847 259-7286
Arlington Heights (G-828)
Reconserve of Illinois Inc ....E .... 708 354-4641
Hodgkins (G-11981)
Roanoke Milling Co ....G .... 309 923-5731
Roanoke (G-18054)
▲ Sem Minerals LP ....D .... 217 224-8766
Quincy (G-17890)
▲ Siemer Enterprises Inc ....E .... 217 857-3171
Teutopolis (G-20855)
T C4 Inc ....F .... 618 335-3486
Vandalia (G-21127)
Tate Lyle Ingrdnts Amricas LLC ....G .... 309 473-2721
Heyworth (G-11766)
Transagra International Inc ....G .... 312 856-1010
Chicago (G-6757)
Trouw Nutrition Usa LLC ....E .... 618 651-1521
Highland (G-11814)
▲ Trouw Nutrition Usa LLC ....E .... 618 654-2070
Highland (G-11815)
Trouw Nutrition Usa LLC ....E .... 618 654-2070
Highland (G-11816)
Trouw Nutrition Usa LLC ....E .... 618 654-2070
Highland (G-11817)
Veal Tech Inc ....G .... 630 554-0410
Oswego (G-16938)
Wagners LLC ....E .... 815 889-4101
Milford (G-14815)
Western Yeast Company Inc ....E .... 309 274-3160
Chillicothe (G-7172)
Westway Feed Products LLC ....F .... 309 654-2211
Cordova (G-7380)
White International Inc ....E .... 630 377-9966
Saint Charles (G-19295)
White Owl Winery Incorporated ....G .... 618 928-2898
Flat Rock (G-10199)
Zoetis LLC ....D .... 708 757-2592
Chicago Heights (G-7137)

## 2051 Bread, Bakery Prdts Exc Cookies & Crackers

2 Figs Baking Co Inc ....G .... 847 778-2936
Des Plaines (G-8135)

SIC SECTION 20 FOOD AND KINDRED PRODUCTS

**Ace Bakeries** F 312 225-4973
Chicago *(G-3726)*

**American Blue Rbbon Hldngs LLC** D 708 687-7650
Oak Forest *(G-16573)*

**American Kitchen Delights Inc** D 708 210-3200
Harvey *(G-11656)*

**Amling Donuts Inc** E 847 426-5327
Carpentersville *(G-3274)*

**Anns Bakery Inc** G 773 384-5562
Chicago *(G-3912)*

▲ **Arlington Specialties Inc** G 847 545-9500
Elk Grove Village *(G-9313)*

**Athenian Foods Co** F 708 343-6700
Melrose Park *(G-14596)*

**Auntie Mmmms** G 217 509-6012
Camp Point *(G-2971)*

**B N K Inc** G 630 231-5640
West Chicago *(G-21664)*

**B&L Services Inc** G 630 257-1688
Lemont *(G-13226)*

**Baker & Nosh** G 773 989-7393
Chicago *(G-4029)*

**Bakery Crescent Corporation** G 847 956-6470
Arlington Heights *(G-722)*

**Bays English Muffin Corp** E 312 829-5253
Chicago *(G-4059)*

**Bays Michigan Corp** E 312 346-5757
Chicago *(G-4060)*

**Bear-Stewart Corporation** E 773 276-0400
Chicago *(G-4065)*

**Bellwood Dunkin Donuts** F 708 401-5601
Bellwood *(G-1695)*

**Bimbo Bakeries Usa Inc** E 773 254-3578
Chicago *(G-4107)*

**Bimbo Bakeries Usa Inc** D 815 626-6797
Rock Falls *(G-18127)*

**Bimbo Bakeries Usa Inc** E 309 797-4968
Moline *(G-14919)*

**Bodines Baking Company** G 217 853-7707
Decatur *(G-7846)*

**Bom Bon Corp** G 773 277-8777
Chicago *(G-4140)*

**Brown & Meyers Inc** G 618 524-3838
Metropolis *(G-14752)*

**Bullards Bakery** G 618 842-6666
Fairfield *(G-10137)*

**Butera Finer Foods Inc** D 708 456-5939
Norridge *(G-16097)*

**By Dozen Bakery Inc** G 815 636-0668
Machesney Park *(G-14063)*

**C & C Bakery Inc** G 773 276-4233
Chicago *(G-4199)*

**Callies Cuties Inc** G 815 566-6885
Plainfield *(G-17583)*

**Caribbean American Bkg Co Inc** G 773 761-0700
Chicago *(G-4244)*

**Casa Nostra Bakery Co Inc** F 847 455-5175
Franklin Park *(G-10424)*

**Cathys Sweet Creations** G 815 886-6769
Plainfield *(G-17585)*

**Cbc Restaurant Corp** D 773 463-0665
Chicago *(G-4260)*

**Charles Cicero Fingerhut** F 708 652-3643
Chicago *(G-4290)*

**Charleston County Market** D 217 345-7031
Charleston *(G-3593)*

**Chateau Food Products Inc** F 708 863-4207
Chicago *(G-4296)*

**Chicago Bread Company** F 630 620-1849
Addison *(G-73)*

**Chicago Pastry Inc** C 630 972-0404
Bolingbrook *(G-2286)*

**Chicago Pastry Inc** D 630 529-6161
Bloomingdale *(G-2100)*

**Christys Kitchen** G 815 735-6791
La Salle *(G-12768)*

▼ **Cloverhill Pastry-Vend LLC** D 773 745-9800
Chicago *(G-4408)*

**Cookie Dough Creations Co** E 630 369-4833
Naperville *(G-15635)*

**Creative Cakes LLC** E 708 614-9755
Tinley Park *(G-20904)*

**Cub Foods Inc** C 309 689-0140
Peoria *(G-17347)*

**Cupcakeologist LLC** G 630 656-2272
Bolingbrook *(G-2294)*

**DAmatos Bakery** F 312 733-5456
Chicago *(G-4547)*

**DAmatos Bakery Inc** G 312 733-6219
Chicago *(G-4548)*

**Dessertwerks Inc** G 847 487-8239
Libertyville *(G-13319)*

**Dimples Donuts** G 630 406-0303
Batavia *(G-1438)*

**Dinkels Bakery Inc** E 773 281-7300
Chicago *(G-4605)*

**Distinctive Foods LLC** E 847 459-3600
Bensenville *(G-1880)*

**Dixie Cream Donut Shop** E 618 937-4866
West Frankfort *(G-21806)*

**Do-Rite Donuts** G 312 422-0150
Chicago *(G-4619)*

**Dominicks Finer Foods Inc** D 630 584-1750
Saint Charles *(G-19173)*

**Dominos Pastries Inc** G 773 889-3549
Hickory Hills *(G-11769)*

**Donut Palace** G 618 692-0532
Edwardsville *(G-8795)*

**Doughnut Boy** E 773 463-6328
Lincolnshire *(G-13444)*

**Dunajec Bakery & Deli** F 773 585-9611
Bridgeview *(G-2485)*

**Dunkin Donuts** E 708 460-3088
Orland Park *(G-16857)*

▼ **Earthgrains Refrigertd Dough P** A 630 455-5200
Downers Grove *(G-8438)*

**East Balt Bakery of Florida** B 407 933-2222
Chicago *(G-4680)*

**East Balt Commissary LLC** G 773 376-4444
Chicago *(G-4681)*

**El Moro De Letran Churros & Ba** F 312 733-3173
Chicago *(G-4708)*

**Emack & Bolios** G 309 682-3530
Peoria *(G-17357)*

**Enjoy Life Natural Brands LLC** E 773 632-2163
Chicago *(G-4756)*

**Entrust Services LLC** G 630 699-9132
Naperville *(G-15654)*

**European Classic Bakery** G 773 774-8755
Chicago *(G-4783)*

**Express Donuts Enterprise Inc** F 630 510-9310
Wheaton *(G-21947)*

**Father Marcellos & Son** C 312 654-2565
Chicago *(G-4820)*

**Faustos Bakery** G 847 255-9049
Arlington Heights *(G-753)*

**Flirty Cupcakes LLC** G 312 545-1096
Chicago *(G-4862)*

**Folsoms Bakery Inc** F 815 622-7870
Rock Falls *(G-18132)*

**Fortuna Baking Company** G 630 681-3000
Carol Stream *(G-3154)*

**G & K Baking LLC** G 630 415-8687
Oak Brook *(G-16517)*

**Gadgetworld Enterprises Inc** G 773 703-0796
Chicago *(G-4907)*

**Gold Coast Baking Co** G 630 620-1849
Addison *(G-137)*

**Gold Standard Baking Inc** C 773 523-2333
Chicago *(G-4971)*

**Golosinas El Canto** G 847 625-5103
Waukegan *(G-21564)*

▲ **Gonnella Baking Co** D 312 733-2020
Schaumburg *(G-19539)*

**Gonnella Baking Co** D 312 733-2020
Schaumburg *(G-19540)*

**Gonnella Baking Co** D 630 820-3433
Aurora *(G-1020)*

**Gonnella Baking Co** D 847 884-8829
Schaumburg *(G-19541)*

**Gonnella Frozen Products LLC** C 847 884-8829
Schaumburg *(G-19542)*

**Gordon Hann** E 630 761-1835
Batavia *(G-1451)*

**Gourmet Frog Pastry Shop** G 847 433-7038
Highland Park *(G-11837)*

◆ **Grecian Delight Foods Inc** C 847 364-1010
Elk Grove Village *(G-9511)*

**Happy Dog Barkery** F 630 512-0822
Downers Grove *(G-8453)*

**Harners Bakery Restaurant** D 630 892-5545
North Aurora *(G-16133)*

**Hearthside Food Solutions LLC** B 815 853-4348
Wenona *(G-21648)*

**Herbs Bakery Inc** F 847 741-0249
Elgin *(G-9065)*

**Herman Seekamp Inc** C 630 628-6555
Addison *(G-145)*

**Hermanitas Cupcakes** G 708 620-9396
Calumet City *(G-2943)*

**Highland Baking Company Inc** A 847 677-2789
Northbrook *(G-16270)*

**Hillshire Brands Company** F 630 991-5100
Downers Grove *(G-8458)*

▼ **Hillshire Brands Company** B 312 614-6000
Chicago *(G-5089)*

**Home Cut Donuts Inc** G 815 726-2132
Joliet *(G-12511)*

**Homer Vintage Bakery** G 217 896-2538
Homer *(G-12075)*

**Honey Fluff Doughnuts** G 708 579-1826
Countryside *(G-7431)*

**Illinois Baking** G 773 995-7200
Chicago *(G-5154)*

**Jay Elka** F 847 540-7776
Lake Zurich *(G-13091)*

**Jewel Osco Inc** C 773 728-7730
Chicago *(G-5299)*

**Jewel Osco Inc** C 773 784-1922
Chicago *(G-5300)*

**Jewel Osco Inc** C 708 352-0120
Countryside *(G-7435)*

**Jewel Osco Inc** D 630 859-1212
Aurora *(G-1177)*

**Jewel Osco Inc** C 847 854-2692
Algonquin *(G-395)*

**Jewel Osco Inc** C 847 677-3331
Skokie *(G-20019)*

**Jewel Osco Inc** C 630 584-4594
Saint Charles *(G-19202)*

**Jewel Osco Inc** C 847 428-3547
West Dundee *(G-21798)*

**Jewel Osco Inc** C 630 355-2172
Naperville *(G-15681)*

**Jewel Osco Inc** D 630 226-1892
Bolingbrook *(G-2328)*

**Jewel Osco Inc** C 815 464-5352
Frankfort *(G-10336)*

**Jewel-Osco Inc** C 847 296-7786
Des Plaines *(G-8216)*

**Jr Bakery** E 773 465-6733
Chicago *(G-5331)*

**K & A Bread LLC** D 708 757-7750
Chicago Heights *(G-7107)*

**Kellogg Company** C 630 941-0300
Elmhurst *(G-9897)*

**Kerry Inc** G 847 595-1003
Elk Grove Village *(G-9572)*

**Kerry Ingredients & Flavours** F 847 595-1003
Elk Grove Village *(G-9573)*

▲ **Keystone Bakery Holdings LLC** G 603 792-3113
Deerfield *(G-8024)*

**Kim & Sctts Grmet Pretzels Inc** D 800 578-9478
Chicago *(G-5383)*

**Korinek & Co Inc** G 708 652-2870
Cicero *(G-7210)*

**Kroger Co** C 309 694-6298
East Peoria *(G-8722)*

**Kroger Co** C 815 332-7267
Rockford *(G-18457)*

**Kronos Foods Corp** B 773 847-2250
Glendale Heights *(G-11039)*

**La Bella Chrstnas Kitchens Inc** G 815 801-1600
German Valley *(G-10891)*

**La Chicanita Bakery** F 630 499-8845
Aurora *(G-1180)*

**La Conchita Bakery** G 847 623-4094
Waukegan *(G-21578)*

**La Dolce Bella Cupcakes** G 847 987-3738
Lockport *(G-13725)*

**La Luc Bakery Inc** G 847 740-0303
Round Lake *(G-19061)*

**Labaquette Kedzie Inc** G 773 925-0455
Chicago *(G-5429)*

▲ **Labriola Baking Company LLC** C 708 377-0400
Alsip *(G-483)*

**Le Petit Pain Holdings LLC** G 312 981-3770
Chicago *(G-5478)*

**Leas Baking Company LLC** G 708 710-3404
Homer Glen *(G-12082)*

**Leesons Cakes Inc** G 708 429-1330
Tinley Park *(G-20930)*

**Leonards Bakery** G 847 564-4977
Northbrook *(G-16294)*

**Lewis Brothers Bakeries Inc** G 618 833-5185
Anna *(G-607)*

**Liborio Baking Co Inc** G 708 452-7222
River Grove *(G-18010)*

**Linx Enterprises LLC** G 224 409-2206
Chicago *(G-5516)*

S I C

Employee Codes: A=Over 500 employees, B=251-500
C=101-250, D=51-100, E=20-50, F=10-19, G=3-9

2017 Harris Illinois
Industrial Directory

919

20 FOOD AND KINDRED PRODUCTS SIC SECTION

**Lucksfood** ........ G ...... 773 878-7778
Chicago *(G-5557)*
**Maiers Bakery** ........ G ...... 847 967-8042
Morton Grove *(G-15216)*
**Mandys Kitchen & Grill** ........ G ...... 630 348-2264
Bolingbrook *(G-2339)*
**Mangel and Co** ........ F ...... 847 634-0730
Long Grove *(G-13894)*
**▲ Manna Organics LLC** ........ F ...... 630 795-0500
Lisle *(G-13618)*
**Maplehurst Bakeries LLC** ........ E ...... 773 826-1245
Chicago *(G-5610)*
**Marconi Bakery Company** ........ F ...... 708 757-6315
Chicago Heights *(G-7111)*
**Mariegold Bake Shoppe** ........ G ...... 773 561-1978
Chicago *(G-5617)*
**Marzeya Bakery Inc** ........ G ...... 773 374-7855
Chicago *(G-5642)*
**Mel-O-Cream Donuts** ........ G ...... 217 528-2303
Springfield *(G-20477)*
**Mel-O-Cream Donuts** ........ F ...... 217 544-4644
Springfield *(G-20476)*
**Melinda I Rhodes** ........ G ...... 815 569-2789
Capron *(G-2997)*
**Milano Bakery Inc** ........ E ...... 815 727-2253
Joliet *(G-12542)*
**Miss Joans Cupcakes** ........ G ...... 630 881-5707
Bolingbrook *(G-2343)*
**Morningfields** ........ G ...... 847 309-8460
Park Ridge *(G-17209)*
**Mybread LLC** ........ G ...... 312 600-9633
Chicago *(G-5843)*
**▲ Nablus Sweets Inc** ........ G ...... 708 529-3911
Bridgeview *(G-2513)*
**Nak Won Korean Bakery** ........ G ...... 773 588-8769
Chicago *(G-5850)*
**Narima Inc** ........ G ...... 847 818-9620
Rolling Meadows *(G-18748)*
**National Biscuit Company** ........ G ...... 773 925-0654
Chicago *(G-5860)*
**Nauvoo Mill & Bakery** ........ G ...... 217 453-6734
Nauvoo *(G-15854)*
**Neuman Bakery Specialties Inc** ........ F ...... 630 916-8909
Addison *(G-227)*
**New Chicago Wholesale Bky Inc** ........ E ...... 847 981-1600
Elk Grove Village *(G-9650)*
**Niemann Foods Foundation** ........ C ...... 217 222-0190
Quincy *(G-17862)*
**Niemann Foods Foundation** ........ C ...... 217 793-4091
Springfield *(G-20487)*
**OBrothers Bakery Inc** ........ G ...... 847 249-0091
Waukegan *(G-21597)*
**Original Ferrara Inc** ........ F ...... 312 666-2200
Chicago *(G-6011)*
**Orland Park Bakery Ltd** ........ E ...... 708 349-8516
Orland Park *(G-16881)*
**Piemonte Bakery Company Inc** ........ E ...... 815 962-4833
Rockford *(G-18536)*
**Pin Hsiao & Associates LLC** ........ E ...... 206 818-0155
Flossmoor *(G-10227)*
**Pinnacle Foods Group LLC** ........ B ...... 217 235-3181
Mattoon *(G-14406)*
**Quality Croutons Inc** ........ E ...... 773 927-8200
Chicago *(G-6246)*
**Rain Creek Baking Corp** ........ G ...... 559 347-9960
Glendale Heights *(G-11063)*
**Red Hen Bread Inc** ........ E ...... 773 342-6823
Elmhurst *(G-9927)*
**Red Hen Corporation** ........ G ...... 312 433-0436
Elmhurst *(G-9928)*
**River City Cupcake LLC** ........ G ...... 309 613-1312
Pekin *(G-17287)*
**Riverside Bake Shop** ........ E ...... 815 385-0044
McHenry *(G-14552)*
**◆ Rjl Inc** ........ C ...... 708 385-4884
Alsip *(G-521)*
**Roesers Bakery** ........ E ...... 773 489-6900
Chicago *(G-6379)*
**Rolfs Patisserie Inc** ........ C ...... 847 675-6565
Lincolnwood *(G-13534)*
**Roma Bakeries Inc** ........ F ...... 815 964-6737
Rockford *(G-18596)*
**Royal Oak Farm Inc** ........ F ...... 815 648-4141
Harvard *(G-11646)*
**Rubschlager Baking Corporation** ........ G ...... 773 826-1245
Chicago *(G-6413)*
**Sara Lee Baking Group** ........ G ...... 217 585-3462
Springfield *(G-20518)*
**Say Cheese Cake** ........ G ...... 618 532-6001
Centralia *(G-3431)*
**Schnuck Markets Inc** ........ C ...... 618 466-0825
Godfrey *(G-11237)*
**▲ Schulze and Burch Biscuit Co** ........ B ...... 773 927-6622
Chicago *(G-6455)*
**Smallcakes Cupcakery of South** ........ G ...... 773 433-0059
South Barrington *(G-20132)*
**Spunky Dunker Donuts** ........ G ...... 847 358-7935
Palatine *(G-17076)*
**Streamlined Baking Co** ........ F ...... 773 227-2635
Chicago *(G-6603)*
**Sugar Monkey Cupcakes Inc** ........ G ...... 630 527-1869
Naperville *(G-15829)*
**Sunset Food Mart Inc** ........ C ...... 847 234-0854
Lake Forest *(G-12964)*
**Superior Baking Stone Inc** ........ G ...... 815 726-4610
Joliet *(G-12580)*
**Sweet Annies Bakery Inc** ........ F ...... 708 297-7066
Flossmoor *(G-10231)*
**Sweet Temptations Cupcake** ........ G ...... 309 212-2637
Bloomington *(G-2228)*
**Swirlcup** ........ G ...... 847 229-2200
Lincolnshire *(G-13483)*
**Tags Bakery Inc** ........ E ...... 847 328-1200
Evanston *(G-10100)*
**Tam Tav Bakery Inc** ........ E ...... 773 764-8877
Chicago *(G-6669)*
**Tarte Cupcakery Company** ........ G ...... 312 898-2103
Lansing *(G-13189)*
**Thats So Sweet** ........ G ...... 903 331-7221
Lexington *(G-13294)*
**▲ Todays Temptations Inc** ........ F ...... 773 385-5355
Chicago *(G-6733)*
**▼ Tonys Bakery** ........ G ...... 847 599-1590
Waukegan *(G-21630)*
**Tortilleria Atotonilco Inc** ........ E ...... 773 523-0800
Chicago *(G-6749)*
**Treasure Island Foods Inc** ........ D ...... 312 642-1105
Chicago *(G-6765)*
**Treasure Island Foods Inc** ........ C ...... 773 880-8880
Chicago *(G-6764)*
**Treasure Island Foods Inc** ........ D ...... 312 440-1144
Chicago *(G-6763)*
**Two Figs Baking Co** ........ G ...... 847 233-0500
Franklin Park *(G-10614)*
**Unity Baking Company LLC** ........ G ...... 630 360-6099
Aurora *(G-1228)*
**Walter & Kathy Anczerewicz** ........ G ...... 708 448-3676
Palos Heights *(G-17113)*
**Walter Lagestee Inc** ........ C ...... 708 957-2974
Homewood *(G-12106)*
**▼ Wholesome Harvest Baking LLC** ........ E ...... 800 550-6810
Des Plaines *(G-8305)*
**◆ Zb Importing Inc** ........ D ...... 708 222-8330
Cicero *(G-7248)*
**Zeldaco Ltd** ........ F ...... 847 679-0033
Skokie *(G-20116)*

## *2052 Cookies & Crackers*

**Baked By Betsy Inc** ........ G ...... 847 292-1434
Wilmette *(G-22242)*
**Blissful Brownies Inc** ........ G ...... 541 308-0226
Lake Forest *(G-12887)*
**Carols Cookies Inc** ........ G ...... 847 831-4500
Northbrook *(G-16217)*
**Casa Nostra Bakery Co Inc** ........ F ...... 847 455-5175
Franklin Park *(G-10424)*
**Charleston County Market** ........ D ...... 217 345-7031
Charleston *(G-3593)*
**Cheryl & Co** ........ C ...... 708 386-1255
Oak Park *(G-16658)*
**Chicago Pastry Inc** ........ D ...... 630 529-6161
Bloomingdale *(G-2100)*
**▲ Chipita America Inc** ........ E ...... 708 731-2434
Westchester *(G-21832)*
**Christian Wolf Inc** ........ G ...... 618 667-9522
Bartelso *(G-1314)*
**Cookie Dough Creations Co** ........ E ...... 630 369-4833
Naperville *(G-15635)*
**Cookie Kingdom Inc** ........ D ...... 815 883-3331
Oglesby *(G-16747)*
**DAmatos Bakery Inc** ........ G ...... 312 733-6219
Chicago *(G-4548)*
**Deerfield Bakery** ........ G ...... 847 520-0068
Buffalo Grove *(G-2683)*
**Dinkels Bakery Inc** ........ E ...... 773 281-7300
Chicago *(G-4605)*
**Dobake Bakeries Inc** ........ F ...... 630 620-1849
Addison *(G-96)*
**▲ Fortella Company Inc** ........ G ...... 312 567-9000
Chicago *(G-4876)*
**Golden Dragon Fortune Cookies** ........ F ...... 312 842-8199
Chicago *(G-4973)*
**Griffin Industries LLC** ........ G ...... 815 357-8200
Seneca *(G-19886)*
**◆ Harvest Valley Bakery Inc** ........ E ...... 815 224-9030
La Salle *(G-12774)*
**Herman Seekamp Inc** ........ C ...... 630 628-6555
Addison *(G-145)*
**▲ Hop Kee Incorporated** ........ E ...... 312 791-9111
Chicago *(G-5109)*
**Jewel Osco Inc** ........ C ...... 847 677-3331
Skokie *(G-20019)*
**Jewel Osco Inc** ........ C ...... 630 355-2172
Naperville *(G-15681)*
**Jr Bakery** ........ E ...... 773 465-6733
Chicago *(G-5331)*
**Katys LLC** ........ G ...... 708 522-9814
Oak Park *(G-16672)*
**Keebler Company** ........ E ...... 630 820-9457
Aurora *(G-1039)*
**Keebler Foods Company** ........ E ...... 630 833-2900
Elmhurst *(G-9896)*
**Kellogg Company** ........ C ...... 630 941-0300
Elmhurst *(G-9897)*
**Kroger Co** ........ C ...... 815 332-7267
Rockford *(G-18457)*
**Lofthouse Bakery Products Inc** ........ G ...... 630 455-5229
Downers Grove *(G-8479)*
**Maiers Bakery** ........ G ...... 847 967-8042
Morton Grove *(G-15216)*
**Market Square Food Company** ........ F ...... 847 599-6070
Park City *(G-17166)*
**Matts Cookie Company** ........ G ...... 847 537-3888
Wheeling *(G-22103)*
**Mondelez Global LLC** ........ E ...... 773 925-4300
Chicago *(G-5793)*
**▲ Mondelez Global LLC** ........ C ...... 847 943-4000
Deerfield *(G-8037)*
**Mondelez Global LLC** ........ B ...... 630 369-1909
Naperville *(G-15699)*
**Mybread LLC** ........ G ...... 312 600-9633
Chicago *(G-5843)*
**Old Colony Baking Company Inc** ........ G ...... 847 498-5434
Spring Valley *(G-20377)*
**P Double Corporation** ........ F ...... 630 585-7160
Aurora *(G-1061)*
**Paleo Prime LLC** ........ G ...... 312 659-6596
Chicago *(G-6059)*
**Pures Food Specialties LLC** ........ E ...... 708 344-8884
Broadview *(G-2605)*
**◆ Quaker Oats Company** ........ A ...... 312 821-1000
Chicago *(G-6242)*
**Quality Croutons Inc** ........ E ...... 773 927-8200
Chicago *(G-6246)*
**Roma Bakeries Inc** ........ F ...... 815 964-6737
Rockford *(G-18596)*
**▲ Schulze and Burch Biscuit Co** ........ B ...... 773 927-6622
Chicago *(G-6455)*
**Stress Free Cookies Inc** ........ G ...... 312 856-7686
Chicago *(G-6605)*
**Sugar/Spice Extraordinry Treat** ........ G ...... 847 864-7800
Evanston *(G-10098)*
**Tags Bakery Inc** ........ E ...... 847 328-1200
Evanston *(G-10100)*
**Th Foods Inc** ........ G ...... 702 565-2816
Loves Park *(G-14000)*
**▲ Th Foods Inc** ........ C ...... 800 896-2396
Loves Park *(G-14001)*
**Treehouse Private Brands Inc** ........ C ...... 815 389-2745
South Beloit *(G-20170)*
**Treehouse Private Brands Inc** ........ F ...... 630 455-5265
Downers Grove *(G-8534)*
**Walter Lagestee Inc** ........ C ...... 708 957-2974
Homewood *(G-12106)*
**Wex Distributors Inc** ........ G ...... 847 691-5823
Antioch *(G-663)*
**Wildlife Cookie Company** ........ G ...... 630 377-6196
Saint Charles *(G-19296)*

## *2053 Frozen Bakery Prdts*

**Aryzta LLC** ........ C ...... 708 498-2300
Northlake *(G-16428)*
**Bear-Stewart Corporation** ........ E ...... 773 276-0400
Chicago *(G-4065)*
**Caramel-A Bakery Ltd** ........ E ...... 773 227-2635
Chicago *(G-4235)*
**▼ Cloverhill Pastry-Vend LLC** ........ D ...... 773 745-9800
Chicago *(G-4408)*
**Conagra Brands Inc** ........ D ...... 630 455-5200
Downers Grove *(G-8417)*

## SIC SECTION
## 20 FOOD AND KINDRED PRODUCTS

▼ Earthgrains Refrigertd Dough P .....A....... 630 455-5200
  Downers Grove *(G-8438)*
▼ Elis Cheesecake Company .............C....... 773 205-3800
  Chicago *(G-4730)*
Forno Palese Baking Company ..........F....... 630 595-5502
  Bartlett *(G-1348)*
Goldies Baking Inc ...........................F....... 224 757-0820
  Volo *(G-21313)*
Griffin Industries LLC .......................G....... 815 357-8200
  Seneca *(G-19886)*
Herman Seekamp Inc .......................C....... 630 628-6555
  Addison *(G-145)*
▼ Hillshire Brands Company ..............B....... 312 614-6000
  Chicago *(G-5089)*
Imanis Original Bean Pies & F ..........G....... 773 716-7007
  Chicago *(G-5163)*
K & A Bread LLC .............................D....... 708 757-7750
  Chicago Heights *(G-7107)*
▲ Keystone Bakery Holdings LLC .....G....... 603 792-3113
  Deerfield *(G-8024)*
Mel-O-Cream Donuts Intl Inc ...........D....... 217 483-1825
  Springfield *(G-20478)*
New Chicago Wholesale Bky Inc ......E....... 847 981-1600
  Elk Grove Village *(G-9650)*
Quality Bakeries LLC .......................F....... 630 553-7377
  Saint Charles *(G-19247)*
Rich Products Corporation ..............A....... 815 729-4509
  Crest Hill *(G-7466)*
Rich Products Corporation ..............A....... 309 886-2465
  Washington *(G-21390)*
Soublend Technologies LLC ............G....... 815 534-5778
  Frankfort *(G-10364)*
Sweet Creation By Sheila ................G....... 708 754-7938
  Glenwood *(G-11220)*
▼ Vienna Beef Ltd ............................E....... 773 278-7800
  Chicago *(G-6896)*
Wilseys Handmade Sweets LLC ......G....... 314 504-0851
  Edwardsville *(G-8818)*

### 2061 Sugar, Cane

Nablus Sweets Inc ..........................E....... 708 205-6534
  Chicago *(G-5847)*
Westway Feed Products LLC ..........F....... 309 654-2211
  Cordova *(G-7380)*

### 2062 Sugar, Cane Refining

Domino Foods Inc ...........................E....... 773 254-8282
  Chicago *(G-4624)*
Inter-Trade Global LLC ....................G....... 618 954-6119
  Belleville *(G-1637)*
Lee Gilster-Mary Corporation ..........B....... 618 965-3449
  Steeleville *(G-20562)*
▲ Necta Sweet Inc ..........................E....... 847 215-9955
  Buffalo Grove *(G-2742)*
▲ Pullman Sugar LLC .....................E....... 773 260-9180
  Chicago *(G-6225)*

### 2063 Sugar, Beet

Inter-Trade Global LLC ....................G....... 618 954-6119
  Belleville *(G-1637)*
Jo Snow Inc .....................................G....... 773 732-3045
  Chicago *(G-5308)*
Lee Gilster-Mary Corporation ..........B....... 618 965-3449
  Steeleville *(G-20562)*
Merisant Us Inc ...............................C....... 815 929-2700
  Manteno *(G-14188)*
Sweet Specialty Solutions LLC ........E....... 630 739-9151
  Lemont *(G-13265)*

### 2064 Candy & Confectionery Prdts

▲ Affy Tapple LLC ..........................E....... 773 338-1100
  Niles *(G-15958)*
Alabaster Box Creations LLC ..........F....... 708 473-6880
  Oak Forest *(G-16572)*
All American Nut & Candy Corp .......F....... 630 595-6473
  Bensenville *(G-1823)*
American Convenience Inc .............F....... 815 344-6040
  McHenry *(G-14480)*
Amy Wertheim .................................G....... 309 830-4361
  Atlanta *(G-946)*
Andersons Candy Shop Inc .............F....... 815 678-6000
  Richmond *(G-17957)*
Andrews Caramel LLC .....................F....... 773 286-2224
  Chicago *(G-3904)*
Andrews Caramel Apples Inc ..........F....... 773 286-2224
  Libertyville *(G-13303)*
Arndts Stores Inc ............................G....... 618 783-2511
  Newton *(G-15937)*

Baileys Fudge & Fine Gifts Inc .........G....... 217 231-3834
  Quincy *(G-17799)*
Baldi Candy Co ...............................E....... 773 463-7600
  Chicago *(G-4031)*
Belgian Chocolatier Piron Inc ...........G....... 847 864-5504
  Evanston *(G-10014)*
Bobbie Haycraft ..............................G....... 217 856-2194
  Humboldt *(G-12128)*
Cambridge Brands Mfg Inc ..............C....... 773 838-3400
  Chicago *(G-4221)*
▲ Candy Tech LLC .........................G....... 847 229-1011
  Park Ridge *(G-17186)*
Candyality .......................................G....... 773 472-7800
  Chicago *(G-4226)*
▲ Capol LLC ..................................G....... 224 545-5095
  Deerfield *(G-7993)*
Cellas Confections Inc ....................D....... 773 838-3400
  Chicago *(G-4267)*
CGC Corporation .............................D....... 773 838-3400
  Chicago *(G-4284)*
Chocolate Potpourri Ltd ..................G....... 847 729-8878
  Glenview *(G-11112)*
▼ Colleens Confection ....................G....... 630 653-2231
  Carol Stream *(G-3133)*
Creative Confections Inc .................G....... 847 724-0990
  Glenview *(G-11117)*
▲ Das Foods LLC ...........................G....... 224 715-9289
  Chicago *(G-4561)*
Deli Star Ventures Inc .....................F....... 618 233-0400
  Belleville *(G-1624)*
Double Good LLC ............................F....... 630 568-5544
  Burr Ridge *(G-2837)*
◆ Doumak Inc .................................G....... 800 323-0318
  Bensenville *(G-1881)*
Doumak Inc .....................................D....... 630 594-5400
  Bensenville *(G-1882)*
Doumak Inc .....................................D....... 847 981-2180
  Elk Grove Village *(G-9433)*
Eat Investments LLC ......................E....... 618 624-5350
  O Fallon *(G-16467)*
Element Bars Inc ............................F....... 888 411-3536
  Chicago *(G-4723)*
Fannie May Cnfctons Brands Inc ....F....... 773 693-9100
  Melrose Park *(G-14635)*
◆ Ferrara Candy Company ............B....... 708 366-0500
  Oakbrook Terrace *(G-16707)*
Ferrara Candy Company ..................B....... 630 366-0500
  Forest Park *(G-10244)*
Ferrara Candy Company ..................G....... 630 378-4197
  Bolingbrook *(G-2309)*
Ferrara Candy Company ..................F....... 708 432-4407
  Bellwood *(G-1705)*
Ferrara Candy Company ..................B....... 708 488-1892
  Forest Park *(G-10245)*
Forbidden Sweets Inc .....................G....... 847 838-9692
  Antioch *(G-633)*
Galenas Kandy Kitchen ...................G....... 815 777-0241
  Galena *(G-10723)*
Gary Poppins LLC ...........................G....... 847 455-2200
  Franklin Park *(G-10476)*
Goelitz Confectionery Company ......C....... 847 689-2225
  North Chicago *(G-16181)*
Healthful Habits LLC .......................G....... 224 489-4256
  West Chicago *(G-21714)*
Hershey Company ..........................A....... 618 544-3111
  Robinson *(G-18064)*
Hollingworth Candies Inc ................E....... 815 838-2275
  Lockport *(G-13721)*
▲ Imaginings 3 Inc .........................E....... 847 647-1370
  Niles *(G-15987)*
Jelly Belly Candy Company .............C....... 847 689-2225
  North Chicago *(G-16183)*
Jessis Hideout .................................G....... 618 343-4346
  Caseyville *(G-3398)*
◆ John B Sanfilippo & Son Inc .....C....... 847 289-1800
  Elgin *(G-9083)*
Killeen Confectionery LLC ..............G....... 312 804-0009
  Wilmette *(G-22258)*
La Sweet Inc ...................................F....... 252 340-0390
  Lincolnwood *(G-13520)*
Larry Ragan ....................................G....... 618 698-1041
  Belleville *(G-1648)*
▲ Long Grove Confectionery Co ....E....... 847 459-3100
  Buffalo Grove *(G-2728)*
Mars Chocolate North Amer LLC .....A....... 662 335-8000
  Chicago *(G-5630)*
Mars Chocolate North Amer LLC .....C....... 630 850-9898
  Burr Ridge *(G-2864)*
McCleary Inc ...................................G....... 815 389-3053
  South Beloit *(G-20160)*

▲ Mederer Group ............................G....... 630 860-4587
  Bensenville *(G-1948)*
Mexicandy Distributor Inc ...............G....... 773 847-0024
  Chicago *(G-5708)*
Mix Match LLC ................................F....... 708 201-0009
  Dolton *(G-8373)*
Mondelez Global LLC ......................G....... 815 877-8081
  Loves Park *(G-13968)*
▲ Monogram Creative Group Inc ...G....... 312 802-1433
  Glenview *(G-11170)*
Morkes Inc ......................................G....... 847 359-3511
  Palatine *(G-17057)*
MSI Green Inc .................................G....... 312 421-6550
  Chicago *(G-5826)*
Nature S American Co ....................G....... 630 246-4776
  Lombard *(G-13832)*
Nestle Usa Inc .................................D....... 847 957-7850
  Franklin Park *(G-10541)*
Nestle Usa Inc .................................D....... 847 808-5300
  Buffalo Grove *(G-2748)*
▲ Office Snax Inc ............................G....... 630 789-1783
  Oak Brook *(G-16552)*
Orbit Room .....................................G....... 773 588-8540
  Chicago *(G-6004)*
Peases Inc ......................................F....... 217 523-3721
  Springfield *(G-20501)*
Peases Inc ......................................F....... 217 529-2912
  Springfield *(G-20502)*
Peerless Confection Company ........D....... 773 281-6100
  Lincolnwood *(G-13529)*
▲ Primrose Candy Co ....................C....... 800 268-9522
  Chicago *(G-6188)*
▲ Princess Foods Inc .....................F....... 847 933-1820
  Skokie *(G-20060)*
◆ Quaker Oats Company ...............A....... 312 821-1000
  Chicago *(G-6242)*
Rebel Brands LLC ...........................B....... 312 804-0009
  Wilmette *(G-22264)*
▲ Ruckers Mkin Batch Candies Inc ...E....... 618 945-7778
  Bridgeport *(G-2455)*
▲ Silvestri Sweets Inc ....................F....... 630 232-2500
  Geneva *(G-10867)*
Sweet Company ..............................F....... 815 462-4586
  Mokena *(G-14909)*
Taylors Candy Inc ...........................E....... 708 371-0332
  Alsip *(G-534)*
▼ Terri Lynn Inc ...............................C....... 847 741-1900
  Elgin *(G-9210)*
Toffee Time .....................................G....... 309 788-2466
  Rock Island *(G-18208)*
Tootsie Roll Company Inc ...............A....... 773 838-3400
  Chicago *(G-6741)*
◆ Tootsie Roll Industries Inc ..........A....... 773 838-3400
  Chicago *(G-6742)*
Tootsie Roll Industries LLC .............G....... 773 245-4202
  Chicago *(G-6743)*
Tri International Co .........................A....... 773 838-3400
  Chicago *(G-6769)*
▲ Universal Holdings I LLC ...........D....... 773 847-1005
  Chicago *(G-6832)*
We Love Soy Inc .............................G....... 630 629-9667
  Lombard *(G-13881)*
White Stokes Company Inc ............E....... 773 254-5000
  Lincolnwood *(G-13543)*
Windy City Gold Popcorn Inc .........G....... 708 596-9940
  Alsip *(G-544)*
▼ Wm Wrigley Jr Company ............B....... 312 280-4710
  Chicago *(G-7012)*
Wm Wrigley Jr Company ..................A....... 312 644-2121
  Chicago *(G-7014)*
Wrigley Manufacturing Co LLC ........B....... 630 553-4800
  Yorkville *(G-22677)*
◆ Zb Importing Inc .........................D....... 708 222-8330
  Cicero *(G-7248)*
Zeldaco Ltd .....................................F....... 847 679-0033
  Skokie *(G-20116)*

### 2066 Chocolate & Cocoa Prdts

American Convenience Inc .............F....... 815 344-6040
  McHenry *(G-14480)*
Andersons Candy Shop Inc .............F....... 815 678-6000
  Richmond *(G-17957)*
Baldi Candy Co ...............................D....... 773 267-5770
  Chicago *(G-4032)*
Barry Callebaut USA LLC ................G....... 312 496-7300
  Chicago *(G-4047)*
◆ Barry Callebaut USA LLC ...........B....... 312 496-7300
  Chicago *(G-4048)*
Belgian Chocolatier Piron Inc ...........G....... 847 864-5504
  Evanston *(G-10014)*

## 20 FOOD AND KINDRED PRODUCTS

▲ Blommer Chocolate Company ..........D...... 800 621-1606
  Chicago  (G-4123)
Cargill Cocoa & Chocolate Inc ...........G...... 815 578-2000
  Island Lake  (G-12213)
Chocolat By Daniel ..............................G...... 815 969-7990
  Rockford  (G-18307)
Chocolate Potpourri  Ltd ......................F...... 847 729-8878
  Glenview  (G-11112)
Cora Lee Candies Inc ...........................F...... 847 724-2754
  Glenview  (G-11115)
Dekalb Confectionary Inc ....................F...... 815 758-5990
  Dekalb  (G-8086)
Galenas Kandy Kitchen .......................G...... 815 777-0241
  Galena  (G-10723)
Gayety Candy Co Inc ..........................E...... 708 418-0062
  Lansing  (G-13163)
Godiva Chocolatier Inc ........................G...... 630 820-5842
  Aurora  (G-1019)
Godiva Chocolatier Inc ........................F...... 847 329-8620
  Skokie  (G-20004)
Godiva Chocolatier Inc ........................F...... 312 280-1133
  Chicago  (G-4968)
Godiva Chocolatier Inc ........................E...... 847 918-0124
  Vernon Hills  (G-21167)
Hershey Company ..............................G...... 800 468-1714
  Deerfield  (G-8011)
Hershey Company ..............................A...... 618 544-3111
  Robinson  (G-18064)
Inside Beverages ................................C...... 847 438-1338
  Lake Zurich  (G-13088)
◆ John B Sanfilippo & Son  Inc ............C...... 847 289-1800
  Elgin  (G-9083)
Joyce Greiner .....................................G...... 618 654-9340
  Highland  (G-11799)
Kruger North America  Inc .................F...... 708 851-3670
  Oak Park  (G-16673)
Mars Chocolate North Amer LLC .........C...... 630 850-9898
  Burr Ridge  (G-2864)
Mars Chocolate North Amer LLC .........A...... 662 335-8000
  Chicago  (G-5630)
▲ Mondelez Global LLC .....................C...... 847 943-4000
  Deerfield  (G-8037)
Morkes Inc .........................................F...... 847 359-3511
  Palatine  (G-17057)
Peases Inc .........................................F...... 217 529-2912
  Springfield  (G-20502)
Sweet Endeavors Inc .........................G...... 224 653-2700
  Schaumburg  (G-19748)
▲ Vosges  Ltd ....................................D...... 773 388-5560
  Chicago  (G-6915)
▲ Worlds Finest Chocolate  Inc ..........B...... 773 847-4600
  Chicago  (G-7033)

### 2067 Chewing Gum

Ford Gum & Machine Company Inc .....F...... 847 955-0003
  Buffalo Grove  (G-2698)
Mid Pack ............................................G...... 773 626-3500
  Chicago  (G-5726)
▲ Mondelez Global LLC .....................C...... 847 943-4000
  Deerfield  (G-8037)
▼ Wm Wrigley Jr Company ................B...... 312 280-4710
  Chicago  (G-7012)
Wm Wrigley Jr Company ....................C...... 312 644-2121
  Romeoville  (G-18880)
Wm Wrigley Jr Company ....................E...... 312 205-2300
  Chicago  (G-7013)
Wm Wrigley Jr Company ....................A...... 312 644-2121
  Chicago  (G-7014)
▲ Wrigley Manufacturing Co LLC .......A...... 312 644-2121
  Chicago  (G-7038)
Wrigley Manufacturing Co LLC ............B...... 630 553-4800
  Yorkville  (G-22677)
Wrigley Manufacturing Co LLC ............A...... 312 644-2121
  Chicago  (G-7039)
▼ Wrigley Sales Company  LLC .........F...... 312 644-2121
  Chicago  (G-7040)

### 2068 Salted & Roasted Nuts & Seeds

▲ Anton-Argires  Inc .........................G...... 708 388-6250
  Alsip  (G-434)
Beer Nuts Inc ....................................C...... 309 827-8580
  Bloomington  (G-2147)
Completely Nuts Inc ..........................G...... 847 394-4312
  Chicago  (G-4439)
Illinois Foundation Seeds Inc ..............F...... 217 485-6420
  Tolono  (G-20971)
◆ John B Sanfilippo & Son  Inc ............C...... 847 289-1800
  Elgin  (G-9083)
John B Sanfilippo & Son  Inc ................C...... 847 690-8432
  Elgin  (G-9084)

Peases Inc .........................................F...... 217 529-2912
  Springfield  (G-20502)
◆ Regal Health Foods Intl Inc .............E...... 773 252-1044
  Chicago  (G-6321)
▲ Sesame Solutions  LLC ...................E...... 630 427-3400
  Bolingbrook  (G-2366)
Specialty Nut & Bky Sup Co Inc ..........G...... 630 268-8500
  Addison  (G-297)
▼ Terri Lynn  Inc ................................C...... 847 741-1900
  Elgin  (G-9210)
Treehouse Private Brands  Inc ............G...... 630 455-5265
  Downers Grove  (G-8534)

### 2074 Cottonseed Oil Mills

◆ Archer-Daniels-Midland Company .....A...... 312 634-8100
  Chicago  (G-3941)
Archer-Daniels-Midland Company .......E...... 217 424-5413
  Decatur  (G-7835)
Lee Gilster-Mary Corporation .............G...... 618 533-4808
  Centralia  (G-3421)
Maxs One Stop .................................G...... 618 235-4005
  Belleville  (G-1653)

### 2075 Soybean Oil Mills

Archer-Daniels-Midland Company .......D...... 217 424-5882
  Decatur  (G-7833)
Archer-Daniels-Midland Company .......D...... 217 424-5200
  Decatur  (G-7836)
Archer-Daniels-Midland Company .......F...... 217 224-1800
  Quincy  (G-17795)
Archer-Daniels-Midland Company .......E...... 217 424-5858
  Decatur  (G-7837)
◆ Archer-Daniels-Midland Company .....A...... 312 634-8100
  Chicago  (G-3941)
Archer-Daniels-Midland Company .......E...... 217 424-5413
  Decatur  (G-7835)
Archer-Daniels-Midland Company .......F...... 217 224-1800
  Quincy  (G-17794)
Bunge North America Foundation .......C...... 217 784-8261
  Gibson City  (G-10898)
Cargill  Incorporated ...........................E...... 309 827-7100
  Bloomington  (G-2153)
Cargill  Incorporated ...........................G...... 815 942-0932
  Morris  (G-15099)
◆ Clarkson Soy Products  LLC ............G...... 217 763-9511
  Cerro Gordo  (G-3439)
Devansoy Inc .....................................G...... 712 792-9665
  Rock City  (G-18125)
▲ Incobrasa Industries  Ltd .................C...... 815 265-4803
  Gilman  (G-10944)
Pioneer Hi-Bred Intl Inc .......................F...... 309 962-2931
  Le Roy  (G-13209)
◆ Solae ..............................................F...... 217 784-8261
  Gibson City  (G-10907)
Solae ..................................................G...... 217 784-2085
  Gibson City  (G-10908)
Solae LLC ..........................................C...... 219 261-2124
  Gibson City  (G-10909)

### 2076 Vegetable Oil Mills

Abitec Corporation .............................E...... 217 465-8577
  Paris  (G-17139)
Bio Fuels By American Farmers ..........F...... 561 859-6251
  Benton  (G-2023)
Bunge Oils  Inc ...................................E...... 815 523-8129
  Bradley  (G-2414)
Dawn Food Products Inc ....................C...... 815 933-0600
  Bradley  (G-2419)
Syngenta Seeds  Inc ..........................F...... 217 253-5646
  Tuscola  (G-21024)

### 2077 Animal, Marine Fats & Oils

Abitec Corporation .............................E...... 217 465-8577
  Paris  (G-17139)
Ace Grease Service  Inc ....................G...... 618 781-1207
  Millstadt  (G-14820)
Ace Grease Service  Inc ....................G...... 618 337-0974
  Millstadt  (G-14821)
Bunge Oils  Inc ...................................E...... 815 939-3631
  Bradley  (G-2415)
Darling Ingredients Inc .......................E...... 773 376-5550
  Chicago  (G-4559)
Darling Ingredients Inc .......................E...... 618 271-8190
  National Stock Yards  (G-15850)
Darling Ingredients Inc .......................E...... 217 482-3261
  Mason City  (G-14363)
Darling Ingredients Inc .......................E...... 309 476-8111
  Lynn Center  (G-14016)

Kostelac Grease Service Inc ...............E...... 314 436-7166
  Belleville  (G-1646)
McShares  Inc ....................................E...... 217 762-2561
  Monticello  (G-15079)
Mendota Agri-Products  Inc ...............G...... 815 539-5633
  Mendota  (G-14724)
▲ Micro Surface Corporation ..............F...... 815 942-4221
  Morris  (G-15116)
Millstadt Rendering Company ............E...... 618 538-5312
  Belleville  (G-1659)
MW Hopkins & Sons  Inc ...................G...... 847 458-1010
  Lake In The Hills  (G-13000)
Potter Rendering Co .........................G...... 580 924-2414
  Buffalo Grove  (G-2755)
▲ Sdr Corp .........................................G...... 773 638-1800
  Chicago  (G-6463)
South Chicago Packing LLC ...............D...... 708 589-2400
  Chicago  (G-6546)
Specialized Separators Inc ................F...... 815 316-0626
  Rockford  (G-18625)
Sustainable Sourcing LLC ..................F...... 815 714-8055
  Mokena  (G-14908)

### 2079 Shortening, Oils & Margarine

A-F Acquisition  LLC ..........................F...... 773 978-5130
  Chicago  (G-3695)
Ach Food Companies  Inc ..................C...... 708 458-8690
  Summit Argo  (G-20759)
All Fresh Food Products .....................G...... 847 864-5030
  Evanston  (G-10007)
Allfresh Food Products Inc ................G...... 847 869-3100
  Evanston  (G-10008)
Archer-Daniels-Midland Company .......D...... 217 224-1875
  Quincy  (G-17796)
Archer-Daniels-Midland Company .......F...... 217 224-1800
  Quincy  (G-17794)
▲ Avatar Corporation .........................D...... 708 534-5511
  University Park  (G-21042)
Beatrice Companies Inc .....................E...... 602 225-2000
  Chicago  (G-4069)
Bunge Oils Inc ....................................G...... 815 939-3631
  Bradley  (G-2415)
Cargill  Incorporated ...........................F...... 773 375-7255
  Chicago  (G-4243)
▼ Cfc  Inc ............................................D...... 847 257-8920
  Des Plaines  (G-8163)
Darling Ingredients Inc .......................E...... 217 482-3261
  Mason City  (G-14363)
Dawn Food Products  Inc ...................C...... 815 933-0600
  Bradley  (G-2419)
Fgfi  LLC ............................................E...... 708 598-0909
  Countryside  (G-7424)
▲ Grante Foods International LLC .......F...... 773 751-9551
  Elk Grove Village  (G-9507)
Loders Croklaan BV ...........................C...... 815 730-5200
  Channahon  (G-3577)
▲ Loders Croklaan Usa LLC ...............C...... 815 730-5200
  Channahon  (G-3578)
Mahoney Environmental Inc ...............E...... 815 730-2087
  Joliet  (G-12535)
Midwest Processing Company ...........D...... 217 424-5200
  Decatur  (G-7916)
Old Town Oil Evanston ......................G...... 312 787-9595
  Evanston  (G-10082)
Olive and Vinnies ...............................G...... 630 534-6457
  Glen Ellyn  (G-10984)
Olive Leclaire Oil Co ...........................G...... 888 255-1867
  Yorkville  (G-22666)
Olive Oil Market Place ........................G...... 618 304-3769
  Godfrey  (G-11231)
Olive Oil Marketplace Inc ....................G...... 618 304-3769
  Alton  (G-586)
Olive Oil Store  Inc .............................G...... 630 262-0210
  Geneva  (G-10856)
Olive Oils & More  LLC .......................G...... 618 656-4645
  Edwardsville  (G-8811)
▲ Olive Spartathlon Oil & Gre .............G...... 312 782-9855
  Chicago  (G-5983)
Pastorelli Food Products  Inc ..............G...... 312 455-1006
  Chicago  (G-6089)
▼ South Chicago Packing LLC ............D...... 708 589-2400
  South Holland  (G-20305)
South Chicago Packing LLC ...............D...... 708 589-2400
  Chicago  (G-6546)
Stevie S Italian Foods  Inc .................G...... 217 793-9693
  Springfield  (G-20538)
Stratas Foods LLC .............................E...... 217 424-5660
  Decatur  (G-7945)
▲ V Formusa Co .................................F...... 224 938-9360
  Des Plaines  (G-8296)

SIC SECTION | 20 FOOD AND KINDRED PRODUCTS

**Ventura Foods LLC** ....... E ....... 708 877-5150
Thornton *(G-20876)*

## 2082 Malt Beverages

**Aero Alehouse** ....... G ....... 815 977-5602
Loves Park *(G-13914)*
**Alao Temitope** ....... F ....... 331 454-3333
Collinsville *(G-7313)*
**Aldi Inc** ....... F ....... 815 877-0861
Machesney Park *(G-14055)*
**Ale Syndicate Brewers LLC** ....... G ....... 773 340-2337
Chicago *(G-3799)*
**Anheuser-Busch LLC** ....... C ....... 708 206-2881
Country Club Hills *(G-7404)*
**Anheuser-Busch LLC** ....... C ....... 630 512-9002
Lisle *(G-13561)*
**Apple Rush Company** ....... G ....... 847 730-5324
Glenview *(G-11104)*
**Argus Brewery** ....... G ....... 773 941-4050
Chicago *(G-3944)*
**Blue Island Beer Co** ....... G ....... 708 954-8085
Blue Island *(G-2239)*
**Bob C Beverages LLC** ....... G ....... 847 520-7582
Wheeling *(G-22016)*
**Breakroom Brewery** ....... G ....... 773 564-9534
Chicago *(G-4160)*
**Carlyle Brewing Co** ....... G ....... 815 963-2739
Rockford *(G-18297)*
**Caulfields Restaurant Ltd** ....... E ....... 708 798-1599
Flossmoor *(G-10223)*
**▲ Chicago Beverage Systems LLC** ....... E ....... 773 826-4100
Chicago *(G-4305)*
**Church Street Brewing Co LLC** ....... G ....... 630 438-5725
Itasca *(G-12244)*
**Cicerone Certification Program** ....... G ....... 773 549-4800
Chicago *(G-4377)*
**City Beverage LLC** ....... D ....... 708 333-4360
Markham *(G-14302)*
**Colleagues of Beer Inc** ....... G ....... 847 727-3318
Grayslake *(G-11327)*
**Crushed Grapes Ltd** ....... G ....... 618 659-3530
Millstadt *(G-14822)*
**Crystal Lake Beer Company** ....... F ....... 779 220-9288
Crystal Lake *(G-7559)*
**▲ Dept 28 Inc** ....... G ....... 847 285-1343
Schaumburg *(G-19502)*
**Dj Liquors Inc** ....... G ....... 815 645-1145
Davis Junction *(G-7810)*
**Drewrys Brewing Company** ....... G ....... 815 385-9115
McHenry *(G-14498)*
**Emmetts Tavern & Brewing Co** ....... G ....... 630 434-8500
Downers Grove *(G-8441)*
**Emmetts Tavern & Brewing Co** ....... G ....... 630 480-7181
Wheaton *(G-21945)*
**Emmetts Tavern & Brewing Co** ....... F ....... 847 359-1533
Palatine *(G-17025)*
**Emmetts Tavern & Brewing Co** ....... E ....... 847 428-4500
West Dundee *(G-21796)*
**Finchs Beer Company LLC** ....... G ....... 773 919-8012
Chicago *(G-4844)*
**Forbidden Root A Benefit LLC** ....... G ....... 312 464-7910
Chicago *(G-4871)*
**▲ Fulton Street Brewery LLC** ....... E ....... 312 915-0071
Chicago *(G-4896)*
**Glazers Stoller Distrg LLC** ....... G ....... 847 350-3200
Franklin Park *(G-10479)*
**Golden Eagle Distributing LLC** ....... F ....... 618 993-8900
Marion *(G-14263)*
**Goose Holdings Inc** ....... E ....... 312 226-1119
Chicago *(G-4979)*
**▲ Half Acre Beer Company** ....... F ....... 773 248-4038
Chicago *(G-5035)*
**Haymarket Brewing Company LLC** ....... G ....... 312 638-0700
Chicago *(G-5056)*
**La Casa Del Tequila Corp** ....... G ....... 708 652-3640
Cicero *(G-7212)*
**Lagunitas Brewing Company** ....... C ....... 773 522-1308
Chicago *(G-5438)*
**Libertyville Brewing Company** ....... D ....... 847 362-6688
Libertyville *(G-13343)*
**Lincoln Park Brewery Inc** ....... D ....... 312 915-0071
Chicago *(G-5507)*
**Metropolitan Brewing LLC** ....... G ....... 773 474-6893
Chicago *(G-5707)*
**◆ Millercoors LLC** ....... A ....... 312 496-2700
Chicago *(G-5760)*
**Millercoors LLC** ....... E ....... 312 496-2700
Chicago *(G-5761)*
**Only Child Brewing Company LLC** ....... G ....... 847 877-9822
Gurnee *(G-11481)*
**Pyramid** ....... G ....... 708 468-8140
Tinley Park *(G-20940)*
**▲ Resco 8 LLC** ....... D ....... 773 772-4422
Chicago *(G-6336)*
**Rock Bottom Minneapolis Inc** ....... D ....... 312 755-9339
Chicago *(G-6373)*
**Rolling Meadows Brewery LLC** ....... G ....... 217 725-2492
Springfield *(G-20514)*
**St Nicholas Brewing Co** ....... G ....... 618 318-3556
Du Quoin *(G-8558)*
**Tenth and Blake Beer Company** ....... F ....... 312 496-2759
Chicago *(G-6702)*
**▲ Wirtz Beverage Illinois LLC** ....... C ....... 847 228-9000
Cicero *(G-7246)*

## 2083 Malt

**Archer-Daniels-Midland Company** ....... D ....... 217 424-5200
Decatur *(G-7836)*
**◆ Archer-Daniels-Midland Company** ....... A ....... 312 634-8100
Chicago *(G-3941)*
**Archer-Daniels-Midland Company** ....... E ....... 217 424-5413
Decatur *(G-7835)*
**▲ Mid Country Malt Supply** ....... G ....... 708 339-7005
South Holland *(G-20291)*
**Muntons Malted Ingredients Inc** ....... G ....... 630 812-1600
Lombard *(G-13830)*
**Warner Harvey Lee Farm Inc** ....... G ....... 217 849-2548
Toledo *(G-20970)*

## 2084 Wine & Brandy

**A Hardy/U S A Ltd** ....... G ....... 847 298-2358
Des Plaines *(G-8138)*
**Acquaviva Winery LLC** ....... G ....... 630 365-0333
Maple Park *(G-14197)*
**Alto Vinyards Inc** ....... F ....... 618 893-4898
Alto Pass *(G-556)*
**Aquaviva Winery** ....... G ....... 815 899-4444
Sycamore *(G-20787)*
**▲ August Hill Winery** ....... G ....... 815 224-8199
Peru *(G-17501)*
**Augusthill Winery Co** ....... G ....... 815 667-5211
Utica *(G-21106)*
**Barrington Cardinal Whse LLC** ....... G ....... 847 387-3676
Barrington *(G-1270)*
**Baxter Vineyards** ....... G ....... 217 453-2528
Nauvoo *(G-15852)*
**Bella Terra Winery LLC** ....... F ....... 618 658-8882
Creal Springs *(G-7453)*
**Benessere Vineyard Inc** ....... G ....... 708 560-9840
Oak Brook *(G-16492)*
**Beverage Art Inc** ....... G ....... 773 881-9463
Chicago *(G-4096)*
**Blue Sky Vineyard** ....... G ....... 618 995-9463
Makanda *(G-14162)*
**Bluffs Vineyard & Winery L L C** ....... G ....... 618 763-4447
Murphysboro *(G-15572)*
**Bonanno Vintners LLC** ....... G ....... 773 477-8351
Chicago *(G-4141)*
**Broken Earth Winery** ....... F ....... 847 383-5052
Long Grove *(G-13888)*
**Cellar LLC** ....... G ....... 618 956-9900
Carterville *(G-3311)*
**▲ Coopers Hawk Production LLC** ....... G ....... 708 839-2920
Countryside *(G-7419)*
**Coopers Hwk Intermedte Holdng** ....... C ....... 708 839-2920
Countryside *(G-7420)*
**Coopers Hwk Intermedte Holdng** ....... F ....... 708 215-5674
Countryside *(G-7421)*
**Crushed Grapes Ltd** ....... G ....... 618 659-3530
Millstadt *(G-14822)*
**D C Estate Winery** ....... G ....... 815 218-0573
South Beloit *(G-20143)*
**▲ De Vine Distributors LLC** ....... G ....... 773 248-7005
Chicago *(G-4567)*
**Diageo North America Inc** ....... E ....... 815 267-4400
Plainfield *(G-17591)*
**Distillery Wine & Allied** ....... G ....... 309 347-1444
Pekin *(G-17259)*
**Edrington Group Usa LLC** ....... E ....... 630 701-9202
Oak Brook *(G-16505)*
**Famous Fossil Vinyard & Winery** ....... G ....... 815 563-4665
Freeport *(G-10655)*
**Fox Creek Vineyards** ....... G ....... 618 395-3325
Olney *(G-16768)*
**Fox Valley Home Brew & Winery** ....... G ....... 630 892-0742
Aurora *(G-1154)*
**Fox Valley Winery Inc** ....... G ....... 630 554-0404
Oswego *(G-16919)*
**Galena Cellars Winery** ....... G ....... 815 777-3330
Galena *(G-10720)*
**Galena Cellars Winery** ....... E ....... 815 777-3429
Galena *(G-10721)*
**Glazers Stoller Distrg LLC** ....... G ....... 847 350-3200
Franklin Park *(G-10479)*
**Glunz Fmly Winery Cellars Inc** ....... E ....... 847 548-9463
Grayslake *(G-11342)*
**Hidden Lake Winery Ltd** ....... E ....... 618 228-9111
Aviston *(G-1244)*
**Hogg Hollow Winery LLC** ....... G ....... 618 695-9463
Golconda *(G-11239)*
**Illinois River Winery Inc** ....... G ....... 815 691-8031
Willowbrook *(G-22216)*
**Kickapoo Creek Winery** ....... G ....... 309 495-9463
Edwards *(G-8782)*
**Klehm Family Winery LLC** ....... G ....... 847 609-9997
Hampshire *(G-11552)*
**Lau Nae Winery Inc** ....... G ....... 618 282-9463
Red Bud *(G-17944)*
**Lavender Crest Winery** ....... E ....... 309 949-2565
Colona *(G-7344)*
**Lincoln Heritage Winery LLC** ....... G ....... 618 833-3783
Cobden *(G-7302)*
**▲ Lynfred Winery Inc** ....... E ....... 630 529-9463
Roselle *(G-18953)*
**Main Street Market Roscoe Inc** ....... G ....... 815 623-6328
Roscoe *(G-18905)*
**▲ Mary McHelle Winery Vinyrd LLC** ....... F ....... 217 942-6250
Carrollton *(G-3308)*
**Old Mill Vineyard LLC** ....... G ....... 309 258-9954
Metamora *(G-14746)*
**Orchard View Winery** ....... G ....... 618 547-9911
Alma *(G-422)*
**Pheasant Hollow Winery Inc** ....... G ....... 618 629-2302
Whittington *(G-22188)*
**Pomona Winery** ....... G ....... 618 893-2623
Pomona *(G-17694)*
**Pour It Again Sam Inc** ....... G ....... 708 474-1744
Lynwood *(G-14023)*
**Prp Wine International Inc** ....... F ....... 630 995-4500
Naperville *(G-15734)*
**Rapid Displays Inc** ....... D ....... 773 927-1500
Chicago *(G-6292)*
**Rustle Hill Winery LLC** ....... G ....... 618 893-2700
Cobden *(G-7303)*
**Shale Lake LLC** ....... G ....... 618 637-2470
Staunton *(G-20558)*
**Shawnee Grapevines LLC** ....... G ....... 618 893-9463
Cobden *(G-7304)*
**Shawnee Winery** ....... G ....... 618 658-8400
Vienna *(G-21225)*
**Southern Ill Wine Trail Nfp** ....... G ....... 618 695-9463
Golconda *(G-11242)*
**Tavern On Prospect Ltd** ....... G ....... 309 693-8677
Peoria *(G-17466)*
**▲ Terlato Wine Group Ltd** ....... E ....... 847 604-8900
Lake Bluff *(G-12867)*
**Terraneo Merchants Inc** ....... G ....... 312 753-9134
Lincolnwood *(G-13539)*
**Valentino Vineyards Inc** ....... G ....... 847 634-2831
Long Grove *(G-13904)*
**Villa Marie Wine & Banquet Ctr** ....... G ....... 618 345-3100
Maryville *(G-14347)*
**Village Vintner Winery Brewry** ....... G ....... 847 658-4900
Algonquin *(G-410)*
**Vins & Vignobles LLC** ....... G ....... 312 375-7656
Mount Prospect *(G-15383)*
**▲ Vma Group Inc** ....... G ....... 847 877-7039
Vernon Hills *(G-21215)*
**Von Jakob Vineyard Limited** ....... G ....... 618 893-4500
Pomona *(G-17695)*
**Walnut St Winery Plus Saunas** ....... G ....... 217 498-9800
Rochester *(G-18123)*
**Waterman Winery & Vineyards** ....... G ....... 815 264-3268
Waterman *(G-21411)*
**Willetts Winery & Cellar** ....... G ....... 309 968-7070
Manito *(G-14177)*
**Wyldewood Cellars 2 LLC** ....... G ....... 217 469-9463
Saint Joseph *(G-19319)*

## 2085 Liquors, Distilled, Rectified & Blended

**▲ 773 LLC** ....... G ....... 312 707-8780
Chicago *(G-3675)*
**Agave Loco LLC** ....... F ....... 847 383-6052
Vernon Hills *(G-21142)*
**▲ Apostrophe Brands** ....... F ....... 312 832-0300
Chicago *(G-3924)*
**◆ Beam Global Spirits & Wine LLC** ....... C ....... 847 948-8888
Deerfield *(G-7990)*
**◆ Beam Suntory Inc** ....... C ....... 847 948-8888
Deerfield *(G-7991)*

S I C

20 FOOD AND KINDRED PRODUCTS SIC SECTION

▲ **Callison Distributing LLC** D 618 277-4300
Belleville *(G-1616)*
**Cliffords Pub Inc** G 847 259-3000
Palatine *(G-17011)*
**Diageo North America Inc** E 815 267-4400
Plainfield *(G-17591)*
**Dtrs Enterprises Inc** G 630 296-6890
Bolingbrook *(G-2302)*
**Glunz Fmly Winery Cellars Inc** E 847 548-9463
Grayslake *(G-11342)*
**Illinois Corn Processing LLC** D 309 353-3990
Pekin *(G-17268)*
◆ **Jim Beam Brands Co** B 847 948-8903
Deerfield *(G-8019)*
**JK Williams Distilling LLC** G 309 839-0591
East Peoria *(G-8717)*
**Kats Meow** G 815 747-2113
East Dubuque *(G-8618)*
▲ **Koval Inc** F 773 944-0089
Chicago *(G-5408)*
**Mega International Ltd** G 309 764-5310
Moline *(G-14956)*
**Mgp Ingredients Illinois Inc** C 309 353-3990
Pekin *(G-17274)*
**Mgpi Processing Inc** C 309 353-3990
Pekin *(G-17275)*
**Mid-Oak Distillery Inc** G 708 925-9318
Crestwood *(G-7495)*
**North Shore Distillery LLC** G 847 574-2499
Libertyville *(G-13363)*
**Podhalanska LLC** G 630 247-9256
Lemont *(G-13256)*
**Rumshine Distilling LLC** G 217 446-6960
Tilton *(G-20882)*
▲ **Sazerac North America Inc** E 502 423-5225
Chicago *(G-6448)*
**Udv North America Inc** G 815 267-4400
Plainfield *(G-17659)*
**Whiskey Acres Distilling Co** F 815 739-8711
Dekalb *(G-8132)*

## 2086 Soft Drinks

**A Barr Ftn Beverage Sls & Svc** G 708 442-2000
Lyons *(G-14028)*
**AD Huesing Corporation** D 309 788-5652
Rock Island *(G-18157)*
**American Bottling Company** E 217 356-0577
Champaign *(G-3448)*
**American Bottling Company** B 708 947-5000
Northlake *(G-16426)*
**American Bottling Company** E 815 877-7777
Loves Park *(G-13919)*
**American Bottling Company** E 309 693-2777
Edwards *(G-8781)*
**Amwell** G 630 898-6900
Aurora *(G-1108)*
▲ **Balon International Corp** E 773 379-7779
Chicago *(G-4034)*
**Berner Food & Beverage LLC** B 815 563-4222
Dakota *(G-7694)*
**Bottle-Free Water** G 630 462-6807
Carol Stream *(G-3119)*
**Brewers Bottlers & Bev Corp** G 773 262-9711
Chicago *(G-4163)*
**Chicago Bottling Industries** G 847 885-8093
Hoffman Estates *(G-11999)*
▲ **Clover Club Bottling Co Inc** F 773 261-7100
Chicago *(G-4406)*
**Coca Cola** G 630 588-8786
Carol Stream *(G-3132)*
**Coca Cola Fleet Service** G 847 600-2279
Niles *(G-15970)*
**Coca-Cola Bottling Co Cnsld** E 217 223-5183
Quincy *(G-17814)*
**Coca-Cola Btlg Wisconsin Del** B 847 647-0200
Niles *(G-15971)*
**Coca-Cola Company** D 847 647-0200
Niles *(G-15972)*
**Coca-Cola Refreshments USA Inc** C 630 513-5247
Saint Charles *(G-19158)*
**Coca-Cola Refreshments USA Inc** C 708 597-6700
Alsip *(G-450)*
**Coca-Cola Refreshments USA Inc** D 815 636-7300
Machesney Park *(G-14067)*
**Coca-Cola Refreshments USA Inc** D 847 647-0200
Niles *(G-15973)*
**Coca-Cola Refreshments USA Inc** E 309 787-1700
Rock Island *(G-18167)*
**Coca-Cola Refreshments USA Inc** D 708 597-4700
Chicago *(G-4415)*
**Coca-Cola Refreshments USA Inc** E 815 933-2653
Kankakee *(G-12605)*
**Coca-Cola Refreshments USA Inc** E 217 544-4892
Springfield *(G-20420)*
**Coca-Cola Refreshments USA Inc** E 217 367-1761
Urbana *(G-21078)*
**Coca-Cola Refreshments USA Inc** C 618 542-2101
Du Quoin *(G-8552)*
**Coca-Cola Refreshments USA Inc** F 217 348-1001
Charleston *(G-3595)*
**Cocacola Bottling Co** G 815 220-3100
Peru *(G-17505)*
**Crisp Container Corporation** D 618 998-0400
Marion *(G-14257)*
**Decatur Bottling Co** D 217 429-5415
Decatur *(G-7870)*
**Dr Pepper Snapple Group Inc** D 708 947-5000
Northlake *(G-16434)*
**Dr Pepper/7 Up Bottling Group** G 217 585-1496
Springfield *(G-20430)*
**Drivnn LLC** G 815 222-4447
Loves Park *(G-13937)*
**Ds Services of America Inc** C 773 586-8600
Chicago *(G-4645)*
**Ds Services of America Inc** F 800 322-6272
Rockford *(G-18352)*
**Ds Services of America Inc** E 815 469-7100
Frankfort *(G-10314)*
**Dynamic Nutritionals Inc** G 815 545-9171
New Lenox *(G-15878)*
**E & J Gallo Winery** E 630 505-4000
Lisle *(G-13584)*
**Egg Cream America Inc** G 847 559-2700
Northbrook *(G-16248)*
▼ **Emmert John** F 773 292-6580
Chicago *(G-4744)*
◆ **Essen Nutrition Corporation** E 630 739-6700
Romeoville *(G-18820)*
**Excel Bottling Co** G 618 526-7159
Breese *(G-2443)*
**Fast Forward Energy Inc** G 312 860-0978
Chicago *(G-4815)*
**Florida Fruit Juices Inc** E 773 586-6200
Chicago *(G-4863)*
**Flowers Distributing Inc** E 618 255-1021
East Alton *(G-8601)*
▼ **Gatorade Company** A 312 821-1000
Chicago *(G-4918)*
**Ginger Bliss Juice LLC** G 773 456-0181
Hinsdale *(G-11949)*
**Great Lakes Coca-Cola Dist LLC** C 847 227-6500
Rosemont *(G-19004)*
**Green Planet Bottling LLC** F 312 962-4444
Vernon Hills *(G-21168)*
**Henderson Water District** G 618 498-6418
Jerseyville *(G-12424)*
▲ **Hinckley & Schmitt Inc** A 773 586-8600
Chicago *(G-5091)*
**Home Juice Corp** G 708 681-2678
Melrose Park *(G-14654)*
**Hydrive Sales** G 708 478-8194
Mokena *(G-14870)*
**Kalena LLC** G 773 598-0033
Chicago *(G-5354)*
**Key Colony Inc** G 630 783-8572
Lemont *(G-13237)*
**Kraft Heinz Foods Company** B 618 512-9100
Granite City *(G-11290)*
**Lee Gilster-Mary Corporation** D 815 472-6456
Momence *(G-14983)*
**Mountain Valley Spring Co LLC** A 618 242-4963
Mount Vernon *(G-15430)*
**Nestle Waters North Amer Inc** D 630 271-7300
Woodridge *(G-22505)*
**P-Americas LLC** B 773 893-2300
Chicago *(G-6042)*
**P-Americas LLC** C 309 266-2400
Morton *(G-15173)*
**P-Americas LLC** C 773 451-4499
Chicago *(G-6043)*
**P-Americas LLC** D 312 821-2266
Chicago *(G-6044)*
**P-Americas LLC** C 773 624-8013
Chicago *(G-6045)*
**Pepsi Cola Gen Bttlers of Lima** G 847 253-1000
Rolling Meadows *(G-18761)*
**Pepsi Mid America** G 217 826-8118
Marshall *(G-14327)*
**Pepsi Midamerica** G 618 242-6285
Mount Vernon *(G-15439)*
**Pepsi Midamerica Co** A 618 997-1377
Marion *(G-14277)*
**Pepsi-Cola Chmpign Urbana Btlr** D 217 352-4126
Champaign *(G-3523)*
▼ **Pepsi-Cola Gen Bottlers Inc** B 847 598-3000
Schaumburg *(G-19688)*
**Pepsi-Cola General Bottlers VA** B 847 253-1000
Rolling Meadows *(G-18762)*
**Pepsico Inc** G 312 821-1000
Chicago *(G-6105)*
**Powercoco LLC** G 614 323-5890
Chicago *(G-6159)*
**Prairie Pure Bottled Water** G 217 774-7873
Shelbyville *(G-19912)*
**Premium Waters Inc** D 217 222-0213
Quincy *(G-17871)*
**Pure Flo Bottling Inc** G 815 963-4797
Rockford *(G-18544)*
**Pursuit Beverage Company LLC** G 888 606-3353
Lake Zurich *(G-13119)*
◆ **Quaker Oats Company** A 312 821-1000
Chicago *(G-6242)*
**Quaker Oats Company** C 708 458-7090
Bridgeview *(G-2521)*
**Rainbow Pure Water Inc** G 618 985-4670
Carbondale *(G-3021)*
**Refreshment Services Inc** F 217 223-8600
Quincy *(G-17886)*
**Refreshment Services Inc** E 217 522-8841
Springfield *(G-20511)*
**Refreshment Services Inc** E 217 429-5415
Decatur *(G-7933)*
**Rockys Beverages LLC** F 312 561-3182
Glenview *(G-11194)*
**Rorke & Riley Specialty B** G 773 929-2522
Chicago *(G-6393)*
**Springfield Pepsi Cola Btlg Co** E 217 522-8841
Springfield *(G-20530)*
**Team Sider Inc** G 847 767-0107
Highland Park *(G-11877)*
**Tst/Impreso Inc** G 630 775-9555
Addison *(G-330)*
▲ **Vision Sales & Marketing Inc** G 708 496-6016
Chicago *(G-6904)*
**Vita-V Energy Co Inc** G 630 999-8961
Glendale Heights *(G-11089)*
▲ **West Water Inc** G 312 326-7480
Chicago *(G-6962)*
**Win Soon Chicago Inc** C 630 585-7090
Oswego *(G-16940)*
**Wis - Pak Inc** D 217 224-6800
Quincy *(G-17907)*
**Wonder Tucky Distillery & Btlg** G 224 678-4396
Woodstock *(G-22626)*

## 2087 Flavoring Extracts & Syrups

**A Barr Ftn Beverage Sls & Svc** D 708 442-2000
Lemont *(G-13221)*
**A Barr Ftn Beverage Sls & Svc** G 708 442-2000
Lyons *(G-14028)*
**Abelei Inc** F 630 859-1410
North Aurora *(G-16117)*
▼ **Beverage Flavors Intl LLC** F 773 248-3860
Chicago *(G-4097)*
▲ **Capol LLC** G 224 545-5095
Deerfield *(G-7993)*
**Caravan Ingredients Inc** D 708 849-8590
Dolton *(G-8368)*
**Coca-Cola Refreshments USA Inc** C 618 542-2101
Du Quoin *(G-8552)*
**Conagra Fods Fd Ingrdients Inc** G 630 682-5600
Carol Stream *(G-3135)*
**Culinary Co-Pack Incorporated** E 847 451-1551
Franklin Park *(G-10448)*
**Custom Culinary Inc** D 630 299-0500
Oswego *(G-16912)*
**Dawn Food Products Inc** C 815 933-0600
Bradley *(G-2419)*
**Dennco Inc** G 708 862-0070
Burnham *(G-2816)*
▲ **Edgar A Weber & Company** E 847 215-1980
Wheeling *(G-22043)*
**Edgar A Weber & Company** E 847 215-1980
Wheeling *(G-22044)*
▼ **Edlong Corporation** D 847 439-9230
Elk Grove Village *(G-9449)*
▼ **Equi-Chem International Inc** F 630 784-0432
Carol Stream *(G-3146)*
**FBC Industries Inc** G 847 839-0880
Rochelle *(G-18089)*

# 20 FOOD AND KINDRED PRODUCTS

◆ Flavorchem Corporation...............D...... 630 932-8100
  Downers Grove (G-8443)
Fona.........................................G...... 630 462-1414
  Carol Stream (G-3153)
Fona International Inc...................G...... 630 578-8600
  Saint Charles (G-19185)
▲ Fona International Inc..................E...... 630 578-8600
  Geneva (G-10827)
Fona Uk Ltd................................C...... 331 442-5779
  Geneva (G-10828)
Givaudan Flavors Corporation........E...... 630 773-8484
  Itasca (G-12270)
Green Mountain Flavors Inc..........F...... 630 554-9530
  Oswego (G-16920)
Gycor International Ltd.................F...... 630 754-8070
  Woodridge (G-22492)
H B Taylor Co.............................E...... 773 254-4805
  Chicago (G-5020)
Inside Beverages........................C...... 847 438-1338
  Lake Zurich (G-13088)
Insight Beverages Inc..................G...... 847 438-1598
  Lake Zurich (G-13089)
▼ Insight Beverages Inc.................G...... 847 438-1598
  Lake Zurich (G-13090)
Institutional Foods Packing Co......G...... 847 904-5250
  Glenview (G-11148)
Interntnal Ingredient Mall LLC.......G...... 630 462-1414
  Geneva (G-10839)
◆ Jel Sert Co.................................B...... 630 231-7590
  West Chicago (G-21727)
Jo Snow Inc................................G...... 773 732-3045
  Chicago (G-5308)
Key Colony Inc............................G...... 630 783-8572
  Lemont (G-13237)
Kosto Food Products Company....F...... 847 487-2600
  Wauconda (G-21478)
Kraft Foods Asia PCF Svcs LLC...C...... 847 943-4000
  Deerfield (G-8026)
Kraft Heinz Company...................C...... 847 646-2000
  Glenview (G-11160)
Kruger North America Inc............F...... 708 851-3670
  Oak Park (G-16673)
▲ La Boost Inc..............................C...... 630 444-1755
  Saint Charles (G-19206)
Lansing Wings Inc.......................G...... 708 895-3300
  Lansing (G-13171)
Lee Gilster-Mary Corporation........D...... 618 965-3426
  Steeleville (G-20561)
▲ Lucta U S A Inc..........................G...... 847 996-3400
  Libertyville (G-13345)
Mh/1993/Foods Inc......................F...... 708 331-7453
  South Holland (G-20290)
▲ Mondelez Global LLC..................C...... 847 943-4000
  Deerfield (G-8037)
◆ Mondelez International Inc..........A...... 847 943-4000
  Deerfield (G-8038)
▲ Necta Sweet Inc.........................E...... 847 215-9955
  Buffalo Grove (G-2742)
▲ Neiman Bros Co Inc...................E...... 773 463-3000
  Chicago (G-5882)
Nestle Usa Inc............................D...... 847 808-5404
  Buffalo Grove (G-2747)
NFC Company Inc.......................G...... 773 472-6468
  Chicago (G-5908)
◆ Northwestern Flavors LLC...........E...... 630 231-6111
  West Chicago (G-21752)
Ocean Cliff Corporation................E...... 847 729-9074
  Glenview (G-11176)
Passion Fruit Drink Inc.................G...... 708 769-4749
  South Holland (G-20296)
Pepsico Inc................................G...... 312 821-1000
  Chicago (G-6105)
Roquette America Inc..................D...... 847 360-0886
  Gurnee (G-11501)
▲ Royal Foods & Flavors Inc..........E...... 847 595-9166
  Elk Grove Village (G-9720)
◆ Sensient Flavors LLC..................B...... 317 243-3521
  Hoffman Estates (G-12050)
Sensient Flavors LLC..................F...... 815 857-3691
  Amboy (G-599)
Sensient Technologies Corp.........E...... 708 481-0910
  Matteson (G-14378)
◆ Sethness Products Company......F...... 847 329-2080
  Skokie (G-20083)
▲ Silesia Flavors Inc.....................E...... 847 645-0270
  Hoffman Estates (G-12054)
◆ Stepan Company.........................................847 446-7500
  Northfield (G-16419)
Sterling Extract Company Inc.......G...... 847 451-9728
  Franklin Park (G-10595)

Supreme Juice Co.......................F...... 773 277-5800
  Chicago (G-6639)
▲ Synergy Flavors Inc...................D...... 847 487-1011
  Wauconda (G-21506)
▲ Synergy Flavors NY Company LLC..E...... 585 232-6648
  Wauconda (G-21507)
T Hasegawa USA Inc...................E...... 847 559-6060
  Northbrook (G-16375)
Tampico Beverages Inc................F...... 773 296-0190
  Chicago (G-6670)
◆ Tampico Beverages Inc..............................773 296-0190
  Chicago (G-6671)
▼ Tone Products Inc......................E...... 708 681-3660
  Melrose Park (G-14702)
Treehouse Foods Inc..................B...... 708 483-1300
  Oak Brook (G-16565)
Ur Inc........................................G...... 630 450-5279
  Batavia (G-1513)
Vitamins Inc...............................G...... 773 483-4640
  Carol Stream (G-3262)
Watson Inc.................................E...... 217 824-4440
  Taylorville (G-20846)
White Stokes Company Inc..........F...... 773 254-5000
  Lincolnwood (G-13543)
▼ Wm Wrigley Jr Company.............B...... 312 280-4710
  Chicago (G-7012)
Wm Wrigley Jr Company...............A...... 312 644-2121
  Chicago (G-7014)

## 2091 Fish & Seafoods, Canned & Cured

Kraft Heinz Foods Company.........C...... 847 291-3900
  Northbrook (G-16290)
◆ Sokol and Company....................D...... 708 482-8250
  Countryside (G-7443)
▲ Vita Food Products Inc...............D...... 312 738-4500
  Chicago (G-6906)

## 2092 Fish & Seafoods, Fresh & Frozen

Betty Watters.............................G...... 618 232-1150
  Hamburg (G-11526)
Dar Enterprises Inc.....................G...... 815 961-8748
  Rockford (G-18334)
King Midas Seafood Entps Inc.....G...... 847 566-2192
  Mundelein (G-15516)
Midway Food LLC........................G...... 773 294-0730
  Chicago (G-5738)
Open Waters Seafood Company...E...... 847 329-8585
  Skokie (G-20051)
Rich Products Corporation............D...... 847 581-1749
  Niles (G-16027)
▲ Vanee Foods Company................D...... 708 449-7300
  Berkeley (G-2050)
Wisepak Foods LLC....................E...... 773 772-0072
  Chicago (G-7006)
▲ Worldwide Shrimp Company........E...... 847 433-3500
  Highland Park (G-11883)

## 2095 Coffee

Berner Food & Beverage LLC......B...... 815 563-4222
  Dakota (G-7694)
Central Mountain Coffee LLC.......G...... 309 981-0094
  Galesburg (G-10743)
Coffee Brewmasters Usa LLC......F...... 773 294-9665
  Buffalo Grove (G-2675)
Crushed Grapes Ltd....................G...... 618 659-3530
  Millstadt (G-14822)
Farmer Bros Co..........................G...... 217 787-7565
  Springfield (G-20438)
▲ Fratelli Coffee Company..............G...... 847 671-7300
  Schiller Park (G-19832)
Healthwise Gourmet Coffees........G...... 847 382-3230
  Deer Park (G-7971)
Hillshire Brands Company.............C...... 847 956-7575
  Elk Grove Village (G-9524)
Hmshost Corporation...................E...... 847 678-2098
  Schiller Park (G-19837)
▼ Insight Beverages Inc..................F...... 847 438-1598
  Lake Zurich (G-13090)
Javamania Coffee Roastery Inc....G...... 815 885-3654
  Loves Park (G-13951)
Kraft Foods Asia PCF Svcs LLC...C...... 847 943-4000
  Deerfield (G-8026)
Kraft Heinz Company...................C...... 847 646-2000
  Glenview (G-11160)
Limitless Coffee LLC..................G...... 630 779-3778
  Chicago (G-5505)
◆ Mondelez International Inc...........A...... 847 943-4000
  Deerfield (G-8038)
▲ Napco Inc..................................E...... 630 406-1100
  Batavia (G-1474)

Nuri Corp...................................F...... 847 940-7134
  Deerfield (G-8044)
Sparrow Coffee Roastery.............G...... 321 648-6415
  Westchester (G-21855)
Stewarts Prvate Blend Fods Inc...E...... 773 489-2500
  Carol Stream (G-3250)
Sweet Company..........................E...... 815 462-4586
  Mokena (G-14909)
Trade-Mark Coffee Corporation....F...... 847 382-4200
  North Barrington (G-16155)
▲ Two Brothers Brewing Company...G...... 630 393-2337
  Warrenville (G-21367)

## 2096 Potato Chips & Similar Prdts

Altona Co...................................G...... 815 232-7819
  Freeport (G-10645)
▲ Azteca Foods Inc........................C...... 708 563-6600
  Chicago (G-4012)
▲ Chipita America Inc....................E...... 708 731-2434
  Westchester (G-21832)
Chips Aleeces Pita......................G...... 309 699-8859
  East Peoria (G-8706)
Donkey Brands LLC....................F...... 630 251-2007
  Carol Stream (G-3144)
El Popocatapetl Industries Inc......D...... 773 843-0888
  Chicago (G-4709)
El-Ranchero Food Products..........F...... 773 843-0430
  Chicago (G-4715)
▲ El-Ranchero Food Products........E...... 773 847-9167
  Chicago (G-4716)
Evans Food Group Ltd.................C...... 773 254-7400
  Chicago (G-4786)
▼ Evans Foods Inc........................D...... 773 254-7400
  Chicago (G-4787)
Frito-Lay North America Inc..........C...... 217 532-5040
  Hillsboro (G-11890)
Frito-Lay North America Inc..........C...... 217 776-2320
  Sidney (G-19936)
Frito-Lay North America Inc..........B...... 618 997-2865
  Marion (G-14260)
Gary Poppins LLC.......................G...... 847 455-2200
  Franklin Park (G-10476)
Great American Popcorn Company..G...... 815 777-4116
  Galena (G-10725)
◆ John B Sanfilippo & Son Inc.......C...... 847 289-1800
  Elgin (G-9083)
Kitchen Cooked Inc.....................E...... 309 245-2191
  Farmington (G-10187)
Kitchen Cooked Inc.....................G...... 309 772-2798
  Bushnell (G-2903)
Larry Ragan...............................G...... 618 698-1041
  Belleville (G-1648)
Marianne Strawn........................G...... 309 447-6612
  Deer Creek (G-7965)
Masa Uno Inc.............................G...... 708 749-4866
  Berwyn (G-2068)
McCleary Inc..............................C...... 815 389-3053
  South Beloit (G-20160)
Michaels Dawg House LLC..........G...... 847 485-7600
  Palatine (G-17055)
Mrs Fishers Inc..........................F...... 815 964-9114
  Rockford (G-18511)
Ole Saltys of Rockford Inc...........G...... 815 637-2447
  Rockford (G-18525)
Ole Saltys of Rockford Inc...........G...... 815 637-2447
  Loves Park (G-13970)
Pepsico Inc................................G...... 312 821-1000
  Chicago (G-6105)
◆ Quality Snack Foods Inc.............D...... 708 377-7120
  Alsip (G-515)
R and B Distributors Inc..............G...... 815 433-6843
  Ottawa (G-16981)
Revolution Companies Inc...........E...... 800 826-4083
  Chicago (G-6341)
Safe Fair Food Company LLC.......F...... 904 930-4277
  Chicago (G-6424)
Select Snacks Company Inc........D...... 773 933-2167
  Chicago (G-6475)
Snak-King Corp...........................C...... 815 232-6700
  Freeport (G-10689)
▼ Tee Lee Popcorn Inc...................E...... 815 864-2363
  Shannon (G-19903)
Tpf Liquidation Co......................D...... 847 362-0028
  Lake Forest (G-12971)
Wisconsin Wilderness Food Pdts..G...... 847 735-8661
  Lake Bluff (G-12872)

## 2097 Ice

Carnaghi Towing & Repair Inc......F...... 217 446-0333
  Tilton (G-20878)

---

Employee Codes: A=Over 500 employees, B=251-500
C=101-250, D=51-100, E=20-50, F=10-19, G=3-9

## 20 FOOD AND KINDRED PRODUCTS

Collinsville Ice & Fuel Co .............. F ...... 618 344-3272
  Collinsville *(G-7315)*
Four Seasons Ace Hardware .......... G ...... 618 439-2101
  Benton *(G-2027)*
Home City Ice ............................. F ...... 773 622-9400
  Chicago *(G-5101)*
Home City Ice Company ................ F ...... 217 877-7733
  Decatur *(G-7889)*
International Ice Bagging Syst ........ G ...... 312 633-4000
  Glencoe *(G-11000)*
Just Ice Inc ................................. G ...... 773 301-7323
  Chicago *(G-5337)*
Muller-Pinehurst Dairy Inc ............. C ...... 815 968-0441
  Rockford *(G-18512)*
Pro Rep Sale IL ............................ G ...... 847 382-1592
  Barrington *(G-1299)*
Sisler Dairy Products Company ...... G ...... 815 376-2913
  Ohio *(G-16753)*
Sislers Ice Inc .............................. E ...... 815 756-6903
  Dekalb *(G-8117)*
Tinley Ice Company ...................... E ...... 708 532-8777
  University Park *(G-21064)*

### 2098 Macaroni, Spaghetti & Noodles

▲ Baily International Inc ................ D ...... 618 451-8878
  National Stock Yards *(G-15849)*
▲ Bellaflora Foods Ltd .................. E ...... 773 252-6113
  Chicago *(G-4077)*
Brandon Mtdba Okaeri Noodle Sp ... G ...... 847 966-0991
  Skokie *(G-19969)*
General Mills Inc .......................... B ...... 630 231-1140
  Calumet City *(G-2939)*
▼ Gilster-Mary Lee Corporation ..... A ...... 618 826-2361
  Chester *(G-3657)*
Golden Grain Company ................. G ...... 708 458-7020
  Bridgeview *(G-2495)*
Jim Noodle & Rice ........................ G ...... 773 935-5923
  Chicago *(G-5304)*
Jo MO Enterprises Inc ................... F ...... 708 599-8098
  Bridgeview *(G-2503)*
Kraft Heinz Company .................... B ...... 412 456-5700
  Chicago *(G-5410)*
Kraft Heinz Foods Company .......... D ...... 217 378-1900
  Champaign *(G-3507)*
Lee Gilster-Mary Corporation ......... G ...... 618 826-2361
  Chester *(G-3658)*
Lee Gilster-Mary Corporation ......... E ...... 618 443-5676
  Sparta *(G-20318)*
Lee Gilster-Mary Corporation ......... D ...... 815 472-6456
  Momence *(G-14983)*
Lee Gilster-Mary Corporation ......... B ...... 618 965-3449
  Steeleville *(G-20562)*
Lee Gilster-Mary Corporation ......... D ...... 618 965-3426
  Steeleville *(G-20561)*
M&L Noodle ................................. G ...... 773 878-3333
  Chicago *(G-5589)*
Maki Sushi & Noodle Shop ............ G ...... 847 318-1920
  Park Ridge *(G-17207)*
Mareta Ravioli Inc ........................ F ...... 815 856-2621
  Leonore *(G-13286)*
◆ Mary Lee Packaging Corporation ..... E ...... 618 826-2361
  Chester *(G-3659)*
Noodle Party ............................... G ...... 773 205-0505
  Chicago *(G-5923)*
Oriental Noodle ............................ G ...... 773 279-1595
  Chicago *(G-6009)*
▲ Pastafresh Co .......................... G ...... 773 745-5888
  Chicago *(G-6088)*
Pastificio Inc ................................ G ...... 847 432-5459
  Highwood *(G-11887)*
Pinto Noodle & Rice ..................... G ...... 847 328-8881
  Evanston *(G-10087)*
Sing S Noodle ............................. G ...... 312 225-2882
  Chicago *(G-6515)*
Stevie S Italian Foods Inc ............. G ...... 217 793-9693
  Springfield *(G-20538)*
Thai Noodle ................................ G ...... 217 235-5584
  Mattoon *(G-14410)*
Wah King Noodle Co Inc ............... G ...... 773 684-8000
  Chicago *(G-6933)*
Zapp Noodle ............................... G ...... 618 979-8863
  O Fallon *(G-16482)*

### 2099 Food Preparations, NEC

Aakash Spices & Produce Inc ........ F ...... 773 916-4100
  Chicago *(G-3703)*
Abbas Foods Corp ....................... G ...... 847 213-0093
  Skokie *(G-19944)*
Abelei Inc ................................... F ...... 630 859-1410
  North Aurora *(G-16117)*
▲ Agritech Worldwide Inc ............ F ...... 847 549-6002
  Mundelein *(G-15466)*
Altona Co ................................... G ...... 815 232-7819
  Freeport *(G-10645)*
American Kitchen Delights Inc ...... D ...... 708 210-3200
  Harvey *(G-11656)*
American Tristar Inc .................... D ...... 920 872-2181
  Saint Charles *(G-19136)*
American Tristar Inc .................... D ...... 630 262-5500
  Geneva *(G-10809)*
American Yeast Corp Tennessee ... G ...... 630 932-1290
  Addison *(G-38)*
Archer-Daniels-Midland Company ... D ...... 224 544-5980
  Lake Bluff *(G-12833)*
Archer-Daniels-Midland Company ... E ...... 309 772-2141
  Bushnell *(G-2897)*
▲ Arlington Specialties Inc ........... G ...... 847 545-9500
  Elk Grove Village *(G-9313)*
Arts Tamales ............................... E ...... 309 367-2850
  Metamora *(G-14739)*
Athenian Foods Co ....................... F ...... 708 343-6700
  Melrose Park *(G-14596)*
Avani Spices LLC ........................ G ...... 847 532-1075
  Algonquin *(G-379)*
▲ Azteca Foods Inc .................... C ...... 708 563-6600
  Chicago *(G-4012)*
Baja Sales Inc ............................. G ...... 708 672-9245
  Crete *(G-7508)*
Barkaat Foods LLC ...................... E ...... 773 376-8723
  Chicago *(G-4042)*
Bay Valley Foods LLC .................. E ...... 708 409-5300
  Oak Brook *(G-16491)*
Bear-Stewart Corporation ............. E ...... 773 276-0400
  Chicago *(G-4065)*
Beatrice Companies Inc ............... E ...... 602 225-2000
  Chicago *(G-4069)*
Bellisario Holdings LLC ................ G ...... 847 867-2960
  Park Ridge *(G-17183)*
Bernard Food Industries Inc ......... D ...... 847 869-5222
  Evanston *(G-10015)*
Best Croutons LLC ...................... F ...... 773 927-8200
  Chicago *(G-4091)*
Bn Delfi USA Inc .......................... G ...... 847 280-0447
  Elgin *(G-8968)*
Calma Optima Foods ................... E ...... 847 962-8329
  Franklin Park *(G-10423)*
Canadian Harvest LP ................... F ...... 309 343-7808
  Galesburg *(G-10740)*
Canyon Foods Inc ........................ G ...... 773 890-9888
  Chicago *(G-4228)*
Caravan Ingredients Inc ............... D ...... 708 849-8590
  Dolton *(G-8368)*
Castro Foods Wholesale Inc ......... E ...... 773 869-0641
  Chicago *(G-4253)*
Char Crust Co Inc ........................ G ...... 773 528-0600
  Chicago *(G-4288)*
Chateau Food Products Inc .......... F ...... 708 863-4207
  Chicago *(G-4296)*
Chef Solutions Inc ....................... C ...... 800 877-1157
  Wheeling *(G-22025)*
Chicago Oriental Cnstr Inc ............ G ...... 312 733-9633
  Chicago *(G-4337)*
Christian Wolf Inc ........................ G ...... 618 667-9522
  Bartelso *(G-1314)*
Cindys Pocket Kitchen ................. G ...... 815 388-8385
  Harvard *(G-11627)*
Cipriainis Spaghetti & Sauce Co .... E ...... 708 755-6212
  Chicago Heights *(G-7091)*
Clown Global Brands LLC ............ G ...... 847 564-5950
  Northbrook *(G-16227)*
Coki Foods LLC ........................... G ...... 708 261-5758
  Elmhurst *(G-9852)*
Combined Technologies Inc ......... G ...... 847 968-4855
  Libertyville *(G-13317)*
◆ Conagra Brands Inc ................. C ...... 312 549-5000
  Chicago *(G-4444)*
Conagra Brands Inc .................... G ...... 630 857-1000
  Naperville *(G-15633)*
Consumer Vinegar and Spice ........ G ...... 708 354-1144
  La Grange *(G-12730)*
Contract Packaging Plus Inc ......... G ...... 708 356-1100
  Bensenville *(G-1865)*
◆ Cornfields LLC ........................ C ...... 847 263-7000
  Waukegan *(G-21544)*
Creative Contract Packg LLC ........ D ...... 630 851-6226
  Aurora *(G-987)*
Culinary Co-Pack LLC .................. G ...... 847 451-1551
  Franklin Park *(G-10447)*
Culinary Co-Pack Incorporated ..... E ...... 847 451-1551
  Franklin Park *(G-10448)*
Custom Culinary Inc .................... D ...... 630 928-4898
  Lombard *(G-13787)*
Custom Culinary Inc .................... D ...... 630 299-0500
  Oswego *(G-16912)*
◆ Custom Menu Insights LLC ....... G ...... 312 237-3860
  Chicago *(G-4524)*
▲ Damron Corporation ................ E ...... 773 265-2724
  Chicago *(G-4549)*
Dean Food Products Company ..... E ...... 847 678-1680
  Franklin Park *(G-10455)*
Deja Investments Inc ................... D ...... 630 408-9222
  Bolingbrook *(G-2301)*
Dell Cove Spice Co ...................... G ...... 312 339-8389
  Chicago *(G-4577)*
Delobian Foods ........................... G ...... 773 564-0913
  Chicago *(G-4578)*
Dennco Inc .................................. G ...... 708 862-0070
  Burnham *(G-2816)*
Dfg Confectionary LLC ................. B ...... 847 412-1961
  Northbrook *(G-16241)*
Dkb Industries LLC ...................... F ...... 630 450-4151
  Naperville *(G-15802)*
Dominique Graves ....................... G ...... 773 368-5289
  Chicago *(G-4623)*
Domino Foods Inc ........................ F ...... 773 646-2203
  Chicago *(G-4625)*
E I Du Pont De Nemours & Co ...... G ...... 815 259-3311
  Thomson *(G-20865)*
E3 Artisan Inc ............................. F ...... 815 575-9315
  Woodstock *(G-22564)*
Eckert Orchards Inc .................... C ...... 618 233-0513
  Belleville *(G-1630)*
El Popocatapetl Industries Inc ...... E ...... 312 421-6143
  Chicago *(G-4710)*
El Tradicional ............................. G ...... 773 925-0335
  Chicago *(G-4712)*
▲ El-Milagro Inc ......................... B ...... 773 579-6120
  Chicago *(G-4713)*
El-Milagro Inc ............................. C ...... 773 650-1614
  Chicago *(G-4714)*
▲ El-Ranchero Food Products ..... E ...... 773 847-9167
  Chicago *(G-4716)*
▼ Equi-Chem International Inc .... F ...... 630 784-0432
  Carol Stream *(G-3146)*
◆ Essen Nutrition Corporation .... E ...... 630 739-6700
  Romeoville *(G-18820)*
Euphoria Catering and Events ..... E ...... 630 301-4369
  Aurora *(G-1148)*
Event Catering Group .................. G ...... 708 534-3100
  Chicago Heights *(G-7096)*
Famar Flavor LLC ....................... G ...... 708 926-2951
  Crestwood *(G-7487)*
▲ Far East Food Inc .................... G ...... 312 733-1688
  Chicago *(G-4813)*
Favorite Foods ............................ G ...... 847 401-7126
  Northbrook *(G-16256)*
▲ FBC Industries Inc .................. G ...... 847 241-6143
  Schaumburg *(G-19525)*
FBC Industries Inc ...................... G ...... 847 839-0880
  Rochelle *(G-18089)*
Fema L & L Food Services Inc ..... G ...... 217 835-2018
  Benld *(G-1805)*
Fibergel Technologies Inc ........... G ...... 847 549-6002
  Mundelein *(G-15500)*
Flaherty Incorporated .................. G ...... 773 472-8456
  Skokie *(G-20000)*
Fleischmanns Vinegar Co Inc ...... F ...... 773 523-2817
  Chicago *(G-4856)*
Food Service ............................... D ...... 815 933-0725
  Kankakee *(G-12617)*
Foulds Inc ................................... E ...... 414 964-1428
  Libertyville *(G-13325)*
Fresh Express Incorporated ......... E ...... 630 736-3900
  Streamwood *(G-20656)*
Frito-Lay North America Inc ......... F ...... 815 468-3940
  Manteno *(G-14184)*
Frito-Lay North America Inc ......... C ...... 708 331-7200
  Oak Forest *(G-16582)*
Futuro Foods Inc ......................... G ...... 773 418-2720
  Chicago *(G-4898)*
General Mills Inc ......................... B ...... 630 231-1140
  Calumet City *(G-2939)*
Georgies Greek Tasty Food Inc .... G ...... 773 987-1298
  Chicago *(G-4946)*
Gilster-Mary Lee Corporation ....... G ...... 618 272-3261
  Ridgway *(G-17985)*
▼ Gilster-Mary Lee Corporation ... A ...... 618 826-2361
  Chester *(G-3657)*
Givaudan Flavors Corporation ..... C ...... 630 682-5600
  Carol Stream *(G-3158)*

SIC SECTION 20 FOOD AND KINDRED PRODUCTS

▲ Golden Hill Ingredients LLC G 773 406-3409
Chicago *(G-4974)*

Golden State Foods Corp C 618 537-6121
Lebanon *(G-13215)*

▲ Gonnella Baking Co D 312 733-2020
Schaumburg *(G-19539)*

Good World Noodle Inc G 312 326-0441
Chicago *(G-4977)*

Gourmet Gorilla Inc F 877 219-3663
Chicago *(G-4981)*

Granadino Food Services Corp F 708 717-2930
Lombard *(G-13805)*

Great American Popcorn Company G 815 777-4116
Galena *(G-10725)*

◆ Grecian Delight Foods Inc C 847 364-1010
Elk Grove Village *(G-9511)*

◆ Griffith Foods Group Inc F 708 371-0900
Alsip *(G-467)*

◆ Griffith Foods Inc B 708 371-0900
Alsip *(G-468)*

Griffith Foods Worldwide Inc G 708 371-0900
Alsip *(G-469)*

Gust-John Foods & Pdts Corp G 630 879-8700
Batavia *(G-1453)*

Gycor International Ltd F 630 754-8070
Woodridge *(G-22492)*

H C Schau & Son Inc C 630 783-1000
Woodridge *(G-22493)*

Hensaal Management Group Inc G 312 624-8133
Chicago *(G-5074)*

Herman Seekamp Inc C 630 628-6555
Addison *(G-145)*

Hogback Haven Maple Farm G 815 291-9440
Orangeville *(G-16815)*

Holton Food Products Company F 708 352-5599
La Grange *(G-12736)*

Home Style G 847 455-5000
Franklin Park *(G-10487)*

▲ Hop Kee Incorporated E 312 791-9111
Chicago *(G-5109)*

▲ Ingredients Inc G 847 419-9595
Buffalo Grove *(G-2708)*

▼ Insight Beverages Inc F 847 438-1598
Lake Zurich *(G-13090)*

Instantwhip-Chicago Inc F 773 235-5588
Chicago *(G-5206)*

▲ Italia Foods Inc E 847 397-4479
Schaumburg *(G-19585)*

▲ Ixtapa Foods G 773 788-9701
Chicago *(G-5249)*

▼ Jbc Holding Co G 217 347-7701
Effingham *(G-8841)*

◆ Jel Sert Co B 630 231-7590
West Chicago *(G-21727)*

Jimmybars G 888 676-7971
Chicago *(G-5305)*

Jo MO Enterprises Inc F 708 599-8098
Bridgeview *(G-2503)*

John B Sanfilippo & Son Inc C 847 690-8432
Elgin *(G-9084)*

◆ John B Sanfilippo & Son Inc C 847 289-1800
Elgin *(G-9083)*

John Morrell & Co C 630 993-8763
Bolingbrook *(G-2329)*

Johnny Vans Smokehouse G 773 750-1589
Chicago *(G-5318)*

Josephs Food Products Co Inc C 708 338-4090
Broadview *(G-2589)*

K K Gourmet LLC G 847 727-5858
Spring Grove *(G-20340)*

Kanbo International (us) Inc G 630 873-6320
Oakbrook Terrace *(G-16713)*

Kerry Holding Co D 309 747-3534
Gridley *(G-11408)*

Kerry Inc D 309 747-3534
Gridley *(G-11409)*

Kerry Inc D 708 450-3260
Melrose Park *(G-14666)*

Kosto Food Products Company F 847 487-2600
Wauconda *(G-21478)*

▼ Kraft Food Ingredients Corp D 901 381-6500
Glenview *(G-11159)*

Kraft Heinz Foods Company B 618 451-4820
Granite City *(G-11289)*

Kraft Heinz Foods Company D 217 378-1900
Champaign *(G-3507)*

Kruger North America Inc F 708 851-3670
Oak Park *(G-16673)*

La Criolla Inc E 312 243-8882
Chicago *(G-5424)*

La Mexicana Tortilleria Inc E 773 247-5443
Chicago *(G-5425)*

▲ Land OFrost Inc C 708 474-7100
Lansing *(G-13169)*

Laredo Foods Inc E 773 762-1500
Chicago *(G-5461)*

▼ Lawrence Foods Inc C 847 437-2400
Elk Grove Village *(G-9588)*

Lcv Company G 309 738-6452
East Moline *(G-8685)*

Lee Gilster-Mary Corporation D 618 965-3426
Steeleville *(G-20561)*

Lee Gilster-Mary Corporation G 618 826-2361
Chester *(G-3658)*

Lee Gilster-Mary Corporation E 618 443-5676
Sparta *(G-20318)*

Lee Gilster-Mary Corporation D 815 472-6456
Momence *(G-14983)*

Legacy Foods Mfg LLC G 224 639-5297
Elk Grove Village *(G-9591)*

Liborio Baking Co Inc G 708 452-7222
River Grove *(G-18010)*

Little Lady Foods Inc C 847 806-1440
Elk Grove Village *(G-9597)*

Los Gamas Inc G 872 829-3514
Chicago *(G-5543)*

Ludis Foods Adams Inc G 312 939-2877
Chicago *(G-5558)*

Mangel and Co F 847 634-0730
Long Grove *(G-13894)*

Mangel and Co E 847 459-3100
Buffalo Grove *(G-2730)*

Marges Aunt Potato Salad G 708 612-2300
Brookfield *(G-2637)*

Margies Brands Inc E 773 643-1417
Chicago *(G-5615)*

◆ Mary Lee Packaging Corporation E 618 826-2361
Chester *(G-3659)*

Mead Johnson & Company LLC F 847 832-2420
Chicago *(G-5670)*

Mexico Distributor Inc G
Chicago *(G-5709)*

◆ Mizkan America Inc E 847 590-0059
Mount Prospect *(G-15347)*

◆ Mizkan America Holdings Inc G 847 590-0059
Mount Prospect *(G-15348)*

Mondelez Global LLC E 773 925-4300
Chicago *(G-5793)*

Monterey Mushrooms Inc G 815 875-4436
Princeton *(G-17755)*

Moon Guy Hong Food Inc F 773 927-3233
Chicago *(G-5801)*

Munoz Flour Tortilleria Inc F 773 523-1837
Chicago *(G-5833)*

My Own Meals Inc G 773 378-6505
Chicago *(G-5841)*

▼ My Own Meals Inc G 847 948-1118
Deerfield *(G-8042)*

Nanas Kitchen Inc G 815 363-8500
Johnsburg *(G-12439)*

National Vinegar Co F 618 395-1011
Olney *(G-16785)*

▲ Necta Sweet Inc E 847 215-9955
Buffalo Grove *(G-2742)*

▲ Neiman Bros Co Inc E 773 463-3000
Chicago *(G-5882)*

Nestle Usa Inc D 847 808-5404
Buffalo Grove *(G-2747)*

Nestle Usa Inc C 847 808-5300
Buffalo Grove *(G-2748)*

New Taste Good Noodle Inc G 312 842-8980
Chicago *(G-5897)*

◆ Newly Weds Foods Inc A 773 489-7000
Chicago *(G-5899)*

▼ Nu-World Amaranth Inc G 630 369-6819
Naperville *(G-15717)*

Nutrivo LLC E 630 270-1700
Aurora *(G-1196)*

O Chilli Frozen Foods Inc E 847 562-1991
Northbrook *(G-16321)*

Oakland Noodle Company G 217 346-2322
Oakland *(G-16724)*

▲ On-Cor Frozen Foods LLC E 630 692-2283
Aurora *(G-1199)*

Open Kitchens Inc C 312 666-5334
Chicago *(G-5994)*

Open Kitchens Inc E 312 666-5334
Chicago *(G-5995)*

▲ OSI Group LLC F 630 851-6600
Aurora *(G-1201)*

▲ OSI Industries LLC D 630 851-6600
Aurora *(G-1202)*

Papys Foods Inc E 815 385-3313
McHenry *(G-14542)*

▲ Pastafresh Co G 773 745-5888
Chicago *(G-6088)*

Pastorelli Food Products Inc G 312 455-1006
Chicago *(G-6089)*

Peanut Butter Partners LLC G 847 489-5322
Glen Ellyn *(G-10986)*

Pennant Foods G 708 752-8730
Alsip *(G-506)*

▲ Perfect Pasta Inc G 630 543-8300
Addison *(G-239)*

PO Food Specialists Ltd G 847 517-8315
Hoffman Estates *(G-12040)*

Pop Box LLC F 630 509-2281
Chicago *(G-6156)*

▲ Princess Foods Inc F 847 933-1820
Skokie *(G-20060)*

◆ Prinova Solutions LLC E 630 868-0359
Carol Stream *(G-3221)*

Quaker Oats Company A 217 443-4995
Danville *(G-7761)*

◆ Quaker Oats Company A 312 821-1000
Chicago *(G-6242)*

Qualifresh LLC E 847 337-1483
Lincolnwood *(G-13530)*

R J Van Drunen & Sons Inc D 815 472-3211
Momence *(G-14989)*

◆ R J Van Drunen & Sons Inc D 815 472-3100
Momence *(G-14987)*

R J Van Drunen & Sons Inc E 830 422-2167
Momence *(G-14988)*

Rawnature5 LLC F 312 800-3239
Chicago *(G-6296)*

Real Taste Noodles Mfg Inc G 312 738-1893
Chicago *(G-6303)*

Revolution Brands LLC G 847 902-3320
Huntley *(G-12173)*

Roma Bakeries Inc F 815 964-6737
Rockford *(G-18596)*

Romaine Empire LLC E 312 229-0099
Chicago *(G-6387)*

▲ Royal Foods & Flavors Inc F 847 595-9166
Elk Grove Village *(G-9720)*

Rt Wholesale D 847 678-3663
Schiller Park *(G-19869)*

S&J Food Management Corp G 630 323-9296
Hinsdale *(G-11961)*

Sabinas Food Products Inc E 312 738-2412
Chicago *(G-6423)*

Schau Southeast Sushi Inc E 630 783-1000
Woodridge *(G-22516)*

▲ Schulze and Burch Biscuit Co B 773 927-6622
Chicago *(G-6455)*

▲ Sdr Corp G 773 638-1800
Chicago *(G-6463)*

Seneca Foods Corporation E 309 545-2233
Manito *(G-14176)*

Sensient Technologies Corp E 708 481-0910
Matteson *(G-14378)*

Sentry Seasonings Inc E 630 530-5370
Elmhurst *(G-9938)*

Sims Family Holdings LLC D 847 488-1230
Elgin *(G-9183)*

Snak-King Corp C 815 232-6700
Freeport *(G-10689)*

◆ Sokol and Company D 708 482-8250
Countryside *(G-7443)*

Solo Foods G 800 328-7656
Countryside *(G-7444)*

Sono Italiano Corporation G 817 472-8903
Manteno *(G-14193)*

Sotiros Foods Inc G 708 371-0002
Alsip *(G-529)*

Sparrow Coffee Roastery G 321 648-6415
Westchester *(G-21855)*

Stepan Specialty Products LLC G 847 446-7500
Northfield *(G-16420)*

Stewarts Prvate Blend Fods Inc E 773 489-2500
Carol Stream *(G-3250)*

Sugar Factory Rosemont LLC F 847 349-9161
Rosemont *(G-19034)*

Sunny Day Distributing Inc G 630 779-8466
Cortland *(G-7395)*

Sunny Enterprises Inc F 847 219-1045
Chicago *(G-6627)*

Swagger Foods Corporation E 847 913-1200
Vernon Hills *(G-21205)*

SIC

Employee Codes: A=Over 500 employees, B=251-500
C=101-250, D=51-100, E=20-50, F=10-19, G=3-9

2017 Harris Illinois
Industrial Directory

927

20 FOOD AND KINDRED PRODUCTS SIC SECTION

**Sweet Beginnings LLC** G 773 638-7058
Chicago *(G-6647)*
**Sweetener Supply Corporation** G 708 484-3455
Berwyn *(G-2075)*
**Swiss Products LP** E 773 394-6480
Chicago *(G-6651)*
**Tara International LP** D 708 354-7050
Hodgkins *(G-11984)*
**Taylor Farms Illinois Inc** B 312 226-3328
Chicago *(G-6680)*
▼ **Tee Lee Popcorn Inc** E 815 864-2363
Shannon *(G-19903)*
**Teresa Foods Inc** F 708 258-6200
Peotone *(G-17493)*
**Thomas Proestler** G 630 971-0185
Lisle *(G-13671)*
**Three Guys Pasta LLC** E 708 932-5555
Northlake *(G-16455)*
**Today Gourmet Foods III LLC** G 847 401-9192
Carol Stream *(G-3256)*
**Top Hat Company Inc** G 847 256-6565
Wilmette *(G-22267)*
**Tortilleria Laf Marias LLC** G 224 399-9902
Waukegan *(G-21631)*
**Tpf Liquidation Co** D 847 362-0028
Lake Forest *(G-12971)*
▲ **United Food Ingredients Inc** G 630 655-9494
Burr Ridge *(G-2891)*
▲ **USspice Mill Inc** F 773 378-6800
Chicago *(G-6859)*
▲ **Vanee Foods Company** D 708 449-7300
Berkeley *(G-2050)*
▲ **Wah King Noodle Co Inc** F 323 268-0222
Chicago *(G-6934)*
**Wah King Noodle Co Inc** G 773 684-8000
Chicago *(G-6933)*
**Whitney Foods Inc** F 773 842-8511
Chicago *(G-6976)*
**Wisconsin Wilderness Food Pdts** G 847 735-8661
Lake Bluff *(G-12872)*
▲ **Xena International Inc** G 630 587-2734
Saint Charles *(G-19301)*
▲ **YMC Corp** F 312 842-4900
Chicago *(G-7052)*
▲ **Ys Health Corporation** F 847 391-9122
Mount Prospect *(G-15387)*
▲ **Zaibak Bros** F 312 564-5800
Chicago *(G-7058)*
**Zuchem Inc** G 312 997-2150
Chicago *(G-7075)*

# 21 TOBACCO PRODUCTS

## *2111 Cigarettes*

**8 Electronic Cigarette Inc** G 630 708-6803
Saint Charles *(G-19129)*
**Cigtechs** G 847 802-4586
Algonquin *(G-384)*
**Cigtechs** G 630 855-6513
Roselle *(G-18932)*
**Itg Brands LLC** G 217 529-5746
Springfield *(G-20458)*
**Philip Morris USA Inc** D 847 605-9595
Schaumburg *(G-19689)*
**Royal Smoke Shop** G 815 539-3499
Mendota *(G-14732)*
**Steves Cigarettes** G 630 827-0820
Lombard *(G-13860)*

## *2121 Cigars*

▲ **Burning Leaf Cigars** G 815 267-3570
Geneva *(G-10815)*
**Casa De Monte Cristo** G 708 352-6668
Countryside *(G-7416)*

## *2131 Tobacco, Chewing & Snuff*

**Casa De Puros** G 708 725-7180
Forest Park *(G-10236)*
**Diamond Wholesale Group Inc** G 708 529-7495
Bridgeview *(G-2483)*
**Having A Good Time** G 847 330-8460
Schaumburg *(G-19549)*
▲ **Inter-Continental Trdg USA Inc** D 847 640-1777
Mount Prospect *(G-15339)*
**Paralleldirect LLC** G 847 748-2025
Lincolnshire *(G-13471)*
**Paramount Plastics LLC** D 815 834-4100
Chicago *(G-6078)*
**PS Tobacco Inc** G 630 793-9823
Glen Ellyn *(G-10988)*
**Raze Vapor** G 415 596-2697
Chicago *(G-6298)*
**Republic Group Inc** G 800 288-8888
Glenview *(G-11193)*
▲ **Top Tobacco LP** G 847 832-9700
Glenview *(G-11210)*
**US Smokeless Tob Mfg Co LLC** E 804 274-2000
Franklin Park *(G-10617)*
**Ust Inc** G 847 957-5104
Franklin Park *(G-10618)*

## *2141 Tobacco Stemming & Redrying*

**Kraft Heinz Foods Company** F 630 227-1474
Wood Dale *(G-22386)*

# 22 TEXTILE MILL PRODUCTS

## *2211 Cotton, Woven Fabric*

**A B C Blind Inc** G 708 877-7100
Thornton *(G-20866)*
**Alpha Bedding LLC** F 847 550-5110
Lake Zurich *(G-13039)*
**Anees Upholstery** G 312 243-2919
Chicago *(G-3906)*
**Annas Draperies & Associates** G 773 282-1365
Chicago *(G-3911)*
**Chicor Inc** G 630 953-6154
Oak Brook *(G-16501)*
**City Living Design Inc** G 312 335-0711
Chicago *(G-4383)*
▲ **Dec Art Designs Inc** G 312 329-0553
Northbrook *(G-16240)*
**DLS Custom Embroidery Inc** E 847 593-5957
Elk Grove Village *(G-9431)*
**Dpe Incorporated** G 773 306-0105
Chicago *(G-4640)*
**Drapery Room Inc** F 708 301-3374
Homer Glen *(G-12077)*
**F & L Drapery Inc** G 815 932-8997
Saint Anne *(G-19122)*
**Fresco Plaster Finishes Inc** G 847 277-1484
Barrington *(G-1281)*
**Haakes Awning** G 618 529-4808
Carbondale *(G-3009)*
**Hartmarx Corporation** F 312 357-5325
Chicago *(G-5051)*
▲ **Henry-Lee & Company LLC** F 312 648-1575
Chicago *(G-5073)*
**Home For All Heros Nfp** G 309 808-2789
Bloomington *(G-2180)*
**Hygienic Fabrics & Filters Inc** G 815 493-2502
Lanark *(G-13155)*
**I M M Inc** F 773 767-3700
Chicago *(G-5131)*
▲ **Jacobson Acqstion Holdings LLC** C 847 623-1414
Waukegan *(G-21574)*
**Jo-Ann Stores LLC** F 847 394-9742
Arlington Heights *(G-784)*
**Kempco Window Treatments Inc** E 708 754-4484
Chicago Heights *(G-7108)*
**Lingle Design Group Inc** E 815 369-9155
Lena *(G-13280)*
▲ **Maya Romanoff Corporation** E 773 465-6909
Skokie *(G-20034)*
▲ **Moss Holding Company** C 847 238-4200
Elk Grove Village *(G-9636)*
**Netranix Enterprise** F
Bolingbrook *(G-2350)*
**Nolte & Tyson Inc** F 847 551-3313
Gilberts *(G-10929)*
**Olivia R Aguilar-Camacho** G 773 600-6864
Chicago *(G-5984)*
**Rt Properties & Cnstr Corp** G 708 913-7607
Riverdale *(G-18025)*
▲ **Rubin Manufacturing Inc** B 312 942-1111
Chicago *(G-6412)*
**Sea-Rich Corp** G 773 261-6633
Chicago *(G-6464)*
**Sultry Satchels** G 773 873-5718
Chicago *(G-6615)*
**Terre Haute Tent & Awning Inc** F 812 235-6068
South Holland *(G-20309)*
**Toco** G 618 257-8626
Belleville *(G-1681)*
**Tru-Colour Products LLC** G 630 447-0559
Warrenville *(G-21366)*
**Veltex Corporation** E 312 235-4014
Chicago *(G-6879)*
▲ **Vitel Industries Inc** G 847 299-9750
Des Plaines *(G-8300)*

## *2221 Silk & Man-Made Fiber*

**Accu-Wright Fiberglass Inc** G 618 337-3318
East Saint Louis *(G-8739)*
◆ **BP Amoco Chemical Company** B 630 420-5111
Naperville *(G-15608)*
▲ **Dyne Inc** G 815 521-1111
Minooka *(G-14839)*
**Fiberglass Solutions Corp** G 630 458-0756
Addison *(G-116)*
▲ **Fiberteq LLC** D 217 431-2111
Danville *(G-7719)*
**Funquilts Inc** G 708 445-9871
Oak Park *(G-16665)*
**Girls In White Satin** G 217 245-5400
Jacksonville *(G-12389)*
**Haakes Awning** G 618 529-4808
Carbondale *(G-3009)*
**Jalaa Fiberglass Inc** G 217 923-3433
Greenup *(G-11384)*
▲ **Kabert Industries Inc** G 630 833-2115
Villa Park *(G-21262)*
▲ **Kobawala Poly-Pack Inc** E 312 664-3810
Naperville *(G-15684)*
**Loomcraft Textile & Supply Co** E 847 680-0000
Vernon Hills *(G-21182)*
**Mahans Fiberglass** G 309 562-7349
Easton *(G-8777)*
▲ **Maya Romanoff Corporation** E 773 465-6909
Skokie *(G-20034)*
**MHS Ltd** F 773 736-3333
Chicago *(G-5716)*
▲ **Neptune USA Inc** G 847 987-3804
Schaumburg *(G-19663)*
**Next Gen Manufacturing Inc** G 847 289-8444
Elgin *(G-9120)*
**Ogden Top & Trim Shop Inc** G 708 484-5422
Berwyn *(G-2070)*
**Robert Stern Industries Inc** G 630 983-9765
Naperville *(G-15742)*
**Sea-Rich Corp** G 773 261-6633
Chicago *(G-6464)*
▲ **Seco** G 618 748-9227
Mound City *(G-15257)*
**Srm Industries Inc** G 847 735-0077
Lake Forest *(G-12963)*
**Upholstered Walls By Anne Mari** G 847 202-0642
Palatine *(G-17084)*

## *2231 Wool, Woven Fabric*

▼ **Aurora Spclty Txtles Group Inc** D 800 864-0303
Yorkville *(G-22650)*
**EW Bredemeier and Co** F 773 237-1600
Chicago *(G-4793)*
▲ **Modern Specialties Company** G 312 648-5800
Chicago *(G-5785)*
**Salt Creek Alpacas Inc** G 309 530-7904
Farmer City *(G-10181)*
**Without A Trace Weaver Inc** F 773 588-4922
Chicago *(G-7009)*

## *2241 Fabric Mills, Cotton, Wool, Silk & Man-Made*

**Adhes Tape Technology Inc** G 847 496-7949
Arlington Heights *(G-702)*
**Chase Corporation** E 847 866-8500
Evanston *(G-10022)*
▲ **F Hyman & Co** G 312 664-3810
Chicago *(G-4804)*
**Harbor Village LLC** G 773 338-2222
Chicago *(G-5043)*
**Lea & Sachs Inc** F 847 296-8000
Des Plaines *(G-8221)*
**Phoenix Graphix** G 618 531-3664
Pinckneyville *(G-17551)*
◆ **Ribbon Webbing Corporation** C 773 287-1221
Chicago *(G-6351)*
**Rogers Custom Trims Inc** G 773 745-6577
Chicago *(G-6380)*
**Shoelace Inc** G 847 854-2500
Kildeer *(G-12704)*
**Shoelace Inc** G 847 854-2500
Crystal Lake *(G-7650)*
▲ **Technical Sealants Inc** F 815 777-9797
Galena *(G-10732)*
**UNI-Label and Tag Corporation** E 847 956-8900
Elk Grove Village *(G-9797)*

## 22 TEXTILE MILL PRODUCTS

Voss Belting & Specialty Co .............E...... 847 673-8900
  Lincolnwood *(G-13541)*
W & W Associates Inc .....................G...... 847 719-1760
  Lake Zurich *(G-13142)*

### 2251 Hosiery, Women's Full & Knee Length
▲ Bee Sales Comapny ........................D...... 847 600-4400
  Niles *(G-15965)*
Felice Hosiery Co Inc .........................G...... 312 922-3710
  Chicago *(G-4832)*

### 2252 Hosiery, Except Women's
▲ Bee Sales Comapny ........................D...... 847 600-4400
  Niles *(G-15965)*
Emeelys Socks and More ...................G...... 847 529-3026
  Chicago *(G-4738)*
Felice Hosiery Co Inc .........................G...... 312 922-3710
  Chicago *(G-4832)*
Felice Hosiery Company Inc ..............E...... 312 922-3710
  Chicago *(G-4833)*
Four White Socks LLC .......................G...... 312 257-6456
  Chicago *(G-4879)*
Living Royal ........................................F...... 312 906-7600
  Wheeling *(G-22096)*
Midwest Socks LLC ...........................G...... 773 283-3952
  Chicago *(G-5749)*
Quincy Socks House ..........................G...... 217 506-6106
  Quincy *(G-17880)*
Soy City Sock Co Inc .........................F...... 217 762-2157
  Monticello *(G-15085)*
Your Team Socks ................................G...... 309 713-1044
  Peoria *(G-17479)*

### 2253 Knit Outerwear Mills
A&B Apparel ........................................G...... 815 962-5070
  Rockford *(G-18241)*
Bird Dog Bay Inc ................................G...... 312 631-3108
  Chicago *(G-4111)*
Bxb Intl Inc ..........................................G...... 312 240-1966
  Brookfield *(G-2626)*
Chicago Knitting Mills ........................G...... 773 463-1464
  Chicago *(G-4326)*
Creative Clothing Created 4 U ...........G...... 847 543-0051
  Grayslake *(G-11330)*
Csi Chicago Inc ..................................G...... 773 665-2226
  Chicago *(G-4511)*
▲ Denise Allen Robinson Inc ............F...... 773 275-8080
  Chicago *(G-4582)*
Derbyteescom .....................................G...... 309 264-1033
  Henry *(G-11739)*
Five Brother Inc ..................................G...... 309 663-6323
  Bloomington *(G-2164)*
Heartfelt Gifts Inc ...............................G...... 309 852-2296
  Kewanee *(G-12690)*
M & G Simplicitees .............................G...... 224 372-7426
  Lake Villa *(G-13018)*
Main Street Records ..........................G...... 618 244-2737
  Mount Vernon *(G-15424)*
Mr T Shirt and Dollar Plus ..................G...... 708 596-9150
  Harvey *(G-11674)*
▲ NRR Corp .......................................F...... 630 915-8388
  Oak Brook *(G-16550)*
Rfq LLC ...............................................G...... 815 893-6656
  Crystal Lake *(G-7640)*
Russell Brands LLC ..........................D...... 309 454-6737
  Normal *(G-16087)*
Sue Peterson ......................................G...... 847 730-3035
  Glenview *(G-11207)*
The Lifeguard Store Inc .....................G...... 630 548-5500
  Naperville *(G-15764)*
Yetee LLC ...........................................G...... 630 340-0132
  Aurora *(G-1236)*

### 2254 Knit Underwear Mills
Inkn Tees ............................................G...... 847 244-2266
  Waukegan *(G-21570)*
▲ Top Ace Inc ....................................G...... 847 581-0550
  Morton Grove *(G-15241)*

### 2257 Circular Knit Fabric Mills
Chicago Knitting Mills ........................G...... 773 463-1464
  Chicago *(G-4326)*
Jr Royals Athletics .............................E...... 224 659-2906
  Elgin *(G-9085)*

### 2259 Knitting Mills, NEC
Intelex Usa LLC .................................G...... 847 496-1727
  East Dundee *(G-8647)*

◆ Omar Medical Supplies Inc ............E...... 708 922-4377
  Chicago *(G-5988)*
▲ Tiger Accessory Group LLC ..........G...... 847 821-9630
  Long Grove *(G-13902)*

### 2261 Cotton Fabric Finishers
▼ Aurora Spclty Txtles Group Inc .....D...... 800 864-0303
  Yorkville *(G-22650)*
B and A Screen Printing .....................G...... 217 762-2632
  Monticello *(G-15074)*
Den Graphix Inc .................................F...... 309 962-2000
  Le Roy *(G-13207)*
Expression Wear Inc ..........................G...... 815 732-1556
  Mount Morris *(G-15296)*
Flock It Ltd .........................................G...... 815 247-8775
  Winnebago *(G-22296)*
Frankenstitch Promotions LLC .........G...... 847 459-4840
  Wheeling *(G-22058)*
Holy Cow Sports Incorporated .........F...... 630 852-9001
  Downers Grove *(G-8460)*
M & P Talking Tees Inc ......................F...... 262 495-4000
  Round Lake Beach *(G-19077)*
Meridian Industries Inc .....................D...... 630 892-7651
  Aurora *(G-1186)*
Murphys Pub .......................................G...... 847 526-1431
  Wauconda *(G-21488)*
Player Sports Ltd ...............................G...... 773 764-4111
  Chicago *(G-6140)*
Proell Inc ............................................G...... 630 587-2300
  Saint Charles *(G-19242)*
Saati Americas Corporation ..............F...... 847 296-5090
  Mount Prospect *(G-15371)*
Santana & Daughter Inc ....................G...... 773 237-1818
  Chicago *(G-6441)*
Silk Screening By Selep ....................G...... 847 593-7050
  Des Plaines *(G-8276)*
Tomen America Inc ............................D...... 847 439-8500
  Elk Grove Village *(G-9782)*
Top Notch Silk Screening ..................G...... 773 847-6335
  Chicago *(G-6744)*
Western Pece Dyers Fnshers Inc .....G...... 773 523-7000
  Oak Brook *(G-16569)*

### 2262 Silk & Man-Made Fabric Finishers
David H Pool ......................................G...... 847 695-5007
  Elgin *(G-9009)*
Image Plus Inc ....................................G...... 630 852-4920
  Downers Grove *(G-8463)*
Insignia Design Ltd ............................G...... 301 254-9221
  Rolling Meadows *(G-18734)*
Jdl Graphics Inc .................................G...... 815 694-2979
  Clifton *(G-7274)*
Marathon Sportswear Inc ..................E...... 708 389-5390
  Blue Island *(G-2262)*
Saati Americas Corporation ..............F...... 847 296-5090
  Mount Prospect *(G-15371)*
Silk Screening By Selep ....................G...... 847 593-7050
  Des Plaines *(G-8276)*
Starline Designs .................................G...... 773 683-7506
  Chicago *(G-6577)*
Ultimate Distributing Inc ....................G...... 847 566-2250
  Mundelein *(G-15565)*

### 2269 Textile Finishers, NEC
Chicago Dye Works ............................G...... 847 931-7968
  Elgin *(G-8987)*
Fas-Trak Industries Inc .....................G...... 708 570-0650
  Monee *(G-14994)*
Mount Vernon Mills ............................G...... 618 882-6300
  Highland *(G-11804)*
▲ Sato Lbling Solutions Amer Inc ....D...... 630 771-4200
  Romeoville *(G-18866)*

### 2273 Carpets & Rugs
Aspen Carpet Designs .......................G...... 815 483-8501
  Mokena *(G-14855)*
Baker Avenue Investments Inc ........G...... 309 427-2500
  Washington *(G-21378)*
◆ Blachford Investments Inc ............C...... 630 231-8300
  West Chicago *(G-21671)*
Ds Production LLC ............................G...... 708 873-3142
  Orland Park *(G-16856)*
▲ Eagle Carpet Services Ltd ............G...... 956 971-8560
  Addison *(G-105)*
East West Martial Arts Sups .............G...... 773 878-7711
  Chicago *(G-4682)*
Edward Fields Incorporated .............G...... 312 644-0400
  Chicago *(G-4703)*

Interfaceflor LLC ................................E...... 312 775-6307
  Chicago *(G-5212)*
Interfaceflor LLC ................................E...... 312 836-3389
  Chicago *(G-5213)*
Interfaceflor LLC ................................F...... 312 822-9640
  Chicago *(G-5214)*
L & L Flooring Inc ..............................G...... 773 935-9314
  Chicago *(G-5418)*
Lessy Messy LLC ...............................F...... 708 790-7589
  Naperville *(G-15814)*
Mailbox International Inc ...................G...... 847 541-8466
  Wheeling *(G-22097)*
Mastercraft Rug Design .....................G...... 630 655-3393
  Hinsdale *(G-11952)*
Milliken & Company ...........................F...... 800 241-4826
  Chicago *(G-5763)*
Minasian Rug Corporation .................G...... 847 864-1010
  Evanston *(G-10073)*
Mohawk Industries Inc ......................D...... 630 972-8000
  Bolingbrook *(G-2344)*
Protect Assoc .....................................G...... 847 446-8664
  Northbrook *(G-16348)*
Shaw Industries Group Inc ...............G...... 312 467-1331
  Chicago *(G-6491)*
Shiir Rugs LLC ...................................G...... 312 828-0400
  Chicago *(G-6497)*
Skandia Inc ........................................D...... 815 393-4600
  Davis Junction *(G-7815)*
▲ W J Dennis & Company .................G...... 847 697-4800
  Elgin *(G-9225)*

### 2284 Thread Mills
▲ Advent Tool & Mfg Inc ...................F...... 847 395-9707
  Antioch *(G-613)*
Dan De Tash Knits .............................G...... 708 970-6238
  Maywood *(G-14424)*
Machine Tool Acc & Mfg Co ..............G...... 773 489-0903
  Chicago *(G-5592)*

### 2295 Fabrics Coated Not Rubberized
Ace Anodizing Impregnating Inc ......D...... 708 547-6680
  Hillside *(G-11907)*
▲ Advanced Flxble Composites Inc .D...... 847 658-3938
  Lake In The Hills *(G-12983)*
Allerton Charter Coach .....................G...... 217 344-2600
  Champaign *(G-3445)*
Brasel Products Inc ..........................G...... 630 879-3759
  Batavia *(G-1424)*
Custom Coating Innvations Inc .......F...... 618 808-0500
  Lebanon *(G-13213)*
Engineered Polymr Solutions Inc ....G...... 815 987-3700
  Rockford *(G-18366)*
▲ Engineered Polymr Solutions Inc .G...... 815 568-4205
  Marengo *(G-14226)*
▲ H E Wisdom & Sons Inc ................E...... 847 841-7002
  Elgin *(G-9052)*
J M Fabricating Inc ...........................G...... 815 359-2024
  Harmon *(G-11595)*
Jessup Manufacturing Company ......G...... 847 362-0961
  Lake Bluff *(G-12851)*
Lanmar Inc ........................................G...... 800 233-5520
  Northbrook *(G-16293)*
Metal Impregnating Corp. .................G...... 630 543-3443
  Addison *(G-200)*
Phoenix Leather Goods LLC ............G...... 815 267-3926
  Plainfield *(G-17639)*
Seal Tech Services ...........................G...... 847 776-0043
  Palatine *(G-17072)*
Stickon Adhesive Inds Inc ...............E...... 847 593-5959
  Arlington Heights *(G-844)*
▲ Technical Sealants Inc ..................F...... 815 777-9797
  Galena *(G-10732)*
Vacumet Corp ...................................F...... 708 562-7290
  Northlake *(G-16458)*

### 2296 Tire Cord & Fabric
▲ Advanced Flxble Composites Inc .D...... 847 658-3938
  Lake In The Hills *(G-12983)*
Mc Chemical Company ....................G...... 618 965-3668
  Steeleville *(G-20563)*
Nnm Manufacturing LLC ..................E...... 815 436-9201
  Plainfield *(G-17633)*

### 2297 Fabrics, Nonwoven
Cowtan and Tout Inc ........................F...... 312 644-0717
  Chicago *(G-4485)*
▲ Fibertex Nonwovens LLC ..............D...... 815 349-3200
  Ingleside *(G-12189)*

# 22 TEXTILE MILL PRODUCTS

▲ Midwest Nonwovens LLC .................. E ....... 618 337-9662
  Sauget  (G-19387)

## 2298 Cordage & Twine

▲ Aamstrand Ropes & Twines Inc ......... F ....... 815 468-2100
  Manteno  (G-14179)
All Gear Inc ........................................... G ....... 847 564-9016
  Northbrook  (G-16202)
All Line Inc ............................................ G ....... 630 820-1800
  Naperville  (G-15792)
Calvert Systems .................................... G ....... 309 523-3262
  Port Byron  (G-17719)
Clark Wire & Cable Co Inc .................... E ....... 847 949-9944
  Mundelein  (G-15488)
Columbian Rope Company .................... C ....... 888 593-7999
  Calumet Park  (G-2959)
Douglas Net Company ........................... F ....... 815 427-6350
  Saint Anne  (G-19119)
▲ Erin Rope Corporation ....................... F ....... 708 377-1084
  Blue Island  (G-2250)
◆ Lehigh Consumer Products LLC ....... C ....... 630 851-7330
  Aurora  (G-1045)
Lifting & Components Parts LLC ........... G ....... 224 315-5294
  Schaumburg  (G-19617)
Mac Lean-Fogg Company ..................... C ....... 847 288-2534
  Franklin Park  (G-10519)
MHS Ltd ............................................... F ....... 773 736-3333
  Chicago  (G-5716)
▲ Mighty Hook Inc ............................... E ....... 773 378-1909
  Chicago  (G-5756)
Nichols Net & Twine Inc ....................... G ....... 618 797-0211
  Granite City  (G-11298)
Obies Tackle Co Inc ............................. G ....... 618 234-5638
  Belleville  (G-1662)
◆ Unicord Corporation ........................ E ....... 708 385-7999
  Calumet Park  (G-2964)

## 2299 Textile Goods, NEC

Advantex Inc ......................................... G ....... 618 505-0701
  Troy  (G-21002)
Annaka Enterprises ............................... G ....... 773 768-5490
  Chicago  (G-3910)
▲ Biz Pins Inc ..................................... G ....... 847 695-6212
  Elgin  (G-8967)
C B E Inc .............................................. G ....... 630 571-2610
  Oak Brook  (G-16497)
▲ Cellusuede Products Inc .................. E ....... 815 964-8619
  Rockford  (G-18302)
Conversion Energy Systems Inc ........... G ....... 312 489-8875
  Chicago  (G-4464)
Deelone Distributing Inc ........................ G ....... 309 788-1444
  Rock Island  (G-18172)
Federal Prison Industries ...................... F ....... 618 664-6361
  Greenville  (G-11393)
Federal Prison Industries ...................... C ....... 309 346-8588
  Pekin  (G-17262)
Filter Technology Inc ............................ E ....... 773 523-7200
  Bedford Park  (G-1550)
Fourell Corp ......................................... G ....... 217 742-3186
  Winchester  (G-22279)
Gilday Services ..................................... G ....... 847 395-0853
  Antioch  (G-635)
Glenraven Inc ....................................... G ....... 847 515-1321
  Huntley  (G-12141)
Hugo Boss Usa Inc ............................... F ....... 847 517-1461
  Schaumburg  (G-19559)
Lorton Group LLC ................................ G ....... 844 352-5089
  Wilmette  (G-22260)
▲ Metric Felt Co .................................. G ....... 708 479-7979
  Mokena  (G-14885)
Midwest Carpet Recycling Inc ............... E ....... 855 406-8600
  Lake Villa  (G-13021)
Novipax LLC ......................................... F ....... 630 686-2735
  Oak Brook  (G-16548)
Rainbow Fabrics Inc ............................. G ....... 312 356-9979
  Chicago  (G-6289)
Superior Health Linens LLC ................. D ....... 630 593-5091
  Batavia  (G-1502)
◆ Tex Tana Inc ................................... G ....... 773 561-9270
  Chicago  (G-6705)
Thermohelp Inc .................................... G ....... 847 821-7130
  Buffalo Grove  (G-2781)
Z A W Collections ................................ G ....... 773 568-2031
  Chicago  (G-7056)

# 23 APPAREL AND OTHER FINISHED PRODUCTS MADE FROM FABRICS AND SIMILAR MATERIAL

## 2311 Men's & Boys' Suits, Coats & Overcoats

Compu-Tap Inc ..................................... G ....... 708 594-5773
  Summit Argo  (G-20761)
▲ Demoulin Brothers & Company ........ C ....... 618 664-2000
  Greenville  (G-11391)
Excelled Sheepskin & Lea Coat ............ C ....... 309 852-3341
  Kewanee  (G-12682)
J G Uniforms Inc .................................. G ....... 773 545-4644
  Chicago  (G-5259)
Mancillas International Ltd .................... F ....... 847 441-7748
  Winnetka  (G-22311)
Oxxford Clothes Xx Inc ......................... C ....... 312 829-3600
  Chicago  (G-6034)
▲ Pro-Pak Industries Inc ..................... F ....... 630 876-1050
  West Chicago  (G-21761)
Signature Design & Tailoring ................. F ....... 773 375-4915
  Chicago  (G-6510)
Vertex International Inc ........................ G ....... 312 242-1864
  Oak Brook  (G-16568)

## 2321 Men's & Boys' Shirts

Drywear Apparel LLC ........................... G ....... 847 687-8540
  Kildeer  (G-12699)
Dyna Comp Inc ..................................... G ....... 815 455-5570
  Crystal Lake  (G-7568)
Pvh Corp .............................................. G ....... 217 253-3398
  Tuscola  (G-21022)
Pvh Corp .............................................. G ....... 630 898-7718
  Aurora  (G-1071)
Riddle McIntyre Inc .............................. G ....... 312 782-3317
  Chicago  (G-6355)
Salmons and Brown .............................. G ....... 312 929-6756
  Chicago  (G-6434)
Silk Screen Express Inc ....................... F ....... 708 845-5600
  Tinley Park  (G-20945)

## 2323 Men's & Boys' Neckwear

Besleys Accessories Inc ...................... G ....... 773 561-3300
  Chicago  (G-4089)
Corporate Textiles Inc .......................... G ....... 847 433-4111
  Lincolnwood  (G-13505)
Lee Allison Company Inc ..................... G ....... 773 276-7172
  Chicago  (G-5482)

## 2325 Men's & Boys' Separate Trousers & Casual Slacks

Demetrios Tailor Inc ............................ G ....... 708 974-0304
  Justice  (G-12597)
Guess Inc ............................................ E ....... 312 440-9592
  Chicago  (G-5009)
▲ Kanan Fashions Inc ......................... G ....... 630 240-1234
  Oak Brook  (G-16530)
Levi Strauss & Co ................................ F ....... 773 486-3900
  Chicago  (G-5496)
Levi Strauss & Co ................................ D ....... 847 619-0655
  Schaumburg  (G-19616)
Lucky Brand Dungarees LLC ............... E ....... 847 550-1647
  Deer Park  (G-7972)
Oxxford Clothes Xx Inc ......................... C ....... 312 829-3600
  Chicago  (G-6034)

## 2326 Men's & Boys' Work Clothing

Advance Uniform Company .................. F ....... 312 922-1797
  Chicago  (G-3765)
Ai Ind ................................................... E ....... 773 265-6640
  Chicago  (G-3784)
◆ Apparel Works Intl LLC ................... G ....... 224 235-4240
  Lake Bluff  (G-12832)
Atlas Uniform Company ........................ G ....... 312 492-8527
  Chicago  (G-3985)
▲ Chicago Uniforms Company ............ E ....... 312 913-1006
  Chicago  (G-4361)
▲ Choi Brands Inc .............................. C ....... 773 489-2800
  Chicago  (G-4368)
Cintas Corporation ............................... F ....... 708 424-4747
  Oak Lawn  (G-16611)
Cintas Corporation ............................... D ....... 708 563-2626
  Chicago  (G-4379)
Compu-Tap Inc ..................................... G ....... 708 594-5773
  Summit Argo  (G-20761)
▲ Demoulin Brothers & Company ........ C ....... 618 664-2000
  Greenville  (G-11391)

Federal Uniform LLC ........................... G ....... 847 658-5470
  Chicago  (G-4823)
▲ G & P Products Inc ......................... E ....... 708 442-9667
  Lyons  (G-14039)
▲ Gelscrubs ....................................... G ....... 312 243-4612
  Chicago  (G-4922)
Harris Clothing & Uniforms Inc ............. G ....... 309 671-4543
  Peoria  (G-17380)
▲ High Performance Entp Inc .............. E ....... 773 283-1778
  Chicago  (G-5087)
▲ Iguanamed LLC ............................... G ....... 312 546-4182
  Chicago  (G-5148)
▲ K A & F Group LLC ......................... G ....... 847 780-4600
  Highland Park  (G-11848)
▲ Magid Glove Safety Mfg Co LLC ..... B ....... 773 384-2070
  Romeoville  (G-18841)
Mennon Rubber & Safety Pdts ............. G ....... 847 678-8250
  Schiller Park  (G-19849)
Mighty Mites Awards and Sons ............. G ....... 847 297-0035
  Des Plaines  (G-8233)
Quincy Specialties Company ................. E ....... 217 222-4057
  Quincy  (G-17881)
Rubin Brothers Inc ............................... C ....... 312 942-1111
  Chicago  (G-6411)
Standard Safety Equipment Co .............. E ....... 815 363-8565
  McHenry  (G-14556)
◆ Universal Overall Company .............. E ....... 312 226-3336
  Chicago  (G-6834)
◆ V-Tex Inc ......................................... E ....... 847 325-4140
  Buffalo Grove  (G-2787)
▲ W Diamond Group Corporation ........ A ....... 646 647-2791
  Des Plaines  (G-8301)
Woolenwear Co .................................... F ....... 847 520-9243
  Prospect Heights  (G-17786)

## 2329 Men's & Boys' Clothing, NEC

Athletic Sewing Mfg Co ........................ E ....... 773 589-0361
  Chicago  (G-3975)
Athllete LLC ......................................... F ....... 773 829-3752
  Bolingbrook  (G-2279)
◆ Bell Sports ...................................... G ....... 309 693-2746
  Rantoul  (G-17919)
BMW Sportswear Inc ........................... G ....... 773 265-0110
  Chicago  (G-4133)
▲ Choi Brands Inc .............................. C ....... 773 489-2800
  Chicago  (G-4368)
Cloz Companies Inc ............................. G ....... 773 247-8879
  Skokie  (G-19983)
Columbia Sportswear Company ............ C ....... 312 649-3758
  Chicago  (G-4432)
Curt Smith Sporting Goods Inc ............. E ....... 618 233-5177
  Belleville  (G-1621)
Custom By Lamar Inc ........................... F ....... 312 738-2160
  Chicago  (G-4520)
Da Closet ............................................. G ....... 708 206-1414
  Country Club Hills  (G-7406)
▼ Dnepr Techologies Inc ..................... F ....... 773 603-3360
  Chicago  (G-4617)
Exclusive Pro Sports Ltd ...................... E ....... 815 877-8585
  Rockford  (G-18377)
Express LLC ........................................ E ....... 708 453-0566
  Norridge  (G-16101)
Foot Locker Retail Inc ......................... G ....... 630 678-0155
  Lombard  (G-13801)
Forever Fly LLC .................................. G ....... 312 981-9161
  Chicago  (G-4873)
H & H Fabric Cutters ........................... G ....... 773 772-1904
  Chicago  (G-5018)
Independence Inc ................................. G ....... 312 675-2105
  Chicago  (G-5172)
Jtoor LLC ............................................. G ....... 312 291-8249
  Chicago  (G-5334)
Kims Menswear Ltd ............................. G ....... 773 373-2237
  Chicago  (G-5385)
Lloyd M Hughes Enterprises Inc ........... G ....... 773 363-6331
  Chicago  (G-5527)
M Handelsman & Co ............................ F ....... 312 427-0784
  Chicago  (G-5581)
Moxie Apparel LLC .............................. G ....... 312 243-9040
  Chicago  (G-5819)
On-Target Sports Marketing ................. G ....... 847 458-9360
  Lake In The Hills  (G-13002)
Pro Image ............................................ G ....... 708 422-7471
  Chicago Ridge  (G-7155)
Sansabelt ............................................. G ....... 312 357-5119
  Chicago  (G-6440)
Tfo Group LLC ..................................... G ....... 608 469-7510
  Chicago  (G-6709)
Vertex International Inc ........................ G ....... 312 242-1864
  Oak Brook  (G-16568)

SIC SECTION 23 APPAREL AND OTHER FINISHED PRODUCTS MADE FROM FABRICS AND SIMILAR MATERIAL

**Vmr Chicago LLC** F 312 649-6673
Chicago *(G-6911)*

### *2331 Women's & Misses' Blouses*

◆ **Apparel Works Intl LLC** G 224 235-4240
Lake Bluff *(G-12832)*
**Besleys Accessories Inc** G 773 561-3300
Chicago *(G-4089)*
**Dyna Comp Inc** G 815 455-5570
Crystal Lake *(G-7568)*
**Forever Fly LLC** G 312 981-9161
Chicago *(G-4873)*
**Joriki LLC** G 312 848-1136
Chicago *(G-5325)*
▲ **Yolanda Lorente Ltd** E 773 334-4536
Chicago *(G-7053)*

### *2335 Women's & Misses' Dresses*

▲ **Alyce Designs Inc** E 847 966-6933
Morton Grove *(G-15187)*
**Best Kept Secrets** G 773 431-0353
Blue Island *(G-2238)*
**Caroline Rose Inc** G 708 386-1011
Oak Park *(G-16656)*
**Casa Di Castronovo Inc** G 815 962-4731
Rockford *(G-18299)*
**Chicago Bridal Store Inc** G 773 445-4450
Chicago *(G-4308)*
**Chicagostyle Weddings** G 847 584-2626
Elk Grove Village *(G-9371)*
**Donna Karan Company LLC** C 630 236-8900
Aurora *(G-996)*
**Doris Bridal Boutique** G 847 433-2575
Highwood *(G-11884)*
**Halanick Enterprises Inc** E 708 403-3334
Orland Park *(G-16864)*
**Igar Bridal Inc** G 224 318-2337
Arlington Heights *(G-772)*
**Jane Stodden Bridals** G 815 223-2091
La Salle *(G-12779)*
**Matthew Christopher Inc** G 212 938-6820
Batavia *(G-1468)*
▲ **Mom Dad & ME** G 773 735-9606
Chicago *(G-5791)*
▲ **Prestige Wedding Decoration** G 847 845-0901
Arlington Heights *(G-820)*
**Salmons and Brown** G 312 929-6756
Chicago *(G-6434)*
◆ **SASI Corporation** E 314 922-7432
Collinsville *(G-7340)*
**Urban Outfitters Inc** G 312 573-2573
Chicago *(G-6848)*
▲ **Yolanda Lorente Ltd** E 773 334-4536
Chicago *(G-7053)*

### *2337 Women's & Misses' Suits, Coats & Skirts*

**Advance Uniform Company** F 312 922-1797
Chicago *(G-3765)*
**Atlas Uniform Company** G 312 492-8527
Chicago *(G-3985)*
▲ **Choi Brands Inc** C 773 489-2800
Chicago *(G-4368)*
**Cintas Corporation** D 708 563-2626
Chicago *(G-4379)*
**Cintas Corporation No 2** G 708 424-4747
Oak Lawn *(G-16612)*
▲ **Demoulin Brothers & Company** C 618 664-2000
Greenville *(G-11391)*
**Fashahnn Corporation** G 773 994-3132
Chicago *(G-4814)*
▲ **Iguanamed LLC** G 312 546-4182
Chicago *(G-5148)*
**Mademoiselle Inc** F 773 394-4555
Chicago *(G-5596)*
**Nine West Holdings Inc** F 630 236-9258
Aurora *(G-1057)*
**Tfo Group LLC** G 608 469-7519
Chicago *(G-6709)*
▲ **Yolanda Lorente Ltd** E 773 334-4536
Chicago *(G-7053)*

### *2339 Women's & Misses' Outerwear, NEC*

**Anart Inc** E 708 447-0225
Riverside *(G-18028)*
**Athlete LLC** F 773 829-3752
Bolingbrook *(G-2279)*
**Besleys Accessories Inc** G 773 561-3300
Chicago *(G-4089)*
**Caroline Rose Inc** G 708 386-1011
Oak Park *(G-16656)*
**Chicago Knitting Mills** G 773 463-1464
Chicago *(G-4326)*
▲ **Choi Brands Inc** C 773 489-2800
Chicago *(G-4368)*
**Cintas Corporation** D 708 563-2626
Chicago *(G-4379)*
**Cloz Companies Inc** E 773 247-8879
Skokie *(G-19983)*
**Custom By Lamar Inc** F 312 738-2160
Chicago *(G-4520)*
▲ **Daniel Bruce LLC** F 917 583-1538
Palatine *(G-17019)*
**Demetrios Tailor Inc** G 708 974-0304
Justice *(G-12597)*
▲ **Demoulin Brothers & Company** C 618 664-2000
Greenville *(G-11391)*
**Doughman Don & Assoc** G 312 321-1011
Chicago *(G-4636)*
**Exclusive Pro Sports Ltd** E 815 877-8585
Rockford *(G-18377)*
**Fashahnn Corporation** G 773 994-3132
Chicago *(G-4814)*
▲ **Gennco International Inc** F 847 541-3333
Wheeling *(G-22062)*
**Golda Inc** C 217 895-3602
Neoga *(G-15858)*
**Its A Girl Thing** F 630 232-2778
Geneva *(G-10840)*
**Jenny Capp Co** F 773 217-0057
Chicago *(G-5291)*
▲ **Laqueus Inc** F 773 508-1993
Chicago *(G-5460)*
**Lauren Lein Ltd** E 312 527-1714
Chicago *(G-5468)*
**Leg Up LLC** G 312 282-2725
Chicago *(G-5486)*
**Levi Strauss & Co** F 773 486-3900
Chicago *(G-5496)*
**Little Journeys Limited** G 847 677-0350
Skokie *(G-20030)*
**Lululemon USA Inc** G 773 227-1869
Chicago *(G-5560)*
**Mademoiselle Inc** F 773 394-4555
Chicago *(G-5596)*
**Marena Marena Two Inc** G 773 327-0619
Chicago *(G-5614)*
**Nguyen Chau** G 773 506-1066
Chicago *(G-5909)*
**Paul Sisti** G 773 472-5615
Chicago *(G-6091)*
**Pola Company** G 847 470-1182
Niles *(G-16020)*
**Pro Image** G 708 422-7471
Chicago Ridge *(G-7155)*
**Quincy Specialties Company** G 217 222-4057
Quincy *(G-17881)*
**Second Child** G 773 883-0880
Chicago *(G-6468)*
▲ **Srh Holdings Inc** G 847 583-2295
Niles *(G-16037)*
**Trim Suits By Show-Off Inc** G 630 894-0100
Roselle *(G-18984)*
**Woolenwear Co** F 847 520-9243
Prospect Heights *(G-17786)*
▲ **Yolanda Lorente Ltd** E 773 334-4536
Chicago *(G-7053)*

### *2341 Women's, Misses' & Children's Underwear & Nightwear*

**Aurora Narinder** G 773 275-2100
Chicago *(G-3989)*
**Kai Lee Couture Inc** G 773 426-1668
Chicago *(G-5351)*
**Maidenform LLC** C 630 898-8419
Aurora *(G-1052)*

### *2342 Brassieres, Girdles & Garments*

**Golda Inc** C 217 895-3602
Neoga *(G-15858)*

### *2353 Hats, Caps & Millinery*

**Amenities Home Design** G 312 421-2450
Chicago *(G-3845)*
◆ **American Needle Inc** E 847 215-0011
Buffalo Grove *(G-2657)*
▲ **Bee Sales Comapny** D 847 600-4400
Niles *(G-15965)*
**Bxb Intl Inc** G 312 240-1966
Brookfield *(G-2626)*
**Cap Factory** F 618 273-9662
Eldorado *(G-8919)*
**Choice Cap Inc** G 847 588-3443
Niles *(G-15968)*
**Federal Prison Industries** C 309 346-8588
Pekin *(G-17262)*
**Hats For You** G 773 481-1611
Chicago *(G-5054)*
**Jenny Capp Co** F 773 217-0057
Chicago *(G-5291)*
**Lewa Acquisition Corp** B 847 940-3535
Deerfield *(G-8029)*
**Lids Corporation** G 708 873-9606
Orland Park *(G-16873)*
**Mademoiselle Inc** F 773 394-4555
Chicago *(G-5596)*
**Midway Cap Company** E 773 384-0911
Chicago *(G-5736)*
**Midway Cap Company** E 773 384-0911
Chicago *(G-5737)*

### *2361 Children's & Infants' Dresses & Blouses*

**Carters Inc** G 847 870-0185
Mount Prospect *(G-15316)*
**Carters Inc** G 708 345-6680
Melrose Park *(G-14605)*
**Carters Inc** F 630 690-6182
Wheaton *(G-21939)*
**Dino Design Incorporated** G 773 763-4223
Chicago *(G-4606)*

### *2369 Girls' & Infants' Outerwear, NEC*

▲ **Bee Sales Comapny** D 847 600-4400
Niles *(G-15965)*
**Cloz Companies Inc** E 773 247-8879
Skokie *(G-19983)*
**Elite Kids** G 815 451-9600
Crystal Lake *(G-7572)*
**Goldfish Swim School Lincoln** E 773 588-7946
Chicago *(G-4975)*
**Lauren Lein Ltd** E 312 527-1714
Chicago *(G-5468)*
**Laurenceleste Inc** G 708 383-3432
Oak Park *(G-16674)*
**Little Journeys Limited** G 847 677-0350
Skokie *(G-20030)*
**Moonbeam Babies** G 847 245-7371
Lindenhurst *(G-13548)*
▼ **Slick Sugar Inc** G 815 782-7101
Plainfield *(G-17649)*
**Trim Suits By Show-Off Inc** G 630 894-0100
Roselle *(G-18984)*

### *2371 Fur Goods*

**Excelled Sheepskin & Lea Coat** E 309 852-3341
Kewanee *(G-12683)*

### *2381 Dress & Work Gloves*

▲ **Boss Holdings Inc** D 309 852-2131
Kewanee *(G-12673)*
▲ **Boss Manufacturing Holdings** F 309 852-2781
Kewanee *(G-12675)*
**Illinois Glove Company** G 800 342-5458
Northbrook *(G-16272)*
**Klein Tools Inc** D 847 228-6999
Elk Grove Village *(G-9577)*
**Klein Tools Inc** E 847 821-5500
Lincolnshire *(G-13461)*
▲ **Kunz Glove Co Inc** E 312 733-8780
Chicago *(G-5414)*
▲ **Magid Glove Safety Mfg Co LLC** B 773 384-2070
Romeoville *(G-18841)*
**Magid Glove Safety Mfg Co LLC** B 773 384-2070
Chicago *(G-5601)*
**Nationwide Glove Co Inc** D 618 252-7192
Harrisburg *(G-11602)*
**PW Masonry Inc** G 847 573-0510
Libertyville *(G-13372)*
**Wells Lamont Indust Group LLC** A 800 247-3295
Niles *(G-16046)*

### *2384 Robes & Dressing Gowns*

**Halanick Enterprises Inc** E 708 403-3334
Orland Park *(G-16864)*
**Herff Jones LLC** C 317 612-3705
Hillside *(G-11918)*

SIC

Employee Codes: A=Over 500 employees, B=251-500
C=101-250, D=51-100, E=20-50, F=10-19, G=3-9
2017 Harris Illinois
Industrial Directory
931

## 23 APPAREL AND OTHER FINISHED PRODUCTS MADE FROM FABRICS AND SIMILAR MATERIAL

Maries Custom Made Choir Robes .......... G ....... 773 826-1214
  Chicago (G-5618)
▲ Telegraph Hill Inc .......................... G ....... 415 252-9097
  Vernon Hills (G-21207)

### 2385 Waterproof Outerwear

▲ Boss Holdings Inc .......................... D ....... 309 852-2131
  Kewanee (G-12673)
▲ Boss Manufacturing Holdings .......... F ....... 309 852-2781
  Kewanee (G-12675)
Drug Testing Suppliers Inc .................. G ....... 618 208-3810
  Godfrey (G-11224)
▲ Petra Manufacturing Co .................... D ....... 773 622-1475
  Chicago (G-6113)
Polyconversions Inc .......................... E ....... 217 893-3330
  Rantoul (G-17935)
Ryan Products Inc ............................ G ....... 847 670-9071
  Arlington Heights (G-833)

### 2386 Leather & Sheep Lined Clothing

Excelled Sheepskin & Lea Coat ............ C ....... 309 852-3341
  Kewanee (G-12682)
Excelled Sheepskin & Lea Coat ............ E ....... 309 852-3341
  Kewanee (G-12683)
Keleen Leathers Inc .......................... F ....... 630 590-5300
  Westmont (G-21898)

### 2387 Apparel Belts

Loren Girovich .................................. G ....... 773 334-1444
  Chicago (G-5541)

### 2389 Apparel & Accessories, NEC

Akshar Limited .................................. G ....... 815 942-1433
  Morris (G-15091)
Allen Larson .................................... G ....... 773 454-2210
  Chicago (G-3811)
▲ American Church Supply .................. G ....... 847 464-4140
  Saint Charles (G-19134)
Andrea and ME and ME Too ................ G ....... 708 955-3850
  Richton Park (G-17976)
Andy Dallas & Co ............................ F ....... 217 351-5974
  Champaign (G-3450)
Baxter Healthcare Corporation ............ E ....... 847 578-4671
  Waukegan (G-21529)
▼ Bazaar Inc .................................. D ....... 708 583-1800
  River Grove (G-18006)
Browns Global Exchange .................... D ....... 708 345-0955
  Maywood (G-14421)
C H Millery LLC .............................. F ....... 773 476-7525
  Chicago (G-4204)
Chicago Harley Davidson Inc .............. G ....... 312 274-9666
  Chicago (G-4322)
▲ Chicago Protective Apparel Inc ........ D ....... 847 674-7900
  Skokie (G-19980)
Custom & Hard To Find Wigs .............. F ....... 773 777-0222
  Chicago (G-4519)
▲ Daniel Bruce LLC .......................... F ....... 917 583-1538
  Palatine (G-17019)
▲ Demoulin Brothers & Company .......... C ....... 618 664-2000
  Greenville (G-11391)
Demoulin Brothers & Company ............ E ....... 618 533-3810
  Centralia (G-3411)
Facemakers Inc ................................ F ....... 815 273-3944
  Savanna (G-19398)
Facemakers Inc ................................ G ....... 815 273-3944
  Savanna (G-19399)
Fanfest Corporation .......................... G ....... 847 658-2000
  Crystal Lake (G-7576)
▲ Gennco International Inc ................ F ....... 847 541-3333
  Wheeling (G-22062)
Herff Jones LLC .............................. C ....... 217 268-4543
  Arcola (G-670)
Herff Jones LLC .............................. C ....... 317 612-3705
  Hillside (G-11918)
▲ Jero Medical Eqp & Sups Inc .......... E ....... 773 305-4193
  Chicago (G-5295)
K&G Mens Company Inc .................... G ....... 708 349-2579
  Orland Park (G-16871)
◆ Learning Curve International .......... E ....... 630 573-7200
  Oak Brook (G-16533)
Midwest Pub Safety Outfitters ............ F ....... 866 985-0013
  Poplar Grove (G-17714)
▲ Nali Inc .................................... E ....... 708 442-8710
  Clarendon Hills (G-7259)
New York & Company Inc .................. F ....... 630 232-7693
  Geneva (G-10853)
New York & Company Inc .................. F ....... 630 783-2910
  Bolingbrook (G-2352)

Nu-Life Inc of Illinois ........................ G ....... 618 943-4500
  Lawrenceville (G-13203)
Orr Marketing Corp .......................... F ....... 847 401-5171
  Elgin (G-9130)
Phoebe & Frances ............................ F ....... 847 446-5480
  Winnetka (G-22314)
Pollack Service ................................ D ....... 773 528-8096
  Chicago (G-6149)
Roq Innovation LLC .......................... G ....... 917 770-2403
  Chicago (G-6392)
Sieden Sticker USA Ltd ...................... G ....... 312 280-7711
  Chicago (G-6505)
Songear Holding Company LLC .......... G ....... 630 699-1119
  Elmhurst (G-9939)
▲ Sunnywood Incorporated ................ G ....... 815 675-9777
  Spring Grove (G-20366)
Taitt Burial Garments ........................ G ....... 773 483-7424
  Chicago (G-6667)
▲ Wedding Brand Investors LLC .......... E ....... 847 887-0071
  Wauconda (G-21513)
Wish Collection ................................ G ....... 205 324-0209
  Chicago (G-7007)
▲ Zagone Studio LLC ........................ E ....... 773 509-0610
  Melrose Park (G-14713)

### 2391 Curtains & Draperies

A B Kelly Inc .................................. G ....... 847 639-1022
  Cary (G-3320)
A D Specialty Sewing ........................ G ....... 847 639-0390
  Fox River Grove (G-10285)
ADM International Inc ........................ F ....... 773 774-2400
  North Chicago (G-16173)
Aracon Drpery Vntian Blind Ltd ............ G ....... 773 252-1281
  Chicago (G-3930)
Baker Drapery Corporation .................. G ....... 309 691-3295
  Peoria (G-17313)
Berg Industries Inc .......................... F ....... 815 874-1588
  Rockford (G-18280)
Cdc Group Inc ................................ F ....... 847 480-8830
  Chicago (G-4262)
Dezign Sewing Inc ............................ G ....... 773 549-4336
  Chicago (G-4590)
Dons Drapery Service ........................ G ....... 815 385-4759
  McHenry (G-14497)
Drapery House Inc .......................... G ....... 847 318-1161
  Park Ridge (G-17191)
Drapery Room Inc ............................ F ....... 708 301-3374
  Homer Glen (G-12077)
Draperyland Inc .............................. F ....... 630 521-1000
  Wood Dale (G-22360)
Drexel House of Drapes Inc ................ G ....... 618 624-5415
  Belleville (G-1627)
E J Self Furniture ............................ G ....... 847 394-0899
  Mount Prospect (G-15327)
Indecor Inc .................................... F ....... 773 561-7670
  Morton Grove (G-15202)
Interior Fashions Contract .................. G ....... 847 358-6050
  Palatine (G-17044)
Loraes Drapery Workroom Inc ............ G ....... 847 358-7999
  Palatine (G-17051)
▲ Marvin Feig & Associates Inc .......... F ....... 773 384-5228
  Niles (G-16001)
North-West Drapery Service ................ G ....... 773 282-7117
  Chicago (G-5937)
Olshaws Interior Services .................. G ....... 312 421-3131
  Chicago (G-5985)
Parenteau Studios ............................ E ....... 312 337-8015
  Chicago (G-6081)
Roberts Draperies Center Inc .............. G ....... 847 255-4040
  Mount Prospect (G-15370)
Rogers Custom Trims Inc .................... G ....... 773 745-6577
  Chicago (G-6380)
Shade Aire Company .......................... G ....... 815 623-7597
  Roscoe (G-18921)
Shade Brookline Co .......................... F ....... 773 274-5513
  Chicago (G-6487)
Slagel Drapery Service ...................... G ....... 815 692-3834
  Fairbury (G-10132)
Tailored Inc .................................... G ....... 708 387-9854
  Brookfield (G-2643)
Tazewell Floor Covering Inc ................ G ....... 309 266-6371
  Morton (G-15184)
Tenggren-Mehl Co Inc ........................ G ....... 773 763-3290
  Chicago (G-6700)
Tres Joli Designs Ltd ........................ F ....... 847 520-3903
  Wheeling (G-22168)
Unitex Industries Inc ........................ G ....... 708 524-0664
  Oak Park (G-16690)
Whiteside Drapery Fabricators ............ G ....... 847 746-5300
  Zion (G-22701)

Zirlin Interiors Inc ............................ E ....... 773 334-5530
  Chicago (G-7069)

### 2392 House furnishings: Textile

A D Specialty Sewing ........................ G ....... 847 639-0390
  Fox River Grove (G-10285)
Ameriguard Corporation ...................... G ....... 630 986-1900
  Burr Ridge (G-2822)
Ameritex Industries Inc ...................... F ....... 217 324-4044
  Litchfield (G-13681)
▲ Bean Products Inc .......................... E ....... 312 666-3600
  Chicago (G-4064)
Besleys Accessories Inc .................... G ....... 773 561-3300
  Chicago (G-4089)
Bio Star Films LLC ............................ G ....... 773 254-5959
  Chicago (G-4108)
Caroline Cole Inc ............................ F ....... 618 233-0600
  Belleville (G-1617)
▼ Cotton Goods Manufacturing Co ........ F ....... 773 265-0088
  Chicago (G-4481)
▲ Don Leventhal Group LLC ................ E ....... 618 783-4424
  Newton (G-15939)
Eastern Accents Inc .......................... C ....... 773 604-7300
  Chicago (G-4683)
Encompass Group LLC ........................ E ....... 847 680-3388
  Mundelein (G-15499)
Envision Unlimited ............................ E ....... 773 651-1100
  Chicago (G-4766)
▲ FHP-Berner USA LP ........................ E ....... 630 270-1400
  Aurora (G-1008)
◆ Freudenberg Household Pdts LP ...... C ....... 630 270-1400
  Aurora (G-1010)
Green Energy Solutions Inc ................ F ....... 708 672-1900
  Crete (G-7514)
I M M Inc ...................................... F ....... 773 767-3700
  Chicago (G-5131)
▲ Ileesh Products LLC ...................... E ....... 847 383-6695
  Vernon Hills (G-21172)
▲ Innocor Foam Tech W Chcago LLC .... E ....... 732 945-6222
  West Chicago (G-21722)
Interior Fashions Contract .................. G ....... 847 358-6050
  Palatine (G-17044)
▲ Jab Distributors LLC ...................... E ....... 847 998-6901
  Wheeling (G-22079)
L & W Bedding Inc ............................ G ....... 309 762-6019
  Moline (G-14951)
▲ Libman Company ............................ C ....... 217 268-4200
  Arcola (G-675)
My Konjac Sponge Inc ........................ F ....... 630 345-3653
  North Barrington (G-16154)
Pacific Coast Feather Company .......... G ....... 847 827-1210
  Des Plaines (G-8248)
Personalized Pillows Co ...................... G ....... 847 226-7393
  Wadsworth (G-21325)
Peterson Dermond Design LLC ............ G ....... 414 383-5029
  Evanston (G-10085)
Piccolino Inc .................................. G ....... 708 259-2072
  Hinsdale (G-11957)
▲ Pillow Factory Inc .......................... F ....... 847 680-3388
  Buffalo Grove (G-2752)
Pyar & Company LLC ........................ G ....... 312 451-5073
  Chicago (G-6232)
◆ Qst Industries Inc .......................... E ....... 312 930-9400
  Chicago (G-6237)
Quiltmaster Inc ................................ E ....... 847 426-6741
  Carpentersville (G-3300)
Rome Metal Mfg Inc .......................... G ....... 773 287-1755
  Chicago (G-6389)
Shiir Rugs LLC ................................ G ....... 312 828-0400
  Chicago (G-6497)
Slagel Drapery Service ...................... G ....... 815 692-3834
  Fairbury (G-10132)
Superior Table Pad Co ...................... G ....... 773 248-7232
  Chicago (G-6636)
Tailored Inc .................................... G ....... 708 387-9854
  Brookfield (G-2643)
Unitex Industries Inc ........................ G ....... 708 524-0664
  Oak Park (G-16690)
Van Stockum Kristine ........................ G ....... 847 914-0015
  Deerfield (G-8064)
Vida Enterprises Inc .......................... G ....... 312 808-0088
  Chicago (G-6895)

### 2393 Textile Bags

▲ ABG Bag Inc ................................ F ....... 815 963-9525
  Rockford (G-18247)
Advance Tools LLC .......................... G ....... 855 685-0633
  Glenview (G-11097)
Ajr Enterprises Inc .......................... C ....... 630 377-8886
  Saint Charles (G-19132)

SIC SECTION 23 APPAREL AND OTHER FINISHED PRODUCTS MADE FROM FABRICS AND SIMILAR MATERIAL

▼ **Amcraft Manufacturing Inc** F 847 439-4565
Elk Grove Village *(G-9294)*
▲ **Bearse Manufacturing Co** D 773 235-8710
Chicago *(G-4068)*
**Beas Bags** G 847 486-1943
Glenview *(G-11106)*
▲ **Block and Company Inc** C 847 537-7200
Wheeling *(G-22015)*
**Deady Brian Rfg Inc** G 708 479-8249
Orland Park *(G-16853)*
▲ **Hunter-Nusport Inc** G 815 254-7520
Plainfield *(G-17607)*
**Inventive Concepts Intl LLC** G 847 350-6102
Glendale Heights *(G-11035)*
▲ **J Design Works Inc** G 847 812-0891
Bolingbrook *(G-2326)*
**Jarries Shoe Bags** G 773 379-4044
Chicago *(G-5280)*
**Keeper Thermal Bag Co Inc** G 630 213-0125
Bartlett *(G-1359)*
◆ **Midwesco Filter Resources Inc** C 540 773-4780
Niles *(G-16006)*
▲ **Omg Handbags LLC** G 847 337-9499
Chicago *(G-5989)*
**Ryan Products Inc** G 847 670-9071
Arlington Heights *(G-833)*
**Sea-Rich Corp** G 773 261-6633
Chicago *(G-6464)*
**Terre Haute Tent & Awning Inc** F 812 235-6068
South Holland *(G-20309)*

## *2394 Canvas Prdts*

**A B Kelly Inc** G 847 639-1022
Cary *(G-3320)*
**Acme Awning Co** G 847 446-0153
Highland Park *(G-11822)*
**Air Land and Sea Interiors** G 630 834-1717
Villa Park *(G-21234)*
◆ **Americana Building Pdts Inc** D 618 548-2800
Salem *(G-19326)*
▲ **Awnings By Zip Dee Inc** E 847 640-0460
Elk Grove Village *(G-9326)*
**Berg Industries Inc** F 815 874-1588
Rockford *(G-18280)*
**Blake Co Inc** G 815 962-3852
Rockford *(G-18287)*
**Bloomington Tent & Awning Inc** G 309 828-3411
Bloomington *(G-2150)*
**Brian Robert Awning Co** G 847 679-1140
Skokie *(G-19970)*
**Brumleve Industries Inc** F 217 857-3777
Teutopolis *(G-20847)*
**Canvas Creations Inc** G 309 343-5082
Galesburg *(G-10741)*
**Champaign Cnty Tent & Awng Co** E 217 328-5749
Urbana *(G-21077)*
**Chesterfield Awning Co Inc** F 708 596-4434
South Holland *(G-20256)*
**Chicago Dropcloth Tarpaulin Co** E 773 588-3123
Chicago *(G-4316)*
**Creative Covers Inc** G 708 233-6880
Bridgeview *(G-2480)*
**Custom Canvas LLC** G 847 587-0225
Ingleside *(G-12188)*
**Eclipse Awnings Inc** F 708 636-3160
Evergreen Park *(G-10113)*
**Ed Hill S Custom Canvas** G 815 476-5042
Wilmington *(G-22271)*
**Environetics Inc** F 815 838-8331
Lockport *(G-13715)*
**Evanston Awning Company** F 847 864-4520
Evanston *(G-10032)*
◆ **Event Equipment Sales LLC** F 708 352-0662
Hodgkins *(G-11974)*
**Flex-O-Glass Inc** D 773 261-5200
Chicago *(G-4858)*
**Haakes Awning** G 618 529-4808
Carbondale *(G-3009)*
**Hunzinger Williams Inc** F 847 381-1878
Lake Barrington *(G-12810)*
**Jelinek & Sons Inc** G 630 355-3474
Plainfield *(G-17610)*
**Johnson Seat & Canvas Shop** G 815 756-2037
Cortland *(G-7389)*
**Kankakee Tent & Awning Co** G 815 932-8000
Kankakee *(G-12634)*
**Kastelic Canvas Inc** G 815 436-8160
Plainfield *(G-17615)*
▲ **Kroto Inc** E 800 980-1089
Morton Grove *(G-15210)*
▲ **M Mauritzon & Company Inc** E 773 235-6000
Chicago *(G-5584)*
**M Putterman & Co LLC** G 773 734-1000
Chicago *(G-5586)*
▲ **M Putterman & Co LLC** D 773 927-4120
Chicago *(G-5585)*
**Magna Extrors Intrors Amer Inc** G 847 548-9170
Grayslake *(G-11353)*
**Material Control Inc** F 630 892-4274
Batavia *(G-1467)*
**Midwest Awnings Inc** G 309 762-3339
Cameron *(G-2970)*
**Mpc Containment Systems LLC** D 773 927-4121
Chicago *(G-5822)*
**Mpc Containment Systems LLC** E 773 734-1000
Chicago *(G-5823)*
**Mpc Group LLC** G 773 927-4120
Chicago *(G-5824)*
**Nieman & Considine Inc** F 312 326-1053
Chicago *(G-5914)*
**North Sails Group LLC** G 773 489-1308
Chicago *(G-5936)*
**Nuyen Awning Co** G 630 892-3995
Aurora *(G-1197)*
**Ogden Top & Trim Shop Inc** G 708 484-5422
Berwyn *(G-2070)*
**Ottos Canvas Shop** G 217 543-3307
Arthur *(G-917)*
**Polyair Inter Pack Inc** D 773 995-1818
Chicago *(G-6153)*
**Rehabilitation and Vocational** E 618 833-5344
Anna *(G-608)*
▼ **Seamcraft International LLC** E 773 417-4002
Chicago *(G-6466)*
**Shading Solutions Group Inc** G 630 444-2102
Geneva *(G-10866)*
**Shelter Systems** G 773 281-9270
Chicago *(G-6495)*
**Sleep6 LLC** G 844 375-3376
Chicago *(G-6528)*
**Stritzel Awnng Svc/Aurra Tent** E 630 420-2000
Plainfield *(G-17654)*
**Tarps Manufacturing Inc** F 217 584-1900
Meredosia *(G-14735)*
**Terre Haute Tent & Awning Inc** F 812 235-6068
South Holland *(G-20309)*
**Thatcher Oaks Inc** E 630 833-5700
Elmhurst *(G-9950)*
**Traube Canvas Products Inc** F 618 281-0696
Dupo *(G-8581)*
**Tri City Canvas Products Inc** F 618 797-1662
Granite City *(G-11308)*
**Tri Vantage LLC** F 630 530-5333
Elmhurst *(G-9952)*
**United Canvas Inc** E 847 395-1470
Antioch *(G-661)*

## *2395 Pleating & Stitching For The Trade*

**A B S Embroidery Inc** G 708 597-7785
Alsip *(G-427)*
**A Plus Apparel** G 815 675-2117
Spring Grove *(G-20323)*
**Acme Button & Buttonhole Co** G 773 907-8400
Chicago *(G-3731)*
**Action Screen Print Inc** F 630 393-1990
Warrenville *(G-21340)*
**Advanced Flexible Mtls LLC** F 770 222-6000
Chicago *(G-3769)*
**All In Stitches** G 309 944-4084
Geneseo *(G-10796)*
**All Stars -N- Stitches Inc** G 618 435-5555
Benton *(G-2021)*
**Allstar Embroidery** G 847 913-1133
Buffalo Grove *(G-2655)*
**Alternative TS** G 618 257-0230
Belleville *(G-1608)*
**Ameri-Tex** G 847 247-0777
Mundelein *(G-15469)*
**American EMB & Screen Prtg LLC** G 630 766-2825
Glendale Heights *(G-11008)*
**Art-Flo Shirt & Lettering Co** E 708 656-5422
Chicago *(G-3953)*
**ASap Specialties Inc Del** G 847 223-7699
Grayslake *(G-11321)*
**Athletic Outfitters Inc** G 815 942-6696
Morris *(G-15094)*
**Award Emblem Mfg Co Inc** F 630 739-0800
Bolingbrook *(G-2281)*
**B & B Custom TS & Gifts** G 618 463-0443
Alton *(G-562)*
**B JS Printables** G 618 656-8625
Edwardsville *(G-8789)*
**Barnes & Noble College** E 309 677-2320
Peoria *(G-17314)*
**Bean Stich Inc** G 630 422-1269
Bensenville *(G-1841)*
**Bee Designs Embroidery & Scree** G 815 393-4593
Malta *(G-14165)*
**Blandings Ltd** G 773 478-3542
Chicago *(G-4122)*
**Brownfield Sports Inc** G 217 367-8321
Urbana *(G-21074)*
**Bullseye Imprinting & EMB** G 630 834-8175
Elmhurst *(G-9844)*
**C & C Embroidery Inc** G 815 777-6167
Galena *(G-10715)*
**C & C Sport Stop** G 618 632-7812
O Fallon *(G-16464)*
**Camilles of Canton Inc** G 309 647-7403
Canton *(G-2983)*
**Chicago Knitting Mills** G 773 463-1464
Chicago *(G-4326)*
**Chicago Printing and EMB Inc** F 630 628-1777
Addison *(G-75)*
**Classic Embroidery Inc** F 708 485-7034
Chicago *(G-4392)*
**Cloz Companies Inc** E 773 247-8879
Skokie *(G-19983)*
**Cottage Collage** G 847 541-7205
Buffalo Grove *(G-2681)*
**Cq Industries Inc** G 630 530-0177
Elmhurst *(G-9857)*
**Creative Clothing Created 4 U** G 847 543-0051
Grayslake *(G-11330)*
**Cubby Hole of Carlinville Inc** F 217 854-8511
Carlinville *(G-3035)*
**Custom AP & Promotions Inc** G 815 398-9823
Rockford *(G-18326)*
**Custom Enterprises** G 618 439-6626
Benton *(G-2025)*
**Custom Monogramming** G 815 625-9044
Rock Falls *(G-18130)*
**D & D Embroidery** G 309 266-7092
Morton *(G-15156)*
▲ **D & J International Inc** F 847 966-9260
Niles *(G-15974)*
**Dabel Incorporated** G 217 398-3389
Champaign *(G-3472)*
**Design Loft Imaging Inc** G 847 439-2486
Elk Grove Village *(G-9425)*
**Digistitch Embroidery & Design** G 773 229-8630
Chicago *(G-4598)*
**Dilars Embroidery & Monograms** G 815 338-6066
Woodstock *(G-22560)*
**Donghia Showrooms Inc** G 312 822-0766
Chicago *(G-4627)*
**Doras Spinning Wheel Inc** G 618 466-1900
Alton *(G-571)*
**Downtown Sports** G 815 284-2255
Dixon *(G-8330)*
**Dpe Incorporated** G 773 306-0105
Chicago *(G-4640)*
**Elegant Embroidery Inc** G 847 540-8003
Lake Zurich *(G-13067)*
**Embroidery Choices** G 708 597-9093
Blue Island *(G-2249)*
**Embroidery Experts Inc** E 847 403-0200
Vernon Hills *(G-21160)*
**Embroidery Express Inc** F 630 365-9393
Elburn *(G-8888)*
**Embroidery Services Inc** G 847 588-2660
Niles *(G-15978)*
**Ensign Emblem Ltd** D 217 877-8224
Decatur *(G-7879)*
**Essential Creations** G 773 238-1700
Chicago *(G-4779)*
**Expressions By Christine Inc** F 217 223-2750
Quincy *(G-17827)*
**Fast Lane Threads Custom EMB** G 815 544-9898
Belvidere *(G-1751)*
**Femina Sport Inc** G 630 271-1876
Downers Grove *(G-8442)*
◆ **Fielders Choice** G 618 937-2294
West Frankfort *(G-21807)*
**First Impression** G 815 883-3357
Oglesby *(G-16748)*
**Fitness Wear Inc** G 847 486-1704
Glenview *(G-11125)*
**G and D Enterprises Inc** E 847 981-8661
Arlington Heights *(G-757)*

SIC

Employee Codes: A=Over 500 employees, B=251-500
C=101-250, D=51-100, E=20-50, F=10-19, G=3-9

2017 Harris Illinois
Industrial Directory

933

23 APPAREL AND OTHER FINISHED PRODUCTS MADE FROM FABRICS AND SIMILAR MATERIAL SIC SECTION

**Galaxy Embroidery Inc** ........ G ....... 312 243-8991
Chicago *(G-4908)*
**Gavina Graphics** ........ F ....... 217 345-9228
Charleston *(G-3598)*
**Harlan Vance Company** ........ F ....... 309 888-4804
Normal *(G-16072)*
▲ **Hermans Inc** ........ E ....... 309 206-4892
Rock Island *(G-18181)*
**Hi-Five Sportswear Inc** ........ G ....... 815 637-6044
Machesney Park *(G-14079)*
**Hyperstitch** ........ F ....... 815 568-0590
Marengo *(G-14230)*
**I D Togs** ........ G ....... 618 235-1538
Belleville *(G-1635)*
**Illinois Embroidery Service** ........ G ....... 618 526-8006
Breese *(G-2445)*
**Image Plus Inc** ........ G ....... 630 852-4920
Downers Grove *(G-8463)*
**Initial Choice** ........ F ....... 847 234-5884
Lake Forest *(G-12917)*
**J C Embroidery & Screen Print** ........ G ....... 630 595-4670
Bensenville *(G-1926)*
**James Randall** ........ G ....... 309 444-8765
Washington *(G-21384)*
**Janes Lettering Service Inc** ........ G ....... 309 243-7669
Dunlap *(G-8568)*
**Johnos Inc** ........ G ....... 630 897-6929
Aurora *(G-1178)*
**Keneal Industries Inc** ........ F ....... 815 886-1300
Romeoville *(G-18834)*
**Langa Resource Group Inc** ........ G ....... 618 462-1899
Alton *(G-581)*
**M&M Embroidery Corp** ........ G ....... 847 209-1086
Palatine *(G-17052)*
**Midwest Stitch** ........ G ....... 815 394-1516
Rockford *(G-18507)*
**Midwest Swiss Embroideries Co** ........ E ....... 773 631-7120
Chicago *(G-5750)*
**Minerva Sportswear Inc** ........ F ....... 309 661-2387
Bloomington *(G-2201)*
**Minor League Inc** ........ G ....... 618 548-8040
Salem *(G-19339)*
**Monograms & More** ........ G ....... 630 789-8424
Burr Ridge *(G-2869)*
**Mt Greenwood Embroidery** ........ G ....... 773 779-5798
Chicago *(G-5827)*
**Need To Know Inc** ........ G ....... 309 691-3877
Peoria *(G-17415)*
**Nelson Enterprises Inc** ........ G ....... 815 633-1100
Roscoe *(G-18910)*
**Orland Sports Ltd** ........ G ....... 773 685-3711
Chicago *(G-6014)*
**Personalized Threads** ........ G ....... 815 431-1815
Ottawa *(G-16978)*
**Promotional TS** ........ G ....... 312 243-8991
Chicago *(G-6215)*
**Quilt Merchant** ........ F ....... 630 480-3000
Winfield *(G-22291)*
**Quiltmaster Inc** ........ E ....... 847 426-6741
Carpentersville *(G-3300)*
**Reel Mate Mfg Co** ........ G ....... 708 423-8005
Oak Lawn *(G-16643)*
**Rh Development** ........ F ....... 773 331-3772
Chicago *(G-6347)*
**Rock Tops Inc** ........ G ....... 708 672-1450
Crete *(G-7518)*
**Ronald J Nixon** ........ G ....... 708 748-8130
Park Forest *(G-17175)*
**Roselynn Fashions** ........ G ....... 847 741-6000
Elgin *(G-9167)*
**S & R Monogramming Inc** ........ G ....... 630 369-5468
Winfield *(G-22292)*
**Sango Embroidery** ........ G ....... 773 582-4354
Chicago *(G-6439)*
**Second Chance Inc** ........ F ....... 630 904-5955
Naperville *(G-15826)*
**Select Screen Prints & EMB** ........ F ....... 309 829-6511
Bloomington *(G-2222)*
**Senn Enterprises Inc** ........ G ....... 309 673-4384
Peoria *(G-17451)*
**Senn Enterprises Inc** ........ F ....... 309 637-1147
Peoria *(G-17450)*
**Sewing Salon** ........ G ....... 217 345-3886
Charleston *(G-3611)*
**Shirt Tales** ........ G ....... 618 662-4572
Flora *(G-10216)*
**Signature of Chicago Inc** ........ G ....... 630 271-1876
Downers Grove *(G-8523)*
**Sports Designs & Graphics** ........ E ....... 217 342-2777
Effingham *(G-8859)*
**Stans Sportsworld Inc** ........ G ....... 217 359-8474
Champaign *(G-3547)*
**Star Silkscreen Design Inc** ........ G ....... 217 877-0804
Decatur *(G-7943)*
**Stitch By Stitch Incorporated** ........ G ....... 847 541-2543
Prospect Heights *(G-17784)*
**Stitch Magic Usa Inc** ........ E ....... 847 836-5000
West Dundee *(G-21802)*
**Stitchables Embroidery** ........ G ....... 217 322-3000
Rushville *(G-19096)*
**Stitchin Image** ........ G ....... 815 578-9890
Richmond *(G-17973)*
**T Graphics** ........ G ....... 618 592-4145
Oblong *(G-16735)*
**Time Embroidery** ........ G ....... 847 364-4371
Elk Grove Village *(G-9780)*
**Top Shelf Quilts Inc** ........ G ....... 815 806-1694
Frankfort *(G-10370)*
**Town Hall Sports Inc** ........ F ....... 618 235-9881
Belleville *(G-1682)*
▲ **Trading Square Company Inc** ........ G ....... 630 960-0606
Westmont *(G-21925)*
**Triangle Screen Print Inc** ........ F ....... 847 678-9200
Franklin Park *(G-10612)*
**Trimark Screen Printing Inc** ........ G ....... 630 629-2823
Lombard *(G-13872)*
**Tryad Specialties Inc** ........ F ....... 630 549-0079
Saint Charles *(G-19287)*
**Twin Towers Marketing** ........ G ....... 815 544-5554
Belvidere *(G-1791)*
**U Keep US In Stitches** ........ G ....... 847 427-8127
Mount Prospect *(G-15380)*
**U R On It** ........ G ....... 847 382-0182
Lake Barrington *(G-12826)*
**Ultimate Distributing Inc** ........ G ....... 847 566-2250
Mundelein *(G-15565)*
**USA Embroidery** ........ G ....... 309 692-1391
Peoria *(G-17475)*
**Visual Persuasion Inc** ........ F ....... 815 899-6609
Sycamore *(G-20823)*
**Waist Up Imprntd Sprtswear LLC** ........ G ....... 847 963-1400
Palatine *(G-17086)*
**Waldos Sports Corner Inc** ........ G ....... 309 688-2425
Peoria *(G-17477)*
**Wellspring Investments LLC** ........ G ....... 773 736-1213
Chicago *(G-6955)*
**Welsh Industries Ltd** ........ E ....... 815 756-1111
Dekalb *(G-8131)*
**Winning Stitch** ........ G ....... 217 348-8279
Charleston *(G-3616)*
**Winning Streak Inc** ........ E ....... 618 277-8191
Dupo *(G-8584)*
**Woolenwear Co** ........ F ....... 847 520-9243
Prospect Heights *(G-17786)*

## *2396 Automotive Trimmings, Apparel Findings, Related Prdts*

**A & R Screening LLC** ........ F ....... 708 598-2480
Bridgeview *(G-2457)*
**Action Screen Print Inc** ........ F ....... 630 393-1990
Warrenville *(G-21340)*
**Alternative TS** ........ G ....... 618 257-0230
Belleville *(G-1608)*
**American Enlightenment LLC** ........ G ....... 773 687-8996
Chicago *(G-3856)*
▲ **American Graphic Systems Inc** ........ E ....... 708 614-7007
Tinley Park *(G-20890)*
**American Name Plate & Metal De** ........ E ....... 773 376-1400
Chicago *(G-3867)*
**Angels Heavenly Funeral Home** ........ G ....... 773 239-8700
Chicago *(G-3907)*
**Arbetman & Associates** ........ G ....... 708 386-8586
Oak Park *(G-16653)*
**Art Newvo Incorporated** ........ G ....... 847 838-0304
Antioch *(G-619)*
**Art-Flo Shirt & Lettering Co** ........ E ....... 708 656-5422
Chicago *(G-3953)*
**Ashland Screening Corporation** ........ E ....... 708 758-8800
Chicago Heights *(G-7080)*
**Authority Screenprint & EMB** ........ G ....... 630 236-0289
Plainfield *(G-17581)*
**B & B Custom TS & Gifts** ........ G ....... 618 463-0443
Alton *(G-562)*
**B and A Screen Printing** ........ G ....... 217 762-2632
Monticello *(G-15074)*
**B JS Printables** ........ G ....... 618 656-8625
Edwardsville *(G-8789)*
**Bailleu & Bailleu Printing Inc** ........ G ....... 309 852-2517
Kewanee *(G-12670)*
**Bean Stich Inc** ........ G ....... 630 422-1269
Bensenville *(G-1841)*
**Bikast Graphics Inc** ........ G ....... 847 487-8822
Wauconda *(G-21446)*
**Bobbi Screen Printing** ........ G ....... 773 847-8200
Chicago *(G-4134)*
**Bow Brothers Co Inc** ........ G ....... 217 359-0555
Champaign *(G-3457)*
**Breedlove Sporting Goods Inc** ........ F ....... 309 852-2434
Kewanee *(G-12677)*
**Breedlove Sporting Goods Inc** ........ F ....... 309 852-2434
Kewanee *(G-12678)*
**Brownfield Sports Inc** ........ G ....... 217 367-8321
Urbana *(G-21074)*
**C & C Sport Stop** ........ G ....... 618 632-7812
O Fallon *(G-16464)*
**Carl Gorr Printing Co** ........ G ....... 815 338-3191
Woodstock *(G-22549)*
**Chicago Shirt & Lettering Co** ........ G ....... 773 745-0222
Chicago *(G-4348)*
**Classic Screen Printing Inc** ........ F ....... 708 771-9355
Forest Park *(G-10239)*
**Color Tone Printing** ........ G ....... 708 385-1442
Blue Island *(G-2242)*
**Cook Merritt** ........ G ....... 630 980-3070
Roselle *(G-18934)*
**Creative Clothing Created 4 U** ........ G ....... 847 543-0051
Grayslake *(G-11330)*
**Cubby Hole of Carlinville Inc** ........ F ....... 217 854-8511
Carlinville *(G-3035)*
**Custom Enterprises** ........ G ....... 618 439-6626
Benton *(G-2025)*
**Custom Monogramming** ........ G ....... 815 625-9044
Rock Falls *(G-18130)*
**Custom Telephone Printing Inc** ........ F ....... 815 338-0000
Woodstock *(G-22557)*
**Custom Towels Inc** ........ G ....... 618 539-5005
Freeburg *(G-10634)*
**Custom Trophies** ........ G ....... 217 422-3353
Decatur *(G-7863)*
**Dabel Incorporated** ........ G ....... 217 398-3389
Champaign *(G-3472)*
**Darnall Printing** ........ G ....... 309 827-7212
Bloomington *(G-2161)*
**Desk & Door Nameplate Company** ........ F ....... 815 806-8670
Frankfort *(G-10312)*
▲ **Diemasters Manufacturing Inc** ........ C ....... 847 640-9900
Elk Grove Village *(G-9429)*
**DMarv Design Specialty Prtrs** ........ G ....... 708 389-4420
Blue Island *(G-2246)*
**Earl Ad Inc** ........ G ....... 312 666-7106
Chicago *(G-4673)*
**Enterprise Signs Inc** ........ G ....... 773 614-8324
Chicago *(G-4760)*
**ESP T-Shirt Co Inc** ........ G ....... 630 393-1033
Warrenville *(G-21346)*
▲ **Excel Screen Prtg & EMB Inc** ........ D ....... 847 801-5200
Schiller Park *(G-19830)*
**Fantastic Lettering Inc** ........ G ....... 773 685-7650
Chicago *(G-4812)*
**Fast Lane Threads Custom EMB** ........ G ....... 815 544-9898
Belvidere *(G-1751)*
**Fitness Wear Inc** ........ G ....... 847 486-1704
Glenview *(G-11125)*
**Fresh Concept Enterprises Inc** ........ G ....... 815 254-7295
Plainfield *(G-17601)*
**G and D Enterprises Inc** ........ E ....... 847 981-8661
Arlington Heights *(G-757)*
**Gabriel Enterprises** ........ G ....... 773 342-8705
Chicago *(G-4906)*
**Gcg Corp** ........ G ....... 847 298-2285
Glenview *(G-11128)*
**George Lauterer Corporation** ........ E ....... 312 913-1881
Chicago *(G-4943)*
**Go Van Goghs Tee Shirt** ........ G ....... 309 342-1112
Galesburg *(G-10755)*
**Good Impressions Inc** ........ G ....... 847 831-4317
Highland Park *(G-11836)*
**Graphic Screen Printing Inc** ........ G ....... 708 429-3330
Orland Park *(G-16863)*
**Hamsher Lakeside Funerals** ........ G ....... 847 587-2100
Fox Lake *(G-10277)*
**Hangables Inc** ........ F ....... 847 673-9770
Skokie *(G-20010)*
**Hazen Display Corporation** ........ E ....... 815 248-2925
Davis *(G-7806)*
**Hi-Five Sportswear Inc** ........ G ....... 815 637-6044
Machesney Park *(G-14079)*
**Hole In The Wall Screen Arts** ........ G ....... 217 243-9100
Jacksonville *(G-12391)*

| Company | Code | Phone |
|---|---|---|
| Ikan Creations LLC | G | 312 204-7333 |
| Chicago (G-5150) | | |
| Image Plus Inc | G | 630 852-4920 |
| Downers Grove (G-8463) | | |
| J & D Instant Signs | G | 847 965-2800 |
| Morton Grove (G-15206) | | |
| Johnson Rolan Co Inc | G | 309 674-9671 |
| Peoria (G-17394) | | |
| K and A Graphics Inc | G | 847 244-2345 |
| Gurnee (G-11463) | | |
| Lee-Wel Printing Corporation | G | 630 682-0935 |
| Wheaton (G-21966) | | |
| Linda Levinson Designs Inc | G | 312 951-6943 |
| Chicago (G-5509) | | |
| Lloyd Midwest Graphics | G | 815 282-8828 |
| Machesney Park (G-14089) | | |
| Lochman Ref Silk Screen Co | F | 847 475-6266 |
| Evanston (G-10065) | | |
| Locker Room Screen Printing | G | 630 759-2533 |
| Bolingbrook (G-2337) | | |
| M Wells Printing Co | G | 312 455-0400 |
| Chicago (G-5588) | | |
| Maxs Screen Machine Inc | G | 773 878-4949 |
| Chicago (G-5659) | | |
| Mer-Pla Inc | F | 847 530-9798 |
| Chicago (G-5687) | | |
| Mexacali Silkscreen Inc | G | 630 628-9313 |
| Addison (G-203) | | |
| Mid State Graphics | G | 309 772-3843 |
| Bushnell (G-2906) | | |
| Midwest Stitch | G | 815 394-1516 |
| Rockford (G-18507) | | |
| Mighty Mites Awards and Sons | G | 847 297-0035 |
| Des Plaines (G-8233) | | |
| Minerva Sportswear Inc | F | 309 661-2387 |
| Bloomington (G-2201) | | |
| Nancys Lettering Shop | G | 217 345-6007 |
| Charleston (G-3605) | | |
| Navitor Inc | B | 800 323-0253 |
| Harwood Heights (G-11687) | | |
| Need To Know Inc | G | 309 691-3877 |
| Peoria (G-17415) | | |
| Nu-Art Printing | G | 618 533-9971 |
| Centralia (G-3425) | | |
| Offworld Designs | G | 815 786-7080 |
| Sandwich (G-19372) | | |
| Olympic Trophy and Awards Co | F | 773 631-9500 |
| Chicago (G-5987) | | |
| Outlaw Tees | G | 217 453-2359 |
| Nauvoo (G-15856) | | |
| Paddock Industries Inc | F | 618 277-1580 |
| Smithton (G-20123) | | |
| Papyrus Press Inc | G | 773 342-0700 |
| Chicago (G-6074) | | |
| ▲ Petra Manufacturing Co | G | 773 622-1475 |
| Chicago (G-6113) | | |
| Plastics Printing Group Inc | F | 312 421-7980 |
| Chicago (G-6138) | | |
| Precision Screen Specialties | G | 630 762-9548 |
| Saint Charles (G-19241) | | |
| Printing Works Inc | G | 847 860-1920 |
| Elk Grove Village (G-9698) | | |
| Priority Print | G | 708 485-7080 |
| Brookfield (G-2641) | | |
| ◆ Qst Industries Inc | E | 312 930-9400 |
| Chicago (G-6237) | | |
| Qst Industries Inc | D | 312 930-9400 |
| Chicago (G-6238) | | |
| Quality Spraying Screen Prtg | E | 630 584-8324 |
| Saint Charles (G-19248) | | |
| R J S Silk Screening Co | G | 708 974-3009 |
| Palos Hills (G-17123) | | |
| Rainbow Art Inc | F | 312 421-5600 |
| Chicago (G-6288) | | |
| ▲ Rebel Screeners Inc | G | 312 525-2670 |
| Chicago (G-6310) | | |
| Ribbon Supply Comp | F | 773 237-7979 |
| Chicago (G-6350) | | |
| ▲ Rico Industries Inc | D | 312 427-0313 |
| Niles (G-16028) | | |
| Ronald J Nixon | G | 708 748-8130 |
| Park Forest (G-17175) | | |
| Roselynn Fashions | G | 847 741-6000 |
| Elgin (G-9167) | | |
| RR Donnelley & Sons Company | D | 630 762-7600 |
| Saint Charles (G-19256) | | |
| Russell Doot Inc | G | 312 527-1437 |
| Chicago (G-6415) | | |
| Santana & Daughter Inc | G | 773 237-1818 |
| Chicago (G-6441) | | |
| Scheiwes Print Shop | G | 815 683-2398 |
| Crescent City (G-7456) | | |
| Scorpion Graphics Inc | F | 773 927-3203 |
| Chicago (G-6459) | | |
| Screen Graphics | G | 309 699-8513 |
| Pekin (G-17288) | | |
| Screen Machine Incorporated | G | 847 439-2233 |
| Elk Grove Village (G-9732) | | |
| Select Screen Prints & EMB | F | 309 829-6511 |
| Bloomington (G-2222) | | |
| Sharprint Slkscrn & Grphcs | D | 877 649-2554 |
| Chicago (G-6490) | | |
| ▼ Shree Mahavir Inc | G | 312 408-1080 |
| Chicago (G-6501) | | |
| Signature Label of Illinois | G | 618 283-5145 |
| Vandalia (G-21125) | | |
| Signcraft Screenprint Inc | C | 815 777-3030 |
| Galena (G-10731) | | |
| Signs In Dundee Inc | G | 847 742-9530 |
| Elgin (G-9179) | | |
| Sport Connection | G | 630 980-1787 |
| Roselle (G-18979) | | |
| Stans Sportsworld Inc | G | 217 359-8474 |
| Champaign (G-3547) | | |
| Star Silkscreen Design Inc | G | 217 877-0804 |
| Decatur (G-7943) | | |
| ▲ Stellar Recognition Inc | D | 773 282-8060 |
| Chicago (G-6588) | | |
| Stevens Sign Co Inc | G | 708 562-4888 |
| Northlake (G-16453) | | |
| T J Marche Ltd | G | 618 445-2314 |
| Albion (G-366) | | |
| Team Works By Holzhauer Inc | G | 309 745-9924 |
| Washington (G-21393) | | |
| Teds Shirt Shack Inc | G | 217 224-9705 |
| Quincy (G-17892) | | |
| Think Ink Inc | G | 815 459-4565 |
| Crystal Lake (G-7665) | | |
| Top Notch Silk Screening | G | 773 847-6335 |
| Chicago (G-6744) | | |
| Triangle Screen Print Inc | F | 847 678-9200 |
| Franklin Park (G-10612) | | |
| Trimark Screen Printing Inc | G | 630 629-2823 |
| Lombard (G-13872) | | |
| Type Concepts Inc | G | 708 361-1005 |
| Palos Heights (G-17112) | | |
| Ultimate Distributing Inc | G | 847 566-2250 |
| Mundelein (G-15565) | | |
| ▲ Wagner Zip-Change Inc | E | 708 681-4100 |
| Melrose Park (G-14706) | | |
| Waldos Sports Corner Inc | G | 309 688-2425 |
| Peoria (G-17477) | | |
| Weiskamp Screen Printing | G | 217 398-8428 |
| Champaign (G-3560) | | |
| Wellspring Investments LLC | G | 773 736-1213 |
| Chicago (G-6955) | | |
| Windy City Silkscreening Inc | E | 312 842-0030 |
| Chicago (G-7000) | | |
| Winning Stitch | G | 217 348-8279 |
| Charleston (G-3616) | | |

## 2397 Schiffli Machine Embroideries

| Company | Code | Phone |
|---|---|---|
| Midwest Swiss Embroideries Co | E | 773 631-7120 |
| Chicago (G-5750) | | |

## 2399 Fabricated Textile Prdts, NEC

| Company | Code | Phone |
|---|---|---|
| Action Advertising Inc | G | 312 791-0660 |
| Chicago (G-3740) | | |
| Action Flag Co | G | 800 669-9639 |
| Woodridge (G-22449) | | |
| Ammeraal Beltech Inc | G | 847 673-1736 |
| Skokie (G-19954) | | |
| Bill Weeks Inc | G | 217 523-8735 |
| Springfield (G-20397) | | |
| Deyco Inc | G | 630 553-5666 |
| Yorkville (G-22656) | | |
| Duo North America | G | 312 421-7755 |
| Chicago (G-4652) | | |
| Duracrest Fabrics | G | 847 350-0030 |
| Elk Grove Village (G-9438) | | |
| ▲ E I T Inc | G | 630 359-3543 |
| Naperville (G-15649) | | |
| ▲ Fabric Images Inc | D | 847 488-9877 |
| Elgin (G-9032) | | |
| George Lauterer Corporation | E | 312 913-1881 |
| Chicago (G-4943) | | |
| Girlygirl | G | 708 633-7290 |
| Tinley Park (G-20917) | | |
| Heiman Sign Studio | G | 815 397-6909 |
| Rockford (G-18416) | | |
| Hooker Custom Harness Inc | G | 815 233-5478 |
| Freeport (G-10666) | | |
| ▲ J C Schultz Enterprises Inc | D | 800 323-9127 |
| Batavia (G-1459) | | |
| ▲ Jac US Inc | E | 312 421-2268 |
| Chicago (G-5267) | | |
| Leader Accessories LLC | G | 877 662-9808 |
| Rockton (G-18698) | | |
| McCormicks Enterprises Inc | E | 847 398-8680 |
| Arlington Heights (G-800) | | |
| ▲ Moss Holding Company | C | 847 238-4200 |
| Elk Grove Village (G-9636) | | |
| N Henry & Son Inc | D | 847 870-0797 |
| Itasca (G-12323) | | |
| Rock Tops Inc | G | 708 672-1450 |
| Crete (G-7518) | | |
| Romel Press Inc | G | 708 343-6090 |
| Melrose Park (G-14687) | | |
| Russell Doot Inc | G | 312 527-1437 |
| Chicago (G-6415) | | |
| ▼ Seamcraft International LLC | E | 773 417-4002 |
| Chicago (G-6466) | | |
| ▲ Seasonal Designs Inc | E | 847 688-0280 |
| Waukegan (G-21613) | | |
| Signcraft Screenprint Inc | C | 815 777-3030 |
| Galena (G-10731) | | |
| Tex Trend Inc | E | 847 215-6796 |
| Wheeling (G-22166) | | |
| ▲ Travel Hammock Inc | G | 847 486-0005 |
| Skokie (G-20102) | | |
| W G N Flag & Decorating Co | G | 773 768-8076 |
| Chicago (G-6918) | | |

# 24 LUMBER AND WOOD PRODUCTS, EXCEPT FURNITURE

## 2411 Logging

| Company | Code | Phone |
|---|---|---|
| Beeman & Sons Inc | F | 217 232-4268 |
| Martinsville (G-14332) | | |
| Big Creek Forestry & Logging L | G | 217 822-8282 |
| Marshall (G-14318) | | |
| Billy & Rachel Poignant | G | 309 713-5500 |
| Lacon (G-12785) | | |
| Bourrette Logging | G | 815 591-3761 |
| Hanover (G-11571) | | |
| Brian Kinney | G | 309 206-4219 |
| Rock Island (G-18166) | | |
| Christiansen Sawmill and Log | G | 815 315-7520 |
| Caledonia (G-2931) | | |
| Cnv Enterprises Inc | G | 815 405-6762 |
| Plainfield (G-17589) | | |
| Dust Logging LLC | G | 217 844-2305 |
| Effingham (G-8834) | | |
| Ericson S Log & Lumber Co | G | 309 667-2147 |
| New Windsor (G-15931) | | |
| Frank E Galloway | G | 618 948-2578 |
| Sumner (G-20770) | | |
| G & C Enterprises Inc | G | 618 747-2272 |
| Jonesboro (G-12591) | | |
| Heartland Hardwoods Inc | E | 217 844-3312 |
| Effingham (G-8838) | | |
| Illiana Real Log Homes Inc | G | 815 471-4004 |
| Milford (G-14813) | | |
| Jack Shepard Logging | G | 618 845-3496 |
| Ullin (G-21031) | | |
| K D Custom Sawing Logging | G | 309 231-4805 |
| Green Valley (G-11379) | | |
| Kelly & Son Forestry & Log LLC | G | 815 275-6877 |
| Crystal Lake (G-7598) | | |
| Larry Musgrave Logging | G | 618 842-6386 |
| Fairfield (G-10148) | | |
| Loneoak Timber & Veneere Co | G | 618 426-3065 |
| Ava (G-1239) | | |
| Lonnie Hickam | G | 618 893-4223 |
| Pomona (G-17693) | | |
| Mid-State Timber & Veneer Co | G | 618 423-2619 |
| Ramsey (G-17914) | | |
| Poignant Logging | G | 309 246-5647 |
| Lacon (G-12791) | | |
| Powell Tree Care Inc | G | 847 364-1181 |
| Elk Grove Village (G-9689) | | |
| Rlw Inc | G | 309 352-2499 |
| Green Valley (G-11380) | | |
| Russell Ferrell | G | 217 847-3954 |
| Hamilton (G-11540) | | |
| Tallwood | G | 815 786-8186 |
| Plano (G-17676) | | |
| W Bozarth Logging | G | 618 658-4016 |
| Vienna (G-21226) | | |

Employee Codes: A=Over 500 employees, B=251-500
C=101-250, D=51-100, E=20-50, F=10-19, G=3-9

# 24 LUMBER AND WOOD PRODUCTS, EXCEPT FURNITURE

Warrior Logging & Perforagine .............G....... 618 662-7373
  Flora *(G-10220)*
Warrior Well Services Inc .............G....... 618 662-7710
  Flora *(G-10221)*

## 2421 Saw & Planing Mills

Alstat Wood Products .............F....... 618 684-5167
  Murphysboro *(G-15571)*
Autumn Mill .............G....... 217 795-3399
  Argenta *(G-689)*
Bach Timber & Pallet Inc .............G....... 815 885-3774
  Caledonia *(G-2930)*
Bailey Business Group .............G....... 618 548-3566
  Salem *(G-19327)*
Bond Brothers Hardwoods .............G....... 618 272-4811
  Ridgway *(G-17983)*
Botkin Lumber Company Inc .............E....... 217 287-2127
  Taylorville *(G-20834)*
Boyd Sawmill .............G....... 618 735-2056
  Dix *(G-8317)*
Bull Valley Hardwood .............G....... 815 701-9400
  Woodstock *(G-22548)*
Burks Sawmill .............F....... 618 432-5451
  Vernon *(G-21139)*
Cairo Dry Kilns Inc .............E....... 618 734-1039
  Cairo *(G-2928)*
Carpenters Millwork Co .............F....... 708 339-7707
  South Holland *(G-20255)*
Carpenters Millwork Co .............G....... 708 339-7707
  Villa Park *(G-21241)*
Charles K Eichen .............G....... 217 854-9751
  Carlinville *(G-3034)*
Christiansen Sawmill and Log .............G....... 815 315-7520
  Caledonia *(G-2931)*
Clarence Hancock Sawmill Inc .............G....... 618 854-2232
  Noble *(G-16050)*
Corsaw Hardwood Lumber Inc .............F....... 309 293-2055
  Smithfield *(G-20119)*
Crooked Trails Sawmill .............G....... 618 244-1547
  Opdyke *(G-16810)*
Custom Lumbermill Works .............G....... 309 875-3534
  Maquon *(G-14216)*
Darrell Fickas Sawmill .............G....... 618 676-1200
  Clay City *(G-7263)*
Don Poore Saw Mill Inc .............G....... 618 757-2240
  Springerton *(G-20382)*
E-Z Tree Recycling Inc .............G....... 773 493-8600
  Chicago *(G-4670)*
Eichen Lumber Co Inc .............G....... 217 854-9751
  Carlinville *(G-3037)*
Ericson S Log & Lumber Co .............G....... 309 667-2147
  New Windsor *(G-15931)*
Farrow Lumber Co .............G....... 618 734-0255
  Cairo *(G-2929)*
Forestech Wood Products .............G....... 217 279-3659
  West Union *(G-21826)*
Francis L Morris .............G....... 618 676-1724
  Clay City *(G-7264)*
Fraser Millwork Inc .............G....... 708 447-3262
  Lyons *(G-14038)*
G L Beaumont Lumber Company .............F....... 618 423-2323
  Ramsey *(G-17913)*
Georgia-Pacific Bldg Pdts LLC .............G....... 630 449-7200
  Aurora *(G-1015)*
Goodman Sawmill .............G....... 309 547-3597
  Lewistown *(G-13289)*
▲ Great Northern Lumber Inc .............D....... 708 388-1818
  Blue Island *(G-2254)*
▲ Griffard & Associates LLC .............G....... 217 316-1732
  Quincy *(G-17832)*
Heartland Hardwoods Inc .............E....... 217 844-3312
  Effingham *(G-8838)*
Hites Hardwood Lumber Inc .............F....... 618 723-2136
  Noble *(G-16051)*
J M Lustig Custom Cabinets Co .............F....... 217 342-6661
  Effingham *(G-8840)*
Jefferies Orchard Sawmill .............G....... 217 487-7582
  Springfield *(G-20463)*
Jht Robertson Lumber Inc .............G....... 618 842-2004
  Fairfield *(G-10146)*
▲ K&S International Inc .............G....... 847 229-0202
  Buffalo Grove *(G-2714)*
Kirkland Sawmill Inc .............G....... 815 522-6150
  Kirkland *(G-12714)*
Kniffen Brothers Sawmill .............G....... 618 629-2437
  Whittington *(G-22187)*
Koppers Industries Inc .............G....... 309 343-5157
  Galesburg *(G-10763)*
▲ Lamboo Inc .............E....... 866 966-2999
  Litchfield *(G-13692)*

Larry Musgrave Logging .............G....... 618 842-6386
  Fairfield *(G-10148)*
Liese Lumber Co Inc .............G....... 618 234-0105
  Belleville *(G-1649)*
Lohrberg Lumber .............F....... 618 473-2061
  Waterloo *(G-21402)*
Lumberyard Suppliers Inc .............G....... 618 931-0315
  Granite City *(G-11291)*
M D Harmon Inc .............F....... 618 662-8925
  Xenia *(G-22644)*
Marvin Suckow .............G....... 618 483-5570
  Mason *(G-14361)*
◆ Mechanics Planing Mill Inc .............F....... 618 288-3000
  Glen Carbon *(G-10954)*
Midwest Wood Inc .............G....... 815 273-3333
  Savanna *(G-19402)*
Mulvain Woodworks .............G....... 815 248-2305
  Durand *(G-8587)*
Oltenia Inc .............G....... 773 987-2888
  Norridge *(G-16107)*
Png Transport LLC .............G....... 312 218-8116
  Chicago *(G-6144)*
Rjt Wood Services .............G....... 815 858-2081
  Galena *(G-10730)*
Sawmill Construction Inc .............G....... 815 937-0037
  Bourbonnais *(G-2406)*
Schrocks Sawmill .............G....... 217 268-3632
  Arcola *(G-684)*
Simonton Hardwood Lumber LLC .............F....... 618 594-2132
  Carlyle *(G-3059)*
Southeast Wood Treating Inc .............F....... 815 562-5007
  Rochelle *(G-18110)*
▲ Towerleaf LLC .............G....... 847 985-1937
  Schaumburg *(G-19766)*
Tree-O Lumber Inc .............E....... 618 357-2576
  Pinckneyville *(G-17553)*
Triezenberg Millwork Co .............G....... 708 489-9062
  Crestwood *(G-7506)*
Tronox Incorporated .............E....... 203 705-3704
  Madison *(G-14154)*
Twin City Wood Recycling Corp .............G....... 309 827-9663
  Bloomington *(G-2234)*
Weatherguard Buildings .............G....... 217 894-6213
  Clayton *(G-7270)*
Westrock CP LLC .............G....... 630 655-6951
  Burr Ridge *(G-2893)*
Westrock CP LLC .............D....... 312 346-6600
  Chicago *(G-6967)*
Willenborg Hardwood Inds Inc .............F....... 217 844-2082
  Effingham *(G-8863)*
Willowbrook Sawmill .............G....... 618 592-3806
  Oblong *(G-16737)*
Wooded Wonderland .............G....... 815 777-1223
  Galena *(G-10735)*

## 2426 Hardwood Dimension & Flooring Mills

Access Flooring Co Inc .............G....... 847 781-0100
  Hoffman Estates *(G-11989)*
Art Jewel Enterprises Ltd .............F....... 630 260-0400
  Carol Stream *(G-3106)*
Bond Brothers Hardwoods .............G....... 618 272-4811
  Ridgway *(G-17983)*
Boyd Sawmill .............G....... 618 735-2056
  Dix *(G-8317)*
▲ Builders Warehouse Inc .............G....... 309 672-1760
  Peoria *(G-17320)*
Central Illinois Hardwood .............G....... 309 352-2363
  Green Valley *(G-11378)*
Christiansen Sawmill and Log .............G....... 815 315-7520
  Caledonia *(G-2931)*
▼ Connor Sports Flooring LLC .............D....... 847 290-9020
  Elk Grove Village *(G-9389)*
Eichen Lumber Co Inc .............G....... 217 854-9751
  Carlinville *(G-3037)*
Enterprise Pallet Inc .............F....... 815 928-8546
  Bourbonnais *(G-2395)*
Ericson S Log & Lumber Co .............G....... 309 667-2147
  New Windsor *(G-15931)*
Flooring Warehouse Direct Inc .............G....... 815 730-6767
  Homer Glen *(G-12078)*
G L Beaumont Lumber Company .............F....... 618 423-2323
  Ramsey *(G-17913)*
Grads Inc .............G....... 847 426-3904
  East Dundee *(G-8641)*
▲ Great Northern Lumber Inc .............D....... 708 388-1818
  Blue Island *(G-2254)*
Greatlakes Architectural Millw .............G....... 312 829-7110
  Chicago *(G-5000)*
▲ Hakwood .............G....... 630 219-3388
  Naperville *(G-15669)*

Hardwood Lumber Products Co .............G....... 309 538-4411
  Kilbourne *(G-12697)*
Heartland Hardwoods Inc .............E....... 217 844-3312
  Effingham *(G-8838)*
Historic Timber & Plank Inc .............E....... 618 372-4546
  Brighton *(G-2542)*
Lohrberg Lumber .............F....... 618 473-2061
  Waterloo *(G-21402)*
Moultrie County Hardwoods LLC .............G.......
  Arthur *(G-912)*
New Line Hardwoods Inc .............D....... 309 657-7621
  Beardstown *(G-1524)*
Outdoors Synergy Products Tech .............D....... 630 552-3111
  Plano *(G-17670)*
Plano Synergy Holding Inc .............E....... 630 552-3111
  Plano *(G-17674)*
Redbox Workshop Ltd .............E....... 773 478-7077
  Chicago *(G-6316)*
▲ Ridgefield Industries Co LLC .............E....... 800 569-0316
  Crystal Lake *(G-7641)*
Riverside Custom Woodworking .............G....... 815 589-3608
  Fulton *(G-10705)*
▲ Signature Innovations LLC .............E....... 847 758-9600
  Elk Grove Village *(G-9739)*
Silvacor Inc .............G....... 630 897-9211
  Aurora *(G-1218)*
Simonton Hardwood Lumber LLC .............F....... 618 594-2132
  Carlyle *(G-3059)*
T J P Investments Inc .............G....... 309 673-8383
  Peoria *(G-17465)*
Tree-O Lumber Inc .............E....... 618 357-2576
  Pinckneyville *(G-17553)*
Unity Hardwoods LLC .............G....... 708 701-2943
  Chicago *(G-6830)*
Vlasici Hardwood Floors Co .............G....... 815 505-4308
  Romeoville *(G-18876)*
Wooded Wonderland .............G....... 815 777-1223
  Galena *(G-10735)*
Woodmac Industries Inc .............F....... 708 755-3545
  S Chicago Hts *(G-19116)*
▲ Woodworkers Shop Inc .............E....... 309 347-5111
  Pekin *(G-17296)*
Woodx Lumber Inc .............G....... 331 979-2171
  Elmhurst *(G-9962)*

## 2429 Special Prdt Sawmills, NEC

▲ Iko Midwest Inc .............D....... 815 936-9600
  Kankakee *(G-12624)*

## 2431 Millwork

A & M Wood Products Inc .............G....... 630 323-2555
  Burr Ridge *(G-2818)*
A and J Development Plus LLC .............G....... 630 470-9539
  Plainfield *(G-17575)*
Ability Cabinet Co Inc .............G....... 847 678-6678
  Franklin Park *(G-10383)*
Absolute Windows Inc .............E....... 708 599-9191
  Oak Lawn *(G-16594)*
Accurate Cstm Sash Mllwk Corp .............G....... 708 423-0423
  Oak Lawn *(G-16595)*
Adams Street Iron Inc .............F....... 312 733-3229
  Evergreen Park *(G-10109)*
Agusta Mill Works .............G....... 309 787-4616
  Milan *(G-14773)*
All American Wood Register Co .............F....... 815 356-1000
  Crystal Lake *(G-7528)*
Alliance Door and Hardware LLC .............G....... 630 451-7070
  Bridgeview *(G-2461)*
Allie Woodworking .............G....... 847 244-1919
  Waukegan *(G-21522)*
Allied Garage Door Inc .............E....... 630 279-0795
  Addison *(G-29)*
American Custom Woodworking .............F....... 847 526-5900
  Wauconda *(G-21440)*
American Woodworks .............G....... 630 279-1629
  Sleepy Hollow *(G-20117)*
▲ Americscan Designs Inc .............D....... 773 542-1291
  Chicago *(G-3886)*
Amron Stair Works Inc .............F....... 847 426-4800
  Gilberts *(G-10912)*
Anderson Awning & Shutter .............G....... 815 654-1155
  Machesney Park *(G-14056)*
Architectual Woodworking .............G....... 847 259-3331
  Prospect Heights *(G-17772)*
Arlen-Jacob Manufacturing Co .............E....... 815 485-4777
  New Lenox *(G-15870)*
Aspen Shutters Inc .............G....... 847 979-0166
  Schaumburg *(G-19447)*
Bailey Hardwoods Inc .............G....... 217 529-6800
  Springfield *(G-20394)*

## 24 LUMBER AND WOOD PRODUCTS, EXCEPT FURNITURE

Baker Elements Inc .................................F 630 660-8100
  Oak Park (G-16654)
Barrington Millwork LLC ........................G 847 304-0791
  Lake Barrington (G-12800)
Barsanti Woodwork Corporation ...............E 773 284-6888
  Chicago (G-4050)
Becker Jules D Wood Products ................G 847 526-8002
  Wauconda (G-21445)
Beloit Pattern Works ..............................F 815 389-2578
  South Beloit (G-20140)
Benchmark Cabinets & Mllwk Inc .............E 309 697-5855
  Peoria (G-17316)
▲ Bernhard Woodwork Ltd .....................E 847 291-1040
  Northbrook (G-16214)
Blue Chip Construction Inc .....................F 630 208-5254
  Geneva (G-10812)
Blueberry Woodworking Inc ....................G 773 230-7179
  Franklin Park (G-10414)
Bond Brothers Hardwoods .....................G 618 272-4811
  Ridgway (G-17983)
Boom Company Inc ..............................G 847 459-6199
  Wheeling (G-22018)
Botti Studio of Architectural ....................E 847 869-5933
  Evanston (G-10017)
▲ Brown Wood Products Company .........F 847 673-4780
  Lincolnwood (G-13503)
Brown Woodworking .............................G 815 477-8333
  Crystal Lake (G-7544)
Byttow Enterprises Inc ..........................G 708 754-4995
  Steger (G-20570)
C A Larson & Son Inc ..........................G 847 717-6010
  Maple Park (G-14199)
CA Custom Woodworking .....................G 630 201-6154
  Oswego (G-16906)
Cabinets Doors and More LLC ...............G 847 395-6334
  Antioch (G-627)
Cain Millwork Inc ................................D 815 561-9700
  Rochelle (G-18082)
Caldwell Woodworks ............................G 217 566-2434
  Williamsville (G-22190)
Carpenters Millwork Co .........................F 708 339-7707
  South Holland (G-20255)
Carpenters Millwork Co .........................G 708 339-7707
  Villa Park (G-21241)
Central Illinois Door .............................G 309 828-0087
  Bloomington (G-2154)
Central Wood LLC ...............................G 217 543-2662
  Arcola (G-666)
Chicago School Woodworking LLC .........G 773 275-1170
  Chicago (G-4346)
Christos Woodworking ..........................G 708 975-5045
  Alsip (G-448)
City Screen Inc ...................................G 773 588-5642
  Chicago (G-4388)
Classic Windows Inc ............................F 847 362-3100
  Libertyville (G-13315)
Clopay Building Pdts Co Inc ..................G 708 346-0901
  Chicago Ridge (G-7143)
Cmp Millwork Co .................................G 630 832-6462
  Elmhurst (G-9851)
Contract Industries Inc .........................E 708 458-8150
  Bedford Park (G-1545)
Cooper Lake Millworks Inc ....................G 217 847-2681
  Hamilton (G-11530)
Corsaw Hardwood Lumber Inc ...............F 309 293-2055
  Smithfield (G-20119)
Crea and Crea .....................................G 630 292-5625
  Bartlett (G-1339)
Creswell Woodworking CA ....................G 847 381-9222
  Woodstock (G-22556)
Curtis Woodworking Inc ........................G 815 544-3543
  Belvidere (G-1748)
Custom Crafted Door Inc ......................F 309 527-5075
  El Paso (G-8867)
Custom Railz & Stairz Inc .....................G 773 592-7210
  Chicago (G-4525)
Custom Window Accents ......................F 815 943-7651
  Harvard (G-11629)
Custom Wood Creations .......................G 618 346-2208
  Collinsville (G-7318)
Custom Woodworking Inc .....................G 630 584-7106
  Saint Charles (G-19166)
Customwood Stairs Inc ........................E 630 739-5252
  Romeoville (G-18815)
Dandurand Custom Woodworking .........G 708 489-6440
  Posen (G-17729)
▲ Daniel M Powers & Assoc Ltd ............D 630 685-8400
  Bolingbrook (G-2299)
Decorators Supply Corporation ..............E 773 847-6300
  Chicago (G-4571)

Decore-Ative Specialties ......................B 630 947-6294
  Cary (G-3334)
Deem Woodworks ...............................G 217 832-9614
  Villa Grove (G-21227)
▲ Del Great Frame Up Systems Inc ......F 847 808-1955
  Franklin Park (G-10456)
Demeter Millwork LLC .........................G 312 224-4440
  Chicago (G-4581)
Der Holtzmacher Ltd ............................G 815 895-4887
  Sycamore (G-20792)
Designed Stairs Inc .............................E 815 786-2021
  Sandwich (G-19361)
Designer Decks By Mj Inc ....................G 815 744-7914
  Morris (G-15106)
Doctors Interior Plantscaping ................G 708 333-3323
  South Holland (G-20262)
Douglas County Mil Moldings ...............G 217 268-4689
  Arcola (G-667)
Duhack Lehn & Associates Inc .............G 815 777-3460
  Galena (G-10719)
Dunigan Custom Woodworking ............G 708 351-5213
  Homewood (G-12095)
Eiesland Builders Inc ...........................E 847 998-1731
  Glenview (G-11123)
Elite Custom Woodworking ..................G 630 888-4322
  Batavia (G-1446)
ERA Development Group Inc ...............G 708 252-6979
  Northbrook (G-16251)
European Wood Works Inc ..................G 773 662-6607
  Carol Stream (G-3148)
Extreme Woodworking Inc ...................G 224 338-8179
  Round Lake (G-19055)
FM Woodworking .................................G 847 533-1545
  Lake Zurich (G-13074)
Four Acre Wood Products ....................F 217 543-2971
  Arthur (G-900)
Fraser Millwork Inc ..............................G 708 447-3262
  Lyons (G-14038)
▲ Furniture Services Inc ......................G 847 520-9490
  Wheeling (G-22060)
G & M Woodworking Inc ......................G 708 425-4013
  Oak Lawn (G-16622)
Gavin Woodworking Inc .......................G 815 786-2242
  Sandwich (G-19365)
Geo J Rothan Co .................................E 309 674-5189
  Peoria (G-17371)
George Drowne Cabinet Sand ..............G 847 234-1487
  Lake Bluff (G-12846)
Georgia-Pacific LLC ............................D 847 885-3920
  Hoffman Estates (G-12014)
Gingerich Custom Woodworking ...........F 217 578-3491
  Arthur (G-902)
Glendale Woodworking .........................G 630 545-1520
  Glendale Heights (G-11027)
Gmk Finishing .....................................G 630 837-0568
  Bartlett (G-1351)
Grays Cabinet Co ................................G 618 948-2211
  Saint Francisville (G-19313)
Greatlakes Architectural Millw ...............E 312 829-7110
  Chicago (G-5000)
H & H Custom Woodworking Inc ..........E 815 932-6820
  Bourbonnais (G-2398)
H & M Woodworks ...............................G 608 289-3141
  Hamilton (G-11536)
Harold Prefinished Wood Inc ................F 618 548-1414
  Salem (G-19336)
Heartland Hardwoods Inc .....................E 217 844-3312
  Effingham (G-8838)
Hill Design Products Inc .......................F 815 344-3333
  McHenry (G-14513)
Hilling Services Inc ..............................G 618 667-2005
  Troy (G-21008)
Historic Timber & Plank Inc ..................E 618 372-4546
  Brighton (G-2542)
HK Woodwork ......................................G 773 964-2468
  Wheeling (G-22071)
Hogan Woodwork Inc ...........................G 708 354-4525
  Countryside (G-7429)
Hylan Design Ltd .................................G 312 243-7341
  Chicago (G-5129)
Ideal Cabinet Solutions Inc ..................G 618 514-7087
  Alhambra (G-418)
Imperial Store Fixtures Inc ...................G 773 348-1137
  Chicago (G-5168)
▲ Imperial Woodworking Entps Inc .......E 847 358-6920
  Palatine (G-17040)
J K Custom Countertops .....................G 630 495-2324
  Lombard (G-13813)
J&E Storm Services Inc ......................G 630 401-3793
  Tinley Park (G-20925)

Janik Custom Millwork Inc ....................G 708 482-4844
  Hodgkins (G-11977)
Jay A Morris ........................................G 815 432-6440
  Watseka (G-21420)
Jeld-Wen Inc .......................................D 217 893-4444
  Rantoul (G-17930)
Jelinek & Sons Inc ..............................G 630 355-3474
  Plainfield (G-17610)
Jj Wood Working ..................................G 708 426-6854
  Bridgeview (G-2502)
Jlm Woodworking ................................G 309 275-8259
  Normal (G-16074)
Jmi Crafted Coml Mllwk Inc ..................F 708 331-6331
  Harvey (G-11673)
John Tobin Millwork Co ........................G 630 832-3780
  Villa Park (G-21260)
Just Sashes ........................................G 773 205-1429
  Chicago (G-5338)
Kabinet Kraft .......................................F 618 395-1047
  Olney (G-16775)
◆ Kempner Company Inc ......................F 312 733-1606
  Chicago (G-5376)
Kencor Stairs & Woodworking ..............G 630 279-8980
  Villa Park (G-21263)
Kep Woodworking ................................F 847 480-9545
  Northbrook (G-16286)
Kite Woodworking Co ..........................G 217 728-4346
  Sullivan (G-20750)
Kozin Woodwork US ............................G 815 568-8918
  Marengo (G-14234)
L Surges Custom Woodwork ................G 815 774-9663
  Joliet (G-12529)
Lake Shore Stair Co Inc ......................E 815 363-7777
  Ingleside (G-12192)
Landquist & Son Inc ...........................E 847 674-6600
  Mokena (G-14878)
Leggett & Platt Incorporated ................G 708 458-1800
  Chicago (G-5490)
Lyko Woodworking & Cnstr ..................G 773 583-4561
  Chicago (G-5573)
M & R Custom Millwork ........................G 815 547-8549
  Belvidere (G-1768)
Majestic Archtctural Wdwrk Inc ............G 708 240-8484
  Bellwood (G-1713)
Manufacturing / Woodworking ..............G 847 730-4823
  Des Plaines (G-8226)
Masonite Corporation ...........................D 630 584-6330
  West Chicago (G-21740)
Master Cabinets ..................................G 847 639-1323
  Cary (G-3359)
May Wood Industries Inc .....................F 708 489-1515
  Chicago (G-5660)
Mc Dist & Mfg Co ................................F 630 628-5180
  Addison (G-195)
Menard Inc ..........................................D 815 474-6767
  Plano (G-17666)
Menard Inc ..........................................D 708 346-9144
  Evergreen Park (G-10117)
Menard Inc ..........................................D 715 876-5911
  Plano (G-17667)
Menard Inc ..........................................E 708 780-0260
  Cicero (G-7220)
Merkel Woodworking Inc ......................F 630 458-0700
  Addison (G-199)
Metal Products Sales Corp ...................G 708 301-6844
  Lockport (G-13732)
▲ Metrie ..............................................E 815 717-2660
  New Lenox (G-15895)
▲ Middletons Mouldings Inc ..................D 517 278-6610
  Schaumburg (G-19646)
Midwest Woodcrafters Inc ....................G 630 665-0901
  Carol Stream (G-3199)
Miller Whiteside Wood Working ............G 309 827-6470
  Mc Lean (G-14463)
Minimill Technologies Inc .....................G 315 857-7107
  Chicago (G-5768)
Missouri Wood Craft Inc ......................G 217 453-2204
  Nauvoo (G-15853)
Mjf Woodworking .................................G 815 679-6700
  McHenry (G-14537)
▲ Monda Window & Door Corp .............E 773 254-8888
  Chicago (G-5792)
Monticello Design & Mfg ......................G 217 762-8551
  Monticello (G-15081)
Moonlight Woodworking ........................G 815 728-9121
  Ringwood (G-17992)
▲ Motion Access LLC ...........................E 847 357-8832
  Elk Grove Village (G-9638)
Mulvain Woodworks .............................G 815 248-2305
  Durand (G-8587)

---

Employee Codes: A=Over 500 employees, B=251-500
C=101-250, D=51-100, E=20-50, F=10-19, G=3-9

**Navillus Woodworks LLC** G 312 375-2680
Chicago *(G-5874)*
**Neisewander Enterprises Inc** A 815 288-1431
Dixon *(G-8337)*
**Nelson Door Co** G 217 543-3489
Arthur *(G-913)*
**Olivet Woodworking** G 773 505-5225
Lake Zurich *(G-13111)*
**Omega Moulding North Amer Inc** G 630 509-2397
Elk Grove Village *(G-9664)*
**Onsite Woodwork Corporation** D 815 633-6400
Loves Park *(G-13971)*
**Original Shutter Man** G 773 966-7160
Chicago *(G-6013)*
**Orstrom Woodworking Ltd** G 847 697-1163
Elgin *(G-9131)*
**Osmer Woodworking Inc** G 815 973-5809
Dixon *(G-8338)*
**Overhead Door Corporation** G 630 775-9118
Itasca *(G-12338)*
**Parenti & Raffaelli Ltd** C 847 253-5550
Mount Prospect *(G-15361)*
**Pella Corporation** B 309 663-7132
Bloomington *(G-2211)*
**Pella Corporation** B 309 663-7132
Bloomington *(G-2212)*
**Pella Corporation** B 309 663-7132
Bloomington *(G-2213)*
**Pella Corporation** B 309 663-7132
Bloomington *(G-2214)*
**Performance Lawn & Power** G 217 857-3717
Teutopolis *(G-20854)*
**Peters Construction** G 773 489-5555
Chicago *(G-6110)*
**Phoenix Art Woodworks** G 847 279-1576
Wheeling *(G-22122)*
**Pinnacle Wood Products Inc** G 815 385-0792
McHenry *(G-14544)*
**Pio Woodworking Inc** G 630 628-6900
Addison *(G-241)*
**Prairie Woodworks Inc** G 309 378-2418
Downs *(G-8547)*
**Pro Woodworking** G 708 508-5948
Bedford Park *(G-1576)*
**R W G Manufacturing Inc** G 708 755-8035
S Chicago Hts *(G-19112)*
**Ramar Industries Inc** G 847 451-0445
Franklin Park *(G-10569)*
◆ **Raynor Mfg Co** A 815 288-1431
Dixon *(G-8341)*
**Remmert Studios Inc** G 815 933-4867
Orland Park *(G-16887)*
**Rhyme or Reason Woodworking** G 217 678-8301
Bement *(G-1802)*
**Richard King and Sons** G 815 654-0226
Loves Park *(G-13982)*
▲ **River City Millwork Inc** D 800 892-9297
Rockford *(G-18556)*
**Riverside Custom Woodworking** G 815 589-3608
Fulton *(G-10705)*
**Roseland II LLC** G 708 479-5010
Orland Park *(G-16888)*
**ROW Window Company** G 815 725-5491
Plainfield *(G-17647)*
**Royal Stairs Co** G 630 860-2223
Bensenville *(G-1980)*
**Rs Woodworking** G 815 476-1818
Wilmington *(G-22275)*
**S R Door Inc** E 815 227-1148
Rockford *(G-18603)*
**Sandwich Millworks Inc** G 815 786-2700
Sandwich *(G-19377)*
**Scheffler Custom Woodworking** G 815 284-6564
Dixon *(G-8348)*
**Schrocks Woodworking** G 217 578-3259
Arthur *(G-921)*
**Scott Lind Owner** G 847 323-9140
Lake In The Hills *(G-13005)*
**Skokie Millwork Inc** G 847 673-7868
Skokie *(G-20087)*
**Stairsland** G 708 853-9593
Lyons *(G-14045)*
**Stancy Woodworking Co Inc** F 847 526-0252
Island Lake *(G-12219)*
**Star Moulding & Trim Company** E 708 458-1040
Bedford Park *(G-1586)*
**Step One Stairworks Inc** F 815 286-7464
Hinckley *(G-11937)*
**Stine Woodworking LLC** G 618 885-2229
Dow *(G-8383)*
**Stovers Fine Woodworking Inc** G 630 557-0072
Maple Park *(G-14203)*
**Sugarcreek Woodworking** G 618 584-3817
Flat Rock *(G-10198)*
**Sunburst Shutters Illinois** F 847 697-4000
Elgin *(G-9196)*
**Suzy Cabinet Company Inc** G 708 705-1259
Bellwood *(G-1724)*
**Temp-Tech Industries Inc** E 773 586-2800
Chicago *(G-6694)*
**Thomas Fine Stairs Inc** G 708 387-9506
Brookfield *(G-2645)*
**Torblo Inc** G 815 941-2684
Morris *(G-15135)*
**Tree-O Lumber Inc** E 618 357-2576
Pinckneyville *(G-17553)*
**Tri State Aluminum Products** F 815 877-6081
Loves Park *(G-14003)*
**Triezenberg Millwork Co** G 708 489-9062
Crestwood *(G-7506)*
**Tru-Guard Manufacturing Co** G 773 568-5264
Chicago *(G-6784)*
**Unimode Inc** G 773 343-6754
Burr Ridge *(G-2890)*
**US Lbm Ridout Holdings LLC** G 877 787-5267
Buffalo Grove *(G-2786)*
**Vista Woodworking** G 815 922-2297
Joliet *(G-12587)*
**Wagners Custom Wood Design** G 847 487-2788
Island Lake *(G-12221)*
**Wampach Woodwork Inc** F 847 742-1900
South Elgin *(G-20232)*
**Washington Woodworking** G 309 339-0913
Washington *(G-21395)*
**Wenger Woodcraft** G 217 578-3440
Tuscola *(G-21030)*
**West Zwick Corp** G 217 222-0228
Quincy *(G-17903)*
**Wiegmann Woodworking** G 618 248-1300
Damiansville *(G-7700)*
**Willard R Schorck** F 217 543-2160
Arthur *(G-924)*
**Wills Milling and Hardwood Inc** E 217 854-9056
Carlinville *(G-3048)*
**Wm Huber Cabinet Works** E 773 235-7660
Chicago *(G-7011)*
▲ **Wood Creations Incorporated** G 773 772-1375
Chicago *(G-7022)*
**Wood Creations Incorporated** G 773 772-1375
Chicago *(G-7023)*
**Wood Cutters Lane LLC** G 847 847-2263
Hainesville *(G-11525)*
**Wooden World of Richmond Inc** G 815 405-4503
Richmond *(G-17974)*
**Woodwork Apts LLC** G 224 595-9691
Streamwood *(G-20681)*
**Yuenger Wood Moulding Inc** G 773 735-7100
Naperville *(G-15788)*

## 2434 Wood Kitchen Cabinets

**57th Street Bookcase & Cabinet** G 312 867-1669
Chicago *(G-3674)*
**Aba Custom Woodworking** G 815 356-9663
Crystal Lake *(G-7525)*
**Ability Cabinet Co Inc** G 847 678-6678
Franklin Park *(G-10383)*
**Action Cabinet Sales Inc** G 847 717-0011
Elgin *(G-8935)*
**Adams Street Iron Inc** F 312 733-3229
Evergreen Park *(G-10109)*
**Aji Custom Cabinets** G 847 312-7847
McHenry *(G-14478)*
**Allie Woodworking** G 847 244-1919
Waukegan *(G-21522)*
**Allwood Cabinet** G 773 778-1242
Chicago *(G-3825)*
**Amberleaf Cabinetry Inc** F 773 247-8282
Chicago *(G-3844)*
**American Custom Woodworking** F 847 526-5900
Wauconda *(G-21440)*
**American Fixture** G 217 429-1300
Decatur *(G-7832)*
▲ **Americsan Designs Inc** D 773 542-1291
Chicago *(G-3886)*
**Anderson & Marter Cabinets** G 630 406-9840
Batavia *(G-1415)*
**Anliker Custom Wood** F 815 657-7510
Forrest *(G-10260)*
**Aspen Cabinet Dist Corp** G 847 381-4241
Barrington *(G-1268)*
**Austin-Westran LLC** C 815 234-2811
Montgomery *(G-15029)*
**Autumn Woods Ltd** G 630 868-3535
Wheaton *(G-21937)*
**Autumn Woods Ltd** E 630 668-2080
Carol Stream *(G-3109)*
**B & B Formica Appliers Inc** F 773 804-1015
Chicago *(G-4014)*
**Becker Jules D Wood Products** G 847 526-8002
Wauconda *(G-21445)*
**Bell Cabinet & Millwork Co** G 708 425-1200
Evergreen Park *(G-10110)*
**Benchmark Cabinets & Mllwk Inc** E 309 697-5855
Peoria *(G-17316)*
**Birom Cabinetry LLC** G 312 286-7132
Addison *(G-56)*
**Bolhuis Woodworking Co** G 708 333-5100
Manhattan *(G-14168)*
**Brakur Custom Cabinetry Inc** C 630 355-2244
Shorewood *(G-19923)*
**Brian Bequette Cabinetry** G 618 670-5427
Staunton *(G-20554)*
**Bridgeview Custom Kit Cabinets** F 708 598-1221
Bridgeview *(G-2472)*
**Brighton Cabinetry Inc** F 217 235-1978
Mattoon *(G-14385)*
**Brighton Cabinetry Inc** F 217 895-3000
Neoga *(G-15857)*
**Brown Woodworking** G 815 477-8333
Crystal Lake *(G-7544)*
**Byttow Enterprises Inc** G 708 754-4995
Steger *(G-20570)*
**C M Sell Woodwork** G 847 526-3627
Wauconda *(G-21451)*
▲ **C S C Inc** E 217 925-5908
Dieterich *(G-8312)*
**C-V Cstom Cntrtops Cbinets Inc** F 708 388-5066
Blue Island *(G-2241)*
**Cabinet Broker Ltd** G 847 352-1898
Elk Grove Village *(G-9354)*
**Cabinet Designs** G 708 614-8603
Oak Forest *(G-16575)*
▲ **Cabinets & Granite Direct LLC** F 630 588-8886
Carol Stream *(G-3121)*
**Cabinets By Custom Craft Inc** G 815 637-4001
Roscoe *(G-18891)*
**Cabinets Doors and More LLC** G 847 395-6334
Antioch *(G-627)*
**Carpenters Millwork Co** F 708 339-7707
South Holland *(G-20255)*
**Carpenters Millwork Co** G 708 339-7707
Villa Park *(G-21241)*
**Cassini Cabinetry** G 847 244-9755
Waukegan *(G-21535)*
▲ **Charles N Benner Inc** E 312 829-4300
Chicago *(G-4293)*
**Choice Cabinet Chicago** G 630 599-1099
Glendale Heights *(G-11016)*
**Closet Works LLC** G 630 832-4422
Elmhurst *(G-9850)*
**Con-Temp Cabinets Inc** F 630 892-7300
North Aurora *(G-16123)*
**Contract Industries Inc** E 708 458-8150
Bedford Park *(G-1545)*
**Cooper Lake Millworks Inc** G 217 847-2681
Hamilton *(G-11530)*
**Counter Craft Inc** G 847 336-8205
Waukegan *(G-21545)*
**County Line Inc** E 217 268-5056
Arthur *(G-892)*
**Creative Cabinetry Inc** G 708 460-2900
Orland Park *(G-16851)*
**Creative Cabinets Countertops** F 217 446-6406
Danville *(G-7710)*
▲ **Creative Designs Kitc** E 773 327-8400
Chicago *(G-4497)*
**Crestwood Custom Cabinets** G 708 385-3167
Crestwood *(G-7485)*
**Crown Coverings Inc** E 630 546-2959
Roselle *(G-18937)*
**Crown Custom Cabinetry Inc** G 815 942-0432
Morris *(G-15104)*
**Custom Cabinet Refacers Inc** G 847 695-8800
Elgin *(G-9006)*
**Custom Wood Designs Inc** G 708 799-3439
Crestwood *(G-7486)*
**Custom Woodwork & Interiors** E 217 546-0006
Springfield *(G-20427)*
**Cws Cabinets** G 847 258-4468
Elk Grove Village *(G-9407)*

**D & D Counter Tops Co Inc** G
Machesney Park *(G-14070)*

▲ **Daniel M Powers & Assoc Ltd** D 630 685-8400
Bolingbrook *(G-2299)*

**David Hayes** G 815 238-7690
Steward *(G-20623)*

**Decams Cabinets Inc** G 847 360-4970
Lincolnshire *(G-13442)*

**Der Holtzmacher Ltd** G 815 895-4887
Sycamore *(G-20792)*

**Design Woodworks** G 847 566-6603
Mundelein *(G-15493)*

**Dicks Custom Cabinet Shop** G 815 358-2663
Cornell *(G-7381)*

**Dilaberto Co Inc** G 630 892-8448
Aurora *(G-1141)*

**Donald Kranz** G 847 428-1616
Carpentersville *(G-3283)*

**Dpcac LLC** F 630 741-7900
Itasca *(G-12253)*

**Dvoraks Creations Inc** G 815 838-2214
Lockport *(G-13713)*

▲ **Eagle Cabinet Inc** G 847 289-9992
Elgin *(G-9018)*

**Eddie Gapastione** G 708 430-3881
Bridgeview *(G-2487)*

**Edgars Custom Cabinets** G 847 928-0922
Franklin Park *(G-10463)*

**Edward Hull Cabinet Shop** G 217 864-3011
Mount Zion *(G-15450)*

**Ellers Custom Cabinets Inc** F 309 633-0101
Groveland *(G-11415)*

**En Pointe Cabinetry** G 847 787-0777
Elk Grove Village *(G-9457)*

**Encon Environmental Concepts** F 630 543-1583
Addison *(G-111)*

**Euro-Tech Cabinetry Rmdlg Corp** G 815 254-3876
Plainfield *(G-17596)*

**Forest City Counter Tops Inc** F 815 633-8602
Loves Park *(G-13942)*

**Four Acre Wood Products** F 217 543-2971
Arthur *(G-900)*

**Fra-Milco Cabinets Co Inc** G
Frankfort *(G-10323)*

**Fraser Millwork Inc** G 708 447-3262
Lyons *(G-14038)*

**Garver Inc** G 217 932-2441
Casey *(G-3383)*

**Glenview Custom Cabinets Inc** G 847 345-5754
Glenview *(G-11130)*

**Gold Seal Cabinets Countertops** E 630 906-0366
Aurora *(G-1163)*

**Grays Cabinet Co** G 618 948-2211
Saint Francisville *(G-19313)*

**Hansen Custom Cabinet Inc** G 847 356-1100
Lake Villa *(G-13015)*

**Hci Cabinetry and Design Inc** G 630 584-0266
Saint Charles *(G-19190)*

**Helmuth Custom Kitchens LLC** E 217 543-3588
Arthur *(G-904)*

**Hester Cabinets & Millwork** G 815 634-4555
Coal City *(G-7293)*

**Hickory Street Cabinets** G 618 667-9676
Troy *(G-21007)*

**Hidalgo Fine Cabinetry** G 630 753-9323
Naperville *(G-15809)*

**Hylan Design Ltd** G 312 243-7341
Chicago *(G-5129)*

**I Kustom Cabinets Inc** G 773 343-6858
Highwood *(G-11885)*

**Ideal Cabinet Solutions Inc** G 618 514-7087
Alhambra *(G-418)*

**J K Custom Countertops** G 630 495-2324
Lombard *(G-13813)*

**J M Lustig Custom Cabinets Co** F 217 342-6661
Effingham *(G-8840)*

**Janik Custom Millwork Inc** G 708 482-4844
Hodgkins *(G-11977)*

**Johnson Custom Cabinets** G 815 675-9690
Spring Grove *(G-20339)*

**Joliet Cabinet Company Inc** E 815 727-4096
Lockport *(G-13724)*

**Jones Design Group Ltd** G 630 462-9340
Winfield *(G-22286)*

**Kabinet Kraft** F 618 395-1047
Olney *(G-16775)*

**Kanneberg Custom Kitchens Inc** G 815 654-1110
Machesney Park *(G-14084)*

**Kaufmans Custom Cabinets** F 217 268-4330
Arcola *(G-673)*

◆ **Kempner Company Inc** F 312 733-1606
Chicago *(G-5376)*

**Kessmanns Cabinet Shop & Cnstr** G 618 654-2538
Highland *(G-11800)*

**Kitchen Krafters Inc** G 815 675-6061
Spring Grove *(G-20341)*

**Koala Cabinets** G 630 818-1289
West Chicago *(G-21730)*

**Kowal Custom Cabinet & Furn** G 708 597-3367
Blue Island *(G-2260)*

**Kraft Custom Design Inc** G 815 485-5506
New Lenox *(G-15890)*

**Krafty Kabinets** G 815 369-5250
Lena *(G-13276)*

**Kunz Carpentry** G 618 224-7892
Trenton *(G-20994)*

▲ **Lacava LLC** E 773 637-9600
Chicago *(G-5432)*

**Lyko Woodworking & Cnstr** G 773 583-4561
Chicago *(G-5573)*

**M & R Custom Millwork** G 815 547-8549
Belvidere *(G-1768)*

**Manufacturing / Woodworking** G 847 730-4823
Des Plaines *(G-8226)*

**Markham Cabinet Works Inc** G 708 687-3074
Midlothian *(G-14767)*

**Markus Cabinet Manufacturing** E 618 228-7376
Aviston *(G-1246)*

**Masco Corporation** D 847 303-3088
Schaumburg *(G-19633)*

**Master Cabinets** G 847 639-1323
Cary *(G-3359)*

**Masterbrand Cabinets Inc** B 217 543-3311
Arthur *(G-909)*

**Masterbrand Cabinets Inc** G 217 543-3466
Arthur *(G-910)*

**Masterbrand Cabinets Inc** G 503 241-4964
Arthur *(G-911)*

**Masters Shop** G 217 643-7826
Thomasboro *(G-20860)*

**Mc Laminated Cabinets** G 773 301-0393
Franklin Park *(G-10525)*

**Metro Cabinet Refinishers** G 217 498-7174
Rochester *(G-18120)*

**Mica Furniture Mfg Inc** G 708 430-1150
Addison *(G-205)*

▲ **Middletons Mouldings Inc** D 517 278-6610
Schaumburg *(G-19646)*

**Midwest Woodcrafters Inc** G 630 665-0901
Carol Stream *(G-3199)*

**Millcraft** G 618 426-9819
Campbell Hill *(G-2977)*

**Miller Whiteside Wood Working** G 309 827-6470
Mc Lean *(G-14463)*

**Mirek Cabinets** G 630 350-8336
Franklin Park *(G-10535)*

**Monarch Mfg Corp Amer** E 217 728-2552
Sullivan *(G-20753)*

**Monticello Design & Mfg** G 217 762-8551
Monticello *(G-15081)*

**Mueller Custom Cabinetry Inc** G 815 448-5448
Mazon *(G-14439)*

**Multiplex Display Fixture Co** E 800 325-3350
Dupo *(G-8574)*

**Murray Cabinetry & Tops Inc** G 815 672-6992
Streator *(G-20696)*

**Northstar Custom Cabinetry** G 708 597-2099
Posen *(G-17733)*

**Northwest Marble Products** E 630 860-2288
Hoffman Estates *(G-12072)*

**OGorman Son Carpentry Contrs** E 815 485-8997
New Lenox *(G-15898)*

**Okaw Valley Woodworking LLC** F 217 543-5180
Arthur *(G-916)*

**Orchard Hill Cabinetry Inc** E 312 829-4300
Chicago *(G-6005)*

**Pac Team US Productions LLC** G 773 360-8960
Chicago *(G-6049)*

◆ **Pace Industries Inc** D 312 226-5500
Chicago *(G-6051)*

**Parenti & Raffaelli Ltd** C 847 253-5550
Mount Prospect *(G-15361)*

**Perkins Construction** G 815 233-9655
Freeport *(G-10678)*

**Pintas Cultured Marble** E 708 385-3360
Alsip *(G-509)*

**Planks Cabinet Shop Inc** G 217 543-2687
Arthur *(G-918)*

**Plas-Co Inc** F 618 476-1761
Millstadt *(G-14832)*

**Prairie Woodworks Inc** G 309 378-2418
Downs *(G-8547)*

**Pro Cabinets Inc** G 618 993-0008
Marion *(G-14284)*

**R & R Custom Cabinet Making** G 847 358-6188
Palatine *(G-17065)*

**Rapp Cabinets & Woodworks Inc** F 618 736-2955
Dahlgren *(G-7692)*

**Raymond Earl Fine Woodworking** G 309 565-7661
Hanna City *(G-11570)*

**Regency Custom Woodworking** F 815 689-2117
Cullom *(G-7683)*

**Richard King and Sons** G 815 654-0226
Loves Park *(G-13982)*

**Richard Schrock** G 217 543-3111
Arthur *(G-920)*

**Riverside Custom Woodworking** G 815 589-3608
Fulton *(G-10705)*

▲ **Riverton Cabinet Company** E 815 462-5300
New Lenox *(G-15908)*

▲ **Rogan Granitindustrie Inc** G 708 758-0050
Lynwood *(G-14025)*

**Romar Cabinet & Top Co Inc** D 815 467-4452
Channahon *(G-3584)*

**Roncin Custom Design** G 847 669-0260
Huntley *(G-12175)*

**Ronnie P Faber** G 815 626-4561
Sterling *(G-20610)*

**Royal Fabricators Inc** F 847 775-7466
Wadsworth *(G-21327)*

**Santelli Custom Cabinetry** G 708 771-3884
River Forest *(G-18000)*

**Schrock Custom Woodworking** G 217 849-3375
Toledo *(G-20965)*

**Seigles Cabinet Center LLC** G 224 535-7034
Elgin *(G-9174)*

**Seneca Custom Cabinetry** G 815 357-1322
Seneca *(G-19890)*

**Shews Custom Woodworking** G 217 737-5543
Lincoln *(G-13419)*

**Sleeping Bear Inc** G 630 541-7220
Lisle *(G-13656)*

**Snaidero USA** G 312 644-6662
Chicago *(G-6538)*

**Space Organization Ltd** F 312 654-1400
Chicago *(G-6548)*

**Specialized Woodwork Inc** G 630 627-0450
Lombard *(G-13854)*

**Stancy Woodworking Co Inc** F 847 526-0252
Island Lake *(G-12219)*

**Stonetree Fabrication Inc** E 618 332-1700
East Saint Louis *(G-8771)*

**T and T Cabinet Co** G 815 245-6322
McHenry *(G-14566)*

▲ **T2 Cabinets Inc** F 312 593-1507
Chicago *(G-6664)*

**Teds Custom Cabinets Inc** G 773 581-4455
Chicago *(G-6687)*

**Trademark Cabinet Corporation** G 847 478-9393
Lincolnshire *(G-13486)*

**Tri Star Cabinet & Top Co Inc** D 815 485-2564
New Lenox *(G-15922)*

**Val Custom Cabinets & Flrg Inc** G 708 790-8373
Elk Grove Village *(G-9803)*

**Van Cleave Woodworking Inc** G 847 424-8200
Northbrook *(G-16382)*

**Vanities Inc** G 847 483-0240
Arlington Heights *(G-862)*

**Viking Metal Cabinet Co LLC** D 800 776-7767
Montgomery *(G-15069)*

**Viking Metal Cabinet Company** D 630 863-7234
Montgomery *(G-15070)*

**Wheaton Cabinetry** G 815 729-1085
Lockport *(G-13750)*

**Wilcor Solid Surface Inc** F 630 350-7703
Elk Grove Village *(G-9813)*

**Wolf Cabinetry & Ganite** G 847 358-9922
Palatine *(G-17091)*

**Wolters Custom Cabinets LLC** G 618 282-3158
Evansville *(G-10108)*

**Wood Shop** G 773 994-6666
Chicago *(G-7024)*

**Wood Specialties Incorporated** F 217 678-8420
Bement *(G-1803)*

**Woodhill Cabinetry Design Inc** G 815 431-0545
Ottawa *(G-16992)*

**Woodways Industries LLC** E 616 956-3070
Chicago *(G-7026)*

**Zenter Custom Cabinets Inc** F 847 488-0744
Elgin *(G-9240)*

## 2435 Hardwood Veneer & Plywood

▲ **Aircraft Plywood Mfg Inc** ... G ... 618 654-6740
Highland *(G-11775)*
▲ **Challinor Wood Products Inc** ... G ... 847 256-8828
Wilmette *(G-22250)*
**Chalon Wood Products Inc** ... G ... 630 243-9793
Lemont *(G-13231)*
▲ **Great Northern Lumber Inc** ... D ... 708 388-1818
Blue Island *(G-2254)*
**Klaman Hardwood** ... G ... 217 972-7888
Decatur *(G-7903)*
**L Land Hardwoods** ... G ... 708 496-9000
Bedford Park *(G-1561)*
**Lumberyard Suppliers Inc** ... E ... 217 965-4911
Virden *(G-21298)*
**R S Bacon Veneer Company** ... G ... 331 777-4762
Lisle *(G-13649)*
◆ **R S Bacon Veneer Company** ... C ... 630 323-1414
Lisle *(G-13648)*
**R-Squared Construction Inc** ... G ... 815 232-7433
Freeport *(G-10682)*
**Veneer Specialties Inc** ... F ... 630 754-8550
Lemont *(G-13267)*
**Walnut Creek Hardwood** ... G ... 815 389-3317
South Beloit *(G-20173)*
**Westrock CP LLC** ... D ... 312 346-6600
Chicago *(G-6967)*

## 2436 Softwood Veneer & Plywood

**Westrock CP LLC** ... D ... 312 346-6600
Chicago *(G-6967)*

## 2439 Structural Wood Members, NEC

**Alexander Lumber Co** ... G ... 815 754-1000
Cortland *(G-7383)*
**Anderson Truss Company** ... G ... 618 982-9228
Pittsburg *(G-17559)*
**Atlas Building Components Inc** ... E ... 618 639-0222
Jerseyville *(G-12418)*
**Atlas Components Inc** ... E ... 815 332-4904
Cherry Valley *(G-3638)*
**Bear Creek Truss Inc** ... E ... 217 543-3329
Tuscola *(G-21016)*
**Cedar Creek LLC** ... E ... 618 797-1220
Granite City *(G-11269)*
**Central Illinois Truss** ... F ... 309 447-6644
Deer Creek *(G-7961)*
**Central Wood LLC** ... G ... 217 543-2662
Arcola *(G-666)*
▼ **Connor Sports Flooring LLC** ... D ... 847 290-9020
Elk Grove Village *(G-9389)*
**Cooper Lake Millworks Inc** ... G ... 217 847-2681
Hamilton *(G-11530)*
**Jesse B Holt Inc** ... D ... 618 783-3075
Newton *(G-15942)*
**Lamboo Technologies LLC** ... G ... 866 966-2999
Litchfield *(G-13693)*
**Lumberyard Suppliers Inc** ... E ... 217 965-4911
Virden *(G-21298)*
**Okaw Truss Inc** ... B ... 217 543-3371
Arthur *(G-915)*
**Rehkemper & Sons Inc** ... E ... 618 526-2269
Breese *(G-2447)*
**Ruff Quality Components** ... E ... 309 662-0425
Bloomington *(G-2221)*
**Southern Truss Inc** ... E ... 618 252-8144
Harrisburg *(G-11604)*
**Strat-O-Span Buildings Inc** ... G ... 618 526-4566
Breese *(G-2448)*
▲ **Tempo Wood Products Inc** ... D ... 815 568-7315
Marengo *(G-14242)*
**Triumph Truss & Steel Company** ... F ... 815 522-6000
Elgin *(G-9216)*
**Truss Components Inc** ... F ... 800 678-7877
Columbia *(G-7365)*
**W Kost Manufacturing Co Inc** ... C ... 847 428-0600
Chicago *(G-6919)*
**WW Timbers Inc** ... G ... 708 423-9112
Chicago Ridge *(G-7159)*

## 2441 Wood Boxes

**Arrowtech Pallet & Crating** ... D ... 815 547-9300
Belvidere *(G-1734)*
**Botkin Lumber Company Inc** ... E ... 217 287-2127
Taylorville *(G-20834)*
◆ **BP Shipping** ... F ... 630 393-1032
Naperville *(G-15610)*
**Central Wood Products Inc** ... E ... 217 728-4412
Sullivan *(G-20742)*
**Chicago Export Packing Co** ... E ... 773 247-8911
Chicago *(G-4318)*
**Chrometec LLC** ... G ... 630 792-8777
Lombard *(G-13778)*
**Community Support Systems** ... D ... 217 705-4300
Teutopolis *(G-20850)*
**D/C Export & Domestic Pkg Inc** ... E ... 847 593-4200
Elk Grove Village *(G-9415)*
**Dexton Enterprises** ... G ... 309 788-1881
Rock Island *(G-18174)*
**Du-Call Miller Plastics Inc** ... F ... 630 964-6020
Batavia *(G-1443)*
**Elm Street Industries Inc** ... F ... 309 854-7000
Kewanee *(G-12681)*
**Export Packaging Co Inc** ... A ... 309 756-4288
Milan *(G-14786)*
▲ **Extreme Tools Inc** ... G ... 630 202-8324
Naperville *(G-15656)*
**Fca LLC** ... E ... 309 949-3999
Coal Valley *(G-7296)*
**Fca LLC** ... E ... 309 385-2588
Princeville *(G-17765)*
**Jordan Paper Box Company** ... F ... 773 287-5362
Chicago *(G-5323)*
**Kccdd Inc** ... D ... 309 344-2030
Galesburg *(G-10762)*
**Kunde Woodwork Inc** ... G ... 847 669-2030
Huntley *(G-12156)*
**Nefab Packaging N Centl LLC** ... C ...
Elk Grove Village *(G-9649)*
▲ **Ockerlund Industries Inc** ... E ... 630 620-1269
Addison *(G-232)*
▲ **Pak Source Inc** ... E ... 309 786-7374
Rock Island *(G-18191)*
**Pierce Packaging Co** ... F ... 815 636-5650
Loves Park *(G-13974)*
**Pierce Packaging Co** ... G ... 815 636-5656
Peoria *(G-17428)*
**Pierce Packaging Co** ... F ... 815 636-5656
Loves Park *(G-13975)*
**R & H Products Inc** ... G ... 815 744-4110
Rockdale *(G-18229)*
**Specialty Box Corp** ... F ... 630 897-7278
North Aurora *(G-16145)*
**Trade Industries** ... E ... 618 643-4321
Mc Leansboro *(G-14469)*
▲ **Upham & Walsh Lumber Co** ... G ... 847 519-1010
Hoffman Estates *(G-12067)*
**Wesling Products Inc** ... G ... 773 533-2850
Chicago *(G-6959)*
**Western Illinois Enterprises** ... G ... 309 342-5185
Galesburg *(G-10779)*

## 2448 Wood Pallets & Skids

**3v Pallet** ... G ... 708 620-7790
South Holland *(G-20237)*
**3v Pallet** ... G ... 708 333-1113
Harvey *(G-11649)*
**815 Pallets Inc** ... E ... 815 678-0012
Richmond *(G-17954)*
**A & F Pallet Service Inc** ... F ... 773 767-9500
Chicago *(G-3680)*
**AA Pallet Inc** ... E ... 773 536-3699
Chicago *(G-3697)*
**ADP Pallet Inc** ... F ... 773 638-3800
Chicago *(G-3755)*
**Advance Pallet Incorporated** ... E ... 847 697-5700
South Elgin *(G-20179)*
**AGCO Recycling LLC** ... F ... 217 224-9048
Quincy *(G-17790)*
▲ **Aldon Co** ... F ... 847 623-8800
Waukegan *(G-21521)*
**All Pallet Service** ... G ... 618 451-7545
Granite City *(G-11262)*
**American Pallet Co Inc** ... D ... 847 662-5525
Waukegan *(G-21525)*
**Amerigreen Pallets** ... G ... 309 698-3463
East Peoria *(G-8700)*
**Arrows Up Inc** ... G ... 847 305-2550
Arlington Heights *(G-717)*
**Arrowtech Pallet & Crating** ... D ... 815 547-9300
Belvidere *(G-1734)*
**ASAP Pallets Inc** ... F ... 630 350-7689
Franklin Park *(G-10402)*
**ASAP Pallets Inc** ... G ... 630 917-0180
Bellwood *(G-1694)*
**Ash Pallet Management Inc** ... D ... 847 473-5700
Antioch *(G-620)*
**Ash Pallet Management Inc** ... E ... 847 473-5700
Franklin Park *(G-10403)*
**Bach Timber & Pallet Inc** ... G ... 815 885-3774
Caledonia *(G-2930)*
**Badger Pallet Inc** ... G ... 815 943-1147
Harvard *(G-11623)*
**Best Pallet Company LLC** ... F ... 815 637-1500
Loves Park *(G-13924)*
**Best Pallet Company LLC** ... G ... 312 242-4009
Chicago *(G-4094)*
**Blue Comet Transport Inc** ... G ... 773 617-9512
Chicago *(G-4125)*
**Bob Ulrichs Pallets** ... G ... 217 224-2568
Quincy *(G-17806)*
**Botkin Lumber Company Inc** ... E ... 217 287-2127
Taylorville *(G-20834)*
**Caisson Inc** ... E ... 815 547-5925
Belvidere *(G-1741)*
**Cantarero Pallets Inc** ... G ... 773 413-7017
Chicago *(G-4227)*
**Cardinal Pallet Co** ... E ... 773 725-5387
Chicago *(G-4240)*
▼ **Cargois Inc** ... F ... 847 357-1901
Elk Grove Village *(G-9356)*
**Central States Pallets** ... G ... 217 494-2710
Chatham *(G-3617)*
**Central Wood Products Inc** ... E ... 217 728-4412
Sullivan *(G-20742)*
**Champion Wood Pallets Inc** ... G ... 630 801-8036
Aurora *(G-1127)*
**Chicago Heights Pallets Co** ... F ... 708 757-7641
Chicago Heights *(G-7088)*
**Chicago Pallet Service Inc** ... E ... 847 439-8754
Elk Grove Village *(G-9368)*
**Chicago Pallet Service II Inc** ... E ... 847 439-8330
Elk Grove Village *(G-9369)*
▲ **Cimc Leasing Usa Inc** ... G ... 630 785-6875
Oakbrook Terrace *(G-16702)*
**Cleary Pallet Sales Inc** ... E ... 815 784-3048
Genoa *(G-10876)*
**Cole Pallet Services Corp** ... E ... 815 758-3226
Dekalb *(G-8077)*
**Commercial Pallet Inc** ... E ... 312 226-6699
Chicago *(G-4435)*
**Community Support Systems** ... D ... 217 705-4300
Teutopolis *(G-20850)*
**Corr-Pak Corporation** ... E ... 708 442-7806
Mc Cook *(G-14447)*
**Corsaw Hardwood Lumber Inc** ... F ... 309 293-2055
Smithfield *(G-20119)*
**Craft Pallet Inc** ... G ... 618 437-5382
INA *(G-12184)*
**Crossroad Crating & Pallet** ... G ... 815 657-8409
Forrest *(G-10261)*
**D & E Pallet Inc** ... G ... 708 891-4307
Chicago *(G-4532)*
**D and D Pallets** ... F ... 630 800-1102
Aurora *(G-1136)*
◆ **Darios Pallets Corp** ... E ... 312 421-3413
Chicago *(G-4558)*
**Decatur Wood Products LLC** ... G ... 217 424-2602
Decatur *(G-7874)*
**Dexton Enterprises** ... G ... 309 788-1881
Rock Island *(G-18174)*
**Dg Wood Processing** ... F ... 217 543-2128
Arthur *(G-894)*
**Diaz Pallets** ... G ... 630 340-3736
Aurora *(G-1140)*
**Dixon Pallet Service** ... G ... 773 238-9569
Chicago *(G-4614)*
**Eam Pallets** ... G ... 708 333-0596
Harvey *(G-11664)*
**Earthwise Recycled Pallet** ... G ... 618 286-6015
Dupo *(G-8570)*
**Edgar Pallets** ... G ... 773 454-8919
Chicago *(G-4695)*
**Edison Pallet & Wood Products** ... G ... 630 653-3416
Winfield *(G-22285)*
**Eds Pallet Service** ... F ... 618 248-5386
Albers *(G-353)*
**Enterprise Pallet Inc** ... F ... 815 928-8546
Bourbonnais *(G-2395)*
▼ **Equustock LLC** ... F ... 866 962-4686
Loves Park *(G-13940)*
**Export Packaging Co Inc** ... A ... 309 756-4288
Milan *(G-14786)*
**F and L Pallets Inc** ... G ... 773 364-0798
Chicago *(G-4801)*
**Fca LLC** ... E ... 309 385-2588
Princeville *(G-17765)*
**Fca LLC** ... E ... 309 792-3444
Moline *(G-14939)*

Fulton County Rehabilitation ........E ....... 309 647-6510
Canton (G-2987)

G & S Pallets ........G ....... 630 574-2741
Oak Brook (G-16518)

General Pallet ........G ....... 773 660-8550
Chicago (G-4930)

Georgetown Wood and Pallet Co ........E ....... 217 662-2563
Georgetown (G-10887)

Glitter Your Pallet ........G ....... 708 516-8494
Homer Glen (G-12080)

Go Jo Pallets & Supplies Inc ........F ....... 815 254-1631
Plainfield (G-17603)

▲ Graphic Pallet & Transport ........E ....... 630 904-4951
Plainfield (G-17604)

Great Lakes Lumber and Pallet ........G ....... 773 243-6839
Park Ridge (G-17200)

Guero Pallets ........G ....... 312 593-4276
Chicago (G-5008)

Hammer Enterprises Inc ........F ....... 217 662-8225
Georgetown (G-10888)

Hardwood Lumber Products Co ........G ....... 309 538-4411
Kilbourne (G-12697)

Harvey Pallets Inc ........C ....... 708 293-1831
Blue Island (G-2255)

Hill Top Pallet ........G ....... 618 426-9810
Ava (G-1237)

HMM Pallets Inc ........G ....... 773 927-3448
Chicago (G-5095)

Hope Pallet Inc ........G ....... 815 412-4606
Rockdale (G-18220)

Human Svc Ctr Southern Metro E ........E ....... 618 282-6233
Red Bud (G-17942)

Ifco ........G ....... 630 226-0650
Bolingbrook (G-2318)

Illinois Pallets Inc ........G ....... 773 640-9228
Willow Springs (G-22197)

Industrial Pallets LLC ........G ....... 708 351-8783
Glendale Heights (G-11034)

Industrial Service Pallet Inc ........G ....... 708 655-4963
Melrose Park (G-14658)

J & J Quality Pallets Inc ........G ....... 618 262-6426
Mount Carmel (G-15269)

J&A Pallets Service Inc ........F ....... 708 333-6601
Chicago Heights (G-7104)

Jjm Products LLC ........G ....... 630 319-9325
Westmont (G-21894)

Jo Go Pallet & Supplies ........F ....... 815 254-1631
Plainfield (G-17613)

Joliet Pallets ........G .......
Joliet (G-12524)

Joseph B Krisher ........G ....... 618 677-2016
Mascoutah (G-14354)

Kccdd Inc ........D ....... 309 344-2030
Galesburg (G-10762)

Kirk Wood Products Inc ........E ....... 309 829-6661
Bloomington (G-2190)

Lake Street Pallets ........G ....... 773 889-2266
Chicago (G-5441)

Lakeland Pallets Inc ........G ....... 616 949-9515
Geneva (G-10844)

Los Primos Pallets Inc ........G ....... 773 418-3584
Chicago (G-5545)

Lottus Inc ........G ....... 847 691-9464
Glenview (G-11166)

M & M Paltech Inc ........D ....... 630 350-7890
Belvidere (G-1767)

M and M Pallet Inc ........G ....... 708 272-4447
Blue Island (G-2261)

Malvaes Solutions Incorporated ........G ....... 773 823-1034
Chicago (G-5608)

McKean Pallet Co ........G ....... 309 246-7543
Lacon (G-12788)

Mental Health Ctrs Centl Ill ........D ....... 217 735-1413
Lincoln (G-13415)

Midwest Wood Inc ........F ....... 815 273-3333
Savanna (G-19402)

Mills Pallet ........F ....... 773 533-6458
Chicago (G-5765)

Mobile Pallet Service Inc ........F ....... 630 231-6597
West Chicago (G-21745)

Momence Pallet Corporation ........E ....... 815 472-6451
Momence (G-14985)

Morris Pallet Skids Inc ........G ....... 618 786-2241
Dow (G-8382)

Muro Pallets Corp ........G ....... 773 640-8606
Chicago (G-5835)

Murrihy Pallet Co ........E ....... 615 370-7000
Chicago (G-5837)

Nefab Packaging N Centl LLC ........C .......
Elk Grove Village (G-9649)

Newport Pallet ........G ....... 217 662-6577
Georgetown (G-10889)

Northern Illinois Pallet Inc ........G ....... 815 236-9242
Fox Lake (G-10280)

Northern Pallet and Supply Co ........F ....... 847 716-1400
Northfield (G-16412)

▲ Northwest Pallet Supply Co ........C ....... 815 544-6001
Belvidere (G-1777)

▲ Pak Source Inc ........E ....... 309 786-7374
Rock Island (G-18191)

Pallet Base LLC ........G ....... 312 316-6137
Chicago (G-6063)

Pallet Recyclers Inc ........G ....... 815 432-4022
Watseka (G-21424)

Pallet Solution ........G ....... 773 837-8677
Streamwood (G-20669)

Pallet Solution Inc ........E ....... 618 445-2316
Albion (G-364)

Pallet Wrapz ........F ....... 847 729-5850
Glenview (G-11178)

Pallet Wrapz Inc ........G ....... 847 729-5850
Glenview (G-11179)

Palletmaxx Inc ........G ....... 708 385-9595
Crestwood (G-7497)

Pallets International Holding ........G ....... 773 391-7223
South Holland (G-20294)

Pallets Plus Inc ........G ....... 847 318-1853
Park Ridge (G-17215)

Pallets Shop ........G ....... 618 920-6875
Springfield (G-20497)

▲ Pallett Wilson ........G ....... 217 543-3555
Sullivan (G-20757)

Piece Works Specialists Inc ........F ....... 309 266-7016
Morton (G-15177)

Premium Pallets ........G ....... 217 974-0155
Springfield (G-20507)

Progressive Recycling Systems ........G ....... 217 291-0009
Jacksonville (G-12410)

Quality Pallets Inc ........E ....... 217 459-2655
Windsor (G-22282)

R & H Products Inc ........G ....... 815 744-4110
Rockdale (G-18229)

R & R Services Illinois Inc ........G ....... 217 424-2602
Decatur (G-7930)

R K J Pallets Inc ........F ....... 708 493-0701
Bellwood (G-1717)

Raildecks Intermodal ........G ....... 630 442-7676
Downers Grove (G-8512)

Rbj Inc ........F ....... 309 344-5066
Galesburg (G-10772)

Rock Valley Pallet Company ........G ....... 815 654-4850
Machesney Park (G-14102)

Rose Pallet LLC ........G ....... 708 333-3000
Bridgeview (G-2525)

Round Lake Pallets Inc ........G ....... 847 637-6162
Round Lake (G-19065)

S & S Pallet Corp ........E ....... 618 219-3218
Granite City (G-11301)

Schroeders Pallet Service ........G ....... 708 371-9046
Blue Island (G-2269)

Simonton Hardwood Lumber LLC ........F ....... 618 594-2132
Carlyle (G-3059)

Singleton Pallets Co ........G ....... 708 687-7006
Oak Forest (G-16588)

Sotos Pallets Inc ........G ....... 815 338-7750
Woodstock (G-22613)

◆ Sterling Lumber Company ........C ....... 708 388-2223
Phoenix (G-17542)

Steve Forrest ........F ....... 815 765-9040
Poplar Grove (G-17717)

Timberline Pallet & Skid Inc ........F ....... 309 752-1770
East Moline (G-8695)

Trade Industries ........E ....... 618 643-4321
Mc Leansboro (G-14469)

Try Our Pallets Inc ........G ....... 708 343-0166
Maywood (G-14436)

Twin City Wood Recycling Corp ........G ....... 309 827-9663
Bloomington (G-2234)

Universal Pallet Inc ........G ....... 815 928-8546
Bradley (G-2436)

▲ Upham & Walsh Lumber Co ........G ....... 847 519-1010
Hoffman Estates (G-12067)

Walnut Grove Packaging ........G ....... 217 268-5112
Arcola (G-687)

Workshop Ltd Inc ........G ....... 708 458-3222
Bedford Park (G-1594)

## 2449 Wood Containers, NEC

A & M Wood Products Inc ........G ....... 630 323-2555
Burr Ridge (G-2818)

Caisson Inc ........E ....... 815 547-5925
Belvidere (G-1741)

Caisson Industries Inc ........F ....... 815 568-6554
Marengo (G-14221)

Central Wood Products Inc ........E ....... 217 728-4412
Sullivan (G-20742)

Chicago Crate Inc ........G ....... 708 380-4716
Downers Grove (G-8409)

Chicago Floral Planters Inc ........G ....... 708 423-2754
Chicago Ridge (G-7141)

Cole Pallet Services Corp ........E ....... 815 758-3226
Dekalb (G-8077)

D/C Export & Domestic Pkg Inc ........E ....... 847 593-4200
Elk Grove Village (G-9415)

Elm Street Industries Inc ........F ....... 309 854-7000
Kewanee (G-12681)

Hart - Clayton Inc ........F ....... 217 525-1610
Springfield (G-20448)

Induspac Rtp Inc ........E ....... 919 484-9484
Bridgeview (G-2500)

Midwest Mktg/Pdctn Mfg Co ........G ....... 217 256-3414
Warsaw (G-21370)

Nefab Packaging N Centl LLC ........C .......
Elk Grove Village (G-9649)

Ockerlund Wood Products Co ........E ....... 630 620-1269
Addison (G-233)

▲ Pallett Wilson ........G ....... 217 543-3555
Sullivan (G-20757)

Polamer Inc ........G ....... 773 774-3600
Chicago (G-6148)

Production Manufacturing ........G ....... 217 256-4211
Warsaw (G-21371)

R & H Products Inc ........G ....... 815 744-4110
Rockdale (G-18229)

Specialty Crate Factory ........G ....... 708 756-2100
Steger (G-20576)

▼ T2 Site Amenities Incorporated ........G ....... 847 579-9003
Highland Park (G-11876)

▲ U S Storage Group LLC ........F ....... 618 482-8000
Madison (G-14155)

Van Voorst Lumber Company Inc ........E ....... 815 426-2544
Union Hill (G-21039)

Wesling Products Inc ........G ....... 773 533-2850
Chicago (G-6959)

## 2451 Mobile Homes

Carlin Mfg A Div Grs Holdg LLC ........E ....... 559 276-0123
Naperville (G-15617)

Gerald Graff ........E ....... 312 343-2612
Lincolnwood (G-13514)

▲ Innovative Mobile Marketing ........F ....... 815 929-1029
Bourbonnais (G-2400)

Mobil Trailer Transport Inc ........E ....... 630 993-1200
Villa Park (G-21270)

Shur Co of Illinois ........G ....... 217 877-8277
Decatur (G-7940)

Skiman Sales Inc ........G ....... 847 888-8200
Elgin (G-9187)

Southmoor Estates Inc ........G ....... 815 756-1299
Dekalb (G-8121)

Superior Mobile Home Service ........G ....... 708 672-7799
Crete (G-7520)

## 2452 Prefabricated Wood Buildings & Cmp-nts

Alply Insulated Panels LLC ........G ....... 217 324-6700
Litchfield (G-13680)

Ashton Diversified Enterprises ........G ....... 630 739-0981
Lemont (G-13225)

Bitter End Yacht Club Intl ........F ....... 312 506-6205
Chicago (G-4115)

Coach House Inc ........E ....... 217 543-3761
Arthur (G-888)

Contempri Industries Inc ........E ....... 618 357-5361
Pinckneyville (G-17545)

Cook Sales Inc ........E ....... 618 893-2114
Cobden (G-7301)

Csi Manufacturing Inc ........E ....... 309 937-2653
Cambridge (G-2967)

Dave White ........G ....... 618 898-1130
Cisne (G-7251)

Everlast Portable Buildings ........G ....... 217 543-4080
Sullivan (G-20745)

Faze Change Produx ........E ....... 217 728-2184
Sullivan (G-20746)

Frederking Construction Co ........G ....... 618 483-5031
Altamont (G-551)

Grs Holding LLC ........G ....... 630 355-1660
Naperville (G-15666)



Employee Codes: A=Over 500 employees, B=251-500
C=101-250, D=51-100, E=20-50, F=10-19, G=3-9

2017 Harris Illinois
Industrial Directory

941

**Homeway Homes Inc** ........ D ....... 309 965-2312
Deer Creek *(G-7964)*
**Jack Bartlett** ........ G ....... 217 659-3575
Dallas City *(G-7697)*
**K & K Storage Barns LLC** ........ F ....... 618 927-0533
Ewing *(G-10120)*
**Lester Building Systems LLC** ........ E ....... 217 348-7676
Charleston *(G-3603)*
**McDonnell Components Inc** ........ D ....... 815 547-9555
Belvidere *(G-1770)*
**Norridge Jewelry** ........ G ....... 312 984-1036
Chicago *(G-5929)*
**Omni-Tech Systems Inc** ........ E ....... 309 962-2281
Le Roy *(G-13208)*
**Otten Construction Co Inc** ........ G ....... 618 768-4310
Addieville *(G-13)*
**R & N Components Co** ........ G ....... 217 543-3495
Tuscola *(G-21023)*
**Schrocks Wood Shop** ........ G ....... 217 773-3842
Mount Sterling *(G-15394)*
**Snagamon Valley Log Builders** ........ G ....... 217 632-7609
Petersburg *(G-17538)*
**Steel Span Inc** ........ F ....... 815 943-9071
Harvard *(G-11648)*
**Strat-O-Span Buildings Inc** ........ G ....... 618 526-4566
Breese *(G-2448)*
**Tuff Shed Inc** ........ F ....... 847 704-1147
Palatine *(G-17083)*
**W Kost Manufacturing Co Inc** ........ C ....... 847 428-0600
Chicago *(G-6919)*
**Walnut Custom Homes Inc** ........ E ....... 815 379-2151
Walnut *(G-21332)*
**West Salem Knox County Htchy** ........ G ....... 618 456-3601
West Salem *(G-21825)*
**Yoders Portable Buildings LLC** ........ G ....... 618 936-2419
Sumner *(G-20773)*

## 2491 Wood Preserving

**Chicago Flameproof WD Spc Corp** ........ E ....... 630 859-0009
Montgomery *(G-15037)*
**Great Lakes Art Foundry Inc** ........ G ....... 847 213-0800
Skokie *(G-20006)*
▲ **Great Northern Lumber Inc** ........ D ....... 708 388-1818
Blue Island *(G-2254)*
**John A Biewer Lumber Company** ........ F ....... 815 357-6792
Seneca *(G-19887)*
**Koppers Industries Inc** ........ E ....... 309 343-5157
Galesburg *(G-10763)*
**Marshall Bauer** ........ G ....... 847 236-1847
Bannockburn *(G-1260)*
**Midwest Intgrted Companies LLC** ........ C ....... 847 426-6354
Gilberts *(G-10926)*
**Miller Whiteside Wood Working** ........ G ....... 309 827-6470
Mc Lean *(G-14463)*
**Northern Illinois Lumber Spc** ........ E ....... 630 859-3226
Montgomery *(G-15064)*
**Northwest Snow Timber Svc Ltd** ........ G ....... 847 778-4998
Glenview *(G-11175)*
**Nu Again** ........ F ....... 630 564-5590
Bartlett *(G-1364)*
**Perma-Treat of Illinois Inc** ........ F ....... 618 997-5646
Marion *(G-14278)*
**Southeast Wood Treating Inc** ........ F ....... 815 562-5007
Rochelle *(G-18110)*
**T P I Inc** ........ G ....... 847 888-0232
Elgin *(G-9201)*
**Tronox Incorporated** ........ E ....... 203 705-3704
Madison *(G-14154)*

## 2493 Reconstituted Wood Prdts

**Claridge Products and Eqp Inc** ........ G ....... 847 991-8822
Elgin *(G-8992)*
◆ **Craftmaster Manufacturing Inc** ........ A ....... 800 405-2233
Chicago *(G-4490)*
**Geneva Wood Fuels LLC** ........ E ....... 773 296-0700
Chicago *(G-4936)*
**Georgia-Pacific Bldg Pdts LLC** ........ G ....... 630 449-7200
Aurora *(G-1015)*
**Iten Industries Inc** ........ G ....... 630 543-2820
Addison *(G-155)*
**Jeld-Wen Inc** ........ C ....... 312 544-5041
Chicago *(G-5287)*
▲ **Vecchio Manufacturing of Ill** ........ F ....... 847 742-8429
Elgin *(G-9224)*

## 2499 Wood Prdts, NEC

▲ **A & M Products Company** ........ G ....... 815 875-2667
Princeton *(G-17740)*
**A Jule Enterprise Inc** ........ G ....... 312 243-6950
Chicago *(G-3689)*
**Aba Custom Woodworking** ........ G ....... 815 356-9663
Crystal Lake *(G-7525)*
**Adel Woodworks** ........ G ....... 815 886-9006
Romeoville *(G-18790)*
**All American Wood Register Co** ........ F ....... 815 356-1000
Crystal Lake *(G-7528)*
▲ **Aph Custom Wood & Metal Pdts** ........ G ....... 708 410-1274
Broadview *(G-2558)*
**Archi-Cepts** ........ G ....... 618 594-8810
Carlyle *(G-3052)*
**Artistic Framing Inc** ........ C ....... 847 808-0200
Wheeling *(G-22007)*
**Axis Design Architectual Mllwk** ........ F ....... 630 466-4549
Sugar Grove *(G-20717)*
**Bergeron Group Inc** ........ E ....... 815 741-1635
Joliet *(G-12464)*
**Better Built Buildings** ........ G ....... 217 267-7824
Westville *(G-21928)*
**Borns Picture Frames** ........ G ....... 630 876-1709
West Chicago *(G-21673)*
**Bravura Moulding Company** ........ G ....... 262 633-1882
Lake Bluff *(G-12838)*
▲ **Brown Wood Products Company** ........ F ....... 847 673-4780
Lincolnwood *(G-13503)*
**Brown Woodworking** ........ G ....... 815 477-8333
Crystal Lake *(G-7544)*
**Caldwell Woodworks** ........ G ....... 217 566-2434
Williamsville *(G-22190)*
▲ **Chicago Dowel Company Inc** ........ D ....... 773 622-2000
Chicago *(G-4315)*
**Christian Cnty Mntal Hlth Assn** ........ D ....... 217 824-9675
Taylorville *(G-20836)*
**Cma Inc** ........ E ....... 847 848-0674
Joliet *(G-12474)*
**Cma Inc** ........ E ....... 630 551-3100
Oswego *(G-16909)*
**Colberts Custom Framing** ........ F ....... 630 717-1448
Naperville *(G-15632)*
**Country Stone Inc** ........ E ....... 309 787-1744
Milan *(G-14781)*
**Curtis Woodworking Inc** ........ G ....... 815 544-3543
Belvidere *(G-1748)*
**Danlee Wood Products Inc** ........ G ....... 815 938-9016
Forreston *(G-10268)*
**Delleman Associates & Corp** ........ G ....... 708 345-9520
Maywood *(G-14425)*
**Dusty Lane Wood Products** ........ G ....... 618 426-9045
Campbell Hill *(G-2975)*
**E-Z Tree Recycling Inc** ........ G ....... 773 493-8600
Chicago *(G-4670)*
▲ **Edgewater Products Company Inc** ........ F ....... 708 345-9200
Melrose Park *(G-14629)*
**Elegant Concepts Ltd** ........ G ....... 708 456-9590
Elmwood Park *(G-9968)*
▼ **Equustock LLC** ........ F ....... 866 962-4686
Loves Park *(G-13940)*
▲ **Excel Group Holdings Inc** ........ E ....... 630 773-1815
Itasca *(G-12261)*
▲ **Fac Enterprises Inc** ........ D ....... 847 844-4000
Elgin *(G-9034)*
**Forest Awards & Engraving** ........ G ....... 630 595-2242
Wood Dale *(G-22371)*
**Frame Game** ........ G ....... 573 754-2385
Pleasant Hill *(G-17680)*
**Frame House Inc** ........ G ....... 708 383-1616
Oak Park *(G-16663)*
**Frame Mart Inc** ........ G ....... 309 452-0658
Normal *(G-16071)*
▲ **Frank A Edmunds & Co Inc** ........ F ....... 773 586-2772
Chicago *(G-4883)*
**Frederics Frame Studio Inc** ........ F ....... 312 243-2950
Chicago *(G-4886)*
**Gavin Woodworking Inc** ........ G ....... 815 786-2242
Sandwich *(G-19365)*
▲ **Global Decor Inc** ........ E ....... 847 437-9600
Elk Grove Village *(G-9500)*
**Golden Valley Hardscapes LLC** ........ G ....... 309 654-2261
Cordova *(G-7376)*
**Greencycle of Indiana Inc** ........ G ....... 847 441-6606
Northfield *(G-16400)*
▲ **Grohe America Inc** ........ D ....... 630 582-7711
Roselle *(G-18944)*
**Herschberger Wood Working** ........ G ....... 217 543-4075
Arthur *(G-905)*
**Hexacomb Corporation** ........ G ....... 847 955-7984
Buffalo Grove *(G-2704)*
**House of Color** ........ F ....... 708 352-3222
Countryside *(G-7432)*
**House On The Hill Inc** ........ G ....... 630 279-4455
Wheaton *(G-21953)*
**Illinois Tool Works Inc** ........ G ....... 708 720-7070
Frankfort *(G-10332)*
**Illinois Wood Fiber Products** ........ G ....... 847 836-6176
Carpentersville *(G-3288)*
**Inlaid Woodcraft Co** ........ F ....... 815 784-6386
Genoa *(G-10880)*
**Iron Castle Inc** ........ F ....... 773 890-0575
Chicago *(G-5238)*
**J R Husar Inc** ........ F ....... 312 243-7888
Chicago *(G-5263)*
**Jack Ruch Quality Homes Inc** ........ G ....... 309 663-6595
Bloomington *(G-2185)*
**Jacobs Reproduction** ........ G ....... 618 374-2198
Elsah *(G-9976)*
**John Joda Post 54** ........ G ....... 815 692-3222
Fairbury *(G-10128)*
**Jones Wood Products** ........ G ....... 618 826-2682
Rockwood *(G-18704)*
**Jorh Frame & Moulding Co Inc** ........ G ....... 708 747-3440
Matteson *(G-14374)*
**Joseph Woodworking Corporation** ........ F ....... 847 233-9766
Schiller Park *(G-19841)*
**Kaufman Woodworking** ........ G ....... 217 543-3607
Arthur *(G-906)*
**Kaufmans Custom Cabinets** ........ F ....... 217 268-4330
Arcola *(G-673)*
**Kohout Woodwork Inc** ........ G ....... 630 628-6257
Addison *(G-172)*
**Larson-Juhl US LLC** ........ D ....... 630 307-9700
Roselle *(G-18951)*
**Lee Armand & Co Ltd** ........ E ....... 312 455-1200
Chicago *(G-5483)*
**Liftseat Corporation** ........ E ....... 630 424-2840
Oak Brook *(G-16537)*
**Linwood LLC** ........ G ....... 217 446-1110
Danville *(G-7748)*
**Little Creek Woodworking** ........ G ....... 217 543-2815
Arthur *(G-908)*
**M & R Custom Millwork** ........ G ....... 815 547-8549
Belvidere *(G-1768)*
**Macks Wood Working** ........ G ....... 630 953-2559
Lombard *(G-13823)*
**Masterpiece Framing** ........ G ....... 630 893-4390
Bloomingdale *(G-2116)*
**Mc Mechanical Contractors Inc** ........ G ....... 708 460-0075
Orland Park *(G-16874)*
▲ **Melyx Inc** ........ F ....... 309 654-2551
Cordova *(G-7379)*
**Mercurys Green LLC** ........ E ....... 708 865-9134
Franklin Park *(G-10528)*
**Mhwp** ........ G ....... 618 228-7600
Aviston *(G-1247)*
**Michels Frame Shop** ........ G ....... 847 647-7366
Niles *(G-16004)*
**Midwest Lifting Products Inc** ........ G ....... 214 356-7102
Granite City *(G-11294)*
**Mike Meier & Sons Fence Mfg** ........ E ....... 847 587-1111
Spring Grove *(G-20347)*
**Mulch Center LLC** ........ E ....... 847 459-7200
Deerfield *(G-8041)*
▲ **Naegele Inc** ........ G ....... 708 388-7766
Alsip *(G-496)*
**New SBL Inc** ........ E ....... 773 376-8280
Chicago *(G-5893)*
**Nielsen & Bainbridge LLC** ........ D ....... 708 546-2135
Bridgeview *(G-2514)*
**Nikwood Products Inc** ........ G ....... 309 658-2341
Hillsdale *(G-11902)*
**Northwest Frame Company Inc** ........ G ....... 847 359-0987
Palatine *(G-17059)*
▲ **Nu-Dell Manufacturing Co Inc** ........ F ....... 847 803-4500
Chicago *(G-5953)*
**Orren Pickell Builders Inc** ........ F ....... 847 572-5200
Northfield *(G-16415)*
**Pearl Design Group LLC** ........ E ....... 630 295-8401
Bloomingdale *(G-2128)*
**Picture Frame Fulfillment LLC** ........ D ....... 847 260-5071
Franklin Park *(G-10550)*
**Powers Woodworking** ........ G ....... 630 663-9644
Woodridge *(G-22509)*
**Premium Wood Products Inc** ........ E ....... 815 787-3669
Dekalb *(G-8113)*
**Quality Plus** ........ F ....... 618 779-4931
Litchfield *(G-13695)*
**R Maderite Inc** ........ G ....... 773 235-1515
Chicago *(G-6268)*
◆ **R S Bacon Veneer Company** ........ C ....... 630 323-1414
Lisle *(G-13648)*
**Rainbow Farms Enterprises Inc** ........ G ....... 708 534-1070
Monee *(G-14999)*

# 25 FURNITURE AND FIXTURES

Reynolds Holdings Inc .................G....... 630 739-0110
  Romeoville *(G-18863)*
Rkb Distributors .............................G....... 847 970-6880
  Mundelein *(G-15552)*
Roselle Custom Woodwork LLC .....G....... 630 980-5655
  Roselle *(G-18969)*
◆ Sarj USA Inc ................................E....... 708 865-9134
  Franklin Park *(G-10582)*
Shawcraft Sign Co ........................G....... 815 282-4105
  Machesney Park *(G-14107)*
Silver Line ....................................G....... 708 832-9100
  Calumet City *(G-2954)*
Springfield Woodworks ..................G....... 217 483-7234
  Chatham *(G-3625)*
Stancy Woodworking Co Inc ..........F....... 847 526-0252
  Island Lake *(G-12219)*
Star Cabinetry ...............................G....... 773 725-4651
  Chicago *(G-6575)*
Supreme Frame & Moulding Co .....F....... 312 930-9056
  Chicago *(G-6638)*
Swagath Group Inc ......................G....... 847 640-6446
  Arlington Heights *(G-849)*
Tender Loving Care Inds Inc ..........D....... 847 891-0230
  Schaumburg *(G-19759)*
Tepromark International Inc ..........G....... 847 329-7881
  Chicago *(G-6703)*
Todd Scanlan ...............................G....... 217 585-1717
  Springfield *(G-20545)*
Vas Design Inc .............................G....... 773 794-1368
  Chicago *(G-6876)*
▲ Vaughan & Bushnell Mfg Co .......F....... 815 648-2446
  Hebron *(G-11730)*
Weathertop Woodcraft ..................G
  Carol Stream *(G-3265)*
Werner Co ....................................E....... 815 459-6020
  Crystal Lake *(G-7676)*
Wood Shop ...................................G....... 773 994-6666
  Chicago *(G-7024)*
Woodlogic Custom Millwork Inc .....E....... 847 640-4500
  Elk Grove Village *(G-9815)*
Woodmac Industries Inc ................G....... 708 755-3545
  S Chicago Hts *(G-19116)*
Woodwind Specialists ...................G....... 217 423-4122
  Decatur *(G-7960)*
Wyman and Company ...................G....... 708 532-9064
  Tinley Park *(G-20956)*

## 25 FURNITURE AND FIXTURES

### 2511 Wood Household Furniture

A Closet Wholesaler .....................F....... 312 654-1400
  Chicago *(G-3685)*
AB&d Custom Furniture Inc ...........E....... 708 922-9061
  Homewood *(G-12090)*
Aba Custom Woodworking .............G....... 815 356-9663
  Crystal Lake *(G-7525)*
Acrylic Ventures Inc .....................F....... 847 901-4440
  Glenview *(G-11094)*
Addison Interiors Company ...........F....... 630 628-1345
  Addison *(G-23)*
Allie Woodworking ........................G....... 847 244-1919
  Waukegan *(G-21522)*
Amish Country Heirlooms LLC ......G....... 217 253-9200
  Tuscola *(G-21015)*
▲ Amtab Manufacturing Corp .........D....... 630 301-7600
  Aurora *(G-1107)*
Athletic & Sports Seating ..............G....... 630 837-5566
  Streamwood *(G-20644)*
Bell Cabinet & Millwork Co ............G....... 708 425-1200
  Evergreen Park *(G-10110)*
Bender Mat Fctry Fton Slepshop ....G....... 217 328-1700
  Urbana *(G-21071)*
Bill Weeks Inc ...............................G....... 217 523-8735
  Springfield *(G-20397)*
Bright Designs Inc ........................G....... 847 428-6012
  Dundee *(G-8559)*
Butcher Block Furn By Oneill .........G....... 312 666-9144
  Chicago *(G-4193)*
Cabinets Doors and More LLC .......G....... 847 395-6334
  Antioch *(G-627)*
Carson Properties Inc ...................E....... 630 832-5322
  Elmhurst *(G-9845)*
Chicago Booth Mfg Inc ..................F....... 773 378-8400
  Chicago *(G-4307)*
Chicago Honeymooners LLC .........G....... 312 399-5699
  Chicago *(G-4323)*
▲ Chicago Wicker & Trading Co ....E....... 708 563-2890
  Alsip *(G-447)*
Chicagoland Closets LLC ..............G....... 630 906-0000
  Aurora *(G-1130)*

Chicagos Finest Ironworks ............G....... 708 895-4484
  Lansing *(G-13159)*
◆ Chillin Products Inc ...................G....... 815 725-7253
  Rockdale *(G-18217)*
▲ Choice Furnishings Inc ..............F....... 847 329-0004
  Skokie *(G-19982)*
▲ Churchill Cabinet Company .......G....... 708 780-0070
  Cicero *(G-7182)*
City Living Design Inc ...................G....... 312 335-0711
  Chicago *(G-4383)*
Closet Works Inc ..........................E....... 630 832-3322
  Elmhurst *(G-9849)*
Country Workshop ........................G....... 217 543-4094
  Arthur *(G-891)*
Creative Wood Concepts Inc .........G....... 773 384-9960
  Chicago *(G-4502)*
Custom Designs By Georgio ..........F....... 847 233-0410
  Franklin Park *(G-10449)*
Custom Window Accents ...............F....... 815 943-7651
  Harvard *(G-11629)*
Custom Wood Designs Inc ............G....... 708 799-3439
  Crestwood *(G-7486)*
▲ D D G Inc ..................................G....... 847 412-0277
  Northbrook *(G-16236)*
Debcor Inc ...................................G....... 708 333-2191
  South Holland *(G-20261)*
Dicks Custom Cabinet Shop ..........G....... 815 358-2663
  Cornell *(G-7381)*
Diebolds Cabinet Shop ..................G....... 773 772-3076
  Chicago *(G-4597)*
Douglas County Wood Products ....G....... 217 543-2888
  Arthur *(G-896)*
E J Self Furniture .........................G....... 847 394-0899
  Mount Prospect *(G-15327)*
Eddie Gapastione ..........................G....... 708 430-3881
  Bridgeview *(G-2487)*
Five Star Industries Inc ................E....... 618 542-4880
  Du Quoin *(G-8554)*
Fredman Bros Furniture Co Inc .....E....... 309 674-2011
  Peoria *(G-17366)*
Gavin Woodworking Inc .................G....... 815 786-2242
  Sandwich *(G-19365)*
Glober Manufacturing Company ....F....... 847 829-4883
  Cary *(G-3349)*
Grant Wood Works ........................G....... 847 328-4349
  Evanston *(G-10046)*
Great Spirit Hardwoods LLC ..........G....... 224 801-1969
  East Dundee *(G-8642)*
Green Gables Country Store ..........D....... 309 897-7160
  Bradford *(G-2411)*
Gro Products Inc ..........................G....... 815 308-5423
  Woodstock *(G-22570)*
Guess Whackit & Hope Inc ............G....... 773 342-4273
  Chicago *(G-5010)*
Hanley Design Inc .........................G....... 309 682-9665
  Peoria *(G-17378)*
Human Svc Ctr Southern Metro ....E....... 618 282-6233
  Red Bud *(G-17942)*
Hylan Design Ltd ..........................G....... 312 243-7341
  Chicago *(G-5129)*
Imperial Kitchens & Bath Inc .........F....... 708 485-0020
  Brookfield *(G-2635)*
Innovative Fix Solutions LLC .........D....... 815 395-8500
  Rockford *(G-18436)*
Innovative Mktg Solutions Inc .......F....... 630 227-4300
  Schaumburg *(G-19568)*
International Wood Design Inc ......G....... 773 227-9270
  Chicago *(G-5224)*
J & J Woodwork Furniture Inc .......G....... 708 563-9581
  Chicago *(G-5253)*
▲ J & M Representatives Inc ........D....... 217 268-4504
  Arcola *(G-672)*
J M Lustig Custom Cabinets Co ....F....... 217 342-6661
  Effingham *(G-8840)*
▲ JAm International Co Ltd ..........G....... 847 827-6391
  Deerfield *(G-8016)*
▼ Jbc Holding Co .........................G....... 217 347-7701
  Effingham *(G-8841)*
Joliet Cabinet Company Inc ..........E....... 815 727-4096
  Lockport *(G-13724)*
Kaufmans Custom Cabinets ..........G....... 217 268-4330
  Arcola *(G-673)*
Kinser Woodworks ........................G....... 618 549-4540
  Makanda *(G-14163)*
Kowal Custom Cabinet & Furn ......G....... 708 597-3367
  Blue Island *(G-2260)*
Kunz Carpentry .............................G....... 618 224-7892
  Trenton *(G-20994)*
Laverns Wood Items .....................G....... 217 268-4544
  Arcola *(G-674)*

Lee Weitzman Furniture Inc ..........G....... 312 243-3009
  Chicago *(G-5485)*
Legacy Woodwork Inc ...................G....... 847 451-7602
  Franklin Park *(G-10515)*
Leggett & Platt Incorporated .........E....... 630 801-0609
  North Aurora *(G-16138)*
M Inc .............................................G....... 312 853-0512
  Chicago *(G-5582)*
Master Cabinets ............................G....... 847 639-1323
  Cary *(G-3359)*
Mastercraft Furn Rfnishing Inc ......F....... 773 722-5730
  Chicago *(G-5647)*
Meadowbrook LLC ........................G....... 312 475-9903
  Chicago *(G-5672)*
Meier Granite Company ................G....... 847 678-7300
  Franklin Park *(G-10527)*
Mica Furniture Mfg Inc ..................G....... 708 430-1150
  Addison *(G-205)*
▲ Michael Scott Inc ......................F....... 847 965-8700
  Deerfield *(G-8036)*
Miller Whiteside Wood Working .....G....... 309 827-6470
  Mc Lean *(G-14463)*
Mobilia Inc ....................................E....... 708 865-0700
  Bellwood *(G-1715)*
Morningside Woodcraft .................G....... 217 268-4313
  Arcola *(G-679)*
Muhs Funiture Manufacturing ........G....... 618 723-2590
  Noble *(G-16052)*
O & I Woodworking .......................G....... 217 543-3155
  Arthur *(G-914)*
Okaw Valley Woodworking LLC .....F....... 217 543-5180
  Arthur *(G-916)*
Old Blue Illinois Inc .......................F....... 309 289-7921
  Knoxville *(G-12722)*
ONeill Products Inc .......................G....... 312 243-3413
  Chicago *(G-5991)*
Patio Plus .....................................G....... 815 433-2399
  Ottawa *(G-16977)*
Pfingsten Partners Fund IV LP ......B....... 312 222-8707
  Chicago *(G-6116)*
▲ Philip Reinisch Company ...........F....... 312 644-6776
  Naperville *(G-15726)*
Planks Cabinet Shop Inc ...............G....... 217 543-2687
  Arthur *(G-918)*
Prairie Woodworks Inc ..................G....... 309 378-2418
  Downs *(G-8547)*
Quesse Moving & Storage Inc ......G....... 815 223-0253
  Peru *(G-17525)*
R Maderite Inc ..............................G....... 847 785-0875
  North Chicago *(G-16186)*
Riverside Custom Woodworking ....G....... 815 589-3608
  Fulton *(G-10705)*
Roncin Custom Design ..................G....... 847 669-0260
  Huntley *(G-12175)*
Rooms Redux Chicago Inc ............F....... 312 835-1192
  Chicago *(G-6390)*
Rose Custom Cabinets Inc ............E....... 847 816-4800
  Mundelein *(G-15553)*
Royal Fabricators Inc ....................F....... 847 775-7466
  Wadsworth *(G-21327)*
Shews Custom Woodworking .........G....... 217 737-5543
  Lincoln *(G-13419)*
▲ Signature Innovations LLC ........G....... 847 758-9600
  Elk Grove Village *(G-9739)*
South Side HM Kit Emporium Inc ..G....... 217 322-3708
  Rushville *(G-19095)*
Specialized Woodwork Inc ............G....... 630 627-0450
  Lombard *(G-13854)*
Spirit Concepts Inc .......................G....... 708 388-4500
  Crestwood *(G-7503)*
Stancy Woodworking Co Inc .........F....... 847 526-0252
  Island Lake *(G-12219)*
◆ Stevens Cabinets Inc ................B....... 217 857-7100
  Teutopolis *(G-20856)*
Suburban Laminating Inc ..............G....... 708 389-6106
  Melrose Park *(G-14697)*
T J Kellogg Inc .............................G....... 815 969-0524
  Rockford *(G-18640)*
Tables Inc ....................................G....... 630 365-0741
  Elburn *(G-8912)*
Tender Loving Care Inds Inc ..........D....... 847 891-0230
  Schaumburg *(G-19759)*
▲ Trendler Inc ..............................E....... 773 284-6600
  Chicago *(G-6768)*
United Woodworking Inc ................G....... 847 352-3066
  Schaumburg *(G-19782)*
▲ Urban Home Furniture & ACC Inc ...E... 630 761-3200
  Batavia *(G-1514)*
Van Cleave Woodworking Inc .......G....... 847 424-8200
  Northbrook *(G-16382)*

Employee Codes: A=Over 500 employees, B=251-500
C=101-250, D=51-100, E=20-50, F=10-19, G=3-9

## 25 FURNITURE AND FIXTURES

Verlo Mattress of Lake Geneva ...........G....... 815 455-2570
  Crystal Lake (G-7673)
◆ Waco Manufacturing Co Inc ...........F....... 312 733-0054
  Chicago (G-6931)
What We Make Inc ...........G....... 331 442-4830
  Hampshire (G-11566)
Whitacres Country Oaks Shop ...........G....... 309 726-1305
  Hudson (G-12127)
▲ Wicks Organ Company ...........E....... 618 654-2191
  Highland (G-11819)
Wooden World of Richmond Inc ...........G....... 815 405-4503
  Richmond (G-17974)

### 2512 Wood Household Furniture, Upholstered

Addison Interiors Company ...........F....... 630 628-1345
  Addison (G-23)
Booths and Upholstery By Ray ...........G....... 773 523-3355
  Chicago (G-4144)
Brusic-Rose Inc ...........E....... 708 458-9900
  Bedford Park (G-1542)
Coles Appliance & Furn Co ...........G....... 773 525-1797
  Chicago (G-4422)
Custom Cabinet Man Inc ...........G....... 847 249-0007
  Gurnee (G-11436)
Custom Craft Cabinetry ...........G....... 630 897-2334
  Aurora (G-1135)
E J Self Furniture ...........G....... 847 394-0899
  Mount Prospect (G-15327)
E M C Industry ...........G....... 217 543-2894
  Arthur (G-898)
▼ Groupe Lacasse LLC ...........E....... 312 670-9100
  Chicago (G-5006)
Knapp Industrial Wood ...........F....... 815 657-8854
  Forrest (G-10263)
La-Z-Boy Incorporated ...........C....... 773 384-4440
  Chicago (G-5428)
M & R Custom Millwork ...........G....... 815 547-8549
  Belvidere (G-1768)
New Image Upholstery ...........F....... 630 542-5560
  South Elgin (G-20221)
Nolte & Tyson Inc ...........F....... 847 551-3313
  Gilberts (G-10929)
Parenteau Studios ...........E....... 312 337-8015
  Chicago (G-6081)
Patrick Cabinetry Inc ...........G....... 630 307-9333
  Bloomingdale (G-2126)
Scibor Upholstering & Gallery ...........G....... 708 671-9700
  Chicago (G-6457)
▲ Sherwood Industries Inc ...........F....... 847 626-0300
  Niles (G-16032)
Shoppe De Lee Inc ...........G....... 847 350-0580
  Elk Grove Village (G-9736)
Tables Inc ...........G....... 630 365-0741
  Elburn (G-8912)
▲ Trp Acquisition Corp ...........G....... 630 261-2380
  Lombard (G-13873)
Vinyl Life North ...........G....... 630 906-9686
  North Aurora (G-16149)

### 2514 Metal Household Furniture

▲ Austin-Westran LLC ...........C....... 815 234-2811
  Byron (G-2912)
Austin-Westran LLC ...........C....... 815 234-2811
  Montgomery (G-15029)
▲ Chicago American Mfg LLC ...........C....... 773 376-0100
  Chicago (G-4302)
Chicagos Finest Ironworks ...........G....... 708 895-4484
  Lansing (G-13159)
Dixline Corporation ...........F....... 309 932-2011
  Galva (G-10787)
Dpcac LLC ...........F....... 630 741-7900
  Itasca (G-12253)
Durable Design Products Inc ...........G....... 708 707-1147
  River Forest (G-17997)
European Ornamental Iron Works ...........G....... 630 705-9300
  Addison (G-113)
Evan Lewis Inc ...........G....... 773 539-0402
  Chicago (G-4784)
Glober Manufacturing Company ...........F....... 847 829-4883
  Cary (G-3349)
▲ Henry Crown and Company ...........C....... 312 236-6300
  Chicago (G-5072)
Melvin Wolf and Associates Inc ...........G....... 847 433-9098
  Highland Park (G-11853)
▲ Metal Box International Inc ...........C....... 847 455-8500
  Franklin Park (G-10529)
◆ Pace Industries Inc ...........D....... 312 226-5500
  Chicago (G-6051)

Parenteau Studios ...........E....... 312 337-8015
  Chicago (G-6081)
Richardson Ironworks LLC ...........G....... 217 359-3333
  Champaign (G-3533)
▲ Smart Solar Inc ...........F....... 813 343-5770
  Libertyville (G-13382)
Tesko Welding & Mfg Co ...........D....... 708 452-0045
  Norridge (G-16109)
US Foods Culinary Eqp Sups LLC ...........G....... 847 720-8000
  Rosemont (G-19039)
Viking Metal Cabinet Co LLC ...........D....... 800 776-7767
  Montgomery (G-15069)
Viking Metal Cabinet Company ...........D....... 630 863-7234
  Montgomery (G-15070)

### 2515 Mattresses & Bedsprings

▲ Bedding Group Inc ...........E....... 309 788-0401
  Rock Island (G-18162)
Bemco Mattress Inc ...........E....... 217 529-0777
  Springfield (G-20395)
Bender Mat Fctry Fton Slepshop ...........G....... 217 328-1700
  Urbana (G-21071)
Corsicana Bedding LLC ...........C....... 630 264-0032
  Aurora (G-1134)
▲ Estee Bedding Company ...........E....... 800 521-7378
  Chicago (G-4780)
Fredman Bros Furniture Co Inc ...........G....... 309 674-2011
  Peoria (G-17366)
HMK Mattress Holdings LLC ...........G....... 773 472-7390
  Chicago (G-5094)
HMK Mattress Holdings LLC ...........G....... 847 798-8023
  Schaumburg (G-19557)
HMK Mattress Holdings LLC ...........G....... 708 429-0704
  Orland Park (G-16865)
▲ Hospitology Products LLC ...........E....... 630 359-5075
  Addison (G-149)
Illini Mattress Company Inc ...........G....... 217 359-0156
  Champaign (G-3498)
Innocor Inc ...........B....... 630 231-0622
  West Chicago (G-21721)
▲ Kolcraft Enterprises Inc ...........D....... 312 361-6315
  Chicago (G-5402)
L A Bedding Corp ...........G....... 773 715-9641
  Chicago (G-5420)
Leggett & Platt Incorporated ...........D.......
  Chicago (G-5488)
Leggett & Platt Incorporated ...........G....... 708 458-1800
  Chicago (G-5489)
Leggett & Platt Incorporated ...........G....... 815 233-0022
  Freeport (G-10672)
Leggett & Platt Incorporated ...........E....... 630 801-0609
  North Aurora (G-16138)
Luna Mattress Transport Inc ...........F....... 773 847-1812
  Chicago (G-5568)
Made Rite Bedding Company ...........F....... 847 349-5886
  Franklin Park (G-10520)
Magic Sleep Mattress Co Inc ...........E....... 815 795-6942
  Marseilles (G-14314)
My Bed Inc ...........F....... 800 326-9233
  Lockport (G-13734)
▲ National Bedding Company LLC ...........G....... 847 645-0200
  Hoffman Estates (G-12028)
National Bedding Company LLC ...........G....... 847 645-0200
  Hoffman Estates (G-12027)
Pace Foundation ...........E....... 309 691-3553
  Peoria (G-17422)
Parenteau Studios ...........E....... 312 337-8015
  Chicago (G-6081)
Piersons Mattress Inc ...........G....... 309 637-8455
  Peoria (G-17429)
◆ Quality Sleep Shop Inc ...........G....... 708 246-2224
  La Grange Highlands (G-12750)
Robin Hood Mat & Quilting Corp ...........G....... 312 953-2960
  Chicago (G-6371)
Royal Bedding Company Inc ...........D....... 847 645-0200
  Hoffman Estates (G-12045)
Sealy Inc ...........C....... 630 879-8011
  Batavia (G-1495)
▲ Serta Inc ...........C....... 847 645-0200
  Hoffman Estates (G-12051)
▲ Shevick Sales Corp ...........G....... 312 487-2865
  Niles (G-16033)
Ther A Pedic Midwest Inc ...........G....... 309 788-0401
  Rock Island (G-18206)
US Specialty Packaging Inc ...........F....... 847 836-1115
  Elgin (G-9221)
Verlo Mat of Skokie-Evanston ...........G....... 847 966-9988
  Morton Grove (G-15243)
Verlo Mattress of Lake Geneva ...........G....... 815 455-2570
  Crystal Lake (G-7673)

Visionary Sleep LLC ...........C....... 224 829-0440
  Hoffman Estates (G-12068)
Wicoff Inc ...........G....... 618 988-8888
  Herrin (G-11758)

### 2517 Wood T V, Radio, Phono & Sewing Cabinets

Anderson & Marter Cabinets ...........G....... 630 406-9840
  Batavia (G-1415)
C M Sell Woodwork ...........G....... 847 526-3627
  Wauconda (G-21451)
Cabinets By Custom Craft Inc ...........G....... 815 637-4001
  Roscoe (G-18891)
Cooper Lake Millworks Inc ...........G....... 217 847-2681
  Hamilton (G-11530)
Creative Wood Concepts Inc ...........G....... 773 384-9960
  Chicago (G-4502)
Crestwood Custom Cabinets ...........G....... 708 385-3167
  Crestwood (G-7485)
Der Holtzmacher Ltd ...........G....... 815 895-4887
  Sycamore (G-20792)
Eddie Gapastione ...........G....... 708 430-3881
  Bridgeview (G-2487)
Elm Street Industries Inc ...........F....... 309 854-7000
  Kewanee (G-12681)
Grays Cabinet Co ...........G....... 618 948-2211
  Saint Francisville (G-19313)
HI Tech ...........G....... 708 957-4210
  Homewood (G-12100)
Manufacturing / Woodworking ...........G....... 847 730-4823
  Des Plaines (G-8226)
Midwest Woodcrafters Inc ...........G....... 630 665-0901
  Carol Stream (G-3199)
Monticello Design & Mfg ...........G....... 217 762-8551
  Monticello (G-15081)
Roncin Custom Design ...........G....... 847 669-0260
  Huntley (G-12175)
Spirit Concepts Inc ...........G....... 708 388-4500
  Crestwood (G-7503)
Timberside Woodworking ...........G....... 217 578-3201
  Arthur (G-922)
Woodhill Cabinetry Design Inc ...........G....... 815 431-0545
  Ottawa (G-16992)
Zenith Electronics Corporation ...........E....... 847 941-8000
  Lincolnshire (G-13496)

### 2519 Household Furniture, NEC

Albert Vivo Upholstery Co Inc ...........G....... 312 226-7779
  Burr Ridge (G-2821)
American Trade & Coml Svc LLC ...........F....... 202 910-8808
  Chicago (G-3879)
▲ Avista Group Corporation ...........F....... 877 772-8826
  Elk Grove Village (G-9324)
Bi State Furniture Inc ...........G....... 309 662-6562
  Bloomington (G-2148)
Bw Dallas LLC ...........G....... 847 441-1892
  Northfield (G-16394)
Gensler Gardens Inc ...........G....... 815 874-9634
  Davis Junction (G-7813)
Glass Artistry ...........G....... 847 998-5800
  Northbrook (G-16265)
Glober Manufacturing Company ...........F....... 847 829-4883
  Cary (G-3349)
▼ House of Rattan Inc ...........G....... 630 627-8160
  Lombard (G-13810)
Jagoli ...........G....... 312 563-0583
  Chicago (G-5271)
▲ Ligo Products Inc ...........E....... 708 478-1800
  Mokena (G-14881)
Mitchel Home ...........G....... 773 205-9902
  Chicago (G-5773)
Patio Plus ...........G....... 815 433-2399
  Ottawa (G-16977)
Petro Enterprises Inc ...........G....... 708 425-1551
  Chicago Ridge (G-7153)
Rustic Woodcrafts ...........G....... 618 584-3912
  Flat Rock (G-10196)
▲ Standard Container Co of Edgar ...........E....... 847 438-1510
  Lake Zurich (G-13134)
◆ Suncast Corporation ...........G....... 630 879-2050
  Batavia (G-1501)
▲ Thomas Monahan Company ...........F....... 217 268-5771
  Arcola (G-686)
Westerling Group ...........G....... 708 547-8488
  Berkeley (G-2052)
Zenith Electronics Corporation ...........E....... 847 941-8000
  Lincolnshire (G-13496)

## 2521 Wood Office Furniture

- **AB&d Custom Furniture Inc** .... E .... 708 922-9061 — Homewood *(G-12090)*
- **Aba Custom Woodworking** .... G .... 815 356-9663 — Crystal Lake *(G-7525)*
- **Accurate Custom Cabinets Inc** .... E .... 630 458-0460 — Addison *(G-17)*
- **Almacen Inc** .... G .... 847 934-7955 — Inverness *(G-12201)*
- ▲ **Amtab Manufacturing Corp** .... D .... 630 301-7600 — Aurora *(G-1107)*
- **B & B Formica Appliers Inc** .... F .... 773 804-1015 — Chicago *(G-4014)*
- ◆ **Bretford Manufacturing Inc** .... B .... 847 678-2545 — Franklin Park *(G-10416)*
- **C-V Cstom Cntrtops Cbinets Inc** .... F .... 708 388-5066 — Blue Island *(G-2241)*
- **Cabinet Gallery LLC** .... G .... 618 882-4801 — Highland *(G-11776)*
- **Castle Craft Products Inc** .... F .... 630 279-7494 — Villa Park *(G-21242)*
- ▲ **Chicago Stool and Chair Inc** .... G .... 847 289-9955 — Elgin *(G-8988)*
- **Cmp Millwork Co** .... G .... 630 832-6462 — Elmhurst *(G-9851)*
- **Complete Custom Woodworks** .... G .... 309 644-1911 — Coal Valley *(G-7294)*
- **Crestwood Custom Cabinets** .... G .... 708 385-3167 — Crestwood *(G-7485)*
- ▲ **Daniel M Powers & Assoc Ltd** .... D .... 630 685-8400 — Bolingbrook *(G-2299)*
- **Debcor Inc** .... G .... 708 333-2191 — South Holland *(G-20261)*
- **Diebolds Cabinet Shop** .... G .... 773 772-3076 — Chicago *(G-4597)*
- ▲ **Dirtt Envmtl Solutions Inc** .... C .... 312 245-2870 — Chicago *(G-4609)*
- **Djr Inc** .... F .... 773 581-5204 — Chicago *(G-4615)*
- **Donald Kranz** .... G .... 847 428-1616 — Carpentersville *(G-3283)*
- **Eddie Gapastione** .... G .... 708 430-3881 — Bridgeview *(G-2487)*
- **Egan Visual/West Inc** .... G .... 800 266-2387 — Chicago *(G-4704)*
- **Gianni Incorporated** .... D .... 708 863-6696 — Cicero *(G-7198)*
- **Global Industries Inc** .... F .... 630 681-2818 — Glendale Heights *(G-11028)*
- **Grays Cabinet Co** .... G .... 618 948-2211 — Saint Francisville *(G-19313)*
- ▼ **Groupe Lacasse LLC** .... E .... 312 670-9100 — Chicago *(G-5006)*
- **Herner-Geissler Wdwkg Corp** .... D .... 312 226-3400 — Chicago *(G-5081)*
- **Ideal Cabinet Solutions Inc** .... G .... 618 514-7087 — Alhambra *(G-418)*
- **J K Custom Countertops** .... G .... 630 495-2324 — Lombard *(G-13813)*
- **J M Lustig Custom Cabinets Co** .... F .... 217 342-6661 — Effingham *(G-8840)*
- ▼ **K-Log Inc** .... E .... 847 872-6611 — Zion *(G-22690)*
- **Kessmanns Cabinet Shop & Cnstr** .... G .... 618 654-2538 — Highland *(G-11800)*
- ▲ **Lacava LLC** .... E .... 773 637-9600 — Chicago *(G-5432)*
- ◆ **Magnuson Group Inc** .... F .... 630 783-8100 — Woodridge *(G-22501)*
- **Manufacturing / Woodworking** .... G .... 847 730-4823 — Des Plaines *(G-8226)*
- **Marcy Enterprises Inc** .... G .... 708 352-7220 — La Grange Park *(G-12758)*
- **Marvel Group Inc** .... C .... 773 523-4804 — Chicago *(G-5639)*
- **Mastercraft Furn Rfnishing Inc** .... F .... 773 722-5730 — Chicago *(G-5647)*
- ◆ **Mayline Investments Inc** .... G .... 847 948-9340 — Northbrook *(G-16307)*
- ▼ **Mlp Seating Corp** .... E .... 847 956-1700 — Elk Grove Village *(G-9633)*
- **Mobilia Inc** .... E .... 708 865-0700 — Bellwood *(G-1715)*
- **Newtec Window & Door Inc** .... E .... 773 869-9888 — Chicago *(G-5905)*
- **Nightingale Corp** .... D .... 800 363-8954 — Chicago *(G-5916)*
- ▲ **Nova Solutions Inc** .... E .... 217 342-7070 — Effingham *(G-8851)*
- **Pio Woodworking Inc** .... G .... 630 628-6900 — Addison *(G-241)*
- **Regency Custom Woodworking** .... F .... 815 689-2117 — Cullom *(G-7683)*
- **Rieke Office Interiors Inc** .... D .... 847 622-9711 — Elgin *(G-9165)*
- **Roevolution 226 LLC** .... G .... 773 658-4022 — Riverwoods *(G-18042)*
- **S & J Woodproducts** .... G .... 815 973-1970 — Rockford *(G-18601)*
- **Stay Straight Manufacturing** .... G .... 312 226-2137 — Chicago *(G-6579)*
- **Steelcase Inc** .... F .... 312 321-3720 — Chicago *(G-6581)*
- ▲ **Systems Unlimited Inc** .... C .... 630 285-0010 — Itasca *(G-12363)*
- **Vertisse Inc** .... G .... 224 532-5145 — Lake In The Hills *(G-13009)*
- **Wm Huber Cabinet Works** .... E .... 773 235-7660 — Chicago *(G-7011)*
- **Woodhill Cabinetry Design Inc** .... G .... 815 431-0545 — Ottawa *(G-16992)*

## 2522 Office Furniture, Except Wood

- **Accurate Custom Cabinets Inc** .... E .... 630 458-0460 — Addison *(G-17)*
- **Almacen Inc** .... G .... 847 934-7955 — Inverness *(G-12201)*
- ▲ **Amtab Manufacturing Corp** .... D .... 630 301-7600 — Aurora *(G-1107)*
- **Austin-Westran LLC** .... C .... 815 234-2811 — Montgomery *(G-15029)*
- **Baker Avenue Investments Inc** .... G .... 309 427-2500 — Washington *(G-21378)*
- ◆ **Bretford Manufacturing Inc** .... B .... 847 678-2545 — Franklin Park *(G-10416)*
- **C-V Cstom Cntrtops Cbinets Inc** .... F .... 708 388-5066 — Blue Island *(G-2241)*
- **Capitol Carton Company** .... E .... 312 563-9690 — Chicago *(G-4229)*
- **Central Radiator Cabinet Co** .... G .... 773 539-1700 — Lena *(G-13274)*
- **Debcor Inc** .... G .... 708 333-2191 — South Holland *(G-20261)*
- ▲ **Dirtt Envmtl Solutions Inc** .... C .... 312 245-2870 — Chicago *(G-4609)*
- **Durable Design Products Inc** .... G .... 708 707-1147 — River Forest *(G-17997)*
- ▲ **Edsal Manufacturing Co Inc** .... A .... 773 475-3020 — Chicago *(G-4699)*
- **Edsal Manufacturing Co Inc** .... D .... 773 475-3013 — Chicago *(G-4700)*
- **Fanmar Inc** .... E .... 708 563-0505 — Elk Grove Village *(G-9475)*
- **Fellowes Trading Company** .... G .... 630 893-1600 — Itasca *(G-12262)*
- ▼ **Groupe Lacasse LLC** .... E .... 312 670-9100 — Chicago *(G-5006)*
- **Hanley Design Inc** .... G .... 309 682-9665 — Peoria *(G-17378)*
- ▲ **IMS Engineered Products LLC** .... C .... 847 391-8100 — Des Plaines *(G-8211)*
- **Ise Inc** .... E .... 703 319-0390 — Chicago *(G-5241)*
- **J & E Seating LLC** .... E .... 847 956-1700 — Elk Grove Village *(G-9556)*
- ▼ **K-Log Inc** .... E .... 847 872-6611 — Zion *(G-22690)*
- **Kimball Office Inc** .... F .... 800 349-9827 — Chicago *(G-5384)*
- **L & D Group Inc** .... B .... 630 892-8941 — Montgomery *(G-15051)*
- **Lincoln Office LLC** .... D .... 309 427-2500 — Washington *(G-21385)*
- **Marvel Group Inc** .... C .... 773 523-4804 — Chicago *(G-5639)*
- ▲ **Marvel Group Inc** .... C .... 773 523-4804 — Chicago *(G-5640)*
- **Marvel Group Inc** .... F .... 773 523-4804 — Chicago *(G-5641)*
- ◆ **Mayline Investments Inc** .... G .... 847 948-9340 — Northbrook *(G-16307)*
- ▲ **Metal Box International Inc** .... C .... 847 455-8500 — Franklin Park *(G-10529)*
- ▼ **Mlp Seating Corp** .... E .... 847 956-1700 — Elk Grove Village *(G-9633)*
- **MT Case Company** .... F .... 630 227-1019 — Wood Dale *(G-22402)*
- **Niedermaier Inc** .... E .... 312 492-9400 — Chicago *(G-5913)*
- **Nightingale Corp** .... D .... 800 363-8954 — Chicago *(G-5916)*
- **Oak Creek Distribution LLC** .... E .... 800 244-5263 — Waukegan *(G-21596)*
- ▲ **Ortho Seating LLC** .... F .... 773 276-3539 — Chicago *(G-6017)*
- ▲ **Paoli Inc** .... G .... 312 644-5509 — Chicago *(G-6070)*
- ▲ **Pointe International Company** .... F .... 847 550-7001 — Lake Zurich *(G-13115)*
- ▲ **Richardson Seating Corporation** .... E .... 312 829-4040 — Chicago *(G-6352)*
- **Rome Metal Mfg Inc** .... G .... 773 287-1755 — Chicago *(G-6389)*
- ◆ **Rwi Manufacturing Inc** .... C .... 800 277-1699 — Aurora *(G-1212)*
- **Steel Solutions USA** .... G .... 815 432-4938 — Watseka *(G-21428)*
- **Steelcase Inc** .... F .... 312 321-3720 — Chicago *(G-6581)*
- **T J Van Der Bosch & Associates** .... E .... 815 344-3210 — McHenry *(G-14567)*
- ▼ **T2 Site Amenities Incorporated** .... G .... 847 579-9003 — Highland Park *(G-11876)*
- **Tables Inc** .... G .... 630 365-0741 — Elburn *(G-8912)*
- **Techline Studio** .... G .... 212 674-1813 — Palatine *(G-17080)*
- **Vertisse Inc** .... G .... 224 532-5145 — Lake In The Hills *(G-13009)*
- **Viking Metal Cabinet Co LLC** .... D .... 800 776-7767 — Montgomery *(G-15069)*
- **Viking Metal Cabinet Company** .... D .... 630 863-7234 — Montgomery *(G-15070)*
- ◆ **Waco Manufacturing Co Inc** .... F .... 312 733-0054 — Chicago *(G-6931)*

## 2531 Public Building & Related Furniture

- **Abundant Living Christian Ctr** .... G .... 708 896-6181 — Dolton *(G-8362)*
- **Adient US LLC** .... C .... 815 895-2095 — Sycamore *(G-20785)*
- **Atwood-Hamlin Mfg Co Inc** .... F .... 815 678-7291 — Richmond *(G-17958)*
- **B/E Aerospace Inc** .... C .... 561 791-5000 — Hanover Park *(G-11576)*
- ◆ **Belson Outdoors LLC** .... E .... 630 897-8489 — North Aurora *(G-16120)*
- **Booths and Upholstery By Ray** .... G .... 773 523-3355 — Chicago *(G-4144)*
- **Center-111 W Burnham Wash LLC** .... E .... 312 368-5320 — Chicago *(G-4269)*
- ▲ **Chicago American Mfg LLC** .... C .... 773 376-0100 — Chicago *(G-4302)*
- **Chicago Booth Mfg Inc** .... F .... 773 378-8400 — Chicago *(G-4307)*
- **Claridge Products and Eqp Inc** .... G .... 847 991-8822 — Elgin *(G-8992)*
- **Correctional Technologies Inc** .... F .... 630 455-0811 — Willowbrook *(G-22207)*
- **Egan Visual/West Inc** .... G .... 800 266-2387 — Chicago *(G-4704)*
- **Fbsa LLC** .... C .... 773 524-2440 — Chicago *(G-4822)*
- ▲ **Fortune Brands Home & SEC Inc** .... C .... 847 484-4400 — Deerfield *(G-8007)*
- ▲ **Freedman Seating Company** .... C .... 773 524-2440 — Chicago *(G-4887)*
- **Hanley Design Inc** .... G .... 309 682-9665 — Peoria *(G-17378)*
- **Harrier Interior Products** .... G .... 847 934-1310 — Palatine *(G-17033)*
- ▲ **Heritage Rstoration Design Inc** .... G .... 309 637-5404 — Peoria *(G-17382)*
- **Ill Dept Natural Resources** .... G .... 217 498-9208 — Rochester *(G-18118)*
- **Innovtive Design Solutions LLC** .... G .... 708 547-1942 — Bellwood *(G-1709)*
- **Inter Swiss Ltd** .... F .... 773 379-0400 — Chicago *(G-5210)*
- **Irwin Seating Company** .... C .... 618 483-6157 — Altamont *(G-553)*
- **J C Decaux New York Inc** .... E .... 312 456-2999 — Chicago *(G-5258)*
- **James Howard Co** .... G .... 815 497-2831 — Compton *(G-7366)*
- **Jcdecaux Chicago LLC** .... E .... 312 456-2999 — Chicago *(G-5285)*
- **Johnson Controls Inc** .... C .... 815 288-3859 — Dixon *(G-8335)*

S I C

Employee Codes: A=Over 500 employees, B=251-500 C=101-250, D=51-100, E=20-50, F=10-19, G=3-9

2017 Harris Illinois Industrial Directory

945

# 25 FURNITURE AND FIXTURES

Johnson Controls Inc .................... E ...... 309 427-2800
East Peoria (G-8719)
Johnson Controls Inc .................... D ...... 630 573-0897
Oak Brook (G-16527)
Johnson Controls Inc .................... G ...... 331 212-3800
Aurora (G-1038)
Johnson Controls Inc .................... E ...... 847 364-1500
Arlington Heights (G-785)
Johnson Controls Inc .................... D ...... 630 279-0050
Elmhurst (G-9892)
Johnson Controls Inc .................... G ...... 630 351-9407
Bloomingdale (G-2110)
▼ K-Log Inc .................................... E ...... 847 872-6611
Zion (G-22690)
▲ Kinsman Enterprises Inc .......... G ...... 618 932-3838
West Frankfort (G-21810)
Library Furniture Intl .................... G ...... 847 564-9497
Northbrook (G-16295)
Mfp Holding Co .............................. G ...... 312 666-3366
Chicago (G-5714)
Norfolk Southern Corporation ...... G ...... 773 933-5698
Chicago (G-5927)
▲ Nu-Dell Manufacturing Co Inc ... F ...... 847 803-4500
Chicago (G-5953)
Partners Resource Inc ................. G ...... 630 620-9161
Glen Ellyn (G-10985)
Patio Plus ...................................... G ...... 815 433-2399
Ottawa (G-16977)
Pep Industries Inc ......................... F ...... 630 833-0404
Villa Park (G-21276)
Picnic Tables Inc .......................... G ...... 630 482-6200
Batavia (G-1482)
▲ Pointe International Company ... F ...... 847 550-7001
Lake Zurich (G-13115)
Redbox Workshop Ltd .................. E ...... 773 478-7077
Chicago (G-6316)
Roberts and Downey Chapel Eqp ........ 217 795-2391
Argenta (G-692)
Sage Clover .................................. G ...... 630 220-9600
Winfield (G-22293)
▲ Sandlock Sandbox LLC ............ G ...... 630 963-9422
Westmont (G-21919)
▲ Sedia Systems Inc .................... G ...... 312 212-8010
Chicago (G-6471)
Serious Energy Inc ....................... E ...... 312 515-4606
Chicago (G-6478)
◆ Stevens Cabinets Inc ............... B ...... 217 857-7100
Teutopolis (G-20856)
▼ T2 Site Amenities Incorporated ... G ...... 847 579-9003
Highland Park (G-11876)
▲ Tao Trading Corporation ........... G ...... 773 764-6542
Chicago (G-6675)
◆ The United Group Inc ............... E ...... 847 816-7100
Lake Forest (G-12970)
▲ Vecchio Manufacturing of Ill .... F ...... 847 742-8429
Elgin (G-9224)
◆ Waco Manufacturing Co Inc .... F ...... 312 733-0054
Chicago (G-6931)
Wise Co Inc ................................... C ...... 618 594-4091
Carlyle (G-3061)
Yanfeng US Automotive ............... A ...... 779 552-7300
Belvidere (G-1798)

## 2541 Wood, Office & Store Fixtures

57th Street Bookcase & Cabinet ... F ...... 773 363-3038
Chicago (G-3673)
AB&d Custom Furniture Inc ......... E ...... 708 922-9061
Homewood (G-12090)
Ability Cabinet Co Inc .................. G ...... 847 678-6678
Franklin Park (G-10383)
Abitzy Inc ....................................... G ...... 847 659-9228
Lombard (G-13757)
Action Cabinet Sales Inc .............. G ...... 847 717-0011
Elgin (G-8935)
Akrylix Inc ..................................... F ...... 773 869-9005
Frankfort (G-10291)
Alex Displays & Co ....................... F ...... 312 829-2948
Chicago (G-3802)
Alexander Lumber Co .................. G ...... 217 429-2729
Decatur (G-7827)
All Stone Inc .................................. G ...... 815 529-1754
Romeoville (G-18793)
All-Style Custom Tops .................. G ...... 708 532-6606
Tinley Park (G-20887)
Allie Woodworking ....................... G ...... 847 244-1919
Waukegan (G-21522)
American Fixture ........................... G ...... 217 429-1300
Decatur (G-7832)
Anderson & Marter Cabinets ....... G ...... 630 406-9840
Batavia (G-1415)

B & B Formica Appliers Inc ......... F ...... 773 804-1015
Chicago (G-4014)
▲ Bards Products Inc .................... F ...... 800 323-5499
Mundelein (G-15475)
Beachys Counter Tops Inc .......... F ...... 217 543-2143
Arthur (G-882)
▲ Bernhard Woodwork Ltd .......... E ...... 847 291-1040
Northbrook (G-16214)
Bolhuis Woodworking Co ............ G ...... 708 333-5100
Manhattan (G-14168)
Booths and Upholstery By Ray ........... 773 523-3355
Chicago (G-4144)
Brakur Custom Cabinetry Inc ............. 630 355-2244
Shorewood (G-19923)
Brothers Leal LLC ........................ G ...... 708 385-4400
Alsip (G-443)
C-V Cstom Cntrtops Cbinets Inc ... G ...... 708 388-5066
Blue Island (G-2241)
Cabinet Designs ........................... G ...... 708 614-8603
Oak Forest (G-16575)
Cabinets By Custom Craft Inc .............. 815 637-4001
Roscoe (G-18891)
▲ Capitol Wood Works LLC ........ G ...... 217 522-5553
Springfield (G-20408)
Castle Craft Products Inc ............ F ...... 630 279-7494
Villa Park (G-21242)
Central Illinois Counter Tops ....... G ...... 309 579-3550
Mossville (G-15252)
Chicago Booth Mfg Inc ................ F ...... 773 378-8400
Chicago (G-4307)
▲ Churchill Cabinet Company ..... E ...... 708 780-0070
Cicero (G-7182)
Clover Custom Counters Inc ....... G ...... 708 598-8912
Bridgeview (G-2478)
Collinsville Custom Kitchens ....... F ...... 618 288-2000
Maryville (G-14340)
▲ Colony Inc .................................. E ...... 847 426-5300
Elgin (G-8994)
Con-Temp Cabinets Inc .............. F ...... 630 892-7300
North Aurora (G-16123)
Contempo Marble & Granite Inc ... G ...... 312 455-0022
Chicago (G-4456)
Continental Marketing Inc ............ F ...... 773 467-8300
Chicago (G-4458)
Contract Industries Inc ................ E ...... 708 458-8150
Bedford Park (G-1545)
Cooper Lake Millworks Inc .......... G ...... 217 847-2681
Hamilton (G-11530)
Coordinated Kitchen Dev Inc ............. 847 847-7692
Lake Zurich (G-13057)
Counter Craft Inc .......................... G ...... 847 336-8205
Waukegan (G-21545)
Countertop Creations ................... F ...... 618 736-2700
Dahlgren (G-7689)
Creative Cabinetry Inc ................. G ...... 708 460-2900
Orland Park (G-16851)
Crown Coverings Inc ................... G ...... 630 546-2959
Roselle (G-18937)
Custom Countertop Creations .... F ...... 847 695-8800
South Elgin (G-20192)
Custom Window Accents ............ F ...... 815 943-7651
Harvard (G-11629)
Custom Woodwork & Interiors ... F ...... 217 546-0006
Springfield (G-20427)
Cut - To - Size Technology Inc .... E ...... 630 543-8328
Addison (G-85)
D & D Counter Tops Co Inc ........ G
Machesney Park (G-14070)
▲ Daniel M Powers & Assoc Ltd ... D ...... 630 685-8400
Bolingbrook (G-2299)
Der Holtzmacher Ltd ................... G ...... 815 895-4887
Sycamore (G-20792)
Design Woodworks ..................... G ...... 847 566-6603
Mundelein (G-15493)
Dieter Construction Inc ............... G ...... 630 960-9662
Woodridge (G-22470)
▲ Display Worldwide LLC ........... G ...... 815 439-2695
Plainfield (G-17592)
DK Knutsen .................................. G ...... 815 626-4388
Sterling (G-20589)
Dpcac LLC .................................... F ...... 630 741-7900
Itasca (G-12253)
Drieselman Manufacturing Co .... E ...... 217 222-1986
Quincy (G-17822)
▲ Dunhill Corp .............................. F ...... 815 806-8600
Frankfort (G-10315)
▲ Duo Usa Incorporated .............. G ...... 312 421-7755
Chicago (G-4653)
Durable Design Products Inc ..... G ...... 708 707-1147
River Forest (G-17997)

▲ Durable Office Products Corp ... G ...... 847 787-0100
Des Plaines (G-8187)
Eddie Gapastione .......................... G ...... 708 430-3881
Bridgeview (G-2487)
Forest City Counter Tops Inc ...... F ...... 815 633-8602
Loves Park (G-13942)
Fra-Milco Cabinets Co Inc ........... G
Frankfort (G-10323)
Gerali Custom Design Inc ........... D ...... 847 760-0500
Elgin (G-9044)
Glenview Custom Cabinets Inc ... G ...... 847 345-5754
Glenview (G-11130)
Granite Xperts Inc ........................ G ...... 847 364-1900
Franklin Park (G-10481)
Graniteworks ................................. G ...... 815 288-3350
Dixon (G-8333)
Greenberg Casework Company Inc ... E ...... 815 624-0288
South Beloit (G-20150)
Hallmark Cabinet Company ......... D ...... 708 757-7807
Chicago Heights (G-7102)
Hanley Design Inc ........................ G ...... 309 682-9665
Peoria (G-17378)
Hansen Custom Cabinet Inc ....... G ...... 847 356-1100
Lake Villa (G-13015)
Harts Top and Cabinet Shop ...... G ...... 708 957-4666
Country Club Hills (G-7408)
Hickory Street Cabinets .............. G ...... 618 667-9676
Troy (G-21007)
Hire-Nelson Company Inc ........... E ...... 630 543-9400
Addison (G-146)
Hylan Design Ltd .......................... G ...... 312 243-7341
Chicago (G-5129)
Imperial Kitchens & Bath Inc ....... F ...... 708 485-0020
Brookfield (G-2635)
▲ Imperial Woodworking Company ... D ...... 847 221-2107
Palatine (G-17039)
J & W Counter Tops Inc .............. E ...... 217 544-0876
Springfield (G-20460)
J K Custom Countertops ............. G ...... 630 495-2324
Lombard (G-13813)
Janik Custom Millwork Inc .......... G ...... 708 482-4844
Hodgkins (G-11977)
▼ Jbc Holding Co ......................... G ...... 217 347-7701
Effingham (G-8841)
John F Mate Co ............................ G ...... 847 381-8131
Lake Barrington (G-12812)
K & D Counter Tops Inc .............. E ...... 618 224-9630
Trenton (G-20992)
Kabinet Kraft ................................. F ...... 618 395-1047
Olney (G-16775)
Kewaunee Scientific Corp ........... E ...... 847 675-7744
Highland Park (G-11850)
Kitchen Krafters Inc ..................... G ...... 815 675-6061
Spring Grove (G-20341)
Kraft Custom Design Inc ............. G ...... 815 485-5506
New Lenox (G-15890)
▲ Laminated Components Inc .... E ...... 815 648-4811
Hebron (G-11723)
Laminated Designs Countertops ... G ...... 815 877-7222
Machesney Park (G-14088)
M & R Custom Millwork ............... G ...... 815 547-8549
Belvidere (G-1768)
Marcy Enterprises Inc .................. G ...... 708 352-7220
La Grange Park (G-12758)
Markham Cabinet Works Inc ...... G ...... 708 687-3074
Midlothian (G-14767)
Marmon Retail Services Inc ....... G ...... 312 332-0317
Chicago (G-5629)
◆ Marv-O-Lus Manufacturing Co ... F ...... 773 826-1717
Chicago (G-5636)
▲ Max Resources Inc .................. G ...... 708 478-5656
Mokena (G-14884)
Maxwell Counters Inc .................. E ...... 309 928-2848
Farmer City (G-10179)
Meier Granite Company ............... G ...... 847 678-7300
Franklin Park (G-10527)
◆ Midwest Custom Case Inc ...... G ...... 708 672-2900
University Park (G-21057)
Midwest Display & Mfg Inc ......... G ...... 815 962-2199
Rockford (G-18505)
Midwest Fabrication-Countertop ... G ...... 217 528-0571
Springfield (G-20483)
Miller Manufacturing Co Inc ........ D ...... 636 343-5700
Dupo (G-8573)
Miller Whiteside Wood Working .. G ...... 309 827-6470
Mc Lean (G-14463)
Monticello Design & Mfg ............. G ...... 217 762-8551
Monticello (G-15081)
▲ Morgan Li LLC .......................... E ...... 708 758-5300
Chicago Heights (G-7114)

▲ Moss Holding Company ..... C ..... 847 238-4200
Elk Grove Village *(G-9636)*
Multiplex Display Fixture Co ..... E ..... 800 325-3350
Dupo *(G-8574)*
Murray Cabinetry & Tops Inc ..... G ..... 815 672-6992
Streator *(G-20696)*
Nelson - Harkins Inds Inc ..... E ..... 773 478-6243
Chicago *(G-5884)*
▲ New Age Surfaces LLC ..... G ..... 630 226-0011
Romeoville *(G-18853)*
Northwest Marble Products ..... E ..... 630 860-2288
Hoffman Estates *(G-12072)*
OGorman Son Carpentry Contrs ..... E ..... 815 485-8997
New Lenox *(G-15898)*
Omni Craft Inc ..... G ..... 815 838-1285
Lockport *(G-13736)*
Pac Team US Productions LLC ..... G ..... 773 360-8960
Chicago *(G-6049)*
Perfection Custom Closets & Co ..... F ..... 847 647-6461
Niles *(G-16017)*
Proto Productions Inc ..... E ..... 630 628-6626
Addison *(G-260)*
Quantum Storage Systems ..... G ..... 630 274-6610
Elk Grove Village *(G-9704)*
R & R Custom Cabinet Making ..... G ..... 847 358-6188
Palatine *(G-17065)*
▲ Randal Wood Displays Inc ..... D ..... 630 761-0400
Batavia *(G-1490)*
Rapp Cabinets & Woodworks Inc ..... F ..... 618 736-2955
Dahlgren *(G-7692)*
Rays Countertop Shop Inc ..... F ..... 217 483-2514
Glenarm *(G-10997)*
Redbox Workshop Ltd ..... E ..... 773 478-7077
Chicago *(G-6316)*
Regency Custom Woodworking ..... F ..... 815 689-2117
Cullom *(G-7683)*
Roncin Custom Design ..... G ..... 847 669-0260
Huntley *(G-12175)*
Royal Fabricators Inc ..... F ..... 847 775-7466
Wadsworth *(G-21327)*
Schrock Custom Woodworking ..... G ..... 217 849-3375
Toledo *(G-20965)*
Shelving and Bath Unlimited ..... G ..... 815 378-3328
Cherry Valley *(G-3647)*
Specialized Woodwork Inc ..... G ..... 630 627-0450
Lombard *(G-13854)*
Stone Fabricators Company ..... G ..... 847 788-8296
Arlington Heights *(G-845)*
Suburban Fabricators Inc ..... G ..... 847 729-0866
Glenview *(G-11206)*
Suburban Fix & Installation ..... G ..... 847 823-4047
Park Ridge *(G-17225)*
Suburban Laminating Inc ..... G ..... 708 389-6106
Melrose Park *(G-14697)*
Surface Solutions Illinois Inc ..... G ..... 708 571-3449
Mokena *(G-14907)*
Swan Surfaces LLC ..... C ..... 618 532-5673
Centralia *(G-3435)*
T J Kellogg Inc ..... G ..... 815 969-0524
Rockford *(G-18640)*
Tremont Kitchen Tops Inc ..... G ..... 309 925-5736
Tremont *(G-20987)*
Unistrut International Corp ..... D ..... 630 773-3460
Addison *(G-334)*
Valley Custom Woodwork Inc ..... E ..... 815 544-3939
Belvidere *(G-1793)*
Wilcor Solid Surface Inc ..... F ..... 630 350-7703
Elk Grove Village *(G-9813)*
Wilson Kitchens Inc ..... D ..... 618 253-7449
Harrisburg *(G-11606)*
Wind Point Partners Vi LP ..... G ..... 312 255-4800
Chicago *(G-6993)*
Windy Hill Woodworking Inc ..... G ..... 309 275-2415
Towanda *(G-20979)*
Woodhill Cabinetry Design Inc ..... G ..... 815 431-0545
Ottawa *(G-16992)*
Woodworking Unlimited Inc ..... F ..... 630 469-7023
Carol Stream *(G-3269)*
Ww Displays Inc ..... F ..... 847 566-6979
Mundelein *(G-15568)*

## *2542 Partitions & Fixtures, Except Wood*

▲ 555 International Inc ..... D ..... 773 869-0555
Chicago *(G-3672)*
▲ Acco Brands Inc ..... A ..... 847 541-9500
Lake Zurich *(G-13032)*
▲ Accurate Partitions Corp ..... G ..... 708 442-6801
Mc Cook *(G-14444)*
Acrylic Service Inc ..... G ..... 630 543-0336
Addison *(G-20)*
Advert Display Products Inc ..... G ..... 815 513-5432
Morris *(G-15090)*
◆ Alessco Inc ..... F ..... 773 327-7919
Chicago *(G-3801)*
American Rack Company ..... E ..... 773 763-7309
Chicago *(G-3870)*
Apex Wire Products Company Inc ..... F ..... 847 671-1830
Franklin Park *(G-10397)*
Armbrust Paper Tubes Inc ..... E ..... 773 586-3232
Chicago *(G-3945)*
Art Wire Works Inc ..... F ..... 708 458-3993
Bedford Park *(G-1538)*
Associated Rack Corporation ..... F ..... 616 554-6004
Chicago *(G-3970)*
Astoria Wire Products Inc ..... D ..... 708 496-9950
Bedford Park *(G-1539)*
B Andrews Inc ..... G ..... 847 381-7444
Barrington *(G-1269)*
B-O-F Corporation ..... E ..... 630 585-0020
Aurora *(G-967)*
Bar Stool Depotcom ..... G ..... 815 727-7294
Joliet *(G-12460)*
Bark Project Management Inc ..... G ..... 630 964-5876
Woodridge *(G-22455)*
Bel Mar Wire Products Inc ..... F ..... 773 342-3800
Chicago *(G-4073)*
Bilt-Rite Metal Products Inc ..... E ..... 815 495-2211
Leland *(G-13218)*
Builders United Sales Co Inc ..... G ..... 815 467-2224
Minooka *(G-14837)*
Bunzl Retail LLC ..... F ..... 847 733-1469
Morton Grove *(G-15190)*
C-V Cstom Cntrtops Cbinets Inc ..... F ..... 708 388-5066
Blue Island *(G-2241)*
Cabinet Designs ..... G ..... 708 614-8603
Oak Forest *(G-16575)*
Cameo Container Corporation ..... C ..... 773 254-1030
Chicago *(G-4222)*
Capitol Carton Company ..... E ..... 312 563-9690
Chicago *(G-4229)*
▲ Capitol Wood Works LLC ..... D ..... 217 522-5553
Springfield *(G-20408)*
◆ Carl Stahl Decorcble Innovtns ..... F ..... 312 454-2996
Burr Ridge *(G-2828)*
Central Sheet Metal Pdts Inc ..... E ..... 773 583-2424
Skokie *(G-19976)*
▲ Chicago American Mfg LLC ..... C ..... 773 376-0100
Chicago *(G-4302)*
▲ Colony Inc ..... E ..... 847 426-5300
Elgin *(G-8994)*
Consolidated Displays Co Inc ..... G ..... 630 851-8666
Oswego *(G-16911)*
Creative Metal Products ..... F ..... 773 638-3200
Chicago *(G-4500)*
DAmico Associates Inc ..... G ..... 847 291-7446
Northbrook *(G-16239)*
▲ Diversified Metal Products Inc ..... E ..... 847 753-9595
Northbrook *(G-16244)*
Easyshow LLC ..... G ..... 847 480-7177
Northbrook *(G-16245)*
▲ Edsal Manufacturing Co Inc ..... A ..... 773 475-3020
Chicago *(G-4699)*
Edsal Manufacturing Co Inc ..... D ..... 773 475-3013
Chicago *(G-4700)*
Enclosures Inc ..... G ..... 847 678-2020
Schiller Park *(G-19824)*
◆ Ets-Lindgren Inc ..... C ..... 630 307-7200
Wood Dale *(G-22363)*
▲ Fixture Hardware Co ..... E ..... 773 777-6100
Chicago *(G-4855)*
Forest City Counter Tops Inc ..... F ..... 815 633-8602
Loves Park *(G-13942)*
▲ Geneva Manufacturing Co ..... F ..... 847 697-1161
South Elgin *(G-20199)*
Gerali Custom Design Inc ..... D ..... 847 760-0500
Elgin *(G-9044)*
Harder Signs Inc ..... F ..... 815 874-7777
Rockford *(G-18413)*
▲ HMC Holdings LLC ..... E ..... 847 541-5070
Buffalo Grove *(G-2705)*
Idx Corporation ..... F ..... 312 600-9783
Chicago *(G-5143)*
Illinois Rack Enterprises Inc ..... E ..... 815 385-5750
Lakemoor *(G-13144)*
Imperial Marble Corp ..... C ..... 815 498-2303
Somonauk *(G-20126)*
Imperial Store Fixtures Inc ..... G ..... 773 348-1137
Chicago *(G-5168)*
▲ IMS Engineered Products LLC ..... C ..... 847 391-8100
Des Plaines *(G-8211)*
▼ Industrial Enclosure Corp ..... E ..... 630 898-7499
Aurora *(G-1171)*
Innovative Mktg Solutions Inc ..... F ..... 630 227-4300
Schaumburg *(G-19568)*
Inter-Market Inc ..... G ..... 847 729-5330
Glenview *(G-11149)*
Interlake Mecalux Inc ..... C ..... 815 844-7191
Pontiac *(G-17703)*
◆ Interlake Mecalux Inc ..... B ..... 708 344-9999
Melrose Park *(G-14659)*
▲ Inventive Display Group LLC ..... F ..... 847 588-1100
Niles *(G-15990)*
▲ Iretired LLC ..... E ..... 630 285-9500
Itasca *(G-12287)*
Ivan Carlson Associates Inc ..... E ..... 312 829-4616
Chicago *(G-5248)*
▼ Jbc Holding Co ..... G ..... 217 347-7701
Effingham *(G-8841)*
Jet Rack Corp ..... E ..... 773 586-2150
Chicago *(G-5298)*
John H Best & Sons Inc ..... E ..... 309 932-2124
Galva *(G-10791)*
Kewaunee Scientific Corp ..... G ..... 847 675-7744
Highland Park *(G-11850)*
Keystone Display Inc ..... D ..... 815 648-2456
Hebron *(G-11721)*
Klein Tools Inc ..... D ..... 847 228-6999
Elk Grove Village *(G-9577)*
Klein Tools Inc ..... E ..... 847 821-5500
Lincolnshire *(G-13461)*
L & D Group Inc ..... B ..... 630 892-8941
Montgomery *(G-15051)*
Liam Brex ..... G ..... 630 848-0222
Naperville *(G-15688)*
▲ Lyon LLC ..... C ..... 630 892-8941
Montgomery *(G-15057)*
Lyon Workspace Products Inc ..... G ..... 630 892-8941
Montgomery *(G-15058)*
Maasscorp Inc ..... G ..... 763 383-1400
Rockford *(G-18478)*
Macon Metal Products Co ..... E ..... 217 824-7205
Taylorville *(G-20842)*
Mailbox International Inc ..... G ..... 847 541-8466
Wheeling *(G-22097)*
Marmon Retail Services Inc ..... G ..... 312 332-0317
Chicago *(G-5629)*
◆ Marv-O-Lus Manufacturing Co ..... F ..... 773 826-1717
Chicago *(G-5636)*
▲ Material Control Systems Inc ..... F ..... 309 523-3774
Port Byron *(G-17721)*
Material Control Systems Inc ..... G ..... 309 654-9031
Cordova *(G-7378)*
▲ Metal Box International Inc ..... C ..... 847 455-8500
Franklin Park *(G-10529)*
▲ Middletons Mouldings Inc ..... D ..... 517 278-6610
Schaumburg *(G-19646)*
Midland Metal Products Co ..... D ..... 773 927-5700
Chicago *(G-5735)*
Mikron Designs Inc ..... G ..... 847 726-3990
Lake Zurich *(G-13103)*
Multiplex Display Fixture Co ..... E ..... 800 325-3350
Dupo *(G-8574)*
Murray Cabinetry & Tops Inc ..... G ..... 815 672-6992
Streator *(G-20696)*
Nycor Products Inc ..... G ..... 815 727-9883
Joliet *(G-12547)*
Organized Home ..... G ..... 217 698-6460
Springfield *(G-20494)*
Plas-Co Inc ..... F ..... 618 476-1761
Millstadt *(G-14832)*
Proto Productions Inc ..... E ..... 630 628-6626
Addison *(G-260)*
R B White Inc ..... E ..... 309 452-5816
Normal *(G-16086)*
Rack Builders Inc ..... G ..... 217 214-9482
Quincy *(G-17884)*
▼ REB Steel Equipment Corp ..... E ..... 773 252-0400
Chicago *(G-6309)*
Roberts Sheet Metal Works Inc ..... E ..... 773 626-3811
Chicago *(G-6370)*
Rome Metal Mfg Inc ..... G ..... 773 287-1755
Chicago *(G-6389)*
▲ Room Dividers Now LLC ..... G ..... 847 224-7900
Barrington *(G-1303)*
Royal Fabricators Inc ..... F ..... 847 775-7466
Wadsworth *(G-21327)*
RTC Industries Inc ..... D ..... 847 640-2400
Chicago *(G-6409)*
Rwi Holdings Inc ..... F ..... 630 897-6951
Aurora *(G-1211)*

SIC

## 25 FURNITURE AND FIXTURES

| Company | Code | Phone |
|---|---|---|
| Ryan Metal Products Inc | E | 815 936-0700 |
| Kankakee (G-12647) | | |
| ▼ Schaumburg Specialties Co | G | 847 451-0070 |
| Schaumburg (G-19721) | | |
| ▲ Southern Imperial Inc | B | 815 877-7041 |
| Rockford (G-18623) | | |
| T and D Metal Products LLC | G | 815 432-4938 |
| Watseka (G-21430) | | |
| Tesko Welding & Mfg Co | D | 708 452-0045 |
| Norridge (G-16109) | | |
| ▲ Tts Granite Inc | E | 708 755-5200 |
| Steger (G-20579) | | |
| ◆ United Wire Craft Inc | C | 847 375-3800 |
| Des Plaines (G-8291) | | |
| West Zwick Corp | G | 217 222-0228 |
| Quincy (G-17903) | | |
| Wilson Kitchens Inc | D | 618 253-7449 |
| Harrisburg (G-11606) | | |
| Wind Point Partners Vi LP | G | 312 255-4800 |
| Chicago (G-6993) | | |
| ▲ Wiremasters Incorporated | E | 773 254-3700 |
| Chicago (G-7005) | | |
| Wm F Meyer Co | E | 773 772-7272 |
| Chicago (G-7010) | | |
| ◆ Workspace Lyon Products LLC | B | 630 892-8941 |
| Montgomery (G-15073) | | |
| Ww Displays Inc | F | 847 566-6979 |
| Mundelein (G-15568) | | |
| ▲ Yetter Manufacturing Company | D | 309 776-3222 |
| Colchester (G-7309) | | |

### 2591 Drapery Hardware, Window Blinds & Shades

| Company | Code | Phone |
|---|---|---|
| ▲ 21st Century Us-Sino Services | G | 312 808-9328 |
| Chicago (G-3664) | | |
| 9161 Corporation | G | 847 470-8828 |
| Niles (G-15953) | | |
| A B C Blind Inc | G | 708 877-7100 |
| Thornton (G-20866) | | |
| Aracon Drpery Vntian Blind Ltd | G | 773 252-1281 |
| Chicago (G-3930) | | |
| Baker Drapery Corporation | G | 309 691-3295 |
| Peoria (G-17313) | | |
| Bills Shade & Blind Service | G | 773 493-5000 |
| Chicago (G-4106) | | |
| Blind Connection Inc | G | 630 728-6275 |
| Lake In The Hills (G-12989) | | |
| Blind Williamson & Drapery | G | 309 694-7339 |
| East Peoria (G-8702) | | |
| Carol Andrzejewski | G | 630 369-9711 |
| Naperville (G-15618) | | |
| Chicago Blind Company | G | 815 553-5525 |
| Joliet (G-12472) | | |
| Chicago Shade Makers Inc | G | 708 597-5590 |
| Alsip (G-446) | | |
| ▲ Clear View Shade Inc | F | 708 535-8631 |
| Orland Park (G-16847) | | |
| Custom Window Accents | F | 815 943-7651 |
| Harvard (G-11629) | | |
| Dezign Sewing Inc | G | 773 549-4336 |
| Chicago (G-4590) | | |
| Dons Drapery Service | G | 815 385-4759 |
| McHenry (G-14497) | | |
| Draperyland Inc | F | 630 521-1000 |
| Wood Dale (G-22360) | | |
| Ensembles Inc | G | 630 527-0004 |
| Naperville (G-15805) | | |
| Excitingwindows By Susan Day | G | 217 652-2821 |
| Springfield (G-20436) | | |
| ▲ EZ Blinds and Drapery Inc | F | 708 246-6600 |
| La Grange (G-12731) | | |
| ▲ Fixture Hardware Co | E | 773 777-6100 |
| Chicago (G-4855) | | |
| Going Vertical Inc | G | 847 669-3377 |
| Huntley (G-12142) | | |
| Hansens Mfrs Win Coverings | F | 815 935-0010 |
| Bradley (G-2424) | | |
| House of Atlas LLC | G | 847 491-1800 |
| Evanston (G-10054) | | |
| Illinois Window Shade Co | G | 773 743-6025 |
| Chicago (G-5159) | | |
| Image Custom Drapery | G | 630 837-0107 |
| Bartlett (G-1354) | | |
| Jack Beall Vertical Service In | G | 847 426-7958 |
| Carpentersville (G-3289) | | |
| Levolor Window Furnishings Inc | G | 800 346-3278 |
| Oak Brook (G-16534) | | |
| ▲ Marvin Feig & Associates Inc | F | 773 384-5228 |
| Niles (G-16001) | | |
| Matiss Inc | F | 773 418-1895 |
| Chicago (G-5653) | | |
| National Temp-Trol Products | G | 630 920-1919 |
| Willowbrook (G-22226) | | |
| ◆ Newell Operating Company | C | 815 235-4171 |
| Freeport (G-10675) | | |
| Offsprings Inc | G | 773 525-1800 |
| Chicago (G-5969) | | |
| Olshaws Interior Services | G | 312 421-3131 |
| Chicago (G-5985) | | |
| Ottos Drapery Service Inc | G | 773 777-7755 |
| Chicago (G-6024) | | |
| Regent Window Fashions LLC | G | 773 871-6400 |
| Chicago (G-6324) | | |
| Robert E Bolton | G | 815 725-7120 |
| Joliet (G-12569) | | |
| Roberts Draperies Center Inc | G | 847 255-4040 |
| Mount Prospect (G-15370) | | |
| Sage Vertical Grdn Systems LLC | F | 312 234-9655 |
| Chicago (G-6428) | | |
| Shade Aire Company | G | 815 623-7597 |
| Roscoe (G-18921) | | |
| Shade Brookline Co | G | 773 274-5513 |
| Chicago (G-6487) | | |
| Ultrasonic Blind Co | G | 847 579-8084 |
| Libertyville (G-13393) | | |
| UNI-Glide Corp | G | 773 235-2100 |
| Chicago (G-6811) | | |
| Unitex Industries Inc | G | 708 524-0664 |
| Oak Park (G-16690) | | |
| Vertical Tower Partner | G | 217 819-3040 |
| Champaign (G-3554) | | |
| Vertidrapes Manufacturing Inc | G | 773 478-9272 |
| Chicago (G-6889) | | |
| Window Tech Inc | G | 847 272-0739 |
| Northbrook (G-16388) | | |
| Zirlin Interiors Inc | G | 773 334-5530 |
| Chicago (G-7069) | | |
| Znl Corporation | G | 815 654-0870 |
| Loves Park (G-14011) | | |

### 2599 Furniture & Fixtures, NEC

| Company | Code | Phone |
|---|---|---|
| 3rd Base Bar | G | 217 644-2424 |
| Charleston (G-3589) | | |
| ▲ Aero Products Holdings Inc | E | 847 485-3200 |
| Schaumburg (G-19424) | | |
| ▲ Akerue Industries LLC | E | 847 395-3300 |
| Antioch (G-615) | | |
| ▲ Aline International LLC | G | 708 478-2471 |
| Mokena (G-14850) | | |
| ◆ American Metalcraft Inc | D | 800 333-9133 |
| Franklin Park (G-10391) | | |
| Amk Kitchen Bar | G | 773 270-4115 |
| Chicago (G-3891) | | |
| Anderson & Marter Cabinets | G | 630 406-9840 |
| Batavia (G-1415) | | |
| Baker Elements Inc | F | 630 660-8100 |
| Oak Park (G-16654) | | |
| Be McGonagle Inc | G | 847 394-0413 |
| Arlington Heights (G-724) | | |
| Booths and Upholstery By Ray | G | 773 523-3355 |
| Chicago (G-4144) | | |
| Buhlworth Design Guild | G | 630 325-5340 |
| Oak Brook (G-16495) | | |
| Campeche Restaurant Inc | G | 815 776-9950 |
| Galena (G-10716) | | |
| Chicago Booth Mfg Inc | G | 773 378-8400 |
| Chicago (G-4307) | | |
| Classic Remix | G | 312 915-0521 |
| Chicago (G-4394) | | |
| ▲ Co-Rect Products Inc | E | 763 542-9200 |
| Lincolnshire (G-13438) | | |
| Concord Cabinets Inc | F | 217 894-6507 |
| Clayton (G-7269) | | |
| Continental Usa Inc | G | 847 823-0958 |
| Park Ridge (G-17188) | | |
| Contract Industries Inc | E | 708 458-8150 |
| Bedford Park (G-1545) | | |
| Custom Wood & Laminate Ltd | G | 815 727-4168 |
| Joliet (G-12481) | | |
| Display Plan Lpdg | G | 773 525-3787 |
| Chicago (G-4612) | | |
| DLM Manufacturing Inc | F | 815 964-3800 |
| Rockford (G-18348) | | |
| E-J Industries Inc | D | 312 226-5023 |
| Chicago (G-4669) | | |
| Eaton Inflatable LLC | G | 312 664-7867 |
| Chicago (G-4685) | | |
| Eddies Cousin Inc | G | 217 679-5777 |
| Springfield (G-20432) | | |
| ▲ Edsal Manufacturing Co Inc | A | 773 475-3020 |
| Chicago (G-4699) | | |
| Edsal Manufacturing Co Inc | D | 773 475-3013 |
| Chicago (G-4700) | | |
| ◆ Euromarket Designs Inc | A | 847 272-2888 |
| Northbrook (G-16252) | | |
| Finishing Touch | G | 309 789-6444 |
| Cuba (G-7680) | | |
| ▲ Fortune Brands Home & SEC Inc | C | 847 484-4400 |
| Deerfield (G-8007) | | |
| Glenview Custom Cabinets Inc | G | 847 345-5754 |
| Glenview (G-11130) | | |
| Hixsters Upper Deck | G | 815 745-2700 |
| Warren (G-21335) | | |
| Hometown Hangout LLC | G | 309 639-2108 |
| Williamsfield (G-22189) | | |
| Hylan Design Ltd | G | 312 243-7341 |
| Chicago (G-5129) | | |
| Jackhammer | G | 773 743-5772 |
| Chicago (G-5268) | | |
| Jeleniz | G | 217 235-6789 |
| Mattoon (G-14395) | | |
| Joe Anthony & Associates | G | 708 935-0804 |
| Richton Park (G-17978) | | |
| K K O Inc | G | 815 569-2324 |
| Capron (G-2995) | | |
| Kci Satellite | G | 800 664-2602 |
| Pittsfield (G-17571) | | |
| Kewaunee Scientific Corp | G | 847 675-7744 |
| Highland Park (G-11850) | | |
| ▲ Kinsman Enterprises Inc | G | 618 932-3838 |
| West Frankfort (G-21810) | | |
| ▲ Kreg Medical Inc | C | 312 829-8904 |
| Melrose Park (G-14668) | | |
| L & D Group Inc | B | 630 892-8941 |
| Montgomery (G-15051) | | |
| Lacava | G | 773 637-9600 |
| Chicago (G-5431) | | |
| Lena Mercantile | F | 815 369-9955 |
| Lena (G-13278) | | |
| M L Rongo Inc | E | 630 540-1120 |
| Bartlett (G-1360) | | |
| Macon Metal Products Co | E | 217 824-7205 |
| Taylorville (G-20842) | | |
| Marks Custom Seating | G | 630 980-8270 |
| Roselle (G-18956) | | |
| Marmon Ret & End User Tech Inc | G | 312 372-9500 |
| Chicago (G-5628) | | |
| Marshall Furniture Inc | G | 847 395-9350 |
| Antioch (G-643) | | |
| Michael Goss Custom Cabinets | G | 217 864-4600 |
| Argenta (G-690) | | |
| Mizrahi Grill | F | 847 831-1400 |
| Highland Park (G-11855) | | |
| Montauk Chicago Inc | G | 312 951-5688 |
| Chicago (G-5797) | | |
| ▼ Mpd Medical Systems Inc | G | 815 477-0707 |
| Crystal Lake (G-7616) | | |
| Muffys Inc | G | 815 433-6839 |
| Ottawa (G-16971) | | |
| ▲ Norix Group Inc | E | 630 231-1331 |
| West Chicago (G-21751) | | |
| OfficeMax Incorporated | G | 877 969-6629 |
| Itasca (G-12334) | | |
| Perfection Custom Closets & Co | F | 847 647-6461 |
| Niles (G-16017) | | |
| Phoenix Woodworking Corp | G | 815 338-9338 |
| Woodstock (G-22599) | | |
| Pollard Bros Mfg Co | F | 773 763-6868 |
| Chicago (G-6150) | | |
| ▲ Polygroup Services NA Inc | G | 847 851-9995 |
| East Dundee (G-8653) | | |
| Precision Service | G | 618 345-2047 |
| Collinsville (G-7337) | | |
| ▲ Railcraft Nexim Design | G | 309 937-2360 |
| Cambridge (G-2969) | | |
| ▲ Regal Manufacturing Co | E | 630 628-6867 |
| Addison (G-273) | | |
| Route 45 Wayside | G | 217 867-2000 |
| Pesotum (G-17533) | | |
| ▲ RTC Industries Inc | B | 847 640-2400 |
| Rolling Meadows (G-18775) | | |
| S L Fixtures Inc | G | 217 423-9907 |
| Decatur (G-7937) | | |
| ▲ Seats & Stools Inc | G | 773 348-7900 |
| Chicago (G-6467) | | |
| Skokie House | G | 847 679-4570 |
| Skokie (G-20086) | | |
| Sport Incentives Inc | F | 847 427-8650 |
| Elk Grove Village (G-9748) | | |

# 26 PAPER AND ALLIED PRODUCTS

| Company | Code | Phone |
|---|---|---|
| Suzy Cabinet Company Inc — Bellwood (G-1724) | G | 708 705-1259 |
| Tads — Loves Park (G-13996) | G | 815 654-3500 |
| Vinyl Life North — North Aurora (G-16149) | G | 630 906-9686 |
| ◆ Waco Manufacturing Co Inc — Chicago (G-6931) | F | 312 733-0054 |
| Wag Industries Inc — Skokie (G-20109) | F | 847 329-8932 |
| X Hale — Harwood Heights (G-11693) | G | 847 884-6250 |

## 26 PAPER AND ALLIED PRODUCTS

### 2611 Pulp Mills

| Company | Code | Phone |
|---|---|---|
| Better Earth Premium Compost — Peoria (G-17317) | G | 309 697-0963 |
| BFI Waste Systems N Amer Inc — Elgin (G-8965) | E | 847 429-7370 |
| Bruce Klapman Inc — Northbrook (G-16215) | G | 847 657-8880 |
| Buster Services Inc — Chicago (G-4191) | E | 773 247-2070 |
| C & M Recycling Inc — North Chicago (G-16176) | G | 847 578-1066 |
| Cicero Iron Metal & Paper Inc — Cicero (G-7183) | G | 708 863-8601 |
| Coyote Transportation Inc — Bensenville (G-1869) | G | 630 204-5729 |
| Fibre-TEC Partitions LLC — Chicago (G-4842) | E | 773 436-4028 |
| Illinois Recovery Group I — Braceville (G-2410) | G | 815 230-7920 |
| International Paper Company — Itasca (G-12286) | E | 630 250-1300 |
| International Paper Company — Lincoln (G-13411) | C | 217 735-1221 |
| JKS Ventures Inc — Melrose Park (G-14663) | G | 708 338-3408 |
| Kaskaskia Mechanical Insul Co — Mascoutah (G-14355) | E | 618 768-4526 |
| Lake Area Disposal Service Inc — Springfield (G-20466) | E | 217 522-9271 |
| Larckers Recycling Svcs Inc — Naperville (G-15813) | F | 630 922-0759 |
| M J Kull LLC — Lerna (G-13288) | G | 217 246-5952 |
| Norm Gordon & Associates Inc — Glenview (G-11174) | G | 847 564-7022 |
| Ohio Pulp Mills Inc — Chicago (G-5974) | F | 312 337-7822 |
| Paper Moon Recycling Inc — Grayslake (G-11358) | G | 847 548-8875 |
| ◆ Profile Products LLC — Buffalo Grove (G-2756) | F | 847 215-1144 |
| R & J Trucking and Recycl Inc — Chicago (G-6263) | F | 708 563-2600 |
| Regenex Corp — Spring Valley (G-20378) | F | 815 663-2003 |
| Tri State Recycling Service — Northlake (G-16456) | E | 708 865-9939 |
| Vida Enterprises Inc — Chicago (G-6895) | G | 312 808-0088 |
| Westrock CP LLC — Chicago (G-6967) | D | 312 346-6600 |
| Weyerhaeuser Company — Naperville (G-15784) | D | 630 778-7070 |

### 2621 Paper Mills

| Company | Code | Phone |
|---|---|---|
| Advantage Printing Inc — Lombard (G-13760) | G | 630 627-7468 |
| Ahlstrom Filtration LLC — Taylorville (G-20831) | D | 217 824-9611 |
| AIM Distribution Inc — Rockford (G-18258) | F | 815 986-2770 |
| Alsip Minimill LLC — Alsip (G-432) | F | 708 272-8700 |
| ◆ Amcor Flexibles LLC — Buffalo Grove (G-2656) | C | 224 313-7000 |
| ▲ Amic Global Inc — Buffalo Grove (G-2659) | G | 847 600-3590 |
| Ashleys Inc — Hinsdale (G-11939) | G | 630 794-0804 |
| Brothers Decorating — Hebron (G-11715) | G | 815 648-2214 |
| Chartwell Studio Inc — Evanston (G-10021) | G | 847 868-8674 |
| ▲ Colorkraft Roll Products Inc — Martinsville (G-14333) | E | 217 382-4967 |
| Cousins Packaging Inc — Peotone (G-17487) | G | 708 258-0063 |
| Cowtan and Tout Inc — Chicago (G-4485) | F | 312 644-0717 |
| ▲ Danco Converting — Chicago (G-4551) | G | 847 718-0448 |
| Dean Patterson — Bridgeview (G-2482) | G | 708 430-0477 |
| Deines-Nitz Solutions LLC — Erie (G-9991) | E | 309 658-9985 |
| Dude Products Inc — Chicago (G-4647) | G | 773 661-1126 |
| ◆ Essentra Packaging US Inc — Westchester (G-21841) | G | 704 418-8692 |
| Evolution Sorbent Products LLC — West Chicago (G-21698) | G | 630 293-8055 |
| ◆ Evolution Sorbent Products LLC — West Chicago (G-21699) | F | 630 293-8055 |
| First State Bank — Champaign (G-3486) | G | 217 239-3000 |
| Gordon Caplan Inc — Chicago (G-4980) | F | 773 489-3300 |
| Hollingsworth & Vose Company — Arlington Heights (G-767) | G | 847 222-9228 |
| Illinois Tool Works Inc — Glenview (G-11142) | G | 847 657-4639 |
| International Paper Company — Belleville (G-1638) | F | 618 233-5460 |
| International Paper Company — Elgin (G-9079) | C | |
| International Paper Company — Lincoln (G-13411) | C | 217 735-1221 |
| International Paper Company — Aurora (G-1031) | G | 630 449-7200 |
| International Paper Company — Aurora (G-1032) | F | 630 585-3300 |
| International Paper Company — Carol Stream (G-3173) | F | 630 653-3500 |
| International Paper Company — Des Plaines (G-8213) | E | 847 390-1300 |
| International Paper Company — Elk Grove Village (G-9552) | C | 847 228-7227 |
| International Paper Company — Itasca (G-12286) | E | 630 250-1300 |
| K C Printing Services Inc — Lake Barrington (G-12814) | F | 847 382-8822 |
| ▼ K-Log Inc — Zion (G-22690) | E | 847 872-6611 |
| ▼ Kapstone Kraft Paper Corp — Northbrook (G-16284) | F | 252 533-6000 |
| ▼ Kapstone Paper and Packg Corp — Northbrook (G-16285) | D | 847 239-8800 |
| ▲ Kdm Enterprises LLC — Carpentersville (G-3290) | E | 877 591-9768 |
| Kimberly-Clark Corporation — Deerfield (G-8025) | D | 312 371-5166 |
| Kimberly-Clark Corporation — Romeoville (G-18835) | C | 815 886-7872 |
| Kimberly-Clark Corporation — Northlake (G-16441) | E | 708 409-8500 |
| Lsc Communications Inc — Chicago (G-5552) | G | 773 272-9200 |
| Lsc Communications Us LLC — Chicago (G-5553) | B | 844 572-5720 |
| Master Mechanic Mfg Inc — Mundelein (G-15524) | G | 847 573-3812 |
| ▲ Matt Pak Inc — Franklin Park (G-10523) | D | 847 451-4018 |
| Meyer Enterprises LLC — East Peoria (G-8725) | G | 309 698-0062 |
| ◆ Michael Lewis Company — Mc Cook (G-14453) | G | 708 688-2200 |
| ▲ Midwest Converting Inc — Bedford Park (G-1564) | D | 708 924-1510 |
| Mii Inc — Batavia (G-1471) | F | 630 879-3000 |
| Millennium Printing Inc — Arlington Heights (G-802) | G | 847 590-8182 |
| ◆ Norkol Converting Corporation — Melrose Park (G-14678) | C | 708 531-1000 |
| Pactiv Intl Holdings Inc — Lake Forest (G-12934) | G | 847 482-2000 |
| Pactiv LLC — Jacksonville (G-12404) | C | 217 479-1144 |
| Paper Machine Services Inc — South Beloit (G-20163) | G | 608 365-8095 |
| Paper Spot — Frankfort (G-10347) | G | 815 464-8533 |
| Pen At Hand — Northbrook (G-16337) | G | 847 498-9174 |
| Pontiac Recyclers Inc — Pontiac (G-17708) | G | 815 844-6419 |
| Ripa LLC — Broadview (G-2609) | G | 708 938-1600 |
| Roll Source Paper — Itasca (G-12350) | G | 630 875-0308 |
| ▲ S and K Packaging Incorporated — East Dubuque (G-8621) | G | 563 582-8895 |
| ◆ Schwarz Paper Company LLC — Morton Grove (G-15235) | C | 847 966-2550 |
| Semper/Exeter Paper Co LLC — Bloomingdale (G-2136) | G | 630 775-9500 |
| ◆ Simu Ltd — Wood Dale (G-22422) | F | 630 350-1060 |
| Sj Converting LLC — West Chicago (G-21774) | G | 630 262-6640 |
| Snow & Graham LLC — Chicago (G-6539) | G | 773 665-9000 |
| Stergo Roofing — Mount Prospect (G-15375) | E | 312 640-9008 |
| Ted Muller — Chicago (G-6686) | G | 312 435-0978 |
| ▲ Transpac USA — Schaumburg (G-19768) | G | 847 605-1616 |
| Tst/Impreso Inc — Addison (G-330) | G | 630 775-9555 |
| ▲ Upm-Kymmene Inc — Naperville (G-15771) | D | 630 922-2500 |
| Voyager Enterprise Inc — Plainfield (G-17661) | G | 815 436-2431 |
| W/S Packaging Group Inc — Algonquin (G-411) | G | 847 658-7363 |
| Welch Packaging LLC — Lombard (G-13882) | G | 630 916-8090 |
| Westrock CP LLC — Waukegan (G-21641) | G | 847 625-8284 |
| Westrock CP LLC — Chicago (G-6967) | D | 312 346-6600 |
| Westrock Rkt Company — Chicago (G-6969) | A | 312 346-6600 |
| Weyerhaeuser Company — Rockford (G-18680) | G | 815 987-0395 |
| Windy City Word — Chicago (G-7001) | G | 773 378-0261 |

### 2631 Paperboard Mills

| Company | Code | Phone |
|---|---|---|
| Accord Packaging LLC — Alsip (G-429) | E | 708 272-3050 |
| Apak Packaging Group Inc — Algonquin (G-377) | G | 630 616-7275 |
| Armbrust Paper Tubes Inc — Chicago (G-3945) | E | 773 586-3232 |
| Artistic Carton Company — Elgin (G-8958) | E | 847 741-0247 |
| ▲ Barrington Packaging Systems — Barrington (G-1272) | G | 847 382-8063 |
| Berry Global Inc — Schaumburg (G-19461) | C | 847 884-1200 |
| C F Anderson & Co — Chicago (G-4203) | G | 312 341-0850 |
| Campus Cardboard — Northbrook (G-16216) | G | 847 373-7673 |
| Capitol Carton Company — Chicago (G-4229) | E | 312 563-9690 |
| Combined Technologies Inc — Libertyville (G-13317) | G | 847 968-4855 |
| Coveris Holding Corp — Chicago (G-4483) | G | 773 877-3300 |
| Grafcor Packaging Inc — Loves Park (G-13945) | F | 815 639-2380 |
| Grafcor Packaging Inc — Rockford (G-18404) | F | 815 963-1300 |
| Graphic Packaging Corporation — Franklin Park (G-10483) | C | 847 451-7400 |
| Graphic Packaging Holding Co — Carol Stream (G-3161) | B | 630 260-6500 |
| Graphic Packaging Intl Inc — Carol Stream (G-3162) | G | 630 260-6500 |
| Graphic Packaging Intl Inc — Elk Grove Village (G-9509) | B | 847 437-1700 |
| Graphic Packaging Intl Inc — Elk Grove Village (G-9510) | A | 847 354-3554 |
| Graphic Packaging Intl Inc — Carol Stream (G-3163) | G | 630 260-6500 |
| Imperial Packaging Corporation — Willowbrook (G-22217) | G | 847 486-0800 |
| International Paper Company — Shelbyville (G-19909) | A | 217 774-2176 |
| International Paper Company — Lincoln (G-13411) | C | 217 735-1221 |

Employee Codes: A=Over 500 employees, B=251-500
C=101-250, D=51-100, E=20-50, F=10-19, G=3-9

**Jsc Products Inc** G 847 290-9520 Elk Grove Village *(G-9566)*
**KJK Corp** G 815 389-0566 South Beloit *(G-20156)*
▲ **Logan Graphic Products Inc** D 847 526-5515 Wauconda *(G-21479)*
▲ **Mac American Corporation** G 847 277-9450 Barrington *(G-1288)*
**Midwest Cortland Inc** E 847 671-0376 Addison *(G-211)*
▲ **Nefab Inc** G 705 748-4888 Chicago *(G-5880)*
**Ox Paperboard LLC** D 309 346-4118 Pekin *(G-17277)*
▲ **Packaging Corporation America** C 847 482-3000 Lake Forest *(G-12933)*
**Pactiv LLC** C Lincolnshire *(G-13469)*
**Pactiv LLC** C 708 534-6595 University Park *(G-21059)*
**PCA Corrugated and Display LLC** G 847 482-3000 Lake Forest *(G-12940)*
**Pekin Paperboard Company LP** E 309 346-4118 Pekin *(G-17281)*
**Portable Mvg Stor Cntl Ill Inc** G 309 693-7637 Peoria *(G-17431)*
**Pulver Inc** E 847 734-9000 Elk Grove Village *(G-9701)*
▼ **Rjg Enterprises Ltd** G 847 752-2065 Grayslake *(G-11362)*
**Rocktenn** F 773 254-1030 Chicago *(G-6376)*
**Rocktenn Cp LLC** E 630 587-9429 Saint Charles *(G-19253)*
**RTS Packaging LLC** C 708 338-2800 Hillside *(G-11932)*
**Sho Pak LLC** G 618 876-1597 Venice *(G-21137)*
**Siebs Die Cutting Specialty Co** G 217 735-1432 Lincoln *(G-13420)*
**Signode Industrial Group LLC** E 815 939-0033 Kankakee *(G-12650)*
**Simon Box Mfg Co** G 815 722-6661 Lockport *(G-13745)*
**Sonoco Products Company** D 630 231-1489 West Chicago *(G-21775)*
**Sonoco Prtective Solutions Inc** D 847 398-0110 Arlington Heights *(G-842)*
**Stevenson Paper Co Inc** G 630 879-5000 Batavia *(G-1498)*
▲ **The Calumet Carton Company** D 708 331-7910 South Holland *(G-20310)*
**Westrock Cp LLC** D 708 458-8100 Bridgeview *(G-2539)*
**Westrock Cp LLC** E 630 924-0104 Bartlett *(G-1325)*
**Westrock Cp LLC** D 630 260-3500 Carol Stream *(G-3267)*
**Westrock Cp LLC** C 309 342-0121 Galesburg *(G-10780)*
**Westrock CP LLC** D 630 443-3538 Saint Charles *(G-19294)*
**Westrock CP LLC** G 773 264-3516 Chicago *(G-6966)*
**Westrock CP LLC** D 312 346-6600 Chicago *(G-6967)*
**Westrock CP LLC** G 847 625-8284 Waukegan *(G-21641)*
**Westrock CP LLC** D 630 924-0054 Bartlett *(G-1326)*
**Westrock CP LLC** D 708 458-5288 Bedford Park *(G-1593)*
**Westrock Mwv LLC** C 773 221-9015 Chicago *(G-6968)*
**Westrock Mwv LLC** E 217 442-2247 Danville *(G-7784)*
**Westrock Mwv LLC** C 630 289-8537 Bartlett *(G-1386)*
**Westrock Rkt Company** A 312 346-6600 Chicago *(G-6969)*

## 2652 Set-Up Paperboard Boxes

**Armbrust Paper Tubes Inc** E 773 586-3232 Chicago *(G-3945)*
**Bierdeman Box LLC** E 847 256-0302 Wilmette *(G-22244)*
▲ **Colbert Packaging Corporation** C 847 367-5990 Lake Forest *(G-12892)*
▲ **Elegant Acquisition LLC** D 708 652-3400 Cicero *(G-7194)*
**International Paper Company** E 708 728-1000 Bedford Park *(G-1557)*
**Jordan Paper Box Company** F 773 287-5362 Chicago *(G-5323)*
**Master Paper Box Company Inc** C 773 927-0252 Chicago *(G-5643)*
**Racine Paper Box Manufacturing** E 773 227-3900 Chicago *(G-6278)*
**Reddi-Pac Inc** F 847 657-5222 Glenview *(G-11191)*
**Wabash Container Corporation** E 618 263-3586 Mount Carmel *(G-15287)*

## 2653 Corrugated & Solid Fiber Boxes

**A Trustworthy Sup Source Inc** G 773 480-0255 Chicago *(G-3693)*
**Aira Enterprise Inc** E 708 458-4360 Bedford Park *(G-1534)*
**Akers Packaging Service Inc** D 773 731-2900 Chicago *(G-3790)*
**Akers Packaging Solutions Inc** E 217 468-2396 Oreana *(G-16816)*
**All-Pak Manufacturing Corp** D 630 851-5859 Aurora *(G-1103)*
**Alois Box Co Inc** E 708 681-4090 Melrose Park *(G-14590)*
**American Boxboard LLC** E 708 924-9810 Batavia *(G-1413)*
**Ameriguard Corporation** G 630 986-1900 Burr Ridge *(G-2822)*
**APAC Unlimited Inc** G 847 441-4282 Northfield *(G-16390)*
**Armbrust Paper Tubes Inc** E 773 586-3232 Chicago *(G-3945)*
**Batavia Container Inc** C 630 879-2100 Batavia *(G-1419)*
**Blackhawk Corrugated LLC** E 844 270-2296 Carol Stream *(G-3115)*
**Blackhawk Courtyards LLC** G 416 298-8101 Carol Stream *(G-3116)*
**Box Manufacturing Inc** G 309 637-6228 Peoria *(G-17319)*
**Box USA** G 708 562-6000 Northlake *(G-16429)*
**Cameo Container Corporation** C 773 254-1030 Chicago *(G-4222)*
**Cano Container Corporation** E 630 585-7500 Aurora *(G-980)*
**Capitol Carton Company** E 312 563-9690 Chicago *(G-4229)*
**Capitol Carton Company** E 312 491-2220 Chicago *(G-4230)*
**Cascades Plastics Inc** E 450 469-3389 Aurora *(G-981)*
**Combined Technologies Inc** G 847 968-4855 Libertyville *(G-13317)*
**Compak Inc** E 815 399-2699 Rockford *(G-18320)*
**Corr-Pak Corporation** E 708 442-7806 Mc Cook *(G-14447)*
▲ **Corrugated Supplies Co LLC** E 708 458-5525 Bedford Park *(G-1546)*
**Cross Container Corporation** E 847 844-3200 Carpentersville *(G-3281)*
**D/C Export & Domestic Pkg Inc** E 847 593-4200 Elk Grove Village *(G-9415)*
**DDN Industries Inc** G 847 885-8595 Hoffman Estates *(G-12004)*
**Dexton Enterprises** G 309 788-1881 Rock Island *(G-18174)*
**Elm Street Industries Inc** F 309 854-7000 Kewanee *(G-12681)*
**Fca LLC** E 309 949-3999 Coal Valley *(G-7296)*
**Forest Packaging Corporation** E 847 981-7000 Elk Grove Village *(G-9485)*
**Georg-Pcific Corrugated IV LLC** C 630 896-3610 Aurora *(G-1014)*
**Georgia-Pacific LLC** C 217 999-2511 Mount Olive *(G-15302)*
**Georgia-Pacific Bldg Pdts LLC** G 630 449-7200 Aurora *(G-1015)*
**Glass Haus** G 815 459-5849 McHenry *(G-14510)*
**Grafcor Packaging Inc** F 815 639-2380 Loves Park *(G-13945)*
**Graphic Packaging Holding Co** B 630 260-6500 Carol Stream *(G-3161)*
**Greif Inc** E 708 371-4777 Alsip *(G-466)*
**Greif Inc** D 217 468-2396 Oreana *(G-16817)*
**H Field & Sons Inc** F 847 434-0970 Arlington Heights *(G-761)*
**Heritage Packaging LLC** E 217 735-4406 Lincoln *(G-13410)*
▲ **Ideal Box Co** C 708 594-3100 Chicago *(G-5140)*
**Illinois Valley Container Inc** E 815 223-7200 Peru *(G-17513)*
**Inglese Box Co Ltd** E 847 669-1700 Huntley *(G-12149)*
**International Paper Company** C 708 728-8200 Chicago *(G-5222)*
**International Paper Company** C 630 896-2061 Montgomery *(G-15050)*
**International Paper Company** C 815 398-2100 Rockford *(G-18439)*
**International Paper Company** D 708 562-6000 Northlake *(G-16440)*
**International Paper Company** C 630 585-3400 Aurora *(G-1033)*
**International Paper Company** C 217 735-1221 Lincoln *(G-13411)*
**J H H of Illinois Inc** F 630 293-0739 West Chicago *(G-21726)*
**J Wallace & Associates Inc** G 630 960-4221 Downers Grove *(G-8467)*
▼ **John J Monaco Products Co Inc** E 708 344-3333 Melrose Park *(G-14664)*
**Jordan Paper Box Company** F 773 287-5362 Chicago *(G-5323)*
**Kindlon Enterprises Inc** G 708 367-4000 Aurora *(G-1043)*
**Kodiak LLC** E 248 545-7520 Chicago *(G-5398)*
**Kodiak LLC** E 773 284-9975 Chicago *(G-5399)*
**Liberty Diversified Intl Inc** E 217 935-8361 Clinton *(G-7285)*
**Liberty Diversified Intl Inc** C 309 787-6161 Rock Island *(G-18186)*
**Menasha Packaging Company LLC** C 773 227-6000 Chicago *(G-5685)*
**Menasha Packaging Company LLC** B 312 880-4620 Chicago *(G-5686)*
**Menasha Packaging Company LLC** F 618 931-7805 Edwardsville *(G-8807)*
**Menasha Packaging Company LLC** C 708 728-0372 Bridgeview *(G-2507)*
**Menasha Packaging Company LLC** C 618 501-6040 Edwardsville *(G-8808)*
**Menasha Packaging Company LLC** C 815 639-0144 Bolingbrook *(G-2340)*
**Menasha Packaging Company LLC** B 309 787-1747 Rock Island *(G-18188)*
**Midwest Fibre Products Inc** E 309 596-2955 Viola *(G-21292)*
**Midwest Packaging & Cont Inc** D 815 633-6800 Machesney Park *(G-14093)*
▲ **Murnane Specialties Inc** E 708 449-1200 Northlake *(G-16444)*
▲ **Nation Inc** E 847 844-7300 Carpentersville *(G-3292)*
▲ **Ockerlund Industries Inc** E 630 620-1269 Addison *(G-232)*
**Orbis Rpm LLC** F 630 844-9255 North Aurora *(G-16139)*
**Orora North America** D 630 613-2600 Lombard *(G-13839)*
**Orora Packaging Solutions** D 815 895-2343 Sycamore *(G-20812)*
**Packaging Corporation America** F 847 388-6000 Mundelein *(G-15540)*
**Packaging Corporation America** G 618 934-3100 Trenton *(G-20995)*
**Packaging Corporation America** D 708 821-1600 Chicago *(G-6053)*
**Packaging Corporation America** G 773 378-8700 Chicago *(G-6054)*
**Packaging Corporation America** D 708 594-5260 Bedford Park *(G-1570)*
**Packaging Corporation America** G 618 662-6700 Flora *(G-10213)*
▲ **Packaging Corporation America** C 847 482-3000 Lake Forest *(G-12933)*
**Packaging Design Corporation** E 630 323-1354 Burr Ridge *(G-2873)*
▲ **Pak Source Inc** E 309 786-7374 Rock Island *(G-18191)*

# SIC SECTION

# 26 PAPER AND ALLIED PRODUCTS

▲ Patti Group Incorporated .............F ...... 630 243-6320
  Lemont *(G-13251)*
PCA International Inc .....................G ...... 847 482-3000
  Lake Forest *(G-12941)*
Pierce Box & Paper Corporation ........E ...... 815 547-0117
  Belvidere *(G-1778)*
Precision Die Cutting & Finish .........G ...... 773 252-5625
  Chicago *(G-6169)*
▲ Premier Packaging Systems Inc ....G ...... 847 996-6860
  Mundelein *(G-15548)*
Pry-Bar Company .............................F ...... 815 436-3383
  Joliet *(G-12558)*
▲ Reliable Container Inc .................E ...... 630 543-6131
  Addison *(G-274)*
Rex Carton Company Inc ................E ...... 773 581-4115
  Chicago *(G-6342)*
Royal Box Group LLC .....................B ...... 708 656-2020
  Cicero *(G-7225)*
Royal Box Group LLC .....................E ...... 630 543-4464
  Addison *(G-281)*
Royal Box Group LLC .....................E ...... 708 222-4650
  Cicero *(G-7226)*
Rudd Container Corporation ............D ...... 773 847-7600
  Chicago *(G-6414)*
Ruscorr LLC ....................................G ...... 708 458-5525
  Bedford Park *(G-1580)*
Sauk Valley Container Corp .............F ...... 815 626-9657
  Sterling *(G-20611)*
SCI Box LLC ....................................E ...... 618 244-7244
  Mount Vernon *(G-15444)*
Siebs Die Cutting Specialty Co .........G ...... 217 735-1432
  Lincoln *(G-13420)*
Sisco Corporation ............................E ...... 618 327-3066
  Nashville *(G-15847)*
Sonoco Display & Packaging LLC ....F ...... 630 789-1111
  Westmont *(G-21922)*
Sonoco Products Company ..............D ...... 630 231-1489
  West Chicago *(G-21775)*
Specialty Box Corp ..........................F ...... 630 897-7278
  North Aurora *(G-16145)*
Stand Fast Group LLC ....................D ...... 630 600-0900
  Carol Stream *(G-3246)*
Stand Fast Packaging Pdts Inc ........D ...... 630 600-0900
  Carol Stream *(G-3247)*
Stitch TEC Co Inc ............................G ...... 618 327-8054
  Nashville *(G-15848)*
▲ Strive Converting Corporation .......C ...... 773 227-6000
  Chicago *(G-6607)*
Sycamore Containers Inc ................D ...... 815 895-2343
  Sycamore *(G-20818)*
▲ The Calumet Carton Company ......D ...... 708 331-7910
  South Holland *(G-20310)*
Tuscola Packaging Group LLC ........D ...... 734 268-2877
  Tuscola *(G-21027)*
United Container Corporation ..........E ...... 773 342-2200
  Chicago *(G-6822)*
Vangard Distribution Inc .................G ...... 708 484-9895
  Berwyn *(G-2077)*
▲ Vangard Distribution Inc ..............G ...... 708 588-8400
  Brookfield *(G-2646)*
Wehrle Lumber Co Inc ....................F ...... 618 283-4859
  Vandalia *(G-21131)*
Welch Packaging LLC .....................D ...... 708 813-1520
  Countryside *(G-7451)*
Wertheimer Box & Paper Corp .........D ...... 312 829-4545
  Mc Cook *(G-14461)*
Westrock Company ..........................C ...... 630 429-2400
  Aurora *(G-1233)*
Westrock Cp LLC ............................C ...... 309 342-0121
  Galesburg *(G-10780)*
Westrock Cp LLC ............................C ...... 847 689-4200
  North Chicago *(G-16190)*
Westrock Cp LLC ............................D ...... 630 384-5200
  Carol Stream *(G-3266)*
Westrock CP LLC ............................C ...... 618 654-2141
  Highland *(G-11818)*
Westrock CP LLC ............................D ...... 630 924-0054
  Bartlett *(G-1326)*
Westrock CP LLC ............................D ...... 708 458-5288
  Bedford Park *(G-1593)*
Westrock Rkt Company ...................C ...... 847 649-9231
  Melrose Park *(G-14709)*
Westrock Rkt Company ...................E ...... 630 325-9670
  Burr Ridge *(G-2894)*
Westrock Rkt Company ...................A ...... 312 346-6600
  Chicago *(G-6969)*
Weyerhaeuser Company ..................... ...... 847 439-1111
  Elk Grove Village *(G-9811)*
York Corrugated Container Corp ......D ...... 630 260-2900
  Glendale Heights *(G-11093)*

## 2655 Fiber Cans, Tubes & Drums

Advantage Structures LLC ................G ...... 773 734-9305
  Chicago *(G-3775)*
Armbrust Paper Tubes Inc ................E ...... 773 586-3232
  Chicago *(G-3945)*
Capitol Carton Company ...................E ...... 312 563-9690
  Chicago *(G-4229)*
Caraustar Industrial and Con .............D ...... 217 323-5225
  Beardstown *(G-1521)*
▲ Chicago Mailing Tube Company .....E ...... 312 243-6050
  Chicago *(G-4330)*
Ehs Solutions LLC ............................G ...... 309 282-9121
  Peoria *(G-17353)*
Fibre Drum Company ........................E ...... 815 933-3222
  Kankakee *(G-12616)*
G T Express Ltd ................................G ...... 708 338-0303
  Northlake *(G-16437)*
Greif Inc ............................................E ...... 630 961-9786
  Naperville *(G-15664)*
Greif Inc ............................................E ...... 630 961-1842
  Naperville *(G-15665)*
Illiana Cores Inc ................................E ...... 618 586-9800
  Palestine *(G-17093)*
Paper Tube LLC ................................G ...... 847 477-0563
  Wheeling *(G-22119)*
Precision Paper Tube Company ........E ...... 847 537-4250
  Wheeling *(G-22128)*
Resinite Corporation .........................C ...... 847 537-4250
  Wheeling *(G-22138)*
▲ Rolled Edge Inc .............................E ...... 773 283-9500
  Chicago *(G-6385)*
Sonoco Products Company ...............D ...... 630 231-1489
  West Chicago *(G-21775)*
Staffco Inc .........................................G ...... 309 688-3223
  Peoria *(G-17460)*
T J Assemblies Inc ...........................E ...... 847 671-0060
  Franklin Park *(G-10603)*

## 2656 Sanitary Food Containers

▲ Best Diamond Plastics LLC ...........F ...... 773 336-3485
  Chicago *(G-4092)*
Box Form Inc .....................................E ...... 773 927-8808
  Chicago *(G-4151)*
▼ Earthgrains Refrigertd Dough P .....A ...... 630 455-5200
  Downers Grove *(G-8438)*
International Paper Company ............C ...... 217 735-1221
  Lincoln *(G-13411)*
Pactiv LLC .........................................C ...... 219 924-4120
  Lake Forest *(G-12936)*
Pactiv LLC .........................................C ...... 630 262-6335
  Saint Charles *(G-19233)*
Party Plate LLC .................................G ...... 708 268-4571
  Lemont *(G-13249)*
SCC Holding Company LLC .............A ...... 847 444-5000
  Lake Forest *(G-12958)*
▼ SF Holdings Group Inc ...................D ...... 847 831-4800
  Lincolnshire *(G-13479)*
▼ Solo Cup Company ........................E ...... 847 831-4800
  Lincolnshire *(G-13480)*
▲ Solo Cup Company LLC .................E ...... 847 444-5000
  Lincolnshire *(G-13481)*
▼ Solo Cup Investment Corp .............D ...... 847 831-4800
  Highland Park *(G-11872)*
▼ Solo Cup Operating Corporation ....D ...... 847 444-5000
  Lincolnshire *(G-13482)*
◆ Tetra Pak US Holdings Inc ............C ...... 940 565-8800
  Vernon Hills *(G-21210)*

## 2657 Folding Paperboard Boxes

Accord Carton Co ..............................C ...... 708 272-3050
  Alsip *(G-428)*
Artistic Carton Company ....................E ...... 847 741-0247
  Elgin *(G-8958)*
Box Form Inc .....................................E ...... 773 927-8808
  Chicago *(G-4151)*
Capitol Carton Company ...................E ...... 312 563-9690
  Chicago *(G-4229)*
Caraustar Industries Inc ....................E ...... 773 308-7622
  Chicago *(G-4236)*
▼ Cartoncraft Inc ...............................D ...... 630 377-1230
  Saint Charles *(G-19151)*
▲ Colbert Packaging Corporation ......C ...... 847 367-5990
  Lake Forest *(G-12892)*
Combined Technologies Inc .............G ...... 847 968-4855
  Libertyville *(G-13317)*
Fox Valley Printing Co Inc ................F ...... 419 232-3348
  Montgomery *(G-15043)*
General Converting Inc ....................D ...... 630 378-9800
  Bolingbrook *(G-2312)*
Graphic Packaging Holding Co .........B ...... 630 260-6500
  Carol Stream *(G-3161)*
Graphic Packaging Intl Inc ................D ...... 618 533-2721
  Centralia *(G-3416)*
H Field & Sons Inc ............................F ...... 847 434-0970
  Arlington Heights *(G-761)*
Impac Group Inc ...............................A ...... 708 344-9100
  Melrose Park *(G-14655)*
Jordan Paper Box Company .............F ...... 773 287-5362
  Chicago *(G-5323)*
▲ Knight Paper Box Company ..........F ...... 773 585-2035
  Chicago *(G-5390)*
Master Paper Box Company Inc .......C ...... 773 927-0252
  Chicago *(G-5643)*
▲ MB Box Inc ....................................G ...... 815 589-3043
  Fulton *(G-10703)*
Midwest Fibre Products Inc .............E ...... 309 596-2955
  Viola *(G-21292)*
▲ Nosco Inc ......................................B ...... 847 336-4200
  Waukegan *(G-21595)*
Pactiv LLC .........................................C ...... 630 262-6335
  Saint Charles *(G-19233)*
▲ Plasticrest Products Inc ................F ...... 773 826-2163
  Chicago *(G-6136)*
Pure Skin LLC ...................................C ...... 217 679-6267
  Springfield *(G-20509)*
Racine Paper Box Manufacturing ......C ...... 773 227-3900
  Chicago *(G-6278)*
Rex Carton Company Inc .................E ...... 773 581-4115
  Chicago *(G-6342)*
Specialty Box Corp ...........................F ...... 630 897-7278
  North Aurora *(G-16145)*
Tegrant Corporation ..........................D ...... 630 879-0121
  Batavia *(G-1505)*
▲ The Calumet Carton Company ......D ...... 708 331-7910
  South Holland *(G-20310)*
▲ Thermal Bags By Ingrid Inc ..........F ...... 847 836-4400
  Gilberts *(G-10938)*
United Press Inc (del) .......................F ...... 847 482-0597
  Lincolnshire *(G-13487)*
Westrock Cp LLC ..............................C ...... 309 342-0121
  Galesburg *(G-10780)*
Winkler Products Inc ........................G ...... 314 421-1926
  Edwardsville *(G-8819)*

## 2671 Paper Coating & Laminating for Packaging

Acorn Diversified Inc ........................F ...... 708 478-1051
  Orland Park *(G-16837)*
Allegra Print & Imaging Inc ..............G ...... 847 697-1434
  Elgin *(G-8942)*
◆ Amcor Flexibles LLC .....................C ...... 224 313-7000
  Buffalo Grove *(G-2656)*
American Graphics Network Inc .......F ...... 847 729-7220
  Glenview *(G-11100)*
American Name Plate & Metal De ....E ...... 773 376-1400
  Chicago *(G-3867)*
Ampac Flexicon LLC ........................C ...... 630 439-3160
  Hanover Park *(G-11575)*
▲ Ampac Flexicon LLC .....................D ...... 847 639-3530
  Cary *(G-3325)*
Applied Products Inc ........................E ...... 815 633-3825
  Machesney Park *(G-14057)*
Arcadia Press Inc .............................F ...... 847 451-6390
  Franklin Park *(G-10398)*
Avery Dnnson Ret Info Svcs LLC ....G ...... 626 304-2000
  Chicago *(G-4000)*
B & B Printing Company ...................G ...... 217 285-6072
  Pittsfield *(G-17561)*
▲ Bagcraftpapercon I LLC ...............C ...... 620 856-2800
  Chicago *(G-4025)*
Bemis Packaging Inc ........................E ...... 708 544-1600
  Bellwood *(G-1697)*
Bucktown Polymers ..........................C ...... 312 436-1460
  Chicago *(G-4181)*
Burgopak Limited ..............................E ...... 312 255-0827
  Chicago *(G-4185)*
Catty Corporation ..............................D ...... 815 943-2143
  Harvard *(G-11626)*
▲ Clear Lam Packaging Inc .............B ...... 847 439-8570
  Elk Grove Village *(G-9376)*
Dart Container Michigan LLC ...........G ...... 312 221-1245
  Chicago *(G-4560)*
▲ Daubert Cromwell LLC ..................E ...... 708 293-7750
  Alsip *(G-456)*
Deco Adhesive Pdts 1985 Ltd ..........E ...... 847 472-2100
  Elk Grove Village *(G-9420)*
Dresbach Distributing Co .................G ...... 815 223-0116
  Peru *(G-17507)*

## 26 PAPER AND ALLIED PRODUCTS

Elite Extrusion Technology Inc .......... G .... 630 485-2020
  Saint Charles *(G-19180)*
Ennis Inc ............................................. E .... 815 875-2000
  Princeton *(G-17748)*
▲ Fisher Container Corp ..................... D .... 847 541-0000
  Buffalo Grove *(G-2694)*
Fisher Container Holdings LLC .......... G .... 847 541-0000
  Buffalo Grove *(G-2695)*
Flex-O-Glass Inc ............................... E .... 815 288-1424
  Dixon *(G-8331)*
▲ Forestree Inc ................................... G .... 708 598-8789
  Oak Brook *(G-16516)*
Formel Industries Inc ........................ E .... 847 928-5100
  Franklin Park *(G-10471)*
▲ Framarx Corporation ....................... E .... 708 755-3530
  Steger *(G-20572)*
▲ General Packaging Products Inc ..... D .... 312 226-5611
  Chicago *(G-4929)*
Great Midwest Packaging LLC .......... F .... 847 395-4500
  Waukegan *(G-21565)*
Griffith Solutions Inc .......................... G .... 847 384-1810
  Park Ridge *(G-17201)*
▲ H S Crocker Company Inc .............. D .... 847 669-3600
  Huntley *(G-12143)*
Hanlon Group Ltd .............................. G .... 773 525-3666
  Chicago *(G-5042)*
Hexacomb Corporation ..................... G .... 847 955-7984
  Buffalo Grove *(G-2704)*
Iam Acquisition LLC .......................... E .... 847 259-7800
  Wheeling *(G-22073)*
Illinois Tag Co ................................... E .... 773 626-0542
  Carol Stream *(G-3169)*
Ken Don LLC ..................................... G .... 708 596-4910
  Markham *(G-14303)*
Label Graphics Co Inc ....................... F .... 815 648-2478
  Hebron *(G-11722)*
Labels Unlimited Incorporated .......... E .... 773 523-7500
  Chicago *(G-5430)*
Lasons Label Co ................................ G .... 773 775-2606
  Chicago *(G-5464)*
▲ Lbp Manufacturing LLC ................... D .... 800 545-6200
  Cicero *(G-7215)*
MEI LLC ............................................. G .... 630 285-1505
  Itasca *(G-12313)*
Midwest Lminating Coatings Inc ....... E .... 708 653-9500
  Alsip *(G-493)*
Miller Products Inc ............................ E .... 708 534-5111
  University Park *(G-21058)*
Miracle Press Company ..................... F .... 773 722-6176
  Chicago *(G-5770)*
Multi Packaging Solutions Inc ........... G .... 773 283-9500
  Chicago *(G-5832)*
Nashua Corporation ........................... D .... 847 692-9130
  Park Ridge *(G-17211)*
▲ Nation Inc ........................................ E .... 847 844-7300
  Carpentersville *(G-3292)*
▲ Navis Industries Inc ........................ G .... 224 293-2000
  Elgin *(G-9117)*
No Surrender Inc ............................... G .... 773 929-7920
  Chicago *(G-5920)*
Noor International Inc ........................ G .... 847 985-2300
  Bartlett *(G-1320)*
Odra Inc ............................................. G .... 847 249-2910
  Gurnee *(G-11478)*
▲ Packaging Dynamics Corporation ... B .... 773 254-8000
  Chicago *(G-6055)*
Packaging Dynamics Oper Co ........... G .... 773 843-8000
  Chicago *(G-6056)*
Packaging Prtg Specialists Inc .......... F .... 630 513-8060
  Saint Charles *(G-19232)*
Perryco Inc ........................................ F .... 815 436-2431
  Plainfield *(G-17638)*
▲ Petra Manufacturing Co .................. D .... 773 622-1475
  Chicago *(G-6113)*
Photo Techniques Corp ..................... E .... 630 690-9360
  Carol Stream *(G-3213)*
▼ Pioneer Labels Inc ......................... C .... 618 546-5418
  Robinson *(G-18068)*
Polyair Inter Pack Inc ......................... D .... 773 995-1818
  Chicago *(G-6153)*
Preferred Printing Service ................. G .... 312 421-2343
  Chicago *(G-6175)*
Pregis Holding I Corporation ............. F .... 847 597-2200
  Deerfield *(G-8046)*
Pregis Innovative Packg LLC ............. E .... 847 597-2200
  Deerfield *(G-8047)*
Pregis LLC ......................................... F .... 847 597-2200
  Deerfield *(G-8049)*
Pregis LLC ......................................... D .... 618 934-4311
  Trenton *(G-20997)*

Prime Label & Packaging LLC ........... D .... 630 227-1300
  Wood Dale *(G-22414)*
Prime Label Group LLC ..................... D .... 773 630-8793
  Batavia *(G-1486)*
Printpack Inc ..................................... C .... 847 888-7150
  Elgin *(G-9148)*
▲ Pro-Pak Industries Inc .................... F .... 630 876-1050
  West Chicago *(G-21761)*
Quality Bags Inc ................................ F .... 630 543-9800
  Addison *(G-263)*
◆ Rapak LLC ....................................... C .... 630 296-2000
  Romeoville *(G-18862)*
RR Donnelley & Sons Company ........ D .... 630 762-7600
  Saint Charles *(G-19256)*
RTC Industries Inc ............................ D .... 847 640-2400
  Chicago *(G-6409)*
◆ Selig Sealing Products Inc ............. G .... 815 785-2100
  Forrest *(G-10266)*
◆ Seshin USA Inc ............................... G .... 847 550-5556
  Lake Zurich *(G-13130)*
Signature Label of Illinois ................. C .... 618 283-5145
  Vandalia *(G-21125)*
▲ Signode Industrial Group LLC ........ E .... 847 724-7500
  Glenview *(G-11198)*
Signode Industrial Group LLC ........... E .... 815 939-6192
  Kankakee *(G-12649)*
Signode Industrial Group LLC ........... E .... 847 724-6100
  Glenview *(G-11200)*
Signode Intl Holdings LLC ................. F .... 800 648-8864
  Glenview *(G-11202)*
◆ SJS Packaging Inc .......................... G .... 630 855-4755
  Streamwood *(G-20673)*
◆ Stepac USA Corporation ................. G .... 630 296-2000
  Romeoville *(G-18870)*
Stephen Fossler Company ................. D .... 847 635-7200
  Des Plaines *(G-8281)*
Surface Guard Inc ............................. D .... 630 236-8250
  Aurora *(G-1084)*
▼ Tegrant Corporation ........................ B .... 815 756-8451
  Dekalb *(G-8125)*
Tetra Pak Inc ..................................... D .... 815 873-1222
  Rockford *(G-18645)*
Tetra Pak Inc ..................................... E .... 847 955-6000
  Vernon Hills *(G-21208)*
◆ Tetra Pak Materials LP .................... E .... 847 955-6000
  Vernon Hills *(G-21209)*
Transparent Container Co Inc ............ D .... 708 449-8520
  Addison *(G-323)*
Transparent Container Co Inc ............ E .... 630 860-2666
  Bensenville *(G-2006)*
Triumph Packaging Georgia LLC ....... E .... 312 251-9600
  Lake Forest *(G-12972)*
Triumph Packaging Group ................. E .... 312 251-9600
  Lake Forest *(G-12973)*
UNI-Label and Tag Corporation ......... E .... 847 956-8900
  Elk Grove Village *(G-9797)*
Waxstar Inc ........................................ G .... 708 755-3530
  S Chicago Hts *(G-19115)*
◆ Westrock Cnsmr Packg Group LLC . A .... 804 444-1000
  Melrose Park *(G-14708)*
World Contract Packagers Inc ........... G .... 815 624-6501
  South Beloit *(G-20177)*
▲ Xshredders Inc ................................ G .... 847 205-1875
  Northbrook *(G-16389)*
▲ Zacros America Inc ......................... G .... 847 397-6191
  Schaumburg *(G-19795)*

## 2672 Paper Coating & Laminating, Exc for Packaging

◆ Acco Brands Corporation ................ A .... 847 541-9500
  Lake Zurich *(G-13033)*
American Name Plate & Metal De ...... E .... 773 376-1400
  Chicago *(G-3867)*
Arcadia Press Inc .............................. F .... 847 451-6390
  Franklin Park *(G-10398)*
Avery Dennison Corporation ............. E .... 847 824-7450
  Mount Prospect *(G-15312)*
Avery Dennison Corporation ............. D .... 877 214-0909
  Niles *(G-15962)*
Basswood Associates Inc ................. F .... 312 240-9400
  Chicago *(G-4053)*
Bisco Intl Inc ..................................... D .... 708 544-6308
  Hillside *(G-11911)*
Brasel Products Inc ........................... D .... 630 879-3759
  Batavia *(G-1424)*
▲ Budnick Converting Inc ................... C .... 618 281-8090
  Columbia *(G-7353)*
Cenveo Inc ........................................ G .... 217 243-4258
  Jacksonville *(G-12383)*

◆ Channeled Resources Inc ............... E .... 312 733-4200
  Chicago *(G-4287)*
Charles H Luck Envelope Inc ............ E .... 847 451-1500
  Franklin Park *(G-10427)*
Chase Corporation ............................. E .... 847 866-8500
  Evanston *(G-10022)*
Classique Signs & Engrv Inc ............. E .... 217 228-7446
  Quincy *(G-17813)*
Coding Solutions Inc ......................... F .... 630 377-5825
  Saint Charles *(G-19159)*
Condor Labels Inc ............................. G .... 708 429-0707
  Tinley Park *(G-20902)*
▲ Continental Datalabel Inc ............... E .... 847 742-1600
  Elgin *(G-9001)*
Cushing and Company ....................... E .... 312 266-8228
  Chicago *(G-4518)*
Cypress Multigraphics LLC ............... E .... 708 633-1166
  Tinley Park *(G-20907)*
Daubert Vci Inc .................................. F .... 630 203-6800
  Burr Ridge *(G-2835)*
Diversfied Lbling Slutions Inc ........... D .... 630 625-1225
  Itasca *(G-12252)*
Fedex Office & Print Svcs Inc ........... E .... 847 329-9464
  Lincolnwood *(G-13510)*
Fedex Office & Print Svcs Inc ........... E .... 309 685-4093
  Peoria *(G-17359)*
Gallas Label & Decal ......................... F .... 773 775-1000
  Chicago *(G-4909)*
General Laminating Company ............ G .... 847 639-8770
  Cary *(G-3347)*
▲ H S Crocker Company Inc .............. D .... 847 669-3600
  Huntley *(G-12143)*
Healthcare Labels Inc ........................ E .... 847 382-3993
  North Barrington *(G-16151)*
▲ Highland Supply Corporation .......... B .... 618 654-2161
  Highland *(G-11794)*
◆ Holden Industries Inc ...................... F .... 847 940-1500
  Deerfield *(G-8013)*
▲ Hollymatic Corporation ................... D .... 708 579-3700
  Countryside *(G-7430)*
Hugh Courtright & Co Ltd ................. F .... 708 534-8400
  Monee *(G-14997)*
Identco International Corp ................. D .... 815 385-0011
  Ingleside *(G-12190)*
Intertape Polymer Corp ...................... D .... 618 549-2131
  Carbondale *(G-3013)*
J & D Instant Signs ........................... G .... 847 965-2800
  Morton Grove *(G-15206)*
Keneal Industries Inc ......................... F .... 815 886-1300
  Romeoville *(G-18834)*
Knight Prtg & Litho Svc Ltd .............. G .... 847 487-7700
  Island Lake *(G-12217)*
L & S Label Printing Inc .................... G .... 815 964-6753
  Cherry Valley *(G-3646)*
Label Graphics Co Inc ....................... F .... 815 648-2478
  Hebron *(G-11722)*
Label Tek Inc ..................................... F .... 630 820-8499
  Aurora *(G-1044)*
Labels Unlimited Incorporated .......... E .... 773 523-7500
  Chicago *(G-5430)*
Lasons Label Co ................................ G .... 773 775-2606
  Chicago *(G-5464)*
Line Craft Inc .................................... F .... 630 932-1182
  Lombard *(G-13819)*
M & R Graphics Inc ........................... F .... 708 534-6621
  University Park *(G-21054)*
Mich Enterprises Inc ......................... F .... 630 616-9000
  Wood Dale *(G-22399)*
Midwest Lminating Coatings Inc ....... E .... 708 653-9500
  Alsip *(G-493)*
Miller Products Inc ............................ E .... 708 534-5111
  University Park *(G-21058)*
Nashua Corporation ........................... D .... 847 692-9130
  Park Ridge *(G-17211)*
National Data-Label Corp ................... E .... 630 616-9595
  Bensenville *(G-1954)*
Navitor Inc ......................................... B .... 800 323-0253
  Harwood Heights *(G-11687)*
Noor International Inc ........................ G .... 847 985-2300
  Bartlett *(G-1320)*
Off The Press .................................... G .... 815 436-9612
  Plainfield *(G-17634)*
▼ Pioneer Labels Inc ......................... C .... 618 546-5418
  Robinson *(G-18068)*
▲ Plitek ............................................... D .... 847 827-6680
  Des Plaines *(G-8257)*
Prairie State Graphics Inc ................. D .... 847 801-3100
  Franklin Park *(G-10556)*
▲ Prairie State Impressions LLC ........ D .... 847 801-3100
  Franklin Park *(G-10557)*

# SIC SECTION
## 26 PAPER AND ALLIED PRODUCTS

Preferred Printing Service................G........ 312 421-2343
  Chicago *(G-6175)*
Primedia Source  LLC .....................G........ 630 553-8451
  Yorkville *(G-22670)*
Print-O-Tape Inc ..............................E........ 847 362-6433
  Mundelein *(G-15550)*
Printing Etc Inc ................................G........ 815 562-6151
  Rochelle *(G-18102)*
Pro Patch Systems Inc ..................G........ 847 356-8100
  Lake Villa *(G-13024)*
Punch Products Manufacturing ....E........ 773 533-2800
  Chicago *(G-6226)*
Qualified Innovation Inc ..................F........ 630 556-4136
  Sugar Grove *(G-20732)*
S & K Label Co ................................G........ 630 307-2577
  Bloomingdale *(G-2132)*
Service Packaging Design  Inc .....G........ 847 966-6592
  Morton Grove *(G-15236)*
Sheer Graphics Inc .........................G........ 630 654-4422
  Westmont *(G-21920)*
Signature Label of Illinois ...............G........ 618 283-5145
  Vandalia *(G-21125)*
Signcraft Screenprint  Inc ...............C........ 815 777-3030
  Galena *(G-10731)*
Specialty Tape & Label Co Inc ......E........ 708 863-3800
  Lyons *(G-14044)*
Stephen Fossler Company .............D........ 847 635-7200
  Des Plaines *(G-8281)*
▲ Strata-Tac Inc ..............................F........ 630 879-9388
  Saint Charles *(G-19272)*
▲ Tek Pak Inc .................................D........ 630 406-0560
  Batavia *(G-1506)*
Upm Raflatac  Inc ............................C........ 815 285-6100
  Dixon *(G-8357)*
Voss Belting & Specialty Co .........E........ 847 673-8900
  Lincolnwood *(G-13541)*
Walter Barr  Inc ................................G........ 630 325-7265
  Willowbrook *(G-22238)*
◆ Weber Marking Systems Inc ......B........ 847 364-8500
  Arlington Heights *(G-871)*
William Holloway Ltd ......................G........ 847 866-9520
  Evanston *(G-10106)*
▲ Zebra Technologies Corporation ..B........ 847 634-6700
  Lincolnshire *(G-13494)*
▲ Zih Corp ......................................B........ 847 634-6700
  Lincolnshire *(G-13497)*

## 2673 Bags: Plastics, Laminated & Coated

Aargus Industries  Inc ....................G........ 847 325-4444
  Wheeling *(G-21994)*
▲ Aargus Plastics  Inc ...................C........ 847 325-4444
  Wheeling *(G-21995)*
▲ ABG Bag Inc ..............................F........ 815 963-9525
  Rockford *(G-18247)*
Advanced Custom Shapes ............F........ 618 684-2222
  Murphysboro *(G-15570)*
▲ Ampac Flexibles  LLC ...............D........ 630 439-3160
  Hanover Park *(G-11574)*
Ampac Holdings  LLC ....................F........ 847 639-3530
  Cary *(G-3326)*
Bag and Barrier Corporation .........G........ 217 849-3271
  Toledo *(G-20961)*
▲ Bagcraftpapercon I  LLC ..........C........ 620 856-2800
  Chicago *(G-4025)*
◆ Bagmakers  Inc ..........................B........ 815 923-2247
  Union *(G-21033)*
Bio Industries Inc ............................D........ 847 215-8999
  Wheeling *(G-22014)*
Brohman Industries  Inc .................F........ 630 761-8160
  Chicago *(G-4174)*
Closet Concept ................................G........ 217 375-4214
  Milford *(G-14811)*
▲ Colonial Bag Corporation ..........D........ 630 690-3999
  Carol Stream *(G-3134)*
Coveris Holding Corp .....................G........ 773 877-3300
  Chicago *(G-4483)*
Dart Container Michigan LLC ........G........ 312 221-1245
  Chicago *(G-4560)*
▲ Diamond Cellophane Pdts Inc ..E........ 847 418-3000
  Northbrook *(G-16242)*
Drumheller Bag Corporation ..........G........ 309 676-1006
  Peoria *(G-17350)*
Duro Hilex Poly  LLC .....................D........ 708 385-8674
  Alsip *(G-459)*
▲ E-Z Products Inc ........................F........ 847 551-9199
  Gilberts *(G-10918)*
▲ Engineered Materials  Inc ..........F........ 847 821-8280
  Buffalo Grove *(G-2691)*
Envision Inc ......................................G........ 847 735-0789
  Lake Forest *(G-12897)*

◆ Essentra Packaging US Inc .......G........ 704 418-8692
  Westchester *(G-21841)*
▲ Fischer Paper Products  Inc .....D........ 847 395-6060
  Antioch *(G-632)*
▲ Fisher Container Corp ...............D........ 847 541-0000
  Buffalo Grove *(G-2694)*
Fisher Container Holdings  LLC ...G........ 847 541-0000
  Buffalo Grove *(G-2695)*
Flex-O-Glass Inc ..............................D........ 773 261-5200
  Chicago *(G-4858)*
Flex-Pak Packaging Products .......F........ 630 761-3335
  Batavia *(G-1448)*
◆ Foodhandler Inc ..........................D........ 866 931-3613
  Elk Grove Village *(G-9484)*
▲ Golden Bag Company Inc .........F........ 847 836-7766
  East Dundee *(G-8639)*
▲ Highland Supply Corporation ....B........ 618 654-2161
  Highland *(G-11794)*
▲ Jacobson Acqstion Holdings LLC ..C........ 847 623-1414
  Waukegan *(G-21574)*
▲ Kam Group Inc ............................F........ 630 679-9668
  Bolingbrook *(G-2330)*
Kapak Company Inc .......................G........ 952 541-0750
  Hanover Park *(G-11584)*
▲ Keenpac LLC ..............................G........ 845 291-8680
  Morton Grove *(G-15209)*
Kleer Pak Mfg Co  Inc ....................E........ 630 543-0208
  Addison *(G-169)*
▲ Laminet Cover Company ...........E........ 773 622-6700
  Chicago *(G-5451)*
▲ Lawrence Packaging Intl ............G........ 630 682-2600
  Wheaton *(G-21965)*
▲ McCook Cold Storage Corp .....E........ 708 387-2585
  Mc Cook *(G-14452)*
Morris Packaging  LLC ..................G........ 309 663-9100
  Bloomington *(G-2204)*
Natural Packaging Inc ....................G........ 708 246-3420
  La Grange *(G-12740)*
Packaging Personified  Inc ............G........ 630 653-1655
  Carol Stream *(G-3210)*
Pactiv Intl Holdings Inc ...................G........ 847 482-2000
  Lake Forest *(G-12934)*
Pactiv LLC ........................................C........ 317 390-5306
  Grant Park *(G-11312)*
Pactiv LLC ........................................C........ 708 924-2402
  Bridgeview *(G-2518)*
Pactiv LLC ........................................G........ 815 469-2112
  Frankfort *(G-10346)*
Pactiv LLC ........................................C........ 217 479-1144
  Jacksonville *(G-12404)*
Pactiv LLC ........................................B........ 217 243-3311
  Jacksonville *(G-12405)*
Pactiv LLC ........................................C
  Lincolnshire *(G-13469)*
◆ Pactiv LLC ...................................A........ 847 482-2000
  Lake Forest *(G-12935)*
▲ Pak Source Inc ............................E........ 309 786-7374
  Rock Island *(G-18191)*
Peelmaster Packaging Corp .........E........ 847 966-6161
  Niles *(G-16015)*
Plastics D-E-F .................................G........ 312 226-4337
  Chicago *(G-6137)*
▼ Pliant LLC ....................................A........ 812 424-2904
  Rolling Meadows *(G-18763)*
Poly Plastics Films Corp ................G........ 815 636-0821
  Machesney Park *(G-14098)*
Pregis LLC .......................................A........ 847 597-2200
  Deerfield *(G-8049)*
Pride Packaging  LLC ....................G........ 309 663-9100
  Bloomington *(G-2215)*
Printpack Inc ....................................C........ 847 888-7150
  Elgin *(G-9148)*
◆ Procon Pacific  LLC ....................G........ 630 575-0551
  Oak Brook *(G-16556)*
Quality Bags  Inc .............................F........ 630 543-9800
  Addison *(G-263)*
R Popernik Co  Inc ..........................F........ 773 434-4300
  Chicago *(G-6269)*
◆ Renew Packaging  LLC ..............G........ 312 421-6699
  Chicago *(G-6333)*
Silgan Plastics LLC .........................C........ 618 662-4471
  Flora *(G-10217)*
Vej Holdings LLC ............................G........ 630 219-1582
  Naperville *(G-15774)*
Vida Enterprises  Inc ......................G........ 312 808-0088
  Chicago *(G-6895)*
▼ Vilutis and Co  Inc ......................E........ 815 469-2116
  Frankfort *(G-10374)*
Vonco Products  LLC .....................E........ 847 356-2323
  Lake Villa *(G-13029)*

Waxstar Inc ......................................G........ 708 755-3530
  S Chicago Hts *(G-19115)*

## 2674 Bags: Uncoated Paper & Multiwall

Bag and Barrier Corporation .........G........ 217 849-3271
  Toledo *(G-20961)*
▲ Bagcraftpapercon I  LLC ..........C........ 620 856-2800
  Chicago *(G-4025)*
◆ Bagmakers  Inc ..........................B........ 815 923-2247
  Union *(G-21033)*
Bulk Lift International  LLC ............G........ 847 428-6059
  Carpentersville *(G-3277)*
Duro Hilex Poly  LLC .....................D........ 708 385-8674
  Alsip *(G-459)*
▲ Fischer Paper Products  Inc .....D........ 847 395-6060
  Antioch *(G-632)*
▲ Gateway Packaging Company ..C........ 618 451-0010
  Granite City *(G-11279)*
▲ Gateway Packaging Company LLC ..C........ 618 415-0010
  Granite City *(G-11280)*
Graphic Packaging Intl Inc ............G........ 630 260-6500
  Carol Stream *(G-3163)*
Langston Bag of Peoria  LLC ........D........ 309 676-1006
  Peoria *(G-17399)*
▲ Lexington Leather Goods Co .....F........ 773 287-5500
  Chicago *(G-5499)*
◆ Midwesco Filter Resources Inc ..C........ 540 773-4780
  Niles *(G-16006)*
◆ Mondi Romeoville  Inc ...............G........ 630 378-9886
  Romeoville *(G-18850)*
Morris Packaging  LLC ..................G........ 309 663-9100
  Bloomington *(G-2204)*
Pride Packaging  LLC ....................G........ 309 663-9100
  Bloomington *(G-2215)*
▲ Studley Products  Inc ................C........ 309 663-2313
  Bloomington *(G-2226)*
Waxstar Inc ......................................G........ 708 755-3530
  S Chicago Hts *(G-19115)*
Westrock Rkt Company .................A........ 312 346-6600
  Chicago *(G-6969)*

## 2675 Die-Cut Paper & Board

11th Street Express Prtg Inc .........F........ 815 968-0208
  Rockford *(G-18235)*
◆ Acco Brands USA LLC ..............B........ 800 222-6462
  Lake Zurich *(G-13034)*
Acco Brands USA LLC ..................D........ 847 272-3700
  Lincolnshire *(G-13423)*
▲ Ade Inc .......................................E........ 773 646-3400
  Chicago *(G-3746)*
Alloyd Brands ..................................G........ 843 383-7000
  Batavia *(G-1408)*
Andrews Converting  LLC ..............C........ 708 352-2555
  La Grange *(G-12725)*
Animated Advg Techniques Inc ....G........ 312 372-4694
  Chicago *(G-3908)*
Anselmo Die and Index Co Inc .....F........ 847 397-1200
  Schaumburg *(G-19443)*
Artistic Carton Company ................E........ 847 741-0247
  Elgin *(G-8958)*
B Allan Graphics  Inc .....................F........ 708 396-1704
  Alsip *(G-438)*
Business Forms Finishing Svc .....G........ 773 229-0230
  Chicago *(G-4187)*
Butler Bros Steel Rule Die Co ......G........ 815 630-4629
  Shorewood *(G-19924)*
Capital Prtg & Die Cutng Inc ........G........ 630 896-5520
  Aurora *(G-1124)*
Carson Printing Inc ........................G........ 847 836-0900
  East Dundee *(G-8629)*
Classic Packaging Corporation ....G........ 224 723-5157
  Northbrook *(G-16226)*
Creative Label  Inc .........................E........ 847 981-3800
  Elk Grove Village *(G-9399)*
Creative Lithocraft Inc ....................G........ 847 352-7002
  Schaumburg *(G-19489)*
Deco Adhesive Pdts 1985 Ltd ......E........ 847 472-2100
  Elk Grove Village *(G-9420)*
Delta Press  Inc ...............................E........ 847 671-3200
  Palatine *(G-17022)*
Diecrafters  Inc ................................E........ 708 656-3336
  Cicero *(G-7190)*
Global Abrasive Products  Inc ......E........ 630 543-9466
  Addison *(G-136)*
▲ Graphic Arts Finishing Company ..D........ 708 345-8484
  Melrose Park *(G-14648)*
▲ Graphic Converting  Inc ............B........ 630 758-4100
  Elmhurst *(G-9880)*
Impression Printing .........................F........ 708 614-8660
  Oak Forest *(G-16583)*

---

Employee Codes: A=Over 500 employees, B=251-500
C=101-250, D=51-100, E=20-50, F=10-19, G=3-9

# 26 PAPER AND ALLIED PRODUCTS

Intra-Cut Die Cutting Inc ..................F...... 773 775-6228
 Chicago *(G-5228)*
Lee-Wel Printing Corporation ............G...... 630 682-0935
 Wheaton *(G-21966)*
M S A Printing Co ..............................G...... 847 593-5699
 Elk Grove Village *(G-9604)*
M Wells Printing Co ...........................G...... 312 455-0400
 Chicago *(G-5588)*
McGrath Press Inc .............................E...... 815 356-5246
 Crystal Lake *(G-7607)*
Mich Enterprises Inc ..........................F...... 630 616-9000
 Wood Dale *(G-22399)*
Midwest Cortland Inc .........................E...... 847 671-0376
 Addison *(G-211)*
Midwest Index Inc .............................D...... 847 995-8425
 Addison *(G-212)*
▼ Murnane Packaging Corporation .....E...... 708 449-1200
 Northlake *(G-16443)*
Plastics Printing Group Inc .................F...... 312 421-7980
 Chicago *(G-6138)*
PMC Converting Corp ........................G...... 773 481-2269
 Chicago *(G-6142)*
◆ Potomac Corporation .....................C...... 847 259-0546
 Wheeling *(G-22126)*
Precision Die Cutting & Finish .............G...... 773 252-5625
 Chicago *(G-6169)*
Pry-Bar Company ...............................F...... 815 436-3383
 Joliet *(G-12558)*
Quick Tabs Inc ....................................G...... 630 969-7737
 Westmont *(G-21915)*
Racine Paper Box Manufacturing ......E...... 773 227-3900
 Chicago *(G-6278)*
▲ Rapid Displays Inc .........................C...... 773 927-5000
 Chicago *(G-6291)*

Review Printing Co Inc ......................G...... 309 788-7094
 Rock Island *(G-18199)*
Rhopac Fabricated Products LLC .....E...... 847 362-3300
 Libertyville *(G-13376)*
Rohrer Corporation .............................D...... 847 961-5920
 Huntley *(G-12174)*
Ross-Gage Inc ....................................F...... 708 347-3659
 Homewood *(G-12105)*
RTS Packaging LLC ...........................C...... 708 338-2800
 Hillside *(G-11932)*
Sales Midwest Prtg & Packg Inc .......G...... 309 764-5544
 Moline *(G-14968)*
Siebs Die Cutting Specialty Co ..........G...... 217 735-1432
 Lincoln *(G-13420)*
Stevenson Paper Co Inc ....................G...... 630 879-5000
 Batavia *(G-1498)*
Village Press Inc ................................G...... 847 362-1856
 Libertyville *(G-13399)*
▲ Warwick Publishing Company .......D...... 630 584-3871
 Saint Charles *(G-19291)*
◆ Weber Marking Systems Inc ..........B...... 847 364-8500
 Arlington Heights *(G-871)*
▲ Young Shin USA Limited ................G...... 847 598-3611
 Schaumburg *(G-19793)*

## 2676 Sanitary Paper Prdts

Barrington Company ..........................G...... 815 933-3233
 Bradley *(G-2413)*
Best Institutional Supply Co ...............G...... 708 216-0000
 Maywood *(G-14419)*
Bottoms Up Inc ...................................G...... 847 336-0040
 Waukegan *(G-21530)*
Dude Products Inc .............................G...... 773 661-1126
 Chicago *(G-4647)*
EPS Solutions Incorporated ...............A...... 815 206-0868
 Woodstock *(G-22566)*
Evergreen Manufacturing Inc ............E...... 217 382-5108
 Martinsville *(G-14335)*
Georgia-Pacific LLC ............................F...... 815 423-9990
 Elwood *(G-9981)*
Johnson & Johnson ............................G...... 847 640-5400
 Elk Grove Village *(G-9563)*
Microweb ..............................................G...... 309 426-2385
 Roseville *(G-19046)*
Sonoco Prtective Solutions Inc .........E...... 708 946-3244
 Beecher *(G-1602)*
US Specialty Packaging Inc ..............G...... 847 836-1115
 Elgin *(G-9221)*
Wells Janitorial Service Inc ................G...... 872 226-9983
 Chicago *(G-6953)*

## 2677 Envelopes

American Graphics Network Inc ........F...... 847 729-7220
 Glenview *(G-11100)*

Cenveo Inc ..........................................D...... 773 267-1717
 Chicago *(G-4279)*
Cenveo Corporation ...........................C...... 312 286-6400
 Chicago *(G-4281)*
Diamond Envelope Corporation .........D...... 630 499-2800
 Aurora *(G-995)*
▲ Federal Envelope Company ...........D...... 630 595-2000
 Bensenville *(G-1896)*
Forest Envelope Company .................G...... 630 515-1200
 Bolingbrook *(G-2311)*
Gaw-Ohara Envelope Co ...................E...... 773 638-1200
 Chicago *(G-4920)*
Gluetech Inc ........................................E...... 847 455-2707
 Wood Dale *(G-22377)*
Gordon Caplan Inc .............................G...... 773 489-3300
 Chicago *(G-4980)*
Graphic Industries Inc ........................E...... 847 357-9870
 South Elgin *(G-20201)*
Mackay Mitchell Envelope Co ............G...... 847 418-3866
 Northbrook *(G-16304)*
Managed Marketing Inc .....................G...... 847 279-8260
 Wheeling *(G-22098)*
Overt Press Inc ...................................F...... 773 284-0909
 Chicago *(G-6029)*
Roodhouse Envelope Co ...................D...... 217 589-4321
 Roodhouse *(G-18884)*
Royal Envelope Corporation ..............D...... 773 376-1212
 Chicago *(G-6401)*
Service Envelope Corporation ............E...... 847 559-0004
 Northbrook *(G-16362)*
▲ The Calumet Carton Company .......D...... 708 331-7910
 South Holland *(G-20310)*
Trekon Company Inc ..........................G...... 309 925-7942
 Tremont *(G-20986)*
Unique Envelope Corporation ............E...... 773 586-0330
 Chicago *(G-6819)*

## 2678 Stationery Prdts

Assemble and Mail Group Inc ............G...... 309 473-2006
 Heyworth *(G-11764)*
▲ Carl Manufacturing USA Inc ..........F...... 847 884-2842
 Itasca *(G-12242)*
Chicago Contract Bridge Assn ..........G...... 630 355-5560
 Naperville *(G-15626)*
Discount Computer Supply Inc ..........G...... 847 883-8743
 Buffalo Grove *(G-2688)*
Dove Foundation ................................G...... 312 217-3683
 Chicago *(G-4637)*
House of Doolittle Ltd ........................E...... 847 593-3417
 Arlington Heights *(G-769)*
▲ Mudlark Papers Inc ........................E...... 630 717-7616
 Naperville *(G-15702)*
Tjmj Inc ................................................F...... 312 315-7780
 Chicago *(G-6731)*

## 2679 Converted Paper Prdts, NEC

All Weather Products Co LLC ............F...... 847 981-0386
 Elk Grove Village *(G-9285)*
Ameri Label Company ........................F...... 847 895-8000
 Bartlett *(G-1315)*
▲ Ar-En Party Printers Inc .................F...... 847 673-7390
 Skokie *(G-19958)*
Brohman Industries Inc ......................F...... 630 761-8160
 Chicago *(G-4174)*
Bypak Inc .............................................G...... 815 933-2870
 Bradley *(G-2416)*
▲ Chicago Tag & Label Inc ................D...... 847 362-5100
 Libertyville *(G-13314)*
Coding Solutions Inc ..........................F...... 630 443-9602
 Saint Charles *(G-19160)*
Corydon Converting Company Inc ....F...... 630 898-9896
 Naperville *(G-15637)*
◆ Corydon Converting Company Inc ..E.... 630 983-1900
 Naperville *(G-15638)*
▲ Crescent Cardboard Company LLC .C... 888 293-3956
 Wheeling *(G-22032)*
Dean Patterson ...................................G...... 708 430-0477
 Bridgeview *(G-2482)*
Deco Adhesive Pdts 1985 Ltd ...........E...... 847 472-2100
 Elk Grove Village *(G-9420)*
Deco Labels & Tags Ltd ....................G...... 847 472-2100
 Wood Dale *(G-22358)*
Dietzgen Corporation .........................F...... 217 348-8111
 Charleston *(G-3596)*
Diversfied Lbling Slutions Inc ............D...... 630 625-1225
 Itasca *(G-12252)*
Franch & Sons Trnsp Inc ...................G...... 630 392-3307
 Addison *(G-123)*
▲ Gateway Packaging Company .......C...... 618 451-0010
 Granite City *(G-11279)*

General Laminating Company ............G...... 847 639-8770
 Cary *(G-3347)*
Gro-Mar Industries Inc .......................F...... 708 343-5901
 Melrose Park *(G-14649)*
H Hal Kramer Co .................................G...... 773 539-9648
 Chicago *(G-5021)*
Hospital Hlth Care Systems Inc .........F...... 708 863-3400
 Lyons *(G-14041)*
I M M Inc .............................................F...... 773 767-3700
 Chicago *(G-5131)*
Identco West LLC ..............................G...... 815 385-0011
 Ingleside *(G-12191)*
Identi-Graphics Inc .............................G...... 630 801-4845
 Montgomery *(G-15049)*
Illinois Tag Co .....................................E...... 773 626-0542
 Carol Stream *(G-3169)*
▲ Integrated Label Corporation ..........F...... 815 874-2500
 Rockford *(G-18437)*
K & N Laboratories Inc ......................F...... 708 482-3240
 La Grange *(G-12739)*
Lewis Paper Place Inc ........................G...... 847 808-1343
 Wheeling *(G-22093)*
Linn West Paper Company ................G...... 773 561-3839
 Chicago *(G-5514)*
Loyola Paper Company ......................E...... 847 956-7770
 Elk Grove Village *(G-9598)*
Lucky Games Inc ................................G...... 773 549-9051
 Northbrook *(G-16300)*
Lucky Games Inc ................................G...... 773 549-9051
 Northbrook *(G-16301)*
▼ Midland Davis Corporation ............D...... 309 637-4491
 Moline *(G-14957)*
▲ Mudlark Papers Inc ........................E...... 630 717-7616
 Naperville *(G-15702)*
Nashua Corporation ...........................D...... 847 692-9130
 Park Ridge *(G-17211)*
▼ New-Indy IVEX LLC ........................E...... 309 686-3830
 Peoria *(G-17417)*
Norkol Inc ...........................................C...... 708 531-1000
 Northlake *(G-16445)*
Norwood Industries Inc ......................F...... 773 788-1508
 Chicago *(G-5946)*
Oakland Enterprises Inc ....................G...... 630 377-1121
 Saint Charles *(G-19225)*
Oce-Van Der Grinten NV ...................E...... 217 348-8111
 Charleston *(G-3606)*
Pactiv LLC ...........................................D...... 618 934-4311
 Trenton *(G-20996)*
▲ Pap-R Products Company .............D...... 775 828-4141
 Martinsville *(G-14339)*
Phoenix Paper Products Inc ..............F...... 815 368-3343
 Lostant *(G-13907)*
◆ Potomac Corporation .....................C...... 847 259-0546
 Wheeling *(G-22126)*
Quality Paper Inc ................................F...... 847 258-3999
 Elk Grove Village *(G-9702)*
River Valley Mechanical Inc ...............G...... 309 364-3776
 Putnam *(G-17788)*
Roosevelt Paper Company .................E...... 708 653-5121
 Alsip *(G-523)*
Rotary Paper Manifold ........................G...... 847 758-7800
 Elk Grove Village *(G-9719)*
RTS Packaging LLC ...........................C...... 708 338-2800
 Hillside *(G-11932)*
Schwab Paper Products Company ...E...... 815 372-2233
 Romeoville *(G-18867)*
Seabee Supply Co ..............................G...... 630 860-1293
 Wood Dale *(G-22421)*
Service Packaging Design Inc ...........G...... 847 966-6592
 Morton Grove *(G-15236)*
▲ Sev-Rend Corporation ....................F...... 618 301-4130
 Collinsville *(G-7341)*
Signode Industrial Group LLC ...........E...... 815 939-0033
 Kankakee *(G-12650)*
Signode Industrial Group LLC ...........E...... 708 371-9050
 Blue Island *(G-2270)*
Spectra Jet ..........................................G...... 847 669-9094
 Huntley *(G-12177)*
◆ Stanford Products LLC ...................E...... 618 548-2600
 Salem *(G-19354)*
◆ Stevens Cabinets Inc .....................B...... 217 857-7100
 Teutopolis *(G-20856)*
Tag Diamond & Label .........................E...... 630 844-9395
 Aurora *(G-1221)*
Terrapin Xpress Inc ............................G...... 866 823-7323
 Palos Heights *(G-17111)*
Trade Label & Decal ...........................G...... 630 773-0447
 Itasca *(G-12367)*
▼ Tricel Corporation ...........................F...... 847 336-1321
 Gurnee *(G-11515)*

**Trimaco LLC** ... E ... 919 674-3476
Elk Grove Village *(G-9793)*
**▲ USA Technologies Inc** ... C ... 309 495-0829
Peoria *(G-17476)*
**▲ Wexford Home Corp** ... G ... 847 922-5738
Northbrook *(G-16386)*
**▲ Xertrex International Inc** ... E ... 630 773-4020
Itasca *(G-12375)*
**▲ Zebra Technologies Corporation** ... B ... 847 634-6700
Lincolnshire *(G-13494)*

## 27 PRINTING, PUBLISHING, AND ALLIED INDUSTRIES

### *2711 Newspapers: Publishing & Printing*

**22nd Century Media** ... G ... 847 272-4565
Northbrook *(G-16194)*
**22nd Century Media** ... E ... 708 326-9170
Orland Park *(G-16836)*
**5 Star Publishing Inc** ... G ... 217 285-1355
Pittsfield *(G-17560)*
**Abington Argus-Sentinel** ... G ... 309 462-3189
Abingdon *(G-9)*
**Acm Publishing** ... G ... 217 498-7500
Rochester *(G-18114)*
**Acres of Sky Communications** ... G ... 815 493-2560
Lanark *(G-13149)*
**Ada Holding Company Inc** ... F ... 312 440-2897
Chicago *(G-3742)*
**Advertising Advice Inc** ... F ... 847 272-0707
Northbrook *(G-16200)*
**Advocate** ... G ... 815 694-2122
Clifton *(G-7272)*
**Agri-News Publications Inc** ... D ... 815 223-2558
La Salle *(G-12760)*
**All Star Publishing** ... G ... 630 428-1515
Naperville *(G-15597)*
**Altamont News** ... G ... 618 483-6176
Altamont *(G-548)*
**Amboy News** ... G ... 815 857-2311
Amboy *(G-597)*
**American Classifieds Inc** ... F ... 217 356-4804
Champaign *(G-3449)*
**American Publishing Co Inc** ... G ... 815 692-2366
Fairbury *(G-10121)*
**Americn Foreign Lang Newspaper** ... E ... 312 368-4815
Chicago *(G-3885)*
**Amerikos Lietuvis Corp** ... G ... 708 924-0403
Oak Lawn *(G-16602)*
**Andrew Distribution Inc** ... E ... 708 410-2400
Broadview *(G-2557)*
**APAC 90 Texas Holding Inc** ... G ... 312 321-2299
Chicago *(G-3920)*
**Arcola Record Herald** ... G ... 217 268-4950
Arcola *(G-665)*
**Arthur Graphic Clarion** ... G ... 217 543-2151
Arthur *(G-881)*
**Augusta Eagle** ... G ... 217 392-2715
Augusta *(G-951)*
**B & B Publishing Co Inc** ... F ... 815 933-1131
Bourbonnais *(G-2388)*
**B F Shaw Printing Company** ... E ... 815 875-4461
Princeton *(G-17744)*
**B F Shaw Printing Company** ... C ... 815 625-3600
Sterling *(G-20584)*
**B F Shaw Printing Company** ... G ... 815 732-6166
Oregon *(G-16819)*
**Baier Publishing Company** ... G ... 815 457-2245
Cissna Park *(G-7254)*
**Bar Code Dr Inc** ... G ... 815 547-1001
Cherry Valley *(G-3639)*
**Bar Stool Depotcom** ... G ... 815 727-7294
Joliet *(G-12460)*
**Bas Success Express Inc** ... G ... 847 258-5550
Des Plaines *(G-8155)*
**Beacon Solutions Inc** ... F ... 303 513-0469
Chicago *(G-4063)*
**Beardstown Newspapers Inc** ... G ... 217 323-1010
Beardstown *(G-1520)*
**Belair Hd Studios LLC** ... E ... 312 254-5188
Chicago *(G-4075)*
**Belvidere Daily Republican Co** ... E ... 815 547-0084
Belvidere *(G-1737)*
**Benton Evening News Co** ... G ... 618 438-5611
Benton *(G-2022)*
**Best Newspapers In Illinois** ... G ... 217 728-7381
Sullivan *(G-20740)*
**Better News Papers Inc** ... G ... 618 566-8282
Mascoutah *(G-14348)*
**Better News Papers Inc** ... G ... 618 483-6176
Altamont *(G-550)*
**Blue Island Sun** ... G ... 708 388-9033
Blue Island *(G-2240)*
**Bond & Fayette County Shopper** ... G ... 618 664-4566
Greenville *(G-11388)*
**Bond Broadcasting Inc** ... F ... 618 664-3300
Greenville *(G-11389)*
**Boone County Shopper Inc** ... F ... 815 544-2166
Belvidere *(G-1739)*
**▼ Breese Publishing Co Inc** ... G ... 618 526-7211
Breese *(G-2440)*
**Breeze Printing Co** ... F ... 217 824-2233
Taylorville *(G-20835)*
**Bulletin** ... G ... 618 553-9764
Oblong *(G-16729)*
**Bunker Hill Publication** ... G ... 618 585-4411
Bunker Hill *(G-2804)*
**Bureau Valley Chief** ... G ... 815 646-4731
Tiskilwa *(G-20958)*
**C & C Publications** ... G ... 815 723-0325
Joliet *(G-12469)*
**Cambridge Chronicle** ... G ... 309 937-3303
Cambridge *(G-2965)*
**Campbell Publishing Co Inc** ... F ... 618 498-1234
Jerseyville *(G-12419)*
**Campbell Publishing Co Inc** ... F ... 217 285-2345
Pittsfield *(G-17564)*
**Campbell Publishing Inc** ... G ... 217 742-3313
Winchester *(G-22278)*
**Carbondale Night Life** ... F ... 618 549-2799
Carbondale *(G-3002)*
**Carmi Times** ... F ... 618 382-4176
Carmi *(G-3064)*
**Carroll County Review** ... G ... 815 259-2131
Thomson *(G-20864)*
**Carterville Courier** ... G ... 618 985-6187
Carterville *(G-3310)*
**Catalyst Paper** ... G ... 224 307-2650
Evanston *(G-10019)*
**Catholic Press Assn of The US** ... G ... 312 380-6789
Chicago *(G-4258)*
**Central Ill Communications LLC** ... F ... 217 753-2226
Springfield *(G-20413)*
**Central Illinois Newspapers** ... G ... 217 935-3171
Clinton *(G-7279)*
**Central Newspaper Incorporated** ... G ... 630 416-4191
Naperville *(G-15624)*
**Centralia Morning Sentinel** ... D ... 618 532-5601
Centralia *(G-3407)*
**Centralia Press Ltd** ... D ... 618 532-5604
Centralia *(G-3408)*
**Centralia Press Ltd** ... F ... 618 246-2000
Mount Vernon *(G-15403)*
**Chgo Daily Law Bulletin** ... G ... 217 525-6735
Springfield *(G-20417)*
**▲ Chicago Chinese Times** ... G ... 630 717-4567
Naperville *(G-15625)*
**Chicago Citizen Newsppr Group** ... F ... 773 783-1251
Chicago *(G-4311)*
**Chicago Crusader News Group** ... G ... 773 752-2500
Chicago *(G-4313)*
**Chicago Defender Publishing Co** ... E ... 312 225-2400
Chicago *(G-4314)*
**Chicago Deportivo Group Inc** ... G ... 708 387-7724
Brookfield *(G-2627)*
**Chicago Group Acquisition LLC** ... G ... 312 755-0720
Chicago *(G-4321)*
**Chicago Jewish News** ... F ... 847 966-0606
Skokie *(G-19979)*
**Chicago News LLC** ... G
Arlington Heights *(G-734)*
**Chicago Sun-Times Features Inc** ... A ... 312 321-3000
Chicago *(G-4351)*
**Chicago Sun-Times Features Inc** ... F ... 312 321-2043
Chicago *(G-4352)*
**Chicago Tribune** ... G ... 773 910-6462
Chicago *(G-4356)*
**▲ Chicago Tribune Company** ... A ... 312 222-3232
Chicago *(G-4357)*
**Chicago Tribune Company** ... G ... 312 222-3232
Chicago *(G-4358)*
**Chicago Tribune Company** ... G ... 312 222-8611
Chicago *(G-4359)*
**Chicago Weekly** ... G ... 773 702-7718
Chicago *(G-4362)*
**Chinese American News** ... G ... 312 225-5600
Chicago *(G-4367)*
**Chrisman Leader** ... G ... 217 269-2811
Chrisman *(G-7173)*
**Chronicle Newspapers Inc** ... G ... 630 845-5247
Geneva *(G-10817)*
**Civitas Media LLC** ... D ... 217 245-6121
Jacksonville *(G-12384)*
**Classified Ventures** ... G ... 847 472-2718
Elk Grove Village *(G-9375)*
**Clay County Advocate Press** ... G ... 618 662-6397
Flora *(G-10204)*
**Clinton Topper Newspaper** ... E ... 815 654-4850
Machesney Park *(G-14065)*
**Cnlc-Stc Inc** ... A ... 312 321-3000
Chicago *(G-4412)*
**Coal City Courant** ... G ... 815 634-0315
Coal City *(G-7291)*
**Community Newsppr Holdings Inc** ... F ... 217 774-2161
Shelbyville *(G-19906)*
**Copley Press Inc** ... F ... 217 732-2101
Lincoln *(G-13408)*
**Cornerstone Media** ... G ... 779 529-0108
Manteno *(G-14182)*
**Crain Communications Inc** ... C ... 312 649-5200
Chicago *(G-4494)*
**Custom Boxes Inc** ... G ... 630 364-3944
Bolingbrook *(G-2295)*
**Czech American TV Herald** ... G ... 708 813-0028
Willowbrook *(G-22208)*
**Daily Dollar Savings LLC** ... G ... 860 883-0351
Morton Grove *(G-15193)*
**Daily Egyptian Siu Newspaper** ... D ... 618 536-3311
Carbondale *(G-3005)*
**Daily General LLC** ... G ... 217 273-0719
Chicago *(G-4542)*
**Daily Kratom** ... G ... 815 768-7104
Joliet *(G-12482)*
**Daily Lawrenceville Record** ... F ... 618 943-2331
Lawrenceville *(G-13198)*
**Daily Lawrenceville Record** ... G ... 618 544-2101
Robinson *(G-18059)*
**Daily Money Matters LLC** ... G ... 847 729-8393
Glenview *(G-11119)*
**Daily News Condominium Assn** ... E ... 312 492-8526
Chicago *(G-4543)*
**Daily News Tribune Inc** ... C ... 815 223-2558
La Salle *(G-12770)*
**Daily News Tribune Inc** ... G ... 815 539-5200
Mendota *(G-14719)*
**Daily Projects** ... G ... 224 209-8636
Algonquin *(G-385)*
**Daily Robinson News Inc** ... E ... 618 544-2101
Robinson *(G-18060)*
**Daily Whale** ... G ... 312 787-5204
Chicago *(G-4544)*
**Dancyn Recovery Systems** ... G ... 309 829-5450
Bloomington *(G-2160)*
**De Boer & Associates** ... G ... 630 972-1600
Bolingbrook *(G-2300)*
**Debbie Harshman** ... G ... 217 335-2112
Barry *(G-1311)*
**Delavan Times** ... G ... 309 244-7111
Delavan *(G-8133)*
**Democrat Company Corp** ... G ... 217 357-2149
Carthage *(G-3313)*
**Democrat Message** ... G ... 217 773-3371
Mount Sterling *(G-15392)*
**Des Plaines Journal Inc** ... D ... 847 299-5511
Des Plaines *(G-8184)*
**Dmi Information Process Center** ... E ... 773 378-2644
Chicago *(G-4616)*
**Double D Printing Inc** ... G ... 630 406-8666
Batavia *(G-1441)*
**Dow Jones & Company Inc** ... E ... 618 651-2300
Highland *(G-11784)*
**Dow Jones & Company Inc** ... D ... 312 580-1023
Chicago *(G-4639)*
**E & L Communication** ... G ... 773 890-1656
Chicago *(G-4663)*
**Ea Mackay Enterprises Inc** ... E ... 630 627-7010
Lombard *(G-13793)*
**Eagle Publications** ... G ... 309 462-5758
Abingdon *(G-10)*
**Eagle Publications Inc** ... E ... 618 345-5400
Collinsville *(G-7321)*
**Ear Hustle 411 LLC** ... G ... 773 616-3598
Chicago *(G-4672)*
**Early Edition** ... G ... 312 345-0786
Chicago *(G-4676)*
**East Central Communications Co** ... E ... 217 892-9613
Rantoul *(G-17926)*
**Echo Prophetstown** ... G ... 815 537-5107
Prophetstown *(G-17768)*



Employee Codes: A=Over 500 employees, B=251-500
C=101-250, D=51-100, E=20-50, F=10-19, G=3-9
2017 Harris Illinois Industrial Directory
955

**Edwardsville Publishing Co**...D... 618 656-4700
Edwardsville *(G-8799)*
**Eisenhower High School - Blue**...G... 708 385-6815
Blue Island *(G-2248)*
**El Dia Newspaper**...G... 708 956-7282
Berwyn *(G-2063)*
**El Paso Journal**...G... 309 527-8595
El Paso *(G-8869)*
**El Sol Dechicago Newspaper**...G... 773 235-7655
Chicago *(G-4711)*
**Elise S Allen**...G... 309 673-2613
Peoria *(G-17354)*
**Elliott Publishing Inc**...G... 217 645-3033
Liberty *(G-13295)*
**Elliott Publishing Inc**...G... 217 593-6515
Camp Point *(G-2972)*
**Ethnic Media LLC**...G... 224 676-0778
Wheeling *(G-22049)*
**Evanston Sentinel Corporation**...G... 847 492-0177
Evanston *(G-10034)*
**Examiner Publications Inc**...G... 630 830-4145
Bartlett *(G-1347)*
**Experimental Aircraft Examiner**...G... 847 226-0777
Cary *(G-3339)*
**Fanboys Games & Movies LLC**...G... 847 894-6448
Park Ridge *(G-17192)*
**Farina News**...G... 618 245-6216
Farina *(G-10176)*
**Farm Week**...E... 309 557-3140
Bloomington *(G-2163)*
**Final Call Inc**...F... 773 602-1230
Chicago *(G-4843)*
**Fisher Printing Inc**...C... 708 598-9266
Bridgeview *(G-2490)*
**Food Service Publishing Co**...F... 847 699-3300
Des Plaines *(G-8200)*
**Forrest Consulting**...G... 630 730-9619
Glen Ellyn *(G-10971)*
**Four Winds Music Pubg LLC**...G... 618 699-1356
Vandalia *(G-21114)*
**Fox Valley Labor News Inc**...G... 630 897-4022
Aurora *(G-1156)*
**Fox Valley Park District**...D... 630 892-1550
Aurora *(G-1157)*
**Fra No 3800 W Division**...G... 708 338-0690
Stone Park *(G-20635)*
**Free Press Newspapers**...E... 815 476-7966
Wilmington *(G-22272)*
**Free Press Progress Inc**...G... 217 563-2115
Nokomis *(G-16056)*
**Freeburg Printing & Publishing**...G... 618 539-3320
Freeburg *(G-10635)*
**Freedom Communications Inc**...G... 217 245-6121
Jacksonville *(G-12387)*
**Freeshopper Ad Paper Inc**...G... 847 675-2783
Lincolnwood *(G-13511)*
**G-W Communications Inc**...G... 815 476-7966
Wilmington *(G-22273)*
**Ganji Klames**...G... 773 478-9000
Chicago *(G-4914)*
**Gannett Satellite Info Netwrk**...G... 312 216-1407
Chicago *(G-4915)*
**Gannett Stllite Info Ntwrk LLC**...C... 630 629-1280
Aurora *(G-1013)*
**Gatehouse Media LLC**...F... 309 852-2181
Kewanee *(G-12686)*
**Gatehouse Media LLC**...G... 618 783-2324
Newton *(G-15940)*
**Gatehouse Media LLC**...B... 217 788-1300
Springfield *(G-20445)*
**Gatehouse Media LLC**...E... 618 393-2931
Olney *(G-16769)*
**Gatehouse Media LLC**...E... 618 937-2850
West Frankfort *(G-21809)*
**Gatehouse Media LLC**...D... 585 598-0030
Oakbrook Terrace *(G-16708)*
**Gatehouse Media LLC**...E... 815 842-1153
Pontiac *(G-17701)*
**Gatehouse Media LLC**...E... 618 253-7146
Harrisburg *(G-11600)*
**Gatehouse Media LLC**...E... 309 734-3164
Monmouth *(G-15013)*
**Gatehouse Media III Holdings**...G... 585 598-0030
Peoria *(G-17368)*
**Gatehouse Media Illinois Ho**...B... 217 788-1300
Springfield *(G-20446)*
**Gazette**...F... 815 777-0105
Galena *(G-10724)*
**Gazette Democrat**...E... 618 833-2150
Anna *(G-603)*

**Gazette Printing Co**...G... 309 389-2811
Glasford *(G-10951)*
**Gazette-Democrat**...E... 618 833-2158
Anna *(G-604)*
**▲ Geomentum Inc**...B... 630 729-7500
Downers Grove *(G-8447)*
**Geomentum Inc**...G... 630 729-7500
Downers Grove *(G-8448)*
**German American Nat Congress**...G... 773 561-9181
Chicago *(G-4948)*
**Gilman Star Inc**...G... 815 265-7332
Gilman *(G-10942)*
**Gmd Mobile Pressure Wshg Svcs**...G... 773 826-1903
Chicago *(G-4964)*
**Gold Nugget Publications Inc**...E... 217 965-3355
Virden *(G-21297)*
**Golda House**...G... 773 927-0140
Chicago *(G-4972)*
**Golden Prairie News**...G... 217 226-3721
Assumption *(G-931)*
**Golf Gazette**...G... 815 838-0184
Lockport *(G-13718)*
**Goreville Gazette**...G... 618 995-9445
Goreville *(G-11253)*
**Greene Jersey Shoppers**...G... 217 942-3626
Carrollton *(G-3307)*
**Greenup Press Inc**...G... 217 923-3704
Greenup *(G-11383)*
**Greenville Advocate Inc**...G... 618 664-3144
Greenville *(G-11394)*
**Hancock County Shopper**...G... 217 847-6628
Hamilton *(G-11538)*
**Hardin County Independent**...G... 618 287-2361
Elizabethtown *(G-9246)*
**Hartman Publishing Group Ltd**...F... 312 822-0202
Chicago *(G-5050)*
**Hearst Communications Inc**...C... 309 829-9000
Bloomington *(G-2177)*
**Henderson Hancock Quill Inc**...G... 309 924-1871
Stronghurst *(G-20713)*
**Henry News Republican**...G... 309 364-3250
Henry *(G-11743)*
**Herald Mount Olive**...G... 217 999-3941
Mount Olive *(G-15303)*
**Herald Newspapers Inc**...E... 773 643-8533
Chicago *(G-5076)*
**Herald Publications**...F... 618 566-8282
Mascoutah *(G-14353)*
**Herald Whig Quincy**...G... 217 222-7600
Quincy *(G-17835)*
**Heritage Media Svcs Co of Ill**...G... 708 594-9340
Summit Argo *(G-20763)*
**Highland News Leader**...G... 618 654-2366
Highland *(G-11790)*
**Hillsboro Journal Inc**...E... 217 532-3933
Hillsboro *(G-11895)*
**Home Shopper Publishing**...G... 309 742-2521
Elmwood *(G-9963)*
**Hometown News Group LP**...G... 815 246-4600
Earlville *(G-8595)*
**Horizon Publications Inc**...C... 618 993-1711
Marion *(G-14265)*
**Horizon Publications (2003)**...G... 618 993-1711
Marion *(G-14266)*
**Hpc of Pennsylvania Inc**...D... 618 993-1711
Marion *(G-14268)*
**Hs Technology Inc**...G... 630 572-7650
Oak Brook *(G-16522)*
**Illini Media Co**...B... 217 337-8300
Champaign *(G-3499)*
**Illinois Agrinews Inc**...G... 815 223-7448
La Salle *(G-12775)*
**Illinois Newspaper In Educatn**...F... 847 427-4388
Springfield *(G-20455)*
**Illinois Valley Press East**...G... 217 586-2512
Mahomet *(G-14159)*
**Inde Enterprises Inc**...E... 815 338-8844
Woodstock *(G-22574)*
**Independent News**...G... 217 662-6001
Danville *(G-7738)*
**India Tribune Ltd**...G... 773 588-5077
Chicago *(G-5174)*
**Indiana Agri-News Inc**...G... 317 726-5391
La Salle *(G-12777)*
**Inn Intl Newspaper Network**...G... 309 764-5314
Moline *(G-14943)*
**International News**...G... 773 283-8323
Chicago *(G-5221)*
**John Dagys Media LLC**...G... 708 373-0180
Palos Park *(G-17129)*

**Joliet Herald Newspaper**...E... 815 280-4100
Joliet *(G-12523)*
**▲ Joong-Ang Daily News**...E... 847 228-7200
Elk Grove Village *(G-9564)*
**Journal News**...G... 217 532-3933
Hillsboro *(G-11896)*
**Journal News**...G... 217 324-6604
Litchfield *(G-13690)*
**Journal of Banking and Fin**...G... 618 203-9074
Glen Carbon *(G-10953)*
**Journal Standard**...G... 815 232-1171
Freeport *(G-10670)*
**Journal Star-Peoria**...G... 309 833-2449
Macomb *(G-14126)*
**Jury Verdict Reporter**...G... 312 644-7800
Chicago *(G-5336)*
**Kane County Cronicle**...G... 815 895-7033
Sycamore *(G-20805)*
**Kaneland Publications Inc**...F... 630 365-6446
Saint Charles *(G-19203)*
**Kankakee Daily Journal Co LLC**...C... 815 937-3300
Kankakee *(G-12632)*
**Kaplan Inc**...E... 312 263-4344
Chicago *(G-5359)*
**Kendall County Record**...E... 630 553-7034
Yorkville *(G-22662)*
**Kerala Express Newspaper**...G... 773 465-5359
Chicago *(G-5377)*
**KK Stevens Publishing Co**...E... 309 329-2151
Astoria *(G-934)*
**Korea Daily News**...E... 847 545-1767
Elk Grove Village *(G-9579)*
**▲ Korea Times**...D... 847 626-0388
Glenview *(G-11157)*
**Korea Times Chicago Inc**...E... 847 626-0388
Glenview *(G-11158)*
**Korea Tribune Inc**...G... 847 956-9101
Mount Prospect *(G-15343)*
**▲ Korean Media Group LLC**...F... 847 391-4112
Northbrook *(G-16289)*
**La Raza Chicago Inc**...E... 312 870-7000
Chicago *(G-5426)*
**Lambda Publications Inc**...F... 773 871-7610
Chicago *(G-5448)*
**Lawndale Press Inc**...G... 708 656-6900
Cicero *(G-7214)*
**Leader**...G... 217 469-0045
Saint Joseph *(G-19316)*
**Lee Enterprises Incorporated**...F... 309 829-9000
Bloomington *(G-2193)*
**Lee Enterprises Incorporated**...G... 217 421-8955
Decatur *(G-7905)*
**Lee Enterprises Incorporated**...E... 309 743-0800
Moline *(G-14954)*
**Lee Enterprises Incorporated**...G... 618 998-8499
Marion *(G-14270)*
**Lee Enterprises Incorporated**...C... 217 421-6920
Decatur *(G-7906)*
**Lee Enterprises Incorporated**...C... 618 529-5454
Carbondale *(G-3014)*
**Lee Enterprises Incorporated**...G... 217 421-8940
Decatur *(G-7907)*
**Liberty Group Publishing**...F... 309 944-1779
Geneseo *(G-10802)*
**Liberty Group Publishing**...G... 618 937-2850
West Frankfort *(G-21812)*
**Liberty Group Publishing**...G... 309 937-3303
Cambridge *(G-2968)*
**Lincolndailynewscom**...G... 217 732-7443
Lincoln *(G-13414)*
**Litchfield News Herald Inc**...F... 217 324-2121
Litchfield *(G-13694)*
**Lithuanian Catholic Press**...E... 773 585-9500
Chicago *(G-5519)*
**Live Daily LLC**...G... 312 286-6706
Chicago *(G-5523)*
**Long View Publishing Co Inc**...F... 773 446-9920
Chicago *(G-5537)*
**Losangeles Features Syndicate**...G... 847 446-4082
Winnetka *(G-22310)*
**Lumber Specialists Inc**...F... 217 351-5311
Urbana *(G-21093)*
**Lumber Specialists Inc**...G... 217 762-2511
Monticello *(G-15078)*
**Lumber Specialists Inc**...F... 217 443-8484
Danville *(G-7750)*
**Macoupin County Enquirer Inc**...E... 217 854-2534
Carlinville *(G-3042)*
**Madison County Publications**...E... 618 344-0265
Collinsville *(G-7332)*

SIC SECTION 27 PRINTING, PUBLISHING, AND ALLIED INDUSTRIES

**Madison County Publications**.................F ....... 618 344-0264
Collinsville *(G-7333)*
**Mahoney Publishing Inc**.........................G....... 815 369-5384
Lena *(G-13281)*
**Marengo Union Times** ............................G....... 815 568-5400
Marengo *(G-14237)*
**Martin Publishing Co**..............................G....... 309 647-9501
Canton *(G-2989)*
**Martin Publishing Co**..............................E ....... 309 543-2000
Havana *(G-11698)*
**Martin Publishing Co**..............................F ....... 309 647-9501
Canton *(G-2990)*
**Mason City Banner Times**......................F ....... 217 482-3276
Mason City *(G-14365)*
**McClatchy Newspapers Inc**...................B ....... 618 239-2624
Belleville *(G-1655)*
**McClatchy Newspapers Inc**...................D ....... 618 654-2366
Highland *(G-11802)*
**Megamedia Enterprises Inc** ...................F ....... 773 889-0880
Chicago *(G-5680)*
**Mendota Reporter**...................................F ....... 815 539-9396
Mendota *(G-14726)*
**Messenger**...............................................G....... 618 235-9601
Belleville *(G-1657)*
▲ **Midwest Suburban Publishing**..........A ....... 708 633-6880
Tinley Park *(G-20933)*
**Migala Report**..........................................G....... 312 948-0260
Chicago *(G-5755)*
**Military Medical News**.............................E ....... 312 368-4860
Chicago *(G-5759)*
**Mirror-Democrat**......................................G....... 815 244-2411
Mount Carroll *(G-15292)*
**ML Content**...............................................G....... 847 212-8824
Wauconda *(G-21485)*
**Moline Dispatch Publishing Co** .............G....... 309 764-4344
Moline *(G-14959)*
**Monitor Newspaper Inc** ..........................G....... 618 271-0468
East Saint Louis *(G-8761)*
**Morris Publishing Company** ..................A ....... 815 942-3221
Morris *(G-15120)*
**Mountaineer Newspapers Inc** ...............E ....... 815 562-2061
Rochelle *(G-18099)*
**Mt Carmel Register Co Inc** .....................E ....... 618 262-5144
Mount Carmel *(G-15276)*
**Nadig Newspapers Inc**............................F ....... 773 286-6100
Chicago *(G-5849)*
**Nashville News**........................................F ....... 618 327-3411
Nashville *(G-15844)*
**Nationwide News Monitor** ......................G....... 312 424-4224
Skokie *(G-20044)*
**New City Communications**.....................E ....... 312 243-8786
Chicago *(G-5891)*
**New Herald News LLC** ............................G....... 217 651-8064
Lincoln *(G-13417)*
**News & Letters**........................................G....... 312 663-0839
Chicago *(G-5901)*
**News Gazette Inc** ....................................C ....... 217 351-5252
Champaign *(G-3517)*
**News Media Corporation**........................E ....... 815 562-2061
Rochelle *(G-18100)*
**News Metropolis** .....................................G....... 618 524-2141
Metropolis *(G-14760)*
**News-Gazette Inc** ....................................G....... 217 351-8128
Champaign *(G-3518)*
**News-Gazette Inc** ....................................B ....... 217 351-5252
Champaign *(G-3519)*
**Newspaper 7 Days** ..................................G....... 847 272-2212
Wheeling *(G-22107)*
**Newspaper Holding Inc** ..........................D ....... 618 242-0113
Mount Vernon *(G-15434)*
**Newspaper Holding Inc** ..........................G....... 618 643-2387
Mc Leansboro *(G-14466)*
**Newspaper Holding Inc** ..........................E ....... 217 446-1000
Danville *(G-7758)*
**Newspaper Holding Inc** ..........................D ....... 217 347-7151
Effingham *(G-8850)*
**Newspaper National Network** ...............G....... 312 644-1142
Chicago *(G-5902)*
**Newspaper Solutions Inc** ........................G....... 773 930-3404
Chicago *(G-5903)*
**Newsprint Ink Inc**......................................F ....... 618 667-3111
Troy *(G-21010)*
**Nikkei America Holdings Inc**.................G....... 312 263-8877
Chicago *(G-5919)*
**Normalite Newspaper**.............................F ....... 309 454-5476
Normal *(G-16080)*
**North County News Inc** ...........................G....... 618 282-3803
Red Bud *(G-17945)*
**Northwestern Illinois Farmer**.................G....... 815 369-2811
Lena *(G-13282)*

**Nuestro Mundo Newspaper** ....................G....... 773 446-9920
Chicago *(G-5955)*
**Nuevos Semana Newspaper**...................G....... 847 991-3939
Palatine *(G-17060)*
**Ocs America Inc**.......................................E ....... 630 595-0111
Wood Dale *(G-22409)*
**Ogle County Life**......................................G....... 815 732-2156
Oregon *(G-16829)*
**Okawville Times**.......................................G....... 618 243-5563
Okawville *(G-16754)*
**Old Gary Inc**..............................................F ....... 219 648-3000
Chicago *(G-5979)*
**Osborne Publications Inc**.......................G....... 217 422-9702
Decatur *(G-7924)*
**Ottawa Publishing Co Inc**.......................C ....... 815 433-2000
Ottawa *(G-16975)*
**Ottawa Publishing Co Inc**.......................F ....... 815 434-3330
Ottawa *(G-16976)*
**Paddock Publications Inc** .......................B ....... 847 427-4300
Arlington Heights *(G-815)*
**Paddock Publications Inc** .......................C ....... 847 608-2700
Elgin *(G-9133)*
**Paddock Publications Inc** .......................C ....... 847 427-5545
Schaumburg *(G-19680)*
**Paddock Publications Inc** .......................E ....... 847 680-5800
Libertyville *(G-13365)*
**Paddock Publications Inc** .......................D ....... 630 955-3500
Lisle *(G-13638)*
**Pakistan News**..........................................G....... 773 271-6400
Chicago *(G-6058)*
**Pana News Inc**...........................................F ....... 217 562-2111
Pana *(G-17137)*
**Pantagraph Publishing Co**.......................F ....... 309 829-9000
Bloomington *(G-2209)*
**Paper**..........................................................E ....... 815 584-1901
Dwight *(G-8590)*
**Paris Beacon News**..................................E ....... 217 465-6424
Paris *(G-17156)*
**Peg N Reds**................................................G....... 618 586-2015
New Lenox *(G-15900)*
**People & Places Newspaper**....................G....... 847 804-6985
Schiller Park *(G-19858)*
**Peoples Tribune**........................................E ....... 773 486-3551
Chicago *(G-6103)*
▲ **Peoria Journal Star Inc**........................C ....... 585 598-0030
Peoria *(G-17423)*
**Peoria Post Inc**..........................................F ....... 309 688-3628
Peoria *(G-17426)*
**Perryco Inc**.................................................E ....... 303 652-8282
Downers Grove *(G-8501)*
**Perryco Inc**.................................................F ....... 815 436-2431
Plainfield *(G-17638)*
**Perryco Inc**.................................................G....... 217 322-3321
Rushville *(G-19094)*
**Petersburg Observer Co Inc** ....................G....... 217 632-2236
Petersburg *(G-17537)*
**Pike County Express** .................................F ....... 217 285-5415
Pittsfield *(G-17574)*
**Pinoy Monthly** ............................................G....... 847 329-1073
Skokie *(G-20055)*
**Pioneer Newspapers Inc** ...........................C ....... 847 486-0600
Chicago *(G-6126)*
**Pioneer Newspapers Inc** ...........................E ....... 708 383-3200
Oak Park *(G-16679)*
**Pioneer Newspapers Inc** ...........................E ....... 630 887-0600
Hinsdale *(G-11958)*
**Porterville Recorder Inc**............................G....... 559 784-5000
Marion *(G-14281)*
**Printed Blog Inc** .........................................G....... 312 924-1040
Chicago *(G-6191)*
**Prints Chicago Inc** ......................................G....... 312 243-6481
Chicago *(G-6197)*
**Progress Reporter Inc**................................G....... 815 472-2000
Momence *(G-14986)*
**Publishing Properties LLC**........................G....... 312 321-2299
Chicago *(G-6223)*
**Puro Futbol Newspaper**.............................G....... 847 858-7493
Gurnee *(G-11495)*
**Quincy Herald-Whig LLC**..........................F ....... 217 223-5100
Quincy *(G-17878)*
**Quincy Media Inc** .......................................C ....... 217 223-5100
Quincy *(G-17879)*
**Rachel Switall Mag Group Nfp**..................G....... 773 344-7123
Chicago *(G-6277)*
**Ramsey News Journal**................................G....... 618 423-2411
Ramsey *(G-17915)*
**Randolph County Herald Tribune**..........F ....... 618 826-2385
Chester *(G-3660)*
**Rankin Publishing Inc** ................................F ....... 217 268-4959
Arcola *(G-683)*

**RCP Publications Inc**..................................G....... 773 227-4066
Chicago *(G-6299)*
**Rd Daily Enterprises**..................................G....... 847 872-7632
Winthrop Harbor *(G-22320)*
**Reach Chicago LLC** ....................................G....... 312 923-1028
Chicago *(G-6301)*
**Real Times Inc of Illinois** ..........................F ....... 312 225-2400
Chicago *(G-6304)*
**Real Times II LLC** .......................................G....... 312 225-2400
Chicago *(G-6305)*
**Realclearpolitics** .........................................G....... 773 255-5846
Chicago *(G-6306)*
**Record Inc** ...................................................G....... 312 985-7270
Chicago *(G-6312)*
**Red Nose Inc**................................................G....... 309 925-7313
Tremont *(G-20985)*
**Red Streak Holdings Company** ................G....... 312 321-3000
Chicago *(G-6315)*
**Refined Haystack LLC**...............................G....... 773 627-3534
Chicago *(G-6319)*
**Reflejos Publications LLC**.........................E ....... 847 806-1111
Arlington Heights *(G-829)*
**Register Publishing Co** ..............................E ....... 618 253-7146
Harrisburg *(G-11603)*
**Register-Mail** ..............................................C ....... 309 343-7181
Galesburg *(G-10773)*
**Reporter Inc**.................................................E ....... 217 932-5211
Casey *(G-3391)*
**Republic Times LLC** ...................................G....... 618 939-3814
Waterloo *(G-21406)*
**Review**..........................................................G....... 309 659-2761
Erie *(G-9993)*
**Review**..........................................................G....... 618 997-2222
Marion *(G-14285)*
**Rickard Publishing** ......................................G....... 309 968-6705
Manito *(G-14175)*
**Riverton Register**........................................G....... 217 629-9247
Riverton *(G-18035)*
**Robert McCormick Tribune Lbrry**...........G....... 847 619-7980
Schaumburg *(G-19713)*
**Rochelle Newspapers Inc**...........................E ....... 815 562-2061
Rochelle *(G-18106)*
**Rochelle Newspapers Inc**...........................E ....... 815 562-4171
Rochelle *(G-18107)*
**Rock River Times**........................................F ....... 815 964-9767
Rockford *(G-18563)*
**Rock Valley Publishing LLC**......................E ....... 815 467-6397
Machesney Park *(G-14103)*
**Rock Valley Publishing LLC**......................G....... 815 234-4821
Byron *(G-2919)*
**Rockford Newspapers Inc**..........................B ....... 815 987-1200
Rockford *(G-18580)*
**Roosevelt Torch** ..........................................F ....... 312 281-3242
Chicago *(G-6391)*
**Russell Publications Inc**.............................E ....... 708 258-3473
Peotone *(G-17492)*
**S & R Media LLC** .........................................F ....... 618 375-7502
Grayville *(G-11376)*
**Salem Times-Commoner Pubg Co** ........E ....... 618 548-3330
Salem *(G-19349)*
**Sauk Valley Shopper Inc** ...........................C ....... 815 625-6700
Sterling *(G-20612)*
**Savanna Times Journal**..............................G....... 815 273-2277
Savanna *(G-19406)*
**Schaumburg Review**...................................F ....... 847 998-3400
Chicago *(G-6450)*
**Senate Democrat Leader Office**..............G....... 708 687-9696
Springfield *(G-20522)*
**Shaw Suburban Media Group Inc**...........C ....... 815 459-4040
Crystal Lake *(G-7649)*
**Shazak Productions**...................................G....... 773 406-9880
Chicago *(G-6493)*
**Shoppers Guide** ..........................................G....... 815 369-4112
Lena *(G-13284)*
**Slack Publications** ......................................G....... 217 268-4950
Arcola *(G-685)*
**Small Newspaper Group** ............................G....... 708 258-3410
Kankakee *(G-12651)*
**Small Newspaper Group** ............................C ....... 815 937-3300
Kankakee *(G-12652)*
**South County Publications**.......................F ....... 217 438-6155
Auburn *(G-949)*
**Southland Voice** ..........................................E ....... 708 214-8582
Crete *(G-7519)*
**Southtown Star Newspapers** ...................G....... 708 633-4800
Tinley Park *(G-20946)*
**Southwest Messenger Press Inc** ..............E ....... 708 388-2425
Midlothian *(G-14769)*
**Spanish Amercn Languag Newspap**......E ....... 312 368-4840
Chicago *(G-6550)*

S I C

# 27 PRINTING, PUBLISHING, AND ALLIED INDUSTRIES SIC SECTION

| Company | Code | Phone |
|---|---|---|
| Springfield Publishers Inc | G | 217 726-6600 |
| Springfield (G-20532) | | |
| Star Media Group | G | 847 674-7827 |
| Skokie (G-20091) | | |
| Star-Times Publishing Co Inc | G | 618 635-2000 |
| Staunton (G-20559) | | |
| Stark County Communications | G | 309 286-4444 |
| Toulon (G-20977) | | |
| Steven Brownstein | G | 847 909-6677 |
| Morton Grove (G-15238) | | |
| Streetwise | F | 773 334-6600 |
| Chicago (G-6604) | | |
| Strohm Newspapers Inc | G | 217 826-3600 |
| Marshall (G-14329) | | |
| Students Publishing Company In | G | 847 491-7206 |
| Evanston (G-10097) | | |
| Suburban Chicago Newspapers | G | 847 336-7000 |
| Naperville (G-15756) | | |
| Suburban Life Publication | D | 630 368-1100 |
| Downers Grove (G-8528) | | |
| Suburban Newspapers of Greater | E | 618 281-7691 |
| Collinsville (G-7342) | | |
| Success Journal Corp | G | 847 583-9000 |
| Morton Grove (G-15240) | | |
| Sumner Press | G | 618 936-2212 |
| Sumner (G-20772) | | |
| Sun Times News Agency | G | 815 672-1260 |
| Streator (G-20706) | | |
| Sun- Tmes Mdia Productions LLC | G | 312 321-2299 |
| Chicago (G-6620) | | |
| Sun-Times Media LLC | D | 312 321-3000 |
| Chicago (G-6621) | | |
| Sun-Times Media LLC | F | 312 321-2299 |
| Chicago (G-6622) | | |
| Sun-Times Media Group Inc | G | 618 273-3379 |
| Eldorado (G-8923) | | |
| Sun-Times Media Group Inc | D | 312 321-2299 |
| Chicago (G-6623) | | |
| Sun-Times Media Holdings LLC | E | 312 321-2299 |
| Chicago (G-6624) | | |
| Sun-Times Media Operations LLC | G | 312 321-2299 |
| Chicago (G-6625) | | |
| T R Communications Inc | F | 773 238-3366 |
| Chicago (G-6663) | | |
| Tegna Inc | C | 847 490-6657 |
| Hoffman Estates (G-12064) | | |
| Teleguia Inc | E | 708 656-6675 |
| Cicero (G-7237) | | |
| The Times | G | 815 433-2000 |
| Ottawa (G-16986) | | |
| Times Record Company | E | 309 582-5112 |
| Aledo (G-373) | | |
| Times Republic | E | 815 432-5227 |
| Watseka (G-21431) | | |
| Times Republic | G | 217 283-5111 |
| Hoopeston (G-12119) | | |
| Times-Press Publishing Co | E | 815 673-3771 |
| Streator (G-20708) | | |
| Tini Martini | G | 773 269-2900 |
| Chicago (G-6729) | | |
| Tne McDonough Democrat Inc | G | 309 837-3343 |
| Macomb (G-14133) | | |
| Todays Advantage Inc | F | 618 463-0612 |
| Alton (G-593) | | |
| Toledo Democrat | G | 217 849-2000 |
| Toledo (G-20967) | | |
| Tonica News | G | 815 442-8419 |
| Tonica (G-20975) | | |
| Trenton Sun | G | 618 224-9422 |
| Trenton (G-20998) | | |
| Tribune Finance Service Center | G | 312 595-0783 |
| Chicago (G-6772) | | |
| Tribune Media Company | G | 708 498-0584 |
| Lisle (G-13673) | | |
| Tribune Publishing Company LLC | E | 312 222-9100 |
| Chicago (G-6773) | | |
| Tribune Publishing Company LLC | D | 312 832-6711 |
| Chicago (G-6774) | | |
| Tribune Tower | F | 312 981-7200 |
| Chicago (G-6775) | | |
| Tronc Inc | C | 312 222-9100 |
| Chicago (G-6781) | | |
| Tuscola Journal Incorporated | G | 217 253-5086 |
| Tuscola (G-21026) | | |
| United Communications Corp | C | 847 746-1515 |
| Zion (G-22698) | | |
| United Communications Corp | E | 847 746-4700 |
| Zion (G-22699) | | |
| Urdu Times | G | 773 274-3100 |
| Chicago (G-6851) | | |
| USA Today Inc | G | 815 987-1400 |
| Rockford (G-18665) | | |
| Vernon Township Offices | E | 847 634-4600 |
| Buffalo Grove (G-2789) | | |
| Village of Mt Zion | F | 217 864-4212 |
| Mount Zion (G-15457) | | |
| Voice | G | 630 966-8642 |
| Aurora (G-1230) | | |
| Vondrak Publishing Co Inc | E | 773 476-4800 |
| Summit Argo (G-20768) | | |
| Want ADS of Champaign Inc | G | 217 356-4804 |
| Champaign (G-3558) | | |
| Waseet America | G | 708 430-1950 |
| Bedford Park (G-1591) | | |
| Washington Courier | F | 309 444-3139 |
| Washington (G-21394) | | |
| Waverly Journal | G | 217 435-9221 |
| Waverly (G-21645) | | |
| Wayne County Press Inc | E | 618 842-2662 |
| Fairfield (G-10159) | | |
| Wednesday Journal Inc | D | 708 386-5555 |
| Oak Park (G-16691) | | |
| Weekly James | G | 815 786-8203 |
| Sandwich (G-19380) | | |
| Weekly Journals | G | 815 459-4040 |
| Crystal Lake (G-7675) | | |
| Weekly Visitor | G | 815 845-2328 |
| Scales Mound (G-19416) | | |
| West Suburban Journal | G | 708 344-5975 |
| Bloomingdale (G-2141) | | |
| Wheels & Deals | G | 217 423-6333 |
| Decatur (G-7959) | | |
| Willis Publishing | F | 618 497-8272 |
| Percy (G-17496) | | |
| Wjez Thunder 93 7 Wjbc Wbnq B1 | G | 815 842-6515 |
| Pontiac (G-17712) | | |
| Wns Publications Inc | G | 815 772-7244 |
| Morrison (G-15149) | | |
| Wnta Studio Line | G | 815 874-7861 |
| Rockford (G-18687) | | |
| World Journal LLC | F | 312 842-8005 |
| Chicago (G-7030) | | |
| World Journal LLC | F | 312 842-8080 |
| Chicago (G-7031) | | |
| Wrapports LLC | G | 312 321-3000 |
| Chicago (G-7035) | | |
| Wyzz Inc | D | 217 753-5620 |
| Springfield (G-20548) | | |
| Zweibel Worldwide Productions | F | 312 751-0503 |
| Chicago (G-7076) | | |

## 2721 Periodicals: Publishing & Printing

| Company | Code | Phone |
|---|---|---|
| A To Z Offset Prtg & Pubg Inc | G | 847 966-3016 |
| Skokie (G-19943) | | |
| Aais Services Corporation | G | 630 457-3263 |
| Lisle (G-13552) | | |
| Aana Publishing Inc | G | 847 692-7050 |
| Park Ridge (G-17177) | | |
| Abc Inc | E | 312 980-1000 |
| Chicago (G-3707) | | |
| Acm Publishing | G | 217 498-7500 |
| Rochester (G-18114) | | |
| Ada Holding Company Inc | E | 312 440-2897 |
| Chicago (G-3742) | | |
| Alali Enterprises Inc | G | 630 827-9231 |
| Carol Stream (G-3095) | | |
| ▲ Alarm Press | E | 312 341-1290 |
| Schaumburg (G-19427) | | |
| Allen Entertainment Management | E | 630 752-0903 |
| Carol Stream (G-3096) | | |
| Allured Publishing Corporation | E | 630 653-2155 |
| Carol Stream (G-3097) | | |
| American Assn Endodontists | E | 312 266-7255 |
| Chicago (G-3849) | | |
| American Assn Insur Svcs | E | 630 681-8347 |
| Lisle (G-13557) | | |
| American Assn Nurosurgeons Inc | E | 847 378-0500 |
| Rolling Meadows (G-18709) | | |
| American Bar Association | A | 312 988-5000 |
| Chicago (G-3851) | | |
| American Catholic Press Inc | F | 708 331-5485 |
| South Holland (G-20242) | | |
| American City Bus Journals Inc | G | 312 873-2200 |
| Chicago (G-3855) | | |
| American Cllege Chest Physcans | D | 224 521-9800 |
| Glenview (G-11099) | | |
| American Custom Publishing | G | 847 816-8660 |
| Libertyville (G-13302) | | |
| American Hosp Assn Svcs Del | E | 312 422-2000 |
| Chicago (G-3858) | | |
| American Library Association | E | 312 280-5718 |
| Chicago (G-3860) | | |
| American Medical Association | E | 312 464-2555 |
| Chicago (G-3864) | | |
| American Medical Association | A | 312 464-5000 |
| Chicago (G-3863) | | |
| American Nurseryman Pubg Co | E | 847 234-5867 |
| Lake Forest (G-12878) | | |
| American Soc HM Inspectors Inc | F | 847 759-2820 |
| Des Plaines (G-8147) | | |
| American Soc Plastic Surgeons | D | 847 228-9900 |
| Arlington Heights (G-710) | | |
| American Trade Magazines LLC | G | 312 497-7707 |
| Chicago (G-3880) | | |
| Anderson House Foundation | G | 630 461-7254 |
| Glen Ellyn (G-10959) | | |
| Andover Junction Publications | G | 815 538-3060 |
| Mendota (G-14716) | | |
| Another Vision | G | 847 884-7325 |
| Schaumburg (G-19442) | | |
| Antigua Casa Sherry-Brener | G | 773 737-1711 |
| Chicago (G-3916) | | |
| API Publishing Services LLC | E | 312 644-6610 |
| Chicago (G-3922) | | |
| Applied Tech Publications Inc | F | 847 382-8100 |
| Willowbrook (G-22199) | | |
| Area Marketing Inc | G | 815 806-8844 |
| Frankfort (G-10297) | | |
| Art In Print Review | G | 773 697-9478 |
| Chicago (G-3950) | | |
| Ashton Gill Publishing LLC | F | 847 673-8675 |
| Evanston (G-10013) | | |
| Associated Equipment Distrs | E | 630 574-0650 |
| Schaumburg (G-19448) | | |
| ▲ Associated Publications Inc | F | 312 266-8680 |
| Chicago (G-3969) | | |
| Association Management Center | D | 847 375-4700 |
| Chicago (G-3971) | | |
| At Home Magazine | G | 217 351-5282 |
| Champaign (G-3453) | | |
| Banner Publications | G | 309 338-3294 |
| Cuba (G-7679) | | |
| Baptist General Conference | D | 800 323-4215 |
| Arlington Heights (G-723) | | |
| Barks Publications Inc | F | 312 321-9440 |
| Chicago (G-4044) | | |
| Be Group Inc | G | 312 436-0301 |
| Chicago (G-4061) | | |
| Bhs Media LLC | E | 312 701-0000 |
| Chicago (G-4102) | | |
| Bi-State Biking LLC | G | 618 531-0432 |
| Fairview Heights (G-10166) | | |
| ▲ Bible Truth Publishers Inc | G | 630 543-1441 |
| Addison (G-55) | | |
| BNP Media Inc | D | 630 690-4200 |
| Deerfield (G-7992) | | |
| Boland Hill Media LLC | G | 877 658-0418 |
| Hoffman Estates (G-11997) | | |
| Bowen Guerrero & Howe LLC | D | 312 447-2370 |
| Chicago (G-4150) | | |
| Bowtie Inc | G | 630 515-9493 |
| Lombard (G-13773) | | |
| Business Insurance | E | 877 812-1587 |
| Chicago (G-4188) | | |
| C and H Publishing Co | G | 618 625-2711 |
| Sesser (G-19894) | | |
| C2 Publishing Inc | F | 630 834-4994 |
| Hillside (G-11912) | | |
| Caduceus Communications Inc | G | 773 549-4800 |
| Chicago (G-4211) | | |
| CAM Systems | G | 800 208-3244 |
| Chicago (G-4220) | | |
| Canvas Communication | G | 815 464-5947 |
| Frankfort (G-10306) | | |
| Cap Today | F | 847 832-7377 |
| Northfield (G-16395) | | |
| Care Education Group Inc | G | 708 361-4110 |
| Palos Park (G-17127) | | |
| ▲ CCH Incorporated | A | 847 267-7000 |
| Riverwoods (G-18037) | | |
| Central Illinois Bus Publs Inc | G | 309 683-3060 |
| Peoria (G-17336) | | |
| ▲ Central Illinois Homes Guide | G | 309 688-6419 |
| Peoria (G-17337) | | |
| Challenge Publications L T D | G | 309 421-0392 |
| Macomb (G-14121) | | |
| Chambers Marketing Options | G | 847 584-2626 |
| Elk Grove Village (G-9364) | | |
| Chas Levy Circulating Co | G | 630 353-2500 |
| Lisle (G-13574) | | |

**Chester White Swine Rcord Assn** G 309 691-0151 Peoria *(G-17341)*
**CHI Home Improvement Mag Inc** G 630 801-7788 Aurora *(G-1128)*
**Chicago Agent Magazine** G 773 296-6001 Chicago *(G-4300)*
**Chicago Boating Publications** G 312 266-8400 Chicago *(G-4306)*
**Chicago Sports Media Inc** G 847 676-1900 Skokie *(G-19981)*
**▲ China Journal Inc** G 312 326-3228 Chicago *(G-4366)*
**▲ Christian Century** F 312 263-7510 Chicago *(G-4370)*
**Christianity Today Intl** C 630 260-6200 Carol Stream *(G-3128)*
**Church of Brethren Inc** D 847 742-5100 Elgin *(G-8990)*
**College Bound Publications** G 773 262-5810 Chicago *(G-4424)*
**Community Magazine Group** G 312 880-0370 Chicago *(G-4437)*
**Consource LLC** G 847 382-8100 Willowbrook *(G-22206)*
**Construction Bus Media LLC** G 847 359-6493 Palatine *(G-17017)*
**Consumers Dgest Cmmnctions LLC** F 847 607-3000 Deerfield *(G-8000)*
**Cook Communications Minis** D 847 741-5168 Elgin *(G-9003)*
**Cook Communications Ministries** C 847 741-0800 Elgin *(G-9004)*
**Copyline** G 773 375-8127 Chicago *(G-4466)*
**Corbett Accel Healthcare Grp C** G 312 475-2505 Chicago *(G-4467)*
**Cornerstone Communications** E 773 989-2087 Chicago *(G-4471)*
**Cosmopolitan Foot Care** G 312 984-5111 Chicago *(G-4479)*
**Country Journal Publishing Co** F 217 877-9660 Decatur *(G-7860)*
**▲ Crain Communications Inc** E 312 649-5200 Chicago *(G-4492)*
**Crain Communications Inc** E 312 649-5411 Chicago *(G-4493)*
**Crain Communications Inc** C 312 649-5200 Chicago *(G-4494)*
**CSP Information Group Inc** E 630 574-5075 Oak Brook *(G-16503)*
**Cube Tomato Inc** G 224 653-2655 Schaumburg *(G-19494)*
**Cupcake Holdings LLC** C 800 794-5866 Woodridge *(G-22466)*
**◆ Dadant & Sons Inc** D 217 847-3324 Hamilton *(G-11533)*
**Damien Corporation** G 630 369-3549 Naperville *(G-15644)*
**Desert Southwest Fitness Inc** G 520 292-0011 Champaign *(G-3474)*
**Dobinski Marketing** G 773 248-5880 Chicago *(G-4620)*
**Dorenfest Group Ltd** D 312 464-3000 Chicago *(G-4632)*
**Dow Jones & Company Inc** D 312 580-1023 Chicago *(G-4639)*
**Dreamland** G 847 524-6060 Schaumburg *(G-19508)*
**Eagle Forum** G 618 462-5415 Alton *(G-572)*
**Earl G Graves Ltd** G 312 664-8667 Chicago *(G-4674)*
**Earl G Graves Pubg Co Inc** G 312 274-0682 Chicago *(G-4675)*
**Elliott Jsj & Associates Inc** G 847 242-0412 Glencoe *(G-10999)*
**Entrepreneur Media Inc** G 312 923-0818 Chicago *(G-4762)*
**Eqes Inc** G 630 858-6161 Glen Ellyn *(G-10969)*
**Evang Lthn Ch Dr Mrtn Luth KG** F 773 380-2540 Chicago *(G-4785)*
**Evangelical Missions Info Svc** G 630 752-7158 Wheaton *(G-21946)*
**Express Publishing Inc** G 773 725-6218 Chicago *(G-4797)*
**Fabricators & Mfrs Assn Intl** E 815 399-8700 Elgin *(G-9033)*
**Fanning Communications Inc** G 708 293-1430 Crestwood *(G-7488)*
**Farm Progress Companies Inc** C 630 690-5600 Saint Charles *(G-19183)*
**Fellowship Black Light** G 773 826-7790 Chicago *(G-4834)*
**Filmfax Magazine Inc** G 847 866-7155 Evanston *(G-10037)*
**Fma Communicatons Inc** D 815 227-8284 Elgin *(G-9038)*
**Food Service Publishing Co** F 847 699-3300 Des Plaines *(G-8200)*
**Frank R Walker Company** G 630 613-9312 Lombard *(G-13802)*
**Free Press Progress Inc** G 217 563-2115 Nokomis *(G-16056)*
**Futures Magazine Inc** G 312 846-4600 Chicago *(G-4897)*
**Gail McGrath & Associates Inc** F 847 770-4620 Northbrook *(G-16262)*
**Gannett Stllite Info Ntwrk Inc** D 847 839-1700 Hoffman Estates *(G-12012)*
**▲ Gary Grimm & Associates Inc** G 217 357-3401 Carthage *(G-3314)*
**Gazette** F 815 777-0105 Galena *(G-10724)*
**Gemworld International Inc** G 847 657-0555 Northbrook *(G-16264)*
**Genesis Comics Group** G 312 544-7473 Chicago *(G-4934)*
**Germain Saint Press Inc** G 847 882-7400 Schaumburg *(G-19536)*
**Glancer Magazine** G 630 428-4387 Sugar Grove *(G-20726)*
**Global Telephony Magazine** E 312 840-8405 Chicago *(G-4961)*
**Good Sam Enterprises LLC** E 847 229-6720 Lincolnshire *(G-13450)*
**Gospel Synergy Magazine Inc** G 708 272-6640 Calumet Park *(G-2961)*
**Grandstand Publishing LLC** G 847 491-6440 Evanston *(G-10045)*
**H & S Publications Inc** G 309 344-1333 Wataga *(G-21398)*
**Half Price Bks Rec Mgzines Inc** E 847 588-2286 Niles *(G-15986)*
**Halper Publishing Company** G 847 542-9793 Evanston *(G-10049)*
**Healthleaders Inc** E 312 932-0848 Chicago *(G-5062)*
**Hearst Corporation** E 312 984-5166 Chicago *(G-5064)*
**Hearst Corporation** E 312 984-5100 Chicago *(G-5065)*
**HH Backer Associates Inc** F 312 578-1818 Chicago *(G-5084)*
**Home School Enrichment Inc** G 309 347-1392 Pekin *(G-17267)*
**Homeland** G 708 415-4555 Homer Glen *(G-12081)*
**Homewood-Flossmoor Chronicle** G 630 728-2661 Homewood *(G-12101)*
**Homnay Magazine** G 773 334-6655 Chicago *(G-5104)*
**Hotel Amerika** G 219 508-9418 Chicago *(G-5119)*
**Hw Holdco LLC** D 773 824-2400 Rosemont *(G-19005)*
**Icd Publications Inc** G 847 913-8295 Lincolnshire *(G-13456)*
**Icon Acquisition Holdings LP** G 312 751-8000 Chicago *(G-5136)*
**◆ Ideal Media LLC** G 312 456-2822 Chicago *(G-5141)*
**Ieg LLC** E 312 944-1727 Chicago *(G-5144)*
**Illini Media Co** B 217 337-8300 Champaign *(G-3499)*
**Imagination Publishing LLC** E 312 887-1000 Chicago *(G-5161)*
**Inc 1105 Media** G 847 358-7272 Palatine *(G-17041)*
**India Tribune Ltd** G 773 588-5077 Chicago *(G-5174)*
**Industrial Market Place** E 847 676-1900 Skokie *(G-20015)*
**Ink Spots Prtg & Meida Design** G 708 754-1300 Homewood *(G-12102)*
**Inside Council** F 312 654-3500 Chicago *(G-5204)*
**Inside Track Trading** G 630 585-9218 Aurora *(G-1030)*
**Institute For Public Affairs** F 773 772-0100 Chicago *(G-5207)*
**Instrumentalists Inc** F 847 446-5000 Northbrook *(G-16278)*
**International College Surgeons** G 312 642-6502 Chicago *(G-5220)*
**Investment Information Svcs** G 312 669-1650 Chicago *(G-5232)*
**Irish Dancing Magazine** G 630 279-7521 Elmhurst *(G-9889)*
**▼ J S Paluch Co Inc** C 847 678-9300 Franklin Park *(G-10502)*
**Jinny Corp** G 773 588-7200 Chicago *(G-5306)*
**John C Grafft** F 847 842-9200 Lake Barrington *(G-12811)*
**Johnson Press America Inc** E 815 844-5161 Pontiac *(G-17704)*
**▼ Johnson Publishing Company LLC** C 312 322-9200 Chicago *(G-5320)*
**Key One Graphics Services Inc** G West Dundee *(G-21799)*
**Keystone Printing & Publishing** G 815 678-2591 Richmond *(G-17965)*
**Kitbuilders Magazine LLC** G 618 588-5232 New Baden *(G-15862)*
**▲ Korea Times** D 847 626-0388 Glenview *(G-11157)*
**Lakeland Boating Magazine** G 312 276-0610 Evanston *(G-10063)*
**Lakeside Publishing Co LLC** G 847 491-6440 Evanston *(G-10064)*
**Lambda Publications Inc** F 773 871-7610 Chicago *(G-5448)*
**Lawrence Rgan Cmmnications Inc** E 312 960-4100 Chicago *(G-5472)*
**Lightner Publishing Corp** F 312 939-4767 Naperville *(G-15691)*
**Lightworks Communcation Inc** G 847 966-1110 Morton Grove *(G-15214)*
**Lithuanian Catholic Press** E 773 585-9500 Chicago *(G-5519)*
**Lithuanian Press Inc** G 773 776-3399 Chicago *(G-5520)*
**Livingstone Corporation** F 630 871-1212 Wheaton *(G-21967)*
**Lsc Communications Inc** D 773 272-9200 Chicago *(G-5552)*
**Lsc Communications Us LLC** A 815 844-5181 Pontiac *(G-17705)*
**Lsc Communications Us LLC** B 844 572-5720 Chicago *(G-5553)*
**Luby Publishing Inc** F 312 341-1110 Chicago *(G-5556)*
**M & B Supply Inc** F 309 944-3206 Geneseo *(G-10803)*
**M I T Financial Group Inc** E 847 205-3000 Northbrook *(G-16303)*
**Magazine Plus** G 773 281-4106 Chicago *(G-5599)*
**Maher Publications Inc** F 630 941-2030 Elmhurst *(G-9906)*
**Mariah Media Inc** G 312 222-1100 Chicago *(G-5616)*
**▲ Marketing & Technology Group** E 312 266-3311 Chicago *(G-5622)*
**Mdm Communications Inc** G 708 582-9667 Skokie *(G-20036)*
**Mediatec Publishing Inc** E 312 676-9900 Chicago *(G-5678)*
**Mediatec Publishing Inc** F 510 834-0100 Chicago *(G-5679)*
**Medical Liability Monitor Inc** G 312 944-7900 Elmwood Park *(G-9973)*
**Medtext Inc** G 630 325-3277 Burr Ridge *(G-2866)*
**Meredith Corp** D 312 580-1623 Chicago *(G-5689)*
**Metal Center News** F 630 571-1067 Oak Brook *(G-16542)*
**Metro Printing & Pubg Inc** F 618 476-9587 Millstadt *(G-14829)*
**Midwest Law Printing Co Inc** G 312 431-0185 Chicago *(G-5745)*
**Midwest Outdoors Ltd** E 630 887-7722 Burr Ridge *(G-2867)*
**Midwestern Family Magazine LLC** G 309 303-7309 Peoria *(G-17409)*
**Modern Luxury Media LLC** E 312 274-2500 Chicago *(G-5783)*

S I C

Employee Codes: A=Over 500 employees, B=251-500 C=101-250, D=51-100, E=20-50, F=10-19, G=3-9
2017 Harris Illinois Industrial Directory
959

# 27 PRINTING, PUBLISHING, AND ALLIED INDUSTRIES

Modern Trade Communications .......... F .... 847 674-2200
  Skokie (G-20041)
Monitor Publishing Inc .......... G .... 773 205-0303
  Chicago (G-5795)
Moody Bible Inst of Chicago .......... E .... 312 329-2102
  Chicago (G-5800)
MTS Publishing Co .......... F .... 630 955-9750
  Naperville (G-15701)
Narda Inc .......... F .... 312 648-2300
  Chicago (G-5853)
National Association Realtors .......... C .... 800 874-6500
  Chicago (G-5857)
National Association Realtors .......... C .... 800 874-6500
  Chicago (G-5858)
National Bus Trader Inc .......... F .... 815 946-2341
  Polo (G-17689)
National Publishing Company .......... F .... 630 837-2044
  Streamwood (G-20667)
National Safety Council .......... B .... 630 285-1121
  Itasca (G-12324)
National Sporting Goods Assn .......... F .... 847 296-6742
  Mount Prospect (G-15353)
New Life Printing & Publishing .......... G .... 847 658-4111
  Algonquin (G-402)
Nickelodeon Magazines Inc .......... G .... 312 836-0668
  Chicago (G-5912)
Northern Illinois Real Estate .......... G .... 630 257-2480
  Lemont (G-13244)
Northwest Publishing LLC .......... G .... 312 329-0600
  Chicago (G-5941)
Novo Card Publishers Inc .......... G .... 847 947-8090
  Chicago (G-5949)
NV Business Publishers Corp .......... G .... 847 441-5645
  Northfield (G-16413)
One Accord Unity Nfp .......... G .... 630 649-0793
  Bolingbrook (G-2355)
Onion Inc .......... F .... 312 751-0503
  Chicago (G-5992)
Onion Inc .......... F .... 312 751-0503
  Chicago (G-5993)
Outdoor Notebook Publishing .......... F .... 630 257-6534
  Lemont (G-13246)
P&L Group Ltd .......... F .... 773 660-1930
  Chicago (G-6041)
Pam Printers and Publs Inc .......... F .... 217 222-4030
  Quincy (G-17866)
Parade Publications Inc .......... F .... 312 661-1620
  Chicago (G-6075)
Penton Media Inc .......... G .... 212 204-4200
  Chicago (G-6100)
Pierce Crandell & Co Inc .......... G .... 847 549-6015
  Libertyville (G-13368)
Pinnacle Publishing Inc .......... F .... 218 444-2180
  Chicago (G-6124)
Pitchfork Media Inc .......... E .... 773 395-5937
  Chicago (G-6130)
Poetry Foundation .......... E .... 312 787-7070
  Chicago (G-6146)
Practical Communications Inc .......... E .... 773 754-3250
  Schaumburg (G-19699)
Practice Law Management Mag .......... F .... 312 988-6114
  Chicago (G-6165)
Preferred Bus Publications Inc .......... G .... 815 717-6399
  New Lenox (G-15902)
Profile Network Inc .......... E .... 847 673-0592
  Skokie (G-20063)
Progressive Publications Inc .......... G .... 847 697-9181
  Elgin (G-9150)
◆ Publications International Ltd .......... B .... 847 676-3470
  Morton Grove (G-15229)
▼ Putman Media Inc .......... D .... 630 467-1301
  Schaumburg (G-19705)
R L D Communications Inc .......... G .... 312 338-7007
  Chicago (G-6267)
Randall Publications .......... E .... 847 437-6604
  Elk Grove Village (G-9708)
Randall Publishing Inc .......... F .... 847 437-6604
  Elk Grove Village (G-9709)
Rankin Publishing Inc .......... F .... 217 268-4959
  Arcola (G-683)
Rasmussen Press Inc .......... G ....
  Bensenville (G-1976)
RCP Publications Inc .......... F .... 773 227-4066
  Chicago (G-6299)
Real Estate News Corp .......... G .... 773 866-9900
  Chicago (G-6302)
Realtor Magazine .......... F .... 312 329-1928
  Chicago (G-6308)
Reilly Communication Group .......... F .... 630 756-1225
  Arlington Heights (G-831)

Relx Inc .......... E .... 309 689-1000
  Peoria (G-17441)
Rochelle Newspapers Inc .......... G .... 815 562-2061
  Rochelle (G-18106)
Rodale Inc .......... F .... 312 726-0365
  Chicago (G-6378)
Rookie LLC .......... G .... 708 278-1628
  Oak Park (G-16682)
RSM International .......... F .... 312 634-4762
  Chicago (G-6408)
Rylin Media LLC .......... G .... 708 246-7599
  Western Springs (G-21873)
S R Bastien Co .......... F .... 847 858-1175
  Evanston (G-10093)
Sagamore Publishing LLC .......... F .... 217 359-5940
  Urbana (G-21102)
Saltzman Printers Inc .......... E .... 708 344-4500
  Melrose Park (G-14690)
Sanderson and Associates .......... F .... 312 829-4350
  Chicago (G-6437)
◆ Scranton Glltte Cmmnctions Inc .......... D .... 847 391-1000
  Arlington Heights (G-836)
SGC Horizon LLC .......... E .... 847 391-1000
  Arlington Heights (G-839)
Sherman Media Company Inc .......... E .... 312 335-1962
  Lake Forest (G-12959)
Silent W Communications Inc .......... G .... 630 978-2050
  Oswego (G-16934)
Specialty Publishing Company .......... F .... 630 933-0844
  Carol Stream (G-3243)
Stagnito Partners LLC .......... D .... 224 632-8200
  Deerfield (G-8056)
Steven Fisher .......... G .... 847 317-1128
  Riverwoods (G-18044)
▲ Summitt Media Group Inc .......... E .... 312 222-1010
  Chicago (G-6617)
Surplus Record LLC .......... F .... 312 372-9077
  Chicago (G-6642)
Tails Inc .......... F .... 773 564-9300
  Chicago (G-6666)
▲ Talcott Communications Corp .......... E .... 312 849-2220
  Chicago (G-6668)
Target Market News Inc .......... G .... 312 408-1881
  Chicago (G-6676)
Tegna Inc .......... C .... 847 490-6657
  Hoffman Estates (G-12064)
Tele-Guia Inc .......... F .... 708 656-9800
  Cicero (G-7236)
Theosophical Society In Amer .......... G .... 630 665-0130
  Wheaton (G-21984)
Theosophical Society In Amer .......... F .... 630 665-0123
  Wheaton (G-21985)
This Week In Chicago Inc .......... F .... 312 943-0838
  Chicago (G-6716)
Thomson Reuters (legal) Inc .......... E .... 312 873-6800
  Chicago (G-6718)
Tmb Publishing Inc .......... G .... 847 564-1127
  Niles (G-16043)
Transportation Eqp Advisors .......... D .... 847 318-7575
  Rosemont (G-19037)
Trend Publishing Inc .......... E .... 312 654-2300
  Chicago (G-6767)
Tribune Publishing Company LLC .......... D .... 312 832-6711
  Chicago (G-6774)
Trmg LLP .......... F .... 847 441-4122
  Northfield (G-16422)
Tube & Pipe Association Intl .......... D .... 815 399-8700
  Elgin (G-9217)
University of Chicago .......... B .... 773 702-1722
  Chicago (G-6836)
US Catholic Magazine .......... G .... 312 236-7782
  Chicago (G-6853)
Utility Business Media Inc .......... G .... 815 459-1796
  Crystal Lake (G-7671)
Verone Publishing Inc .......... G .... 773 866-0811
  Chicago (G-6886)
Vertical Web Media LLC .......... E .... 312 362-0076
  Chicago (G-6888)
Vietnow National Headquarters .......... G .... 815 395-8484
  Rockford (G-18670)
W Whorton & Co .......... G .... 773 445-2400
  Chicago (G-6927)
Walnecks Inc .......... G .... 630 985-2097
  Downers Grove (G-8541)
Watt Publishing Co .......... E .... 815 966-5400
  Rockford (G-18674)
Watt Publishing Co .......... E .... 815 966-5400
  Rockford (G-18675)
Wenner Media LLC .......... G .... 312 660-3040
  Chicago (G-6957)

Willis Stein & Partners Manage .......... E .... 312 422-2400
  Northbrook (G-16387)
Willow Group Inc .......... G .... 847 277-9400
  Chicago (G-6988)
◆ Wilton Brands LLC .......... B .... 630 963-7100
  Woodridge (G-22526)
▼ Wilton Holdings Inc .......... G .... 630 963-7100
  Woodridge (G-22527)
◆ Wilton Industries Inc .......... B .... 630 963-7100
  Woodridge (G-22528)
Wilton Industries Inc .......... F .... 815 834-9390
  Romeoville (G-18879)
Windy City Media Group .......... G .... 773 871-7610
  Chicago (G-6997)
Winsight LLC .......... E .... 312 876-0004
  Chicago (G-7003)
◆ Wolters Kluwer US Inc .......... E .... 847 580-5000
  Riverwoods (G-18046)

## 2731 Books: Publishing & Printing

3b Media Inc .......... F .... 312 563-9363
  Chicago (G-3667)
A To Z Offset Prtg & Pubg Inc .......... G .... 847 966-3016
  Skokie (G-19943)
A Trustworthy Sup Source Inc .......... G .... 773 480-0255
  Chicago (G-3693)
Acta Publications .......... G .... 773 989-3036
  Chicago (G-3739)
Advantage Press Inc .......... G .... 630 960-5305
  Lisle (G-13553)
Adventures Unlimited .......... G .... 815 253-6390
  Kempton (G-12661)
AJS Publications .......... G .... 847 526-5027
  Island Lake (G-12212)
▲ Albert Whitman & Company .......... E .... 847 232-2800
  Park Ridge (G-17180)
▼ Allegro Publishing Inc .......... G .... 847 565-9083
  Chicago (G-3810)
American Association of Indivi .......... E .... 312 280-0170
  Chicago (G-3850)
American Bar Association .......... A .... 312 988-5000
  Chicago (G-3851)
American Catholic Press Inc .......... F .... 708 331-5485
  South Holland (G-20242)
American Chamber of .......... E .... 312 960-9400
  Chicago (G-3854)
American Hosp Assn Svcs Del .......... E .... 312 422-2000
  Chicago (G-3858)
◆ American Labelmark Company .......... C .... 773 478-0900
  Chicago (G-3859)
American Nurseryman Pubg Co .......... E .... 847 234-5867
  Lake Forest (G-12878)
American Supply Association .......... F .... 630 467-0000
  Itasca (G-12228)
Antigua Casa Sherry-Brener .......... G .... 773 737-1711
  Chicago (G-3916)
▲ Art Media Resources Inc .......... G .... 312 663-5351
  Chicago (G-3951)
Arthur Coyle Press .......... G .... 773 465-8418
  Chicago (G-3955)
Audio Tech Bus Bk Summaries .......... G .... 630 734-0500
  Oak Brook (G-16490)
Baptist General Conference .......... D .... 800 323-4215
  Arlington Heights (G-723)
Bar List Publishing Co .......... G .... 847 498-0100
  Northbrook (G-16210)
Barks Publications Inc .......... F .... 312 321-9440
  Chicago (G-4044)
Barnes & Noble College .......... G .... 708 209-3173
  River Forest (G-17996)
Beloved Characters Ltd .......... G .... 773 599-0073
  Chicago (G-4079)
Bendinger Bruce Crtve Comm In .......... G .... 773 871-1179
  Chicago (G-4082)
Bestwords Org Corp .......... G .... 618 939-4324
  Columbia (G-7352)
BGF Performance Systems LLC .......... G .... 773 539-7099
  Chicago (G-4101)
▲ Bolchazy-Carducci Publishers .......... F .... 847 526-4344
  Mundelein (G-15479)
Book Power Inc .......... G .... 630 790-4144
  Glen Ellyn (G-10961)
Bookends Publishing .......... G .... 312 988-1500
  Chicago (G-4143)
Brainworx Studio .......... F .... 773 743-8200
  Chicago (G-4157)
Broken Oar Inc .......... G .... 847 639-9468
  Port Barrington (G-17718)
Brown & Miller Literary Assoc .......... G .... 312 922-3063
  Chicago (G-4177)

# 27 PRINTING, PUBLISHING, AND ALLIED INDUSTRIES

| Company | Code | Phone |
|---|---|---|
| C M S Publishing Inc | G | 708 839-9201 |
| Willow Springs (G-22193) | | |
| C W Publications Inc | G | 800 554-5537 |
| Sterling (G-20586) | | |
| ▲ Carus Publishing Company | G | 603 924-7209 |
| Chicago (G-4246) | | |
| Carus Publishing Company | F | 312 701-1720 |
| Chicago (G-4247) | | |
| Castlegate Publishers Inc | G | 847 382-6420 |
| Barrington (G-1275) | | |
| Catalyst Chicago | G | 312 427-4830 |
| Chicago (G-4256) | | |
| Caxton Club | G | 312 266-8825 |
| Chicago (G-4259) | | |
| ▲ CCH Incorporated | A | 847 267-7000 |
| Riverwoods (G-18037) | | |
| Charles C Thomas Publisher | F | 217 789-8980 |
| Springfield (G-20416) | | |
| Charles H Kerr Publishing Co | G | 773 262-1329 |
| Chicago (G-4291) | | |
| Chicago Prvnce of The Soc Jsus | E | 773 281-1818 |
| Chicago (G-4343) | | |
| ▲ Chicago Review Press Inc | E | 312 337-0747 |
| Chicago (G-4344) | | |
| Christian National Womans | G | 847 864-1396 |
| Evanston (G-10024) | | |
| ▲ Christianica Center | G | 847 657-3818 |
| Glenview (G-11113) | | |
| City of Chicago | G | 773 581-8000 |
| Chicago (G-4386) | | |
| Common Ground Publishing LLC | E | 217 328-0405 |
| Champaign (G-3468) | | |
| Computer Industry Almanac Inc | G | 847 758-1926 |
| Arlington Heights (G-738) | | |
| ▲ Continental Sales Inc | G | 847 381-6530 |
| Barrington (G-1277) | | |
| Contractors Register Inc | G | 630 519-3480 |
| Lombard (G-13784) | | |
| Cook Communications Minis | D | 847 741-5168 |
| Elgin (G-9003) | | |
| Cook Communications Ministries | G | 847 741-0800 |
| Elgin (G-9004) | | |
| Cornerstone Community Outreach | F | 773 506-4904 |
| Chicago (G-4472) | | |
| Cornerstones Publishing I | E | 847 998-4746 |
| Glenview (G-11116) | | |
| Creative Curricula Inc | G | 815 363-9419 |
| McHenry (G-14491) | | |
| Crown Kandy Enterprise Ltd | F | 708 580-6494 |
| Westchester (G-21837) | | |
| ▲ Crystal Productions Co | F | 847 657-8144 |
| Northbrook (G-16235) | | |
| Cupcake Holdings LLC | G | 800 794-5866 |
| Woodridge (G-22466) | | |
| Curbside Splendor | G | 224 515-6512 |
| Chicago (G-4517) | | |
| ▲ Dalkey Archive Press | G | 217 244-5700 |
| Champaign (G-3473) | | |
| Damien Corporation | G | 630 369-3549 |
| Naperville (G-15644) | | |
| Dasher Dependable Reindeer LLC | G | 630 513-7737 |
| Saint Charles (G-19167) | | |
| Deagostini Publishing USA Inc | A | 212 432-4070 |
| Woodstock (G-22559) | | |
| Deerpath Publishing Co Inc | G | 847 234-3385 |
| Lake Forest (G-12895) | | |
| Delair Publishing Company Inc | C | 708 345-7000 |
| Melrose Park (G-14614) | | |
| Do You See What I See Entertai | G | 773 612-1269 |
| Chicago (G-4618) | | |
| Eagle Forum | G | 618 462-5415 |
| Alton (G-572) | | |
| Ebonyenergy Publishing Inc Nfp | G | 773 851-5159 |
| Chicago (G-4689) | | |
| Ebooks2go | G | 847 598-1145 |
| Schaumburg (G-19512) | | |
| Elliot Institute For Social SC | G | 217 525-8202 |
| Springfield (G-20434) | | |
| Empowered Press LLC | G | 630 400-3127 |
| Oswego (G-16915) | | |
| ▲ Encyclopaedia Britannica Inc | G | 847 777-2241 |
| Chicago (G-4749) | | |
| Final Call Inc | F | 773 602-1230 |
| Chicago (G-4843) | | |
| Foundation Lithuanian Minor | G | 630 969-1316 |
| Downers Grove (G-8445) | | |
| Frank R Walker Company | G | 630 613-9312 |
| Lombard (G-13802) | | |
| ▲ Gary Grimm & Associates Inc | G | 217 357-4501 |
| Carthage (G-3314) | | |
| Germain Saint Press Inc | G | 847 882-7400 |
| Schaumburg (G-19536) | | |
| ◆ Good News Publishers | E | 630 868-6025 |
| Wheaton (G-21951) | | |
| Goodheart-Willcox Company Inc | D | 708 687-0315 |
| Tinley Park (G-20919) | | |
| Gordon Burke John Publisher | G | 847 866-8625 |
| Evanston (G-10044) | | |
| Gorman & Associates | G | 309 691-9087 |
| Peoria (G-17373) | | |
| GPA Media Inc | G | 773 968-3728 |
| Calumet City (G-2940) | | |
| ◆ Grace & Truth Inc | G | 217 442-1120 |
| Danville (G-7727) | | |
| Graphic Score Book Co Inc | G | 847 823-7382 |
| Park Ridge (G-17199) | | |
| ▲ Great Books Foundation | E | 312 332-5870 |
| Chicago (G-4994) | | |
| Greek Art Printing & Pubg Co | G | 847 724-8860 |
| Chicago (G-11133) | | |
| Guildhall Publishers Ltd | G | 309 693-9232 |
| Peoria (G-17374) | | |
| H G Acquisition Corp | G | 630 382-1000 |
| Burr Ridge (G-2848) | | |
| ▲ Heimburger House Pubg Co Inc | G | 708 366-1973 |
| Forest Park (G-10248) | | |
| Helivalues | G | 847 487-8258 |
| Wauconda (G-21466) | | |
| Holder Publishing Corporation | G | 309 828-7533 |
| Bloomington (G-2179) | | |
| Home Design Alternatives Inc | E | 314 731-1427 |
| Schaumburg (G-19558) | | |
| Hope Publishing Company | F | 630 665-3200 |
| Carol Stream (G-3167) | | |
| Houghton Mifflin Harcourt Co | G | 630 467-6049 |
| Itasca (G-12275) | | |
| Houghton Mifflin Harcourt Pubg | C | 630 208-5704 |
| Geneva (G-10833) | | |
| Houghton Mifflin Harcourt Pubg | B | 630 467-6095 |
| Itasca (G-12276) | | |
| Houghton Mifflin Harcourt Pubg | B | 847 869-2300 |
| Evanston (G-10052) | | |
| Houghton Mifflin Harcourt Pubg | B | 708 869-2300 |
| Evanston (G-10053) | | |
| Human Factor RES Group Inc | G | 618 476-3200 |
| Millstadt (G-14826) | | |
| IB Source Inc | G | 312 698-7062 |
| Chicago (G-5134) | | |
| Ifpra Inc | G | 708 410-0100 |
| Westchester (G-21843) | | |
| Illinois Inst Cntng Legl Ed | E | 217 787-2080 |
| Springfield (G-20454) | | |
| Information Usa Inc | G | 312 943-6288 |
| Chicago (G-5189) | | |
| Intervrsity Chrstn Fllwshp/Usa | D | 630 734-4000 |
| Westmont (G-21893) | | |
| ▼ J S Paluch Co Inc | C | 847 678-9300 |
| Franklin Park (G-10502) | | |
| Jameson Books Inc | G | 815 434-7905 |
| Ottawa (G-16963) | | |
| Jgc United Publishing Corps | G | 815 968-6601 |
| Rockford (G-18444) | | |
| ▼ Johnson Publishing Company LLC | G | 312 322-9200 |
| Chicago (G-5320) | | |
| ▲ Kidsbooks LLC | G | 773 509-0707 |
| Chicago (G-5382) | | |
| Kishknows Inc | G | 708 252-3648 |
| Richton Park (G-17979) | | |
| Koza | G | 773 646-0958 |
| Chicago (G-5409) | | |
| Lifetouch Services Inc | G | 815 633-3881 |
| Loves Park (G-13961) | | |
| Linmore Publishing Co | G | 847 382-7606 |
| Barrington (G-1286) | | |
| LMS Innovations Inc | G | 312 613-2345 |
| Chicago (G-5528) | | |
| Manufctrers Claring Hse of Ill | G | 773 545-6300 |
| Chicago (G-5609) | | |
| Marantha Wrld Rvval Ministries | G | 773 384-7717 |
| Chicago (G-5611) | | |
| Marytown | E | 847 367-7800 |
| Libertyville (G-13347) | | |
| Media Associates Intl Inc | F | 630 260-9063 |
| Carol Stream (G-3192) | | |
| Medical Memories LLC | G | 847 478-0078 |
| Buffalo Grove (G-2734) | | |
| Michael A Greenberg MD Ltd | F | 847 364-4711 |
| Elk Grove Village (G-9625) | | |
| Monitor Publishing Inc | G | 773 205-0303 |
| Chicago (G-5795) | | |
| Moody Bible Inst of Chicago | E | 312 329-2102 |
| Chicago (G-5800) | | |
| ◆ Moody Bible Inst of Chicago | A | 312 329-4000 |
| Chicago (G-5799) | | |
| Motamed Medical Publishing Co | G | 773 761-6667 |
| Chicago (G-5812) | | |
| Movie Facts Inc | E | 847 299-9700 |
| Des Plaines (G-8238) | | |
| Multi Packaging Solutions Inc | G | 773 283-9500 |
| Chicago (G-5832) | | |
| National Bus Trader Inc | F | 815 946-2341 |
| Polo (G-17689) | | |
| National School Services Inc | G | 847 438-3859 |
| Long Grove (G-13899) | | |
| Nature House Inc | D | 217 833-2393 |
| Griggsville (G-11413) | | |
| Neal-Schuman Publishers Inc | F | 312 944-6780 |
| Chicago (G-5879) | | |
| Need To Know Inc | G | 309 691-3877 |
| Peoria (G-17415) | | |
| Nexus Supply Consortium Inc | G | 630 649-2868 |
| Bolingbrook (G-2353) | | |
| Oasis Audio LLC | G | 630 668-5367 |
| Carol Stream (G-3208) | | |
| Oasis International Limited | G | 630 326-0045 |
| Geneva (G-10855) | | |
| Omega Publishing Services Inc | G | 630 968-0440 |
| Downers Grove (G-8498) | | |
| Pamacheyon Publishing Inc | G | 815 395-0101 |
| Rockford (G-18529) | | |
| Partner Health LLC | G | 847 208-6074 |
| Lake Forest (G-12939) | | |
| Permissions Group Inc | G | 847 635-6550 |
| Glenview (G-11181) | | |
| Perry Johnson Inc | F | 847 635-0010 |
| Rosemont (G-19021) | | |
| ▲ Phoenix Intl Publications Inc | B | 312 739-4400 |
| Chicago (G-6119) | | |
| Pieces of Learning Inc | G | 618 964-9426 |
| Marion (G-14279) | | |
| Pinnacle Publishing Inc | F | 218 444-2180 |
| Chicago (G-6124) | | |
| Pipestone Passages | G | 773 735-2488 |
| Chicago (G-6129) | | |
| ▲ Pivot Point Usa Inc | D | 800 886-4247 |
| Chicago (G-6133) | | |
| Polonia Book Store Inc | G | 773 481-6968 |
| Chicago (G-6151) | | |
| Practice Management Info Corp | E | 800 633-7467 |
| Downers Grove (G-8508) | | |
| Press Syndication Group LLC | G | 646 325-3221 |
| Chicago (G-6181) | | |
| ◆ Preston Industries Inc | C | 847 647-2900 |
| Niles (G-16022) | | |
| Print Rite Inc | G | 773 625-0792 |
| Chicago (G-6189) | | |
| Psytec Inc | G | 815 758-1415 |
| Dekalb (G-8114) | | |
| ◆ Publications International Ltd | B | 847 676-3470 |
| Morton Grove (G-15229) | | |
| ▼ Putman Media Inc | D | 630 467-1301 |
| Schaumburg (G-19705) | | |
| Raven Tree Press LLC | G | 800 323-8270 |
| Crystal Lake (G-7637) | | |
| Research Press Company | F | 217 352-3273 |
| Champaign (G-3532) | | |
| Respect Incorporated | G | 815 806-1907 |
| Manhattan (G-14170) | | |
| Rite-TEC Communications | G | 815 459-7712 |
| Crystal Lake (G-7643) | | |
| Rohrer Graphic Arts Inc | F | 630 832-3434 |
| Elmhurst (G-9930) | | |
| Rookie LLC | G | 708 278-1628 |
| Oak Park (G-16682) | | |
| Royal Publishing Inc | G | 309 343-4007 |
| Galesburg (G-10775) | | |
| Royal Publishing Inc | G | 815 220-0400 |
| Peru (G-17526) | | |
| S R Bastien Co | F | 847 858-1175 |
| Evanston (G-10093) | | |
| Sagamore Publishing LLC | F | 217 359-5940 |
| Urbana (G-21102) | | |
| Scholastic Inc | E | 630 443-8197 |
| Saint Charles (G-19261) | | |
| Scholastic Inc | E | 630 671-0601 |
| Roselle (G-18974) | | |
| ▲ Shure Products Inc | G | 773 227-1001 |
| Chicago (G-6504) | | |
| ▲ Sourcebooks Inc | D | 630 961-3900 |
| Naperville (G-15751) | | |

Employee Codes: A=Over 500 employees, B=251-500
C=101-250, D=51-100, E=20-50, F=10-19, G=3-9

# 27 PRINTING, PUBLISHING, AND ALLIED INDUSTRIES — SIC SECTION

| Company | Code | Phone |
|---|---|---|
| Springfield Printing Inc — Springfield (G-20531) | G | 217 787-3500 |
| Sterling Books Limited — Hinsdale (G-11965) | G | 630 325-3853 |
| Students Publishing Company In — Evanston (G-10097) | G | 847 491-7206 |
| Success Publishing Group Inc — Chicago (G-6611) | F | 708 565-2681 |
| Surrey Books Inc — Evanston (G-10099) | G | 847 475-4457 |
| Taylor Enterprises Inc — Libertyville (G-13389) | G | 847 367-1032 |
| Templegate Publishers — Springfield (G-20543) | G | 217 522-3353 |
| Theosophical Society In Amer — Wheaton (G-21985) | F | 630 665-0123 |
| Theosophical Society In Amer — Wheaton (G-21984) | G | 630 665-0130 |
| Third Wrld Press Fundation Inc — Chicago (G-6715) | F | 773 651-0700 |
| Thomson Reuters (markets) LLC — Palatine (G-17082) | B | 847 705-7929 |
| Thomson Reuters Corporation — Chicago (G-6719) | D | 312 288-4654 |
| Thrice Publishing Nfp — Roselle (G-18982) | G | 630 776-0478 |
| ◆ Triumph Books Corp — Chicago (G-6780) | E | 312 337-0747 |
| Twain Media Mark Publishing — Quincy (G-17901) | G | 217 223-7008 |
| ◆ Tyndale House Publishers Inc — Carol Stream (G-3257) | C | 630 668-8300 |
| Tyndale House Publishers Inc — Carol Stream (G-3258) | D | 630 668-8300 |
| U S Naval Institute — University Park (G-21065) | G | 800 233-8764 |
| United Educators Inc — Lake Bluff (G-12868) | F | 847 234-3700 |
| University of Chicago — Chicago (G-6836) | B | 773 702-1722 |
| Urantia Corp — Chicago (G-6844) | F | 773 248-6616 |
| Urantia Foundation — Chicago (G-6845) | F | 773 525-3319 |
| Urban Research Press Inc — Chicago (G-6850) | F | 773 994-7200 |
| Venture Publishing Inc — Urbana (G-21104) | G | 217 359-5940 |
| ▲ Wedding Brand Investors LLC — Wauconda (G-21513) | E | 847 887-0071 |
| West Publishing Corporation — Chicago (G-6961) | D | 312 894-1690 |
| ◆ Wilton Brands LLC — Woodridge (G-22526) | B | 630 963-7100 |
| ▼ Wilton Holdings Inc — Woodridge (G-22527) | G | 630 963-7100 |
| ◆ Wilton Industries Inc — Woodridge (G-22528) | B | 630 963-7100 |
| Wilton Industries Inc — Romeoville (G-18879) | F | 815 834-9390 |
| Windsong Press Ltd — Grayslake (G-11368) | G | 847 223-4586 |
| Windy City Publishers LLC — Palatine (G-17090) | G | 847 925-9434 |
| ◆ Wolters Kluwer US Inc — Riverwoods (G-18046) | E | 847 580-5000 |
| ▲ World Book Inc — Chicago (G-7028) | E | 312 729-5800 |

## 2732 Book Printing, Not Publishing

| Company | Code | Phone |
|---|---|---|
| Advance Instant Printing Co — Chicago (G-3760) | G | 312 346-0986 |
| Andover Junction Publications — Mendota (G-14716) | G | 815 538-3060 |
| Award/Visionps Inc — Chicago (G-4003) | G | 331 318-7800 |
| Bostic Publishing Company — Chicago (G-4149) | G | 773 551-7065 |
| Bronte Press — Bourbonnais (G-2390) | G | 815 932-5192 |
| Charles C Thomas Publisher — Springfield (G-20416) | F | 217 789-8980 |
| Cook Communications Ministries — Elgin (G-9004) | C | 847 741-0800 |
| Copies Overnight Inc — Carol Stream (G-3136) | F | 630 690-2000 |
| Creasey Printing Services Inc — Springfield (G-20425) | G | 217 787-1055 |
| Finishing Group — Schaumburg (G-19528) | G | 847 884-4890 |
| Greek Art Printing & Pubg Co — Glenview (G-11133) | G | 847 724-8860 |
| Hopper Graphics Inc — Palos Heights (G-17107) | G | 708 489-0459 |
| In-Print Graphics Inc — Oak Forest (G-16584) | E | 708 396-1010 |
| Ink Spots Prtg & Meida Design — Homewood (G-12102) | G | 708 754-1300 |
| Interntnal Awkening Ministries — Wheaton (G-21958) | G | 630 653-8616 |
| Johnson Press America Inc — Pontiac (G-17704) | E | 815 844-5161 |
| Kellogg Printing Co — Monmouth (G-15016) | F | 309 734-8388 |
| Kjellberg Printing — Chicago (G-21960) | F | 630 653-2244 |
| KK Stevens Publishing Co — Astoria (G-934) | E | 309 329-2151 |
| ◆ Lake Book Manufacturing Inc — Melrose Park (G-14669) | E | 708 345-7000 |
| Lsc Communications Inc — Chicago (G-5552) | D | 773 272-9200 |
| Lsc Communications Us LLC — Chicago (G-5553) | B | 844 572-5720 |
| Marty Gannon — Schaumburg (G-19632) | E | 847 895-1059 |
| Morgen Transportation Inc — Chicago (G-5805) | G | 773 405-1250 |
| Palmer Printing Inc — Chicago (G-6065) | E | 312 427-7150 |
| Pantagraph Printing and Sty Co — Bloomington (G-2208) | F | 309 829-1071 |
| Quad/Graphics Inc — Mount Morris (G-15297) | A | 815 734-4121 |
| R R Donnelley & Sons Company — Pontiac (G-17710) | A | 815 844-5181 |
| R R Donnelley & Sons Company — Chicago (G-6270) | B | 312 326-8000 |
| R R Donnelley & Sons Company — Dwight (G-8591) | A | 815 584-2770 |
| Rasmussen Press Inc — Bensenville (G-1976) | G | |
| Roger Fritz & Associates Inc — Naperville (G-15744) | G | 630 355-2614 |
| RR Donnelley & Sons Company — Saint Charles (G-19255) | D | 630 513-4681 |
| RR Donnelley & Sons Company — Lisle (G-13653) | B | 630 588-5000 |
| RR Donnelley & Sons Company — Chicago (G-6404) | C | 312 236-8000 |
| Sandes Quynetta — Freeport (G-10687) | G | 815 275-4876 |
| ▲ Sunrise Hitek Group LLC — Chicago (G-6629) | E | 773 792-8880 |
| ▲ TPS Enterprises Inc — Newton (G-15950) | E | 618 783-2978 |
| ▲ Tvp Color Graphics Inc — Streamwood (G-20679) | G | 630 837-3600 |
| ▲ United Graphics Llc — Mattoon (G-14412) | C | 217 235-7161 |
| University of Chicago — Chicago (G-6837) | G | 773 702-7000 |
| Versa Press Inc — East Peoria (G-8738) | C | 309 822-0260 |
| Vision Integrated Graphics — Bolingbrook (G-2380) | F | 708 570-7900 |
| Wctu Press — Evanston (G-10105) | G | 847 864-1396 |
| Wold Printing Services Ltd — Volo (G-21320) | E | 847 546-3110 |

## 2741 Misc Publishing

| Company | Code | Phone |
|---|---|---|
| ◆ 24land Express Inc — Elk Grove Village (G-9247) | G | 630 766-2424 |
| A J Express Power Tools — Schiller Park (G-19796) | G | 847 678-8200 |
| About Learning Inc — Wauconda (G-21436) | F | 847 487-1800 |
| Aerodine Magazine — Inverness (G-12200) | G | 847 358-4355 |
| ▲ Agate Publishing Inc — Evanston (G-10005) | G | 847 475-4457 |
| Allured Publishing Corporation — Carol Stream (G-3097) | G | 630 653-2155 |
| Am-Don Partnership — Champaign (G-3447) | G | 217 355-7750 |
| American Bar Foundation — Chicago (G-3852) | D | 312 988-6500 |
| American Custom Publishing — Libertyville (G-13302) | G | 847 816-8660 |
| American Marketing & Pubg LLC — Dekalb (G-8074) | E | 815 756-2840 |
| Amnet Systems LLC — Urbana (G-21069) | F | 217 954-0130 |
| Anash Educational Institute — Chicago (G-3900) | G | 773 338-7704 |
| Angle Press Inc — Arlington Heights (G-714) | G | 847 439-6388 |
| Art In Print Review — Chicago (G-3950) | G | 773 697-9478 |
| Arthur Coyle Press — Chicago (G-3955) | G | 773 465-8418 |
| AT&T Corp — Lombard (G-13765) | G | 630 693-5000 |
| AT&T Teleholdings Inc — Chicago (G-3973) | G | 800 257-0902 |
| ▲ Avenir Publishing Inc — Chicago (G-3998) | E | 312 577-7200 |
| Award/Visionps Inc — Chicago (G-4003) | G | 331 318-7800 |
| B A I Publishers — Wheeling (G-22010) | G | 847 537-1300 |
| Baka Vitaliy — Chicago (G-4027) | G | 773 370-5522 |
| ◆ Ball Publishing — West Chicago (G-21665) | F | 630 208-9080 |
| Ballotready Inc — Chicago (G-4033) | G | 301 706-0708 |
| Band of Shoppers Inc — Chicago (G-4035) | G | 312 857-4250 |
| Bar List Publishing Co — Northbrook (G-16210) | G | 847 498-0100 |
| ◆ Bass-Mollett Publishers Inc — Greenville (G-11387) | D | 618 664-3141 |
| Beardstown Newspapers Inc — Beardstown (G-1520) | G | 217 323-1010 |
| Bendinger Bruce Crtve Comm In — Chicago (G-4082) | G | 773 871-1179 |
| Bishop Engineering Company — Lisle (G-13569) | F | 630 305-9538 |
| Biz 3 Publicity — Chicago (G-4116) | G | 773 342-3331 |
| Book Power Inc — Glen Ellyn (G-10961) | G | 630 790-4144 |
| Boone County Shopper Inc — Belvidere (G-1739) | F | 815 544-2166 |
| Brilliant Color Corp — Libertyville (G-13310) | G | 847 367-3300 |
| Buhl Press — Berkeley (G-2044) | E | 708 449-8989 |
| Bureau of National Affairs — Chicago (G-4184) | G | 773 775-8801 |
| Businessmine LLC — Lombard (G-13774) | G | 630 541-8480 |
| C W Publications Inc — Sterling (G-20586) | G | 800 554-5537 |
| Cab Communications Inc — Palatine (G-17007) | G | 847 963-8740 |
| Cade Communications Inc — Chicago (G-4210) | G | 773 477-7184 |
| Cambridge Business — Westmont (G-21879) | G | 800 619-6473 |
| Cammun LLC — Chicago (G-4224) | G | 312 628-1201 |
| Carlberg Design Inc — Petersburg (G-17534) | G | 217 341-3291 |
| Cash House Music Group LLC — Indian Creek (G-12185) | G | 847 471-7401 |
| Catalog Designers Inc — Elk Grove Village (G-9359) | G | 847 228-0025 |
| ▲ Central Illinois Homes Guide — Peoria (G-17337) | G | 309 688-6419 |
| Centup Industries LLC — Chicago (G-4274) | G | 312 291-1687 |
| ▲ Chase Group LLC — Northbrook (G-16219) | F | 847 564-2000 |
| Chesley Limited — Northbrook (G-16220) | G | 847 562-9292 |
| Chicago Sports Media Inc — Skokie (G-19981) | G | 847 676-1900 |
| Chicago Sun-Times Features Inc — Chicago (G-4352) | F | 312 321-2043 |
| China Ying Inc — Naperville (G-15629) | G | 630 428-2638 |
| Christian Specialized Services — Springfield (G-20418) | G | 217 546-7338 |
| Cirrus Products — Addison (G-77) | G | 630 501-1881 |
| Cision US Inc — Chicago (G-4381) | C | 312 922-2400 |

**Consumerbase LLC** ........ C ....... 312 600-8000
Chicago *(G-4455)*
**Cottage Door Press LLC** ........ F ....... 224 228-6000
Barrington *(G-1278)*
**Creasey Printing Services Inc** ........ G ....... 217 787-1055
Springfield *(G-20425)*
**Creative Directory Inc** ........ G ....... 773 427-7777
Chicago *(G-4498)*
**Creative Ideas Inc** ........ G ....... 217 245-1378
Jacksonville *(G-12386)*
**Cross Express Company** ........ G ....... 847 439-7457
Elk Grove Village *(G-9401)*
**Custom Design Services & Assoc** ........ F ....... 815 226-9747
Rockford *(G-18327)*
**Damien Corporation** ........ G ....... 630 369-3549
Naperville *(G-15644)*
**Debbie Harshman** ........ G ....... 217 335-2112
Barry *(G-1311)*
**Deshamusic Inc** ........ G ....... 818 257-2716
Chicago *(G-4585)*
**▲ Devils Due Publishing** ........ G ....... 773 412-6427
Chicago *(G-4588)*
**Dex Media Inc** ........ F ....... 312 240-6000
Chicago *(G-4589)*
**Dino Publishing LLC** ........ G ....... 312 822-9266
Chicago *(G-4607)*
**Doody Enterprises Inc** ........ G ....... 312 239-6226
Oak Park *(G-16660)*
**Dramatic Publishing Company** ........ F ....... 815 338-7170
Woodstock *(G-22563)*
**Ea Mackay Enterprises Inc** ........ E ....... 630 627-7010
Lombard *(G-13793)*
**Eagle Publications Inc** ........ E ....... 618 345-5400
Collinsville *(G-7321)*
**Earthcomber LLC** ........ F ....... 708 366-1600
Oak Park *(G-16662)*
**▲ East Wisconsin LLC** ........ E ....... 618 224-9133
Trenton *(G-20991)*
**Ebsco Industries Inc** ........ F ....... 800 245-7224
South Holland *(G-20264)*
**Ebsco Industries Inc** ........ E ....... 847 244-1800
Waukegan *(G-21556)*
**Edge Communication** ........ G ....... 708 749-7818
Berwyn *(G-2062)*
**Educational Directories Inc** ........ G ....... 847 891-1250
Schaumburg *(G-19513)*
**Element Collection** ........ G ....... 217 898-5175
Allerton *(G-421)*
**Elite Publishing and Design** ........ G ....... 888 237-8119
Peoria *(G-17355)*
**Elliot Institute For Social SC** ........ G ....... 217 525-8202
Springfield *(G-20434)*
**Exclusive Publications Inc** ........ G ....... 847 963-0400
Hoffman Estates *(G-12008)*
**F & F Publishing Inc** ........ G ....... 847 480-0330
Highland Park *(G-11831)*
**F M Aquisition Corp** ........ G ....... 773 728-8351
Chicago *(G-4806)*
**Farm Week** ........ E ....... 309 557-3140
Bloomington *(G-2163)*
**Fleming Music Technology Ctr** ........ G ....... 708 316-8662
Wheaton *(G-21948)*
**Food Service Publishing Co** ........ G ....... 847 699-3300
Park Ridge *(G-17195)*
**Food Service Publishing Co** ........ F ....... 847 699-3300
Des Plaines *(G-8200)*
**Foodservice Database Co Inc** ........ F ....... 773 745-9400
Chicago *(G-4870)*
**Frank R Walker Company** ........ G ....... 630 613-9312
Lombard *(G-13802)*
**Fresh Facs** ........ G ....... 618 357-9697
Pinckneyville *(G-17548)*
**▲ G I A Publications Inc** ........ E ....... 708 496-3800
Chicago *(G-4901)*
**▲ G R Leonard & Co Inc** ........ E ....... 847 797-8101
Arlington Heights *(G-758)*
**Gatehouse Media III Holdings** ........ G ....... 585 598-0030
Peoria *(G-17368)*
**Glorius Renditions** ........ G ....... 815 315-0177
Leaf River *(G-13211)*
**Gold-Slvr-Bronze Medal Mus Inc** ........ G ....... 847 272-6854
Gurnee *(G-11453)*
**Graphic Communicators Inc** ........ G ....... 708 385-7550
Palos Heights *(G-17106)*
**Graphic Press** ........ G ....... 312 909-6100
Chicago *(G-4991)*
**Haggin Marketing Inc** ........ F ....... 312 343-2611
Chicago *(G-5031)*
**Halper Publishing Company** ........ G ....... 847 542-9793
Evanston *(G-10049)*

**Hancock County Shopper** ........ G ....... 217 847-6628
Hamilton *(G-11538)*
**Haute Noir Media Group Inc** ........ G ....... 312 869-4526
Chicago *(G-5055)*
**Health Administration Press** ........ D ....... 312 424-2800
Chicago *(G-5058)*
**Heartland Publications Inc** ........ G ....... 217 529-9506
Springfield *(G-20450)*
**Heritage Products Corporation** ........ G ....... 847 419-8835
Buffalo Grove *(G-2703)*
**Hermitage Group Inc** ........ E ....... 773 561-3773
Chicago *(G-5080)*
**Holder Publishing Corporation** ........ G ....... 309 828-7533
Bloomington *(G-2179)*
**Holsolutions Inc** ........ G ....... 888 847-5467
Frankfort *(G-10327)*
**Holt Publications Inc** ........ G ....... 618 654-6206
Highland *(G-11796)*
**Hope Publishing Company** ........ F ....... 630 665-3200
Carol Stream *(G-3167)*
**Hospital & Physician Pubg** ........ G ....... 618 997-9375
Marion *(G-14267)*
**◆ Houghton Mifflin Harcourt** ........ E ....... 928 467-9599
Geneva *(G-10832)*
**HP Interactive Inc** ........ G ....... 773 681-4440
Chicago *(G-5124)*
**Hunting Network LLC** ........ G ....... 847 659-8200
Huntley *(G-12145)*
**▲ I P G Warehouse Ltd** ........ E ....... 773 722-5527
Chicago *(G-5132)*
**Illini Media Co** ........ B ....... 217 337-8300
Champaign *(G-3499)*
**Imagination Publishing LLC** ........ E ....... 312 887-1000
Chicago *(G-5161)*
**Imedia Network Inc** ........ G ....... 847 331-1774
Chicago *(G-5164)*
**Inn Partners LLC** ........ D ....... 309 743-0800
Moline *(G-14944)*
**Inter-State Studio & Pubg Co** ........ D ....... 815 874-0342
Rockford *(G-18438)*
**J C Communications Company** ........ G ....... 312 236-5122
Chicago *(G-5257)*
**▼ J S Paluch Co Inc** ........ C ....... 847 678-9300
Franklin Park *(G-10502)*
**Janelle Publications Inc** ........ G ....... 815 756-2300
Dekalb *(G-8100)*
**JAS Express Inc** ........ G ....... 847 836-7984
Union *(G-21035)*
**Java Express** ........ G ....... 217 525-2430
Springfield *(G-20462)*
**John C Graff** ........ F ....... 847 842-9200
Lake Barrington *(G-12811)*
**▲ Joong-Ang Daily News** ........ E ....... 847 228-7200
Elk Grove Village *(G-9564)*
**JW Express** ........ G ....... 630 697-1037
Elk Grove Village *(G-9567)*
**Kae Dj Publishing** ........ G ....... 773 233-2609
Chicago *(G-5350)*
**Kaelco Entrmt Holdings Inc** ........ G ....... 217 600-7815
Champaign *(G-3505)*
**Keane Gillette Publishing LLC** ........ G ....... 630 279-7521
Elmhurst *(G-9895)*
**Key One Graphics Services Inc** ........ G .......
West Dundee *(G-21799)*
**Km Press Incorporated** ........ G ....... 618 277-1222
Belleville *(G-1644)*
**Knighthouse Media Inc** ........ G ....... 312 676-1100
Chicago *(G-5391)*
**L A M Inc De** ........ G ....... 630 860-9700
Wood Dale *(G-22388)*
**Labelquest Inc** ........ E ....... 630 833-9400
Elmhurst *(G-9900)*
**Law Bulletin Publishing Co** ........ C ....... 312 416-1860
Chicago *(G-5470)*
**Law Bulletin Publishing Co** ........ F ....... 847 883-9100
Buffalo Grove *(G-2722)*
**Lee Enterprises Incorporated** ........ G ....... 217 421-8940
Decatur *(G-7907)*
**Leonard Publishing Co** ........ F ....... 773 486-2737
Norridge *(G-16104)*
**Liberty Group Publishing** ........ F ....... 309 944-1779
Geneseo *(G-10802)*
**Lifetouch Services Inc** ........ C ....... 815 633-3881
Loves Park *(G-13961)*
**Line of Advance Nfp** ........ G ....... 312 768-0043
Chicago *(G-5510)*
**LMS Innovations Inc** ........ G ....... 312 613-2345
Chicago *(G-5528)*
**Loyalty Publishing Inc** ........ E ....... 309 693-0840
Bartonville *(G-1396)*

**Luby Publishing Inc** ........ F ....... 312 341-1110
Chicago *(G-5556)*
**Luna Azul Communications Inc** ........ E ....... 773 616-0007
Deerfield *(G-8030)*
**M & G Graphics Inc** ........ E ....... 773 247-1596
Chicago *(G-5576)*
**M M Marketing** ........ G ....... 815 459-7968
Crystal Lake *(G-7603)*
**Make It Better LLC** ........ G ....... 847 256-4642
Wilmette *(G-22261)*
**Manufacturers News Inc** ........ D ....... 847 864-7000
Evanston *(G-10068)*
**Marshall Pubg & Promotions** ........ G ....... 224 238-3530
Barrington *(G-1289)*
**McIlvaine Co** ........ E ....... 847 784-0012
Northfield *(G-16408)*
**▲ McX Press** ........ G ....... 630 784-4325
Bloomingdale *(G-2117)*
**Medallion Press Inc** ........ G ....... 630 513-8316
Aurora *(G-1053)*
**Mediatec Publishing Inc** ........ E ....... 312 676-9900
Chicago *(G-5678)*
**Mendota Reporter** ........ F ....... 815 539-9396
Mendota *(G-14726)*
**Merit Emplyment Assssment Svcs** ........ G ....... 815 320-3680
New Lenox *(G-15894)*
**▲ Midwest Suburban Publishing** ........ A ....... 708 633-6880
Tinley Park *(G-20933)*
**Modern Trade Communications** ........ F ....... 847 674-2200
Skokie *(G-20041)*
**Morris Cody & Assoc** ........ G ....... 847 945-8050
Deerfield *(G-8040)*
**Nas Media Group Inc** ........ G ....... 312 371-7499
Olympia Fields *(G-16803)*
**Nas Media Group Inc** ........ F ....... 773 824-0242
Chicago *(G-5855)*
**Nascar Car Wash** ........ G ....... 630 236-3400
Aurora *(G-1055)*
**New Millenium Directories** ........ E ....... 815 626-5737
Sterling *(G-20601)*
**New Millennium Investment** ........ G ....... 708 358-1512
Oak Park *(G-16676)*
**▲ New Wave Express Inc** ........ G ....... 630 238-3129
Bensenville *(G-1955)*
**Nice Card Company** ........ G ....... 773 467-8450
Park Ridge *(G-17212)*
**Norskobok Press** ........ G ....... 847 516-0085
Cary *(G-3362)*
**North American Press Inc** ........ G ....... 847 515-3882
Huntley *(G-12164)*
**▲ Norwood House Press Inc** ........ G ....... 866 565-2900
Chicago *(G-5945)*
**▼ Oag Aviation Worldwide LLC** ........ G ....... 630 515-5300
Lisle *(G-13635)*
**Odx Media LLC** ........ G ....... 847 868-0548
Evanston *(G-10080)*
**Olney Daily Mail** ........ E ....... 618 393-2931
Olney *(G-16787)*
**Omni Publishing Co** ........ G ....... 847 483-9668
Wheeling *(G-22113)*
**Pacific Press Technologies LP** ........ G ....... 618 262-8666
Mount Carmel *(G-15280)*
**Paddock Publications Inc** ........ E ....... 847 680-5800
Libertyville *(G-13365)*
**Palm International Inc** ........ G ....... 630 357-1437
Naperville *(G-15721)*
**Panache Editions Ltd** ........ G ....... 847 921-8574
Glencoe *(G-11005)*
**Paperworks** ........ G ....... 630 969-3218
Downers Grove *(G-8499)*
**Payment Pathways Inc** ........ G ....... 312 346-9400
Chicago *(G-6092)*
**Peoria Post Inc** ........ F ....... 309 688-3628
Peoria *(G-17426)*
**Perq/Hci LLC** ........ C ....... 847 375-5000
Rosemont *(G-19020)*
**Perspecto Map Company Inc** ........ G ....... 815 356-1288
Village of Lakewood *(G-21291)*
**Phoenix Press Inc** ........ G ....... 630 833-2281
Villa Park *(G-21277)*
**▲ Phoenix Tree Publishing Inc** ........ G ....... 773 251-0309
Chicago *(G-6120)*
**Pierce Crandell & Co Inc** ........ G ....... 847 549-6015
Libertyville *(G-13368)*
**Premier Travel Media** ........ G ....... 630 794-0696
Willowbrook *(G-22228)*
**Press Dough Inc** ........ G ....... 630 243-6900
Lemont *(G-13257)*
**Press On Inc** ........ G ....... 630 628-1630
Addison *(G-255)*

SIC

# 27 PRINTING, PUBLISHING, AND ALLIED INDUSTRIES

Prime Publishing LLC .................................. D .... 847 205-9435
　Northbrook (G-16343)
Publishing Task Force ................................. F .... 312 670-4360
　Chicago (G-6224)
Qt Info Systems Inc ................................... F .... 800 240-8761
　Chicago (G-6239)
Quarasan Group Inc ................................... D .... 312 981-2540
　Chicago (G-6254)
Quincy Media Inc ...................................... C .... 217 223-5100
　Quincy (G-17879)
R L Allen Industries .................................... G .... 618 667-2544
　Troy (G-21011)
R R Donnelley & Sons Company ............... C .... 847 393-3000
　Libertyville (G-13373)
R R Donnelley & Sons Company ............... A .... 815 584-2770
　Dwight (G-8591)
Rain Publication Inc .................................... G .... 312 284-2444
　Chicago (G-6287)
▲ Rand McNally & Company ..................... B .... 847 329-8100
　Skokie (G-20069)
Rand McNally International Co .................. G .... 847 329-8100
　Skokie (G-20070)
Rapid Circular Press Inc ............................. F .... 312 421-5611
　Chicago (G-6290)
Redshelf Inc ............................................... G .... 312 878-8586
　Chicago (G-6317)
Reid Communications Inc .......................... E .... 847 741-9700
　Elgin (G-9163)
Rickard Publishing ..................................... F .... 217 482-3276
　Mason City (G-14366)
▲ Rm Acquisition LLC ............................... C .... 847 329-8100
　Skokie (G-20077)
Robert-Leslie Publishing LLC ..................... G .... 773 935-8358
　Chicago (G-6369)
Rockford Map Publishers Inc ..................... F .... 815 708-6324
　Rockford (G-18579)
Roger Fritz & Associates Inc ..................... G .... 630 355-2614
　Naperville (G-15744)
RR Donnelley Logistics SE ........................ G .... 630 672-2500
　Roselle (G-18970)
Rs Ductless Technical Support ................. G .... 815 223-7949
　La Salle (G-12784)
Sauk Valley Shopper Inc ........................... C .... 815 625-6700
　Sterling (G-20612)
Scars Publications .................................... G .... 847 281-9070
　Gurnee (G-11502)
Scholastic Testing Service ........................ F .... 630 766-7150
　Bensenville (G-1988)
Schumaker Publications Inc ...................... G .... 309 365-7105
　Lexington (G-13293)
Serbian Yellow Pages Inc ......................... F .... 847 588-0555
　Niles (G-16031)
SGS International LLC .............................. C .... 309 690-5231
　Peoria (G-17453)
Shiftgig Inc ................................................ E .... 312 763-3003
　Chicago (G-6496)
Shoppers Guide ........................................ G .... 815 369-4112
　Lena (G-13284)
Shoppers Review ...................................... F .... 618 654-4459
　Highland (G-11811)
Shoppers Weekly Inc ................................ F .... 618 533-7283
　Centralia (G-3433)
Sim Partners Inc ....................................... E .... 800 260-3380
　Chicago (G-6512)
Simon Global Services LLC ...................... G .... 773 334-7794
　Chicago (G-6513)
Simple Solutions ........................................ G .... 618 932-6177
　West Frankfort (G-21819)
Slaymaker Fine Art Ltd ............................. G .... 773 348-1450
　Chicago (G-6526)
Sony/Atv Music Publishing LLC ............... E .... 630 739-8129
　Bolingbrook (G-2374)
Spudnik Press Cooperative ..................... F .... 312 563-0302
　Chicago (G-6564)
St Johns United Church Christ ................ G .... 847 491-6686
　Evanston (G-10195)
▲ Sunrise Hitek Service Inc ..................... E .... 773 792-8880
　Chicago (G-6630)
T D C Inc .................................................. F .... 815 229-7064
　Rockford (G-18639)
T R Communications Inc ......................... F .... 773 238-3366
　Chicago (G-6663)
Techno - Grphics Trnsltons Inc ............... E .... 708 331-3433
　South Holland (G-20308)
Tele Guia Spanish TV Guide ................... E .... 708 656-9800
　Cicero (G-7235)
Tele-Guia Inc ............................................ F .... 708 656-9800
　Cicero (G-7236)
Thomas Publishing Printing Div ............... G .... 618 351-6655
　Carbondale (G-3025)

Tighe Publishing Services Inc ................. F .... 773 281-9100
　Chicago (G-6726)
Totalworks Inc .......................................... F .... 773 489-4313
　Chicago (G-6750)
Translucent Publishing Corp .................... F .... 312 447-5450
　Chicago (G-6762)
Trottie Publishing Group Inc .................... G .... 708 344-5975
　Westchester (G-21859)
Truequest Communications LLC ............. G .... 312 356-9900
　Chicago (G-6788)
TWT Marketing Inc .................................. G .... 773 274-4470
　Chicago (G-6799)
U S Free Press LLC ................................ G .... 217 847-3361
　Hamilton (G-11541)
United Press International Inc ................. G .... 847 864-9450
　Evanston (G-10104)
Van Meter Graphx Inc ............................. G .... 847 465-0600
　Wheeling (G-22177)
Varsity Publications Inc .......................... G .... 309 353-4570
　Pekin (G-17292)
Veritiv Operating Company .................... G .... 800 347-9279
　Des Plaines (G-8298)
Vision Integrated Graphics .................... C .... 708 570-7900
　Bolingbrook (G-2380)
Vondrak Publishing Co Inc ..................... E .... 773 476-4800
　Summit Argo (G-20768)
Vortex Media Group Inc ......................... G .... 630 717-9541
　Naperville (G-15778)
W-F Professional Assoc Inc .................. G .... 847 945-8050
　Deerfield (G-8067)
Wabash Publishing Co Inc .................... G .... 312 939-5900
　Chicago (G-6930)
Want ADS of Champaign Inc ................ G .... 217 356-4804
　Champaign (G-3558)
Wealth Partners Publishing Inc ............. F .... 312 854-2522
　Chicago (G-6946)
White Picket Media Inc .......................... F .... 773 769-8400
　Chicago (G-6973)
Wireless Express Inc Central ................ G .... 309 689-9933
　Peoria (G-17478)
Wolfsword Press ................................... G .... 773 403-1144
　Chicago (G-7021)
◆ Wolters Kluwer US Inc ....................... E .... 847 580-5000
　Riverwoods (G-18046)
Wonderlic Inc ........................................ D .... 847 680-4900
　Vernon Hills (G-21218)
Wordspace Press Limited .................... G .... 773 292-0292
　Chicago (G-7027)
▲ World Book Inc ................................ G .... 312 729-5800
　Chicago (G-7028)
World Library Publications .................. C .... 847 678-9300
　Franklin Park (G-10631)
▲ Zaptel Corporation .......................... G .... 847 386-8050
　Elk Grove Village (G-9824)

## 2752 Commercial Printing: Lithographic

11th Street Express Prtg Inc ................ F .... 815 968-0208
　Rockford (G-18235)
360 Digital Print Inc ............................. G .... 630 682-3601
　Carol Stream (G-3086)
A & B Printing Service Inc ................... G .... 217 789-9034
　Springfield (G-20383)
A & H Lithoprint Inc ............................. F .... 708 345-1196
　Broadview (G-2551)
A & J Printers Inc ................................ G .... 847 909-9609
　Elk Grove Village (G-9249)
A A Swift Print Inc ................................ G .... 847 301-1122
　Schaumburg (G-19418)
A and K Prtg & Graphic Design ........... G .... 618 244-3525
　Mount Vernon (G-3099)
A To Z Offset Prtg & Pubg Inc ............. G .... 847 966-3016
　Skokie (G-19943)
A+ Printing Co ..................................... G .... 815 968-8181
　Rockford (G-18242)
A-Reliable Printing .............................. G .... 630 790-2525
　Glen Ellyn (G-10956)
Abbotts Minute Printing Inc ................. G .... 708 339-6010
　South Holland (G-20239)
▼ ABS Graphics Inc ........................... G .... 630 495-2400
　Itasca (G-12223)
Accurate Business Controls Inc .......... G .... 815 633-5500
　Machesney Park (G-14051)
▲ Ace Graphics Inc ........................... E .... 630 357-2244
　Naperville (G-15589)
Acres of Sky Communications ........... G .... 815 493-2560
　Lanark (G-13149)
Active Graphics Inc ............................ E .... 708 656-8900
　Cicero (G-7176)
Ad Works Inc ...................................... G .... 217 342-9688
　Effingham (G-8821)

Adams Printing Co .............................. G .... 618 529-2396
　Carbondale (G-3000)
Adcraft Printers Inc ............................. F .... 815 932-6432
　Kankakee (G-12601)
Addvalue2print LLC ........................... G .... 847 551-1570
　East Dundee (G-8628)
Advance Instant Printing Co ............. G .... 312 346-0986
　Chicago (G-3760)
Advantage Printing Inc ..................... G .... 630 627-7468
　Lombard (G-13760)
Advocate ............................................ G .... 815 694-2122
　Clifton (G-7272)
◆ Ah Tensor International LLC ......... G .... 630 739-9600
　Woodridge (G-22450)
Aires Press Inc .................................. G .... 847 698-6813
　Park Ridge (G-17179)
Ajs Premier Printing Inc .................... G .... 847 838-6350
　Antioch (G-614)
All Printing & Graphics Inc ............... G .... 773 553-3049
　Chicago (G-3807)
All Printing & Graphics Inc ............... F .... 708 450-1512
　Broadview (G-2555)
All Purpose Prtg & Bus Forms .......... G .... 708 389-9192
　Alsip (G-431)
All-Ways Quick Print ......................... G .... 708 403-8422
　Orland Park (G-16841)
Allegra Network LLC ........................ G .... 815 877-3400
　Belvidere (G-1730)
Allegra Network LLC ........................ G .... 630 801-9335
　Aurora (G-1104)
Allegra Print & Imaging .................... G .... 630 963-9100
　Lisle (G-13554)
Allegra Print & Imaging .................... G .... 815 524-3902
　Romeoville (G-18794)
Allegra Print & Imaging Inc .............. G .... 847 697-1434
　Elgin (G-8942)
Alliance Creative Group Inc ............. E .... 847 885-1800
　Schaumburg (G-19431)
Alliance Graphics .............................. G .... 312 280-8000
　Chicago (G-3814)
Alliance Investment Corp ................. F .... 847 933-0400
　Skokie (G-19949)
▲ Allied Graphics Inc ...................... G .... 847 419-8833
　Buffalo Grove (G-2654)
Allprint Graphics Inc ......................... G .... 847 519-9898
　Schaumburg (G-19432)
Allstate Printing Inc .......................... G .... 847 640-4401
　Elk Grove Village (G-9288)
Alphadigital Inc ................................. G .... 708 482-4488
　La Grange Park (G-12752)
AlphaGraphics .................................. F .... 630 261-1227
　Oakbrook Terrace (G-16694)
AlphaGraphics Printshops .............. G .... 630 964-9600
　Lisle (G-13555)
Alta Vista Graphic Corporation ...... F .... 773 267-2530
　Chicago (G-3835)
Althea Crutex Inc ............................ G .... 630 595-7200
　Wood Dale (G-22337)
Alwan Printing Inc .......................... F .... 708 598-9600
　Bridgeview (G-2462)
Amboy News ................................... G .... 815 857-2311
　Amboy (G-597)
America Printing Inc ...................... G .... 847 229-8358
　Wheeling (G-22002)
American Inks and Coatings Co ... G .... 630 226-0994
　Romeoville (G-18795)
◆ American Labelmark Company .. C .... 773 478-0900
　Chicago (G-3859)
American Litho Incorporated ......... A .... 630 682-0600
　Carol Stream (G-3099)
▲ American Litho Incorporated ...... B .... 630 462-1700
　Carol Stream (G-3100)
American Quick Print Inc ............... G .... 847 253-2700
　Wauconda (G-21441)
American Reprographics Co LLC . D .... 847 647-1131
　Niles (G-15960)
American Slide-Chart Co ............... D .... 630 665-3333
　Carol Stream (G-3102)
American Speedy Printing Ctrs ..... E .... 847 806-0135
　Elk Grove Village (G-9298)
Amric Resources ............................ G .... 309 664-0391
　Bloomington (G-2144)
Anikam Inc ....................................... G .... 708 385-0200
　Alsip (G-433)
Apollo Printing Inc .......................... G .... 815 741-3065
　Homewood (G-12091)
Apple Graphics Inc ......................... G .... 630 389-2222
　Batavia (G-1416)
Apple Press Inc ............................... G .... 815 224-1451
　Peru (G-17500)

SIC SECTION
27 PRINTING, PUBLISHING, AND ALLIED INDUSTRIES

**Apple Printing Center** ............ G ....... 630 932-9494
Addison *(G-41)*
**Arby Graphic Service Inc** ............ F ....... 847 763-0900
Niles *(G-15961)*
**Arch Printing Inc** ............ G ....... 630 966-0235
Aurora *(G-1110)*
**Arla Graphics Inc** ............ G ....... 847 470-0005
Deerfield *(G-7978)*
**Art Newvo Incorporated** ............ G ....... 847 838-0304
Antioch *(G-619)*
**Art-Craft Printers** ............ G ....... 847 455-2201
Franklin Park *(G-10401)*
**Arthur Graphic Clarion** ............ G ....... 217 543-2151
Arthur *(G-881)*
**Arthur R Baker Inc** ............ G ....... 708 301-4828
Homer Glen *(G-12076)*
**Asa Inc** ............ E ....... 847 446-1856
Northfield *(G-16391)*
**Associated Printers Inc** ............ G ....... 847 548-8929
Antioch *(G-621)*
**▲ Athena Design Group Inc** ............ E ....... 312 733-2828
Chicago *(G-3974)*
**Atlantic Press Inc** ............ D ....... 708 496-2400
Chicago *(G-3977)*
**Augusta Label Corp** ............ G ....... 630 537-1961
Burr Ridge *(G-2823)*
**Aurora Fastprint Inc** ............ G ....... 630 896-5980
Aurora *(G-1116)*
**Austin Graphic** ............ G ....... 815 432-4983
Watseka *(G-21414)*
**Available Business Group Inc** ............ D ....... 773 247-4141
Chicago *(G-3995)*
**Avid of Illinois Inc** ............ F ....... 847 698-2775
Saint Charles *(G-19140)*
**Avsec Printing Inc** ............ G ....... 815 722-2961
Joliet *(G-12458)*
**Award/Visionps Inc** ............ G ....... 331 318-7800
Chicago *(G-4003)*
**Azusa Inc** ............ G ....... 618 244-6591
Mount Vernon *(G-15399)*
**B & B Printing Company** ............ G ....... 217 285-6072
Pittsfield *(G-17561)*
**B Allan Graphics Inc** ............ F ....... 708 396-1704
Alsip *(G-438)*
**B F Shaw Printing Company** ............ C ....... 815 625-3600
Sterling *(G-20584)*
**B F Shaw Printing Company** ............ E ....... 815 875-4461
Princeton *(G-17744)*
**B P I Printing & Duplicating** ............ F ....... 773 327-7300
Chicago *(G-4020)*
**B P I Printing & Duplicating** ............ E ....... 773 822-0111
Chicago *(G-4021)*
**Babak Inc** ............ G ....... 312 419-8686
Chicago *(G-4024)*
**Bach & Associates** ............ G ....... 618 277-1652
Belleville *(G-1610)*
**Bailleu & Bailleu Printing Inc** ............ G ....... 309 852-2517
Kewanee *(G-12670)*
**Bally Foil Graphics Inc** ............ G ....... 847 427-1509
Elk Grove Village *(G-9333)*
**Balsley Printing Inc** ............ F ....... 815 624-7515
Rockton *(G-18692)*
**Balsley Printing Inc** ............ G ....... 815 637-8787
Rockton *(G-18691)*
**Bardash & Bukowski Inc** ............ G ....... 312 829-2080
Chicago *(G-4041)*
**Barnaby Inc** ............ F ....... 815 895-6555
Sycamore *(G-20789)*
**Barrel Maker Printing** ............ G ....... 773 490-3065
Chicago *(G-4046)*
**Barrington Print & Copy Inc** ............ G ....... 847 382-1185
Barrington *(G-1273)*
**Basswood Associates Inc** ............ F ....... 312 240-9400
Chicago *(G-4053)*
**Bat Business Services Inc** ............ G ....... 630 801-9335
Aurora *(G-1118)*
**Batavia Instant Print** ............ G ....... 630 262-0370
West Chicago *(G-21668)*
**Beans Printing Inc** ............ G ....... 217 223-5555
Quincy *(G-17800)*
**Beardsley Printery Inc** ............ G ....... 309 788-4041
Rock Island *(G-18161)*
**Bell Litho Inc** ............ D ....... 847 952-3300
Elk Grove Village *(G-9338)*
**Bell Litho Inc** ............ G ....... 847 290-9300
Elk Grove Village *(G-9339)*
**Belmonte Printing Co** ............ G ....... 847 352-8841
Schaumburg *(G-19459)*
**Belrock Printing Inc** ............ G ....... 815 547-1096
Belvidere *(G-1735)*

**Benton Evening News Co** ............ G ....... 618 438-5611
Benton *(G-2022)*
**Benzinger Printing** ............ G ....... 815 784-6560
Genoa *(G-10875)*
**Berland Printing Inc** ............ E ....... 773 702-1999
Chicago *(G-4086)*
**Best Advertising Spc & Prtg** ............ G ....... 708 448-1110
Worth *(G-22633)*
**Bfc Forms Service Inc** ............ C ....... 630 879-9240
Batavia *(G-1422)*
**Bfc Print** ............ F ....... 630 879-9240
Batavia *(G-1423)*
**Bikast Graphics Inc** ............ G ....... 847 487-8822
Wauconda *(G-21446)*
**Biller Press & Manufacturing** ............ G ....... 847 395-4111
Antioch *(G-623)*
**Bitforms Inc** ............ G ....... 630 595-6800
Wood Dale *(G-22345)*
**Bloom-Norm Printing Inc** ............ G ....... 309 663-8545
Normal *(G-16065)*
**Bloomington Offset Process Inc** ............ D ....... 309 662-3395
Bloomington *(G-2149)*
**Blue Island Newspaper Prtg Inc** ............ D ....... 708 333-1006
Harvey *(G-11661)*
**Bmt Prnting Crtgraph Espclists** ............ G ....... 773 646-4700
Chicago *(G-4132)*
**Bond Brothers & Co** ............ F ....... 708 442-5510
Lyons *(G-14032)*
**Brads Printing Inc** ............ G ....... 847 662-0447
Waukegan *(G-21531)*
**Branstiter Printing Co** ............ G ....... 217 245-6533
Jacksonville *(G-12381)*
**Breaker Press Co Inc** ............ G ....... 773 927-1666
Chicago *(G-4159)*
**▼ Breese Publishing Co Inc** ............ G ....... 618 526-7211
Breese *(G-2440)*
**Brian Paul Inc** ............ E ....... 847 398-8677
Buffalo Grove *(G-2670)*
**Brilliant Color Corp** ............ G ....... 847 367-3300
Libertyville *(G-13310)*
**Brokers Print Mail Rsource Inc** ............ G ....... 708 532-9900
Tinley Park *(G-20900)*
**Bros Lithographing Company** ............ G ....... 312 666-0919
Chicago *(G-4176)*
**Budget Printing Center** ............ G ....... 618 655-1636
Edwardsville *(G-8793)*
**Bureau Valley Chief** ............ G ....... 815 646-4731
Tiskilwa *(G-20958)*
**Burstan Inc** ............ G ....... 847 787-0380
Elk Grove Village *(G-9349)*
**Business Card Systems Inc** ............ F ....... 815 877-0990
Machesney Park *(G-14061)*
**Business Cards Tomorrow** ............ F ....... 815 877-0990
Machesney Park *(G-14062)*
**Button Man Printing Inc** ............ G ....... 630 549-0438
Saint Charles *(G-19146)*
**C & L Printing Company** ............ F ....... 312 235-0380
Chicago *(G-4201)*
**C E Dienberg Printing Company** ............ G ....... 708 848-4406
Oak Park *(G-16655)*
**C F C Interantional** ............ G ....... 708 753-0679
Chicago Heights *(G-7085)*
**C M J Associates Inc** ............ G ....... 708 636-2995
Oak Lawn *(G-16608)*
**C2 Imaging LLC** ............ E ....... 847 439-7834
Elk Grove Village *(G-9353)*
**Cadore-Miller Printing Inc** ............ F ....... 708 430-7091
Hickory Hills *(G-11768)*
**Caldwell Letter Service Inc** ............ E ....... 773 847-0708
Chicago *(G-4214)*
**Cambrdg Printing Corp** ............ G ....... 630 510-2100
Carol Stream *(G-3123)*
**Camera Ready Copies Inc** ............ E ....... 847 215-8611
Prospect Heights *(G-17773)*
**Cameron Printing Inc** ............ G ....... 630 231-3301
West Chicago *(G-21677)*
**Campbell Publishing Inc** ............ G ....... 217 742-3313
Winchester *(G-22278)*
**Cannon Ball Marketing Inc** ............ G ....... 630 971-2127
Lisle *(G-13573)*
**Capital Prtg & Die Cutng Inc** ............ G ....... 630 896-5520
Aurora *(G-1124)*
**Capitol Impressions Inc** ............ E ....... 309 633-1400
Peoria *(G-17322)*
**Card Prsnlzation Solutions LLC** ............ E ....... 630 543-2630
Glendale Heights *(G-11014)*
**Cardinal Colorprint Prtg Corp** ............ E ....... 630 467-1000
Itasca *(G-12241)*
**Carey Color Inc** ............ G ....... 630 761-2605
West Chicago *(G-21678)*

**Carson Printing Inc** ............ G ....... 847 836-0900
East Dundee *(G-8629)*
**Carter Printing Co Inc** ............ G ....... 217 227-4464
Farmersville *(G-10183)*
**Case Paluch & Associates Inc** ............ G ....... 773 465-0098
Chicago *(G-4248)*
**Catalina Graphics Inc** ............ G ....... 773 973-7780
Chicago *(G-4255)*
**Cavco Printers** ............ G ....... 618 988-8011
Energy *(G-9985)*
**CCL Label (chicago) Inc** ............ E ....... 630 406-9991
Batavia *(G-1427)*
**▲ CDI Corp** ............ F ....... 773 205-2960
Chicago *(G-4264)*
**CDs Office Systems Inc** ............ F ....... 630 305-9034
Springfield *(G-20411)*
**Central Illinois Newspapers** ............ G ....... 217 935-3171
Clinton *(G-7279)*
**Central Printers & Graphics** ............ G ....... 773 586-3711
Bedford Park *(G-1543)*
**Century Printing** ............ G ....... 618 632-2486
O Fallon *(G-16465)*
**Cenveo Inc** ............ D ....... 636 240-5817
Chicago *(G-4278)*
**Cenveo Inc** ............ D ....... 773 539-0411
Chicago *(G-4280)*
**Cenveo Inc** ............ G ....... 217 243-4258
Jacksonville *(G-12383)*
**Challenge Printers** ............ G ....... 773 252-0212
Chicago *(G-4285)*
**Charles C Thomas Publisher** ............ F ....... 217 789-8980
Springfield *(G-20416)*
**Charles Chauncey Wells Inc** ............ G ....... 708 524-0695
Oak Park *(G-16657)*
**CHI-Town Printing Inc** ............ G ....... 773 577-2500
Chicago *(G-4299)*
**Chicago Envelope Inc** ............ E ....... 630 668-0400
Carol Stream *(G-3127)*
**Chicago Mltlingua Graphics Inc** ............ F ....... 847 386-7187
Northfield *(G-16397)*
**Chicago Press Corporation** ............ E ....... 773 276-1500
Chicago *(G-4342)*
**Chicago Sun-Times Features Inc** ............ A ....... 312 321-3000
Chicago *(G-4351)*
**Child Evngelism Fellowship Inc** ............ E ....... 630 983-7708
Naperville *(G-15628)*
**Christopher R Cline Prtg Ltd** ............ F ....... 847 981-0500
Elk Grove Village *(G-9372)*
**Christopher Wagner** ............ G ....... 630 205-9200
Oswego *(G-16907)*
**Chromatech Printing Inc** ............ F ....... 847 699-0333
Des Plaines *(G-8168)*
**Cifuentes Luis & Nicole Inc** ............ G ....... 847 490-3660
Schaumburg *(G-19472)*
**Cjs Printing** ............ G ....... 309 968-6585
Manito *(G-14172)*
**Classic Color Inc** ............ C ....... 708 484-0000
Broadview *(G-2568)*
**Classic Printery Inc** ............ G ....... 847 546-6555
Hainesville *(G-11522)*
**Classic Printing Co Inc** ............ G ....... 217 428-1733
Decatur *(G-7857)*
**Classic Prtg Thermography Inc** ............ G ....... 630 595-7765
Wood Dale *(G-22352)*
**Clear Print Inc** ............ G ....... 815 795-6225
Ottawa *(G-16954)*
**Clementi Printing Inc** ............ G ....... 773 622-0795
Chicago *(G-4401)*
**Cloverdale Corporation** ............ G ....... 847 296-9225
Des Plaines *(G-8171)*
**Clyde Printing Company** ............ F ....... 773 847-5900
Chicago *(G-4410)*
**Cmb Printing Inc** ............ F ....... 630 323-1110
Burr Ridge *(G-2830)*
**▼ Color Communications Inc** ............ C ....... 773 638-1400
Chicago *(G-4426)*
**Color Tone Printing** ............ G ....... 708 385-1442
Blue Island *(G-2242)*
**Colorwave Graphics LLC** ............ G ....... 815 397-4293
Loves Park *(G-13925)*
**Colvin Printing** ............ G ....... 708 331-4580
Blue Island *(G-2243)*
**Comet Conection Inc** ............ G ....... 312 243-5400
Alsip *(G-451)*
**Commercial Copy Printing Ctr** ............ F ....... 847 981-8590
Elk Grove Village *(G-9384)*
**Commercial Fast Print** ............ G ....... 815 673-1196
Streator *(G-20685)*
**Commercial Prtg of Rockford** ............ G ....... 815 965-4759
Rockford *(G-18317)*

S I C

27 PRINTING, PUBLISHING, AND ALLIED INDUSTRIES SIC SECTION

Communication Technologies Inc.........E....... 630 384-0900
Glendale Heights (G-11017)
Component Sales Incorporated.............F....... 630 543-9666
Addison (G-79)
Congress Printing Company .................F....... 312 733-6599
Chicago (G-4448)
Conrad Press Ltd....................................G.....
Columbia (G-7356)
Consolidated Carqueville Prtg...............C....... 630 246-6451
Streamwood (G-20649)
Consolidated Printing Co Inc.................F....... 773 631-2800
Chicago (G-4453)
Consulate General Lithuania .................G....... 312 397-0382
Chicago (G-4454)
▲ Continental Web Press Inc................C....... 630 773-1903
Itasca (G-12247)
Continental Web Press KY Inc...............C....... 630 773-1903
Itasca (G-12248)
▲ Continental Web Press KY Inc..........D....... 859 485-1500
Itasca (G-12249)
Cook JV Printing.....................................F....... 708 799-0007
Country Club Hills (G-7405)
Cook Printing Co Inc ..............................G....... 217 345-2514
Mattoon (G-14387)
Copy Express Inc....................................F....... 815 338-7161
Woodstock (G-22555)
Copy Mat Printing...................................G....... 309 452-1392
Bloomington (G-2155)
▲ Copy-Mor Inc.......................................E....... 312 666-4000
Elmhurst (G-9856)
▲ Copyco Printing Inc .............................E....... 847 824-4400
Des Plaines (G-8175)
Corporate Business Card Ltd.................E....... 847 455-5760
Franklin Park (G-10442)
Corporate Graphics America Inc...........F....... 773 481-2100
Chicago (G-4474)
Corporation Supply Co Inc .....................E....... 312 726-3375
Chicago (G-4476)
Corwin Printing .......................................G....... 618 263-3936
Mount Carmel (G-15263)
Coyle Print Group Inc.............................G....... 847 784-1080
Skokie (G-19987)
Cpr Printing Inc......................................F....... 630 377-8420
Geneva (G-10821)
Craftsmen Printing..................................G....... 217 283-9574
Hoopeston (G-12108)
Creasey Printing Services Inc ...............G....... 217 787-1055
Springfield (G-20425)
Creative Graphic Arts Inc.......................G....... 847 498-2678
Northbrook (G-16234)
Creative Lithocraft Inc............................F....... 847 352-7002
Schaumburg (G-19488)
Creative Lithocraft Inc............................G....... 847 352-7002
Schaumburg (G-19489)
Crossmark Printing Inc ...........................F....... 708 532-8263
Tinley Park (G-20906)
Crosswind Printing..................................G....... 847 356-1009
Lindenhurst (G-13546)
Custom Calendar Corp............................G....... 708 547-6191
Lombard (G-13786)
Custom Telephone Printing Inc..............F....... 815 338-0000
Woodstock (G-22557)
Cynlar Inc................................................G....... 630 820-2200
Aurora (G-992)
Cypress Multigraphics LLC ....................E....... 708 633-1166
Tinley Park (G-20907)
D & D Business Inc..................................G....... 630 935-3522
Willowbrook (G-22209)
D & D Printing Inc ...................................G....... 708 425-2080
Oak Lawn (G-16615)
D & R Press.............................................G....... 708 452-0500
Elmwood Park (G-9966)
D E Asbury Inc ........................................F....... 217 222-0617
Hamilton (G-11532)
D E Signs & Storage LLC........................G....... 618 939-8050
Waterloo (G-21401)
D G Brandt Inc.........................................G....... 815 942-4064
Morris (G-15105)
D L V Printing Service Inc ......................F....... 773 626-1661
Chicago (G-4537)
Dale K Brown...........................................G....... 815 338-0222
Woodstock (G-22558)
Dallas Corporation..................................F....... 630 322-8000
Downers Grove (G-8424)
Dandelion Distributors Inc .....................G....... 815 675-9800
Grayslake (G-11332)
Dans Printing & Off Sups Inc..................F....... 708 687-3055
Oak Forest (G-16577)
Dark Matter Printing................................G....... 217 791-4059
Decatur (G-7866)
Darnall Printing .......................................G....... 309 827-7212
Bloomington (G-2161)
David H Vander Ploeg.............................G....... 708 331-7700
South Holland (G-20260)
Dbp Communications..............................F....... 312 263-1569
Chicago (G-4565)
Dbp Communications Inc.......................G....... 312 263-1569
Chicago (G-4566)
DE Asbury Inc .........................................E....... 217 222-0617
Quincy (G-17820)
Deadline Prtg Clor Copying LLC ...........G....... 847 437-9000
Elk Grove Village (G-9419)
Dean Printing Systems............................G....... 847 526-9545
Island Lake (G-12214)
Debbie Harshman ....................................G....... 217 335-2112
Barry (G-1311)
Decatur Blue Print Company .................G....... 217 423-7589
Decatur (G-7869)
▲ Deluxe Johnson ...................................F....... 847 635-7200
Des Plaines (G-8182)
Deluxe Printing........................................G....... 312 225-0061
Chicago (G-4580)
Demis Printing Inc ..................................G....... 773 282-9128
Park Ridge (G-17189)
Denor Graphics Inc..................................F....... 847 364-1130
Elk Grove Village (G-9423)
Dependable Graphics & Services.........G....... 630 231-2746
West Chicago (G-21691)
Des Plaines Journal Inc...........................D....... 847 299-5511
Des Plaines (G-8184)
Des Plaines Printing LLC .......................F....... 847 465-3300
Buffalo Grove (G-2686)
Design Graphics Inc................................G....... 815 462-3323
New Lenox (G-15875)
Designation Inc .......................................F....... 847 367-9100
Mundelein (G-15494)
Di-Carr Printing Company......................G....... 708 863-0069
Cicero (G-7189)
Diamond Envelope Corporation ............D....... 630 499-2800
Aurora (G-995)
Diamond Graphics of Berwyn................G....... 708 749-2500
Berwyn (G-2060)
Diamond Web Printing LLC ...................F....... 630 663-0350
Downers Grove (G-8428)
Dicianni Graphics Incorporated ............F....... 630 833-5100
Addison (G-91)
Diversified Print Group...........................G....... 630 893-8920
Bloomingdale (G-2104)
Dixon Direct LLC.....................................C....... 815 284-2211
Dixon (G-8328)
Dla Document Services..........................F....... 618 256-4686
Scott Air Force Base (G-19885)
DMarv Design Specialty Prtrs................G....... 708 389-4420
Blue Island (G-2246)
Donnelley Financial LLC ........................F....... 312 326-8000
Chicago (G-4629)
Donnells Printing & Off Pdts..................G....... 815 842-6541
Pontiac (G-17698)
Dos Bro Corp...........................................G....... 773 334-1919
Chicago (G-4633)
DOT Sharper Printing Inc........................G....... 847 581-9033
Morton Grove (G-15194)
Double Image Press Inc .........................F....... 630 893-6777
Glendale Heights (G-11020)
Doubletake Marketing Inc .....................G....... 845 598-3175
Evanston (G-10029)
Douglas Press Inc...................................C....... 800 323-0705
Bellwood (G-1704)
Dps Digital Print Svc...............................G....... 847 836-7734
East Dundee (G-8632)
Drake Envelope Printing Co...................G....... 217 374-2772
White Hall (G-22184)
Dreamwrks Grphic Cmmnctons LLC ....D....... 847 679-6710
Glenview (G-11121)
Dsr Screenprinting..................................G....... 630 855-2790
Streamwood (G-20652)
Dun-Wel Lithograph Co Inc....................G....... 773 327-8811
Chicago (G-4650)
Duo Graphics ..........................................G....... 847 228-7080
Elk Grove Village (G-9436)
Dupli Group Inc ......................................F....... 773 549-5285
Chicago (G-4654)
Dyna-Tone Litho Inc...............................G....... 630 595-1073
Bensenville (G-1886)
E & D Web Inc..........................................C....... 815 562-5800
Rochelle (G-18086)
E & H Graphic Service ............................G....... 708 748-5656
Matteson (G-14371)
E A A Enterprises Inc..............................G....... 630 279-0150
Villa Park (G-21249)
Eagle Printing Company ........................G....... 309 762-0771
Moline (G-14936)
East Central Communications Co.........E....... 217 892-9613
Rantoul (G-17926)
East Moline Herald Print Inc ..................G....... 309 755-5224
East Moline (G-8678)
Eastrich Printing & Sales........................G....... 815 232-4216
Freeport (G-10654)
Ed Garvey and Company .......................E....... 847 647-1900
Niles (G-15976)
Edwardsville Publishing Co....................D....... 618 656-4700
Edwardsville (G-8799)
Einstein Crest..........................................G....... 847 965-7791
Niles (G-15977)
Elgin Instant Print ...................................G....... 847 931-9006
Elgin (G-9024)
Elise S Allen ...........................................G....... 309 673-2613
Peoria (G-17354)
Elliott Publishing Inc ..............................G....... 217 645-3033
Liberty (G-13295)
Elmhurst Enterprise Group Inc..............G....... 847 228-5945
Arlington Heights (G-749)
Emerald Printing & Promotions.............G....... 815 344-3303
McHenry (G-14502)
Ennis Inc..................................................E....... 815 875-2000
Princeton (G-17748)
Envelopes Only Inc.................................E....... 630 213-2500
Streamwood (G-20655)
◆ Essentra Packaging US Inc ...............G....... 704 418-8692
Westchester (G-21841)
Eugene Ewbank ......................................G....... 630 705-0400
Oswego (G-16917)
▲ Evanston Graphic Imaging Inc .........G....... 847 869-7446
Evanston (G-10033)
Ever-Redi Printing Inc ............................G....... 708 352-4378
Hinsdale (G-11945)
Evergreen Printing..................................G....... 708 499-0688
Evergreen Park (G-10115)
Excel Forms Inc ......................................G....... 630 801-1936
Aurora (G-1150)
Express Print Champaign LLC ..............G....... 217 693-7079
Urbana (G-21083)
Express Printing Ctr of Libert.................G....... 847 675-0659
Skokie (G-19998)
Express Prtg & Promotions Inc..............G....... 847 498-9640
Northbrook (G-16253)
Expri Publishing & Printing ...................G....... 773 274-5955
Chicago (G-4798)
F C L Graphics Inc..................................C....... 708 867-5500
Harwood Heights (G-11684)
F Weber Printing Co Inc .........................G....... 815 468-6152
Manteno (G-14183)
Faith Printing..........................................G....... 217 675-2191
Franklin (G-10379)
Falcon Press Inc .....................................G....... 815 455-9099
Crystal Lake (G-7575)
Far West Print Solutions LLC ................G....... 630 879-9500
North Aurora (G-16130)
Fast Print Shop .......................................G....... 618 997-1976
Marion (G-14259)
Fast Printing of Joliet Inc.......................G....... 815 723-0080
Joliet (G-12492)
Fastway Printing Inc...............................G....... 847 882-0950
Schaumburg (G-19524)
Faulstich Printing Company Inc.............G....... 217 442-4994
Danville (G-7718)
Fedex Corporation ..................................F....... 847 918-7730
Vernon Hills (G-21163)
Fedex Office & Print Svcs Inc................G....... 708 345-0984
Melrose Park (G-14637)
Fedex Office & Print Svcs Inc................G....... 312 492-8355
Chicago (G-4825)
Fedex Office & Print Svcs Inc................G....... 630 469-2677
Glen Ellyn (G-10970)
Fedex Office & Print Svcs Inc................G....... 773 472-3066
Chicago (G-4826)
Fedex Office & Print Svcs Inc................G....... 847 292-7176
Rosemont (G-19001)
Fedex Office & Print Svcs Inc................G....... 708 799-5323
Homewood (G-12098)
Fedex Office & Print Svcs Inc................F....... 312 341-9644
Chicago (G-4827)
Fedex Office & Print Svcs Inc................F....... 312 755-0325
Chicago (G-4828)
Fedex Office & Print Svcs Inc................F....... 312 595-0768
Chicago (G-4829)
Fedex Office & Print Svcs Inc................F....... 312 663-1149
Chicago (G-4830)
Fedex Office & Print Svcs Inc................F....... 630 894-1800
Bloomingdale (G-2108)

# 27 PRINTING, PUBLISHING, AND ALLIED INDUSTRIES

Fernwood Printers Ltd .................. G ...... 630 964-9449
  Oak Forest *(G-16581)*
▲ Fgs Inc ...................................... F ...... 312 421-3060
  Chicago *(G-4839)*
Fgs-IL LLC .................................... C ...... 630 375-8500
  Aurora *(G-1007)*
Fidelity Bindery Company ............. E ...... 708 343-6833
  Broadview *(G-2578)*
Fidelity Print Cmmncations LLC ... E ...... 708 343-6833
  Broadview *(G-2579)*
Financial and Professional Reg .... G ...... 217 782-2127
  Springfield *(G-20439)*
Fine Line Printing .......................... G ...... 773 582-9709
  Chicago *(G-4846)*
Fisher Printing Inc ......................... C ...... 708 598-1500
  Bridgeview *(G-2489)*
Fisher Printing Inc ......................... G ...... 708 598-9266
  Bridgeview *(G-2490)*
Fisheye Services Incorporated .... G ...... 773 942-6314
  Chicago *(G-4852)*
Five Star Printing Inc .................... G ...... 217 965-3355
  Virden *(G-21296)*
FL 1 ............................................... F ...... 847 956-9400
  Elk Grove Village *(G-9479)*
Flash Printing Inc .......................... G ...... 847 288-9101
  Franklin Park *(G-10470)*
Fleetwood Press Inc ..................... G ...... 708 485-6811
  Brookfield *(G-2632)*
Floden Enterprises ........................ G ...... 847 566-7898
  Mundelein *(G-15502)*
▲ Flow-Eze Company ................... F ...... 815 965-1062
  Rockford *(G-18383)*
Flyerinc Corporation ..................... G ...... 630 655-3400
  Oak Brook *(G-16515)*
FM Graphic Impressions Inc ......... E ...... 630 897-8788
  Aurora *(G-1153)*
Forcerl ........................................... G ...... 847 432-7588
  Highland Park *(G-11833)*
Forest Printing Co ......................... F ...... 708 366-5100
  Forest Park *(G-10247)*
Forms Design Plus Coleman Prtg ... G ...... 309 685-6000
  Peoria *(G-17365)*
Forms Specialist Inc ..................... G ...... 847 298-2868
  Lincolnshire *(G-13449)*
Forrest Press Inc .......................... G ...... 847 381-1621
  Barrington *(G-1280)*
Fort Dearborn Company ............... D ...... 847 357-2300
  Elk Grove Village *(G-9487)*
Fortman & Associates Ltd ........... G ...... 847 524-0741
  Elk Grove Village *(G-9488)*
Fox Valley Printing Co Inc ............ F ...... 419 232-3348
  Montgomery *(G-15043)*
Franz Stationery Company Inc .... G ...... 847 593-0060
  Lake Barrington *(G-12807)*
French Studio Ltd ......................... G ...... 618 942-5328
  Herrin *(G-11748)*
Frye-Williamson Press Inc ........... E ...... 217 522-7744
  Springfield *(G-20444)*
Full Court Press Inc ...................... G ...... 773 779-1135
  Chicago *(G-4894)*
Full Line Printing Inc .................... G ...... 312 642-8080
  Chicago *(G-4895)*
Fuse LLC ....................................... C ...... 708 449-8989
  Berkeley *(G-2045)*
G & G Studios /Broadway Prtg .... F ...... 815 933-8181
  Bradley *(G-2422)*
G F Printing .................................. G ...... 618 797-0576
  Granite City *(G-11278)*
G T Services of Illinois Inc .......... G ...... 309 925-5111
  Tremont *(G-20982)*
Gallas Label & Decal .................... F ...... 773 775-1000
  Chicago *(G-4909)*
Gallery Office Pdts & Prtrs ........... G ...... 708 798-2220
  Homewood *(G-12099)*
Gametime Screen Printing ........... G ...... 815 297-5263
  Freeport *(G-10660)*
Gamma Alpha Visual .................... G ...... 847 956-0633
  Elk Grove Village *(G-9496)*
Gammon Group Inc ...................... G ...... 815 722-6400
  Shorewood *(G-19927)*
Gannon Graphics ......................... G ...... 847 895-1043
  Schaumburg *(G-19535)*
Gatehouse Media LLC ................. G ...... 217 788-1300
  Springfield *(G-20445)*
Gatling Printing Inc ...................... G ...... 708 388-4746
  Blue Island *(G-2252)*
Gazette Printing Co ..................... G ...... 309 389-2811
  Glasford *(G-10951)*
Gemini Digital Inc ........................ G ...... 630 894-9430
  Roselle *(G-18942)*

Generation Copy Inc ..................... G ...... 847 866-0469
  Evanston *(G-10041)*
Genesis Press Inc ........................ G ...... 630 467-1000
  Itasca *(G-12268)*
Genoa Business Forms Inc .......... E ...... 815 895-2800
  Sycamore *(G-20798)*
George Press Inc .......................... G ...... 217 324-2242
  Litchfield *(G-13687)*
George Vaggelatos ....................... G ...... 847 361-3880
  Itasca *(G-12269)*
Gerard Printing Company ............. G ...... 847 437-6442
  Elk Grove Village *(G-9499)*
Gh Printing Co Inc ........................ E ...... 630 960-4115
  Downers Grove *(G-8449)*
Go Calendars ................................ G ...... 847 816-1563
  Vernon Hills *(G-21166)*
Goalgetters Inc ............................. F ...... 708 579-9800
  La Grange *(G-12733)*
Golden Prairie News ..................... G ...... 217 226-3721
  Assumption *(G-931)*
Goose Printing Co ........................ G ...... 847 673-1414
  Evanston *(G-10043)*
Gossett Printing Inc ..................... G ...... 618 548-2583
  Salem *(G-19335)*
Graf Ink Printing Inc ..................... G ...... 618 273-4231
  Harrisburg *(G-11601)*
Grand Forms & Systems Inc ........ G ...... 847 259-4600
  Arlington Heights *(G-760)*
Grand Printing & Graphics Inc ..... F ...... 312 218-6780
  Chicago *(G-4984)*
Grandcentral Enterprises Inc ....... G ...... 309 287-5362
  Bloomington *(G-2171)*
Granja & Sons Printing ................ F ...... 773 762-3840
  Chicago *(G-4987)*
Graphic Arts Studio Inc ................ E ...... 847 381-1105
  Barrington *(G-1282)*
Graphic Image Corporation .......... F ...... 312 829-7800
  Chicago *(G-4989)*
Graphic Packaging Corporation ... C ...... 847 451-7400
  Franklin Park *(G-10483)*
Graphic Partners ........................... E ...... 847 872-9445
  Zion *(G-22686)*
Graphic Promotions Inc ................ F ...... 815 726-3288
  Shorewood *(G-19928)*
Graphic Source Group Inc ........... G ...... 847 854-2670
  Lake In The Hills *(G-12995)*
Graphics & Technical Systems .... G ...... 708 974-3806
  Palos Hills *(G-17118)*
Graphics Group LLC ..................... D ...... 708 867-5500
  Chicago *(G-4992)*
Graphics Plus Inc ......................... F ...... 630 968-9073
  Lisle *(G-13597)*
Grasso Graphics Inc .................... G ...... 708 489-2060
  Alsip *(G-465)*
Gray Wolf Graphics Inc ................ F ...... 815 356-0895
  Crystal Lake *(G-7584)*
Great Impressions Inc .................. G ...... 847 367-6725
  Libertyville *(G-13327)*
Greek Art Printing & Pubg Co ...... G ...... 847 724-8860
  Glenview *(G-11133)*
Greenup Press Inc ........................ G ...... 217 923-3704
  Greenup *(G-11383)*
Griffith Solutions Inc .................... G ...... 847 384-1810
  Park Ridge *(G-17201)*
Grovak Instant Printing Co .......... G ...... 847 675-2414
  Mount Prospect *(G-15334)*
Grove Design & Advertising Inc .. G ...... 815 459-4552
  Crystal Lake *(G-7585)*
Grphic Richards Communications ... F ...... 708 547-6000
  Bellwood *(G-1707)*
H B H Print Co .............................. F ...... 847 662-2233
  Gurnee *(G-11456)*
H2o Ltd ......................................... G ...... 217 762-7441
  Monticello *(G-15077)*
Haapanen Brothers Inc ................ D ...... 847 662-2233
  Gurnee *(G-11457)*
Hafner Printing Co Inc ................. F ...... 312 362-0120
  Chicago *(G-5030)*
▲ Hako Minuteman Inc ................. G ...... 630 627-6900
  Addison *(G-140)*
Hal Mather & Sons Incorporated ... E ...... 815 338-4000
  Woodstock *(G-22573)*
Hammond Printing ........................ G ...... 847 724-1539
  Glenview *(G-11135)*
Hansen Printing Co Inc ................ E ...... 708 599-1500
  Bridgeview *(G-2496)*
Harlan Vance Company ............... F ...... 309 888-4804
  Normal *(G-16072)*
Harrison Martha Print Studio ...... G ...... 949 290-8630
  Crystal Lake *(G-7587)*

Harry Otto Printing Company ...... F ...... 630 365-6111
  Elburn *(G-8889)*
Havana Printing & Mailing ........... F ...... 309 543-2000
  Havana *(G-11695)*
Hawthorne Press ........................... G ...... 708 652-9000
  Cicero *(G-7201)*
Hawthorne Press Inc .................... G ...... 847 587-0582
  Spring Grove *(G-20336)*
Heart Printing Inc ......................... G ...... 847 259-2100
  Arlington Heights *(G-764)*
Heavenly Enterprises ................... G ...... 773 783-2981
  Hickory Hills *(G-11770)*
Hempel Group Inc ........................ G ...... 630 389-2222
  Batavia *(G-1454)*
Henderson Family ........................ G ...... 309 236-6783
  Aledo *(G-370)*
Henry Printing Inc ........................ G ...... 618 529-3040
  Carbondale *(G-3010)*
Heritage Press Inc ....................... G ...... 847 362-9699
  Libertyville *(G-13330)*
Heritage Printing .......................... G ...... 815 537-2372
  Prophetstown *(G-17770)*
Hermitage Group Inc ................... E ...... 773 561-3773
  Chicago *(G-5080)*
▲ Hertzberg Ernst & Sons ............ E ...... 773 525-3518
  Chicago *(G-5082)*
Higgins Quick Print ...................... G ...... 847 635-7700
  Des Plaines *(G-8204)*
Highland Printers .......................... G ...... 618 654-5880
  Highland *(G-11791)*
Hillsboro Journal Inc .................... E ...... 217 532-3933
  Hillsboro *(G-11895)*
◆ Holden Industries Inc ............... F ...... 847 940-1500
  Deerfield *(G-8013)*
Holland Printing Inc ..................... F ...... 708 596-9000
  South Holland *(G-20278)*
Horizon Graphics .......................... G ...... 309 699-4287
  East Peoria *(G-8712)*
House of Doolittle Ltd .................. G ...... 847 593-3417
  Arlington Heights *(G-769)*
House of Graphics ........................ G ...... 630 682-0810
  Carol Stream *(G-3168)*
Howard Press Printing Inc ........... G ...... 708 345-7437
  Northlake *(G-16439)*
Howard Sportswear Graphics ..... E ...... 847 695-8195
  Elgin *(G-9067)*
Hq Printers Inc ............................. G ...... 312 782-2020
  Chicago *(G-5125)*
Hts Hancock Transcriptions Svc ... E ...... 217 379-9241
  Paxton *(G-17237)*
Hub Printing Company Inc .......... F ...... 815 562-7057
  Rochelle *(G-18094)*
Hunt Enterprises Inc .................... G ...... 708 354-8464
  Countryside *(G-7433)*
Huston-Patterson Corporation .... D ...... 217 429-5161
  Decatur *(G-7890)*
Ideal Advertising & Printing ........ F ...... 815 965-1713
  Rockford *(G-18426)*
Illini Digital Printing Co ................ G ...... 618 271-6622
  East Saint Louis *(G-8756)*
Illinois Office Sup Elect Prtg ....... G ...... 815 434-0186
  Ottawa *(G-16962)*
Image Pact Printing ..................... E ...... 708 460-6070
  Tinley Park *(G-20923)*
Image Print Inc ............................. G ...... 815 672-1068
  Streator *(G-20691)*
Impact Prtrs & Lithographers ...... G ...... 847 981-9676
  Elk Grove Village *(G-9542)*
Impossible Objects LLC .............. G ...... 847 400-9582
  Northbrook *(G-16275)*
Impression Printing ...................... F ...... 708 614-8660
  Oak Forest *(G-16583)*
In Color Graphics Coml Prtg ....... F ...... 847 697-0003
  Elgin *(G-9075)*
In-Print Graphics Inc ................... E ...... 708 396-1010
  Oak Forest *(G-16584)*
Indigo Digital Printing LLC .......... G ...... 312 753-3025
  Chicago *(G-5175)*
Informative Systems Inc ............. F ...... 217 523-8422
  Springfield *(G-20457)*
Ink Enterprises Inc ...................... G ...... 815 547-5515
  Belvidere *(G-1764)*
Ink Spot Printing .......................... G ...... 773 528-0288
  Chicago *(G-5194)*
Ink Spot Silk Screen .................... G ...... 847 724-6234
  Glenview *(G-11147)*
Ink Spots Prtg & Meida Design ... G ...... 708 754-1300
  Homewood *(G-12102)*
Ink Well ......................................... G ...... 618 398-1427
  Fairview Heights *(G-10169)*

Employee Codes: A=Over 500 employees, B=251-500
C=101-250, D=51-100, E=20-50, F=10-19, G=3-9

2017 Harris Illinois
Industrial Directory

**Ink Well Printing**....G....815 224-1366
Peru *(G-17514)*
**Ink Well Printing & Design Ltd**....G....847 923-8060
Schaumburg *(G-19566)*
**Inkdot LLC**....G....630 768-6415
Chicago *(G-5195)*
**Inkpartners Corporation**....G....773 843-1786
Chicago *(G-5197)*
**Inky Printers**....G....815 235-3700
Freeport *(G-10668)*
▲ **Innerworkings Inc**....D....312 642-3700
Chicago *(G-5198)*
**Innova Print Fulfillment Inc**....G....630 845-3215
Geneva *(G-10837)*
**Innovtive Design Graphics Corp**....G....847 475-7772
Evanston *(G-10057)*
**Inoprints**....G....312 994-2351
Chicago *(G-5202)*
**Insty Prints Palatine Inc**....F....847 963-0000
Palatine *(G-17042)*
**Insty-Prints of Champaign Inc**....G....217 356-6166
Champaign *(G-3501)*
**Instyprints of Waukegan Inc**....G....847 336-5599
Waukegan *(G-21571)*
**Integra Graphics and Forms Inc**....F....708 385-0950
Crestwood *(G-7490)*
**Integrated Print Graphics Inc**....D....847 695-6777
South Elgin *(G-20206)*
**Integrated Print Graphics Inc**....C....847 888-2880
South Elgin *(G-20207)*
**Integrity Prtg McHy Svcs LLC**....G....847 834-9484
Hoffman Estates *(G-12019)*
**Intel Printing Inc**....G....708 343-1144
Broadview *(G-2587)*
**International Graphics & Assoc**....F....630 584-2248
Saint Charles *(G-19199)*
**Intersports Screen Printing**....G....773 489-7383
Chicago *(G-5226)*
**Irving Press Inc**....E....847 595-6650
Elk Grove Village *(G-9555)*
**J & J Mr Quick Print Inc**....G....773 767-7776
Chicago *(G-5251)*
**J and K Printing**....G....708 229-9558
Oak Lawn *(G-16627)*
**J D Graphic Co Inc**....E....847 364-4000
Elk Grove Village *(G-9557)*
**J F Wagner Printing Co**....G....847 564-0017
Northbrook *(G-16280)*
**J Gooch & Associates Inc**....G....217 522-7575
Springfield *(G-20461)*
▲ **J J Collins Sons Inc**....E....630 960-2525
Woodridge *(G-22499)*
**J J Collins Sons Inc**....D....217 345-7606
Charleston *(G-3601)*
**J K Printing & Mailing Inc**....G....847 432-7717
Highland Park *(G-11846)*
**J M Printers Inc**....F....815 727-1579
Crest Hill *(G-7459)*
**J Oshana & Son Printing**....G....773 283-8311
Chicago *(G-5261)*
**J S Printing Inc**....G....847 678-6300
Franklin Park *(G-10503)*
**Jade Screen Printing**....G....618 463-2325
Alton *(G-579)*
**Jamali Kopy Kat Printing Inc**....G....708 544-6164
Bellwood *(G-1711)*
**James Ray Monroe Corporation**....F....618 532-4575
Centralia *(G-3420)*
▲ **James W Smith Printing Company**....E....847 244-6486
Gurnee *(G-11461)*
**Jamether Incorporated**....G....815 444-9971
Crystal Lake *(G-7593)*
**Jans Graphics Inc**....F....312 644-4700
Chicago *(G-5278)*
**Janssen Avenue Boys Inc**....G....630 627-0202
North Aurora *(G-16136)*
**Jarr Printing Co**....F....815 363-5435
McHenry *(G-14515)*
**Jay Printing**....G....847 934-6103
Palatine *(G-17046)*
**Jds Printing Inc**....G....630 208-1195
Glendale Heights *(G-11037)*
**Jjm Printing Inc**....G....815 499-3067
Sterling *(G-20595)*
▲ **JL Clark LLC**....C....815 961-5609
Rockford *(G-18447)*
**Joes Printing**....G....773 545-6063
Chicago *(G-5309)*
**Jofas Print Corporation**....G....815 534-5725
Frankfort *(G-10337)*

▲ **John S Swift Company Inc**....E....847 465-3300
Buffalo Grove *(G-2713)*
**Johns-Byrne Company**....D....847 583-3100
Niles *(G-15992)*
**Johnsbyrne Graphic Tech Corp**....G....847 583-3100
Niles *(G-15993)*
**Johnson Press America Inc**....E....815 844-5161
Pontiac *(G-17704)*
**Johnson Printing**....G....630 595-8815
Bensenville *(G-1930)*
**Johnsons Screen Printing**....G....630 262-8210
Geneva *(G-10843)*
**Josco Inc**....G....708 867-7189
Chicago *(G-5326)*
**Josephs Printing Service**....G....847 724-4429
Glenview *(G-11154)*
**Jost & Kiefer Printing Company**....E....217 222-5145
Quincy *(G-17842)*
**Jph Enterprises Inc**....G....847 390-0900
Des Plaines *(G-8217)*
**Jsn Printing Inc**....G....815 582-4014
Joliet *(G-12525)*
**Jsolo Corp**....G....847 964-9188
Deerfield *(G-8023)*
**July 25th Corporation**....F....309 664-6444
Bloomington *(G-2186)*
**Juskie Printing Corp**....G....630 663-8833
Downers Grove *(G-8468)*
**K & J Phillips Corporation**....G....630 355-0660
Naperville *(G-15682)*
**K & M Printing Company Inc**....D....847 884-1100
Schaumburg *(G-19595)*
**K Chae Corp**....F....847 763-0077
Lincolnwood *(G-13518)*
**K R O Enterprises Ltd**....G....309 797-2213
Moline *(G-14949)*
**KB Publishing Inc**....D....708 331-6352
South Holland *(G-20282)*
**KB Publishing Inc**....E....708 331-6352
South Holland *(G-20283)*
**Kellogg Printing Co**....F....309 734-8388
Monmouth *(G-15016)*
**Kelly Printing Co Inc**....E....217 443-1792
Danville *(G-7741)*
**Kelvyn Press Inc**....D....708 343-0448
Broadview *(G-2591)*
**Kelvyn Press Inc**....E....630 585-8160
Aurora *(G-1040)*
**Kendall Printing Co**....G....630 553-9200
Yorkville *(G-22663)*
**Keneal Industries Inc**....F....815 886-1300
Romeoville *(G-18834)*
**Kenilworth Press Incorporated**....G....847 256-5210
Wilmette *(G-22256)*
**Kens Quick Print Inc**....F....847 831-4410
Highland Park *(G-11849)*
**Kevin Kewney**....G....217 228-7444
Quincy *(G-17844)*
**Key Printing**....G....815 933-1800
Kankakee *(G-12635)*
**Keystone Printing & Publishing**....G....815 678-2591
Richmond *(G-17965)*
**Keystone Printing Services**....G....773 622-7210
Chicago *(G-5380)*
**Kingery Printing Company**....C....217 347-5151
Effingham *(G-8842)*
**Kingsbury Enterprises Inc**....G....708 535-7590
Oak Forest *(G-16586)*
**Kjellberg Printing**....F....630 653-2244
Wheaton *(G-21960)*
**KK Stevens Publishing Co**....E....309 329-2151
Astoria *(G-934)*
**Klein Printing Inc**....G....773 235-2121
Chicago *(G-5387)*
**Klh Printing Corp**....G....847 459-0115
Wheeling *(G-22086)*
**Knight Prtg & Litho Svc Ltd**....G....847 487-7700
Island Lake *(G-12217)*
**Kon Printing Inc**....G....630 879-2211
Batavia *(G-1461)*
**Kram Digital Solutions Inc**....G....312 222-0431
Glenview *(G-11164)*
**Krueger International Inc**....F....312 467-6850
Chicago *(G-5413)*
**Kwik Print Inc**....G....630 773-3225
Itasca *(G-12299)*
**L & S Label Printing Inc**....G....815 964-6753
Cherry Valley *(G-3646)*
**L P M Inc**....G....847 866-9777
Evanston *(G-10062)*

**Labels Unlimited Incorporated**....E....773 523-7500
Chicago *(G-5430)*
**LAC Enterprises Inc**....G....815 455-5044
Crystal Lake *(G-7601)*
**Lake Media Services Inc**....G....312 739-0423
Chicago *(G-5439)*
**Lake Shore Printing**....G....847 679-4110
Skokie *(G-20024)*
**Lakes Reg Prtg & Graphics LLC**....G....847 838-5838
Antioch *(G-639)*
▼ **Lakeside Lithography LLC**....E....312 243-3001
Chicago *(G-5445)*
**Lans Printing Inc**....G....708 895-6226
Lynwood *(G-14021)*
**Lazare Printing Co Inc**....G....773 871-2500
Chicago *(G-5475)*
**Lebolt Print Service Inc**....G....847 681-1210
Highwood *(G-11886)*
**Lee Enterprises Incorporated**....C....618 529-5454
Carbondale *(G-3014)*
**Lee-Wel Printing Corporation**....G....630 682-0935
Wheaton *(G-21966)*
**Legend Promotions**....G....847 438-3528
Lake Zurich *(G-13095)*
**Legislative Printing**....G....217 782-7312
Springfield *(G-20469)*
**Leonard A Unes Printing Co**....G....309 674-4942
Peoria *(G-17400)*
**Leonard Emerson**....G....217 628-3441
Divernon *(G-8316)*
**Leonard Publishing Co**....F....773 486-2737
Norridge *(G-16104)*
**Liberty Lithographers Inc**....C....708 633-7450
Tinley Park *(G-20931)*
**Lincoln Printers Inc**....G....217 732-3121
Lincoln *(G-13413)*
**Lincolnshire Printing Inc**....G....815 578-0740
McHenry *(G-14523)*
**Lind-Remsen Printing Co Inc**....F....815 969-0610
Rockford *(G-18470)*
**Link-Letters Ltd**....F....847 459-1199
Wheeling *(G-22094)*
**Lists & Letters**....F....847 520-5207
Wheeling *(G-22095)*
**Lith Liqure**....G....847 458-5180
Lake In The Hills *(G-12998)*
**Litho Type LLC**....E....708 895-3720
Lansing *(G-13173)*
**Lithographic Industries Inc**....E....773 921-7955
Broadview *(G-2594)*
**Lithoprint Inc**....G....630 964-9200
Westmont *(G-21900)*
**Lithotype Company Inc**....F....630 771-1920
Bolingbrook *(G-2336)*
**Lithuanian Catholic Press**....E....773 585-9500
Chicago *(G-5519)*
**Little Doloras**....G....708 331-1330
South Holland *(G-20286)*
**Little Village Printing Inc**....G....708 749-4414
Berwyn *(G-2067)*
**Lloyd Midwest Graphics**....G....815 282-8828
Machesney Park *(G-14089)*
▲ **Lsk Import**....G....847 342-8447
Chicago *(G-5554)*
▲ **Luke Graphics Inc**....F....773 775-6733
Chicago *(G-5559)*
**Lure Group LLC**....G....630 222-6515
Bolingbrook *(G-2338)*
**Lutheran General Printing Svcs**....G....847 298-8040
Mount Prospect *(G-15344)*
**Luxon Printing Inc**....F....630 293-7710
West Chicago *(G-21734)*
**Lynns Printing Co**....G....618 465-7701
Alton *(G-583)*
**M & R Printing Inc**....G....847 398-2500
Rolling Meadows *(G-18742)*
**M C F Printing Company**....G....630 279-0301
Elmhurst *(G-9904)*
**M L S Printing Co Inc**....G....847 948-8902
Deerfield *(G-8033)*
**M M Marketing**....G....815 459-7968
Crystal Lake *(G-7603)*
**M O W Printing Inc**....F....618 345-5525
Collinsville *(G-7331)*
**M S A Printing Co**....G....847 593-5699
Elk Grove Village *(G-9604)*
**M Wells Printing Co**....G....312 455-0400
Chicago *(G-5588)*
**M13 Inc**....E....847 310-1913
Schaumburg *(G-19629)*

**Mac Graphics Group Inc** ........ G ....... 630 620-7200
Oakbrook Terrace *(G-16716)*

**Macoupin County Enquirer Inc** ........ E ....... 217 854-2534
Carlinville *(G-3042)*

◆ **Madden Communications Inc** ........ C ....... 630 787-2200
Wood Dale *(G-22394)*

**Madden Communications Inc** ........ E ....... 630 784-4325
Bloomingdale *(G-2114)*

**Mag Tag** ........ G ....... 847 647-6255
Niles *(G-15999)*

**Makkah Printing** ........ G ....... 630 980-2315
Glendale Heights *(G-11045)*

**Mall Graphic Inc** ........ F ....... 847 668-7600
Huntley *(G-12161)*

**Mallof Abruzino Nash Mktg Inc** ........ E ....... 630 929-5200
Carol Stream *(G-3188)*

**Mar Graphics** ........ D ....... 618 935-2111
Valmeyer *(G-21112)*

**Marc Business Forms Inc** ........ F ....... 847 568-9200
Lincolnwood *(G-13524)*

**Marcus Press** ........ G ....... 630 351-1857
Bloomingdale *(G-2115)*

**Marjo Graphics Inc** ........ G ....... 847 367-1305
Libertyville *(G-13346)*

**Mark Twain Press Inc** ........ G ....... 847 255-2700
Mundelein *(G-15523)*

**Marking Specialists/Poly** ........ F ....... 847 793-8100
Buffalo Grove *(G-2731)*

**Marnic Inc** ........ G ....... 309 343-1418
Galesburg *(G-10766)*

**Marquardt Printing Company** ........ E ....... 630 887-8500
Willowbrook *(G-22220)*

**Martinez Printing LLC** ........ G ....... 773 732-8108
Chicago *(G-5633)*

**Marty Gannon** ........ E ....... 847 895-1059
Schaumburg *(G-19632)*

**Mason City Banner Times** ........ F ....... 217 482-3276
Mason City *(G-14365)*

**Master Graphics LLC** ........ D ....... 815 562-5800
Rochelle *(G-18098)*

**Mattoon Printing Center** ........ G ....... 217 234-3100
Mattoon *(G-14400)*

**Maximum Prtg & Graphics Inc** ........ F ....... 630 737-0270
Downers Grove *(G-8484)*

**Mc Adams Multigraphics Inc** ........ G ....... 630 990-1707
Oak Brook *(G-16539)*

**McDonough Democrat Inc** ........ F ....... 309 772-2129
Bushnell *(G-2905)*

**McGrath Press Inc** ........ E ....... 815 356-5246
Crystal Lake *(G-7607)*

**McIntyre & Associates** ........ G ....... 847 639-8050
Fox Lake *(G-10278)*

**Media Unlimited Inc** ........ G ....... 630 527-0900
Naperville *(G-15816)*

**Medical Records Co** ........ G ....... 847 662-6373
Waukegan *(G-21588)*

**Mencarini Enterprises Inc** ........ F ....... 815 398-9565
Rockford *(G-18491)*

**Menus To Go** ........ G ....... 630 483-0848
Streamwood *(G-20666)*

▲ **Merrill Fine Arts Engrv Inc** ........ D ....... 312 786-6300
Chicago *(G-5697)*

**Merritt & Edwards Corporation** ........ F ....... 309 828-4741
Bloomington *(G-2196)*

**Metro Printing & Pubg Inc** ........ F ....... 618 476-9587
Millstadt *(G-14829)*

**Metropolitan Graphic Arts Inc** ........ E ....... 847 566-9502
Gurnee *(G-11471)*

**Metropolitan Printers** ........ G ....... 309 694-1114
East Peoria *(G-8724)*

**Meyercord Revenue Inc** ........ E ....... 630 682-6200
Carol Stream *(G-3194)*

**Mgsolutions Inc** ........ G ....... 630 530-2005
Elmhurst *(G-9912)*

**Mi-Te Fast Printers Inc** ........ G ....... 312 236-3278
Glencoe *(G-11002)*

**Mi-Te Fast Printers Inc** ........ E ....... 312 236-8352
Chicago *(G-5718)*

**Mich Enterprises Inc** ........ F ....... 630 616-9000
Wood Dale *(G-22399)*

**Michael Burza** ........ G ....... 815 909-0233
Cortland *(G-7393)*

**Michael Zimmerman** ........ G ....... 847 272-5560
Northbrook *(G-16311)*

**Microdynamics Corporation** ........ C ....... 630 276-0527
Naperville *(G-15697)*

**Microprint Inc** ........ G ....... 630 969-1710
Romeoville *(G-18846)*

**Mid Central Printing & Mailing** ........ F ....... 847 251-4040
Wilmette *(G-22262)*

**Mid City Printing Service** ........ G ....... 773 777-5400
Chicago *(G-5725)*

**Mid-Central Business Forms** ........ G ....... 309 692-9090
Peoria *(G-17406)*

**MidAmerican Prtg Systems Inc** ........ E ....... 312 663-4720
Chicago *(G-5732)*

**Midwest Graphic Industries** ........ F ....... 630 509-2972
Bensenville *(G-1952)*

**Midwest Law Printing Co Inc** ........ G ....... 312 431-0185
Chicago *(G-5745)*

**Midwest Outdoors Ltd** ........ E ....... 630 887-7722
Burr Ridge *(G-2867)*

**Midwest Sign & Lighting Inc** ........ G ....... 708 365-5555
Country Club Hills *(G-7410)*

▲ **Midwest Suburban Publishing** ........ A ....... 708 633-6880
Tinley Park *(G-20933)*

**Minute Man Press** ........ G ....... 847 839-9600
Hoffman Estates *(G-12023)*

**Minute Men Inc** ........ E ....... 630 692-1583
Aurora *(G-1191)*

**Minuteman Press** ........ G ....... 708 524-4940
Oak Park *(G-16675)*

**Minuteman Press** ........ G ....... 708 598-4915
Hickory Hills *(G-11773)*

**Minuteman Press** ........ G ....... 630 541-9122
Countryside *(G-7437)*

**Minuteman Press** ........ G ....... 630 584-7383
Saint Charles *(G-19223)*

**Minuteman Press** ........ G ....... 630 279-0438
Lombard *(G-13827)*

**Minuteman Press Inc** ........ G ....... 847 577-2411
Arlington Heights *(G-803)*

**Minuteman Press Intl Inc** ........ G ....... 630 574-0090
Oak Brook *(G-16545)*

**Minuteman Press Morton Grove** ........ G ....... 847 470-0212
Morton Grove *(G-15221)*

**Minuteman Press of Countryside** ........ G ....... 708 354-2190
Countryside *(G-7438)*

**Minuteman Press of Lansing** ........ G ....... 708 895-0505
Lansing *(G-13177)*

**Minuteman Press of Rockford** ........ G ....... 815 633-2992
Loves Park *(G-13967)*

**Minuteman Press of Waukegan** ........ G ....... 847 244-6288
Gurnee *(G-11474)*

**Miracle Press Company** ........ F ....... 773 722-6176
Chicago *(G-5770)*

**Mission of Our Lady of Mercy** ........ G ....... 312 738-7568
Chicago *(G-5771)*

**Mission Press Inc** ........ G ....... 312 455-9501
Chicago *(G-5772)*

**MJM Graphics** ........ G ....... 847 234-1802
Lake Forest *(G-12927)*

**Mmpcu Limited** ........ G ....... 217 355-0500
Champaign *(G-3516)*

**Modern Printing of Quincy** ........ F ....... 217 223-1063
Quincy *(G-17861)*

**Modern Trade Communications** ........ F ....... 847 674-2200
Skokie *(G-20041)*

**Moline Dispatch Publishing Co** ........ G ....... 309 764-4344
Moline *(G-14959)*

**Moran Graphics Inc** ........ E ....... 312 226-3900
Chicago *(G-5803)*

▲ **Morton Suggestion Company LLC** .. G ....... 847 255-4770
Mount Prospect *(G-15351)*

**Motr Grafx LLC** ........ G ....... 847 600-5656
Niles *(G-16009)*

**MPE Business Forms Inc** ........ E ....... 815 748-3676
Dekalb *(G-8106)*

▲ **MPS Chicago Inc** ........ C ....... 630 932-9000
Downers Grove *(G-8492)*

**Msf Graphics Inc** ........ G ....... 847 446-6900
Des Plaines *(G-8239)*

**Mt Carmel Register Co Inc** ........ E ....... 618 262-5144
Mount Carmel *(G-15276)*

**Multi Art Press** ........ G ....... 773 775-0515
Chicago *(G-5831)*

**Multicopy Corp** ........ G ....... 847 446-7015
Northfield *(G-16410)*

**N Bujarski Inc** ........ G ....... 847 884-1600
Schaumburg *(G-19660)*

**N P D Inc** ........ G ....... 708 424-6788
Oak Lawn *(G-16636)*

**Naco Printing Co Inc** ........ G ....... 618 664-0423
Greenville *(G-11400)*

**Nature House Inc** ........ D ....... 217 833-2393
Griggsville *(G-11413)*

**Nedras Printing Inc** ........ G ....... 618 846-3853
Shobonier *(G-19922)*

**Need To Know Inc** ........ G ....... 309 691-3877
Peoria *(G-17415)*

**Negs & Litho Inc** ........ G ....... 847 647-7770
Chicago *(G-5881)*

**Network Printing Inc** ........ G ....... 847 566-4146
Mundelein *(G-15537)*

**New City Communications** ........ E ....... 312 243-8786
Chicago *(G-5891)*

**New Life Printing & Publishing** ........ G ....... 847 658-4111
Algonquin *(G-402)*

**New Vision Print & Marketing** ........ G ....... 630 406-0509
Naperville *(G-15713)*

**Newell & Haney Inc** ........ F ....... 618 277-3660
Belleville *(G-1660)*

**Newsweb Corporation** ........ E ....... 773 975-5727
Chicago *(G-5904)*

▲ **Nissha Usa Inc** ........ E ....... 847 413-2665
Schaumburg *(G-19666)*

**Nite Owl Prints LLC** ........ G ....... 630 541-6273
Downers Grove *(G-8496)*

**North County News Inc** ........ G ....... 618 282-3803
Red Bud *(G-17945)*

**North Shore Printers Inc** ........ F ....... 847 623-0037
Waukegan *(G-21593)*

**Northstar Group Inc** ........ F ....... 847 726-0880
Lake Zurich *(G-13110)*

**Northwest Premier Printing** ........ G ....... 773 736-1882
Chicago *(G-5940)*

**Northwest Printing Inc** ........ G ....... 815 943-7977
Harvard *(G-11642)*

▲ **Nosco Inc** ........ B ....... 847 336-4200
Waukegan *(G-21595)*

**Nosco Inc** ........ D ....... 847 336-4200
Gurnee *(G-11476)*

**Nova Printing and Litho Co** ........ F ....... 773 486-8500
Mount Prospect *(G-15355)*

**Novak Business Forms Inc** ........ E ....... 630 932-9850
Lombard *(G-13834)*

**Npn360** ........ E ....... 847 215-7300
Wheeling *(G-22109)*

**Nu-Art Printing** ........ G ....... 618 533-9971
Centralia *(G-3425)*

**Off The Press** ........ G ....... 815 436-9612
Plainfield *(G-17634)*

**Office Assistants Inc** ........ G ....... 708 346-0505
Oak Lawn *(G-16637)*

**Officers Printing Inc** ........ G ....... 847 480-4663
Northbrook *(G-16323)*

**Ogden Minuteman Inc** ........ G ....... 773 542-6917
Chicago *(G-5972)*

**Ogden Offset Printers Inc** ........ G ....... 773 284-7797
Chicago *(G-5973)*

**Olde Print Shoppe Inc** ........ G ....... 618 395-3833
Olney *(G-16786)*

**Om Printing Corporation** ........ G ....... 708 482-4750
Alsip *(G-503)*

▲ **Omega Printing Inc** ........ E ....... 630 595-6344
Bensenville *(G-1958)*

**Omega Royal Graphics Inc** ........ F ....... 847 952-8000
Elk Grove Village *(G-9665)*

**On Time Printing and Finishing** ........ G ....... 708 544-4500
Hillside *(G-11929)*

**Oneims Printing LLC** ........ G ....... 773 297-2050
Skokie *(G-20050)*

▲ **Only For One Printers** ........ F ....... 847 947-4119
Wheeling *(G-22114)*

**Original Smith Printing Inc** ........ D ....... 309 663-0325
Bloomington *(G-2207)*

**Orion Star Corp** ........ F ....... 847 776-2300
Palatine *(G-17061)*

**Orora Visual TX LLC** ........ B ....... 847 647-1900
Niles *(G-16014)*

**Osbon Lithographers** ........ G ....... 847 825-7727
Park Ridge *(G-17214)*

**Ottawa Publishing Co Inc** ........ C ....... 815 433-2000
Ottawa *(G-16975)*

**Overt Press Inc** ........ E ....... 773 284-0909
Chicago *(G-6029)*

▼ **P & P Press Inc** ........ E ....... 309 691-8511
Peoria *(G-17420)*

**P & S Cochran Printers Inc** ........ E ....... 309 691-6668
Peoria *(G-17421)*

**P F Pettibone & Co** ........ G ....... 815 344-7811
Crystal Lake *(G-7624)*

**P H C Enterprises Inc** ........ G ....... 847 816-7373
Vernon Hills *(G-21186)*

**P P Graphics Inc** ........ G ....... 708 343-2530
Westchester *(G-21852)*

**Paap Printing** ........ G ....... 217 345-6878
Charleston *(G-3607)*

**Pace Print Plus** ........ G ....... 847 381-1720
Barrington *(G-1296)*

SIC

Employee Codes: A=Over 500 employees, B=251-500
C=101-250, D=51-100, E=20-50, F=10-19, G=3-9

2017 Harris Illinois
Industrial Directory

969

Palmer Printing Inc ....E.... 312 427-7150
Chicago (G-6065)
Palwaukee Printing Company ....G.... 847 459-0240
Wheeling (G-22117)
Pamco Printed Tape Label Inc ....C.... 847 803-2200
Des Plaines (G-8249)
Pana News Inc ....F.... 217 562-2111
Pana (G-17137)
Panda Graphics Inc ....G.... 312 666-7642
Chicago (G-6068)
Pantagraph Printing and Sty Co ....F.... 309 829-1071
Bloomington (G-2208)
▲ Pap-R Products Company ....D.... 775 828-4141
Martinsville (G-14339)
Papiros Graphics ....G.... 773 581-3000
Chicago (G-6072)
Papyrus Press Inc ....F.... 773 342-0700
Chicago (G-6074)
Paragon Print & Mail Prod Inc ....G.... 630 671-2222
Bloomingdale (G-2125)
▲ Park Printing Inc ....G.... 708 430-4878
Palos Hills (G-17120)
Parkway Printers ....G.... 217 525-2485
Springfield (G-20499)
Parrot Press ....G.... 773 376-6333
Chicago (G-6087)
Patrick Impressions LLC ....G.... 630 257-9336
Lemont (G-13250)
Patton Printing and Graphics ....G.... 217 347-0220
Effingham (G-8852)
Paul D Burton ....G.... 309 467-2613
Eureka (G-10000)
Paulson Press Inc ....E.... 847 290-0080
Elk Grove Village (G-9671)
Peacock Printing Inc ....G.... 618 242-3157
Mount Vernon (G-15437)
Pebblefork Partners Inc ....D.... 708 449-8989
Berkeley (G-2047)
▲ Perfect Plastic Printing Corp ....C.... 630 584-1600
Saint Charles (G-19234)
Performance Mailing & Prtg Inc ....G.... 847 549-0500
Libertyville (G-13366)
Perma Graphics Printers ....G.... 815 485-6955
New Lenox (G-15901)
Perryco Inc ....F.... 815 436-2431
Plainfield (G-17638)
Petersburg Observer Co Inc ....G.... 217 632-2236
Petersburg (G-17537)
Peterson Publication Services ....G.... 630 469-6732
Glen Ellyn (G-10987)
Phoenix Business Solutions LLC ....E.... 708 388-1330
Alsip (G-508)
Phoenix Press Inc ....G.... 630 833-2281
Villa Park (G-21277)
Photo Graphic Design Service ....G.... 815 672-4417
Streator (G-20700)
▼ Physicians Record Co Inc ....D.... 800 323-9268
Berwyn (G-2074)
Pinney Printing Company ....G.... 815 626-2727
Sterling (G-20603)
Pinney Printing Company ....E.... 815 626-2727
Sterling (G-20604)
Pioneer Printing Service Inc ....G.... 312 337-4283
Chicago (G-6127)
PIP Printing ....G.... 847 998-6330
Glenview (G-11182)
PIP Printing Inc ....G.... 815 464-0075
Frankfort (G-10349)
Plum Grove Printers Inc ....E.... 847 882-4020
Hoffman Estates (G-12039)
Poets Study Inc ....G.... 773 286-1355
Chicago (G-6147)
Poll Enterprises Inc ....F.... 708 756-1120
Chicago Heights (G-7117)
Polpress Inc ....G.... 773 792-1200
Chicago (G-6152)
Power Graphics & Print Inc ....G.... 847 568-1808
Skokie (G-20057)
Prairieland Printing ....G.... 309 647-5425
Washington (G-21387)
Precision Dialogue Direct Inc ....D.... 773 237-2264
Chicago (G-6168)
Precision Printing Inc ....G.... 630 737-0075
Lombard (G-13844)
Precision Reproductions Inc ....F.... 847 724-0182
Glenview (G-11184)
Preferred Press Inc ....G.... 630 980-9799
Glendale Heights (G-11059)
Preferred Printing & Graphics ....G.... 708 547-6880
Berkeley (G-2049)
Preferred Printing Service ....G.... 312 421-2343
Chicago (G-6175)
▲ Press America Inc ....E.... 847 228-0333
Elk Grove Village (G-9696)
Press Proof Printing ....G.... 847 466-7156
Carpentersville (G-3298)
Press Tech Inc ....F.... 847 824-4485
Des Plaines (G-8263)
Pride In Graphics Inc ....F.... 312 427-2000
Chicago (G-6184)
Prime Printing Inc ....G.... 847 299-9960
Des Plaines (G-8264)
Print & Design Services LLC ....G.... 847 317-9001
Bannockburn (G-1264)
Print & Mailing Solutions LLC ....G.... 708 544-9400
Romeoville (G-18861)
Print and Mktg Solutions Group ....E.... 847 498-9640
Northbrook (G-16344)
Print Butler Inc ....F.... 312 296-2804
Grayslake (G-11359)
Print King Inc ....F.... 708 499-3777
Oak Lawn (G-16641)
Print Rite Inc ....G.... 773 625-0792
Chicago (G-6189)
Print Service & Dist Assn Psda ....G.... 312 321-5120
Chicago (G-6190)
Print Shop ....G.... 815 786-8278
Sandwich (G-19375)
Print Source For Business Inc ....G.... 847 356-0190
Lake Villa (G-13023)
Print Turnaround Inc ....F.... 847 228-1762
Arlington Heights (G-822)
Print Xpress ....G.... 847 677-5555
Skokie (G-20061)
Printech of Illinois Inc ....G.... 815 356-1195
Crystal Lake (G-7631)
Printed Impressions Inc ....G.... 773 604-8585
Villa Park (G-21279)
Printed Word Inc ....G.... 847 328-1511
Evanston (G-10091)
Printers Ink of Paris Inc ....G.... 217 463-2552
Paris (G-17158)
Printers Mark ....G.... 309 732-1174
Rock Island (G-18193)
Printers Quill Inc ....G.... 708 429-3636
Mokena (G-14897)
Printers Row LLC ....G.... 312 435-0411
Chicago (G-6192)
Printers Row Loft ....G.... 312 431-1019
Chicago (G-6193)
Printers Square Condo Assn ....G.... 312 765-8794
Chicago (G-6194)
Printing Arts Cmmnications LLC ....E.... 708 938-1600
Broadview (G-2604)
Printing By Joseph ....G.... 708 479-2669
Mokena (G-14898)
Printing Craftsmen of Joliet ....G.... 815 254-3982
Joliet (G-12555)
Printing Craftsmen of Pontiac ....G.... 815 844-7118
Pontiac (G-17709)
Printing Dimensions ....G.... 847 439-7521
Arlington Heights (G-823)
Printing Etc Inc ....G.... 815 562-6151
Rochelle (G-18102)
Printing Impression Direc ....G.... 815 385-6688
Lakemoor (G-13147)
Printing On Ashland Inc ....G.... 773 488-4707
Chicago (G-6196)
Printing Plant ....G.... 618 529-3115
Carbondale (G-3019)
Printing Plus ....G.... 708 301-3900
Lockport (G-13739)
Printing Plus of Roselle Inc ....G.... 630 893-0410
Roselle (G-18963)
Printing Press of Joliet Inc ....G.... 815 725-0018
Joliet (G-12556)
Printing Source Inc ....G.... 773 588-2930
Morton Grove (G-15228)
Printing Store Inc ....F.... 708 383-3638
Oak Park (G-16681)
Printing Works Inc ....G.... 847 860-1920
Elk Grove Village (G-9698)
Printmeisters Inc ....G.... 708 474-8400
Lansing (G-13180)
Printsmart Printing & Graphics ....G.... 630 434-2000
Woodridge (G-22510)
Printsource Plus Inc ....G.... 708 389-6252
Blue Island (G-2265)
Priority Print ....G.... 708 485-7080
Brookfield (G-2641)
Priority Printing ....G.... 773 889-6021
Chicago (G-6198)
Prism Commercial Printing Ctrs ....G.... 630 834-4443
Chicago (G-6199)
Prism Commercial Printing Ctrs ....G.... 773 229-2620
Chicago (G-6200)
Prism Commercial Printing Ctrs ....G.... 773 735-5400
Chicago (G-6201)
Prism Commercial Printing Ctrs ....G.... 630 834-4443
Addison (G-257)
Pro Graphics Ink ....G.... 309 647-2526
Canton (G-2992)
Pro-Type Printing Inc ....G.... 217 379-4715
Paxton (G-17244)
Production Press Inc ....E.... 217 243-3353
Jacksonville (G-12409)
Professional Printers ....G.... 630 739-7761
Bolingbrook (G-2361)
Professnal Mling Prtg Svcs Inc ....F.... 630 510-1000
Carol Stream (G-3222)
Proform ....G.... 309 676-2535
Peoria (G-17437)
Proforma Awards Print & Promot ....G.... 630 897-9848
Montgomery (G-15065)
Proforma Quality Business Svcs ....G.... 847 356-1959
Gurnee (G-11492)
Progress Printing Corporation ....E.... 773 927-0123
Chicago (G-6210)
Progressive Systems Netwrk Inc ....G.... 312 382-8383
Chicago (G-6214)
Progrssive Imprssions Intl Inc ....C.... 309 664-0444
Bloomington (G-2216)
▼ Promoframes LLC ....G.... 866 566-7224
Schaumburg (G-19701)
Provena Enterprises Inc ....E.... 708 478-3230
Kankakee (G-12643)
Qaprintscom ....G.... 312 404-2130
Chicago (G-6236)
Qg LLC ....B.... 217 347-7721
Effingham (G-8854)
◆ Qst Industries Inc ....E.... 312 930-9400
Chicago (G-6237)
Quad City Press ....F.... 309 764-8142
Moline (G-14965)
Quad/Graphics Inc ....A.... 815 734-4121
Mount Morris (G-15297)
Quad/Graphics Inc ....A.... 630 343-4400
Bolingbrook (G-2362)
Quality Blue & Offset Printing ....G.... 630 759-8035
Bolingbrook (G-2363)
Quality Quickprint Inc ....F.... 815 439-3430
Joliet (G-12560)
Quality Quickprint Inc ....G.... 815 723-0941
Lemont (G-13258)
Quality Quickprint Inc ....F.... 815 838-1784
Lockport (G-13740)
Quantum Color Graphics LLC ....C.... 847 967-3600
Morton Grove (G-15231)
Quebecor Wrld Mt Morris II LLC ....F.... 815 734-4121
Mount Morris (G-15298)
Quick Print Shoppe ....G.... 309 694-1204
East Peoria (G-8729)
Quickprinters ....G.... 309 833-5250
Macomb (G-14130)
Quik Impressions Group Inc ....E.... 630 495-7845
Addison (G-265)
Quincy Media Inc ....C.... 217 223-5100
Quincy (G-17879)
Quinn Print Inc ....G.... 847 823-9100
Park Ridge (G-17218)
▲ R & R Creative Graphics Inc ....G.... 630 208-4724
Geneva (G-10861)
R & S Screen Printing Inc ....G.... 815 337-3935
Woodstock (G-22604)
R N R Photographers Inc ....G.... 708 453-1868
River Grove (G-18013)
R R Donnelley & Sons Company ....A.... 815 584-2770
Dwight (G-8591)
R R Donnelley & Sons Company ....A.... 815 844-5181
Pontiac (G-17710)
R R Donnelley & Sons Company ....B.... 312 326-8000
Chicago (G-6270)
R T P Inc ....G.... 312 664-6150
Chicago (G-6274)
R W Wilson Printing Company ....G.... 630 584-4100
Saint Charles (G-19249)
Rainbow Manufacturing Inc ....E.... 847 824-9600
Mundelein (G-15551)
Rapid Circular Press Inc ....F.... 312 421-5611
Chicago (G-6290)

# 27 PRINTING, PUBLISHING, AND ALLIED INDUSTRIES

Rapid Copy & Duplicating Co ............ G ... 312 733-3353
 Elmwood Park (G-9974)
Rapid Print ......................................... G ... 309 673-0826
 Peoria (G-17440)
Rasmussen Press Inc ........................ G
 Bensenville (G-1976)
Ready Press ..................................... ... 847 358-8655
 Palatine (G-17066)
Redline Press .................................... ... 630 690-9828
 Lisle (G-13650)
Register-Mail .................................... C ... 309 343-7181
 Galesburg (G-10773)
Reign Print Solutions Inc .................. ... 847 590-7091
 Arlington Heights (G-830)
Reliable Mail Services Inc ................ F ... 847 677-6245
 Skokie (G-20073)
Remke Printing Inc ........................... ... 847 520-7300
 Wheeling (G-22137)
Repro-Graphics Inc .......................... D ... 847 439-1775
 Elk Grove Village (G-9714)
Review Graphics Inc ........................ ... 815 623-2570
 Roscoe (G-18913)
Review Printing Co Inc .................... G ... 309 788-7094
 Rock Island (G-18199)
▲ Ribbon Print Company .................. G ... 847 421-8208
 Highland Park (G-11865)
Richardson & Edwards Inc .............. E ... 630 543-1818
 Oak Brook (G-16559)
Rick Styfer ........................................ G ... 630 734-3244
 Burr Ridge (G-2877)
Rider Dickerson Inc ......................... D ... 312 427-2926
 Bellwood (G-1718)
Rieger Printing Inc ........................... ... 773 229-2095
 Bedford Park (G-1578)
Rightsource Digital Svcs Inc ........... F ... 888 774-2201
 Chicago (G-6357)
Rightway Printing Inc ...................... F ... 630 790-0444
 Glendale Heights (G-11064)
River Bend Printing .......................... ... 217 324-6056
 Litchfield (G-13696)
Rivershore Press ............................. ... 847 516-8105
 Cary (G-3368)
Riverside Graphics Corporation ...... G ... 312 372-3766
 Chicago (G-6363)
Riverview Printing Inc ..................... ... 815 987-1425
 Rockford (G-18558)
Ro-Web Inc ....................................... ... 309 688-2155
 Peoria (G-17444)
Rockford Newspapers Inc ............... B ... 815 987-1200
 Rockford (G-18580)
Rodin Enterprises Inc ...................... ... 847 412-1370
 Wheeling (G-22142)
Rohrer Graphic Arts Inc .................. F ... 630 832-3434
 Elmhurst (G-9930)
Rohrer Litho Inc ............................... G ... 630 833-6610
 Elmhurst (G-9931)
Romel Press Inc ............................... G ... 708 343-6090
 Melrose Park (G-14687)
Rose Business Forms & Printing .... G ... 618 533-3032
 Centralia (G-6405)
Rosette Printing LLC ....................... G ... 630 295-8500
 Bloomingdale (G-2131)
Roskuszka & Sons Inc .................... F ... 630 851-3400
 Aurora (G-1210)
RR Donnelley & Sons Company ..... C ... 217 935-2113
 Clinton (G-7288)
RR Donnelley & Sons Company ..... D ... 630 762-7600
 Saint Charles (G-19256)
RR Donnelley & Sons Company ..... E ... 312 332-4345
 Chicago (G-6402)
RR Donnelley Printing Co LP ........... A ... 217 235-0561
 Mattoon (G-14408)
▲ RR Donnelley Printing Co LP ....... G ... 312 326-8000
 Chicago (G-6405)
Rrr Graphics & Film Corp ................ G ... 708 478-4573
 Mokena (G-14901)
Rt Associates Inc ............................. D ... 847 577-0700
 Wheeling (G-22143)
Rudin Printing Company Inc ........... F ... 217 528-5111
 Springfield (G-20515)
Rush Printing On Oak ...................... ... 815 344-8880
 McHenry (G-14553)
Rusty & Angela Buzzard ................. G ... 217 342-9841
 Effingham (G-8857)
Rutledge Printing Co ....................... F ... 708 479-8282
 Orland Park (G-16889)
S G C M Corp .................................... G ... 630 953-2428
 Oakbrook Terrace (G-16720)
S G S Inc ........................................... G ... 708 544-6061
 Downers Grove (G-8517)

▲ S M C Graphics ............................. G ... 708 754-8973
 Chicago Heights (G-7125)
Safeguard 201 Corp ......................... G ... 630 241-0370
 Westmont (G-21918)
Saints Volo & Olha Uk Cath Par ...... ... 312 829-5209
 Chicago (G-6430)
Salem Times-Commoner Pubg Co ... E ... 618 548-3330
 Salem (G-19349)
Sales Midwest Prtg & Packg Inc ..... G ... 309 764-5544
 Moline (G-14968)
Salsedo Press Inc ............................ F ... 773 533-9900
 Chicago (G-6435)
Saltzman Printers Inc ...................... E ... 708 344-4500
 Melrose Park (G-14690)
Samecwei Inc ................................... G ... 630 897-7888
 Aurora (G-1214)
Save On Printing Inc ....................... G ... 847 922-7855
 Elk Grove Village (G-9729)
Savino Enterprises ........................... G ... 708 385-5277
 Blue Island (G-2268)
Scarzone Printing Services ............. ... 630 595-2690
 Wood Dale (G-22419)
Scheiwes Print Shop ........................ G ... 815 683-2398
 Crescent City (G-7456)
Schiele Graphics Inc ........................ D ... 847 434-5455
 Elk Grove Village (G-9731)
Schneider Graphics Inc ................... G ... 847 550-4310
 Lake Zurich (G-13126)
Schommer Inc .................................. G ... 815 344-1404
 McHenry (G-14554)
Schwartzkopf Printing Inc ............... F ... 618 463-0747
 Alton (G-589)
Screen Graphics .............................. G ... 309 699-8513
 Pekin (G-17288)
Screen Machine Incorporated ......... G ... 847 439-2233
 Elk Grove Village (G-9732)
Screen Print Plus Inc ....................... G ... 630 236-0260
 Naperville (G-15825)
Segerdahl Corp ................................ C ... 847 541-1080
 Wheeling (G-22146)
Segerdahl Corp ................................ D ... 847 850-8811
 Wheeling (G-22147)
▲ Segerdahl Graphics Inc ................ B ... 847 541-1080
 Wheeling (G-22148)
Selnar Inc ......................................... G ... 309 699-3977
 East Peoria (G-8733)
Semper FI Printing LLC ................... G ... 847 640-7737
 Arlington Heights (G-838)
Service Packaging Design Inc ........ G ... 847 966-6592
 Morton Grove (G-15236)
Service Printing Corporation .......... G ... 847 669-9620
 Huntley (G-12176)
Shanin Company .............................. D ... 847 676-1200
 Lincolnwood (G-13537)
Sharp Graphics Inc .......................... G ... 847 966-7000
 Skokie (G-20085)
Shawver Press Inc ........................... G ... 815 772-4700
 Morrison (G-15148)
Sheer Graphics Inc .......................... G ... 630 654-4422
 Westmont (G-21920)
Sheet Wise Printing ......................... ... 815 664-3025
 Spring Valley (G-20381)
Shoppers Guide ............................... G ... 815 369-4112
 Lena (G-13284)
Shoreline Graphics Inc .................... ... 847 587-4804
 Ingleside (G-12198)
▼ Shree Mahavir Inc ....................... G ... 312 408-1080
 Chicago (G-6501)
Shree Printing Corp ......................... G ... 773 267-9500
 Chicago (G-6502)
Sigley Printing & Off Sup Co ........... G ... 618 997-5304
 Marion (G-14287)
Sigma Graphics Inc ......................... F ... 815 433-1000
 Ottawa (G-16984)
Signcraft Screenprint Inc ................ C ... 815 777-3030
 Galena (G-10731)
Signs In Dundee Inc ........................ G ... 847 742-9530
 Elgin (G-9179)
Signs Today Inc ............................... G ... 847 934-9777
 Palatine (G-17074)
Silk 21 Screen Printing and Em ...... ... 630 972-4250
 Bolingbrook (G-2370)
Simple Solutions .............................. G ... 618 932-6917
 West Frankfort (G-21819)
Sir Speedy Printing ......................... G ... 312 337-0774
 Chicago (G-6518)
Sir Speedy Printing Cntr 6129 ........ G ... 708 349-7789
 Orland Park (G-16891)
Sir Speedy Printing Ctr 6080 .......... G ... 708 351-8841
 Schaumburg (G-19728)

Six Color Print LLC .......................... F ... 847 336-3287
 Waukegan (G-21618)
Sleepeck Printing Company ........... C ... 708 544-8900
 Chicago (G-6529)
Small Newspaper Group .................. C ... 815 937-3300
 Kankakee (G-12652)
Smart Office Services Inc ............... ... 773 227-1121
 Chicago (G-6532)
Snegde Deep .................................... G ... 630 351-7111
 Roselle (G-18978)
Snow Printing LLC ........................... ... 618 233-0712
 Belleville (G-1676)
Solid Impressions Inc ..................... G ... 630 543-7300
 Carol Stream (G-3241)
Solution 3 Graphics Inc .................. ... 773 233-3600
 Chicago (G-6542)
Solution Printing Inc ....................... G ... 217 529-9700
 Springfield (G-20528)
Sommers & Fahrenbach Inc ........... F ... 773 478-3033
 Chicago (G-6543)
Sons Enterprises ............................. F ... 847 677-4444
 Skokie (G-20088)
Southern Illinois University ............. F ... 618 453-2268
 Carbondale (G-3024)
Southwest Printing Co .................... G ... 708 389-0800
 Alsip (G-530)
Specialty Printing Midwest ............. G ... 618 799-8472
 Roxana (G-19086)
▲ Specialty Promotions Inc ............. B ... 847 588-2580
 Niles (G-16036)
Spectrum Graphic Services Inc ...... E ... 630 766-7673
 Elmhurst (G-9941)
Speed Ink Printing .......................... G ... 773 539-9700
 Chicago (G-6556)
Speedpro North Shore ..................... ... 847 983-0095
 Skokie (G-20089)
Speedys Quick Print ........................ G ... 217 431-0510
 Danville (G-7766)
Spell It With Color Inc ..................... G ... 630 961-5617
 Naperville (G-15753)
Sphere Inc ........................................ G ... 847 566-4800
 Mundelein (G-15560)
Springfield Printing Inc ................... ... 217 787-3500
 Springfield (G-20531)
Sprinter Coml Print Label Corp ...... G ... 630 460-3492
 Naperville (G-15828)
Stark Printing Company .................. ... 847 234-8430
 Round Lake (G-19068)
State Attorney Appellate ................. ... 217 782-3397
 Springfield (G-20536)
Stecker Graphics Inc ....................... ... 309 786-4973
 Rock Island (G-18204)
Steiner Impressions Inc .................. ... 815 633-4135
 Loves Park (G-13994)
Stellato Printing Inc ......................... ... 815 725-1057
 Crest Hill (G-7468)
Steve Bortman ................................. G ... 708 442-1669
 Lyons (G-14046)
Steve O Inc ....................................... ... 847 473-4466
 North Chicago (G-16187)
Stevens Group LLC ......................... E ... 331 209-2100
 Elmhurst (G-9945)
Stix Envelope & Mfg Co .................. ... 217 589-5122
 Roodhouse (G-18886)
Strathmore Company ...................... ... 630 232-9677
 Geneva (G-10870)
▲ Stromberg Allen and Company .... F ... 773 847-7131
 Tinley Park (G-20947)
Suburban Press Inc ......................... E ... 847 255-2240
 Arlington Heights (G-847)
Suncraft Technologies Inc .............. C ... 630 369-7900
 Naperville (G-15757)
Sung Ji USA ..................................... ... 847 956-9400
 Elk Grove Village (G-9760)
▲ Sunrise Hitek Service Inc ............. E ... 773 792-8880
 Chicago (G-6630)
Sunrise Printing Inc ........................ F ... 847 928-1800
 Schiller Park (G-19877)
Superior Business Solutions .......... G ... 815 787-1333
 Dekalb (G-8123)
Superior Print Services Inc ............. G ... 630 257-7012
 Lemont (G-13264)
Swift Impressions Inc ..................... G ... 312 263-3800
 Chicago (G-6650)
Swifty Print ...................................... ... 630 584-9063
 Saint Charles (G-19276)
T & C Graphics Inc .......................... E ... 630 532-5050
 South Elgin (G-20227)
T C W F Inc ...................................... E ... 630 369-1360
 Naperville (G-15759)

Employee Codes: A=Over 500 employees, B=251-500
C=101-250, D=51-100, E=20-50, F=10-19, G=3-9

**T F N W Inc** ... G ... 630 584-7383
Saint Charles *(G-19277)*
**T K O Quality Offset Printing** ... G ... 847 709-0455
Arlington Heights *(G-850)*
**Tampico Press** ... G ... 312 243-5448
Chicago *(G-6672)*
**Tarco Printing Inc** ... G ... 630 467-1000
Itasca *(G-12364)*
**Taykit Inc** ... E ... 847 888-1150
Elgin *(G-9202)*
**Team Cncept Prtg Thrmgrphy Inc** ... E ... 630 653-8326
Carol Stream *(G-3252)*
**Techprint Inc** ... F ... 847 616-0109
Elk Grove Village *(G-9774)*
**Tele Print** ... G ... 630 941-7877
Elmhurst *(G-9949)*
**Temper Enterprises Inc** ... G ... 815 553-0374
Crest Hill *(G-7469)*
**Tempo Holdings Inc** ... E ... 630 462-8200
Carol Stream *(G-3254)*
**Thermo-Craft Inc** ... G ... 618 281-7055
Columbia *(G-7363)*
**Thiessen Communications Inc** ... E ... 847 884-0980
Schaumburg *(G-19761)*
**Thomas Printing & Sty Co** ... G ... 618 435-2801
Benton *(G-2041)*
**Thompson & Walsh LLC** ... G ... 847 734-1770
Arlington Heights *(G-855)*
**Three Angels Printing Svcs Inc** ... F ... 630 333-4305
Addison *(G-313)*
**Three Castle Press Inc** ... G ... 630 540-0120
Streamwood *(G-20676)*
**Three-Z Printing Co** ... B ... 217 857-3153
Teutopolis *(G-20857)*
**Thrift n Swift** ... G ... 847 455-1350
Franklin Park *(G-10606)*
**Tidd Printing Co** ... G ... 708 749-1200
Berwyn *(G-2076)*
**Times Record Company** ... E ... 309 582-5112
Aledo *(G-373)*
**Times Republic** ... E ... 815 432-5227
Watseka *(G-21431)*
**Timothy Helgoth** ... G ... 217 224-8008
Quincy *(G-17894)*
**Tlm Enterprises Inc** ... G ... 815 284-5040
Dixon *(G-8356)*
**Toledo Democrat** ... G ... 217 849-2000
Toledo *(G-20967)*
**Topweb LLC** ... E ... 773 975-0400
Chicago *(G-6746)*
**Tora Print Svcs** ... G ... 773 252-1000
Chicago *(G-6747)*
**Total Graphics Services Inc** ... G ... 847 675-0800
Skokie *(G-20101)*
**Tower Printing & Design** ... G ... 630 495-1976
Lombard *(G-13870)*
**Trafficcom** ... G ... 773 997-8351
Chicago *(G-6755)*
**Tree Towns Reprographics Inc** ... E ... 630 832-0209
Elmhurst *(G-9951)*
**Trenton Sun** ... G ... 618 224-9422
Trenton *(G-20998)*
**Treudt Corporation** ... G ... 630 293-0500
West Chicago *(G-21785)*
**Tri-Tower Printing Inc** ... G ... 847 640-6633
Rolling Meadows *(G-18785)*
**Triangle Printers Inc** ... E ... 847 675-3700
Skokie *(G-20103)*
**Trump Printing Inc** ... F ... 217 429-9001
Decatur *(G-7954)*
**Trymark Print Production LLC** ... G ... 630 668-7800
Glendale Heights *(G-11086)*
**Turner Jct Prtg & Litho Svc** ... G ... 630 293-1377
West Chicago *(G-21786)*
▲ **Tvp Color Graphics Inc** ... G ... 630 837-3600
Streamwood *(G-20679)*
**Two JS Copies Now Inc** ... G ... 847 292-2679
Chicago *(G-6797)*
**Tylka Printing Inc** ... G ... 773 767-3775
Chicago *(G-6801)*
**Type Concepts Inc** ... G ... 708 361-1005
Palos Heights *(G-17112)*
**Unique Prtrs Lithographers Inc** ... D ... 708 656-8900
Cicero *(G-7240)*
**Unique/Active LLC** ... E ... 708 656-8900
Cicero *(G-7241)*
**United Graphics Indiana Inc** ... F ... 217 235-7161
Mattoon *(G-14413)*
**United Letter Service Inc** ... F ... 312 408-2404
Bensenville *(G-2009)*
**United Lithograph Inc** ... G ... 847 803-1700
Des Plaines *(G-8290)*
**United Press Inc (del)** ... F ... 847 482-0597
Lincolnshire *(G-13487)*
**University of Illinois** ... E ... 217 333-9350
Champaign *(G-3552)*
**University Printing Co Inc** ... G ... 773 525-2400
Chicago *(G-6839)*
**Up North Printing Inc** ... G ... 630 584-8675
Saint Charles *(G-19290)*
**Urban Imaging Group Inc** ... G ... 773 961-7500
Chicago *(G-6847)*
**V C P Inc** ... E ... 847 658-5090
Algonquin *(G-409)*
**Valee Inc** ... G ... 847 364-6464
Elk Grove Village *(G-9804)*
**Valid Usa Inc** ... G ... 630 852-8200
Lisle *(G-13675)*
**Van Lancker Steven** ... G ... 309 764-2221
Moline *(G-14975)*
**Van Meter Graphx Inc** ... G ... 847 465-0600
Wheeling *(G-22177)*
**Venus Printing Inc** ... G ... 847 985-7510
Schaumburg *(G-19785)*
**Vigil Printing Inc** ... G ... 773 794-8808
Chicago *(G-6898)*
**Viking Printing & Copying Inc** ... G ... 312 341-0985
Chicago *(G-6899)*
**Village Press Inc** ... G ... 847 362-1856
Libertyville *(G-13399)*
**Vis-O-Graphic Inc** ... E ... 630 590-6100
Addison *(G-341)*
**Vision Integrated Graphics** ... E ... 312 373-6300
Chicago *(G-6903)*
**Vision Integrated Graphics** ... C ... 708 570-7900
Bolingbrook *(G-2380)*
**Voris Communication Co Inc** ... C ... 630 898-4268
Berkeley *(G-2051)*
**Voris Communication Co Inc** ... D ... 630 231-2425
West Chicago *(G-21791)*
**W R S Inc** ... G ... 630 279-0400
Elmhurst *(G-9959)*
**W W Barthel & Co** ... G ... 847 392-5643
Arlington Heights *(G-869)*
**Wagner Printing Co** ... E ... 630 941-7961
Freeport *(G-10698)*
**Warner Offset Inc** ... E ... 847 695-9400
South Elgin *(G-20233)*
▲ **Warwick Publishing Company** ... D ... 630 584-3871
Saint Charles *(G-19291)*
**Washburn Graficolor Inc** ... G ... 630 596-0880
Naperville *(G-15781)*
**Wayne Printing Company** ... E ... 309 691-2496
Edwards *(G-8785)*
**Wayne Printing Company** ... E ... 309 691-2496
Edwards *(G-8786)*
**We-B-Print Inc** ... G ... 309 353-8801
Pekin *(G-17293)*
**Weakley Printing & Sign Shop** ... G ... 847 473-4466
North Chicago *(G-16189)*
**Weary & Baity Inc** ... G ... 312 943-6197
Chicago *(G-6947)*
**Webb-Mason Inc** ... F ... 630 428-5838
Naperville *(G-15782)*
**Weber Press Inc** ... G ... 773 561-9815
Chicago *(G-6949)*
**Weimer Design & Print Ltd Inc** ... G ... 630 393-3334
Warrenville *(G-21368)*
**West Vly Graphics & Print Inc** ... G ... 630 377-7575
Saint Charles *(G-19293)*
**Westrock Mwv LLC** ... E ... 217 442-2247
Danville *(G-7784)*
**Whipples Printing Press Inc** ... G ... 309 787-3538
Milan *(G-14808)*
**Willert Company** ... G ... 630 860-1620
Franklin Park *(G-10630)*
**William Holloway Ltd** ... G ... 847 866-9520
Evanston *(G-10106)*
**Williamsburg Press Inc** ... G ... 630 229-0228
North Aurora *(G-16150)*
**Willis Publishing** ... F ... 618 497-8272
Percy *(G-17496)*
**Wilson Printing Inc** ... G ... 847 949-7800
Mundelein *(G-15567)*
**Windward Print Star Inc** ... G ... 309 787-8853
Milan *(G-14810)*
**Wold Printing Services Ltd** ... G ... 847 546-3110
Volo *(G-21320)*
**Wood Labeling Systems Inc** ... G ... 815 344-8733
Johnsburg *(G-12444)*
**Wood River Printing & Pubg Co** ... F ... 618 254-3134
Wood River *(G-22446)*
**Woogl Corporation** ... E ... 847 806-1160
Elk Grove Village *(G-9816)*
**Woow Sushi Orland Park LLC** ... F ... 815 469-5189
Frankfort *(G-10377)*
**Wortman Printing Company Inc** ... G ... 217 347-3775
Effingham *(G-8864)*
**Wyckoff Advertising Inc** ... G ... 630 260-2525
Wheaton *(G-21990)*
**Wyka LLC** ... F ... 847 298-0740
Des Plaines *(G-8306)*
**Yeast Printing Inc** ... G ... 309 833-2845
Macomb *(G-14137)*
**Yorke Printe Shoppe Inc** ... E ... 630 627-4960
Lombard *(G-13885)*
**Zone Inc** ... G ... 630 887-8585
Willowbrook *(G-22240)*

## *2754 Commercial Printing: Gravure*

**A Cut Above Engraving Inc** ... G ... 708 671-9800
Palos Park *(G-17126)*
◆ **American Labelmark Company** ... C ... 773 478-0900
Chicago *(G-3859)*
**Arcadia Press Inc** ... F ... 847 451-6390
Franklin Park *(G-10398)*
**C2 Imaging LLC** ... E ... 312 238-3800
Chicago *(G-4206)*
**Chicago Producers Inc** ... F ... 312 226-6900
Forest Park *(G-10237)*
**Cook Communications Minis** ... D ... 847 741-5168
Elgin *(G-9003)*
**Donnells Printing & Off Pdts** ... G ... 815 842-6541
Pontiac *(G-17698)*
**Field Holdings LLC** ... G ... 847 509-2250
Northbrook *(G-16257)*
▲ **Gc Packaging LLC** ... D ... 630 758-4100
Elmhurst *(G-9874)*
▲ **General Packaging Products Inc** ... D ... 312 226-5611
Chicago *(G-4929)*
**Graphic Industries Inc** ... E ... 847 357-9870
South Elgin *(G-20201)*
**Illinois Tool Works Inc** ... D ... 630 752-4000
Carol Stream *(G-3170)*
**Integrated Media Inc** ... F ... 217 854-6260
Carlinville *(G-3040)*
**International Graphics & Assoc** ... F ... 630 584-2248
Saint Charles *(G-19199)*
**Kl Watch Service Inc** ... G ... 847 368-8780
Mount Prospect *(G-15342)*
**Label Tek Inc** ... F ... 630 820-8499
Aurora *(G-1044)*
**Larsen Envelope Co Inc** ... E ... 847 952-9020
Elk Grove Village *(G-9584)*
**Pingotopia Inc** ... F ... 847 503-9333
Northbrook *(G-16338)*
▼ **Pioneer Labels Inc** ... C ... 618 546-5418
Robinson *(G-18068)*
**Proforma-Ppg Inc** ... G ... 847 429-9349
Elgin *(G-9149)*
**Qg LLC** ... D ... 217 347-7721
Effingham *(G-8855)*
**Quad/Graphics Inc** ... A ... 815 734-4121
Mount Morris *(G-15297)*
**R R Donnelley & Sons Company** ... B ... 312 326-8000
Chicago *(G-6270)*
**Rogers Loose Leaf Co** ... F ... 312 226-1947
Chicago *(G-6381)*
**RR Donnelley & Sons Company** ... E ... 217 258-2675
Mattoon *(G-14407)*
**RR Donnelley & Sons Company** ... E ... 847 622-1026
Elgin *(G-9169)*
**RR Donnelley & Sons Company** ... C ... 312 236-8000
Chicago *(G-6404)*
**RR Donnelley & Sons Company** ... B ... 630 588-5000
Lisle *(G-13653)*
**RR Donnelley Printing Co LP** ... A ... 217 235-0561
Mattoon *(G-14408)*
▲ **RR Donnelley Printing Co LP** ... G ... 312 326-8000
Chicago *(G-6405)*
**Rrd Netherlands LLC** ... F ... 312 326-8000
Chicago *(G-6406)*
**Standard Register Inc** ... F ... 630 467-8300
Itasca *(G-12359)*
**Ted Holum & Associates Inc** ... G ... 630 543-9355
Addison *(G-309)*
**Tst/Impreso Inc** ... G ... 630 775-9555
Addison *(G-330)*
**Unique Envelope Corporation** ... E ... 773 586-0330
Chicago *(G-6819)*

**United Engravers Inc** E 847 301-3740
Schaumburg *(G-19780)*

**White Graphics Printing Svcs** G 630 629-9300
Downers Grove *(G-8545)*

**Xpress Printing & Copying Co** G 630 980-9600
Roselle *(G-18987)*

**Zipwhaa Inc** G 630 898-4330
Palatine *(G-17092)*

## *2759 Commercial Printing*

**3 Penguins Ltd** G 630 528-7086
Batavia *(G-1401)*

**A & R Screening LLC** F 708 598-2480
Bridgeview *(G-2457)*

**A Corporate Printing Service** F 630 515-0432
Woodridge *(G-22447)*

**A-Creations Inc** G 630 541-5801
Woodridge *(G-22448)*

**Abbey Copying Support Svcs Inc** G 618 466-3300
Godfrey *(G-11221)*

**Abbott Label Inc** F 630 773-3614
Itasca *(G-12222)*

**Able Printing Service** G 708 788-7115
Berwyn *(G-2054)*

**▼ ABS Graphics Inc** C 630 495-2400
Itasca *(G-12223)*

**Accord Carton Co** C 708 272-3050
Alsip *(G-428)*

**▲ Accurate Printing Inc** G 708 824-0058
Crestwood *(G-7473)*

**Ace Printing Co** G 618 259-2711
East Alton *(G-8598)*

**Acj Partners LLC** G 630 745-1335
Chicago *(G-3729)*

**Acres of Sky Communications** G 815 493-2560
Lanark *(G-13149)*

**Active Graphics Inc** E 708 656-8900
Cicero *(G-7176)*

**Ad Images** G 847 956-1887
Elk Grove Village *(G-9269)*

**Ad Works Inc** G 217 342-9688
Effingham *(G-8821)*

**Advance Instant Printing Co** G 312 346-0986
Chicago *(G-3760)*

**Advance Press Sign Inc** G 630 833-1600
Villa Park *(G-21233)*

**▲ Aim Screen Printing Supply LLC** G 630 357-4293
Naperville *(G-15791)*

**Ajs Premier Printing Inc** G 847 838-6350
Antioch *(G-614)*

**All She Wrote** F 773 529-0100
Chicago *(G-3808)*

**All Stars -N- Stitches Inc** G 618 435-5555
Benton *(G-2021)*

**Allan Brooks & Associates Inc** F 847 537-7500
Lake Villa *(G-13010)*

**Allegra Marketing Print Mail** G 630 790-0444
Schaumburg *(G-19430)*

**Alliance Envelope & Print LLC** G 847 446-4079
Winnetka *(G-22301)*

**▲ Allied Graphics Inc** G 847 419-8830
Buffalo Grove *(G-2654)*

**Allied Printing Inc** G 773 334-5200
Chicago *(G-3817)*

**Allprint Graphics Inc** G 847 519-9898
Schaumburg *(G-19432)*

**Alphabet Shop Inc** E 847 888-3150
Elgin *(G-8946)*

**AlphaGraphics** F 630 261-1227
Oakbrook Terrace *(G-16694)*

**Alta Vista Solutions Inc** F 312 473-3050
Chicago *(G-3836)*

**Altec Printing LLC** G 708 489-2484
Crestwood *(G-7476)*

**▲ American Ad Bag Company Inc** C 815 338-0300
Woodstock *(G-22538)*

**American Advertising Assoc Inc** G 773 312-5110
Chicago *(G-3847)*

**American Bell Screen Prtg Co** G 815 623-5522
Roscoe *(G-18890)*

**American Campaigns** G 773 261-6800
Chicago *(G-3853)*

**American Color Alticor** G 847 472-7500
Elk Grove Village *(G-9295)*

**▲ American Graphic Systems Inc** E 708 614-7007
Tinley Park *(G-20890)*

**American Graphics Network Inc** F 847 729-7220
Glenview *(G-11100)*

**American Label Company** G 630 830-4444
Schaumburg *(G-19438)*

**American Litho Incorporated** A 630 682-0600
Carol Stream *(G-3099)*

**American Outfitters Ltd** E 847 623-3959
Waukegan *(G-21524)*

**American Spcalty Advg Prtg Co** G 847 272-5255
Northbrook *(G-16203)*

**Americas Community Bankers** E 312 644-3100
Chicago *(G-3884)*

**Amy Schutt** G 618 994-7405
Carrier Mills *(G-3305)*

**◆ Anatol Equipment Mfg Co** E 847 367-9760
Lake Bluff *(G-12831)*

**Anns Printing & Copying Co** G 618 656-6878
Edwardsville *(G-8788)*

**Apple Press Inc** G 815 224-1451
Peru *(G-17500)*

**Arcadia Press Inc** F 847 451-6390
Franklin Park *(G-10398)*

**Arch Printing** G 630 896-6610
North Aurora *(G-16118)*

**Arjay Instant Printing** G 847 438-9059
Mundelein *(G-15471)*

**Arroweye Solutions Inc** E 312 253-9400
Chicago *(G-3948)*

**Art-Craft Printers** G 847 455-2201
Franklin Park *(G-10401)*

**Art-Flo Shirt & Lettering Co** E 708 656-5422
Chicago *(G-3953)*

**▼ Artisan Handprints Inc** G 773 725-1799
Chicago *(G-3956)*

**Artistry Engraving & Embossing** G 773 775-4888
Chicago *(G-3957)*

**Artline Screen Printing Inc** G 815 963-8125
Rockford *(G-18271)*

**Artpol Printing Inc** G 773 622-0498
Chicago *(G-3958)*

**Artsonia LLC** F 224 538-5060
Gurnee *(G-11429)*

**Artwear** G 618 234-5522
Belleville *(G-1609)*

**Ashland Screening Corporation** E 708 758-8800
Chicago Heights *(G-7080)*

**Aspen Printing Services LLC** G 630 357-3203
Naperville *(G-15601)*

**Associated Design Inc** F 708 974-9100
Palos Hills *(G-17114)*

**Astro Plastic Containers Inc** F 708 458-7100
Bedford Park *(G-1540)*

**AT&I Resources LLC** G 918 925-0154
Addison *(G-47)*

**Athletic Image** G 217 347-7377
Effingham *(G-8825)*

**Authority Screenprint & EMB** G 630 236-0289
Plainfield *(G-17581)*

**Available Business Group Inc** D 773 247-4141
Chicago *(G-3995)*

**Award/Visionps Inc** G 331 318-7800
Chicago *(G-4003)*

**B & B Printing Company** G 217 285-6072
Pittsfield *(G-17561)*

**B Allan Graphics Inc** F 708 396-1704
Alsip *(G-438)*

**B Creative Screen Print Co** G 815 806-3037
Frankfort *(G-10298)*

**B D Enterprises** G 618 462-5861
Alton *(G-563)*

**B F Shaw Printing Company** E 815 875-4461
Princeton *(G-17744)*

**▲ Bagcraftpapercon I LLC** C 620 856-2800
Chicago *(G-4025)*

**Bailleu & Bailleu Printing Inc** G 309 852-2517
Kewanee *(G-12670)*

**Baker La Russo** G 630 788-5108
Naperville *(G-15602)*

**Bally Foil Graphics Inc** G 847 427-1509
Elk Grove Village *(G-9333)*

**Bar Code Graphics Inc** F 312 664-0700
Chicago *(G-4038)*

**Barnaby Inc** F 815 895-6555
Sycamore *(G-20789)*

**◆ Bass-Mollett Publishers Inc** D 618 664-3141
Greenville *(G-11387)*

**Batavia Instant Print** G 630 262-0370
West Chicago *(G-21668)*

**Bdc Capital Enterprises LLC** G 847 908-0650
Schaumburg *(G-19457)*

**Bee Designs Embroidery & Scree** G 815 393-4593
Malta *(G-14165)*

**Belboz Corp** G 708 856-6099
Dolton *(G-8366)*

**Bellen Container Corporation** E 847 741-5600
Elgin *(G-8964)*

**Belmonte Printing Co** G 847 352-8841
Schaumburg *(G-19459)*

**Benzinger Printing** G 815 784-6560
Genoa *(G-10875)*

**Bes Designs & Associates Inc** G 217 443-4619
Danville *(G-7705)*

**Bikast Graphics Inc** G 847 487-8822
Wauconda *(G-21446)*

**Biller Press & Manufacturing** G 847 395-4111
Antioch *(G-623)*

**Bizbash Media Inc** G 312 436-2525
Chicago *(G-4117)*

**Blazing Color Inc** G 618 826-3001
Chester *(G-3651)*

**Bobs Tshirt Store** G 618 567-1730
Mascoutah *(G-14349)*

**Bond Brothers & Co** F 708 442-5510
Lyons *(G-14032)*

**▲ Bradley Industries Inc** E 815 469-2314
Frankfort *(G-10304)*

**Brads Printing Inc** G 847 662-0447
Waukegan *(G-21531)*

**Branstiter Printing Co** G 217 245-6533
Jacksonville *(G-12381)*

**Brooke Graphics LLC** E 847 593-1300
Elk Grove Village *(G-9346)*

**Brownfield Sports Inc** G 217 367-8321
Urbana *(G-21074)*

**Business Cards Tomorrow** F 815 877-0990
Machesney Park *(G-14062)*

**Business Identity Spc Inc** G 847 669-1946
Huntley *(G-12134)*

**C & E Specialties Inc** E 815 229-9230
Rockford *(G-18294)*

**C E Dienberg Printing Company** G 708 848-4406
Oak Park *(G-16655)*

**C F C Interantional** G 708 753-0679
Chicago Heights *(G-7085)*

**C L Graphics Inc** E 815 455-0900
Crystal Lake *(G-7547)*

**C2 Imaging LLC** E 312 238-3800
Chicago *(G-4206)*

**Campbell Publishing Inc** G 217 742-3313
Winchester *(G-22278)*

**Campus Sportswear Incorporated** F 217 344-0944
Champaign *(G-3460)*

**Cannon Ball Marketing Inc** G 630 971-2127
Lisle *(G-13573)*

**Capital Prtg & Die Cutng Inc** G 630 896-5520
Aurora *(G-1124)*

**Capitol Impressions Inc** E 309 633-1400
Peoria *(G-17322)*

**Card Prsnlzation Solutions LLC** E 630 543-2630
Glendale Heights *(G-11014)*

**Carl Gorr Printing Co** G 815 338-3191
Woodstock *(G-22549)*

**Carlberg Design Inc** G 217 341-3291
Petersburg *(G-17534)*

**Carson Printing Inc** G 847 836-0900
East Dundee *(G-8629)*

**Carter Printing Co Inc** G 217 227-4464
Farmersville *(G-10183)*

**Castle-Printech Inc** G 815 758-5484
Dekalb *(G-8076)*

**Catalog Designers Inc** G 847 228-0025
Elk Grove Village *(G-9359)*

**Cavco Printers** G 618 988-8011
Energy *(G-9985)*

**CDs Office Systems Inc** F 217 351-5046
Champaign *(G-3464)*

**Central Decal Company Inc** D 630 325-9892
Burr Ridge *(G-2829)*

**Central IL Business Magazine** G 217 351-5281
Champaign *(G-3465)*

**Century Printing** G 618 632-2486
O Fallon *(G-16465)*

**Cenveo Inc** G 217 243-4258
Jacksonville *(G-12383)*

**Challenge Printers** G 773 252-0212
Chicago *(G-4285)*

**Cherry Street Printing & Award** G 618 252-6814
Harrisburg *(G-11597)*

**Chicago Print Partners LLC** F 312 525-2015
Addison *(G-74)*

**Chicago Printing and EMB Inc** F 630 628-1777
Addison *(G-75)*

**Churchill Wilmslow Corporation** G 312 759-8911
Chicago *(G-4374)*

Employee Codes: A=Over 500 employees, B=251-500
C=101-250, D=51-100, E=20-50, F=10-19, G=3-9

2017 Harris Illinois
Industrial Directory

973

**Cifuentes Luis & Nicole Inc** G 847 490-3660
Schaumburg *(G-19472)*
**Cityblue Technologies LLC** F 309 676-6633
Peoria *(G-17343)*
**Clark Printing & Marketing** G 217 363-5300
Champaign *(G-3467)*
**Classic Impressions Inc** G
Oswego *(G-16908)*
**Classique Signs & Engrv Inc** G 217 228-7446
Quincy *(G-17813)*
**Cloz Companies Inc** E 773 247-8879
Skokie *(G-19983)*
**Clyde Printing Company** F 773 847-5900
Chicago *(G-4410)*
**Color Tone Printing** G 708 385-1442
Blue Island *(G-2242)*
**Color4** F 847 996-6880
Libertyville *(G-13316)*
**Colvin Printing** G 708 331-4580
Blue Island *(G-2243)*
**Com-Graphics Inc** D 312 226-0900
Chicago *(G-4434)*
**Condor Labels Inc** G 708 429-0707
Tinley Park *(G-20902)*
**Continent Corp** G 773 733-1584
Bolingbrook *(G-2287)*
**Cook Printing Co Inc** G 217 345-2514
Mattoon *(G-14387)*
**Corporate Business Card Ltd** E 847 455-5760
Franklin Park *(G-10442)*
**Corporate Promotions Inc** G 630 964-5000
Lisle *(G-13577)*
**Corporation Supply Co Inc** E 312 726-3375
Chicago *(G-4476)*
**Corwin Printing** G 618 263-3936
Mount Carmel *(G-15263)*
**Cpg Printing & Graphics** G 309 820-1392
Bloomington *(G-2156)*
**Craftsmen Printing** G 217 283-9574
Hoopeston *(G-12108)*
**Creative Lithocraft Inc** F 847 352-7002
Schaumburg *(G-19488)*
**Creative Lithocraft Inc** G 847 352-7002
Schaumburg *(G-19489)*
**Creative Prtg & Smart Ideas** G 773 481-6522
Chicago *(G-4501)*
**Crest Greetings Inc** F 708 210-0800
Chicago *(G-4503)*
**Crossmark Printing Inc** G 708 754-4000
Chicago Heights *(G-7094)*
**Culture Studio LLC** E 312 243-8304
Chicago *(G-4515)*
**Custom Graphics Inc** E 309 633-0850
Bartonville *(G-1393)*
**Custom Screen Printing** G 217 543-3691
Arthur *(G-893)*
**D & R Press** G 708 452-0500
Elmwood Park *(G-9966)*
**D G Brandt Inc** G 815 942-4064
Morris *(G-15105)*
**D G Printing Inc** E 847 397-7779
Schaumburg *(G-19498)*
**D L V Printing Service Inc** F 773 626-1661
Chicago *(G-4537)*
**Dale K Brown** G 815 338-0222
Woodstock *(G-22558)*
**Damy Corp** F 847 233-0515
Schiller Park *(G-19819)*
**Dans Printing & Off Sups Inc** F 708 687-3055
Oak Forest *(G-16577)*
▲ **Darwill Inc** C 708 449-7770
Hillside *(G-11914)*
**Data Com PLD Inc** G 708 839-9620
Willow Springs *(G-22195)*
▲ **Decal Works LLC** E 815 784-4000
Kingston *(G-12706)*
**Decorative Industries Inc** E 773 229-0015
Chicago *(G-4570)*
**Delta Label Inc** G 618 233-8984
Belleville *(G-1625)*
**Deluxe Corporation** C 847 635-7200
Des Plaines *(G-8181)*
**Deluxe Printing** G 312 225-0061
Chicago *(G-4580)*
**Design Graphics Inc** G 815 462-3323
New Lenox *(G-15875)*
**Desitalk Chicago LLC** E 773 856-0545
Chicago *(G-4586)*
**Dg Digital Printing** G 815 961-0000
Rockford *(G-18340)*
**Diamond Screen Process Inc** G 847 439-6200
Elk Grove Village *(G-9426)*
**Diamond Web Printing LLC** F 630 663-0350
Downers Grove *(G-8428)*
**Diaz Printing** G 773 887-3366
Chicago *(G-4595)*
**Digital Hub LLC** E 312 943-6161
Chicago *(G-4602)*
**Digital Prtg & Total Graphics** G 630 627-7400
Lombard *(G-13792)*
**Display Link Inc** G 815 968-0778
Rockford *(G-18346)*
**DMarv Design Specialty Prtrs** G 708 389-4420
Blue Island *(G-2246)*
**Document Publishing Group** E 847 783-0670
Elgin *(G-9011)*
**Dolls Lettering Inc** G 815 467-8000
Minooka *(G-14838)*
**Domino Amjet Inc** E 847 662-3148
Gurnee *(G-11439)*
**Donnells Printing & Off Pdts** G 815 842-6541
Pontiac *(G-17698)*
**DOT Press LLC** G 312 421-0293
Chicago *(G-4635)*
**Dpe Incorporated** G 773 306-0105
Chicago *(G-4640)*
**Drake Envelope Printing Co** G 217 374-2772
White Hall *(G-22184)*
**Duckys Formal Wear Inc** G 309 342-5914
Galesburg *(G-10748)*
**Duo Graphics** G 847 228-7080
Elk Grove Village *(G-9436)*
**Dynagraphics Incorporated** E 217 876-9950
Decatur *(G-7878)*
▲ **Dynamesh Inc** E 630 293-5454
Batavia *(G-1444)*
**E & D Web Inc** C 815 562-5800
Rochelle *(G-18086)*
**E & H Graphic Service** G 708 748-5656
Matteson *(G-14371)*
**E K Kuhn Inc** G 815 899-9211
Sycamore *(G-20795)*
**E&D Printing Services Inc** G 815 609-8222
Plainfield *(G-17593)*
**Eagle Express Mail LLC** G 618 377-6245
Bethalto *(G-2081)*
**Eagle Screen Print Inds Inc** F 708 579-0454
Countryside *(G-7423)*
**Earl Ad Inc** G 312 666-7106
Chicago *(G-4673)*
**East Central Communications Co** E 217 892-9613
Rantoul *(G-17926)*
**East Moline Herald Print Inc** G 309 755-5224
East Moline *(G-8678)*
**Edwards Creative Services LLC** F 309 756-0199
Milan *(G-14784)*
**Elegant Embroidery Inc** G 847 540-8003
Lake Zurich *(G-13067)*
**Elite Die & Finishing Inc** G 708 389-4848
South Holland *(G-20265)*
**Elite Impressions & Graphics** G 847 695-3730
South Elgin *(G-20195)*
**Elliott Publishing Inc** G 217 645-3033
Liberty *(G-13295)*
**Embossed Graphics Inc** D 630 236-4000
Aurora *(G-1002)*
**Embroid ME** G 815 485-4155
New Lenox *(G-15880)*
▲ **Emsur USA LLC** E 847 274-9450
Elk Grove Village *(G-9456)*
**Energy Tees** G 708 771-0000
Forest Park *(G-10240)*
**Envision Graphics LLC** D 630 825-1200
Bloomingdale *(G-2107)*
**ESP T-Shirt Co Inc** G 630 393-1033
Warrenville *(G-21346)*
**Ethan Company Incorporated** G 815 715-2283
Shorewood *(G-19925)*
**Eugene Ewbank** G 630 705-0400
Oswego *(G-16917)*
▲ **Evanston Graphic Imaging Inc** G 847 869-7446
Evanston *(G-10033)*
▲ **Everwill Inc** G 847 357-0446
Elk Grove Village *(G-9466)*
**Excel Glass Inc** G 847 801-5200
Schiller Park *(G-19829)*
**Expression Wear Inc** G 815 732-1556
Mount Morris *(G-15296)*
**F & F Publishing Inc** G 847 480-0330
Highland Park *(G-11831)*
**F & S Engraving Inc** E 847 870-8400
Mount Prospect *(G-15328)*
**F C D Inc** E 847 498-3711
Northbrook *(G-16255)*
**F Weber Printing Co Inc** G 815 468-6152
Manteno *(G-14183)*
**F-C Enterprises Inc** G 815 254-7295
Plainfield *(G-17598)*
**Falcon Press Inc** G 815 455-9099
Crystal Lake *(G-7575)*
**Fantastic Lettering Inc** G 773 685-7650
Chicago *(G-4812)*
**Fast Print Shop** G 618 997-1976
Marion *(G-14259)*
**Fast Track Printing Inc** G 773 761-9400
Chicago *(G-4817)*
**Father & Daughters Printing** G 708 749-8286
Berwyn *(G-2064)*
**Faulstich Printing Company Inc** G 217 442-4994
Danville *(G-7718)*
**Fedex Ground Package Sys Inc** G 800 463-3339
Glendale Heights *(G-11023)*
**Fedex Office & Print Svcs Inc** G 630 759-5784
Bolingbrook *(G-2308)*
**Fedex Office & Print Svcs Inc** G 847 670-7283
Mount Prospect *(G-15329)*
**Fedex Office & Print Svcs Inc** E 217 355-3400
Champaign *(G-3485)*
**Fedex Office & Print Svcs Inc** E 309 685-4093
Peoria *(G-17359)*
**Fedex Office & Print Svcs Inc** E 708 452-0149
Elmwood Park *(G-9970)*
**Fedex Office & Print Svcs Inc** F 312 670-4460
Chicago *(G-4831)*
▲ **Fgs Inc** F 312 421-3060
Chicago *(G-4839)*
**Financial Graphic Services Inc** D 708 343-0448
Broadview *(G-2580)*
**Fine Arts Engraving Co** G 800 688-4400
Chicago *(G-4845)*
**Fine Line Printing** G 773 582-9709
Chicago *(G-4846)*
**First Impression** G 815 883-3357
Oglesby *(G-16748)*
**First Impression of Chicago** G 773 224-3434
Chicago *(G-4849)*
**First String Enterprises Inc** E 708 614-1200
Tinley Park *(G-20913)*
**Fisheye Services Incorporated** G 773 942-6314
Chicago *(G-4852)*
**Fleetwood Press Inc** G 708 485-6811
Brookfield *(G-2632)*
**Flexografix Inc** F 630 350-0100
Carol Stream *(G-3152)*
**Floden Enterprises** G 847 566-7898
Mundelein *(G-15502)*
▲ **Flow-Eze Company** F 815 965-1062
Rockford *(G-18383)*
**FM Graphic Impressions Inc** E 630 897-8788
Aurora *(G-1153)*
**Forest Envelope Company** E 630 515-1200
Bolingbrook *(G-2311)*
**Forms Specialist Inc** G 847 298-2868
Lincolnshire *(G-13449)*
**Forrest Press Inc** G 847 381-1621
Barrington *(G-1280)*
**Fort Dearborn Company** C 773 774-4321
Niles *(G-15979)*
**Forte Print Corporation** G 773 391-0105
Chicago *(G-4875)*
**Fox Valley Printing Co Inc** F 419 232-3348
Montgomery *(G-15043)*
**Freddie Bear Sports** F 708 532-4133
Tinley Park *(G-20916)*
**Freeburg Printing & Publishing** G 618 539-3320
Freeburg *(G-10635)*
**Freedom Design & Decals Inc** G 815 806-8172
Mokena *(G-14864)*
**Freeport Press Inc** G 815 232-1181
Freeport *(G-10658)*
**Fresh Concept Enterprises Inc** G 815 254-7295
Plainfield *(G-17601)*
**Frye-Williamson Press Inc** E 217 522-7744
Springfield *(G-20444)*
**G and D Enterprises Inc** E 847 981-8661
Arlington Heights *(G-757)*
**G F Printing** G 618 797-0576
Granite City *(G-11278)*
**G Y Industries LLC** F 708 210-1300
Chicago *(G-4902)*

**Gallas Label & Decal** F 773 775-1000 Chicago *(G-4909)*
**Galleon Industries Inc** G 708 478-5444 Joliet *(G-12499)*
**Gallimore Industries Inc** F 847 356-3331 Lake Villa *(G-13014)*
▲ **General Packaging Products Inc** D 312 226-5611 Chicago *(G-4929)*
**Genesis Print & Copy Svcs Inc** G 773 374-1020 Chicago *(G-4935)*
**George Press Inc** G 217 324-2242 Litchfield *(G-13687)*
**Gfx Dynamic** G 847 543-4600 Grayslake *(G-11339)*
**Gfx International Inc** C 847 543-7179 Grayslake *(G-11340)*
▲ **Globe Ticket** G 847 258-1000 Carol Stream *(G-3160)*
**Goalgetters Inc** F 708 579-9800 La Grange *(G-12733)*
**Golden Plastics LLC** F 847 836-7766 East Dundee *(G-8640)*
**Golden Prairie News** G 217 226-3721 Assumption *(G-931)*
**Good Impressions Inc** G 847 831-4317 Highland Park *(G-11836)*
**Good News Printing** G 708 389-1127 Palos Heights *(G-17105)*
**Grace Enterprises Inc** E 773 465-5300 Chicago *(G-4982)*
**Grace Enterprises Inc** G 773 465-5300 Chicago *(G-4983)*
**Grace Printing and Mailing** F 847 423-2100 Skokie *(G-20005)*
**Grand Forms & Systems Inc** F 847 259-4600 Arlington Heights *(G-760)*
**Granja & Sons Printing** F 773 762-3840 Chicago *(G-4987)*
**Graphic Arts Services Inc** E 630 629-7770 Villa Park *(G-21256)*
**Graphic Press Inc** G 847 272-6000 Morton Grove *(G-15199)*
**Graphic Screen Printing Inc** G 708 429-3330 Orland Park *(G-16863)*
**Graphics Group LLC** D 708 867-5500 Chicago *(G-4992)*
**Great Display Company Llc** F 309 821-1037 Bloomington *(G-2172)*
**Greek Art Printing & Pubg Co** G 847 724-8860 Glenview *(G-11133)*
**Griffin John** G 708 301-2316 Lockport *(G-13720)*
▲ **Gsi Technologies LLC** D 630 325-8181 Burr Ridge *(G-2847)*
**H & H Graphics Illinois Inc** E 847 383-6285 Vernon Hills *(G-21170)*
**H & H Printing** G 847 866-9520 Evanston *(G-10048)*
**H A Friend & Company Inc** E 847 746-1248 Zion *(G-22687)*
**Hafner Printing Co Inc** F 312 362-0120 Chicago *(G-5030)*
**Hal Mather & Sons Incorporated** E 815 338-4000 Woodstock *(G-22573)*
**Harry Otto Printing Company** F 630 365-6111 Elburn *(G-8889)*
**Hastings Printing** G 217 253-5086 Tuscola *(G-21020)*
**Hawthorne Press** G 708 652-9000 Cicero *(G-7201)*
**Hazen Display Corporation** E 815 248-2925 Davis *(G-7806)*
**Heart Printing Inc** G 847 259-2100 Arlington Heights *(G-764)*
**Heartland Labels Inc** E 217 826-8324 Marshall *(G-14323)*
**Helene Printing Inc** G 630 482-3300 Bensenville *(G-1915)*
**Henry News Republican** G 309 364-3250 Henry *(G-11743)*
**Hermitage Group Inc** E 773 561-3773 Chicago *(G-5080)*
**Hi-Five Sportswear Inc** G 815 637-6044 Machesney Park *(G-14079)*
**High-5 Printwear Inc** G 847 818-0081 Arlington Heights *(G-765)*
**Highland Journal Printing Inc** G 618 654-4131 Highland *(G-11787)*
**Hillsboro Journal Inc** E 217 532-3933 Hillsboro *(G-11895)*
**Hole In The Wall Screen Arts** G 217 243-9100 Jacksonville *(G-12391)*
**Hopper Graphics Inc** G 708 489-0459 Palos Heights *(G-17107)*
**Howard Press Printing Inc** G 708 345-7437 Northlake *(G-16439)*
**Hub Printing Company Inc** F 815 562-7057 Rochelle *(G-18094)*
**Huetone Imprints Inc** G 630 694-9610 Elk Grove Village *(G-9528)*
**ID Label Inc** E 847 265-1200 Lake Villa *(G-13016)*
**Ideal Advertising & Printing** F 815 965-1713 Rockford *(G-18426)*
**Identi-Graphics Inc** G 630 801-4845 Montgomery *(G-15049)*
**Iemco Corporation** G 773 728-4400 Chicago *(G-5145)*
◆ **Illini/Altco Inc** D 847 549-0321 Vernon Hills *(G-21173)*
**Illinois Office Sup Elect Prtg** E 815 434-0186 Ottawa *(G-16962)*
**Illinois Printing Services Inc** G 217 728-2786 Sullivan *(G-20749)*
**Illinois Tag Co** E 773 626-0542 Carol Stream *(G-3169)*
**Illinois Valley Printing Inc** G 309 674-4942 Peoria *(G-17388)*
**Image Plus Inc** G 630 852-4920 Downers Grove *(G-8463)*
**Impress Printing** G 630 933-8966 Wheaton *(G-21956)*
**Impress Printing & Design Inc** G 815 730-9440 Joliet *(G-12514)*
**Impression Printing** F 708 614-8660 Oak Forest *(G-16583)*
**Impressive Impressions** G 312 432-0501 Chicago *(G-5170)*
**Impro International Inc** G 847 398-3870 Arlington Heights *(G-776)*
**Imtran Industries Inc** D 630 752-4000 Carol Stream *(G-3172)*
**In Color Graphics Coml Prtg** F 847 697-0003 Elgin *(G-9075)*
**Ink Spots Prtg & Meida Design** G 708 754-1300 Homewood *(G-12102)*
**Ink Spots Prtg Mdia Design Inc** G 708 754-1300 Glenwood *(G-11216)*
**Integra Graphics and Forms Inc** F 708 385-0950 Crestwood *(G-7490)*
**Interstate Graphics Inc** E 815 877-6777 Machesney Park *(G-14083)*
**Invitation Creations Inc** G 847 432-4441 Highland Park *(G-11844)*
**J & J Express Envelopes Inc** G 847 253-7146 South Elgin *(G-20209)*
**J & J Silk Screening** G 773 838-9000 Chicago *(G-5252)*
**J F Wagner Printing Co** G 847 564-0017 Northbrook *(G-16280)*
**J J Collins Sons Inc** E 309 664-5404 Bloomington *(G-2184)*
**J S Printing Inc** G 847 678-6300 Franklin Park *(G-10503)*
**Jbl Marketing Inc** G 847 266-1080 Highland Park *(G-11847)*
**Jem Associates Ltd** G 847 808-8377 Chicago *(G-5289)*
**JLJ Corp** G 847 726-9795 Lake Zurich *(G-13092)*
**Joes Printing** G 773 545-6063 Chicago *(G-5309)*
**Johnson Printing** G 630 595-8815 Bensenville *(G-1930)*
**Joliet Pattern Works Inc** D 815 726-5373 Crest Hill *(G-7460)*
◆ **Jordan Industries Inc** F 847 945-5591 Deerfield *(G-8020)*
**Jph Enterprises Inc** G 847 390-0900 Des Plaines *(G-8217)*
**K & S Printing Services** G 815 899-2923 Sycamore *(G-20804)*
**K and A Graphics Inc** G 847 244-2345 Gurnee *(G-11463)*
**Kara Graphics Inc** G 630 964-8122 Woodridge *(G-22500)*
**Kellogg Printing Co** F 309 734-8388 Monmouth *(G-15016)*
**Kelly Printing Co Inc** E 217 443-1792 Danville *(G-7741)*
**Keneal Industries Inc** F 815 886-1300 Romeoville *(G-18834)*
**Kens Quick Print Inc** F 847 831-4410 Highland Park *(G-11849)*
**Kestler Digital Printing Inc** F 773 581-5918 Chicago *(G-5379)*
**Kevin Kewney** G 217 228-7444 Quincy *(G-17844)*
**Kevron Printing & Design Inc** G 708 229-7725 Hickory Hills *(G-11772)*
**Kjellberg Printing** F 630 653-2244 Wheaton *(G-21960)*
**Klein Printing Inc** G 773 235-2121 Chicago *(G-5387)*
**Klh Printing Corp** G 847 459-0115 Wheeling *(G-22086)*
**Klimko Ink Inc** G 815 459-5066 Crystal Lake *(G-7599)*
**Kmf Enterprises Inc** G 630 858-2210 Wheaton *(G-21961)*
**Knight Prtg & Litho Svc Ltd** G 847 487-7700 Island Lake *(G-12217)*
**Kon Printing Inc** G 630 879-2211 Batavia *(G-1461)*
▲ **Korea Times** D 847 626-0388 Glenview *(G-11157)*
**Kwik Print Inc** G 630 773-3225 Itasca *(G-12299)*
**Label Printers LP** D 630 897-6970 Aurora *(G-1181)*
**Label Tek Inc** F 630 820-8499 Aurora *(G-1044)*
**Labels Unlimited Incorporated** E 773 523-7500 Chicago *(G-5430)*
**Lampe Publications** G 309 741-9790 Elmwood *(G-9964)*
**Landmarx Screen Printing** F 217 223-4601 Quincy *(G-17853)*
**Laninver USA Inc** G 847 367-8787 Elk Grove Village *(G-9583)*
**Lans Printing Inc** G 708 895-6226 Lynwood *(G-14021)*
◆ **Lasersketch Ltd** F 630 243-6360 Romeoville *(G-18837)*
**Lasons Label Co** G 773 775-2606 Chicago *(G-5464)*
**Last Minute Prtg & Copy Ctr** G 888 788-2965 Tinley Park *(G-20929)*
**Laughing Dog Graphics** G 309 392-3330 Minier *(G-14833)*
**Lazare Printing Co Inc** G 773 871-2500 Chicago *(G-5475)*
**Lee-Wel Printing Corporation** G 630 682-0935 Wheaton *(G-21966)*
**Legacy Prints** G 815 946-9112 Polo *(G-17688)*
**Legend Promotions** G 847 438-3528 Lake Zurich *(G-13095)*
**Leonard Publishing Co** F 773 486-2737 Norridge *(G-16104)*
**Liberty Group Publishing** G 309 937-3303 Cambridge *(G-2968)*
**Lighthouse Marketing Services** G 630 482-9900 Batavia *(G-1464)*
**Lighthouse Printing Inc** G 708 479-7776 New Lenox *(G-15891)*
**Lincoln Square Printing** G 773 334-9030 Chicago *(G-5508)*
**Lincolnshire Printing Inc** G 815 578-0740 McHenry *(G-14523)*
**Lithuanian Catholic Press** E 773 585-9500 Chicago *(G-5519)*
**Little Doloras** G 708 331-1330 South Holland *(G-20286)*
**Little Shop of Papers Ltd** G 847 382-7733 Barrington *(G-1287)*
**Livegift Inc** G 312 725-4514 Chicago *(G-5524)*
**Lloyd Midwest Graphics** G 815 282-8828 Machesney Park *(G-14089)*
**Locker Room Screen Printing** G 630 759-2533 Bolingbrook *(G-2337)*
**Logo Wear Unlimited Inc** G 309 367-2333 Metamora *(G-14743)*
**Logo Works** G 815 942-4700 Morris *(G-15113)*
**Ltb Graphics Inc** G 630 238-1754 Wood Dale *(G-22391)*
**M & G Graphics Inc** E 773 247-1596 Chicago *(G-5576)*

Employee Codes: A=Over 500 employees, B=251-500
C=101-250, D=51-100, E=20-50, F=10-19, G=3-9
2017 Harris Illinois
Industrial Directory
975

**M & R Graphics Inc** F 708 534-6621
University Park *(G-21054)*
**M L S Printing Co Inc** G 847 948-8902
Deerfield *(G-8033)*
**M S A Printing Co** G 847 593-5699
Elk Grove Village *(G-9604)*
**M Wells Printing Co** G 312 455-0400
Chicago *(G-5588)*
**Mac Graphics Group Inc** G 630 620-7200
Oakbrook Terrace *(G-16716)*
**Macoupin County Enquirer Inc** E 217 854-2534
Carlinville *(G-3042)*
**Madmaxmar Group Inc** E 630 320-3700
Itasca *(G-12308)*
**Managed Marketing Inc** G 847 279-8260
Wheeling *(G-22098)*
**Market Connect Inc** G 847 726-6788
Kildeer *(G-12702)*
**Maro Carton Inc** G 708 649-9982
Bellwood *(G-1714)*
**Mason City Banner Times** F 217 482-3276
Mason City *(G-14365)*
**Master Engraving** G 217 965-5885
Virden *(G-21299)*
**Master Engraving Inc** G 217 627-3279
Girard *(G-10948)*
▲ **Master Marketing Intl Inc** E 630 653-5525
Carol Stream *(G-3190)*
**Master Print** G 708 499-4037
Oak Lawn *(G-16633)*
**Master Tape Printers Inc** E 773 283-8273
Chicago *(G-5645)*
**Matrix Press** G 847 885-7076
Schaumburg *(G-19637)*
**Mattoon Printing Center** G 217 234-3100
Mattoon *(G-14400)*
**Mbh Promotions Inc** G 847 634-2411
Buffalo Grove *(G-2733)*
◆ **McCracken Label Co** E 773 581-8860
Chicago *(G-5666)*
**McGrath Press Inc** E 815 356-5246
Crystal Lake *(G-7607)*
**McKillip Industries Inc** E 815 439-1050
Yorkville *(G-22664)*
**McKnights Long Term Care News** G 847 559-2884
Northbrook *(G-16308)*
**Melon Ink Screen Print** G 847 726-0003
Lake Zurich *(G-13101)*
**Meridian** E 815 885-4646
Loves Park *(G-13964)*
**Merrill Corporation** C 312 263-3524
Chicago *(G-5695)*
**Merrill Corporation** C 312 386-2200
Chicago *(G-5696)*
▲ **Merrill Fine Arts Engrv Inc** D 312 786-6300
Chicago *(G-5697)*
**Meto-Grafics Inc** F 847 639-0044
Crystal Lake *(G-7609)*
**Mexacali Silkscreen Inc** G 630 628-9313
Addison *(G-203)*
**Mi-Te Fast Printers Inc** G 312 236-3278
Glencoe *(G-11002)*
◆ **Michael Lewis Company** C 708 688-2200
Mc Cook *(G-14453)*
**Microdynamics Corporation** C 630 276-0527
Naperville *(G-15697)*
**Mid City Printing Service** G 773 777-5400
Chicago *(G-5725)*
**MidAmerican Prtg Systems Inc** E 312 663-4720
Chicago *(G-5732)*
**Midwest Gold Stampers Inc** F 773 775-5253
Chicago *(G-5744)*
**Midwest Labels & Decals Inc** G 630 543-7556
Addison *(G-213)*
**Midwest Law Printing Co Inc** G 312 431-0185
Chicago *(G-5745)*
**Midwest Silkscreening Inc** G 217 892-9596
Rantoul *(G-17934)*
**Miller Products Inc** E 708 534-5111
University Park *(G-21058)*
**Minerva Sportswear Inc** F 309 661-2387
Bloomington *(G-2201)*
**Minuteman Press** G 630 541-9122
Countryside *(G-7437)*
**Minuteman Press** G 630 584-7383
Saint Charles *(G-19223)*
**Minuteman Press Inc** G 847 577-2411
Arlington Heights *(G-803)*
**MJM Graphics** G 847 234-1802
Lake Forest *(G-12927)*
**Mjt Design and Prtg Entps Inc** G 708 240-4323
Hillside *(G-11926)*
**Modagrafics Inc** D 800 860-3169
Rolling Meadows *(G-18746)*
**Modern Methods Creative Inc** G 309 263-4100
Peoria *(G-17410)*
**Modern Methods LLC** G 309 263-4100
Morton *(G-15165)*
**Modern Printing of Quincy** F 217 223-1063
Quincy *(G-17861)*
**Mortgage Market Info Svcs** E 630 834-7555
Villa Park *(G-21272)*
**Moss Inc** G 800 341-1557
Elk Grove Village *(G-9637)*
**Motr Grafx LLC** G 847 600-5656
Niles *(G-16009)*
**MPS Chicago Inc** E 630 932-5583
Bolingbrook *(G-2347)*
**Msf Graphics Inc** G 847 446-6900
Des Plaines *(G-8239)*
**Muir Omni Graphics Inc** E 309 673-7034
Peoria *(G-17413)*
**Multi Art Press** G 773 775-0515
Chicago *(G-5831)*
**Multi Packaging Solutions Inc** G 773 283-9500
Chicago *(G-5832)*
**Murray Printing Service Inc** G 847 310-8959
Schaumburg *(G-19658)*
**Nancy J Perkins** G 815 748-7121
Dekalb *(G-8107)*
**National Data Svcs Chicago Inc** C 630 597-9100
Carol Stream *(G-3204)*
**National Data-Label Corp** E 630 616-9595
Bensenville *(G-1954)*
**Nbs Systems Inc** E 217 999-3472
Mount Olive *(G-15306)*
**Newport Printing Services Inc** G 847 632-1000
Schaumburg *(G-19664)*
**Next Generneration** F 630 261-1477
Lombard *(G-13833)*
▲ **NGS Printing Inc** E 847 741-4411
Elgin *(G-9122)*
▲ **Nissha Usa Inc** E 847 413-2665
Schaumburg *(G-19666)*
**Noor International Inc** G 847 985-2300
Bartlett *(G-1320)*
**Northwest Premier Printing** G 773 736-1882
Chicago *(G-5940)*
**Northwestern Illinois Farmer** G 815 369-2811
Lena *(G-13282)*
**Norway Press Inc** G 773 846-9422
Chicago *(G-5944)*
**Nosco Inc** D 847 336-4200
Gurnee *(G-11476)*
**Nu-Art Printing** G 618 533-9971
Centralia *(G-3425)*
▲ **Oec Graphics-Chicago LLC** E 630 455-6700
Willowbrook *(G-22227)*
**OfficeMax North America Inc** E 815 748-3007
Dekalb *(G-8111)*
**Offworld Designs** G 815 786-7080
Sandwich *(G-19372)*
**Olde Print Shoppe Inc** G 618 395-3833
Olney *(G-16786)*
**Olympic Trophy and Awards Co** F 773 631-9500
Chicago *(G-5987)*
**On Time Envelopes & Printing** G 630 682-0466
Carol Stream *(G-3209)*
**Osborne Publications Inc** G 217 422-9702
Decatur *(G-7924)*
**Ottawa Publishing Co Inc** F 815 434-3330
Ottawa *(G-16976)*
**Outbreak Designs** G 217 370-5418
South Jacksonville *(G-20311)*
**Overt Press Inc** E 773 284-0909
Chicago *(G-6029)*
▲ **P & L Mark-It Inc** E 630 879-7590
Batavia *(G-1478)*
**P H C Enterprises Inc** G 847 816-7373
Vernon Hills *(G-21186)*
**Packaging Prtg Specialists Inc** F 630 513-8060
Saint Charles *(G-19232)*
**Pamco Printed Tape Label Inc** C 847 803-2200
Des Plaines *(G-8249)*
**Pana News Inc** F 217 562-2111
Pana *(G-17137)*
**Panda Graphics Inc** G 312 666-7642
Chicago *(G-6068)*
**Pantagraph Printing and Sty Co** F 309 829-1071
Bloomington *(G-2208)*
**Panther Products** G 618 664-1071
Greenville *(G-11402)*
**Papyrus Press Inc** F 773 342-0700
Chicago *(G-6074)*
**Park Press Inc** F 708 331-6352
South Holland *(G-20295)*
**Patrick Impressions LLC** G 630 257-9336
Lemont *(G-13250)*
**Paul D Burton** G 309 467-2613
Eureka *(G-10000)*
**Pcbl Retail Holdings LLC** G 610 761-4838
Northbrook *(G-16331)*
**Peacock Printing Inc** G 618 242-3157
Mount Vernon *(G-15437)*
**Pelegan Inc** G 708 442-9797
Riverside *(G-18033)*
**Perryco Inc** F 815 436-2431
Plainfield *(G-17638)*
**Petersburg Observer Co Inc** G 217 632-2236
Petersburg *(G-17537)*
**PHI Group Inc** C 847 824-5610
Mount Prospect *(G-15364)*
**Phoenix Graphics Inc** G 847 699-9520
Des Plaines *(G-8255)*
**Phoenix Marketing Services** F 630 616-8000
Mundelein *(G-15546)*
**Photo Techniques Corp** E 630 690-9360
Carol Stream *(G-3212)*
**Photo Techniques Corp** E 630 690-9360
Carol Stream *(G-3213)*
▼ **Physicians Record Co Inc** D 800 323-9268
Berwyn *(G-2074)*
**Pinney Printing Company** E 815 626-2727
Sterling *(G-20604)*
**Pioneer Forms Inc** G 773 539-8587
Chicago *(G-6125)*
**Pioneer Printing Service Inc** G 312 337-4283
Chicago *(G-6127)*
**Plastics Printing Group Inc** F 312 421-7980
Chicago *(G-6138)*
**Poets Study Inc** G 773 286-1355
Chicago *(G-6147)*
**Pontiac Engraving** G 630 834-4424
Bensenville *(G-1965)*
**Positive Impressions** G 618 438-7030
Benton *(G-2038)*
**Precision Screen Specialties** G 630 762-9548
Saint Charles *(G-19241)*
**Preferred Printing Service** G 312 421-2343
Chicago *(G-6175)*
**Premier Printing & Promotions** F 815 282-3890
Machesney Park *(G-14100)*
**Premier Printing and Packaging** G 847 970-9434
Rolling Meadows *(G-18769)*
**Premier Printing Illinois Inc** D 217 359-2219
Champaign *(G-3529)*
**Prime Label & Packaging LLC** D 630 227-1300
Wood Dale *(G-22414)*
**Primedia Source LLC** G 630 553-8451
Yorkville *(G-22670)*
**Print & Design Services LLC** G 847 317-9001
Bannockburn *(G-1264)*
**Print Graphics** G 847 249-1007
Beach Park *(G-1519)*
**Print Management Partners Inc** E 847 699-2999
Des Plaines *(G-8265)*
**Print Shop of Morris** G 815 710-5030
Morris *(G-15126)*
**Print Tech Inc** F 847 949-5400
Mundelein *(G-15549)*
**Printer Connection** G 217 268-3252
Arcola *(G-682)*
**Printforce Inc** G 618 395-7746
Olney *(G-16793)*
**Printing Craftsmen of Joliet** G 815 254-3982
Joliet *(G-12555)*
**Printing Craftsmen of Pontiac** G 815 844-7118
Pontiac *(G-17709)*
**Printing In Remebrance Inc** F 773 874-8700
Chicago *(G-6195)*
**Printing Press of Joliet Inc** G 815 725-0018
Joliet *(G-12556)*
**Printing System** G 630 339-5900
Glendale Heights *(G-11060)*
**Printing Works Inc** G 847 860-1920
Elk Grove Village *(G-9698)*
**Printing You Can Trust** G 224 676-0482
Deerfield *(G-8050)*
**Printlink Enterprises Inc** G 847 753-9800
Northbrook *(G-16345)*

**Printmeisters Inc**.....G..... 708 474-8400
Lansing *(G-13180)*
**Printsource Plus Inc**.....G..... 708 389-6252
Blue Island *(G-2265)*
**Printwise Inc**.....G..... 630 833-2845
Wheaton *(G-21972)*
**Printworld**.....G..... 815 544-1000
Belvidere *(G-1781)*
**Priority Print**.....G..... 708 485-7080
Brookfield *(G-2641)*
**Prismatec Inc**.....G..... 847 562-9022
Northbrook *(G-16346)*
**Pro Image Promotions Inc**.....G..... 773 292-1111
Chicago *(G-6202)*
▲ **Pro Tuff Decal Inc**.....E..... 815 356-9160
Crystal Lake *(G-7633)*
**Process Graphics Corp**.....E..... 815 637-2500
Rockford *(G-18542)*
**Productive Portable Disp Inc**.....G..... 630 458-9100
Addison *(G-259)*
**Proell Inc**.....G..... 630 587-2300
Saint Charles *(G-19242)*
**Progress Printing Corporation**.....E..... 773 927-0123
Chicago *(G-6210)*
**Progrssive Imprssions Intl Inc**.....C..... 309 664-0444
Bloomington *(G-2216)*
**Project Te Inc**.....G..... 217 344-9833
Urbana *(G-21100)*
**Promark Advertising Specialtie**.....G..... 618 483-6025
Altamont *(G-554)*
**Pryde Graphics Plus**.....G..... 630 882-5103
Plano *(G-17675)*
**Publishers Graphics LLC**.....E..... 630 221-1850
Carol Stream *(G-3223)*
**Q B F Graphic Group**.....G..... 708 781-9580
Tinley Park *(G-20941)*
**Qg LLC**.....D..... 217 347-7721
Effingham *(G-8855)*
**Quad/Graphics Inc**.....A..... 815 734-4121
Mount Morris *(G-15297)*
**Quality Bags Inc**.....F..... 630 543-9800
Addison *(G-263)*
**Quality Blue & Offset Printing**.....G..... 630 759-8035
Bolingbrook *(G-2363)*
▼ **Quality Logo Products Inc**.....E..... 630 896-1627
Aurora *(G-1207)*
**Quickprinters**.....G..... 309 833-5250
Macomb *(G-14130)*
**R & R Printnserve Inc**.....G..... 630 654-4044
Hinsdale *(G-11960)*
**R L Allen Industries**.....G..... 618 667-2544
Troy *(G-21011)*
**R N R Photographers Inc**.....G..... 708 453-1868
River Grove *(G-18013)*
**R Popernik Co Inc**.....F..... 773 434-4300
Chicago *(G-6269)*
**R R Donnelley & Sons Company**.....B..... 312 326-8000
Chicago *(G-6270)*
**R R Donnelley & Sons Company**.....A..... 815 584-2770
Dwight *(G-8591)*
**R W Wilson Printing Company**.....G..... 630 584-4100
Saint Charles *(G-19249)*
**Rainbow Art Inc**.....F..... 312 421-5600
Chicago *(G-6288)*
**Rapid Circular Press Inc**.....F..... 312 421-5611
Chicago *(G-6290)*
**Ready Inc**.....F..... 630 501-1352
Elmhurst *(G-9926)*
**Redeen Engraving Inc**.....G..... 847 593-6500
Elk Grove Village *(G-9712)*
**Reel Life Dvd LLC**.....G..... 708 579-1360
Western Springs *(G-21872)*
**Reid Communications Inc**.....E..... 847 741-9700
Elgin *(G-9163)*
**Remke Printing Inc**.....G..... 847 520-7300
Wheeling *(G-22137)*
**Review Printing Co Inc**.....G..... 309 788-7094
Rock Island *(G-18199)*
**Richco Graphics Inc**.....G..... 847 367-7277
Northbrook *(G-16356)*
**Rick Styfer**.....G..... 630 734-3244
Burr Ridge *(G-2877)*
**Rightway Printing Inc**.....F..... 630 790-0444
Glendale Heights *(G-11064)*
**Ripa LLC**.....G..... 708 938-1600
Broadview *(G-2609)*
**Robal Company Inc**.....F..... 630 393-0777
Warrenville *(G-21361)*
**Rodin Enterprises Inc**.....G..... 847 412-1370
Wheeling *(G-22142)*
▲ **Roeda Signs Inc**.....E..... 708 333-3021
South Holland *(G-20302)*
**Rohner Engraving Inc**.....G..... 773 244-8343
Chicago *(G-6382)*
**Rohner Letterpress Inc**.....F..... 773 248-0800
Chicago *(G-6383)*
**Rose Business Forms & Printing**.....G..... 618 533-3032
Centralia *(G-3429)*
**Roseri Business Forms Inc**.....G..... 847 381-8012
Inverness *(G-12211)*
**Roshan Ag Inc**.....G..... 773 267-1635
Chicago *(G-6397)*
**Rotary Forms and Systems Inc**.....G..... 847 843-8585
Hoffman Estates *(G-12044)*
**Rowboat Creative LLC**.....F..... 773 675-2628
Chicago *(G-6400)*
**RR Donnelley & Sons Company**.....E..... 847 622-1026
Elgin *(G-9169)*
**RR Donnelley & Sons Company**.....C..... 312 236-8000
Chicago *(G-6404)*
**RR Donnelley & Sons Company**.....B..... 630 588-5000
Lisle *(G-13653)*
**RR Donnelley Logistics SE**.....G..... 630 672-2500
Roselle *(G-18970)*
**Rt Associates Inc**.....D..... 847 577-0700
Wheeling *(G-22143)*
▲ **Ruco USA Inc**.....E..... 866 373-7912
Wood Dale *(G-22417)*
**Rush Impressions Inc**.....G..... 847 671-0622
Schiller Park *(G-19870)*
**Russell Doot Inc**.....G..... 312 527-1437
Chicago *(G-6415)*
**Rusty & Angela Buzzard**.....G..... 217 342-9841
Effingham *(G-8857)*
**Rv Enterprises Ltd**.....F..... 847 509-8710
Niles *(G-16030)*
**S V C Printing Co**.....G..... 773 286-2219
Chicago *(G-6422)*
**Salzman Printing**.....G..... 309 745-3016
Washington *(G-21391)*
**Samecwei Inc**.....G..... 630 897-7888
Aurora *(G-1214)*
**Sass-N-Class Inc**.....G..... 630 655-2420
Hinsdale *(G-11962)*
▲ **Sato Lbling Solutions Amer Inc**.....D..... 630 771-4200
Romeoville *(G-18866)*
**Sauk Valley Printing**.....G..... 815 284-2222
Dixon *(G-8347)*
**Scheiwes Print Shop**.....G..... 815 683-2398
Crescent City *(G-7456)*
**Schellhorn Photo Techniques**.....F..... 773 267-5141
Chicago *(G-6451)*
**Scholl Communications Inc**.....G..... 847 945-1891
Deerfield *(G-8051)*
**Schultz Brothers Inc**.....G..... 630 458-1437
Addison *(G-283)*
**Screen Graphics**.....G..... 309 699-8513
Pekin *(G-17288)*
**Scribes Inc**.....G..... 630 654-3800
Burr Ridge *(G-2879)*
**Sebis Direct Inc**.....E..... 312 243-9300
Bedford Park *(G-1584)*
▲ **Selah USA Inc**.....G..... 847 758-0702
Elk Grove Village *(G-9733)*
**Select Screen Prints & EMB**.....F..... 309 829-6511
Bloomington *(G-2222)*
**Selective Label & Tabs Inc**.....F..... 630 466-0091
Sugar Grove *(G-20735)*
**Selective Label & Tabs Inc**.....G..... 630 466-0091
Sugar Grove *(G-20736)*
**Selnar Inc**.....G..... 309 699-3977
East Peoria *(G-8733)*
**Sentro Printing Equip N Movers**.....G..... 779 423-0255
Rockton *(G-18702)*
**Seritex Inc**.....G..... 201 755-3002
Addison *(G-287)*
**Sew Wright Embroidery Inc**.....G..... 309 691-5780
Peoria *(G-17452)*
**Shamrock Scientific**.....D..... 800 323-0249
Bellwood *(G-1720)*
**Shanin Company**.....D..... 847 676-1200
Lincolnwood *(G-13537)*
**Shawver Press Inc**.....G..... 815 772-4700
Morrison *(G-15148)*
**Sheer Graphics Inc**.....G..... 630 654-4422
Westmont *(G-21920)*
**Shetley Management Inc**.....G..... 618 548-1556
Salem *(G-19351)*
▼ **Shree Mahavir Inc**.....G..... 312 408-1080
Chicago *(G-6501)*
**Sigley Printing & Off Sup Co**.....G..... 618 997-5304
Marion *(G-14287)*
**Signs In Dundee Inc**.....G..... 847 742-9530
Elgin *(G-9179)*
**Silkworm Inc**.....D..... 618 687-4077
Murphysboro *(G-15583)*
◆ **Simu Ltd**.....F..... 630 350-1060
Wood Dale *(G-22422)*
**Sir Cooper Inc**.....G..... 630 279-0162
Villa Park *(G-21285)*
**Skyline**.....G..... 312 300-4700
Mc Cook *(G-14458)*
**Skyline Printing Sales**.....G..... 847 412-1931
Northbrook *(G-16363)*
**Snegde Deep**.....G..... 630 351-7111
Roselle *(G-18978)*
**Southwest Printing Co**.....G..... 708 389-0800
Alsip *(G-530)*
**Spectrum Media Inc**.....G..... 217 234-2044
Mattoon *(G-14409)*
**Speedpro Imaging**.....G..... 847 856-8220
Gurnee *(G-11506)*
**Spirit Warrior Inc**.....G..... 708 614-0020
Orland Park *(G-16895)*
**Sportdecals Sport & Spirit Pro**.....D..... 800 435-6110
Spring Grove *(G-20365)*
**Sports All Sorts AP & Design**.....G..... 815 756-9910
Dekalb *(G-8122)*
**Sprectra Graphics Inc**.....G..... 618 624-6776
O Fallon *(G-16479)*
**Squeegee Brothers Inc**.....F..... 630 510-9152
Carol Stream *(G-3244)*
▲ **Ssn LLC**.....G..... 815 978-8729
Byron *(G-2922)*
**Standard Register Inc**.....E..... 847 783-1040
Elgin *(G-9191)*
**Star-Times Publishing Co Inc**.....G..... 618 635-2000
Staunton *(G-20559)*
**Stationary Studio LLC**.....G..... 847 541-2499
Buffalo Grove *(G-2777)*
▲ **Stellar Recognition Inc**.....D..... 773 282-8060
Chicago *(G-6588)*
**Stephen Fossler Company**.....D..... 847 635-7200
Des Plaines *(G-8281)*
**Strathmore Press**.....E..... 513 483-3600
Saint Charles *(G-19273)*
▲ **Stromberg Allen and Company**.....E..... 773 847-7131
Tinley Park *(G-20947)*
**Studio Color Inc**.....F..... 630 766-3333
Bensenville *(G-1999)*
**Sunburst Sportswear Inc**.....F..... 630 717-8680
Glendale Heights *(G-11079)*
**Sunny Direct LLC**.....G..... 630 795-0800
Woodridge *(G-22519)*
▲ **Sunrise Hitek Service Inc**.....E..... 773 792-8880
Chicago *(G-6630)*
**Sweet TS LLC**.....G..... 618 943-5729
Lawrenceville *(G-13204)*
**Swifty Print**.....G..... 630 584-9063
Saint Charles *(G-19276)*
**Systematics Screen Printing**.....F..... 630 521-1123
Itasca *(G-12362)*
**T F N W Inc**.....G..... 630 584-7383
Saint Charles *(G-19277)*
**T Graphics**.....G..... 618 592-4145
Oblong *(G-16735)*
**Tailored Printing Inc**.....G..... 217 522-6287
Rochester *(G-18122)*
**Tampico Press**.....G..... 312 243-5448
Chicago *(G-6672)*
**Te Shurt Shop Inc**.....F..... 217 344-1226
Champaign *(G-3549)*
**Team Cncept Prtg Thrmgrphy Inc**.....E..... 630 653-8326
Carol Stream *(G-3252)*
**Team Impressions Inc**.....E..... 847 357-9270
Elk Grove Village *(G-9769)*
**Tease**.....G..... 630 960-4950
Downers Grove *(G-8530)*
▲ **Techgraphic Solutions Inc**.....F..... 309 693-9400
Peoria *(G-17467)*
**Technicraft Supply Co**.....G..... 309 495-5245
Peoria *(G-17468)*
**Techprint Inc**.....F..... 847 616-0109
Elk Grove Village *(G-9774)*
**Teds Shirt Shack Inc**.....G..... 217 224-9705
Quincy *(G-17892)*
**Teeatude Inc**.....G..... 312 324-3554
Chicago *(G-6688)*
**Tees Ink**.....G..... 815 462-7300
New Lenox *(G-15919)*

**Temper Enterprises Inc** G 815 553-0374
Crest Hill *(G-7469)*
**Thermo-Craft Inc** G 618 281-7055
Columbia *(G-7363)*
**Thermo-Graphic LLC** E 630 350-2226
Bensenville *(G-2001)*
**Thia & Co** G 630 510-9770
Wheaton *(G-21986)*
**Think Ink Inc** G 815 459-4565
Crystal Lake *(G-7665)*
**Thomas Printing & Sty Co** G 618 435-2801
Benton *(G-2041)*
**Thomas Publishing Printing Div** G 618 351-6655
Carbondale *(G-3025)*
**Thomas Tees Inc** G 217 488-2288
New Berlin *(G-15866)*
**Three Castle Press Inc** G 630 540-0120
Streamwood *(G-20676)*
**Tidd Printing Co** G 708 749-1200
Berwyn *(G-2076)*
**Tiem Engineering Corporation** F 630 553-7484
Yorkville *(G-22672)*
**Time Out Chicago Partners Lllp** E 312 924-9555
Chicago *(G-6727)*
**Times Republic** E 815 432-5227
Watseka *(G-21431)*
**Toledo Democrat** G 217 849-2000
Toledo *(G-20967)*
**Toms Signs** G 630 377-8525
Saint Charles *(G-19284)*
**Town Square Publications LLC** G 847 427-4633
Arlington Heights *(G-856)*
**Tree Towns Reprographics Inc** E 630 832-0209
Elmhurst *(G-9951)*
**Trendy Screenprinting** G 815 895-0081
Sycamore *(G-20821)*
**Tri Star Plowing** G 847 584-5070
Schaumburg *(G-19771)*
**Tri-City Sports Inc** G 217 224-2489
Quincy *(G-17899)*
**Tri-Tower Printing Inc** G 847 640-6633
Rolling Meadows *(G-18785)*
**Triangle Screen Print Inc** F 847 678-9200
Franklin Park *(G-10612)*
**Trimark Screen Printing Inc** G 630 629-2823
Lombard *(G-13872)*
**Tst/Impreso Inc** G 630 775-9555
Addison *(G-330)*
**Type Concepts Inc** G 708 361-1005
Palos Heights *(G-17112)*
**Ultimate Distributing Inc** G 847 566-2250
Mundelein *(G-15565)*
**UNI-Label and Tag Corporation** E 847 956-8900
Elk Grove Village *(G-9797)*
**▲ Unique Assembly & Decorating** E 630 241-4300
Downers Grove *(G-8535)*
**Unique Envelope Corporation** E 773 586-0330
Chicago *(G-6819)*
**United Printers Inc** G 773 376-1955
Chicago *(G-6825)*
**Universal Digital Printing** G 708 389-0133
Midlothian *(G-14771)*
**UPS Authorized Retailer** G 708 354-8772
La Grange *(G-12748)*
**USA Printworks LLC** E 815 206-0854
Woodstock *(G-22620)*
**Usmss Inc** G 708 409-9010
Westchester *(G-21861)*
**Valee Inc** G 847 364-6464
Elk Grove Village *(G-9804)*
**Valid Secure Solutions LLC** F 260 633-0728
Lisle *(G-13674)*
**Van Lancker Steven** G 309 764-2221
Moline *(G-14975)*
**Var Graphics** G 708 456-2028
Elmwood Park *(G-9975)*
**Victor Envelope Mfg Corp** C 630 616-2750
Bensenville *(G-2012)*
**Village Press Inc** G 847 362-1856
Libertyville *(G-13399)*
**Vision Integrated Graphics** C 708 570-7900
Bolingbrook *(G-2380)*
**Voris Communication Co Inc** D 630 231-2425
West Chicago *(G-21791)*
**Vr Printing Co Inc** G 630 980-2315
Glendale Heights *(G-11090)*
**W W Barthel & Co** G 847 392-5643
Arlington Heights *(G-869)*
**Wagner International LLC** G 224 619-9247
Vernon Hills *(G-21216)*
**Waist Up Imprntd Sprtswear LLC** G 847 963-1400
Palatine *(G-17086)*
**Walter Barr Inc** G 630 325-7265
Willowbrook *(G-22238)*
**Washington Courier** F 309 444-3139
Washington *(G-21394)*
**Weakley Enterprises Inc** G 815 498-3429
Somonauk *(G-20130)*
**Weakley Printing & Sign Shop** G 847 473-4466
North Chicago *(G-16189)*
**Webe Ink** G 618 498-7620
Jerseyville *(G-12429)*
**Weber Press Inc** G 773 561-9815
Chicago *(G-6949)*
**Weiskamp Screen Printing** G 217 398-8428
Champaign *(G-3560)*
**Wes Tech Printing Graphic** G 630 520-9041
West Chicago *(G-21792)*
**White Graphics Inc** F 630 791-0232
Downers Grove *(G-8544)*
**White Graphics Printing Svcs** G 630 629-9300
Downers Grove *(G-8545)*
**Wide Image Incorporated** G 773 279-9183
Schaumburg *(G-19789)*
**William Holloway Ltd** G 847 866-9520
Evanston *(G-10106)*
**Williamsburg Press Inc** G 630 229-0228
North Aurora *(G-16150)*
**Winnetka Sign Co Inc** G 847 473-9378
North Chicago *(G-16191)*
**Winning Streak Inc** E 618 277-8191
Dupo *(G-8584)*
**Wold Printing Services Ltd** G 847 546-3110
Volo *(G-21320)*
**Wolfam Holdings Corporation** G 312 407-0100
Chicago *(G-7020)*
**◆ Wolters Kluwer US Inc** E 847 580-5000
Riverwoods *(G-18046)*
**Wood River Printing & Pubg Co** F 618 254-3134
Wood River *(G-22446)*
**Woolenwear Co** F 847 520-9243
Prospect Heights *(G-17786)*
**Workplace Ink Inc** G 312 939-0296
Park Ridge *(G-17229)*
**Workshop** E 815 777-2211
Galena *(G-10736)*
**Wortman Printing Company Inc** G 217 347-3775
Effingham *(G-8864)*
**Wyka LLC** F 847 298-0740
Des Plaines *(G-8306)*
**Xtreme Dzignz** G 309 633-9311
Bartonville *(G-1400)*
**Yes Print Management Inc** G 312 226-4444
Chicago *(G-7049)*
**Your Images Group Inc** G 847 437-6688
Schaumburg *(G-19794)*
**Your Logo Here** G 708 258-6666
Peotone *(G-17494)*
**Z Print Inc** G 773 685-4878
Chicago *(G-7057)*
**Zell Co** G 312 226-9191
Chicago *(G-7062)*
**Zoe Publications LLC** G 636 625-6622
Peoria *(G-17482)*
**Zorch International Inc** E 312 751-8010
Chicago *(G-7072)*

## 2761 Manifold Business Forms

**◆ Acco Brands Corporation** A 847 541-9500
Lake Zurich *(G-13033)*
**◆ Acco Brands USA LLC** B 800 222-6462
Lake Zurich *(G-13034)*
**Acco Brands USA LLC** D 847 272-3700
Lincolnshire *(G-13423)*
**Advance Instant Printing Co** G 312 346-0986
Chicago *(G-3760)*
**American Graphics Network Inc** F 847 729-7220
Glenview *(G-11100)*
**Azusa Inc** G 618 244-6591
Mount Vernon *(G-15399)*
**B & B Printing Company** G 217 285-6072
Pittsfield *(G-17561)*
**▲ Block and Company Inc** C 847 537-7200
Wheeling *(G-22015)*
**Certified Business Forms Inc** G 773 286-8194
Chicago *(G-4283)*
**Computer Business Forms Co** G 773 775-0155
Chicago *(G-4440)*
**Eklunds Typesetting & Prtg LLC** G 630 924-0057
Roselle *(G-18940)*
**Ennis Inc** E 815 875-2000
Princeton *(G-17748)*
**Fast Print Shop** G 618 997-1976
Marion *(G-14259)*
**▲ Forms Etc By Marty Walsh** G 708 499-6767
Oak Lawn *(G-16620)*
**Forms Specialist Inc** G 847 298-2868
Lincolnshire *(G-13449)*
**Frank R Walker Company** G 630 613-9312
Lombard *(G-13802)*
**Gem Acquisition Company Inc** F 773 735-3300
Chicago *(G-4923)*
**Genoa Business Forms Inc** E 815 895-2800
Sycamore *(G-20798)*
**Grand Forms & Systems Inc** F 847 259-4600
Arlington Heights *(G-760)*
**Integrated Print Graphics Inc** D 847 695-6777
South Elgin *(G-20206)*
**J Gooch & Associates Inc** G 217 522-7575
Springfield *(G-20461)*
**K R O Enterprises Ltd** G 309 797-2213
Moline *(G-14949)*
**Kellogg Printing Co** F 309 734-8388
Monmouth *(G-15016)*
**Keneal Industries Inc** F 815 886-1300
Romeoville *(G-18834)*
**Little Doloras** G 708 331-1330
South Holland *(G-20286)*
**M L S Printing Co Inc** G 847 948-8902
Deerfield *(G-8033)*
**M Wells Printing Co** G 312 455-0400
Chicago *(G-5588)*
**Marc Business Forms Inc** F 847 568-9200
Lincolnwood *(G-13524)*
**Midwest Graphic Industries** F 630 509-2972
Bensenville *(G-1952)*
**Moore North America Fin Inc** G 847 607-6000
Chicago *(G-5802)*
**Multi Packaging Solutions Inc** G 773 283-9500
Chicago *(G-5832)*
**N Bujarski Inc** G 847 884-1600
Schaumburg *(G-19660)*
**Nbs Systems Inc** E 217 999-3472
Mount Olive *(G-15306)*
**Novak Business Forms Inc** E 630 932-9850
Lombard *(G-13834)*
**▲ Perftech Inc** E 630 554-0010
North Aurora *(G-16141)*
**▼ Physicians Record Co Inc** D 800 323-9268
Berwyn *(G-2074)*
**Proform** G 309 676-2535
Peoria *(G-17437)*
**R & L Business Forms Inc** F 618 939-6535
Waterloo *(G-21404)*
**RR Donnelley & Sons Company** C 630 377-2586
Saint Charles *(G-19254)*
**RR Donnelley & Sons Company** D 312 326-8000
Chicago *(G-6403)*
**RR Donnelley & Sons Company** C 217 935-2113
Clinton *(G-7288)*
**Safeguard Scientifics Inc** G 312 234-9828
Chicago *(G-6427)*
**Shanin Company** D 847 676-1200
Lincolnwood *(G-13537)*
**Springfield Printing Inc** G 217 787-3500
Springfield *(G-20531)*
**Standard Register Inc** G 309 693-3700
Peoria *(G-17462)*
**Standard Register Inc** F 815 432-4203
Watseka *(G-21427)*
**Standard Register Inc** F 630 784-6833
Chicago *(G-6571)*
**Standard Register Inc** G 217 793-1900
Springfield *(G-20535)*
**Standard Register Inc** G 708 560-7600
Oak Forest *(G-16589)*
**Standard Register Inc** G 630 368-0336
Oak Brook *(G-16561)*
**Standard Register Inc** E 815 439-1050
Plainfield *(G-17652)*
**Standard Register Inc** C 630 784-6810
Carol Stream *(G-3248)*

## 2771 Greeting Card Publishing

**Advantage Printing Inc** G 630 627-7468
Lombard *(G-13760)*
**Alex Smart Inc** G 773 244-9275
Chicago *(G-3803)*
**Cardthartic LLC** F 217 239-5895
Champaign *(G-3461)*

# 27 PRINTING, PUBLISHING, AND ALLIED INDUSTRIES

Cook Communications Ministries .......... C ...... 847 741-0800
  Elgin (G-9004)
Crest Greetings Inc .......... F ...... 708 210-0800
  Chicago (G-4503)
▲ Florists Transworld Dlvry Inc .......... A ...... 630 719-7800
  Downers Grove (G-8444)
Fsg Crest LLC .......... F ...... 708 210-0800
  Lake In The Hills (G-12993)
▲ Ggc Corp .......... D ...... 847 671-6500
  Schiller Park (G-19834)
Gram Colossal Inc .......... G ...... 847 223-5757
  Grayslake (G-11343)
Harry Otto Printing Company .......... F ...... 630 365-6111
  Elburn (G-8889)
K Chae Corp .......... F ...... 847 763-0077
  Lincolnwood (G-13518)
Karen Young .......... F ...... 312 202-0142
  Chicago (G-5360)
Marketing Card Technology LLC .......... D ...... 630 985-7900
  Darien (G-7799)
National Gift Card Corp .......... E ...... 815 477-4288
  Crystal Lake (G-7617)
▲ P S Greetings Inc .......... C ...... 708 831-5340
  Chicago (G-6040)
P S Greetings Inc .......... F ...... 847 673-7255
  Skokie (G-20052)
▲ Recycled Paper Greetings Inc .......... E ...... 773 348-6410
  Chicago (G-6314)
▲ Salamander Studios Chicago Inc .......... F ...... 773 379-2211
  Chicago (G-6431)
United Press Inc (del) .......... F ...... 847 482-0597
  Lincolnshire (G-13487)

## 2782 Blankbooks & Looseleaf Binders

◆ Acco Brands Corporation .......... A ...... 847 541-9500
  Lake Zurich (G-13033)
Advance Bindery Co .......... F ...... 847 662-2418
  Waukegan (G-21518)
Americas Community Bankers .......... E ...... 312 644-3100
  Chicago (G-3884)
Assemble and Mail Group Inc .......... G ...... 309 473-2006
  Heyworth (G-11764)
Beta Pak Inc .......... F ...... 708 466-7844
  Sugar Grove (G-20718)
Bindery Maintenance Services .......... G ...... 618 945-7480
  Bridgeport (G-2449)
▲ Bound + D Termined Inc .......... G ...... 847 696-1501
  Park Ridge (G-17185)
▲ Carousel Checks Inc .......... F ...... 708 599-8576
  Bridgeview (G-2474)
Chartwell Studio Inc .......... G ...... 847 868-8674
  Evanston (G-10021)
Counter Cft Svc Systems & Pdts .......... G ...... 630 629-7336
  Lombard (G-13785)
Deluxe Corporation .......... C ...... 847 635-7200
  Des Plaines (G-8181)
Deluxe Express .......... F ...... 847 756-0429
  Plainfield (G-17590)
Funeral Register Books Inc .......... F ...... 217 627-3235
  Girard (G-10946)
General Loose Leaf Bindery Inc .......... E ...... 847 244-9700
  Waukegan (G-21562)
▲ General Products .......... E ...... 773 463-2424
  Chicago (G-4932)
George S Music Room .......... G ...... 773 767-4676
  Chicago (G-4945)
Got 2b Scrappin .......... G ...... 217 347-3600
  Effingham (G-8837)
Harris Bmo Bank National Assn .......... E ...... 815 886-1900
  Romeoville (G-18830)
Heart & Soul Memories Inc .......... F ...... 847 478-1931
  Buffalo Grove (G-2702)
▲ Howard Medical Company .......... G ...... 773 278-1440
  Chicago (G-5122)
J-Industries Inc .......... F ...... 815 654-0055
  Loves Park (G-13949)
▲ Jacobson Acqstion Holdings LLC .......... C ...... 847 623-1414
  Waukegan (G-21574)
▲ Johnson Diaries .......... G ...... 708 478-2882
  Mokena (G-14877)
Jpmorgan Chase Bank Nat Assn .......... E ...... 630 653-1270
  Carol Stream (G-3177)
K & L Looseleaf Products Inc .......... D ...... 847 357-9733
  Elk Grove Village (G-9568)
Medcal Sales LLC .......... G ...... 847 837-2771
  Mundelein (G-15527)
◆ Michael Lewis Company .......... C ...... 708 688-2200
  Mc Cook (G-14453)
▲ Multi Swatch Corporation .......... D ...... 708 344-9440
  Broadview (G-2600)

Polyvinyl Record Co .......... G ...... 217 403-1752
  Champaign (G-3527)
Post Press Production Inc .......... F ...... 630 860-9833
  Elk Grove Village (G-9688)
Protek Inc .......... G ...... 888 536-5466
  Saint Charles (G-19243)
◆ Simu Ltd .......... G ...... 630 350-1060
  Wood Dale (G-22422)
Systems Service & Supply .......... G ...... 815 725-1836
  Joliet (G-12581)
Tower Plastics Mfg Inc .......... G ...... 847 788-1700
  Burr Ridge (G-2885)
Webcrafters Inc .......... G ...... 847 658-6661
  Algonquin (G-414)
Zookbinders Inc .......... D ...... 847 272-5745
  Deerfield (G-8070)

## 2789 Bookbinding

11th Street Express Prtg Inc .......... F ...... 815 968-0208
  Rockford (G-18235)
A A Swift Print Inc .......... G ...... 847 301-1122
  Schaumburg (G-19418)
A To Z Engraving Co Inc .......... G ...... 847 526-7396
  Wauconda (G-21435)
A To Z Offset Prtg & Pubg Inc .......... G ...... 847 966-3016
  Skokie (G-19943)
A+ Printing Co .......... G ...... 815 968-8181
  Rockford (G-18242)
▼ ABS Graphics Inc .......... C ...... 630 495-2400
  Itasca (G-12223)
Accord Carton Co .......... C ...... 708 272-3050
  Alsip (G-428)
Accurate Die Cutting Inc .......... G ...... 847 437-7215
  Elk Grove Village (G-9261)
Acres of Sky Communications .......... G ...... 815 493-2560
  Lanark (G-13149)
Adams Printing Inc .......... F ...... 618 529-2396
  Carbondale (G-3000)
Adcraft Printers Inc .......... F ...... 815 932-6432
  Kankakee (G-12601)
Advertisers Bindery Inc .......... F ...... 312 939-4995
  Chicago (G-3776)
All Printing & Graphics Inc .......... F ...... 708 450-1512
  Broadview (G-2555)
All-Ways Quick Print .......... G ...... 708 403-8422
  Orland Park (G-16841)
Allegra Network LLC .......... G ...... 630 801-9335
  Aurora (G-1104)
Allegra Print & Imaging Inc .......... G ...... 847 697-1434
  Elgin (G-8942)
Alphadigital Inc .......... G ...... 708 482-4488
  La Grange Park (G-12752)
AlphaGraphics .......... F ...... 630 261-1227
  Oakbrook Terrace (G-16694)
AlphaGraphics Printshops .......... G ...... 630 964-9600
  Lisle (G-13555)
American Litho Incorporated .......... A ...... 630 682-0600
  Carol Stream (G-3099)
American Quick Print Inc .......... G ...... 847 253-2700
  Wauconda (G-21441)
Apple Graphics Inc .......... G ...... 630 389-2222
  Batavia (G-1416)
Apple Press Inc .......... G ...... 815 224-1451
  Peru (G-17500)
Apple Printing Center .......... G ...... 630 932-9494
  Addison (G-41)
Arch Printing Inc .......... G ...... 630 966-0235
  Aurora (G-1110)
Art Bookbinders of America .......... E ...... 312 226-4100
  Chicago (G-3949)
Avid of Illinois Inc .......... F ...... 847 698-2775
  Saint Charles (G-19140)
B & B Printing Company .......... G ...... 217 285-6072
  Pittsfield (G-17561)
B F Shaw Printing Company .......... E ...... 815 875-4461
  Princeton (G-17744)
B J Plastic Molding Co .......... G ...... 630 766-3200
  Franklin Park (G-10408)
Bailleu & Bailleu Printing Inc .......... G ...... 309 852-2517
  Kewanee (G-12670)
Barnaby Inc .......... F ...... 815 895-6555
  Sycamore (G-20789)
Bb Services LLC .......... G ...... 630 941-8122
  Elmhurst (G-9837)
Bell Litho Inc .......... D ...... 847 952-3300
  Elk Grove Village (G-9338)
Benzinger Printing .......... G ...... 815 784-6560
  Genoa (G-10875)
Bikast Graphics Inc .......... G ...... 847 487-8822
  Wauconda (G-21446)

Biller Press & Manufacturing .......... G ...... 847 395-4111
  Antioch (G-623)
Bindery & Distribution Service .......... G ...... 847 550-7000
  South Barrington (G-20131)
Brads Printing Inc .......... G ...... 847 662-0447
  Waukegan (G-21531)
Branstiter Printing Co .......... G ...... 217 245-6533
  Jacksonville (G-12381)
Business Forms Finishing Svc .......... G ...... 773 229-0230
  Chicago (G-4187)
Cadore-Miller Printing Inc .......... F ...... 708 430-7091
  Hickory Hills (G-11768)
Camera Ready Copies Inc .......... F ...... 847 215-8611
  Prospect Heights (G-17773)
Cameron Printing Inc .......... G ...... 630 231-3301
  West Chicago (G-21677)
Cannon Ball Marketing Inc .......... G ...... 630 971-2127
  Lisle (G-13573)
Capitol Impressions Inc .......... E ...... 309 633-1400
  Peoria (G-17322)
Cardinal Colorprint Prtg Corp .......... G ...... 630 467-1000
  Itasca (G-12241)
Carter Printing Co Inc .......... G ...... 217 227-4464
  Farmersville (G-10183)
Case Paluch & Associates Inc .......... G ...... 773 465-0098
  Chicago (G-4248)
Century Printing .......... G ...... 618 632-2486
  O Fallon (G-16465)
Cenveo Inc .......... G ...... 217 243-4258
  Jacksonville (G-12383)
Challenge Printers .......... G ...... 773 252-0212
  Chicago (G-4285)
Christopher R Cline Prtg Ltd .......... F ...... 847 981-0500
  Elk Grove Village (G-9372)
Cifuentes Luis & Nicole Inc .......... G ...... 847 490-3660
  Schaumburg (G-19472)
Cjs Printing .......... G ...... 309 968-6585
  Manito (G-14172)
Cloverdale Corporation .......... G ...... 847 296-9225
  Des Plaines (G-8171)
Cmb Printing Inc .......... F ...... 630 323-1110
  Burr Ridge (G-2830)
Commercial Copy Printing Ctr .......... F ...... 847 981-8590
  Elk Grove Village (G-9384)
Continental Bindery Corp .......... D ...... 847 439-6811
  Elk Grove Village (G-9390)
Copy Mat Printing .......... G ...... 309 452-1392
  Bloomington (G-2155)
Copy Service Inc .......... G ...... 815 758-1151
  Dekalb (G-8079)
▲ Copy-Mor Inc .......... E ...... 312 666-4000
  Elmhurst (G-9856)
Cpr Printing Inc .......... G ...... 630 377-8420
  Geneva (G-10821)
Craftsmen Printing .......... G ...... 217 283-9574
  Hoopeston (G-12108)
Creative Label Inc .......... D ...... 847 981-3800
  Elk Grove Village (G-9399)
Creative Lithocraft Inc .......... G ...... 847 352-7002
  Schaumburg (G-19489)
Crossmark Printing Inc .......... F ...... 708 532-8263
  Tinley Park (G-20906)
D E Asbury Inc .......... G ...... 217 222-0617
  Hamilton (G-11532)
D G Brandt Inc .......... G ...... 815 942-4064
  Morris (G-15105)
D L V Printing Service Inc .......... F ...... 773 626-1661
  Chicago (G-4537)
Dale K Brown .......... G ...... 815 338-0222
  Woodstock (G-22558)
Darnall Printing .......... G ...... 309 827-7212
  Bloomington (G-2161)
▲ Darwill Inc .......... C ...... 708 449-7770
  Hillside (G-11914)
David H Vander Ploeg .......... G ...... 708 331-7700
  South Holland (G-20260)
DE Asbury Inc .......... E ...... 217 222-0617
  Quincy (G-17820)
Deadline Prtg Clor Copying LLC .......... G ...... 847 437-9000
  Elk Grove Village (G-9419)
▲ Deluxe Johnson .......... F ...... 847 635-7200
  Des Plaines (G-8182)
Demis Printing Inc .......... G ...... 773 282-9128
  Park Ridge (G-17189)
Denor Graphics Inc .......... F ...... 847 364-1130
  Elk Grove Village (G-9423)
Design Graphics Inc .......... G ...... 815 462-3323
  New Lenox (G-15875)
Diamond Graphics of Berwyn .......... G ...... 708 749-2500
  Berwyn (G-2060)

## 27 PRINTING, PUBLISHING, AND ALLIED INDUSTRIES

| Company | Code | Phone |
|---|---|---|
| DMarv Design Specialty Prtrs — Blue Island (G-2246) | G | 708 389-4420 |
| Donnells Printing & Off Pdts — Pontiac (G-17698) | G | 815 842-6541 |
| E & H Graphic Service — Matteson (G-14371) | G | 708 748-5656 |
| Eastrich Printing & Sales — Freeport (G-10654) | G | 815 232-4216 |
| Einstein Crest — Niles (G-15977) | G | 847 965-7791 |
| Elgin Instant Print — Elgin (G-9024) | G | 847 931-9006 |
| Elliott Publishing Inc — Liberty (G-13295) | G | 217 645-3033 |
| Elmhurst Enterprise Group Inc — Arlington Heights (G-749) | G | 847 228-5945 |
| Excellent Bindery Inc — Bensenville (G-1894) | E | 630 766-9050 |
| F Weber Printing Co Inc — Manteno (G-14183) | G | 815 468-6152 |
| Fast Printing of Joliet Inc — Joliet (G-12492) | G | 815 723-0080 |
| Fastway Printing Inc — Schaumburg (G-19524) | G | 847 882-0950 |
| Fedex Office & Print Svcs Inc — Champaign (G-3485) | E | 217 355-3400 |
| Fedex Office & Print Svcs Inc — Evanston (G-10036) | F | 847 475-8650 |
| Fedex Office & Print Svcs Inc — Rockford (G-18380) | F | 815 229-0033 |
| Fedex Office & Print Svcs Inc — Lincolnwood (G-13510) | F | 847 329-9464 |
| Fedex Office & Print Svcs Inc — Glenview (G-11124) | F | 847 729-3030 |
| Fedex Office & Print Svcs Inc — Peoria (G-17359) | E | 309 685-4093 |
| Fedex Office & Print Svcs Inc — Buffalo Grove (G-2693) | E | 847 459-8008 |
| Fedex Office & Print Svcs Inc — Elmwood Park (G-9970) | E | 708 452-0149 |
| Fedex Office & Print Svcs Inc — Park Ridge (G-17193) | G | 847 823-9360 |
| Fedex Office & Print Svcs Inc — Bloomingdale (G-2108) | F | 630 894-1800 |
| Fedex Office & Print Svcs Inc — Arlington Heights (G-754) | E | 847 670-4100 |
| Fedex Office & Print Svcs Inc — Chicago (G-4831) | E | 312 670-4460 |
| Fernwood Printers Ltd — Oak Forest (G-16581) | G | 630 964-9449 |
| Fidelity Bindery Company — Broadview (G-2578) | E | 708 343-6833 |
| First Impression of Chicago — Chicago (G-4849) | G | 773 224-3434 |
| First String Enterprises Inc — Tinley Park (G-20913) | E | 708 614-1200 |
| Fisheye Services Incorporated — Chicago (G-4852) | G | 773 942-6314 |
| Flash Printing Inc — Franklin Park (G-10470) | G | 847 288-9101 |
| Fleetwood Press Inc — Brookfield (G-2632) | G | 708 485-6811 |
| Floden Enterprises — Mundelein (G-15502) | G | 847 566-7898 |
| FM Graphic Impressions Inc — Aurora (G-1153) | E | 630 897-8788 |
| Forman Co Inc — Monmouth (G-15012) | G | 309 734-3413 |
| Forms Design Plus Coleman Prtg — Peoria (G-17365) | G | 309 685-6000 |
| French Studio Ltd — Herrin (G-11748) | E | 618 942-5328 |
| G F Printing — Granite City (G-11278) | G | 618 797-0576 |
| Gamma Alpha Visual — Elk Grove Village (G-9496) | G | 847 956-0633 |
| GM Laminating & Mounting Corp — Elmhurst (G-9878) | G | 630 941-7979 |
| Gossett Printing Inc — Salem (G-19335) | G | 618 548-2583 |
| Graphic Arts Bindery LLC — Rochelle (G-18092) | D | 708 416-4290 |
| Graphics Group LLC — Chicago (G-4992) | D | 708 867-5500 |
| Grasso Graphics Inc — Alsip (G-465) | G | 708 489-2060 |
| Griffith Solutions Inc — Park Ridge (G-17201) | G | 847 384-1810 |
| Group O Inc — Milan (G-14790) | E | 309 736-8100 |
| Grovak Instant Printing Co — Mount Prospect (G-15334) | G | 847 675-2414 |
| Harris Bookbinding LLC — Downers Grove (G-8454) | G | 773 287-9414 |
| Harry Otto Printing Company — Elburn (G-8889) | F | 630 365-6111 |
| Hawthorne Press — Cicero (G-7201) | G | 708 652-9000 |
| Hawthorne Press Inc — Spring Grove (G-20336) | G | 847 587-0582 |
| Heart Printing Inc — Arlington Heights (G-764) | G | 847 259-2100 |
| Heritage Press Inc — Libertyville (G-13330) | G | 847 362-9699 |
| Highland Printers — Highland (G-11791) | G | 618 654-5880 |
| Homan Bindery — Chicago (G-5100) | E | 773 276-1500 |
| Hopkins Printing & Envelope Co — Addison (G-148) | F | 630 543-8227 |
| House of Graphics — Carol Stream (G-3168) | E | 630 682-0810 |
| Hq Printers Inc — Chicago (G-5125) | G | 312 782-2020 |
| Hub Printing Company Inc — Rochelle (G-18094) | F | 815 562-7057 |
| Ideal Advertising & Printing — Rockford (G-18426) | F | 815 965-1713 |
| Illinois Office Sup Elect Prtg — Ottawa (G-16962) | E | 815 434-0186 |
| Illinois Tool Works Inc — Frankfort (G-10333) | G | 708 720-0300 |
| Image Print Inc — Streator (G-20691) | G | 815 672-1068 |
| Impression Printing — Oak Forest (G-16583) | F | 708 614-8660 |
| In A Bind Assembly Fulfillment — Marengo (G-14231) | E | 815 568-6952 |
| In-Print Graphics Inc — Oak Forest (G-16584) | E | 708 396-1010 |
| Ink Well Printing — Peru (G-17514) | G | 815 224-1366 |
| Ink Well Printing & Design Ltd — Schaumburg (G-19566) | G | 847 923-8060 |
| Instant Collating Service Inc — Chicago (G-5205) | F | 312 243-4703 |
| Insty Prints Palatine Inc — Palatine (G-17042) | F | 847 963-0000 |
| Insty-Prints of Champaign Inc — Champaign (G-3501) | G | 217 356-6166 |
| Instyprints of Waukegan Inc — Waukegan (G-21571) | G | 847 336-5599 |
| Integra Graphics and Forms Inc — Crestwood (G-7490) | F | 708 385-0950 |
| International Graphics & Assoc — Saint Charles (G-19199) | F | 630 584-2248 |
| J & J Mr Quick Print Inc — Chicago (G-5251) | G | 773 767-7776 |
| J D Graphic Co Inc — Elk Grove Village (G-9557) | G | 847 364-4000 |
| J F Wagner Printing Co — Northbrook (G-16280) | G | 847 564-0017 |
| J R Finishers Inc — Schaumburg (G-19586) | D | 847 301-2556 |
| Jay Printing — Palatine (G-17046) | G | 847 934-6103 |
| Joes Printing — Chicago (G-5309) | G | 773 545-6063 |
| Johns-Byrne Company — Niles (G-15992) | D | 847 583-3100 |
| Johnson Press America Inc — Pontiac (G-17704) | E | 815 844-5161 |
| Josco Inc — Chicago (G-5326) | G | 708 867-7189 |
| Jph Enterprises Inc — Des Plaines (G-8217) | G | 847 390-0900 |
| Juskie Printing Corp — Downers Grove (G-8468) | G | 630 663-8833 |
| K & M Printing Company Inc — Schaumburg (G-19595) | D | 847 884-1100 |
| K O G Mfg & Bindery Corp — Waukegan (G-21576) | F | 847 263-5050 |
| K R O Enterprises Ltd — Moline (G-14949) | G | 309 797-2213 |
| Kelly Printing Co Inc — Danville (G-7741) | E | 217 443-1792 |
| Kendall Printing Co — Yorkville (G-22663) | G | 630 553-9200 |
| Kens Quick Print Inc — Highland Park (G-11849) | F | 847 831-4410 |
| Kevin Kewney — Quincy (G-17844) | G | 217 228-7444 |
| Key Printing — Kankakee (G-12635) | G | 815 933-1800 |
| Klein Printing Inc — Chicago (G-5387) | G | 773 235-2121 |
| Klh Printing Corp — Wheeling (G-22086) | G | 847 459-0115 |
| Koehler Bindery Inc — Chicago (G-5401) | G | 773 539-7979 |
| Kwik Print Inc — Itasca (G-12299) | G | 630 773-3225 |
| LAC Enterprises Inc — Crystal Lake (G-7601) | G | 815 455-5044 |
| Lake Shore Printing — Skokie (G-20024) | G | 847 679-4110 |
| Lans Printing Inc — Lynwood (G-14021) | G | 708 895-6226 |
| Lasons Label Co — Chicago (G-5464) | G | 773 775-2606 |
| Lee-Wel Printing Corporation — Wheaton (G-21966) | G | 630 682-0935 |
| Leonard Emerson — Divernon (G-8316) | G | 217 628-3441 |
| Lind-Remsen Printing Co Inc — Rockford (G-18470) | F | 815 969-0610 |
| Link-Letters Ltd — Wheeling (G-22094) | F | 847 459-1199 |
| Lists & Letters — Wheeling (G-22095) | F | 847 520-5207 |
| Lynns Printing Co — Alton (G-583) | G | 618 465-7701 |
| M & G Graphics Inc — Chicago (G-5576) | E | 773 247-1596 |
| M O W Printing Inc — Collinsville (G-7331) | F | 618 345-5525 |
| Macoupin County Enquirer Inc — Carlinville (G-3042) | E | 217 854-2534 |
| Mall Graphic Inc — Huntley (G-12161) | F | 847 668-7600 |
| Marcus Press — Bloomingdale (G-2115) | G | 630 351-1857 |
| Mark Twain Press Inc — Mundelein (G-15523) | G | 847 255-2700 |
| Marquardt Printing Company — Willowbrook (G-22220) | E | 630 887-8500 |
| Mason City Banner Times — Mason City (G-14365) | F | 217 482-3276 |
| Master Engraving — Virden (G-21299) | G | 217 965-5885 |
| Mattoon Printing Center — Mattoon (G-14400) | G | 217 234-3100 |
| McGrath Press Inc — Crystal Lake (G-7607) | E | 815 356-5246 |
| Mencarini Enterprises Inc — Rockford (G-18491) | F | 815 398-9565 |
| Merritt & Edwards Corporation — Bloomington (G-2196) | F | 309 828-4741 |
| Metro Printing & Pubg Inc — Millstadt (G-14829) | F | 618 476-9587 |
| Michael Zimmerman — Northbrook (G-16311) | G | 847 272-5560 |
| Mid Central Printing & Mailing — Wilmette (G-22262) | G | 847 251-4040 |
| Mid City Printing Service — Chicago (G-5725) | G | 773 777-5400 |
| Midwest Gold Stampers Inc — Chicago (G-5744) | F | 773 775-5253 |
| Minuteman Press — Countryside (G-7437) | G | 630 541-9122 |
| Minuteman Press — Lombard (G-13827) | G | 630 279-0438 |
| Minuteman Press — Arlington Heights (G-803) | G | 847 577-2411 |
| Minuteman Press Morton Grove — Morton Grove (G-15221) | G | 847 470-0212 |
| Minuteman Press of Rockford — Loves Park (G-13967) | G | 815 633-2992 |
| Modern Printing of Quincy — Quincy (G-17861) | F | 217 223-1063 |
| Msf Graphics Inc — Des Plaines (G-8239) | G | 847 446-6900 |
| Multi Art Press — Chicago (G-5831) | G | 773 775-0515 |
| Multicopy Corp — Northfield (G-16410) | G | 847 446-7015 |
| N Bujarski Inc — Schaumburg (G-19660) | G | 847 884-1600 |
| N P D Inc — Oak Lawn (G-16636) | G | 708 424-6788 |

## SIC SECTION — 27 PRINTING, PUBLISHING, AND ALLIED INDUSTRIES

| Company | Code | Phone |
|---|---|---|
| National Binding Sups Eqp Inc — Geneva (G-10851) | G | 630 801-7600 |
| New Life Printing & Publishing — Algonquin (G-402) | G | 847 658-4111 |
| Newell & Haney Inc — Belleville (G-1660) | F | 618 277-3660 |
| Northwest Premier Printing — Chicago (G-5940) | G | 773 736-1882 |
| Northwest Printing Inc — Harvard (G-11642) | G | 815 943-7977 |
| Nu-Art Printing — Centralia (G-3425) | G | 618 533-9971 |
| Off The Press — Plainfield (G-17634) | G | 815 436-9612 |
| Office Assistants Inc — Oak Lawn (G-16637) | G | 708 346-0505 |
| Ogden Offset Printers Inc — Chicago (G-5973) | G | 773 284-7797 |
| Olde Print Shoppe Inc — Olney (G-16786) | G | 618 395-3833 |
| Olympic Bindery Inc — Arlington Heights (G-813) | D | 847 577-8132 |
| On Time Printing and Finishing — Hillside (G-11929) | G | 708 544-4500 |
| Osbon Lithographers — Park Ridge (G-17214) | G | 847 825-7727 |
| P & S Cochran Printers Inc — Peoria (G-17421) | E | 309 691-6668 |
| P H C Enterprises Inc — Vernon Hills (G-21186) | G | 847 816-7373 |
| P P Graphics Inc — Westchester (G-21852) | G | 708 343-2530 |
| Parrot Press — Chicago (G-6087) | G | 773 376-6333 |
| Patrick Impressions LLC — Lemont (G-13250) | G | 630 257-9336 |
| Patton Printing and Graphics — Effingham (G-8852) | G | 217 347-0220 |
| Perma Graphics Printers — New Lenox (G-15901) | G | 815 485-6955 |
| Perryco Inc — Plainfield (G-17638) | F | 815 436-2431 |
| Phoenix Binding Corp — Elk Grove Village (G-9678) | G | 847 981-1111 |
| Pinney Printing Company — Sterling (G-20603) | G | 815 626-2727 |
| Pinney Printing Company — Sterling (G-20604) | E | 815 626-2727 |
| PIP Printing — Glenview (G-11182) | G | 847 998-6330 |
| PIP Printing Inc — Frankfort (G-10349) | G | 815 464-0075 |
| Prairieland Printing — Washington (G-21387) | G | 309 647-5425 |
| Precision Die Cutting & Finish — Chicago (G-6169) | G | 773 252-5625 |
| Preferred Printing Service — Chicago (G-6175) | G | 312 421-2343 |
| Print & Design Services LLC — Bannockburn (G-1264) | G | 847 317-9001 |
| Print King Inc — Oak Lawn (G-16641) | F | 708 499-3777 |
| Print Turnaround Inc — Arlington Heights (G-822) | F | 847 228-1762 |
| Printed Word Inc — Evanston (G-10091) | G | 847 328-1511 |
| Printing By Joseph — Mokena (G-14898) | G | 708 479-2669 |
| Printing Craftsmen of Joliet — Joliet (G-12555) | G | 815 254-3982 |
| Printing Etc Inc — Rochelle (G-18102) | G | 815 562-6151 |
| Printing Plus — Lockport (G-13739) | G | 708 301-3900 |
| Printing Plus of Roselle Inc — Roselle (G-18963) | G | 630 893-0410 |
| Printing Press of Joliet Inc — Joliet (G-12556) | G | 815 725-0018 |
| Printing Source Inc — Morton Grove (G-15228) | G | 773 588-2930 |
| Printing Works Inc — Elk Grove Village (G-9698) | G | 847 860-1920 |
| Printmeisters Inc — Lansing (G-13180) | G | 708 474-8400 |
| Printsource Plus Inc — Blue Island (G-2265) | G | 708 389-6252 |
| Prism Commercial Printing Ctrs — Chicago (G-6199) | G | 630 834-4443 |
| Pro-Type Printing Inc — Paxton (G-17244) | G | 217 379-4715 |
| Progress Printing Corporation — Chicago (G-6210) | E | 773 927-0123 |
| Quad City Press — Moline (G-14965) | F | 309 764-8142 |
| Quad/Graphics Inc — Mount Morris (G-15297) | A | 815 734-4121 |
| Quality Quickprint Inc — Joliet (G-12560) | G | 815 439-3430 |
| Quality Quickprint Inc — Lockport (G-13740) | F | 815 838-1784 |
| Quickprinters — Macomb (G-14130) | G | 309 833-5250 |
| Quinn Print Inc — Park Ridge (G-17218) | G | 847 823-9100 |
| R & R Bindery Service Inc — Girard (G-10949) | C | 217 627-2143 |
| R R Donnelley & Sons Company — Dwight (G-8591) | A | 815 584-2770 |
| R R Donnelley & Sons Company — Pontiac (G-17710) | A | 815 844-5181 |
| Rapid Print — Peoria (G-17440) | G | 309 673-0826 |
| Rasmussen Press Inc — Bensenville (G-1976) | G | |
| Ready Press — Palatine (G-17066) | G | 847 358-8655 |
| Redline Press — Lisle (G-13650) | G | 630 690-9828 |
| Remke Printing Inc — Wheeling (G-22137) | G | 847 520-7300 |
| Reprographics — Crystal Lake (G-7638) | G | 815 477-1018 |
| Review Printing Co Inc — Rock Island (G-18199) | G | 309 788-7094 |
| Rickard Circular Folding Co — Chicago (G-6353) | D | 312 243-6300 |
| Ricter Corporation — Broadview (G-2608) | F | 708 344-3300 |
| Rider Dickerson Inc — Bellwood (G-1718) | D | 312 427-2926 |
| Rightway Printing Inc — Glendale Heights (G-11064) | F | 630 790-0444 |
| River Bend Printing — Litchfield (G-13696) | G | 217 324-6056 |
| Rkf Enterprises — Chicago (G-6364) | G | 773 723-7038 |
| Ro-Web Inc — Peoria (G-17444) | G | 309 688-2155 |
| Robal Company Inc — Warrenville (G-21361) | F | 630 393-0777 |
| Rodin Enterprises Inc — Wheeling (G-22142) | G | 847 412-1370 |
| Rohrer Litho Inc — Elmhurst (G-9931) | G | 630 833-6610 |
| Rose Business Forms & Printing — Centralia (G-3429) | G | 618 533-3032 |
| Rrr Graphics & Film Corp — Mokena (G-14901) | G | 708 478-4573 |
| Rudin Printing Company Inc — Springfield (G-20515) | F | 217 528-5111 |
| Rusty & Angela Buzzard — Effingham (G-8857) | G | 217 342-9841 |
| S B Liquidating Company — Elk Grove Village (G-9723) | D | 847 758-9500 |
| Salem Times-Commoner Pubg Co — Salem (G-19349) | E | 618 548-3330 |
| Samecwei Inc — Aurora (G-1214) | G | 630 897-7888 |
| Scheiwes Print Shop — Crescent City (G-7456) | G | 815 683-2398 |
| Schommer Inc — McHenry (G-14554) | G | 815 344-1404 |
| Service Printing Corporation — Huntley (G-12176) | G | 847 669-9620 |
| Shawver Press Inc — Morrison (G-15148) | G | 815 772-4700 |
| Shoreline Graphics Inc — Ingleside (G-12198) | G | 847 587-4804 |
| ▼ Shree Mahavir Inc — Chicago (G-6501) | G | 312 408-1080 |
| Shree Printing Corp — Chicago (G-6502) | G | 773 267-9500 |
| Sigley Printing & Off Sup Co — Marion (G-14287) | G | 618 997-5304 |
| Sir Speedy Printing — Chicago (G-6518) | G | 312 337-0774 |
| Sommers & Fahrenbach Inc — Chicago (G-6543) | F | 773 478-3033 |
| Speedys Quick Print — Danville (G-7766) | G | 217 431-0510 |
| Springfield Printing Inc — Springfield (G-20531) | G | 217 787-3500 |
| Stark Printing Company — Round Lake (G-19068) | G | 847 234-8430 |
| Stearns Printing of Charleston — Charleston (G-3613) | G | 217 345-7518 |
| Steve Bortman — Lyons (G-14046) | G | 708 442-1669 |
| Swifty Print — Saint Charles (G-19276) | G | 630 584-9063 |
| T F N W Inc — Saint Charles (G-19277) | G | 630 584-7383 |
| Techprint Inc — Elk Grove Village (G-9774) | F | 847 616-0109 |
| Thomas Printing & Sty Co — Benton (G-2041) | G | 618 435-2801 |
| Tidd Printing Co — Berwyn (G-2076) | G | 708 749-1200 |
| Tower Printing & Design — Lombard (G-13870) | G | 630 495-1976 |
| Tree Towns Reprographics Inc — Elmhurst (G-9951) | E | 630 832-0209 |
| Tri-Tower Printing Inc — Rolling Meadows (G-18785) | G | 847 640-6633 |
| Trump Printing Inc — Decatur (G-7954) | F | 217 429-9001 |
| ▲ United Bindery Service — Chicago (G-6821) | E | 312 243-0240 |
| United Lithograph Inc — Des Plaines (G-8290) | G | 847 803-1700 |
| Viking Printing & Copying Inc — Chicago (G-6899) | G | 312 341-0985 |
| Voris Communication Co Inc — Berkeley (G-2051) | C | 630 898-4268 |
| Wagner Printing Co — Freeport (G-10698) | E | 630 941-7961 |
| We-B-Print Inc — Pekin (G-17293) | G | 309 353-8801 |
| Weakley Printing & Sign Shop — North Chicago (G-16189) | G | 847 473-4466 |
| Weimer Design & Print Ltd Inc — Warrenville (G-21368) | G | 630 393-3334 |
| West Vly Graphics & Print Inc — Saint Charles (G-19293) | G | 630 377-7575 |
| Whitson Bindery Services — Round Lake (G-19071) | F | 847 515-8371 |
| William Holloway Ltd — Evanston (G-10106) | G | 847 866-9520 |
| Wood River Printing & Pubg Co — Wood River (G-22446) | F | 618 254-3134 |
| Woogl Corporation — Elk Grove Village (G-9816) | E | 847 806-1160 |
| Wortman Printing Company Inc — Effingham (G-8864) | G | 217 347-3775 |

### 2791 Typesetting

| Company | Code | Phone |
|---|---|---|
| 11th Street Express Prtg Inc — Rockford (G-18235) | F | 815 968-0208 |
| A and K Prtg & Graphic Design — Mount Vernon (G-15396) | G | 618 244-3525 |
| A To Z Type & Graphic Inc — Chicago (G-3692) | G | 312 587-1887 |
| A+ Printing Co — Rockford (G-18242) | G | 815 968-8181 |
| Acres of Sky Communications — Lanark (G-13149) | G | 815 493-2560 |
| Adcraft Printers Inc — Kankakee (G-12601) | F | 815 932-6432 |
| All Purpose Prtg & Bus Forms — Alsip (G-431) | G | 708 389-9192 |
| All-Ways Quick Print — Orland Park (G-16841) | G | 708 403-8422 |
| Allegra Print & Imaging Inc — Elgin (G-8942) | G | 847 697-1434 |
| Alphadigital Inc — La Grange Park (G-12752) | G | 708 482-4488 |
| AlphaGraphics — Oakbrook Terrace (G-16694) | G | 630 261-1227 |
| AlphaGraphics Printshops — Lisle (G-13555) | G | 630 964-9600 |
| Amboy News — Amboy (G-597) | G | 815 857-2311 |
| American Graphics Network Inc — Glenview (G-11100) | F | 847 729-7220 |
| American Quick Print Inc — Wauconda (G-21441) | G | 847 253-2700 |
| Apple Graphics Inc — Batavia (G-1416) | G | 630 389-2222 |
| Apple Press Inc — Peru (G-17500) | G | 815 224-1451 |

Employee Codes: A=Over 500 employees, B=251-500, C=101-250, D=51-100, E=20-50, F=10-19, G=3-9

## 27 PRINTING, PUBLISHING, AND ALLIED INDUSTRIES

Apple Printing Center .................... G ...... 630 932-9494
  Addison (G-41)
Apr Graphics Inc ........................... G ...... 847 329-7800
  Skokie (G-19957)
Arby Graphic Service Inc ............... F ...... 847 763-0900
  Niles (G-15961)
Arcadia Press Inc .......................... F ...... 847 451-6390
  Franklin Park (G-10398)
Arch Printing Inc ........................... G ...... 630 966-0235
  Aurora (G-1110)
Artistry Engraving & Embossing ..... G ...... 773 775-4888
  Chicago (G-3957)
Avid of Illinois Inc ......................... F ...... 847 698-2775
  Saint Charles (G-19140)
Azusa Inc ...................................... G ...... 618 244-6591
  Mount Vernon (G-15399)
B & B Printing Company ............... G ...... 217 285-6072
  Pittsfield (G-17561)
B Allan Graphics Inc ..................... F ...... 708 396-1704
  Alsip (G-438)
B F Shaw Printing Company ......... E ...... 815 875-4461
  Princeton (G-17744)
Babak Inc ...................................... G ...... 312 419-8686
  Chicago (G-4024)
Bailleu & Bailleu Printing Inc ........ G ...... 309 852-2517
  Kewanee (G-12670)
Bally Foil Graphics Inc .................. G ...... 847 427-1509
  Elk Grove Village (G-9333)
Banner Publications ...................... G ...... 309 338-3294
  Cuba (G-7679)
Barnaby Inc ................................... F ...... 815 895-6555
  Sycamore (G-20789)
Baseline Graphics Inc ................... G ...... 630 964-9566
  Downers Grove (G-8395)
Belmonte Printing Co .................... G ...... 847 352-8841
  Schaumburg (G-19459)
Benzinger Printing ........................ G ...... 815 784-6560
  Genoa (G-10875)
Bikast Graphics Inc ...................... G ...... 847 487-8822
  Wauconda (G-21446)
Biller Press & Manufacturing ........ G ...... 847 395-4111
  Antioch (G-623)
Blazing Color Inc .......................... G ...... 618 826-3001
  Chester (G-3651)
Bond Brothers & Co ...................... F ...... 708 442-5510
  Lyons (G-14032)
Brads Printing Inc ......................... G ...... 847 662-0447
  Waukegan (G-21531)
Branstiter Printing Co ................... G ...... 217 245-6533
  Jacksonville (G-12381)
Breaker Press Co Inc .................... G ...... 773 927-1666
  Chicago (G-4159)
Budget Printing Center ................. G ...... 618 655-1636
  Edwardsville (G-8793)
Cameron Printing Inc .................... G ...... 630 231-3301
  West Chicago (G-21677)
Cardinal Colorprint Prtg Corp ........ E ...... 630 467-1000
  Itasca (G-12241)
Carson Printing Inc ....................... G ...... 847 836-0900
  East Dundee (G-8629)
Carter Printing Co Inc ................... G ...... 217 227-4464
  Farmersville (G-10183)
Case Paluch & Associates Inc ...... G ...... 773 465-0098
  Chicago (G-4248)
Century Printing ........................... G ...... 618 632-2486
  O Fallon (G-16465)
Cenveo Inc .................................... G ...... 217 243-4258
  Jacksonville (G-12383)
Challenge Printers ........................ G ...... 773 252-0212
  Chicago (G-4285)
Charleston Graphics Inc ............... G
  Charleston (G-3594)
Chicago Citizen Newsppr Group ... F ...... 773 783-1251
  Chicago (G-4311)
Chicago Mltlingua Graphics Inc .... F ...... 847 386-7187
  Northfield (G-16397)
Christopher R Cline Prtg Ltd ......... F ...... 847 981-0500
  Elk Grove Village (G-9372)
Cifuentes Luis & Nicole Inc .......... G ...... 847 490-3660
  Schaumburg (G-19472)
Cjs Printing .................................... G ...... 309 968-6585
  Manito (G-14172)
Clementi Printing Inc .................... G ...... 773 622-0795
  Chicago (G-4401)
Clyde Printing Company ............... G ...... 773 847-5900
  Chicago (G-4410)
Cmb Printing Inc .......................... G ...... 630 323-1110
  Burr Ridge (G-2830)
Color Smiths Inc ........................... E ...... 708 562-0061
  Elmhurst (G-9853)

Commercial Copy Printing Ctr ....... F ...... 847 981-8590
  Elk Grove Village (G-9384)
Commercial Fast Print .................. G ...... 815 673-1196
  Streator (G-20685)
Composing Room Inc ................... G ...... 708 795-7523
  Berwyn (G-2059)
Composition One Inc ................... E ...... 630 588-1900
  Roselle (G-18933)
Conrad Press Ltd .......................... G
  Columbia (G-7356)
Copy Express Inc .......................... F ...... 815 338-7161
  Woodstock (G-22555)
Copy Mat Printing ......................... G ...... 309 452-1392
  Bloomington (G-2155)
Copy Service Inc ........................... G ...... 815 758-1151
  Dekalb (G-8079)
▲ Copy-Mor Inc ........................... E ...... 312 666-4000
  Elmhurst (G-9856)
Copyset Shop Inc .......................... G ...... 847 768-2679
  Des Plaines (G-8176)
Corwin Printing ............................ G ...... 618 263-3936
  Mount Carmel (G-15263)
Cpr Printing Inc ............................ F ...... 630 377-8420
  Geneva (G-10821)
Craftsmen Printing ....................... G ...... 217 283-9574
  Hoopeston (G-12108)
Crossmark Printing Inc ................ F ...... 708 532-8263
  Tinley Park (G-20906)
Crosstech Communications Inc .... E ...... 312 382-0111
  Chicago (G-4506)
Custom Direct Inc ......................... F ...... 630 529-1936
  Roselle (G-18938)
Custom Graphics ........................... G ...... 309 828-0717
  Bloomington (G-2158)
D E Asbury Inc .............................. F ...... 217 222-0617
  Hamilton (G-11532)
D L V Printing Service Inc ............ F ...... 773 626-1661
  Chicago (G-4537)
Dale K Brown ................................ G ...... 815 338-0222
  Woodstock (G-22558)
Darnall Printing ............................ G ...... 309 827-7212
  Bloomington (G-2161)
David H Vander Ploeg ................... G ...... 708 331-7700
  South Holland (G-20260)
DE Asbury Inc ............................... E ...... 217 222-0617
  Quincy (G-17820)
▲ Deluxe Johnson ....................... F ...... 847 635-7200
  Des Plaines (G-8182)
Demis Printing Inc ........................ G ...... 773 282-9128
  Park Ridge (G-17189)
Denor Graphics Inc ....................... F ...... 847 364-1130
  Elk Grove Village (G-9423)
Des Plaines Journal Inc ................ D ...... 847 299-5511
  Des Plaines (G-8184)
Design Graphics Inc ..................... G ...... 815 462-3323
  New Lenox (G-15875)
Diamond Graphics of Berwyn ....... G ...... 708 749-2500
  Berwyn (G-2060)
Donnas House of Type Inc ........... G ...... 217 522-5050
  Athens (G-938)
Donnells Printing & Off Pdts ........ G ...... 815 842-6541
  Pontiac (G-17698)
DOT Black Group ......................... G ...... 312 204-8000
  Chicago (G-4634)
Dupli Group Inc ............................ F ...... 773 549-5285
  Chicago (G-4654)
E & H Graphic Service .................. G ...... 708 748-5656
  Matteson (G-14371)
Early Bird Advertising Inc ............. G ...... 847 253-1423
  Prospect Heights (G-17777)
East Moline Herald Print Inc ......... G ...... 309 755-5224
  East Moline (G-8678)
Edwardsville Publishing Co .......... D ...... 618 656-4700
  Edwardsville (G-8799)
Einstein Crest .............................. G ...... 847 965-7791
  Niles (G-15977)
Eklunds Typesetting & Prtg LLC ... G ...... 630 924-0057
  Roselle (G-18940)
Elgin Instant Print ........................ G ...... 847 931-9006
  Elgin (G-9024)
Elmhurst Enterprise Group Inc ..... G ...... 847 228-5945
  Arlington Heights (G-749)
Everything Xclusive ...................... G ...... 309 370-7450
  Peoria (G-17358)
F Weber Printing Co Inc ............... G ...... 815 468-6152
  Manteno (G-14183)
Fedex Office & Print Svcs Inc ....... G ...... 847 475-8650
  Evanston (G-10036)
Fedex Office & Print Svcs Inc ....... F ...... 815 229-0033
  Rockford (G-18380)

## SIC SECTION

Fedex Office & Print Svcs Inc ....... F ...... 847 329-9464
  Lincolnwood (G-13510)
Fedex Office & Print Svcs Inc ....... E ...... 847 729-3030
  Glenview (G-11124)
Fedex Office & Print Svcs Inc ....... G ...... 847 459-8008
  Buffalo Grove (G-2693)
Fedex Office & Print Svcs Inc ....... E ...... 708 452-0149
  Elmwood Park (G-9970)
Fedex Office & Print Svcs Inc ....... G ...... 847 823-9360
  Park Ridge (G-17193)
Fedex Office & Print Svcs Inc ....... F ...... 630 894-1800
  Bloomingdale (G-2108)
Fedex Office & Print Svcs Inc ....... E ...... 312 670-4460
  Chicago (G-4831)
Fedex Office & Print Svcs Inc ....... E ...... 309 685-4093
  Peoria (G-17359)
Fine Line Printing ......................... G ...... 773 582-9709
  Chicago (G-4846)
First Impression of Chicago .......... G ...... 773 224-3434
  Chicago (G-4849)
Fisheye Services Incorporated ..... G ...... 773 942-6314
  Chicago (G-4852)
Flash Printing Inc ......................... G ...... 847 288-9101
  Franklin Park (G-10470)
Fleetwood Press Inc ..................... G ...... 708 485-6811
  Brookfield (G-2632)
FM Graphic Impressions Inc ........ E ...... 630 897-8788
  Aurora (G-1153)
French Studio Ltd ......................... G ...... 618 942-5328
  Herrin (G-11748)
G F Printing .................................. G ...... 618 797-0576
  Granite City (G-11278)
Gamma Alpha Visual .................... G ...... 847 956-0633
  Elk Grove Village (G-9496)
Gatehouse Media LLC .................. B ...... 217 788-1300
  Springfield (G-20445)
Gazette Printing Co ...................... G ...... 309 389-2811
  Glasford (G-10951)
Gorman & Associates .................. G ...... 309 691-9087
  Peoria (G-17373)
Gossett Printing Inc ..................... G ...... 618 548-2583
  Salem (G-19335)
Graphic Image Corporation .......... F ...... 312 829-7800
  Chicago (G-4989)
Graphics Group LLC ..................... D ...... 708 867-5500
  Chicago (G-4992)
Graphics Plus Inc ......................... F ...... 630 968-9073
  Lisle (G-13597)
Grasso Graphics Inc .................... G ...... 708 489-2060
  Alsip (G-465)
Greenup Press Inc ........................ G ...... 217 923-3704
  Greenup (G-11383)
Griffith Solutions Inc .................... G ...... 847 384-1810
  Park Ridge (G-17201)
Group 329 LLC ............................ G ...... 312 828-0200
  Chicago (G-5005)
▲ Gsi Technologies LLC .............. D ...... 630 325-8181
  Burr Ridge (G-2847)
Hawthorne Press Inc .................... G ...... 847 587-8222
  Spring Grove (G-20336)
Heart Printing Inc ......................... G ...... 847 259-2100
  Arlington Heights (G-764)
Henderson Co Inc ......................... F ...... 773 628-7216
  Chicago (G-5070)
Heritage Media Svcs Co of Ill ....... G ...... 708 594-9340
  Summit Argo (G-20763)
Heritage Press Inc ........................ G ...... 847 362-9699
  Libertyville (G-13330)
Heritage Printing .......................... G ...... 815 537-2372
  Prophetstown (G-17770)
Highland Printers .......................... G ...... 618 654-5880
  Highland (G-11791)
House of Graphics ........................ E ...... 630 682-0810
  Carol Stream (G-3168)
Hq Printers Inc ............................. G ...... 312 782-2020
  Chicago (G-5125)
Hub Printing Company Inc ........... F ...... 815 562-7057
  Rochelle (G-18094)
Huston-Patterson Corporation ..... D ...... 217 429-5161
  Decatur (G-7890)
Ideal Advertising & Printing ......... F ...... 815 965-1713
  Rockford (G-18426)
Ideal/Mikron Inc ........................... G ...... 847 873-0254
  Mount Prospect (G-15336)
Illinois Office Sup Elect Prtg ........ E ...... 815 434-0186
  Ottawa (G-16962)
Image Print Inc ............................. G ...... 815 672-1068
  Streator (G-20691)
Informative Systems Inc .............. F ...... 217 523-8422
  Springfield (G-20457)

**Ink Spot Printing**....G....773 528-0288
Chicago *(G-5194)*
**Ink Well Printing**....G....815 224-1366
Peru *(G-17514)*
**Ink Well Printing & Design Ltd**....G....847 923-8060
Schaumburg *(G-19566)*
**Inky Printers**....G....815 235-3700
Freeport *(G-10668)*
**Innovtive Design Graphics Corp**....G....847 475-7772
Evanston *(G-10057)*
**Insty Prints Palatine Inc**....F....847 963-0000
Palatine *(G-17042)*
**Instyprints of Waukegan Inc**....G....847 336-5599
Waukegan *(G-21571)*
**International Graphics & Assoc**....F....630 584-2248
Saint Charles *(G-19199)*
**J & J Mr Quick Print Inc**....G....773 767-7776
Chicago *(G-5251)*
**J F Wagner Printing Co**....G....847 564-0017
Northbrook *(G-16280)*
**J Oshana & Son Printing**....G....773 283-8311
Chicago *(G-5261)*
**J P Printing Inc**....G....773 626-5222
Chicago *(G-5262)*
**James Ray Monroe Corporation**....F....618 532-4575
Centralia *(G-3420)*
**Jay Printing**....G....847 934-6103
Palatine *(G-17046)*
**JD Pro Productions Inc**....G....708 485-2126
Brookfield *(G-2636)*
**Jds Printing Inc**....G....630 208-1195
Glendale Heights *(G-11037)*
**Johns-Byrne Company**....D....847 583-3100
Niles *(G-15992)*
**Johnson Press America Inc**....E....815 844-5161
Pontiac *(G-17704)*
**Josco Inc**....G....708 867-7189
Chicago *(G-5326)*
**Josephs Printing Service**....G....847 724-4429
Glenview *(G-11154)*
**Jph Enterprises Inc**....G....847 390-0900
Des Plaines *(G-8217)*
**July 25th Corporation**....F....309 664-6444
Bloomington *(G-2186)*
**Just Your Type Inc**....G....847 864-8890
Evanston *(G-10060)*
**K & M Printing Company Inc**....D....847 884-1100
Schaumburg *(G-19595)*
**K R O Enterprises Ltd**....G....309 797-2213
Moline *(G-14949)*
**Kelly Printing Co Inc**....E....217 443-1792
Danville *(G-7741)*
**Kendall Printing Co**....G....630 553-9200
Yorkville *(G-22663)*
**Kenilworth Press Incorporated**....G....847 256-5210
Wilmette *(G-22256)*
**Kens Quick Print Inc**....F....847 831-4410
Highland Park *(G-11849)*
**Kevin Kewney**....G....217 228-7444
Quincy *(G-17844)*
**Key One Graphics Services Inc**....G....
West Dundee *(G-21799)*
**KK Stevens Publishing Co**....E....309 329-2151
Astoria *(G-934)*
**Klein Printing Inc**....G....773 235-2121
Chicago *(G-5387)*
**Klh Printing Corp**....G....847 459-0115
Wheeling *(G-22086)*
▲ **Korea Times**....D....847 626-0388
Glenview *(G-11157)*
**LAC Enterprises Inc**....G....815 455-5044
Crystal Lake *(G-7601)*
**Lake County Press Inc**....C....847 336-4333
Waukegan *(G-21580)*
**Lake Shore Printing**....G....847 679-4110
Skokie *(G-20024)*
**Lans Printing Inc**....G....708 895-6226
Lynwood *(G-14021)*
**Laser Expressions Ltd**....G....847 419-9600
Buffalo Grove *(G-2721)*
**Legend Promotions**....G....847 438-3528
Lake Zurich *(G-13095)*
**Leonard Emerson**....G....217 628-3441
Divernon *(G-8316)*
**Link-Letters Ltd**....F....847 459-1199
Wheeling *(G-22094)*
**Lists & Letters**....F....847 520-5207
Wheeling *(G-22095)*
**Lithuanian Catholic Press**....E....773 585-9500
Chicago *(G-5519)*
**Lloyd Midwest Graphics**....G....815 282-8828
Machesney Park *(G-14089)*
**Lynns Printing Co**....G....618 465-7701
Alton *(G-583)*
**M & R Printing Inc**....G....847 398-2500
Rolling Meadows *(G-18742)*
**M M Marketing**....G....815 459-7968
Crystal Lake *(G-7603)*
**M O W Printing Inc**....F....618 345-5525
Collinsville *(G-7331)*
**Macoupin County Enquirer Inc**....E....217 854-2534
Carlinville *(G-3042)*
**Marcus Press**....G....630 351-1857
Bloomingdale *(G-2115)*
**Mark Twain Press Inc**....G....847 255-2700
Mundelein *(G-15523)*
**Mason City Banner Times**....F....217 482-3276
Mason City *(G-14365)*
**Mattoon Printing Center**....G....217 234-3100
Mattoon *(G-14400)*
**Mc Adams Multigraphics Inc**....G....630 990-1707
Oak Brook *(G-16539)*
**McGrath Press Inc**....E....815 356-5246
Crystal Lake *(G-7607)*
**Mencarini Enterprises Inc**....F....815 398-9565
Rockford *(G-18491)*
**Metro Printing & Pubg Inc**....F....618 476-9587
Millstadt *(G-14829)*
**Metropolitan Graphic Arts Inc**....E....847 566-9502
Gurnee *(G-11471)*
**Michael Zimmerman**....G....847 272-5560
Northbrook *(G-16311)*
**Mid City Printing Service**....G....773 777-5400
Chicago *(G-5725)*
**Midwest Outdoors Ltd**....E....630 887-7722
Burr Ridge *(G-2867)*
**Minuteman Press**....G....630 541-9122
Countryside *(G-7437)*
**Minuteman Press**....G....630 279-0438
Lombard *(G-13827)*
**Minuteman Press**....G....630 584-7383
Saint Charles *(G-19223)*
**Minuteman Press of Rockford**....G....815 633-2992
Loves Park *(G-13967)*
**Minuteman Press of Waukegan**....G....847 244-6288
Gurnee *(G-11474)*
**Multicopy Corp**....G....847 446-7015
Northfield *(G-16410)*
**N & M Type & Design**....G....630 834-3696
Elmhurst *(G-9914)*
**N Bujarski Inc**....G....847 884-1600
Schaumburg *(G-19660)*
**N P D Inc**....G....708 424-6788
Oak Lawn *(G-16636)*
**Negs & Litho Inc**....G....847 647-7770
Chicago *(G-5881)*
**New City Communications**....E....312 243-8786
Chicago *(G-5891)*
**New Life Printing & Publishing**....G....847 658-4111
Algonquin *(G-402)*
**Newell & Haney Inc**....F....618 277-3660
Belleville *(G-1660)*
**Northwest Premier Printing**....G....773 736-1882
Chicago *(G-5940)*
**Northwest Printing Inc**....G....815 943-7977
Harvard *(G-11642)*
**Nu-Art Printing**....G....618 533-9971
Centralia *(G-3425)*
**Off The Press**....G....815 436-9612
Plainfield *(G-17634)*
**Office Assistants Inc**....G....708 346-0505
Oak Lawn *(G-16637)*
**Okawville Times**....G....618 243-5563
Okawville *(G-16754)*
**Olde Print Shoppe Inc**....G....618 395-3833
Olney *(G-16786)*
**Omni Craft Inc**....G....815 838-1285
Lockport *(G-13736)*
**On Time Printing and Finishing**....G....708 544-4500
Hillside *(G-11929)*
**Osborne Publications Inc**....G....217 422-9702
Decatur *(G-7924)*
**P & S Cochran Printers Inc**....E....309 691-6668
Peoria *(G-17421)*
**P H C Enterprises Inc**....G....847 816-7373
Vernon Hills *(G-21186)*
**P P Graphics Inc**....G....708 343-2530
Westchester *(G-21852)*
**Papyrus Press Inc**....F....773 342-0700
Chicago *(G-6074)*
▲ **Park Printing Inc**....G....708 430-4878
Palos Hills *(G-17120)*
**Patrick Impressions LLC**....G....630 257-9336
Lemont *(G-13250)*
**Patton Printing and Graphics**....G....217 347-0220
Effingham *(G-8852)*
**Perma Graphics Printers**....G....815 485-6955
New Lenox *(G-15901)*
**Perryco Inc**....F....815 436-2431
Plainfield *(G-17638)*
**Photo Graphic Design Service**....G....815 672-4417
Streator *(G-20700)*
**Pinney Printing Company**....E....815 626-2727
Sterling *(G-20604)*
**PIP Printing Inc**....G....815 464-0075
Frankfort *(G-10349)*
**Poets Study Inc**....G....773 286-1355
Chicago *(G-6147)*
**Precision Language & Graphics**....G....847 413-1688
Schaumburg *(G-19700)*
**Preferred Printing Service**....G....312 421-2343
Chicago *(G-6175)*
**Prime Market Targeting Inc**....E....815 469-4555
Frankfort *(G-10353)*
**Print & Design Services LLC**....G....847 317-9001
Bannockburn *(G-1264)*
**Print King Inc**....F....708 499-3777
Oak Lawn *(G-16641)*
**Print Turnaround Inc**....F....847 228-1762
Arlington Heights *(G-822)*
**Print Xpress**....G....847 677-5555
Skokie *(G-20061)*
**Printed Impressions Inc**....G....773 604-8585
Villa Park *(G-21279)*
**Printed Word Inc**....G....847 328-1511
Evanston *(G-10091)*
**Printing By Joseph**....G....708 479-2669
Mokena *(G-14898)*
**Printing Craftsmen of Joliet**....G....815 254-3982
Joliet *(G-12555)*
**Printing Etc Inc**....G....815 562-6151
Rochelle *(G-18102)*
**Printing Plus of Roselle Inc**....G....630 893-0410
Roselle *(G-18963)*
**Printing Press of Joliet Inc**....G....815 725-0018
Joliet *(G-12556)*
**Printing Source Inc**....G....773 588-2930
Morton Grove *(G-15228)*
**Printing Works Inc**....G....847 860-1920
Elk Grove Village *(G-9698)*
**Printmeisters Inc**....G....708 474-8400
Lansing *(G-13180)*
**Printsource Plus Inc**....G....708 389-6252
Blue Island *(G-2265)*
**Prism Commercial Printing Ctrs**....G....630 834-4443
Chicago *(G-6199)*
**Pro-Type Printing Inc**....G....217 379-4715
Paxton *(G-17244)*
**Progress Printing Corporation**....E....773 927-0123
Chicago *(G-6210)*
**Quad City Press**....F....309 764-8142
Moline *(G-14965)*
**Quality Quickprint Inc**....F....815 439-3430
Joliet *(G-12560)*
**Quality Quickprint Inc**....F....815 838-1784
Lockport *(G-13740)*
**Quickprinters**....G....309 833-5250
Macomb *(G-14130)*
**Quinn Print Inc**....G....847 823-9100
Park Ridge *(G-17218)*
**R N R Photographers Inc**....G....708 453-1868
River Grove *(G-18013)*
**Rapid Circular Press Inc**....F....312 421-5611
Chicago *(G-6290)*
**Redline Press**....G....630 690-9828
Lisle *(G-13650)*
**Remke Printing Inc**....G....847 520-7300
Wheeling *(G-22137)*
**Reprographics**....G....815 477-1018
Crystal Lake *(G-7638)*
**Review Graphics Inc**....G....815 623-2570
Roscoe *(G-18913)*
**Review Printing Co Inc**....G....309 788-7094
Rock Island *(G-18199)*
**Rider Dickerson Inc**....D....312 427-2926
Bellwood *(G-1718)*
**Rightway Printing Inc**....F....630 790-0444
Glendale Heights *(G-11064)*
**Rite-TEC Communications**....G....815 459-7712
Crystal Lake *(G-7643)*

S I C

Employee Codes: A=Over 500 employees, B=251-500
C=101-250, D=51-100, E=20-50, F=10-19, G=3-9
2017 Harris Illinois
Industrial Directory
983

**River Bend Printing** G 217 324-6056
Litchfield *(G-13696)*
**Ro-Web Inc** G 309 688-2155
Peoria *(G-17444)*
**Rodin Enterprises Inc** G 847 412-1370
Wheeling *(G-22142)*
**Rohrer Graphic Arts Inc** F 630 832-3434
Elmhurst *(G-9930)*
**Rohrer Litho Inc** G 630 833-6610
Elmhurst *(G-9931)*
**Rose Business Forms & Printing** G 618 533-3032
Centralia *(G-3429)*
**Rrr Graphics & Film Corp** G 708 478-4573
Mokena *(G-14901)*
**Rt Associates Inc** D 847 577-0700
Wheeling *(G-22143)*
**Rudin Printing Company Inc** F 217 528-5111
Springfield *(G-20515)*
**Rusty & Angela Buzzard** G 217 342-9841
Effingham *(G-8857)*
**▲ S M C Graphics** G 708 754-8973
Chicago Heights *(G-7125)*
**Salem Times-Commoner Pubg Co** E 618 548-3330
Salem *(G-19349)*
**Samecwei Inc** G 630 897-7888
Aurora *(G-1214)*
**Schellhorn Photo Techniques** F 773 267-5141
Chicago *(G-6451)*
**Schiele Graphics Inc** D 847 434-5455
Elk Grove Village *(G-9731)*
**Schommer Inc** G 815 344-1404
McHenry *(G-14554)*
**Sharp Graphics Inc** G 847 966-7000
Skokie *(G-20085)*
**Shawver Press Inc** G 815 772-4700
Morrison *(G-15148)*
**Sheer Graphics Inc** G 630 654-4422
Westmont *(G-21920)*
**Shoreline Graphics Inc** G 847 587-4804
Ingleside *(G-12198)*
**▼ Shree Mahavir Inc** G 312 408-1080
Chicago *(G-6501)*
**Shree Printing Corp** G 773 267-9500
Chicago *(G-6502)*
**Sigley Printing & Off Sup Co** G 618 997-5304
Marion *(G-14287)*
**Sir Speedy Printing** G 312 337-0774
Chicago *(G-6518)*
**Small Newspaper Group** C 815 937-3300
Kankakee *(G-12652)*
**Solid Impressions Inc** G 630 543-7300
Carol Stream *(G-3241)*
**Sommers & Fahrenbach Inc** F 773 478-3033
Chicago *(G-6543)*
**Sons Enterprises** F 847 677-4444
Skokie *(G-20088)*
**Speedys Quick Print** G 217 431-0510
Danville *(G-7766)*
**Stark Printing Company** G 847 234-8430
Round Lake *(G-19068)*
**Stearns Printing of Charleston** G 217 345-7518
Charleston *(G-3613)*
**Steve Bortman** G 708 442-1669
Lyons *(G-14046)*
**Swifty Print** G 630 584-9063
Saint Charles *(G-19276)*
**T F N W Inc** G 630 584-7383
Saint Charles *(G-19277)*
**T R Communications Inc** F 773 238-3366
Chicago *(G-6663)*
**Tele-Guia Inc** F 708 656-9800
Cicero *(G-7236)*
**Tidd Printing Co** G 708 749-1200
Berwyn *(G-2076)*
**Times Record Company** E 309 582-5112
Aledo *(G-373)*
**Times Republic** E 815 432-5227
Watseka *(G-21431)*
**Tlm Enterprises Inc** G 815 284-5040
Dixon *(G-8356)*
**Toledo Democrat** G 217 849-2000
Toledo *(G-20967)*
**Tower Printing & Design** G 630 495-1976
Lombard *(G-13870)*
**Trenton Sun** G 618 224-9422
Trenton *(G-20998)*
**Tri-Tower Printing Inc** G 847 640-6633
Rolling Meadows *(G-18785)*
**Trump Printing Inc** F 217 429-9001
Decatur *(G-7954)*
**Type Concepts Inc** G 708 361-1005
Palos Heights *(G-17112)*
**Unicomp Typography Inc** G 847 821-0221
Buffalo Grove *(G-2784)*
**United Lithograph Inc** G 847 803-1700
Des Plaines *(G-8290)*
**V C P Inc** E 847 658-5090
Algonquin *(G-409)*
**Valee Inc** G 847 364-6464
Elk Grove Village *(G-9804)*
**Viking Printing & Copying Inc** G 312 341-0985
Chicago *(G-6899)*
**Village Typographers Inc** G 618 235-6756
Belleville *(G-1687)*
**Voris Communication Co Inc** C 630 898-4268
Berkeley *(G-2051)*
**W R Typesetting Co** G 847 966-1315
Morton Grove *(G-15244)*
**Washburn Graficolor Inc** G 630 596-0880
Naperville *(G-15781)*
**Weakley Printing & Sign Shop** G 847 473-4466
North Chicago *(G-16189)*
**Weber Press Inc** G 773 561-9815
Chicago *(G-6949)*
**Weimer Design & Print Ltd Inc** G 630 393-3334
Warrenville *(G-21368)*
**Westrock Mwv LLC** E 217 442-2247
Danville *(G-7784)*
**Woogl Corporation** E 847 806-1160
Elk Grove Village *(G-9816)*
**World Journal LLC** F 312 842-8005
Chicago *(G-7030)*
**Wortman Printing Company Inc** G 217 347-3775
Effingham *(G-8864)*
**Yeast Printing Inc** G 309 833-2845
Macomb *(G-14137)*

## 2796 Platemaking & Related Svcs

**A Jule Enterprise Inc** G 312 243-6950
Chicago *(G-3689)*
**Apr Graphics Inc** G 847 329-7800
Skokie *(G-19957)*
**Artistry Engraving & Embossing** G 773 775-4888
Chicago *(G-3957)*
**▲ Associates Engraving Company** D 217 523-4565
Springfield *(G-20389)*
**Autotype Americas Incorporated** G 847 818-8262
Rolling Meadows *(G-18713)*
**B Allan Graphics Inc** F 708 396-1704
Alsip *(G-438)*
**B F Shaw Printing Company** E 815 875-4461
Princeton *(G-17744)*
**Banner Moulded Products** E 708 452-0033
River Grove *(G-18005)*
**Best Machine & Welding Co Inc** E 708 343-4455
Woodridge *(G-22456)*
**Blooming Color Inc** E 630 705-9200
Lombard *(G-13772)*
**Brilliant Color Corp** G 847 367-3300
Libertyville *(G-13310)*
**C F C Interantional** G 708 753-0679
Chicago Heights *(G-7085)*
**Cardinal Colorprint Prtg Corp** E 630 467-1000
Itasca *(G-12241)*
**Carson Printing Inc** G 847 836-0900
East Dundee *(G-8629)*
**Chicago Prepress Color Inc** G 708 385-3465
Midlothian *(G-14765)*
**▲ Chromium Industries Inc** E 773 287-3716
Chicago *(G-4373)*
**Clodfelter Engraving Inc** G 314 968-8418
Alton *(G-566)*
**Color Smiths Inc** E 708 562-0061
Elmhurst *(G-9853)*
**Color Works Graphics Inc** E 847 383-5270
Chicago *(G-4427)*
**Commercial Copy Printing Ctr** F 847 981-8590
Elk Grove Village *(G-9384)*
**Cpr Printing Inc** F 630 377-8420
Geneva *(G-10821)*
**Creative Label Inc** D 847 981-3800
Elk Grove Village *(G-9399)*
**Creative Lithocraft Inc** G 847 352-7002
Schaumburg *(G-19489)*
**Crossmark Printing Inc** F 708 532-8263
Tinley Park *(G-20906)*
**Crosstech Communications Inc** E 312 382-0111
Chicago *(G-4506)*
**Delta Press Inc** E 847 671-3200
Palatine *(G-17022)*
**Dupli Group Inc** F 773 549-5285
Chicago *(G-4654)*
**E C Schultz & Co Inc** F 847 640-1190
Elk Grove Village *(G-9442)*
**Eugene Ewbank** G 630 705-0400
Oswego *(G-16917)*
**Excel Color Corporation** G 847 734-1270
Elk Grove Village *(G-9467)*
**Expercolor Inc** E 773 465-3400
Skokie *(G-19997)*
**Graphic Arts Studio Inc** E 847 381-1105
Barrington *(G-1282)*
**Graphic Engravers Inc** E 630 595-0400
Bensenville *(G-1913)*
**Graphic Image Corporation** F 312 829-7800
Chicago *(G-4989)*
**Graphics Plus Inc** F 630 968-9073
Lisle *(G-13597)*
**Henderson Co Inc** F 773 628-7216
Chicago *(G-5070)*
**Hurst Chemical Company** G 815 964-0451
Rockford *(G-18424)*
**Ideal/Mikron Inc** G 847 873-0254
Mount Prospect *(G-15336)*
**Iemco Corporation** G 773 728-4400
Chicago *(G-5145)*
**Impression Printing** F 708 614-8660
Oak Forest *(G-16583)*
**Instyprints of Waukegan Inc** G 847 336-5599
Waukegan *(G-21571)*
**J D Graphic Co Inc** E 847 364-4000
Elk Grove Village *(G-9557)*
**Jph Enterprises Inc** G 847 390-0900
Des Plaines *(G-8217)*
**Lasons Label Co** G 773 775-2606
Chicago *(G-5464)*
**Lincoln Electric Company** F 630 783-3600
Bolingbrook *(G-2335)*
**Lloyd Midwest Graphics** G 815 282-8828
Machesney Park *(G-14089)*
**Luttrell Engraving Inc** E 708 489-3800
Alsip *(G-485)*
**M & G Graphics Inc** E 773 247-1596
Chicago *(G-5576)*
**M L S Printing Co Inc** G 847 948-8902
Deerfield *(G-8033)*
**M S A Printing Co** G 847 593-5699
Elk Grove Village *(G-9604)*
**Marcus Press** G 630 351-1857
Bloomingdale *(G-2115)*
**Multicopy Corp** G 847 446-7015
Northfield *(G-16410)*
**N Bujarski Inc** G 847 884-1600
Schaumburg *(G-19660)*
**Naco Printing Co Inc** G 618 664-0423
Greenville *(G-11400)*
**▲ Oec Graphics-Chicago LLC** E 630 455-6700
Willowbrook *(G-22227)*
**Pamarco Global Graphics Inc** E 630 879-7300
Batavia *(G-1479)*
**Pamarco Global Graphics Inc** F 847 459-6000
Wheeling *(G-22118)*
**Pontiac Engraving** G 630 834-4424
Bensenville *(G-1965)*
**Precision Die Cutting & Finish** G 773 252-5625
Chicago *(G-6169)*
**Prime Market Targeting Inc** E 815 469-4555
Frankfort *(G-10353)*
**Priority Printing** G 773 889-6021
Chicago *(G-6198)*
**Prism Commercial Printing Ctrs** G 630 834-4443
Chicago *(G-6199)*
**Rohrer Graphic Arts Inc** F 630 832-3434
Elmhurst *(G-9930)*
**Rohrer Litho Inc** G 630 833-6610
Elmhurst *(G-9931)*
**Rotation Dynamics Corporation** E 630 769-9700
Chicago *(G-6398)*
**Rotation Dynamics Corporation** D 773 247-5600
Chicago *(G-6399)*
**Saltzman Printers Inc** E 708 344-4500
Melrose Park *(G-14690)*
**Servi-Sure Corporation** E 773 271-5900
Chicago *(G-6480)*
**Southern Graphic Systems LLC** E 847 695-9515
Elgin *(G-9189)*
**Splash Graphics Inc** F 630 230-5775
Willowbrook *(G-22232)*
**▲ Sunrise Hitek Service Inc** E 773 792-8880
Chicago *(G-6630)*

# 28 CHEMICALS AND ALLIED PRODUCTS

Tanic Rubber Plate Co .................G...... 630 896-2122
  Aurora *(G-1223)*
Village Press Inc .........................G...... 847 362-1856
  Libertyville *(G-13399)*
Voss Pattern Works Inc ...............G...... 618 233-4242
  Belleville *(G-1689)*
West Vly Graphics & Print Inc .....G...... 630 377-7575
  Saint Charles *(G-19293)*
Woogl Corporation .......................E...... 847 806-1160
  Elk Grove Village *(G-9816)*

## 28 CHEMICALS AND ALLIED PRODUCTS

### 2812 Alkalies & Chlorine

Arkema Inc ..................................C...... 708 396-3001
  Alsip *(G-435)*
Arkema Inc ..................................C...... 708 385-2188
  Alsip *(G-436)*
▲ Aspen API Inc ..........................F...... 847 635-0985
  Des Plaines *(G-8152)*
Champion Packaging & Dist Inc ..C...... 630 755-4220
  Woodridge *(G-22460)*
Clorox Products Mfg Co .............C...... 847 229-5500
  Wheeling *(G-22028)*
Coral Chemical Company ............E...... 847 246-6666
  Zion *(G-22680)*
Korex Chicago LLC .....................E...... 708 458-4890
  Chicago *(G-5406)*
Occidental Chemical Corp ...........F...... 618 482-6346
  Sauget *(G-19388)*
Olin Corporation ..........................E...... 618 258-5668
  East Alton *(G-8607)*
◆ Petra Industries Inc ..................F...... 618 271-0022
  East Saint Louis *(G-8765)*

### 2813 Industrial Gases

Aeropres Corporation ..................G...... 815 478-3266
  Manhattan *(G-14167)*
Air Products and Chemicals Inc ..E...... 618 452-5335
  Granite City *(G-11260)*
Air Products and Chemicals Inc ..E...... 815 223-2924
  La Salle *(G-12761)*
Air Products and Chemicals Inc ..D...... 618 451-0577
  Granite City *(G-11261)*
Air Products and Chemicals Inc ..E...... 815 423-5032
  Channahon *(G-3564)*
Airgas Inc ....................................G...... 773 785-3000
  Chicago *(G-3787)*
Airgas Inc ....................................G...... 773 785-3000
  Chicago *(G-3786)*
Airgas USA LLC ..........................C...... 708 482-8400
  Countryside *(G-7413)*
Airgas USA LLC ..........................E...... 630 231-9260
  West Chicago *(G-21653)*
Airgas USA LLC ..........................E...... 708 354-0813
  Countryside *(G-7412)*
Airgas USA LLC ..........................G...... 618 439-7207
  Benton *(G-2020)*
Amer Nitrogen Co .......................E...... 847 681-1068
  Highland Park *(G-11823)*
AmeriGas .....................................D...... 708 544-1131
  Hillside *(G-11909)*
Boc Global Helium Inc ................C...... 630 897-1900
  Montgomery *(G-15032)*
Brewer Company .........................F...... 708 339-9000
  Harvey *(G-11662)*
C P Contractor ............................G...... 630 235-2381
  Hanover Park *(G-11577)*
◆ Chase Products Co ..................D...... 708 865-1000
  Broadview *(G-2566)*
Claire-Sprayway Inc ....................D...... 630 628-3000
  Downers Grove *(G-8413)*
Continental Carbonic Pdts Inc ....G...... 217 428-2080
  Decatur *(G-7858)*
Continental Carbonic Pdts Inc ....E...... 217 428-2068
  Decatur *(G-7859)*
Continental Carbonic Pdts Inc ....E...... 309 346-7515
  Pekin *(G-17257)*
▲ Custom Blending & Pckaging of F...... 618 286-1140
  Dupo *(G-8569)*
◆ Diversified CPC Intl Inc ...........E...... 815 423-5991
  Channahon *(G-3571)*
Dixie Carbonic Inc .......................D...... 217 428-2068
  Decatur *(G-7876)*
Full-Fill Industries LLC ................E...... 217 286-3532
  Henning *(G-11737)*
Gano Welding Supplies Inc ........F...... 217 345-3770
  Charleston *(G-3597)*

Hands To Work Railroading ........G...... 708 489-9776
  Alsip *(G-470)*
◆ Ilmo Products Company ..........E...... 217 245-2183
  Jacksonville *(G-12394)*
Industrial Gas Products Inc .........G...... 618 337-1030
  East Saint Louis *(G-8757)*
K-G Spray-Pak Inc .......................G...... 630 543-7600
  Downers Grove *(G-8469)*
Linde Gas North America LLC ...F...... 630 857-6460
  Broadview *(G-2592)*
Linde LLC .....................................E...... 630 515-2576
  Naperville *(G-15692)*
Linde LLC .....................................E...... 618 251-5217
  Hartford *(G-11611)*
Linde LLC .....................................F...... 630 690-3010
  Carol Stream *(G-3185)*
Linde North America Inc ..............G...... 309 353-9717
  Pekin *(G-17273)*
Linde North America Inc ..............E...... 630 257-3612
  Lockport *(G-13726)*
Maccarb Inc .................................G...... 877 427-2499
  Elgin *(G-9098)*
Matheson Tri-Gas Inc ..................F...... 309 697-1933
  Mapleton *(G-14213)*
Matheson Tri-Gas Inc ..................E...... 815 727-2202
  Joliet *(G-12539)*
Neon Moon Ltd ............................G...... 847 849-3200
  Algonquin *(G-401)*
Neon Nights Dj Svc .....................G...... 309 820-9000
  Bloomington *(G-2205)*
Nitrogen Labs Inc ........................G...... 312 504-8134
  Champaign *(G-3520)*
Plz Aeroscience Corporation ......G...... 630 628-3000
  Downers Grove *(G-8505)*
Praxair Inc ...................................E...... 847 428-3405
  Gilberts *(G-10932)*
Praxair Distribution Inc ................E...... 314 664-7900
  Cahokia *(G-2924)*
Quality Neon Service ...................G...... 847 299-2969
  Des Plaines *(G-8266)*
Shinn Enterprises ........................G...... 217 698-3344
  Springfield *(G-20523)*
Slide Products Inc .......................F...... 847 541-7220
  Wheeling *(G-22153)*
▲ We Are Done LLC ...................E...... 708 598-7100
  Bridgeview *(G-2538)*
▼ Weldstar Company ..................E...... 630 859-3100
  Aurora *(G-1232)*

### 2816 Inorganic Pigments

Accel Corporation .......................E...... 630 579-6961
  Batavia *(G-1402)*
Allegheny Color Corporation ......E...... 815 741-1391
  Rockdale *(G-18213)*
◆ American Chemet Corporation F...... 847 948-0800
  Deerfield *(G-7975)*
▲ Chromium Industries Inc .........E...... 773 287-3716
  Chicago *(G-4373)*
Color Corporation of America ....D...... 815 987-3700
  Rockford *(G-18314)*
Colors For Plastics Inc ................G...... 847 437-0033
  Elk Grove Village *(G-9381)*
Colors For Plastics Inc ................G...... 847 437-0033
  Elk Grove Village *(G-9382)*
▲ Fortune International Tech LLC G...... 847 429-9791
  Hoffman Estates *(G-12011)*
Huntsman P&A Americas LLC ...E...... 618 646-2119
  East Saint Louis *(G-8755)*
Kasha Industries Inc ...................E...... 618 375-2511
  Grayville *(G-11372)*
Kasha Industries Inc ...................F...... 618 375-2511
  Grayville *(G-11373)*
P M S Consolidated ....................G...... 847 364-0011
  Elk Grove Village *(G-9668)*
▲ Plastics Color Corp Illinois ......D...... 708 868-3800
  Calumet City *(G-2950)*
Polyone Corporation ...................D...... 847 364-0011
  Elk Grove Village *(G-9686)*
Prince Minerals LLC ....................G...... 646 747-4222
  Quincy *(G-17873)*
Prince Minerals LLC ....................G...... 646 747-4200
  Quincy *(G-17874)*
◆ Rust-Oleum Corporation ..........C...... 847 367-7700
  Vernon Hills *(G-21195)*
▲ Scientific Colors Inc ................F...... 815 741-1391
  Rockdale *(G-18232)*
▲ Solomon Colors Inc ................D...... 217 522-3112
  Springfield *(G-20527)*
Toyal America Inc .......................G...... 630 505-2160
  Naperville *(G-15766)*

◆ Toyal America Inc ....................D...... 815 740-3000
  Lockport *(G-13749)*
Valspar Corporation ....................F...... 815 962-9986
  Rockford *(G-18667)*
Versatile Materials Inc ................G...... 773 924-3700
  Chicago *(G-6887)*

### 2819 Indl Inorganic Chemicals, NEC

AA-Gem Corporation ..................G...... 773 539-9303
  Chicago *(G-3699)*
▲ Acl Inc ....................................G...... 773 285-0295
  Chicago *(G-3730)*
Advanced Diamond Tech Inc .....E...... 815 293-0900
  Romeoville *(G-18791)*
◆ Akzo Nobel Inc .......................C...... 312 544-7000
  Chicago *(G-3793)*
◆ American Chemet Corporation F...... 847 948-0800
  Deerfield *(G-7975)*
Americo Chemical Products Inc .E...... 630 588-0830
  Carol Stream *(G-3103)*
Amnetic LLC ................................G...... 877 877-3678
  Des Plaines *(G-8149)*
Aquion Partners Ltd Partnr .........G...... 847 437-9400
  Elk Grove Village *(G-9311)*
Arch Chemicals Inc ....................E...... 630 955-0401
  Naperville *(G-15600)*
Arcturus Performance Pdts LLC G...... 630 204-0211
  Saint Charles *(G-19137)*
▲ Bellman-Melcor Holdings Inc ...F...... 708 532-5000
  Tinley Park *(G-20896)*
▼ Big River Zinc Corporation ......F...... 618 274-5000
  Sauget *(G-19382)*
Boyer Corporation .......................G...... 708 352-2553
  La Grange *(G-12727)*
◆ BP Amoco Chemical Company B...... 630 420-5111
  Naperville *(G-15608)*
Brainerd Chemical Midwest LLC G...... 918 622-1214
  Danville *(G-7707)*
Bullen Midwest Inc .....................E...... 773 785-2300
  Chicago *(G-4183)*
C & S Chemicals Inc .................G...... 815 722-6671
  Joliet *(G-12470)*
Cabot Corporation ......................C...... 217 253-3370
  Tuscola *(G-21017)*
Cabot Microelectronics Corp ......C...... 630 375-6631
  Aurora *(G-979)*
Calgon Carbon Corporation .......G...... 815 741-5452
  Rockdale *(G-18215)*
Campbell Camie Inc ...................E...... 314 968-3222
  Downers Grove *(G-8403)*
Campbell Science Corp .............F...... 815 962-7415
  Rockford *(G-18295)*
▲ Carus Corporation ..................D...... 815 223-1500
  Peru *(G-17503)*
Carus Corporation ......................C...... 815 223-1500
  La Salle *(G-12766)*
Carus Corporation ......................D...... 815 223-1565
  La Salle *(G-12767)*
Carus Group Inc .........................D...... 815 223-1500
  Peru *(G-17504)*
◆ Catalytic Products Intl Inc .......E...... 847 438-0334
  Lake Zurich *(G-13050)*
▲ Cater Chemical Co .................G...... 630 980-2300
  Roselle *(G-18930)*
Chemtech Services Inc ..............F...... 815 838-4800
  Lockport *(G-13709)*
Chemtrade Chemicals US LLC ..E...... 618 274-4363
  East Saint Louis *(G-8746)*
Circle Systems Inc .....................F...... 815 286-3271
  Hinckley *(G-11934)*
Clorox Products Mfg Co .............C...... 708 728-4200
  Chicago *(G-4404)*
▲ Dauber Company Inc .............E...... 815 442-3569
  Tonica *(G-20973)*
Delta Products Group Inc ...........F...... 630 357-5544
  Aurora *(G-1139)*
Dfg Mercury Corp .......................E...... 847 869-7800
  Evanston *(G-10028)*
Dow Chemical Company ............E...... 847 439-2240
  Elk Grove Village *(G-9434)*
Dow Chemical Company ............C...... 815 653-2411
  Ringwood *(G-17989)*
Dow Chemical Company ............D...... 815 933-8900
  Kankakee *(G-12610)*
▲ DSM Desotech Inc .................C...... 847 697-0400
  Elgin *(G-9013)*
Elemental Art Jewelry ................G...... 773 844-4812
  Chicago *(G-4725)*
Elements Group .........................G...... 312 664-2252
  Chicago *(G-4726)*

---

Employee Codes: A=Over 500 employees, B=251-500
C=101-250, D=51-100, E=20-50, F=10-19, G=3-9

## 28 CHEMICALS AND ALLIED PRODUCTS

Emco Chemical Distributors Inc .............. C  262 427-0400
 North Chicago (G-16178)
Entrust Services LLC .............................. G  630 699-9132
 Naperville (G-15654)
Equa Star Chemical Corp ........................ G  815 942-7011
 Morris (G-15107)
◆ Esma Inc .............................................. G  708 331-0456
 South Holland (G-20267)
Essential Elmnts Therapeutic M ............... G  815 623-6810
 Roscoe (G-18896)
Eureka Chemical Labs Inc ....................... G  773 847-9672
 Chicago (G-4782)
▲ Finoric LLC ........................................ G  773 829-5811
 Naperville (G-15658)
Frank Miller & Sons Inc .......................... E  708 201-7200
 Mokena (G-14863)
Fusion Chemical Corporation .................. G  847 656-5285
 Park Ridge (G-17197)
Gcp Applied Technologies ...................... C  410 531-4000
 Bannockburn (G-1259)
Gmm Holdings LLC ................................ F  312 255-9830
 Chicago (G-4966)
Gycor International Ltd .......................... E  630 754-8070
 Woodridge (G-22492)
H A Gartenberg & Company .................... F  847 821-7590
 Buffalo Grove (G-2700)
Helena Chemical Company ..................... F  217 382-4241
 Martinsville (G-14336)
Helena Chemical Company ..................... G  217 234-2726
 Mattoon (G-14391)
Honeywell International Inc .................... B  618 524-2111
 Metropolis (G-14754)
Hussain Shaheen ................................... G  630 405-8009
 Bolingbrook (G-2317)
▲ Hydrox Chemical Company Inc ............ D  847 468-9400
 Elgin (G-9069)
Incon Industries Inc ................................ G  630 728-4014
 Saint Charles (G-19196)
Incon Processing LLC ............................. E  630 305-8556
 Batavia (G-1456)
Innophos Inc .......................................... C  708 757-6111
 Chicago Heights (G-7103)
Innophos Inc .......................................... G  773 468-2300
 Chicago (G-5199)
▲ Interra Global Corporation ................... F  847 292-8600
 Park Ridge (G-17204)
J B Watts Company Inc ........................... G  773 643-1855
 Chicago (G-5256)
J Stilling Enterprises Inc ......................... G  630 584-5050
 Saint Charles (G-19201)
JM Huber Corporation ............................. E  217 224-1100
 Quincy (G-17841)
◆ Kafko International Ltd ....................... E  847 763-0333
 Skokie (G-20021)
Klean-Ko Inc ........................................... D  630 620-1860
 Lombard (G-13816)
Konzen Chemicals Inc ............................ F  708 878-7636
 Matteson (G-14375)
Lattice Energy LLC ................................. G  312 861-0115
 Chicago (G-5466)
Lonza Inc ............................................... D  309 697-7200
 Mapleton (G-14212)
▲ Maclee Chemical Company Inc ............ G  847 480-0953
 Northbrook (G-16305)
Magrabar LLC ........................................ F  847 965-7550
 Morton Grove (G-15215)
▲ Mason Chemical Company .................. F  847 290-1621
 Arlington Heights (G-799)
Masters Co Inc ....................................... E  630 238-9292
 Wood Dale (G-22396)
McClendon Holdings LLC ....................... G  773 251-2314
 Chicago (G-5664)
McShares Inc ......................................... E  217 762-2561
 Monticello (G-15079)
Merichem Chem Rfinery Svcs LLC ........... F  847 285-3850
 Schaumburg (G-19643)
Metal Finishing Research Corp ............... F  773 373-0800
 Chicago (G-5699)
Milliken & Company ............................... D  312 666-2015
 Chicago (G-5764)
Murdock Company Inc ............................ G  847 566-0050
 Mundelein (G-15535)
▲ Nanochem Solutions Inc ..................... G  708 563-9200
 Naperville (G-15708)
Nanochem Solutions Inc ......................... G  815 224-8480
 Peru (G-17521)
National Interchem LLC .......................... G  708 597-7777
 Blue Island (G-2264)
▲ Nikkin Flux Corp ................................ G  618 656-2125
 Edwardsville (G-8810)

▲ NNt Enterprises Incorporated ............... E  630 875-9600
 Itasca (G-12332)
◆ Old World Global LLC ......................... G  800 323-5440
 Northbrook (G-16324)
Old World Inds Holdings LLC .................. G  800 323-5440
 Northbrook (G-16325)
Orica USA Inc ........................................ E  815 357-8711
 Morris (G-15125)
◆ Pcs Phosphate Company Inc ............... D  847 849-4200
 Northbrook (G-16336)
Pharmasyn Inc ....................................... G  847 752-8405
 Libertyville (G-13367)
Phosphate Resource Ptrs ....................... A  847 739-1200
 Lake Forest (G-12945)
◆ Plaze Inc ............................................ C  630 628-4240
 Downers Grove (G-8503)
▼ Potash Corp Ssktchewan Fla Inc .......... G  847 849-4200
 Northbrook (G-16339)
Potash Corp Ssktchewan Fla Inc ............. C  847 849-4200
 Northbrook (G-16340)
Powerlab Inc .......................................... G  815 273-7718
 Savanna (G-19404)
PQ Corporation ...................................... G  815 667-4241
 Utica (G-21107)
PQ Corporation ...................................... G  847 662-8566
 Gurnee (G-11488)
Pure Element ......................................... G  309 269-7823
 Moline (G-14963)
PVS Chemical Solutions Inc ................... E  773 933-8800
 Chicago (G-6231)
Radco Industries Inc .............................. G  630 232-7966
 Elburn (G-8908)
Radco Industries Inc .............................. G  630 232-7966
 Batavia (G-1489)
Reagent Chemical & RES Inc .................. F  618 271-8140
 East Saint Louis (G-8766)
Regis Technologies Inc .......................... D  847 967-6000
 Morton Grove (G-15232)
Remuriate LLC ....................................... G  815 220-5050
 La Salle (G-12783)
▲ Rend Lake Carbide Inc ....................... G  618 438-0160
 Benton (G-2039)
Rhone-Poulenc Basic Chem Co .............. G  708 757-6111
 Chicago Heights (G-7121)
◆ Rockform Tooling & Machinery ............ E  770 345-4624
 Rockford (G-18591)
Sanford Chemical Co Inc ....................... F  847 437-3530
 Elk Grove Village (G-9727)
◆ Scholle Ipn Corporation ...................... F  708 562-7290
 Northlake (G-16450)
Schwanog LLC ...................................... G  847 289-1055
 Elgin (G-9172)
Solvay Chemicals Inc ............................. G  618 274-0755
 East Saint Louis (G-8769)
Solvay USA Inc ...................................... C  708 441-6041
 Chicago Heights (G-7126)
Solvay USA Inc ...................................... G  708 371-2000
 Blue Island (G-2271)
Spartan Flame Retardants Inc ................ F  815 459-8500
 Crystal Lake (G-7653)
Stellar Manufacturing Company .............. D  618 823-3761
 Cahokia (G-2926)
Toyal America Inc .................................. G  630 505-2160
 Naperville (G-15766)
Trico Technologies Inc ........................... G  847 662-9224
 Gurnee (G-11516)
▲ U Op .................................................. G  847 391-2000
 Des Plaines (G-8289)
Universal Chem & Coatings Inc .............. E  847 297-2001
 Elk Grove Village (G-9801)
◆ Universial Cat LLC .............................. E  708 753-8070
 S Chicago Hts (G-19114)
UOP LLC ............................................... C  708 442-3681
 Chicago (G-6840)
UOP LLC ............................................... G  847 391-2540
 Des Plaines (G-8294)
UOP LLC ............................................... G  708 442-7400
 Mc Cook (G-14460)
US Silica ............................................... F  312 589-7539
 Chicago (G-6856)
Vacumet Corp ........................................ F  708 562-7290
 Northlake (G-16458)
▲ Velsicol Chemical LLC ....................... F  847 813-7888
 Rosemont (G-19040)
Vernon Micheal ...................................... G  217 735-4005
 Lincoln (G-13421)
Vertex Chemical Corporation .................. F  618 286-5207
 Dupo (G-8583)
▲ Vital Chemicals USA LLC ................... G  630 778-0330
 Naperville (G-15777)

W R Grace & Co ..................................... C  708 458-0340
 Chicago (G-6921)
W R Grace & Co ..................................... G  773 838-3200
 Chicago (G-6920)
W R Grace & Co- Conn ........................... F  708 458-9700
 Chicago (G-6924)
Washington Mills Tonawanda .................. D  815 925-7302
 Hennepin (G-11736)
Xena International Inc ............................ E  815 946-2626
 Polo (G-17691)
▲ Xingfa USA Corporation ..................... G  360 720-9256
 Naperville (G-15786)

### 2821 Plastics, Mtrls & Nonvulcanizable Elastomers

A Schulman Inc ...................................... E  847 426-3350
 Carpentersville (G-3270)
Aabbitt Adhesives Inc ............................ D  773 227-2700
 Chicago (G-3701)
Acomtech Mold Inc ................................ G  847 741-3537
 Elgin (G-8933)
▲ Ade Inc .............................................. E  773 646-3400
 Chicago (G-3746)
▲ Advanced Prototype Molding .............. G  847 202-4200
 Palatine (G-16998)
Akrylix Inc ............................................. G  773 869-9005
 Frankfort (G-10291)
◆ Akshar Plastic Inc .............................. E  815 635-3536
 Bloomington (G-2142)
Akzo Nobel Coatings Inc ........................ E  630 792-1619
 Lombard (G-13763)
▼ Amcol Hlth Buty Solutions Inc ............. F  847 851-1300
 Hoffman Estates (G-11990)
◆ Amcor Flexibles LLC .......................... C  224 313-7000
 Buffalo Grove (G-2656)
Americas Styrenics LLC ......................... D  815 418-6403
 Channahon (G-3565)
Ameriflon Ltd ......................................... G  847 541-6000
 Wheeling (G-22004)
Ashland Chemical Incorporated .............. G  708 891-0760
 Calumet City (G-2935)
▲ Atlas Fibre Company .......................... D  847 674-1234
 Northbrook (G-16208)
Atsp Innovations LLC ............................. G  217 239-1703
 Champaign (G-3454)
BASF Corporation .................................. B  815 932-9863
 Kankakee (G-12603)
Bayer Corporation .................................. G  847 725-6320
 Elk Grove Village (G-9335)
◆ BP Amoco Chemical Company ............ B  630 420-5111
 Naperville (G-15608)
Brinkman Company Inc .......................... G  630 595-3640
 Bensenville (G-1847)
Camryn Industries LLC .......................... C  815 544-1900
 Belvidere (G-1743)
Catlyst Reaction LLC ............................. G  708 941-4616
 Markham (G-14301)
Chicago Latex Products Inc ................... G  815 459-9680
 Crystal Lake (G-7552)
Clarich Mold Corp .................................. F  708 865-8120
 Westchester (G-21833)
Clear Lam Packaging Inc ....................... D  847 378-1200
 Elk Grove Village (G-9377)
Color Corporation of America ................. D  815 987-3700
 Rockford (G-18314)
Cope Plastics Inc .................................. G  309 787-4465
 Rock Island (G-18168)
Corro-Shield International Inc ................. F  847 298-7770
 Elk Grove Village (G-9397)
Creative Marble Inc ............................... G  217 359-7271
 Champaign (G-3471)
▲ Crown Premiums Inc .......................... F  815 469-8789
 Frankfort (G-10311)
Custom Films Inc ................................... F  217 826-2326
 Marshall (G-14320)
David Teplica M D .................................. G  773 296-9900
 Chicago (G-4564)
▼ De Enterprises Inc ............................. F  708 345-8088
 Broadview (G-2571)
Dip Seal Plastics Inc ............................. G  815 398-3533
 Rockford (G-18345)
Dmr International Inc ............................. G  815 704-5678
 Woodstock (G-22561)
Dow Chemical Company ........................ D  217 784-2093
 Gibson City (G-10900)
Dow Chemical Company ........................ C  815 423-5921
 Channahon (G-3572)
Dow Chemical Company ........................ D  815 476-9688
 Wilmington (G-22270)

**Dow Chemical Company** ........ E ....... 847 439-2240
Elk Grove Village ***(G-9434)***

**Dow Chemical Company** ........ C ....... 815 653-2411
Ringwood ***(G-17989)***

**Dow Chemical Company** ........ D ....... 815 933-8900
Kankakee ***(G-12610)***

**Drum Manufacturing** ........ F ....... 217 923-5625
Greenup ***(G-11381)***

▲ **DSM Desotech Inc** ........ C ....... 847 697-0400
Elgin ***(G-9013)***

◆ **Dynachem Inc** ........ D ....... 217 662-2136
Westville ***(G-21929)***

**Ecologic LLC** ........ F ....... 630 869-0495
Oakbrook Terrace ***(G-16706)***

▲ **Elevator Cable & Supply Co** ........ E ....... 708 338-9700
Broadview ***(G-2574)***

**Emerald Performance Mtls LLC** ........ D ....... 309 364-2311
Henry ***(G-11741)***

**Ems Acrylics & Silk Screener** ........ F ....... 773 777-5656
Chicago ***(G-4747)***

**Evergreen Scale Models Inc** ........ F ....... 224 567-8099
Des Plaines ***(G-8191)***

**Excelsior Inc** ........ E ....... 815 987-2900
Rockford ***(G-18375)***

▲ **Fitz Chem Corporation** ........ E ....... 630 467-8383
Itasca ***(G-12264)***

**Flex-O-Glass Inc** ........ E ....... 815 288-1424
Dixon ***(G-8331)***

**Flint Hlls Rsources Joliet LLC** ........ G ....... 815 224-5232
Peru ***(G-17510)***

**Gallagher Corporation** ........ D ....... 847 249-3440
Gurnee ***(G-11451)***

**Hanlon Group Ltd** ........ G ....... 773 525-3666
Chicago ***(G-5042)***

▲ **Harry J Bosworth Company** ........ E ....... 847 679-3400
Evanston ***(G-10050)***

**Hexion Inc** ........ E ....... 708 728-8834
Bedford Park ***(G-1554)***

**Huntsman Expndable Polymers Lc** ........ C ....... 815 224-5463
Peru ***(G-17512)***

**Huntsman International LLC** ........ D ....... 815 653-1500
Ringwood ***(G-17991)***

**ID Additives Inc** ........ G ....... 708 588-0081
La Grange ***(G-12737)***

▼ **Ineos Bio USA LLC** ........ E ....... 630 857-7000
Lisle ***(G-13604)***

**Ineos New Planet Bioenergy LLC** ........ D ....... 630 857-7143
Lisle ***(G-13605)***

▼ **Ineos Silicas Americas LLC** ........ D ....... 815 727-3651
Joliet ***(G-12517)***

▲ **Innocor Foam Tech W Chcago LLC** ........ E ....... 732 945-6222
West Chicago ***(G-21722)***

▲ **Innovative Hess Products LLC** ........ B ....... 847 676-3260
Arlington Heights ***(G-778)***

▲ **Itasca Plastics Inc** ........ E ....... 630 443-4446
Saint Charles ***(G-19200)***

**Iten Industries Inc** ........ G ....... 630 543-2820
Addison ***(G-155)***

**J L M Plastics Corporation** ........ F ....... 815 722-0066
Joliet ***(G-12520)***

**Jakes World Design** ........ G ....... 217 348-3043
Lerna ***(G-13287)***

**Kns Companies Inc** ........ F ....... 630 665-9010
Carol Stream ***(G-3181)***

**Kunz Industries Inc** ........ G ....... 708 596-7717
South Holland ***(G-20285)***

**Lanxess Solutions US Inc** ........ F ....... 309 633-9480
Mapleton ***(G-14211)***

**LL Display Group Ltd** ........ E ....... 847 982-0231
Lincolnwood ***(G-13522)***

**Lyondell Chemical Company** ........ B ....... 815 942-7011
Morris ***(G-15114)***

**Mapei Corporation** ........ D ....... 630 293-5800
West Chicago ***(G-21737)***

**Maxwell Counters Inc** ........ E ....... 309 928-2848
Farmer City ***(G-10179)***

**Midwest Innovative Pdts LLC** ........ E ....... 888 945-4545
Frankfort ***(G-10343)***

▲ **Miner Elastomer Products Corp** ........ E ....... 630 232-3000
Geneva ***(G-10848)***

**Minova USA Inc** ........ D ....... 618 993-2611
Marion ***(G-14274)***

**Mossan Inc** ........ G ....... 857 247-4122
Schaumburg ***(G-19650)***

▲ **MRC Polymers Inc** ........ D ....... 773 890-9000
Chicago ***(G-5825)***

▼ **Nanocor LLC** ........ E ....... 847 851-1900
Hoffman Estates ***(G-12026)***

▼ **National Casein of California** ........ D ....... 773 846-7300
Chicago ***(G-5863)***

**Natural Polymers LLC** ........ G ....... 888 563-3111
West Chicago ***(G-21749)***

**Nova Chemicals Inc** ........ D ....... 815 224-1525
Peru ***(G-17523)***

**Novipax LLC** ........ F ....... 630 686-2735
Oak Brook ***(G-16548)***

**Nypro Inc** ........ F ....... 630 773-3341
Hanover Park ***(G-11587)***

**Oly Ola Edging Inc** ........ F ....... 630 833-3033
Villa Park ***(G-21274)***

**Owens Corning Sales LLC** ........ D ....... 815 226-4627
Rockford ***(G-18527)***

**Pactiv LLC** ........ B ....... 715 723-4181
Lake Forest ***(G-12938)***

**Pintas Cultured Marble** ........ E ....... 708 385-3360
Alsip ***(G-509)***

**Plastics Color & Compounding** ........ D ....... 708 868-3800
Calumet City ***(G-2949)***

**Poly-Resyn Inc** ........ F ....... 847 428-4031
West Dundee ***(G-21801)***

**Polybilt Body Company LLC** ........ G ....... 708 345-8050
Itasca ***(G-12343)***

**Polycast** ........ F ....... 815 648-4438
Hebron ***(G-11725)***

**Polyconversions Inc** ........ E ....... 217 893-3330
Rantoul ***(G-17935)***

◆ **Polyform Products Company** ........ E ....... 847 427-0020
Elk Grove Village ***(G-9685)***

**Polymax Thermoplastic** ........ E ....... 847 316-9900
Waukegan ***(G-21602)***

▲ **Polynt Composites USA Inc** ........ C ....... 847 428-2657
Carpentersville ***(G-3296)***

**Polyone Corporation** ........ D ....... 815 385-8500
McHenry ***(G-14548)***

**Polyone Corporation** ........ C ....... 309 364-2154
Henry ***(G-11746)***

**Polyone Corporation** ........ D ....... 630 972-0505
Romeoville ***(G-18859)***

**PPG Architectural Finishes Inc** ........ B ....... 217 584-1323
Meredosia ***(G-14734)***

**PPG Architectural Finishes Inc** ........ D ....... 773 523-6333
Chicago ***(G-6161)***

**Raytech Machining Fabrication** ........ E ....... 618 932-2511
West Frankfort ***(G-21816)***

**Resin Exchange Inc** ........ E ....... 630 628-7266
Addison ***(G-276)***

**Rhopac Fabricated Products LLC** ........ E ....... 847 362-3300
Libertyville ***(G-13376)***

**Rohm and Haas Company** ........ C ....... 847 426-3245
Elgin ***(G-9166)***

**Rohm and Haas Company** ........ D ....... 815 935-7725
Kankakee ***(G-12646)***

**Sabic Innovative Plas US LLC** ........ B ....... 815 434-7000
Ottawa ***(G-16982)***

◆ **Scholle Ipn Corporation** ........ F ....... 708 562-7290
Northlake ***(G-16450)***

◆ **Senior Holdings Inc** ........ C ....... 630 837-1811
Bartlett ***(G-1373)***

**Serionix** ........ G ....... 651 503-3930
Champaign ***(G-3537)***

▲ **Sherman Plastics Corp** ........ E ....... 630 369-6170
Naperville ***(G-15746)***

**Snyder Industries Inc** ........ D ....... 630 773-9510
Bensenville ***(G-1993)***

**Solvay USA Inc** ........ E ....... 708 235-7200
University Park ***(G-21062)***

**Standard Rubber Products Co** ........ E ....... 847 593-5630
Elk Grove Village ***(G-9751)***

**Star Thermoplastic Alloys and** ........ E ....... 708 343-1100
Broadview ***(G-2613)***

**Star Thermoplastic Alloys and** ........ F ....... 708 343-1100
Broadview ***(G-2614)***

▲ **Stellar Performance Mfg LLC** ........ F ....... 312 951-2311
Chicago ***(G-6587)***

◆ **Stepan Company** ........ B ....... 847 446-7500
Northfield ***(G-16419)***

**Stepan Company** ........ B ....... 815 727-4944
Elwood ***(G-9982)***

**Sunemco Technologies Inc** ........ G ....... 630 369-8947
Naperville ***(G-15758)***

▲ **Tangent Technologies LLC** ........ E ....... 630 264-1110
Aurora ***(G-1222)***

**Tech-Mate Inc** ........ G ....... 847 352-9690
Elk Grove Village ***(G-9772)***

**Technique Eng Inc** ........ F ....... 847 816-1870
Waukegan ***(G-21621)***

**Tenneco Packaging** ........ G ....... 847 482-2000
Lake Forest ***(G-12969)***

▼ **Thermoflex Corp** ........ D ....... 847 473-9001
Waukegan ***(G-21626)***

**Thermoflex Corp** ........ G ....... 847 473-9001
Waukegan ***(G-21627)***

**Total Plastics Inc** ........ F ....... 847 593-5000
Elk Grove Village ***(G-9785)***

**Underground Devices Inc** ........ F ....... 847 205-9000
Northbrook ***(G-16379)***

**United Gilsonite Laboratories** ........ E ....... 217 243-7878
Jacksonville ***(G-12415)***

**Vacumet Corp** ........ F ....... 708 562-7290
Northlake ***(G-16458)***

**Valspar Corporation** ........ G ....... 815 987-3701
Rockford ***(G-18668)***

**Voss Belting & Specialty Co** ........ E ....... 847 673-8900
Lincolnwood ***(G-13541)***

**Wilcor Solid Surface Inc** ........ F ....... 630 350-7703
Elk Grove Village ***(G-9813)***

## *2822 Synthetic Rubber (Vulcanizable Elastomers)*

**Advanced Polymer Alloys LLC** ........ G ....... 847 836-8119
Carpentersville ***(G-3272)***

▲ **Advanced Prototype Molding** ........ G ....... 847 202-4200
Palatine ***(G-16998)***

▲ **Allstates Rubber & Tool Corp** ........ F ....... 708 342-1030
Tinley Park ***(G-20888)***

**Bamberger Polymers Inc** ........ F ....... 630 773-8626
Itasca ***(G-12233)***

▼ **Custom Seal & Rubber Products** ........ G ....... 888 356-2966
Mount Morris ***(G-15295)***

**Elas Tek Molding Inc** ........ E ....... 815 675-9012
Spring Grove ***(G-20335)***

**Excelsior Inc** ........ E ....... 815 987-2900
Rockford ***(G-18375)***

**Hallstar Company** ........ D ....... 708 594-5947
Bedford Park ***(G-1552)***

**J6 Polymers LLC** ........ G ....... 815 517-1179
Dekalb ***(G-8099)***

**Mexichem Specialty Resins Inc** ........ F ....... 309 364-2154
Henry ***(G-11744)***

▲ **Modern Silicone Tech Inc** ........ F ....... 727 507-9800
Bannockburn ***(G-1262)***

**Moriteq Rubber Co** ........ F ....... 847 734-0970
Arlington Heights ***(G-806)***

▲ **Morton International LLC** ........ C ....... 312 807-2696
Chicago ***(G-5807)***

◆ **Morton Salt Inc** ........ C ....... 312 807-2000
Chicago ***(G-5809)***

**Nauvoo Products Inc** ........ F ....... 217 453-2817
Nauvoo ***(G-15855)***

**Parker-Hannifin Corporation** ........ C ....... 630 427-2020
Woodridge ***(G-22508)***

**Plastic Specialties & Tech Inc** ........ E ....... 847 781-2414
Schaumburg ***(G-19693)***

**Polymax Thermoplastic** ........ E ....... 847 316-9900
Waukegan ***(G-21602)***

**Star Thermoplastic Alloys and** ........ F ....... 708 343-1100
Broadview ***(G-2614)***

**T9 Group LLC** ........ G ....... 847 912-8862
Hawthorn Woods ***(G-11705)***

**Vibracoustic Usa Inc** ........ E ....... 618 382-5891
Carmi ***(G-3081)***

**Voss Belting & Specialty Co** ........ E ....... 847 673-8900
Lincolnwood ***(G-13541)***

▲ **Weiler Rubber Technologies LLC** ........ G ....... 773 826-8900
Chicago ***(G-6951)***

## *2823 Cellulosic Man-Made Fibers*

**Higgins Bros Inc** ........ F ....... 773 523-0124
Chicago ***(G-5086)***

**Iten Industries Inc** ........ G ....... 630 543-2820
Addison ***(G-155)***

**Lanxess Corporation** ........ E ....... 630 789-8440
Willowbrook ***(G-22219)***

## *2824 Synthetic Organic Fibers, Exc Cellulosic*

**Acrylic Design Works Inc** ........ F ....... 773 843-1300
Chicago ***(G-3738)***

**Fairfield Processing Corp** ........ E ....... 618 452-8404
Granite City ***(G-11276)***

**Gig Karasek LLC** ........ F ....... 630 549-0394
Saint Charles ***(G-19189)***

**Honeywell International Inc** ........ E .....
Danville ***(G-7733)***

**Magnetic Occasions & More Inc** ........ G ....... 815 462-4141
New Lenox ***(G-15892)***

▲ **RITA Corporation** ........ E ....... 815 337-2500
Crystal Lake ***(G-7642)***

SIC

Employee Codes: A=Over 500 employees, B=251-500
C=101-250, D=51-100, E=20-50, F=10-19, G=3-9

2017 Harris Illinois
Industrial Directory

987

**Vinylworks Inc**.....G..... 815 477-9680
Crystal Lake *(G-7674)*

## *2833 Medicinal Chemicals & Botanical Prdts*

**▲ Animal Center International**.....G..... 217 214-0536
Quincy *(G-17792)*
**Archer-Daniels-Midland Company**.....D..... 217 424-5200
Decatur *(G-7840)*
**Ataraxia LLC**.....E..... 618 446-3219
Albion *(G-355)*
**▲ Bean Products Inc**.....E..... 312 666-3600
Chicago *(G-4064)*
**Biomerieux Inc**.....E..... 630 628-6055
Lombard *(G-13771)*
**▲ Chemblend of America LLC**.....F..... 630 521-1600
Bensenville *(G-1857)*
**▲ Chemsci Technologies Inc**.....G..... 815 608-9135
Belvidere *(G-1746)*
**◆ Daito Pharmaceuticals Amer Inc**.....G..... 847 205-0800
Northbrook *(G-16238)*
**Dashire Inc**.....F..... 847 236-0776
Deerfield *(G-8003)*
**▼ Dawes LLC**.....F..... 847 577-2020
Arlington Heights *(G-745)*
**Frontida Biopharm Inc**.....G..... 215 620-3527
Aurora *(G-1012)*
**▲ GE Healthcare Holdings Inc**.....A..... 847 398-8400
Arlington Heights *(G-759)*
**GE Healthcare Inc**.....F..... 312 243-0787
Burr Ridge *(G-2844)*
**GE Healthcare Inc**.....E..... 630 595-6642
Wood Dale *(G-22376)*
**Glanbia Performance Ntrtn Inc**.....E..... 630 256-7445
Aurora *(G-1016)*
**Glanbia Performance Ntrtn Inc**.....D..... 630 236-3126
Aurora *(G-1017)*
**◆ Glanbia Performance Ntrtn Inc**.....C..... 630 236-0097
Downers Grove *(G-8451)*
**Herbaland Inc**.....G..... 773 267-7225
Chicago *(G-5077)*
**Janssen Pharmaceutica Inc**.....F..... 312 750-0507
Chicago *(G-5279)*
**Jewel Osco Inc**.....C..... 847 882-6477
Hoffman Estates *(G-12020)*
**Lonza Inc**.....D..... 309 697-7200
Mapleton *(G-14212)*
**Medimmune LLC**.....G..... 847 356-3274
Lindenhurst *(G-13547)*
**▼ Natures Best Inc**.....E..... 631 232-3355
Downers Grove *(G-8493)*
**Natures Healing Remedies Inc**.....F..... 773 589-9996
Chicago *(G-5871)*
**▲ North Amrcn Herb Spice Ltd LLC**.....F..... 847 367-6070
Lake Forest *(G-12930)*
**Nutritional Institute LLC**.....G..... 847 223-7699
Grayslake *(G-11357)*
**Obiter Research LLC**.....F..... 217 359-1626
Champaign *(G-3521)*
**Orchard Products Inc**.....G..... 847 818-6760
Mount Prospect *(G-15359)*
**Organnica Inc**.....G..... 312 925-7272
Berwyn *(G-2071)*
**◆ Pelron Corporation**.....E..... 708 442-9100
Mc Cook *(G-14455)*
**▲ Premier Health Concepts LLC**.....G..... 630 575-1059
Carol Stream *(G-3216)*
**Resolution Systems Inc**.....G..... 616 392-8001
Wilmette *(G-22265)*
**▲ RITA Corporation**.....E..... 815 337-2500
Crystal Lake *(G-7642)*
**Synchem Inc**.....F..... 847 298-2436
Elk Grove Village *(G-9764)*
**UOP LLC**.....D..... 708 442-7400
Mc Cook *(G-14460)*
**Vidasym Inc**.....G..... 847 680-6072
Libertyville *(G-13398)*
**Vitamins Inc**.....G..... 773 483-4640
Carol Stream *(G-3262)*
**Wellmark Int Farnam Co**.....B..... 925 948-4000
Schaumburg *(G-19787)*
**▲ Ys Health Corporation**.....F..... 847 391-9122
Mount Prospect *(G-15387)*
**Zoetis LLC**.....D..... 708 757-2592
Chicago Heights *(G-7137)*

## *2834 Pharmaceuticals*

**1717 Chemall Corporation**.....G..... 224 864-4180
Mundelein *(G-15460)*
**A-S Medication Solutions LLC**.....D..... 847 680-3515
Libertyville *(G-13297)*
**◆ Aardvark Pharma LLC**.....E..... 630 248-2380
Oakbrook Terrace *(G-16693)*
**▲ Abbott Health Products Inc**.....D..... 847 937-6100
North Chicago *(G-16157)*
**▲ Abbott Laboratories**.....A..... 224 667-6100
Abbott Park *(G-1)*
**Abbott Laboratories**.....A..... 224 667-6100
North Chicago *(G-16158)*
**Abbott Laboratories**.....A..... 224 330-0271
Libertyville *(G-13298)*
**Abbott Laboratories**.....A..... 847 937-2210
Chicago *(G-3705)*
**Abbott Laboratories**.....G..... 847 921-9455
Lindenhurst *(G-13545)*
**Abbott Laboratories**.....A..... 847 735-0573
Mettawa *(G-14762)*
**Abbott Laboratories**.....A..... 847 937-7970
North Chicago *(G-16159)*
**Abbott Laboratories**.....A..... 847 937-6100
North Chicago *(G-16160)*
**Abbott Laboratories**.....C..... 847 937-6100
North Chicago *(G-16161)*
**Abbott Laboratories**.....A..... 847 938-8717
North Chicago *(G-16163)*
**Abbott Laboratories**.....A..... 847 935-8130
Gurnee *(G-11417)*
**Abbott Laboratories**.....A..... 847 937-6100
Des Plaines *(G-8140)*
**Abbott Laboratories**.....A..... 847 937-6100
Abbott Park *(G-3)*
**Abbott Laboratories**.....A..... 847 937-6100
North Chicago *(G-16164)*
**◆ Abbott Laboratories Inc**.....A..... 224 668-2076
Abbott Park *(G-4)*
**◆ Abbott Laboratories PCF Ltd**.....F..... 847 937-6100
North Chicago *(G-16165)*
**Abbott Nutrition Mfg Inc**.....G..... 614 624-6083
Abbott Park *(G-5)*
**▲ Abbott Products Inc**.....B..... 847 937-6100
Abbott Park *(G-7)*
**Abbvie Holdings Inc**.....D..... 847 937-7632
Abbott Park *(G-8)*
**Abbvie Inc**.....G..... 847 367-7621
Vernon Hills *(G-21141)*
**Abbvie Inc**.....G..... 847 735-0573
Mettawa *(G-14763)*
**◆ Abbvie Inc**.....B..... 847 932-7900
North Chicago *(G-16166)*
**Abbvie Inc**.....D..... 847 932-7900
North Chicago *(G-16167)*
**Abbvie Inc**.....E..... 847 473-4787
Waukegan *(G-21517)*
**Abbvie Inc**.....G..... 847 938-2042
North Chicago *(G-16168)*
**Abbvie Products LLC**.....B..... 847 937-6100
North Chicago *(G-16169)*
**Abbvie Respiratory LLC**.....G..... 847 937-6100
North Chicago *(G-16170)*
**▲ Abbvie US LLC**.....C..... 800 255-5162
North Chicago *(G-16171)*
**Abraxis Bioscience LLC**.....G..... 310 437-7715
Elk Grove Village *(G-9258)*
**Abraxis Bioscience LLC**.....G..... 310 883-1300
Melrose Park *(G-14582)*
**Accelerated Pharma Inc**.....G..... 773 517-0789
Burr Ridge *(G-2819)*
**Access Medical Supply Inc**.....G..... 847 891-6210
Schaumburg *(G-19420)*
**Aceva LLC**.....G..... 201 978-7928
Peoria *(G-17301)*
**Actavis Pharma Inc**.....G..... 847 377-5480
Gurnee *(G-11418)*
**Actavis Pharma Inc**.....C..... 847 855-0812
Gurnee *(G-11419)*
**Acura Pharmaceuticals Inc**.....F..... 847 705-7709
Palatine *(G-16996)*
**Adello Biologics LLC**.....G..... 312 235-3665
Chicago *(G-3748)*
**Aeropharm Technology LLC**.....G..... 847 937-6100
North Chicago *(G-16174)*
**Akorn Inc**.....F..... 847 625-1100
Gurnee *(G-11425)*
**▲ Akorn Inc**.....C..... 847 279-6100
Lake Forest *(G-12876)*
**Akorn Inc**.....C..... 217 423-9715
Decatur *(G-7826)*
**Akorn Inc**.....G..... 847 279-6166
Vernon Hills *(G-21143)*
**◆ Akzo Nobel Inc**.....C..... 312 544-7000
Chicago *(G-3793)*
**Allergan Inc**.....G..... 714 246-4500
Gurnee *(G-11426)*
**Altathera Pharmaceuticals LLC**.....G..... 312 445-8900
Chicago *(G-3837)*
**Alva/Amco Pharmacal Companies**.....E..... 847 663-0700
Niles *(G-15959)*
**▲ Am2pat Inc**.....G..... 847 726-9443
Chicago *(G-3842)*
**American Phrm Partners Inc**.....E..... 847 969-2700
Schaumburg *(G-19440)*
**Amerisourcebergen Corporation**.....E..... 815 221-3600
Romeoville *(G-18797)*
**▲ Anritsu Infivis Inc**.....E..... 847 419-9729
Elk Grove Village *(G-9309)*
**Apser Laboratory Inc**.....D..... 630 543-3333
Addison *(G-42)*
**Aptimmune Biologics Inc**.....G..... 217 377-8866
Champaign *(G-3451)*
**Archer-Daniels-Midland Company**.....D..... 217 424-5200
Decatur *(G-7840)*
**Ashland ABC Choice Inc**.....G..... 773 488-7800
Chicago *(G-3960)*
**▲ Aspen API Inc**.....F..... 847 635-0985
Des Plaines *(G-8152)*
**Astellas Pharma Inc**.....E..... 800 695-4321
Northbrook *(G-16205)*
**Astellas US Holding Inc**.....E..... 224 205-8800
Northbrook *(G-16206)*
**Astellas US LLC**.....C..... 800 888-7704
Deerfield *(G-7979)*
**Astellas US Technologies Inc**.....B..... 847 317-8800
Deerfield *(G-7980)*
**Athenex Pharmaceutical Div LLC**.....E..... 847 922-8041
Schaumburg *(G-19449)*
**Avocet Polymer Tech Inc**.....G..... 773 523-2872
Chicago *(G-4001)*
**B & H Biotechnologies LLC**.....G..... 630 915-3227
Willowbrook *(G-22200)*
**▼ Baxalta Export Corporation**.....G..... 224 948-2000
Deerfield *(G-7981)*
**Baxalta Incorporated**.....B..... 224 940-2000
Bannockburn *(G-1256)*
**Baxalta World Trade LLC**.....G..... 224 948-2000
Deerfield *(G-7982)*
**Baxalta Worldwide LLC**.....G..... 224 948-2000
Deerfield *(G-7983)*
**▼ Baxter Global Holdings II Inc**.....E..... 847 948-2000
Deerfield *(G-7984)*
**Baxter Healthcare Corporation**.....B..... 847 522-8600
Vernon Hills *(G-21147)*
**Baxter Healthcare Corporation**.....G..... 847 270-4757
Wonder Lake *(G-22321)*
**Baxter Healthcare Corporation**.....B..... 847 948-4251
Lincolnshire *(G-13432)*
**Baxter Healthcare Corporation**.....B..... 847 940-6599
Round Lake *(G-19054)*
**Baxter International Inc**.....A..... 224 948-2000
Deerfield *(G-7988)*
**Baxter World Trade Corporation**.....F..... 224 948-2000
Deerfield *(G-7989)*
**Becton Dickinson and Company**.....G..... 630 428-3499
Naperville *(G-15604)*
**Bella Pharmaceuticals Inc**.....G..... 773 279-5350
Chicago *(G-4076)*
**Bio-Bridge Science Inc**.....E..... 630 328-0213
Oakbrook Terrace *(G-16699)*
**Black Start Labs Inc**.....G..... 630 444-1800
Saint Charles *(G-19144)*
**◆ Blistex Inc**.....C..... 630 571-2870
Oak Brook *(G-16493)*
**Blistex Inc**.....G..... 630 571-2870
Oak Brook *(G-16494)*
**Bridgeport Pharmacy Inc**.....G..... 312 326-3200
Chicago *(G-4166)*
**Care Solutions Incorporated**.....F..... 815 301-4034
Crystal Lake *(G-7550)*
**Catalent Pharma Solutions Inc**.....C..... 815 338-9500
Woodstock *(G-22550)*
**Celerity Pharmaceuticals LLC**.....G..... 847 999-0131
Rosemont *(G-18992)*
**Celgene Corporation**.....E..... 908 673-9000
Melrose Park *(G-14607)*
**Chicago Dscovery Solutions LLC**.....G..... 815 609-2071
Plainfield *(G-17586)*
**Clarus Therapeutics Inc**.....G..... 847 562-4300
Northbrook *(G-16225)*
**Coretechs Corp**.....F..... 847 295-3720
Lake Forest *(G-12894)*
**Cour Pharmaceuticals Dev**.....G..... 773 621-3241
Northbrook *(G-16233)*

SIC SECTION 28 CHEMICALS AND ALLIED PRODUCTS

**Curatek Pharmaceuticals Ltd** ......G....... 847 806-7674
Elk Grove Village *(G-9402)*
◆ **Daito Pharmaceuticals Amer Inc**......G....... 847 205-0800
Northbrook *(G-16238)*
▲ **Daniels Sharpsmart Inc** ......E....... 312 546-8900
Chicago *(G-4554)*
▲ **Dental Technologies Inc** ......D....... 847 677-5500
Lincolnwood *(G-13507)*
**Dr Earles LLC** ......G....... 312 225-7200
Chicago *(G-4641)*
**Drug Source Company LLC** ......G....... 708 236-1768
Westchester *(G-21838)*
**Earths Healing Cafe LLC** ......G....... 773 728-0598
Chicago *(G-4678)*
**East West Intergrated Therapys** ......G....... 815 788-0574
Crystal Lake *(G-7570)*
**Elgin Center Pharmacy Inc** ......F....... 847 697-1600
Elgin *(G-9022)*
**Elim Pdtric Phrmaceuticals Inc** ......G....... 412 266-5968
Rolling Meadows *(G-18727)*
**Elorac Inc** ......F....... 847 362-8200
Vernon Hills *(G-21159)*
**Espee** ......G....... 224 256-9570
Schaumburg *(G-19519)*
▲ **Espee Biopharma & Finechem LLC** .G....... 888 851-6667
Schaumburg *(G-19520)*
**Finish Line Horse Products Inc** ......E....... 630 694-0000
Bensenville *(G-1897)*
▲ **First Priority Inc** ......D....... 847 531-1215
Elgin *(G-9037)*
**Flexxsonic Corporation** ......G....... 847 452-7226
Mount Prospect *(G-15330)*
**Fresenius Kabi Usa Inc** ......C....... 708 410-4761
Melrose Park *(G-14641)*
▲ **Fresenius Kabi Usa Inc** ......B....... 847 969-2700
Lake Zurich *(G-13076)*
**Fresenius Kabi Usa Inc** ......C....... 708 450-7509
Melrose Park *(G-14642)*
**Fresenius Kabi Usa Inc** ......C....... 708 345-6170
Melrose Park *(G-14643)*
**Fresenius Kabi Usa Inc** ......B....... 708 450-7500
Melrose Park *(G-14640)*
▲ **Fresenius Kabi Usa LLC** ......A....... 847 550-2300
Lake Zurich *(G-13077)*
**Fresenius Kabi Usa LLC** ......E....... 847 983-7100
Skokie *(G-20002)*
**Fresenius Kabi USA LLC** ......E....... 847 550-2300
Lake Zurich *(G-13078)*
**Fresenius Kabi USA LLC** ......E....... 708 343-6100
Melrose Park *(G-14644)*
**Fresenius Usa Inc** ......E....... 773 262-7147
Chicago *(G-4890)*
**Glendale Incorporated** ......F....... 630 770-1965
Villa Park *(G-21255)*
**Glenview Pharma Inc** ......F....... 773 856-3205
Chicago *(G-4956)*
**Global Medical Services LLC** ......G....... 847 460-8086
Plainfield *(G-17602)*
**Global Pharma Device Solutions** ......G....... 708 212-5801
Chicago *(G-4959)*
▼ **Globepharm Inc** ......G....... 847 914-0922
Deerfield *(G-8009)*
**Golden Health Products Inc** ......G....... 217 223-3209
Quincy *(G-17831)*
**H3 Life Science Corporation** ......F....... 708 705-1299
Westchester *(G-21842)*
**Healthy Life Nutraceutics Inc** ......G....... 201 253-9053
Deerfield *(G-8010)*
**Hepalink USA Inc** ......G....... 630 206-1788
Chicago *(G-5075)*
**Horizon Pharma Inc** ......D....... 224 383-3000
Lake Forest *(G-12906)*
**Horizon Therapeutics Inc** ......D....... 224 383-3000
Lake Forest *(G-12907)*
◆ **Hospira Inc** ......A....... 224 212-2000
Lake Forest *(G-12908)*
**Hospira Inc** ......C....... 224 212-6244
Lake Forest *(G-12909)*
**Hot Shots Nm LLC** ......G....... 815 484-0500
Rockford *(G-18423)*
▲ **Hydrox Chemical Company Inc** ......D....... 847 468-9400
Elgin *(G-9069)*
**Hznp Usa Inc** ......F....... 224 383-3000
Lake Forest *(G-12913)*
**Illinois Tool Works Inc** ......E....... 847 593-8811
Elk Grove Village *(G-9535)*
**Inpharmco Inc** ......G....... 708 596-9262
South Holland *(G-20281)*
**International Drug Dev Cons** ......G....... 847 634-9586
Long Grove *(G-13892)*
**Iterative Therapeutics Inc** ......G....... 773 455-7203
Chicago *(G-5246)*
**Iterum Therapeutics US Limited** ......G....... 312 763-3975
Chicago *(G-5247)*
**Jewel Osco Inc** ......C....... 630 948-6000
Itasca *(G-12291)*
**Johnson & Johnson** ......D....... 815 282-5671
Loves Park *(G-13954)*
**Joseph B Pigato MD Ltd** ......G....... 815 937-2122
Kankakee *(G-12631)*
**Kastle Therapeutics LLC** ......G....... 312 883-5695
Chicago *(G-5364)*
**Lake Consumer Products** ......G....... 847 793-0230
Vernon Hills *(G-21180)*
**Lodaat LLC** ......G....... 630 248-2380
Oakbrook Terrace *(G-16715)*
**Lodaat LLC** ......D....... 630 852-7544
Downers Grove *(G-8478)*
▲ **Lundbeck LLC** ......C....... 847 282-1000
Deerfield *(G-8031)*
**Lundbeck Pharmaceuticals LLC** ......A....... 847 282-1000
Deerfield *(G-8032)*
**Mab Pharmacy Inc** ......G....... 773 342-5878
Chicago *(G-5591)*
**Mar Cor Purification Inc** ......G....... 630 435-1017
Downers Grove *(G-8483)*
**Mayne Pharma USA Inc** ......G....... 224 212-2660
Lake Forest *(G-12925)*
**Mead Johnson & Company LLC** ......F....... 847 832-2420
Chicago *(G-5670)*
**Mead Johnson Nutrition Company** ......E....... 312 466-5800
Chicago *(G-5671)*
**Meda Pharmaceuticals Inc** ......D....... 217 424-8400
Decatur *(G-7912)*
**Medimmune LLC** ......G....... 618 235-8730
Belleville *(G-1656)*
**Meitheal Pharmaceuticals Inc** ......G....... 773 951-6542
Des Plaines *(G-8232)*
**Meridian Healthcare** ......G....... 815 633-5326
Rockford *(G-18492)*
**Meridian Laboratories Inc** ......G....... 847 808-0081
Buffalo Grove *(G-2735)*
**Merix Pharmaceutical Corp** ......G....... 847 277-1111
Barrington *(G-1290)*
▲ **Mgp Holding Corp** ......B....... 847 967-5600
Morton Grove *(G-15220)*
**Midwest Biofluids Inc** ......G....... 630 790-9708
Glen Ellyn *(G-10981)*
**Midwest Research Labs LLC** ......G....... 847 283-9176
Lake Forest *(G-12926)*
▲ **Morton Grove Phrmceuticals Inc** ......B....... 847 967-5600
Morton Grove *(G-15223)*
**Nantpharma LLC** ......G....... 847 243-1200
Rolling Meadows *(G-18747)*
**Naurex Inc** ......G....... 847 871-0377
Evanston *(G-10078)*
**Neurotherapeutics Pharma Inc** ......G....... 773 444-4180
Chicago *(G-5889)*
**Newhealth Solutions LLC** ......G....... 803 627-8378
Brookfield *(G-2638)*
**Novalex Therapeutics Inc** ......G....... 630 750-9334
Chicago *(G-5947)*
**Novum Pharma LLC** ......F....... 877 404-4724
Chicago *(G-5950)*
▲ **Now Health Group Inc** ......A....... 630 545-9098
Bloomingdale *(G-2122)*
**Now Health Group Inc** ......A....... 888 669-3663
Bloomingdale *(G-2123)*
**Ocularis Pharma** ......G....... 708 712-6263
Riverside *(G-18032)*
**Oncquest** ......G....... 847 682-4703
Zion *(G-22694)*
▲ **Ortho Molecular Products Inc** ......E....... 815 337-0089
Woodstock *(G-22596)*
**Pal Midwest Ltd** ......G....... 815 965-2981
Rockford *(G-18528)*
**Patrin Pharma Inc** ......E....... 800 936-3088
Skokie *(G-20053)*
▲ **Pfanstiehl Inc** ......G....... 847 623-0370
Waukegan *(G-21601)*
**Pfizer Inc** ......G....... 847 506-8895
Mount Prospect *(G-15363)*
▲ **Pharma Logistics** ......D....... 847 388-3104
Mundelein *(G-15545)*
**Pharmaceutical Labs and Cons I** ......G....... 630 359-3831
Addison *(G-240)*
**Pharmanutrients Inc** ......G....... 847 234-2334
Lake Bluff *(G-12862)*
**Pharmdium Hlthcare Hldings Inc** ......G....... 800 523-7749
Lake Forest *(G-12943)*
**Pharmedium Healthcare Corp** ......E....... 847 457-2300
Lake Forest *(G-12944)*
**Phillips Pharmaceuticals Inc** ......G....... 630 328-0016
Naperville *(G-15727)*
**Porche Pharmaceutical Staffing** ......G....... 312 259-3982
Park Ridge *(G-17217)*
**Powbab Inc** ......G....... 630 481-6140
Oak Brook *(G-16555)*
**Power Partners LLC** ......G....... 773 465-8688
Chicago *(G-6158)*
**Professional Packaging Corp** ......E....... 630 896-0574
Aurora *(G-1205)*
**Ravens Wood Pharmacy** ......G....... 708 667-0525
Chicago *(G-6295)*
**Redd Remedies Inc** ......F....... 815 614-2083
Bradley *(G-2430)*
**Renaissance SSP Holdings Inc** ......G....... 210 476-8194
Lake Forest *(G-12951)*
▲ **Respa Pharmaceuticals Inc** ......E....... 630 543-3333
Addison *(G-277)*
**Riverside Medi-Center Inc** ......G....... 815 932-6632
Kankakee *(G-12645)*
**Roundtble Hlthcare Partners LP** ......E....... 847 482-9275
Lake Forest *(G-12954)*
**Sagent Logistics LP** ......F....... 847 908-1600
Schaumburg *(G-19716)*
▲ **Sagent Pharmaceuticals Inc** ......D....... 847 908-1600
Schaumburg *(G-19717)*
**Sams West Inc** ......G....... 618 622-0507
O Fallon *(G-16477)*
**Savind Inc** ......G....... 217 687-2710
Seymour *(G-19898)*
**Senior Care Pharmacy LLC** ......G....... 847 579-0093
Highland Park *(G-11868)*
**Sfc Chemicals Ltd** ......G....... 847 221-2152
Chicago *(G-6486)*
**Shaars International Inc** ......G....... 815 315-0717
Rockford *(G-18614)*
**Sterling Phrm Svcs LLC** ......F....... 618 286-4116
East Carondelet *(G-8615)*
**Sterling Phrm Svcs LLC** ......G....... 618 286-6060
Dupo *(G-8578)*
**Strategic Applications Inc** ......G....... 847 680-9385
Lake Villa *(G-13027)*
◆ **Sukgyung At Inc** ......G....... 847 298-6570
Des Plaines *(G-8282)*
▲ **Sunstar Pharmaceutical Inc** ......D....... 773 777-4000
Elgin *(G-9198)*
**Superior Biologics II Inc** ......G....... 847 469-2400
Schaumburg *(G-19745)*
**Symbria Rx Services LLC** ......E....... 630 981-8000
Woodridge *(G-22520)*
**Takeda Dev Ctr Americas Inc** ......A....... 224 554-6500
Deerfield *(G-8058)*
**Takeda Pharmaceuticals NA** ......G....... 972 819-5353
Deerfield *(G-8059)*
▲ **Takeda Pharmaceuticals USA Inc** ......A....... 224 554-6500
Deerfield *(G-8060)*
**Takeda Phrmaceuticals Amer Inc** ......A....... 224 554-6500
Deerfield *(G-8061)*
**Therapeutic Skin Care** ......G....... 630 244-1833
Lombard *(G-13868)*
**Trudeau Approved Products Inc** ......G....... 312 924-7230
Hinsdale *(G-11967)*
**Unichem International Inc** ......E....... 847 669-6552
Huntley *(G-12181)*
**Vitamins Inc** ......G....... 773 483-4640
Carol Stream *(G-3262)*
**Wellness Center Usa Inc** ......G....... 847 925-1885
Hoffman Estates *(G-12069)*
▼ **Winlind Skincare LLC** ......G....... 630 789-9408
Burr Ridge *(G-2896)*
**Winston Pharmaceuticals Inc** ......G....... 847 362-8200
Vernon Hills *(G-21217)*
**Wockhardt Holding Corp** ......B....... 847 967-5600
Morton Grove *(G-15246)*
▲ **Xttrium Laboratories Inc** ......D....... 773 268-5800
Mount Prospect *(G-15386)*
**Zoetis LLC** ......D....... 708 757-2592
Chicago Heights *(G-7137)*

## *2835 Diagnostic Substances*

**3primedx Inc** ......G....... 312 621-0643
Chicago *(G-3668)*
**Abbott Laboratories** ......F....... 847 937-6100
Abbott Park *(G-2)*
**Abbott Laboratories** ......G....... 224 361-7129
Elk Grove Village *(G-9254)*
▲ **Abbott Laboratories** ......A....... 224 667-6100
Abbott Park *(G-1)*

SIC

Employee Codes: A=Over 500 employees, B=251-500
C=101-250, D=51-100, E=20-50, F=10-19, G=3-9
2017 Harris Illinois
Industrial Directory
989

**Abbott Laboratories** A 847 938-8717
North Chicago *(G-16163)*
**Abbott Laboratories** A 847 937-6100
North Chicago *(G-16164)*
**Abbott Molecular Inc** G 224 361-7800
Des Plaines *(G-8141)*
▲ **Abbott Molecular Inc** D 224 361-7800
Des Plaines *(G-8142)*
**Aid For Women Northern Lk Cnty** F 847 249-2700
Gurnee *(G-11421)*
**Amoco Technology Company (del)** C 312 861-6000
Chicago *(G-3892)*
▼ **Baxalta Export Corporation** G 224 948-2000
Deerfield *(G-7981)*
**Baxalta US Inc** F 312 648-2244
Chicago *(G-4056)*
**Baxalta US Inc** D 847 948-2000
Round Lake *(G-19052)*
**Baxalta World Trade LLC** G 224 948-2000
Deerfield *(G-7982)*
**Baxalta Worldwide LLC** G 224 948-2000
Deerfield *(G-7983)*
**Baxter Healthcare Corporation** C 847 948-3206
Spring Grove *(G-20328)*
**Baxter Healthcare Corporation** E 847 578-4671
Waukegan *(G-21529)*
**Baxter International Inc** A 224 948-2000
Deerfield *(G-7988)*
**Bion Enterprises Ltd** E 847 544-5044
Des Plaines *(G-8159)*
**Cairo Diagnostic Center** F 618 734-1500
Cairo *(G-2927)*
**Chem-Impex International Inc** E 630 350-5015
Wood Dale *(G-22351)*
**Chemprobe Inc** G 847 231-4534
Grayslake *(G-11326)*
**Cooper Equipment Company Inc** G 708 367-1291
Crete *(G-7511)*
**Fox Valley Pregnancy Center** G 847 697-0200
South Elgin *(G-20197)*
▲ **GE Healthcare Holdings Inc** A 847 398-8400
Arlington Heights *(G-759)*
**Glucosentient Inc** G 217 487-4087
Champaign *(G-3490)*
**Guardian Angel Outreach** G 815 672-4567
Streator *(G-20689)*
**Innovative Molecular Diagnosti** G 630 845-8246
Geneva *(G-10838)*
**Kim Laboratories Inc** G 217 337-6666
Rantoul *(G-17932)*
**Macneal Hospital** G 773 581-2199
Chicago *(G-5594)*
**Muhammad Sotavia** G 708 966-2262
Orland Park *(G-16877)*
**Nuclin Diagnostics Inc** G 847 498-5210
Northbrook *(G-16320)*
**Ohmx Corporation** F 847 491-8500
Evanston *(G-10081)*
**Open Advanced Mri Crystl** G 815 444-1330
Crystal Lake *(G-7623)*
**Ortho-Clinical Diagnostics Inc** C 618 281-3882
Columbia *(G-7362)*
**Petnet Solutions Inc** G 847 297-3721
Des Plaines *(G-8252)*
**Prenosis Inc** G 949 246-3113
Champaign *(G-3530)*
**Pyramid Sciences Inc** G 630 974-6110
Burr Ridge *(G-2876)*
**Regis Technologies Inc** D 847 967-6000
Morton Grove *(G-15232)*
**Tri Cnty Prgnncy Prenting Svcs** G 847 231-4651
Grayslake *(G-11364)*
**Voyant Diagnostics Inc** G 630 456-6340
Chicago *(G-6916)*

## 2836 Biological Prdts, Exc Diagnostic Substances

**3abn** G 618 627-4651
Thompsonville *(G-20861)*
◆ **Abbvie Inc** B 847 932-7900
North Chicago *(G-16166)*
▲ **Abbvie US LLC** C 800 255-5162
North Chicago *(G-16171)*
▲ **Aspen API Inc** F 847 635-0985
Des Plaines *(G-8152)*
**Avexis Inc** F 847 572-8280
Bannockburn *(G-1254)*
**Baxter Healthcare Corporation** C 800 422-9837
Deerfield *(G-7985)*
**Bioaffinity Inc** G 815 988-5077
Rockford *(G-18285)*
**Bioforce Nanosciences Inc** G 515 233-8333
Chicago *(G-4110)*
**Biologos Inc** G 630 801-4740
Montgomery *(G-15031)*
**Bn National Trail** G 618 783-8709
Newton *(G-15938)*
**C & S Chemicals Inc** G 815 722-6671
Joliet *(G-12470)*
**Charles River Laboratories Inc** D 309 923-7122
Roanoke *(G-18049)*
**Cislak Manufacturing Inc** E 847 647-1819
Niles *(G-15969)*
**Csl Behring LLC** B 815 932-6773
Bradley *(G-2418)*
**Csl Plasma Inc** E 708 343-8845
Melrose Park *(G-14612)*
**Grifols Shared Svcs N Amer Inc** G 309 827-3031
Bloomington *(G-2173)*
**Laboratory Media Corporation** F 630 897-8000
Montgomery *(G-15053)*
**Midwest Bio Manufacturing Div** F 815 542-6417
Tampico *(G-20828)*
**Northern Ill Blood Bnk Inc** D 815 965-8751
Rockford *(G-18520)*
**Octapharma Plasma Inc** G 708 409-0900
Northlake *(G-16446)*
**Octapharma Plasma Inc** G 630 375-0028
Aurora *(G-1198)*
**Octapharma Plasma Inc** G 217 546-8605
Springfield *(G-20491)*
**Protide Pharmaceuticals Inc** G 847 726-3100
Lake Zurich *(G-13117)*
**Ptm Biolabs Inc** G 312 802-6843
Chicago *(G-6221)*
**Quorum Labs LLC** G 618 525-5600
Eldorado *(G-8921)*
**Roy Winnett** G 309 367-4867
Metamora *(G-14748)*
**Spherotech Inc** F 847 680-8922
Lake Forest *(G-12961)*
**Splash Dog Therapy Inc** G 847 296-4007
Des Plaines *(G-8279)*
▲ **W-R Industries Inc** G 312 733-5200
Chicago *(G-6929)*
▼ **West Laboratories Inc** E 815 935-1630
Kankakee *(G-12658)*

## 2841 Soap & Detergents

**A & H Manufacturing Inc** F 630 543-5900
Addison *(G-14)*
**Afton Chemical Corporation** B 618 583-1000
East Saint Louis *(G-8740)*
◆ **Akzo Nobel Chemicals LLC** C 312 544-7000
Chicago *(G-3791)*
**AM Harper Products Inc** F 312 767-8283
Chicago *(G-3841)*
▲ **Apco Packaging Inc** E 708 430-7333
Bridgeview *(G-2467)*
**Ashley Lauren** G 847 733-9470
Evanston *(G-10012)*
◆ **Atm America Corp** E 800 298-0030
Chicago *(G-3986)*
▲ **Avatar Corporation** D 708 534-5511
University Park *(G-21042)*
▲ **Blachford Corporation** E 815 464-2100
Frankfort *(G-10301)*
▲ **Black Swan Manufacturing Co** F 773 227-3700
Chicago *(G-4121)*
**Blast Products Inc** G 618 452-4700
Madison *(G-14140)*
**Blew Chemical Company** G 708 448-5780
Palos Heights *(G-17100)*
**Bullen Midwest Inc** E 773 785-2300
Chicago *(G-4183)*
▲ **Cater Chemical Co** G 630 980-2300
Roselle *(G-18930)*
▲ **Cedar Concepts Corporation** E 773 890-5790
Chicago *(G-4265)*
**Chemstation Chicago LLC** E 630 279-2857
Elmhurst *(G-9846)*
◆ **Chemtool Incorporated** C 815 957-4140
Rockton *(G-18694)*
**Chemtool Incorporated** D 815 459-1250
Crystal Lake *(G-7551)*
▲ **Combe Laboratories Inc** C 217 893-4490
Rantoul *(G-17923)*
▲ **Custom Blending & Pckaging of** F 618 286-1140
Dupo *(G-8569)*
**Custom Chemical Inc** G 217 529-0878
Springfield *(G-20426)*
▲ **Cygnus Corporation** D 773 785-2845
Chicago *(G-4530)*
**Dairy Dynamics LLC** F 847 758-7300
Elk Grove Village *(G-9416)*
**Damco Products Inc** G 618 452-4700
Madison *(G-14141)*
**Dial Corporation** C 630 892-4381
Montgomery *(G-15041)*
**Ecolab Ff Aperion Care St** G 618 829-5581
Saint Elmo *(G-19306)*
**Ecp Incorporated** D 630 754-4200
Woodridge *(G-22474)*
**First Ayd Corporation** D 847 622-0001
Elgin *(G-9036)*
**Floor-Chem Inc** G 630 789-2152
Romeoville *(G-18825)*
**Formulations Inc** G 847 674-9141
Skokie *(G-20001)*
**Gea Farm Technologies Inc** E 630 759-1063
Romeoville *(G-18828)*
◆ **Gea Farm Technologies Inc** C 630 548-8200
Naperville *(G-15662)*
**Getex Corporation** G 630 993-1300
Hinsdale *(G-11948)*
▼ **Gurtler Chemicals Inc** E 708 331-2550
South Holland *(G-20273)*
**Henkel Consumer Goods Inc** D 847 426-4552
Elgin *(G-9063)*
▼ **Interflo Industries Inc** G 847 228-0606
Elk Grove Village *(G-9551)*
**Karimi Saifuddin** G 630 379-9344
Plainfield *(G-17614)*
▲ **Kik Custom Products Inc** B 217 442-1400
Danville *(G-7743)*
**Lasalle Chemical & Supply Co** F 847 470-1234
Morton Grove *(G-15211)*
**Marietta Corporation** C 773 816-5137
Chicago *(G-5619)*
▼ **Nataz Specialty Coatings Inc** F 773 247-7030
Chicago *(G-5856)*
**People Against Dirty Mfg Pbc** D 415 568-4600
Chicago *(G-6101)*
**PLC Corp** G 847 247-1900
Lake Bluff *(G-12863)*
▼ **Progressive Solutions Corp** G 847 639-7272
Algonquin *(G-405)*
**Rock River Blending** G 815 968-7860
Rockford *(G-18562)*
**Sanford Chemical Co Inc** F 847 437-3530
Elk Grove Village *(G-9727)*
▲ **Solab Inc** F 708 544-2200
Bellwood *(G-1722)*
**Standard Indus & Auto Eqp Inc** E 630 289-9500
Hanover Park *(G-11590)*
**Sweet Thyme Soaps** G 708 848-0234
Oak Park *(G-16688)*
**Tri Sect Corporation** F 847 524-1119
Schaumburg *(G-19770)*
**Unichem Corporation** F 773 376-8872
Chicago *(G-6812)*
▲ **Vantage Oleochemicals Inc** C 773 376-9000
Chicago *(G-6873)*
◆ **Venus Laboratories Inc** E 630 595-1900
Addison *(G-339)*
▲ **Vvf Illinois Services LLC** B 630 892-4381
Montgomery *(G-15071)*
**Westfalia-Surge Inc** G 630 759-7346
Romeoville *(G-18878)*

## 2842 Spec Cleaning, Polishing & Sanitation Preparations

▲ **300 Below Inc** G 217 423-3070
Decatur *(G-7819)*
**A J Funk & Co** G 847 741-6760
Elgin *(G-8929)*
▲ **Acl Inc** F 773 285-0295
Chicago *(G-3730)*
**Advanage Diversified Pdts Inc** F 708 331-8390
Harvey *(G-11650)*
**Anytime Window Cleaning Inc** G 773 235-5677
Chicago *(G-3919)*
**Apco Enterprises Inc** G 708 430-7333
Bridgeview *(G-2466)*
◆ **Apex Engineering Products Corp** F 630 820-8888
Aurora *(G-958)*
◆ **Atm America Corp** E 800 298-0030
Chicago *(G-3986)*

# 28 CHEMICALS AND ALLIED PRODUCTS

Bass Brother Incorporated .............. G ...... 773 638-7628
  Chicago *(G-4052)*
Blue Light Inc .............................. E ...... 630 400-4539
  Lisle *(G-13570)*
Boyer Corporation ......................... G ...... 708 352-2553
  La Grange *(G-12727)*
Brite Site Supply Inc ...................... G ...... 773 772-7300
  Chicago *(G-4171)*
Bullen Midwest Inc ........................ E ...... 773 785-2300
  Chicago *(G-4183)*
Bumper Scuffs .............................. G ...... 847 489-7926
  Lake Villa *(G-13011)*
Cabot Microelectronics Corp ............. D ...... 630 375-6631
  Aurora *(G-977)*
Calumet Lubr Co Ltd Partnr ............... F ...... 708 832-2463
  Burnham *(G-2815)*
▲ Cater Chemical Co ....................... G ...... 630 980-2300
  Roselle *(G-18930)*
Champion Packaging & Dist Inc ........ C ...... 630 755-4220
  Woodridge *(G-22460)*
Chemical Specialties Mfg Corp .......... G ...... 309 697-5400
  Mapleton *(G-14207)*
Chemix Corp ................................. F ...... 708 754-2150
  Glenwood *(G-11215)*
◆ Chemtool Incorporated .................. C ...... 815 957-4140
  Rockton *(G-18694)*
Chemtool Incorporated ................... E ...... 815 459-1250
  Crystal Lake *(G-7551)*
Circle K Industries Inc .................... F ...... 847 949-0363
  Mundelein *(G-15487)*
City of Chicago ............................. E ...... 312 744-0940
  Chicago *(G-4384)*
City of Chicago ............................. E ...... 312 746-6583
  Chicago *(G-4387)*
▼ Claire-Sprayway Inc ..................... E ...... 630 628-3000
  Downers Grove *(G-8412)*
Claire-Sprayway Inc ...................... D ...... 630 628-3000
  Downers Grove *(G-8413)*
CLC Lubricants Company ................. E ...... 630 232-7900
  Geneva *(G-10818)*
Clifton Chemical Company .............. G ...... 815 697-2343
  Chebanse *(G-3630)*
Clorox Company ........................... G ...... 510 271-7000
  Willowbrook *(G-22204)*
Clorox Hidden Valley Mfg ............... F ...... 847 229-5500
  Wheeling *(G-22027)*
Clorox Products Mfg Co ................. C ...... 708 728-4200
  Chicago *(G-4404)*
◆ Clorox Products Mfg Co ............... E ...... 708 728-4200
  Chicago *(G-4405)*
Clorox Products Mfg Co ................. G ...... 847 229-5500
  Wheeling *(G-22028)*
Colorex Chemical Co Inc ................ G ...... 630 238-3124
  Bensenville *(G-1862)*
▲ Concept Laboratories Inc .............. D ...... 773 395-7300
  Chicago *(G-4446)*
Coral Chemical Company ................ E ...... 847 246-6666
  Zion *(G-22680)*
▲ CPC Aeroscience Inc ................... G ...... 954 974-5440
  Downers Grove *(G-8421)*
Creative Metal Products ................. F ...... 773 638-3200
  Chicago *(G-4500)*
Damco Products Inc ...................... G ...... 618 452-4700
  Madison *(G-14141)*
Detrex Corporation ........................ G ...... 708 345-3806
  Melrose Park *(G-14616)*
Dial Corporation ............................ C ...... 630 892-4381
  Montgomery *(G-15041)*
Diversey Inc ................................. D ...... 262 631-4001
  Bartlett *(G-1341)*
◆ Dober Chemical Corp ................... C ...... 630 410-7300
  Woodridge *(G-22471)*
Doris Company ............................. G ...... 224 302-5605
  Waukegan *(G-21553)*
▼ Dura Wax Company ..................... F ...... 815 385-5000
  McHenry *(G-14499)*
Duraclean International Inc ............. F ...... 847 704-7100
  Arlington Heights *(G-748)*
Ecolab Inc .................................... E ...... 815 389-8132
  Roscoe *(G-18895)*
Ecolab Inc .................................... E ...... 815 729-7334
  Joliet *(G-12488)*
Ecolab Inc .................................... E ...... 847 350-2229
  Elk Grove Village *(G-9448)*
Ecolab Inc .................................... E ...... 815 389-4063
  South Beloit *(G-20144)*
Ecp Incorporated ........................... G ...... 630 754-4200
  Woodridge *(G-22474)*
▲ Elco Laboratories Inc .................... D ...... 708 534-3000
  University Park *(G-21047)*

Electro-Glo Distribution Inc ............ G ...... 815 224-4030
  La Salle *(G-12771)*
First Ayd Corporation .................... D ...... 847 622-0001
  Elgin *(G-9036)*
First Mate Yacht Detailing .............. G ...... 847 249-7654
  Waukegan *(G-21560)*
Floor-Chem Inc ............................. G ...... 630 789-2152
  Romeoville *(G-18825)*
Fola Community Action Services ..... F ...... 773 487-4310
  Chicago *(G-4868)*
Formulations Inc .......................... G ...... 847 674-9141
  Skokie *(G-20001)*
▲ Fox Valley Chemical Company ...... G ...... 815 653-2660
  Ringwood *(G-17990)*
Frank Miller & Sons Inc ................. E ...... 708 201-7200
  Mokena *(G-14863)*
Future Environmental Inc ............... C ...... 708 479-6900
  Mokena *(G-14865)*
Gea Farm Technologies Inc ............ E ...... 630 759-1063
  Romeoville *(G-18828)*
◆ Gea Farm Technologies Inc .......... C ...... 630 548-8200
  Naperville *(G-15662)*
Getex Corporation ........................ G ...... 630 993-1300
  Hinsdale *(G-11948)*
Houghton International Inc ............. F ...... 610 666-4000
  Chicago *(G-5121)*
Hurst Chemical Company .............. G ...... 815 964-0451
  Rockford *(G-18424)*
Imagination Products Corp ............ G ...... 309 274-6223
  Chillicothe *(G-7167)*
▼ Interflo Industries Inc .................. G ...... 847 228-0606
  Elk Grove Village *(G-9551)*
Ivanhoe Industries Inc ................... E ...... 847 872-3311
  Zion *(G-22688)*
Jacob Hay Co .............................. G ...... 847 215-8880
  Wheeling *(G-22080)*
Jaffee Investment Partnr LP ........... C ...... 312 321-1515
  Chicago *(G-5270)*
Johnnys Little LLC ........................ G ...... 217 243-2570
  Jacksonville *(G-12399)*
◆ Kafko International Ltd ................ G ...... 847 763-0333
  Skokie *(G-20021)*
▲ Kik Custom Products Inc ............. B ...... 217 442-1400
  Danville *(G-7743)*
Kik International Inc ..................... F ...... 905 660-0444
  Carol Stream *(G-3178)*
Kocour Co ................................... E ...... 773 847-1111
  Chicago *(G-5397)*
Korex Corporation ........................ G ...... 708 458-4890
  Chicago *(G-5407)*
Lasalle Chemical & Supply Co ........ F ...... 847 470-1234
  Morton Grove *(G-15211)*
▼ Lundmark Inc ............................. F ...... 630 628-1199
  Addison *(G-184)*
Mackenzie Johnson ...................... G ...... 630 244-2367
  Maywood *(G-14428)*
◆ Mat Holdings Inc ........................ D ...... 847 821-9630
  Long Grove *(G-13897)*
▲ Matchless Metal Polish Company .. E ...... 773 924-1515
  Chicago *(G-5649)*
◆ Minuteman International Inc ......... C ...... 630 627-6900
  Pingree Grove *(G-17556)*
Newby Oil Company Inc ................ G ...... 815 756-7688
  Sycamore *(G-20810)*
▲ Odorite International Inc .............. F ...... 816 920-5000
  Saint Charles *(G-19227)*
Oil-Dri Corporation America ........... D ...... 312 321-1515
  Chicago *(G-5975)*
Oil-Dri Corporation America ........... D ...... 618 745-6881
  Mounds *(G-15259)*
▼ Penray Companies Inc ................. D ...... 800 323-6329
  Wheeling *(G-22120)*
Pete Frcano Sons Cstm HM Bldrs ... F ...... 847 258-4626
  Elk Grove Village *(G-9675)*
PLC Corp .................................... E ...... 847 247-1900
  Lake Bluff *(G-12863)*
Premium Oil Company .................. F ...... 815 963-3800
  Rockford *(G-18540)*
Princeton Sealing Wax Co ............. G ...... 815 875-1943
  Princeton *(G-17760)*
◆ Protective Products Intl ............... F ...... 847 526-1180
  Wauconda *(G-21495)*
▲ Purdy Products Company ............. F ...... 847 526-5505
  Wauconda *(G-21497)*
▼ Qualitex Company ...................... F ...... 773 506-8112
  Chicago *(G-6244)*
R E Z Packaging Inc ..................... G ...... 773 247-0800
  Chicago *(G-6266)*
R R Street & Co Inc ..................... E ...... 773 247-1190
  Chicago *(G-6271)*

R R Street & Co Inc ..................... E ...... 630 416-4244
  Naperville *(G-15736)*
R R Street & Co Inc ..................... F ...... 773 254-1277
  Chicago *(G-6272)*
Rainbow Cleaners ......................... G ...... 630 789-6989
  Westmont *(G-21916)*
Reed-Union Corporation ................ G ...... 312 644-3200
  Chicago *(G-6318)*
Rock-Tred 2 LLC .......................... E ...... 888 762-5873
  Waukegan *(G-21610)*
◆ Rust-Oleum Corporation .............. C ...... 847 367-7700
  Vernon Hills *(G-21195)*
◆ Rycoline Products LLC ................ C ...... 773 775-6755
  Chicago *(G-6417)*
▲ Sandstrom Products Company ...... E ...... 309 523-2121
  Port Byron *(G-17723)*
Sandstrom Products Company ....... F ...... 309 523-2121
  Port Byron *(G-17724)*
Science Solutions LLC .................. G ...... 773 261-1197
  Chicago *(G-6458)*
Scs Company ............................... E ...... 708 203-4955
  Crestwood *(G-7501)*
Stellar Blending & Packaging ......... F ...... 314 520-7318
  Dupo *(G-8577)*
Teitelbaum Brothers Inc ................ G ...... 847 729-3490
  Glenview *(G-11208)*
▲ Tiger Accessory Group LLC ......... G ...... 847 821-9630
  Long Grove *(G-13902)*
◆ Treatment Products Ltd ............... E ...... 773 626-8888
  Chicago *(G-6766)*
Tri Sect Corporation ..................... F ...... 847 524-1119
  Schaumburg *(G-19770)*
◆ Turtle Wax Inc ........................... B ...... 630 455-3700
  Addison *(G-331)*
Umf Corporation ........................... G ...... 224 251-7822
  Niles *(G-16045)*
▲ Umf Corporation ......................... F ...... 847 920-0370
  Skokie *(G-20104)*
◆ United Laboratories Inc ............... D ...... 630 377-0900
  Saint Charles *(G-19289)*
Vanguard Chemical Corporation ..... F ...... 312 751-0717
  Chicago *(G-6871)*
◆ Venus Laboratories Inc ................ E ...... 630 595-1900
  Addison *(G-339)*
Voodoo Ride LLC ......................... G ...... 312 944-0465
  Chicago *(G-6914)*
West Agro Inc ............................. E ...... 847 298-5505
  Des Plaines *(G-8303)*
Zoes Mfgco LLC ........................... F ...... 312 666-4018
  Chicago *(G-7071)*

## 2843 Surface Active & Finishing Agents, Sulfonated Oils

▲ Avatar Corporation ...................... D ...... 708 534-5511
  University Park *(G-21042)*
▲ Cedar Concepts Corporation ........ E ...... 773 890-5790
  Chicago *(G-4265)*
▲ Custom Blending & Pckaging of ... F ...... 618 286-1140
  Dupo *(G-8569)*
Griffin Industries LLC ................... G ...... 815 357-8200
  Seneca *(G-19886)*
Houghton International Inc ............. F ...... 610 666-4000
  Chicago *(G-5121)*
Ilf Technologies LLC ..................... G ...... 630 789-9770
  Willowbrook *(G-22215)*
▲ ISachs Sons Inc .......................... G ...... 312 733-2815
  Chicago *(G-5240)*
▲ Ivanhoe Industries Inc ................. F ...... 847 566-7170
  Mundelein *(G-15512)*
▲ Kik Custom Products Inc ............. B ...... 217 442-1400
  Danville *(G-7743)*
Sadelco USA Corp ........................ G ...... 847 781-8844
  Hoffman Estates *(G-12048)*
Sanford Chemical Co Inc .............. F ...... 847 437-3530
  Elk Grove Village *(G-9727)*
Solvay USA Inc ............................ E ...... 708 371-2000
  Blue Island *(G-2271)*
◆ Stepan Company ......................... B ...... 847 446-7500
  Northfield *(G-16419)*
Union Drainage District ................. G ...... 618 445-2843
  Mount Erie *(G-15294)*
Vantage Specialties Inc ................. F ...... 847 244-3410
  Chicago *(G-6875)*

## 2844 Perfumes, Cosmetics & Toilet Preparations

4 Elements Company ..................... G ...... 773 236-2284
  Mundelein *(G-15461)*

---

Employee Codes: A=Over 500 employees, B=251-500
C=101-250, D=51-100, E=20-50, F=10-19, G=3-9

**A & H Manufacturing Inc** ...F ... 630 543-5900
Addison *(G-14)*
**A&B Apparel** ...G ... 815 962-5070
Rockford *(G-18241)*
**Abbott Laboratories** ...A ... 847 937-6100
North Chicago *(G-16164)*
**Abyss Salon Inc** ...G ... 312 880-0263
Chicago *(G-3713)*
**Affirmed LLC** ...G ... 847 550-0170
Lake Zurich *(G-13037)*
**Amedico Laboratories LLC** ...G ... 347 857-7546
Oakbrook Terrace *(G-16696)*
**▲ American Blending & Filling Co** ...D ... 847 689-1000
Waukegan *(G-21523)*
**Anjel Scents LLC** ...G ... 313 729-0719
Chicago *(G-3909)*
**Art of Shaving - Fl LLC** ...G ... 847 568-0881
Skokie *(G-19959)*
**Art of Shaving - Fl LLC** ...G ... 312 527-1604
Chicago *(G-3952)*
**Art of Shaving - Fl LLC** ...G ... 630 684-0277
Oak Brook *(G-16489)*
**◆ Atm America Corp** ...E ... 800 298-0030
Chicago *(G-3986)*
**Aveda Corporation** ...G ... 847 413-0438
Schaumburg *(G-19453)*
**◆ Avlon Industries Inc** ...D ... 708 344-0709
Melrose Park *(G-14598)*
**Bad Girlz Enterprises Inc** ...C ... 618 215-1428
East Saint Louis *(G-8743)*
**Bdi Enterprises** ...G ... 773 354-6433
Westchester *(G-21830)*
**Be Products Inc** ...G ... 312 201-9669
Chicago *(G-4062)*
**Belle-Aire Fragrances Inc** ...E ... 847 816-3500
Mundelein *(G-15476)*
**Bethany Pharmacol Co Inc** ...G ... 217 665-3395
Bethany *(G-2084)*
**▼ Biocare Labs Inc** ...G ... 708 496-8657
Bedford Park *(G-1541)*
**Bioelements Inc** ...F ... 773 525-3509
Chicago *(G-4109)*
**BMC 1092 Inc** ...E ... 708 544-2200
Broadview *(G-2563)*
**▲ Cedar Concepts Corporation** ...E ... 773 890-5790
Chicago *(G-4265)*
**Clintex Laboratories Inc** ...E ... 773 493-9777
Chicago *(G-4403)*
**Collagen Usa Inc** ...G ... 708 716-0251
Chicago *(G-4423)*
**▲ Colorlab Cosmetics Inc** ...E ... 815 965-0026
Rockford *(G-18315)*
**▲ Combe Laboratories Inc** ...C ... 217 893-4490
Rantoul *(G-17923)*
**Common Scents Mom** ...G ... 309 389-3216
Mapleton *(G-14208)*
**▲ Concept Laboratories Inc** ...D ... 773 395-7300
Chicago *(G-4446)*
**Conopco Inc** ...C ... 773 916-4400
Chicago *(G-4452)*
**D-Orum Corporation** ...F ... 773 567-2064
Chicago *(G-4538)*
**Dallas Scrub** ...G ... 312 651-6012
Chicago *(G-4546)*
**▲ Delta Laboratories Inc** ...G ... 630 351-1798
Elk Grove Village *(G-9421)*
**Deputante Inc** ...G ... 773 545-9531
Chicago *(G-4584)*
**Dhaliwal Labs Illinois LLC** ...D ... 312 690-7734
Bedford Park *(G-1548)*
**Dial Corporation** ...C ... 630 892-4381
Montgomery *(G-15041)*
**Dzro-Bans International Inc** ...G ... 779 324-2740
Homewood *(G-12096)*
**▲ Ecoco Inc** ...E ... 773 745-7700
Chicago *(G-4693)*
**Emlin Cosmetics Inc** ...E ... 630 860-5773
Bensenville *(G-1892)*
**Formulations Inc** ...G ... 847 674-9141
Skokie *(G-20001)*
**Garcoa Inc** ...D ... 708 905-5118
Brookfield *(G-2633)*
**◆ Geka Manufacturing Corporation** ...E ... 224 238-5080
Elgin *(G-9043)*
**Givaudan Fragrances Corp** ...G ... 847 735-0221
Lake Forest *(G-12900)*
**H N C Products Inc** ...E ... 217 935-9100
Clinton *(G-7281)*
**Healing Scents** ...G ... 815 874-0924
Rockford *(G-18415)*
**Holland Specialty Co** ...E ... 309 697-9262
Peoria *(G-17383)*
**▼ Hollywood International Co** ...E ... 708 926-9437
Blue Island *(G-2256)*
**▲ Hydrox Chemical Company Inc** ...D ... 847 468-9400
Elgin *(G-9069)*
**▲ Jindilli Beverages LLC** ...G ... 630 581-5697
Burr Ridge *(G-2860)*
**▼ Johnson Publishing Company LLC** ...C ... 312 322-9200
Chicago *(G-5320)*
**Juvenesse By Elaine Gayle Inc** ...G ... 312 944-1211
Chicago *(G-5340)*
**Kellyjo Makes Scents** ...G ... 618 281-4241
Columbia *(G-7359)*
**▲ Kik Custom Products Inc** ...B ... 217 442-1400
Danville *(G-7743)*
**▲ Lab TEC Cosmt By Marzena Inc** ...F ... 630 396-3970
Addison *(G-176)*
**Lakeview Oral and Maxillofacia** ...G ... 773 327-9500
Chicago *(G-5447)*
**Lasner Bros Inc** ...G ... 773 935-7383
Chicago *(G-5463)*
**◆ Luster Products Inc** ...B ... 773 579-1800
Chicago *(G-5569)*
**Luxis International Inc** ...G ... 800 240-1473
Dekalb *(G-8104)*
**Luxurious Lathers Ltd** ...G ... 844 877-7627
Hinsdale *(G-11951)*
**▲ Marcy Laboratories Inc** ...E ... 630 377-6655
West Chicago *(G-21738)*
**Market Ready Inc** ...G ... 847 689-1000
Waukegan *(G-21586)*
**Master Well Comb Co Inc** ...F ... 847 540-8300
Chicago *(G-5646)*
**Maynard Inc** ...G ... 773 235-5225
Chicago *(G-5661)*
**Michael Christopher Ltd** ...G ... 815 308-5018
Woodstock *(G-22589)*
**Mseed Group LLC** ...G ... 847 226-1147
South Holland *(G-20292)*
**Multi-Pack Solutions LLC** ...D ... 847 635-6772
Mount Prospect *(G-15352)*
**◆ Namaste Laboratories LLC** ...D ... 708 824-1393
Chicago *(G-5851)*
**▲ Natural Beginnings** ...G ... 773 457-0509
Plainfield *(G-17630)*
**New Avon LLC** ...A ... 847 966-0200
Morton Grove *(G-15224)*
**Oak Court Creations** ...G ... 815 467-7676
Minooka *(G-14845)*
**One Love** ...G ... 708 832-1740
Calumet City *(G-2947)*
**Paket Corporation** ...E ... 773 221-7300
Chicago *(G-6057)*
**Pal Midwest Ltd** ...G ... 815 965-2981
Rockford *(G-18528)*
**Pivotal Production LLC** ...G ... 773 726-7706
Chicago *(G-6134)*
**Prevention Health Sciences Inc** ...G ... 618 252-6922
Raleigh *(G-17910)*
**Princeton Chemicals Inc** ...G ... 847 975-6210
Highland Park *(G-11862)*
**Pro-Line Winning Ways & Penlan** ...G ... 309 745-8530
Washington *(G-21388)*
**Punch Skin Care Inc** ...E ... 702 333-2510
Chicago *(G-6227)*
**Pure Essential Supply Inc** ...G ...
Saint Charles *(G-19245)*
**▲ RITA Corporation** ...E ... 815 337-2500
Crystal Lake *(G-7642)*
**◆ Rna Corporation** ...D ... 708 597-7777
Blue Island *(G-2267)*
**Rochester Midland Corporation** ...E ... 630 896-8543
Montgomery *(G-15066)*
**Rose Laboratories Inc** ...E ... 815 740-1121
Joliet *(G-12571)*
**Safe Effective Alternatives** ...F ... 618 236-2727
Belleville *(G-1675)*
**San Telmo Ltd** ...G ... 847 842-9115
Barrington *(G-1304)*
**Schmit Laboratories Inc** ...E ... 773 476-0072
Glendale Heights *(G-11066)*
**▼ Selected Chemical Products Co** ...E ... 847 623-2224
Waukegan *(G-21614)*
**▲ Sigan America LLC** ...E ... 815 431-9830
Ottawa *(G-16983)*
**▲ Signature Nail Systems LLC** ...G ... 888 445-2786
Quincy *(G-17891)*
**◆ Skyline Beauty Supply Inc** ...F ... 773 275-6003
Franklin Park *(G-10589)*
**Smile Aromatics Inc** ...E ... 847 759-0350
Des Plaines *(G-8277)*
**▲ Solab Inc** ...F ... 708 544-2200
Bellwood *(G-1722)*
**Special Scents Inc** ...E ... 708 596-9370
Harvey *(G-11676)*
**Spike Nanotech Inc** ...G ... 847 504-6273
Matteson *(G-14379)*
**Summit Laboratories Inc** ...E ... 708 333-2995
Harvey *(G-11677)*
**▲ Sunstar Pharmaceutical Inc** ...D ... 773 777-4000
Elgin *(G-9198)*
**Suretint Technologies LLC** ...F ... 847 509-3625
Mount Prospect *(G-15377)*
**Takasago Intl Corp USA** ...G ... 815 479-5030
Crystal Lake *(G-7659)*
**Techpack Inc** ...E ... 847 439-8220
Elk Grove Village *(G-9773)*
**Tja Health LLC** ...G ...
Joliet *(G-12582)*
**▲ Tru Fragrance & Beauty LLC** ...E ... 630 563-4110
Willowbrook *(G-22235)*
**True Royalty Scents** ...G ... 309 992-0688
Peoria *(G-17471)*
**Trumans Brands LLC** ...F ... 224 302-5605
Waukegan *(G-21633)*
**Unilever Manufacturing US Inc** ...G ... 847 541-8868
Wheeling *(G-22170)*
**◆ Universal Beauty Products Inc** ...E ... 847 805-4100
Glendale Heights *(G-11088)*
**Vee Pak LLC** ...D ... 708 482-8881
Hodgkins *(G-11986)*
**Vee Pak LLC** ...C ... 708 482-8881
Countryside *(G-7449)*
**Vies Nails** ...G ... 773 281-6485
Chicago *(G-6897)*
**▲ W-R Industries Inc** ...G ... 312 733-5200
Chicago *(G-6929)*
**Zanfel Laboratories Inc** ...G ... 309 683-3500
Peoria *(G-17480)*
**Zotos International Inc** ...C ... 847 390-0984
Rosemont *(G-19044)*

## *2851 Paints, Varnishes, Lacquers, Enamels*

**Acm Inc** ...G ... 847 473-1991
North Chicago *(G-16172)*
**Agi Corp** ...F ... 815 708-0502
Loves Park *(G-13915)*
**Akzo Nobel Coatings Inc** ...E ... 630 792-1619
Lombard *(G-13763)*
**Akzo Nobel Coatings Inc** ...F ... 847 623-4200
Waukegan *(G-21520)*
**◆ Akzo Nobel Inc** ...C ... 312 544-7000
Chicago *(G-3793)*
**▲ Alpha Coating Technologies LLC** ...E ... 630 268-8787
Addison *(G-30)*
**▲ Alvar Inc** ...F ... 309 248-7523
Washburn *(G-21374)*
**▲ American Powder Coatings Inc** ...E ... 630 762-0100
Saint Charles *(G-19135)*
**American Rack Company** ...E ... 773 763-7309
Chicago *(G-3870)*
**Armitage Industries Inc** ...F ... 847 288-9090
Franklin Park *(G-10400)*
**Ata Finishing Corp** ...G ... 847 677-8560
Skokie *(G-19960)*
**▲ Atlas Putty Products Co** ...D ... 708 429-5858
Tinley Park *(G-20895)*
**Automatic Anodizing Corp** ...E ... 773 478-3304
Chicago *(G-3991)*
**Autonomic Materials Inc** ...F ... 217 863-2023
Champaign *(G-3455)*
**Basement Dewatering Systems** ...F ... 309 647-0331
Canton *(G-2981)*
**BASF Construction Chem LLC** ...G ... 847 249-4080
Gurnee *(G-11431)*
**Behr Process Corporation** ...D ... 630 289-6247
Bartlett *(G-1336)*
**Behr Process Corporation** ...D ... 708 753-0136
Chicago Heights *(G-7082)*
**Behr Process Corporation** ...D ... 708 753-1820
Lynwood *(G-14018)*
**Behr Process Corporation** ...C ... 708 757-6350
Chicago Heights *(G-7083)*
**Belzona Gateway Inc** ...G ... 888 774-2984
Caseyville *(G-3393)*
**Benjamin Moore & Co** ...C ... 708 343-6000
Carol Stream *(G-3114)*
**▲ Black Swan Manufacturing Co** ...F ... 773 227-3700
Chicago *(G-4121)*

Buster Snow Inc ........ G ....... 847 673-4275
Lincolnwood *(G-13504)*
C2 Premium Paint ........ G ....... 847 251-6906
Wilmette *(G-22248)*
Carbit Corporation ........ E ....... 312 280-2300
Chicago *(G-4237)*
Cavero Coatings Company LLC ........ G ....... 630 616-2868
Bensenville *(G-1853)*
Central Chemical and Service ........ F ....... 630 653-9200
Carol Stream *(G-3126)*
Chase Corporation ........ E ....... 847 866-8500
Evanston *(G-10022)*
◆ Chase Products Co ........ D ....... 708 865-1000
Broadview *(G-2566)*
Chemix Corp ........ F ....... 708 754-2150
Glenwood *(G-11215)*
Chicago Latex Products Inc ........ F ....... 815 459-9680
Crystal Lake *(G-7552)*
▲ Chromium Industries Inc ........ E ....... 773 287-3716
Chicago *(G-4373)*
CIS Systems Inc ........ G ....... 847 827-0747
Glenview *(G-11114)*
Clariant Plas Coatings USA Inc ........ D ....... 630 562-9700
West Chicago *(G-21682)*
▲ Coatings International Inc ........ E ....... 847 455-1400
Franklin Park *(G-10439)*
Color Corporation of America ........ D ....... 815 987-3700
Rockford *(G-18314)*
Continental Supply Co ........ G ....... 708 448-2728
Palos Heights *(G-17102)*
Contract Transportation Sys Co ........ C ....... 217 342-5757
Effingham *(G-8831)*
Crest Chemical Industries Ltd ........ G ....... 815 485-2138
New Lenox *(G-15873)*
Custom Chemical Inc ........ G ....... 217 529-0878
Springfield *(G-20426)*
D and R Tech ........ G ....... 224 353-6693
Schaumburg *(G-19497)*
Dick Blick Company ........ C ....... 309 343-6181
Galesburg *(G-10747)*
Dip Seal Plastics Inc ........ G ....... 815 398-3533
Rockford *(G-18345)*
▲ DSM Desotech Inc ........ C ....... 847 697-0400
Elgin *(G-9013)*
Dunamis International ........ G ....... 773 504-5733
Chicago *(G-4651)*
Dyco-TEC Products Ltd ........ G ....... 630 837-6410
Bartlett *(G-1342)*
Eli Morris Group LLC ........ G ....... 773 314-7173
Chicago *(G-4729)*
Enginered Polymr Solutions Inc ........ E ....... 815 987-3700
Rockford *(G-18366)*
F H Leinweber Co Inc ........ E ....... 773 568-7722
Chicago *(G-4803)*
▲ Federated Paint Mfg Co ........ F ....... 708 345-4848
Chicago *(G-4824)*
Finishes Unlimited Inc ........ F ....... 630 466-4881
Sugar Grove *(G-20724)*
Finishing Company ........ C ....... 630 559-0808
Addison *(G-117)*
▼ G J Nikolas & Co Inc ........ E ....... 708 544-0320
Bellwood *(G-1706)*
▲ Gibraltar Chemical Works Inc ........ F ....... 708 333-0600
South Holland *(G-20270)*
Hallstar Company ........ D ....... 708 594-5947
Bedford Park *(G-1552)*
Hentzen Coatings Inc ........ E ....... 414 353-4200
Batavia *(G-1455)*
Hlh Associates ........ F ....... 773 646-5900
Chicago *(G-5092)*
I Pulloma Paints ........ F ....... 847 426-4140
Carpentersville *(G-3287)*
◆ ICP Industrial Inc ........ E ....... 630 227-1692
Itasca *(G-12278)*
If Walls Could Talk ........ G ....... 847 219-5527
South Elgin *(G-20205)*
Inhance Technologies LLC ........ E ....... 630 231-7515
West Chicago *(G-21719)*
▲ Ink Solutions LLC ........ F ....... 847 593-5200
Elk Grove Village *(G-9546)*
International Paint LLC ........ F ....... 847 623-4200
Waukegan *(G-21572)*
Jet Rack Corp ........ E ....... 773 586-2150
Chicago *(G-5298)*
Jfb Hart Coatings Inc ........ F ....... 949 724-9737
Plainfield *(G-17611)*
Jfb Hart Coatings Inc ........ F ....... 630 783-1917
Plainfield *(G-17612)*
Knott So Shabby ........ G ....... 618 281-6002
Columbia *(G-7360)*
Kns Companies Inc ........ F ....... 630 665-9010
Carol Stream *(G-3181)*
▲ Lawter Inc ........ E ....... 312 662-5700
Chicago *(G-5473)*
▲ Magnum International Inc ........ G ....... 708 889-9999
Lansing *(G-13175)*
Mate Technologies Inc ........ F ....... 847 289-1010
Elgin *(G-9103)*
Metro Paint Supplies ........ G ....... 708 385-7701
Crestwood *(G-7494)*
▲ Mid-Amrica Prtctive Ctings Inc ........ G ....... 630 628-4501
Addison *(G-210)*
Midwest Ground Effects ........ G ....... 708 516-5874
Plainfield *(G-17625)*
▲ Midwest Powder Coatings Inc ........ E ....... 630 587-2918
Saint Charles *(G-19222)*
Miller Purcell Co Inc ........ G ....... 815 485-2142
New Lenox *(G-15897)*
Mla Franklin Park Inc ........ F ....... 847 451-0279
Franklin Park *(G-10536)*
▲ Morton International LLC ........ C ....... 312 807-2696
Chicago *(G-5807)*
Morton Nippon Coatings ........ G ....... 708 868-7403
Lansing *(G-13178)*
◆ Morton Salt Inc ........ C ....... 312 807-2000
Chicago *(G-5809)*
▼ Nataz Specialty Coatings Inc ........ F ....... 773 247-7030
Chicago *(G-5856)*
▲ National Coatings Inc ........ E ....... 309 342-4184
Galesburg *(G-10769)*
▲ Nb Coatings Inc ........ C ....... 800 323-3224
Lansing *(G-13179)*
Neverstrip LLC ........ G ....... 708 588-9707
Hinsdale *(G-11955)*
Nu-Puttie Corporation ........ E ....... 708 681-1040
Maywood *(G-14433)*
One Shot LLC ........ E ....... 773 646-5900
Chicago *(G-5990)*
Owens Corning Sales LLC ........ E ....... 708 594-6935
Argo *(G-695)*
▼ Penray Companies Inc ........ D ....... 800 323-6329
Wheeling *(G-22120)*
Petrochem Inc ........ G ....... 630 513-6350
Saint Charles *(G-19235)*
Pioneer Powder Coatings LLC ........ E ....... 847 671-1100
Franklin Park *(G-10552)*
Plastic Services and Products ........ D ....... 708 868-3800
Calumet City *(G-2948)*
▲ Plastics Color Corp Illinois ........ D ....... 708 868-3800
Calumet City *(G-2950)*
Polymer Nation LLC ........ G ....... 847 972-2157
Waukegan *(G-21603)*
Polyone Corporation ........ D ....... 847 364-0011
Elk Grove Village *(G-9686)*
Polyone Corporation ........ D ....... 630 972-0505
Romeoville *(G-18859)*
▲ Polyurethane Products Corp ........ E ....... 630 543-6700
Addison *(G-246)*
Porcelain Enamel Finishers ........ G ....... 312 808-1560
Chicago *(G-6157)*
Powder Coat Plus ........ G ....... 217 228-0081
Quincy *(G-17868)*
PPG Architectural Finishes Inc ........ G ....... 309 673-3761
Peoria *(G-17432)*
PPG Industries Inc ........ E ....... 773 646-5900
Chicago *(G-6162)*
PPG Industries Inc ........ E ....... 630 879-5100
Batavia *(G-1485)*
PPG Industries Inc ........ E ....... 773 646-5900
Chicago *(G-6163)*
PPG Industries Inc ........ G ....... 708 597-7044
Alsip *(G-512)*
PPG Industries Inc ........ E ....... 847 742-3340
Elgin *(G-9145)*
PPG Industries Inc ........ G ....... 618 206-2250
O Fallon *(G-16475)*
PPG Industries Inc ........ E ....... 312 666-2277
Chicago *(G-6164)*
PPG Industries Inc ........ E ....... 847 991-0620
Rolling Meadows *(G-18766)*
PPG Industries Inc ........ E ....... 217 757-9080
Springfield *(G-20506)*
PPG Industries Inc ........ G ....... 708 345-1515
Stone Park *(G-20636)*
PPG Industries Inc ........ G ....... 630 960-3600
Westmont *(G-21913)*
Premium Products Inc ........ F ....... 630 553-6160
Yorkville *(G-22669)*
Prescription Plus Ltd ........ F ....... 618 537-6202
Lebanon *(G-13216)*
Quality Coating Co ........ F ....... 815 875-3228
Princeton *(G-17761)*
R C Industries Inc ........ F ....... 773 378-1118
Chicago *(G-6265)*
Richards Company II Inc ........ F ....... 708 385-6633
Alsip *(G-520)*
Rock-Tred 2 LLC ........ E ....... 888 762-5873
Waukegan *(G-21610)*
Rust-Oleum Corporation ........ D ....... 815 967-4258
Rockford *(G-18600)*
◆ Rust-Oleum Corporation ........ C ....... 847 367-7700
Vernon Hills *(G-21195)*
▲ Sandstrom Products Company ........ E ....... 309 523-2121
Port Byron *(G-17723)*
Sandstrom Products Company ........ F ....... 309 523-2121
Port Byron *(G-17724)*
Sarco Putty Company ........ G ....... 773 735-5577
Chicago *(G-6444)*
Sectional Snow Plow ........ E ....... 815 932-7569
Bradley *(G-2432)*
◆ Seymour of Sycamore Inc ........ C ....... 815 895-9101
Sycamore *(G-20815)*
Sherwin-Williams Company ........ C ....... 618 662-4415
Flora *(G-10215)*
Sherwin-Williams Company ........ G ....... 847 573-0240
Libertyville *(G-13380)*
Sherwin-Williams Company ........ G ....... 815 337-0942
Woodstock *(G-22611)*
Sherwin-Williams Company ........ G ....... 847 478-0677
Long Grove *(G-13901)*
Sherwin-Williams Company ........ G ....... 708 409-4728
Westchester *(G-21854)*
Sherwin-Williams Company ........ G ....... 815 254-3559
Romeoville *(G-18868)*
Shunk Corp ........ G ....... 217 398-2636
Champaign *(G-3538)*
Snow Command Incorporated ........ G ....... 708 991-7004
Flossmoor *(G-10228)*
Snow Control Inc ........ G ....... 708 670-6269
Orland Park *(G-16892)*
Systems Al Snow ........ G ....... 312 846-6026
Chicago *(G-6661)*
Tamms Industries Inc ........ D ....... 815 522-3394
Kirkland *(G-12719)*
Technical Coatings Co ........ E ....... 708 343-6000
Melrose Park *(G-14701)*
Tennant Company ........ E ....... 773 376-7132
Chicago *(G-6701)*
▲ Testor Corporation ........ D ....... 815 962-6654
Rockford *(G-18644)*
Tms Manufacturing Co ........ G ....... 847 353-8000
Alsip *(G-535)*
Topiarius ........ G ....... 773 475-7784
Chicago *(G-6745)*
Tru Serv Corp ........ F ....... 773 695-5674
Chicago *(G-6783)*
True Value Company ........ G ....... 847 639-5383
Cary *(G-3378)*
▼ True Value Company ........ B ....... 773 695-5000
Chicago *(G-6786)*
U S Colors & Coatings Inc ........ G ....... 630 879-8898
Batavia *(G-1512)*
United Gilsonite Laboratories ........ E ....... 217 243-7878
Jacksonville *(G-12415)*
▼ Universal Chem & Coatings Inc ........ E ....... 847 931-1700
Elgin *(G-9219)*
Universal Chem & Coatings Inc ........ E ....... 847 297-2001
Elk Grove Village *(G-9801)*
V J Dolan & Company Inc ........ E ....... 773 237-0100
Chicago *(G-6867)*
▲ Valspar ........ G ....... 815 962-9969
Rockford *(G-18666)*
Valspar ........ G ....... 309 743-7133
East Moline *(G-8696)*
Valspar Corporation ........ C ....... 815 933-5561
Kankakee *(G-12657)*
Valspar Corporation ........ D ....... 708 469-7194
Hodgkins *(G-11985)*
Valspar Corporation ........ D ....... 847 541-9000
Wheeling *(G-22175)*
Valspar Corporation ........ C ....... 708 720-0600
Matteson *(G-14380)*
Valspar Corporation ........ D ....... 847 541-9000
Wheeling *(G-22176)*
Valspar Corporation ........ D ....... 815 962-9986
Rockford *(G-18669)*
Vanex Inc ........ E ....... 618 244-1413
Mount Vernon *(G-15448)*
▲ Voges Inc ........ D ....... 618 233-2760
Belleville *(G-1688)*



Employee Codes: A=Over 500 employees, B=251-500
C=101-250, D=51-100, E=20-50, F=10-19, G=3-9
2017 Harris Illinois
Industrial Directory
993

# 28 CHEMICALS AND ALLIED PRODUCTS

◆ Willims-Hyward Intl Ctings Inc .......... E ...... 708 563-5182
  Summit Argo *(G-20769)*
Willims-Hyward Intl Ctings Inc .......... F ...... 708 458-0015
  Argo *(G-698)*

## 2861 Gum & Wood Chemicals

Bradley Smoker USA Inc .......... F ...... 309 343-1124
  Galesburg *(G-10739)*
Ryano Resins Inc .......... G ...... 630 621-5677
  Aurora *(G-1076)*

## 2865 Cyclic-Crudes, Intermediates, Dyes & Org Pigments

Allegheny Color Corporation .......... E ...... 815 741-1391
  Rockdale *(G-18213)*
Apex Colors .......... G ...... 219 764-3301
  Chicago *(G-3921)*
◆ BP Amoco Chemical Company .......... B ...... 630 420-5111
  Naperville *(G-15608)*
Clariant Plas Coatings USA Inc .......... D ...... 630 562-9700
  West Chicago *(G-21682)*
Colors For Plastics Inc .......... G ...... 847 437-0033
  Elk Grove Village *(G-9381)*
Colors For Plastics Inc .......... D ...... 847 437-0033
  Elk Grove Village *(G-9382)*
Discount Computer Supply Inc .......... G ...... 847 883-8743
  Buffalo Grove *(G-2688)*
▲ General Press Colors Ltd .......... E ...... 630 543-7878
  Chicago *(G-4931)*
HI Tech Colorants .......... G ...... 630 762-0368
  Saint Charles *(G-19192)*
Huntsman P&A Americas LLC .......... E ...... 618 646-2119
  East Saint Louis *(G-8755)*
Koppers Industries Inc .......... E ...... 708 656-5900
  Cicero *(G-7209)*
Miller Purcell Co Inc .......... G ...... 815 485-2142
  New Lenox *(G-15897)*
Navran Advncd Nanoprdcts Dev .......... G ...... 847 331-0809
  Hoffman Estates *(G-12029)*
▲ Nb Coatings Inc .......... C ...... 800 323-3224
  Lansing *(G-13179)*
Polyone Corporation .......... D ...... 847 364-0011
  Elk Grove Village *(G-9686)*
Polyone Corporation .......... D ...... 630 972-0505
  Romeoville *(G-18859)*
▲ Rite Systems East Inc .......... E ...... 630 293-9174
  West Chicago *(G-21765)*
▲ Scientific Colors Inc .......... F ...... 815 741-1391
  Rockdale *(G-18232)*
Scientific Colors Inc .......... C ...... 815 744-5650
  Rockdale *(G-18233)*
Stepan Company .......... B ...... 815 727-4944
  Elwood *(G-9982)*
◆ Stepan Company .......... B ...... 847 446-7500
  Northfield *(G-16419)*
U S Colors & Coatings Inc .......... G ...... 630 879-8898
  Batavia *(G-1512)*

## 2869 Industrial Organic Chemicals, NEC

▲ AB Specialty Silicones LLC .......... E ...... 908 273-8015
  Waukegan *(G-21516)*
Adkins Energy LLC .......... E ...... 815 369-9173
  Lena *(G-13272)*
Afs Inc .......... F ...... 847 437-2345
  Arlington Heights *(G-703)*
Afton Chemical Corporation .......... B ...... 618 583-1000
  East Saint Louis *(G-8740)*
▲ Akzo Nobel Functional Chem LLC .......... D ...... 312 544-7000
  Chicago *(G-3792)*
◆ Akzo Nobel Inc .......... C ...... 312 544-7000
  Chicago *(G-3793)*
◆ Akzo Nobel Surfc Chemistry LLC .......... F ...... 312 544-7000
  Chicago *(G-3794)*
AMP Americas LLC .......... F ...... 312 300-6700
  Chicago *(G-3893)*
▲ Amtex Chemicals LLC .......... G ...... 630 268-0085
  Lombard *(G-13764)*
Archer-Daniels-Midland Company .......... C ...... 309 673-7828
  Peoria *(G-17309)*
Arvens Technology Inc .......... G ...... 650 776-5443
  Peoria *(G-17311)*
Ashland Fuel & Quick Lube .......... G ...... 773 434-8870
  Chicago *(G-3962)*
▲ Aspen API Inc .......... F ...... 847 635-0985
  Des Plaines *(G-8152)*
▼ AST Industries Inc .......... F ...... 847 455-2300
  Franklin Park *(G-10405)*
Austins Saloon & Eatery .......... G ...... 847 549-1972
  Libertyville *(G-13305)*

▲ Avatar Corporation .......... D ...... 708 534-5511
  University Park *(G-21042)*
Aventine Renewable Energy .......... G ...... 309 347-9200
  Pekin *(G-17255)*
Bada Beans .......... G ...... 630 655-0693
  Hinsdale *(G-11940)*
Bala & Anula Fuels Inc .......... G ...... 630 766-1807
  Bensenville *(G-1840)*
BASF Corporation .......... B ...... 815 932-9863
  Kankakee *(G-12603)*
◆ Bell Flavors & Fragrances Inc .......... C ...... 847 291-8300
  Northbrook *(G-16213)*
Belle-Aire Fragrances Inc .......... E ...... 847 816-3500
  Mundelein *(G-15476)*
Big River Prairie Gold LLC .......... G ...... 319 753-1100
  Galva *(G-10783)*
Big River Resources Galva LLC .......... G ...... 309 932-2033
  Galva *(G-10784)*
Big Rver Rsrces W Brlngton LLC .......... G ...... 309 734-8423
  Monmouth *(G-15010)*
Biovantage Fuels LLC .......... G ...... 815 544-6028
  Belvidere *(G-1738)*
◆ BP Amoco Chemical Company .......... B ...... 630 420-5111
  Naperville *(G-15608)*
Bps Fuels Inc .......... G ...... 217 452-7608
  Virginia *(G-21304)*
Breakfast Fuel LLC .......... G ...... 847 251-3835
  Wilmette *(G-22247)*
Bullen Midwest Inc .......... E ...... 773 785-2300
  Chicago *(G-4183)*
▲ C U Plastic LLC .......... G ...... 888 957-9993
  Rochelle *(G-18081)*
Campbell Camie Inc .......... G ...... 314 968-3222
  Downers Grove *(G-8403)*
▲ Cedar Concepts Corporation .......... E ...... 773 890-5790
  Chicago *(G-4265)*
Center Ethanol Company LLC .......... G ...... 618 875-3008
  Sauget *(G-19384)*
Cheers Food and Fuel 240 .......... G ...... 618 995-9153
  Goreville *(G-11250)*
Cheers Food Fuel .......... G ...... 618 827-4836
  Dongola *(G-8379)*
Chem Free Solutions .......... G ...... 630 541-7931
  Darien *(G-7791)*
Chrisman Fuel .......... G ...... 217 463-3400
  Paris *(G-17144)*
Clean Motion Inc .......... F ...... 607 323-1778
  Chicago *(G-4397)*
Compania Brasileira De T .......... G ...... 319 550-6440
  Mount Olive *(G-15301)*
Cooper Oil Co .......... G ...... 708 349-2893
  Orland Park *(G-16850)*
Covachem LLC .......... F ...... 815 714-8421
  Loves Park *(G-13927)*
Custom Chemical Inc .......... G ...... 217 529-0878
  Springfield *(G-20426)*
Dubois Chemicals Group Inc .......... G ...... 708 458-2000
  Chicago *(G-4646)*
◆ Dynachem Inc .......... D ...... 217 662-2136
  Westville *(G-21929)*
Ecolocap Solutions Inc .......... G ...... 866 479-7041
  Barrington *(G-1279)*
Eden Fuels LLC .......... G ...... 847 676-9470
  Skokie *(G-19991)*
◆ Elevance Rnewable Sciences Inc .......... C ...... 630 296-8880
  Woodridge *(G-22476)*
Elona Biotechnologies Inc .......... F ...... 317 865-4770
  Chicago *(G-4735)*
Emerald Biofuels LLC .......... G ...... 847 420-0898
  Chicago *(G-4739)*
Emerald One LLC .......... G ...... 601 529-6793
  Chicago *(G-4741)*
Entrust Services LLC .......... D ...... 630 699-9132
  Naperville *(G-15654)*
Envirox LLC .......... E ...... 217 442-8596
  Danville *(G-7716)*
▼ Enzymes Incorporated .......... G ...... 847 487-5401
  Wauconda *(G-21460)*
Equistar Chemicals LP .......... E ...... 217 253-3311
  Tuscola *(G-21019)*
Ethyl Corp .......... G ...... 618 583-1292
  East Saint Louis *(G-8751)*
Evonik Corporation .......... G ...... 309 697-6220
  Mapleton *(G-14209)*
Evonik Corporation .......... G ...... 630 230-0176
  Burr Ridge *(G-2841)*
Executive Performance Fuel LLC .......... B ...... 847 364-1933
  Elk Grove Village *(G-9471)*
FBC Industries Inc .......... G ...... 847 839-0880
  Rochelle *(G-18089)*

Flavorfocus LLC .......... D ...... 630 520-9060
  Addison *(G-118)*
Franmar Chemical .......... G ...... 309 829-5952
  Bloomington *(G-2166)*
Freedom Fuel & Food Inc .......... G ...... 773 233-5350
  Chicago *(G-4888)*
Friends Fuel .......... G ...... 773 434-9387
  Chicago *(G-4892)*
▲ Frigid Fluid Company .......... E ...... 708 836-1215
  Melrose Park *(G-14645)*
▲ Fryer To Fuel Inc .......... G ...... 309 654-2875
  Cordova *(G-7375)*
Fuel Fitness .......... G ...... 708 367-0707
  Crete *(G-7513)*
Fuel Research & Instrument Co .......... G ...... 630 953-2459
  Lombard *(G-13804)*
Gateway Fuels Inc .......... G ...... 618 248-5000
  Albers *(G-354)*
Givaudan Flavors Corporation .......... E ...... 630 773-8484
  Itasca *(G-12270)*
Givaudan Flavors Corporation .......... C ...... 847 608-6200
  Elgin *(G-9047)*
Global Water Technology Inc .......... E ...... 708 349-9991
  Orland Park *(G-16862)*
Green Plains Madison LLC .......... G ...... 618 451-8195
  Madison *(G-14147)*
Green Plains Partners LP .......... F ...... 618 451-4420
  Madison *(G-14148)*
H A Gartenberg & Company .......... F ...... 847 821-7590
  Buffalo Grove *(G-2700)*
H&Z Fuel & Food Inc .......... G ...... 815 399-9108
  Rockford *(G-18410)*
▲ Ha-International LLC .......... E ...... 630 575-5700
  Westmont *(G-21888)*
Ha-International LLC .......... E ...... 815 732-3898
  Oregon *(G-16826)*
Ha-Usa Inc .......... G ...... 630 575-5700
  Westmont *(G-21889)*
▲ Hallstar Company .......... G ...... 312 554-7400
  Chicago *(G-5036)*
Hallstar Company .......... D ...... 708 594-5947
  Bedford Park *(G-1552)*
Hallstar Services Corp .......... G ...... 312 554-7400
  Chicago *(G-5037)*
Harvey Fuels .......... G ...... 708 339-0777
  Harvey *(G-11669)*
Havanah Fuel .......... G ...... 309 543-2211
  Havana *(G-11696)*
Hinman Specialty Fuels .......... G ...... 847 868-6026
  Evanston *(G-10051)*
Honeywell International Inc .......... B ...... 618 524-2111
  Metropolis *(G-14754)*
Horizon Fuel Cell Americas .......... G ...... 312 316-8050
  Chicago *(G-5112)*
Houghton International Inc .......... F ...... 610 666-4000
  Chicago *(G-5121)*
Hucks Food Fuel .......... F ...... 618 286-5111
  Dupo *(G-8571)*
Hudson Technologies Inc .......... E ...... 217 373-1414
  Champaign *(G-3496)*
Hurst Chemical Company .......... G ...... 815 964-0451
  Rockford *(G-18424)*
▲ Hydrox Chemical Company Inc .......... C ...... 847 468-9400
  Elgin *(G-9069)*
Illini Fs Inc .......... G ...... 217 442-4737
  Potomac *(G-17738)*
▼ Illinois River Energy LLC .......... D ...... 815 561-0650
  Rochelle *(G-18095)*
▼ Indorama Ventures Oxide & Glyl .......... E ...... 800 365-0794
  Riverwoods *(G-18039)*
Ineos Styrolution America LLC .......... G ...... 815 423-5541
  Channahon *(G-3576)*
◆ Ineos Styrolution America LLC .......... C ...... 630 820-9500
  Aurora *(G-1028)*
▲ Interface Protein Tech Inc .......... D ...... 630 963-8809
  Lisle *(G-13607)*
Ivanhoe Industries Inc .......... E ...... 847 872-3311
  Zion *(G-22688)*
Jada Specialties Inc .......... G ...... 847 272-7799
  Northbrook *(G-16282)*
Jagjita Corp .......... G ...... 217 374-6016
  White Hall *(G-22185)*
K&H Fuel .......... G ...... 815 405-4364
  Frankfort *(G-10338)*
Koppers Industries Inc .......... E ...... 708 656-5900
  Cicero *(G-7209)*
L & W Fuels .......... G ...... 815 848-8360
  Fairbury *(G-10130)*
▲ La Boost Inc .......... G ...... 630 444-1755
  Saint Charles *(G-19206)*

## SIC SECTION
## 28 CHEMICALS AND ALLIED PRODUCTS

Lakeview Energy LLC ..................E....... 312 386-5897
  Chicago *(G-5446)*
▲ Lanzatech Inc .............................D....... 630 439-3050
  Skokie *(G-20025)*
Lincolnland Agri-Energy LLC .......E....... 618 586-2321
  Palestine *(G-17094)*
Liquid Resin International ............E....... 618 392-3590
  Olney *(G-16777)*
LLC Ethersonic Techno ................G...... 708 441-4730
  Matteson *(G-14376)*
Lonza Inc .......................................D....... 309 697-7200
  Mapleton *(G-14212)*
▲ Lucta U S A Inc ...........................G...... 847 996-3400
  Libertyville *(G-13345)*
Lyondell Chemical Company .......B....... 815 942-7011
  Morris *(G-15114)*
◆ Marquis Energy LLC .....................G...... 815 925-7300
  Hennepin *(G-11734)*
▼ Merisant Company .......................F....... 312 840-6000
  Chicago *(G-5691)*
▲ Merisant Foreign Holdings I .........F....... 312 840-6000
  Chicago *(G-5692)*
◆ Merisant Us Inc ............................B....... 312 840-6000
  Chicago *(G-5693)*
Merisant Us Inc ............................C....... 815 929-2700
  Manteno *(G-14188)*
Mgp Ingredients Illinois Inc ..........C....... 309 353-3990
  Pekin *(G-17274)*
Mgpi Processing Inc ....................C....... 309 353-3990
  Pekin *(G-17275)*
Midtown Fuels ...............................G...... 217 347-7191
  Effingham *(G-8846)*
Midwest Bio Fuel Inc ....................G...... 309 965-2612
  Goodfield *(G-11247)*
Midwest Biodiesel Products LLC ..F....... 618 254-2920
  South Roxana *(G-20313)*
Miwon NA ......................................G...... 630 568-5850
  Willowbrook *(G-22224)*
National Interchem LLC ...............G...... 708 597-7777
  Blue Island *(G-2264)*
Natures Appeal Mfg Corp .............G...... 630 880-6222
  Addison *(G-226)*
Natures Sources LLC ...................G...... 847 663-9168
  Niles *(G-16013)*
▲ Necta Sweet Inc ...........................E....... 847 215-9955
  Buffalo Grove *(G-2742)*
Nikli Fuels Inc ...............................G...... 309 363-2425
  Pekin *(G-17276)*
◆ Nufarm Americas Inc ....................D....... 708 377-1330
  Alsip *(G-501)*
Numat Technologies Inc ..............G...... 301 233-5329
  Skokie *(G-20047)*
▲ Nutrasweet Company ...................E....... 312 873-5000
  Chicago *(G-5956)*
Omega Partners ...........................G...... 618 254-0603
  Hartford *(G-11613)*
One Earth Energy LLC .................E....... 217 784-5321
  Gibson City *(G-10905)*
Onyx Environmental Svcs LLC ....E....... 630 218-1500
  Lombard *(G-13838)*
Pacific Ethanol Canton LLC .........G...... 309 347-9200
  Pekin *(G-17278)*
Pacific Ethanol Pekin Inc .............C....... 309 347-9200
  Pekin *(G-17279)*
Paradigm Bioaviation LLC ............G...... 309 663-2303
  Bloomington *(G-2210)*
Patriot Fuels LLC ..........................G...... 847 551-5946
  East Dundee *(G-8651)*
Patriot Renewable Fuels LLC ......D....... 309 935-5700
  Annawan *(G-611)*
▼ Penray Companies Inc .................D....... 800 323-6329
  Wheeling *(G-22120)*
◆ Pmp Fermentation Products Inc ...E....... 309 637-0400
  Peoria *(G-17430)*
Polyenviro Labs Inc .....................G...... 708 489-0195
  Mokena *(G-14896)*
PPG Architectural Finishes Inc ....D....... 773 523-6333
  Chicago *(G-6161)*
◆ Prinova Solutions LLC ..................E....... 630 868-0359
  Carol Stream *(G-3221)*
Pro Fuel Nine Inc ..........................G...... 309 867-3375
  Oquawka *(G-16813)*
▲ Purecircle USA Inc .......................E....... 866 960-8242
  Oak Brook *(G-16557)*
PVS Chemical Solutions Inc .......E....... 773 933-8800
  Chicago *(G-6231)*
R & P Fuels ...................................G...... 630 855-2358
  Hoffman Estates *(G-12042)*
▲ Rahn USA Corp .............................E....... 630 851-4220
  Aurora *(G-1072)*

Reg Seneca LLC ..........................E....... 888 734-8686
  Seneca *(G-19889)*
Regis Technologies Inc ................D....... 847 967-6000
  Morton Grove *(G-15232)*
▲ Reliance Specialty Pdts Inc .........F....... 847 640-8923
  Elk Grove Village *(G-9713)*
▲ RHO Chemical Company Inc .......F....... 815 727-4791
  Joliet *(G-12568)*
▲ RJ Distributing Co ........................E....... 309 685-2794
  East Peoria *(G-8731)*
Rocket Fuel Inc .............................F....... 207 520-9075
  Chicago *(G-6374)*
Roquette America Inc ...................D....... 847 360-0886
  Gurnee *(G-11501)*
Rsb Fuels Inc ................................G...... 217 999-4409
  Mount Olive *(G-15307)*
Saint Mary Fuel Company ............G...... 773 918-1681
  Chicago *(G-6429)*
▲ SB Boron Corporation ..................D....... 708 547-9002
  Bellwood *(G-1719)*
Sensient Flavors ...........................C....... 847 645-7002
  Hoffman Estates *(G-12049)*
Solvay Chemicals Inc ..................E....... 618 274-0755
  East Saint Louis *(G-8769)*
Solvay USA Inc .............................E....... 708 371-2000
  Blue Island *(G-2271)*
Solvay USA Inc .............................E....... 708 235-7200
  University Park *(G-21062)*
Speedway .....................................G...... 815 463-0840
  New Lenox *(G-15912)*
Standard Rubber Products Co .....E....... 847 593-5630
  Elk Grove Village *(G-9751)*
Stateline Renewable Fuels LLC ...F....... 608 931-4634
  Buffalo Grove *(G-2776)*
Stepan Company ..........................B....... 815 727-4944
  Elwood *(G-9982)*
Strebor Specialties LLC ...............E....... 618 286-1140
  Dupo *(G-8580)*
Swi Energy LLC ............................E....... 618 465-7277
  Alton *(G-592)*
Swissport Fueling Incorpo ...........G...... 773 203-5419
  Chicago *(G-6652)*
Tate Lyle Ingrdnts Amricas LLC ...G...... 309 473-2721
  Heyworth *(G-11766)*
Tempil Inc ......................................G...... 908 757-8300
  Elk Grove Village *(G-9775)*
Union Carbide Corporation ..........D....... 708 396-3000
  Alsip *(G-538)*
United Fuel Savers LLC ...............G...... 312 725-4993
  Chicago *(G-6824)*
Uzhavoor Fuels Inc .......................G...... 630 401-6173
  Dixon *(G-8358)*
▲ Vantage Oleochemicals Inc .........G...... 773 376-9000
  Chicago *(G-6873)*
◆ Vantage Specialties Inc ................G...... 847 244-3410
  Gurnee *(G-11518)*
Water & Oil Technologies Inc ......G...... 630 892-2007
  Montgomery *(G-15072)*
Wenona Food & Fuel ....................G...... 815 853-4141
  Wenona *(G-21649)*
West Fuels Inc ..............................G...... 708 488-8880
  Forest Park *(G-10257)*
Wieman Fuels LP Gas Company ..G...... 618 632-4015
  Belleville *(G-1691)*
Xena International Inc ..................E....... 815 946-2626
  Polo *(G-17691)*

## 2873 Nitrogenous Fertilizers

Amsoil Inc .....................................G...... 630 595-8385
  Bensenville *(G-1835)*
Bio Green Inc ................................G...... 847 740-9637
  Volo *(G-21308)*
◆ CF Industries Inc ..........................B....... 847 405-2400
  Deerfield *(G-7994)*
CF Industries Inc ..........................D....... 309 654-2218
  Albany *(G-352)*
CF Industries Enterprises Inc .....C....... 847 405-2400
  Deerfield *(G-7995)*
CF Industries Holdings Inc .........B....... 847 405-2400
  Deerfield *(G-7996)*
CF Industries Nitrogen LLC ........F....... 847 405-2400
  Deerfield *(G-7998)*
CF Industries Nitrogen Llc ..........C....... 847 405-2400
  Deerfield *(G-7997)*
CF Industries Sales LLC .............B....... 847 405-2400
  Deerfield *(G-7999)*
Crop Production Services Inc ....G...... 815 853-4078
  Wenona *(G-21647)*
E N P Inc ........................................G...... 800 255-4906
  Mendota *(G-14720)*

E N P Inc ........................................G...... 815 539-7471
  Mendota *(G-14721)*
▲ East Dbque Ntrgn Frtlizers LLC ...C....... 815 747-3101
  East Dubuque *(G-8617)*
Fertilizer Inc .................................G...... 708 458-8615
  Chicago *(G-4838)*
Fertilizer Inc .................................G...... 708 458-8615
  Bedford Park *(G-1549)*
Gateway Fs Inc .............................G...... 618 824-6631
  Venedy *(G-21136)*
Gold Star Fs Inc ...........................G...... 309 659-2801
  Erie *(G-9992)*
Harbach Gillan & Nixon Inc .........F....... 217 935-8378
  Clinton *(G-7282)*
Harbach Gillan & Nixon Inc .........F....... 217 794-5117
  Maroa *(G-14305)*
Hyponex Corporation ...................G...... 815 772-2167
  Morrison *(G-15144)*
I A E Inc ........................................G...... 219 882-2400
  Oak Park *(G-16670)*
Michel Fertilizer & Equipment .....G...... 618 242-6000
  Mount Vernon *(G-15425)*
◆ Pcs Nitrogen Inc ...........................D....... 847 849-4200
  Northbrook *(G-16332)*
Pcs Nitrogen Fertilizer LP ............F....... 847 849-4200
  Northbrook *(G-16333)*
Pcs Nitrogen Trinidad Corp .........C....... 847 849-4200
  Northbrook *(G-16334)*
▲ Pcs Ntrgen Frtlzer Oprtons Inc ...C....... 847 849-4200
  Northbrook *(G-16335)*
▼ Potash Corp Ssktchewan Fla Inc ..C....... 847 849-4200
  Northbrook *(G-16339)*
Potash Corp Ssktchewan Fla Inc ..C....... 847 849-4200
  Northbrook *(G-16340)*
Pro Ag Inc ......................................G...... 815 365-2353
  Reddick *(G-17952)*
Rentech Development Corp ........C....... 815 747-3101
  East Dubuque *(G-8620)*
Scotts Company LLC ....................E....... 630 343-4070
  Woodridge *(G-22517)*
Scotts Company LLC ....................E....... 815 467-1605
  Channahon *(G-3585)*
Scotts Company LLC ....................E....... 847 777-0700
  Buffalo Grove *(G-2764)*
Solution Designs Inc ...................G...... 847 680-7788
  Vernon Hills *(G-21203)*
Sun Ag Inc .....................................G...... 309 726-1331
  Hudson *(G-12126)*
Sunrise AG Service Company .....G...... 309 538-4287
  Kilbourne *(G-12698)*
▲ Terra Nitrogen Company LP ........F....... 847 405-2400
  Deerfield *(G-8062)*
Tri-County Chemical Inc .............F....... 618 273-2071
  Eldorado *(G-8925)*
Veolia Es Industrial Svcs Inc ......F....... 708 652-0575
  Cicero *(G-7244)*

## 2874 Phosphatic Fertilizers

◆ CF Industries Inc ..........................B....... 847 405-2400
  Deerfield *(G-7994)*
CF Industries Holdings Inc .........B....... 847 405-2400
  Deerfield *(G-7996)*
CF Industries Nitrogen LLC ........F....... 847 405-2400
  Deerfield *(G-7998)*
Gateway Fs Inc .............................G...... 618 824-6631
  Venedy *(G-21136)*
Innophos Inc .................................G...... 773 468-2300
  Chicago *(G-5199)*
Innophos Inc .................................C....... 708 757-6111
  Chicago Heights *(G-7103)*
Occidental Chemical Corp ..........F....... 773 284-0079
  Chicago *(G-5965)*
◆ Pcs Nitrogen Inc ...........................D....... 847 849-4200
  Northbrook *(G-16332)*
◆ Pcs Phosphate Company Inc .......D....... 847 849-4200
  Northbrook *(G-16336)*
Phosphate Resource Ptrs ............A....... 847 739-1200
  Lake Forest *(G-12945)*
▼ Potash Corp Ssktchewan Fla Inc ..C....... 847 849-4200
  Northbrook *(G-16339)*
Potash Corp Ssktchewan Fla Inc ..C....... 847 849-4200
  Northbrook *(G-16340)*
Sun Ag Inc .....................................G...... 309 726-1331
  Hudson *(G-12126)*

## 2875 Fertilizers, Mixing Only

Allerton Supply Company ............F....... 217 896-2522
  Homer *(G-12074)*
Anp Inc ..........................................G...... 309 757-0372
  Moline *(G-14918)*

Employee Codes: A=Over 500 employees, B=251-500
C=101-250, D=51-100, E=20-50, F=10-19, G=3-9

# 28 CHEMICALS AND ALLIED PRODUCTS

Archer-Daniels-Midland Company .....G..... 618 483-6171
 Altamont (G-549)
Better Earth Premium Compost .........G..... 309 697-0963
 Peoria (G-17317)
Bio Green Inc .....................................G..... 847 740-9637
 Volo (G-21308)
▲ Brandt Consolidated Inc ................E..... 217 547-5800
 Springfield (G-20399)
Brandt Consolidated Inc ....................... 217 626-1123
 Farmer City (G-10178)
Brandt Consolidated Inc ...................G..... 309 365-7201
 Lexington (G-13291)
Brandt Consolidated Inc ...................F..... 217 438-6158
 Auburn (G-948)
CF Industries Nitrogen Llc .................C..... 847 405-2400
 Deerfield (G-7997)
Country Stone Inc ..............................E..... 309 787-1744
 Milan (G-14781)
Crop Production Services Inc ...........G..... 217 427-2181
 Catlin (G-3401)
E N P Inc ............................................G..... 815 539-7471
 Mendota (G-14721)
E N P Inc ............................................G..... 800 255-4906
 Mendota (G-14720)
Evergreen Fs Inc ...............................G..... 815 934-5422
 Cullom (G-7681)
F S Gateway Inc .................................G..... 618 458-6588
 Fults (G-10709)
Garden Prairie Organics LLC ............G..... 815 597-1318
 Garden Prairie (G-10794)
Green Earth Technologies Inc ..........G..... 847 991-0436
 Palatine (G-17031)
Green Organics Inc ............................F..... 630 871-0108
 Carol Stream (G-3164)
Harbach Gillan & Nixon Inc ...............F..... 217 935-8378
 Clinton (G-7282)
Hayden Mills Inc .................................E..... 618 962-3136
 Omaha (G-16807)
Hyponex Corporation ........................E..... 815 772-2167
 Morrison (G-15144)
Kimmy Compost Inc ..........................G..... 847 372-9201
 Evanston (G-10061)
Kreider Services Incorporated .........D..... 815 288-6691
 Dixon (G-8336)
Lebanon Seaboard Corporation ........E..... 217 446-0983
 Danville (G-7746)
◆ Masterblend International LLC ......F..... 815 423-5551
 Morris (G-15115)
Midwest Intgrted Companies LLC ....C..... 847 426-6354
 Gilberts (G-10926)
Miller Fertilizer Inc ...........................G..... 217 382-4241
 Casey (G-3390)
Millers Fertilizer & Feed ....................F..... 217 783-6321
 Cowden (G-7452)
Myers Inc ..........................................G..... 309 725-3710
 Varna (G-21135)
Pearl Valley Organix Inc ....................F..... 815 443-2170
 Pearl City (G-17249)
Piatt County Service Co ....................G..... 217 678-5511
 Bement (G-1801)
Piatt County Service Co ....................G..... 217 489-2411
 Mansfield (G-14178)
Prairieland Fs Inc ..............................G..... 309 329-2162
 Astoria (G-936)
Randolph Agricultural Services ........G..... 309 473-3256
 Heyworth (G-11765)
South Central Fs Inc ..........................F..... 217 849-2242
 Toledo (G-20966)
South Central Fs Inc ..........................E..... 618 283-1557
 Vandalia (G-21126)
Van Diest Supply Company ...............G..... 815 232-6053
 Freeport (G-10697)
Veteran Greens LLC ..........................G..... 773 599-9689
 Chicago (G-6891)
Wabash Valley Service Co ................F..... 618 393-2971
 Olney (G-16800)
Wedgworths Inc .................................E..... 863 682-2153
 Northbrook (G-16385)
West Central Fs Inc ...........................G..... 309 375-6904
 Wataga (G-21399)

## 2879 Pesticides & Agricultural Chemicals, NEC

Agriscience Inc ..................................G..... 212 365-4214
 Peoria (G-17304)
Agrochem Inc .....................................F..... 847 564-1304
 Northbrook (G-16201)
◆ Alpha AG Inc ...................................G..... 217 546-2724
 Pleasant Plains (G-17681)

Cardinal Professional Products ........G..... 714 761-3292
 Decatur (G-7850)
◆ Chase Products Co .........................D..... 708 865-1000
 Broadview (G-2566)
Claire-Sprayway Inc ..........................D..... 630 628-3000
 Downers Grove (G-8413)
Clarke Aquatic Services Inc .............G..... 630 894-2000
 Saint Charles (G-19154)
Clarke Group Inc ...............................G..... 630 894-2000
 Saint Charles (G-19155)
◆ Clarke Mosquito Ctrl Pdts Inc .........C..... 630 894-2000
 Saint Charles (G-19156)
Crop Production Services Inc ...................217 466-5430
 Kansas (G-12659)
Dow Agrosciences LLC .....................D..... 630 428-8494
 Naperville (G-15648)
Dow Agrosciences LLC ............................. 815 844-3128
 Pontiac (G-17699)
Dow Chemical Company ...................E..... 815 933-5514
 Kankakee (G-12611)
Du Pont Delaware Inc .......................G..... 630 285-2700
 Itasca (G-12255)
E I Du Pont De Nemours & Co .........E..... 309 527-5115
 El Paso (G-8868)
E N P Inc ............................................G..... 800 255-4906
 Mendota (G-14720)
FMC Corporation ................................E..... 309 695-2571
 Wyoming (G-22638)
Frank Miller & Sons Inc ....................E..... 708 201-7200
 Mokena (G-14863)
Gard Rogard Inc .................................D..... 847 836-7700
 Carpentersville (G-3284)
Harbach Nixon & Willson Inc ...................217 935-8378
 Clinton (G-7283)
Isky North America Inc .....................G..... 937 641-1368
 Chicago (G-5243)
J Stewart & Co ........................................... 847 419-9595
 Buffalo Grove (G-2712)
Maplehurst Farms Inc .......................F..... 815 562-8723
 Rochelle (G-18097)
Monsanto Company ...........................D..... 309 829-6640
 Bloomington (G-2202)
Monsanto Company ................................. 815 264-8153
 Waterman (G-21408)
Nufarm Americas Inc ................................ 708 756-2010
 Chicago Heights (G-7115)
◆ Nufarm Americas Inc .............................. 708 377-1330
 Alsip (G-501)
Pfizer Inc ............................................D..... 847 639-3020
 Cary (G-3363)
▲ Precision Laboratories LLC ..........E..... 800 323-6280
 Waukegan (G-21606)
Pro-Tek Products Inc ........................G..... 630 293-5100
 Wheaton (G-21973)
Sanford Chemical Co Inc ..................F..... 847 437-3530
 Elk Grove Village (G-9727)
▲ Sem Minerals LP ............................D..... 217 224-8766
 Quincy (G-17890)
Smithereen Company .........................D..... 800 340-1888
 Niles (G-16034)
Smithereen Company Del ..................D..... 847 675-0010
 Niles (G-16035)
Tri-County Chemical Inc ...........................618 268-4318
 Galatia (G-10713)
◆ Valent Biosciences Corporation ....D..... 847 968-4700
 Libertyville (G-13397)
Van Diest Supply Company ...............G..... 815 232-6053
 Freeport (G-10697)
Wellmark Int Farnam Co ....................B..... 925 948-4000
 Schaumburg (G-19787)
West Agro Inc ....................................E..... 847 298-5505
 Des Plaines (G-8303)
Westmin Corporation ........................G..... 217 224-4570
 Quincy (G-17904)

## 2891 Adhesives & Sealants

A J Adhesives Inc .............................G..... 708 210-1111
 South Holland (G-20238)
Aabbitt Adhesives Inc .......................D..... 773 227-2700
 Chicago (G-3701)
Aabbitt Adhesives Inc .......................E..... 773 723-6780
 Chicago (G-3702)
◆ Adco Global Inc ..............................G..... 847 282-3485
 Lincolnshire (G-13424)
Advanced Extruder Tech Inc .............E..... 847 238-9651
 Elk Grove Village (G-9275)
Alhencam Seal Coat Inc ...........................217 422-4605
 Decatur (G-7829)
All Weather Courts Inc .............................217 364-4546
 Dawson (G-7816)

Armitage Industries Inc .....................F..... 847 288-9090
 Franklin Park (G-10400)
▲ AST Industries Inc .........................F..... 847 455-2300
 Franklin Park (G-10405)
▲ Black Swan Manufacturing Co ......F..... 773 227-3700
 Chicago (G-4121)
Bradley Adhsive Applctions Inc .......C..... 630 443-8424
 Saint Charles (G-19145)
Campbell Camie Inc ..........................E..... 314 968-3222
 Downers Grove (G-8403)
Chase Corporation .............................E..... 847 866-8500
 Evanston (G-10022)
Chem Spec Corporation ....................G..... 847 891-2133
 Elburn (G-8879)
Chicago Adhesive Products ..............G..... 630 978-7766
 Aurora (G-983)
Chicago Latex Products Inc .............F..... 815 459-9680
 Crystal Lake (G-7552)
▲ Chromium Industries Inc ...............G..... 773 287-3716
 Chicago (G-4373)
CP Moyen Co .....................................G..... 847 673-6866
 Skokie (G-19988)
◆ Cyberbond LLC ...............................E..... 630 761-0341
 Batavia (G-1436)
▲ D & K Group Inc ..............................E..... 847 956-0160
 Elk Grove Village (G-9409)
D & K International Inc ......................E..... 847 439-3423
 Elk Grove Village (G-9410)
◆ Daubert Industries Inc ...................G..... 630 203-6800
 Burr Ridge (G-2834)
Dental Sealants & More .....................G..... 309 692-6435
 Peoria (G-17348)
Dip Seal Plastics Inc .........................G..... 815 398-3533
 Rockford (G-18345)
Eagle Enterprises Inc ........................G..... 618 643-2588
 Mc Leansboro (G-14464)
▲ Eco-Pur Solutions LLC ..................E..... 630 917-8789
 Chicago (G-4692)
Eco-Pur Solutions LLC ......................G..... 630 226-2300
 Romeoville (G-18818)
Ecool LLC ...........................................G..... 309 966-3701
 Champaign (G-3477)
▲ Emecole Inc .....................................F..... 815 372-2493
 Romeoville (G-18819)
Emulsicoat Inc ....................................F..... 217 344-7775
 Urbana (G-21081)
Essentra International LLC ...............G..... 866 800-0775
 Westchester (G-21840)
F H Leinweber Co Inc ........................E..... 708 424-7000
 Oak Lawn (G-16619)
F H Leinweber Co Inc ........................E..... 773 568-7722
 Chicago (G-4803)
▲ Fitz Chem Corporation ...................E..... 630 467-8383
 Itasca (G-12264)
Fontana Associates Inc .....................G..... 888 707-8273
 Arlington Heights (G-755)
▼ G J Nikolas & Co Inc .......................E..... 708 544-0320
 Bellwood (G-1706)
Glue Inc ..............................................F..... 312 451-4018
 Chicago (G-4962)
Green Products LLC ..........................F..... 815 407-0900
 Romeoville (G-18829)
H A Gartenberg & Company ..............F..... 847 821-7590
 Buffalo Grove (G-2700)
H E Wisdom & Sons Inc ....................G..... 847 841-7002
 Elgin (G-9053)
▲ H E Wisdom & Sons Inc .................E..... 847 841-7002
 Elgin (G-9052)
HB Fuller Adhesives LLC ..................E..... 815 357-6726
 Morris (G-15110)
◆ HB Fuller Cnstr Pdts Inc ................C..... 630 978-7766
 Aurora (G-1023)
HB Fuller Cnstr Pdts Inc ...................F..... 847 776-4375
 Palatine (G-17035)
HB Fuller Company ............................G..... 847 358-9555
 Aurora (G-1024)
Henkel Corporation ............................D..... 847 468-9200
 Elgin (G-9064)
▲ Highland Supply Corporation ........B..... 618 654-2161
 Highland (G-11794)
Illinois Tool Works Inc ......................C..... 708 342-6000
 Mokena (G-14872)
Illinois Tool Works Inc ......................B..... 847 724-7500
 Glenview (G-11141)
Illinois Tool Works Inc ......................C..... 630 372-2150
 Bartlett (G-1353)
Illinois Tool Works Inc ......................G..... 847 783-5500
 Elgin (G-9072)
ITW Dynatec .......................................G..... 847 657-4830
 Glenview (G-11151)

| Company | Code | Phone |
|---|---|---|
| J & J Industries Inc | G | 630 595-8878 |
| Bensenville (G-1925) | | |
| JB Enterprises II Inc | E | 630 372-8300 |
| Streamwood (G-20660) | | |
| Jjc Epoxy Inc | G | 630 231-5600 |
| West Chicago (G-21728) | | |
| JW Sealants Inc | G | 630 398-1010 |
| Bartlett (G-1358) | | |
| ◆ La-Co Industries Inc | C | 847 427-3220 |
| Elk Grove Village (G-9582) | | |
| ▲ Lectro Stik Corp | E | 630 894-1355 |
| Glendale Heights (G-11040) | | |
| ▲ Lintec of America Inc | E | 847 229-0547 |
| Schaumburg (G-19619) | | |
| ▲ Mafomsic Incorporated | F | 630 279-2005 |
| Elmhurst (G-9905) | | |
| Mapei Corporation | | 630 293-5800 |
| West Chicago (G-21737) | | |
| Miller Purcell Co Inc | G | 815 485-2142 |
| New Lenox (G-15897) | | |
| ▲ Morton International LLC | C | 312 807-2696 |
| Chicago (G-5807) | | |
| Morton Intl Inc Adhsves Spclty | G | 815 653-2042 |
| Ringwood (G-17993) | | |
| ◆ Morton Salt Inc | C | 312 807-2000 |
| Chicago (G-5809) | | |
| Morton Yokohama Inc | F | 312 807-2000 |
| Chicago (G-5810) | | |
| ◆ Nalco Company LLC | A | 630 305-1000 |
| Naperville (G-15703) | | |
| ▼ Nataz Specialty Coatings Inc | F | 773 247-7030 |
| Chicago (G-5856) | | |
| ▲ National Casein Company | E | 773 846-7300 |
| Chicago (G-5861) | | |
| ▲ National Casein New Jersey Inc | G | 773 846-7300 |
| Chicago (G-5862) | | |
| ▲ National Casein of California | D | 773 846-7300 |
| Chicago (G-5863) | | |
| ND Industries Inc | E | 847 498-3600 |
| Northbrook (G-16318) | | |
| Nolan Sealants Inc | G | 630 774-5713 |
| Bloomingdale (G-2121) | | |
| North Shore Consultants Inc | E | 847 290-1599 |
| Elk Grove Village (G-9655) | | |
| Npc Sealants | F | 708 681-1040 |
| Maywood (G-14431) | | |
| Nu-Puttie Corporation | E | 708 681-1040 |
| Maywood (G-14433) | | |
| Olon Industries Inc (us) | E | 630 232-4705 |
| Geneva (G-10858) | | |
| ◆ Opticote Inc | E | 847 678-8900 |
| Franklin Park (G-10544) | | |
| Owens Corning Sales LLC | E | 708 594-6935 |
| Argo (G-695) | | |
| Palm Labs Adhesives LLC | G | 773 799-8470 |
| Chicago (G-6064) | | |
| Pierce & Stevens Chemical | G | 630 653-3800 |
| Carol Stream (G-3214) | | |
| Porcelain Enamel Finishers | G | 312 808-1560 |
| Chicago (G-6157) | | |
| PPG Architectural Finishes Inc | D | 773 523-6333 |
| Chicago (G-6161) | | |
| PPG Architectural Finishes Inc | G | 847 336-2355 |
| Gurnee (G-11487) | | |
| PPG Architectural Finishes Inc | E | 630 773-8484 |
| Itasca (G-12344) | | |
| PPG Architectural Finishes Inc | E | 630 820-8692 |
| Aurora (G-1067) | | |
| PPG Architectural Finishes Inc | B | 217 584-1323 |
| Meredosia (G-14734) | | |
| PPG Industries Inc | E | 773 646-5900 |
| Chicago (G-6163) | | |
| Princeton Sealing Wax Co | G | 815 875-1943 |
| Princeton (G-17760) | | |
| ◆ Protective Products Intl | G | 847 526-1180 |
| Wauconda (G-21495) | | |
| ▲ Remet Corporation | | 480 766-3464 |
| Palatine (G-17067) | | |
| Rhopac Fabricated Products LLC | E | 847 362-3300 |
| Libertyville (G-13376) | | |
| Right/Pointe Company | D | 815 754-5700 |
| Dekalb (G-8115) | | |
| RM Lucas Co | E | 773 523-4300 |
| Chicago (G-6365) | | |
| ▼ RM Lucas Co | E | 773 523-4300 |
| Alsip (G-522) | | |
| Roanoke Companies Group Inc | G | 630 499-5870 |
| Aurora (G-1074) | | |
| ▲ Roanoke Companies Group Inc | D | 630 375-0324 |
| Aurora (G-1075) | | |
| ▲ Roman Decorating Products LLC | E | 708 891-0770 |
| Calumet City (G-2952) | | |
| Roman Holdings Corporation | D | 708 891-0770 |
| Calumet City (G-2953) | | |
| ◆ Rust-Oleum Corporation | C | 847 367-7700 |
| Vernon Hills (G-21195) | | |
| Rust-Oleum Corporation | F | 815 967-4258 |
| Rockford (G-18600) | | |
| Saf-T-Lok International Corp | E | 630 495-2001 |
| Lombard (G-13850) | | |
| Safety Compound Corporation | E | 630 953-1515 |
| Lombard (G-13851) | | |
| ▲ Sandstrom Products Company | E | 309 523-2121 |
| Port Byron (G-17723) | | |
| Sandstrom Products Company | F | 309 523-2121 |
| Port Byron (G-17724) | | |
| ◆ Sanford LP | A | 770 418-7000 |
| Downers Grove (G-8518) | | |
| Sanford Chemical Co Inc | F | 847 437-3530 |
| Elk Grove Village (G-9727) | | |
| Sarco Putty Company | G | 773 735-5577 |
| Chicago (G-6444) | | |
| Sigma Coatings Inc | G | 630 628-5305 |
| Addison (G-290) | | |
| Sika Corporation | G | 815 431-1080 |
| Ottawa (G-16985) | | |
| Simpson Strong-Tie Company Inc | E | 630 293-2800 |
| West Chicago (G-21773) | | |
| ▲ Simpson Strong-Tie Company Inc | E | 630 613-5100 |
| Addison (G-293) | | |
| Ski Seal Coating Inc | E | 708 246-5656 |
| Countryside (G-7442) | | |
| ▲ Spartan Adhesives Coatings Co | F | 815 459-8500 |
| Crystal Lake (G-7652) | | |
| ◆ Specialty Cnstr Brands Inc | F | 630 851-0782 |
| Aurora (G-1081) | | |
| Spl-Usa LLC | E | 312 807-2000 |
| Chicago (G-6562) | | |
| Strytech Adhesives | G | 847 509-7566 |
| Northbrook (G-16373) | | |
| Surebond Inc | E | 630 762-0606 |
| Saint Charles (G-19275) | | |
| Surebonder Adhesives Inc | G | 847 487-4583 |
| Wauconda (G-21505) | | |
| ◆ Tape Case Ltd | E | 847 299-7880 |
| Elk Grove Village (G-9768) | | |
| Tempel Steel Company | A | 773 250-8000 |
| Chicago (G-6698) | | |
| ▲ Testor Corporation | D | 815 962-6654 |
| Rockford (G-18644) | | |
| ▲ Therm-O-Web Inc | E | 847 520-5200 |
| Wheeling (G-22167) | | |
| ◆ Tsv Adhesive Systems Inc | E | 815 464-5606 |
| Frankfort (G-10373) | | |
| United Adhesives Inc | G | 224 436-0077 |
| Buffalo Grove (G-2785) | | |
| United Gilsonite Laboratories | E | 217 243-7878 |
| Jacksonville (G-12415) | | |
| ▼ Universal Chem & Coatings Inc | E | 847 931-1700 |
| Elgin (G-9219) | | |
| Universal Chem & Coatings Inc | E | 847 297-2001 |
| Elk Grove Village (G-9801) | | |
| US Adhesives | G | 312 829-7438 |
| Chicago (G-6852) | | |
| Versatile Materials Inc | G | 773 924-3700 |
| Chicago (G-6887) | | |
| Vibracoustic Usa Inc | E | 618 382-5891 |
| Carmi (G-3081) | | |
| W R Grace & Co- Conn | F | 708 458-9700 |
| Chicago (G-6924) | | |
| Wisdom Adhesives | G | 847 841-7002 |
| Elgin (G-9238) | | |
| WW Henry Company LP | D | 815 933-8059 |
| Bourbonnais (G-2409) | | |

## 2892 Explosives

| Company | Code | Phone |
|---|---|---|
| Buckley Powder Co | F | 217 285-5531 |
| Pittsfield (G-17562) | | |
| Dyno Nobel Inc | F | 217 285-5621 |
| Barry (G-1312) | | |
| Dyno Nobel Inc | E | 217 285-5531 |
| Detroit (G-8309) | | |
| Evenson Explosives LLC | E | 815 942-5800 |
| Morris (G-15108) | | |
| General Dynamics Ordnance | C | 618 985-8211 |
| Marion (G-14261) | | |
| Hanley Industries Inc | E | 618 465-8892 |
| Alton (G-577) | | |
| Orica USA Inc | E | 815 357-8711 |
| Morris (G-15125) | | |

## 2893 Printing Ink

| Company | Code | Phone |
|---|---|---|
| ▲ ABM Marking Ltd | F | 618 277-3773 |
| Belleville (G-1606) | | |
| Actega North America Inc | G | 847 690-9310 |
| Elk Grove Village (G-9267) | | |
| ▲ Alden & Ott Printing Inks Co | D | 847 956-6830 |
| Arlington Heights (G-706) | | |
| Alden & Ott Printing Inks Co | F | 847 364-6817 |
| Mount Prospect (G-15309) | | |
| Buzz Sales Company Inc | G | 815 459-1170 |
| Crystal Lake (G-7546) | | |
| ▲ Central Ink Corporation | E | 630 231-6500 |
| West Chicago (G-21679) | | |
| CIS Systems Inc | G | 847 827-0747 |
| Glenview (G-11114) | | |
| Cudner & OConnor Co | F | 773 826-0200 |
| Chicago (G-4514) | | |
| Domino Holdings Inc | D | 847 244-2501 |
| Gurnee (G-11441) | | |
| Environmental Inks & Coding | G | 630 231-7313 |
| West Chicago (G-21696) | | |
| ▲ Environmental Specialties Inc | G | 630 860-7070 |
| Itasca (G-12259) | | |
| Flint Group US LLC | G | 630 526-9903 |
| Batavia (G-1450) | | |
| Flint Group US LLC | F | 618 349-8384 |
| Saint Peter (G-19322) | | |
| Gibbon America Inc | F | 847 931-1255 |
| Elgin (G-9045) | | |
| ▲ Gibbon America II Corp | F | 847 931-1255 |
| Elgin (G-9046) | | |
| ▲ Graphic Chemical & Ink Co | F | 630 832-6004 |
| Villa Park (G-21257) | | |
| Hostmann Steinberg Inc | F | 502 968-5961 |
| Kankakee (G-12622) | | |
| Hostmann Steinberg Inc | F | 815 401-5493 |
| Bourbonnais (G-2399) | | |
| ▲ Hubergroup Usa Inc | D | 815 929-9293 |
| Kankakee (G-12623) | | |
| Hurst Chemical Company | G | 815 964-0451 |
| Rockford (G-18424) | | |
| Hydro Ink Corp | F | 847 674-0057 |
| Skokie (G-20014) | | |
| ▲ I C T W Ink | G | 630 893-4658 |
| Roselle (G-18945) | | |
| ▲ I Q Infinity LLC | G | 773 651-2556 |
| Chicago (G-5133) | | |
| ▲ I S C America Inc | G | 630 616-1331 |
| Wood Dale (G-22380) | | |
| Ink Systems Inc | G | 847 427-2200 |
| Elk Grove Village (G-9547) | | |
| ◆ INX Digital International Co | F | 630 382-1800 |
| Schaumburg (G-19576) | | |
| INX Group Ltd | G | 708 799-1993 |
| Homewood (G-12103) | | |
| ◆ INX Group Ltd | E | 630 382-1800 |
| Schaumburg (G-19577) | | |
| ◆ INX International Ink Co | D | 630 382-1800 |
| Schaumburg (G-19578) | | |
| INX International Ink Co | E | 630 681-7200 |
| West Chicago (G-21724) | | |
| INX International Ink Co | E | 708 496-3600 |
| Chicago (G-5235) | | |
| INX International Ink Co | | 800 233-4657 |
| Schaumburg (G-19579) | | |
| INX International Ink Co | E | 630 382-1800 |
| Schaumburg (G-19580) | | |
| INX International Ink Co | E | 630 382-1800 |
| Schaumburg (G-19581) | | |
| INX International Ink Co | E | 630 681-7100 |
| West Chicago (G-21725) | | |
| ▼ Kolorcure Corporation | E | 630 879-9050 |
| Batavia (G-1460) | | |
| L P S Express Inc | G | 217 636-7683 |
| Springfield (G-20465) | | |
| Laser Technology Group Inc | F | 847 524-4088 |
| Elk Grove Village (G-9586) | | |
| ▲ Midwest Ink Co | E | 708 345-7177 |
| Broadview (G-2595) | | |
| Paper Graphics Inc | G | 847 276-2727 |
| Lincolnshire (G-13470) | | |
| Precision Ink Corporation | F | 847 952-1500 |
| Elk Grove Village (G-9694) | | |
| ▼ R A Kerley Ink Engineers Inc | E | 708 344-1295 |
| Broadview (G-2606) | | |
| Scientific Colors Inc | C | 815 744-5650 |
| Rockdale (G-18233) | | |
| Springbox Inc | G | 708 921-9944 |
| Flossmoor (G-10229) | | |

**Sun Chemical Corporation** ..... C ..... 708 562-0550
Northlake *(G-16454)*

**Sun Chemical Corporation** ..... D ..... 815 939-0136
Kankakee *(G-12655)*

◆ **Thrall Enterprises Inc** ..... F ..... 312 621-8200
Chicago *(G-6722)*

**Toyo Ink International Corp** ..... F ..... 630 930-5100
Addison *(G-320)*

◆ **Toyo Ink International Corp** ..... F ..... 866 969-8696
Wood Dale *(G-22432)*

**U S Colors & Coatings Inc** ..... G ..... 630 879-8898
Batavia *(G-1512)*

**Wikoff Color Corporation** ..... G ..... 847 487-2704
Wauconda *(G-21515)*

## *2895 Carbon Black*

**Cabot Corporation** ..... D ..... 217 253-5752
Tuscola *(G-21018)*

## *2899 Chemical Preparations, NEC*

▲ **300 Below Inc** ..... G ..... 217 423-3070
Decatur *(G-7819)*

**Abbott Laboratories** ..... F ..... 847 937-6100
Abbott Park *(G-2)*

▲ **ABM Marking Ltd** ..... F ..... 618 277-3773
Belleville *(G-1606)*

**Accusol Incorporated** ..... G ..... 773 283-4686
Oak Lawn *(G-16597)*

**Advanced Finishing** ..... G ..... 815 964-3367
Belvidere *(G-1728)*

**Advantech Limited** ..... G ..... 815 397-9133
Aurora *(G-1102)*

**Afton Chemical Corporation** ..... E ..... 708 728-1546
Bedford Park *(G-1533)*

**Afton Chemical Corporation** ..... B ..... 618 583-1000
East Saint Louis *(G-8740)*

▲ **Aldridge Electric Inc** ..... B ..... 847 680-5200
Libertyville *(G-13300)*

▲ **All American Chemical Co Inc** ..... E ..... 847 297-2840
Melrose Park *(G-14586)*

**Alloy Chrome Inc** ..... G ..... 847 678-2880
Schiller Park *(G-19800)*

▲ **American Chemical & Eqp Inc** ..... G ..... 815 675-9199
Northlake *(G-16427)*

**American Colloid Company** ..... F ..... 815 547-5369
Belvidere *(G-1731)*

**American Colloid Company** ..... E ..... 618 452-8143
Granite City *(G-11263)*

**American Colloid Company** ..... F ..... 304 882-2123
Elgin *(G-8947)*

◆ **American Colloid Company** ..... E ..... 847 851-1700
Hoffman Estates *(G-11992)*

**Americlean Inc** ..... F ..... 314 741-8901
Wood River *(G-22440)*

**An Environmental Inks** ..... F ..... 800 728-8200
West Chicago *(G-21659)*

◆ **Apex Engineering Products Corp** ..... F ..... 630 820-8888
Aurora *(G-958)*

**Arbor Products** ..... G ..... 847 653-6210
Park Ridge *(G-17182)*

**Arch Chemicals Inc** ..... G ..... 630 365-1720
Elburn *(G-8876)*

**Arch Chemicals Inc** ..... F ..... 630 955-0401
Naperville *(G-15600)*

**BASF Construction Chem LLC** ..... G ..... 847 249-4080
Gurnee *(G-11431)*

**BASF Corporation** ..... B ..... 815 932-9863
Kankakee *(G-12603)*

▲ **Bird-X Inc** ..... E ..... 312 226-2473
Chicago *(G-4112)*

▲ **Black Swan Manufacturing Co** ..... F ..... 773 227-3700
Chicago *(G-4121)*

▲ **Bmi Products Northern Ill Inc** ..... E ..... 847 395-7110
Antioch *(G-625)*

**Bonsal American Inc** ..... D ..... 847 678-6220
Franklin Park *(G-10415)*

**Brite Site Supply Inc** ..... G ..... 773 772-7300
Chicago *(G-4171)*

**Bromine Systems Inc** ..... G ..... 630 624-3303
Addison *(G-61)*

▲ **Butterfield Color Inc** ..... E ..... 630 906-1980
Aurora *(G-1122)*

**Buzz Sales Company Inc** ..... G ..... 815 459-1170
Crystal Lake *(G-7546)*

**C & S Chemicals Inc** ..... G ..... 815 722-6671
Joliet *(G-12470)*

**C & S Fabrication Services Inc** ..... G ..... 815 363-8510
Johnsburg *(G-12431)*

**Cabot Corporation** ..... D ..... 217 253-5752
Tuscola *(G-21018)*

**Campbell Camie Inc** ..... E ..... 314 968-3222
Downers Grove *(G-8403)*

◆ **Castrol Industrial N Amer Inc** ..... C ..... 877 641-1600
Naperville *(G-15620)*

▲ **Cater Chemical Co** ..... G ..... 630 980-2300
Roselle *(G-18930)*

◆ **CCI Manufacturing IL Corp** ..... E ..... 630 685-7534
Lemont *(G-13230)*

**CD Magic Inc** ..... G ..... 708 582-3496
Roselle *(G-18931)*

**Central Chemical and Service** ..... F ..... 630 653-9200
Carol Stream *(G-3126)*

▲ **Chem Trade Global** ..... G ..... 847 675-2682
Skokie *(G-19978)*

**Chemical Processing & Acc** ..... G ..... 847 793-2387
Lincolnshire *(G-13437)*

**Chemix Corp** ..... F ..... 708 754-2150
Glenwood *(G-11215)*

**Chemsong Inc** ..... F
Glen Ellyn *(G-10962)*

◆ **Chemtool Incorporated** ..... C ..... 815 957-4140
Rockton *(G-18694)*

**Chemtool Incorporated** ..... D ..... 815 459-1250
Crystal Lake *(G-7551)*

**Circle Systems Inc** ..... F ..... 815 286-3271
Hinckley *(G-11934)*

**Claire-Sprayway Inc** ..... D ..... 630 628-3000
Downers Grove *(G-8413)*

**CLC Lubricants Company** ..... E ..... 630 232-7900
Geneva *(G-10818)*

◆ **Colloid Envmtl Tech Co LLC** ..... C ..... 847 851-1500
Hoffman Estates *(G-12002)*

**Compass Minerals Intl Inc** ..... F ..... 773 978-7258
Chicago *(G-4438)*

**Crosslink Coatings Corporation** ..... G ..... 815 467-7970
Channahon *(G-3568)*

**Custom Chemical Inc** ..... G ..... 217 529-0878
Springfield *(G-20426)*

**D and I Analyst Inc** ..... F ..... 217 636-7500
Athens *(G-937)*

◆ **Daubert Industries Inc** ..... F ..... 630 203-6800
Burr Ridge *(G-2834)*

**Dayton Superior Corporation** ..... E ..... 815 732-3136
Oregon *(G-16821)*

**Dayton Superior Corporation** ..... C ..... 815 936-3300
Kankakee *(G-12609)*

▼ **De Enterprises Inc** ..... F ..... 708 345-8088
Broadview *(G-2571)*

**Debourg Corp** ..... G ..... 815 338-7852
Bull Valley *(G-2798)*

◆ **Dober Chemical Corp** ..... C ..... 630 410-7300
Woodridge *(G-22471)*

**Domino Amjet Inc** ..... E ..... 847 662-3148
Gurnee *(G-11439)*

◆ **Domino Amjet Inc** ..... D ..... 847 244-2501
Gurnee *(G-11440)*

**Dynacron** ..... G ..... 773 378-0736
Chicago *(G-4659)*

**Ecp Incorporated** ..... D ..... 630 754-4200
Woodridge *(G-22474)*

**Emerald Polymer Additives LLC** ..... D ..... 309 364-2311
Henry *(G-11742)*

**Enterprise Oil Co** ..... E ..... 312 487-2025
Chicago *(G-4759)*

▲ **Enviro Tech International Inc** ..... G ..... 708 343-6641
Melrose Park *(G-14634)*

▲ **Environmental Specialties Inc** ..... G ..... 630 860-7070
Itasca *(G-12259)*

**Express Care** ..... G ..... 815 521-2185
Channahon *(G-3575)*

**First Step Womens Center** ..... G ..... 217 523-0100
Springfield *(G-20441)*

▲ **Fragrance Island** ..... G ..... 773 488-2700
Chicago *(G-4881)*

**Frank Miller & Sons Inc** ..... E ..... 708 201-7200
Mokena *(G-14863)*

◆ **Fuchs Corporation** ..... G ..... 800 323-7755
Harvey *(G-11667)*

**Garratt-Callahan Company** ..... G ..... 630 543-4411
Addison *(G-128)*

**GE Betz Inc** ..... E ..... 630 543-8480
Addison *(G-129)*

▲ **Gelita USA Chicago** ..... F ..... 708 891-8400
Calumet City *(G-2938)*

**Getex Corporation** ..... G ..... 630 993-1300
Hinsdale *(G-11948)*

**Gillette Company** ..... D ..... 847 689-3111
North Chicago *(G-16180)*

**Girard Chemical Company** ..... G ..... 630 293-5886
Bensenville *(G-1909)*

**Global Water Technology Inc** ..... E ..... 708 349-9991
Orland Park *(G-16862)*

**Graphic Sciences Inc** ..... G ..... 630 226-0994
Bolingbrook *(G-2314)*

**H A Gartenberg & Company** ..... F ..... 847 821-7590
Buffalo Grove *(G-2700)*

**H-O-H Water Technology Inc** ..... E ..... 847 358-7400
Palatine *(G-17032)*

**Harcros Chemicals Inc** ..... G ..... 815 740-9971
Thornton *(G-20872)*

**Hawkins Inc** ..... G ..... 708 258-3797
Peotone *(G-17489)*

**HIG Chemicals Holdings** ..... C ..... 773 376-9000
Chicago *(G-5085)*

▲ **Holland LP** ..... C ..... 708 672-2300
Crete *(G-7515)*

**Honeywell International Inc** ..... G ..... 630 554-5342
Oswego *(G-16921)*

**Houghton International Inc** ..... F ..... 610 666-4000
Chicago *(G-5121)*

▲ **I S C America Inc** ..... G ..... 630 616-1331
Wood Dale *(G-22380)*

**I W M Corporation** ..... G ..... 847 695-0700
Elgin *(G-9070)*

**Illinois Oil Products Inc** ..... F ..... 309 788-1896
Rock Island *(G-18183)*

**Illinois Tool Works Inc** ..... E ..... 847 350-0193
Elk Grove Village *(G-9536)*

▲ **In3gredients Inc** ..... G ..... 312 577-4275
Chicago *(G-5171)*

**Industrial Specialty Chem Inc** ..... E ..... 708 339-1313
South Holland *(G-20280)*

**Industrial Waste Elimination** ..... F ..... 312 498-0880
Peoria *(G-17390)*

**Industrial Water Trtmnt Soltns** ..... G ..... 708 339-1313
Harvey *(G-11672)*

**Ineos Americas LLC** ..... G ..... 630 857-7463
Naperville *(G-15673)*

**Ineos Americas LLC** ..... G ..... 630 857-7000
Lisle *(G-13603)*

**Ingersoll-Rand Company** ..... E ..... 704 655-4000
Chicago *(G-5191)*

**Ink Smart Inc** ..... G ..... 708 349-9555
Orland Park *(G-16868)*

**Interactive Inks Coatings Corp** ..... F ..... 847 289-8710
South Elgin *(G-20208)*

▲ **Interra Global Corporation** ..... F ..... 847 292-8600
Park Ridge *(G-17204)*

**INX International Ink Co** ..... E ..... 630 681-7200
West Chicago *(G-21724)*

**INX International Ink Co** ..... F ..... 630 382-1800
Schaumburg *(G-19581)*

**INX International Ink Co** ..... E ..... 630 681-7100
West Chicago *(G-21725)*

▲ **Ivanhoe Industries Inc** ..... G ..... 847 566-7170
Mundelein *(G-15512)*

◆ **Jackson Marking Products Co** ..... F ..... 618 242-7901
Mount Vernon *(G-15417)*

**Jamaica Pyrotechnics** ..... G ..... 217 649-2902
Philo *(G-17539)*

**Jeanblanc International Inc** ..... G ..... 815 598-3400
Elizabeth *(G-9242)*

**JM Huber Corporation** ..... E ..... 217 224-1100
Quincy *(G-17841)*

▲ **Johnny Rckets Firewrks Display** ..... G ..... 847 501-1270
Chicago *(G-5317)*

**K+s Montana Holdings LLC** ..... G ..... 312 807-2000
Chicago *(G-5346)*

**K+s Salt LLC** ..... G ..... 844 789-3991
Chicago *(G-5347)*

**Klein Tools Inc** ..... D ..... 847 228-6999
Elk Grove Village *(G-9577)*

**Klein Tools Inc** ..... E ..... 847 821-5500
Lincolnshire *(G-13461)*

**Kona Blackbird Inc** ..... F ..... 815 792-8750
Serena *(G-19892)*

**Kop-Coat Inc** ..... F ..... 847 272-2278
Buffalo Grove *(G-2719)*

◆ **La-Co Industries Inc** ..... C ..... 847 427-3220
Elk Grove Village *(G-9582)*

**Lamar Owings** ..... G ..... 630 232-0564
Geneva *(G-10845)*

▲ **Lawter Inc** ..... E ..... 312 662-5700
Chicago *(G-5473)*

**Litho Research Incorporated** ..... G ..... 630 860-7070
Itasca *(G-12307)*

**Lubrication Enterprises LLC** ..... G ..... 800 537-7683
Plainfield *(G-17623)*

**Lubrizol Corporation** ..... F ..... 630 355-3605
Naperville *(G-15694)*

| Company | Code | Phone |
|---|---|---|
| Lumina Inc | G | 312 829-8970 |
| Chicago (G-5565) | | |
| ▲ Luster Leaf Products Inc | | 815 337-5560 |
| Woodstock (G-22586) | | |
| ◆ M R O Solutions LLC | E | 847 588-2480 |
| Niles (G-15998) | | |
| Macdermid Enthone Inc | | 708 598-3210 |
| Bridgeview (G-2505) | | |
| Magnetic Inspection Lab Inc | D | 847 437-4488 |
| Elk Grove Village (G-9606) | | |
| Mapei Corporation | D | 630 293-5800 |
| West Chicago (G-21737) | | |
| Master Fog LLC | | 773 918-9080 |
| Plainfield (G-17624) | | |
| Mc Chemical Company | G | 618 965-3668 |
| Steeleville (G-20563) | | |
| Mc Chemical Company | E | 815 964-7687 |
| Rockford (G-18487) | | |
| Metal Finishing Research Corp | F | 773 373-0800 |
| Chicago (G-5699) | | |
| ▲ Micro Surface Corporation | | 815 942-4221 |
| Morris (G-15116) | | |
| ▲ Mid America Intl Inc | | 847 635-8303 |
| Glenview (G-11169) | | |
| Miller Purcell Co Inc | | 815 485-2142 |
| New Lenox (G-15897) | | |
| ▲ Mineral Masters Corporation | F | 630 293-7727 |
| West Chicago (G-21744) | | |
| ▲ Modern Printing Colors Inc | F | 708 681-5678 |
| Broadview (G-2597) | | |
| ▲ Morton International LLC | C | 312 807-2696 |
| Chicago (G-5807) | | |
| ◆ Morton Salt Inc | C | 312 807-2000 |
| Chicago (G-5809) | | |
| ◆ Nalco Company LLC | A | 630 305-1000 |
| Naperville (G-15703) | | |
| ◆ Nalco Holding Company | D | 630 305-1000 |
| Naperville (G-15706) | | |
| ◆ Nalco Holdings LLC | A | 630 305-1000 |
| Naperville (G-15707) | | |
| ▼ Nataz Specialty Coatings Inc | | 773 247-7030 |
| Chicago (G-5856) | | |
| ▲ Nostalgia Pyrotechnics Inc | | 309 522-5136 |
| Osco (G-16900) | | |
| Ochem Inc | G | 847 403-7044 |
| Des Plaines (G-8246) | | |
| Ochem Inc | F | 847 403-7044 |
| Chicago (G-5967) | | |
| Opsdirt LLC | | 773 412-1179 |
| Chicago (G-5996) | | |
| Opw Fueling Components Inc | | 708 485-4200 |
| Hodgkins (G-11980) | | |
| ▼ Penray Companies Inc | D | 800 323-6329 |
| Wheeling (G-22120) | | |
| ▲ Philos Technologies Inc | G | 630 945-2933 |
| Buffalo Grove (G-2751) | | |
| Phoenix Inks and Coatings LLC | F | 630 972-2500 |
| Lemont (G-13255) | | |
| Planet Earth Antifreeze Inc | | 815 282-2463 |
| Loves Park (G-13976) | | |
| ▲ Plating International Inc | F | 847 451-2101 |
| Franklin Park (G-10554) | | |
| Polyenviro Labs Inc | | 708 489-0195 |
| Mokena (G-14896) | | |
| PPG Architectural Finishes Inc | F | 847 699-8400 |
| Des Plaines (G-8259) | | |
| PQ Corporation | E | 815 667-4241 |
| Utica (G-21107) | | |
| Pressure Vessel Service Inc | F | 773 913-7700 |
| Chicago (G-6182) | | |
| Prestone Products Corporation | D | 708 371-3000 |
| Alsip (G-513) | | |
| Prestone Products Corporation | | 203 731-8185 |
| Lake Forest (G-12948) | | |
| ▼ Prestone Products Corporation | C | 847 482-2045 |
| Lake Forest (G-12949) | | |
| Pro TEC Metal Finishing Corp | | 773 384-7853 |
| Chicago (G-6203) | | |
| Producers Chemical Company | E | 630 466-4584 |
| Sugar Grove (G-20731) | | |
| ▼ Progressive Solutions Corp | G | 847 639-7272 |
| Algonquin (G-405) | | |
| PVS Chemical Solutions Inc | E | 773 933-8800 |
| Chicago (G-6231) | | |
| ▲ Qualitek International Inc | E | 630 628-8083 |
| Addison (G-262) | | |
| Quikrete Chicago | D | 630 557-8252 |
| Elburn (G-8906) | | |
| Rampro Facilities Svcs Corp | G | 224 639-6378 |
| Gurnee (G-11498) | | |
| Rda Inc | F | 815 427-8444 |
| Saint Anne (G-19125) | | |
| Right/Pointe Company | D | 815 754-5700 |
| Dekalb (G-8115) | | |
| Rockford Chemical Co | G | 815 544-3476 |
| Belvidere (G-1783) | | |
| ▲ RPS Products Inc | G | 847 683-3400 |
| Hampshire (G-11562) | | |
| Rust-Oleum (canada) Ltd | B | 847 367-7700 |
| Vernon Hills (G-21194) | | |
| ◆ Rust-Oleum Corporation | C | 847 367-7700 |
| Vernon Hills (G-21195) | | |
| ◆ Rycoline Products LLC | C | 773 775-6755 |
| Chicago (G-6417) | | |
| Safety Compound Corporation | E | 630 953-1515 |
| Lombard (G-13851) | | |
| Samuel Rowell | G | 618 942-6970 |
| Herrin (G-11754) | | |
| ▼ Sanchem Inc | E | 312 733-6100 |
| Chicago (G-6436) | | |
| Sanford Chemical Co Inc | | 847 437-3530 |
| Elk Grove Village (G-9727) | | |
| Sensory Essence Inc | | 847 526-3645 |
| Island Lake (G-12218) | | |
| ◆ Seymour of Sycamore Inc | C | 815 895-9101 |
| Sycamore (G-20815) | | |
| Siemens Industry Inc | | 618 451-1205 |
| Granite City (G-11303) | | |
| Sika Corporation | G | 815 431-1080 |
| Ottawa (G-16985) | | |
| Solazyme | | 309 258-5695 |
| Peoria (G-17457) | | |
| Solutia Inc | A | 618 482-6536 |
| Sauget (G-19390) | | |
| Solvay Chemicals Inc | E | 618 274-0755 |
| East Saint Louis (G-8769) | | |
| Solvay USA Inc | | 708 235-7200 |
| University Park (G-21062) | | |
| ◆ Specialty Cnstr Brands Inc | F | 630 851-0782 |
| Aurora (G-1081) | | |
| Steroids Ltd | G | 312 996-2364 |
| Chicago (G-6593) | | |
| ▲ Stutz Company | | 773 287-1068 |
| Chicago (G-6610) | | |
| Sun Chemical Corporation | C | 630 513-5348 |
| Saint Charles (G-19274) | | |
| Super-Dri Corp | G | 708 599-8700 |
| Bridgeview (G-2532) | | |
| Swanson Water Treatment Inc | G | 847 680-1113 |
| Libertyville (G-13386) | | |
| Swenson Technology Inc | F | 708 587-2300 |
| Monee (G-15003) | | |
| T D J Group Inc | | 847 639-1113 |
| Cary (G-3374) | | |
| T K O Waterproof Coating LLP | G | 815 338-2006 |
| Woodstock (G-22618) | | |
| Tamms Industries Inc | D | 815 522-3394 |
| Kirkland (G-12719) | | |
| Techdrive Inc | G | 312 567-3910 |
| Chicago (G-6684) | | |
| Technic Inc | | 773 262-2662 |
| Arlington Heights (G-852) | | |
| Technical Ordnance Inc | | 630 969-0620 |
| Downers Grove (G-8531) | | |
| Ted Muller | G | 312 435-0978 |
| Chicago (G-6686) | | |
| The Euclid Chemical Company | F | 815 522-2308 |
| Kirkland (G-12720) | | |
| Tower Oil & Technology Co | E | 773 927-6161 |
| Chicago (G-6752) | | |
| Uniqema Americas | | 773 376-9000 |
| Chicago (G-6818) | | |
| United Gilsonite Laboratories | E | 217 243-7878 |
| Jacksonville (G-12415) | | |
| ◆ Vantage Oleochemicals Inc | E | 773 376-9000 |
| Chicago (G-6872) | | |
| Vantage Oleochemicals Inc | | 773 376-9000 |
| Chicago (G-6874) | | |
| Varn International Inc | E | 630 406-6501 |
| Batavia (G-1516) | | |
| W R Grace & Co | | 414 354-4400 |
| Chicago (G-6922) | | |
| W R Grace & Co - Conn | C | 708 458-0340 |
| Chicago (G-6923) | | |
| W R Grace & Co- Conn | F | 708 458-9700 |
| Chicago (G-6924) | | |
| Wenesco Inc | F | 773 283-3004 |
| Chicago (G-6956) | | |
| Winn Star Inc | G | 618 964-1811 |
| Carbondale (G-3028) | | |
| ▼ Wm Wrigley Jr Company | B | 312 280-4710 |
| Chicago (G-7012) | | |
| Wm Wrigley Jr Company | A | 312 644-2121 |
| Chicago (G-7014) | | |
| Zeller + Gmelin Corporation | | 630 443-8800 |
| Saint Charles (G-19302) | | |

## 29 PETROLEUM REFINING AND RELATED INDUSTRIES

### 2911 Petroleum Refining

| Company | Code | Phone |
|---|---|---|
| 4200 Kirchoff Corp | G | 773 551-1541 |
| Rolling Meadows (G-18705) | | |
| Airgas Inc | F | 773 785-3000 |
| Chicago (G-3786) | | |
| Apple Lube Center | G | 217 787-7035 |
| Springfield (G-20387) | | |
| Arland Clean Fuels LLC | G | 847 868-8580 |
| Evanston (G-10011) | | |
| Blackhawk Biofuels LLC | E | 217 431-6600 |
| Freeport (G-10649) | | |
| ▲ BP America Inc | A | 630 420-5111 |
| Warrenville (G-21344) | | |
| BP Products North America Inc | | 630 420-4300 |
| Naperville (G-15609) | | |
| BP Products North America Inc | D | 312 594-7689 |
| Chicago (G-4153) | | |
| Caibros Americas LLC | | 312 593-3128 |
| Highland Park (G-11826) | | |
| Cartel Holdings Inc | | 815 334-0250 |
| Harvard (G-11625) | | |
| Chicap Pipeline | G | 618 432-5311 |
| Vernon (G-21140) | | |
| Citation Oil & Gas Corp | E | 618 966-2101 |
| Crossville (G-7521) | | |
| Citgo Petroleum Corporation | | 847 818-1800 |
| Downers Grove (G-8411) | | |
| Citgo Petroleum Corporation | | 847 229-1159 |
| Wheeling (G-22026) | | |
| Citgo Petroleum Corporation | F | 847 734-7611 |
| Lemont (G-13233) | | |
| Commax Inc | | 847 995-0994 |
| Schaumburg (G-19476) | | |
| Drig Corporation | G | 312 265-1509 |
| Chicago (G-4644) | | |
| E Z Lube | | 815 439-3980 |
| Joliet (G-12487) | | |
| Equilon Enterprises LLC | F | 312 733-1849 |
| Chicago (G-4768) | | |
| Esi Fuel & Energy Group LLC | G | 716 465-4289 |
| Collinsville (G-7324) | | |
| ET Products LLC | | 800 325-5746 |
| Burr Ridge (G-2839) | | |
| Exxonmobil Pipeline Company | F | 815 423-5571 |
| Elwood (G-9980) | | |
| Gateway Propane LLC | G | 618 286-3005 |
| East Carondelet (G-8614) | | |
| Hydrophi Tech Group Inc | G | 630 981-0098 |
| Oak Brook (G-16523) | | |
| Indilab Inc | E | 847 928-1050 |
| Franklin Park (G-10496) | | |
| Koch Industries Inc | | 312 867-1295 |
| Chicago (G-5394) | | |
| Koppers Industries Inc | E | 708 656-5900 |
| Cicero (G-7209) | | |
| Lamson Oil Company | | 815 226-8090 |
| Rockford (G-18461) | | |
| Lub-Tek Petroleum Products | G | 815 741-0414 |
| Joliet (G-12534) | | |
| Matheson Tri-Gas Inc | E | 815 727-2202 |
| Joliet (G-12539) | | |
| Murphy Oil Usa Inc | | 217 442-7882 |
| Danville (G-7757) | | |
| North American Refining Co | G | 708 762-5117 |
| Mc Cook (G-14454) | | |
| Oxbow Carbon LLC | | 630 257-7751 |
| Lemont (G-13247) | | |
| Oxbow Midwest Calcining LLC | D | 630 257-7751 |
| Lemont (G-13248) | | |
| ▲ Patriot Fuels Biodiesel LLC | F | 309 935-5700 |
| Annawan (G-610) | | |
| Pdv Midwest Refining LLC | A | 630 257-7761 |
| Lemont (G-13254) | | |
| Phillips 66 | D | 618 251-2800 |
| Hartford (G-11614) | | |
| Power Lube LLC | | 847 806-7022 |
| Elk Grove Village (G-9690) | | |
| Raymond D Wright | | 618 783-2206 |
| Newton (G-15947) | | |

Employee Codes: A=Over 500 employees, B=251-500
C=101-250, D=51-100, E=20-50, F=10-19, G=3-9

**Saco Dps/Morris Wax** ....G.... 815 462-0939
New Lenox *(G-15909)*
**Seneca Petroleum Co Inc** ....E.... 708 396-1100
Crestwood *(G-7502)*
**Shell Oil Company** ....C.... 618 254-7371
Wood River *(G-22445)*
**South West Oil Inc** ....F.... 815 416-0400
Morris *(G-15130)*
**Southern Illinois Power Coop** ....G.... 618 995-2371
Buncombe *(G-2799)*
◆ **Standard Oil Company** ....E.... 630 836-5000
Warrenville *(G-21362)*
◆ **Suma America Inc** ....G.... 847 427-7880
Wood Dale *(G-22425)*
**Synsel Energy Inc** ....G.... 630 516-1284
Elmhurst *(G-9947)*
**Vertec Biosolvents Inc** ....G.... 630 960-0600
Downers Grove *(G-8537)*
▲ **W R B Refinery LLC** ....E.... 618 255-2345
Roxana *(G-19087)*

## 2951 Paving Mixtures & Blocks

**Advanced Asphalt Co** ....E.... 815 872-9911
Princeton *(G-17741)*
**All Pro Paving Inc** ....F.... 815 806-2222
Steger *(G-20566)*
**Allied Asphalt Paving Co Inc** ....F.... 847 824-2848
Franklin Park *(G-10390)*
**Allied Asphalt Paving Co Inc** ....E.... 630 289-6080
Elgin *(G-8943)*
**Ambraw Asphalt Materials Inc** ....E.... 618 943-4716
Lawrenceville *(G-13194)*
**Anytime Blacktopping** ....G.... 618 931-6958
Granite City *(G-11266)*
**Arrow Asphalt Paving** ....G.... 618 277-3009
Swansea *(G-20774)*
**Arrow Road Construction Co** ....C.... 847 437-0700
Mount Prospect *(G-15310)*
**Arrow Road Construction Co** ....G.... 847 658-1140
Algonquin *(G-378)*
**Asphalt Maintenance** ....G.... 815 234-7325
Byron *(G-2911)*
**Asphalt Products Inc** ....E.... 618 943-4716
Lawrenceville *(G-13195)*
**Bonsal American Inc** ....D.... 847 678-6220
Franklin Park *(G-10415)*
**Byron Blacktop Inc** ....G.... 815 234-2225
Byron *(G-2913)*
**Certified Asphalt Paving** ....G.... 847 441-5000
Northfield *(G-16396)*
**Cgk Enterprises Inc** ....G.... 847 888-1362
Elgin *(G-8985)*
**Cgk Enterprises Inc** ....E.... 815 942-0080
Morris *(G-15102)*
**Charles E Mahoney Company** ....E.... 618 235-3355
Swansea *(G-20776)*
**Chaulsetts Painting** ....G.... 618 931-6958
Granite City *(G-11270)*
**Christ Bros Products LLC** ....G.... 618 537-6174
Lebanon *(G-13212)*
**Clean Sweep Environmental Inc** ....G.... 630 879-8750
Batavia *(G-1431)*
**Consolidated Paving Inc** ....G.... 309 693-3505
Peoria *(G-17346)*
**Cope & Sons Asphalt** ....G.... 618 462-2207
Alton *(G-567)*
**Corrective Asphalt Mtls LLC** ....G.... 618 254-3855
South Roxana *(G-20312)*
**County Asphalt Inc** ....G.... 618 224-9033
Trenton *(G-20990)*
**Crowley-Sheppard Asphalt Inc** ....F.... 708 499-2900
Chicago Ridge *(G-7145)*
**Cullinan & Sons Inc** ....E.... 309 925-2711
Tremont *(G-20981)*
**Curran Contracting Company** ....E.... 815 455-5100
Crystal Lake *(G-7562)*
**Curran Contracting Company** ....G.... 815 758-8113
Dekalb *(G-8081)*
**Don Anderson Co** ....G.... 618 495-2511
Hoffman *(G-11988)*
**Done Rite Sealcoating Inc** ....G.... 630 830-5310
Streamwood *(G-20651)*
**Dougherty E J Oil & Stone Sup** ....G.... 618 271-4414
East Saint Louis *(G-8748)*
**Du-Kane Asphalt Co** ....G.... 630 953-1500
Addison *(G-101)*
**Emulsicoat Inc** ....F.... 217 344-7775
Urbana *(G-21081)*
**Emulsions Inc** ....G.... 618 943-2615
Lawrenceville *(G-13199)*
**ET Simonds Materials Company** ....E.... 618 457-8191
Carbondale *(G-3007)*
**Fahrner Asphalt Sealers LLC** ....G.... 815 986-1180
Rockford *(G-18379)*
**Ferro Asphalt Company** ....G.... 815 744-6633
Rockdale *(G-18219)*
**Frank S Johnson & Company** ....G.... 847 492-1660
Evanston *(G-10039)*
**Freesen Inc** ....E.... 309 827-4554
Bloomington *(G-2167)*
**Fuller Asphalt & Landscape** ....G.... 618 797-1169
Granite City *(G-11277)*
**G & S Asphalt Inc** ....F.... 217 826-2421
Marshall *(G-14322)*
**General Contractor Inc** ....G.... 618 533-5213
Sandoval *(G-19357)*
**Geneva Construction Company** ....G.... 630 892-6536
North Aurora *(G-16132)*
**Geske and Sons Inc** ....G.... 815 459-2407
Crystal Lake *(G-7582)*
**Geske and Sons Inc** ....F.... 815 459-2407
Crystal Lake *(G-7581)*
**Gorman Brothers Ready Mix Inc** ....F.... 618 498-2173
Jerseyville *(G-12422)*
**Hassebrock Asphalt Sealing** ....G.... 618 566-7214
Mascoutah *(G-14352)*
**Hillyer Inc** ....D.... 309 837-6434
Macomb *(G-14125)*
**Howell Asphalt Company** ....G.... 217 234-8877
Mattoon *(G-14393)*
**Illinois Road Contractors Inc** ....E.... 217 245-6181
Jacksonville *(G-12393)*
**Illinois Valley Paving Co** ....E.... 217 422-1010
Elwin *(G-9977)*
**Jax Asphalt Company Inc** ....F.... 618 244-0500
Mount Vernon *(G-15418)*
▲ **Lafarge North America Inc** ....C.... 703 480-3600
Chicago *(G-5435)*
**Louis Marsch Inc** ....E.... 217 526-3723
Morrisonville *(G-15151)*
**Marathon Petroleum Company LP** ....G.... 618 829-3288
Saint Elmo *(G-19308)*
**Maul Asphalt Sealcoating Inc** ....E.... 630 420-8765
Naperville *(G-15695)*
**Orange Crush LLC** ....E.... 708 544-9440
Hillside *(G-11930)*
**Orange Crush LLC** ....G.... 847 428-6176
East Dundee *(G-8650)*
**Orange Crush LLC** ....G.... 630 739-5560
Romeoville *(G-18856)*
**Orange Crush LLC** ....G.... 847 537-7900
Wheeling *(G-22115)*
**Owens Corning Sales LLC** ....E.... 708 594-6935
Argo *(G-695)*
**Peter Baker & Son Co** ....D.... 847 362-3663
Lake Bluff *(G-12861)*
**Plote Construction Inc** ....D.... 847 695-9300
Hoffman Estates *(G-12036)*
**Plote Inc** ....D.... 847 695-9467
Hoffman Estates *(G-12037)*
**Pothole Pros** ....G.... 847 815-5789
Elgin *(G-9144)*
**Prosser Construction Co** ....F.... 217 774-5032
Shelbyville *(G-19913)*
**Quikrete Companies Inc** ....F.... 309 346-1184
Pekin *(G-17285)*
**Reliable Asphalt Corporation** ....F.... 773 254-1121
Chicago *(G-6328)*
**Reliable Asphalt Corporation** ....G.... 630 497-8700
Bartlett *(G-1368)*
**Rock Road Companies Inc** ....F.... 815 874-2441
Rockford *(G-18564)*
**Route 66 Asphalt Company** ....G.... 630 739-6633
Lemont *(G-13260)*
**Sandeno Inc** ....G.... 815 730-9415
Rockdale *(G-18231)*
**Savanna Quarry Inc** ....G.... 815 273-4208
Savanna *(G-19405)*
**Schulze & Schulze Inc** ....G.... 618 687-1106
Murphysboro *(G-15582)*
**Sealmaster Inc** ....F.... 847 480-7325
Northbrook *(G-16360)*
**Sealmaster/Alsip** ....G.... 708 489-0900
Alsip *(G-527)*
**Seneca Petroleum Co Inc** ....E.... 630 257-2268
Lemont *(G-13262)*
**Sherwin Industries Inc** ....E.... 815 234-8007
Byron *(G-2921)*
**St Clair Tennis Club LLC** ....G.... 618 632-1400
O Fallon *(G-16480)*
**Streator Asphalt Inc** ....G.... 815 672-8683
Streator *(G-20703)*
**Taft Street Company Inc** ....G.... 217 544-3471
Springfield *(G-20541)*
**Terry Terri Mulgrew** ....G.... 815 747-6248
East Dubuque *(G-8625)*
**Thorworks Industries Inc** ....G.... 815 969-0664
Rockford *(G-18650)*
**Tmw Enterprises Paving & Maint** ....E.... 630 350-7717
Bensenville *(G-2004)*
**Tri-State Asphalt LLC** ....G.... 815 942-0080
Morris *(G-15136)*
**Veterans Parking Lot Maint** ....G.... 815 245-7584
Woodstock *(G-22621)*
**William Charles Cnstr Co LLC** ....D.... 815 654-4700
Loves Park *(G-14007)*

## 2952 Asphalt Felts & Coatings

**Allied Asphalt Paving Co Inc** ....E.... 630 289-6080
Elgin *(G-8943)*
**American Asp Surfc Recycl Inc** ....F.... 708 448-9540
Orland Park *(G-16842)*
**American Grinders Inc** ....G.... 815 943-4902
Harvard *(G-11620)*
**Asphalt Maint Systems Inc** ....F.... 815 986-6977
South Beloit *(G-20139)*
**Atlas Roofing Corporation** ....E.... 309 752-7121
East Moline *(G-8670)*
**Black Rock Milling and Pav Co** ....F.... 847 952-0700
Arlington Heights *(G-726)*
**Bonsal American Inc** ....D.... 847 678-6220
Franklin Park *(G-10415)*
**Brewer Company** ....F.... 708 339-9000
Harvey *(G-11662)*
**Co-Fair Corporation** ....E.... 847 626-1500
Skokie *(G-19984)*
**Cofair Products Inc** ....G.... 847 626-1500
Skokie *(G-19985)*
**Complete Asphalt Service Co** ....E.... 217 285-6099
Pittsfield *(G-17567)*
**Complete Flashings Inc** ....G.... 630 595-9725
Bensenville *(G-1864)*
**Cornerstone Building Products** ....G.... 217 543-2829
Arthur *(G-889)*
**Crosscom Inc** ....F.... 630 871-5500
Wheaton *(G-21942)*
**Crown Coatings Company** ....F.... 630 365-9925
Elburn *(G-8881)*
**D N M Sealcoating Inc** ....G.... 630 365-1816
Elburn *(G-8882)*
**Deks North America Inc** ....G.... 312 219-2110
Chicago *(G-4574)*
**Don Anderson Co** ....G.... 618 495-2511
Hoffman *(G-11988)*
**Emulsicoat Inc** ....F.... 217 344-7775
Urbana *(G-21081)*
▼ **Green Roof Solutions Inc** ....G.... 847 297-7936
Glenview *(G-11134)*
**Harsco Corporation** ....F.... 217 237-4335
Pawnee *(G-17234)*
**J and J Prfmce Powdr Coating** ....G.... 309 376-4340
Carlock *(G-3051)*
**Jax Asphalt Company Inc** ....F.... 618 244-0500
Mount Vernon *(G-15418)*
**Jesus People USA Full Gos** ....G.... 773 989-2083
Chicago *(G-5296)*
**Karnak Midwest LLC** ....F.... 708 338-3388
Broadview *(G-2590)*
**Lakefront Roofing Supply** ....E.... 773 509-0400
Chicago *(G-5443)*
**Lifetime Rooftile Company** ....G.... 630 355-7922
Naperville *(G-15689)*
**Miller Purcell Co Inc** ....G.... 815 485-2142
New Lenox *(G-15897)*
▼ **Nataz Specialty Coatings Inc** ....F.... 773 247-7030
Chicago *(G-5856)*
**Nu-Puttie Corporation** ....E.... 708 681-1040
Maywood *(G-14433)*
**Omnimax International Inc** ....E.... 309 747-2937
Gridley *(G-11410)*
**Owens Corning Sales LLC** ....B.... 708 594-6911
Argo *(G-694)*
**Owens Corning Sales LLC** ....E.... 708 594-6935
Argo *(G-695)*
**Plote Inc** ....D.... 847 695-9467
Hoffman Estates *(G-12037)*
**Pure Asphalt Company** ....F.... 773 247-7030
Chicago *(G-6228)*
**R E Burke Roofing Co Inc** ....F.... 847 675-5010
Skokie *(G-20068)*

▼ **RM Lucas Co** E 773 523-4300
Alsip *(G-522)*
▲ **Sales Stretcher Enterprises** F 815 223-9681
Peru *(G-17527)*
**Sheet Metal Supply Ltd** G 847 478-8500
Mundelein *(G-15557)*
**St Louis Flexicore Inc** F 618 531-8691
East Saint Louis *(G-8770)*
**Ted Muller** G 312 435-0978
Chicago *(G-6686)*
**TMJ Architectural LLC** G 815 388-7820
Crystal Lake *(G-7666)*

## 2992 Lubricating Oils & Greases

**Ameriflon Ltd** G 847 541-6000
Wheeling *(G-22004)*
**Amsoil Inc** G 630 595-8385
Bensenville *(G-1835)*
◆ **Atm America Corp** E 800 298-0030
Chicago *(G-3986)*
▲ **Avatar Corporation** D 708 534-5511
University Park *(G-21042)*
**Bioblend Lubricants Intl** G 630 227-1800
Joliet *(G-12466)*
**Boyer Corporation** G 708 352-2553
La Grange *(G-12727)*
**Calumet Lubr Co Ltd Partnr** F 708 832-2463
Burnham *(G-2815)*
**CAM Tek Lubricants Inc** G 708 477-3000
Orland Park *(G-16846)*
**Campbell Camie Inc** E 314 968-3222
Downers Grove *(G-8403)*
**Cargill Incorporated** F 773 375-7255
Chicago *(G-4243)*
**Cartel Holdings Inc** G 815 334-0250
Harvard *(G-11625)*
◆ **Castrol Industrial N Amer Inc** C 877 641-1600
Naperville *(G-15620)*
**Chemix Corp** F 708 754-2150
Glenwood *(G-11215)*
◆ **Chemtool Incorporated** C 815 957-4140
Rockton *(G-18694)*
**Chemtool Incorporated** D 815 459-1250
Crystal Lake *(G-7551)*
**Claire-Sprayway Inc** D 630 628-3000
Downers Grove *(G-8413)*
**CLC Lubricants Company** E 630 232-7900
Geneva *(G-10818)*
**Clean Harbors Wichita LLC** G 815 675-1272
Spring Grove *(G-20330)*
**Comet Supply Inc** G 309 444-2712
Washington *(G-21381)*
**Darling Ingredients Inc** E 217 482-3261
Mason City *(G-14363)*
**Ecli Products LLC** E 630 449-5000
Aurora *(G-1000)*
**Enterprise Oil Co** E 312 487-2025
Chicago *(G-4759)*
**Famous Lubricants Inc** G 773 268-2555
Chicago *(G-4811)*
**Filter Kleen Inc** G 708 447-4666
Lyons *(G-14037)*
◆ **Fuchs Corporation** G 800 323-7755
Harvey *(G-11667)*
**Growmark Energy LLC** G 309 557-6000
Bloomington *(G-2174)*
**Gtx Inc** G 847 699-7421
Des Plaines *(G-8203)*
**Harris Lubricants** G 708 849-1935
Dolton *(G-8370)*
**Havoline Xpress Lube LLC** G 847 221-5724
Palatine *(G-17034)*
**Havoline Xpress Lube LLC** F 224 757-5628
Round Lake *(G-19060)*
**High Performance Lubr LLC** G 815 468-3535
Manteno *(G-14185)*
**Houghton International Inc** F 610 666-4000
Chicago *(G-5121)*
**Huels Oil Company** F 877 338-6277
Carlyle *(G-3054)*
▲ **Ideas Inc** G 630 620-2010
Lombard *(G-13812)*
**Ideas Inc** G 708 596-1055
Harvey *(G-11671)*
▲ **Illini Coolant Management Corp** F 847 966-1079
Morton Grove *(G-15201)*
**Illinois Oil Products Inc** F 309 788-1896
Rock Island *(G-18183)*
**Jcl Specialty Products Inc** G 815 806-2202
Mokena *(G-14876)*
▲ **Jx Nippon Oil & Energy Lubrica** F 847 413-2188
Schaumburg *(G-19594)*
**K & J Synthetic Lubricants** G 630 628-1011
Addison *(G-162)*
**Konzen Chemicals Inc** F 708 878-7636
Matteson *(G-14375)*
**Kostelac Grease Service Inc** E 314 436-7166
Belleville *(G-1646)*
**Lsp Industries Inc** F 815 226-8090
Rockford *(G-18474)*
**Lub-Tek Petroleum Products** G 815 741-0414
Joliet *(G-12534)*
**Lube Rite** G 217 267-7766
Westville *(G-21930)*
▲ **Lubrication Technology Inc** G 740 574-5150
Aurora *(G-1048)*
**Marathon Petroleum Company LP** A 618 544-2121
Robinson *(G-18066)*
**Midwest Recycling Co** E 815 744-4922
Rockdale *(G-18227)*
**Mistic Metal Mover Inc** G 815 875-1371
Princeton *(G-17754)*
**Motor Oil Inc** F 847 956-7550
Elk Grove Village *(G-9639)*
**Mullen Circle Brand Inc** F 847 676-1880
Skokie *(G-20042)*
◆ **Nalco Company LLC** A 630 305-1000
Naperville *(G-15703)*
◆ **Nalco Holding Company** D 630 305-1000
Naperville *(G-15706)*
▲ **Nalco Holdings LLC** A 630 305-1000
Naperville *(G-15707)*
▼ **Nanolube Inc** G 630 706-1250
Lombard *(G-13831)*
**Olympic Petroleum Corporation** D 847 995-0996
Schaumburg *(G-19674)*
◆ **Olympic Petroleum Corporation** D 708 876-7900
Cicero *(G-7223)*
**Pdv Midwest Refining LLC** A 630 257-7761
Lemont *(G-13254)*
**Perkins Products Inc** E 708 458-2000
Bedford Park *(G-1572)*
▲ **Polartech Additives Inc** E 708 458-8450
Bedford Park *(G-1573)*
**Polyenviro Labs Inc** G 708 489-0195
Mokena *(G-14896)*
**Premium Oil Company** F 815 963-3800
Rockford *(G-18540)*
**Rilco Fluid Care** E 309 788-1854
Rock Island *(G-18200)*
**Rock Valley Oil & Chemical Co** E 815 654-2400
Loves Park *(G-13983)*
**Rs Used Oil Services Inc** G 618 781-1717
Roxana *(G-19085)*
**Safety-Kleen Systems Inc** G 618 875-8050
East Saint Louis *(G-8768)*
**Sandstrom Products Company** F 309 523-2121
Port Byron *(G-17724)*
▲ **Shima American Corporation** F 630 760-4330
Itasca *(G-12353)*
**Spartacus Group Inc** F 815 637-1574
Machesney Park *(G-14108)*
**Specialized Separators Inc** F 815 316-0626
Rockford *(G-18625)*
**Speedco Inc** G 618 931-1575
Granite City *(G-11304)*
**Strebor Specialties LLC** E 618 286-1140
Dupo *(G-8580)*
**Superior Graphite Co** E 708 458-0006
Chicago *(G-6633)*
▲ **Syn-Tech Ltd** E 630 628-3044
Addison *(G-303)*
**Tower Oil & Technology Co** E 773 927-6161
Chicago *(G-6752)*
**Truckers Oil Pros Inc** F 773 523-8990
Chicago *(G-6785)*
▲ **Uberlube Inc** G 847 372-3127
Evanston *(G-10103)*
▲ **Viscosity Oil Company** E 630 850-4000
Willowbrook *(G-22237)*
**William Ingram** G 217 442-5075
Danville *(G-7785)*

## 2999 Products Of Petroleum & Coal, NEC

**Chemalloy Company LLC** E
Rosemont *(G-18993)*
**Koch Industries Inc** E 773 375-3700
Chicago *(G-5395)*
**Price Tech Group Illinois LLC** G 815 521-4667
Channahon *(G-3583)*
**Raven Energy LLC** G 217 532-3983
Hillsboro *(G-11899)*

# 30 RUBBER AND MISCELLANEOUS PLASTICS PRODUCTS

## 3011 Tires & Inner Tubes

**Best Designs Inc** F 618 985-4445
Carterville *(G-3309)*
▲ **Brahlers Truckers Supply Inc** E 217 243-6471
Jacksonville *(G-12380)*
**Bridgestone Americas** F 309 452-4411
Normal *(G-16066)*
**Bridgestone Ret Operations LLC** F 630 893-6336
Glendale Heights *(G-11012)*
**C&C Sealants** F 708 717-0686
Elgin *(G-8975)*
**Continental Tire Americas LLC** G 618 242-7100
Mount Vernon *(G-15407)*
**Continental Tire Americas LLC** G 618 246-2585
Mascoutah *(G-14351)*
**Continental Tire Americas LLC** A 618 246-2466
Mount Vernon *(G-15406)*
**Dealer Tire LLC** G 847 671-0683
Franklin Park *(G-10454)*
**Dyneer Corporation** B 217 228-6011
Quincy *(G-17823)*
**Joseph Coppolino** G 773 735-8647
Chicago *(G-5328)*
**Kraly Tire Repair Materials** G 708 863-5981
Cicero *(G-7211)*
**Liberty Tire Recycling LLC** G 773 871-6360
Chicago *(G-5502)*
**Mecanica En General Santoyo** G 708 652-2217
Cicero *(G-7219)*
▲ **Otr Wheel Engineering Inc** E 217 223-7705
Quincy *(G-17864)*
▲ **Stop & Go International Inc** G 815 455-9080
Crystal Lake *(G-7654)*
**Tbc Corporation** G 630 428-2233
Naperville *(G-15760)*
◆ **Titan International Inc** B 217 228-6011
Quincy *(G-17896)*
**Titan Tire Corporation** B 217 228-6011
Quincy *(G-17897)*
**Titan Tyre Corporation** G 217 228-6011
Freeport *(G-10692)*

## 3021 Rubber & Plastic Footwear

**Crocs Inc** F 630 820-3572
Aurora *(G-988)*
**Honeywell Safety Pdts USA Inc** C 309 786-7741
Rock Island *(G-18182)*
▲ **Leos Dancewear Inc** D 773 889-7700
River Forest *(G-17998)*
**Nike Inc** E 773 846-5460
Chicago *(G-5918)*
**Nike Inc** E 630 585-9568
Aurora *(G-1056)*
**Plastic Specialists America** G 847 406-7547
Gurnee *(G-11486)*
**Polyconversions Inc** E 217 893-3330
Rantoul *(G-17935)*
**Standard Safety Equipment Co** E 815 363-8565
McHenry *(G-14556)*
**Vans Inc** G 847 673-0628
Skokie *(G-20108)*

## 3052 Rubber & Plastic Hose & Belting

◆ **Ammeraal Beltech Inc** D 847 673-6720
Skokie *(G-19953)*
◆ **Bando Usa Inc** E 630 773-6600
Itasca *(G-12234)*
▲ **Behabelt USA** G 630 521-9835
Bensenville *(G-1842)*
**Bristol Hose & Fitting Inc** E 708 492-3456
Northlake *(G-16430)*
**Bristol Transport Inc** E 708 343-6411
Northlake *(G-16431)*
**Caterpillar Inc** A 309 578-2473
Mossville *(G-15250)*
**Chemi-Flex LLC** E 630 627-9650
Lombard *(G-13776)*
**Gates Corporation** C 309 343-7171
Galesburg *(G-10752)*
**Geib Industries Inc** E 847 455-4550
Bensenville *(G-1906)*
**Gusco Silicone Rbr & Svcs LLC** G 773 770-5008
Aurora *(G-1165)*

S I C

Employee Codes: A=Over 500 employees, B=251-500
C=101-250, D=51-100, E=20-50, F=10-19, G=3-9
2017 Harris Illinois
Industrial Directory
1001

**Industrial Rubber & Sup Entp** G 217 429-3747
Decatur *(G-7895)*
▲ **Jason of Illinois Inc** E 630 752-0600
Carol Stream *(G-3176)*
▲ **Kanaflex Corporation Illinois** G 847 634-6100
Vernon Hills *(G-21177)*
**Kemper Industries** G 217 826-5712
Marshall *(G-14324)*
▲ **Kuriyama of America Inc** D 847 755-0360
Schaumburg *(G-19608)*
**Lanmar Inc** G 800 233-5520
Northbrook *(G-16293)*
**Molds & Tooling** G 630 627-9650
Lombard *(G-13828)*
**Pix North America Inc** E 217 516-8348
Danville *(G-7760)*
▲ **Power Port Products Inc** E 630 628-9102
Addison *(G-249)*
**Quad City Hose** E 563 386-8936
Taylor Ridge *(G-20830)*
**Robbi Joy Eklow** G 847 223-0460
Third Lake *(G-20858)*
**Royal Brass Inc** G 618 439-6341
Benton *(G-2040)*
◆ **Suncast Corporation** A 630 879-2050
Batavia *(G-1501)*
▲ **Team Products Inc** F 815 244-6100
Mount Carroll *(G-15293)*
▲ **Tigerflex Corporation** A 847 439-1766
Elk Grove Village *(G-9779)*
**Voss Belting & Specialty Co** E 847 673-8900
Lincolnwood *(G-13541)*
▲ **W J Dennis & Company** F 847 697-4800
Elgin *(G-9225)*
**Western Consolidated Tech Inc** G 815 334-3684
Woodstock *(G-22623)*

## *3053 Gaskets, Packing & Sealing Devices*

▲ **Advantage Seal Inc** F 630 226-0200
Bolingbrook *(G-2277)*
**All American Washer Werks Inc** E 847 566-9091
Mundelein *(G-15468)*
**All-State Industries Inc** D 847 350-0460
Elk Grove Village *(G-9286)*
▲ **American Gasket Tech Inc** D 630 543-1510
Addison *(G-36)*
**Better Gaskets Inc** G 847 276-7635
Ingleside *(G-12187)*
▲ **Black Swan Manufacturing Co** F 773 227-3700
Chicago *(G-4121)*
**Cal-Ill Gasket Co** F 773 287-9605
Chicago *(G-4213)*
▲ **CFC International Corporation** C 708 323-4131
Chicago Heights *(G-7087)*
**Chambers Gasket & Mfg Co** E 773 626-8800
Chicago *(G-4286)*
▲ **Chicago-Wilcox Mfg Co** E 708 339-5000
South Holland *(G-20257)*
**Dana Sealing Manufacturing LLC** B 618 544-8651
Robinson *(G-18061)*
**Dike-O-Seal Incorporated** F 773 254-3224
Chicago *(G-4603)*
**Excelsior Inc** G 815 987-2900
Rockford *(G-18376)*
**Excelsior Inc** E 815 987-2900
Rockford *(G-18375)*
**Federal-Mogul Corporation** A 847 674-7700
Skokie *(G-19999)*
**Federal-Mogul Corporation** E 248 354-7700
Berwyn *(G-2065)*
**Flatout Group Llc** G 847 837-9200
Mundelein *(G-15501)*
**Flowserve Fsd Corporation** D 630 783-1468
Woodridge *(G-22479)*
**Flowserve US Inc** E 630 655-5700
Burr Ridge *(G-2842)*
▲ **Fluid-Aire Dynamics Inc** E 847 678-8388
Schaumburg *(G-19531)*
▲ **Gasket & Seal Fabricators Inc** E 314 241-3673
East Saint Louis *(G-8752)*
◆ **Grumen Manufacturing Inc** G 847 473-2233
Gurnee *(G-11455)*
**Hennig Gasket & Seals Inc** G 312 243-8270
Chicago *(G-5071)*
**Illinois Tool Works Inc** C 708 325-2300
Bridgeview *(G-2498)*
**Ilpea Industries Inc** D 309 343-3332
Galesburg *(G-10760)*
**Innovative Automation** G 708 418-8720
Lansing *(G-13166)*
**Inpro/Seal LLC** C 309 787-8940
Rock Island *(G-18184)*
▲ **Intech Industries Inc** F 847 487-5599
Wauconda *(G-21473)*
**J & J Industries Inc** G 630 595-8878
Bensenville *(G-1925)*
▲ **James Walker Mfg Co** E 708 754-4020
Glenwood *(G-11217)*
▲ **John Crane Inc** A 312 605-7800
Chicago *(G-5313)*
**John Crane Inc** G 847 967-2400
Morton Grove *(G-15207)*
▲ **Jsn Inc** E 708 410-1800
Maywood *(G-14426)*
**L A D Specialties** G 708 430-1588
Oak Lawn *(G-16630)*
**Lamons Gasket Company** G 815 744-3902
Joliet *(G-12532)*
**M Cor Inc** F 630 860-1150
Bensenville *(G-1943)*
**McAllister Equipment Co** E 217 789-0351
Lincolnshire *(G-13464)*
**Midwest Sealing Products Inc** E 847 459-2202
Buffalo Grove *(G-2737)*
▲ **Modern Silicone Tech Inc** F 727 507-9800
Bannockburn *(G-1262)*
▲ **Non-Metals Inc** G 630 378-9866
Bolingbrook *(G-2354)*
**Plastic Specialties & Tech Inc** E 847 781-2414
Schaumburg *(G-19693)*
▲ **Plitek** D 847 827-6680
Des Plaines *(G-8257)*
▲ **Pres-On Corporation** E 630 628-2255
Bolingbrook *(G-2360)*
**Punch Products Manufacturing** E 773 533-2800
Chicago *(G-6226)*
◆ **Qcc LLC** C 708 867-5400
Harwood Heights *(G-11689)*
**Rhopac Fabricated Products LLC** E 847 362-3300
Libertyville *(G-13376)*
▲ **Rt Enterprises Inc** F 847 675-1444
Skokie *(G-20080)*
**Rutgers Enterprises Inc** G 847 674-7666
Lincolnwood *(G-13535)*
**Seals & Components Inc** G 708 895-5222
Lansing *(G-13182)*
**Sealtec** F 630 692-0633
Oswego *(G-16932)*
**SKF USA Inc** D 847 742-0700
Elgin *(G-9184)*
**SKF USA Inc** D 847 742-0700
Elgin *(G-9185)*
**SKF USA Inc** D 847 742-0700
Elgin *(G-9186)*
**Southland Industries Inc** E 757 543-5701
Bannockburn *(G-1265)*
**Standard Rubber Products Co** E 847 593-5630
Elk Grove Village *(G-9751)*
**Supreme Felt & Abrasives Inc** E 708 344-0134
Cicero *(G-7234)*
**Transco Products Inc** E 815 672-2197
Streator *(G-20709)*
**Trellborg Sling Sltions US Inc** D 630 289-1500
Streamwood *(G-20677)*
▲ **Triseal Corporation** E 815 648-2473
Hebron *(G-11728)*
▲ **Union Street Tin Co** G 312 379-8200
Park Ridge *(G-17227)*
**Unipaq Inc** G 773 252-3000
Chicago *(G-6817)*
▲ **United Gasket Corporation** D 708 656-3700
Cicero *(G-7242)*
**Vangard Distribution Inc** G 708 484-9895
Berwyn *(G-2077)*
▲ **Vangard Distribution Inc** G 708 588-8400
Brookfield *(G-2646)*
**Vanseal Corporation** D 618 283-4700
Vandalia *(G-21130)*
**Vibracoustic Usa Inc** C 618 382-2318
Carmi *(G-3082)*
**Winner Cutting & Stamping Co** F 630 963-1800
Downers Grove *(G-8546)*
**Woods Manufacturing Co Inc** G 630 595-6620
Wood Dale *(G-22438)*

## *3061 Molded, Extruded & Lathe-Cut Rubber Mechanical Goods*

**All-State Industries Inc** D 847 350-0460
Elk Grove Village *(G-9286)*
**Andrews Automotive Company** F 773 768-1122
Chicago *(G-3903)*
**Aztec Products** G 217 726-8631
Springfield *(G-20393)*
**Calumet Rubber Corp** G 773 536-6350
Chicago *(G-4219)*
▼ **Custom Seal & Rubber Products** G 888 356-2966
Mount Morris *(G-15295)*
**Elk Grove Rubber & Plastic Co** F 630 543-5656
Addison *(G-109)*
**Excelsior Inc** E 815 987-2900
Rockford *(G-18375)*
▲ **Fairchild Industries Inc** E 847 550-9580
Lake Zurich *(G-13071)*
▲ **Fmi Inc** D 847 350-1535
Elk Grove Village *(G-9481)*
**Industrial Roller Co** F 618 234-0740
Smithton *(G-20121)*
▲ **James Walker Mfg Co** E 708 754-4020
Glenwood *(G-11217)*
▲ **Kokoku Rubber Inc** G 847 517-6770
Schaumburg *(G-19601)*
◆ **Mac Lean-Fogg Company** D 847 566-0010
Mundelein *(G-15521)*
▲ **Modern Silicone Tech Inc** F 727 507-9800
Bannockburn *(G-1262)*
**Nilan/Primarc Tool & Mold Inc** F 847 885-2300
Hoffman Estates *(G-12030)*
**Rotation Dynamics Corporation** D 773 247-5600
Chicago *(G-6399)*
▲ **Rt Enterprises Inc** F 847 675-1444
Skokie *(G-20080)*
**Sage Products LLC** G 815 455-4700
Crystal Lake *(G-7645)*
**Sanyo Seiki America Corp** F 630 876-8270
West Chicago *(G-21768)*
**Smart Solutions Inc** G 630 775-1517
Itasca *(G-12354)*
**Standard Rubber Products Co** E 847 593-5630
Elk Grove Village *(G-9751)*
**Systems By Lar Inc** G 815 694-3141
Clifton *(G-7275)*
**Vibracoustic Usa Inc** E 618 382-5891
Carmi *(G-3081)*
**Vibracoustic Usa Inc** C 618 382-2318
Carmi *(G-3082)*
**Weiland Fast Trac Inc** G 847 438-7996
Long Grove *(G-13905)*

## *3069 Fabricated Rubber Prdts, NEC*

▲ **A Lakin & Sons Inc** E 773 871-6360
Montgomery *(G-15026)*
**A R B C Inc** F 815 777-6006
Galena *(G-10714)*
**Access Casters** G 773 881-4186
Chicago *(G-3714)*
▲ **Accurate Products Incorporated** E 773 878-2200
Chicago *(G-3722)*
**Adapt Seals Co** G 309 463-2482
Varna *(G-21132)*
**Adhes Tape Technology Inc** G 847 496-7949
Arlington Heights *(G-702)*
▲ **Aero Rubber Company Inc** E 800 662-1009
Tinley Park *(G-20886)*
◆ **Alessco Inc** F 773 327-7919
Chicago *(G-3801)*
**Arizon Strctures Worldwide LLC** E 618 451-7250
Granite City *(G-11267)*
**Aztec Products** G 217 726-8631
Springfield *(G-20393)*
**Balloon Art By Dj** G 815 736-6123
Newark *(G-15932)*
▲ **Barriersafe Solutions Intl Inc** E 847 735-0163
Lake Forest *(G-12884)*
◆ **Bls Enterprises Inc** F 630 766-1300
Bensenville *(G-1844)*
**Boss Balloon Company Inc** G 309 852-2131
Kewanee *(G-12672)*
▲ **Boss Holdings Inc** D 309 852-2131
Kewanee *(G-12673)*
▲ **Bows Arts Inc** F 847 501-3161
Glenview *(G-11109)*
**Caroline Cole Inc** F 618 233-0600
Belleville *(G-1617)*
**Central Rbr Extrusions Ill Inc** G 618 654-1171
Highland *(G-11778)*
▲ **CTI Industries Corporation** C 847 382-1000
Lake Barrington *(G-12804)*
**CTI Industries Corporation** D 800 284-5605
Lake Zurich *(G-13060)*

▲ **Custom Product Innovations** ............G ....... 618 628-0111
Lebanon *(G-13214)*
▼ **Custom Seal & Rubber Products** .....G ....... 888 356-2966
Mount Morris *(G-15295)*
**Dans Rubber Stamp & Signs** ................G ....... 815 964-5603
Rockford *(G-18333)*
**Davis Athletic Equipment Co** ................F ....... 708 563-9006
Bedford Park *(G-1547)*
**Day International Group Inc** .................D ....... 630 406-6501
Batavia *(G-1437)*
**Dennis Carnes** ......................................G ....... 618 244-1770
Mount Vernon *(G-15410)*
**Diamond Tool & Mold Inc** .....................G ....... 630 543-7011
Addison *(G-90)*
**Dyneer Corporation** ..............................B ....... 217 228-6011
Quincy *(G-17823)*
▲ **Edgewater Products Company Inc** ...F ....... 708 345-9200
Melrose Park *(G-14629)*
▲ **Essentra Specialty Tapes Inc** ...........C ....... 708 488-1025
Forest Park *(G-10242)*
**Excelsior Inc** .........................................E ....... 815 987-2900
Rockford *(G-18375)*
**Female Health Company** .......................E ....... 312 595-9123
Chicago *(G-4835)*
▲ **Fenwal Inc** ............................................B ....... 847 550-2300
Lake Zurich *(G-13072)*
**Fenwal Holdings Inc** ..............................B ....... 847 550-2300
Lake Zurich *(G-13073)*
**Finzer Holding LLC** ...............................G ....... 847 390-6200
Des Plaines *(G-8198)*
◆ **Finzer Roller Inc** .................................E ....... 847 390-6200
Des Plaines *(G-8199)*
▲ **Flexan LLC** ...........................................C ....... 773 685-6446
Chicago *(G-4860)*
▲ **Flexicraft Industries Inc** ......................F ....... 312 738-3588
Chicago *(G-4861)*
**Go Steady LLC** .......................................G ....... 630 293-3243
West Chicago *(G-21709)*
**Gusco Silicone Rbr & Svcs LLC** ...........G ....... 773 770-5008
Aurora *(G-1165)*
**Hst Materials Inc** ...................................F ....... 847 640-1803
Elk Grove Village *(G-9527)*
**Hydac Rubber Manufacturing** ...............E ....... 618 233-2129
Smithton *(G-20120)*
**Industrial Roller Co** ................................F ....... 618 234-0740
Smithton *(G-20121)*
**Industrial Roller Co** ................................F ....... 618 234-0740
Smithton *(G-20122)*
**James Ray Monroe Corporation** ............F ....... 618 532-4575
Centralia *(G-3420)*
**Jessup Manufacturing Company** ..........E ....... 847 362-0961
Lake Bluff *(G-12851)*
▼ **Jvi Inc** ....................................................E ....... 847 675-1560
Lincolnwood *(G-13517)*
▲ **Kelco Industries Inc** ............................G ....... 815 334-3600
Woodstock *(G-22577)*
**Lakin General Corporation** ....................D ....... 773 871-6360
Montgomery *(G-15054)*
**Ljm Equipment Co** .................................G ....... 847 291-0162
Northbrook *(G-16297)*
**Lochman Ref Silk Screen Co** ................F ....... 847 475-6266
Evanston *(G-10065)*
▲ **Loop Attachment Co** ...........................G ....... 847 922-0642
Chicago *(G-5538)*
**Medical Resource Inc** ............................G ....... 847 249-0854
Gurnee *(G-11470)*
**Menges Roller Co Inc** ............................E ....... 847 487-8877
Wauconda *(G-21482)*
**Midwest Sealing Products Inc** ..............E ....... 847 459-2202
Buffalo Grove *(G-2737)*
**Moon Jump Inc** .......................................G ....... 630 983-0953
Addison *(G-219)*
**Morrow Shoe and Boot Inc** ....................G ....... 217 342-6833
Effingham *(G-8848)*
**Omni Products Inc** .................................G ....... 815 344-3100
McHenry *(G-14539)*
**Pamarco Global Graphics Inc** ...............F ....... 847 459-6000
Wheeling *(G-22118)*
**Polyonics Rubber Co** ............................G ....... 815 765-2033
Poplar Grove *(G-17716)*
**Praire State Floor Covering** ..................G ....... 309 253-5982
Pekin *(G-17283)*
**Prestige Motor Works Inc** ......................G ....... 630 780-6439
Naperville *(G-15823)*
**Pro Form Industries Inc** ........................G ....... 815 923-2555
Union *(G-21038)*
**Rahco Rubber Inc** .................................D ....... 847 298-4200
Des Plaines *(G-8267)*
▲ **RDF Inc** ..................................................F ....... 618 273-4141
Eldorado *(G-8922)*
**Rehling & Associates Inc** ......................G ....... 630 941-3560
Elmhurst *(G-9929)*
**Reilly Foam Corp** ...................................E ....... 630 392-2680
Naperville *(G-15740)*
**Roho Inc** .................................................C ....... 618 277-9173
Belleville *(G-1672)*
**Roho Inc** .................................................C ....... 618 234-4899
Belleville *(G-1673)*
**Rotation Dynamics Corporation** ............E ....... 630 679-7053
Romeoville *(G-18865)*
**Rutgers Enterprises Inc** .........................G ....... 847 674-7666
Lincolnwood *(G-13535)*
**Secon Rubber and Plastics Inc** .............E ....... 618 282-7700
Red Bud *(G-17948)*
**Shore Capital Partners LLC** ..................F ....... 312 348-7580
Chicago *(G-6499)*
**Smith Industrial Rubber & Plas** .............F ....... 815 874-5364
Rockford *(G-18622)*
**Southland Industries Inc** .......................E ....... 757 543-5701
Bannockburn *(G-1265)*
◆ **Sponge-Cushion Inc** ............................D ....... 815 942-2300
Morris *(G-15131)*
**Standard Rubber Products Co** ..............E ....... 847 593-5630
Elk Grove Village *(G-9751)*
**Superior Bumpers Inc** ...........................G ....... 630 932-4910
Lombard *(G-13862)*
▲ **Superior Mfg Group - Europe** ..............F ....... 708 458-4600
Chicago *(G-6635)*
**Tholeo Design Inc** ..................................G ....... 630 325-3792
Clarendon Hills *(G-7260)*
**Tools Aviation LLC** .................................G ....... 630 377-7260
Saint Charles *(G-19285)*
**Traeyne Corporation** .............................G ....... 309 936-7878
Atkinson *(G-945)*
**Verona Rubber Works Inc** .....................F ....... 815 673-2929
Blackstone *(G-2089)*
**Verona Rubber Works Inc** .....................F ....... 815 673-2929
Blackstone *(G-2090)*
**Vestitrak Intl Inc** .....................................E ....... 312 236-7100
Chicago *(G-6890)*
**Voss Belting & Specialty Co** .................E ....... 847 673-8900
Lincolnwood *(G-13541)*
▲ **W J Dennis & Company** ........................F ....... 847 697-4800
Elgin *(G-9225)*
**Weiland Fast Trac Inc** ............................G ....... 847 438-7996
Long Grove *(G-13905)*
**Winfield Technology Inc** ........................F ....... 630 584-0475
Saint Charles *(G-19297)*
**Winfun Usa LLC** .....................................G ....... 630 942-8464
Glen Ellyn *(G-10995)*

## *3081 Plastic Unsupported Sheet & Film*

**A B Kelly Inc** ...........................................G ....... 847 639-1022
Cary *(G-3320)*
▲ **Aargus Plastics Inc** ..............................C ....... 847 325-4444
Wheeling *(G-21995)*
**Abbott Plastics & Supply Co** .................E ....... 815 874-8500
Rockford *(G-18246)*
**Alpha Industries MGT Inc** .....................D ....... 773 359-8000
Chicago *(G-3828)*
◆ **Amcor Flexibles LLC** ............................C ....... 224 313-7000
Buffalo Grove *(G-2656)*
**Avery Dennison Corporation** ..................D ....... 877 214-0909
Niles *(G-15962)*
▲ **Bema Inc** ...............................................D ....... 630 279-7800
Elmhurst *(G-9839)*
**Berry Global Films LLC** ..........................D ....... 708 239-4619
Alsip *(G-442)*
**C M F Enterprises Inc** ............................F ....... 847 526-9499
Wauconda *(G-21450)*
**Cadillac Products Packaging Co** ...........C ....... 217 463-1444
Paris *(G-17142)*
**Camo Clad Inc** ........................................F ....... 618 342-6860
Mounds *(G-15258)*
**Cast Films Inc** .........................................F ....... 847 808-0363
Wheeling *(G-22024)*
**Catalina Coating & Plas Inc** ...................F ....... 847 806-1340
Elk Grove Village *(G-9358)*
**CFC International Inc** .............................G ....... 708 891-3456
Chicago Heights *(G-7086)*
▲ **CFC International Corporation** .............C ....... 708 323-4131
Chicago Heights *(G-7087)*
▲ **Clear Focus Imaging Inc** ......................E ....... 707 544-7990
Franklin Park *(G-10436)*
**Clear Pack Company** ..............................C ....... 847 957-6282
Franklin Park *(G-10437)*
**Clorox Company** .....................................E ....... 510 271-7000
Willowbrook *(G-22204)*
▲ **Co-Ordinated Packaging Inc** ................F ....... 847 559-8877
Northbrook *(G-16228)*
**Cope Plastics Inc** ....................................F ....... 630 226-1664
Bolingbrook *(G-2288)*
◆ **Cosmo Films Inc** ...................................E ....... 630 458-5200
Addison *(G-82)*
**Custom Films Inc** ....................................F ....... 217 826-2326
Marshall *(G-14320)*
**Custom Plastics of Peoria** ......................G ....... 309 697-2888
Bartonville *(G-1394)*
▼ **Design Packaging Company Inc** .........E ....... 847 835-3327
Glencoe *(G-10998)*
▲ **E-Z Products Inc** ...................................F ....... 847 551-9199
Gilberts *(G-10918)*
**Environetics Inc** ......................................F ....... 815 838-8331
Lockport *(G-13715)*
▲ **Exclusively Expo** ...................................E ....... 630 378-4600
Romeoville *(G-18821)*
▲ **Fisher Container Corp** ..........................D ....... 847 541-0000
Buffalo Grove *(G-2694)*
**Fisher Container Holdings LLC** ..............G ....... 847 541-0000
Buffalo Grove *(G-2695)*
**Flex-O-Glass Inc** .....................................D ....... 773 261-5200
Chicago *(G-4858)*
**Flex-O-Glass Inc** .....................................G ....... 773 379-7878
Chicago *(G-4859)*
**Flex-O-Glass Inc** .....................................E ....... 815 288-1424
Dixon *(G-8331)*
**Formco Plastics Inc** ................................F ....... 630 860-7998
Bensenville *(G-1901)*
**Fox Enterprises Inc** .................................G ....... 630 513-9010
Saint Charles *(G-19188)*
**G-P Manufacturing Co Inc** ......................E ....... 847 473-9001
Waukegan *(G-21561)*
**H H Interantional Inc** ...............................G ....... 847 697-7805
Elgin *(G-9054)*
▲ **Highland Mfg & Sls Co** ..........................D ....... 618 654-2161
Highland *(G-11789)*
▲ **Highland Supply Corporation** ...............B ....... 618 654-2161
Highland *(G-11794)*
**Huntsman Expndable Polymers Lc** .........C ....... 815 224-5463
Peru *(G-17512)*
**Jordan Specialty Plastics Inc** .................G ....... 847 945-5591
Deerfield *(G-8021)*
**Kns Companies Inc** .................................F ....... 630 665-9010
Carol Stream *(G-3181)*
**Kw Plastics** ..............................................F ....... 708 757-5140
Chicago *(G-5415)*
**Letters Unlimited Inc** ...............................G ....... 847 891-7811
Schaumburg *(G-19615)*
**Major Prime Plastics Inc** ..........................G ....... 630 953-4111
Addison *(G-189)*
◆ **Midwest Canvas Corp** ...........................C ....... 773 287-4400
Chicago *(G-5742)*
**Midwest Lminating Coatings Inc** .............E ....... 708 653-9500
Alsip *(G-493)*
**Midwest Marketing Distrs Inc** .................G ....... 309 663-6972
Bloomington *(G-2199)*
▲ **Midwest Marketing Distrs Inc** ...............F ....... 309 688-8858
Peoria *(G-17408)*
▲ **Minigrip Inc** .............................................D ....... 845 680-2710
Ottawa *(G-16969)*
▲ **Morton Group Ltd** ...................................G ....... 847 831-2766
Highland Park *(G-11857)*
**Multi-Plastics Inc** .....................................E ....... 630 226-0580
Bolingbrook *(G-2348)*
▲ **Multifilm Packaging Corp** ......................D ....... 847 695-7600
Elgin *(G-9116)*
▲ **Neptune USA Inc** ....................................G ....... 847 987-3804
Schaumburg *(G-19663)*
**Orbis Rpm LLC** ........................................F ....... 217 876-8655
Decatur *(G-7922)*
**Orbis Rpm LLC** ........................................G ....... 309 697-1549
Bartonville *(G-1398)*
**Orbis Rpm LLC** ........................................G ....... 773 376-9775
Chicago *(G-6003)*
**Packaging AM Inc** ....................................G ....... 630 568-9506
Burr Ridge *(G-2872)*
**Perfect Circle Projectiles LLC** .................F ....... 847 367-8960
Lake Forest *(G-12942)*
▲ **Piper Plastics Inc** ...................................D ....... 847 367-0110
Libertyville *(G-13369)*
▼ **Pliant LLC** ...............................................A ....... 812 424-2904
Rolling Meadows *(G-18763)*
**Pliant Corp International** .........................G ....... 847 969-3300
Rolling Meadows *(G-18764)*
**Pliant Corporation of Canada** ..................G ....... 847 969-3300
Schaumburg *(G-19695)*
**Pliant Investment Inc** ...............................G ....... 847 969-3300
Schaumburg *(G-19696)*
**Pliant Solutions Corporation** ...................E ....... 847 969-3300
Schaumburg *(G-19697)*

S
I
C

# 30 RUBBER AND MISCELLANEOUS PLASTICS PRODUCTS

▲ Poli-Film America Inc .................. D ...... 847 453-8104
  Hampshire (G-11559)
Poly Films Inc .................................. G ...... 708 547-7963
  Hillside (G-11931)
Polyair Inter Pack Inc ..................... D ...... 773 995-1818
  Chicago (G-6153)
Printpack Inc .................................. C ...... 847 888-7150
  Elgin (G-9148)
◆ Protective Products Intl ................ G ...... 847 526-1180
  Wauconda (G-21495)
Realt Images Inc ............................ G ...... 217 567-3487
  Tower Hill (G-20980)
Reynolds Food Packaging LLC ....... C ...... 847 482-3500
  Lake Forest (G-12953)
Sandee Manufacturing Co .............. G ...... 847 671-1335
  Franklin Park (G-10581)
◆ Scholle Ipn Corporation ............... F ...... 708 562-7290
  Northlake (G-16450)
Senoplast USA ............................... G ...... 630 898-0731
  Aurora (G-1077)
Signode Industrial Group LLC ........ E ...... 847 483-1490
  Glenview (G-11199)
Sisco Corporation .......................... E ...... 618 327-3066
  Nashville (G-15847)
Sofiflex LLC ................................... F ...... 847 261-4849
  Schiller Park (G-19874)
Sonoco Products Company ............ C ...... 847 957-6282
  Franklin Park (G-10591)
▲ Summit Plastics Inc ..................... G ...... 815 578-8700
  McHenry (G-14558)
▲ Sun Process Converting Inc ........ D ...... 847 593-5656
  Mount Prospect (G-15376)
▲ Tee Group Films Inc ................... D ...... 815 894-2331
  Ladd (G-12792)
Thermal Industries Inc ................... E ...... 800 237-0560
  Wood Dale (G-22430)
◆ Transcendia Inc .......................... C ...... 847 678-1800
  Franklin Park (G-10609)
Transilwrap Company Inc .............. E ...... 847 678-1800
  Franklin Park (G-10611)
▼ Transworld Plastic Films Inc ....... F ...... 815 561-7117
  Rochelle (G-18112)
Tredegar Film Products Corp ......... E ...... 847 438-2111
  Lake Zurich (G-13138)
Unique Blister Company ................. F ...... 630 289-1232
  Bartlett (G-1383)
Vacumet Corp ................................ F ...... 708 562-7290
  Northlake (G-16458)
W R Grace & Co ............................ C ...... 773 838-3200
  Chicago (G-6920)
Western Plastics Inc ...................... F ...... 630 629-3034
  Addison (G-342)

## 3082 Plastic Unsupported Profile Shapes

Abbott Plastics & Supply Co .......... E ...... 815 874-8500
  Rockford (G-18246)
▲ Advanced Plastic Corp ................ D ...... 847 674-2070
  Lincolnwood (G-13501)
▲ Atlas Fibre Company .................. D ...... 847 674-1234
  Northbrook (G-16208)
Custom Films Inc ........................... F ...... 217 826-2326
  Marshall (G-14320)
Custom Plastics of Peoria .............. G ...... 309 697-2888
  Bartonville (G-1394)
▲ Engineered Plastic Systems LLC ... F ...... 800 480-2327
  Elgin (G-9029)
Flex-O-Glass Inc ............................ D ...... 773 261-5200
  Chicago (G-4858)
Flex-O-Glass Inc ............................ G ...... 773 379-7878
  Chicago (G-4859)
Flex-O-Glass Inc ............................ E ...... 815 288-1424
  Dixon (G-8331)
G-P Manufacturing Co Inc ............. E ...... 847 473-9001
  Waukegan (G-21561)
Jabat Inc ........................................ E ...... 618 392-3010
  Olney (G-16773)
Polytec Plastics Inc ........................ E ...... 630 584-8282
  Saint Charles (G-19236)
Rampart LLC .................................. G ...... 847 367-8960
  Lake Forest (G-12950)
Resinite Corporation ...................... C ...... 847 537-4250
  Wheeling (G-22138)
Sandee Manufacturing Co .............. G ...... 847 671-1335
  Franklin Park (G-10581)
Shape Master Inc ........................... G ...... 217 582-2638
  Ogden (G-16744)
Shape Master Inc ........................... F ...... 217 469-7027
  Saint Joseph (G-19318)
Sonoco Plastics Inc ........................ F ...... 630 628-5859
  Addison (G-295)

Springfield Plastics Inc ................... E ...... 217 438-6167
  Auburn (G-950)
Streamwood Plastics Ltd ............... G ...... 847 895-9190
  Schaumburg (G-19741)

## 3083 Plastic Laminated Plate & Sheet

◆ Acco Brands Corporation ............ A ...... 847 541-9500
  Lake Zurich (G-13033)
▲ Accurate Partitions Corp ............. G ...... 708 442-6801
  Mc Cook (G-14444)
▲ American Louver Company ......... E ...... 847 470-0400
  Skokie (G-19950)
American Name Plate & Metal De ... E ...... 773 376-1400
  Chicago (G-3867)
▲ Ameriscan Designs Inc ............... D ...... 773 542-1291
  Chicago (G-3886)
▲ Atlas Fibre Company .................. D ...... 847 674-1234
  Northbrook (G-16208)
B & B Formica Appliers Inc ............ F ...... 773 804-1015
  Chicago (G-4014)
▲ C Line Products Inc ................... D ...... 847 827-6661
  Mount Prospect (G-15315)
▲ Card Dynamix LLC ..................... C ...... 630 685-4060
  Romeoville (G-18806)
Carl Gorr Printing Co ..................... G ...... 815 338-3191
  Woodstock (G-22549)
Catalina Coating & Plas Inc ............ F ...... 847 806-1340
  Elk Grove Village (G-9358)
CFC International Inc ..................... G ...... 708 891-3456
  Chicago Heights (G-7086)
Coilform Company ......................... G ...... 630 232-8000
  Geneva (G-10820)
▲ Cortube Products Co ................. G ...... 708 429-6700
  Tinley Park (G-20903)
Credit Card Systems Inc ................ F ...... 847 459-8320
  Wheeling (G-22031)
Custom Films Inc ........................... F ...... 217 826-2326
  Marshall (G-14320)
Custom Plastics of Peoria .............. G ...... 309 697-2888
  Bartonville (G-1394)
Dana Plastic Container Corp ......... E ...... 630 529-7878
  Roselle (G-18939)
Designed Plastics Inc .................... E ...... 630 694-7300
  Bensenville (G-1879)
▲ Diamond Cellophane Pdts Inc .... E ...... 847 418-3000
  Northbrook (G-16242)
E-Jay Plastics Co ........................... G ...... 630 543-4000
  Addison (G-104)
Field Ventures LLC ........................ D ...... 847 509-2250
  Northbrook (G-16258)
Glazed Structures Inc .................... F ...... 847 223-4560
  Grayslake (G-11341)
Iten Industries Inc .......................... G ...... 630 543-2820
  Addison (G-155)
James Injection Molding Co ........... E ...... 847 564-3820
  Northbrook (G-16283)
John Manely Company ................... C ...... 773 254-0617
  Chicago (G-5316)
▲ Lakone Company ........................ D ...... 630 892-4251
  Montgomery (G-15055)
◆ Laminart Inc ............................... E ...... 800 323-7624
  Schaumburg (G-19612)
Npi Holding Corp ........................... E ...... 217 391-1229
  Springfield (G-20488)
Nudo Products Inc ......................... E ...... 217 528-5636
  Springfield (G-20489)
▲ Nudo Products Inc ..................... E ...... 217 528-5636
  Springfield (G-20490)
Nypro Hanover Park ...................... G ...... 630 868-3517
  Roselle (G-18961)
Oberthur Tech Amer Corp .............. D ...... 630 551-0792
  Naperville (G-15718)
▲ Olon Industries Inc (us) ............. E ...... 630 232-4705
  Geneva (G-10857)
Olon Industries Inc (us) ................. E ...... 630 232-4705
  Geneva (G-10858)
Photo Techniques Corp .................. D ...... 630 690-9360
  Carol Stream (G-3213)
Pro Glass Corporation ................... G ...... 630 553-3141
  Bristol (G-2549)
R & R Custom Cabinet Making ....... G ...... 847 358-6188
  Palatine (G-17065)
Rainbow Colors Inc ....................... F ...... 847 640-7700
  Elk Grove Village (G-9707)
Richard Tindall .............................. E ...... 618 433-8107
  Godfrey (G-11233)
Stark Standard Co ......................... G ...... 847 916-2636
  Franklin Park (G-10593)
Suburban Laminating Inc ............... G ...... 708 389-6106
  Melrose Park (G-14697)

# SIC SECTION

▲ Sun Process Converting Inc ........ D ...... 847 593-5656
  Mount Prospect (G-15376)
T J Kellogg Inc ............................... G ...... 815 969-0524
  Rockford (G-18640)
Tb Cardworks Llc ........................... E ...... 847 229-9990
  Palatine (G-17079)
Technologies Dvlpmnt .................... G ...... 815 943-9922
  Crystal Lake (G-7662)
Tempel Steel Company .................. A ...... 773 250-8000
  Chicago (G-6698)
Transcendia Inc ............................. E ...... 847 678-1800
  Franklin Park (G-10610)
Unique Designs ............................. G ...... 309 454-1226
  Normal (G-16092)
Upm Raflatac Inc ........................... C ...... 815 285-6100
  Dixon (G-8357)
▲ Vecchio Manufacturing of Ill ....... F ...... 847 742-8429
  Elgin (G-9224)

## 3084 Plastic Pipe

Blackburn Sampling Inc ................. G ...... 309 342-8429
  Galesburg (G-10738)
Eastern Illinois Clay Company ....... F ...... 815 427-8144
  Saint Anne (G-19120)
Eastern Illinois Clay Company ....... E ...... 815 427-8106
  Saint Anne (G-19121)
Fusibond Piping Systems Inc ......... F ...... 630 969-4488
  Downers Grove (G-8446)
George W Pierson Company .......... E ...... 815 726-3351
  Joliet (G-12501)

## 3085 Plastic Bottles

Alpha Packaging Minnesota Inc ..... G ...... 507 454-3830
  Chicago (G-3829)
Amcor Rigid Plastics Usa LLC ........ E ...... 630 406-3500
  Batavia (G-1411)
Amcor Rigid Plastics Usa LLC ........ D ...... 630 773-3235
  Itasca (G-12227)
American National Can Co ............. G ...... 630 406-3500
  Batavia (G-1414)
▲ CCL Dispensing Systems LLC .... D ...... 847 816-9400
  Libertyville (G-13312)
Consolidated Container Co LLC ..... C ...... 630 231-7150
  West Chicago (G-21686)
Container Specialties Inc .............. E ...... 708 615-1400
  Franklin Park (G-10441)
▲ Dana Plastic Container Corp ...... G ...... 847 670-0650
  Arlington Heights (G-744)
Dana Plastic Container Corp ......... E ...... 630 529-7878
  Roselle (G-18939)
▲ Fitpac Co Ltd ............................. G ...... 630 428-9077
  Bensenville (G-1899)
Graham Packaging Co Europe LLC ... C ...... 630 562-5912
  West Chicago (G-21711)
Graham Packaging Co Europe LLC ... B ...... 630 231-0850
  West Chicago (G-21712)
Graham Packaging Company LP ... G ...... 630 739-9150
  Woodridge (G-22490)
Harbison Corporation .................... D ...... 815 224-2633
  Peru (G-17511)
▲ Illinois Bottle Mfg Co ................. D ...... 847 595-9000
  Elk Grove Village (G-9533)
Inhance Technologies LLC ............. E ...... 630 231-7515
  West Chicago (G-21719)
Innocor Foam Technologies LLC .... F ...... 630 293-0780
  West Chicago (G-21723)
Isovac Products LLC ..................... G ...... 630 679-1740
  Romeoville (G-18831)
Lexi Group Inc ............................... G ...... 866 675-1683
  Chicago (G-5498)
Liquid Container Inc ...................... E ...... 630 562-5812
  West Chicago (G-21733)
Logoplaste Chicago LLC ................ G ...... 815 230-6961
  Plainfield (G-17619)
Logoplaste Fort Worth LLC ............ G ...... 815 230-6961
  Plainfield (G-17620)
Logoplaste Racine LLC .................. G ...... 815 230-6961
  Plainfield (G-17621)
▲ Logoplaste Usa Inc .................... D ...... 815 230-6961
  Plainfield (G-17622)
Petainer Manufacturing USA Inc .... F ...... 630 326-9921
  Batavia (G-1481)
Phoenix Unlimited Ltd ................... G ...... 847 515-1263
  Huntley (G-12167)
▲ Plastic Container Corporation .... E ...... 217 352-2722
  Urbana (G-21098)
Plastipak Packaging Inc ................ B ...... 217 398-1832
  Champaign (G-3526)
Plastipak Packaging Inc ................ C ...... 708 385-0721
  Alsip (G-510)

# 30 RUBBER AND MISCELLANEOUS PLASTICS PRODUCTS

Pvc Container Corporation ............... C ....... 217 463-6600
  Paris *(G-17159)*
Ring Container Tech LLC ................. E ....... 217 875-5084
  Decatur *(G-7934)*
Ring Container Tech LLC ................. E ....... 815 229-9110
  Rockford *(G-18555)*
Ringwood Containers LP .................. E ....... 815 939-7270
  Kankakee *(G-12644)*
Silgan Plastics LLC ......................... D ....... 618 662-4471
  Flora *(G-10217)*
Southeastern Container Inc ............. E ....... 217 342-9600
  Effingham *(G-8858)*
Wheaton Plastic Products ................ G ....... 847 298-5626
  Des Plaines *(G-8304)*
Whitney Products Inc ...................... F ....... 847 966-6161
  Niles *(G-16047)*

## 3086 Plastic Foam Prdts

▲ Ade Inc ....................................... E ....... 773 646-3400
  Chicago *(G-3746)*
All Foam Products Co .................... G ....... 847 913-9341
  Buffalo Grove *(G-2653)*
▲ All-Vac Industries Inc .................. F ....... 847 675-2290
  Skokie *(G-19948)*
Armacell LLC .................................. D ....... 708 596-9501
  South Holland *(G-20246)*
Atlas Roofing Corporation .............. E ....... 309 752-7121
  East Moline *(G-8670)*
◆ Blachford Investments Inc ........... C ....... 630 231-8300
  West Chicago *(G-21671)*
Centro Inc ...................................... G ....... 309 751-9700
  East Moline *(G-8672)*
▲ Co-Ordinated Packaging Inc ........ F ....... 847 559-8877
  Northbrook *(G-16228)*
Cpg Finance Inc ............................. A ....... 773 877-3300
  Chicago *(G-4487)*
Cushioneer Inc ............................... D ....... 815 748-5505
  Dekalb *(G-8083)*
Custom Foam Works Inc ................ G ....... 618 920-2810
  Troy *(G-21005)*
Dart Container Corp Illinois ............ D ....... 630 896-4631
  North Aurora *(G-16126)*
Dart Container Corp Illinois ............ C ....... 630 896-4631
  North Aurora *(G-16127)*
▲ DC Works Inc .............................. G ....... 847 464-4280
  Hampshire *(G-11546)*
Dow Chemical Company ................. C ....... 815 423-5921
  Channahon *(G-3572)*
Eagle Panel System Inc .................. G ....... 618 326-7132
  Mulberry Grove *(G-15459)*
▲ Elongated Plastics Inc ................. E ....... 224 456-0559
  Northbrook *(G-16249)*
Engineered Foam Solutions Inc ...... G ....... 708 769-4130
  South Holland *(G-20266)*
Engineered Plastic Components ..... C ....... 217 892-2026
  Rantoul *(G-17927)*
Epe Industries Usa Inc ................... F ....... 800 315-0336
  Elk Grove Village *(G-9462)*
▲ Essentra Specialty Tapes Inc ....... C ....... 708 488-1025
  Forest Park *(G-10242)*
▲ Evergreen Resource Inc .............. G ....... 630 428-9077
  Naperville *(G-15655)*
Excelsior Inc .................................. E ....... 815 987-2900
  Rockford *(G-18375)*
▲ Focus Poly ................................. G ....... 847 981-6890
  Elk Grove Village *(G-9483)*
▲ Form Plastics Company .............. D ....... 630 443-1400
  Saint Charles *(G-19187)*
Free-Flow Packaging Intl Inc .......... D ....... 708 589-6500
  Thornton *(G-20869)*
General Foam Plastics Corp ........... G ....... 847 851-9995
  East Dundee *(G-8637)*
Grafcor Packaging Inc ................... G ....... 815 963-1300
  Rockford *(G-18404)*
Greg Waters .................................. G ....... 618 798-9758
  Granite City *(G-11282)*
Hunter Panels LLC ......................... D ....... 847 671-2516
  Franklin Park *(G-10492)*
Illinois Tool Works Inc ................... E ....... 217 345-2166
  Charleston *(G-3599)*
Insulco Inc .................................... F ....... 309 353-6145
  Pekin *(G-17270)*
▲ K & S Service & Rental Corp ....... F ....... 630 279-4292
  Elmhurst *(G-9893)*
Mailbox Plus .................................. G ....... 847 577-1737
  Mount Prospect *(G-15345)*
Master Containers Inc ................... F ....... 863 425-5571
  Lake Forest *(G-12924)*
Meadoworks LLC ........................... F ....... 847 640-8580
  Schaumburg *(G-19638)*

Midpoint Packaging LLC ................ G ....... 630 613-9922
  Downers Grove *(G-8487)*
Minnesota Diversified Pdts Inc ....... E ....... 815 539-3106
  Mendota *(G-14728)*
Northern Products Company .......... D ....... 708 597-8501
  Alsip *(G-500)*
Owens Corning Sales LLC ............. D ....... 815 226-4627
  Rockford *(G-18527)*
Polar Tech Industries Inc ............... E ....... 815 784-9000
  Genoa *(G-10882)*
Polyair Inter Pack Inc .................... D ....... 773 995-1818
  Chicago *(G-6153)*
▲ Positive Packaging Inc ............... G ....... 847 392-4405
  Rolling Meadows *(G-18765)*
Pregis LLC .................................... G ....... 331 425-6264
  Aurora *(G-1068)*
◆ Pregis LLC .................................. E ....... 847 597-9330
  Deerfield *(G-8048)*
Pregis LLC .................................... A ....... 847 597-2200
  Deerfield *(G-8049)*
▲ Pres-On Corporation ................... D ....... 630 628-2255
  Bolingbrook *(G-2360)*
Punch Products Manufacturing ...... E ....... 773 533-2800
  Chicago *(G-6226)*
Quality Pallets Inc ......................... E ....... 217 459-2655
  Windsor *(G-22282)*
Remco Technology Inc .................. F ....... 847 329-8090
  Skokie *(G-20074)*
Rock-Tenn Company ...................... E ....... 815 756-8913
  Dekalb *(G-8116)*
Sales Midwest Prtg & Packg Inc ..... G ....... 309 764-5544
  Moline *(G-14968)*
Sealed Air Corporation .................. D ....... 708 352-8700
  Hodgkins *(G-11982)*
▲ Silgan Equipment Company ........ E ....... 847 336-0552
  Waukegan *(G-21617)*
◆ Simonton Holdings Inc ................ F ....... 304 428-8261
  Deerfield *(G-8055)*
Sonoco Display & Packaging LLC .. D ....... 630 972-1990
  Bolingbrook *(G-2373)*
Sonoco Protective Solutions .......... E ....... 847 398-0110
  Arlington Heights *(G-841)*
Superb Packaging Inc ................... E ....... 847 579-1870
  Highland Park *(G-11874)*
▲ Tek Pak Inc ................................ D ....... 630 406-0560
  Batavia *(G-1506)*
◆ Thermos LLC .............................. E ....... 847 439-7821
  Schaumburg *(G-19760)*
◆ Tkk USA Inc ................................ G ....... 847 439-7821
  Rolling Meadows *(G-18783)*
▲ Volflex Inc .................................. E ....... 708 478-1117
  Mokena *(G-14915)*
W R Grace & Co- Conn .................. F ....... 708 458-9700
  Chicago *(G-6924)*
Westrock Converting Company ...... E ....... 630 783-6700
  Bolingbrook *(G-2383)*
Wrap & Send Services ................... E ....... 847 329-2559
  Skokie *(G-20115)*
Wrapping Inc ................................. G ....... 773 871-2898
  Chicago *(G-7034)*

## 3087 Custom Compounding Of Purchased Plastic Resins

Aabbitt Adhesives Inc .................... D ....... 773 227-2700
  Chicago *(G-3701)*
Ameriflon Ltd ................................. G ....... 847 541-6000
  Wheeling *(G-22004)*
Bach Plastic Works Inc .................. G ....... 847 680-4342
  Libertyville *(G-13306)*
▲ Bulk Molding Compounds Inc ..... D ....... 630 377-1065
  West Chicago *(G-21675)*
Cdj Technologies Inc ..................... G ....... 321 277-7807
  Wilmette *(G-22249)*
Chicago Latex Products Inc ........... F ....... 815 459-9680
  Crystal Lake *(G-7552)*
Cream Team Logistics LLC ............ F ....... 708 541-9128
  Phoenix *(G-17540)*
Elastocon Tpe Technologies Inc .... E ....... 217 498-8500
  Springfield *(G-20433)*
Enbarr LLC .................................... D ....... 630 217-2101
  Bartlett *(G-1346)*
Lyondell Chemical Company .......... B ....... 815 942-7011
  Morris *(G-15114)*
◆ Major-Prime Plastics Inc ............. E ....... 630 834-9400
  Villa Park *(G-21267)*
Parker-Hannifin Corporation .......... D ....... 847 836-6859
  Elgin *(G-9135)*
▲ Poly Compounding LLC ............... G ....... 847 488-0683
  Elgin *(G-9143)*

Polyone Corporation ...................... D ....... 630 972-0505
  Romeoville *(G-18859)*
Polyone Corporation ...................... G ....... 815 385-8500
  McHenry *(G-14548)*
▲ Shannon Industrial Corporation ... F ....... 815 337-2349
  Woodstock *(G-22609)*
Standard Rubber Products Co ........ E ....... 847 593-5630
  Elk Grove Village *(G-9751)*
Tom McCowan Enterprises Inc ....... G ....... 217 369-9352
  Urbana *(G-21103)*

## 3088 Plastic Plumbing Fixtures

BCI Acrylic Inc .............................. G ....... 847 963-8827
  Libertyville *(G-13307)*
Carstin Brands Inc ........................ D ....... 217 543-3331
  Arthur *(G-885)*
◆ Danze Inc .................................. G ....... 630 754-0277
  Woodridge *(G-22467)*
Fiber Winders Inc ......................... G ....... 618 548-6388
  Salem *(G-19332)*
G K L Corporation ......................... D ....... 815 886-5900
  Romeoville *(G-18826)*
Industrial Fiberglass Inc ................ F ....... 708 681-2707
  Melrose Park *(G-14657)*
Jalaa Fiberglass Inc ...................... G ....... 217 923-3433
  Greenup *(G-11384)*
▲ Lordahl Manufacturing Co .......... G ....... 847 244-0448
  Waukegan *(G-21584)*
▲ Luxury Bath Liners Inc ............... E ....... 630 295-9084
  Glendale Heights *(G-11042)*
Northwest Marble Products ............ G ....... 630 860-2288
  Hoffman Estates *(G-12072)*
Rht Inc ......................................... G ....... 630 227-1737
  Roselle *(G-18967)*
Staffco Inc ................................... G ....... 309 688-3223
  Peoria *(G-17460)*
Swan Surfaces LLC ...................... C ....... 618 532-5673
  Centralia *(G-3435)*
T J Van Der Bosch & Associates ... E ....... 815 344-3210
  McHenry *(G-14567)*

## 3089 Plastic Prdts

A P L Plastics ............................... G ....... 773 265-1370
  Chicago *(G-3691)*
A To Z Engraving Co Inc ................ G ....... 847 526-7396
  Wauconda *(G-21435)*
A W Enterprises Inc ...................... F ....... 708 458-8989
  Bedford Park *(G-1531)*
AAA Trash .................................... E ....... 618 775-1365
  Odin *(G-16738)*
Abba Plastics Inc .......................... G ....... 630 385-2156
  Yorkville *(G-22647)*
Abbacus Inc .................................. E ....... 815 637-9222
  Machesney Park *(G-14048)*
Abbacus Injection Molding Inc ....... E ....... 815 637-9222
  Machesney Park *(G-14049)*
Abbott Plastics & Supply Co .......... G ....... 815 874-8500
  Rockford *(G-18246)*
Aberdeen Technologies Inc ............ F ....... 630 665-8590
  Carol Stream *(G-3088)*
Able American Plastics Inc ............ F ....... 815 678-4646
  Richmond *(G-17956)*
◆ Acco Brands USA LLC ................ B ....... 800 222-6462
  Lake Zurich *(G-13034)*
Acco Brands USA LLC ................... D ....... 847 272-3700
  Lincolnshire *(G-13423)*
Accubow LLC ................................ G ....... 815 250-0607
  Peru *(G-17498)*
▲ Accurate Carriers Inc ................. F ....... 630 790-3430
  Glendale Heights *(G-11007)*
Ace Plastics Inc ............................ F ....... 815 635-1368
  Chatsworth *(G-3626)*
Acme Awning Co Inc ..................... G ....... 847 446-0153
  Lake Zurich *(G-13035)*
Acrylic Service Inc ........................ G ....... 630 543-0336
  Addison *(G-20)*
▲ Adams Apple Distributing LP ....... E ....... 847 832-9900
  Glenview *(G-11095)*
▲ Admo ......................................... G ....... 847 741-5777
  Elgin *(G-8936)*
Advance Design Inc ....................... G ....... 815 338-0843
  Woodstock *(G-22534)*
Advance Plastic Corp .................... G ....... 773 637-5922
  Chicago *(G-3761)*
Advanced Drainage Systems Inc ... F ....... 815 539-2160
  Mendota *(G-14714)*
Advanced Molding Tech Inc ........... D ....... 847 334-3600
  Woodstock *(G-22535)*
▲ Advanced Prototype Molding ....... G ....... 847 202-4200
  Palatine *(G-16998)*

Employee Codes: A=Over 500 employees, B=251-500
C=101-250, D=51-100, E=20-50, F=10-19, G=3-9

30 RUBBER AND MISCELLANEOUS PLASTICS PRODUCTS SIC SECTION

**Advanced Window Corp** ........ E ....... 773 379-3500
Chicago *(G-3773)*
**Advangene Consumables Inc** ........ G ....... 847 283-9780
Lake Bluff *(G-12827)*
▲ **Advantech Plastics LLC** ........ D ....... 815 338-8383
Woodstock *(G-22536)*
**Advert Display Products Inc** ........ G ....... 815 513-5432
Morris *(G-15090)*
**AEP Inc** ........ G ....... 618 466-7668
Alton *(G-558)*
**Agriplastics LLC** ........ G ....... 847 604-8847
Lake Bluff *(G-12828)*
▲ **AGS Technology Inc** ........ E ....... 847 534-6600
Batavia *(G-1407)*
**Air Diffusion Systems A John** ........ G ....... 847 782-0044
Gurnee *(G-11422)*
**Akrylix Inc** ........ F ....... 773 869-9005
Frankfort *(G-10291)*
**Albea** ........ G ....... 847 439-8220
Elk Grove Village *(G-9283)*
**Algus Packaging Inc** ........ D ....... 815 756-1881
Dekalb *(G-8073)*
**All Star Injection Molders Inc** ........ G ....... 630 978-4046
Naperville *(G-15793)*
◆ **All West Plastics Inc** ........ D ....... 847 395-8830
Antioch *(G-616)*
**Alliance Plastics** ........ G ....... 888 643-1432
Bensenville *(G-1824)*
▼ **Allmetal Inc** ........ D ....... 630 250-8090
Itasca *(G-12225)*
**Allmetal Inc** ........ F ....... 630 766-1407
Bensenville *(G-1826)*
**Alltech Plastics Inc** ........ G ....... 847 352-2309
Schaumburg *(G-19433)*
**Alpha Acrylic Design** ........ G ....... 847 818-8178
Arlington Heights *(G-708)*
▼ **Alpha Omega Plastics Company** ........ D ....... 847 956-8777
Elk Grove Village *(G-9289)*
**Alpha Star Tool and Mold Inc** ........ F ....... 815 455-2802
Crystal Lake *(G-7529)*
▲ **Altamont Co** ........ D ....... 800 626-5774
Thomasboro *(G-20859)*
**Amcor Phrm Packg USA LLC** ........ C ....... 847 298-5626
Des Plaines *(G-8146)*
▲ **American Gasket Tech Inc** ........ D ....... 630 543-1510
Addison *(G-36)*
**American Molding Tech Inc** ........ E ....... 847 437-6900
Elk Grove Village *(G-9297)*
**Amtec Molded Products Inc** ........ E ....... 815 226-0187
Elgin *(G-8952)*
▲ **Amtec Precision Products Inc** ........ D ....... 847 695-8030
Elgin *(G-8953)*
**Amtech Industries LLC** ........ D ....... 847 202-3488
Palatine *(G-17001)*
**Andrews Automotive Company** ........ F ....... 773 768-1122
Chicago *(G-3903)*
▲ **Anfinsen Plastic Moulding Inc** ........ E ....... 630 554-4100
Oswego *(G-16904)*
**APAC II LLC** ........ G ....... 618 426-1338
Campbell Hill *(G-2974)*
▲ **Apollo Plastics Corporation** ........ D ....... 773 282-9222
Chicago *(G-3923)*
**Applied Arts & Sciences Inc** ........ G ....... 407 288-8228
Mokena *(G-14853)*
**Applied Polymer System Inc** ........ G ....... 847 301-1712
Schaumburg *(G-19445)*
**Aptargroup Inc** ........ E ....... 779 220-4430
Crystal Lake *(G-7534)*
◆ **Aptargroup Inc** ........ B ....... 815 477-0424
Crystal Lake *(G-7535)*
**Aptargroup Inc** ........ E ....... 847 462-3900
McHenry *(G-14481)*
**Aptargroup International LLC** ........ G ....... 815 477-0424
Crystal Lake *(G-7536)*
**Armbrust Paper Tubes Inc** ........ E ....... 773 586-3232
Chicago *(G-3945)*
**Armin Molding Corp** ........ E ....... 847 742-1864
South Elgin *(G-20182)*
**Arnel Industries Inc** ........ E ....... 630 543-6500
Addison *(G-45)*
**Aztec Plastic Company** ........ E ....... 312 733-0900
Chicago *(G-4011)*
**B & M Plastic Inc** ........ F ....... 847 258-4437
Elk Grove Village *(G-9328)*
**B J Plastic Molding Co** ........ E ....... 630 766-3200
Franklin Park *(G-10408)*
**B J Plastic Molding Co** ........ E ....... 630 766-8750
Bensenville *(G-1839)*
**Badger Molding Inc** ........ F ....... 847 483-9005
Wheeling *(G-22011)*

▲ **Bankier Companies Inc** ........ C ....... 847 647-6565
Niles *(G-15963)*
**Bannon Enterprises Inc** ........ G ....... 847 529-9265
Geneva *(G-10811)*
▲ **Baps Investors Group LLC** ........ E ....... 847 818-8444
Rolling Meadows *(G-18716)*
▲ **Bay Plastics** ........ F ....... 847 299-2045
Des Plaines *(G-8156)*
**Bee Boat Co Inc** ........ G ....... 217 379-2605
Paxton *(G-17236)*
**Berry Global Inc** ........ C ....... 815 334-5225
Woodstock *(G-22544)*
**Berry Global Inc** ........ G .......
Lake Bluff *(G-12836)*
**Berry Global Inc** ........ C ....... 847 541-7900
Buffalo Grove *(G-2663)*
**Berry Global Inc** ........ B ....... 708 396-1470
Alsip *(G-441)*
**Bfw Coating** ........ G ....... 847 639-2155
Cary *(G-3328)*
**Bird Dog Diversified** ........ E ....... 847 741-0700
Elgin *(G-8966)*
**BJ Mold & Die Inc** ........ G ....... 630 595-1797
Wood Dale *(G-22346)*
**Black Rhino Concealment** ........ G ....... 847 783-6499
Gilberts *(G-10913)*
◆ **Blackhawk Molding Co Inc** ........ D ....... 630 628-6218
Addison *(G-58)*
**Bli Legacy Inc** ........ E ....... 847 428-6059
Carpentersville *(G-3276)*
▲ **Boss Manufacturing Holdings** ........ F ....... 309 852-2781
Kewanee *(G-12675)*
▲ **Box Enclsres Assembly Svcs Inc** ........ G ....... 847 932-4700
Libertyville *(G-13309)*
**Bway Corporation** ........ C ....... 847 956-0750
Elk Grove Village *(G-9351)*
**Bway Corporation** ........ C ....... 773 254-8700
Chicago *(G-4194)*
**Bway Parent Company Inc** ........ F ....... 773 890-3300
Chicago *(G-4195)*
▲ **C Line Products Inc** ........ D ....... 847 827-6661
Mount Prospect *(G-15315)*
▲ **C R Plastics Inc** ........ G ....... 847 541-3601
Wheeling *(G-22021)*
**Cal-Ill Gasket Co** ........ F ....... 773 287-9605
Chicago *(G-4213)*
▲ **Calumet Container Corp** ........ F ....... 773 646-3653
Chicago *(G-4218)*
▲ **Capsonic Group LLC** ........ B ....... 847 888-7264
Elgin *(G-8980)*
**Carroll Tool & Manufacturing** ........ G ....... 630 766-3363
Bensenville *(G-1852)*
▲ **Centech Plastics Inc** ........ C ....... 847 364-4433
Elk Grove Village *(G-9361)*
**Central Molded Products LLC** ........ F ....... 773 622-4000
Chicago *(G-4271)*
**Century Mold & Tool Co** ........ E ....... 847 364-5858
Elk Grove Village *(G-9362)*
▲ **Century Molded Plastics Inc** ........ E ....... 847 729-3455
Glenview *(G-11111)*
**Certified Polymers Inc** ........ G ....... 630 515-0007
Western Springs *(G-21865)*
▲ **Chatham Plastics Inc** ........ G ....... 217 483-1481
Chatham *(G-3618)*
**Chem-Tainer Industries Inc** ........ G ....... 630 932-7778
Lombard *(G-13775)*
▲ **Chemtech Plastics Inc** ........ D ....... 630 503-6000
Elgin *(G-8986)*
**Chicago Molding Outlet** ........ G ....... 773 471-6870
Chicago *(G-4335)*
**Chicago Plastic Systems Inc** ........ E ....... 815 455-4599
Crystal Lake *(G-7553)*
**Cicero Plastic Products Inc** ........ E ....... 815 886-9522
Romeoville *(G-18811)*
**Cim-Tech Plastics Inc** ........ F ....... 847 350-0900
Elk Grove Village *(G-9373)*
▲ **Circle Caster Engineering Co** ........ G ....... 847 455-2206
Franklin Park *(G-10432)*
▲ **Circle Engineering Company** ........ G ....... 847 455-2204
Franklin Park *(G-10433)*
▲ **Classic Fasteners LLC** ........ G ....... 630 605-0195
Saint Charles *(G-19157)*
**Classic Midwest Die Mold Inc** ........ F ....... 773 227-8000
Chicago *(G-4393)*
**Classic Molding Co Inc** ........ D ....... 847 671-7888
Schiller Park *(G-19814)*
**Clear Pack Company** ........ C ....... 847 957-6282
Franklin Park *(G-10437)*
**Clover Plastics LLC** ........ G ....... 630 473-6488
West Chicago *(G-21683)*

▲ **Cmt International Inc** ........ G ....... 618 549-1829
Murphysboro *(G-15575)*
**Collapsible Core Inc** ........ G ....... 630 408-1693
Romeoville *(G-18814)*
▲ **Com-Pac International Inc** ........ C ....... 618 529-2421
Carbondale *(G-3004)*
▲ **Commercial Plastics Company** ........ C ....... 847 566-1700
Mundelein *(G-15490)*
▲ **Component Plastics Inc** ........ D ....... 847 695-9200
Elgin *(G-8995)*
**Computhink Inc** ........ E ....... 630 705-9050
Lombard *(G-13783)*
**Condor Tool & Manufacturing** ........ F ....... 630 628-8200
Addison *(G-81)*
**Consolidated Container Co LLC** ........ C ....... 815 943-7828
Harvard *(G-11628)*
▲ **Consolidated Foam Inc** ........ F ....... 847 850-5011
Buffalo Grove *(G-2678)*
▼ **Continental Window and GL Corp** ........ E ....... 773 794-1600
Chicago *(G-4461)*
**Conwed Plastics** ........ D ....... 630 293-3737
West Chicago *(G-21687)*
**Core-Mark International Inc** ........ G ....... 847 593-1800
Elk Grove Village *(G-9396)*
**Cortina Companies Inc** ........ E ....... 847 455-2800
Franklin Park *(G-10443)*
▲ **Cortina Tool & Molding Co** ........ C ....... 847 455-2800
Franklin Park *(G-10444)*
◆ **Crane Composites Inc** ........ B ....... 815 467-8600
Channahon *(G-3566)*
**Crane Composites Inc** ........ D ....... 630 378-9580
Bolingbrook *(G-2289)*
**Crane Composites Inc** ........ C ....... 815 467-1437
Channahon *(G-3567)*
**Creative Concepts Fabrication** ........ F ....... 630 940-0500
Saint Charles *(G-19165)*
**Creative Conveniences By K&E** ........ G ....... 847 975-8526
Lake Zurich *(G-13059)*
**Crestwood Industries Inc** ........ F ....... 847 680-9088
Mundelein *(G-15492)*
▲ **Crystal Die and Mold Inc** ........ E ....... 847 658-6535
Rolling Meadows *(G-18724)*
▲ **CTI Industries Corporation** ........ C ....... 847 382-1000
Lake Barrington *(G-12804)*
**CTI Industries Corporation** ........ D ....... 800 284-5605
Lake Zurich *(G-13060)*
**CTS Automotive LLC** ........ E ....... 815 385-9480
McHenry *(G-14493)*
▲ **CTS Automotive LLC** ........ C ....... 630 614-7201
Lisle *(G-13578)*
**Custom Blow Molding** ........ G ....... 630 820-9700
Aurora *(G-990)*
**Custom Films Inc** ........ F ....... 217 826-2326
Marshall *(G-14320)*
▲ **Custom Plastics Inc** ........ C ....... 847 439-6770
Elk Grove Village *(G-9404)*
**Custom Plastics Inc** ........ F ....... 847 640-4723
Elk Grove Village *(G-9405)*
**Cwi** ........ G ....... 618 443-2030
Sparta *(G-20316)*
**D & D Manufacturing** ........ G ....... 815 339-9100
Hennepin *(G-11733)*
▲ **D & J Plastics Inc** ........ G ....... 847 534-0601
Schaumburg *(G-19496)*
**D & M Custom Injection M** ........ D ....... 847 683-2054
Burlington *(G-2811)*
**D and S Molding & Dctg Inc** ........ G ....... 815 399-2734
Rockford *(G-18332)*
**D&W Fine Pack Holdings LLC** ........ G ....... 847 378-1200
Elk Grove Village *(G-9413)*
**D&W Fine Pack LLC** ........ G ....... 800 323-0422
Lake Zurich *(G-13061)*
▲ **D&W Fine Pack LLC** ........ A ....... 847 378-1200
Elk Grove Village *(G-9414)*
▲ **Damron Corporation** ........ E ....... 773 265-2724
Chicago *(G-4549)*
**Dana Molded** ........ G ....... 847 783-1800
Carpentersville *(G-3282)*
▲ **Davies Molding LLC** ........ C ....... 630 510-8188
Carol Stream *(G-3141)*
**Dayton Superior Corporation** ........ C ....... 815 936-3300
Kankakee *(G-12609)*
**Designed Plastics Inc** ........ E ....... 630 694-7300
Bensenville *(G-1879)*
▲ **Deslauriers Inc** ........ E ....... 708 544-4455
La Grange Park *(G-12754)*
**Detroit Forming Inc** ........ D ....... 630 820-0500
Aurora *(G-994)*
**Dice Mold & Engineering Inc** ........ E ....... 630 773-3595
Itasca *(G-12250)*

# SIC SECTION
## 30 RUBBER AND MISCELLANEOUS PLASTICS PRODUCTS

| Company | Code | Phone |
|---|---|---|
| Dike-O-Seal Incorporated, Chicago (G-4603) | F | 773 254-3224 |
| ▲ Dimension Molding Corporation, Addison (G-94) | E | 630 628-0777 |
| Dirk Vander Noot, Prospect Heights (G-17776) | G | 224 558-1878 |
| Dordan Manufacturing Company, Woodstock (G-22562) | E | 815 334-0087 |
| Dove Products Inc, Lockport (G-13711) | E | 815 727-4683 |
| DRG Molding & Pad Printing Inc, Round Lake Beach (G-19075) | G | 847 223-3398 |
| Drummond Industries Inc, Bensenville (G-1884) | E | 773 637-1264 |
| Dsign In Plastics Inc, Franklin Park (G-10459) | F | 847 288-8085 |
| Dss Rapak Inc, Romeoville (G-18817) | G | 630 296-2000 |
| ▲ Dti Molding Technologies Inc, Addison (G-100) | D | 630 543-3600 |
| Du-Call Miller Plastics Inc, Batavia (G-1443) | F | 630 964-6020 |
| Dukane Ias LLC, Saint Charles (G-19176) | D | 630 797-4900 |
| Dunham Designs Inc, New Lenox (G-15877) | G | 815 462-0100 |
| Dura Operating LLC, Stockton (G-20631) | C | 815 947-3333 |
| Duratech Corporation, Centralia (G-3412) | G | 618 533-8891 |
| ▲ E A M & J Inc, Elgin (G-9017) | E | 847 622-9200 |
| E & T Plastic Mfg Co Inc, Addison (G-103) | F | 630 628-9048 |
| E-Jay Plastics Co, Addison (G-104) | F | 630 543-4000 |
| E-Z Rotational Molder Inc, Elk Grove Village (G-9445) | G | 847 806-1327 |
| Eagle Plastics & Supply Inc, South Holland (G-20263) | G | 708 331-6232 |
| ▲ Eakas Corporation, Peru (G-17508) | B | 815 223-8811 |
| Eco-Tech Plastics LLC, Northbrook (G-16247) | E | 262 539-3811 |
| Elas Tek Molding Inc, Spring Grove (G-20335) | E | 815 675-9012 |
| ▲ Electroform Company, Machesney Park (G-14072) | E | 815 633-1113 |
| Elgin Die Mold Co, Pingree Grove (G-17555) | D | 847 464-0140 |
| ▲ Elgin Molded Plastics Inc, Elgin (G-9025) | D | 847 931-2455 |
| ▲ EMC Innovations Inc, Joliet (G-12490) | G | 815 741-2546 |
| Ems Acrylics & Silk Screener, Chicago (G-4747) | F | 773 777-5656 |
| ◆ Energy Absorption Systems Inc, Chicago (G-4750) | E | 312 467-6750 |
| Engineered Plastic Components, Rantoul (G-17927) | C | 217 892-2026 |
| Engineered Plastic Pdts Corp, Elk Grove Village (G-9460) | E | 847 952-8400 |
| Enginred Molding Solutions Inc, McHenry (G-14503) | E | 815 363-9600 |
| Entrigue Designs, Homewood (G-12097) | G | 708 647-6159 |
| Essentra Components Inc, Forest Park (G-10241) | C | 815 943-6487 |
| Evans Tool & Manufacturing, Aurora (G-1149) | G | 630 897-8656 |
| ▼ Extruded Solutions Inc, Carol Stream (G-3149) | G | 630 871-6450 |
| F & R Plastics Inc, Waukegan (G-21558) | F | 847 336-1330 |
| ▲ Fabrik Industries Inc, McHenry (G-14505) | B | 815 385-9480 |
| Fanplastic Molding Co, Marengo (G-14228) | G | 815 923-6950 |
| Fasteners For Retail Inc, Des Plaines (G-8194) | C | 847 296-5511 |
| Fiber Winders Inc, Salem (G-19332) | G | 618 548-6388 |
| Fiberbasin Inc, Aurora (G-1151) | F | 630 978-0705 |
| Fiberglass Innovations LLC, Rockford (G-18381) | F | 815 962-9338 |
| Field Manufacturing Corp, Crystal Lake (G-7578) | D | 815 455-5596 |
| ◆ Filtertek Inc, Hebron (G-11719) | B | 815 648-2410 |
| ▲ First Amrcn Plstic Mlding Entp, South Beloit (G-20145) | D | 815 624-8538 |
| Flex-N-Gate Chicago LLC, Urbana (G-21084) | G | 217 255-5098 |
| Flex-N-Gate Corporation, Danville (G-7721) | G | 217 442-4018 |
| Flextronics Intl USA Inc, Buffalo Grove (G-2696) | F | 847 383-1529 |
| Fliptabs Inc, Wonder Lake (G-22323) | G | 815 701-2584 |
| Floline Archtctral Systems LLC, Plainfield (G-17600) | F | 815 733-5044 |
| Flotek Inc, Cary (G-3342) | G | 815 943-6816 |
| ▲ Flow-Eze Company, Rockford (G-18383) | F | 815 965-1062 |
| Foreman Tool & Mold Corp, Saint Charles (G-19186) | E | 630 377-6389 |
| Foremost Plastic Pdts Co Inc, Elmwood Park (G-9971) | E | 708 452-5300 |
| Forreston Tool Inc, Forreston (G-10269) | F | 815 938-3626 |
| Four Seasons Gutter Prote, East Peoria (G-8710) | G | 309 694-4565 |
| ▲ Four Star Tool Inc, Rolling Meadows (G-18729) | D | 224 735-2419 |
| ▲ Fox Valley Molding Inc, Plano (G-17665) | C | 630 552-3176 |
| Frederics Frame Studio Inc, Chicago (G-4886) | F | 312 243-2950 |
| Furnel Inc, Addison (G-124) | G | 630 543-0885 |
| G A I M Plastics Incorporated, Bensenville (G-1903) | F | 630 350-9500 |
| GAim Plastics Incorporated, Bensenville (G-1904) | F | 630 350-9500 |
| Gayton Group Inc, Schiller Park (G-19833) | G | 847 233-0509 |
| GE Polymers LLC, Hinsdale (G-11947) | G | 312 674-7434 |
| Genesis Mold Corp, Libertyville (G-13326) | G | 847 573-9431 |
| ▼ Gilster-Mary Lee Corporation, Chester (G-3657) | A | 618 826-2361 |
| Glasstek Inc, Naperville (G-15807) | G | 630 978-9897 |
| ▲ Global Contract Mfg Inc, Chicago (G-4957) | D | 312 432-6200 |
| Gmt Inc, Elgin (G-9049) | E | 847 697-8161 |
| Golden Plastics LLC, East Dundee (G-8640) | F | 847 836-7766 |
| Goodco Products LLC, Countryside (G-7428) | G | 630 258-6384 |
| ▲ Gord Industrial Plastics Inc, Sandwich (G-19366) | F | 815 786-9494 |
| Goudie Tool and Engrg Del, Lake Zurich (G-13079) | E | 847 438-4597 |
| Graham Packaging Co Europe LLC, West Chicago (G-21710) | A | 630 293-8616 |
| Graham Packaging Company LP, Woodridge (G-22490) | E | 630 739-9150 |
| ▲ Graphic Tool Corp, Itasca (G-12272) | E | 630 250-9800 |
| Great Midwest Packaging LLC, Waukegan (G-21565) | F | 847 395-4500 |
| Greenwood Inc, Danville (G-7729) | E | 217 431-6034 |
| ▲ Greenwood Inc, Danville (G-7728) | F | 800 798-4900 |
| Greif Inc, Lockport (G-13719) | G | 815 838-7210 |
| Greif Inc, Bradley (G-2423) | G | 815 935-7575 |
| Gy Packaging LLC, Northbrook (G-16267) | F | 847 272-8803 |
| H E Associates Inc, Yorkville (G-22661) | G | 630 553-6382 |
| Han-Win Products Inc, Aurora (G-1166) | E | 630 897-1591 |
| Hangables Inc, Skokie (G-20010) | F | 847 673-9770 |
| ▲ Hansen Plastics Corp, Elgin (G-9055) | D | 847 741-4510 |
| Hansen Plastics Corp, Elgin (G-9056) | G | 847 741-4510 |
| Harbison Corporation, Peru (G-17511) | G | 815 224-2633 |
| Hardwood Line Manufacturing Co, Chicago (G-5045) | E | 773 463-2600 |
| Hawk Molding Inc, Harvard (G-11636) | G | 224 523-2888 |
| Hazen Display Corporation, Davis (G-7806) | E | 815 248-2925 |
| ▲ Hbp Inc, Freeport (G-10662) | D | 815 235-3000 |
| ▲ Heathrow Scientific LLC, Vernon Hills (G-21171) | F | 847 816-5070 |
| Heidts Automotive LLC, Lake Zurich (G-13083) | G | 847 487-0150 |
| Hemmerle Jr Irvin, Naperville (G-15670) | G | 630 334-4392 |
| Heritage Products Corporation, Buffalo Grove (G-2703) | G | 847 419-8835 |
| Herschberger Window Mfg, Tuscola (G-21021) | G | 217 543-2106 |
| Hi-Tech Plastics Inc, Wheeling (G-22070) | E | 847 577-1805 |
| Hi-Tech Polymers Inc, Loves Park (G-13946) | G | 815 282-2272 |
| ▲ Hmt Manufacturing Inc, North Chicago (G-16182) | E | 847 473-2310 |
| ◆ Hoffer Plastics Corporation, South Elgin (G-20203) | G | 847 741-5740 |
| ◆ Home Pdts Intl - N Amer Inc, Chicago (G-5102) | B | 773 890-1010 |
| Husky Injection Molding, Mokena (G-14869) | F | 708 479-9049 |
| Hy Tech Cnc Machining Inc, Schaumburg (G-19561) | G | |
| I T W Deltar/Diamed Corp, Elk Grove Village (G-9529) | E | 847 593-8811 |
| I TW Deltar Insert Molded Pdts, Elk Grove Village (G-9530) | E | 847 593-8811 |
| ▲ Iceberg Enterprises LLC, Des Plaines (G-8207) | F | 847 685-9500 |
| ICI Fiberite, Orland Park (G-16866) | G | 708 403-3788 |
| Id3 Inc, Arlington Heights (G-771) | F | 847 734-9781 |
| Identatronics Inc, Crystal Lake (G-7591) | E | 847 437-2654 |
| ▲ Identification Products Mfg Co, Lake Forest (G-12914) | F | 847 367-6452 |
| ▲ Illinois Bottle Mfg Co, Elk Grove Village (G-9533) | D | 847 595-9000 |
| Illinois Electro Deburring Co, Franklin Park (G-10494) | F | 847 678-5010 |
| Illinois Pro-Turn Inc, Cary (G-3353) | G | 847 462-1870 |
| Illinois Tool Works Inc, Glenview (G-11141) | B | 847 724-7500 |
| Illinois Tool Works Inc, Bartlett (G-1353) | C | 630 372-2150 |
| Illinois Tool Works Inc, Itasca (G-12280) | E | 630 773-9300 |
| Illinois Tool Works Inc, Frankfort (G-10330) | D | 708 720-0300 |
| Illinois Tool Works Inc, Itasca (G-12282) | E | 630 773-9301 |
| Illinois Tool Works Inc, Elk Grove Village (G-9534) | D | 630 787-3298 |
| Illinois Tool Works Inc, Carol Stream (G-3171) | C | 630 315-2150 |
| Illinois Tool Works Inc, Richton Park (G-17977) | D | 708 720-7800 |
| Illinois Tool Works Inc, Des Plaines (G-8209) | C | 847 299-2222 |
| Illinois Tool Works Inc, Mokena (G-14873) | C | 708 479-7200 |
| Illinois Tool Works Inc, Glenview (G-11144) | B | 847 724-6100 |
| Illinois Tool Works Inc, Elgin (G-9072) | E | 847 783-5500 |
| Illinois Tool Works Inc, Mazon (G-14438) | C | 815 448-7300 |
| Illinois Tool Works Inc, Buffalo Grove (G-2707) | D | 847 724-7500 |
| Illinois Tool Works Inc, Tinley Park (G-20922) | C | 708 479-7200 |
| Illinois Tool Works Inc, Glenview (G-11145) | D | 847 657-4022 |
| Illinois Tool Works Inc, Roselle (G-18946) | C | 630 595-3500 |
| Ilpea Industries Inc, Galesburg (G-10760) | D | 309 343-3332 |
| Indiana Precision Inc, Danville (G-7739) | F | 765 361-0247 |
| ▲ Inland Plastics Inc, Kankakee (G-12625) | G | 815 933-3500 |

Employee Codes: A=Over 500 employees, B=251-500, C=101-250, D=51-100, E=20-50, F=10-19, G=3-9

# 30 RUBBER AND MISCELLANEOUS PLASTICS PRODUCTS

◆ Innovative Components Inc .........E ...... 847 885-9050
Schaumburg *(G-19567)*
Innovative Plastech Inc .........D ...... 630 232-1808
Batavia *(G-1458)*
▲ Innoware Plastic Inc .........C ...... 678 690-5100
Lake Forest *(G-12918)*
Inplex Custom Extruders LLC .........D ...... 847 827-7046
Naperville *(G-15676)*
◆ Insertech LLC .........D ...... 847 516-6184
Cary *(G-3354)*
Insertech International Inc .........E ...... 847 416-6184
Cary *(G-3355)*
Intec-Mexico LLC .........B ...... 847 358-0088
Palatine *(G-17043)*
Intergrted Thrmforming Systems .........F ...... 630 906-6895
Aurora *(G-1172)*
Intermolding Technology LLC .........F ...... 847 376-8517
Des Plaines *(G-8212)*
International Automotive .........B ...... 815 544-2102
Belvidere *(G-1765)*
International Mold & Prod LLC .........G ...... 313 617-5251
Grayslake *(G-11347)*
▲ Intrepid Molding Inc .........E ...... 847 526-9477
Wauconda *(G-21474)*
▲ Iplastics LLC .........D ...... 309 444-8884
Washington *(G-21383)*
▲ Ironwood Industries Inc .........G ...... 847 362-8681
Libertyville *(G-13338)*
Isovac Products LLC .........G ...... 630 679-1740
Romeoville *(G-18831)*
Iten Industries Inc .........G ...... 630 543-2820
Addison *(G-155)*
ITW International Holdings LLC .........F ...... 847 724-7500
Glenview *(G-11153)*
J and K Molding .........G ...... 224 276-3355
Volo *(G-21314)*
J C Products Inc .........G ...... 847 208-9616
Algonquin *(G-394)*
Jalaa Fiberglass Inc .........G ...... 217 923-3433
Greenup *(G-11384)*
James Injection Molding Co .........E ...... 847 564-3820
Northbrook *(G-16283)*
▼ Janler Corporation .........E ...... 773 774-0166
Chicago *(G-5277)*
Jarden Corporation .........D ...... 201 836-7070
Aurora *(G-1036)*
Jay Cee Plastic Fabricators .........F ...... 773 276-1920
Chicago *(G-5284)*
Jdi Mold and Tool LLC .........F ...... 815 759-5646
Johnsburg *(G-12437)*
▲ Jeffrey Jae Inc .........E ...... 847 394-1313
Arlington Heights *(G-782)*
▲ Jessup Manufacturing Company .........D ...... 815 385-6650
Mchenry *(G-14517)*
▲ Jigsaw Solutions Inc .........G ...... 630 926-1948
Romeoville *(G-18832)*
JL Clark LLC .........G ...... 815 961-5677
Rockford *(G-18446)*
▲ JL Clark LLC .........C ...... 815 961-5609
Rockford *(G-18447)*
Jodi Maurer .........G ...... 847 961-5347
Lake In The Hills *(G-12996)*
John Thomas Inc .........E ...... 815 288-2343
Dixon *(G-8334)*
Johnson Bag Co Inc .........F ...... 847 438-2424
Lake Zurich *(G-13093)*
◆ Jordan Industries Inc .........F ...... 847 945-5591
Deerfield *(G-8020)*
Jordan Specialty Plastics Inc .........G ...... 847 945-5591
Deerfield *(G-8021)*
Jr Plastics LLC .........C ...... 773 523-5454
Chicago *(G-5333)*
Jtec Industries Inc .........E ...... 309 698-9301
East Peoria *(G-8720)*
Jth Enterprises Inc .........E ...... 847 394-3355
Arlington Heights *(G-787)*
K B Tool Inc .........G ...... 630 595-4340
Bensenville *(G-1932)*
K H M Dist & Mfg Inc .........E ...... 847 249-4910
Gurnee *(G-11464)*
▲ Kalle USA Inc .........G ...... 847 775-0781
Gurnee *(G-11466)*
▲ Kastalon Inc .........D ...... 708 389-2210
Alsip *(G-478)*
Katco Enterprises LLC .........G ...... 217 429-5855
Decatur *(G-7901)*
Kevs Kans Inc .........G ...... 309 303-3999
Roanoke *(G-18051)*
▲ Ki Industries Inc .........E ...... 708 449-1990
Berkeley *(G-2046)*

Kipp Manufacturing Company Inc .........F ...... 630 768-9051
Wauconda *(G-21477)*
Klein Plastics Company LLC .........D ...... 616 863-9900
Lincolnshire *(G-13459)*
▲ Knight Plastics LLC .........C ...... 815 334-1240
Woodstock *(G-22579)*
▲ L & P Guarding LLC .........C ...... 708 325-0400
Bedford Park *(G-1560)*
L C Mold Inc .........E ...... 847 593-5004
Rolling Meadows *(G-18740)*
Lake Pacific Partners LLC .........B ...... 312 578-1110
Chicago *(G-5440)*
Lakeland Plastics Inc .........E ...... 847 680-1550
Mundelein *(G-15517)*
▲ Lakone Company .........D ...... 630 892-4251
Montgomery *(G-15055)*
Laminarp .........E ...... 847 884-9298
Schaumburg *(G-19611)*
Lee Gilster-Mary Corporation .........E ...... 618 826-2361
Chester *(G-3658)*
Lee Gilster-Mary Corporation .........E ...... 618 443-5676
Sparta *(G-20318)*
Lee Gilster-Mary Corporation .........E ...... 815 472-6456
Momence *(G-14983)*
Legacy Plastics Inc .........G ...... 815 226-3013
Rockford *(G-18465)*
Lens Lenticlear Lenticular .........E ...... 630 467-0900
Itasca *(G-12303)*
Leroys Plastic Co Inc .........E ...... 630 898-7006
Aurora *(G-1182)*
▲ Lewis Acquisition Corp .........D ...... 773 486-5660
Addison *(G-180)*
Lily-Canada Holding Corp .........G ...... 847 831-4800
Highland Park *(G-11852)*
▲ Limitless Innovations Inc .........E ...... 855 843-4828
McHenry *(G-14522)*
▲ Logan Square Aluminum Sup Inc .........D ...... 773 235-2500
Chicago *(G-5530)*
Loop Automotive LLC .........E ...... 847 912-9090
Chicago *(G-5539)*
Lordahl Manufacturing Co .........D ...... 847 244-0448
Long Grove *(G-13893)*
M F K Enterprises Inc .........F ...... 630 516-1230
Villa Park *(G-21266)*
▲ M Putterman & Co LLC .........D ...... 773 927-4120
Chicago *(G-5585)*
◆ Mac Lean-Fogg Company .........F ...... 847 566-0010
Mundelein *(G-15521)*
Magenta LLC .........D ...... 773 777-5050
Lockport *(G-13730)*
Mako Mold Corporation .........G ...... 630 377-9010
Saint Charles *(G-19212)*
▲ Makray Manufacturing Company .........D ...... 708 456-7100
Norridge *(G-16106)*
▲ Mark Power International .........F ...... 815 877-5984
Machesney Park *(G-14090)*
Martinez Management Inc .........G ...... 847 822-7202
Algonquin *(G-399)*
◆ Mary Lee Packaging Corporation .........E ...... 618 826-2361
Chester *(G-3659)*
▲ Master Molded Products LLC .........C ...... 847 695-9700
Elgin *(G-9102)*
▼ Mastermolding Inc .........E ...... 815 741-1230
Joliet *(G-12538)*
Mat Capital LLC .........G ...... 847 821-9630
Long Grove *(G-13895)*
Mate Technologies Inc .........F ...... 847 289-1010
Elgin *(G-9103)*
Material Control Inc .........D ...... 630 892-4274
Batavia *(G-1467)*
▲ Matrix IV Inc .........E ...... 815 338-4500
Woodstock *(G-22588)*
Matrix Packaging Inc .........G ...... 630 458-1942
Addison *(G-193)*
Matrix Tooling Inc .........D ...... 630 595-6144
Wood Dale *(G-22397)*
Maxon Plastics Inc .........D ...... 630 761-3667
Batavia *(G-1469)*
Mc Dist & Mfg Co .........F ...... 630 628-5180
Addison *(G-195)*
MCS Midwest LLC .........G ...... 630 393-7402
Aurora *(G-1185)*
Medplast Group Inc .........B ...... 630 706-5500
Oak Brook *(G-16541)*
▲ Mega Corporation .........E ...... 847 985-1900
Schaumburg *(G-19640)*
▲ Mercury Plastics Inc .........E ...... 888 884-1864
Chicago *(G-5688)*
Met Plastics .........E ...... 847 228-5070
Elk Grove Village *(G-9618)*

Met-L-Flo Inc .........F ...... 630 409-9860
Sugar Grove *(G-20729)*
Met2plastic LLC .........E ...... 847 228-5070
Elk Grove Village *(G-9619)*
Mgs Group North America Inc .........D ...... 847 371-1158
Libertyville *(G-13357)*
Mgs Mfg Group Inc .........E ...... 847 968-4335
Libertyville *(G-13358)*
Michael Clesen .........G ...... 630 377-3075
Saint Charles *(G-19220)*
Micron Mold & Mfg Inc .........G ...... 630 871-9531
Carol Stream *(G-3196)*
Microthincom Inc .........F ...... 630 543-0501
Bensenville *(G-1950)*
Mid Oaks Investments LLC .........E ...... 847 215-3475
Buffalo Grove *(G-2736)*
Mid-America Plastic Company .........E ...... 815 938-3110
Forreston *(G-10270)*
Midland Plastics Inc .........E ...... 262 938-7000
Roselle *(G-18958)*
Midland Plastics Inc .........G ...... 815 282-4079
Machesney Park *(G-14091)*
Midwest Blow Molding LLC .........G ...... 618 283-9223
Vandalia *(G-21117)*
◆ Midwest Canvas Corp .........C ...... 773 287-4400
Chicago *(G-5742)*
▲ Midwest Exchange Entps Inc .........E ...... 847 599-9595
Gurnee *(G-11472)*
Midwest Molding Inc .........D ...... 224 208-1110
Bartlett *(G-1363)*
▲ Midwest Molding Solutions .........F ...... 309 663-7374
Bloomington *(G-2200)*
Midwest Tropical Entps Inc .........E ...... 847 679-6666
Skokie *(G-20040)*
Millennium Mold Design Inc .........G ...... 815 344-9790
McHenry *(G-14535)*
▲ Mjsrf Inc .........F ...... 888 677-6175
Mount Prospect *(G-15349)*
◆ Mold-Rite Plastics LLC .........E ...... 518 561-1812
Chicago *(G-5790)*
Molded Displays .........G ...... 773 892-4098
Highland Park *(G-11856)*
Molding Services Group Inc .........E ...... 847 931-1491
South Elgin *(G-20220)*
▲ Molding Services Illinois Inc .........E ...... 618 395-3888
Olney *(G-16782)*
Moldtronics Inc .........E ...... 630 968-7000
Downers Grove *(G-8488)*
▲ Molor Products Company .........F ...... 630 375-5999
Oswego *(G-16927)*
▲ Monahan Filaments LLC .........D ...... 217 268-4957
Arcola *(G-677)*
▲ Monda Window & Door Corp .........E ...... 773 254-8888
Chicago *(G-5792)*
Moore-Addison Co .........E ...... 630 543-6744
Addison *(G-220)*
Mountain Horizions Inc .........E ...... 630 501-0190
Addison *(G-222)*
Mpc Group LLC .........G ...... 773 927-4120
Chicago *(G-5824)*
◆ MPD Inc .........E ...... 847 489-7705
Lake Forest *(G-12928)*
▲ Mpr Plastics Inc .........E ...... 847 468-9950
Elgin *(G-9115)*
Mueller Door Company .........E ...... 815 385-8550
Wauconda *(G-21487)*
Multi Packaging Solutions Inc .........G ...... 773 283-9500
Chicago *(G-5832)*
Multi-Plastics Inc .........E ...... 630 226-0580
Bolingbrook *(G-2348)*
Mvs Molding Inc .........G ...... 847 740-7700
Round Lake *(G-19063)*
Nascote Industries Inc .........D ...... 419 324-3392
Belvidere *(G-1774)*
National Emergency Med ID Inc .........E ...... 847 366-1267
Spring Grove *(G-20351)*
Navitor Inc .........B ...... 800 323-0253
Harwood Heights *(G-11687)*
Nebraska Plastics Incorporated .........E ...... 217 423-9007
Decatur *(G-7921)*
▲ Neil Enterprises Inc .........E ...... 847 549-0321
Vernon Hills *(G-21184)*
▲ Neil International Inc .........E ...... 847 549-7627
Vernon Hills *(G-21185)*
Neomek Incorporated .........F ...... 630 879-5400
Batavia *(G-1475)*
◆ Newell Operating Company .........C ...... 815 235-4171
Freeport *(G-10675)*
Newovo Plastics LLC .........G ...... 224 535-8183
Elgin *(G-9119)*

**Nissei America Inc** G 847 228-5000
Elk Grove Village *(G-9652)*

▲ **North Amercn Acquisition Corp** C 847 695-8030
Elgin *(G-9125)*

**North America Packaging Corp** C 630 845-8726
Peotone *(G-17491)*

▼ **North America Packaging Corp** E 630 203-4100
Oak Brook *(G-16547)*

▲ **North American Fund III LP** G 312 332-4950
Chicago *(G-5932)*

▲ **Northern Precision Plas Inc** E 815 544-8099
Belvidere *(G-1776)*

**Northstar Trading LLC** F 224 422-6050
Romeoville *(G-18855)*

**Northwestern Cup & Logo Inc** G 773 874-8000
Chicago *(G-5942)*

**Npi Holding Corp** G 217 391-1229
Springfield *(G-20488)*

▲ **Nu-Dell Manufacturing Co Inc** F 847 803-4500
Chicago *(G-5953)*

▲ **Nudo Products Inc** C 217 528-5636
Springfield *(G-20490)*

**Nypro Inc** E 630 671-2000
Hanover Park *(G-11588)*

**Nypromold Inc** C 847 855-2200
Gurnee *(G-11477)*

▲ **Oak Technical LLC** G 931 455-7011
Matteson *(G-14377)*

▲ **Oakridge Products LLC** G 815 363-4700
McHenry *(G-14538)*

**Oberthur Tech Amer Corp** D 630 551-0792
Naperville *(G-15718)*

**Odra Inc** G 847 249-2910
Gurnee *(G-11478)*

**Olcott Plastics Inc** D 630 584-0555
Saint Charles *(G-19228)*

▼ **One Way Solutions LLC** G 847 446-0872
Northfield *(G-16414)*

**Owen Plastics LLC** E 847 683-2054
Burlington *(G-2813)*

**P & P Industries Inc** D 815 623-3297
Sterling *(G-20602)*

**Pactiv Intl Holdings Inc** G 847 482-2000
Lake Forest *(G-12934)*

**Pactiv LLC** B 715 723-4181
Lake Forest *(G-12938)*

**Pactiv LLC** B 847 459-8049
Wheeling *(G-22116)*

**Pactiv LLC** C 708 496-2900
Bedford Park *(G-1571)*

**Pactiv LLC** C 847 451-1480
Franklin Park *(G-10545)*

◆ **Pactiv LLC** A 847 482-2000
Lake Forest *(G-12935)*

**Pactiv LLC** C 815 469-2112
Frankfort *(G-10346)*

**Pactiv LLC** C 217 479-1144
Jacksonville *(G-12404)*

**Paragon Manufacturing Inc** D 708 345-1717
Melrose Park *(G-14681)*

**Paramount Plastics Inc** D 815 834-4100
Chicago *(G-6077)*

**Parting Line Tool Inc** F 847 669-0331
Huntley *(G-12166)*

**Peeps Inc** G 708 935-4201
Palos Hills *(G-17121)*

▲ **Perfect Plastic Printing Corp** C 630 584-1600
Saint Charles *(G-19234)*

**Perfect Shutters Inc** E 815 648-2401
Hebron *(G-11724)*

**Performance Gear Systems Inc** E 630 739-6666
Plainfield *(G-17637)*

**Peritus Plastics LLC** E 815 448-2005
Mazon *(G-14440)*

▲ **Pexco LLC** C 847 296-5511
Des Plaines *(G-8253)*

▲ **Phoenix Electric Mfg Co** E 773 477-8855
Chicago *(G-6118)*

**Pimco Plastics Inc** G 815 675-6464
Spring Grove *(G-20356)*

**Plano Metal Specialties Inc** F 630 552-8510
Plano *(G-17672)*

◆ **Plano Molding Company LLC** G 630 552-3111
Plano *(G-17673)*

**Plano Molding Company LLC** C 630 552-9557
Sandwich *(G-19373)*

**Plano Molding Company LLC** C 815 538-3111
Mendota *(G-14730)*

**Plano Molding Company LLC** C 815 786-3331
Sandwich *(G-19374)*

◆ **Plaspros Inc** D 815 430-2300
McHenry *(G-14546)*

**Plaspros Inc** G 847 639-6492
Cary *(G-3364)*

**Plastech Inc** F 630 595-7222
Bensenville *(G-1964)*

**Plastech Molding Inc** G 847 398-0355
Wheeling *(G-22123)*

▲ **Plastic Container Corporation** D 217 352-2722
Urbana *(G-21098)*

**Plastic Designs Inc** E 217 379-9214
Paxton *(G-17243)*

▲ **Plastic Film Corp America Inc** F 630 887-0800
Romeoville *(G-18857)*

▲ **Plastic Parts Intl Inc** E 815 637-9222
Machesney Park *(G-14097)*

**Plastic Power Corporation** G 847 233-9601
Franklin Park *(G-10553)*

**Plastic Powerdrive Pdts LLC** F 847 637-5233
Elgin *(G-9139)*

**Plastic Products Company Inc** C 309 762-6532
Moline *(G-14962)*

**Plastic Products Inc** E 847 874-3440
Schaumburg *(G-19692)*

**Plastic Services Group** G 847 368-1444
Arlington Heights *(G-818)*

▲ **Plasticrest Products Inc** F 773 826-2163
Chicago *(G-6136)*

**Plastics** G 847 931-9391
Elgin *(G-9141)*

**Plastipak Packaging Inc** C 630 231-7650
West Chicago *(G-21757)*

**Plastipak Packaging Inc** B 217 398-1832
Champaign *(G-3526)*

**Plastipak Packaging Inc** C 708 385-0721
Alsip *(G-510)*

**Plastival Inc** B 847 931-4771
Elgin *(G-9142)*

▲ **Platt Luggage Inc** D 773 838-2000
Chicago *(G-6139)*

▼ **Pliant LLC** A 812 424-2904
Rolling Meadows *(G-18763)*

▲ **Plitek** D 847 827-6680
Des Plaines *(G-8257)*

▲ **Plustech Inc** G 847 490-8130
Schaumburg *(G-19698)*

**Pnc Inc** D 815 946-2328
Polo *(G-17690)*

**Polar Tech Industries Inc** E 815 784-9000
Genoa *(G-10882)*

**Polydesigns Ltd** G 847 433-9920
Highland Park *(G-11861)*

**Polymer Plnfeld Hldings US Inc** C 815 436-5671
Plainfield *(G-17641)*

**Polytech Industries Inc** E 630 443-6030
Saint Charles *(G-19237)*

**Portola Packaging LLC** E 630 515-8383
Downers Grove *(G-8506)*

**Powerpath Microproducts Inc** G 847 827-6330
Des Plaines *(G-8258)*

▼ **Prairie Packaging Inc** E 708 496-1172
Bedford Park *(G-1575)*

**Prairie Packaging Inc** F 708 496-2900
Chicago *(G-6166)*

**Prairie Packaging Inc** G 708 563-8670
Bridgeview *(G-2520)*

**Precision Container Inc** G 618 548-2830
Salem *(G-19344)*

**Precision Custom Molders Inc** E 815 675-1370
Spring Grove *(G-20357)*

**Precision Molded Concepts** F 815 675-0060
Spring Grove *(G-20358)*

**Precision Plastic Products** G 217 784-4920
Gibson City *(G-10906)*

**Prestige Motor Works Inc** G 630 780-6439
Naperville *(G-15823)*

▲ **Prismier LLC** E 630 592-4515
Woodridge *(G-22511)*

**Process Systems Inc** G 217 563-2872
Nokomis *(G-16060)*

**Profile Plastics Inc** D 847 256-1623
Lake Bluff *(G-12864)*

**Prommar Plastics Inc** G 815 770-0555
Harvard *(G-11645)*

**Prototek Tool & Mold Inc** G 847 487-2708
Wauconda *(G-21496)*

**Psa Equity LLC** F 847 478-6000
Buffalo Grove *(G-2757)*

**Pylon Plastics Inc** G 630 968-6374
Lisle *(G-13646)*

**Q C H Incorporated** D 630 820-5550
Oswego *(G-16929)*

▲ **Quad Inc** E 815 624-8538
South Beloit *(G-20166)*

◆ **Qualitas Manufacturing Inc** D 630 529-7111
Itasca *(G-12346)*

**Quality Custom Closets** G 773 307-1105
Glenview *(G-11185)*

**Quality Plastic Products Inc** G 630 766-7593
Bensenville *(G-1972)*

◆ **Quixote Corporation** E 312 705-8400
Chicago *(G-6259)*

**Quixote Transportation Safety** D 312 467-6750
Chicago *(G-6260)*

◆ **R and R Brokerage Co** C 847 438-4600
Lake Zurich *(G-13121)*

**R C Sales & Manufacturing Inc** G 815 645-8898
Stillman Valley *(G-20626)*

**R T P Company** G 618 286-6100
Dupo *(G-8576)*

**Rackow Polymers Corporation** E 630 766-3982
Bensenville *(G-1975)*

**Railshop Inc** G 847 816-0925
Libertyville *(G-13374)*

**Ram Plastic Corp** G 847 669-8003
Huntley *(G-12172)*

**Rand Manufacturing Network Inc** G 847 299-8884
Wheeling *(G-22132)*

▲ **Ravenscroft Inc** G 630 513-9911
Saint Charles *(G-19250)*

**Really Useful Boxes Inc** F 847 238-0444
Elk Grove Village *(G-9710)*

**Rensel-Chicago Inc** F 773 235-2100
Chicago *(G-6334)*

**Resins Inc** G 847 884-0025
Hoffman Estates *(G-12043)*

**Resource Plastics Inc** D 708 389-3558
Alsip *(G-519)*

▲ **Reum Corporation** C 847 625-7386
Chicago *(G-6340)*

▲ **Revcor Inc** B 847 428-4411
Carpentersville *(G-3301)*

**Revcor Inc** G 847 428-4411
Carpentersville *(G-3302)*

**Rf Plastics Co** G 630 628-6033
Addison *(G-278)*

**Ricon Colors Inc** F 630 562-9000
West Chicago *(G-21764)*

▲ **Riken Corporation of America** C 847 673-1400
Skokie *(G-20076)*

**Ring Container Tech LLC** E 217 875-5084
Decatur *(G-7934)*

**Rockford Molded Products Inc** D 815 637-0585
Loves Park *(G-13985)*

**Rohrer Corporation** D 847 961-5920
Huntley *(G-12174)*

▲ **Ropak Central Inc** D 847 956-0750
Elk Grove Village *(G-9718)*

**Royal Touch Carwash** G 847 808-8600
Buffalo Grove *(G-2760)*

**RPI Extrusion Co** G 708 389-2584
Alsip *(G-524)*

▲ **RPS Products Inc** E 847 683-3400
Hampshire *(G-11562)*

**Rust-Oleum Corporation** D 815 967-4258
Rockford *(G-18600)*

**Rway Plastics Ltd** F 815 476-5252
Wilmington *(G-22276)*

**S & S Mold Corporation** G 815 385-0818
Woodstock *(G-22606)*

▲ **S4 Industries Inc** F 224 699-9674
East Dundee *(G-8656)*

**Safe-T-Quip Corporation** F 773 235-2100
Chicago *(G-6425)*

**Safeway Products Inc** F 815 226-8322
Rockford *(G-18606)*

▲ **Sakamoto Kanagata Usa Inc** G 224 856-2008
South Elgin *(G-20225)*

**Sandee Manufacturing Co** G 847 671-1335
Franklin Park *(G-10581)*

▲ **Sap Acquisition Co LLC** E 847 229-1600
Buffalo Grove *(G-2761)*

**SCC Holding Company LLC** A 847 444-5000
Lake Forest *(G-12958)*

◆ **Scholle Ipn Corporation** F 708 562-7290
Northlake *(G-16450)*

◆ **Scholle Ipn Packaging Inc** B 708 562-7290
Northlake *(G-16451)*

**Scholle Packaging Inc** G 708 273-3792
Northlake *(G-16452)*

S I C

Employee Codes: A=Over 500 employees, B=251-500
C=101-250, D=51-100, E=20-50, F=10-19, G=3-9

2017 Harris Illinois
Industrial Directory

1009

30 RUBBER AND MISCELLANEOUS PLASTICS PRODUCTS | SIC SECTION

**Schweppe Inc** ... G ... 630 627-3550
Addison *(G-284)*

**Scimitar Prototyping Inc** ... G ... 630 483-3875
Streamwood *(G-20672)*

**Seals & Components Inc** ... G ... 708 895-5222
Lansing *(G-13182)*

**Security Molding Inc** ... F ... 630 543-8607
Addison *(G-285)*

▲ **Sek Corporation** ... E ... 630 762-0606
Saint Charles *(G-19262)*

**Selig S LLC** ... G ... 815 785-2100
Forrest *(G-10264)*

**Selig Sealing Holdings Inc** ... G ... 815 785-2100
Forrest *(G-10265)*

**Shamrock Plastics Inc** ... E ... 309 243-7723
Peoria *(G-17454)*

**Shannon Industries Inc** ... G ... 815 338-8960
Woodstock *(G-22610)*

**Sherwood Tool Inc** ... F ... 815 648-1463
Hebron *(G-11726)*

▲ **Signode Packaging Systems Corp** ... D ... 800 323-2464
Glenview *(G-11203)*

**Sikora Precision Inc** ... G ... 847 468-0900
Elgin *(G-9180)*

**Silgan Plastics LLC** ... D ... 618 662-4471
Flora *(G-10217)*

**Silgan Plastics LLC** ... C ... 815 334-1200
Woodstock *(G-22612)*

**Silver Line Building Pdts LLC** ... B ... 708 474-9100
Lansing *(G-13184)*

**Simonton Building Products Inc** ... B ... 217 466-2851
Paris *(G-17162)*

◆ **Simonton Holdings Inc** ... F ... 304 428-8261
Deerfield *(G-8055)*

**Simonton Windows Inc** ... G ... 217 466-2851
Paris *(G-17163)*

**Simplomatic Manufacturing Co** ... E ... 773 342-7757
Elgin *(G-9181)*

**Smt LLC** ... E ... 630 961-3000
Naperville *(G-15747)*

**Sno Gem Inc** ... F ... 888 766-4367
McHenry *(G-14555)*

**Snyder Industries Inc** ... D ... 630 773-9510
Bensenville *(G-1993)*

▼ **Solo Cup Company** ... C ... 847 831-4800
Lincolnshire *(G-13480)*

▲ **Solo Cup Company LLC** ... C ... 847 444-5000
Lincolnshire *(G-13481)*

▼ **Solo Cup Investment Corp** ... E ... 847 831-4800
Highland Park *(G-11872)*

▼ **Solo Cup Operating Corporation** ... D ... 847 444-5000
Lincolnshire *(G-13482)*

**Solo Cup Operating Corporation** ... C ... 847 444-5000
Chicago *(G-6541)*

**Sonoco Products Company** ... C ... 847 957-6282
Franklin Park *(G-10591)*

**Sparx EDM Inc** ... G ... 847 722-7577
Streamwood *(G-20674)*

**Specialized Woodwork Inc** ... G ... 630 627-0450
Lombard *(G-13854)*

**Spinner Medical Products Inc** ... B ... 312 944-8700
Chicago *(G-6560)*

▲ **Spintex Inc** ... G ... 847 608-5411
Elgin *(G-9190)*

**Spirit Foodservice Inc** ... C ... 214 634-1393
Lake Forest *(G-12962)*

**Stanger Tool & Mold Inc** ... G ... 847 426-5826
Belvidere *(G-1785)*

▲ **Star Die Molding Inc** ... D ... 847 766-7952
Elk Grove Village *(G-9754)*

**Steel Guard Inc** ... F ... 773 342-6265
Chicago *(G-6580)*

**Stellar Plastics Corporation** ... D ... 630 443-1200
Saint Charles *(G-19270)*

**Stevens Plastic Inc** ... E ... 847 885-2378
Hoffman Estates *(G-12060)*

**Stock Gears Inc** ... F ... 224 653-9489
Elk Grove Village *(G-9758)*

**Studio Moulding** ... G ... 217 523-2101
Springfield *(G-20539)*

▲ **Suburban Plastics Co** ... B ... 847 741-4900
Elgin *(G-9194)*

**Sullivan Tool and Repair Inc** ... G ... 224 856-5867
Elgin *(G-9195)*

**Sun Dome Inc** ... F ... 773 890-5350
Chicago *(G-6618)*

**Sun Pattern & Model Inc** ... E ... 630 293-3366
West Chicago *(G-21777)*

**Superior American Plastics Co** ... E ... 847 229-1600
Buffalo Grove *(G-2778)*

**Survyvn Ltd** ... G ... 847 977-8665
Ringwood *(G-17995)*

**T C I Vacuum Forming Company** ... E ... 847 622-9100
Elgin *(G-9200)*

**T L Swint Industries Inc** ... G ... 847 358-3834
Inverness *(G-12206)*

**Taico Design Products Inc** ... G ... 773 871-9086
Chicago *(G-6665)*

**Target Plastics Tech Corp** ... D ... 630 545-1776
Glendale Heights *(G-11083)*

**Team Technologies Inc** ... D ... 630 937-0380
Batavia *(G-1504)*

**Technatool Inc** ... G ... 847 398-0355
Wheeling *(G-22165)*

**Technimold Tool Corporation** ... F ... 847 639-4226
Cary *(G-3376)*

◆ **Technipaq Inc** ... C ... 815 477-1800
Crystal Lake *(G-7661)*

**Techny Plastics Corp** ... E ... 847 498-2212
Northbrook *(G-16377)*

**Teepak Usa LLC** ... G ... 217 446-6460
Danville *(G-7767)*

**Tegrant Alloyd Brands Inc** ... B ... 815 756-8451
Dekalb *(G-8124)*

**Tegrant Holding Corp** ... A ... 815 756-8451
Dekalb *(G-8126)*

**Tempco Products Co** ... D ... 618 544-3175
Robinson *(G-18074)*

▲ **Tenex Corporation** ... E ... 847 504-0400
Buffalo Grove *(G-2780)*

**Teraco-II Inc** ... E ... 630 539-4400
Roselle *(G-18981)*

▲ **Testor Corporation** ... D ... 815 962-6654
Rockford *(G-18644)*

**Tex Trend Inc** ... E ... 847 215-6796
Wheeling *(G-22166)*

▲ **The Intec Group Inc** ... C ... 847 358-0088
Palatine *(G-17081)*

**Thermal-Tech Systems Inc** ... E ... 630 639-5115
West Chicago *(G-21780)*

▼ **Thermform Engineered Qulty LLC** ... D ... 847 669-5291
Huntley *(G-12179)*

**Thermo-Graphic LLC** ... E ... 630 350-2226
Bensenville *(G-2001)*

**Thermo-Pak Co** ... E ... 630 860-1303
Wood Dale *(G-22431)*

**Three R Plastics Inc** ... F ... 815 675-0844
Spring Grove *(G-20368)*

**Thurow Tool Works Inc** ... G ... 630 377-6403
Saint Charles *(G-19283)*

**Time Records Publishing and Bo** ... G ... 618 996-3803
Marion *(G-14291)*

▲ **Tinex Technology Corp** ... G ... 630 904-5368
Naperville *(G-15830)*

▲ **Tmf Plastic Solutions LLC** ... D ... 630 552-7575
Plano *(G-17677)*

**Tmf Polymer Solutions Inc** ... F ... 630 552-7575
Plano *(G-17678)*

▲ **Tmf Polymer Solutions Inc** ... G ... 541 479-7484
Plano *(G-17679)*

▲ **Tni Packaging Inc** ... G ... 630 293-3030
West Chicago *(G-21781)*

**TNT Plastics Inc** ... F ... 847 895-6921
Schaumburg *(G-19764)*

**Tomco Die & Kellering Co** ... G ... 847 678-8113
Franklin Park *(G-10608)*

**Transparent Container Co Inc** ... E ... 708 449-8520
Addison *(G-321)*

**Transparent Container Co Inc** ... D ... 630 543-1818
Addison *(G-322)*

**Transparent Container Co Inc** ... D ... 708 449-8520
Addison *(G-323)*

**Transparent Container Co Inc** ... E ... 630 860-2666
Bensenville *(G-2006)*

**Tredegar Film Products Corp** ... C ... 847 438-2111
Lake Zurich *(G-13138)*

**Trellborg Sling Sltions US Inc** ... F ... 630 539-5500
Schaumburg *(G-19769)*

**Trend Technologies LLC** ... C ... 847 640-2382
Elk Grove Village *(G-9789)*

**Tri Guards Inc** ... F ... 847 537-8444
Elk Grove Village *(G-9790)*

**Tri-Par Die and Mold Corp** ... E ... 630 232-8800
South Elgin *(G-20229)*

**Tri-Tech Molding** ... G ... 847 263-7769
Lake Villa *(G-13028)*

▲ **Trident Manufacturing Inc** ... E ... 847 464-0140
Pingree Grove *(G-17557)*

▲ **Trim-Tex Inc** ... D ... 847 679-3000
Lincolnwood *(G-13540)*

**True Line Mold and Engrg Corp** ... E ... 815 648-2739
Hebron *(G-11729)*

◆ **Tuf-Tite Inc** ... F ... 847 550-1011
Lake Zurich *(G-13139)*

**Tuscola Packaging Group LLC** ... G ... 734 268-2877
Tuscola *(G-21027)*

**Uniphase Inc** ... E ... 630 584-4747
Saint Charles *(G-19288)*

▲ **Unique Assembly & Decorating** ... E ... 630 241-4300
Downers Grove *(G-8535)*

**Universal Hovercraft Amer Inc** ... F ... 815 963-1200
Rockford *(G-18664)*

**Upward Bound** ... G ... 773 265-1370
Chicago *(G-6843)*

**Urban Services of America** ... G ... 847 278-3210
Schaumburg *(G-19783)*

**Urpoint LLC** ... G ... 773 919-9002
New Lenox *(G-15925)*

▲ **US Acrylic LLC** ... D ... 847 837-4800
Libertyville *(G-13395)*

**Uwd Inc** ... F ... 815 316-3080
Roscoe *(G-18925)*

**Vac-Matic Corporation** ... G ... 630 543-4518
Addison *(G-336)*

**Van Norman Molding Company LLC** ... E ... 708 430-4343
Oak Lawn *(G-16647)*

**Vector Mold & Tool Inc** ... G ... 847 437-0110
Des Plaines *(G-8297)*

◆ **Vector USA Inc** ... F ... 630 434-0040
Oak Brook *(G-16567)*

**Veejay Plastics Inc** ... F ... 847 683-2954
Burlington *(G-2814)*

**Vega Molded Products Inc** ... G ... 847 428-7761
Gilberts *(G-10940)*

▲ **Versatile Card Technology Inc** ... C ... 630 852-5600
Downers Grove *(G-8536)*

**Viscofan Usa Inc** ... D ... 217 444-8000
Danville *(G-7779)*

▲ **Vision Sales & Marketing Inc** ... G ... 708 496-6016
Chicago *(G-6904)*

◆ **Viskase Companies Inc** ... D ... 630 874-0700
Lombard *(G-13879)*

▼ **Viskase Corporation** ... D ... 630 874-0700
Lombard *(G-13880)*

**Vp Plastics and Engrg Inc** ... E ... 847 689-8900
Waukegan *(G-21638)*

▲ **W J Dennis & Company** ... F ... 847 697-4800
Elgin *(G-9225)*

▲ **W M Plastics Inc** ... D ... 815 578-8888
McHenry *(G-14570)*

**Wedco Molded Products** ... G ... 630 455-6711
Willowbrook *(G-22239)*

**Werner Co** ... E ... 815 459-6020
Crystal Lake *(G-7676)*

**Wesdar Technologies Inc** ... G ... 630 761-0965
Aurora *(G-1096)*

**Westrock Dspensing Systems Inc** ... G ... 847 310-3073
Schaumburg *(G-19788)*

**White Eagle Brands Inc** ... G ... 773 631-1764
Chicago *(G-6971)*

**Will County Waste** ... G ... 708 489-9718
Blue Island *(G-2272)*

◆ **Wind Point Partners LP** ... F ... 312 255-4800
Chicago *(G-6992)*

▲ **Winzeler Inc** ... E ... 708 867-7971
Harwood Heights *(G-11692)*

▲ **Wise Plastics Technologies Inc** ... C ... 630 584-2307
Saint Charles *(G-19298)*

**Wise Plastics Technologies Inc** ... G ... 847 697-2840
West Chicago *(G-21793)*

**WJ Die Mold Inc** ... F ... 847 895-6561
Schaumburg *(G-19791)*

**Woodland Engineering Company** ... G ... 847 362-0110
Lake Bluff *(G-12873)*

▼ **Woodland Plastics Corp** ... E ... 630 543-1144
Addison *(G-345)*

**Woojin Plaimm Inc** ... F ... 708 606-5536
Mount Prospect *(G-15385)*

▼ **Work Area Protection Corp** ... D ... 630 377-9100
Saint Charles *(G-19299)*

▲ **Xcell International Corp** ... D ... 630 323-0107
Lemont *(G-13271)*

◆ **Yoshino America Corporation** ... E ... 708 534-1141
University Park *(G-21067)*

◆ **Zeller Plastik Usa Inc** ... C ... 847 247-7900
Libertyville *(G-13403)*

**Zender Enterprises Ltd** ... G ... 773 282-2293
Chicago *(G-7063)*

# 31 LEATHER AND LEATHER PRODUCTS

### 3111 Leather Tanning & Finishing

**Angelo Bruni** ....G.... 773 754-5422
Aurora *(G-957)*
**Brighton Collectibles LLC** ....E.... 847 674-6719
Skokie *(G-19971)*
**Darling Ingredients Inc** ....E.... 618 271-8190
National Stock Yards *(G-15850)*
**Excelled Sheepskin & Lea Coat** ....C.... 309 852-3341
Kewanee *(G-12682)*
▲ **Horween Leather Company** ....C.... 773 772-2026
Chicago *(G-5115)*
▲ **Sukie Group Inc** ....F.... 773 521-1800
Chicago *(G-6613)*
**Tyson Fresh Meats Inc** ....F.... 847 836-5550
Elgin *(G-9218)*
**Unidex Packaging LLC** ....F.... 630 735-7040
Hanover Park *(G-11592)*
**United Rawhide Mfg Co** ....G.... 847 692-2791
Park Ridge *(G-17228)*
**Zoes Mfgco LLC** ....F.... 312 666-4018
Chicago *(G-7071)*

### 3131 Boot & Shoe Cut Stock & Findings

**Counter** ....G.... 312 666-5335
Chicago *(G-4482)*
**Counter Creations LLC** ....G.... 815 568-1000
Marengo *(G-14223)*
**Counter-Intelligence** ....G.... 708 974-3326
Palos Hills *(G-17115)*
**Cupcake Counter LLC** ....G.... 312 422-0800
Chicago *(G-4516)*
**Curt Herrmann Construction Inc** ....G.... 815 748-0531
Dekalb *(G-8082)*
**D R Walters** ....G.... 618 926-6337
Norris City *(G-16113)*
**Fifth Quarter** ....G.... 618 346-6659
Saint Jacob *(G-19315)*
**Fishermans Quarters** ....G.... 217 791-5104
Decatur *(G-7882)*
**French Qrter Prof Off Bldg LLC** ....G.... 815 972-0681
Joliet *(G-12498)*
**Hanigs Footwear Inc** ....G.... 773 248-1977
Wilmette *(G-22253)*
**Illinois Hand & Upper Extremit** ....G.... 847 956-0099
Arlington Heights *(G-774)*
**Painted Quarter Ridge** ....G.... 618 534-9734
Ava *(G-1241)*
**Quarters Concessions Inc** ....G.... 847 343-4864
Carpentersville *(G-3299)*
**Rays Countertop Shop Inc** ....F.... 217 483-2514
Glenarm *(G-10997)*
**Upper Deck Sports Bar** ....G.... 815 517-0682
Dekalb *(G-8129)*
**Upper Urban Green Prprty Maint** ....G.... 312 218-5903
Chicago *(G-6841)*
**Uppercase Living - Indepndent** ....G.... 309 657-3054
Mapleton *(G-14214)*
**Zoes Mfgco LLC** ....F.... 312 666-4018
Chicago *(G-7071)*

### 3143 Men's Footwear, Exc Athletic

◆ **Belleville Shoe Mfg Co** ....B.... 618 233-5600
Belleville *(G-1612)*
▲ **Leos Dancewear Inc** ....D.... 773 889-7700
River Forest *(G-17998)*
**London Shoe Shop & Western Wr** ....G.... 618 345-9570
Collinsville *(G-7330)*
**Springfield Sales Assoc Inc** ....G.... 217 529-6987
Springfield *(G-20533)*
**Steven Madden Ltd** ....D.... 773 276-5486
Chicago *(G-6594)*

### 3144 Women's Footwear, Exc Athletic

**Bone & Rattle Inc** ....G.... 312 813-8830
Chicago *(G-4142)*
**Horse Creek Outfitters** ....G.... 217 544-2740
Springfield *(G-20452)*
▲ **Leos Dancewear Inc** ....D.... 773 889-7700
River Forest *(G-17998)*
**Springfield Sales Assoc Inc** ....G.... 217 529-6987
Springfield *(G-20533)*

### 3149 Footwear, NEC

**Red Wing Brands America Inc** ....G.... 815 394-1328
Rockford *(G-18552)*

### 3151 Leather Gloves & Mittens

▲ **Boss Holdings Inc** ....D.... 309 852-2131
Kewanee *(G-12673)*
▲ **Boss Manufacturing Company** ....D.... 309 852-2131
Kewanee *(G-12674)*
▲ **Boss Manufacturing Holdings** ....F.... 309 852-2781
Kewanee *(G-12675)*
▲ **Kunz Glove Co Inc** ....E.... 312 733-8780
Chicago *(G-5414)*
▲ **Magid Glove Safety Mfg Co LLC** ....B.... 773 384-2070
Romeoville *(G-18841)*
**Magid Glove Safety Mfg Co LLC** ....B.... 773 384-2070
Chicago *(G-5601)*
**Nationwide Glove Co Inc** ....D.... 618 252-7192
Harrisburg *(G-11602)*
**Nexx Business Solutions Inc** ....G.... 708 252-1958
Oakbrook Terrace *(G-16717)*

### 3161 Luggage

**A W Enterprises Inc** ....E.... 708 458-8989
Bedford Park *(G-1531)*
**Art Jewel Enterprises Ltd** ....F.... 630 260-0400
Carol Stream *(G-3106)*
**Custom Case Co Inc** ....E.... 773 585-1164
Chicago *(G-4521)*
**Du-Call Miller Plastics Inc** ....F.... 630 964-6020
Batavia *(G-1443)*
**Hartmann** ....G.... 618 684-6814
Murphysboro *(G-15576)*
**Ips & Luggage Co Inc** ....G.... 630 894-2414
Roselle *(G-18948)*
**J-Industries Inc** ....F.... 815 654-0055
Loves Park *(G-13949)*
▲ **Jacobson Acqstion Holdings LLC** ....C.... 847 623-1414
Waukegan *(G-21574)*
**Jans** ....G.... 815 722-9360
Joliet *(G-12521)*
▲ **Jelco Inc** ....F.... 847 459-5207
Wheeling *(G-22082)*
▲ **Kingport Industries LLC** ....G.... 847 480-5745
Northbrook *(G-16287)*
▲ **LC Industries Inc** ....E.... 312 455-0500
Elk Grove Village *(G-9589)*
▲ **McKlein Company LLC** ....F.... 773 235-0600
Chicago *(G-5668)*
**Mechanical Music Corp** ....F.... 847 398-5444
Arlington Heights *(G-801)*
**Mfz Ventures Inc** ....G.... 773 247-4611
Chicago *(G-5715)*
**Midwest Fibre Products Inc** ....E.... 309 596-2955
Viola *(G-21292)*
**Plano Molding Company LLC** ....C.... 815 786-3331
Sandwich *(G-19374)*
▲ **Platt Luggage Inc** ....D.... 773 838-2000
Chicago *(G-6139)*
▼ **Seamcraft International LLC** ....E.... 773 417-4002
Chicago *(G-6466)*
**Service & Manufacturing Corp** ....E.... 773 287-5500
Chicago *(G-6481)*
▲ **Sukie Group Inc** ....F.... 773 521-1800
Chicago *(G-6613)*
**Sultry Satchels Inc** ....G.... 312 810-1081
Chicago *(G-6616)*
▲ **Travel Caddy Inc** ....E.... 847 621-7000
Elk Grove Village *(G-9788)*

### 3171 Handbags & Purses

**Coach Inc** ....F.... 630 232-0667
Geneva *(G-10819)*
**Coach Inc** ....E.... 708 349-1053
Orland Park *(G-16848)*
**Ipurse Inc** ....F.... 312 344-3449
Chicago *(G-5236)*

### 3172 Personal Leather Goods

**A W Enterprises Inc** ....E.... 708 458-8989
Bedford Park *(G-1531)*
▲ **Elegant Acquisition LLC** ....D.... 708 652-3400
Cicero *(G-7194)*
▲ **Hertzberg Ernst & Sons** ....E.... 773 525-3518
Chicago *(G-5082)*
**J-Industries Inc** ....F.... 815 654-0055
Loves Park *(G-13949)*
**Loren Girovich** ....G.... 773 334-1444
Chicago *(G-5541)*
**Medacta Usa Inc** ....D.... 312 878-2381
Chicago *(G-5675)*
▲ **Plasticrest Products Inc** ....F.... 773 826-2163
Chicago *(G-6136)*

◆ **Randa Accessories Lea Gds LLC** ....D.... 847 292-8300
Rosemont *(G-19026)*
▲ **Rico Industries Inc** ....D.... 312 427-0313
Niles *(G-16028)*
**Tia Tynette Designs Inc** ....G.... 219 440-2859
Olympia Fields *(G-16806)*
**Toshware Inc** ....E.... 217 896-2437
Monticello *(G-15087)*
▲ **World Richman Mfg Corp** ....F.... 847 468-8898
Elgin *(G-9239)*

### 3199 Leather Goods, NEC

**American Trade & Coml Svc LLC** ....F.... 202 910-8808
Chicago *(G-3879)*
▲ **Boston Leather Inc** ....E.... 815 622-1635
Sterling *(G-20585)*
▲ **Choice Usa LLC** ....G.... 847 428-2252
Gilberts *(G-10915)*
**Cocajo Blades & Leather** ....G.... 217 370-6634
Franklin *(G-10378)*
**Elite Manufacturer LLC** ....G.... 779 777-3857
Streamwood *(G-20653)*
▲ **Hertzberg Ernst & Sons** ....E.... 773 525-3518
Chicago *(G-5082)*
◆ **Klein Tools Inc** ....B.... 847 821-5500
Lincolnshire *(G-13460)*
**Klein Tools Inc** ....D.... 847 228-6999
Elk Grove Village *(G-9577)*
**Klein Tools Inc** ....E.... 847 821-5500
Lincolnshire *(G-13461)*
**Mast Harness Shop** ....E.... 217 543-3463
Campbell Hill *(G-2976)*
**Spirit Industries Inc** ....G.... 217 285-4500
Griggsville *(G-11414)*
**W W Belt Inc** ....G.... 708 788-1855
Berwyn *(G-2078)*

# 32 STONE, CLAY, GLASS, AND CONCRETE PRODUCTS

### 3211 Flat Glass

**Allpro Fleet Maint Systems** ....G.... 708 430-1400
Burbank *(G-2806)*
▲ **Cat I Manufacturing Inc** ....C.... 847 931-1200
South Elgin *(G-20188)*
▲ **Chicago Tempered Glass Inc** ....F.... 773 583-2300
Chicago *(G-4354)*
**Crystal Win & Door Systems Ltd** ....E.... 773 376-6688
Chicago *(G-4510)*
**Duo Plex Glass Ltd** ....G.... 708 532-4422
Orland Park *(G-16858)*
**Energy-Glazed Systems Inc** ....F.... 847 223-4500
Grayslake *(G-11334)*
**Engineered Glass Products LLC** ....D.... 312 326-4710
Chicago *(G-4752)*
**Engineered Glass Products LLC** ....E.... 773 843-1964
Chicago *(G-4753)*
▲ **Euroview Enterprises LLC** ....E.... 630 227-3300
Elmhurst *(G-9869)*
**Fuyao Glass Illinois Inc** ....C.... 217 864-2392
Decatur *(G-7883)*
**Glass America Midwest Inc** ....G.... 203 932-0248
Elmhurst *(G-9876)*
**Glazed Structures Inc** ....F.... 847 223-4560
Grayslake *(G-11341)*
**Great Lakes GL & Mirror Corp** ....G.... 847 647-1036
Niles *(G-15984)*
**Harmon Inc** ....D.... 312 726-5050
Chicago *(G-5046)*
**Higgins Glass Studio LLC** ....G.... 708 447-2787
Riverside *(G-18031)*
▲ **Horan Glass Block Inc** ....G.... 773 586-4808
Chicago *(G-5111)*
**Jacksonville Art Glass Inc** ....G.... 217 245-0500
Jacksonville *(G-12395)*
**Lang Exterior Inc** ....D.... 773 737-4500
Chicago *(G-5458)*
**Montrose Glass & Mirror Corp** ....G.... 773 478-6433
Chicago *(G-5798)*
**Pilkington North America Inc** ....C.... 630 545-0063
Glendale Heights *(G-11057)*
**Pilkington North America Inc** ....C.... 815 433-0932
Ottawa *(G-16979)*
**Pittsburgh Glass Works LLC** ....C.... 630 879-5100
Batavia *(G-1483)*
**Pontiac Recyclers Inc** ....G.... 815 844-6419
Pontiac *(G-17708)*
**S R Door Inc** ....E.... 815 227-1148
Rockford *(G-18603)*

S I C

Thermal Ceramics Inc E 217 627-2101
Girard (G-10950)
◆ Tru Vue Inc C 708 485-5080
Countryside (G-7448)
Willow Ridge Glass Inc F 630 910-8300
Woodridge (G-22525)

### 3221 Glass Containers

Alexander Technique G 847 337-7926
Evanston (G-10006)
Amcor Phrm Packg USA LLC C 847 298-5626
Des Plaines (G-8146)
Anchor Glass Container Corp E 815 672-7761
Streator (G-20683)
Ardagh Glass Inc C 217 732-1796
Lincoln (G-13405)
Ardagh Glass Inc D 708 849-4010
Dolton (G-8363)
Ball Foster Glass Container G 708 849-1500
Dolton (G-8365)
Ball Foster Glass Container Co G 217 735-1511
Lincoln (G-13406)
Bc International G 847 674-7384
Skokie (G-19962)
◆ Enviro-Safe Refrigerants Inc E 309 346-1110
Pekin (G-17261)
▲ Fitpac Co Ltd G 630 428-9077
Bensenville (G-1899)
▲ Fri Jado Inc G 630 633-7944
Woodridge (G-22480)
Gerresheimer Glass Inc C 708 757-6853
Chicago Heights (G-7098)
Glass Haus G 815 459-5849
McHenry (G-14510)
Kavalierglass North Amer Inc F 847 364-7303
Elk Grove Village (G-9571)
Libation Container Inc F 312 287-4524
Chicago (G-5501)
Owens-Brockway Glass Cont Inc C 815 672-3141
Streator (G-20699)
Teamdance Illinois G 815 463-9044
Geneva (G-10871)
Wis - Pak Inc D 217 224-6800
Quincy (G-17907)

### 3229 Pressed & Blown Glassware, NEC

Advanced Fiber Products LLC G 847 768-9001
Des Plaines (G-8144)
Alpha Precision Inc F 630 553-7331
Yorkville (G-22648)
Altamira Art Glass G 708 848-3799
Oak Park (G-16652)
Amkine Inc F 847 526-7088
Wauconda (G-21442)
Arttig Art G 847 804-8001
Wheeling (G-22008)
Barcor Inc F 847 940-0750
Bannockburn (G-1255)
Cleavenger Associates Inc G 630 221-0007
Winfield (G-22284)
Elite Fiber Optics LLC E 630 225-9454
Oak Brook (G-16506)
Finer Line Inc F 847 884-1611
Schaumburg (G-19527)
▲ Harris Potteries LP G 847 564-5544
Northbrook (G-16268)
▲ Hunter Mfg LLP D 859 254-7573
Lake Forest (G-12912)
Industrial Fiberglass Inc F 708 681-2707
Melrose Park (G-14657)
James R Wilbat Glass Studio G 847 940-0015
Deerfield (G-8017)
Lang Exterior Inc D 773 737-4500
Chicago (G-5458)
Libation Container Inc F 312 287-4524
Chicago (G-5501)
Libbey Inc C 630 818-3400
West Chicago (G-21731)
Lotton Art Glass Co G 708 672-1400
Crete (G-7516)
Mac Lean-Fogg Company C 847 288-2534
Franklin Park (G-10519)
Mattarusky Inc G 630 469-4125
Glen Ellyn (G-10980)
Montclare Scientific Glass G 847 255-6870
Arlington Heights (G-805)
Neolight Labs LLC G 312 242-1773
Ingleside (G-12195)
▲ Nippon Electric Glass Amer Inc G 630 285-8323
Schaumburg (G-19665)
Norman P Moeller G 847 991-3933
Lake Barrington (G-12821)
OBrien Scntfic GL Blowing LLC G 217 762-3636
Monticello (G-15082)
Prairie Fire Glass Inc G 217 762-3332
Monticello (G-15083)
Punch Products Manufacturing E 773 533-2800
Chicago (G-6226)
Quality Coating Co F 815 875-3228
Princeton (G-17761)
Sotish Ltd G 708 476-2017
La Grange (G-12746)
Spectragen Incorporated G 847 982-0481
Naperville (G-15752)
Tacom Hq Inc G 630 251-8919
Sheridan (G-19919)
▲ Tadd LLC F 847 380-3540
Cary (G-3375)
Thermal Ceramics Inc E 217 627-2101
Girard (G-10950)
▲ Waters Industries Inc E 847 783-5900
West Dundee (G-21803)
◆ Wki Holding Company Inc D 847 233-8600
Rosemont (G-19041)
◆ World Kitchen LLC C 847 233-8600
Rosemont (G-19042)

### 3231 Glass Prdts Made Of Purchased Glass

Alfred Robinson G 773 487-5777
Chicago (G-3804)
▼ Art Crystal II Enterprises Inc E 630 739-0222
Lyons (G-14030)
▲ Bards Products Inc F 800 323-5499
Mundelein (G-15475)
Bertco Enterprises Inc G 618 234-9283
Belleville (G-1614)
Besco Awards & Embroidery G 847 395-4862
Antioch (G-622)
Biomerieux Inc E 630 628-6055
Lombard (G-13771)
Boom Company Inc G 847 459-6199
Wheeling (G-22018)
Botti Studio of Architectural E 847 869-5933
Evanston (G-10017)
Brenda Miller G 618 678-2639
Xenia (G-22643)
Central Illinois Glass & G 309 367-4242
Metamora (G-14741)
Circle Studio Stained Glass G 847 432-7249
Highland Park (G-11827)
Circle Studio Stained Glass G 773 588-4848
Chicago (G-4380)
Clear View Industries Inc G 815 267-3593
Plainfield (G-17588)
▲ Cristaux Inc G 773 775-6020
Elk Grove Village (G-9400)
Crystal Cave F 847 251-1160
Glenview (G-11118)
Diamond J Glass G 847 973-2741
Fox Lake (G-10276)
Doralco Inc E 708 388-9324
Alsip (G-458)
Dorma Usa Inc D 717 336-3881
Steeleville (G-20560)
Dorma Usa Inc D 847 295-2700
Lake Bluff (G-12840)
Drehobl Art Glass Company G 773 286-2566
Chicago (G-4643)
Duo Plex Glass Ltd G 708 532-4422
Orland Park (G-16858)
Enameled Steel and Sign Co E 773 481-2270
Chicago (G-4748)
Energy-Glazed Systems Inc F 847 223-4500
Grayslake (G-11334)
Engineered Glass Products LLC C 312 326-4710
Chicago (G-4754)
Engineered Glass Products LLC D 312 326-4710
Chicago (G-4752)
Engineered Glass Products LLC E 773 843-1964
Chicago (G-4753)
G & R Stained Glass G 847 455-7026
Franklin Park (G-10474)
Geneva Glassworks Inc G 630 232-1200
Geneva (G-10830)
Gerresheimer Glass Inc C 708 757-6853
Chicago Heights (G-7098)
Glass America Midwest Inc G 877 743-7237
Elmhurst (G-9875)
Glass Concepts LLC F 773 650-0520
Chicago (G-4954)
Glass Dimensions Inc F 708 410-2305
Melrose Park (G-14647)
Glass Fx G 217 359-0048
Champaign (G-3488)
Glass Haus G 815 459-5849
McHenry (G-14510)
Glazed Structures Inc F 847 223-4560
Grayslake (G-11341)
Harmon Inc D 312 726-5050
Chicago (G-5046)
Henry Baron Enterprises Inc G 847 681-2755
Highland Park (G-11840)
Hillside Industries Inc C 708 498-1100
Hillside (G-11920)
▲ Howw Manufacturing Company Inc E 847 382-4380
Lake Barrington (G-12809)
Hunter Manufacturing Group Inc G 859 254-7573
Lake Forest (G-12911)
Illinois Valley Glass & Mirror F 309 682-6603
Peoria (G-17387)
J K Custom Countertops G 630 495-2324
Lombard (G-13813)
Lead n Glass Tm F 847 255-2074
Wheeling (G-22090)
Legend Dynamix Inc G 847 789-7007
Antioch (G-641)
▲ Lester L Brossard Co F 815 338-7825
Woodstock (G-22585)
Lotton Art Glass Co G 708 672-1400
Crete (G-7516)
Martin Glass Company F 618 277-1946
Belleville (G-1652)
Metal Products Sales Corp G 708 301-6844
Lockport (G-13732)
Meyer Glass Design Inc F 847 675-7219
Evanston (G-10071)
Midwest Tropical Entps Inc E 847 679-6666
Skokie (G-20040)
▲ Monogram of Evanston Inc G 847 864-8100
Evanston (G-10074)
Montclare Scientific Glass G 847 255-6870
Arlington Heights (G-805)
Montrose Glass & Mirror Corp G 773 478-6433
Chicago (G-5798)
Mth Enterprises LLC D 708 498-1100
Hillside (G-11928)
Norman P Moeller G 847 991-3933
Lake Barrington (G-12821)
OBrien Scntfic GL Blowing LLC G 217 762-3636
Monticello (G-15082)
OHara Autoglass Inc G 217 323-2300
Beardstown (G-1525)
▲ Oi Glass Containers Oi G9 G 815 672-1548
Streator (G-20698)
Oldcastle Buildingenvelope Inc G 773 523-8400
Chicago (G-5981)
Oldcastle Buildingenvelope Inc E 630 250-7270
Elk Grove Village (G-9663)
▲ Ostrom & Co Inc F 503 281-6469
Winfield (G-22288)
Panel Window Co Inc G 708 485-0310
Brookfield (G-2640)
Pilkington North America Inc C 815 433-0932
Ottawa (G-16979)
Precision Screen Specialties G 630 762-9548
Saint Charles (G-19241)
Pro Glass Corporation G 630 553-3141
Bristol (G-2549)
Pure 111 G 618 558-7888
Caseyville (G-3400)
▲ Quality Glass and Mirror Inc G 847 290-1707
Mount Prospect (G-15366)
▲ River City Millwork Inc D 800 892-9297
Rockford (G-18556)
Roscoe Glass Co G 815 623-6268
Roscoe (G-18916)
S P Industries Inc E 847 228-2851
Elk Grove Village (G-9724)
Safelite Glass Corp G 815 436-6333
Crest Hill (G-7467)
Safelite Glass Corp G 877 800-2727
Decatur (G-7938)
Safelite Glass Corp G 877 800-2727
Champaign (G-3535)
◆ Sarj USA Inc E 708 865-9134
Franklin Park (G-10582)
▲ See All Industries Inc F 773 927-3232
Chicago (G-6472)
Sharp Bullet Resistant Pdts G 815 726-2626
Joliet (G-12574)

**Sheri Law Art Glass Ltd** ......G...... 708 301-2800
Homer Glen *(G-12086)*
**Shoreline Glass Co Inc** ......E...... 312 829-9500
Hillside *(G-11933)*
◆ **Skyline Design Inc** ......D...... 773 278-4660
Chicago *(G-6524)*
◆ **Slee Corporation** ......E...... 773 777-2444
Chicago *(G-6527)*
**Southern Glass Co** ......G...... 618 532-4281
Centralia *(G-3434)*
**Stained Glass of Peoria** ......G...... 309 674-7929
Peoria *(G-17461)*
**Strategic Materials Inc** ......G...... 773 523-2200
Chicago *(G-6602)*
**Supertek Scientific LLC** ......G...... 630 345-3450
Villa Park *(G-21287)*
**Sure Plus Manufacturing Co** ......D...... 708 756-3100
Chicago Heights *(G-7128)*
**Temp-Tech Industries Inc** ......E...... 773 586-2800
Chicago *(G-6694)*
**Tiffany Stained Glass Ltd** ......G...... 312 642-0680
Forest Park *(G-10255)*
**Tonjon Company** ......F...... 630 208-1173
Geneva *(G-10873)*
▲ **Torstenson Glass Co** ......E...... 773 525-0435
Chicago *(G-6748)*
**Total Look** ......G...... 847 382-6646
Barrington *(G-1310)*
▼ **Tuminello Enterprizes Inc** ......G...... 815 416-1007
Morris *(G-15137)*
**Tuminello Enterprizes Inc** ......G...... 815 416-1007
Morris *(G-15138)*
**Weathertop Woodcraft** ......G ....
Carol Stream *(G-3265)*
**Will Hamms Stained Glass** ......F...... 847 255-2230
Arlington Heights *(G-872)*

## 3241 Cement, Hydraulic

**Bonsal American Inc** ......D...... 847 678-6220
Franklin Park *(G-10415)*
**Buzzi Unicem USA Inc** ......E...... 815 768-3660
Joliet *(G-12468)*
**Cemex Cement Inc** ......G...... 773 995-5100
Chicago *(G-4268)*
**Coal City Redi-Mix Co Inc** ......F...... 815 634-4455
Coal City *(G-7292)*
**Essroc Cement Corp** ......G...... 708 388-0797
Riverdale *(G-18019)*
**GBS Liquidating Corp** ......G...... 309 342-4155
Galesburg *(G-10753)*
**Holcim (us) Inc** ......G...... 773 721-8352
Chicago *(G-5097)*
**Holcim (us) Inc** ......E...... 773 731-1320
Chicago *(G-5098)*
▲ **Illinois Cement Company LLC** ......C...... 815 224-2112
La Salle *(G-12776)*
**Kona Blackbird Inc** ......F...... 815 792-8750
Serena *(G-19892)*
▲ **Lafarge Building Materials Inc** ......D...... 678 746-2000
Chicago *(G-5434)*
**Lafarge North America Inc** ......E...... 630 892-1616
North Aurora *(G-16137)*
▲ **Lafarge North America Inc** ......C...... 703 480-3600
Chicago *(G-5435)*
**Lafarge North America Inc** ......E...... 847 742-6060
South Elgin *(G-20213)*
**Lafarge North America Inc** ......E...... 815 741-2090
Rockdale *(G-18224)*
**Lafarge North America Inc** ......E...... 618 289-3404
Cave In Rock *(G-3403)*
**Lafarge North America Inc** ......E...... 773 372-1000
Golconda *(G-11240)*
**Lafarge North America Inc** ......C...... 618 543-7541
Grand Chain *(G-11256)*
**Lafarge North America Inc** ......F...... 847 599-0391
Waukegan *(G-21579)*
**Lafarge North America Inc** ......E...... 773 372-1000
Chicago *(G-5436)*
**Lafarge North America Inc** ......G...... 773 646-5228
Chicago *(G-5437)*
**Lone Star Industries Inc** ......G...... 815 883-3173
Oglesby *(G-16751)*
**Red-E-Mix Transportation LLC** ......E...... 618 654-2166
Highland *(G-11809)*
**Skyway Cement Company LLC** ......F...... 800 643-1808
Chicago *(G-6525)*
**Southfield Corporation** ......C...... 815 284-3357
Dixon *(G-8352)*
**Sport Redi-Mix LLC** ......E...... 217 355-4222
Champaign *(G-3545)*
**Sport Redi-Mix LLC** ......E...... 217 892-4222
Rantoul *(G-17937)*
**Sport Redi-Mix LLC** ......G...... 217 582-2555
Ogden *(G-16745)*
**St Marys Cement Inc (us)** ......E...... 313 842-4600
Dixon *(G-8354)*

## 3251 Brick & Structural Clay Tile

**Arrowhead Brick Pavers Inc** ......E...... 630 393-1584
Warrenville *(G-21342)*
**Building Products Corp** ......E...... 618 233-4427
Belleville *(G-1615)*
**Complete Lawn and Snow Service** ......F...... 847 776-7287
Palatine *(G-17014)*
**Kona Blackbird Inc** ......F...... 815 792-8750
Serena *(G-19892)*
**Miller Tiling Co Inc** ......G...... 217 971-4709
Virden *(G-21300)*
**Red-E-Mix LLC** ......D...... 618 654-2166
Highland *(G-11808)*
**Richards Brick Company** ......D...... 618 656-0230
Edwardsville *(G-8812)*
**Selee Corporation** ......E...... 847 428-4455
Gilberts *(G-10937)*
**Southfield Corporation** ......F...... 217 398-4300
Champaign *(G-3543)*

## 3253 Ceramic Tile

**American Bullnose Co Midw** ......G...... 630 238-1300
Wood Dale *(G-22340)*
◆ **Curran Group Inc** ......E...... 815 455-5100
Crystal Lake *(G-7563)*
▲ **M H Detrick Company** ......E...... 708 479-5085
Mokena *(G-14882)*
**Meier Granite Company** ......G...... 847 678-7300
Franklin Park *(G-10527)*
**Mosaicos Inc** ......G...... 773 777-8453
Chicago *(G-5811)*
**Pilla Exec Inc** ......G...... 312 882-8263
Chicago *(G-6122)*
▲ **Stonepeak Ceramics Inc** ......E...... 312 335-0321
Chicago *(G-6599)*

## 3255 Clay Refractories

▲ **Bmi Products Northern Ill Inc** ......E...... 847 395-7110
Antioch *(G-625)*
**Cimentos N Votorantim Amer Inc** ......E...... 708 458-0400
Bridgeview *(G-2477)*
**Great Lakes Clay & Supply Inc** ......G...... 224 535-8127
Elgin *(G-9051)*
**Harbisonwalker Intl Inc** ......G...... 708 474-5350
Calumet City *(G-2941)*
▲ **Holland Manufacturing Corp** ......E...... 708 849-1000
Dolton *(G-8371)*
**Maxi-Mix Inc** ......G...... 773 489-6747
Chicago *(G-5658)*
**Thermal Ceramics Inc** ......E...... 217 627-2101
Girard *(G-10950)*
**V J Mattson Company** ......D...... 708 479-1990
New Lenox *(G-15926)*

## 3259 Structural Clay Prdts, NEC

**C & L Tiling Inc** ......D...... 217 773-3357
Timewell *(G-20884)*
◆ **Colloid Envmtl Tech Co LLC** ......C...... 847 851-1500
Hoffman Estates *(G-12002)*
**Coon Run Drainage & Levee Dst** ......G...... 217 248-5511
Arenzville *(G-688)*

## 3261 China Plumbing Fixtures & Fittings

▲ **BBC Innovation Corporation** ......G...... 847 458-2334
Crystal Lake *(G-7540)*
▲ **Cfpg Ltd** ......C...... 630 679-1420
Woodridge *(G-22459)*
**Coronado Conservation Inc** ......G...... 301 512-4671
Chicago *(G-4473)*
**Elkay Manufacturing Company** ......B...... 708 681-1880
Broadview *(G-2575)*
▲ **Gerber Plumbing Fixtures LLC** ......D...... 630 679-1420
Woodridge *(G-22482)*
◆ **Globe Union Group Inc** ......D...... 630 679-1420
Woodridge *(G-22487)*
**Kohler Co** ......D...... 847 734-1777
Huntley *(G-12155)*
▲ **Lacava LLC** ......E...... 773 637-9600
Chicago *(G-5432)*
**Sterline Manufacturing Corp** ......E...... 847 244-1234
Gurnee *(G-11509)*
**Swan Surfaces LLC** ......C...... 618 532-5673
Centralia *(G-3435)*
▲ **Wells Sinkware Corp** ......G...... 312 850-3466
Chicago *(G-6954)*
**Wonder Kids Inc** ......G...... 773 437-8025
Evanston *(G-10107)*

## 3262 China, Table & Kitchen Articles

▲ **Pickard Incorporated** ......D...... 847 395-3800
Antioch *(G-650)*
▲ **Spring (usa) Corporation** ......F...... 630 527-8600
Naperville *(G-15754)*

## 3263 Earthenware, Whiteware, Table & Kitchen Articles

**Antioch Fine Arts Foundation** ......G...... 847 838-2274
Antioch *(G-617)*

## 3264 Porcelain Electrical Splys

**Arnold Magnetic Tech Corp** ......E...... 815 568-2000
Marengo *(G-14219)*
**Dpcac LLC** ......F...... 630 741-7900
Itasca *(G-12253)*
**Ferro Corporation** ......C...... 847 623-0370
Waukegan *(G-21559)*
**Hitachi Metals America LLC** ......F...... 847 364-7200
Arlington Heights *(G-766)*
**Johnson Sign Co** ......G...... 847 678-2092
Franklin Park *(G-10509)*
**Permacor Inc** ......E...... 708 422-3353
Oak Lawn *(G-16639)*
**Porcelain Enamel Finishers** ......G...... 312 808-1560
Chicago *(G-6157)*
**Senna Design LLC** ......G...... 847 821-7877
Vernon Hills *(G-21201)*
▲ **TSC Pyroferric International** ......C...... 217 849-2230
Toledo *(G-20969)*
▲ **Voges Inc** ......D...... 618 233-2760
Belleville *(G-1688)*

## 3269 Pottery Prdts, NEC

▲ **BSC Imports Incorporated** ......G...... 773 844-4788
Chicago *(G-4180)*
**C & L Manufacturing Entps** ......G...... 618 465-7623
Alton *(G-565)*
▲ **Haeger Industries Inc** ......D...... 847 426-3441
West Dundee *(G-21797)*
**In The Attic Inc** ......G...... 847 949-5077
Mundelein *(G-15509)*
**Ipsen Inc** ......E...... 815 239-2385
Pecatonica *(G-17252)*
**Richard Ochwat Specialty Entp** ......G...... 630 682-0800
Carol Stream *(G-3228)*
**Spouts of Water Inc** ......G...... 303 570-5104
Des Plaines *(G-8280)*
**Ws Incorporated of Manmouth** ......F...... 309 734-2161
Monmouth *(G-15024)*

## 3271 Concrete Block & Brick

**Artistries By Tommy Musto Inc** ......G...... 630 674-8667
Bloomingdale *(G-2094)*
**Atlas Concrete Products Co** ......F...... 217 528-7368
Springfield *(G-20390)*
**Beelman Ready-Mix Inc** ......G...... 618 247-3866
Sandoval *(G-19355)*
**Bricks Inc** ......F...... 773 523-5718
Chicago *(G-4164)*
**Bricks Inc** ......G...... 630 897-6926
Aurora *(G-1121)*
**Building Products Corp** ......E...... 618 233-4427
Belleville *(G-1615)*
**Contractors Ready-Mix Inc** ......G...... 217 482-5530
Mason City *(G-14362)*
**County Materials Corp** ......E...... 217 352-4181
Champaign *(G-3470)*
**County Materials Corp** ......E...... 217 544-4607
Springfield *(G-20422)*
**Elston Materials LLC** ......G...... 773 235-3100
Chicago *(G-4736)*
**Fireplace & Chimney Authority** ......E...... 630 279-8500
Elmhurst *(G-9872)*
**Glen-Gery Corporation** ......D...... 815 795-6911
Marseilles *(G-14309)*
**Hamilton Concrete Products Co** ......G...... 217 847-3118
Hamilton *(G-11537)*
**Harvey Cement Products Inc** ......F...... 708 333-1900
Harvey *(G-11668)*
▲ **Lafarge Building Materials Inc** ......D...... 678 746-2000
Chicago *(G-5434)*

S I C

▲ **Lafarge North America Inc** ... C ... 703 480-3600
Chicago *(G-5435)*

**Lion Ornamental Concrete Pdts** ... G ... 630 892-7304
Montgomery *(G-15056)*

**M & M Exposed Aggregate Co** ... G ... 847 551-1818
Carpentersville *(G-3291)*

**Macomb Concrete Products Inc** ... G ... 309 772-3826
Bushnell *(G-2904)*

**Mef Construction Inc** ... G ... 847 741-8601
Elgin *(G-9105)*

**Meno Stone Co Inc** ... E ... 630 257-9220
Lemont *(G-13241)*

**Midwest Cement Products Inc** ... G ... 815 284-2342
Woosung *(G-22630)*

**Monmouth Ready Mix Corp** ... G ... 309 734-3211
Monmouth *(G-15021)*

**New Panel Brick Company of Ill** ... G ... 847 696-1686
Glenview *(G-11173)*

**North Shore Paving Inc** ... G ... 847 201-1710
Round Lake Heights *(G-19082)*

▼ **Northfield Block Company** ... C ... 847 816-9000
Mundelein *(G-15538)*

**Northfield Block Company** ... E ... 815 941-4100
Morris *(G-15123)*

**Northfield Block Company** ... E ... 847 949-3600
Mundelein *(G-15539)*

**Northfield Block Company** ... G ... 708 458-8130
Berwyn *(G-2069)*

**Paveloc Industries Inc** ... F ... 815 568-4700
Marengo *(G-14238)*

**Quikrete Companies Inc** ... F ... 309 346-1184
Pekin *(G-17285)*

**R & D Concrete Products Inc** ... E ... 309 787-0264
Rock Island *(G-18195)*

**Rockford Cement Products Co** ... F ... 815 965-0537
Rockford *(G-18571)*

**Sesser Concrete Products Co** ... F ... 618 625-2811
Sesser *(G-19895)*

**Southfield Corporation** ... F ... 217 875-5455
Decatur *(G-7941)*

**Southfield Corporation** ... E ... 708 458-0400
Oak Lawn *(G-16644)*

**Swansea Building Products Inc** ... F ... 618 874-6282
East Saint Louis *(G-8772)*

**Terrell Materials Corporation** ... E ... 312 376-0105
Rosemont *(G-19036)*

**Tison & Hall Concrete Products** ... F ... 618 253-7808
Harrisburg *(G-11605)*

**Top Block & Brick Inc** ... F ... 815 747-3159
East Dubuque *(G-8626)*

**US Paving Inc** ... E ... 630 653-4900
Glen Ellyn *(G-10992)*

**Valley View Industries Hc Inc** ... E ... 800 323-9369
Crestwood *(G-7507)*

## *3272 Concrete Prdts*

**A&J Paving Inc** ... G ... 773 889-9133
Chicago *(G-3694)*

**Abel Vault & Monument Co Inc** ... G ... 309 647-0105
Canton *(G-2980)*

**American Cast Stone** ... F ... 630 291-0250
Lemont *(G-13223)*

**American Wilbert Vault Corp** ... F ... 773 238-2746
Chicago *(G-3883)*

**American Wilbert Vault Corp** ... F ... 708 366-3210
Bridgeview *(G-2464)*

**American Wilbert Vault Corp** ... G ... 847 824-4415
Des Plaines *(G-8148)*

**American Wilbert Vault Corp** ... G ... 847 741-3089
Elgin *(G-8951)*

▲ **Aqua Control Inc** ... E ... 815 664-4900
Spring Valley *(G-20374)*

**Architectural Cast Ston** ... E ... 630 377-4800
West Chicago *(G-21661)*

**Architectural Distributors** ... G ... 847 223-5800
Grayslake *(G-11320)*

**Atlas Concrete Products Co** ... F ... 217 528-7368
Springfield *(G-20390)*

**Atmi Dynacore LLC** ... G ... 815 838-9492
Lockport *(G-13704)*

**Atmi Precast Inc** ... E ... 630 897-0577
Aurora *(G-1113)*

**Atmi Precast Inc** ... E ... 630 897-0577
Aurora *(G-1114)*

**Avan Precast Concrete Pdts Inc** ... F ... 708 757-6200
Lynwood *(G-14017)*

**Beauty Vault LLC** ... G ... 773 621-5189
Chicago *(G-4070)*

**Bernard Cffey Vtrans Fundation** ... G ... 630 687-0033
Naperville *(G-15605)*

**Blue Linx Corporation** ... F ... 708 235-4200
University Park *(G-21045)*

**Blue Pearl Stone Tech LLC** ... G ... 708 698-5700
La Grange *(G-12726)*

**Bobs Market & Greenhouse** ... G ... 217 442-8155
Danville *(G-7706)*

**Bonsal American Inc** ... D ... 847 678-6220
Franklin Park *(G-10415)*

**Bricks Inc** ... G ... 630 897-6926
Aurora *(G-1121)*

**C & L Tiling Inc** ... D ... 217 773-3357
Timewell *(G-20885)*

**C L Vault & Safe Srv** ... G ... 708 237-0039
Oak Lawn *(G-16607)*

**Casey Stone Co** ... G ... 217 857-3425
Teutopolis *(G-20849)*

**Central Concrete Products** ... F ... 217 523-7964
Springfield *(G-20412)*

**Central Concrete Products** ... F ... 217 673-6111
Woodson *(G-22530)*

**Chimney King LLC** ... G ... 847 244-8860
Waukegan *(G-21537)*

**Christopher Concrete Products** ... G ... 618 724-2951
Buckner *(G-2647)*

**Classical Statuary & Decor** ... G ... 815 462-3408
New Lenox *(G-15871)*

**Clay Vollmar Products Co** ... F ... 773 774-1234
Chicago *(G-4396)*

**Clay Vollmar Products Co** ... G ... 847 540-5850
Lake Zurich *(G-13054)*

**Cline Concrete Products** ... F ... 217 283-5012
Hoopeston *(G-12107)*

**Component Precast Supply Inc** ... G ... 630 483-2900
West Chicago *(G-21685)*

**Concrete & Marble Polishing &** ... G ... 773 968-6897
Prospect Heights *(G-17774)*

**Concrete Products** ... G ... 815 339-6395
Granville *(G-11317)*

**Concrete Specialities Co Inc** ... E ... 847 608-1200
Elgin *(G-8998)*

▼ **Concrete Specialties Co** ... E ... 847 608-1200
Elgin *(G-8999)*

**Concrete Unit Step Co Inc** ... G ... 618 344-7256
Collinsville *(G-7317)*

▼ **Connelly-Gpm Inc** ... E ... 773 247-7231
Chicago *(G-4451)*

▼ **Construction Equipment** ... G ... 618 345-0799
Belleville *(G-1619)*

**Contractors Ready-Mix Inc** ... F ... 217 735-2565
Lincoln *(G-13407)*

**Cortelyou Excavating** ... G ... 309 772-2922
Bushnell *(G-2901)*

**County Materials Corp** ... E ... 217 352-4181
Champaign *(G-3470)*

**Creative Inds Terrazzo Pdts** ... G ... 773 235-9088
Chicago *(G-4499)*

**Details Etc** ... F ... 708 932-5543
Mokena *(G-14860)*

**Di Cicco Concrete Products** ... F ... 708 754-5691
Chicago Heights *(G-7095)*

**Doty & Sons Concrete Products** ... F ... 815 895-2884
Sycamore *(G-20793)*

**Eagle Burial Vault** ... G ... 815 722-8660
Frankfort *(G-10318)*

**Eagle Stone and Brick Inc** ... G ... 618 282-6722
Red Bud *(G-17940)*

**Electric Conduit Cnstr Co** ... C ... 630 293-4474
Elburn *(G-8886)*

**Elite Monument Co** ... G ... 217 532-6080
Hillsboro *(G-11889)*

**Elmhurst-Chicago Stone Company** ... F ... 630 557-2446
Kaneville *(G-12599)*

**Elmhurst-Chicago Stone Company** ... E ... 630 832-4000
Elmhurst *(G-9865)*

**Elmhurst-Chicago Stone Company** ... E ... 630 983-6410
Bolingbrook *(G-2305)*

**Elmos Tombstone Service** ... G ... 773 643-0200
Chicago *(G-4733)*

**Energy Vault LLC** ... G ... 847 722-1128
Chicago *(G-4751)*

**Englewood Co Op** ... G ... 773 873-1201
Chicago *(G-4755)*

**Euro Marble Supply Ltd** ... G ... 847 233-0700
Schiller Park *(G-19828)*

**F H Leinweber Co Inc** ... E ... 773 568-7722
Chicago *(G-4803)*

**Farmington Wilbert Vault Corp** ... F ... 309 245-2133
Farmington *(G-10186)*

**Ferber George & Sons** ... G ... 217 733-2184
Fairmount *(G-10163)*

**Fischer Stone & Materials LLC** ... G ... 815 233-3232
Freeport *(G-10656)*

**Forrest Redi-Mix Inc** ... G ... 815 657-8241
Forrest *(G-10262)*

**Forsyth Brothers Concrete Pdts** ... G ... 217 548-2770
Fithian *(G-10193)*

▲ **Forterra Pressure Pipe Inc** ... E ... 815 389-4800
South Beloit *(G-20147)*

**Forterra Pressure Pipe Inc** ... C ... 815 389-4800
South Beloit *(G-20148)*

**Fountain Technologies Ltd** ... E ... 847 537-3677
Wheeling *(G-22057)*

**G P Concrete & Iron Works** ... G ... 815 842-2270
Pontiac *(G-17700)*

**Gary & Larry Brown Trucking** ... G ... 618 268-6377
Raleigh *(G-17909)*

**GBS Liquidating Corp** ... G ... 309 342-4155
Galesburg *(G-10753)*

**George Pagels Company** ... G ... 708 478-7036
Mokena *(G-14867)*

**George W Pierson Company** ... E ... 815 726-3351
Joliet *(G-12501)*

**Graber Concrete Pipe Company** ... E ... 630 894-5950
Bloomingdale *(G-2109)*

**Great Lakes Envmtl Mar Del** ... G ... 312 332-3377
Chicago *(G-4996)*

**Great Lakes Lifting** ... G ... 815 931-4825
Country Club Hills *(G-7407)*

**Hahn Industries** ... G ... 815 689-2133
Cullom *(G-7682)*

**Hallen Burial Vault Inc** ... G ... 815 544-6138
Belvidere *(G-1761)*

**Hamel Tire and Concrete Pdts** ... G ... 618 633-2405
Hamel *(G-11529)*

**Hamilton Concrete Products Co** ... G ... 217 847-3118
Hamilton *(G-11537)*

**Hanson Aggregates East LLC** ... E ... 815 398-2300
Rockford *(G-18412)*

**Hinckley Concrete Products Co** ... G ... 815 286-3235
Hinckley *(G-11935)*

**Hoosier Precast LLC** ... G ... 815 459-4545
Crystal Lake *(G-7588)*

**Hulse Excavating** ... G ... 815 796-4106
Flanagan *(G-10194)*

**Illini Precast LLC** ... F ... 708 562-7700
Westchester *(G-21844)*

**Illinois Cast Stone** ... G ... 815 943-6050
Harvard *(G-11637)*

**Imco Precast LLC** ... G ... 217 742-5300
Winchester *(G-22280)*

**Impact Polymer LLC** ... G ... 847 441-2394
Northfield *(G-16402)*

**J E Tomes & Associates Inc** ... F ... 708 653-5100
Blue Island *(G-2258)*

**J P Vincent & Sons Inc** ... G ... 815 777-2365
Galena *(G-10727)*

**Jgr Commercial Solutions Inc** ... G ... 847 669-7010
Huntley *(G-12152)*

**Kelley Vault Co Inc** ... F ... 217 355-5551
Champaign *(G-3506)*

**Kieft Bros Inc** ... E ... 630 832-8090
Elmhurst *(G-9898)*

**Kienstra Pipe & Precast LLC** ... E ... 618 482-3283
Madison *(G-14151)*

**Knauer Industries Ltd** ... E ... 815 725-0246
Joliet *(G-12528)*

**Kodiak Concrete Forms Inc** ... G ... 630 773-9339
Itasca *(G-12298)*

**Kohnens Concrete Products Inc** ... E ... 618 277-2120
Germantown *(G-10892)*

**Kowalski Memorials Inc** ... G ... 630 462-7226
Carol Stream *(G-3182)*

**Kw Precast LLC** ... F ... 708 562-7700
Westchester *(G-21846)*

▲ **Lafarge North America Inc** ... C ... 703 480-3600
Chicago *(G-5435)*

**Lane Construction Corporation** ... F ... 815 846-4466
Shorewood *(G-19929)*

**Legacy Vulcan LLC** ... G ... 773 890-2360
Chicago *(G-5487)*

**Legacy Vulcan LLC** ... G ... 217 963-2196
Decatur *(G-7908)*

**Leonards Unit Step Co** ... G ... 815 744-1263
Rockdale *(G-18225)*

**Leonards Unit Step of Moline** ... G ... 309 792-9641
Colona *(G-7345)*

**Lifetime Rooftile Company** ... G ... 630 355-7922
Naperville *(G-15689)*

**Lion Ornamental Concrete Pdts** ... G ... 630 892-7304
Montgomery *(G-15056)*

Lombard Archtctral Prcast Pdts ............ E ...... 708 389-1060
  Chicago *(G-5535)*
Lombard Investment Company ............ D ...... 708 389-1060
  Alsip *(G-484)*
M & M Exposed Aggregate Co ............ G ...... 847 551-1818
  Carpentersville *(G-3291)*
Macomb Concrete Products Inc ............ G ...... 309 772-3826
  Bushnell *(G-2904)*
▼ Material Haulers Inc ............ G ...... 815 857-4336
  Schaumburg *(G-19636)*
Material Service Corporation ............ E ...... 815 838-2400
  Romeoville *(G-18842)*
McCann Concrete Products Inc ............ G ...... 618 377-3888
  Dorsey *(G-8381)*
Meatball Vault Original ............ G ...... 312 285-2090
  Chicago *(G-5673)*
Merz Vault Company Inc ............ G ...... 618 548-2859
  Salem *(G-19338)*
Meyer Material Co Merger Corp ............ D ...... 815 943-2605
  Harvard *(G-11641)*
Mid-Illinois Concrete Inc ............ G ...... 217 382-6650
  Martinsville *(G-14338)*
Mid-Illinois Concrete Inc ............ G ...... 618 664-1340
  Greenville *(G-11399)*
Mid-Illinois Concrete Inc ............ F ...... 618 283-1600
  Vandalia *(G-21116)*
Mid-Illinois Concrete Inc ............ G ...... 217 345-6404
  Charleston *(G-3604)*
Mid-Illinois Concrete Inc ............ E ...... 217 235-5858
  Mattoon *(G-14404)*
▲ Mid-States Concrete Inds LLC ............ D ...... 815 389-2277
  South Beloit *(G-20162)*
Midwest Cement Products Inc ............ G ...... 815 284-2342
  Woosung *(G-22630)*
Midwest Perma-Column Inc ............ G ...... 309 589-7949
  Edwards *(G-8783)*
MK Tile Ink ............ G ...... 773 964-8905
  Chicago *(G-5778)*
Monumental Art Works ............ G ...... 708 389-3038
  Blue Island *(G-2263)*
National Concrete Pipe Co ............ E ...... 630 766-3600
  Franklin Park *(G-10539)*
Northern Illinois Wilbert Vlt ............ G ...... 815 544-3355
  Belvidere *(G-1775)*
Northfield Block Company ............ G ...... 708 458-8130
  Berwyn *(G-2069)*
Oakwood Memorial Park Inc ............ G ...... 815 433-0313
  Ottawa *(G-16973)*
▲ Orlandi Statuary Company ............ D ...... 773 489-0303
  Chicago *(G-6015)*
Ozinga Concrete Products Inc ............ E ...... 847 426-0920
  Elgin *(G-9132)*
Ozinga Concrete Products Inc ............ G ...... 708 479-9050
  Hampshire *(G-11557)*
Ozinga Ready Mix Concrete Inc ............ E ...... 708 326-4200
  Mokena *(G-14892)*
Peoria Wilbert Vault Co Inc ............ F ...... 309 383-2882
  Metamora *(G-14747)*
Perfection Vault Co Inc ............ F ...... 217 673-6111
  Woodson *(G-22531)*
Peter Baker & Son Co ............ D ...... 847 362-3663
  Lake Bluff *(G-12861)*
Prestress Engineering Company ............ E ...... 815 586-4239
  Blackstone *(G-2088)*
Prestress Engineering Company ............ G ...... 815 459-4545
  Crystal Lake *(G-7630)*
Price Brothers Co ............ D ...... 815 389-4800
  South Beloit *(G-20165)*
Prosser Construction Co ............ F ...... 217 774-5032
  Shelbyville *(G-19913)*
Quad Cities Concrete Pdts LLC ............ G ...... 309 787-4919
  Milan *(G-14799)*
Quick Building Systems Inc ............ G ...... 708 598-6733
  Palos Hills *(G-17122)*
Quikrete Chicago ............ D ...... 630 557-8252
  Elburn *(G-8906)*
Quikrete Companies Inc ............ F ...... 309 346-1184
  Pekin *(G-17285)*
Rex Vault Co ............ F ...... 618 783-2416
  Newton *(G-15948)*
Rochelle Vault Co ............ G ...... 815 562-6484
  Rochelle *(G-18108)*
Rockford Cement Products Co ............ F ...... 815 965-0537
  Rockford *(G-18571)*
Rockford Sewer Co Inc ............ G ...... 815 877-9060
  Loves Park *(G-13987)*
Royal Corinthian Inc ............ E ...... 630 876-8899
  West Chicago *(G-21767)*
S & M Basements ............ G ...... 618 533-1939
  Centralia *(G-3430)*

Safe Sheds Inc ............ G ...... 888 556-1531
  Alma *(G-423)*
Schmalz Precast Concrete Mfg ............ G ...... 815 747-3939
  East Dubuque *(G-8622)*
Sebens Concrete Products Inc ............ G ...... 217 864-2824
  Decatur *(G-7939)*
Shrine Memorial Mausoleum Co ............ G ...... 618 283-0153
  Vandalia *(G-21123)*
Skelcher Concrete Products ............ G ...... 618 457-2930
  Carbondale *(G-3023)*
Slavish Inc ............ G ...... 309 754-8233
  Matherville *(G-14367)*
Southern Ill Wilbert Vlt Co ............ F ...... 618 942-5845
  Herrin *(G-11756)*
Southern Illinois Redimix Inc ............ F ...... 618 993-3600
  Marion *(G-14290)*
Southern Illinois Stone Co ............ F ...... 573 334-5261
  Buncombe *(G-2800)*
Southern Illinois Vault Co Inc ............ G ...... 270 554-4436
  Herrin *(G-11757)*
Southfield Corporation ............ F ...... 217 875-5455
  Decatur *(G-7941)*
Spacil Construction Co ............ G ...... 708 448-3809
  Palos Heights *(G-17110)*
Spence Monuments Co ............ G ...... 217 348-5992
  Charleston *(G-3612)*
St Louis Flexicore Inc ............ F ...... 618 531-8691
  East Saint Louis *(G-8770)*
Sterling Vault Company ............ F ...... 815 625-0077
  Sterling *(G-20616)*
Stockdale Block Systems LLC ............ G ...... 815 416-1030
  Morris *(G-15132)*
Stone Installation & Maint Inc ............ G ...... 630 545-2326
  Glendale Heights *(G-11077)*
Stonecraft Cast Stone LLC ............ G ...... 708 653-1477
  Steger *(G-20577)*
Super Mix of Wisconsin Inc ............ G ...... 262 859-9000
  McHenry *(G-14564)*
Surtreat Construction Svcs LLC ............ G ...... 630 986-0780
  Schaumburg *(G-19746)*
Sws ............ G ...... 815 267-7378
  Plainfield *(G-17656)*
Tagitsold Inc ............ G ...... 630 724-1800
  Downers Grove *(G-8529)*
Tanya Shipley ............ G ...... 708 476-0433
  Mokena *(G-14910)*
Taurus Safety Products Inc ............ G ...... 630 620-7940
  Lombard *(G-13865)*
Tickle Asphalt Co Ltd ............ G ...... 309 787-1308
  Milan *(G-14806)*
Unique Concrete Concepts Inc ............ F ...... 618 466-0700
  Jerseyville *(G-12427)*
Unit Step Company of Peoria ............ G ...... 309 674-4392
  Metamora *(G-14751)*
US Fireplace Products Inc ............ G ...... 888 290-8181
  Lake Bluff *(G-12869)*
Utility Concrete Products LLC ............ E ...... 815 416-1000
  Morris *(G-15140)*
V & N Concrete Products Inc ............ F ...... 815 293-0315
  Romeoville *(G-18875)*
▲ Van-Packer Co ............ E ...... 309 895-2311
  Buda *(G-2648)*
Vault Arts Collective ............ G ...... 217 599-1215
  Tuscola *(G-21029)*
Vault Shop ............ G ...... 630 699-0307
  Lisle *(G-13677)*
Vcna Prairie Inc ............ A ...... 312 733-0094
  Chicago *(G-6877)*
Vcna Prairie Indiana Inc ............ E ...... 708 458-0400
  Bridgeview *(G-2537)*
Vitelli Concrete Products Inc ............ G ...... 708 754-5846
  Chicago Heights *(G-7136)*
▲ Welch Bros Inc ............ C ...... 847 741-6134
  Elgin *(G-9233)*
Welch Bros Inc ............ G ...... 815 547-3000
  Belvidere *(G-1796)*
West Lake Concrete & Rmdlg LLC ............ G ...... 847 477-8667
  Chicago *(G-6960)*
White Star Silo ............ G ...... 618 523-4735
  Germantown *(G-10894)*
Wilbert Quincy Vault Co ............ G ...... 217 224-8557
  Quincy *(G-17905)*
Wilbert Shultz Vault Co Inc ............ F ...... 815 672-2049
  Streator *(G-20711)*
Wilbert Vault Company ............ F ...... 309 787-5281
  Milan *(G-14809)*
Windo Well Cover Co ............ G ...... 630 554-0366
  Oswego *(G-16941)*
Wolfe Burial Vault Co Inc ............ G ...... 815 697-2012
  Chebanse *(G-3632)*

### 3273 Ready-Mixed Concrete

A & L Construction Inc ............ E ...... 708 343-1660
  Melrose Park *(G-14577)*
Advanced On-Site Concrete Inc ............ E ...... 773 622-7836
  Chicago *(G-3771)*
Atlas Ready Mix Inc ............ G ...... 618 271-0774
  East Saint Louis *(G-8741)*
Aztec Material Service Corp ............ G ...... 773 521-0909
  Chicago *(G-4010)*
Ballard Bros Inc ............ F ...... 217 374-2137
  White Hall *(G-22183)*
Barnett Redi-Mix Inc ............ G ...... 618 276-4298
  Junction *(G-12593)*
Bee Line Service Inc ............ G ...... 815 233-1812
  Freeport *(G-10648)*
Beelman Ready-Mix Inc ............ G ...... 618 357-6120
  Pinckneyville *(G-17544)*
Beelman Ready-Mix Inc ............ G ...... 618 646-5300
  East Saint Louis *(G-8744)*
Beelman Ready-Mix Inc ............ G ...... 618 244-9600
  Mount Vernon *(G-15400)*
Beelman Ready-Mix Inc ............ G ...... 618 247-3866
  Sandoval *(G-19355)*
Beelman Ready-Mix Inc ............ G ...... 618 478-2044
  Nashville *(G-15834)*
Beelman Ready-Mix Inc ............ F ...... 618 526-0260
  Breese *(G-2439)*
Biochemical Lab ............ G ...... 708 447-3923
  Riverside *(G-18029)*
Bleigh Construction Company ............ G ...... 217 222-5005
  Quincy *(G-17805)*
Blomberg Bros Inc ............ F ...... 618 245-6321
  Farina *(G-10174)*
▲ Bmi Products Northern Ill Inc ............ E ...... 847 395-7110
  Antioch *(G-625)*
Bob Barnett Redi-Mix Inc ............ F ...... 618 252-3581
  Harrisburg *(G-11596)*
Breckenridge Material Company ............ F ...... 618 398-4141
  Caseyville *(G-3394)*
Builders Ready-Mix Co ............ G ...... 847 866-6300
  Evanston *(G-10018)*
Canton Redi-Mix Inc ............ F ...... 309 668-2261
  Canton *(G-2984)*
Canton Redi-Mix Inc ............ G ...... 309 647-0019
  Canton *(G-2985)*
Capitol Ready-Mix Inc ............ E ...... 217 528-1100
  Springfield *(G-20407)*
CCI Redi Mix ............ E ...... 217 342-2299
  Effingham *(G-8829)*
Charleston Concrete Supply Co ............ F ...... 217 345-6404
  Charleston *(G-3592)*
Chris Dj Mix LLC ............ G ...... 312 725-3838
  Chicago *(G-4369)*
Cigar Mix & Detail Shop ............ G ...... 708 396-1826
  Calumet Park *(G-2957)*
Clinard Ready Mix Inc ............ E ...... 217 773-3965
  Mount Sterling *(G-15391)*
Clinton County Materials Corp ............ F ...... 618 533-4252
  Centralia *(G-3409)*
Coal City Redi-Mix Co Inc ............ F ...... 815 634-4455
  Coal City *(G-7292)*
Community Rady Mix of Pttsfeld ............ F ...... 217 285-5548
  Pittsfield *(G-17566)*
Community Readymix Inc ............ F ...... 217 245-6668
  Jacksonville *(G-12385)*
Concrete 1 Inc ............ G ...... 630 357-1329
  Naperville *(G-15634)*
Concrete Supply LLC ............ G ...... 618 646-5300
  East Saint Louis *(G-8747)*
Concrete Supply Tolono Inc ............ G ...... 217 485-3100
  Urbana *(G-21079)*
Condominiums Northbrook Cort 1 ............ G ...... 847 498-1640
  Lincolnshire *(G-13439)*
Continental Materials Corp ............ F ...... 312 541-7200
  Chicago *(G-4459)*
Contractors Ready-Mix Inc ............ F ...... 217 482-5530
  Mason City *(G-14362)*
Contractors Ready-Mix Inc ............ F ...... 217 735-2565
  Lincoln *(G-13407)*
Country Stone Inc ............ E ...... 309 787-1744
  Milan *(G-14781)*
County Materials Corp ............ E ...... 217 544-4607
  Springfield *(G-20422)*
County Materials Corp ............ E ...... 217 352-4181
  Champaign *(G-3470)*
Crazy Horse Concrete Inc ............ E ...... 217 523-4420
  Springfield *(G-20423)*
Curry Ready Mix of Petersburg ............ G ...... 217 632-2516
  Petersburg *(G-17535)*

# 32 STONE, CLAY, GLASS, AND CONCRETE PRODUCTS — SIC SECTION

Curry Ready-Mix of Decatur ............... F ...... 217 428-7177
  Decatur (G-7862)
Cyrulik Inc ............................................ G ...... 217 935-6969
  Clinton (G-7280)
David Yates .......................................... G ...... 618 656-7879
  Edwardsville (G-8794)
Diamond Ready Mix Inc ...................... F ...... 630 355-5414
  Naperville (G-15645)
Dollar Mix ............................................ G ...... 773 582-7110
  Chicago (G-4622)
Edwards County Concrete LLC ........... G ...... 618 445-2711
  Albion (G-361)
Elmhurst-Chicago Stone Company ..... E ...... 630 832-4000
  Elmhurst (G-9865)
Elmhurst-Chicago Stone Company ..... E ...... 630 983-6410
  Bolingbrook (G-2305)
Fairfield Ready Mix Inc ........................ G ...... 618 842-9462
  Fairfield (G-10141)
Fehrenbacher Ready-Mix Inc .............. G ...... 618 395-2306
  Olney (G-16766)
Ferber George & Sons ........................ G ...... 217 733-2184
  Fairmount (G-10163)
Fishstone Studio Inc ........................... G ...... 815 276-0299
  Crystal Lake (G-7579)
Flora Ready Mix Inc ............................. G ...... 618 662-4818
  Flora (G-10207)
Fnh Ready Mix Inc ............................... F ...... 815 235-1400
  Freeport (G-10657)
Forrest Redi-Mix Inc ........................... G ...... 815 657-8241
  Forrest (G-10262)
Fox Redi-Mix Inc .................................. G ...... 217 774-2110
  Shelbyville (G-19907)
Franklin Park Building Mtls .................. G ...... 847 455-3985
  Franklin Park (G-10472)
Fuller Brothers Ready Mix ................... G ...... 217 532-2422
  Hillsboro (G-11891)
Gary & Larry Brown Trucking .............. G ...... 618 268-6377
  Raleigh (G-17909)
GBS Liquidating Corp .......................... G ...... 309 342-4155
  Galesburg (G-10753)
Goreville Concrete Inc ......................... E ...... 618 995-2670
  Goreville (G-11252)
Gorman Brothers Ready Mix Inc ......... F ...... 618 498-2173
  Jerseyville (G-12422)
Great River Ready Mix Inc ................... F ...... 217 847-3515
  Hamilton (G-11535)
Grohne Concrete Products Co ............. G ...... 217 877-4197
  Decatur (G-7886)
Gunther Construction Co ..................... G ...... 309 343-1032
  Galesburg (G-10756)
H J Mohr & Sons Company .................. F ...... 708 366-0338
  Oak Park (G-16667)
Hahn Ready-Mix Company ................... G ...... 309 582-2436
  Aledo (G-369)
Hamilton County Concrete Co .............. G ...... 618 643-4333
  Mc Leansboro (G-14465)
Herman Bade & Sons ........................... G ...... 217 832-9444
  Villa Grove (G-21228)
Illini Concrete Inc ................................. F ...... 618 235-4141
  Belleville (G-1636)
Illini Concrete Inc ................................. G ...... 618 398-4141
  Caseyville (G-3397)
Illini Ready Mix Inc ............................... G ...... 618 833-7321
  Anna (G-605)
Illini Ready Mix Inc ............................... G ...... 618 734-0287
  Carbondale (G-3011)
Illini Ready Mix Inc ............................... G ...... 618 529-1626
  Carbondale (G-3012)
Info Corner Materials Inc ..................... F ...... 217 566-3561
  Springfield (G-20456)
J W Ossola Company Inc ..................... G ...... 815 339-6112
  Granville (G-11318)
J&J Ready Mix Inc ............................... G ...... 309 676-0579
  East Peoria (G-8716)
Jerry Berry Contracting Co ................. G ...... 618 594-3339
  Carlyle (G-3055)
Joe Hatzer & Son Inc ........................... G ...... 815 673-5571
  Streator (G-20692)
Joe Hatzer & Son Inc ........................... G ...... 815 672-2161
  Streator (G-20693)
JW Ossola Co Inc ................................. G ...... 815 339-6113
  Granville (G-11319)
Kendall County Concrete Inc ............... E ...... 630 851-9197
  Aurora (G-1041)
▲ Lafarge Building Materials Inc ......... D ...... 678 746-2000
  Chicago (G-5434)
▲ Lafarge North America Inc .............. C ...... 703 480-3600
  Chicago (G-5435)
Lahood Construction Inc ..................... E ...... 309 699-5080
  East Peoria (G-8723)

Langheim Ready Mix Inc ..................... G ...... 217 625-2351
  Girard (G-10947)
Material Service Corporation ............... E ...... 815 838-2400
  Romeoville (G-18842)
Max Miller ............................................ F ...... 708 758-7760
  S Chicago Hts (G-19107)
Maxheimer Construction Inc ................ G ...... 309 444-4200
  Washington (G-21386)
McLean County Asphalt Co .................. D ...... 309 827-6115
  Bloomington (G-2194)
Menoni & Mocogni Inc ......................... F ...... 847 432-0850
  Highland Park (G-11854)
Mertel Gravel Company Inc ................. G ...... 815 223-0468
  Peru (G-17518)
Metropolis Ready Mix Inc .................... E ...... 618 524-8221
  Metropolis (G-14758)
Meyer Material Co Merger Corp .......... E ...... 847 824-4111
  Elburn (G-8892)
Meyer Material Co Merger Corp .......... E ...... 815 568-6119
  Elburn (G-8893)
Meyer Material Co Merger Corp .......... E ...... 815 385-4920
  Elburn (G-8894)
Meyer Material Co Merger Corp .......... E ...... 847 689-9200
  Lake Bluff (G-12857)
Meyer Material Co Merger Corp .......... E ...... 815 568-7205
  Elburn (G-8895)
Meyer Material Co Merger Corp .......... D ...... 815 943-2605
  Harvard (G-11641)
Meyer Material Handling ...................... E ...... 414 768-1631
  Elburn (G-8896)
Mid-Illinois Concrete Inc ...................... E ...... 217 235-5858
  Mattoon (G-14404)
Mid-Illinois Concrete Inc ...................... G ...... 217 382-6650
  Martinsville (G-14338)
Mid-Illinois Concrete Inc ...................... G ...... 618 664-1340
  Greenville (G-11399)
Mid-Illinois Concrete Inc ...................... G ...... 618 283-1600
  Vandalia (G-21116)
Mindful Mix ........................................... G ...... 847 284-4404
  Lake Zurich (G-13105)
Mix Foods LLC ..................................... G ...... 224 338-0377
  Ingleside (G-12194)
Mix Kitchen .......................................... G ...... 312 649-0330
  Chicago (G-5776)
Mix N Mingle ........................................ G ...... 815 308-5170
  Woodstock (G-22592)
Moeller Ready Mix Inc ......................... F ...... 217 243-7471
  Jacksonville (G-12402)
Moline Consumers Co ......................... F ...... 309 757-8289
  Moline (G-14958)
Monmouth Ready Mix Corp ................. G ...... 309 734-3211
  Monmouth (G-15021)
Moultrie County Redi-Mix Co ............... F ...... 217 728-2334
  Sullivan (G-20755)
Mt Crmel Stblzation Group Inc ............. E ...... 618 262-5118
  Mount Carmel (G-15277)
Myers Concrete & Construction ........... G ...... 815 732-2591
  Oregon (G-16828)
Narvick Bros Lumber Co Inc ................ G ...... 815 521-1173
  Minooka (G-14844)
Narvick Bros Lumber Co Inc ................ G ...... 815 942-1173
  Morris (G-15121)
Newton Ready Mix Inc ......................... F ...... 618 783-8611
  Newton (G-15944)
ODaniel Trucking Co ............................ D ...... 618 382-5371
  Carmi (G-3076)
Odum Concrete Products Inc .............. G ...... 618 942-4572
  Herrin (G-11751)
Odum Concrete Products Inc .............. E ...... 618 993-6211
  Marion (G-14275)
Oltman & Sons Inc ............................... G ...... 309 364-2849
  Henry (G-11745)
Ozinga Bros Inc ................................... E ...... 708 326-4200
  Mokena (G-14889)
Ozinga Bros Inc ................................... D ...... 708 326-4200
  Chicago Heights (G-7116)
Ozinga Chicago Ready Mix Con .......... E ...... 708 479-9050
  Alsip (G-504)
Ozinga Chicago Ready Mix Con .......... E ...... 312 432-5700
  Chicago (G-6035)
Ozinga Chicago Ready Mix Con .......... E ...... 773 862-2817
  Chicago (G-6036)
Ozinga Chicago Ready Mix Con .......... E ...... 847 447-0353
  Chicago (G-6037)
Ozinga Chicago Ready Mix Con .......... E ...... 312 432-5700
  Chicago (G-6038)
Ozinga Indiana Rdymx Con Inc ........... E ...... 708 479-9050
  Mokena (G-14890)
Ozinga Materials Inc ............................ F ...... 309 364-3401
  Mokena (G-14891)

Ozinga Ready Mix Concrete Inc .......... E ...... 708 326-4200
  Mokena (G-14892)
Ozinga S Subn Rdymx Con Inc ........... F ...... 708 479-3080
  Mokena (G-14893)
Ozinga S Subn Rdymx Con Inc ........... D ...... 708 326-4201
  Mokena (G-14894)
Paxton Ready Mix Inc .......................... E ...... 217 379-2303
  Paxton (G-17242)
Pbi Redi Mix & Trucking ...................... E ...... 217 562-3717
  Pana (G-17138)
Peoples Coal and Lumber Co .............. F ...... 815 432-2456
  Watseka (G-21425)
Pike County Concrete Inc ................... E ...... 217 285-5548
  Pittsfield (G-17573)
Poggenpohl LLC ................................. G ...... 217 229-3411
  Raymond (G-17939)
Poggenpohl LLC ................................. G ...... 217 824-2020
  Taylorville (G-20844)
Point Ready Mix LLC .......................... G ...... 815 578-9100
  McHenry (G-14547)
Prairie Central Ready Mix ................... G ...... 217 877-5210
  Decatur (G-7928)
Prairie Group Management LLC ......... D ...... 708 458-0400
  Bridgeview (G-2519)
Prairie Materials Group ....................... G ...... 815 207-6750
  Shorewood (G-19930)
Prarie Material Sales Inc ..................... G ...... 847 733-8809
  Evanston (G-10090)
Princeton Ready-Mix Inc ..................... F ...... 815 875-3359
  Princeton (G-17759)
Quad County Ready Mix Swansea ..... G ...... 618 257-9530
  Swansea (G-20779)
Quad-County Ready Mix Corp ............ G ...... 618 243-6430
  Okawville (G-16755)
Quad-County Ready Mix Corp ............ F ...... 618 588-4656
  New Baden (G-15863)
Quad-County Ready Mix Corp ............ G ...... 618 526-7130
  Breese (G-2446)
Quad-County Ready Mix Corp ............ E ...... 618 244-6973
  Mount Vernon (G-15442)
Quad-County Ready Mix Corp ............ F ...... 618 327-3748
  Nashville (G-15846)
Quad-County Ready Mix Corp ............ G ...... 618 594-2732
  Carlyle (G-3057)
Quad-County Ready Mix Corp ............ G ...... 618 548-2477
  Salem (G-19346)
Quad-County Ready Mix Corp ............ G ...... 618 295-3000
  Marissa (G-14297)
Quality Ready Mix Concrete Co .......... G ...... 815 589-2013
  Fulton (G-10704)
Quality Ready Mix Concrete Co .......... F ...... 815 772-7181
  Morrison (G-15147)
Quality Ready Mix Concrete Co .......... F ...... 815 625-0750
  Sterling (G-20608)
Quality Ready Mix Concrete Co .......... G ...... 815 288-6416
  Dixon (G-8340)
R & L Ready Mix Inc ............................ F ...... 618 544-7514
  Robinson (G-18070)
Ranger Redi-Mix & Mtls Inc ................ G ...... 815 337-2662
  Woodstock (G-22605)
Rapco Ltd ............................................ G ...... 618 249-6614
  Richview (G-17981)
Regional Ready Mix LLC .................... F ...... 815 562-1901
  Rochelle (G-18104)
Riber Construction Inc ........................ F ...... 815 584-3337
  Dwight (G-8592)
River Redi Mix Inc ............................... G ...... 815 795-2025
  Marseilles (G-14317)
Riverstone Group Inc .......................... G ...... 309 757-8297
  Moline (G-14967)
Riverstone Group Inc .......................... F ...... 309 788-9543
  Rock Island (G-18202)
Roanoke Concrete Products Co .......... F ...... 309 698-7882
  East Peoria (G-8732)
Rock River Ready Mix Inc ................... G ...... 815 625-1139
  Dixon (G-8345)
Rock River Ready-Mix ......................... E ...... 815 288-2269
  Dixon (G-8346)
Rogers Ready Mix & Mtls Inc .............. D ...... 815 234-8212
  Byron (G-2920)
Rogers Ready Mix & Mtls Inc .............. G ...... 815 234-8044
  Oregon (G-16831)
Rogers Ready Mix & Mtls Inc .............. E ...... 815 874-6626
  Rockford (G-18595)
Rogers Ready Mix & Mtls Inc .............. F ...... 815 389-2223
  Roscoe (G-18915)
Rogers Redi-Mix Inc ............................ F ...... 618 282-3844
  Ruma (G-19088)
Roscoe Ready-Mix Inc ........................ G ...... 815 389-0888
  Roscoe (G-18917)

**Silver Bros Inc**..........G....... 217 283-7751
Hoopeston *(G-12117)*
**Southern Illinois Redimix Inc**..........F....... 618 993-3600
Marion *(G-14290)*
**Southfield Corporation**..........D....... 708 345-0030
Melrose Park *(G-14694)*
**Southfield Corporation**..........D....... 708 563-4056
Addison *(G-296)*
**Southfield Corporation**..........D....... 309 676-6121
Morton *(G-15181)*
**Southfield Corporation**..........E....... 708 362-2520
Bridgeview *(G-2529)*
**Southfield Corporation**..........C....... 815 284-3357
Dixon *(G-8352)*
**Southfield Corporation**..........F....... 217 877-5210
Decatur *(G-7942)*
**Southfield Corporation**..........D....... 708 458-0400
Bridgeview *(G-2530)*
**Southfield Corporation**..........E....... 309 829-1087
Bloomington *(G-2225)*
**Southfield Corporation**..........E....... 309 676-0576
Peoria *(G-17459)*
**Southfield Corporation**..........E....... 708 458-0400
Oak Lawn *(G-16644)*
**Speedy Redi Mix LLC**..........E....... 773 487-2000
Chicago *(G-6557)*
**Spicy Mix Asian and American**..........G....... 773 295-5765
Chicago *(G-6559)*
**Stahl Lumber Company**..........F....... 309 695-4331
Wyoming *(G-22640)*
**Stahl Lumber Company**..........F....... 309 385-2552
Wyoming *(G-22641)*
**Staley Concrete Co**..........E....... 217 356-9533
Champaign *(G-3546)*
**Sterling-Rock Falls Ready Mix**..........F....... 815 288-3135
Dixon *(G-8355)*
**Super Mix Inc**..........E....... 815 544-9100
McHenry *(G-14561)*
**Super Mix Inc**..........D....... 815 578-9100
McHenry *(G-14562)*
**Super Mix Concrete LLC**..........G....... 262 742-2892
McHenry *(G-14563)*
**Super Mix of Wisconsin Inc**..........F....... 815 578-9100
McHenry *(G-14565)*
**T H Davidson & Co Inc**..........E....... 815 464-2000
Oak Forest *(G-16591)*
**T H Davidson & Co Inc**..........G....... 815 941-0280
Morris *(G-15134)*
**Thelen Sand & Gravel Inc**..........F....... 847 662-0760
Waukegan *(G-21625)*
**Thelen Sand & Gravel Inc**..........D....... 847 838-8800
Antioch *(G-656)*
**Tri-City Ready-Mix**..........G....... 618 439-2071
Benton *(G-2042)*
**Tri-County Concrete Inc**..........G....... 815 786-2179
Sandwich *(G-19378)*
**Triangle Concrete Co Inc**..........G....... 309 853-4334
Kewanee *(G-12695)*
**Twin Cities Ready Mix Inc**..........F....... 309 862-1500
Normal *(G-16090)*
**United Ready Mix Inc**..........E....... 309 676-3287
Peoria *(G-17473)*
**Upchurch Ready Mix Concrete**..........G....... 618 235-6222
Belleville *(G-1684)*
**Upchurch Ready Mix Concrete**..........G....... 618 286-4808
Dupo *(G-8582)*
**Upland Concrete**..........G....... 224 699-9909
East Dundee *(G-8661)*
**Urban RE Mix LLC**..........G....... 312 360-0011
Chicago *(G-6849)*
**Valley Concrete Inc**..........D....... 815 725-2422
Joliet *(G-12586)*
**Vcna Prairie Inc**..........D....... 708 458-0400
Bridgeview *(G-2535)*
**Vcna Prairie Illinois Inc**..........F....... 708 458-0400
Bridgeview *(G-2536)*
**Wayland Ready Mix Concrete Svc**..........F....... 309 833-2064
Macomb *(G-14134)*
**Westmore Supply Co**..........F....... 630 627-0278
Lombard *(G-13883)*
**Westville Ready Mix Inc**..........G....... 217 267-2082
Westville *(G-21931)*
**Wille Bros Co**..........E....... 815 464-1300
Monee *(G-15009)*
**Wille Bros Co**..........D....... 708 388-9000
Chicago *(G-6982)*
**Winnetka Mews Condominium Assn**..........G....... 847 501-2770
Winnetka *(G-22316)*

## 3274 Lime

**Heisler Stone Co Inc**..........G....... 815 244-2685
Mount Carroll *(G-15291)*
**Jacobs Trucking**..........G....... 618 687-3578
Murphysboro *(G-15577)*
▲ **Lafarge Building Materials Inc**..........D....... 678 746-2000
Chicago *(G-5434)*
**Mineral Products Inc**..........G....... 618 433-3150
Galatia *(G-10712)*

## 3275 Gypsum Prdts

**Continental Studios Inc**..........E....... 773 542-0309
Chicago *(G-4460)*
**Creative Perky Cuisine LLC**..........G....... 312 870-0282
Tinley Park *(G-20905)*
**Georgia-Pacific Bldg Pdts LLC**..........G....... 630 449-7200
Aurora *(G-1015)*
**Ken Matthews & Associates Inc**..........G....... 630 628-6470
Addison *(G-165)*
**New Ngc Inc**..........D....... 847 623-8100
Waukegan *(G-21592)*
**Owens Corning Sales LLC**..........D....... 815 226-4627
Rockford *(G-18527)*
**Patrick Industries Inc**..........D....... 630 595-0595
Franklin Park *(G-10548)*
◆ **United States Gypsum Company**..........B....... 312 606-4000
Chicago *(G-6829)*
**USG Corporation**..........F....... 847 970-5200
Libertyville *(G-13396)*
**USG Corporation**..........B....... 312 436-4000
Chicago *(G-6858)*

## 3281 Cut Stone Prdts

**AA Rigoni Brothers Inc**..........E....... 815 838-9770
Lockport *(G-13701)*
**Absolute Stoneworks Inc**..........G....... 708 652-7600
Cicero *(G-7175)*
▲ **Accorn Gran Natural Stone Inc**..........G....... 312 663-5000
Chicago *(G-3718)*
**Acme Marble Co Inc**..........G....... 630 964-7162
Darien *(G-7786)*
**All Saints Monument Co Inc**..........G....... 847 824-1248
Des Plaines *(G-8145)*
**American Marble & Granite Inc**..........G....... 815 741-1710
Crest Hill *(G-7457)*
**American Monument Co**..........G....... 618 993-8968
Marion *(G-14253)*
**Argyle Cut Stone Co**..........E....... 847 456-6210
Des Plaines *(G-8151)*
**Arnold Monument Co Inc**..........G....... 217 546-2102
Springfield *(G-20388)*
**Beutel Corporation**..........G....... 309 786-8134
Rock Island *(G-18164)*
▲ **Bevel Granite Co Inc**..........D....... 708 388-9060
Merrionette Park *(G-14736)*
**Botti Studio of Architectural**..........E....... 847 869-5933
Evanston *(G-10017)*
**Brombereks Flagstone Co Inc**..........G....... 630 257-0686
Lemont *(G-13228)*
**Carrera Stone Systems of Chica**..........E....... 847 566-2277
Mundelein *(G-15483)*
▲ **Central Illinois Granite Inc**..........G....... 309 263-6880
Morton *(G-15155)*
**Cline Concrete Products**..........F....... 217 283-5012
Hoopeston *(G-12107)*
**Clugston Tibbitts Funeral Home**..........G....... 309 833-2188
Macomb *(G-14122)*
▲ **Condor Granites Intl Inc**..........G....... 847 635-7214
Elgin *(G-9000)*
**Contempo Marble & Granite Inc**..........G....... 312 455-0022
Chicago *(G-4456)*
**Contemporary Marble Inc**..........G....... 618 281-6200
Columbia *(G-7357)*
**Contractors Ready-Mix Inc**..........G....... 217 482-5530
Mason City *(G-14362)*
▲ **Cosmos Granite & Marble Corp**..........G....... 630 595-8025
Wood Dale *(G-22355)*
**Country Stone Inc**..........E....... 309 787-1744
Milan *(G-14781)*
**Creative Cabinetry Inc**..........G....... 708 460-2900
Orland Park *(G-16851)*
**Creative Inds Terrazzo Pdts**..........G....... 773 235-9088
Chicago *(G-4499)*
**Creative Marble Inc**..........G....... 217 359-7271
Champaign *(G-3471)*
**Custom Stone Wrks Acqstion Inc**..........G....... 630 669-1119
Cortland *(G-7386)*
**Czarnik Memorials Inc**..........G....... 708 458-4443
Justice *(G-12596)*

**D & H Granite and Marble Sup**..........E....... 773 869-9988
Chicago *(G-4533)*
**Daprato Rigali Inc**..........E....... 773 763-5511
Chicago *(G-4557)*
▲ **Dtk Construction Inc**..........G....... 312 296-2762
Wheeling *(G-22037)*
**Earth Stone Products III Inc**..........G....... 847 671-3000
Schiller Park *(G-19822)*
**Effingham Monument Co Inc**..........G....... 217 857-6085
Effingham *(G-8835)*
▲ **Euro Marble & Granite Inc**..........F....... 847 233-0700
Schiller Park *(G-19827)*
**F Lee Charles & Sons Inc**..........G....... 815 547-7141
Kirkland *(G-12712)*
▲ **Factory Plaza Inc**..........E....... 630 616-9999
Bensenville *(G-1895)*
**G & L Counter Tops Corporation**..........F....... 815 786-2244
Sandwich *(G-19364)*
**Gallasi Cut Stone & Marble LLC**..........E....... 708 479-9494
Mokena *(G-14866)*
**Galloy and Van Etten Inc**..........E....... 773 928-4800
Chicago *(G-4911)*
**Gast Monuments Inc**..........G....... 773 262-2400
Chicago *(G-4916)*
**GBS Liquidating Corp**..........G....... 309 342-4155
Galesburg *(G-10753)*
▲ **Geokat Granite**..........G....... 773 265-1423
Chicago *(G-4940)*
**Global Stone Inc**..........G....... 847 718-1418
Elk Grove Village *(G-9502)*
**Granite Designs of Ilinois**..........G....... 773 772-5300
Chicago *(G-4985)*
**Granite Mountain Inc**..........G....... 708 774-1442
New Lenox *(G-15884)*
▲ **Granite Works LLC**..........G....... 847 837-1688
Mundelein *(G-15503)*
**Granitex Corp**..........G....... 630 888-1838
Elmhurst *(G-9879)*
▲ **Heartland Granite Inc**..........E....... 630 499-8000
Aurora *(G-1025)*
**Heisler Stone Co Inc**..........G....... 815 244-2685
Mount Carroll *(G-15291)*
▲ **House Granite & Marble Corp**..........G....... 847 928-1111
Schiller Park *(G-19839)*
**Imperial Marble Corp**..........C....... 815 498-2303
Somonauk *(G-20126)*
**Insignia Stone**..........G....... 815 463-9802
New Lenox *(G-15886)*
**J W Reynolds Monument Co Inc**..........G....... 618 833-6014
Anna *(G-606)*
**Jack R Phillips**..........G....... 618 242-8411
Mount Vernon *(G-15416)*
**Jacksonville Monument Co**..........G....... 217 245-2514
Jacksonville *(G-12397)*
**Keepes Funeral Home Inc**..........F....... 618 262-5200
Mount Carmel *(G-15271)*
**King & Sons Monuments**..........G....... 815 786-6321
Sandwich *(G-19371)*
▲ **Kitchen Transformation Inc**..........F....... 847 758-1905
Elk Grove Village *(G-9574)*
**Lansing Cut Stone Co**..........F....... 708 474-7515
Lansing *(G-13170)*
**Liberty Limestone Inc**..........G....... 815 385-5011
McHenry *(G-14521)*
▲ **Lonnies Stonecrafters Inc**..........E....... 815 316-6565
Rockford *(G-18473)*
**Luxury MBL & Gran Design Inc**..........G....... 773 656-2125
Chicago *(G-5570)*
**Machine & Design**..........G....... 630 858-6416
Glen Ellyn *(G-10979)*
▲ **Marble Emporium Inc**..........E....... 847 205-4000
Northbrook *(G-16306)*
**Material Service Corporation**..........E....... 847 658-4559
Algonquin *(G-400)*
**Material Service Corporation**..........E....... 708 447-1100
Westchester *(G-21849)*
**Material Service Corporation**..........E....... 217 732-2117
Athens *(G-939)*
**Meier Granite Company**..........G....... 847 678-7300
Franklin Park *(G-10527)*
**Mendota Monument Co**..........G....... 815 539-7276
Mendota *(G-14725)*
**Meno Stone Co Inc**..........E....... 630 257-9220
Lemont *(G-13241)*
**Midwest Stone Sales Inc**..........F....... 815 254-6600
Plainfield *(G-17628)*
**Milano Direct**..........G....... 847 566-1387
Mundelein *(G-15532)*
**Monumental Art Works**..........G....... 708 389-3038
Blue Island *(G-2263)*



Employee Codes: A=Over 500 employees, B=251-500
C=101-250, D=51-100, E=20-50, F=10-19, G=3-9
2017 Harris Illinois
Industrial Directory
1017

## 32 STONE, CLAY, GLASS, AND CONCRETE PRODUCTS

Monumental Manufacturing Co .......... D .... 708 544-0916
  Hillside (G-11927)
Moore Memorials ..................................... F .... 708 636-6532
  Chicago Ridge (G-7152)
Nashville Memorial Co ......................... G .... 618 327-8492
  Nashville (G-15843)
Natural Stone Inc ................................... G .... 847 735-1129
  Lake Bluff (G-12858)
Newton Ready Mix Inc ......................... F .... 618 783-8611
  Newton (G-15944)
▲ Nu-Dell Manufacturing Co Inc ......... F .... 847 803-4500
  Chicago (G-5953)
Old Capitol Monument Works Inc ...... G .... 217 324-5673
  Vandalia (G-21118)
▲ Optimum Granite & Marble Inc ...... G .... 800 920-6033
  South Elgin (G-20222)
Pana Monument Co .............................. G .... 217 562-5121
  Pana (G-17136)
Patterson Products ............................... G .... 618 723-2688
  Noble (G-16053)
Pep Industries Inc ................................. G .... 630 833-0404
  Villa Park (G-21276)
Peter Troost Monument Co ................ G .... 773 585-0242
  Chicago (G-6109)
Pintas Cultured Marble ........................ E .... 708 385-3360
  Alsip (G-509)
Pontiac Granite Company Inc ............. F .... 815 842-1384
  Pontiac (G-17707)
Primo Granito LLC ................................ F .... 773 282-6391
  Chicago (G-6187)
Regal Cut Stone LLC ........................... F .... 773 826-8796
  Chicago (G-6320)
Reynolds Rock of Ages ....................... F .... 618 658-2911
  Vienna (G-21224)
Rogan Granitindustrie Inc ................... G .... 708 758-0050
  Merrionette Park (G-14737)
▲ Rogan Granitindustrie Inc ............... G .... 708 758-0050
  Lynwood (G-14025)
Rogan Group Inc .................................. G .... 708 371-4191
  Merrionette Park (G-14738)
Spence Monuments Co ....................... G .... 217 348-5992
  Charleston (G-3612)
St Charles Memorial Works Inc ......... G .... 630 584-0183
  Saint Charles (G-19268)
▲ Standard Marble & Granite ............. F .... 773 533-0450
  Chicago (G-6570)
Stone Center Inc .................................. G .... 630 971-2060
  Lisle (G-13664)
Stone Design Inc .................................. F .... 630 790-5715
  Glendale Heights (G-11075)
▲ Stone Design Inc ............................. E .... 630 790-5715
  Glendale Heights (G-11076)
▲ Stonecasters LLC ............................ D .... 847 526-5200
  Wauconda (G-21504)
▲ Stonecrafters Inc ............................. E .... 815 363-8730
  Lakemoor (G-13148)
Stylenquaza LLC .................................. G .... 847 981-0191
  Elk Grove Village (G-9759)
Superior Home Products Inc .............. G .... 217 726-9300
  Springfield (G-20540)
Tisch Monuments Inc .......................... G .... 618 233-3017
  Belleville (G-1680)
Tri-State Cut Stone Co ........................ E .... 815 469-7550
  Frankfort (G-10371)
▲ Unilock Chicago Inc ........................ D .... 630 892-9191
  Aurora (G-1227)
United Granite & Marble ..................... G .... 815 582-3345
  Joliet (G-12584)
▲ Vecchio Manufacturing of Ill .......... F .... 847 742-8429
  Elgin (G-9224)
Venetian Monument Company ........... F .... 312 829-9622
  Chicago (G-6880)
Wasowski Jacek ................................... G .... 847 693-1878
  Palatine (G-17087)
▲ Weiss Monument Works Inc ......... G .... 618 398-1811
  Belleville (G-1690)
▲ Wendell Adams ................................ E .... 217 345-9587
  Charleston (G-3615)
Wienmar Inc .......................................... C .... 847 742-9222
  South Elgin (G-20235)
Wilson & Wilson Monument Co ......... F .... 618 775-6488
  Odin (G-16742)
World Granite Inc ................................. G .... 815 288-3350
  Dixon (G-8359)
Worldwide Tiles Ltd Inc ....................... G .... 708 389-2992
  Alsip (G-545)
Zoia Monument Company ................... G .... 815 338-0358
  Woodstock (G-22629)

### 3291 Abrasive Prdts

A Wheels Inc ......................................... G .... 847 699-7000
  Des Plaines (G-8139)
▲ Abrasic 90 Inc .................................. E .... 800 447-4248
  Niles (G-15955)
Abrasive Rubber Wheel Co ................ G .... 847 587-0900
  Fox Lake (G-10273)
Abrasive Technology Inc .................... E .... 847 888-7100
  Elgin (G-8930)
Abrasive-Form LLC .............................. E .... 630 220-3437
  Bloomingdale (G-2091)
◆ Agsco Corporation ........................... E .... 847 520-4455
  Wheeling (G-21999)
▲ American Buff Intl Inc ..................... F .... 217 465-1411
  Paris (G-17141)
Anchor Abrasives Company ............... G .... 708 444-4300
  Tinley Park (G-20893)
Arcelor Mittal USA LLC ....................... G .... 312 899-3500
  Chicago (G-3932)
Avec Inc ................................................. G .... 217 670-0439
  Naperville (G-15799)
▲ Bates Abrasive Products Inc ......... E .... 773 586-8700
  Chicago (G-4054)
C M C Industries Inc ............................ F .... 630 377-0530
  Saint Charles (G-19147)
Carbco Manufacturing Inc ................... G .... 630 377-1410
  Saint Charles (G-19150)
Covidien LP ........................................... C .... 815 744-3766
  Joliet (G-12478)
Diagrind Inc .......................................... F .... 708 460-4333
  Orland Park (G-16854)
▼ Dura Wax Company ........................ G .... 815 385-5000
  McHenry (G-14499)
Electro-Glo Distribution Inc ................ G .... 815 224-4030
  La Salle (G-12771)
▲ Engis Corporation ........................... E .... 847 808-9400
  Wheeling (G-22047)
▲ Global Material Tech Inc ................ C .... 847 495-4700
  Buffalo Grove (G-2699)
Global Material Tech Inc ..................... C .... 773 247-6000
  Chicago (G-4958)
▲ Grier Abrasive Co Inc ..................... C .... 708 333-6445
  South Holland (G-20271)
Harsco Corporation .............................. F .... 217 237-4335
  Pawnee (G-17234)
Hayes Abrasives Inc ............................ G .... 217 532-6850
  Hillsboro (G-11892)
Higman LLC .......................................... F .... 618 785-2545
  Baldwin (G-1251)
Ideal Industries Inc ............................... C .... 815 895-1108
  Sycamore (G-20801)
K & K Abrasives & Supplies ............... G .... 773 582-9500
  Chicago (G-5341)
Kona Blackbird Inc ............................... F .... 815 792-8750
  Serena (G-19892)
▲ Marvel Abrasives Products LLC ... F .... 800 621-0673
  Chicago (G-5637)
▲ Matchless Metal Polish Company .. E .... 773 924-1515
  Chicago (G-5649)
Meinhardt Diamond Tool Co ............... G .... 773 267-3260
  Chicago (G-5681)
▲ Modern Abrasive Corp ................... C .... 815 675-2352
  Spring Grove (G-20349)
◆ Radiac Abrasives Inc ...................... C .... 618 548-4200
  Salem (G-19347)
Radiac Abrasives Inc ........................... E .... 630 898-0315
  Oswego (G-16931)
Rh Preyda Company ............................ F .... 212 880-1477
  Chicago (G-6348)
▲ Rock Solid Imports LLC .................. G .... 331 472-4522
  Naperville (G-15743)
S & J Industrial Supply Corp .............. F .... 708 339-1708
  South Holland (G-20303)
Saint-Gobain Abrasives Inc ................ C .... 630 238-3300
  Carol Stream (G-3231)
Saint-Gobain Abrasives Inc ................ E .... 630 868-8060
  Carol Stream (G-3232)
▲ Sand-Rite Manufacturing Co .......... G .... 312 997-2200
  Melrose Park (G-14691)
▲ Sandtech Inc .................................... E .... 847 470-9595
  Morton Grove (G-15234)
Schram Enterprises Inc ....................... G .... 708 345-2252
  Melrose Park (G-14693)
◆ Severstal US Holdings II Inc .......... F .... 708 756-0400
  Hinsdale (G-11964)
Superior Joining Tech Inc ................... E .... 815 282-7581
  Machesney Park (G-14109)
U S Silica Company ............................. C .... 815 434-0188
  Ottawa (G-16988)
▲ Uk Abrasives Inc ............................. E .... 847 291-3566
  Northbrook (G-16378)
Ultramatic Equipment Co .................... E .... 630 543-4565
  Addison (G-333)
▲ US Minerals Inc ............................... F .... 219 864-0909
  Tinley Park (G-20954)
US Minerals Inc .................................... F .... 618 785-2217
  Baldwin (G-1252)
US Minerals Inc .................................... F .... 217 534-2370
  Coffeen (G-7306)
▲ Washington Mills Hennepin Inc .... D .... 815 925-7302
  Hennepin (G-11735)
Washington Mills Tonawanda ............. D .... 815 925-7302
  Hennepin (G-11736)

### 3292 Asbestos products

Asbestos Control & Envmtl Svc ......... F .... 630 690-0189
  Eola (G-9988)
Celtic Environmental ............................ G .... 708 442-5823
  Chicago Ridge (G-7140)
Wise Construction Services ................ G .... 630 553-6350
  Yorkville (G-22676)

### 3295 Minerals & Earths: Ground Or Treated

▲ Aero Industries Inc .......................... F .... 815 943-7818
  Harvard (G-11618)
Beelman Slag Sales ............................. B .... 618 452-8120
  Madison (G-14139)
C-E Minerals Inc ................................... F .... 618 285-6558
  Rosiclare (G-19047)
▲ Dauber Company Inc ...................... G .... 815 442-3569
  Tonica (G-20973)
Harsco Corporation .............................. F .... 217 237-4335
  Pawnee (G-17234)
Holcim (us) Inc ..................................... E .... 773 731-1320
  Chicago (G-5098)
Jaffee Investment Partnr LP ............... C .... 312 321-1515
  Chicago (G-5270)
John Crane Inc ..................................... E .... 815 459-0420
  Crystal Lake (G-7596)
Littleson Inc .......................................... G .... 815 968-8349
  Rockford (G-18471)
Material Service Corporation .............. D .... 708 877-6540
  Thornton (G-20875)
McGill Asphalt Construction Co ......... G .... 708 924-1755
  Chicago (G-5667)
▲ Mid River Minerals Inc ................... G .... 815 941-7524
  Morris (G-15117)
Mineral Products Inc ........................... G .... 618 433-3150
  Galatia (G-10712)
Minerals Technologies Inc .................. E .... 847 851-1500
  Hoffman Estates (G-12022)
Oil-Dri Corporation America ............... D .... 312 321-1515
  Chicago (G-5975)
Oil-Dri Corporation America ............... D .... 618 745-6881
  Mounds (G-15259)
Oil-Dri Corporation America ............... B .... 312 321-1516
  Chicago (G-5976)
Phoenix Services LLC ......................... E .... 708 849-3527
  Riverdale (G-18022)
◆ Polyform Products Company ......... E .... 847 427-0020
  Elk Grove Village (G-9685)
▼ Prince Minerals Inc ......................... F .... 618 285-6558
  Rosiclare (G-19049)
▲ Sem Minerals LP ............................. D .... 217 224-8766
  Quincy (G-17890)
◆ Superior Graphite Co ...................... E .... 312 559-2999
  Chicago (G-6632)
Superior Graphite Co ........................... E .... 708 458-0006
  Chicago (G-6633)
Superior Graphite Co ........................... E .... 773 890-4100
  Chicago (G-6634)
Tms International LLC ......................... E .... 618 451-7840
  Granite City (G-11307)
Tms International LLC ......................... G .... 815 939-9460
  Bourbonnais (G-2408)
Unimin Corporation .............................. E .... 815 667-5102
  Utica (G-21109)
Washington Mills Tonawanda ............. D .... 815 925-7302
  Hennepin (G-11736)

### 3296 Mineral Wool

Advance Thermal Corp ........................ E .... 630 595-5150
  Wood Dale (G-22331)
▲ Advance Thermal Corp ................... D .... 630 595-5150
  Wood Dale (G-22332)
Atlas Roofing Corporation ................... E .... 309 752-7121
  East Moline (G-8670)
Fbm Galaxy Inc ..................................... E .... 847 362-0925
  Lake Bluff (G-12843)

# 33 PRIMARY METAL INDUSTRIES

J & J Industries Inc .................................. G .... 630 595-8878
  Bensenville *(G-1925)*
Johns Manville Corporation .................... C .... 815 744-1545
  Rockdale *(G-18221)*
Mary E Fisher ........................................... G .... 618 964-1528
  Marion *(G-14273)*
Owens Corning Sales LLC ....................... B .... 708 594-6911
  Argo *(G-694)*
Owens-Corning Fiberglass Tech ............. G .... 708 563-9091
  Argo *(G-696)*
Safe-T-Quip Corporation ......................... F .... 773 235-2100
  Chicago *(G-6425)*
◆ Silbrico Corporation ............................ D .... 708 354-3350
  Hodgkins *(G-11983)*
Tex Trend Inc ........................................... E .... 847 215-6796
  Wheeling *(G-22166)*
▲ Transco Products Inc .......................... D .... 312 427-2818
  Chicago *(G-6758)*
USG Corporation ...................................... F .... 847 970-5200
  Libertyville *(G-13396)*
USG Corporation ...................................... B .... 312 436-4000
  Chicago *(G-6858)*

## 3297 Nonclay Refractories

Ipsen Inc .................................................... E .... 815 239-2385
  Pecatonica *(G-17252)*
▲ M H Detrick Company .......................... E .... 708 479-5085
  Mokena *(G-14882)*
Magneco Inc .............................................. D .... 630 543-6660
  Addison *(G-186)*
Magneco Inc .............................................. G .... 630 543-6660
  Addison *(G-187)*
▼ Magneco/Metrel Inc ............................ E .... 630 543-6660
  Addison *(G-188)*
Miller Purcell Co Inc ................................. G .... 815 485-2142
  New Lenox *(G-15897)*
▲ Vesuvius Crucible Company ............... C .... 217 351-5000
  Champaign *(G-3555)*
Vesuvius U S A Corporation .................... D .... 708 757-7880
  Chicago Heights *(G-7135)*
Vesuvius U S A Corporation .................... C .... 217 897-1145
  Fisher *(G-10192)*
Vesuvius U S A Corporation .................... C .... 217 345-7044
  Charleston *(G-3614)*
◆ Vesuvius U S A Corporation ............... C .... 217 351-5000
  Champaign *(G-3556)*

## 3299 Nonmetallic Mineral Prdts, NEC

Better Earth LLC ....................................... G .... 844 243-6333
  Chicago *(G-4095)*
Budget Signs ............................................. F .... 618 259-4460
  Wood River *(G-22441)*
Continental Studios Inc ............................ E .... 773 542-0309
  Chicago *(G-4460)*
Daprato Rigali Inc ..................................... E .... 773 763-5511
  Chicago *(G-4557)*
Decorators Supply Corporation .............. E .... 773 847-6300
  Chicago *(G-4571)*
Depth Action Marketing Group ............... G .... 847 475-7122
  Evanston *(G-10027)*
Espe Manufacturing Co ........................... F .... 847 678-8950
  Schiller Park *(G-19826)*
▲ Ghp Group Inc ..................................... E .... 847 324-5900
  Niles *(G-15983)*
GL Downs Inc ........................................... G .... 618 993-9777
  Marion *(G-14262)*
Image Systems Bus Slutions LLC .......... E .... 847 378-8249
  Elk Grove Village *(G-9539)*
Lakefront Sculpture Exhibit .................... G .... 312 719-0207
  Chicago *(G-5444)*
Nanophase Technologies Corp .............. F .... 630 771-6708
  Burr Ridge *(G-2870)*
Nanophase Technologies Corp .............. E .... 630 771-6708
  Romeoville *(G-18852)*
▲ Orlandi Statuary Company ................. D .... 773 489-0303
  Chicago *(G-6015)*
Pillar Enterprises Inc ............................... G .... 630 966-2566
  North Aurora *(G-16142)*
Quality Molding Products LLC ............... G .... 224 308-4167
  Grayslake *(G-11360)*
Sand Sculpture Co ................................... G .... 815 334-9101
  Woodstock *(G-22607)*
Thermal Ceramics Inc ............................. E .... 217 627-2101
  Girard *(G-10950)*
▲ Thermionics Corp ............................... F .... 800 800-5728
  Springfield *(G-20544)*

# 33 PRIMARY METAL INDUSTRIES

## 3312 Blast Furnaces, Coke Ovens, Steel & Rolling Mills

A & A Steel Fabricating Co ...................... F .... 708 389-4499
  Posen *(G-17726)*
A 2 Steel Sales LLC .................................. G .... 708 924-1200
  Bedford Park *(G-1529)*
◆ A Finkl & Sons Co ............................... B .... 773 975-2510
  Chicago *(G-3687)*
Aap Metals LLC ........................................ D .... 847 916-1220
  Elk Grove Village *(G-9252)*
Accurate Metals Illinois LLC .................. F .... 815 966-6320
  Rockford *(G-18254)*
Adams Elevator Equipment Co .............. E .... 847 581-2900
  Chicago *(G-3743)*
▼ Advance Steel Services Inc ............... G .... 773 619-2977
  Chicago *(G-3764)*
Advantage Tool and Mold Inc ................ G .... 847 301-9020
  Elk Grove Village *(G-9280)*
AK Steel Corporation .............................. B .... 815 267-3838
  Plainfield *(G-17577)*
▲ Aldon Co ............................................... F .... 847 623-8800
  Waukegan *(G-21521)*
Allegheny Ludlum LLC ........................... F .... 708 974-8801
  Bridgeview *(G-2460)*
Alter Trading Corporation ...................... F .... 309 828-6084
  Bloomington *(G-2143)*
▲ Alton Steel Inc .................................... B .... 618 463-4490
  Alton *(G-560)*
Apex Material Technologies LLC .......... G .... 815 727-3010
  Joliet *(G-12456)*
Arcanum Alloy Design Inc ..................... G .... 219 508-5531
  Chicago *(G-3931)*
◆ Arcelormittal USA LLC ...................... B .... 312 346-0300
  Chicago *(G-3935)*
Archer Industries & Supplies ................ G .... 773 777-2698
  Chicago *(G-3937)*
Archer Metal & Paper Co ....................... F .... 773 585-3030
  Chicago *(G-3939)*
Arntzen Corporation ............................... E .... 815 334-0788
  Woodstock *(G-22541)*
Automation Design & Mfg Inc ............... G .... 630 896-4206
  Aurora *(G-1117)*
Bar Processing Corporation .................. E .... 708 757-4570
  Chicago Heights *(G-7081)*
◆ Bevstream Corp .................................. G .... 630 761-0060
  Batavia *(G-1421)*
Block Steel Corp ..................................... E .... 847 965-6700
  Skokie *(G-19965)*
Brass Creations Inc ............................... G .... 773 237-7755
  Chicago *(G-4158)*
Bretmar Steel Industry ........................... G .... 847 382-5940
  Barrington *(G-1274)*
C & F Forge Company ............................ G .... 847 455-6609
  Franklin Park *(G-10420)*
Cambridge Pattern Works ..................... G .... 309 937-5370
  Cambridge *(G-2966)*
Carpenter Technology Corp .................. G .... 630 771-1020
  Bolingbrook *(G-2284)*
Caster Warehouse Inc ........................... F .... 847 836-5712
  Carpentersville *(G-3279)*
▲ Central Wire Inc ................................ C .... 815 923-2131
  Union *(G-21034)*
▲ CFC Wire Forms Inc ........................ G .... 630 879-7575
  Batavia *(G-1428)*
Chicago Metal Fabricators Inc .............. D .... 773 523-5755
  Chicago *(G-4332)*
Chicago Pipe Bending & Coil Co ........... F .... 773 379-1918
  Chicago *(G-4339)*
▲ Chromium Industries Inc ................. E .... 773 287-3716
  Chicago *(G-4373)*
▼ CHS Acquisition Corp ...................... C .... 708 756-5648
  Chicago Heights *(G-7090)*
Cisne Iron Works Inc ............................ F .... 618 673-2188
  Cisne *(G-7250)*
Cobraa Inc ............................................. G .... 618 228-7380
  Aviston *(G-1243)*
Combined Metals Holding Inc ............. C .... 708 547-8800
  Bellwood *(G-1701)*
Commercial Metals Company ............. G .... 815 928-9600
  Kankakee *(G-12606)*
Commercial Stainless Services ........... F .... 847 349-1560
  Elk Grove Village *(G-9387)*
▼ Connelly-Gpm Inc ............................. E .... 773 247-7231
  Chicago *(G-4451)*
▲ Consolidated Mill Supply Inc ......... G .... 847 706-6715
  Palatine *(G-17016)*
Contour Tool Works Inc ....................... G .... 847 947-4700
  Palatine *(G-17018)*

Covey Machine Inc ............................... F .... 773 650-1530
  Chicago *(G-4484)*
▼ Craftsman Custom Metals LLC ..... D .... 847 655-0040
  Schiller Park *(G-19817)*
▲ D R Sperry & Co .............................. D .... 630 892-4361
  Aurora *(G-1137)*
Earthsafe Systems Inc ........................ F .... 312 226-7600
  Chicago *(G-4679)*
Economy Iron Inc ................................ F .... 708 343-1777
  Melrose Park *(G-14628)*
Elg Metals Inc ..................................... F .... 773 374-1500
  Chicago *(G-4728)*
▲ Evraz Inc NA ................................... C .... 312 533-3621
  Chicago *(G-4792)*
Fabricating Machinery Sales ............ E .... 630 350-2266
  Wood Dale *(G-22366)*
▲ Ferralloy Corporation .................... E .... 503 286-8869
  Chicago *(G-4836)*
Forza Customs ................................... G .... 708 474-6625
  Lansing *(G-13162)*
▲ Fox Valley Iron & Metal Corp ....... F .... 630 897-5907
  Aurora *(G-1155)*
Franks Maintenance & Engrg ........... E .... 847 475-1003
  Evanston *(G-10040)*
Frazer Manufacturing Corp .............. G .... 815 625-5411
  Rock Falls *(G-18133)*
Gerald R Page Corporation ............... F .... 847 398-5575
  Prospect Heights *(G-17779)*
Grab Brothers Ir Works Co Corp ...... F .... 847 288-1055
  Franklin Park *(G-10480)*
▲ Guardian Construction Pdts Inc .. E .... 630 820-8899
  Naperville *(G-15808)*
Heidtman Steel Products Inc .......... F .... 618 451-0052
  Granite City *(G-11284)*
Heidtman Steel Products Inc .......... F .... 618 451-0052
  Granite City *(G-11285)*
HI Tek Tool & Machining Inc ............ G .... 847 836-6422
  Algonquin *(G-392)*
Highland Southern Wire Inc ............ E .... 618 654-2161
  Highland *(G-11792)*
Hoosier Stamping & Mfg Corp ......... G .... 812 426-2778
  Grayville *(G-11370)*
▲ Illinois Engineered Pdts Inc ........ G .... 312 850-3710
  Chicago *(G-5156)*
Illinois Steel Service Inc .................. D .... 312 926-7440
  Chicago *(G-5158)*
Illinois Weld & Machine Inc ............. F .... 309 565-0533
  Hanna City *(G-11568)*
Illinois Weld & Machine Inc ............. F .... 309 565-0533
  Hanna City *(G-11569)*
Industrial Pipe and Supply Co ........ E .... 708 652-7511
  Chicago *(G-5179)*
Jacobs Boiler & Mech Inds Inc ....... F .... 773 385-9900
  Chicago *(G-5269)*
Jamco Products Inc ......................... D .... 815 624-0400
  South Beloit *(G-20152)*
Joe Zsido Sales & Design Inc ........ E .... 618 435-2605
  Benton *(G-2032)*
John Maneely Company .................. C .... 773 254-0617
  Chicago *(G-5316)*
▲ Kaltband North America Inc ....... F .... 773 248-6684
  Chicago *(G-5355)*
▲ Keats Manufacturing Co ............. F .... 847 520-1133
  Wheeling *(G-22083)*
Keystone Consolidated Inds Inc .... E .... 309 697-7020
  Peoria *(G-17396)*
Keystone Consolidated Inds Inc .... E .... 708 753-1200
  Chicago Heights *(G-7109)*
Keystone-Calumet Inc ..................... E .... 708 753-1200
  Chicago Heights *(G-7110)*
Korhumel Inc .................................... G .... 847 330-0335
  Schaumburg *(G-19604)*
Kusmierek Industries Inc ............... E .... 708 258-3100
  Peotone *(G-17490)*
Lawndale Forging & Tool Works .... G .... 773 277-2800
  Chicago *(G-5471)*
Leeco Steel Products ...................... G .... 630 427-2100
  Lisle *(G-13617)*
Lexington Steel Corporation .......... F .... 708 594-9200
  Oak Brook *(G-16536)*
▲ Main Steel LLC ............................ D .... 847 916-1220
  Elk Grove Village *(G-9607)*
Marias Chicken ATI Atihan ............. F .... 847 699-3113
  Niles *(G-16000)*
Marqutte Stl Sup Fbrcation Inc ..... F .... 815 433-0178
  Ottawa *(G-16968)*
Matcon Manufacturing Inc ............. E .... 309 755-1020
  Cordova *(G-7377)*
Mc Chemical Company ................... E .... 815 964-7687
  Rockford *(G-18487)*

Employee Codes: A=Over 500 employees, B=251-500
C=101-250, D=51-100, E=20-50, F=10-19, G=3-9

# 33 PRIMARY METAL INDUSTRIES

Metal Resources Inc .................... G ..... 630 616-1850
  Hinsdale *(G-11953)*
Metal-Matic Inc ........................... C ..... 708 594-7553
  Bedford Park *(G-1562)*
Mexinox USA Inc ......................... D ..... 224 533-6700
  Bannockburn *(G-1261)*
Middletown Coke Company LLC ... G ..... 630 284-1755
  Lisle *(G-13623)*
Midstates Cutting Tools Inc ......... E ..... 630 595-0700
  Bensenville *(G-1951)*
Midwest Wheel Covers Inc ........... G ..... 847 609-9980
  Barrington *(G-1291)*
▲ Mittal Steel USA Inc .................. F ..... 312 899-3440
  Chicago *(G-5775)*
Modern Tube LLC ........................ G ..... 877 848-3300
  Bloomingdale *(G-2118)*
Mt Tool and Manufacturing Inc .... G ..... 847 985-6211
  Schaumburg *(G-19655)*
Multiple Metal Production ........... G ..... 847 679-1510
  Skokie *(G-20043)*
Multiplex Industries Inc ............... G ..... 630 906-9780
  Montgomery *(G-15062)*
Multitech Industries .................... G ..... 815 206-0015
  Woodstock *(G-22594)*
Nacme Steel Processing LLC ...... G ..... 847 806-7226
  Elk Grove Village *(G-9644)*
Nacme Steel Processing LLC ...... D ..... 773 468-3309
  Chicago *(G-5848)*
National Material LP .................... E ..... 773 646-6300
  Chicago *(G-5864)*
▲ New C F & I Inc ......................... A ..... 312 533-3555
  Chicago *(G-5890)*
▲ Nucor Steel Kankakee Inc ......... B ..... 815 937-3131
  Bourbonnais *(G-2403)*
▲ O & K American Corp ................ D ..... 773 767-2500
  Chicago *(G-5957)*
O & W Wire Co Inc ...................... F ..... 773 776-5919
  Chicago *(G-5958)*
Offko Tool Inc ............................. G ..... 815 933-9474
  Kankakee *(G-12641)*
Olympic Steel Inc ........................ E ..... 847 584-4000
  Schaumburg *(G-19675)*
Omega Products Inc .................... G ..... 618 939-3445
  Waterloo *(G-21403)*
Outokumpu Stainless Usa LLC .... D ..... 847 405-6604
  Deerfield *(G-8045)*
Outokumpu Stainless Usa LLC .... B ..... 847 317-1400
  Bannockburn *(G-1263)*
P B A Corp .................................. F ..... 312 666-7370
  Chicago *(G-6039)*
Paragon Spring Company ............ E ..... 773 489-6300
  Chicago *(G-6076)*
Penn Aluminum Intl LLC .............. C ..... 618 684-2146
  Murphysboro *(G-15579)*
Phillips & Johnston Inc ............... F ..... 815 778-3355
  Lyndon *(G-14014)*
▲ Pinnacle Metals Inc ................... E ..... 815 232-1600
  Freeport *(G-10679)*
Prairie Profile ............................. G ..... 618 846-2116
  Vandalia *(G-21120)*
Precise Stamping Inc .................. E ..... 630 897-6477
  North Aurora *(G-16143)*
▲ Processed Steel Company ......... B ..... 815 459-2400
  Crystal Lake *(G-7635)*
Production Cutting Services ....... D ..... 815 264-3505
  Waterman *(G-21409)*
Production Tooling and Automtn .. G ..... 217 283-7373
  Hoopeston *(G-12114)*
Progress Rail Services Corp ....... E ..... 309 963-4425
  Danvers *(G-7701)*
Ptc Group Holdings Corp ............ D ..... 708 757-4747
  Chicago Heights *(G-7118)*
Ptc Tubular Products LLC ........... C ..... 815 692-4900
  Fairbury *(G-10131)*
R & E Quality Mfg Co .................. G ..... 773 286-6846
  Chicago *(G-6262)*
R M Tool & Manufacturing Co ..... G ..... 847 888-0433
  Elgin *(G-9160)*
▲ Raco Steel Company ................. E ..... 708 339-2958
  Markham *(G-14304)*
Rain Cii Carbon LLC ................... E ..... 618 544-2193
  Robinson *(G-18071)*
Residntial Stl Fabricators Inc ...... E ..... 847 695-4800
  South Elgin *(G-20223)*
Revere Metals LLC ..................... G ..... 708 945-3992
  Frankfort *(G-10357)*
Rmi Inc ....................................... F ..... 708 756-5640
  Chicago Heights *(G-7122)*
S 4 Global Inc ............................. G ..... 708 325-1236
  Bedford Park *(G-1581)*

SE Steel Inc ................................ G ..... 847 350-9618
  Antioch *(G-654)*
Seraph Industries LLC ................ G ..... 815 222-9686
  Caledonia *(G-2934)*
Service Sheet Metal Works Inc .... F ..... 773 229-0031
  Chicago *(G-6483)*
Shapiro Bros of Illinois Inc ......... E ..... 618 244-3168
  Mount Vernon *(G-15445)*
South Shore Iron Works Inc ........ E ..... 773 264-2267
  Chicago *(G-6547)*
▲ Southern Steel and Wire Inc ...... E ..... 618 654-2161
  Highland *(G-11812)*
▲ Ssab Enterprises LLC ................ G ..... 630 810-4800
  Lisle *(G-13661)*
Ssab US Holding Inc ................... G ..... 630 810-4800
  Lisle *(G-13662)*
St Louis Scrap Trading LLC ....... G ..... 618 307-9002
  Edwardsville *(G-8815)*
Steel Fabrication and Welding .... G ..... 773 343-0731
  Cicero *(G-7230)*
◆ Steel Whse Quad Cities LLC ..... E ..... 309 756-1089
  Rock Island *(G-18205)*
Stein Inc ..................................... F ..... 815 626-9355
  Sterling *(G-20613)*
Stein Inc ..................................... D ..... 618 452-0836
  Granite City *(G-11305)*
▲ Sterling Steel Company LLC ...... B ..... 815 548-7000
  Sterling *(G-20614)*
Strictly Stainless Inc ................... G ..... 847 885-2890
  Hoffman Estates *(G-12061)*
Summit Stinless Stl Holdg Corp .. F ..... 732 297-9500
  Rosemont *(G-19035)*
▲ Sun Coke International Inc ........ D ..... 630 824-1000
  Lisle *(G-13665)*
Suncoke Energy Inc .................... B ..... 630 824-1000
  Lisle *(G-13666)*
Suncoke Energy Partners LP ...... F ..... 630 824-1000
  Lisle *(G-13667)*
Suncoke Technology and Dev LLC ... G ..... 630 824-1000
  Lisle *(G-13668)*
Superior Piling Inc ...................... G ..... 708 496-1196
  Bridgeview *(G-2533)*
Tdy Industries LLC ..................... D ..... 847 564-0700
  Northbrook *(G-16376)*
Titan International Inc ................. A ..... 217 221-4498
  Quincy *(G-17895)*
◆ Titan International Inc ................ B ..... 217 228-6011
  Quincy *(G-17896)*
Tj Tool Inc .................................. F ..... 630 543-3595
  Addison *(G-315)*
Tj Wire Forming Inc .................... G ..... 630 628-9209
  Addison *(G-316)*
Tomko Machine Works Inc .......... G ..... 630 244-0902
  Lemont *(G-13266)*
▲ Tritech International LLC ........... G ..... 847 888-0333
  Elgin *(G-9215)*
▲ TSA Processing Chicago Inc ..... G ..... 630 860-5900
  Bensenville *(G-2007)*
United States Steel Corp ............ D ..... 618 451-3456
  Granite City *(G-11310)*
United Toolers of Illinois ............. F ..... 779 423-0548
  Loves Park *(G-14005)*
Valbruna Stainless Inc ................ G ..... 630 871-5524
  Carol Stream *(G-3260)*
Venus Processing & Storage ...... D ..... 847 455-0496
  Franklin Park *(G-10621)*
Waters Wire EDM Service ........... G ..... 630 640-3534
  Downers Grove *(G-8542)*
Westwood Lands Inc .................. G ..... 618 877-4990
  Madison *(G-14156)*
Wheel Worx North LLC ............... G ..... 309 346-3535
  Pekin *(G-17294)*
Woodards LLC DBA Custom Wroug ... G ..... 773 283-8113
  Chicago *(G-7025)*
Works In Progress Foundation .... G ..... 847 997-8338
  Lake Villa *(G-13031)*

### 3313 Electrometallurgical Prdts

Hickman Williams & Company .... F ..... 630 574-2150
  Oak Brook *(G-16521)*
Masters & Alloy LLC ................... G ..... 312 582-1880
  Alsip *(G-489)*
▲ Miller and Company LLC ........... G ..... 847 696-2400
  Rosemont *(G-19017)*
Prince Minerals LLC ................... G ..... 646 747-4222
  Quincy *(G-17873)*
Prince Minerals LLC ................... G ..... 646 747-4200
  Quincy *(G-17874)*
▲ SWB Inc ..................................... G ..... 847 438-1800
  Lake Zurich *(G-13136)*

Tempel Steel Company ............... A ..... 773 250-8000
  Chicago *(G-6697)*
Tempel Steel Company ............... F ..... 847 244-5330
  Old Mill Creek *(G-16756)*
▲ Tempel Steel Company ............. A ..... 773 250-8000
  Chicago *(G-6696)*
Tempel Steel Company ............... A ..... 773 250-8000
  Chicago *(G-6698)*

### 3315 Steel Wire Drawing & Nails & Spikes

Accurate Wire Strip Frming Inc ... F ..... 630 260-1000
  Carol Stream *(G-3089)*
Ace Custom Upholstery & Rod Sp ... G ..... 618 842-2913
  Fairfield *(G-10135)*
Aif Inc ......................................... E ..... 630 495-0077
  Addison *(G-27)*
Allform Manufacturing Co ........... G ..... 847 680-0144
  Libertyville *(G-13301)*
▲ Ansonia Copper & Brass Inc ..... C ..... 866 607-7066
  Chicago *(G-3914)*
Apex Wire Products Company Inc ... F ..... 847 671-1830
  Franklin Park *(G-10397)*
Arcelormittal South Chicago ....... G ..... 312 899-3300
  Chicago *(G-3933)*
Atlantis Products Inc .................. G ..... 630 971-9680
  Bolingbrook *(G-2280)*
Berens Inc .................................. G ..... 815 935-3237
  Saint Anne *(G-19118)*
Blue Ridge Forge Inc .................. G ..... 309 274-5377
  Chillicothe *(G-7162)*
C & L Manufacturing Entps ......... G ..... 618 465-7623
  Alton *(G-565)*
Central Steel and Wire Company ... D ..... 773 471-3800
  Chicago *(G-4272)*
▲ Central Wire Inc ........................ C ..... 815 923-2131
  Union *(G-21034)*
City Ornamental Iron Works ....... G ..... 847 888-8898
  Elgin *(G-8991)*
Combined Metals Chicago LLC ... G ..... 847 683-0500
  Hampshire *(G-11545)*
Dayton Superior Corporation ..... E ..... 219 476-4106
  Kankakee *(G-12607)*
Dayton Superior Corporation ..... C ..... 815 936-3300
  Kankakee *(G-12609)*
E H Baare Corporation ................ C ..... 618 546-1575
  Robinson *(G-18062)*
EDM Dept Inc .............................. F ..... 630 736-0531
  Bartlett *(G-1343)*
Estad Stamping & Mfg Co .......... E ..... 217 442-4600
  Danville *(G-7717)*
▲ Excel Specialty Corp ................. G ..... 773 262-7575
  Lake Forest *(G-12898)*
Fairbanks Wire Corporation ....... E ..... 847 683-2600
  Hampshire *(G-11550)*
▲ Hamalot Inc ............................... E ..... 847 944-1500
  Schaumburg *(G-19547)*
Hangables Inc ............................. F ..... 847 673-9770
  Skokie *(G-20010)*
◆ Heico Companies LLC ................ C ..... 312 419-8220
  Chicago *(G-5068)*
Highland Wire Inc ....................... F ..... 618 654-2161
  Highland *(G-11795)*
Hohmann & Barnard Illinois LLC ... E ..... 773 586-6700
  Chicago Ridge *(G-7150)*
Ideal Industries Inc .................... D ..... 815 758-2656
  Dekalb *(G-8098)*
▲ Ifastgroupe Usa LLC .................. G ..... 450 658-7148
  Downers Grove *(G-8462)*
▲ Illinois Engineered Pdts Inc ...... E ..... 312 850-3710
  Chicago *(G-5156)*
Illinois Tool Works Inc ................ G ..... 847 821-2170
  Vernon Hills *(G-21174)*
▲ ITW Bldg Components Group .... G ..... 847 634-1900
  Glenview *(G-11150)*
▲ Krueger and Company ............... G ..... 630 833-5650
  Elmhurst *(G-9899)*
▲ L & J Industrial Staples Inc ....... E ..... 815 864-3337
  Shannon *(G-19899)*
Lift-All Company Inc ................... E ..... 630 534-6860
  Glendale Heights *(G-11041)*
Major Wire Incorporated ............. F ..... 708 457-0121
  Norridge *(G-16105)*
Mapes & Sprowl Steel LLC ......... G ..... 800 777-1025
  Elk Grove Village *(G-9610)*
Master-Halco Inc ........................ E ..... 618 395-4365
  Olney *(G-16780)*
Master-Halco Inc ........................ G ..... 630 293-5560
  West Chicago *(G-21741)*
McCarthy Enterprises Inc ............ G ..... 847 367-5718
  Libertyville *(G-13351)*

SIC SECTION 33 PRIMARY METAL INDUSTRIES

Moffat Wire & Display Inc....F....630 458-8560
Addison (G-218)
National Material Company LLC....E....847 806-7200
Elk Grove Village (G-9646)
▲ Pneu Fast Inc....F....847 866-8787
Evanston (G-10089)
▲ Powernail Company....E....800 323-1653
Lake Zurich (G-13116)
▲ Raajrtna Stinless Wire USA Inc....F....847 923-8000
Schaumburg (G-19711)
Reino Tool & Manufacturing Co....F....773 588-5800
Chicago (G-6326)
▲ Rockford Rigging Inc....F....309 263-0566
Roscoe (G-18914)
Salzgitter International....G....847 692-6312
Rosemont (G-19029)
Southwire Company LLC....D....618 662-8341
Flora (G-10219)
Stephens Pipe & Steel LLC....E....800 451-2612
North Aurora (G-16146)
▲ Taubensee Steel & Wire Company....C....847 459-5100
Wheeling (G-22164)
The Parts House....G....309 343-0146
Galesburg (G-10777)
◆ Vargyas Networks Inc....F....630 929-3610
Lisle (G-13676)
▲ Vision Sales Incorporated....G....630 483-1900
Bartlett (G-1385)
▲ W H Maze Company....E....815 223-1742
Peru (G-17530)
W H Maze Company....D....815 223-8290
Peru (G-17531)
W R Pabich Manufacturing Co....F....773 486-4141
Chicago (G-6925)
William Dach....F....815 962-3455
Rockford (G-18683)
Wiretech Inc....G....815 986-9614
Rockford (G-18686)

## 3316 Cold Rolled Steel Sheet, Strip & Bars

A & A Steel Fabricating Co....F....708 389-4499
Posen (G-17726)
▲ Arcelormittal Riverdale Inc....B....708 849-8803
Riverdale (G-18014)
◆ Arcelormittal USA LLC....B....312 346-0300
Chicago (G-3935)
Bonell Manufacturing Company....E....708 849-1770
Riverdale (G-18016)
▲ Capitol Coil Inc....F....847 891-1390
Schaumburg (G-19468)
Chase Fasteners Inc....E....708 345-0335
Melrose Park (G-14608)
◆ Clingan Steel Inc....D....847 228-6200
Elk Grove Village (G-9378)
Combined Metals Chicago LLC....G....847 683-0500
Hampshire (G-11545)
▲ Corey Steel Company....C....800 323-2750
Cicero (G-7185)
▲ Deringer-Ney Inc....E....847 566-4100
Vernon Hills (G-21157)
Design Manufacturing & Eqp Co....F....217 824-9219
Taylorville (G-20837)
Expandable Habitats....G....815 624-6784
Rockton (G-18696)
Gartech Manufacturing Co....E....217 324-6527
Litchfield (G-13686)
Harris Steel Company....D....708 656-5500
Cicero (G-7200)
▲ Krueger and Company....E....630 833-5650
Elmhurst (G-9899)
▲ Lapham-Hickey Steel Corp....C....708 496-6111
Chicago (G-5459)
Madison Inds Holdings LLC....G....312 277-0156
Chicago (G-5598)
Mid-State Industries Oper Inc....E....217 268-3900
Arcola (G-676)
Mid-States Wire Proc Corp....F....773 379-3775
Chicago (G-5730)
Multiplex Industries Inc....G....630 906-9780
Montgomery (G-15062)
Multitech Industries....G....815 206-0015
Woodstock (G-22594)
▲ Nelsen Steel and Wire LP....D....847 671-9700
Franklin Park (G-10540)
Niagara Lasalle Corporation....C....708 596-2700
South Holland (G-20293)
▲ Petersen Aluminum Corporation....D....847 228-7150
Elk Grove Village (G-9676)
Phillip C Cowen....E....630 208-1848
Geneva (G-10859)

Ptc Group Holdings Corp....D....708 757-4747
Chicago Heights (G-7118)
Rockford Secondary Co....G....815 398-0401
Rockford (G-18586)
Sandvik Inc....D....847 519-1737
Schaumburg (G-19718)
▲ Screws Industries Inc....D....630 539-9200
Glendale Heights (G-11068)
Skach Manufacturing Co Inc....E....847 395-3560
Antioch (G-655)
Soudan Metals Company Inc....C....773 548-7600
Chicago (G-6545)
▲ Taubensee Steel & Wire Company....C....847 459-5100
Wheeling (G-22164)
▲ Tempel Steel Company....A....773 250-8000
Chicago (G-6696)
Tinsley Steel Inc....G....618 656-5231
Edwardsville (G-8817)
Welding Apparatus Company....E....773 252-7670
Fox Lake (G-10284)
▲ Worth Steel and Machine Co....E....708 388-6300
Alsip (G-546)

## 3317 Steel Pipe & Tubes

Addison Precision Tech LLC....G....773 626-4747
Chicago (G-3745)
▲ Advanced Valve Tech Inc....E....847 364-3700
Elk Grove Village (G-9278)
◆ Allied Tube & Conduit Corp....A....708 339-1610
Harvey (G-11652)
Allied Tube and Conduit....G....708 225-2955
Harvey (G-11653)
▲ American Diesel Tube Corp....F....630 628-1830
Addison (G-35)
Arntzen Corporation....E....815 334-0788
Woodstock (G-22541)
▲ Atkore International Inc....E....708 339-1610
Harvey (G-11657)
▲ Atlas ABC Corporation....B....773 646-4500
Chicago (G-3978)
◆ Atlas Holding Inc....F....773 646-4500
Chicago (G-3980)
▼ Atlas Tube (chicago) LLC....B....773 646-4500
Chicago (G-3984)
B & B Fabrications LLC....G....217 620-3210
Sullivan (G-20739)
Bull Moose Tube Company....D....708 757-7700
Chicago Heights (G-7084)
Chicago Tube and Iron Company....E....815 834-2500
Romeoville (G-18810)
▲ D D G Inc....G....847 412-0277
Northbrook (G-16236)
▲ Durabilt Dyvex Inc....F....708 397-4673
Broadview (G-2573)
E & H Tubing Inc....F....773 522-3100
Chicago (G-4662)
Eagle Tubular Products Inc....E....618 463-1702
Alton (G-573)
Epix Tube Co Inc....E....630 844-0960
Aurora (G-1146)
▲ Evraz Inc NA....C....312 533-3621
Chicago (G-4792)
▲ Forterra Pressure Pipe Inc....E....815 389-4800
South Beloit (G-20147)
▲ Gerlin Inc....G....630 653-5232
Carol Stream (G-3157)
Great Lakes Precision Tube Inc....E....630 859-8940
Aurora (G-1164)
Hanna Steel Corporation....C....309 478-3800
Pekin (G-17265)
Harris William & Company Inc....E....312 621-0590
Chicago (G-5048)
Illinois Meter Inc....G....618 438-6039
Benton (G-2030)
Illinois Ni Cast LLC....G....217 398-3200
Champaign (G-3500)
Illinois Steel Service Inc....D....312 926-7440
Chicago (G-5158)
◆ Independence Tube Corporation....D....708 496-0380
Chicago (G-5173)
Independence Tube Corporation....D....815 795-4400
Marseilles (G-14311)
John Maneely Company....C....773 254-0617
Chicago (G-5316)
Kroh-Wagner Inc....E....773 252-2031
Chicago (G-5412)
▲ Lapham-Hickey Steel Corp....C....708 496-6111
Chicago (G-5459)
▲ Leading Edge Group Inc....C....815 316-3500
Rockford (G-18464)

Legacy International Assoc LLC....G....847 823-1602
Park Ridge (G-17206)
Lex Holding Co....G....708 594-9200
Oak Brook (G-16535)
M C Steel Inc....E....847 350-9618
Antioch (G-642)
Manning Material Services Inc....F....847 669-5750
Huntley (G-12162)
Maruichi Leavitt Pipe Tube LLC....G....800 532-8488
Chicago (G-5634)
▲ Maruichi Leavitt Pipe Tube LLC....C....773 239-7700
Chicago (G-5635)
Metal-Matic Inc....C....708 594-7553
Bedford Park (G-1562)
▲ National Metalwares LP....C....630 892-9000
Aurora (G-1194)
Naylor Pipe Company....C....773 721-9400
Chicago (G-5876)
Nelson Global Products Inc....F....309 263-8914
Morton (G-15171)
Northwest Pipe Company....C....312 587-8702
Chicago (G-5939)
◆ Plymouth Tube Company....E....630 393-3550
Warrenville (G-21355)
Plymouth Tube Company....D....773 489-0226
Chicago (G-6141)
Plymouth Tube Company....D....262 642-8201
Warrenville (G-21356)
Ptc Group Holdings Corp....D....708 757-4747
Chicago Heights (G-7118)
Ptc Tubular Products LLC....C....815 692-4900
Fairbury (G-10131)
▲ Roll McHning Tech Slutions Inc....E....815 372-9100
Romeoville (G-18864)
▲ Structural Steel Systems Limi....F....815 937-3800
Bradley (G-2434)
▲ Tmk Ipsco....E....630 874-0078
Downers Grove (G-8533)
Welding Apparatus Company....E....773 252-7670
Fox Lake (G-10284)
Whi Capital Partners....G....312 621-0590
Chicago (G-6970)
Zapp Tooling Alloys Inc....G....847 599-0351
Gurnee (G-11521)
Zekelman Industries Inc....E....312 275-1600
Chicago (G-7061)
Zero Ground LLC....F....847 360-9500
Waukegan (G-21644)

## 3321 Gray Iron Foundries

Ae Sewer & Septics Inc....G....847 289-9084
Elgin (G-8938)
Alstom Transportation Inc....E....630 369-2201
Naperville (G-15598)
▲ American Electronic Pdts Inc....F....630 889-9977
Oak Brook (G-16488)
◆ Amsted Industries Incorporated....B....312 645-1700
Chicago (G-3896)
Anchor Brake Shoe Company LLC....G....630 293-1110
West Chicago (G-21660)
Burgess-Norton Mfg Co Inc....E....630 232-4100
Geneva (G-10814)
Castwell Products LLC....C....847 966-9552
Skokie (G-19974)
Caterpillar Inc....A....309 633-8788
Mapleton (G-14205)
▲ Charter Dura-Bar Inc....E....815 338-3900
Woodstock (G-22551)
Charter Dura-Bar Inc....C....815 338-7800
Woodstock (G-22552)
Charter Dura-Bar Inc....D....847 854-1044
Algonquin (G-383)
Decatur Foundry Inc....D....217 429-5261
Decatur (G-7871)
Demco Products Inc....F....708 636-6240
Oak Lawn (G-16616)
E H Baare Corporation....C....618 546-1575
Robinson (G-18062)
E Rowe Foundry & Machine Co....D....217 382-4135
Martinsville (G-14334)
Ej Usa Inc....F....815 740-1640
New Lenox (G-15879)
F J Murphy & Son Inc....D....217 787-3477
Springfield (G-20437)
Fast Pipe Lining Inc....G....815 712-8646
La Salle (G-12772)
Galesburg Castings Inc....D....309 343-6178
Galesburg (G-10749)
Group Industries Inc....E....708 877-6200
Thornton (G-20871)

S I C

# 33 PRIMARY METAL INDUSTRIES

▼ Gunite EMI Corporation .................. B ... 815 964-7124
  Rockford (G-18409)
Illini Foundry Co Inc ........................... G ... 309 697-3142
  Peoria (G-17385)
Johnston & Jennings Inc .................... G ... 708 757-5375
  Chicago Heights (G-7106)
Kettler Casting Co Inc ........................ E ... 618 234-5303
  Belleville (G-1642)
Lemfco Inc .......................................... E ... 815 777-0242
  Galena (G-10729)
▲ M H Detrick Company ..................... E ... 708 479-5085
  Mokena (G-14882)
Meta TEC of Illinois Inc ...................... D ... 309 246-2960
  Lacon (G-12790)
▲ Perfect Pipe & Supply Corp ............ G ... 630 628-6728
  Elgin (G-9137)
Ptc Tubular Products LLC .................. C ... 815 692-4900
  Fairbury (G-10131)
Reynolds Manufacturing Company ..... E ... 309 787-8600
  Milan (G-14803)
▼ Rj Link International Inc .................. F ... 815 874-8110
  Rockford (G-18559)
Russell Enterprises Inc ....................... E ... 847 692-6050
  Park Ridge (G-17221)
◆ Standard Car Truck Company .......... E ... 847 692-6050
  Rosemont (G-19033)
State Line Foundries Inc .................... D ... 815 389-3921
  Roscoe (G-18922)
▲ Sunrise Distributors Inc .................. G ... 630 400-8786
  Elk Grove Village (G-9761)
Timkensteel Corporation .................... G ... 708 263-6868
  Tinley Park (G-20948)
Tmb Industries Inc ............................. F ... 312 280-2565
  Chicago (G-6732)
USP Holdings Inc ............................... A ... 847 604-6100
  Des Plaines (G-8295)
Waupaca Foundry Inc ......................... C ... 217 347-0600
  Effingham (G-8862)
Westwick Foundry Ltd ........................ E ... 815 777-0815
  Galena (G-10734)
Winnebago Foundry Inc ...................... D ... 815 389-3533
  South Beloit (G-20176)

## 3322 Malleable Iron Foundries

Advanced Pattern Works LLC ............ G ... 618 346-9039
  Collinsville (G-7312)
Du Page Precision Products Co .......... D ... 630 849-2940
  Aurora (G-998)
▲ M H Detrick Company ..................... E ... 708 479-5085
  Mokena (G-14882)
Wirco Inc ............................................ D ... 217 398-3200
  Champaign (G-3561)

## 3324 Steel Investment Foundries

Fisher & Ludlow Inc ........................... G ... 217 324-6106
  Litchfield (G-13684)

## 3325 Steel Foundries, NEC

Alloys Tech Inc ................................... G ... 708 248-5041
  S Chicago Hts (G-19099)
Allquip Co Inc ..................................... G ... 309 944-6153
  Geneseo (G-10797)
Ameri Rolls and Guides ...................... G ... 815 588-0486
  Lockport (G-13703)
◆ Amsted Industries Incorporated ..... B ... 312 645-1700
  Chicago (G-3896)
Arcelormittal USA LLC ....................... C ... 312 899-3400
  Chicago (G-3934)
◆ Arcelormittal USA LLC .................... B ... 312 346-0300
  Chicago (G-3935)
Cast Rite Steel Casting Corp .............. F ... 312 738-2900
  Chicago (G-4251)
Colson Group Holdings LLC ............... G ... 630 613-2941
  Oakbrook Terrace (G-16704)
Combined Metals Holding Inc ............ C ... 708 547-8800
  Bellwood (G-1701)
Componenta USA LLC ........................ G ... 309 691-7000
  Peoria (G-17345)
Dee Erectors Inc ................................. G ... 630 327-1185
  Downers Grove (G-8426)
Devco Casting ..................................... G ... 312 456-0076
  Chicago (G-4587)
Du Page Precision Products Co .......... D ... 630 849-2940
  Aurora (G-998)
E H Baare Corporation ....................... C ... 618 546-1575
  Robinson (G-18062)
▲ Evraz Inc NA .................................... C ... 312 533-3621
  Chicago (G-4792)
FMC Corporation ................................ D ... 815 824-2153
  Lee (G-13217)

Illinois Ni Cast LLC ............................ G ... 217 398-3200
  Champaign (G-3500)
Jame Roll Form Products Inc ............. E ... 847 455-0496
  Franklin Park (G-10506)
▲ Kaltband North America Inc ........... F ... 773 248-6684
  Chicago (G-5355)
Lmt Usa Inc ........................................ G ... 630 969-5412
  Waukegan (G-21583)
▲ Metal Resources Intl LLC ................ E ... 847 806-7200
  Elk Grove Village (G-9622)
Micro Thread Corporation .................. F ... 773 775-1200
  Chicago (G-5723)
Monett Metals Inc .............................. G ... 773 478-8888
  Chicago (G-5794)
Neenah Foundry Co ............................ G ... 800 558-5075
  Frankfort (G-10345)
Nisshin Holding Inc ............................ G ... 847 290-5100
  Rolling Meadows (G-18750)
Scot Forge Company .......................... D ... 847 678-6000
  Franklin Park (G-10584)
Set Enterprises of Mi Inc ................... F ... 708 758-1111
  Sauk Village (G-19393)
▲ T & H Lemont Inc ........................... D ... 708 482-1800
  Countryside (G-7446)
Universal Electric Foundry Inc ........... G ... 312 421-7233
  Chicago (G-6831)
US Tsubaki Power Transm LLC ......... C ... 847 459-9500
  Wheeling (G-22173)
▲ Voestlpine Precision Strip LLC ...... D ... 847 227-5272
  Elk Grove Village (G-9810)

## 3331 Primary Smelting & Refining Of Copper

◆ Ampco Metal Incorporated .............. E ... 847 437-6000
  Arlington Heights (G-711)
▲ Ansonia Copper & Brass Inc .......... C ... 866 607-7066
  Chicago (G-3914)
◆ Cerro Flow Products LLC ................ E ... 618 337-6000
  Sauget (G-19385)
Inter-Trade Global LLC ....................... G ... 618 954-6119
  Belleville (G-1637)
Mahoney Foundries Inc ...................... E ... 309 784-2311
  Vermont (G-21138)

## 3334 Primary Production Of Aluminum

▲ Century Aluminum Company .......... C ... 312 696-3101
  Chicago (G-4275)
Duval Group Ltd ................................. G ... 847 949-7001
  Mundelein (G-15495)
Huml Industries Inc ........................... G ... 847 426-8061
  Gilberts (G-10923)
New Century Performance Inc ........... G ... 618 466-6383
  Godfrey (G-11230)
Penn Aluminum Intl LLC ................... G ... 618 684-2146
  Murphysboro (G-15579)
Reynolds Packaging Kama Inc ........... C ... 815 468-8300
  Manteno (G-14192)

## 3339 Primary Nonferrous Metals, NEC

Academy Corp ..................................... G ... 847 359-3000
  Palatine (G-16995)
AG Medical Systems Inc .................... F ... 847 458-3100
  Lake In The Hills (G-12984)
Ames Metal Products Company ......... F ... 773 523-3230
  Wheeling (G-22005)
AMS Store and Shred LLC ................. F ... 847 458-3100
  Lake In The Hills (G-12985)
▼ Big River Zinc Corporation .............. G ... 618 274-5000
  Sauget (G-19382)
Cambridge-Lee Industries LLC .......... F ... 708 388-0121
  Alsip (G-444)
Chicago Precious Mtls Exch LLC ...... G ... 312 854-7084
  Chicago (G-4341)
Elite Precious Metals Inc ................... G ... 312 929-3055
  Chicago (G-4732)
Horizon Metals Inc ............................ F ... 773 478-8888
  Chicago (G-5113)
Horsehead Corporation ...................... G ... 773 933-9260
  Chicago (G-5114)
Jason Incorporated ............................ C ... 847 362-8300
  Libertyville (G-13340)
Mayco Manufacturing LLC ................. E ... 618 451-4400
  Granite City (G-11292)
Powerlab Inc ....................................... G ... 815 273-7718
  Savanna (G-19404)
RE Met Corp ....................................... G ... 312 733-6700
  Chicago (G-6300)
Refiners House ................................... E ... 708 922-0772
  Olympia Fields (G-16805)
▲ Rockford Rigging Inc ...................... F ... 309 263-0566
  Roscoe (G-18914)

▲ Sipi Metals Corp .............................. C ... 773 276-0070
  Chicago (G-6517)
Tanaka Kikinzoku Intl Amer Inc ......... G ... 224 653-8309
  Schaumburg (G-19752)
Tanaka Kknzoku Intrnational Kk ........ G ... 224 653-8309
  Schaumburg (G-19753)
TPC Metals LLC .................................. G ... 330 479-9510
  Willowbrook (G-22234)

## 3341 Secondary Smelting & Refining Of Non-ferrous Metals

A Miller & Co ...................................... F ... 309 637-7756
  Peoria (G-17298)
Abco Metals Corporations .................. F ... 773 881-1504
  Chicago (G-3708)
▲ Allied Metal Co ............................... C ... 312 225-2800
  Chicago (G-3816)
Alter Trading Corporation .................. G ... 309 697-6161
  Bartonville (G-1390)
Alter Trading Corporation .................. F ... 217 223-0156
  Quincy (G-17791)
Ames Metal Products Company ......... F ... 773 523-3230
  Wheeling (G-22005)
Archer Metal & Paper Co .................... F ... 773 585-3030
  Chicago (G-3939)
Azcon Inc ........................................... C ... 312 559-3100
  Chicago (G-4009)
Belson Steel Center Scrap Inc ........... G ... 815 932-7416
  Bourbonnais (G-2389)
BFI Waste Systems N Amer Inc ......... E ... 847 429-7370
  Elgin (G-8965)
▼ Big River Zinc Corporation .............. G ... 618 274-5000
  Sauget (G-19382)
C & M Recycling Inc ........................... E ... 847 578-1066
  North Chicago (G-16176)
C&R Scrap Iron & Metal ..................... E ... 847 459-9815
  Wheeling (G-22022)
Cicero Iron Metal & Paper Inc ............ E ... 708 863-8601
  Cicero (G-7183)
Columbia Aluminum Recycl Ltd ......... E ... 708 758-8888
  Chicago Heights (G-7093)
▲ D R Sperry & Co ............................. D ... 630 892-4361
  Aurora (G-1137)
Dels Metal Co ..................................... F ... 309 788-1993
  Rock Island (G-18173)
Elg Metals Inc .................................... E ... 773 374-1500
  Chicago (G-4728)
Enviro-Chem Inc ................................. G ... 847 549-7797
  Vernon Hills (G-21161)
▲ Fox Valley Iron & Metal Corp .......... F ... 630 897-5907
  Aurora (G-1155)
Galva Iron and Metal Co Inc .............. G ... 309 932-3450
  Galva (G-10789)
◆ Gbc Metals LLC ............................... G ... 618 258-2350
  East Alton (G-8603)
Global Brass and Copper Inc ............. G ... 502 873-3000
  East Alton (G-8604)
Global Brass Cop Holdings Inc .......... E ... 847 240-4700
  Schaumburg (G-19537)
GM Scrap Metals ................................ G ... 618 259-8570
  Cottage Hills (G-7397)
▲ H Kramer & Co ................................ C ... 312 226-6600
  Chicago (G-5022)
▲ Imperial Zinc Corp .......................... D ... 773 264-5900
  Chicago (G-5169)
▲ International Proc Co Amer ............ E ... 847 437-8400
  Elk Grove Village (G-9553)
Lake Area Disposal Service Inc ......... E ... 217 522-9271
  Springfield (G-20466)
Lemont Scrap Processing ................... G ... 630 257-6532
  Lemont (G-13239)
M Buckman & Son Co ......................... G ... 815 663-9411
  Spring Valley (G-20375)
Mahoney Foundries Inc ...................... E ... 309 784-2311
  Vermont (G-21138)
Mervis Industries Inc ......................... F ... 217 235-5575
  Mattoon (G-14402)
Mervis Industries Inc ......................... E ... 217 753-1492
  Springfield (G-20480)
Metal Management Inc ....................... E ... 773 721-1100
  Chicago (G-5700)
Metal Management Inc ....................... E ... 773 489-1800
  Chicago (G-5701)
▼ Midland Davis Corporation .............. D ... 309 637-4491
  Moline (G-14957)
Midstate Salvage Corp ....................... G ... 217 824-6047
  Taylorville (G-20843)
▼ Midwest Fiber Inc Decatur .............. E ... 217 424-9460
  Decatur (G-7915)

National Material Company LLC ....E .... 847 806-7200
Elk Grove Village (G-9646)

Pontiac Recyclers Inc ....G .... 815 844-6419
Pontiac (G-17708)

Precious Metal Ref Svcs Inc ....G .... 847 756-2700
Barrington (G-1298)

Real Alloy Recycling Inc ....D .... 708 758-8888
Chicago Heights (G-7120)

Reclamation LLC ....G .... 510 441-2305
Chicago (G-6311)

Rondout Iron & Metal Co Inc ....G .... 847 362-2750
Lake Bluff (G-12865)

S & S Metal Recyclers Inc ....F .... 630 844-3344
Aurora (G-1213)

Serlin Iron & Metal Co Inc ....F .... 773 227-3826
Chicago (G-6479)

Shapiro Bros of Illinois Inc ....E .... 618 244-3168
Mount Vernon (G-15445)

Sims Rcycl Sltons Holdings Inc ....C .... 847 455-8800
Franklin Park (G-10587)

Sims Recycling Solutions Inc ....G .... 847 455-8800
Franklin Park (G-10588)

▲ Sipi Metals Corp ....C .... 773 276-0070
Chicago (G-6517)

Springfield Iron & Metal Co ....G .... 217 544-7131
Springfield (G-20529)

T & C Metal Co ....G .... 815 459-4445
Crystal Lake (G-7658)

T J Metal Co ....G .... 708 388-6191
Alsip (G-532)

Tms International LLC ....G .... 815 939-9460
Bourbonnais (G-2408)

Top Metal Buyers Inc ....F .... 314 421-2721
East Saint Louis (G-8773)

Tower Metal Products LP ....G .... 847 806-7200
Elk Grove Village (G-9787)

Trialco Inc ....E .... 708 757-4200
Chicago Heights (G-7132)

United Conveyor Supply Company ....E .... 708 344-8050
Melrose Park (G-14703)

▲ Waukegan Architectural Inc ....G .... 847 746-9077
Zion (G-22700)

Weco Trading Inc ....G .... 847 615-1020
Lake Bluff (G-12871)

## 3351 Rolling, Drawing & Extruding Of Copper

American Bare Conductor Inc ....E .... 815 224-3422
La Salle (G-12762)

◆ Ampco Metal Incorporated ....E .... 847 437-6000
Arlington Heights (G-711)

▲ Ansonia Copper & Brass Inc ....C .... 866 607-7066
Chicago (G-3914)

◆ Cerro Flow Products LLC ....C .... 618 337-6000
Sauget (G-19385)

▲ Chicago Hardware and Fix Co ....D .... 847 455-6609
Franklin Park (G-10429)

Demco Products Inc ....F .... 708 636-6240
Oak Lawn (G-16616)

▲ Empire Bronze Corp ....F .... 630 916-9722
Lombard (G-13796)

Ems Industrial and Service Co ....E .... 815 678-2700
Richmond (G-17961)

Fairbanks Wire Corporation ....G .... 847 683-2600
Hampshire (G-11550)

Gbc Metals LLC ....F .... 618 258-2350
East Alton (G-8602)

◆ Gbc Metals LLC ....G .... 618 258-2350
East Alton (G-8603)

General Cable Industries Inc ....D .... 618 542-4761
Du Quoin (G-8556)

Global Brass and Copper Inc ....G .... 502 873-3000
East Alton (G-8604)

Global Brass Cop Holdings Inc ....E .... 847 240-4700
Schaumburg (G-19537)

▲ Industrial Wire Cable II Corp ....F .... 847 726-8910
Lake Zurich (G-13087)

Kroh-Wagner Inc ....E .... 773 252-2031
Chicago (G-5412)

◆ Marmon Holdings Inc ....D .... 312 372-9500
Chicago (G-5625)

Materion Brush Inc ....F .... 630 832-9650
Elmhurst (G-9909)

◆ Midwest Model Aircraft Co ....F .... 773 229-0740
Chicago (G-5747)

Mueller Industries Inc ....C .... 847 290-1108
Elk Grove Village (G-9641)

▲ Nehring Electrical Works Co ....C .... 815 756-2741
Dekalb (G-8110)

Olin Corporation ....G .... 618 258-2245
Brighton (G-2543)

Universal Electric Foundry Inc ....E .... 312 421-7233
Chicago (G-6831)

▲ Wieland Metals Inc ....C .... 847 537-3990
Wheeling (G-22182)

## 3353 Aluminum Sheet, Plate & Foil

Arconic Inc ....D .... 217 431-3800
Danville (G-7703)

Ashland Aluminum Company Inc ....F .... 773 278-6440
Chicago (G-3961)

▲ Climco Coils Company ....C .... 815 772-3717
Morrison (G-15143)

Coatings Applications Inc ....E .... 847 238-9408
Elk Grove Village (G-9380)

Comet Roll & Machine Company ....E .... 630 268-1407
Saint Charles (G-19161)

Country Cast Products ....F .... 815 777-1070
Galena (G-10718)

J-TEC Metal Products Inc ....F .... 630 875-1300
Itasca (G-12288)

◆ Mandel Metals Inc ....D .... 847 455-6606
Franklin Park (G-10521)

Midwest Lminating Coatings Inc ....E .... 708 653-9500
Alsip (G-493)

▲ Monda Window & Door Corp ....E .... 773 254-8888
Chicago (G-5792)

Nichols Aluminum LLC ....C .... 847 634-3150
Lincolnshire (G-13467)

Pactiv LLC ....E .... 847 482-2000
Lake Forest (G-12937)

Pechiney Cast Plate ....C .... 847 299-0220
Chicago (G-6094)

▲ Petersen Aluminum Corporation ....D .... 847 228-7150
Elk Grove Village (G-9676)

Quanex Homeshield LLC ....F .... 815 635-3171
Chatsworth (G-3629)

Reynolds Consumer Products LLC ....E .... 217 479-1126
Jacksonville (G-12411)

Reynolds Consumer Products LLC ....G .... 217 479-1466
Jacksonville (G-12412)

◆ Reynolds Consumer Products LLC ....B .... 847 482-3500
Lake Forest (G-12952)

Reynolds Food Packaging ....F .... 815 465-2115
Grant Park (G-11314)

Sea Converting Inc ....F .... 630 694-9178
Wood Dale (G-22420)

Security Metal Products Inc ....G .... 815 933-3307
Bradley (G-2433)

Transco Products Inc ....E .... 815 672-2197
Streator (G-20709)

Werner Co ....A .... 847 455-8001
Itasca (G-12374)

## 3354 Aluminum Extruded Prdts

Afco Industries Inc ....G .... 618 742-6469
Olmsted (G-16757)

Al3 Inc ....G .... 847 441-7888
Winnetka (G-22300)

American Alum Extrusion Co LLC ....G .... 877 896-2236
Roscoe (G-18889)

Architctural Grilles Sunshades ....F .... 708 479-9458
Mokena (G-14854)

Bending Specialists LLC ....E .... 815 726-6281
Lockport (G-13706)

Central Tool Specialities Co ....G .... 630 543-6351
Addison (G-72)

Crown Cork & Seal Usa Inc ....C .... 815 933-9351
Bradley (G-2417)

Custom Aluminum Products Inc ....D .... 847 717-5000
Genoa (G-10877)

▲ Custom Aluminum Products Inc ....B .... 847 717-5000
South Elgin (G-20191)

▲ Durable Inc ....A .... 847 541-4400
Wheeling (G-22039)

Efco Corporation ....E .... 630 378-4720
Bolingbrook (G-2303)

Imageworks Manufacturing Inc ....E .... 708 503-1122
Park Forest (G-17172)

JM Circle Enterprise Inc ....G .... 708 946-3333
Beecher (G-1598)

Kloeckner Metals Corporation ....F .... 773 646-6363
Chicago (G-5388)

▲ Maytec Inc ....G .... 847 429-0321
Dundee (G-8564)

Metal Impact South LLC ....F .... 847 718-9300
Elk Grove Village (G-9621)

◆ Midwest Model Aircraft Co ....F .... 773 229-0740
Chicago (G-5747)

▲ Monda Window & Door Corp ....E .... 773 254-8888
Chicago (G-5792)

Nichols Aluminum LLC ....C .... 847 634-3150
Lincolnshire (G-13467)

▼ Peerless America Incorporated ....C .... 217 342-0400
Effingham (G-8853)

Penn Aluminum Intl LLC ....C .... 618 684-2146
Murphysboro (G-15579)

▲ Petersen Aluminum Corporation ....D .... 847 228-7150
Elk Grove Village (G-9676)

◆ Plymouth Tube Company ....E .... 630 393-3550
Warrenville (G-21355)

Plymouth Tube Company ....D .... 773 489-0226
Chicago (G-6141)

Plymouth Tube Company ....D .... 262 642-8201
Warrenville (G-21356)

Rotation Dynamics Corporation ....E .... 630 769-9700
Chicago (G-6398)

Sapa Extrusions Inc ....E .... 847 233-9105
Rosemont (G-19030)

▲ Sapa Extrusions Inc ....C .... 877 710-7272
Rosemont (G-19031)

Sapa Extrusions North Amer LLC ....G .... 877 922-7272
Rosemont (G-19032)

Signa Group Inc ....G .... 847 386-7639
Northfield (G-16417)

Sno Gem Inc ....F .... 888 766-4367
McHenry (G-14555)

▲ Sternberg Lanterns Inc ....C .... 847 588-3400
Roselle (G-18980)

T A U Inc ....G .... 708 841-5757
Dolton (G-8377)

Transco Products Inc ....E .... 815 672-2197
Streator (G-20709)

Werner Co ....A .... 847 455-8001
Itasca (G-12374)

William Dach ....F .... 815 962-3455
Rockford (G-18683)

## 3355 Aluminum Rolling & Drawing, NEC

American Alum Extrusion Co LLC ....G .... 877 896-2236
Roscoe (G-18889)

Ashland Aluminum Company Inc ....F .... 773 278-6440
Chicago (G-3961)

▲ Conex Cable LLC ....E .... 800 877-8089
Dekalb (G-8078)

◆ Corus America Inc ....E .... 847 585-2599
Schaumburg (G-19486)

▲ Lapham-Hickey Steel Corp ....C .... 708 496-6111
Chicago (G-5459)

Meyer Metal Systems Inc ....F .... 847 468-0500
Elgin (G-9109)

Msystems Group LLC ....G .... 630 567-3930
Saint Charles (G-19224)

▲ Nehring Electrical Works Co ....C .... 815 756-2741
Dekalb (G-8110)

Plastic Power Extrusions Corp ....E .... 847 233-9901
Schiller Park (G-19859)

Southwire Company LLC ....D .... 618 662-8341
Flora (G-10219)

Werner Co ....E .... 815 459-6020
Crystal Lake (G-7676)

▼ Windy City Wire and Connectivi ....D .... 630 633-4500
Bolingbrook (G-2384)

## 3356 Rolling, Drawing-Extruding Of Nonferrous Metals

Alloy Rod Products Inc ....G .... 815 562-8200
Aurora (G-1105)

Alloy Rod Products Inc ....F .... 815 562-8200
Rochelle (G-18078)

Alpha Assembly Solutions Inc ....C .... 847 426-4241
Elgin (G-8944)

American Titanium Works LLC ....G .... 312 327-3178
Chicago (G-3878)

▲ American/Jebco Corporation ....C .... 847 455-3150
Franklin Park (G-10394)

Ames Metal Products Company ....F .... 773 523-3230
Wheeling (G-22005)

◆ Arcelormittal USA LLC ....B .... 312 346-0300
Chicago (G-3935)

Armor Coated Technology Corp ....G .... 815 636-7200
Machesney Park (G-14058)

AWI / Titanium ....G .... 708 263-9970
Oak Forest (G-16574)

▼ Big River Zinc Corporation ....G .... 618 274-5000
Sauget (G-19382)

Chicago Magnesium ....G .... 708 926-9531
Dixmoor (G-8319)

◆ Cooper B-Line Inc ....A .... 618 654-2184
Highland (G-11780)

S
I
C

Employee Codes: A=Over 500 employees, B=251-500
C=101-250, D=51-100, E=20-50, F=10-19, G=3-9

Daniel J Nickel & Assocs PC ................G....... 312 345-1850
Chicago (G-4553)
Double Nickel Holdings LLC ................G....... 618 476-3200
Millstadt (G-14824)
Dupage Products Group ................D....... 630 969-7200
Downers Grove (G-8435)
◆ Elektron N Magnesium Amer Inc ......D....... 618 452-5190
Madison (G-14144)
Elgiloy Specialty Metals ................G....... 847 683-0500
Hampshire (G-11549)
Guardian Rollform LLC ................D....... 847 382-8074
Lake Barrington (G-12808)
Hadley Gear Manufacturing Co ................F....... 773 722-1030
Chicago (G-5028)
Horizon Metals Inc ................F....... 773 478-8888
Chicago (G-5113)
IL International LLC ................G....... 773 276-0070
Chicago (G-5151)
Industrial Titanium Corp ................G....... 847 272-2730
Northbrook (G-16277)
International Titanium Powder ................G....... 815 834-2112
Lockport (G-13723)
Kester Inc ................G....... 630 616-6882
Itasca (G-12293)
◆ Kester Inc ................C....... 630 616-4000
Itasca (G-12294)
▲ Mayco-Granite City Inc ................E....... 618 451-4400
Granite City (G-11293)
MBA Marketing Inc ................G....... 847 566-2555
Mundelein (G-15526)
◆ Midland Industries Inc ................E....... 312 664-7300
Chicago (G-5734)
Nickel Putter ................G....... 312 337-7888
Chicago (G-5911)
Nickels Electric ................G....... 309 676-1350
Peoria (G-17418)
Nickels Quarters LLC ................G....... 630 514-5779
Downers Grove (G-8495)
Nippon Yakin America Inc ................G....... 847 685-6644
Des Plaines (G-8243)
Nuclear Power Outfitters LLC ................F....... 630 963-0320
Lisle (G-13634)
Pat 24 Inc ................G....... 708 336-8671
Burbank (G-2809)
Red Devil Manufacturing Co ................G....... 847 215-1377
Wheeling (G-22134)
Suburban Industries Inc ................F....... 630 766-3773
Franklin Park (G-10597)
Tin HLA Health Svcs ................G....... 708 633-0426
Tinley Park (G-20949)
Tin Man Heating & Cooling Inc ................E....... 630 267-3232
Aurora (G-1225)
Tin Maung ................G....... 217 233-1405
Decatur (G-7953)
Tin Tree Gifts ................G....... 630 935-8086
Aurora (G-1086)
Tinsley Steel Inc ................G....... 618 656-5231
Edwardsville (G-8817)
Titanium Insulation Inc ................G....... 708 932-5927
Midlothian (G-14770)
Titanium Ventures Group LLC ................G....... 312 375-3526
Chicago (G-6730)
Townley Engrg & Mfg Co Inc ................F....... 618 273-8271
Eldorado (G-8924)
▲ TSC Pyroferric International ................C....... 217 849-2230
Toledo (G-20969)
▲ Wagner Zip-Change Inc ................E....... 708 681-4100
Melrose Park (G-14706)
Wooden Nickel Pub and Grill ................G....... 618 288-2141
Glen Carbon (G-10955)

## 3357 Nonferrous Wire Drawing

All Line Inc ................G....... 630 820-1800
Naperville (G-15792)
▲ Amerline Enterprises Co Inc ................E....... 847 671-6554
Schiller Park (G-19802)
Andrew Corporation ................E....... 779 435-6000
Joliet (G-12454)
Andrew New Zealand Inc ................E....... 708 873-3507
Orland Park (G-16843)
▲ ARI Industries Inc ................D....... 630 953-9100
Addison (G-44)
Arris Group Inc ................E....... 630 281-3000
Lisle (G-13564)
▲ Belford Electronics Inc ................E....... 630 705-3020
Addison (G-52)
C & L Manufacturing Entps ................G....... 618 465-7623
Alton (G-565)
C R V Electronics Corp ................D....... 815 675-6500
Spring Grove (G-20329)
▲ Central Rubber Company ................E....... 815 544-2191
Belvidere (G-1745)
Charles Industries Ltd ................D....... 217 826-2318
Marshall (G-14319)
Chase Security Systems Inc ................G....... 773 594-1919
Chicago (G-4295)
▲ Chicago Car Seal Company ................G....... 773 278-9400
Chicago (G-4310)
Circom Inc ................E....... 630 595-4460
Bensenville (G-1859)
Coleman Cable LLC ................G....... 847 672-2300
Waukegan (G-21541)
Coleman Cable LLC ................D....... 847 672-2300
Waukegan (G-21543)
◆ Coleman Cable LLC ................D....... 847 672-2300
Waukegan (G-21542)
◆ Commscope Technologies LLC ................A....... 708 236-6600
Westchester (G-21835)
Commscope Technologies LLC ................B....... 779 435-6000
Joliet (G-12476)
D & S Wire Inc ................F....... 847 766-5520
Elk Grove Village (G-9412)
Digi Cell Communications ................G....... 847 808-7900
Wheeling (G-22035)
▲ Erin Rope Corporation ................F....... 708 377-1084
Blue Island (G-2250)
Essex Group Inc ................D....... 630 628-7841
Addison (G-112)
▲ Excel Specialty Corp ................E....... 773 262-7575
Lake Forest (G-12898)
▲ Gepco International Inc ................E....... 847 795-9555
Des Plaines (G-8201)
▲ Heil Sound Ltd ................F....... 618 257-3000
Fairview Heights (G-10168)
▲ Industrial Wire & Cable Corp ................E....... 847 726-8910
Lake Zurich (G-13086)
▲ Industrial Wire Cable II Corp ................F....... 847 726-8910
Lake Zurich (G-13087)
▲ Insulation Solutions Inc ................F....... 309 698-0062
East Peoria (G-8714)
Julian Elec Svc & Engrg Inc ................E....... 630 920-8950
Westmont (G-21895)
Live Wire & Cable Co ................G....... 847 577-5483
Arlington Heights (G-794)
Lkq Broadway Auto Parts Inc ................G....... 312 621-1950
Chicago (G-5526)
Major Wire Incorporated ................F....... 708 457-0121
Norridge (G-16105)
Methode Development Co ................D....... 708 867-6777
Chicago (G-5703)
▲ Molex LLC ................A....... 630 969-4550
Lisle (G-13625)
Molex LLC ................G....... 630 527-4363
Bolingbrook (G-2345)
Molex LLC ................F....... 630 512-8787
Downers Grove (G-8489)
▲ Molex International Inc ................F....... 630 969-4550
Lisle (G-13627)
▲ Molex Premise Networks Inc ................A....... 866 733-6659
Lisle (G-13628)
Neolight Technologies LLC ................G....... 773 561-1410
Ingleside (G-12196)
P M Mfg Services Inc ................G....... 630 553-6924
Yorkville (G-22668)
SITech Inc ................F....... 630 761-3640
Batavia (G-1496)
Sterling Brands LLC ................E....... 847 229-1600
Wheeling (G-22156)
Teledyne Reynolds Inc ................C....... 630 754-3300
Woodridge (G-22522)
Unified Wire and Cable Company ................E....... 815 748-4876
Dekalb (G-8128)
United Universal Inds Inc ................E....... 815 727-4445
Joliet (G-12585)
▲ Woodhead Industries LLC ................B....... 847 353-2500
Lincolnshire (G-13490)

## 3363 Aluminum Die Castings

Able Die Casting Corporation ................D....... 847 678-1991
Schiller Park (G-19797)
▲ Acme Alliance LLC ................C....... 847 272-9520
Northbrook (G-16196)
▲ Acme Die Casting LLC ................G....... 847 272-9520
Northbrook (G-16197)
ADC Diecasting LLC ................C....... 847 541-3030
Elk Grove Village (G-9271)
ADC Diecasting LLC ................G....... 847 541-3030
Elk Grove Village (G-9272)
▲ Aluminum Castings Corporation ................E....... 309 343-8910
Galesburg (G-10737)
▲ American Electronic Pdts Inc ................F....... 630 889-9977
Oak Brook (G-16488)
Ames Metal Products Company ................F....... 773 523-3230
Wheeling (G-22005)
Anderson Casting Company Inc ................G....... 312 733-1185
Chicago (G-3901)
Arrow Aluminum Castings Inc ................G....... 815 338-4480
Woodstock (G-22542)
Belden Energy Solutions Inc ................G....... 800 235-3361
Elmhurst (G-9838)
Burgess-Norton Mfg Co Inc ................E....... 630 232-4100
Geneva (G-10814)
C B & A Inc ................F....... 815 561-0255
Rochelle (G-18080)
Carroll Tool & Manufacturing ................G....... 630 766-3363
Bensenville (G-1852)
▲ Cast Aluminum Solutions LLC ................D....... 630 482-5325
Batavia (G-1426)
◆ Chicago White Metal Cast Inc ................C....... 630 595-4424
Bensenville (G-1858)
Continental Automation Inc ................E....... 630 584-5100
Saint Charles (G-19162)
▲ Crown Premiums Inc ................F....... 815 469-8789
Frankfort (G-10311)
Curto-Ligonier Foundries Co ................E....... 708 345-2250
Melrose Park (G-14613)
Dart Castings Inc ................E....... 708 388-4914
Alsip (G-455)
Dixline Corporation ................F....... 309 932-2011
Galva (G-10787)
Dixline Corporation ................D....... 309 932-2011
Galva (G-10788)
Duro Cast Inc ................G....... 815 498-2317
Somonauk (G-20125)
Dynacast Inc ................C....... 847 608-2200
Elgin (G-9015)
▲ Federal Equipment & Svcs Inc ................F....... 847 731-9002
Zion (G-22685)
G & M Die Casting Company Inc ................D....... 630 595-2340
Wood Dale (G-22374)
G & W Electric Company ................E....... 708 389-8307
Blue Island (G-2251)
Lovejoy Industries Inc ................G....... 859 873-6828
Northbrook (G-16299)
Mahoney Foundries Inc ................E....... 309 784-2311
Vermont (G-21138)
Master-Cast Inc ................E....... 630 879-3866
Carol Stream (G-3191)
▲ Mattoon Precision Mfg ................C....... 217 235-6000
Mattoon (G-14399)
▲ Monnex International Inc ................E....... 847 850-5263
Buffalo Grove (G-2738)
OFallon Pressure Cast Co ................G....... 618 632-8694
O Fallon (G-16472)
Precision Entps Fndry Mch Inc ................G....... 815 797-1000
Somonauk (G-20128)
Precision Entps Fndry Mch Inc ................E....... 815 498-2317
Somonauk (G-20129)
▲ Prismier LLC ................E....... 630 592-4515
Woodridge (G-22511)
RCM Industries Inc ................C....... 847 455-1950
Franklin Park (G-10571)
RCM Industries Inc ................C....... 847 455-1950
Wheeling (G-22133)
Rockbridge Casting Inc ................G....... 618 753-3188
Rockbridge (G-18212)
Soldy Manufacturing Inc ................D....... 847 671-3396
Schiller Park (G-19875)
◆ Spartan Light Metal Pdts Inc ................E....... 618 443-4346
Sparta (G-20321)
Spartan Light Metal Pdts Inc ................A....... 618 443-4346
Sparta (G-20322)
▲ Tek-Cast Inc ................D....... 630 422-1458
Elgin (G-9205)
Tompkins Aluminum Foundry Inc ................G....... 815 438-5578
Rock Falls (G-18154)

## 3364 Nonferrous Die Castings, Exc Aluminum

Accucast Inc ................G....... 815 394-1875
Rockford (G-18253)
▲ Acme Die Casting LLC ................G....... 847 272-9520
Northbrook (G-16197)
▲ Allied Die Casting Corporation ................E....... 815 385-9330
McHenry (G-14479)
Amcast Inc ................F....... 630 766-7450
Bensenville (G-1831)
▲ American Cast Products Inc ................F....... 708 895-5152
Lansing (G-13156)

# 33 PRIMARY METAL INDUSTRIES

Anderson Casting Company Inc .......... G ...... 312 733-1185
  Chicago *(G-3901)*
▲ Cast Products Inc ........................... C ...... 708 457-1500
  Norridge *(G-16098)*
Chicago Die Casting Mfg Co ............... E ...... 847 671-5010
  Franklin Park *(G-10428)*
◆ Chicago White Metal Cast Inc .......... C ...... 630 595-4424
  Bensenville *(G-1858)*
Condor Tool & Manufacturing ............. F ...... 630 628-8200
  Addison *(G-81)*
Continental Automation Inc ................ G ...... 630 584-5100
  Saint Charles *(G-19162)*
Craft Die Casting Corporation ............ E ...... 773 237-9710
  Chicago *(G-4488)*
Curto-Ligonier Foundries Co ............... E ...... 708 345-2250
  Melrose Park *(G-14613)*
Dart Castings Inc ............................ E ...... 708 388-4914
  Alsip *(G-455)*
Dynacast Inc ................................... C ...... 847 608-2200
  Elgin *(G-9015)*
Edge Mold Corporation ...................... G ...... 630 616-8108
  Bensenville *(G-1889)*
G & W Electric Company .................... G ...... 708 389-8307
  Blue Island *(G-2251)*
Gary W Berger ................................. G ...... 708 588-0200
  Countryside *(G-7427)*
GM Casting House Inc ....................... F ...... 312 782-7160
  Chicago *(G-4963)*
Hub Manufacturing Company Inc ......... E ...... 773 252-1373
  Chicago *(G-5127)*
Lovejoy Industries Inc ....................... G ...... 859 873-6828
  Northbrook *(G-16299)*
Mahoney Foundries Inc ...................... E ...... 309 784-2311
  Vermont *(G-21138)*
Micro Industries Inc .......................... E ...... 815 625-8000
  Rock Falls *(G-18143)*
Polar Container Corp Inc .................... G ...... 847 299-5030
  Rosemont *(G-19024)*
Quality Die Casting Co ....................... F ...... 847 214-8840
  Elgin *(G-9156)*
▲ Quality Metal Finishing Co ............. C ...... 815 234-2711
  Byron *(G-2918)*
Rockbridge Casting Inc ..................... G ...... 618 753-3188
  Rockbridge *(G-18212)*
Serv-All Die & Tool Company .............. E ...... 815 459-2900
  Crystal Lake *(G-7647)*
Soldy Manufacturing Inc .................... D ...... 847 671-3396
  Schiller Park *(G-19875)*
◆ Spartan Light Metal Pdts Inc ........... E ...... 618 443-4346
  Sparta *(G-20321)*
Spartan Light Metal Pdts Inc .............. A ...... 618 443-4346
  Sparta *(G-20322)*
Taurus Die Casting LLC ..................... F ...... 815 316-6160
  Rockford *(G-18642)*
TI Squared Technologies Inc .............. F ...... 541 367-2929
  Schaumburg *(G-19763)*
Universal Die Cast Corporation ........... G ...... 815 633-1702
  Machesney Park *(G-14115)*
Vogel/Hill Corporation ....................... E ...... 773 235-6916
  Chicago *(G-6912)*

## 3365 Aluminum Foundries

Able Die Casting Corporation ............. D ...... 847 678-1991
  Schiller Park *(G-19797)*
▲ Acme Die Casting LLC .................... G ...... 847 272-9520
  Northbrook *(G-16197)*
▲ Alcast Company ............................ D ...... 309 691-5513
  Peoria *(G-17306)*
Alcast Company ............................... D ...... 309 691-5513
  Peoria *(G-17307)*
Altman & Koehler Foundry ................. G ...... 773 373-7737
  Chicago *(G-3838)*
Altman Pattern and Foundry Co .......... F ...... 773 586-9100
  Chicago *(G-3839)*
Alu-Bra Foundry Inc ......................... D ...... 630 766-3112
  Bensenville *(G-1829)*
Amcast Inc ...................................... F ...... 630 766-7450
  Bensenville *(G-1831)*
AMS LLC .......................................... G ...... 773 904-7740
  Chicago *(G-3895)*
Anderson Casting Company Inc .......... G ...... 312 733-1185
  Chicago *(G-3901)*
Arrow Aluminum Castings Inc ............. G ...... 815 338-4480
  Woodstock *(G-22542)*
Atherton Foundry Products Inc ........... E ...... 708 849-4615
  Riverdale *(G-18015)*
Becks Light Gauge Aluminum Co ......... F ...... 847 290-9990
  Elk Grove Village *(G-9337)*
Bio Services Inc ............................... G ...... 630 808-2125
  Hillside *(G-11910)*

Cast Technologies Inc ....................... C ...... 309 676-1715
  Peoria *(G-17323)*
Chester Brass and Aluminum .............. F ...... 618 826-2391
  Chester *(G-3652)*
Chicago Alum Castings Co Inc ............ G ...... 773 762-3009
  Chicago *(G-4301)*
Country Cast Products ....................... F ...... 815 777-1070
  Galena *(G-10718)*
Curto-Ligonier Foundries Co ............... E ...... 708 345-2250
  Melrose Park *(G-14613)*
Custom Fabrications Inc .................... F ...... 847 531-5912
  Elgin *(G-9007)*
▲ D R Sperry & Co ........................... D ...... 630 892-4361
  Aurora *(G-1137)*
Du Page Precision Products Co .......... D ...... 630 849-2940
  Aurora *(G-998)*
Dynacast Inc ................................... C ...... 847 608-2200
  Elgin *(G-9015)*
Illini Foundry Co Inc ......................... G ...... 309 697-3142
  Peoria *(G-17385)*
Jsp Mold ......................................... G ...... 815 225-7110
  Milledgeville *(G-14817)*
Kellermann Manufacturing Inc ............. F ...... 847 526-7266
  Wauconda *(G-21476)*
Komet America Holding Inc ................ G ...... 847 923-8400
  Schaumburg *(G-19602)*
Kvk Foundry Inc ............................... F ...... 815 695-5212
  Millington *(G-14819)*
Louis Meskan Brass Foundry Inc ......... C ...... 773 237-7662
  Chicago *(G-5547)*
Marble Machine Inc ........................... G ...... 217 442-0746
  Danville *(G-7752)*
Martin Tool Works Inc ........................ G ...... 847 923-8400
  Schaumburg *(G-19631)*
Master Foundry Inc ........................... F ...... 217 223-7396
  Quincy *(G-17856)*
Nelson - Harkins Inds Inc ................... E ...... 773 478-6243
  Chicago *(G-5884)*
◆ Newell Operating Company ............. C ...... 815 235-4171
  Freeport *(G-10675)*
Olson Aluminum Castings Ltd ............. E ...... 815 229-3292
  Rockford *(G-18526)*
Precision Entps Fndry Mch Inc ............ E ...... 815 498-2317
  Somonauk *(G-20129)*
Quincy Foundry & Pattern Co .............. G ...... 217 222-0718
  Quincy *(G-17877)*
R&R Racing of Palm Beach Inc ........... F ...... 618 937-6767
  West Frankfort *(G-21815)*
RCM Industries Inc ........................... E ...... 847 455-1950
  Wheeling *(G-22133)*
Reynolds Manufacturing Company ....... E ...... 309 787-8600
  Milan *(G-14803)*
Robert Kellerman & Co ...................... F ...... 847 526-7266
  Wauconda *(G-21500)*
Rockford Foundries Inc ...................... F ...... 815 965-7243
  Rockford *(G-18574)*
▲ Rome Industries Inc ...................... G ...... 309 691-7120
  Peoria *(G-17448)*
Sonoco Prtective Solutions Inc ........... E ...... 815 787-5244
  Dekalb *(G-8119)*
◆ Spartan Light Metal Pdts Inc ........... E ...... 618 443-4346
  Sparta *(G-20321)*
Tazewell Machine Works Inc ............... G ...... 309 347-3181
  Pekin *(G-17291)*
Tompkins Aluminum Foundry Inc ......... G ...... 815 438-5578
  Rock Falls *(G-18154)*
Tricast/Presfore Corporation .............. G ...... 815 459-1820
  Crystal Lake *(G-7669)*
Trio Foundry Inc ............................... G ...... 815 786-6616
  Sandwich *(G-19379)*
Trio Foundry Inc ............................... E ...... 630 892-1676
  Montgomery *(G-15068)*
Universal Electric Foundry Inc ............ E ...... 312 421-7233
  Chicago *(G-6831)*
Wagner Brass Foundry Inc .................. G ...... 773 276-7907
  Chicago *(G-6932)*
◆ World Kitchen LLC ......................... E ...... 847 233-8600
  Rosemont *(G-19042)*

## 3366 Copper Foundries

▲ Aetna Bearing Company ................. E ...... 630 694-0024
  Franklin Park *(G-10386)*
AJ Oster LLC .................................... C ...... 630 260-0950
  Carol Stream *(G-3094)*
Altman Pattern and Foundry Co .......... F ...... 773 586-9100
  Chicago *(G-3839)*
Alu-Bra Foundry Inc ......................... D ...... 630 766-3112
  Bensenville *(G-1829)*
Amcast Inc ...................................... F ...... 630 766-7450
  Bensenville *(G-1831)*

American Bare Conductor Inc ............. E ...... 815 224-3422
  La Salle *(G-12762)*
◆ Ampco Metal Incorporated .............. F ...... 847 437-6000
  Arlington Heights *(G-711)*
Amsted Rail Company Inc .................. A ...... 618 452-2111
  Granite City *(G-11264)*
Anderson Casting Company Inc .......... G ...... 312 733-1185
  Chicago *(G-3901)*
Art Casting of IL Inc ......................... G ...... 815 732-7777
  Oregon *(G-16818)*
Atherton Foundry Products Inc ........... E ...... 708 849-4615
  Riverdale *(G-18015)*
◆ Aurora Metals Division LLC .............. G ...... 630 844-4900
  Montgomery *(G-15028)*
▲ Bearing Sales Corporation ............. E ...... 773 282-8686
  Chicago *(G-4066)*
C B & A Inc .................................... F ...... 815 561-0255
  Rochelle *(G-18080)*
Calumet Brass Foundry Inc ................ F ...... 708 849-3040
  Dolton *(G-8367)*
Cast Technologies Inc ....................... C ...... 309 676-1715
  Peoria *(G-17323)*
Chester Brass and Aluminum .............. F ...... 618 826-2391
  Chester *(G-3652)*
Covey Machine Inc ........................... F ...... 773 650-1530
  Chicago *(G-4484)*
F Kreutzer & Co ............................... G ...... 773 826-5767
  Chicago *(G-4805)*
Fiberlink LLC ................................... E ...... 312 951-8500
  Chicago *(G-4841)*
▲ General Products Intl Ltd ............... G ...... 847 458-6357
  Lake In The Hills *(G-12994)*
Illini Foundry Co Inc ......................... G ...... 309 697-3142
  Peoria *(G-17385)*
Imperial Punch & Manufacturing ......... F ...... 815 226-8200
  Rockford *(G-18428)*
▲ Intermet Metals Services Inc .......... E ...... 847 605-1300
  Schaumburg *(G-19571)*
Kvk Foundry Inc ............................... F ...... 815 695-5212
  Millington *(G-14819)*
Louis Meskan Brass Foundry Inc ......... C ...... 773 237-7662
  Chicago *(G-5547)*
Mahoney Foundries Inc ...................... E ...... 309 784-2311
  Vermont *(G-21138)*
Petro Prop Inc ................................. F ...... 630 910-4738
  Downers Grove *(G-8502)*
Propeller Hr Solutions Inc .................. G ...... 312 342-7355
  Western Springs *(G-21871)*
Reynolds Manufacturing Company ....... E ...... 309 787-8600
  Milan *(G-14803)*
Rockford Foundries Inc ...................... F ...... 815 965-7243
  Rockford *(G-18574)*
Tilton Pattern Works Inc .................... F ...... 217 442-1502
  Danville *(G-7776)*
Tricast/Presfore Corporation .............. G ...... 815 459-1820
  Crystal Lake *(G-7669)*
Trio Foundry Inc ............................... E ...... 630 892-1676
  Montgomery *(G-15068)*
Universal Electric Foundry Inc ............ E ...... 312 421-7233
  Chicago *(G-6831)*
Wagner Brass Foundry Inc .................. G ...... 773 276-7907
  Chicago *(G-6932)*

## 3369 Nonferrous Foundries: Castings, NEC

Able Die Casting Corporation ............. D ...... 847 678-1991
  Schiller Park *(G-19797)*
▲ Acme Die Casting LLC .................... G ...... 847 272-9520
  Northbrook *(G-16197)*
Altman & Koehler Foundry ................. G ...... 773 373-7737
  Chicago *(G-3838)*
Amcast Inc ...................................... F ...... 630 766-7450
  Bensenville *(G-1831)*
Ames Metal Products Company ........... F ...... 773 523-3230
  Wheeling *(G-22005)*
Anderson Casting Company Inc .......... G ...... 312 733-1185
  Chicago *(G-3901)*
Avan Tool & Die Co Inc ...................... F ...... 773 287-1670
  Chicago *(G-3996)*
Batavia Foundry and Machine Co ........ G ...... 630 879-1319
  Batavia *(G-1420)*
▼ Big River Zinc Corporation .............. F ...... 618 274-5000
  Sauget *(G-19382)*
Caterpillar Inc ................................. C ...... 706 779-4620
  Mapleton *(G-14206)*
Charter Dura-Bar Inc ........................ G ...... 815 338-7800
  Woodstock *(G-22552)*
Clark Tashaunda .............................. G ...... 708 247-8274
  Calumet Park *(G-2958)*
Clinkenbeard & Associates Inc ........... E ...... 815 226-0291
  Rockford *(G-18313)*

Curto-Ligonier Foundries Co ....E.... 708 345-2250
Melrose Park (G-14613)
Darda Enterprises Inc ....F.... 847 270-0410
Palatine (G-17020)
Du Page Precision Products Co ....D.... 630 849-2940
Aurora (G-998)
Dynacast Inc ....C.... 847 608-2200
Elgin (G-9015)
G & W Electric Company ....E.... 708 389-8307
Blue Island (G-2251)
Illini Foundry Co Inc ....G.... 309 697-3142
Peoria (G-17385)
Impro Industries Usa Inc ....G.... 630 759-0280
Bolingbrook (G-2320)
Ipsen Inc ....E.... 815 239-2385
Pecatonica (G-17252)
▲ Kabert Industries Inc ....G.... 630 833-2115
Villa Park (G-21262)
Kettler Casting Co Inc ....E.... 618 234-5303
Belleville (G-1642)
Knock On Metal Inc ....G.... 312 372-4569
Chicago (G-5392)
Kraig Corporation ....E.... 847 928-0630
Franklin Park (G-10514)
▲ Laurel Manufacturing LLC ....G.... 773 961-8545
Chicago (G-5467)
Lemfco Inc ....E.... 815 777-0242
Galena (G-10729)
Libco Industries Inc ....F.... 815 623-7677
Roscoe (G-18902)
Mahoney Foundries Inc ....E.... 309 784-2311
Vermont (G-21138)
Marble Machine Inc ....G.... 217 442-0746
Danville (G-7752)
Master Foundry Inc ....F.... 217 223-7396
Quincy (G-17856)
Quincy Foundry & Pattern Co ....G.... 217 222-0718
Quincy (G-17877)
Reynolds Manufacturing Company ....E.... 309 787-8600
Milan (G-14803)
Robert Kellerman & Co ....G.... 847 526-7266
Wauconda (G-21500)
Rockbridge Casting Inc ....G.... 618 753-3188
Rockbridge (G-18212)
Rockford Foundries Inc ....F.... 815 965-7243
Rockford (G-18574)
Sarcol ....G.... 773 533-3000
Chicago (G-6445)
◆ Spartan Light Metal Pdts Inc ....E.... 618 443-4346
Sparta (G-20321)
▲ Tempco Electric Heater Corp ....B.... 630 350-2252
Wood Dale (G-22429)
Tompkins Aluminum Foundry Inc ....G.... 815 438-5578
Rock Falls (G-18154)
Tricast/Presfore Corporation ....G.... 815 459-1820
Crystal Lake (G-7669)
Trio Foundry Inc ....E.... 815 786-6616
Sandwich (G-19379)
Trio Foundry Inc ....E.... 630 892-1676
Montgomery (G-15068)
Universal Electric Foundry Inc ....E.... 312 421-7233
Chicago (G-6831)
Wagner Brass Foundry Inc ....G.... 773 276-7907
Chicago (G-6932)
Wishzing ....E.... 217 413-8469
Dalton City (G-7699)

## 3398 Metal Heat Treating

▲ 300 Below Inc ....G.... 217 423-3070
Decatur (G-7819)
Advanced Heat Treating Inc ....E.... 815 877-8593
Loves Park (G-13913)
Advanced Thermal Processing ....G.... 630 595-9000
Bensenville (G-1820)
▲ Arrow Gear Company ....C.... 630 969-7640
Downers Grove (G-8389)
▲ Axletech International ....D.... 773 264-1234
Chicago (G-4006)
Beechner Heat Treating Co Inc ....G.... 815 397-4314
Rockford (G-18279)
Bodycote Thermal Proc Inc ....D.... 708 236-5360
Melrose Park (G-14601)
Bonell Manufacturing Company ....E.... 708 849-1770
Riverdale (G-18016)
Bulaw Welding & Engineering Co ....D.... 630 228-8300
Itasca (G-12239)
Bwt LLC ....E.... 708 410-8000
Northlake (G-16432)
Bwt LLC ....E.... 630 210-4577
Rockford (G-18293)
C/B Machine Tool Corp ....G.... 847 288-1807
Franklin Park (G-10422)
Certified Heat Treating Co ....F.... 309 693-7711
Peoria (G-17340)
Chem-Plate Industries Inc ....E.... 708 345-3588
Maywood (G-14422)
Chem-Plate Industries Inc ....D.... 847 640-1600
Elk Grove Village (G-9366)
▲ Cooley Wire Products Mfg Co ....E.... 847 678-8585
Schiller Park (G-19816)
Curtis Metal Finishing Company ....F.... 815 282-1433
Machesney Park (G-14068)
Diamond Heat Treat Inc ....E.... 815 873-1348
Rockford (G-18343)
DK Surface Hardening Inc ....G.... 708 233-9095
Bridgeview (G-2484)
Eklund Metal Treating Inc ....E.... 815 877-7436
Loves Park (G-13939)
F P M LLC ....C.... 847 228-2525
Elk Grove Village (G-9473)
F P M LLC ....D.... 815 332-4961
Cherry Valley (G-3643)
Fpm Heat Treating ....F.... 815 332-4961
Cherry Valley (G-3644)
Fpm Heat Treatment ....G.... 847 274-7269
Itasca (G-12267)
General Surface Hardening ....E.... 312 226-5472
Chicago (G-4933)
Golfers Family Corporation ....E.... 815 968-0094
Rockford (G-18401)
▲ Horizon Steel Treating Inc ....D.... 847 639-4030
Cary (G-3351)
Howell Welding Corporation ....G.... 630 616-1100
Franklin Park (G-10489)
Hudapack Mtal Treating Ill Inc ....E.... 630 793-1916
Glendale Heights (G-11031)
Induction Heat Treating Corp ....E.... 815 477-7788
Crystal Lake (G-7592)
▲ International Proc Co Amer ....E.... 847 437-8400
Elk Grove Village (G-9553)
K V F Company ....E.... 847 437-5100
Elk Grove Village (G-9569)
K V F Company ....F.... 847 437-5019
Elk Grove Village (G-9570)
▲ Lapham-Hickey Steel Corp ....C.... 708 496-6111
Chicago (G-5459)
Met Co Industries Inc ....E.... 630 584-5100
Saint Charles (G-19218)
Metal Improvement Company LLC ....E.... 630 543-4950
Addison (G-201)
Metals Technology Corporation ....C.... 630 221-2500
Carol Stream (G-3193)
Metform LLC ....E.... 815 273-0230
Savanna (G-19401)
Morgan Ohare Inc ....D.... 630 543-6780
Addison (G-221)
Mp Steel Chicago LLC ....E.... 773 242-0853
Chicago (G-5820)
Nitrex Inc ....E.... 630 851-5880
Aurora (G-1058)
Precision Chrome Inc ....E.... 847 587-1515
Fox Lake (G-10282)
Precision Metal Technologies ....F.... 847 228-6630
Rolling Meadows (G-18768)
Progressive Steel Treating Inc ....E.... 815 877-2571
Loves Park (G-13979)
R-M Industries Inc ....F.... 630 543-3071
Addison (G-267)
Riverdale Pltg Heat Trting LLC ....E.... 708 849-2050
Riverdale (G-18024)
Rockford Heat Treaters Inc ....E.... 815 874-0089
Rockford (G-18575)
Rogers Metal Services Inc ....E.... 847 679-4642
Skokie (G-20078)
Rogers Metal Services Inc ....E.... 847 679-4642
Skokie (G-20079)
▼ Salman Metal ....G.... 630 359-5110
Elmhurst (G-9933)
Scientific Metal Treating Co ....E.... 630 582-0071
Roselle (G-18975)
Standard Heat Treating LLC ....E.... 773 242-0853
Cicero (G-7229)
Standard Heat Treating Co Inc ....D.... 708 447-7504
Chicago (G-6569)
Superheat Fgh Services Inc ....G.... 708 478-0205
New Lenox (G-15915)
Supertech Holdings Inc ....G.... 708 478-0205
New Lenox (G-15916)
▼ Tc Industries Inc ....C.... 815 459-2401
Crystal Lake (G-7660)
▲ Tempel Steel Company ....A.... 773 250-8000
Chicago (G-6696)
Terra Cotta Holdings Co ....E.... 815 459-2400
Crystal Lake (G-7664)
Thermo Techniques LLC ....E.... 217 446-1407
Danville (G-7768)
Tri-City Heat Treat Co Inc ....D.... 309 786-2689
Rock Island (G-18209)
Wec Welding and Machining LLC ....G.... 847 680-8100
Lake Bluff (G-12870)

## 3399 Primary Metal Prdts, NEC

A2 Sales LLC ....D.... 708 924-1200
Bedford Park (G-1532)
Accurate Finishers ....G.... 630 543-8575
Addison (G-18)
◆ American Metal Fibers Inc ....E.... 847 295-8166
Lake Bluff (G-12830)
▲ Bearing Sales Corporation ....E.... 773 282-8686
Chicago (G-4066)
Binzel Industries LLC ....G.... 847 506-0003
Lockport (G-13707)
▲ Burgess-Norton Mfg Co Inc ....B.... 630 232-4100
Geneva (G-10813)
▼ Connelly-Gpm Inc ....E.... 773 247-7231
Chicago (G-4451)
Controlled Thermal Processing ....G.... 847 651-5511
Streamwood (G-20650)
Dippit Inc ....G.... 630 762-6500
West Chicago (G-21693)
Direct Selling Strategies ....G.... 847 993-3188
Rosemont (G-18999)
◆ Duo-Fast Corporation ....E.... 847 944-2288
Glenview (G-11122)
Dva Metal Fabrication Inc ....G.... 224 577-8217
Elk Grove Village (G-9440)
Eagle Chassis Inc ....G.... 217 525-1941
Springfield (G-20431)
▲ Ecf Holdings LLC ....G.... 224 723-5524
Northbrook (G-16246)
Ferguson Enterprises Inc ....G.... 217 425-7262
Decatur (G-7880)
Filter Technology Inc ....E.... 773 523-7200
Bedford Park (G-1550)
Finish Line USA Inc ....F.... 847 608-7800
Elgin (G-9035)
Forge Resources Group LLC ....C.... 815 758-6400
Dekalb (G-8091)
Forge Resources Group LLC ....C.... 815 758-6400
Dekalb (G-8092)
Forge Resources Group LLC ....G.... 815 758-6400
Dekalb (G-8093)
Gemco ....E.... 217 446-7900
Danville (G-7726)
Hall Fabrication Inc ....G.... 217 322-2212
Rushville (G-19091)
Hilti Inc ....G.... 847 364-9818
Elmhurst (G-9882)
Illinois Block and Tackle Inc ....G.... 618 451-8696
Granite City (G-11288)
J D M Coatings Inc ....G.... 708 755-6300
Steger (G-20574)
Jjj Brass and Aluminum Foundry ....G.... 608 363-9225
South Beloit (G-20153)
▲ L & J Industrial Staples Inc ....G.... 815 864-3337
Shannon (G-19899)
Lindsay Metal Madness Inc ....G.... 815 568-4560
Marengo (G-14235)
Midwest Finishers Pwdrctng ....G.... 217 536-9098
Effingham (G-8847)
Mount Vernon Iron Works LLC ....G.... 618 244-2313
Mount Vernon (G-15428)
MSC Pre Finish Metals Egv Inc ....C.... 847 439-2210
Elk Grove Village (G-9640)
Mueller Company Plant 4 ....G.... 217 425-7424
Decatur (G-7919)
Nanophase Technologies Corp ....E.... 630 771-6708
Romeoville (G-18852)
Nanophase Technologies Corp ....F.... 630 771-6747
Burr Ridge (G-2870)
National Material Company LLC ....E.... 847 806-7200
Elk Grove Village (G-9646)
Orion Metals Co ....G.... 847 412-9532
Glenview (G-11177)
Perfect Powder Coating ....G.... 847 322-6666
Gurnee (G-11484)
Permacor Inc ....E.... 708 422-3353
Oak Lawn (G-16639)
Phillip C Cowen ....E.... 630 208-1848
Geneva (G-10859)

## SIC SECTION — 34 FABRICATED METAL PRODUCTS, EXCEPT MACHINERY AND TRANSPORTATION EQUIPMENT

Polaris Laser Laminations LLC .............G..... 630 444-0760
  West Chicago *(G-21758)*
Progress Rail Services Corp .................G..... 309 343-6176
  Galesburg *(G-10771)*
Protek ...........................................G..... 815 773-2280
  Joliet *(G-12557)*
Sales Specialty Metal ........................G..... 217 864-1496
  Mount Zion *(G-15456)*
Senju Comtek Corp .............................G..... 847 549-5690
  Mundelein *(G-15555)*
Stein Inc ......................................D..... 618 452-0836
  Granite City *(G-11305)*
Tempel Steel Company .........................A..... 773 250-8000
  Chicago *(G-6698)*
▲ Topy Precision Mfg Inc ....................D..... 847 228-5902
  Elk Grove Village *(G-9784)*
Toyal America Inc ............................G..... 630 505-2160
  Naperville *(G-15766)*
◆ Toyal America Inc ..........................D..... 815 740-3000
  Lockport *(G-13749)*
Winning Colors .................................G..... 815 462-4810
  Manhattan *(G-14171)*

## 34 FABRICATED METAL PRODUCTS, EXCEPT MACHINERY AND TRANSPORTATION EQUIPMENT

### 3411 Metal Cans

All Container Inc ..............................G..... 847 677-2100
  Lincolnwood *(G-13502)*
Amcor Rigid Plastics Usa LLC .............F..... 630 406-3500
  Batavia *(G-1412)*
Ardagh Metal Beverage USA Inc .........D..... 773 399-3000
  Chicago *(G-3943)*
Ball Corporation .............................C.....
  Elgin *(G-8963)*
Best Metal Corporation ......................E..... 815 337-0420
  Woodstock *(G-22545)*
Brockway Standard Inc .......................G..... 773 893-2100
  Chicago *(G-4173)*
Bway Corporation ..............................C..... 847 956-0750
  Elk Grove Village *(G-9351)*
Bway Corporation ..............................C..... 773 254-8700
  Chicago *(G-4194)*
Bway Parent Company Inc ....................F..... 773 890-3300
  Chicago *(G-4195)*
▲ Central Can Company Inc ..................C..... 773 254-8700
  Chicago *(G-4270)*
Centric Co Inc .................................G..... 708 728-9061
  Downers Grove *(G-8407)*
Certified Tank & Mfg LLC ....................E..... 217 525-1433
  Springfield *(G-20415)*
Chicago Mtal Sup Fbrcation Inc ...........F..... 773 227-6200
  Chicago *(G-4336)*
Cooler Concepts Inc ..........................G..... 815 462-3866
  New Lenox *(G-15872)*
Creative Metal Products ....................F..... 773 638-3200
  Chicago *(G-4500)*
Crown Cork & Seal Usa Inc .................C..... 708 239-5555
  Alsip *(G-452)*
Crown Cork & Seal Usa Inc .................G..... 815 933-9351
  Bradley *(G-2417)*
Crown Cork & Seal Usa Inc .................C..... 708 239-5000
  Alsip *(G-453)*
Crown Cork & Seal Usa Inc .................D..... 217 672-3533
  Warrensburg *(G-21338)*
Crown Cork & Seal Usa Inc .................C..... 217 872-6100
  Decatur *(G-7861)*
Crown Cork & Seal Usa Inc .................E..... 630 851-7774
  Aurora *(G-989)*
D & B Fabricators & Distrs ................F..... 630 325-3811
  Lemont *(G-13234)*
▲ Ds Containers Inc ..........................C..... 630 406-9600
  Batavia *(G-1442)*
▲ Fitpac Co Ltd ...............................G..... 630 428-9077
  Bensenville *(G-1899)*
Great Lakes Art Foundry Inc ..............G..... 847 213-0800
  Skokie *(G-20006)*
Ideal Fabricators Inc .......................F..... 217 999-7017
  Mount Olive *(G-15304)*
▲ Ignite Usa LLC ..............................E..... 312 432-6223
  Chicago *(G-5147)*
Jamiel Inc .....................................G..... 217 423-1000
  Decatur *(G-7898)*
▲ JL Clark LLC ................................C..... 815 961-5609
  Rockford *(G-18447)*
Jlo Metal Products Co A Corp ............D..... 773 889-6242
  Chicago *(G-5307)*

Justrite Manufacturing Co LLC ..........C..... 217 234-7486
  Mattoon *(G-14396)*
Kraft Heinz Company .........................C..... 847 646-2000
  Glenview *(G-11160)*
▲ Metraflex Company .........................D..... 312 738-3800
  Chicago *(G-5706)*
Midway Food LLC ..............................  773 294-0730
  Chicago *(G-5738)*
◆ Rexam Beverage Can Company ..........C..... 773 399-3000
  Chicago *(G-6344)*
Rexam Beverage Can Company .............  773 247-4646
  Chicago *(G-6345)*
Rexam Beverage Can Company .............C..... 847 228-3200
  Elk Grove Village *(G-9715)*
◆ Shenglong Intl Group Corp ..............G..... 312 388-2345
  Glenview *(G-11195)*
Silgan Containers LLC .......................D..... 815 562-1250
  Rochelle *(G-18109)*
Silgan Containers Mfg Corp ...............C..... 217 283-5501
  Hoopeston *(G-12116)*
Silgan Containers Mfg Corp ...............E..... 847 336-0552
  Waukegan *(G-21616)*
▲ Silgan Equipment Company ..............E..... 847 336-0552
  Waukegan *(G-21617)*
Silgan White Cap Americas LLC .........F..... 630 515-8383
  Downers Grove *(G-8524)*
Silgan White Cap Corporation ............C..... 217 398-1600
  Champaign *(G-3539)*
Staffco Inc ....................................G..... 309 688-3223
  Peoria *(G-17460)*
Willow Farm Product Inc ...................G..... 630 395-9246
  Darien *(G-7804)*

### 3412 Metal Barrels, Drums, Kegs & Pails

American Rack Company .....................E..... 773 763-7309
  Chicago *(G-3870)*
Arrows Up Inc .................................G..... 847 305-2550
  Arlington Heights *(G-717)*
▲ Central Can Company Inc ................C..... 773 254-8700
  Chicago *(G-4270)*
Chicago Steel Container Corp ............E..... 773 277-2244
  Chicago *(G-4350)*
Cleveland Steel Container Corp .........E..... 708 258-0700
  Peotone *(G-17486)*
D & B Fabricators & Distrs ................F..... 630 325-3811
  Lemont *(G-13234)*
Grafcor Packaging Inc ......................G..... 815 639-2380
  Loves Park *(G-13945)*
Greif Inc ......................................E..... 815 935-7575
  Bradley *(G-2423)*
Higgins Bros Inc ..............................F..... 773 523-0124
  Chicago *(G-5086)*
Liberty Diversified Intl Inc ..............E..... 217 935-8361
  Clinton *(G-7285)*
Mauser Usa LLC ...............................G..... 773 261-2332
  Chicago *(G-5657)*
Meyer Steel Drum Inc ........................G..... 773 522-3030
  Chicago *(G-5712)*
▲ Meyer Steel Drum Inc ....................C..... 773 376-8376
  Chicago *(G-5713)*
Mobile Mini Inc ...............................E..... 708 297-2004
  Calumet Park *(G-2963)*
Production Manufacturing ..................  217 256-4211
  Warsaw *(G-21371)*
Staffco Inc ....................................G..... 309 688-3223
  Peoria *(G-17460)*
◆ Van Leer Containers Inc .................C..... 708 371-4777
  Alsip *(G-539)*
Westrock Cp LLC ..............................C..... 847 689-4200
  North Chicago *(G-16190)*
Woods Equipment Company ..................D..... 815 732-2141
  Oregon *(G-16834)*
▼ Zorin Material Handling Co ............G..... 773 342-3818
  Chicago *(G-7073)*

### 3421 Cutlery

Alps Group Inc ................................G..... 815 469-3800
  Frankfort *(G-10293)*
Alps Group Inc ................................G..... 815 469-3800
  Chicago *(G-3833)*
▲ Anjay Traders Inc .........................G..... 847 888-8562
  Elgin *(G-8954)*
Art Jewel Enterprises Ltd .................F..... 630 260-0400
  Carol Stream *(G-3106)*
Bubble Bubble Inc ...........................G..... 815 455-2366
  Crystal Lake *(G-7545)*
Burrito Beach LLC ............................F..... 312 861-1986
  Chicago *(G-4186)*
Cafetine Panio ................................G..... 773 697-8007
  Chicago *(G-4212)*

Carbon On Chicago LLC ......................G..... 312 225-3200
  Chicago *(G-4238)*
Choochs ........................................  847 888-0211
  Elgin *(G-8989)*
Custom Cutting Tools Inc ..................G..... 815 986-0320
  Loves Park *(G-13931)*
Delicias Brianna .............................G..... 773 409-4394
  Chicago *(G-4576)*
Edgewell Per Care Brands LLC ...........B..... 708 544-5550
  Melrose Park *(G-14630)*
▲ Estwing Manufacturing Co Inc ........B..... 815 397-9521
  Rockford *(G-18370)*
Goodco Products LLC ........................G..... 630 258-6384
  Countryside *(G-7428)*
Harris Precision Tools Inc ................G..... 708 422-5808
  Chicago Ridge *(G-7149)*
Irwin Industrial Tool Company ..........G..... 815 235-4171
  Freeport *(G-10669)*
Joseph Taylor Inc ............................G..... 309 762-5323
  Moline *(G-14948)*
Just Turkey ...................................G..... 708 957-2222
  Chicago *(G-5339)*
Kernel Kutter Inc ............................  815 877-1515
  Machesney Park *(G-14085)*
Kilt of Schaumburg .........................G..... 847 413-2000
  Schaumburg *(G-19597)*
La Autentica Michoacana Never .........G..... 630 516-1888
  Addison *(G-175)*
Lulus ...........................................  773 865-8978
  Chicago *(G-5561)*
Mburger II ....................................  312 428-3548
  Chicago *(G-5663)*
▲ Modern Specialties Company ...........G..... 312 648-5800
  Chicago *(G-5785)*
Moes River North LLC .......................G..... 312 245-2000
  Chicago *(G-5787)*
Olive Tree Foods Inc ........................G..... 847 872-2762
  Zion *(G-22693)*
Pactiv LLC .....................................  708 496-2900
  Bedford Park *(G-1571)*
▼ Prairie Packaging Inc ...................E..... 708 496-1172
  Bedford Park *(G-1575)*
Prairie Packaging Inc ......................F..... 708 496-2900
  Chicago *(G-6166)*
River Bend Wild Game & Sausage ........G..... 217 688-3337
  Saint Joseph *(G-19317)*
SCC Holding Company LLC ..................A..... 847 444-5000
  Lake Forest *(G-12958)*
Seadog ..........................................G..... 773 235-8100
  Chicago *(G-6465)*
Shaws Shack ..................................  618 669-2220
  Pocahontas *(G-17685)*
▼ Solo Cup Company .........................  847 831-4800
  Lincolnshire *(G-13480)*
▲ Solo Cup Company LLC ...................  847 444-5000
  Lincolnshire *(G-13481)*
▼ Solo Cup Investment Corp ..............E..... 847 831-4800
  Highland Park *(G-11872)*
Solo Cup Operating Corporation .........  847 444-5000
  Chicago *(G-6541)*
▲ Speco Inc ..................................E..... 847 678-4240
  Schiller Park *(G-19876)*
Summervlle Consulting Svcs LLC .......  618 547-7142
  Alma *(G-424)*
▲ Superior Knife Inc ......................E..... 847 982-2280
  Skokie *(G-20095)*
▲ W A Whitney Co ............................  815 964-6771
  Rockford *(G-18671)*
▲ Wallace/Haskin Corp ....................  630 789-2882
  Downers Grove *(G-8540)*
▲ Whitney Roper LLC .......................D..... 815 962-3011
  Rockford *(G-18681)*
▲ Whitney Roper Rockford Inc ..........D..... 815 962-3011
  Rockford *(G-18682)*
Wings of Roselle LLC ........................  630 529-5700
  Roselle *(G-18985)*
◆ World Kitchen LLC ........................C..... 847 233-8600
  Rosemont *(G-19042)*

### 3423 Hand & Edge Tools

A To Z Tool Inc ...............................G..... 630 787-0478
  Villa Park *(G-21231)*
Adel Tool Co LLP .............................G..... 708 867-8530
  Chicago *(G-3747)*
▲ Adjustable Clamp Company .............C..... 312 666-0640
  Chicago *(G-3751)*
▲ Advance Equipment Mfg Co ............F..... 773 287-8220
  Chicago *(G-3759)*
▲ Ajax Tool Works Inc ......................D..... 847 455-5420
  Franklin Park *(G-10387)*

Employee Codes: A=Over 500 employees, B=251-500
C=101-250, D=51-100, E=20-50, F=10-19, G=3-9

34 FABRICATED METAL PRODUCTS, EXCEPT MACHINERY AND TRANSPORTATION EQUIPMENT SIC SECTION

▲ **Aldon Co** F 847 623-8800
Waukegan *(G-21521)*

**Atlas Die LLC** D 630 351-5140
Glendale Heights *(G-11009)*

▲ **Beno J Gundlach Company** E 618 233-1781
Belleville *(G-1613)*

▲ **Bit Brokers International Ltd** G 618 435-5811
West Frankfort *(G-21804)*

**Brian Burcar** G 815 856-2271
Leonore *(G-13285)*

**Builders Ironworks Inc** G 708 754-4092
Steger *(G-20569)*

**C K North America Inc** F 815 524-4246
Romeoville *(G-18804)*

**Chicago Grinding & Machine Co** E 708 343-4399
Melrose Park *(G-14610)*

**Custom Cutting Tools Inc** G 815 986-0320
Loves Park *(G-13931)*

▲ **Dasco Pro Inc** D 815 962-3727
Rockford *(G-18335)*

**Dobratz Sales Company Inc** G 224 569-3081
Lake In The Hills *(G-12990)*

**Doerock Inc** G 217 543-2101
Arthur *(G-895)*

▲ **Durabilt Dyvex Inc** F 708 397-4673
Broadview *(G-2573)*

**E J Welch Co Inc** E 847 238-0100
Elk Grove Village *(G-9443)*

▼ **Eklind Tool Co** C 847 994-8550
Franklin Park *(G-10464)*

**Ergo Help Inc** G 847 593-0722
Arlington Heights *(G-750)*

▲ **Estwing Manufacturing Co Inc** B 815 397-9521
Rockford *(G-18370)*

▲ **Galaxy Industries Inc** D 847 639-8580
Cary *(G-3345)*

**Gartech Manufacturing Co** E 217 324-6527
Litchfield *(G-13686)*

**Gaunt Industries Inc** G 847 671-0776
Franklin Park *(G-10477)*

**Greenfield Products LLC** E 708 596-5200
Hazel Crest *(G-11707)*

**H E Associates Inc** F 630 553-6382
Yorkville *(G-22661)*

**H R Slater Co Inc** F 312 666-1855
Chicago *(G-5023)*

**H&H Die Manufacturing Inc** G 708 479-6267
Frankfort *(G-10326)*

▲ **Hand Tool America** G 847 947-2866
Buffalo Grove *(G-2701)*

**Hollywood Tools LLC** G 773 793-3119
West Chicago *(G-21715)*

**Hydra Fold Auger Inc** G 217 379-2614
Loda *(G-13751)*

**Hyponex Corporation** E 815 772-2167
Morrison *(G-15144)*

**I D Rockford Shop Inc** G 815 335-1150
Winnebago *(G-22297)*

**Ideal Industries Inc** C 815 895-1108
Sycamore *(G-20801)*

**Illinois Tool Works Inc** G 847 821-2170
Vernon Hills *(G-21174)*

◆ **Ironwood Mfg Inc** G 630 778-8963
Naperville *(G-15679)*

**Irwin Industrial Tool Company** C 815 235-4171
Freeport *(G-10669)*

**K-C Tool Co** G 630 983-5960
Naperville *(G-15683)*

**Kishwaukee Forge Company** E 815 758-4451
Cortland *(G-7391)*

◆ **Klein Tools Inc** B 847 821-5500
Lincolnshire *(G-13460)*

**Klein Tools Inc** D 847 228-6999
Elk Grove Village *(G-9577)*

**Klein Tools Inc** E 847 821-5500
Lincolnshire *(G-13461)*

▲ **Knipex Tools LP** F 847 398-8520
Arlington Heights *(G-789)*

**Lawndale Forging & Tool Works** G 773 277-2800
Chicago *(G-5471)*

**Line Group Inc** E 847 593-6810
Arlington Heights *(G-793)*

▲ **Link Tools Intl (usa) Inc** G 773 549-3000
Chicago *(G-5512)*

▲ **Lmt Onsrud LP** C 847 362-1560
Waukegan *(G-21582)*

**Lorette Dies Inc** G 630 279-9682
Elmhurst *(G-9902)*

**Lsp Industries Inc** F 815 226-8090
Rockford *(G-18474)*

▲ **Luster Leaf Products Inc** G 815 337-5560
Woodstock *(G-22586)*

**M E Barber Co Inc** G 217 428-4591
Decatur *(G-7909)*

◆ **Marmon Holdings Inc** D 312 372-9500
Chicago *(G-5625)*

▲ **Modern Specialties Company** G 312 648-5800
Chicago *(G-5785)*

**Nextstep Commercial Products** G 217 379-2377
Paxton *(G-17239)*

**Northern Ordinance Corporation** G 815 675-6400
Spring Grove *(G-20352)*

**P K Neuses Incorporated** G 847 253-6555
Rolling Meadows *(G-18756)*

**Packers Supplies & Eqp LLC** G 630 543-5810
Addison *(G-236)*

▲ **Patterson Avenue Tool Company** G 847 949-8100
Long Grove *(G-13900)*

▲ **Perkins Manufacturing Co** E 708 482-9500
Bolingbrook *(G-2358)*

▲ **Power House Tool Inc** E 815 727-6301
Joliet *(G-12552)*

▲ **Pratt-Read Tools LLC** G 815 895-1121
Sycamore *(G-20813)*

**Precision Industrial Knife** G 630 350-7898
Wood Dale *(G-22412)*

**Precision Instruments Inc** D 847 824-4194
Des Plaines *(G-8261)*

◆ **Precision Products Inc** C 217 735-1590
Lincoln *(G-13418)*

**Precision Tool** F 815 464-2428
Frankfort *(G-10351)*

▲ **Proton Multimedia Inc** G 847 531-8664
Elgin *(G-9152)*

▲ **Pullr Holding Company LLC** E 224 366-2500
Schaumburg *(G-19704)*

**Ravco Incorporated** G 815 725-9095
Joliet *(G-12564)*

▲ **Rhino Tool Company** F 309 853-5555
Kewanee *(G-12694)*

**Richardson Enterprises** G 309 833-5395
Macomb *(G-14131)*

▲ **Rieco-Titan Products Inc** E 815 464-7400
Frankfort *(G-10358)*

◆ **Rothenberger USA LLC** D 815 397-7617
Rockford *(G-18598)*

▲ **Ryeson Corporation** D 847 455-8677
Carol Stream *(G-3230)*

**S & G Step Tool Inc** G 773 992-0808
Chicago *(G-6420)*

▲ **Sab Tool Supply Co** G 847 634-3700
Vernon Hills *(G-21196)*

**Sk Hand Tool LLC** F 815 895-7701
Sycamore *(G-20816)*

▲ **Stanley Hartco Co** E 847 967-1122
Skokie *(G-20090)*

**Stark Tools and Supply Inc** G 847 772-8974
Elk Grove Village *(G-9756)*

**Stuhr Manufacturing Co** F 815 398-2460
Rockford *(G-18636)*

▲ **Sws Industries Inc** E 904 482-0091
Woodstock *(G-22616)*

**Thread & Gage Co Inc** G 815 675-2305
Spring Grove *(G-20367)*

**Toby Small Engine Repair** G 708 699-6021
Richton Park *(G-17980)*

◆ **Tuxco Corporation** F 847 244-2220
Gurnee *(G-11517)*

▲ **Vaughan & Bushnell Mfg Co** F 815 648-2446
Hebron *(G-11730)*

**Vaughan & Bushnell Mfg Co** C 309 772-2131
Bushnell *(G-2909)*

**Wenco Manufacturing Co Inc** E 630 377-7474
Elgin *(G-9235)*

▲ **Whitney Roper LLC** D 815 962-3011
Rockford *(G-18681)*

▲ **Whitney Roper Rockford Inc** D 815 962-3011
Rockford *(G-18682)*

**Woodland Engineering Company** G 847 362-0110
Lake Bluff *(G-12873)*

**Zah Group Inc** G 847 821-5500
Lincolnshire *(G-13492)*

**Zim Manufacturing Co** E 773 622-2500
Chicago *(G-7067)*

## 3425 Hand Saws & Saw Blades

**Allkut Tool Incorporated** G 815 476-9656
Wilmington *(G-22269)*

▲ **Amv International Inc** F 815 282-9990
Loves Park *(G-13920)*

◆ **Contour Saws Inc** C 800 259-6834
Des Plaines *(G-8174)*

**Custom Blades & Tools Inc** G 630 860-7650
Bensenville *(G-1875)*

▲ **Estwing Manufacturing Co Inc** B 815 397-9521
Rockford *(G-18370)*

**Fiskars Brands Inc** B 309 690-2200
Peoria *(G-17363)*

**Jaeger Saw and Cutter Inc** G 815 963-0313
Rockford *(G-18442)*

**Midwest Saw Inc** G 630 293-4252
West Chicago *(G-21743)*

**Milwaukee Electric Tool Corp** B 847 588-3356
Niles *(G-16008)*

**R & S Cutterhead Mfg Co** F 815 678-2611
Richmond *(G-17969)*

▲ **Roentgen USA LLC** G 847 787-0135
Schiller Park *(G-19868)*

**S & J Industrial Supply Corp** F 708 339-1708
South Holland *(G-20303)*

**Saws Unlimited Inc** G 847 640-7450
Elk Grove Village *(G-9730)*

**Supreme Saw & Service Co** G 708 396-1125
Wheeling *(G-22160)*

**Techniks LLC** E 815 689-2748
Cullom *(G-7685)*

**Trac Equipment Company Inc** G 309 647-5066
Canton *(G-2993)*

**Tru-Cut Tool & Supply Co** F 708 396-1122
Wheeling *(G-22169)*

**Unicut Corporation** G 773 525-4210
Chicago *(G-6813)*

▲ **Wallace/Haskin Corp** G 630 789-2882
Downers Grove *(G-8540)*

▲ **Wikus Saw Technology Corp** E 630 766-0960
Addison *(G-343)*

## 3429 Hardware, NEC

**9161 Corporation** G 847 470-8828
Niles *(G-15953)*

**A Ashland Lock Company** F 773 348-5106
Chicago *(G-3684)*

**Aco Inc** E 773 774-5200
Chicago *(G-3735)*

**Adams Machine Shop** G 630 851-6060
Naperville *(G-15590)*

▲ **Adjustable Clamp Company** C 312 666-0640
Chicago *(G-3751)*

▼ **Advanced Machine & Engrg Co** C 815 962-6076
Rockford *(G-18257)*

▲ **Afc Cable Systems Inc** B 508 998-1131
Harvey *(G-11651)*

**Agena Manufacturing Co** E 630 668-5086
Carol Stream *(G-3093)*

**Alan Manufacturing Corp** G 815 568-6836
Marengo *(G-14217)*

▲ **Aldon Co** F 847 623-8800
Waukegan *(G-21521)*

**Allegion S&S US Holding Co** C 815 875-3311
Princeton *(G-17742)*

**Allquip Co Inc** G 309 944-6153
Geneseo *(G-10797)*

**Amazing Cabinets & Design Corp** G 773 405-0174
Elk Grove Village *(G-9292)*

▲ **American Couplings Co** G 630 323-4442
Westmont *(G-21875)*

**American Partsmith Inc** G 630 520-0432
West Chicago *(G-21656)*

▲ **Amos Industries Inc** F 630 393-0606
Warrenville *(G-21341)*

**Antolin Interiors Usa Inc** B 618 327-4416
Nashville *(G-15833)*

▲ **Architctral Bldrs Hdwr Mfg Inc** E 630 875-9900
Itasca *(G-12230)*

**Ashland Door Solutions LLC** G 773 348-5106
Elk Grove Village *(G-9315)*

**Avoca Ridge Ltd** G 815 692-4772
Fairbury *(G-10122)*

**Baker Drapery Corporation** G 309 691-3295
Peoria *(G-17313)*

◆ **Baron Manufacturing Co LLC** E 630 628-9110
Itasca *(G-12235)*

**Berens Inc** G 815 932-0913
Kankakee *(G-12604)*

**Braun Manufacturing Co Inc** E 847 635-2050
Mount Prospect *(G-15313)*

▼ **Capital Rubber Corporation** F 630 595-6644
Bensenville *(G-1851)*

**Caterpillar Inc** A 309 578-2473
Mossville *(G-15250)*

SIC SECTION 34 FABRICATED METAL PRODUCTS, EXCEPT MACHINERY AND TRANSPORTATION EQUIPMENT

Chas O Larson Co....E....815 625-0503
Rock Falls *(G-18129)*
▲ Chicago Car Seal Company....G....773 278-9400
Chicago *(G-4310)*
▲ Chicago Hardware and Fix Co....D....847 455-6609
Franklin Park *(G-10429)*
Cleats Mfg Inc....F....773 521-0300
Chicago *(G-4399)*
▲ Compx Security Products Inc....D....847 234-1864
Grayslake *(G-11329)*
◆ Cooper B-Line Inc....A....618 654-2184
Highland *(G-11780)*
Creative Steel Fabricators....G....847 803-2090
Des Plaines *(G-8177)*
Crosby Group LLC....G....708 333-3005
Harvey *(G-11663)*
▲ Crown Metal Manufacturing Co....E....630 279-9800
Elmhurst *(G-9859)*
Custom Stainless Steel Inc....F....618 435-2605
Benton *(G-2026)*
Del Storm Products Inc....F....217 446-3377
Danville *(G-7715)*
Dixline Corporation....D....309 932-2011
Galva *(G-10788)*
Dixline Corporation....F....309 932-2011
Galva *(G-10787)*
Dorma Usa Inc....D....717 336-3881
Steeleville *(G-20560)*
Driv-Lok Inc....G....815 895-8161
Sycamore *(G-20794)*
▲ Du Bro Products Inc....E....847 526-2136
Wauconda *(G-21456)*
Dumore Supplies Inc....F....312 949-6260
Chicago *(G-4649)*
Dura Operating LLC....C....815 947-3333
Stockton *(G-20631)*
▲ Durabilt Dyvex Inc....F....708 397-4673
Broadview *(G-2573)*
Duratrack Inc....E....847 806-0202
Elk Grove Village *(G-9439)*
E R Wagner Manufacturing Co....C....708 485-3400
Brookfield *(G-2630)*
Eastern Company....C....847 537-1800
Wheeling *(G-22041)*
▼ Engert Co Inc....E....847 673-1633
Skokie *(G-19993)*
Estad Stamping & Mfg Co....E....217 442-4600
Danville *(G-7717)*
▲ Estwing Manufacturing Co Inc....B....815 397-9521
Rockford *(G-18370)*
Expert Locksmith Inc....G....917 751-9267
Chicago *(G-4796)*
F B Williams Co....G....773 233-4255
Chicago *(G-4802)*
Fenix Manufacturing LLC....G....815 208-0755
Fulton *(G-10700)*
▲ First Choice Building Pdts Inc....F....630 350-2770
Wood Dale *(G-22368)*
Focus Marketing Group Inc....G....815 363-2525
Johnsburg *(G-12434)*
▲ Fort Lock Corporation....E....708 456-1100
Grayslake *(G-11338)*
▲ Fortune Brands Home & SEC Inc....C....847 484-4400
Deerfield *(G-8007)*
Freeman Products Inc....G....847 439-1000
Elk Grove Village *(G-9490)*
Geib Industries Inc....E....847 455-4550
Bensenville *(G-1906)*
General Machinery & Mfg Co....F....773 235-3700
Chicago *(G-4928)*
Grand Specialties Co....F....630 629-8000
Oak Brook *(G-16520)*
Haddock Tool & Manufacturing....G....815 786-2739
Sandwich *(G-19367)*
▲ Heckmann Building Products Inc....E....708 865-2403
Melrose Park *(G-14652)*
Hendrickson International Corp....C....815 727-4031
Joliet *(G-12510)*
HM Manufacturing Inc....F....847 487-8700
Wauconda *(G-21469)*
Hunter-Stevens Company Inc....F....847 671-5014
Franklin Park *(G-10493)*
Hyspan Precision Products Inc....E....773 277-0700
South Holland *(G-20279)*
I Hardware Direct Inc....G....708 325-0000
Westmont *(G-21892)*
Illinois Fibre Specialty Co....E....773 376-1122
Chicago *(G-5157)*
Illinois Steel Service Inc....D....312 926-7440
Chicago *(G-5158)*

Illinois Tool Works Inc....E....708 681-3891
Broadview *(G-2585)*
In Midwest Service Enterprises....G....217 224-1932
Quincy *(G-17839)*
Industrial Rubber & Sup Entp....G....217 429-3747
Decatur *(G-7895)*
▲ Inland Fastener Inc....F....630 293-3800
West Chicago *(G-21720)*
Innerweld Cover Co....F....847 497-3009
Mundelein *(G-15511)*
◆ Innovative Components Inc....E....847 885-9050
Schaumburg *(G-19567)*
Jerome Remien Corporation....F....847 806-0888
Elk Grove Village *(G-9561)*
Kemper Industries....G....217 826-5712
Marshall *(G-14324)*
Kraig Corporation....E....847 928-0630
Franklin Park *(G-10514)*
Kwikset Corporation....G....630 577-0500
Lisle *(G-13616)*
L & M Hardware Ltd....G....312 805-2752
Downers Grove *(G-8471)*
▲ Leatherneck Hardware Inc....E....217 431-3096
Danville *(G-7745)*
Lovatt & Radcliffe Ltd....G....815 568-9797
Skokie *(G-20031)*
Max Fire Training Inc....F....618 210-2079
Godfrey *(G-11228)*
Metal Mfg LLC....C....815 432-4595
Watseka *(G-21423)*
Meyer Engineering Co....G....847 746-1500
Winthrop Harbor *(G-22319)*
MHS Ltd....F....773 736-3333
Chicago *(G-5716)*
Midwest Group Dist & Svcs Inc....G....708 597-0059
Alsip *(G-492)*
▲ Midwest Keyless Inc....G....815 675-0404
Spring Grove *(G-20346)*
Neisewander Enterprises Inc....A....815 288-1431
Dixon *(G-8337)*
Norforge and Machining Inc....D....309 772-3124
Bushnell *(G-2907)*
Nova Wildcat Amerock LLC....F....815 266-6416
Freeport *(G-10677)*
▲ OBerry Enterprises Inc....G....815 728-9480
Ringwood *(G-17994)*
▲ Peerless Industries Inc....B....630 375-5100
Aurora *(G-1063)*
◆ Plews Inc....C....815 288-3344
Dixon *(G-8339)*
Practechal Marketing....G....847 486-8600
Glenview *(G-11183)*
▲ Prater Industries Inc....D....630 679-3200
Bolingbrook *(G-2359)*
◆ Precision Brand Products Inc....E....630 969-7200
Downers Grove *(G-8509)*
Quality Hnge A Div Spreme Hnge....E....708 534-7801
University Park *(G-21061)*
▲ Reichel Hardware Company Inc....G....630 762-7394
Saint Charles *(G-19252)*
Reliable Machine Company....E....815 968-8803
Rockford *(G-18554)*
▲ Remin Laboratories Inc....D....815 723-1940
Joliet *(G-12566)*
▲ Rockford Process Control Inc....C....815 966-2000
Rockford *(G-18583)*
Royal Brass Inc....G....618 439-6341
Benton *(G-2040)*
Royal Kitchen & Bathroom Cabin....G....847 588-0011
Niles *(G-16029)*
▲ Rutland Inc....E....217 245-7810
Jacksonville *(G-12413)*
S & D Products Inc....E....630 372-2325
Bartlett *(G-1370)*
S L Fixtures Inc....G....217 423-9907
Decatur *(G-7937)*
Seamless Gutter Corp....E....630 495-9800
Lombard *(G-13852)*
Shapco Inc....G....847 229-1439
Wheeling *(G-22149)*
Slick Locks LLC....G....815 838-3557
Homer Glen *(G-12088)*
SPEP Acquisition Corp....E....310 608-0693
Bolingbrook *(G-2375)*
Standard Truck Parts Inc....G....815 726-4486
Joliet *(G-12578)*
▲ Stanley Hartco Co....E....847 967-1122
Skokie *(G-20090)*
Stanley Security Solutions Inc....F....877 476-4968
Lombard *(G-13859)*

Stock Gears Inc....F....224 653-9489
Elk Grove Village *(G-9758)*
▲ Strut & Supply Inc....G....847 756-4337
Lake Barrington *(G-12824)*
▲ Stucchi Usa Inc....F....847 956-9720
Romeoville *(G-18871)*
▲ Sweet Manufacturing Corp....E....847 546-5575
Chicago *(G-6648)*
Tables Inc....G....630 365-0741
Elburn *(G-8912)*
Tekni-Plex Inc....E....217 935-8311
Clinton *(G-7289)*
▲ Termax Corporation....C....847 519-1500
Lake Zurich *(G-13137)*
◆ Thermos LLC....E....847 439-7821
Schaumburg *(G-19760)*
◆ Tkk USA Inc....G....847 439-7821
Rolling Meadows *(G-18783)*
Tolerance Manufacturing Inc....F....847 244-8836
Waukegan *(G-21629)*
Top Gallant Inc....F....847 981-5521
Elk Grove Village *(G-9783)*
Treetop Marketing Inc....G....877 249-0479
Batavia *(G-1510)*
U S Tool & Manufacturing Co....E....630 953-1000
Addison *(G-332)*
▲ Unistrut International Corp....C....800 882-5543
Harvey *(G-11679)*
▲ United Steel & Fasteners Inc....E....630 250-0900
Itasca *(G-12370)*
V & N Metal Products Inc....G....773 436-1855
Chicago *(G-6863)*
Value Engineered Products....E....708 867-6777
Rolling Meadows *(G-18787)*
Van Craft Industry of Del Edel....G....708 430-6670
Oak Lawn *(G-16646)*
Venturedyne Ltd....E....708 597-7550
Chicago *(G-6884)*
▲ W J Dennis & Company....F....847 697-4800
Elgin *(G-9225)*
▲ Weiland Metal Products Company....G....773 631-4210
Chicago *(G-6950)*
◆ William Dudek Manufacturing Co....E....773 622-2727
Chicago *(G-6983)*
Wind Point Partners Vi LP....G....312 255-4800
Chicago *(G-6993)*
Wozniak Industries Inc....C....708 458-1220
Bedford Park *(G-1595)*
Zirlin Interiors Inc....E....773 334-5530
Chicago *(G-7069)*
Zsi-Foster Inc....G....800 323-7053
Chicago *(G-7074)*

## 3431 Enameled Iron & Metal Sanitary Ware

Aldo-Shane Corporation....D....714 361-4830
Lanark *(G-13150)*
Elkay Manufacturing Company....B....708 681-1880
Broadview *(G-2575)*
Elkay Manufacturing Company....G....630 574-8484
Broadview *(G-2576)*
Elkay Manufacturing Company....B....815 273-7001
Savanna *(G-19397)*
▲ Elkay Plumbing Products Co....D....630 574-8484
Oak Brook *(G-16507)*
Hajoca Corporation....F....309 663-7524
Bloomington *(G-2176)*
▲ Just Manufacturing Company....C....847 678-5151
Franklin Park *(G-10510)*
Kohler Co....E....630 323-7674
Burr Ridge *(G-2861)*
Kohler Co....E....847 635-8071
Glenview *(G-11156)*
Kohler Co....D....847 734-1777
Huntley *(G-12155)*
▲ Lenova Inc....G....312 733-1098
Hillside *(G-11924)*
Swan Surfaces LLC....C....618 532-5673
Centralia *(G-3435)*
T J M & Associates Inc....G....847 382-1993
Lake Barrington *(G-12825)*

## 3432 Plumbing Fixture Fittings & Trim, Brass

▲ Anderson Copper & Brass Co LLC....E....708 535-9030
Frankfort *(G-10295)*
Anderson Copper & Brass Co LLC....F....815 469-8201
Frankfort *(G-10296)*
▲ Black Swan Manufacturing Co....F....773 227-3700
Chicago *(G-4121)*
Caldwell Plumbing Co....F....630 588-8900
Wheaton *(G-21938)*

Employee Codes: A=Over 500 employees, B=251-500
C=101-250, D=51-100, E=20-50, F=10-19, G=3-9
2017 Harris Illinois
Industrial Directory
1029

34 FABRICATED METAL PRODUCTS, EXCEPT MACHINERY AND TRANSPORTATION EQUIPMENT SIC SECTION

**▲ Cfpg Ltd** C 630 679-1420
Woodridge *(G-22459)*

**▲ Chicago Faucet Company** D 847 803-5000
Des Plaines *(G-8165)*

**Chicago Faucet Federal Cr Un** F 847 803-5000
Des Plaines *(G-8166)*

**▲ Couplings Company Inc** F 847 634-8990
Lincolnshire *(G-13440)*

**Deks North America Inc** G 312 219-2110
Chicago *(G-4574)*

**Elkay Manufacturing Company** B 708 681-1880
Broadview *(G-2575)*

**Fiskars Brands Inc** F 800 635-7668
Peoria *(G-17362)*

**Fiskars Brands Inc** B 309 690-2200
Peoria *(G-17363)*

**G B Holdings Inc** C 773 265-3000
Chicago *(G-4899)*

**◆ Globe Union Group Inc** D 630 679-1420
Woodridge *(G-22487)*

**▲ Guardian Equipment Inc** E 312 447-8100
Chicago *(G-5007)*

**Iodon Inc** G 708 799-4062
Country Club Hills *(G-7409)*

**Isenberg Bath Corporation** G 972 510-5916
Bensenville *(G-1924)*

**Kamco Representatives Inc** G 630 516-0417
Elmhurst *(G-9894)*

**▲ Ki Industries Inc** E 708 449-1990
Berkeley *(G-2046)*

**Kieft Bros Inc** E 630 832-8090
Elmhurst *(G-9898)*

**▲ Kkt Chillers Inc** F 847 734-1600
Elk Grove Village *(G-9575)*

**Kohler Co** D 847 734-1777
Huntley *(G-12155)*

**▲ Lacava LLC** E 773 637-9600
Chicago *(G-5432)*

**Lavell General Handyman Svcs** G 773 691-3101
Chicago *(G-5469)*

**▲ LDR Global Industries LLC** D 773 265-3000
Chicago *(G-5477)*

**Leyden Lawn Sprinklers** E 630 665-5520
Glen Ellyn *(G-10976)*

**▲ Mifab Inc** E 773 341-3030
Chicago *(G-5754)*

**Performance Pro Plumbing Inc** G 630 566-5207
Westmont *(G-21910)*

**Plumbers Supply Co St Louis** G 618 624-5151
O Fallon *(G-16474)*

**▲ PSI Systems North America Inc** G 630 830-9435
Bartlett *(G-1366)*

**Royale Innovation Group Ltd** G 312 339-1406
Itasca *(G-12351)*

**Schulhof Company** F 773 348-1123
Richmond *(G-17971)*

**Sergio Barajas** G 708 238-7614
La Grange *(G-12744)*

**◆ Sloan Valve Company** G 847 671-4300
Franklin Park *(G-10590)*

**Sterline Manufacturing Corp** E 847 244-1234
Gurnee *(G-11509)*

**◆ Suncast Corporation** A 630 879-2050
Batavia *(G-1501)*

**▲ Water Saver Faucet Co** C 312 666-5500
Chicago *(G-6941)*

**▲ White Racker Co Inc** G 847 758-1640
Elk Grove Village *(G-9812)*

## 3433 Heating Eqpt

**Aldrico Inc** E 309 695-2311
Wyoming *(G-22636)*

**All American Wood Register Co** F 815 356-1000
Crystal Lake *(G-7528)*

**All Wood or Metal Radiator Cov** G 773 973-7328
Chicago *(G-3809)*

**American Fuel Economy Inc** G 815 433-3226
Ottawa *(G-16946)*

**▲ BP Solar International Inc** A 301 698-4200
Naperville *(G-15611)*

**Cruise Boiler and Repr Co Inc** F 630 279-7111
Elmhurst *(G-9860)*

**Custom Linear Grille Inc** G 847 520-5511
Wheeling *(G-22033)*

**Dva Mayday Corporation** G 847 848-7555
Village of Lakewood *(G-21290)*

**▲ Easy Heat Inc** E 847 268-6000
Rosemont *(G-19000)*

**◆ Eclipse Inc** D 815 877-3031
Rockford *(G-18356)*

**▲ Eclipse Combustion Inc** C 815 877-3031
Rockford *(G-18357)*

**▲ Empire Comfort Systems Inc** C 618 233-7420
Belleville *(G-1631)*

**Filtran Holdings LLC** G 847 635-6670
Des Plaines *(G-8196)*

**◆ Filtran LLC** C 847 635-6670
Des Plaines *(G-8197)*

**Goose Island Mfg & Supply Corp** G 708 343-4225
Lansing *(G-13164)*

**▼ Grieve Corporation** D 847 546-8225
Round Lake *(G-19059)*

**Guntner US** G 847 781-0900
Schaumburg *(G-19545)*

**Hardy Radiator Repair** F 217 223-8320
Quincy *(G-17834)*

**Industries Publication Inc** E 630 357-5269
Lisle *(G-13602)*

**Ipsen Inc** E 815 239-2385
Pecatonica *(G-17252)*

**Mfi Industries Inc** F 708 841-0727
Riverdale *(G-18021)*

**▲ Midco International Inc** E 773 604-8700
Chicago *(G-5733)*

**Polyair Inter Pack Inc** D 773 995-1818
Chicago *(G-6153)*

**R & D Electronics Inc** G 847 583-9080
Niles *(G-16024)*

**▲ Spirotherm Inc** G 630 307-2662
Glendale Heights *(G-11071)*

**Sunbird Solar LLC** G 847 509-8888
Northbrook *(G-16374)*

**▲ Sws Industries Inc** E 904 482-0091
Woodstock *(G-22616)*

**Tri-State Food Equipment** G 217 228-1550
Quincy *(G-17900)*

## 3441 Fabricated Structural Steel

**A & A Steel Fabricating Co** F 708 389-4499
Posen *(G-17726)*

**A & B Metal Polishing Inc** F 773 847-1077
Chicago *(G-3678)*

**A & S Steel Specialties Inc** E 815 838-8188
Lockport *(G-13700)*

**A Lucas & Sons** E 309 673-8547
Peoria *(G-17297)*

**AAA Galvanizing - Joliet Inc** E 815 284-5001
Dixon *(G-8321)*

**Aak Mechanical Inc** D 217 935-8501
Clinton *(G-7276)*

**Abitzy Inc** G 847 800-8666
Lake In The Hills *(G-12981)*

**Ablaze Welding & Fabricating** G 815 965-0046
Rockford *(G-18248)*

**Accurate Fabricators Inc** G 618 451-1886
Granite City *(G-11258)*

**Accurate Fabricators Svcs Inc** G 618 530-7883
Granite City *(G-11259)*

**Accurate Metal Fabricating LLC** D 773 235-0400
Chicago *(G-3720)*

**Ace Metal Crafts Company** C 847 455-1010
Bensenville *(G-1815)*

**Adams Steel Service Inc** E 815 385-9100
McHenry *(G-14477)*

**Adams Street Iron Inc** F 312 733-3229
Evergreen Park *(G-10109)*

**Addison Steel Inc** G 847 998-9445
Glenview *(G-11096)*

**Adermanns Welding & Mch & Co** G 217 342-3234
Effingham *(G-8822)*

**Advance Iron Works Inc** F 708 798-3540
East Hazel Crest *(G-8663)*

**Advanced Steel Fabrication** G 847 956-6565
Elk Grove Village *(G-9277)*

**Advanced Welding Ltd** F 708 205-4559
Addison *(G-26)*

**▲ Ae2009 Technologies Inc** E 708 331-0025
South Holland *(G-20240)*

**Aetna Engineering Works Inc** E 773 785-0489
Chicago *(G-3778)*

**Affton Fabg & Wldg Co Inc** F 314 781-4100
Sauget *(G-19381)*

**Alert Tubing Fabricators Inc** G 847 253-7237
Schaumburg *(G-19429)*

**Alfredos Iron Works Inc** E 815 748-1177
Cortland *(G-7384)*

**Allen Popovich** G 815 712-7404
Custer Park *(G-7686)*

**▼ Alliance Steel Corporation** E 708 924-1200
Bedford Park *(G-1535)*

**Alloy Specialties Inc** F 815 586-4728
Blackstone *(G-2087)*

**Allquip Co Inc** G 309 944-6153
Geneseo *(G-10797)*

**Alro Steel Corporation** G 708 534-5400
Park Forest *(G-17176)*

**Alton Sheet Metal Corp** F 618 462-0609
Alton *(G-559)*

**Ambassador Steel Corporation** G 815 876-9089
Princeton *(G-17743)*

**Ambassador Steel Corporation** F 815 929-3770
Bourbonnais *(G-2387)*

**American Industrial Werks Inc** F 847 477-2648
Schaumburg *(G-19437)*

**American Piping Group Inc** D 815 772-7470
Morrison *(G-15141)*

**Anamet Inc** G 217 234-8844
Glen Ellyn *(G-10958)*

**Anchor Welding & Fabrication** G 815 937-1640
Aroma Park *(G-878)*

**Andersen Machine & Welding Inc** G 815 232-4664
Freeport *(G-10647)*

**Andscot Co Inc** G 847 455-5800
Franklin Park *(G-10396)*

**Archer General Contg & Fabg** G 708 757-7902
Steger *(G-20568)*

**Area Fabricators** G 217 455-3426
Coatsburg *(G-7300)*

**Arlington Strl Stl Co Inc** E 847 577-2200
Arlington Heights *(G-716)*

**Arnette Pattern Co Inc** E 618 451-7700
Granite City *(G-11268)*

**AS Fabricating Inc** G 618 242-7438
Mount Vernon *(G-15398)*

**▲ Aspen Industries Inc** F 630 238-0611
Bensenville *(G-1836)*

**Atkore International Group Inc** A 708 339-1610
Harvey *(G-11658)*

**Atkore Intl Holdings Inc** G 708 225-2051
Harvey *(G-11659)*

**Auburn Iron Works Inc** F 708 422-7330
Palos Heights *(G-17099)*

**B & B Fabrications LLC** G 217 620-3210
Sullivan *(G-20739)*

**Baron-Blakeslee Sfc Inc** E 847 796-0822
Northbrook *(G-16212)*

**Bartell Grinding and Mch LLC** G 708 408-1700
Mc Cook *(G-14445)*

**Best Machine & Welding Co Inc** E 708 343-4455
Woodridge *(G-22456)*

**▼ Best Manufacturing & Wldg Inc** E 815 562-4107
Rochelle *(G-18079)*

**Bi State Steel Co** G 309 755-0668
East Moline *(G-8671)*

**Biewer Fabricating Inc** G 630 530-8922
Villa Park *(G-21238)*

**Birdsell Machine & Orna Inc** G 217 243-5849
Jacksonville *(G-12379)*

**BJs Welding Services Etc Co** G 773 964-5836
Chicago *(G-4118)*

**BR Machine Inc** F 815 434-0427
Ottawa *(G-16950)*

**Bridge City Mechanical Inc** F 309 944-4873
Geneseo *(G-10799)*

**Bridgeport Steel Sales Inc** F 312 326-4800
Chicago *(G-4167)*

**Btd Manufacturing Inc** E 309 444-1268
Washington *(G-21379)*

**Byus Steel Inc** E 630 879-2200
Batavia *(G-1425)*

**C & S Fabrication Services Inc** G 815 363-8510
Johnsburg *(G-12431)*

**C Keller Manufacturing Inc** E 630 833-5593
Villa Park *(G-21240)*

**▲ C M I Novacast Inc** F 847 699-9020
Des Plaines *(G-8161)*

**Canam Steel Corporation** C 815 224-9588
Peru *(G-17502)*

**Carpenter Contractors Amer Inc** B 815 544-1699
Belvidere *(G-1744)*

**▲ Catapult Global LLC** F 847 364-8149
Elk Grove Village *(G-9360)*

**Cem LLC** D 708 333-3761
Barrington *(G-1276)*

**Central Ill Fbrcation Whse Inc** F 217 367-2323
Urbana *(G-21076)*

**Central Illinois Steel Company** E 217 854-3251
Carlinville *(G-3032)*

**Cervones Welding Service Inc** ..... G ..... 847 985-6865
Schaumburg *(G-19470)*

**Challenger Fabricators Inc** ..... G ..... 815 704-0077
South Beloit *(G-20142)*

**Charter Dura-Bar Inc** ..... C ..... 815 338-7800
Woodstock *(G-22552)*

**Chicago Grinding & Machine Co** ..... E ..... 708 343-4399
Melrose Park *(G-14610)*

**Chicago Metal Fabricators Inc** ..... D ..... 773 523-5755
Chicago *(G-4332)*

**◆ Chicago Metal Rolled Pdts Co** ..... D ..... 773 523-5757
Chicago *(G-4333)*

**Chicagoland Metal Fabricators** ..... G ..... 847 260-5320
Franklin Park *(G-10430)*

**Circle Metal Specialties Inc** ..... E ..... 708 597-1700
Alsip *(G-449)*

**Cisne Iron Works Inc** ..... F ..... 618 673-2188
Cisne *(G-7250)*

**CJ Drilling Inc** ..... E ..... 847 854-3888
Dundee *(G-8560)*

**Clarkwestern Dietrich Building** ..... E ..... 815 561-2360
Rochelle *(G-18083)*

**Cokel Dj Welding Bay & Muffler** ..... G ..... 309 385-4567
Princeville *(G-17763)*

**Comet Fabricating & Welding Co** ..... E ..... 815 229-0468
Rockford *(G-18316)*

**Commercial Fabricators Inc** ..... G ..... 708 594-1199
Bridgeview *(G-2479)*

**Commercial Metals Company** ..... G ..... 815 928-9600
Kankakee *(G-12606)*

**◆ Cooper B-Line Inc** ..... A ..... 618 654-2184
Highland *(G-11780)*

**Corsetti Structural Steel Inc** ..... E ..... 815 726-0186
Joliet *(G-12477)*

**Cortelyou Machine & Welding** ..... G ..... 618 592-3961
Oblong *(G-16730)*

**Covey Machine Inc** ..... F ..... 773 650-1530
Chicago *(G-4484)*

**Creative Steel Fabricators** ..... G ..... 847 803-2090
Des Plaines *(G-8177)*

**Crest Metal Craft Inc** ..... G ..... 773 978-0950
Chicago *(G-4504)*

**Custom Fbrication Coatings Inc** ..... D ..... 618 452-9540
Granite City *(G-11271)*

**Custom Feeder Co of Rockford** ..... E ..... 815 654-2444
Loves Park *(G-13932)*

**Cyclops Welding Co** ..... G ..... 815 223-0685
La Salle *(G-12769)*

**D & M Welding Inc** ..... G ..... 708 233-6080
Bridgeview *(G-2481)*

**D L Austin Steel Supply Corp** ..... G ..... 618 345-7200
Collinsville *(G-7319)*

**D5 Design Met Fabrication LLC** ..... G ..... 773 770-4705
Chicago *(G-4539)*

**Dams Inc** ..... F ..... 708 385-3092
Alsip *(G-454)*

**Dayton Superior Corporation** ..... E ..... 219 476-4106
Kankakee *(G-12608)*

**Decatur Aeration Inc** ..... F ..... 217 422-6828
Decatur *(G-7868)*

**Delta Erectors Inc** ..... F ..... 708 267-9721
Villa Park *(G-21248)*

**▲ Delta Structures Inc** ..... F ..... 630 694-8700
Lombard *(G-13789)*

**Design Metals Fabrication Inc** ..... G ..... 630 752-9060
Carol Stream *(G-3143)*

**▲ Dicke Tool Company** ..... E ..... 630 969-0050
Downers Grove *(G-8429)*

**Dietrich Industries Inc** ..... E ..... 815 207-0110
Joliet *(G-12485)*

**Dill Brothers Inc** ..... F ..... 847 746-8323
Zion *(G-22682)*

**▲ DSI Spaceframes Inc** ..... E ..... 630 607-0045
Addison *(G-99)*

**◆ E B Inc** ..... F ..... 815 758-6646
De Kalb *(G-7817)*

**Ed Stan Fabricating Co** ..... G ..... 708 863-7668
Chicago *(G-4694)*

**▲ Ekstrom Carlson Fabricating Co** ..... G ..... 815 226-1511
Rockford *(G-18360)*

**Emco Metalworks Co** ..... E ..... 708 222-1011
Cicero *(G-7195)*

**▲ Ermak Usa Inc** ..... F ..... 847 640-7765
Des Plaines *(G-8190)*

**Esi Steel & Fabrication** ..... F ..... 618 548-3017
Salem *(G-19331)*

**European Ornamental Iron Works** ..... G ..... 630 705-9300
Addison *(G-113)*

**▲ Ex-Cell Kaiser LLC** ..... E ..... 847 451-0451
Franklin Park *(G-10467)*

**Exo Fabrication Inc** ..... G ..... 630 501-1136
Addison *(G-114)*

**F K Pattern & Foundry Company** ..... G ..... 847 578-5260
North Chicago *(G-16179)*

**F Kreutzer & Co** ..... G ..... 773 826-5767
Chicago *(G-4805)*

**F Vogelmann and Company** ..... F ..... 815 469-2285
Frankfort *(G-10321)*

**Fabco Enterprises Inc** ..... G ..... 708 333-4644
Harvey *(G-11666)*

**Fabmax Inc** ..... F ..... 630 766-0370
Wood Dale *(G-22365)*

**Fabricated Metal Systems Inc** ..... G ..... 815 886-6200
Romeoville *(G-18824)*

**Fabricating & Welding Corp** ..... E ..... 773 928-2050
Chicago *(G-4809)*

**Famaco Corp** ..... E ..... 217 442-4412
Tilton *(G-20881)*

**Fanmar Inc** ..... E ..... 708 563-0505
Elk Grove Village *(G-9475)*

**Fbs Group Inc** ..... F ..... 773 229-8675
Chicago *(G-4821)*

**Fehring Ornamental Iron Works** ..... F ..... 217 483-6727
Chatham *(G-3620)*

**First Stage Fabrication Inc** ..... G ..... 618 282-8320
Red Bud *(G-17941)*

**Fisher & Ludlow Inc** ..... D ..... 217 324-6106
Litchfield *(G-13685)*

**▲ Flex-Weld Inc** ..... D ..... 815 334-3662
Woodstock *(G-22567)*

**Floyd Steel Erectors Inc** ..... F ..... 630 238-8383
Wood Dale *(G-22369)*

**Funk Linko Group Inc** ..... F ..... 708 757-7421
Monee *(G-14995)*

**▼ G & F Manufacturing Co Inc** ..... E ..... 708 424-4170
Oak Lawn *(G-16621)*

**G & M Fabricating Inc** ..... G ..... 815 282-1744
Roscoe *(G-18898)*

**Gallon Industries Inc** ..... E ..... 630 628-1020
Addison *(G-127)*

**Garbe Iron Works Inc** ..... E ..... 630 897-5100
Aurora *(G-1160)*

**Gcs Steel Installers Inc** ..... G ..... 630 487-6736
Montgomery *(G-15044)*

**Gemini Steel Inc** ..... G ..... 815 472-4462
Momence *(G-14981)*

**Gentner Fabrication Inc** ..... F ..... 773 523-2505
Chicago *(G-4937)*

**Gerdau Ameristeel US Inc** ..... E ..... 815 547-0400
Belvidere *(G-1757)*

**Gma Inc** ..... G ..... 630 595-1255
Bensenville *(G-1910)*

**Gooder-Henrichsen Company Inc** ..... D ..... 708 757-5030
Chicago Heights *(G-7100)*

**Greg Lambert Construction** ..... E ..... 815 468-7361
Bourbonnais *(G-2397)*

**Gremp Steel Co** ..... E ..... 708 389-7393
Posen *(G-17731)*

**Grimm Metal Fabricators Inc** ..... E ..... 630 792-1710
Lombard *(G-13807)*

**Grover Welding Company** ..... G ..... 847 966-3119
Skokie *(G-20007)*

**Gsi Group LLC** ..... C ..... 217 463-1612
Paris *(G-17148)*

**Harmony Metal Fabrication Inc** ..... E ..... 847 426-8900
Gilberts *(G-10920)*

**Hercules Iron Works Inc** ..... E ..... 312 226-2405
Chicago *(G-5078)*

**Hi-Tech Towers Inc** ..... E ..... 217 784-5212
Gibson City *(G-10902)*

**High Standard Fabricating Inc** ..... E ..... 815 965-6517
Rockford *(G-18419)*

**Hofmeister Wldg & Fabrication** ..... F ..... 217 833-2451
Griggsville *(G-11412)*

**◆ Holden Industries Inc** ..... F ..... 847 940-1500
Deerfield *(G-8013)*

**Huntley & Associates Inc** ..... G ..... 224 381-8500
Lake Zurich *(G-13085)*

**Hyspan Precision Products Inc** ..... E ..... 773 277-0700
South Holland *(G-20279)*

**Ideal Fabricators Inc** ..... F ..... 217 999-7017
Mount Olive *(G-15304)*

**▲ Igm Solutions Inc** ..... E ..... 847 918-1790
Libertyville *(G-13336)*

**Illinois Steel Service Inc** ..... D ..... 312 926-7440
Chicago *(G-5158)*

**Industrial Mint Wldg Machining** ..... D ..... 773 376-6526
Chicago *(G-5178)*

**Industrial Steel Cnstr Inc** ..... G ..... 630 232-7473
Geneva *(G-10835)*

**Industrial Steel Cnstr Inc** ..... D ..... 219 885-7600
Hodgkins *(G-11976)*

**Innotech Manufacturing LLC** ..... E ..... 618 244-6261
Mount Vernon *(G-15415)*

**▲ Integrated Mfg Tech LLC** ..... E ..... 618 282-8306
Red Bud *(G-17943)*

**Ireco LLC** ..... F ..... 630 741-0155
Elmhurst *(G-9888)*

**ITW Blding Cmponents Group Inc** ..... E ..... 217 324-0303
Litchfield *(G-13689)*

**J & G Fabricating Inc** ..... G ..... 708 385-9147
Blue Island *(G-2257)*

**J B Metal Works Inc** ..... G ..... 847 824-4253
Des Plaines *(G-8215)*

**J H Botts LLC** ..... E ..... 815 726-5885
Joliet *(G-12519)*

**Jalor Company** ..... G ..... 847 202-1172
Elgin *(G-9082)*

**▲ James Walker Mfg Co** ..... E ..... 708 754-4020
Glenwood *(G-11217)*

**Jameson Steel Fabrication Inc** ..... G ..... 217 354-2205
Oakwood *(G-16725)*

**Jarvis Welding Co** ..... G ..... 309 647-0033
Canton *(G-2988)*

**Jay RS Steel & Welding Inc** ..... G ..... 847 949-9353
Mundelein *(G-15514)*

**JB & S Machining** ..... G ..... 815 258-4007
Bourbonnais *(G-2401)*

**Jet Industries Inc** ..... E ..... 773 586-8900
Chicago *(G-5297)*

**K & K Iron Works LLC** ..... D ..... 708 924-0000
Mc Cook *(G-14449)*

**K Three Welding Service Inc** ..... G ..... 708 563-2911
Chicago *(G-5344)*

**K&R Enterprises I Inc** ..... D ..... 847 502-3371
Lake Barrington *(G-12815)*

**K-Met Industries Inc** ..... F ..... 708 534-3300
Monee *(G-14998)*

**Kemper Industries** ..... G ..... 217 826-5712
Marshall *(G-14324)*

**Kim Gough** ..... G ..... 309 734-3511
Monmouth *(G-15017)*

**King Metal Co** ..... G ..... 708 388-3845
Alsip *(G-479)*

**Kingery Steel Fabricators Inc** ..... E ..... 708 474-6665
Lansing *(G-13168)*

**Kmk Metal Fabricators Inc** ..... E ..... 618 224-2000
Trenton *(G-20993)*

**Knoll Steel Inc** ..... F ..... 815 675-9400
Spring Grove *(G-20342)*

**Kroh-Wagner Inc** ..... E ..... 773 252-2031
Chicago *(G-5412)*

**Ksem Inc** ..... G ..... 618 656-5388
Edwardsville *(G-8805)*

**Kso Metalfab Inc** ..... E ..... 630 372-1200
Streamwood *(G-20663)*

**L & M Steel Services Inc** ..... F ..... 309 755-3713
East Moline *(G-8684)*

**Laser Plus Technologies LLC** ..... G ..... 847 787-9017
Elk Grove Village *(G-9585)*

**Laystrom Manufacturing Co** ..... D ..... 773 342-4800
Chicago *(G-5474)*

**Leroys Welding & Fabg Inc** ..... F ..... 847 215-6151
Wheeling *(G-22092)*

**Lesker Company Inc** ..... E ..... 708 343-2277
Bensenville *(G-1940)*

**▼ Liberty Machinery Company** ..... F ..... 847 276-2761
Lincolnshire *(G-13463)*

**Lichtnwald - Johnston Ir Works** ..... E ..... 847 966-1100
Morton Grove *(G-15212)*

**Lickenbrock & Sons Inc** ..... G ..... 618 632-4977
O Fallon *(G-16470)*

**Linear Kinetics Inc** ..... G ..... 630 365-0075
Maple Park *(G-14201)*

**▲ Littell International Inc** ..... E ..... 630 622-4950
Schaumburg *(G-19621)*

**Lizotte Sheet Metal Inc** ..... G ..... 618 656-3066
Edwardsville *(G-8806)*

**LPI Worldwide Inc** ..... G ..... 773 826-8600
Chicago *(G-5550)*

**Mace Iron Works Inc** ..... E ..... 708 479-2456
Frankfort *(G-10341)*

**Marcmetals** ..... G ..... 847 905-0018
Evanston *(G-10069)*

**Marco Lighting Components Inc** ..... F ..... 312 829-6900
Chicago *(G-5613)*

**Marqutte Stl Sup Fbrcation Inc** ..... F ..... 815 433-0178
Ottawa *(G-16968)*

**▲ Matcor Mtal Fbrication Ill Inc** ..... E ..... 309 263-1707
Morton *(G-15163)*

SIC

Employee Codes: A=Over 500 employees, B=251-500
C=101-250, D=51-100, E=20-50, F=10-19, G=3-9

2017 Harris Illinois
Industrial Directory

1031

**Max Fire Training Inc** F 618 210-2079<br>Godfrey *(G-11228)*

**Mc Kinney Steel & Sales Inc** E 847 746-3344<br>Zion *(G-22691)*

**McLaughlin Body Co** C 309 736-6105<br>East Moline *(G-8687)*

▲ **McLaughlin Body Co** D 309 762-7755<br>Moline *(G-14955)*

▲ **Mead Products LLC** G 847 541-9500<br>Lake Zurich *(G-13100)*

**Mechanical Indus Stl Svcs Inc** E 815 521-1725<br>Channahon *(G-3580)*

**Mellish & Murray Co** F 312 733-3513<br>Chicago *(G-5683)*

**Meno Stone Co Inc** E 630 257-9220<br>Lemont *(G-13241)*

**Metal Tech Inc** E 630 529-7400<br>Roselle *(G-18957)*

**Metals & Metals LLC** G 630 866-4200<br>Bolingbrook *(G-2341)*

**Metaltek Fabricating Inc** F 708 534-9102<br>University Park *(G-21056)*

▲ **Metamora Industries LLC** E 309 367-2368<br>Metamora *(G-14745)*

▲ **Metraflex Company** D 312 738-3800<br>Chicago *(G-5706)*

**Michelmann Steel Cnstr Co** E 217 222-0555<br>Quincy *(G-17857)*

**Midwest Metals Inc** G 618 295-3444<br>Marissa *(G-14296)*

**Mj Snyder Ironworks Inc** G 217 826-6440<br>Marshall *(G-14326)*

**Mobile Mini Inc** E 708 297-2004<br>Calumet Park *(G-2963)*

**Mold Shields Inc** G 708 983-5931<br>Villa Park *(G-21271)*

**Moline Welding Inc** F 309 756-0643<br>Milan *(G-14795)*

**Montefusco Heating & Shtmtl Co** G 309 691-7400<br>Peoria *(G-17412)*

**Morey Industries Inc** C 708 343-3220<br>Broadview *(G-2598)*

**Morris Construction Inc** E 618 544-8504<br>Robinson *(G-18067)*

**Mrt Sureway Inc** D 847 801-3010<br>Franklin Park *(G-10537)*

**Mutual Svcs Highland Pk Inc** F 847 432-3815<br>Highland Park *(G-11858)*

▲ **National Cycle Inc** C 708 343-0400<br>Maywood *(G-14430)*

**National Machine Repair Inc** F 708 672-7711<br>Crete *(G-7517)*

◆ **National Metal Fabricators LLC** E 847 439-5321<br>Elk Grove Village *(G-9647)*

**Neiweem Industries Inc** G 847 487-1239<br>Oakwood Hills *(G-16727)*

**New Metal Fabrication Corp** E 618 532-9000<br>Centralia *(G-3424)*

**Newman Welding & Machine Shop** G 618 435-5591<br>Benton *(G-2037)*

**Nicks Metal Fabg & Sons** F 708 485-1170<br>Brookfield *(G-2639)*

**North Chicago Iron Works Inc** E 847 689-2000<br>North Chicago *(G-16185)*

◆ **Northwestern Corporation** E 815 942-1300<br>Morris *(G-15124)*

**Nowfab** G 815 675-2916<br>Spring Grove *(G-20353)*

**Nu Mill Inc** G 630 458-8950<br>Addison *(G-231)*

**OBrien Architectural Mtls Inc** F 773 868-1065<br>Chicago *(G-5964)*

**Okaw Truss Inc** B 217 543-3371<br>Arthur *(G-915)*

**Old Style Iron Works Inc** G 773 265-5787<br>Chicago *(G-5980)*

**Olympic Steel Inc** E 847 584-4000<br>Schaumburg *(G-19675)*

▲ **Onkens Incorporated** F 309 562-7477<br>Easton *(G-8778)*

**Oostman Fabricating & Wldg Inc** F 630 241-1315<br>Westmont *(G-21909)*

**Ornamental Metalworks Inc** G 217 424-2326<br>Decatur *(G-7923)*

▲ **Orsolinis Welding & Fabg** F 773 722-9855<br>Chicago *(G-6016)*

**Osbornes Mch Weld Fabrication** G 217 795-4716<br>Argenta *(G-691)*

**Owens Welding & Fabricating** F 773 265-9900<br>Chicago *(G-6032)*

**P R Manufacturing Co** G 309 596-2986<br>Viola *(G-21293)*

**Paco Corporation** F 708 430-2424<br>Bridgeview *(G-2517)*

**Palatine Welding Company** E 847 358-1075<br>Rolling Meadows *(G-18757)*

**Parkway Metal Products Inc** D 847 789-4000<br>Des Plaines *(G-8251)*

**Patrick Holdings Inc** F 815 874-5300<br>Rockford *(G-18531)*

**Paul Wever Construction Eqp Co** F 309 965-2005<br>Goodfield *(G-11248)*

**Performance Industries Inc** E 972 393-6881<br>Carpentersville *(G-3294)*

**Phoenix Fabrication & Sup Inc** G 708 754-5901<br>S Chicago Hts *(G-19110)*

**Phoenix Welding Co Inc** F 630 616-1700<br>Franklin Park *(G-10549)*

**Pittsfield Mch Tl & Wldg Co** G 217 656-4000<br>Payson *(G-17246)*

**Pools Welding Inc** G 309 787-2083<br>Milan *(G-14798)*

**Prairie State Industries Inc** F 847 428-3641<br>Carpentersville *(G-3297)*

**Pro-Fab Metals Inc** G 618 283-2986<br>Vandalia *(G-21121)*

**Pro-Tech Metal Specialties Inc** E 630 279-7094<br>Elmhurst *(G-9923)*

**Pro-Tran Inc** G 217 348-9353<br>Charleston *(G-3608)*

**Professional Metal Works LLC** F 618 539-2214<br>Freeburg *(G-10639)*

**R & B Metal Products Inc** E 815 338-1890<br>Woodstock *(G-22603)*

**R C Industrial Inc** G 309 756-3724<br>Milan *(G-14801)*

**R W Bradley Supply Company** G 217 528-8438<br>Springfield *(G-20510)*

**Rail Exchange Inc** E 708 757-3317<br>Chicago Heights *(G-7119)*

**Reber Welding Service** G 217 774-3441<br>Shelbyville *(G-19914)*

**Redi-Weld & Mfg Co Inc** G 815 455-4460<br>Lake In The Hills *(G-13004)*

▲ **Ri-Del Mfg Inc** D 312 829-8720<br>Chicago *(G-6349)*

**Ricar Industries Inc** G 847 914-9083<br>Northbrook *(G-16355)*

**Rockford Ornamental Iron Inc** F 815 633-1162<br>Rockford *(G-18581)*

**Rohn Products LLC** D 309 697-4400<br>Peoria *(G-17446)*

**Rohn Products LLC** E 309 566-3000<br>Peoria *(G-17447)*

▼ **Romero Steel Company Inc** E 708 216-0001<br>Melrose Park *(G-14688)*

**Rrb Fabrication Inc** F 815 977-5603<br>Loves Park *(G-13989)*

**S & S Welding & Fabrication** G 847 742-7344<br>Elgin *(G-9170)*

**Selvaggio Orna & Strl Stl Inc** E 217 528-4077<br>Springfield *(G-20521)*

**Shamrock Manufacturing Co Inc** G 708 331-7776<br>South Holland *(G-20304)*

**Sheas Iron Works Inc** E 847 356-2922<br>Lake Villa *(G-13026)*

**Sheet Metal Supply Ltd** G 847 478-8500<br>Mundelein *(G-15557)*

**Sheets & Cylinder Welding Inc** G 800 442-2200<br>Chicago *(G-6494)*

**Shew Brothers Inc** G 618 997-4414<br>Marion *(G-14286)*

**Silver Machine Shop Inc** G 217 359-5717<br>Champaign *(G-3540)*

**Simion Fabrication Inc** G 618 724-7331<br>Christopher *(G-7174)*

**Sivco Welding Company** G 309 944-5171<br>Geneseo *(G-10804)*

▼ **Skyjack Equipment Inc** E 630 797-3299<br>Saint Charles *(G-19263)*

**Smf Inc** C 309 432-2586<br>Minonk *(G-14834)*

**Smith Brothers Fabricating** G 618 498-5612<br>Jerseyville *(G-12426)*

**South Subn Wldg & Fabg Co Inc** G 708 385-7160<br>Posen *(G-17736)*

**Spectracrafts Ltd** G 847 824-4117<br>Lombard *(G-13856)*

**Spg International LLC** E 815 233-0022<br>Freeport *(G-10690)*

**Spider Company Inc** D 815 961-8200<br>Rockford *(G-18628)*

**Square 1 Precision Ltg Inc** G 708 343-1500<br>Melrose Park *(G-14695)*

**Stairs & Rales Inc** G 708 216-0078<br>Melrose Park *(G-14696)*

**Standard Sheet Metal Works Inc** E 309 633-2300<br>Peoria *(G-17463)*

**Steel Construction Svcs Inc** G 815 678-7509<br>Richmond *(G-17972)*

**Steel Management Inc** G 630 397-5083<br>Geneva *(G-10869)*

**Steel Span Inc** F 815 943-9071<br>Harvard *(G-11648)*

**Steelfab Inc** E 815 935-6540<br>Kankakee *(G-12654)*

**Steelwerks of Chicago LLC** G 312 792-9593<br>Chicago *(G-6582)*

**Stevenson Fabrication Svcs Inc** G 815 468-7941<br>Manteno *(G-14195)*

**Strat-O-Span Buildings Inc** G 618 526-4566<br>Breese *(G-2448)*

**Structural Design Corp** G 847 816-3816<br>Libertyville *(G-13385)*

**Sturdee Metal Products Inc** G 773 523-3074<br>New Lenox *(G-15913)*

**Sturdi Iron Inc** G 815 464-1173<br>Frankfort *(G-10365)*

**Summit Metal Products Inc** G 630 879-7008<br>Batavia *(G-1500)*

**Superior Fabrication & Machine** G 217 762-5512<br>Monticello *(G-15086)*

**Superior Joining Tech Inc** E 815 282-7581<br>Machesney Park *(G-14109)*

**Syr-Tech Perforating Co** E 630 942-7300<br>Glendale Heights *(G-11081)*

▲ **T & L Mfg Corporation** E 630 898-7100<br>Aurora *(G-1220)*

**Taylor Off Road Racing** G 815 544-4500<br>Belvidere *(G-1788)*

**Testa Steel Constructors Inc** F 815 729-4777<br>Channahon *(G-3587)*

**Tgm Fabricating Inc** G 708 533-0857<br>Chicago Heights *(G-7131)*

**Thybar Corporation** E 630 543-5300<br>Addison *(G-314)*

**Tinsley Steel Inc** G 618 656-5231<br>Edwardsville *(G-8817)*

**Titan Industries Inc** G 309 440-1010<br>Deer Creek *(G-7966)*

**Titan Steel Corporation** E 815 726-4900<br>New Lenox *(G-15920)*

**Tmz Metal Fabricating Inc** G 815 230-3071<br>Plainfield *(G-17658)*

▲ **Tni Packaging Inc** G 630 293-3030<br>West Chicago *(G-21781)*

**Tonys Welding Service Inc** G 618 532-9353<br>Centralia *(G-3436)*

**Total Engineered Products Inc** G 630 543-9006<br>Addison *(G-319)*

**Tri-Cunty Wldg Fabrication LLC** E 217 543-3304<br>Arthur *(G-923)*

**Trifab Inc** G 847 838-2083<br>Antioch *(G-660)*

**Trinity Structural Towers Inc** F 217 935-7900<br>Clinton *(G-7290)*

**Triton Industries Inc** C 773 384-3700<br>Chicago *(G-6779)*

**Ultra Stamping & Assembly Inc** E 815 874-9888<br>Rockford *(G-18660)*

▲ **Unistrut International Corp** C 800 882-5543<br>Harvey *(G-11679)*

**Unistrut International Corp** D 630 773-3460<br>Addison *(G-334)*

**United Conveyor Supply Company** E 708 344-8050<br>Melrose Park *(G-14703)*

**United Industries Illinois Ltd** G 847 526-9485<br>Wauconda *(G-21511)*

**US Fabg & Mine Svcs Inc** G 618 983-7850<br>Johnston City *(G-12448)*

**V & N Metal Products Inc** G 773 436-1855<br>Chicago *(G-6863)*

**V A Robinson Ltd** G 773 205-4364<br>Chicago *(G-6866)*

**Valmont Industries Inc** D 773 625-0354<br>Franklin Park *(G-10619)*

**Van Pelt Corporation** E 313 365-3600<br>East Moline *(G-8697)*

**Vent Products Co Inc** E 773 521-1900<br>Chicago *(G-6881)*

**Veritas Steel LLC** ........ C ....... 630 423-8708
Lisle *(G-13678)*

▲ **Voges Inc** ........ D ....... 618 233-2760
Belleville *(G-1688)*

**Walnut Custom Homes Inc** ........ E ....... 815 379-2151
Walnut *(G-21333)*

**Walt Ltd** ........ E ....... 312 337-2756
Chicago *(G-6936)*

**Walters Metal Fabrication Inc** ........ D ....... 618 931-5551
Granite City *(G-11311)*

**Waukegan Steel LLC** ........ E ....... 847 662-2810
Waukegan *(G-21639)*

**WEb Production & Fabg Inc** ........ F ....... 312 733-6800
Chicago *(G-6948)*

**Weld-Rite Service Inc** ........ E ....... 708 458-6000
Bedford Park *(G-1592)*

**Westmont Metal Mfg LLC** ........ F ....... 708 343-0214
Broadview *(G-2620)*

**Wherry Machine & Welding Inc** ........ G ....... 309 828-5423
Bloomington *(G-2235)*

◆ **Whiting Corporation** ........ C ....... 708 587-2000
Monee *(G-15007)*

**Willow Farm Products Inc** ........ G ....... 630 430-7491
Lemont *(G-13270)*

**Wilmouth Machine Works Inc** ........ G ....... 618 372-3189
Brighton *(G-2546)*

**Wsw Industrial Maintenance** ........ F ....... 773 721-0675
Chicago *(G-7041)*

### *3442 Metal Doors, Sash, Frames, Molding & Trim*

**555 International Inc** ........ E ....... 773 847-1400
Chicago *(G-3670)*

**A-Ok Inc** ........ E ....... 815 943-7431
Harvard *(G-11616)*

**Adams Street Iron Inc** ........ F ....... 312 733-3229
Evergreen Park *(G-10109)*

▲ **Advantage Manufacturing Inc** ........ F ....... 773 626-2200
Chicago *(G-3774)*

**All Style Awning Corporation** ........ G ....... 708 343-2323
Melrose Park *(G-14587)*

**Alliance Door and Hardware LLC** ........ G ....... 630 451-7070
Bridgeview *(G-2461)*

**Allied Garage Door Inc** ........ E ....... 630 279-0795
Addison *(G-29)*

**Allmetal Inc** ........ E ....... 630 766-8500
Bensenville *(G-1825)*

**Allmetal Inc** ........ F ....... 630 766-1407
Bensenville *(G-1826)*

**Allmetal Inc** ........ E ....... 630 350-2524
Wood Dale *(G-22335)*

▲ **Aluminite of Paris** ........ G ....... 217 463-2233
Paris *(G-17140)*

**Anchor Welding & Fabrication** ........ G ....... 815 937-1640
Aroma Park *(G-878)*

**Assa Abloy Entrance Systems US** ........ F ....... 847 228-5600
Elk Grove Village *(G-9316)*

**Barneys Aluminum Specialties** ........ G ....... 815 723-5341
Joliet *(G-12462)*

**Boom Company Inc** ........ G ....... 847 459-6199
Wheeling *(G-22018)*

**Builders Chicago Corporation** ........ D ....... 224 654-2122
Rosemont *(G-18991)*

**C B M Plastics Inc** ........ F ....... 217 543-3870
Arthur *(G-883)*

◆ **C H I Overhead Doors Inc** ........ B ....... 217 543-2135
Arthur *(G-884)*

**Carroll Tool & Manufacturing** ........ G ....... 630 766-3363
Bensenville *(G-1852)*

▲ **Center North America Inc** ........ E ....... 630 957-1000
Aurora *(G-982)*

**Charles Sheridan and Sons** ........ G ....... 847 903-7209
Evanston *(G-10020)*

◆ **CHi Doors Holdings Inc** ........ G ....... 217 543-2135
Arthur *(G-887)*

**Chicago Iron Works Corporation** ........ F ....... 312 829-1062
Chicago *(G-4324)*

**Chicagone Developers Inc** ........ G ....... 773 783-2105
Chicago *(G-4364)*

**City Screen Inc** ........ G ....... 773 588-5642
Chicago *(G-4388)*

**Climate Sltion Wndows Dors Inc** ........ E ....... 847 233-9800
Franklin Park *(G-10438)*

**Continental Window South Inc** ........ F ....... 773 767-1300
Chicago *(G-4462)*

**Custom Aluminum Products Inc** ........ D ....... 847 717-5000
Genoa *(G-10877)*

▲ **Custom Aluminum Products Inc** ........ B ....... 847 717-5000
South Elgin *(G-20191)*

**Defender Steel Door & Window** ........ E ....... 708 780-7320
Cicero *(G-7188)*

▲ **Del Great Frame Up Systems Inc** ........ F ....... 847 808-1955
Franklin Park *(G-10456)*

**Del Storm Products Inc** ........ F ....... 217 446-3377
Danville *(G-7715)*

**Dorbin Metal Strip Mfg Co Inc** ........ F ....... 708 656-2333
Cicero *(G-7191)*

**Dorma Usa Inc** ........ D ....... 847 295-2700
Lake Bluff *(G-12840)*

▲ **Dynaco Usa Inc** ........ E ....... 847 562-4910
Mundelein *(G-15497)*

**Efco Corporation** ........ E ....... 630 378-4720
Bolingbrook *(G-2303)*

**Erect-A-Tube Inc** ........ E ....... 815 943-4091
Harvard *(G-11632)*

**Eric Harr** ........ E ....... 618 538-7889
East Carondelet *(G-8613)*

**Fix It Fast Ltd** ........ F ....... 708 401-8320
Midlothian *(G-14766)*

**G P Concrete & Iron Works** ........ G ....... 815 842-2270
Pontiac *(G-17700)*

**Group Industries Inc** ........ E ....... 708 877-6200
Thornton *(G-20871)*

**Harmon Inc** ........ D ....... 312 726-5050
Chicago *(G-5046)*

▲ **Hormann LLC** ........ C ....... 877 654-6762
Montgomery *(G-15047)*

**Hormann LLC** ........ G ....... 630 859-3000
Montgomery *(G-15048)*

**Huntley & Associates Inc** ........ G ....... 224 381-8500
Lake Zurich *(G-13085)*

**Imageworks Manufacturing Inc** ........ E ....... 708 503-1122
Park Forest *(G-17172)*

**Insulators Supply Inc** ........ G ....... 847 394-2836
Prospect Heights *(G-17780)*

**Kawneer Company Inc** ........ D ....... 815 224-2708
Peru *(G-17515)*

**Kramer Window Co** ........ G ....... 708 343-4780
Maywood *(G-14427)*

**Kroh-Wagner Inc** ........ E ....... 773 252-2031
Chicago *(G-5412)*

**La Force Inc** ........ G ....... 630 325-1950
Willowbrook *(G-22218)*

**La Force Inc** ........ E ....... 847 415-5107
Vernon Hills *(G-21179)*

**Lang Exterior Inc** ........ D ....... 773 737-4500
Chicago *(G-5458)*

**Logan Square Aluminum Sup Inc** ........ D ....... 847 985-1700
Schaumburg *(G-19622)*

**Logan Square Aluminum Sup Inc** ........ F ....... 847 676-4767
Lincolnwood *(G-13523)*

**Logan Square Aluminum Sup Inc** ........ E ....... 773 846-8300
Chicago *(G-5531)*

**Logan Square Aluminum Sup Inc** ........ C ....... 773 278-3600
Chicago *(G-5532)*

▲ **Marathon Manufacturing Inc** ........ E ....... 630 543-6262
Addison *(G-191)*

◆ **Mechanics Planing Mill Inc** ........ E ....... 618 288-3000
Glen Carbon *(G-10954)*

**Metal Products Sales Corp** ........ G ....... 708 301-6844
Lockport *(G-13732)*

**Michelmann Steel Cnstr Co** ........ E ....... 217 222-0555
Quincy *(G-17857)*

▲ **Middletons Mouldings Inc** ........ D ....... 517 278-6610
Schaumburg *(G-19646)*

**Midway Industries Inc** ........ C ....... 708 594-2600
Chicago *(G-5740)*

**Midwest Detention Systems Inc** ........ G ....... 815 521-4580
Minooka *(G-14843)*

**Midwest Screens LLC** ........ G ....... 847 557-5015
Antioch *(G-646)*

**Mold Seekers** ........ G ....... 847 650-8025
Grayslake *(G-11355)*

**Moldtronics Inc** ........ E ....... 630 968-7000
Downers Grove *(G-8488)*

**Mueller Door Company** ........ E ....... 815 385-8550
Wauconda *(G-21487)*

**Neisewander Enterprises Inc** ........ A ....... 815 288-1431
Dixon *(G-8337)*

**Nelson Sash Systems Inc** ........ G ....... 708 385-5815
Alsip *(G-498)*

**Overhead Door Corporation** ........ G ....... 630 775-9118
Itasca *(G-12338)*

**Overhead Door Solutions Inc** ........ G ....... 847 359-3667
Palatine *(G-17062)*

**Pegas Window Inc** ........ G ....... 773 394-6466
Chicago *(G-6097)*

**Pittco Architectural Mtls Inc** ........ G ....... 800 992-7488
Elk Grove Village *(G-9682)*

**Power-Sonic Corporation** ........ G ....... 309 752-7750
East Moline *(G-8690)*

**Qh Inc** ........ E ....... 708 534-7801
University Park *(G-21060)*

◆ **Qualitas Manufacturing Inc** ........ D ....... 630 529-7111
Itasca *(G-12346)*

**Quanex Screens LLC** ........ G ....... 217 463-2233
Paris *(G-17160)*

◆ **Raynor Mfg Co** ........ A ....... 815 288-1431
Dixon *(G-8341)*

**Raynor Mfg Co** ........ D ....... 815 288-1431
Dixon *(G-8342)*

▲ **River City Millwork Inc** ........ D ....... 800 892-9297
Rockford *(G-18556)*

**Ryans Glass & Metal Inc** ........ G ....... 708 430-7790
Bridgeview *(G-2526)*

**S R Door Inc** ........ E ....... 815 227-1148
Rockford *(G-18603)*

**Sheraton Road Lumber** ........ F ....... 309 691-0858
Peoria *(G-17455)*

**Shoreline Glass Co Inc** ........ E ....... 312 829-9500
Hillside *(G-11933)*

**Silver Line Building Pdts LLC** ........ B ....... 708 474-9100
Lansing *(G-13184)*

▼ **Steel-Guard Safety Corp** ........ G ....... 708 589-4588
South Holland *(G-20306)*

**Steele & Loeber Lumber** ........ G ....... 708 544-8383
Bellwood *(G-1723)*

**Summit Window Co Inc** ........ G ....... 708 594-3200
Summit Argo *(G-20767)*

**Supreme Frame & Moulding Co** ........ F ....... 312 930-9056
Chicago *(G-6638)*

**Supreme Hinge Inc** ........ G ....... 708 534-7801
University Park *(G-21063)*

**Temp-Tech Industries Inc** ........ E ....... 773 586-2800
Chicago *(G-6694)*

**Tempco Products Co** ........ D ....... 618 544-3175
Robinson *(G-18074)*

**Thermal Industries Inc** ........ E ....... 800 237-0560
Wood Dale *(G-22430)*

**Tri State Aluminum Products** ........ F ....... 815 877-6081
Loves Park *(G-14003)*

**Tru-Guard Manufacturing Co** ........ G ....... 773 568-5264
Chicago *(G-6784)*

**Vent Products Co Inc** ........ E ....... 773 521-1900
Chicago *(G-6881)*

**Wall-Fill Company -** ........ G ....... 630 668-3400
Wheaton *(G-21988)*

▲ **Waukegan Architectural Inc** ........ G ....... 847 746-9077
Zion *(G-22700)*

**Wunderlich Doors Inc** ........ E ....... 815 727-6430
Joliet *(G-12590)*

**YKK AP America Inc** ........ F ....... 630 582-9602
Roselle *(G-18988)*

### *3443 Fabricated Plate Work*

**3d Flight Simulation Co** ........ G ....... 708 560-0701
Oak Forest *(G-16571)*

**A & A Steel Fabricating Co** ........ F ....... 708 389-4499
Posen *(G-17726)*

**Abbey Metal Services Inc** ........ F ....... 773 568-0330
Chicago *(G-3704)*

**Ablaze Welding & Fabricating** ........ G ....... 815 965-0046
Rockford *(G-18248)*

**Accurate Fabricators Svcs Inc** ........ G ....... 618 530-7883
Granite City *(G-11259)*

▲ **Ae2009 Technologies Inc** ........ E ....... 708 331-0025
South Holland *(G-20240)*

**Alfa Laval Inc** ........ C ....... 630 354-6090
Wood Dale *(G-22334)*

**Allquip Co Inc** ........ G ....... 309 944-6153
Geneseo *(G-10797)*

**Alum-I-Tank Inc** ........ D ....... 815 943-6649
Harvard *(G-11619)*

**Amag Manufacturing Inc** ........ G ....... 773 667-5184
Chicago *(G-3843)*

**Ameralloy Steel Corporation** ........ E ....... 847 967-0600
Morton Grove *(G-15188)*

**American Chute Systems Inc** ........ G ....... 815 723-7632
Joliet *(G-12452)*

**American Rack Company** ........ E ....... 773 763-7309
Chicago *(G-3870)*

**Ameropan Oil Corp** ........ F ....... 773 847-4400
Chicago *(G-3887)*

**Amex Nooter LLC** ........ G ....... 708 429-8300
Tinley Park *(G-20892)*

◆ **Amsted Industries Incorporated** ........ B ....... 312 645-1700
Chicago *(G-3896)*

**Amsted Industries Incorporated** ........ F ....... 312 645-1700
Chicago *(G-3897)*

SIC

Employee Codes: A=Over 500 employees, B=251-500
C=101-250, D=51-100, E=20-50, F=10-19, G=3-9

**Anchor Welding & Fabrication** .... G .... 815 937-1640
Aroma Park *(G-878)*
**Anderson Awning & Shutter** .... G .... 815 654-1155
Machesney Park *(G-14056)*
**Arthur Custom Tank LLC** .... G .... 217 543-4022
Arthur *(G-880)*
**AS Fabricating Inc** .... G .... 618 242-7438
Mount Vernon *(G-15398)*
**Associated Rack Corporation** .... F .... 616 554-6004
Chicago *(G-3970)*
**Atlas Boiler & Welding Company** .... G .... 815 963-3360
Elgin *(G-8960)*
▲ **Atlas Tool & Die Works Inc** .... D .... 708 442-1661
Lyons *(G-14031)*
**Barker Metal Craft Inc** .... G .... 773 588-9300
Chicago *(G-4043)*
**Beaver Creek Enterprises Inc** .... F .... 815 723-9455
Joliet *(G-12463)*
**Befco Manufacturing Co Inc** .... F .... 708 424-4170
Oak Lawn *(G-16606)*
**Bennu Group Inc** .... F .... 708 331-0025
South Holland *(G-20250)*
**Blommer Machinery Company** .... G .... 312 226-7700
Chicago *(G-4124)*
**BR Concepts International Inc** .... G .... 847 674-9481
Skokie *(G-19968)*
**BR Machine Inc** .... F .... 815 434-0427
Ottawa *(G-16950)*
**Brenner Tank Services LLC** .... G .... 773 468-6390
Chicago *(G-4161)*
**Bulk Lift International LLC** .... G .... 847 428-6059
Carpentersville *(G-3277)*
▲ **Burns Machine Company** .... E .... 815 434-1660
Ottawa *(G-16953)*
**C J Holdings Inc** .... G .... 309 274-3141
Chillicothe *(G-7163)*
▲ **Cablofil Inc** .... B .... 618 566-3230
Mascoutah *(G-14350)*
**Captain Hook Inc** .... G .... 309 565-7676
Hanna City *(G-11567)*
**CB&i LLC** .... G .... 815 936-5440
Bourbonnais *(G-2392)*
**Central Manufacturing Company** .... G .... 309 387-6591
East Peoria *(G-8705)*
**Chadwick Manufacturing Ltd** .... G .... 815 684-5152
Chadwick *(G-3440)*
**Chicago Tank Lining Sales** .... G .... 847 328-0500
Evanston *(G-10023)*
**Chips Manufacturing Inc** .... D .... 630 682-4477
West Chicago *(G-21681)*
**Colfax Welding & Fabricating** .... G .... 847 359-4433
Palatine *(G-17013)*
▲ **Component Parts Company** .... G .... 815 477-2323
Crystal Lake *(G-7556)*
**Contech Engnered Solutions LLC** .... E .... 217 529-5461
Springfield *(G-20421)*
◆ **Cooper B-Line Inc** .... A .... 618 654-2184
Highland *(G-11780)*
**Corrugated Converting Eqp** .... F .... 618 532-2138
Centralia *(G-3410)*
**CST Industries Inc** .... C .... 815 756-1551
Dekalb *(G-8080)*
**Cyclops Welding Co** .... G .... 815 223-0685
La Salle *(G-12769)*
**D & D Manufacturing** .... G .... 815 339-9100
Hennepin *(G-11733)*
**D & P Construction Co Inc** .... E .... 773 714-9330
Chicago *(G-4535)*
**D C Cooper Corporation** .... G .... 309 924-1941
Stronghurst *(G-20712)*
**Debcor Inc** .... G .... 708 333-2191
South Holland *(G-20261)*
▼ **Dee Concrete Accessories** .... F .... 708 452-0250
Norridge *(G-16099)*
**Deere & Company** .... E .... 309 765-8000
Moline *(G-14930)*
**Diesel Radiator Co** .... D .... 708 865-7299
Melrose Park *(G-14619)*
**Dill Brothers Inc** .... F .... 847 746-8323
Zion *(G-22682)*
**Dip Seal Plastics Inc** .... G .... 815 398-3533
Rockford *(G-18345)*
**E H Baare Corporation** .... C .... 618 546-1575
Robinson *(G-18062)*
**Eastland Fabrication LLC** .... G .... 815 493-8399
Lanark *(G-13152)*
**EC Harms Met Fabricators Inc** .... F .... 309 385-2132
Princeville *(G-17764)*
◆ **Eclipse Inc** .... D .... 815 877-3031
Rockford *(G-18356)*
**Ed Stan Fabricating Co** .... G .... 708 863-7668
Chicago *(G-4694)*
**Edmik Inc** .... E .... 847 263-0460
Gurnee *(G-11445)*
▲ **Eirich Machines Inc** .... D .... 847 336-2444
Gurnee *(G-11446)*
▲ **Ekstrom Carlson Fabricating Co** .... G .... 815 226-1511
Rockford *(G-18360)*
**Elite Fabrication Inc** .... G .... 773 274-4474
Chicago *(G-4731)*
**Elkay Manufacturing Company** .... B .... 815 273-7001
Savanna *(G-19397)*
**Energy Solutions Inc** .... G .... 618 465-5404
Alton *(G-575)*
**Erq Systems Inc** .... E .... 815 469-1072
Chicago *(G-4773)*
**Evapco Inc** .... E .... 410 756-2600
Chicago *(G-4788)*
**Evapco Inc** .... C .... 217 923-3431
Greenup *(G-11382)*
**Fabricated Products Co Inc** .... F .... 630 898-6460
Aurora *(G-1006)*
▲ **Fabtek Aero Ltd** .... F .... 630 552-3622
Plano *(G-17664)*
**Faspro Technologies Inc** .... D .... 847 392-9500
Arlington Heights *(G-752)*
**Ferguson Enterprises Inc** .... G .... 217 425-7262
Decatur *(G-7881)*
**G & M Fabricating Inc** .... G .... 815 282-1744
Roscoe *(G-18898)*
▲ **G E Mathis Company** .... D .... 773 586-3800
Chicago *(G-4900)*
▲ **G K Enterprises Inc** .... G .... 708 587-2150
Monee *(G-14996)*
**G&M Metal** .... G .... 630 616-1126
Elk Grove Village *(G-9492)*
**Gateway Fabricators Inc** .... G .... 618 271-5700
East Saint Louis *(G-8754)*
**Gears Gears Gears Inc** .... G .... 708 366-6555
Harwood Heights *(G-11685)*
▼ **Gpe Controls Inc** .... F .... 708 236-6000
Hillside *(G-11917)*
**Great Lakes Art Foundry Inc** .... G .... 847 213-0800
Skokie *(G-20006)*
▼ **H A Phillips & Co** .... E .... 630 377-0050
Dekalb *(G-8095)*
▲ **HEF Corporation** .... E .... 708 343-0866
Melrose Park *(G-14653)*
▲ **Hoerbiger-Origa Corporation** .... D .... 800 283-1377
Glendale Heights *(G-11030)*
▲ **Howe Corporation** .... E .... 773 235-0200
Chicago *(G-5123)*
**Hudson Boiler & Tank Company** .... F .... 312 666-4780
Lockport *(G-13722)*
**Ideal Fabricators Inc** .... F .... 217 999-7017
Mount Olive *(G-15304)*
▼ **Ifh Group Inc** .... D .... 800 435-7003
Rock Falls *(G-18138)*
**Ifh Group Inc** .... G .... 815 380-2367
Galt *(G-10781)*
**Illinois Oil Marketing Eqp Inc** .... E .... 309 347-1819
Pekin *(G-17269)*
**Illinois Oil Marketing Eqp Inc** .... F .... 217 935-5107
Clinton *(G-7284)*
**Illinois Rack Enterprises Inc** .... E .... 815 385-5750
Lakemoor *(G-13144)*
**Illinois Tool Works Inc** .... C .... 708 325-2300
Bridgeview *(G-2498)*
**Imbert Construction Inds Inc** .... G .... 847 588-3170
Niles *(G-15988)*
**Industrial Maintenance & McHy** .... G .... 815 726-0030
Mokena *(G-14874)*
**ITW Blding Cmponents Group Inc** .... E .... 217 324-0303
Litchfield *(G-13689)*
**J & G Fabricating Inc** .... G .... 708 385-9147
Blue Island *(G-2257)*
**J B Metal Works Inc** .... G .... 847 824-4253
Des Plaines *(G-8215)*
**J H Botts LLC** .... E .... 815 726-5885
Joliet *(G-12519)*
**Jet Rack Corp** .... E .... 773 586-2150
Chicago *(G-5298)*
**Jiffy Metal Products Inc** .... G .... 773 626-8090
Chicago *(G-5303)*
**JM Industries LLC** .... E .... 708 849-4700
Riverdale *(G-18020)*
**Jodi Maurer** .... G .... 847 961-5347
Lake In The Hills *(G-12996)*
**JT Cullen Co Inc** .... D .... 815 589-2412
Fulton *(G-10702)*
**Kennamtal Tricon Mtls Svcs Inc** .... E .... 708 235-0563
University Park *(G-21053)*
**Kodiak Concrete Forms Inc** .... G .... 630 773-9339
Itasca *(G-12298)*
**Kohnens Concrete Products Inc** .... E .... 618 277-2120
Germantown *(G-10892)*
**Lake Process Systems Inc** .... E .... 847 381-7663
Lake Barrington *(G-12817)*
**Lawndale Forging & Tool Works** .... G .... 773 277-2800
Chicago *(G-5471)*
**Lee Industries Inc** .... C .... 847 462-1865
Elk Grove Village *(G-9590)*
**Lewis Process Systems Inc** .... F .... 630 510-8200
Carol Stream *(G-3184)*
**Lizotte Sheet Metal Inc** .... G .... 618 656-3066
Edwardsville *(G-8806)*
**Luebbers Welding & Mfg Inc** .... F .... 618 594-2489
Carlyle *(G-3056)*
**Maccarb Inc** .... G .... 877 427-2499
Elgin *(G-9098)*
**Mach Mechanical Group LLC** .... G .... 630 674-6224
Naperville *(G-15815)*
**Madison Inds Holdings LLC** .... G .... 312 277-0156
Chicago *(G-5598)*
**Mailbox International Inc** .... G .... 847 541-8466
Wheeling *(G-22097)*
**Matrix Service Inc** .... F .... 618 466-4862
Alton *(G-585)*
**Melters and More** .... G .... 815 419-2043
Chenoa *(G-3634)*
**Mendota Welding & Mfg** .... G .... 815 539-6944
Mendota *(G-14727)*
**Metal Improvement Company LLC** .... E .... 630 620-6808
Lombard *(G-13825)*
**Mid-State Tank Co Inc** .... D .... 217 728-8383
Sullivan *(G-20751)*
◆ **Midwest Can Company** .... E .... 708 615-1400
Melrose Park *(G-14673)*
**Midwest Hydra-Line Inc** .... G .... 309 674-6570
Peoria *(G-17407)*
**Midwest Hydra-Line Inc** .... F .... 309 342-6171
Galesburg *(G-10768)*
**Midwest Imperial Steel** .... F .... 815 469-1072
Oak Lawn *(G-16635)*
**Midwest Pipe Supports Inc** .... G .... 630 665-6400
Bartlett *(G-1319)*
**Mj Snyder Ironworks Inc** .... G .... 217 826-6440
Marshall *(G-14326)*
**Montefusco Heating & Shtmtl Co** .... G .... 309 691-7400
Peoria *(G-17412)*
**Mt Carmel Machine Shop Inc** .... F .... 618 262-4591
Mount Carmel *(G-15275)*
**Murdock Company Inc** .... G .... 847 566-0050
Mundelein *(G-15535)*
**Newman Welding & Machine Shop** .... G .... 618 435-5591
Benton *(G-2037)*
**Nuair Filter Company LLC** .... F .... 309 888-4331
Normal *(G-16081)*
**Osbornes Mch Weld Fabrication** .... G .... 217 795-4716
Argenta *(G-691)*
▲ **Paasche Airbrush Co** .... D .... 773 867-9191
Chicago *(G-6048)*
**Paul D Stark & Associates** .... G .... 630 964-7111
Downers Grove *(G-8500)*
▼ **Peerless America Incorporated** .... C .... 217 342-0400
Effingham *(G-8853)*
**Petro Chem Echer Erhardt LLC** .... G .... 773 847-7535
Chicago *(G-6114)*
**Pools Welding Inc** .... G .... 309 787-2083
Milan *(G-14798)*
**Powerone Corp** .... G .... 630 443-6500
Saint Charles *(G-19239)*
**Precision Ibc Inc** .... F .... 708 396-0750
Crestwood *(G-7498)*
**Precision Tank & Equipment Co** .... F .... 217 636-7023
Athens *(G-942)*
**Pro-Fab Inc** .... E .... 309 263-8454
Morton *(G-15178)*
**Pro-Tran Inc** .... G .... 217 348-9353
Charleston *(G-3608)*
▼ **Pryco Inc** .... E .... 217 364-4467
Mechanicsburg *(G-14574)*
▲ **Pureline Treatment Systems LLC** .... E .... 847 963-8465
Bensenville *(G-1970)*
**R & B Metal Products Inc** .... E .... 815 338-1890
Woodstock *(G-22603)*
**R L Hoener Co** .... E .... 217 223-2190
Quincy *(G-17883)*
**R-M Industries Inc** .... F .... 630 543-3071
Addison *(G-267)*

Rayes Boiler & Welding Ltd ... G ... 847 675-6655
Skokie (G-20072)
▲ Realwheels Corporation ... E ... 847 662-7722
Gurnee (G-11499)
Redi-Weld & Mfg Co Inc ... G ... 815 455-4460
Lake In The Hills (G-13004)
Reino Tool & Manufacturing Co ... F ... 773 588-5800
Chicago (G-6326)
▲ Resist-A-Line Industries Inc ... G ... 815 650-3177
Joliet (G-12567)
Rmb Engineered Products Inc ... G ... 847 382-0100
Barrington (G-1301)
Rockford Air Devices Inc ... F ... 815 654-3330
Machesney Park (G-14104)
Rome Metal Mfg Inc ... G ... 773 287-1755
Chicago (G-6389)
Roney Machine Works Inc ... E ... 618 462-4113
Alton (G-588)
Ross and White Company ... F ... 847 516-3900
Cary (G-3369)
Rotary Airlock LLC ... E ... 800 883-8955
Rock Falls (G-18150)
Ryan Manufacturing Inc ... G ... 815 695-5310
Newark (G-15934)
▲ S+s Inspection Inc ... G ... 770 493-9332
Bartlett (G-1371)
Sendra Service Corp ... G ... 815 462-0061
New Lenox (G-15910)
Shew Brothers Inc ... G ... 618 997-4414
Marion (G-14286)
▼ Simplex Inc ... C ... 217 483-1600
Springfield (G-20526)
South Subn Wldg & Fabg Co Inc ... G ... 708 385-7160
Posen (G-17736)
Specialized Separators Inc ... F ... 815 316-0626
Rockford (G-18625)
Spectrum Technologies Intl Ltd ... G ... 630 961-5244
Woodridge (G-22518)
SPX Cooling Technologies Inc ... D ... 815 873-3767
Rockford (G-18630)
SPX Corporation ... C ... 847 593-8855
Elk Grove Village (G-9749)
SPX Corporation ... B ... 815 874-5556
Rockford (G-18631)
Squibb Tank Company ... F ... 618 548-0141
Salem (G-19352)
Staffco Inc ... G ... 309 688-3223
Peoria (G-17460)
◆ Streator Industrial Hdlg Inc ... D ... 815 672-0551
Streator (G-20704)
Superior Fabrication & Machine ... G ... 217 762-5512
Monticello (G-15086)
Tacknologies ... G ... 630 729-9900
Woodridge (G-22521)
Tech-Weld Inc ... F ... 630 365-3000
Elburn (G-8913)
▲ Temprite Company ... E ... 630 293-5910
West Chicago (G-21778)
Tinsley Steel Inc ... G ... 618 656-5231
Edwardsville (G-8817)
Titan US LLC ... G ... 331 212-5953
Aurora (G-1088)
Traco Industries Inc ... G ... 815 675-6603
Spring Grove (G-20371)
▲ Tranter Phe Inc ... F ... 217 227-3470
Farmersville (G-10184)
Ucc Holdings Corporation ... F ... 847 473-5900
Waukegan (G-21634)
Unistrut International Corp ... D ... 630 773-3460
Addison (G-334)
▲ United Conveyor Supply Company ... D ... 847 672-5100
Waukegan (G-21636)
United Conveyor Supply Company ... E ... 708 344-8050
Melrose Park (G-14703)
V & N Metal Products Inc ... G ... 773 436-1855
Chicago (G-6863)
▲ Vapor Corporation ... B ... 847 777-6400
Buffalo Grove (G-2788)
◆ VPI Acquisition Company LLC ... E ... 630 694-5500
Franklin Park (G-10624)
Wastequip LLC ... E ... 618 271-6250
East Saint Louis (G-8775)
Waves Fluid Solutions LLC ... G ... 630 765-7533
Carol Stream (G-3264)
◆ Whiting Corporation ... C ... 708 587-2000
Monee (G-15007)
Wilkos Industries ... G ... 563 249-6691
Savanna (G-19407)
WW Engineering Company LLC ... F ... 773 376-9494
Chicago (G-7042)
▲ Yinlun Usa Inc ... G ... 309 291-0843
Morton (G-15185)
Youngberg Industries Inc ... D ... 815 544-2177
Belvidere (G-1799)

## 3444 Sheet Metal Work

3 D Concrete Design Inc ... G ... 847 297-7968
Des Plaines (G-8136)
555 International Inc ... E ... 773 847-1400
Chicago (G-3670)
A & A Steel Fabricating Co ... F ... 708 389-4499
Posen (G-17726)
A D Skylights Inc ... G ... 847 854-2900
Algonquin (G-376)
A G Welding ... G ... 773 261-0575
Chicago (G-3688)
A Hartlett & Sons Inc ... G ... 815 338-0109
Woodstock (G-22533)
A J Wagner & Son ... F ... 773 935-1414
Wauconda (G-21434)
A&S Machining & Welding Inc ... E ... 708 442-4544
Mc Cook (G-14443)
▲ Abbott Scott Manufacturing Co ... E ... 773 342-7200
Chicago (G-3706)
▲ Ability Fasteners Inc ... F ... 847 593-4230
Elk Grove Village (G-9256)
Ablaze Welding & Fabricating ... G ... 815 965-0046
Rockford (G-18248)
Ace Metal Spinning Inc ... F ... 708 389-5635
Alsip (G-430)
Adler Norco Inc ... F ... 847 473-3600
Mundelein (G-15464)
Advance Awnair Corp ... F ... 708 422-2730
Orland Park (G-16838)
Advanced Metalcraft Inc ... F ... 847 451-0771
Franklin Park (G-10384)
Aetna Engineering Works Inc ... E ... 773 785-0489
Chicago (G-3778)
▲ Afc Cable Systems Inc ... B ... 508 998-1131
Harvey (G-11651)
Agena Manufacturing Co ... E ... 630 668-5086
Carol Stream (G-3093)
Air Caddy ... G ... 708 383-5541
Oak Park (G-16650)
Air Vent Inc ... G ... 309 692-6969
Peoria (G-17305)
Albert J Wagner & Son LLC ... F ... 815 459-1287
Crystal Lake (G-7527)
Alert Tubing Fabricators Inc ... G ... 847 253-7237
Schaumburg (G-19429)
All Seasons Heating & AC ... G ... 217 429-2022
Decatur (G-7831)
All Style Awning Corporation ... G ... 708 343-2323
Melrose Park (G-14587)
▲ All-Vac Industries Inc ... F ... 847 675-2290
Skokie (G-19948)
Allmetal Inc ... E ... 630 350-2524
Wood Dale (G-22335)
Alloy Welding Corp ... E ... 708 345-6756
Melrose Park (G-14588)
Allquip Co Inc ... G ... 309 944-6153
Geneseo (G-10797)
▼ Allstate Metal Fabricators Inc ... G ... 630 860-1500
Wood Dale (G-22336)
Alumafloor & More Inc ... G ... 630 628-0226
Addison (G-31)
American Chute Systems Inc ... G ... 815 723-7632
Joliet (G-12452)
American Fuel Economy Inc ... G ... 815 433-3226
Ottawa (G-16946)
American Home Aluminium Co ... G ... 773 925-9442
Calumet Park (G-2956)
American Metal Installers & FA ... G ... 630 993-0812
Villa Park (G-21236)
American Shtmtl Fbricators Inc ... F ... 708 877-7200
Thornton (G-20867)
◆ Americana Building Pdts Inc ... D ... 618 548-2800
Salem (G-19326)
Anchor Welding & Fabrication ... G ... 815 937-1640
Aroma Park (G-878)
Anderson Awning & Shutter ... G ... 815 654-1155
Machesney Park (G-14056)
Angle Metal Manufacturing Co ... G ... 847 437-8666
Elk Grove Village (G-9306)
Anytime Heating & AC ... F ... 630 851-6696
Naperville (G-15796)
Aquarius Metal Products Inc ... F ... 847 659-9266
Huntley (G-12132)
Archer Industries & Supplies ... G ... 773 777-2698
Chicago (G-3937)
Arntzen Corporation ... E ... 815 334-0788
Woodstock (G-22541)
Arrow Sheet Metal Company ... E ... 815 455-2019
Crystal Lake (G-7538)
Art Wire Works Inc ... F ... 708 458-3993
Bedford Park (G-1538)
AS Fabricating Inc ... G ... 618 242-7438
Mount Vernon (G-15398)
Associated Rack Corporation ... F ... 616 554-6004
Chicago (G-3970)
Astoria Wire Products Inc ... D ... 708 496-9950
Bedford Park (G-1539)
▲ Austin-Westran LLC ... C ... 815 234-2811
Byron (G-2912)
Austin-Westran LLC ... C ... 815 234-2811
Montgomery (G-15029)
Avenue Metal Manufacturing Co ... F ... 312 243-3483
Chicago (G-3999)
Awnings Over Chicagoland Inc ... G ... 847 233-0310
Franklin Park (G-10406)
Awnings Unlimited Inc ... G ... 708 485-6769
Brookfield (G-2622)
B & D Independence Inc ... E ... 618 262-7117
Mount Carmel (G-15260)
B & G Sheet Metal ... G ... 773 265-6121
Chicago (G-4015)
B & J Wire Inc ... E ... 877 787-9473
Chicago (G-4016)
B M I Inc ... C ... 847 839-6000
Schaumburg (G-19456)
Barker Metal Craft Inc ... G ... 773 588-9300
Chicago (G-4043)
Bartec Orb Inc ... E ... 773 927-8600
Chicago (G-4051)
▲ Bella Architectural Products ... G ... 708 339-4782
Harvey (G-11660)
Belvin J & F Sheet Metal Co ... G ... 312 666-5222
Chicago (G-4081)
Berridge Manufacturing Company ... G ... 630 231-7495
West Chicago (G-21669)
Beverly Shear Mfg Corporation ... G ... 773 233-2063
Chicago (G-4098)
Bill West Enterprises Inc ... G ... 217 886-2591
Jacksonville (G-12378)
Bilt-Rite Metal Products Inc ... E ... 815 495-2211
Leland (G-13218)
Bing Engineering Inc ... C ... 708 228-8005
Frankfort (G-10300)
Boekeloo Heating & Sheet Metal ... G ... 708 877-6560
Thornton (G-20868)
Brex-Arlington Incorporated ... F ... 847 255-6284
Arlington Heights (G-729)
Brian Burcar ... G ... 815 856-2271
Leonore (G-13285)
▲ Busatis Inc ... G ... 630 844-9803
Montgomery (G-15034)
Buww Coverings Incorporated ... E ... 815 394-1985
Rockford (G-18292)
C J Holdings Inc ... G ... 309 274-3141
Chillicothe (G-7163)
C Keller Manufacturing Inc ... E ... 630 833-5593
Villa Park (G-21240)
Carroll Distrg & Cnstr Sup Inc ... G ... 815 464-0100
Frankfort (G-10308)
Carroll Distrg & Cnstr Sup Inc ... G ... 630 892-4855
Aurora (G-1125)
Carroll Distrg & Cnstr Sup Inc ... G ... 630 243-0272
Lemont (G-13229)
Carroll Distrg & Cnstr Sup Inc ... G ... 815 941-1548
Morris (G-15100)
Carroll Distrg & Cnstr Sup Inc ... G ... 309 449-6044
Hopedale (G-12121)
Carroll Distrg & Cnstr Sup Inc ... G ... 217 223-8126
Quincy (G-17810)
Carroll Distrg & Cnstr Sup Inc ... F ... 630 369-6520
Naperville (G-15619)
Carroll International Corp ... F ... 630 983-5979
Lake Forest (G-12890)
Castle Metal Products Corp ... G ... 847 806-4540
Glendale Heights (G-11015)
▲ CCS Contractor Eqp & Sup Inc ... E ... 630 393-9020
Naperville (G-15622)
Central Machining Service ... G ... 217 422-7472
Decatur (G-7855)
Central Radiator Cabinet Co ... G ... 773 539-1700
Lena (G-13274)
Central Sheet Metal Pdts Inc ... E ... 773 583-2424
Skokie (G-19976)
Cgi Automated Mfg Inc ... E ... 815 221-5300
Romeoville (G-18808)



Employee Codes: A=Over 500 employees, B=251-500
C=101-250, D=51-100, E=20-50, F=10-19, G=3-9
2017 Harris Illinois
Industrial Directory
1035

**Charles Atwater Assoc Inc** ..... G ..... 815 678-4813
Richmond *(G-17959)*
**Charles Industries Ltd** ..... D ..... 217 893-8335
Rantoul *(G-17922)*
**Chesterfield Awning Co Inc** ..... F ..... 708 596-4434
South Holland *(G-20256)*
**◆ Chicago Metal Rolled Pdts Co** ..... D ..... 773 523-5757
Chicago *(G-4333)*
**Chicagoland Metal Fabricators** ..... G ..... 847 260-5320
Franklin Park *(G-10430)*
**▲ Chris Industries Inc** ..... E ..... 847 729-9292
Northbrook *(G-16222)*
**Christensen Precision Products** ..... G ..... 630 543-6525
Addison *(G-76)*
**City Screen Inc** ..... G ..... 773 588-5642
Chicago *(G-4388)*
**Classic Sheet Metal Inc** ..... D ..... 630 694-0300
Franklin Park *(G-10435)*
**Cleats Mfg Inc** ..... F ..... 773 521-0300
Chicago *(G-4399)*
**Cleats Mfg Inc** ..... F ..... 773 542-0453
Chicago *(G-4400)*
**▲ Cobra Metal Works Inc** ..... C ..... 847 214-8400
Elgin *(G-8993)*
**Colfax Welding & Fabricating** ..... G ..... 847 359-4433
Palatine *(G-17013)*
**Columbus Industries Inc** ..... F ..... 309 245-1010
Fairview *(G-10165)*

**Comet Roll & Machine Company** ..... E ..... 630 268-1407
Saint Charles *(G-19161)*
**Contech Engnered Solutions LLC** ..... G ..... 630 573-1110
Oak Brook *(G-16502)*
**Control Equipment Company Inc** ..... F ..... 847 891-7500
Schaumburg *(G-19482)*
**◆ Cooper B-Line Inc** ..... A ..... 618 654-2184
Highland *(G-11780)*
**Corrpak Inc** ..... G ..... 618 758-2755
Coulterville *(G-7399)*
**Corrugated Metals Inc** ..... F ..... 815 323-1310
Belvidere *(G-1747)*
**▼ Craftsman Custom Metals LLC** ..... D ..... 847 655-0040
Schiller Park *(G-19817)*
**Crawford Heating & Cooling Co** ..... D ..... 309 788-4573
Rock Island *(G-18169)*
**Creative Steel Fabricators** ..... G ..... 847 803-2090
Des Plaines *(G-8177)*
**Crown Concepts Corporation** ..... E ..... 815 941-1081
Morris *(G-15103)*
**Custom Fabricating Htg & Coolg** ..... G ..... 815 726-0477
Joliet *(G-12480)*
**Custom Fit Shtmetal Roofg Corp** ..... F ..... 773 227-9019
Chicago *(G-4522)*
**Custom Linear Grille Inc** ..... G ..... 847 520-5511
Wheeling *(G-22033)*
**Cyclops Welding Co** ..... G ..... 815 223-0685
La Salle *(G-12769)*
**D & J Metalcraft Company Inc** ..... F ..... 773 878-6446
Chicago *(G-4534)*
**D L Sheet Metal** ..... G ..... 708 599-5538
Palos Hills *(G-17116)*
**D W Terry Welding Company** ..... G ..... 618 433-9722
Alton *(G-570)*
**Dadant & Sons Inc** ..... F ..... 217 852-3324
Dallas City *(G-7696)*
**Daniel & Sons Mech Contrs Inc** ..... F ..... 618 997-2822
Marion *(G-14258)*
**Daniel Mfg Inc** ..... F ..... 309 963-4227
Carlock *(G-3050)*
**Daves Welding Service Inc** ..... G ..... 630 655-3224
Darien *(G-7792)*
**▼ Dayton Superior Corporation** ..... A ..... 847 391-4700
Elk Grove Village *(G-9418)*
**▼ Dee Concrete Accessories** ..... F ..... 708 452-0250
Norridge *(G-16099)*
**Delaney Sheet Metal Co** ..... G ..... 847 991-9579
Palatine *(G-17021)*
**Demco Inc** ..... F ..... 708 345-4822
Melrose Park *(G-14615)*
**Depue Mechanical Inc** ..... E ..... 815 447-2267
Depue *(G-8134)*
**▲ Diemasters Manufacturing Inc** ..... C ..... 847 640-9900
Elk Grove Village *(G-9429)*
**Diversified Cnstr Svcs LLC** ..... G ..... 708 344-4900
Melrose Park *(G-14620)*
**Duroweld Company Inc** ..... E ..... 847 680-3064
Lake Bluff *(G-12841)*
**Dynacoil Inc** ..... E ..... 847 731-3300
Zion *(G-22683)*
**E-M Metal Fabricator** ..... G ..... 847 593-9970
Elk Grove Village *(G-9444)*

**Eclipse Awnings Inc** ..... F ..... 708 636-3160
Evergreen Park *(G-10113)*
**Ed Stan Fabricating Co** ..... G ..... 708 863-7668
Chicago *(G-4694)*
**Eikenberry Sheet Metal Works** ..... G ..... 815 625-0955
Sterling *(G-20590)*
**▲ Ekstrom Carlson Fabricating Co** ..... G ..... 815 226-1511
Rockford *(G-18360)*
**Elgin Sheet Metal Co** ..... E ..... 847 742-3486
South Elgin *(G-20194)*
**Elite Machining Co** ..... G ..... 708 308-0947
Bridgeview *(G-2488)*
**▲ Elite Manufacturing Tech Inc** ..... C ..... 630 351-5757
Bloomingdale *(G-2106)*
**Elk Grove Custom Sheet Metal** ..... F ..... 847 352-2845
Elk Grove Village *(G-9451)*
**Elk Heating & Sheet Metal Inc** ..... F ..... 618 251-4747
Wood River *(G-22442)*
**Emerald Machine Inc** ..... G ..... 773 924-3659
Chicago *(G-4740)*
**EMR Manufacturing Inc** ..... E ..... 630 766-3366
Wood Dale *(G-22362)*
**Energy Culvert Co Inc** ..... G ..... 618 942-7381
Energy *(G-9986)*
**Enterprise AC & Htg Co** ..... G ..... 708 430-2212
Chicago Ridge *(G-7147)*
**Epic Metals Corporation** ..... G ..... 847 803-6411
Des Plaines *(G-8189)*
**Esi Steel & Fabrication** ..... F ..... 618 548-3017
Salem *(G-19331)*
**Estes Laser & Mfg Inc** ..... F ..... 847 301-8231
Schaumburg *(G-19522)*
**◆ Ets-Lindgren Inc** ..... C ..... 630 307-7200
Wood Dale *(G-22363)*
**Evans Heating and Air Inc** ..... G ..... 217 483-8440
Chatham *(G-3619)*
**Expanded Metal Products Corp** ..... F ..... 773 735-4500
Chicago *(G-4795)*
**Exton Corp** ..... C ..... 847 391-8100
Des Plaines *(G-8192)*
**Extreme Manufacturing Inc** ..... G ..... 630 350-8566
Wood Dale *(G-22364)*
**▲ Ezee Roll Manufacturing Co** ..... G ..... 217 339-2279
Hoopeston *(G-12110)*
**Eztech Manufacturing Inc** ..... F ..... 630 293-0010
West Chicago *(G-21700)*
**F Kreutzer & Co** ..... G ..... 773 826-5767
Chicago *(G-4805)*
**F Vogelmann and Company** ..... F ..... 815 469-2285
Frankfort *(G-10321)*
**Fab Werks Inc** ..... E ..... 815 724-0317
Crest Hill *(G-7458)*
**Fab-Rite Sheet Metal** ..... F ..... 847 228-0300
Des Plaines *(G-8193)*
**Fabricating Machinery Sales** ..... E ..... 630 350-2266
Wood Dale *(G-22366)*
**Famaco Corp** ..... E ..... 217 442-4412
Tilton *(G-20881)*
**Fanmar Inc** ..... E ..... 708 563-0505
Elk Grove Village *(G-9475)*
**▲ Farmweld Inc** ..... E ..... 217 857-6423
Teutopolis *(G-20852)*
**Fbs Group Inc** ..... F ..... 773 229-8675
Chicago *(G-4821)*
**▲ Feralloy Corporation** ..... E ..... 503 286-8869
Chicago *(G-4836)*
**Forming America Ltd** ..... E ..... 888 993-1304
West Chicago *(G-21706)*
**Formtec Inc** ..... E ..... 630 752-9700
Glendale Heights *(G-11024)*
**Fox Metal Services Inc** ..... F ..... 847 439-9696
Carol Stream *(G-3155)*
**Fracar Sheet Metal Mfg Co Inc** ..... E ..... 847 678-1600
Schiller Park *(G-19831)*
**Fulton Metal Works Inc** ..... G ..... 217 476-8223
Ashland *(G-926)*
**G & M Fabricating Inc** ..... G ..... 815 282-1744
Roscoe *(G-18898)*
**G Branch Corp** ..... D ..... 630 458-1909
Addison *(G-125)*
**General Machinery & Mfg Co** ..... F ..... 773 235-3700
Chicago *(G-4928)*
**▲ Genesis Inc** ..... D ..... 630 351-4400
Roselle *(G-18943)*
**Gengler-Lowney Laser Works** ..... F ..... 630 801-4840
Aurora *(G-1161)*
**Gerdau Ameristeel US Inc** ..... E ..... 815 547-0400
Belvidere *(G-1757)*
**Giovanini Metals Corp** ..... G ..... 815 842-0500
Pontiac *(G-17702)*

**Glazed Structures Inc** ..... F ..... 847 223-4560
Grayslake *(G-11341)*
**GLC Industries Inc** ..... E ..... 630 628-5870
Addison *(G-135)*
**Gma Inc** ..... G ..... 630 595-1255
Bensenville *(G-1910)*
**Goose Island Mfg & Supply Corp** ..... G ..... 708 343-4225
Lansing *(G-13164)*
**Grimm Metal Fabricators Inc** ..... E ..... 630 792-1710
Lombard *(G-13807)*
**GROsse&sons Htg &SHeet Met Inc** ..... G ..... 708 447-8397
Lyons *(G-14040)*
**Group Industries Inc** ..... E ..... 708 877-6200
Thornton *(G-20871)*
**▲ Helander Metal Spinning Co** ..... E ..... 630 268-9292
Lombard *(G-13808)*
**Hemingway Chimney Inc** ..... G ..... 708 333-0355
South Holland *(G-20275)*
**Hendrick Metal Products LLC** ..... D ..... 847 742-7002
Elgin *(G-9062)*
**Hennessy Sheet Metal** ..... G ..... 708 754-6342
S Chicago Hts *(G-19104)*
**▲ Hennig Inc** ..... G ..... 815 636-9900
Machesney Park *(G-14078)*
**Heritage Sheet Metal Inc** ..... G ..... 847 724-8449
Glenview *(G-11137)*
**▼ Hi-Grade Welding and Mfg LLC** ..... E ..... 847 640-8172
Schaumburg *(G-19553)*
**Highland Mch & Screw Pdts Co** ..... D ..... 618 654-2103
Highland *(G-11788)*
**Hogg Welding Inc** ..... G ..... 708 339-0033
Harvey *(G-11670)*
**Hohlflder A H Shtmtl Htg Coolg** ..... G ..... 815 965-9134
Rockford *(G-18420)*
**▲ Hontech International Corp** ..... F ..... 847 364-9800
Elk Grove Village *(G-9525)*
**Hot Food Boxes Inc** ..... E ..... 773 533-5912
Chicago *(G-5117)*
**◆ Hovi Industries Incorporated** ..... E ..... 815 512-7500
Bolingbrook *(G-2316)*
**▼ Howler Fabrication & Wldg Inc** ..... E ..... 630 293-9300
West Chicago *(G-21716)*
**Hpl Stampings Inc** ..... E ..... 847 540-1400
Lake Zurich *(G-13084)*
**I F & G Metal Craft Co** ..... G ..... 847 488-0630
South Elgin *(G-20204)*
**Ibbotson Heating Co** ..... E ..... 847 253-0866
Arlington Heights *(G-770)*
**Icon Metalcraft Inc** ..... C ..... 630 766-5600
Wood Dale *(G-22381)*
**Illinois Valley Glass & Mirror** ..... F ..... 309 682-6603
Peoria *(G-17387)*
**Illinois Valley Gutters Inc** ..... G ..... 309 698-8140
East Peoria *(G-8713)*
**ILmachine Company Inc** ..... F ..... 847 243-9900
Wheeling *(G-22074)*
**Imperial Glass Structures Co** ..... F ..... 847 253-6150
Wheeling *(G-22075)*
**Imperial Mfg Group Inc** ..... F ..... 618 465-3133
Alton *(G-578)*
**▼ IMS Companies LLC** ..... D ..... 847 391-8100
Des Plaines *(G-8210)*
**▲ IMS Engineered Products LLC** ..... C ..... 847 391-8100
Des Plaines *(G-8211)*
**International Source Solutions** ..... G ..... 847 251-8265
Wilmette *(G-22255)*
**Ironform Holdings Co** ..... F ..... 312 374-4810
Chicago *(G-5239)*
**J & G Fabricating Inc** ..... G ..... 708 385-9147
Blue Island *(G-2257)*
**▲ J & I Son Tool Company Inc** ..... G ..... 847 455-4200
Franklin Park *(G-10500)*
**J & M Fab Metals Inc** ..... G ..... 815 758-0354
Marengo *(G-14232)*
**J B Metal Works Inc** ..... G ..... 847 824-4253
Des Plaines *(G-8215)*
**J F Schroeder Company Inc** ..... E ..... 847 357-8600
Arlington Heights *(G-781)*
**J K Manufacturing Co** ..... D ..... 708 563-2500
Bedford Park *(G-1558)*
**J Mac Metals Inc** ..... G ..... 309 822-2023
Galva *(G-10790)*
**J-TEC Metal Products Inc** ..... F ..... 630 875-1300
Itasca *(G-12288)*
**John J Rickhoff Shtmtl Co Inc** ..... F ..... 708 331-2970
Phoenix *(G-17541)*
**Joiner Sheet Metal & Roofing** ..... G ..... 618 664-9488
Greenville *(G-11396)*
**JT Cullen Co Inc** ..... D ..... 815 589-2412
Fulton *(G-10702)*

1036 2017 Harris Illinois Industrial Directory

K & K Tool & Die Inc ....F ....309 829-4479
Bloomington (G-2187)
K B Metal Company ....G ....309 248-7355
Washburn (G-21376)
K Three Welding Service Inc ....G ....708 563-2911
Chicago (G-5344)
Kaiser Manufacturing Co ....C ....773 235-4705
Chicago (G-5352)
Kcp Metal Fabrications Inc ....E ....773 775-0318
Chicago (G-5367)
Keil-Forness Comfort Systems ....G ....618 233-3039
Belleville (G-1640)
Kelley Construction Inc ....B ....217 422-1800
Decatur (G-7902)
Kemper Industries ....G ....217 826-5712
Marshall (G-14324)
Key West Metal Industries Inc ....C ....708 371-1470
Crestwood (G-7491)
Kier Mfg Co ....G ....630 953-9500
Addison (G-168)
Kim Gough ....G ....309 734-3511
Monmouth (G-15017)
▲ Kipp Manufacturing Company Inc ....F ....630 768-9051
Wauconda (G-21477)
Kirby Sheet Metal Works Inc ....E ....773 247-6477
Chicago (G-5386)
Kormex Metal Craft Inc ....E ....630 953-8856
Lombard (G-13818)
Kroh-Wagner Inc ....E ....773 252-2031
Chicago (G-5412)
L M Sheet Metal Inc ....E ....815 654-1837
Loves Park (G-13957)
L R Gregory and Son Inc ....E ....847 247-0216
Lake Bluff (G-12852)
L/J Fabricators Inc ....E ....815 397-9099
Rockford (G-18460)
Lakefront Roofing Supply ....G ....312 275-0270
Chicago (G-5442)
Lakefront Roofing Supply ....E ....773 509-0400
Chicago (G-5443)
Lamco Slings & Rigging Inc ....E ....309 764-7400
Moline (G-14952)
Laser Center Corporation ....E ....630 422-1975
Bensenville (G-1938)
Laystrom Manufacturing Co ....D ....773 342-4800
Chicago (G-5474)
Lemanski Heating & AC ....G ....815 232-4519
Freeport (G-10673)
Lewis Process Systems Inc ....F ....630 510-8200
Carol Stream (G-3184)
Licon Inc ....G ....618 485-2222
Ashley (G-927)
▲ Lindemann Chimney Service Inc ....F ....847 918-7994
Lake Bluff (G-12854)
Litt Aluminium & Shtmtl Co ....G ....708 366-4720
Westchester (G-21847)
Lizotte Sheet Metal Inc ....G ....618 656-3066
Edwardsville (G-8806)
Lmt Usa Inc ....G ....630 969-5412
Waukegan (G-21583)
Logan Square Aluminum Sup Inc ....D ....847 985-1700
Schaumburg (G-19622)
Luebbers Welding & Mfg Inc ....F ....618 594-2489
Carlyle (G-3056)
Mac-Ster Inc ....F ....847 830-7013
Addison (G-185)
Macari Service Center Inc ....G ....217 774-4214
Shelbyville (G-19910)
Macon Metal Products Co ....E ....217 824-7205
Taylorville (G-20842)
Mailbox International Inc ....G ....847 541-8466
Wheeling (G-22097)
Marcres Manufacturing Inc ....E ....847 439-1808
Mount Prospect (G-15346)
Marsha Lega Studio Inc ....G
Joliet (G-12537)
MB Machine Inc ....F ....815 864-3555
Shannon (G-19900)
▼ Mech-Tronics Corporation ....D ....708 344-9823
Melrose Park (G-14671)
Mellish & Murray Co ....F ....312 733-3513
Chicago (G-5683)
Mellish & Murray Co ....F ....312 379-0335
Chicago (G-5684)
Mendota Welding & Mfg ....G ....815 539-6944
Mendota (G-14727)
Merz Air Conditioning and Htg ....E ....217 342-2323
Effingham (G-8845)
▲ Metal Box International Inc ....C ....847 455-8500
Franklin Park (G-10529)

Metal Culverts Inc ....E ....309 543-2271
Havana (G-11699)
Metal Sales Manufacturing Corp ....E ....309 787-1200
Rock Island (G-18189)
Metal Spinners Inc ....E ....815 625-0390
Rock Falls (G-18142)
Metal Strip Buiding Products ....G ....847 742-8500
Itasca (G-12314)
Metal-Rite Inc ....F ....708 656-3832
Cicero (G-7221)
Metalex Corporation ....C ....847 362-5400
Libertyville (G-13355)
▲ Metals and Services Inc ....D ....630 627-2900
Addison (G-202)
Midwest Awnings Inc ....G ....309 762-3339
Cameron (G-2970)
Midwest Manufacturing & Distrg ....F ....773 866-1010
Chicago (G-5746)
Midwest Skylite Company Inc ....E ....847 214-9505
South Elgin (G-20219)
Midwest Skylite Service Inc ....G ....847 214-9505
Schaumburg (G-19648)
▲ Mj Celco International LLC ....E ....847 671-1900
Schiller Park (G-19852)
Mj Snyder Ironworks Inc ....G ....217 826-6440
Marshall (G-14326)
Monmouth Metal Culvert Co ....G ....309 734-7723
Monmouth (G-15020)
Montana Metal Products LLC ....C ....847 803-6600
Des Plaines (G-8234)
Montefusco Heating & Shtmtl Co ....G ....309 691-7400
Peoria (G-17412)
Morton Metalcraft Co PA ....E ....309 266-7176
Morton (G-15169)
Mucci Kirkpatrick Sheet Metal ....G ....815 433-3350
Ottawa (G-16970)
Multimetal Products Corp ....E ....847 662-9110
Gurnee (G-11475)
National Metal Works Inc ....G ....815 282-5533
Loves Park (G-13969)
Nature House Inc ....D ....217 833-2393
Griggsville (G-11413)
Nelson Manufacturing Co Inc ....F ....815 229-0161
Rockford (G-18519)
Neomek Incorporated ....F ....630 879-5400
Batavia (G-1475)
Nesterowicz & Associates Inc ....G ....815 522-4469
Kirkland (G-12715)
North Shore Truck & Equipment ....G ....847 887-0200
Lake Bluff (G-12860)
▲ Northstar Industries Inc ....D ....630 446-7800
Glendale Heights (G-11052)
▼ Nova Metals Inc ....F ....630 690-4300
Carol Stream (G-3206)
Npi Holding Corp ....G ....217 391-1229
Springfield (G-20488)
▲ Nu-Way Industries Inc ....C ....847 298-7710
Des Plaines (G-8244)
▲ Nudo Products Inc ....C ....217 528-5636
Springfield (G-20490)
Odin Industries Inc ....F ....630 365-2475
Elburn (G-8901)
Olympia Manufacturing Inc ....G ....309 387-2633
East Peoria (G-8727)
Omega Products Inc ....G ....618 939-3445
Waterloo (G-21403)
Omnimax International Inc ....E ....309 747-2937
Gridley (G-11410)
Omnimax International Inc ....E ....770 449-7066
Bedford Park (G-1569)
Osbornes Mch Weld Fabrication ....G ....217 795-4716
Argenta (G-691)
▲ Paasche Airbrush Co ....D ....773 867-9191
Chicago (G-6048)
Parker Fabrication Inc ....E ....309 266-8413
Morton (G-15174)
Pate Company Inc ....E ....630 705-1920
Lombard (G-13843)
Pearson Industries Inc ....G ....847 963-9633
Rolling Meadows (G-18759)
Pep Industries Inc ....F ....630 833-0404
Villa Park (G-21276)
Peter Lehman Inc ....G ....847 395-7997
Antioch (G-649)
Peter Perella & Co ....F ....815 727-4526
Joliet (G-12550)
Pittsfield Mch Tl & Wldg Co ....G ....217 656-4000
Payson (G-17246)
Pools Welding Inc ....G ....309 787-2083
Milan (G-14798)

Powdered Metal Tech LLC ....G ....630 852-0500
Downers Grove (G-8507)
Prairie State Industries Inc ....F ....847 428-3641
Carpentersville (G-3297)
Precision Metal Products Inc ....F ....630 458-0100
Addison (G-252)
Premier Manufacturing Corp ....F ....847 640-6644
Addison (G-254)
Prince Fabricators Inc ....E ....630 588-0088
Carol Stream (G-3219)
▲ Prismier LLC ....E ....630 592-4515
Woodridge (G-22511)
Pro-Bilt Buildings LLC ....F ....217 532-9331
Hillsboro (G-11898)
Pro-Tech Metal Specialties Inc ....E ....630 279-7094
Elmhurst (G-9923)
Pro-Tran Inc ....G ....217 348-9353
Charleston (G-3608)
Production Fabg & Stamping Inc ....F ....708 755-5468
S Chicago Hts (G-19111)
Production Manufacturing ....G ....217 256-4211
Warsaw (G-21371)
Professional Metal Company ....E ....630 983-9777
Naperville (G-15733)
Progressive Sheet Metal Inc ....G ....773 376-1155
Chicago (G-6213)
▲ Pyramid Manufacturing Corp ....D ....630 443-0141
Saint Charles (G-19246)
Quad-Metal Inc ....F ....630 953-0907
Addison (G-261)
Quality Fabricators Inc ....D ....630 543-0540
Addison (G-264)
Quality Metal Works Inc ....G ....309 379-5311
Stanford (G-20552)
Quanex Homeshield LLC ....E ....815 635-3171
Chatsworth (G-3628)
Quicksilver Mechanical Inc ....G ....847 577-1564
Arlington Heights (G-824)
R & B Metal Products Inc ....E ....815 338-1890
Woodstock (G-22603)
R B Hayward Company ....E ....847 671-0400
Schiller Park (G-19864)
R B White Inc ....E ....309 452-5816
Normal (G-16086)
R E Burke Roofing Co Inc ....F ....847 675-5010
Skokie (G-20068)
R&R Rf Inc ....E ....847 669-3720
Rock Falls (G-18147)
▼ Ready Access Inc ....E ....800 621-5045
West Chicago (G-21763)
Redi-Weld & Mfg Co Inc ....G ....815 455-4460
Lake In The Hills (G-13004)
Reliable Autotech Usa LLC ....G ....815 945-7838
Chenoa (G-3635)
▲ Remin Laboratories Inc ....D ....815 723-1940
Joliet (G-12566)
Rettick Enterprises Inc ....G ....309 275-4967
Bloomington (G-2218)
Rijon Manufacturing Company ....G ....708 388-2295
Blue Island (G-2266)
▲ Rogers Precision Machining ....F ....815 233-0065
Freeport (G-10685)
Rollex Corporation ....C ....847 437-3000
Elk Grove Village (G-9717)
Rome Metal Mfg Inc ....G ....773 287-1755
Chicago (G-6389)
▲ RPS Engineering Inc ....F ....847 931-1950
Elgin (G-9168)
S & S Heating & Sheet Metal ....G ....815 933-1993
Bradley (G-2431)
S & S Welding & Fabrication ....G ....847 742-7344
Elgin (G-9170)
Safe-Air of Illinois Inc ....E ....708 652-9100
Cicero (G-7227)
San Mateo Inc ....E ....630 860-6991
Bensenville (G-1985)
Schubert Environmental Eqp Inc ....F ....630 307-9400
Glendale Heights (G-11067)
Seamless Gutter Corp ....E ....630 495-9800
Lombard (G-13852)
Service Metal Enterprises ....G ....630 628-1444
Addison (G-288)
Service Sheet Metal Works Inc ....F ....773 229-0031
Chicago (G-6483)
Shademaker Products Corp ....G ....773 955-0998
Chicago (G-6488)
Shamrock Manufacturing Co Inc ....G ....708 331-7776
South Holland (G-20304)
Shannon & Sons Welding ....G ....630 898-7778
Aurora (G-1215)

Sheas Iron Works Inc ... E ... 847 356-2922
Lake Villa *(G-13026)*

Sheet Metal Connectors Inc ... F ... 815 874-4600
Rockford *(G-18615)*

Sheet Metal Supply Ltd ... G ... 847 478-8500
Mundelein *(G-15557)*

Sheet Metal Werks Inc ... D ... 847 827-4700
Arlington Heights *(G-840)*

Sheets & Cylinder Welding Inc ... G ... 800 442-2200
Chicago *(G-6494)*

Shew Brothers Inc ... G ... 618 997-4414
Marion *(G-14286)*

Silgan White Cap Americas LLC ... F ... 630 515-8383
Downers Grove *(G-8524)*

Silver Machine Shop Inc ... G ... 217 359-5717
Champaign *(G-3540)*

Smid Heating & Air ... G ... 815 467-0362
Channahon *(G-3586)*

South Subn Wldg & Fabg Co Inc ... G ... 708 385-7160
Posen *(G-17736)*

Southwick Machine & Design Co ... G ... 309 949-2868
Colona *(G-7348)*

Spartan Sheet Metal Inc ... G ... 773 895-7266
Chicago *(G-6553)*

▲ Spiral-Helix Inc ... F ... 224 659-7870
Bensenville *(G-1996)*

▲ Stack-On Products Co ... C ... 847 526-1611
Wauconda *(G-21502)*

▲ Stainless Specialties Inc ... G ... 618 654-7723
Pocahontas *(G-17686)*

Standing Water Solutions Inc ... G ... 847 469-8876
Wauconda *(G-21503)*

▲ Star Forge Inc ... D ... 815 235-7750
Freeport *(G-10691)*

Starmont Manufacturing Co ... G ... 815 939-1041
Kankakee *(G-12653)*

Steel Services Enterprises ... E ... 708 259-1181
Lansing *(G-13187)*

Steel Span Inc ... F ... 815 943-9071
Harvard *(G-11648)*

Stuecklen Manufacturing Co ... G ... 847 678-5130
Franklin Park *(G-10596)*

Sturdee Metal Products Inc ... G ... 773 523-3074
New Lenox *(G-15913)*

Suburban Welding & Steel LLC ... F ... 847 678-1264
Franklin Park *(G-10599)*

Sudholt Sheet Metal Inc ... G ... 618 228-7351
Aviston *(G-1248)*

Sugar River Machine Shop ... E ... 815 624-0214
South Beloit *(G-20169)*

Summit Sheet Metal Specialists ... F ... 708 458-8622
Summit Argo *(G-20766)*

Superior Fabrication & Machine ... G ... 217 762-5512
Monticello *(G-15086)*

Superior Joining Tech Inc ... E ... 815 282-7581
Machesney Park *(G-14109)*

Synergy Mechanical Inc ... G ... 708 410-1004
Westchester *(G-21857)*

T & L Sheet Metal Inc ... F ... 630 628-7960
Addison *(G-304)*

T/J Fabricators Inc ... D ... 630 543-2293
Addison *(G-305)*

Tandem Industries Inc ... G ... 630 761-6615
Saint Charles *(G-19279)*

▲ Tassos Metal Inc ... E ... 630 953-1333
Lombard *(G-13864)*

Tcr Systems LLC ... D ... 217 877-5622
Decatur *(G-7951)*

Tella Tool & Mfg Co ... D ... 630 495-0545
Lombard *(G-13867)*

Temp Excel Properties LLC ... G ... 847 844-3845
Elgin *(G-9207)*

Tewell Bros Machine Inc ... F ... 217 253-6303
Tuscola *(G-21025)*

Thomas Engineering Inc ... E ... 815 398-0280
Rockford *(G-18648)*

Thybar Corporation ... E ... 630 543-5300
Addison *(G-314)*

Thyssenkrupp Materials NA Inc ... G ... 630 563-3365
Bolingbrook *(G-2378)*

Tin Mans Garage Inc ... G ... 630 262-0752
Elburn *(G-8916)*

Tinsley Steel Inc ... G ... 618 656-5231
Edwardsville *(G-8817)*

Tlk Industries Inc ... D ... 847 359-3200
East Dundee *(G-8659)*

Traco Industries Inc ... G ... 815 675-6603
Spring Grove *(G-20371)*

Transco Products Inc ... E ... 815 672-2197
Streator *(G-20709)*

Tri City Sheet Metal ... G ... 630 232-4255
Geneva *(G-10874)*

Tri State Aluminum Products ... F ... 815 877-6081
Loves Park *(G-14003)*

Troxel Industries Inc ... E ... 217 431-8674
Tilton *(G-20883)*

Tru-Way Inc ... E ... 708 562-3690
Northlake *(G-16457)*

Tu-Star Manufacturing Co Inc ... G ... 815 338-5760
Woodstock *(G-22619)*

Two J S Sheet Metal Works Inc ... G ... 773 436-9424
Chicago *(G-6796)*

Ultratech Inc ... E ... 630 539-3578
Bloomingdale *(G-2140)*

Unifab Mfg Inc ... E ... 630 682-8970
Carol Stream *(G-3259)*

Unique Checkout Systems ... F ... 773 522-4400
Franklin Park *(G-10615)*

Unistrut International Corp ... D ... 630 773-3460
Addison *(G-334)*

United Canvas Inc ... E ... 847 395-1470
Antioch *(G-661)*

United Conveyor Supply Company ... E ... 708 344-8050
Melrose Park *(G-14703)*

United Skys LLC ... F ... 847 546-7776
Round Lake *(G-19069)*

US Post Co Inc ... G ... 815 675-9313
Spring Grove *(G-20373)*

V & N Metal Products Inc ... G ... 773 436-1855
Chicago *(G-6863)*

Vanfab Inc ... E ... 815 426-2544
Union Hill *(G-21040)*

Vent Products Co Inc ... E ... 773 521-1900
Chicago *(G-6881)*

Venus Processing & Storage ... D ... 847 455-0496
Franklin Park *(G-10621)*

Viking Metal Cabinet Co LLC ... D ... 800 776-7767
Montgomery *(G-15069)*

Viking Metal Cabinet Company ... D ... 630 863-7234
Montgomery *(G-15070)*

Vorteq Coil Finishers LLC ... E ... 847 455-7200
Franklin Park *(G-10623)*

▲ W A Whitney Co ... C ... 815 964-6771
Rockford *(G-18671)*

W L Engler Distributing Inc ... G ... 630 898-5400
Aurora *(G-1093)*

▲ Wagner Zip-Change Inc ... E ... 708 681-4100
Melrose Park *(G-14706)*

Wallfill Co ... F ... 630 499-9591
Aurora *(G-1094)*

▲ Waukegan Architectural Inc ... G ... 847 746-9077
Zion *(G-22700)*

Welding Specialties ... G ... 708 798-5388
East Hazel Crest *(G-8667)*

White Sheet Metal ... G ... 217 465-3195
Paris *(G-17164)*

◆ William Dudek Manufacturing Co ... E ... 773 622-2727
Chicago *(G-6983)*

Wilson Railing & Metal Fabg Co ... G ... 847 662-1747
Park City *(G-17167)*

Wiltek Inc ... G ... 630 922-9200
Naperville *(G-15832)*

Wirfs Industries Inc ... F ... 815 344-0635
McHenry *(G-14571)*

Woodlawn Engineering Co Inc ... E ... 630 543-3550
Addison *(G-346)*

Woods Mfg and Machining Co ... F ... 847 982-9585
Skokie *(G-20112)*

◆ Wozniak Industries Inc ... G ... 630 954-3400
Oakbrook Terrace *(G-16723)*

Wright Metals Inc ... G ... 847 267-1212
Bannockburn *(G-1267)*

## *3446 Architectural & Ornamental Metal Work*

555 International Inc ... E ... 773 847-1400
Chicago *(G-3670)*

▲ Accurate Partitions Corp ... G ... 708 442-6801
Mc Cook *(G-14444)*

Aetna Engineering Works Inc ... E ... 773 785-0489
Chicago *(G-3778)*

Aj Welding Services ... G ... 708 843-2701
Oak Park *(G-16651)*

Alert Tubing Fabricators Inc ... G ... 847 253-7237
Schaumburg *(G-19429)*

Alfredos Iron Works Inc ... E ... 815 748-1177
Cortland *(G-7384)*

▲ All-Steel Structures Inc ... E ... 708 210-1313
South Holland *(G-20241)*

American Stair Corporation Inc ... D ... 815 886-9600
Romeoville *(G-18796)*

Amron Stair Works Inc ... F ... 847 426-4800
Gilberts *(G-10912)*

Anchor Welding & Fabrication ... G ... 815 937-1640
Aroma Park *(G-878)*

◆ Ancient Graffiti Inc ... E ... 847 726-5800
Lake Zurich *(G-13040)*

Architectural Metals LLC ... F ... 815 654-2370
Loves Park *(G-13922)*

AS Fabricating Inc ... G ... 618 242-7438
Mount Vernon *(G-15398)*

Atkore International Group Inc ... A ... 708 339-1610
Harvey *(G-11658)*

Atkore Intl Holdings Inc ... G ... 708 225-2051
Harvey *(G-11659)*

Atlantis Products Inc ... G ... 630 971-9680
Bolingbrook *(G-2280)*

Bailey Hardwoods Inc ... G ... 217 529-6800
Springfield *(G-20394)*

Barker Metal Craft Inc ... G ... 773 588-9300
Chicago *(G-4043)*

▲ Barnett-Bates Corporation ... F ... 815 726-5223
Joliet *(G-12461)*

Birdsell Machine & Orna Inc ... G ... 217 243-5849
Jacksonville *(G-12379)*

Botti Studio of Architectural ... E ... 847 869-5933
Evanston *(G-10017)*

Brian Hobbs ... G ... 618 758-1303
Coulterville *(G-7398)*

Builders Ironworks Inc ... G ... 708 672-1047
Crete *(G-7509)*

▲ Capitol Wood Works LLC ... D ... 217 522-5553
Springfield *(G-20408)*

Chase Security Systems Inc ... G ... 773 594-1919
Chicago *(G-4295)*

Chicago Iron Works Corporation ... F ... 312 829-1062
Chicago *(G-4324)*

◆ Chicago Metal Rolled Pdts Co ... D ... 773 523-5757
Chicago *(G-4333)*

▲ Chicago Metallic Company LLC ... C ... 708 563-4600
Chicago *(G-4334)*

Chicago Ornamental Iron Inc ... E ... 773 321-9635
Chicago *(G-4338)*

Chicagos Finest Iron Works ... F ... 773 646-4484
Chicago *(G-4365)*

Chicagos Finest Ironworks ... G ... 708 895-4484
Lansing *(G-13159)*

Christopher Glass & Aluminum ... D ... 312 256-8500
Chicago *(G-4372)*

City Ornamental Iron Works ... G ... 847 888-8898
Elgin *(G-8991)*

City Screen Inc ... G ... 773 588-5642
Chicago *(G-4388)*

Concrete Unit Step Co Inc ... G ... 618 344-7256
Collinsville *(G-7317)*

Cooper B-Line Inc ... C ... 618 357-5353
Pinckneyville *(G-17546)*

Crosstree Inc ... G ... 773 227-1234
Chicago *(G-4507)*

Custom Linear Grille Inc ... G ... 847 520-5511
Wheeling *(G-22033)*

Custom Railz & Stairs Inc ... G ... 773 592-7210
Oak Lawn *(G-16613)*

D5 Design Met Fabrication LLC ... G ... 773 770-4705
Chicago *(G-4539)*

Daves Welding Service Inc ... G ... 630 655-3224
Darien *(G-7792)*

David Architectural Metals Inc ... E ... 773 376-3200
Chicago *(G-4563)*

▲ DSI Spaceframes Inc ... E ... 630 607-0045
Addison *(G-99)*

Dynamic Iron Inc ... G ... 708 672-7617
Park Forest *(G-17171)*

Economy Iron Inc ... F ... 708 343-1777
Melrose Park *(G-14628)*

Ed Stan Fabricating Co ... G ... 708 863-7668
Chicago *(G-4694)*

Electrostatic Concepts Inc ... F ... 630 585-5080
Naperville *(G-15804)*

▲ Empire Bronze Corp ... F ... 630 916-9722
Lombard *(G-13796)*

Essential Flooring Inc ... G ... 630 788-3121
Oswego *(G-16916)*

European Ornamental Iron Works ... G ... 630 705-9300
Addison *(G-113)*

Fariss John ... G ... 815 433-3803
Moline *(G-14938)*

Fastrack Stairs & Rails Ltd ... G ... 847 531-6252
Dekalb *(G-8090)*

Fbs Group Inc ... F ... 773 229-8675
Chicago *(G-4821)*

SIC SECTION 34 FABRICATED METAL PRODUCTS, EXCEPT MACHINERY AND TRANSPORTATION EQUIPMENT

**Fehring Ornamental Iron Works**............F....... 217 483-6727
Chatham *(G-3620)*
**▲ First Alert Inc**....................G....... 630 499-3295
Aurora *(G-1009)*
**Fisher & Ludlow Inc**....................D....... 815 932-1200
Bourbonnais *(G-2396)*
**Fisher & Ludlow Inc**....................D....... 217 324-6106
Litchfield *(G-13685)*
**G & M Fabricating Inc**....................G....... 815 282-1744
Roscoe *(G-18898)*
**G P Concrete & Iron Works**....................G....... 815 842-2270
Pontiac *(G-17700)*
**Gemini Steel Inc**....................G....... 815 472-4462
Momence *(G-14981)*
**Gilco Real Estate Company**....................E....... 847 298-1717
Des Plaines *(G-8202)*
**Glitech Inc**....................F....... 708 753-1220
Chicago Heights *(G-7099)*
**Goose Island Mfg & Supply Corp**....................G....... 708 343-4225
Lansing *(G-13164)*
**Greene Welding & Hardware Inc**....................E....... 217 375-4244
East Lynn *(G-8668)*
**▼ Gs Metals Corp**....................C....... 618 357-5353
Pinckneyville *(G-17550)*
**▲ Handi Products Inc**....................E....... 847 816-7525
Libertyville *(G-13329)*
**Hart & Cooley Inc**....................C....... 630 665-5549
Carol Stream *(G-3165)*
**Hercules Iron Works Inc**....................F....... 312 226-2405
Chicago *(G-5078)*
**Ibarra Group LLC**....................G....... 773 650-0503
Chicago *(G-5135)*
**Imperial Stone Collection**....................G....... 847 640-8817
Elk Grove Village *(G-9543)*
**Industrial Fence Inc**....................E....... 773 521-9900
Chicago *(G-5176)*
**Iron Castle Inc**....................F....... 773 890-0575
Chicago *(G-5238)*
**ITW Blding Cmponents Group Inc**....................E....... 217 324-0303
Litchfield *(G-13689)*
**J B Metal Works Inc**....................G....... 847 824-4253
Des Plaines *(G-8215)*
**▲ J C Schultz Enterprises Inc**....................D....... 800 323-9127
Batavia *(G-1459)*
**J H Botts LLC**....................E....... 815 726-5885
Joliet *(G-12519)*
**Jack Ruch Quality Homes Inc**....................G....... 309 663-6595
Bloomington *(G-2185)*
**John F Mate Co**....................G....... 847 381-8131
Lake Barrington *(G-12812)*
**K & K Iron Works LLC**....................D....... 708 924-0000
Mc Cook *(G-14449)*
**K D Iron Works**....................G....... 847 991-3039
Palatine *(G-17047)*
**K Three Welding Service Inc**....................G....... 708 563-2911
Chicago *(G-5344)*
**Kelley Ornamental Iron LLC**....................E....... 309 697-9870
East Peoria *(G-8721)*
**Kelley Ornamental Iron LLC**....................F....... 309 820-7540
Bloomington *(G-2189)*
**Kencor Stairs & Woodworking**....................G....... 630 279-8980
Villa Park *(G-21263)*
**▲ Ki Industries Inc**....................E....... 708 449-1990
Berkeley *(G-2046)*
**King Metal Co**....................G....... 708 388-3845
Alsip *(G-479)*
**Krum Kreations**....................G....... 815 772-8296
Morrison *(G-15145)*
**Lamonica Ornamental Iron Works**....................G....... 773 638-6633
Chicago *(G-5452)*
**Lawndale Forging & Tool Works**....................G....... 773 277-2800
Chicago *(G-5471)*
**Leggs Manufacturing**....................G....... 618 842-9847
Fairfield *(G-10149)*
**Legna Iron Works Inc**....................E....... 630 894-8056
Roselle *(G-18952)*
**Leonards Unit Step Co**....................G....... 815 744-1263
Rockdale *(G-18225)*
**Leonards Unit Step of Moline**....................G....... 309 792-9641
Colona *(G-7345)*
**Lickenbrock & Sons Inc**....................G....... 618 632-4977
O Fallon *(G-16470)*
**Lizotte Sheet Metal Inc**....................G....... 618 656-3066
Edwardsville *(G-8806)*
**Mechanical Indus Stl Svcs Inc**....................E....... 815 521-1725
Channahon *(G-3580)*
**Merchants Metals LLC**....................G....... 847 249-4086
Waukegan *(G-21590)*
**Metal Edge Inc**....................F....... 708 756-4696
S Chicago Hts *(G-19108)*

**Metalex Corporation**....................C....... 847 362-5400
Libertyville *(G-13355)*
**Midwest Cage Company**....................G....... 815 806-0005
Frankfort *(G-10342)*
**Midwest Stair Parts**....................G....... 630 723-3991
Naperville *(G-15817)*
**Mike Meier & Sons Fence Mfg**....................E....... 847 587-1111
Spring Grove *(G-20347)*
**Milk Design Company**....................G....... 312 563-6455
Posen *(G-17732)*
**Millers Eureka Inc**....................F....... 312 666-9383
Chicago *(G-5762)*
**Mj Snyder Ironworks Inc**....................G....... 217 826-6440
Marshall *(G-14326)*
**Montefusco Heating & Shtmtl Co**....................G....... 309 691-7400
Peoria *(G-17412)*
**▲ Mrk Industries Inc**....................E....... 847 362-8720
Libertyville *(G-13361)*
**Mueller Orna Ir Works Inc**....................F....... 847 758-9941
Elk Grove Village *(G-9643)*
**Nci Group Inc**....................D....... 309 527-3095
El Paso *(G-8871)*
**Neiweem Industries Inc**....................G....... 847 487-1239
Oakwood Hills *(G-16727)*
**Nelson - Harkins Inds Inc**....................E....... 773 478-6243
Chicago *(G-5884)*
**Nicks Metal Fabg & Sons**....................F....... 708 485-1170
Brookfield *(G-2639)*
**North Chicago Iron Works Inc**....................E....... 847 689-2000
North Chicago *(G-16185)*
**Old Style Iron Works Inc**....................G....... 773 265-5787
Chicago *(G-5980)*
**Oldcastle Precast Inc**....................F....... 309 661-4608
Normal *(G-16082)*
**Ornamental Iron Shop**....................G....... 618 281-6072
Columbia *(G-7361)*
**▲ Orsolinis Welding & Fabg**....................F....... 773 722-9855
Chicago *(G-6016)*
**Osorio Iron Works**....................F....... 773 772-4060
Chicago *(G-6022)*
**Otis Elevator Company**....................D....... 312 454-1616
Chicago *(G-6023)*
**P & M Ornamental Ir Works Inc**....................F....... 708 267-2868
Melrose Park *(G-14680)*
**▲ P & P Artec Inc**....................F....... 630 860-2990
Wood Dale *(G-22410)*
**P I W Corporation**....................F....... 708 301-5100
Homer Glen *(G-12085)*
**Paco Corporation**....................F....... 708 430-2424
Bridgeview *(G-2517)*
**Palo Verde Suspension Inc**....................G....... 815 939-2196
Bourbonnais *(G-2405)*
**Patrick Holdings Inc**....................F....... 815 874-5300
Rockford *(G-18531)*
**Paul D Metal Products Inc**....................D....... 773 847-1400
Chicago *(G-6090)*
**Pep Industries Inc**....................F....... 630 833-0404
Villa Park *(G-21276)*
**Quality Iron Works Inc**....................F....... 630 766-0885
Bensenville *(G-1971)*
**R & B Metal Products Inc**....................E....... 815 338-1890
Woodstock *(G-22603)*
**R & I Ornamental Iron Inc**....................E....... 847 836-6934
Gilberts *(G-10933)*
**Rockford Ornamental Iron Inc**....................F....... 815 633-1162
Rockford *(G-18581)*
**Royal Stairs Co**....................G....... 847 685-9448
Park Ridge *(G-17220)*
**S & G Iron Works**....................G.....
Zion *(G-22697)*
**Sandoval Fences Corp**....................G....... 773 287-0279
Chicago *(G-6438)*
**Selco Industries**....................G....... 708 499-1060
Chicago Ridge *(G-7158)*
**Selvaggio Orna & Strl Stl Inc**....................E....... 217 528-4077
Springfield *(G-20521)*
**Sheas Iron Works Inc**....................E....... 847 356-2922
Lake Villa *(G-13026)*
**Sno Gem Inc**....................F....... 888 766-4367
McHenry *(G-14555)*
**South Subn Wldg & Fabg Co Inc**....................G....... 708 385-7160
Posen *(G-17736)*
**Steel Construction Svcs Inc**....................G....... 815 678-7509
Richmond *(G-17972)*
**Steel Guard Inc**....................F....... 773 342-6265
Chicago *(G-6580)*
**Steelwerks of Chicago LLC**....................G....... 312 792-9593
Chicago *(G-6582)*
**Stevenson Fabrication Svcs Inc**....................G....... 815 468-7941
Manteno *(G-14195)*

**Technetics Group LLC**....................G....... 708 887-6080
Harwood Heights *(G-11691)*
**▲ Tim Detwiler Enterprises Inc**....................G....... 815 758-9950
Dekalb *(G-8127)*
**Tinsley Steel Inc**....................G....... 618 656-5231
Edwardsville *(G-8817)*
**Tru-Guard Manufacturing Co**....................G....... 773 568-5264
Chicago *(G-6784)*
**Tuschall Engineering Co Inc**....................E....... 630 655-9100
Burr Ridge *(G-2888)*
**▲ Uncommon Usa Inc**....................F....... 630 268-9672
Lombard *(G-13876)*
**▲ Unistrut International Corp**....................C....... 800 882-5543
Harvey *(G-11679)*
**United Conveyor Supply Company**....................E....... 708 344-8050
Melrose Park *(G-14703)*
**United Fence Co Inc**....................G....... 773 924-0773
Chicago *(G-6823)*
**V & N Metal Products Inc**....................G....... 773 436-1855
Chicago *(G-6863)*
**▲ Vector Custom Fabricating Inc**....................F....... 312 421-5161
Chicago *(G-6878)*
**W G N Flag & Decorating Co**....................F....... 773 768-8076
Chicago *(G-6918)*
**▲ Waukegan Architectural Inc**....................G....... 847 746-9077
Zion *(G-22700)*
**Waukegan Steel LLC**....................E....... 847 662-2810
Waukegan *(G-21639)*
**WEb Production & Fabg Inc**....................F....... 312 733-6800
Chicago *(G-6948)*
**Weber Metals Inc**....................G....... 847 951-7920
Libertyville *(G-13400)*
**Werner Co**....................A....... 847 455-8001
Itasca *(G-12374)*
**Werner Co**....................E....... 815 459-6020
Crystal Lake *(G-7676)*
**Wilson Railing & Metal Fabg Co**....................G....... 847 662-1747
Park City *(G-17167)*
**Winters Welding Inc**....................G....... 773 860-7735
Chicago *(G-7004)*

### *3448 Prefabricated Metal Buildings & Cmpnts*

**Alvarez & Marsal Inc**....................E....... 312 601-4220
Chicago *(G-3840)*
**American Buildings Company**....................C....... 309 527-5420
El Paso *(G-8865)*
**American Deck & Sunroom C**....................G....... 217 586-4840
Mahomet *(G-14157)*
**American Fixture**....................G....... 217 429-1300
Decatur *(G-7832)*
**American Steel Carports Inc**....................F....... 800 487-4010
Kewanee *(G-12669)*
**◆ Americana Building Pdts Inc**....................D....... 618 548-2800
Salem *(G-19326)*
**◆ Arrow Shed LLC**....................E....... 618 526-4546
Breese *(G-2437)*
**Arrow Shed LLC**....................C....... 618 526-4546
Breese *(G-2438)*
**Associated Group Holdings LLC**....................G....... 312 662-5488
Chicago *(G-3968)*
**Atkore International Group Inc**....................A....... 708 339-1610
Harvey *(G-11658)*
**Atkore Intl Holdings Inc**....................G....... 708 225-2051
Harvey *(G-11659)*
**Bluescope Buildings N Amer Inc**....................E....... 217 348-7676
Charleston *(G-3590)*
**Cardinal Enterprises**....................G....... 618 994-4454
Stonefort *(G-20637)*
**Chicago Enclosures**....................G....... 708 344-6600
Melrose Park *(G-14609)*
**Chicago Panel & Truss Inc**....................E....... 630 870-1300
Aurora *(G-1129)*
**▼ Comforts Home Services Inc**....................G....... 847 856-8002
Montgomery *(G-15040)*
**▼ Craig Industries Inc**....................D....... 217 228-2421
Quincy *(G-17816)*
**CST Industries Inc**....................C....... 815 756-1551
Dekalb *(G-8080)*
**D & D Construction Co LLC**....................G....... 217 852-6631
Dallas City *(G-7695)*
**Dspc Company**....................E....... 815 997-1116
Rockford *(G-18353)*
**Eagle Companies Inc**....................F....... 309 686-9054
Chillicothe *(G-7164)*
**▼ Elfi LLC**....................E....... 815 439-1833
Chicago *(G-4727)*
**Esi Steel & Fabrication**....................F....... 618 548-3017
Salem *(G-19331)*

S I C

# 34 FABRICATED METAL PRODUCTS, EXCEPT MACHINERY AND TRANSPORTATION EQUIPMENT

Fehring Ornamental Iron Works............F......217 483-6727
  Chatham (G-3620)
◆ Heico Companies LLC............................F......312 419-8220
  Chicago (G-5068)
Jack Walters & Sons Corp......................E......618 842-2642
  Fairfield (G-10145)
Kravet Inc............................................G......847 870-1414
  Arlington Heights (G-790)
McElroy Metal Mill Inc..........................E......217 935-9421
  Clinton (G-7287)
Medieval Builders LLC..........................G......331 245-7791
  Schaumburg (G-19639)
Minority Auto Hdlg Specialists..............F......708 757-8758
  Chicago Heights (G-7113)
Mobile Mini Inc....................................E......708 297-2004
  Calumet Park (G-2963)
Morton Buildings Inc............................G......217 357-3713
  Carthage (G-3317)
Morton Buildings Inc............................F......630 904-1122
  Streator (G-20695)
Morton Buildings Inc............................F......309 936-7282
  Atkinson (G-944)
Nci Group Inc......................................D......309 527-3095
  El Paso (G-8871)
Optimal Construction Svcs Inc..............G......630 365-5050
  Elburn (G-8902)
Penstock Construction Services............G......630 816-2456
  Plainfield (G-17636)
▲ Petersen Aluminum Corporation..........D......847 228-7150
  Elk Grove Village (G-9676)
Renegade Steel....................................G......716 903-2506
  Chicago (G-6332)
▲ Rv6 Performance..............................G......630 346-7998
  Wheaton (G-21978)
▼ Safety Storage Inc............................D......217 345-4422
  Charleston (G-3610)
Signa Development Group Inc..............G......773 418-4506
  Norridge (G-16108)
Singer Safety Company........................F......773 235-2100
  Chicago (G-6516)
Steel Span Inc....................................F......815 943-9071
  Harvard (G-11648)
Strat-O-Span Buildings Inc..................G......618 526-4566
  Breese (G-2448)
Tandem Industries Inc.........................G......630 761-6615
  Saint Charles (G-19279)
▲ Unistrut International Corp...............C......800 882-5543
  Harvey (G-11679)
Ward Cnc Machining............................G......815 637-1490
  Loves Park (G-14006)
White Star Silo....................................G......618 523-4735
  Germantown (G-10894)

## 3449 Misc Structural Metal Work

A & S Steel Specialties Inc...................E......815 838-8188
  Lockport (G-13700)
Advance Welding & Equipment.............F......630 759-3334
  Countryside (G-7411)
Advanced Assembly.............................G......630 379-6158
  Streamwood (G-20639)
▲ All-Steel Structures Inc....................E......708 210-1313
  South Holland (G-20241)
American Classic Rebar Corp...............G......708 225-1010
  South Holland (G-20243)
American Steel Fabricators Inc.............F......847 807-4200
  Melrose Park (G-14593)
Bergst Special Tools Inc......................G......630 543-1020
  Addison (G-53)
Bohler................................................G......630 883-3000
  Elgin (G-8969)
▼ Central Steel Fabricators..................E......708 652-2037
  Broadview (G-2565)
◆ Chicago Metal Rolled Pdts Co............D......773 523-5757
  Chicago (G-4333)
Chicago Ornamental Iron Inc...............E......773 321-9635
  Chicago (G-4338)
▲ Crown Premiums Inc.......................F......815 469-8789
  Frankfort (G-10311)
Dayton Superior Corporation...............E......219 476-4106
  Kankakee (G-12608)
Delta Erectors Inc..............................F......708 267-9721
  Villa Park (G-21248)
Dixline Corporation.............................D......309 932-2011
  Galva (G-10788)
Dixline Corporation.............................F......309 932-2011
  Galva (G-10787)
Duroweld Company Inc.......................E......847 680-3064
  Lake Bluff (G-12841)
▼ Elfi LLC..........................................E......815 439-1833
  Chicago (G-4727)

Expanded Metal Products Corp............F......773 735-4500
  Chicago (G-4795)
Fabco Enterprises Inc.........................G......708 333-4644
  Harvey (G-11666)
FHB Lighting Inc................................G......888 364-8802
  Palatine (G-17028)
Gerdau Ameristeel US Inc...................F......815 544-9651
  Belvidere (G-1756)
Gerdau Ameristeel US Inc...................G......815 547-0400
  Belvidere (G-1757)
Gmh Metal Fabrication Inc..................G......309 253-6429
  East Peoria (G-8711)
Great Lakes Stair & Steel Inc..............G......708 430-2323
  Chicago Ridge (G-7148)
H3 Group LLC....................................F......309 222-6027
  Peoria (G-17377)
Harmon Inc........................................G......630 759-8060
  Bolingbrook (G-2315)
Headhunter2000 Inc..........................G......708 533-3769
  Northlake (G-16438)
HI Metals LLC....................................G......312 590-3360
  Winnetka (G-22307)
Illinois Steel Service Inc.....................D......312 926-7440
  Chicago (G-5158)
J and D Installers Inc........................G......847 288-0783
  Franklin Park (G-10501)
Jason Incorporated.............................C......847 362-8300
  Libertyville (G-13340)
JC Metalcrafters Inc...........................F......815 942-9891
  Morris (G-15111)
Kroh-Wagner Inc................................E......773 252-2031
  Chicago (G-5412)
▲ L & M Welding Inc..........................F......773 237-8500
  Chicago (G-5419)
▲ Ladder Industries Inc......................E......800 360-6789
  Deerfield (G-8027)
Lockport Steel Fabricators LLC.............D......815 726-6281
  Lockport (G-13728)
Ltc Holdings Inc.................................C......847 249-5900
  Waukegan (G-21585)
Luren Precision Chicago Co Ltd...........G......847 882-1388
  Schaumburg (G-19624)
Marsha Lega Studio Inc......................G
  Joliet (G-12537)
MB Steel Company Inc.......................F......618 877-7000
  Madison (G-14152)
MBI Tools LLC....................................G......815 844-0937
  Pontiac (G-17706)
Mercedes Fabrication..........................F......708 709-9240
  Chicago Heights (G-7112)
Metal Strip Buiding Products...............G......847 742-8500
  Itasca (G-12314)
▲ Metalex Corporation........................C......847 362-8300
  Libertyville (G-13354)
▲ Metals and Services Inc..................D......630 627-2900
  Addison (G-202)
MMC Precision Holdings Corp.............G......309 266-7176
  Morton (G-15164)
▲ Morton Industrial Group Inc............G......309 266-7176
  Morton (G-15167)
Morton Metalcraft Co PA.....................E......309 266-7176
  Morton (G-15169)
▲ Nucor Steel Kankakee Inc...............B......815 937-3131
  Bourbonnais (G-2403)
Olin Engineered Systems Inc..............F......618 258-2874
  East Alton (G-8609)
OMalley Welding and Fabg..................G......630 553-1604
  Yorkville (G-22667)
On Target Grinding and Mfg................G......708 418-3905
  Lynwood (G-14022)
R W Bradley Supply Company.............F......217 528-8438
  Springfield (G-20510)
Schmolz Bckenbach USA Holdings.......G......630 682-3900
  Carol Stream (G-3236)
Sitexpedite LLC..................................E......847 245-2185
  Lindenhurst (G-13549)
Steel Fabricating Inc..........................F......815 977-5355
  Rockford (G-18633)
Steel Rebar Manufacturing LLC...........G......618 920-2748
  Centreville (G-3438)
Steelwerks of Chicago LLC..................E......312 792-9593
  Chicago (G-6582)
Superior Metalcraft Inc.......................F......708 418-8940
  Lansing (G-13188)
Thirteen Rf Inc..................................E......618 687-1313
  Murphysboro (G-15585)
Trinity Machined Products Inc.............E......630 876-6992
  Aurora (G-1090)
Van Pelt Corporation..........................E......313 365-3600
  East Moline (G-8697)

▲ Vermilion Steel Fabrication...............G......217 442-5300
  Danville (G-7778)
Ziglers Mch & Met Works Inc..............G......815 652-7518
  Dixon (G-8360)

## 3451 Screw Machine Prdts

A E Micek Engineering Corp................E......847 455-8181
  Franklin Park (G-10381)
Abbco Inc..........................................E......630 595-7115
  Elk Grove Village (G-9253)
▲ Abbott Scott Manufacturing Co........E......773 342-7200
  Chicago (G-3706)
▲ Abbott-Interfast Corporation............D......847 459-6200
  Wheeling (G-21996)
▲ Ability Fasteners Inc.......................F......847 593-4230
  Elk Grove Village (G-9256)
Accumation Inc..................................F......815 455-6250
  Crystal Lake (G-7526)
Acme Screw Co..................................F......815 332-7548
  Cherry Valley (G-3637)
Advance Screw Products Inc...............F......773 237-0034
  Chicago (G-3763)
Afco Products Incorporated.................F......847 299-1055
  Lake Zurich (G-13036)
▲ Afi Industries Inc............................E......630 462-0400
  Carol Stream (G-3092)
Alert Scrw Products Inc......................G......847 587-1360
  Fox Lake (G-10274)
Alpha Swiss Industries Inc..................G......815 455-3031
  Crystal Lake (G-7530)
AM Swiss Screw Mch Pdts Inc............F......847 468-9300
  South Elgin (G-20181)
American Machine Pdts & Svcs...........G......708 743-9088
  Mokena (G-14852)
American Precision Machine................F......847 428-5950
  Carpentersville (G-3273)
American Screw Machine Co...............G......847 455-4308
  Franklin Park (G-10393)
▲ American/Jebco Corporation............C......847 455-3150
  Franklin Park (G-10394)
Ampex Screw Mfg Inc........................G......847 228-1202
  Arlington Heights (G-712)
Anpec Industries Inc..........................E......815 239-2303
  Pecatonica (G-17250)
Archer Engineering Company..............G......773 247-3501
  Chicago (G-3936)
Arrow Gear Company..........................G......630 969-7640
  Downers Grove (G-8390)
Astro-Craft Inc..................................E......815 675-1500
  Spring Grove (G-20326)
▲ Automatic Precision Inc..................E......708 867-1116
  Chicago (G-3992)
Automatic Swiss Corporation...............E......630 543-3888
  Addison (G-49)
Automation Systems Inc....................E......847 671-9515
  Melrose Park (G-14597)
Autonamic Corporation.......................G......815 675-6300
  Spring Grove (G-20327)
Autonetics Inc...................................F......847 426-8525
  Carpentersville (G-3275)
Avan Tool & Die Co Inc......................F......773 287-1670
  Chicago (G-3996)
Avanti Engineering Inc.......................F......630 260-1333
  Glendale Heights (G-11011)
B & M Screw Machine Inc..................G......815 432-5892
  Watseka (G-21415)
B Radtke and Sons Inc......................G......847 546-3999
  Round Lake Park (G-19083)
Belrich Inc........................................G
  Chicago (G-4080)
Bensenville Screw Products.................G......630 860-5222
  Bensenville (G-1843)
Bradley Machining Inc........................F......630 543-2875
  Addison (G-59)
Calcon Machine Inc............................G......815 495-9227
  Leland (G-13219)
Calumet Screw Machine Products.......D......708 479-1660
  Mokena (G-14856)
Camco Manufacturing Inc...................F......708 597-4288
  Crestwood (G-7478)
Camcraft Inc......................................C......630 582-6001
  Hanover Park (G-11578)
Camshop Industrial LLC.....................G......708 597-4288
  Crestwood (G-7478)
Central Autmtc Screw Pdts Inc...........G......630 766-7966
  Bensenville (G-1854)
Chase Fasteners Inc..........................E......708 345-0335
  Melrose Park (G-14608)

SIC SECTION — 34 FABRICATED METAL PRODUCTS, EXCEPT MACHINERY AND TRANSPORTATION EQUIPMENT

**Chicago Rivet & Machine Co** ....C.... 630 357-8500
Naperville *(G-15627)*
▼ **Chicago Turnrite Co Inc** ....E.... 773 626-8404
Chicago *(G-4360)*
**Cnc Swiss Inc** ....G.... 630 543-9595
Addison *(G-78)*
**Continental Automation Inc** ....E.... 630 584-5100
Saint Charles *(G-19162)*
**Continental Midland** ....G.... 708 441-1000
Calumet Park *(G-2960)*
**Continental Screws Mch Pdts** ....E.... 847 459-7766
Wheeling *(G-22030)*
**Contour Screw Products Inc** ....E.... 847 357-1190
Arlington Heights *(G-739)*
**CP Screw Machine Products** ....F.... 630 766-2313
Bensenville *(G-1870)*
**Demco Products Inc** ....F.... 708 636-6240
Oak Lawn *(G-16616)*
▲ **Devon Precision Machine Pdts** ....F.... 847 233-9700
Franklin Park *(G-10458)*
**Dune Manufacturing Company** ....F.... 708 681-2905
Melrose Park *(G-14622)*
**Durite Screw Corporation** ....E.... 773 622-3410
Chicago *(G-4656)*
▲ **E J Basler Co** ....D.... 847 678-8880
Schiller Park *(G-19821)*
**Eastview Manufacturing Inc** ....G.... 847 741-2514
Elgin *(G-9019)*
**Ella Engineering Incorporated** ....G.... 847 354-4767
Elk Grove Village *(G-9453)*
**Empire Screw Manufacturing Co** ....F.... 630 833-7060
Villa Park *(G-21251)*
**Engineered Plastic Pdts Corp** ....E.... 847 952-8400
Elk Grove Village *(G-9460)*
**F and F Screw Products** ....G.... 815 968-7330
Rockford *(G-18378)*
**Forster Tool & Mfg Co Inc** ....E.... 630 616-8177
Bensenville *(G-1902)*
**Francis Screw Products Co Inc** ....G.... 847 647-9462
Niles *(G-15980)*
**Franklin Screw Products Inc** ....G.... 815 784-8500
Genoa *(G-10878)*
**Fsp LLC** ....G.... 773 992-2600
Gurnee *(G-11450)*
**G & E Automatic** ....G.... 815 654-7766
Machesney Park *(G-14077)*
**G Messmore Company** ....G.... 708 343-8114
Broadview *(G-2581)*
**Gage Manufacturing Inc** ....F.... 847 228-7300
Elk Grove Village *(G-9493)*
**General Engineering Works** ....E.... 630 543-8000
Addison *(G-131)*
**General Fas Acquisition Co** ....E.... 630 960-3360
Woodridge *(G-22481)*
**Global Turnings Inc** ....G.... 630 562-0946
West Chicago *(G-21708)*
**Globe Precision Machining Inc** ....G.... 815 389-4586
South Beloit *(G-20149)*
**Greg Screw Machine Products** ....G.... 630 694-8875
Wood Dale *(G-22378)*
**Groth Manufacturing** ....E.... 847 428-5950
Carpentersville *(G-3286)*
**H & M Thread Rolling Co Inc** ....G.... 847 451-1570
Franklin Park *(G-10485)*
**Hi-Tech Welding Services Inc** ....G.... 630 595-8160
Bensenville *(G-1917)*
**Highland Mch & Screw Pdts Co** ....D.... 618 654-2103
Highland *(G-11788)*
**Highland Metal Inc** ....E.... 708 544-6641
Hillside *(G-11919)*
**I D Rockford Shop Inc** ....G.... 815 335-1150
Winnebago *(G-22297)*
**Illinois Tool Works Inc** ....E.... 815 654-1510
Machesney Park *(G-14080)*
**Illinois Tool Works Inc** ....E.... 847 741-7900
Elgin *(G-9071)*
▲ **J N R Custo-Matic Screw Inc** ....D.... 630 260-1333
Glendale Heights *(G-11036)*
**JB Mfg & Screw Machine** .... 630 850-6978
Burr Ridge *(G-2859)*
**JB Mfg & Screw Machine PR** ....G.... 847 451-0892
Franklin Park *(G-10507)*
**Jedi Corporation** ....G.... 815 344-5334
Mchenry *(G-14516)*
**Jefco Screw Machine Products** ....F.... 815 282-2000
Loves Park *(G-13952)*
**Jim Sterner Machines** ....G.... 815 962-8983
Rockford *(G-18445)*
**Jmd Screw Products** ....G.... 815 505-9113
Belvidere *(G-1766)*
**Jt Products Co** ....G.... 773 378-4550
Melrose Park *(G-14665)*
**Kadon Precision Machining Inc** ....D.... 815 874-5850
Rockford *(G-18452)*
**Kenent Screw Machine Products** ....F.... 815 624-7216
Rockton *(G-18697)*
**Kiel Machine Products** ....G....
Elgin *(G-9088)*
▲ **Kksp Precision Machining LLC** ....D.... 630 260-1735
Glendale Heights *(G-11038)*
**L & W Tool & Screw Mch Pdts** ....E.... 847 238-1212
Itasca *(G-12300)*
**L D Redmer Screw Pdts Inc** ....E.... 630 787-0504
Bensenville *(G-1935)*
**L D Redmer Screw Products** ....G.... 630 787-0507
Naperville *(G-15685)*
**Lab Ten LLC** ....E.... 815 877-1410
Machesney Park *(G-14087)*
**Lafox Screw Products Inc** ....G.... 847 695-1732
South Elgin *(G-20214)*
**Lakeside Screw Products Inc** ....C.... 630 495-1606
Addison *(G-178)*
**Lakeview Prcsion Machining Inc** ....F.... 847 742-7170
South Elgin *(G-20215)*
**Lawrence Screw Products Inc** ....G.... 217 735-1230
Lincoln *(G-13412)*
**Lombard Swiss Screw Company** ....E.... 630 576-5096
Addison *(G-183)*
**Lsl Precision Machining Inc** ....E.... 815 633-4701
Loves Park *(G-13962)*
◆ **Mac Lean-Fogg Company** ....D.... 847 566-0010
Mundelein *(G-15521)*
**Magnet-Schultz Amer Holdg LLC** ....G.... 630 789-0600
Westmont *(G-21901)*
▲ **Magnet-Schultz America Inc** ....D.... 630 789-0600
Westmont *(G-21902)*
**Magnus Screw Products Co** ....E.... 773 889-2344
Chicago *(G-5603)*
**Makerite Mfg Co Inc** ....E.... 815 389-3902
Roscoe *(G-18906)*
**Masters Yates Inc** ....G.... 815 227-9585
Rockford *(G-18486)*
**Mc Henry Screw Products Inc** ....G.... 815 344-4638
McHenry *(G-14529)*
▲ **Meaden Precision Machined Pdts** ....D.... 630 655-0888
Burr Ridge *(G-2865)*
**Meador Industries Inc** ....E.... 847 671-5042
Franklin Park *(G-10526)*
▲ **Metomic Corporation** ....E.... 773 247-4716
Chicago *(G-5705)*
**Micro Screw Machine Co Inc** ....G.... 815 397-2115
Rockford *(G-18501)*
**Mid-West Screw Products Inc** ....E.... 773 283-6032
Chicago *(G-5731)*
**Midway Machine Products & Svcs** ....G.... 847 860-8180
Elk Grove Village *(G-9628)*
**Minic Precision Inc** ....F.... 815 675-0451
Spring Grove *(G-20348)*
▲ **Monnex International Inc** ....E.... 847 850-5263
Buffalo Grove *(G-2738)*
▲ **Multitech Cold Forming LLC** ....E.... 630 949-8200
Carol Stream *(G-3201)*
**National Cap and Set Screw Co** ....F.... 815 675-2363
Spring Grove *(G-20350)*
▲ **National Cycle Inc** ....C.... 708 343-0400
Maywood *(G-14430)*
**Nelson & Lavold Manufacturing** ....G.... 312 943-6300
Chicago *(G-5883)*
**North Amercn Acquisition Corp** ....D.... 847 695-8030
Elgin *(G-9124)*
**Nu-Metal Products Inc** ....F.... 815 459-2075
Crystal Lake *(G-7622)*
**Nyclo Screw Machine Pdts Inc** ....F.... 815 229-7900
Rockford *(G-18523)*
**Pioneer Service Inc** ....E.... 630 628-0249
Addison *(G-242)*
▲ **Precise Products Inc** ....E.... 630 393-9698
Warrenville *(G-21357)*
▲ **Precision McHned Cmponents Inc** ....E.... 630 759-5555
Romeoville *(G-18860)*
**Precision Screw Machining Co** ....F.... 773 205-4280
Chicago *(G-6172)*
▲ **Precision Steel Warehouse Inc** ....C.... 800 323-0740
Franklin Park *(G-10560)*
**Precision-Tek Mfg Inc** ....E.... 847 364-7800
Arlington Heights *(G-819)*
**Preferred Fasteners Inc** ....G.... 630 510-0200
Carol Stream *(G-3215)*
**Princeton Industrial Products** ....F.... 847 839-8500
Hoffman Estates *(G-12041)*
**Process Screw Products Inc** ....E.... 815 864-2220
Shannon *(G-19901)*
**Progressive Turnings Inc** ....F.... 630 898-3072
Aurora *(G-1206)*
◆ **Qcc LLC** ....C.... 708 867-5400
Harwood Heights *(G-11689)*
**R & N Machine Co** ....F.... 708 841-5555
Riverdale *(G-18023)*
**R B Evans Co** ....G.... 630 365-3554
Elburn *(G-8907)*
**Red Devil Manufacturing Co** ....G.... 847 215-1377
Wheeling *(G-22134)*
**Reino Tool & Manufacturing Co** ....F.... 773 588-5800
Chicago *(G-6326)*
**RF Mau Co** ....F.... 847 329-9731
Lincolnwood *(G-13533)*
**Roberts Swiss Inc** ....E.... 630 467-9100
Itasca *(G-12348)*
**Rockford Ball Screw Company** ....D.... 815 961-7700
Rockford *(G-18566)*
**Royal Machining Corporation** ....G.... 708 338-3387
Melrose Park *(G-14689)*
▲ **S & W Manufacturing Co Inc** ....E.... 630 595-5044
Bensenville *(G-1984)*
**SA Industries 2 Inc** ....G.... 815 381-6200
Rockford *(G-18604)*
**Saturn Manufacturing Company** ....G.... 630 860-8474
Bensenville *(G-1986)*
**Screw Machine Engrg Co Inc** ....E.... 773 631-7600
Chicago *(G-6461)*
▲ **Screws Industries Inc** ....D.... 630 539-9200
Glendale Heights *(G-11068)*
▲ **Security Locknut LLC** ....E.... 847 970-4050
Vernon Hills *(G-21200)*
**Special Fastener Operations** ....G.... 815 544-6449
Belvidere *(G-1784)*
**St Charles Screw Products Inc** ....G.... 815 943-8060
Harvard *(G-11647)*
**Starro Precision Products Inc** ....E.... 847 741-9400
Elgin *(G-9192)*
**Suburban Screw Machine Pdts** ....G.... 815 337-0434
Woodstock *(G-22614)*
**Supreme Manufacturing Company** ....E.... 847 297-8212
Des Plaines *(G-8283)*
**Supreme Screw Products** ....G.... 708 579-3500
Countryside *(G-7445)*
**Swebco Mfg Inc** ....E.... 815 636-7160
Machesney Park *(G-14110)*
**Swiss Automation Inc** ....D.... 847 381-4405
Barrington *(G-1306)*
▲ **Swiss Precision Machining Inc** ....D.... 847 647-7111
Wheeling *(G-22162)*
**Swisstronics Corp** ....G.... 708 403-8877
Orland Park *(G-16897)*
**T R Jones Machine Co Inc** ....G.... 815 356-5000
Machesney Park *(G-14111)*
**Tanko Scrw Prd Corp** ....G.... 708 418-0300
Chicago Heights *(G-7130)*
**Toledo Screw Machine Products** ....G.... 815 877-8213
Rockford *(G-18652)*
**Tri-Part Screw Products Inc** ....E.... 815 654-7311
Machesney Park *(G-14114)*
**Turnco Inc** ....G.... 708 756-6565
Chicago Heights *(G-7133)*
**Ty Precision Automatics Inc** ....F.... 815 963-9668
Rockford *(G-18658)*
**Uca Group Inc** ....E.... 847 742-7151
South Elgin *(G-20231)*
**Vandeventer Mfg Co Inc** ....E.... 630 879-2511
Batavia *(G-1515)*
**Vanguard Tool & Engineering Co** ....E.... 847 981-9595
Mount Prospect *(G-15382)*
**Vek Screw Machine Products** ....G.... 630 543-5557
Addison *(G-338)*
**Weber Metal Products Inc** ....F.... 815 844-3169
Chenoa *(G-3636)*
**Wenlyn Screw Company Inc** ....G.... 630 766-0050
Bensenville *(G-2013)*
**Wilmette Screw Products** ....G.... 773 725-2626
Chicago *(G-6989)*
**Wilson Mfg Screw Mch Pdts** ....F.... 815 964-8724
Rockford *(G-18684)*
**Worley Machining Inc** ....F.... 630 801-9198
Aurora *(G-1234)*
**X-L-Engineering Corp** ....E.... 847 965-3030
Niles *(G-16048)*
**X-L-Engineering Corp** ....E.... 847 364-4750
Elk Grove Village *(G-9820)*

SIC

Employee Codes: A=Over 500 employees, B=251-500
C=101-250, D=51-100, E=20-50, F=10-19, G=3-9
2017 Harris Illinois
Industrial Directory
1041

34 FABRICATED METAL PRODUCTS, EXCEPT MACHINERY AND TRANSPORTATION EQUIPMENT SIC SECTION

### 3452 Bolts, Nuts, Screws, Rivets & Washers

**A J Horne Inc** ....G.... 630 231-8686
West Chicago *(G-21651)*
**A J Kay Co** ....F.... 224 475-0370
Mundelein *(G-15462)*
▲ **Abbott-Interfast Corporation** ....D.... 847 459-6200
Wheeling *(G-21996)*
▲ **Ability Fasteners Inc** ....F.... 847 593-4230
Elk Grove Village *(G-9256)*
**Accurate Rivet Manufacturing** ....G.... 630 766-3401
Wood Dale *(G-22330)*
▲ **Acme Screw Co** ....D.... 630 665-2200
Wheaton *(G-21933)*
**Acument Global Techologies** ....F.... 815 544-7574
Belvidere *(G-1727)*
▼ **Advanced Machine & Engrg Co** ....C.... 815 962-6076
Rockford *(G-18257)*
▲ **Afi Industries Inc** ....E.... 630 462-0400
Carol Stream *(G-3092)*
**Alan Manufacturing Corp** ....G.... 815 568-6836
Marengo *(G-14217)*
**All American Washer Werks Inc** ....E.... 847 566-9091
Mundelein *(G-15468)*
**Allied Rivet Inc** ....F.... 630 208-0120
Geneva *(G-10808)*
▲ **Allstar Fasteners Inc** ....E.... 847 640-7827
Elk Grove Village *(G-9287)*
**Alltec Gates Inc** ....G.... 708 301-9361
Tinley Park *(G-20889)*
**Amber Engineering and Mfg Co** ....D.... 847 595-6966
Elk Grove Village *(G-9293)*
▲ **American/Jebco Corporation** ....C.... 847 455-3150
Franklin Park *(G-10394)*
**Ames Metal Products Company** ....F.... 773 523-3230
Wheeling *(G-22005)*
**Ampex Screw Mfg Inc** ....G.... 847 228-1202
Arlington Heights *(G-712)*
▲ **Archer Screw Products Inc** ....D.... 847 451-1150
Franklin Park *(G-10399)*
**Arrow Pin and Products Inc** ....F.... 708 755-7575
S Chicago Hts *(G-19100)*
**Aspen Manufacturing Company** ....G.... 630 495-0922
Addison *(G-46)*
**Aww 10 Inc** ....D.... 630 595-7600
Bensenville *(G-1837)*
▲ **Aztech Engineering Inc** ....E.... 630 236-3200
Aurora *(G-964)*
**BBC Fasteners Inc** ....E.... 708 597-9100
Alsip *(G-439)*
**Borny Enterprise Corp** ....G.... 646 662-1514
Chicago *(G-4146)*
▲ **Brynolf Manufacturing Inc** ....E.... 815 873-8878
Rockford *(G-18291)*
▲ **Burgess-Norton Mfg Co Inc** ....B.... 630 232-4100
Geneva *(G-10813)*
**Burgess-Norton Mfg Co Inc** ....E.... 630 232-4100
Geneva *(G-10814)*
**Camcar LLC** ....D.... 815 544-7574
Belvidere *(G-1742)*
**Century Fasteners & Mch Co Inc** ....F.... 773 463-3900
Skokie *(G-19977)*
**Chas O Larson Co** ....E.... 815 625-0503
Rock Falls *(G-18129)*
**Chase Fasteners Inc** ....E.... 708 345-0335
Melrose Park *(G-14608)*
▲ **Chicago Fastener Inc** ....F.... 708 479-9770
Mokena *(G-14857)*
▲ **Chicago Hardware and Fix Co** ....D.... 847 455-6609
Franklin Park *(G-10429)*
**Chicago Rivet & Machine Co** ....C.... 630 357-8500
Naperville *(G-15627)*
▲ **Chicago-Wilcox Mfg Co** ....E.... 708 339-5000
South Holland *(G-20257)*
▲ **Classic Fasteners LLC** ....G.... 630 605-0195
Saint Charles *(G-19157)*
**Component Hardware Inc** ....G.... 847 458-8181
Gilberts *(G-10916)*
**Continental/Midland LLC** ....C.... 708 747-1200
Park Forest *(G-17169)*
◆ **Cooper B-Line Inc** ....A.... 618 654-2184
Highland *(G-11780)*
**CSM Fastener Products Co** ....G.... 630 350-8282
Bensenville *(G-1874)*
**Custom Metal Products Corp** ....E.... 815 397-3306
Rockford *(G-18328)*
**Dayton Superior Corporation** ....E.... 219 476-4106
Kankakee *(G-12607)*
**Dayton Superior Corporation** ....C.... 815 936-3300
Kankakee *(G-12609)*
**Deco Manufacturing Company** ....E.... 217 872-6450
Decatur *(G-7875)*
▲ **Deringer-Ney Inc** ....E.... 847 566-4100
Vernon Hills *(G-21157)*
▲ **Dml Distribution Inc** ....F.... 630 839-9041
Schaumburg *(G-19507)*
▲ **Du Bro Products Inc** ....E.... 847 526-2136
Wauconda *(G-21456)*
▲ **Elite Fasteners Inc** ....E.... 815 397-8848
Rockford *(G-18363)*
**Essentra Components Inc** ....C.... 815 943-6487
Forest Park *(G-10241)*
▲ **Fastron Co** ....E.... 630 766-5000
Melrose Park *(G-14636)*
**Folkerts Manufacturing Inc** ....G.... 815 968-7426
Rockford *(G-18385)*
**Forest City Industry Inc** ....F.... 815 877-4084
Loves Park *(G-13943)*
**Formed Fastener Mfg Inc** ....E.... 708 496-1219
Bridgeview *(G-2492)*
**Freedom Fastener Inc** ....G.... 847 891-3686
Schaumburg *(G-19533)*
**Freeway-Rockford Inc** ....E.... 815 397-6425
Rockford *(G-18393)*
**G-Fast Distribution Inc** ....G.... 847 926-0722
Highland Park *(G-11834)*
▲ **Gateway Screw & Rivet Inc** ....E.... 630 539-2232
Glendale Heights *(G-11026)*
**Global Fastener Engrg Inc** ....F.... 847 929-9563
Volo *(G-21312)*
▲ **Great Lakes Washer Company** ....F.... 630 887-7447
Burr Ridge *(G-2846)*
▲ **Hadady Corporation** ....E.... 219 322-7417
South Holland *(G-20274)*
**Haddock Tool & Manufacturing** ....G.... 815 786-2739
Sandwich *(G-19367)*
**Hadley Gear Manufacturing Co** ....F.... 773 722-1030
Chicago *(G-5028)*
**Hill Holdings Inc** ....E.... 815 625-6600
Rock Falls *(G-18135)*
▲ **Holbrook Mfg Inc** ....D.... 847 229-1999
Wheeling *(G-22072)*
**Hunter-Stevens Company Inc** ....F.... 847 671-5014
Franklin Park *(G-10493)*
**Illinois Tool Works Inc** ....C.... 630 595-3500
Itasca *(G-12281)*
**Illinois Tool Works Inc** ....C.... 708 720-2600
Frankfort *(G-10331)*
**Illinois Tool Works Inc** ....E.... 847 741-7900
Elgin *(G-9071)*
**Illinois Tool Works Inc** ....F.... 708 343-0728
Broadview *(G-2586)*
**Illinois Tool Works Inc** ....F.... 815 654-1510
Machesney Park *(G-14081)*
**Illinois Tool Works Inc** ....C.... 847 766-9000
Elk Grove Village *(G-9537)*
▲ **Image Industries Inc** ....E.... 847 659-0100
Huntley *(G-12147)*
▲ **Imperial Rivets & Fasteners Co** ....G.... 630 964-0208
Darien *(G-7797)*
▲ **Inland Fastener Inc** ....F.... 630 293-3800
West Chicago *(G-21720)*
**J H Botts LLC** ....E.... 815 726-5885
Joliet *(G-12519)*
**Jeffrey Jae Inc** ....E.... 847 808-2002
Wheeling *(G-22081)*
▲ **Jeffrey Jae Inc** ....E.... 847 394-1313
Arlington Heights *(G-782)*
**Jupiter Industries Inc** ....G.... 847 925-5120
Schaumburg *(G-19592)*
**JW Fasteners Inc** ....G.... 815 963-2658
Rockford *(G-18450)*
**Kanebridge Corporation** ....E....
Elgin *(G-9087)*
**Kdk Upset Forging Co** ....E.... 708 388-8770
Blue Island *(G-2259)*
**Kile Machine & Tool Inc** ....G.... 217 446-8616
Danville *(G-7744)*
▲ **Komar Screw Corp** ....E.... 847 965-9090
Niles *(G-15995)*
**L & M Screw Machine Products** ....F.... 630 801-0455
Montgomery *(G-15052)*
**Laundry Services Company** ....G.... 630 327-9329
Downers Grove *(G-8473)*
**Lawndale Forging & Tool Works** ....G.... 773 277-2800
Chicago *(G-5471)*
◆ **Lehigh Consumer Products LLC** ....C.... 630 851-7330
Aurora *(G-1045)*
▲ **Locknut Technology Inc** ....F.... 630 628-5330
Addison *(G-182)*
▲ **Lre Products Inc** ....E.... 630 238-8321
Bensenville *(G-1942)*
◆ **Mac Lean-Fogg Company** ....D.... 847 566-0010
Mundelein *(G-15521)*
**Machine Tool Acc & Mfg Co** ....G.... 773 489-0903
Chicago *(G-5592)*
**Marengo Tool & Die Works Inc** ....E.... 815 568-7411
Marengo *(G-14236)*
▲ **Marmon Group LLC** ....G.... 312 372-9500
Chicago *(G-5624)*
**Matthew Warren Inc** ....E.... 847 364-5000
Elk Grove Village *(G-9614)*
**Matthew Warren Inc** ....F.... 630 860-7766
Bensenville *(G-1946)*
**Maxi-Vac Inc** ....G.... 224 699-9760
Addison *(G-194)*
**Medalist Industries Inc** ....G.... 847 766-9000
Elk Grove Village *(G-9617)*
**Metform LLC** ....C.... 815 273-2201
Savanna *(G-19400)*
**Metform LLC** ....E.... 815 273-0230
Savanna *(G-19401)*
▲ **Mid-Continent Fastener Inc** ....G.... 815 625-1081
Rock Falls *(G-18144)*
▲ **Mid-States Screw Corporation** ....E.... 815 397-2440
Rockford *(G-18503)*
▲ **Mighty Hook Inc** ....E.... 773 378-1909
Chicago *(G-5756)*
**MNP Precision Parts LLC** ....C.... 815 391-5256
Rockford *(G-18509)*
▲ **Multitech Cold Forming LLC** ....E.... 630 949-8200
Carol Stream *(G-3201)*
▲ **National Bolt & Nut Corp** ....F.... 630 307-8800
Bloomingdale *(G-2119)*
**National Cap and Set Screw Co** ....F.... 815 675-2363
Spring Grove *(G-20350)*
**ND Industries Inc** ....E.... 847 498-3600
Northbrook *(G-16318)*
**Nekg Holdings Inc** ....G.... 815 383-1379
Channahon *(G-3582)*
**Nelson Stud Welding Inc** ....G.... 708 430-3770
Tinley Park *(G-20934)*
**Nylok Fastener Corporation** ....D.... 847 674-9680
Lincolnwood *(G-13528)*
▲ **Parker International Pdts Inc** ....D.... 815 524-5831
Vernon Hills *(G-21188)*
**Pearson Fastener Corporation** ....F.... 815 397-4460
Rockford *(G-18532)*
**Philly Fasteners Corp** ....G.... 847 584-9408
Schaumburg *(G-19690)*
**Pin Up Tattoo** ....G.... 815 477-7515
Crystal Lake *(G-7625)*
**Pins & Needles Consignment** ....G.... 217 299-7365
Pawnee *(G-17235)*
**Pontiac Engraving** ....G.... 630 834-4424
Bensenville *(G-1965)*
▲ **Prairie State Screw & Bolt Co** ....F.... 847 858-9551
Northbrook *(G-16342)*
**R & N Machine Co** ....F.... 708 841-5555
Riverdale *(G-18023)*
**Rail Forge** ....G.... 630 561-4989
Chicago *(G-6285)*
**Red Devil Manufacturing Co** ....G.... 847 215-1377
Wheeling *(G-22134)*
**Reino Tool & Manufacturing Co** ....F.... 773 588-5800
Chicago *(G-6326)*
**Roberts Swiss Inc** ....E.... 630 467-9100
Itasca *(G-12348)*
**Rockford Bolt & Steel Co** ....E.... 815 968-0514
Rockford *(G-18567)*
**Saint Technologies Inc** ....G.... 815 864-3035
Shannon *(G-19902)*
**Sanco Industries Inc** ....F.... 847 243-8675
Kildeer *(G-12703)*
**Schmid Tool & Engineering Corp** ....E.... 630 333-1733
Villa Park *(G-21283)*
▲ **Screws Industries Inc** ....D.... 630 539-9200
Glendale Heights *(G-11068)*
▲ **Security Locknut LLC** ....E.... 847 970-4050
Vernon Hills *(G-21200)*
▲ **Semblex Corporation** ....D.... 630 833-2880
Elmhurst *(G-9936)*
**Semblex Corporation** ....E.... 630 833-2880
Elmhurst *(G-9937)*
▲ **Set Screw & Mfg Co** ....E.... 847 717-3700
Elgin *(G-9176)*
▲ **Si Enterprises Inc** ....G.... 630 539-9200
Glendale Heights *(G-11069)*
▲ **Simpson Strong-Tie Company Inc** ....E.... 630 613-5100
Addison *(G-293)*

SIC SECTION 34 FABRICATED METAL PRODUCTS, EXCEPT MACHINERY AND TRANSPORTATION EQUIPMENT

**Skach Manufacturing Co Inc**.................E ....... 847 395-3560
Antioch *(G-655)*
▲ **Slidematic Industries Inc**.................C ....... 815 986-0500
Rockford *(G-18620)*
▲ **Slidemtic Prcsion Cmpnents Inc**......G....... 815 986-0500
Rockford *(G-18621)*
◆ **Slsb LLC**................................D ....... 618 219-4115
Madison *(G-14153)*
**Southern Imperial Inc**..........................G....... 815 877-7041
Loves Park *(G-13993)*
▲ **Specialty Screw Corporation**...........D....... 815 969-4100
Rockford *(G-18626)*
▲ **Stanley Hartco Co**.............................E ....... 847 967-1122
Skokie *(G-20090)*
**Stelfast Inc**.............................................F ....... 847 783-0161
Elgin *(G-9193)*
**Steloc Fastener Co**..................................F ....... 847 459-6200
Wheeling *(G-22155)*
**Suburban Industries Inc**.........................F ....... 630 766-3773
Franklin Park *(G-10597)*
**Thread & Gage Co Inc**...........................G....... 815 675-2305
Spring Grove *(G-20367)*
**Tour Industries Inc**.................................G....... 847 854-9400
Lake In The Hills *(G-13008)*
▲ **Unytite Inc**.............................................C ....... 815 224-2221
Peru *(G-17529)*
**Valley Fastener Group LLC**...................E ....... 630 548-5679
Naperville *(G-15772)*
▲ **Valley Fastener Group LLC**.............E ....... 630 299-8910
Aurora *(G-1229)*
**Valley Fastener Group LLC**...................F ....... 708 343-2496
Melrose Park *(G-14704)*
**Venturedyne Ltd**.....................................E ....... 708 597-7550
Chicago *(G-6884)*
▲ **Weiland Metal Products Company**...G....... 773 631-4210
Chicago *(G-6950)*
**Wenco Manufacturing Co Inc**................E ....... 630 377-7474
Elgin *(G-9235)*
**Wenlyn Screw Company Inc**..................G....... 630 766-0050
Bensenville *(G-2013)*
**Willie Washer Mfg Co**..........................C ....... 847 956-1344
Elk Grove Village *(G-9814)*

## 3462 Iron & Steel Forgings

**Adrian Orgas Gheorghe**..........................G....... 773 355-1200
Palatine *(G-16997)*
**Allied Gear Co**.........................................G....... 773 287-8742
Chicago *(G-3815)*
▲ **Anderson Shumaker Company**.........E ....... 773 287-0874
Chicago *(G-3902)*
**Andrew McDonald**...................................G....... 618 867-2323
De Soto *(G-7818)*
▲ **Arrow Gear Company**........................C ....... 630 969-7640
Downers Grove *(G-8389)*
**Blaz-Man Gear Inc**..................................G....... 708 599-9700
Bridgeview *(G-2471)*
**C & F Forge Company**............................G....... 847 455-6609
Franklin Park *(G-10420)*
**Carmona Gear Cutting**............................G....... 815 963-8236
Rockford *(G-18298)*
**Caterpillar Inc**.........................................G....... 815 729-5511
Rockdale *(G-18216)*
**Caterpillar Inc**.........................................G....... 309 675-4408
Peoria *(G-17329)*
**Chicago Clamp Company**.......................G....... 708 343-8311
Broadview *(G-2567)*
▲ **Chicago Hardware and Fix Co**..........D ....... 847 455-6609
Franklin Park *(G-10429)*
**Clark Gear Works Inc**.............................G....... 630 561-2320
Carol Stream *(G-3130)*
**Cleveland Hdwr & Forging Co**...............D ....... 630 896-9850
Aurora *(G-1132)*
▲ **Core Pipe Products Inc**.....................C ....... 630 690-7000
Carol Stream *(G-3138)*
**Cornell Forge Company**..........................D ....... 708 458-1582
Chicago *(G-4470)*
**Danfoss Power Solutions US Co**............C ....... 815 233-4200
Freeport *(G-10652)*
**Dayton Superior Corporation**.................C ....... 815 936-3300
Kankakee *(G-12609)*
**Deer Creek Flange Pipe Co Inc**..............G....... 309 447-6981
Deer Creek *(G-7963)*
**Dekalb Forge Company**..........................D ....... 815 756-3538
Dekalb *(G-8087)*
**E M Glabus Co Inc**..................................F ....... 630 766-3027
Bensenville *(G-1887)*
**Eagle Gear & Manufacturing Co**............F ....... 630 628-6100
Addison *(G-106)*
**Emco Gears Inc**.......................................E ....... 847 220-4327
Elk Grove Village *(G-9454)*
**Engelhardt Enterprises Inc**.....................G....... 847 277-7070
Inverness *(G-12208)*
▲ **Excel Gear Inc**......................................E ....... 815 623-3414
Roscoe *(G-18897)*
**Exelon Corporation**................................A ....... 815 357-6761
Marseilles *(G-14308)*
**Forge Resources Group LLC**..................G....... 815 758-6400
Dekalb *(G-8093)*
**Forgings & Stampings Inc**.....................E ....... 815 962-5597
Rockford *(G-18390)*
**Gear & Repair**.........................................G....... 708 387-0144
Brookfield *(G-2634)*
**Gear Products & Mfg Inc**.......................G....... 708 344-0875
Bridgeview *(G-2493)*
**Gears Gears Gears Inc**...........................G....... 708 366-6555
Harwood Heights *(G-11685)*
**General Forging Die Co Inc**...................E ....... 815 874-4224
Rockford *(G-18397)*
**Great Lakes Forge Company**.................G....... 773 277-2800
Chicago *(G-4997)*
**Group Industries Inc**..............................E ....... 708 877-6200
Thornton *(G-20871)*
**Hadley Gear Manufacturing Co**.............F ....... 773 722-1030
Chicago *(G-5028)*
**HM Manufacturing Inc**...........................F ....... 847 487-8700
Wauconda *(G-21469)*
**Hurst Enterprises Inc**.............................G....... 708 344-9291
Glendale Heights *(G-11032)*
**I Forge Company LLC**............................G....... 815 535-0600
Rock Falls *(G-18137)*
**Innovative Rack & Gear Company**........F ....... 630 766-2652
Wood Dale *(G-22382)*
**J & L Gear Incorporated**........................F ....... 630 832-1880
Villa Park *(G-21259)*
**Jernberg Industries LLC**.........................C ....... 773 268-3004
Chicago *(G-5294)*
**Jernberg Industries LLC**.........................C ....... 630 972-7000
Bolingbrook *(G-2327)*
**Kautzmann Machine Works Inc**.............G....... 847 455-9105
Franklin Park *(G-10511)*
**Kd Steel Inc**.............................................G....... 630 201-1619
Westmont *(G-21897)*
**Kdk Upset Forging Co**...........................E ....... 708 388-8770
Blue Island *(G-2259)*
**Keller Group Inc**.....................................B ....... 847 446-7550
Northfield *(G-16405)*
**Ken Elliott Co Inc**...................................G....... 618 466-8200
Godfrey *(G-11226)*
**Kishwaukee Forge Company**..................E ....... 815 758-4451
Cortland *(G-7391)*
**Lawndale Forging & Tool Works**...........G....... 773 277-2800
Chicago *(G-5471)*
◆ **Lehigh Consumer Products LLC**......C ....... 630 851-7330
Aurora *(G-1045)*
**Loch Precision Technologies**................G....... 847 438-1400
Lake Zurich *(G-13096)*
**Machine Tool Acc & Mfg Co**..................G....... 773 489-0903
Chicago *(G-5592)*
**Malca-Amit North America Inc**.............G....... 312 346-1507
Chicago *(G-5606)*
**Master Guard Security Co**.....................G....... 618 398-7749
East Saint Louis *(G-8760)*
**Metform LLC**..........................................C ....... 815 273-2201
Savanna *(G-19400)*
▲ **Metform LLC**......................................G....... 847 566-0010
Mundelein *(G-15531)*
**Metform LLC**..........................................E ....... 815 273-0230
Savanna *(G-19401)*
**Mitsutoyo-Kiko USA Inc**.......................G....... 847 981-5200
Rolling Meadows *(G-18745)*
**Modern Gear & Machine Inc**..................F ....... 630 350-9173
Bensenville *(G-1953)*
▲ **Moline Forge Inc**................................D ....... 309 762-5506
Moline *(G-14960)*
**Moore-Addison Co**.................................E ....... 630 543-6744
Addison *(G-220)*
**Norforge and Machining Inc**..................D ....... 309 772-3124
Bushnell *(G-2907)*
**Northeast Illinois Regional**...................A ....... 708 246-0304
Western Springs *(G-21870)*
▲ **Park-Hio Frged McHned Pdts LLC**...D ....... 708 652-6691
Chicago *(G-6084)*
**Phoenix Trading Chicago Inc**................G....... 847 304-5181
Lake Barrington *(G-12822)*
◆ **Prime Stainless Products LLC**.........G....... 847 678-0800
Schiller Park *(G-19863)*
**Process Screw Products Inc**..................E ....... 815 864-2220
Shannon *(G-19901)*
**Productigear Inc**.....................................E ....... 773 847-4505
Chicago *(G-6205)*
**Products In Motion Inc**..........................G....... 815 213-7251
Rock Falls *(G-18146)*
**Rail Exchange Inc**...................................E ....... 708 757-3317
Chicago Heights *(G-7119)*
**Raycar Gear & Machine Company**........E ....... 815 874-3948
Rockford *(G-18549)*
▼ **Rj Link International Inc**...................F ....... 815 874-8110
Rockford *(G-18559)*
**Rockford Drop Forge Company**.............D ....... 815 963-9611
Rockford *(G-18572)*
**Rockford Jobbing Service Inc**................G....... 815 398-8661
Rockford *(G-18576)*
**RT Blackhawk Mch Pdts Inc**..................G....... 815 389-3632
South Beloit *(G-20167)*
**Sbic America Inc**....................................G....... 847 303-5430
Schaumburg *(G-19719)*
▲ **Schafer Gear Works Roscoe LLC**....C ....... 815 874-4327
Roscoe *(G-18920)*
**Schmid Tool & Engineering Corp**..........E ....... 630 333-1733
Villa Park *(G-21283)*
▲ **Scot Forge Company**..........................B ....... 815 675-1000
Spring Grove *(G-20364)*
**Scot Forge Company**..............................D ....... 847 678-6000
Franklin Park *(G-10584)*
▲ **Simpson Strong-Tie Company Inc**...E ....... 630 613-5100
Addison *(G-293)*
▲ **Stanley Hartco Co**...............................E ....... 847 967-1122
Skokie *(G-20090)*
▲ **Star Forge Inc**......................................D ....... 815 235-7750
Freeport *(G-10691)*
**Stock Gears Inc**......................................F ....... 224 653-9489
Elk Grove Village *(G-9758)*
**Sumitomo Machinery Corp Amer**..........E ....... 630 752-0200
Glendale Heights *(G-11078)*
**Thyssenkrupp Crankshaft Co LLC**........C ....... 217 444-5400
Danville *(G-7772)*
◆ **Thyssenkrupp Crankshaft Co LLC**...C ....... 217 431-0060
Danville *(G-7770)*
**Thyssenkrupp Crankshaft Co LLC**........C ....... 217 444-5500
Danville *(G-7773)*
◆ **Timken Drives LLC**............................C ....... 815 589-2211
Fulton *(G-10706)*
**Timken Drives LLC**................................G....... 312 274-9710
Chicago *(G-6728)*
**Tomek Iron Originals**.............................G....... 773 788-1750
Chicago *(G-6738)*
**Tomko Machine Works Inc**....................G....... 630 244-0902
Lemont *(G-13266)*
**US Tsubaki Power Transm LLC**.............C ....... 847 459-9500
Wheeling *(G-22173)*
**Velocity International Inc**......................G....... 773 570-6441
Lake Forest *(G-12979)*
**Welch Steel Products Inc**.......................F ....... 847 741-2623
Elgin *(G-9234)*
▲ **Weldbend Corporation**.......................C ....... 708 594-1700
Argo *(G-697)*
**Wozniak Industries Inc**..........................C ....... 708 458-1220
Bedford Park *(G-1595)*
◆ **Wozniak Industries Inc**......................G....... 630 954-3400
Oakbrook Terrace *(G-16723)*

## 3463 Nonferrous Forgings

**Acme Screw Co**.......................................F ....... 815 332-7548
Cherry Valley *(G-3637)*
**Anchor-Harvey Components LLC**.........D ....... 815 233-3833
Freeport *(G-10646)*
▲ **Anderson Shumaker Company**.........E ....... 773 287-0874
Chicago *(G-3902)*
**Boler Ventures LLC**................................G....... 630 773-9111
Itasca *(G-12237)*
**Burgess-Norton Mfg Co Inc**...................E ....... 630 232-4100
Geneva *(G-10814)*
**Genacc LLC**............................................G....... 309 253-9034
Peoria *(G-17370)*
**Jernberg Industries LLC**.........................C ....... 773 268-3004
Chicago *(G-5294)*
**Midwest Brass Forging Co**.....................E ....... 847 678-7023
Franklin Park *(G-10532)*
▲ **Standard Precision Grinding Co**.......F ....... 708 474-1211
Lansing *(G-13185)*
**Voss Engineering Inc**.............................E ....... 847 673-8900
Lincolnwood *(G-13542)*

## 3465 Automotive Stampings

**Ada Metal Products Inc**..........................E ....... 847 673-1190
Lincolnwood *(G-13500)*
**Amis Inc**..................................................G....... 708 598-9700
Bridgeview *(G-2465)*
**Autogenesis LLC**....................................G....... 630 851-9424
Aurora *(G-963)*

S I C

**Borgwarner Inc** ... C ... 815 288-1462
Dixon *(G-8324)*

**Borgwarner Transm Systems** ... A ... 708 547-2600
Bellwood *(G-1700)*

**Bosch Auto Svc Solutions Inc** ... F ... 815 407-3900
Romeoville *(G-18803)*

**Clay Cnty Rhbilitation Ctr Inc** ... F ... 618 662-6607
Flora *(G-10203)*

**Ford Motor Company** ... A ... 708 757-5700
Ford Heights *(G-10233)*

**G & M Manufacturing Corp** ... E ... 815 455-1900
Crystal Lake *(G-7580)*

◆ **G T Motoring Inc** ... G ... 847 466-7463
Elk Grove Village *(G-9491)*

**Grace Auto Body Frame** ... G ... 847 963-1234
Palatine *(G-17030)*

**Gs Custom Works Inc** ... G ... 815 233-4724
Freeport *(G-10661)*

**Illinois Tool Works Inc** ... G ... 708 720-3541
Frankfort *(G-10334)*

**Inland Tool Company** ... E ... 217 792-3206
Mount Pulaski *(G-15389)*

**ITW Dynatec** ... G ... 847 657-4830
Glenview *(G-11151)*

▲ **Kipp Manufacturing Company Inc** ... F ... 630 768-9051
Wauconda *(G-21477)*

**Laystrom Manufacturing Co** ... D ... 773 342-4800
Chicago *(G-5474)*

◆ **Marmon Industries LLC** ... G ... 312 372-9500
Chicago *(G-5627)*

▲ **Mercury Products Corp** ... C ... 847 524-4400
Schaumburg *(G-19641)*

**Mercury Products Corp** ... C ... 847 524-4400
Schaumburg *(G-19642)*

**Mmma** ... F ... 309 888-8765
Normal *(G-16078)*

**MNP Precision Parts LLC** ... C ... 815 391-5256
Rockford *(G-18509)*

▲ **Perfection Spring Stmping Corp** ... D ... 847 437-3900
Mount Prospect *(G-15362)*

▲ **Plastic Technologies Inc** ... E ... 847 841-8610
Elgin *(G-9140)*

**Rhino Pros** ... G ... 815 235-7767
Freeport *(G-10684)*

**SPX Corporation** ... F ... 815 407-3915
Romeoville *(G-18869)*

**T R Z Motorsports Inc** ... G ... 815 806-0838
Frankfort *(G-10367)*

**Taurus Die Casting LLC** ... F ... 815 316-6160
Rockford *(G-18642)*

▲ **Topy Precision Mfg Inc** ... D ... 847 228-5902
Elk Grove Village *(G-9784)*

**Tower Automotive Operations I** ... B ... 773 646-6550
Chicago *(G-6751)*

**Tsm Inc** ... G ... 815 544-5012
Belvidere *(G-1790)*

**Waupaca Foundry Inc** ... C ... 217 347-0600
Effingham *(G-8862)*

## 3466 Crowns & Closures

**Alcon Tool & Mfg Co Inc** ... F ... 773 545-8742
Chicago *(G-3798)*

◆ **Amcor Flexibles LLC** ... C ... 224 313-7000
Buffalo Grove *(G-2656)*

▲ **American Flange & Mfg Co Inc** ... E ... 630 665-7900
Carol Stream *(G-3098)*

**Galena Manufacturing Co Inc** ... G ... 815 777-2078
Galena *(G-10722)*

**Kile Machine & Tool Inc** ... G ... 217 446-8616
Danville *(G-7744)*

▲ **Kipp Manufacturing Company Inc** ... F ... 630 768-9051
Wauconda *(G-21477)*

**Product Service Craft Inc** ... F ... 630 964-5160
Downers Grove *(G-8511)*

▲ **Sorini Manufacturing Corp** ... E ... 773 247-5858
Chicago *(G-6544)*

▲ **Walter H Jelly & Co Inc** ... G ... 847 455-4235
Franklin Park *(G-10626)*

## 3469 Metal Stampings, NEC

**10 4 Irp Inc** ... G ... 708 485-1040
Brookfield *(G-2621)*

**A & M Tool Co Inc** ... E ... 847 215-8140
Wheeling *(G-21993)*

**Aable License Consultants** ... G ... 708 836-1235
Westchester *(G-21827)*

▲ **Abbott Scott Manufacturing Co** ... E ... 773 342-7200
Chicago *(G-3706)*

**Able Barmilling & Mfg Co Inc** ... F ... 708 343-5666
Melrose Park *(G-14580)*

**Accurate CNc Machining Inc** ... G ... 815 623-6516
Roscoe *(G-18888)*

**Accurate Perforating Co Inc** ... D ... 773 254-3232
Chicago *(G-3721)*

**Accurate Wire Strip Frming Inc** ... F ... 630 260-1000
Carol Stream *(G-3089)*

**Ace Metal Spinning Inc** ... F ... 708 389-5635
Alsip *(G-430)*

**Ace Plating Company** ... E ... 773 376-1800
Chicago *(G-3727)*

▲ **Acme Spinning Company Inc** ... F ... 773 927-2711
Chicago *(G-3734)*

**Action Tool & Mfg Inc** ... E ... 815 874-5775
Rockford *(G-18256)*

**Adler Norco Inc** ... F ... 847 473-3600
Mundelein *(G-15464)*

**Air-Drive Inc** ... E ... 847 625-0226
Gurnee *(G-11423)*

▼ **Alagor Industries Incorporated** ... F ... 630 766-2910
Bensenville *(G-1822)*

**Alan Manufacturing Corp** ... G ... 815 568-6836
Marengo *(G-14217)*

**Alcon Tool & Mfg Co Inc** ... F ... 773 545-8742
Chicago *(G-3798)*

**All American Spring Stamping** ... G ... 847 928-9468
Franklin Park *(G-10389)*

**All American Washer Werks Inc** ... E ... 847 566-9091
Mundelein *(G-15468)*

**Allied Production Drilling** ... F ... 815 969-0940
Rockford *(G-18259)*

▲ **Alpha Products Inc** ... E ... 708 594-3883
Bedford Park *(G-1536)*

**AM Metal Spinning Co Inc** ... G ... 630 616-8634
Bensenville *(G-1830)*

**American Industrial Company** ... F ... 847 855-9200
Gurnee *(G-11427)*

**American Metal Perforating Inc** ... F ... 773 523-8884
Chicago *(G-3866)*

**American Partsmith Inc** ... G ... 630 520-0432
West Chicago *(G-21656)*

**Amity Die and Stamping Co** ... E ... 847 680-6600
Lake Forest *(G-12879)*

**Ammentorp Tool Company Inc** ... G ... 847 671-9290
Franklin Park *(G-10395)*

▲ **Amtec Precision Products Inc** ... D ... 847 695-8030
Elgin *(G-8953)*

**Angle Tool Company** ... G ... 847 593-7572
Elk Grove Village *(G-9307)*

**Animated Manufacturing Company** ... F ... 708 333-6688
South Holland *(G-20245)*

**Apex Wire Products Company Inc** ... F ... 847 671-1830
Franklin Park *(G-10397)*

**Archer Manufacturing Corp** ... E ... 773 585-7181
Chicago *(G-3938)*

▲ **Ark Technologies Inc** ... C ... 630 377-8855
Saint Charles *(G-19138)*

**Aro Metal Stamping Company Inc** ... E ... 630 351-7676
Roselle *(G-18927)*

**Ascent Mfg Co** ... E ... 847 806-6600
Elk Grove Village *(G-9314)*

◆ **Ask Products Inc** ... D ... 630 896-4056
Aurora *(G-1111)*

**Astoria Wire Products Inc** ... D ... 708 496-9950
Bedford Park *(G-1539)*

**Atlantic Engineering** ... G ... 847 782-1762
Zion *(G-22679)*

▲ **Atlas Tool & Die Works Inc** ... D ... 708 442-1661
Lyons *(G-14031)*

**Austin Tool & Die Co** ... D ... 847 509-5800
Northbrook *(G-16209)*

**Available Spring and Mfg Co** ... G ... 847 520-4854
Wheeling *(G-22009)*

**B & D Murray Manufacturing Co** ... G ... 815 568-6176
Marengo *(G-14220)*

**B M I Inc** ... C ... 847 839-6000
Schaumburg *(G-19456)*

**B Radtke and Sons Inc** ... G ... 847 546-3999
Round Lake Park *(G-19083)*

▲ **Barco Stamping Co** ... E ... 630 293-5155
West Chicago *(G-21666)*

**Barrington Automation Ltd** ... E ... 847 458-0900
Lake In The Hills *(G-12987)*

**Bel-Air Manufacturing Inc** ... F ... 773 276-7550
Chicago *(G-4074)*

▼ **Bellota Agrsltions Tls USA LLC** ... E ... 309 787-2491
Milan *(G-14775)*

**Berny Metal Products Inc** ... G ... 847 742-8500
South Elgin *(G-20187)*

▲ **Bi-Link Metal Specialties Inc** ... C ... 630 858-5900
Bloomingdale *(G-2096)*

▲ **Big 3 Precision Products Inc** ... C ... 618 533-3251
Centralia *(G-3405)*

**Bilt-Rite Metal Products Inc** ... E ... 815 495-2211
Leland *(G-13218)*

**Bingaman-Precision Metal Spini** ... E ... 847 392-5620
Rolling Meadows *(G-18718)*

▲ **Block and Company Inc** ... C ... 847 537-7200
Wheeling *(G-22015)*

**Blue Chip Mfg LLC** ... G ... 630 553-6321
Oswego *(G-16905)*

**Bomel Tool Manufacturing Co** ... C ... 708 343-3663
Broadview *(G-2564)*

**Borgwarner Transm Systems** ... A ... 708 547-2600
Bellwood *(G-1700)*

**Braun Manufacturing Co Inc** ... E ... 847 635-2050
Mount Prospect *(G-15313)*

**Briergate Tool & Engrg Co** ... F ... 630 766-7050
Bensenville *(G-1846)*

▲ **Buhrke Industries LLC** ... B ... 847 981-7550
Arlington Heights *(G-732)*

**Burnex Corporation** ... E ... 815 728-1317
Ringwood *(G-17988)*

**C & C Can Co Inc** ... G ... 312 421-2372
Chicago *(G-4200)*

▲ **C & J Metal Products Inc** ... F ... 847 455-0766
Franklin Park *(G-10421)*

**C E R Machining & Tooling Ltd** ... G ... 708 442-9614
Lyons *(G-14034)*

**C J Holdings Inc** ... G ... 309 274-3141
Chillicothe *(G-7163)*

**C Keller Manufacturing Inc** ... E ... 630 833-5593
Villa Park *(G-21240)*

**C M Holding Co Inc** ... G ... 847 438-2171
Lake Zurich *(G-13048)*

**C N C HI-Tech Inc** ... G ... 847 201-8151
Volo *(G-21309)*

**Cac Corporation** ... E ... 630 221-5200
Carol Stream *(G-3122)*

**Cap & Seal Co** ... E ... 847 741-3101
Elgin *(G-8976)*

**Cardinal Engineering Inc** ... G ... 309 342-7474
Galesburg *(G-10742)*

**Carlson Capitol Mfg Co** ... F ... 815 398-3110
Rockford *(G-18296)*

**Central Radiator Cabinet Co** ... G ... 773 539-1700
Lena *(G-13274)*

**Central Tool Specialities Co** ... G ... 630 543-6351
Addison *(G-72)*

**Century Metal Spinning Co Inc** ... E ... 630 595-3900
Bensenville *(G-1855)*

▲ **Chicago Car Seal Company** ... G ... 773 278-9400
Chicago *(G-4310)*

▲ **Chicago Cutting Die Co** ... D ... 847 509-5800
Northbrook *(G-16221)*

**Chicago Metal Fabricators Inc** ... D ... 773 523-5755
Chicago *(G-4332)*

**Chirch Global Mfg LLC** ... F ... 815 385-5600
Cary *(G-3330)*

**Cicero Plastic Products Inc** ... E ... 815 886-9522
Romeoville *(G-18811)*

**City of Danville** ... G ... 217 442-1564
Tilton *(G-20879)*

**Classic Sheet Metal Inc** ... D ... 630 694-0300
Franklin Park *(G-10435)*

**Columbia Metal Spinning Co** ... D ... 773 685-2800
Chicago *(G-4431)*

**Component Tool & Mfg Co** ... F ... 708 672-5505
Crete *(G-7510)*

**Craft Metal Spinning Co** ... F ... 773 685-4700
Chicago *(G-4489)*

▼ **Craftsman Custom Metals LLC** ... D ... 847 655-0040
Schiller Park *(G-19817)*

**Creative Metal Products** ... F ... 773 638-3200
Chicago *(G-4500)*

**Creative Steel Fabricators** ... G ... 847 803-2090
Des Plaines *(G-8177)*

**Crystal Precision Drilling** ... G ... 815 633-5460
Loves Park *(G-13930)*

**CSI Cutting Specialist Inc** ... D ... 731 352-5351
East Alton *(G-8600)*

**Culen Tool & Manufacturing Co** ... G ... 708 387-1580
Brookfield *(G-2629)*

**Custom Machinery Inc** ... G ... 847 678-3033
Schiller Park *(G-19818)*

**Custom Metal Products Corp** ... E ... 815 397-3306
Rockford *(G-18328)*

**D & B Fabricators & Distrs** ... F ... 630 325-3811
Lemont *(G-13234)*

**D & D Tooling and Mfg Inc** ... D ... 888 300-6869
Bolingbrook *(G-2297)*

D & J Machine Shop Inc ... G ... 815 472-6057
Momence (G-14979)
Dadum Inc ... G ... 847 541-7851
Buffalo Grove (G-2682)
Dart Technology Inc ... G ... 847 534-0357
Schaumburg (G-19499)
Delta Metal Products Co ... G ... 773 745-9220
Chicago (G-4579)
Derby Industries LLC ... E ... 309 344-0547
Galesburg (G-10746)
▲ Deringer-Ney Inc ... E ... 847 566-4100
Vernon Hills (G-21157)
Desk & Door Nameplate Company ... F ... 815 806-8670
Frankfort (G-10312)
Dial Tool Industries Inc ... D ... 630 543-3600
Addison (G-88)
▲ Diemasters Manufacturing Inc ... C ... 847 640-9900
Elk Grove Village (G-9429)
Dixline Corporation ... F ... 309 932-2011
Galva (G-10787)
Dixline Corporation ... D ... 309 932-2011
Galva (G-10788)
▲ Domeny Tool & Stamping Company F ... 847 526-5700
Wauconda (G-21454)
Dovee Manufacturing Inc ... F ... 847 437-8122
Elgin (G-9012)
▲ Dudek & Bock Spring Mfg Co ... C ... 773 379-4100
Chicago (G-4648)
E H Baare Corporation ... C ... 618 546-1575
Robinson (G-18062)
Ed Stan Fabricating Co ... G ... 708 863-7668
Chicago (G-4694)
▲ Elburn Metal Stamping Inc ... E ... 630 365-2500
Elburn (G-8885)
Elkay Vrgnia Dcrative Surfaces ... F ... 630 574-8484
Oak Brook (G-16508)
Ems Industrial and Service Co ... E ... 815 678-2700
Richmond (G-17961)
Equinox Group Inc ... F ... 312 226-7002
Chicago (G-4769)
▼ Equipto Electronics Corp ... E ... 630 897-4691
Aurora (G-1147)
ERA Tool and Manufacturing Co ... E ... 847 298-6333
Zion (G-22684)
Erickson Tool & Machine Co ... G ... 815 397-2653
Rockford (G-18369)
▲ Erva Tool & Die Company ... G ... 773 533-7806
Chicago (G-4775)
Estad Stamping & Mfg Co ... E ... 217 442-4600
Danville (G-7717)
◆ Ets-Lindgren Inc ... C ... 630 307-7200
Wood Dale (G-22363)
Exclusive Stone ... G ... 847 593-6963
Elk Grove Village (G-9470)
Exton Corp ... C ... 847 391-8100
Des Plaines (G-8192)
F B Williams Co ... G ... 773 233-4255
Chicago (G-4802)
Fabricating Machinery Sales ... E ... 630 350-2266
Wood Dale (G-22366)
Fabricators Unlimited Inc ... G ... 847 223-7986
Grayslake (G-11337)
Fanmar Inc ... E ... 708 563-0505
Elk Grove Village (G-9475)
▲ FIC America Corp ... A ... 630 871-7609
Carol Stream (G-3151)
Force Manufacturing Inc ... G ... 847 265-6500
Lake Villa (G-13013)
Ford Motor Company ... A ... 708 757-5700
Ford Heights (G-10233)
Form-All Spring Stamping Inc ... E ... 630 595-8833
Bensenville (G-1900)
Formco Metal Products Inc ... E ... 630 766-4441
Wood Dale (G-22372)
Forster Tool & Mfg Co Inc ... E ... 630 616-8177
Bensenville (G-1902)
▲ Fortune Brands Home & SEC Inc ... C ... 847 484-4400
Deerfield (G-8007)
Fountain Products Inc ... G ... 630 991-7237
Elgin (G-9039)
▲ Four Star Tool Inc ... D ... 224 735-2419
Rolling Meadows (G-18729)
Fox Valley Stamping Company ... F ... 847 741-2277
South Elgin (G-20198)
Fulton Corporation ... D ... 815 589-3211
Fulton (G-10701)
G & M Manufacturing Corp ... E ... 815 455-1900
Crystal Lake (G-7580)
G & M Metal Fabricators Inc ... D ... 847 678-6501
Franklin Park (G-10473)
G & Z Industries Inc ... E ... 847 215-2300
Wheeling (G-22061)
G T L Technologies Inc ... G ... 630 469-9818
Glendale Heights (G-11025)
◆ Gbc Metals LLC ... G ... 618 258-2350
East Alton (G-8603)
General Machinery & Mfg Co ... F ... 773 235-3700
Chicago (G-4928)
▲ General Products Intl Ltd ... G ... 847 458-6357
Lake In The Hills (G-12994)
▲ Gilbert Spring Corporation ... E ... 773 486-6030
Chicago (G-4952)
Gingrich Enterprises Inc ... E ... 309 923-7312
Roanoke (G-18050)
Global Brass and Copper Inc ... G ... 502 873-3000
East Alton (G-8604)
Global Brass Cop Holdings Inc ... E ... 847 240-4700
Schaumburg (G-19537)
Graphic Parts Intl Inc ... F ... 773 725-4900
Chicago (G-4990)
Haddock Tool & Manufacturing ... G ... 815 786-2739
Sandwich (G-19367)
▲ Harig Manufacturing Corp ... E ... 847 647-9500
Skokie (G-20011)
Harrington King Prforating Inc ... C ... 773 626-1800
Chicago (G-5047)
Headly Manufacturing Co ... D ... 708 338-0800
Broadview (G-2583)
Headly Manufacturing Co ... D ... 708 338-0800
Broadview (G-2584)
▲ Helander Metal Spinning Co ... E ... 630 268-9292
Lombard (G-13808)
Highland Southern Wire Inc ... G ... 618 654-2161
Highland (G-11792)
▲ HMC Holdings LLC ... E ... 847 541-5070
Buffalo Grove (G-2705)
Hoosier Stamping & Mfg Corp ... E ... 618 375-2057
Grayville (G-11371)
Horizon Die Company Inc ... E ... 847 426-8558
East Dundee (G-8643)
Hpl Stampings Inc ... E ... 847 540-1400
Lake Zurich (G-13084)
Hub Manufacturing Company Inc ... E ... 773 252-1373
Chicago (G-5127)
Hudson Tool & Die Co ... F ... 847 678-8710
Franklin Park (G-10491)
I C Universal Inc ... G ... 630 766-1169
Bensenville (G-1918)
▲ Icon Power Roller Inc ... E ... 630 545-2345
Marseilles (G-14310)
Illinois Tool Works Inc ... F ... 708 343-0728
Broadview (G-2586)
Illinois Tool Works Inc ... C ... 847 299-2222
Des Plaines (G-8209)
▼ IMS Companies LLC ... D ... 847 391-8100
Des Plaines (G-8210)
▲ IMS Engineered Products LLC ... C ... 847 391-8100
Des Plaines (G-8211)
IMS Olson LLC ... D ... 630 969-9400
Downers Grove (G-8464)
▼ Industrial Enclosure Corp ... E ... 630 898-7499
Aurora (G-1171)
Industrial Park Machine & Tool ... F ... 708 754-7080
S Chicago Hts (G-19105)
Inland Tool Company ... E ... 217 792-3206
Mount Pulaski (G-15389)
Integrity Manufacturing Inc ... G ... 815 514-8230
New Lenox (G-15887)
International Spring Company ... D ... 847 470-8170
Morton Grove (G-15203)
▼ Interplex Daystar Inc ... D ... 847 455-2424
Franklin Park (G-10499)
Ironform Holdings Co ... F ... 312 374-4810
Chicago (G-5239)
J F Schroeder Company Inc ... E ... 847 357-8600
Arlington Heights (G-781)
J-TEC Metal Products Inc ... F ... 630 875-1300
Itasca (G-12288)
Jason Incorporated ... C ... 630 627-7000
Addison (G-158)
▲ JD Norman Industries Inc ... D ... 630 458-3700
Addison (G-159)
Jenco Metal Products Inc ... F ... 847 956-0550
Mount Prospect (G-15340)
Jiffy Metal Products Inc ... G ... 773 626-8090
Chicago (G-5303)
Jlo Metal Products Co A Corp ... D ... 773 889-6242
Chicago (G-5307)
Johnson Tool Company ... G ... 708 453-8600
Huntley (G-12154)
▲ Jsn Inc ... E ... 708 410-1800
Maywood (G-14426)
K-Metal Products Incorporated ... G ... 773 476-2700
Chicago (G-5349)
Kaman Tool Corporation ... G ... 708 652-9023
Cicero (G-7208)
Kaskaskia Tool and Machine Inc ... E ... 618 475-3301
New Athens (G-15860)
▲ Kenmode Tool and Engrg Inc ... C ... 847 658-5041
Algonquin (G-396)
Kensen Tool & Die Inc ... F ... 847 455-0150
Franklin Park (G-10512)
Kernel Kutter Inc ... G ... 815 877-1515
Machesney Park (G-14085)
Kier Mfg Co ... G ... 630 953-9500
Addison (G-168)
King Tool and Die Inc ... G ... 630 787-0799
Bensenville (G-1934)
▲ Kipp Manufacturing Company Inc ... F ... 630 768-9051
Wauconda (G-21477)
Kleen Cut Tool Inc ... G ... 630 447-7020
Warrenville (G-21349)
Klein Tools Inc ... D ... 847 228-6999
Elk Grove Village (G-9577)
Klein Tools Inc ... E ... 847 821-5500
Lincolnshire (G-13461)
Knapheide Manufacturing Co ... E ... 217 223-1848
Quincy (G-17847)
Kosmos Tool Inc ... F ... 815 675-2200
Spring Grove (G-20343)
Kr Machine ... G ... 815 248-2250
Durand (G-8586)
Kuester Tool & Die Inc ... E ... 217 223-1955
Quincy (G-17851)
▲ Lakeview Metals Inc ... E ... 847 838-9800
Antioch (G-640)
▲ Lamination Specialties Corp ... D ... 312 243-2181
Chicago (G-5449)
Lamination Specialties Corp ... E ... 773 254-7500
Chicago (G-5450)
▲ Larsen Manufacturing LLC ... C ... 847 970-9600
Mundelein (G-15519)
Laystrom Manufacturing Co ... D ... 773 342-4800
Chicago (G-5474)
Lew-El Tool & Manufacturing Co ... F ... 773 804-1133
Chicago (G-5497)
Lewis Spring and Mfg Company ... E ... 847 588-7030
Niles (G-15996)
Lindy Manufacturing Company ... E ... 630 963-4126
Downers Grove (G-8476)
Line Group Inc ... E ... 847 593-6810
Arlington Heights (G-793)
Lorbern Mfg Inc ... E ... 847 301-8600
Schaumburg (G-19623)
▲ Lsa United Inc ... C ... 773 476-7439
Lombard (G-13822)
Lyon LLC ... C ... 815 432-4595
Watseka (G-21421)
▲ M J Celco Inc ... D ... 847 671-1900
Schiller Park (G-19843)
M Lizen Manufacturing Co ... E ... 708 755-7213
University Park (G-21055)
M Ward Manufacturing Co Inc ... E ... 847 864-4786
Evanston (G-10067)
Macon Metal Products Co ... E ... 217 824-7205
Taylorville (G-20842)
Major Die & Engineering Co ... E ... 630 773-3444
Itasca (G-12309)
Manor Tool and Mfg Co ... E ... 847 678-2020
Schiller Park (G-19845)
Marengo Tool & Die Works Inc ... E ... 815 568-7411
Marengo (G-14236)
Mark Development Corporation ... C ... 815 339-2226
Mark (G-14298)
Marlboro Wire Ltd ... E ... 217 224-7989
Quincy (G-17855)
Masonite Corporation ... D ... 630 584-6330
West Chicago (G-21740)
Mayfair Metal Spinning Co Inc ... G ... 847 358-7450
Palatine (G-17054)
McCarthy Enterprises Inc ... G ... 847 367-5718
Libertyville (G-13351)
▲ Mercury Products Corp ... C ... 847 524-4400
Schaumburg (G-19641)
Mercury Products Corp ... C ... 847 524-4400
Schaumburg (G-19642)
▲ Meridian Parts Inc ... G ... 630 718-1995
Naperville (G-15696)
Metal Spinners Inc ... E ... 815 625-0390
Rock Falls (G-18142)

SIC

Employee Codes: A=Over 500 employees, B=251-500
C=101-250, D=51-100, E=20-50, F=10-19, G=3-9
2017 Harris Illinois
Industrial Directory
1045

34 FABRICATED METAL PRODUCTS, EXCEPT MACHINERY AND TRANSPORTATION EQUIPMENT SIC SECTION

**Metal Technology Solutions** G 630 587-1450 Saint Charles *(G-19219)*
▲ **Metalex Corporation** C 847 362-8300 Libertyville *(G-13354)*
▲ **Metalstamp Inc** E 815 467-7800 Minooka *(G-14842)*
**Mfz Ventures Inc** G 773 247-4611 Chicago *(G-5715)*
**Micromatic Spring Stamping Inc** E 630 607-0141 Addison *(G-208)*
**Mid-West Spring & Stamping Inc** G 630 739-3800 Romeoville *(G-18847)*
**Midland Stamping and** G 847 678-7573 Schiller Park *(G-19850)*
**Midland Stamping and Fabg Corp** D 847 678-7573 Schiller Park *(G-19851)*
**Midwest Nameplate Corp** G 708 614-0606 Orland Park *(G-16875)*
**Milans Machining & Mfg Co Inc** D 708 780-6600 Cicero *(G-7222)*
**Millenia Metals LLC** D 630 458-0401 Itasca *(G-12317)*
▲ **Millenia Products Group Inc** C 630 458-0401 Itasca *(G-12318)*
**Millenia Specialty Metals LLC** G 630 458-0401 Itasca *(G-12319)*
**Millenia Trucking LLC** E 630 458-0401 Itasca *(G-12320)*
**Mint Masters Inc** E 847 451-1133 Franklin Park *(G-10534)*
**Mity Inc** G 630 365-5030 Elburn *(G-8898)*
▲ **Mj Celco International LLC** E 847 671-1900 Schiller Park *(G-19852)*
**MNP Precision Parts LLC** C 815 391-5256 Rockford *(G-18509)*
**Moline Welding Inc** F 309 756-0643 Milan *(G-14795)*
**Moline Welding Inc** G 309 756-0643 Milan *(G-14796)*
**Mueller Mfg Corp** E 847 640-1666 Elk Grove Village *(G-9642)*
**My-Lin Manufacturing Co Inc** E 630 897-4100 Aurora *(G-1192)*
**Natural Products Inc** F 847 509-5835 Northbrook *(G-16317)*
**Navitor Inc** B 800 323-0253 Harwood Heights *(G-11687)*
**Nelson Manufacturing Co Inc** F 815 229-0161 Rockford *(G-18519)*
**New Dimension Models** G 815 935-1001 Aroma Park *(G-879)*
**New Process Steel LP** D 708 389-3482 Alsip *(G-499)*
**Newko Tool & Engineering Co** E 847 359-1670 Palatine *(G-17058)*
▲ **North Amercn Acquisition Corp** C 847 695-8030 Elgin *(G-9125)*
**North Star Stamping & Tool Inc** F 847 658-9400 Lake In The Hills *(G-13001)*
▲ **Northfield Holdings LLC** E 847 755-0700 Schaumburg *(G-19669)*
◆ **Northwestern Corporation** E 815 942-1300 Morris *(G-15124)*
▲ **Nu-Way Industries Inc** C 847 298-7710 Des Plaines *(G-8244)*
**Octavia Tool & Gage Company** G 847 913-9233 Elk Grove Village *(G-9661)*
**Odm Tool & Mfg Co Inc** D 708 485-6130 Hodgkins *(G-11978)*
**Offko Tool Inc** G 815 933-9474 Kankakee *(G-12641)*
**OHare Spring Company Inc** E 847 298-1360 Elk Grove Village *(G-9662)*
**Olson Metal Products LLC** F 847 981-7550 Arlington Heights *(G-812)*
▲ **Omiotek Coil Spring Co** D 630 495-4056 Lombard *(G-13837)*
**P T L Manufacturing Inc** E 618 277-6789 Belleville *(G-1663)*
**P-K Tool & Mfg Co** D 773 235-4700 Chicago *(G-6046)*
**Paddock Industries Inc** F 618 277-1580 Smithton *(G-20123)*
**Paragon Spring Company** E 773 489-6300 Chicago *(G-6076)*
**Paris Metal Products LLC** D 217 465-6321 Paris *(G-17157)*
**Park Manufacturing Corp Inc** F 708 345-6090 Melrose Park *(G-14682)*
**Parkway Metal Products Inc** D 847 789-4000 Des Plaines *(G-8251)*
**Patko Tool & Manufacturing** G 630 616-8802 Bensenville *(G-1963)*
**PDQ Tool & Stamping Co** E 708 841-3000 Dolton *(G-8374)*
**Pecora Tool Service Inc** G 847 524-1275 Schaumburg *(G-19687)*
▲ **Perfection Spring Stmping Corp** D 847 437-3900 Mount Prospect *(G-15362)*
▲ **Performance Stamping Co Inc** E 847 426-2233 Carpentersville *(G-3295)*
**Plano Molding Company LLC** C 815 538-3111 Mendota *(G-14730)*
▲ **Plasticrest Products Inc** F 773 826-2163 Chicago *(G-6136)*
**Polymer Plnfeld Hldings US Inc** C 815 436-5671 Plainfield *(G-17641)*
**Porcelain Enamel Finishers** G 312 808-1560 Chicago *(G-6157)*
**Precise Stamping Inc** E 630 897-6477 North Aurora *(G-16143)*
**Precision Forming Stamping Co** E 773 489-6868 Chicago *(G-6170)*
**Precision Metal Spinning Corp** E 847 392-5672 Rolling Meadows *(G-18767)*
**Precision Metal Technologies** F 847 228-6630 Rolling Meadows *(G-18768)*
**Precision Resource Inc** C 847 383-1300 Vernon Hills *(G-21190)*
▲ **Precision Stamping Pdts Inc** E 847 678-0800 Schiller Park *(G-19862)*
**Premier Metal Works Inc** G 312 226-7414 Chicago *(G-6178)*
**Prikos & Becker LLC** D 847 675-3910 Skokie *(G-20059)*
▲ **Principal Manufacturing Corp** B 708 865-7500 Broadview *(G-2603)*
▲ **Prismier LLC** E 630 592-4515 Woodridge *(G-22511)*
**Pro Machining Inc** F 815 633-4140 Loves Park *(G-13978)*
**Pro-Tech Metal Specialties Inc** E 630 279-7094 Elmhurst *(G-9923)*
**Production Fabg & Stamping Inc** F 708 755-5468 S Chicago Hts *(G-19111)*
**Production Stampings Inc** G 815 495-2800 Leland *(G-13220)*
**Prospect Tool Company LLC** G 630 766-2200 Franklin Park *(G-10564)*
**Pt Holdings Inc** G 217 691-1793 Springfield *(G-20508)*
**R B White Inc** E 309 452-5816 Normal *(G-16086)*
**R C Coil Spring Mfg Co Inc** E 630 790-3500 Glendale Heights *(G-11062)*
**R Hansel & Son Inc** G 815 784-5500 Genoa *(G-10883)*
**R Z Tool Inc** F 847 647-2350 Niles *(G-16025)*
**Radiad Manufacturing** G 847 678-5808 Franklin Park *(G-10568)*
**Rail Exchange Inc** E 708 757-3317 Chicago Heights *(G-7119)*
**Ramcel Engineering Co** D 847 272-6980 Northbrook *(G-16353)*
▲ **Realwheels Corporation** E 847 662-7722 Gurnee *(G-11499)*
**Reliable Die Service Inc** F 708 458-5155 Bedford Park *(G-1577)*
**Reliable Machine Company** E 815 968-8803 Rockford *(G-18554)*
▲ **Reliable Metal Stamping Co Inc** F 773 625-1177 Franklin Park *(G-10572)*
**Reliance Tool & Mfg Co** E 847 695-1235 Elgin *(G-9164)*
▲ **Ri-Del Mfg Inc** D 312 829-8720 Chicago *(G-6349)*
**Rijon Manufacturing Company** G 708 388-2295 Blue Island *(G-2266)*
◆ **Rittal Corp** A 847 240-4600 Schaumburg *(G-19712)*
**Riverfront Machine Inc** D 815 663-5000 Spring Valley *(G-20379)*
▲ **Rj Stuckel Co Inc** E 800 789-7220 Elk Grove Village *(G-9716)*
**Rockford Toolcraft Inc** C 815 398-5507 Rockford *(G-18589)*
▲ **Rockwell Metal Products Inc** G 773 762-7030 Chicago *(G-6377)*
▲ **Royal Die & Stamping Co Inc** C 630 766-2685 Carol Stream *(G-3229)*
**Rtm Trend Industries Inc** E 847 455-4350 Franklin Park *(G-10578)*
**Runge Enterprises Inc** G 630 365-2000 Elburn *(G-8909)*
**Rursch Specialties Inc** G 309 795-1502 Reynolds *(G-17953)*
**S & L Tool Co Inc** G 847 455-5550 Franklin Park *(G-10579)*
▼ **S & S Hinge Company** E 630 582-9500 Bloomingdale *(G-2133)*
**S & S Keytax Inc** F 708 656-9221 Chicago *(G-6421)*
▲ **S & W Manufacturing Co Inc** E 630 595-5044 Bensenville *(G-1984)*
▲ **Sealco Industries Inc** E 847 741-3101 Elgin *(G-9173)*
**Secretary of State Illinois** G 217 466-5220 Paris *(G-17161)*
**Secretary of State Illinois** G 217 782-4850 Springfield *(G-20520)*
**Secretary of State Illinois** G 708 388-9199 Midlothian *(G-14768)*
**Secretary of State Illinois** G 217 243-4327 Jacksonville *(G-12414)*
**Secretary of State Illinois** F 773 660-4963 Chicago *(G-6469)*
**Senna Design LLC** G 847 821-7877 Vernon Hills *(G-21201)*
**Service Sheet Metal Works Inc** F 773 229-0031 Chicago *(G-6483)*
**Service Stampings of IL Inc** E 630 894-7880 Roselle *(G-18977)*
**Simplomatic Manufacturing Co** E 773 342-7757 Elgin *(G-9181)*
**Skill-Di Inc** F 708 544-6080 Bellwood *(G-1721)*
**Slidematic Products Co** E 773 545-4213 Chicago *(G-6530)*
▲ **Smith & Richardson Mfg Co** E 630 232-2581 Geneva *(G-10868)*
**Smithco Fabricators Inc** F 847 678-1619 Schiller Park *(G-19873)*
**Spannagel Tool & Die** E 630 969-7575 Downers Grove *(G-8526)*
▲ **Spare Part Solutions Inc** F 815 637-1490 Rockford *(G-18624)*
**Spectracrafts Ltd** G 847 824-4117 Lombard *(G-13856)*
**St Charles Stamping Inc** F 630 584-2029 Saint Charles *(G-19269)*
▲ **Stack-On Products Co** C 847 526-1611 Wauconda *(G-21502)*
▲ **Stanley Spring & Stamping Corp** D 773 777-2600 Chicago *(G-6572)*
**Stanron Corporation** D 773 777-2600 Chicago *(G-6573)*
**Starmont Manufacturing Co** G 815 939-1041 Kankakee *(G-12653)*
**Starmont Manufacturing Inc** F 708 758-2525 Chicago Heights *(G-7127)*
**Steibel License Service** G 618 233-7555 Swansea *(G-20783)*
▲ **Sterling Metal Craft Inc** F 708 652-4590 Cicero *(G-7231)*
**Stuecklen Manufacturing Co** G 847 678-5130 Franklin Park *(G-10596)*
**Stumpfoll Tool & Mfg** G 312 733-2632 Chicago *(G-6609)*
**Style Rite Restaurant Eqp Co** G 630 628-0940 Addison *(G-299)*
▲ **Sundstrom Pressed Steel Co** E 773 721-2237 Chicago *(G-6626)*
**Superior Metal Products Inc** F 630 466-1150 Sugar Grove *(G-20737)*
**Sure-Way Die Designs Inc** F 630 323-0370 Westmont *(G-21924)*
▲ **Sweet Manufacturing Corp** E 847 546-5575 Chicago *(G-6648)*
**T A U Inc** G 708 841-5757 Dolton *(G-8377)*
**T and D Metal Products LLC** G 815 432-4938 Watseka *(G-21430)*
◆ **T H K Holdings of America LLC** G 847 310-1111 Schaumburg *(G-19750)*
**T N T Industries Inc** F 630 879-1522 Batavia *(G-1503)*
**Tarney Inc** E 773 235-0331 Chicago *(G-6677)*

SIC SECTION
34 FABRICATED METAL PRODUCTS, EXCEPT MACHINERY AND TRANSPORTATION EQUIPMENT

**Tauber Brothers Tool & Die Co** ....E.... 708 867-9100
Chicago *(G-6679)*
**Technical Metals Inc** ....D.... 815 692-4643
Fairbury *(G-10133)*
**Tellenar Inc** ....F.... 815 356-8044
Crystal Lake *(G-7663)*
**Tempel Holdings Inc** ....G.... 773 250-8000
Chicago *(G-6695)*
▲ **Tempel Steel Company** ....A.... 773 250-8000
Chicago *(G-6696)*
**Three Star Mfg Co Inc** ....G.... 847 526-2222
Wauconda *(G-21510)*
**Thryselius Stamping Inc** ....G.... 630 232-0795
Geneva *(G-10872)*
**Tj Wire Forming Inc** ....G.... 630 628-9209
Addison *(G-316)*
▲ **Tlk Tool & Stamping Inc** ....G.... 224 293-6941
East Dundee *(G-8660)*
**Tool Automation Enterprises** ....G.... 708 799-6847
East Hazel Crest *(G-8666)*
**Trinity Machined Products Inc** ....E.... 630 876-6992
Aurora *(G-1090)*
**Trio Wire Products Inc** ....G.... 815 469-2148
Frankfort *(G-10372)*
**Triton Industries Inc** ....C.... 773 384-3700
Chicago *(G-6779)*
**Tro Manufacturing Company Inc** ....E.... 847 455-3755
Franklin Park *(G-10613)*
**Tru-Machine Co Inc** ....G.... 815 675-6735
Spring Grove *(G-20372)*
**Tru-Way Inc** ....E.... 708 562-3690
Northlake *(G-16457)*
**TRW Automotive US LLC** ....B.... 217 826-3011
Marshall *(G-14330)*
**Tryson Metal Stampg & Mfg Inc** ....G.... 630 628-6570
Addison *(G-328)*
**Tryson Metal Stampg & Mfg Inc** ....E.... 630 458-0591
Addison *(G-329)*
**Tu-Star Manufacturing Co Inc** ....G.... 815 338-5760
Woodstock *(G-22619)*
**Tvh Parts Co** ....E.... 847 223-1000
Grayslake *(G-11365)*
**Twinplex Manufacturing Co** ....F.... 630 595-2040
Wood Dale *(G-22435)*
**Ultra Stamping & Assembly Inc** ....E.... 815 874-9888
Rockford *(G-18660)*
**Unified Tool Die & Mfg Co Inc** ....F.... 847 678-3773
Schiller Park *(G-19878)*
**United Standard Industries Inc** ....D.... 847 724-0350
Glenview *(G-11212)*
**United Steel Perforating/ARC** ....E.... 630 942-7300
Glendale Heights *(G-11087)*
**United Tool and Engineering Co** ....D.... 815 389-3021
South Beloit *(G-20171)*
▲ **USA Technologies Inc** ....C.... 309 495-0829
Peoria *(G-17476)*
**Vanart Engineering Company** ....E.... 847 678-6255
Franklin Park *(G-10620)*
▲ **Vindee Industries Inc** ....E.... 815 469-3300
Frankfort *(G-10375)*
**Voco Tool & Mfg Inc** ....G.... 708 771-3800
Forest Park *(G-10256)*
▲ **Voges Inc** ....D.... 618 233-2760
Belleville *(G-1688)*
**Wardzala Industries Inc** ....F.... 847 288-9909
Franklin Park *(G-10627)*
**Wauconda Tool & Engineering Co** ....E.... 847 608-0602
Elgin *(G-9231)*
**Wauconda Tool & Engrg LLC** ....D.... 847 658-4588
Algonquin *(G-412)*
**Wenco Manufacturing Co Inc** ....E.... 630 377-7474
Elgin *(G-9235)*
**Wesco Spring Company** ....E.... 773 838-3350
Chicago *(G-6958)*
◆ **William Dudek Manufacturing Co** ....E.... 773 622-2727
Chicago *(G-6983)*
**Willie Washer Mfg Co** ....C.... 847 956-1344
Elk Grove Village *(G-9814)*
**Wireformers Inc** ....E.... 847 718-1920
Mount Prospect *(G-15384)*
◆ **Wki Holding Company Inc** ....D.... 847 233-8600
Rosemont *(G-19041)*
◆ **World Kitchen LLC** ....C.... 847 233-8600
Rosemont *(G-19042)*
**World Washer & Stamping Inc** ....F.... 630 543-6749
Addison *(G-347)*
**Wozniak Industries Inc** ....C.... 630 820-4052
Aurora *(G-1100)*
◆ **Wozniak Industries Inc** ....G.... 630 954-3400
Oakbrook Terrace *(G-16723)*

## *3471 Electroplating, Plating, Polishing, Anodizing & Coloring*

**A & B Metal Polishing Inc** ....F.... 773 847-1077
Chicago *(G-3678)*
**A & J Finishers** ....G.... 847 352-5408
Schaumburg *(G-19417)*
**A & L Drilling Inc** ....F.... 815 962-7538
Rockford *(G-18238)*
**A and R Custom Chrome** ....G.... 708 728-1005
Chicago *(G-3683)*
**AAA Mold Finishers Inc** ....G.... 773 775-3977
Chicago *(G-3700)*
**AAM-Ro Corporation** ....F.... 708 343-5543
Broadview *(G-2552)*
**Aaro Roller Corp** ....G.... 815 398-7655
Rockford *(G-18244)*
**Accent Metal Finishing Inc** ....F.... 847 678-7420
Schiller Park *(G-19798)*
**Accurate Metal Finishing Co** ....G.... 847 428-7705
Gilberts *(G-10911)*
**Ace Anodizing Impregnating Inc** ....D.... 708 547-6680
Hillside *(G-11907)*
**Ace Metal Refinishers Inc** ....F.... 800 323-7147
Oak Brook *(G-16484)*
▲ **Ace Metal Refinishers Inc** ....F.... 630 778-9200
Lombard *(G-13758)*
**Ace Plating Company** ....E.... 773 376-1800
Chicago *(G-3727)*
**Ace Sandblast Company (del)** ....F.... 773 777-6654
Chicago *(G-3728)*
**Advanced Graphics Tech Inc** ....C.... 817 481-8561
Darien *(G-7787)*
**Aggresive Motor Sports** ....G.... 630 761-1550
Batavia *(G-1405)*
**Al Bar Laboratories Inc** ....F.... 847 251-1218
Wilmette *(G-22241)*
**All-Brite Anodizing Co Inc** ....E.... 708 562-0502
Northlake *(G-16425)*
**Alliance Specialties Corp** ....F.... 847 487-1945
Wauconda *(G-21439)*
▼ **Alliance Steel Corporation** ....E.... 708 924-1200
Bedford Park *(G-1535)*
**Alloy Chrome Inc** ....G.... 847 678-2880
Schiller Park *(G-19800)*
**Alton Industries Inc** ....F.... 708 865-2000
Broadview *(G-2556)*
▲ **Aluminum Coil Anodizing Corp** ....C.... 630 837-4000
Streamwood *(G-20641)*
**American Nickel Works Inc** ....E.... 312 942-0070
Chicago *(G-3868)*
**American Plating & Mfg Co** ....F.... 773 890-4907
Chicago *(G-3869)*
**Ameriplate Inc** ....E.... 815 744-8585
Joliet *(G-12453)*
**Anodizing Specialists Ltd** ....G.... 847 437-9495
Elk Grove Village *(G-9308)*
**Archer Tinning & Re-Tinning Co** ....F.... 773 927-7240
Chicago *(G-3940)*
▲ **Arlington Plating Company** ....C.... 847 359-1490
Palatine *(G-17003)*
**Arnold Monument Co Inc** ....G.... 217 546-2102
Springfield *(G-20388)*
**Ata Finishing Corp** ....G.... 847 677-8560
Skokie *(G-19960)*
**Automatic Anodizing Corp** ....E.... 773 478-3304
Chicago *(G-3991)*
**B & T Polishing Co** ....E.... 847 658-6415
Chicago *(G-4018)*
**Bales Mold Service Inc** ....E.... 630 852-4665
Downers Grove *(G-8394)*
**Bar Processing Corporation** ....E.... 708 757-4570
Chicago Heights *(G-7081)*
**Baroque Silversmith Inc** ....G.... 312 357-2813
Chicago *(G-4045)*
**Barron Metal Finishing LLC** ....F.... 815 962-8053
Rockford *(G-18277)*
**Bellows Shoppe** ....G.... 847 446-5533
Winnetka *(G-22303)*
**Bellwood Industries Inc** ....G.... 773 522-1002
Chicago *(G-4078)*
**Belmont Plating Works Inc** ....C.... 847 678-0200
Franklin Park *(G-10410)*
**Berge Plating Works Inc** ....G.... 309 788-2831
Rock Island *(G-18163)*
**Berteau-Lowell Pltg Works Inc** ....E.... 773 276-3135
Chicago *(G-4088)*
**Bobco Enterprises Inc Del** ....E.... 773 722-1700
Bloomingdale *(G-2097)*
**Bright Metals Finishing Corp** ....G.... 773 486-2312
Chicago *(G-4169)*
**Brite One Inc** ....G.... 708 481-8005
Matteson *(G-14368)*
**Bucthel Metal Finishing Corp** ....F.... 847 427-8704
Elk Grove Village *(G-9347)*
**Budding Polishing & Met Finshg** ....G.... 708 396-1166
South Holland *(G-20254)*
▲ **Capron Mfg Co** ....D.... 815 569-2301
Capron *(G-2994)*
**Cardon Mold Finishing Inc** ....G.... 630 543-5431
Addison *(G-69)*
**Castle Metal Finishing Corp** ....F.... 847 678-6041
Schiller Park *(G-19811)*
**Celinco Inc** ....G.... 815 964-2256
Rockford *(G-18301)*
**Chem Processing Inc** ....D.... 815 874-8118
Rockford *(G-18305)*
**Chem Processing Inc** ....F.... 815 965-1037
Rockford *(G-18306)*
**Chem-Plate Industries Inc** ....E.... 708 345-3588
Maywood *(G-14422)*
**Chem-Plate Industries Inc** ....D.... 847 640-1600
Elk Grove Village *(G-9366)*
**Chemix Corp** ....F.... 708 754-2150
Glenwood *(G-11215)*
**Chemtool Incorporated** ....D.... 815 459-1250
Crystal Lake *(G-7551)*
**Chris Plating Inc** ....E.... 847 729-9271
Northbrook *(G-16223)*
▲ **Chromium Industries Inc** ....E.... 773 287-3716
Chicago *(G-4373)*
**Chromold Plating Inc** ....G.... 815 344-8644
McHenry *(G-14486)*
**Circle Studio Stained Glass** ....G.... 847 432-7249
Highland Park *(G-11827)*
**Circle Studio Stained Glass** ....G.... 773 588-4848
Chicago *(G-4380)*
**Ciske & Dresch** ....G.... 630 251-9200
Batavia *(G-1430)*
**Classic Metal Company Inc** ....G.... 815 252-0104
Mendota *(G-14718)*
**Clybourn Metal Finishing Co** ....E.... 773 525-8162
Chicago *(G-4409)*
**Cmp Associates Inc** ....F.... 847 956-1313
Elk Grove Village *(G-9379)*
**Coating Specialty Inc** ....G.... 708 754-3311
S Chicago Hts *(G-19101)*
**Cody Metal Finishing Inc** ....F.... 773 252-2026
Chicago *(G-4417)*
▲ **Cooley Wire Products Mfg Co** ....E.... 847 678-8585
Schiller Park *(G-19816)*
**Cornerstone Polishing Company** ....G.... 618 777-2754
Ozark *(G-16993)*
**Courtesy Metal Polishing** ....G.... 630 832-1862
Villa Park *(G-21246)*
**Craftsman Pltg & Tinning Corp** ....E.... 773 477-1040
Chicago *(G-4491)*
**Curtis Metal Finishing Company** ....D.... 815 633-6693
Machesney Park *(G-14069)*
**Custom Chrome & Polishing** ....G.... 618 885-9499
Jerseyville *(G-12420)*
**Custom Hard Chrome Service Co** ....G.... 847 759-1420
Rosemont *(G-18996)*
**D & N Deburring Co Inc** ....G.... 847 451-7702
Franklin Park *(G-10452)*
**Dana Anodizing Inc** ....F.... 773 486-2312
Chicago *(G-4550)*
**De Kalb Plating Co Inc** ....G.... 815 756-6112
Dekalb *(G-8085)*
**Decatur Plating & Mfg Co** ....F.... 217 422-8514
Decatur *(G-7873)*
**Deep Coat LLC** ....E.... 630 466-1505
Sugar Grove *(G-20722)*
**Delta Secondary Inc** ....E.... 630 766-1180
Bensenville *(G-1878)*
**Diamond Blast Corporation** ....F.... 708 681-2640
Melrose Park *(G-14617)*
**Diamond Plating Company Inc** ....E.... 618 451-7740
Madison *(G-14142)*
▲ **Diamond Spray Painting Inc** ....G.... 630 513-5600
Saint Charles *(G-19171)*
**Dixline Corporation** ....D.... 309 932-2011
Galva *(G-10788)*
**Dixline Corporation** ....F.... 309 932-2011
Galva *(G-10787)*
**Dover Industrial Chrome Inc** ....G.... 773 478-2022
Chicago *(G-4638)*
**DS Polishing & Metal Finshg** ....G.... 309 755-0544
East Moline *(G-8677)*
**Duro-Chrome Industries Inc** ....E.... 847 487-2900
Wauconda *(G-21457)*

# 34 FABRICATED METAL PRODUCTS, EXCEPT MACHINERY AND TRANSPORTATION EQUIPMENT — SIC SECTION

Duroweld Company Inc .......... E ...... 847 680-3064
Lake Bluff *(G-12841)*

Durr - All Corporation .......... G ...... 815 943-1032
Harvard *(G-11631)*

Dyna-Burr Chicago Inc .......... F ...... 708 250-6744
Northlake *(G-16435)*

Ej Somerville Plating Co .......... E ...... 708 345-5100
Melrose Park *(G-14631)*

Electro-Glo Distribution Inc .......... G ...... 815 224-4030
La Salle *(G-12771)*

Electro-Max Inc .......... E ...... 847 683-4100
Hampshire *(G-11548)*

Electrohone Technologies Inc .......... G ...... 815 363-5536
McHenry *(G-14501)*

Electrolizing Inc .......... G ...... 815 758-6657
Dekalb *(G-8089)*

Electronic Plating Co .......... E ...... 708 652-8100
Cicero *(G-7193)*

Ellwood Group Inc .......... F ...... 815 725-9030
Joliet *(G-12489)*

Empire Hard Chrome Inc .......... C ...... 773 762-3156
Chicago *(G-4745)*

Empire Hard Chrome Inc .......... C ...... 312 226-7548
Chicago *(G-4746)*

▲ En-Chro Plating Inc .......... E ...... 708 450-1250
Melrose Park *(G-14633)*

Enameled Steel and Sign Co .......... E ...... 773 481-2270
Chicago *(G-4748)*

▲ Engis Corporation .......... E ...... 847 808-9400
Wheeling *(G-22047)*

Envirocoat Inc .......... G ...... 847 673-3649
Skokie *(G-19995)*

Expert Metal Finishing Inc .......... F ...... 708 583-2550
River Grove *(G-18008)*

▲ Feralloy Corporation .......... E ...... 503 286-8869
Chicago *(G-4836)*

FHP Inc .......... G ...... 708 452-4100
Northlake *(G-16436)*

Finished Metals Incorporated .......... F ...... 773 229-1600
Chicago *(G-4847)*

Finishing Company .......... C ...... 630 559-0808
Addison *(G-117)*

▲ Finishing Company .......... D ...... 630 521-9635
Bensenville *(G-1898)*

Finishing Touch Inc .......... F ...... 773 774-7349
Chicago *(G-4848)*

Floor-Chem Inc .......... G ...... 630 789-2152
Romeoville *(G-18825)*

Forest Plating Co .......... G ...... 708 366-2071
Forest Park *(G-10246)*

Formulations Inc .......... G ...... 847 674-9141
Skokie *(G-20001)*

Fox Valley Sandblasting Inc .......... G ...... 630 553-6050
Yorkville *(G-22659)*

▲ G L Tool and Manufacturing Co .......... F ...... 630 628-1992
Addison *(G-126)*

Gatto Industrial Platers Inc .......... C ...... 773 287-0100
Chicago *(G-4919)*

General Plating Co Inc .......... G ...... 630 543-0088
Addison *(G-133)*

Glass Fx .......... G ...... 217 359-0048
Champaign *(G-3488)*

Great Lakes Finishing Eqp Inc .......... G ...... 708 345-5300
South Elgin *(G-20202)*

Griffin Plating Co Inc .......... G ...... 773 342-5181
Chicago *(G-5003)*

Grove Plating Company Inc .......... F ...... 847 639-7651
Fox River Grove *(G-10287)*

Gyro Processing Inc .......... E ...... 800 491-0733
Chicago *(G-5016)*

Hanson Metal Finishing Inc .......... G ...... 847 520-1463
Wheeling *(G-22068)*

Hausner Hard - Chrome Inc .......... E ...... 847 439-6010
Elk Grove Village *(G-9518)*

Heidtman Steel Products Inc .......... D ...... 618 451-0052
Granite City *(G-11284)*

Heidtman Steel Products Inc .......... D ...... 618 451-0052
Granite City *(G-11285)*

Human Svc Ctr Southern Metro E .......... E ...... 618 282-6233
Red Bud *(G-17942)*

Illinois Electro Deburring Co .......... F ...... 847 678-5010
Franklin Park *(G-10494)*

Imperial Plating Company III .......... E ...... 773 586-3500
Chicago *(G-5167)*

Industrial Hard Chrome Ltd .......... C ...... 630 208-7000
Geneva *(G-10834)*

▲ International Proc Co Amer .......... E ...... 847 437-8400
Elk Grove Village *(G-9553)*

International Silver Plating .......... G ...... 847 835-0705
Glencoe *(G-11001)*

Interntional Metal Finshg Svcs .......... G ...... 815 234-5254
Byron *(G-2917)*

Irmko Tool Works Inc .......... E ...... 630 350-7550
Bensenville *(G-1923)*

▲ J & M Plating Inc .......... C ...... 815 964-4975
Rockford *(G-18441)*

J D Plating Works Inc .......... G ...... 847 662-6484
Waukegan *(G-21573)*

James Precious Metals Plating .......... F ...... 773 774-8700
Chicago *(G-5274)*

Jensen Plating Works Inc .......... E ...... 773 252-7733
Chicago *(G-5292)*

Jensen Plating Works Inc .......... E ...... 773 252-7733
Chicago *(G-5293)*

Jhelsa Metal Polsg Fabrication .......... G ...... 773 385-6628
Chicago *(G-5302)*

Jvk Precision Hard Chrome Inc .......... G ...... 630 628-0810
Addison *(G-161)*

K & P Industries Inc .......... G ...... 630 628-6676
Addison *(G-163)*

K V F Company .......... E ...... 847 437-5100
Elk Grove Village *(G-9569)*

K V F Company .......... F ...... 847 437-5019
Elk Grove Village *(G-9570)*

Kobac .......... E ...... 847 520-6000
Buffalo Grove *(G-2716)*

Koderhandt Inc .......... E ...... 618 233-4808
Belleville *(G-1645)*

Krel Laboratories Inc .......... F ...... 773 826-4487
Chicago *(G-5411)*

▲ Krueger and Company .......... E ...... 630 833-5650
Elmhurst *(G-9899)*

Lbs Marketing Ltd .......... E ...... 815 965-5234
Rockford *(G-18463)*

Lee Quigley Company .......... G ...... 708 563-1600
Fox Lake *(G-5484)*

M & B Services Ltd Inc .......... F ...... 217 463-2162
Paris *(G-17153)*

Magnetic Inspection Lab Inc .......... D ...... 847 437-4488
Elk Grove Village *(G-9606)*

▲ Main Steel Polishing Co Inc .......... E ...... 847 916-1220
Elk Grove Village *(G-9608)*

Manner Plating Inc .......... G ...... 815 877-7791
Loves Park *(G-13963)*

Marjan Inc .......... G ...... 630 906-0053
Montgomery *(G-15060)*

Markham Industry Inc .......... G ...... 815 338-0116
Woodstock *(G-22587)*

Master Polishing & Buffing .......... G ...... 773 731-3883
Chicago *(G-5644)*

Masters Plating Co Inc .......... G ...... 815 226-8846
Rockford *(G-18485)*

MBA Manufacturing Inc .......... G ...... 847 566-2555
Mundelein *(G-15525)*

Meminger Metal Finishing Inc .......... F ...... 309 582-3363
Aledo *(G-371)*

Metal Arts Finishing Inc .......... E ...... 630 892-6744
Aurora *(G-1187)*

Metal Finishing Pros Corp .......... G ...... 630 883-8339
Elgin *(G-9107)*

Metal Images Inc .......... G ...... 847 488-9877
Elgin *(G-9108)*

Metco Treating and Dev Co .......... D ...... 773 277-1600
Chicago *(G-5702)*

Meto-Grafics Inc .......... F ...... 847 639-0044
Crystal Lake *(G-7609)*

Metokote Corporation .......... E ...... 815 223-1190
Peru *(G-17519)*

Mexicali Hard Chrome Corp .......... E ...... 630 543-0646
Addison *(G-204)*

▲ Micro Surface Corporation .......... F ...... 815 942-4221
Morris *(G-15116)*

Midwest Galvanizing Inc .......... F ...... 773 434-2682
Chicago *(G-5743)*

▲ Midwestern Rust Proof Inc .......... D ...... 773 725-6636
Chicago *(G-5753)*

Mikes Anodizing Co .......... E ...... 773 722-5778
Chicago *(G-5758)*

▲ Modern Plating Corporation .......... G ...... 815 235-1790
Freeport *(G-10674)*

Morgan Ohare Inc .......... D ...... 630 543-6780
Addison *(G-221)*

MSC Pre Finish Metals Egv Inc .......... C ...... 847 439-2210
Elk Grove Village *(G-9640)*

Nb Finishing Inc .......... F ...... 847 364-7500
Melrose Park *(G-14677)*

Neiland Custom Products .......... G ...... 815 825-2233
Malta *(G-14166)*

Nobert Plating Co .......... G ...... 312 421-4040
Chicago *(G-5921)*

North American EN Inc .......... F ...... 847 952-3680
Elk Grove Village *(G-9654)*

▲ Nova-Chrome Inc .......... F ...... 847 455-8200
Franklin Park *(G-10542)*

▲ Oerlikon Blzers Cating USA Inc .......... F ...... 847 619-5541
Schaumburg *(G-19673)*

Omega Plating Inc .......... F ...... 708 389-5410
Crestwood *(G-7496)*

P B A Corp .......... F ...... 312 666-7370
Chicago *(G-6039)*

Pannon Mord Polishing .......... G ...... 630 893-9252
Bloomingdale *(G-2124)*

Paradigm Coatings LLC .......... E ...... 847 961-6466
Huntley *(G-12165)*

Pariso Inc .......... F ...... 773 889-4383
Chicago *(G-6082)*

Perfection Plating Inc .......... C ...... 847 593-6506
Elk Grove Village *(G-9673)*

Performance Auto Salon Inc .......... E ...... 815 468-6882
Manteno *(G-14189)*

Petersen Finishing Corporation .......... G ...... 847 228-7150
Elk Grove Village *(G-9677)*

Plano Metal Specialties Inc .......... F ...... 630 552-8510
Plano *(G-17672)*

▲ Plating International Inc .......... E ...... 847 451-2101
Franklin Park *(G-10554)*

Polyenviro Labs Inc .......... G ...... 708 489-0195
Mokena *(G-14896)*

Possehl Connector Svcs SC Inc .......... E ...... 803 366-8316
Elk Grove Village *(G-9687)*

Powers Paint Shop Inc .......... G ...... 815 338-3619
Woodstock *(G-22600)*

▲ Precise Finishing Co Inc .......... E ...... 847 451-2077
Franklin Park *(G-10558)*

Precision Chrome Inc .......... E ...... 847 587-1515
Fox Lake *(G-10282)*

Precision Finishing Systems In .......... F ...... 847 907-4266
Wheeling *(G-22127)*

Precision Plating of Quincy .......... F ...... 217 223-6590
Quincy *(G-17870)*

Pro TEC Metal Finishing Corp .......... G ...... 773 384-7853
Chicago *(G-6203)*

Production Chemical Co Inc .......... E ...... 847 455-8450
Franklin Park *(G-10563)*

Quality Plating .......... G ...... 815 626-5223
Sterling *(G-20607)*

R C Industries Inc .......... F ...... 773 378-1118
Chicago *(G-6265)*

R&R Research Inc .......... G ...... 847 345-5051
Mount Prospect *(G-15368)*

Rainbow Art Inc .......... F ...... 312 421-5600
Chicago *(G-6288)*

Redi-Strip Company .......... G ...... 630 529-2442
Roselle *(G-18966)*

Reliable Plating Corporation .......... D ...... 312 421-4747
Chicago *(G-6330)*

Riverdale Pltg Heat Trting LLC .......... E ...... 708 849-2050
Riverdale *(G-18024)*

Rockford Metal Polishing Co .......... G ...... 815 282-4448
Loves Park *(G-13984)*

Saporito Finishing Co .......... D ...... 708 222-5300
Cicero *(G-7228)*

Saporito Finishing Co .......... E ...... 708 222-5300
Chicago *(G-6443)*

Scot Industries Inc .......... D ...... 630 466-7591
Sugar Grove *(G-20734)*

Selective Plating Inc .......... E ...... 630 543-1380
Addison *(G-286)*

Skilled Plating Corp .......... F ...... 773 227-0262
Chicago *(G-6520)*

South Holland Met Finshg Inc .......... D ...... 708 235-0842
Monee *(G-15002)*

Southern Plating Inc .......... G ...... 618 983-6350
Johnston City *(G-12447)*

Specialty Pntg Soda Blastg Inc .......... G ...... 815 577-0006
Plainfield *(G-17651)*

Specified Plating Co .......... E ...... 773 826-4501
Chicago *(G-6555)*

Spider Company Inc .......... G ...... 815 961-8200
Rockford *(G-18629)*

Sterling Plating Inc .......... E ...... 708 867-6587
Chicago *(G-6590)*

Streamwood Plating Co .......... G ...... 630 830-6363
Streamwood *(G-20675)*

Superior Metal Finishing .......... F ...... 815 282-8888
Loves Park *(G-13995)*

Surcom Industries Inc .......... G ...... 773 378-0736
Chicago *(G-6640)*

Sure Shine Polishing .......... G ...... 217 853-4888
Decatur *(G-7946)*

SIC SECTION 34 FABRICATED METAL PRODUCTS, EXCEPT MACHINERY AND TRANSPORTATION EQUIPMENT

**Surface Manufacturing Company** F 815 569-2362
Capron *(G-2998)*
▲ **Swd Inc** D 630 543-3003
Addison *(G-302)*
**T M T Industries Inc** E 815 562-0111
Rochelle *(G-18111)*
**TFC Group LLC** D 630 559-0808
Addison *(G-311)*
**Thomson Steel Polishing Corp** G 773 586-2345
Chicago *(G-6720)*
**Thornton Welding Service Inc** E 217 877-0610
Decatur *(G-7952)*
**Three JS Industries Inc** F 847 640-6080
Elk Grove Village *(G-9777)*
**Transcend Corp** G 847 395-6630
Antioch *(G-658)*
**Tru Coat Plating and Finishing** F 708 544-3940
Bellwood *(G-1725)*
**Twr Service Corporation** F 847 923-0692
Schaumburg *(G-19776)*
**Ultra Polishing Inc** E 630 635-2926
Schaumburg *(G-19777)*
**Unitech Industries Inc** F 847 357-8800
Elk Grove Village *(G-9798)*
**Universal Coatings Inc** G 708 756-7000
Steger *(G-20581)*
**Universal-Spc Inc** G 847 742-4400
Elgin *(G-9220)*
**US Chrome Corp Illinois** E 815 544-3487
Kingston *(G-12708)*
**US Plating Co Inc** F 773 522-7300
Chicago *(G-6855)*
**V and L Polishing Co** G 630 543-5999
Addison *(G-335)*
**V P Anodizing Inc** G 773 622-9100
Chicago *(G-6868)*
**Vision Pickling and Proc Inc** F 815 264-7755
Waterman *(G-21410)*
**W D Mold Finishing Inc** G 847 678-8449
Schiller Park *(G-19882)*
**Wear Cote International Inc** E 309 793-1250
Rock Island *(G-18211)*
**West Town Plating Inc** E 708 652-1600
Cicero *(G-7245)*
▲ **White Racker Co Inc** G 847 758-1640
Elk Grove Village *(G-9812)*
**Xd Industries Inc** F 630 766-2843
Bensenville *(G-2019)*

## *3479 Coating & Engraving, NEC*

**A R C Electro Refinishers Inc** G 708 681-5535
Bellwood *(G-1692)*
**AAA Galvanizing - Joliet Inc** E 815 284-5001
Dixon *(G-8321)*
▲ **AAA Galvanizing - Joliet Inc** D 815 723-5000
Joliet *(G-12449)*
▲ **AAA Galvanizing - Peoria Inc** E 309 697-4100
Peoria *(G-17299)*
**ABC Coating Company Inc** E 708 258-9633
Manteno *(G-14180)*
**Accent Metal Finishing Inc** F 847 678-7420
Schiller Park *(G-19798)*
**Accurate Metallizing Inc** G 708 424-7747
Oak Lawn *(G-16596)*
**Ace Engraving & Specialties Co** G 815 759-2093
McHenry *(G-14476)*
**Acme Finishing Company Inc** D 847 640-7890
Elk Grove Village *(G-9265)*
**Acme Metallizing Co Inc** F 773 767-7000
Chicago *(G-3733)*
**Addison Engraving Inc** G 630 833-9123
Villa Park *(G-21232)*
**Advance Enameling Co** E 773 737-7356
Chicago *(G-3758)*
**Advanced Graphics Tech Inc** C 817 481-8561
Darien *(G-7787)*
**Aggressive Motorsports Inc** G 847 846-7488
Batavia *(G-1406)*
**Ambrotos Inc** G 815 355-8217
Crystal Lake *(G-7532)*
**Amerigraphics Corp** G 630 543-9790
Addison *(G-39)*
**Amex Nooter LLC** G 708 429-8300
Tinley Park *(G-20892)*
**Applied Thermal Coatings** F 815 372-4305
Romeoville *(G-18799)*
**Aqua Coat Inc** G 815 209-0808
Elgin *(G-8955)*
**Armoloy of Illinois Inc** E 815 758-6657
Dekalb *(G-8075)*
**Art Clay World Usa Inc** G 708 857-8800
Oak Lawn *(G-16604)*
**B&B Awards and Recognition Inc** G 309 828-9698
Bloomington *(G-2146)*
**Bertco Enterprises Inc** G 618 234-9283
Belleville *(G-1614)*
**Bishops Engrv & Trophy Svc Inc** G 773 777-5014
Chicago *(G-4114)*
**Blue Brothers Coatings** G 847 265-5400
Round Lake Beach *(G-19073)*
**Britt Industries Inc** E 847 640-1177
Arlington Heights *(G-731)*
**Casting Impregnators Inc** F 847 455-1000
Franklin Park *(G-10425)*
**Chem Processing Inc** D 815 874-8118
Rockford *(G-18305)*
**Chem Processing Inc** F 815 965-1037
Rockford *(G-18306)*
**Chicago Anodizing Company** D 773 533-3737
Chicago *(G-4303)*
**Chicago Tank Lining Sales** G 847 328-0500
Evanston *(G-10023)*
**Clad-Rex Steel LLC** E 847 455-7373
Franklin Park *(G-10434)*
**Coating Methods Incorporated** F 847 428-8800
Carpentersville *(G-3280)*
**Coatings Applications Inc** E 847 238-9408
Elk Grove Village *(G-9380)*
▲ **Comet Die & Engraving Company** D 630 833-5600
Elmhurst *(G-9854)*
**Commercial Finishes Co Ltd** E 847 981-9222
Elk Grove Village *(G-9385)*
**Construction Solutions LLC** G 630 834-1929
Villa Park *(G-21244)*
**Core Finishing Inc** E 630 521-9635
Bensenville *(G-1866)*
**Crosslink Coatings Corporation** G 815 467-7970
Channahon *(G-3568)*
**Crown Trophy** G 309 699-1766
East Peoria *(G-8707)*
**Curtis Metal Finishing Company** D 815 633-6693
Machesney Park *(G-14069)*
**D N D Coating** G 309 379-3021
Stanford *(G-20551)*
▲ **Diamond Spray Painting Inc** G 630 513-5600
Saint Charles *(G-19171)*
**DLP Coatings Inc** E 847 350-0113
Elk Grove Village *(G-9430)*
**Dover Industrial Chrome Inc** G 773 478-2022
Chicago *(G-4638)*
▼ **Downey Investments Inc** B 708 345-8000
Broadview *(G-2572)*
**Dt Metronic Inc** G 847 593-0945
Mount Prospect *(G-15326)*
**Durable Engravers Inc** E 630 766-6420
Franklin Park *(G-10461)*
**E & R Powder Coatings Inc** E 773 523-9510
Chicago *(G-4664)*
**Economic Plastic Coating Inc** F 708 343-2216
Melrose Park *(G-14627)*
▲ **Eifeler Coatings Tech Inc** E 630 587-1220
Saint Charles *(G-19178)*
**Electrostatic Concepts Inc** F 630 585-5080
Naperville *(G-15804)*
**Enameled Steel and Sign Co** E 773 481-2270
Chicago *(G-4748)*
**Envirocoat Inc** G 847 673-3649
Skokie *(G-19995)*
**Epscca** E 815 568-3020
Marengo *(G-14227)*
**Etch-Tech Inc** G 630 833-4234
Elmhurst *(G-9868)*
**Faspro Technologies Inc** F 847 364-9999
Elk Grove Village *(G-9476)*
**Finer Line Inc** F 847 884-1611
Schaumburg *(G-19527)*
▲ **Finishing Company** D 630 521-9635
Bensenville *(G-1898)*
**Finishing Company** C 630 559-0808
Addison *(G-117)*
**Forest Awards & Engraving** G 630 595-2242
Wood Dale *(G-22371)*
**Fresh Look & Sons** G 815 325-9692
Morris *(G-15109)*
**Group O Inc** B 309 736-8311
Milan *(G-14789)*
**Hoeing Die & Mold Engraving** G 630 543-0006
Addison *(G-147)*
**Iemco Corporation** G 773 728-4400
Chicago *(G-5145)*
**Industrial Cstm Pwdr Cting Inc** F 217 423-4272
Decatur *(G-7894)*
**Industrial Finishing Inc** F 847 451-4230
Franklin Park *(G-10497)*
**Jet Finishers Inc** D 847 718-0501
Addison *(G-160)*
**Jet Rack Corp** E 773 586-2150
Chicago *(G-5298)*
**Johnos Inc** G 630 897-6929
Aurora *(G-1178)*
**Joseph Kristan** G 847 731-3131
Zion *(G-22689)*
**Kobelco Advnced Cting Amer Inc** A 847 520-6000
Buffalo Grove *(G-2717)*
▲ **Krueger and Company** E 630 833-5650
Elmhurst *(G-9899)*
**Kvf-Quad Corporation** E 563 529-1916
East Moline *(G-8683)*
**Legend Dynamix Inc** G 847 789-7007
Antioch *(G-641)*
**Lifetime Creations** G 708 895-2770
Lansing *(G-13172)*
**Lo-Ko Performance Coatings** G 708 424-7863
Oak Lawn *(G-16632)*
**Long Construction Services** G 217 443-2876
Danville *(G-7749)*
**M J Burton Engraving Co** G 217 223-7273
Quincy *(G-17854)*
**Macon Metal Products Co** E 217 824-7205
Taylorville *(G-20842)*
**Marie Gere Corporation** C 847 540-1154
Lake Zurich *(G-13099)*
**Material Sciences Corporation** E 847 439-2210
Elk Grove Village *(G-9613)*
**Metal Impregnating Corp** G 630 543-3443
Addison *(G-200)*
**Metal Prep Services Inc** G 815 874-7631
Rockford *(G-18496)*
**Meto-Grafics Inc** F 847 639-0044
Crystal Lake *(G-7609)*
**Metokote Corporation** E 815 223-1190
Peru *(G-17519)*
**Micron Metal Finishing LLC** E 708 599-0055
Bridgeview *(G-2508)*
**Midwest Coatings Inc** G 815 717-8914
New Lenox *(G-15896)*
**Midwest Galvanizing Inc** F 773 434-2682
Chicago *(G-5743)*
**Midwest Metal Coatings LLC** E 618 451-2971
Granite City *(G-11295)*
**Midwest Nameplate Corp** G 708 614-0606
Orland Park *(G-16875)*
**Mobile Air Inc** F 847 755-0586
Glendale Heights *(G-11049)*
▲ **Monogram of Evanston Inc** G 847 864-8100
Evanston *(G-10074)*
**MSC Pre Finish Metals Egv Inc** C 847 439-2210
Elk Grove Village *(G-9640)*
**Nameplate Robinson & Precision** G 847 678-2255
Franklin Park *(G-10538)*
**National Rubber Stamp Co Inc** G 773 281-6522
Chicago *(G-5868)*
**Neiland Custom Products** G 815 825-2233
Malta *(G-14166)*
**Nickel Composite Coatings Inc** E 708 563-2780
Chicago *(G-5910)*
**Oerlikon** F 847 619-5541
Schaumburg *(G-19672)*
▲ **Oerlikon Blzers Cating USA Inc** F 847 619-5541
Schaumburg *(G-19673)*
**Oerlikon Blzers Cating USA Inc** E 847 695-5200
Elgin *(G-9127)*
**Omega Plating Inc** F 708 389-5410
Crestwood *(G-7496)*
▲ **Ostrom & Co Inc** F 503 281-6469
Winfield *(G-22288)*
**Paradigm Coatings LLC** G 847 961-6466
Huntley *(G-12165)*
**Petersburg Power Washing Inc** G 217 415-9013
Springfield *(G-20504)*
**Photo Techniques Corp** E 630 690-9360
Carol Stream *(G-3213)*
**Plastisol Products Inc** E 630 543-1770
Addison *(G-243)*
**Polaris Laser Laminations LLC** G 630 444-0760
West Chicago *(G-21758)*
**Porcelain Enamel Finishers** G 312 808-1560
Chicago *(G-6157)*
**Powers Paint Shop Inc** G 815 338-3619
Woodstock *(G-22600)*

S I C

# 34 FABRICATED METAL PRODUCTS, EXCEPT MACHINERY AND TRANSPORTATION EQUIPMENT

▲ Pre Fnish Mtals Mrrisville Inc .......... D ...... 847 439-2211
   Elk Grove Village *(G-9691)*
Precoat Metals .......... D ...... 618 451-0909
   Granite City *(G-11300)*
Production Chemical Co Inc .......... E ...... 847 455-8450
   Franklin Park *(G-10563)*
Progressive Coating Corp .......... F ...... 773 261-8900
   Chicago *(G-6212)*
Protective Coatings & Waterpro .......... G ...... 708 403-7650
   Orland Park *(G-16886)*
▲ Qc Finishers Inc .......... E ...... 847 678-2660
   Franklin Park *(G-10565)*
Qc Powder Inc .......... E ...... 630 832-0606
   Villa Park *(G-21281)*
Quality Coating Co .......... F ...... 815 875-3228
   Princeton *(G-17761)*
R & B Powder Coatings Inc .......... E ...... 773 247-8300
   Chicago *(G-6261)*
R & O Specialties Incorporated .......... D ...... 309 736-8660
   Milan *(G-14800)*
Rainbow Art Inc .......... F ...... 312 421-5600
   Chicago *(G-6288)*
Rebechini Studio Inc .......... F ...... 847 364-8600
   Elk Grove Village *(G-9711)*
Reliable Autotech Usa LLC .......... G ...... 815 945-7838
   Chenoa *(G-3635)*
Reliable Galvanizing Company .......... E ...... 773 651-2500
   Chicago *(G-6329)*
Ro Pal Grinding Inc .......... F ...... 815 964-5894
   Rockford *(G-18561)*
Rogers Brothers Co .......... D ...... 815 965-5132
   Rockford *(G-18594)*
S & B Finishing Co Inc .......... D ...... 773 533-0033
   Chicago *(G-6418)*
Safeway Services Rockford Inc .......... E ...... 815 986-1504
   Rockford *(G-18607)*
Salt Creek Rural Park District .......... F ...... 847 259-6890
   Palatine *(G-17071)*
Sealtronix Inc .......... F ...... 800 878-9864
   Franklin Park *(G-10585)*
Slipmate Co .......... E ...... 847 289-9200
   Elgin *(G-9188)*
Smithco Fabricators Inc .......... F ...... 847 678-1619
   Schiller Park *(G-19873)*
Specialty Pntg Soda Blastg Inc .......... G ...... 815 577-0006
   Plainfield *(G-17651)*
Specified Plating Co .......... E ...... 773 826-4501
   Chicago *(G-6555)*
Stripmasters Illinois Inc .......... E ...... 618 452-1060
   Granite City *(G-11306)*
Sub Source Inc .......... E ...... 815 968-7800
   Rockford *(G-18637)*
Superior Coating Corporation .......... E ...... 815 544-3340
   Belvidere *(G-1786)*
Surface Solutions Group LLC .......... D ...... 773 427-2084
   Chicago *(G-6641)*
▲ Sycamore Precision .......... D ...... 815 784-5151
   Genoa *(G-10884)*
Thomson Steel Polishing Corp .......... G ...... 773 586-2345
   Chicago *(G-6720)*
▲ Transco Products Inc .......... D ...... 312 427-2818
   Chicago *(G-6758)*
Trophies and Awards Plus .......... G ...... 708 754-7127
   Steger *(G-20578)*
Tru-Tone Finishing Inc .......... E ...... 630 543-5520
   Addison *(G-327)*
Viking Awards Inc .......... G ...... 630 833-1733
   Elmhurst *(G-9957)*
▲ Voges Inc .......... D ...... 618 233-2760
   Belleville *(G-1688)*
Wear Cote International Inc .......... E ...... 309 793-1250
   Rock Island *(G-18211)*
Wheaton Trophy & Engravers .......... G ...... 630 682-4200
   Wheaton *(G-21989)*
Wheeling Service & Supply .......... F ...... 815 338-6410
   Woodstock *(G-22624)*
Willis Stein & Partners Manage .......... E ...... 312 422-2400
   Northbrook *(G-16387)*
Zegers Inc .......... F ...... 708 474-7700
   Lansing *(G-13193)*

## 3482 Small Arms Ammunition

A & S Arms Inc .......... G ...... 224 267-5670
   Antioch *(G-612)*
◆ Aerostar Global Logistics Inc .......... F ...... 630 396-7890
   Lombard *(G-13761)*
Civilian Force Arms Inc .......... G ...... 630 926-6982
   Yorkville *(G-22652)*
Rampart LLC .......... G ...... 847 367-8960
   Lake Forest *(G-12950)*
RR Defense Systems Inc .......... G ...... 312 446-9167
   Elk Grove Village *(G-9721)*

## 3483 Ammunition, Large

Alanson Manufacturing LLC .......... F ...... 773 762-2530
   Chicago *(G-3795)*
General Dynamics Ordnance .......... C ...... 618 985-8211
   Marion *(G-14261)*
Maxon Shooters Supplies Inc .......... G ...... 847 298-4867
   Des Plaines *(G-8228)*

## 3484 Small Arms

A & S Arms Inc .......... G ...... 224 267-5670
   Antioch *(G-612)*
Ar1510 LLC .......... F ...... 309 944-6939
   Geneseo *(G-10798)*
Art Jewel Enterprises Ltd .......... F ...... 630 260-0400
   Carol Stream *(G-3106)*
Civilian Force Arms Inc .......... G ...... 630 926-6982
   Yorkville *(G-22652)*
D S Arms Incorporated .......... F ...... 847 277-7258
   Lake Barrington *(G-12805)*
Devil Dog Arms Inc .......... G ...... 847 790-4004
   Lake Zurich *(G-13062)*
Double Nickel LLC .......... G ...... 618 476-3200
   Millstadt *(G-14823)*
Dynamic Door Service Inc .......... G ...... 847 885-4751
   Elgin *(G-9016)*
Fim Engineering LLC .......... G ...... 773 880-8841
   Milford *(G-14812)*
Gregory Martin .......... 815 265-4527
   Gilman *(G-10943)*
McGowen Rifle Barrels .......... G ...... 815 937-9816
   Saint Anne *(G-19123)*
▲ Nelson-Whittaker Ltd .......... E ...... 815 459-6000
   Crystal Lake *(G-7618)*
Northern Ordinance Corporation .......... G ...... 815 675-6400
   Spring Grove *(G-20352)*
Oglesby & Oglesby Gunmakers .......... G ...... 217 487-7100
   Springfield *(G-20492)*
Olin Corporation .......... C ...... 618 258-2000
   East Alton *(G-8608)*
Phalanx Training Inc .......... G ...... 847 859-9156
   Evanston *(G-10086)*
Pro Tech Engineering .......... G ...... 309 475-2502
   Saybrook *(G-19414)*
▼ Rock River Arms Inc .......... D ...... 309 792-5780
   Colona *(G-7347)*
RR Defense Systems Inc .......... G ...... 312 446-9167
   Elk Grove Village *(G-9721)*
▲ Springfield Inc .......... C ...... 309 944-5631
   Geneseo *(G-10805)*

## 3489 Ordnance & Access, NEC

Contract Assembly Partners .......... F ...... 217 960-3352
   Hillsboro *(G-11888)*
Devil Dog Arms Inc .......... G ...... 847 790-4004
   Lake Zurich *(G-13062)*
General Dynamics Ordnance .......... C ...... 618 985-8211
   Marion *(G-14261)*
◆ United Tactical Systems LLC .......... E ...... 877 887-3773
   Lake Forest *(G-12978)*

## 3491 Industrial Valves

Advanced Automation Systems .......... G ...... 815 877-1075
   Loves Park *(G-13912)*
Advanced Valve Tech Inc .......... E ...... 877 489-4909
   Blue Island *(G-2237)*
Aptargroup Inc .......... B ...... 847 639-2124
   Cary *(G-3327)*
▲ Aquatrol Inc .......... F ...... 630 365-2363
   Elburn *(G-8875)*
Asco Valve Inc .......... F ...... 630 789-2082
   Arlington Heights *(G-718)*
◆ Corken Inc .......... D ...... 405 946-5576
   Lake Bluff *(G-12839)*
Cyrus Shank Company .......... G ...... 630 618-4732
   Aurora *(G-993)*
Cyrus Shank Company .......... 708 652-2700
   Cicero *(G-7187)*
Deltrol Corp .......... 708 547-0500
   Bellwood *(G-1703)*
Dezurik Inc .......... F ...... 847 985-5580
   Schaumburg *(G-19503)*
Dresser Inc .......... D ...... 847 437-5940
   Elk Grove Village *(G-9435)*
▲ Emerson Process Management .......... D ...... 708 535-5120
   Oak Forest *(G-16580)*
Engineered Fluid Inc .......... C ...... 618 533-1351
   Centralia *(G-3413)*
Ergo-Tech Incorporated .......... G ...... 630 773-2222
   Itasca *(G-12260)*
Evsco Inc .......... F ...... 847 362-7068
   McHenry *(G-14504)*
Fisher Controls Intl LLC .......... D ...... 847 956-8020
   Chicago *(G-4851)*
Fkavpc Inc .......... D ...... 847 524-9000
   Schaumburg *(G-19530)*
▲ Flocon Inc .......... E ...... 815 444-1500
   Cary *(G-3341)*
General Assembly & Mfg Corp .......... E ...... 847 516-6462
   Cary *(G-3346)*
▼ Gpe Controls Inc .......... F ...... 708 236-6000
   Hillside *(G-11917)*
▼ H A Phillips & Co .......... E ...... 630 377-0050
   Dekalb *(G-8095)*
▲ Henry Pratt Company LLC .......... C ...... 630 844-4000
   Aurora *(G-1168)*
▲ Henry Technologies Inc .......... G ...... 217 483-2406
   Chatham *(G-3621)*
▲ Honeywell Analytics Inc .......... F ...... 847 955-8200
   Lincolnshire *(G-13454)*
Hydra-Stop LLC .......... E ...... 708 389-5111
   Burr Ridge *(G-2852)*
Keckley Manufacturing Company .......... E ...... 847 674-8422
   Skokie *(G-20022)*
L & J Holding Company Ltd .......... D ...... 708 236-6000
   Hillside *(G-11923)*
▲ Lilly Industries Inc .......... F ...... 630 773-2222
   Itasca *(G-12306)*
▲ Midland Manufacturing Corp .......... C ...... 847 677-0333
   Skokie *(G-20039)*
Midwest Water Group Inc .......... G ...... 866 526-6558
   McHenry *(G-14534)*
New Tech Marketing Inc .......... F ...... 630 378-4300
   Romeoville *(G-18854)*
▲ O C Keckley Company .......... E ...... 847 674-8422
   Skokie *(G-20048)*
Parker-Hannifin Corporation .......... E ...... 708 681-6300
   Broadview *(G-2601)*
Pioneer Pump and Packing Inc .......... G ...... 217 791-5293
   Decatur *(G-7927)*
▲ Pressure Specialist Inc .......... E ...... 815 477-0007
   Crystal Lake *(G-7629)*
Rebuilders Enterprises Inc .......... G ...... 708 430-0030
   Bridgeview *(G-2523)*
▲ Rhino Tool Company .......... F ...... 309 853-5555
   Kewanee *(G-12694)*
Schrader-Bridgeport Intl Inc .......... G ...... 815 288-3344
   Dixon *(G-8349)*
SMC Corporation of America .......... E ...... 630 449-0600
   Aurora *(G-1080)*
Spirax Sarco Inc .......... F ...... 630 493-4525
   Lisle *(G-13660)*
Strahman Valves Inc .......... E ...... 630 208-9343
   Lafox *(G-12797)*
▲ Sycamore Precision .......... D ...... 815 784-5151
   Genoa *(G-10884)*
USP Holdings Inc .......... A ...... 847 604-6100
   Des Plaines *(G-8295)*
◆ Val-Matic Valve & Mfg Corp .......... C ...... 630 941-7600
   Elmhurst *(G-9956)*
Val-Matic Valve and Mfg Corp .......... E ...... 630 993-4078
   Addison *(G-337)*
Vonberg Valve Inc .......... E ...... 847 259-3800
   Rolling Meadows *(G-18788)*
Waves Fluid Solutions LLC .......... G ...... 630 765-7533
   Carol Stream *(G-3264)*

## 3492 Fluid Power Valves & Hose Fittings

A Len Radiator Shoppe Inc .......... G ...... 630 852-5445
   Downers Grove *(G-8384)*
Adair Enterprises Inc .......... F ...... 847 640-7789
   Elk Grove Village *(G-9270)*
All Type Hydraulics Corp .......... G ...... 618 585-4844
   Bunker Hill *(G-2803)*
Bristol Hose & Fitting Inc .......... E ...... 708 492-3456
   Northlake *(G-16430)*
Bristol Transport Inc .......... E ...... 708 343-6411
   Northlake *(G-16431)*
▲ Ckd USA Corporation .......... E ...... 847 368-0539
   Rolling Meadows *(G-18722)*
Crane Nuclear Inc .......... E ...... 630 226-4900
   Bolingbrook *(G-2290)*
▲ Delta Power Company .......... G ...... 815 397-6628
   Rockford *(G-18339)*
Deltrol Corp .......... C ...... 708 547-0500
   Bellwood *(G-1703)*

SIC SECTION
34 FABRICATED METAL PRODUCTS, EXCEPT MACHINERY AND TRANSPORTATION EQUIPMENT

◆ **Deublin Company** C 847 689-8600
Waukegan *(G-21551)*
▲ **Flexitech Inc** C 309 664-7828
Bloomington *(G-2165)*
**Flow Valves International LLC** G 847 866-1188
Evanston *(G-10038)*
**Fluid Logic Inc** G 847 459-2202
Buffalo Grove *(G-2697)*
**Hurst Manufacturing Co** F 309 756-9960
Milan *(G-14791)*
▲ **Hydraforce Inc** B 847 793-2300
Lincolnshire *(G-13455)*
**J C Hose & Tube Inc** G 630 543-4747
Addison *(G-157)*
▲ **James Walker Mfg Co** E 708 754-4020
Glenwood *(G-11217)*
▲ **Jason of Illinois Inc** E 630 752-0600
Carol Stream *(G-3176)*
**Kepner Products Company** D 630 279-1550
Villa Park *(G-21264)*
**Kocsis Technologies Inc** F 708 597-4177
Alsip *(G-481)*
**Kocsis Technologies Inc** G 708 597-4177
Alsip *(G-482)*
**Lsl Precision Machining Inc** E 815 633-4701
Loves Park *(G-13962)*
◆ **Mac Lean-Fogg Company** D 847 566-0010
Mundelein *(G-15521)*
◆ **Marmon Industrial LLC** G 312 372-9500
Chicago *(G-5626)*
**MEA Inc** E 847 766-9040
Elk Grove Village *(G-9616)*
▲ **Mead Fluid Dynamics Inc** E 773 685-6800
Chicago *(G-5669)*
▲ **Milliken Valve LLC** G 610 861-8803
Aurora *(G-1190)*
**Mj Works Hose & Fitting LLC** G 708 995-5723
Mokena *(G-14886)*
▲ **Nagano International Corp** G 847 537-0011
Buffalo Grove *(G-2741)*
**Nanco Sales Co Inc** G 630 892-9820
Aurora *(G-1193)*
**Parker-Hannifin Corporation** C 847 258-6200
Elk Grove Village *(G-9670)*
◆ **Plews Inc** C 815 288-3344
Dixon *(G-8339)*
**Quad City Hose** E 563 386-8936
Taylor Ridge *(G-20830)*
**Reber Welding Service** G 217 774-3441
Shelbyville *(G-19914)*
▲ **Rehobot Inc** G 815 385-7777
McHenry *(G-14550)*
◆ **Robertshaw Controls Company** C 630 260-3400
Itasca *(G-12349)*
**Rotary Ram Inc** E 618 466-2651
Godfrey *(G-11236)*
**Royal Brass Inc** G 618 439-6341
Benton *(G-2040)*
**Seals & Components Inc** G 708 895-5222
Lansing *(G-13182)*
**SMC Corporation of America** E 630 449-0600
Aurora *(G-1080)*
**Standard Truck Parts Inc** G 815 726-4486
Joliet *(G-12578)*
**T & T Distribution Inc** E 815 223-0715
Peru *(G-17528)*
**Trellborg Sling Sltions US Inc** D 630 289-1500
Streamwood *(G-20677)*
**Vonberg Valve Inc** E 847 259-3800
Rolling Meadows *(G-18788)*
**Vrg Controls LLC** G 773 230-1543
Highland Park *(G-11879)*
▲ **Wandfluh of America Inc** F 847 566-5700
Mundelein *(G-15566)*
▲ **Whitley Products Inc** F 574 267-7114
Chicago *(G-6975)*
**Woods Manufacturing Co Inc** G 630 595-6620
Wood Dale *(G-22438)*

## *3493 Steel Springs, Except Wire*

**A J Kay Co** F 224 475-0370
Mundelein *(G-15462)*
▲ **Alco Spring Industries Inc** D 708 755-0438
Chicago Heights *(G-7078)*
▲ **All-Rite Spring Co** E 815 675-1350
Spring Grove *(G-20325)*
**Baumbach Manufacturing** G 630 941-0505
Elmhurst *(G-9836)*
◆ **Boler Company** F 630 773-9111
Itasca *(G-12236)*
**Burnex Corporation** E 815 728-1317
Ringwood *(G-17988)*
▲ **Capitol Coil Inc** F 847 891-1390
Schaumburg *(G-19468)*
**Casey Spring Co Inc** F 708 867-8949
Harwood Heights *(G-11682)*
▲ **Classic Products Inc** E 815 344-0051
McHenry *(G-14487)*
▲ **Dudek & Bock Spring Mfg Co** C 773 379-4100
Chicago *(G-4648)*
▲ **Gilbert Spring Corporation** E 773 486-6030
Chicago *(G-4952)*
**High-Life Products Inc** G 847 991-9449
Palatine *(G-17036)*
**Highland Spring & Specialty** F 618 654-3831
Highland *(G-11793)*
**Johnson Tool Company** G 708 453-8600
Huntley *(G-12154)*
**Kankakee Spring and Alignment** G 815 932-6718
Kankakee *(G-12633)*
**Kdk Upset Forging Co** E 708 388-8770
Blue Island *(G-2259)*
▲ **Khc Corporation** E 815 337-7630
Woodstock *(G-22578)*
**Lew-El Tool & Manufacturing Co** F 773 804-1133
Chicago *(G-5497)*
**Lewis Spring and Mfg Company** E 847 588-7030
Niles *(G-15996)*
**Lrm Grinding Co Inc** D 708 458-7878
Bridgeview *(G-2504)*
**Matthew Warren Inc** E 847 349-5760
Rosemont *(G-19015)*
**Matthew Warren Inc** D 773 539-5600
Chicago *(G-5656)*
**Mid-West Spring & Stamping Inc** G 630 739-3800
Romeoville *(G-18848)*
**Mid-West Spring & Stamping Inc** G 630 739-3800
Romeoville *(G-18847)*
**Mid-West Spring Mfg Co** G 630 739-3800
Romeoville *(G-18849)*
▲ **Omiotek Coil Spring Co** D 630 495-4056
Lombard *(G-13837)*
**Paragon Spring Company** E 773 489-6300
Chicago *(G-6076)*
**Park Manufacturing Corp Inc** F 708 345-6090
Melrose Park *(G-14682)*
**Patrick Manufacturing Inc** E 847 697-5920
Elgin *(G-9136)*
**R & G Spring Co Inc** G 847 228-5640
Elk Grove Village *(G-9706)*
▲ **Smalley Steel Ring Co** C 847 537-7600
Lake Zurich *(G-13132)*
**Spirolox Inc** B 847 719-5900
Lake Zurich *(G-13133)*
**Spring R-R Corporation** E 630 543-7445
Addison *(G-298)*
**Spring Specialist Corporation** G 815 562-7991
Kings *(G-12705)*
▲ **Stanley Spring & Stamping Corp** D 773 777-2600
Chicago *(G-6572)*
**United Spring & Manufacturing** E 773 384-8464
Chicago *(G-6826)*
**Wesco Spring Company** E 773 838-3350
Chicago *(G-6958)*
◆ **William Dudek Manufacturing Co** E 773 622-2727
Chicago *(G-6983)*
**York Spring Co** E 847 695-5978
South Elgin *(G-20236)*

## *3494 Valves & Pipe Fittings, NEC*

**ADS LLC** D 256 430-3366
Burr Ridge *(G-2820)*
**Advanced Plbg & Pipe Fitting** G 618 554-2677
Newton *(G-15936)*
**American Rack Company** E 773 763-7309
Chicago *(G-3870)*
▲ **Aquatrol Inc** F 630 365-2363
Elburn *(G-8875)*
**Arnel Industries Inc** E 630 543-6500
Addison *(G-45)*
**B&B Machining Incorporated** F 630 898-3009
Aurora *(G-966)*
**Barrington Automation Ltd** E 847 458-0900
Lake In The Hills *(G-12987)*
**Bi-Torq Valve Automation Inc** G 630 208-9343
Lafox *(G-12793)*
▲ **C U Services LLC** G 847 439-2303
Elk Grove Village *(G-9352)*
**Catching Hydraulics Co Ltd** E 708 344-2334
Melrose Park *(G-14606)*
**Caterpillar Inc** B 815 729-5511
Joliet *(G-12471)*
**Certified Power Inc** E 847 573-3800
Mundelein *(G-15485)*
**Chicago Pipe Bending & Coil Co** F 773 379-1918
Chicago *(G-4339)*
**Control Equipment Company Inc** F 847 891-7500
Schaumburg *(G-19482)*
**Cooper Smith International Inc** D 847 595-7572
Elk Grove Village *(G-9395)*
▲ **Couplings Company Inc** F 847 634-8990
Lincolnshire *(G-13440)*
**Deltrol Corp** C 708 547-0500
Bellwood *(G-1703)*
◆ **Deublin Company** C 847 689-8600
Waukegan *(G-21551)*
▲ **Dixon Brass** E 630 323-3716
Westmont *(G-21885)*
**Dooley Brothers Plumbing & Htg** G 309 852-2720
Kewanee *(G-12680)*
**Dresser Inc** D 847 437-5940
Elk Grove Village *(G-9435)*
**Dvcc Inc** E 630 323-3105
Westmont *(G-21886)*
◆ **Eclipse Inc** D 815 877-3031
Rockford *(G-18356)*
**Eg Group Inc** G 309 692-0968
Peoria *(G-17352)*
▲ **Emerson Process Management** D 708 535-5120
Oak Forest *(G-16580)*
**Evsco Inc** F 847 362-7068
McHenry *(G-14504)*
**Flocon Inc** G 815 943-5893
Harvard *(G-11633)*
▲ **Henry Technologies Inc** G 217 483-2406
Chatham *(G-3621)*
**Hoosier Stamping & Mfg Corp** E 618 375-2057
Grayville *(G-11371)*
▲ **Illinois Tool Works** E 815 648-2416
Hebron *(G-11720)*
**Instrument & Valve Services Co** D 708 535-5120
Oak Forest *(G-16585)*
▲ **Intech Industries Inc** F 847 487-5599
Wauconda *(G-21473)*
▲ **J/B Industries Inc** D 630 851-9444
Aurora *(G-1174)*
**Keckley Manufacturing Company** E 847 674-8422
Skokie *(G-20022)*
▲ **Kelco Industries Inc** G 815 334-3600
Woodstock *(G-22577)*
**Kepner Products Company** D 630 279-1550
Villa Park *(G-21264)*
**Lewis Process Systems Inc** F 630 510-8200
Carol Stream *(G-3184)*
▲ **Lilly Industries Inc** F 630 773-2222
Itasca *(G-12306)*
**M CA Chicago** G 312 384-1220
Burr Ridge *(G-2863)*
▲ **Mead Fluid Dynamics Inc** E 773 685-6800
Chicago *(G-5669)*
**Mechanical Engineering Pdts** G 312 421-3375
Chicago *(G-5674)*
▲ **Metraflex Company** D 312 738-3800
Chicago *(G-5706)*
▲ **Midland Manufacturing Corp** C 847 677-0333
Skokie *(G-20039)*
**Mity Inc** G 630 365-5030
Elburn *(G-8898)*
**MRC Global (us) Inc** F 815 729-7742
Joliet *(G-12544)*
**Newman-Green Inc** D 630 543-6500
Addison *(G-228)*
▲ **O C Keckley Company** E 847 674-8422
Skokie *(G-20048)*
**Oso Technologies Inc** G 844 777-2575
Urbana *(G-21096)*
**Pokorney Manufacturing Co** G 630 458-0406
Addison *(G-245)*
**Pro-Quip Incorporated** F 708 352-5732
La Grange Park *(G-12759)*
**Process Piping Inc** G 708 717-0513
Tinley Park *(G-20939)*
**Process Screw Products Inc** E 815 864-2220
Shannon *(G-19901)*
**RF Mau Co** F 847 329-9731
Lincolnwood *(G-13533)*
◆ **Sloan Valve Company** G 847 671-4300
Franklin Park *(G-10590)*
**Solomon Plumbing** G 847 498-6388
Glenview *(G-11205)*

Employee Codes: A=Over 500 employees, B=251-500
C=101-250, D=51-100, E=20-50, F=10-19, G=3-9
2017 Harris Illinois
Industrial Directory
1051

34 FABRICATED METAL PRODUCTS, EXCEPT MACHINERY AND TRANSPORTATION EQUIPMENT SIC SECTION

**Spirax Sarco Inc** F 630 493-4525
Lisle *(G-13660)*
**Spreader Inc** G 217 568-7219
Gifford *(G-10910)*
**SPX Flow US LLC** G 815 874-5556
Rockford *(G-18632)*
**Steamgard LLC** E 847 913-8400
Vernon Hills *(G-21204)*
**Strahman Valves Inc** E 630 208-9343
Lafox *(G-12797)*
**Victaulic Company** B 630 585-2919
Aurora *(G-1092)*
**Vonberg Valve Inc** E 847 259-3800
Rolling Meadows *(G-18788)*
**▲ World Wide Fittings Inc** C 847 588-2200
Vernon Hills *(G-21219)*
**▲ Wrap-On Company LLC** E 708 496-2150
Alsip *(G-547)*

## *3495 Wire Springs*

**A J Kay Co** F 224 475-0370
Mundelein *(G-15462)*
**All American Spring Stamping** G 847 928-9468
Franklin Park *(G-10389)*
**▲ All-Rite Spring Co** E 815 675-1350
Spring Grove *(G-20325)*
**▲ Ark Technologies Inc** C 630 377-8855
Saint Charles *(G-19138)*
**Ascent Mfg Co** E 847 806-6600
Elk Grove Village *(G-9314)*
**Available Spring and Mfg Co** G 847 520-4854
Wheeling *(G-22009)*
**Beall Manufacturing Inc** E 618 259-8154
East Alton *(G-8599)*
**▲ Capitol Coil Inc** F 847 891-1390
Schaumburg *(G-19468)*
**Century Spring Corporation** G 800 237-5225
Chicago *(G-4277)*
**▲ CFC Wire Forms Inc** E 630 879-7575
Batavia *(G-1428)*
**David V Michals** D 847 671-6767
Schiller Park *(G-19820)*
**Form-All Spring Stamping Inc** E 630 595-8833
Bensenville *(G-1900)*
**▲ Gerb Vibration Control Systems** G 630 724-1660
Lisle *(G-13595)*
**Highland Spring & Specialty** F 618 654-3831
Highland *(G-11793)*
**▲ Innocor Foam Tech W Chcago LLC** E 732 945-6222
West Chicago *(G-21722)*
**International Spring Company** D 847 470-8170
Morton Grove *(G-15203)*
**Jackson Spring & Mfg Co** D 847 952-8850
Elk Grove Village *(G-9559)*
**▲ JD Norman Industries Inc** D 630 458-3700
Addison *(G-159)*
**Johnson Tool Company** G 708 453-8600
Huntley *(G-12154)*
**Kan-Du Manufacturing Co Inc** G 708 681-0370
Riverwoods *(G-18040)*
**Kaylen Industries Inc** D 847 671-6767
Schiller Park *(G-19842)*
**Lew-El Tool & Manufacturing Co** F 773 804-1133
Chicago *(G-5497)*
**Lewis Spring and Mfg Company** E 847 588-7030
Niles *(G-15996)*
**M Lizen Manufacturing Co** E 708 755-7213
University Park *(G-21055)*
**Majestic Spring Inc** F 847 593-8887
Elk Grove Village *(G-9609)*
**Master Spring & Wire Form Co** E 708 453-2570
Itasca *(G-12312)*
**Matthew Warren Inc** G 847 671-6767
Schiller Park *(G-19847)*
**Matthew Warren Inc** D 773 539-5600
Chicago *(G-5656)*
**Micromatic Spring Stamping Inc** E 630 607-0141
Addison *(G-208)*
**Mid-West Spring & Stamping Inc** G 630 739-3800
Romeoville *(G-18847)*
**Mid-West Spring & Stamping Inc** G 630 739-3800
Romeoville *(G-18848)*
**Mid-West Spring Mfg Co** G 630 739-3800
Romeoville *(G-18849)*
**OHare Spring Company Inc** E 847 298-1360
Elk Grove Village *(G-9662)*
**Paragon Spring Company** E 773 489-6300
Chicago *(G-6076)*
**▲ Perfection Spring Stmping Corp** D 847 437-3900
Mount Prospect *(G-15362)*
**R & G Spring Co Inc** G 847 228-5640
Elk Grove Village *(G-9706)*
**R C Coil Spring Mfg Co Inc** E 630 790-3500
Glendale Heights *(G-11062)*
**▲ Rich Industries Inc** E 630 766-9150
Bensenville *(G-1978)*
**Riverside Spring Company** G 815 963-3334
Rockford *(G-18557)*
**Sanco Industries Inc** F 847 243-8675
Kildeer *(G-12703)*
**▲ Schaff International LLC** E 847 438-4560
Lake Zurich *(G-13125)*
**▲ Smalley Steel Ring Co** C 847 537-7600
Lake Zurich *(G-13132)*
**▲ Solar Spring Company** C 847 437-7838
Elk Grove Village *(G-9742)*
**Spirolox Inc** B 847 719-5900
Lake Zurich *(G-13133)*
**Spring Specialist Corporation** G 815 562-7991
Kings *(G-12705)*
**▲ Stanley Spring & Stamping Corp** D 773 777-2600
Chicago *(G-6572)*
**Sterling Spring LLC** D 773 582-6464
Chicago *(G-6591)*
**Sterling Spring LLC** E 773 777-4647
Bedford Park *(G-1587)*
**Sterling Spring LLC** E 773 772-9331
Chicago *(G-6592)*
**▲ Taycorp Inc** E 708 629-0921
Alsip *(G-533)*
**United Spring & Manufacturing** E 773 384-8464
Chicago *(G-6826)*
**Wesco Spring Company** E 773 838-3350
Chicago *(G-6958)*
**White Eagle Spring &** F 773 384-4455
Chicago *(G-6972)*
**Willdon Corp** E 773 276-7080
Chicago *(G-6981)*

## *3496 Misc Fabricated Wire Prdts*

**A J Kay Co** F 224 475-0370
Mundelein *(G-15462)*
**◆ Acco Brands USA LLC** B 800 222-6462
Lake Zurich *(G-13034)*
**Acco Brands USA LLC** D 847 272-3700
Lincolnshire *(G-13423)*
**Accurate Wire Strip Frming Inc** F 630 260-1000
Carol Stream *(G-3089)*
**▲ Acme Wire Products LLC** E 708 345-4430
Broadview *(G-2553)*
**▼ Acorn Wire and Iron Works LLC** E 312 243-6414
Chicago *(G-3736)*
**▲ Advantage Components Inc** E 815 725-8644
Joliet *(G-12450)*
**Agena Manufacturing Co** E 630 668-5086
Carol Stream *(G-3093)*
**▼ Alagor Industries Incorporated** F 630 766-2910
Bensenville *(G-1822)*
**Alecto Industries Inc** E 708 344-1488
Maywood *(G-14414)*
**All Rite Industries Inc** E 847 540-0300
Lake Zurich *(G-13038)*
**Allform Manufacturing Co** G 847 680-0144
Libertyville *(G-13301)*
**▲ Alloy Sling Chains Inc** D 708 647-4900
East Hazel Crest *(G-8664)*
**▲ Altak Inc** D 630 622-0300
Bloomingdale *(G-2092)*
**Amag Manufacturing Inc** G 773 667-5184
Chicago *(G-3843)*
**Ameriguard Corporation** G 630 986-1900
Burr Ridge *(G-2822)*
**Ammeraal Beltech Inc** D 847 673-6720
Skokie *(G-19955)*
**Amsysco Inc** E 630 296-8383
Romeoville *(G-18798)*
**Androck Hardware Corporation** F 815 229-1144
Rockford *(G-18268)*
**Apex Wire Products Company Inc** F 847 671-1830
Franklin Park *(G-10397)*
**▲ Archer Wire International Corp** C 708 563-1700
Bedford Park *(G-1537)*
**Arcon Ring and Specialty Corp** F 630 682-5252
Carol Stream *(G-3104)*
**Art Wire Works Inc** F 708 458-3993
Bedford Park *(G-1538)*
**Ascent Mfg Co** E 847 806-6600
Elk Grove Village *(G-9314)*
**Astoria Wire Products Inc** D 708 496-9950
Bedford Park *(G-1539)*
**Atkore International Group Inc** A 708 339-1610
Harvey *(G-11658)*
**Atkore Intl Holdings Inc** G 708 225-2051
Harvey *(G-11659)*
**Available Spring and Mfg Co** G 847 520-4854
Wheeling *(G-22009)*
**Axelent Inc** F 708 745-3128
Lockport *(G-13705)*
**B & J Wire Inc** E 877 787-9473
Chicago *(G-4016)*
**B M I Inc** C 847 839-6000
Schaumburg *(G-19456)*
**Bel Mar Wire Products Inc** F 773 342-3800
Chicago *(G-4073)*
**Bergeron Group Inc** E 815 741-1635
Joliet *(G-12464)*
**Bristar** G 847 678-5000
Franklin Park *(G-10417)*
**Burnex Corporation** E 815 728-1317
Ringwood *(G-17988)*
**▲ C & J Metal Products Inc** F 847 455-0766
Franklin Park *(G-10421)*
**C R V Electronics Corp** D 815 675-6500
Spring Grove *(G-20329)*
**Cal-Ill Gasket Co** F 773 287-9605
Chicago *(G-4213)*
**▲ Capitol Coil Inc** F 847 891-1390
Schaumburg *(G-19468)*
**Casey Spring Co Inc** F 708 867-8949
Harwood Heights *(G-11682)*
**Cda Industries Inc** G 630 357-7654
Naperville *(G-15623)*
**▲ CFC Wire Forms Inc** E 630 879-7575
Batavia *(G-1428)*
**Chas O Larson Co** E 815 625-0503
Rock Falls *(G-18129)*
**▲ Chicago Car Seal Company** G 773 278-9400
Chicago *(G-4310)*
**▲ Chicago Hardware and Fix Co** D 847 455-6609
Franklin Park *(G-10429)*
**Chicago Wire Design Inc** E 773 342-4220
Chicago *(G-4363)*
**Chicagos Finest Ironworks** G 708 895-4484
Lansing *(G-13159)*
**Circle K Industries Inc** F 847 949-0363
Mundelein *(G-15487)*
**City Screen Inc** G 773 588-5642
Chicago *(G-4388)*
**Contractors Ready-Mix Inc** G 217 482-5530
Mason City *(G-14362)*
**▲ Cooley Wire Products Mfg Co** E 847 678-8585
Schiller Park *(G-19816)*
**Cutting Edge Industries Inc** G 847 678-1777
Franklin Park *(G-10451)*
**Darbe Products Company Inc** G 630 985-0769
Woodridge *(G-22468)*
**Dayton Superior Corporation** E 815 732-3136
Oregon *(G-16821)*
**Dayton Superior Corporation** C 815 936-3300
Kankakee *(G-12609)*
**Dove Industries Inc** F 618 234-4509
Belleville *(G-1626)*
**▲ Dudek & Bock Spring Mfg Co** C 773 379-4100
Chicago *(G-4648)*
**▲ Durabilt Dyvex Inc** F 708 397-4673
Broadview *(G-2573)*
**E H Baare Corporation** C 618 546-1575
Robinson *(G-18062)*
**Economy Iron Inc** F 708 343-1777
Melrose Park *(G-14628)*
**Elite Wireworks Corporation** F 630 837-9100
Bartlett *(G-1345)*
**Essentra Components Inc** C 815 943-6487
Forest Park *(G-10241)*
**European Ornamental Iron Works** G 630 705-9300
Addison *(G-113)*
**Expandable Habitats** G 815 624-6784
Rockton *(G-18696)*
**Exterior Services** G 773 660-1457
Chicago *(G-4799)*
**Fbs Group Inc** F 773 229-8675
Chicago *(G-4821)*
**▲ Franklin Display Group Inc** D 815 544-6676
Belvidere *(G-1752)*
**Franklin Wire Works Inc** G 815 544-6676
Belvidere *(G-1753)*
**▲ G F Ltd** E 708 333-8300
South Holland *(G-20269)*
**Galena Manufacturing Co Inc** G 815 777-2078
Galena *(G-10722)*

Gall Machine Co ... F ... 708 352-2800
Countryside (G-7426)

Gateway Construction Company ... E ... 708 868-2926
Chicago (G-4917)

Guide Line Industries Inc ... F ... 815 777-3722
Scales Mound (G-19415)

▲ Hamalot Inc ... E ... 847 944-1500
Schaumburg (G-19547)

Highland Southern Wire Inc ... G ... 618 654-2161
Highland (G-11792)

Hohmann & Barnard Illinois LLC ... E ... 773 586-6700
Chicago Ridge (G-7150)

Hudson Tool & Die Co ... F ... 847 678-8710
Franklin Park (G-10491)

Illinois Tool Works Inc ... G ... 847 821-2170
Vernon Hills (G-21174)

▲ Industrial Wire & Cable Corp ... E ... 847 726-8910
Lake Zurich (G-13086)

Innovation Specialists Inc ... G ... 815 372-9001
New Lenox (G-15885)

Innovative Fix Solutions LLC ... F ... 815 395-8500
Rockford (G-18435)

Jason Incorporated ... C ... 630 627-7000
Addison (G-158)

▲ JD Norman Industries Inc ... D ... 630 458-3700
Addison (G-159)

Jenco Metal Products Inc ... F ... 847 956-0550
Mount Prospect (G-15340)

Johnson Tool Company ... G ... 708 453-8600
Huntley (G-12154)

▲ Jsn Inc ... E ... 708 410-1800
Maywood (G-14426)

Kan-Du Manufacturing Co Inc ... G ... 708 681-0370
Riverwoods (G-18040)

▲ Keats Manufacturing Co ... D ... 847 520-1133
Wheeling (G-22083)

Keystone Consolidated Inds Inc ... E ... 309 697-7020
Peoria (G-17396)

Klimp Industries Inc ... G ... 630 682-0752
Carol Stream (G-3179)

Klimp Industries Inc ... G ... 630 790-0600
Carol Stream (G-3180)

◆ L & P Guarding LLC ... C ... 708 325-0400
Bedford Park (G-1560)

▲ Lake Cable LLC ... C ... 888 518-8086
Bensenville (G-1937)

Lamco Slings & Rigging Inc ... E ... 309 764-7400
Moline (G-14952)

Lee Jensen Sales Co Inc ... E ... 815 459-0929
Crystal Lake (G-7602)

▲ Letraw Manufacturing Co ... G ... 815 987-9670
Rockford (G-18469)

Lew-El Tool & Manufacturing Co ... F ... 773 804-1133
Chicago (G-5497)

Lewis Spring and Mfg Company ... E ... 847 588-7030
Niles (G-15996)

Lodan Electronics Inc ... C ... 847 398-5311
Arlington Heights (G-795)

▲ Logan Graphic Products Inc ... D ... 847 526-5515
Wauconda (G-21479)

▲ Manufasteners House Iq Inc ... G ... 847 705-6538
Palatine (G-17053)

Marcal Rope & Rigging Inc ... E ... 618 462-0172
Alton (G-584)

Marcal Rope & Rigging Inc ... G ... 618 462-0172
Metropolis (G-14756)

Marlboro Wire Ltd ... E ... 217 224-7989
Quincy (G-17855)

Master Spring & Wire Form Co ... E ... 708 453-2570
Itasca (G-12312)

Master-Halco Inc ... E ... 618 395-4365
Olney (G-16780)

▲ Mazel & Co Inc ... F ... 773 533-1600
Chicago (G-5662)

MHS Ltd ... F ... 773 736-3333
Chicago (G-5716)

Midwest Color ... F ... 847 647-1364
Niles (G-16007)

▲ Midwest Tungsten Service Inc ... E ... 630 325-1001
Willowbrook (G-22223)

Midwest Wire Works ... F ... 815 874-1701
Rockford (G-18508)

▲ Minerallac Company ... E ... 630 543-7080
Hampshire (G-11554)

Myco Inc ... C ... 815 395-8500
Rockford (G-18513)

▼ Nixalite of America Inc ... F ... 309 755-8771
East Moline (G-8689)

OHare Spring Company Inc ... E ... 847 298-1360
Elk Grove Village (G-9662)

Paragon Spring Company ... E ... 773 489-6300
Chicago (G-6076)

Paramount Wire Specialties ... F ... 773 252-5636
Chicago (G-6080)

Park Manufacturing Corp Inc ... F ... 708 345-6090
Melrose Park (G-14682)

Partex Marking Systems Inc ... G ... 630 516-0400
Lombard (G-13842)

▲ Perfection Spring Stmping Corp ... D ... 847 437-3900
Mount Prospect (G-15362)

Prairie State Industries Inc ... F ... 847 428-3641
Carpentersville (G-3297)

Precision Forming Stamping Co ... E ... 773 489-6868
Chicago (G-6170)

▲ Precision Steel Warehouse Inc ... C ... 800 323-0740
Franklin Park (G-10560)

▲ Precitec Corporation ... D ... 847 949-2800
Mundelein (G-15547)

Rapid Wire Forms Inc ... G ... 773 586-6600
Chicago (G-6294)

Reino Tool & Manufacturing Co ... F ... 773 588-5800
Chicago (G-6326)

▲ Remin Laboratories Inc ... D ... 815 723-1940
Joliet (G-12566)

Riverside Spring Company ... G ... 815 963-3334
Rockford (G-18557)

▲ Rockford Rigging Inc ... F ... 309 263-0566
Roscoe (G-18914)

Sanco Industries Inc ... F ... 847 243-8675
Kildeer (G-12703)

▲ Schaff International LLC ... E ... 847 438-4560
Lake Zurich (G-13125)

▲ Solar Spring Company ... C ... 847 437-7838
Elk Grove Village (G-9742)

▲ Southern Steel and Wire Inc ... G ... 618 654-2161
Highland (G-11812)

Spring Specialist Corporation ... G ... 815 562-7991
Kings (G-12705)

▲ Stanley Hartco Co ... E ... 847 967-1122
Skokie (G-20090)

Steel Guard Inc ... F ... 773 342-6265
Chicago (G-6580)

Sterling Wire Products Inc ... G ... 815 625-3015
Rock Falls (G-18153)

▲ SWB Inc ... G ... 847 438-1800
Lake Zurich (G-13136)

The Parts House ... G ... 309 343-0146
Galesburg (G-10777)

Trico Belting & Supply Company ... F ... 773 261-0988
Chicago (G-6776)

Trio Wire Products Inc ... G ... 815 469-2148
Frankfort (G-10372)

◆ Tru Vue Inc ... C ... 708 485-5080
Countryside (G-7448)

Tru-Guard Manufacturing Co ... G ... 773 568-5264
Chicago (G-6784)

▲ Unistrut International Corp ... C ... 800 882-5543
Harvey (G-11679)

Wardzala Industries Inc ... F ... 847 288-9909
Franklin Park (G-10627)

Wesco Spring Company ... E ... 773 838-3350
Chicago (G-6958)

White Eagle Spring & ... F ... 773 384-4455
Chicago (G-6972)

Will Don Corp ... D ... 773 276-7081
Chicago (G-6980)

Willdon Corp ... E ... 773 276-7080
Chicago (G-6981)

William Dach ... F ... 815 962-3455
Rockford (G-18683)

◆ William Dudek Manufacturing Co ... E ... 773 622-2727
Chicago (G-6983)

Wirco Inc ... D ... 217 398-3200
Champaign (G-3561)

Wire Mesh LLC ... G ... 815 579-8597
Oglesby (G-16752)

Wireformers Inc ... E ... 847 718-1920
Mount Prospect (G-15384)

▲ Wiremasters Incorporated ... E ... 773 254-3700
Chicago (G-7005)

Woodland Fence Forest Pdts Inc ... G ... 630 393-2220
Warrenville (G-21369)

## *3497 Metal Foil & Leaf*

▲ Bagcraftpapercon I LLC ... C ... 620 856-2800
Chicago (G-4025)

C M Holding Co Inc ... G ... 847 438-2171
Lake Zurich (G-13048)

D W Machine Products Inc ... G ... 618 654-2161
Highland (G-11782)

▲ Durable Inc ... A ... 847 541-4400
Wheeling (G-22039)

▲ Handi-Foil Corp ... A ... 847 520-1000
Wheeling (G-22065)

Handi-Foil Corp ... E ... 847 520-5742
Wheeling (G-22066)

◆ Hfa Inc ... A ... 847 520-1000
Wheeling (G-22069)

▲ Highland Supply Corporation ... B ... 618 654-2161
Highland (G-11794)

Kurz Transfer Products LP ... G ... 847 228-0001
Elk Grove Village (G-9580)

Pactiv LLC ... E ... 847 482-2000
Lake Forest (G-12937)

Pactiv LLC ... C ... 217 479-1144
Jacksonville (G-12404)

◆ R and R Brokerage Co ... C ... 847 438-4600
Lake Zurich (G-13121)

▲ Tinscape LLC ... G ... 630 236-7236
Aurora (G-1087)

Winpak Heat Seal Corp ... D ... 309 477-6600
Pekin (G-17295)

## *3498 Fabricated Pipe & Pipe Fittings*

Acrofab ... G ... 630 350-7941
Bensenville (G-1816)

ADS LLC ... D ... 256 430-3366
Burr Ridge (G-2820)

▲ Alconix Usa Inc ... G ... 847 717-7407
Elk Grove Village (G-9284)

Alert Tubing Fabricators Inc ... G ... 815 633-5065
Loves Park (G-13917)

Alert Tubing Fabricators Inc ... G ... 847 253-7237
Schaumburg (G-19429)

▲ American Diesel Tube Corp ... F ... 630 628-1830
Addison (G-35)

American Piping Group Inc ... D ... 815 772-7470
Morrison (G-15141)

American Piping Products Inc ... E ... 708 339-1753
South Holland (G-20244)

Americhem Systems Inc ... F ... 630 495-9300
Aurora (G-1106)

▲ Anamet Electrical Inc ... C ... 217 234-8844
Mattoon (G-14382)

Anvil International LLC ... D ... 708 534-1414
Tinley Park (G-20894)

Arntzen Corporation ... E ... 815 334-0788
Woodstock (G-22541)

Art Wire Works Inc ... F ... 708 458-3993
Bedford Park (G-1538)

Bessco Tube Bending Pipe Fabg ... G ... 708 339-3977
South Holland (G-20251)

Boyce Industries Inc ... F ... 708 345-0455
Melrose Park (G-14604)

Cain Tubular Products Inc ... G ... 630 584-5330
Saint Charles (G-19149)

◆ Cerro Flow Products LLC ... C ... 618 337-6000
Sauget (G-19385)

Chicago Metal Fabricators Inc ... D ... 773 523-5755
Chicago (G-4332)

◆ Chicago Metal Rolled Pdts Co ... D ... 773 523-5757
Chicago (G-4333)

Chicago Pipe Bending & Coil Co ... F ... 773 379-1918
Chicago (G-4339)

Chicago Tube and Iron Company ... E ... 815 834-2500
Romeoville (G-18810)

Chicago Tube and Iron Company ... E ... 309 787-4947
Milan (G-14779)

▲ Cortube Products Co ... G ... 708 429-6700
Tinley Park (G-20903)

▲ D & W Mfg Co Inc ... E ... 773 533-1542
Chicago (G-4536)

D B M Services Corp ... G ... 630 964-5678
Lisle (G-13581)

◆ Deublin Company ... C ... 847 689-8600
Waukegan (G-21551)

Dove Steel Inc ... F ... 815 588-3772
Lockport (G-13712)

▲ Duraflex Inc ... E ... 847 462-1007
Cary (G-3336)

Eg Group Inc ... G ... 309 692-0968
Peoria (G-17352)

▲ Flex-Weld Inc ... D ... 815 334-3662
Woodstock (G-22567)

▲ Flexicraft Industries Inc ... F ... 312 738-3588
Chicago (G-4861)

Fulton Metal Works Inc ... G ... 217 476-8223
Ashland (G-926)

Geib Industries Inc ... E ... 847 455-4550
Bensenville (G-1906)

S I C

Employee Codes: A=Over 500 employees, B=251-500 C=101-250, D=51-100, E=20-50, F=10-19, G=3-9

2017 Harris Illinois Industrial Directory

1053

▲ **Gerlin Inc** G 630 653-5232
Carol Stream *(G-3157)*
**Global Maintenance LLC** F 270 933-1281
Metropolis *(G-14753)*
▲ **Howe Corporation** E 773 235-0200
Chicago *(G-5123)*
**Hub Manufacturing Company Inc** E 773 252-1373
Chicago *(G-5127)*
**Hyspan Precision Products Inc** E 773 277-0700
South Holland *(G-20279)*
**Icon Mech Cnstr & Engrg LLC** C 618 452-0035
Granite City *(G-11287)*
**Illco Inc** G 815 725-9100
Joliet *(G-12513)*
**Industrial Pipe and Supply Co** E 708 652-7511
Chicago *(G-5179)*
▲ **Integrated Mfg Tech LLC** E 618 282-8306
Red Bud *(G-17943)*
**James L Tracey Co** F 630 907-8999
Aurora *(G-1176)*
**John Maneely Company** C 773 254-0617
Chicago *(G-5316)*
**K & K Metal Works Inc** F 618 271-4680
East Saint Louis *(G-8758)*
**L M K Fabrication Inc** F 815 433-1530
Ottawa *(G-16965)*
**Lafox Manufacturing Corp** G 630 232-0266
Lafox *(G-12794)*
▲ **Leading Edge Group Inc** C 815 316-3500
Rockford *(G-18464)*
**Machine Tool Acc & Mfg Co** G 773 489-0903
Chicago *(G-5592)*
▲ **Manufactured Specialties Inc** F 630 444-1992
Saint Charles *(G-19213)*
▲ **Metamora Industries LLC** E 309 367-2368
Metamora *(G-14745)*
**Midwest Pipe Supports Inc** G 630 665-6400
Bartlett *(G-1319)*
**Monco Fabricators Inc** G 630 293-0063
West Chicago *(G-21746)*
**Morris Construction Inc** E 618 544-8504
Robinson *(G-18067)*
▲ **Morton Industries LLC** B 309 263-2590
Morton *(G-15168)*
▲ **National Metalwares LP** C 630 892-9000
Aurora *(G-1194)*
**Parker Fabrication Inc** E 309 266-8413
Morton *(G-15174)*
▼ **Peerless America Incorporated** C 217 342-0400
Effingham *(G-8853)*
**Pekay Machine & Engrg Co Inc** F 312 829-5530
Chicago *(G-6098)*
▲ **Peoria Tube Forming Corp** D 309 822-0274
Morton *(G-15176)*
▲ **Perma-Pipe Inc** E 847 966-2190
Niles *(G-16018)*
**Ptc Tubular Products LLC** C 815 692-4900
Fairbury *(G-10131)*
▲ **Rovanco Piping Systems Inc** D 815 741-6700
Joliet *(G-12572)*
**Scot Industries Inc** D 630 466-7591
Sugar Grove *(G-20734)*
**Service Sheet Metal Works Inc** F 773 229-0031
Chicago *(G-6483)*
**Sharlen Electric Co** E 773 721-0700
Chicago *(G-6489)*
**Shew Brothers Inc** G 618 997-4414
Marion *(G-14286)*
**Strait-O-Flex** G 815 965-2625
Stillman Valley *(G-20628)*
**Superior Pipe Standards Inc** G 708 656-0208
Cicero *(G-7233)*
**Tech-Weld Inc** F 630 365-3000
Elburn *(G-8913)*
**Tesko Welding & Mfg Co** D 708 452-0045
Norridge *(G-16109)*
**Traco Industries Inc** G 815 675-6603
Spring Grove *(G-20371)*
**Tubular Steel Inc** G 630 515-5000
Westmont *(G-21926)*
▲ **Vindee Industries Inc** E 815 469-3300
Frankfort *(G-10375)*
▲ **Whitley Products Inc** F 574 267-7114
Chicago *(G-6975)*
◆ **Zeman Mfg Co** E 630 960-2300
Lisle *(G-13679)*

## *3499 Fabricated Metal Prdts, NEC*

**A - Square Manufacturing Inc** F 800 628-6720
Chicago *(G-3681)*
**A - Square Manufacturing Inc** E 800 628-6720
Chicago *(G-3682)*
**Abct Corporation** G 773 427-1010
Lincolnwood *(G-13499)*
▲ **About Face Designs Inc** G 847 914-9040
Highland Park *(G-11821)*
**Adk Products Inc** G 847 710-0021
Elk Grove Village *(G-9274)*
**Afar Imports & Interiors Inc** G 217 744-3262
Springfield *(G-20386)*
▲ **All Right Sales Inc** G 773 558-4800
West Chicago *(G-21654)*
**All Star Custom Awards** G 630 428-1515
Naperville *(G-15596)*
◆ **Alpina Manufacturing LLC** E 773 202-8887
Chicago *(G-3832)*
**American Machine** G 815 539-6558
Mendota *(G-14715)*
**American Metal Mfg Inc** G 847 651-6097
Chicago *(G-3865)*
**American Partsmith Inc** G 630 520-0432
West Chicago *(G-21656)*
**American Trophy & Award Co Inc** G 312 939-3252
Chicago *(G-3881)*
**Aptargroup Inc** B 847 639-2124
Cary *(G-3327)*
◆ **Aptargroup Inc** B 815 477-0424
Crystal Lake *(G-7535)*
**Artistic Framing Inc** C 847 808-0200
Wheeling *(G-22007)*
**Austin-Westran LLC** C 815 234-2811
Montgomery *(G-15029)*
**Award Designs Inc** G 815 227-1264
Rockford *(G-18273)*
**Awards and More Inc** G 773 581-7771
Chicago *(G-4004)*
**Berkshire Investments LLC** D 708 656-7900
Cicero *(G-7180)*
▲ **Black Mountain Products Inc** G 224 655-5955
McHenry *(G-14482)*
**Bronze Memorial Inc** G 773 276-7972
Chicago *(G-4175)*
**Builders Chicago Corporation** D 224 654-2122
Rosemont *(G-18991)*
**Cardinal Engineering Inc** G 309 342-7474
Galesburg *(G-10742)*
**Chadwick Manufacturing Ltd** G 815 684-5152
Chadwick *(G-3440)*
▲ **Chicago-Wilcox Mfg Co** E 708 339-5000
South Holland *(G-20257)*
**Crabtree & Evelyn Ltd** G 630 898-3478
Aurora *(G-985)*
▲ **Durabilt Dyvex Inc** F 708 397-4673
Broadview *(G-2573)*
**Dva Metal Fabrication Inc** G 224 577-8217
Mundelein *(G-15496)*
◆ **Energy Absorption Systems Inc** E 312 467-6750
Chicago *(G-4750)*
▲ **First Alert Inc** G 630 499-3295
Aurora *(G-1009)*
**Fotofab LLC** E 773 463-6211
Chicago *(G-4877)*
**Fox Metal Services Inc** F 847 439-9696
Carol Stream *(G-3155)*
**Framery** G 618 656-5749
Edwardsville *(G-8802)*
**Frederics Frame Studio Inc** F 312 243-2950
Chicago *(G-4886)*
**G & M Fabricating Inc** G 815 282-1744
Roscoe *(G-18898)*
**G & M Metal Fabricators Inc** D 847 678-6501
Franklin Park *(G-10473)*
▲ **Gpi Manufacturing Inc** E 847 615-8900
Lake Bluff *(G-12847)*
**Group Industries Inc** E 708 877-6200
Thornton *(G-20871)*
▲ **Hadady Corporation** E 219 322-7417
South Holland *(G-20274)*
◆ **Home Pdts Intl - N Amer Inc** B 773 890-1010
Chicago *(G-5102)*
**Illinois Tool Works Inc** C 708 458-7320
Bridgeview *(G-2499)*
**Illinois Tool Works Inc** C 708 342-6000
Mokena *(G-14872)*
**Illinois Tool Works Inc** E 847 215-8925
Buffalo Grove *(G-2706)*
**Illinois Tool Works Inc** B 847 724-7500
Glenview *(G-11141)*
**Illinois Tool Works Inc** C 630 372-2150
Bartlett *(G-1353)*
**Illinois Tool Works Inc** C 847 783-5500
Elgin *(G-9072)*
**Infrastructure Def Tech LLC** G 800 379-1822
Belvidere *(G-1763)*
**Innerweld Cover Co** F 847 497-3009
Mundelein *(G-15511)*
**J&A Mtchell Stl Fbricators Inc** G 815 939-2144
Kankakee *(G-12629)*
**Jerome Remien Corporation** F 847 806-0888
Elk Grove Village *(G-9561)*
▲ **JL Clark LLC** C 815 961-5609
Rockford *(G-18447)*
**JMS Metals Inc** G 618 443-1000
Sparta *(G-20317)*
**John Thomas Inc** E 815 288-2343
Dixon *(G-8334)*
**Kenneth W Templeman** G 847 912-2740
Volo *(G-21315)*
**Key West Metal Industries Inc** C 708 371-1470
Crestwood *(G-7491)*
◆ **Knaack LLC** D 815 459-6020
Crystal Lake *(G-7600)*
**Laird Technologies Inc** C 847 839-6900
Schaumburg *(G-19610)*
▲ **Lechler Inc** D 630 377-6611
Saint Charles *(G-19208)*
**Lindsay Metal Madness Inc** G 815 568-4560
Marengo *(G-14235)*
**Livingston Innovations LLC** G 847 808-0900
Buffalo Grove *(G-2727)*
**Louisville Ladder Inc** G 309 692-1895
Peoria *(G-17402)*
**Lynda Hervas** G 847 985-1690
Schaumburg *(G-19627)*
**Macholl Metal Fabrication** G 815 597-1908
Garden Prairie *(G-10795)*
▼ **Manufacturers Inv Group LLC** E 630 285-0800
Itasca *(G-12310)*
**Mc Metals & Fabricating Inc** G 847 961-5242
Huntley *(G-12163)*
▲ **McLean Manufacturing Company** G 847 277-9912
Lake Barrington *(G-12819)*
**Metal Strip Buiding Products** G 847 742-8500
Itasca *(G-12314)*
**Mfz Ventures Inc** G 773 247-4611
Chicago *(G-5715)*
**Midland Metal Products Co** D 773 927-5700
Chicago *(G-5735)*
**Midland Stamping and Fabg Corp** D 847 678-7573
Schiller Park *(G-19851)*
**Mighty Mites Awards and Sons** G 847 297-0035
Des Plaines *(G-8233)*
▲ **Millenia Products Group Inc** C 630 458-0401
Itasca *(G-12318)*
**Millenia Specialty Metals LLC** G 630 458-0401
Itasca *(G-12319)*
**Millenia Trucking LLC** E 630 458-0401
Itasca *(G-12320)*
**Morris Magnetics Inc** E 847 487-0829
Wauconda *(G-21486)*
▲ **MPS Chicago Inc** C 630 932-9000
Downers Grove *(G-8492)*
**Nafisco Inc** F 815 372-3300
Romeoville *(G-18851)*
**Naked Army USA LLC** G 630 456-8738
Glen Ellyn *(G-10982)*
**Newman-Green Inc** D 630 543-6500
Addison *(G-228)*
**Noise Barriers LLC** E 847 843-0500
Libertyville *(G-13362)*
▲ **North American Safety Products** G 815 469-1144
Mokena *(G-14888)*
**Ojedas Welding Co** G 708 595-3799
Maywood *(G-14434)*
**Olympic Trophy and Awards Co** F 773 631-9500
Chicago *(G-5987)*
**Orient Machining & Welding Inc** E 708 371-3500
Dixmoor *(G-8320)*
**Panek Precision Products Co** C 847 291-9755
Northbrook *(G-16330)*
▲ **Planter Inc** D 773 637-7777
Chicago *(G-6135)*
**Pma Friction Products Inc** D 630 406-9119
Batavia *(G-1484)*
◆ **Precision Brand Products Inc** E 630 969-7200
Downers Grove *(G-8509)*
▲ **Precision Steel Warehouse Inc** C 800 323-0740
Franklin Park *(G-10560)*
**Product Service Craft Inc** F 630 964-5160
Downers Grove *(G-8511)*

# 35 INDUSTRIAL AND COMMERCIAL MACHINERY AND COMPUTER EQUIPMENT

Progressive Bronze Works Inc .......... E ...... 773 463-5500
  Chicago *(G-6211)*
Promus Equity Partners LLC .......... F ...... 312 784-3990
  Chicago *(G-6216)*
PSM Industries Inc .......... E ...... 815 337-8800
  Woodstock *(G-22602)*
Quinceanerboutiquecom Inc .......... G ...... 779 324-5468
  Frankfort *(G-10356)*
Quixote Transportation Safety .......... D ...... 312 467-6750
  Chicago *(G-6260)*
▲ R S Owens & Co Inc .......... B ...... 773 282-6000
  Chicago *(G-6273)*
Renner & Co .......... F ...... 847 639-4900
  Cary *(G-3366)*
Robin L Barnhouse .......... G ...... 309 737-5431
  Joy *(G-12592)*
Roll Roll Met Fabricators Inc .......... G ...... 773 434-1315
  Chicago *(G-6384)*
◆ Samuel Strapping Systems Inc .......... D ...... 630 783-8900
  Woodridge *(G-22515)*
Serra Laser Precision LLC .......... D ...... 847 367-0282
  Libertyville *(G-13379)*
◆ Signode Corporation .......... A ...... 800 527-1499
  Glenview *(G-11197)*
▲ Signode Packaging Systems Corp .... D ...... 800 323-2464
  Glenview *(G-11203)*
Signode Supply Corporation .......... C ...... 708 458-7320
  Bridgeview *(G-2528)*
Skol Mfg Co .......... E ...... 773 878-5959
  Chicago *(G-6522)*
▲ Spraying Systems Co .......... A ...... 630 665-5000
  Glendale Heights *(G-11072)*
Spraying Systems Co .......... F ...... 630 665-5001
  Aurora *(G-1082)*
◆ Spraying Systems Midwest Inc .......... G ...... 630 665-5000
  Glendale Heights *(G-11073)*
Strebor Specialties LLC .......... E ...... 618 286-1140
  Dupo *(G-8580)*
Suburban Metalcraft Inc .......... G ...... 847 678-7550
  Franklin Park *(G-10598)*
Supreme Frame & Moulding Co .......... F ...... 312 930-9056
  Chicago *(G-6638)*
▲ Talaris Inc .......... C ...... 630 577-1000
  Lisle *(G-13669)*
▼ Tc Industries Inc .......... C ...... 815 459-2401
  Crystal Lake *(G-7660)*
▲ Techny Advisors LLC .......... F ...... 630 771-0095
  Burr Ridge *(G-2883)*
Terra Cotta Holdings Co .......... E ...... 815 459-2400
  Crystal Lake *(G-7664)*
Titan Metals Inc .......... E ...... 630 752-9700
  Glendale Heights *(G-11085)*
◆ Titan Wheel Corp Illinois .......... A ...... 217 228-6023
  Quincy *(G-17898)*
▲ Trendler Inc .......... E ...... 773 284-6600
  Chicago *(G-6768)*
TSC International Inc .......... F ...... 847 249-4900
  Wadsworth *(G-21328)*
Tu-Star Manufacturing Co Inc .......... G ...... 815 338-5760
  Woodstock *(G-22619)*
Tvh Parts Co .......... E ...... 847 223-1000
  Grayslake *(G-11365)*
Two Four Seven Metal Laser .......... G ...... 847 250-5199
  Itasca *(G-12369)*
V & N Metal Products Inc .......... G ...... 773 436-1855
  Chicago *(G-6863)*
Variable Operations Tech Inc .......... G ...... 815 479-8528
  Crystal Lake *(G-7672)*
▲ Vibro/Dynamics Corporation .......... E ...... 708 345-2050
  Broadview *(G-2619)*
Viking Metal Cabinet Co LLC .......... D ...... 800 776-7767
  Montgomery *(G-15069)*
Viking Metal Cabinet Company .......... D ...... 630 863-7234
  Montgomery *(G-15070)*
Voss Pattern Works Inc .......... E ...... 618 233-4242
  Belleville *(G-1689)*
▲ Vulcan Ladder Usa LLC .......... G ...... 847 526-6321
  Island Lake *(G-12220)*
▲ Webster-Hoff Corporation .......... D ...... 630 858-8030
  Glendale Heights *(G-11091)*
Wehrli Custom Fabrication .......... F ...... 630 277-8239
  Sycamore *(G-20825)*
▼ Welding Company of America .......... E ...... 630 806-2000
  Aurora *(G-1231)*
Werner Co .......... E ...... 815 459-6020
  Crystal Lake *(G-7676)*
▲ Wiremasters Incorporated .......... E ...... 773 254-3700
  Chicago *(G-7005)*
Zenith Fabricating Company .......... E ...... 773 622-2601
  Chicago *(G-7064)*

## 35 INDUSTRIAL AND COMMERCIAL MACHINERY AND COMPUTER EQUIPMENT

### 3511 Steam, Gas & Hydraulic Turbines & Engines

ABB Inc .......... F ...... 630 759-7428
  Bolingbrook *(G-2276)*
Acciona Windpower N Amer LLC .......... G ...... 319 643-9463
  Chicago *(G-3717)*
Action Turbine Repair Svc Inc .......... F ...... 708 924-9601
  Summit Argo *(G-20760)*
Angel Wind Energy Inc .......... G ...... 815 471-2020
  Onarga *(G-16808)*
▲ Area Diesel Service Inc .......... E ...... 217 854-2641
  Carlinville *(G-3030)*
B N Blance Enrgy Solutions LLC .......... G ...... 847 287-7466
  Palatine *(G-17005)*
Babcock & Wilcox Powr Generatn .......... F ...... 630 719-5120
  Downers Grove *(G-8392)*
Broadwind Energy Inc .......... C ...... 708 780-4800
  Cicero *(G-7181)*
Catching Hydraulics Co Ltd .......... E ...... 708 344-2334
  Melrose Park *(G-14606)*
◆ Caterpillar Inc .......... A ...... 309 675-1000
  Peoria *(G-17326)*
Caterpillar Inc .......... G ...... 815 729-5511
  Rockdale *(G-18216)*
Caterpillar Inc .......... B ...... 888 614-4328
  Peoria *(G-17328)*
Caterpillar Inc .......... B ...... 309 675-6590
  Peoria *(G-17333)*
Doncasters Inc .......... C ...... 217 465-6500
  Paris *(G-17146)*
Energy Parts Solutions Inc .......... F ...... 224 653-9412
  Schaumburg *(G-19516)*
Gds Enterprises .......... G ...... 217 543-3681
  Arthur *(G-901)*
Invenergy .......... G ...... 815 795-4964
  Marseilles *(G-14312)*
ITT Water & Wastewater USA Inc .......... F ...... 708 342-0484
  Tinley Park *(G-20924)*
ITT Water & Wastewater USA Inc .......... G ...... 847 966-3700
  Morton Grove *(G-15205)*
Lee Industries Inc .......... C ...... 847 462-1865
  Elk Grove Village *(G-9590)*
Mag-Drive LLC .......... G ...... 847 690-0871
  Arlington Heights *(G-797)*
Marty Lundeen .......... G ...... 630 250-8917
  Itasca *(G-12311)*
Michael Wilton Cstm Homes Inc .......... G ...... 630 508-1200
  Willowbrook *(G-22221)*
◆ Nordex Usa Inc .......... D ...... 208 383-6500
  Chicago *(G-5925)*
Ntpwind Power Inc .......... G ...... 815 345-1931
  Crystal Lake *(G-7621)*
Pne Wind Usa Inc .......... G ...... 773 329-3705
  Chicago *(G-6143)*
Rebuilders Enterprises Inc .......... G ...... 708 430-0030
  Bridgeview *(G-2523)*
Rockwind Venture Partners LLC .......... G ...... 630 881-6664
  Rockford *(G-18593)*
Siemens Energy Inc .......... F ...... 618 357-6360
  Pinckneyville *(G-17552)*
Solar Turbines Incorporated .......... E ...... 630 527-1700
  Naperville *(G-15748)*
▲ Sur-Fit Corporation .......... E ...... 815 301-5815
  Crystal Lake *(G-7656)*
Suzlon Wind Energy Corporation .......... G ...... 773 328-5077
  Elgin *(G-9199)*
▲ Suzlon Wind Energy Corporation .......... C ...... 773 328-5077
  Chicago *(G-6645)*
▼ Union Iron Inc .......... E ...... 217 429-5148
  Decatur *(G-7955)*
University of Chicago .......... F ...... 773 702-9780
  Chicago *(G-6838)*
▲ Usway Corporation .......... G ...... 773 338-9688
  Chicago *(G-6860)*
◆ VPI Acquisition Company LLC .......... E ...... 630 694-5500
  Franklin Park *(G-10624)*

### 3519 Internal Combustion Engines, NEC

American Speed Enterprises .......... G ...... 309 764-3601
  Moline *(G-14917)*
B & M Automotive .......... G ...... 309 637-4977
  Peoria *(G-17312)*
B & S Auto Rebuilders Inc .......... G ...... 773 283-3763
  Chicago *(G-4017)*
Boley Tool & Machine Works Inc .......... C ...... 309 694-2722
  East Peoria *(G-8703)*
◆ Brunswick Corporation .......... B ...... 847 735-4700
  Lake Forest *(G-12888)*
Brunswick International Ltd .......... G ...... 847 735-4700
  Lake Forest *(G-12889)*
C & M Engineering .......... G ...... 815 932-3388
  Bourbonnais *(G-2391)*
Caterpillar Gb LLC .......... G ...... 309 675-1000
  Peoria *(G-17325)*
◆ Caterpillar Inc .......... A ...... 309 675-1000
  Peoria *(G-17326)*
Caterpillar Inc .......... G ...... 815 729-5511
  Rockdale *(G-18216)*
Caterpillar Inc .......... B ...... 888 614-4328
  Peoria *(G-17328)*
Caterpillar Inc .......... B ...... 309 675-6590
  Peoria *(G-17333)*
Chicago Jet Group LLC .......... E ...... 630 466-3600
  Sugar Grove *(G-20719)*
▲ Concentric Itasca Inc .......... D ...... 630 268-1528
  Itasca *(G-12246)*
Conley Precision Engines Inc .......... F ...... 630 858-3160
  Glen Ellyn *(G-10964)*
◆ Cummins - Allison Corp .......... B ...... 847 759-6403
  Mount Prospect *(G-15320)*
Cummins - Allison Corp .......... D ...... 847 299-9550
  Mount Prospect *(G-15321)*
Cummins - Allison Corp .......... G ...... 847 299-9550
  Mount Prospect *(G-15322)*
Cummins - Allison Corp .......... F ...... 630 833-2285
  Elmhurst *(G-9862)*
Cummins Crosspoint LLC .......... E ...... 309 452-4454
  Normal *(G-16068)*
Cummins Dist Holdco Inc .......... G ...... 309 787-4300
  Rock Island *(G-18170)*
Cummins Inc .......... E ...... 309 787-4300
  Rock Island *(G-18171)*
Cummins Npower LLC .......... G ...... 708 579-9222
  Hodgkins *(G-11973)*
Cummins-American Corp .......... G ...... 847 299-9550
  Mount Prospect *(G-15323)*
◆ Diesel Radiator Co .......... E ...... 708 345-2839
  Melrose Park *(G-14618)*
Diesel Radiator Co .......... D ...... 708 865-7299
  Melrose Park *(G-14619)*
Dura Products Corporation .......... G ...... 815 939-1399
  Bradley *(G-2420)*
Engine Efficiency Systems LLC .......... F ...... 630 590-5241
  Burr Ridge *(G-2838)*
▲ Global Cmpnent Tech Amrcas Inc .... E ...... 815 568-4507
  Marengo *(G-14229)*
◆ Heavy Quip Incorporated .......... F ...... 312 368-7997
  Chicago *(G-5067)*
Honeywell International Inc .......... A ...... 847 391-2000
  Des Plaines *(G-8205)*
Iet-Meco .......... C ...... 217 465-6575
  Paris *(G-17150)*
Jasiek Motor Rebuilding Inc .......... G ...... 815 883-3678
  Oglesby *(G-16750)*
Jimmy Diesel Inc .......... G ...... 708 482-4500
  Wheaton *(G-21959)*
L S Diesel Repair Inc .......... G ...... 217 283-5537
  Hoopeston *(G-12112)*
Lv Ventures Inc .......... G ...... 312 993-1800
  Chicago *(G-5571)*
Marine Engine and Drive S .......... G ...... 630 606-6124
  West Chicago *(G-21739)*
Navistar Inc .......... C
  Melrose Park *(G-14675)*
Navistar Inc .......... B ...... 317 352-4500
  Melrose Park *(G-14676)*
◆ Navistar Inc .......... C ...... 331 332-5000
  Lisle *(G-13629)*
◆ Navistar International Corp .......... A ...... 331 332-5000
  Lisle *(G-13633)*
Nelson Enterprises Inc .......... G ...... 815 633-1100
  Roscoe *(G-18910)*
Npt Automotive Machine Shop .......... E ...... 618 233-1344
  Belleville *(G-1661)*
Performance Diesel Service .......... G ...... 217 375-4429
  Hoopeston *(G-12113)*
▲ Perkins Engines Inc .......... E ...... 309 578-7364
  Mossville *(G-15254)*
Precision Engine Rebuilders .......... G ...... 815 254-2333
  Plainfield *(G-17642)*
◆ Progress Rail Locomotive Inc .......... A ...... 800 255-5355
  Mc Cook *(G-14456)*
Progress Rail Locomotive Inc .......... F ...... 708 387-5510
  Mc Cook *(G-14457)*

---

Employee Codes: A=Over 500 employees, B=251-500
C=101-250, D=51-100, E=20-50, F=10-19, G=3-9

## 35 INDUSTRIAL AND COMMERCIAL MACHINERY AND COMPUTER EQUIPMENT

Quincy Compressor LLC .................. C ...... 217 222-7700
  Quincy *(G-17875)*
R & C Auto Supply Corp .................. G ...... 815 625-4414
  Sterling *(G-20609)*
▲ Sierra International LLC .................. C ...... 217 324-9400
  Litchfield *(G-13698)*
Speed Tech Technology Inc .................. G ...... 847 516-2001
  Cary *(G-3372)*
▲ Tpr America Inc .................. G ...... 847 446-5336
  Schaumburg *(G-19767)*
◆ Unicarriers Americas Corp .................. B ...... 800 871-5438
  Marengo *(G-14244)*
Waymore Power Co Inc .................. F ...... 618 729-3876
  Piasa *(G-17543)*
Wuebbels Repair & Sales LLC .................. G ...... 618 648-2227
  Mc Leansboro *(G-14470)*

### 3523 Farm Machinery & Eqpt

360 Yield Center LLC .................. E ...... 309 263-4360
  Morton *(G-15152)*
A & P Grain Systems Inc .................. F ...... 815 827-3079
  Maple Park *(G-14196)*
AGCO Corporation .................. E ...... 630 406-3248
  Batavia *(G-1404)*
Alamo Group (il) Inc .................. E ...... 217 784-4261
  Gibson City *(G-10897)*
Alvarez & Marsal Inc .................. E ...... 312 601-4220
  Chicago *(G-3840)*
▲ Aqua Control Inc .................. E ...... 815 664-4900
  Spring Valley *(G-20374)*
Arrows Up Inc .................. G ...... 847 305-2550
  Arlington Heights *(G-717)*
▲ Avant Tecno USA Inc .................. E ...... 847 380-9822
  Arlington Heights *(G-720)*
B J Fehr Machine Co .................. G ...... 309 923-8691
  Roanoke *(G-18048)*
B T Brown Manufacturing .................. G ...... 815 947-3633
  Kent *(G-12665)*
Beall Manufacturing Inc .................. E ...... 618 259-8154
  East Alton *(G-8599)*
▼ Bellota Agrsltions Tls USA LLC .................. E ...... 309 787-2491
  Milan *(G-14775)*
Bill Peterson .................. G ...... 815 378-8633
  Harvard *(G-11624)*
Birkeys Farm Store Inc .................. E ...... 217 337-1772
  Urbana *(G-21073)*
Blue Ridge Land and Cattle .................. E ...... 217 762-9652
  Monticello *(G-15075)*
Brian Burcar .................. G ...... 815 856-2271
  Leonore *(G-13285)*
Brian Lindstrom .................. G ...... 309 463-2388
  Varna *(G-21133)*
▲ Bushnell Illinois Tank Co .................. D ...... 309 772-3106
  Bushnell *(G-2898)*
▲ Calmer Corn Heads Inc .................. E ...... 309 629-9000
  Lynn Center *(G-14015)*
Cardinal Cattle .................. G ...... 309 479-1302
  Wyoming *(G-22637)*
▼ Caterpillar Brazil LLC .................. G ...... 309 675-1000
  Peoria *(G-17324)*
Charles Crane .................. G ...... 815 258-5375
  Clifton *(G-7273)*
Christopher Concrete Products .................. G ...... 618 724-2951
  Buckner *(G-2647)*
Circle K Industries Inc .................. F ...... 847 949-0363
  Mundelein *(G-15487)*
Cline Concrete Products .................. F ...... 217 283-5012
  Hoopeston *(G-12107)*
Cnh Capital America LLC .................. E ...... 630 887-2233
  Burr Ridge *(G-2831)*
Cnh Industrial America LLC .................. E ...... 847 263-5793
  Waukegan *(G-21539)*
Cnh Industrial America LLC .................. E ...... 309 965-2233
  Goodfield *(G-11244)*
Cnh Industrial America LLC .................. C ...... 309 965-2217
  Goodfield *(G-11245)*
Cnh Industrial America LLC .................. C ...... 630 887-2233
  Burr Ridge *(G-2833)*
Cnh Industrial America LLC .................. E ...... 706 629-5572
  Burr Ridge *(G-2832)*
Coster Company .................. C ...... 312 541-7200
  Chicago *(G-4480)*
Coyote Transportation Inc .................. G ...... 630 204-5729
  Bensenville *(G-1869)*
Cronkhite Industries Inc .................. F ...... 217 443-3700
  Danville *(G-7711)*
CST Industries Inc .................. C ...... 815 756-1551
  Dekalb *(G-8080)*
Custom Grain Systems LLC .................. G ...... 812 881-8175
  Lawrenceville *(G-13197)*

Custom Millers Supply Inc .................. G ...... 309 734-6312
  Monmouth *(G-15011)*
D & B Fabricators & Distrs .................. F ...... 630 325-3811
  Lemont *(G-13234)*
D M Manufacturing 2 Inc .................. G ...... 618 455-3550
  Sainte Marie *(G-19323)*
Davenport Tractor Inc .................. G ...... 309 781-8305
  Milan *(G-14782)*
David Taylor .................. E ...... 217 222-6480
  Quincy *(G-17819)*
Davidson Grain Incorporated .................. E ...... 815 384-3208
  Creston *(G-7471)*
Davis Welding & Manfctg Inc .................. E ...... 217 784-5480
  Gibson City *(G-10899)*
Dawn Equipment Company Inc .................. F ...... 815 899-8000
  Sycamore *(G-20791)*
Deere & Company .................. A ...... 309 765-8000
  Moline *(G-14925)*
Deere & Company .................. E ...... 309 765-8000
  East Moline *(G-8673)*
Deere & Company .................. A ...... 309 748-0580
  Moline *(G-14926)*
Deere & Company .................. G ...... 309 765-3177
  Moline *(G-14927)*
Deere & Company .................. G ...... 309 765-8000
  Moline *(G-14928)*
Deere & Company .................. A ...... 800 765-9588
  East Moline *(G-8674)*
Deere & Company .................. G ...... 309 765-8000
  East Moline *(G-8675)*
Deere & Company .................. D ...... 309 765-8275
  Moline *(G-14929)*
Deere & Company .................. G ...... 309 748-8260
  Moline *(G-14931)*
Deere & Company .................. F ...... 309 765-8000
  Moline *(G-14932)*
Deere & Company .................. A ...... 309 765-8277
  Moline *(G-14934)*
Deere & Company .................. G ...... 309 765-7310
  Moline *(G-14935)*
Design Manufacturing & Eqp Co .................. F ...... 217 824-9219
  Taylorville *(G-20837)*
▼ Doyle Equipment Mfg Co .................. D ...... 217 222-1592
  Quincy *(G-17821)*
Dsi Inc .................. G ...... 309 965-5110
  Goodfield *(G-11246)*
Dspc Company .................. E ...... 815 997-1116
  Rockford *(G-18353)*
Dutch Prairie Conveyors .................. G ...... 618 349-6177
  Shobonier *(G-19921)*
▲ Dutch Valley Partners LLC .................. E ...... 815 937-8812
  Bourbonnais *(G-2394)*
▲ E Z Trail Inc .................. G ...... 217 543-3471
  Arthur *(G-899)*
Ecoturf Midwest Inc .................. G ...... 630 350-9500
  Bensenville *(G-1888)*
▲ Factory Direct Worldwide LLC .................. F ...... 847 272-6464
  Wheeling *(G-22053)*
▲ Farmweld Inc .................. E ...... 217 857-6423
  Teutopolis *(G-20852)*
Feeder Corporation of America .................. F ...... 708 343-4900
  Melrose Park *(G-14638)*
▲ Fehr Cab Interiors .................. G ...... 815 692-3355
  Fairbury *(G-10124)*
◆ Gea Farm Technologies Inc .................. C ...... 630 548-8200
  Naperville *(G-15662)*
Genwoods Holdco LLC .................. A ...... 815 732-2141
  Oregon *(G-16825)*
Globetec Midwest Partners LLC .................. G ...... 847 608-9300
  South Elgin *(G-20200)*
Gsi Group LLC .................. E ...... 217 226-4401
  Assumption *(G-932)*
Gsi Group LLC .................. C ...... 217 287-6244
  Taylorville *(G-20839)*
▼ Gsi Holdings Corp .................. G ...... 217 226-4421
  Assumption *(G-933)*
H W Hostetler & Sons .................. E ...... 815 438-7816
  Deer Grove *(G-7967)*
◆ Hcc Inc .................. C ...... 815 539-9371
  Mendota *(G-14722)*
◆ HD Hudson Manufacturing Co .................. E ...... 312 644-2830
  Chicago *(G-5057)*
Henry A Engelhart .................. G ...... 217 563-2176
  Nokomis *(G-16057)*
Hipro Manufacturing Inc .................. G ...... 815 432-5271
  Watseka *(G-21418)*
Hypermax Engineering Inc .................. F ...... 847 428-5655
  Gilberts *(G-10924)*
Ideal Turf Inc .................. G ...... 309 691-3362
  Peoria *(G-17384)*

J & J Equipment Inc .................. G ...... 309 449-5442
  Hopedale *(G-12122)*
John Deere AG Holdings Inc .................. G ...... 309 765-8000
  Moline *(G-14946)*
John Deere Cnstr & For Co .................. F ...... 309 765-8000
  Moline *(G-14947)*
JWT Farms Inc .................. G ...... 618 664-3429
  Pocahontas *(G-17684)*
Keller Grain & Livestock Inc .................. G ...... 618 455-3634
  Willow Hill *(G-22192)*
Kinast Inc .................. G ...... 217 852-3525
  Dallas City *(G-7698)*
King Systems Inc .................. G ...... 309 879-2668
  Dahinda *(G-7688)*
▲ Kongskilde Industries Inc .................. C ...... 309 452-3300
  Hudson *(G-12124)*
Korhumel Inc .................. G ...... 847 330-0335
  Schaumburg *(G-19604)*
Ksem Inc .................. G ...... 618 656-5388
  Edwardsville *(G-8805)*
Ksi Conveyor Inc .................. D ...... 815 457-2403
  Cissna Park *(G-7255)*
Kuchar Combine Performance .................. G ...... 217 854-9838
  Carlinville *(G-3041)*
Lakeview Energy LLC .................. E ...... 312 386-5897
  Chicago *(G-5446)*
Lawrence Allen .................. G ...... 618 786-3794
  Grafton *(G-11255)*
Licon Inc .................. G ...... 618 485-2222
  Ashley *(G-927)*
◆ Lmt Inc .................. F ...... 309 932-3311
  Galva *(G-10792)*
▲ Malthandlingcom LLC .................. G ...... 773 888-7718
  Chicago *(G-5607)*
Manitou Americas Inc .................. G ...... 262 334-9461
  Belvidere *(G-1769)*
Mathews Company .................. D ...... 815 459-2210
  Crystal Lake *(G-7606)*
▲ McLaughlin Body Co .................. D ...... 309 762-7755
  Moline *(G-14955)*
Mega International Ltd .................. G ...... 309 764-5310
  Moline *(G-14956)*
Meinhart Grain Farm Inc .................. G ...... 217 683-2692
  Montrose *(G-15089)*
Meteer Inc .................. G ...... 217 636-7280
  Athens *(G-940)*
◆ Midwest Bio-Systems Inc .................. F ...... 815 438-7200
  Tampico *(G-20829)*
Midwest Sport Turf Systems LLC .................. F ...... 630 923-8342
  Plainfield *(G-17627)*
Ndy Manufacturing Inc .................. G ...... 815 426-2330
  Bonfield *(G-2385)*
▲ Neuero Corporation .................. F ...... 630 231-9020
  West Chicago *(G-21750)*
Newton Implement Partnership .................. E ...... 618 783-8716
  Newton *(G-15943)*
▲ Ogden Metalworks Inc .................. F ...... 217 582-2552
  Ogden *(G-16743)*
Outdoor Space LLC .................. G ...... 773 857-5296
  Chicago *(G-6026)*
◆ P & H Manufacturing Co .................. D ...... 217 774-2123
  Shelbyville *(G-19911)*
Paw Paw Co-Operative Grain .................. G ...... 815 627-2071
  Paw Paw *(G-17233)*
Phelps Farms .................. G ...... 815 624-7263
  Rockton *(G-18701)*
Polar Container Corp Inc .................. G ...... 847 299-5030
  Rosemont *(G-19024)*
Prairie Land Mllwrght Svcs Inc .................. F ...... 815 538-3085
  Mendota *(G-14731)*
▲ Prater Industries Inc .................. D ...... 630 679-3200
  Bolingbrook *(G-2359)*
Precision Tank & Equipment Co .................. E ...... 217 452-7228
  Virginia *(G-21307)*
Quality Metal Works Inc .................. G ...... 309 379-5311
  Stanford *(G-20552)*
R K Products Inc .................. G ...... 309 792-1927
  East Moline *(G-8693)*
R&R Flight Service .................. G ...... 815 538-2599
  Earlville *(G-8596)*
R-Tech Feeders Inc .................. E ...... 815 874-2990
  Rockford *(G-18546)*
Robert Swaar .................. G ...... 217 968-2232
  Greenview *(G-11386)*
S & P Farms .................. G ...... 309 772-3936
  Bushnell *(G-2908)*
▼ Seedburo Equipment Company Inc .................. F ...... 312 738-3700
  Des Plaines *(G-8271)*
◆ Shoup Manufacturing Co Inc .................. E ...... 815 933-4439
  Kankakee *(G-12648)*

## 35 INDUSTRIAL AND COMMERCIAL MACHINERY AND COMPUTER EQUIPMENT

Sopher Design & Manufacturing ............G..... 309 699-6419
 East Peoria (G-8735)
◆ Speeco Incorporated ............................C..... 303 279-5544
 Oregon (G-16832)
Spreader Inc ...........................................G..... 217 568-7219
 Gifford (G-10910)
▲ Star Forge Inc .....................................D..... 815 235-7750
 Freeport (G-10691)
Stephens Pipe & Steel LLC ...................E..... 800 451-2612
 North Aurora (G-16146)
Straightline AG Inc ................................G..... 217 963-1270
 Harristown (G-11608)
Tft Inc .....................................................G..... 309 531-2012
 Colfax (G-7311)
Trusty Warns Inc ....................................E..... 630 766-9015
 Wood Dale (G-22434)
▼ Union Iron Inc ....................................E..... 217 429-5148
 Decatur (G-7955)
▲ W A Rice Seed Company ...................G..... 618 498-5538
 Jerseyville (G-12428)
Waipuna USA Inc ...................................G..... 630 514-0364
 Downers Grove (G-8539)
Weaver Equipment LLC .........................G..... 618 833-5521
 Buncombe (G-2802)
Wernze Farms Inc ..................................G..... 618 569-4820
 Annapolis (G-609)
▲ Whalen Manufacturing Company .......G..... 309 836-1438
 Macomb (G-14136)
Wilder Farms .........................................G..... 309 537-3218
 New Boston (G-15867)
Woods Equipment Company .................D..... 815 732-2141
 Rockford (G-18688)
▼ Yargus Manufacturing Inc .................E..... 217 826-6352
 Marshall (G-14331)
▲ Yetter Manufacturing Company .........D..... 309 776-3222
 Colchester (G-7309)
Yoder John ..............................................G..... 217 676-3430
 Blue Mound (G-2274)

### 3524 Garden, Lawn Tractors & Eqpt

A Yard Materials Co ...............................G..... 815 385-4560
 Mchenry (G-14474)
▼ Alpha Omega Profile Extrusion .........F..... 847 956-8777
 Elk Grove Village (G-9290)
▲ Amerisun Inc .....................................F..... 800 791-9458
 Itasca (G-12229)
Bartonville Equipment Rental ................G..... 309 633-0227
 Bartonville (G-1392)
Beall Manufacturing Inc ........................E..... 618 259-8154
 East Alton (G-8599)
Coleman Lawn Equipment Inc ..............G..... 618 529-0181
 Carbondale (G-3003)
Contempo Industries Inc .......................D..... 815 337-6267
 Woodstock (G-22553)
David Taylor ...........................................E..... 217 222-6480
 Quincy (G-17819)
Deere & Company ..................................A..... 309 765-8000
 Moline (G-14925)
◆ Echo Incorporated .............................A..... 847 540-8400
 Lake Zurich (G-13064)
Echo Incorporated .................................E..... 847 540-3500
 Lake Zurich (G-13065)
Fiskars Brands Inc .................................B..... 309 690-2200
 Peoria (G-17363)
Grower Equipment & Supply Co ............F..... 847 223-3100
 Hainesville (G-11523)
Hevco Industries ....................................G..... 708 344-1342
 Aurora (G-1169)
Hipro Manufacturing Inc ........................E..... 815 432-5271
 Watseka (G-21418)
Hyponex Corporation .............................E..... 815 772-2167
 Morrison (G-15144)
◆ Jeffs Small Engine Inc ......................G..... 630 904-6840
 Plainfield (G-17609)
John Deere AG Holdings Inc .................G..... 309 765-8000
 Moline (G-14946)
▼ Kunz Engineering Inc .......................G..... 815 539-6954
 Mendota (G-14723)
Lutz Corp ................................................G..... 800 203-7740
 Normal (G-16075)
M Martinez Inc .......................................G..... 847 740-6364
 Round Lake Heights (G-19081)
Oldcastle Lawn & Garden Inc ...............F..... 618 274-1222
 East Saint Louis (G-8763)
◆ Precision Products Inc .....................G..... 217 735-1590
 Lincoln (G-13418)
Randys Exper-Clean ...............................G..... 217 423-1975
 Decatur (G-7931)
Ryan Manufacturing Inc .........................G..... 815 695-5310
 Newark (G-15934)

Sawier .....................................................E..... 630 297-8588
 Downers Grove (G-8519)
◆ Tuthill Corporation ............................E..... 630 382-4900
 Burr Ridge (G-2889)
Valley View Industries Hc Inc ................E..... 800 323-9369
 Crestwood (G-7507)
▲ Vaughan & Bushnell Mfg Co .............F..... 815 648-2446
 Hebron (G-11730)
▼ Yanmar (usa) Inc .............................G..... 847 541-1900
 Buffalo Grove (G-2796)
Zuma Corporation ..................................G..... 815 288-7269
 Dixon (G-8361)

### 3531 Construction Machinery & Eqpt

Aaron Engnered Process Eqp Inc .........G..... 630 350-2200
 Bensenville (G-1809)
Allegion S&S US Holding Co .................C..... 815 875-3311
 Princeton (G-17742)
▲ APL Logistics Americas Ltd .............E..... 630 783-0200
 Woodridge (G-22453)
Associated Professionals ......................G..... 847 931-0095
 Elgin (G-8959)
Avanti Motor Carriers Inc ......................G..... 630 313-9160
 Naperville (G-15798)
Baird Inc .................................................G..... 217 526-3407
 Morrisonville (G-15150)
Bergstrom Electrified Systems ..............G..... 815 874-7821
 Rockford (G-18282)
▲ Bergstrom Inc ....................................B..... 815 874-7821
 Rockford (G-18283)
▲ Bergstrom Parts LLC ........................G..... 815 874-7821
 Rockford (G-18284)
Black-Jack Grout Pumps Inc ................G..... 815 494-2904
 Rockford (G-18286)
Bonnell Industries Inc ............................G..... 815 284-3819
 Dixon (G-8323)
Brave Products Inc ................................G..... 815 672-0551
 Streator (G-20684)
Brunner & Lay Inc ..................................C..... 847 678-3232
 Elmhurst (G-9843)
Byron Blacktop Inc .................................G..... 815 234-8115
 Byron (G-2914)
▲ C S O Corp .........................................E..... 630 365-6600
 Virgil (G-21302)
Caterpillar Global Mining LLC ...............G..... 618 378-3441
 Norris City (G-16112)
◆ Caterpillar Inc ...................................A..... 309 675-1000
 Peoria (G-17326)
Caterpillar Inc ........................................B..... 815 729-5511
 Joliet (G-12471)
Caterpillar Inc ........................................A..... 630 859-5000
 Montgomery (G-15036)
Caterpillar Inc ........................................B..... 309 675-1000
 East Peoria (G-8704)
Caterpillar Inc ........................................B..... 815 584-4887
 Dwight (G-8588)
Caterpillar Inc ........................................G..... 309 675-5681
 Peoria (G-17327)
Caterpillar Inc ........................................B..... 309 578-2086
 Washington (G-21380)
Caterpillar Inc ........................................B..... 217 424-1809
 Decatur (G-7854)
Caterpillar Inc ........................................B..... 309 266-4294
 Mossville (G-15248)
Caterpillar Inc ........................................B..... 903 712-4505
 Mossville (G-15249)
Caterpillar Inc ........................................B..... 888 614-4328
 Peoria (G-17328)
Caterpillar Inc ........................................A..... 309 578-2473
 Mossville (G-15250)
Caterpillar Inc ........................................E..... 309 675-1000
 Peoria (G-17330)
Caterpillar Inc ........................................B..... 309 578-8250
 Peoria (G-17331)
Caterpillar Inc ........................................B..... 309 675-1000
 Peoria (G-17332)
Caterpillar Inc ........................................B..... 309 494-0138
 East Peoria (G-8699)
Caterpillar Inc ........................................B..... 309 675-6590
 Peoria (G-17333)
Caterpillar Inc ........................................A..... 217 475-4000
 Decatur (G-7853)
▲ Caterpillar Luxembourg LLC ............G..... 309 675-1000
 Peoria (G-17334)
Caterpillar Power Systems ....................G..... 309 675-1000
 Peoria (G-17335)
Central Township Road & Bridge ..........G..... 618 704-5517
 Greenville (G-11390)
▼ Chartrand Equipment Co Inc ............G..... 618 853-2314
 Ellis Grove (G-9826)

Chicago Materials Corporation ..............E..... 630 257-5600
 Lemont (G-13232)
Clarke Equipment Company .................G..... 701 241-8700
 Woodridge (G-22461)
Cnh Industrial America LLC ..................E..... 706 629-5572
 Burr Ridge (G-2832)
▼ Coast Crane Company .....................C..... 847 215-6500
 Buffalo Grove (G-2674)
▲ Cougar Industries Inc .......................E..... 815 224-1200
 Peru (G-17506)
▼ CPM Co Inc .......................................E..... 815 385-7700
 McHenry (G-14490)
▲ CTS Advanced Materials LLC ..........E..... 630 226-9080
 Bolingbrook (G-2293)
Czarnik Precision Grinding Mch ............G..... 708 229-9639
 Oak Lawn (G-16614)
D & B Fabricators & Distrs ....................F..... 630 325-3811
 Lemont (G-13234)
Deere & Company ..................................A..... 309 765-8000
 Moline (G-14925)
Division 5 Metals Inc .............................G..... 815 901-5001
 Kirkland (G-12711)
Dlc Inc ....................................................F..... 224 567-8656
 Park Ridge (G-17190)
Doosan Infracore America Corp ............G..... 847 437-1010
 Elk Grove Village (G-9432)
Dover Europe Inc ...................................G..... 630 541-1540
 Downers Grove (G-8433)
Dun-Rite Tool & Machine Co .................E..... 815 758-5464
 Cortland (G-7388)
ED Etnyre & Co ......................................E..... 815 732-2116
 Oregon (G-16822)
▲ Eirich Machines Inc ..........................E..... 847 336-2444
 Gurnee (G-11446)
Engineered Fluid Pwr Con Cons ............G..... 815 332-3344
 Cherry Valley (G-3641)
◆ Etnyre International Ltd ...................B..... 815 732-2116
 Oregon (G-16823)
Flink Company .......................................E..... 815 673-4321
 Streator (G-20688)
◆ Flsmidth Pekin LLC ...........................D..... 309 347-3031
 Pekin (G-17263)
▲ Fluid Mnagement Operations LLC ....G..... 847 537-0880
 Wheeling (G-22056)
▲ G&D Intgrted Mfg Logistics Inc ........B..... 309 284-6700
 Morton (G-15160)
Gayton Enterprises LLC .........................G..... 847 462-4030
 Algonquin (G-391)
Gemtar Inc ..............................................G..... 618 548-1353
 Salem (G-19334)
Genesis III Inc ........................................E..... 815 537-7900
 Prophetstown (G-17769)
◆ Global Track Property USA Inc ........G..... 630 213-6863
 Bartlett (G-1350)
Harig Products Inc .................................F..... 847 695-1000
 Elgin (G-9057)
◆ Heico Companies LLC ......................F..... 312 419-8220
 Chicago (G-5068)
Henderson Products Inc ........................F..... 847 836-4996
 Gilberts (G-10921)
High Point Recovery Company ..............G..... 217 821-7777
 Toledo (G-20964)
Illinois Tool Works Inc ............................F..... 847 918-6473
 Libertyville (G-13337)
Inertia Machine Corporation ..................E..... 815 233-1619
 Freeport (G-10667)
▲ Interntional Eqp Solutions LLC ........D..... 630 570-6880
 Oak Brook (G-16526)
Interstate Mechanical Inc ......................G..... 312 961-9291
 Chicago (G-5227)
▲ Ism Machinery Incorporated ............G..... 847 231-8002
 Libertyville (G-13339)
Jamesons Asphalt Service ....................G..... 630 830-7266
 Streamwood (G-20659)
Jcb Inc ....................................................G..... 912 704-2995
 Aurora (G-1037)
John Deere AG Holdings Inc .................G..... 309 765-8000
 Moline (G-14946)
Jordan Services .....................................G..... 630 416-6701
 Lisle (G-13611)
Jrb Attachments LLC .............................G..... 319 378-3696
 Oak Brook (G-16529)
▲ K R Komarek Inc ...............................E..... 847 956-0060
 Wood Dale (G-22384)
Koflo Corporation ...................................F..... 847 516-3700
 Cary (G-3356)
◆ Komatsu America Corp .....................B..... 847 437-5800
 Rolling Meadows (G-18737)
◆ Kress Corporation .............................D..... 309 446-3395
 Brimfield (G-2547)

Kvd Enterprises LLC ....G....618 726-5114
O Fallon (G-16469)
L & N Structures Inc ....E....815 426-2164
Herscher (G-11759)
L T Properties Inc....G....217 423-8772
Decatur (G-7904)
▼ Lanco International Inc....B....708 596-5200
Hazel Crest (G-11709)
Lanigan Holdings LLC....F....708 596-5200
Hazel Crest (G-11710)
Lee Industries Inc....C....847 462-1865
Elk Grove Village (G-9590)
▲ Machine Solution Providers Inc....D....630 717-7040
Downers Grove (G-8481)
Maimin Technology Group Inc....E....847 263-8200
Gurnee (G-11468)
Manitou Americas Inc....G....262 334-9461
Belvidere (G-1769)
Marine Canada Acquisition....G....630 513-5809
Saint Charles (G-19215)
Mega International Ltd....G....309 764-5310
Moline (G-14956)
Mfs Holdings LLC....E....815 385-7700
McHenry (G-14532)
◆ Mi-Jack Products Inc....B....708 596-5200
Hazel Crest (G-11711)
Midwest Cnstr Svcs Inc Peoria....F....309 697-1000
Bartonville (G-1397)
Midwest Mixing Inc....G....708 422-8100
Chicago Ridge (G-7151)
Millstadt Township....G....618 476-3592
Millstadt (G-14831)
Mineral Products Inc....G....618 433-3150
Galatia (G-10712)
Mj Snyder Ironworks Inc....G....217 826-6440
Marshall (G-14326)
Mjmc Inc....E....708 596-5200
Hazel Crest (G-11713)
▲ National Tractor Parts Inc....E....630 552-4235
Plano (G-17668)
North Point Investments Inc....G....312 977-4386
Chicago (G-5935)
Omg Inc....E....630 228-8377
Addison (G-235)
Ovis Loader Attachments Inc....G....618 203-2757
Carbondale (G-3017)
▲ Paladin Brands International H....G....319 378-3696
Oak Brook (G-16554)
Paul Wever Construction Eqp Co....F....309 965-2005
Goodfield (G-11248)
Paver Protector Inc....G....630 488-0069
Gilberts (G-10931)
Peter Baker & Son Co....F....815 344-1640
Mc Henry (G-14462)
Pilot Township Road District....G....815 426-6221
Herscher (G-11761)
Pioneer Pavers Inc....G....847 833-9866
McHenry (G-14545)
Prella Technologies Inc....G....630 400-0626
Huntley (G-12168)
Prime Group Inc....G....312 922-3883
Chicago (G-6186)
Ramsplitter Log Splitters Inc....G....815 398-4726
Rockford (G-18547)
▲ Rdi Group Inc....C....630 773-4900
Itasca (G-12347)
Reload Sales Inc....E....618 588-2866
New Baden (G-15864)
▲ Rhino Tool Company....F....309 853-5555
Kewanee (G-12694)
▲ Ringwood Company....D....708 458-6000
Bedford Park (G-1579)
Roadsafe Traffic Systems Inc....G....217 629-7139
Riverton (G-18036)
Rockford Rigging Inc....G....309 263-0566
Morton (G-15180)
S & S Maintenance....G....815 725-9263
Wilmington (G-22277)
S&S Recovery....G....217 538-2206
Fillmore (G-10189)
Sauber Manufacturing Company....D....630 365-6600
Virgil (G-21303)
Sebens Backhoe Service Inc....G....217 762-7365
Monticello (G-15084)
Sibor Express Ltd....G....773 499-8707
La Grange (G-12745)
▼ Skyjack Equipment Inc....E....630 797-3299
Saint Charles (G-19263)
Skyjack Inc....G....630 262-0005
Saint Charles (G-19264)

Snook Equipment Crane Inc....G....815 223-0003
Joliet (G-12577)
◆ Speeco Incorporated....C....303 279-5544
Oregon (G-16832)
Spreader Inc....G....217 568-7219
Gifford (G-10910)
Steuben Township....F....309 208-7073
Sparland (G-20315)
Stevenson Sales & Service LLC....G....630 972-0330
Bolingbrook (G-2376)
Streator Asphalt Inc....G....815 426-2164
Herscher (G-11762)
Streator Asphalt Inc....G....815 672-8683
Streator (G-20703)
▲ Swenson Spreader LLC....C....815 393-4455
Lindenwood (G-13551)
T J S Equipment Inc....G....618 656-8046
Edwardsville (G-8816)
Teleweld Inc....F....815 672-4561
Streator (G-20707)
Terramac LLC....G....630 365-4800
Elburn (G-8914)
Tim Wallace Ldscp Sup Co Inc....F....630 759-6813
Bolingbrook (G-2379)
Troxel Industries Inc....E....217 431-8674
Tilton (G-20883)
U S Railway Services....G....708 468-8343
Tinley Park (G-20952)
Uesco Industries Inc....G....708 385-7700
Alsip (G-536)
▲ US Shredder Castings Group Inc....G....309 359-3151
Peoria (G-17474)
▲ USA Hoist Company Inc....E....815 740-1890
Crest Hill (G-7470)
USA Star Group of Company....G....773 456-6677
Chicago (G-6857)
Utica Terminal Inc....G....815 667-5131
Utica (G-21111)
▼ W N G S Inc....E....847 451-1224
Franklin Park (G-10625)
W R Grace & Co- Conn....F....708 458-9700
Chicago (G-6924)
Walter Payton Power Eqp LLC....E....708 656-7700
Riverdale (G-18027)
Washington URS Div....G....309 578-8113
Mossville (G-15255)
Wehrli Equipment Co Inc....F....630 717-4150
Naperville (G-15783)
West Lake Concrete & Rmdlg LLC....G....847 477-8667
Chicago (G-6960)
West Side Tractor Sales Co....E....815 961-3160
Rockford (G-18678)
Wille Bros Co....D....708 535-4101
Monee (G-15008)
Woods Equipment Company....D....815 732-2141
Oregon (G-16834)

## 3532 Mining Machinery & Eqpt

Alpha Services II Inc....E....618 997-9999
Marion (G-14252)
▲ American Equipment & Mch Inc....D....618 533-3857
Centralia (G-3404)
Braden Rock Bit....G....618 435-4519
Benton (G-2024)
Carroll International Corp....F....630 983-5979
Lake Forest (G-12890)
Caterpillar Globl Min Amer LLC....D....618 982-9000
Carrier Mills (G-3306)
◆ Centrifugal Services Inc....D....618 268-4850
Raleigh (G-17908)
◆ Diager USA Inc....G....630 762-8443
Saint Charles (G-19170)
▼ Drumbeaters of America Inc....F....630 365-5527
Elburn (G-8883)
◆ Dry Systems Technologies LLC....E....630 427-2051
Woodridge (G-22473)
Dry Systems Technologies LLC....F....618 658-3000
Vienna (G-21222)
Elgin Equipment Group LLC....G....630 434-7200
Downers Grove (G-8439)
◆ Elgin National Industries Inc....F....630 434-7200
Downers Grove (G-8440)
▲ Fibro Inc....F....815 229-1300
Rockford (G-18382)
Fox International Corp....F....773 465-3634
Chicago (G-4880)
Freedom Material Resources Inc....D....618 937-6415
West Frankfort (G-21808)
G&D Integrated Services Inc....E....309 284-6700
Morton (G-15159)

GE Fairchild Mining Equipment....D....618 559-3216
Du Quoin (G-8555)
▲ Gundlach Equipment Corporation....D....618 233-7208
Belleville (G-1633)
Hydra Fold Auger Inc....G....217 379-2614
Loda (G-13751)
Kennametal Inc....C....815 226-0650
Rockford (G-18454)
Komatsu America Corp....C....309 672-7000
Peoria (G-17397)
◆ Komatsu America Corp....B....847 437-5800
Rolling Meadows (G-18737)
Lashcon Inc....G....217 742-3186
Winchester (G-22281)
Logan Actuator Co....G....815 943-9500
Harvard (G-11640)
◆ Martin Engineering Company....C....309 852-2384
Neponset (G-15859)
Midwest Machine Tool Inc....G....815 427-8665
Saint Anne (G-19124)
O-Cedar Commercial....G....217 379-2377
Paxton (G-17240)
▲ Rend Lake Carbide Inc....G....618 438-0160
Benton (G-2039)
Roe Machine Inc....E....618 983-5524
West Frankfort (G-21817)
▲ Sollami Company....E....618 988-1521
Herrin (G-11755)
Terrasource Global Corporation....D....618 641-6985
Belleville (G-1678)
Townley Engrg & Mfg Co Inc....F....618 273-8271
Eldorado (G-8924)
▲ Wallace Auto Parts & Svcs Inc....E....618 268-4446
Raleigh (G-17912)

## 3533 Oil Field Machinery & Eqpt

Arid Technologies Inc....E....630 681-8500
Wheaton (G-21936)
Azcon Inc....F....815 548-7000
Sterling (G-20583)
Bartec Orb Inc....E....773 927-8600
Chicago (G-4051)
Big Als Machines Inc....G....618 963-2619
Enfield (G-9987)
Cortelyou Machine & Welding....G....618 592-3961
Oblong (G-16730)
Country Side Woodworking....F....217 543-4190
Arthur (G-890)
Dnow LP....G....618 842-9176
Fairfield (G-10139)
▲ Dover Artificial Lift Intl LLC....F....630 743-2563
Downers Grove (G-8430)
◆ Dover Corporation....C....630 541-1540
Downers Grove (G-8431)
Emerson Electric Co....E....312 803-4321
Chicago (G-4742)
FMC Subsea Service Inc....G....312 861-6174
Chicago (G-4864)
Gemtar Inc....G....618 548-1353
Salem (G-19334)
Green Investment Group Inc....G....618 465-7277
Alton (G-576)
H & H Drilling Co....G....618 529-3697
Carbondale (G-3008)
▼ Hutchens-Bit Service Inc....F....618 439-9485
Benton (G-2029)
Innerweld Cover Co....F....847 497-3009
Mundelein (G-15511)
▲ Maass Midwest Mfg Inc....E....847 669-5135
Huntley (G-12160)
Mueller Co LLC....E....217 423-4471
Decatur (G-7918)
Oil Filter Recyclers Inc....E....309 329-2131
Astoria (G-935)
Proppant Frac Sand LLC....G....815 942-2467
Morris (G-15128)
▲ Rend Lake Carbide Inc....G....618 438-0160
Benton (G-2039)
Robit Inc....G....708 667-7892
Chicago (G-6372)
Royal Brass Inc....G....618 439-6341
Benton (G-2040)
Squibb Tank Company....F....618 548-0141
Salem (G-19352)
Triad Oil Inc....G....815 485-9535
New Lenox (G-15923)
Trusty Warns Inc....E....630 766-9015
Wood Dale (G-22434)
U O P Equitec Services Inc....A....847 391-2000
Des Plaines (G-8288)

## 3534 Elevators & Moving Stairways

**Ace Action Elevator Services** ...G... 773 708-1666
Chicago *(G-3725)*

**Adams Elevator Equipment Co** ...E... 847 581-2900
Chicago *(G-3743)*

▲ **Bella Elevator LLC** ...F... 410 685-0344
Peoria *(G-17315)*

**Cabworks LLC** ...E... 773 588-1731
Chicago *(G-4209)*

**CJ Anderson & Company** ...E... 708 867-4002
Harwood Heights *(G-11683)*

**Colley Elevator Company** ...E... 630 766-7230
Bensenville *(G-1861)*

▼ **D A Matot Inc** ...D... 708 547-1888
Bellwood *(G-1702)*

**Dover Europe Inc** ...G... 630 541-1540
Downers Grove *(G-8433)*

▲ **Elevator Cable & Supply Co** ...E... 708 338-9700
Broadview *(G-2574)*

**Elevators USA Incorporated** ...G... 847 847-1856
Lake Zurich *(G-13068)*

**Fixture Company** ...G... 847 214-3100
Chicago *(G-4854)*

▲ **Formula Systems North America** ...G... 847 350-0655
Elk Grove Village *(G-9486)*

**Harris Companies Inc** ...F... 217 578-2231
Atwood *(G-947)*

▲ **Hollister-Whitney Elev Corp** ...C... 217 222-0466
Quincy *(G-17836)*

**Home Mobility Solutions Inc** ...G... 630 800-7800
Downers Grove *(G-8461)*

**Integrated Display Systems** ...F... 708 298-9661
Cicero *(G-7206)*

**Kafka Manufacturing Co** ...G... 708 771-0970
Forest Park *(G-10250)*

▲ **Kone Elevator** ...C... 309 764-6771
Moline *(G-14950)*

▲ **Kone Inc** ...A... 630 577-1650
Lisle *(G-13614)*

**Kone Inc** ...C... 309 945-4961
Coal Valley *(G-7297)*

**Lifts of Illinois Inc** ...G... 309 923-7450
Roanoke *(G-18052)*

**Long Elevator and Mch Co Inc** ...D... 217 629-9648
Springfield *(G-20472)*

▲ **Mid-American Elevator Co Inc** ...C... 773 486-6900
Chicago *(G-5727)*

**Mid-American Elevator Co Inc** ...E... 815 740-1204
Joliet *(G-12541)*

**Mitsubishi Electric Us Inc** ...E... 708 354-2900
Countryside *(G-7439)*

**North Shore Stairs** ...G... 847 295-7906
Lake Bluff *(G-12859)*

**Otis Elevator Company** ...D... 312 454-1616
Chicago *(G-6023)*

**Otis Elevator Company** ...F... 618 529-3411
Carbondale *(G-3016)*

**Phoenix Modular Elevator Inc** ...F... 618 244-2314
Mount Vernon *(G-15441)*

▲ **Quality Elevator Products Inc** ...E... 847 581-0085
Niles *(G-16023)*

**Thyssenkrupp Elevator Corp** ...D... 312 733-8025
Chicago *(G-6724)*

**United Technologies Corp** ...B... 815 226-6000
Rockford *(G-18663)*

◆ **Vator Accessories Inc** ...G... 630 876-8370
West Chicago *(G-21788)*

## 3535 Conveyors & Eqpt

**Acro Magnetics Inc** ...G... 815 943-5018
Harvard *(G-11617)*

**Align Production Systems LLC** ...E... 217 423-6001
Decatur *(G-7830)*

▲ **Astec Mobile Screens Inc** ...C... 815 626-6374
Sterling *(G-20582)*

**Automatic Feeder Company Inc** ...F... 847 534-2300
Schaumburg *(G-19450)*

◆ **Automotion Inc** ...C... 708 229-3700
Oak Lawn *(G-16605)*

**Avasarala Inc** ...G... 847 969-0630
Palatine *(G-17004)*

**Bankmark Inc** ...F... 847 683-9834
Hampshire *(G-11542)*

**Barrington Automation Ltd** ...E... 847 458-0900
Lake In The Hills *(G-12987)*

▼ **Barry-Whmller Cont Systems Inc** ...C... 630 759-6800
Romeoville *(G-18802)*

▼ **Birnberg Machinery Inc** ...G... 847 673-5242
Skokie *(G-19964)*

**Bost Corporation** ...E... 708 344-7023
Maywood *(G-14420)*

**Canconex Inc** ...F... 847 458-9955
Algonquin *(G-382)*

**Central Manufacturing Company** ...G... 309 387-6591
East Peoria *(G-8705)*

**Chicago Can Conveyor Corp** ...G... 708 430-0988
Bridgeview *(G-2476)*

**Chicago Chain and Transm Co** ...E... 630 482-9000
Countryside *(G-7417)*

**Cmd Conveyor Inc** ...E... 708 237-0996
Chicago Ridge *(G-7144)*

**Confab Systems Inc** ...F... 708 388-4103
Posen *(G-17728)*

**Container Hdlg Systems Corp** ...E... 708 482-9900
Countryside *(G-7418)*

**Container Service Group Inc** ...F... 815 744-8693
Rockdale *(G-18218)*

**Conveyor Installations Inc** ...F... 630 859-8900
Batavia *(G-1433)*

**Conveyors Plus Inc** ...G... 708 361-1512
Orland Park *(G-16849)*

**Cosveyor Inc** ...F... 630 859-8900
Batavia *(G-1434)*

**Custom Machinery Inc** ...G... 847 678-3033
Schiller Park *(G-19818)*

**Dematic Corp** ...F... 630 852-9200
Lisle *(G-13583)*

**Deyco Inc** ...G... 630 553-5666
Yorkville *(G-22656)*

**Diversatech Metalfab LLC** ...E... 309 747-4159
Gridley *(G-11404)*

**Diversified Fleet MGT Inc** ...E... 815 578-1051
McHenry *(G-14496)*

▲ **Dover Artificial Lift Intl LLC** ...F... 630 743-2563
Downers Grove *(G-8430)*

**Dspc Company** ...E... 815 997-1116
Rockford *(G-18353)*

**Duravant** ...G... 630 635-3910
Downers Grove *(G-8436)*

◆ **Duravant LLC** ...F... 630 635-3910
Downers Grove *(G-8437)*

**Eaglestone Inc** ...F... 630 587-1115
Saint Charles *(G-19177)*

▲ **Eirich Machines Inc** ...D... 847 336-2444
Gurnee *(G-11446)*

**Engineered Plumbing Spc LLC** ...E... 630 682-1555
Joliet *(G-12491)*

**Engineering Products Company** ...G... 815 436-9055
Plainfield *(G-17595)*

**Erect - O -Veyor Corporation** ...F... 630 766-1200
Franklin Park *(G-10465)*

▲ **Ewab Engineering Inc** ...E... 847 247-0015
Libertyville *(G-13321)*

**Forbo Siegling LLC** ...F... 630 595-4031
Wood Dale *(G-22370)*

▲ **Forte Automation Systems Inc** ...E... 815 316-6247
Machesney Park *(G-14076)*

**Frantz Manufacturing Company** ...D... 815 564-0991
Sterling *(G-20593)*

**Gammerler US Corp** ...E... 941 465-4400
Mount Prospect *(G-15332)*

**GE Fairchild Mining Equipment** ...D... 618 559-3216
Du Quoin *(G-8555)*

**GMI Packaging Co** ...E... 734 972-7389
Chicago *(G-4965)*

**Gsi Group LLC** ...C... 217 463-1612
Paris *(G-17148)*

**Icon Co** ...G... 630 545-2345
Glen Ellyn *(G-10973)*

▼ **Industrial Kinetics Inc** ...E... 630 655-0300
Downers Grove *(G-8466)*

▲ **Industrial Motion Control LLC** ...C... 847 459-5200
Wheeling *(G-22076)*

**Intelligrated Systems Inc** ...B... 630 985-4350
Woodridge *(G-22495)*

**J W Todd Co** ...G... 630 406-5715
Aurora *(G-1173)*

**Joy Technologies Inc** ...E... 618 242-3650
Mount Vernon *(G-15419)*

**Kamflex Conveyor Corporation** ...G... 630 682-1555
Joliet *(G-12526)*

**Kanetic Inc** ...E... 847 382-9922
Lake Barrington *(G-12816)*

**Kelly Systems Inc** ...E... 312 733-3224
Chicago *(G-5374)*

**Kimco USA Inc** ...F... 800 788-1133
Marshall *(G-14325)*

▲ **Kongskilde Industries Inc** ...C... 309 452-3300
Hudson *(G-12124)*

**Krygier Design Inc** ...F... 620 766-1001
Wood Dale *(G-22387)*

▲ **L M C Inc** ...G... 815 758-3514
Dekalb *(G-8101)*

**Lake Fabrication Inc** ...G... 217 832-2761
Villa Grove *(G-21229)*

▲ **Loma International Inc** ...D... 630 588-0900
Carol Stream *(G-3186)*

**Loop Belt Industries Inc** ...G... 630 469-1300
Glen Ellyn *(G-10978)*

**Machinex Technologies Inc** ...D... 773 867-8801
Chicago *(G-5593)*

▲ **Mallard Handling Solutions LLC** ...E... 815 625-9491
Sterling *(G-20596)*

**Marvco Tool & Manufacturing** ...G... 847 437-4900
Elk Grove Village *(G-9612)*

**Matrix Design LLC** ...D... 847 841-8260
South Elgin *(G-20217)*

**Measured Plastics Inc** ...G... 815 939-4408
Bourbonnais *(G-2402)*

**Mid States Corporation** ...E... 708 754-1760
S Chicago Hts *(G-19109)*

▲ **Mid-American Elevator Co Inc** ...C... 773 486-6900
Chicago *(G-5727)*

**Mid-American Elevator Co Inc** ...E... 815 740-1204
Joliet *(G-12541)*

**Morrison Timing Screw Company** ...D... 708 331-6600
Glenwood *(G-11219)*

▲ **Neuero Corporation** ...F... 630 231-9020
West Chicago *(G-21750)*

**Panasonic Corp North America** ...C... 847 637-9700
Buffalo Grove *(G-2750)*

**Payson Casters Inc** ...C... 847 336-5033
Gurnee *(G-11483)*

**Pre Pack Machinery Inc** ...G... 217 352-1010
Champaign *(G-3528)*

**Precision Conveyor and Erct Co** ...F... 779 324-5269
Frankfort *(G-10350)*

**Quantum Services Inc** ...G... 815 230-5893
Joliet *(G-12561)*

**Roll-A-Way Conveyors Inc** ...G... 847 336-5033
Gurnee *(G-11500)*

◆ **Rotec Industries Inc** ...D... 630 279-3300
Hampshire *(G-11561)*

▲ **RPS Engineering Inc** ...F... 847 931-1950
Elgin *(G-9168)*

◆ **Rwi Manufacturing Inc** ...C... 800 277-1699
Aurora *(G-1212)*

**SA Nat Industrial Cnstr Co Inc** ...E... 618 246-9402
Mount Vernon *(G-15443)*

▲ **Sardee Industries Inc** ...G... 630 824-4200
Lisle *(G-13654)*

◆ **SBS Steel Belt Systems USA Inc** ...F... 847 841-3300
Gilberts *(G-10935)*

▼ **Smart Motion Robotics Inc** ...E... 815 895-8550
Sycamore *(G-20817)*

**Special Tool Engineering Co** ...F... 773 767-6690
Chicago *(G-6554)*

▲ **Stanford Bettendorf Inc** ...D... 618 548-3555
Salem *(G-19353)*

**Superior Industries Inc** ...A... 309 346-1742
Pekin *(G-17290)*

**Total Conveyor Services Inc** ...G... 630 860-2471
Bensenville *(G-2005)*

**Tracoinsa USA** ...G... 309 287-7046
Gridley *(G-11411)*

**Translogic Corporation** ...F... 847 392-3700
Rolling Meadows *(G-18784)*

◆ **Tricon Inds Mfg & Eqp Sls** ...E... 815 379-2090
Walnut *(G-21331)*

▲ **United Conveyor Corporation** ...C... 847 473-5900
Waukegan *(G-21635)*

**United Systems Incorporated** ...F... 708 479-1450
Mokena *(G-14914)*

**US Conveyor Tech Mfg Inc** ...E... 309 359-4088
Mackinaw *(G-14119)*

◆ **US Conveyor Technologies** ...F... 309 359-4088
Mackinaw *(G-14120)*

**V & C Converters** ...G... 708 251-5635
Lansing *(G-13191)*

**Wes-Tech Automtn Solutions LLC** ...D... 847 541-5070
Buffalo Grove *(G-2794)*

▲ **William W Meyer and Sons** ...D... 847 918-0111
Libertyville *(G-13402)*

▲ **Witron Intgrated Logistics Inc** ...C... 847 398-6130
Arlington Heights *(G-873)*

▲ **Wynright Corporation** ...D... 847 595-9400
Elk Grove Village *(G-9819)*



Employee Codes: A=Over 500 employees, B=251-500
C=101-250, D=51-100, E=20-50, F=10-19, G=3-9

2017 Harris Illinois
Industrial Directory

1059

## 35 INDUSTRIAL AND COMMERCIAL MACHINERY AND COMPUTER EQUIPMENT

### 3536 Hoists, Cranes & Monorails

| Company | Code | Phone |
|---|---|---|
| ▲ Aldon Co | F | 847 623-8800 |
| Waukegan (G-21521) | | |
| Bucket Mart Inc | G | 813 390-8626 |
| Marion (G-14256) | | |
| Columbus McKinnon Corporation | C | 800 548-2930 |
| Eureka (G-9995) | | |
| Columbus McKinnon Corporation | G | 630 783-2188 |
| Woodridge (G-22462) | | |
| Columbus McKinnon Corporation | E | 630 783-1195 |
| Woodridge (G-22463) | | |
| Crane Equipment & Services Inc | E | 309 467-6262 |
| Eureka (G-9996) | | |
| ▲ G K Enterprises Inc | G | 708 587-2150 |
| Monee (G-14996) | | |
| Gemtar Inc | G | 618 548-1353 |
| Salem (G-19334) | | |
| ▲ Gh Cranes Corporation | G | 815 277-5328 |
| Frankfort (G-10325) | | |
| H & B Machine Corporation | G | 312 829-4850 |
| Chicago (G-5017) | | |
| Handling Systems Inc | E | 708 352-1213 |
| La Grange (G-12735) | | |
| Hyster Co | G | 217 443-7000 |
| Danville (G-7735) | | |
| ▼ Lanco International Inc | B | 708 596-5200 |
| Hazel Crest (G-11709) | | |
| ▼ Lift Systems Inc | D | 309 764-9842 |
| East Moline (G-8686) | | |
| Liftex Corporation | E | 847 782-0572 |
| Gurnee (G-11467) | | |
| Logan Actuator Co | G | 815 943-9500 |
| Harvard (G-11640) | | |
| ▲ Manitex International Inc | C | 708 430-7500 |
| Bridgeview (G-2506) | | |
| ▲ Matcon Usa Inc | F | 856 256-1330 |
| Elmhurst (G-9908) | | |
| Peerless Chain Company | E | 708 339-0545 |
| South Holland (G-20297) | | |
| Ramseys Machine Co | G | 217 824-2320 |
| Taylorville (G-20845) | | |
| Sievert Electric Svc & Sls Co | D | 708 771-1600 |
| Forest Park (G-10253) | | |
| Uesco Industries Inc | E | 800 325-8372 |
| Alsip (G-537) | | |
| Uesco Industries Inc | G | 708 385-7700 |
| Alsip (G-536) | | |
| ▲ Vector Engineering & Mfg Corp | E | 708 474-3900 |
| Lansing (G-13192) | | |
| ◆ Whiting Corporation | C | 708 587-2000 |
| Monee (G-15007) | | |
| WW Engineering Company LLC | F | 773 376-9494 |
| Chicago (G-7042) | | |
| Zg3 Systems LLC | G | 309 745-3398 |
| Washington (G-21397) | | |

### 3537 Indl Trucks, Tractors, Trailers & Stackers

| Company | Code | Phone |
|---|---|---|
| A Lift Above Inc | G | 630 758-1023 |
| Elmhurst (G-9829) | | |
| A1 Skilled Staffing | E | 309 281-1400 |
| East Moline (G-8669) | | |
| ▲ AAR Corp | D | 630 227-2000 |
| Wood Dale (G-22328) | | |
| Aidar Express Inc | G | 773 757-3447 |
| Chicago (G-3785) | | |
| Align Production Systems LLC | E | 217 423-6001 |
| Decatur (G-7830) | | |
| ▲ All-Vac Industries Inc | F | 847 675-2290 |
| Skokie (G-19948) | | |
| Always There Express Corp | E | 773 931-3744 |
| Downers Grove (G-8386) | | |
| ◆ Anthony Liftgates Inc | G | 815 842-3383 |
| Pontiac (G-17696) | | |
| Barnes Industrial Equipment | G | 630 213-9240 |
| Streamwood (G-20645) | | |
| ▲ Big Lift LLC | F | 630 916-2600 |
| Lombard (G-13768) | | |
| Blue Nile Trucking LLC | G | 618 215-1077 |
| East Saint Louis (G-8745) | | |
| ▲ Bolzoni Auramo Inc | E | 708 957-8809 |
| Homewood (G-12092) | | |
| ▲ Brennan Equipment and Mfg Inc | D | 708 534-5500 |
| University Park (G-21046) | | |
| C C P Express Inc | G | 773 315-0317 |
| Berwyn (G-2058) | | |
| Caples-El Transport Inc | G | 708 300-2727 |
| Calumet City (G-2936) | | |
| Caterpillar Inc | A | 630 859-5000 |
| Montgomery (G-15036) | | |
| Centralia Machine & Fab Inc | G | 618 533-9010 |
| Centralia (G-3406) | | |
| Chevron Commercial Inc | G | 618 654-5555 |
| Highland (G-11779) | | |
| Chicago Pallet Service Inc | E | 847 439-8330 |
| Maywood (G-14423) | | |
| Cif Industries Inc | F | 618 635-2010 |
| Staunton (G-20556) | | |
| Clark Caster Co | G | 708 366-1913 |
| Forest Park (G-10238) | | |
| Conveyors Plus Inc | G | 708 361-1512 |
| Orland Park (G-16849) | | |
| Crown Equipment Corporation | C | 847 397-1900 |
| Schaumburg (G-19492) | | |
| Crown Equipment Corporation | C | 815 773-0022 |
| Joliet (G-12479) | | |
| Crown Equipment Corporation | F | 309 663-9200 |
| Bloomington (G-2157) | | |
| Daco Products LLC | G | 630 373-2245 |
| North Aurora (G-16125) | | |
| ▲ Dfk America Inc | G | 630 324-6793 |
| Downers Grove (G-8427) | | |
| Dicom Transportation Group LP | G | 312 255-4800 |
| Chicago (G-4596) | | |
| ED Etnyre & Co | B | 815 732-2116 |
| Oregon (G-16822) | | |
| Edward J Warren Jr | G | 630 882-8817 |
| Yorkville (G-22657) | | |
| ▲ Ezee Roll Manufacturing Co | G | 217 339-2279 |
| Hoopeston (G-12110) | | |
| F and S Enterprises Plainfield | G | 815 439-9655 |
| Plainfield (G-17597) | | |
| Frahtex Inc | G | 773 796-7914 |
| Chicago (G-4882) | | |
| Freight Car Services Inc | B | 217 443-4106 |
| Danville (G-7722) | | |
| Grand Specialties Co | G | 630 629-8000 |
| Oak Brook (G-16520) | | |
| Grant J Grapperhaus | G | 618 410-4428 |
| Highland (G-11786) | | |
| Green Valley Mfg III Inc | G | 217 864-4125 |
| Mount Zion (G-15452) | | |
| H & B Machine Corporation | G | 312 829-4850 |
| Chicago (G-5017) | | |
| H R Slater Co Inc | F | 312 666-1855 |
| Chicago (G-5023) | | |
| Handling Systems Inc | E | 708 352-1213 |
| La Grange (G-12735) | | |
| Henderson Products Inc | G | 847 515-3482 |
| Huntley (G-12144) | | |
| Hendrickson Usa LLC | C | 630 874-9700 |
| Itasca (G-12274) | | |
| ◆ Hoist Liftruck Mfg Inc | E | 708 458-2200 |
| Bedford Park (G-1555) | | |
| ◆ Holland Applied Technologies | E | 630 325-5130 |
| Burr Ridge (G-2851) | | |
| Hyster-Yale Group Inc | G | 217 443-7416 |
| Danville (G-7736) | | |
| ▼ I80 Equipment LLC | F | 309 949-3701 |
| Colona (G-7343) | | |
| ◆ Illinois Lift Equipment Inc | G | 888 745-0577 |
| West Chicago (G-21717) | | |
| Integrity Material Hdlg Svcs | G | 847 669-6233 |
| Huntley (G-12150) | | |
| Interstate Cargo Inc | E | 630 701-7744 |
| Bolingbrook (G-2324) | | |
| It Transportation Company | F | 773 383-5073 |
| Chicago (G-5245) | | |
| J W Todd Co | G | 630 406-5715 |
| Aurora (G-1173) | | |
| Jcb Inc | G | 912 704-2995 |
| Aurora (G-1037) | | |
| ▲ Jeffrey Elevator Co Inc | F | 847 524-2400 |
| Schaumburg (G-19587) | | |
| John Bean Technologies Corp | E | 312 861-5900 |
| Chicago (G-5310) | | |
| ▲ Komatsu Forklift USA LLC | F | 847 437-5800 |
| Rolling Meadows (G-18738) | | |
| ▼ Lanco International Inc | B | 708 596-5200 |
| Hazel Crest (G-11709) | | |
| Lexpress Inc | G | 773 517-7095 |
| Prospect Heights (G-17783) | | |
| ▼ Littell LLC | E | 630 916-6662 |
| Schaumburg (G-19620) | | |
| Loso Trucking Inc | G | 312 601-2231 |
| Chicago (G-5546) | | |
| M&J Hauling Inc | G | 312 342-6596 |
| Chicago (G-5590) | | |
| Mailbox International Inc | G | 847 541-8466 |
| Wheeling (G-22097) | | |
| Majesty Cases Inc | E | 847 546-2558 |
| Ingleside (G-12193) | | |
| ▲ Manitex International Inc | C | 708 430-7500 |
| Bridgeview (G-2506) | | |
| Marcells Pallet Inc | G | 773 265-1200 |
| Chicago (G-5612) | | |
| Marvel Industries Incorporated | G | 847 325-2930 |
| Buffalo Grove (G-2732) | | |
| Mh Equipment Company | D | 217 443-7210 |
| Danville (G-7755) | | |
| MHS Ltd | F | 773 736-3333 |
| Chicago (G-5716) | | |
| Midaco Corporation | G | 847 593-8420 |
| Elk Grove Village (G-9626) | | |
| Mike Simon Trucking LLC | G | 618 659-8755 |
| Edwardsville (G-8809) | | |
| ▲ Neuero Corporation | F | 630 231-9020 |
| West Chicago (G-21750) | | |
| New Cie Inc | E | 815 224-1511 |
| Peru (G-17522) | | |
| ▲ Pallet Repair Systems Inc | F | 217 291-0009 |
| Jacksonville (G-12406) | | |
| Pools Welding Inc | G | 309 787-2083 |
| Milan (G-14798) | | |
| Preflight LLC | G | 312 935-2804 |
| Chicago (G-6176) | | |
| Pwf | G | 815 967-0218 |
| Rockford (G-18545) | | |
| Sam Solutions Inc | G | 708 594-0480 |
| Summit Argo (G-20765) | | |
| ▲ Sardee Industries Inc | G | 630 824-4200 |
| Lisle (G-13654) | | |
| ▲ Schaeff Lift Truck Inc | E | 708 430-5301 |
| Bridgeview (G-2527) | | |
| Scott Janczak | G | 773 545-7233 |
| Chicago (G-6460) | | |
| Spec Check LLC | G | 773 270-0003 |
| Mundelein (G-15559) | | |
| Specialized Liftruck Svcs LLC | E | 708 552-2705 |
| Bedford Park (G-1585) | | |
| STI Holdings Inc | F | 630 789-2713 |
| Burr Ridge (G-2882) | | |
| Superior Truck Dock Services | G | 630 978-1697 |
| Aurora (G-1083) | | |
| ▼ Swingmaster Corporation | E | 847 451-1224 |
| Franklin Park (G-10601) | | |
| Synergy Power Group LLC | E | 618 247-3200 |
| Sandoval (G-19359) | | |
| Systems Equipment Services | G | 708 535-1273 |
| Oak Forest (G-16590) | | |
| T & E Enterprises Herscher Inc | F | 815 426-2761 |
| Herscher (G-11763) | | |
| Tarnow Logistics Inc | G | 773 844-3203 |
| Melrose Park (G-14700) | | |
| Tdr Express Inc | G | 224 805-0070 |
| Chicago (G-6760) | | |
| Tewell Bros Machine Inc | F | 217 253-6303 |
| Tuscola (G-21025) | | |
| Transco Railway Products Inc | D | 419 562-1031 |
| Chicago (G-6760) | | |
| Transfer Logistics Inc | G | 773 646-0529 |
| Chicago (G-6761) | | |
| Tri County Lift Trucks Inc | E | 847 838-0183 |
| Antioch (G-659) | | |
| ◆ Tri-Cam Inc | F | 815 226-9200 |
| Rockford (G-18656) | | |
| Triad Trucking LLC | G | 847 833-9276 |
| Elk Grove Village (G-9792) | | |
| Triple B Manufacturing Co Inc | G | 618 566-2888 |
| Mascoutah (G-14360) | | |
| Tvh Parts Co | E | 847 223-1000 |
| Grayslake (G-11365) | | |
| Twin Mills Timber & Tie Co Inc | E | 618 932-3662 |
| West Frankfort (G-21821) | | |
| ◆ Unicarriers Americas Corp | B | 800 871-5438 |
| Marengo (G-14244) | | |
| Universal Feeder Inc | G | 815 633-0752 |
| Machesney Park (G-14116) | | |
| ▼ Upstaging Inc | C | 815 899-9888 |
| Sycamore (G-20822) | | |
| ◆ Vactor Manufacturing Inc | A | 815 672-3171 |
| Streator (G-20710) | | |
| Wastequip Saint Louis | E | 216 292-0625 |
| East Saint Louis (G-8776) | | |
| ▲ William W Meyer and Sons | D | 847 918-0111 |
| Libertyville (G-13402) | | |
| Yes Equipment & Services LLC | G | 866 799-7743 |
| Itasca (G-12376) | | |
| Yusraa Inc | G | 312 608-1916 |
| Dolton (G-8378) | | |

# SIC SECTION
## 35 INDUSTRIAL AND COMMERCIAL MACHINERY AND COMPUTER EQUIPMENT

### 3541 Machine Tools: Cutting

▲ 1883 Properties Inc .................D....... 847 537-8800
  Lincolnshire *(G-13422)*
A&W Tool Inc ..............................G....... 815 653-1700
  Ringwood *(G-17986)*
Abbco Inc ....................................E....... 630 595-7115
  Elk Grove Village *(G-9253)*
Above & Beyond Black Oxiding ..........G....... 708 345-7100
  Melrose Park *(G-14581)*
ABRA Enterprises Inc ..................G....... 847 866-6903
  Evanston *(G-10001)*
AC Precision Tool Inc .................G....... 630 797-5161
  Saint Charles *(G-19131)*
Accelrted Mch Design Engrg LLC .......F....... 815 316-6381
  Rockford *(G-18251)*
Acsys Lasertechnik US Inc ...........G....... 224 699-9572
  Elgin *(G-8934)*
ADK Arms Inc ............................G....... 847 981-9800
  Elk Grove Village *(G-9273)*
ADS LLC .....................................D....... 256 430-3366
  Burr Ridge *(G-2820)*
▼ Advanced Machine & Engrg Co .......C....... 815 962-6076
  Rockford *(G-18257)*
AG Precision Inc ........................G....... 847 724-7786
  Glenview *(G-11098)*
Air Mite Devices Inc ....................E....... 224 338-0071
  Round Lake *(G-19051)*
Alliance Tool & Manufacturing .......F....... 708 345-5444
  Maywood *(G-14415)*
▼ American Machine Tools Inc .......G....... 773 775-6285
  Chicago *(G-3861)*
Automatic Production Equipment .....G....... 847 439-1448
  Elk Grove Village *(G-9321)*
B & B Machine Inc ......................G....... 309 786-3279
  Rock Island *(G-18160)*
Belcar Products Inc ....................G....... 630 462-1950
  Carol Stream *(G-3113)*
Belden Machine Corporation .........F....... 708 344-4600
  Broadview *(G-2561)*
▲ Bertsche Engineering Corp ........F....... 847 537-8757
  Buffalo Grove *(G-2664)*
Beverly Shear Mfg Corporation ......G....... 773 233-2063
  Chicago *(G-4098)*
Bilz Tool Company ......................F....... 630 495-3996
  Lombard *(G-13770)*
Blackhawk Industrial Dist Inc .......F....... 773 736-9600
  Carol Stream *(G-3117)*
▲ Bley LLC ................................D....... 847 290-0117
  Elk Grove Village *(G-9344)*
Bos Machine Tool Services Inc .....F....... 309 658-2223
  Hillsdale *(G-11901)*
Bourn & Bourn Inc .....................C....... 815 965-4013
  Rockford *(G-18289)*
▲ Bourn & Koch Inc ...................D....... 815 965-4013
  Rockford *(G-18290)*
Branson Ultrasonics Corp ............G....... 847 229-0800
  Buffalo Grove *(G-2669)*
▲ Bystronic Inc ..........................C....... 847 214-0300
  Elgin *(G-8974)*
C D T Manufacturing Inc .............G....... 847 679-2361
  Skokie *(G-19972)*
Cdv Corp ....................................F....... 815 397-3903
  Rockford *(G-18300)*
CH Machining Company ..............G....... 630 595-1050
  Bensenville *(G-1856)*
Chad Mazeika .............................G....... 815 298-8118
  Rockford *(G-18303)*
Charlotte Dmg Inc ......................G....... 630 227-3900
  Itasca *(G-12243)*
Chicago Cnc Machining Co ..........G....... 708 352-1255
  Hodgkins *(G-11972)*
Chicago Grinding & Machine Co ....E....... 708 343-4399
  Melrose Park *(G-14610)*
Circle Cutting Tools Inc ...............G....... 815 398-4153
  Rockford *(G-18310)*
Composite Cutter Tech Inc ..........G....... 847 740-6875
  Volo *(G-21311)*
Condor Machine Tool ..................G....... 773 767-5985
  Chicago *(G-4447)*
Crown Tool Company Inc .............G....... 630 766-3050
  Bensenville *(G-1872)*
Crw Finishing .............................E....... 630 495-4994
  Addison *(G-84)*
Ctc Machine Service Inc .............G....... 630 876-5120
  West Chicago *(G-21688)*
Custom Cutting Tools Inc ............G....... 815 986-0320
  Loves Park *(G-13931)*
Custom Tool Inc .........................F....... 217 465-8538
  Paris *(G-17145)*

Cutting Tool Innovations Inc .......G....... 630 766-4839
  Bensenville *(G-1877)*
▲ Dainichi Machinery Inc ............G....... 630 681-1572
  Carol Stream *(G-3139)*
Dearborn Tool & Mfg Inc .............E....... 630 655-1260
  Burr Ridge *(G-2836)*
Del-Co-West Inc .........................F....... 309 799-7543
  Milan *(G-14783)*
Diamond Edge Manufacturing ......G....... 630 458-1630
  Addison *(G-89)*
▲ Dmg Charlotte LLC ..................F....... 704 583-1193
  Hoffman Estates *(G-12005)*
▲ Dmg Mori Usa Inc ...................D....... 847 593-5400
  Hoffman Estates *(G-12006)*
Dynamic Automation Inc .............G....... 312 782-8555
  Lincolnwood *(G-13508)*
E H Wachs ..................................G....... 815 943-4785
  Lincolnshire *(G-13446)*
Edmpartscom Inc ........................G....... 630 427-1603
  Darien *(G-7794)*
▲ Electron Beam Technologies Inc ..C....... 815 935-2211
  Kankakee *(G-12612)*
Emhart Teknologies LLC ..............F....... 877 364-2781
  Chicago *(G-4743)*
Endofix Ltd ................................G....... 708 715-3472
  Brookfield *(G-2631)*
◆ Engineered Abrasives Inc .........E....... 662 582-4143
  Alsip *(G-462)*
Engineered Mills Inc ...................G....... 847 548-0044
  Grayslake *(G-11335)*
▲ Engis Corporation ...................C....... 847 808-9400
  Wheeling *(G-22047)*
Extrude Hone LLC .......................E....... 847 669-5355
  Huntley *(G-12139)*
Fives Landis Corp .......................D....... 815 389-2251
  South Beloit *(G-20146)*
Folkerts Manufacturing Inc .........G....... 815 968-7426
  Rockford *(G-18385)*
Fordoc Incorporated ...................G....... 708 452-8400
  River Grove *(G-18009)*
Form Relief Tool Co Inc ..............F....... 815 393-4263
  Davis Junction *(G-7812)*
Gail E Stephens .........................G....... 618 372-0140
  Brighton *(G-2540)*
Glaser USA Inc ..........................G....... 847 362-7878
  Lake Forest *(G-12901)*
▲ Greenlee Textron Inc ...............D....... 815 397-7070
  Rockford *(G-18405)*
▲ Grindal Company .....................E....... 630 250-8950
  Itasca *(G-12273)*
Gymtek Incorporated ..................G....... 815 547-0771
  Belvidere *(G-1760)*
Harris Precision Tools Inc ..........G....... 708 422-5808
  Chicago Ridge *(G-7149)*
Hartland Cutting Tools Inc ..........F....... 847 639-9400
  Cary *(G-3350)*
Hausermann Abrading Process Co ..F....... 630 543-6688
  Addison *(G-142)*
Hfd Manufacturing Inc ................G....... 847 263-5050
  Waukegan *(G-21568)*
Hi-Tech Manufacturing LLC .........G....... 847 678-1616
  Schiller Park *(G-19836)*
Hobsource ..................................G....... 847 229-9120
  Mount Prospect *(G-15335)*
▲ Hoffman J&M Farm Holdings Inc ..D....... 847 671-6280
  Schiller Park *(G-19838)*
◆ Holden Industries Inc ..............F....... 847 940-1500
  Deerfield *(G-8013)*
Honor Med Maskiner Corp ...........G....... 847 741-9400
  Elgin *(G-9066)*
Hottinger Bldwin Msrements Inc ...E....... 217 328-5359
  Champaign *(G-3495)*
Huml Industries Inc ....................G....... 847 426-8061
  Gilberts *(G-10923)*
Hyundai Wia Machine Amer Corp ..E....... 201 636-5600
  Itasca *(G-12277)*
I-N-I Machining Inc ....................G....... 309 496-1002
  East Moline *(G-8682)*
Ibanum Manufacturing LLC .........G....... 815 262-5373
  Rockford *(G-18425)*
Illinois Broaching Co ..................G....... 847 678-3080
  Schiller Park *(G-19840)*
Illinois Electro Deburring Co .......F....... 847 678-5010
  Franklin Park *(G-10494)*
◆ Ingersoll Machine Tools Inc .....C....... 815 987-6000
  Rockford *(G-18433)*
▲ Ingersoll Prod Systems LLC .....D....... 815 637-8500
  Rockford *(G-18434)*
Inland Broaching and TI Co LLC ..G....... 847 233-0033
  Elgin *(G-9077)*

Intrepid Tool Industries LLC .......E....... 773 467-4200
  Chicago *(G-5229)*
Isewan USA Inc ..........................G....... 630 561-2807
  Schaumburg *(G-19584)*
J & L Gear Incorporated ..............F....... 630 832-1880
  Villa Park *(G-21259)*
J Francis & Assoc .......................G....... 309 697-5931
  Bartonville *(G-1395)*
▲ J Schneerberger Corp ..............G....... 847 888-3498
  Elgin *(G-9081)*
Jakes McHning Rbilding Svc Inc ..G....... 630 892-3291
  Aurora *(G-1175)*
John Crane Inc ...........................E....... 815 459-0420
  Crystal Lake *(G-7596)*
◆ Jtekt Toyoda Americas Corp .....C....... 847 253-0340
  Arlington Heights *(G-786)*
Kautzmann Machine Works Inc ....G....... 847 455-9105
  Franklin Park *(G-10511)*
▲ Kiene Diesel Accessories Inc ...E....... 630 543-7170
  Addison *(G-167)*
Kmp Tool Grinding Inc ................G....... 847 205-9640
  Northbrook *(G-16288)*
Komet America Holding Inc ........G....... 847 923-8400
  Schaumburg *(G-19602)*
▲ Komet of America Inc ..............C....... 847 923-8400
  Schaumburg *(G-19603)*
▲ Laser Technologies Inc ............G....... 630 761-1200
  Naperville *(G-15686)*
▲ Lc Holdings of Delaware Inc ....G....... 847 940-3550
  Deerfield *(G-8028)*
▲ Logan Graphic Products Inc .....G....... 847 526-5515
  Wauconda *(G-21479)*
M & M Tooling Inc ......................G....... 630 595-8834
  Wood Dale *(G-22392)*
Machine Medics LLC ...................G....... 309 633-5454
  Peoria *(G-17404)*
Machine Technology Inc ..............G....... 815 795-6818
  Marseilles *(G-14313)*
▼ Magnetrol International Inc ......C....... 630 723-6600
  Aurora *(G-1051)*
Manan Tool & Manufacturing .......A....... 847 637-3333
  Wheeling *(G-22100)*
Master Machine Group .................G....... 847 472-9940
  Elgin *(G-9101)*
Meadoweld Machine Inc .............G....... 815 623-3939
  South Beloit *(G-20161)*
▲ Metal Cutting Tools Corp .........C....... 815 226-0650
  Rockford *(G-18495)*
Micro Lapping & Grinding Co ......G....... 847 455-5446
  Franklin Park *(G-10531)*
Micro Machines Intl LLC .............G....... 815 985-3652
  Rockford *(G-18499)*
Mid-West Millwork Wholesale ......G....... 618 407-5940
  Mascoutah *(G-14356)*
Midwest Machine Tool Inc ..........G....... 815 427-8665
  Saint Anne *(G-19124)*
Midwest Turned Products LLC ....G....... 847 551-4482
  Gilberts *(G-10927)*
▲ Miyano Machinery USA Inc ......G....... 630 766-4141
  Elk Grove Village *(G-9631)*
Modern Gear & Machine Inc ........F....... 630 350-9173
  Bensenville *(G-1953)*
▲ Modern Specialties Company ...G....... 312 648-5800
  Chicago *(G-5785)*
N W Horizontal Boring ................G....... 618 566-9117
  Mascoutah *(G-14358)*
▲ Nicholas Machine & Tool Inc ...G....... 847 298-2035
  Rosemont *(G-19018)*
▲ NNt Enterprises Incorporated ...E....... 630 875-9600
  Itasca *(G-12332)*
Onsrud Machine Corp .................G....... 847 520-5300
  Northbrook *(G-16327)*
OSG Power Tools Inc ..................C....... 630 561-4008
  Bensenville *(G-1960)*
▲ OSG Usa Inc ...........................G....... 630 790-1400
  Glendale Heights *(G-11054)*
◆ Peddinghaus Corporation .........C....... 815 937-3800
  Bradley *(G-2428)*
Pioneer Service Inc ....................E....... 630 628-0249
  Addison *(G-242)*
Port Byron Machine Inc ..............G....... 309 523-9111
  Port Byron *(G-17722)*
Ppt Industrial Machines Inc ........E....... 800 851-3586
  Mount Carmel *(G-15281)*
▲ Prater Industries Inc ................D....... 630 679-3200
  Bolingbrook *(G-2359)*
▲ Precise Lapping Grinding Corp ..F....... 708 615-0240
  Melrose Park *(G-14683)*
Precision Chrome Inc .................G....... 847 587-1515
  Fox Lake *(G-10282)*

Employee Codes: A=Over 500 employees, B=251-500
C=101-250, D=51-100, E=20-50, F=10-19, G=3-9

2017 Harris Illinois
Industrial Directory

- ▲ **Precision McHned Cmponents Inc** ... E ... 630 759-5555 — Romeoville *(G-18860)*
- **Precision Tool & Die Company** ... F ... 217 864-3371 — Mount Zion *(G-15455)*
- **Process Screw Products Inc** ... E ... 815 864-2220 — Shannon *(G-19901)*
- **Prototype & Production Co** ... E ... 847 419-1553 — Wheeling *(G-22130)*
- **R B Evans Co** ... G ... 630 365-3554 — Elburn *(G-8907)*
- **R T M Precision Machining Inc** ... G ... 630 595-0946 — Carol Stream *(G-3226)*
- **Rabbit Tool USA Inc** ... G ... 309 793-4375 — Rock Island *(G-18196)*
- **Radiac Abrasives Inc** ... E ... 630 898-0315 — Oswego *(G-16931)*
- **Ramco Group LLC** ... F ... 847 639-9899 — Crystal Lake *(G-7636)*
- ▲ **Raymond Alstom** ... G ... 630 369-3700 — Naperville *(G-15739)*
- **Rdh Inc of Rockford** ... F ... 815 874-9421 — Rockford *(G-18550)*
- **Redin Parts Inc** ... G ... 815 398-1010 — Rockford *(G-18553)*
- **Reliance Tool & Mfg Co** ... E ... 847 695-1235 — Elgin *(G-9164)*
- **Reliance Tool & Mfg Co** ... E ... 847 455-4350 — Franklin Park *(G-10573)*
- **Resco Products Co** ... G ... 847 455-3776 — Franklin Park *(G-10574)*
- **Robbins Hdd LLC** ... F ... 847 955-0050 — Lake Zurich *(G-13123)*
- ◆ **Robert Bosch LLC** ... B ... 248 876-1000 — Broadview *(G-2610)*
- **Roberts Swiss Inc** ... E ... 630 467-9100 — Itasca *(G-12348)*
- **Rockford Broach Inc** ... F ... 815 484-0409 — Rockford *(G-18568)*
- **Rodifer Enterprises Inc** ... G ... 815 678-0100 — Richmond *(G-17970)*
- **Roll Rite Inc** ... G ... 815 645-8600 — Davis Junction *(G-7814)*
- **Rothenberger Usa Inc** ... E ... 815 397-7617 — Loves Park *(G-13988)*
- **S & S Tool Company** ... G ... 847 891-0780 — Schaumburg *(G-19715)*
- **Sacco-Camex Inc** ... G ... 630 595-8090 — Franklin Park *(G-10580)*
- **Schram Enterprises Inc** ... E ... 708 345-2252 — Melrose Park *(G-14693)*
- **Serien Manufacturing Inc** ... G ... 815 337-1447 — Woodstock *(G-22608)*
- **Service Machine Jobs** ... G ... 815 986-3033 — Rockford *(G-18613)*
- **Specialty Enterprises Inc** ... G ... 630 595-7808 — Franklin Park *(G-10592)*
- **Spencer and Krahn Mch Tl Sls** ... G ... 815 282-3300 — Rockford *(G-18627)*
- ▲ **Sterling Gear Inc** ... F ... 815 438-4327 — Deer Grove *(G-7968)*
- **Stuhr Manufacturing Co** ... F ... 815 398-2460 — Rockford *(G-18636)*
- **Swisstronics Corp** ... G ... 708 403-8877 — Orland Park *(G-16897)*
- **Synax Inc** ... F ... 224 352-2927 — Buffalo Grove *(G-2779)*
- **T&J Turning Inc** ... G ... 309 738-8762 — Colona *(G-7349)*
- **Tauber Brothers Tool & Die Co** ... E ... 708 867-9100 — Chicago *(G-6679)*
- **Technox Machine & Mfg Inc** ... E ... 773 745-6800 — Chicago *(G-6685)*
- **Thread & Gage Co Inc** ... G ... 815 675-2305 — Spring Grove *(G-20367)*
- **Tiger Tool Inc** ... G ... 888 551-4490 — Glendale Heights *(G-11084)*
- **Tooling Solutions Inc** ... G ... 847 472-9940 — Elgin *(G-9212)*
- **Total Tooling Technology Inc** ... F ... 847 437-5135 — Elk Grove Village *(G-9786)*
- ◆ **Tri-Cam Inc** ... F ... 815 226-9200 — Rockford *(G-18656)*
- **Trigon International Corp** ... E ... 630 978-9990 — Aurora *(G-1089)*
- ◆ **TT Technologies Inc** ... D ... 630 851-8200 — Aurora *(G-1091)*
- **Tvo Acquisition Corporation** ... E ... 708 656-4240 — Cicero *(G-7239)*
- **Ty Miles Incorporated** ... E ... 708 344-5480 — Westchester *(G-21860)*
- **Ultramatic Equipment Co** ... E ... 630 543-4565 — Addison *(G-333)*
- **Umt Wind Down Co** ... E ... 815 467-7900 — Minooka *(G-14848)*
- **United Tool and Engineering Co** ... D ... 815 389-3021 — South Beloit *(G-20171)*
- **Universal Broaching Inc** ... F ... 847 228-1440 — Elk Grove Village *(G-9800)*
- **USA Machine Rebuilders** ... G ... 815 547-6542 — Belvidere *(G-1792)*
- ▲ **Usach Technologies Inc** ... E ... 847 888-0148 — Elgin *(G-9222)*
- **Variable Operations Tech Inc** ... E ... 815 479-8528 — Crystal Lake *(G-7672)*
- **Vaughn & Sons Machine Shop** ... G ... 618 842-9048 — Fairfield *(G-10157)*
- **Versatility Tl Works Mfg Inc** ... F ... 708 389-8909 — Alsip *(G-541)*
- ▲ **Voortman USA Corp** ... F ... 815 468-6300 — Monee *(G-15006)*
- **Walega Precision Company Inc** ... G ... 630 682-5000 — Carol Stream *(G-3263)*
- **Walter Tool & Mfg Inc** ... F ... 847 697-7230 — Elgin *(G-9227)*
- ▲ **We Innovex Inc** ... G ... 847 291-3553 — Northbrook *(G-16384)*
- **Wec Welding and Machining LLC** ... G ... 847 680-8100 — Lake Bluff *(G-12870)*
- **West Precision Tool Inc** ... F ... 630 766-8304 — Bensenville *(G-2014)*

## 3542 Machine Tools: Forming

- **10x Microstructures LLC** ... G ... 847 215-7448 — Wheeling *(G-21991)*
- **A & A Magnetics Inc** ... F ... 815 338-6054 — Woodstock *(G-22532)*
- **A J Carbide Grinding** ... G ... 847 675-5112 — Skokie *(G-19942)*
- **Accu-Cut Diamond Bore Sizing** ... F ... 708 457-8800 — Norridge *(G-16094)*
- **Accurate Spring Tech Inc** ... F ... 815 344-3333 — McHenry *(G-14475)*
- ▲ **Advanced Prototype Molding** ... G ... 847 202-4200 — Palatine *(G-16998)*
- ▲ **Ajax Tool Works Inc** ... D ... 847 455-5420 — Franklin Park *(G-10387)*
- **Alan Manufacturing Corp** ... G ... 815 568-6836 — Marengo *(G-14217)*
- ▲ **Altman Manufacturing Co Inc** ... F ... 630 963-0031 — Lisle *(G-13556)*
- ▼ **American Machine Tools Inc** ... G ... 773 775-6285 — Chicago *(G-3861)*
- **Ardagh Conversion Systems Inc** ... G ... 847 438-4100 — Lake Zurich *(G-13043)*
- **Bohl Machine & Tool Company** ... E ... 309 799-5122 — Milan *(G-14777)*
- **Bourn & Bourn Inc** ... C ... 815 965-4013 — Rockford *(G-18289)*
- ▲ **Ceg Subsidiary LLC** ... D ... 618 262-8666 — Mount Carmel *(G-15262)*
- **Centric Mfg Solutions Inc** ... G ... 815 315-9258 — Chicago *(G-4273)*
- **Chicago Rivet & Machine Co** ... C ... 630 357-8500 — Naperville *(G-15627)*
- ▲ **Clements National Company** ... G ... 708 594-5890 — Broadview *(G-2569)*
- ▲ **Cloos Robotic Welding Inc** ... F ... 847 923-9988 — Schaumburg *(G-19474)*
- **Continental Automation Inc** ... E ... 630 584-5100 — Saint Charles *(G-19162)*
- ▼ **Crd Enterprises Inc** ... G ... 847 438-4299 — Lake Zurich *(G-13058)*
- **Cutting Edge Industries Inc** ... G ... 847 678-1777 — Franklin Park *(G-10451)*
- ▲ **D R Sperry & Co** ... D ... 630 892-4361 — Aurora *(G-1137)*
- ▲ **Deringer-Ney Inc** ... E ... 847 566-4100 — Vernon Hills *(G-21157)*
- **Die Cast Machinery LLC** ... F ... 847 360-9170 — Waukegan *(G-21552)*
- **DJB Corporation** ... G ... 815 469-7533 — Frankfort *(G-10313)*
- **Dover Europe Inc** ... G ... 630 541-1540 — Downers Grove *(G-8433)*
- ▲ **Dreis and Krump Mfg Co** ... E ... 708 258-1200 — Peotone *(G-17488)*
- ◆ **Duo-Fast Corporation** ... E ... 847 944-2288 — Glenview *(G-11122)*
- **Ebe Industrial LLC** ... F ... 815 379-2400 — Walnut *(G-21330)*
- ▲ **Elgalabwater LLC** ... G ... 630 343-5251 — Woodridge *(G-22477)*
- **Epcor Industrial Inc** ... G ... 847 545-9212 — Elk Grove Village *(G-9461)*
- **First Header Die Inc** ... E ... 815 282-5161 — Machesney Park *(G-14075)*
- ▲ **Formtek Inc** ... F ... 630 285-1500 — Lisle *(G-13589)*
- ▲ **Geo T Schmidt Inc** ... D ... 847 647-7117 — Niles *(G-15982)*
- **Giant Globes Inc** ... G ... 773 772-2917 — Chicago *(G-4950)*
- **Hastings Manufacturing Inc** ... E ... 800 338-8688 — Millstadt *(G-14825)*
- ▲ **Hersheys Metal Meister LLC** ... E ... 217 234-4700 — Claremont *(G-7256)*
- **Illinois Tool Works Inc** ... C ... 630 595-3500 — Itasca *(G-12281)*
- **Infinity Metal Spinning Inc** ... G ... 773 731-4467 — Chicago *(G-5183)*
- **Ingenious Concepts Inc** ... G ... 630 539-8059 — Medinah *(G-14576)*
- **Innovate Technologies Inc** ... G ... 630 587-4220 — Saint Charles *(G-19197)*
- ▼ **Integral Automation Inc** ... F ... 630 654-4300 — Burr Ridge *(G-2856)*
- **Ives-Way Products Inc** ... G ... 847 740-0658 — Round Lake Beach *(G-19076)*
- **John J Rickhoff Shtmtl Co Inc** ... F ... 708 331-2970 — Phoenix *(G-17541)*
- **Kaufman-Worthen Machinery Inc** ... G ... 847 360-9170 — Waukegan *(G-21577)*
- **Kazmier Tooling Inc** ... G ... 773 586-0300 — Chicago *(G-5366)*
- ▲ **Kipp Manufacturing Company Inc** ... F ... 630 768-9051 — Wauconda *(G-21477)*
- ▲ **Komori America Corporation** ... D ... 847 806-9000 — Rolling Meadows *(G-18739)*
- ▲ **Kwalyti Tling McHy Rblding Inc** ... F ... 630 761-8040 — Batavia *(G-1463)*
- **Kwik Mark Inc** ... G ... 815 363-8268 — McHenry *(G-14519)*
- ▼ **Kwm Gutterman Inc** ... E ... 815 725-9205 — Rockdale *(G-18223)*
- ▲ **L M C Inc** ... G ... 815 758-3514 — Dekalb *(G-8101)*
- **Lens Lenticlear Lenticular** ... F ... 630 467-0900 — Itasca *(G-12303)*
- ▲ **Littell International Inc** ... E ... 630 622-4950 — Schaumburg *(G-19621)*
- **Lotus Creative Innovations LLC** ... G ... 815 440-8999 — Compton *(G-7367)*
- ▲ **Madison Capital Partners Corp** ... G ... 312 277-0323 — Chicago *(G-5597)*
- ▼ **Marsh Shipping Supply Co LLC** ... F ... 618 343-1006 — Collinsville *(G-7335)*
- **MB Corp & Associates** ... F ... 847 214-8843 — South Elgin *(G-20218)*
- ▲ **Mead Products LLC** ... G ... 847 541-9500 — Lake Zurich *(G-13100)*
- ▲ **Mechanical Tool & Engrg Co** ... C ... 815 397-4701 — Rockford *(G-18489)*
- **Metro Tool Company** ... G ... 847 673-6790 — Skokie *(G-20037)*
- **Mgb Engineering Company** ... E ... 847 956-7444 — Elk Grove Village *(G-9624)*
- **Mikes Machinery Rebuilders** ... G ... 630 543-6400 — Addison *(G-215)*
- **Mzm Manufacturing Inc** ... G ... 815 624-8666 — Roscoe *(G-18909)*
- **New Lenox Machine Co Inc** ... F ... 815 584-4866 — Dwight *(G-8589)*
- **Nor Service Inc** ... E ... 815 232-8379 — Freeport *(G-10676)*
- **Ocm Inc** ... G ... 847 462-4258 — Wauconda *(G-21490)*
- **Park Engineering Inc** ... E ... 847 455-1424 — Franklin Park *(G-10546)*
- ▲ **Petrak Industries Incorporated** ... E ... 815 483-2290 — Joliet *(G-12551)*
- **Ppt Industrial Machines Inc** ... E ... 800 851-3586 — Mount Carmel *(G-15281)*
- **Precision Entps Fndry Mch Inc** ... G ... 815 797-1000 — Somonauk *(G-20128)*
- **Precision Header Tooling Inc** ... F ... 815 874-9116 — Rockford *(G-18538)*
- **Precision Service Mtr Inc** ... F ... 630 628-9900 — Addison *(G-253)*
- **Press Brakes** ... G ... 630 916-1494 — Lombard *(G-13845)*

# 35 INDUSTRIAL AND COMMERCIAL MACHINERY AND COMPUTER EQUIPMENT

Punch Products Manufacturing ............E ...... 773 533-2800
  Chicago (G-6226)
R-K Press Brake Dies Inc ..................F ...... 708 371-1756
  Chicago (G-6275)
Rae Products and Chem Corp .............G ...... 708 396-1984
  Alsip (G-517)
Rapid Air ......................................G ...... 815 397-2578
  Rockford (G-18548)
Riteway Brake Dies Inc ......................F ...... 708 430-0795
  Bridgeview (G-2524)
Rock Valley Die Sinking Inc .................F ...... 815 874-5511
  Rockford (G-18565)
Roll Rite Inc .................................G ...... 815 645-8600
  Davis Junction (G-7814)
Service Machine Jobs .......................G ...... 815 986-3033
  Rockford (G-18613)
Seward Screw Acquisition LLC ............G ...... 312 498-9933
  Chicago (G-6484)
Seward Screw Operating LLC ..............C ...... 312 498-9933
  Chicago (G-6485)
Sieber Tool Engineering LP .................F ...... 630 462-9370
  Carol Stream (G-3240)
Simpson Technologies .......................E ...... 630 978-2700
  Aurora (G-1078)
Slidecraft Inc ...............................G ...... 630 628-1218
  Addison (G-294)
▲ Sloan Industries Inc ........................E ...... 630 350-1614
  Wood Dale (G-22423)
◆ Sterling Products Inc ......................D ...... 847 273-7700
  Schaumburg (G-19740)
Straightline Erectors Inc ....................G ...... 708 430-5426
  Oak Lawn (G-16645)
Summit Tooling Inc ..........................F ...... 815 385-7500
  McHenry (G-14559)
Sure-Way Die Designs Inc ...................F ...... 630 323-0370
  Westmont (G-21924)
Terry Tool & Machining Corp ...............G ...... 847 289-1054
  East Dundee (G-8658)
Tox- Pressotechnik LLC ......................G ...... 630 447-4600
  Warrenville (G-21365)
▲ Uniflex of America Ltd .....................G ...... 847 519-1100
  Schaumburg (G-19779)
Venturedyne Ltd ............................E ...... 708 597-7550
  Chicago (G-6884)
Versatech LLC ...............................C ...... 217 342-3500
  Effingham (G-8860)
▲ W A Whitney Co ............................C ...... 815 964-6771
  Rockford (G-18671)
Wardzala Industries Inc .....................F ...... 847 288-9909
  Franklin Park (G-10627)
▲ Whitney Roper LLC .........................D ...... 815 962-3011
  Rockford (G-18681)
▲ Whitney Roper Rockford Inc ..............D ...... 815 962-3011
  Rockford (G-18682)
Williams White & Company .................C ...... 309 797-7650
  Moline (G-14977)
Woodstock Special Machining ..............G ...... 815 338-7383
  Woodstock (G-22628)

## 3543 Industrial Patterns

Advanced Pattern Works LLC .............E ...... 618 346-9039
  Collinsville (G-7312)
Alang Pattern Inc ...........................G ...... 773 722-9481
  Cicero (G-7177)
Apex Pattern Works ........................G ...... 309 346-2905
  Pekin (G-17254)
Arnette Pattern Co Inc ....................E ...... 618 451-7700
  Granite City (G-11268)
Beloit Pattern Works .......................F ...... 815 389-2578
  South Beloit (G-20140)
Cambridge Pattern Works ..................G ...... 309 937-5370
  Cambridge (G-2966)
Capital Pttern Model Works Inc ...........G ...... 630 469-8200
  Glendale Heights (G-11013)
Carroll Industrial Molds Inc ................F ...... 815 225-7250
  Milledgeville (G-14816)
Chem-Cast Ltd .............................C ...... 217 443-5532
  Danville (G-7709)
Clinkenbeard & Associates Inc ...........E ...... 815 226-0291
  Rockford (G-18313)
Cores For You Inc .........................E ...... 217 847-3233
  Hamilton (G-11531)
Curto-Ligonier Foundries Co ..............E ...... 708 345-2250
  Melrose Park (G-14613)
D & M Pattern Co ..........................G ...... 217 877-0064
  Decatur (G-7864)
E & E Pattern Works Inc ...................E ...... 847 689-1088
  North Chicago (G-16177)
Johnson Pattern & Mch Works ............E ...... 815 433-2775
  Ottawa (G-16964)

Jsp Mold .....................................G ...... 815 225-7110
  Milledgeville (G-14817)
Kerrigan Corporation Inc ..................G ...... 847 251-8994
  Wilmette (G-22257)
Koswell Pattern Works Inc .................G ...... 708 757-5225
  Lynwood (G-14020)
Master Foundry Inc ........................F ...... 217 223-7396
  Quincy (G-17856)
Microtek Pattern Inc .......................G ...... 217 428-0433
  Decatur (G-7913)
Midstate Core Co ..........................E ...... 217 429-2673
  Decatur (G-7914)
Midwest Patterns Inc ......................C ...... 217 228-6900
  Quincy (G-17859)
Modern Pattern Works Inc .................G ...... 309 676-2157
  Peoria (G-17411)
N & S Pattern Co ...........................F ...... 815 874-6166
  Rockford (G-18514)
Nosko Manufacturing Inc ..................F ...... 847 678-0813
  Schiller Park (G-19854)
Olson Aluminum Castings Ltd ............E ...... 815 229-3292
  Rockford (G-18526)
P & H Pattern Inc ..........................G ...... 815 795-2449
  Marseilles (G-14315)
Park Products Inc ..........................G ...... 630 543-2474
  Addison (G-237)
Precision Entps Fndry Mch Inc ............G ...... 815 797-1000
  Somonauk (G-20128)
Precision Foundry Tooling Ltd .............F ...... 217 847-3233
  Hamilton (G-11539)
Prs Inc ......................................G ...... 630 620-7259
  Lombard (G-13846)
Quincy Foundry & Pattern Co .............G ...... 217 222-0718
  Quincy (G-17877)
R & C Pattern Works Inc ...................G ...... 708 331-1882
  South Holland (G-20299)
R C Castings Inc ...........................G ...... 708 331-1882
  South Holland (G-20300)
Rockbridge Casting Inc ....................G ...... 618 753-3188
  Rockbridge (G-18212)
Spectron Manufacturing ...................G ...... 720 879-7605
  Bloomingdale (G-2138)
Sun Pattern & Model Inc ...................E ...... 630 293-3366
  West Chicago (G-21777)
Tilton Pattern Works Inc ...................F ...... 217 442-1502
  Danville (G-7776)
Voss Pattern Works Inc ....................G ...... 618 233-4242
  Belleville (G-1689)

## 3544 Dies, Tools, Jigs, Fixtures & Indl Molds

3-D Mold & Tool Inc ........................G ...... 847 870-7150
  Wheeling (G-21992)
3d Industries Inc ...........................E ...... 630 616-8702
  Bensenville (G-1808)
A & B Machine Shop .......................G ...... 815 397-0495
  Rockford (G-18237)
▲ A & C Mold Company Inc .................E ...... 630 587-0177
  Saint Charles (G-19130)
A J Carbide Grinding .......................G ...... 847 675-5112
  Skokie (G-19942)
A K Tool & Manufacturing Inc .............G ...... 630 889-9220
  Lombard (G-13756)
A M Tool & Die .............................E ...... 847 398-7530
  Rolling Meadows (G-18706)
A R Tech & Tool Inc ........................G ...... 708 599-5745
  Bridgeview (G-2458)
A&S Machining & Welding Inc ............E ...... 708 442-4544
  Mc Cook (G-14443)
▲ A-1 Tool Corporation ......................D ...... 708 345-5000
  Melrose Park (G-14579)
A-B Die Mold Inc ...........................F ...... 847 658-1199
  Bartlett (G-1327)
Aberdeen Technologies Inc ................F ...... 630 665-8590
  Carol Stream (G-3088)
Ability Tool Co .............................E ...... 815 633-5909
  Machesney Park (G-14050)
Able Die & Mold Inc .......................G ...... 773 282-3652
  Chicago (G-3709)
AC Precision Tool Inc ......................G ...... 630 797-5161
  Saint Charles (G-19131)
Accurate Grinding Co Inc ..................F ...... 708 371-1887
  Posen (G-17727)
Accurate Tool & Mfg Corp .................F ...... 708 652-4266
  Chicago (G-3723)
Ace Plating Company ......................G ...... 773 376-1800
  Chicago (G-3727)
Acomtech Mold Inc ........................G ...... 847 741-3537
  Elgin (G-8933)
Action Rotary Die Inc ......................E ...... 630 628-6830
  Addison (G-21)

Action Tool & Mfg Inc .....................E ...... 815 874-5775
  Rockford (G-18256)
▲ Admo ......................................D ...... 847 741-5777
  Elgin (G-8936)
Advance Design Inc .......................G ...... 815 338-0843
  Woodstock (G-22534)
Advanced Digital & Mold Inc ..............G ...... 630 595-8242
  Bensenville (G-1818)
Advanced Molding Tech Inc ...............D ...... 815 334-3600
  Woodstock (G-22535)
▲ Airo Tool & Manufacturing Inc ...........F ...... 815 547-7588
  Belvidere (G-1729)
Alcon Tool & Mfg Co Inc ..................G ...... 773 545-8742
  Chicago (G-3798)
Algen Enterprises Ltd .....................E ...... 217 428-4888
  Decatur (G-7828)
Allen Popovich ............................G ...... 815 712-7404
  Custer Park (G-7686)
Allstar Tool & Molds Inc ..................F ...... 630 766-0162
  Bensenville (G-1828)
Alm Materials Handling LLC ..............E ...... 815 673-5546
  Streator (G-20682)
Alm Positioners Inc .......................G ...... 309 787-6200
  Rock Island (G-18159)
Alpha Star Tool and Mold Inc .............G ...... 815 455-2802
  Crystal Lake (G-7529)
Alpha Tool & Die Inc ......................F ...... 847 622-8849
  Elgin (G-8945)
▲ Altman Manufacturing Co Inc ............F ...... 630 963-0031
  Lisle (G-13556)
▲ American Die Supplies Acquisit ..........G ...... 630 766-6226
  Wood Dale (G-22341)
▼ American Engraving Inc ..................G ...... 630 543-2525
  Bensenville (G-1833)
American Total Engine Co .................G ...... 847 623-2737
  Ingleside (G-12186)
▲ Ameriken Die Supply Inc .................E ...... 630 766-6226
  Wood Dale (G-22342)
Amity Die and Stamping Co ...............E ...... 847 680-6600
  Lake Forest (G-12879)
Ammentorp Tool Company Inc ...........G ...... 847 671-9290
  Franklin Park (G-10395)
Amt (additive Mfg Tech Inc ................G ...... 847 258-4475
  Elk Grove Village (G-9304)
Amtech Inc .................................F ...... 815 962-0500
  Rockford (G-18266)
Andersson Tool & Die LLP .................F ...... 847 746-8866
  Zion (G-22678)
Angle Tool Company .......................G ...... 847 593-7572
  Elk Grove Village (G-9307)
Apex Pattern Works ........................G ...... 309 346-2905
  Pekin (G-17254)
▲ Apex Tool Works Inc ......................E ...... 847 394-5810
  Rolling Meadows (G-18710)
Apollo Machine & Manufacturing .........G ...... 847 677-6444
  Skokie (G-19956)
APT Tool Inc ...............................G ...... 815 337-0051
  Woodstock (G-22540)
ARC Industries Inc ........................G ...... 847 303-5005
  Schaumburg (G-19446)
Armin Tool and Mfg Co ....................D ...... 847 742-1864
  South Elgin (G-20183)
Arrow Engineering Inc ....................G ...... 815 397-0862
  Rockford (G-18270)
Assurance Clg Restoration LLC ...........F ...... 630 444-3600
  Saint Charles (G-19139)
Astro Tool Co Inc ..........................G ...... 630 876-3402
  West Chicago (G-21663)
Atlantic Engineering ......................G ...... 847 782-1762
  Zion (G-22679)
Atlas Die LLC ..............................D ...... 630 351-5140
  Glendale Heights (G-11009)
▲ Atlas Tool & Die Works Inc ...............D ...... 708 442-1661
  Lyons (G-14031)
Atomic Engineering Co ....................F ...... 847 228-1387
  Elk Grove Village (G-9320)
Atomoweld Co .............................G ...... 773 736-5577
  Chicago (G-3987)
Austin Tool & Die Co ......................G ...... 847 509-5800
  Northbrook (G-16209)
Automation Design & Mfg Inc .............G ...... 630 896-4206
  Aurora (G-1117)
Avan Tool & Die Co Inc ....................F ...... 773 287-1670
  Chicago (G-3996)
Azimuth Cnc Inc ...........................G ...... 815 399-4433
  Rockford (G-18274)
B & B Tool Co .............................G ...... 815 229-5792
  Rockford (G-18275)
B & D Murray Manufacturing Co ..........G ...... 815 568-6176
  Marengo (G-14220)

35 INDUSTRIAL AND COMMERCIAL MACHINERY AND COMPUTER EQUIPMENT SIC SECTION

**B A Die Mold Inc** F 630 978-4747
Aurora *(G-965)*

**B C Die & Mold Inc** G 630 543-5090
Addison *(G-50)*

**B L I Tool & Die Inc** G 217 434-9106
Fowler *(G-10272)*

**B Radtke and Sons Inc** G 847 546-3999
Round Lake Park *(G-19083)*

**B&H Machine Inc** F 618 281-3737
Columbia *(G-7351)*

**Bahr Tool & Die Co** G 847 392-4447
Wheeling *(G-22012)*

**Ballek Die Mold Inc** F 847 885-2300
Hoffman Estates *(G-11993)*

**Banner Moulded Products** E 708 452-0033
River Grove *(G-18005)*

▲ **Barco Stamping Co** E 630 293-5155
West Chicago *(G-21666)*

**Bel-Air Manufacturing Inc** F 773 276-7550
Chicago *(G-4074)*

**Bennett Metal Products Inc** D 618 244-1911
Mount Vernon *(G-15401)*

**Bergst Special Tools Inc** G 630 543-1020
Addison *(G-53)*

**Best Brake Die Inc** G 708 388-1896
Crestwood *(G-7477)*

▲ **Best Cutting Die Co** C 847 675-5522
Skokie *(G-19963)*

**Best Metal Extrusions Inc** E 847 981-0797
Elk Grove Village *(G-9341)*

**Bg Die Mold Inc** G 847 961-5861
Huntley *(G-12133)*

▲ **Bi-Link Metal Specialties Inc** C 630 858-5900
Bloomingdale *(G-2096)*

▲ **Big 3 Precision Products Inc** C 618 533-3251
Centralia *(G-3405)*

**Binder Tool Inc** G 847 678-4222
Franklin Park *(G-10412)*

▲ **Bluco Corporation** F 630 637-1820
Aurora *(G-970)*

**Bohl Machine & Tool Company** E 309 799-5122
Milan *(G-14777)*

**Bomel Tool Manufacturing Co** C 708 343-3663
Broadview *(G-2564)*

**Briergate Tool & Engrg Co** F 630 766-7050
Bensenville *(G-1846)*

**Bronson & Bratton Inc** C 630 986-1815
Burr Ridge *(G-2825)*

**BT & E Co** G 815 544-6431
Belvidere *(G-1740)*

**Burns Machine Company** E 815 434-3131
Ottawa *(G-16952)*

**C & S Steel Rule Die Co Inc** G 773 254-4027
Chicago *(G-4202)*

**C Tri Co** E 309 467-4715
Eureka *(G-9994)*

**C/B Machine Tool Corp** G 847 288-1807
Franklin Park *(G-10422)*

**Cabot McRlectronics Polsg Corp** E 630 543-6682
Addison *(G-67)*

**Cac Corporation** E 630 221-5200
Carol Stream *(G-3122)*

**Cameo Mold Corp** F 630 876-1340
West Chicago *(G-21676)*

▲ **Canny Tool & Mold Corporation** G 847 548-1573
Grayslake *(G-11324)*

**Capitol City Tool & Design** G 217 544-9250
Springfield *(G-20406)*

**Cardon Mold Finishing Inc** G 630 543-5431
Addison *(G-69)*

**Carroll Industrial Molds Inc** F 815 225-7250
Milledgeville *(G-14816)*

**Carroll Tool & Manufacturing** G 630 766-3363
Bensenville *(G-1852)*

**Cdv Corp** F 815 397-3903
Rockford *(G-18300)*

**Celco Tool & Engineering Inc** F 847 671-2520
Schiller Park *(G-19812)*

**Center Tool Company Inc** G 847 683-7559
Hampshire *(G-11544)*

**Central Tool Specialities Co** G 630 543-6351
Addison *(G-72)*

**Century Mold & Tool Co** E 847 364-5858
Elk Grove Village *(G-9362)*

**CGR Technologies Inc** E 847 934-7622
Palatine *(G-17010)*

**Challenge Tool Co** G 847 640-8085
Elk Grove Village *(G-9363)*

◆ **Chase Products Co** D 708 865-1000
Broadview *(G-2566)*

**Chelar Tool & Die Inc** D 618 234-6550
Belleville *(G-1618)*

**Chem-Cast Ltd** C 217 443-5532
Danville *(G-7709)*

▲ **Chicago Cutting Die Co** D 847 509-5800
Northbrook *(G-16221)*

▲ **Chicago Heights Star Tool and** F 708 758-2525
Chicago Heights *(G-7089)*

**Chicago Mold Engrg Co Inc** D 630 584-1311
Saint Charles *(G-19152)*

**Chicago Quadrill Co** G 847 824-4196
Des Plaines *(G-8167)*

**Chicago Roll Co Inc** E 630 627-8888
Lombard *(G-13777)*

**Chirch Global Mfg LLC** F 815 385-5600
Cary *(G-3330)*

**CJCwood Products Inc** E 815 479-5190
Crystal Lake *(G-7554)*

**CMC Tool Manufacturing** G 630 350-0300
Bensenville *(G-1860)*

▲ **Comet Die & Engraving Company** D 630 833-5600
Elmhurst *(G-9854)*

**Complete Mold Polishing Inc** G 630 406-7668
Batavia *(G-1432)*

**Component Tool & Mfg Co** F 708 672-5505
Crete *(G-7510)*

**Comtec Industries Ltd** G 630 759-9000
Woodridge *(G-22465)*

**Con Mold** G 708 442-6002
Hillside *(G-11913)*

**Condor Tool & Manufacturing** F 630 628-8200
Addison *(G-81)*

**Conform Industries Inc** F 630 285-0272
Schaumburg *(G-19479)*

▲ **Converting Technology Inc** D 847 290-0590
Elk Grove Village *(G-9392)*

▲ **Correct Tool Inc** F 630 595-6055
Bensenville *(G-1867)*

**Corrugated Converting Eqp** F 618 532-2138
Centralia *(G-3410)*

**Country Cast Products** F 815 777-1070
Galena *(G-10718)*

**County Tool & Die** G 217 324-6527
Litchfield *(G-13683)*

**Craftsman Tool & Mold Co** E 630 851-8700
Aurora *(G-986)*

**Creative Steel Rule Dies Inc** F 630 307-8880
Glendale Heights *(G-11019)*

**Crown Tool Company Inc** G 630 766-3050
Bensenville *(G-1872)*

▲ **Crystal Die and Mold Inc** E 847 658-6535
Rolling Meadows *(G-18724)*

**Custom Machining & Design LLC** G 847 364-2601
Elk Grove Village *(G-9403)*

**Custom Mold Services** E 847 364-6589
Mount Prospect *(G-15324)*

**Custom Tool & Gage Co Inc** G 847 671-5306
Franklin Park *(G-10450)*

**Custom Tool Inc** F 217 465-8538
Paris *(G-17145)*

**Cut Rite Die Co** G 847 394-0492
Arlington Heights *(G-742)*

**Cutting Edge Industries Inc** G 847 678-1777
Franklin Park *(G-10451)*

**D & D Tooling Inc** C 630 759-0015
Bolingbrook *(G-2298)*

**D & H Precision Tooling Co** G 815 653-9611
Wonder Lake *(G-22322)*

**D & J Machine Shop Inc** G 815 472-6057
Momence *(G-14979)*

**D & M Tool Llc** G 847 731-3600
Zion *(G-22681)*

**D C T/Precision LLC** F 217 475-0141
Decatur *(G-7865)*

▲ **D E Specialty Tool & Mfg Inc** E 847 678-0004
Franklin Park *(G-10453)*

**D M C Mold & Tool Corp** G 847 639-3098
Cary *(G-3332)*

**D S Precision Tool Company** G 630 627-0696
Downers Grove *(G-8423)*

**Dadum Inc** G 847 541-7851
Buffalo Grove *(G-2682)*

**Dagger Tool Co Inc** G 630 279-5050
Addison *(G-86)*

**Daley Automation LLC** G 630 384-9900
Naperville *(G-15642)*

**Dangios** G 773 533-3000
Chicago *(G-4552)*

**Davis Machine Company Inc** G 815 723-9121
Joliet *(G-12484)*

**Davitz Mold Co Inc** G 847 426-4848
East Dundee *(G-8631)*

**Dax Steel Rule Dies Inc** G 708 448-4436
Orland Park *(G-16852)*

**Dearborn Tool & Mfg Inc** E 630 655-1260
Burr Ridge *(G-2836)*

**Dec Tool Corp** E 630 513-9883
Saint Charles *(G-19169)*

**Decore Tool & Mfg Inc** F 630 681-9760
Carol Stream *(G-3142)*

**Design Systems Inc** E 309 263-7706
Morton *(G-15157)*

**Dial Tool Industries Inc** D 630 543-3600
Addison *(G-88)*

**Dice Mold & Engineering Inc** E 630 773-3595
Itasca *(G-12250)*

**Die Craft Metal Products** G 847 593-1433
Elk Grove Village *(G-9427)*

**Die Cut Group Inc** F 630 629-9211
Lombard *(G-13790)*

**Die Darrell** G 309 282-9112
Eureka *(G-9997)*

**Die Mold Jig Grinding & Mfg** G 847 228-1444
Elk Grove Village *(G-9428)*

**Die Pros Inc** G 630 543-2025
Addison *(G-93)*

**Die Specialty Co** G 312 303-5738
La Grange Park *(G-12755)*

**Die World Steel Rule Dies** G 815 399-8675
Rockford *(G-18344)*

▲ **Diemasters Manufacturing Inc** C 847 640-9900
Elk Grove Village *(G-9429)*

**Dies Plus Inc** F 630 285-1065
Itasca *(G-12251)*

**Dike-O-Seal Incorporated** F 773 254-3224
Chicago *(G-4603)*

**Dms Inc** F 847 726-2828
Lake Zurich *(G-13063)*

**Do-Rite Die & Engineering Co** F 708 754-4355
S Chicago Hts *(G-19103)*

**Dodge Machine Tool** G 815 544-0967
Belvidere *(G-1749)*

▲ **Domeny Tool & Stamping Company** F 847 526-5700
Wauconda *(G-21454)*

**Dooling Machine Products Inc** G 618 254-0724
Hartford *(G-11610)*

**Doral Inc** G 630 543-5523
Addison *(G-97)*

**Double M Machine Inc** F 815 692-4676
Fairbury *(G-10123)*

**Dovee Manufacturing Inc** F 847 437-8122
Elgin *(G-9012)*

**Dragon Die Mold Inc** G 630 836-0699
Warrenville *(G-21345)*

**Durabuilt Die Corp** G 847 437-2086
Elk Grove Village *(G-9437)*

**E C Schultz & Co Inc** F 847 640-1190
Elk Grove Village *(G-9442)*

**E-Lite Tool & Mfg Co** E 618 236-1580
Belleville *(G-1628)*

**Eagle Tool Us LLC** G 815 459-4177
Crystal Lake *(G-7569)*

**East Side Tool & Die Co Inc** F 618 397-1633
Caseyville *(G-3395)*

**East West Martial Arts Sups** G 773 878-7711
Chicago *(G-4682)*

**Eberle Manufacturing Company** F 847 215-0100
Wheeling *(G-22042)*

**Edge Mold Corporation** G 630 616-8108
Bensenville *(G-1889)*

▼ **Ehrhardt Tool & Machine LLC** C 314 436-6900
Granite City *(G-11274)*

**Elba Tool Co Inc** F 847 895-4100
Bloomingdale *(G-2105)*

**Elite Die & Finishing Inc** G 708 389-4848
South Holland *(G-20265)*

**Elm Tool and Manufacturing Co** G 847 455-6805
Melrose Park *(G-14632)*

**Embeddedkits** G 847 401-7488
Streamwood *(G-20654)*

**Emerson Industries LLC** F 630 279-0920
Villa Park *(G-21250)*

**Emt International Inc** G 630 655-4145
Westmont *(G-21887)*

**Engineering Design & Dev Inc** E 309 266-6298
Morton *(G-15158)*

**ERA Tool and Manufacturing Co** E 847 298-6333
Zion *(G-22684)*

**Erickson Tool & Machine Co** G 815 397-2653
Rockford *(G-18369)*

SIC SECTION 35 INDUSTRIAL AND COMMERCIAL MACHINERY AND COMPUTER EQUIPMENT

▲ **Erowa Technology Inc** ........ F ....... 847 290-0295
Arlington Heights ***(G-751)***
▲ **Erva Tool & Die Company** ........ G ....... 773 533-7806
Chicago ***(G-4775)***
**Essentra Components Inc** ........ C ....... 815 943-6487
Forest Park ***(G-10241)***
**Etch-Tech Inc** ........ G ....... 630 833-4234
Elmhurst ***(G-9868)***
**Ever Ready Pin & Manufacturing** ........ D ....... 815 874-4949
Rockford ***(G-18371)***
▲ **Ewikon Molding Tech Inc** ........ G ....... 815 874-7270
Rockford ***(G-18373)***
**Exact Tool Company Inc** ........ G ....... 847 632-1140
Wheeling ***(G-22051)***
**Extrusion Tooling Technology** ........ G ....... 847 526-1606
Wauconda ***(G-21461)***
**F & R Plastics Inc** ........ G ....... 847 336-1330
Waukegan ***(G-21558)***
**F & S Engraving Inc** ........ E ....... 847 870-8400
Mount Prospect ***(G-15328)***
**Fabricating Machinery Sales** ........ E ....... 630 350-2266
Wood Dale ***(G-22366)***
▲ **Fabrik Industries Inc** ........ B ....... 815 385-9480
McHenry ***(G-14505)***
**Famaco Corp** ........ E ....... 217 442-4412
Tilton ***(G-20881)***
◆ **Federal Signal Corporation** ........ D ....... 630 954-2000
Oak Brook ***(G-16510)***
▲ **Fidelity Tool & Mold Ltd** ........ F ....... 630 879-2300
Batavia ***(G-1447)***
**First Header Die Inc** ........ E ....... 815 282-5161
Machesney Park ***(G-14075)***
**Flores Precision Products** ........ G ....... 630 264-2222
Aurora ***(G-1152)***
**Ford Tool & Machining Inc** ........ D ....... 815 633-5727
Loves Park ***(G-13941)***
**Form Walern Grinding Inc** ........ G ....... 815 874-7000
Rockford ***(G-18391)***
**Forster Products Inc** ........ E ....... 815 493-6360
Lanark ***(G-13154)***
**Forster Tool & Mfg Co Inc** ........ E ....... 630 616-8177
Bensenville ***(G-1902)***
▼ **Fosbinder Fabrication Inc** ........ E ....... 309 764-0913
Moline ***(G-14940)***
**Frankfort Machine & Tools Inc** ........ G ....... 815 469-9902
Frankfort ***(G-10324)***
**Furnel Inc** ........ E ....... 630 543-0885
Addison ***(G-124)***
**Future Tool Inc** ........ F ....... 815 395-0012
Rockford ***(G-18394)***
**G & M Die Casting Company Inc** ........ D ....... 630 595-2340
Wood Dale ***(G-22374)***
**Gage Tool & Manufacturing Inc** ........ G ....... 847 640-1069
Elk Grove Village ***(G-9494)***
**Gail E Stephens** ........ G ....... 618 372-0140
Brighton ***(G-2540)***
**Galaxy Precision Mfg Inc** ........ F ....... 847 238-9066
Elk Grove Village ***(G-9495)***
**Gc Dies LLC** ........ E ....... 630 758-4100
Elmhurst ***(G-9873)***
**Gemini Tool & Manufacturing** ........ F ....... 847 678-5000
Franklin Park ***(G-10478)***
**General Forging Die Co Inc** ........ E ....... 815 874-4224
Rockford ***(G-18397)***
**General Machinery & Mfg Co** ........ F ....... 773 235-3700
Chicago ***(G-4928)***
▲ **Geo T Schmidt Inc** ........ D ....... 847 647-7117
Niles ***(G-15982)***
**George Hansen & Co Inc** ........ F ....... 630 628-8700
Addison ***(G-134)***
**Gerhard Designing & Mfg Inc** ........ E ....... 708 599-4664
Bridgeview ***(G-2494)***
**Glenwood Tool & Mold Inc** ........ F ....... 630 289-3400
Bartlett ***(G-1349)***
**Glo-Mold Inc** ........ F ....... 847 671-1762
Schiller Park ***(G-19835)***
**Global Tool & Die Inc** ........ G ....... 847 956-1200
Elk Grove Village ***(G-9503)***
**Graffs Tooling Center Inc** ........ G ....... 618 357-5005
Pinckneyville ***(G-17549)***
**Great Lakes Tool & Mold Inc** ........ G ....... 630 964-7121
Woodridge ***(G-22491)***
**Grinding Specialty Co Inc** ........ E ....... 847 724-6493
West Chicago ***(G-21713)***
**Grove Plastic Inc** ........ F ....... 847 678-8244
Franklin Park ***(G-10484)***
**H & B Quality Tooling Inc** ........ F ....... 217 223-2387
Quincy ***(G-17833)***
**H & R Tool & Machine Co** ........ G ....... 618 344-7683
Caseyville ***(G-3396)***

**H B Products Incorporated** ........ G ....... 773 735-0936
Chicago ***(G-5019)***
**H&H Die Manufacturing Inc** ........ G ....... 708 479-6267
Frankfort ***(G-10326)***
**Haaker Mold Co Inc** ........ G ....... 847 253-8103
Arlington Heights ***(G-762)***
**Hansels Custom Tech Inc** ........ G ....... 815 496-2345
Sheridan ***(G-19918)***
**Harbor Manufacturing Inc** ........ D ....... 708 614-6400
Tinley Park ***(G-20920)***
▲ **Harig Manufacturing Corp** ........ E ....... 847 647-9500
Skokie ***(G-20011)***
**Hastings Manufacturing Inc** ........ E ....... 800 338-8688
Millstadt ***(G-14825)***
**Hatcher Associates Inc** ........ F ....... 773 252-2171
Chicago ***(G-5053)***
**Hattan Tool Company** ........ G ....... 708 597-9308
Alsip ***(G-471)***
**Hausermann Die & Machine Co** ........ F ....... 630 543-6688
Addison ***(G-144)***
**Header Die and Tool Inc** ........ D ....... 815 397-0123
Rockford ***(G-18414)***
**Headly Manufacturing Co** ........ D ....... 708 338-0800
Broadview ***(G-2584)***
**Headly Manufacturing Co** ........ D ....... 708 338-0800
Broadview ***(G-2583)***
**Heat Seal Tooling Corporation** ........ G ....... 815 626-6009
Rock Falls ***(G-18134)***
**Helm Tool Company Incorporated** ........ E ....... 847 952-9528
Elk Grove Village ***(G-9522)***
**Henning Machine & Die Works** ........ G ....... 217 286-3393
Henning ***(G-11738)***
**Henry Tool & Die Co** ........ G ....... 847 671-1361
Franklin Park ***(G-10486)***
**Heritage Mold Incorporated** ........ F ....... 815 397-1117
Rockford ***(G-18417)***
**Hl Prcision Tl Makers McHy Inc** ........ G ....... 630 694-0200
Bensenville ***(G-1916)***
**Hill Engineering Inc** ........ E ....... 630 315-5070
Carol Stream ***(G-3166)***
**Hoffman Tool Inc** ........ E ....... 815 692-4643
Fairbury ***(G-10125)***
**Hoffman Tool & Die Inc** ........ E ....... 815 692-2628
Fairbury ***(G-10126)***
**Horizon Die Company Inc** ........ E ....... 847 426-8558
East Dundee ***(G-8643)***
**Howell Welding Corporation** ........ G ....... 630 616-1100
Franklin Park ***(G-10489)***
**Icon Metalcraft Inc** ........ C ....... 630 766-5600
Wood Dale ***(G-22381)***
**Idea Tool & Manufacturing Co** ........ D ....... 312 476-1080
Chicago ***(G-5139)***
**Iemco Corporation** ........ G ....... 773 728-4400
Chicago ***(G-5145)***
**Illinois Broaching Co** ........ G ....... 847 678-3080
Schiller Park ***(G-19840)***
**Illinois Mold Builders Inc** ........ F ....... 847 526-0400
Wauconda ***(G-21471)***
**Illinois Tool Works Inc** ........ C ....... 708 479-7200
Mokena ***(G-14873)***
**Illinois Tool Works Inc** ........ G ....... 708 479-7200
Tinley Park ***(G-20922)***
**Imperial Punch & Manufacturing** ........ F ....... 815 226-8200
Rockford ***(G-18428)***
**IMS Olson LLC** ........ D ....... 630 969-9400
Downers Grove ***(G-8464)***
**Inc Midwest Die Mold** ........ G ....... 224 353-6417
Schaumburg ***(G-19564)***
**Indiana Precision Inc** ........ F ....... 765 361-0247
Danville ***(G-7739)***
**Industrial Modern Pattern** ........ G ....... 847 296-4930
Rosemont ***(G-19006)***
**Industrial Molded Products** ........ G ....... 847 358-2160
Mundelein ***(G-15510)***
▲ **Industrial Molds Inc** ........ D ....... 815 397-2971
Rockford ***(G-18430)***
**Industrial Park Machine & Tool** ........ F ....... 708 754-7080
S Chicago Hts ***(G-19105)***
**Inland Tool Company** ........ E ....... 217 792-3206
Mount Pulaski ***(G-15389)***
**International Cutting Die Inc** ........ E ....... 708 343-3333
Melrose Park ***(G-14660)***
**Inventive Mfg Inc** ........ F ....... 847 647-9500
Skokie ***(G-20018)***
▲ **Iplastics LLC** ........ D ....... 309 444-8884
Washington ***(G-21383)***
▲ **J & J Carbide & Tool Inc** ........ E ....... 708 489-0300
Alsip ***(G-475)***
**J & S Tool Inc** ........ G .....
Chicago ***(G-5254)***

**J F Schroeder Company Inc** ........ E ....... 847 357-8600
Arlington Heights ***(G-781)***
**J H Benedict Co Inc** ........ D ....... 309 694-3111
East Peoria ***(G-8715)***
**J M Resources Inc** ........ F ....... 630 690-7337
Elgin ***(G-9080)***
**J R Mold Inc** ........ G ....... 630 289-2192
Streamwood ***(G-20658)***
**Jamco Tool & Cams Inc** ........ F ....... 847 678-0280
Franklin Park ***(G-10505)***
▼ **Janler Corporation** ........ E ....... 773 774-0166
Chicago ***(G-5277)***
**Jbw Machining Inc** ........ F ....... 847 451-0276
Franklin Park ***(G-10508)***
**JC Automation Inc** ........ E ....... 309 270-7000
Rock Island ***(G-18185)***
**JC Tool and Mold Inc** ........ G ....... 630 483-2203
Streamwood ***(G-20661)***
**Jenco Metal Products Inc** ........ F ....... 847 956-0550
Mount Prospect ***(G-15340)***
**Jensen and Son Inc** ........ G ....... 815 895-3855
Sycamore ***(G-20803)***
**Jjs High TEC Machining Inc** ........ G ....... 618 775-8840
Odin ***(G-16740)***
**JM Die Tooling Co** ........ E ....... 630 616-7776
Bensenville ***(G-1928)***
**JM Tool & Die LLC** ........ G ....... 630 595-1274
Bensenville ***(G-1929)***
**Johnson Steel Rule Die Co** ........ F ....... 773 921-4334
Chicago ***(G-5321)***
**Jsp Mold** ........ G ....... 815 225-7110
Milledgeville ***(G-14817)***
**K & B Machining** ........ G ....... 847 663-9534
Morton Grove ***(G-15208)***
**K & H Tool Co** ........ G ....... 630 766-4588
Bensenville ***(G-1931)***
**K B Tool Inc** ........ G ....... 630 595-4340
Bensenville ***(G-1932)***
**K P Enterprises Inc** ........ G ....... 630 509-2174
Bensenville ***(G-1933)***
▲ **K-B-K Tool and Mfg Inc** ........ F ....... 847 674-3636
Skokie ***(G-20020)***
**Kam Tool and Mold** ........ G ....... 815 338-8360
Woodstock ***(G-22576)***
**Kaskaskia Tool and Machine Inc** ........ E ....... 618 475-3301
New Athens ***(G-15860)***
▲ **Kelco Industries Inc** ........ G ....... 815 334-3600
Woodstock ***(G-22577)***
▲ **Kenmode Tool and Engrg Inc** ........ C ....... 847 658-5041
Algonquin ***(G-396)***
**Kensen Tool & Die Inc** ........ F ....... 847 455-0150
Franklin Park ***(G-10512)***
**King Tool and Die Inc** ........ G ....... 630 787-0799
Bensenville ***(G-1934)***
**Kleen Cut Tool Inc** ........ G ....... 630 447-7020
Warrenville ***(G-21349)***
▲ **Knight Tool Works Inc** ........ F ....... 847 678-1237
Elgin ***(G-9091)***
**Kosmos Tool Inc** ........ F ....... 815 675-2200
Spring Grove ***(G-20343)***
**Koson Tool Inc** ........ G ....... 815 277-2107
Frankfort ***(G-10340)***
**Kreis Tool & Mfg Co Inc** ........ E ....... 847 289-3700
Elgin ***(G-9092)***
▲ **Kyowa Industrial Co Ltd USA** ........ F ....... 847 459-3500
Wheeling ***(G-22087)***
**L & M Tool & Die Co Inc** ........ G ....... 847 364-9760
Elk Grove Village ***(G-9581)***
**L & M Tool & Die Works** ........ G ....... 815 625-3256
Rock Falls ***(G-18140)***
**L C Mold Inc** ........ E ....... 847 593-5004
Rolling Meadows ***(G-18740)***
**L E D Tool & Die Inc** ........ G ....... 708 597-2505
Chicago ***(G-5422)***
**L T L Co** ........ F ....... 815 874-0913
Rockford ***(G-18459)***
**L-V Industries Inc** ........ F ....... 630 595-9251
Bensenville ***(G-1936)***
**Lah Inc** ........ G ....... 815 282-4939
Loves Park ***(G-13958)***
**Lake County Tool Works North** ........ G ....... 847 662-4542
Wadsworth ***(G-21324)***
**Lane Tool & Mfg Co Inc** ........ E ....... 847 622-1506
South Elgin ***(G-20216)***
**Lauber Tool Co Inc** ........ G ....... 847 228-5969
Elk Grove Village ***(G-9587)***
**Laystrom Manufacturing Co** ........ D ....... 773 342-4800
Chicago ***(G-5474)***
**Lehman Fast Tech** ........ G ....... 847 742-5202
Elgin ***(G-9094)***

SIC

## 35 INDUSTRIAL AND COMMERCIAL MACHINERY AND COMPUTER EQUIPMENT

| Company | Code | Phone |
|---|---|---|
| Lenhardt Tool and Die Company<br>Alton *(G-582)* | D | 618 462-1075 |
| Lens Lenticlear Lenticular<br>Itasca *(G-12303)* | F | 630 467-0900 |
| Lew-El Tool & Manufacturing Co<br>Chicago *(G-5497)* | F | 773 804-1133 |
| Libco Industries Inc<br>Roscoe *(G-18902)* | F | 815 623-7677 |
| Line Group Inc<br>Arlington Heights *(G-793)* | E | 847 593-6810 |
| Lion Tool & Die Co<br>Algonquin *(G-397)* | F | 847 658-8898 |
| Lmt Usa Inc<br>Waukegan *(G-21583)* | G | 630 969-5412 |
| Loren Tool & Manufacturing Co<br>Franklin Park *(G-10517)* | G | 630 595-0100 |
| Lorette Dies Inc<br>Elmhurst *(G-9902)* | G | 630 279-9682 |
| Lovejoy Industries Inc<br>Northbrook *(G-16299)* | G | 859 873-6828 |
| Lv Ventures Inc<br>Chicago *(G-5571)* | G | 312 993-1800 |
| Lv Ventures Inc<br>Chicago *(G-5572)* | E | 312 993-1758 |
| M S Tool & Engineering<br>West Chicago *(G-21735)* | F | 630 876-3437 |
| M Ward Manufacturing Co Inc<br>Evanston *(G-10067)* | E | 847 864-4786 |
| M-1 Tool Works Inc<br>McHenry *(G-14525)* | E | 815 344-1275 |
| Machine Works Inc<br>Alsip *(G-487)* | F | 708 597-1665 |
| Magic Mold Removal<br>Aurora *(G-1183)* | G | 630 486-0912 |
| Major Die & Engineering Co<br>Itasca *(G-12309)* | F | 630 773-3444 |
| ▲ Makray Manufacturing Company<br>Norridge *(G-16106)* | D | 708 456-7100 |
| Manor Tool and Mfg Co<br>Schiller Park *(G-19845)* | E | 847 678-2020 |
| Manufcture Dsign Innvation Inc<br>West Chicago *(G-21736)* | G | 773 526-7773 |
| Marathon Cutting Die Inc<br>Wheeling *(G-22101)* |  | 847 398-5165 |
| Marengo Tool & Die Works Inc<br>Marengo *(G-14236)* | E | 815 568-7411 |
| Marshall Mold Inc<br>Glendale Heights *(G-11046)* | G | 630 582-1800 |
| Master Tech Tool Inc<br>McHenry *(G-14528)* |  | 815 363-4001 |
| Masterite Tool & Mfg<br>Wheaton *(G-21969)* | G | 630 653-2028 |
| Matrix Tooling Inc<br>Wood Dale *(G-22397)* | D | 630 595-6144 |
| Maverick Tool Company Inc<br>Bensenville *(G-1947)* | E | 630 766-2313 |
| Mbs Manufacturing<br>Franklin Park *(G-10524)* | G | 630 227-0300 |
| McCurdy Tool & Machining Co<br>Caledonia *(G-2933)* | D | 815 765-2117 |
| ▲ Mennies Machine Company<br>Mark *(G-14299)* | C | 815 339-2226 |
| Merit Tool Engineering Co Inc<br>Chicago *(G-5694)* | G | 773 283-1114 |
| Met Plastics<br>Elk Grove Village *(G-9618)* | G | 847 228-5070 |
| Meta-Meg Tool Corporation<br>Elgin *(G-9106)* | G | 847 742-3600 |
| Metal Impact LLC<br>Elk Grove Village *(G-9620)* | D | 847 718-0192 |
| Method Molds Inc<br>Loves Park *(G-13965)* | G | 815 877-0191 |
| Metro Tool Company<br>Skokie *(G-20037)* | G | 847 673-6790 |
| Micro Mold Corporation<br>Addison *(G-207)* | G | 630 628-0777 |
| Micro Punch & Die Co<br>Rockford *(G-18500)* | F | 815 874-5544 |
| Micron Engineering Co<br>Crystal Lake *(G-7611)* | G | 815 455-2888 |
| Mid-City Die & Mold Corp<br>Chicago *(G-5729)* | G | 773 278-4844 |
| Mid-States Forging Die-Tool<br>Rockford *(G-18502)* | G | 815 226-2313 |
| Midwest Machine Tool Inc<br>Saint Anne *(G-19124)* | G | 815 427-8665 |
| Midwest Press Brake Dies Inc<br>Bridgeview *(G-2510)* | F | 708 598-3860 |
| Midwest Tool Technology<br>Elburn *(G-8897)* | G | 630 207-6076 |
| Mik Tool & Die Co Inc<br>Wauconda *(G-21484)* | G | 847 487-4311 |
| Milans Machining & Mfg Co Inc<br>Cicero *(G-7222)* | D | 708 780-6600 |
| Millennium Mold & Tool<br>Lake Zurich *(G-13104)* | G | 847 438-5600 |
| Millennium Mold Design Inc<br>McHenry *(G-14535)* | G | 815 344-9790 |
| Miller Midwestern Die Co<br>Woodstock *(G-22591)* | G | 815 338-6686 |
| Mold Express Inc<br>Chicago *(G-5789)* | G | 773 766-0874 |
| Monarch Manufacturing<br>Lombard *(G-13829)* | G | 630 519-4580 |
| Monarch Tool & Die Co<br>Elmhurst *(G-9913)* | E | 630 530-8886 |
| Mp Mold Inc<br>Addison *(G-223)* | G | 630 613-8086 |
| Mt Vernon Mold Works Inc<br>Mount Vernon *(G-15431)* | F | 618 242-6040 |
| Mushro Machine & Tool Co<br>Streator *(G-20697)* | G | 815 672-5848 |
| National Component Sales Inc<br>Arlington Heights *(G-808)* | F | 847 439-0333 |
| National Header Die Corp<br>Rockford *(G-18516)* | F | 815 636-7201 |
| Natural Products Inc<br>Northbrook *(G-16317)* | F | 847 509-5835 |
| Nemeth Tool Inc<br>Wood Dale *(G-22404)* | G | 630 595-0409 |
| Newko Tool & Engineering Co<br>Palatine *(G-17058)* | E | 847 359-1670 |
| ▲ Nicholas Machine & Tool Inc<br>Rosemont *(G-19018)* | G | 847 298-2035 |
| North America O M C G Inc<br>Bensenville *(G-1956)* | G | 630 860-1016 |
| North American Die Castng Assn<br>Chicago *(G-5931)* |  | 773 202-1000 |
| Northern Illinois Mold Corp<br>Dundee *(G-8565)* | F | 847 669-2100 |
| Octavia Tool & Gage Company<br>Elk Grove Village *(G-9661)* | G | 847 913-9233 |
| Odm Tool & Mfg Co Inc<br>Hodgkins *(G-11978)* | D | 708 485-6130 |
| Odom Tool and Technology Inc<br>Sycamore *(G-20811)* | G | 815 895-8545 |
| Ontario Die USA<br>Batavia *(G-1477)* | F | 630 761-6562 |
| Oostman Fabricating & Wldg Inc<br>Westmont *(G-21909)* | E | 630 241-1315 |
| P & L Tool & Manufacturing Co<br>Steger *(G-20575)* | G | 708 754-4777 |
| ▲ P M Mold Company<br>Schaumburg *(G-19678)* | E | 847 923-5400 |
| P M Mold Company<br>Schaumburg *(G-19679)* | E | 847 923-5400 |
| Panzer Tool Corp<br>Lombard *(G-13841)* | G | 630 519-5214 |
| Park Products Inc<br>Addison *(G-237)* | G | 630 543-2474 |
| Park Tool & Machine Co Inc<br>Villa Park *(G-21275)* | G | 630 530-5110 |
| Parker Tool & Die Co<br>Mundelein *(G-15541)* | G | 847 566-2229 |
| Parting Line Tool Inc<br>Huntley *(G-12166)* | F | 847 669-0331 |
| Partners Manufacturing Inc<br>Schaumburg *(G-19685)* | G | 847 352-1080 |
| Paul & Ron Manufacturing Inc<br>Viola *(G-21294)* | F | 309 596-2986 |
| PDQ Tool & Stamping Co<br>Dolton *(G-8374)* | G | 708 841-3000 |
| Pecora Tool & Die Co Inc<br>Schaumburg *(G-19686)* | G | 847 524-1275 |
| Pelco Tool & Mold Inc<br>Glendale Heights *(G-11056)* | G | 630 871-1010 |
| Performance Design Inc<br>Lake Zurich *(G-13113)* | G | 847 719-1535 |
| ▲ Performance Stamping Co Inc<br>Carpentersville *(G-3295)* | E | 847 426-2233 |
| ▲ Phoenix Tool Corp<br>Elk Grove Village *(G-9679)* | G | 847 956-1886 |
| Plastic Products Company Inc<br>Moline *(G-14962)* | G | 309 762-6532 |
| Plaza Tool & Mold Co<br>Wheeling *(G-22125)* | G | 847 537-2320 |
| Pontiac Engraving<br>Bensenville *(G-1965)* | G | 630 834-4424 |
| ▲ Power House Tool Inc<br>Joliet *(G-12552)* | E | 815 727-6301 |
| Precise Rotary Die Inc<br>Schiller Park *(G-19861)* | E | 847 678-0001 |
| Precision Engineering & Dev Co<br>Villa Park *(G-21278)* |  | 630 834-5956 |
| Precision Header Tooling Inc<br>Rockford *(G-18538)* | F | 815 874-9116 |
| Precision Process Corp<br>Elk Grove Village *(G-9695)* | E | 847 640-9820 |
| Precision Resource Inc<br>Vernon Hills *(G-21190)* | C | 847 383-1300 |
| Precision Tool & Die Company<br>Mount Zion *(G-15455)* | F | 217 864-3371 |
| Pro Built Tool & Mold Inc<br>Plainfield *(G-17645)* | G | 815 436-9088 |
| Pro-Mold Incorporated<br>Roselle *(G-18964)* | D | 630 893-3594 |
| Pro-Tech Metal Specialties Inc<br>Elmhurst *(G-9923)* | G | 630 279-7094 |
| Procraft Engraving Inc<br>Skokie *(G-20062)* | G | 847 673-1500 |
| Production Fabg & Stamping Inc<br>S Chicago Hts *(G-19111)* | F | 708 755-5468 |
| Prototek Tool & Mold Inc<br>Wauconda *(G-21496)* | G | 847 487-2708 |
| Prototype & Production Co<br>Wheeling *(G-22130)* | E | 847 419-1553 |
| Quad City Engineering Company<br>East Moline *(G-8692)* | E | 309 755-9762 |
| Qualitek Manufacturing Inc<br>Gurnee *(G-11496)* | G | 847 336-7570 |
| Quality Tool & Machine Inc<br>Chicago *(G-6248)* | G | 773 721-8655 |
| Quantum Engineering Inc<br>Elk Grove Village *(G-9703)* | G | 847 640-1340 |
| R & R Machining Inc<br>Benld *(G-1806)* | G | 217 835-4579 |
| R M Tool & Manufacturing Co<br>Elgin *(G-9160)* | G | 847 888-0433 |
| R-K Press Brake Dies Inc<br>Chicago *(G-6275)* | F | 708 371-1756 |
| ▲ Raco Steel Company<br>Markham *(G-14304)* | E | 708 339-2958 |
| Radius Machine & Tool Inc<br>Gurnee *(G-11497)* | F | 847 662-7690 |
| Rajner Quality Machine Works<br>Wheeling *(G-22131)* | G | 847 394-8999 |
| Ralph Cody Gravrok<br>Addison *(G-269)* | G | 630 628-9570 |
| ▲ RAO Design International Inc<br>Schiller Park *(G-19865)* |  | 847 671-6182 |
| Rapid Manufacturing Inc<br>Algonquin *(G-406)* | G | 847 458-0888 |
| Ravco Incorporated<br>Joliet *(G-12564)* | G | 815 725-9095 |
| Ray Tool & Engineering Inc<br>Saint Charles *(G-19251)* | E | 630 587-0000 |
| Redeen Engraving Inc<br>Elk Grove Village *(G-9712)* | G | 847 593-6500 |
| Reliable Die Service Inc<br>Bedford Park *(G-1577)* | F | 708 458-5155 |
| Republic Drill<br>Melrose Park *(G-14686)* | G | 708 865-7666 |
| Resinite Corporation<br>Wheeling *(G-22138)* | C | 847 537-4250 |
| Reynolds Manufacturing Company<br>Milan *(G-14803)* | E | 309 787-8600 |
| Rijon Manufacturing Company<br>Blue Island *(G-2266)* | G | 708 388-2295 |
| Risk Never Die Inc<br>Chicago *(G-6360)* | G | 708 240-4194 |
| Riverside Tool & Die Co<br>Peoria *(G-17443)* | F | 309 689-0104 |
| ▲ Rj Stuckel Co Inc<br>Elk Grove Village *(G-9716)* |  | 800 789-7220 |
| Roanoke Companies Group Inc<br>Aurora *(G-1074)* | G | 630 499-5870 |
| Rock Valley Die Sinking Inc<br>Rockford *(G-18565)* | F | 815 874-5511 |
| Rockford Carbide Die & Tool<br>Rockford *(G-18570)* | G | 815 394-0645 |
| Rockford Tool and Mfg Co<br>Rockford *(G-18588)* | F | 815 398-5876 |
| Rockford Toolcraft Inc<br>Rockford *(G-18589)* | C | 815 398-5507 |
| Rogus Tool Inc<br>Des Plaines *(G-8268)* | G | 847 824-5939 |
| Roscoe Tool & Manufacturing<br>Roscoe *(G-18918)* | E | 815 633-8808 |
| Roto-Die Company Inc<br>Lombard *(G-13848)* | G | 630 932-8605 |

| | | | |
|---|---|---|---|
| **Belcar Products Inc** | G | 630 462-1950 | Carol Stream *(G-3113)* |
| ◆ **Belden Tools Inc** | E | 708 344-4600 | Broadview *(G-2562)* |
| ▲ **Bertsche Engineering Corp** | F | 847 537-8757 | Buffalo Grove *(G-2664)* |
| **Besly Cutting Tools Inc** | F | 815 389-2231 | South Beloit *(G-20141)* |
| **Big Kser Precision Tooling Inc** | E | 847 228-7660 | Hoffman Estates *(G-11996)* |
| **Blackhawk Industrial Dist Inc** | F | 773 736-9600 | Carol Stream *(G-3117)* |
| **Bourn & Bourn Inc** | C | 815 965-4013 | Rockford *(G-18289)* |
| **Bradley Machining Inc** | F | 630 543-2875 | Addison *(G-59)* |
| **Brunner & Lay Inc** | C | 847 678-3232 | Elmhurst *(G-9843)* |
| **Burnex Corporation** | E | 815 728-1317 | Ringwood *(G-17988)* |
| **C & C Tooling Inc** | F | 630 543-5523 | Addison *(G-63)* |
| **Cams Inc** | G | 773 929-3656 | Chicago *(G-4225)* |
| **Carbco Manufacturing Inc** | F | 630 377-1410 | Saint Charles *(G-19150)* |
| **Center Tool Company Inc** | G | 847 683-7559 | Hampshire *(G-11544)* |
| **Central Illinois Scale Co** | G | 309 697-0033 | Peoria *(G-17338)* |
| ▲ **Champion Chisel Works Inc** | F | 815 535-0647 | Rock Falls *(G-18128)* |
| ▲ **Chicago Hardware and Fix Co** | D | 847 455-6609 | Franklin Park *(G-10429)* |
| **Chicago Quadrill Co** | G | 847 824-4196 | Des Plaines *(G-8167)* |
| **Circle Cutting Tools Inc** | G | 815 398-4153 | Rockford *(G-18310)* |
| ▲ **Cjt Koolcarb Inc** | C | 630 690-5933 | Carol Stream *(G-3129)* |
| ▲ **Comet Tool Inc** | E | 847 956-0126 | Elk Grove Village *(G-9383)* |
| **Coordinate Machine Company** | E | 630 894-9880 | Roselle *(G-18935)* |
| **Craftstech Inc** | E | 847 758-3100 | Elk Grove Village *(G-9398)* |
| **Crown Tool Company Inc** | G | 630 766-3050 | Bensenville *(G-1872)* |
| **Custom Cutting Tools Inc** | G | 815 986-0320 | Loves Park *(G-13931)* |
| **Custom Cuttingedge Tool Inc** | G | 847 622-0457 | Batavia *(G-1435)* |
| **Custom Feeder Co of Rockford** | E | 815 654-2444 | Loves Park *(G-13932)* |
| **Custom Machining & Design LLC** | G | 847 364-2601 | Elk Grove Village *(G-9403)* |
| **Custom Tool & Gage Co Inc** | G | 847 671-5306 | Franklin Park *(G-10450)* |
| **Custom Tool Inc** | F | 217 465-8538 | Paris *(G-17145)* |
| **D & R Ekstrom Carlson Co** | G | 815 394-1744 | Rockford *(G-18331)* |
| ▲ **Damen Carbide Tool Company Inc** | E | 630 766-7875 | Wood Dale *(G-22357)* |
| **David Linderholm** | G | 847 336-3755 | Waukegan *(G-21548)* |
| **Del-Co-West Inc** | F | 309 799-7543 | Milan *(G-14783)* |
| **Design Systems Inc** | E | 309 263-7706 | Morton *(G-15157)* |
| **Die Specialty Co** | G | 312 303-5738 | La Grange Park *(G-12755)* |
| ▲ **Dmg Mori Usa Inc** | D | 847 593-5400 | Hoffman Estates *(G-12006)* |
| **Dover Energy Automation LLC** | E | 630 541-1540 | Downers Grove *(G-8432)* |
| **Dundick Corporation** | E | 708 656-6363 | Cicero *(G-7192)* |
| **Dynacut Industries Inc** | E | 630 462-1900 | Carol Stream *(G-3145)* |
| **Edmik Inc** | E | 847 263-0460 | Gurnee *(G-11445)* |
| **EJ Cady & Company** | G | 847 537-2239 | Wheeling *(G-22045)* |
| **Electro-Matic Products Co** | F | 773 235-4010 | Chicago *(G-4720)* |
| **Elgin CAM Co** | G | 847 741-1757 | Elgin *(G-9021)* |
| **Emtech Machining & Grinding** | G | 815 338-1580 | Woodstock *(G-22565)* |
| **Engineering Products Company** | G | 815 436-9055 | Plainfield *(G-17595)* |
| ▲ **Engis Corporation** | C | 847 808-9400 | Wheeling *(G-22047)* |
| ▲ **Eri America Inc** | G | 847 550-9710 | Lake Zurich *(G-13070)* |
| ▲ **Estwing Manufacturing Co Inc** | B | 815 397-9521 | Rockford *(G-18370)* |
| ◆ **Federal Signal Corporation** | D | 630 954-2000 | Oak Brook *(G-16510)* |
| **Forster Products Inc** | E | 815 493-6360 | Lanark *(G-13154)* |
| **Fotofabrication Corp** | E | 773 463-6211 | Chicago *(G-4878)* |
| **Fox Machine & Tool Inc** | G | 847 357-1845 | Elk Grove Village *(G-9489)* |
| **Fulton Corporation** | D | 815 589-3211 | Fulton *(G-10701)* |
| **G & S Manufacturing Inc** | F | 847 674-7666 | Bannockburn *(G-1258)* |
| **Gage Assembly Co** | D | 847 679-5180 | Lincolnwood *(G-13512)* |
| ▲ **Galaxy Industries Inc** | D | 847 639-8580 | Cary *(G-3345)* |
| ▲ **Galaxy Sourcing Inc** | G | 630 532-5003 | Villa Park *(G-21254)* |
| ▲ **Gator Products Inc** | G | 847 836-0581 | Gilberts *(G-10919)* |
| **General Cutng Tl Svc & Mfg Inc** | F | 847 677-8770 | Lincolnwood *(G-13513)* |
| **Gki Incorporated** | E | 815 459-2330 | Rockford *(G-18398)* |
| **Glen Products** | G | 847 998-1361 | Glenview *(G-11129)* |
| **Greenlee Diamond Tool Co** | E | 866 451-3316 | Elk Grove Village *(G-9512)* |
| **Grove Industrial** | G | 815 385-4800 | Johnsburg *(G-12435)* |
| **Guide Line Industries Inc** | F | 815 777-3722 | Scales Mound *(G-19415)* |
| **H R Slater Co Inc** | F | 312 666-1855 | Chicago *(G-5023)* |
| ▲ **Haimer Usa LLC** | G | 630 833-1500 | Villa Park *(G-21258)* |
| ▲ **Hallmark Industries Inc** | F | 847 301-8050 | Schaumburg *(G-19546)* |
| ▲ **Harig Manufacturing Corp** | E | 847 647-9500 | Skokie *(G-20011)* |
| **Harris Precision Tools Inc** | G | 708 422-5808 | Chicago Ridge *(G-7149)* |
| **Hartland Cutting Tools Inc** | F | 847 639-9400 | Cary *(G-3350)* |
| ▲ **Heidenhain Holding Inc** | G | 716 661-1700 | Schaumburg *(G-19552)* |
| ▲ **Heim Group** | G | 708 496-7403 | Chicago *(G-5069)* |
| ▲ **Henry Technologies Inc** | G | 217 483-2406 | Chatham *(G-3621)* |
| ▲ **Hg-Farley Laserlab USA Inc** | G | 815 874-1400 | Rockford *(G-18418)* |
| **Hilti Inc** | G | 847 364-9818 | Elmhurst *(G-9882)* |
| ◆ **Holden Industries Inc** | F | 847 940-1500 | Deerfield *(G-8013)* |
| **Ideal Industries Inc** | C | 815 895-1108 | Sycamore *(G-20801)* |
| **Illinois Broaching Co** | G | 847 678-3080 | Schiller Park *(G-19840)* |
| **Illinois Carbide Tool Co Inc** | F | 847 244-1110 | Waukegan *(G-21569)* |
| **Imprex International Inc** | G | 847 364-4930 | Arlington Heights *(G-775)* |
| ▲ **Industrial Diamond Products** | E | 847 272-7840 | Northbrook *(G-16276)* |
| **Industrial Instrument Svc Corp** | G | 773 581-3355 | Chicago *(G-5177)* |
| ▲ **Infinity Tool Mfg LLC** | G | 618 439-4042 | Benton *(G-2031)* |
| ▲ **Ingersoll Cutting Tool Company** | B | 815 387-6600 | Rockford *(G-18432)* |
| ◆ **Ingersoll Machine Tools Inc** | C | 815 987-6000 | Rockford *(G-18433)* |
| **Inland Tool Company** | E | 217 792-3206 | Mount Pulaski *(G-15389)* |
| ▲ **Intech Industries Inc** | F | 847 487-5599 | Wauconda *(G-21473)* |
| **Intrepid Tool Industries LLC** | E | 773 467-4200 | Chicago *(G-5229)* |
| **Irwin Industrial Tool Company** | C | 815 235-4171 | Freeport *(G-10669)* |
| **Ivan Schwenker** | G | 630 543-7798 | Addison *(G-156)* |
| ▲ **J & J Carbide & Tool Inc** | E | 708 489-0300 | Alsip *(G-475)* |
| **J H Benedict Co Inc** | D | 309 694-3111 | East Peoria *(G-8715)* |
| **J M Resources Inc** | F | 630 690-7337 | Elgin *(G-9080)* |
| **Jamco Tool & Cams Inc** | F | 847 678-0280 | Franklin Park *(G-10505)* |
| ▲ **Jerhen Industries Inc** | D | 815 397-0400 | Rockford *(G-18443)* |
| **Johnson Pattern & Mch Works** | E | 815 433-2775 | Ottawa *(G-16964)* |
| ▲ **Jrm International Inc** | G | 815 282-9330 | Loves Park *(G-13955)* |
| **K Systems Corporation** | G | 708 449-0400 | Hillside *(G-11921)* |
| **K-C Tool Co** | G | 630 983-5960 | Naperville *(G-15683)* |
| **Kaydon Acquisition Xii Inc** | E | 217 443-3592 | Danville *(G-7740)* |
| **Kennametal Inc** | F | 309 578-1888 | Mossville *(G-15253)* |
| **Kennametal Inc** | E | 630 963-2910 | Lisle *(G-13613)* |
| **Kennametal Inc** | C | 815 226-0650 | Rockford *(G-18454)* |
| **Keonix Corporation** | G | 847 259-9430 | Arlington Heights *(G-788)* |
| ▲ **Keson Industries Inc** | E | 630 820-4200 | Aurora *(G-1042)* |
| **Kile Machine & Tool Inc** | G | 217 446-8616 | Danville *(G-7744)* |
| ▲ **Kitagawa Usa Inc** | E | 847 310-8198 | Schaumburg *(G-19599)* |
| ▲ **Kitagawa-Northtech Inc** | E | 847 310-8787 | Schaumburg *(G-19600)* |
| ▲ **Kitamura Machinery USA Inc** | F | 847 520-7755 | Wheeling *(G-22084)* |
| **Klein Tools Inc** | G | 815 282-0530 | Machesney Park *(G-14086)* |
| **Kmp Tool Grinding Inc** | G | 847 205-9640 | Northbrook *(G-16288)* |
| **Kut-Rite Tool Company** | F | 630 837-8130 | Streamwood *(G-20664)* |
| **L & M Screw Machine Products** | F | 630 801-0455 | Montgomery *(G-15052)* |
| **L S Starrett Co** | G | 847 816-9999 | Vernon Hills *(G-21178)* |
| ▲ **LFA Industries Inc** | G | 630 762-7391 | Saint Charles *(G-19210)* |
| ▲ **Lmt Onsrud LP** | C | 847 362-1560 | Waukegan *(G-21582)* |
| **Lmt Usa Inc** | G | 630 969-5412 | Waukegan *(G-21583)* |
| **Logan Actuator Co** | G | 815 943-9500 | Harvard *(G-11640)* |
| ▲ **Logan Graphic Products Inc** | D | 847 526-5515 | Wauconda *(G-21479)* |
| ▲ **Machine Technology Inc** | G | 815 444-4837 | Crystal Lake *(G-7604)* |
| **Machine Tool Acc & Mfg Co** | G | 773 489-0903 | Chicago *(G-5592)* |
| ▼ **Magna-Lock Usa Inc** | F | 815 962-8700 | Rockford *(G-18480)* |
| **Matheu Tool Works Inc** | G | 773 327-9274 | Chicago *(G-5652)* |
| **Maverick Tool Company Inc** | E | 630 766-2313 | Bensenville *(G-1947)* |
| **Meinhardt Diamond Tool Co** | G | 773 267-3260 | Chicago *(G-5681)* |
| **Merit Tool Engineering Co Inc** | G | 773 283-1114 | Chicago *(G-5694)* |
| **Method Molds Inc** | G | 815 877-0191 | Loves Park *(G-13965)* |
| **Metrom LLC (not Llc)** | G | 847 847-7233 | Lake Zurich *(G-13102)* |
| **Mid-West Feeder Inc** | E | 815 544-2994 | Belvidere *(G-1771)* |
| ▲ **Midland Manufacturing Corp** | C | 847 677-0333 | Skokie *(G-20039)* |
| **Midwest Machine Tool Inc** | G | 815 427-8665 | Saint Anne *(G-19124)* |
| **Midwest Tool & Manufacturing** | G | 815 282-6754 | Machesney Park *(G-14094)* |
| ▲ **Mincon Inc** | E | 618 435-3404 | Benton *(G-2035)* |
| **Mitsubishi Materials USA Corp** | F | 847 519-1601 | Schaumburg *(G-19649)* |

SIC SECTION — 35 INDUSTRIAL AND COMMERCIAL MACHINERY AND COMPUTER EQUIPMENT

▲ Royal Die & Stamping Co Inc ..........C....... 630 766-2685
Carol Stream *(G-3229)*

S & S Tool Company ..........G....... 847 891-0780
Schaumburg *(G-19715)*

Schwarz Bros Manufacturing Co ..........G....... 309 342-5814
Galesburg *(G-10776)*

Select Tool & Die Inc ..........G....... 630 372-0300
Bartlett *(G-1372)*

Select Tool & Die Inc ..........G....... 630 980-8458
Roselle *(G-18976)*

Serv-All Die & Tool Company ..........E....... 815 459-2900
Crystal Lake *(G-7647)*

Service Machine Jobs ..........G....... 815 986-3033
Rockford *(G-18613)*

Sharp Metal Products ..........G....... 847 439-5393
Elk Grove Village *(G-9735)*

Shelby Tool & Die Inc ..........G....... 217 774-2189
Shelbyville *(G-19915)*

Shup Tool & Machine Co ..........G....... 618 931-2596
Granite City *(G-11302)*

Sieber Tool Engineering LP ..........F....... 630 462-9370
Carol Stream *(G-3240)*

Sierra Manufacturing Corp ..........G....... 630 458-8830
Addison *(G-289)*

Smithco Fabricators Inc ..........F....... 847 678-1619
Schiller Park *(G-19873)*

Soldy Manufacturing Inc ..........D....... 847 671-3396
Schiller Park *(G-19875)*

Sonoco Prtective Solutions Inc ..........E....... 815 787-5244
Dekalb *(G-8119)*

Sopher Design & Manufacturing ..........G....... 309 699-6419
East Peoria *(G-8735)*

Southern Mold Finishing Inc ..........F....... 618 983-5049
Johnston City *(G-12446)*

▲ Southern Steel and Wire Inc ..........G....... 618 654-2161
Highland *(G-11812)*

Spannagel Tool & Die ..........E....... 630 969-7575
Downers Grove *(G-8526)*

Special Fastener Operations ..........G....... 815 544-6449
Belvidere *(G-1784)*

Specific Press Brake Dies Inc ..........F....... 708 478-1776
Mokena *(G-14904)*

▲ Speco Inc ..........E....... 847 678-4240
Schiller Park *(G-19876)*

Spectron Manufacturing ..........G....... 720 879-7605
Bloomingdale *(G-2138)*

Standard Machine & Tool Corp ..........F....... 309 762-6431
Moline *(G-14972)*

Standex International Corp ..........E....... 630 588-0400
Carol Stream *(G-3249)*

Stanick Tool Manufacturing Co ..........G....... 847 726-7090
Lake Zurich *(G-13135)*

▲ Stanley Hartco Co ..........E....... 847 967-1122
Skokie *(G-20090)*

▲ Star Die Molding Inc ..........D....... 847 766-7952
Elk Grove Village *(G-9754)*

Sterling Die Inc ..........G....... 216 267-1300
Glendale Heights *(G-11074)*

Sterling Tool & Manufacturing ..........G....... 847 304-1800
Barrington *(G-1305)*

Stumpfoll Tool & Mfg ..........G....... 312 733-2632
Chicago *(G-6609)*

Sure-Way Die Designs Inc ..........F....... 630 323-0370
Westmont *(G-21924)*

Surfacetec Corp ..........F....... 630 521-0001
Franklin Park *(G-10600)*

▲ Suruga USA Corp ..........E....... 630 628-0989
Schaumburg *(G-19747)*

▲ Sws Industries Inc ..........E....... 904 482-0091
Woodstock *(G-22616)*

▲ T & H Lemont Inc ..........D....... 708 482-1800
Countryside *(G-7446)*

T & K Tool & Manufacturing Co ..........G....... 815 338-0954
Woodstock *(G-22617)*

T M T Industries Inc ..........E....... 815 562-0111
Rochelle *(G-18111)*

T N T Industries Inc ..........F....... 630 879-1522
Batavia *(G-1503)*

T R Jones Machine Co Inc ..........G....... 815 356-5000
Machesney Park *(G-14111)*

Tapco USA Inc ..........G....... 815 877-4039
Loves Park *(G-13998)*

Tauber Brothers Tool & Die Co ..........E....... 708 867-9100
Chicago *(G-6679)*

Taylor Design Inc ..........G....... 815 389-3991
Roscoe *(G-18924)*

Technical Tool Enterprise ..........G....... 630 893-3390
Addison *(G-307)*

Technique Engineering Inc ..........F....... 847 816-1870
Waukegan *(G-21622)*

Tella Tool & Mfg Co ..........D....... 630 495-0545
Lombard *(G-13867)*

Ternkirst Tl & Die & Mch Works ..........F....... 847 437-8360
Elk Grove Village *(G-9776)*

Terry Tool & Machining Corp ..........G....... 847 289-1054
East Dundee *(G-8658)*

Three Star Mfg Co Inc ..........G....... 847 526-2222
Wauconda *(G-21510)*

Titan Tool Company Inc ..........G....... 847 671-0045
Franklin Park *(G-10607)*

Tomco Die & Kellering Co ..........G....... 847 678-8113
Franklin Park *(G-10608)*

Tool-Masters Tool & Stamp Inc ..........G....... 815 465-6830
Grant Park *(G-11316)*

Top Notch Tool & Supply Inc ..........G....... 815 633-6295
Cherry Valley *(G-3648)*

Tower Tool & Engineering Inc ..........F....... 815 654-1115
Machesney Park *(G-14112)*

Treasure Keeper Inc ..........G....... 630 761-1500
Batavia *(G-1509)*

Trend Technologies LLC ..........C....... 847 640-2382
Elk Grove Village *(G-9789)*

Tri-Par Die and Mold Corp ..........E....... 630 232-8800
South Elgin *(G-20229)*

Tri-Star Engineering Inc ..........E....... 847 595-3377
Elk Grove Village *(G-9791)*

▲ Triangle Dies and Supplies Inc ..........D....... 630 454-3200
Batavia *(G-1511)*

Triumph Twist Drill Co Inc ..........B....... 815 459-6250
Crystal Lake *(G-7670)*

Turbo Tool & Mold Co ..........G....... 708 615-1730
Broadview *(G-2618)*

U S Machine & Tool ..........G....... 847 740-0077
Hainesville *(G-11524)*

Ultra Polishing Inc ..........E....... 630 635-2926
Schaumburg *(G-19777)*

Ultra Specialty Holdings Inc ..........E....... 847 437-8110
Elk Grove Village *(G-9796)*

Ultra-Metric Tool Co ..........F....... 773 281-4200
Chicago *(G-6808)*

Unified Tool Die & Mfg Co Inc ..........F....... 847 678-3773
Schiller Park *(G-19878)*

United Craftsmen Ltd ..........F....... 815 626-7802
Sterling *(G-20618)*

United Skilled Inc ..........G....... 815 874-9696
Rockford *(G-18661)*

United Tool and Engineering Co ..........D....... 815 389-3021
South Beloit *(G-20171)*

Urway Design and Manufacturing ..........G....... 847 674-7464
Skokie *(G-20106)*

V & S Tool Co ..........G....... 847 891-0780
Schaumburg *(G-19784)*

V-Cam Inc ..........F....... 217 835-4381
Benld *(G-1807)*

Vanart Engineering Company ..........E....... 847 678-6255
Franklin Park *(G-10620)*

Vector Mold & Tool Inc ..........G....... 847 437-0110
Des Plaines *(G-8297)*

Vega Molded Products Inc ..........G....... 847 428-7761
Gilberts *(G-10940)*

▲ Vhd Inc ..........E....... 815 544-2169
Belvidere *(G-1794)*

Vicma Tool Co ..........G....... 847 541-0177
Wheeling *(G-22178)*

Voco Tool & Mfg Inc ..........G....... 708 771-3800
Forest Park *(G-10256)*

Voss Pattern Works Inc ..........G....... 618 233-4242
Belleville *(G-1689)*

▲ W A Whitney Co ..........C....... 815 964-6771
Rockford *(G-18671)*

Walt Ltd ..........E....... 312 337-2756
Chicago *(G-6936)*

Wand Enterprises Inc ..........F....... 847 433-0231
Highland Park *(G-11880)*

Wand Tool Enterprise ..........G....... 847 433-0231
Highland Park *(G-11881)*

Wapro Inc ..........G....... 888 927-8677
Chicago *(G-6938)*

Wardzala Industries Inc ..........F....... 847 288-9909
Franklin Park *(G-10627)*

Wauconda Tool & Engineering Co ..........E....... 847 608-0602
Elgin *(G-9231)*

Wauconda Tool & Engrg LLC ..........D....... 847 658-4588
Algonquin *(G-412)*

West End Tool & Die Inc ..........G....... 815 462-3040
New Lenox *(G-15927)*

Westwood Machine & Tool Co ..........F....... 815 626-5090
Sterling *(G-20622)*

White Jig Grinding ..........G....... 847 888-2260
South Elgin *(G-20234)*

▲ Whitney Roper LLC ..........D....... 815 962-3011
Rockford *(G-18681)*

▲ Whitney Roper Rockford Inc ..........D....... 815 962-3011
Rockford *(G-18682)*

William J Kline & Co Inc ..........F....... 815 338-2055
Woodstock *(G-22625)*

Windy City Cutting Die Inc ..........E....... 630 521-9410
Bensenville *(G-2016)*

Wirco Inc ..........D....... 217 398-3200
Champaign *(G-3561)*

Wireformers Inc ..........E....... 847 718-1920
Mount Prospect *(G-15384)*

Wisniwski Rchard Stl Rule Dies ..........G....... 773 282-1144
Chicago *(G-7008)*

Witte Kendel Die & Mold ..........G....... 815 233-9270
Freeport *(G-10699)*

World Wide Rotary Die ..........G....... 630 521-9410
Bensenville *(G-2018)*

Wright Tool & Die Inc ..........F....... 815 669-2020
McHenry *(G-14573)*

Z-Tech Inc ..........G....... 815 335-7395
Winnebago *(G-22299)*

Zender Enterprises Ltd ..........G....... 773 282-2293
Chicago *(G-7063)*

## 3545 Machine Tool Access

▲ 2I Technologies LLC ..........G....... 312 526-3900
Chicago *(G-3666)*

3d Manufacturing Corporation ..........G....... 815 806-9200
Frankfort *(G-10290)*

A J Manufacturing Co Inc ..........G....... 630 832-2828
Elmhurst *(G-9828)*

A R Tech & Tool Inc ..........G....... 708 599-5745
Bridgeview *(G-2458)*

A&W Tool Inc ..........G....... 815 653-1700
Ringwood *(G-17986)*

Abbco Inc ..........E....... 630 595-7115
Elk Grove Village *(G-9253)*

Ability Tool Co ..........E....... 815 633-5909
Machesney Park *(G-14050)*

Accu-Cut Diamond Tool Company ..........F....... 708 457-8800
Norridge *(G-16095)*

Accu-Grind Manufacturing Inc ..........F....... 847 526-2700
Wauconda *(G-21437)*

▼ Acme Industrial Company ..........C....... 847 428-3911
Carpentersville *(G-3271)*

Active Grinding & Mfg Co ..........F....... 708 344-0510
Broadview *(G-2554)*

▲ Adjustable Clamp Company ..........C....... 312 666-0640
Chicago *(G-3751)*

ADS LLC ..........D....... 256 430-3366
Burr Ridge *(G-2820)*

Advanced Machine Co Inc ..........G....... 773 545-9790
Chicago *(G-3770)*

▲ Advent Tool & Mfg Inc ..........F....... 847 395-9707
Antioch *(G-613)*

▲ Air Gage Company ..........C....... 847 695-0911
Elgin *(G-8941)*

Alcon Tool & Mfg Co Inc ..........F....... 773 545-8742
Chicago *(G-3798)*

Alfa Mfg Industries Inc ..........E....... 847 470-9595
Morton Grove *(G-15186)*

Alliance Tool & Manufacturing ..........F....... 708 345-5444
Maywood *(G-14415)*

Allkut Tool Incorporated ..........G....... 815 476-9656
Wilmington *(G-22269)*

Alpha Swiss Industries Inc ..........G....... 815 455-3031
Crystal Lake *(G-7530)*

▼ American Machine Tools Inc ..........G....... 773 775-6285
Chicago *(G-3861)*

Ammentorp Tool Company Inc ..........G....... 847 671-9290
Franklin Park *(G-10395)*

Arrow Engineering Inc ..........E....... 815 397-0862
Rockford *(G-18270)*

Asko Inc ..........E....... 773 785-4515
South Holland *(G-20248)*

Assurance Technologies Inc ..........F....... 630 550-5000
Bartlett *(G-1331)*

◆ Atm America Corp ..........E....... 800 298-0030
Chicago *(G-3986)*

▲ Auto Meter Products Inc ..........C....... 815 991-2292
Sycamore *(G-20788)*

Autocut Machine Co ..........G....... 815 436-1900
Elwood *(G-9978)*

▲ Automatic Precision Inc ..........E....... 708 867-1116
Chicago *(G-3992)*

Balanstar Corporation ..........F....... 773 261-5034
Chicago *(G-4030)*

Barcor Inc ..........F....... 847 940-0750
Bannockburn *(G-1255)*

S I C

Employee Codes: A=Over 500 employees, B=251-500
C=101-250, D=51-100, E=20-50, F=10-19, G=3-9

2017 Harris Illinois
Industrial Directory

1067

SIC SECTION 35 INDUSTRIAL AND COMMERCIAL MACHINERY AND COMPUTER EQUIPMENT

Miyanohitec Machinery Inc ....G.... 847 382-2794
Barrington (G-1292)
Moldtronics Inc ....E.... 630 968-7000
Downers Grove (G-8488)
National Bushing & Mfg ....G.... 847 847-1553
Lake Zurich (G-13108)
◆ New World Products Inc ....G.... 630 690-5625
Carol Stream (G-3205)
Nex Gen Manufacturing Inc ....G.... 847 487-7077
Wauconda (G-21489)
▲ NNt Enterprises Incorporated ....E.... 630 875-9600
Itasca (G-12332)
OSG Usa Inc ....C.... 630 274-2100
Bensenville (G-1961)
P K Neuses Incorporated ....G.... 847 253-6555
Rolling Meadows (G-18756)
P-K Tool & Mfg Co ....D.... 773 235-4700
Chicago (G-6046)
▲ Pace Machinery Group Inc ....F.... 630 377-1750
Wasco (G-21373)
Palmgren Steel Products Inc ....F.... 773 265-5700
Chicago (G-6066)
Park Products Inc ....G.... 630 543-2474
Addison (G-237)
PDQ Machine Inc ....G.... 815 282-7575
Machesney Park (G-14096)
▲ Pfeifer Industries LLC ....G.... 630 596-9000
Naperville (G-15725)
Pixel Pushers Incorporated ....G.... 847 550-6560
Lake Zurich (G-13114)
Pontiac Engraving ....G.... 630 834-4424
Bensenville (G-1965)
Porcelain Enamel Finishers ....G.... 312 808-1560
Chicago (G-6157)
Port Byron Machine Inc ....G.... 309 523-9111
Port Byron (G-17722)
▲ Powertronics Surgitech USA Inc ....G.... 630 305-4261
Naperville (G-15731)
◆ Precision Brand Products Inc ....E.... 630 969-7200
Downers Grove (G-8509)
◆ Precision Dormer LLC ....C.... 800 877-3745
Elgin (G-9146)
◆ Precision Gage Company ....F.... 630 655-2121
Burr Ridge (G-2875)
Precision Header Tooling Inc ....F.... 815 874-9116
Rockford (G-18538)
Precision Masters ....E.... 815 397-3894
Rockford (G-18539)
Precision Prismatic Inc ....G.... 708 424-0905
Chicago Ridge (G-7154)
Precision Tool & Die Company ....F.... 217 864-3371
Mount Zion (G-15455)
▲ Prince Industries Inc ....C.... 630 588-0088
Carol Stream (G-3220)
▲ Progrssive Cmponents Intl Corp ....D.... 847 487-1000
Wauconda (G-21494)
▼ Proto-Cutter Inc ....F.... 815 232-2300
Freeport (G-10681)
Prototype & Production Co ....E.... 847 419-1553
Wheeling (G-22130)
Quality Tech Tool Inc ....E.... 847 690-9643
Bensenville (G-1973)
Rdh Inc of Rockford ....F.... 815 874-9421
Rockford (G-18550)
▲ Regal Cutting Tools Inc ....C.... 815 389-3461
Roscoe (G-18912)
▲ Reichel Hardware Company Inc ....G.... 630 762-7394
Saint Charles (G-19252)
Reino Tool & Manufacturing Co ....F.... 773 588-5800
Chicago (G-6326)
▲ Rend Lake Carbide Inc ....G.... 618 438-0160
Benton (G-2039)
Retondo Enterprises Inc ....G.... 630 837-8130
Streamwood (G-20671)
Rockford Jobbing Service Inc ....G.... 815 398-8661
Rockford (G-18576)
Rockform Tooling & Machinery ....G.... 815 398-7650
Rockford (G-18592)
▲ Roll McHning Tech Slutions Inc ....E.... 815 372-9100
Romeoville (G-18864)
Roll Rite Inc ....G.... 815 645-8600
Davis Junction (G-7814)
Roscoe Tool & Manufacturing ....E.... 815 633-8808
Roscoe (G-18918)
▲ Ryeson Corporation ....D.... 847 455-8677
Carol Stream (G-3230)
S & J Industrial Supply Corp ....F.... 708 339-1708
South Holland (G-20303)
▲ S & W Manufacturing Co Inc ....E.... 630 595-5044
Bensenville (G-1984)

S Vs Industries Inc ....G.... 630 408-1083
Hoffman Estates (G-12047)
Sacco-Camex Inc ....G.... 630 595-8090
Franklin Park (G-10580)
Saint-Gobain Abrasives Inc ....C.... 630 868-8060
Carol Stream (G-3232)
▲ Sandtech Inc ....F.... 847 470-9595
Morton Grove (G-15234)
Scale-Tronix Inc ....F.... 630 653-3377
Carol Stream (G-3235)
Schaefer Technologies LLC ....G.... 630 406-9377
Batavia (G-1493)
▲ Sensible Products Inc ....G.... 773 774-7400
Chicago (G-6477)
▲ Shape-Master Tool Co ....E.... 815 522-6186
Kirkland (G-12718)
Shelby Tool & Die Inc ....G.... 217 774-2189
Shelbyville (G-19915)
▲ Shinwa Measuring Tools Corp ....G.... 847 598-3701
Schaumburg (G-19726)
Sieber Tool Engineering LP ....F.... 630 462-9370
Carol Stream (G-3240)
▲ Sollami Company ....E.... 618 988-1521
Herrin (G-11755)
Spectris Holdings Inc ....F.... 847 680-3709
Libertyville (G-13383)
▲ Spie Tool Co ....E.... 847 891-6556
Schaumburg (G-19738)
Stock Gears Inc ....F.... 224 653-9489
Elk Grove Village (G-9758)
Stuhr Manufacturing Co ....F.... 815 398-2460
Rockford (G-18636)
Tag Sales Co Inc ....G.... 630 990-3434
Hinsdale (G-11966)
Tag Tool Services Incorporated ....E.... 309 694-2400
East Peoria (G-8736)
Tapco Cutting Tools Inc ....G.... 815 877-4039
Loves Park (G-13997)
Tapco USA Inc ....G.... 815 877-4039
Loves Park (G-13998)
Team Cnc Inc ....G.... 630 377-2723
Saint Charles (G-19280)
Technical Tool Enterprise ....G.... 630 893-3390
Addison (G-307)
Techniks LLC ....E.... 815 689-2748
Cullom (G-7685)
Techny Precision Mfg Inc ....F.... 630 543-7065
Addison (G-308)
Thermal-Tech Systems Inc ....E.... 630 639-5115
West Chicago (G-21780)
Thermoplastec Inc ....F.... 815 873-9288
Rockford (G-18647)
▲ Thomas Packaging LLC ....F.... 847 392-1652
Rolling Meadows (G-18782)
Thomas-Zientz Group Inc ....G.... 847 395-2363
Antioch (G-657)
Thread & Gage Co Inc ....G.... 815 675-2305
Spring Grove (G-20367)
Tool Engrg Consulting Mfg LLC ....G.... 815 316-2304
Rockford (G-18654)
Toolmasters LLC ....E.... 815 968-0961
Rockford (G-18655)
Toolmasters LLC ....F.... 815 645-2224
Stillman Valley (G-20629)
Top Notch Tool & Supply Inc ....G.... 815 633-6295
Cherry Valley (G-3648)
▲ Tornos Technologies US Corp ....G.... 630 812-2040
Lombard (G-13869)
Tox- Pressotechnik LLC ....G.... 630 447-4600
Warrenville (G-21365)
Tri-Star Engineering Inc ....E.... 847 595-3377
Elk Grove Village (G-9791)
Triad Cutting Tools Svc & Mfg ....G.... 847 352-0459
Schaumburg (G-19772)
Triumph Twist Drill Co Inc ....B.... 815 459-6250
Crystal Lake (G-7670)
▲ Tru-Cut Inc ....D.... 847 639-2090
Cary (G-3377)
Udce Limited ....G.... 630 495-9940
Lombard (G-13875)
Universal Broaching Inc ....F.... 847 228-1440
Elk Grove Village (G-9800)
Universal Feeder Inc ....G.... 815 633-0752
Machesney Park (G-14116)
Vanguard Tool & Engineering Co ....E.... 847 981-9595
Mount Prospect (G-15382)
▲ Vhd Inc ....E.... 815 544-2169
Belvidere (G-1794)
▲ W A Whitney Co ....C.... 815 964-6771
Rockford (G-18671)

Wema Vogtland America LLC ....F.... 815 544-0526
Rockford (G-18677)
Wenco Manufacturing Co Inc ....E.... 630 377-7474
Elgin (G-9235)
West Precision Tool Inc ....F.... 630 766-8304
Bensenville (G-2014)
Willow Farm Products Inc ....G.... 630 430-7491
Lemont (G-13270)
Wozniak Industries Inc ....C.... 708 458-1220
Bedford Park (G-1595)
Wunderlich Diamond Tool Corp ....F.... 847 437-9904
Elk Grove Village (G-9818)
Yana House ....G.... 773 874-7120
Chicago (G-7047)
Z-Patch Inc ....E.... 618 529-2431
Carbondale (G-3029)

## 3546 Power Hand Tools

A J Horne Inc ....G.... 630 231-8686
West Chicago (G-21651)
▲ Ajax Tool Works Inc ....D.... 847 455-5420
Franklin Park (G-10387)
Allegion S&S US Holding Co ....C.... 815 875-3311
Princeton (G-17742)
Ally Global Corporation ....G.... 773 822-3373
Chicago (G-3826)
Black & Decker Corporation ....F.... 630 521-1097
Addison (G-57)
Brunner & Lay Inc ....C.... 847 678-3232
Elmhurst (G-9843)
▲ Champion Chisel Works Inc ....F.... 815 535-0647
Rock Falls (G-18128)
Chicago Quadrill Co ....G.... 847 824-4196
Des Plaines (G-8167)
Corless Equipment Co ....G.... 773 776-8383
Chicago (G-4469)
Custom Cutting Tools Inc ....G.... 815 986-0320
Loves Park (G-13931)
▲ Damen Carbide Tool Company Inc ....E.... 630 766-7875
Wood Dale (G-22357)
Decatur Custom Tool Inc ....G.... 618 244-4078
Mount Vernon (G-15408)
◆ Duo-Fast Corporation ....E.... 847 944-2288
Glenview (G-11122)
Ed Hartwig Trucking & Excvtg ....G.... 309 364-3672
Henry (G-11740)
▲ Estwing Manufacturing Co Inc ....B.... 815 397-9521
Rockford (G-18370)
Federal Prison Industries ....C.... 309 346-8588
Pekin (G-17262)
▲ Gator Products Inc ....G.... 847 836-0581
Gilberts (G-10919)
Gbj I LLC ....F.... 815 877-4041
Rockford (G-18396)
Gentry Small Engine Repair ....G.... 217 849-3378
Toledo (G-20963)
Gibson Insurance Inc ....G.... 217 864-4877
Mount Zion (G-15451)
▲ Greenlee Textron Inc ....D.... 815 397-7070
Rockford (G-18405)
Groff Testing Corporation ....G.... 815 939-1153
Kankakee (G-12619)
Harris Precision Tools Inc ....G.... 708 422-5808
Chicago Ridge (G-7149)
Hopkins Saws & Karts Inc ....G.... 618 756-2778
Belle Rive (G-1605)
Industrial Instrument Svc Corp ....G.... 773 581-3355
Chicago (G-5177)
Ivan Schwenker ....G.... 630 543-7798
Addison (G-156)
K-C Tool Co ....G.... 630 983-5960
Naperville (G-15683)
Kaser Power Equipment Inc ....G.... 309 289-2176
Knoxville (G-12721)
▲ Link Tools Intl (usa) Inc ....G.... 773 549-3000
Chicago (G-5512)
Marvco Tool & Manufacturing ....G.... 847 437-4900
Elk Grove Village (G-9612)
Michaels Equipment Co ....G.... 618 524-8560
Metropolis (G-14759)
Milwaukee Electric Tool Corp ....B.... 847 588-3356
Niles (G-16008)
National Detroit Inc ....E.... 815 877-4041
Rockford (G-18515)
▲ NNt Enterprises Incorporated ....E.... 630 875-9600
Itasca (G-12332)
Outdoor Power Inc ....F.... 217 228-9890
Quincy (G-17865)
Owen Walker ....G.... 217 285-4012
Pittsfield (G-17572)

SIC

# 35 INDUSTRIAL AND COMMERCIAL MACHINERY AND COMPUTER EQUIPMENT

▲ Paslode Corp .................................. G ...... 641 672-2515
   Glenview (G-11180)
Peoria Midwest Equipment Inc ........ G ...... 309 454-6800
   Normal (G-16083)
Pgi Mfg LLC ..................................... G ...... 815 398-0313
   Rockford (G-18533)
▲ Powernail Company ....................... E ...... 800 323-1653
   Lake Zurich (G-13116)
R & S Cutterhead Mfg Co ................ F ...... 815 678-2611
   Richmond (G-17969)
Ralph Cody Gravrok ......................... G ...... 630 628-9570
   Addison (G-269)
Rdh Inc of Rockford ......................... F ...... 815 874-9421
   Rockford (G-18550)
▲ Rhino Tool Company ..................... F ...... 309 853-5555
   Kewanee (G-12694)
◆ Robert Bosch Tool Corporation ..... A ...... 224 232-2000
   Mount Prospect (G-15369)
▲ Rockford Commercial Whse Inc ..... G ...... 815 623-8400
   Machesney Park (G-14105)
S & J Industrial Supply Corp ............ F ...... 708 339-1708
   South Holland (G-20303)
Saws Unlimited Inc .......................... G ...... 847 640-7450
   Elk Grove Village (G-9730)
Sierra Manufacturing Corp ............... G ...... 630 458-8830
   Addison (G-289)
▲ Sollami Company ........................... E ...... 618 988-1521
   Herrin (G-11755)
Stange Industrial Group ................... G ...... 847 640-8470
   Elk Grove Village (G-9752)
▲ T & T Carbide ................................ G ...... 618 439-7253
   Logan (G-13755)
Tapco USA Inc ................................. G ...... 815 877-4039
   Loves Park (G-13998)
Technical Tool Enterprise ................ G ...... 630 893-3390
   Addison (G-307)
Toolmasters LLC .............................. F ...... 815 645-2224
   Stillman Valley (G-20629)
Total Tooling Technology Inc ........... F ...... 847 437-5135
   Elk Grove Village (G-9786)
Triumph Twist Drill Co Inc ................ B ...... 815 459-6250
   Crystal Lake (G-7670)
▲ Tru-Cut Inc .................................... D ...... 847 639-2090
   Cary (G-3377)
Unicut Corporation ........................... G ...... 773 525-4210
   Chicago (G-6813)
▲ Wallace/Haskin Corp ..................... G ...... 630 789-2882
   Downers Grove (G-8540)
Welliver & Sons Inc ......................... E ...... 815 874-2400
   Rockford (G-18676)
▲ Whitney Roper LLC ....................... D ...... 815 962-3011
   Rockford (G-18681)
▲ Whitney Roper Rockford Inc ......... D ...... 815 962-3011
   Rockford (G-18682)
Wodack Electric Tool Corp ............... F ...... 773 287-9866
   Chicago (G-7019)

## 3547 Rolling Mill Machinery & Eqpt

Bonell Manufacturing Company ....... E ...... 708 849-1770
   Riverdale (G-18016)
Chicago Roll Co Inc ......................... E ...... 630 627-8888
   Lombard (G-13777)
Combined Metals Chicago LLC ........ G ...... 847 683-0500
   Hampshire (G-11545)
▲ Fkm Usa LLC ................................ F ...... 815 469-2473
   Frankfort (G-10322)
Frame Material Supply Inc .............. G ...... 309 362-2323
   Trivoli (G-20999)
▲ K R Komarek Inc .......................... E ...... 847 956-0060
   Wood Dale (G-22384)
▲ Leading Edge Group Inc ............... C ...... 815 316-3500
   Rockford (G-18464)
▲ Littell LLC ..................................... E ...... 630 916-6662
   Schaumburg (G-19620)
Nor Service Inc ................................ E ...... 815 232-8379
   Freeport (G-10676)
▲ Nucor Steel Kankakee Inc ............. B ...... 815 937-3131
   Bourbonnais (G-2403)
Vision Pickling and Proc Inc ............ F ...... 815 264-7755
   Waterman (G-21410)
▲ Worth Steel and Machine Co ........ E ...... 708 388-6300
   Alsip (G-546)

## 3548 Welding Apparatus

Adams Steel Service Inc ................. E ...... 815 385-9100
   McHenry (G-14477)
Airgas Inc ........................................ F ...... 773 785-3000
   Chicago (G-3786)
Airgas Usa LLC ............................... G ...... 815 935-7750
   Bradley (G-2412)
Airgas USA LLC ............................... E ...... 630 231-9260
   West Chicago (G-21653)
▲ American Vacuum Co ................... G ...... 847 674-8383
   Skokie (G-19951)
Associate General Labs Inc ............. G ...... 847 678-2717
   Franklin Park (G-10404)
▼ Automation International Inc ......... D ...... 217 446-9500
   Danville (G-7704)
Branson Ultrasonics Corp ................ G ...... 847 229-0800
   Buffalo Grove (G-2669)
▲ C M Industries Inc ........................ E ...... 847 550-0033
   Lake Zurich (G-13049)
Coakley Mfg & Metrology ................ F ...... 847 202-9331
   Palatine (G-17012)
D & G Welding Supply Company ..... G ...... 815 675-9890
   Spring Grove (G-20332)
▲ Electron Beam Technologies Inc ... C ...... 815 935-2211
   Kankakee (G-12612)
▲ Ezee Roll Manufacturing Co ......... G ...... 217 339-2279
   Hoopeston (G-12110)
Fanuc America Corporation ............. E ...... 847 898-5000
   Hoffman Estates (G-12009)
Globaltech International LLC ........... G ...... 630 327-6909
   Aurora (G-1018)
▲ Image Industries Inc ..................... E ...... 847 659-0100
   Huntley (G-12147)
Industrial Welder Rebuilders ........... G ...... 708 371-5688
   Alsip (G-473)
Kopp Welding Inc ............................ G ...... 847 593-2070
   Elk Grove Village (G-9578)
Kriese Mfg ....................................... G ...... 815 748-2683
   Cortland (G-7392)
▲ Littell International Inc .................. E ...... 630 622-4950
   Schaumburg (G-19621)
Marvel Electric Corporation ............. E ...... 847 671-0632
   Schiller Park (G-19846)
Melissa A Miller ............................... G ...... 708 529-7786
   New Lenox (G-15893)
Praxair Distribution Inc ................... G ...... 309 346-3164
   Pekin (G-17284)
Reber Welding Service .................... G ...... 217 774-3441
   Shelbyville (G-19914)
▲ Sommer Products Company Inc ... G ...... 309 697-1216
   Peoria (G-17458)
Steelwerks of Chicago LLC .............. G ...... 312 792-9593
   Chicago (G-6582)
Weldstar Company ........................... G ...... 708 534-6419
   University Park (G-21066)
Wenesco Inc .................................... F ...... 773 283-3004
   Chicago (G-6956)

## 3549 Metalworking Machinery, NEC

Accelrted Mch Design Engrg LLC .... F ...... 815 316-6381
   Rockford (G-18251)
Active Automation Inc ..................... F ...... 847 427-8100
   Elk Grove Village (G-9268)
Advanced Robotics Research .......... G ...... 630 544-0040
   Naperville (G-15591)
Advantage Machining Inc ................ E ...... 630 897-1220
   Aurora (G-1101)
Amber Engineering and Mfg Co ...... D ...... 847 595-6966
   Elk Grove Village (G-9293)
▲ Arcam Cad To Metal Inc ............... G ...... 630 357-5700
   Naperville (G-15599)
◆ Ats Sortimat USA LLC ................... D ...... 847 925-1234
   Rolling Meadows (G-18711)
Automation Systems Inc ................. E ...... 847 671-9515
   Melrose Park (G-14597)
Bams Manufacturing Co Inc ............ G ...... 800 206-0613
   Elk Grove Village (G-9334)
Bartell Corporation ........................... G ...... 847 854-3232
   Algonquin (G-380)
Beverly Shear Mfg Corporation ....... G ...... 773 233-2063
   Chicago (G-4098)
◆ Blachford Enterprises Inc .............. E ...... 630 231-8300
   West Chicago (G-21670)
▲ Black Bros Co ............................... G ...... 815 539-7451
   Mendota (G-14717)
▲ Braner Usa Inc .............................. E ...... 847 671-6210
   Schiller Park (G-19809)
Burns Machine Company ................. G ...... 815 434-3131
   Ottawa (G-16952)
▲ C B Ferrari Incorporated ............... G ...... 847 756-4100
   Lake Barrington (G-12801)
C E R Machining & Tooling Ltd ....... G ...... 708 442-9614
   Lyons (G-14034)
Canny Innovative Solutions Inc ....... G ...... 847 323-1271
   Grayslake (G-11323)
Central Machines Inc ...................... E ...... 847 634-6900
   Lincolnshire (G-13435)
Continental Automation Inc ............. E ...... 630 584-5100
   Saint Charles (G-19162)
Court & Slope Inc ............................ G ...... 847 697-3600
   Elgin (G-9005)
▲ Crl Industries Inc .......................... G ...... 847 940-3550
   Deerfield (G-8002)
▲ Custom Assembly Solutions Inc ... F ...... 847 224-5800
   Schaumburg (G-19495)
Custom Machinery Inc ..................... G ...... 847 678-3033
   Schiller Park (G-19818)
Darda Enterprises Inc ..................... F ...... 847 270-0410
   Palatine (G-17020)
◆ Deluxe Stitcher Company Inc ....... D ...... 847 455-4400
   Franklin Park (G-10457)
▲ Dmtg North America LLC ............. G ...... 815 637-8500
   Rockford (G-18349)
Dooling Machine Products Inc ........ G ...... 618 254-0724
   Hartford (G-11610)
▲ Drawing Technology Inc ............... G ...... 815 877-5133
   Rockford (G-18351)
◆ Engineered Abrasives Inc ............. G ...... 662 582-4143
   Alsip (G-462)
Feeder Corporation of America ....... F ...... 708 343-4900
   Melrose Park (G-14638)
Gerhard Designing & Mfg Inc ......... E ...... 708 599-4664
   Bridgeview (G-2494)
GMC Technologies Inc ..................... G ...... 847 426-8618
   East Dundee (G-8638)
▲ Greenlee Textron Inc .................... D ...... 815 397-7070
   Rockford (G-18405)
Hansel Walter J & Assoc Inc ........... G ...... 815 678-6065
   Richmond (G-17963)
Hilscher North America Inc ............. F ...... 630 505-5301
   Lisle (G-13600)
Illinois Tool Works Inc ..................... D ...... 618 997-1716
   Marion (G-14269)
▲ International Technologies Inc ...... G ...... 847 301-9005
   Schaumburg (G-19573)
J & C Premier Concepts Inc ............ G ...... 309 523-2344
   Port Byron (G-17720)
Jardis Industries Inc ....................... F ...... 630 773-5600
   Itasca (G-12290)
▲ Jerhen Industries Inc ................... D ...... 815 397-0400
   Rockford (G-18443)
Junker Inc ....................................... G ...... 630 231-3770
   West Chicago (G-21729)
▲ K R Komarek Inc .......................... E ...... 847 956-0060
   Wood Dale (G-22384)
Kormex Metal Craft Inc ................... E ...... 630 953-8856
   Lombard (G-13818)
Lane Tool & Mfg Co Inc ................... E ...... 847 622-1506
   South Elgin (G-20216)
▲ Lc Holdings of Delaware Inc ......... G ...... 847 940-3550
   Deerfield (G-8028)
Leggett & Platt Incorporated .......... D ...... 847 768-6139
   Des Plaines (G-8223)
Lester Manufacturing Inc ................ E ...... 815 986-1172
   Rockford (G-18468)
Lipscomb Engineering Inc ............... G ...... 630 231-3833
   West Chicago (G-21732)
▲ Littell LLC ..................................... E ...... 630 916-6662
   Schaumburg (G-19620)
▲ Littell International Inc .................. E ...... 630 622-4950
   Schaumburg (G-19621)
▲ Magnum Steel Works Inc ............. D ...... 618 244-5190
   Mount Vernon (G-15423)
Marvco Tool & Manufacturing ......... E ...... 847 437-4900
   Elk Grove Village (G-9612)
Master Machine Craft Inc ................ E ...... 815 874-3078
   Rockford (G-18484)
Master Manufacturing Co ................ F ...... 630 833-7060
   Villa Park (G-21269)
Meadoweld Machine Inc .................. G ...... 815 623-3939
   South Beloit (G-20161)
Medford Aero Arms LLC ................... G ...... 773 961-7686
   Chicago (G-5676)
Merit Tool Engineering Co Inc ......... G ...... 773 283-1114
   Chicago (G-5694)
Mfw Services Inc ............................. G ...... 708 522-5879
   South Holland (G-20289)
Navillus Woodworks LLC ................. G ...... 312 375-2680
   Chicago (G-5874)
North America O M C G Inc ............. E ...... 630 860-1016
   Bensenville (G-9)
▲ Omiotek Coil Spring Co ................ D ...... 630 495-4056
   Lombard (G-13837)
Onsrud Machine Corp ...................... E ...... 847 520-5300
   Northbrook (G-16327)
P-K Tool & Mfg Co ........................... D ...... 773 235-4700
   Chicago (G-6046)

**Park Tool & Machine Co Inc** ....... G ....... 630 530-5110
Villa Park *(G-21275)*
**Performance Design Inc** ....... G ....... 847 719-1535
Lake Zurich *(G-13113)*
**Precision Tool & Die Company** ....... F ....... 217 864-3371
Mount Zion *(G-15455)*
**Prototype & Production Co** ....... E ....... 847 419-1553
Wheeling *(G-22130)*
**Qc Service Associates Inc** ....... E ....... 309 755-6785
East Moline *(G-8691)*
**▼ R+d Custom Automation Inc** ....... E ....... 847 395-3330
Lake Villa *(G-13025)*
**▼ Red Bud Industries Inc** ....... C ....... 618 282-3801
Red Bud *(G-17947)*
**Remington Industries Inc** ....... F ....... 815 385-1987
Johnsburg *(G-12441)*
**Robert Brysiewicz Incorporated** ....... G ....... 630 289-0903
Bartlett *(G-1369)*
**Rockford Systems LLC** ....... D ....... 815 874-7891
Rockford *(G-18587)*
**Schaffer Tool & Design Inc** ....... G ....... 630 876-3800
West Chicago *(G-21769)*
**Schmid Tool & Engineering Corp** ....... E ....... 630 333-1733
Villa Park *(G-21283)*
**Sigmatron International Inc** ....... G ....... 847 586-5200
Elgin *(G-9178)*
**▲ Sigmatron International Inc** ....... G ....... 847 956-8000
Elk Grove Village *(G-9737)*
**▼ Sortimat Technology LP** ....... D ....... 847 925-1234
Rolling Meadows *(G-18780)*
**Spinco Tool & Fabe** ....... G ....... 815 578-8600
Wonder Lake *(G-22325)*
**Stalex Inc** ....... G ....... 630 627-9401
Lombard *(G-13858)*
**T & K Tool & Manufacturing Co** ....... G ....... 815 338-0954
Woodstock *(G-22617)*
**Tellenar Inc** ....... F ....... 815 356-8044
Crystal Lake *(G-7663)*
**Titan Tool Company Inc** ....... G ....... 847 671-0045
Franklin Park *(G-10607)*
**Tool Rite Industries Inc** ....... G ....... 630 406-6161
Batavia *(G-1508)*
**Ty Miles Incorporated** ....... E ....... 708 344-5480
Westchester *(G-21860)*
**▲ U S Concepts Inc** ....... F ....... 630 876-3110
West Chicago *(G-21787)*
**Ultramatic Equipment Co** ....... E ....... 630 543-4565
Addison *(G-333)*
**◆ United Automation Inc** ....... G ....... 847 394-7903
Wheeling *(G-22171)*
**Used Solutions Inc** ....... G ....... 815 759-5000
Algonquin *(G-408)*
**Variable Operations Tech Inc** ....... E ....... 815 479-8528
Crystal Lake *(G-7672)*
**▲ Vindee Industries Inc** ....... E ....... 815 469-3300
Frankfort *(G-10375)*
**▲ W A Whitney Co** ....... C ....... 815 964-6771
Rockford *(G-18671)*
**Wes-Tech Automtn Solutions LLC** ....... D ....... 847 541-5070
Buffalo Grove *(G-2794)*
**Z-Tech Inc** ....... G ....... 815 335-7395
Winnebago *(G-22299)*
**Zj Industries Inc** ....... F ....... 630 543-6400
Addison *(G-351)*

## 3552 Textile Machinery

**▼ Birnberg Machinery Inc** ....... G ....... 847 673-5242
Skokie *(G-19964)*
**Cargill Incorporated** ....... F ....... 217 872-7653
Decatur *(G-7851)*
**▲ Cy Laser LLC** ....... G ....... 630 208-1931
Geneva *(G-10822)*
**David H Pool** ....... G ....... 847 695-5007
Elgin *(G-9009)*
**Forest Lee LLC** ....... G ....... 312 379-0032
Chicago *(G-4872)*
**▲ Forte Automation Systems Inc** ....... E ....... 815 316-6247
Machesney Park *(G-14076)*
**▲ Handy Button Machine Co** ....... E ....... 847 459-0900
Wheeling *(G-22067)*
**Initial Impressions Inc** ....... G ....... 630 208-9399
Geneva *(G-10836)*
**Initially Ewe** ....... G ....... 708 246-7777
Western Springs *(G-21868)*
**Innovo Corp** ....... F ....... 847 616-0063
Elk Grove Village *(G-9548)*
**Lmk Technologies LLC** ....... D ....... 815 433-1530
Ottawa *(G-16967)*
**▲ M & R Printing Equipment Inc** ....... B ....... 800 736-6431
Roselle *(G-18954)*
**▲ M&R Holdings Inc** ....... C ....... 630 858-6101
Roselle *(G-18955)*
**Manufacturers Alliance Corp** ....... F ....... 847 696-1600
Villa Park *(G-21268)*
**Modern Graphic Systems Inc** ....... G ....... 773 476-6898
Chicago *(G-5781)*
**Natural Fiber Welding Inc** ....... G ....... 309 685-3591
Peoria *(G-17414)*
**On Time Decorations Inc** ....... F ....... 708 357-6072
Cicero *(G-7224)*
**Peerless** ....... G ....... 773 294-2667
Chicago *(G-6096)*
**Signature Label of Illinois** ....... G ....... 618 283-5145
Vandalia *(G-21125)*
**Summit Graphics Inc** ....... F ....... 309 799-5100
Moline *(G-14973)*

## 3553 Woodworking Machinery

**▲ Black Bros Co** ....... D ....... 815 539-7451
Mendota *(G-14717)*
**Bona Fide Corp** ....... G ....... 847 970-8693
Wheeling *(G-22017)*
**Bw Exhibits** ....... G ....... 847 697-9224
Gilberts *(G-10914)*
**Coalesse** ....... F ....... 312 622-6269
Chicago *(G-4413)*
**▲ Crl Industries Inc** ....... G ....... 847 940-3550
Deerfield *(G-8002)*
**D M O Inc** ....... G ....... 815 756-3638
Cortland *(G-7387)*
**Doll Furniture Co Inc** ....... G ....... 309 452-2606
Normal *(G-16070)*
**Elliott Aviation Arcft Sls Inc** ....... G ....... 309 799-3183
Milan *(G-14785)*
**▲ Lc Holdings of Delaware Inc** ....... G ....... 847 940-3550
Deerfield *(G-8028)*
**Little Creek Woodworking** ....... G ....... 217 543-2815
Arthur *(G-908)*
**Marvco Tool & Manufacturing** ....... G ....... 847 437-4900
Elk Grove Village *(G-9612)*
**Onsrud Machine Corp** ....... E ....... 847 520-5300
Northbrook *(G-16327)*
**Prairie State Machine LLC** ....... G ....... 217 543-3768
Arthur *(G-919)*
**Quality Cove** ....... G ....... 618 684-5900
Murphysboro *(G-15581)*
**SA Industries Inc** ....... G ....... 847 730-4823
Des Plaines *(G-8269)*
**▲ Sand-Rite Manufacturing Co** ....... G ....... 312 997-2200
Melrose Park *(G-14691)*
**Sawmill Hydraulics** ....... F ....... 309 245-2448
Farmington *(G-10188)*
**Total Tooling Technology Inc** ....... F ....... 847 437-5135
Elk Grove Village *(G-9786)*
**White Oak Technology** ....... G ....... 309 228-4201
Germantown Hills *(G-10896)*
**Yazdan Essie** ....... G ....... 847 675-7916
Lincolnwood *(G-13544)*
**Your Custom Cabinetry Corp** ....... G ....... 773 290-7247
Melrose Park *(G-14712)*

## 3554 Paper Inds Machinery

**▼ Birnberg Machinery Inc** ....... G ....... 847 673-5242
Skokie *(G-19964)*
**▲ Black Bros Co** ....... D ....... 815 539-7451
Mendota *(G-14717)*
**C F Anderson & Co** ....... F ....... 312 341-0850
Chicago *(G-4203)*
**Culmac Inc** ....... E ....... 309 944-5197
Geneseo *(G-10800)*
**Emt International Inc** ....... G ....... 630 655-4145
Westmont *(G-21887)*
**▲ Finishers Exchange** ....... G ....... 847 462-0533
Fox River Grove *(G-10286)*
**Gt Flow Technology Inc** ....... G ....... 815 636-9982
Roscoe *(G-18899)*
**Gy Packaging LLC** ....... F ....... 847 272-8803
Northbrook *(G-16267)*
**Hfd Manufacturing Inc** ....... G ....... 847 263-5050
Waukegan *(G-21568)*
**◆ Keene Technology Inc** ....... D ....... 815 624-8989
South Beloit *(G-20155)*
**Mayatech Corporation** ....... E ....... 847 297-0930
Des Plaines *(G-8229)*
**Midwest Gold Stampers Inc** ....... F ....... 773 775-5253
Chicago *(G-5744)*
**▲ Paperchine Inc** ....... C ....... 815 389-8200
Rockton *(G-18700)*
**▲ Platit Inc** ....... G ....... 847 680-5270
Libertyville *(G-13370)*
**Quality Converting Inc** ....... G ....... 847 669-9094
Huntley *(G-12169)*
**▲ Quipp Inc** ....... F ....... 305 623-8700
Glenview *(G-11186)*
**▲ Ringwood Company** ....... D ....... 708 458-6000
Bedford Park *(G-1579)*
**▲ Rosenthal Manufacturing Co Inc** ....... E ....... 847 714-0404
Northbrook *(G-16358)*
**Ultra Packaging Inc** ....... G ....... 630 595-9820
Bensenville *(G-2008)*
**▲ United Gasket Corporation** ....... D ....... 708 656-3700
Cicero *(G-7242)*

## 3555 Printing Trades Machinery & Eqpt

**▲ 2m Control Systems Inc** ....... G ....... 630 709-6225
West Chicago *(G-21650)*
**4l Technologies Inc** ....... D ....... 815 431-8100
Ottawa *(G-16944)*
**▲ A-Korn Roller Inc** ....... E ....... 773 254-5700
Chicago *(G-3696)*
**Aaxis Engravers Inc** ....... G ....... 224 629-4045
Bensenville *(G-1811)*
**Able Engravers Inc** ....... G ....... 847 676-3737
Skokie *(G-19945)*
**Accu-Chem Industries Inc** ....... G ....... 708 344-0900
Melrose Park *(G-14584)*
**▲ Advance World Trade Inc** ....... D ....... 773 777-7100
Chicago *(G-3767)*
**Altair Corporation (del)** ....... E ....... 847 634-9540
Lincolnshire *(G-13426)*
**▲ Anderson & Vreeland-Illinois** ....... F ....... 847 255-2110
Arlington Heights *(G-713)*
**▲ Baldwin OXY-Dry Corporation** ....... D ....... 630 595-3651
Addison *(G-51)*
**Banner Moulded Products** ....... E ....... 708 452-0033
River Grove *(G-18005)*
**Bisco Intl Inc** ....... G ....... 708 544-6308
Hillside *(G-11911)*
**C & C Printing Controls Inc** ....... G ....... 630 810-0484
Downers Grove *(G-8401)*
**C CN Chicago Corp** ....... G ....... 847 671-3319
Addison *(G-64)*
**C F Anderson & Co** ....... F ....... 312 341-0850
Chicago *(G-4203)*
**Cdj Technologies Inc** ....... G ....... 321 277-7807
Wilmette *(G-22249)*
**▲ Central Graphics Corp** ....... F ....... 630 759-1696
Romeoville *(G-18807)*
**Chatham Corporation** ....... F ....... 847 634-5506
Lincolnshire *(G-13436)*
**Color Smiths Inc** ....... E ....... 708 562-0061
Elmhurst *(G-9853)*
**Container Graphics Corp** ....... E ....... 847 584-0299
Schaumburg *(G-19481)*
**Culmac Inc** ....... E ....... 309 944-5197
Geneseo *(G-10800)*
**Cy-Tec Inc** ....... G ....... 815 756-8416
Dekalb *(G-8084)*
**▲ D & K Custom Machine Design** ....... E ....... 847 956-4757
Elk Grove Village *(G-9408)*
**▲ D & K Group Inc** ....... E ....... 847 956-0160
Elk Grove Village *(G-9409)*
**Distribution Enterprises Inc** ....... F ....... 847 582-9276
Lake Forest *(G-12896)*
**Dms Inc** ....... F ....... 847 726-2828
Lake Zurich *(G-13063)*
**◆ Domino Amjet Inc** ....... D ....... 847 244-2501
Gurnee *(G-11440)*
**Donnelley and Sons Co R R** ....... G ....... 708 924-6200
Chicago *(G-4628)*
**Ebway Industries Inc** ....... E ....... 630 860-5959
Itasca *(G-12256)*
**Emt International Inc** ....... G ....... 630 655-4145
Westmont *(G-21887)*
**▲ Environmental Specialties Inc** ....... G ....... 630 860-7070
Itasca *(G-12259)*
**Global Brass and Copper Inc** ....... G ....... 618 258-5330
East Alton *(G-8605)*
**▲ Global Web Systems Inc** ....... F ....... 630 782-9690
Elk Grove Village *(G-9504)*
**◆ Goss International LLC** ....... E ....... 630 796-7560
Woodridge *(G-22488)*
**GP Liquidation Inc** ....... G ....... 630 784-9736
Addison *(G-138)*
**◆ Graphic Innovators Inc** ....... E ....... 847 718-1516
Elk Grove Village *(G-9508)*
**Group 3 Envelope F & S Type** ....... G ....... 630 766-1230
Bensenville *(G-1914)*
**H R Slater Co Inc** ....... F ....... 312 666-1855
Chicago *(G-5023)*



Employee Codes: A=Over 500 employees, B=251-500
C=101-250, D=51-100, E=20-50, F=10-19, G=3-9
2017 Harris Illinois
Industrial Directory
1071

Heidelberg USA Inc....D....847 550-0915
Barrington (G-1284)
▲ I S C America Inc....G....630 616-1331
Wood Dale (G-22380)
Ilf Technologies LLC....F....630 759-1776
Cicero (G-7204)
Imtran Industries Inc....D....630 752-4000
Carol Stream (G-3172)
Intersol Industries Inc....F....630 238-0385
Bensenville (G-1922)
▲ Jardis Industries Inc....E....630 860-5959
Itasca (G-12289)
K and A Graphics Inc....G....847 244-2345
Gurnee (G-11463)
Kiwi Coders Corp....E....847 541-4511
Wheeling (G-22085)
◆ Klai-Co Idntification Pdts Inc....E....847 573-0375
Lake Forest (G-12921)
▲ Komori America Corporation....D....847 806-9000
Rolling Meadows (G-18739)
◆ Laser Reproductions Inc....E....847 410-0397
Skokie (G-20026)
Luttrell Engraving Inc....E....708 489-3800
Alsip (G-485)
▲ M & R Printing Equipment Inc....B....800 736-6431
Roselle (G-18954)
▲ Manroland Inc....E....630 920-2000
Westmont (G-21903)
▲ Manroland Web Systems Inc....E....630 920-5850
Lisle (G-13619)
▼ Mark Bst-Pro Inc....D....630 833-9900
Elmhurst (G-9907)
◆ Martin Automatic Inc....C....815 654-4800
Rockford (G-18483)
Midwest Index Inc....D....847 995-8425
Addison (G-212)
Milans Machining & Mfg Co Inc....D....708 780-6600
Cicero (G-7222)
Mmpcu Limited....G....217 355-0500
Champaign (G-3516)
Nama Graphics E LLC....G....262 966-3853
Homer Glen (G-12083)
▲ Oec Graphics-Chicago LLC....E....630 455-6700
Willowbrook (G-22227)
Ortman-Mccain Co....G....312 666-2244
Chicago (G-6018)
Pamarco Global Graphics Inc....E....630 879-7300
Batavia (G-1479)
Pamarco Global Graphics Inc....F....847 459-6000
Wheeling (G-22118)
Paper Benders Supply Inc....G....815 577-7583
Plainfield (G-17635)
Paw Office Machines Inc....G....815 363-9780
McHenry (G-14543)
Plate and Pre-Press Management....G....847 352-0462
Schaumburg (G-19694)
Polyurthane Engrg Tchnques Inc....E....847 362-1820
Lake Forest (G-12947)
Precision Screen Specialties....G....630 762-9548
Saint Charles (G-19241)
Printers Parts Inc....G....847 288-9000
Franklin Park (G-10561)
▼ Printers Repair Parts Inc....E....847 288-9000
Franklin Park (G-10562)
Quipp Systems Inc....G....305 304-1985
Glenview (G-11187)
Quipp Systems Inc....E....305 623-8700
Glenview (G-11188)
Resinite Corporation....C....847 537-4250
Wheeling (G-22138)
Rotation Dynamics Corporation....D....773 247-5600
Chicago (G-6399)
◆ Rycoline Products LLC....C....773 775-6755
Chicago (G-6417)
Saati Americas Corporation....F....847 296-5090
Mount Prospect (G-15371)
Schellhorn Photo Techniques....F....773 267-5141
Chicago (G-6451)
Schlesinger Machinery Inc....G....630 766-4074
Bensenville (G-1987)
▲ Smart Inc....G....847 464-4160
Hampshire (G-11563)
Sopher Design & Manufacturing....G....309 699-6419
East Peoria (G-8735)
▲ Southern Illinois McHy Co Inc....D....217 868-5431
Shumway (G-19935)
Special Tool Engineering Co....F....773 767-6690
Chicago (G-6554)
Stolp Gore Company....G....630 904-5180
Plainfield (G-17653)
▼ Sun Graphic Inc....E....773 775-6755
Chicago (G-6619)
Tamarack Products Inc....E....847 526-9333
Wauconda (G-21508)
Tanic Rubber Plate Co....G....630 896-2122
Aurora (G-1223)
▲ Technotrans America Inc....E....847 227-9200
Mount Prospect (G-15378)
◆ Thermal Care Inc....C....847 966-2260
Niles (G-16041)
Vm Electronics LLC....G....847 663-9310
Chicago (G-6910)
Web Printing Controls Co Inc....D....618 842-2664
Arlington Heights (G-870)
Web Printing Controls Co Inc....C....618 842-2664
Fairfield (G-10161)
◆ Weber Marking Systems Inc....B....847 364-8500
Arlington Heights (G-871)
▲ Western Printing Machinery Co....E....847 678-1740
Schiller Park (G-19883)
Western Printing Machinery Co....E....847 678-1740
Schiller Park (G-19884)
Wpc Machinery Corp....E....630 231-7721
Arlington Heights (G-874)
Zebra Outlet....F....312 416-1518
Chicago (G-7059)

## 3556 Food Prdts Machinery

5 Rabbit Cerveceria Inc....F....312 265-8316
Chicago (G-3669)
▲ Aaron Process Equipment Co Inc....E....630 350-2200
Bensenville (G-1810)
▲ Alberti Enterprises Inc....G....847 810-7610
Lake Forest (G-12877)
◆ American Extrusion Intl Corp....E....815 624-6616
South Beloit (G-20138)
American Metal Installers & FA....G....630 993-0812
Villa Park (G-21236)
Angel Equipment LLC....G....815 455-4320
Glenview (G-11101)
APV Consolidated Inc....F....847 678-4300
Schiller Park (G-19804)
▼ Armour-Eckrich Meats LLC....B....630 281-5000
Lisle (G-13563)
▲ Bauermeister Inc....G....901 363-0921
Vernon Hills (G-21146)
▼ Beacon Inc....F....708 544-9900
Alsip (G-440)
Blommer Machinery Company....G....312 226-7700
Chicago (G-4124)
▲ Bravilor Bonamat LLC....F....630 423-9400
Aurora (G-973)
Carrier Commercial Rfrgn Inc....A....815 624-8333
Rockton (G-18693)
Cartpac Inc....E....630 283-8979
Carol Stream (G-3125)
Choice Treat Equipment Mfg....G....708 442-2004
Lyons (G-14035)
▲ CMC America Corporation....F....815 726-4337
Joliet (G-12475)
◆ Cobatco Inc....F....309 676-2663
Peoria (G-17344)
Colborne Acquisition Co LLC....E....847 371-0101
Lake Forest (G-12893)
Comtec Industries Ltd....G....630 759-9000
Woodridge (G-22465)
◆ Cornelius Inc....B....630 539-6850
Glendale Heights (G-11018)
Corrigan Corporation America....F....800 462-6478
Gurnee (G-11435)
Cozzini LLC....C....773 478-9700
Chicago (G-4486)
Crm North America LLC....G....708 603-3475
Franklin Park (G-10446)
Custom Systems Inc....G....314 355-4575
Granite City (G-11272)
◆ Cvp Systems Inc....D....630 852-1190
Downers Grove (G-8422)
D W Ram Manufacturing Co....E....708 633-7900
Tinley Park (G-20908)
Davenport Dryer L L C....G....309 786-1500
Moline (G-14923)
Dons Meat Market....G....309 968-6026
Manito (G-14174)
▲ Dontech Industries Inc....F....847 428-8222
Gilberts (G-10917)
◆ Dover Prtg Identification Inc....D....630 541-1540
Downers Grove (G-8434)
▲ E-Quip Manufacturing Co....E....815 464-0053
Frankfort (G-10317)
▲ Eirich Machines Inc....D....847 336-2444
Gurnee (G-11446)
F & S Engraving Inc....E....847 870-8400
Mount Prospect (G-15328)
Felste Co Inc....G....217 283-4884
Hoopeston (G-12111)
Formax Inc....E....708 479-3000
Mokena (G-14862)
Frigid Coil/Frick Inc....G....630 562-4602
West Chicago (G-21707)
▲ G K Enterprises Inc....G....708 587-2150
Monee (G-14996)
Galena Garlic Co....G....331 248-0342
Geneva (G-10829)
Gilberts Craft Sausages LLC....G....630 923-8969
Wheaton (G-21950)
Great Lakes Service Chicago....G....630 627-4022
Lombard (G-13806)
Gregor Jonsson Associates Inc....E....847 247-4200
Lake Forest (G-12904)
Gsi Group LLC....D....618 283-9792
Vandalia (G-21115)
▲ HC Duke & Son LLC....C....309 755-4553
East Moline (G-8681)
Heat and Control Inc....D....309 342-5518
Galesburg (G-10758)
▲ Hollymatic Corporation....D....708 579-3700
Countryside (G-7430)
▲ Home Fires Inc....G....815 967-4100
Rockford (G-18421)
Hot Food Boxes Inc....E....773 533-5912
Chicago (G-5117)
Houpt Revolving Cutters Inc....G....618 395-1913
Olney (G-16771)
▲ IMI McR Inc....E....309 734-6282
Monmouth (G-15014)
Institutional Equipment Inc....E....630 771-0990
Bolingbrook (G-2321)
John Bean Technologies Corp....E....312 861-5900
Chicago (G-5310)
Keating of Chicago Inc....E....815 569-2324
Capron (G-2996)
Kitchy Koo Gourmet Co....G....708 499-5236
Oak Lawn (G-16629)
Lee Industries Inc....C....847 462-1865
Elk Grove Village (G-9590)
Mario Escobar....G....773 202-8497
Chicago (G-5621)
◆ Marshall Middleby Inc....C....847 289-0204
Elgin (G-9100)
◆ Mc Brady Engineering Inc....F....815 744-8900
Rockdale (G-18226)
Mc Cleary Equipment Inc....G....815 389-3053
South Beloit (G-20159)
Middleby Corporation....E....847 741-3300
Elgin (G-9110)
Middleby Corporation....E....847 741-3300
Elgin (G-9111)
◆ Middleby Worldwide Inc....G....847 741-3300
Elgin (G-9112)
Miles Bros....G....618 937-4115
West Frankfort (G-21814)
Modern Food Concepts Inc....G....815 534-5747
Frankfort (G-10344)
Modern Process Equipment Inc....E....773 254-3929
Chicago (G-5784)
Mww Food Processing USA LLC....G....800 582-1574
Chicago (G-5838)
▲ Nimco Corporation....D....815 459-4200
Crystal Lake (G-7619)
▼ Optimal Automatics Co....G....847 439-9110
Elk Grove Village (G-9667)
Packers Supplies & Eqp LLC....G....630 543-5810
Addison (G-236)
▲ Practical Baker Equipment....G....815 943-8730
Harvard (G-11644)
▲ Prater Industries Inc....D....630 679-3200
Bolingbrook (G-2359)
Pre Pack Machinery Inc....G....217 352-1010
Champaign (G-3528)
Precision Service....G....618 345-2047
Collinsville (G-7337)
◆ Primedge Inc....C....224 265-6600
Elk Grove Village (G-9697)
Q-Matic Technologies Inc....G....847 263-7324
Carol Stream (G-3224)
▲ R S Cryo Equipment Inc....G....815 468-6115
Manteno (G-14191)
◆ Rancilio North America Inc....E....630 427-1703
Woodridge (G-22513)

# 35 INDUSTRIAL AND COMMERCIAL MACHINERY AND COMPUTER EQUIPMENT

◆ Rantoul Foods LLC .................. B ...... 217 892-4178
Rantoul *(G-17936)*
▲ Rational Cooking Systems Inc ...... D ...... 224 366-3500
Rolling Meadows *(G-18772)*
Rockdale Controls Co Inc .................. F ...... 815 436-6181
Plainfield *(G-17646)*
S G Acquisition Inc .................. G ...... 815 624-6501
South Beloit *(G-20168)*
▼ Savage Bros Company .................. D ...... 847 981-3000
Elk Grove Village *(G-9728)*
▲ Sojuz Ent .................. G ...... 847 215-9400
Bensenville *(G-1994)*
▲ Solo Cup Operating Corporation ...... D ...... 847 444-5000
Lincolnshire *(G-13482)*
▲ Speco Inc .................. E ...... 847 678-4240
Schiller Park *(G-19876)*
▲ Stanford Bettendorf Inc .................. D ...... 618 548-3555
Salem *(G-19353)*
Stephen Paoli Mfg Corp .................. F ...... 815 965-0621
Rockford *(G-18634)*
TEC Systems Inc .................. F ...... 815 722-2800
New Lenox *(G-15917)*
Terrace Holding Company .................. A ...... 708 652-5600
Cicero *(G-7238)*
Titan Injection Parts & Svc .................. G ...... 630 882-8455
Yorkville *(G-22673)*
Towne Machine Tool Company ...... F ...... 217 442-4910
Danville *(G-7777)*
Tyson Fresh Meats Inc .................. G ...... 847 836-5550
Elgin *(G-9218)*
▼ Vilutis and Co Inc .................. E ...... 815 469-2116
Frankfort *(G-10374)*
Vision Machine & Fabrication .................. G ...... 618 965-3199
Steeleville *(G-20564)*
Wag Industries Inc .................. F ...... 847 329-8932
Skokie *(G-20109)*
▲ Wallace/Haskin Corp .................. G ...... 630 789-2882
Downers Grove *(G-8540)*
▲ Weidenmiller Co .................. F ...... 630 250-2500
Itasca *(G-12373)*
Wemco Inc .................. F ...... 708 388-1980
Alsip *(G-543)*
World Cup Packaging Inc .................. G ...... 815 624-6501
South Beloit *(G-20178)*

## 3559 Special Ind Machinery, NEC

Accelrted Mch Design Engrg LLC ...... F ...... 815 316-6381
Rockford *(G-18251)*
Ace Machine & Tool .................. G ...... 815 793-5077
Dekalb *(G-8072)*
Acro Magnetics Inc .................. G ...... 815 943-5018
Harvard *(G-11617)*
All Metal Recycling Company ...... G ...... 847 530-4825
Villa Park *(G-21235)*
▼ American Industrial Direct LLC ...... E ...... 800 382-1200
Elgin *(G-8948)*
American Rack Company .................. E ...... 773 763-7309
Chicago *(G-3870)*
Americlean Inc .................. F ...... 314 741-8901
Wood River *(G-22440)*
▼ Amiberica Inc .................. E ...... 773 247-3600
Chicago *(G-3888)*
Arcoa Group Inc .................. E ...... 847 693-7519
Waukegan *(G-21527)*
Asahi Kasei Bioprocess Inc .................. E ...... 847 834-0800
Glenview *(G-11105)*
Asta Service Inc .................. G ...... 630 271-0960
Lisle *(G-13565)*
Atlas Maintenance Service Inc ...... G ...... 773 486-3386
Chicago *(G-3981)*
Bailey Business Group .................. G ...... 618 548-3566
Salem *(G-19327)*
▲ Black Bros Co .................. D ...... 815 539-7451
Mendota *(G-14717)*
Black Market Parts Inc .................. G ...... 630 562-9400
West Chicago *(G-21672)*
Brown Metal Products Ltd .................. G ...... 309 936-7384
Atkinson *(G-943)*
▲ Bystronic Inc .................. C ...... 847 214-0300
Elgin *(G-8974)*
Calser Corp .................. G ...... 618 277-0329
Swansea *(G-20775)*
Carlson Sti Inc .................. G ...... 630 232-2460
Elgin *(G-8982)*
▲ Carlson Tool & Machine Company ...... F ...... 630 232-2460
Elgin *(G-8983)*
◆ CDL Technology Inc .................. E ...... 630 543-5240
Addison *(G-70)*
Chatham Corporation .................. F ...... 847 634-5506
Lincolnshire *(G-13436)*

Chemtech Services Inc .................. F ...... 815 838-4800
Lockport *(G-13709)*
Chicago Kiln Service .................. G ...... 847 436-0919
Rolling Meadows *(G-18720)*
▲ CIC North America Inc .................. G ...... 847 873-0860
Rolling Meadows *(G-18721)*
Cortes Enterprise Inc .................. G ...... 779 777-1061
Cortland *(G-7385)*
CR Laurence Co Inc .................. D ...... 773 242-2871
Cicero *(G-7186)*
Credit Card Systems Inc .................. F ...... 847 459-8320
Wheeling *(G-22031)*
Crw Finishing Inc .................. E ...... 630 495-4994
Addison *(G-84)*
Cryogenic Systems Equipment ...... E ...... 708 385-4216
Blue Island *(G-2244)*
▲ D R Sperry & Co .................. D ...... 630 892-4361
Aurora *(G-1137)*
▲ Dabrico Inc .................. E ...... 815 939-0580
Bourbonnais *(G-2393)*
Desco Inc .................. G ...... 847 439-2130
Elk Grove Village *(G-9424)*
▲ Disa Holding Corp .................. G ...... 630 820-3000
Oswego *(G-16913)*
▲ Dover Artificial Lift Intl LLC ...... F ...... 630 743-2563
Downers Grove *(G-8430)*
◆ Duravant LLC .................. F ...... 630 635-3910
Downers Grove *(G-8437)*
E P M Sales Co Inc .................. G ...... 630 761-2051
Batavia *(G-1445)*
▼ Effective Energy Assoc LLC ...... G ...... 815 248-9280
Davis *(G-7805)*
▲ Eirich Machines Inc .................. G ...... 847 336-2444
Gurnee *(G-11446)*
Electro-Glo Distribution Inc ...... G ...... 815 224-4030
La Salle *(G-12771)*
▲ Engineering Finshg Systems LLC ...... E ...... 815 893-6090
Elmhurst *(G-9866)*
ER&r Inc .................. G ...... 847 791-5671
Northbrook *(G-16250)*
▲ Etel Inc .................. G ...... 847 519-3380
Schaumburg *(G-19523)*
▲ Ewikon Molding Tech Inc .................. G ...... 815 874-7270
Rockford *(G-18373)*
Fanuc America Corporation ...... E ...... 847 898-5000
Hoffman Estates *(G-12009)*
◆ Federal Signal Corporation ...... D ...... 630 954-2000
Oak Brook *(G-16510)*
Felix Partners LLC .................. F ...... 847 648-8449
Rolling Meadows *(G-18728)*
◆ Fluid Management Inc .................. B ...... 847 537-0880
Wheeling *(G-22055)*
Fortune Metal Midwest LLC ...... E ...... 630 778-7776
Sandwich *(G-19363)*
▲ G K Enterprises Inc .................. G ...... 708 587-2150
Monee *(G-14996)*
▲ Gaither Tool Co .................. G ...... 217 245-0545
Jacksonville *(G-12388)*
Gisco Inc .................. G ...... 630 910-3000
Darien *(G-7795)*
Globe Lift LLC .................. G ...... 630 844-4247
Aurora *(G-1162)*
Gone For Good .................. E ...... 217 753-0414
Springfield *(G-20447)*
▲ Graymills Corporation .................. D ...... 773 477-4100
Broadview *(G-2582)*
Guzzler Manufacturing Inc .................. C ...... 815 672-3171
Streator *(G-20690)*
▲ Hackett Precision Company Inc ...... E ...... 615 227-3136
Chicago *(G-5027)*
Hanjitech Inc .................. G ...... 847 707-5611
Chicago *(G-5041)*
Hardwood Line Manufacturing Co ...... E ...... 773 463-2600
Chicago *(G-5045)*
Harris Metals & Recycling .................. G ...... 217 235-1808
Mattoon *(G-14390)*
Hastings Manufacturing Inc ...... E ...... 800 338-8688
Millstadt *(G-14825)*
Haussermann Usa LLC .................. F ...... 847 272-9850
Northbrook *(G-16269)*
▲ Hmt Manufacturing Inc .................. E ...... 847 473-2310
North Chicago *(G-16182)*
◆ Hunter Foundry Machinery Corp ...... D ...... 847 397-5100
Schaumburg *(G-19560)*
Hygeia Industries Inc .................. F ...... 847 380-2030
Glenview *(G-11139)*
▲ I T R Inc .................. E ...... 217 245-4478
Jacksonville *(G-12392)*
Industrial Phrm Resources Inc ...... F ...... 630 823-4700
Bartlett *(G-1357)*

International Molding Mch Co ...... G ...... 708 354-1380
La Grange Park *(G-12757)*
Isis3d LLC .................. G ...... 516 426-5410
Chicago *(G-5242)*
▲ K R Komarek Inc .................. E ...... 847 956-0060
Wood Dale *(G-22384)*
K&J Finishing Inc .................. F ...... 815 965-9655
Rockford *(G-18451)*
Kinast Inc .................. G ...... 217 852-3525
Dallas City *(G-7698)*
▲ Kirby Lester LLC .................. D ...... 847 984-3377
Lake Forest *(G-12920)*
Koflo Corporation .................. G ...... 847 516-3700
Cary *(G-3356)*
Kps Capital Partners LP .................. G ...... 630 972-7000
Bolingbrook *(G-2333)*
▼ Kuusakoski Philadelphia LLC ...... D ...... 215 533-8323
Plainfield *(G-17616)*
▲ LAB Equipment Inc .................. G ...... 630 595-4288
Itasca *(G-12301)*
Leonard Associates Inc .................. E ...... 815 226-9609
Rockford *(G-18467)*
▲ Maac Machinery Co Inc .................. E ...... 630 665-1700
Carol Stream *(G-3187)*
▲ Mamata Enterprises Inc .................. G ...... 941 205-0227
Montgomery *(G-15059)*
Maren Engineering Corporation ...... E ...... 708 333-6250
South Holland *(G-20287)*
Masterfeed Corporation .................. G ...... 630 879-1133
Batavia *(G-1466)*
▲ McLaughlin Body Co .................. D ...... 309 762-7755
Moline *(G-14955)*
Meminger Metal Finishing Inc ...... G ...... 309 582-3363
Aledo *(G-371)*
Mgb Engineering Company ...... E ...... 847 956-7444
Elk Grove Village *(G-9624)*
Midwest Electronics Recycling ...... G ...... 847 249-7011
Waukegan *(G-21591)*
Midwest Innovations Inc .................. G ...... 815 578-1401
McHenry *(G-14533)*
Midwest Mixing Inc .................. G ...... 708 422-8100
Chicago Ridge *(G-7151)*
Morrell Incorporated .................. F ...... 630 858-4600
Glendale Heights *(G-11050)*
▲ Multitech Industries Inc .................. G ...... 630 784-9200
Carol Stream *(G-3202)*
▲ Multitech McHned Cmponents LLC ...... E ...... 630 949-8200
Carol Stream *(G-3203)*
Nal Worldwide Holdings Inc ...... G ...... 630 261-3100
Addison *(G-225)*
◆ Nalco Company LLC .................. A ...... 630 305-1000
Naperville *(G-15703)*
Nalco Company LLC .................. G ...... 630 305-2451
Naperville *(G-15705)*
▲ Nalco Holdings LLC .................. A ...... 630 305-1000
Naperville *(G-15707)*
Norchem Inc .................. F ...... 708 478-4777
Mokena *(G-14887)*
Nu-Recycling Technology Inc ...... F ...... 630 904-5237
Naperville *(G-15820)*
Ozonology Inc .................. G ...... 847 998-8808
Northbrook *(G-16329)*
Parking Systems Inc .................. E ...... 847 891-3819
Schaumburg *(G-19684)*
Parkson Corporation .................. E ...... 847 816-3700
Vernon Hills *(G-21189)*
Pekay Machine & Engrg Co Inc ...... F ...... 312 829-5530
Chicago *(G-6098)*
Plastics Color Corporation ...... E ...... 708 868-3800
Calumet City *(G-2951)*
▲ Pollmann North America Inc ...... E ...... 815 834-1122
Romeoville *(G-18858)*
▲ Prater Industries Inc .................. D ...... 630 679-3200
Bolingbrook *(G-2359)*
Prinsco Inc .................. F ...... 815 635-3131
Chatsworth *(G-3627)*
Pro Tools & Equipment Inc ...... G ...... 847 838-6666
Antioch *(G-652)*
▲ Processing Tech Intl LLC .................. D ...... 630 585-5800
Aurora *(G-1070)*
Quality Fastener Products Inc ...... G ...... 224 330-3162
Elgin *(G-9157)*
R & G Machine Shop Inc .................. F ...... 217 342-6622
Effingham *(G-8856)*
▲ Ransburg Corporation .................. B ...... 847 724-7500
Glenview *(G-11190)*
▲ RAO Design International Inc ...... G ...... 847 671-6182
Schiller Park *(G-19865)*
Rapid Electroplating Process ...... G ...... 708 344-2504
Melrose Park *(G-14685)*

Employee Codes: A=Over 500 employees, B=251-500
C=101-250, D=51-100, E=20-50, F=10-19, G=3-9

2017 Harris Illinois
Industrial Directory

Rapid Line Industries Inc ........F ....... 815 727-4362
Joliet (G-12563)
Rdn Manufacturing Company Inc ........E ....... 630 893-4500
Bloomingdale (G-2130)
Renu Electronics Private Ltd ........G ....... 630 879-8412
Batavia (G-1491)
Rex Morioka ........G ....... 847 651-9400
Schiller Park (G-19867)
ROC Industries Inc ........G ....... 618 277-6044
Belleville (G-1670)
Saint-Gobain Abrasives Inc ........C ....... 630 868-8060
Carol Stream (G-3232)
Schold Machine Corporation ........E ....... 708 458-3788
Chicago (G-6454)
◆ Simpson Technologies Corp ........E ....... 630 978-2700
Aurora (G-1079)
Six Oaks Company ........G ....... 312 343-4037
Chicago (G-6519)
SMC Corporation of America ........E ....... 630 449-0600
Aurora (G-1080)
SMS Technical Services LLC ........G ....... 708 479-1333
Mokena (G-14903)
▲ Spacesaver Parking Company ........G ....... 773 486-6900
Chicago (G-6549)
Speed Bleeder Products Co ........G ....... 815 736-6296
Newark (G-15935)
Spf Supplies Inc ........G ....... 847 454-9081
Elk Grove Village (G-9746)
Srmd Solutions LLC ........G ....... 217 925-5773
Dieterich (G-8315)
Star Cutter Co ........G ....... 231 264-5661
Hoffman Estates (G-12058)
◆ Sterling Products Inc ........D ....... 847 273-7700
Schaumburg (G-19740)
▲ Sterling Systems Sales Corp ........G ....... 630 584-3580
Saint Charles (G-19271)
▲ Stutz Company ........F ....... 773 287-1068
Chicago (G-6610)
▲ Substrate Technology Inc ........F ....... 815 941-4800
Morris (G-15133)
T & S Business Group LLC ........F ....... 815 432-7084
Watseka (G-21429)
▲ Tek Pak Inc ........D ....... 630 406-0560
Batavia (G-1506)
▲ Therma-Kleen Inc ........G ....... 630 718-0212
Plainfield (G-17657)
▲ Thomas Engineering Inc ........D ....... 847 358-5800
Hoffman Estates (G-12065)
Thomas Engineering Inc ........E ....... 815 398-0280
Rockford (G-18648)
Tuskin Equipment Corporation ........G ....... 630 466-5590
Sugar Grove (G-20738)
Ultramatic Equipment Co ........E ....... 630 543-4565
Addison (G-333)
▲ Union Special LLC ........C ....... 847 669-5101
Huntley (G-12182)
United Validation & Com ........G ....... 815 953-6068
Watseka (G-21432)
Unitel Technologies Inc ........F ....... 847 297-2265
Mount Prospect (G-15381)
Vacudyne Incorporated ........E ....... 708 757-5200
Chicago Heights (G-7134)
◆ Vst America Inc ........G ....... 847 952-3800
Arlington Heights (G-868)
▲ Wagner Systems Inc ........E ....... 630 503-2400
Elgin (G-9226)
Waupaca Foundry Inc ........C ....... 217 347-0600
Effingham (G-8862)
WEI TO Associates Inc ........G ....... 708 747-6660
Matteson (G-14381)
▲ Weiler Engineering Inc ........D ....... 847 697-4900
Elgin (G-9232)
Yer Kiln Me LLC ........G ....... 309 606-9007
Wyoming (G-22642)

## 3561 Pumps & Pumping Eqpt

A-L-L Equipment Company ........G ....... 815 877-7000
Loves Park (G-13911)
▲ Action Pump Co ........F ....... 847 516-3636
Cary (G-3322)
Allegion S&S US Holding Co ........C ....... 815 875-3311
Princeton (G-17742)
Aptargroup Inc ........B ....... 847 639-2124
Cary (G-3327)
▲ Aqua Control Inc ........E ....... 815 664-4900
Spring Valley (G-20374)
Automax Corporation ........G ....... 630 972-1919
Woodridge (G-22454)
▲ Basement Flood Protector Inc ........F ....... 847 438-6770
Lake Zurich (G-13045)
Canada Organization & Dev LLC ........G ....... 630 743-2563
Downers Grove (G-8404)
Century Fasteners & Mch Co Inc ........F ....... 773 463-3900
Skokie (G-19977)
Certified Power Inc ........E ....... 847 573-3800
Mundelein (G-15485)
Chicago Industrial Pump Co ........G ....... 847 214-8988
South Elgin (G-20189)
Cool Fluidics Inc ........G ....... 815 861-4063
Woodstock (G-22554)
◆ Corken Inc ........D ....... 405 946-5576
Lake Bluff (G-12839)
Davis Welding & Manfctg Inc ........F ....... 217 784-5480
Gibson City (G-10899)
▲ Dover Artificial Lift Intl LLC ........F ....... 630 743-2563
Downers Grove (G-8430)
Dover Energy Automation LLC ........E ....... 630 541-1540
Downers Grove (G-8432)
◆ Emco Wheaton Usa Inc ........E ....... 281 856-1300
Quincy (G-17825)
Engineered Fluid Inc ........C ....... 618 533-1351
Centralia (G-3413)
Engineered Fluid Inc ........D ....... 618 533-1351
Centralia (G-3414)
▲ Ergoseal Inc ........E ....... 630 462-9600
Carol Stream (G-3147)
◆ Evac North America Inc ........E ....... 815 654-8300
Cherry Valley (G-3642)
◆ Fairbanks Morse Pump Corp ........B ....... 630 859-7000
North Aurora (G-16129)
FH Ayer Manufacturing Co ........E ....... 708 755-0550
Chicago Heights (G-7097)
Flow Control US Holding Corp ........F ....... 630 307-3000
Hanover Park (G-11582)
Flowserve Corporation ........E ....... 630 762-4100
West Chicago (G-21704)
Flowserve Corporation ........E ....... 630 762-4100
West Chicago (G-21705)
Flowserve Corporation ........E ....... 630 435-9596
Lombard (G-13799)
Flowserve Corporation ........E ....... 630 260-1310
Wheaton (G-21949)
Fluid Handling LLC ........B ....... 773 267-1600
Morton Grove (G-15198)
Fna Ip Holdings Inc ........D ....... 847 348-1500
Elk Grove Village (G-9482)
Georgetown Waste Water ........G ....... 217 662-2525
Georgetown (G-10886)
▲ Graymills Corporation ........D ....... 773 477-4100
Broadview (G-2582)
▲ Grundfos Water Utility Inc ........D ....... 630 236-5500
Aurora (G-1021)
Guzzler Manufacturing Inc ........C ....... 815 672-3171
Streator (G-20690)
Heidolph NA LLC ........F ....... 224 265-9600
Elk Grove Village (G-9520)
Hidrostal LLC ........F ....... 630 240-6271
Aurora (G-1026)
Idex Corporation ........B ....... 847 498-7070
Lake Forest (G-12915)
Industrial Filter Pump Mfg Co ........D ....... 708 656-7800
Bedford Park (G-1556)
Ingersoll-Rand Company ........E ....... 704 655-4000
Chicago (G-5191)
Inman Electric Motors Inc ........E ....... 815 223-2288
La Salle (G-12778)
ITT Bell & Gossett ........E ....... 847 966-3700
Morton Grove (G-15204)
ITT Water & Wastewater USA Inc ........F ....... 708 342-0484
Tinley Park (G-20924)
Jn Pump Holdings Inc ........F ....... 708 754-2940
Chicago Heights (G-7105)
▲ Johnson Pumps America Inc ........E ....... 847 671-7867
Rockford (G-18449)
Knox Capital Holdings LLC ........G ....... 312 402-1425
Chicago (G-5393)
L V Barnhouse & Sons ........G ....... 309 586-5404
Galesburg (G-10764)
▲ Lubeq Corporation ........F ....... 847 931-1020
Elgin (G-9096)
▲ March Manufacturing Inc ........D ....... 847 729-5300
Glenview (G-11167)
Mechanical Engineering Pdts ........G ....... 312 421-3375
Chicago (G-5674)
▲ Metropolitan Industries Inc ........C ....... 815 886-9200
Romeoville (G-18845)
Midwest Fuel Injction Svc Corp ........F ....... 847 991-7867
Palatine (G-17056)
Murdock Company Inc ........G ....... 847 566-0050
Mundelein (G-15535)
▲ Nexpump Inc ........G ....... 630 365-4639
Elburn (G-8900)
O Adjust Matic Pump Company ........G ....... 630 766-1490
Wood Dale (G-22408)
Olive Mount Mart ........G ....... 773 476-4964
Chicago (G-5982)
▲ Omni Pump Repairs Inc ........F ....... 847 451-0000
Franklin Park (G-10543)
Park Engineering Inc ........E ....... 847 455-1424
Franklin Park (G-10546)
Pentair Flow Technologies LLC ........C ....... 630 859-7000
North Aurora (G-16140)
Pokorney Manufacturing Co ........G ....... 630 458-0406
Addison (G-245)
Polar Container Corp Inc ........G ....... 847 299-5030
Rosemont (G-19024)
Pump House ........G ....... 618 216-2404
Wood River (G-22444)
Pump Solutions Group ........D ....... 630 487-2240
Oakbrook Terrace (G-16719)
Quincy Compressor LLC ........C ....... 217 222-7700
Quincy (G-17875)
R S Corcoran Co ........E ....... 815 485-2156
New Lenox (G-15905)
Roy E Roth Company ........G ....... 309 787-1791
Milan (G-14805)
Rrp Enterprises Inc ........G ....... 847 455-5674
Franklin Park (G-10577)
Ruthman Pump and Engineering ........G ....... 708 754-2940
Chicago Heights (G-7124)
▲ S C C Pumps Inc ........G ....... 847 593-8495
Arlington Heights (G-834)
S-P-D Incorporated ........G ....... 847 882-9820
Palatine (G-17070)
Simpson Well & Pump Company ........G ....... 708 301-0826
Lockport (G-13746)
Spirax Sarco Inc ........F ....... 630 493-4525
Lisle (G-13660)
▲ Swaby Manufacturing Company ........G ....... 773 626-1400
Chicago (G-6646)
Tacmina USA Corporation ........G ....... 312 810-8128
Schaumburg (G-19751)
Thermo Fisher Scientific Inc ........D ....... 847 381-7050
Bartlett (G-1380)
Thomas Pump Company ........F ....... 630 851-9393
Aurora (G-1085)
Townley Engrg & Mfg Co Inc ........F ....... 618 273-8271
Eldorado (G-8924)
Toyo Pump North America ........G ....... 815 806-1414
New Lenox (G-15921)
Tramco Pump Co ........E ....... 312 243-5800
Chicago (G-6756)
Trd Manufacturing Inc ........E ....... 815 654-7775
Machesney Park (G-14113)
Trusty Warns Inc ........E ....... 630 766-9015
Wood Dale (G-22434)
Tuskin Equipment Corporation ........G ....... 630 466-5590
Sugar Grove (G-20738)
◆ Tuthill Corporation ........E ....... 630 382-4900
Burr Ridge (G-2889)
Unique Indoor Comfort ........F ....... 847 362-1910
Libertyville (G-13394)
W S Darley & Co ........F ....... 630 735-3500
Itasca (G-12372)
Wagner Pump & Supply Co Inc ........G ....... 847 526-8573
Wauconda (G-21512)
Waves Fluid Solutions LLC ........G ....... 630 765-7533
Carol Stream (G-3264)
◆ Yamada America Inc ........E ....... 847 228-9063
Arlington Heights (G-877)

## 3562 Ball & Roller Bearings

Allegion S&S US Holding Co ........C ....... 815 875-3311
Princeton (G-17742)
▲ Alternative Bearings Corp ........G ....... 847 240-9630
Schaumburg (G-19435)
▲ American NTN Bearing Mfg Corp ........B ....... 847 741-4545
Elgin (G-8950)
American NTN Bearing Mfg Corp ........E ....... 847 671-5450
Schiller Park (G-19801)
Bearings Manufacturing Company ........F ....... 773 583-6703
Chicago (G-4067)
Beauticontrol ........G ....... 217 223-0382
Quincy (G-17801)
Caster Warehouse Inc ........F ....... 847 836-5712
Carpentersville (G-3279)
▲ Ccty USA Bearing Co ........G ....... 847 540-8196
Lake Zurich (G-13051)
▲ Frantz Manufacturing Company ........G ....... 815 625-3333
Sterling (G-20591)

**Frantz Manufacturing Company** D 815 625-7063
Sterling *(G-20592)*
**▲ HRB America Corporation** G 630 513-1800
Saint Charles *(G-19195)*
**▲ Mechanical Power Inc** E 847 487-0070
Wauconda *(G-21481)*
**NTN Bearing Corporation** G 847 298-7500
Macomb *(G-14127)*
**▼ NTN USA Corporation** C 847 298-4652
Mount Prospect *(G-15357)*
**◆ NTN-Bower Corporation** G 309 837-0440
Macomb *(G-14128)*
**NTN-Bower Corporation** A 309 837-0322
Macomb *(G-14129)*
**▲ Pacific Bearing Corp** C 815 389-5600
Roscoe *(G-18911)*
**▲ Pan Pac International Inc** G 847 222-9077
Arlington Heights *(G-816)*
**▲ Payson Casters Inc** C 847 336-6200
Gurnee *(G-11482)*
**▲ Peer Bearing Company** C 877 600-7337
Waukegan *(G-21600)*
**Precision Plastic Ball Co** G 847 678-2255
Franklin Park *(G-10559)*
**Roberts Swiss Inc** E 630 467-9100
Itasca *(G-12348)*
**SKF USA Inc** D 847 742-0700
Elgin *(G-9185)*
**SKF USA Inc** D 847 742-0700
Elgin *(G-9186)*
**▲ Thomson Linear LLC** C 815 568-8001
Marengo *(G-14243)*
**Timken Company** G 309 692-8150
Peoria *(G-17469)*

## 3563 Air & Gas Compressors

**Agro-Chem Inc** F 309 475-8311
Saybrook *(G-19413)*
**Allegion S&S US Holding Co** C 815 875-3311
Princeton *(G-17742)*
**Atlas Copco Compressors LLC** F 847 640-6067
Elk Grove Village *(G-9319)*
**Atlas Copco Compressors LLC** F 281 590-7500
Chicago *(G-3979)*
**Atlas Copco Comptec Inc** G 847 726-9866
Hawthorn Woods *(G-11701)*
**Bridgeport Air Comprsr & Tl Co** G 618 945-7163
Bridgeport *(G-2450)*
**Brock Equipment Company** E 815 459-4210
Woodstock *(G-22547)*
**Buell Manufacturing Company** G 708 447-6320
Lyons *(G-14033)*
**Compressed Air Advisors Inc** G 877 247-2381
Westchester *(G-21836)*
**◆ Corken Inc** D 405 946-5576
Lake Bluff *(G-12839)*
**◆ Cvp Systems Inc** D 630 852-1190
Downers Grove *(G-8422)*
**Demarco Industrial Vacuum Corp** G 815 344-2222
Crystal Lake *(G-7567)*
**Ecothermics Corporation** G 217 621-2402
Peoria *(G-17483)*
**▲ Fluid-Aire Dynamics Inc** E 847 678-8388
Schaumburg *(G-19531)*
**Fna Ip Holdings Inc** D 847 348-1500
Elk Grove Village *(G-9482)*
**▲ G H Meiser & Co** E 708 388-7867
Posen *(G-17730)*
**Gardner Denver Inc** F 209 823-0356
Princeton *(G-17749)*
**Gardner Denver Inc** D 217 222-5400
Quincy *(G-17828)*
**Gardner Denver Inc** D 815 875-3321
Princeton *(G-17750)*
**◆ Harris Equipment Corporation** E 708 343-0866
Melrose Park *(G-14651)*
**▲ Howe Corporation** E 773 235-0200
Chicago *(G-5123)*
**Idex Corporation** B 847 498-7070
Lake Forest *(G-12915)*
**Industrial Vacuum** G 630 357-7700
Maple Park *(G-14200)*
**Ingersoll-Rand Company** E 704 655-4000
Chicago *(G-5191)*
**▲ J/B Industries Inc** D 630 851-9444
Aurora *(G-1174)*
**Master Manufacturing Co** F 630 833-7060
Villa Park *(G-21269)*
**◆ Mat Holdings Inc** D 847 821-9630
Long Grove *(G-13897)*
**◆ Mat Industries LLC** G 847 821-9630
Long Grove *(G-13898)*
**▲ Mayekawa USA Inc** F 773 516-5070
Elk Grove Village *(G-9615)*
**Meyer Tool & Manufacturing Inc** E 708 425-9080
Oak Lawn *(G-16634)*
**Nordson Corporation** E 815 784-5025
Genoa *(G-10881)*
**◆ Ohio Medical LLC** D 847 855-0500
Gurnee *(G-11479)*
**On-Line Compressor Inc** G 847 497-9750
Johnsburg *(G-12440)*
**Ortman-Mccain Co** G 312 666-2244
Chicago *(G-6018)*
**▲ Paasche Airbrush Co** D 773 867-9191
Chicago *(G-6048)*
**Quincy Compressor LLC** C 217 222-7700
Quincy *(G-17875)*
**Rebuilders Enterprises Inc** G 708 430-0030
Bridgeview *(G-2523)*
**Resolute Industrial LLC** E 800 537-9675
Wheeling *(G-22139)*
**Rietschle Inc** G 410 712-4100
Quincy *(G-17888)*
**Rpk Technologies Inc** G 630 595-0911
Bensenville *(G-1981)*
**Ryan Manufacturing Inc** G 815 695-5310
Newark *(G-15934)*
**Scrollex Corporation** G 630 887-8817
Willowbrook *(G-22230)*
**Standard Car Truck Company** D 630 860-5511
Bensenville *(G-1998)*
**▲ Standard Lifts & Equipment Inc** G 414 444-1000
Hanover Park *(G-11591)*
**Thomas Gardner Denver Inc** E 217 222-5400
Quincy *(G-17893)*
**▲ William W Meyer and Sons** D 847 918-0111
Libertyville *(G-13402)*

## 3564 Blowers & Fans

**Aen Industries Inc** F 708 758-3000
Chicago Heights *(G-7077)*
**Aeropulse LLC** G 215 245-7600
Romeoville *(G-18792)*
**Altair Corporation (del)** E 847 634-9540
Lincolnshire *(G-13426)*
**American Air Filter Co Inc** D 502 637-0011
Chicago *(G-3848)*
**Architectural Fan Coil Inc** G 312 399-1203
Chicago *(G-3942)*
**Bact Process Systems Inc** G 847 577-0950
Arlington Heights *(G-721)*
**Basement Dewatering Systems** F 309 647-0331
Canton *(G-2981)*
**Bee Clean Specialties LLC** G 847 451-0844
Schaumburg *(G-19458)*
**Bisco Enterprise Inc** F 630 628-1831
Schaumburg *(G-19463)*
**Blowers LLC** E 708 594-1800
Elmhurst *(G-9841)*
**▲ Bofa Americas Inc** G 618 205-5007
Staunton *(G-20553)*
**Bost Corporation** E 708 344-7023
Maywood *(G-14420)*
**Bost Corporation** F 708 450-9234
Melrose Park *(G-14603)*
**C P Environmental Inc** F 630 759-8866
Romeoville *(G-18805)*
**Calutech Inc** G 708 614-0228
Orland Park *(G-16845)*
**Camfil USA Inc** D 815 459-6600
Crystal Lake *(G-7549)*
**Car - Mon Products Inc** E 847 695-9000
Elgin *(G-8981)*
**◆ Catalytic Products Intl Inc** E 847 438-0334
Lake Zurich *(G-13050)*
**Chatham Corporation** F 847 634-5506
Lincolnshire *(G-13436)*
**Chicago Plastic Systems Inc** E 815 455-4599
Crystal Lake *(G-7553)*
**Clean and Science USA Co Ltd** G 847 461-9292
Schaumburg *(G-19473)*
**Communication Coil Inc** D 847 671-1333
Schiller Park *(G-19815)*
**◆ Conservation Technology Ltd** D 847 559-5500
Northbrook *(G-16232)*
**Creasey Construction Ill Inc** F 217 546-1277
Springfield *(G-20424)*
**▲ Custom Filter LLC** D 630 906-2100
Aurora *(G-991)*
**Custom Systems Inc** G 314 355-4575
Granite City *(G-11272)*
**Df Fan Services Inc** F 630 876-1495
West Chicago *(G-21692)*
**Diablo Furnaces LLC** F 815 636-7502
Machesney Park *(G-14071)*
**Donaldson Company Inc** E 815 288-3374
Dixon *(G-8329)*
**Durable Manufacturing Company** F 630 766-0398
Bensenville *(G-1885)*
**Dust Patrol Inc** G 309 676-1161
Peoria *(G-17351)*
**E I P Inc** G 847 885-3615
Hoffman Estates *(G-12007)*
**◆ Eclipse Inc** D 815 877-3031
Rockford *(G-18356)*
**Filter Friend Z Inc** G 847 824-4049
Des Plaines *(G-8195)*
**◆ Filtertek Inc** B 815 648-2410
Hebron *(G-11719)*
**Filtration Group Corporation** D 815 726-4600
Joliet *(G-12494)*
**Filtration Group LLC** D 630 968-1563
Oak Brook *(G-16512)*
**Filtration Group LLC** E 815 726-4600
Joliet *(G-12495)*
**Flanders Corporation** C 815 472-4230
Momence *(G-14980)*
**Freedom Air Filtration Inc** G 815 744-8999
Joliet *(G-12497)*
**▼ Frequency Devices Inc** F 815 434-7800
Ottawa *(G-16960)*
**◆ Fuel Tech Inc** C 630 845-4500
Warrenville *(G-21348)*
**G T C Industries Inc** G 708 369-9815
Naperville *(G-15661)*
**Goose Island Mfg & Supply Corp** G 708 343-4225
Lansing *(G-13164)*
**Greenlees Filter LLC** D 708 366-3256
Vernon Hills *(G-21169)*
**H D A Fans Inc** G 630 627-2087
Elk Grove Village *(G-9514)*
**Heidolph NA LLC** F 224 265-9600
Elk Grove Village *(G-9520)*
**Henderson Engineering Co Inc** G 815 786-9471
Sandwich *(G-19368)*
**▲ Henry Technologies Inc** G 217 483-2406
Chatham *(G-3621)*
**▲ Homewerks Worldwide LLC** E 877 319-3757
Lake Bluff *(G-12849)*
**▲ Hydrosil International Ltd** G 847 741-1600
East Dundee *(G-8645)*
**▲ Illinois Blower Inc** D 847 639-5500
Cary *(G-3352)*
**Industrial Fiberglass Inc** F 708 681-2707
Melrose Park *(G-14657)*
**Industrial Filter Pump Mfg Co** D 708 656-7800
Bedford Park *(G-1556)*
**Jacobs Boiler & Mech Inds Inc** E 773 385-9900
Chicago *(G-5269)*
**Jan-Air Inc** E 815 678-4516
Richmond *(G-17964)*
**Kap Holdings LLC** F 708 948-0226
Oak Park *(G-16671)*
**Keating of Chicago Inc** E 815 569-2324
Capron *(G-2996)*
**▲ Kturbo USA Inc** G 630 406-1473
Batavia *(G-1462)*
**Lilly Air Systems Co Inc** F 630 773-2225
Itasca *(G-12305)*
**Marvel Electric Corporation** D 773 327-2644
Chicago *(G-5638)*
**Mason Engineering & Designing** E 630 595-5000
Inverness *(G-12209)*
**Master Manufacturing Co** F 630 833-7060
Villa Park *(G-21269)*
**Mellish & Murray Co** F 312 733-3513
Chicago *(G-5683)*
**Met-Pro Technologies LLC** E 630 775-0707
Wood Dale *(G-22398)*
**Midwest Air Pro Inc** G 773 622-4566
Chicago *(G-5741)*
**Mity Inc** G 630 365-5030
Elburn *(G-8898)*
**Monoxivent Systems Inc** G 309 764-9605
Rock Island *(G-18190)*
**Muffler** G 217 344-1676
Urbana *(G-21095)*
**Murdock Company Inc** G 847 566-0050
Mundelein *(G-15535)*

SIC

## 35 INDUSTRIAL AND COMMERCIAL MACHINERY AND COMPUTER EQUIPMENT

New York Blower Company .........D 217 347-3233
  Effingham *(G-8849)*
Paul D Stark & Associates .........G 630 964-7111
  Downers Grove *(G-8500)*
◆ Perma-Pipe Intl Holdings Inc .........C 847 966-1000
  Niles *(G-16019)*
▲ Permatron Corporation .........E 847 434-1421
  Elk Grove Village *(G-9674)*
Promark Associates Inc .........G 847 676-1894
  Skokie *(G-20064)*
Quality Cleaning Fluids Inc .........G 847 451-1190
  Franklin Park *(G-10566)*
▲ Revcor Inc .........B 847 428-4411
  Carpentersville *(G-3301)*
Revcor Inc .........G 847 428-4411
  Carpentersville *(G-3302)*
Robko Flock Coating Company .........G 847 272-6202
  Northbrook *(G-16357)*
▲ Robuschi Usa Inc .........G 704 424-1018
  Quincy *(G-17889)*
▲ Sanders Inc .........E 815 634-4611
  Morris *(G-15129)*
Schubert Environmental Eqp Inc .........F 630 307-9400
  Glendale Heights *(G-11067)*
Scott Industrial Blower Co .........F 847 426-8800
  Gilberts *(G-10936)*
Scrubair Systems Inc .........E 847 550-8061
  Lake Zurich *(G-13129)*
▲ Smith Filter Corporation .........E 309 764-8324
  Moline *(G-14971)*
▲ Solberg International Ltd .........G 630 616-4400
  Itasca *(G-12355)*
◆ Solberg Mfg Inc .........D 630 616-4400
  Itasca *(G-12356)*
Solberg Mfg Inc .........E 630 773-1363
  Itasca *(G-12357)*
▲ Storms Industries Inc .........E 312 243-7480
  Chicago *(G-6601)*
Terre Haute Tent & Awning Inc .........F 812 235-6068
  South Holland *(G-20309)*
Tri-Dim Filter Corporation .........E 847 695-5822
  Elgin *(G-9213)*
Universal Air Filter Company .........E 618 271-7300
  East Saint Louis *(G-8774)*
Vent Products Co Inc .........E 773 521-1900
  Chicago *(G-6881)*
▲ William W Meyer and Sons .........D 847 918-0111
  Libertyville *(G-13402)*

### 3565 Packaging Machinery

Algus Packaging Inc .........D 815 756-1881
  Dekalb *(G-8073)*
▲ All-Vac Industries Inc .........F 847 675-2290
  Skokie *(G-19948)*
American Packaging McHy Inc .........E 815 337-8580
  Woodstock *(G-22539)*
◆ Arpac LLC .........C 847 678-9034
  Schiller Park *(G-19805)*
◆ Ats Sortimat USA LLC .........D 847 925-1234
  Rolling Meadows *(G-18711)*
Automtc Lquid Pckg Sltons LLC .........E 847 372-3336
  Arlington Heights *(G-719)*
▲ Barrington Packaging Systems .........G 847 382-8063
  Barrington *(G-1272)*
▼ Birnberg Machinery Inc .........G 847 673-5242
  Skokie *(G-19964)*
Bms Manufacturing Company Inc .........E 309 787-3158
  Milan *(G-14776)*
◆ Bprex Healthcare Packaging Inc .........D 800 537-0178
  Buffalo Grove *(G-2667)*
▲ British Cnvrtng Sltns Nrth AME .........E 281 764-6651
  Elmhurst *(G-9842)*
Burghof Engineering & Mfg Co .........E 847 634-0737
  Lincolnshire *(G-13433)*
C N C Central Inc .........G 630 595-1453
  Bensenville *(G-1849)*
Cartpac Inc .........E 630 283-8979
  Carol Stream *(G-3125)*
Combined Technologies Inc .........G 847 968-4855
  Libertyville *(G-13317)*
Competitive Edge Opportunities .........G 815 322-2164
  Lakemoor *(G-13143)*
◆ Cvp Systems Inc .........D 630 852-1190
  Downers Grove *(G-8422)*
▲ Diamond Machine Werks Inc .........E 847 437-0665
  Arlington Heights *(G-746)*
Dover Europe Inc .........G 630 541-1540
  Downers Grove *(G-8433)*
◆ Dover Prtg Identification Inc .........D 630 541-1540
  Downers Grove *(G-8434)*

Duravant .........G 630 635-3910
  Downers Grove *(G-8436)*
◆ Duravant LLC .........G 630 635-3910
  Downers Grove *(G-8437)*
Econopin .........G 708 599-5002
  Bridgeview *(G-2486)*
▼ Eoe Inc .........F 847 550-1665
  Lake Zurich *(G-13069)*
F C D Inc .........G 847 498-3711
  Northbrook *(G-16255)*
▲ Frings America Inc .........G 630 851-5826
  Aurora *(G-1011)*
▲ Fromm Airpad Inc .........F 630 393-9790
  Warrenville *(G-21347)*
▲ Fuji Impulse American Corp .........G 847 236-9190
  Deerfield *(G-8008)*
▲ Gama Electronics Inc .........F 815 356-9600
  Woodstock *(G-22569)*
▲ Gateway Packaging Company LLC .........C 618 415-0010
  Granite City *(G-11280)*
Graphbury Machines LLC .........G 754 779-4285
  Chicago *(G-4988)*
Henkelman Inc .........G 331 979-2013
  Elmhurst *(G-9881)*
I T W Inc .........C 847 657-6171
  Glenview *(G-11140)*
Illinois Tool Works Inc .........E 708 720-0300
  Frankfort *(G-10333)*
Illinois Tool Works Inc .........F 847 215-8925
  Buffalo Grove *(G-2706)*
Illinois Tool Works Inc .........E 217 345-2166
  Charleston *(G-3599)*
Illinois Tool Works Inc .........D 618 997-1716
  Marion *(G-14269)*
◆ Integrated Packg & Fastener .........D 847 439-5730
  Elk Grove Village *(G-9550)*
Jescorp Inc .........D 847 378-1200
  Elk Grove Village *(G-9562)*
John R Nalbach Engineering Co .........E 708 579-9100
  Countryside *(G-7436)*
Knight Packaging Group Inc .........G 773 585-2035
  Chicago *(G-5389)*
▲ Korpack Inc .........F 630 213-3600
  Bloomingdale *(G-2111)*
Libco Industries Inc .........F 815 623-7677
  Roscoe *(G-18902)*
▲ Mamata Enterprises Inc .........E 941 205-0227
  Montgomery *(G-15059)*
Marquette Enterprises LLC .........G 877 689-0001
  Waukegan *(G-21587)*
▼ Marsh Shipping Supply Co LLC .........F 618 343-1006
  Collinsville *(G-7335)*
◆ Martin Automatic Inc .........C 815 654-4800
  Rockford *(G-18483)*
MB Corp & Associates .........F 847 214-8843
  South Elgin *(G-20218)*
Mid America Ems Industries .........G 630 916-8203
  Schaumburg *(G-19645)*
Midwest Mobile Canning LLC .........E 815 861-4515
  Crystal Lake *(G-7612)*
Mii Inc .........F 630 879-3000
  Batavia *(G-1471)*
Millwood Inc .........F 708 343-7341
  Melrose Park *(G-14674)*
Mssc LLC .........F 618 343-1006
  Collinsville *(G-7336)*
Nortech Packaging LLC .........E 847 884-1805
  Schaumburg *(G-19668)*
Pandaderia El Acambaro .........D 312 666-6316
  Chicago *(G-6069)*
Park Lawn Association Inc .........F 708 425-7377
  Oak Lawn *(G-16638)*
Pioneer Container McHy Inc .........F 618 533-7833
  Centralia *(G-3427)*
PMI Cartoning Inc .........D 847 437-1427
  Elk Grove Village *(G-9684)*
▲ Point Five Packaging LLC .........G 847 678-5016
  Schiller Park *(G-19860)*
Pre Pack Machinery Inc .........F 217 352-1010
  Champaign *(G-3528)*
Prototype Equipment Corp .........D 847 596-9000
  Waukegan *(G-21609)*
Purchasing Services Ltd Inc .........E 618 566-8100
  Mascoutah *(G-14359)*
R P Grollman Co Inc .........G 847 607-0294
  Highland Park *(G-11864)*
◆ Robert Bosch LLC .........B 248 876-1000
  Broadview *(G-2610)*
Robert L Murphy .........G 708 424-0277
  Evergreen Park *(G-10118)*

Robey Packaging Eqp & Svc .........G 708 758-8250
  Chicago Heights *(G-7123)*
Rollstock Inc .........G 708 579-3700
  Countryside *(G-7441)*
▲ Rosenthal Manufacturing Co Inc .........E 847 714-0404
  Northbrook *(G-16358)*
S G Acquisition Inc .........G 815 624-6501
  South Beloit *(G-20168)*
▲ Sardee Industries Inc .........G 630 824-4200
  Lisle *(G-13654)*
▲ Serac Inc .........E 630 510-9343
  Carol Stream *(G-3239)*
◆ Signode Corporation .........A 800 527-1499
  Glenview *(G-11197)*
Signode Industrial Group LLC .........E 847 483-1490
  Glenview *(G-11199)*
Signode Industrial Group LLC .........G 630 268-9999
  Glenview *(G-11201)*
Sj Converting LLC .........G 630 262-6640
  West Chicago *(G-21774)*
▲ Sjd Direct Midwest LLC .........G 618 931-2151
  Edwardsville *(G-8814)*
Suburban Machine Corporation .........E 847 808-9095
  Wheeling *(G-22158)*
T & T Machinery Inc .........G 708 366-8747
  River Forest *(G-18002)*
▲ Taisei Lamick USA Inc .........F 847 258-3283
  Elk Grove Village *(G-9767)*
Tegrant Alloyd Brands Inc .........B 815 756-8451
  Dekalb *(G-8124)*
Tegrant Holding Corp .........A 815 756-8451
  Dekalb *(G-8126)*
Terco Inc .........E 630 894-8828
  Bloomingdale *(G-2139)*
Tetra Pak Inc .........F 847 955-6000
  Vernon Hills *(G-21208)*
◆ Trebor Sales Corporation .........F 630 434-0040
  Oak Brook *(G-16564)*
Triangle Package Machinery Co .........C 773 889-0200
  Chicago *(G-6771)*
▲ Triangle Technologies Inc .........G 630 736-3318
  Streamwood *(G-20678)*
Ultra Packaging Inc .........G 630 595-9820
  Bensenville *(G-2008)*
Unique Blister Company .........F 630 289-1232
  Bartlett *(G-1383)*
Weigh Right Automatic Scale Co .........G 815 726-4626
  Joliet *(G-12588)*
Winpak Portion Packaging Inc .........F 708 753-5700
  Sauk Village *(G-19394)*
World Cup Packaging Inc .........G 815 624-6501
  South Beloit *(G-20178)*
◆ Yeaman Machine Tech Inc .........F 847 758-0500
  Elk Grove Village *(G-9823)*
◆ Z Automation Company .........F 847 357-0120
  Mundelein *(G-15569)*
Zitropack Ltd .........F 630 543-1016
  Addison *(G-350)*

### 3566 Speed Changers, Drives & Gears

Afton Chemical Corporation .........B 618 583-1000
  East Saint Louis *(G-8740)*
Allied Gear Co .........G 773 287-8742
  Chicago *(G-3815)*
▲ Arrow Gear Company .........C 630 969-7640
  Downers Grove *(G-8389)*
Brad Foote Gear Works Inc .........G 708 298-1100
  Naperville *(G-15612)*
Brock Equipment Company .........E 815 459-4210
  Woodstock *(G-22547)*
▲ Circle Gear & Machine Co Inc .........E 708 652-1000
  Cicero *(G-7184)*
▲ Diequa Corporation .........D 630 980-1133
  Bloomingdale *(G-2103)*
Dynamic Manufacturing Inc .........E 708 343-8753
  Melrose Park *(G-14626)*
▲ Dynomax Inc .........D 847 680-8833
  Wheeling *(G-22040)*
Engelhardt Gear Co .........E 847 766-7070
  Elk Grove Village *(G-9458)*
Gam Enterprises Inc .........E 847 649-2500
  Mount Prospect *(G-15331)*
Geitek Automation Inc .........D 815 385-3500
  McHenry *(G-14509)*
▲ GKN Stromag Inc .........E 937 433-3882
  Woodridge *(G-22485)*
Hadley Gear Manufacturing Co .........F 773 722-1030
  Chicago *(G-5028)*
▲ Hydraulicnet LLC .........E 630 543-7630
  Addison *(G-151)*

## 35 INDUSTRIAL AND COMMERCIAL MACHINERY AND COMPUTER EQUIPMENT

▲ Industrial Motion Control LLC .........C...... 847 459-5200
  Wheeling  (G-22076)
◆ LI Gear Inc ..................................G...... 630 226-1688
  Romeoville  (G-18840)
Martin Sprocket & Gear Inc ...............F...... 847 298-8844
  Des Plaines  (G-8227)
Midwest Converters Inc .....................F...... 815 229-9808
  Rockford  (G-18504)
▲ Mitsubishi Elc Automtn Inc .............C...... 847 478-2100
  Vernon Hills  (G-21183)
▲ Nidec-Shimpo America Corp ............E...... 630 924-7138
  Itasca  (G-12331)
Omni Gear and Machine Corp ............F...... 815 723-4327
  Joliet  (G-12548)
▲ Overton Chicago Gear Corp ............D...... 773 638-0508
  Chicago  (G-6030)
Productigear Inc .................................E...... 773 847-4505
  Chicago  (G-6205)
Prophet Gear Co ................................E...... 815 537-2002
  Prophetstown  (G-17771)
Quad Plus LLC ...................................E...... 815 740-0860
  Joliet  (G-12559)
Quincy Torque Converter Inc ..............E...... 217 228-0852
  Quincy  (G-17882)
Raycar Gear & Machine Company ......E...... 815 874-3948
  Rockford  (G-18549)
▲ Reliance Gear Corporation ...............D...... 630 543-6640
  Addison  (G-275)
▲ Rhino Tool Company ........................F...... 309 853-5555
  Kewanee  (G-12694)
▼ Rj Link International Inc ...................F...... 815 874-8110
  Rockford  (G-18559)
Rockford Jobbing Service Inc .............G...... 815 398-8661
  Rockford  (G-18576)
Sfc of Illinois Inc .................................E...... 815 745-2100
  Warren  (G-21336)
Siemens Industry Inc .........................E...... 847 931-1990
  Elgin  (G-9177)
Siemens Industry Inc .........................C......
  West Chicago  (G-21771)
Sumitomo Machinery Corp Amer ........E...... 630 752-0200
  Glendale Heights  (G-11078)
Surge Clutch & Drive Line Co .............G...... 708 331-1352
  South Holland  (G-20307)
Timken Gears & Services Inc ..............F...... 708 720-9400
  Mokena  (G-14911)
Weldon Corporation ............................E...... 708 343-4700
  Maywood  (G-14437)
▲ Wittenstein Inc ................................E...... 630 540-5300
  Bartlett  (G-1388)
◆ Yaskawa America Inc .......................C...... 847 887-7000
  Waukegan  (G-21642)

### 3567 Indl Process Furnaces & Ovens

Acra Electric Corporation ....................D...... 847 678-8870
  Schiller Park  (G-19799)
▲ Akinsun Heat Co Inc ........................F...... 630 289-9506
  Streamwood  (G-20640)
▼ Amiberica Inc ...................................E...... 773 247-3600
  Chicago  (G-3888)
Anderson Msnry Refr Spcialists ..........G...... 847 540-8885
  Lake Zurich  (G-13041)
◆ Armil/Cfs Inc ....................................E...... 708 339-6810
  South Holland  (G-20247)
▲ Austin-Westran LLC ........................C...... 815 234-2811
  Byron  (G-2912)
Burdett Burner Mfg Inc .......................G...... 630 617-5060
  Villa Park  (G-21239)
Calco Controls Inc .............................F...... 847 639-3858
  Crystal Lake  (G-7548)
Campbell International Inc .................E...... 408 661-0794
  Wauconda  (G-21452)
◆ Catalytic Products Intl Inc ................E...... 847 438-0334
  Lake Zurich  (G-13050)
▼ Chicago Brick Oven LLC ..................G...... 630 359-4793
  Elmhurst  (G-9847)
Coating & Systems Integration ..........F...... 312 335-1848
  Chicago  (G-4414)
Dane Industries LLC ..........................D...... 815 234-2811
  Byron  (G-2915)
Delta-Therm Corporation ....................F...... 847 526-2407
  Crystal Lake  (G-7566)
Durex Industries Inc ...........................G...... 847 462-2706
  Cary  (G-3337)
▲ Durex International Corp .................C...... 847 639-5600
  Cary  (G-3338)
◆ Elastec Inc ......................................C...... 618 382-2525
  Carmi  (G-3066)
Enders Process Equipment Corp .........G...... 630 469-3787
  Glendale Heights  (G-11022)

▲ Fast Heat Inc ...................................C...... 630 359-6300
  Elmhurst  (G-9871)
Fish Oven and Equipment Corp ..........E...... 847 526-8686
  Wauconda  (G-21463)
G & M Fabricating Inc .........................G...... 815 282-1744
  Roscoe  (G-18898)
Goodman Distribution Inc ...................G...... 773 376-8214
  Chicago  (G-4978)
▼ Grieve Corporation ...........................D...... 847 546-8225
  Round Lake  (G-19059)
Henderson Engineering Co Inc ............G...... 815 786-9471
  Sandwich  (G-19368)
▲ Henry Technologies Inc ...................E...... 217 483-2406
  Chatham  (G-3621)
Hts Chicago Inc .................................G...... 630 352-3690
  Wheaton  (G-21954)
IDI Fabrication Inc ..............................G...... 630 783-2246
  Lemont  (G-13236)
Infratrol LLC ......................................E...... 779 475-3098
  Byron  (G-2916)
◆ Ipsen Inc .........................................G...... 815 332-4941
  Cherry Valley  (G-3645)
Ipsen Inc ...........................................G...... 815 239-2385
  Pecatonica  (G-17252)
▲ J N Machinery Corp .........................G...... 224 699-9161
  East Dundee  (G-8648)
Lv Ventures Inc .................................E...... 312 993-1758
  Chicago  (G-5572)
▲ M H Detrick Company ......................E...... 708 479-5085
  Mokena  (G-14882)
▼ McEnglevan Indus Frnc Mfg Inc .......G...... 217 446-0941
  Danville  (G-7753)
Mellish & Murray Co ..........................F...... 312 379-0335
  Chicago  (G-5684)
▲ Midco International Inc ....................E...... 773 604-8700
  Chicago  (G-5733)
Moffitt Co ..........................................G...... 847 678-5450
  Schiller Park  (G-19853)
Northpoint Heating & Air Cond ...........G...... 847 731-1067
  Zion  (G-22692)
Oakley Industrial McHy Inc .................E...... 847 966-0052
  Elk Grove Village  (G-9660)
Oxytech Systems Inc .........................F...... 847 888-8611
  Carpentersville  (G-3293)
Paul D Stark & Associates .................G...... 630 964-7111
  Downers Grove  (G-8500)
Pioneer Express .................................E...... 217 236-3022
  Perry  (G-17497)
Precision Chrome Inc .........................E...... 847 587-1515
  Fox Lake  (G-10282)
Precision Quincy Ovens LLC ..............E...... 302 602-8738
  South Beloit  (G-20164)
Quincy Lab Inc ..................................E...... 773 622-2428
  Chicago  (G-6258)
▲ Tempco Electric Heater Corp ...........B...... 630 350-2252
  Wood Dale  (G-22429)
▲ Tempro International Corp ...............G...... 847 677-5370
  Skokie  (G-20100)
Thermal Solutions Inc ........................G...... 217 352-7019
  Savoy  (G-19412)
Tks Control Systems Inc ....................F...... 630 554-3020
  Oswego  (G-16937)
Tutco Inc ...........................................C...... 630 833-5400
  Elmhurst  (G-9953)
Uic Inc ...............................................G...... 815 744-4477
  Rockdale  (G-18234)
Westran Thermal Processing LLC .......E...... 815 634-1001
  South Beloit  (G-20175)
◆ Zeman Mfg Co .................................E...... 630 960-2300
  Lisle  (G-13679)

### 3568 Mechanical Power Transmission Eqpt, NEC

A Fischer Phase Drives .......................G...... 815 759-6928
  McHenry  (G-14473)
Active Tool and Machine Inc ..............F...... 708 599-0022
  Oak Lawn  (G-16598)
Air802 LLC ........................................G...... 630 585-6383
  Aurora  (G-955)
Allied Gear Co ....................................G...... 773 287-8742
  Chicago  (G-3815)
Allied-Locke Industries Inc .................E...... 800 435-7752
  Dixon  (G-8322)
▲ Arens Controls Company LLc ..........D...... 847 844-4700
  Arlington Heights  (G-715)
▲ Arrow Gear Company .......................C...... 630 969-7640
  Downers Grove  (G-8389)
▲ Aurora Bearing Company ..................B...... 630 897-8941
  Montgomery  (G-15027)

▲ Babbitting Service Inc .....................D...... 847 841-8008
  South Elgin  (G-20184)
▲ Bearing Sales Corporation ...............E...... 773 282-8686
  Chicago  (G-4066)
Bearings Manufacturing Company .....F...... 773 583-6703
  Chicago  (G-4067)
Borgwarner Transm Systems ..............A...... 708 547-2600
  Bellwood  (G-1700)
Chicago Die Casting Mfg Co ...............E...... 847 671-5010
  Franklin Park  (G-10428)
▲ Composite Bearings Mfg .................E...... 630 595-8334
  Wood Dale  (G-22354)
◆ Deublin Company .............................E...... 847 689-8600
  Waukegan  (G-21551)
Dyneer Corporation ............................B...... 217 228-6011
  Quincy  (G-17823)
▲ E N M Company ...............................D...... 773 775-8400
  Chicago  (G-4667)
Eastview Manufacturing Inc ...............G...... 847 741-2514
  Elgin  (G-9019)
◆ Flex-Weld Inc ..................................D...... 815 334-3662
  Woodstock  (G-22567)
Flowserve Corporation .......................E...... 630 543-4240
  Addison  (G-120)
▲ Forbo Siegling LLC ..........................F...... 630 595-4031
  Wood Dale  (G-22370)
Force America Inc ..............................E...... 815 730-3600
  Joliet  (G-12496)
Frantz Manufacturing Company ..........D...... 815 564-0991
  Sterling  (G-20593)
▲ Galaxy Sourcing Inc ........................E...... 630 532-5003
  Villa Park  (G-21254)
Gears Gears Gears Inc .......................G...... 708 366-6555
  Harwood Heights  (G-11685)
▲ GKN Stromag Inc .............................E...... 937 433-3882
  Woodridge  (G-22485)
▲ GKN Walterscheid Inc ......................C...... 630 972-9300
  Woodridge  (G-22486)
Grayslake Feed Sales Inc ...................G...... 847 223-4855
  Grayslake  (G-11344)
Hadley Gear Manufacturing Co ...........F...... 773 722-1030
  Chicago  (G-5028)
Hyspan Precision Products Inc ...........E...... 773 277-0700
  South Holland  (G-20279)
▲ Industrial Motion Control LLC .........C...... 847 459-5200
  Wheeling  (G-22076)
Innovative Mag Drive LLC ..................E...... 630 543-4240
  Chicago  (G-5200)
Innovative Mag-Drive LLC ..................E...... 630 543-4240
  Addison  (G-153)
J T C Inc ............................................F...... 773 292-9262
  Chicago  (G-5264)
▲ John King Usa Inc ...........................G...... 309 698-9250
  East Peoria  (G-8718)
La Salle Co Esda ................................G...... 815 433-5622
  Ottawa  (G-16966)
▲ Lovejoy Inc ......................................C...... 630 852-0500
  Downers Grove  (G-8480)
Lv Ventures Inc .................................E...... 312 993-1800
  Chicago  (G-5571)
Marland Clutch ..................................G...... 800 216-3515
  South Beloit  (G-20157)
Martin Sprocket & Gear Inc ...............F...... 847 298-8844
  Des Plaines  (G-8227)
Mathis Energy LLC ............................G...... 309 925-3177
  Tremont  (G-20984)
Metal Ceramics Inc ............................G...... 847 678-2293
  Franklin Park  (G-10530)
Naylor Automotive Engrg Co Inc .........F...... 773 582-6900
  Chicago  (G-5875)
▲ Nb Corporation of America ..............E...... 630 295-8880
  Hanover Park  (G-11586)
▼ NTN USA Corporation ......................E...... 847 298-4652
  Mount Prospect  (G-15357)
NTN-Bower Corporation .....................A...... 309 837-0322
  Macomb  (G-14129)
Process Screw Products Inc ...............E...... 815 864-2220
  Shannon  (G-19901)
Productigear Inc .................................E...... 773 847-4505
  Chicago  (G-6205)
Prophet Gear Co ................................E...... 815 537-2002
  Prophetstown  (G-17771)
Raycar Gear & Machine Company ......E...... 815 874-3948
  Rockford  (G-18549)
▲ Reliance Gear Corporation ...............D...... 630 543-6640
  Addison  (G-275)
Rexnord Industries LLC .....................D...... 847 520-1428
  Downers Grove  (G-8514)
Rexnord Industries LLC .....................G...... 630 969-1770
  Downers Grove  (G-8515)

35 INDUSTRIAL AND COMMERCIAL MACHINERY AND COMPUTER EQUIPMENT SIC SECTION

▲ Ringspann Corporation....F....847 678-3581
Franklin Park (G-10575)
Rockford Jobbing Service Inc....G....815 398-8661
Rockford (G-18576)
S&R Precision Machine LLC....F....815 469-6544
Frankfort (G-10360)
SKF USA Inc....D....847 742-0700
Elgin (G-9186)
Stock Gears Inc....F....224 653-9489
Elk Grove Village (G-9758)
Surge Clutch & Drive Line Co....G....708 331-1352
South Holland (G-20307)
▲ Technymon Technology USA Inc....G....630 787-0501
Wood Dale (G-22428)
▲ Thk America Inc....C....847 310-1111
Schaumburg (G-19762)
Timken Company....E....618 594-4545
Carlyle (G-3060)
▲ US Tsubaki Holdings Inc....C....847 459-9500
Wheeling (G-22172)
US Tsubaki Power Transm LLC....C....847 459-9500
Wheeling (G-22173)
Wrench....G....773 609-1698
Chicago (G-7036)

### 3569 Indl Machinery & Eqpt, NEC

Aberdon Enterprises....F....847 228-1300
Elk Grove Village (G-9255)
Accelrted Mch Design Engrg LLC....F....815 316-6381
Rockford (G-18251)
◆ Advanced Engneered Systems Inc....E....815 624-7797
South Beloit (G-20135)
All Metal Recycling Company....G....847 530-4825
Villa Park (G-21235)
American Precision Machining....F....847 455-1720
Franklin Park (G-10392)
▲ Amkus Inc....E....630 515-1800
Downers Grove (G-8387)
Apf US Inc....G....217 304-0027
Danville (G-7702)
Aquagreen Dispositions LLC....G....708 606-0211
Monee (G-14992)
Aquarius Fluid Products Inc....G....847 289-9090
Elgin (G-8957)
▲ Arrow Pneumatics Inc....D....708 343-6177
Broadview (G-2559)
Assemtech Inc....E....630 876-4990
West Chicago (G-21662)
Atlas Material Tstg Tech LLC....E....773 327-4520
Chicago (G-3983)
▲ Atlas Material Tstg Tech LLC....C....773 327-4520
Mount Prospect (G-15311)
◆ Ats Sortimat USA LLC....D....847 925-1234
Rolling Meadows (G-18711)
Automatic Feeder Company Inc....F....847 534-2300
Schaumburg (G-19450)
Automatic Fire Sprinkler LLC....F....309 862-2724
Normal (G-16064)
Automation Systems Inc....E....847 671-9515
Melrose Park (G-14597)
Averus Usa Inc....D....800 913-7034
Elgin (G-8961)
Barrington Automation Ltd....E....847 458-0900
Lake In The Hills (G-12987)
Bjs Enterprises Inc....G....815 432-5176
Watseka (G-21416)
Boley Tool & Machine Works Inc....C....309 694-2722
East Peoria (G-8703)
Bowl Doctors Inc....G....815 282-6009
Machesney Park (G-14060)
Camfil USA Inc....D....815 459-6600
Crystal Lake (G-7549)
Centec Automation Inc....G....847 791-9430
Palatine (G-17009)
Central Hydraulics Inc....G....309 527-5238
El Paso (G-8866)
Century Filter Products Inc....G....773 477-1790
Chicago (G-4276)
Champion Laboratories Inc....A....618 445-6011
Albion (G-357)
Cintas Corporation....E....309 821-1920
Normal (G-16067)
Citizenprime LLC....G....708 995-1241
Mokena (G-14859)
▲ Classic Fasteners LLC....G....630 605-0195
Saint Charles (G-19157)
Cleavenger Associates Inc....G....630 221-0007
Winfield (G-22284)
▲ Component Products Inc....E....847 301-1000
Schaumburg (G-19477)
Concep Machine Co Inc....E....847 498-9740
Northbrook (G-16230)
Concept and Design Services....G....847 259-1675
Mount Prospect (G-15317)
▼ Csiteq LLC....D....312 265-1509
Chicago (G-4512)
Cylinder Maintenance & Sup Inc....F....708 754-5040
Steger (G-20571)
▲ Diamond Machine Werks Inc....E....847 437-0665
Arlington Heights (G-746)
▲ Disa Holding Corp....G....630 820-3000
Oswego (G-16913)
Doms Incorporated....E....847 838-6723
Antioch (G-630)
Dtc Products Inc....G....630 513-3323
Saint Charles (G-19174)
DTS America Inc....G....847 783-0401
East Dundee (G-8633)
Eberle Manufacturing Company....F....847 215-0100
Wheeling (G-22042)
Egd Manufacturing Inc....G....815 964-2900
Rockford (G-18359)
◆ Ets-Lindgren Inc....C....630 307-7200
Wood Dale (G-22363)
Evac Systems Fire & Rescue....F....309 764-7812
Moline (G-14937)
Evoqua Water Technologies LLC....G....618 451-1205
Granite City (G-11275)
Fanuc America Corporation....E....847 898-5000
Hoffman Estates (G-12009)
Filter Monkey LLC....G....630 773-4402
Itasca (G-12263)
Filter Renew Tecnologies....G....815 344-2200
McCullom Lake (G-14471)
Filters To You....G....815 939-0700
Bradley (G-2421)
Fire Systems Holdings Inc....F....708 333-4130
Mokena (G-14861)
Flame Guard Usa LLC....G....815 219-4074
Lake Barrington (G-12806)
▲ Flow Pro Products Inc....F....815 836-1900
Bolingbrook (G-2310)
G & W Technical Corporation....G....847 487-0990
Island Lake (G-12215)
Gaunt Industries Inc....G....847 671-0776
Franklin Park (G-10477)
Gutter Masters....G....309 686-1234
Peoria (G-17376)
H2o Filter Inc....G....630 963-3303
Lisle (G-13598)
◆ Helix International Inc....G....847 709-0666
Elk Grove Village (G-9521)
Higman LLC....G....618 785-2545
Baldwin (G-1251)
ICC Intrntonal Celsius Concept....G....773 993-4405
Cicero (G-7203)
Iindigenous Railroad Svcs LLC....G....630 517-8207
Wheaton (G-21955)
Illini Hi-Reach Inc....F....847 428-3311
East Dundee (G-8646)
Illinois Tool Works Inc....F....708 720-0300
Frankfort (G-10329)
Industrial Filter Pump Mfg Co....D....708 656-7800
Bedford Park (G-1556)
Industrial Filter Pump Mfg Co....G....708 656-7800
Cicero (G-7205)
Industrial Pipe and Supply Co....E....708 652-7511
Chicago (G-5179)
▲ Inlet & Pipe Protection Inc....G....630 355-3288
Naperville (G-15811)
Innovative Industrial Svcs LLC....F....309 527-2035
El Paso (G-8870)
▲ Intech Industries Inc....F....847 487-5599
Wauconda (G-21473)
Intellgent Prcsses Automtn Inc....G....630 656-1215
Addison (G-154)
International Filter Mfg Corp....F....217 324-2303
Litchfield (G-13688)
Intertech Development Company....D....847 679-3377
Skokie (G-20017)
J2sys LLC....F....630 542-1342
Clarendon Hills (G-7257)
Jahns Structure Jacking System....G....630 365-2455
Elburn (G-8890)
Komax Systems Rockford Inc....D....815 885-8800
Loves Park (G-13956)
LDI Industries Inc....D....847 669-7510
Huntley (G-12157)
Leaffilter North LLC....E....630 595-9605
Wood Dale (G-22390)
Linear Kinetics Inc....G....630 365-0075
Maple Park (G-14201)
Lsp Industries Inc....F....815 226-8090
Rockford (G-18474)
Marion Fire Sprnklr Alarm Inc....F....618 889-9106
Marion (G-14272)
▲ Mavea LLC....G....905 712-2045
Elgin (G-9104)
Miller Carbonic Inc....F....773 624-5651
Aurora (G-1189)
Mity Inc....G....630 365-5030
Elburn (G-8898)
▼ Norman Filter Company LLC....D....708 233-5521
Bridgeview (G-2515)
▲ Nsk-America Corporation....F....847 843-7664
Hoffman Estates (G-12031)
Numerical Control Incorporated....G....708 389-8140
Alsip (G-502)
Online Inc....F....815 363-8008
McHenry (G-14540)
Oregon Fire Protection Dst....E....815 732-7214
Oregon (G-16830)
PAcrimson Fire Risk Svcs Inc....G....630 424-3400
Lombard (G-13840)
▲ Paratech Incorporated....D....815 469-3911
Frankfort (G-10348)
◆ Perma-Pipe Intl Holdings Inc....C....847 966-1000
Niles (G-16019)
Pro Techmation Inc....G....815 459-5909
Crystal Lake (G-7632)
Progressive Recovery Inc....D....618 286-5000
Dupo (G-8575)
▲ Pulsarlube USA Inc....G....847 593-5300
Elk Grove Village (G-9700)
Quality Cleaning Fluids Inc....G....847 451-1190
Franklin Park (G-10566)
Rainmaker....G....847 998-0838
Glenview (G-11189)
▲ Rehobot Inc....G....815 385-7777
McHenry (G-14550)
Robko Flock Coating Company....G....847 272-6202
Northbrook (G-16357)
Roodhouse Fire Protection Dst....E....217 589-5134
Roodhouse (G-18885)
Rotospray Mfg Inc....G....708 478-3307
Mokena (G-14900)
Saicor Inc....G....630 530-0350
Villa Park (G-21282)
Smb Toolroom Inc....G....309 353-7396
Pekin (G-17289)
Smith Power Transmission Co....G....773 526-5512
Chicago (G-6535)
Specialized Separators Inc....F....815 316-0626
Rockford (G-18625)
Standard Indus & Auto Eqp Inc....E....630 289-9500
Hanover Park (G-11590)
State Line International Inc....G....708 251-5772
Lansing (G-13186)
Superheat Fgh Services Inc....G....618 251-9450
New Lenox (G-15914)
Systems Piping....G....847 948-1373
Deerfield (G-8057)
Tampotech Decorating Inc....G....847 515-2968
Huntley (G-12178)
Textile Industries Inc....G....312 829-3112
Chicago (G-6706)
▲ Tomermo Inc....E....815 229-5077
Rockford (G-18653)
Tri-Dim Filter Corporation....E....847 695-5822
Elgin (G-9213)
Trueline Inc....E....309 378-2571
Downs (G-8548)
U S Filter Products....G....618 451-1205
Granite City (G-11309)
U S Filters....G....815 932-8154
Bradley (G-2435)
United States Filter/Iwt....G....815 877-3041
Rockford (G-18662)
Walach Manufacturing Co Inc....F....773 836-2060
Chicago (G-6935)
Water Products Company Ill Inc....E....630 553-0840
Yorkville (G-22675)
Waves Fluid Solutions LLC....G....630 765-7533
Carol Stream (G-3264)
▲ Western Slate Company....D....847 683-4400
Hampshire (G-11565)
Wm W Nugent & Co Inc....E....847 673-8109
Skokie (G-20111)

SIC SECTION — 35 INDUSTRIAL AND COMMERCIAL MACHINERY AND COMPUTER EQUIPMENT

## 3571 Electronic Computers

**Accelerated Assemblies Inc** ... E ... 630 616-6680
Elk Grove Village *(G-9259)*
**Ace Pcb Design Inc** ... G ... 847 674-8745
Skokie *(G-19946)*
**Alegria Company** ... C ... 608 726-2336
Chicago *(G-3800)*
**Antares Computer Systems Inc** ... G ... 773 783-8855
Chicago *(G-3915)*
**Apollo Computer Solutions Inc** ... G ... 312 671-3575
Downers Grove *(G-8388)*
**Apple Express** ... G ... 708 483-8168
Maywood *(G-14416)*
**Baked Apple Pancake House** ... G ... 630 515-9000
Downers Grove *(G-8393)*
**Bio-Logic Systems Corp** ... D ... 847 949-0456
Mundelein *(G-15478)*
**Derbytech Inc** ... E ... 309 755-2662
East Moline *(G-8676)*
**Easy Pay & Data Inc** ... G ... 217 398-9729
Champaign *(G-3476)*
**Election Systems & Sftwr LLC** ... F ... 815 397-8144
Rockford *(G-18362)*
◆ **Emac Inc** ... E ... 618 529-4525
Carbondale *(G-3006)*
**Enghouse Interactive Inc** ... G ... 630 472-9669
Oak Brook *(G-16509)*
**Fourier Systems Inc** ... G ... 708 478-5333
Homer Glen *(G-12079)*
**General Dynamics Adv Inf Sys** ... C ... 703 876-3000
Chicago *(G-4926)*
**George Electronics Inc** ... G ... 708 331-1983
Orland Park *(G-16860)*
**George Press Inc** ... G ... 217 324-2242
Litchfield *(G-13687)*
**Gld Industries Inc** ... G ... 217 390-9594
Champaign *(G-3489)*
**HP Inc** ... D ... 847 342-2000
Elk Grove Village *(G-9526)*
**HP Inc** ... G ... 847 207-9118
Palatine *(G-17038)*
**ICC Intrntonal Celsius Concept** ... G ... 773 993-4405
Cicero *(G-7203)*
**Integrity Technologies LLC** ... G ... 850 240-6089
Elgin *(G-9078)*
**International Bus Mchs Corp** ... A ... 847 706-3461
Schaumburg *(G-19572)*
**Interntional Cmpt Concepts Inc** ... E ... 847 808-7789
Northbrook *(G-16279)*
**Inverom Corporation** ... G ... 630 568-5609
Burr Ridge *(G-2858)*
**Jets Computing Inc** ... G ... 618 585-6676
Bunker Hill *(G-2805)*
**Koi Computers Inc** ... G ... 630 627-8811
Lombard *(G-13817)*
**Konica Minolta** ... G ... 630 893-8238
Roselle *(G-18950)*
**Konica Minolta Business Soluti** ... E ... 309 671-1360
Peoria *(G-17398)*
**Monroe Associates Inc** ... G ... 217 665-3898
Bethany *(G-2085)*
**Motorola Solutions Inc** ... G ... 847 341-3485
Oak Brook *(G-16546)*
**Motorola Solutions Inc** ... C ... 847 576-8600
Schaumburg *(G-19652)*
**Nano Technologies Inc** ... G ... 630 517-8824
Wheaton *(G-21970)*
**National Micro Systems Inc** ... G ... 312 566-0414
Chicago *(G-5865)*
**Northrop Grumman Systems Corp** ... A ... 847 259-9600
Rolling Meadows *(G-18753)*
▲ **Okamura Corp** ... G ... 312 645-0115
Chicago *(G-5977)*
**Perkins Enterprise Inc** ... G ... 708 560-3837
South Holland *(G-20298)*
**Pinehurst Bus Solutions Corp** ... G ... 630 842-6155
Winfield *(G-22290)*
◆ **Retailout Inc** ... E ... 312 786-4312
Chicago *(G-6339)*
**Rico Computers Enterprises Inc** ... F ... 708 594-7426
Chicago *(G-6354)*
**RMC Imaging Inc** ... G ... 815 885-4521
Rockford *(G-18560)*
**Royer Systems Inc** ... G ... 217 965-3699
Virden *(G-21301)*
**Tech Global Inc** ... G ... 224 623-2000
Elgin *(G-9204)*
**Texmac Inc** ... G ... 630 244-4702
Mundelein *(G-15564)*
**Toggle Inc** ... G ... 323 882-6339
Chicago *(G-6734)*
**Tri-Cor Industries Inc** ... D ... 618 589-9890
O Fallon *(G-16481)*
**Tunnel Vision Consulting Group** ... G ... 773 367-7292
Chicago *(G-6791)*
**Urban Apple LLC** ... G ... 312 912-1377
Chicago *(G-6846)*
**W S C Inc** ... G ... 312 372-1121
Chicago *(G-6926)*

## 3572 Computer Storage Devices

**10th Magnitude LLC** ... E ... 224 628-9047
Chicago *(G-3661)*
**Ally Global Corporation** ... G ... 773 822-3373
Chicago *(G-3826)*
**Amaitis and Associates Inc** ... F ... 847 428-1269
Wood Dale *(G-22338)*
▲ **Ckd USA Corporation** ... E ... 847 368-0539
Rolling Meadows *(G-18722)*
▲ **Dickson/Unigage Inc** ... E ... 630 543-3747
Addison *(G-92)*
**E Mc** ... G ... 217 228-1280
Quincy *(G-17824)*
▲ **E N M Company** ... D ... 773 775-8400
Chicago *(G-4667)*
**EMC** ... G ... 480 225-5498
Channahon *(G-3573)*
**File System Labs LLC** ... F ... 617 431-4313
Northbrook *(G-16259)*
**Illinoi Eye Surgns/Quantm Visn** ... G ... 618 315-6560
Mount Vernon *(G-15414)*
**International Bus Mchs Corp** ... C ... 312 423-6640
Chicago *(G-5219)*
**Interntional Cmpt Concepts Inc** ... E ... 847 808-7789
Northbrook *(G-16279)*
**Invision Software Inc** ... F ... 312 474-7767
Lisle *(G-13608)*
**Loop Limited** ... G ... 312 612-1010
Evanston *(G-10066)*
**Numeridex Incorporated** ... F ... 847 541-8840
Wheeling *(G-22111)*
**Pinehurst Bus Solutions Corp** ... G ... 630 842-6155
Winfield *(G-22290)*
**Quantum Corporation** ... D ... 312 372-2857
Chicago *(G-6250)*
**Quantum Healing** ... G ... 217 414-2412
Mechanicsburg *(G-14575)*
**Quantum Legal LLC** ... G ... 847 433-4500
Highland Park *(G-11863)*
**Quantum Marketing LLC** ... F ... 630 257-7012
Lemont *(G-13259)*
**Quantum Mechanical LLC** ... G ... 773 480-8200
Huntley *(G-12170)*
**Quantum Meruit LLC** ... G ... 630 283-3555
Glendale Heights *(G-11061)*
**Quantum Nova Technologies** ... G ... 773 386-6816
Chicago *(G-6251)*
**Quantum Partners LLC** ... G ... 312 725-4668
Chicago *(G-6252)*
**Quantum Vision Centers** ... G ... 618 656-7774
Swansea *(G-20780)*
**Quantum9 Inc** ... G ... 888 716-0404
Chicago *(G-6253)*
**Western Digital Tech Inc** ... G ... 949 672-7000
Chicago *(G-6963)*
**Wevaultcom LLC** ... E ... 877 938-2858
Crystal Lake *(G-7677)*
**Xlogotech Inc** ... G ... 888 244-5152
Arlington Heights *(G-875)*

## 3575 Computer Terminals

▲ **American Gaming & Elec Inc** ... G ... 708 290-2100
Countryside *(G-7414)*
**Art Cnc Machining LLC** ... G ... 708 907-3090
Bridgeview *(G-2468)*
**Blue Gem Computers Inc** ... G ... 708 562-5524
Morris *(G-15098)*
**CBS Broadcasting Inc** ... E ... 708 206-2900
Homewood *(G-12094)*
**Charles Industries Ltd** ... D ... 217 932-5294
Casey *(G-3382)*
▲ **Grayhill Inc** ... B ... 708 354-1040
La Grange *(G-12734)*
▲ **Kristel Limited Partnership** ... D ... 630 443-1290
Saint Charles *(G-19205)*
**Lightfoot Technologies Inc** ... G ... 331 302-1297
Naperville *(G-15690)*
**Luna It Services** ... G ... 213 537-2764
Chicago *(G-5567)*
◆ **Nec Display Solutions Amer Inc** ... C ... 630 467-3000
Itasca *(G-12328)*
**Pacap LLC** ... G ... 773 754-7089
Chicago *(G-6050)*
**Stepping Stones Gps LLC** ... G ... 217 529-6697
Springfield *(G-20537)*
**T 26 Inc** ... G ... 773 862-1201
Chicago *(G-6662)*
**Teledyne Lecroy Inc** ... E ... 847 888-0450
Elgin *(G-9206)*
**Tunnel Vision Consulting Group** ... G ... 773 367-7292
Chicago *(G-6791)*
▲ **Ziv USA Inc** ... G ... 224 735-3961
Rolling Meadows *(G-18789)*

## 3577 Computer Peripheral Eqpt, NEC

**Adazon Inc** ... G ... 847 235-2700
Lake Forest *(G-12874)*
**Allied Telesis Inc** ... D ... 312 726-1990
Chicago *(G-3818)*
▲ **Ambir Technology Inc** ... G ... 630 530-5400
Wood Dale *(G-22339)*
**American Digital Corporation** ... E ... 847 637-4300
Elk Grove Village *(G-9296)*
**Andrew New Zealand Inc** ... E ... 708 873-3507
Orland Park *(G-16843)*
**Antares Computer Systems Inc** ... G ... 773 783-8855
Chicago *(G-3915)*
**Applus Technologies Inc** ... E ... 312 661-1604
Chicago *(G-3927)*
**Arba Retail Systems Corp** ... G ... 630 620-8566
Naperville *(G-15797)*
**Automated Systems & Control Co** ... G ... 847 735-8310
Lake Bluff *(G-12834)*
▲ **Bar Codes Inc** ... F ... 800 351-9962
Chicago *(G-4039)*
**Barcodesource Inc** ... G ... 630 545-9590
West Chicago *(G-21667)*
**Bigtime Fantasy Sports Inc** ... G ... 630 605-7544
Lombard *(G-13769)*
**Bishop Image Group Inc** ... G ... 312 735-8153
Chicago *(G-4113)*
**Black Box Corporation** ... F ... 312 656-8807
Tinley Park *(G-20899)*
**Bowe Bell + Hwell Scanners LLC** ... E ... 847 675-7600
Wheeling *(G-22020)*
**Bycap Inc** ... E ... 773 561-4976
Chicago *(G-4196)*
**CDI Computers (us) Corp** ... G ... 888 226-5727
Chicago *(G-4263)*
**CDs Office Systems Inc** ... D ... 800 367-1508
Springfield *(G-20410)*
**Cim Bar Code Technology Inc** ... G ... 847 559-9776
Northbrook *(G-16224)*
**Cisco Systems Inc** ... B ... 847 678-6600
Des Plaines *(G-8170)*
**Cisco Systems Inc** ... G ... 217 363-4500
Champaign *(G-3466)*
**Cobius Halthcare Solutions LLC** ... G ... 847 656-8700
Northbrook *(G-16229)*
**Colorjar LLC** ... F ... 312 489-8510
Chicago *(G-4428)*
**Commscope Technologies LLC** ... B ... 779 435-6000
Joliet *(G-12476)*
**Computerprox** ... F ... 847 516-8560
Elgin *(G-8997)*
◆ **Contemporary Ctrl Systems Inc** ... E ... 630 963-1993
Downers Grove *(G-8419)*
**Corporate Graphics Inc** ... G ... 630 762-9000
Saint Charles *(G-19164)*
**Current Works Inc** ... G ... 847 497-9650
Johnsburg *(G-12433)*
**Dennis Wright** ... G ... 847 816-6110
Vernon Hills *(G-21156)*
▲ **Digital Check Corp** ... E ... 847 446-2285
Northbrook *(G-16243)*
**Display Graphics Systems LLC** ... G ... 800 706-9670
Chicago *(G-4611)*
**Domino Amjet Inc** ... E ... 847 662-3148
Gurnee *(G-11439)*
**Domino Lasers Inc** ... E ... 847 855-1364
Gurnee *(G-11442)*
◆ **Dover Corporation** ... C ... 630 541-1540
Downers Grove *(G-8431)*
**Elfring Fonts Inc** ... G ... 630 377-3520
Saint Charles *(G-19179)*
**Epix Inc** ... G ... 847 465-1818
Buffalo Grove *(G-2692)*
**Gb Marketing Inc** ... F ... 847 367-0101
Vernon Hills *(G-21164)*

Employee Codes: A=Over 500 employees, B=251-500
C=101-250, D=51-100, E=20-50, F=10-19, G=3-9
2017 Harris Illinois
Industrial Directory
1079

Hafner Duplicating Company.....G.....312 362-0120
Chicago (G-5029)
Hausermann Die & Machine Co.....F.....630 543-6688
Addison (G-144)
▲ Hoffman J&M Farm Holdings Inc.....D.....847 671-6280
Schiller Park (G-19838)
Ibs Conversions Inc.....D.....630 571-9100
Oak Brook (G-16524)
Illinois Tool Works Inc.....D.....618 997-1716
Marion (G-14269)
Illinois Tool Works Inc.....C.....847 876-9400
Des Plaines (G-8208)
Imageworks Manufacturing Inc.....E.....708 503-1122
Park Forest (G-17172)
Intermec Technologies Corp.....G.....312 475-0106
Chicago (G-5216)
John Harland Company.....G.....815 293-4350
Romeoville (G-18833)
Lexmark International Inc.....E.....847 318-5700
Rosemont (G-19009)
Mediarecall Holdings LLC.....G.....847 513-6710
Northbrook (G-16309)
Mextell Inc.....E.....630 595-4146
Elmhurst (G-9911)
Micros Systems Inc.....F.....443 285-6000
Itasca (G-12316)
Oceancomm Incorporated.....G.....800 757-3266
Champaign (G-3522)
Omex Technologies Inc.....G.....847 850-5858
Wheeling (G-22112)
▲ Omni Vision Inc.....E.....630 893-1720
Glendale Heights (G-11053)
Peradata Technology Corp.....E.....631 588-2216
Chicago (G-6106)
Pos Plus LLC.....F.....618 993-7587
Marion (G-14282)
Poynting Products Inc.....G.....708 386-2139
Oak Park (G-16680)
Precision Computer Methods.....G.....630 208-8000
Elburn (G-8904)
▲ Printjet Corporation.....F.....815 877-7511
Machesney Park (G-14101)
Richardson Electronics Ltd.....C.....630 208-2278
Lafox (G-12795)
Scadaware Inc.....F.....309 665-0135
Normal (G-16088)
Sg2.....G.....847 779-5500
Skokie (G-20084)
Singer Data Products Inc.....G.....630 860-6500
Bensenville (G-1991)
Somat Corporation.....E.....800 578-4260
Champaign (G-3541)
Source Software Inc.....G.....815 922-7717
Lockport (G-13747)
▲ Spartanics Ltd.....E.....847 394-5700
Rolling Meadows (G-18781)
Sparton Aydin LLC.....G.....800 772-7866
Schaumburg (G-19733)
Speedpro of Dupage.....G.....630 812-5080
Lombard (G-13857)
Tangent Systems Inc.....F.....847 882-3833
Hoffman Estates (G-12062)
▲ Tech Global Inc.....F.....847 532-4882
Elgin (G-9203)
Teledyne Lecroy Inc.....E.....847 888-0450
Elgin (G-9206)
Timeout Devices Inc.....F.....847 729-6543
Glenview (G-11209)
Tomantron Inc.....F.....708 532-2456
Tinley Park (G-20950)
Tri-Cor Industries Inc.....D.....618 589-9890
O Fallon (G-16481)
◆ Trippe Manufacturing Company.....B.....773 869-1111
Chicago (G-6778)
United Universal Inds Inc.....E.....815 727-4445
Joliet (G-12585)
Verdasee Solutions Inc.....G.....847 265-9441
Gurnee (G-11519)
Wam Ventures Inc.....G.....312 214-6136
Chicago (G-6937)
Xerox Corporation.....E.....630 573-1000
Hinsdale (G-11969)
Yfy Jupiter Inc.....E.....312 419-8565
Chicago (G-7050)
▲ Zebra Technologies Corporation.....B.....847 634-6700
Lincolnshire (G-13494)
Zebra Technologies Corporation.....B.....847 634-6700
Chicago (G-7060)
◆ Zebra Technologies Intl LLC.....G.....847 634-6700
Lincolnshire (G-13495)
▲ Zih Corp.....G.....847 634-6700
Lincolnshire (G-13497)
Zih Corp.....E.....847 634-6700
Lincolnshire (G-13498)

## 3578 Calculating & Accounting Eqpt

Alliance Service Co.....G.....708 746-5026
Frankfort (G-10292)
Asai Chicago.....F.....708 239-0133
Alsip (G-437)
B & M Machine Inc.....G.....630 350-8950
Bensenville (G-1838)
Barcodesource Inc.....G.....630 545-9590
West Chicago (G-21667)
Business Valuation Group Inc.....G.....312 595-1900
Chicago (G-4190)
Creative Merchandising Systems.....G.....847 955-9990
Lincolnshire (G-13441)
◆ Cummins - Allison Corp.....B.....847 759-6403
Mount Prospect (G-15320)
Diebold Incorporated.....D.....847 598-3300
Schaumburg (G-19504)
Harvard State Bank.....G.....815 943-4400
Harvard (G-11635)
Jpmorgan Chase Bank Nat Assn.....G.....847 392-1600
Prospect Heights (G-17781)
Jpmorgan Chase Bank Nat Assn.....G.....708 868-1274
Calumet City (G-2944)
Jpmorgan Chase Bank Nat Assn.....G.....815 462-2800
New Lenox (G-15889)
Jpmorgan Chase Bank Nat Assn.....G.....847 726-4000
Lake Zurich (G-13094)
Jpmorgan Chase Bank Nat Assn.....G.....847 663-1235
Niles (G-15994)
Jpmorgan Chase Bank Nat Assn.....G.....217 353-4234
Champaign (G-3504)
Kahuna LLC.....F.....888 357-8472
Bloomington (G-2188)
Micros Systems Inc.....F.....443 285-6000
Itasca (G-12316)
OHare Shell Partners Inc.....G.....847 678-1900
Schiller Park (G-19855)
◆ Pfingsten Partners LLC.....F.....312 222-8707
Chicago (G-6115)
PNC Financial Svcs Group Inc.....G.....630 420-8400
Naperville (G-15728)
Pos Plus LLC.....F.....618 993-7587
Marion (G-14282)
Singer Data Products Inc.....G.....630 860-6500
Bensenville (G-1991)
▲ Talaris Inc.....C.....630 577-1000
Lisle (G-13669)
▲ Ultramark Inc.....G.....847 981-0400
Arlington Heights (G-860)

## 3579 Office Machines, NEC

Acco Brands USA LLC.....E.....708 280-4702
Addison (G-16)
American Perforator Company.....G.....815 469-4300
Frankfort (G-10294)
▲ Astro Machine Corporation.....E.....847 364-6363
Elk Grove Village (G-9318)
▲ Bowe Bell + Hwell Holdings Inc.....A.....312 541-9300
Wheeling (G-22019)
Copar Corporation.....E.....708 496-1859
Burbank (G-2807)
Cummins - Allison Corp.....D.....847 299-9550
Mount Prospect (G-15321)
Cummins - Allison Corp.....C.....847 299-9550
Mount Prospect (G-15322)
Cummins - Allison Corp.....F.....630 833-2285
Elmhurst (G-9862)
◆ Deluxe Stitcher Company Inc.....D.....847 455-4400
Franklin Park (G-10457)
Direct Mail Equipment Services.....G.....815 485-7010
New Lenox (G-15876)
H N C Products Inc.....E.....217 935-9100
Clinton (G-7281)
▲ Identification Products Mfg Co.....G.....847 367-6452
Lake Forest (G-12914)
Inscerco Mfg Inc.....E.....708 597-8777
Crestwood (G-7489)
Intermail Direct Marketing.....G.....630 274-6333
Bensenville (G-1920)
◆ Klai-Co Idntification Pdts Inc.....E.....847 573-0375
Lake Forest (G-12921)
Laminting Bnding Solutions Inc.....G.....847 573-0375
Lake Forest (G-12922)
Lane Industries Inc.....E.....847 498-6650
Northbrook (G-16292)
Lason Inc.....G.....217 893-1515
Rantoul (G-17933)
Multimail Solutions.....G.....847 516-9977
Cary (G-3361)
Neopost R Meadows.....G.....630 467-0604
Itasca (G-12329)
Pitney Bowes Inc.....E.....312 209-2216
Schaumburg (G-19691)
Pitney Bowes Inc.....E.....773 755-5808
Chicago (G-6131)
Pitney Bowes Inc.....F.....312 419-7114
Chicago (G-6132)
Pitney Bowes Inc.....D.....630 435-7476
Lisle (G-13640)
Pitney Bowes Inc.....D.....630 435-7500
Lisle (G-13641)
Pitney Bowes Inc.....E.....800 784-4224
Itasca (G-12341)
▲ Plastic Binding Laminating Inc.....G.....847 573-0375
Lake Forest (G-12946)
▲ SBA Wireless Inc.....E.....847 215-8720
Buffalo Grove (G-2762)
Singer Data Products Inc.....G.....630 860-6500
Bensenville (G-1991)
Stenograph LLC.....D.....630 532-5100
Elmhurst (G-9942)
▲ Sws Industries Inc.....E.....904 482-0091
Woodstock (G-22616)
Taloc Usa Inc.....G.....847 665-8222
Libertyville (G-13388)
Videojet Technologies Inc.....D.....630 238-3900
Elk Grove Village (G-9808)
Videojet Technologies Inc.....C.....618 235-6804
Belleville (G-1686)
◆ Videojet Technologies Inc.....A.....630 860-7300
Wood Dale (G-22436)
▲ Your Supply Depot Limited.....G.....815 568-4115
Marengo (G-14245)

## 3581 Automatic Vending Machines

Advanced Technologies Inc.....G.....847 329-9875
Park Ridge (G-17178)
Classic Vending Inc.....E.....773 252-7000
Chicago (G-4395)
Jax Amusements.....G.....618 887-4761
Alhambra (G-419)
Laurel Metal Products Inc.....E.....847 674-0064
Skokie (G-20027)
▲ Manufctrng-Resourcing Intl Inc.....F.....217 821-3733
Shumway (G-19933)
◆ Northwestern Corporation.....E.....815 942-1300
Morris (G-15124)
▲ Partec Inc.....C.....847 678-9520
Franklin Park (G-10547)
▲ Seaga Manufacturing Inc.....C.....815 297-9500
Freeport (G-10688)
Singer Data Products Inc.....G.....630 860-6500
Bensenville (G-1991)
Success Vending Mfg Co LLC.....E.....773 262-1685
Chicago (G-6612)

## 3582 Commercial Laundry, Dry Clean & Pressing Mchs

B-Clean Laundromat Inc.....G.....678 983-5492
Chicago (G-4022)
◆ Chicago Dryer Company.....C.....773 235-4430
Chicago (G-4317)
▼ Cmv Sharper Finish Inc.....E.....773 276-4800
Chicago (G-4411)
▲ Ellis Corporation.....D.....630 250-9222
Itasca (G-12258)
Eminent Technologies LLC.....G.....630 416-2311
Naperville (G-15653)
Extractor Corporation.....F.....847 742-3532
South Elgin (G-20196)
Jetin Systems Inc.....F.....815 726-4686
Joliet (G-12522)
L T P LLC.....C.....815 723-9400
Joliet (G-12530)
New Spin Cycle.....G.....773 952-7490
Chicago (G-5895)
▼ Qualitex Company.....F.....773 506-8112
Chicago (G-6244)
Rkc Cleaner I Corp.....F.....630 904-0477
Naperville (G-15824)
Ross and White Company.....F.....847 516-3900
Cary (G-3369)

**Solvair LLC** ....F .... 630 416-4244
Naperville *(G-15749)*

## 3585 Air Conditioning & Heating Eqpt

**Air Duct Manufacturing Inc** ....G .... 630 620-9866
Addison *(G-28)*
**Airdronic Test & Balance Inc** ....G .... 815 561-0339
Rochelle *(G-18077)*
**Alfa Laval Inc** ....C .... 630 354-6090
Wood Dale *(G-22334)*
**American Fuel Economy Inc** ....G .... 815 433-3226
Ottawa *(G-16946)*
**American Soda Ftn Exch Inc** ....F .... 312 733-5000
Chicago *(G-3875)*
◆ **Amsted Industries Incorporated** ....B .... 312 645-1700
Chicago *(G-3896)*
**Anderson - Snow Corp** ....E .... 847 678-2084
Schiller Park *(G-19803)*
**Baer Heating & Cooling Inc** ....G .... 618 224-7344
Trenton *(G-20989)*
▲ **Banner Equipment Co** ....E .... 815 941-9600
Morris *(G-15097)*
**Bergesch Heating & Cooling** ....G .... 618 259-4620
Alton *(G-564)*
▲ **Bergstrom Climate Systems LLC** ....B .... 815 874-7821
Rockford *(G-18281)*
**Bernard Cffey Vtrans Fundation** ....G .... 630 687-0033
Naperville *(G-15605)*
◆ **Bevstream Corp** ....G .... 630 761-0060
Batavia *(G-1421)*
**Big M Manufacturing LLC** ....G .... 217 824-9372
Taylorville *(G-20833)*
**Brunet Snow Service Company** ....G .... 847 846-0037
Wood Dale *(G-22347)*
**Buell Manufacturing Company** ....G .... 708 447-6320
Lyons *(G-14033)*
**Cardinal Construction Co** ....G .... 618 842-5553
Fairfield *(G-10138)*
◆ **Cerro Flow Products LLC** ....C .... 618 337-6000
Sauget *(G-19385)*
**Cisco Heating & Cooling** ....G .... 309 637-6809
Peoria *(G-17342)*
**Commercial Rfrgn Centl Ill Inc** ....E .... 217 235-5016
Mattoon *(G-14386)*
**Continental Materials Corp** ....F .... 312 541-7200
Chicago *(G-4459)*
◆ **Cornelius Inc** ....B .... 630 539-6850
Glendale Heights *(G-11018)*
◆ **Custom Innovation LLC** ....G .... 847 847-7100
Long Grove *(G-13890)*
**Dupage Mechanical** ....G .... 630 620-1122
Wheeling *(G-22038)*
**Durable Manufacturing Company** ....F .... 630 766-0398
Bensenville *(G-1885)*
**Eclipse Usa Inc** ....G .... 773 816-0886
Elmwood Park *(G-9967)*
**Ecool LLC** ....G .... 309 966-3701
Champaign *(G-3477)*
**Elkay Manufacturing Company** ....C .... 815 493-8850
Lanark *(G-13153)*
**Elkay Manufacturing Company** ....B .... 708 681-1880
Broadview *(G-2575)*
**Elkay Manufacturing Company** ....B .... 815 273-7001
Savanna *(G-19397)*
▼ **Enertech Global LLC** ....E .... 618 664-9010
Greenville *(G-11392)*
**Evapco Inc** ....C .... 217 923-3431
Greenup *(G-11382)*
**EZ Comfort Heating & AC** ....G .... 630 289-2020
Elgin *(G-9031)*
**Flinn & Dreffein Engrg Co** ....E .... 847 272-6374
Northbrook *(G-16260)*
▲ **Frigel North America Inc** ....F .... 847 540-0160
East Dundee *(G-8636)*
**Galmar Enterprises Inc** ....G .... 815 463-9826
New Lenox *(G-15883)*
**Gateway Industrial Power Inc** ....C .... 888 865-8675
Collinsville *(G-7327)*
**Gateway Industrial Power Inc** ....G .... 309 821-1035
Bloomington *(G-2169)*
**Goose Island Mfg & Supply Corp** ....G .... 708 343-4225
Lansing *(G-13164)*
▲ **Green Box America Inc** ....G .... 630 616-5400
Schaumburg *(G-19543)*
▼ **H A Phillips & Co** ....E .... 630 377-0050
Dekalb *(G-8095)*
**Habegger Corporation** ....F .... 309 793-7172
Rock Island *(G-18178)*
**Haggerty Corporation** ....G .... 309 793-4328
Rock Island *(G-18179)*
**Haskris Co** ....D .... 847 956-6420
Elk Grove Village *(G-9517)*
**Heatcraft Rfrgn Pdts LLC** ....B .... 217 446-3710
Danville *(G-7731)*
**Henry Technologies Inc** ....D .... 217 483-2406
Chatham *(G-3622)*
▲ **Henry Technologies Inc** ....G .... 217 483-2406
Chatham *(G-3621)*
**Hohlfider A H Shtmtl Htg Coolg** ....G .... 815 965-9134
Rockford *(G-18420)*
**Honeywell International Inc** ....D .... 847 797-4000
Arlington Heights *(G-768)*
▲ **Howe Corporation** ....E .... 773 235-0200
Chicago *(G-5123)*
**ICC Intrntonal Celsius Concept** ....G .... 773 993-4405
Cicero *(G-7203)*
**Illinois Tool Works Inc** ....B .... 847 724-7500
Glenview *(G-11141)*
**Illinois Tool Works Inc** ....C .... 630 372-2150
Bartlett *(G-1353)*
**Illinois Tool Works Inc** ....C .... 847 783-5500
Elgin *(G-9072)*
**J D Refrigeration** ....G .... 618 345-0041
Collinsville *(G-7328)*
**John Bean Technologies Corp** ....E .... 312 861-5900
Chicago *(G-5310)*
**John F Mate Co** ....G .... 847 381-8131
Lake Barrington *(G-12812)*
**Kackert Enterprises Inc** ....G .... 630 898-9339
Aurora *(G-1179)*
**Kap Holdings LLC** ....F .... 708 948-0226
Oak Park *(G-16671)*
▲ **Kelco Industries Inc** ....G .... 815 334-3600
Woodstock *(G-22577)*
**Kool Technologies Inc** ....G .... 630 483-2256
Streamwood *(G-20662)*
◆ **Krack Corporation** ....E .... 630 250-0187
Bolingbrook *(G-2334)*
**Lennox Industries Inc** ....D .... 630 378-7054
Romeoville *(G-18839)*
**M & I Heating and Cooling Inc** ....G .... 773 743-7073
Chicago *(G-5577)*
◆ **Maid O Mist LLC** ....E .... 773 685-7300
Chicago *(G-5604)*
◆ **Marshall Middleby Inc** ....C .... 847 289-0204
Elgin *(G-9100)*
**Marvin Schumaker Plbg Inc** ....G .... 815 626-8130
Sterling *(G-20597)*
▲ **Mayekawa USA Inc** ....F .... 773 516-5070
Elk Grove Village *(G-9615)*
▲ **Natural Choice Corporation** ....F .... 815 874-4444
Rockford *(G-18518)*
**Oceanaire Inc** ....F .... 847 583-0311
Morton Grove *(G-15225)*
**Optimal Energy LLC** ....G ....
Arlington Heights *(G-814)*
**Parks Industries LLC** ....F .... 618 997-9608
Marion *(G-14276)*
▼ **Peerless America Incorporated** ....C .... 217 342-0400
Effingham *(G-8853)*
**Perfection Equipment Inc** ....E .... 847 244-7200
Gurnee *(G-11485)*
◆ **Polyscience Inc** ....D .... 847 647-0611
Niles *(G-16021)*
**Prost Heating & Cooling LLC** ....G .... 618 344-3749
Collinsville *(G-7338)*
**Pure N Natural Systems Inc** ....F .... 630 372-9681
Morton Grove *(G-15230)*
**Quality Filter Services** ....G .... 618 654-3716
Highland *(G-11807)*
**Reedy Industries Inc** ....F .... 847 729-9450
Glenview *(G-11192)*
**Ring Sheet Metal Heating & AC** ....G .... 309 289-4213
Knoxville *(G-12723)*
**Rowald Refrigeration Systems** ....G .... 815 397-7733
Rockford *(G-18599)*
**Ruyle Incorporated** ....E .... 309 674-6644
Springfield *(G-20516)*
**Scotsman Group Inc** ....D .... 847 215-4500
Vernon Hills *(G-21197)*
**Scotsman Ice Systems** ....E .... 847 215-4500
Vernon Hills *(G-21198)*
▲ **Scotsman Industries Inc** ....D .... 847 215-4501
Vernon Hills *(G-21199)*
**Sendra Service Corp** ....G .... 815 462-0061
New Lenox *(G-15910)*
**SGS Refrigeration Inc** ....E .... 815 284-2700
Dixon *(G-8351)*
▲ **Sigma Coachair Group (us) Inc** ....G .... 847 541-4446
Wheeling *(G-22151)*
▲ **Spirotherm Inc** ....G .... 630 307-2662
Glendale Heights *(G-11071)*
**Standing Water Solutions Inc** ....G .... 847 469-8876
Wauconda *(G-21503)*
**Support Central Inc** ....G .... 702 202-3500
Skokie *(G-20096)*
**Synergy Mech Solutions Inc** ....G .... 847 437-4500
Elk Grove Village *(G-9765)*
**Temp-Air Inc** ....F .... 847 931-7700
Elgin *(G-9208)*
**Temperature Equipment Corp** ....G .... 815 229-2935
Rockford *(G-18643)*
◆ **Thermal Care Inc** ....C .... 847 966-2260
Niles *(G-16041)*
**Thermal Care Inc** ....F .... 847 929-1207
Niles *(G-16042)*
**Trane US Inc** ....G .... 309 691-4224
Peoria *(G-17470)*
**Trane US Inc** ....G .... 708 532-8004
Tinley Park *(G-20951)*
**United Technologies Corp** ....B .... 815 226-6000
Rockford *(G-18663)*
**Ventfabrics Inc** ....F .... 773 775-4477
Chicago *(G-6883)*
▲ **Voges Inc** ....D .... 618 233-2760
Belleville *(G-1688)*
**York International Corporation** ....D .... 815 946-2351
Polo *(G-17692)*

## 3586 Measuring & Dispensing Pumps

◆ **Cornelius Inc** ....B .... 630 539-6850
Glendale Heights *(G-11018)*
◆ **Dover Corporation** ....C .... 630 541-1540
Downers Grove *(G-8431)*
**Franklin Fueling Systems Inc** ....G .... 207 283-0156
Chicago *(G-4885)*
**Gfi Innovations LLC** ....G .... 847 263-9000
Antioch *(G-634)*
▲ **March Manufacturing Inc** ....D .... 847 729-5300
Glenview *(G-11167)*
▲ **Standard Lifts & Equipment Inc** ....G .... 414 444-1000
Hanover Park *(G-11591)*
◆ **Tuthill Corporation** ....E .... 630 382-4900
Burr Ridge *(G-2889)*

## 3589 Service Ind Machines, NEC

▲ **A J Antunes & Co** ....C .... 630 784-1000
Carol Stream *(G-3087)*
**A La Cart Inc** ....E .... 847 256-4102
Highland Park *(G-11820)*
**AC Nalco Chemical Co** ....F .... 630 305-1000
Naperville *(G-15587)*
**Addison Business Systems Inc** ....G .... 708 371-5454
Palos Heights *(G-17098)*
**Advanage Diversified Pdts Inc** ....F .... 708 331-8390
Harvey *(G-11650)*
**Ali Group North America Corp** ....E .... 847 215-6565
Vernon Hills *(G-21144)*
**Alternative Wastewater Systems** ....G .... 630 761-8720
Batavia *(G-1409)*
**Amber Soft Inc** ....F .... 630 377-6945
Lake Barrington *(G-12799)*
**Ambi-Design Incorporated** ....G .... 815 964-7568
Rockford *(G-18261)*
▲ **American Vacuum Co** ....G .... 847 674-8383
Skokie *(G-19951)*
**American Watersource LLC** ....E .... 630 778-9900
Naperville *(G-15794)*
**Amsoil Inc** ....G .... 630 595-8385
Bensenville *(G-1835)*
◆ **Aquion Inc** ....D .... 847 725-3000
Roselle *(G-18926)*
**Arbortech Corporation** ....G .... 847 462-1111
Johnsburg *(G-12430)*
**Area Disposal Service Inc** ....F .... 217 935-1300
Clinton *(G-7278)*
**Asbestos Control & Envmtl Svc** ....F .... 630 690-0189
Eola *(G-9988)*
▲ **Avw Equipment Company Inc** ....E .... 708 343-7738
Maywood *(G-14417)*
**Azcon Inc** ....F .... 815 548-7000
Sterling *(G-20583)*
**Best Way Carpet & Uphl Clg** ....G .... 618 544-8585
Robinson *(G-18057)*
**Big R Car Wash Inc** ....G .... 217 367-4958
Urbana *(G-21072)*
**Bissell Inc** ....G .... 815 423-1300
Elwood *(G-9979)*
▼ **Blastline USA Inc** ....G .... 630 871-0147
Carol Stream *(G-3118)*

S I C

Employee Codes: A=Over 500 employees, B=251-500
C=101-250, D=51-100, E=20-50, F=10-19, G=3-9
2017 Harris Illinois
Industrial Directory
1081

## 35 INDUSTRIAL AND COMMERCIAL MACHINERY AND COMPUTER EQUIPMENT

| Company | Code | Phone |
|---|---|---|
| Brite-O-Matic Mfg Inc — Arlington Heights (G-730) | D | 847 956-1100 |
| Brochem Industries Inc — East Hazel Crest (G-8665) | G | 708 206-2874 |
| Bunn-O-Matic Corporation — Springfield (G-20401) | G | 217 528-8739 |
| Bunn-O-Matic Corporation — Springfield (G-20402) | G | 217 529-6601 |
| Butterfield Cleaners — Mundelein (G-15480) | G | 847 816-7060 |
| ◆ C Cretors & Co — Wood Dale (G-22348) | D | 847 616-6900 |
| C2 Water Inc — Kenilworth (G-12662) | G | 312 550-1159 |
| ▲ Calco Ltd — Bartlett (G-1316) | F | 630 539-1800 |
| Carlinville Waste Water Plants — Carlinville (G-3031) | G | 217 854-6506 |
| Carney Flow Technics LLC — Frankfort (G-10307) | G | 815 277-2600 |
| ▲ Carter Hoffmann LLC — Mundelein (G-15484) | G | 847 362-5500 |
| ▲ Charger Water Conditioning Inc — Morton Grove (G-15192) | F | 847 967-9558 |
| Chemical Pump — Frankfort (G-10309) | G | 815 464-1908 |
| Clements National Company — Broadview (G-2570) | E | 708 594-5890 |
| Coe Equipment Inc — Rochester (G-18116) | G | 217 498-7200 |
| Countryside Pure Water Solutio — Arlington Heights (G-740) | G | 847 255-5524 |
| Covington Service Installation — Carlock (G-3049) | G | 309 376-4921 |
| ◆ Culligan International Company — Rosemont (G-18994) | C | 847 430-2800 |
| Culligan International Company — Libertyville (G-13318) | E | 847 430-1338 |
| ▲ D R Sperry & Co — Aurora (G-1137) | D | 630 892-4361 |
| Detrex Corporation — Melrose Park (G-14616) | G | 708 345-3806 |
| Diskin Systems Inc — Algonquin (G-387) | G | 815 276-7288 |
| Dml LLC — West Chicago (G-21694) | G | 630 231-8873 |
| ▲ Dontech Industries Inc — Gilberts (G-10917) | F | 847 428-8222 |
| Dun-Rite Tool & Machine Co — Cortland (G-7388) | E | 815 758-5464 |
| Durable Manufacturing Company — Bensenville (G-1885) | F | 630 766-0398 |
| Earthwise Environmental Inc — Wood Dale (G-22361) | G | 630 475-3070 |
| ◆ Ecodyne Water Treatment LLC — Naperville (G-15650) | E | 630 961-5043 |
| Edwardsville Water Treatment — Edwardsville (G-8800) | G | 618 692-7053 |
| ▲ Ellis Corporation — Itasca (G-12258) | D | 630 250-9222 |
| Enterprises One Stop — Chicago (G-4761) | G | 773 924-5506 |
| Ep Purification Inc — Champaign (G-3481) | F | 217 693-7950 |
| ◆ Evac North America Inc — Cherry Valley (G-3642) | E | 815 654-8300 |
| ▲ Everblast Inc — Crystal Lake (G-7574) | G | 815 788-8660 |
| Evoqua Water Technologies LLC — Rockford (G-18372) | F | 815 921-8325 |
| Evoqua Water Technologies LLC — Granite City (G-11275) | G | 618 451-1205 |
| Extol Hydro Technologies Inc — Palos Park (G-17128) | F | 708 717-4371 |
| Fna Ip Holdings Inc — Elk Grove Village (G-9482) | D | 847 348-1500 |
| ◆ Food Equipment Technologies Co — Lake Zurich (G-13075) | C | 847 719-3000 |
| Galesburg Manufacturing Co — Galesburg (G-10750) | E | 309 342-3173 |
| Garretts & Sons Inc — McHenry (G-14508) | G | 815 385-3821 |
| ▲ Gehrke Technology Group Inc — Wauconda (G-21464) | F | 847 498-7320 |
| Getz Fire Equipment Co — Peoria (G-17372) | E | 309 637-1440 |
| Gillespie City Water — Gillespie (G-10941) | G | 217 839-3279 |
| H-O-H Water Technology Inc — Palatine (G-17032) | E | 847 358-7400 |
| Heat Transfer Laboratories — Oakbrook Terrace (G-16709) | G | 708 715-4300 |
| ◆ Heico Companies LLC — Chicago (G-5068) | F | 312 419-8220 |
| ◆ Holden Industries Inc — Deerfield (G-8013) | F | 847 940-1500 |
| Hpd LLC — Plainfield (G-17606) | C | 815 436-3013 |
| Hurley Chicago Company Inc — Momence (G-14982) | G | 815 472-0087 |
| Hydrotec Systems Company Inc — Tiskilwa (G-20959) | G | 815 624-6644 |
| ▲ Illinois Water Tech Inc — Roscoe (G-18901) | E | 815 636-8884 |
| Industrial Specialty Chem Inc — South Holland (G-20280) | E | 708 339-1313 |
| Industrial Water Trtmnt Soltns — Harvey (G-11672) | G | 708 339-1313 |
| ▲ Inlet & Pipe Protection Inc — Naperville (G-15811) | G | 630 355-3288 |
| International Water Werks Inc — Huntley (G-12151) | G | 847 669-1902 |
| J II Inc — Highland Park (G-11845) | D | 847 432-8979 |
| James A Freund LLC — Oswego (G-16923) | G | 630 664-7692 |
| Jetin Systems Inc — Joliet (G-12522) | F | 815 726-4686 |
| K & S Manufacturing Co Inc — Freeport (G-10671) | F | 815 232-7519 |
| Keating of Chicago Inc — Capron (G-2996) | G | 815 569-2324 |
| Lane Industries Inc — Northbrook (G-16292) | G | 847 498-6650 |
| Lee Industries Inc — Elk Grove Village (G-9590) | C | 847 462-1865 |
| ▲ Liquitech Inc — Lombard (G-13821) | F | 630 693-0500 |
| M & M Pump Co — Clinton (G-7286) | G | 217 935-2517 |
| Markham Division 9 Inc — Park Forest (G-17174) | E | 708 503-0657 |
| ◆ Marmon Holdings Inc — Chicago (G-5625) | D | 312 372-9500 |
| ◆ Marmon Industrial LLC — Chicago (G-5626) | G | 312 372-9500 |
| McDowell Inc — Eureka (G-9999) | | 309 467-2335 |
| ▼ McNish Corporation — Aurora (G-1184) | D | 630 892-7921 |
| ▲ Meyer Machine & Equipment Inc — Antioch (G-645) | F | 847 395-2970 |
| ▲ Midco International Inc — Chicago (G-5733) | G | 773 604-8700 |
| Middleby Corporation — Elgin (G-9110) | E | 847 741-3300 |
| Middleby Corporation — Elgin (G-9111) | E | 847 741-3300 |
| ◆ Minuteman International Inc — Pingree Grove (G-17556) | F | 630 627-6900 |
| Minuteman International Inc — Hampshire (G-11555) | D | 847 683-5210 |
| Nalco Company LLC — Naperville (G-15704) | G | |
| Nano Gas Technologies Inc — Deerfield (G-8043) | G | 586 229-2656 |
| ▲ Natural Choice Corporation — Rockford (G-18518) | F | 815 874-4444 |
| Newater International Inc — Bloomingdale (G-2120) | E | 630 894-5000 |
| Nijhuis Water Technology Inc — Chicago (G-5917) | G | 312 466-9900 |
| ◆ Nikro Industries Inc — Villa Park (G-21273) | E | 630 530-0558 |
| North Shore Wtr Rclamation Dst — Waukegan (G-21594) | E | 847 623-6060 |
| ▼ Omni Containment Systems LLC — Elgin (G-9129) | G | 847 468-1772 |
| ▼ Optimal Automatics Co — Elk Grove Village (G-9667) | G | 847 439-9110 |
| Original Systems — Riverwoods (G-18041) | G | 847 945-7660 |
| Palmyra Modesto Water Comm — Palmyra (G-17097) | G | 217 436-2519 |
| ▲ Pentair Fltrtion Solutions LLC — Hanover Park (G-11589) | E | 630 307-3000 |
| Pentair Fltrtion Solutions LLC — Bartlett (G-1321) | E | 630 307-3000 |
| Pond Alliance Inc — Naperville (G-15729) | G | 877 377-8131 |
| ▼ Powerboss Inc — Hampshire (G-11560) | C | 910 944-2105 |
| ◆ Prince Castle LLC — Carol Stream (G-3218) | C | 630 462-8800 |
| Princeton Fast Stop — Princeton (G-17758) | F | 815 872-0706 |
| Prinzings of Rockford — Rockford (G-18541) | | 815 874-9654 |
| Pristine Water Solutions Inc — Waukegan (G-21607) | F | 847 689-1100 |
| Producers Envmtl Pdts LLC — Batavia (G-1487) | | 630 482-5995 |
| Pure N Natural Systems Inc — Morton Grove (G-15230) | | 630 372-9681 |
| ▲ Pureline Treatment Systems LLC — Bensenville (G-1970) | E | 847 963-8465 |
| Quantum Technical Services Inc — Frankfort (G-10355) | | 815 464-1540 |
| Rays Power Wshg Svc Peggy Ray — Waterloo (G-21405) | G | 618 939-6306 |
| Regency Hand Laundry — Chicago (G-6322) | G | 773 871-3950 |
| Regunathan & Assoc Inc — Wheaton (G-21975) | | 630 653-0387 |
| River North Hand — Chicago (G-6362) | G | 312 335-9669 |
| Ross and White Company — Cary (G-3369) | F | 847 516-3900 |
| ▲ RPS Products Inc — Hampshire (G-11562) | | 847 683-3400 |
| ▲ Safe Water Technologies Inc — Elgin (G-9171) | | 847 888-6900 |
| Selrok Inc — West Chicago (G-21770) | | 630 876-8322 |
| Servetech Water Solutions Inc — Wheaton (G-21980) | G | 630 784-9050 |
| Sewer Equipment Co America — Dixon (G-8350) | C | 815 835-5566 |
| Siemens Industry Inc — Streator (G-20702) | | 815 672-2653 |
| Siemens Industry Inc — Rockford (G-18616) | D | 815 877-3041 |
| Sparkle Express — Oswego (G-16935) | | 630 375-9801 |
| ▲ Spartan Tool LLC — Mendota (G-14733) | E | 815 539-7411 |
| Star Industries Inc — Highland Park (G-11873) | E | 708 240-4862 |
| Superior Water Services Inc — Peoria (G-17464) | | 309 691-9287 |
| Tenco Hydro Inc of Illinois — Brookfield (G-2644) | G | 708 387-0700 |
| Tkg Sweeping & Services LLC — Waukegan (G-21628) | G | 847 505-1400 |
| Toppert Jetting Service Inc — Hillsdale (G-11904) | | 309 755-2240 |
| ▲ Tornado Industries LLC — West Chicago (G-21783) | D | 817 551-6507 |
| Triplex Sales Company Inc — Schaumburg (G-19774) | G | 847 839-8442 |
| Triwater Holdings LLC — Lake Forest (G-12974) | G | 847 457-1812 |
| Twh Water Treatment Industries — Rosemont (G-19038) | D | 847 457-1813 |
| U Wash Equipment Co — Alton (G-594) | G | 618 466-9442 |
| Umf Corporation — Niles (G-16045) | G | 224 251-7822 |
| ▲ Umf Corporation — Skokie (G-20104) | F | 847 920-0370 |
| Walter Louis Chem & Assoc Inc — Quincy (G-17902) | F | 217 223-2017 |
| Water Dynamics Inc — Saint Charles (G-19292) | G | 630 584-8475 |
| Water Inc — Sterling (G-20621) | G | 815 626-8844 |
| We Clean — Oak Forest (G-16593) | | 708 574-2551 |
| ▲ Wet & Forget Usa A New Zeaind — Elgin (G-9236) | G | 847 428-3894 |
| Will County Well & Pump Co Inc — New Lenox (G-15928) | | 815 485-2413 |
| William N Pasulka — Peru (G-17532) | G | 815 339-6300 |
| ▲ William W Meyer and Sons — Libertyville (G-13402) | D | 847 918-0111 |

### 3592 Carburetors, Pistons, Rings & Valves

| Company | Code | Phone |
|---|---|---|
| Borgwarner Inc — Dixon (G-8324) | C | 815 288-1462 |

▲ **Burgess-Norton Mfg Co Inc** ............B ....... 630 232-4100
Geneva *(G-10813)*
**Extreme Force Valve Inc** ............G ....... 618 494-5795
Jerseyville *(G-12421)*
**Hantemp Corporation** ............G ....... 630 537-1049
Westmont *(G-21890)*
▲ **Helio Precision Products Inc** ............C ....... 847 473-1300
Lake Bluff *(G-12848)*
**Milliken Valve Co Inc** ............G ....... 217 425-7410
Decatur *(G-7917)*
**Mueller Co LLC** ............E ....... 217 423-4471
Decatur *(G-7918)*
**Research and Testing Worx Inc** ............G ....... 815 734-7346
Mount Morris *(G-15299)*
▲ **Riken Corporation of America** ............C ....... 847 673-1400
Skokie *(G-20076)*
**United Carburetor Inc** ............E ....... 773 777-1223
Schiller Park *(G-19879)*
▲ **United Remanufacturing Co Inc** ............G ....... 773 777-1223
Schiller Park *(G-19880)*
**United Remanufacturing Co Inc** ............E ....... 847 678-2233
Schiller Park *(G-19881)*
▲ **Yeary & Associates Inc** ............G ....... 312 335-1012
Chicago *(G-7048)*

### 3593 Fluid Power Cylinders & Actuators

**Advance Automation Company** ............F ....... 773 539-7633
Chicago *(G-3757)*
▲ **Bimba Manufacturing Company** ............B ....... 708 534-8544
University Park *(G-21044)*
**Bimba Manufacturing Company** ............E ....... 708 534-7997
Manteno *(G-14181)*
**Bimba Manufacturing Company** ............E ....... 708 534-8544
Frankfort *(G-10299)*
▲ **Blac Inc** ............D ....... 630 279-6400
Elmhurst *(G-9840)*
**Brake Parts Inc LLC** ............G ....... 217 324-2161
Litchfield *(G-13682)*
**Catching Hydraulics Co Ltd** ............E ....... 708 344-2334
Melrose Park *(G-14606)*
**Custom Cylinder Inc** ............E ....... 847 516-6467
Cary *(G-3331)*
◆ **Dover Prtg Identification Inc** ............D ....... 630 541-1540
Downers Grove *(G-8434)*
**Dresser Inc** ............D ....... 847 437-5940
Elk Grove Village *(G-9435)*
**Ergo Help Inc** ............G ....... 847 593-0722
Arlington Heights *(G-750)*
▼ **Gpe Controls Inc** ............F ....... 708 236-6000
Hillside *(G-11917)*
**Hadady Machining Company Inc** ............F ....... 708 474-8620
Lansing *(G-13165)*
**Illinois Pneumatic Inc** ............G ....... 815 654-9301
Roscoe *(G-18900)*
**Ken Elliott Co Inc** ............G ....... 618 466-8200
Godfrey *(G-11226)*
▲ **Kitagawa Usa Inc** ............E ....... 847 310-8198
Schaumburg *(G-19599)*
**Kocsis Technologies Inc** ............F ....... 708 597-4177
Alsip *(G-481)*
**Kocsis Technologies Inc** ............G ....... 708 597-4177
Alsip *(G-482)*
**Manitowoc Lifts and Mfg LLC** ............G ....... 815 748-9500
Dekalb *(G-8105)*
**Master Hydraulics & Machining** ............F ....... 847 895-5578
Schaumburg *(G-19635)*
**MEA Inc** ............E ....... 847 766-9040
Elk Grove Village *(G-9616)*
▲ **Mead Fluid Dynamics Inc** ............E ....... 773 685-6800
Chicago *(G-5669)*
**Mpc Products Corporation** ............G ....... 847 673-8300
Niles *(G-16011)*
**Ortman Fluid Power Inc** ............E ....... 217 277-0321
Quincy *(G-17863)*
**Parker-Hannifin Corporation** ............D ....... 815 636-4100
Machesney Park *(G-14095)*
**Parker-Hannifin Corporation** ............C ....... 847 298-2400
Des Plaines *(G-8250)*
▲ **Rdc Linear Enterprises LLC** ............F ....... 815 547-1106
Belvidere *(G-1782)*
**RE-Do-It Corp** ............G ....... 708 343-7125
Broadview *(G-2607)*
**Regent Automotive Engineering** ............G ....... 773 889-5744
Chicago *(G-6323)*
▲ **Rehobot Inc** ............G ....... 815 385-7777
McHenry *(G-14550)*
◆ **Sarco Hydraulics Inc** ............E ....... 217 324-6577
Litchfield *(G-13697)*
**SMC Corporation of America** ............E ....... 630 449-0600
Aurora *(G-1080)*
**T J Brooks Co** ............G ....... 847 680-0350
Libertyville *(G-13387)*
**T Mac Cylinders Inc** ............G ....... 815 877-7090
Roscoe *(G-18923)*
◆ **Tuxco Corporation** ............F ....... 847 244-2220
Gurnee *(G-11517)*
**Walach Manufacturing Co Inc** ............F ....... 773 836-2060
Chicago *(G-6935)*

### 3594 Fluid Power Pumps & Motors

▲ **American Electronic Pdts Inc** ............F ....... 630 889-9977
Oak Brook *(G-16488)*
▲ **Applied Hydraulic Services** ............G ....... 773 638-8500
Chicago *(G-3925)*
**Applied Hydraulics Corporation** ............G ....... 773 638-8500
Chicago *(G-3926)*
**Brock Equipment Company** ............E ....... 815 459-4210
Woodstock *(G-22547)*
**Bucher Hydraulics Inc** ............G ....... 847 429-0700
Elgin *(G-8973)*
**Caterpillar Inc** ............B ....... 815 729-5511
Joliet *(G-12471)*
**Central Hydraulics Inc** ............G ....... 309 527-5238
El Paso *(G-8866)*
**Concentric Rockford Inc** ............C ....... 815 398-4400
Rockford *(G-18322)*
**Danfoss Power Solutions US Co** ............C ....... 815 233-4200
Freeport *(G-10652)*
**Deltrol Corp** ............C ....... 708 547-0500
Bellwood *(G-1703)*
**Grand Specialties Co** ............F ....... 630 629-8000
Oak Brook *(G-16520)*
**Highland Mch & Screw Pdts Co** ............D ....... 618 654-2103
Highland *(G-11788)*
▲ **Hydro-Gear Inc** ............C ....... 217 728-2581
Sullivan *(G-20748)*
**Idex Corporation** ............B ....... 847 498-7070
Lake Forest *(G-12915)*
▼ **Ifh Group Inc** ............D ....... 800 435-7003
Rock Falls *(G-18138)*
**Ifh Group Inc** ............G ....... 815 380-2367
Galt *(G-10781)*
**Kocsis Technologies Inc** ............G ....... 708 597-4177
Alsip *(G-482)*
▲ **Leading Edge Group Inc** ............C ....... 815 316-3500
Rockford *(G-18464)*
**Mandus Group Ltd** ............F ....... 309 786-1507
Rock Island *(G-18187)*
**Mechanical Engineering Pdts** ............G ....... 312 421-3375
Chicago *(G-5674)*
▲ **Mechanical Tool & Engrg Co** ............C ....... 815 397-4701
Rockford *(G-18489)*
**Mechanical Tool & Engrg Co** ............C ....... 815 397-4701
Rockford *(G-18490)*
**New Dimensions Precision Mac** ............D ....... 815 923-8300
Union *(G-21037)*
**Parker-Hannifin Corporation** ............C ....... 847 955-5000
Lincolnshire *(G-13472)*
**Rdh Inc of Rockford** ............F ....... 815 874-9421
Rockford *(G-18550)*
▲ **Rehobot Inc** ............G ....... 815 385-7777
McHenry *(G-14550)*
▲ **Rhino Tool Company** ............F ....... 309 853-5555
Kewanee *(G-12694)*
▲ **S C C Pumps Inc** ............G ....... 847 593-8495
Arlington Heights *(G-834)*
**Settima Usa Inc** ............G ....... 630 812-1433
Mount Prospect *(G-15373)*
**Sunsource Holdings Inc** ............G ....... 630 317-2700
Addison *(G-300)*
**Tomenson Machine Works Inc** ............D ....... 630 377-7670
West Chicago *(G-21782)*
**Tramco Pump Co** ............E ....... 312 243-5800
Chicago *(G-6756)*
◆ **Tuxco Corporation** ............F ....... 847 244-2220
Gurnee *(G-11517)*
**Wes-Tech Inc** ............G ....... 847 541-5070
Buffalo Grove *(G-2793)*

### 3596 Scales & Balances, Exc Laboratory

**Advanced Weighing Systems Inc** ............G ....... 630 916-6179
Addison *(G-25)*
**Belt-Way Scales Inc** ............E ....... 815 625-5573
Rock Falls *(G-18126)*
**Brian Burcar** ............G ....... 815 856-2271
Leonore *(G-13285)*
**Control Weigh** ............G ....... 847 540-8260
Buffalo Grove *(G-2679)*
◆ **Doran Scales Inc** ............E ....... 630 879-1200
Batavia *(G-1440)*
**E Rowe Foundry & Machine Co** ............D ....... 217 382-4135
Martinsville *(G-14334)*
**EJ Cady & Company** ............G ....... 847 537-2239
Wheeling *(G-22045)*
**G & H Balancer Service** ............G ....... 773 509-1988
Glenview *(G-11127)*
▲ **Glenview Systems Inc** ............F ....... 847 724-2691
Glenview *(G-11132)*
▲ **Heng Tuo Usa Inc** ............G ....... 630 705-1898
Oakbrook Terrace *(G-16710)*
**Integrated Measurement Systems** ............G ....... 847 956-1940
Elk Grove Village *(G-9549)*
▲ **Lifespan Brands LLC** ............F ....... 630 315-3300
Elk Grove Village *(G-9595)*
▲ **Loadsense Technologies LLC** ............G ....... 312 239-0146
Chicago *(G-5529)*
◆ **Medela LLC** ............C ....... 800 435-8316
McHenry *(G-14531)*
**Meto-Grafics Inc** ............F ....... 847 639-0044
Crystal Lake *(G-7609)*
**Morrison Weighing Systems Inc** ............G ....... 309 799-7311
Milan *(G-14797)*
◆ **Newell Operating Company** ............C ....... 815 235-4171
Freeport *(G-10675)*
◆ **Pelstar LLC** ............E ....... 708 377-0600
Countryside *(G-7440)*
**Scale-Tronix Inc** ............F ....... 630 653-3377
Carol Stream *(G-3235)*
**Southern Illinois Scale Servc** ............G ....... 618 723-2303
Noble *(G-16054)*
▲ **Taylor Precision Products Inc** ............F ....... 630 954-1250
Oak Brook *(G-16563)*

### 3599 Machinery & Eqpt, Indl & Commercial, NEC

**2 M Tool Company Inc** ............F ....... 773 282-0722
Chicago *(G-3662)*
**3-V Industries Inc** ............G ....... 217 835-4453
Benld *(G-1804)*
**3d Industries Inc** ............E ....... 630 616-8702
Bensenville *(G-1808)*
**A & A Machine Co Inc** ............G ....... 847 985-4619
Elk Grove Village *(G-9248)*
**A & B Machine Shop** ............G ....... 815 397-0495
Rockford *(G-18237)*
**A & B Machine Works Inc** ............G ....... 312 733-7888
Chicago *(G-3677)*
**A & L Drilling Inc** ............F ....... 815 962-7538
Rockford *(G-18238)*
**A & R Machine Inc** ............G ....... 708 388-4764
Alsip *(G-426)*
**A J Horne Inc** ............G ....... 630 231-8686
West Chicago *(G-21651)*
**A J Machining Inc** ............E ....... 708 563-2580
Bedford Park *(G-1530)*
**A K Tool & Manufacturing Inc** ............G ....... 630 889-9220
Lombard *(G-13756)*
**A R Tech & Tool Inc** ............G ....... 708 599-5745
Bridgeview *(G-2458)*
**A&S Machining & Welding Inc** ............E ....... 708 442-4544
Mc Cook *(G-14443)*
**A-1 Lapping & Machine Inc** ............F ....... 815 398-1465
Rockford *(G-18243)*
**AAA Tool and Machine Co** ............G ....... 618 632-6718
O Fallon *(G-16459)*
**Aarmen Tool & Manufacturing** ............G ....... 815 678-4818
Richmond *(G-17955)*
**Aarstar Precision Grinding** ............G ....... 847 678-4880
Franklin Park *(G-10382)*
**Abacus Manufacturing Group Inc** ............G ....... 815 654-7050
Rockford *(G-18245)*
▲ **Abbott Machine Co** ............F ....... 618 465-1898
Alton *(G-557)*
▲ **Abbott Scott Manufacturing Co** ............E ....... 773 342-7200
Chicago *(G-3706)*
**Abet Industries Corporation** ............G ....... 708 482-8282
La Grange Park *(G-12751)*
**Able Metal Hose Inc** ............F ....... 630 543-9620
Addison *(G-15)*
**ABS Tool & Machine Inc** ............G ....... 815 968-4630
Rockford *(G-18249)*
**Absolute Grinding and Mfg** ............F ....... 815 964-1999
Rockford *(G-18250)*
**Absolute Turn Inc** ............E ....... 847 459-4629
Wheeling *(G-21997)*
**Accro Precision Grinding Inc** ............G ....... 708 681-0520
Melrose Park *(G-14583)*
**Accurate Metal Components Inc** ............F ....... 847 520-5900
Niles *(G-15957)*

SIC

Employee Codes: A=Over 500 employees, B=251-500
C=101-250, D=51-100, E=20-50, F=10-19, G=3-9

2017 Harris Illinois
Industrial Directory

1083

# 35 INDUSTRIAL AND COMMERCIAL MACHINERY AND COMPUTER EQUIPMENT

Accurate Metal Fabricating LLC .... D ..... 773 235-0400
 Chicago *(G-3720)*
Accurate Metallizing Inc .... G ..... 708 424-7747
 Oak Lawn *(G-16596)*
Accurate Tool & Mfg Corp .... F ..... 708 652-4266
 Chicago *(G-3723)*
Accutech Machining Inc .... E ..... 630 350-2066
 Bensenville *(G-1814)*
Ace Coating Enterprises Inc .... F ..... 708 547-6680
 Hillside *(G-11908)*
Ace Machining of Rockford Inc .... 815 398-3200
 Rockford *(G-18255)*
Ace Precision Tool & Mfg Co .... G ..... 847 690-0111
 Elk Grove Village *(G-9263)*
Ace Sandblast Company (del) .... F ..... 773 777-6654
 Chicago *(G-3728)*
Acme Grinding & Manufacturing .... C ..... 815 323-1380
 Belvidere *(G-1726)*
▲ Acme Industries Inc .... C ..... 847 296-3346
 Elk Grove Village *(G-9266)*
Action Carbide Grinding Co .... 847 891-9026
 Schaumburg *(G-19422)*
Active Grinding & Mfg Co .... F ..... 708 344-0510
 Broadview *(G-2554)*
▲ Adam Tool & Mfg Co Inc .... F ..... 630 530-8810
 Elmhurst *(G-9830)*
Addison Precision Products .... F ..... 815 857-4466
 Amboy *(G-596)*
Adermanns Welding & Mch & Co .... G ..... 217 342-3234
 Effingham *(G-8822)*
Advance Machining .... 630 521-9392
 Bensenville *(G-1817)*
Advance Printers Machine Shop .... G ..... 773 588-3169
 Chicago *(G-3762)*
▲ Advanced Filtration Systems Inc .... C ..... 217 351-3073
 Champaign *(G-3444)*
▼ Advanced Machine & Engrg Co .... C ..... 815 962-6076
 Rockford *(G-18257)*
Advanced Machine Products Inc .... G ..... 618 254-4112
 Hartford *(G-11609)*
Advanced Prcsion Machining Ltd .... 630 860-2549
 Bensenville *(G-1819)*
Advantage Machining Inc .... E ..... 630 897-1220
 Aurora *(G-1101)*
Aero Apmc Inc .... F ..... 630 766-0910
 Franklin Park *(G-10385)*
▲ Afc Cable Systems Inc .... B ..... 508 998-1131
 Harvey *(G-11651)*
Affri Inc .... G ..... 224 374-0931
 Wood Dale *(G-22333)*
AGS Machine Co Inc .... G ..... 630 766-7777
 Bensenville *(G-1821)*
Air Caster LLC .... E ..... 217 877-1237
 Decatur *(G-7824)*
▲ Air Stamping Inc .... F ..... 217 342-1283
 Effingham *(G-8823)*
▲ Airo Tool & Manufacturing Inc .... F ..... 815 547-7588
 Belvidere *(G-1729)*
Algen Enterprises Ltd .... F ..... 217 428-4888
 Decatur *(G-7828)*
Alicona Manufacturing Inc .... 630 736-2718
 Bartlett *(G-1330)*
Alin Machining Company Inc .... D ..... 708 345-8600
 Oswego *(G-16903)*
All Cnc Solutions Inc .... G ..... 847 972-1139
 Skokie *(G-19947)*
All Cut Inc .... G ..... 630 910-6505
 Darien *(G-7788)*
Allans Welding & Machine Inc .... G ..... 618 392-3708
 Olney *(G-16758)*
Allen Popovich .... 815 712-7404
 Custer Park *(G-7686)*
Allied Machine Tool & Dye .... G ..... 708 388-7676
 Crestwood *(G-7475)*
Allied Welding Inc .... E ..... 309 274-6227
 Chillicothe *(G-7161)*
Alpha Machine Corp .... E ..... 708 532-2313
 New Lenox *(G-15869)*
Alpine Amusement Co Inc .... G ..... 708 233-9131
 Oak Lawn *(G-16600)*
Alsip Mfg Inc .... E ..... 708 333-4446
 Harvey *(G-11654)*
Alster Machining Corp .... F ..... 773 384-2370
 Chicago *(G-3834)*
▲ AM Precision Machine Inc .... E ..... 847 439-9955
 Elk Grove Village *(G-9291)*
American Calibration Inc .... F ..... 815 356-5839
 Crystal Lake *(G-7533)*
American Cnc Machine Co Inc .... E ..... 630 628-6490
 Addison *(G-34)*

American Drilling Inc .... E ..... 847 850-5090
 Wheeling *(G-22003)*
▼ American Engraving Inc .... G ..... 630 543-2525
 Bensenville *(G-1833)*
American Grinding & Machine Co .... D ..... 773 889-4343
 Chicago *(G-3857)*
American Machining Inc .... 815 498-1593
 Somonauk *(G-20124)*
▲ American Machining & Wldg Inc .... E ..... 773 586-2585
 Chicago *(G-3862)*
American Precision Machine .... F ..... 847 428-5950
 Carpentersville *(G-3273)*
American Quality Mfg Inc .... E ..... 815 226-9301
 Rockford *(G-18263)*
American Total Engine Co .... E ..... 847 623-2737
 Ingleside *(G-12186)*
Anah Machine Mfg Co .... F ..... 847 228-6450
 Elk Grove Village *(G-9305)*
Anamet Inc .... G ..... 217 234-8844
 Glen Ellyn *(G-10958)*
Anderson Tage Co .... E ..... 815 397-3040
 Rockford *(G-18267)*
Andersson Tool & Die LLP .... F ..... 847 746-8866
 Zion *(G-22678)*
Andrew Toschak .... G ..... 630 553-3434
 Yorkville *(G-22649)*
Antler Inn Manufactory Inc .... E ..... 309 799-1132
 Milan *(G-14774)*
AP Machine Inc .... F ..... 708 450-1010
 Melrose Park *(G-14594)*
Apex Manufacturing Inc .... G ..... 815 728-0108
 Ringwood *(G-17987)*
Aphelion Precision Tech Corp .... E ..... 847 215-7285
 Elk Grove Village *(G-9310)*
Apollo Machine & Manufacturing .... G ..... 847 677-6444
 Skokie *(G-19956)*
Archer Manufacturing Corp .... E ..... 773 585-7181
 Chicago *(G-3938)*
Ardekin Precision LLC .... F ..... 815 397-1069
 Rockford *(G-18269)*
▲ Argo Manufacturing Co .... F ..... 630 377-1750
 Wasco *(G-21372)*
Armitage Machine Co Inc .... F ..... 309 697-9050
 Peoria *(G-17310)*
Arnette Pattern Co Inc .... E ..... 618 451-7700
 Granite City *(G-11268)*
Aro Metal Stamping Company Inc .... E ..... 630 351-7676
 Roselle *(G-18927)*
Arrow Edm Inc .... F ..... 217 893-4277
 Rantoul *(G-17918)*
Asteroid Grinding & Mfg Inc .... E ..... 847 298-8109
 Des Plaines *(G-8153)*
Astro-Craft Inc .... E ..... 815 675-1500
 Spring Grove *(G-20326)*
Atlas Manufacturing Ltd .... F ..... 815 943-1400
 Harvard *(G-11622)*
Atlas Material Tstg Tech LLC .... E ..... 773 327-4520
 Chicago *(G-3983)*
▲ Atlas Material Tstg Tech LLC .... C ..... 773 327-4520
 Mount Prospect *(G-15311)*
Atomic Engineering Co .... F ..... 847 228-1387
 Elk Grove Village *(G-9320)*
◆ Ats Sortimat USA LLC .... E ..... 847 925-1234
 Rolling Meadows *(G-18711)*
Aura Systems Inc .... E ..... 217 423-4100
 Decatur *(G-7842)*
Aurora Custom Machining Inc .... D ..... 630 859-2638
 Aurora *(G-1115)*
◆ Aurora Metals Division LLC .... C ..... 630 844-4900
 Montgomery *(G-15028)*
Austin Tool & Die Co .... D ..... 847 509-5800
 Northbrook *(G-16209)*
Auto Head and Engine Exchange .... G ..... 708 448-8762
 Worth *(G-22632)*
Autocut Machine Co .... G ..... 815 436-1900
 Elwood *(G-9978)*
Automated Design Corp .... G ..... 630 783-1150
 Romeoville *(G-18801)*
Automated Mfg Solutions Inc .... F ..... 815 477-2428
 Crystal Lake *(G-7539)*
Automation Design & Mfg Inc .... E ..... 630 896-4206
 Aurora *(G-1117)*
Automotive Engine Specialties .... G ..... 847 956-1244
 Elk Grove Village *(G-9322)*
Avan Tool & Die Co Inc .... F ..... 773 287-1670
 Chicago *(G-3996)*
Avers Machine & Mfg Inc .... F ..... 847 447-3430
 Schiller Park *(G-19807)*
Awerkamp Machine Co .... E ..... 217 222-3480
 Quincy *(G-17797)*

Awerkamp Machine Co .... F ..... 217 222-3490
 Quincy *(G-17798)*
Axis Manufacturing Inc .... E ..... 847 350-0200
 Elk Grove Village *(G-9327)*
Azimuth Cnc Inc .... F ..... 815 399-4433
 Rockford *(G-18274)*
B & B Specialty Company Inc .... G ..... 708 652-9234
 Cicero *(G-7179)*
B & B Tool Co .... E ..... 815 229-5792
 Rockford *(G-18275)*
B & G Machine Inc .... E ..... 618 262-2269
 Mount Carmel *(G-15261)*
B & R Grinding Co .... E ..... 630 595-7789
 Franklin Park *(G-10407)*
B & W Machine Company Inc .... G ..... 847 364-4500
 Elk Grove Village *(G-9329)*
B A P Enterprises Inc .... E ..... 708 849-0900
 Dolton *(G-8364)*
B M S Enterprise .... G ..... 815 730-3450
 Rockdale *(G-18214)*
B M W Inc .... E ..... 847 439-0095
 Elk Grove Village *(G-9331)*
B Radtke and Sons Inc .... G ..... 847 546-3999
 Round Lake Park *(G-19083)*
B S Grinding Inc .... E ..... 847 787-0770
 Elk Grove Village *(G-9332)*
▲ B T M Industries Inc .... G ..... 815 338-6464
 Woodstock *(G-22543)*
B&B Machining Incorporated .... F ..... 630 898-3009
 Aurora *(G-966)*
Baley Enterprises Inc .... G ..... 708 681-0900
 Melrose Park *(G-14599)*
▲ Ballco Manufacturing Co Inc .... D ..... 630 898-1600
 Aurora *(G-968)*
Bams Manufacturing Co Inc .... G ..... 800 206-0613
 Elk Grove Village *(G-9334)*
▲ Banner Service Corporation .... C ..... 630 653-7500
 Carol Stream *(G-3112)*
Barnes Machine Shop LLC .... G ..... 217 774-5308
 Shelbyville *(G-19905)*
Bartech Precision Machining Co .... F ..... 618 243-9068
 Lemont *(G-13227)*
▲ Barton Manufacturing LLC .... E ..... 217 428-0711
 Decatur *(G-7843)*
▲ Bbs Automation Chicago Inc .... C ..... 630 351-3000
 Bartlett *(G-1335)*
Bc Machine .... E ..... 815 962-7884
 Rockford *(G-18278)*
Bedford Rakim .... G ..... 773 749-3086
 Lansing *(G-13157)*
Bem Mold Inc .... E ..... 847 805-9750
 Schaumburg *(G-19460)*
Berndt & Thacker Inc .... F ..... 630 628-1934
 Addison *(G-54)*
Best Machine & Welding Co Inc .... E ..... 708 343-4455
 Woodridge *(G-22456)*
▲ Big 3 Precision Products Inc .... C ..... 618 533-3251
 Centralia *(G-3405)*
▲ Bills Machine & Power Transm .... E ..... 618 392-2500
 Olney *(G-16763)*
Bitzer Products Company .... E ..... 708 345-0795
 Naperville *(G-15606)*
Bk Production Specialties .... G ..... 847 526-5150
 Wauconda *(G-21447)*
Blue Chip Industries Inc .... F ..... 309 854-7100
 Kewanee *(G-12671)*
Bold Machine Works Inc .... F ..... 217 428-6644
 Decatur *(G-7847)*
Boley Tool & Machine Works Inc .... C ..... 309 694-2722
 East Peoria *(G-8703)*
Boring Industries .... F ..... 815 986-1172
 Rockford *(G-18288)*
BR Machine Inc .... G ..... 815 434-0427
 Ottawa *(G-16950)*
Bradley Machining Inc .... F ..... 630 543-2875
 Addison *(G-59)*
Brenco Machine and Tool Inc .... E ..... 815 356-5100
 Crystal Lake *(G-7543)*
Brian Burcar .... G ..... 815 856-2271
 Leonore *(G-13285)*
Bridgeview Machining Inc .... G ..... 708 599-4060
 Bridgeview *(G-2473)*
Brock Industrial Services LLC .... E ..... 815 730-3350
 Joliet *(G-12467)*
Brucher Machining Inc .... F ..... 630 876-1661
 West Chicago *(G-21674)*
▲ Bryco Machine Inc .... E ..... 708 614-1900
 Tinley Park *(G-20901)*
BSB International Corp .... G ..... 847 791-9272
 Bensenville *(G-1848)*

Budapest Tool ........G....... 630 250-0711
Itasca *(G-12238)*
Burdzy Tool & Die Co ........F....... 847 671-6666
Schiller Park *(G-19810)*
Burgess Manufacturing Inc........F....... 847 680-1724
Libertyville *(G-13311)*
Burke Tool & Manufacturing Inc........G....... 618 542-6441
Du Quoin *(G-8551)*
Burmac Manufacturing Inc........G....... 815 434-1660
Ottawa *(G-16951)*
Burns Machine Company........E....... 815 434-3131
Ottawa *(G-16952)*
▲ Burns Machine Company........E....... 815 434-1660
Ottawa *(G-16953)*
Byrne & Schaefer Inc........G....... 815 727-5000
Lockport *(G-13708)*
C & D Machining Inc........F....... 815 778-4946
Lyndon *(G-14013)*
C & F Machine Corp........F....... 630 924-0300
Bloomingdale *(G-2098)*
C D Tools Machining Inc........G....... 773 859-2028
Addison *(G-65)*
C E R Machining & Tooling Ltd........G....... 708 442-9614
Lyons *(G-14034)*
C N C Central Inc........G....... 630 595-1453
Bensenville *(G-1849)*
C Tri Co........E....... 309 467-4715
Eureka *(G-9994)*
C/B Machine Tool Corp........G....... 847 288-1807
Franklin Park *(G-10422)*
Cadillac Tank Met Fbrctors Inc........E....... 630 543-2600
Addison *(G-68)*
Caffero Tool & Mfg........D....... 224 293-2600
Streamwood *(G-20647)*
Calco Controls Inc........F....... 847 639-3858
Crystal Lake *(G-7548)*
▲ CAM Co Inc........F....... 630 556-3110
Big Rock *(G-2086)*
Camco Manufacturing Inc........F....... 708 597-4288
Crestwood *(G-7478)*
Cams Inc........G....... 773 929-3656
Chicago *(G-4225)*
Capitol City Machine........G....... 217 529-0293
Springfield *(G-20405)*
Car Shop Inc........G....... 309 797-4188
Moline *(G-14920)*
Carmona Gear Cutting........G....... 815 963-8236
Rockford *(G-18298)*
Carr Machine & Tool Inc........G....... 847 593-8003
Elk Grove Village *(G-9357)*
Casward Tool Works Inc........G....... 773 486-4900
Chicago *(G-4254)*
Catapult Marketing........D....... 312 216-4460
Chicago *(G-4257)*
Celinco Inc........G....... 815 964-2256
Rockford *(G-18301)*
Centerless Grinding Co........F....... 847 455-7660
Franklin Park *(G-10426)*
▲ Central Illinois Mfg Co........D....... 217 762-8184
Bement *(G-1800)*
Central Machining Inc........G....... 217 854-6646
Carlinville *(G-3033)*
Central Machining Service........G....... 217 422-7472
Decatur *(G-7855)*
CF Gear Holdings LLC........F....... 847 376-8322
Des Plaines *(G-8162)*
Chadwick Manufacturing Ltd........G....... 815 684-5152
Chadwick *(G-3440)*
Chamfermatic Inc........G....... 815 636-5082
Machesney Park *(G-14064)*
Chicago Copper & Iron Works........G....... 773 327-2780
Chicago *(G-4312)*
Chicago Grinding & Machine Co........E....... 708 343-4399
Melrose Park *(G-14610)*
Chicago Park District........D....... 708 857-2653
Chicago Ridge *(G-7142)*
▼ Chicago Powdered Metal Pdts Co....D....... 847 678-2836
Schiller Park *(G-19813)*
Chicago Waterjet Inc........G....... 847 350-1898
Elk Grove Village *(G-9370)*
▲ Chrome Crankshaft Company LLC ..F....... 815 725-9030
Joliet *(G-12473)*
Cimino Machine Corp........F....... 773 767-7000
Chicago *(G-4378)*
Circle Boring & Machine Co........G....... 815 398-4150
Rockford *(G-18308)*
Circle Boring & Machine Co........G....... 815 397-3040
Rockford *(G-18309)*
Class A Grinding........G....... 815 874-2118
Rockford *(G-18311)*
Classic Automation & Tool........G....... 708 388-6311
Crestwood *(G-7482)*
Clean and Science USA Co Ltd........G....... 847 461-9292
Schaumburg *(G-19473)*
Clinkenbeard & Associates Inc........E....... 815 226-0291
Rockford *(G-18313)*
Cmg Precision Machining Co Inc........G....... 630 759-8080
Romeoville *(G-18813)*
Cnh Industrial America LLC........E....... 309 965-2233
Goodfield *(G-11244)*
Cobalt Tool & Manufacturing........G....... 630 530-8898
Villa Park *(G-21243)*
▲ Cold Headers Inc........F....... 773 775-7900
Chicago *(G-4421)*
Comet Roll & Machine Company........E....... 630 268-1407
Saint Charles *(G-19161)*
Commercial Dynamics Inc........G....... 847 439-5300
Arlington Heights *(G-737)*
Commercial Machine Services........F....... 847 806-1901
Elk Grove Village *(G-9386)*
Compak Inc........E....... 815 399-2699
Rockford *(G-18320)*
▲ Component Products Inc........E....... 847 301-1000
Schaumburg *(G-19477)*
▲ Component Specialty Inc........E....... 847 742-4400
Elgin *(G-8996)*
Component Tool & Mfg Co........F....... 708 672-5505
Crete *(G-7510)*
Concepts and Controls Inc........F....... 847 478-9296
Buffalo Grove *(G-2676)*
Concorde Mfg & Fabrication Inc........F....... 815 344-3788
McHenry *(G-14488)*
Conform Industries Inc........F....... 630 285-0272
Schaumburg *(G-19479)*
Connell Mc Machine & Welding........G....... 815 868-2275
Mc Connell *(G-14442)*
Contour Machining Inc........G....... 847 364-0111
Elk Grove Village *(G-9391)*
Contour Screw Products Inc........E....... 847 357-1190
Arlington Heights *(G-739)*
Cope Plastics Inc........D....... 618 466-0221
Alton *(G-568)*
Corrigan Manufacturing Co........F....... 815 399-9326
Rockford *(G-18324)*
Cortelyou Machine & Welding........G....... 618 592-3961
Oblong *(G-16730)*
Cosmopolitan Machine Rebuilder........G....... 630 595-8141
Bensenville *(G-1868)*
County Tool & Die........G....... 217 324-6527
Litchfield *(G-13683)*
▲ Creative Machining Tech LLC........D....... 309 755-7700
Highland Park *(G-11829)*
Crown Machine Inc........E....... 815 877-7700
Rockford *(G-18325)*
Crv Industries Inc........F....... 630 595-3777
Bensenville *(G-1873)*
Custom Cut EDM Inc........G....... 847 647-9500
Skokie *(G-19989)*
Custom Machine Inc........G....... 815 284-3820
Dixon *(G-8327)*
Custom Machinery Inc........G....... 847 678-3033
Schiller Park *(G-19818)*
Custom Machining Company........G....... 630 766-2600
Bensenville *(G-1876)*
Custom Millers Supply Inc........G....... 309 734-6312
Monmouth *(G-15011)*
Custom Superfinishing Grinding........G....... 847 699-9710
Rosemont *(G-18997)*
Cutting Edge Machining Inc........G....... 847 427-1392
Elk Grove Village *(G-9406)*
D & H Precision Tooling Co........G....... 815 653-9611
Wonder Lake *(G-22322)*
D & J Machine Shop Inc........G....... 815 472-6057
Momence *(G-14979)*
D & K Machine and Tool Inc........G....... 847 439-8691
Elk Grove Village *(G-9411)*
D & M Tool Llc........G....... 847 731-3600
Zion *(G-22681)*
D & R Autochuck Inc........E....... 815 398-9131
Rockford *(G-18330)*
D & R Machine Company Inc........G....... 618 465-5611
Alton *(G-569)*
D & S Manufacturing Inc........G....... 815 637-8889
Loves Park *(G-13933)*
D and K Plastics........G....... 712 723-5372
Yorkville *(G-22653)*
▲ D E Specialty Tool & Mfg Inc........E....... 847 678-0004
Franklin Park *(G-10453)*
D Machine Inc........G....... 815 877-5991
Loves Park *(G-13934)*
▲ Daco Incorporated........F....... 630 897-8797
North Aurora *(G-16124)*
Dagger Tool Co Inc........G....... 630 279-5050
Addison *(G-86)*
Daley Automation LLC........G....... 630 384-9900
Naperville *(G-15642)*
Dan Horenberger........F....... 818 394-0028
Marengo *(G-14224)*
Dart Technology Inc........G....... 847 534-0357
Schaumburg *(G-19499)*
Datum Machine Works Inc........F....... 815 877-8502
Rockford *(G-18336)*
Datum Tool and Mfg Inc........F....... 847 742-4092
South Elgin *(G-20193)*
Daves Auto Repair........G....... 630 682-4411
Carol Stream *(G-3140)*
David L Knoche........G....... 618 466-7120
Godfrey *(G-11223)*
Davis Machine Company Inc........G....... 815 723-9121
Joliet *(G-12484)*
Deedrick Machine Inc........E....... 217 598-2366
Sadorus *(G-19117)*
▲ Delta Design Inc........F....... 708 424-9400
Evergreen Park *(G-10111)*
Dempsey Tool Inc........G....... 815 210-4896
Schaumburg *(G-19501)*
Dendick Engineering and Mch Co........G....... 815 464-6100
Palos Heights *(G-17103)*
Design Enhanced Mfg Co........G....... 815 946-3562
Polo *(G-17687)*
Device Technologies Inc........G....... 630 553-7178
Yorkville *(G-22655)*
Dial Industries Inc........F....... 815 397-7994
Rockford *(G-18341)*
Dial Machine Inc........E....... 815 397-6660
Rockford *(G-18342)*
Diamond Industrial Sales Ltd........G....... 630 858-3687
Glen Ellyn *(G-10966)*
Dill Brothers Inc........F....... 847 746-8323
Zion *(G-22682)*
Direct Automation Inc........F....... 815 675-0588
Spring Grove *(G-20333)*
Disco Machine & Mfg Inc........E....... 708 456-0835
Norridge *(G-16100)*
Diversified Machining Inc........G....... 815 316-8561
Rockford *(G-18347)*
Djw Machining Inc........G....... 847 956-5330
Arlington Heights *(G-747)*
DK Precision Inc........G....... 847 985-8008
Schaumburg *(G-19506)*
DMS Industries Inc........F....... 708 895-8000
Lansing *(G-13160)*
DNp Enterprises Inc........G....... 630 628-7210
Addison *(G-95)*
Donaldson Company Inc........C....... 309 667-2885
New Windsor *(G-15930)*
Donaldson Company Inc........E....... 815 288-3374
Dixon *(G-8329)*
Donnelly Automotive Machine........F....... 217 428-7414
Decatur *(G-7877)*
Donson Machine........G....... 708 468-8392
Orland Park *(G-16855)*
▲ Donson Machine Company........D....... 708 388-0880
Alsip *(G-457)*
Dooling Machine Products Inc........G....... 618 254-0724
Hartford *(G-11610)*
Double-Disc Grinding Corp........F....... 708 410-1770
Melrose Park *(G-14621)*
Dovin Machine Shop........G....... 815 672-5247
Streator *(G-20687)*
Dowell Lynnea........G....... 309 543-3854
Havana *(G-11694)*
Du Page Precision Products Co........F....... 630 849-2940
Aurora *(G-997)*
Du Page Precision Products Co........D....... 630 849-2940
Aurora *(G-998)*
Dundick Corporation........E....... 708 656-6363
Cicero *(G-7192)*
Dunteman and Co........G....... 309 772-2166
Bushnell *(G-2902)*
Dura Feed Inc........G....... 815 395-1115
Loves Park *(G-13938)*
▲ Duraflex Inc........E....... 847 462-1007
Cary *(G-3336)*
Durr - All Corporation........G....... 815 943-1032
Harvard *(G-11631)*
Dyers Machine Service Inc........G....... 708 496-8100
Summit Argo *(G-20762)*
Dynamac Inc........E....... 630 543-0033
Addison *(G-102)*



Employee Codes: A=Over 500 employees, B=251-500
C=101-250, D=51-100, E=20-50, F=10-19, G=3-9
2017 Harris Illinois
Industrial Directory
1085

35 INDUSTRIAL AND COMMERCIAL MACHINERY AND COMPUTER EQUIPMENT SIC SECTION

Dynamic Machining Inc G 815 675-3330
Spring Grove (G-20334)
Dynamic Precision Products F 847 526-2054
Wauconda (G-21458)
E & E Machine & Engineering Co G 708 841-5208
Riverdale (G-18018)
▲ E & F Tool Company Inc F 815 729-1305
Joliet (G-12486)
E & J Precision Machining Inc F 815 363-2522
McHenry (G-14500)
E B Bronson & Co Inc E 708 385-3600
Blue Island (G-2247)
E C Machining Inc E 708 496-0116
Justice (G-12598)
E M Glabus Co Inc F 630 766-3027
Bensenville (G-1887)
Eagle Machine Company G 312 243-7407
Chicago (G-4671)
Eaglestone Inc F 630 587-1115
Saint Charles (G-19177)
Eastwood Enterprises Inc D 847 940-4008
Deerfield (G-8004)
Eaton Tool & Machine Inc G 815 874-6664
Rockford (G-18355)
Ed Hartwig Trucking & Excvtg G 309 364-3672
Henry (G-11740)
Ed Weitekamp Inc G 217 229-4239
Raymond (G-17938)
EDM Scorpio Inc G 847 931-5164
Elgin (G-9020)
Edwardsville Mch & Wldg Co Inc G 618 656-5145
Edwardsville (G-8798)
Eenigenburg Mfg Inc G 708 474-0850
Lansing (G-13161)
◆ Elastec Inc C 618 382-2525
Carmi (G-3066)
▲ Elburn Metal Stamping Inc E 630 365-2500
Elburn (G-8885)
▲ Electri-Flex Company (del) D 630 307-1095
Roselle (G-18941)
▲ Electroform Company E 815 633-1113
Machesney Park (G-14072)
Elite McHning of Chicago Ridge G 708 423-0767
Chicago Ridge (G-7146)
Elliott Machine & Tool Corp G 630 543-6755
Addison (G-110)
EM Smith & Co E 309 691-6812
Peoria (G-17356)
EMC Machining Inc F 630 860-7076
Bensenville (G-1891)
Emerald Machine Inc G 773 924-3659
Chicago (G-4740)
Empire Crankshafts G 847 640-8101
Elk Grove Village (G-9455)
Empire Hard Chrome Inc C 773 762-3156
Chicago (G-4745)
Emtech Machining & Grinding G 815 338-1580
Woodstock (G-22565)
Engineering Design & Dev Inc E 309 266-6298
Morton (G-15158)
Engle Manufacturing Co F 815 738-2282
Leaf River (G-13210)
ENR General Machining Co E 773 523-2944
Chicago (G-4757)
▲ ERA Industries Inc C 847 357-1320
Elk Grove Village (G-9463)
Erickson Tool & Machine Co G 815 397-2653
Rockford (G-18369)
Eton Machine Co Ltd F 847 426-3380
Elgin (G-9030)
Eww Enterprise Inc G 815 463-9607
New Lenox (G-15881)
Exact Machine Company Inc F 815 963-7905
Rockford (G-18374)
Excel Machine & Tool G 815 467-1177
Channahon (G-3574)
Excel Machining Inc G 773 585-6666
Chicago (G-4794)
Express Grinding Inc G 847 434-5827
Elk Grove Village (G-9472)
Express Machining & Molds G 630 350-8480
Franklin Park (G-10468)
F N Smith Corporation E 815 732-2171
Oregon (G-16824)
▲ Fabricated Metals Co C 847 718-1300
Elk Grove Village (G-9474)
Fabricators Unlimited Inc G 847 223-7986
Grayslake (G-11337)
Fabtec Manufacturing Inc F 847 671-4888
Franklin Park (G-10469)
Famaco Corp E 217 442-4412
Tilton (G-20881)
Fanmar Inc E 708 563-0505
Elk Grove Village (G-9475)
Felde Tool & Machine Co Inc F 309 692-5870
Peoria (G-17360)
Fern Manufacturing Company G 630 260-9350
Carol Stream (G-3150)
FH Ayer Manufacturing Co E 708 755-0550
Chicago Heights (G-7097)
Field Works Inc G 847 658-8200
Algonquin (G-389)
▲ Flex-Weld Inc D 815 334-3662
Woodstock (G-22567)
Flextron Inc F 630 543-5995
Addison (G-119)
Flores Precision Products G 630 264-2222
Aurora (G-1152)
Focus Mfg G 815 877-6043
Rockford (G-18384)
Folk Race Cars G 815 629-2418
Durand (G-8585)
Folkerts Manufacturing Inc G 815 968-7426
Rockford (G-18385)
Forest City Grinding Inc G 815 874-2424
Rockford (G-18388)
Form Walern Grinding Inc G 815 874-7000
Rockford (G-18391)
Formar Inc F 630 543-1151
Addison (G-122)
▼ Fosbinder Fabrication Inc E 309 764-0913
Moline (G-14940)
Four-Tech Industries Co G 708 444-8230
Tinley Park (G-20915)
Fox Machine & Tool Inc G 847 357-1845
Elk Grove Village (G-9489)
Fox Tool & Manufacturing Inc F 815 338-3046
Woodstock (G-22568)
Fox Valley Machining Co Inc E 630 859-0700
North Aurora (G-16131)
▲ Franklin Automation Inc F 630 466-1900
Sugar Grove (G-20725)
Frey Wiss Prcsion McHining Inc E 630 595-9073
Wood Dale (G-22373)
Furry Inc F 217 446-0084
Danville (G-7724)
Future Tool Inc F 815 395-0012
Rockford (G-18394)
G G Premier Precision Inc E 708 588-1234
La Grange Park (G-12756)
G L Doemelt F 217 268-4243
Arcola (G-669)
G Messmore Company G 708 343-8114
Broadview (G-2581)
G P Cole Inc F 217 431-3029
Danville (G-7725)
G&G Machine Shop Inc G 217 892-9696
Rantoul (G-17928)
G&R Machining Inc G 847 526-7364
Island Lake (G-12216)
Gage Grinding Company Inc F 847 639-3888
Cary (G-3344)
Gail E Stephens G 618 372-0140
Brighton (G-2540)
Galactic Tool Co G 815 962-3420
Rockford (G-18395)
Galaxy Precision Mfg Inc F 847 238-9066
Elk Grove Village (G-9495)
Gardner Products Inc F 815 562-6011
Rochelle (G-18091)
Gartech Manufacturing Co E 217 324-6527
Litchfield (G-13686)
Gates Inc G 217 335-2378
Barry (G-1313)
Gavin Woodworking Inc G 815 786-2242
Sandwich (G-19365)
Gebco Machine Inc F 618 452-6120
Granite City (G-11281)
General Electric Company D 708 924-5055
Bedford Park (G-1551)
General Grind & Machine Inc C 309 582-5959
Aledo (G-368)
General Grinding Co G 630 543-9088
Addison (G-132)
General Machine Inc E 618 234-1919
Freeburg (G-10636)
General Machine & Tl Works Inc F 312 337-2177
Chicago (G-4927)
General Machine and Tool Inc G 815 727-4342
Lockport (G-13717)
General Machining Service Inc G 708 636-4848
Oak Lawn (G-16623)
▲ Geo T Schmidt Inc D 847 647-7117
Niles (G-15982)
Gett Industries Ltd D 309 799-5131
Milan (G-14787)
Gibbs Machine Corp E 815 336-9000
Coleta (G-7310)
Gibson Insurance Inc G 217 864-4877
Mount Zion (G-15451)
Gki Incorporated E 815 459-2330
Rockford (G-18398)
Glenview Grind G 847 729-0111
Glenview (G-11131)
Goellner Inc C 815 962-6076
Rockford (G-18400)
Gordys Machine and Tool Inc F 618 842-9331
Fairfield (G-10143)
Goreville Auto Parts & Mch Sp G 618 995-2375
Goreville (G-11251)
GPI Industries Incorporated D 708 877-8200
Thornton (G-20870)
GPM Mfg Inc F 847 550-8200
Lake Zurich (G-13080)
Gray Machine & Welding Inc F 309 788-2501
Rock Island (G-18177)
Grebner Machine & Tool Inc G 309 248-7768
Washburn (G-21375)
Greens Machine Shop G 618 532-4631
Centralia (G-3417)
Griffin Machining Inc G 847 360-0098
Waukegan (G-21566)
Grind Lap Services Inc E 630 458-1111
Addison (G-139)
Griswold Machine Co G 708 333-4258
South Holland (G-20272)
Gti Spindle Technology Inc F 309 820-7887
Bloomington (G-2175)
H & B Machine Corporation G 312 829-4850
Chicago (G-5017)
H & D Motor Service G 217 342-3262
Altamont (G-552)
H & H Machining G 309 365-7010
Lexington (G-13292)
H & M Thread Rolling Co Inc G 847 451-1570
Franklin Park (G-10485)
H & R Tool & Machine Co G 618 344-7683
Caseyville (G-3396)
H B Products Incorporated G 773 735-0936
Chicago (G-5019)
H Borre & Sons Inc G 847 524-8890
Lake Zurich (G-13081)
H M C Products Inc E 815 885-1900
Caledonia (G-2932)
H&S Machine & Tools Inc G 618 451-0164
Granite City (G-11283)
Hadady Machining Company Inc F 708 474-8620
Lansing (G-13165)
Hadco Tool Co LLC G 847 677-6263
Skokie (G-20009)
Halter Machine Shop Inc G 618 943-2224
Lawrenceville (G-13201)
Harbor Manufacturing Inc D 708 614-6400
Tinley Park (G-20920)
Harmony Metal Fabrication Inc E 847 426-8900
Gilberts (G-10920)
▲ Harvard Factory Automation Inc F 815 943-1195
Harvard (G-11634)
Hattan Tool Company G 708 597-9308
Alsip (G-471)
◆ Haumiller Engineering Company C 847 695-9111
Elgin (G-9060)
Headco Industries Inc F 847 640-6490
Elk Grove Village (G-9519)
Headco Industries Inc G 815 729-4016
Joliet (G-12509)
Heartland Machine and Sup LLC F 217 543-2678
Arthur (G-903)
Hefke Machines & Machining G 630 896-6617
Aurora (G-1167)
Henning Machine & Die Works G 217 286-3393
Henning (G-11738)
Hess Machine Inc G 618 887-4444
Marine (G-14246)
Hfo Chicago LLC F 847 258-2850
Elk Grove Village (G-9523)
▲ Hfr Precision Machining Inc E 630 556-4325
Sugar Grove (G-20727)
HI Tech Machining & Welding G 708 331-3608
South Holland (G-20277)

SIC SECTION 35 INDUSTRIAL AND COMMERCIAL MACHINERY AND COMPUTER EQUIPMENT

Hidden Hollow Stables Inc ....G ....309 243-7979
Dunlap (G-8567)
Highland Mch & Screw Pdts Co ....D ....618 654-2103
Highland (G-11788)
Highland Metal Inc ....E ....708 544-6641
Hillside (G-11919)
Hillers Sheet Metal Works ....G ....217 532-2595
Hillsboro (G-11893)
Holmes Bros Inc ....E ....217 442-1430
Danville (G-7732)
Holshouser Machine & Tool Inc ....G ....618 451-0164
Granite City (G-11286)
Hopkins Machine Corporation ....G ....773 772-2800
Chicago (G-5110)
Hottenrott Company Inc ....G ....618 473-2531
Hecker (G-11732)
HPp Precision Machine Co Inc ....G ....815 469-2608
Frankfort (G-10328)
Hurst Enterprises Inc ....G ....708 344-9291
Glendale Heights (G-11032)
Hy Tech Cnc Machining Inc ....G ....
Schaumburg (G-19561)
▲ Hy-Tek Manufacturing Co Inc ....E ....630 466-7664
Sugar Grove (G-20728)
I D Rockford Shop Inc ....G ....815 335-1150
Winnebago (G-22297)
▲ Idex Mpt Inc ....D ....630 530-3333
Elmhurst (G-9884)
▲ Illiana Machine & Mfg Corp ....D ....708 479-1333
Mokena (G-14871)
Illini Precision Machining Inc ....G ....217 425-5780
Decatur (G-7892)
Illinois Valley Machine Sp Inc ....F ....815 586-4511
Ransom (G-17916)
IMI Manufacturing Inc ....G ....630 771-0003
Bolingbrook (G-2319)
In-Place Machining Co Inc ....G ....847 669-3006
Huntley (G-12148)
Indar Ventures LLC ....F ....708 343-4900
Melrose Park (G-14656)
Indiana Precision Inc ....F ....765 361-0247
Danville (G-7739)
Industra Sharp Inc ....G ....708 877-1200
Thornton (G-20873)
Industrial Maintenance & McHy ....G ....815 726-0030
Mokena (G-14874)
Industrial Tool and Repair ....G ....309 633-0939
Peoria (G-17389)
Innovative Gringing Inc ....G ....630 766-4567
Bensenville (G-1919)
Innovative Machine Inc ....G ....309 945-9445
Geneseo (G-10801)
▲ Insync Manufacturing LLC ....F ....815 304-6300
Kankakee (G-12626)
Inventive Mfg Inc ....F ....847 647-9500
Skokie (G-20018)
Irmko Tool Works Inc ....E ....630 350-7550
Bensenville (G-1923)
J & A Sheet Metal Shop Inc ....E ....773 276-3739
Chicago (G-5250)
▲ J & I Son Tool Company Inc ....G ....847 455-4200
Franklin Park (G-10500)
J & L Thread Grinding Inc ....G ....815 389-4644
South Beloit (G-20151)
J & S Machine Works Inc ....G ....708 344-2101
Melrose Park (G-14661)
J & S Tool Inc ....G ....
Chicago (G-5254)
J D Machining ....G ....847 428-8690
Gilberts (G-10925)
J K Manufacturing Co ....D ....708 563-2500
Bedford Park (G-1558)
J T Fennell Co Inc ....D ....309 274-2145
Chillicothe (G-7168)
J-Marcs Corporation ....F ....815 786-2293
Sandwich (G-19369)
Jacksonville Machine Inc ....D ....217 243-1119
Jacksonville (G-12396)
Jaday Industries ....F ....847 928-1033
Franklin Park (G-10504)
Jakes McHning Rbilding Svc Inc ....E ....630 892-3291
Aurora (G-1175)
▲ James Walker Mfg Co ....E ....708 754-4020
Glenwood (G-11217)
Janssen Machine Inc ....F ....815 877-9901
Loves Park (G-13950)
Jav Machine Craft Inc ....G ....708 867-8608
Chicago (G-5283)
Jay RS Steel & Welding Inc ....G ....847 949-9353
Mundelein (G-15514)
Jbw Machining Inc ....F ....847 451-0276
Franklin Park (G-10508)
Jda Aqua Cutting Inc ....G ....815 485-8028
New Lenox (G-15888)
▲ Jdb Machining Inc ....G ....708 749-9596
Forest View (G-10258)
▲ Jdb Manufacturing Company ....G ....708 749-9596
Forest View (G-10259)
Jem Tool & Manufacturing Co ....F ....630 595-1686
Bensenville (G-1927)
Jen-Sko-Vec Machining & Engrg ....G ....773 776-7400
Chicago (G-5290)
Jet Grinding & Manufacturing ....F ....847 956-8646
Arlington Heights (G-783)
Jet Industries Inc ....E ....773 586-8900
Chicago (G-5297)
Jewel Machine Inc ....G ....815 765-3636
Poplar Grove (G-17713)
Jim Sterner Machines ....G ....815 962-8983
Rockford (G-18445)
JMr Precision Machining Inc ....G ....847 279-3982
Mundelein (G-15515)
John & Helen Inc ....F ....815 654-1070
Loves Park (G-13953)
John H Best & Sons Inc ....E ....309 932-2124
Galva (G-10791)
Johnson Pattern & Mch Works ....E ....815 433-2775
Ottawa (G-16964)
Jones Garrison Sons Mch Works ....G ....618 847-2161
Fairfield (G-10147)
Jr Tech Inc ....G ....847 214-8860
Elgin (G-9086)
K & A Precision Machine Inc ....D ....847 998-1933
Glenview (G-11155)
K & B Machining ....G ....847 663-9534
Morton Grove (G-15208)
K & H Tool Co ....G ....630 766-4588
Bensenville (G-1931)
K & K Tool & Die Inc ....F ....309 829-4479
Bloomington (G-2187)
K D Industries Illinois Inc ....G ....309 854-7100
Kewanee (G-12691)
K D L Machining Inc ....G ....309 477-3036
Pekin (G-17271)
K P Enterprises Inc ....G ....630 509-2174
Bensenville (G-1933)
K R J Inc ....G ....309 925-5123
Tremont (G-20983)
K R N Machine and Laser Center ....G ....618 942-6064
Herrin (G-11750)
K&R Enterprises I Inc ....D ....847 502-3371
Lake Barrington (G-12815)
▲ K-B-K Tool and Mfg Inc ....F ....847 674-3636
Skokie (G-20020)
▲ K1 Speed-Illinois Inc ....G ....847 941-9400
Buffalo Grove (G-2715)
▲ Kaas Industries Inc ....G ....847 298-9106
Rosemont (G-19008)
Kaman Tool Corporation ....G ....708 652-9023
Cicero (G-7208)
Kaskaskia Tool and Machine Inc ....E ....618 475-3301
New Athens (G-15860)
Keene Technology Inc ....F ....815 624-8988
South Beloit (G-20154)
Keeper Corp ....G ....630 773-9393
Itasca (G-12292)
Kegley Machine Co ....G ....309 346-8914
Pekin (G-17272)
▲ Kelco Industries Inc ....G ....815 334-3600
Woodstock (G-22577)
Kemp Manufacturing Company ....E ....309 682-7292
Peoria (G-17395)
Kemper Industries ....G ....217 826-5712
Marshall (G-14324)
Kern Precision ....G ....331 979-0954
Addison (G-166)
KLM Tool Company ....E ....630 458-1700
Addison (G-170)
▲ Kocsis Brothers Machine Co ....D ....708 597-8110
Alsip (G-480)
Koenig Machine & Welding Inc ....G ....217 228-6538
Quincy (G-17849)
Koerner Aviation Inc ....G ....815 932-4222
Kankakee (G-12636)
Kohlert Manufacturing Corp ....G ....630 584-0013
Saint Charles (G-19204)
▲ Komax Corporation ....D ....847 537-6640
Buffalo Grove (G-2718)
Kopis Machine Co Inc ....E ....630 543-4138
Addison (G-173)
Kormex Metal Craft Inc ....E ....630 953-8856
Lombard (G-13818)
Kreis Tool & Mfg Co Inc ....E ....847 289-3700
Elgin (G-9092)
Kremer Precision Machine Inc ....F ....217 868-2627
Shumway (G-19932)
Kresser Precision Inds Inc ....G ....815 899-2202
Sycamore (G-20806)
▲ Kris Dee and Associates Inc ....D ....630 503-4093
South Elgin (G-20211)
Krygier Machine Company Inc ....G ....708 331-5255
South Holland (G-20284)
Kuester Tool & Die Inc ....E ....217 223-1955
Quincy (G-17851)
L A T Enterprise Inc ....G ....630 543-5533
Addison (G-174)
L K Beutel Machining Co Inc ....G ....847 895-5310
Schaumburg (G-19609)
L M C Automotive Inc ....G ....618 235-5242
Belleville (G-1647)
L M Machine Shop Inc ....G ....815 625-3256
Rock Falls (G-18141)
L T D Industries Inc ....E ....309 547-3251
Lewistown (G-13290)
L T Properties Inc ....G ....217 423-8772
Decatur (G-7904)
▲ L W Schneider Inc ....E ....815 875-3835
Princeton (G-17752)
L-V Industries Inc ....F ....630 595-9251
Bensenville (G-1936)
Lake County Technologies Inc ....G ....847 658-1330
Barrington (G-1285)
Lake County Tool Works North ....G ....847 662-4542
Wadsworth (G-21324)
Lake Sara Properties LLC ....G ....708 267-1187
Tinley Park (G-20928)
Lancer Manufacturing Inc ....F ....630 595-1150
Wood Dale (G-22389)
Lane Tool & Mfg Co Inc ....E ....847 622-1506
South Elgin (G-20216)
Lays Mining Service Inc ....E ....618 244-6570
Mount Vernon (G-15421)
▲ Leading Edge Group Inc ....C ....815 316-3500
Rockford (G-18464)
Lehman Fast Tech ....G ....847 742-5202
Elgin (G-9094)
Lemke Machine Products Inc ....F ....815 338-1560
Woodstock (G-22584)
Lenrok Industries Inc ....G ....630 628-1946
Addison (G-179)
Leppala Machining Inc ....G ....847 625-0270
Beach Park (G-1518)
▼ Lewis Machine & Tool Co ....D ....309 787-7151
Milan (G-14792)
Licon Inc ....G ....618 485-2222
Ashley (G-927)
Line Craft Tool Company Inc ....C ....630 932-1182
Lombard (G-13820)
Linne Machine Company Inc ....G ....217 446-5746
Danville (G-7747)
Lion Tool & Die Co ....F ....847 658-8898
Algonquin (G-397)
▲ Littell LLC ....E ....630 916-6662
Schaumburg (G-19620)
Livingston Products Inc ....F ....847 808-0900
Waukegan (G-21581)
Lorbern Mfg Inc ....E ....847 301-8600
Schaumburg (G-19623)
Lrm Grinding Co Inc ....D ....708 458-7878
Bridgeview (G-2504)
Luebbers Welding & Mfg Inc ....F ....618 594-2489
Carlyle (G-3056)
Lunquist Manufacturing Corp ....E ....815 874-2437
Rockford (G-18475)
M & J Manufacturing Co Inc ....F ....847 364-6066
Elk Grove Village (G-9601)
▲ M & R Precision Machining Inc ....E ....847 364-1050
Elk Grove Village (G-9602)
M & S Industrial Co Inc ....E ....773 252-1616
Chicago (G-5578)
M & W Grinding of Rockford ....G ....815 874-9481
Rockford (G-18476)
M S —action Machining Corp ....E ....815 344-3770
McHenry (G-14524)
Mac-Weld Inc ....G ....618 529-1828
Carbondale (G-3015)
Machine & Design ....G ....630 858-6416
Glen Ellyn (G-10979)
Machine Technology Inc ....F ....815 795-6818
Marseilles (G-14313)

S I C

Employee Codes: A=Over 500 employees, B=251-500
C=101-250, D=51-100, E=20-50, F=10-19, G=3-9
2017 Harris Illinois
Industrial Directory
1087

35 INDUSTRIAL AND COMMERCIAL MACHINERY AND COMPUTER EQUIPMENT SIC SECTION

**Machine Tool Acc & Mfg Co** ......G...... 773 489-0903
Chicago *(G-5592)*
**Machine Works of Decatur Inc** ......G...... 217 428-3896
Decatur *(G-7910)*
**Machined Concepts LLC** ......G...... 847 708-4923
Elgin *(G-9099)*
**Machined Metals Manufacturing** ......E...... 847 364-6116
Elk Grove Village *(G-9605)*
**Machinex Manufacturing Co Inc** ......G...... 630 766-4210
Bensenville *(G-1944)*
**Machining Systems Corporation** ......G...... 708 385-7903
Crestwood *(G-7493)*
▼ **Machining Technology Inc** ......G...... 815 469-0400
Lemont *(G-13240)*
**Madden Ventures Inc** ......G...... 847 487-0644
Mundelein *(G-15522)*
▼ **Magna-Lock Usa Inc** ......F...... 815 962-8700
Rockford *(G-18480)*
**Magnet-Schultz Amer Holdg LLC** ......G...... 630 789-0600
Westmont *(G-21901)*
▲ **Magnet-Schultz America Inc** ......D...... 630 789-0600
Westmont *(G-21902)*
▲ **Mah Machine Company** ......C...... 708 656-1826
Cicero *(G-7217)*
**Main Source Machining** ......G...... 815 962-8770
Rockford *(G-18481)*
**Mar-Fre Manufacturing Co** ......F...... 630 377-1022
Saint Charles *(G-19214)*
**Marathon Technologies Inc** ......E...... 847 378-8572
Elk Grove Village *(G-9611)*
**Marble Machine Inc** ......E...... 217 431-3014
Danville *(G-7751)*
**Marion Tool & Die Inc** ......D...... 309 266-6551
Morton *(G-15162)*
**Mark Lahey** ......G...... 217 243-4433
Jacksonville *(G-12401)*
**Marvel Machining Co Inc** ......G...... 630 350-0075
Bensenville *(G-1945)*
**Master Cut E D M Inc** ......G...... 847 534-0343
Schaumburg *(G-19634)*
**Master Hydraulics & Machining** ......F...... 847 895-5578
Schaumburg *(G-19635)*
**Matrix Machine & Tool Mfg** ......G...... 708 452-8707
River Grove *(G-18011)*
**Matrix Precision Corporation** ......G...... 773 283-1739
Chicago *(G-5655)*
▲ **Mattsn/Witt Precision Pdts Inc** ......E...... 847 382-7810
Lake Barrington *(G-12818)*
**MB Machine Inc** ......F...... 815 864-3555
Shannon *(G-19900)*
**MBR Tool Inc** ......G...... 847 671-4491
Schiller Park *(G-19848)*
**Mc Henry Machine Co Inc** ......G...... 815 875-1953
Princeton *(G-17753)*
**McArthur Machining Inc** ......G...... 847 838-6998
Antioch *(G-644)*
**McBride & Shoff Inc** ......E...... 309 367-4193
Metamora *(G-14744)*
▲ **Mechanical Devices Company** ......G...... 309 663-2843
Bloomington *(G-2195)*
▲ **Mechanical Products Corp** ......F...... 630 543-4842
Addison *(G-196)*
**Mechanical Tool & Engrg Co** ......C...... 815 397-4701
Rockford *(G-18490)*
**Medco Inc** ......F...... 847 296-3021
Des Plaines *(G-8231)*
**Merit Tool Engineering Co Inc** ......G...... 773 283-1114
Chicago *(G-5694)*
**Messer Machine** ......G...... 815 398-6248
Rockford *(G-18494)*
▲ **Meta TEC Development Inc** ......G...... 309 246-2960
Lacon *(G-12789)*
**Meta TEC of Illinois Inc** ......D...... 309 246-2960
Lacon *(G-12790)*
**Metal Component Machining** ......F...... 815 643-2207
Malden *(G-14164)*
**Metal Works Machine Inc** ......G...... 217 868-5111
Shumway *(G-19934)*
**Metals USA Rockford** ......F...... 815 874-8536
Rockford *(G-18497)*
**Meteer Manufacturing Co** ......G...... 217 636-8109
Athens *(G-941)*
**Metric Machine Shop Inc** ......G...... 847 439-9891
Elk Grove Village *(G-9623)*
**Metro East Manufacturing** ......F...... 618 233-0182
Swansea *(G-20778)*
**Micro Craft Manufacturing Co** ......F...... 847 679-2022
Skokie *(G-20038)*
**Microlution Inc** ......E...... 773 282-6495
Chicago *(G-5724)*
**Microtech Machine Inc** ......E...... 847 870-0707
Wheeling *(G-22104)*
**Midaco Corporation** ......E...... 847 593-8420
Elk Grove Village *(G-9626)*
**Midstate Manufacturing Company** ......C...... 309 342-9555
Galesburg *(G-10767)*
**Midway Grinding Inc** ......E...... 847 439-7424
Elk Grove Village *(G-9627)*
**Midway Machine & Tool Co Inc** ......G...... 708 385-3450
Alsip *(G-491)*
**Midwest Design & Automtn Inc** ......G...... 618 392-2892
Olney *(G-16781)*
**Midwest EDM Specialties Inc** ......G...... 815 521-2130
Channahon *(G-3581)*
**Midwest Hardfacing LLC** ......F...... 815 622-9420
Rock Falls *(G-18145)*
▲ **Midwest Machine Company Ltd** ......G...... 630 628-0485
Addison *(G-214)*
**Midwest Machine Service Inc** ......F...... 708 229-1122
Alsip *(G-494)*
**Midwest Machine Tool Inc** ......G...... 815 427-8665
Saint Anne *(G-19124)*
**Midwestern Mch Hydraulics Inc** ......F...... 618 246-9440
Mount Vernon *(G-15426)*
**Milans Machining & Mfg Co Inc** ......D...... 708 780-6600
Cicero *(G-7222)*
**Milco Precision Machining Inc** ......F...... 630 628-5730
Addison *(G-216)*
**Miller Roger Weston** ......G...... 217 352-0476
Champaign *(G-3514)*
**Mills Machine Inc** ......G...... 815 273-4707
Savanna *(G-19403)*
**Mills Machining** ......G...... 815 933-9193
Bradley *(G-2426)*
**Mitsubishi Heavy Inds Amer Inc** ......F...... 630 693-4700
Addison *(G-217)*
**Mk Systems Incorporated** ......F...... 847 709-6180
Elk Grove Village *(G-9632)*
**Moore Machine Works** ......G...... 815 625-0536
Sterling *(G-20600)*
**Moore-Addison Co** ......E...... 630 543-6744
Addison *(G-220)*
**Moran Auto Parts and Mch Sp** ......F...... 309 663-6449
Bloomington *(G-2203)*
▲ **Morgan Bronze Products Inc** ......D...... 847 526-6000
Lake Zurich *(G-13106)*
**Moultri Cnty Hstrcl/Gnlgcl Sct** ......F...... 217 728-4085
Sullivan *(G-20754)*
**Mt Carmel Machine Shop Inc** ......F...... 618 262-4591
Mount Carmel *(G-15275)*
**Mtech Cnc Machining Inc** ......G...... 224 848-0818
Lake Zurich *(G-13107)*
▲ **Multax Corporation** ......D...... 309 266-9765
Morton *(G-15170)*
**Mushro Machine & Tool Co** ......F...... 815 672-5848
Streator *(G-20697)*
**N Contour Concepts Inc** ......G...... 708 599-9571
Bridgeview *(G-2512)*
**N J Tech Inc** ......G...... 847 428-1001
Gilberts *(G-10928)*
**N K C Inc** ......G...... 630 628-9159
Addison *(G-224)*
**Napier Machine & Welding Inc** ......G...... 217 525-8740
Springfield *(G-20486)*
**National Component Sales Inc** ......F...... 847 439-0333
Arlington Heights *(G-808)*
**National Machine Repair Inc** ......F...... 708 672-7711
Crete *(G-7517)*
**National Tool & Machine Co** ......F...... 618 271-6445
East Saint Louis *(G-8762)*
**National Tool & Mfg Co** ......D...... 847 806-9800
Wheeling *(G-22105)*
**Natural Products Inc** ......F...... 847 509-5835
Northbrook *(G-16317)*
**ND Manifold** ......G...... 815 923-4305
Union *(G-21036)*
**Nelson-Rose Inc** ......D...... 760 744-7400
Hinsdale *(G-11954)*
**New Cie Inc** ......E...... 815 224-1511
Peru *(G-17522)*
**New Lenox Machine Co Inc** ......F...... 815 584-4866
Dwight *(G-8589)*
**Newssor Manufacturing Inc** ......G...... 618 259-1174
East Alton *(G-8606)*
▲ **Nicholas Machine & Tool Inc** ......G...... 847 298-2035
Rosemont *(G-19018)*
**Niese Walter Machine Mfg Co** ......G...... 773 774-7337
Chicago *(G-5915)*
**Njc Machine Co** ......F...... 708 442-6004
Lyons *(G-14042)*
**Nor Service Inc** ......E...... 815 232-8379
Freeport *(G-10676)*
**Northwest Mold & Machine Corp** ......G...... 847 690-1501
Elk Grove Village *(G-9656)*
**Northwest Tool Co Inc** ......G...... 630 350-4770
Bensenville *(G-1957)*
▲ **Norton Machine Co** ......G...... 217 748-6115
Rossville *(G-19050)*
**NS Precision Lathe Inc** ......G...... 708 867-5023
Maywood *(G-14432)*
▲ **Nu-Way Industries Inc** ......C...... 847 298-7710
Des Plaines *(G-8244)*
▲ **Numalliance - North Amer Inc** ......G...... 847 439-4500
Elk Grove Village *(G-9658)*
**O & L Machine Inc** ......G...... 815 963-6600
Rockford *(G-18524)*
**O Brien Bill** ......G...... 630 980-5571
Geneva *(G-10854)*
**O K Jobbers Inc** ......G...... 217 728-7378
Sullivan *(G-20756)*
**Octane Motorsports LLC** ......G...... 224 419-5460
Waukegan *(G-21598)*
**OHare Precision Metals LLC** ......E...... 847 640-6050
Arlington Heights *(G-811)*
**Oldendorf Machining & Fabg** ......G...... 708 946-2498
Beecher *(G-1600)*
**Olney Machine & Design Inc** ......F...... 618 392-6634
Olney *(G-16788)*
**Olon Industries Inc (us)** ......E...... 630 232-4705
Geneva *(G-10858)*
**Olson Machining Inc** ......E...... 815 675-2900
Spring Grove *(G-20354)*
**Oostman Fabricating & Wldg Inc** ......F...... 630 241-1315
Westmont *(G-21909)*
**Orat Inc** ......G...... 630 567-6728
Saint Charles *(G-19230)*
**Orbit Machining Company** ......E...... 847 678-1050
Schiller Park *(G-19856)*
**Orient Machining & Welding Inc** ......E...... 708 371-3500
Dixmoor *(G-8320)*
**Orion Tool Die & Machine Co** ......E...... 309 526-3303
Orion *(G-16835)*
**Osbornes Mch Weld Fabrication** ......G...... 217 795-4716
Argenta *(G-691)*
**P & A Driveline & Machine Inc** ......F...... 630 860-7474
Bensenville *(G-1962)*
**P & G Machine & Tool Inc** ......G...... 618 283-0273
Vandalia *(G-21119)*
◆ **P & H Manufacturing Co** ......D...... 217 774-2123
Shelbyville *(G-19911)*
**P M Armor Inc** ......E...... 847 797-9940
Mount Prospect *(G-15360)*
**P M Mfg Services Inc** ......G...... 630 553-6924
Yorkville *(G-22668)*
▲ **Pacific Bearing Corp** ......C...... 815 389-5600
Roscoe *(G-18911)*
**Paragon Automation Inc** ......F...... 847 593-0434
Elk Grove Village *(G-9669)*
**Parallel Machine Products Inc** ......F...... 847 359-1012
Palatine *(G-17063)*
**Paramount Sintered Pdts LLP** ......G...... 847 746-8866
Zion *(G-22695)*
**Park Engineering Inc** ......E...... 847 455-1424
Franklin Park *(G-10546)*
**Park Tool & Machine Co Inc** ......G...... 630 530-5110
Villa Park *(G-21275)*
**Parker Tool & Die Co** ......G...... 847 566-2229
Mundelein *(G-15541)*
**Parsons Company Inc** ......C...... 309 467-9100
Roanoke *(G-18053)*
**Part Stop Inc** ......G...... 618 377-5238
Bethalto *(G-2082)*
**Patkus Machine Co** ......G...... 815 398-7818
Rockford *(G-18530)*
**Patlin Enterprises Inc** ......F...... 815 675-6606
Spring Grove *(G-20355)*
▲ **Pauls Machine & Welding Corp** ......D...... 217 832-2541
Villa Grove *(G-21230)*
**PDQ Machine Inc** ......G...... 815 282-7575
Machesney Park *(G-14096)*
**Peoria Manufacturing Co Inc** ......G...... 708 429-4200
Tinley Park *(G-20938)*
**Performance Automotive** ......G...... 618 377-0020
Bethalto *(G-2083)*
**Performance Pattern & Mch Inc** ......E...... 309 676-0907
Peoria *(G-17427)*
**Peters Machine Inc** ......F...... 217 875-2578
Decatur *(G-7926)*
**Peters Machine Works Inc** ......F...... 708 496-3005
Oak Lawn *(G-16640)*

SIC SECTION 35 INDUSTRIAL AND COMMERCIAL MACHINERY AND COMPUTER EQUIPMENT

**Pgi Mfg LLC** D 800 821-3475
Rockford *(G-18534)*
**PH Tool Manufacturing** G 847 952-9441
Des Plaines *(G-8254)*
**Phillip Rodgers** G 815 877-5461
Loves Park *(G-13973)*
▲ **Phoenix Tool Corp** F 847 956-1886
Elk Grove Village *(G-9679)*
**Pioneer Grinding & Mfg Co** G 847 678-6565
Franklin Park *(G-10551)*
▲ **Piper Plastics Inc** D 847 367-0110
Libertyville *(G-13369)*
**Pittsfield Mch Tl & Wldg Co** G 217 656-4000
Payson *(G-17246)*
▲ **Planter Inc** D 773 637-7777
Chicago *(G-6135)*
**Plastak Inc** G 630 466-4100
Sugar Grove *(G-20730)*
**Playing With Fusion Inc** G 309 258-7259
Mackinaw *(G-14118)*
**PM Machine Shop** G 217 854-3504
Carlinville *(G-3046)*
**Pmb Industries Inc** G 708 442-4515
La Grange *(G-12742)*
**Popular Ridge Machine Met Cft** G 618 687-1656
Murphysboro *(G-15580)*
**Port Byron Machine Inc** G 309 523-9111
Port Byron *(G-17722)*
**Prairie Manufacturing Inc** G 815 498-1593
Somonauk *(G-20127)*
**Precision Dynamics Inc** F 815 877-1592
Machesney Park *(G-14099)*
**Precision Engineering & Dev Co** E 630 834-5956
Villa Park *(G-21278)*
**Precision Grinding and Mch Inc** G
Joliet *(G-12553)*
**Precision Grinding Inc** G 847 238-1000
Elk Grove Village *(G-9692)*
**Precision Ground** F 815 578-2613
Lakemoor *(G-13146)*
**Precision Inc** G 847 593-2947
Elk Grove Village *(G-9693)*
**Precision Laser Marking Inc** G 630 628-8575
Addison *(G-251)*
**Precision Machine and** F 618 997-8795
Marion *(G-14283)*
**Precision Machine Products** G 630 860-0861
Wood Dale *(G-22413)*
**Precision Machining & Tool Co** G 847 674-7111
Skokie *(G-20058)*
**Precision Masters** E 815 397-3894
Rockford *(G-18539)*
**Precision Metal Crafters Inc** F 847 816-3244
Libertyville *(G-13371)*
**Precision Metal Crafts Inc** G 815 254-2306
Plainfield *(G-17643)*
**Precision Plus Products Inc** G 815 459-1351
Crystal Lake *(G-7628)*
▲ **Premier Fabrication LLC** C 309 448-2338
Congerville *(G-7369)*
**Premier Tool & Machine Inc** G 618 445-9066
Albion *(G-365)*
**Premium Manufacturing Inc** E 309 787-3882
Rock Island *(G-18192)*
**Price Machine Inc** G 217 892-8958
Dewey *(G-8311)*
**Pride Machine & Tool Co Inc** F 708 343-7190
Melrose Park *(G-14684)*
**Pro Arc Inc** E 815 877-1804
Loves Park *(G-13977)*
**Pro-Qua Inc** G 630 543-5644
Addison *(G-258)*
**Production Manufacturing** G 217 256-4211
Warsaw *(G-21371)*
▲ **Production Tool Companies LLC** E 773 288-4400
Chicago *(G-6206)*
▲ **Prosco Inc** G 847 336-1323
Gurnee *(G-11493)*
**Prospan Manufacturing Co** G 630 860-1930
Bensenville *(G-1967)*
**Prospect Grinding Incorporated** G 847 229-9240
Wheeling *(G-22129)*
**Protech Design & Manufacturing** G 815 398-7520
Rockford *(G-18543)*
**Pull X Machines Inc 933** G 847 952-9977
Elgin *(G-9153)*
**Puskar Precision Machining Co** F 847 888-2929
Elgin *(G-9154)*
**Qc Components & Sales Inc** F 630 268-0644
Lombard *(G-13847)*
**Quadrant Tool and Mfg Co** E 847 352-6977
Schaumburg *(G-19707)*
**Quality Circle Machine Inc** G 708 474-1160
Lynwood *(G-14024)*
**Quality Cnc Incorporated** F 630 406-0101
Batavia *(G-1488)*
**Quality Fabricators Inc** D 630 543-0540
Addison *(G-264)*
**Quality Machine** G 708 499-0021
Oak Lawn *(G-16642)*
**Quality Machine Tool Services** G 847 776-0073
Schaumburg *(G-19708)*
**Quality Metal Products Inc** C 309 692-8014
Peoria *(G-17438)*
**Quality Metal Works Inc** G 309 379-5311
Stanford *(G-20552)*
▲ **Quality Tool Inc** G 847 288-9330
Franklin Park *(G-10567)*
**R & B Metal Products Inc** E 815 338-1890
Woodstock *(G-22603)*
**R & D Machine LLC** G 618 282-6262
Red Bud *(G-17946)*
**R & N Machine Co** F 708 841-5555
Riverdale *(G-18023)*
**R & S Steel Corporation** G 309 448-2645
Congerville *(G-7370)*
**R A E Tool and Manufacturing** G 815 485-2506
New Lenox *(G-15904)*
**R A R Machine & Manufacturing** E 630 260-9591
Chicago *(G-6264)*
**R C Sales & Manufacturing Inc** G 815 645-8898
Stillman Valley *(G-20626)*
**R D S Co** G 630 893-2990
Bloomingdale *(G-2129)*
**R G Hanson Company Inc** F 309 661-9200
Bloomington *(G-2217)*
**R K Precision Machine Inc** G 574 293-0231
Alsip *(G-516)*
**R L Lewis Industries Inc** E 309 353-7670
Pekin *(G-17286)*
**R M Armstrong & Son Inc** G 847 669-3988
Huntley *(G-12171)*
**R M Tool & Manufacturing Co** G 847 888-0433
Elgin *(G-9160)*
**R Machining Inc** G 217 532-2174
Butler *(G-2910)*
**R-M Industries Inc** F 630 543-3071
Addison *(G-267)*
**R/K Industries Inc** F 847 526-2222
Wauconda *(G-21498)*
**Radius Machine & Tool Inc** F 847 662-7690
Gurnee *(G-11497)*
**Rah Enterprises Inc** G 217 223-1970
Quincy *(G-17885)*
**Rajner Quality Machine Works** G 847 394-8999
Wheeling *(G-22131)*
**Ramco Tool & Manufacturing** F 847 639-9899
Cary *(G-3365)*
**Rand Jig Boring Inc** G 847 678-7416
Franklin Park *(G-10570)*
**Rapco Ltd** G 618 249-6614
Richview *(G-17981)*
**Raycar Gear & Machine Company** E 815 874-3948
Rockford *(G-18549)*
**Rays Machine & Mfg Co Inc** F 309 699-2121
East Peoria *(G-8730)*
**Reba Machine Corp** G 630 595-1272
Wood Dale *(G-22416)*
**Rebco Machine Specialties Inc** F 630 852-3419
Westmont *(G-21917)*
**Regent Automotive Engineering** G 773 889-5744
Chicago *(G-6323)*
**Reliance Tool Inc** G 815 636-2770
Loves Park *(G-13981)*
**Remmers Welding and Machine** G 815 689-2765
Cullom *(G-7684)*
**Reyco Precision Welding Inc** F 847 593-2947
Lake Zurich *(G-13122)*
**Reynolds Manufacturing Company** E 309 787-8600
Milan *(G-14803)*
**RF Mau Co** F 847 329-9731
Lincolnwood *(G-13533)*
▲ **Ri-Del Mfg Inc** D 312 829-8720
Chicago *(G-6349)*
**Rice Precision Machining** F 630 543-7220
Addison *(G-279)*
**Richard A Anderson** G 815 895-5627
Sycamore *(G-20814)*
**Richardson Manufacturing Co** D 217 546-2249
Springfield *(G-20513)*
**Riser Machine Corp** F 708 532-2313
New Lenox *(G-15907)*
**Rix Enterprise Inc** G 618 996-8237
Creal Springs *(G-7454)*
**Rj Cnc Works Inc** G 847 671-9120
Franklin Park *(G-10576)*
▼ **Rj Link International Inc** F 815 874-8110
Rockford *(G-18559)*
**RMH Enterprises** G 630 525-5552
Wheaton *(G-21976)*
**Rnw Machining Co Inc** G 847 635-6560
Rosemont *(G-19028)*
**Robert C Weisheit Co Inc** E 630 766-1213
Glendale Heights *(G-11065)*
**Rockford Burrall Mch Co Inc** E 815 877-7428
Rockford *(G-18569)*
**Rockford Jobbing Service Inc** G 815 398-8661
Rockford *(G-18576)*
**Rockford Linear Actuation** G 815 986-4400
Rockford *(G-18577)*
**Rockford Precision Machine** F 815 873-1018
Rockford *(G-18582)*
**Rockford Secondary Co** G 815 398-0401
Rockford *(G-18586)*
**Rockford Tool and Mfg Co** F 815 398-5876
Rockford *(G-18588)*
**Roe Machine Inc** E 618 983-5524
West Frankfort *(G-21817)*
▲ **Rogers Precision Machining** F 815 233-0065
Freeport *(G-10685)*
**Rogus Tool Inc** G 847 824-5939
Des Plaines *(G-8268)*
**Rohbi Enterprises Inc** G 708 343-2004
Broadview *(G-2611)*
**Roll Rite Inc** G 815 645-8600
Davis Junction *(G-7814)*
**Roll-Kraft Northern Inc** G 815 469-0205
Frankfort *(G-10359)*
**Romed Industries Corporation** G 847 362-3900
Lake Zurich *(G-13124)*
**Romtech Machining Inc** G 630 543-7039
Addison *(G-280)*
**Roscoe Tool & Manufacturing** E 815 633-8808
Roscoe *(G-18918)*
**Royal Machine Works Inc** G 815 465-6879
Grant Park *(G-11315)*
**RT Blackhawk Mch Pdts Inc** G 815 389-3632
South Beloit *(G-20167)*
**Runge Enterprises Inc** G 630 365-2000
Elburn *(G-8909)*
**Rusco Manufacturing Inc** F 815 654-3930
Machesney Park *(G-14106)*
**Rutherford & Associates** G 630 365-5263
Saint Charles *(G-19257)*
**S & B Jig Grinding** G 815 654-7907
Loves Park *(G-13990)*
**S & D Development & Prototype** F 847 872-7257
Zion *(G-22696)*
**S & J Machine Inc** G 815 297-1594
Freeport *(G-10686)*
**S & K Boring Inc** G 815 227-4394
Rockford *(G-18602)*
**S & S Machining Services Inc** G 708 758-8300
Lynwood *(G-14026)*
**S & W Machine Works Inc** G 708 597-6043
Alsip *(G-526)*
**S D Custom Machining** G 618 544-7007
Robinson *(G-18072)*
**S&R Precision Machine LLC** F 815 469-6544
Frankfort *(G-10360)*
**Saliba Industries Inc** G 847 680-2266
Lake Forest *(G-12955)*
▼ **Sandbagger LLC** D 630 876-2400
Elmhurst *(G-9934)*
**Sandbagger Corp** F 630 876-2400
Elmhurst *(G-9935)*
**Sandoval Machine Works Inc** G 618 247-3588
Sandoval *(G-19358)*
**Sanks Machining Inc** G 618 635-8279
Staunton *(G-20557)*
**Sas Industrial Machinery Inc** G 847 455-5526
Franklin Park *(G-10583)*
**Schmid Tool & Engineering Corp** E 630 333-1733
Villa Park *(G-21283)*
**Schram Enterprises Inc** E 708 345-2252
Melrose Park *(G-14693)*
**Schultes Precision Mfg Inc** D 847 465-0300
Buffalo Grove *(G-2763)*
**Scot Industries Inc** D 630 466-7591
Sugar Grove *(G-20734)*

SIC

Employee Codes: A=Over 500 employees, B=251-500
C=101-250, D=51-100, E=20-50, F=10-19, G=3-9
2017 Harris Illinois
Industrial Directory
1089

35 INDUSTRIAL AND COMMERCIAL MACHINERY AND COMPUTER EQUIPMENT SIC SECTION

**SEC Design Technologies Inc** ............F ....... 847 680-0439
Libertyville *(G-13378)*
◆ **Senior Holdings Inc**............C ....... 630 837-1811
Bartlett *(G-1373)*
**Senior Operations LLC**............A ....... 630 837-1811
Bartlett *(G-1374)*
▲ **Senior Operations LLC**............B ....... 630 837-1811
Bartlett *(G-1375)*
**Senior PLC**............G ....... 630 372-3511
Bartlett *(G-1376)*
**Service Auto Supply**............F ....... 309 444-9704
Washington *(G-21392)*
**Service Machine Company Inc**............F ....... 815 654-2310
Loves Park *(G-13992)*
**Service Machine Jobs**............G ....... 815 986-3033
Rockford *(G-18613)*
**Share Machine Inc**............F ....... 630 906-1810
Aurora *(G-1216)*
▲ **Shredderhotlinecom Company**............C ....... 815 674-5802
Streator *(G-20701)*
**Sigma Tool & Machining**............G ....... 815 874-0500
Rockford *(G-18617)*
**Sikora Automation Incorporated**............G ....... 630 833-0298
Addison *(G-291)*
**Sikora Precision Inc**............G ....... 847 468-0900
Elgin *(G-9180)*
**Silver Machine Shop Inc**............G ....... 217 359-5717
Champaign *(G-3540)*
**Skild Manufacturing Inc**............E ....... 847 437-1717
Elk Grove Village *(G-9741)*
**Smith and Son Machine Shop**............G ....... 217 260-3257
Broadlands *(G-2550)*
**Sobot Tool & Manufacturing Co**............E ....... 847 480-0560
Northbrook *(G-16365)*
▲ **Sollami Company**............E ....... 618 988-1521
Herrin *(G-11755)*
**Solutions Manufacturing Inc**............E ....... 847 310-4506
Hoffman Estates *(G-12057)*
**Sonic Manufacturing Corp**............F ....... 847 228-0015
Elk Grove Village *(G-9743)*
**Source United LLC**............G ....... 847 956-1459
Elk Grove Village *(G-9745)*
**Southern IL Crankshaft Inc**............F ....... 618 282-4100
Red Bud *(G-17949)*
**Southern IL Precision**............G ....... 618 643-3340
Mc Leansboro *(G-14467)*
**Southern Illinois Crankshafts**............F ....... 618 282-4100
Ruma *(G-19089)*
**Southwest Tool & Machine**............G ....... 708 349-4441
Orland Park *(G-16894)*
**Southwick Machine & Design Co**............G ....... 309 949-2868
Colona *(G-7348)*
**Sparks Fiberglass Inc**............F ....... 309 848-0077
Port Byron *(G-17725)*
**Spec Check LLC**............G ....... 773 270-0003
Mundelein *(G-15559)*
**Specialty Enterprises Inc**............G ....... 630 595-7808
Franklin Park *(G-10592)*
**Spectrum Machining Co**............E ....... 630 562-9400
West Chicago *(G-21776)*
**Spyco Industries Inc**............E ....... 630 655-5900
Burr Ridge *(G-2881)*
**Spytek Aerospace Corporation**............G ....... 847 318-7515
Bensenville *(G-1997)*
▲ **Sst Forming Roll Inc**............G ....... 847 215-6812
Buffalo Grove *(G-2775)*
**St Charles Screw Products Inc**............G ....... 815 943-8060
Harvard *(G-11647)*
**Standard Machine & Tool Corp**............F ....... 309 762-6431
Moline *(G-14972)*
▲ **Stanley Machining & Tool Corp**............D ....... 847 426-4560
Carpentersville *(G-3303)*
**Starmont Manufacturing Co**............G ....... 815 939-1041
Kankakee *(G-12653)*
**Sterling Tool & Manufacturing**............G ....... 847 304-1800
Barrington *(G-1305)*
**Steve Green**............G ....... 847 623-6327
Waukegan *(G-21619)*
**Strategic Mfg Partner LLC**............G ....... 262 878-5213
Northbrook *(G-16372)*
**Streator Machine Company**............G ....... 815 672-2436
Streator *(G-20705)*
**Stuart Moore Racing Ltd**............G ....... 847 949-9100
Mundelein *(G-15561)*
**Stuhlman Family LLC**............G ....... 815 436-2432
Plainfield *(G-17655)*
**Suburban Indus Tl & Mfg Co**............F ....... 708 597-7788
Alsip *(G-531)*
**Suburban Machine & Tool**............G ....... 815 469-2221
Mokena *(G-14906)*
**Suburban Machine Corporation**............E ....... 847 808-9095
Wheeling *(G-22158)*
**Sugar River Machine Shop**............E ....... 815 624-0214
South Beloit *(G-20169)*
**Summit Mold Inc**............G ....... 815 865-5809
Davis *(G-7807)*
**Supreme Manufacturing Company**............E ....... 847 297-8212
Des Plaines *(G-8283)*
**Swebco Mfg Inc**............E ....... 815 636-7160
Machesney Park *(G-14110)*
**Swiss E D M Wirecut Inc**............F ....... 847 459-4310
Prospect Heights *(G-17785)*
▲ **Sycamore Precision**............D ....... 815 784-5151
Genoa *(G-10884)*
**Symbol Tool Inc**............G ....... 847 674-1080
Skokie *(G-20098)*
**T & K Precision Grinding**............G ....... 708 450-0565
Melrose Park *(G-14699)*
**T & K Tool & Manufacturing Co**............G ....... 815 338-0954
Woodstock *(G-22617)*
▲ **T & L Mfg Corporation**............E ....... 630 898-7100
Aurora *(G-1220)*
**T & T Machine Shop**............G ....... 847 244-2020
Gurnee *(G-11511)*
**T R Machine Inc**............E ....... 815 865-5711
Davis *(G-7808)*
**T/J Fabricators Inc**............D ....... 630 543-2293
Addison *(G-305)*
**Tag-Barton LLC**............G ....... 217 428-0711
Decatur *(G-7948)*
**Tait Machine Tool Inc**............G ....... 815 932-2011
Kankakee *(G-12656)*
**Tal Mar Custom Met Fabricators**............D ....... 708 371-0333
Crestwood *(G-7505)*
**Tane Corporation**............G ....... 847 705-7125
Palatine *(G-17078)*
**Tanko Bros Screw Mch Pdts Corp**............F ....... 708 755-8823
S Chicago Hts *(G-19113)*
**Tar-B Precision Machining Corp**............G ....... 630 521-9771
Bensenville *(G-2000)*
**Target Laser & Machining Inc**............E ....... 815 963-6706
Rockford *(G-18641)*
**Tarney Inc**............E ....... 773 235-0331
Chicago *(G-6677)*
**Taylor Design Inc**............G ....... 815 389-3991
Roscoe *(G-18924)*
**Taylor Made Machining Inc**............G ....... 815 339-6267
Mark *(G-14300)*
**Tazewell Machine Works Inc**............C ....... 309 347-3181
Pekin *(G-17291)*
**Tbw Machining Inc**............F ....... 847 524-1501
Schaumburg *(G-19754)*
**TDS Machining Inc**............F ....... 630 964-0004
Darien *(G-7803)*
**Tech-Max Machine Inc**............E ....... 630 875-0054
Itasca *(G-12365)*
**Technical Metals Inc**............D ....... 815 692-4643
Fairbury *(G-10133)*
**Telco Machine & Manufacturing**............E ....... 773 725-4441
Chicago *(G-6689)*
**Telco Machine & Manufacturing**............G ....... 773 725-4441
Chicago *(G-6690)*
**Temco Grinding Inc**............F ....... 815 282-9405
Loves Park *(G-13999)*
**Tent Maker Industrial Sup Inc**............G ....... 847 469-6070
Wauconda *(G-21509)*
**Ter-Son Corporation**............D ....... 309 274-6227
Chillicothe *(G-7171)*
**Ternkirst Tl & Die & Mch Works**............F ....... 847 437-8360
Elk Grove Village *(G-9776)*
**Thomason Machine Works Inc**............G ....... 815 874-8217
Rockford *(G-18649)*
**Thompson Industries Inc**............E ....... 815 899-6670
Sycamore *(G-20819)*
**Threads Up Inc**............G ....... 630 595-2297
Bensenville *(G-2002)*
**Thryselius Machining Inc**............F ....... 630 365-9191
Elburn *(G-8915)*
**Thunder Tool Corp**............F ....... 708 544-4742
Broadview *(G-2616)*
**Thunderbird LLC**............G ....... 847 718-9300
Elk Grove Village *(G-9778)*
**Tibor Machine Products Inc**............D ....... 708 499-0017
Bridgeview *(G-2534)*
**Tibor Machine Products Inc**............E ....... 309 786-3052
Rock Island *(G-18207)*
**Tinney Tool & Machine Co**............G ....... 618 236-7273
Belleville *(G-1679)*
**Titan Tool Works LLC**............F ....... 630 221-1080
Carol Stream *(G-3255)*
**Tnp Machinery Co Inc**............G ....... 708 344-7750
Westchester *(G-21858)*
**Tolerance Manufacturing Inc**............F ....... 847 244-8836
Waukegan *(G-21629)*
**Tolerances Grinding Co Inc**............E ....... 630 543-6066
Addison *(G-317)*
**Tomenson Machine Works Inc**............D ....... 630 377-7670
West Chicago *(G-21782)*
**Tomko Machine Works Inc**............G ....... 630 244-0902
Lemont *(G-13266)*
**Tomsons Products Inc**............G ....... 708 479-7030
Mokena *(G-14912)*
**Tool Rite Industries Inc**............G ....... 630 406-6161
Batavia *(G-1508)*
**Toolex Corporation**............G ....... 630 458-0001
Addison *(G-318)*
**Top Notch Tool & Supply Inc**............G ....... 815 633-6295
Cherry Valley *(G-3648)*
▲ **Torrence Machine & Tool Co**............G ....... 815 469-1850
Mokena *(G-14913)*
**Total Titanium Inc**............E ....... 618 473-2429
Red Bud *(G-17950)*
**Toth Automotive**............F ....... 708 474-5137
Lansing *(G-13190)*
**Tower Tool & Engineering Inc**............F ....... 815 654-1115
Machesney Park *(G-14112)*
**Traco Industries Inc**............G ....... 815 675-6603
Spring Grove *(G-20371)*
**Trailers Inc**............G ....... 217 472-6000
Chapin *(G-3588)*
▲ **Transcedar Limited**............E ....... 618 262-4153
Mount Carmel *(G-15284)*
▲ **Traxco Inc**............G ....... 847 669-1545
Huntley *(G-12180)*
**Trident Machine Co**............G ....... 815 968-1585
Rockford *(G-18657)*
**Trinity Machined Products Inc**............E ....... 630 876-6992
Aurora *(G-1090)*
**Triple Edge Manufacturing Inc**............G ....... 847 468-9156
South Elgin *(G-20230)*
**Triwire Inc**............G ....... 815 633-7707
Loves Park *(G-14004)*
**Tru-Cut Machine Incorporated**............G ....... 815 422-5047
Saint Anne *(G-19127)*
**Tru-Cut Production Inc**............G ....... 815 335-2215
Winnebago *(G-22298)*
**Tru-Vu Monitors Inc**............G ....... 847 259-2344
Arlington Heights *(G-859)*
▲ **Trufab Group USA LLC**............E ....... 630 994-3286
Schaumburg *(G-19775)*
**Tsd Manufacturing Co Inc**............F ....... 630 238-8750
Elk Grove Village *(G-9794)*
**Turbo Tool & Mold Co**............G ....... 708 615-1730
Broadview *(G-2618)*
**U S Machine & Tool**............G ....... 847 740-0077
Hainesville *(G-11524)*
**Uhlar Inc**............G ....... 815 961-0970
Rockford *(G-18659)*
**Uhlir Manufacturing Corp**............G ....... 773 376-5289
Chicago *(G-6804)*
▲ **Ulrich Kaeppler**............G ....... 847 290-0220
Elk Grove Village *(G-9795)*
**Ultimate Machining & Engrg Inc**............E ....... 815 439-8361
Plainfield *(G-17660)*
**Ultra Specialty Holdings Inc**............E ....... 847 437-8110
Elk Grove Village *(G-9796)*
**Ultra-Metric Tool Co**............F ....... 773 281-4200
Chicago *(G-6808)*
**Umw Inc**............F ....... 847 352-5252
Schaumburg *(G-19778)*
**United Craftsmen Ltd**............F ....... 815 626-7802
Sterling *(G-20618)*
**United Machine Works Inc**............G ....... 847 352-5252
Schaumburg *(G-19781)*
**United Maint Wldg & McHy C**............F ....... 708 458-1705
Bedford Park *(G-1588)*
**Universal-Spc Inc**............G ....... 847 742-4400
Elgin *(G-9220)*
◆ **US Hose Corp**............D ....... 815 886-1140
Romeoville *(G-18874)*
**USA Industrial Export Corp**............G ....... 312 391-5552
Northbrook *(G-16381)*
**V & A Manufacturing**............G ....... 630 595-1072
Bensenville *(G-2011)*
**V & L Enterprises Inc**............F ....... 847 541-1760
Wheeling *(G-22174)*
**V Brothers Machine Co**............E ....... 708 652-0062
Cicero *(G-7243)*
**V W Broaching Service Inc**............F ....... 773 533-9000
Chicago *(G-6869)*

# 36 ELECTRONIC AND OTHER ELECTRICAL EQUIPMENT AND COMPONENTS, EXCEPT COMPUTER

Vandeventer Mfg Co Inc .......................... E ...... 630 879-2511
Batavia *(G-1515)*
Vari-Op Company ................................. G ...... 847 623-7667
Waukegan *(G-21637)*
Variable Operations Tech Inc ................... E ...... 815 479-8528
Crystal Lake *(G-7672)*
▲ Vector Engineering & Mfg Corp ............... E ...... 708 474-3900
Lansing *(G-13192)*
Vek Screw Machine Products ................... G ...... 630 543-5557
Addison *(G-338)*
Vicari Tool & Plastics Inc ........................ G ...... 847 671-9430
Franklin Park *(G-10622)*
Visos Machine Shop & Mfg ...................... G ...... 630 372-3925
Streamwood *(G-20680)*
W & K Machining Inc ............................. G ...... 708 430-9000
Alsip *(G-542)*
W-D Tool Engineering Company ............... F ...... 773 638-2688
Chicago *(G-6928)*
Wabel Tool Company ............................. E ...... 217 429-3656
Decatur *(G-7958)*
Wachs Technical Services Inc .................. E ...... 847 537-8800
Wheeling *(G-22179)*
Walach Manufacturing Co Inc .................. F ...... 773 836-2060
Chicago *(G-6935)*
▲ Walco Tool & Engineering Corp ............. D ...... 815 834-0225
Romeoville *(G-18877)*
Wallys Precision Machining ..................... G ...... 708 205-2950
Melrose Park *(G-14707)*
Walt Machine and Tool Inc ...................... G ...... 815 754-6484
Cortland *(G-7396)*
Walter Tool & Mfg Inc ............................. F ...... 847 697-7230
Elgin *(G-9227)*
▲ Warner Industries Inc .......................... D ...... 708 458-0627
Bedford Park *(G-1590)*
Warner Machine Products Inc .................. G ...... 815 338-2100
Woodstock *(G-22622)*
Weber Metal Products Inc ....................... G ...... 815 844-3169
Chenoa *(G-3636)*
West Machine Products Inc .................... E ...... 847 740-2404
Round Lake *(G-19070)*
▲ West Side Machine Inc ........................ F ...... 630 243-1069
Lemont *(G-13269)*
Whale Manufacturing Inc ........................ G ...... 847 357-9192
Lombard *(G-13884)*
Wherry Machine & Welding Inc ................ G ...... 309 828-5423
Bloomington *(G-2235)*
▲ White Racker Co Inc ........................... G ...... 847 758-1640
Elk Grove Village *(G-9812)*
Wilczak Industrial Parts Inc ..................... G ...... 847 260-5559
Franklin Park *(G-10629)*
William Davis & Co ................................ G ...... 847 395-6860
Antioch *(G-664)*
Willoughbys Auto & Mch Sp .................... G ...... 815 448-2281
Mazon *(G-14441)*
Wilmouth Machine Works Inc .................. G ...... 618 372-3189
Brighton *(G-2546)*
Wilson Tool Corporation ......................... E ...... 815 226-0147
Rockford *(G-18685)*
Wirco Inc ............................................ D ...... 217 398-3200
Champaign *(G-3561)*
Wk Machine ........................................ G ...... 618 426-3423
Campbell Hill *(G-2979)*
Woods Mfg and Machining Co ................. F ...... 847 982-9585
Skokie *(G-20112)*
World Class Tool & Machine .................... G ...... 815 962-2081
Sterling *(G-18689)*
Wright Technologies Inc ......................... G ...... 847 439-4150
Elk Grove Village *(G-9817)*
▲ X-Cel Technologies Inc ........................ E ...... 708 802-7400
Tinley Park *(G-20957)*
X-Tech Innovations Inc ........................... G ...... 815 962-4127
Rockford *(G-18690)*
Xact Wire EDM Corp .............................. F ...... 847 516-0903
Cary *(G-3379)*
▼ Z & L Machining Inc ........................... E ...... 847 623-9500
Waukegan *(G-21643)*
Z-Tech Inc .......................................... G ...... 815 335-7395
Winnebago *(G-22299)*
Zeco Inc ............................................. G ...... 847 446-1413
Northfield *(G-16423)*

## 36 ELECTRONIC AND OTHER ELECTRICAL EQUIPMENT AND COMPONENTS, EXCEPT COMPUTER

### 3612 Power, Distribution & Specialty Transformers

A J Smoy Co Inc .................................. E ...... 773 775-8282
Schaumburg *(G-19419)*
Actown-Electrocoil Inc ........................... G
Spring Grove *(G-20324)*
Aldonex Inc ........................................ F ...... 708 547-5663
Bellwood *(G-1693)*
American Cips .................................... G ...... 618 393-5641
Olney *(G-16759)*
Anderson Engrg New Prague Inc ............. G ...... 630 736-0900
Streamwood *(G-20643)*
Audio Video Electronics LLC ................... G ...... 847 983-4761
Skokie *(G-19961)*
Coiltechnic Inc .................................... F ...... 815 675-9260
Spring Grove *(G-20331)*
Communication Coil Inc ......................... D ...... 847 671-1333
Schiller Park *(G-19815)*
Cymatics Inc ....................................... G ...... 630 420-7117
Naperville *(G-15640)*
Dresser Inc ........................................ D ...... 847 437-5940
Elk Grove Village *(G-9435)*
Dual Voltage Distributors ....................... G ...... 847 519-1201
Schaumburg *(G-19509)*
Equus Power I LP ................................. F ...... 847 908-2878
Schaumburg *(G-19518)*
▲ Ferrite International Company ............. E ...... 847 249-4900
Wadsworth *(G-21322)*
Forest Electric Company ........................ E ...... 708 681-0180
Melrose Park *(G-14639)*
Gsg Industries .................................... F ...... 618 544-7976
Robinson *(G-18063)*
Hubbell Power Systems Inc .................... F ...... 618 797-5000
Edwardsville *(G-8803)*
Ibt Inc ............................................... G ...... 618 244-5353
Mount Vernon *(G-15413)*
▲ Inglot Electronics Corp ....................... D ...... 773 286-5881
Chicago *(G-5192)*
▲ Intermatic Incorporated ...................... A ...... 815 675-2321
Spring Grove *(G-20337)*
Invenergy Wind Fin Co III LLC ................. G ...... 312 224-1400
Chicago *(G-5231)*
Ipr Systems Inc ................................... G ...... 708 385-7500
Alsip *(G-474)*
▲ Lenco Electronics Inc ......................... E ...... 815 344-2900
McHenry *(G-14520)*
▲ Light To Form LLC ............................. E ...... 847 498-5832
Northbrook *(G-16296)*
▲ Lumenergi Inc .................................. E ...... 866 921-4652
Chicago *(G-5564)*
Magnetic Coil Manufacturing Co .............. E ...... 630 787-1948
Wood Dale *(G-22395)*
Magnetic Devices Inc ............................ G ...... 815 459-0077
Crystal Lake *(G-7605)*
Marvel Electric Corporation .................... D ...... 773 327-2644
Chicago *(G-5638)*
Marvel Electric Corporation .................... E ...... 847 671-0632
Schiller Park *(G-19846)*
Methode Development Co ...................... D ...... 708 867-6777
Chicago *(G-5703)*
Micron Engineering Co .......................... G ...... 815 455-2888
Crystal Lake *(G-7611)*
▲ Micron Industries Corporation .............. F ...... 630 516-1222
Oak Brook *(G-16544)*
Micron Industries Corporation ................. D ...... 815 380-2222
Sterling *(G-20599)*
▲ Mitsubishi Elc Automtn Inc .................. C ...... 847 478-2100
Vernon Hills *(G-21183)*
▲ Newhaven Display Intl Inc ................... E ...... 847 844-8795
Elgin *(G-9118)*
◆ Olsun Electrics Corporation .................. G ...... 815 678-2421
Richmond *(G-17968)*
Pactra Corp ........................................ G ...... 847 281-0308
Vernon Hills *(G-21187)*
Peterson Elc Panl Mfg Co Inc .................. F ...... 708 449-2270
Berkeley *(G-2048)*
Powell Industries Inc ............................. F ...... 708 409-1200
Northlake *(G-16449)*
▲ Power House Tool Inc ......................... E ...... 815 727-6301
Joliet *(G-12552)*
Precision Components Inc ...................... D ...... 630 462-9110
Saint Charles *(G-19240)*

Psytronics Inc ..................................... G ...... 847 719-1371
Lake Zurich *(G-13118)*
▲ Radionic Industries Inc ....................... C ...... 773 804-0100
Chicago *(G-6282)*
Relay Services Mfg Corp ....................... F ...... 773 252-2700
Chicago *(G-6327)*
▲ Robertson Transformer Co ................... E ...... 708 388-2315
Crestwood *(G-7500)*
▲ Saachi Inc ....................................... G ...... 630 775-1700
Roselle *(G-18971)*
Saturn Electrical Services Inc .................. G ...... 630 980-0300
Roselle *(G-18973)*
▼ Simplex Inc ..................................... C ...... 217 483-1600
Springfield *(G-20526)*
Storage Battery Systems LLC ................. G ...... 630 221-1700
Carol Stream *(G-3251)*
▲ Thomas Research Products LLC ........... F ...... 224 654-8626
Elgin *(G-9211)*
▲ Transformer Manufacturers Inc ............. E ...... 708 457-1200
Norridge *(G-16110)*
U S Co-Tronics Corp ............................. E ...... 815 692-3204
Fairbury *(G-10134)*
▲ V and F Transformer Corp .................... G ...... 630 497-8070
Bartlett *(G-1384)*
Wicc Ltd ............................................ D ...... 309 444-4125
Washington *(G-21396)*

### 3613 Switchgear & Switchboard Apparatus

A C Gentrol Inc ................................... E ...... 309 274-5486
Chillicothe *(G-7160)*
▲ Accu-Fab Incorporated ....................... E ...... 847 541-4230
Wheeling *(G-21998)*
Agnes & Chris Gulik ............................. G ...... 847 931-9641
Elgin *(G-8940)*
AKD Controls Inc ................................. G ...... 815 633-4586
Machesney Park *(G-14053)*
▲ Appleton Grp LLC .............................. E ...... 847 268-6000
Rosemont *(G-18989)*
Automated Systems & Control Co ............ G ...... 847 735-8310
Lake Bluff *(G-12834)*
◆ Boltswitch Inc .................................. E ...... 815 459-6900
Crystal Lake *(G-7542)*
Cable Electric Company Inc .................... G ...... 708 458-8900
Oak Lawn *(G-16609)*
Calo Corporation .................................. E ...... 630 879-2202
North Aurora *(G-16122)*
CCI Power Supplies LLC ........................ E ...... 847 362-6500
Palatine *(G-17008)*
Chicago Switchboard Co Inc ................... E ...... 630 833-2266
Elmhurst *(G-9848)*
Clark Tashaunda .................................. G ...... 708 247-8274
Calumet Park *(G-2958)*
Control Panels Inc ................................ F ...... 815 654-6000
Rockford *(G-18323)*
▲ Control Solutions LLC ........................ D ...... 630 806-7062
Aurora *(G-984)*
Control Works Inc ................................ G ...... 630 444-1942
Saint Charles *(G-19163)*
Custom Power Products Inc .................... F ...... 309 249-2704
Edelstein *(G-8779)*
Cymatics Inc ....................................... G ...... 630 420-7117
Naperville *(G-15640)*
D/C Industries LLC ............................... G ...... 630 876-1100
West Chicago *(G-21689)*
David Jeskey ...................................... G ...... 630 659-6337
Saint Charles *(G-19168)*
Deif Inc ............................................. G ...... 970 530-2261
Wood Dale *(G-22359)*
Don Johns Inc ..................................... E ...... 630 326-9650
Batavia *(G-1439)*
▲ E N M Company ................................ D ...... 773 775-8400
Chicago *(G-4667)*
Eaton Corporation ................................ A ...... 217 732-3131
Lincoln *(G-13409)*
Elcon Inc ........................................... E ...... 815 467-9500
Minooka *(G-14840)*
◆ Elenco Electronics Inc ........................ E ...... 847 541-3800
Wheeling *(G-22046)*
Elm Products Corp ............................... G ...... 847 336-0020
Waukegan *(G-21557)*
◆ Emac Inc ........................................ E ...... 618 529-4525
Carbondale *(G-3006)*
◆ Enercon Engineering Inc ..................... C ...... 800 218-8831
East Peoria *(G-8708)*
Enercon Engineering Inc ....................... C ...... 309 694-1418
East Peoria *(G-8709)*
Engineered Fluid Inc ............................. F ...... 618 533-1351
Centralia *(G-3413)*
Eunice Larry ....................................... G ...... 708 339-5678
South Holland *(G-20268)*

# 36 ELECTRONIC AND OTHER ELECTRICAL EQUIPMENT AND COMPONENTS, EXCEPT COMPUTER

Excel Ltd Inc .................................... G ...... 847 543-9138
 Grayslake (G-11336)
Fixture Company ............................... G ...... 847 214-3100
 Chicago (G-4854)
Fox Controls Inc ................................ E ...... 847 464-5096
 Elgin (G-9040)
Fuseco ............................................... G ...... 847 749-4158
 Rolling Meadows (G-18731)
▼ G & F Manufacturing Co Inc ............ E ...... 708 424-4170
 Oak Lawn (G-16621)
General Electric Company ................. E ...... 630 334-0054
 Oak Brook (G-16519)
General Electric Company ................. C ...... 309 664-1513
 Bloomington (G-2170)
▲ Grayhill Inc .................................... B ...... 708 354-1040
 La Grange (G-12734)
▲ Gus Berthold Electric Company ..... E ...... 312 243-5767
 Chicago (G-5013)
Honeywell International Inc ................ G ...... 815 235-5500
 Freeport (G-10664)
Honeywell International Inc ................ D ...... 815 235-5500
 Freeport (G-10665)
Hubbell Power Systems Inc ............... G ...... 618 797-5000
 Edwardsville (G-8804)
Illinois Switchboard Corp .................... F ...... 630 543-0910
 Addison (G-152)
Illinois Tool Works Inc ........................ C ...... 847 876-9400
 Des Plaines (G-8208)
Industrial Electric Svc Inc ................... G ...... 708 997-2090
 Bartlett (G-1356)
Inland Tech Holdings LLC .................. G ...... 618 476-7678
 Millstadt (G-14827)
Inman Electric Motors Inc .................. G ...... 815 223-2288
 La Salle (G-12778)
Its Solar LLC ..................................... G ...... 618 476-7678
 Millstadt (G-14828)
ITT Water & Wastewater USA Inc ...... G ...... 847 966-3700
 Morton Grove (G-15205)
J & A Sheet Metal Shop Inc ............... E ...... 773 276-3739
 Chicago (G-5250)
Jemison Elc Box Swtchboard Inc ....... G ...... 815 459-4060
 Crystal Lake (G-7594)
Julian Elec Svc & Engrg Inc ............... G ...... 630 920-8950
 Westmont (G-21895)
Kinney Electrical Mfg Co .................... D ...... 847 742-9600
 Elgin (G-9090)
◆ Kms Industries LLC ....................... G ...... 331 225-2671
 Addison (G-171)
Kosmos Tool Inc ................................ F ...... 815 675-2200
 Spring Grove (G-20343)
Langham Engineering ........................ G ...... 815 223-5250
 Peru (G-17516)
Littelfuse Inc ....................................... A ...... 773 628-1000
 Chicago (G-5521)
Lumenite Control Technology ............. F ...... 847 455-1450
 Franklin Park (G-10518)
Machine Control Systems Inc ............ G ...... 708 597-1200
 Alsip (G-486)
Machine Control Systems Inc ............ G ...... 708 389-2160
 Palos Heights (G-17108)
Marshall Electric Inc ........................... F ...... 618 382-3932
 Carmi (G-3074)
◆ Marshall Wolf Automation Inc ........ G ...... 847 658-8130
 Algonquin (G-398)
Methode Electronics Inc .................... A ...... 217 357-3941
 Carthage (G-3316)
Meto-Grafics Inc ................................ F ...... 847 639-0044
 Crystal Lake (G-7609)
Midwest Control Corp ......................... F ...... 708 599-1331
 Bridgeview (G-2509)
▲ Mitsubishi Elc Automtn Inc ............ C ...... 847 478-2100
 Vernon Hills (G-21183)
Morton Automatic Electric Co ............. G ...... 309 263-7577
 Morton (G-15166)
▲ Motec Inc ....................................... G ...... 630 241-9595
 Downers Grove (G-8490)
Mpc Products Corporation ................. G ...... 847 673-8300
 Niles (G-16012)
New Cie Inc ....................................... F ...... 815 224-1485
 La Salle (G-12781)
Northwest Instrumentation Inc ............ E ...... 847 825-0699
 Park Ridge (G-17213)
Numerical Control Incorporated ......... G ...... 708 389-8140
 Alsip (G-502)
▼ Nutherm International Inc ............... E ...... 618 244-6000
 Mount Vernon (G-15435)
Oakland Industries Ltd ....................... E ...... 847 827-7600
 Mount Prospect (G-15358)
Panel Authority Inc ............................ F ...... 815 838-0488
 Lockport (G-13738)

Panelshopnet Inc ................................ G ...... 630 692-0214
 Naperville (G-15821)
Peterson Elc Panl Mfg Co Inc ............ F ...... 708 449-2270
 Berkeley (G-2048)
Platt Industrial Control Inc ................. G ...... 630 833-4388
 Addison (G-244)
Power Distribution Eqp Co Inc ........... F ...... 847 455-2500
 Franklin Park (G-10555)
▲ Prater Industries Inc ...................... D ...... 630 679-3200
 Bolingbrook (G-2359)
Product Service Craft Inc ................... F ...... 630 964-5160
 Downers Grove (G-8511)
Protection Controls Inc ...................... E ...... 773 763-3110
 Skokie (G-20066)
Quantum Design Inc .......................... G ...... 815 885-1300
 Loves Park (G-13980)
R G Controls Inc ................................ G ...... 847 438-3981
 Barrington (G-1300)
Rauckman High Voltage Sales .......... G ...... 618 239-0399
 Swansea (G-20781)
RLC Industries Inc ............................. G ...... 708 837-7300
 La Grange (G-12743)
▲ Robotics Technologies Inc ............. E ...... 815 722-7650
 Joliet (G-12570)
Ronk Electrical Industries Inc ............. E ...... 217 563-8333
 Nokomis (G-16061)
RWS Design and Controls Inc .......... G ...... 815 654-6000
 Roscoe (G-18919)
◆ S & C Electric Company ................. A ...... 773 338-1000
 Chicago (G-6419)
▲ SAI Advanced Pwr Solutions Inc .... E ...... 708 450-0990
 Elmhurst (G-9932)
Schneider Electric Usa Inc ................. C ...... 630 428-3849
 Schiller Park (G-19871)
Schneider Electric Usa Inc ................. C ...... 312 697-4770
 Chicago (G-6452)
Schneider Electric Usa Inc ................. G ...... 847 925-7773
 Downers Grove (G-8520)
Schneider Electric Usa Inc ................. C ...... 847 441-2526
 Schaumburg (G-19723)
Schubert Controls Corporation .......... G ...... 847 526-8200
 Wauconda (G-21501)
▼ Simplex Inc ..................................... C ...... 217 483-1600
 Springfield (G-20526)
Smart Surveillance Inc ...................... G ...... 630 968-5075
 Lisle (G-13657)
▲ Switchcraft Inc ............................... B ...... 773 792-2700
 Chicago (G-6653)
▲ Switchcraft Holdco Inc ................... G ...... 773 792-2700
 Chicago (G-6654)
Texas Instruments Incorporated ........ D ...... 630 836-2827
 Warrenville (G-21363)
Venture Design Incorporated ............. F ...... 630 369-1148
 Naperville (G-15775)
Venturedyne Ltd ................................ E ...... 708 597-7550
 Chicago (G-6884)
▲ Woodward Controls Inc ................. C ...... 847 673-8300
 Skokie (G-20114)

## 3621 Motors & Generators

▲ A E Iskra Inc ................................... G ...... 815 874-4022
 Rockford (G-18239)
Active Tool and Machine Inc .............. F ...... 708 599-0022
 Oak Lawn (G-16598)
Advanced Ozone Tech Inc ................. F ...... 630 964-1300
 Downers Grove (G-8385)
Al Cook Electric Motors ...................... G ...... 309 653-2337
 Adair (G-11)
◆ Alfa Controls Inc ............................. G ...... 847 978-9245
 Wheeling (G-22001)
▲ Alin Machining Company Inc ......... C ...... 708 681-1043
 Melrose Park (G-14585)
Alternative Technologies .................... G ...... 888 858-4678
 Melrose Park (G-14592)
▲ Altorfer Power Systems ................. G ...... 309 697-1234
 Bartonville (G-1391)
▲ American Electronic Pdts Inc ........ F ...... 630 889-9977
 Oak Brook (G-16488)
American Rotors Inc .......................... E ...... 847 263-1300
 Gurnee (G-11428)
American Total Engine Co ................. G ...... 847 623-2737
 Ingleside (G-12186)
Applied Mechanical Tech LLC ........... E ...... 815 472-2700
 Momence (G-14978)
Atlas Copco Compressors LLC ......... G ...... 281 590-7500
 Chicago (G-3979)
Awem Corporation ............................. G ...... 217 670-1451
 Springfield (G-20392)
Baldor Electric Company ................... C ...... 630 296-1400
 Bolingbrook (G-2282)

Becsis LLC ......................................... G ...... 630 400-6454
 South Elgin (G-20186)
Belmont Electro Co Inc ...................... G ...... 773 472-4641
 Brookfield (G-2623)
Bill West Enterprises Inc .................... G ...... 217 886-2591
 Jacksonville (G-12378)
▲ Bison Gear & Engineering Corp .... C ...... 630 377-0153
 Saint Charles (G-19143)
▲ Bodine Electric Company .............. G ...... 773 478-3515
 Northfield (G-16393)
▲ Bolingbrook Communications Inc .. A ...... 630 759-9500
 Lisle (G-13571)
Broad Ocean Motors LLC .................. E ...... 630 908-4720
 Westmont (G-21877)
Brook Crompton Usa Inc ................... G ...... 708 893-0690
 South Holland (G-20252)
▲ Brown Line Metal Works LLC ........ G ...... 312 884-7644
 Chicago (G-4178)
C & D Rebuilders ............................... G ...... 618 273-9862
 Eldorado (G-8918)
▲ Calumet Armature and Elc LLC ..... E ...... 708 841-6880
 Riverdale (G-18017)
Cemec Inc ......................................... G ...... 630 495-9696
 Downers Grove (G-8405)
Charles Industries Ltd ........................ D ...... 217 826-2318
 Marshall (G-14319)
Charles R Frontczak .......................... G ...... 224 392-4151
 Rockford (G-18304)
Coilform Company .............................. G ...... 630 232-8000
 Geneva (G-10820)
Communication Coil Inc ..................... D ...... 847 671-1333
 Schiller Park (G-19815)
Con-Trol-Cure Inc .............................. F ...... 773 248-0099
 Chicago (G-4442)
D C Grove Electric Inc ....................... G ...... 847 587-0864
 Fox Lake (G-10275)
Ddu Magnetics Inc ............................. G ...... 708 325-6587
 Lynwood (G-14019)
Digitaldrive Tech ................................ G ...... 630 510-1580
 Wheaton (G-21944)
Djh Industries Inc .............................. E ...... 309 246-8456
 Lacon (G-12786)
▲ Dlt Electric LLC .............................. G ...... 630 552-4115
 Plano (G-17663)
Eastview Manufacturing Inc ............... G ...... 847 741-2514
 Elgin (G-9019)
Eco Green Analytics LLC .................. G ...... 847 691-1148
 Deerfield (G-8005)
Ees Inc .............................................. G ...... 708 343-1800
 Stone Park (G-20633)
◆ Electric Motor Corp ......................... E ...... 773 725-1050
 Chicago (G-4719)
▲ Electric Vehicle Technologies ........ E ...... 847 673-8330
 Skokie (G-19992)
Elm Products Corp ............................. E ...... 847 336-0020
 Waukegan (G-21557)
Encap Technologies Inc ..................... F ...... 510 337-2700
 Palatine (G-17026)
Encap Technologies Inc ..................... B ...... 510 337-2700
 Palatine (G-17027)
Engine Rebuilders & Supply .............. G ...... 708 338-1113
 Stone Park (G-20634)
Federal Prison Industries ................... G ...... 309 346-8588
 Pekin (G-17262)
Flolo Corporation ............................... G ...... 847 249-0880
 Gurnee (G-11448)
▲ Forest City Auto Electric Co .......... F ...... 815 963-4350
 Rockford (G-18386)
▲ Fulling Motor USA Inc .................... G ...... 847 894-6238
 Park Ridge (G-17196)
Geitek Automation Inc ....................... G ...... 815 385-3500
 McHenry (G-14509)
▲ General Manufacturing LLC ........... D ...... 708 345-8600
 Melrose Park (G-14646)
Ghetzler Aero-Power Corp ................. G ...... 224 513-5636
 Vernon Hills (G-21165)
▲ GKN Stromag Inc ........................... E ...... 937 433-3882
 Woodridge (G-22485)
▲ Hallmark Industries Inc .................. F ...... 847 301-8050
 Schaumburg (G-19546)
Haran Technologies LLC ................... G ...... 217 239-1628
 Champaign (G-3492)
Haran Ventures LLC .......................... G ...... 217 239-1628
 Champaign (G-3493)
Hardin Industries LLC ........................ E ...... 309 246-8456
 Lacon (G-12787)
Harvey Bros Inc ................................. F ...... 309 342-3137
 Galesburg (G-10757)
▲ Heng Tuo Usa Inc .......................... G ...... 630 705-1898
 Oakbrook Terrace (G-16710)

**Hopcroft Electric Inc**.....G..... 618 288-7302
Glen Carbon *(G-10952)*
▲ **Howland Technology Inc**.....F..... 847 965-9808
Morton Grove *(G-15200)*
**Illinois Tool Works Inc**.....C..... 847 876-9400
Des Plaines *(G-8208)*
**Industrial Welder Rebuilders**.....G..... 708 371-5688
Alsip *(G-473)*
▲ **Inglot Electronics Corp**.....D..... 773 286-5881
Chicago *(G-5192)*
**Inman Electric Motors Inc**.....E..... 815 223-2288
La Salle *(G-12778)*
**Innova Global LLC**.....G..... 630 568-5609
Burr Ridge *(G-2853)*
**Integrated Power Services LLC**.....E..... 708 877-5310
Thornton *(G-20874)*
**International Supply Co**.....D..... 309 249-6211
Edelstein *(G-8780)*
**ITT Water & Wastewater USA Inc**.....G..... 847 966-3700
Morton Grove *(G-15205)*
**Jardis Industries Inc**.....F..... 630 773-5600
Itasca *(G-12290)*
**Jasiek Motor Rebuilding Inc**.....G..... 815 883-3678
Oglesby *(G-16750)*
**Jomar Electric Coil Mfg Inc**.....G..... 630 279-1494
Villa Park *(G-21261)*
◆ **Jordan Industries Inc**.....F..... 847 945-5591
Deerfield *(G-8020)*
**Kackert Enterprises Inc**.....G..... 630 898-9339
Aurora *(G-1179)*
**Kaman Automation Inc**.....F..... 847 273-9050
Schaumburg *(G-19596)*
**Kap Holdings LLC**.....F..... 708 948-0226
Oak Park *(G-16671)*
**Kaybee Engineering Company Inc**.....E..... 630 968-7100
Westmont *(G-21896)*
**L & H Company Inc**.....F..... 630 571-7200
Oak Brook *(G-16532)*
**Lakeview Energy LLC**.....E..... 312 386-5897
Chicago *(G-5446)*
**Lenhardt Tool and Die Company**.....D..... 618 462-1075
Alton *(G-582)*
**Lionheart Critical Pow**.....E..... 847 291-1413
Huntley *(G-12159)*
◆ **Luon Energy LLC**.....G..... 217 419-2678
Savoy *(G-19411)*
**M R Glenn Electric Inc**.....E..... 708 479-9200
Lockport *(G-13729)*
**Magnetic Coil Manufacturing Co**.....E..... 630 787-1948
Wood Dale *(G-22395)*
**Magnetic Devices Inc**.....G..... 815 459-0077
Crystal Lake *(G-7605)*
◆ **Marmon Industries LLC**.....G..... 312 372-9500
Chicago *(G-5627)*
**Maurey Instrument Corp**.....F..... 708 388-9898
Alsip *(G-490)*
◆ **Mecc Alte Inc**.....F..... 815 344-0530
McHenry *(G-14530)*
▲ **Moons Industries America Inc**.....A..... 630 833-5940
Itasca *(G-12322)*
**Morrell Incorporated**.....F..... 630 858-4600
Glendale Heights *(G-11050)*
**Motormakers De Kalb Credit Un**.....G..... 815 756-6331
Chicago *(G-5814)*
◆ **Mpc Products Corporation**.....A..... 847 673-8300
Niles *(G-16010)*
**Mpc Products Corporation**.....G..... 847 673-8300
Niles *(G-16011)*
**Nelco Coil Supply Company**.....E..... 847 259-7517
Mount Prospect *(G-15354)*
**Netgain Motors Inc**.....G..... 630 243-9100
Lockport *(G-13735)*
**Nidec Motor Corporation**.....D..... 847 439-3760
Elk Grove Village *(G-9651)*
**Nidec Motor Corporation**.....B..... 847 585-8430
Elgin *(G-9123)*
**North Point Investments Inc**.....G..... 312 977-4386
Chicago *(G-5935)*
**Northrop Grumman Systems Corp**.....A..... 847 259-9600
Rolling Meadows *(G-18753)*
**Performance Battery Group Inc**.....G..... 630 293-5505
West Chicago *(G-21755)*
**Power Enclosures Inc**.....F..... 309 274-9000
Chillicothe *(G-7170)*
**Powersource Generator Rentals**.....G..... 847 587-3991
Fox Lake *(G-10281)*
▲ **Pre Fnish Mtals Mrrisville Inc**.....D..... 847 439-2211
Elk Grove Village *(G-9691)*
◆ **Progress Rail Locomotive Inc**.....A..... 800 255-5355
Mc Cook *(G-14456)*
**Progress Rail Locomotive Inc**.....F..... 708 387-5510
Mc Cook *(G-14457)*
**Provisur Technologies**.....G..... 312 284-4698
Chicago *(G-6219)*
**Qcircuits Inc**.....E..... 618 662-8365
Flora *(G-10214)*
**R&R Equipment Plus1 Inc**.....F..... 708 529-3931
Chicago Ridge *(G-7157)*
**Rathje Enterprises Inc**.....F..... 217 443-0022
Danville *(G-7763)*
▲ **Robertson Transformer Co**.....E..... 708 388-2315
Crestwood *(G-7500)*
**Ronk Electrical Industries Inc**.....E..... 217 563-8333
Nokomis *(G-16061)*
**Ronk Electrical Industries Inc**.....E..... 217 563-8333
Nokomis *(G-16062)*
**Rotary Dryer Parts Inc**.....G..... 217 877-2787
Decatur *(G-7936)*
**Rsf Electronics Inc**.....F..... 847 490-0351
Schaumburg *(G-19714)*
▲ **Saco USA (il)inc**.....G..... 815 877-8832
Rockford *(G-18605)*
**Santucci Enterprises**.....G..... 773 286-5629
Chicago *(G-6442)*
▲ **Schneider Elc Buildings LLC**.....B..... 815 381-5000
Rockford *(G-18608)*
▲ **Schneider Elc Holdings Inc**.....A..... 717 944-5460
Schaumburg *(G-19722)*
**Sexton Wind Power LLC**.....G..... 224 212-1250
Lake Bluff *(G-12866)*
**Sfc of Illinois Inc**.....E..... 815 745-2100
Warren *(G-21336)*
▲ **Spg Usa Inc**.....G..... 847 439-4949
Elk Grove Village *(G-9747)*
**Stable Beginning Corporation**.....E..... 815 745-2100
Warren *(G-21337)*
**Stanton Wind Energy LLC**.....F..... 312 224-1400
Chicago *(G-6574)*
**Switched Source LLC**.....G..... 708 207-1479
Chicago *(G-6655)*
**Synergy Power Group LLC**.....E..... 618 247-3200
Sandoval *(G-19359)*
**Teledyne Lecroy Inc**.....E..... 847 888-0450
Elgin *(G-9206)*
▲ **Torqeedo Inc**.....G..... 815 444-8806
Crystal Lake *(G-7667)*
**Tracy Electric Inc**.....E..... 618 943-6205
Lawrenceville *(G-13206)*
▲ **Transformer Manufacturers Inc**.....E..... 708 457-1200
Norridge *(G-16110)*
**Trinity Structural Towers Inc**.....F..... 217 935-7900
Clinton *(G-7290)*
**U S Co-Tronics Corp**.....E..... 815 692-3204
Fairbury *(G-10134)*
▼ **Ultrasonic Power Corporation**.....E..... 815 235-6020
Freeport *(G-10695)*
**UOP LLC**.....G..... 847 391-2000
Des Plaines *(G-8293)*
**UPS Power Management Inc**.....F..... 844 877-2288
Chicago *(G-6842)*
**Vestas-American Wind Tech Inc**.....G..... 815 646-4280
Tiskilwa *(G-20960)*
**Voss Electric Inc**.....G..... 708 596-6000
Harvey *(G-11680)*
**Wagenate Entps Holdings LLC**.....G..... 773 503-1306
Riverdale *(G-18026)*
▲ **Warfield Electric Company Inc**.....E..... 815 469-4094
Frankfort *(G-10376)*
**Waves Fluid Solutions LLC**.....G..... 630 765-7533
Carol Stream *(G-3264)*
**Weldon Corporation**.....E..... 708 343-4700
Maywood *(G-14437)*
**Wellington Drive Tech US**.....G..... 847 922-5098
Buffalo Grove *(G-2792)*
▲ **Western Motor Mfg Co**.....G..... 815 986-2214
Rockford *(G-18679)*
**Willow Creek Energy LLC**.....G..... 312 224-1400
Chicago *(G-6987)*
**Wodack Electric Tool Corp**.....F..... 773 287-9866
Chicago *(G-7019)*
**Xform Power and Eqp Sups LLC**.....G..... 773 260-0209
Chicago *(G-7044)*
◆ **Yaskawa America Inc**.....C..... 847 887-7000
Waukegan *(G-21642)*
**Yaskawa America Inc**.....C..... 847 887-7909
Des Plaines *(G-8307)*

## *3624 Carbon & Graphite Prdts*

▲ **Aero Industries Inc**.....F..... 815 943-7818
Harvard *(G-11618)*
**AMS Seals Inc**.....G..... 815 609-4977
Plainfield *(G-17580)*
**Becker Brothers Graphite Corp**.....G..... 708 410-0700
Maywood *(G-14418)*
**Cabot Corporation**.....D..... 217 253-5752
Tuscola *(G-21018)*
**Carbon Solutions Group LLC**.....F..... 312 638-9077
Chicago *(G-4239)*
**Frantz Manufacturing Company**.....D..... 815 625-7063
Sterling *(G-20592)*
◆ **Graphtek LLC**.....F..... 847 279-1925
Northbrook *(G-16266)*
**Hausermann Die & Machine Co**.....F..... 630 543-6688
Addison *(G-144)*
**Hickman Williams & Company**.....F..... 708 656-8818
Cicero *(G-7202)*
**Industrial Graphite Products**.....G..... 630 350-0155
Franklin Park *(G-10498)*
**Industrial Graphite Sales LLC**.....G..... 815 943-5502
Harvard *(G-11638)*
**J Ream Manufacturing**.....G..... 630 983-6945
Naperville *(G-15680)*
**Kirkman Composites**.....G..... 309 734-5606
Monmouth *(G-15018)*
**Process Engineering Corp**.....F..... 815 459-1734
Crystal Lake *(G-7634)*
**Rnfl Acquisition LLC**.....E..... 651 442-6011
Chicago *(G-6366)*
**Seal Operation S L**.....G..... 847 537-8100
Wheeling *(G-22145)*
▲ **Starex Inc**.....G..... 847 918-5555
Libertyville *(G-13384)*
**Superior Graphite Co**.....E..... 708 458-0006
Chicago *(G-6633)*

## *3625 Relays & Indl Controls*

▲ **7 Mile Solutions Inc**.....E..... 847 588-2280
Niles *(G-15952)*
**ABRA Enterprises Inc**.....G..... 847 866-6903
Evanston *(G-10001)*
◆ **Advanced Engineered Systems Inc**.....E..... 815 624-7797
South Beloit *(G-20135)*
**Advanced Technologies Inc**.....G..... 847 329-9875
Park Ridge *(G-17178)*
**American Control Elec LLC**.....G..... 815 624-6950
South Beloit *(G-20137)*
**American Controls & Automation**.....G..... 630 293-8841
West Chicago *(G-21655)*
**Automated Systems & Control Co**.....G..... 847 735-8310
Lake Bluff *(G-12834)*
**Autotech Tech Ltd Partnr**.....G..... 563 359-7501
Carol Stream *(G-3107)*
**Autotech Tech Ltd Partnr**.....E..... 563 359-7501
Chicago *(G-3994)*
**Autotech Tech Ltd Partnr**.....E..... 630 668-8886
Carol Stream *(G-3108)*
**Avg Advanced Technologies LP**.....A..... 630 668-3900
Carol Stream *(G-3110)*
◆ **Blachford Investments Inc**.....C..... 630 231-8300
West Chicago *(G-21671)*
▲ **Bodine Electric Company**.....C..... 773 478-3515
Northfield *(G-16393)*
**Box of Rain Ltd**.....G..... 847 640-6996
Arlington Heights *(G-727)*
**BTR Controls Inc**.....G..... 847 608-9500
Elgin *(G-8972)*
**Burke Tool & Manufacturing Inc**.....G..... 618 542-6441
Du Quoin *(G-8551)*
**C-Storm Electronic LLC**.....F..... 630 406-1353
Saint Charles *(G-19148)*
**Capable Controls Inc**.....D..... 630 860-6514
Bensenville *(G-1850)*
**Capsonic Automotive Inc**.....F..... 847 888-7300
Elgin *(G-8978)*
▲ **Capsonic Automotive Inc**.....F..... 847 888-7300
Elgin *(G-8979)*
**Capsonic Automotive Inc**.....B..... 915 872-3585
Chicago *(G-4232)*
**Caterpillar Inc**.....B..... 815 729-5511
Joliet *(G-12471)*
◆ **Chamberlain Manufacturing Corp**.....A..... 630 279-3600
Oak Brook *(G-16500)*
▲ **Comet Tool Inc**.....E..... 847 956-0126
Elk Grove Village *(G-9383)*
**Competition Electronics Inc**.....G..... 815 874-8001
Rockford *(G-18321)*
**Con-Trol-Cure Inc**.....F..... 773 248-0099
Chicago *(G-4442)*
**Connor-Winfield Corp**.....C..... 630 851-4722
Aurora *(G-1133)*

S I C

Employee Codes: A=Over 500 employees, B=251-500
C=101-250, D=51-100, E=20-50, F=10-19, G=3-9
2017 Harris Illinois
Industrial Directory
1093

## 36 ELECTRONIC AND OTHER ELECTRICAL EQUIPMENT AND COMPONENTS, EXCEPT COMPUTER

Continental Auto Systems Inc ............. G ..... 847 862-5000
Deer Park (G-7969)
Control Designs Inc ............................ G ..... 847 918-9347
Gurnee (G-11434)
Control Masters Inc ............................ G ..... 630 968-2390
Downers Grove (G-8420)
Control Research Inc .......................... G ..... 847 352-4920
Schaumburg (G-19483)
▲ Control Solutions LLC ..................... D ..... 630 806-7062
Aurora (G-984)
Control Systems Inc ........................... G ..... 847 438-6228
Long Grove (G-13889)
Controllink Incorporated .................... E ..... 847 622-1100
Elgin (G-9002)
Copar Corporation .............................. E ..... 708 496-1859
Burbank (G-2807)
Core Components Inc ......................... F ..... 630 690-0520
Carol Stream (G-3137)
Crane Dorray Corporation ................... G ..... 630 893-7553
Addison (G-83)
Creative Controls Systems Inc ............ G ..... 815 629-2358
Rockton (G-18695)
▲ CTS Automotive LLC ...................... G ..... 630 614-7201
Lisle (G-13578)
CTS Automotive LLC .......................... E ..... 815 385-9480
McHenry (G-14493)
D C Grove Electric Inc ......................... G ..... 847 587-0864
Fox Lake (G-10275)
▲ Danfoss Inc .................................... G ..... 815 639-8600
Loves Park (G-13935)
Danfoss LLC ....................................... C ..... 888 326-3677
Loves Park (G-13936)
Deltrol Corp ........................................ C ..... 708 547-0500
Bellwood (G-1703)
Dgm Electronics Inc ............................ G ..... 815 389-2040
Roscoe (G-18894)
Domino Engineering Corp ................... F ..... 217 824-9441
Taylorville (G-20838)
Don Johns Inc .................................... E ..... 630 326-9650
Batavia (G-1439)
Dresser Inc ......................................... D ..... 847 437-5940
Elk Grove Village (G-9435)
▲ E N M Company .............................. D ..... 773 775-8400
Chicago (G-4667)
Eaton Corporation ............................... C ..... 815 398-6585
Rockford (G-18354)
Eaton Corporation ............................... C ..... 815 562-2107
Rochelle (G-18087)
Eaton Hydraulics LLC .......................... G ..... 618 667-2553
Troy (G-21006)
Elcon Inc ............................................. E ..... 815 467-9500
Minooka (G-14840)
▲ Electric Vehicle Technologies ......... E ..... 847 673-8330
Skokie (G-19992)
Electro-Matic Products Co .................. F ..... 773 235-4010
Chicago (G-4720)
Elemech Inc ........................................ E ..... 630 417-2845
Aurora (G-1001)
◆ Elenco Electronics Inc ..................... E ..... 847 541-3800
Wheeling (G-22046)
Elm Products Corp ............................. E ..... 847 336-0020
Waukegan (G-21557)
Enercon Engineering Inc .................... G ..... 309 694-1418
East Peoria (G-8709)
◆ Enercon Engineering Inc ................. C ..... 800 218-8831
East Peoria (G-8708)
Envirnmntal Ctrl Solutions Inc ............ G ..... 217 793-8966
Springfield (G-20435)
▲ Environmental Specialties Inc ......... G ..... 630 860-7070
Itasca (G-12259)
▲ Essex Electro Engineers Inc ............ E ..... 847 891-4444
Schaumburg (G-19521)
Fivecubits Inc ..................................... F ..... 925 273-1862
Oak Brook (G-16514)
Flolo Corporation ................................ G ..... 847 249-0880
Gurnee (G-11448)
FSI Technologies Inc .......................... E ..... 630 932-9380
Lombard (G-13803)
Garen Eaton Farms LLC ..................... G ..... 217 228-0324
Quincy (G-17829)
Geitek Automation Inc ........................ D ..... 815 385-3500
McHenry (G-14509)
General Electric Company ................... C ..... 309 664-1513
Bloomington (G-2170)
▼ Gpe Controls Inc ............................ F ..... 708 236-6000
Hillside (G-11917)
▲ Grayhill Inc ...................................... B ..... 708 354-1040
La Grange (G-12734)
Guardian Consolidated Tech Inc ......... G ..... 815 334-3600
Woodstock (G-22571)

▲ Guardian Electric Mfg Co ................. D ..... 815 334-3600
Woodstock (G-22572)
▲ Harrington Signal Inc ...................... G ..... 309 762-0731
Moline (G-14942)
Harris Precision Tools Inc .................. G ..... 708 422-5808
Chicago Ridge (G-7149)
Harvey Bros Inc .................................. F ..... 309 342-3137
Galesburg (G-10757)
Hauhinco LP ....................................... E ..... 618 993-5399
Marion (G-14264)
Hausermann Controls Co ................... F ..... 630 543-6688
Addison (G-143)
Hausermann Die & Machine Co .......... F ..... 630 543-6688
Addison (G-144)
Hella Corporate Center USA Inc ......... B ..... 734 414-0900
Flora (G-10208)
Hella Corporate Center USA Inc ......... B ..... 618 662-4402
Flora (G-10209)
Hella Electronics Corporation ............. A ..... 618 662-5186
Flora (G-10210)
Honeywell International Inc ................ G ..... 815 235-5500
Freeport (G-10664)
Hurletron Incorporated ....................... F ..... 847 680-7022
Libertyville (G-13335)
▲ I P C Automation Inc ...................... G ..... 815 759-3934
McHenry (G-14514)
Ideal Industries Inc ............................ C ..... 815 895-1108
Sycamore (G-20801)
Imperial Fabricators Co ...................... E ..... 773 463-5522
Franklin Park (G-10495)
Industrial Controls Inc ........................ G ..... 630 752-8100
Batavia (G-1457)
▲ Industrial Motion Control LLC ......... C ..... 847 459-5200
Wheeling (G-22076)
Industrial Service Solutions ............... F ..... 917 609-6979
Chicago (G-5180)
Instrmntation Ctrl Systems Inc ........... F ..... 630 543-6200
Roselle (G-18947)
Intersol Industries Inc ........................ F ..... 630 238-0385
Bensenville (G-1922)
Interstate Industrial Tech ................... E ..... 618 286-4900
Dupo (G-8572)
Invektek Llc ........................................ E ..... 312 343-0600
Chicago (G-5230)
▲ Italvibras Usa Inc ............................ G ..... 815 872-1350
Princeton (G-17751)
Jemison Elc Box Swtchboard Inc ....... G ..... 815 459-4060
Crystal Lake (G-7594)
Joliet Technologies LLC ..................... G ..... 815 725-9696
Crest Hill (G-7461)
◆ Jordan Industries Inc ...................... F ..... 847 945-5591
Deerfield (G-8020)
◆ Jtekt Toyoda Americas Corp ........... G ..... 847 253-0340
Arlington Heights (G-786)
Julian Elec Svc & Engrg Inc ................ E ..... 630 920-8950
Westmont (G-21895)
K & W Auto Electric ............................ F ..... 217 857-1717
Teutopolis (G-20853)
Kackert Enterprises Inc ...................... G ..... 630 898-9339
Aurora (G-1179)
▲ Kelco Industries Inc ........................ G ..... 815 334-3600
Woodstock (G-22577)
Keonix Corporation ............................ G ..... 847 259-9430
Arlington Heights (G-788)
Knowles Elec Holdings Inc ................. A ..... 630 250-5100
Itasca (G-12296)
▲ Las Systems Inc .............................. E ..... 847 462-8100
Woodstock (G-22582)
Light of Mine LLC ............................... G ..... 312 840-8570
Chicago (G-5503)
Littelfuse Inc ...................................... E ..... 773 628-1000
Chicago (G-5522)
Loda Electronics Co ........................... E ..... 217 386-2554
Loda (G-13752)
Lumec Control Products Inc ............... G ..... 309 691-4747
Peoria (G-17403)
Lumenite Control Technology ............. F ..... 847 455-1450
Franklin Park (G-10518)
M-1 Tool Works Inc ............................ E ..... 815 344-1275
McHenry (G-14525)
Machine Control Systems Inc ............. G ..... 708 389-2160
Palos Heights (G-17108)
Machine Control Systems Inc ............. G ..... 708 597-1200
Alsip (G-486)
Magnet-Schultz Amer Holdg LLC ........ G ..... 630 789-0600
Westmont (G-21901)
▲ Magnet-Schultz America Inc ........... D ..... 630 789-0600
Westmont (G-21902)
▼ Magnetrol International Inc ............ C ..... 630 723-6600
Aurora (G-1051)

◆ Martin Automatic Inc ...................... C ..... 815 654-4800
Rockford (G-18483)
▼ Master Control Systems Inc ........... E ..... 847 295-1010
Lake Bluff (G-12856)
Maurey Instrument Corp ..................... F ..... 708 388-9898
Alsip (G-490)
Meister Industries Inc ........................ G ..... 815 623-8919
Roscoe (G-18907)
Mektronix Technology Inc .................. G ..... 847 680-3300
Libertyville (G-13353)
Methode Electronics Inc ..................... A ..... 217 357-3941
Carthage (G-3316)
Meto-Grafics Inc ................................ G ..... 847 639-0044
Crystal Lake (G-7609)
Meyer Electronic Mfg Svcs Inc ........... G ..... 309 808-4100
Normal (G-16076)
Meyer Systems .................................. G ..... 815 436-7077
Joliet (G-12540)
Microware Inc ..................................... G ..... 847 943-9113
Glenview (G-11168)
Mission Control Systems Inc ............. F ..... 847 956-7650
Elk Grove Village (G-9630)
▲ Mitsubishi Elc Automtn Inc ............. G ..... 847 478-2100
Vernon Hills (G-21183)
Morton Automatic Electric Co ............. G ..... 309 263-7577
Morton (G-15166)
Mpc Products Corporation .................. G ..... 847 673-8300
Niles (G-16012)
Mpc Products Corporation .................. G ..... 847 673-8300
Niles (G-16011)
◆ Mpc Products Corporation .............. A ..... 847 673-8300
Niles (G-16010)
▲ National Control Holdings .............. B ..... 630 231-5900
West Chicago (G-21748)
Network Merchants LLC ..................... G ..... 847 352-4850
Roselle (G-18959)
New Cie Inc ........................................ F ..... 815 224-1485
La Salle (G-12781)
Niles Auto Parts ................................. G ..... 847 215-2549
Lincolnshire (G-13468)
▲ O C Keckley Company ..................... E ..... 847 674-8422
Skokie (G-20048)
▲ Ohmite Holding LLC ........................ E ..... 847 258-0300
Warrenville (G-21352)
▲ Olympic Controls Corp .................... E ..... 847 742-3566
Elgin (G-9128)
▲ Omron Automotive Elec Inc ............ A ..... 630 443-6800
Saint Charles (G-19229)
Panatrol Corporation .......................... E ..... 630 655-4700
Burr Ridge (G-2874)
Parker-Hannifin Corporation ............... C ..... 309 266-2200
Morton (G-15175)
Parking Systems Inc ........................... E ..... 847 891-3819
Schaumburg (G-19684)
Pilz Automtn Safety Ltd Partnr ........... G ..... 734 354-0272
Chicago (G-6123)
Power-Io Inc ...................................... E ..... 630 717-7335
Naperville (G-15730)
Pro-Quip Incorporated ........................ F ..... 708 352-5732
La Grange Park (G-12759)
Process and Control Systems ............. F ..... 708 293-0557
Alsip (G-514)
Process Technologies Group .............. G ..... 630 393-4777
Warrenville (G-21360)
Protection Controls Inc ...................... E ..... 773 763-3110
Skokie (G-20066)
▲ Questek Manufacturing Corp ........... D ..... 847 428-0300
Elgin (G-9159)
R & D Electronics Inc ......................... G ..... 847 583-9080
Niles (G-16024)
Relay Services Mfg Corp .................... F ..... 773 252-2700
Chicago (G-6327)
Rensel-Chicago Inc ............................ G ..... 773 235-2100
Chicago (G-6334)
Robert Higgins .................................... D ..... 217 337-0734
Urbana (G-21101)
Rockdale Controls Co Inc ................... F ..... 815 436-6181
Plainfield (G-17646)
Rockwell Automation Inc ................... C ..... 217 373-0800
Champaign (G-3534)
Rockwell Automation Inc ................... D ..... 414 382-3662
Burr Ridge (G-2878)
◆ S & C Electric Company .................. A ..... 773 338-1000
Chicago (G-6419)
S & N Manufacturing Inc .................... E ..... 630 232-0275
Geneva (G-10865)
▲ Schneider Elc Buildings LLC ........... B ..... 815 381-5000
Rockford (G-18608)
▲ Schneider Elc Holdings Inc ............. A ..... 717 944-5460
Schaumburg (G-19722)

Scientific Instruments Inc ........ G ....... 847 679-1242
Skokie (G-20082)
▲ SE Relays LLC ........ G ....... 847 827-9880
Schaumburg (G-19724)
Siemens Industry Inc ........ C .....
West Chicago (G-21771)
◆ Siemens Industry Inc ........ A ....... 847 215-1000
Buffalo Grove (G-2767)
▼ Simplex Inc ........ C ....... 217 483-1600
Springfield (G-20526)
Smart Surveillance Inc ........ G ....... 630 968-5075
Lisle (G-13657)
▲ Smart Systems Inc ........ E ....... 630 343-3333
Bolingbrook (G-2372)
Sound Seal Inc ........ E ....... 630 844-1999
North Aurora (G-16144)
Sparton Aydin LLC ........ G ....... 800 772-7866
Schaumburg (G-19733)
▲ Spectrum Cos International ........ G ....... 630 879-8008
Batavia (G-1497)
▼ Steel-Guard Safety Corp ........ G ....... 708 589-4588
South Holland (G-20306)
Sterling Systems & Controls ........ F ....... 815 625-0852
Sterling (G-20615)
Sumitomo Machinery Corp Amer ........ E ....... 630 752-0200
Glendale Heights (G-11078)
Tc Electric Controls LLC ........ G ....... 847 598-3508
Schaumburg (G-19755)
Terex Utilities Inc ........ G ....... 847 515-7030
Addison (G-310)
▲ Thomson Linear LLC ........ C ....... 815 568-8001
Marengo (G-14243)
Tomantron Inc ........ F ....... 708 532-2456
Tinley Park (G-20950)
Tough Electric Inc ........ G ....... 630 236-8332
Aurora (G-1226)
Trend Machinery Inc ........ G ....... 630 655-0030
Burr Ridge (G-2887)
Unitrol Electronics Inc ........ E ....... 847 480-0115
Northbrook (G-16380)
USA Drives Inc ........ E ....... 630 323-1282
Burr Ridge (G-2892)
Value Added Services & Tech ........ G ....... 847 888-8232
Elgin (G-9223)
Warming Systems ........ G ....... 800 663-7831
Lake Villa (G-13030)
Warner Electric LLC ........ E ....... 815 566-4683
Belvidere (G-1795)
Web Printing Controls Co Inc ........ C ....... 618 842-2664
Fairfield (G-10161)
▲ Wilkes & McLean Ltd ........ G ....... 847 381-3872
North Barrington (G-16156)
Win Technologies Incorporated ........ E ....... 630 236-1020
Aurora (G-1099)
Woodward Inc ........ F ....... 847 673-8300
Skokie (G-20113)
Woodward Inc ........ G ....... 815 877-7441
Rockton (G-18703)
▲ Woodward Controls Inc ........ C ....... 847 673-8300
Skokie (G-20114)
Xylem Inc ........ D ....... 847 966-3700
Morton Grove (G-15247)
◆ Yaskawa America Inc ........ C ....... 847 887-7000
Waukegan (G-21642)
Z-Tech Inc ........ G ....... 815 335-7395
Winnebago (G-22299)

## 3629 Electrical Indl Apparatus, NEC

A J R International Inc ........ D ....... 800 232-3965
Glendale Heights (G-11006)
▲ American Electronic Pdts Inc ........ F ....... 630 889-9977
Oak Brook (G-16488)
Ametek Inc ........ C ....... 847 596-7000
Waukegan (G-21526)
B&Bimc LLC ........ D ....... 815 433-5100
Ottawa (G-16948)
Brigitflex Inc ........ F ....... 847 741-1452
Elgin (G-8971)
◆ Charles Industries Ltd ........ D ....... 847 806-6300
Rolling Meadows (G-18719)
Charles Industries Ltd ........ D ....... 217 932-2068
Casey (G-3381)
Dalec Electronics Inc ........ G ....... 847 671-7676
South Holland (G-20259)
▲ Delta-Unibus Corp ........ C ....... 708 409-1200
Northlake (G-16433)
Ees Inc ........ G ....... 708 343-1800
Stone Park (G-20633)
Electro-Matic Products Co ........ F ....... 773 235-4010
Chicago (G-4720)
▲ Elpac Electronics Inc ........ C ....... 708 316-4407
Westchester (G-21839)
◆ Engineered Abrasives Inc ........ E ....... 662 582-4143
Alsip (G-462)
Hauhinco LP ........ E ....... 618 993-5399
Marion (G-14264)
Heico Ohmite LLC ........ F ....... 847 258-0300
Rolling Meadows (G-18733)
Innovation Plus Power Systems ........ F ....... 630 457-1105
Saint Charles (G-19198)
▲ Inventus Power Inc ........ C ....... 630 410-7900
Woodridge (G-22496)
Jf Industries Inc ........ G ....... 773 775-8840
Chicago (G-5301)
▲ La Marche Mfg Co ........ C ....... 847 299-1188
Des Plaines (G-8220)
▼ Master Control Systems Inc ........ E ....... 847 295-1010
Lake Bluff (G-12856)
▲ Motor Capacitors Inc ........ F ....... 773 774-6666
Wood Dale (G-22401)
Nexergy Tauber LLC ........ A ....... 708 316-4407
Westchester (G-21851)
Nova Tronics Inc ........ G ....... 630 455-1034
Burr Ridge (G-2871)
Panatrol Corporation ........ E ....... 630 655-4700
Burr Ridge (G-2874)
Powell Electrical Systems Inc ........ C ....... 708 409-1200
Northlake (G-16447)
Powell Electrical Systems Inc ........ C ....... 708 409-1200
Northlake (G-16448)
Powerone Corp ........ G ....... 630 443-6500
Saint Charles (G-19239)
◆ Powervar Inc ........ C ....... 847 596-7000
Waukegan (G-21604)
Powervar Holdings LLC ........ C ....... 800 369-7179
Waukegan (G-21605)
Radionic Hi-Tech Inc ........ D ....... 773 804-0100
Chicago (G-6281)
▲ Ransburg Corporation ........ B ....... 847 724-7500
Glenview (G-11190)
▲ Richardson Rfpd Inc ........ G ....... 630 262-6800
Geneva (G-10862)
Ronken Industries Inc ........ E ....... 815 664-5306
Spring Valley (G-20380)
Safecharge LLC ........ G ....... 248 866-9428
Chicago (G-6426)
◆ Schumacher Electric Corp ........ D ....... 847 385-1600
Mount Prospect (G-15372)
Schumacher Electric Corp ........ E ....... 217 283-5551
Hoopeston (G-12115)
▲ Slaughter Company Inc ........ E ....... 847 932-3662
Lake Forest (G-12960)
▲ Synergistic Tech Solutions Inc ........ G ....... 224 360-6165
Mundelein (G-15562)
▲ We International ........ G ....... 618 549-1784
Carbondale (G-3026)

## 3631 Household Cooking Eqpt

▲ Apache Supply ........ G ....... 708 409-1040
Melrose Park (G-14595)
▲ Axis International Marketing ........ C ....... 847 297-0744
Des Plaines (G-8154)
◆ Belson Outdoors LLC ........ E ....... 630 897-8489
North Aurora (G-16120)
BR Machine Inc ........ F ....... 815 434-0427
Ottawa (G-16950)
Chadwick Manufacturing Ltd ........ G ....... 815 684-5152
Chadwick (G-3440)
▲ Empire Comfort Systems Inc ........ C ....... 618 233-7420
Belleville (G-1631)
▲ Global Contract Mfg Inc ........ G ....... 312 432-6200
Chicago (G-4957)
Home & Leisure Lifestyles LLC ........ G ....... 618 651-0358
Highland (G-11797)
Homefire Hearth Inc ........ G ....... 815 997-1123
Rockford (G-18422)
▼ Kalamazoo Outdoor Gourmet LLC .. G ....... 312 423-8770
Chicago (G-5353)
◆ Marshall Middleby Inc ........ C ....... 847 289-0204
Elgin (G-9100)
Microwave RES & Applications ........ G ....... 630 480-7456
Carol Stream (G-3197)
▲ Peerless-Premier Appliance Co ........ D ....... 618 233-0475
Belleville (G-1666)
Sun Ovens International Inc ........ F ....... 630 208-7273
Elburn (G-8911)
◆ Weber-Stephen Products LLC ........ B ....... 847 934-5700
Palatine (G-17088)
Weber-Stephen Products LLC ........ G ....... 224 836-8536
Palatine (G-17089)
Weber-Stephen Products LLC ........ F ....... 847 669-4900
Huntley (G-12183)

## 3632 Household Refrigerators & Freezers

▼ Craig Industries Inc ........ D ....... 217 228-2421
Quincy (G-17816)
◆ Dover Corporation ........ C ....... 630 541-1540
Downers Grove (G-8431)
Flurida Group Inc ........ G ....... 310 513-0888
Naperville (G-15806)
▼ H A Phillips & Co ........ E ....... 630 377-0050
Dekalb (G-8095)
Lambright Distributors ........ G ....... 217 543-2083
Arthur (G-907)
▲ Scotsman Industries Inc ........ D ....... 847 215-4501
Vernon Hills (G-21199)
Sphinx Panel and Door Inc ........ G ....... 618 351-9266
Cobden (G-7305)
Tri-State Food Equipment ........ G ....... 217 228-1550
Quincy (G-17900)

## 3633 Household Laundry Eqpt

C Streeter Enterprise ........ G ....... 773 858-4388
Chicago (G-4205)
Coin Macke Laundry ........ G ....... 847 459-1109
Wheeling (G-22029)
Eastgate Cleaners ........ G ....... 630 627-9494
Lombard (G-13794)
Iron-A-Way LLC ........ E ....... 309 266-7232
Morton (G-15161)

## 3634 Electric Household Appliances

▲ Akinsun Heat Co Inc ........ F ....... 630 289-9506
Streamwood (G-20640)
Alpha Bedding LLC ........ F ....... 847 550-5110
Lake Zurich (G-13039)
▲ American Dryer Inc ........ E ....... 734 421-2400
Berkeley (G-2043)
American Fuel Economy Inc ........ G ....... 815 433-3226
Ottawa (G-16946)
Baier Home Center ........ G ....... 815 457-2300
Cissna Park (G-7253)
▲ Bath Solutions Inc ........ F ....... 817 429-2318
Chicago (G-4055)
Beck Shoe Products Company ........ G ....... 618 656-5819
Edwardsville (G-8792)
▲ Bestair Pro ........ G ....... 847 683-3400
Hampshire (G-11543)
▲ Blueair Inc ........ F ....... 888 258-3247
Chicago (G-4127)
▲ Boneco North America Corp ........ G ....... 630 983-3294
Naperville (G-15607)
Cabot Microelectronics Corp ........ D ....... 630 375-6631
Aurora (G-978)
▲ Clements National Company ........ G ....... 708 594-5890
Broadview (G-2569)
◆ Conair Corporation ........ E ....... 203 351-9000
Rantoul (G-17924)
▲ Dyson B2b Inc ........ E ....... 312 469-5950
Chicago (G-4661)
Expo Engineered Inc ........ G ....... 708 780-7155
Cicero (G-7196)
Extractor Corporation ........ F ....... 847 742-3532
South Elgin (G-20196)
General Electric Company ........ F ....... 708 780-2600
Cicero (G-7197)
Hamilton Beach Brands Inc ........ E ....... 847 252-7036
Hoffman Estates (G-12015)
Hotvapes Ltd ........ F ....... 775 468-8273
Chicago (G-5120)
Keating of Chicago Inc ........ E ....... 815 569-2324
Capron (G-2996)
▲ Matthews-Gerbar Ltd ........ G ....... 847 680-9043
Libertyville (G-13348)
Matthewsgerbar Ltd ........ G ....... 847 680-9043
Libertyville (G-13349)
▲ Menk Usa LLC ........ E ....... 815 626-9730
Sterling (G-20598)
Mh Equipment Company ........ D ....... 217 443-7210
Danville (G-7755)
▲ Newhaven Display Intl Inc ........ E ....... 847 844-8795
Elgin (G-9118)
▲ O2cool LLC ........ E ....... 312 951-6700
Chicago (G-5960)
▲ Power Industries Inc ........ G ....... 630 443-0671
Saint Charles (G-19238)
Quick Nic Juice LLC ........ F ....... 815 315-8523
Sandwich (G-19376)
Radovent Illinois LLC ........ G ....... 847 637-0297
Arlington Heights (G-827)



Employee Codes: A=Over 500 employees, B=251-500
C=101-250, D=51-100, E=20-50, F=10-19, G=3-9
2017 Harris Illinois
Industrial Directory
1095

## 36 ELECTRONIC AND OTHER ELECTRICAL EQUIPMENT AND COMPONENTS, EXCEPT COMPUTER

▲ Sensible Designs Online Inc ............G....... 708 267-8924
 Orland Park (G-16890)
Sun Ovens International Inc ..............F....... 630 208-7273
 Elburn (G-8911)
▲ Tempro International Corp ..............G....... 847 677-5370
 Skokie (G-20100)
▲ Thermosoft International Corp ........E....... 847 279-3800
 Vernon Hills (G-21211)
Tifb Media Group Inc .........................G....... 844 862-4391
 Burbank (G-2810)
Tonjon Company ..................................F....... 630 208-1173
 Geneva (G-10873)
▲ Tri-Lite Inc .........................................G....... 773 384-7765
 Chicago (G-6770)
Upper Limits Midwest Inc ..................G....... 217 679-4315
 Springfield (G-20547)
Western Auto Associate Str Co .........G....... 618 357-5555
 Pinckneyville (G-17554)
▲ World Dryer Corporation ...................E....... 708 449-6950
 Berkeley (G-2053)
◆ Xfpg LLC ............................................B....... 224 513-2010
 Lincolnshire (G-13491)

### 3635 Household Vacuum Cleaners

Aerotech Inc ........................................D....... 618 942-5131
 Energy (G-9984)
Aerus Electrolux .................................G....... 847 949-4222
 Mundelein (G-15465)
▲ Dyson Inc ...........................................D....... 312 469-5950
 Chicago (G-4660)
Lee Sauzek .........................................G....... 618 539-5815
 Freeburg (G-10638)
Wodack Electric Tool Corp ................F....... 773 287-9866
 Chicago (G-7019)

### 3639 Household Appliances, NEC

Appliance Repair .................................G....... 708 456-1020
 Norridge (G-16096)
◆ Belson Outdoors LLC .......................E....... 630 897-8489
 North Aurora (G-16120)
◆ Mic Quality Service Inc .....................E....... 847 778-5676
 Chicago (G-5719)
Quantum Precision Inc ......................E....... 630 692-1545
 West Chicago (G-12762)
Rampro Facilities Svcs Corp .............G....... 224 639-6378
 Gurnee (G-11498)
Rivercrest Sewing Center .................G....... 708 385-2516
 Crestwood (G-7499)
◆ Tablecraft Products Co Inc ..............D....... 847 855-9000
 Gurnee (G-11512)
Threads of Time ..................................G....... 217 431-9202
 Danville (G-7769)
Unique Indoor Comfort ......................F....... 847 362-1910
 Libertyville (G-13394)

### 3641 Electric Lamps

▲ AAA Press Specialists Inc ...............F....... 847 818-1100
 Arlington Heights (G-701)
Acculight LLC .....................................G....... 630 847-1000
 Elk Grove Village (G-9260)
Aco Inc .................................................E....... 773 774-5200
 Chicago (G-3735)
▲ Advanced Micro Lites Inc ................G....... 630 365-5450
 Elburn (G-8874)
▲ Advanced Strobe Products Inc ......D....... 708 867-3100
 Chicago (G-3772)
▲ Aero-Tech Light Bulb Co .................F....... 847 534-6580
 Schaumburg (G-19425)
▲ American Light Bulb Mfg Inc ..........D....... 843 464-0755
 Schaumburg (G-19439)
▲ Amglo Kemlite Laboratories Inc ....D....... 630 238-3031
 Bensenville (G-1834)
Anixter Inc ...........................................C....... 800 323-8167
 Glenview (G-11103)
Bz Bearing & Power Inc ....................G....... 877 850-3993
 Hickory Hills (G-11767)
▲ Cec Industries Ltd ............................E....... 847 821-1199
 Lincolnshire (G-13434)
Comet Neon ........................................G....... 630 668-6366
 Lombard (G-13782)
Ddk Scientific Corporation ...............G....... 618 235-2849
 Belleville (G-1623)
▲ Dontech Industries Inc ....................F....... 847 428-8222
 Gilberts (G-10917)
Eden Park Illumination Inc ...............G....... 217 403-1866
 Champaign (G-3478)
General Electric Company .................C....... 217 235-4081
 Mattoon (G-14389)
Keating of Chicago Inc ......................E....... 815 569-2324
 Capron (G-2996)

▲ Lampholders Assemblies Inc ..........G....... 773 205-0005
 Chicago (G-5453)
▲ Light Matrix Inc .................................G....... 847 590-0856
 Palatine (G-17050)
Malcolite Corporation ........................D....... 847 562-1350
 Deerfield (G-8034)
▲ Mattson Lamp Plant .........................G....... 217 258-9390
 Mattoon (G-14401)
Modern Lighting Tech LLC ................G....... 312 624-9267
 Chicago (G-5782)
National Direct Lighting ....................E....... 708 371-4950
 Alsip (G-497)
North American Lighting Inc ............A....... 618 548-6249
 Salem (G-19340)
Orion Media Logistics Inc .................G....... 847 866-6215
 Evanston (G-10084)
Radionic Hi-Tech Inc .........................D....... 773 804-0100
 Chicago (G-6281)
▼ Royal Haeger Lamp Co ....................E....... 309 837-9966
 Macomb (G-14132)
S A W Co ..............................................G....... 630 678-5400
 Lombard (G-13849)
Santas Best .........................................F....... 847 459-3301
 Riverwoods (G-18043)
Universal Lighting Corporation ........G....... 773 927-2000
 Chicago (G-6833)

### 3643 Current-Carrying Wiring Devices

2d2c Inc ...............................................G....... 847 543-0980
 Gurnee (G-11416)
Aco Inc .................................................E....... 773 774-5200
 Chicago (G-3735)
Advantage Direct Inc ........................F....... 847 427-1185
 Elk Grove Village (G-9279)
Alan Manufacturing Corp ..................G....... 815 568-6836
 Marengo (G-14217)
Alcon Tool & Mfg Co Inc ...................F....... 773 545-8742
 Chicago (G-3798)
▲ Aldridge Electric Inc ........................B....... 847 680-5200
 Libertyville (G-13300)
Allied Instrument Service Inc ...........F....... 708 788-1912
 Berwyn (G-2056)
American Bare Conductor Inc .........E....... 815 224-3422
 La Salle (G-12762)
▲ Americor Electronics Ltd ................F....... 847 956-6200
 Elk Grove Village (G-9300)
▲ Amerline Enterprises Co Inc ..........E....... 847 671-6554
 Schiller Park (G-19802)
▲ Amphenol Eec Inc .............................E....... 773 463-8343
 Chicago (G-3894)
▲ Appleton Grp LLC .............................C....... 847 268-6000
 Rosemont (G-18989)
Belden Energy Solutions Inc ...........G....... 800 235-3361
 Elmhurst (G-9838)
▲ Central Rubber Company ................E....... 815 544-2191
 Belvidere (G-1745)
Chicago Freight Car Leasing Co ......D....... 847 318-8000
 Schaumburg (G-19471)
Christiana Industries Inc ..................C....... 773 465-6330
 Chicago (G-4371)
Cinch Connectors Inc .......................D....... 630 705-6001
 Lombard (G-13780)
Cinch Connectors Inc .......................B....... 630 705-6001
 Lombard (G-13781)
▲ Clements National Company ..........G....... 708 594-5890
 Broadview (G-2569)
Coleman Cable LLC ...........................F....... 847 672-2508
 Waukegan (G-21540)
◆ Coleman Cable LLC ...........................D....... 847 672-2300
 Waukegan (G-21542)
Connector Concepts Inc ...................F....... 847 541-4020
 Mundelein (G-15491)
Connomac Corporation ....................E....... 708 482-3434
 La Grange (G-12729)
Cooper B-Line Inc ..............................F....... 618 667-6779
 Troy (G-21004)
▲ CTS Automotive LLC ........................G....... 630 614-7201
 Lisle (G-13578)
Cutshaw Instls Inc ..............................G....... 847 426-9208
 East Dundee (G-8630)
Data Cable Technologies Inc ...........F....... 630 226-5600
 Romeoville (G-18816)
David Jeskey .......................................G....... 630 659-6337
 Saint Charles (G-19168)
Dcx-Chol Enterprises Inc .................F....... 309 353-4455
 Pekin (G-17258)
▲ Deringer-Ney Inc ...............................E....... 847 566-4100
 Vernon Hills (G-21157)
Dollar Express ....................................G....... 815 399-9719
 Rockford (G-18350)

Dqm Inc ................................................F....... 630 692-0633
 Oswego (G-16914)
Eagle Connector Corporation ..........F....... 847 593-8737
 Elk Grove Village (G-9446)
▲ Eastco Inc ...........................................G....... 708 499-1701
 Oak Lawn (G-16617)
▲ Excel Specialty Corp .........................E....... 773 262-7575
 Lake Forest (G-12898)
▲ Flex-Weld Inc .....................................D....... 815 334-3662
 Woodstock (G-22567)
French Corporation ............................E....... 708 354-9000
 La Grange (G-12732)
◆ Garvin Industries Inc .......................E....... 847 455-0188
 Franklin Park (G-10475)
Gateway Cable Inc ............................G....... 630 766-7969
 Lisle (G-13592)
General Electric Company .................E....... 309 664-1513
 Bloomington (G-2170)
▲ GKN Stromag Inc ..............................E....... 937 433-3882
 Woodridge (G-22485)
Grayhill Inc ..........................................C....... 847 428-6990
 Carpentersville (G-3285)
▲ Grayhill Inc .........................................B....... 708 354-1040
 La Grange (G-12734)
▲ Gus Berthold Electric Company ......E....... 312 243-5767
 Chicago (G-5013)
▲ Harger Inc ...........................................E....... 847 548-8700
 Grayslake (G-11345)
Hauhinco LP ........................................E....... 618 993-5399
 Marion (G-14264)
▲ Heil Sound Ltd ..................................F....... 618 257-3000
 Fairview Heights (G-10168)
Hubbell Incorporated ........................F....... 972 756-1184
 Aurora (G-1170)
Ideal Industries Inc ............................C....... 815 895-1108
 Sycamore (G-20801)
Ideal Industries Inc ............................C....... 815 895-5181
 Sycamore (G-20802)
▲ Ideal Industries Inc ..........................C....... 815 895-5181
 Sycamore (G-20800)
Ideal Industries Inc ............................D....... 815 758-2656
 Dekalb (G-8098)
Illinois Tool Works Inc ......................C....... 847 876-9400
 Des Plaines (G-8208)
Imperial Fabricators Co ....................E....... 773 463-5522
 Franklin Park (G-10495)
▲ Inglot Electronics Corp ....................D....... 773 286-5881
 Chicago (G-5192)
Itron Corporation Del .........................F....... 708 222-5320
 Cicero (G-3207)
J P Goldenne Incorporated ..............F....... 847 776-5063
 Palatine (G-17045)
▲ Ki Industries Inc ................................E....... 708 449-1990
 Berkeley (G-2046)
Leviton Manufacturing Co Inc .........D....... 630 539-0249
 Bloomingdale (G-2113)
Leviton Manufacturing Co Inc .........C....... 630 443-0500
 Saint Charles (G-19209)
Leviton Manufacturing Co Inc .........B....... 630 350-2656
 Bensenville (G-1941)
◆ Lumisource LLC ................................E....... 847 699-8988
 Elk Grove Village (G-9600)
▲ Lutamar Electrical Assemblies ......E....... 847 679-5400
 Skokie (G-20032)
M E Barber Co Inc ..............................G....... 217 428-4591
 Decatur (G-7909)
Mac Lean-Fogg Company ..................C....... 847 288-2534
 Franklin Park (G-10519)
◆ Maclean Senior Industries LLC .......E....... 630 350-1600
 Wood Dale (G-22393)
▼ Magnetrol International Inc ............C....... 630 723-6600
 Aurora (G-1051)
Methode Development Co ................D....... 708 867-6777
 Chicago (G-5703)
Methode Electronics Inc ...................C....... 847 577-9545
 Rolling Meadows (G-18744)
Methode Electronics Inc ...................E....... 217 357-3941
 Carthage (G-3316)
▲ Methode Electronics Inc .................B....... 708 867-6777
 Chicago (G-5704)
Micro West Ltd ....................................G....... 630 766-7160
 Bensenville (G-1949)
Midwest Fiber Solutions ...................G....... 217 971-7400
 Springfield (G-20484)
▲ Molex LLC ..........................................A....... 630 969-4550
 Lisle (G-13625)
Molex LLC ............................................E....... 630 527-4363
 Bolingbrook (G-2345)
Molex LLC ............................................F....... 630 512-8787
 Downers Grove (G-8489)

SIC SECTION 36 ELECTRONIC AND OTHER ELECTRICAL EQUIPMENT AND COMPONENTS, EXCEPT COMPUTER

▲ **Molex International Inc** F 630 969-4550 Lisle *(G-13627)*
▲ **Molex Premise Networks Inc** A 866 733-6659 Lisle *(G-13628)*
**Morrell Incorporated** F 630 858-4600 Glendale Heights *(G-11050)*
**Mpc Products Corporation** G 847 673-8300 Niles *(G-16012)*
**Pancon Illinois LLC** G 630 972-6400 Bolingbrook *(G-2356)*
**Panduit Corp** E 815 836-1800 Lockport *(G-13737)*
**Porch Electric LLC** G 815 368-3230 Lostant *(G-13908)*
**Possehl Connector Svcs SC Inc** E 803 366-8316 Elk Grove Village *(G-9687)*
**Process Screw Products Inc** E 815 864-2220 Shannon *(G-19901)*
**Radionic Hi-Tech Inc** D 773 804-0100 Chicago *(G-6281)*
▲ **Remke Industries Inc** D 847 541-3780 Wheeling *(G-22135)*
**Remke Industries Inc** D 847 325-7835 Wheeling *(G-22136)*
▲ **Rockford Rigging Inc** F 309 263-0566 Roscoe *(G-18914)*
**Rrp Enterprises Inc** G 847 455-5674 Franklin Park *(G-10577)*
◆ **S & C Electric Company** A 773 338-1000 Chicago *(G-6419)*
**S-P Products Inc** F 847 593-8595 Elk Grove Village *(G-9725)*
▲ **Safco LLC** E 847 677-3204 Skokie *(G-20081)*
**Schneider Electric Usa Inc** E 847 441-2526 Schaumburg *(G-19723)*
**Shattuc Cord Specialties Inc** F 847 360-9500 Waukegan *(G-21615)*
▲ **Sicame Corp** D 630 238-6680 Aurora *(G-1217)*
**Simmons Lightning Protection** G 217 746-3971 Burnside *(G-2817)*
▲ **Simple Assemblies Inc** G 708 212-7494 New Lenox *(G-15911)*
▼ **Simplex Inc** C 217 483-1600 Springfield *(G-20526)*
**Skach Manufacturing Co Inc** E 847 395-3560 Antioch *(G-655)*
**Special Mine Services Inc** D 618 932-2151 West Frankfort *(G-21820)*
▲ **Switchcraft Inc** B 773 792-2700 Chicago *(G-6653)*
▲ **Switchcraft Holdco Inc** G 773 792-2700 Chicago *(G-6654)*
**Telegartner Inc** E 630 616-7600 Franklin Park *(G-10605)*
**Triton Manufacturing Co Inc** D 708 587-4000 Monee *(G-15004)*
**Twin City Electric Inc** E 309 827-0636 Bloomington *(G-2233)*
**U S Tool & Manufacturing Co** E 630 953-1000 Addison *(G-332)*
**United Universal Inds Inc** E 815 727-4445 Joliet *(G-12585)*
**Unlimited Svcs Wisconsin Inc** E 815 399-0282 Machesney Park *(G-14117)*
**Western-Cullen-Hayes Inc** D 773 254-9600 Chicago *(G-6964)*
▲ **Woodhead Industries LLC** B 847 353-2500 Lincolnshire *(G-13490)*
▲ **Woodward Controls Inc** C 847 673-8300 Skokie *(G-20114)*

## 3644 Noncurrent-Carrying Wiring Devices

**Aco Inc** E 773 774-5200 Chicago *(G-3735)*
▲ **Anamet Electrical Inc** C 217 234-8844 Mattoon *(G-14382)*
**Anamet Inc** G 217 234-8844 Glen Ellyn *(G-10958)*
▲ **Appleton Grp LLC** C 847 268-6000 Rosemont *(G-18989)*
▼ **Atlas Tube (chicago) LLC** B 773 646-4500 Chicago *(G-3984)*
▲ **Beacon Fas & Components Inc** E 847 541-0404 Wheeling *(G-22013)*
▲ **Cable Management Products Inc** G 630 723-0470 Aurora *(G-976)*
**Chase Corporation** F 630 752-3622 Wheaton *(G-21940)*
**Chase Corporation** F 708 385-4679 Palos Heights *(G-17101)*
**Chicago Switchboard Co Inc** E 630 833-2266 Elmhurst *(G-9848)*
**Chicagoland Raceway** G 708 203-8003 Downers Grove *(G-8410)*
**Dells Raceway Park Inc** G 815 494-0074 Roscoe *(G-18893)*
**Eaton Corporation** A 217 732-3131 Lincoln *(G-13409)*
▲ **Electri-Flex Company (del)** D 630 307-1095 Roselle *(G-18941)*
**Electric Conduit Cnstr Co** C 630 293-4474 Elburn *(G-8886)*
**Electric Conduit Construction** F 630 859-9310 Elburn *(G-8887)*
▲ **Excel Specialty Corp** E 773 262-7575 Lake Forest *(G-12898)*
**Guardian Energy Tech Inc** F 800 516-0949 Riverwoods *(G-18038)*
**Honeywell International Inc** G 815 235-5500 Freeport *(G-10664)*
▲ **Hubbell Wiegmann Inc** B 618 539-3542 Freeburg *(G-10637)*
**Illinois Tool Works Inc** D 847 537-8800 Lincolnshire *(G-13457)*
**Imperial Fabricators Co** E 773 463-5522 Franklin Park *(G-10495)*
**J & A Sheet Metal Shop Inc** E 773 276-3739 Chicago *(G-5250)*
**John Maneely Company** C 773 254-0617 Chicago *(G-5316)*
**Jpmorgan Chase & Co** F 773 978-3408 Chicago *(G-5329)*
**Jpmorgan Chase Bank Nat Assn** G 773 994-2490 Chicago *(G-5330)*
**Jpmorgan Chase Bank Nat Assn** G 847 685-0490 Park Ridge *(G-17205)*
▲ **Lew Electric Fittings Co** F 630 665-2075 Carol Stream *(G-3183)*
▲ **Lutamar Electrical Assemblies** E 847 679-5400 Skokie *(G-20032)*
◆ **Maclean Senior Industries LLC** E 630 350-1600 Wood Dale *(G-22393)*
**Methode Development Co** D 708 867-6777 Chicago *(G-5703)*
**Midwest-Design Inc** G 708 615-1572 Broadview *(G-2596)*
▲ **Minerallac Company** E 630 543-7080 Hampshire *(G-11554)*
**Panduit Corp** C 708 460-1800 Orland Park *(G-16882)*
**Panduit Corp** E 815 836-1800 Lockport *(G-13737)*
◆ **Panduit Corp** A 708 532-1800 Tinley Park *(G-20937)*
**Party Fantasy** G 847 837-0010 Mundelein *(G-15542)*
▲ **Questek Manufacturing Corp** D 847 428-0300 Elgin *(G-9159)*
**Raceway Electric Company Inc** G 630 501-1180 Elmhurst *(G-9924)*
**Resinite Corporation** C 847 537-4250 Wheeling *(G-22138)*
**Southern IL Raceway** G 618 201-0500 Marion *(G-14288)*
**Taurus Safety Products Inc** G 630 620-7940 Lombard *(G-13865)*
**Vertiv Group Corporation** E 630 579-5000 Lombard *(G-13878)*

## 3645 Residential Lighting Fixtures

▲ **Advanced Micro Lites Inc** G 630 365-5450 Elburn *(G-8874)*
◆ **Afx Inc** C 847 249-5970 Waukegan *(G-21519)*
**Astral Power Systems Inc** G 630 518-1741 Aurora *(G-1112)*
**Cooper Lighting LLC** G 312 595-2770 Elk Grove Village *(G-9393)*
**Cooper Lighting LLC** D 847 956-8400 Elk Grove Village *(G-9394)*
**Cosas Inc** G 312 492-6100 Chicago *(G-4477)*
▲ **Eclipse Lighting Inc** E 847 260-0333 Schiller Park *(G-19823)*
▲ **Elcast Manufacturing Inc** E 630 628-1992 Addison *(G-107)*
**Fanmar Inc** E 708 563-0505 Elk Grove Village *(G-9475)*
**Fli Products LLC** G 630 520-0017 West Chicago *(G-21702)*
▲ **Gerber Manufacturing (gm) LLC** F 708 478-0100 Mokena *(G-14868)*
**Greencast Services Inc** G 630 723-8000 Hinsdale *(G-11950)*
**Grow Masters** G 224 399-9877 Gurnee *(G-11454)*
▲ **H A Framburg & Company** E 708 547-5757 Bellwood *(G-1708)*
**H E Associates Inc** F 630 553-6382 Yorkville *(G-22661)*
▲ **Intermatic Incorporated** A 815 675-2321 Spring Grove *(G-20337)*
▲ **Io Lighting LLC** E 847 735-7000 Vernon Hills *(G-21176)*
▲ **K&I Light Kandi Led Inc** G 773 745-1533 Chicago *(G-5345)*
**Lamp Co of America Inc** G 630 584-4001 Saint Charles *(G-19207)*
▲ **Lampshade Inc** F 773 522-2300 Chicago *(G-5454)*
**Larentia Led LLC** F 312 291-9111 Chicago *(G-5462)*
▲ **Lifespan Brands LLC** F 630 315-3300 Elk Grove Village *(G-9595)*
**Lightolier Genlyte Inc** D 847 364-8250 Elk Grove Village *(G-9596)*
▲ **Lumenart Ltd** G 773 254-0744 Chicago *(G-5563)*
▲ **Lumenart Ltd** G 773 254-0744 Chicago *(G-5562)*
**McAteers Wholesale** G 618 233-3400 Belleville *(G-1654)*
▲ **Metomic Corporation** E 773 247-4716 Chicago *(G-5705)*
**Midwest Sun-Ray Lighting & Sig** F 618 656-2884 Granite City *(G-11296)*
▲ **New Metal Crafts Inc** E 312 787-6991 Lincolnwood *(G-13526)*
◆ **Pace Industries Inc** D 312 226-5500 Chicago *(G-6051)*
**Paramount Wire Specialties** F 773 252-5636 Chicago *(G-6080)*
▲ **Productworks LLC** G 224 406-8810 Northbrook *(G-16347)*
▲ **Rgb Lights Inc** F 312 421-6080 Chicago *(G-6346)*
▼ **Royal Haeger Lamp Co** E 309 837-9966 Macomb *(G-14132)*
▲ **Smart Solar Inc** F 813 343-5770 Libertyville *(G-13382)*
▲ **Sternberg Lanterns Inc** C 847 588-3400 Roselle *(G-18980)*
**Stone Lighting LLC** F 312 240-0400 Flossmoor *(G-10230)*
▲ **Uncommon Radiant** G 773 640-1674 Chicago *(G-6810)*
▲ **Vaxcel International Co Ltd** E 630 260-0067 Carol Stream *(G-3261)*
**Western Lighting Inc** F 847 451-7200 Franklin Park *(G-10628)*

## 3646 Commercial, Indl & Institutional Lighting Fixtures

**555 International Inc** E 773 869-0555 Chicago *(G-3671)*
**555 International Inc** E 773 847-1400 Chicago *(G-3670)*
▲ **Advanced Specialty Lighting** C 708 867-3140 Harwood Heights *(G-11681)*
◆ **Afx Inc** C 847 249-5970 Waukegan *(G-21519)*
**Amerilights Inc** G 847 219-1476 Bloomingdale *(G-2093)*
▲ **Appleton Grp LLC** C 847 268-6000 Rosemont *(G-18989)*
**Astral Power Systems Inc** G 630 518-1741 Aurora *(G-1112)*
**Avtec Inc** F 618 337-7800 East Saint Louis *(G-8742)*
**Blackjack Lighting** G 847 941-0588 Buffalo Grove *(G-2666)*
▲ **Challenger Lighting Co Inc** E 847 717-4700 Batavia *(G-1429)*
**Conservation Tech III LLC** G 847 559-5500 Northbrook *(G-16231)*
◆ **Conservation Technology Ltd** D 847 559-5500 Northbrook *(G-16232)*

S I C

36 ELECTRONIC AND OTHER ELECTRICAL EQUIPMENT AND COMPONENTS, EXCEPT COMPUTER SIC SECTION

**Contemprary Enrgy Slutions LLC** F 630 768-3743
Naperville *(G-15801)*

**Cooper Lighting LLC** D 847 956-8400
Elk Grove Village *(G-9394)*

**Dado Lighting LLC** G 877 323-6584
Western Springs *(G-21866)*

**Dva Mayday Corporation** G 847 848-7555
Village of Lakewood *(G-21290)*

▲ **Eclipse Lighting Inc** E 847 260-0333
Schiller Park *(G-19823)*

◆ **Esco Lighting Inc** E 773 427-7000
Chicago *(G-4776)*

▲ **Eti Solid State Lighting Inc** E 855 384-7754
Vernon Hills *(G-21162)*

**Everlights Inc** F 773 734-9873
Skokie *(G-19996)*

**First Light Inc** G 630 520-0017
West Chicago *(G-21701)*

**Fli Products LLC** G 630 520-0017
West Chicago *(G-21702)*

**Focal Point Lighting Inc** C 773 247-9494
Chicago *(G-4866)*

▲ **Focal Point LLC** C 773 247-9494
Chicago *(G-4867)*

▲ **Glamox Aqua Signal Corporation** F 847 639-6412
Cary *(G-3348)*

▲ **H A Framburg & Company** E 708 547-5757
Bellwood *(G-1708)*

▲ **Holiday Bright Lights Inc** G 312 226-8281
Chicago *(G-5099)*

**Jarvis Corp** E 800 363-1075
Elk Grove Village *(G-9560)*

**Lamp Co of America Inc** G 630 584-4001
Saint Charles *(G-19207)*

**Larentia Led LLC** F 312 291-9111
Chicago *(G-5462)*

**Leading Energy Designs Ltd** G 815 382-8852
Woodstock *(G-22583)*

**Led Business Solutions LLC** F 844 464-5337
Downers Grove *(G-8474)*

◆ **Led Lighting Inc** F 847 412-4880
Buffalo Grove *(G-2723)*

**Lighting Design By Michael Ant** G 708 289-4783
Mokena *(G-14880)*

▲ **Louvers International Inc** E 630 782-9977
Elmhurst *(G-9903)*

**Morris Kurtzon Incorporated** E 773 277-2121
Chicago *(G-5806)*

◆ **Neptun Light Inc** G 847 735-8330
Lake Forest *(G-12929)*

▲ **New Metal Crafts Inc** E 312 787-6991
Lincolnwood *(G-13526)*

▲ **New Star Custom Lighting Co** E 773 254-7827
Chicago *(G-5896)*

▲ **North Star Lighting LLC** D 708 681-4330
Elmhurst *(G-9915)*

**Paul D Metal Products Inc** D 773 847-1400
Chicago *(G-6090)*

**Philips Lighting N Amer Corp** C 800 825-5844
Rosemont *(G-19022)*

▲ **Productworks LLC** G 224 406-8810
Northbrook *(G-16347)*

▲ **Pure Lighting LLC** F 773 770-1130
Chicago *(G-6229)*

◆ **Rainbow Lighting** E 847 480-1136
Northbrook *(G-16352)*

▲ **Rgb Lights Inc** F 312 421-6080
Chicago *(G-6346)*

**S-P Products Inc** F 847 593-8595
Elk Grove Village *(G-9725)*

▲ **Security Lighting Systems Inc** E 800 544-4848
Rolling Meadows *(G-18778)*

**Square 1 Precision Ltg Inc** G 708 343-1500
Melrose Park *(G-14695)*

▲ **Sternberg Lanterns Inc** C 847 588-3400
Roselle *(G-18980)*

**Sustanble Sltions Amer Led LLC** F 866 323-3494
Chicago *(G-6644)*

▲ **Tri-Lite Inc** E 773 384-7765
Chicago *(G-6770)*

**Twin Supplies Ltd** F 630 590-5138
Oak Brook *(G-16566)*

▲ **Waldmann Lighting Company** E 847 520-1060
Wheeling *(G-22180)*

▲ **Wallace/Haskin Corp** G 630 789-2882
Downers Grove *(G-8540)*

**Western Lighting Inc** F 847 451-7200
Franklin Park *(G-10628)*

## 3647 Vehicular Lighting Eqpt

**Elc Industries Corp** C 630 851-1616
Aurora *(G-1143)*

▲ **Elc Industries Corp** E 630 851-1616
Aurora *(G-1144)*

**Els Electronic Lighting Spc** G 708 453-3666
Elmwood Park *(G-9969)*

◆ **Federal Signal Corporation** D 630 954-2000
Oak Brook *(G-16510)*

▲ **Glamox Aqua Signal Corporation** F 847 639-6412
Cary *(G-3348)*

**L & T Services Inc** G 815 397-6260
Rockford *(G-18458)*

▲ **Lecip Inc** G 312 626-2525
Bensenville *(G-1939)*

**Mellish & Murray Co** F 312 733-3513
Chicago *(G-5683)*

▲ **North American Lighting Inc** A 217 465-6600
Paris *(G-17155)*

**North American Lighting Inc** A 618 548-6249
Salem *(G-19340)*

**North American Lighting Inc** B 618 662-4483
Flora *(G-10212)*

◆ **Progress Rail Locomotive Inc** A 800 255-5355
Mc Cook *(G-14456)*

**Progress Rail Locomotive Inc** F 708 387-5510
Mc Cook *(G-14457)*

**River View Motor Sports Inc** G 309 467-4569
Congerville *(G-7371)*

▲ **Tiger Accessory Group LLC** G 847 821-9630
Long Grove *(G-13902)*

**Tool Automation Enterprises** G 708 799-6847
East Hazel Crest *(G-8666)*

▲ **Tri-Lite Inc** E 773 384-7765
Chicago *(G-6770)*

## 3648 Lighting Eqpt, NEC

**A Burst of Sun Inc** G 815 335-2331
Winnebago *(G-22294)*

▲ **Advanced Cstm Enrgy Sltons Inc** D 312 428-9540
Chicago *(G-3768)*

**Afterdark Outdoor Lighting** G 708 243-1228
Lockport *(G-13702)*

▲ **APL Engineered Materials Inc** E 217 367-1340
Urbana *(G-21070)*

**Apolinski John** G 847 696-3156
Park Ridge *(G-17181)*

**Artemide Inc** G 312 475-0100
Chicago *(G-3954)*

▲ **Big Beam Emergency Systems Inc** E 815 459-6100
Crystal Lake *(G-7541)*

**Bilt-Rite Metal Products Inc** E 815 495-2211
Leland *(G-13218)*

**Boston Warehouse Trading Corp** G 630 992-5604
Aurora *(G-972)*

▲ **Carmen Matthew LLC** D 630 784-7500
Elgin *(G-8984)*

**City of Pekin** F 309 477-2325
Pekin *(G-17256)*

▲ **Clements National Company** G 708 594-5890
Broadview *(G-2569)*

**Comcast Corporation** E 217 498-3274
Quincy *(G-17815)*

**Cyclops Industrial Inc** G 815 962-1984
Rockford *(G-18329)*

**D2 Lighting LLC** G 708 243-9059
La Grange Highlands *(G-12749)*

**David Michael Productions** F 630 972-9640
Woodridge *(G-22469)*

**Designed For Just For You** G 309 221-2667
Macomb *(G-14124)*

**Duroweld Company Inc** E 847 680-3064
Lake Bluff *(G-12841)*

**Eagle High Mast Ltg Co Inc** G 847 473-3800
Waukegan *(G-21555)*

**Efficient Energy Lighting Inc** G 630 272-9388
Sycamore *(G-20796)*

▲ **Elcast Manufacturing Inc** E 630 628-1992
Addison *(G-107)*

**Est Lighting Inc** G 847 612-1705
Richmond *(G-17962)*

**F G Lighting Inc** G 847 295-0445
Lake Bluff *(G-12842)*

▲ **First Alert Inc** G 630 499-3295
Aurora *(G-1009)*

**First-Light Usa LLC** F 217 687-4048
Seymour *(G-19897)*

**Flex Lighting II LLC** G 312 929-3488
Chicago *(G-4857)*

**Golden Road Productions** G 217 335-2606
New Canton *(G-15868)*

▲ **Good Earth Lighting Inc** E 847 808-1133
Mount Prospect *(G-15333)*

**Group O Inc** D 309 736-8660
Milan *(G-14788)*

▲ **Ilight Technologies Inc** F 312 876-8630
Chicago *(G-5152)*

**Illuminight Lighting LLC** F 312 685-4448
Highland Park *(G-11843)*

**Intex Lighting LLC** G 847 380-2027
Schaumburg *(G-19575)*

**Jr Lighting Design Inc** G 708 460-6319
Tinley Park *(G-20926)*

**Lakeshore Lighting LLC** G 847 989-5843
Mundelein *(G-15518)*

▲ **Lampholders Assemblies Inc** G 773 205-0005
Chicago *(G-5453)*

▲ **Lbl Lighting LLC** F 708 755-2100
Skokie *(G-20028)*

▲ **Lighting Innovations Inc** E 630 889-8100
Saint Charles *(G-19211)*

**Lightitech LLC** G 847 910-4177
Chicago *(G-5504)*

**Lightscape Inc** E 847 247-8800
Libertyville *(G-13344)*

**Litetronics Technologies Inc** G 708 333-6707
Chicago *(G-5518)*

**Microlite Corporation** G 630 876-0500
West Chicago *(G-21742)*

**Midwest Sign & Lighting Inc** G 708 365-5555
Country Club Hills *(G-7410)*

▲ **Modern Home Products Corp** E 847 395-6556
Antioch *(G-647)*

**Musco Sports Lighting LLC** E 630 876-0500
Batavia *(G-1473)*

▲ **North American Signal Co** E 847 537-8888
Wheeling *(G-22108)*

**Northern Lighting & Power Inc** G 708 383-9926
Oak Park *(G-16677)*

**Patty Style Shop** G 618 654-2015
Highland *(G-11805)*

▲ **Plastic Technologies Inc** E 847 841-8610
Elgin *(G-9140)*

**Poem Lighting Company** G 847 395-1768
Antioch *(G-651)*

▲ **Press A Light Corporation** F 630 231-6566
West Chicago *(G-21760)*

▲ **Productworks LLC** G 224 406-8810
Northbrook *(G-16347)*

**Promier Products Inc** F 815 223-3393
Peru *(G-17524)*

**Radionic Hi-Tech Inc** D 773 804-0100
Chicago *(G-6281)*

**SC Lighting** G 630 849-3384
Schaumburg *(G-19720)*

▲ **Schreder Lighting LLC** E 847 621-5130
Addison *(G-282)*

▲ **Sensio America LLC** F 877 501-5337
Carol Stream *(G-3238)*

**Shinetoo Lighting America LLC** G 877 957-7317
Des Plaines *(G-8274)*

▲ **Soleil Systems Inc** E 847 427-0428
Schaumburg *(G-19731)*

**Spotlight Youth Theater** G 847 516-2298
Cary *(G-3373)*

**Spurt Inc** G 847 571-6497
Northbrook *(G-16370)*

**Square 1 Precision Ltg Inc** G 708 343-1500
Melrose Park *(G-14695)*

▲ **Sternberg Lanterns Inc** C 847 588-3400
Roselle *(G-18980)*

**Tactical Lighting Systems Inc** F 800 705-0518
Addison *(G-306)*

**Track Master Inc** G 815 675-6603
Spring Grove *(G-20370)*

**Transco Products Inc** E 815 672-2197
Streator *(G-20709)*

▲ **Tri-Lite Inc** E 773 384-7765
Chicago *(G-6770)*

**Twin Supplies Ltd** F 630 590-5138
Oak Brook *(G-16566)*

**Western Lighting Inc** F 847 451-7200
Franklin Park *(G-10628)*

## 3651 Household Audio & Video Eqpt

**A and T Labs Incorporated** G 630 668-8562
Wheaton *(G-21932)*

**Aco Inc** E 773 774-5200
Chicago *(G-3735)*

SIC SECTION 36 ELECTRONIC AND OTHER ELECTRICAL EQUIPMENT AND COMPONENTS, EXCEPT COMPUTER

◆ **Acoustic Avenue Inc** ....F .... 217 544-9810
Springfield *(G-20385)*
**Advance Tools LLC** ....G .... 855 685-0633
Glenview *(G-11097)*
**Advanced Audio Devices LLC** ....G .... 847 604-9630
Lake Forest *(G-12875)*
**Alexander Brewster LLC** ....G .... 618 346-8580
Collinsville *(G-7314)*
▲ **Alumapro Inc** ....G .... 224 569-3650
Huntley *(G-12131)*
▲ **Amplivox Sound Systems LLC** ....E .... 800 267-5486
Northbrook *(G-16204)*
▲ **Audio Installers Inc** ....F .... 815 969-7500
Loves Park *(G-13923)*
**Audio Supply Inc** ....G .... 847 549-6086
Mundelein *(G-15472)*
**Audio Video Electronics LLC** ....G .... 847 983-4761
Skokie *(G-19961)*
**AVI-Spl Employee** ....B .... 847 437-7712
Schaumburg *(G-19454)*
▲ **Bem Wireless LLC** ....F .... 815 337-0541
Algonquin *(G-381)*
**Bose Corporation** ....G .... 630 575-8044
Hinsdale *(G-11942)*
**Bose Corporation** ....G .... 630 585-6654
Aurora *(G-971)*
◆ **Bretford Manufacturing Inc** ....B .... 847 678-2545
Franklin Park *(G-10416)*
**Buzzfire Incorporated** ....F .... 630 572-9200
Oak Brook *(G-16496)*
**Cco Holdings LLC** ....G .... 618 505-3505
Troy *(G-21003)*
**Cco Holdings LLC** ....G .... 618 651-6486
Highland *(G-11777)*
◆ **Chamberlain Manufacturing Corp** ....A .... 630 279-3600
Oak Brook *(G-16500)*
**Cinemaquest Inc** ....G .... 847 603-7649
Gurnee *(G-11433)*
**Connecteriors LLC** ....G .... 773 549-3333
Chicago *(G-4449)*
**Crystal Partners Inc** ....G .... 847 882-0467
Schaumburg *(G-19493)*
**Decibel Audio Inc** ....G .... 773 862-6700
Chicago *(G-4569)*
**Delta Design Inc** ....F .... 708 424-9400
Evergreen Park *(G-10112)*
**Digital Living Inc** ....G .... 708 434-1197
Oak Park *(G-16659)*
▲ **Elexa Consumer Products Inc** ....B .... 773 794-1300
Deerfield *(G-8006)*
**Epic Eye** ....G .... 309 210-6212
Grand Ridge *(G-11257)*
**Fire CAM LLC** ....G .... 618 416-8390
Belleville *(G-1632)*
▲ **Foster Electric (usa) Inc** ....F .... 847 310-8200
Schaumburg *(G-19532)*
**G T C Industries Inc** ....G .... 708 369-9815
Naperville *(G-15661)*
**Gier Radio & Television Inc** ....G .... 815 722-8514
Joliet *(G-12502)*
**Guys Hi-Def Inc** ....G .... 708 261-7487
Joliet *(G-12506)*
▲ **Hammond Suzuki Usa Inc** ....E .... 630 543-0277
Addison *(G-141)*
▲ **Heil Sound Ltd** ....F .... 618 257-3000
Fairview Heights *(G-10168)*
**Home Specialty Connection Inc** ....G .... 815 363-1934
Chicago *(G-5103)*
**Identatronics Inc** ....E .... 847 437-2654
Crystal Lake *(G-7591)*
**Ionit Technologies Inc** ....E .... 847 205-9651
Northfield *(G-16403)*
**J P Goldenne Incorporated** ....F .... 847 776-5063
Palatine *(G-17045)*
**John Hardy Co** ....G .... 847 864-8060
Evanston *(G-10059)*
**K C Audio** ....G .... 708 636-4928
Alsip *(G-477)*
**Key Car Stereo** ....G .... 217 446-4556
Oakwood *(G-16726)*
**Knowles Corporation** ....D .... 630 250-5100
Itasca *(G-12295)*
**Knowles Elec Holdings Inc** ....A .... 630 250-5100
Itasca *(G-12296)*
**Linx Enterprises LLC** ....G .... 224 409-2206
Chicago *(G-5516)*
▲ **Maxxsonics Usa Inc** ....E .... 847 540-7700
Libertyville *(G-13350)*
**Mechanical Music Corp** ....F .... 847 398-5444
Arlington Heights *(G-801)*
**Mitek Corporation** ....C .... 608 328-5560
Winslow *(G-22317)*
**Mitek Corporation** ....C .... 815 367-3000
Winslow *(G-22318)*
▲ **Nantsound Inc** ....F .... 847 939-6101
Park Ridge *(G-17210)*
▲ **Newhaven Display Intl Inc** ....E .... 847 844-8795
Elgin *(G-9118)*
**Northrop Grumman Systems Corp** ....A .... 847 259-9600
Rolling Meadows *(G-18753)*
**Nueva Vida Productions Inc** ....G .... 708 444-8474
Tinley Park *(G-20935)*
**Organized Noise Inc** ....G .... 630 820-9855
Aurora *(G-1059)*
**Peterson Intl Entp Ltd** ....F .... 847 541-3700
Wheeling *(G-22121)*
**Philips Lighting N Amer Corp** ....E .... 708 307-3000
Roselle *(G-18962)*
**Prager Associates** ....G .... 309 691-1565
Peoria *(G-17433)*
▲ **Precision Electronics Inc** ....F .... 847 599-1799
Gurnee *(G-11490)*
**Prescotts Inc** ....G .... 815 626-2996
Sterling *(G-20605)*
**Pyar & Company LLC** ....G .... 312 451-5073
Chicago *(G-6232)*
▲ **Quam-Nichols Company** ....C .... 773 488-5800
Chicago *(G-6249)*
**Relay Systems America Inc** ....F .... 815 730-0100
Joliet *(G-12565)*
**Rf Communications Inc** ....F .... 630 420-8882
Naperville *(G-15741)*
▲ **Robotics Technologies Inc** ....E .... 815 722-7650
Joliet *(G-12570)*
**Sansui America Inc** ....C .... 618 392-7000
Olney *(G-16796)*
▲ **SBA Wireless Inc** ....E .... 847 215-8720
Buffalo Grove *(G-2762)*
▲ **Senario LLC** ....F .... 847 882-0677
Schaumburg *(G-19725)*
**Shockyave Customs** ....G .... 815 469-9141
Frankfort *(G-10363)*
**Shure Incorporated** ....F .... 847 520-4404
Wheeling *(G-22150)*
**Sonic Low Voltage** ....G .... 815 790-4400
Johnsburg *(G-12442)*
**Sonistic** ....G .... 217 377-9698
Champaign *(G-3542)*
**Sony Electronics Inc** ....C .... 630 773-7500
Carol Stream *(G-3242)*
▲ **Sound Enhancement Products Inc** ....E .... 847 639-4646
Glendale Heights *(G-11070)*
**Studio Technologies Inc** ....F .... 847 676-9177
Skokie *(G-20093)*
**Sytek Audio Systems Corp** ....F .... 847 345-6971
Palatine *(G-17077)*
**Tech Upgraders** ....G .... 877 324-8940
Maywood *(G-14435)*
**Techpol Automation Inc** ....G .... 847 347-4765
Des Plaines *(G-8285)*
**Touchtunes Music Corporation** ....E .... 847 253-8708
Schaumburg *(G-19765)*
**United States Audio Corp** ....F .... 312 316-2929
Glenview *(G-11213)*
**United States Audio Corp** ....G .... 312 316-2929
Chicago *(G-6827)*
**Van L Speakerworks Inc** ....G .... 773 769-0773
Chicago *(G-6870)*
**Victoria Amplifier Company** ....F .... 630 369-3527
Naperville *(G-15831)*
**Vidicon LLC** ....G .... 815 756-9600
Dekalb *(G-8130)*
**William N Pasulka** ....G .... 815 339-6300
Peru *(G-17532)*
▲ **Wireless Chamberlain Products** ....E .... 800 282-6225
Elmhurst *(G-9961)*
**Wirelessusa Inc** ....G .... 217 222-4300
Quincy *(G-17906)*
**Zenith Electronics Corporation** ....E .... 847 941-8000
Lincolnshire *(G-13496)*

## *3652 Phonograph Records & Magnetic Tape*

**Acta Publications** ....G .... 773 989-3036
Chicago *(G-3739)*
**Advanced Audio Technology Inc** ....G .... 630 665-3344
Carol Stream *(G-3090)*
▼ **Alligator Rec & Artist MGT Inc** ....F .... 773 973-7736
Chicago *(G-3819)*
**Aztec Corporation** ....G ....
Downers Grove *(G-8391)*
◆ **B D C Inc** ....E .... 847 741-2233
Elgin *(G-8962)*
**Cedille Chicago Nfp** ....G .... 773 989-2515
Chicago *(G-4266)*
**Chicago Producers Inc** ....F .... 312 226-6900
Forest Park *(G-10237)*
**Corporate Disk Company** ....D .... 800 634-3475
McHenry *(G-14489)*
**Crusade Enterprises Inc** ....G .... 618 662-4461
Flora *(G-10205)*
**Datasis Corporation** ....F .... 847 427-0909
Elk Grove Village *(G-9417)*
▲ **Drag City** ....G .... 312 455-1015
Chicago *(G-4642)*
**Idea Media Services LLC** ....F .... 312 226-2900
Chicago *(G-5138)*
**Lion Productions LLC** ....G .... 630 845-1610
Geneva *(G-10846)*
**Private Studios** ....G .... 217 367-3530
Urbana *(G-21099)*
**Replay S Disc Cook-Kankaee LLC** ....F .... 312 371-5018
Monee *(G-15000)*
**Robert Koester** ....G .... 773 539-5001
Chicago *(G-6368)*
**Solid Sound Inc** ....G .... 847 490-2101
Hoffman Estates *(G-12055)*
**Sparrow Sound Design** ....G .... 773 281-8510
Chicago *(G-6552)*
**Spectape of Midwest Inc** ....G .... 630 682-8600
Glen Ellyn *(G-10990)*
**Tony Patterson** ....G .... 773 487-4000
Chicago *(G-6740)*
▲ **Towers Media Holdings Inc** ....D .... 312 993-1550
Northfield *(G-16421)*
**United Cmra Binocular Repr LLC** ....E .... 630 595-2525
Elk Grove Village *(G-9799)*

## *3661 Telephone & Telegraph Apparatus*

**A T Products Inc** ....G .... 815 943-3590
Harvard *(G-11615)*
**Acn Indpndent Bus Rprsentative** ....G .... 618 623-4238
O Fallon *(G-16460)*
**Addax Sound Company** ....F .... 847 412-0000
Northbrook *(G-16198)*
**Advantage Optics Inc** ....F .... 630 548-9870
Naperville *(G-15592)*
**Airbus Ds Communications Inc** ....G .... 708 450-1911
Westchester *(G-21828)*
**Alcatel-Lucent USA Inc** ....E .... 630 979-0210
Naperville *(G-15594)*
**Alltemated Inc** ....E .... 847 394-5800
Arlington Heights *(G-707)*
▲ **American Comm & Networks** ....E .... 630 241-2800
Lisle *(G-13558)*
**Arris Group Inc** ....E .... 630 281-3000
Lisle *(G-13564)*
**AT&T Corp** ....F .... 312 602-4108
Chicago *(G-3972)*
**Autotech Tech Ltd Partnr** ....E .... 630 668-8886
Carol Stream *(G-3108)*
**Avg Advanced Technologies LP** ....A .... 630 668-3900
Carol Stream *(G-3110)*
**Axon Telecom LLC** ....G .... 618 278-4606
Dorsey *(G-8380)*
**Ayla Group Inc** ....G .... 630 954-9432
Bartlett *(G-1334)*
▲ **Best-Tronics Mfg Inc** ....C .... 708 802-9677
Tinley Park *(G-20898)*
**Brocade Cmmnctions Systems Inc** ....F .... 630 273-5530
Schaumburg *(G-19466)*
◆ **Charles Industries Ltd** ....D .... 847 806-6300
Rolling Meadows *(G-18719)*
**Charles Industries Ltd** ....D .... 217 826-2318
Marshall *(G-14319)*
**Charles Industries Ltd** ....D .... 217 893-8335
Rantoul *(G-17922)*
**Charles Industries Ltd** ....D .... 217 932-2068
Casey *(G-3381)*
**Charles Industries Ltd** ....D .... 217 932-5294
Casey *(G-3382)*
**Cml Technologies Inc** ....G .... 708 450-1911
Westchester *(G-21834)*
◆ **Coleman Cable LLC** ....D .... 847 672-2300
Waukegan *(G-21542)*
**Coleman Cable LLC** ....D .... 847 672-2300
Waukegan *(G-21543)*
**Comprehensive Convgnt Solut** ....F .... 847 558-1401
Lake Zurich *(G-13056)*
▲ **Coriant Operations Inc** ....E .... 847 382-8817
Naperville *(G-15636)*

S I C

Employee Codes: A=Over 500 employees, B=251-500
C=101-250, D=51-100, E=20-50, F=10-19, G=3-9
2017 Harris Illinois
Industrial Directory
1099

# 36 ELECTRONIC AND OTHER ELECTRICAL EQUIPMENT AND COMPONENTS, EXCEPT COMPUTER

| Company | Code | Phone |
|---|---|---|
| Create USA Modem Eight | G | 630 519-3403 |
| Oakbrook Terrace (G-16705) | | |
| Cronus Technologies Inc | D | 847 839-0088 |
| Schaumburg (G-19491) | | |
| Cutting Edge Communications | G | 815 788-9419 |
| Crystal Lake (G-7564) | | |
| ▲ D & S Communications Inc | D | 847 468-8082 |
| Elgin (G-9008) | | |
| Eks Fiber Optics LP | G | 312 291-4482 |
| Chicago (G-4706) | | |
| Elanza Technologies Inc | E | 312 396-4187 |
| Chicago (G-4717) | | |
| ▲ Elexa Consumer Products Inc | B | 773 794-1300 |
| Deerfield (G-8006) | | |
| Elite Fiber Optics LLC | E | 630 225-9454 |
| Oak Brook (G-16506) | | |
| ▲ Etcon Corp | F | 630 325-6100 |
| Burr Ridge (G-2840) | | |
| ▲ Firefly Mobile Inc | E | 305 538-2777 |
| Schaumburg (G-19529) | | |
| H K Tellabs Limited | G | 630 445-5333 |
| Naperville (G-15668) | | |
| HI Tech | G | 708 957-4210 |
| Homewood (G-12100) | | |
| IL Green Pastures Fiber Co-Op | G | 815 751-0887 |
| Kirkland (G-12713) | | |
| Integrated Dna Tech Modem | F | 847 745-1700 |
| Skokie (G-20016) | | |
| ▲ Isco International LLC | E | 847 391-9400 |
| Schaumburg (G-19583) | | |
| Kuna Corp | G | 815 675-0140 |
| Spring Grove (G-20344) | | |
| Ledcor Construction Inc | F | 630 916-1200 |
| Oakbrook Terrace (G-16714) | | |
| Mar-Don Corporation | G | 847 823-4958 |
| Park Ridge (G-17208) | | |
| Medical Cmmnctions Systems Inc | G | 708 895-4500 |
| Lansing (G-13176) | | |
| Mitel Networks Inc | F | 312 479-9000 |
| Chicago (G-5774) | | |
| Motorola Solutions Inc | G | 847 523-5000 |
| Libertyville (G-13359) | | |
| Motorola Solutions Inc | C | 847 576-5000 |
| Chicago (G-5818) | | |
| Motorola Solutions Inc | C | 847 576-8600 |
| Schaumburg (G-19652) | | |
| Netgear Inc | G | 630 955-0080 |
| Naperville (G-15712) | | |
| ◆ Parts Specialists Inc | G | 708 371-2444 |
| Posen (G-17734) | | |
| Pentegra Systems LLC | E | 630 941-6000 |
| Addison (G-238) | | |
| Pitney Bowes Inc | E | 800 784-4224 |
| Itasca (G-12341) | | |
| Precision Components Inc | D | 630 462-9110 |
| Saint Charles (G-19240) | | |
| Quen-Tel Communication Svc Inc | G | 815 463-1800 |
| New Lenox (G-15903) | | |
| Quintum Technologies Inc | F | 847 348-7730 |
| Schaumburg (G-19710) | | |
| Sandmancom Inc | G | 630 980-7710 |
| Roselle (G-18972) | | |
| Siemens AG | G | 708 345-7290 |
| Palos Park (G-17131) | | |
| Siemens Corporation | E | 630 850-6973 |
| Westmont (G-21921) | | |
| Smart Choice Mobile Inc | F | 708 933-6851 |
| Calumet City (G-2955) | | |
| Smart Choice Mobile Inc | F | 708 581-4904 |
| Hickory Hills (G-11774) | | |
| Stellar Manufacturing Company | D | 618 823-3761 |
| Cahokia (G-2926) | | |
| ▲ Switchcraft Inc | B | 773 792-2700 |
| Chicago (G-6653) | | |
| ▲ Switchcraft Holdco Inc | G | 773 792-2700 |
| Chicago (G-6654) | | |
| Tancher Corp | F | 847 668-8765 |
| Park Ridge (G-17226) | | |
| Tekno Industries Inc | F | 630 766-6960 |
| Naperville (G-15761) | | |
| ▲ Telefonix Incorporated | D | 847 244-4500 |
| Waukegan (G-21624) | | |
| ▲ Tellabs Inc | E | 630 798-8800 |
| Naperville (G-15762) | | |
| Tellabs Mexico Inc | F | 630 445-5333 |
| Naperville (G-15763) | | |
| Unified Solutions Corp | E | 847 478-9100 |
| Arlington Heights (G-861) | | |
| Vertiv Group Corporation | E | 630 579-5000 |
| Lombard (G-13878) | | |
| Wescom Products | G | 217 932-5292 |
| Casey (G-3392) | | |
| ▲ Westell Inc | G | 630 898-2500 |
| Aurora (G-1097) | | |
| Westell Technologies Inc | E | 630 898-2500 |
| Aurora (G-1098) | | |
| ▲ Wireless Chamberlain Products | G | 800 282-6225 |
| Elmhurst (G-9961) | | |

## 3663 Radio & T V Communications, Systs & Eqpt, Broadcast/Studio

| Company | Code | Phone |
|---|---|---|
| 4g Antenna Shop Inc | G | 815 496-0444 |
| Aurora (G-952) | | |
| Acp Tower Holdings LLC | G | 800 835-8527 |
| Chicago (G-3737) | | |
| Advance Technologies Inc | G | 815 297-1771 |
| Freeport (G-10644) | | |
| AF Antronics Inc | G | 217 328-0800 |
| Urbana (G-21068) | | |
| Ale USA Inc | G | 630 713-5194 |
| Naperville (G-15595) | | |
| Allcom Products Illinois LLC | E | 847 468-8830 |
| South Elgin (G-20180) | | |
| American Data Centre Inc | G | 847 358-7111 |
| Palatine (G-17000) | | |
| ◆ Amphenol Antenna Solutions Inc | C | 815 399-0001 |
| Rockford (G-18265) | | |
| ▲ Amphenol T&M Antennas Inc | F | 847 478-5600 |
| Lincolnshire (G-13428) | | |
| ▲ Amplivox Sound Systems LLC | G | 800 267-5486 |
| Northbrook (G-16204) | | |
| Andrew International Svcs Corp | A | 779 435-6000 |
| Joliet (G-12455) | | |
| Andrew New Zealand Inc | E | 708 873-3507 |
| Orland Park (G-16843) | | |
| ▲ Antenex Inc | D | 847 839-6910 |
| Schaumburg (G-19444) | | |
| Anywave Communication Tech Inc | F | 847 415-2258 |
| Lincolnshire (G-13429) | | |
| Arris Group Inc | E | 630 281-3000 |
| Lisle (G-13564) | | |
| AVI-Spl Employee | B | 847 437-7712 |
| Schaumburg (G-19454) | | |
| Ayla Group Inc | G | 630 954-9432 |
| Bartlett (G-1334) | | |
| ▲ Bar Codes Inc | F | 800 351-9962 |
| Chicago (G-4039) | | |
| BEI Electronics LLC | C | 217 224-9600 |
| Quincy (G-17802) | | |
| BEI Holding Corporation | C | 217 224-9600 |
| Quincy (G-17803) | | |
| Big Ten Network Services LLC | D | 312 329-3666 |
| Chicago (G-4104) | | |
| Boeing Company | B | 312 544-2000 |
| Chicago (G-4136) | | |
| Boeing Irving Company | A | 312 544-2000 |
| Chicago (G-4137) | | |
| ▲ Bolingbrook Communications Inc | A | 630 759-9500 |
| Lisle (G-13571) | | |
| ◆ Broadcast Electronics Inc | C | 217 224-9600 |
| Quincy (G-17809) | | |
| ▲ Cable Company | E | 847 437-5267 |
| Elk Grove Village (G-9355) | | |
| ▲ Callpod Inc | F | 312 829-2680 |
| Chicago (G-4217) | | |
| Cco Holdings LLC | E | 618 505-3505 |
| Troy (G-21003) | | |
| Cco Holdings LLC | E | 618 651-6486 |
| Highland (G-11777) | | |
| Charles Electronics LLC | G | 815 244-7981 |
| Mount Carroll (G-15290) | | |
| Checkpoint Systems Inc | D | 630 771-4240 |
| Romeoville (G-18809) | | |
| Clearchoice Mobility Inc | G | 847 986-6313 |
| Round Lake Beach (G-19074) | | |
| Coleman Cable LLC | A | 847 672-2300 |
| Waukegan (G-21543) | | |
| Colt Technology Services LLC | G | 312 465-2484 |
| Chicago (G-4430) | | |
| Comlink Technologies Inc | F | 630 279-5445 |
| Bensenville (G-1863) | | |
| ◆ Commscope Technologies LLC | A | 708 236-6600 |
| Westchester (G-21835) | | |
| Commscope Technologies LLC | B | 779 435-6000 |
| Joliet (G-12476) | | |
| Community Advantage Network | G | 847 376-8943 |
| Des Plaines (G-8173) | | |
| ▲ Crescend Technologies LLC | E | 847 908-5400 |
| Schaumburg (G-19490) | | |
| D W Ram Manufacturing Co | E | 708 633-7900 |
| Tinley Park (G-20908) | | |
| Driver Services | G | 505 267-8686 |
| Bensenville (G-1883) | | |
| Dtv Innovations LLC | F | 847 919-3550 |
| Elgin (G-9014) | | |
| Easy Trac Gps Inc | G | 630 359-5804 |
| Berwyn (G-2061) | | |
| Ed Co | E | 708 614-0695 |
| Tinley Park (G-20909) | | |
| ▲ Evanston Graphic Imaging Inc | G | 847 869-7446 |
| Evanston (G-10033) | | |
| Fleet Management Solutions Inc | E | 805 787-0508 |
| Glenview (G-11126) | | |
| Forest City Satellite | G | 815 639-0500 |
| Davis Junction (G-7811) | | |
| Fred Kennerly | G | 815 398-6861 |
| Rockford (G-18392) | | |
| FSI Technologies Inc | G | 630 932-9380 |
| Lombard (G-13803) | | |
| Gatesair Inc | C | 217 222-8200 |
| Quincy (G-17830) | | |
| Gogo Intermediate Holdings LLC | G | 630 647-1400 |
| Itasca (G-12271) | | |
| Gogo LLC | B | 630 647-1400 |
| Chicago (G-4970) | | |
| Gogo LLC | D | 630 647-1400 |
| Bensenville (G-1911) | | |
| Grass Valley Usa LLC | G | 847 803-8060 |
| Rosemont (G-19003) | | |
| Healthcom Inc | E | 217 728-8331 |
| Sullivan (G-20747) | | |
| ◆ Heico Companies LLC | F | 312 419-8220 |
| Chicago (G-5068) | | |
| ▲ Heil Sound Ltd | F | 618 257-3000 |
| Fairview Heights (G-10168) | | |
| Hi-Def Communications | G | 217 258-6679 |
| Mattoon (G-14392) | | |
| Iheartcommunications Inc | G | 312 255-5100 |
| Chicago (G-5149) | | |
| Iic Acquisitions II LLC | G | 217 224-9600 |
| Quincy (G-17838) | | |
| ▲ Inclusion Solutions LLC | F | 847 869-2500 |
| Evanston (G-10055) | | |
| Intelligent Designs LLC | G | 630 235-7965 |
| Wheaton (G-21957) | | |
| Invisio Communications Inc | G | 412 327-6578 |
| Chicago (G-5234) | | |
| Isco International Inc | G | 630 283-3100 |
| Schaumburg (G-19582) | | |
| Jai-S Record Label | G | 708 351-4279 |
| Park Forest (G-17173) | | |
| Jklein Enterprises Inc | G | 618 664-4554 |
| Greenville (G-11395) | | |
| Kokes Kid Zone | G | 217 483-4615 |
| Chatham (G-3624) | | |
| Kvh Industries Inc | G | 708 444-2800 |
| Tinley Park (G-20927) | | |
| L3 Technologies Inc | F | 212 697-1111 |
| Rolling Meadows (G-18741) | | |
| Langham Engineering | G | 815 223-5250 |
| Peru (G-17516) | | |
| ▲ Las Systems Inc | E | 847 462-8100 |
| Woodstock (G-22582) | | |
| Latino Arts & Communications | G | 773 501-0029 |
| Chicago (G-5465) | | |
| Lemko Corporation | E | 630 948-3025 |
| Itasca (G-12302) | | |
| Linear Industries Inc | F | 847 428-5793 |
| Elgin (G-9095) | | |
| LL Electronics | G | 217 586-6477 |
| Mahomet (G-14160) | | |
| Metro Service Center | B | 618 524-8583 |
| Metropolis (G-14757) | | |
| Moran Cristobalian | G | 630 506-4777 |
| Batavia (G-1472) | | |
| ▲ Motorola Mobility Holdings LLC | G | 847 523-5000 |
| Chicago (G-5815) | | |
| ▲ Motorola Mobility LLC | B | 800 668-6765 |
| Chicago (G-5817) | | |
| Motorola Solutions Inc | C | 847 576-5000 |
| Chicago (G-5818) | | |
| Motorola Solutions Inc | G | 847 538-6959 |
| Northbrook (G-16316) | | |
| Motorola Solutions Inc | G | 847 341-3485 |
| Oak Brook (G-16546) | | |
| Motorola Solutions Inc | C | 630 308-9394 |
| Hoffman Estates (G-12025) | | |
| Motorola Solutions Inc | G | 630 353-8000 |
| Downers Grove (G-8491) | | |

SIC SECTION 36 ELECTRONIC AND OTHER ELECTRICAL EQUIPMENT AND COMPONENTS, EXCEPT COMPUTER

**Motorola Solutions Inc** ....C ....847 576-8600
Schaumburg *(G-19652)*

**Motorola Solutions Inc** ....C ....847 540-8815
Arlington Heights *(G-807)*

**Motorola Solutions Inc** ....G ....847 523-5000
Libertyville *(G-13360)*

**Motorola Solutions Inc** ....E ....847 541-1014
West Chicago *(G-21747)*

**Motorola Solutions Inc** ....C ....708 476-8226
Schaumburg *(G-19653)*

**Motorola Solutions Inc** ....C ....800 331-6456
Schaumburg *(G-19654)*

**Motorola Solutions Inc** ....C ....847 576-5000
Elgin *(G-9114)*

**Mr Dvr Llc** ....G ....708 827-5030
Worth *(G-22634)*

**Nielsen & Bainbridge LLC** ....D ....708 546-2135
Bridgeview *(G-2514)*

**Nokia Slutions Networks US LLC** ....F ....224 248-8204
Arlington Heights *(G-809)*

**Nokia Slutions Networks US LLC** ....G ....630 979-9572
Naperville *(G-15716)*

**Northern Information Tech** ....F ....800 528-4343
Rolling Meadows *(G-18752)*

**Northrop Grumman Systems Corp** ....A ....847 259-9600
Rolling Meadows *(G-18753)*

**Nucurrent Inc** ....G ....312 575-0388
Chicago *(G-5954)*

**OEM Solutions Inc** ....G ....708 574-8893
Oak Brook *(G-16551)*

**▲ Omni Vision Inc** ....E ....630 893-1720
Glendale Heights *(G-11053)*

**Portable Cmmnctons Spclsts** ....G ....630 458-1800
Addison *(G-247)*

**Prime Time Sports LLC** ....F ....847 637-3500
Arlington Heights *(G-821)*

**Qaboss Partners** ....B ....312 203-4290
Chicago *(G-6235)*

**Radio Frequency Systems Inc** ....E ....800 321-4700
Naperville *(G-15737)*

**Ram Systems & Communication** ....G ....847 487-7575
Wauconda *(G-21499)*

**Research In Motion Rf Inc** ....G ....815 444-1095
Crystal Lake *(G-7639)*

**Roscor Corporation** ....D ....847 299-8080
Chicago *(G-6394)*

**Safemobile Inc** ....F ....847 818-1649
Rolling Meadows *(G-18776)*

**Saga Communications Inc** ....G ....248 631-8099
Springfield *(G-20517)*

**Satellite Certified Inc** ....G ....815 230-3877
Joliet *(G-12573)*

**◆ Scrn LLC** ....G ....847 513-4082
Chicago *(G-6462)*

**Simpson Electric Company** ....E ....847 697-2260
Elgin *(G-9182)*

**▲ Spectrum Cos International** ....G ....630 879-8008
Batavia *(G-1497)*

**State of Illinois** ....C ....312 836-9500
Chicago *(G-6578)*

**▼ STC Inc** ....E ....618 643-2555
Mc Leansboro *(G-14468)*

**Studio Technologies Inc** ....F ....847 676-9177
Skokie *(G-20093)*

**▲ Switchcraft Inc** ....B ....773 792-2700
Chicago *(G-6653)*

**▲ Switchcraft Holdco Inc** ....G ....773 792-2700
Chicago *(G-6654)*

**T-Mobile Usa Inc** ....F ....847 289-9988
South Elgin *(G-20228)*

**Tanklink Corporation** ....E ....312 379-8397
Chicago *(G-6673)*

**Team Cast Inc** ....G ....312 263-0033
Chicago *(G-6682)*

**▲ Telular Corporation** ....D ....800 835-8527
Chicago *(G-6692)*

**Temco Japan Co Ltd** ....G ....847 359-3277
South Barrington *(G-20134)*

**▼ Tower Works Inc** ....F ....630 557-2221
Maple Park *(G-14204)*

**▲ Tribeam Inc** ....G ....847 409-9497
Arlington Heights *(G-857)*

**U-Tracking International Inc** ....E ....312 242-6003
Chicago *(G-6803)*

**Vincor Ltd** ....F ....708 534-0008
Monee *(G-15005)*

**▲ Visiplex Inc** ....E ....847 918-0250
Buffalo Grove *(G-2790)*

**▼ Visiplex Inc** ....F ....847 229-0250
Buffalo Grove *(G-2791)*

**West Star Aviation LLC** ....G ....618 259-3230
East Alton *(G-8612)*

**▲ Wireless Chamberlain Products** ....E ....800 282-6225
Elmhurst *(G-9961)*

**▲ Xentris Wireless LLC** ....D ....630 693-9700
Addison *(G-348)*

**Zenith Electronics Corporation** ....E ....847 941-8000
Lincolnshire *(G-13496)*

## *3669 Communications Eqpt, NEC*

**All Tech Systems & Install** ....G ....815 609-0685
Plainfield *(G-17579)*

**Ametek Inc** ....E ....630 621-3121
West Chicago *(G-21658)*

**AR Concepts USA Inc** ....G ....847 392-4608
Palatine *(G-17002)*

**AVI-Spl Employee** ....B ....847 437-7712
Schaumburg *(G-19454)*

**◆ Brk Brands Inc** ....C ....630 851-7330
Aurora *(G-975)*

**Buell Manufacturing Company** ....G ....708 447-6320
Lyons *(G-14033)*

**Data Comm For Business Inc** ....F ....217 897-1741
Dewey *(G-8310)*

**Extentel Wrless Communications** ....G ....847 809-3131
Inverness *(G-12203)*

**◆ Federal Signal Corporation** ....D ....630 954-2000
Oak Brook *(G-16510)*

**▲ Fire Sentry Corporation** ....E ....714 694-0823
Lincolnshire *(G-13448)*

**▲ First Alert Inc** ....G ....630 499-3295
Aurora *(G-1009)*

**Global Fire Control Inc** ....G ....309 314-0919
East Moline *(G-8680)*

**▲ Harrington Signal Inc** ....E ....309 762-0731
Moline *(G-14942)*

**▲ Jeron Electronic Systems Inc** ....D ....773 275-1900
Niles *(G-15991)*

**John Thomas Inc** ....E ....815 288-2343
Dixon *(G-8334)*

**Km Enterprises Inc** ....F ....618 204-0888
Mount Vernon *(G-15420)*

**Lares Technologies LLC** ....G ....630 408-4368
Oswego *(G-16925)*

**▲ Lecip Inc** ....G ....312 626-2525
Bensenville *(G-1939)*

**▼ Lund Industries Inc** ....E ....847 459-1460
Northbrook *(G-16302)*

**Magnum Machining LLC** ....G ....815 678-6800
Richmond *(G-17967)*

**▲ Marine Technologies Inc** ....E ....847 546-9001
Volo *(G-21318)*

**McC Technology Inc** ....F ....630 377-7200
Saint Charles *(G-19216)*

**▲ Minelab Americas Inc** ....F ....630 401-8150
Lisle *(G-13624)*

**Motorola Mobility LLC** ....G ....847 523-5000
Chicago *(G-5816)*

**N E S Traffic Safety** ....F ....312 603-7444
Chicago *(G-5846)*

**Nafisco Inc** ....F ....815 372-3300
Romeoville *(G-18851)*

**Neovision Usa Inc** ....F ....847 533-0541
Deer Park *(G-7973)*

**▲ North American Signal Co** ....E ....847 537-8888
Wheeling *(G-22108)*

**▲ Pacific Electronics Corp** ....F ....815 206-5450
Woodstock *(G-22598)*

**▲ Pro Intercom LLC** ....F ....224 406-7108
Algonquin *(G-404)*

**▲ Procomm Inc Hoopeston Illinois** ....E ....815 268-4303
Onarga *(G-16809)*

**Quality Service & Installation** ....G ....847 352-4000
Schaumburg *(G-19709)*

**Regional Emrgncy Dispatch Ctr** ....F ....847 498-5748
Northbrook *(G-16354)*

**▲ RF Technologies Inc** ....E ....618 377-2654
Buffalo Grove *(G-2759)*

**Securecom Inc** ....G ....219 314-4537
Lansing *(G-13183)*

**◆ Siemens Industry Inc** ....A ....847 215-1000
Buffalo Grove *(G-2767)*

**Signalmasters Inc** ....F ....708 534-3330
Monee *(G-15001)*

**Simplexgrinnell LP** ....B ....630 268-1863
Addison *(G-292)*

**Simplexgrinnell LP** ....D ....309 694-8000
East Peoria *(G-8734)*

**Stenograph LLC** ....D ....630 532-5100
Elmhurst *(G-9942)*

**▲ Synergistic Tech Solutions Inc** ....G ....224 360-6165
Mundelein *(G-15562)*

**Talk-A-Phone Co** ....D ....773 539-1100
Niles *(G-16039)*

**Tool Automation Enterprises** ....G ....708 799-6847
East Hazel Crest *(G-8666)*

**Traffco Products LLC** ....G ....773 374-6645
Chicago *(G-6754)*

**▲ Tri-Lite Inc** ....E ....773 384-7765
Chicago *(G-6770)*

**Vpnvantagecom** ....G ....877 998-4678
Arlington Heights *(G-867)*

**Western Remac Inc** ....E ....630 972-7770
Woodridge *(G-22524)*

**Western-Cullen-Hayes Inc** ....D ....773 254-9600
Chicago *(G-6964)*

**Windy City Detectors Sales** ....G ....773 774-5445
Chicago *(G-6994)*

**▲ Wireless Chamberlain Products** ....E ....800 282-6225
Elmhurst *(G-9961)*

**Xomi Instruments Co Ltd** ....G ....847 660-4614
Vernon Hills *(G-21220)*

## *3671 Radio & T V Receiving Electron Tubes*

**Dcx-Chol Enterprises Inc** ....E ....309 353-4455
Pekin *(G-17258)*

**F & L Electronics LLC** ....F ....217 586-2132
Mahomet *(G-14158)*

**King S Court Exterior** ....G ....630 904-4305
Naperville *(G-15812)*

**Light of Mine LLC** ....G ....312 840-8570
Chicago *(G-5503)*

**Northrop Grumman Systems Corp** ....A ....847 259-9600
Rolling Meadows *(G-18753)*

**Rcl Electronics** ....G ....630 834-0156
Addison *(G-271)*

**Richardson Electronics Ltd** ....C ....630 208-2200
Lafox *(G-12796)*

**Starfire Industries LLC** ....E ....217 721-4165
Champaign *(G-3548)*

**Teledyne Monitor Labs Inc** ....G ....303 792-3300
Chicago *(G-6691)*

**Thomas Electronics Inc** ....E ....315 923-2051
Addison *(G-312)*

**Zenith Electronics Corporation** ....E ....847 941-8000
Lincolnshire *(G-13496)*

## *3672 Printed Circuit Boards*

**ABRA Enterprises Inc** ....G ....847 866-6903
Evanston *(G-10001)*

**Accelerated Assemblies Inc** ....E ....630 616-6680
Elk Grove Village *(G-9259)*

**Accutrace Inc** ....F ....847 290-9900
Elk Grove Village *(G-9262)*

**▲ Advanced Electronics Inc** ....D ....630 293-3300
West Chicago *(G-21652)*

**▲ Aerotronic Controls Co** ....F ....847 228-6504
Elk Grove Village *(G-9282)*

**▲ Alpha Circuit Corporation** ....E ....630 617-5555
Elmhurst *(G-9833)*

**▲ Alpha Pcb Designs Inc** ....G ....773 631-5543
Chicago *(G-3831)*

**American Circuit Services Inc** ....G ....847 895-0500
Schaumburg *(G-19436)*

**American Circuit Systems Inc** ....E ....630 543-4450
Addison *(G-33)*

**American Controls & Automation** ....G ....630 293-8841
West Chicago *(G-21655)*

**American Prgrssive Crcuits Inc** ....E ....630 495-6900
Addison *(G-37)*

**▲ American Standard Circuits Inc** ....C ....630 639-5444
West Chicago *(G-21657)*

**▲ Amitron Inc** ....C ....847 290-9800
Elk Grove Village *(G-9302)*

**Ampel Incorporated** ....E ....847 952-1900
Elk Grove Village *(G-9303)*

**▲ ARC-Tronics Inc** ....C ....847 437-0211
Elk Grove Village *(G-9312)*

**Assembly International Inc** ....F ....847 437-3120
Elk Grove Village *(G-9317)*

**Astral Power Systems Inc** ....G ....630 518-1741
Aurora *(G-1112)*

**▲ Aurora Circuits Inc** ....D ....630 978-3830
Aurora *(G-960)*

**▲ Aurora Circuits LLC** ....D ....630 978-3830
Aurora *(G-961)*

**Avg Advanced Technologies LP** ....A ....630 668-3900
Carol Stream *(G-3110)*

**B M I Inc** ....C ....847 839-6000
Schaumburg *(G-19456)*

SIC

Employee Codes: A=Over 500 employees, B=251-500
C=101-250, D=51-100, E=20-50, F=10-19, G=3-9

2017 Harris Illinois
Industrial Directory

1101

Bandjwet Enterprises Inc....E.... 847 797-9250
Rolling Meadows *(G-18715)*
Bartec Orb Inc....E.... 773 927-8600
Chicago *(G-4051)*
Benchmark Electronics Inc....B.... 309 822-8587
Metamora *(G-14740)*
Bestproto Inc....F.... 224 387-3280
Rolling Meadows *(G-18717)*
Bishop Engineering Company....F.... 630 305-9538
Lisle *(G-13569)*
Bobco Enterprises Inc Del....E.... 773 722-1700
Bloomingdale *(G-2097)*
Buildex Electronics Inc....F.... 847 437-2299
Elk Grove Village *(G-9348)*
C & C Electronics Inc....F.... 847 550-0177
Mundelein *(G-15481)*
▲ Cck Automations Inc....E.... 217 243-6040
Jacksonville *(G-12382)*
Chicago Circuits Corporation....F.... 847 238-1623
Elk Grove Village *(G-9367)*
Circom Inc....E.... 630 595-4460
Bensenville *(G-1859)*
▲ Circuit Engineering LLC....E.... 847 806-7777
Elk Grove Village *(G-9374)*
▲ Circuit Works Corporation....D.... 847 283-8600
Waukegan *(G-21538)*
▲ Circuit World Inc....E.... 630 250-1100
Itasca *(G-12245)*
Circuitronics....E.... 630 668-5407
Wheaton *(G-21941)*
Creative Hi-Tech Ltd....E.... 224 653-4000
Schaumburg *(G-19487)*
Current Works Inc....G.... 847 497-9650
Johnsburg *(G-12433)*
Daves Electronic Service....F.... 217 283-5010
Hoopeston *(G-12109)*
Delta Circuits Inc....E.... 630 876-0691
West Chicago *(G-21690)*
Delta Design Inc....F.... 708 424-9400
Evergreen Park *(G-10112)*
▲ Delta Precision Circuits Inc....E.... 847 758-8000
Elk Grove Village *(G-9422)*
Eagle Electronics Inc....D.... 847 891-5800
Schaumburg *(G-19511)*
Edgo Technical Sales Inc....G.... 630 961-8398
Naperville *(G-15803)*
Elcon Inc....E.... 815 467-9500
Minooka *(G-14840)*
Electro-Circuits Inc....E.... 630 339-3389
Schaumburg *(G-19515)*
Electronic Assembly Corp....D.... 847 793-4400
Buffalo Grove *(G-2690)*
Electronic Design & Mfg Inc....D.... 847 550-1912
Lake Zurich *(G-13066)*
Electronic Interconnect Corp....D.... 847 364-4848
Elk Grove Village *(G-9450)*
Electronic Resources Corp....G.... 630 620-0725
Lombard *(G-13795)*
▲ Emerge Technology Group LLC....G.... 800 613-1501
Wauconda *(G-21459)*
Excel Electro Assembly Inc....F.... 847 621-2500
Elk Grove Village *(G-9468)*
▲ Excell Electronics Corporation....E.... 847 766-7455
Elk Grove Village *(G-9469)*
▲ Galaxy Circuits Inc....E.... 630 462-1010
Carol Stream *(G-3156)*
General Electro Corporation....F.... 630 595-8989
Bensenville *(G-1908)*
Hytel Group Inc....E.... 847 683-9800
Hampshire *(G-11551)*
Illinois Tool Works Inc....E.... 630 825-7900
Glendale Heights *(G-11033)*
Image Circuit Inc....G.... 847 622-3300
Elk Grove Village *(G-9538)*
Image Technology Inc....F.... 847 622-3300
Elgin *(G-9074)*
▲ Imagineering Inc....E.... 847 806-0003
Elk Grove Village *(G-9541)*
▲ International Control Svcs Inc....C.... 217 422-6700
Decatur *(G-7896)*
Intratek Inc....G.... 847 640-0007
Elk Grove Village *(G-9554)*
Journey Circuits Inc....G.... 630 283-0604
Schaumburg *(G-19591)*
▲ K Trox Sales Inc....G.... 815 568-1521
Marengo *(G-14233)*
Kay & Cee....G.... 773 425-9169
Calumet Park *(G-2962)*
King Circuit....E.... 630 629-7300
Schaumburg *(G-19598)*

Lectro Graphics Inc....G.... 847 537-3592
Wheeling *(G-22091)*
Light of Mine LLC....G.... 312 840-8570
Chicago *(G-5503)*
▲ M-Wave International LLC....E.... 630 562-5550
Glendale Heights *(G-11043)*
Manu Industries Inc....F.... 847 891-6412
Schaumburg *(G-19630)*
Manu-TEC of Illinois LLC....F.... 630 543-3022
Addison *(G-190)*
▲ Mega Circuit Inc....D.... 630 543-8460
Addison *(G-198)*
Mektronix Technology Inc....G.... 847 680-3300
Libertyville *(G-13353)*
Methode Development Co....D.... 708 867-6777
Chicago *(G-5703)*
▲ Methode Electronics Inc....B.... 708 867-6777
Chicago *(G-5704)*
Michele Terrell....G.... 312 305-0876
Evanston *(G-10072)*
Micro Circuit Inc....F.... 630 628-5760
Addison *(G-206)*
Microsun Electronics Corp....F.... 630 410-7900
Woodridge *(G-22502)*
Midwest Cad Design Inc....G.... 847 397-0220
Schaumburg *(G-19647)*
Milplex Circuits Inc....C.... 630 250-1580
Itasca *(G-12321)*
◆ National Technology Inc....E.... 847 506-1300
Rolling Meadows *(G-18749)*
Ncab Group Usa Inc....F.... 630 562-5550
Itasca *(G-12326)*
▲ Novatronix Inc....E.... 630 860-4300
Wood Dale *(G-22407)*
On Time Circuits Inc....E.... 630 955-1110
Lisle *(G-13636)*
Online Electronics Inc....E.... 847 871-1700
Elk Grove Village *(G-9666)*
▲ Paramount Laminates Inc....G.... 630 594-1840
Wood Dale *(G-22411)*
Parth Consultants Inc....E.... 847 758-1400
Rolling Meadows *(G-18758)*
▲ Patriot Materials LLC....G.... 630 501-0260
Elmhurst *(G-9920)*
Pcb Express Inc....G.... 847 952-8896
Elk Grove Village *(G-9672)*
Plexus Corp....G.... 630 250-1074
Itasca *(G-12342)*
Plexus Corp....B.... 847 793-4400
Buffalo Grove *(G-2754)*
Price Circuits LLC....E.... 847 742-4700
Elgin *(G-9147)*
Printing Circuit Boards....F.... 630 543-3453
Addison *(G-256)*
▲ Qcircuits Inc....E.... 847 797-6678
Rolling Meadows *(G-18771)*
Qcircuits Inc....E.... 618 662-8365
Flora *(G-10214)*
Quality Surface Mount Inc....E.... 630 350-8556
Wood Dale *(G-22415)*
▲ R B Manufacturing Inc....E.... 815 522-3100
Kirkland *(G-12716)*
▲ RB Manufacturing & Electronics....E.... 815 522-3100
Kirkland *(G-12717)*
▲ Righthand Technologies Inc....E.... 773 774-7600
Chicago *(G-6356)*
Rw Technologies US LLC....F.... 815 444-6887
Crystal Lake *(G-7644)*
S & M Group Inc....F.... 630 766-1000
Wood Dale *(G-22418)*
Siemens Manufacturing Co Inc....D.... 618 539-3000
Freeburg *(G-10641)*
Siemens Manufacturing Co Inc....C.... 618 475-3325
New Athens *(G-15861)*
Sigenics Inc....F.... 312 448-8000
Chicago *(G-6506)*
Sigmatron International Inc....G.... 847 586-5200
Elgin *(G-9178)*
▲ Sigmatron International Inc....G.... 847 956-8000
Elk Grove Village *(G-9737)*
▲ Sparton Corporation....B.... 847 762-5800
Schaumburg *(G-19734)*
Sparton Design Services LLC....G.... 847 762-5800
Schaumburg *(G-19735)*
Sparton led LLC....D.... 847 762-5800
Schaumburg *(G-19737)*
Star Acquisition Inc....G.... 847 439-0605
Elk Grove Village *(G-9753)*
Star Electronics Corp....E.... 847 439-0605
Elk Grove Village *(G-9755)*

Summit Design Solutions Inc....G.... 847 836-8183
East Dundee *(G-8657)*
▲ Sunrise Electronics Inc....E.... 847 357-0500
Elk Grove Village *(G-9762)*
▲ Surya Electronics Inc....C.... 630 858-8000
Glendale Heights *(G-11080)*
▲ SWB Inc....G.... 847 438-1800
Lake Zurich *(G-13136)*
Taranda Specialties Inc....G.... 815 469-3041
Frankfort *(G-10368)*
▲ Tecnova Electronics Inc....D.... 847 336-6160
Waukegan *(G-21623)*
Triad Circuits Inc....E.... 847 283-8600
Waukegan *(G-21632)*
▲ United Electronics Corp Inc....D.... 847 671-6034
Franklin Park *(G-10616)*
Universal Scientific Ill Inc....E.... 847 228-6464
Elk Grove Village *(G-9802)*
Wand Enterprises Inc....F.... 847 433-0231
Highland Park *(G-11880)*
▲ Y 2 K Electronics Inc....F.... 847 238-9024
Elk Grove Village *(G-9821)*

## 3674 Semiconductors

Accelerated Assemblies Inc....E.... 630 616-6680
Elk Grove Village *(G-9259)*
Akhan Semiconductor Inc....G.... 847 855-8400
Gurnee *(G-11424)*
American Led Ltg Solutions LLC....G.... 847 931-1900
Elgin *(G-8949)*
Amoco Technology Company (del)....C.... 312 861-6000
Chicago *(G-3892)*
Analog Devices Inc....G.... 847 519-3669
Schaumburg *(G-19441)*
Angela Yang Chingjui....G.... 630 724-0596
Darien *(G-7790)*
▲ B+b Smartworx Inc....D.... 815 433-5100
Ottawa *(G-16949)*
Bare Development Inc....F.... 708 352-2273
Countryside *(G-7415)*
▲ BP Solar International Inc....A.... 301 698-4200
Naperville *(G-15611)*
Capsonic Automotive Inc....G.... 847 888-0930
Elgin *(G-8977)*
▲ Capsonic Automotive Inc....F.... 847 888-7300
Elgin *(G-8979)*
Chicago Pixels Mulitmedia Nfp....G.... 312 513-7949
Chicago *(G-4340)*
Coinstar Procurement LLC....G.... 630 424-4788
Oakbrook Terrace *(G-16703)*
▲ Components Express Inc....E.... 630 257-0605
Woodridge *(G-22464)*
Convergent Advisors....G.... 312 971-2602
Chicago *(G-4463)*
Convergent Bill Ete Ort T....G.... 847 387-4059
Hoffman Estates *(G-12003)*
Convergent Group LLC....G.... 847 274-6336
Deerfield *(G-8001)*
▲ CPA Systems Incorporated....G.... 630 858-3057
Glen Ellyn *(G-10965)*
Csi2d Inc....G.... 312 282-7407
Hoffman Estates *(G-12071)*
▲ CTS Automotive LLC....C.... 630 614-7201
Lisle *(G-13578)*
▲ CTS Corporation....C.... 630 577-8800
Lisle *(G-13579)*
▲ Dauber Company Inc....E.... 815 442-3569
Tonica *(G-20973)*
Digital Optics Tech Inc....G.... 847 358-2592
Rolling Meadows *(G-18725)*
◆ Dover Corporation....C.... 630 541-1540
Downers Grove *(G-8431)*
Dynawave Corporation....F.... 630 232-4945
Geneva *(G-10826)*
Effimax Solar....G.... 217 550-2422
Champaign *(G-3479)*
Epir Inc....G.... 630 842-0893
Bolingbrook *(G-2306)*
Epir Technologies Inc....E.... 630 771-0203
Bolingbrook *(G-2307)*
▲ Epiworks Inc....D.... 217 373-1590
Champaign *(G-3483)*
FSI Technologies Inc....E.... 630 932-9380
Lombard *(G-13803)*
GBA Systems Integrators LLC....G.... 913 492-0400
Moline *(G-14941)*
Hoku Solar Power I LLC....F.... 312 803-4972
Chicago *(G-5096)*
Hytel Group Inc....E.... 847 683-9800
Hampshire *(G-11551)*

SIC SECTION
36 ELECTRONIC AND OTHER ELECTRICAL EQUIPMENT AND COMPONENTS, EXCEPT COMPUTER

**Inland Tech Holdings LLC** ....E.... 618 476-7678
Millstadt *(G-14827)*
**Integrated Lighting Tech Inc** ....G.... 630 750-3786
Bolingbrook *(G-2322)*
**Intel Americas Inc** ....E.... 847 706-5779
Schaumburg *(G-19570)*
**Intel Corp** ....G.... 847 602-1170
Long Grove *(G-13891)*
**Intel Corporation** ....D.... 408 765-8080
Chicago *(G-5209)*
**Intel East** ....G.... 312 725-2014
Mount Prospect *(G-15338)*
**▼ Interplex Daystar Inc** ....D.... 847 455-2424
Franklin Park *(G-10499)*
**Ipr Systems Inc** ....G.... 708 385-7500
Alsip *(G-474)*
**ITT Water & Wastewater USA Inc** ....G.... 847 966-3700
Morton Grove *(G-15205)*
**JAD Group Inc** ....G.... 847 223-1804
Grayslake *(G-11348)*
**Jql Electronics Inc** ....F.... 630 873-2020
Rolling Meadows *(G-18736)*
**Konekt Inc** ....G.... 773 733-0471
Chicago *(G-5403)*
**▲ Led Industries Inc** ....E.... 888 700-7815
Spring Grove *(G-20345)*
**LED Rite LLC** ....G.... 847 683-8000
Hampshire *(G-11553)*
**Linear Dimensions Inc** ....F.... 312 321-1810
Chicago *(G-5511)*
**▲ Methode Electronics Inc** ....B.... 708 867-6777
Chicago *(G-5704)*
**Microchip Technology Inc** ....E.... 630 285-0071
Itasca *(G-12315)*
**Microlink Devices Inc** ....E.... 847 588-3001
Niles *(G-16005)*
**Moline Semicon LLC** ....G.... 309 755-0433
East Moline *(G-8688)*
**Motorola International Capital** ....G.... 847 576-5000
Schaumburg *(G-19651)*
**Motorola Solutions Inc** ....G.... 847 341-3485
Oak Brook *(G-16546)*
**Motorola Solutions Inc** ....C.... 847 576-8600
Schaumburg *(G-19652)*
**Mp Technologies LLC** ....G.... 847 491-4253
Evanston *(G-10076)*
**Nhanced Semiconductors Inc** ....F.... 408 759-4060
Naperville *(G-15715)*
**Nxp Usa Inc** ....B.... 847 843-6824
Hoffman Estates *(G-12032)*
**▲ Power Electronics Intl Inc** ....E.... 847 836-2071
East Dundee *(G-8654)*
**Precision Technologies Inc** ....G.... 847 439-5447
Glendale Heights *(G-11058)*
**Printovate Technologies Inc** ....G.... 847 962-3106
Palatine *(G-17064)*
**River West Radiation Center L** ....G.... 630 264-8580
Aurora *(G-1209)*
**Seasonal Magnets** ....G.... 708 499-3235
Evergreen Park *(G-10119)*
**Shakthi Solar Inc** ....G.... 630 842-0893
Bolingbrook *(G-2367)*
**Sigenics Inc** ....F.... 312 448-8000
Chicago *(G-6506)*
**Smart Controls LLC** ....G.... 618 394-0300
Fairview Heights *(G-10171)*
**▲ Solid State Luminaires LLC** ....G.... 877 775-4733
Saint Charles *(G-19266)*
**Sparton Aubrey LLC** ....E.... 386 740-5381
Schaumburg *(G-19732)*
**▲ Sparton Corporation** ....B.... 847 762-5800
Schaumburg *(G-19734)*
**Sparton Design Services LLC** ....G.... 847 762-5800
Schaumburg *(G-19735)*
**Sparton Emt LLC** ....G.... 800 772-7866
Schaumburg *(G-19736)*
**Sparton Ied LLC** ....D.... 847 762-5800
Schaumburg *(G-19737)*
**Systems Intel** ....G.... 847 842-0120
Barrington *(G-1307)*
**Tagore Technology Inc** ....G.... 847 790-3799
Arlington Heights *(G-851)*
**Tech Oasis International Inc** ....F.... 847 302-1590
Gurnee *(G-11513)*
**Telehealth Sensors LLC** ....E.... 630 879-3101
North Aurora *(G-16147)*
**▲ Tempro International Corp** ....G.... 847 677-5370
Skokie *(G-20100)*
**Thermoelectric Coolg Amer Corp** ....G.... 773 342-4900
Chicago *(G-6713)*
**Toshiba America Electronic** ....G.... 847 484-2400
Buffalo Grove *(G-2782)*
**▲ Touchsensor Technologies LLC** ....B.... 630 221-9000
Wheaton *(G-21987)*
**Value Engineered Products** ....E.... 708 867-6777
Rolling Meadows *(G-18787)*
**Vega Wave Systems Inc** ....G.... 630 562-9433
West Chicago *(G-21789)*
**Visco Technologies Usa Inc** ....G.... 847 993-3047
Arlington Heights *(G-865)*
**▲ Wanxiang New Energy LLC** ....F.... 815 226-0884
Rockford *(G-18672)*
**Wilmar Group LLC** ....G.... 847 421-6595
Lake Forest *(G-12980)*
**Worth Door Company** ....G.... 877 379-4947
Mchenry *(G-14572)*
**Xtremedata Inc** ....E.... 847 871-0379
Schaumburg *(G-19792)*
**Zenith Electronics Corporation** ....E.... 847 941-8000
Lincolnshire *(G-13496)*

## 3675 Electronic Capacitors

**Aisin Light Metals LLC** ....G.... 618 997-7900
Marion *(G-14249)*
**Bycap Inc** ....E.... 773 561-4976
Chicago *(G-4196)*
**▲ Elpac Electronics Inc** ....C.... 708 316-4407
Westchester *(G-21839)*
**▲ Jbsmwg Corp** ....F.... 847 675-1865
Lincolnwood *(G-13516)*
**Knowles Corporation** ....D.... 630 250-5100
Itasca *(G-12295)*
**▲ Motor Capacitors Inc** ....F.... 773 774-6666
Wood Dale *(G-22401)*
**Murata Electronics N Amer Inc** ....G.... 847 330-9200
Schaumburg *(G-19657)*
**Pei/Genesis Inc** ....G.... 215 673-0400
Rolling Meadows *(G-18760)*
**Standard Condenser Corporation** ....F.... 847 965-2722
Morton Grove *(G-15237)*
**▲ United Chemi-Con Inc** ....E.... 847 696-2000
Rolling Meadows *(G-18786)*

## 3676 Electronic Resistors

**Autotech Tech Ltd Partnr** ....E.... 630 668-8886
Carol Stream *(G-3108)*
**▲ CTS Corporation** ....C.... 630 577-8800
Lisle *(G-13579)*
**Elematec USA Corporation** ....G.... 847 466-1451
Itasca *(G-12257)*
**Maurey Instrument Corp** ....F.... 708 388-9898
Alsip *(G-490)*
**▲ Methode Electronics Inc** ....B.... 708 867-6777
Chicago *(G-5704)*
**◆ Mpc Products Corporation** ....A.... 847 673-8300
Niles *(G-16010)*
**Mpc Products Corporation** ....G.... 847 673-8300
Niles *(G-16011)*
**Pei/Genesis Inc** ....G.... 215 673-0400
Rolling Meadows *(G-18760)*
**Voltronics Inc** ....F.... 773 625-1779
Chicago *(G-6913)*
**Waveteam LLC** ....G.... 630 323-0277
Hinsdale *(G-11968)*

## 3677 Electronic Coils & Transformers

**A J Smoy Co Inc** ....E.... 773 775-8282
Schaumburg *(G-19419)*
**Actown-Electrocoil Inc** ....G....
Spring Grove *(G-20324)*
**▲ Altran Corp** ....E.... 815 455-5650
Crystal Lake *(G-7531)*
**▲ Arnold Engineering Co** ....D.... 815 568-2000
Marengo *(G-14218)*
**AT&T Corp** ....F.... 312 602-4108
Chicago *(G-3972)*
**Barnes International Inc** ....C.... 815 964-8661
Rockford *(G-18276)*
**▲ Becker Specialty Corporation** ....F.... 847 766-3555
Elk Grove Village *(G-9336)*
**Bias Power Technology Inc** ....G.... 847 991-2427
Palatine *(G-17006)*
**Blocksmoy Inc** ....F.... 847 260-9070
Franklin Park *(G-10413)*
**Cemec Inc** ....G.... 630 495-9696
Downers Grove *(G-8405)*
**◆ Charles Industries Ltd** ....D.... 847 806-6300
Rolling Meadows *(G-18719)*
**Charles Industries Ltd** ....D.... 217 826-2318
Marshall *(G-14319)*
**Coilcraft Incorporated** ....G.... 815 879-4408
Princeton *(G-17745)*
**Coilcraft Incorporated** ....D.... 815 732-6834
Oregon *(G-16820)*
**Coilcraft Incorporated** ....D.... 815 288-7051
Dixon *(G-8326)*
**Coilform Company** ....G.... 630 232-8000
Geneva *(G-10820)*
**Communication Coil Inc** ....D.... 847 671-1333
Schiller Park *(G-19815)*
**Custom Magnetics Inc** ....E.... 773 463-6500
Chicago *(G-4523)*
**Daly Engineered Filtration Inc** ....G.... 708 355-1550
Naperville *(G-15643)*
**Eis** ....G.... 630 530-7500
Elmhurst *(G-9863)*
**Erbeck One Chem & Lab Sup Inc** ....G.... 312 203-0078
Manhattan *(G-14169)*
**◆ Ets-Lindgren Inc** ....C.... 630 307-7200
Wood Dale *(G-22363)*
**Everpurse Inc** ....G.... 650 204-3212
Chicago *(G-4790)*
**Federal-Mogul Corporation** ....C.... 815 271-9600
McHenry *(G-14506)*
**Forest Electric Company** ....E.... 708 681-0180
Melrose Park *(G-14639)*
**Gsg Industries** ....F.... 618 544-7976
Robinson *(G-18063)*
**▲ Induction Innovations Inc** ....G.... 847 836-6933
Elgin *(G-9076)*
**▲ Inglot Electronics Corp** ....D.... 773 286-5881
Chicago *(G-5192)*
**Ipr Systems Inc** ....G.... 708 385-7500
Alsip *(G-474)*
**▲ Lenco Electronics Inc** ....E.... 815 344-2900
McHenry *(G-14520)*
**Magnetic Coil Manufacturing Co** ....E.... 630 787-1948
Wood Dale *(G-22395)*
**Magnetic Devices Inc** ....G.... 815 459-0077
Crystal Lake *(G-7605)*
**Marvel Electric Corporation** ....D.... 773 327-2644
Chicago *(G-5638)*
**Marvel Electric Corporation** ....E.... 847 671-0632
Schiller Park *(G-19846)*
**MEI Realty Ltd** ....G.... 847 358-5000
Inverness *(G-12205)*
**Michele Terrell** ....G.... 312 305-0876
Evanston *(G-10072)*
**◆ Muntz Industries Inc** ....E.... 847 949-8280
Mundelein *(G-15534)*
**Nelco Coil Supply Company** ....E.... 847 259-7517
Mount Prospect *(G-15354)*
**◆ Netcom Inc** ....C.... 847 537-6300
Wheeling *(G-22106)*
**North Point Investments Inc** ....G.... 312 977-4386
Chicago *(G-5935)*
**▲ Olympic Controls Corp** ....E.... 847 742-3566
Elgin *(G-9128)*
**◆ Perma-Pipe Intl Holdings Inc** ....C.... 847 966-1000
Niles *(G-16019)*
**Permacor Inc** ....E.... 708 422-3353
Oak Lawn *(G-16639)*
**Pnc Inc** ....D.... 815 946-2328
Polo *(G-17690)*
**▲ Power House Tool Inc** ....E.... 815 727-6301
Joliet *(G-12552)*
**▲ Power-Volt Inc** ....E.... 630 628-9999
Addison *(G-250)*
**▲ Qcircuits Inc** ....E.... 847 797-6678
Rolling Meadows *(G-18771)*
**Qcircuits Inc** ....E.... 618 662-8365
Flora *(G-10214)*
**▲ Qse Inc** ....E.... 815 432-5281
Watseka *(G-21426)*
**Santucci Enterprises** ....G.... 773 286-5629
Chicago *(G-6442)*
**◆ Schumacher Electric Corp** ....D.... 847 385-1600
Mount Prospect *(G-15372)*
**Sigmatron International Inc** ....G.... 847 586-5200
Elgin *(G-9178)*
**▲ Sigmatron International Inc** ....G.... 847 956-8000
Elk Grove Village *(G-9737)*
**Starfire Industries LLC** ....E.... 217 721-4165
Champaign *(G-3548)*
**▼ STC Inc** ....E.... 618 643-2555
Mc Leansboro *(G-14468)*
**Stryde Technologies Inc** ....G.... 510 786-8890
Evanston *(G-10096)*
**Taycorp Inc** ....E.... 630 530-7500
Elmhurst *(G-9948)*

SIC

▲ **Taycorp Inc** ........ E ....... 708 629-0921
Alsip ***(G-533)***
**Te Connectivity Corporation** ........ D ....... 847 680-7400
Mundelein ***(G-15563)***
▲ **Transformer Manufacturers Inc** ........ E ....... 708 457-1200
Norridge ***(G-16110)***
**U S Co-Tronics Corp** ........ E ....... 815 692-3204
Fairbury ***(G-10134)***
▲ **V and F Transformer Corp** ........ D ....... 630 497-8070
Bartlett ***(G-1384)***
◆ **Wattcore Inc** ........ G ....... 571 482-6777
Morton Grove ***(G-15245)***

### *3678 Electronic Connectors*

▲ **Advantage Components Inc** ........ E ....... 815 725-8644
Joliet ***(G-12450)***
**Amphenol Corporation** ........ D ....... 800 944-6446
Lisle ***(G-13559)***
**Amphenol Corporation** ........ G ....... 847 478-5600
Lincolnshire ***(G-13427)***
▲ **Amphenol Fiber Optic Products** ........ E ....... 630 960-1010
Lisle ***(G-13560)***
**B M I Inc** ........ C ....... 847 839-6000
Schaumburg ***(G-19456)***
**Belden Energy Solutions Inc** ........ G ....... 800 235-3361
Elmhurst ***(G-9838)***
**Bragi NA LLC** ........ D ....... 708 717-5000
Frankfort ***(G-10305)***
**C D T Manufacturing Inc** ........ G ....... 847 679-2361
Skokie ***(G-19972)***
▲ **Central Rubber Company** ........ E ....... 815 544-2191
Belvidere ***(G-1745)***
▲ **Cinch Cnnctivity Solutions Inc** ........ C ....... 847 739-0300
Lombard ***(G-13779)***
**Cinch Connectors Inc** ........ D ....... 630 705-6001
Lombard ***(G-13780)***
**Continental Automation Inc** ........ E ....... 630 584-5100
Saint Charles ***(G-19162)***
**Conxall Corporation** ........ C ....... 630 834-7504
Villa Park ***(G-21245)***
▲ **CTS Corporation** ........ C ....... 630 577-8800
Lisle ***(G-13579)***
▲ **Custom Assembly LLC** ........ C ....... 630 595-4855
Wood Dale ***(G-22356)***
**Data Accessories Inc** ........ G ....... 847 669-3640
Huntley ***(G-12136)***
**David Jeskey** ........ G ....... 630 659-6337
Saint Charles ***(G-19168)***
▲ **Eastco Inc** ........ G ....... 708 499-1701
Oak Lawn ***(G-16617)***
**Element14 Inc** ........ E ....... 773 784-5100
Chicago ***(G-4724)***
**Evoys Corp** ........ G ....... 773 736-4200
Chicago ***(G-4791)***
**Gage Applied Technologies LLC** ........ E ....... 815 838-0005
Lockport ***(G-13716)***
**Glenair Inc** ........ E ....... 847 679-8833
Lincolnwood ***(G-13515)***
▲ **Hale Devices Inc** ........ G ....... 305 394-4119
Chicago ***(G-5034)***
**Harting Inc of North America** ........ E ....... 847 741-2700
Elgin ***(G-9058)***
▲ **Harting Inc of North America** ........ E ....... 847 741-1500
Elgin ***(G-9059)***
**Hirose Electric (usa) Inc** ........ D ....... 630 282-6700
Downers Grove ***(G-8459)***
▲ **Iconn Systems LLC** ........ E ....... 630 827-6000
Lombard ***(G-13811)***
▲ **Ip Media Holdings** ........ E ....... 847 714-1177
Wheeling ***(G-22078)***
**Kylon Midwest** ........ G ....... 773 699-3640
Chicago ***(G-5416)***
◆ **Mac Lean-Fogg Company** ........ D ....... 847 566-0010
Mundelein ***(G-15521)***
**Methode Development Co** ........ D ....... 708 867-6777
Chicago ***(G-5703)***
▲ **Methode Electronics Inc** ........ B ....... 708 867-6777
Chicago ***(G-5704)***
**Methode Electronics Inc** ........ C ....... 847 577-9545
Rolling Meadows ***(G-18744)***
**Methode Electronics Inc** ........ A ....... 217 357-3941
Carthage ***(G-3316)***
**Microway Systems Inc** ........ E ....... 847 679-8833
Lincolnwood ***(G-13525)***
**Molex LLC** ........ F ....... 847 353-2500
Lincolnshire ***(G-13466)***
**Molex LLC** ........ G ....... 630 527-4357
Lisle ***(G-13626)***
**Molex LLC** ........ E ....... 630 969-4747
Bolingbrook ***(G-2346)***
**Molex LLC** ........ F ....... 630 512-8787
Downers Grove ***(G-8489)***
**Molex Incorporated** ........ F ....... 630 969-4550
Naperville ***(G-15698)***
▲ **Molex International Inc** ........ F ....... 630 969-4550
Lisle ***(G-13627)***
**Nec Display Solutions Amer Inc** ........ G ....... 630 467-5000
Itasca ***(G-12327)***
**Newko Tool & Engineering Co** ........ E ....... 847 359-1670
Palatine ***(G-17058)***
▲ **Nobility Corporation** ........ E ....... 847 677-3204
Skokie ***(G-20045)***
**P K Neuses Incorporated** ........ G ....... 847 253-6555
Rolling Meadows ***(G-18756)***
▲ **Switchcraft Inc** ........ B ....... 773 792-2700
Chicago ***(G-6653)***
▲ **Switchcraft Holdco Inc** ........ G ....... 773 792-2700
Chicago ***(G-6654)***
**Te Connectivity Corporation** ........ D ....... 847 680-7400
Mundelein ***(G-15563)***
**United Universal Inds Inc** ........ E ....... 815 727-4445
Joliet ***(G-12585)***
▲ **Woodhead Industries LLC** ........ B ....... 847 353-2500
Lincolnshire ***(G-13490)***

### *3679 Electronic Components, NEC*

**Absolute Process Instruments** ........ E ....... 847 918-3510
Libertyville ***(G-13299)***
**Accelerated Assemblies Inc** ........ E ....... 630 616-6680
Elk Grove Village ***(G-9259)***
▲ **Access Assembly LLC** ........ G ....... 847 894-1047
Mundelein ***(G-15463)***
▲ **Advanced Strobe Products Inc** ........ D ....... 708 867-3100
Chicago ***(G-3772)***
**Advanced Technologies Inc** ........ G ....... 847 329-9875
Park Ridge ***(G-17178)***
▲ **Aerotronic Controls Co** ........ F ....... 847 228-6504
Elk Grove Village ***(G-9282)***
▲ **Aimtron Corporation** ........ D ....... 630 372-7500
Palatine ***(G-16999)***
▲ **Air802 Corporation** ........ G ....... 630 428-3108
Aurora ***(G-956)***
▲ **American Precision Elec Inc** ........ D ....... 630 510-8080
Carol Stream ***(G-3101)***
**Americut Wire Edm Inc** ........ F ....... 847 675-1754
Skokie ***(G-19952)***
**Andrew New Zealand Inc** ........ E ....... 708 873-3507
Orland Park ***(G-16843)***
**Andrew Technologies Inc** ........ E ....... 847 520-5770
Wheeling ***(G-22006)***
▲ **ARC-Tronics Inc** ........ C ....... 847 437-0211
Elk Grove Village ***(G-9312)***
**Aria Corporation** ........ G ....... 847 918-9329
Libertyville ***(G-13304)***
**Avg Group of Companies** ........ F ....... 630 668-8886
Carol Stream ***(G-3111)***
◆ **B D C Inc** ........ E ....... 847 741-2233
Elgin ***(G-8962)***
▲ **Bem Wireless LLC** ........ F ....... 815 337-0541
Algonquin ***(G-381)***
▲ **Bestar Technologies Inc** ........ G ....... 520 439-9204
Saint Charles ***(G-19142)***
▲ **Bias Power Inc** ........ G ....... 847 419-9180
Buffalo Grove ***(G-2665)***
**Big Joes Sealcoati** ........ G ....... 630 935-7032
Lisle ***(G-13568)***
▲ **Bircher America Inc** ........ G ....... 847 952-3730
Schaumburg ***(G-19462)***
▲ **Blockmaster Electronics Inc** ........ G ....... 847 956-1680
Elk Grove Village ***(G-9345)***
**Bozki Inc** ........ G ....... 312 767-2122
Chicago ***(G-4152)***
**Bryton Technology Inc** ........ E ....... 309 995-3379
Toulon ***(G-20976)***
**C & B Services** ........ G ....... 847 462-8484
Cary ***(G-3329)***
**C & C Electronics Inc** ........ F ....... 847 550-0177
Mundelein ***(G-15481)***
**C Hofbauer Inc** ........ G ....... 630 920-1222
Burr Ridge ***(G-2826)***
**C L Greenslade Sales Inc** ........ G ....... 847 593-3450
Arlington Heights ***(G-733)***
**C R V Electronics Corp** ........ D ....... 815 675-6500
Spring Grove ***(G-20329)***
**Cal-Tronics Systems Inc** ........ E ....... 630 350-0044
Wood Dale ***(G-22350)***
**Camtek Inc** ........ D ....... 309 661-0348
Bloomington ***(G-2151)***
**Capital Advanced Technologies** ........ G ....... 630 690-1696
Carol Stream ***(G-3124)***
▲ **Capsonic Automotive Inc** ........ F ....... 847 888-7300
Elgin ***(G-8979)***
**Casco Manufacturing Inc** ........ E ....... 630 771-9555
Bolingbrook ***(G-2285)***
**Central Industries of Indiana** ........ G ....... 618 943-2311
Lawrenceville ***(G-13196)***
▲ **Central Rubber Company** ........ E ....... 815 544-2191
Belvidere ***(G-1745)***
**Chicago Cardinal Communication** ........ F ....... 708 424-1446
Oak Lawn ***(G-16610)***
**Chicago Technical Sales Inc** ........ G ....... 630 889-7121
Oakbrook Terrace ***(G-16701)***
▲ **Cinch Cnnctivity Solutions Inc** ........ C ....... 847 739-0300
Lombard ***(G-13779)***
**Circom Inc** ........ E ....... 630 595-4460
Bensenville ***(G-1859)***
▲ **Cita Technologies LLC** ........ G ....... 847 419-9118
Buffalo Grove ***(G-2673)***
**Cmetrix Inc** ........ G ....... 630 595-9800
Wood Dale ***(G-22353)***
◆ **Commscope Technologies LLC** ........ A ....... 708 236-6600
Westchester ***(G-21835)***
**Commscope Technologies LLC** ........ B ....... 779 435-6000
Joliet ***(G-12476)***
**Compu Doc Inc** ........ G ....... 630 554-5800
Oswego ***(G-16910)***
**Connor-Winfield Corp** ........ C ....... 630 851-4722
Aurora ***(G-1133)***
▲ **Consolidated Elec Wire & Cable** ........ D ....... 847 455-8830
Franklin Park ***(G-10440)***
▲ **Continental Assembly Inc** ........ F ....... 773 472-8004
Chicago ***(G-4457)***
▲ **CTS Corporation** ........ C ....... 630 577-8800
Lisle ***(G-13579)***
▲ **Daesam Corporation** ........ G ....... 917 653-2000
Grayslake ***(G-11331)***
**Dalco Marketing Services** ........ G ....... 630 961-3366
Naperville ***(G-15641)***
▲ **De Amertek Corporation Inc** ........ E ....... 630 572-0800
Lombard ***(G-13788)***
**Delta Circuits Inc** ........ E ....... 630 876-0691
West Chicago ***(G-21690)***
**Delta Design Inc** ........ F ....... 708 424-9400
Evergreen Park ***(G-10112)***
▲ **Delta Design Inc** ........ F ....... 708 424-9400
Evergreen Park ***(G-10111)***
**Dynomax Inc** ........ E ....... 224 542-1031
Lincolnshire ***(G-13445)***
▲ **Dynomax Inc** ........ D ....... 847 680-8833
Wheeling ***(G-22040)***
**E Solutions Business** ........ E ....... 855 324-3339
Chicago ***(G-4668)***
▲ **Elan Industries Inc** ........ F ....... 630 679-2000
Bolingbrook ***(G-2304)***
**Electronic Design & Mfg Inc** ........ D ....... 847 550-1912
Lake Zurich ***(G-13066)***
**Elgo Electronic Inc** ........ G ....... 630 626-1639
Bartlett ***(G-1344)***
▲ **Elpac Electronics Inc** ........ C ....... 708 316-4407
Westchester ***(G-21839)***
▲ **Entropy International Inc USA** ........ F ....... 630 834-3872
Elmhurst ***(G-9867)***
▲ **Essex Electro Engineers Inc** ........ E ....... 847 891-4444
Schaumburg ***(G-19521)***
▲ **Excel Specialty Corp** ........ E ....... 773 262-7575
Lake Forest ***(G-12898)***
**Excelitas Technologies Corp** ........ E ....... 847 537-4277
Wheeling ***(G-22052)***
**Flp Industries LLC** ........ F ....... 847 215-8650
Wheeling ***(G-22054)***
**Formcraft Tool Company** ........ F ....... 773 476-8727
Chicago ***(G-4874)***
▲ **Four Star Tool Inc** ........ D ....... 224 735-2419
Rolling Meadows ***(G-18729)***
▲ **Futaba Corporation of America** ........ E ....... 847 884-1444
Schaumburg ***(G-19534)***
**G T C Industries Inc** ........ G ....... 708 369-9815
Naperville ***(G-15661)***
**Gateway Cable Inc** ........ G ....... 630 766-7969
Bensenville ***(G-1905)***
**Gil Instruments Co** ........ G ....... 815 459-8764
Crystal Lake ***(G-7583)***
▲ **Global Display Solutions Inc** ........ E ....... 815 282-2328
Rockford ***(G-18399)***
◆ **Grand Products Inc** ........ C ....... 800 621-6101
Elk Grove Village ***(G-9506)***
**Grayhill Inc** ........ C ....... 847 428-6990
Carpentersville ***(G-3285)***
▲ **Grayhill Inc** ........ B ....... 708 354-1040
La Grange ***(G-12734)***

▲ **Guardian Electric Mfg Co** D 815 334-3600
Woodstock *(G-22572)*
**Gulf Coast Switching Co LLC** G 312 324-7353
Chicago *(G-5011)*
**Hart Electric LLC** E 815 368-3341
Lostant *(G-13906)*
▲ **Hi-Tech Elctronic Pdts Mfg Inc** E 815 220-1543
Oglesby *(G-16749)*
**His Company Inc** G 847 885-2922
Schaumburg *(G-19556)*
**Honeywell International Inc** C 815 777-2780
Galena *(G-10726)*
**Hubbell Power Systems Inc** F 618 797-5000
Edwardsville *(G-8803)*
▲ **Ikonix Group Inc** G 847 367-4671
Lake Forest *(G-12916)*
**Illinois Tool Works Inc** C 847 876-9400
Des Plaines *(G-8208)*
▼ **IMS Companies LLC** D 847 391-8100
Des Plaines *(G-8210)*
**Innolux Technology USA Inc** G 847 490-5315
Hoffman Estates *(G-12018)*
**Integrated Circuits Research** G 630 830-9024
Hanover Park *(G-11583)*
**Ipr Systems Inc** G 708 385-7500
Alsip *(G-474)*
**Jds Labs Inc** G 618 366-0475
Collinsville *(G-7329)*
**John Hauter Dremel** G 800 437-3635
Mount Prospect *(G-15341)*
**Joseph C Rakers** G 618 670-6995
Pocahontas *(G-17683)*
**Journey Circuits Inc** G 630 283-0604
Schaumburg *(G-19591)*
**Julian Elec Svc & Engrg Inc** E 630 920-8950
Westmont *(G-21895)*
**Knowles Elec Holdings Inc** A 630 250-5100
Itasca *(G-12296)*
▲ **Knowles Electronics LLC** A 630 250-5100
Itasca *(G-12297)*
**Kp Performance Inc** G 780 809-1908
Melrose Park *(G-14667)*
**Kraus & Naimer Inc** G 847 298-2450
Des Plaines *(G-8219)*
◆ **L I K Inc** F 630 213-1282
Streamwood *(G-20665)*
**Lace Technologies Inc** F 630 762-3865
Addison *(G-177)*
▲ **Lane Technical Sales Inc** E 773 775-1613
Chicago *(G-5457)*
**Lifesafety Power Inc** F 224 324-4240
Mundelein *(G-15520)*
▲ **Light To Form LLC** E 847 498-5832
Northbrook *(G-16296)*
▲ **Limitless Innovations Inc** E 855 843-4828
McHenry *(G-14522)*
**Littelfuse Inc** A 773 628-1000
Chicago *(G-5521)*
**Loda Electronics Co** G 217 386-2554
Loda *(G-13752)*
**Manu-TEC of Illinois LLC** F 630 543-3022
Addison *(G-190)*
**Matrix Circuits LLC** G 319 367-5000
Lake Villa *(G-13020)*
**Midwest Aero Support Inc** E 815 398-9202
Machesney Park *(G-14092)*
▲ **Millennium Electronics Inc** D 815 479-9755
Crystal Lake *(G-7613)*
**Mk Test Systems Americas Inc** G 773 569-3778
Lake Barrington *(G-12820)*
▲ **Molex LLC** A 630 969-4550
Lisle *(G-13625)*
**Molex LLC** G 630 527-4363
Bolingbrook *(G-2345)*
**Molex LLC** F 630 512-8787
Downers Grove *(G-8489)*
▲ **Molex International Inc** F 630 969-4550
Lisle *(G-13627)*
▲ **Molex Premise Networks Inc** A 866 733-6659
Lisle *(G-13628)*
▲ **Monnex International Inc** E 847 850-5263
Buffalo Grove *(G-2738)*
▲ **Motec Inc** G 630 241-9595
Downers Grove *(G-8490)*
**Murata Electronics N Amer Inc** G 847 330-9200
Schaumburg *(G-19657)*
**Navatek Resources Inc** G 847 301-0174
Schaumburg *(G-19662)*
**Navitas Electronics Corp** E 702 293-4670
Woodridge *(G-22504)*
▲ **Nep Electronics Inc** C 630 595-8500
Wood Dale *(G-22405)*
◆ **Netcom Inc** C 847 537-6300
Wheeling *(G-22106)*
**Northrop Grumman Systems Corp** A 847 259-9600
Rolling Meadows *(G-18753)*
**Novel Electronic Designs Inc** G 309 224-9945
Chillicothe *(G-7169)*
**Nu-Way Electronics Inc** E 847 437-7120
Elk Grove Village *(G-9657)*
**Nusource Inc** F 847 201-8934
Round Lake *(G-19064)*
**Omnitronix Corporation** F 630 837-1400
Streamwood *(G-20668)*
**On Time Circuits Inc** E 630 955-1110
Lisle *(G-13636)*
**Ot Systems Limited** G 630 554-9178
Plano *(G-17669)*
**Panasonic Corp North America** G 630 801-0359
Aurora *(G-1062)*
▲ **Partec Inc** C 847 678-9520
Franklin Park *(G-10547)*
**Perfectvision Mfg Inc** C 630 226-9890
Bolingbrook *(G-2357)*
▲ **Peterson Elctr-Msical Pdts Inc** E 708 388-3311
Alsip *(G-507)*
◆ **Pfingsten Partners LLC** F 312 222-8707
Chicago *(G-6115)*
**Pintsch Tiefenbach Us Inc** G 618 993-8513
Marion *(G-14280)*
**Polyera Corporation** E 847 677-7517
Skokie *(G-20056)*
**Power Equipment Company** E 815 754-4090
Cortland *(G-7394)*
**Precision Circuits Inc** F 630 515-9100
Downers Grove *(G-8510)*
▲ **Puls LP** E 630 587-9780
Saint Charles *(G-19244)*
▲ **Qcircuits Inc** E 847 797-6678
Rolling Meadows *(G-18771)*
**Quality Cable & Components Inc** E 309 695-3435
Wyoming *(G-22639)*
▲ **R B Manufacturing Inc** E 815 522-3100
Kirkland *(G-12716)*
**Relay Services Mfg Corp** F 773 252-2700
Chicago *(G-6327)*
**Richardson Electronics Ltd** C 630 208-2278
Lafox *(G-12795)*
▲ **Rubicon Technology Inc** C 847 295-7000
Bensenville *(G-1983)*
**Safemobile Inc** F 847 818-1649
Rolling Meadows *(G-18776)*
**Sandes Quynetta** G 815 275-4876
Freeport *(G-10687)*
**Satellink Inc** G 618 983-5555
Johnston City *(G-12445)*
**Seaco Data Systems Inc** D 630 876-2169
Carol Stream *(G-3237)*
**Seagon Inc** G 630 541-5460
Lisle *(G-13655)*
**Sentral Assemblies LLC** D 847 478-9720
Lincolnshire *(G-13477)*
**Sentral Group LLC** G 847 478-9720
Lincolnshire *(G-13478)*
**Sigmatron International Inc** G 847 586-5200
Elgin *(G-9178)*
▲ **Sigmatron International Inc** G 847 956-8000
Elk Grove Village *(G-9737)*
**Simple Circuits Inc** G 708 671-9600
Palos Park *(G-17132)*
▲ **Skyline International Inc** E 847 357-9077
Downers Grove *(G-8525)*
**Sota Service Ctr By Bodinets** G 608 538-3500
Dekalb *(G-8120)*
▲ **Sub-Sem Inc** E 815 459-4139
Crystal Lake *(G-7655)*
▲ **Sumida America Components Inc** F 847 545-6700
Schaumburg *(G-19742)*
**Sumida America Inc** E 847 545-6700
Schaumburg *(G-19743)*
▲ **Switchcraft Inc** B 773 792-2700
Chicago *(G-6653)*
▲ **Switchcraft Holdco Inc** G 773 792-2700
Chicago *(G-6654)*
**Switchee Bandz Usa LLC** G 312 415-1100
Highland Park *(G-11875)*
▲ **T&L International Mfg/Dist Inc** G 309 830-7238
Farmer City *(G-10182)*
**Tanvas Inc** G 773 295-6220
Chicago *(G-6674)*
**Tech Star Design and Mfg** F 847 290-8676
Elk Grove Village *(G-9771)*
**Tedds Cstm Installations Inc** G 815 485-6800
New Lenox *(G-15918)*
◆ **Teejet Technologies LLC** D 630 665-5002
Springfield *(G-20542)*
◆ **Tellurian Technologies Inc** C 847 934-4141
Arlington Heights *(G-854)*
▲ **The Syntek Group Inc** G 773 279-0131
Chicago *(G-6710)*
**Triton Manufacturing Co Inc** D 708 587-4000
Monee *(G-15004)*
**TRW Automotive US LLC** B 217 826-3011
Marshall *(G-14330)*
**Tvh Parts Co** E 847 223-1000
Grayslake *(G-11365)*
◆ **Uico LLC** E 630 592-4400
Elmhurst *(G-9954)*
**Unlimited Svcs Wisconsin Inc** E 815 399-0282
Machesney Park *(G-14117)*
**Value Link 1 Enterprises** G 630 833-6243
Villa Park *(G-21289)*
**Vl Inc** G 618 277-8703
Belleville *(G-1685)*
**Weldon Corporation** E 708 343-4700
Maywood *(G-14437)*
▲ **Woodhead Industries LLC** B 847 353-2500
Lincolnshire *(G-13490)*
**Zero Ground LLC** F 847 360-9500
Waukegan *(G-21644)*

### *3691 Storage Batteries*

**A123 Systems LLC** G 617 778-5700
Elgin *(G-8930)*
▲ **Advanced Battery LLC** F 309 755-7775
Milan *(G-14772)*
▲ **All Cell Technologies LLC** E 773 922-1155
Chicago *(G-3805)*
**Batteries Plus 287** G 630 279-3478
Villa Park *(G-21237)*
**Bell City Battery Mfg Inc** G 618 233-0437
Belleville *(G-1611)*
**Crown Battery Manufacturing Co** G 630 530-8060
Villa Park *(G-21247)*
**Crown Battery Manufacturing Co** G 708 946-2535
Beecher *(G-1597)*
**Duracell Company** G 203 796-4000
Chicago *(G-4655)*
**Ecolocap Solutions Inc** G 866 479-7041
Barrington *(G-1279)*
**Enersys** D 630 455-4872
Lisle *(G-13587)*
**Exide Technologies** C 630 862-2200
Aurora *(G-1005)*
**Exide Technologies** D 678 566-9000
Lombard *(G-13798)*
**Firefly International Enrgy Co** G 781 937-0619
Peoria *(G-17361)*
**Hubbell Power Systems Inc** F 618 797-5000
Edwardsville *(G-8803)*
**Ill Battery Spxcialists L** G 773 478-8600
Chicago *(G-5153)*
**Interstate All Battery Center** F 217 214-1069
Quincy *(G-17840)*
**Interstate Battery System Intl** G 708 424-2288
Oak Lawn *(G-16626)*
**Inventus Power Holdings Inc** D 630 410-7900
Woodridge *(G-22498)*
▲ **Iterna LLC** E 630 585-7400
Aurora *(G-1035)*
**Johnson Contrls Btry Group Inc** B 630 232-4270
Geneva *(G-10842)*
▲ **National Power Corp** E 773 685-2662
Chicago *(G-5867)*
**Newly Weds Foods Inc** D 773 628-6900
Chicago *(G-5900)*
**P L R Sales Inc** G 217 733-2245
Fairmount *(G-10164)*
**Palladium Energy Group Inc** D 630 410-7900
Woodridge *(G-22507)*
**Performance Battery Group Inc** G 630 293-5505
West Chicago *(G-21755)*
**Spectrum Brands Inc** G 815 285-6500
Dixon *(G-8353)*
**Storage Battery Systems LLC** G 630 221-1700
Carol Stream *(G-3251)*
▲ **Technical Power Systems Inc** E 630 719-1471
Lisle *(G-13670)*

SIC

Employee Codes: A=Over 500 employees, B=251-500
C=101-250, D=51-100, E=20-50, F=10-19, G=3-9
2017 Harris Illinois
Industrial Directory
1105

### 3692 Primary Batteries: Dry & Wet

**Exide Technologies** ....C.... 630 862-2200
Aurora *(G-1005)*
**Exide Technologies** ....D.... 678 566-9000
Lombard *(G-13798)*
**Larrys Better Built Battery** ....G.... 618 758-2011
Coulterville *(G-7401)*

### 3694 Electrical Eqpt For Internal Combustion Engines

**A and D Industrial Ignition** ....G.... 773 992-4040
Franklin Park *(G-10380)*
**A E Iskra Inc** ....G.... 815 874-4022
Rockford *(G-18240)*
**▲ A E Iskra Inc** ....G.... 815 874-4022
Rockford *(G-18239)*
**Aerodyne Incorporated** ....G.... 773 588-2905
Chicago *(G-3777)*
**Aeromotive Services Inc** ....F.... 224 535-9220
Elgin *(G-8939)*
**▲ Amerline Enterprises Co Inc** ....E.... 847 671-6554
Schiller Park *(G-19802)*
**Appliance Information and Repr** ....G.... 217 698-8858
Rochester *(G-18115)*
**▲ Ark Technologies Inc** ....C.... 630 377-8855
Saint Charles *(G-19138)*
**▲ Barcar Manufacturing Inc** ....G.... 630 365-5200
Elburn *(G-8877)*
**Bill West Enterprises Inc** ....G.... 217 886-2591
Jacksonville *(G-12378)*
**Borgwarner Transm Systems Inc** ....F.... 708 731-4540
Melrose Park *(G-14602)*
**C & D Rebuilders** ....G.... 618 273-9862
Eldorado *(G-8918)*
**▲ Carnation Enterprises** ....G.... 847 804-5928
Niles *(G-15967)*
**Charlotte Louise Tate** ....G.... 773 849-3236
Chicago *(G-4294)*
**Continental Automotive Inc** ....E.... 847 862-6300
Deer Park *(G-7970)*
**▲ County Packaging Inc** ....D.... 708 597-1100
Crestwood *(G-7484)*
**D C Grove Electric Inc** ....G.... 847 587-0864
Fox Lake *(G-10275)*
**Dale Schawitsch** ....G.... 217 224-5161
Quincy *(G-17817)*
**Egan Wagner Corporation** ....G.... 630 985-8007
Woodridge *(G-22475)*
**Elc Industries Corp** ....C.... 630 851-1616
Aurora *(G-1143)*
**▲ Elc Industries Corp** ....E.... 630 851-1616
Aurora *(G-1144)*
**▲ Excel Specialty Corp** ....E.... 773 262-7575
Lake Forest *(G-12898)*
**◆ Fram Group Operations LLC** ....B.... 800 890-2075
Lake Forest *(G-12899)*
**General Air Compressor Inc** ....G.... 630 860-1717
Bensenville *(G-1907)*
**H R Larke Corp** ....G.... 847 204-2776
Crystal Lake *(G-7586)*
**Harvey Bros Inc** ....F.... 309 342-3137
Galesburg *(G-10757)*
**Innovation Specialists Inc** ....G.... 815 372-9001
New Lenox *(G-15885)*
**J & B Truck Services Ltd** ....G.... 708 430-8760
Bridgeview *(G-2501)*
**Joes Automotive Inc** ....G.... 815 937-9281
Kankakee *(G-12630)*
**Julian Elec Svc & Engrg Inc** ....E.... 630 920-8950
Westmont *(G-21895)*
**K & W Auto Electric** ....F.... 217 857-1717
Teutopolis *(G-20853)*
**▼ Kold-Ban International Ltd** ....E.... 847 658-8561
Lake In The Hills *(G-12997)*
**Kromray Hydraulic McHy Inc** ....G.... 630 257-8655
Lemont *(G-13238)*
**Major Wire Incorporated** ....F.... 708 457-0121
Norridge *(G-16105)*
**▲ Mat Engine Technologies LLC** ....G.... 847 821-9630
Long Grove *(G-13896)*
**▲ Midtronics Inc** ....D.... 630 323-2800
Willowbrook *(G-22222)*
**Midwest Aero Support Inc** ....E.... 815 398-9202
Machesney Park *(G-14092)*
**Monona Holdings LLC** ....G.... 630 946-0630
Naperville *(G-15700)*
**Motion Industries Inc** ....G.... 847 760-6630
Elgin *(G-9113)*
**Motorola Solutions Inc** ....C.... 847 576-8600
Schaumburg *(G-19652)*
**▲ MTA USA Corp** ....G.... 847 847-5503
Schaumburg *(G-19656)*
**NGK Spark Plugs (usa) Inc** ....E.... 630 595-7894
Wood Dale *(G-22406)*
**Nidec Motor Corporation** ....D.... 847 439-3760
Des Plaines *(G-8241)*
**Niles Auto Parts** ....G.... 847 215-2549
Lincolnshire *(G-13468)*
**Northrop Grmmn Spce & Mssn Sys** ....F.... 630 773-6900
Itasca *(G-12333)*
**▲ P & G Keene Elec Rbldrs LLC** ....E.... 708 430-5770
Bridgeview *(G-2516)*
**Plasmatreat USA Inc** ....F.... 847 783-0622
Elgin *(G-9138)*
**Powermaster** ....G.... 630 957-4019
West Chicago *(G-21759)*
**Quick Start Pdts & Solutions** ....F.... 815 562-5414
Rochelle *(G-18103)*
**◆ Robert Bosch LLC** ....B.... 248 876-1000
Broadview *(G-2610)*
**Sentral Group LLC** ....G.... 847 478-9720
Lincolnshire *(G-13478)*
**Sk Express Inc** ....C.... 815 748-4388
Dekalb *(G-8118)*
**Southern Ill Auto Elec Inc** ....F.... 618 587-3308
Tilden *(G-20877)*
**Thyssenkrupp Presta Cold Forgi** ....E.... 217 431-4212
Danville *(G-7774)*
**UNI Electric Enterprise Inc** ....G.... 630 372-6312
Bartlett *(G-1323)*
**Xenia Mfg Inc** ....C.... 618 678-2218
Xenia *(G-22645)*
**Xenia Mfg Inc** ....E.... 618 392-7212
Olney *(G-16801)*

### 3695 Recording Media

**Acro Magnetics Inc** ....G.... 815 943-5018
Harvard *(G-11617)*
**Acta Publications** ....G.... 773 989-3036
Chicago *(G-3739)*
**Adsensa Corporation** ....G.... 312 559-2881
Chicago *(G-3756)*
**Arba Retail Systems Corp** ....G.... 630 620-8566
Naperville *(G-15797)*
**Ats Commercial Group LLC** ....F.... 815 686-2705
Piper City *(G-17558)*
**Bpn Chicago** ....E.... 312 799-4100
Chicago *(G-4154)*
**Computers At Work Inc** ....G.... 815 776-9470
Galena *(G-10717)*
**Error Free Software LLC** ....E.... 312 461-0300
Chicago *(G-4774)*
**Estad Stamping & Mfg Co** ....E.... 217 442-4600
Danville *(G-7717)*
**Imperial Technical Services** ....F.... 708 403-1564
Orland Park *(G-16867)*
**◆ Jvc Advanced Media USA Inc** ....G.... 630 237-2439
Schaumburg *(G-19593)*
**Lssp Corporation** ....G.... 630 428-0099
Naperville *(G-15693)*
**M K Advantage Inc** ....F.... 773 902-5272
Chicago *(G-5583)*
**Magna-Flux International** ....G.... 815 623-7634
Roscoe *(G-18904)*
**Magnetic Occasions & More Inc** ....G.... 815 462-4141
New Lenox *(G-15892)*
**Mak-System Corp** ....F.... 847 803-4863
Des Plaines *(G-8225)*
**Paragon Group Inc** ....G.... 847 526-1800
Wauconda *(G-21491)*
**▲ Rinda Technologies Inc** ....F.... 773 736-6633
Chicago *(G-6358)*
**Sammy USA Corp** ....E.... 847 364-9787
Elk Grove Village *(G-9726)*
**Stenograph LLC** ....D.... 630 532-5100
Elmhurst *(G-9943)*
**Tdm Systems Inc** ....G.... 847 605-1269
Schaumburg *(G-19756)*

### 3699 Electrical Machinery, Eqpt & Splys, NEC

**2d2c Inc** ....G.... 847 543-0980
Gurnee *(G-11416)*
**Access Japan LLC** ....G.... 773 583-7183
Chicago *(G-3716)*
**Accu Cut Inc** ....G.... 815 229-3525
Rockford *(G-18252)*
**Accurate Security & Lock Corp** ....G.... 815 455-0133
Lake In The Hills *(G-12982)*
**Aemm A Electric** ....G.... 708 403-6700
Orland Park *(G-16839)*
**Agrowtek Inc** ....G.... 847 380-3009
Gurnee *(G-11420)*
**Aim Inc** ....G.... 630 941-0027
Elmhurst *(G-9831)*
**▲ Alliance Laser Sales Inc** ....E.... 847 487-1945
Wauconda *(G-21438)*
**▼ Allmetal Inc** ....D.... 630 250-8090
Itasca *(G-12225)*
**Ambient Lightning and Electric** ....G.... 708 529-3434
Oak Lawn *(G-16601)*
**American Holiday Lights Inc** ....G.... 630 769-9999
Woodridge *(G-22451)*
**Amt (additive Mfg Tech Inc** ....G.... 847 258-4475
Elk Grove Village *(G-9304)*
**▲ Appleton Grp LLC** ....C.... 847 268-6000
Rosemont *(G-18989)*
**Asco Power Technologies LP** ....G.... 630 505-4050
Warrenville *(G-21343)*
**Assa Abloy Entrance Systems US** ....F.... 847 228-5600
Elk Grove Village *(G-9316)*
**Associate General Labs Inc** ....G.... 847 678-2717
Franklin Park *(G-10404)*
**Axon Electric LLC** ....G.... 630 834-4090
Lake In The Hills *(G-12986)*
**Azilsa Inc** ....E.... 312 919-1741
Schaumburg *(G-19455)*
**Azz Incorporated** ....D.... 815 723-5000
Joliet *(G-12459)*
**▲ Bechara Sim** ....F.... 847 913-9950
Buffalo Grove *(G-2662)*
**Best Rep Company Corporation** ....G.... 847 451-6644
Franklin Park *(G-10411)*
**Bin Long & Electric** ....G.... 309 758-5407
Adair *(G-12)*
**Blustor Pmc Inc** ....G.... 312 265-3058
Chicago *(G-4131)*
**Branson Ultrasonics Corp** ....G.... 847 229-0800
Buffalo Grove *(G-2669)*
**Brighter Electric Inc** ....G.... 630 325-4915
Willowbrook *(G-22202)*
**Burr Ridge Lighting Inc** ....G.... 630 323-4850
Westmont *(G-21878)*
**Buss Boyz Customs Inc** ....G.... 815 369-2803
Lena *(G-13273)*
**▲ Bystronic Inc** ....C.... 847 214-0300
Elgin *(G-8974)*
**Calx Trading Corporation** ....E.... 630 456-6721
Naperville *(G-15800)*
**Carey Electric Co Inc** ....G.... 847 949-9294
Grayslake *(G-11325)*
**Cdc Enterprises Inc** ....G.... 815 790-4205
Johnsburg *(G-12432)*
**Cecomp Electronics Inc** ....E.... 847 918-3510
Libertyville *(G-13313)*
**Chamberlain Group Inc** ....G.... 630 833-0618
Oak Brook *(G-16498)*
**▲ Chamberlain Group Inc** ....B.... 630 279-3600
Oak Brook *(G-16499)*
**◆ Chamberlain Manufacturing Corp** ....A.... 630 279-3600
Oak Brook *(G-16500)*
**Charlotte Dmg Inc** ....G.... 630 227-3900
Itasca *(G-12243)*
**Chase Security Systems Inc** ....G.... 773 594-1919
Chicago *(G-4295)*
**Checkpoint Systems Inc** ....D.... 630 771-4240
Romeoville *(G-18809)*
**Cipher Technology Solution** ....G.... 630 892-2355
Montgomery *(G-15038)*
**Coating & Systems Integration** ....F.... 312 335-1848
Chicago *(G-4414)*
**Coles Craft Corporation** ....G.... 630 858-8171
Glen Ellyn *(G-10963)*
**◆ Commscope Technologies LLC** ....A.... 708 236-6600
Westchester *(G-21835)*
**Compx International Inc** ....G.... 847 543-4583
Grayslake *(G-11328)*
**Connor Electric Services Inc** ....E.... 630 823-8230
Schaumburg *(G-19480)*
**Corporate Electric Inc** ....G.... 847 963-2800
Schaumburg *(G-19485)*
**Current Plus Electric LLC** ....G.... 618 394-4827
Belleville *(G-1620)*
**Custom Tool Inc** ....F.... 217 465-8538
Paris *(G-17145)*
**D & D Manufacturing Inc** ....G.... 888 300-6869
Bolingbrook *(G-2296)*
**Dalmatian Fire Equipment Ltd** ....G.... 708 201-1730
Dolton *(G-8369)*
**Delta-Therm Corporation** ....F.... 847 526-2407
Crystal Lake *(G-7566)*

SIC SECTION 36 ELECTRONIC AND OTHER ELECTRICAL EQUIPMENT AND COMPONENTS, EXCEPT COMPUTER

**Domino Amjet Inc** ....E.... 847 662-3148
Gurnee *(G-11439)*
**Domino Lasers Inc** ....E.... 847 855-1364
Gurnee *(G-11442)*
▲ **Dukane Corporation** ....C.... 630 797-4900
Saint Charles *(G-19175)*
**Duvas USA Limited** ....G.... 312 266-1420
Chicago *(G-4658)*
▲ **E N M Company** ....D.... 773 775-8400
Chicago *(G-4667)*
**East West Martial Arts Sups** ....G.... 773 878-7711
Chicago *(G-4682)*
**Eazypower Corporation** ....E.... 773 278-5000
Chicago *(G-4686)*
▲ **Eazypower Corporation** ....G.... 773 278-5000
Chicago *(G-4687)*
**Edison Electric** ....G.... 815 464-1006
Frankfort *(G-10319)*
**Elec Easel** ....G.... 815 444-9700
Crystal Lake *(G-7571)*
▲ **Electri-Flex Company (del)** ....D.... 630 307-1095
Roselle *(G-18941)*
**Electric Grand** ....G.... 630 363-8893
Montgomery *(G-15042)*
**Electro-Technic Products Inc** ....F.... 773 561-2349
Chicago *(G-4721)*
◆ **Elenco Electronics Inc** ....E.... 847 541-3800
Wheeling *(G-22046)*
**Elite Access Systems Inc** ....D.... 800 528-5880
Elmhurst *(G-9864)*
**Engineered Security & Sound** ....G.... 630 876-8853
West Chicago *(G-21695)*
**Enginuity Communications Corp** ....E.... 630 444-0778
Saint Charles *(G-19182)*
**Excarb Inc** ....G.... 217 493-8477
Champaign *(G-3484)*
**Eztech Manufacturing Inc** ....F.... 630 293-0010
West Chicago *(G-21700)*
▲ **Fisa North America Inc** ....G.... 847 593-2080
Elk Grove Village *(G-9478)*
**Fortitud Inc** ....G.... 312 919-4938
Algonquin *(G-390)*
**Foulk Electric Inc** ....G.... 309 435-7006
Canton *(G-2986)*
**Fryman Electric** ....G.... 309 387-6540
Pekin *(G-17264)*
**Gate Systems Corporation** ....G.... 847 731-6700
Gurnee *(G-11452)*
**Genesis Electric & Tech Inc** ....G.... 847 258-5218
Elk Grove Village *(G-9498)*
**Gerardo and Quintana Auto Elc** ....G.... 773 424-0634
Chicago *(G-4947)*
**Giba Electric** ....G.... 773 685-4420
Chicago *(G-4951)*
**Gilbert Electric** ....G.... 618 458-7235
Fults *(G-10710)*
**Global Manufacturing** ....G.... 630 908-7633
Willowbrook *(G-22213)*
**Hardt Electric** ....G.... 312 822-0869
Chicago *(G-5044)*
**Herrmann Ultrasonics Inc** ....E.... 630 626-1626
Bartlett *(G-1352)*
▲ **Heuft Usa Inc** ....F.... 630 395-9521
Downers Grove *(G-8457)*
▲ **HK America Inc** ....G.... 630 916-0200
Lombard *(G-13809)*
**Hopcroft Electric Inc** ....G.... 618 288-7302
Glen Carbon *(G-10952)*
**Hs Technology Inc** ....G.... 630 572-7650
Oak Brook *(G-16522)*
**Hubbell Power Systems Inc** ....F.... 618 797-5000
Edwardsville *(G-8803)*
▲ **I C Dynamics Inc** ....G.... 708 922-0501
Plainfield *(G-17608)*
▲ **Image Industries Inc** ....E.... 847 659-0100
Huntley *(G-12147)*
▲ **IMS Engineered Products LLC** ....C.... 847 391-8100
Des Plaines *(G-8211)*
▼ **Industrial Enclosure Corp** ....E.... 630 898-7499
Aurora *(G-1171)*
**Interior Tectonics LLC** ....G.... 312 515-7779
Chicago *(G-5215)*
**Intermountain Electronics Inc** ....G.... 618 339-6743
Centralia *(G-3419)*
**Intown Electric** ....G.... 847 305-4816
Arlington Heights *(G-779)*
▲ **Inventus Power (illinois) LLC** ....C.... 630 410-7900
Woodridge *(G-22497)*
**Invisible Fencing of Quad City** ....G.... 309 797-1688
Moline *(G-14945)*

**James J Sandoval** ....G.... 734 717-7555
Lombard *(G-13814)*
**Jardis Industries Inc** ....F.... 630 773-5600
Itasca *(G-12290)*
**Jarvis Electric** ....G.... 618 806-2767
O Fallon *(G-16468)*
**Jescorp Inc** ....D.... 847 378-1200
Elk Grove Village *(G-9562)*
**Jess Electric** ....G.... 217 243-7946
Jacksonville *(G-12398)*
**Jk Audio Inc** ....F.... 815 786-2929
Sandwich *(G-19370)*
**Kamstra Door Service Inc** ....G.... 708 895-9990
Lansing *(G-13167)*
**Kavanaugh Electric Inc** ....G.... 708 503-1310
Frankfort *(G-10339)*
**Kaybee Engineering Company Inc** ....E.... 630 968-7100
Westmont *(G-21896)*
**Kidde Fire Triner Holdings LLC** ....G.... 312 219-7900
Chicago *(G-5381)*
**Klass Electric Company Inc** ....F.... 847 437-5555
Elk Grove Village *(G-9576)*
**Kohns Electric** ....G.... 309 463-2331
Varna *(G-21134)*
**Laser Energy Systems** ....G.... 815 282-8200
Loves Park *(G-13959)*
▲ **Lecip Inc** ....G.... 312 626-2525
Bensenville *(G-1939)*
**Lee Electric** ....G.... 618 244-6810
Mount Vernon *(G-15422)*
**Littelfuse Inc** ....G.... 217 531-3100
Champaign *(G-3511)*
▲ **Lutamar Electrical Assemblies** ....E.... 847 679-5400
Skokie *(G-20032)*
**M P V Inc** ....G.... 847 234-3960
Lake Zurich *(G-13097)*
**Mac Lean-Fogg Company** ....C.... 847 288-2534
Franklin Park *(G-10519)*
**Maco-Sys LLC** ....F.... 779 888-3260
Rockford *(G-18479)*
▼ **Magnetrol International Inc** ....C.... 630 723-6600
Aurora *(G-1051)*
▲ **Marantec America Corporation** ....E.... 847 596-6400
Gurnee *(G-11469)*
◆ **Marbil Enterprises Inc** ....G.... 618 257-1810
Belleville *(G-1651)*
**Marmon Engineered Components** ....G.... 312 372-9500
Chicago *(G-5623)*
**Maxi-Vac Inc** ....G.... 630 620-6669
East Dundee *(G-8649)*
**Mi-Jack Systems & Tech LLC** ....F.... 708 596-3780
Hazel Crest *(G-11712)*
**Midwest Assembly & Packg Inc** ....G....
Wauconda *(G-21483)*
**Midwest Tool Inc** ....G.... 773 588-1313
Chicago *(G-5751)*
**Midwest Treasure Detectors** ....G.... 217 223-4769
Quincy *(G-17860)*
**Migatron Corporation** ....E.... 815 338-5800
Woodstock *(G-22590)*
**Mikus Elc & Generators Inc** ....G.... 224 757-5534
Volo *(G-21319)*
**Mkc Electric** ....G.... 630 844-9700
Montgomery *(G-15061)*
**Mobiloc LLC** ....G.... 773 742-1329
Alsip *(G-495)*
**Moog Inc** ....E.... 770 987-7550
Northbrook *(G-16313)*
**Motor Sport Marketing Group** ....E.... 618 654-6750
Highland *(G-11803)*
**Natures Best Christmas Trees** ....G.... 815 765-2960
Poplar Grove *(G-17715)*
▲ **Newhaven Display Intl Inc** ....E.... 847 844-8795
Elgin *(G-9118)*
▲ **Nitek International LLC** ....G.... 847 259-8900
Rolling Meadows *(G-18751)*
**Northern Illi Electrcl Jnt App** ....F.... 815 969-8484
Rockford *(G-18521)*
**Nova Systems Ltd** ....G.... 630 879-2296
Aurora *(G-1195)*
**Novanta Inc** ....G.... 781 266-5700
Newton *(G-15945)*
**O R Lasertechnology Inc** ....G.... 847 593-5711
Elk Grove Village *(G-9659)*
**Occly LLC** ....G.... 773 969-5080
Chicago *(G-5966)*
**Omron Electronics LLC** ....C.... 847 843-7900
Hoffman Estates *(G-12033)*
**P & J Technologies** ....G.... 847 995-1108
Schaumburg *(G-19677)*

◆ **Panduit Corp** ....A.... 708 532-1800
Tinley Park *(G-20937)*
**Panduit Corp** ....E.... 815 836-1800
Lockport *(G-13737)*
**Penco Electric** ....G.... 847 423-2159
Niles *(G-16016)*
**Perimeter Access Sys Svcs Inc** ....F.... 630 556-4283
Elburn *(G-8903)*
**Pipeline Trading Systems LLC** ....G.... 312 212-4288
Chicago *(G-6128)*
**Plug-In Electric Charge Inc** ....G.... 224 856-5229
Hoffman Estates *(G-12038)*
▲ **Polygroup Services NA Inc** ....G.... 847 851-9995
East Dundee *(G-8653)*
▲ **Power Port Products Inc** ....E.... 630 628-9102
Addison *(G-249)*
**Presentation Studios Intl LLC** ....F.... 312 733-8160
Chicago *(G-6180)*
**Prime Devices Corporation** ....F.... 847 729-2550
Willow Springs *(G-22198)*
▲ **Pro Access Systems Inc** ....F.... 630 426-0022
Elburn *(G-8905)*
▲ **Probotix** ....G.... 309 691-2643
Peoria *(G-17436)*
**Protection Controls Inc** ....E.... 773 763-3110
Skokie *(G-20066)*
**Quality Intgrted Solutions Inc** ....G.... 815 464-4772
Tinley Park *(G-20942)*
◆ **Raynor Mfg Co** ....A.... 815 288-1431
Dixon *(G-8341)*
**Rein Electric** ....G.... 224 433-6936
Libertyville *(G-13375)*
**Rent-A-Center Inc** ....G.... 773 376-8883
Chicago *(G-6335)*
**Request Electric** ....G.... 217 629-7789
Riverton *(G-18034)*
▲ **Rf Ideas Inc** ....D.... 847 870-1723
Rolling Meadows *(G-18774)*
**Rockford Linear Motion LLC** ....G.... 815 961-7900
Rockford *(G-18578)*
**Roman Electric** ....G.... 773 777-9246
Chicago *(G-6388)*
**Roundtble Hlthcare Partners LP** ....E.... 847 482-9275
Lake Forest *(G-12954)*
**Rtenergy LLC** ....F.... 773 975-2598
Chicago *(G-6410)*
**RTS Sentry Inc** ....F.... 618 257-7100
Belleville *(G-1674)*
**S & S Electric Service** ....G.... 708 366-5800
Forest Park *(G-10252)*
**Santas Best** ....F.... 847 459-3301
Riverwoods *(G-18043)*
**Sciaky Inc** ....E.... 708 594-3841
Chicago *(G-6456)*
**Scis Air Security Corporation** ....G.... 847 671-9502
Schiller Park *(G-19872)*
**Service King Plbg Htg Colg Elc** ....G.... 847 458-8900
Lake In The Hills *(G-13007)*
**Shield Electronics LLC** ....G.... 815 467-4134
Minooka *(G-14847)*
▼ **Simformotion LLC** ....F.... 309 263-7595
Peoria *(G-17456)*
**Simulation Technology LLC** ....G.... 630 365-3400
Elburn *(G-8910)*
**Sound Design Inc** ....G.... 630 548-7000
Plainfield *(G-17650)*
▲ **Spartanics Ltd** ....E.... 847 394-5700
Rolling Meadows *(G-18781)*
**Spurt Inc** ....G.... 847 571-6497
Northbrook *(G-16370)*
**SRC Electric LLC** ....G.... 224 404-6103
Elk Grove Village *(G-9750)*
**Stabiloc LLC** ....G.... 586 412-1147
Carol Stream *(G-3245)*
**Stanley Security Solutions Inc** ....F.... 630 724-3600
Lisle *(G-13663)*
**Superior One Electric Inc** ....G.... 630 655-3300
Westchester *(G-21856)*
**Sustanable Infrastructures Inc** ....G.... 815 341-1447
Frankfort *(G-10366)*
**Swiatek Electric** ....G.... 331 225-3052
Elmhurst *(G-9946)*
▲ **Temple Display Ltd** ....G.... 630 851-3331
Oswego *(G-16936)*
▼ **Tenneco Automotive Oper Co Inc** ....C.... 847 482-5000
Lake Forest *(G-12965)*
**Thomas & Betts Corp** ....G.... 630 444-2151
Saint Charles *(G-19282)*
**Three Hands Technologies** ....G.... 847 680-5358
Vernon Hills *(G-21212)*

S I C

**Tii Technical Educatn Systems** ....G.... 847 428-3085
Gilberts *(G-10939)*
**Toho Technology Inc** ....G.... 773 583-7183
Chicago *(G-6735)*
**▼ Trafficguard Direct LLC** ....G.... 815 899-8471
Sycamore *(G-20820)*
**Tricor International Inc** ....E.... 630 629-1213
Lombard *(G-13871)*
**Tricor Systems Inc** ....E.... 847 742-5542
Elgin *(G-9214)*
**Trigon International Corp** ....E.... 630 978-9990
Aurora *(G-1089)*
**Tylu Wireless Technology LLC** ....G.... 312 260-7934
Chicago *(G-6802)*
**Unified Tool Die & Mfg Co Inc** ....F.... 847 678-3773
Schiller Park *(G-19878)*
**▲ United Amercn Healthcare Corp** ....F.... 313 393-4571
Chicago *(G-6820)*
**United Technologies Corp** ....B.... 815 226-6000
Rockford *(G-18663)*
**United Universal Inds Inc** ....E.... 815 727-4445
Joliet *(G-12585)*
**▲ Vasco Data Security Inc (de)** ....G.... 630 932-8844
Oakbrook Terrace *(G-16721)*
**Victoria Amplifier Company** ....F.... 630 369-3527
Naperville *(G-15831)*
**Visco Electric LLC** ....G.... 630 336-7824
West Chicago *(G-21790)*
**Vlahos Electric Service Dr** ....G.... 224 764-2335
Arlington Heights *(G-866)*
**Weg Electric Motors** ....G.... 630 226-5688
Bolingbrook *(G-2381)*
**Wesco International Inc** ....G.... 630 513-4864
Elmhurst *(G-9960)*
**▲ Wildlife Materials Inc** ....E.... 618 687-3505
Murphysboro *(G-15586)*
**Windy City Laser Service Inc** ....G.... 773 995-0188
Chicago *(G-6996)*
**Wittenstein Arspc Smlation Inc** ....G.... 630 540-5300
Bartlett *(G-1389)*
**Yale Security Inc** ....D.... 704 283-2101
Franklin Park *(G-10632)*

# 37 TRANSPORTATION EQUIPMENT

## *3711 Motor Vehicles & Car Bodies*

**4x4 Headquarters LLC** ....G.... 217 540-5337
Effingham *(G-8820)*
**Alcon Components** ....G.... 847 788-0901
Arlington Heights *(G-705)*
**Alexis Fire Equipment Company** ....D.... 309 482-6121
Alexis *(G-375)*
**Amerex Corporation** ....E.... 309 382-4389
North Pekin *(G-16192)*
**Android Indstres- Blvidere LLC** ....C.... 815 547-3742
Belvidere *(G-1732)*
**Automotive Metal Specialist** ....G.... 309 383-2980
Germantown Hills *(G-10895)*
**Bergstrom Inc** ....D.... 847 394-4013
Joliet *(G-12465)*
**Bill West Enterprises Inc** ....G.... 217 886-2591
Jacksonville *(G-12378)*
**Blackjack Customs** ....G.... 847 361-5225
North Chicago *(G-16175)*
**Brunos Automotive Products** ....G.... 630 458-0043
Addison *(G-62)*
**▼ Chassis Service Unlimited** ....G.... 847 336-2305
Waukegan *(G-21536)*
**Chicago Motorcars** ....E.... 630 221-1800
West Chicago *(G-21680)*
**Crete Twp** ....G.... 708 672-3111
Crete *(G-7512)*
**Dakkota Integrated Systems LLC** ....D.... 517 694-6500
Chicago *(G-4545)*
**Dierzen-Kewanee Heavy Inds** ....D.... 309 853-2316
Kewanee *(G-12679)*
**Direct Dimension Inc** ....G.... 815 479-1936
Algonquin *(G-386)*
**ED Etnyre & Co** ....B.... 815 732-2116
Oregon *(G-16822)*
**▼ Elgin Sweeper Company** ....B.... 847 741-5370
Elgin *(G-9026)*
**Enterprise Service Corporation** ....G.... 773 589-2727
Des Plaines *(G-8188)*
**FCA US LLC** ....G.... 630 724-2321
Lisle *(G-13588)*
**Federal Signal Corporation** ....E.... 708 534-4756
University Park *(G-21048)*
**◆ Federal Signal Corporation** ....D.... 630 954-2000
Oak Brook *(G-16510)*
**Federal Signal Corporation** ....E.... 708 534-3400
University Park *(G-21050)*
**Federal Signal Credit Corp** ....G.... 630 954-2000
Oak Brook *(G-16511)*
**Folk Race Cars** ....G.... 815 629-2418
Durand *(G-8585)*
**◆ Fs Depot Inc** ....G.... 847 468-2350
University Park *(G-21051)*
**Heartland Classics Inc** ....G.... 618 783-4444
Newton *(G-15941)*
**▼ Heat Armor LLC** ....F.... 773 938-1030
Chicago *(G-5066)*
**Hertz Corporation** ....G.... 630 897-0956
Montgomery *(G-15046)*
**High Speed Welding Inc** ....G.... 630 971-8929
Westmont *(G-21891)*
**Hopperstad Customs** ....G.... 815 547-7534
Belvidere *(G-1762)*
**Hot Rod Chassis & Cycle Inc** ....G.... 630 458-0808
Addison *(G-150)*
**Illinois Sterling Ltd** ....G.... 847 526-5151
Wauconda *(G-21472)*
**Innova Uev LLC** ....F.... 630 568-5609
Burr Ridge *(G-2855)*
**Jenner Precision Inc** ....F.... 815 692-6655
Fairbury *(G-10127)*
**John Beyer Race Cars** ....G.... 773 779-5313
Chicago *(G-5311)*
**Jorge A Cruz** ....G.... 773 722-2828
Chicago *(G-5324)*
**Kens Street Rod Repair** ....G.... 815 874-1811
Rockford *(G-18455)*
**Koenig Body & Equipment Inc** ....E.... 309 673-7435
West Peoria *(G-21823)*
**Kurts Carstar Collision Ctr** ....F.... 618 345-4519
Maryville *(G-14343)*
**Legend Racing Enterprises Inc** ....G.... 847 923-8979
Schaumburg *(G-19614)*
**Liberty Coach Inc** ....D.... 847 578-4600
North Chicago *(G-16184)*
**Light of Mine LLC** ....G.... 312 840-8570
Chicago *(G-5503)*
**Mares Service Inc** ....G.... 708 656-1660
Cicero *(G-7218)*
**Maxim Inc** ....F.... 217 544-7015
Springfield *(G-20475)*
**Mickey Truck Bodies Inc** ....F.... 309 827-8227
Bloomington *(G-2197)*
**Midwest Coach Builders Inc** ....G.... 630 690-1420
Carol Stream *(G-3198)*
**Midwest Hot Rods Inc** ....F.... 815 254-7637
Plainfield *(G-17626)*
**Midwest Remanufacturing LLC** ....G.... 708 496-9100
Bedford Park *(G-1565)*
**Mobilty Works** ....G.... 815 254-2000
Plainfield *(G-17629)*
**Motor Coach Inds Intl Inc** ....C.... 847 285-2000
Des Plaines *(G-8235)*
**Motor Coach Industries** ....G.... 847 285-2000
Des Plaines *(G-8236)*
**◆ Navistar Inc** ....C.... 331 332-5000
Lisle *(G-13629)*
**Navistar Inc** ....D.... 630 963-0769
Downers Grove *(G-8494)*
**Navistar Inc** ....D.... 331 332-5000
Lisle *(G-13630)*
**Navistar Inc** ....C.... 331 332-5000
Joliet *(G-12545)*
**◆ Navistar International Corp** ....A.... 331 332-5000
Lisle *(G-13633)*
**▲ Nippon Sharyo Mfg LLC** ....G.... 815 562-8600
Rochelle *(G-18101)*
**Odin Fire Protection District** ....E.... 618 775-8292
Odin *(G-16741)*
**Park License Service Inc** ....G.... 815 633-5511
Loves Park *(G-13972)*
**Performance Military Group Inc** ....G.... 847 325-4450
Lincolnshire *(G-13473)*
**Peters Body Shop & Towing Inc** ....G.... 217 223-5250
Quincy *(G-17867)*
**Phils Auto Body** ....G.... 773 847-7156
Chicago *(G-6117)*
**▲ Powertrain Technology Inc** ....G.... 847 458-2323
Algonquin *(G-403)*
**Prince Race Car Engineering** ....G.... 815 625-8116
Sterling *(G-20606)*
**◆ R/A Hoerr Inc** ....E.... 309 691-8789
Edwards *(G-8784)*
**Rahn Equipment Company** ....G.... 217 431-1232
Danville *(G-7762)*
**Restorations Unlimited II Inc** ....G.... 847 639-5818
Cary *(G-3367)*
**Rj Race Cars Inc** ....F.... 309 343-7575
Galesburg *(G-10774)*
**SAE Customs Inc** ....G.... 855 723-2878
Round Lake *(G-19066)*
**Sentinel Emrgncy Solutions LLC** ....E.... 618 539-3863
Freeburg *(G-10640)*
**Subaru of America Inc** ....E.... 630 250-4740
Itasca *(G-12361)*
**T J Van Der Bosch & Associates** ....E.... 815 344-3210
McHenry *(G-14567)*
**T R Z Motorsports Inc** ....G.... 815 806-0838
Frankfort *(G-10367)*
**Taylor Off Road Racing** ....G.... 815 544-4500
Belvidere *(G-1788)*
**Tenneco Intl Holdg Corp** ....G.... 847 482-5000
Lake Forest *(G-12968)*
**Tesla Motors Inc** ....F.... 312 733-9780
Chicago *(G-6704)*
**Tm Autoworks** ....G.... 630 766-8250
Bensenville *(G-2003)*
**Vanderbosch Tj & Assoc Inc** ....G.... 815 344-3210
McHenry *(G-14568)*
**Vuteq Usa Inc** ....C.... 309 452-9933
Normal *(G-16093)*
**Workhorse Custom Chassis LLC** ....G.... 765 964-4000
Highland Park *(G-11882)*

## *3713 Truck & Bus Bodies*

**▲ ATI Oldco Inc** ....C.... 630 860-5600
Bartlett *(G-1332)*
**▲ Auto Truck Group LLC** ....C.... 630 860-5600
Bartlett *(G-1333)*
**Automotive Metal Specialist** ....G.... 309 383-2980
Germantown Hills *(G-10895)*
**Biddison Autobody** ....G.... 309 673-6277
Peoria *(G-17318)*
**C I F Industries Inc** ....F.... 618 635-2010
Staunton *(G-20555)*
**▲ C S O Corp** ....E.... 630 365-6600
Virgil *(G-21302)*
**Campbell International Inc** ....E.... 408 661-0794
Wauconda *(G-21452)*
**Caterpillar Inc** ....A.... 217 475-4000
Decatur *(G-7853)*
**City Utility Equipment** ....F.... 815 254-6673
Plainfield *(G-17587)*
**Dierzen Trailer Co** ....D.... 815 695-5291
Newark *(G-15933)*
**Donermen LLC** ....G.... 773 430-2828
Chicago *(G-4626)*
**Erie Vehicle Company** ....F.... 773 536-6300
Chicago *(G-4772)*
**Fricker Machine Shop & Salvage** ....G.... 618 285-3271
Elizabethtown *(G-9245)*
**▲ Gvw Group LLC** ....G.... 847 681-8417
Highland Park *(G-11839)*
**Herr Display Vans Inc** ....G.... 708 755-7926
Steger *(G-20573)*
**Imperial Oil Inc** ....G.... 773 866-1235
Chicago *(G-5166)*
**Independent Antique RAD Mfg** ....G.... 847 458-7400
Algonquin *(G-393)*
**Instar Auto Carriers LLC** ....G.... 708 428-6318
Orland Park *(G-16869)*
**Knapheide Manufacturing Co** ....F.... 217 222-7134
Quincy *(G-17846)*
**Kurts Carstar Collision Ctr** ....F.... 618 345-4519
Maryville *(G-14343)*
**L & M Manufacturing Inc** ....F.... 309 734-3009
Kewanee *(G-12692)*
**Lacy Enterprises Inc** ....G.... 773 264-2557
Chicago *(G-5433)*
**MCI Service Parts Inc** ....D.... 419 994-4141
Des Plaines *(G-8230)*
**▲ McLaughlin Body Co** ....D.... 309 762-7755
Moline *(G-14955)*
**Mickey Truck Bodies Inc** ....F.... 309 827-8227
Bloomington *(G-2197)*
**Mid City Truck Bdy & Equipmemt** ....F.... 630 628-9080
Addison *(G-209)*
**Mid-America Truck Corporation** ....D.... 815 672-3211
Streator *(G-20694)*
**Motor Coach Inds Intl Inc** ....C.... 847 285-2000
Des Plaines *(G-8235)*
**Navistar Inc** ....B.... 662 494-3421
Lisle *(G-13631)*
**Navistar Inc** ....G.... 815 230-0060
Plainfield *(G-17631)*

◆ Navistar International Corp ... A ... 331 332-5000
Lisle *(G-13633)*
Newf LLC ... G ... 630 330-5462
Naperville *(G-15714)*
Paramount Truck Body Co Inc ... E ... 312 666-6441
Chicago *(G-6079)*
Phils Auto Body ... G ... 773 847-7156
Chicago *(G-6117)*
Polar Corporation ... E ... 618 548-3660
Salem *(G-19343)*
Pools Welding Inc ... G ... 309 787-2083
Milan *(G-14798)*
Quad County Fire Equipment ... G ... 815 832-4475
Saunemin *(G-19395)*
R & L Truck Service Inc ... F ... 847 489-7135
Wadsworth *(G-21326)*
Robinsport LLC ... G ... 630 724-9280
Woodridge *(G-22514)*
Sauber Manufacturing Company ... D ... 630 365-6600
Virgil *(G-21303)*
Summit Tank & Equipment Co ... F ... 708 594-3040
Mc Cook *(G-14459)*
Thule Inc ... C ... 847 455-2420
Forest Park *(G-10254)*
Tondinis Wrecker Service ... G ... 618 997-9884
Marion *(G-14292)*
▲ Triseal Corporation ... E ... 815 648-2473
Hebron *(G-11728)*
Wag Industries Inc ... F ... 847 329-8932
Skokie *(G-20109)*

## 3714 Motor Vehicle Parts & Access

▲ A&G Manufacturing Inc ... E ... 815 562-2107
Rochelle *(G-18076)*
Accurate Auto Manufacturing Co ... G ... 618 244-0727
Mount Vernon *(G-15397)*
Accurate Engine & Machine Inc ... G ... 773 237-4942
Chicago *(G-3719)*
Accuride Corporation ... C ... 630 454-4299
Batavia *(G-1403)*
Accuride Corporation ... C ... 630 568-3914
Hinsdale *(G-11938)*
Acme Auto Electric Co ... G ... 708 754-5420
S Chicago Hts *(G-19098)*
▲ Advance Wheel Corporation ... D ... 773 471-5734
Chicago *(G-3766)*
Advanced Machine Products Inc ... G ... 618 254-4112
Hartford *(G-11609)*
Air Land and Sea Interiors ... G ... 630 834-1717
Villa Park *(G-21234)*
Air-X Remanufacturing Corp ... G ... 708 598-0044
Bridgeview *(G-2459)*
Airbrake Products Inc ... F ... 708 594-1110
Orland Park *(G-16840)*
▲ Aircraft Gear Corporation ... D ... 815 877-7473
Loves Park *(G-13916)*
◆ Aisin Electronics Illinois LLC ... C ... 618 997-9800
Marion *(G-14248)*
Aisin Mfg Illinois LLC ... D ... 618 998-8333
Marion *(G-14250)*
▲ Aisin Mfg Illinois LLC ... A ... 618 998-8333
Marion *(G-14251)*
Alloy Tech ... G ... 217 253-3939
Tuscola *(G-21014)*
Aluminum Drive Line Products ... G ... 708 946-9777
Beecher *(G-1596)*
Amerex Corporation ... E ... 309 382-4389
North Pekin *(G-16192)*
▲ American Diesel Tube Corp ... F ... 630 628-1830
Addison *(G-35)*
American Gear Inc ... F ... 815 537-5111
Prophetstown *(G-17767)*
American Speed Enterprises ... G ... 309 764-3601
Moline *(G-14917)*
▲ American Vulko Tread Corp ... F ... 847 956-1300
Elk Grove Village *(G-9299)*
American Wheel Corp ... E ... 708 458-9141
Chicago *(G-3882)*
Amsoil Inc ... G ... 630 595-8385
Bensenville *(G-1835)*
▲ Amtec Precision Products Inc ... D ... 847 695-8030
Elgin *(G-8953)*
Andersen Machine & Welding Inc ... G ... 815 232-4664
Freeport *(G-10647)*
◆ Anthony Liftgates Inc ... C ... 815 842-3383
Pontiac *(G-17696)*
Antolin Interiors Usa Inc ... B ... 618 327-4416
Nashville *(G-15833)*
Appleton Rack & Pinions Inc ... F ... 815 467-9583
Minooka *(G-14836)*
Arco Automotive Elec Svc Co ... G ... 708 422-2976
Oak Lawn *(G-16603)*
▲ Area Diesel Service Inc ... E ... 217 854-2641
Carlinville *(G-3030)*
▲ Arrow Gear Company ... C ... 630 969-7640
Downers Grove *(G-8389)*
Arsco ... F ... 708 755-1733
Chicago Heights *(G-7079)*
▲ Auto Meter Products Inc ... C ... 815 991-2292
Sycamore *(G-20788)*
◆ Autonomoustuff LLC ... G ... 314 270-2123
Morton *(G-15153)*
Autoparts Holdings Ltd ... A ... 203 830-7800
Lake Forest *(G-12883)*
Axletech International LLC ... F ... 877 547-3907
Chicago *(G-4007)*
Bedford Rakim ... G ... 773 759-3947
South Holland *(G-20249)*
Bergstrom Inc ... D ... 847 394-4013
Joliet *(G-12465)*
▲ Bi-Phase Technologies LLC ... F ... 952 886-6450
Wood Dale *(G-22344)*
Bill Weeks Inc ... G ... 217 523-8735
Springfield *(G-20397)*
▲ Bison Gear & Engineering Corp ... C ... 630 377-0153
Saint Charles *(G-19143)*
◆ Boler Company ... F ... 630 773-9111
Itasca *(G-12236)*
Boler Company ... C ... 630 910-2800
Woodridge *(G-22457)*
Borgwarner Inc ... E ... 248 754-9200
Bellwood *(G-1699)*
Borgwarner Inc ... E ... 248 754-9200
Frankfort *(G-10302)*
▲ Borgwarner Inc ... G ... 815 288-1462
Dixon *(G-8325)*
Borgwarner Inc ... C ... 815 288-1462
Dixon *(G-8324)*
Borgwarner Transm Systems ... A ... 708 547-2600
Bellwood *(G-1700)*
Borgwarner Transm Systems Inc ... B ... 815 469-2721
Frankfort *(G-10303)*
Borgwarner Transm Systems Inc ... B ... 815 469-7819
Chicago *(G-4145)*
Boyce Industries Inc ... F ... 708 345-0455
Melrose Park *(G-14604)*
Bpi Holdings International Inc ... C ... 815 363-9000
McHenry *(G-14483)*
◆ Brake Parts Inc India LLC ... F ... 815 363-9000
McHenry *(G-14484)*
◆ Brake Parts Inc LLC ... C ... 815 363-9000
McHenry *(G-14485)*
Brake Parts Inc LLC ... G ... 217 324-2161
Litchfield *(G-13682)*
▲ Bremskerl North America Inc ... G ... 847 289-3460
Bartlett *(G-1337)*
Brunos Automotive Products ... G ... 630 458-0043
Addison *(G-62)*
Buell Manufacturing Company ... G ... 708 447-6320
Lyons *(G-14033)*
C & M Engineering ... G ... 815 932-3388
Bourbonnais *(G-2391)*
California Muffler and Brakes ... G ... 773 776-8990
Chicago *(G-4215)*
Caterpillar Inc ... B ... 815 842-6000
Pontiac *(G-17697)*
Cavanaugh Government Group LLC ... F ... 630 210-8668
Bridgeview *(G-2475)*
CC Distributing Services Inc ... G ... 800 931-2668
Crestwood *(G-7480)*
Central Hydraulics Inc ... G ... 309 527-5238
El Paso *(G-8866)*
◆ Champion Laboratories Inc ... A ... 618 445-6011
Albion *(G-356)*
Champion Laboratories Inc ... B ... 803 684-3205
Albion *(G-358)*
Champion Laboratories Inc ... A ... 618 445-6011
Albion *(G-359)*
Champion Laboratories Inc ... C ... 618 445-6011
Albion *(G-360)*
Chicago Drive Line Inc ... G ... 708 385-1900
Alsip *(G-445)*
Chicago Transmission Parts ... G ... 773 427-6100
Chicago *(G-4355)*
Chucking Machine Products Inc ... D ... 847 678-1192
Franklin Park *(G-10431)*
City Subn Auto Svc Goodyear ... G ... 773 355-5550
Chicago *(G-4389)*
CK Acquisition Holdings Inc ... F ... 773 646-0115
Chicago *(G-4391)*
Clement Industries Inc Del ... E ... 708 458-9141
Bedford Park *(G-1544)*
Cloyes Gear and Products Inc ... E ... 630 420-0900
Naperville *(G-15630)*
Clutch Systems Inc ... G ... 815 282-7960
Machesney Park *(G-14066)*
Cnh Industrial America LLC ... E ... 309 965-2233
Goodfield *(G-11244)*
▲ Cosmos Manufacturing Inc ... C ... 708 756-1400
S Chicago Hts *(G-19102)*
▲ Cross Tread Industries Inc ... F ... 630 850-7100
Willow Springs *(G-22194)*
▲ CTS Automotive LLC ... C ... 630 614-7201
Lisle *(G-13578)*
Cummins Filtration Inc ... G ... 931 526-9551
Crystal Lake *(G-7561)*
Dana Auto Systems Group LLC ... D ... 630 960-4200
Lisle *(G-13582)*
Dana Driveshaft Mfg LLC ... E ... 815 626-6700
Sterling *(G-20588)*
Dana Sealing Manufacturing LLC ... B ... 618 544-8651
Robinson *(G-18061)*
Danfoss Power Solutions US Co ... C ... 815 233-4200
Freeport *(G-10652)*
Delphi Automotive Systems LLC ... E ... 847 391-2000
Des Plaines *(G-8180)*
▲ Doga USA Corporation ... F ... 847 669-8529
Huntley *(G-12138)*
Dow Chemical Company ... E ... 815 933-5514
Kankakee *(G-12611)*
Drive Shaft Unlimited Inc ... G ... 708 447-2211
Lyons *(G-14036)*
Dura Products Corporation ... G ... 815 939-1399
Bradley *(G-2420)*
▲ Dynamic Manufacturing Inc ... D ... 708 343-8753
Melrose Park *(G-14623)*
Dynamic Manufacturing Inc ... D ... 708 681-0682
Melrose Park *(G-14624)*
Dynamic Manufacturing Inc ... D ... 708 547-7081
Hillside *(G-11915)*
Dynamic Manufacturing Inc ... E ... 708 343-8753
Melrose Park *(G-14625)*
Dynamic Manufacturing Inc ... B ... 708 547-9011
Hillside *(G-11916)*
▲ Eagle Wings Industries Inc ... B ... 217 892-4322
Rantoul *(G-17925)*
Eaton Corporation ... C ... 815 562-2107
Rochelle *(G-18087)*
Eberspaecher North America Inc ... G ... 815 544-1421
Belvidere *(G-1750)*
▲ Elgin Industries Inc ... C ... 847 742-1720
Elgin *(G-9023)*
Engine Rebuilders & Supply ... G ... 708 338-1113
Stone Park *(G-20634)*
▲ Engine Solutions Inc ... G ... 815 979-2312
Rockford *(G-18365)*
Express Motor and Lift Parts ... G ... 630 327-2000
Frankfort *(G-10320)*
▲ Ezee Roll Manufacturing Co ... G ... 217 339-2279
Hoopeston *(G-12110)*
FCA US LLC ... A ... 630 637-3000
Naperville *(G-15657)*
FCA US LLC ... G ... 630 724-2321
Lisle *(G-13588)*
Federal-Mogul Corporation ... E ... 248 354-7700
Berwyn *(G-2065)*
Federal-Mogul Corporation ... C ... 815 271-9600
McHenry *(G-14506)*
Finish Line Transmission Inc ... G ... 630 350-7776
Wood Dale *(G-22367)*
Fire Chariot LLC ... G ... 815 561-3688
Rochelle *(G-18090)*
Flex-N-Gate Corporation ... D ... 217 442-4018
Danville *(G-7720)*
▲ Flex-N-Gate Corporation ... B ... 217 384-6600
Urbana *(G-21085)*
Flex-N-Gate Corporation ... B ... 217 384-6600
Urbana *(G-21086)*
Flex-N-Gate Corporation ... A ... 217 255-5025
Urbana *(G-21087)*
Flex-N-Gate Corporation ... A ... 217 278-2400
Urbana *(G-21088)*
Fox Enterprises Inc ... G ... 630 513-9010
Saint Charles *(G-19188)*
◆ Fram Group Operations LLC ... B ... 800 890-2075
Lake Forest *(G-12899)*
Frantz Manufacturing Company ... D ... 815 564-0991
Sterling *(G-20593)*
Freeman Products Inc ... G ... 847 439-1000
Elk Grove Village *(G-9490)*



Employee Codes: A=Over 500 employees, B=251-500
C=101-250, D=51-100, E=20-50, F=10-19, G=3-9
2017 Harris Illinois
Industrial Directory
1109

**Ft Motors Inc** ....... F ....... 773 737-5581
Chicago *(G-4893)*
**Gates Corporation** ....... C ....... 309 343-7171
Galesburg *(G-10752)*
**Gem Manufacturing Corporation** ....... G ....... 630 458-0014
Addison *(G-130)*
**General Motors LLC** ....... C ....... 815 733-0668
Bolingbrook *(G-2313)*
**Genuine Parts Company** ....... F ....... 630 293-1300
Chicago *(G-4938)*
**Ggb North America LLC** ....... E ....... 847 775-1859
Waukegan *(G-21563)*
**◆ GKN America Corp** ....... F ....... 630 972-9300
Woodridge *(G-22483)*
**◆ GKN North America Services Inc** ....... F ....... 630 972-9300
Woodridge *(G-22484)*
**◆ GKN Rockford Inc** ....... C ....... 815 633-7460
Loves Park *(G-13944)*
**▲ GKN Stromag Inc** ....... E ....... 937 433-3882
Woodridge *(G-22485)*
**Glk Enterprises Inc** ....... G ....... 847 395-7368
Antioch *(G-636)*
**▲ Global Gear & Machining LLC** ....... C ....... 630 969-9400
Downers Grove *(G-8452)*
**Gray Machine & Welding Inc** ....... F ....... 309 788-2501
Rock Island *(G-18177)*
**Great Lakes Forge Company** ....... G ....... 773 277-2800
Chicago *(G-4997)*
**Grupo Antolin Illinois Inc** ....... C ....... 815 544-8020
Belvidere *(G-1759)*
**Gs Custom Works Inc** ....... G ....... 815 233-4724
Freeport *(G-10661)*
**▲ Gunite Corporation** ....... B ....... 815 490-6260
Rockford *(G-18407)*
**Gunite Corporation** ....... B ....... 815 964-3301
Rockford *(G-18408)*
**▼ Gunite EMI Corporation** ....... B ....... 815 964-7124
Rockford *(G-18409)*
**Harbison-Fischer Inc** ....... G ....... 618 375-3841
Grayville *(G-11369)*
**Hardy Radiator Repair** ....... F ....... 217 223-8320
Quincy *(G-17834)*
**Hendrickson International Corp** ....... C ....... 815 727-4031
Joliet *(G-12510)*
**Hendrix Industrial Gastrux Inc** ....... G ....... 847 526-1700
Wauconda *(G-21467)*
**High Impact Fabricating LLC** ....... G ....... 708 235-8912
University Park *(G-21052)*
**HM Manufacturing Inc** ....... F ....... 847 487-8700
Wauconda *(G-21469)*
**Hoosier Stamping & Mfg Corp** ....... E ....... 618 375-2057
Grayville *(G-11371)*
**Iggys Auto Parts** ....... F ....... 708 452-9790
Norridge *(G-16102)*
**Illinois Tool Works Inc** ....... D ....... 630 993-9990
Elmhurst *(G-9885)*
**Illinois Tool Works Inc** ....... C ....... 708 479-7200
Mokena *(G-14873)*
**Illinois Tool Works Inc** ....... C ....... 815 448-7300
Mazon *(G-14438)*
**Illinois Tool Works Inc** ....... G ....... 708 479-7200
Tinley Park *(G-20922)*
**▼ IMS Companies LLC** ....... D ....... 847 391-8100
Des Plaines *(G-8210)*
**Independent Antique RAD Mfg** ....... G ....... 847 458-7400
Algonquin *(G-393)*
**Infinitybox LLC** ....... G ....... 847 232-1991
Elk Grove Village *(G-9545)*
**Interstate Power Systems Inc** ....... F ....... 630 871-1111
Carol Stream *(G-3174)*
**Interstate Power Systems Inc** ....... D ....... 952 854-2044
Rockford *(G-18440)*
**◆ ITW Deltar Seat Component** ....... E ....... 630 993-9990
Elmhurst *(G-9890)*
**ITW Global Investments Inc** ....... G ....... 847 724-7500
Glenview *(G-11152)*
**Jasiek Motor Rebuilding Inc** ....... G ....... 815 883-3678
Oglesby *(G-16750)*
**Jimmy Diesel Inc** ....... G ....... 708 482-4500
Wheaton *(G-21959)*
**Johnson Controls Inc** ....... G ....... 312 829-5956
Chicago *(G-5319)*
**Johnson Controls Inc** ....... D ....... 630 279-0050
Elmhurst *(G-9892)*
**▲ Johnson Power Ltd** ....... E ....... 708 345-4300
Broadview *(G-2588)*
**◆ Jordan Industries Inc** ....... F ....... 847 945-5591
Deerfield *(G-8020)*
**▲ Jsn Inc** ....... E ....... 708 410-1800
Maywood *(G-14426)*
**Julian Elec Svc & Engrg Inc** ....... E ....... 630 920-8950
Westmont *(G-21895)*
**▲ Just Parts Inc** ....... G ....... 815 756-2184
Cortland *(G-7390)*
**K & W Auto Electric** ....... F ....... 217 857-1717
Teutopolis *(G-20853)*
**Kackert Enterprises Inc** ....... G ....... 630 898-9339
Aurora *(G-1179)*
**Kama Enterprises Inc** ....... G ....... 773 551-9642
Chicago *(G-5356)*
**Kay Manufacturing Company** ....... C ....... 708 862-6800
Calumet City *(G-2945)*
**Kccdd Inc** ....... D ....... 309 344-2030
Galesburg *(G-10762)*
**▲ Kiene Diesel Accessories Inc** ....... E ....... 630 543-7170
Addison *(G-167)*
**Kleinhoffer Manufacturing Inc** ....... G ....... 815 725-3638
Joliet *(G-12527)*
**▲ Koehler Enterprises Inc** ....... G ....... 847 451-4966
Franklin Park *(G-10513)*
**L & M Screw Machine Products** ....... F ....... 630 801-0455
Montgomery *(G-15052)*
**Larry Pontnack** ....... G ....... 815 732-7751
Oregon *(G-16827)*
**Lemfco Inc** ....... E ....... 815 777-0242
Galena *(G-10729)*
**Lgb Industries** ....... G ....... 847 639-1691
Cary *(G-3357)*
**Line Craft Tool Company Inc** ....... C ....... 630 932-1182
Lombard *(G-13820)*
**Little Egypt Gas A & Wldg Sups** ....... G ....... 618 937-2271
West Frankfort *(G-21813)*
**▲ Mag Daddy LLC** ....... G ....... 847 719-5600
Lake Zurich *(G-13098)*
**Magna Exteriors America Inc** ....... A ....... 618 327-4381
Nashville *(G-15837)*
**Magna Extrors Intrors Amer Inc** ....... B ....... 618 327-2136
Nashville *(G-15838)*
**Makerite Mfg Co Inc** ....... E ....... 815 389-3902
Roscoe *(G-18906)*
**Mann+hummel Filtration Tech** ....... F ....... 800 407-9263
McHenry *(G-14526)*
**Mann+hummel Filtration Technol** ....... G ....... 815 759-7744
McHenry *(G-14527)*
**◆ Marmon Industries LLC** ....... G ....... 312 372-9500
Chicago *(G-5627)*
**◆ Mat Holdings Inc** ....... D ....... 847 821-9630
Long Grove *(G-13897)*
**Matrix International Ltd** ....... G ....... 815 389-3771
South Beloit *(G-20158)*
**▲ Mattoon Precision Mfg** ....... C ....... 217 235-6000
Mattoon *(G-14399)*
**Maxim Inc** ....... F ....... 217 544-7015
Springfield *(G-20475)*
**MCI Service Parts Inc** ....... D ....... 419 994-4141
Des Plaines *(G-8230)*
**Mendota Welding & Mfg** ....... G ....... 815 539-6944
Mendota *(G-14727)*
**▲ Mercury Products Corp** ....... C ....... 847 524-4400
Schaumburg *(G-19641)*
**Mercury Products Corp** ....... C ....... 847 524-4400
Schaumburg *(G-19642)*
**Methode Electronics Inc** ....... A ....... 217 357-3941
Carthage *(G-3316)*
**▲ Methods Distrs & Mfrs Inc** ....... G ....... 847 973-1449
Fox Lake *(G-10279)*
**Michelangelo & Donata Burdi** ....... F ....... 773 427-1437
Chicago *(G-5722)*
**Mid-Illinois Caliper Co Inc** ....... F
Springfield *(G-20482)*
**Midamerica Industries Inc** ....... G ....... 309 787-5119
Milan *(G-14793)*
**Midwest Converters Inc** ....... F ....... 815 229-9808
Rockford *(G-18504)*
**Midwest Driveshaft Inc** ....... G ....... 630 513-9292
Saint Charles *(G-19221)*
**▲ Molor Products Company** ....... F ....... 630 375-5999
Oswego *(G-16927)*
**▲ Morse Automotive Corporation** ....... A ....... 773 843-9000
Buffalo Grove *(G-2739)*
**▲ Motec Inc** ....... G ....... 630 241-9595
Downers Grove *(G-8490)*
**Motor Coach Inds Intl Inc** ....... C ....... 847 285-2000
Des Plaines *(G-8235)*
**Motor Row Development Corp** ....... G ....... 773 525-3311
Chicago *(G-5813)*
**Mr Auto Electric** ....... G ....... 217 523-3659
Springfield *(G-20485)*
**Murrays Disc Auto Stores Inc** ....... G ....... 847 458-7179
Lake In The Hills *(G-12999)*
**▲ Nascote Industries Inc** ....... A ....... 618 327-3286
Nashville *(G-15840)*
**Nascote Industries Inc** ....... C ....... 618 478-2092
Nashville *(G-15841)*
**▲ National Cycle Inc** ....... C ....... 708 343-0400
Maywood *(G-14430)*
**National Porges Radiator Corp** ....... F ....... 773 224-3000
Chicago *(G-5866)*
**◆ Navistar Inc** ....... C ....... 331 332-5000
Lisle *(G-13629)*
**◆ Navistar International Corp** ....... A ....... 331 332-5000
Lisle *(G-13633)*
**Naylor Automotive Engrg Co Inc** ....... F ....... 773 582-6900
Chicago *(G-5875)*
**▲ North Amercn Acquisition Corp** ....... C ....... 847 695-8030
Elgin *(G-9125)*
**▲ Nta Precision Axle Corporation** ....... B ....... 630 690-6300
Carol Stream *(G-3207)*
**Ogden Top & Trim Shop Inc** ....... G ....... 708 484-5422
Berwyn *(G-2070)*
**▲ Omron Automotive Elec Inc** ....... A ....... 630 443-6800
Saint Charles *(G-19229)*
**▲ Otr Wheel Engineering Inc** ....... E ....... 217 223-7705
Quincy *(G-17864)*
**Pack 2000 Inc** ....... G ....... 217 529-4408
Springfield *(G-20496)*
**Pactiv LLC** ....... C
Lincolnshire *(G-13469)*
**Parker Fabrication Inc** ....... E ....... 309 266-8413
Morton *(G-15174)*
**Performance Manufacturing** ....... G ....... 630 231-8099
West Chicago *(G-21756)*
**Php Racengines Inc** ....... G ....... 847 526-9393
Wauconda *(G-21492)*
**Piston Automotive LLC** ....... C ....... 313 541-8789
Belvidere *(G-1779)*
**◆ Plews Inc** ....... C ....... 815 288-3344
Dixon *(G-8339)*
**▲ Power Plus Products Inc** ....... F ....... 773 788-9794
Bedford Park *(G-1574)*
**Precision Cnncting Rod Svc Inc** ....... F ....... 708 345-3700
Broadview *(G-2602)*
**▲ Precision Governors LLC** ....... E ....... 815 229-5300
Rockford *(G-18537)*
**Precision Remanufacturing Inc** ....... F ....... 773 489-7225
Chicago *(G-6171)*
**Precision Truck Products Inc** ....... E ....... 618 548-9011
Salem *(G-19345)*
**Premiere Auto Service** ....... G ....... 773 275-8785
Chicago *(G-6179)*
**Premiere Motorsports LLC** ....... G ....... 708 634-0007
Plainfield *(G-17644)*
**Premium Components** ....... G ....... 630 521-1700
Bensenville *(G-1966)*
**Prestige Motor Works Inc** ....... G ....... 630 780-6439
Naperville *(G-15823)*
**▼ Pryco Inc** ....... E ....... 217 364-4467
Mechanicsburg *(G-14574)*
**Quarter Master Industries Inc** ....... E ....... 847 540-8999
Lake Zurich *(G-13120)*
**Quincy Torque Converter Inc** ....... G ....... 217 228-0852
Quincy *(G-17882)*
**Qwik-Tip Inc** ....... G ....... 847 640-7387
Elk Grove Village *(G-9705)*
**R & R Engines and Parts Inc** ....... G ....... 630 628-1545
Addison *(G-266)*
**◆ Randall Manufacturing LLC** ....... D ....... 630 782-0001
Elmhurst *(G-9925)*
**RE-Do-It Corp** ....... G ....... 708 343-7125
Broadview *(G-2607)*
**▲ Realwheels Corporation** ....... E ....... 847 662-7722
Gurnee *(G-11499)*
**Rebuilders Enterprises Inc** ....... G ....... 708 430-0030
Bridgeview *(G-2523)*
**Rj Race Cars Inc** ....... F ....... 309 343-7575
Galesburg *(G-10774)*
**◆ Robert Bosch LLC** ....... B ....... 248 876-1000
Broadview *(G-2610)*
**Rock Valley Antique Auto Parts** ....... G ....... 815 645-2272
Stillman Valley *(G-20627)*
**▲ S A Gear Company Inc** ....... E ....... 708 496-0395
Bedford Park *(G-1582)*
**SKF USA Inc** ....... D ....... 847 742-0700
Elgin *(G-9186)*
**Somic America Inc** ....... G ....... 630 274-4423
Bensenville *(G-1995)*
**▲ Strange Engineering Inc** ....... D ....... 847 663-1701
Morton Grove *(G-15239)*
**Suburban Driveline Inc** ....... G ....... 630 941-7101
Villa Park *(G-21286)*

# 37 TRANSPORTATION EQUIPMENT

Sumitomo Machinery Corp Amer .......... E ...... 630 752-0200
　Glendale Heights (G-11078)
Sure Plus Manufacturing Co .................. D ...... 708 756-3100
　Chicago Heights (G-7128)
Surge Clutch & Drive Line Co ............... G ...... 708 331-1352
　South Holland (G-20307)
Symbol Tool Inc ..................................... G ...... 847 674-1080
　Skokie (G-20098)
T & T Machine Shop .............................. G ...... 847 244-2020
　Gurnee (G-11511)
T G Automotive ...................................... E ...... 630 916-7818
　Lombard (G-13863)
T J Van Der Bosch & Associates ......... G ...... 815 344-3210
　McHenry (G-14567)
▲ T/CCI Manufacturing LLC ................. C ...... 217 423-0066
　Decatur (G-7947)
▲ Taap Corp ........................................... F ...... 224 676-0653
　Wheeling (G-22163)
Taw Enterprises LLC ............................. G ...... 618 466-0134
　Godfrey (G-11238)
▼ Tenneco Automotive Oper Co Inc .... C ...... 847 482-5000
　Lake Forest (G-12965)
Tenneco Automotive Oper Co Inc ........ G ...... 847 821-0757
　Lincolnshire (G-13485)
Tenneco Global Holdings Inc ............... F ...... 847 482-5000
　Lake Forest (G-12966)
◆ Tenneco Inc ........................................ D ...... 847 482-5000
　Lake Forest (G-12967)
Tenneco Intl Holdg Corp ....................... G ...... 847 482-5000
　Lake Forest (G-12968)
Tesla Motors Inc .................................... F ...... 312 733-9780
　Chicago (G-6704)
◆ Thyssenkrupp Crankshaft Co LLC ... C ...... 217 431-0060
　Danville (G-7770)
Thyssenkrupp Crankshaft Co LLC ....... E ...... 217 444-5230
　Danville (G-7771)
Thyssenkrupp Crankshaft Co LLC ....... C ...... 217 444-5500
　Danville (G-7773)
Thyssenkrupp North America Inc ........ E ...... 312 525-2800
　Chicago (G-6725)
◆ Thyssnkrupp Prsta Danville LLC ...... B ...... 217 444-5500
　Danville (G-7775)
◆ Titan International Inc ........................ E ...... 217 228-6011
　Quincy (G-17896)
▲ TKT Enterprises Inc .......................... E ...... 630 307-9355
　Roselle (G-18983)
Torque-Traction Integration .................. G ...... 815 759-7388
　Sterling (G-20617)
▲ Toyo USA Manufacturing Inc ........... F ...... 309 827-8836
　Bloomington (G-2232)
▲ Toyota Boshoku Illinois LLC ............. B ...... 618 943-5300
　Lawrenceville (G-13205)
▲ Transcedar Limited ........................... E ...... 618 262-4153
　Mount Carmel (G-15284)
◆ Tuxco Corporation ............................. F ...... 847 244-2220
　Gurnee (G-11517)
U S Tool & Manufacturing Co ............... E ...... 630 953-1000
　Addison (G-332)
▲ UCI International Inc ......................... E ...... 847 941-0965
　Lake Forest (G-12975)
▲ Ugn Inc ............................................... D ...... 773 437-2400
　Tinley Park (G-20953)
United Carburetor Inc ............................ E ...... 773 777-1223
　Schiller Park (G-19879)
◆ United Components LLC .................. E ...... 812 867-4516
　Lake Forest (G-12977)
▲ United Gasket Corporation ............... D ...... 708 656-3700
　Cicero (G-7242)
▲ United Remanufacturing Co Inc ...... G ...... 773 777-1223
　Schiller Park (G-19880)
United Remanufacturing Co Inc ........... E ...... 847 678-2233
　Schiller Park (G-19881)
United States Gear Corporation ........... G ...... 773 821-5450
　Chicago (G-6828)
US Tsubaki Power Transm LLC ........... C ...... 847 459-9500
　Wheeling (G-22173)
◆ Vehicle Improvement Pdts Inc ......... G ...... 847 395-7250
　Antioch (G-662)
Velasquez & Sons Muffler Shop .......... G ...... 847 740-6990
　Round Lake Beach (G-19080)
Vfn Fiberglass Inc .................................. F ...... 630 543-0232
　Addison (G-340)
Vibracoustic Usa Inc ............................. E ...... 618 382-2318
　Carmi (G-3082)
Vogel Manufacturing Co Inc ................. G ...... 217 536-6946
　Effingham (G-8861)
Vuteq Usa Inc ........................................ C ...... 309 452-9933
　Normal (G-16093)
Walters Distributing Company ............. G ...... 847 468-0941
　Elgin (G-9228)

▲ Waltz Brothers Inc ............................. E ...... 847 520-1122
　Wheeling (G-22181)
▲ Wanxiang USA Holdings Corp ........ F ...... 847 622-8838
　Elgin (G-9229)
▲ Warner Electric LLC .......................... C ...... 815 389-4300
　South Beloit (G-20174)
Windy City Engineering Inc .................. C ...... 773 254-8113
　Chicago (G-6995)
Winhere Brake Parts Inc ....................... G ...... 630 307-0158
　Bartlett (G-1387)
Ycl International Inc .............................. G ...... 630 873-0768
　Woodridge (G-22529)
Zeigler Chrysler Dodge .......................... E ...... 708 956-7700
　Berwyn (G-2079)
ZF Chassis Components LLC ............... B ...... 773 371-4550
　Chicago (G-7065)
ZF Chassis Systems Chicago LLC ...... C ...... 773 371-4550
　Chicago (G-7066)
ZF Services LLC ................................... G ...... 734 416-6200
　Vernon Hills (G-21221)

## 3715 Truck Trailers

A & S Steel Specialties Inc ................... E ...... 815 838-8188
　Lockport (G-13700)
A & Z Sas Express Inc .......................... G ...... 847 451-0851
　Melrose Park (G-14578)
Advanced Mobility & ............................. E ...... 708 235-2800
　Monee (G-14991)
Azcon Inc ............................................... F ...... 815 548-7000
　Sterling (G-20583)
Barrington Financial Services .............. G ...... 847 404-1767
　Lake In The Hills (G-12988)
Barron 2m Inc ........................................ G ...... 847 219-3650
　Schiller Park (G-19808)
Classic Roadliner Corporation ............. G ...... 708 769-0666
　Justice (G-12595)
▲ Coras Welding Shop Inc .................. G ...... 815 672-7950
　Streator (G-20686)
D D Sales Inc ......................................... E ...... 217 857-3196
　Teutopolis (G-20851)
Dolche Truckload Corp ......................... G ...... 800 719-4921
　Palatine (G-17024)
Dundee Truck & Trlr Works LLC .......... G ...... 224 484-8182
　East Dundee (G-8635)
Fleetpride Inc ......................................... C ...... 708 430-2081
　Bridgeview (G-2491)
Great Dane Limited Partnership ........... C ...... 309 854-0407
　Kewanee (G-12687)
Great Dane Limited Partnership ........... B ...... 309 854-0407
　Kewanee (G-12688)
Great Dane Limited Partnership ........... D ...... 773 254-5533
　Kewanee (G-12689)
▼ Great Dane Limited Partnership ...... D ...... 773 254-5533
　Chicago (G-4995)
Groovy Logistics Inc ............................. G ...... 847 946-1491
　Joliet (G-12505)
Haynes Express Inc .............................. G ...... 309 793-6080
　Rock Island (G-18180)
Imperial Group Mfg Inc ......................... B ...... 615 325-9224
　Chicago (G-5165)
Imperial Trailer Mfg Inc ......................... E ...... 618 395-2414
　Olney (G-16772)
K B K Truck and Trlr Repr Co .............. G ...... 630 422-7265
　Wood Dale (G-22383)
Load Redi Inc ........................................ G ...... 217 784-4200
　Gibson City (G-10904)
Maple Park Trucking Inc ....................... G ...... 815 899-1958
　Maple Park (G-14202)
Matt Snell and Sons .............................. G ...... 618 695-3555
　Vienna (G-21223)
Mickey Truck Bodies Inc ...................... G ...... 309 827-8227
　Bloomington (G-2197)
Mid City Truck Bdy & Equipmemt ........ F ...... 630 628-9080
　Addison (G-209)
▲ Midland Manufacturing Corp .......... C ...... 847 677-0333
　Skokie (G-20039)
Paramount Truck Body Co Inc ............. E ...... 312 666-6441
　Chicago (G-6079)
Peter Built ............................................... E ...... 618 337-4000
　East Saint Louis (G-8764)
Pk Corporation ....................................... G ...... 847 879-1070
　Elk Grove Village (G-9683)
Polar Corporation .................................. E ...... 618 548-3660
　Salem (G-19343)
Quality Trailer Sales Inc ....................... G ...... 630 739-2495
　Morton (G-15179)
Roadex Carriers Inc .............................. G ...... 773 454-8772
　Wheeling (G-22141)
Robert Davis & Son Inc ........................ G ...... 815 889-4168
　Milford (G-14814)

Schantz Mfg Inc ..................................... E ...... 618 654-1523
　Highland (G-11810)
Seat Trans Inc ....................................... G ...... 224 522-1007
　Lake In The Hills (G-13006)
STI Holdings Inc .................................... F ...... 630 789-2713
　Burr Ridge (G-2882)
Summit Tank & Equipment Co ............. F ...... 708 594-3040
　Mc Cook (G-14459)
Timpte Industries Inc ............................ D ...... 309 820-1095
　Bloomington (G-2231)

## 3716 Motor Homes

Mobilty Works ........................................ G ...... 815 254-2000
　Plainfield (G-17629)

## 3721 Aircraft

A R B C Inc ............................................. F ...... 815 777-6006
　Galena (G-10714)
Aerostars Inc ......................................... G ...... 847 736-8171
　Cary (G-3323)
Aviation Services Group Inc ................. G ...... 708 425-4700
　Chicago Ridge (G-7139)
Boeing Aerospace - Tams Inc .............. C ...... 312 544-2000
　Chicago (G-4135)
Boeing Company ................................... B ...... 312 544-2000
　Chicago (G-4136)
Boeing Company ................................... G ...... 847 240-0767
　Schaumburg (G-19465)
Boeing LTS Inc ...................................... B ...... 312 544-2000
　Chicago (G-4138)
Calumet Motorsports Inc ...................... G ...... 708 895-0398
　Lansing (G-13158)
Donath Aircraft Service ........................ G ...... 217 528-6667
　Springfield (G-20429)
Elan Express Inc ................................... E ...... 815 713-1190
　Rockford (G-18361)
Gulfstream Aerospace Corp ................. A ...... 630 470-9146
　Naperville (G-15667)
Helivalues ............................................... G ...... 847 487-8258
　Wauconda (G-21466)
Ibanum Manufacturing LLC .................. G ...... 815 262-5373
　Rockford (G-18425)
Illini Aerofab Inc .................................... G ...... 217 425-2971
　Decatur (G-7891)
Jet Aviation St Louis Inc ...................... E ...... 618 646-8000
　Cahokia (G-2923)
Kaman Industrial Tech Corp ................ E ...... 317 248-8355
　Wood Dale (G-22385)
Learjet Inc .............................................. B ...... 847 553-0172
　Des Plaines (G-8222)
Mitchell Arcft Expendables LLC .......... E ...... 847 516-3773
　Cary (G-3360)
Northstar Aerospace (usa) Inc ............. C ...... 708 728-2000
　Bedford Park (G-1567)
Olivers Helicopters Inc ......................... G ...... 847 697-7346
　Gilberts (G-10930)
Quad City Ultralight Aircraft ................. F ...... 309 764-3515
　Moline (G-14966)
SC Aviation Inc ...................................... G ...... 800 416-4176
　Saint Charles (G-19259)
▲ Strauss Facter Assoc Inc ................ G ...... 847 759-1100
　Park Ridge (G-17224)
Textron Aviation Inc .............................. G ...... 630 443-5080
　West Chicago (G-21779)
Textron Inc ............................................. B ...... 815 961-5293
　Rockford (G-18646)
United Technologies Corp .................... B ...... 815 226-6000
　Rockford (G-18663)

## 3724 Aircraft Engines & Engine Parts

AAR Aircraft Services Inc .................... E ...... 630 227-2000
　Wood Dale (G-22326)
▲ AAR Corp ........................................... D ...... 630 227-2000
　Wood Dale (G-22328)
▼ Aero-Cables Corp ............................. G ...... 815 609-6600
　Oswego (G-16902)
Air International C W T US ................... E ...... 217 422-1896
　Decatur (G-7825)
▲ Area Diesel Service Inc .................... E ...... 217 854-2641
　Carlinville (G-3030)
▲ Arrow Gear Company ....................... G ...... 630 969-7640
　Downers Grove (G-8389)
Chemring Energetic Devices Inc ......... C ...... 630 969-0620
　Downers Grove (G-8408)
▲ CTS Electronic Components Inc ..... D ...... 630 577-8800
　Lisle (G-13580)
Danville Metal Stamping Co Inc ........... F ...... 217 446-0647
　Danville (G-7712)
Danville Metal Stamping Co Inc ........... F ...... 217 446-0647
　Danville (G-7713)

# 37 TRANSPORTATION EQUIPMENT

Danville Metal Stamping Co Inc .......... G ...... 217 446-0647
  Danville *(G-7714)*
Doncasters Inc .......... C ...... 217 465-6500
  Paris *(G-17146)*
▲ Essex Electro Engineers Inc .......... E ...... 847 891-4444
  Schaumburg *(G-19521)*
General Machinery & Mfg Co .......... F ...... 773 235-3700
  Chicago *(G-4928)*
Heligear Acquisition Co .......... C ...... 708 728-2000
  Bedford Park *(G-1553)*
Heligear Acquisition Co .......... G ...... 708 728-2055
  Burr Ridge *(G-2850)*
Honeywell .......... E ...... 815 235-5500
  Freeport *(G-10663)*
Honeywell International Inc .......... A ...... 630 960-5282
  Darien *(G-7796)*
Honeywell International Inc .......... A ...... 630 922-0138
  Naperville *(G-15810)*
Honeywell International Inc .......... A ...... 480 353-3020
  Chicago *(G-5106)*
Honeywell International Inc .......... A ...... 847 701-3038
  Palatine *(G-17037)*
Honeywell International Inc .......... B ...... 630 377-6580
  Saint Charles *(G-19193)*
Honeywell International Inc .......... A ...... 973 455-2000
  Chicago *(G-5107)*
Honeywell International Inc .......... A ...... 309 383-4045
  Metamora *(G-14742)*
Honeywell International Inc .......... G ...... 217 431-3710
  Danville *(G-7734)*
I D Rockford Shop Inc .......... G ...... 815 335-1150
  Winnebago *(G-22297)*
▲ Ihi Turbo America Co .......... D ...... 217 774-9571
  Shelbyville *(G-19908)*
Innovative Design and RES Inc .......... G ...... 217 322-3907
  Rushville *(G-19093)*
Jetpower LLC .......... F ...... 847 856-8359
  Gurnee *(G-11462)*
Midwest Fuel Injction Svc Corp .......... F ...... 847 991-7867
  Palatine *(G-17056)*
Precoat Metals .......... D ...... 618 451-0909
  Granite City *(G-11300)*
Superior Joining Tech Inc .......... E ...... 815 282-7581
  Machesney Park *(G-14109)*
United Technologies Corp .......... B ...... 630 516-3460
  Elmhurst *(G-9955)*
United Technologies Corp .......... B ...... 815 226-6000
  Rockford *(G-18663)*
Universal Trnspt Systems LLC .......... F ...... 312 994-2349
  Chicago *(G-6835)*
UOP LLC .......... D ...... 303 791-0311
  Des Plaines *(G-8292)*
Woodward Inc .......... A ...... 815 877-7441
  Loves Park *(G-14009)*
Woodward International Inc .......... G ...... 815 877-7441
  Loves Park *(G-14010)*

## 3728 Aircraft Parts & Eqpt, NEC

A J R Industries Inc .......... E ...... 847 439-0380
  Elk Grove Village *(G-9250)*
AAR Allen Services Inc .......... D ...... 630 227-2410
  Wood Dale *(G-22327)*
▲ AAR Supply Chain Inc .......... C ...... 630 227-2000
  Wood Dale *(G-22329)*
Advanced Precision Mfg Inc .......... E ...... 847 981-9800
  Elk Grove Village *(G-9276)*
Aertrade LLC .......... G ...... 630 428-4440
  Aurora *(G-954)*
Air Land and Sea Interiors .......... G ...... 630 834-1717
  Villa Park *(G-21234)*
▲ Aircraft Gear Corporation .......... D ...... 815 877-7473
  Loves Park *(G-13916)*
Airport Aviation Professionals .......... G ...... 773 948-6631
  Chicago *(G-3788)*
American Concorde Systems .......... F ...... 773 342-9951
  Streamwood *(G-20642)*
American Science and Tech Corp .......... G ...... 312 433-3800
  Chicago *(G-3872)*
Armstrong Aerospace Inc .......... D ...... 630 285-0200
  Itasca *(G-12232)*
Auxitrol SA .......... G ...... 815 874-2471
  Rockford *(G-18272)*
Azimuth Cnc Inc .......... F ...... 815 399-4433
  Rockford *(G-18274)*
Beringer Aero Usa Inc .......... G ...... 708 667-7891
  Chicago *(G-4085)*
Boeing Company .......... B ...... 312 544-2000
  Chicago *(G-4136)*
Brunswick International Ltd .......... G ...... 847 735-4700
  Lake Forest *(G-12889)*
Calport Aviation Company .......... G ...... 630 588-8091
  Bartlett *(G-1317)*
CEF Industries LLC .......... C ...... 630 628-2299
  Addison *(G-71)*
Chucking Machine Products Inc .......... D ...... 847 678-1192
  Franklin Park *(G-10431)*
CMC Electronics Aurora LLC .......... G ...... 630 556-9619
  Sugar Grove *(G-20720)*
Cyn Industries Inc .......... F ...... 773 895-4324
  Chicago *(G-4531)*
Electronica Aviation LLC .......... G ...... 407 498-1092
  Chicago *(G-4722)*
Engineering Prototype Inc .......... F ...... 708 447-3155
  Riverside *(G-18030)*
Fgc Plasma Solutions LLC .......... G ...... 954 591-1429
  Lemont *(G-13235)*
Fiberforge Corporation .......... G ...... 970 945-9377
  Chicago *(G-4840)*
▲ Frasca International Inc .......... C ...... 217 344-9200
  Urbana *(G-21089)*
Gail E Stephens .......... G ...... 618 372-0140
  Brighton *(G-2540)*
▼ Gpe Controls Inc .......... F ...... 708 236-6000
  Hillside *(G-11917)*
Hamilton Sundstrand Corp .......... A ...... 815 226-6000
  Rockford *(G-18411)*
Ibanum Manufacturing LLC .......... G ...... 815 262-5373
  Rockford *(G-18425)*
Ingenium Aerospace LLC .......... F ...... 815 525-2000
  Rockford *(G-18431)*
Jetpower LLC .......... F ...... 847 856-8359
  Gurnee *(G-11462)*
▲ Jsn Inc .......... G ...... 708 410-1800
  Maywood *(G-14426)*
Kemell Enterprises LLC .......... G ...... 618 671-1513
  Belleville *(G-1641)*
Logan Actuator Co .......... G ...... 815 943-9500
  Harvard *(G-11640)*
Makerite Mfg Co Inc .......... E ...... 815 389-3902
  Roscoe *(G-18906)*
Mitchell Aircraft Products .......... G ...... 815 331-8609
  McHenry *(G-14536)*
◆ Mpc Products Corporation .......... A ...... 847 673-8300
  Niles *(G-16010)*
Mpc Products Corporation .......... A ...... 847 673-8300
  Niles *(G-16011)*
▲ Multax Corporation .......... D ...... 309 266-9765
  Morton *(G-15170)*
▲ Nsa (chi) Liquidating Corp .......... F ...... 708 728-2000
  Elmhurst *(G-9916)*
Prograf LLC .......... G ...... 815 234-4848
  Villa Park *(G-21280)*
Quad City Ultralight Aircraft .......... F ...... 309 764-3515
  Moline *(G-14966)*
Qualiseal Technology LLC .......... D ...... 708 887-6080
  Harwood Heights *(G-11690)*
S I A Inc .......... G ...... 708 361-3100
  Palos Heights *(G-17109)*
▼ Seginus Inc .......... G ...... 630 800-2795
  Oswego *(G-16933)*
Shadowtech Labs Inc .......... G ...... 630 413-4478
  Willowbrook *(G-22231)*
Skandia Inc .......... G ...... 815 393-4600
  Davis Junction *(G-7815)*
South Subn Logistics Sups Corp .......... G ...... 312 804-3401
  Harvey *(G-11675)*
Systems & Electronics Inc .......... E ...... 847 228-0985
  Elk Grove Village *(G-9766)*
Textron Aviation Inc .......... G ...... 630 443-5080
  West Chicago *(G-21779)*
Thales Visionix Inc .......... D ...... 630 375-2008
  Aurora *(G-1224)*
TI International Ltd .......... G ...... 847 689-0233
  North Chicago *(G-16188)*
Titus Enterprises LLC .......... G ...... 773 441-7222
  Warrenville *(G-21364)*
Trident Machine Co .......... G ...... 815 968-1585
  Rockford *(G-18657)*
▲ Usac Aeronautics Ria-Jmtc .......... E ...... 949 680-8167
  Rock Island *(G-18210)*
Vesterqaard Company Inc .......... G ...... 815 759-9102
  McHenry *(G-14569)*
◆ Video Refurbishing Svcs Inc .......... E ...... 847 844-7366
  Carpentersville *(G-3304)*
Vonberg Valve Inc .......... F ...... 847 259-3800
  Rolling Meadows *(G-18788)*
Wittenstein Arspc Smlation Inc .......... G ...... 630 540-5300
  Bartlett *(G-1389)*
Woodward Inc .......... B ...... 815 877-7441
  Loves Park *(G-14008)*
Xclusive Auto Sales & Security .......... G ...... 708 897-9990
  Blue Island *(G-2273)*

## 3731 Shipbuilding & Repairing

▲ Chicago Flyhouse Incorporated .......... F ...... 773 533-1590
  Chicago *(G-4320)*
Chips Marine .......... G ...... 217 728-2610
  Sullivan *(G-20743)*
▲ Midland Manufacturing Corp .......... C ...... 847 677-0333
  Skokie *(G-20039)*
▲ Mikes Inc .......... D ...... 618 254-4491
  South Roxana *(G-20314)*
▲ National Maint & Repr Inc .......... C ...... 618 254-7451
  Hartford *(G-11612)*
Pactiv LLC .......... C ......
  Lincolnshire *(G-13469)*
Rinker Boat Company .......... E ...... 574 457-5731
  Chicago *(G-6359)*
Senformatics LLC .......... G ...... 217 419-2571
  Champaign *(G-3536)*
Swath International Limited .......... G ...... 815 654-4800
  Rockford *(G-18638)*
Triplex Marine Ltd .......... G ...... 815 485-0202
  New Lenox *(G-15924)*
Williamson J Hunter & Company .......... G ...... 847 441-7888
  Winnetka *(G-22315)*

## 3732 Boat Building & Repairing

Advocations Inc .......... G ...... 815 568-7505
  Woodstock *(G-22537)*
Air Land and Sea Interiors .......... G ...... 630 834-1717
  Villa Park *(G-21234)*
ARS Marine Inc East Location .......... G ...... 815 942-2600
  Morris *(G-15093)*
◆ Brunswick Corporation .......... B ...... 847 735-4700
  Lake Forest *(G-12888)*
Brunswick International Ltd .......... G ...... 847 735-4700
  Lake Forest *(G-12889)*
▼ Chicago Sea Ray Inc .......... E ...... 815 385-2720
  Volo *(G-21310)*
Crowleys Yacht Yard Lakeside .......... F ...... 773 221-9990
  Chicago *(G-4509)*
Custom Fiberglass of Illinois .......... G ...... 309 344-7727
  Galesburg *(G-10744)*
Elite Power Boats Inc .......... G ...... 618 654-6292
  Highland *(G-11785)*
Final Finish Boat Works .......... G ...... 847 603-1345
  Antioch *(G-631)*
Karma Yacht Sales LLC .......... G ...... 773 254-0200
  Chicago *(G-5362)*
Landcraft Auto & Marine Inc .......... F ...... 708 385-0717
  Crestwood *(G-7492)*
▼ Leisure Properties LLC .......... A ...... 618 937-6426
  West Frankfort *(G-21811)*
Metro East Fiberglass Repair .......... G ...... 618 235-9217
  Belleville *(G-1658)*
▼ Nautic Global Group LLC .......... G ...... 574 457-5731
  Chicago *(G-5872)*
Oquawka Boats and Fabrications .......... G ...... 309 867-2213
  Oquawka *(G-16812)*
Outback USA Inc .......... G ...... 863 699-2220
  Saint Charles *(G-19231)*
P W C Sports .......... G ...... 708 516-6183
  Tinley Park *(G-20936)*
Purity Select Inc .......... G ...... 847 275-3821
  Northbrook *(G-16349)*
Rinalli Boat Co Inc .......... G ...... 618 467-8850
  Godfrey *(G-11234)*
Scf Services LLC .......... E ...... 314 436-7559
  Sauget *(G-19389)*
Seavivor Boats .......... G ...... 847 297-5953
  Des Plaines *(G-8270)*
Sereen LLC .......... G ...... 386 527-4876
  Rockford *(G-18612)*
Tls Windsled Inc .......... G ...... 815 262-5791
  Belvidere *(G-1789)*
Union Ave Auto Inc .......... G ...... 708 754-3899
  Steger *(G-20580)*
Waypoint Enterprises .......... G ...... 847 551-9213
  Algonquin *(G-413)*

## 3743 Railroad Eqpt

A & S Steel Specialties Inc .......... E ...... 815 838-8188
  Lockport *(G-13700)*
▲ Aldon Co .......... F ...... 847 623-8800
  Waukegan *(G-21521)*
Alliance Wheel Services LLC .......... G ...... 309 444-4334
  Washington *(G-21377)*
American Sea and Air .......... F ...... 773 262-5960
  Chicago *(G-3873)*

▼ Amfab LLC ..... G ..... 630 783-2570
Lemont *(G-13224)*
◆ Amsted Industries Incorporated ..... B ..... 312 645-1700
Chicago *(G-3896)*
Amsted Rail Company Inc ..... D ..... 312 258-8000
Chicago *(G-3898)*
◆ Amsted Rail Company Inc ..... B ..... 312 922-4501
Chicago *(G-3899)*
Amsted Rail Company Inc ..... B ..... 618 225-6463
Granite City *(G-11265)*
Anchor Brake Shoe Company LLC ..... G ..... 630 293-1110
West Chicago *(G-21660)*
▲ Avtec (usa) Powertrain Corp ..... G ..... 773 708-9686
Chicago *(G-4002)*
▲ Cardwell Westinghouse Company ..... D ..... 773 483-7575
Chicago *(G-4241)*
Eagle Freight Inc ..... G ..... 708 202-0651
Franklin Park *(G-10462)*
Freight Car Services Inc ..... B ..... 217 443-4106
Danville *(G-7722)*
◆ Freightcar America Inc ..... D ..... 800 458-2235
Chicago *(G-4889)*
Freightcar America Inc ..... C ..... 217 443-4106
Danville *(G-7723)*
Fugiel Railroad Supply Corp ..... G ..... 847 516-6862
Cary *(G-3343)*
▲ G K Enterprises Inc ..... G ..... 708 587-2150
Monee *(G-14996)*
G&E Transportation Inc ..... E ..... 404 350-6497
Chicago *(G-4903)*
Gateway Rail Services Inc ..... F ..... 618 451-0100
Madison *(G-14146)*
Geismar ..... G ..... 847 697-7510
Elgin *(G-9042)*
Greenbrier Companies Inc ..... G ..... 847 838-1435
Antioch *(G-637)*
Gunderson Rail Services LLC ..... E ..... 309 676-1597
Peoria *(G-17375)*
Gunderson Rail Services LLC ..... E ..... 866 858-3919
Chicago Heights *(G-7101)*
▲ Hadady Corporation ..... E ..... 219 322-7417
South Holland *(G-20274)*
Heavy Equipment Products ..... G ..... 630 377-3005
Saint Charles *(G-19191)*
▲ Holland LP ..... C ..... 708 672-2300
Crete *(G-7515)*
▲ Illini Castings LLC ..... F ..... 217 446-6365
Danville *(G-7737)*
Illinois Central Gulf Car Shop ..... D ..... 618 533-8281
Centralia *(G-3418)*
▲ Illinois Transit Assembly Corp ..... F ..... 618 451-0100
Madison *(G-14150)*
Jaix Leasing Company ..... G ..... 312 928-0850
Chicago *(G-5273)*
▲ Maclean Fastener Services LLC ..... G ..... 847 353-8402
Buffalo Grove *(G-2729)*
◆ Marmon Holdings Inc ..... D ..... 312 372-9500
Chicago *(G-5625)*
◆ Marmon Industrial LLC ..... G ..... 312 372-9500
Chicago *(G-5626)*
Meadoweld Machine Inc ..... G ..... 815 623-3939
South Beloit *(G-20161)*
Midland Railway Supply Inc ..... E ..... 618 467-6305
Godfrey *(G-11229)*
Midwest Railcar Corporation ..... F ..... 618 288-2233
Maryville *(G-14344)*
Milano Railcar Services LLC ..... G ..... 618 242-4004
Mount Vernon *(G-15427)*
◆ Miner Enterprises Inc ..... C ..... 630 232-3000
Geneva *(G-10849)*
Narita Manufacturing Inc ..... F ..... 248 345-1777
Belvidere *(G-1773)*
National Railway Equipment Co ..... C ..... 618 242-6590
Mount Vernon *(G-15432)*
National Railway Equipment Co ..... C ..... 309 755-6800
Silvis *(G-19939)*
National Railway Equipment Co ..... G ..... 618 241-9270
Mount Vernon *(G-15433)*
▲ National Trackwork Inc ..... E ..... 630 250-0600
Itasca *(G-12325)*
Pintsch Tiefenbach Us Inc ..... G ..... 618 993-8513
Marion *(G-14280)*
Precision Screw Machining Co ..... F ..... 773 205-4280
Chicago *(G-6172)*
Rail Exchange Inc ..... E ..... 708 757-3317
Chicago Heights *(G-7119)*
Railway & Industrial Svcs Inc ..... C ..... 815 726-4224
Crest Hill *(G-7465)*
Railway Program Services Inc ..... G ..... 708 552-4000
Chicago *(G-6286)*
Relco Locomotives Inc ..... D ..... 630 968-0670
Lisle *(G-13651)*
Rescar Industries Inc ..... G ..... 618 875-3234
East Saint Louis *(G-8767)*
Rescar Industries Inc ..... E ..... 630 963-1114
Downers Grove *(G-8513)*
Russell Enterprises Inc ..... E ..... 847 692-6050
Park Ridge *(G-17221)*
Salco Products Inc ..... D ..... 630 783-2570
Lemont *(G-13261)*
Seec Trasportation Corp ..... G ..... 800 215-4003
Chicago *(G-6474)*
◆ Standard Car Truck Company ..... E ..... 847 692-6050
Rosemont *(G-19033)*
Standard Car Truck Company ..... D ..... 630 860-5511
Bensenville *(G-1998)*
Steven E Wasko & Associates ..... G ..... 773 693-2330
Park Ridge *(G-17223)*
Teleweld Inc ..... F ..... 815 672-4561
Streator *(G-20707)*
Tenneco Intl Holdg Corp ..... G ..... 847 482-5000
Lake Forest *(G-12968)*
▲ Transco Railway Products Inc ..... G ..... 312 427-2818
Chicago *(G-6759)*
Transco Railway Products Inc ..... D ..... 419 562-1031
Chicago *(G-6760)*
Union Pacific Railroad Company ..... G ..... 309 637-9322
Peoria *(G-17472)*
◆ Union Tank Car Company ..... C ..... 312 431-3111
Chicago *(G-6815)*
Union Tank Car Company ..... G ..... 815 942-7391
Morris *(G-15139)*
Union Tank Car Company ..... C ..... 312 431-3111
Chicago *(G-6816)*
UTC Railcar Repair Svcs LLC ..... A ..... 312 431-5053
Chicago *(G-6861)*
▲ Vapor Corporation ..... B ..... 847 777-6400
Buffalo Grove *(G-2788)*
Voestalpine Nortrak Inc ..... D ..... 217 876-9160
Decatur *(G-7957)*
Wallace Industries Inc ..... G ..... 815 389-8999
South Beloit *(G-20172)*
▲ Western Railway Devices Corp ..... G ..... 847 625-8500
Waukegan *(G-21640)*
Western-Cullen-Hayes Inc ..... D ..... 773 254-9600
Chicago *(G-6964)*
Westinghouse A Brake Tech Corp ..... E ..... 708 596-6730
Chicago *(G-6965)*
◆ Whiting Corporation ..... C ..... 708 587-2000
Monee *(G-15007)*
Willims-Hyward Intl Ctings Inc ..... F ..... 708 458-0015
Argo *(G-698)*

### 3751 Motorcycles, Bicycles & Parts

Biker Threads Inc ..... G ..... 618 993-3046
Marion *(G-14255)*
Black Magic Customs Inc ..... G ..... 815 786-1977
Sandwich *(G-19360)*
Brg Sports Inc ..... F ..... 217 893-9300
Rantoul *(G-17921)*
▲ Brg Sports Inc ..... C ..... 831 461-7500
Rosemont *(G-18990)*
BV USA Enterprises ..... G ..... 224 619-7888
Elk Grove Village *(G-9350)*
Chopper Mm LLC ..... G ..... 309 875-3544
Maquon *(G-14215)*
▲ Colnago America Inc ..... G ..... 312 239-6666
Chicago *(G-4425)*
David Taylor ..... E ..... 217 222-6480
Quincy *(G-17819)*
DFT Inc ..... G ..... 630 628-8352
Addison *(G-87)*
Franks Maintenance & Engrg ..... G ..... 847 475-1003
Evanston *(G-10040)*
▲ Genuine Scooters LLC ..... G ..... 773 271-8514
Chicago *(G-4939)*
Gs Custom Works Inc ..... G ..... 815 233-4724
Freeport *(G-10661)*
Jh Choppers LLC ..... G ..... 618 420-2500
Maryville *(G-14342)*
▲ Joe Hunt ..... G ..... 618 392-2000
Olney *(G-16774)*
Midwest Recumbent Bicycles ..... G ..... 618 343-1885
Mascoutah *(G-14357)*
Monahan Partners Inc ..... F ..... 217 268-5758
Arcola *(G-678)*
▲ Mx Tech Inc ..... G ..... 815 936-6277
Bradley *(G-2427)*
▲ N Fly Cycle Inc ..... G ..... 815 562-4620
Ashton *(G-929)*
▲ National Cycle Inc ..... C ..... 708 343-0400
Maywood *(G-14430)*
Pacific Cycle Inc ..... C ..... 618 393-2508
Olney *(G-16789)*
Pruett Enterprises Inc ..... G ..... 618 235-6184
Belleville *(G-1667)*
Quality Plating ..... G ..... 815 626-5223
Sterling *(G-20607)*
▲ Sram LLC ..... D ..... 312 664-8800
Chicago *(G-6565)*
T G Enterprises Inc ..... F ..... 309 662-0508
Bloomington *(G-2229)*
Taurus Cycle ..... G ..... 309 454-1565
Bloomington *(G-2230)*
Valley Racing Inc ..... G ..... 708 946-1440
Beecher *(G-1603)*
W L & J Enterprises Inc ..... G ..... 708 946-0999
Beecher *(G-1604)*
World of Soul Inc ..... G ..... 773 840-4839
Chicago *(G-7032)*
Wrench ..... G ..... 773 609-1698
Chicago *(G-7036)*

### 3761 Guided Missiles & Space Vehicles

Boeing Company ..... B ..... 312 544-2000
Chicago *(G-4136)*
Boeing Company ..... G ..... 847 240-0767
Schaumburg *(G-19465)*
Branmark Strategy Group LLC ..... G ..... 847 849-9080
Glenview *(G-11110)*
National Def Intelligence Inc ..... G ..... 630 757-4007
Naperville *(G-15818)*

### 3764 Guided Missile/Space Vehicle Propulsion Units & parts

Boeing Company ..... B ..... 312 544-2000
Chicago *(G-4136)*
Starfire Industries LLC ..... E ..... 217 721-4165
Champaign *(G-3548)*

### 3769 Guided Missile/Space Vehicle Parts & Eqpt, NEC

Azimuth Cnc Inc ..... F ..... 815 399-4433
Rockford *(G-18274)*
▲ Duraflex Inc ..... E ..... 847 462-1007
Cary *(G-3336)*
Spytek Aerospace Corporation ..... G ..... 847 318-7515
Bensenville *(G-1997)*
Wilson Tool Corporation ..... E ..... 815 226-0147
Rockford *(G-18685)*

### 3792 Travel Trailers & Campers

A & S Steel Specialties Inc ..... E ..... 815 838-8188
Lockport *(G-13700)*
Arthur Leo Kuhl ..... G ..... 618 752-5473
Ingraham *(G-12199)*
Boyd Spotting Inc ..... G ..... 217 669-2418
Cisco *(G-7249)*
Brumleve Industries Inc ..... F ..... 217 857-3777
Teutopolis *(G-20847)*
▲ Davison Co Ltd ..... G ..... 815 966-2905
Rockford *(G-18337)*
Dedicated Tcs LLC ..... F ..... 815 467-9560
Channahon *(G-3569)*
Hanna Hopper Trlr Sls & Rv Ctr ..... G ..... 217 243-3374
Jacksonville *(G-12390)*
I94 Rv LLC ..... F ..... 847 395-9500
Russell *(G-19097)*
Lakeshore Lacrosse LLC ..... G ..... 773 350-4356
Wheaton *(G-21963)*
Midwest Trailer Mfg LLC ..... G ..... 309 897-8216
Kewanee *(G-12693)*
▲ Rieco-Titan Products Inc ..... E ..... 815 464-7400
Frankfort *(G-10358)*
▲ Travel Caddy Inc ..... E ..... 847 621-7000
Elk Grove Village *(G-9788)*

### 3795 Tanks & Tank Components

Certified Tank & Mfg LLC ..... E ..... 217 525-1433
Springfield *(G-20415)*
Chelsea Framing Products Inc ..... G ..... 847 550-5556
Lake Zurich *(G-13053)*
▲ Mid-States Industrial Inc ..... F ..... 815 357-1663
Seneca *(G-19888)*
▲ Protectoseal Company ..... D ..... 630 595-0800
Bensenville *(G-1969)*

S I C

### 3799 Transportation Eqpt, NEC

▲ **Advance Metalworking Company**.....E....... 309 853-3387
Kewanee *(G-12668)*
**Andy Wurst**.....G....... 630 964-4410
Darien *(G-7789)*
**Brewer Utility Systems Inc**.....G....... 217 224-5975
Quincy *(G-17808)*
**Custom Millers Supply Inc**.....G....... 309 734-6312
Monmouth *(G-15011)*
**Equity Lifestyle Prpts Inc**.....G....... 815 857-3333
Amboy *(G-598)*
**Ervin Equipments**.....G....... 217 849-3125
Toledo *(G-20962)*
**FL West Corporation**.....G....... 708 342-0500
Tinley Park *(G-20914)*
**General RV Center Inc**.....C....... 847 669-5570
Huntley *(G-12140)*
**Great Lakes Forge Company**.....G....... 773 277-2800
Chicago *(G-4997)*
**Grs Holding LLC**.....G....... 630 355-1660
Naperville *(G-15666)*
▲ **Howland Technology Inc**.....F....... 847 965-9808
Morton Grove *(G-15200)*
▲ **Kerins Industries Inc**.....G....... 630 515-9111
Darien *(G-7798)*
**Knight Bros Inc**.....E....... 618 439-9626
Benton *(G-2033)*
**New World Trnsp Systems**.....G....... 773 509-5931
Chicago *(G-5898)*
**Prompt Usa Inc**.....G....... 309 660-0222
Minooka *(G-14846)*
**Quiller Outboard Sls Svcs LLC**.....G....... 618 232-1218
Hamburg *(G-11527)*
▲ **Scaletta Moloney Armoring**.....D....... 708 924-0099
Bedford Park *(G-1583)*
▲ **Smart Solar Inc**.....F....... 813 343-5770
Libertyville *(G-13382)*
**T & E Enterprises Herscher Inc**.....F....... 815 426-2761
Herscher *(G-11763)*
**T and D Metal Products LLC**.....G....... 815 432-4938
Watseka *(G-21430)*
**Triple B Manufacturing Co Inc**.....G....... 618 566-2888
Mascoutah *(G-14360)*
◆ **Wise Equipment & Rentals Inc**.....F....... 847 895-5555
Schaumburg *(G-19790)*
**Woodstock Powersports**.....G....... 815 308-5705
Woodstock *(G-22627)*

## 38 MEASURING, ANALYZING AND CONTROLLING INSTRUMENTS; PHOTOGRAPHIC, MEDICAL AN

### 3812 Search, Detection, Navigation & Guidance Systs & Instrs

▲ **Ability Metal Company**.....E....... 847 437-7040
Elk Grove Village *(G-9257)*
▲ **Acl Inc**.....F....... 773 285-0295
Chicago *(G-3730)*
**Advanced Precision Mfg Inc**.....E....... 847 981-9800
Elk Grove Village *(G-9276)*
**Andrew New Zealand Inc**.....E....... 708 873-3507
Orland Park *(G-16843)*
**ARINC Incorporated**.....E....... 800 633-6882
O Fallon *(G-16463)*
**Armstrong Aerospace Inc**.....G....... 847 250-5132
Itasca *(G-12231)*
**Auxitrol SA**.....G....... 815 874-2471
Rockford *(G-18272)*
▲ **Binks Industries Inc**.....G....... 630 801-1100
Montgomery *(G-15030)*
**Bizstarterscom LLC**.....G....... 847 305-4626
Arlington Heights *(G-725)*
**Boeing Company**.....G....... 847 240-0767
Schaumburg *(G-19465)*
**Boeing Company**.....B....... 312 544-2000
Chicago *(G-4136)*
▲ **Bolingbrook Communications Inc**.....A....... 630 759-9500
Lisle *(G-13571)*
**Brunswick International Ltd**.....G....... 847 735-4700
Lake Forest *(G-12889)*
**Cadicam Inc**.....E....... 847 394-3610
Wheeling *(G-22023)*
▲ **CAM Co Inc**.....F....... 630 556-3110
Big Rock *(G-2086)*
**CEF Industries LLC**.....C....... 630 628-2299
Addison *(G-71)*
**Checkpoint Systems Inc**.....D....... 630 771-4240
Romeoville *(G-18809)*
**Chemring Energetic Devices Inc**.....C....... 630 969-0620
Downers Grove *(G-8408)*
◆ **Commscope Technologies LLC**.....A....... 708 236-6600
Westchester *(G-21835)*
▼ **Csiteq LLC**.....D....... 312 265-1509
Chicago *(G-4512)*
**Ctg Advanced Materials LLC**.....E....... 630 226-9080
Bolingbrook *(G-2292)*
**D W Terry Welding Company**.....G....... 618 433-9722
Alton *(G-570)*
**Ecolotech Asl Inc**.....G....... 630 859-0485
Aurora *(G-1142)*
**Electro-Technic Products Inc**.....F....... 773 561-2349
Chicago *(G-4721)*
**Engility Corporation**.....G....... 847 583-1216
Skokie *(G-19994)*
**Engility Corporation**.....G....... 708 596-8245
Harvey *(G-11665)*
**Epir Technologies Inc**.....E....... 630 771-0203
Bolingbrook *(G-2307)*
**FSI Technologies Inc**.....E....... 630 932-9380
Lombard *(G-13803)*
**GKN Aerospace Inc**.....G....... 630 737-1456
Lisle *(G-13596)*
**Graceland Custom Products Inc**.....F....... 630 616-4143
Bensenville *(G-1912)*
**Honeywell International Inc**.....G....... 815 235-5500
Freeport *(G-10664)*
**Intex Systems Corp**.....G....... 630 636-6594
Oswego *(G-16922)*
**Kaney Group LLC**.....G....... 815 986-4359
Rockford *(G-18453)*
**Korean Air**.....G....... 773 686-2730
Chicago *(G-5405)*
**Kvh Industries Inc**.....E....... 708 444-2800
Tinley Park *(G-20927)*
**L A M Inc De**.....G....... 630 860-9700
Wood Dale *(G-22388)*
**Lg Innotek USA Inc**.....G....... 847 941-8713
Lincolnshire *(G-13462)*
▲ **Marine Technologies Inc**.....E....... 847 546-9001
Volo *(G-21318)*
▲ **Metrasens Inc**.....E....... 603 541-6509
Lisle *(G-13622)*
**MidAmerican Technology Inc**.....G....... 815 496-2400
Serena *(G-19893)*
**Midwest Aero Support Inc**.....E....... 815 398-9202
Machesney Park *(G-14092)*
**Motorola Solutions Inc**.....G....... 847 341-3485
Oak Brook *(G-16546)*
**Motorola Solutions Inc**.....C....... 847 576-8600
Schaumburg *(G-19652)*
◆ **Mpc Products Corporation**.....A....... 847 673-8300
Niles *(G-16010)*
**Mpc Products Corporation**.....G....... 847 673-8300
Niles *(G-16011)*
**Municipal Electronics Inc**.....G....... 217 877-8601
Decatur *(G-7920)*
**National Aerospace Corp**.....G....... 847 566-5834
Hawthorn Woods *(G-11704)*
**Navigo Technologies LLC**.....G....... 312 560-9257
Geneva *(G-10852)*
▲ **Navigon Inc**.....D....... 312 268-1500
Chicago *(G-5873)*
◆ **Navistar Defense LLC**.....E....... 331 332-3500
Lisle *(G-13632)*
▲ **Navman Wireless Holdings LP**.....D....... 866 527-9896
Glenview *(G-11171)*
▲ **Navman Wireless North Amer Ltd**.....E....... 866 527-9896
Glenview *(G-11172)*
**Northrop Grumman Technical**.....C....... 847 259-2396
Rolling Meadows *(G-18754)*
**Oceancomm Incorporated**.....G....... 800 757-3266
Champaign *(G-3522)*
**Progressive Electronics**.....G....... 217 672-8434
Warrensburg *(G-21339)*
**Quartix Inc**.....F....... 855 913-6663
Chicago *(G-6255)*
**Raytheon Company**.....B....... 630 295-6394
Rolling Meadows *(G-18773)*
**Research In Motion Rf Inc**.....G....... 815 444-1095
Crystal Lake *(G-7639)*
**S Flying Inc**.....F....... 618 586-9999
Palestine *(G-17095)*
**Sextant Company**.....G....... 847 680-6550
Gurnee *(G-11503)*
**Smart Pixel Inc**.....G....... 630 771-0206
Bolingbrook *(G-2371)*
**Trident Machine Co**.....G....... 815 968-1585
Rockford *(G-18657)*
▲ **Waltz Brothers Inc**.....E....... 847 520-1122
Wheeling *(G-22181)*
**Whisco Component Engrg Inc**.....F....... 630 790-9785
Glendale Heights *(G-11092)*
**Winn Star Inc**.....G....... 618 964-1811
Carbondale *(G-3028)*
**Zebra Entp Solutions Corp**.....E....... 847 634-6700
Lincolnshire *(G-13493)*

### 3821 Laboratory Apparatus & Furniture

**1 Federal Supply Source Inc**.....G....... 708 964-2222
Steger *(G-20565)*
**Aalborg Company**.....G....... 708 246-8858
Western Springs *(G-21862)*
**Amity Hospital Services Inc**.....G....... 708 206-3970
Country Club Hills *(G-7403)*
**Amoco Technology Company (del)**.....C....... 312 861-6000
Chicago *(G-3892)*
▲ **Atlas Material Tstg Tech LLC**.....C....... 773 327-4520
Mount Prospect *(G-15311)*
**B T Technology Inc**.....G....... 217 322-3768
Rushville *(G-19090)*
**Biosynergy Inc**.....G....... 847 956-0471
Elk Grove Village *(G-9342)*
**Blair Company**.....G....... 847 439-3980
Elk Grove Village *(G-9343)*
**Carlson Scientific Inc**.....G....... 708 258-6377
Peotone *(G-17485)*
**Celinco Inc**.....G....... 815 964-2256
Rockford *(G-18301)*
**Chicago Lab Products**.....G....... 312 942-0730
Chicago *(G-4327)*
**Cole-Parmer Instrument Co LLC**.....C....... 847 381-7050
Lake Barrington *(G-12802)*
**Colormetric Laboratories Inc**.....G....... 847 803-3737
Des Plaines *(G-8172)*
**Cymatics Inc**.....G....... 630 420-7117
Naperville *(G-15640)*
**Daigger Scientific Inc**.....E....... 800 621-7193
Vernon Hills *(G-21155)*
**David Martin**.....G....... 217 564-2440
Ivesdale *(G-12377)*
**Dual Mfg Co Inc**.....F....... 773 267-4457
Franklin Park *(G-10460)*
◆ **Flinn Scientific Inc**.....C....... 800 452-1261
Batavia *(G-1449)*
**Florida Metrology LLC**.....F....... 630 833-3800
Villa Park *(G-21252)*
**Gardner Denver Inc**.....E....... 847 676-8800
Niles *(G-15981)*
▼ **Grieve Corporation**.....D....... 847 546-8225
Round Lake *(G-19059)*
**Hcs Hahn Calibration Service**.....G....... 847 567-2500
Lincolnshire *(G-13453)*
**Heidolph NA LLC**.....F....... 224 265-9600
Elk Grove Village *(G-9520)*
◆ **Humboldt Mfg Co**.....E....... 708 456-6300
Elgin *(G-9068)*
**Illinois Tool Works Inc**.....C....... 847 295-6500
Lake Bluff *(G-12850)*
**Innovative Projects Lab Inc**.....G....... 847 605-2125
Schaumburg *(G-19569)*
**Intermerican Clinical Svcs Inc**.....G....... 773 252-1147
Chicago *(G-5217)*
**K H Steuernagel Technical Ltg**.....G....... 773 327-4520
Chicago *(G-5343)*
**Kewaunee Scientific Corp**.....G....... 847 675-7744
Highland Park *(G-11850)*
**L A M Inc De**.....G....... 630 860-9700
Wood Dale *(G-22388)*
▲ **Laboratory Builders Inc**.....G....... 630 598-0216
Burr Ridge *(G-2862)*
▲ **Leica Microsystems Inc**.....C....... 847 405-0123
Buffalo Grove *(G-2726)*
**Leybold USA Inc**.....E....... 724 327-5700
Chicago *(G-5500)*
**Ludwig Medical Inc**.....G....... 217 342-6570
Effingham *(G-8844)*
**Modernfold Doors of Chicago**.....G....... 630 654-4560
Westmont *(G-21908)*
**Norman P Moeller**.....G....... 847 991-3933
Lake Barrington *(G-12821)*
**Novel Products Inc**.....G....... 815 624-4888
Rockton *(G-18699)*
**OBrien Scntfic GL Blowing LLC**.....G....... 217 762-3636
Monticello *(G-15082)*
▼ **Parr Instrument Company**.....D....... 309 762-7716
Moline *(G-14961)*
**Perez Health Incorporated**.....G....... 708 788-0101
Berwyn *(G-2072)*

SIC SECTION 38 MEASURING, ANALYZING AND CONTROLLING INSTRUMENTS; PHOTOGRAPHIC, MEDICAL AN

▲ **Perten Instruments Inc** E 217 585-9440
Springfield ***(G-20503)***

▲ **Preferred Freezer Services of** F 773 254-9500
Chicago ***(G-6174)***

◆ **Preston Industries Inc** C 847 647-2900
Niles ***(G-16022)***

◆ **Prime Industries Inc** E 630 833-6821
Lisle ***(G-13645)***

**Quincy Lab Inc** E 773 622-2428
Chicago ***(G-6258)***

**R L Kolbi Company** F 847 506-1440
Arlington Heights ***(G-826)***

◆ **Reviss Services Inc** G 847 680-4522
Vernon Hills ***(G-21192)***

**Scanlab America Inc** G 630 797-2044
Saint Charles ***(G-19260)***

**Scientific Instruments Inc** G 847 679-1242
Skokie ***(G-20082)***

**Sirius Automation Inc** F 847 607-9378
Buffalo Grove ***(G-2773)***

**Sterigenics US LLC** E 847 855-0727
Gurnee ***(G-11508)***

**Sterigenics US LLC** E
Willowbrook ***(G-22233)***

▼ **Suburban Surgical Co** C 847 537-9320
Wheeling ***(G-22159)***

**Supertek Scientific LLC** G 630 345-3450
Villa Park ***(G-21287)***

**Swenson Technology Inc** F 708 587-2300
Monee ***(G-15003)***

**Vac Serve Inc** G 224 766-6445
Skokie ***(G-20107)***

▲ **Wrightwood Technologies Inc** G 312 238-9512
Chicago ***(G-7037)***

### *3822 Automatic Temperature Controls*

**233 Skydeck LLC** G 312 875-9448
Chicago ***(G-3665)***

**A&B Reliable** G 708 228-6148
Lemont ***(G-13222)***

**All Precision Mfg LLC** F 217 563-7070
Nokomis ***(G-16055)***

**Automatic Building Contrls LLC** E 847 296-4000
Rolling Meadows ***(G-18712)***

**Automax Corporation** G 630 972-1919
Woodridge ***(G-22454)***

**Avg Advanced Technologies LP** A 630 668-3900
Carol Stream ***(G-3110)***

**Beneficial Reuse MGT LLC** F 312 784-0300
Chicago ***(G-4083)***

**Biosynergy Inc** G 847 956-0471
Elk Grove Village ***(G-9342)***

**Boyleston 21st Century LLC** G 708 387-2012
Brookfield ***(G-2625)***

▲ **Braeburn Systems LLC** F 866 268-8892
Montgomery ***(G-15033)***

▲ **Candy Mfg Co Inc** F 847 588-2639
Niles ***(G-15966)***

◆ **Catalytic Products Intl Inc** E 847 438-0334
Lake Zurich ***(G-13050)***

**Caterpillar Inc** B 815 729-5511
Joliet ***(G-12471)***

**Caviton Inc** G 217 621-5746
Urbana ***(G-21075)***

**Cdc Enterprises Inc** G 815 790-4205
Johnsburg ***(G-12432)***

**Chicago Sensor Inc** G 773 252-9660
Chicago ***(G-4347)***

**Chicago Tank Removal Inc** G 312 214-6144
Chicago ***(G-4353)***

**Control Equipment Company Inc** F 847 891-7500
Schaumburg ***(G-19482)***

**Crandall Stats and Sensors Inc** E 815 979-3340
Loves Park ***(G-13929)***

**Creative Controls Systems Inc** G 815 629-2358
Rockton ***(G-18695)***

▲ **Dickson/Unigage Inc** E 630 543-3747
Addison ***(G-92)***

**Dundee Design LLC** G 847 494-2360
East Dundee ***(G-8634)***

**E+e Elektronik Corporation** G 508 530-3068
Schaumburg ***(G-19510)***

◆ **Eclipse Inc** D 815 877-3031
Rockford ***(G-18356)***

**Eg Group Inc** G 309 692-0968
Peoria ***(G-17352)***

**Elcon Inc** E 815 467-9500
Minooka ***(G-14840)***

**Emerson Electric Co** D 847 585-8300
Elgin ***(G-9027)***

▲ **Global Green Products LLC** G 708 341-3670
Orland Park ***(G-16861)***

**Goodrich Sensor Systems** G 847 546-5749
Round Lake ***(G-19058)***

**Green Ladder Technologies LLC** E 630 457-1872
Batavia ***(G-1452)***

▲ **Gus Berthold Electric Company** E 312 243-5767
Chicago ***(G-5013)***

**Gypsoil Pelletized Pdts LLC** F 312 784-0300
Chicago ***(G-5015)***

▼ **H A Phillips & Co** E 630 377-0050
Dekalb ***(G-8095)***

◆ **Hansen Technologies Corp** D 706 335-5551
Burr Ridge ***(G-2849)***

▲ **Holland Safety Equipment Inc** G 847 680-9930
Libertyville ***(G-13332)***

**Homecontrolplus Incorporated** G 847 823-8414
Park Ridge ***(G-17202)***

**Honeywell International Inc** G 815 235-5500
Freeport ***(G-10664)***

**Indesco Oven Products Inc** G 217 622-6345
Petersburg ***(G-17536)***

▲ **Intech Industries Inc** F 847 487-5599
Wauconda ***(G-21473)***

**Interactive Bldg Solutions LLC** F 815 724-0525
Joliet ***(G-12518)***

**ITW Motion** F 708 720-0300
Frankfort ***(G-10335)***

**Johnson Controls Inc** E 815 397-5147
Rockford ***(G-18448)***

**Johnson Controls Inc** F 217 793-8858
Springfield ***(G-20464)***

**Jql Electronics Inc** F 630 873-2020
Rolling Meadows ***(G-18736)***

**Lopez Plumbing Systems Inc** G 773 424-8225
Chicago ***(G-5540)***

**Marine Canada Acquisition** G 630 513-5809
Saint Charles ***(G-19215)***

▲ **Mitsubishi Elc Automtn Inc** C 847 478-2100
Vernon Hills ***(G-21183)***

**Precision Control Systems** D 630 521-0234
Lisle ***(G-13643)***

**Professional Freezing Svcs LLC** G 773 847-7500
Chicago ***(G-6208)***

**R & D Electronics Inc** G 847 583-9080
Niles ***(G-16024)***

**Reliable Appliance and Ref** G 847 581-9520
Morton Grove ***(G-15233)***

◆ **Robertshaw Controls Company** C 630 260-3400
Itasca ***(G-12349)***

**Ronald Allen** F 314 568-1446
Cahokia ***(G-2925)***

▲ **Schneider Elc Buildings LLC** B 815 381-5000
Rockford ***(G-18608)***

**Schneider Elc Buildings LLC** E 815 227-4000
Rockford ***(G-18609)***

▲ **Schneider Elc Holdings Inc** A 717 944-5460
Schaumburg ***(G-19722)***

**Scientific Instruments Inc** G 847 679-1242
Skokie ***(G-20082)***

**Siemens Industry Inc** D 847 520-9084
Buffalo Grove ***(G-2766)***

◆ **Siemens Industry Inc** A 847 215-1000
Buffalo Grove ***(G-2767)***

**Siemens Industry Inc** G 309 664-2460
Bloomington ***(G-2223)***

**Siemens Industry Inc** D 847 215-1000
Buffalo Grove ***(G-2768)***

**Siemens Industry Inc** D 301 419-2600
Hoffman Estates ***(G-12052)***

**SMC Corporation of America** E 630 449-0600
Aurora ***(G-1080)***

▲ **Solidyne Corporation** F 847 394-3333
Rolling Meadows ***(G-18779)***

**Solidyne Corporation** G 847 394-3333
Hoffman Estates ***(G-12056)***

**Sonne Industries LLC** G 630 235-6734
Naperville ***(G-15750)***

**Spring Brook Nature Center** G 630 773-5572
Itasca ***(G-12358)***

**Temperature Equipment Corp** G 847 429-0818
Elgin ***(G-9209)***

▲ **Temprite Company** E 630 293-5910
West Chicago ***(G-21778)***

▲ **Tempro International Corp** G 847 677-5370
Skokie ***(G-20100)***

**Unitrol Electronics Inc** E 847 480-0115
Northbrook ***(G-16380)***

**Vanguard Energy Services LLC** E 630 955-1500
Naperville ***(G-15773)***

**Vent Ure Air** G 708 652-7200
Chicago ***(G-6882)***

**Web Printing Controls Co Inc** C 618 842-2664
Fairfield ***(G-10161)***

### *3823 Indl Instruments For Meas, Display & Control*

**Active Grinding & Mfg Co** F 708 344-0510
Broadview ***(G-2554)***

**Advanced Technologies Inc** G 847 329-9875
Park Ridge ***(G-17178)***

▲ **Air Gage Company** C 847 695-0911
Elgin ***(G-8941)***

**Airways Video Inc** G 773 539-8400
Chicago ***(G-3789)***

**Alpha Pages LLC** G 847 733-1740
Chicago ***(G-3830)***

**Altera Corporation** G 847 240-0313
Schaumburg ***(G-19434)***

▲ **ARI Industries Inc** D 630 953-9100
Addison ***(G-44)***

**Ascon Corp** G 630 482-2950
Batavia ***(G-1417)***

▲ **Atlas Material Tstg Tech LLC** C 773 327-4520
Mount Prospect ***(G-15311)***

▲ **Auto Meter Products Inc** C 815 991-2292
Sycamore ***(G-20788)***

**Automated Logic Corporation** F 630 852-1700
Lisle ***(G-13566)***

▲ **Autrol Corporation of America** G 847 779-5000
Schaumburg ***(G-19451)***

**Axode Corp** G 312 578-9897
Chicago ***(G-4008)***

**Azcon Inc** F 815 548-7000
Sterling ***(G-20583)***

**Barcor Inc** F 847 940-0750
Bannockburn ***(G-1255)***

**Benetech Inc** E 630 844-1300
Aurora ***(G-1119)***

**Benetech (taiwan) LLC** G 630 844-1300
Aurora ***(G-1120)***

**Caterpillar Inc** B 815 729-5511
Joliet ***(G-12471)***

▲ **Charnor Inc** D 309 787-2427
Milan ***(G-14778)***

**Chino Works America Inc** G 630 328-0014
Arlington Heights ***(G-735)***

**Claud S Gordon Company** B 815 678-2211
Richmond ***(G-17960)***

**Clean Energy Renewables LLC** E 309 797-4844
Moline ***(G-14922)***

**Cognex Corporation** G 630 505-9990
Naperville ***(G-15631)***

**Competition Electronics Inc** G 815 874-8001
Rockford ***(G-18321)***

**Controlled Thermal Processing** G 847 651-5511
Streamwood ***(G-20650)***

**County of Piatt** G 217 762-7009
Monticello ***(G-15076)***

**Creative Controls Systems Inc** G 815 629-2358
Rockton ***(G-18695)***

**Dadant & Sons Inc** F 217 852-3324
Dallas City ***(G-7696)***

**Dalec Controls Inc** G 847 671-7676
South Holland ***(G-20258)***

**Danaher Corporation** C 815 568-8001
Marengo ***(G-14225)***

**Danfoss LLC** C 888 326-3677
Loves Park ***(G-13936)***

**Decatur Aeration and Temp** F 217 733-2800
Fairmount ***(G-10162)***

▲ **Dickson/Unigage Inc** E 630 543-3747
Addison ***(G-92)***

**Dinamica Generale Us Inc** G 815 751-9916
Elgin ***(G-9010)***

**Doncasters Inc** C 217 465-6500
Paris ***(G-17146)***

**Dots UT Inc** G 217 390-3286
Champaign ***(G-3475)***

▲ **Durex International Corp** C 847 639-5600
Cary ***(G-3338)***

◆ **Eclipse Inc** D 815 877-3031
Rockford ***(G-18356)***

**Electro-Matic Products Co** F 773 235-4010
Chicago ***(G-4720)***

**Electronic System Design Inc** G 847 358-8212
Bensenville ***(G-1890)***

◆ **Emac Inc** E 618 529-4525
Carbondale ***(G-3006)***

S I C

Employee Codes: A=Over 500 employees, B=251-500
C=101-250, D=51-100, E=20-50, F=10-19, G=3-9

2017 Harris Illinois
Industrial Directory

1115

# 38 MEASURING, ANALYZING AND CONTROLLING INSTRUMENTS; PHOTOGRAPHIC, MEDICAL AN

## SIC SECTION

Embedor Technologies Inc .................G....... 202 681-0359
  Champaign (G-3480)
Enerstar Inc .................G....... 847 350-3400
  Bensenville (G-1893)
Erdco Engineering Corporation ...........E....... 847 328-0550
  Evanston (G-10031)
Ffg Restoration Inc .................F....... 708 240-4873
  Broadview (G-2577)
Fjw Optical Systems Inc .................F....... 847 358-2500
  Palatine (G-17029)
Fms USA Inc .................G....... 847 519-4400
  Hoffman Estates (G-12010)
▼ Frequency Devices Inc .................F....... 815 434-7800
  Ottawa (G-16960)
FSI Technologies Inc .................E....... 630 932-9380
  Lombard (G-13803)
◆ Fuel Tech Inc .................C....... 630 845-4500
  Warrenville (G-21348)
▲ Fusion Systems Incorporated .............E....... 630 323-4115
  Burr Ridge (G-2843)
G-M Services .................G....... 618 532-2324
  Centralia (G-3415)
Goodrich Corporation .................D....... 815 226-6000
  Rockford (G-18402)
Goodrich Corporation .................D....... 815 226-6000
  Rockford (G-18403)
Hadady Machining Company Inc .........F....... 708 474-8620
  Lansing (G-13165)
Harry J Trainor .................G....... 630 493-1163
  Downers Grove (G-8455)
Hauhinco LP .................E....... 618 993-5399
  Marion (G-14264)
▲ Heng Tuo Usa Inc .................G....... 630 705-1898
  Oakbrook Terrace (G-16710)
Hexagon Metrology Inc .................G....... 312 624-8786
  Chicago (G-5083)
Honeywell International Inc .................E....... 618 940-0401
  Metropolis (G-14755)
Humidity 2 Optimization LLC .............F....... 847 991-7488
  East Dundee (G-8644)
Imada Inc .................E....... 847 562-0834
  Northbrook (G-16273)
▲ Indev Gauging Systems Inc .................G....... 815 282-4463
  Rockford (G-18429)
Indev Gauging Systems Inc .................G....... 815 282-4463
  Loves Park (G-13948)
Janco Process Controls Inc .................E....... 847 526-0800
  Wauconda (G-21475)
Jjs Global Ventures Inc .................G....... 847 999-4313
  Schaumburg (G-19589)
Lake Electronics Inc .................F....... 847 201-1270
  Volo (G-21317)
▲ Landairsea Systems Inc .................F....... 847 462-8100
  Woodstock (G-22581)
Liveone Inc .................G....... 312 282-2320
  Chicago (G-5525)
Lumenite Control Technology .............F....... 847 455-1450
  Franklin Park (G-10518)
Luse Thermal Technologies LLC .............G....... 630 862-2600
  Aurora (G-1050)
▼ Magnetrol International Inc .............C....... 630 723-6600
  Aurora (G-1051)
Mar-TEC Research Inc .................E....... 630 879-1200
  Batavia (G-1465)
◆ Martin Automatic Inc .................C....... 815 654-4800
  Rockford (G-18483)
▼ Master Control Systems Inc .............E....... 847 295-1010
  Lake Bluff (G-12856)
▼ Mech-Tronics Corporation .............D....... 708 344-9823
  Melrose Park (G-14671)
Metrology Resource Group Inc ............G....... 815 703-3141
  Rockford (G-18498)
Mettler-Toledo LLC .................E....... 630 790-3355
  Aurora (G-1054)
▲ Mid-American Elevator Co Inc .........C....... 773 486-6900
  Chicago (G-5727)
Mid-American Elevator Co Inc .............E....... 815 740-1204
  Joliet (G-12541)
Mid-American Elevator Eqp Co .............E....... 773 486-6900
  Chicago (G-5728)
Midwest Energy Management Inc ..........G....... 630 759-6007
  Lombard (G-13826)
Minnesota Office Technology .............G....... 312 236-0400
  Bolingbrook (G-2342)
Modern Fluid Technology Inc .............G....... 815 356-0001
  Crystal Lake (G-7614)
▲ Monitor Technologies LLC .................E....... 630 365-9403
  Elburn (G-8899)
National Micro Systems Inc .................G....... 312 566-0414
  Chicago (G-5865)

Nordson Asymtek Inc .................C....... 760 431-1919
  Chicago (G-5926)
▲ Northern Technologies Inc .................G....... 440 246-6999
  Warrenville (G-21351)
Oakland Industries Ltd .................E....... 847 827-7600
  Mount Prospect (G-15358)
◆ Omron Healthcare Inc .................D....... 847 680-6200
  Lake Forest (G-12932)
◆ Orochem Technologies Inc .................G....... 630 210-8300
  Naperville (G-15719)
◆ Pan America Environmental Inc .........G....... 847 487-9166
  McHenry (G-14541)
Principal Instruments Inc .................G....... 815 469-8159
  Frankfort (G-10354)
Proceq USA Inc .................G....... 847 623-9570
  Gurnee (G-11491)
Process Mechanical Inc .................G....... 630 416-7021
  Naperville (G-15732)
Process Technologies Group .................G....... 630 393-4777
  Warrenville (G-21360)
Prostat Corporation .................G....... 630 238-8883
  Bensenville (G-1968)
Protection Controls Inc .................E....... 773 763-3110
  Skokie (G-20066)
Robertshaw Controls Company .............E....... 815 591-2417
  Hanover (G-11573)
◆ Robertshaw Controls Company .........C....... 630 260-3400
  Itasca (G-12349)
Rosemount Inc .................G....... 217 877-5278
  Decatur (G-7935)
▲ Schneider Elc Buildings LLC .............B....... 815 381-5000
  Rockford (G-18608)
▲ Schneider Elc Holdings Inc .............A....... 717 944-5460
  Schaumburg (G-19722)
Schrader-Bridgeport Intl Inc .................G....... 815 288-3344
  Dixon (G-8349)
▲ Semler Industries Inc .................E....... 847 671-5650
  Franklin Park (G-10586)
Sendele Wireless Solutions .................G....... 815 227-4212
  Rockford (G-18610)
Sensor Synergy .................G....... 847 353-8200
  Vernon Hills (G-21202)
Silicon Control Inc .................E....... 847 215-7947
  Deerfield (G-8054)
▲ Starhouse Inc .................G....... 630 679-0979
  Lockport (G-13948)
◆ Sterling Products Inc .................E....... 847 273-7700
  Schaumburg (G-19740)
Superior Graphite Co .................F....... 708 458-0006
  Chicago (G-6633)
▲ Surya Electronics Inc .................C....... 630 858-8000
  Glendale Heights (G-11080)
T T T Inc .................G....... 630 860-7499
  Wood Dale (G-22426)
▲ Taylor Precision Products Inc .........F....... 630 954-1250
  Oak Brook (G-16563)
Technical Sales Midwest Inc .................G....... 847 855-2457
  Gurnee (G-11514)
▲ Tecnova Electronics Inc .................D....... 847 336-6160
  Waukegan (G-21623)
▲ Tempro International Corp .................G....... 847 677-5370
  Skokie (G-20100)
Thermo Fisher Scientific Inc .................G.......
  Bannockburn (G-1266)
Thread & Gage Co Inc .................G....... 815 675-2305
  Spring Grove (G-20367)
Tii Technical Educatn Systems .............G....... 847 428-3085
  Gilberts (G-10939)
Tomantron Inc .................F....... 708 532-2456
  Tinley Park (G-20950)
Tricor Systems Inc .................E....... 847 742-5542
  Elgin (G-9214)
Uic Inc .................G....... 815 744-4477
  Rockdale (G-18234)
UOP LLC .................G....... 847 391-2000
  Des Plaines (G-8293)
V2 Flow Controls LLC .................G....... 708 945-9331
  Tinley Park (G-20955)
Veeder-Root Company .................F....... 309 797-1762
  Moline (G-14976)
Village Hampshire Trtmnt Plant .............G....... 847 683-2064
  Hampshire (G-11564)
Village Hebron Water Sewage .............G....... 815 648-2353
  Hebron (G-11731)
Vorne Industries Inc .................E....... 630 250-9378
  Itasca (G-12371)
Xco International Incorporated .............F....... 847 428-2400
  East Dundee (G-8662)
Xisync LLC .................C....... 630 350-9400
  Wood Dale (G-22439)

◆ Yaskawa America Inc .................C....... 847 887-7000
  Waukegan (G-21642)

### 3824 Fluid Meters & Counters

▲ Advance Engineering Corp .................E....... 847 760-9421
  Elgin (G-8937)
▲ ARC-Tronics Inc .................C....... 847 437-0211
  Elk Grove Village (G-9312)
▲ Auto Meter Products Inc .................C....... 815 991-2292
  Sycamore (G-20788)
Avg Advanced Technologies LP .............A....... 630 668-3900
  Carol Stream (G-3110)
Bc Enterprises .................G....... 618 655-0784
  Edwardsville (G-8791)
Danaher Corporation .................F....... 800 866-6659
  Gurnee (G-11437)
▲ Dynapar Corporation .................C....... 847 662-2666
  Gurnee (G-11443)
▲ E N M Company .................D....... 773 775-8400
  Chicago (G-4667)
Erdco Engineering Corporation .............E....... 847 328-0550
  Evanston (G-10031)
Flodyne Inc .................G....... 630 563-3600
  Hanover Park (G-11581)
▲ G H Meiser & Co .................E....... 708 388-7867
  Posen (G-17730)
▲ International Traffic Corp .................C....... 815 675-1430
  Spring Grove (G-20338)
Kinetic Fit Works Inc .................G....... 630 340-5168
  Galena (G-10728)
Langham Engineering .................G....... 815 223-5250
  Peru (G-17516)
Line Group Inc .................E....... 847 593-6810
  Arlington Heights (G-793)
▲ Liquid Controls LLC .................C....... 847 295-1050
  Lake Bluff (G-12855)
▲ Metraflex Company .................D....... 312 738-3800
  Chicago (G-5706)
▲ Nep Electronics Inc .................C....... 630 595-8500
  Wood Dale (G-22405)
▲ O E M Marketing Inc .................F....... 847 985-9490
  Schaumburg (G-19671)
▲ Opw Fuel MGT Systems Inc .................G....... 708 352-9617
  Hodgkins (G-11979)
▼ Otak International Inc .................G....... 630 373-9229
  Melrose Park (G-14679)
Professional Meters Inc .................C....... 815 942-7000
  Morris (G-15127)
▲ Rauckman Utility Products LLC .........G....... 618 234-0001
  Belleville (G-1668)
Shoppertrak Rct Corporation .................F....... 312 529-5300
  Chicago (G-6498)
▲ Spartanics Ltd .................E....... 847 394-5700
  Rolling Meadows (G-18781)
▲ Tml Inc .................G....... 847 382-1550
  Barrington (G-1308)
Walk 4 Life Inc .................F....... 815 439-2340
  Oswego (G-16939)
Woodward Inc .................F....... 847 673-8300
  Skokie (G-20113)

### 3825 Instrs For Measuring & Testing Electricity

ABM Marking Services Ltd .................G....... 618 277-3773
  Belleville (G-1607)
Abundant Venture Innovation AC .........G....... 312 291-1910
  Chicago (G-3712)
Accushim Inc .................G....... 708 442-6448
  Lyons (G-14029)
▲ Acl Inc .................F....... 773 285-0295
  Chicago (G-3730)
Adams Elevator Equipment Co .............E....... 847 581-2900
  Chicago (G-3743)
Agilent Technologies Inc .................E....... 800 227-9770
  Chicago (G-3782)
Agilent Technologies Inc .................A....... 847 690-0431
  Arlington Heights (G-704)
Aiknow Inc .................F....... 312 391-9452
  Naperville (G-15790)
▲ Air Gage Company .................C....... 847 695-0911
  Elgin (G-8941)
Amerinet of Michigan Inc .................G....... 708 466-0110
  Naperville (G-15795)
▲ Associated Research Inc .................E....... 847 367-4077
  Lake Forest (G-12881)
▲ Atlas Material Tstg Tech LLC .............C....... 773 327-4520
  Mount Prospect (G-15311)
▲ Auto Meter Products Inc .................C....... 815 991-2292
  Sycamore (G-20788)

**B T Technology Inc** ... G ... 217 322-3768 Rushville *(G-19090)*
▲ **B+b Smartworx Inc** ... D ... 815 433-5100 Ottawa *(G-16949)*
**Bittle** ... G ... 618 539-6099 Freeburg *(G-10633)*
▲ **Bolingbrook Communications Inc** ... A ... 630 759-9500 Lisle *(G-13571)*
**Brandt Assoc** ... G ... 847 362-0556 Lake Bluff *(G-12837)*
**C E R Machining & Tooling Ltd** ... G ... 708 442-9614 Lyons *(G-14034)*
**Centurion Non Destructive Tstg** ... F ... 630 736-5500 Streamwood *(G-20648)*
**Cobalt Tool & Manufacturing** ... G ... 630 530-8898 Villa Park *(G-21243)*
**Creative Science Activities** ... G ... 847 870-1746 Prospect Heights *(G-17775)*
**CSM Products Inc** ... G ... 815 444-1671 Crystal Lake *(G-7560)*
**Cyber Innovation Labs LLC** ... G ... 847 804-4724 Mount Prospect *(G-15325)*
**Cymatics Inc** ... G ... 630 420-7117 Naperville *(G-15640)*
▲ **Davies Molding LLC** ... C ... 630 510-8188 Carol Stream *(G-3141)*
**Deif Inc** ... G ... 970 530-2261 Wood Dale *(G-22359)*
▲ **Design Technology Inc** ... E ... 630 920-1300 Westmont *(G-21883)*
**Dgm Electronics Inc** ... G ... 815 389-2040 Roscoe *(G-18894)*
**Dytec Midwest Inc** ... G ... 847 255-3200 Rolling Meadows *(G-18726)*
**E2s LLC** ... G ... 708 629-0714 Alsip *(G-460)*
**Eagle Test Systems Inc** ... E ... 847 367-8282 Buffalo Grove *(G-2689)*
**Electronic System Design Inc** ... G ... 847 358-8212 Bensenville *(G-1890)*
◆ **Elenco Electronics Inc** ... E ... 847 541-3800 Wheeling *(G-22046)*
**Erdco Engineering Corporation** ... E ... 847 328-0550 Evanston *(G-10031)*
▲ **Etcon Corp** ... F ... 630 325-6100 Burr Ridge *(G-2840)*
**F T I Inc** ... E ... 312 943-4015 Chicago *(G-4807)*
**Falex Corporation** ... E ... 630 556-3679 Sugar Grove *(G-20723)*
**Fox Meter Inc** ... G ... 630 968-3635 Lisle *(G-13590)*
▼ **Frequency Devices Inc** ... F ... 815 434-7800 Ottawa *(G-16960)*
**FSI Technologies Inc** ... E ... 630 932-9380 Lombard *(G-13803)*
**Gld Industries Inc** ... G ... 217 390-9594 Champaign *(G-3489)*
**Greenlee Textron Inc** ... C ... 815 784-5127 Genoa *(G-10879)*
**Haynes-Bent Inc** ... F ... 630 845-3316 Wilmington *(G-22274)*
◆ **Hd Electric Company** ... E ... 847 473-4980 Waukegan *(G-21567)*
▲ **Heidenhain Corporation** ... D ... 847 490-1191 Schaumburg *(G-19551)*
**Hipskind Tech Sltons Group Inc** ... E ... 630 920-0960 Oakbrook Terrace *(G-16712)*
**Huygen Corporation** ... G ... 815 455-2200 Crystal Lake *(G-7590)*
▲ **I P C Automation Inc** ... G ... 815 759-3934 McHenry *(G-14514)*
▲ **Ideal Industries Inc** ... C ... 815 895-5181 Sycamore *(G-20800)*
**Ideal Industries Inc** ... C ... 815 895-1108 Sycamore *(G-20801)*
**Identcorp Industries** ... E ... 708 896-6407 Dolton *(G-8372)*
**Illinois Tool Works Inc** ... E ... 847 657-5300 Glenview *(G-11143)*
**Illinois Tool Works Inc** ... C ... 847 295-6500 Lake Bluff *(G-12850)*
**Innovative Sports Training Inc** ... G ... 773 244-6470 Chicago *(G-5201)*
▼ **Integral Automation Inc** ... F ... 630 654-4300 Burr Ridge *(G-2856)*
**International Electro Magnetic** ... G ... 847 358-4622 Wheeling *(G-22077)*
▲ **L & B Global Power LLC** ... G ... 847 323-0770 Chicago *(G-5417)*
▲ **LAB Equipment Inc** ... E ... 630 595-4288 Itasca *(G-12301)*
**Langham Engineering** ... G ... 815 223-5250 Peru *(G-17516)*
**Maurey Instrument Corp** ... F ... 708 388-9898 Alsip *(G-490)*
▲ **Methode Electronics Inc** ... B ... 708 867-6777 Chicago *(G-5704)*
▲ **Midtronics Inc** ... D ... 630 323-2800 Willowbrook *(G-22222)*
**Monolithic Industries Inc** ... G ... 630 985-6009 Woodridge *(G-22503)*
**Nanofast Inc** ... E ... 312 943-4223 Chicago *(G-5852)*
**National Technical Systems Inc** ... F ... 815 315-9250 Rockford *(G-18517)*
▲ **Nidec-Shimpo America Corp** ... E ... 630 924-7138 Itasca *(G-12331)*
**Nls Analytics LLC** ... G ... 312 593-0293 Glencoe *(G-11003)*
**Nu Vision Media Inc** ... G ... 773 495-5254 Chicago *(G-5952)*
**Oso Technologies Inc** ... G ... 844 777-2575 Urbana *(G-21096)*
**P K Neuses Incorporated** ... G ... 847 253-6555 Rolling Meadows *(G-18756)*
▲ **Phoenix Converting LLC** ... F ... 630 285-1500 Itasca *(G-12339)*
**Premium Test Equipment Corp** ... G ... 630 400-2681 Warrenville *(G-21358)*
**Professional Meters Inc** ... C ... 815 942-7000 Morris *(G-15127)*
**Prostat Corporation** ... G ... 630 238-8883 Bensenville *(G-1968)*
**Protec Equipment Resources Inc** ... G ... 847 434-5808 Schaumburg *(G-19702)*
**Radio Controlled Models Inc** ... G ... 847 740-8726 Round Lake Beach *(G-19079)*
**S Himmelstein and Company** ... E ... 847 843-3300 Hoffman Estates *(G-12046)*
**Schweitzer Engrg Labs Inc** ... D ... 847 362-8304 Lake Zurich *(G-13128)*
**Sfc of Illinois Inc** ... E ... 815 745-2100 Warren *(G-21336)*
**Sigmatron International Inc** ... G ... 847 586-5200 Elgin *(G-9178)*
▲ **Sigmatron International Inc** ... G ... 847 956-8000 Elk Grove Village *(G-9737)*
**Silicon Control Inc** ... G ... 847 215-7947 Deerfield *(G-8054)*
**Simpson Electric Company** ... E ... 847 697-2260 Elgin *(G-9182)*
**Singer Data Products Inc** ... G ... 630 860-6500 Bensenville *(G-1991)*
**Singer Medical Products Inc** ... G ... 630 860-6500 Bensenville *(G-1992)*
**Sk Hynix America Inc** ... G ... 847 925-0196 Schaumburg *(G-19729)*
**Stevens Instrument Company** ... G ... 847 336-9375 Waukegan *(G-21620)*
**Suffolk Business Group Inc** ... G ... 847 404-2486 Bartlett *(G-1379)*
**TEC Rep Corporation** ... F ... 630 627-9110 Lombard *(G-13866)*
**Telcom Innovations Group LLC** ... E ... 630 350-0700 Itasca *(G-12366)*
**Teledyne Lecroy Inc** ... E ... 847 888-0450 Elgin *(G-9206)*
◆ **Tellurian Technologies Inc** ... C ... 847 934-4141 Arlington Heights *(G-854)*
▲ **Transformer Manufacturers Inc** ... E ... 708 457-1200 Norridge *(G-16110)*
**Wb Tray LLC** ... G ... 618 918-3821 Centralia *(G-3437)*
**Weetech Inc** ... G ... 847 775-7240 Gurnee *(G-11520)*

## *3826 Analytical Instruments*

▲ **Abbott Laboratories** ... A ... 224 667-6100 Abbott Park *(G-1)*
**Abbott Laboratories** ... A ... 847 938-8717 North Chicago *(G-16163)*
**Abbott Molecular Inc** ... G ... 224 361-7800 Des Plaines *(G-8141)*
▲ **Abbott Molecular Inc** ... D ... 224 361-7800 Des Plaines *(G-8142)*
**Ag-Defense Systems Inc** ... G ... 309 495-7258 Peoria *(G-17303)*
◆ **Akzo Nobel Inc** ... C ... 312 544-7000 Chicago *(G-3793)*
**Alexeter Technologies LLC** ... F ... 847 419-1507 Wheeling *(G-22000)*
**Alltech Associates Inc** ... D ... 773 261-2252 Chicago *(G-3824)*
**Amoco Technology Company (del)** ... C ... 312 861-6000 Chicago *(G-3892)*
**Beckman Coulter Inc** ... G ... 800 526-3821 Wood Dale *(G-22343)*
**Bio-RAD Laboratories Inc** ... B ... 847 699-2217 Des Plaines *(G-8158)*
**Blanke Industries Incorporated** ... G ... 847 487-2780 Wauconda *(G-21448)*
**Cambridge Sensors USA LLC** ... G ... 877 374-4062 Plainfield *(G-17584)*
**Cbana Labs Inc** ... G ... 217 819-5201 Champaign *(G-3463)*
**Design Scientific Inc** ... G ... 616 582-5225 Wilmette *(G-22251)*
**Dionex Corporation** ... G ... 847 295-7500 Bannockburn *(G-1257)*
**EJ Cady & Company** ... G ... 847 537-2239 Wheeling *(G-22045)*
**EMD Millipore Corporation** ... C ... 815 937-8270 Kankakee *(G-12613)*
**EMD Millipore Corporation** ... B ... 815 932-9017 Kankakee *(G-12614)*
**Enhanced Plasmonics LLC** ... G ... 904 238-9270 Evanston *(G-10030)*
**Fisher Scientific Company LLC** ... C ... 412 490-8300 Hanover Park *(G-11580)*
**Forest City Diagnostic Imaging** ... E ... 815 398-1300 Rockford *(G-18387)*
**Gaertner Scientific Corp** ... E ... 847 673-5006 Skokie *(G-20003)*
**Hach Company** ... C ... 800 227-4224 Chicago *(G-5026)*
**Huygen Corporation** ... G ... 815 455-2200 Crystal Lake *(G-7590)*
**Igt Testing Systems Inc** ... G ... 847 952-2448 Arlington Heights *(G-773)*
**Illinois Instruments Inc** ... E ... 815 344-6212 Johnsburg *(G-12436)*
**Illinois Tool Works Inc** ... C ... 847 295-6500 Lake Bluff *(G-12850)*
**Imed Glenview** ... G ... 847 298-2200 Glenview *(G-11146)*
◆ **Jrd Labs LLC** ... G ... 847 818-1076 Elk Grove Village *(G-9565)*
**L A M Inc De** ... G ... 630 860-9700 Wood Dale *(G-22388)*
**Lachata Design Ltd** ... G ... 708 946-2757 Beecher *(G-1599)*
**Laser Products Industries Inc** ... G ... 877 679-1300 Romeoville *(G-18836)*
**McCrone Associates Inc** ... G ... 630 887-7100 Westmont *(G-21904)*
**Mk Environmental Inc** ... G ... 630 848-0585 Willowbrook *(G-22225)*
**Moisture Detection Inc** ... G ... 847 426-0464 Hoffman Estates *(G-12024)*
**Morton Grove Med Imaging LLC** ... E ... 847 213-2700 Morton Grove *(G-15222)*
**Networked Robotics Corporation** ... G ... 847 424-8019 Evanston *(G-10079)*
**O2m Technologies LLC** ... G ... 773 910-8533 Chicago *(G-5961)*
**Omex Technologies Inc** ... G ... 847 850-5858 Wheeling *(G-22112)*
▼ **Parr Instrument Company** ... D ... 309 762-7716 Moline *(G-14961)*
**Peoria Open M R I** ... G ... 309 692-7674 Peoria *(G-17425)*
**Pine Environmental Svcs LLC** ... G ... 847 718-1246 Elk Grove Village *(G-9681)*
**Prairie Glen Imaging Ctr LLC** ... G ... 847 296-5366 Des Plaines *(G-8260)*
▲ **Prime Systems Inc** ... E ... 630 681-2100 Carol Stream *(G-3217)*
**Progroup Instrument Inc** ... G ... 618 466-2815 Godfrey *(G-11232)*
**Regis Technologies Inc** ... D ... 847 967-6000 Morton Grove *(G-15232)*
**Scientific Instruments Inc** ... G ... 847 679-1242 Skokie *(G-20082)*
**Sensor 21 Inc** ... G ... 847 561-6233 Mundelein *(G-15556)*
▲ **Sherwood Industries Inc** ... F ... 847 626-0300 Niles *(G-16032)*
**Slipchip Corporation** ... F ... 312 550-5600 Chicago *(G-6531)*



Employee Codes: A=Over 500 employees, B=251-500
C=101-250, D=51-100, E=20-50, F=10-19, G=3-9
2017 Harris Illinois
Industrial Directory
1117

**Smart Scan Mri LLC** .......... G ...... 847 623-4000
Gurnee *(G-11505)*
**Spectroclick Inc** .......... G ...... 217 356-4829
Champaign *(G-3544)*
**St Imaging Inc** .......... F ...... 847 501-3344
Northbrook *(G-16371)*
**Standard Safety Equipment Co** .......... E ...... 815 363-8565
McHenry *(G-14556)*
**Sterigenics US LLC** .......... E ...... 630 285-9121
Itasca *(G-12360)*
**Supertek Scientific LLC** .......... G ...... 630 345-3450
Villa Park *(G-21287)*
▲ **Swan Analytical Usa Inc** .......... F ...... 847 229-1290
Wheeling *(G-22161)*
**UOP LLC** .......... G ...... 847 391-2000
Des Plaines *(G-8293)*
**Verson Enterprises Inc** .......... F ...... 847 364-2600
Elk Grove Village *(G-9806)*
**Warbler of Illinois Company** .......... G ...... 301 520-0438
Champaign *(G-3559)*
**Waters Technologies Corp** .......... F ...... 630 766-6249
Wood Dale *(G-22437)*
**Waters Technologies Corp** .......... F ...... 508 482-8365
Chicago *(G-6942)*
**Westmont Mri Center** .......... G ...... 630 856-4060
Westmont *(G-21927)*

## 3827 Optical Instruments

**Alicona Corporation** .......... G ...... 630 372-9900
Bartlett *(G-1329)*
**Astro-Physics Inc** .......... F ...... 815 282-1513
Machesney Park *(G-14059)*
**Beastgrip Co** .......... G ...... 312 283-5283
Des Plaines *(G-8157)*
**Cabot McRlectronics Polsg Corp** .......... E ...... 630 543-6682
Addison *(G-67)*
**Community Gospel Center** .......... G ...... 773 486-7661
Chicago *(G-4436)*
**Elmed Incorporated** .......... E ...... 630 543-2792
Glendale Heights *(G-11021)*
**Gaertner Scientific Corp** .......... E ...... 847 673-5006
Skokie *(G-20003)*
**H L Clausing Inc** .......... G ...... 847 676-0330
Skokie *(G-20008)*
**Identity Optical Lab** .......... G ...... 309 807-3160
Normal *(G-16073)*
**Illinois Tool Works Inc** .......... C ...... 847 295-6500
Lake Bluff *(G-12850)*
**Intra Action Corp** .......... E ...... 708 547-6644
Bellwood *(G-1710)*
**J A K Enterprises Inc** .......... G ...... 217 422-3881
Decatur *(G-7897)*
**Jme Technologies Inc** .......... G ...... 815 477-8800
Crystal Lake *(G-7595)*
**Karl Lambrecht Corp** .......... E ...... 773 472-5442
Chicago *(G-5361)*
**Kreischer Optics Ltd** .......... F ...... 815 344-4220
McHenry *(G-14518)*
**Laurel Industries Inc** .......... E ...... 847 432-8204
Highland Park *(G-11851)*
**Leica McRosystems Holdings Inc** .......... F ...... 800 248-0123
Buffalo Grove *(G-2724)*
**Leica Microsystems Inc** .......... G ...... 847 405-0123
Buffalo Grove *(G-2725)*
▲ **Leica Microsystems Inc** .......... C ...... 847 405-0123
Buffalo Grove *(G-2726)*
**Lens Lenticlear Lenticular** .......... F ...... 630 467-0900
Itasca *(G-12303)*
**Lenscrafters Crafters** .......... F ...... 618 632-2312
Fairview Heights *(G-10170)*
**McCrone Associates Inc** .......... G ...... 630 887-7100
Westmont *(G-21904)*
**Mitchell Optics Inc** .......... G ...... 217 688-2219
Sidney *(G-19937)*
**Oakley Inc** .......... G ...... 312 787-2545
Chicago *(G-5962)*
**Omex Technologies Inc** .......... G ...... 847 850-5858
Wheeling *(G-22112)*
**Opti-Vue Inc** .......... G ...... 630 274-6121
Bensenville *(G-1959)*
**Precision Vision Inc** .......... G ...... 815 223-2022
Woodstock *(G-22601)*
**Quality Msrement Solutions Inc** .......... G ...... 630 406-1618
Naperville *(G-15735)*
**Quality Optical Inc** .......... G ...... 773 561-0870
Chicago *(G-6247)*
**Scuva Optics Inc** .......... G ...... 815 625-6195
Rock Falls *(G-18152)*
**Solarscope LLC** .......... G ...... 847 579-0024
Highland Park *(G-11871)*
**Strausberger Assoc Sls & Mktg** .......... G ...... 630 553-3447
Yorkville *(G-22671)*
**Tonjon Company** .......... F ...... 630 208-1173
Geneva *(G-10873)*
**Two Tower Frames Inc** .......... G ...... 773 697-6856
Chicago *(G-6798)*
**Vega Technology & Systems** .......... G ...... 630 855-5068
Bartlett *(G-1324)*
**Vibgyor Optical Systems Corp** .......... E ...... 847 818-0788
Arlington Heights *(G-863)*
**Vibgyor Optics Inc** .......... E ...... 847 818-0788
Arlington Heights *(G-864)*
**Wayne Engineering** .......... G ...... 847 674-7166
Skokie *(G-20110)*

## 3829 Measuring & Controlling Devices, NEC

▲ **7 Mile Solutions Inc** .......... E ...... 847 588-2280
Niles *(G-15952)*
**7000 Inc** .......... F ...... 312 800-3612
Bolingbrook *(G-2275)*
**Aixacct Systems Inc** .......... G ...... 952 303-4077
Wheaton *(G-21935)*
**Alphagage** .......... G ...... 815 391-6400
Rockford *(G-18260)*
**Amerex Corporation** .......... E ...... 309 382-4389
North Pekin *(G-16192)*
**Anamet Inc** .......... G ...... 217 234-8844
Glen Ellyn *(G-10958)*
**Asm Sensors Inc** .......... F ...... 630 832-3202
Elmhurst *(G-9834)*
**Assurance Technologies Inc** .......... F ...... 630 550-5000
Bartlett *(G-1331)*
▲ **Auto Meter Products Inc** .......... C ...... 815 991-2292
Sycamore *(G-20788)*
▲ **Autonics USA Inc** .......... G ...... 847 680-8160
Mundelein *(G-15473)*
**Avalign Technologies Inc** .......... E ...... 855 282-5446
Bannockburn *(G-1253)*
▲ **B&W Technologies Inc** .......... G ...... 888 749-8878
Lincolnshire *(G-13430)*
**Barcor Inc** .......... F ...... 847 831-2650
Highland Park *(G-11824)*
**Barcor Inc** .......... F ...... 847 940-0750
Bannockburn *(G-1255)*
**Biosynergy Inc** .......... G ...... 847 956-0471
Elk Grove Village *(G-9342)*
**C & L Manufacturing Entps** .......... G ...... 618 465-7623
Alton *(G-565)*
**Cabot McRlectronics Polsg Corp** .......... E ...... 630 543-6682
Addison *(G-67)*
▲ **CAM Co Inc** .......... F ...... 630 556-3110
Big Rock *(G-2086)*
**Cd LLC** .......... F ...... 312 275-5747
Chicago *(G-4261)*
**Celinco Inc** .......... G ...... 815 964-2256
Rockford *(G-18301)*
**Centurion Non Destructive Tstg** .......... F ...... 630 736-5500
Streamwood *(G-20648)*
▲ **Chicago Dial Indicator Company** .......... E ...... 847 827-7186
Des Plaines *(G-8164)*
**Circle Systems Inc** .......... F ...... 815 286-3271
Hinckley *(G-11934)*
**Clean Energy Renewables LLC** .......... E ...... 309 797-4844
Moline *(G-14922)*
**Coinstar Procurement LLC** .......... G ...... 630 424-4788
Oakbrook Terrace *(G-16703)*
**Converting Systems Inc** .......... G ...... 847 519-0232
Schaumburg *(G-19484)*
▲ **Crain Enterprises Inc** .......... D ...... 618 748-9227
Mound City *(G-15256)*
▲ **CTS Corporation** .......... C ...... 630 577-8800
Lisle *(G-13579)*
**Cubic Trnsp Systems Inc** .......... G ...... 312 257-3242
Chicago *(G-4513)*
▲ **Deatak Inc** .......... F ...... 815 322-2013
McHenry *(G-14494)*
**Deere & Company** .......... E ...... 309 765-2960
Moline *(G-14933)*
▲ **DOD Technologies Inc** .......... G ...... 815 788-5200
Cary *(G-3335)*
**Dual Mfg Co Inc** .......... F ...... 773 267-4457
Franklin Park *(G-10460)*
▲ **Durex International Corp** .......... C ...... 847 639-5600
Cary *(G-3338)*
▼ **Dynamicsignals LLC** .......... E ...... 815 838-0005
Lockport *(G-13714)*
**EJ Cady & Company** .......... G ...... 847 537-2239
Wheeling *(G-22045)*
**Elcon Inc** .......... E ...... 815 467-9500
Minooka *(G-14840)*
**Emissions Systems Incorporated** .......... G ...... 847 669-8044
Lake In The Hills *(G-12991)*
**Erdco Engineering Corporation** .......... E ...... 847 328-0550
Evanston *(G-10031)*
▲ **Ewikon Molding Tech Inc** .......... G ...... 815 874-7270
Rockford *(G-18373)*
**Falex Corporation** .......... E ...... 630 556-3679
Sugar Grove *(G-20723)*
▲ **First Alert Inc** .......... G ...... 630 499-3295
Aurora *(G-1009)*
**Fluid Manufacturing Services** .......... G ...... 800 458-5262
Lake Bluff *(G-12844)*
**Gamma Products Inc** .......... F ...... 708 974-4100
Palos Hills *(G-17117)*
▲ **Geotest Instrument Corp** .......... G ...... 847 869-7645
Burr Ridge *(G-2845)*
**Germann Instruments Inc** .......... G ...... 847 329-9999
Evanston *(G-10042)*
▼ **Gpe Controls Inc** .......... F ...... 708 236-6000
Hillside *(G-11917)*
▲ **H S I Fire and Safety Group** .......... G ...... 847 427-8340
Elk Grove Village *(G-9515)*
**Hamilton-Maurer Intl Inc** .......... G ...... 713 468-6805
Hudson *(G-12123)*
**Holmes Bros Inc** .......... E ...... 217 442-1430
Danville *(G-7732)*
▲ **Honeywell Analytics Inc** .......... C ...... 847 955-8200
Lincolnshire *(G-13454)*
**Honeywell International Inc** .......... G ...... 815 235-5500
Freeport *(G-10664)*
◆ **Humboldt Mfg Co** .......... E ...... 708 456-6300
Elgin *(G-9068)*
▲ **I C Innovations Inc** .......... G ...... 847 279-7888
Highland Park *(G-11842)*
**Illinois Tool Works Inc** .......... E ...... 847 657-5300
Glenview *(G-11143)*
**Illinois Tool Works Inc** .......... C ...... 847 295-6500
Lake Bluff *(G-12850)*
**Industrial Measurement Systems** .......... G ...... 630 236-5901
Aurora *(G-1027)*
▲ **Innoquest Inc** .......... G ...... 815 337-8555
Woodstock *(G-22575)*
**Jones Medical Instrument Co** .......... E ...... 630 571-1980
Oak Brook *(G-16528)*
**Jordan Industrial Controls Inc** .......... E ...... 217 864-4444
Mount Zion *(G-15453)*
**Joseph Ringelstein** .......... G ...... 708 955-7467
Norridge *(G-16103)*
▲ **Keson Industries Inc** .......... E ...... 630 820-4200
Aurora *(G-1042)*
▲ **Kiene Diesel Accessories Inc** .......... E ...... 630 543-7170
Addison *(G-167)*
**Kocour Co** .......... E ...... 773 847-1111
Chicago *(G-5397)*
**L & J Engineering Inc** .......... E ...... 708 236-6000
Hillside *(G-11922)*
**L & J Holding Company Ltd** .......... D ...... 708 236-6000
Hillside *(G-11923)*
**L A M Inc De** .......... G ...... 630 860-9700
Wood Dale *(G-22388)*
**Landauer Inc** .......... C ...... 708 755-7000
Glenwood *(G-11218)*
◆ **Lcr Hallcrest Llc** .......... E ...... 847 998-8580
Glenview *(G-11165)*
**Libco Industries Inc** .......... F ...... 815 623-7677
Roscoe *(G-18902)*
**Linde Gas North America LLC** .......... F ...... 708 345-0894
Broadview *(G-2593)*
◆ **Livorsi Marine Inc** .......... E ...... 847 548-5900
Grayslake *(G-11352)*
▲ **Luster Leaf Products Inc** .......... G ...... 815 337-5560
Woodstock *(G-22586)*
▲ **M I E America Inc** .......... F ...... 847 981-6100
Elk Grove Village *(G-9603)*
◆ **Martin Engineering Company** .......... C ...... 309 852-2384
Neponset *(G-15859)*
**Material Testing Tech Inc** .......... F ...... 847 215-1211
Wheeling *(G-22102)*
**Mech-Tronics Corporation** .......... G ...... 708 344-0202
Melrose Park *(G-14672)*
**Melt Design Inc** .......... F ...... 630 443-4000
Saint Charles *(G-19217)*
**Midwest Ultrasonics Inc** .......... G ...... 630 434-9458
Darien *(G-7800)*
**Migatron Corporation** .......... E ...... 815 338-5800
Woodstock *(G-22590)*
▲ **Mitsubishi Elc Automtn Inc** .......... C ...... 847 478-2100
Vernon Hills *(G-21183)*
**Norman P Moeller** .......... G ...... 847 991-3933
Lake Barrington *(G-12821)*

**Nova Systems Ltd** G 630 879-2296
Aurora *(G-1195)*

**◆ Omron Healthcare Inc** D 847 680-6200
Lake Forest *(G-12932)*

**One Plus Corp** E 847 498-0955
Northbrook *(G-16326)*

**Outdoor Environments LLC** G 847 325-5000
Buffalo Grove *(G-2749)*

**Parking Systems Inc** G 847 891-3819
Schaumburg *(G-19684)*

**Perfection Probes Inc** G 847 726-8868
Lake Zurich *(G-13112)*

**Polmax LLC** C 708 843-8300
Alsip *(G-511)*

**▲ Power House Tool Inc** E 815 727-6301
Joliet *(G-12552)*

**Praxsym Inc** F 217 897-1744
Fisher *(G-10191)*

**Product Feeding Solutions Inc** G 630 709-9546
Chicago Ridge *(G-7156)*

**Prostat Corporation** G 630 238-8883
Bensenville *(G-1968)*

**Psylotech Inc** G 847 328-7100
Evanston *(G-10092)*

**Q Sales Llc** G 708 271-9842
Hazel Crest *(G-11714)*

**R & D Clark Ltd** G 847 749-2061
Arlington Heights *(G-825)*

**Rockford Rams Products Inc** G 815 226-0016
Rockford *(G-18585)*

**Romus Incorporated** G 414 350-6233
Roselle *(G-18968)*

**▲ Ryeson Corporation** D 847 455-8677
Carol Stream *(G-3230)*

**▲ S & W Manufacturing Co Inc** E 630 595-5044
Bensenville *(G-1984)*

**▲ Safersonic Us Inc** G 847 274-1534
Highland Park *(G-11867)*

**Santec Systems Inc** F 847 215-8884
Arlington Heights *(G-835)*

**Schultes Precision Mfg Inc** D 847 465-0300
Buffalo Grove *(G-2763)*

**Schweitzer Engrg Labs Inc** E 847 540-3037
Lake Zurich *(G-13127)*

**Scientific Instruments Inc** G 847 679-1242
Skokie *(G-20082)*

**Siemens Med Solutions USA Inc** D 847 304-7700
Hoffman Estates *(G-12053)*

**Sigenics Inc** F 312 448-8000
Chicago *(G-6506)*

**Sikora Automation Incorporated** G 630 833-0298
Addison *(G-291)*

**Simpson Electric Company** E 847 697-2260
Elgin *(G-9182)*

**SKF USA Inc** D 847 742-0700
Elgin *(G-9186)*

**▼ Sonoscan Inc** D 847 437-6400
Elk Grove Village *(G-9744)*

**Source Technology** G 281 894-6171
Broadview *(G-2612)*

**Ssh Environmental Inds Inc** G 312 573-6413
Chicago *(G-6566)*

**Star Test Dynamometer Inc** G 309 452-0371
Normal *(G-16089)*

**Stevens Instrument Company** G 847 336-9375
Waukegan *(G-21620)*

**▲ Taylor Precision Products Inc** F 630 954-1250
Oak Brook *(G-16563)*

**▲ Technics Inc** G 630 215-3742
Bolingbrook *(G-2377)*

**Teledyne Lecroy Inc** E 847 888-0450
Elgin *(G-9206)*

**▲ Tempco Electric Heater Corp** B 630 350-2252
Wood Dale *(G-22429)*

**▲ Tempro International Corp** G 847 677-5370
Skokie *(G-20100)*

**Touhy Diagnostic At Home LLC** F 847 803-1111
Des Plaines *(G-8287)*

**TRC Environmental Corp** G 630 953-9046
Burr Ridge *(G-2886)*

**Tricor Systems Inc** E 847 742-5542
Elgin *(G-9214)*

**Trinity Brand Industries Inc** F 708 482-4980
Countryside *(G-7447)*

**Tunnel Vision Consulting Group** G 773 367-7292
Chicago *(G-6791)*

**▼ Ultrasonic Power Corporation** E 815 235-6020
Freeport *(G-10695)*

**Venturedyne Ltd** E 708 597-7090
Alsip *(G-540)*

**Vibra-Tech Engineers Inc** G 630 858-0681
Glen Ellyn *(G-10994)*

**Water Services Company of Ill** G 847 697-6623
Elgin *(G-9230)*

**Wellness Center Usa Inc** G 847 925-1885
Hoffman Estates *(G-12069)*

**Wilkens-Anderson Company** E 773 384-4433
Chicago *(G-6979)*

**▲ Worth-Pfaff Innovations Inc** G 847 940-9305
Deerfield *(G-8068)*

## 3841 Surgical & Medical Instrs & Apparatus

**1 Federal Supply Source Inc** G 708 964-2222
Steger *(G-20565)*

**3M Company** B 309 654-2291
Cordova *(G-7374)*

**7000 Inc** F 312 800-3612
Bolingbrook *(G-2275)*

**Abbott Laboratories** B 847 935-5509
North Chicago *(G-16162)*

**Abbott Laboratories** A 847 937-6100
Abbott Park *(G-3)*

**▲ Abbott Laboratories** A 224 667-6100
Abbott Park *(G-1)*

**Abbott Laboratories** A 847 938-8717
North Chicago *(G-16163)*

**◆ Abbott Laboratories Inc** A 224 668-2076
Abbott Park *(G-4)*

**Abbott Point of Care Inc** C 847 937-6100
Abbott Park *(G-6)*

**Abrasive West LLC** G 630 736-0818
Bartlett *(G-1328)*

**Access Medical Supply Inc** G 847 891-6210
Schaumburg *(G-19420)*

**Accessing Your Abilities Inc** G 309 761-4016
Kewanee *(G-12667)*

**Accuro Medical Products LLC** G 800 669-4757
Chicago *(G-3724)*

**Addison Central Pathology** G 847 685-9326
Chicago *(G-3744)*

**Addition Technology Inc** F 847 297-8419
Lombard *(G-13759)*

**Adhereon Corporation** G 312 997-5002
Chicago *(G-3750)*

**Advanced Microderm Inc** E 630 980-3300
Schaumburg *(G-19423)*

**Advanced Retinal Institute Inc** G 617 821-5597
Oak Park *(G-16649)*

**African American Ctr For Hnb** D 618 549-3965
Park Forest *(G-17168)*

**Aksys Ltd** D 847 229-2020
Lincolnshire *(G-13425)*

**◆ Akzo Nobel Inc** C 312 544-7000
Chicago *(G-3793)*

**Alicona Manufacturing Inc** G 630 736-2718
Bartlett *(G-1330)*

**Allcare Inc** G 630 830-7486
Saint Charles *(G-19133)*

**Amar Plastics Inc** F 630 627-4105
Addison *(G-32)*

**▲ American Biooptics LLC** G 847 467-0628
Evanston *(G-10009)*

**American Imaging MGT Inc** E 708 236-8500
Westchester *(G-21829)*

**American Imaging MGT Inc** E 847 564-8500
Deerfield *(G-7976)*

**American Medical Industries** G 847 918-9800
Lake Bluff *(G-12829)*

**▲ Amerisrcbergen Solutions Group** E 847 808-2600
Buffalo Grove *(G-2658)*

**Anchor Products Company** E 630 543-9124
Addison *(G-40)*

**Argentum Medical LLC** E 888 551-0188
Geneva *(G-10810)*

**Atch Inc** G 847 295-5055
Lake Forest *(G-12882)*

**Attune Medical** E 312 994-0174
Chicago *(G-3988)*

**Avalign Technologies Inc** E 855 282-5446
Bannockburn *(G-1253)*

**Bandgrip Inc** G 844 968-6322
Chicago *(G-4036)*

**▼ Baxalta Export Corporation** G 224 948-2000
Deerfield *(G-7981)*

**Baxalta World Trade LLC** G 224 948-2000
Deerfield *(G-7982)*

**Baxalta Worldwide LLC** G 224 948-2000
Deerfield *(G-7983)*

**▲ Baxter Diagnostics Inc** F 201 337-1212
Buffalo Grove *(G-2661)*

**▼ Baxter Global Holdings II Inc** E 847 948-2000
Deerfield *(G-7984)*

**Baxter Healthcare Corporation** A 224 270-6300
Round Lake *(G-19053)*

**Baxter Healthcare Corporation** C 847 367-2544
Vernon Hills *(G-21148)*

**Baxter Healthcare Corporation** E 847 578-4671
Waukegan *(G-21529)*

**Baxter Healthcare Corporation** B 847 948-2000
Deerfield *(G-7986)*

**Baxter Healthcare Corporation** B 847 948-2000
Deerfield *(G-7987)*

**Baxter International Inc** A 224 948-2000
Deerfield *(G-7988)*

**Baxter V Mueller** G 847 774-6800
Niles *(G-15964)*

**Baxter World Trade Corporation** F 224 948-2000
Deerfield *(G-7989)*

**Beaver-Visitec Intl Holdings** B 847 739-3219
Lake Forest *(G-12885)*

**Beaver-Visitec Intl Inc** G 847 739-3219
Lake Forest *(G-12886)*

**Becton Dickinson and Company** G 630 743-2006
Downers Grove *(G-8396)*

**Beecken Petty Okeefe & Co LLC** A 312 435-0300
Chicago *(G-4071)*

**Bio-Logic Systems Corp** D 847 949-0456
Mundelein *(G-15478)*

**Biosynergy Inc** G 847 956-0471
Elk Grove Village *(G-9342)*

**Bold Diagnostics LLC** G 806 543-5743
Chicago *(G-4139)*

**Bosley Medical Institute** G 312 642-5252
Chicago *(G-4148)*

**▲ Brainlab Inc** C 800 784-7700
Westchester *(G-21831)*

**Briteseed LLC** G 206 384-0311
Chicago *(G-4172)*

**C & S Chemicals Inc** G 815 722-6671
Joliet *(G-12470)*

**Cardinal Health Inc** B 847 578-4443
Waukegan *(G-21532)*

**Cardinal Health 200 LLC** C 847 473-3200
Waukegan *(G-21533)*

**Cardinal Health 200 LLC** E 847 689-8410
Waukegan *(G-21534)*

**Carefusion Corporation** D 858 617-2000
Vernon Hills *(G-21153)*

**▲ Carstens Incorporated** D 708 669-1500
Chicago *(G-4245)*

**Cast21 Inc** G 847 772-8547
Champaign *(G-3462)*

**Cell-Safe Life Sciences LLC** G 847 674-7075
Skokie *(G-19975)*

**Chucking Machine Products Inc** D 847 678-1192
Franklin Park *(G-10431)*

**Coeur Inc** F 815 648-1093
Hebron *(G-11717)*

**◆ Corpak Medsystems Inc** C 847 537-4601
Buffalo Grove *(G-2680)*

**Creative Bedding Technologies** G 815 444-9088
Crystal Lake *(G-7558)*

**Csl Behring LLC** B 815 932-6773
Bradley *(G-2418)*

**▲ D-M-S Holdings Inc** C 847 680-6811
Waukegan *(G-21547)*

**Diagnostic Photonics Inc** G 312 320-5478
Chicago *(G-4592)*

**Doctors Choice Inc** G 312 666-1111
Chicago *(G-4621)*

**Eagle Medical Concepts Inc** G 618 475-3671
Fairview Heights *(G-10167)*

**Elas Tek Molding Inc** E 815 675-9012
Spring Grove *(G-20335)*

**Eldest Daughter LLC** G 949 677-7385
Chicago *(G-4718)*

**Elite Imaging** F 618 632-2900
East Saint Louis *(G-8750)*

**Elmed Incorporated** E 630 543-2792
Glendale Heights *(G-11021)*

**Endepth Vision Systems LLC** G 630 329-7909
Lisle *(G-13586)*

**Endofix Ltd** G 708 715-3472
Brookfield *(G-2631)*

**Endotronix Inc** G 630 504-2861
Woodridge *(G-22478)*

**◆ Esma Inc** G 708 331-0456
South Holland *(G-20267)*

**Feelsure Health Corparation** G 847 823-0137
Park Ridge *(G-17194)*

S
I
C

Employee Codes: A=Over 500 employees, B=251-500
C=101-250, D=51-100, E=20-50, F=10-19, G=3-9

2017 Harris Illinois
Industrial Directory

1119

## 38 MEASURING, ANALYZING AND CONTROLLING INSTRUMENTS; PHOTOGRAPHIC, MEDICAL AN

| Company | Code | Phone |
|---|---|---|
| Feelsure Health Corporation | G | 847 446-7881 |
| Winnetka (G-22306) | | |
| Fetzer Surgical LLC | G | 630 635-2520 |
| Schaumburg (G-19526) | | |
| Flexxsonic Corporation | G | 847 452-7226 |
| Mount Prospect (G-15330) | | |
| Gema Inc | G | 773 508-6690 |
| Chicago (G-4924) | | |
| Global Endoscopy Inc | G | 847 910-5836 |
| Elk Grove Village (G-9501) | | |
| ▲ Good Lite Co | G | 847 841-1145 |
| Elgin (G-9050) | | |
| Griffith Company | G | 847 524-4173 |
| Schaumburg (G-19544) | | |
| Hearing Screening Assoc LLC | G | 855 550-9427 |
| Arlington Heights (G-763) | | |
| Hill-Rom Holdings Inc | B | 312 819-7200 |
| Chicago (G-5088) | | |
| ◆ Hollister Incorporated | B | 847 680-1000 |
| Libertyville (G-13333) | | |
| ◆ Hospira Inc | A | 224 212-2000 |
| Lake Forest (G-12908) | | |
| Hospira Inc | C | 224 212-6244 |
| Lake Forest (G-12909) | | |
| ◆ Hospira Worldwide LLC | G | 224 212-2000 |
| Lake Forest (G-12910) | | |
| ▲ Hospital Therapy Products Inc | F | 630 766-7101 |
| Wood Dale (G-22379) | | |
| Inland Midwest Corporation | E | 773 775-2111 |
| Elmhurst (G-9887) | | |
| Integrated Medical Tech Inc | G | 309 662-3614 |
| Bloomington (G-2183) | | |
| Intratherm LLC | G | 630 333-5419 |
| Naperville (G-15677) | | |
| ISS Medical Inc | G | 217 359-8681 |
| Champaign (G-3503) | | |
| ▲ J Stone Inc | F | 847 325-5660 |
| Mundelein (G-15513) | | |
| Janin Group Inc | G | 630 554-8906 |
| Oswego (G-16924) | | |
| Jones Medical Instrument Co | E | 630 571-1980 |
| Oak Brook (G-16528) | | |
| Kdk Upset Forging Co | E | 708 388-8770 |
| Blue Island (G-2259) | | |
| Kimberly-Clark Corporation | C | 815 886-7872 |
| Romeoville (G-18835) | | |
| Labthermics Technologies | E | 217 351-7722 |
| Champaign (G-3509) | | |
| Lakeview Equipment Co | G | 847 548-7705 |
| Round Lake (G-19062) | | |
| Lavezzi Precision Inc | C | 630 582-1230 |
| Bloomingdale (G-2112) | | |
| Leica Microsystems Inc | G | 847 405-0123 |
| Buffalo Grove (G-2725) | | |
| ▲ Leica Microsystems Inc | C | 847 405-0123 |
| Buffalo Grove (G-2726) | | |
| Lemoy International Inc | G | 847 427-0840 |
| Elk Grove Village (G-9594) | | |
| Life Spine Inc | E | 847 884-6117 |
| Huntley (G-12158) | | |
| ▲ Lsl Industries Inc | D | 773 878-1100 |
| Chicago (G-5555) | | |
| Ltc Holdings Inc | C | 847 249-5900 |
| Waukegan (G-21585) | | |
| Ludwig Medical Inc | G | 217 342-6570 |
| Effingham (G-8844) | | |
| Mallinckrodt LLC | E | 618 664-2111 |
| Greenville (G-11397) | | |
| ▲ Manan Medical Products Inc | D | 847 637-3333 |
| Wheeling (G-22099) | | |
| Manan Tool & Manufacturing | A | 847 637-3333 |
| Wheeling (G-22100) | | |
| MD Technologies Inc | F | 815 598-3143 |
| Elizabeth (G-9244) | | |
| Medical Adherence Tech Inc | G | 847 525-6300 |
| Winnetka (G-22312) | | |
| Medical Screening Labs Inc | E | 847 647-7911 |
| Niles (G-16002) | | |
| Medifix Inc | G | 847 965-1898 |
| Morton Grove (G-15219) | | |
| Medigroup Inc | G | 630 554-5533 |
| Oswego (G-16926) | | |
| ◆ Medline Industries Inc | A | 847 949-5500 |
| Northfield (G-16409) | | |
| Medline Industries Inc | B | 847 949-2056 |
| Mundelein (G-15528) | | |
| Medline Industries Inc | B | 847 949-5500 |
| Waukegan (G-21589) | | |
| Medtec Applications Inc | G | 224 353-6752 |
| Glendale Heights (G-11047) | | |
| Medtex Health Services Inc | G | 630 789-0330 |
| Clarendon Hills (G-7258) | | |
| Medtronic Inc | G | 815 444-2500 |
| Crystal Lake (G-7608) | | |
| Medtronic Inc | E | 630 627-6677 |
| Lombard (G-13824) | | |
| Merge Healthcare Incorporated | C | 312 565-6868 |
| Chicago (G-5690) | | |
| Monogen Inc | G | 847 573-6700 |
| Chicago (G-5796) | | |
| Murray Inc | D | 847 620-7990 |
| North Barrington (G-16153) | | |
| ◆ Nemera Buffalo Grove LLC | B | 847 541-7900 |
| Buffalo Grove (G-2743) | | |
| Nemera Buffalo Grove LLC | G | 847 325-3629 |
| Buffalo Grove (G-2744) | | |
| Nemera Buffalo Grove LLC | G | 847 325-3628 |
| Buffalo Grove (G-2745) | | |
| Nemera US Holding Inc | F | 847 325-3620 |
| Buffalo Grove (G-2746) | | |
| ▲ Newmedical Technology Inc | E | 847 412-1000 |
| Northbrook (G-16319) | | |
| Nexhand Inc | G | 619 820-2988 |
| Chicago (G-5906) | | |
| Nordent Manufacturing Inc | E | 847 437-4780 |
| Elk Grove Village (G-9653) | | |
| Northgate Technologies Inc | E | 847 608-8900 |
| Elgin (G-9126) | | |
| Novian Health Inc | G | 312 266-7200 |
| Chicago (G-5948) | | |
| Novo Surgical Inc | G | 877 860-6686 |
| Oak Brook (G-16549) | | |
| Nrtx LLC | G | 224 717-0465 |
| Chicago (G-5951) | | |
| Nuclin Diagnostics Inc | G | 847 498-5210 |
| Northbrook (G-16320) | | |
| ◆ Ohio Medical LLC | D | 847 855-0500 |
| Gurnee (G-11479) | | |
| Omc Investors LLC | G | 847 855-6220 |
| Gurnee (G-11480) | | |
| Omnicare Group Inc | G | 708 949-9802 |
| Homer Glen (G-12084) | | |
| ◆ Omron Healthcare Inc | D | 847 680-6200 |
| Lake Forest (G-12932) | | |
| Opticent Inc | G | 410 829-7384 |
| Evanston (G-10083) | | |
| ▲ Organ Recovery Systems Inc | F | 847 824-2600 |
| Itasca (G-12337) | | |
| ▲ Patterson Medical Products Inc | G | 630 393-6671 |
| Warrenville (G-21353) | | |
| Phenome Technologies Inc | G | 847 962-1273 |
| Lincolnshire (G-13474) | | |
| Philips Medical Systems Clevel | G | 630 585-2000 |
| Aurora (G-1065) | | |
| Photonicare Inc | G | 405 880-7209 |
| Champaign (G-3525) | | |
| Precision Products Mfg Intl | F | 847 299-8500 |
| Des Plaines (G-8262) | | |
| Precision Vision Inc | G | 815 223-2022 |
| Woodstock (G-22601) | | |
| Prodico Technologies LLC | F | 312 498-5152 |
| Chicago (G-6204) | | |
| Provena Randalwood Open Mri | E | 630 587-9917 |
| Geneva (G-10860) | | |
| Resonance Medical LLC | G | 229 292-2094 |
| Chicago (G-6337) | | |
| ▲ Rexam Devices LLC | F | 847 325-3629 |
| Buffalo Grove (G-2758) | | |
| Reznik Instrument Co | G | 847 673-3444 |
| Skokie (G-20075) | | |
| ▼ Richard Wolf Med Instrs Corp | C | 847 913-1113 |
| Vernon Hills (G-21193) | | |
| River Bank Laboratories Inc | F | 630 232-2207 |
| Geneva (G-10863) | | |
| Rockford Wellness & Diagnostic | G | 815 708-0125 |
| Rockford (G-18590) | | |
| Salter Labs | G | 661 854-3166 |
| Lake Forest (G-12956) | | |
| ◆ Salter Labs | E | 847 739-3224 |
| Lake Forest (G-12957) | | |
| Savex Manufacturing Company | G | 630 668-7219 |
| Carol Stream (G-3233) | | |
| Shanks Veterinary Equipment | G | 815 225-7700 |
| Milledgeville (G-14818) | | |
| ▲ Siemens Hlthcare Dgnostics Inc | E | 847 267-5300 |
| Deerfield (G-8052) | | |
| Siemens Med Solutions USA Inc | G | 847 304-7700 |
| Schaumburg (G-19727) | | |
| Simpex Medical Inc | G | 847 757-9928 |
| Mount Prospect (G-15374) | | |
| ▲ Smart Medical Technology Inc | F | 630 964-1689 |
| Darien (G-7802) | | |
| Sonoma Orthopedic Products Inc | F | 847 807-4378 |
| Buffalo Grove (G-2774) | | |
| Spinecraft LLC | F | 630 920-7300 |
| Westmont (G-21923) | | |
| ▲ Star Cushion Products Inc | F | 618 539-7070 |
| Freeburg (G-10643) | | |
| Stereo Optical Company Inc | F | 773 867-0380 |
| Chicago (G-6589) | | |
| Steris Corporation | F | 847 455-2881 |
| Franklin Park (G-10594) | | |
| Stretch CHI | G | 773 420-9355 |
| Chicago (G-6606) | | |
| Stryker Corporation | B | 312 386-9780 |
| Chicago (G-6608) | | |
| ▲ Sunset Hlthcare Solutions Inc | E | 877 578-6738 |
| Chicago (G-6631) | | |
| Superior Surgical Instrumen TS | G | 630 628-8437 |
| Addison (G-301) | | |
| Supertek Scientific LLC | G | 630 345-3450 |
| Villa Park (G-21287) | | |
| ▼ Sysmex America Inc | C | 847 996-4500 |
| Lincolnshire (G-13484) | | |
| Teleflex Incorporated | D | 847 259-7400 |
| Arlington Heights (G-853) | | |
| Thermatome Corporation | G | 312 772-2201 |
| Chicago (G-6712) | | |
| Thermopol Inc | G | 815 422-0400 |
| Saint Anne (G-19126) | | |
| Thrift Medical Products | G | 630 857-3548 |
| Naperville (G-15765) | | |
| Tianhe Stem Cell | F | 630 723-1968 |
| Lisle (G-13672) | | |
| Total Titanium Inc | E | 618 473-2429 |
| Red Bud (G-17950) | | |
| ▲ United Amercn Healthcare Corp | F | 313 393-4571 |
| Chicago (G-6820) | | |
| Uresil LLC | E | 847 982-0200 |
| Skokie (G-20105) | | |
| Vyaire Medical Inc | F | 847 362-8088 |
| Mettawa (G-14764) | | |
| Welkins Inc | G | 877 319-3504 |
| Downers Grove (G-8543) | | |
| Whitney Products Inc | F | 847 966-6161 |
| Niles (G-16942) | | |
| Wholesale Point Inc | F | 630 986-1700 |
| Burr Ridge (G-2895) | | |
| Wisdom Medical Technology LLC | G | 630 803-6383 |
| Oswego (G-16942) | | |
| Woundwear Inc | G | 847 634-1700 |
| Buffalo Grove (G-2795) | | |

### 3842 Orthopedic, Prosthetic & Surgical Appliances/Splys

| Company | Code | Phone |
|---|---|---|
| 1 Federal Supply Source Inc | G | 708 964-2222 |
| Steger (G-20565) | | |
| ▲ 20 20 Medical Systems Inc | G | 815 455-7161 |
| Crystal Lake (G-7524) | | |
| Accuquest Hearing Center Inc | G | 847 588-1895 |
| Niles (G-15956) | | |
| Accurate Radiation Shielding | G | 847 639-5533 |
| Cary (G-3321) | | |
| Accutone Hearing Aid Inc | G | 773 545-3279 |
| Evanston (G-10004) | | |
| Advanced Mbility Solutions LLC | E | 618 658-8580 |
| Marion (G-14247) | | |
| ▲ Anatomical Worldwide LLC | C | 312 224-4772 |
| Evanston (G-10010) | | |
| Argentum Medical LLC | E | 888 551-0188 |
| Geneva (G-10810) | | |
| Artistic Dental Studio Inc | E | 630 679-8686 |
| Bolingbrook (G-2278) | | |
| Audibel Hearing Center | G | 217 670-1183 |
| Springfield (G-20391) | | |
| B & D Independence Inc | E | 618 262-7117 |
| Mount Carmel (G-15260) | | |
| ▼ Baxalta Export Corporation | G | 224 948-2000 |
| Deerfield (G-7981) | | |
| Baxalta World Trade LLC | G | 224 948-2000 |
| Deerfield (G-7982) | | |
| Baxalta Worldwide LLC | G | 224 948-2000 |
| Deerfield (G-7983) | | |
| Baxter Healthcare Corporation | E | 847 578-4671 |
| Waukegan (G-21529) | | |
| Baxter International Inc | A | 224 948-2000 |
| Deerfield (G-7988) | | |
| Becks Medical & Indus Gases | F | 618 273-9019 |
| Eldorado (G-8917) | | |

SIC SECTION 38 MEASURING, ANALYZING AND CONTROLLING INSTRUMENTS; PHOTOGRAPHIC, MEDICAL AN

**Beltone Corporation** ....D ....847 832-3300
Glenview *(G-11107)*

**Bergmann Orthotic Lab Inc** ....G ....847 446-3616
Northfield *(G-16392)*

**Bergmann Orthotic Laboratory** ....G ....847 729-7923
Glenview *(G-11108)*

**Berry Global Inc** ....G ....630 375-0358
Aurora *(G-969)*

**Bioconcepts Inc** ....G ....630 986-0007
Burr Ridge *(G-2824)*

**Blue Sky Bio LLC** ....G ....718 376-0422
Grayslake *(G-11322)*

▲ **Boss Manufacturing Holdings** ....F ....309 852-2781
Kewanee *(G-12675)*

**Brandt Interiors** ....G ....847 251-3543
Wilmette *(G-22246)*

**Brasel Products Inc** ....G ....630 879-3759
Batavia *(G-1424)*

**C & S Chemicals Inc** ....G ....815 722-6671
Joliet *(G-12470)*

**C R Kesner Company** ....G ....630 232-8118
Geneva *(G-10816)*

**Cape Prosthetics-Orthotics Inc** ....G ....618 457-4692
Carbondale *(G-3001)*

**Cera Ltd** ....G ....773 334-1042
Chicago *(G-4282)*

**Clinere Products Inc** ....G ....847 837-4020
Mundelein *(G-15489)*

**Comprhnsive Prsthtics Orthtics** ....F ....708 387-9700
Brookfield *(G-2628)*

**Cosmedent Inc** ....E ....312 644-9388
Chicago *(G-4478)*

**Covidien LP** ....A ....815 444-2500
Crystal Lake *(G-7557)*

**D J Peters Orthopedics Ltd** ....G ....309 664-6930
Bloomington *(G-2159)*

**D ME To ME** ....F ....815 485-3632
New Lenox *(G-15874)*

**Dabir Surfaces Inc** ....F ....708 867-6777
Chicago *(G-4541)*

**Dean Prsthtic Orthtic Svcs Ltd** ....G ....847 475-7080
Evanston *(G-10026)*

**Deborah Morris Gulbrandson Pt** ....F ....847 639-4140
Cary *(G-3333)*

**Delta Molding LLC** ....G ....847 414-7773
Buffalo Grove *(G-2685)*

**Dreher Orthopedic Industries** ....G ....708 848-4646
Oak Park *(G-16661)*

**Dura-Crafts Corp** ....F ....815 464-3561
Frankfort *(G-10316)*

**Duroweld Company Inc** ....E ....847 680-3064
Lake Bluff *(G-12841)*

**E-Z Cuff Inc** ....G ....847 549-1550
Libertyville *(G-13320)*

**East West Martial Arts Sups** ....G ....773 878-7711
Chicago *(G-4682)*

**Ecomed Solutions LLC** ....E ....866 817-7114
Mundelein *(G-15498)*

**Elginex Corporation** ....G ....815 786-8406
Sandwich *(G-19362)*

**Elmed Incorporated** ....E ....630 543-2792
Glendale Heights *(G-11021)*

**Eln Group LLC** ....G ....847 477-1496
Winnetka *(G-22305)*

**Etymotic Research Inc** ....E ....847 228-0006
Elk Grove Village *(G-9465)*

**Fall Protection Systems Inc** ....E ....618 452-7000
Madison *(G-14145)*

◆ **Firm of John Dickinson** ....E ....847 680-1000
Libertyville *(G-13324)*

**G & M Industries Inc** ....G ....618 344-6655
Collinsville *(G-7326)*

**Gema Inc** ....G ....773 508-6690
Chicago *(G-4924)*

**General Bandages Inc** ....F ....847 966-8383
Park Ridge *(G-17198)*

**Go Steady LLC** ....G ....630 293-3243
West Chicago *(G-21709)*

**Gohear LLC** ....G ....847 574-7829
Lake Forest *(G-12902)*

**Gregory Lamar & Assoc Inc** ....G ....312 595-1545
Chicago *(G-5002)*

▲ **Guardian Equipment Inc** ....E ....312 447-8100
Chicago *(G-5007)*

**Hanger Inc** ....E ....847 695-6955
McHenry *(G-14511)*

**Hanger Inc** ....E ....708 679-1006
Matteson *(G-14372)*

**Hanger Prosthetics &** ....G ....217 429-6656
Decatur *(G-7887)*

**Hanger Prosthetics &** ....D ....708 371-9999
Oak Lawn *(G-16624)*

**Hanger Prosthetics &** ....G ....618 997-1451
Herrin *(G-11749)*

**Hanger Prosthetics &** ....G ....847 478-8154
Lincolnshire *(G-13452)*

**Hanger Prosthetics &** ....G ....815 344-3070
McHenry *(G-14512)*

**Hanger Prosthetics &** ....F ....815 937-0241
Joliet *(G-12507)*

**Hanger Prosthetics &** ....G ....847 623-6080
Gurnee *(G-11458)*

**Hanger Prosthetics &** ....G ....630 820-5656
Aurora *(G-1022)*

**Hanger Prosthetics & Orthotics** ....E ....618 288-8920
Maryville *(G-14341)*

**Hanger Prsthetcs & Ortho Inc** ....G ....708 957-0240
Hazel Crest *(G-11708)*

**Hanger Prsthetcs & Ortho Inc** ....G ....815 937-0241
Kankakee *(G-12620)*

**Hanger Prsthetcs & Ortho Inc** ....G ....815 744-9944
Joliet *(G-12508)*

**Hearing Aid Warehouse Inc** ....G ....217 431-4700
Danville *(G-7730)*

**Hearing Associates PC** ....F ....847 662-9300
Gurnee *(G-11459)*

**Heart 4 Heart Inc** ....G ....217 544-2699
Springfield *(G-20449)*

**Hearwell** ....G ....217 824-5210
Taylorville *(G-20840)*

**Hogg Welding Inc** ....G ....708 339-0033
Harvey *(G-11670)*

◆ **Hollister Incorporated** ....B ....847 680-1000
Libertyville *(G-13333)*

**Hollister Wound Care LLC** ....G ....847 996-6000
Libertyville *(G-13334)*

**Howmedica Osteonics Corp** ....G ....309 663-6414
Bloomington *(G-2181)*

**Hoya Lens of Chicago Inc** ....E ....847 678-4700
Franklin Park *(G-10490)*

**Illiana Orthopedics Inc** ....G ....708 532-0061
Tinley Park *(G-20921)*

**Illinois Soc For Rsprtory Care** ....G ....815 742-9367
Rockford *(G-18427)*

**Integrated Medical Tech Inc** ....G ....309 662-3614
Bloomington *(G-2183)*

**Intelliwheels Inc** ....G ....630 341-1942
Champaign *(G-3502)*

**Itus Corporation LLC** ....G ....888 537-5661
Arlington Heights *(G-780)*

**Joliet Orthotics** ....G ....708 798-1767
Flossmoor *(G-10226)*

**JP Orthotics** ....G ....217 885-3047
Quincy *(G-17843)*

**Keller Orthotics Inc** ....F ....773 929-4700
Chicago *(G-5369)*

**Kimberly-Clark Corporation** ....C ....815 886-7872
Romeoville *(G-18835)*

**Kinetic Orthotic Inc** ....G ....708 246-9266
Western Springs *(G-21869)*

▲ **Kinsman Enterprises Inc** ....G ....618 932-3838
West Frankfort *(G-21810)*

▲ **Knowles Electronics LLC** ....A ....630 250-5100
Itasca *(G-12297)*

**Koebers Prosthetic Orthpd Lab** ....G ....309 676-2276
Chicago *(G-5400)*

**Landau Real Estate Svcs LLC** ....G ....312 379-9146
Chicago *(G-5455)*

**Lanterna Medical Tech USA** ....G ....847 446-9995
Winnetka *(G-22309)*

**Lemaitre Vascular Inc** ....F ....847 462-2191
Fox River Grove *(G-10288)*

▲ **Lester L Brossard Co** ....F ....815 338-7825
Woodstock *(G-22585)*

**Lincoln Advanced Tech LLC** ....G ....815 286-3500
Hinckley *(G-11936)*

**Lloyd American Corporation** ....F ....815 964-4191
Rockford *(G-18472)*

**Logan Actuator Co** ....G ....815 943-9500
Harvard *(G-11640)*

▲ **Lsl Industries Inc** ....D ....773 878-1100
Chicago *(G-5555)*

**M2m Enterprises LLC** ....G ....847 899-7565
Elgin *(G-9097)*

▲ **Magid Glove Safety Mfg Co LLC** ....B ....773 384-2070
Romeoville *(G-18841)*

▲ **Manan Medical Products Inc** ....D ....847 637-3333
Wheeling *(G-22099)*

**Mandis Dental Laboratory** ....G ....618 345-3777
Collinsville *(G-7334)*

▲ **Medgyn Products Inc** ....D ....630 627-4105
Addison *(G-197)*

**Medline Industries Inc** ....B ....847 949-5500
Waukegan *(G-21589)*

**Medline Industries Inc** ....E ....847 949-5500
Mundelein *(G-15529)*

**Merry Walker Corporation** ....G ....847 837-9580
Mundelein *(G-15530)*

**Mhub** ....G ....773 580-1485
Chicago *(G-5717)*

**Microguide Inc** ....G ....630 964-3335
Downers Grove *(G-8485)*

**Midwest Orthotic Services LLC** ....E ....773 930-3770
Chicago *(G-5748)*

**Milvia** ....G ....312 527-3403
Chicago *(G-5766)*

**Mimosa Acoustics Inc** ....G ....217 359-9740
Champaign *(G-3515)*

**Mio Med Orthopedics Inc** ....G ....773 477-8991
Chicago *(G-5769)*

**Mobility Connection Inc** ....G ....815 965-8090
Rockford *(G-18510)*

**Modern Aids Inc** ....E ....847 437-8600
Elk Grove Village *(G-9634)*

**Neo Orthotics Inc** ....G ....309 699-0354
East Peoria *(G-8726)*

**New Step Orthotic Lab Inc** ....F ....618 208-4444
Maryville *(G-14345)*

▲ **Newmedical Technology Inc** ....E ....847 412-1000
Northbrook *(G-16319)*

**Norfolk Medical Products Inc** ....F ....847 674-7075
Skokie *(G-20046)*

**Northern Prosthetics** ....G ....815 226-0444
Rockford *(G-18522)*

**O & P Kinetic** ....G ....815 401-7260
Bourbonnais *(G-2404)*

**Opportunity Inc** ....D ....847 831-9400
Highland Park *(G-11860)*

**Optech Ortho & Prosth Svcs** ....G ....708 364-9700
Orland Park *(G-16880)*

**Optech Ortho & Prosth Svcs** ....G ....815 932-8564
Kankakee *(G-12642)*

**Orthotic & Prosthetic Assoc** ....G ....217 789-1450
Springfield *(G-20495)*

▲ **Pal Health Technologies Inc** ....D ....309 347-8785
Pekin *(G-17280)*

**Parkview Orthopaedic Group** ....F ....815 727-3030
New Lenox *(G-15899)*

**Payne Chauna** ....G ....618 580-2584
Belleville *(G-1664)*

**Peoria Neuroinnovations LLC** ....G ....217 899-0443
Peoria *(G-17424)*

**Permobil Inc** ....F ....847 568-0001
Skokie *(G-20054)*

▲ **Phonak LLC** ....A ....630 821-5000
Warrenville *(G-21354)*

**Plastic Specialists America** ....G ....847 406-7547
Gurnee *(G-11486)*

▲ **Pres-On Corporation** ....E ....630 628-2255
Bolingbrook *(G-2360)*

**Pro-Orthotics Inc** ....G ....708 326-1554
Orland Park *(G-16885)*

**Prointegration Tech LLC** ....G ....618 409-3233
Highland *(G-11806)*

**Prosthetic Orthotic Specialist** ....G ....309 454-8733
Normal *(G-16085)*

**Prosthetics Orthotics Han** ....G ....847 695-6955
McHenry *(G-14549)*

**Psyonic Inc** ....G ....773 888-3252
Champaign *(G-3531)*

**Punch Products Manufacturing** ....E ....773 533-2800
Chicago *(G-6226)*

**Quad City Prosthetics Inc** ....F ....309 676-2276
Rock Island *(G-18194)*

**Quincy Lab Inc** ....E ....773 622-2428
Chicago *(G-6258)*

**R W G Manufacturing Inc** ....G ....708 755-8035
S Chicago Hts *(G-19112)*

**Replacement Arts Inc** ....G ....708 922-0580
Posen *(G-17735)*

**Respironics Inc** ....C ....708 923-6200
Palos Park *(G-17130)*

**Rinella Orthotics Inc** ....G ....815 717-8970
New Lenox *(G-15906)*

**Robert B Scott Ocularists Ltd** ....G ....312 782-3558
Chicago *(G-6367)*

**Ronald S Lefors Bs Cpo** ....G ....618 259-1969
East Alton *(G-8610)*

▲ **Rondex Products Incorporated** ....F ....815 226-0452
Rockford *(G-18597)*

SIC

Employee Codes: A=Over 500 employees, B=251-500
C=101-250, D=51-100, E=20-50, F=10-19, G=3-9
2017 Harris Illinois
Industrial Directory
1121

38 MEASURING, ANALYZING AND CONTROLLING INSTRUMENTS; PHOTOGRAPHIC, MEDICAL AN SIC SECTION

◆ Sage Products LLC B 815 455-4700
Cary (G-3370)

▲ Salisbury Elec Safety LLC B 877 406-4501
Bolingbrook (G-2365)

SC Industries Inc G 312 366-3899
Chicago (G-6449)

Scale-Tronix Inc F 630 653-3377
Carol Stream (G-3235)

Scheck & Siress G 708 383-2257
Oak Park (G-16683)

Scheck Siress Prosthetics Inc C 630 424-0392
Oak Park (G-16684)

▲ Sellstrom Manufacturing Co D 800 323-7402
Elgin (G-9175)

Sensaphonics Inc G 312 432-1714
Chicago (G-6476)

Serola Biomechanics Inc F 815 636-2780
Loves Park (G-13991)

▲ Sourcennex International Co G 847 251-5500
Wilmette (G-22266)

Srt Prosthetics Orthotics LLC G 847 855-0030
Gurnee (G-11507)

Standard Safety Equipment Co E 815 363-8565
McHenry (G-14556)

▲ Star Cushion Products Inc F 618 539-7070
Freeburg (G-10643)

▼ Steel-Guard Safety Corp G 708 589-4588
South Holland (G-20306)

▲ Steiner Industries Inc D 773 588-3444
Chicago (G-6585)

Teleflex Incorporated D 847 259-7400
Arlington Heights (G-853)

▲ Tetra Medical Supply Corp F 847 647-0590
Niles (G-16040)

▲ Therafin Corporation E 708 479-7300
Frankfort (G-10369)

Therapeutic Envisions Inc G 720 323-7032
Libertyville (G-13390)

Thor Defense Inc G 630 541-5106
Downers Grove (G-8532)

Tri R G 224 399-7786
Libertyville (G-13392)

Triad Controls Inc E 630 443-9343
Saint Charles (G-19286)

Tuu Duc Le Inc G 630 897-6363
North Aurora (G-16148)

United Seating & Mobility LLC G 309 699-0509
East Peoria (G-8737)

W W Belt Inc G 708 788-1855
Berwyn (G-2078)

▼ Weeb Enterprises LLC G 815 861-2625
Wauconda (G-21514)

Welkins LLC G 877 319-3504
Downers Grove (G-8543)

Wheaton Resource Corp G 630 690-5795
Carol Stream (G-3268)

Whitney Products Inc F 847 966-6161
Niles (G-16047)

▲ Williams Halthcare Systems LLC D 847 741-3650
Elgin (G-9237)

World Class Technologies Inc G 312 758-3114
Chicago (G-7029)

## 3843 Dental Eqpt & Splys

Acquamed Technologies Inc G 630 728-4014
Oswego (G-16901)

Allstar Dental Inc G 847 325-5134
Vernon Hills (G-21145)

▲ American Dental Products Inc E 630 238-0275
Bensenville (G-1832)

Anthony Collins G 847 566-5350
Mundelein (G-15470)

Apex Dental Materials Inc G 847 719-1133
Lake Zurich (G-13042)

Artistic Dental Studio Inc E 630 679-8686
Bolingbrook (G-2278)

▲ Astron Dental Corporation F 847 726-8787
Lake Zurich (G-13044)

Bennett Technologies Inc F 708 389-9501
Tinley Park (G-20897)

▲ Bisco Inc D 847 534-6000
Schaumburg (G-19464)

Brite Dental PC E 773 735-8353
Chicago (G-4170)

Ched Markay Inc G 847 566-3307
Mundelein (G-15486)

Cislak Manufacturing Inc E 847 647-1819
Niles (G-15969)

Coralite Dental Products Inc G 847 679-3400
Skokie (G-19986)

Denbur Inc G 630 986-9667
Westmont (G-21882)

Dental Arts Laboratories Inc G 309 342-3117
Galesburg (G-10745)

Dental Crafts Lab Inc G 815 872-3221
Princeton (G-17746)

Dental Laboratory Inc E 630 262-3700
Geneva (G-10823)

▲ Dental Technologies Inc D 847 677-5500
Lincolnwood (G-13507)

▲ Dental USA Inc F 815 363-8003
McHenry (G-14495)

Dentalez Alabama Inc C 773 624-4330
Chicago (G-4583)

Dentsply Sirona Inc C 847 640-4800
Des Plaines (G-8183)

Dove Dental Studio G 847 679-2434
Niles (G-15975)

Duquoin Dental Associates G 618 542-8832
Du Quoin (G-8553)

Fred Pigg Dental Lab G 618 439-6829
Benton (G-2028)

Fricke Dental Manufacturing Co G 630 540-1900
Streamwood (G-20657)

▲ Fricke International Inc F 630 833-2627
Villa Park (G-21253)

◆ Gc America Inc C 708 597-0900
Alsip (G-463)

Gc Manufacturing America LLC D 708 597-0900
Alsip (G-464)

Goldman Products Inc E 847 526-1166
Wauconda (G-21465)

Harris and Discount Supplies G 847 726-3800
Lake Zurich (G-13082)

▲ Harry J Bosworth Company E 847 679-3400
Evanston (G-10050)

Healthdentl LLC G 800 845-5172
Plainfield (G-17605)

Holland Specialty Co E 309 697-9262
Peoria (G-17383)

▲ Hu-Friedy Mfg Co LLC B 773 975-3975
Chicago (G-5126)

Integrated Medical Tech Inc G 309 662-3614
Bloomington (G-2183)

J L Lawrence & Co G 217 235-3622
Mattoon (G-14394)

James Street Dental P C G 630 232-9535
Geneva (G-10841)

Landman Dental G 312 266-6480
Chicago (G-5456)

◆ Lang Dental Mfg Co Inc F 847 215-6622
Wheeling (G-22089)

Lemoy International Inc G 847 427-0840
Elk Grove Village (G-9594)

Lmpl Management Corporation G 708 636-2443
Oak Lawn (G-16631)

M & N Dental G 815 678-0036
Richmond (G-17966)

Mandis Dental Laboratory G 618 345-3777
Collinsville (G-7334)

Martin Dental Laboratory Inc F 708 597-8880
Lockport (G-13731)

Myerson LLC G 312 432-8200
Chicago (G-5844)

Naper Dental G 630 369-6818
Naperville (G-15709)

Nordent Manufacturing Inc E 847 437-4780
Elk Grove Village (G-9653)

North Halsted Dental Spa G 773 296-0325
Chicago (G-5934)

Northwest Dental Prosthetics G 773 505-9191
Chicago (G-5938)

▲ Odl Inc D 815 434-0655
Ottawa (G-16974)

Oratech Inc E 217 793-2735
Springfield (G-20493)

Perfect Smiles G 708 687-6100
Oak Forest (G-16587)

Prairie Orthodontics PC F 847 249-8800
Gurnee (G-11489)

▲ Prime Dental Manufacturing E 773 283-2914
Chicago (G-6185)

Reliance Dental Mfg Co G 708 597-6694
Alsip (G-518)

Smile Lee Faces G 773 376-9999
Chicago (G-6534)

Smile of Brookfield G 708 485-7754
Brookfield (G-2642)

Spiraltech Superior Dental Imp F 312 440-7777
Chicago (G-6561)

Strictly Dentures G 815 969-0531
Rockford (G-18635)

◆ Sunstar Americas Inc B 773 777-4000
Schaumburg (G-19744)

Tanaka Dental Enterprises Inc F 847 679-1610
Skokie (G-20099)

Underwood Dental Laboratories F 217 398-0090
Champaign (G-3551)

▲ Young Innovations Inc D 847 458-5400
Algonquin (G-415)

Young Innovations Inc D 847 458-5400
Algonquin (G-416)

Young Innovations Holdings LLC G 312 506-5600
Chicago (G-7054)

Young Os LLC E 847 458-5400
Algonquin (G-417)

## 3844 X-ray Apparatus & Tubes

▲ 7 Mile Solutions Inc E 847 588-2280
Niles (G-15952)

Abbott Laboratories A 847 938-8717
North Chicago (G-16163)

Arquilla Inc F 815 455-2470
Crystal Lake (G-7537)

Assurance Technologies Inc F 630 550-5000
Bartlett (G-1331)

Brand X-Ray Company F 630 543-5331
Addison (G-60)

▲ Claymount Americas Corporation E 630 271-9729
Downers Grove (G-8414)

▲ Del Medical Inc F 800 800-6006
Bloomingdale (G-2102)

▲ Dunlee Corporation G 630 585-2100
Aurora (G-999)

Faxitron X-Ray LLC E 847 465-9729
Lincolnshire (G-13447)

▲ Gama Electronics Inc F 815 356-9600
Woodstock (G-22569)

Huestis Pro-Tronics Inc F 847 426-1055
Gilberts (G-10922)

Lixi Inc G 630 620-4646
Downers Grove (G-8477)

Mark Industries G 847 487-8670
Wauconda (G-21480)

Material Control Inc F 630 892-4274
Batavia (G-1467)

Medical Radiation Concepts G 630 289-1515
Bartlett (G-1362)

Midmark Corporation D 847 415-9800
Lincolnshire (G-13465)

Philips Elec N Amer Corp C 630 585-2000
Aurora (G-1064)

Poersch Metal Manufacturing Co F 773 722-0890
Chicago (G-6145)

▲ Sedecal Usa Inc E 847 394-6960
Arlington Heights (G-837)

Starfire Industries LLC E 217 721-4165
Champaign (G-3548)

◆ Summit Industries LLC D 773 353-4000
Niles (G-16038)

Superior X Ray Tube Company G 815 338-4424
Woodstock (G-22615)

Varex Imaging Corporation E 847 279-5121
Lincolnshire (G-13488)

Wallace Enterprises Inc G 309 496-1230
East Moline (G-8698)

▲ X-Ray Cassette Repair Co Inc E 815 356-8181
Crystal Lake (G-7678)

## 3845 Electromedical & Electrotherapeutic Apparatus

7000 Inc F 312 800-3612
Bolingbrook (G-2275)

Acoustic Medsystems Inc G 217 355-8888
Savoy (G-19408)

ADM Imaging Inc G 630 834-7100
Wheaton (G-21934)

Aespheptics Medical Ltd G 630 416-1400
Lombard (G-13762)

Amigo Mobility Center G 630 268-8670
Oakbrook Terrace (G-16697)

Apana Inc G 309 303-4007
Peoria (G-17308)

Arxium Inc C 847 808-2600
Buffalo Grove (G-2660)

Axios Medtech Inc G 312 224-7856
Round Lake Beach (G-19072)

Axiosonic LLC F 217 342-3412
Effingham (G-8826)

**Barrington Clinical Partners**.................G....... 847 508-9737
Barrington *(G-1271)*
**Bio-Logic Systems Corp**......................D....... 847 949-0456
Mundelein *(G-15478)*
**Cardiac Imaging Inc**..............................F....... 630 834-7100
Oakbrook Terrace *(G-16700)*
**Carematix Inc**........................................E....... 312 627-9300
Chicago *(G-4242)*
**Cortek Endoscopy Inc**...........................G....... 847 526-2266
Wauconda *(G-21453)*
**Ctg Advanced Materials LLC**................E....... 630 226-9080
Bolingbrook *(G-2292)*
▲ **CTS Automotive LLC**........................C....... 630 614-7201
Lisle *(G-13578)*
**Dermatique Laser & Skin**......................F....... 630 262-2515
Geneva *(G-10824)*
**Domino Lasers Inc**................................E....... 847 855-1364
Gurnee *(G-11442)*
**Dupage Chropractic Centre Ltd**.............G....... 630 858-9780
Glen Ellyn *(G-10968)*
**Elmed Incorporated**..............................E....... 630 543-2792
Glendale Heights *(G-11021)*
**Fredrick Hoy**.........................................G....... 309 691-4410
Peoria *(G-17367)*
**General Electric Company**....................B....... 847 304-7400
Hoffman Estates *(G-12013)*
**Healthlight LLC**.....................................F....... 224 231-0342
Schaumburg *(G-19550)*
**Henderson Engineering Co Inc**..............G....... 815 786-9471
Sandwich *(G-19368)*
**Intellidrain Inc**......................................G....... 312 725-4332
Evanston *(G-10058)*
**Interexpo Ltd**........................................F....... 847 489-7056
Kildeer *(G-12700)*
**Isovac Products LLC**.............................G....... 630 679-1740
Romeoville *(G-18831)*
**IV & Respiratory Care Services**.............E....... 618 398-2720
Belleville *(G-1639)*
**Jones Medical Instrument Co**................E....... 630 571-1980
Oak Brook *(G-16528)*
**Lifeline Scientific Inc**...........................E....... 847 294-0300
Itasca *(G-12304)*
**Lifewatch Corp**.....................................G....... 847 720-2100
Rosemont *(G-19012)*
**Lifewatch Services Inc**..........................B....... 847 720-2100
Rosemont *(G-19013)*
▲ **Lifewatch Technologies Inc**...............D....... 800 633-3361
Rosemont *(G-19014)*
**Medical Specialties Distrs LLC**...............E....... 630 307-6200
Hanover Park *(G-11585)*
**Medtex Health Services Inc**...................G....... 630 789-0330
Clarendon Hills *(G-7258)*
**Memorial Breast Diagnstc Svcs**.............G....... 217 788-4042
Springfield *(G-20479)*
**Metritrack Inc**.......................................G....... 708 498-3578
Hillside *(G-11925)*
**Mobile Endoscopix LLC**........................G....... 847 380-8992
Northbrook *(G-16312)*
**Nanocytomics LLC**................................G....... 847 467-2868
Evanston *(G-10077)*
**Natus Medical Incorporated**..................F....... 847 949-5200
Mundelein *(G-15536)*
**Northgate Technologies Inc**...................E....... 847 608-8900
Elgin *(G-9126)*
**Olympus America Inc**...........................F....... 630 953-2080
Lombard *(G-13836)*
**Omex Technologies Inc**.........................G....... 847 850-5858
Wheeling *(G-22112)*
◆ **Omron Healthcare Inc**.......................D....... 847 680-6200
Lake Forest *(G-12932)*
**Output Medical Inc**...............................G....... 630 430-8024
Chicago *(G-6027)*
**Positron Corporation**.............................E....... 317 576-0183
Westmont *(G-21912)*
**Retmap Inc**...........................................G....... 312 224-8938
Grayslake *(G-11361)*
**Samel Botros**.........................................G....... 847 466-5905
Bloomingdale *(G-2134)*
**Siemens Med Solutions USA Inc**............F....... 847 793-4429
Buffalo Grove *(G-2769)*
**Siemens Med Solutions USA Inc**............D....... 847 304-7700
Hoffman Estates *(G-12053)*
**Smart Scan Mri LLC**..............................G....... 847 623-4000
Gurnee *(G-11505)*
**Snap Diagnostics LLC**...........................F....... 847 777-0000
Wheeling *(G-22154)*
**Sullivan Home Health Products**..............G....... 217 532-6366
Hillsboro *(G-11900)*
**System Science Corporation**..................G....... 708 214-2264
Chicago *(G-6659)*
**Thermatome Corporation**......................G....... 312 772-2201
Chicago *(G-6712)*
**Thermopol Inc**.......................................G....... 815 422-0400
Saint Anne *(G-19126)*
**Touchpointcare LLC**..............................G....... 866 713-6590
Libertyville *(G-13391)*
**Universal Holdings Inc**..........................F....... 224 353-6198
Hoffman Estates *(G-12066)*
**Verena Solutions LLC**............................G....... 314 651-1908
Chicago *(G-6885)*
**Vestibular Technologies LLC**.................G....... 618 993-7561
Marion *(G-14293)*
**Victory Pharmacy Decatur Inc**...............E....... 217 429-8650
Decatur *(G-7956)*

## *3851 Ophthalmic Goods*

**Alcon Laboratories Inc**..........................E....... 312 751-6200
Chicago *(G-3797)*
**Asico LLC**..............................................F....... 630 986-8032
Westmont *(G-21876)*
**Bahk Eye Center Inc**..............................G....... 773 561-1199
Chicago *(G-4026)*
**Black Spectacles Blog**...........................G....... 312 884-9091
Park Ridge *(G-17184)*
**C & S Chemicals Inc**..............................G....... 815 722-6671
Joliet *(G-12470)*
**Ciba Vision Inc**......................................A....... 847 294-3000
Des Plaines *(G-8169)*
**Clear Sight Inc**.......................................G....... 630 323-3590
Westmont *(G-21880)*
**Dean B Scott**..........................................G....... 630 960-4455
Downers Grove *(G-8425)*
**Edgebrook Eyecare**................................F....... 815 397-5959
Rockford *(G-18358)*
**Essilor Laboratories Amer Inc**................E....... 309 787-2727
Rock Island *(G-18176)*
**Eye Candy Optics Corporation**...............G....... 773 697-7370
Chicago *(G-4800)*
**Eye Surgeons of Libertyville**..................G....... 847 362-3811
Libertyville *(G-13322)*
**Eyewearplanet Com Inc**.........................G....... 847 513-6203
Northbrook *(G-16254)*
**Family Eye Care**.....................................G....... 708 614-2311
Tinley Park *(G-20912)*
**G T Laboratories Inc**..............................G....... 847 998-4776
Lisle *(G-13591)*
**Henderson Eye Center**...........................F....... 217 698-9477
Springfield *(G-20451)*
**Hoya Corporation**..................................C....... 618 281-3344
Columbia *(G-7358)*
**Hoya Lens of Chicago Inc**......................E....... 847 678-4700
Franklin Park *(G-10490)*
**Illinois Retina Institute SC**....................F....... 309 589-1880
Peoria *(G-17386)*
**Illmo R/X Service**..................................F....... 217 877-1192
Decatur *(G-7893)*
**Independent Eyewear Mfg LLC**..............D....... 847 537-0008
Vernon Hills *(G-21175)*
**Innova Systems Inc**................................G....... 630 920-8880
Burr Ridge *(G-2854)*
**Jim Maui Inc**..........................................G....... 888 666-5905
Peoria *(G-17392)*
**Lights Prosthetic Eyes Inc**......................G....... 309 676-3663
Peoria *(G-17401)*
▲ **M & S Technologies Inc**....................F....... 847 763-0500
Niles *(G-15997)*
**Midwest Uncuts Inc**...............................F....... 312 664-3131
Chicago *(G-5752)*
**My Eye Doctor**.......................................G....... 847 325-4440
Buffalo Grove *(G-2740)*
▲ **My Eye Doctor**...................................G....... 312 782-4208
Chicago *(G-5839)*
**Night Vision Corporation**........................G....... 847 677-7611
Lincolnwood *(G-13527)*
**One Way Safety LLC**..............................G....... 708 579-0229
La Grange *(G-12741)*
◆ **Opticote Inc**.......................................E....... 847 678-8900
Franklin Park *(G-10544)*
**Quality Optical Inc**..................................G....... 773 561-0870
Chicago *(G-6247)*
**Reding Optics Inc**...................................G....... 708 301-2020
Lockport *(G-13741)*
**Robert B Scott Ocularists Ltd**..................G....... 312 782-3558
Chicago *(G-6367)*
▲ **Scuba Optics Inc**................................G....... 815 625-7272
Rock Falls *(G-18151)*
**Seoco Inc**...............................................G....... 815 874-9565
Rockford *(G-18611)*
**Spectacle Zoom LLC**..............................G....... 504 352-7237
Des Plaines *(G-8278)*
**Tammy Smith**..........................................G....... 618 372-8410
Brighton *(G-2545)*
**US Vision Inc**..........................................G....... 847 367-0420
Vernon Hills *(G-21214)*
**Vicron Optical Inc**...................................F....... 847 412-5530
Deerfield *(G-8066)*
**Walman Optical Company**.......................E....... 309 787-0000
Milan *(G-14807)*
▲ **Waters Industries Inc**.........................E....... 847 783-5900
West Dundee *(G-21803)*
**Weiner Optical Inc**..................................G....... 708 848-4040
Oak Park *(G-16692)*
**Wesley-Jessen Corporation Del**..............A....... 847 294-3000
Des Plaines *(G-8302)*
**Western Ilinois Optical Inc**.......................G....... 309 837-2000
Macomb *(G-14135)*
**Ziemer Usa Inc**.......................................F....... 618 462-9301
Alton *(G-595)*

## *3861 Photographic Eqpt & Splys*

**2nd Cine Inc**...........................................G....... 773 455-5808
Elgin *(G-8928)*
**A Division of A&A Studios Inc**.................F....... 312 278-1144
Chicago *(G-3686)*
**Alpha Laser of Chicago**...........................G....... 708 478-0464
Mokena *(G-14851)*
▲ **AV Stumpfl Usa Corp**..........................F....... 630 359-0999
Elmhurst *(G-9835)*
**AVI-Spl Employee**...................................B....... 847 437-7712
Schaumburg *(G-19454)*
**Baldwin Graphic Systems Inc**..................E....... 630 261-9180
Lombard *(G-13766)*
**Base-Line II Inc**.......................................G....... 847 336-8403
Gurnee *(G-11430)*
**Bka Inc**....................................................G....... 847 831-3535
Highland Park *(G-11825)*
**Black Point Studios llc**.............................E....... 773 791-2377
Chicago *(G-4120)*
◆ **Bretford Manufacturing Inc**................B....... 847 678-2545
Franklin Park *(G-10416)*
**Canon Solutions America Inc**..................D....... 630 351-1227
Itasca *(G-12240)*
**Cartridge World Sterling**..........................G....... 815 625-2345
Sterling *(G-20587)*
**CDs Office Systems Inc**...........................D....... 800 367-1508
Springfield *(G-20410)*
**Chicago Film Archive Nfp**........................G....... 773 478-3799
Chicago *(G-4319)*
**Clover Global Headquarters**....................G....... 815 431-8100
Hoffman Estates *(G-12000)*
**Clover Technologies Group LLC**..............F....... 815 431-8100
Hoffman Estates *(G-12001)*
◆ **Clover Technologies Group LLC**.........A....... 815 431-8100
Ottawa *(G-16956)*
**Clover Technologies Group LLC**..............B....... 815 431-8100
Ottawa *(G-16957)*
**Colors Chicago Inc**..................................G....... 312 265-1642
Chicago *(G-4429)*
**Cushing and Company**.............................E....... 312 266-8228
Chicago *(G-4518)*
▲ **Dukane Corporation**...........................C....... 630 797-4900
Saint Charles *(G-19175)*
▲ **Essannay Show It Inc**..........................G....... 312 733-5511
Chicago *(G-4778)*
**Fujifilm Hunt Chem USA Inc**....................C....... 847 259-8800
Rolling Meadows *(G-18730)*
**George Wilson**..........................................G....... 847 342-1111
Prospect Heights *(G-17778)*
◆ **Gpa Inc**................................................G....... 773 650-2020
Mc Cook *(G-14448)*
**Imac Motion Control Corp**........................G....... 847 741-4622
Elgin *(G-9073)*
**Imcopex**...................................................G....... 630 980-1015
Bartlett *(G-1355)*
▲ **International Toner Corp**.....................G....... 847 276-2700
Buffalo Grove *(G-2710)*
▲ **Ishot Products Inc**...............................G....... 312 497-4190
Bolingbrook *(G-2325)*
**Kinetic BEI LLC**........................................F....... 847 888-8060
South Elgin *(G-20210)*
**Lanxess Corporation**................................E....... 630 789-8440
Willowbrook *(G-22219)*
**Laser Pro**..................................................G....... 847 742-1055
Elgin *(G-9093)*
**Letter-Rite Express LLC**...........................F....... 847 678-1100
Aurora *(G-1046)*
**Lipsner Smith Co**......................................G....... 847 677-3000
Lincolnwood *(G-13521)*
**Lochman Ref Silk Screen Co**....................F....... 847 475-6266
Evanston *(G-10065)*

S I C

Employee Codes: A=Over 500 employees, B=251-500
C=101-250, D=51-100, E=20-50, F=10-19, G=3-9

2017 Harris Illinois
Industrial Directory

1123

## 38 MEASURING, ANALYZING AND CONTROLLING INSTRUMENTS; PHOTOGRAPHIC, MEDICAL AN

Midwest Laser Incorporated .......... G  708 974-0084
  Palos Hills *(G-17119)*
Moog Inc ........................................ C  847 498-0700
  Northbrook *(G-16314)*
Motus Digital Llc ........................... E  972 943-0008
  Des Plaines *(G-8237)*
Nexus Office Systems Inc ............. F  847 836-1095
  Elgin *(G-9121)*
Norvida USA Inc ........................... G  618 282-2992
  Sparta *(G-20319)*
Nuarc Company Inc ...................... G  847 967-4400
  Roselle *(G-18960)*
Paulmar Industries Inc .................. F  847 395-2520
  Antioch *(G-648)*
Plate and Pre-Press Management ... G  847 352-0462
  Schaumburg *(G-19694)*
Poersch Metal Manufacturing Co ... F  773 722-0890
  Chicago *(G-6145)*
▲ Promark International  Inc .......... D  630 830-2500
  Bartlett *(G-1365)*
Quickset International  Inc ............. D  847 498-0700
  Northbrook *(G-16350)*
Rensel-Chicago Inc ....................... F  773 235-2100
  Chicago *(G-6334)*
Research Technology Intl Co ......... E  847 677-3000
  Lincolnwood *(G-13532)*
Rmf Products Inc ........................... G  630 879-0020
  Batavia *(G-1492)*
▲ Robotics Technologies  Inc ........ E  815 722-7650
  Joliet *(G-12570)*
Rotation Dynamics Corporation ..... E  630 769-9700
  Chicago *(G-6398)*
Screen North Amer Holdings Inc ... F  847 870-7400
  Rolling Meadows *(G-18777)*
Sigma Bio Medics Industries ......... G  847 419-0669
  Buffalo Grove *(G-2770)*
▲ Speedotron Corporation ............. G  630 246-5001
  Bartlett *(G-1378)*
▲ Team Play Inc ............................ F  847 952-7533
  Elk Grove Village *(G-9770)*
Toner Tech Plus ............................. G  815 625-7006
  Rock Falls *(G-18155)*
Trend Setters Ltd .......................... F  309 929-7012
  Tremont *(G-20988)*
▲ Tri Industries Nfp ........................ E  773 754-3100
  Vernon Hills *(G-21213)*
Wesling Products Inc .................... G  773 533-2850
  Chicago *(G-6959)*
Xerox Corporation .......................... D  630 983-0172
  Naperville *(G-15785)*
Xerox Corporation .......................... D  217 355-5460
  Champaign *(G-3563)*
Xerox Corporation .......................... B  847 928-5500
  Rosemont *(G-19043)*
Xerox Corporation .......................... D  630 573-0200
  Oak Brook *(G-16570)*
Xerox Corporation .......................... E  630 573-1000
  Hinsdale *(G-11969)*

### 3873 Watch & Clock Devices & Parts

Chicago Lighthouse Industries ....... D  312 666-1331
  Chicago *(G-4328)*
▲ Hampden Corporation ................ E  312 583-3000
  Chicago *(G-5039)*
Indigo Time .................................... G  847 255-4818
  Mount Prospect *(G-15337)*
Instrument Services Inc ................ G  815 623-2993
  Machesney Park *(G-14082)*
KI Watch Service Inc. .................... G  847 368-8780
  Mount Prospect *(G-15342)*
Lumenite Control Technology ....... F  847 455-1450
  Franklin Park *(G-10518)*
◆ Tellurian Technologies Inc ......... C  847 934-4141
  Arlington Heights *(G-854)*
Zantech Inc .................................... G  309 692-0307
  Peoria *(G-17481)*

## 39 MISCELLANEOUS MANUFACTURING INDUSTRIES

### 3911 Jewelry: Precious Metal

A G Mitchells Jewelers Ltd ............ F  847 394-0820
  Arlington Heights *(G-700)*
A M Lee Inc .................................... G  847 291-1777
  Northbrook *(G-16195)*
Accents By Fred ............................ G  708 366-9850
  Forest Park *(G-10234)*
Afshar Inc ...................................... G  773 645-8922
  Chicago *(G-3781)*

Alan Rocca  Ltd ............................. E  630 323-5800
  Oak Brook *(G-16485)*
▲ Alomar Inc. ................................. G  312 855-0714
  Chicago *(G-3827)*
▲ Award Concepts Inc .................. E  630 513-7801
  Saint Charles *(G-19141)*
Award Emblem Mfg Co Inc ........... G  630 739-0800
  Bolingbrook *(G-2281)*
Azteca Jewelry ............................... G  773 929-0796
  Chicago *(G-4013)*
Bee-Jay Industries Inc ................... F  708 867-4431
  Bloomingdale *(G-2095)*
Bing Yeung Jewelers Inc ............... G  708 749-4800
  Berwyn *(G-2057)*
Blandings Ltd ................................. G  773 478-3542
  Chicago *(G-4122)*
Blando G Mfg Jewelers ................. G  708 387-0014
  Brookfield *(G-2624)*
Bliss Ring Company Inc ................ F  847 446-3440
  Winnetka *(G-22304)*
Burdeens Jewelry Ltd .................... G  847 459-8980
  Buffalo Grove *(G-2671)*
Cabanas Manufacturing Jewelers . G  312 726-0333
  Chicago *(G-4208)*
Casting House  Inc ........................ F  312 782-7160
  Chicago *(G-4252)*
Charles Horberg Jewelers Inc ....... G  312 263-4924
  Chicago *(G-4292)*
D&M Perlman Fine Jwly Gift LLC .. G  847 426-8881
  West Dundee *(G-21795)*
Dalzell & Company ........................ G  815 477-8816
  Crystal Lake *(G-7565)*
David Nelson Exquisite Jewelry .... G  815 741-4702
  Joliet *(G-12483)*
Edgar H Fey Jewelers Inc ............. E  708 352-4115
  Naperville *(G-15651)*
Emerald City Jewelry Inc ............... G  217 222-8896
  Quincy *(G-17826)*
Eve J Alfille Ltd .............................. E  847 869-7920
  Evanston *(G-10035)*
Fashion Craft Corporation ............. E  847 998-0092
  Highland Park *(G-11832)*
Faye Jewellery Chez ..................... G  815 477-1818
  Crystal Lake *(G-7577)*
Fine Gold Mfg Jewelers ................ F  630 323-9600
  Hinsdale *(G-11946)*
Frank S Bender Inc ........................ G  847 441-7370
  Northfield *(G-16399)*
G Blando Jewelers Inc ................... F  630 627-7963
  Countryside *(G-7425)*
General Design Jewelers  Inc ....... G  312 201-9047
  Chicago *(G-4925)*
Georg Jensen Inc. .......................... G  312 642-9160
  Chicago *(G-4941)*
George Erckman Jewelers ............ G  312 263-7380
  Chicago *(G-4942)*
H Watson Jewelry Co .................... G  312 236-1104
  Chicago *(G-5024)*
Hakimian Gem Co ......................... G  312 236-6969
  Chicago *(G-5033)*
Herff Jones  LLC. .......................... F  815 756-4743
  Dekalb *(G-8096)*
Herff Jones  LLC ........................... D  773 463-1144
  Chicago *(G-5079)*
Herff Jones  LLC ........................... E  217 351-9500
  Champaign *(G-3494)*
Herff Jones  LLC ........................... G  708 425-0130
  Oak Lawn *(G-16625)*
Herff Jones  LLC ........................... C  317 612-3705
  Hillside *(G-11918)*
Hustedt Manufacturing Jewelers ... G  217 784-8462
  Gibson City *(G-10903)*
▼ Hy Spreckman & Sons  Inc ....... F  312 236-2173
  Skokie *(G-20013)*
ISA Chicago ................................... G  630 317-7169
  Carol Stream *(G-3175)*
Jamex Jewelry Inc ......................... G  312 726-7867
  Chicago *(G-5275)*
Jason Lau Jewelry ......................... G  312 750-1028
  Chicago *(G-5282)*
John Buechner Inc. ........................ G  312 263-2226
  Chicago *(G-5312)*
Joseph C Wolf ............................... G  312 332-3135
  Chicago *(G-5327)*
Jostens  Inc .................................... G  630 963-3500
  Lisle *(G-13612)*
Jostens Inc ..................................... E  217 483-8989
  Chatham *(G-3623)*
Kaye Lee & Company Inc ............. G  312 236-9686
  Chicago *(G-5365)*

Kesher  Stam ................................. G  773 973-7826
  Chicago *(G-5378)*
La Ron Jewelers ............................ G  312 263-3898
  Chicago *(G-5427)*
Lana Unlimited  Co ........................ G  312 226-7050
  Lake Forest *(G-12923)*
Leo A Bachrach Jewelers Inc ........ G  312 263-3111
  Chicago *(G-5492)*
Lester Lampert  Inc. ....................... E  312 944-6888
  Chicago *(G-5495)*
M B Jewelers Inc ............................ G  312 853-3490
  Chicago *(G-5579)*
Made As Intended Inc ................... G  630 789-3494
  Oak Brook *(G-16538)*
Masud Jewelers Inc ....................... G  312 236-0547
  Chicago *(G-5648)*
Medaowview Ventures II Inc ......... E  847 965-1700
  Morton Grove *(G-15218)*
Mfz Ventures Inc ............................ G  773 247-4611
  Chicago *(G-5715)*
Michael P Jones ............................. G  217 787-7457
  Springfield *(G-20481)*
Michals Accessory Mart Inc .......... G  312 263-0066
  Chicago *(G-5721)*
Mint Masters Inc ............................ E  847 451-1133
  Franklin Park *(G-10534)*
Mtm Jostens Inc ............................. G  815 875-1111
  Princeton *(G-17756)*
Mtm Recognition Corporation ....... C  815 875-1111
  Princeton *(G-17757)*
Norkin Jewelry Co Inc ................... E  312 782-7311
  Chicago *(G-5928)*
Park-Ohio Industries Inc ................ D  708 652-6691
  Chicago *(G-6085)*
Patricia Locke Ltd .......................... F  847 949-2303
  Mundelein *(G-15543)*
Perle & Sons Jewelers Inc ............ G  630 357-3357
  Naperville *(G-15724)*
▲ R S Owens & Co  Inc ................. B  773 282-6000
  Chicago *(G-6273)*
Rahmanims Imports  Inc ............... G  312 236-2200
  Chicago *(G-6284)*
◆ Razny Jewelers  Ltd .................. E  630 932-4900
  Addison *(G-270)*
Richards Fine Jewelry & Design ... G  847 697-4053
  South Elgin *(G-20224)*
Rodger Murphy ............................. G  309 582-2202
  Aledo *(G-372)*
Roger Burke Jewelers Inc ............. F  309 692-0210
  Peoria *(G-17445)*
Rosengard Sue Jwly Design Ltd ... G  312 733-1133
  Chicago *(G-6396)*
Ross Designs Ltd. .......................... G  847 831-7669
  Highland Park *(G-11866)*
S G Nelson & Co ............................ G  630 668-7900
  Wheaton *(G-21979)*
Simon Zelikman ............................. G  847 338-8031
  Oakwood Hills *(G-16728)*
Therese Crowe Design Ltd ........... G  312 269-0039
  Chicago *(G-6711)*
Tommy Ho Jewelers ...................... G  312 368-8593
  Chicago *(G-6739)*
Trebor Enterprises Ltd ................... G  815 235-1700
  Freeport *(G-10693)*
Tri-City Gold Exchange Inc ........... F  708 331-5995
  Harvey *(G-11678)*
Unicorn Designs ............................. G  847 295-5230
  Lake Forest *(G-12976)*
Victor Levy Jewelry Co Inc ........... G  312 782-5297
  Chicago *(G-6894)*
Vintaj Natural Brass Co ................. G  815 776-9300
  Galena *(G-10733)*

### 3914 Silverware, Plated & Stainless Steel Ware

A & J Plating  Inc .......................... G  708 453-9713
  River Grove *(G-18004)*
All American Trophy King Inc ....... F  708 597-2121
  Crestwood *(G-7474)*
AMG International  Inc .................. G  847 439-1001
  Elk Grove Village *(G-9301)*
Baroque Silversmith  Inc ............... G  312 357-2813
  Chicago *(G-4045)*
Budget Signs ................................. F  618 259-4460
  Wood River *(G-22441)*
Captains Emporium Inc ................. G  773 972-7609
  Chicago *(G-4234)*
▲ Empire Bronze Corp ................. F  630 916-9722
  Lombard *(G-13796)*

**Fusion Tech Integrated Inc** D 309 774-4275
Roseville *(G-19045)*
**Mint Masters Inc** E 847 451-1133
Franklin Park *(G-10534)*
**Mtm Recognition Corporation** C 815 875-1111
Princeton *(G-17757)*
▲ **Nelson-Whittaker Ltd** E 815 459-6000
Crystal Lake *(G-7618)*
▲ **RS Owens Div St Regis LLC** D 773 282-6000
Chicago *(G-6407)*
**Rudon Enterprises Inc** G 618 457-0441
Carbondale *(G-3022)*
▲ **Stellar Recognition Inc** D 773 282-8060
Chicago *(G-6588)*
▼ **Suburban Surgical Co** C 847 537-9320
Wheeling *(G-22159)*
▲ **Tri Star Metals LLC** E 815 232-1600
Freeport *(G-10694)*
**Trophies By George** G 630 497-1212
Bartlett *(G-1381)*

### 3915 Jewelers Findings & Lapidary Work

**144 International Inc** F 847 426-8881
West Dundee *(G-21794)*
**Alex and Ani LLC** G 630 574-2329
Oak Brook *(G-16486)*
**Branchfield Casting** E 309 932-2278
Galva *(G-10786)*
▲ **C D Nelson Consulting Inc** G 847 487-4870
Wauconda *(G-21449)*
▲ **Diamond Die & Bevel Cutng LLC** E 224 387-3200
Wheeling *(G-22034)*
**Dimend Scaasi Ltd** G 312 857-1700
Chicago *(G-4604)*
**Edmund D Schmelzie & Sons** G 312 782-7230
Chicago *(G-4697)*
**Israel Levy Diamnd Cutters Inc** E 312 368-8540
Chicago *(G-5244)*
**M B Jewelers Inc** G 312 853-3490
Chicago *(G-5579)*
**Micro Lapping & Grinding Co** E 847 455-5446
Franklin Park *(G-10531)*
**North American Jewelers Inc** D 312 425-9000
Chicago *(G-5933)*
▲ **Precise Lapping Grinding Corp** F 708 615-0240
Melrose Park *(G-14683)*
**S G Nelson & Co** G 630 668-7900
Wheaton *(G-21979)*
**Steinmetz R (us) Ltd** G 312 332-0990
Chicago *(G-6586)*

### 3931 Musical Instruments

**American Plating & Mfg Co** F 773 890-4907
Chicago *(G-3869)*
**Analog Outfitters Inc** G 217 202-6134
Rantoul *(G-17917)*
**Berghaus Pipe Organ Builders** E 708 544-4052
Bellwood *(G-1698)*
▲ **Buzard Pipe Organ Builders LLC** F 217 352-1955
Champaign *(G-3459)*
**C P O Inc** G 630 898-7733
Aurora *(G-1123)*
**Daves Electronic Service** F 217 283-5010
Hoopeston *(G-12109)*
▲ **Engelhardt-Link Inc** G 847 593-5850
Elk Grove Village *(G-9459)*
**Flynn Guitars Inc** G 800 585-9555
Wilmette *(G-22252)*
**Fugate Inc** G 309 472-6830
Washington *(G-21382)*
▲ **Hammond Suzuki Usa Inc** E 630 543-0277
Addison *(G-141)*
**Harrison Harmonicas LLC** G 312 379-9427
Chicago *(G-5049)*
▲ **Intelligent Instrument Sy** G 630 323-3911
Burr Ridge *(G-2857)*
**Interntnal Mscal Suppliers Inc** G 847 774-2938
Glen Ellyn *(G-10974)*
**Lothson Guitars** G 815 756-2031
Dekalb *(G-8102)*
▲ **Lyon & Healy Harps Inc** G 312 786-1881
Chicago *(G-5574)*
▲ **Lyon & Healy Holding Corp** E 312 786-1881
Chicago *(G-5575)*
**Mechanical Music Corp** F 847 398-5444
Arlington Heights *(G-801)*
▲ **Midi Music Center Inc** E 708 352-3388
Wood Dale *(G-22400)*
**Music Connection Inc** G 708 364-7590
Orland Park *(G-16878)*
**Music Solutions** F 630 759-3033
Bolingbrook *(G-2349)*
**North Okaw Woodworking** G 217 856-2178
Humboldt *(G-12129)*
▲ **Peterson Elctr-Msical Pdts Inc** E 708 388-3311
Alsip *(G-507)*
▲ **Pjla Music** G 847 382-3212
Barrington *(G-1297)*
▲ **Schaff International LLC** E 847 438-4560
Lake Zurich *(G-13125)*
**Schilke Music Products Inc** E 708 343-8858
Melrose Park *(G-14692)*
**Schneider Pipe Organs Inc** G 217 871-4807
Kenney *(G-12664)*
**Suntimez Entertainment** G 630 747-0712
Cicero *(G-7232)*
**Tom Crown Mute Co** G 708 352-1039
La Grange *(G-12747)*
**Trick Percussion Products Inc** G 847 342-2019
Arlington Heights *(G-858)*
**Umphreys McGee Inc** G 773 880-0024
Chicago *(G-6809)*
**W & W Musical Instrument Co** E 773 278-4210
Chicago *(G-6917)*
▲ **Wicks Organ Company** E 618 654-2191
Highland *(G-11819)*
▲ **William Harris Lee & Co Inc** E 312 786-0459
Chicago *(G-6984)*
**Windy City Mutes** G 630 616-8634
Bensenville *(G-2017)*

### 3942 Dolls & Stuffed Toys

▲ **First & Main Inc** E 630 587-1000
Saint Charles *(G-19184)*
▲ **Hunter Mfg LLP** D 859 254-7573
Lake Forest *(G-12912)*
▲ **Jiminees Inc** G 630 295-8002
Roselle *(G-18949)*
▲ **North American Bear Co Inc** E 773 376-3457
Chicago *(G-5930)*
**Shawnimals LLC** G 312 235-2625
Chicago *(G-6492)*
**Unique Novelty & Manufacturing** G 217 538-2014
Fillmore *(G-10190)*
**Windy City Parrot Inc** G 312 492-9673
Chicago *(G-6998)*

### 3944 Games, Toys & Children's Vehicles

▲ **Accurail Inc** F 630 365-6400
Elburn *(G-8873)*
▲ **Aeromax Industries Inc** G 847 756-4085
Lake Barrington *(G-12798)*
**AGS Partners LLC** D 630 446-7777
Itasca *(G-12224)*
**Airgun Designs USA Inc** G 847 520-7507
Cary *(G-3324)*
▲ **Amav Enterprises Ltd** G 630 761-3077
Batavia *(G-1410)*
**American Science & Surplus Inc** F 773 763-0313
Chicago *(G-3871)*
**American Specialty Toy** G 312 222-0984
Chicago *(G-3876)*
**Aqua Golf Inc** G 217 824-2097
Taylorville *(G-20832)*
**Arkadian Gaming LLC** G 708 377-5656
Orland Park *(G-16844)*
**Ayla Group Inc** G 630 954-9432
Bartlett *(G-1334)*
**Belco International Toy Co** G 847 256-6818
Wilmette *(G-22243)*
**Branch Lines Ltd** G 847 256-4294
Wilmette *(G-22245)*
**Budd AA Inc** G 630 879-1740
North Aurora *(G-16121)*
**Central RC Hobbies** G 309 686-8004
Peoria *(G-17339)*
**Chicago Contract Bridge Assn** G 630 355-5560
Naperville *(G-15626)*
**Chicago Kite** G 773 467-1428
Chicago *(G-4325)*
**Cino Incorporated** G 630 377-7242
Saint Charles *(G-19153)*
**Circuitron Inc** G 815 886-9010
Romeoville *(G-18812)*
**Citizens Bank National Assn** G 708 755-0741
Chicago Heights *(G-7092)*
▲ **Click-Block Corporation** E 847 749-1651
Rolling Meadows *(G-18723)*
**Conley Precision Engines Inc** F 630 858-3160
Glen Ellyn *(G-10964)*
**Craft World Inc** G 800 654-6114
Loves Park *(G-13928)*
**Diecasm LLC** G 877 343-2276
Buffalo Grove *(G-2687)*
▲ **Du Bro Products Inc** E 847 526-2136
Wauconda *(G-21456)*
**E J Kupjack & Associates Inc** G 847 823-6661
Chicago *(G-4666)*
**Educational Insights Inc** E 847 573-8400
Vernon Hills *(G-21158)*
**Edwin Waldmire & Virginia** G 217 498-9375
Rochester *(G-18117)*
▲ **Fun Incorporated** E 773 745-3837
Wheeling *(G-22059)*
▲ **Gamenamics Inc** F 847 844-7688
Elgin *(G-9041)*
**Gameplan Inc** G 877 284-9180
Northbrook *(G-16263)*
**Gamestop Inc** G 773 568-0457
Chicago *(G-4912)*
**Gamestop Corp** G 618 258-8611
Wood River *(G-22443)*
**Gamestop Corp** G 773 545-9602
Chicago *(G-4913)*
**Great Planes Model Mfg Inc** E 217 367-2707
Urbana *(G-21090)*
**Harris Skokie** G 847 675-6300
Skokie *(G-20012)*
▲ **Henes Usa Inc** D 312 448-6130
Glenview *(G-11136)*
**Hobbico Inc** E 217 367-2707
Urbana *(G-21091)*
**Huff & Puff Industries Ltd** G 847 381-8255
North Barrington *(G-16152)*
**Ing Bank Fsb** G 312 981-1236
Chicago *(G-5190)*
◆ **Jcw Investments Inc** G 708 478-7323
Orland Park *(G-16870)*
▲ **Kaskey Kids Inc** G 847 441-3092
Winnetka *(G-22308)*
**Lake County C V Joints Inc** G 847 537-7588
Wheeling *(G-22088)*
▲ **Liberty Classics Inc** G 847 367-1288
Libertyville *(G-13342)*
**Mackin Group LLC** G 847 245-4201
Lake Villa *(G-13019)*
**Made By Hands Inc** G 773 761-4200
Chicago *(G-5595)*
▲ **Mayfair Games Inc** E 847 677-6655
Skokie *(G-20035)*
▲ **Merlin Technologies Inc** G 630 232-9223
Rockford *(G-18493)*
**Midwest Rail Junction** G 815 963-0200
Rockford *(G-18506)*
**Narita Manufacturing Inc** F 248 345-1777
Belvidere *(G-1773)*
▲ **Neat-OH International LLC** F 847 441-4290
Northfield *(G-16411)*
▲ **Nelson-Whittaker Ltd** E 815 459-6000
Crystal Lake *(G-7618)*
**Non Violent Toys Inc** G 847 835-9066
Glencoe *(G-11004)*
**Novomatic Americas Sales LLC** G 224 802-2974
Mount Prospect *(G-15356)*
**Oakridge Corporation** G 630 435-5900
Lemont *(G-13245)*
**Octura Models Inc** G 847 674-7351
Skokie *(G-20049)*
**Pacific Cycle Inc** C 618 393-2508
Olney *(G-16789)*
**Petronics Inc** G 608 630-6527
Champaign *(G-3524)*
**Picture Perfect Puzzles LLC** G 847 838-0848
Lake Villa *(G-13022)*
**Pro-Line Winning Ways & Penlan** G 309 745-8530
Washington *(G-21388)*
**Puzzles Bus Off Solutions Inc** G 773 891-7688
Chicago *(G-6230)*
**Qsimaginationstation** G 708 928-9622
Dolton *(G-8376)*
**Quicker Engineering** G 815 675-6516
Spring Grove *(G-20360)*
**Racine Paper Box Manufacturing** E 773 227-3900
Chicago *(G-6278)*
▲ **Radio Flyer Inc** E 773 637-7100
Chicago *(G-6279)*
▲ **Rapid Displays Inc** C 773 927-5000
Chicago *(G-6291)*
◆ **Raw Thrills Inc** D 847 679-8373
Skokie *(G-20071)*

S I C

Employee Codes: A=Over 500 employees, B=251-500
C=101-250, D=51-100, E=20-50, F=10-19, G=3-9
2017 Harris Illinois
Industrial Directory
1125

**Reel Life Dvd LLC** G 708 579-1360
Western Springs *(G-21872)*

**Rocking Horse** G 773 486-0011
Chicago *(G-6375)*

**Rust-Oleum Corporation** D 815 967-4258
Rockford *(G-18600)*

**▲ Safe Traffic System Inc** G 847 233-0365
Lincolnwood *(G-13536)*

**Scale Railroad Equipment** G 630 682-9170
Carol Stream *(G-3234)*

**▲ Science Supply Solutions** G 847 981-5500
Bensenville *(G-1989)*

**Sharin Toy Company** E 847 676-1200
Lincolnwood *(G-13538)*

**▲ Shure Products Inc** F 773 227-1001
Chicago *(G-6504)*

**▲ Standard Container Co of Edgar** E 847 438-1510
Lake Zurich *(G-13134)*

**Star Sleigh** F 630 858-2576
Glen Ellyn *(G-10991)*

**Sunburst Technology Corp** G 800 321-7511
Elgin *(G-9197)*

**▲ Sunnywood Incorporated** G 815 675-9777
Spring Grove *(G-20366)*

**▲ Testor Corporation** D 815 962-6654
Rockford *(G-18644)*

**Tractronics** G 630 527-0000
Naperville *(G-15767)*

**▲ Trivial Development Corp** E 630 860-2500
Itasca *(G-12368)*

**Video Gaming Technologies Inc** G 847 776-3516
Palatine *(G-17085)*

**Virtu** G 773 235-3790
Chicago *(G-6900)*

**Wiliams Interactive LLC** C 773 961-1920
Chicago *(G-6978)*

**Zipwhaa Inc** G 630 898-4330
Palatine *(G-17092)*

## 3949 Sporting & Athletic Goods, NEC

**A W H Sales** G 847 869-0950
Niles *(G-15954)*

**Abbacus Inc** E 815 637-9222
Machesney Park *(G-14048)*

**All American Athletics Ltd** G 815 432-8326
Watseka *(G-21413)*

**Allied Scoring Tables Inc** G 815 654-8807
Loves Park *(G-13918)*

**▲ Altamont Co** D 800 626-5774
Thomasboro *(G-20859)*

**◆ Amer Sports Company** B 773 714-6400
Chicago *(G-3846)*

**Andrew C Arnold** G 815 220-0282
Peru *(G-17499)*

**◆ Arachnid 360 LLC** E 815 654-0212
Loves Park *(G-13921)*

**▲ Athletic Specialties Inc** G 847 487-7880
Wauconda *(G-21444)*

**▲ Bell Racing Usa LLC** G 217 239-5355
Champaign *(G-3456)*

**◆ Bell Sports** G 309 693-2746
Rantoul *(G-17919)*

**Bell Sports Inc** D 217 893-9300
Rantoul *(G-17920)*

**Best Technology Systems Inc** F 815 254-9554
Plainfield *(G-17582)*

**◆ Big Dog Treestand Inc** G 309 263-6800
Morton *(G-15154)*

**Biospawn Lure Co** G 773 458-0752
Evanston *(G-10016)*

**Blitz Lures LLC** G 309 256-1574
Dunlap *(G-8566)*

**Bluebird Lanes** G 773 582-2828
Chicago *(G-4128)*

**Bluetown Skateboard Co LLC** G 312 718-4786
Chicago *(G-4130)*

**Bob Folder Lures Co** F 217 787-1116
Springfield *(G-20398)*

**Bobs Business Inc** G 630 238-5790
Bensenville *(G-1845)*

**▲ Boss Manufacturing Holdings** F 309 852-2781
Kewanee *(G-12675)*

**Bowl-Tronics Enterprises Inc** G 847 741-4500
Elgin *(G-8970)*

**Bowlmor AMF Corp** D 708 456-4100
River Grove *(G-18007)*

**Bowlmor AMF Corp** D 847 367-1600
Vernon Hills *(G-21152)*

**Bowtree Inc** G 217 430-8884
Quincy *(G-17807)*

**Brg Sports Inc** F 217 893-9300
Rantoul *(G-17921)*

**▲ Brg Sports Inc** C 831 461-7500
Rosemont *(G-18990)*

**Brg Sports Inc** G 217 819-5187
Champaign *(G-3458)*

**Brunswick Corporation** A 847 288-3300
Franklin Park *(G-10418)*

**Brunswick Corporation** B 847 288-3300
Franklin Park *(G-10419)*

**◆ Brunswick Corporation** B 847 735-4700
Lake Forest *(G-12888)*

**Brunswick International Ltd** G 847 735-4700
Lake Forest *(G-12889)*

**BSN Sports LLC** G 217 788-0914
Springfield *(G-20400)*

**Buffalo Arms** G 630 969-1796
Downers Grove *(G-8399)*

**Burt Coyote Co** F 309 358-1602
Yates City *(G-22646)*

**Cast Industries Inc** E 217 522-8292
Springfield *(G-20409)*

**▲ Ccsi International Inc** E 815 544-8385
Garden Prairie *(G-10793)*

**City Sports & Stage Door Dance** E 708 687-9950
Oak Forest *(G-16576)*

**Collinsville Sports Store** G 618 345-5588
Collinsville *(G-7316)*

**Compound Bow Rifle Sight Inc** G 618 526-4427
Breese *(G-2442)*

**Court & Slope Inc** G 847 697-3600
Elgin *(G-9005)*

**Crooked Creek Outdoors** G 309 837-3000
Macomb *(G-14123)*

**Crown Gym Mats Inc** F 847 381-8282
Lake Barrington *(G-12803)*

**Custom Golf By Tanis** G 708 481-4433
Matteson *(G-14369)*

**Custom Rods By Grandt Ltd** G 847 577-0848
Arlington Heights *(G-741)*

**Dark Speed Works** G 312 772-3275
Wheaton *(G-21943)*

**David Hall** E 309 797-9721
Moline *(G-14924)*

**Davis Athletic Equipment Co** F 708 563-9006
Bedford Park *(G-1547)*

**Dj Illinois River Valley Calls** G 309 348-2112
Pekin *(G-17260)*

**Donaldson & Associates Inc** G 708 633-1090
Lockport *(G-13710)*

**Draves Investment Inc** G 888 678-0251
Effingham *(G-8833)*

**Dreamworld Golf** G 847 803-4757
Des Plaines *(G-8186)*

**EJL Custom Golf Clubs Inc** G 630 654-8887
Willowbrook *(G-22210)*

**▲ Empire Comfort Systems Inc** C 618 233-7420
Belleville *(G-1631)*

**▲ Enjoylife Inc** G 847 966-3377
Morton Grove *(G-15196)*

**Evergreen Pool & Spa LLC** G 618 247-3555
Sandoval *(G-19356)*

**▼ Flex Court International Inc** F 309 852-0899
Kewanee *(G-12684)*

**◆ Flora Bowl** G 618 662-4561
Flora *(G-10206)*

**Freemans Sports Inc** G 630 553-0515
Yorkville *(G-22660)*

**Geneva Running Outfitters LLC** G 331 248-0221
Geneva *(G-10831)*

**▼ Gill Athletics** G 800 637-3090
Champaign *(G-3487)*

**▲ Golfco Inc** E 773 777-7877
Chicago *(G-4976)*

**Good Times Roll** G 217 285-4885
Pittsfield *(G-17569)*

**H2o Pod Inc** G 630 240-1769
Glen Ellyn *(G-10972)*

**Hampster Industries Inc** G 866 280-2287
Mundelein *(G-15507)*

**Headball Inc** G 618 628-2656
Belleville *(G-1634)*

**Heartland Inspection Company** G 630 788-3607
Sycamore *(G-20799)*

**Hunter Marketing Inc** G 630 541-8480
Lisle *(G-13601)*

**▲ Hunter Mfg LLP** D 859 254-7573
Lake Forest *(G-12912)*

**▲ Hunter-Nusport Inc** G 815 254-7520
Plainfield *(G-17607)*

**Illinois State Usbc Wba** G 309 827-6355
Bloomington *(G-2182)*

**Industryreadycom Inc** G 773 575-7001
Chicago *(G-5181)*

**▲ Infiniti Golf** G 630 520-0626
West Chicago *(G-21718)*

**International Wood Products** G 630 530-6164
Aurora *(G-1034)*

**J & C Premier Concepts Inc** G 309 523-2344
Port Byron *(G-17720)*

**Jack & Lidias Resort Inc** G 847 356-1389
Lake Villa *(G-13017)*

**James G Carter** G 309 543-2634
Havana *(G-11697)*

**Jerry H Simpson** G 618 654-3235
Highland *(G-11798)*

**Jerrys Pro Shop Inc** G 708 597-1144
Alsip *(G-476)*

**John Killough Dpm Cws** G 217 348-3339
Charleston *(G-3602)*

**Kayser Lure Corp** G 217 964-2110
Ursa *(G-21105)*

**▲ Kranos Corporation** D 217 324-3978
Litchfield *(G-13691)*

**L L Bean Inc** G 847 568-3600
Skokie *(G-20023)*

**▼ Life Fitness Inc** B 847 288-3300
Rosemont *(G-19010)*

**Life Fitness Inc** G 847 288-3300
Franklin Park *(G-10516)*

**Life Fitness Inc** C 800 494-6344
Rosemont *(G-19011)*

**◆ Litania Sports Group Inc** C 217 367-8438
Champaign *(G-3510)*

**▲ Luck E Strike Corporation** F 630 313-2408
Geneva *(G-10847)*

**Moreno and Sons Inc** G 815 725-8600
Crest Hill *(G-7464)*

**Nameplate Robinson & Precision** G 847 678-2255
Franklin Park *(G-10538)*

**Natural Cedar Products Inc** G 815 416-0223
Morris *(G-15122)*

**▲ New Archery Products LLC** D 708 488-2500
Forest Park *(G-10251)*

**Nichols Net & Twine Inc** G 618 797-0211
Granite City *(G-11298)*

**Normal Cornbelters** G 309 451-3432
Normal *(G-16079)*

**Oak Leaf Outdoors Inc** F 309 691-9653
Brimfield *(G-2548)*

**Oban Composites LLC** G 866 607-0284
Chicago *(G-5963)*

**Obies Tackle Co Inc** G 618 234-5638
Belleville *(G-1662)*

**▲ Official Issue Inc** G 847 795-1066
Harwood Heights *(G-11688)*

**▲ Orthotech Sports - Med Eqp Inc** F 618 942-6611
Herrin *(G-11752)*

**Orvis Company Inc** F 312 440-0662
Chicago *(G-6019)*

**▼ Par Golf Supply Inc** E 847 891-1222
Schaumburg *(G-19681)*

**▲ Park View Manufacturing Corp** D 618 548-9054
Salem *(G-19342)*

**Peak Healthcare Advisors LLC** G 646 479-0005
Chicago *(G-6093)*

**Perry Adult Living Inc** G 618 542-5421
Du Quoin *(G-8557)*

**Pistoleercom LLC** G 618 288-4649
Maryville *(G-14346)*

**Plastech Inc** F 630 595-7222
Bensenville *(G-1964)*

**Platinum Aquatech Ltd** F 847 537-3800
Wheeling *(G-22124)*

**Polyair Inter Pack Inc** D 773 995-1818
Chicago *(G-6153)*

**Pro Circle Golf Centers Inc** G 815 675-2747
Spring Grove *(G-20359)*

**ProAm Sports Products** G 708 841-4200
Dolton *(G-8375)*

**▲ Protactic Golf Enterprises** F 708 209-1120
River Forest *(G-17999)*

**Prototech Industries Inc** G 847 223-9808
Gurnee *(G-11494)*

**Qcfec LLC** G 309 517-1158
Moline *(G-14964)*

**▲ Quality Sport Nets Inc** G 618 533-0700
Centralia *(G-3428)*

**Quality Targets** G 618 245-6515
Farina *(G-10177)*

**Rainbo Sports LLC** G 847 784-9857
Northfield *(G-16416)*

**Rainbo Sports LLC** E 847 998-1000
Northbrook *(G-16351)*

**Rainbow Midwest Inc** G 847 955-9300
Vernon Hills *(G-21191)*

**Rasoi Resturaunt** G 847 455-8888
Roselle *(G-18965)*

**Reagent Chemical & RES Inc** G 618 271-8140
East Saint Louis *(G-8766)*

**Reeves Lure Co** G 217 864-3493
Lovington *(G-14012)*

**Reflex Fitness Products Inc** F 309 756-1050
Milan *(G-14802)*

**Restoring Path** F 773 424-7023
Chicago *(G-6338)*

▲ **Riddell Inc** C 847 292-1472
Rosemont *(G-19027)*

**Road Runner Sports Inc** F 847 719-8941
Palatine *(G-17068)*

**Roger Jolly Skateboards** G 618 277-7113
Belleville *(G-1671)*

**Royal Fiberglass Pools Inc** D 618 266-7089
Dix *(G-8318)*

**Scuba Sports Inc** G 217 787-3483
Springfield *(G-20519)*

**Sentry Pool & Chemical Supply** E 309 797-9721
Moline *(G-14970)*

◆ **Septic Solutions Inc** G 217 925-5992
Dieterich *(G-8314)*

**Shuffle Tech International LLC** G 312 787-7780
Chicago *(G-6503)*

**Siggs Rigs** G 847 456-4012
Crystal Lake *(G-7651)*

**Soccer House** G 847 998-0088
Glenview *(G-11204)*

▲ **South Bend Sporting Goods Inc** E 847 715-1400
Northbrook *(G-16367)*

**Southern Illinois Miners** F 618 969-8506
Marion *(G-14289)*

▲ **Strikeforce Bowling LLC** E 800 297-8555
Broadview *(G-2615)*

**Superior Table Pad Co** G 773 248-7232
Chicago *(G-6636)*

**Terre Haute Tent & Awning Inc** F 812 235-6068
South Holland *(G-20309)*

**The Athletic Equipment Source** E 630 587-9333
Saint Charles *(G-19281)*

**Total Control Sports Inc** G 708 486-5800
Broadview *(G-2617)*

**True Lacrosse LLC** G 630 359-3857
Lombard *(G-13874)*

▲ **Tweeten Fibre Co** E 312 733-7878
Chicago *(G-6795)*

**U Camp Products** G 618 228-5080
Aviston *(G-1249)*

▲ **U S Weight Inc** E 618 392-0408
Olney *(G-16799)*

▲ **Ultra Play Systems Inc** E 618 282-8200
Red Bud *(G-17951)*

**United Sportsmens Company** G 815 599-5690
Freeport *(G-10696)*

▲ **Unlimited Wares Inc** F 773 234-4867
Morton Grove *(G-15242)*

**US Golf Manufacturing** G 309 797-9820
Moline *(G-14974)*

**Varisport Inc** G 847 480-1366
Northbrook *(G-16383)*

**Wagner International LLC** G 224 619-9247
Vernon Hills *(G-21216)*

**Warthog Inc** G 815 540-7197
Rockford *(G-18673)*

**Welkins LLC** G 877 319-3504
Downers Grove *(G-8543)*

**Wilson Sporting Goods Co** C 773 714-6500
Chicago *(G-6991)*

▲ **Wilson Sporting Goods Co** B 773 714-6400
Chicago *(G-6990)*

**Woodland Fence Forest Pdts Inc** G 630 393-2220
Warrenville *(G-21369)*

**World Class Technologies Inc** G 312 758-3114
Chicago *(G-7029)*

**Xmt Solutions LLC** G 703 338-9422
Chicago *(G-7046)*

**Zarc International Inc** F 309 807-2565
Minonk *(G-14835)*

## *3951 Pens & Mechanical Pencils*

**Alexander Manufacturing Co** D 309 728-2224
Towanda *(G-20978)*

▲ **Eversharp Pen Company** E 847 366-5030
Franklin Park *(G-10466)*

**Fayco Enterprises Inc** E 618 283-0638
Vandalia *(G-21113)*

**Pilot Corporation of America** G 773 792-1111
Park Ridge *(G-17216)*

▲ **Premier Packaging Corp** G 815 469-7951
Frankfort *(G-10352)*

◆ **Sanford LP** A 770 418-7000
Downers Grove *(G-8518)*

▲ **Techgraphic Solutions Inc** F 309 693-9400
Peoria *(G-17467)*

▲ **U Mark Inc** E 618 235-7500
Belleville *(G-1683)*

## *3952 Lead Pencils, Crayons & Artist's Mtrls*

**Alexander Manufacturing Co** D 309 728-2224
Towanda *(G-20978)*

▲ **Badger Air Brush Co** D 847 678-3104
Franklin Park *(G-10409)*

**Bio Packaging Films LLC** F 847 566-4444
Mundelein *(G-15477)*

**Chicago Ink & Research Co Inc** G 847 395-1078
Antioch *(G-628)*

**Cushing and Company** E 312 266-8228
Chicago *(G-4518)*

▲ **Duro Art Industries Inc** D 773 743-3430
Chicago *(G-4657)*

◆ **E W Enterprises Inc** G 618 345-2244
Collinsville *(G-7320)*

**Egan Visual/West Inc** G 800 266-2387
Chicago *(G-4704)*

**Erasermitt Incorporated** G 312 842-2855
Chicago *(G-4771)*

**Fernandez Windows Corp** G 773 762-2365
Chicago *(G-4837)*

▲ **Graphic Chemical & Ink Co** F 630 832-6004
Villa Park *(G-21257)*

**Hobbico Inc** E 217 367-2707
Urbana *(G-21091)*

**Hydro Ink Corp** G 847 674-0057
Skokie *(G-20014)*

**James Howard Co** G 815 497-2831
Compton *(G-7366)*

▲ **Lectro Stik Corp** E 630 894-1355
Glendale Heights *(G-11040)*

▲ **Leisure Time Products Inc** G 847 287-2863
Prospect Heights *(G-17782)*

**Miller Pallet** F 217 589-4411
Roodhouse *(G-18883)*

**Moldworks Inc** G 815 520-8819
Roscoe *(G-18908)*

**On Paint It Company** G 219 765-5639
Dekalb *(G-8112)*

▲ **Paasche Airbrush Co** D 773 867-9191
Chicago *(G-6048)*

◆ **Polyform Products Company** E 847 427-0020
Elk Grove Village *(G-9685)*

**Rust-Oleum Corporation** D 815 967-4258
Rockford *(G-18600)*

◆ **Sanford LP** A 770 418-7000
Downers Grove *(G-8518)*

**Stentech Inc** G 630 833-4747
Elmhurst *(G-9944)*

▲ **Testor Corporation** D 815 962-6654
Rockford *(G-18644)*

## *3953 Marking Devices*

**A & E Rubber Stamp Corp** G 312 575-1416
Chicago *(G-3679)*

**A 1 Marking Products** G 309 762-6096
Moline *(G-14916)*

**A To Z Engraving Co Inc** G 847 526-7396
Wauconda *(G-21435)*

**ABM Marking Services Ltd** G 618 277-3773
Belleville *(G-1607)*

**All-Brite Sign Co Inc** F 309 829-1551
Normal *(G-16063)*

**Anderson Safford Mkg Graphics** F 847 827-8968
Des Plaines *(G-8150)*

**B&H Machine Inc** F 618 281-3737
Columbia *(G-7351)*

**Bendsen Signs & Graphics Inc** F 217 877-2345
Decatur *(G-7845)*

**Bertco Enterprises Inc** G 618 234-9283
Belleville *(G-1614)*

**Blue Monkey Graphics Inc** G 708 488-9501
Forest Park *(G-10235)*

▲ **C H Hanson Company** D 630 848-2000
Naperville *(G-15613)*

**C H Hanson Company** F 630 848-2000
Naperville *(G-15614)*

**Chicago Ink & Research Co Inc** G 847 395-1078
Antioch *(G-628)*

**Chicago Silk Screen Sup Co Inc** E 312 666-1213
Chicago *(G-4349)*

**Custom Cut Stencil Company Inc** G 618 277-5077
Belleville *(G-1622)*

**Dans Rubber Stamp & Signs** G 815 964-5603
Rockford *(G-18333)*

**Education Partners Project Ltd** G 773 675-6643
Chicago *(G-4701)*

**Gadge Signs Inc** G 815 462-4490
New Lenox *(G-15882)*

**Hookset Enterprises LLC** G 224 374-1936
Northbrook *(G-16271)*

**Iemco Corporation** G 773 728-4400
Chicago *(G-5145)*

**Illinois Tool Works Inc** D 618 997-1716
Marion *(G-14269)*

◆ **Jackson Marking Products Co** F 618 242-7901
Mount Vernon *(G-15417)*

**Joes Printing** G 773 545-6063
Chicago *(G-5309)*

**K and A Graphics Inc** G 847 244-2345
Gurnee *(G-11463)*

**Kellogg Printing Co** F 309 734-8388
Monmouth *(G-15016)*

**Keneal Industries Inc** F 815 886-1300
Romeoville *(G-18834)*

▲ **Keson Industries Inc** E 630 820-4200
Aurora *(G-1042)*

**Kiwi Coders Corp** E 847 541-4511
Wheeling *(G-22085)*

**Letters Unlimited Inc** G 847 891-7811
Schaumburg *(G-19615)*

**Mich Enterprises Inc** F 630 616-9000
Wood Dale *(G-22399)*

◆ **Millennium Marking Company** E 847 806-1750
Elk Grove Village *(G-9629)*

**Nameplate Robinson & Precision** G 847 678-2255
Franklin Park *(G-10538)*

**Nathan Winston Service Inc** G 815 758-4545
Dekalb *(G-8109)*

**National Rubber Stamp Co Inc** G 773 281-6522
Chicago *(G-5868)*

**Navitor Inc** B 800 323-0253
Harwood Heights *(G-11687)*

**Nelson - Harkins Inds Inc** E 773 478-6243
Chicago *(G-5884)*

▲ **Pro-Pak Industries Inc** F 630 876-1050
West Chicago *(G-21761)*

**Professional Sales Associates** G 847 487-1900
Wauconda *(G-21493)*

▼ **Promoframes LLC** G 866 566-7224
Schaumburg *(G-19701)*

**Pylon Plastics Inc** G 630 968-6374
Lisle *(G-13646)*

**Rebechini Studio Inc** F 847 364-8600
Elk Grove Village *(G-9711)*

**Richards Sthman Rbr Stamps LLC** G 217 522-6801
Springfield *(G-20512)*

**S and S Associates Inc** G 847 584-0033
Elk Grove Village *(G-9722)*

**Shawver Press Inc** G 815 772-4700
Morrison *(G-15148)*

**Take Your Mark Sports LLC** G 708 655-0525
Western Springs *(G-21874)*

▲ **U Mark Inc** E 618 235-7500
Belleville *(G-1683)*

**Village Press Inc** G 847 362-1856
Libertyville *(G-13399)*

▲ **Wagner Zip-Change Inc** E 708 681-4100
Melrose Park *(G-14706)*

**Weakley Printing & Sign Shop** G 847 473-4466
North Chicago *(G-16189)*

## *3955 Carbon Paper & Inked Ribbons*

**Active Office Solutions** F 773 539-3333
Chicago *(G-3741)*

**Aim Graphic Machinery Ltd** F 847 215-8000
Buffalo Grove *(G-2652)*

**Allen Paper Company** G 312 454-4500
Chicago *(G-3812)*

**Alternative TS** G 618 257-0230
Belleville *(G-1608)*

**Cartridge World Decatur** G 217 875-0465
Decatur *(G-7852)*

**Dauphin Enterprise Inc** G 630 893-6300
Bloomingdale *(G-2101)*

Employee Codes: A=Over 500 employees, B=251-500
C=101-250, D=51-100, E=20-50, F=10-19, G=3-9

2017 Harris Illinois
Industrial Directory

1127

**Illinois Tool Works Inc** E 708 720-0300
Frankfort *(G-10333)*
**Ink Stop Inc** G 847 478-0631
Buffalo Grove *(G-2709)*
**Laser Innovations Inc** F 217 522-8580
Springfield *(G-20467)*
**Nashua Corporation** D 847 692-9130
Park Ridge *(G-17211)*
**Next Day Toner Supplies Inc** E 708 478-1000
Orland Park *(G-16879)*
**▲ Rpt Toner LLC** E 630 694-0400
Bensenville *(G-1982)*
**▼ Tonerhead Inc** E 815 331-3200
Spring Grove *(G-20369)*

### *3961 Costume Jewelry & Novelties*

**Acme Button & Buttonhole Co** G 773 907-8400
Chicago *(G-3731)*
**◆ Alessco Inc** F 773 327-7919
Chicago *(G-3801)*
**Anthos and Co LLC** G 773 744-6813
Inverness *(G-12202)*
**Bee-Jay Industries Inc** F 708 867-4431
Bloomingdale *(G-2095)*
**Bird Dog Bay Inc** G 312 631-3108
Chicago *(G-4111)*
**Blandings Ltd** G 773 478-3542
Chicago *(G-4122)*
**D & D Sukach Inc** G 815 895-3377
Sycamore *(G-20790)*
**Dan De Tash Knits** G 708 970-6238
Maywood *(G-14424)*
**Daniels Jewelry & Mfg Co** G 847 998-5222
Glenview *(G-11120)*
**▲ Diamondaire Corp** G 630 355-7464
Saint Charles *(G-19172)*
**Faiths Designs** G 773 768-5804
Chicago *(G-4810)*
**Hustedt Manufacturing Jewelers** G 217 784-8462
Gibson City *(G-10903)*
**Jewerly and Beyond** G 312 833-6785
Schaumburg *(G-19588)*
**Jordan Gold Inc** G 708 430-7008
Oak Lawn *(G-16628)*
**JP Leatherworks Inc** G 847 317-9804
Deerfield *(G-8022)*
**K Fleye Designs** G 773 531-0716
Chicago *(G-5342)*
**Medical ID Fashions Company** G 847 404-6789
Deerfield *(G-8035)*
**Pearl Perfect Inc** E 847 679-6251
Morton Grove *(G-15227)*
**▲ R S Owens & Co Inc** B 773 282-6000
Chicago *(G-6273)*
**Replacement Services LLC** F 618 398-9880
Belleville *(G-1669)*
**Ribbon Supply Comp** F 773 237-7979
Chicago *(G-6350)*
**S & S Keytax Inc** F 708 656-9221
Chicago *(G-6421)*
**Smart Creations Inc** G 847 433-3451
Highland Park *(G-11869)*
**Solari R Mfg Jewelers** G 847 823-4354
Park Ridge *(G-17222)*
**▲ Sunnywood Incorporated** G 815 675-9777
Spring Grove *(G-20366)*
**Swarovski North America Ltd** G 847 680-5150
Vernon Hills *(G-21206)*
**Swarovski US Holding Limited** G 847 679-8670
Skokie *(G-20097)*
**Total Design Jewelry Inc** G 847 433-5333
Highland Park *(G-11878)*
**Ulla of Finland** G 773 763-0700
Chicago *(G-6806)*

### *3965 Fasteners, Buttons, Needles & Pins*

**Accurate Industrial Supply Co** G 708 422-7050
Chicago Ridge *(G-7138)*
**Acme Button & Buttonhole Co** G 773 907-8400
Chicago *(G-3731)*
**Aerofast Inc** E 630 668-6575
Carol Stream *(G-3091)*
**▲ Afi Industries Inc** E 630 462-0400
Carol Stream *(G-3092)*
**▲ American Fas & Components** G 815 397-2698
Rockford *(G-18262)*
**▲ Ample Supply Company** E 815 895-3500
Sycamore *(G-20786)*
**Anixter Inc** E 512 989-4254
Glenview *(G-11102)*
**▲ Blue Ribbon Fastener Company** F 847 673-1248
Skokie *(G-19966)*
**▲ Brighton-Best Intl Inc** G 562 808-8000
Aurora *(G-974)*
**▲ Classic Fasteners LLC** G 630 605-0195
Saint Charles *(G-19157)*
**Component Hardware Inc** G 847 458-8181
Gilberts *(G-10916)*
**Contmid Inc** G 708 747-1200
Park Forest *(G-17170)*
**▲ Ecf Holdings LLC** G 224 723-5524
Northbrook *(G-16246)*
**▲ Engineered Components Co** E 847 985-8000
Elgin *(G-9028)*
**Excell Fastener Solutions Inc** G 630 424-3360
Lombard *(G-13797)*
**Forest City Technologies Inc** E 815 965-5880
Rockford *(G-18389)*
**Greenslade Fastener Svcs LLC** G 815 398-4073
Rockford *(G-18406)*
**▲ H L M Sales Inc** G 815 455-6922
Barrington *(G-1283)*
**▲ Handy Button Machine Co** E 847 459-0900
Wheeling *(G-22067)*
**▲ Hawk Fastener Services** F 708 489-2000
Alsip *(G-472)*
**▲ Ideal Supply Inc** G 847 961-5900
Huntley *(G-12146)*
**Illinois Tool Works Inc** C 708 342-6000
Mokena *(G-14872)*
**Illinois Tool Works Inc** B 847 724-7500
Glenview *(G-11141)*
**Illinois Tool Works Inc** C 630 372-2150
Bartlett *(G-1353)*
**Illinois Tool Works Inc** C 847 783-5500
Elgin *(G-9072)*
**Illinois Tool Works Inc** C 847 299-2222
Des Plaines *(G-8209)*
**▲ Inland Fastener Inc** F 630 293-3800
West Chicago *(G-21720)*
**Jason Incorporated** C 630 627-7000
Addison *(G-158)*
**Jinhap US Corporation** G 630 833-2880
Elmhurst *(G-9891)*
**Just Another Button** F 618 667-8531
Troy *(G-21009)*
**L & M Screw Machine Products** F 630 801-0455
Montgomery *(G-15052)*
**▲ Lawrence Screw Products Inc** D 708 867-5150
Harwood Heights *(G-11686)*
**Leggett & Platt Incorporated** D 847 768-6139
Des Plaines *(G-8223)*
**◆ Lehigh Consumer Products LLC** C 630 851-7330
Aurora *(G-1045)*
**Lhs Inc** G 630 832-3875
Elmhurst *(G-9901)*
**Linda Levinson Designs Inc** G 312 951-6943
Chicago *(G-5509)*
**▲ Lre Products Inc** E 630 238-8321
Bensenville *(G-1942)*
**Magic Solutions Inc** G 312 647-8688
Chicago *(G-5600)*
**◆ Marmon Industrial LLC** G 312 372-9500
Chicago *(G-5626)*
**Matchless Parisian Novelty Inc** G 773 924-1515
Chicago *(G-5650)*
**Matthew Warren Inc** F 630 860-7766
Bensenville *(G-1946)*
**▲ Minigrip Inc** D 845 680-2710
Ottawa *(G-16969)*
**▲ Multitech Cold Forming LLC** E 630 949-8200
Carol Stream *(G-3201)*
**Nbs Corporation** G 847 860-8856
Elk Grove Village *(G-9648)*
**◆ Newell Operating Company** C 815 235-4171
Freeport *(G-10675)*
**▲ Pecson Distributors LLC** G 815 342-7977
Beecher *(G-1601)*
**Peter Fox** G 847 428-2249
East Dundee *(G-8652)*
**◆ R-B Industries Inc** E 847 647-4020
Niles *(G-16026)*
**S & S International Inc III** G 847 304-1890
Lake Barrington *(G-12823)*
**Safety Socket LLC** E 224 484-6222
Gilberts *(G-10934)*
**Sanco Industries Inc** F 847 243-8675
Kildeer *(G-12703)*
**▲ Signode Packaging Systems Corp** D 800 323-2464
Glenview *(G-11203)*
**▲ STA-Rite Ginnie Lou Inc** F 217 774-3921
Shelbyville *(G-19916)*
**Sullivans Inc** F 815 331-8347
McHenry *(G-14557)*
**▲ Supreme Screw Inc** G 630 226-9000
Romeoville *(G-18872)*
**▲ Swd Inc** D 630 543-3003
Addison *(G-302)*
**▲ Vertex Distribution** G 847 437-0400
Elk Grove Village *(G-9807)*

### *3991 Brooms & Brushes*

**Concorde Laboratories Inc** G 630 717-5300
Lisle *(G-13576)*
**▲ Don Leventhal Group LLC** E 618 783-4424
Newton *(G-15939)*
**▲ E Gornell & Sons Inc** E 773 489-2330
Chicago *(G-4665)*
**F B Williams Co** G 773 233-4255
Chicago *(G-4802)*
**Federal Prison Industries** C 309 346-8588
Pekin *(G-17262)*
**◆ Freudenberg Household Pdts LP** C 630 270-1400
Aurora *(G-1010)*
**Gosia Cartage Ltd** G 312 613-8735
Hodgkins *(G-11975)*
**Humboldt Broom Company** G 217 268-3718
Arcola *(G-671)*
**Jim Jolly Sales Inc** G 847 669-7570
Huntley *(G-12153)*
**Jones Software Corp** G 312 952-0011
Chicago *(G-5322)*
**Klm Commercial Sweeping Inc** G 618 978-9276
Belleville *(G-1643)*
**◆ Libman Company** C 217 268-4200
Arcola *(G-675)*
**Luco Mop Company** G 217 235-1992
Mattoon *(G-14398)*
**◆ Newell Operating Company** C 815 235-4171
Freeport *(G-10675)*
**◆ Nexstep Commercial Pdts LLC** G 217 379-2377
Paxton *(G-17238)*
**▲ Quinn Broom Works Inc** E 217 923-3181
Greenup *(G-11385)*
**Rainbow Dusters International** G 770 627-3575
Carol Stream *(G-3227)*
**Re-Maid Incorporated** G 815 315-0500
Freeport *(G-10683)*
**Sherwin-Williams Company** G 847 251-6115
Kenilworth *(G-12663)*
**Team Technologies Inc** D 630 937-0380
Batavia *(G-1504)*
**True Value Company** G 847 639-5383
Cary *(G-3378)*
**▼ True Value Company** B 773 695-5000
Chicago *(G-6786)*
**Zimmerman Brush Co** D 773 761-6331
Chicago *(G-7068)*

### *3993 Signs & Advertising Displays*

**1187 Creative LLC** F 618 457-1187
Carbondale *(G-2999)*
**3-D Resource** G 815 899-8600
Sycamore *(G-20784)*
**A & E Rubber Stamp Corp** G 312 575-1416
Chicago *(G-3679)*
**A & J Signs** F 815 476-0128
Wilmington *(G-22268)*
**A 1 Trophies Awards & Engrv** G 630 837-6000
Streamwood *(G-20638)*
**A Plus Signs Inc** G 708 534-2030
Monee *(G-14990)*
**A To Z Engraving Co Inc** G 847 526-7396
Wauconda *(G-21435)*
**A Trustworthy Sup Source Inc** G 773 480-0255
Chicago *(G-3693)*
**Ability Plastics Inc** E 708 458-4480
Justice *(G-12594)*
**Academy Screenprinting Awards** G 309 686-0026
Peoria *(G-17300)*
**Accurate Metal Fabricating LLC** D 773 235-0400
Chicago *(G-3720)*
**Accurate Repro Inc** F 630 428-4433
Naperville *(G-15588)*
**Ace Sign Co** E 217 522-8417
Springfield *(G-20384)*
**Acrylic Service Inc** G 630 543-0336
Addison *(G-20)*
**Action Graphics and Signs Inc** G 618 939-5755
Columbia *(G-7350)*

**Ad Deluxe Sign Company Inc** ....G....... 815 556-8469
Plainfield *(G-17576)*

**Ad Electric Sign Inc** ....G....... 708 222-8000
Berwyn *(G-2055)*

**Ad Special TZ Inc** ....G....... 847 845-6767
Buffalo Grove *(G-2650)*

**Adams Outdoor Advg Ltd Partnr** ....E....... 309 692-2482
Peoria *(G-17302)*

**Addison Engraving Inc** ....G....... 630 833-9123
Villa Park *(G-21232)*

**Addison Pro Plastics Inc** ....G....... 630 543-6770
Addison *(G-24)*

**Adnama Inc** ....G....... 312 922-0509
Chicago *(G-3754)*

**Advance Press Sign Inc** ....G....... 630 833-1600
Villa Park *(G-21233)*

**Advertising Premiums Inc** ....G....... 888 364-9710
Mount Prospect *(G-15308)*

**Advertising Products Inc** ....G....... 847 758-0415
Elk Grove Village *(G-9281)*

**Albright Enterprises Inc** ....G....... 630 357-2300
Naperville *(G-15593)*

**Alexander Manufacturing Co** ....D....... 309 728-2224
Towanda *(G-20978)*

**Alexander Signs & Designs Inc** ....G....... 815 933-3100
Bourbonnais *(G-2386)*

**All Signs & Wonders Co** ....G....... 630 232-9019
Geneva *(G-10807)*

**▲ All-American Sign Co Inc** ....E....... 708 422-2203
Oak Lawn *(G-16599)*

**All-Brite Sign Co Inc** ....F....... 309 829-1551
Normal *(G-16063)*

**All-Right Sign Inc** ....F....... 708 754-6366
Steger *(G-20567)*

**▲ All-Steel Structures Inc** ....E....... 708 210-1313
South Holland *(G-20241)*

**▲ Allied Die Casting Corporation** ....E....... 815 385-9330
McHenry *(G-14479)*

**Alphabet Shop Inc** ....E....... 847 888-3150
Elgin *(G-8946)*

**▲ AM Ko Oriental Foods** ....G....... 217 398-2922
Champaign *(G-3446)*

**◆ AMD Industries Inc** ....D....... 708 863-8900
Cicero *(G-7178)*

**American Advertising Assoc Inc** ....G....... 773 312-5110
Chicago *(G-3847)*

**American Name Plate & Metal De** ....E....... 773 376-1400
Chicago *(G-3867)*

**▲ American Sign & Lighting Co** ....E....... 847 258-8151
Chicago *(G-3874)*

**Anbek Inc** ....G....... 815 672-6087
La Salle *(G-12763)*

**Anbek Inc** ....F....... 815 223-0734
La Salle *(G-12764)*

**Anbek Inc** ....G....... 815 434-7340
Ottawa *(G-16947)*

**Antolak Management Co Inc** ....G....... 312 464-1800
Chicago *(G-3917)*

**Arrow Signs** ....F....... 618 466-0818
Godfrey *(G-11222)*

**Art & Son Sign Inc** ....F....... 847 526-7205
Wauconda *(G-21443)*

**Art Wire Works Inc** ....F....... 708 458-3993
Bedford Park *(G-1538)*

**Artistic Engraving Corporation** ....G....... 708 409-0149
Broadview *(G-2560)*

**Arts & Letters Marshall Signs** ....G....... 773 927-4442
Chicago *(G-3959)*

**Asi Sign Systems Inc** ....G....... 773 478-5241
Chicago *(G-3963)*

**Associated Attractions Entps** ....F....... 773 376-1900
Chicago *(G-3967)*

**▲ Athena Design Group Inc** ....E....... 312 733-2828
Chicago *(G-3974)*

**Aubrey Sign Co Inc** ....G....... 630 482-9901
Batavia *(G-1418)*

**Aurora Sign Co** ....G....... 630 898-5900
Aurora *(G-962)*

**◆ Authentic Street Signs Inc** ....G....... 618 349-8878
Saint Peter *(G-19320)*

**Award Emblem Mfg Co Inc** ....F....... 630 739-0800
Bolingbrook *(G-2281)*

**Awnings Express** ....G....... 773 579-1437
Chicago *(G-4005)*

**Azusa Inc** ....G....... 618 244-6591
Mount Vernon *(G-15399)*

**B Gunther & Co** ....F....... 630 969-5595
Lisle *(G-13567)*

**▲ B W M Global** ....G....... 847 785-1355
Waukegan *(G-21528)*

**▲ Bards Products Inc** ....F....... 800 323-5499
Mundelein *(G-15475)*

**Barry Signs Inc** ....G....... 773 327-1183
Chicago *(G-4049)*

**Baum Holdings Inc** ....G....... 847 488-0650
South Elgin *(G-20185)*

**Beard Enterprises Inc** ....G....... 630 357-3278
Naperville *(G-15603)*

**Bee-Jay Industries Inc** ....F....... 708 867-4431
Bloomingdale *(G-2095)*

**Bella Sign Co** ....G....... 630 539-0343
Roselle *(G-18928)*

**◆ Benchmarc Display Incorporated** ....E....... 847 541-2828
Vernon Hills *(G-21149)*

**Bendsen Signs & Graphics Inc** ....F....... 217 877-2345
Decatur *(G-7845)*

**Best Advertising Spc & Prtg** ....G....... 708 448-1110
Worth *(G-22633)*

**Best Neon Sign Co Inc** ....F....... 773 586-2700
Chicago *(G-4093)*

**Bick Broadcasting Inc** ....G....... 217 223-9693
Quincy *(G-17804)*

**Biron Studio General Svcs Inc** ....G....... 708 229-2600
Bridgeview *(G-2470)*

**◆ Bish Creative Display Inc** ....E....... 847 438-1500
Lake Zurich *(G-13046)*

**Blue Diamond Athletic Disp Inc** ....G....... 847 414-9971
Downers Grove *(G-8397)*

**Boatman Signs** ....G....... 618 548-6567
Salem *(G-19328)*

**Braeside LLC** ....E....... 847 395-8500
Antioch *(G-626)*

**Bright Light Sign Company Inc** ....G....... 847 550-8902
Lake Zurich *(G-13047)*

**Briscoe Signs LLC** ....G....... 630 529-1616
Roselle *(G-18929)*

**Brownfield Sports Inc** ....G....... 217 367-8321
Urbana *(G-21074)*

**Budget Sign** ....G....... 708 354-7512
La Grange *(G-12728)*

**Budget Signs** ....F....... 618 259-4460
Wood River *(G-22441)*

**C M F Enterprises Inc** ....F....... 847 526-9499
Wauconda *(G-21450)*

**Cachera and Klemm Inc** ....G....... 217 876-7446
Decatur *(G-7849)*

**Cacini Inc** ....G....... 847 884-1162
Schaumburg *(G-19467)*

**Campbell Management Services** ....G....... 847 566-9020
Mundelein *(G-15482)*

**Canham Graphics** ....G....... 217 585-5085
Springfield *(G-20404)*

**Castino & Associates Inc** ....G....... 847 291-7446
Northbrook *(G-16218)*

**Central Illinois Sign Company** ....G....... 217 523-4740
Springfield *(G-20414)*

**Century Signs Inc** ....F....... 217 224-7419
Quincy *(G-17812)*

**Charleston Industries Inc** ....G....... 847 228-7150
Elk Grove Village *(G-9365)*

**Chicago Scenic Studios Inc** ....D....... 312 274-9900
Chicago *(G-4345)*

**▲ Chicago Show Inc** ....E....... 847 955-0200
Buffalo Grove *(G-2672)*

**▲ Chicago Sign Group** ....G....... 847 899-9021
Vernon Hills *(G-21154)*

**Churchill Wilmslow Corporation** ....G....... 312 759-8911
Chicago *(G-4374)*

**City of Chicago** ....G....... 773 686-2254
Chicago *(G-4385)*

**Classic Midwest Die Mold Inc** ....F....... 773 227-8000
Chicago *(G-4393)*

**Classique Signs & Engrv Inc** ....G....... 217 228-7446
Quincy *(G-17813)*

**Clover Signs** ....G....... 773 588-2828
Chicago *(G-4407)*

**CNE Inc** ....G....... 847 534-7135
Schaumburg *(G-19475)*

**▼ Color Communications Inc** ....C....... 773 638-1400
Chicago *(G-4426)*

**Color Signs** ....G....... 847 368-0101
Arlington Heights *(G-736)*

**Compliancesigns Inc** ....D....... 800 578-1245
Chadwick *(G-3441)*

**Concepts Magnet** ....G....... 847 253-3351
Mount Prospect *(G-15318)*

**Consolidated Displays Co Inc** ....G....... 630 851-8666
Oswego *(G-16911)*

**Contempo Autographic & Signs** ....G....... 708 371-5499
Crestwood *(G-7483)*

**Cook Fabrication Signs Graphic** ....G....... 309 360-3805
Deer Creek *(G-7962)*

**Corporate Identification Solut** ....E....... 773 763-9600
Chicago *(G-4475)*

**Corporate Sign Systems Inc** ....F....... 847 882-6100
Roselle *(G-18936)*

**Corpro Screen Tech Inc** ....G....... 815 633-1201
Loves Park *(G-13926)*

**▲ Cosmos Plastics Company** ....E....... 847 451-1307
Franklin Park *(G-10445)*

**Crown Trophy** ....G....... 309 699-1766
East Peoria *(G-8707)*

**Cubby Hole of Carlinville Inc** ....F....... 217 854-8511
Carlinville *(G-3035)*

**Custom Enterprises** ....G....... 618 439-6626
Benton *(G-2025)*

**Custom Sign Consultants Inc** ....G....... 312 533-2302
Chicago *(G-4526)*

**Custom Signs On Metal LLC** ....F....... 217 443-5347
Tilton *(G-20880)*

**Custom Telephone Printing Inc** ....F....... 815 338-0000
Woodstock *(G-22557)*

**Custom Trophies** ....G....... 217 422-3353
Decatur *(G-7863)*

**Cypress Multigraphics LLC** ....E....... 708 633-1166
Tinley Park *(G-20907)*

**D E Signs & Storage LLC** ....G....... 618 939-8050
Waterloo *(G-21401)*

**D&J Arlington Heights Inc** ....G....... 847 577-8200
Arlington Heights *(G-743)*

**DAmico Associates Inc** ....G....... 847 291-7446
Northbrook *(G-16239)*

**Dans Rubber Stamp & Signs** ....G....... 815 964-5603
Rockford *(G-18333)*

**▲ Dard Products Inc** ....C....... 847 328-5000
Evanston *(G-10025)*

**Darnall Printing** ....G....... 309 827-7212
Bloomington *(G-2161)*

**DE Asbury Inc** ....E....... 217 222-0617
Quincy *(G-17820)*

**De Luca Visual Solutions Inc** ....G....... 847 884-6300
Schaumburg *(G-19500)*

**Dean Patterson** ....G....... 708 430-0477
Bridgeview *(G-2482)*

**Demond Signs Inc** ....F....... 618 624-7260
O Fallon *(G-16466)*

**Derse Inc** ....D....... 847 473-2149
Waukegan *(G-21549)*

**Design Group Signage Corp** ....F....... 847 390-0350
Des Plaines *(G-8185)*

**▲ Design Phase Inc** ....E....... 847 473-0077
Waukegan *(G-21550)*

**Designovations Inc** ....G....... 815 645-8598
Stillman Valley *(G-20625)*

**Designs Unlimited** ....G....... 618 357-6728
Pinckneyville *(G-17547)*

**Desk & Door Nameplate Company** ....F....... 815 806-8670
Frankfort *(G-10312)*

**Dewrich Inc** ....G....... 847 249-7445
Gurnee *(G-11438)*

**▲ Dgs Import Inc** ....E....... 847 595-7016
Chicago *(G-4591)*

**▲ Dicke Tool Company** ....E....... 630 969-0050
Downers Grove *(G-8429)*

**Dickey Sign Co** ....G....... 618 797-1262
Granite City *(G-11273)*

**Digital Artz LLC** ....G....... 618 651-1500
Highland *(G-11783)*

**Digital Edge Signs Inc** ....G....... 847 838-4760
Antioch *(G-629)*

**Digital Factory Inc** ....G....... 708 320-9879
Chicago *(G-4599)*

**Digital Greensigns Inc** ....G....... 312 624-8550
Chicago *(G-4600)*

**Digital Minds Inc** ....G....... 847 430-3390
Rosemont *(G-18998)*

**Display Link Inc** ....G....... 815 968-0778
Rockford *(G-18346)*

**Distinctive SIGns& The Neon Ex** ....G....... 847 245-7159
Grayslake *(G-11333)*

**▲ Diversified Adtee Inc** ....E....... 309 454-2555
Normal *(G-16069)*

**Doyle Signs Inc** ....D....... 630 543-9490
Addison *(G-98)*

**Dyna Comp Inc** ....G....... 815 455-5570
Crystal Lake *(G-7568)*

**E A A Enterprises Inc** ....G....... 630 279-0150
Villa Park *(G-21249)*

**E B G B Inc** ....G....... 847 228-9333
Elk Grove Village *(G-9441)*

S I C

Employee Codes: A=Over 500 employees, B=251-500
C=101-250, D=51-100, E=20-50, F=10-19, G=3-9

2017 Harris Illinois
Industrial Directory

1129

## 39 MISCELLANEOUS MANUFACTURING INDUSTRIES

▲ E I T Inc .....................................G...... 630 359-3543
  Naperville *(G-15649)*
E K Kuhn Inc ....................................G...... 815 899-9211
  Sycamore *(G-20795)*
E Z Sign Co Inc ................................G...... 815 469-4080
  Oak Forest *(G-16578)*
East Bank Neon Inc ........................G...... 618 345-9517
  Collinsville *(G-7322)*
East Coast Signs Advertising ........D...... 215 458-9042
  Elk Grove Village *(G-9447)*
Eberhart Sign & Lighting Co ..........G...... 618 656-7256
  Edwardsville *(G-8797)*
Edventure Promotions Inc .............G...... 312 440-1800
  Chicago *(G-4702)*
Effingham Signs & Graphics ..........G...... 217 347-8711
  Effingham *(G-8836)*
Eisendrath Inc .................................G...... 847 432-3899
  Highland Park *(G-11830)*
▲ Electronic Displays Inc ................F...... 630 628-0658
  Addison *(G-108)*
▲ Elk Grove Signs Inc ......................G...... 847 427-0005
  Elk Grove Village *(G-9452)*
Elm Street Design Inc ....................G...... 815 455-3622
  Crystal Lake *(G-7573)*
Enchanted Signs of Rockford ........G...... 815 874-5100
  Rockford *(G-18364)*
Enterprise Signs Inc .......................G...... 773 614-8324
  Chicago *(G-4760)*
Exclusively Expo ..............................F...... 630 378-4600
  Romeoville *(G-18822)*
Exex Holding Corporation ..............G...... 815 703-7295
  Romeoville *(G-18823)*
Express Signs & Lighting Maint .....F...... 815 725-9080
  Shorewood *(G-19926)*
Fast Signs ........................................G...... 773 698-8115
  Chicago *(G-4816)*
Fast Signs ........................................G...... 815 730-7828
  Joliet *(G-12493)*
Fast Signs 590 ................................G...... 815 937-1855
  Kankakee *(G-12615)*
Fastsigns .........................................G...... 312 344-1765
  Chicago *(G-4818)*
Fastsigns .........................................G...... 847 981-1965
  Elk Grove Village *(G-9477)*
Fastsigns .........................................G...... 312 332-7446
  Chicago *(G-4819)*
Fastsigns .........................................G...... 847 675-1600
  Lincolnwood *(G-13509)*
Fastsigns .........................................G...... 847 680-7446
  Libertyville *(G-13323)*
Fastsigns International ...................G...... 847 967-7222
  Morton Grove *(G-15197)*
Federal Heath Sign Company LLC ...F...... 630 887-6800
  Willowbrook *(G-22211)*
Federal Signal Corporation ............D...... 708 534-3400
  University Park *(G-21049)*
Fedex Office & Print Svcs Inc ........E...... 309 685-4093
  Peoria *(G-17359)*
Fedex Office & Print Svcs Inc ........E...... 847 670-4100
  Arlington Heights *(G-754)*
▲ Flow-Eze Company .......................F...... 815 965-1062
  Rockford *(G-18383)*
FM Graphic Impressions Inc .........E...... 630 897-8788
  Aurora *(G-1153)*
Forest Awards & Engraving ...........G...... 630 595-2242
  Wood Dale *(G-22371)*
Fourth Quarter Holdings Inc .........G...... 847 249-7445
  Gurnee *(G-11449)*
Fox Valley Signs Inc .......................G...... 630 896-3113
  Aurora *(G-1158)*
▲ Frank O Carlson & Co Inc ............F...... 773 847-6900
  Chicago *(G-4884)*
Franks Dgtal Prtg Off Sups Inc .....G...... 630 892-2511
  Aurora *(G-1159)*
Friendly Signs Inc ...........................G...... 815 933-7070
  Kankakee *(G-12618)*
Frontier Signs & Lighting ...............G...... 309 694-7300
  Chillicothe *(G-7165)*
▲ Fun Incorporated ...........................E...... 773 745-3837
  Wheeling *(G-22059)*
G & J Associates Inc .....................G...... 847 255-0123
  Arlington Heights *(G-756)*
G and D Enterprises Inc ................E...... 847 981-8661
  Arlington Heights *(G-757)*
G D S Professional Bus Display ...E...... 309 829-3298
  Bloomington *(G-2168)*
G M Sign Inc ...................................D...... 847 546-0424
  Round Lake *(G-19056)*
Gabel & Schubert Bronze ..............F...... 773 878-6800
  Chicago *(G-4905)*

Gadge Signs Inc .............................G...... 815 462-4490
  New Lenox *(G-15882)*
Galesburg Sign & Lighting .............G...... 309 342-9798
  Galesburg *(G-10751)*
Gaytan Signs & Co Inc ...................G...... 815 726-2975
  Joliet *(G-12500)*
Geebees Inc ....................................G...... 309 682-5300
  Peoria *(G-17369)*
Gemcom Inc ....................................G...... 800 871-6840
  Willow Springs *(G-22196)*
▲ Gemini Industries Inc ....................D...... 618 251-3352
  Roxana *(G-1084)*
General Exhibits and Displays ......D...... 847 934-1943
  Inverness *(G-12204)*
General Motor Sign .........................G...... 847 546-0424
  Round Lake *(G-19057)*
George Lauterer Corporation ........E...... 312 913-1881
  Chicago *(G-4943)*
GL Led LLC ......................................G...... 312 600-9363
  Chicago *(G-4953)*
Goalgetters Inc ................................F...... 708 579-9800
  La Grange *(G-12733)*
◆ Granite Gallery Inc .......................G...... 773 279-9200
  Chicago *(G-4986)*
Grate Signs Inc ...............................E...... 815 729-9700
  Joliet *(G-12503)*
Graymon Graphics Inc ...................G...... 773 737-0176
  Chicago *(G-4993)*
Greg Signs ......................................G...... 815 726-5655
  Joliet *(G-12504)*
▲ H L M Sales Inc .............................G...... 815 455-6922
  Barrington *(G-1283)*
▲ Hanover Displays Inc ....................F...... 773 334-9934
  Elk Grove Village *(G-9516)*
Harder Signs Inc .............................F...... 815 874-7777
  Rockford *(G-18413)*
Hardin Signs Inc .............................F...... 309 688-4111
  Peoria *(G-17379)*
Haus Sign Incorporated .................G...... 708 598-8740
  Bridgeview *(G-2497)*
Hazen Display Corporation ...........E...... 815 248-2925
  Davis *(G-7806)*
Heavy Hitters LLC ...........................G...... 630 258-2991
  Calumet City *(G-2942)*
Heiman Sign Studio ........................G...... 815 397-6909
  Rockford *(G-18416)*
Heritage Signs Ltd .........................G...... 847 549-1942
  Libertyville *(G-13331)*
Hermann Gene Signs & Service ...G...... 618 244-3681
  Mount Vernon *(G-15411)*
Heron Bay Inc ................................G...... 309 661-1300
  Bloomington *(G-2178)*
Herrmann Signs & Service ............G...... 618 246-6537
  Mount Vernon *(G-15412)*
▼ HM Witt & Co ...............................E...... 773 250-5000
  Chicago *(G-5093)*
Holland Design Group Inc ............F...... 847 526-8848
  Wauconda *(G-21470)*
Holmes Associates Inc ..................G...... 847 336-4515
  Gurnee *(G-11460)*
Horizon Downing LLC ....................E...... 815 758-6867
  Dekalb *(G-8097)*
House of Doolittle Ltd ...................G...... 847 593-3417
  Arlington Heights *(G-769)*
Howard Displays Inc ......................F......
  Highland Park *(G-11841)*
Hughes & Son Inc ..........................G...... 815 459-1887
  Crystal Lake *(G-7589)*
Icon Identity Solutions Inc ............E...... 847 364-2250
  Elk Grove Village *(G-9531)*
Icon Identity Solutions Inc ............E...... 847 364-2250
  Elk Grove Village *(G-9532)*
▲ Ideal Box Co ..................................C...... 708 594-3100
  Chicago *(G-5140)*
Ideal Sign Solutions LLC ..............G...... 847 695-9091
  Hoffman Estates *(G-12017)*
Idek Graphics LLC ..........................G...... 630 530-1232
  Elmhurst *(G-9883)*
Identiti Resources Ltd ...................E...... 847 301-0510
  Schaumburg *(G-19562)*
Idot North Side Sign Shop ............G...... 847 705-4033
  Schaumburg *(G-19563)*
◆ Illini/Altco Inc ................................D...... 847 549-0321
  Vernon Hills *(G-21173)*
Image Signs Inc .............................F...... 815 282-4141
  Loves Park *(G-13947)*
Imagecare Maintenance Svcs LLC ...G...... 847 631-3306
  Elk Grove Village *(G-9540)*
Images Alive Ltd ............................G...... 847 498-5550
  Northbrook *(G-16274)*

Imageworks Manufacturing Inc ....E...... 708 503-1122
  Park Forest *(G-17172)*
Impact Signs & Graphics Inc ........G...... 708 469-7178
  La Grange *(G-12738)*
Independent Outdoor Ltd ..............G...... 630 960-2460
  Downers Grove *(G-8465)*
Infinity Cmmncations Group Ltd ...F...... 708 352-1086
  Countryside *(G-7434)*
Insight Advertising Inc ...................G...... 847 647-0004
  Niles *(G-15989)*
Insignia Design Ltd ........................G...... 301 254-9221
  Rolling Meadows *(G-18734)*
Integrated Mdsg Systems LLC .....D...... 630 571-2020
  Oak Brook *(G-16525)*
Integrity Sign Company ..................F...... 708 532-5038
  Mokena *(G-14875)*
Isates Inc ........................................G...... 309 691-8822
  Peoria *(G-17391)*
Ivan Carlson Associates Inc .........E...... 312 829-4616
  Chicago *(G-5248)*
J & D Instant Signs ........................G...... 847 965-2800
  Morton Grove *(G-15206)*
J M Signs .........................................G...... 847 945-7446
  Deerfield *(G-8015)*
J R Fridrich Inc ..............................F...... 847 439-1554
  Elk Grove Village *(G-9558)*
▲ Jacobson Acqstion Holdings LLC ...C...... 847 623-1414
  Waukegan *(G-21574)*
Jamali Kopy Kat Printing Inc ........G...... 708 544-6164
  Bellwood *(G-1711)*
▼ Janis Plastics Inc ..........................D...... 847 838-5500
  Antioch *(G-638)*
JAS Dahern Signs ..........................G...... 773 254-0717
  Chicago *(G-5281)*
Jenkins Displays Co ......................G...... 618 335-3874
  Patoka *(G-17232)*
▲ Joans Trophy & Plaque Co ...........E...... 309 674-6500
  Peoria *(G-17393)*
Jodaat Inc .......................................G...... 630 916-7776
  Lombard *(G-13815)*
John Parker Advertising Co ..........G...... 217 892-4118
  Rantoul *(G-17931)*
Johnson Sign Co ............................G...... 847 678-2092
  Franklin Park *(G-10509)*
Joliet Pattern Works Inc ...............D...... 815 726-5373
  Crest Hill *(G-7460)*
Jonem Grp Inc DBA Sign A Rama ..G...... 224 848-4620
  Lake Barrington *(G-12813)*
Joseph D Smithies .........................G...... 618 632-6141
  Caseyville *(G-3399)*
K 9 Tag Company Inc ....................G...... 847 304-8247
  Waukegan *(G-21575)*
K and A Graphics Inc .....................G...... 847 244-2345
  Gurnee *(G-11463)*
K R O Enterprises Ltd ...................G...... 309 797-2213
  Moline *(G-14949)*
K-Display Corp ................................F...... 773 586-2042
  Chicago *(G-5348)*
Kane Graphical Corporation .........E...... 773 384-1200
  Chicago *(G-5358)*
Kellys Sign Shop .............................G...... 217 477-0167
  Danville *(G-7742)*
Ken Young Construction Co .........G...... 847 358-3026
  Hoffman Estates *(G-12021)*
Key Outdoor Inc ..............................G...... 815 224-4742
  La Salle *(G-12780)*
Keyesport Manufacturing Inc .......G...... 618 749-5510
  Keyesport *(G-12696)*
Keystone Display Inc .....................D...... 815 648-2456
  Hebron *(G-11721)*
Keystone Printing & Publishing ...G...... 815 678-2591
  Richmond *(G-17965)*
Kieffer Holding Co ..........................G...... 877 543-3337
  Lincolnshire *(G-13458)*
Kim Gilmore ....................................G...... 847 931-1511
  Elgin *(G-9089)*
Kornick Enterprises LLC ...............G...... 847 884-1162
  Schaumburg *(G-19605)*
Krick Enterprises Inc .....................G...... 630 515-1085
  Downers Grove *(G-8470)*
Ksem Inc .........................................G...... 618 656-5388
  Edwardsville *(G-8805)*
L & C Imaging Inc ...........................G...... 309 829-1802
  Bloomington *(G-2192)*
Lange Sign Group ...........................G...... 815 747-2448
  East Dubuque *(G-8619)*
Laux Grafix Inc ...............................G...... 618 337-4558
  East Saint Louis *(G-8759)*
Legacy 3d LLC ................................F...... 815 727-5454
  Crest Hill *(G-7462)*

Legible Signs Group Corp ....F .... 815 654-0100
Loves Park *(G-13960)*
Lena Sign Shop ....G .... 815 369-9090
Lena *(G-13279)*
Leo Burnett Company Inc ....C .... 312 220-5959
Chicago *(G-5493)*
Leos Sign ....G .... 773 227-2460
Chicago *(G-5494)*
Lettering Specialists Inc ....F .... 847 674-3414
Skokie *(G-20029)*
Lettermen Signage Inc ....G .... 708 479-5161
Mokena *(G-14879)*
Letters Unlimited Inc ....G .... 847 891-7811
Schaumburg *(G-19615)*
Light Waves LLC ....F .... 847 251-1622
Wilmette *(G-22259)*
Lightning Graphic ....G .... 815 623-1937
Roscoe *(G-18903)*
Lincolnland Archtctral Grphics ....G .... 217 629-9009
Glenarm *(G-10996)*
Lonelino Sign Company Inc ....G .... 217 243-2444
Jacksonville *(G-12400)*
Lou Plucinski ....G .... 815 758-7888
Dekalb *(G-8103)*
M & R Media Inc ....G .... 847 884-6300
Schaumburg *(G-19628)*
M G M Displays Inc ....G .... 708 594-3699
Chicago *(G-5580)*
Magnetic Signs ....G .... 773 476-6551
Chicago *(G-5602)*
Main Street Visuals Inc ....G .... 847 869-7446
Morton Grove *(G-15217)*
Mandel Metals Inc ....G .... 847 455-7446
Franklin Park *(G-10522)*
Mark Collins ....G .... 847 324-5500
Skokie *(G-20033)*
Mark Your Space Inc ....G .... 630 289-7082
Bartlett *(G-1361)*
Marking Specialists/Poly ....F .... 847 793-8100
Buffalo Grove *(G-2731)*
Massey Grafix ....G .... 815 644-4620
Watseka *(G-21422)*
Master Marketing Intl Inc ....F .... 630 909-1846
Carol Stream *(G-3189)*
Matrex Exhibits Inc ....D .... 630 628-2233
Addison *(G-192)*
Maxs Screen Machine Inc ....G .... 773 878-4949
Chicago *(G-5659)*
Mbm Business Assistance Inc ....G .... 217 398-6600
Champaign *(G-3512)*
McKernin Exhibits Inc ....F .... 708 333-4500
South Holland *(G-20288)*
Meagher Sign & Graphics Inc ....G .... 618 662-7446
Flora *(G-10211)*
Mekanism Inc ....F .... 415 908-4000
Chicago *(G-5682)*
Mer-Pla Inc ....F .... 847 530-9798
Chicago *(G-5687)*
▲ Mercury Plastics Inc ....E .... 888 884-1864
Chicago *(G-5688)*
▲ Metal Box International Inc ....C .... 847 455-8500
Franklin Park *(G-10529)*
Mich Enterprises Inc ....F .... 630 616-9000
Wood Dale *(G-22399)*
Michael Reggis Clark ....G .... 618 533-3841
Centralia *(G-3422)*
▲ Midway Displays Inc ....E .... 708 563-2323
Bedford Park *(G-1563)*
Midwest Nameplate Corp ....G .... 708 614-0606
Orland Park *(G-16875)*
Midwest Promotional Group Co ....E .... 708 563-0600
Burr Ridge *(G-2868)*
Midwest Sign & Lighting Inc ....G .... 708 365-5555
Country Club Hills *(G-7410)*
Midwest Signs & Structures Inc ....G .... 847 249-8398
Gurnee *(G-11473)*
Midwest Signworks ....G .... 815 942-3517
Morris *(G-15119)*
Midwest Sun-Ray Lighting & Sig ....F .... 618 656-2884
Granite City *(G-11296)*
Minerva Sportswear Inc ....F .... 309 661-2387
Bloomington *(G-2201)*
Mission Signs Inc ....G .... 630 243-6731
Lemont *(G-13242)*
▲ Mk Signs Inc ....E .... 773 545-4444
Chicago *(G-5777)*
Modagrafics Inc ....D .... 800 860-3169
Rolling Meadows *(G-18746)*
Monitor Sign Co ....F .... 217 234-2412
Mattoon *(G-14405)*
Mostert & Ferguson Signs ....G .... 815 485-1212
Orland Park *(G-16876)*
Mount Vernon Neon Sign Co ....C .... 618 242-0645
Mount Vernon *(G-15429)*
My-Signguycom Inc ....G .... 888 223-9703
Chicago *(G-5842)*
N Bujarski Inc ....G .... 847 884-1600
Schaumburg *(G-19660)*
Nafisco Inc ....F .... 815 372-3300
Romeoville *(G-18851)*
Nameplate Robinson & Precision ....G .... 847 678-2255
Franklin Park *(G-10538)*
Nathan Winston Service Inc ....G .... 815 758-4545
Dekalb *(G-8109)*
Navitor Inc ....B .... 800 323-0253
Harwood Heights *(G-11687)*
▲ Neil International Inc ....G .... 847 549-7627
Vernon Hills *(G-21185)*
Nelson - Harkins Inds Inc ....E .... 773 478-6243
Chicago *(G-5884)*
Neon Art ....G .... 773 588-5883
Chicago *(G-5885)*
Neon Design Inc ....G .... 773 880-5020
Chicago *(G-5886)*
Neon Express Signs ....G .... 773 463-7335
Chicago *(G-5887)*
Neon Prism Electric Sign Co ....G .... 630 879-1010
Batavia *(G-1476)*
Neon Shop Inc ....G .... 773 227-0303
Chicago *(G-5888)*
▲ Nevco Inc ....D .... 618 664-0360
Greenville *(G-11401)*
Newport Printing Services Inc ....G .... 847 632-1000
Schaumburg *(G-19664)*
▲ Nimlok Company ....D .... 847 647-1012
Des Plaines *(G-8242)*
Nite Lite Signs & Balloons Inc ....G .... 630 953-2866
Addison *(G-229)*
Nordmeyer Graphics ....G .... 815 697-2634
Chebanse *(G-3631)*
North Shore Sign Company ....E .... 847 816-7020
Libertyville *(G-13364)*
Nsi Signs Inc ....F .... 630 433-3525
Addison *(G-230)*
Nu Glo Sign Company ....F .... 847 223-6160
Grayslake *(G-11356)*
Nu-Art Printing ....G .... 618 533-9971
Centralia *(G-3425)*
▲ Nu-Dell Manufacturing Co Inc ....F .... 847 803-4500
Chicago *(G-5953)*
▲ Nu-Way Signs Inc ....F .... 847 243-0164
Wheeling *(G-22110)*
Nutheme Sign Company ....G .... 847 230-0067
Downers Grove *(G-8497)*
Nycor Products Inc ....G .... 815 727-9883
Joliet *(G-12547)*
O Signs Inc ....G .... 312 888-3386
Chicago *(G-5959)*
Oakley Signs & Graphics Inc ....F .... 224 612-5045
Des Plaines *(G-8245)*
Ogden Offset Printers Inc ....G .... 773 284-7797
Chicago *(G-5973)*
Olympic Signs Inc ....E .... 630 424-6100
Lombard *(G-13835)*
Olympic Trophy and Awards Co ....F .... 773 631-9500
Chicago *(G-5987)*
Omega Sign & Lighting Inc ....E .... 630 237-4397
Addison *(G-234)*
Orbit Enterprises Inc ....G .... 630 469-3405
Oak Brook *(G-16553)*
Outdoor Solutions Team Inc ....E .... 312 446-4220
Northbrook *(G-16328)*
Ozko Sign & Lighting Company ....G .... 224 653-8531
Schaumburg *(G-19676)*
▲ P & L Mark-It Inc ....E .... 630 879-7590
Batavia *(G-1478)*
P N K Ventures Inc ....G .... 630 527-0500
Naperville *(G-15720)*
Paddock Industries Inc ....F .... 618 277-1580
Smithton *(G-20123)*
Paldo Sign and Display Company ....G .... 708 456-1711
River Grove *(G-18012)*
Pan-O-Graphics Inc ....G .... 630 834-7123
Elmhurst *(G-9918)*
Paramount Wire Specialties ....F .... 773 252-5636
Chicago *(G-6080)*
Parvin-Clauss Sign Co Inc ....E .... 866 490-2877
Carol Stream *(G-3211)*
Patt Supply Corporation ....F .... 708 442-3901
Lyons *(G-14043)*
Pellegrini Enterprises Inc ....G .... 815 717-6408
Orland Park *(G-16884)*
Perfection Signs & Graphics ....G .... 708 795-0611
Berwyn *(G-2073)*
▲ Petersen Aluminum Corporation ....D .... 847 228-7150
Elk Grove Village *(G-9676)*
Peterson Brothers Plastics ....F .... 773 286-5666
Chicago *(G-6111)*
Photo Techniques Corp ....E .... 630 690-9360
Carol Stream *(G-3213)*
Piasa Plastics Inc ....G .... 618 372-7516
Brighton *(G-2544)*
Plainfield Signs Inc ....G .... 815 439-1063
Plainfield *(G-17640)*
Plastic Letter & Signs Inc ....G .... 847 251-3719
Wilmette *(G-22263)*
Plus Signs & Banners Inc ....G .... 630 236-6917
Naperville *(G-15822)*
Prairie Display Chicago Inc ....F .... 630 834-8773
Elmhurst *(G-9922)*
Prairie Signs Inc ....F .... 309 452-0463
Normal *(G-16084)*
Precision Neon Glasswork ....G .... 847 428-1200
Crystal Lake *(G-7627)*
Preformance Signs ....G .... 815 544-5044
Belvidere *(G-1780)*
Premier Signs Creations Inc ....G .... 309 637-6890
Peoria *(G-17435)*
Prime Market Targeting Inc ....E .... 815 469-4555
Frankfort *(G-10353)*
Printing Plus of Roselle Inc ....G .... 630 893-0410
Roselle *(G-18963)*
Process Graphics Corp ....E .... 815 637-2500
Rockford *(G-18542)*
Promotional Co of Illinois ....G .... 847 382-0239
Inverness *(G-12210)*
Pronto Signs and Engraving ....G .... 847 249-7874
Waukegan *(G-21608)*
Pry-Bar Company ....F .... 815 436-3383
Joliet *(G-12558)*
Q SC Design ....G .... 815 933-6777
Bradley *(G-2429)*
▲ Quantum Sign Corporation ....F .... 630 466-0372
Sugar Grove *(G-20733)*
Quatum Structure and Design ....F .... 815 741-0733
Rockdale *(G-18228)*
Quick Quality Printing Inc ....G .... 708 895-5885
Lansing *(G-13181)*
Quick Signs ....G .... 618 549-0747
Carbondale *(G-3020)*
Quick Signs Inc ....G .... 630 554-7370
Oswego *(G-16930)*
Quincy Electric & Sign Company ....F .... 217 223-8404
Quincy *(G-17876)*
R & L Signs Inc ....G .... 708 233-0112
Bridgeview *(G-2522)*
▲ R D Niven & Associates Ltd ....E .... 630 580-6000
Carol Stream *(G-3225)*
R N I Industries Inc ....E .... 630 860-9147
Bensenville *(G-1974)*
R-Signs Service and Design Inc ....G .... 815 722-0283
Joliet *(G-12562)*
Ra-Ujamaa Inc ....G .... 773 373-8585
Chicago *(G-6276)*
Rainbow Signs ....F .... 815 675-6750
Spring Grove *(G-20361)*
Real Neon Inc ....F .... 630 543-0995
Addison *(G-272)*
Realt Images Inc ....G .... 217 567-3487
Tower Hill *(G-20980)*
Rebechini Studio Inc ....F .... 847 364-8600
Elk Grove Village *(G-9711)*
▲ Rico Industries Inc ....D .... 312 427-0313
Niles *(G-16028)*
Rkm Enterprises ....G .... 217 348-5437
Charleston *(G-3609)*
Road Ready Signs ....F .... 309 828-1007
Bloomington *(G-2219)*
▲ Roeda Signs Inc ....E .... 708 333-3021
South Holland *(G-20302)*
Roman Signs ....G .... 847 381-3425
Barrington *(G-1302)*
Roth Neon Sign Company Inc ....G .... 618 942-6378
Herrin *(G-11753)*
Rout A Bout Shop Inc ....G .... 309 829-0674
Bloomington *(G-2220)*
Rowdy Star Custom Creations ....G .... 217 497-1789
Danville *(G-7764)*
RTC Industries Inc ....D .... 847 640-2400
Chicago *(G-6409)*

S I C

Employee Codes: A=Over 500 employees, B=251-500
C=101-250, D=51-100, E=20-50, F=10-19, G=3-9
2017 Harris Illinois
Industrial Directory
1131

**Russell Doot Inc** ... G ... 312 527-1437
Chicago *(G-6415)*

**Rutke Signs Inc** ... G ... 708 841-6464
Westchester *(G-21853)*

**S and S Associates Inc** ... G ... 847 584-0033
Elk Grove Village *(G-9722)*

**S D Custom Machining** ... G ... 618 544-7007
Robinson *(G-18072)*

**Sadannah Group LLC** ... G ... 630 357-2300
Naperville *(G-15745)*

**Samsung Sign Corp** ... G ... 847 816-1374
Libertyville *(G-13377)*

**Sandee Manufacturing Co** ... G ... 847 671-1335
Franklin Park *(G-10581)*

**Sandra E Greene** ... G ... 815 469-0092
Frankfort *(G-10361)*

**Saturn Sign** ... G ... 847 520-9009
Wheeling *(G-22144)*

**Savino Displays Inc** ... G ... 630 574-0777
Hinsdale *(G-11963)*

**Schellerer Corporation Inc** ... D ... 630 980-4567
Bloomingdale *(G-2135)*

**Schepel Signs Inc** ... G ... 708 758-1441
Lynwood *(G-14027)*

**Service Sheet Metal Works Inc** ... F ... 773 229-0031
Chicago *(G-6483)*

**SGS International LLC** ... C ... 309 690-5231
Peoria *(G-17453)*

**▲ Sharn Enterprises Inc** ... E ... 815 464-9715
Frankfort *(G-10362)*

**Shawcraft Sign Co** ... G ... 815 282-4105
Machesney Park *(G-14107)*

**Shinn Enterprises** ... G ... 217 698-3344
Springfield *(G-20523)*

**Sign** ... G ... 630 351-8400
Bloomingdale *(G-2137)*

**Sign & Banner Express** ... G ... 630 783-9700
Bolingbrook *(G-2368)*

**Sign A Rama** ... G ... 630 293-7300
West Chicago *(G-21772)*

**Sign A Rama Inc** ... G ... 630 359-5125
Villa Park *(G-21284)*

**Sign America** ... G ... 773 262-7800
Chicago *(G-6507)*

**Sign Appeal Inc** ... G ... 847 587-4300
Fox Lake *(G-10283)*

**Sign Authority** ... G ... 630 462-9850
Wheaton *(G-21981)*

**Sign Central** ... G ... 847 543-7600
Round Lake *(G-19067)*

**Sign Contractors** ... G ... 708 795-1761
Burr Ridge *(G-2880)*

**Sign Express Inc** ... G ... 708 524-8811
Oak Park *(G-16686)*

**Sign Girls Inc** ... G ... 847 336-4002
Gurnee *(G-11504)*

**Sign Identity Inc** ... G ... 630 942-1400
Glen Ellyn *(G-10989)*

**Sign O Rama** ... G ... 815 744-8702
Joliet *(G-12575)*

**Sign Outlet Inc** ... G ... 708 824-2222
Alsip *(G-528)*

**Sign Palace Inc** ... G ... 847 228-7446
Elk Grove Village *(G-9738)*

**Sign Solutions** ... G ... 618 443-6565
Sparta *(G-20320)*

**Sign Team Inc** ... G ... 309 302-0017
East Moline *(G-8694)*

**Sign-A-Rama** ... G ... 312 922-0509
Chicago *(G-6508)*

**Sign-A-Rama of Buffalo Grove** ... G ... 847 215-1535
Buffalo Grove *(G-2771)*

**Signage Plus Ltd** ... G ... 815 485-0300
Lockport *(G-13744)*

**Signarama** ... G ... 847 543-4870
Grayslake *(G-11363)*

**▲ Signco** ... F ... 402 474-6646
Greenville *(G-11403)*

**Signcraft Screenprint Inc** ... C ... 815 777-3030
Galena *(G-10731)*

**Signcrafters Enterprises Inc** ... G ... 815 648-4484
Hebron *(G-11727)*

**Signet Sign Company** ... G ... 630 830-8242
Bartlett *(G-1377)*

**Signkraft Co** ... G ... 217 787-7105
Springfield *(G-20524)*

**Signs By Custom Cutting Inc** ... G ... 630 759-2734
Bolingbrook *(G-2369)*

**Signs By Design** ... G ... 708 599-9970
Palos Hills *(G-17124)*

**Signs By Tomorrow** ... G ... 815 436-0880
Plainfield *(G-17648)*

**Signs For Success Inc** ... F ... 847 800-4870
Buffalo Grove *(G-2772)*

**Signs In Dundee Inc** ... G ... 847 742-9530
Elgin *(G-9179)*

**Signs Now** ... G ... 847 427-0005
Elk Grove Village *(G-9740)*

**Signs Now** ... G ... 800 356-3373
Chicago *(G-6511)*

**Signs of Distinction Inc** ... G ... 847 520-0787
Wheeling *(G-22152)*

**Signs Plus** ... G ... 847 489-9009
Des Plaines *(G-8275)*

**Signs To You** ... G ... 708 429-6783
Tinley Park *(G-20944)*

**Signs Today Inc** ... G ... 847 934-9777
Palatine *(G-17074)*

**Signscapes Inc** ... G ... 847 719-2610
Lake Zurich *(G-13131)*

**◆ Signsdirect Inc** ... G ... 309 820-1070
Bloomington *(G-2224)*

**Signtastic Inc** ... G ... 708 598-4749
Palos Hills *(G-17125)*

**Signwise Inc** ... G ... 630 932-3204
Lombard *(G-13853)*

**Signworx Sign & Lighting Co** ... G ... 217 413-2532
Springfield *(G-20525)*

**Signx Co Inc** ... G ... 847 639-7917
Cary *(G-3371)*

**Simply Signs** ... G ... 309 849-9016
Metamora *(G-14750)*

**Skyward Promotions Inc** ... G ... 815 969-0909
Rockford *(G-18619)*

**Skywide Publicity Solutions** ... G ... 331 425-0341
Aurora *(G-1219)*

**Solar Traffic Systems Inc** ... G ... 331 318-8500
Lemont *(G-13263)*

**South Water Signs LLC** ... E ... 630 333-4900
Elmhurst *(G-9940)*

**Specialty Graphics Supply Inc** ... G ... 630 584-8202
Saint Charles *(G-19267)*

**Square 1 Precision Ltg Inc** ... G ... 708 343-1500
Melrose Park *(G-14695)*

**Staar Bales Lestarge Inc** ... G ... 618 259-6366
East Alton *(G-8611)*

**Stans Sportsworld Inc** ... G ... 217 359-8474
Champaign *(G-3547)*

**Stecker Graphics Inc** ... G ... 309 786-4973
Rock Island *(G-18204)*

**▲ Stellar Recognition Inc** ... D ... 773 282-8060
Chicago *(G-6588)*

**Stelmont Inc** ... G ... 847 870-0200
Arlington Heights *(G-843)*

**Stevens Exhibits & Displays** ... E ... 773 523-3900
Chicago *(G-6595)*

**Stevens Sign Co Inc** ... G ... 708 562-4888
Northlake *(G-16453)*

**Store 409 Inc** ... F ... 708 478-5751
Mokena *(G-14905)*

**Strictly Neon Inc** ... G ... 708 597-1616
Crestwood *(G-7504)*

**▲ Sub-Surface Sign Co Ltd** ... E ... 847 675-6530
Skokie *(G-20094)*

**Summit Signworks Inc** ... G ... 847 870-0937
Arlington Heights *(G-848)*

**Super Sign Service** ... F ... 309 829-9241
Bloomington *(G-2227)*

**Swansea Sign A Rama Inc** ... G ... 618 234-7446
Belleville *(G-1677)*

**T Graphics** ... G ... 618 592-4145
Oblong *(G-16735)*

**T Ham Sign Inc** ... F ... 618 242-2010
Opdyke *(G-16811)*

**T J Marche Ltd** ... G ... 618 445-2314
Albion *(G-366)*

**Targin Sign Systems Inc** ... G ... 630 766-7667
Wood Dale *(G-22427)*

**Technicraft Supply Co** ... G ... 309 495-5245
Peoria *(G-17468)*

**Teds Shirt Shack Inc** ... G ... 217 224-9705
Quincy *(G-17892)*

**Teraco-II Inc** ... E ... 630 539-4400
Roselle *(G-18981)*

**Tfa Signs** ... G ... 773 267-6007
Chicago *(G-6708)*

**Tgrv LLC** ... G ... 815 634-2102
Bourbonnais *(G-2407)*

**Thermo-Graphic LLC** ... E ... 630 350-2226
Bensenville *(G-2001)*

**Timothy Anderson Corporation** ... F ... 815 398-8371
Rockford *(G-18651)*

**Timothy Darrey** ... G ... 847 231-2277
Des Plaines *(G-8286)*

**Toms Signs** ... G ... 630 377-8525
Saint Charles *(G-19284)*

**Traffic Control & Protection** ... E ... 630 293-0026
West Chicago *(G-21784)*

**Transportation Illinois Dept** ... F ... 217 785-0288
Springfield *(G-20546)*

**Trophytime Inc** ... G ... 217 351-7958
Champaign *(G-3550)*

**Turk Electric Sign Co** ... G ... 773 736-9300
Chicago *(G-6793)*

**Turnroth Sign Company Inc** ... F ... 815 625-1155
Rock Falls *(G-18156)*

**Twin City Awards** ... G ... 309 452-9291
Normal *(G-16091)*

**Ultimate Sign Co** ... G ... 773 282-4595
Chicago *(G-6807)*

**Unistrut International Corp** ... D ... 630 773-3460
Addison *(G-334)*

**◆ United Wire Craft Inc** ... C ... 847 375-3800
Des Plaines *(G-8291)*

**Varsity Striping & Cnstr Co** ... E ... 217 352-2203
Champaign *(G-3553)*

**▲ Vindee Industries Inc** ... E ... 815 469-3300
Frankfort *(G-10375)*

**Vinyl Graphics Inc** ... G ... 708 579-1234
Countryside *(G-7450)*

**▲ Visual Marketing Inc** ... E ... 312 664-9177
Chicago *(G-6905)*

**Visual Marketing Solutions** ... G ... 815 589-3848
Fulton *(G-10707)*

**Vital Signs USA** ... G ... 630 832-9600
Elmhurst *(G-9958)*

**W G N Flag & Decorating Co** ... F ... 773 768-8076
Chicago *(G-6918)*

**▲ Wagner Zip-Change Inc** ... E ... 708 681-4100
Melrose Park *(G-14706)*

**Walnut Creek Hardwood** ... G ... 815 389-3317
South Beloit *(G-20173)*

**Warren Wiersema Signs** ... G ... 815 589-3001
Fulton *(G-10708)*

**▲ Watchfire Enterprises Inc** ... E ... 217 442-0611
Danville *(G-7780)*

**◆ Watchfire Signs LLC** ... B ... 217 442-0611
Danville *(G-7781)*

**Watchfire Tech Holdings I Inc** ... G ... 217 442-6971
Danville *(G-7782)*

**Watchfire Tech Holdings II Inc** ... G ... 217 442-0611
Danville *(G-7783)*

**Wave Mechanics Neon** ... G ... 312 829-9283
Chicago *(G-6944)*

**Weakley Printing & Sign Shop** ... G ... 847 473-4466
North Chicago *(G-16189)*

**Weatherford Signs** ... G ... 618 529-2000
Carbondale *(G-3027)*

**Weathertop Woodcraft** ... G ...
Carol Stream *(G-3265)*

**Weiskamp Screen Printing** ... G ... 217 398-8428
Champaign *(G-3560)*

**West Zwick Corp** ... G ... 217 222-0228
Quincy *(G-17903)*

**Western Lighting Inc** ... F ... 847 451-7200
Franklin Park *(G-10628)*

**Western Remac Inc** ... E ... 630 972-7770
Woodridge *(G-22524)*

**White Way Sign & Maint Co** ... C ... 847 391-0200
Chicago *(G-6974)*

**Willdon Corp** ... E ... 773 276-7080
Chicago *(G-6981)*

**◆ William Frick & Company** ... E ... 847 918-3700
Libertyville *(G-13401)*

**Windy City Plastics Inc** ... G ... 773 533-1099
Chicago *(G-6999)*

**▲ Wiremasters Incorporated** ... E ... 773 254-3700
Chicago *(G-7005)*

**Wow Signs Inc** ... G ... 847 910-4405
Deerfield *(G-8069)*

**Wright Quick Signs Inc** ... G ... 708 652-6020
Cicero *(G-7247)*

**Xpressigns Inc** ... G ... 888 303-0640
Arlington Heights *(G-876)*

**Xtrem Graphix Solutions Inc** ... G ... 217 698-6424
Springfield *(G-20549)*

**Ye Olde Sign Shoppe** ... G ... 847 228-7446
Elk Grove Village *(G-9822)*

**Zainab Enterprises Inc** ... G ... 630 739-0110
Romeoville *(G-18881)*

Zimmerman Enterprises Inc .................. F ....... 847 297-3177
Des Plaines (G-8308)

## 3995 Burial Caskets

Dixline Corporation ............................... D ....... 309 932-2011
Galva (G-10788)
Doric Products Inc .............................. D ....... 217 826-6302
Marshall (G-14321)
▲ Greenwood Inc ................................ F ....... 800 798-4900
Danville (G-7728)
Illinois Casket Company ...................... G ....... 773 483-4500
Chicago (G-5155)
Loyal Casket Co ................................. F ....... 773 722-4065
Chicago (G-5549)
Tolar Group LLC ................................. E ....... 847 668-9485
Oak Park (G-16689)

## 3996 Linoleum & Hard Surface Floor Coverings, NEC

Carpets By Kuniej ............................... G ....... 815 232-9060
Freeport (G-10650)
Kitchen & Bath Gallery ......................... G ....... 217 214-0310
Quincy (G-17845)
Owens Corning Sales LLC ................... E ....... 708 594-6935
Argo (G-695)
◆ Surface Shields Inc ......................... E ....... 708 226-9810
Orland Park (G-16896)

## 3999 Manufacturing Industries, NEC

3 Goldenstar Inc .................................. F ....... 847 963-0451
Palatine (G-16994)
312 Aquaponics LLC ........................... G ....... 312 469-0239
Des Plaines (G-8137)
3dp Unlimited ..................................... G ....... 815 389-5667
Roscoe (G-18887)
◆ 3M Dekalb Distribution ..................... G ....... 815 756-5087
Dekalb (G-8071)
425 Manufacturing .............................. G ....... 815 873-7066
Rockford (G-18236)
◆ A and T Cigarettes Imports .............. G ....... 847 836-9134
East Dundee (G-8627)
A Beadtiful Thing ................................ G ....... 630 236-5913
Aurora (G-953)
A Stucki Company ............................... E ....... 618 498-4442
Jerseyville (G-12416)
A Wiley & Associates .......................... G ....... 815 343-7401
Ottawa (G-16945)
ABC Beverage Mfg Inc ........................ G ....... 708 449-2600
Northlake (G-16424)
▲ Accurate Parts Mfg Co .................... E ....... 630 616-4125
Bensenville (G-1813)
Ace Wood Products LLC ..................... G ....... 630 557-2115
Sugar Grove (G-20716)
Aci Plastics Manufacturing .................. G ....... 630 629-0400
Addison (G-19)
Acme Design Inc ................................. G ....... 847 841-7400
Elgin (G-8932)
Acme Finishing Company LLC ............ F ....... 847 640-7890
Elk Grove Village (G-9264)
Advance Manufacturing ....................... G ....... 618 245-6515
Farina (G-10172)
◆ Afam Concept Inc ........................... C ....... 773 838-1336
Chicago (G-3779)
Al Mite Manufacturing Co Inc .............. G ....... 815 654-0720
Machesney Park (G-14054)
Albert F Amling LLC ............................ C ....... 630 333-1720
Elmhurst (G-9832)
All For Dogs Inc .................................. G ....... 708 744-4113
Plainfield (G-17578)
Alliance For Illinois Mfg ....................... G ....... 773 594-9292
Chicago (G-3813)
Alpha Industries Inc ............................ G ....... 847 945-1740
Deerfield (G-7974)
Amerex Corporation ............................ E ....... 309 382-4389
North Pekin (G-16192)
America Display Inc ............................ F ....... 708 430-7000
Bridgeview (G-2463)
American Alum Extrusion Co LLC ....... G ....... 877 896-2236
Roscoe (G-18889)
American Fur Enterprises ................... G ....... 618 542-2018
Du Quoin (G-8550)
American Tape Measures ................... G ....... 312 208-0282
Chicago (G-3877)
Ameriguard Corporation ..................... G ....... 630 986-1900
Burr Ridge (G-2822)
Amk Enterprises Chicago Inc ............. G ....... 312 523-7212
Chicago (G-3890)
Amt Corp ............................................ G ....... 847 459-6177
Deerfield (G-7977)

Andrew C Arnold ................................. G ....... 815 220-0282
Peru (G-17499)
Android Industries LLC ....................... G ....... 815 544-4165
Belvidere (G-1733)
▲ Anfinsen Plastic Moulding Inc ......... E ....... 630 554-4100
Oswego (G-16904)
Aquadine Inc ...................................... G ....... 800 497-3463
Harvard (G-11621)
AR Industries ..................................... G ....... 630 543-0282
Addison (G-43)
Arrow Sales & Service Inc ................... G ....... 815 223-0251
La Salle (G-12765)
▲ Assemblers Inc ............................... C ....... 773 378-3000
Chicago (G-3965)
Associated Design Inc ........................ F ....... 708 974-9100
Palos Hills (G-17114)
▲ Atlas Manufacturing ........................ G ....... 773 327-3005
Chicago (G-3982)
Atlas Match LLC ................................. D ....... 815 469-2314
Western Springs (G-21864)
Auth-Florence Mfg .............................. G .......
Glendale Heights (G-11010)
Awesome Hand Services LLC ............. G ....... 630 445-8695
Rolling Meadows (G-18714)
B and B Amusement Illinois LLC ......... G ....... 309 585-2077
Bloomington (G-2145)
◆ B and K Mueller Industries ............... G ....... 847 290-1108
Elk Grove Village (G-9330)
◆ Badge-A-Minit Ltd ........................... E ....... 815 883-8822
Oglesby (G-16746)
▲ Baker Manufacturing LLC ................ G ....... 847 362-3663
Lake Bluff (G-12835)
Baumbach Manufacturing ................... G ....... 630 941-0505
Elmhurst (G-9836)
Beachwaver ........................................ E ....... 224 513-5817
Libertyville (G-13308)
Bella Casa .......................................... G ....... 630 455-5900
Hinsdale (G-11941)
◆ Belvedere Usa LLC ......................... C ....... 815 544-3131
Belvidere (G-1736)
Bentleys Pet Stuff LLC ....................... G ....... 312 222-1012
Chicago (G-4084)
Bentleys Pet Stuff LLC ....................... F ....... 847 793-0500
Long Grove (G-13886)
Bentleys Pet Stuff LLC ....................... G ....... 224 567-4700
Long Grove (G-13887)
▲ Bestpysanky Inc .............................. G ....... 877 797-2659
Morton Grove (G-15189)
Blast Zone .......................................... F ....... 847 996-0100
Vernon Hills (G-21151)
▼ Bocks Cattle-Identi Co Inc .............. G ....... 217 234-6634
Mattoon (G-14384)
Bodacious Beads Inc .......................... G ....... 847 699-7959
Des Plaines (G-8160)
Bogart Industries LLC ........................ G ....... 224 242-4578
Elburn (G-8878)
Bone A Fide Pet Grooming .................. G ....... 217 872-0907
Decatur (G-7848)
Bork Industries ................................... G ....... 630 365-5517
Maple Park (G-14198)
Borse Industries Inc ........................... G ....... 630 325-1210
Willowbrook (G-22201)
Boss Manufacturing Holdings ............. G ....... 309 852-2131
Kewanee (G-12676)
▲ Bradley Industries Inc ..................... E ....... 815 469-2314
Frankfort (G-10304)
Brees Studio Inc ................................. F ....... 618 687-3331
Murphysboro (G-15573)
Buff & Go Inc ...................................... G ....... 773 719-4436
Chicago (G-4182)
Buh Hines Group LLC ........................ G ....... 847 336-1460
Gurnee (G-11432)
Buhrke Industries LLC ....................... E ....... 847 981-7550
Downers Grove (G-8400)
Burke Whistles Inc ............................. G ....... 618 534-7953
Murphysboro (G-15574)
Busy Beaver Button Company ............ G ....... 773 645-3359
Chicago (G-4192)
Bw Industries ..................................... G ....... 630 784-1020
Winfield (G-22283)
C & J Industries ................................. G ....... 708 757-4495
Sauk Village (G-19391)
C Becky & Company Inc .................... G ....... 847 818-1021
Mount Prospect (G-15314)
▲ C H Hanson Company ..................... D ....... 630 848-2000
Naperville (G-15613)
Candle Enterprises Inc ....................... G ....... 618 526-8070
Breese (G-2441)
Candle-Licious ................................... G ....... 847 488-9982
Morrison (G-15142)

Cane Plus ........................................... G ....... 217 522-4035
Springfield (G-20403)
Capital Pttern Model Works Inc ........... G ....... 630 469-8200
Glendale Heights (G-11013)
Cargo Support Industries Inc .............. G .......
Inverness (G-12207)
Casper Ernest E Hairgoods ................. G ....... 773 545-2800
Chicago (G-4249)
Ccar Industries ................................... E ....... 217 345-3300
Charleston (G-3591)
Cell Parts Manufacturing Co ............... G ....... 847 669-9690
Huntley (G-12135)
Central Service Center ....................... G ....... 217 423-3900
Decatur (G-7856)
Chicago Art Center Co ........................ G ....... 773 817-2725
Chicago (G-4304)
Chicago Candle Company .................. G ....... 773 637-5279
Chicago (G-4309)
Chicago Scenic Studios Inc ................ D ....... 312 274-9900
Chicago (G-4345)
Cindys Nail & Hair Care ...................... G ....... 847 234-0780
Lake Forest (G-12891)
Circle T Mfg ....................................... G ....... 217 728-4834
Sullivan (G-20744)
Cjj Industries Inc ................................ G ....... 708 921-9290
La Grange Park (G-12753)
Clown Global Brands LLC .................. G ....... 847 564-5950
Northbrook (G-16227)
▲ Cobraco Manufacturing Inc ............. E ....... 847 726-5800
Lake Zurich (G-13055)
◆ Conair Corporation .......................... E ....... 203 351-9000
Rantoul (G-17924)
Consolidated Displays Co Inc ............. G ....... 630 851-8666
Oswego (G-16911)
Creative Werks LLC ........................... E ....... 630 860-2222
Bartlett (G-1340)
▲ Creative Werks LLC ........................ E ....... 630 860-2222
Bensenville (G-1871)
Crutcher Mfg ...................................... G ....... 309 725-3545
Cooksville (G-7372)
Crutcher Mfg ...................................... G ....... 309 724-8206
Ellsworth (G-9827)
Crystal Nails McHenry ........................ G ....... 815 363-5498
McHenry (G-14492)
Cultivated Energy Group Inc ............... G ....... 312 203-8833
Hebron (G-11718)
Curlee Mfg .......................................... G ....... 847 268-6517
Rosemont (G-18995)
▲ CWI Displays Corp .......................... F ....... 773 277-0040
Chicago (G-4528)
◆ Dadant & Sons Inc .......................... D ....... 217 847-3324
Hamilton (G-11533)
Dal Acres West Kennel ....................... G ....... 217 793-3647
Springfield (G-20428)
Danko Industries ................................ G ....... 630 882-6070
Yorkville (G-22654)
▼ Delaval Manufacturing .................... G ....... 847 298-5505
Des Plaines (G-8179)
▲ Denoyer - Geppert Science Co ........ E ....... 800 621-1014
Skokie (G-19990)
Design Merchants .............................. G ....... 630 208-1850
Geneva (G-10825)
▲ Design Plus Industries Inc .............. G ....... 309 697-9778
Peoria (G-17349)
Diamond Dogs ................................... G ....... 773 267-0069
Chicago (G-4593)
Diamond Quality Manufacturing .......... G ....... 815 521-4184
Channahon (G-3570)
Discuss Music Education Co .............. G ....... 773 561-2796
Chicago (G-4610)
DMJ Group Inc ................................... G ....... 847 322-7533
Algonquin (G-388)
DPM Solutions LLC ............................ G ....... 630 285-1170
Itasca (G-12254)
Duchossois Industries Inc Non ........... G ....... 630 279-3600
Oak Brook (G-16504)
Dura-Crafts Corp ................................ F ....... 815 464-3561
Frankfort (G-10316)
Dyno Manufacturing Inc ..................... G ....... 618 451-6609
Madison (G-14143)
E J Kupjack & Associates Inc ............. G ....... 847 823-6661
Chicago (G-4666)
E2 Manufacturing Group LLC ............. G ....... 224 399-9608
Waukegan (G-21554)
▲ Ecologic Industries LLC .................. E ....... 847 234-5855
Gurnee (G-11444)
Edmark Visual Identification ............... G ....... 800 923-8333
Chicago (G-4696)
Educational Insights Inc ..................... E ....... 847 573-8400
Vernon Hills (G-21158)

**Elan Furs** F 317 255-6100
Morton Grove *(G-15195)*
**Elia Day Spa** F 708 535-1450
Oak Forest *(G-16579)*
**Elite Industries** G 224 433-6988
Gurnee *(G-11447)*
**Enz (usa) Inc** G 630 692-7880
Aurora *(G-1004)*
**Erell Manufacturing Company** F 847 427-3000
Elk Grove Village *(G-9464)*
**Evergreen Scale Models Inc** F 224 567-8099
Des Plaines *(G-8191)*
**Evo Exhibits LLC** G 630 520-0710
West Chicago *(G-21697)*
**F & A Industries Company LLC** G 630 504-9839
Oak Lawn *(G-16618)*
**Fab Con Industries Inc** G 618 969-9040
Eldorado *(G-8920)*
**Fiberforge Corporation** E 970 945-9377
Chicago *(G-4840)*
▲ **First Alert Inc** G 630 499-3295
Aurora *(G-1009)*
**Flame Guard Usa LLC** G 815 219-4074
Lake Barrington *(G-12806)*
**Floralstar Enterprises** G 847 726-0124
Hawthorn Woods *(G-11702)*
**Flurry Industries Inc** G 630 882-8361
Yorkville *(G-22658)*
**Freitas P Sabah** G 708 386-8934
Oak Park *(G-16664)*
**Fun Industries Inc** F 309 755-5021
East Moline *(G-8679)*
**Fuyao Glass Illinois Inc** C 217 864-2392
Decatur *(G-7883)*
**G & M Industries Inc** G 618 344-6655
Collinsville *(G-7326)*
**Gabel & Schubert Bronze** F 773 878-6800
Chicago *(G-4905)*
**Galvanize Labs Inc** G 630 258-1476
Palos Heights *(G-17104)*
**Gateway Seed Company Inc** G 618 327-8000
Nashville *(G-15836)*
**Gbn Nails LLC** G 773 881-8880
Chicago *(G-4921)*
**General Precision Mfg LLC** G 847 624-4969
Elk Grove Village *(G-9497)*
**Genetics Development Corp** G 847 283-9780
Lake Bluff *(G-12845)*
**Gilster-Mary Lee Corporation** G 618 826-3102
Chester *(G-3656)*
**GM Partners** G 847 895-7627
Schaumburg *(G-19538)*
**Goble Manufacturing Inc** G 217 932-5615
Casey *(G-3384)*
**Godbey Industries** G 773 769-4391
Chicago *(G-4967)*
◆ **Grand Products Inc** C 800 621-6101
Elk Grove Village *(G-9506)*
**Grande Diva Hair Salon** E 217 383-0023
Champaign *(G-3491)*
**Green Giant** G 815 544-0438
Belvidere *(G-1758)*
**Groomsmart Inc** G 847 836-6007
Dundee *(G-8562)*
**H and D Distribution Inc** G 847 247-2011
Libertyville *(G-13328)*
▲ **H Hal Kramer Co** G 847 441-0213
Northfield *(G-16401)*
**H V Manufacturing Vanguar** G 847 229-5502
Wheeling *(G-22063)*
**Hagen Manufacturing Inc** G 224 735-2099
Wheeling *(G-22064)*
**Hairline Creations Inc** F 773 282-5454
Chicago *(G-5032)*
**Hangables Inc** F 847 673-9770
Skokie *(G-20010)*
**Hearthside Food Solutions LLC** C 217 784-4238
Gibson City *(G-10901)*
**Heartland Candle Co** G 815 698-2200
Ashkum *(G-925)*
**Heartland House Designs** G 708 383-2278
Oak Park *(G-16668)*
**Hi-Tech Builidng Systems** G 847 526-5310
Wauconda *(G-21468)*
**Holm Industries** G 309 343-3332
Galesburg *(G-10759)*
**Houghton Mifflin Harcourt Co** G 630 467-6049
Itasca *(G-12275)*
**Hu-Friedy Mfg Co LLC** F 847 257-4500
Des Plaines *(G-8206)*

▲ **Hue Circle Inc** G 224 567-8116
Glenview *(G-11138)*
▲ **Hunter Mfg LLP** D 859 254-7573
Lake Forest *(G-12912)*
**I T C W Inc** B 630 305-8849
Naperville *(G-15671)*
▲ **Idex Mpt Inc** D 630 530-3333
Elmhurst *(G-9884)*
▲ **Ihi Turbo America Co** D 217 774-9571
Shelbyville *(G-19908)*
▲ **Illinois Bottle Mfg Co** D 847 595-9000
Elk Grove Village *(G-9533)*
**Illumivation Studios LLC** G 312 261-5561
Chicago *(G-5160)*
**Imagination Products Corp** G 309 274-6223
Chillicothe *(G-7167)*
**Imagine That Candle Co** G 708 481-6370
Matteson *(G-14373)*
**In Aaw Hair Emporium LLC** G 779 227-1450
Joliet *(G-12515)*
**Indigo Cigar Factory** G 217 348-1514
Charleston *(G-3600)*
**Infamous Industries Inc** G 708 789-2326
Hickory Hills *(G-11771)*
▲ **Inspira Industries Inc** G 630 907-2123
North Aurora *(G-16134)*
**Integrated Industries Inc** G 773 299-1970
Chicago *(G-5208)*
▲ **Integrated Mfg Tech LLC** E 618 282-8306
Red Bud *(G-17943)*
**Interesting Products Inc** G 773 265-1100
Chicago *(G-5211)*
**International Tactical Trainin** G 872 221-4886
Chicago *(G-5223)*
**Interntonal Hair Solutions LLC** G 404 474-3547
Schaumburg *(G-19574)*
◆ **Ironwood Mfg Inc** G 630 778-8963
Naperville *(G-15679)*
▲ **ITW Bldg Components Group** G 847 634-1900
Glenview *(G-11150)*
**J B Burling Group Ltd** G 773 327-5362
Chicago *(G-5255)*
**J Garvin Industries** G 708 819-1148
Evergreen Park *(G-10116)*
**Jail Education Solutions Inc** E 773 263-0718
Chicago *(G-5272)*
◆ **James Coleman Company** F 847 963-8100
Rolling Meadows *(G-18735)*
**Jf Industries Inc** G 773 775-8840
Chicago *(G-5301)*
▲ **Jing MEI Industrial USA Inc** E 847 671-0800
Rosemont *(G-19007)*
**Jr Industries LLC** F 773 908-5317
Chicago *(G-5332)*
▲ **K M I International Corp** G 630 627-6300
Addison *(G-164)*
**Kemis Kollections** G 773 431-2037
Chicago *(G-5375)*
**Kemp Manufacturing Company** E 309 682-7292
Peoria *(G-17395)*
▲ **Keys Manufacturing Company Inc** E 217 465-4001
Paris *(G-17152)*
▲ **Kim Tiffani Institute LLC** D 312 260-9000
Lincolnwood *(G-13519)*
**Kkj Industries LLC** G 630 202-9160
Villa Park *(G-21265)*
**Km4 Manufacturing** G 708 924-5150
Bedford Park *(G-1559)*
▲ **Kmp Products LLC** G 630 956-0438
Westmont *(G-21899)*
**Knapheide Mfg Co** E 217 223-1848
Quincy *(G-17848)*
**Kriese Mfg** G 815 748-2683
Cortland *(G-7392)*
**Kunverji Enterprise Corp** F 847 683-2954
Burlington *(G-2812)*
**Kyjen Company LLC** F 847 504-4010
Northbrook *(G-16291)*
**L & M Hardware Ltd** G 312 805-2752
Downers Grove *(G-8471)*
◆ **Lcg Sales Inc** D 773 378-7455
Chicago *(G-5476)*
▲ **Leapfrog Product Dev LLC** F 312 229-0089
Chicago *(G-5480)*
◆ **Learning Resources Inc** D 847 573-9471
Vernon Hills *(G-21181)*
**Learning Seed LLC** G 847 540-8855
Chicago *(G-5481)*
**Ledretrofitting Inc** G 815 347-5047
Glen Ellyn *(G-10975)*

**Lifts of Illinois Inc** G 309 923-7450
Roanoke *(G-18052)*
**Lincoln Green Mazda Inc** F 217 391-2400
Springfield *(G-20470)*
**Linx** G 847 910-5303
Chicago *(G-5515)*
**Live Love Hair** G 530 554-2471
Lansing *(G-13174)*
**Love Journey Inc** G 773 447-5591
Chicago *(G-5548)*
▲ **Lucky Yuppy Puppy Co Inc** G 847 437-7879
Arlington Heights *(G-796)*
**Luminescence Media Group Nfp** G 312 602-3302
Chicago *(G-5566)*
▲ **Luxury Living Inc** G 847 845-3863
Cary *(G-3358)*
**M & A Grocery** G 708 749-9786
Stickney *(G-20624)*
**M Squared Industries LLC** G 708 606-2603
Chicago *(G-5587)*
**Mac Medical Inc** G 618 719-6757
Belleville *(G-1650)*
**Makray Manufacturing Company** E 847 260-5408
Schiller Park *(G-19844)*
**Manhattan Eyelash EXT Sew On** G 847 818-8774
Arlington Heights *(G-798)*
**Marca Industries Inc** E 773 884-4500
Burbank *(G-2808)*
**Marking Specialists/Poly** F 847 793-8100
Buffalo Grove *(G-2731)*
**Marley Candles** E 815 485-6604
Mokena *(G-14883)*
**Marshall Manufacturing LLC** G 312 914-7288
Chicago *(G-5631)*
**Mat Capital LLC** G 847 821-9630
Long Grove *(G-13895)*
**Mbs Manufacturing** G 630 227-0300
Franklin Park *(G-10524)*
**Medline Industries Inc** F 847 557-2400
Libertyville *(G-13352)*
**Metrom Rail LLC** F 847 874-7233
Crystal Lake *(G-7610)*
**Mgn Tool & Mfg Co Inc** G 630 849-3575
Carol Stream *(G-3195)*
**Midland Product LLC** F 708 444-8200
Tinley Park *(G-20932)*
**Midstate Industries** G 217 268-3900
Sullivan *(G-20752)*
▲ **Midwest Foods Mfg Inc** E 847 455-4636
Franklin Park *(G-10533)*
**Midwest Nameplate Corp** G 708 614-0606
Orland Park *(G-16875)*
▲ **Ming Trading LLC** G 773 442-2221
Chicago *(G-5767)*
**Mint Masters Inc** E 847 451-1133
Franklin Park *(G-10534)*
**Mobilty Works** G 815 254-2000
Plainfield *(G-17629)*
**Models Plus Inc** E 847 231-4300
Grayslake *(G-11354)*
▲ **Modern Specialties Company** G 312 648-5800
Chicago *(G-5785)*
**Modern Sprout LLC** G 312 342-2114
Chicago *(G-5786)*
**Mold Repair and Manufacturing** G 815 477-1332
Crystal Lake *(G-7615)*
▲ **Molor Products Company** F 630 375-5999
Oswego *(G-16927)*
▲ **Mondelez Global LLC** C 847 943-4000
Deerfield *(G-8037)*
**Monty Burcenski** G 815 838-0934
Lockport *(G-13733)*
**Morris Industries Inc** G 630 739-1502
Lemont *(G-13243)*
**Mp Manufacturing Inc** G 815 334-1112
Woodstock *(G-22593)*
▲ **Mpc Containment Intl LLC** D 773 927-4120
Chicago *(G-5821)*
**Murff Enterprises LLC** G 203 685-5556
Chicago *(G-5834)*
▲ **Namco America Inc** E 847 264-5610
Elk Grove Village *(G-9645)*
**Nascote Industries Inc** G 618 327-3286
Nashville *(G-15842)*
**Nature House Inc** D 217 833-2393
Griggsville *(G-11413)*
**Northwoods Wreaths Company** E 847 615-9491
Lake Forest *(G-12931)*
**Northwstern Globl Hlth Fndtion** G 214 207-9485
Chicago *(G-5943)*

Omega Door Frame Products ... E ... 630 773-9900
Itasca (G-12335)
Online Merchant Systems LLC ... G ... 847 973-2337
Ingleside (G-12197)
▲ Orbus LLC ... C ... 630 226-1155
Woodridge (G-22506)
Orbus LLC ... C ... 847 647-1012
Des Plaines (G-8247)
▲ Orlandi Statuary Company ... D ... 773 489-0303
Chicago (G-6015)
Oval Fire Products Corporation ... G ... 630 635-5000
Glendale Heights (G-11055)
Palapa Coatings Inc ... G ... 847 628-6360
Elgin (G-9134)
Paradigm Development Group Inc ... F ... 847 545-9600
Winfield (G-22289)
Partylite Inc ... E ... 630 845-6025
Batavia (G-1480)
Pawz & Klawz ... G ... 630 257-0245
Lemont (G-13252)
◆ PC Successor Inc ... C ... 630 783-2400
Lemont (G-13253)
Pegasus Mfg Inc ... F ... 309 342-9337
Galesburg (G-10770)
Performance Manufacturing ... G ... 630 231-8099
West Chicago (G-21756)
Pet King Brands Inc ... G ... 630 241-3905
Westmont (G-21911)
▲ Petego Egr LLC ... G ... 312 726-1341
Chicago (G-6108)
▲ Petote LLC ... G ... 312 455-0873
Chicago (G-6112)
▲ Phoenix Industries Inc ... G ... 708 478-5474
Mokena (G-14895)
▼ Pioneer Industries Intl Inc ... G ... 630 543-7676
Itasca (G-12340)
▲ Plastic Container Corporation ... D ... 217 352-2722
Urbana (G-21098)
Platinum Touch Industries LLC ... G ... 773 775-9988
Des Plaines (G-8256)
Pollack Manufacturing Co LLC ... G ... 815 520-8415
Crystal Lake (G-7626)
▲ Polycorp Illinois Inc ... D ... 773 847-7575
Chicago (G-6154)
▲ Polygroup Services NA Inc ... G ... 847 851-9995
East Dundee (G-8653)
Potash Holding Company Inc ... G ... 847 849-4200
Northbrook (G-16341)
Pratt Industries ... D ... 630 254-0271
Sauk Village (G-19392)
▲ Prevue Pet Products Inc ... F ... 773 722-1052
Chicago (G-6183)
Prospan Manufacturing ... G ... 847 815-0191
Rosemont (G-19025)
Pru Dent Mfg Inc ... G ... 847 301-1170
Schaumburg (G-19703)
QS Luxurious Hair & Shoes Inc ... G ... 773 556-6092
Bellwood (G-1716)
Quad-Illinois Inc ... F ... 847 836-1115
Elgin (G-9155)
◆ Quality Technology Intl Inc ... E ... 847 649-9300
Elgin (G-9158)
R L Allen Industries ... G ... 618 667-2544
Troy (G-21011)
▲ R S Owens & Co Inc ... B ... 773 282-6000
Chicago (G-6273)
Ramona Sedivy ... G ... 630 983-1902
Naperville (G-15738)
Rebechini Studio Inc ... F ... 847 364-8600
Elk Grove Village (G-9711)
Research Mannikins Inc ... F ... 618 426-3456
Ava (G-1242)
Rexnord Industries LLC ... C ... 630 719-2345
Downers Grove (G-8516)
Ringmaster Mfg ... G ... 815 675-4230
Spring Grove (G-20362)
▲ River City Sign Company Inc ... G ... 309 796-3606
Silvis (G-19940)
River North Industries Inc ... G ... 773 600-4960
Spring Grove (G-20363)
Riverside Memorial Co ... G ... 217 323-1280
Beardstown (G-1527)
Riverview Mfg House SA ... G ... 815 625-1459
Rock Falls (G-18148)
Riviera Tan Spa (del) ... G ... 618 466-1012
Godfrey (G-11235)
▲ Roberts Colonial House Inc ... F ... 708 331-6233
South Holland (G-20301)
Robs Aquatics ... G ... 708 444-7627
Tinley Park (G-20943)
Rock Island Cannon Company ... G ... 309 786-1507
Rock Island (G-18203)
Rockford Quality Grinding Inc ... F ... 815 227-9001
Rockford (G-18584)
Roll-A-Way Conveyors Inc ... G ... 847 336-5033
Gurnee (G-11500)
▲ Rome Industries Inc ... G ... 309 691-7120
Peoria (G-17448)
Roses Moulding By Design Inc ... E ... 847 549-9200
Mundelein (G-15554)
Rudon Enterprises Inc ... G ... 618 457-0441
Carbondale (G-3022)
Ryan Industries ... G ... 708 479-7600
Mokena (G-14902)
S & S Mfg Solutions LLC ... G ... 815 838-1960
Lockport (G-13743)
▲ Sarj Kalidas LLC ... D ... 708 865-9134
Chicago (G-6446)
Sassy Primitives Ltd ... G ... 815 385-9302
McCullom Lake (G-14472)
Schmit Laboratories Inc ... E ... 773 476-0072
Glendale Heights (G-11066)
Scientific Manufacturing Inc ... G ... 847 414-5658
Sleepy Hollow (G-20118)
Scimatco Office ... E ... 630 879-1306
Batavia (G-1494)
Sean Matthew Innovations Inc ... G ... 815 455-4525
Crystal Lake (G-7646)
Sentry Spring & Mfg Co ... G ... 847 584-9391
Elk Grove Village (G-9734)
▲ Seven Mfg Inc ... G ... 815 356-8102
Crystal Lake (G-7648)
Shedrain Corporation ... G ... 708 848-5212
Oak Park (G-16685)
Shermar Industries LLC ... G ... 847 378-8073
Des Plaines (G-8273)
Skin Care Systems ... G ... 312 644-9067
Chicago (G-6521)
SKW Industries LLC ... F ... 773 261-8900
Chicago (G-6523)
▲ Slagel Manufacturing Inc ... E ... 815 688-3318
Forrest (G-10267)
Smh2 Manufacturing LLC ... G ... 773 793-6643
Chicago (G-6533)
Smith Industrial Rubber & Plas ... F ... 815 874-5364
Rockford (G-18622)
Snowball Industries ... G ... 773 316-0051
Chicago (G-6540)
Southern Blooms LLC ... G ... 618 565-1111
Murphysboro (G-15584)
Sport Electronics Inc ... G ... 847 564-5575
Northbrook (G-16369)
Star Lite Mfg ... G ... 630 595-8338
Wood Dale (G-22424)
Starfish Ventures Inc ... E ... 847 490-9334
Hoffman Estates (G-12059)
▲ Stellar Recognition Inc ... D ... 773 282-8060
Chicago (G-6588)
▼ Stern Pinball Inc ... D ... 708 345-7700
Elk Grove Village (G-9757)
Stock Manufacturing Co LLC ... G ... 773 265-6640
Chicago (G-6597)
Sturtevant Inc ... G ... 630 613-8968
Lombard (G-13861)
Sun Pattern & Model Inc ... E ... 630 293-3366
West Chicago (G-21777)
▲ Sunscape Time Inc ... G ... 708 345-8791
Melrose Park (G-14698)
Sustainable Holding Inc ... G ... 773 324-0407
Chicago (G-6643)
Swan Manufacturing Co ... E ... 309 441-6985
Geneseo (G-10806)
Sweet Beginnings LLC ... G ... 773 638-7058
Chicago (G-6647)
Synergetic Industries ... G ... 309 321-8145
Morton (G-15183)
T P R Resources Inc ... G ... 630 443-9060
Saint Charles (G-19278)
Tatine ... G ... 312 733-0173
Chicago (G-6678)
▲ Technical Power Systems Inc ... E ... 630 719-1471
Lisle (G-13670)
Thrilled LLC ... G ... 312 404-1929
Chicago (G-6723)
Tii Technical Educatn Systems ... G ... 847 428-3085
Gilberts (G-10939)
Tishma Engineering LLC ... G ... 847 755-1200
Elk Grove Village (G-9781)
Top Dollar Slots ... G ... 779 210-4884
Loves Park (G-14002)
Trident Industries ... F ... 847 285-1316
Schaumburg (G-19773)
Tropar Trophy Manufacturing Co ... E ... 630 787-1900
Wood Dale (G-22433)
Troy Design & Manufacturing Co ... G ... 773 646-0804
Chicago (G-6782)
Two Consulting ... G ... 630 830-2415
Bartlett (G-1382)
UIC ... F ... 312 413-7697
Chicago (G-6805)
▼ US International Inc ... G ... 312 671-9207
Chicago (G-6854)
Utlx Manufacturing Inc ... G ... 419 698-3820
Chicago (G-6862)
◆ Veeco Manufacturing Inc ... E ... 312 666-0900
Melrose Park (G-14705)
Visionary Solutions Inc ... G ... 847 296-9615
Des Plaines (G-8299)
Vrmc LLC ... G ... 612 210-1868
Downers Grove (G-8538)
Vs Mfg Co ... G ... 224 475-1190
Lake Zurich (G-13141)
▲ W J Dennis & Company ... F ... 847 697-4800
Elgin (G-9225)
◆ Wahl Clipper Corporation ... A ... 815 625-6525
Sterling (G-20619)
Wahl Clipper Corporation ... F ... 815 625-6525
Sterling (G-20620)
Waterway Rv LLC Mfg Home ... G ... 312 207-1835
Chicago (G-6943)
Waxman Candles Inc ... G ... 773 929-3000
Chicago (G-6945)
Western Sand & Gravel Co ... F ... 815 433-1600
Ottawa (G-16991)
Whyte Gate Incorporated ... F ... 847 201-7000
Grayslake (G-11366)
Wielgus Product Models Inc ... E ... 312 432-1950
Chicago (G-6977)
Wikus Technology ... G ... 630 766-0960
Addison (G-344)
Williams Electronic Games De ... B ... 773 961-1000
Chicago (G-6985)
Williams Electronic Games De ... F ... 773 961-1000
Chicago (G-6986)
Wilton Brands Inc ... F ... 815 823-8547
Joliet (G-12589)
Wish Bone Rescue ... G ... 309 212-9210
Bloomington (G-2236)
WMS Games Inc ... F ... 773 728-2300
Chicago (G-7015)
WMS Gaming Inc ... C ... 773 961-1747
Chicago (G-7016)
◆ WMS Gaming Inc ... A ... 773 961-1000
Chicago (G-7017)
WMS Industries Inc ... D ... 847 785-3000
Chicago (G-7018)
Wotkun Group Inc ... G ... 708 396-2121
Posen (G-17737)
Write Stuff ... G ... 630 365-4425
Saint Charles (G-19300)
Xd Industries Inc ... G ... 847 293-0796
Prospect Heights (G-17787)
Xl Manufacture ... G ... 773 271-8900
Chicago (G-7045)
Yetter M Co Inc Emp B Tr ... G ... 309 776-4111
Colchester (G-7308)
Yetter Manufacturing Company ... E ... 309 833-1445
Macomb (G-14138)
Zarc International Inc ... F ... 309 807-2565
Minonk (G-14835)
Zeta Manufacturing Company ... G ... 708 301-3766
Homer Glen (G-12089)
Zing Enterprises LLC ... G ... 608 201-9490
Oswego (G-16943)

# 73 BUSINESS SERVICES

## 7372 Prepackaged Software

4ever Printing Inc ... G ... 847 222-1525
Arlington Heights (G-699)
A M P Software Inc ... G ... 630 240-5922
Elk Grove Village (G-9251)
A Trustworthy Sup Source Inc ... G ... 773 480-0255
Chicago (G-3693)
Abki Tech Service Inc ... F ... 847 818-8403
Des Plaines (G-8143)
Access International Inc ... E ... 312 920-9366
Chicago (G-3715)
Accruent LLC ... G ... 847 425-3600
Evanston (G-10002)

S
I
C

**Accuity Inc** B 847 676-9600
Evanston *(G-10003)*

**Accuware Incorporated** F 630 858-8409
Glen Ellyn *(G-10957)*

**Acp Tower Holdings LLC** G 800 835-8527
Chicago *(G-3737)*

**Acresso Software Inc** G 408 642-3865
Schaumburg *(G-19421)*

**Active Simulations Inc** G 630 747-8393
Oak Park *(G-16648)*

**Adams Telephone Co-Operative** E 217 224-9566
Quincy *(G-17789)*

**Adaptive Insights Inc** E 800 303-6346
Rolling Meadows *(G-18707)*

**Adesso Solutions LLC** F 847 342-1095
Rolling Meadows *(G-18708)*

**Adflow Networks** G 866 423-3569
Chicago *(G-3749)*

**Advanced EMR Solutions Inc** G 877 327-6160
Northbrook *(G-16199)*

**Aeverie Inc** G 844 238-3743
Buffalo Grove *(G-2651)*

**Affinnova Inc** G 781 464-4700
Chicago *(G-3780)*

**Agile Health Technologies Inc** E 630 247-5565
Naperville *(G-15789)*

**Ahead LLC** D 312 924-4492
Chicago *(G-3783)*

▲ **Aldea Technologies Inc** E 800 804-0635
Schaumburg *(G-19428)*

**Allscripts Healthcare LLC** G 312 506-1200
Chicago *(G-3820)*

**Allscripts Healthcare LLC** G 800 334-8534
Chicago *(G-3821)*

**Allscrpts Hlthcare Sltions Inc** C 312 506-1200
Chicago *(G-3822)*

**Allscrpts Hlthcare Sltions Inc** C 312 506-1200
Chicago *(G-3823)*

**Alpine Energy Systems LLC** G 630 581-4840
Oak Brook *(G-16487)*

**Amada America Inc** G 877 262-3287
Itasca *(G-12226)*

◆ **American Labelmark Company** C 773 478-0900
Chicago *(G-3859)*

**Amoco Technology Company (del)** C 312 861-6000
Chicago *(G-3892)*

**Anju Software Inc** E 630 243-9810
Woodridge *(G-22452)*

**Anylogic N Amer Ltd Lblty Co** G 312 635-3344
Chicago *(G-3918)*

**Applied Systems Inc** A 708 534-5575
University Park *(G-21041)*

**Appsanity Advisory LLC** G 847 638-1172
Winnetka *(G-22302)*

**Aprimo US LLC** D 877 794-8556
Chicago *(G-3928)*

**Aptean Holdings Inc** F 773 975-3100
Chicago *(G-3929)*

**Aqueous Solutions LLC** G 217 531-1206
Champaign *(G-3452)*

**AR Inet Corp** G 603 380-3903
Aurora *(G-959)*

**ARC Mobile LLC** F 201 838-3410
Western Springs *(G-21863)*

**Ariba Inc** G 630 649-7600
Lisle *(G-13562)*

**Asset Partners Inc** G 312 224-8300
Chicago *(G-3966)*

**Associate Computer Systems** G 618 997-3653
Marion *(G-14254)*

**Associated Agri-Business Inc** G 618 498-2977
Jerseyville *(G-12417)*

**Associated Agri-Business Inc** G 618 498-2977
Eldred *(G-8927)*

**Audibel Hearing Aid Services** G 217 234-6426
Mattoon *(G-14383)*

**Auto Injury Solutions Inc** C 312 229-2704
Chicago *(G-3990)*

**Autonomy Inc** E 312 580-9100
Chicago *(G-3993)*

**Avaya Inc** F 847 885-3598
Schaumburg *(G-19452)*

**Avectra Inc** E 312 425-9094
Chicago *(G-3997)*

**Bantix Technologies LLC** G 630 446-0886
Glen Ellyn *(G-10960)*

**Banyan Technologies Inc** G 312 967-9885
Chicago *(G-4037)*

**Barclay Business Group Inc** G 847 325-5555
Lincolnshire *(G-13431)*

**Barcodesource Inc** G 630 545-9590
West Chicago *(G-21667)*

**Barcoding Inc** F 847 726-7777
Mundelein *(G-15474)*

**Bc Asi Capital II Inc** A 708 534-5575
University Park *(G-21043)*

**Bi Software Inc** G 224 622-4706
Hoffman Estates *(G-11995)*

**Bighand Inc** F 312 893-5906
Chicago *(G-4105)*

**Blue Software LLC** D 773 957-1669
Chicago *(G-4126)*

**BMC Software Inc** E 331 777-8700
Downers Grove *(G-8398)*

**Bosch Sftwr Innovations Corp** E 312 368-2500
Chicago *(G-4147)*

**Braindok LLC** G 847 877-1586
Buffalo Grove *(G-2668)*

**Brainstorm USA** F 773 509-1227
Chicago *(G-4155)*

**Brainware Company** G 773 250-6465
Chicago *(G-4156)*

**Brevity LLC** F 312 375-3996
Chicago *(G-4162)*

**Bridgeline Digital Inc** G 312 784-5720
Chicago *(G-4165)*

**Business Systems Consultants** F 312 553-1253
Chicago *(G-4189)*

**Buyersvine Inc** G 630 235-6804
Hinsdale *(G-11943)*

**Bytebin LLC** G 312 286-0740
Chicago *(G-4197)*

**C W Publications Inc** G 800 554-5537
Sterling *(G-20586)*

**Ca Inc** G 312 201-8557
Chicago *(G-4207)*

**Ca Inc** D 631 342-6000
Lisle *(G-13572)*

**Call Potential LLC** F 877 552-2557
Naperville *(G-15615)*

**Capers North America LLC** F 708 995-7500
Burr Ridge *(G-2827)*

**Capital Merchant Solutions Inc** F 309 452-5990
Bloomington *(G-2152)*

**Capital Tours & Travel Inc** G 847 274-1138
Skokie *(G-19973)*

**Capsim MGT Simulations Inc** E 312 477-7200
Chicago *(G-4231)*

**Captivision Inc** G 630 235-8763
Bolingbrook *(G-2283)*

**Cassetica Software Inc** G 312 546-3668
Chicago *(G-4250)*

**Catalytic Inc** G 312 927-8750
Naperville *(G-15621)*

**Catapult Communications Corp** G 847 884-0048
Schaumburg *(G-19469)*

**CDK Global Inc** A 847 397-1700
Hoffman Estates *(G-11998)*

**Cengage Learning Inc** G 630 554-0821
Downers Grove *(G-8406)*

**Champion Medical Tech Inc** E 866 803-3720
Lake Zurich *(G-13052)*

**Chartnet Technologies Inc** F 630 385-4100
Yorkville *(G-22651)*

**Chewy Software LLC** G 773 935-2627
Chicago *(G-4298)*

**Chicago Data Solutions Inc** G 847 370-4609
Willowbrook *(G-22203)*

**Chwey Software LLC** E 773 525-6445
Chicago *(G-4376)*

**Citrix Systems Inc** G 847 716-4797
Northfield *(G-16398)*

**Cityzenith LLC** F 312 282-2900
Chicago *(G-4390)*

**Classroom Technologies LLC** G 708 548-1642
Frankfort *(G-10310)*

**Clear Nda LLC** F 470 222-6320
Park Ridge *(G-17187)*

**Cleartrial LLC** F 877 206-4846
Chicago *(G-4398)*

**Cleo Communications Inc** E 815 654-8110
Rockford *(G-18312)*

**Clientloyalty LLC** G 312 307-5716
Chicago *(G-4402)*

**Cliqster LLC** G 847 732-1457
Highland Park *(G-11828)*

**Code Sixfour LLC** G 312 429-4802
Chicago *(G-4416)*

**Cognizant Tech Solutions Corp** E 630 955-0617
Lisle *(G-13575)*

**Common Goal Systems Inc** E 630 592-4200
Elmhurst *(G-9855)*

**Community Cllabration Acquatio** G 815 316-6390
Rockford *(G-18318)*

**Community Collaboration Inc** G 815 316-4660
Rockford *(G-18319)*

**Compsoft Tech Sltons Group Inc** F 847 517-9608
Schaumburg *(G-19478)*

**Comptia Learning LLC** F 630 678-8490
Downers Grove *(G-8415)*

**Compusystems Inc** C 708 344-9070
Downers Grove *(G-8416)*

**Computer Pwr Solutions Ill Ltd** E 618 281-8898
Columbia *(G-7355)*

**Computer Svcs & Consulting Inc** E 855 827-8328
Chicago *(G-4441)*

**Computerized Fleet Analysis** G 630 543-1410
Addison *(G-80)*

**Computhink Inc** E 630 705-9050
Lombard *(G-13783)*

**Computing Integrity Inc** G 217 355-4469
Champaign *(G-3469)*

**Comvigo Inc** G 240 255-4093
Willowbrook *(G-22205)*

**Cona LLC** G 773 750-7485
Chicago *(G-4443)*

**Connectmedia Ventures LLC** G 773 327-3188
Chicago *(G-4450)*

**Connelly & Associates** E 847 372-5001
Palatine *(G-17015)*

**Conscisys Corp** E 630 810-4444
Downers Grove *(G-8418)*

**Coorens Communications Inc** G 773 235-8688
Chicago *(G-4465)*

**Cozent LLC** G 630 781-2822
Naperville *(G-15639)*

**Credit & Management Systems** F 618 654-3500
Highland *(G-11781)*

**Crestwood Associates LLC** F 847 394-8820
Mount Prospect *(G-15319)*

**Crew Beacon LLC** G 888 966-4455
Chicago *(G-4505)*

**Crowdmatrix Fx LLC** G 312 329-1170
Chicago *(G-4508)*

**Crowdsource Solutions Inc** F 855 276-9376
Swansea *(G-20777)*

**CU Info Systems** E 630 607-0300
Elmhurst *(G-9861)*

**Cunningham Electronics Corp** G 618 833-7775
Anna *(G-602)*

**Customergauge USA LLC** G 773 669-5915
Chicago *(G-4527)*

**Cyborg Systems Inc** C 312 279-7000
Chicago *(G-4529)*

**Data Link Communications** G 815 405-2856
Matteson *(G-14370)*

**Datafordummies** G 618 421-2323
Flat Rock *(G-10195)*

**Datair Employee Beneft Systems** E 630 325-2600
Westmont *(G-21881)*

**Datix (usa) Inc** G 312 724-7776
Chicago *(G-4562)*

**Decision Systems Company** G 815 885-3000
Roscoe *(G-18892)*

**Deductly LLC** G 312 945-8265
Chicago *(G-4572)*

**Deep Value Inc** E 312 239-0143
Chicago *(G-4573)*

**Delante Group Inc** G 312 493-4371
Chicago *(G-4575)*

**Dell Software Inc** D 630 836-0503
Buffalo Grove *(G-2684)*

**Designa Access Corporation** G 630 891-3105
Westmont *(G-21884)*

**Diehl Controls North Amer Inc** E 630 955-9055
Naperville *(G-15646)*

**Digi Trax Corporation** E 847 613-2100
Lincolnshire *(G-13443)*

**Digital Ignite LLC** G 630 317-7904
Lombard *(G-13791)*

**Digital Minds Inc** G 847 430-3390
Rosemont *(G-18998)*

**Digital Realty Inc** E 630 428-7979
Naperville *(G-15647)*

**Dimension Data North Amer Inc** F 847 278-6413
Schaumburg *(G-19505)*

**Donr Co** G 773 895-3359
Chicago *(G-4630)*

**Dynami Solutions LLC** G 618 363-2771
Edwardsville *(G-8796)*

SIC SECTION

73 BUSINESS SERVICES

**Earshot Inc** .......... F ....... 773 383-1798
Chicago ***(G-4677)***
**Ecd-Network LLC** .......... G ....... 917 670-0821
Chicago ***(G-4691)***
**Edqu Media LLC** .......... G ....... 773 803-9793
Chicago ***(G-4698)***
**Effici Inc** .......... G ....... 401 584-2266
Schaumburg ***(G-19514)***
**Eighty Nine Robotics LLC** .......... G ....... 512 573-9091
Chicago ***(G-4705)***
**Electronics Boutique Amer Inc** .......... G ....... 618 465-3125
Alton ***(G-574)***
**Elitegen Corp** .......... F ....... 630 637-6917
Naperville ***(G-15652)***
**Embassy Security Group Inc** .......... E ....... 800 627-1325
Orland Park ***(G-16859)***
**Embodied Labs Inc** .......... G ....... 336 971-5886
Chicago ***(G-4737)***
**EMC Corporation** .......... D ....... 630 505-3273
Lisle ***(G-13585)***
**Endure Holdings Inc** .......... G ....... 224 558-1828
Plainfield ***(G-17594)***
**Enrollment Rx LLC** .......... F ....... 847 233-0088
Schiller Park ***(G-19825)***
**Entappia LLC** .......... G ....... 630 546-4531
Aurora ***(G-1003)***
**Entience** .......... G ....... 217 649-2590
Urbana ***(G-21082)***
**Envestnet Inc** .......... C ....... 312 827-2800
Chicago ***(G-4763)***
**Envestnet Rtrment Slutions LLC** .......... G ....... 312 827-7957
Chicago ***(G-4764)***
**Environmental Systems Res Inst** .......... G ....... 312 609-0966
Chicago ***(G-4765)***
▲ **Ep Technology Corporation USA** .......... D ....... 217 351-7888
Champaign ***(G-3482)***
**Epazz Inc** .......... G ....... 312 955-8161
Wheeling ***(G-22048)***
**Eplan Software & Svcs N Ameri** .......... G ....... 517 762-5800
Schaumburg ***(G-19517)***
**Epublishing Inc** .......... G ....... 312 768-6800
Chicago ***(G-4767)***
**Equilibrium Contact Center Inc** .......... G ....... 888 708-1405
Rockford ***(G-18367)***
**Equisoft Inc** .......... G ....... 815 629-2789
Winnebago ***(G-22295)***
**Equity Concepts Co Inc** .......... G ....... 815 226-1300
Rockford ***(G-18368)***
**Esquify Inc** .......... G ....... 917 553-3741
Chicago ***(G-4777)***
**Evention LLC** .......... E ....... 773 733-4256
Chicago ***(G-4789)***
**Eyelation LLC** .......... F ....... 888 308-4703
Tinley Park ***(G-20911)***
**Family Time Computing Inc** .......... F ....... 309 664-1742
Bloomington ***(G-2162)***
**Fantasy Coverage Inc** .......... F ....... 630 592-8082
Elmhurst ***(G-9870)***
**Fast Lane Applications LLC** .......... G ....... 815 245-2145
Cary ***(G-3340)***
**Fivecubits Inc** .......... G ....... 630 749-4182
Oak Brook ***(G-16513)***
**Fleetwood Press Inc** .......... G ....... 708 485-6811
Brookfield ***(G-2632)***
**Flexera Holdings LP** .......... G ....... 847 466-4000
Itasca ***(G-12265)***
**Flexera Software LLC** .......... B ....... 800 374-4353
Itasca ***(G-12266)***
**Floydware LLC** .......... G ....... 630 469-1078
Lombard ***(G-13800)***
**Follett School Solutions Inc** .......... C ....... 815 759-1700
McHenry ***(G-14507)***
**Fooda Inc** .......... E ....... 312 752-4352
Chicago ***(G-4869)***
**Forecast Five** .......... G ....... 630 657-6400
Naperville ***(G-15660)***
**Forte Incorporated** .......... G ....... 815 224-8300
La Salle ***(G-12773)***
**Foster Learning LLC** .......... G ....... 618 656-6836
Edwardsville ***(G-8801)***
**Friedrich Klatt and Associates** .......... G ....... 773 753-1806
Chicago ***(G-4891)***
**G2 Crowd Inc** .......... F ....... 847 748-7559
Chicago ***(G-4904)***
**Galleria Retail Tech Solutions** .......... F ....... 312 822-3437
Chicago ***(G-4910)***
**Gcom Inc** .......... F ....... 217 351-4241
Savoy ***(G-19409)***
**GE Intelligent Platforms Inc** .......... D ....... 630 829-4000
Lisle ***(G-13593)***
**Genisys Decision Corporation** .......... G ....... 708 524-5100
Oak Park ***(G-16666)***
**Glidera Inc** .......... G ....... 773 350-4000
Elmhurst ***(G-9877)***
**Global Tech & Resources Inc** .......... G ....... 630 364-4260
Rolling Meadows ***(G-18732)***
**Goeducation LLC** .......... G ....... 312 800-1838
Chicago ***(G-4969)***
**Govqa Inc** .......... F ....... 630 985-1300
Woodridge ***(G-22489)***
**Great Software Laboratory Inc** .......... G ....... 630 655-8905
Chicago ***(G-4999)***
**Gtx Surgery Inc** .......... G ....... 847 920-8489
Evanston ***(G-10047)***
**H & R Block Inc** .......... F ....... 847 566-5557
Mundelein ***(G-15506)***
**H&R Block Inc** .......... F ....... 773 582-3444
Chicago ***(G-5025)***
**Hands of Many LLC** .......... G ....... 917 841-9969
Flossmoor ***(G-10225)***
**Healthcare Research LLC** .......... F ....... 773 592-3508
Chicago ***(G-5060)***
**Healthengine** .......... G ....... 312 340-8555
Chicago ***(G-5061)***
**Healthware Systems Inc** .......... E ....... 847 783-0670
Elgin ***(G-9061)***
**Healthy-Txt LLC** .......... G ....... 630 945-1787
Chicago ***(G-5063)***
**Hera Cnsltng Interntnl Opratn** .......... F ....... 630 515-8819
Lisle ***(G-13599)***
**Hicx Solutions Inc** .......... E ....... 630 560-3640
Oakbrook Terrace ***(G-16711)***
**High Tech Research Inc** .......... F ....... 847 215-9797
Deerfield ***(G-8012)***
**Hildebrant J Boyd & Co Inc** .......... G ....... 847 839-0850
Schaumburg ***(G-19554)***
**HMS Teach Inc** .......... E ....... 800 624-2926
Hoffman Estates ***(G-12016)***
**Hostforweb Incorporated** .......... G ....... 312 343-4678
Chicago ***(G-5116)***
**Humaginarium LLC** .......... G ....... 312 788-7719
Oak Park ***(G-16669)***
**Hybris (us) Corporation** .......... E ....... 312 265-5010
Chicago ***(G-5128)***
**Hyperera Inc** .......... F ....... 312 842-2288
Chicago ***(G-5130)***
**I2c LLC** .......... G ....... 630 281-2330
Naperville ***(G-15672)***
**Icnet Systems Inc** .......... E ....... 630 836-8073
Deerfield ***(G-8014)***
**Idevconcepts Inc** .......... G ....... 312 351-1615
Chicago ***(G-5142)***
**Iep Quality Inc** .......... G ....... 217 840-0570
Champaign ***(G-3497)***
**Ifs North America Inc** .......... E ....... 888 437-4968
Itasca ***(G-12279)***
**Imaging Systems Inc** .......... F ....... 630 875-1100
Itasca ***(G-12283)***
**Imanage LLC** .......... C ....... 312 667-7000
Chicago ***(G-5162)***
**Imcp Inc** .......... G ....... 630 477-8600
Itasca ***(G-12284)***
**Impact Technologies Inc** .......... G ....... 708 246-5041
Western Springs ***(G-21867)***
**Independent Network Tv LLC** .......... G ....... 312 953-8508
Forest Park ***(G-10249)***
**Industrial Finance Systems** .......... G ....... 847 592-0200
Itasca ***(G-12285)***
**Industrial Phrm Resources Inc** .......... F ....... 630 823-4700
Bartlett ***(G-1357)***
**Infiniscene Inc** .......... G ....... 630 567-0452
Chicago ***(G-5182)***
**Infinite Cnvrgnce Slutions Inc** .......... G ....... 224 764-3400
Arlington Heights ***(G-777)***
**Infogix Inc** .......... C ....... 630 505-1800
Naperville ***(G-15674)***
**Infopro Inc** .......... G ....... 630 978-9231
Aurora ***(G-1029)***
**Infor (us) Inc** .......... D ....... 312 279-1245
Chicago ***(G-5184)***
**Infor (us) Inc** .......... C ....... 312 258-6000
Chicago ***(G-5185)***
**Information Builders Inc** .......... E ....... 630 971-6700
Schaumburg ***(G-19565)***
**Information Resources Inc** .......... G ....... 312 474-3380
Chicago ***(G-5186)***
**Information Resources Inc** .......... A ....... 312 726-1221
Chicago ***(G-5187)***
**Information Resources Inc** .......... B ....... 312 474-3154
Bartlett ***(G-1318)***
**Information Resources Inc** .......... A ....... 312 474-8900
Chicago ***(G-5188)***
**Infosys Limited** .......... E ....... 630 482-5000
Lisle ***(G-13606)***
**Inkling** .......... G ....... 312 376-8129
Chicago ***(G-5196)***
▲ **Innerworkings Inc** .......... D ....... 312 642-3700
Chicago ***(G-5198)***
**Innovations For Learning Inc** .......... G ....... 800 975-3452
Evanston ***(G-10056)***
**Innovative Custom Software Inc** .......... G ....... 630 892-5022
Naperville ***(G-15675)***
**Innovative SEC Systems Inc** .......... F ....... 217 355-6308
Savoy ***(G-19410)***
**Inrule Technology Inc** .......... E ....... 312 648-1800
Chicago ***(G-5203)***
**Intel Corporation** .......... D ....... 408 765-8080
Chicago ***(G-5209)***
**Interscience Technologies Inc** .......... G ....... 630 759-4444
Bolingbrook ***(G-2323)***
**Intersect Healthcare Systems** .......... G ....... 847 457-2159
Lake Forest ***(G-12919)***
**Intravation Inc** .......... G ....... 847 299-6423
Des Plaines ***(G-8214)***
**Invisible Institute** .......... G ....... 415 669-4691
Chicago ***(G-5233)***
**Iq7 Technology Inc** .......... G ....... 917 670-1715
Chicago ***(G-5237)***
**Ironsafe LLC** .......... G ....... 877 297-1833
Naperville ***(G-15678)***
**Isewa LLC** .......... G ....... 847 877-1586
Buffalo Grove ***(G-2711)***
**Isoprime Corporation** .......... G ....... 630 737-0963
Lisle ***(G-13609)***
**Jabber Labs Inc** .......... F ....... 607 227-6353
Chicago ***(G-5266)***
**Janitor Ltd** .......... G ....... 773 936-3389
Chicago ***(G-5276)***
**Jellyvision Inc** .......... D ....... 312 266-0606
Chicago ***(G-5288)***
**Jmk Computerized Tdis Inc** .......... G ....... 217 384-8891
Urbana ***(G-21092)***
**Jones Software Corp** .......... G ....... 312 952-0011
Chicago ***(G-5322)***
**K-Tron Inc** .......... G ....... 708 460-2128
Orland Park ***(G-16872)***
**Kana Software Inc** .......... G ....... 312 447-5600
Chicago ***(G-5357)***
**Kcura LLC** .......... B ....... 312 263-1177
Chicago ***(G-5368)***
**King of Software Inc** .......... G ....... 847 354-8745
Des Plaines ***(G-8218)***
**Knowledgeshift Inc** .......... G ....... 630 221-8759
Wheaton ***(G-21962)***
**Konveau Inc** .......... G ....... 312 476-9385
Chicago ***(G-5404)***
**Kronos Incorporated** .......... F ....... 847 969-6501
Schaumburg ***(G-19606)***
**Ksr Software LLC** .......... G ....... 847 705-0100
Palatine ***(G-17048)***
**L-Data Corporation** .......... E ....... 312 552-7855
Chicago ***(G-5423)***
**Lab Software Inc** .......... G ....... 815 521-9116
Minooka ***(G-14841)***
**Lansa Inc** .......... C ....... 630 874-7042
Downers Grove ***(G-8472)***
**Larsen & Toubro Infotech Ltd** .......... G ....... 847 303-3900
Schaumburg ***(G-19613)***
**Lattice Incorporated** .......... E ....... 630 949-3250
Wheaton ***(G-21964)***
**Lbe Ltd** .......... G ....... 847 907-4959
Kildeer ***(G-12701)***
**Leanoptima LLC** .......... E ....... 847 648-1592
Palatine ***(G-17049)***
**Legal Files Software Inc** .......... E ....... 217 726-6000
Springfield ***(G-20468)***
**Legistek LLC** .......... G ....... 312 399-4891
Chicago ***(G-5491)***
**Lexray LLC** .......... F ....... 630 664-6740
Downers Grove ***(G-8475)***
**Liaison Home Automation LLC** .......... G ....... 888 279-1235
Mount Zion ***(G-15454)***
**Liberty Grove Software Inc** .......... G ....... 630 858-7388
Glen Ellyn ***(G-10977)***
**Linkedhealth Solutions** .......... F ....... 312 600-6684
Chicago ***(G-5513)***
**Linkhouse LLC** .......... G ....... 312 671-2225
Schaumburg ***(G-19618)***
**Liquidfire** .......... G ....... 312 376-7448
Chicago ***(G-5517)***

S I C

Employee Codes: A=Over 500 employees, B=251-500
C=101-250, D=51-100, E=20-50, F=10-19, G=3-9

2017 Harris Illinois
Industrial Directory

1137

# 73 BUSINESS SERVICES

| Company | Location | Code | Phone |
|---|---|---|---|
| Localfix Solutions LLC | Winfield (G-22287) | G | 312 569-0619 |
| Logical Design Solutions Inc | Aurora (G-1047) | G | 630 786-5999 |
| Logicgate Inc | Chicago (G-5533) | F | 312 279-2775 |
| Lonelybrand LLC | Chicago (G-5536) | G | 312 880-7506 |
| M T M Assn For Standards & RES | Des Plaines (G-8224) | G | 847 299-1111 |
| Manscore LLC | Downers Grove (G-8482) | G | 630 297-7502 |
| Manufacturing Tech Group Inc | Rockford (G-18482) | G | 815 966-2300 |
| Marin Software Incorporated | Chicago (G-5620) | G | 312 267-2083 |
| Marketing Analytics Inc | Evanston (G-10070) | D | 847 733-8459 |
| Martin Peter Associates Inc | Chicago (G-5632) | F | 773 478-2400 |
| Marucco Stddard Frenbach Walsh | Springfield (G-20474) | E | 217 698-3535 |
| McConnell Chase Software Works | Chicago (G-5665) | G | 312 540-1508 |
| MCS Management Corp | Hawthorn Woods (G-11703) | G | 847 680-3707 |
| Mealplot Inc | Champaign (G-3513) | G | 217 419-2681 |
| Medcore International LLC | Oak Brook (G-16540) | G | 630 645-9900 |
| Mediafly Inc | Chicago (G-5677) | G | 312 281-5175 |
| Memdem Inc | Elmhurst (G-9910) | G | 571 205-8778 |
| Memorable Inc | Northbrook (G-16310) | G | 847 272-8207 |
| Message Mediums LLC | Chicago (G-5698) | F | 877 450-0075 |
| Metamation Inc | Rolling Meadows (G-18743) | F | 775 826-1717 |
| Mfrontiers LLC | Libertyville (G-13356) | G | 224 513-5312 |
| Michaels Ross and Cole Inc | Oak Brook (G-16543) | F | 630 916-0662 |
| Micrograms Inc | Loves Park (G-13966) | G | 815 877-4455 |
| Microsoft Corporation | Downers Grove (G-8486) | D | 630 725-4000 |
| Microsoft Corporation | Bloomington (G-2198) | D | 309 665-0113 |
| Microsoft Corporation | Northlake (G-16442) | D | 708 409-4759 |
| Microstrategy Incorporated | Schaumburg (G-19644) | G | 703 589-0734 |
| Midway Games Inc | Chicago (G-5739) | E | 773 961-2222 |
| Mirus Research | Normal (G-16077) | E | 309 828-3100 |
| Mlevel Inc | Chicago (G-5779) | E | 888 564-5395 |
| Mobilehop Technology LLC | Chicago (G-5780) | G | 312 504-3773 |
| Moduslink Corporation | Bedford Park (G-1566) | E | 708 496-7800 |
| Monotype Imaging Inc | Mount Prospect (G-15350) | G | 847 718-0400 |
| Monotype Imaging Inc | Elk Grove Village (G-9635) | F | 847 718-0400 |
| Mosaic Construction | Northbrook (G-16315) | G | 847 504-0177 |
| Motivequest LLC | Evanston (G-10075) | F | 847 905-6100 |
| Mu Dai LLC | Chicago (G-5828) | F | 312 982-0040 |
| My Local Beacon Llc | Chicago (G-5840) | G | 888 482-6691 |
| Myeccho LLC | Des Plaines (G-8240) | G | 224 639-3068 |
| Myhomeeq LLC | Chicago (G-5845) | G | 773 328-7034 |
| Nanex LLC | Winnetka (G-22313) | G | 847 501-4787 |
| Napersoft Inc | Naperville (G-15710) | F | 630 420-1515 |
| Narrative Health Network Inc | Chicago (G-5854) | G | 312 600-9154 |
| Nautilus Medical | Barrington (G-1294) | G | 866 520-6477 |
| Navipoint Genomics LLC | Naperville (G-15819) | G | 630 464-4013 |
| Nerd Island Studios LLC | Highland Park (G-11859) | G | 224 619-5361 |
| Network Harbor Inc | Peoria (G-17416) | G | 309 633-9118 |
| New Vision Software Inc | Barrington (G-1295) | G | 847 382-1532 |
| Newera Software Inc | Kingston (G-12707) | G | 815 784-3345 |
| Next Generation Inc | Plainfield (G-17632) | G | 312 953-7514 |
| Nextpoint Inc | Chicago (G-5907) | E | 773 929-4000 |
| Novaspect Inc | Schaumburg (G-19670) | C | 847 956-8020 |
| Oas Software Corp | Saint Charles (G-19226) | F | 630 513-2990 |
| Onefire Media Group Inc | Peoria (G-17419) | E | 309 740-0345 |
| Onx USA LLC | Lisle (G-13637) | E | 630 343-8940 |
| Optimus Advantage LLC | Chicago (G-5997) | E | 847 905-1000 |
| Oracle Corporation | Chicago (G-5998) | B | 773 404-9300 |
| Oracle Corporation | Chicago (G-5999) | | 312 692-5270 |
| Oracle Corporation | Itasca (G-12336) | B | 630 931-6400 |
| Oracle Corporation | Chicago (G-6000) | B | 262 957-3000 |
| Oracle Hcm User Group Inc | Chicago (G-6001) | | 312 222-9350 |
| Oracle Systems Corporation | Chicago (G-6002) | | 312 245-1580 |
| Orbit Enterprises Inc | Oak Brook (G-16553) | | 630 469-3405 |
| Orecx | Chicago (G-6006) | | 312 895-5292 |
| Origami Risk LLC | Chicago (G-6010) | | 312 546-6515 |
| Orinoco Systems LLC | Wheaton (G-21971) | | 630 510-0775 |
| Otus LLC | Chicago (G-6025) | | 312 229-7648 |
| Overgrad Inc | Chicago (G-6028) | G | 312 324-4952 |
| Owanza Corporation | Chicago (G-6031) | | 312 281-2900 |
| Own The Night App | Chicago (G-6033) | G | 773 216-0245 |
| P B R W Enterprises Inc | Woodstock (G-22597) | | 815 337-5519 |
| Pagepath Technologies Inc | Plano (G-17671) | | 630 689-4111 |
| Panatech Computer Management | Schiller Park (G-19857) | G | 847 678-8848 |
| Paragon International Inc | Schaumburg (G-19682) | F | 847 240-2981 |
| Parallel Solutions LLC | Schaumburg (G-19683) | G | 847 708-9227 |
| Patientbond LLC | Elmhurst (G-9919) | E | 312 445-8751 |
| Paylocity Holding Corporation | Arlington Heights (G-817) | | 847 463-3200 |
| Paylocity Holding Corporation | Naperville (G-15722) | C | 331 701-7975 |
| PC Concepts | Round Lake Beach (G-19078) | | 847 223-6490 |
| Pc-Tel Inc | Bloomingdale (G-2127) | | 630 372-6800 |
| Peak Computer Systems Inc | Belleville (G-1665) | E | 618 398-5612 |
| Pendragon Software Corporation | Chicago (G-6099) | G | 847 816-9660 |
| Peopleadmin Inc | Chicago (G-6102) | E | 877 637-5800 |
| Perry Johnson Inc | Rosemont (G-19021) | F | 847 635-0010 |
| Personify | Urbana (G-21097) | F | 217 840-2638 |
| Pervasive Health Inc | Chicago (G-6107) | | 312 257-2967 |
| Phillip Grigalanz | Jerseyville (G-12425) | | 219 628-6706 |
| Physician Software Systems LLC | Lisle (G-13639) | | 630 717-8192 |
| Picis Clinical Solutions Inc | Rosemont (G-19023) | | 847 993-2200 |
| Pinnakle Technologies Inc | Aurora (G-1066) | F | 630 352-0070 |
| Pitney Bowes Inc | Itasca (G-12341) | E | 800 784-4224 |
| Pix2doc LLC | Lisle (G-13642) | G | 312 925-4010 |
| Playground Pointers | Hinsdale (G-11959) | G | 952 200-4168 |
| Pluribus Games LLC | Aurora (G-1204) | G | 630 770-2043 |
| Politech Inc | Trout Valley (G-21001) | G | 847 516-2717 |
| Polysystems Inc | Chicago (G-6155) | D | 312 332-2114 |
| Powerschool Group LLC | Chicago (G-6160) | G | 610 867-9200 |
| Prairie Area Library System | Coal Valley (G-7298) | E | 309 799-3155 |
| Prairie Wi-FI Systems | Chicago (G-6167) | G | 515 988-3260 |
| Precision Software Limited | Lisle (G-13644) | E | 312 239-1630 |
| Premier International Entps | Chicago (G-6177) | E | 312 857-2200 |
| Prime Time Computer Services | Joliet (G-12554) | G | 815 553-0300 |
| Prism Esolutions Dv Andy Frain | Aurora (G-1069) | F | 630 820-3820 |
| Procura LLC | Westmont (G-21914) | G | 801 265-4571 |
| Producepro Inc | Woodridge (G-22512) | G | 630 395-9700 |
| Productive Edge LLC | Chicago (G-6207) | D | 312 561-9000 |
| Proquis Inc | Elgin (G-9151) | F | 847 278-3230 |
| Proship Inc | Chicago (G-6217) | G | 312 332-7447 |
| Protepo Ltd | Elk Grove Village (G-9699) | | 847 466-1023 |
| Psychiatric Assessments Inc | Chicago (G-6220) | G | 312 878-6490 |
| Ptc Inc | Oakbrook Terrace (G-16718) | E | 630 827-4900 |
| Public Good Software Inc | Chicago (G-6222) | F | 877 941-2747 |
| Publishers Row | Skokie (G-20067) | F | 847 568-0593 |
| Pubpal LLC | Washington (G-21389) | G | 309 222-5062 |
| Qad Inc | Lisle (G-13647) | G | 630 964-4030 |
| Quadramed Corporation | Chicago (G-6240) | | 312 396-0700 |
| Quadrant 4 System Corporation | Schaumburg (G-19706) | B | 855 995-7367 |
| Quality Network Solutions Inc | Sullivan (G-20758) | E | 217 728-3155 |
| Questily LLC | Chicago (G-6256) | | 312 636-6657 |
| Questily LLC | Chicago (G-6257) | | 312 636-6657 |
| R & J Systems Inc | Bartlett (G-1322) | G | 630 289-3010 |
| Radiofx Inc | Chicago (G-6280) | G | 773 255-8069 |
| Radius Solutions Incorporated | Chicago (G-6283) | F | 312 648-0800 |
| Rapid Execution Services LLC | Chicago (G-6293) | G | 312 789-4358 |
| Rayalco Inc | Park Ridge (G-17219) | G | 847 692-7422 |
| Raytrans Distribution Svcs Inc | Chicago (G-6297) | F | 708 503-9940 |
| React Computer Services Inc | Willowbrook (G-22229) | D | 630 323-6200 |
| Realize Inc | Chicago (G-6307) | G | 312 566-8759 |
| Recsolu Inc | Chicago (G-6313) | | 312 517-3200 |
| Reflection Software Inc | Aurora (G-1073) | G | 630 585-2300 |
| Reliefwatch Inc | Chicago (G-6331) | G | 646 678-2336 |
| Rivalfly National Network LLC | Chicago (G-6361) | G | 847 867-8660 |
| Rmcis Corporation | Lisle (G-13652) | E | 630 955-1310 |
| Robis Elections Inc | Wheaton (G-21977) | F | 630 752-0220 |
| Roger Cantu & Assocs | Oak Brook (G-16560) | G | 630 573-9215 |

| Company | Code | Phone |
|---|---|---|
| Rosewood Software Inc — Palatine (G-17069) | G | 847 438-2185 |
| Route 40 Media LLC — Peoria (G-17449) | G | 309 370-5809 |
| SAI Info USA — Itasca (G-12352) | G | 630 773-3335 |
| Sales & Marketing Resources — Fox River Grove (G-10289) | G | 847 910-9169 |
| Salesforcecom Inc — Chicago (G-6432) | G | 312 361-3555 |
| Salesforcecom Inc — Chicago (G-6433) | G | 312 288-3600 |
| Savo Group Ltd — Chicago (G-6447) | C | 312 276-7700 |
| Scholarship Solutions LLC — Chicago (G-6453) | F | 847 859-5629 |
| School Town LLC — Northbrook (G-16359) | G | 847 943-9115 |
| Scientific Cmpt Assoc Corp — River Forest (G-18001) | G | 708 771-4567 |
| Sct Alternative Inc — Buffalo Grove (G-2765) | F | 847 215-7488 |
| Secure Data Inc — O Fallon (G-16478) | G | 618 726-5225 |
| Secureslice Inc — Chicago (G-6470) | E | 800 984-0494 |
| Sedona Inc — Moline (G-14969) | C | 309 736-4104 |
| See What You Send Inc — Chicago (G-6473) | | 781 780-1483 |
| Sellers Commerce LLC — Northbrook (G-16361) | F | 858 345-1212 |
| Seoclarity — Des Plaines (G-8272) | F | 773 831-4500 |
| Servicenow Inc — Downers Grove (G-8521) | G | 630 963-4608 |
| Sharpedge Solutions Inc — Naperville (G-15827) | F | 630 792-9639 |
| Showcase Corporation — Chicago (G-6500) | C | 312 651-3000 |
| Siemens Product Life Mgmt Sftw — Downers Grove (G-8522) | E | 630 437-6700 |
| Signal Digital Inc — Chicago (G-6509) | E | 312 685-1911 |
| Signature Business Systems Inc — Deerfield (G-8053) | F | 847 459-8500 |
| Signs & Wonders Unlimited LLC — Libertyville (G-13381) | G | 847 816-9734 |
| Simplement Inc — Northfield (G-16418) | G | 702 560-5332 |
| Simply Computer Software Inc — Rockford (G-18618) | G | 815 231-0063 |
| Sirius Business Software — Palos Park (G-17133) | G | 708 361-5538 |
| Smartbyte Solutions Inc — Palatine (G-17075) | G | 847 925-1870 |
| Smartsignal Corporation — Lisle (G-13658) | D | 630 829-4000 |
| Snaglet LLC — Northbrook (G-16364) | G | 404 449-6394 |
| Social Qnect LLC — Northbrook (G-16366) | G | 847 997-0077 |
| Socialcloak Inc — East Dubuque (G-8624) | G | 650 549-4412 |
| Soft O Soft Inc — Schaumburg (G-19730) | E | 630 741-4414 |
| Softhaus Ltd — Alton (G-590) | G | 618 463-1140 |
| Softlabz Corporation — Highland Park (G-11870) | G | 847 780-7076 |
| Software Support Systems Inc — Saint Charles (G-19265) | G | 630 587-2999 |
| Spend Radar LLC — Chicago (G-6558) | E | 312 265-0764 |
| Spl Software Alliance LLC — Morton (G-15182) | G | 309 266-0304 |
| Spooky Cool Labs LLC — Chicago (G-6563) | E | 773 577-5555 |
| Srv Professional Publications — Schaumburg (G-19739) | G | 847 330-1260 |
| Starlight Software System Inc — Hudson (G-12125) | G | 309 454-7349 |
| Storiant Inc — Chicago (G-6600) | E | 617 431-8000 |
| Streamlinx LLC — Naperville (G-15755) | F | 630 864-3043 |
| Structurepoint LLC — Skokie (G-20092) | F | 847 966-4357 |
| Su Enterprise Inc — Arlington Heights (G-846) | G | 847 394-1656 |
| Sullivan Cgliano Training Ctrs — Chicago (G-6614) | G | 312 422-0009 |
| Sunburst Technology Corp — Elgin (G-9197) | G | 800 321-7511 |
| Sunrise Futures LLC — Chicago (G-6628) | G | 312 612-1041 |
| Supply Vision Inc — Chicago (G-6637) | G | 847 388-0064 |
| Svanaco Inc — Des Plaines (G-8284) | D | 847 699-0300 |
| Swift Education Systems Inc — Chicago (G-6649) | G | 312 257-3751 |
| Swift Technologies Inc — Marengo (G-14241) | G | 815 568-8402 |
| Symantec Corporation — Oak Brook (G-16562) | C | 630 706-4700 |
| Symfact Inc — Chicago (G-6656) | E | 847 380-4174 |
| Synergy Technology Group Inc — Chicago (G-6657) | F | 773 305-3500 |
| Synopsys Inc — Schaumburg (G-19749) | F | 847 706-2000 |
| Systat Software Inc — Chicago (G-6658) | E | 408 876-4508 |
| System Software Associates Del — Chicago (G-6660) | E | 312 258-6000 |
| Systems Live Ltd — Crystal Lake (G-7657) | G | 815 455-3383 |
| Systemslogix LLC — Glendale Heights (G-11082) | G | 630 784-3113 |
| Tagobi LLC — Wheaton (G-21983) | G | 331 444-2951 |
| Teenfitnation LLC — South Barrington (G-20133) | E | 847 322-2953 |
| Tegratecs Development Corp — Schaumburg (G-19757) | G | 847 397-0088 |
| Tegrity Inc — Burr Ridge (G-2884) | E | 800 411-0579 |
| Telemedicine Solutions LLC — Schaumburg (G-19758) | F | 847 519-3500 |
| ▲ Telular Corporation — Chicago (G-6692) | D | 800 835-8527 |
| Tempus Health Inc — Chicago (G-6699) | E | 312 784-4400 |
| Textura Corporation — Deerfield (G-8063) | C | 866 839-8872 |
| Thinkcercacom Inc — Chicago (G-6714) | F | 224 412-3722 |
| Thomas A Doan — Evanston (G-10102) | G | 847 864-8772 |
| Thomson Quantitative Analytics — Chicago (G-6717) | E | 847 610-0574 |
| Thoughtly Corp — Chicago (G-6721) | | 772 559-2008 |
| Timepilot Corporation — Batavia (G-1507) | G | 630 879-6400 |
| Tindall Associates Inc — Orland Park (G-16898) | F | 708 403-7775 |
| ◆ Tom Zosel Associates Ltd — Long Grove (G-13903) | D | 847 540-6543 |
| Topvox Corporation — Barrington (G-1309) | B | 847 842-0900 |
| Torgo Inc — Riverwoods (G-18045) | | 800 360-5910 |
| Track My Foreclosures LLC — Monticello (G-15088) | G | 877 782-8187 |
| Tradevolve Inc — Crystal Lake (G-7668) | G | 847 987-9411 |
| Tradingscreen Inc — Chicago (G-6753) | G | 312 447-0100 |
| Tri-Tech Sltons Consulting Inc — Mount Prospect (G-15379) | G | 847 941-0199 |
| Trident Software Corp — Niles (G-16044) | G | 847 219-8777 |
| Tripnary LLC — Chicago (G-6777) | G | 512 554-1911 |
| Trizetto Corporation — Naperville (G-15768) | C | 630 369-5300 |
| Truepad LLC — Chicago (G-6787) | F | 847 274-6898 |
| Trustwave Holdings Inc — Chicago (G-6789) | G | 312 750-0950 |
| Truth Labs LLC — Chicago (G-6790) | F | 312 291-9035 |
| Tsf Net Inc — Earlville (G-8597) | F | 815 246-7295 |
| Turfmapp Inc — Chicago (G-6792) | | 703 473-5678 |
| Turner Agward — Chicago (G-6794) | G | 773 669-8559 |
| Twocanoes Software Inc — Naperville (G-15769) | G | 630 305-9601 |
| Txticon LLC — Chicago (G-6800) | | 312 860-3378 |
| U4g Group LLC — Buffalo Grove (G-2783) | | 847 821-6061 |
| Uberloop Inc — Naperville (G-15770) | G | 630 707-0567 |
| Ubipass Inc — Willowbrook (G-22236) | | 312 626-4624 |
| Upright Network Services — Bensenville (G-2010) | G | 630 595-5559 |
| Uxm Studio In — Villa Park (G-21288) | G | 773 359-1333 |
| Vanguard Solutions Group Inc — Glen Ellyn (G-10993) | E | 630 545-1600 |
| Varsity Logistics Inc — Deerfield (G-8065) | | 650 392-7979 |
| Vauto Inc — Oakbrook Terrace (G-16722) | E | 630 590-2000 |
| Velocity Software LLC — Lombard (G-13877) | | 800 351-6893 |
| Vertex Inc — Naperville (G-15776) | E | 630 328-2600 |
| Vertex Consulting Services Inc — Schaumburg (G-19786) | F | 313 492-5154 |
| Vertical Software Inc — Bartonville (G-1399) | F | 309 633-0700 |
| Viclarity Inc — Chicago (G-6892) | G | 201 214-5405 |
| Victor Consulting — Lincolnshire (G-13489) | | 847 267-8012 |
| Visibillity Inc — Chicago (G-6901) | | 312 616-5900 |
| Vision I Systems — Chicago (G-6902) | G | 312 326-9188 |
| Visual Information Tech Inc — Champaign (G-3557) | G | 217 841-2155 |
| Viva Solutions Inc — Lemont (G-13268) | G | 312 332-8882 |
| Vivor LLC — Chicago (G-6908) | G | 312 967-6379 |
| Vizr Tech LLC — Chicago (G-6909) | G | 312 420-4466 |
| W A M Computers International — Litchfield (G-13699) | G | 217 324-6926 |
| Warbler Digital Inc — Chicago (G-6939) | E | 312 924-1056 |
| Wargaming (usa) Inc — Chicago (G-6940) | F | 312 258-0500 |
| Webqa Incorporated — Woodridge (G-22523) | G | 630 985-1300 |
| Websolutions Technology Inc — Aurora (G-1095) | E | 630 375-6833 |
| Wincademy Inc — Grayslake (G-11367) | G | 847 445-7886 |
| Winscribe Usa Inc — Chicago (G-7002) | F | 773 399-1608 |
| Wolfram Research Inc — Champaign (G-3562) | C | 217 398-0700 |
| Written Word Inc — Roselle (G-18986) | G | 630 671-9803 |
| Xaptum Inc — Chicago (G-7043) | G | 847 404-6205 |
| Yhlsoft Inc — Naperville (G-15787) | F | 630 355-8033 |
| Yield Management Systems LLC — Chicago (G-7051) | G | 312 665-1595 |
| Youtopia Inc — Chicago (G-7055) | G | 312 593-0859 |
| Zebra Software Inc — Hoffman Estates (G-12070) | G | 847 742-9110 |
| Zirmed Inc — Chicago (G-7070) | F | 312 207-0889 |

# 76 MISCELLANEOUS REPAIR SERVICES

### 7692 Welding Repair

| Company | Code | Phone |
|---|---|---|
| A G Welding — Chicago (G-3688) | G | 773 261-0575 |
| A&S Machining & Welding Inc — Mc Cook (G-14443) | E | 708 442-4544 |
| A-Z Welding — Bethalto (G-2080) | G | 618 259-2515 |
| Ability Welding Service Inc — Bensenville (G-1812) | G | 630 595-3737 |
| Ablaze Welding & Fabricating — Rockford (G-18248) | G | 815 965-0046 |

Employee Codes: A=Over 500 employees, B=251-500, C=101-250, D=51-100, E=20-50, F=10-19, G=3-9

76 MISCELLANEOUS REPAIR SERVICES SIC SECTION

**Accurate Auto Manufacturing Co**..........G....... 618 244-0727
Mount Vernon *(G-15397)*
**Adams Steel Service Inc**..........E....... 815 385-9100
McHenry *(G-14477)*
**Adermanns Welding & Mch & Co**..........G....... 217 342-3234
Effingham *(G-8822)*
**Adler Norco Inc**..........F....... 847 473-3600
Mundelein *(G-15464)*
**Advanced Welding Services**..........G....... 630 759-3334
La Grange *(G-12724)*
**Affton Fabg & Wldg Co Inc**..........F....... 314 781-4100
Sauget *(G-19381)*
**AG Precision Inc**..........G....... 847 724-7786
Glenview *(G-11098)*
**Aileys 3 Welding**..........G....... 815 683-2181
Crescent City *(G-7455)*
**Airgas USA LLC**..........F....... 815 289-1928
Machesney Park *(G-14052)*
**Alberto Daza**..........F....... 773 638-9880
Chicago *(G-3796)*
**Aledo Welding Enterprises Inc**..........G....... 309 582-2019
Aledo *(G-367)*
**All Metal Machine**..........G....... 815 389-0168
South Beloit *(G-20136)*
**Allans Welding & Machine Inc**..........G....... 618 392-3708
Olney *(G-16758)*
**Allen Popovich**..........G....... 815 712-7404
Custer Park *(G-7686)*
**Alloy Welding Corp**..........E....... 708 345-6756
Melrose Park *(G-14588)*
**Alloyweld Inspection Co Inc**..........E....... 630 595-2145
Bensenville *(G-1827)*
**American Grinding & Machine Co**..........D....... 773 889-4343
Chicago *(G-3857)*
▲ **American Machining & Wldg Inc**..........E....... 773 586-2585
Chicago *(G-3862)*
**American Metal Installers & FA**..........G....... 630 993-0812
Villa Park *(G-21236)*
**American Welding & Gas Inc**..........E....... 630 527-2550
Stone Park *(G-20632)*
**Anchor Welding & Fabrication**..........G....... 815 937-1640
Aroma Park *(G-878)*
**Andel Services Inc**..........G....... 630 566-0210
Aurora *(G-1109)*
**Andersen Machine & Welding Inc**..........G....... 815 232-4664
Freeport *(G-10647)*
**Apollo Machine & Manufacturing**..........G....... 847 677-6444
Skokie *(G-19956)*
**Armitage Welding**..........G....... 773 772-1442
Chicago *(G-3946)*
◆ **Arndt Enterprise Ltd**..........G....... 847 234-5736
Lake Forest *(G-12880)*
**AS Fabricating Inc**..........G....... 618 242-7438
Mount Vernon *(G-15398)*
**Ascent Mfg Co**..........E....... 847 806-6600
Elk Grove Village *(G-9314)*
**Assured Welding Service Inc**..........G....... 847 671-1414
Schiller Park *(G-19806)*
**Atlas Boiler & Welding Company**..........G....... 815 963-3360
Elgin *(G-8960)*
**Atomoweld Co**..........G....... 773 736-5577
Chicago *(G-3987)*
◆ **Ats Sortimat USA LLC**..........D....... 847 925-1234
Rolling Meadows *(G-18711)*
**Awerkamp Machine Co**..........E....... 217 222-3480
Quincy *(G-17797)*
**B & W Machine Company Inc**..........G....... 847 364-4500
Elk Grove Village *(G-9329)*
**B J Fehr Machine Co**..........G....... 309 923-8691
Roanoke *(G-18048)*
**B T Brown Manufacturing**..........G....... 815 947-3633
Kent *(G-12665)*
**Bales Mold Service Inc**..........E....... 630 852-4665
Downers Grove *(G-8394)*
**Baley Enterprises Inc**..........G....... 708 681-0900
Melrose Park *(G-14599)*
**Barton Manufacturing LLC**..........F....... 217 428-0726
Decatur *(G-7844)*
**Bc Welding Inc**..........G....... 708 258-0076
Peotone *(G-17484)*
**Bear Mtal Wldg Fabrication Inc**..........G....... 630 261-9353
Lombard *(G-13767)*
**Beaver Creek Enterprises Inc**..........F....... 815 723-9455
Joliet *(G-12463)*
**Bessler Welding Inc**..........F....... 309 699-6224
East Peoria *(G-8701)*
**Best Machine & Welding Co Inc**..........E....... 708 343-4455
Woodridge *(G-22456)*
**Bi State Steel Co**..........G....... 309 755-0668
East Moline *(G-8671)*
**Bierman Welding Inc**..........F....... 217 342-2050
Effingham *(G-8827)*
**Botts Welding and Trck Svc Inc**..........E....... 815 338-0594
Woodstock *(G-22546)*
**Bulaw Welding & Engineering Co**..........D....... 630 228-8300
Itasca *(G-12239)*
**Burgess Manufacturing Inc**..........F....... 847 680-1724
Libertyville *(G-13311)*
**Burke Tool & Manufacturing Inc**..........G....... 618 542-6441
Du Quoin *(G-8551)*
**Burns Machine Company**..........E....... 815 434-3131
Ottawa *(G-16952)*
**Bushnell Welding & Radiator**..........G....... 309 772-9289
Bushnell *(G-2900)*
**C & B Welders Inc**..........G....... 773 722-0097
Chicago *(G-4198)*
**C E R Machining & Tooling Ltd**..........G....... 708 442-9614
Lyons *(G-14034)*
**C I F Industries Inc**..........F....... 618 635-2010
Staunton *(G-20555)*
**C J Holdings Inc**..........G....... 309 274-3141
Chillicothe *(G-7163)*
**C Keller Manufacturing Inc**..........E....... 630 833-5593
Villa Park *(G-21240)*
**C/B Machine Tool Corp**..........G....... 847 288-1807
Franklin Park *(G-10422)*
**Carrolls Welding & Fabrication**..........G....... 217 728-8720
Sullivan *(G-20741)*
**Casward Tool Works Inc**..........G....... 773 486-4900
Chicago *(G-4254)*
**Certiweld Inc**..........G....... 708 389-0148
Crestwood *(G-7481)*
**Cervones Welding Service Inc**..........G....... 847 985-6865
Schaumburg *(G-19470)*
**Chicago Tube and Iron Company**..........E....... 815 834-2500
Romeoville *(G-18810)*
**Cimino Machine Corp**..........F....... 773 767-7000
Chicago *(G-4378)*
**Cisne Iron Works Inc**..........F....... 618 673-2188
Cisne *(G-7250)*
**Cokel Dj Welding Bay & Muffler**..........G....... 309 385-4567
Princeville *(G-17763)*
**Cokel Welding Shop**..........G....... 217 357-3312
Carthage *(G-3312)*
**Colfax Welding & Fabricating**..........G....... 847 359-4433
Palatine *(G-17013)*
**Comers Welding Service Inc**..........G....... 630 892-0168
Montgomery *(G-15039)*
**Comet Fabricating & Welding Co**..........E....... 815 229-0468
Rockford *(G-18316)*
**Commercial Machine Services**..........F....... 847 806-1901
Elk Grove Village *(G-9386)*
**Component Tool & Mfg Co**..........F....... 708 672-5505
Crete *(G-7510)*
**Concept Industries Inc**..........G....... 847 258-3545
Elk Grove Village *(G-9388)*
**Connell Mc Machine & Welding**..........G....... 815 868-2275
Mc Connell *(G-14442)*
**Corrugated Converting Eqp**..........F....... 618 532-2138
Centralia *(G-3410)*
**County Tool & Die**..........G....... 217 324-6527
Litchfield *(G-13683)*
**Custom Machinery Inc**..........G....... 847 678-3033
Schiller Park *(G-19818)*
**Cyclops Welding Co**..........G....... 815 223-0685
La Salle *(G-12769)*
**Cylinder Services Inc**..........G....... 630 466-9820
Sugar Grove *(G-20721)*
**D & H Precision Tooling Co**..........G....... 815 653-9611
Wonder Lake *(G-22322)*
**D & M Welding Inc**..........G....... 708 233-6080
Bridgeview *(G-2481)*
**D M Manufacturing 2 Inc**..........G....... 618 455-3550
Sainte Marie *(G-19323)*
**D N Welding & Fabricating Inc**..........G....... 847 244-6410
Waukegan *(G-21546)*
**D W Terry Welding Company**..........G....... 618 433-9722
Alton *(G-570)*
**Daniel Mfg Inc**..........F....... 309 963-4227
Carlock *(G-3050)*
**Darnell Welding**..........G....... 618 945-9538
Bridgeport *(G-2451)*
**Daves Welding Service Inc**..........G....... 630 655-3224
Darien *(G-7792)*
**David Schutte**..........G....... 217 223-5464
Quincy *(G-17818)*
**Device Technologies Inc**..........G....... 630 553-7178
Yorkville *(G-22655)*
**Dons Welding**..........G....... 847 526-1177
Wauconda *(G-21455)*
**Dooling Machine Products Inc**..........G....... 618 254-0724
Hartford *(G-11610)*
**Duroweld Company Inc**..........E....... 847 680-3064
Lake Bluff *(G-12841)*
**Dyers Machine Service Inc**..........G....... 708 496-8100
Summit Argo *(G-20762)*
**E & E Machine & Engineering Co**..........G....... 708 841-5208
Riverdale *(G-18018)*
**Eagle Machine Company**..........G....... 312 243-7407
Chicago *(G-4671)*
**East Savanna Welding**..........G....... 815 273-7371
Savanna *(G-19396)*
**Edward F Data**..........G....... 708 597-0158
Alsip *(G-461)*
**Edwardsville Mch & Wldg Co Inc**..........G....... 618 656-5145
Edwardsville *(G-8798)*
**Eenigenburg Mfg Inc**..........G....... 708 474-0850
Lansing *(G-13161)*
▼ **Ehrhardt Tool & Machine LLC**..........C....... 314 436-6900
Granite City *(G-11274)*
▲ **Ekstrom Carlson Fabricating Co**..........G....... 815 226-1511
Rockford *(G-18360)*
**Ellners Welding and Machine Sp**..........G....... 618 282-4302
Prairie Du Rocher *(G-17739)*
**Emerald Machine Inc**..........G....... 773 924-3659
Chicago *(G-4740)*
**Emv Welding Inc**..........G....... 630 853-3199
Aurora *(G-1145)*
▲ **Erva Tool & Die Company**..........G....... 773 533-7806
Chicago *(G-4775)*
**Estructuras Inc**..........F....... 773 522-2200
Chicago *(G-4781)*
**Eton Machine Co Ltd**..........F....... 847 426-3380
Elgin *(G-9030)*
**Eveready Welding Service Inc**..........G....... 708 532-2432
Tinley Park *(G-20910)*
**Extreme Welding & Machine Serv**..........G....... 618 272-7237
Ridgway *(G-17984)*
**F Vogelmann and Company**..........F....... 815 469-2285
Frankfort *(G-10321)*
**Fabco Enterprises Inc**..........G....... 708 333-4644
Harvey *(G-11666)*
**Fabricating & Welding Corp**..........E....... 773 928-2050
Chicago *(G-4809)*
▲ **Farmweld Inc**..........E....... 217 857-6423
Teutopolis *(G-20852)*
**Fast Forward Welding Inc**..........G....... 815 254-1901
Plainfield *(G-17599)*
**Fehring Ornamental Iron Works**..........F....... 217 483-6727
Chatham *(G-3620)*
**Felde Tool & Machine Co Inc**..........F....... 309 692-5870
Peoria *(G-17360)*
**Floyds Welding Service**..........G....... 618 395-2414
Olney *(G-16767)*
**Folk Race Cars**..........G....... 815 629-2418
Durand *(G-8585)*
**Force Manufacturing Inc**..........G....... 847 265-6500
Lake Villa *(G-13013)*
**Fox Valley Signs Inc**..........G....... 630 896-3113
Aurora *(G-1158)*
**Franklin Maintenance**..........G....... 815 284-6806
Dixon *(G-8332)*
**Fred Stollenwerk**..........G....... 309 852-3794
Kewanee *(G-12685)*
**Fricker Machine Shop & Salvage**..........G....... 618 285-3271
Elizabethtown *(G-9245)*
**Gengler-Lowney Laser Works**..........F....... 630 801-4840
Aurora *(G-1161)*
**Giovanini Metals Corp**..........G....... 815 842-0500
Pontiac *(G-17702)*
**Global Field Services Intl Inc**..........G....... 847 931-8930
Elgin *(G-9048)*
**Gma Inc**..........G....... 630 595-1255
Bensenville *(G-1910)*
**Golden Hydraulic & Machine**..........G....... 708 597-4265
Blue Island *(G-2253)*
**Graham Welding Inc**..........G....... 217 422-1423
Decatur *(G-7885)*
**Great Lakes Mech Svcs Inc**..........F....... 708 672-5900
Lincolnshire *(G-13451)*
**Greens Machine Shop**..........G....... 618 532-4631
Centralia *(G-3417)*
**Gridley Welding Inc**..........G....... 309 747-2325
Gridley *(G-11406)*
**Grimm Metal Fabricators Inc**..........E....... 630 792-1710
Lombard *(G-13807)*
**Grover Welding Company**..........G....... 847 966-3119
Skokie *(G-20007)*
**H & H Services Inc**..........F....... 618 633-2837
Hamel *(G-11528)*

1140 2017 Harris Illinois
Industrial Directory

SIC SECTION 76 MISCELLANEOUS REPAIR SERVICES

Halter Machine Shop Inc ....G.... 618 943-2224
Lawrenceville (G-13201)
Harbor Manufacturing Inc ....D.... 708 614-6400
Tinley Park (G-20920)
Hattan Tool Company ....G.... 708 597-9308
Alsip (G-471)
HB Coatings LLC ....G.... 618 215-8161
Madison (G-14149)
Heavy Metal Industries LLC ....F.... 309 966-3007
Peoria (G-17381)
Hedricks Welding & Fabrication ....G.... 217 846-3230
Foosland (G-10232)
Heiss Welding Inc ....F.... 815 434-1838
Ottawa (G-16961)
▲ Hfr Precision Machining Inc ....E.... 630 556-4325
Sugar Grove (G-20727)
Higgs Welding LLC ....G.... 217 925-5999
Dieterich (G-8313)
High Speed Welding Inc ....G.... 630 971-8929
Westmont (G-21891)
Hofmeister Wldg & Fabrication ....F.... 217 833-2451
Griggsville (G-11412)
Hogg Welding Inc ....G.... 708 339-0033
Harvey (G-11670)
Holshouser Machine & Tool Inc ....G.... 618 451-0164
Granite City (G-11286)
Holstein Garage Inc ....G.... 630 668-0328
Wheaton (G-21952)
Howell Welding Corporation ....G.... 630 616-1100
Franklin Park (G-10489)
Hutton Welding Service Inc ....G.... 217 932-5585
Casey (G-3386)
ILmachine Company Inc ....F.... 847 243-9900
Wheeling (G-22074)
Incline Construction Inc ....G.... 815 577-8881
Joliet (G-12516)
Indium Corporation of America ....G.... 847 439-9134
Elk Grove Village (G-9544)
Industrial Maintenance & McHy ....G.... 815 726-0030
Mokena (G-14874)
Industrial Mint Wldg Machining ....D.... 773 376-6526
Chicago (G-5178)
Industrial Welding Inc ....F.... 815 535-9300
Rock Falls (G-18139)
▲ J & I Son Tool Company Inc ....G.... 847 455-4200
Franklin Park (G-10500)
J & M Fab Metals Inc ....G.... 815 758-0354
Marengo (G-14232)
Jacksonville Machine Inc ....D.... 217 243-1119
Jacksonville (G-12396)
Jacob Chambliss ....G.... 618 731-6632
Dahlgren (G-7691)
Jacobs Boiler & Mech Inds Inc ....E.... 773 385-9900
Chicago (G-5269)
Jakes McHning Rbilding Svc Inc ....E.... 630 892-3291
Aurora (G-1175)
Jarvis Welding Co ....G.... 309 647-0033
Canton (G-2988)
Jasiek Motor Rebuilding Inc ....G.... 815 883-3678
Oglesby (G-16750)
Jav Machine Craft Inc ....G.... 708 867-8608
Chicago (G-5283)
Jet Industries Inc ....E.... 773 586-8900
Chicago (G-5297)
Jim Cokel Welding ....G.... 309 734-5063
Monmouth (G-15015)
Jones Brothers Mch & Wldg Inc ....G.... 618 945-4609
Bridgeport (G-2453)
JW Welding ....G.... 618 228-7213
Aviston (G-1245)
K & K Metal Works Inc ....F.... 618 271-4680
East Saint Louis (G-8758)
K & K Tool & Die Inc ....F.... 309 829-4479
Bloomington (G-2187)
K & P Welding ....G.... 217 536-5245
Watson (G-21433)
K D Welding Inc ....G.... 815 591-3545
Hanover (G-11572)
K Three Welding Service Inc ....G.... 708 563-2911
Chicago (G-5344)
K&R Enterprises I Inc ....D.... 847 502-3371
Lake Barrington (G-12815)
Karly Iron Works Inc ....G.... 815 477-3430
Crystal Lake (G-7597)
Kemper Industries ....G.... 217 826-5712
Marshall (G-14324)
Kenneth W Templeman ....G.... 847 912-2740
Volo (G-21315)
Kim Gough ....G.... 309 734-3511
Monmouth (G-15017)

Koerner Aviation Inc ....G.... 815 932-4222
Kankakee (G-12636)
Ksem Inc ....G.... 618 656-5388
Edwardsville (G-8805)
L E D Tool & Die Inc ....G.... 708 597-2505
Chicago (G-5422)
L M Machine Shop Inc ....G.... 815 625-3256
Rock Falls (G-18141)
Lake Fabrication Inc ....G.... 217 832-2761
Villa Grove (G-21229)
Larrys Garage & Machine Shop ....G.... 815 968-8416
Rockford (G-18462)
Laystrom Manufacturing Co ....D.... 773 342-4800
Chicago (G-5474)
Lee Brothers Welding Inc ....G.... 309 342-6017
Galesburg (G-10765)
Legna Iron Works Inc ....E.... 630 894-8056
Roselle (G-18952)
Leroys Welding & Fabg Inc ....F.... 847 215-6151
Wheeling (G-22092)
Lewis Process Systems Inc ....F.... 630 510-8200
Carol Stream (G-3184)
Linne Machine Company Inc ....G.... 217 446-5746
Danville (G-7747)
Lion Welding Service Inc ....G.... 630 543-5230
Addison (G-181)
Lous Spring and Welding Shop ....G.... 815 223-4282
Peru (G-17517)
Luebbers Welding & Mfg Inc ....F.... 618 594-2489
Carlyle (G-3056)
M & F Fabrication & Welding ....G.... 217 457-2221
Concord (G-7368)
M & J Manufacturing Co Inc ....F.... 847 364-6066
Elk Grove Village (G-9601)
M & M Welding Inc ....G.... 815 895-3955
Sycamore (G-20808)
Magnetic Inspection Lab Inc ....D.... 847 437-4488
Elk Grove Village (G-9606)
Mar-Fre Manufacturing Co ....F.... 630 377-1022
Saint Charles (G-19214)
Mark Lahey ....G.... 217 243-4433
Jacksonville (G-12401)
Mark S Machine Shop Inc ....G.... 815 895-3955
Sycamore (G-20809)
Marlboro Wire Ltd ....E.... 217 224-7989
Quincy (G-17855)
Mason Welding Inc ....G.... 708 755-0621
S Chicago Hts (G-19106)
Matrix Machine & Tool Mfg ....G.... 708 452-8707
River Grove (G-18011)
MB Machine Inc ....F.... 815 864-3555
Shannon (G-19900)
McCloskey Eyman Mlone Mfg Svcs ....G.... 309 647-4000
Canton (G-2991)
McFarland Welding and Machine ....G.... 618 627-2838
Thompsonville (G-20863)
Meadoweld Machine Inc ....G.... 815 623-3939
South Beloit (G-20161)
Mendota Welding & Mfg ....G.... 815 539-6944
Mendota (G-14727)
Merritt Farm Equipment Inc ....G.... 217 746-5331
Carthage (G-3315)
Metalock Corporation ....F.... 815 666-1560
Crest Hill (G-7463)
Meteer Manufacturing Co ....G.... 217 636-8109
Athens (G-941)
Method Molds Inc ....G.... 815 877-0191
Loves Park (G-13965)
Metzger Welding Service ....G.... 217 234-2851
Mattoon (G-14403)
Mfw Services Inc ....G.... 708 522-5879
South Holland (G-20289)
Midway Machine & Tool Co Inc ....G.... 708 385-3450
Alsip (G-491)
Mihalis Marine ....G.... 773 445-6220
Chicago (G-5757)
Milans Machining & Mfg Co Inc ....D.... 708 780-6600
Cicero (G-7222)
Millers Eureka Inc ....F.... 312 666-9383
Chicago (G-5762)
Misselhorn Welding & Machines ....G.... 618 426-3714
Campbell Hill (G-2978)
Moline Welding Inc ....F.... 309 756-0643
Milan (G-14795)
Moline Welding Inc ....G.... 309 756-0643
Milan (G-14796)
Mt Vernon Mold Works Inc ....E.... 618 242-6040
Mount Vernon (G-15431)
Murphy Brothers Enterprises ....F.... 773 874-9020
Chicago (G-5836)

Mushro Machine & Tool Co ....F.... 815 672-5848
Streator (G-20697)
Napier Machine & Welding Inc ....G.... 217 525-8740
Springfield (G-20486)
National Tool & Machine Co ....F.... 618 271-6445
East Saint Louis (G-8762)
Neals Trailer Sales ....G.... 217 792-5136
Lincoln (G-13416)
Needham Shop Inc ....G.... 630 557-9019
Kaneville (G-12600)
▲ Nehring Electrical Works Co ....C.... 815 756-2741
Dekalb (G-8110)
Newman Welding & Machine Shop ....G.... 618 435-5591
Benton (G-2037)
Njc Machine Co ....F.... 708 442-6004
Lyons (G-14042)
North Shore Truck & Equipment ....G.... 847 887-0200
Lake Bluff (G-12860)
▲ Norton Machine Co ....G.... 217 748-6115
Rossville (G-19050)
Odom Tool and Technology Inc ....G.... 815 895-8545
Sycamore (G-20811)
Oostman Fabricating & Wldg Inc ....F.... 630 241-1315
Westmont (G-21909)
Orient Machining & Welding Inc ....E.... 708 371-3500
Dixmoor (G-8320)
▲ Orsolinis Welding & Fabg ....F.... 773 722-9855
Chicago (G-6016)
Osbornes Mch Weld Fabrication ....G.... 217 795-4716
Argenta (G-691)
P & G Machine & Tool Inc ....G.... 618 283-0273
Vandalia (G-21119)
Papendik Inc ....G.... 708 492-6230
Orland Park (G-16883)
Paramount Wire Specialties ....F.... 773 252-5636
Chicago (G-6080)
Park Tool & Machine Co Inc ....G.... 630 530-5110
Villa Park (G-21275)
Parker Fabrication Inc ....E.... 309 266-8413
Morton (G-15174)
Patkus Machine Co ....G.... 815 398-7818
Rockford (G-18530)
Pekin Weldors Inc ....F.... 309 382-3627
North Pekin (G-16193)
Performance Welding LLC ....G.... 217 412-5722
Maroa (G-14307)
Peters Machine Inc ....F.... 217 875-2578
Decatur (G-7926)
Petri Welding & Prop Repr Inc ....G.... 217 243-1748
Jacksonville (G-12407)
Phoenix Welding Co Inc ....F.... 630 616-1700
Franklin Park (G-10549)
PM Woodwind Repair Inc ....G.... 847 869-7049
Evanston (G-10088)
Precision Tool Welding ....G.... 630 285-9844
Itasca (G-12345)
Pro-Fab Metals Inc ....G.... 618 283-2986
Vandalia (G-21121)
Production Fabg & Stamping Inc ....F.... 708 755-5468
S Chicago Hts (G-19111)
Production Manufacturing ....G.... 217 256-4211
Warsaw (G-21371)
Professional Metal Works LLC ....F.... 618 539-2214
Freeburg (G-10639)
Quality Metal Works Inc ....G.... 309 379-5311
Stanford (G-20552)
Quality Tool & Machine Inc ....G.... 773 721-8655
Chicago (G-6248)
R & R Machining Inc ....G.... 217 835-4579
Bend (G-1806)
R A R Machine & Manufacturing ....E.... 630 260-9591
Chicago (G-6264)
R Machining Inc ....G.... 217 532-2174
Butler (G-2910)
R-M Industries Inc ....F.... 630 543-3071
Addison (G-267)
Ramsey Welding Inc ....E.... 618 483-6248
Altamont (G-555)
Ramseys Machine Co ....G.... 217 824-2320
Taylorville (G-20845)
Rapco Ltd ....G.... 618 249-6614
Richview (G-17981)
Reber Welding Service ....G.... 217 774-3441
Shelbyville (G-19914)
Reco of IL Inc ....G.... 630 898-2010
Aurora (G-1208)
Redi-Weld & Mfg Co Inc ....G.... 815 455-4460
Lake In The Hills (G-13004)
Regal Steel Erectors LLC ....E.... 847 888-3500
Elgin (G-9162)

SIC

Employee Codes: A=Over 500 employees, B=251-500
C=101-250, D=51-100, E=20-50, F=10-19, G=3-9
2017 Harris Illinois
Industrial Directory
1141

76 MISCELLANEOUS REPAIR SERVICES SIC SECTION

**Rex Radiator and Welding Co**...G... 847 428-1112
East Dundee *(G-8655)*
**Rex Radiator and Welding Co**...G... 312 421-1531
Chicago *(G-6343)*
**Rex Radiator and Welding Co**...G... 630 595-4664
Bensenville *(G-1977)*
**Rex Radiator and Welding Co**...G... 815 725-6655
Rockdale *(G-18230)*
▲ **Ri-Del Mfg Inc**...D... 312 829-8720
Chicago *(G-6349)*
**River Valley Mechanical Inc**...G... 309 364-3776
Putnam *(G-17788)*
**Robert Davis & Son Inc**...G... 815 889-4168
Milford *(G-14814)*
**Robertson Repair**...G... 618 895-2593
Sims *(G-19941)*
**Rockford Precision Machine**...F... 815 873-1018
Rockford *(G-18582)*
**Rodney Tite Welding**...G... 618 845-9072
Ullin *(G-21032)*
**Rogers Metal Services Inc**...E... 847 679-4642
Skokie *(G-20079)*
**Rw Welding Inc**...G... 847 541-5508
Arlington Heights *(G-832)*
**S & S Welding & Fabrication**...G... 847 742-7344
Elgin *(G-9170)*
▲ **S & W Manufacturing Co Inc**...E... 630 595-5044
Bensenville *(G-1984)*
**S D Custom Machining**...G... 618 544-7007
Robinson *(G-18072)*
**Sanitary Stainless Services**...G... 618 659-8567
Edwardsville *(G-8813)*
**Service Cutting & Welding**...G... 773 622-8366
Chicago *(G-6482)*
**Service Sheet Metal Works Inc**...F... 773 229-0031
Chicago *(G-6483)*
**Shanks Veterinary Equipment**...G... 815 225-7700
Milledgeville *(G-14818)*
**Shannon & Sons Welding**...G... 630 898-7778
Aurora *(G-1215)*
**Sheas Iron Works Inc**...E... 847 356-2922
Lake Villa *(G-13026)*
**Sheets & Cylinder Welding Inc**...G... 800 442-2200
Chicago *(G-6494)*
**Shup Tool & Machine Co**...G... 618 931-2596
Granite City *(G-11302)*
**Sigel Welding**...G... 217 844-2412
Sigel *(G-19938)*
**Silver Machine Shop Inc**...G... 217 359-5717
Champaign *(G-3540)*
**Sivco Welding Company**...G... 309 944-5171
Geneseo *(G-10804)*
**Smith Welding LLC**...G... 618 829-5414
Saint Elmo *(G-19311)*
**South Side Bler Wldg Works Inc**...G... 708 478-1714
Orland Park *(G-16893)*
**South Subn Wldg & Fabg Co Inc**...G... 708 385-7160
Posen *(G-17736)*
**Southwick Machine & Design Co**...G... 309 949-2868
Colona *(G-7348)*
**Spaeth Welding Inc**...F... 618 588-3596
New Baden *(G-15865)*
**Spannuth Boiler Co**...G... 708 386-1882
Oak Park *(G-16687)*
**Special Tool Engineering Co**...F... 773 767-6690
Chicago *(G-6554)*
**Spencer Welding Service Inc**...G... 847 272-0580
Northbrook *(G-16368)*
**Springfield Welding & Auto Bdy**...E... 217 523-5365
Springfield *(G-20534)*
**Steel Services Enterprises**...E... 708 259-1181
Lansing *(G-13187)*
**Stevenson Fabrication Svcs Inc**...G... 815 468-7941
Manteno *(G-14195)*
**Stuhlman Family LLC**...G... 815 436-2432
Plainfield *(G-17655)*
**Suburban Welding & Steel LLC**...F... 847 678-1264
Franklin Park *(G-10599)*
**Sulzer Pump Services (us) Inc**...F... 815 600-7355
Joliet *(G-12579)*
**Superior Joining Tech Inc**...E... 815 282-7581
Machesney Park *(G-14109)*
**Superior Welding Inc**...F... 618 544-8822
Robinson *(G-18073)*
**Sycamore Welding & Fabg Co**...G... 815 784-2557
Genoa *(G-10885)*
▲ **T & L Mfg Corporation**...E... 630 898-7100
Aurora *(G-1220)*
**Tait Machine Tool Inc**...G... 815 932-2011
Kankakee *(G-12656)*
**Taylor Design Inc**...G... 815 389-3991
Roscoe *(G-18924)*
**Taylor Off Road Racing**...G... 815 544-4500
Belvidere *(G-1788)*
▲ **Technology One Welding Inc**...G... 630 871-1296
Carol Stream *(G-3253)*
**Telza Welding Inc**...G... 773 777-4467
Chicago *(G-6693)*
**Terry Tool & Machining Corp**...G... 847 289-1054
East Dundee *(G-8658)*
**Tewell Bros Machine Inc**...F... 217 253-6303
Tuscola *(G-21025)*
**Thornton Welding Service Inc**...E... 217 877-0610
Decatur *(G-7952)*
**Titan Tool Works LLC**...F... 630 221-1080
Carol Stream *(G-3255)*
**Toledo Machine & Welding Inc**...G... 217 849-2251
Toledo *(G-20968)*
**Tomko Machine Works Inc**...G... 630 244-0902
Lemont *(G-13266)*
**Tony Weishaar**...G... 217 774-2774
Shelbyville *(G-19917)*
**Tonys Welding Service Inc**...G... 618 532-9353
Centralia *(G-3436)*
**Toolweld Inc**...G... 847 854-8013
Algonquin *(G-407)*
▲ **Torrence Machine & Tool Co**...G... 815 469-1850
Mokena *(G-14913)*
**Trailers Inc**...G... 217 472-6000
Chapin *(G-3588)*
**Tri-Cunty Wldg Fabrication LLC**...E... 217 543-3304
Arthur *(G-923)*
**Triplett Entereprises Inc**...G... 708 333-9421
Oak Forest *(G-16592)*
**Trotters Manufacturing Co**...G... 217 364-4540
Buffalo *(G-2649)*
**Tylers Fab & Welding Inc**...G... 217 283-6855
Hoopeston *(G-12120)*
**Uhlar Inc**...G... 815 961-0970
Rockford *(G-18659)*
**United Machine Works Inc**...G... 847 352-5252
Schaumburg *(G-19781)*
**United Maint Wldg & McHy C**...F... 708 458-1705
Bedford Park *(G-1588)*
**United Tool and Engineering Co**...D... 815 389-3021
South Beloit *(G-20171)*
**Universal Broaching Inc**...F... 847 228-1440
Elk Grove Village *(G-9800)*
**V Brothers Machine Co**...E... 708 652-0062
Cicero *(G-7243)*
**Vaughn & Sons Machine Shop**...G... 618 842-9048
Fairfield *(G-10157)*
▲ **Vindee Industries Inc**...E... 815 469-3300
Frankfort *(G-10375)*
**Wachs Technical Services Inc**...E... 847 537-8800
Wheeling *(G-22179)*
▲ **Walco Tool & Engineering Corp**...D... 815 834-0225
Romeoville *(G-18877)*
**Walt Ltd**...E... 312 337-2756
Chicago *(G-6936)*
**Wardzala Industries Inc**...F... 847 288-9909
Franklin Park *(G-10627)*
**WEb Production & Fabg Inc**...F... 312 733-6800
Chicago *(G-6948)*
**Weiland Welding Inc**...G... 815 580-8079
Cherry Valley *(G-3649)*
**Weld-Rite Service Inc**...E... 708 458-6000
Bedford Park *(G-1592)*
▼ **Welding Company of America**...E... 630 806-2000
Aurora *(G-1231)*
**Welding Shop**...G... 773 785-1305
Chicago *(G-6952)*
**Welding Specialties**...G... 708 798-5388
East Hazel Crest *(G-8667)*
**Wemco Inc**...F... 708 388-1980
Alsip *(G-543)*
**West End Tool & Die Inc**...G... 815 462-3040
New Lenox *(G-15927)*
**Wherry Machine & Welding Inc**...G... 309 828-5423
Bloomington *(G-2235)*
**Williams Welding Service**...G... 217 235-1758
Humboldt *(G-12130)*
**Wirfs Industries Inc**...F... 815 344-0635
McHenry *(G-14571)*
**Wissmiller & Evans Road Eqp**...G... 309 725-3598
Cooksville *(G-7373)*
**Wittwer Brothers Inc**...G... 815 522-3589
Monroe Center *(G-15025)*
**Xd Industries Inc**...F... 630 766-2843
Bensenville *(G-2019)*
**Ziglers Mch & Met Works Inc**...G... 815 652-7518
Dixon *(G-8360)*

### *7694 Armature Rewinding Shops*

**Accurate Elc Mtr & Pump Co**...G... 708 448-2792
Worth *(G-22631)*
**Acme Control Service Inc**...E... 773 774-9191
Chicago *(G-3732)*
**Addison Electric Inc**...E... 800 517-4871
Addison *(G-22)*
**Al Cook Electric Motors**...G... 309 653-2337
Adair *(G-11)*
**All Electric Mtr Repr Svc Inc**...F... 773 925-2404
Chicago *(G-3806)*
▲ **Amj Industries Inc**...F... 815 654-9000
Rockford *(G-18264)*
**Anna-Jonesboro Motor Co Inc**...G... 618 833-4486
Anna *(G-601)*
**Automatic Machinery Resources**...G... 630 543-4944
Addison *(G-48)*
**Avana Electric Motors Inc**...F... 847 588-0400
Elk Grove Village *(G-9323)*
**Bak Electric**...G... 708 458-3578
Bridgeview *(G-2469)*
**Bellwood Electric Motors Inc**...G... 708 544-7223
Bellwood *(G-1696)*
**Belmont Electro Co Inc**...G... 773 472-4641
Brookfield *(G-2623)*
**BP Elc Mtrs Pump & Svc Inc**...G... 773 539-4343
Skokie *(G-19967)*
**C and C Machine Tool Service**...G... 630 810-0484
Downers Grove *(G-8402)*
▲ **Calumet Armature and Elc LLC**...E... 708 841-6880
Riverdale *(G-18017)*
**Cameron Electric Motor Corp**...F... 312 939-5770
Chicago *(G-4223)*
**Cox Electric Motor Service**...G... 217 344-2458
Urbana *(G-21080)*
**Decatur Industrial Elc Inc**...E... 618 244-1066
Mount Vernon *(G-15409)*
**Decatur Industrial Elc Inc**...E... 217 428-6621
Decatur *(G-7872)*
**Dependable Electric**...G... 618 592-3314
Oblong *(G-16732)*
**Dreisilker Electric Motors Inc**...C... 630 469-7510
Glen Ellyn *(G-10967)*
**Ebling Electric Company**...F... 312 455-1885
Chicago *(G-4688)*
◆ **Electric Motor Corp**...E... 773 725-1050
Chicago *(G-4719)*
**Elmot Inc**...G... 773 791-7039
Chicago *(G-4734)*
**Endeavor Technologies Inc**...E... 630 562-0300
Saint Charles *(G-19181)*
**Erbes Electric**...G... 815 849-5508
Sublette *(G-20715)*
▲ **Fdf Armature Inc**...G... 630 458-0452
Addison *(G-115)*
**First Electric Motor Shop Inc**...G... 217 698-0672
Springfield *(G-20440)*
**Fleetpride Inc**...F... 630 455-6881
Willowbrook *(G-22212)*
**Flolo Corporation**...E... 630 595-1010
West Chicago *(G-21703)*
**Flolo Corporation**...G... 847 249-0880
Gurnee *(G-11448)*
**Fluid Pump Service Inc**...G... 847 228-0750
Elk Grove Village *(G-9480)*
**Fontela Electric Incorporated**...F... 630 932-1600
Addison *(G-121)*
**Foremost Electric & Transm Inc**...E... 309 699-2200
Peoria *(G-17364)*
**Gem Electric Motor Repair**...G... 815 756-5317
Dekalb *(G-8094)*
**Goding Electric Company**...F... 630 858-7700
Glendale Heights *(G-11029)*
**H & H Motor Service Inc**...G... 708 652-6100
Cicero *(G-7199)*
**Harvey Bros Inc**...F... 309 342-3137
Galesburg *(G-10757)*
**Heise Industries Inc**...G... 847 223-2410
Grayslake *(G-11346)*
**Hills Electric Motor Service**...G... 815 625-0305
Rock Falls *(G-18136)*
**Hopcroft Electric Inc**...G... 618 288-7302
Glen Carbon *(G-10952)*
**Iesco Inc**...E... 708 594-1250
Chicago *(G-5146)*
**Industrial Service Solutions**...F... 917 609-6979
Chicago *(G-5180)*

# 76 MISCELLANEOUS REPAIR SERVICES

Inman Electric Motors Inc .................... E ...... 815 223-2288
　La Salle  *(G-12778)*
Integrated Power Services LLC .............. E ...... 708 877-5310
　Thornton  *(G-20874)*
J & J Electric Motor Repair Sp ................ G ...... 217 529-0015
　Springfield  *(G-20459)*
Jasiek Motor Rebuilding Inc .................... G ...... 815 883-3678
　Oglesby  *(G-16750)*
Joes Automotive Inc .................................. G ...... 815 937-9281
　Kankakee  *(G-12630)*
Kankakee Industrial Tech ........................ F ...... 815 933-6683
　Bradley  *(G-2425)*
Keller United Elc & Mch Co ...................... G ...... 217 382-4521
　Martinsville  *(G-14337)*
L A Motors Incorporated .......................... G ...... 773 736-7305
　Chicago  *(G-5421)*
Lakenburges Motor Co .............................. G ...... 618 523-4231
　Germantown  *(G-10893)*
Lange Electric Inc .................................... G ...... 217 347-7626
　Effingham  *(G-8843)*
Lawrence Maddock .................................. F ...... 847 394-1698
　Arlington Heights  *(G-792)*
Lee Foss Electric Motor Svc .................... G ...... 708 681-5335
　Melrose Park  *(G-14670)*
M H Electric Motor & Ctrl Corp ................ G ...... 630 393-3736
　Warrenville  *(G-21350)*
M R Glenn Electric Inc .............................. E ...... 708 479-9200
　Lockport  *(G-13729)*
Melton Electric Co .................................... G ...... 309 697-1422
　Peoria  *(G-17405)*

Metroeast Motorsports Inc ...................... G ...... 618 628-2466
　O Fallon  *(G-16471)*
Metzka Inc ................................................ G ...... 815 932-6363
　Kankakee  *(G-12638)*
▲ Mid-America Taping Reeling Inc .......... D ...... 630 629-6646
　Glendale Heights  *(G-11048)*
Midwest Elc Mtr Inc Danville .................... G ...... 217 442-5656
　Danville  *(G-7756)*
Midwest Motor Specialists Inc ................ G ...... 815 942-0083
　Morris  *(G-15118)*
Murrays Disc Auto Stores Inc ................ G ...... 847 458-7179
　Lake In The Hills  *(G-12999)*
Murrays Disc Auto Stores Inc ................ G ...... 847 882-4384
　Schaumburg  *(G-19659)*
Murrays Disc Auto Stores Inc ................ G ...... 708 430-8155
　Bridgeview  *(G-2511)*
New Cie Inc .............................................. F ...... 815 224-1485
　La Salle  *(G-12781)*
New Cie Inc .............................................. E ...... 815 224-1511
　Peru  *(G-17522)*
Oreillys Auto Parts Store ........................ G ...... 847 360-0012
　Waukegan  *(G-21599)*
Park Electric Motor Service .................... G ...... 217 442-1977
　Danville  *(G-7759)*
Pauls Mc Culloch Sales .......................... G ...... 217 323-2159
　Beardstown  *(G-1526)*
Pillarhouse USA Inc ................................ F ...... 847 593-9080
　Elk Grove Village  *(G-9680)*
Precision Drive & Control Inc ................ G ...... 815 235-7595
　Freeport  *(G-10680)*

Prompt Motor Rewinding Service .......... G ...... 847 675-7155
　Skokie  *(G-20065)*
Quality Armature Inc ................................ G ...... 773 622-3951
　Chicago  *(G-6245)*
Rathje Enterprises Inc ............................ B ...... 217 423-2593
　Decatur  *(G-7932)*
Richards Electric Motor Co .................... E ...... 217 222-7154
　Quincy  *(G-17887)*
Rockford Electric Equipment Co ............ G ...... 815 398-4096
　Rockford  *(G-18573)*
Sandner Electric Co Inc .......................... G ...... 618 932-2179
　West Frankfort  *(G-21818)*
Schaeffer Electric Co .............................. G ...... 618 592-3231
　Oblong  *(G-16734)*
Service Pro Electric Mtr Repr ................ G ...... 630 766-1215
　Bensenville  *(G-1990)*
Steiner Electric Company ...................... E ...... 312 421-7220
　Chicago  *(G-6584)*
Tracy Electric Inc .................................... E ...... 618 943-6205
　Lawrenceville  *(G-13206)*
Vandalia Electric Mtr Svc Inc ................ G ...... 618 283-0068
　Vandalia  *(G-21128)*
Voss Electric Inc .................................... G ...... 708 596-6000
　Harvey  *(G-11680)*
▲ Warfield Electric Company Inc .......... E ...... 815 469-4094
　Frankfort  *(G-10376)*
◆ Yaskawa America Inc ........................ C ...... 847 887-7000
　Waukegan  *(G-21642)*

# ALPHABETIC SECTION

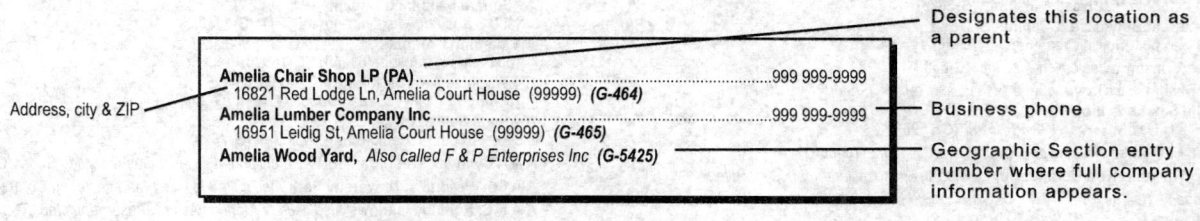

*See footnotes for symbols and codes identification.*
* Companies listed alphabetically.
* Complete physical or mailing address.

**1 Engineering, Batavia** Also called Bevstream Corp *(G-1421)*
**1 Federal Supply Source Inc** ......708 964-2222
  30 E 34th St  Steger  (60475)  *(G-20565)*
**1 Heavy Equipment Loading Inc** ......773 581-7374
  6535 S Austin Ave  Bedford Park  (60638)  *(G-1528)*
**10 4 Irp Inc** ......708 485-1040
  8846 47th St  Brookfield  (60513)  *(G-2621)*
**1035 Kiss, Chicago** Also called Iheartcommunications Inc *(G-5149)*
**10th Magnitude LLC** ......224 628-9047
  20 N Wacker Dr Ste 530  Chicago  (60606)  *(G-3661)*
**10x Microstructures LLC** ......847 215-7448
  420 Harvester Ct  Wheeling  (60090)  *(G-21991)*
**1101 Flavors, Schaumburg** Also called Sweet Endeavors Inc *(G-19748)*
**1187 Creative LLC** ......618 457-1187
  201 E Main St Ste 2-I  Carbondale  (62901)  *(G-2999)*
**11th Street Express Prtg Inc** ......815 968-0208
  2135 11th St  Rockford  (61104)  *(G-18235)*
**13rf Rental & Fabrication, Murphysboro** Also called Thirteen Rf Inc *(G-15585)*
**13th Ward Office, Chicago** Also called City of Chicago *(G-4386)*
**144 International Inc** ......847 426-8881
  740 S 8th St  West Dundee  (60118)  *(G-21794)*
**15679 Wadsworth Inc** ......847 662-4561
  15679 W Wadsworth Rd  Wadsworth  (60083)  *(G-21321)*
**1717 Chemall Corporation** ......224 864-4180
  222 Terrace Dr  Mundelein  (60060)  *(G-15460)*
**1883 Properties Inc (HQ)** ......847 537-8800
  600 Knightsbridge Pkwy  Lincolnshire  (60069)  *(G-13422)*
**2 Figs Baking Co Inc** ......847 778-2936
  229 Leahy Cir S  Des Plaines  (60016)  *(G-8135)*
**2 Koi, Gurnee** Also called Speedpro Imaging *(G-11506)*
**2 M Tool Company Inc** ......773 282-0722
  6530 W Dakin St  Chicago  (60634)  *(G-3662)*
**20 20 Medical Systems Inc** ......815 455-7161
  111 Erick St Ste 125  Crystal Lake  (60014)  *(G-7524)*
**2000plus Groups Inc** ......630 528-3220
  2607 W 22nd St Ste 39  Oak Brook  (60523)  *(G-16483)*
**2000plus Groups Inc (PA)** ......800 939-6268
  4343 W 44th Pl  Chicago  (60632)  *(G-3663)*
**21st Century Us-Sino Services** ......312 808-9328
  500 W 18th St Ste 2  Chicago  (60616)  *(G-3664)*
**22nd Century Media** ......847 272-4565
  60 Revere Dr  Northbrook  (60062)  *(G-16194)*
**22nd Century Media (PA)** ......708 326-9170
  11516 W 183rd St U Sw 3  Orland Park  (60467)  *(G-16836)*
**233 Skydeck LLC** ......312 875-9448
  233 S Wacker Dr  Chicago  (60606)  *(G-3665)*
**24land Express Inc** ......630 766-2424
  1460 Mark St  Elk Grove Village  (60007)  *(G-9247)*
**2d2c Inc (PA)** ......847 543-0980
  1071 Cheswick Dr  Gurnee  (60031)  *(G-11416)*
**2l Technologies LLC** ......312 526-3900
  445 N Franklin St  Chicago  (60654)  *(G-3666)*
**2m Control Systems Inc** ......630 709-6225
  245 W Roosevelt Rd Ste 86  West Chicago  (60185)  *(G-21650)*
**2nd Cine Inc** ......773 455-5808
  637 Frazier St  Elgin  (60123)  *(G-8928)*
**3 Angels, Addison** Also called Three Angels Printing Svcs Inc *(G-313)*
**3 D Concrete Design Inc** ......847 297-7968
  1000 Lee St  Des Plaines  (60016)  *(G-8136)*
**3 Goldenstar Inc** ......847 963-0451
  545 E Dundee Rd  Palatine  (60074)  *(G-16994)*
**3 Penguins Ltd** ......630 528-7086
  609 Millview Dr  Batavia  (60510)  *(G-1401)*
**3-D Mold & Tool Inc** ......847 870-7150
  2078 Foster Ave  Wheeling  (60090)  *(G-21992)*
**3-D Resource** ......815 899-8600
  1005 Brickville Rd  Sycamore  (60178)  *(G-20784)*

**3-V Industries Inc** ......217 835-4453
  110 W Oak St  Benld  (62009)  *(G-1804)*
**300 Below Inc** ......217 423-3070
  2999 E Parkway Dr  Decatur  (62526)  *(G-7819)*
**312 Aquaponics LLC** ......312 469-0239
  711 S River Rd Apt 812  Des Plaines  (60016)  *(G-8137)*
**321 Learning Services, Barrington** Also called New Vision Software Inc *(G-1295)*
**360 Digital Print Inc** ......630 682-3601
  262 Tubeway Dr  Carol Stream  (60188)  *(G-3086)*
**360 Yield Center LLC** ......309 263-4360
  180 Detroit Ave  Morton  (61550)  *(G-15152)*
**3abn** ......618 627-4651
  6020 Green Meadow Rd  Thompsonville  (62890)  *(G-20861)*
**3b Media Inc** ......312 563-9363
  401 N Michigan Ave # 1200  Chicago  (60611)  *(G-3667)*
**3d Flight Simulation Co** ......708 560-0701
  15025 Ridgewood Dr  Oak Forest  (60452)  *(G-16571)*
**3d Industries Inc** ......630 616-8702
  500 Frontier Way  Bensenville  (60106)  *(G-1808)*
**3d Manufacturing Corporation** ......815 806-9200
  9218 Corsair Rd Unit 5  Frankfort  (60423)  *(G-10290)*
**3d Resource, Sycamore** Also called 3-D Resource *(G-20784)*
**3dp Unlimited** ......815 389-5667
  6402 E Rockton Rd  Roscoe  (61073)  *(G-18887)*
**3e Graphics & Printing, Buffalo Grove** Also called Brian Paul Inc *(G-2670)*
**3M Company** ......309 654-2291
  22614 Route 84 N  Cordova  (61242)  *(G-7374)*
**3M Dekalb Distribution** ......815 756-5087
  12101 Barber Greene Rd  Dekalb  (60115)  *(G-8071)*
**3primedx Inc** ......312 621-0643
  191 N Wacker Dr Ste 1500  Chicago  (60606)  *(G-3668)*
**3rd Base Bar** ......217 644-2424
  18263 E County Road 400n  Charleston  (61920)  *(G-3589)*
**3t Imaging Center, Morton Grove** Also called Morton Grove Med Imaging LLC *(G-15222)*
**3v Pallet** ......708 620-7790
  133 W 154th St  South Holland  (60473)  *(G-20237)*
**3v Pallet** ......708 333-1113
  16140 Clinton St  Harvey  (60426)  *(G-11649)*
**4 Elements Company** ......773 236-2284
  520 Cardinal Pl  Mundelein  (60060)  *(G-15461)*
**4 Seasons Sales and Marketing, Park Ridge** Also called Strauss Facter Assoc Inc *(G-17224)*
**4200 Kirchoff Corp** ......773 551-1541
  4200 Kirchoff Rd  Rolling Meadows  (60008)  *(G-18705)*
**425 Manufacturing** ......815 873-7066
  5004 27th Ave  Rockford  (61109)  *(G-18236)*
**4ever Design Studio, Arlington Heights** Also called 4ever Printing Inc *(G-699)*
**4ever Printing Inc** ......847 222-1525
  3401b N Kennicott Ave  Arlington Heights  (60004)  *(G-699)*
**4g Antenna Shop Inc** ......815 496-0444
  2948 Kirk Rd Ste 106  Aurora  (60502)  *(G-952)*
**4l Technologies Inc (PA)** ......815 431-8100
  4200 Columbus St  Ottawa  (61350)  *(G-16944)*
**4l Waterjet, Winchester** Also called Lashcon Inc *(G-22281)*
**4x4 Headquarters LLC** ......217 540-5337
  18086 N Highway 45  Effingham  (62401)  *(G-8820)*
**5 B'S Catering Service, Waterman** Also called William Badal *(G-21412)*
**5 Rabbit Brewery, Chicago** Also called 5 Rabbit Cerveceria Inc *(G-3669)*
**5 Rabbit Cerveceria Inc** ......312 265-8316
  6398 W 74th St  Chicago  (60638)  *(G-3669)*
**5 Star Publishing Inc** ......217 285-1355
  1401 E Washington St  Pittsfield  (62363)  *(G-17560)*
**555 International Inc** ......773 847-1400
  2225 W Pershing Rd  Chicago  (60609)  *(G-3670)*
**555 International Inc** ......773 869-0555
  4000 S Bell Ave  Chicago  (60609)  *(G-3671)*
**555 International Inc (PA)** ......773 869-0555
  4501 S Western Blvd  Chicago  (60609)  *(G-3672)*

(PA)=Parent Co  (HQ)=Headquarters  (DH)=Div Headquarters

**555 MANUFACTURING DIV OF:, Chicago** *Also called 555 International Inc* ***(G-3672)***
**57th Street Bookcase & Cabinet**.....773 363-3038
1455 E 55th Pl Chicago (60637) ***(G-3673)***
**57th Street Bookcase & Cabinet**.....312 867-1669
1443 E 56th St Chicago (60637) ***(G-3674)***
**5inch, Chicago** *Also called T 26 Inc* ***(G-6662)***
**680 Design, Elk Grove Village** *Also called Rebechini Studio Inc* ***(G-9711)***
**7 Mile Solutions Inc**.....847 588-2280
7540 N Caldwell Ave Niles (60714) ***(G-15952)***
**7 Up, East Alton** *Also called Flowers Distributing Inc* ***(G-8601)***
**7-Up-The American Bottling Co, Loves Park** *Also called American Bottling Company* ***(G-13919)***
**7000 Inc**.....312 800-3612
856 Fieldcrest Dr Bolingbrook (60490) ***(G-2275)***
**773 LLC**.....312 707-8780
564 W Randolph St Chicago (60661) ***(G-3675)***
**78 Brand Co**.....312 344-1602
1655 S Blue Island Ave Chicago (60608) ***(G-3676)***
**78 Red Ketchup, Chicago** *Also called 78 Brand Co* ***(G-3676)***
**8 Electronic Cigarette Inc**.....630 708-6803
1830 Wallace Ave Ste 201 Saint Charles (60174) ***(G-19129)***
**8 Electronic Cigarettes, Saint Charles** *Also called 8 Electronic Cigarette Inc* ***(G-19129)***
**815 Pallets Inc**.....815 678-0012
11600 Sterling Pkwy Richmond (60071) ***(G-17954)***
**847 696-9278, Rolling Meadows** *Also called United Chemi-Con Inc* ***(G-18786)***
**89robotics, Chicago** *Also called Eighty Nine Robotics LLC* ***(G-4705)***
**9161 Corporation**.....847 470-8828
9161 N Milwaukee Ave Niles (60714) ***(G-15953)***
**A & A Graphx, Champaign** *Also called Dabel Incorporated* ***(G-3472)***
**A & A Machine Co Inc**.....847 985-4619
1530 Jarvis Ave Elk Grove Village (60007) ***(G-9248)***
**A & A Magnetics Inc**.....815 338-6054
520 Magnet Way Woodstock (60098) ***(G-22532)***
**A & A Steel Fabricating Co**.....708 389-4499
14100 S Harrison Ave Posen (60469) ***(G-17726)***
**A & B Machine Shop**.....815 397-0495
1920 20th Ave Rockford (61104) ***(G-18237)***
**A & B Machine Works Inc**.....312 733-7888
460 N Union Ave Chicago (60654) ***(G-3677)***
**A & B Metal Polishing Inc**.....773 847-1077
1900 S Washtenaw Ave Chicago (60608) ***(G-3678)***
**A & B Printing Service Inc**.....217 789-9034
2122 N Republic St Springfield (62702) ***(G-20383)***
**A & C Mold Company Inc**.....630 587-0177
3870 Swenson Ave Saint Charles (60174) ***(G-19130)***
**A & E Forge, Forest Park** *Also called Clark Caster Co* ***(G-10238)***
**A & E Rubber Stamp Corp**.....312 575-1416
215 N Desplaines St 2n Chicago (60661) ***(G-3679)***
**A & F Pallet Service Inc**.....773 767-9500
4333 S Knox Ave Chicago (60632) ***(G-3680)***
**A & H Bindery, The, Broadview** *Also called Ricter Corporation* ***(G-2608)***
**A & H Lithoprint Inc**.....708 345-1196
2540 S 27th Ave Broadview (60155) ***(G-2551)***
**A & H Manufacturing Inc**.....630 543-5900
200 W Laura Dr Addison (60101) ***(G-14)***
**A & J Finishers**.....847 352-5408
623 Lunt Ave Schaumburg (60193) ***(G-19417)***
**A & J Graphics, Elk Grove Village** *Also called A & J Printers Inc* ***(G-9249)***
**A & J Plating Inc**.....708 453-9713
8058 Grand Ave River Grove (60171) ***(G-18004)***
**A & J Printers Inc**.....847 909-9609
809 Dierking Ter Elk Grove Village (60007) ***(G-9249)***
**A & J Signs**.....815 476-0128
2104 Woodview Dr Wilmington (60481) ***(G-22268)***
**A & L Construction Inc**.....708 343-1660
1951 Cornell Ave Melrose Park (60160) ***(G-14577)***
**A & L Drilling Inc**.....815 962-7538
1453 Hunting Woods Trl Rockford (61102) ***(G-18238)***
**A & M Cabinets, Batavia** *Also called Anderson & Marter Cabinets* ***(G-1415)***
**A & M Products Company**.....815 875-2667
575 Elm Pl Princeton (61356) ***(G-17740)***
**A & M Tool Co Inc**.....847 215-8140
5 W Waltz Dr Wheeling (60090) ***(G-21993)***
**A & M Wood Products Inc**.....630 323-2555
9900 S Madison St Unit A Burr Ridge (60527) ***(G-2818)***
**A & P Grain Systems Inc**.....815 827-3079
410 S County Line Rd Maple Park (60151) ***(G-14196)***
**A & R Machine Inc**.....708 388-4764
12340 S Keeler Ave Alsip (60803) ***(G-426)***
**A & R Screening LLC**.....708 598-2480
8417 Beloit Ave Bridgeview (60455) ***(G-2457)***
**A & S Arms Inc**.....224 267-5670
847 Forest View Way Antioch (60002) ***(G-612)***
**A & S Steel Specialties Inc**.....815 838-8188
1001 Clinton St Ste A Lockport (60441) ***(G-13700)***
**A & W Auto Truck & Trailer, Darien** *Also called Andy Wurst* ***(G-7789)***
**A & Z Sas Express Inc**.....847 451-0851
3051 Lee St Melrose Park (60164) ***(G-14578)***
**A - Square Manufacturing Inc**.....800 628-6720
3939 S Karlov Ave Chicago (60632) ***(G-3681)***
**A - Square Manufacturing Inc (PA)**.....800 628-6720
1100 S Kostner Ave Chicago (60624) ***(G-3682)***
**A 1 Marking Products**.....309 762-6096
1801 5th Ave Moline (61265) ***(G-14916)***
**A 1 Trophies Awards & Engrv**.....630 837-6000
1534 Brandy Pkwy Streamwood (60107) ***(G-20638)***
**A 2 Steel Sales LLC**.....708 924-1200
6499 W 66th Pl Bedford Park (60638) ***(G-1529)***
**A A A Cylinder, West Frankfort** *Also called Little Egypt Gas A & Wldg Sups* ***(G-21813)***
**A A Coil Products, University Park** *Also called M Lizen Manufacturing Co* ***(G-21055)***
**A A N S, Rolling Meadows** *Also called American Assn Nurosurgeons Inc* ***(G-18709)***
**A A Swift Print Inc**.....847 301-1122
30 Standish Ln Schaumburg (60193) ***(G-19418)***
**A and D Industrial Ignition**.....773 992-4040
10330 Front Ave Franklin Park (60131) ***(G-10380)***
**A and J Development Plus LLC**.....630 470-9539
10101 S Mandel St Ste A Plainfield (60585) ***(G-17575)***
**A and K Prtg & Graphic Design**.....618 244-3525
605 S 10th St Mount Vernon (62864) ***(G-15396)***
**A and R Custom Chrome**.....708 728-1005
6528 S Lavergne Ave Chicago (60638) ***(G-3683)***
**A and T Cigarettes Imports**.....847 836-9134
105 Prairie Lake Rd East Dundee (60118) ***(G-8627)***
**A and T Labs Incorporated**.....630 668-8562
1926 Berkshire Pl Wheaton (60189) ***(G-21932)***
**A Arbec Company, Lockport** *Also called Printing Plus* ***(G-13739)***
**A Ashland Lock Company (PA)**.....773 348-5106
2510 N Ashland Ave Chicago (60614) ***(G-3684)***
**A B, Waukegan** *Also called AB Specialty Silicones LLC* ***(G-21516)***
**A B C Blind Inc**.....708 877-7100
108 S Julian St Thornton (60476) ***(G-20866)***
**A B C Truss, Jerseyville** *Also called Atlas Building Components Inc* ***(G-12418)***
**A B Kelly Inc**.....847 639-1022
212 W Main St Ste 5 Cary (60013) ***(G-3320)***
**A B S Embroidery Inc**.....708 597-7785
4814 W 129th St Alsip (60803) ***(G-427)***
**A Barr Ftn Beverage Sls & Svc**.....708 442-2000
4424 Prescott Ave Lyons (60534) ***(G-14028)***
**A Barr Ftn Beverage Sls & Svc**.....708 442-2000
16300 103rd St Lemont (60439) ***(G-13221)***
**A Beadtiful Thing**.....630 236-5913
2406 Wilton Ln Aurora (60502) ***(G-953)***
**A Burst of Sun Inc**.....815 335-2331
817 N Elida St Winnebago (61088) ***(G-22294)***
**A C A, Streamwood** *Also called Aluminum Coil Anodizing Corp* ***(G-20641)***
**A C Gentrol Inc**.....309 274-5486
100 S 4th St Chillicothe (61523) ***(G-7160)***
**A Closet Wholesaler**.....312 654-1400
1155 N Howe St Chicago (60610) ***(G-3685)***
**A Corporate Printing Service**.....630 515-0432
7705 Dalewood Pkwy Woodridge (60517) ***(G-22447)***
**A Cut Above Engraving Inc**.....708 671-9800
12741 S La Grange Rd Palos Park (60464) ***(G-17126)***
**A D Skylights Inc**.....847 854-2900
206 Berg St Algonquin (60102) ***(G-376)***
**A D Specialty Sewing**.....847 639-0390
410 Northwest Hwy Fox River Grove (60021) ***(G-10285)***
**A Division of A&A Studios Inc**.....312 278-1144
350 N Ogden Ave Ste 10 Chicago (60607) ***(G-3686)***
**A Division of TEC, Elgin** *Also called Temperature Equipment Corp* ***(G-9209)***
**A Divison of Da, Montgomery** *Also called Viking Metal Cabinet Company* ***(G-15070)***
**A E Frasz Inc**.....630 232-6223
1n545 Brundige Rd Elburn (60119) ***(G-8872)***
**A E Iskra Inc (PA)**.....815 874-4022
4814 American Rd Rockford (61109) ***(G-18239)***
**A E Iskra Inc**.....815 874-4022
4814 American Rd Rockford (61109) ***(G-18240)***
**A E Micek Engineering Corp**.....847 455-8181
9239 Cherry Ave Franklin Park (60131) ***(G-10381)***
**A F C, Lake In The Hills** *Also called Advanced Flxble Composites Inc* ***(G-12983)***
**A F I, Carol Stream** *Also called Afi Industries Inc* ***(G-3092)***
**A Finkl & Sons Co (HQ)**.....773 975-2510
1355 E 93rd St Chicago (60619) ***(G-3687)***
**A Fischer Phase Drives**.....815 759-6928
4615 Prime Pkwy McHenry (60050) ***(G-14473)***
**A Flores, Aurora** *Also called Flores Precision Products* ***(G-1152)***
**A G Mitchells Jewelers Ltd**.....847 394-0820
10 N Dunton Ave Arlington Heights (60005) ***(G-700)***
**A G Welding**.....773 261-0575
4711 W Lake St Chicago (60644) ***(G-3688)***
**A Hardy/U S A Ltd**.....847 298-2358
1400 E Touhy Ave Ste 120 Des Plaines (60018) ***(G-8138)***
**A Hartlett & Sons Inc**.....815 338-0109
406 N Eastwood Dr Woodstock (60098) ***(G-22533)***
**A I 2, Chicago** *Also called Access International Inc* ***(G-3715)***
**A I I, Danville** *Also called Automation International Inc* ***(G-7704)***

**A I R, Rochester** *Also called Appliance Information and Repr* ***(G-18115)***
**A I Satellite Distributing, Loves Park** *Also called Audio Installers Inc* ***(G-13923)***
**A J Adhesives Inc**.....708 210-1111
15461 La Salle St South Holland (60473) ***(G-20238)***
**A J Antunes & Co**.....630 784-1000
180 Kehoe Blvd Carol Stream (60188) ***(G-3087)***
**A J Carbide Grinding**.....847 675-5112
8509 E Prairie Rd Skokie (60076) ***(G-19942)***
**A J Express Power Tools**.....847 678-8200
4918 River Rd Schiller Park (60176) ***(G-19796)***
**A J Funk & Co**.....847 741-6760
1471 Timber Dr Elgin (60123) ***(G-8929)***
**A J Horne Inc**.....630 231-8686
893 Industrial Dr West Chicago (60185) ***(G-21651)***
**A J Kay Co**.....224 475-0370
304 Washington Blvd Mundelein (60060) ***(G-15462)***
**A J Machining Inc**.....708 563-2580
7229 W 66th St Bedford Park (60638) ***(G-1530)***
**A J Manufacturing Co Inc**.....630 832-2828
437 W Wrightwood Ave Elmhurst (60126) ***(G-9828)***
**A J R Industries Inc**.....847 439-0380
117 Gordon St Elk Grove Village (60007) ***(G-9250)***
**A J R International Inc (PA)**.....800 232-3965
300 Regency Dr Glendale Heights (60139) ***(G-11006)***
**A J Smoy Co Inc**.....773 775-8282
163 Chatsworth Cir Schaumburg (60194) ***(G-19419)***
**A J Wagner & Son**.....773 935-1414
1120 N Rand Rd Frnt 1 Wauconda (60084) ***(G-21434)***
**A Jule Enterprise Inc**.....312 243-6950
2219 W Grand Ave Chicago (60612) ***(G-3689)***
**A K Tool & Manufacturing Inc**.....630 889-9220
260 Cortland Ave Ste 4 Lombard (60148) ***(G-13756)***
**A La Cart Inc**.....847 256-4102
1490 Old Deerfield Rd # 18 Highland Park (60035) ***(G-11820)***
**A Lakin & Sons Inc (PA)**.....773 871-6360
2001 Greenfield Rd Montgomery (60538) ***(G-15026)***
**A Len Complete Auto Svc Ctr, Downers Grove** *Also called A Len Radiator Shoppe Inc* ***(G-8384)***
**A Len Radiator Shoppe Inc**.....630 852-5445
333 Ogden Ave Downers Grove (60515) ***(G-8384)***
**A Lift Above Inc**.....630 758-1023
699 N Walnut St Ste 1 Elmhurst (60126) ***(G-9829)***
**A Lucas & Sons**.....309 673-8547
1328 Sw Washington St Peoria (61602) ***(G-17297)***
**A M Lee Inc**.....847 291-1777
2778 Dundee Rd Northbrook (60062) ***(G-16195)***
**A M P Software Inc**.....630 240-5922
455 Vermont Dr Elk Grove Village (60007) ***(G-9251)***
**A M R, Addison** *Also called Automatic Machinery Resources* ***(G-48)***
**A M T, Elk Grove Village** *Also called American Molding Tech Inc* ***(G-9297)***
**A M Tool, Rolling Meadows** *Also called Precision Metal Spinning Corp* ***(G-18767)***
**A M Tool & Die**.....847 398-7530
1000 Carnegie St Rolling Meadows (60008) ***(G-18706)***
**A Miller & Co**.....309 637-7756
Foot Of Clark St Peoria (61607) ***(G-17298)***
**A New Dairy Company**.....312 421-1234
1234 W Randolph St Chicago (60607) ***(G-3690)***
**A P Deli IV Inc**.....708 335-4462
1925 170th St Hazel Crest (60429) ***(G-11706)***
**A P L Plastics**.....773 265-1370
3501 W Fillmore St Chicago (60624) ***(G-3691)***
**A P M, Nokomis** *Also called All Precision Mfg LLC* ***(G-16055)***
**A P M, Woodstock** *Also called American Packaging McHy Inc* ***(G-22539)***
**A Plus Apparel**.....815 675-2117
9902 Fox Bluff Ln Spring Grove (60081) ***(G-20323)***
**A Plus Signs Inc**.....708 534-2030
25807 S Governors Hwy Monee (60449) ***(G-14990)***
**A Printing, Rockford** *Also called A+ Printing Co* ***(G-18242)***
**A R B C Inc**.....815 777-6006
11440 Dandar St Galena (61036) ***(G-10714)***
**A R C, Chicago** *Also called Leo Burnett Company Inc* ***(G-5493)***
**A R C Electro Refinishers Inc**.....708 681-5535
4113 Butterfield Rd Bellwood (60104) ***(G-1692)***
**A R C O, Skokie** *Also called American Vacuum Co* ***(G-19951)***
**A R K, Saint Charles** *Also called Ark Technologies Inc* ***(G-19138)***
**A R Tech & Tool Inc**.....708 599-5745
8620 S Thomas Ave Bridgeview (60455) ***(G-2458)***
**A Schulman Inc**.....847 426-3350
400 Maple Ave Ste A Carpentersville (60110) ***(G-3270)***
**A Seamless Gutters, Lombard** *Also called Seamless Gutter Corp* ***(G-13852)***
**A Stucki Company**.....618 498-4442
27128 Crystal Lake Rd Jerseyville (62052) ***(G-12416)***
**A T Products Inc**.....815 943-3590
1600 S Division St Harvard (60033) ***(G-11615)***
**A T S, Lawrenceville** *Also called Toyota Boshoku Illinois LLC* ***(G-13205)***
**A To Z Engraving Co Inc**.....847 526-7396
1150 Brown St Ste G Wauconda (60084) ***(G-21435)***
**A To Z Engrvg, Wauconda** *Also called A To Z Engraving Co Inc* ***(G-21435)***
**A To Z Offset Prtg & Pubg Inc**.....847 966-3016
9115 Terminal Ave Skokie (60077) ***(G-19943)***
**A To Z Tool Inc**.....630 787-0478
400 W Saint Charles Rd # 1 Villa Park (60181) ***(G-21231)***
**A To Z Type & Graphic Inc**.....312 587-1887
1703 N Vine St Chicago (60614) ***(G-3692)***
**A Trustworthy Sup Source Inc**.....773 480-0255
6047 N Central Park Ave Chicago (60659) ***(G-3693)***
**A W Enterprises Inc**.....708 458-8989
6543 S Laramie Ave Bedford Park (60638) ***(G-1531)***
**A W H Sales**.....847 869-0950
6001 W Gross Point Rd Niles (60714) ***(G-15954)***
**A Wheels Inc**.....847 699-7000
666 Garland Pl Des Plaines (60016) ***(G-8139)***
**A Wiley & Associates**.....815 343-7401
707 E Dayton Rd Ottawa (61350) ***(G-16945)***
**A Yard Materials Co**.....815 385-4560
Ringwood Rd Mchenry (60051) ***(G-14474)***
**A Z Z, Joliet** *Also called AAA Galvanizing - Joliet Inc* ***(G-12449)***
**A&B Apparel**.....815 962-5070
1029 Broadway Frnt Rockford (61104) ***(G-18241)***
**A&B Reliable**.....708 228-6148
190 Munster Rd Lemont (60439) ***(G-13222)***
**A&E Plastics, Elgin** *Also called E A M & J Inc* ***(G-9017)***
**A&G Manufacturing Inc**.....815 562-2107
200 E Avenue G Rochelle (61068) ***(G-18076)***
**A&J Paving Inc**.....773 889-9133
1911 N Sayre Ave Chicago (60707) ***(G-3694)***
**A&K C.N.C. Machining, Harwood Heights** *Also called Qcc LLC* ***(G-11689)***
**A&S Machining & Welding Inc**.....708 442-4544
4828 Lawndale Ave Ste 3 Mc Cook (60525) ***(G-14443)***
**A&W Tool Inc**.....815 653-1700
5309 Bus Pkwy Unit 101 Ringwood (60072) ***(G-17986)***
**A+ Printing Co**.....815 968-8181
920 2nd Ave Rockford (61104) ***(G-18242)***
**A-1 Food & Liquor, Decatur** *Also called Jamiel Inc* ***(G-7898)***
**A-1 Lapping & Machine Inc**.....815 398-1465
539 Grable St Rockford (61109) ***(G-18243)***
**A-1 Tool Corporation**.....708 345-5000
1425 Armitage Ave Ste 2 Melrose Park (60160) ***(G-14579)***
**A-B Die Mold Inc**.....847 658-1199
5n701 Meadowlark Dr Bartlett (60103) ***(G-1327)***
**A-Creations Inc**.....630 541-5801
8102 Lemont Rd Ste 1500 Woodridge (60517) ***(G-22448)***
**A-F Acquisition LLC**.....773 978-5130
2701 E 100th St Chicago (60617) ***(G-3695)***
**A-Korn Roller Inc (PA)**.....773 254-5700
3545 S Morgan St Chicago (60609) ***(G-3696)***
**A-L-L Equipment Company**.....815 877-7000
5619 Pike Rd Loves Park (61111) ***(G-13911)***
**A-Ok Inc**.....815 943-7431
711 W Brown St Harvard (60033) ***(G-11616)***
**A-Punch Products Mfg Co, Chicago** *Also called Punch Products Manufacturing* ***(G-6226)***
**A-Reliable Printing**.....630 790-2525
604 Roosevelt Rd Glen Ellyn (60137) ***(G-10956)***
**A-S Medication Solutions LLC (PA)**.....847 680-3515
2401 Commerce Dr Libertyville (60048) ***(G-13297)***
**A-Z Stepping Stones, Bolingbrook** *Also called Mandys Kitchen & Grill* ***(G-2339)***
**A-Z Welding**.....618 259-2515
8373 Militello Ln Bethalto (62010) ***(G-2080)***
**A.M.H. Products, Chicago** *Also called AM Harper Products Inc* ***(G-3841)***
**A.P.e, Carol Stream** *Also called American Precision Elec Inc* ***(G-3101)***
**A.W.T. World Trade, Chicago** *Also called Advance World Trade Inc* ***(G-3767)***
**A1 Skilled Staffing**.....309 281-1400
915 15th Ave East Moline (61244) ***(G-8669)***
**A123 Systems LLC**.....617 778-5700
88 Airport Rd Elgin (60123) ***(G-8930)***
**A2 Sales LLC (PA)**.....708 924-1200
6499 W 66th Pl Bedford Park (60638) ***(G-1532)***
**A2z Green Lighting, Bloomingdale** *Also called Amerilights Inc* ***(G-2093)***
**AA Pallet Inc**.....773 536-3699
900 W 49th Pl Chicago (60609) ***(G-3697)***
**AA Rigoni Brothers Inc**.....815 838-9770
112 Connor Ave Lockport (60441) ***(G-13701)***
**AA Superb Food Corporation**.....773 927-3233
3823 S Halsted St Chicago (60609) ***(G-3698)***
**AA-Gem Corporation**.....773 539-9303
4221 N Lawndale Ave Chicago (60618) ***(G-3699)***
**AAA Galvanizing - Joliet Inc**.....815 284-5001
310 E Progress Dr Dixon (61021) ***(G-8321)***
**AAA Galvanizing - Joliet Inc (HQ)**.....815 723-5000
625 Mills Rd Joliet (60433) ***(G-12449)***
**AAA Galvanizing - Peoria Inc**.....309 697-4100
6718 W Plank Rd Ste 2 Peoria (61604) ***(G-17299)***
**AAA Galvanizing of Dixon, Dixon** *Also called AAA Galvanizing - Joliet Inc* ***(G-8321)***
**AAA Mold Finishers Inc**.....773 775-3977
7208 W Pratt Ave Chicago (60631) ***(G-3700)***
**AAA Press International, Arlington Heights** *Also called AAA Press Specialists Inc* ***(G-701)***

A L P H A B E T I C

(PA)=Parent Co (HQ)=Headquarters (DH)=Div Headquarters
2017 Harris Illinois Industrial Directory
1147

**AAA Press Specialists Inc** ....847 818-1100
3160 N Kennicott Ave Arlington Heights (60004) *(G-701)*
**AAA Tool and Machine Co** ....618 632-6718
230 Obernuefemann Rd O Fallon (62269) *(G-16459)*
**AAA Trash** ....618 775-1365
408 S Merritt St Odin (62870) *(G-16738)*
**Aabbitt Adhesives Inc (PA)** ....773 227-2700
2403 N Oakley Ave Chicago (60647) *(G-3701)*
**Aabbitt Adhesives Inc** ....773 723-6780
601 W 81st Chicago (60620) *(G-3702)*
**Aable License Consultants** ....708 836-1235
1938 S Mannheim Rd Westchester (60154) *(G-21827)*
**Aaec, Roscoe** *Also called American Alum Extrusion Co LLC (G-18889)*
**AAF International, Chicago** *Also called American Air Filter Co Inc (G-3848)*
**Aaii, Chicago** *Also called American Association of Indivi (G-3850)*
**Aais Services Corporation** ....630 457-3263
701 Wrrnvlle Rd Ste 100 Lisle (60532) *(G-13552)*
**Aak Mechanical Inc** ....217 935-8501
10962 Riddle Rd Clinton (61727) *(G-7276)*
**Aakash Spices & Produce Inc** ....773 916-4100
6404 N Fairfield Ave Chicago (60645) *(G-3703)*
**Aalborg Company** ....708 246-8858
4521 Harvey Ave Western Springs (60558) *(G-21862)*
**AAM-Ro Corporation** ....708 343-5543
3110 S 26th Ave Broadview (60155) *(G-2552)*
**Aamstrand Ropes & Twines Inc** ....815 468-2100
711 N Grove St Manteno (60950) *(G-14179)*
**Aana Publishing Inc** ....847 692-7050
222 S Prospect Ave Park Ridge (60068) *(G-17177)*
**Aap Metals LLC (HQ)** ....847 916-1220
2200 Pratt Blvd Elk Grove Village (60007) *(G-9252)*
**AAR Aircraft Services Inc (HQ)** ....630 227-2000
1100 N Wood Dale Rd Wood Dale (60191) *(G-22326)*
**AAR Aircraft Svcs - Miami Inc, Wood Dale** *Also called AAR Aircraft Services Inc (G-22326)*
**AAR Allen Services Inc (HQ)** ....630 227-2410
1100 N Wood Dale Rd Wood Dale (60191) *(G-22327)*
**AAR Corp (PA)** ....630 227-2000
1100 N Wood Dale Rd Wood Dale (60191) *(G-22328)*
**AAR Defense Systems Logistics, Wood Dale** *Also called AAR Supply Chain Inc (G-22329)*
**AAR Supply Chain Inc (HQ)** ....630 227-2000
1100 N Wood Dale Rd Wood Dale (60191) *(G-22329)*
**Aardvark Pharma LLC** ....630 248-2380
2 Mid America Plz Ste 800 Oakbrook Terrace (60181) *(G-16693)*
**Aardvark Pharmaceuticals, Oakbrook Terrace** *Also called Aardvark Pharma LLC (G-16693)*
**Aargus Industries, Wheeling** *Also called Aargus Plastics Inc (G-21995)*
**Aargus Industries Inc** ....847 325-4444
540 Allendale Dr Ste 100a Wheeling (60090) *(G-21994)*
**Aargus Plastics Inc** ....847 325-4444
540 Allendale Dr Ste 100a Wheeling (60090) *(G-21995)*
**Aarmen Tool & Manufacturing** ....815 678-4818
11475 Commercial St Richmond (60071) *(G-17955)*
**Aaro Roller Corp** ....815 398-7655
4338 11th St Rockford (61109) *(G-18244)*
**Aaron Co, Lincolnwood** *Also called Gerald Graff (G-13514)*
**Aaron Engnered Process Eqp Inc** ....630 350-2200
735 E Green St Bensenville (60106) *(G-1809)*
**Aaron Process Equipment Co Inc** ....630 350-2200
735 E Green St Bensenville (60106) *(G-1810)*
**Aarstar Precision Grinding** ....847 678-4880
9007 Exchange Ave Franklin Park (60131) *(G-10382)*
**Aat, Carol Stream** *Also called Advanced Audio Technology Inc (G-3090)*
**Aaxis Engravers Inc** ....224 629-4045
230 William St Ste A Bensenville (60106) *(G-1811)*
**AB & D Custom Cabinets, Homewood** *Also called AB&d Custom Furniture Inc (G-12090)*
**AB Specialty Silicones LLC (PA)** ....908 273-8015
3790 Sunset Ave Waukegan (60087) *(G-21516)*
**AB&d Custom Furniture Inc** ....708 922-9061
17200 Palmer Blvd Homewood (60430) *(G-12090)*
**Aba Custom Woodworking** ....815 356-9663
765 Duffy Dr Ste B Crystal Lake (60014) *(G-7525)*
**Abacus Manufacturing Group Inc** ....815 654-7050
516 18th Ave Rockford (61104) *(G-18245)*
**ABB Inc** ....630 759-7428
1 Territorial Ct Ste A Bolingbrook (60440) *(G-2276)*
**Abba Plastics Inc** ....630 385-2156
207 Beaver St Yorkville (60560) *(G-22647)*
**Abbacus Inc** ....815 637-9222
1248 Shappert Dr Machesney Park (61115) *(G-14048)*
**ABBACUS INJECTION MOLDING, Machesney Park** *Also called Abbacus Inc (G-14048)*
**Abbacus Injection Molding Inc** ....815 637-9222
1248 Shappert Dr Machesney Park (61115) *(G-14049)*
**Abbas Foods Corp** ....847 213-0093
8111 Saint Louis Ave Skokie (60076) *(G-19944)*
**Abbco Inc** ....630 595-7115
2401 American Ln Elk Grove Village (60007) *(G-9253)*
**Abbey Copying Support Svcs Inc** ....618 466-3300
3312 Godfrey Rd Godfrey (62035) *(G-11221)*
**Abbey Metal Services Inc** ....773 568-0330
820 W 120th St Chicago (60643) *(G-3704)*
**Abbott Health Products Inc (HQ)** ....847 937-6100
100 Abbott Park Rd North Chicago (60064) *(G-16157)*
**Abbott Label Inc** ....630 773-3614
1414 Norwood Ave Itasca (60143) *(G-12222)*
**Abbott Laboratories (PA)** ....224 667-6100
100 Abbott Park Rd Abbott Park (60064) *(G-1)*
**Abbott Laboratories** ....224 667-6100
100 Abbott Park Rd North Chicago (60064) *(G-16158)*
**Abbott Laboratories** ....224 330-0271
279 Adler Dr Libertyville (60048) *(G-13298)*
**Abbott Laboratories** ....847 937-2210
6235 N Newark Ave Chicago (60631) *(G-3705)*
**Abbott Laboratories** ....847 921-9455
445 Red Rock Dr Lindenhurst (60046) *(G-13545)*
**Abbott Laboratories** ....847 735-0573
26525 N Riverwoods Blvd Mettawa (60045) *(G-14762)*
**Abbott Laboratories** ....847 937-7970
100 Abbott Park Rd North Chicago (60064) *(G-16159)*
**Abbott Laboratories** ....847 937-6100
Mlk Jr Dr Rr 41 North Chicago (60064) *(G-16160)*
**Abbott Laboratories** ....847 937-6100
100 Abbott Park Rd Abbott Park (60064) *(G-2)*
**Abbott Laboratories** ....224 361-7129
1800 Brummel Ave Elk Grove Village (60007) *(G-9254)*
**Abbott Laboratories** ....847 937-6100
100 Abbott Park Rd North Chicago (60064) *(G-16161)*
**Abbott Laboratories** ....847 935-5509
100 Abbott Park Rd North Chicago (60064) *(G-16162)*
**Abbott Laboratories** ....847 938-8717
1401 Sheridan Rd North Chicago (60064) *(G-16163)*
**Abbott Laboratories** ....847 935-8130
1136 Laurel Ln Gurnee (60031) *(G-11417)*
**Abbott Laboratories** ....847 937-6100
215 E Washington St Des Plaines (60016) *(G-8140)*
**Abbott Laboratories** ....847 937-6100
200 Abbott Park Rd Abbott Park (60064) *(G-3)*
**Abbott Laboratories** ....847 937-6100
100 Abbott Park Rd North Chicago (60064) *(G-16164)*
**Abbott Laboratories Inc** ....224 668-2076
200 Abbott Park Rd Abbott Park (60064) *(G-4)*
**Abbott Laboratories PCF Ltd (HQ)** ....847 937-6100
100 Abbott Park Rd North Chicago (60064) *(G-16165)*
**Abbott Labortories Purchasing, North Chicago** *Also called Abbott Laboratories (G-16164)*
**Abbott Machine Co (PA)** ....618 465-1898
700 W Broadway Alton (62002) *(G-557)*
**Abbott Molecular Inc** ....224 361-7800
1300 E Touhy Ave Des Plaines (60018) *(G-8141)*
**Abbott Molecular Inc (HQ)** ....224 361-7800
1300 E Touhy Ave Des Plaines (60018) *(G-8142)*
**Abbott Nutrition Mfg Inc** ....614 624-6083
200 Abbott Park Rd Abbott Park (60064) *(G-5)*
**Abbott Pharmaceutical Corp, Abbott Park** *Also called Abbvie Holdings Inc (G-8)*
**Abbott Plastics & Supply Co** ....815 874-8500
3302 Lonergan Dr Rockford (61109) *(G-18246)*
**Abbott Point of Care Inc** ....847 937-6100
100 Abbott Park Rd Abbott Park (60064) *(G-6)*
**Abbott Products Inc (HQ)** ....847 937-6100
100 Abbott Park Rd Abbott Park (60064) *(G-7)*
**Abbott Scott Manufacturing Co** ....773 342-7200
4215 W Grand Ave Chicago (60651) *(G-3706)*
**Abbott-Interfast Corporation** ....847 459-6200
190 Abbott Dr Wheeling (60090) *(G-21996)*
**Abbotts Minute Printing Inc** ....708 339-6010
611 E 170th St South Holland (60473) *(G-20239)*
**Abbvie Holdings Inc** ....847 937-7632
100 Abbott Park Rd Abbott Park (60064) *(G-8)*
**Abbvie Inc** ....847 367-7621
75 N Fairway Dr Vernon Hills (60061) *(G-21141)*
**Abbvie Inc** ....847 735-0573
26525 N Riverwoods Blvd Mettawa (60045) *(G-14763)*
**Abbvie Inc (PA)** ....847 932-7900
1 N Waukegan Rd North Chicago (60064) *(G-16166)*
**Abbvie Inc** ....847 932-7900
1401 Sheridan Rd North Chicago (60064) *(G-16167)*
**Abbvie Inc** ....847 473-4787
1150 S Northpoint Blvd Waukegan (60085) *(G-21517)*
**Abbvie Inc** ....847 938-2042
1675 Lakeside Ave J23 North Chicago (60064) *(G-16168)*
**Abbvie Products LLC** ....847 937-6100
100 Abbott Park Rd North Chicago (60064) *(G-16169)*
**Abbvie Respiratory LLC** ....847 937-6100
100 Abbott Park Rd North Chicago (60064) *(G-16170)*
**Abbvie US LLC** ....800 255-5162
1 N Waukegan Rd North Chicago (60064) *(G-16171)*
**Abc Inc** ....312 980-1000
190 N State St Fl 7 Chicago (60601) *(G-3707)*
**ABC Beverage Mfg Inc** ....708 449-2600
400 N Wolf Rd Ste A Northlake (60164) *(G-16424)*
**ABC Coating Company Inc** ....708 258-9633
1160 N Boudreau Rd Manteno (60950) *(G-14180)*

**ABC Coating Company Illinois, Manteno** *Also called ABC Coating Company Inc* ***(G-14180)***
**Abco Metals Corporations** ....773 881-1504
1020 W 94th St Chicago (60620) ***(G-3708)***
**Abct Corporation** ....773 427-1010
3924 W Devon Ave Ste 300 Lincolnwood (60712) ***(G-13499)***
**Abel Howe Crane, Woodridge** *Also called Columbus McKinnon Corporation* ***(G-22463)***
**Abel Vault & Monument Co Inc** ....309 647-0105
1001 E Linn St Canton (61520) ***(G-2980)***
**Abelei Inc** ....630 859-1410
194 Alder Dr North Aurora (60542) ***(G-16117)***
**Aberdeen Group, Rosemont** *Also called Hw Holdco LLC* ***(G-19005)***
**Aberdeen Technologies Inc** ....630 665-8590
272 Commonwealth Dr Carol Stream (60188) ***(G-3088)***
**Aberdeen Window Shade Service, Chicago** *Also called Shade Brookline Co* ***(G-6487)***
**Aberdon Enterprises** ....847 228-1300
225 Bond St Elk Grove Village (60007) ***(G-9255)***
**Abet Industries Corporation** ....708 482-8282
111 Kemman Ave La Grange Park (60526) ***(G-12751)***
**ABG Bag Inc** ....815 963-9525
1925 Elmwood Rd Rockford (61103) ***(G-18247)***
**Abh Manufacturing, Itasca** *Also called Architctral Bldrs Hdwr Mfg Inc* ***(G-12230)***
**Ability Cabinet Co Inc** ....847 678-6678
3503 Martens St Franklin Park (60131) ***(G-10383)***
**Ability Engineering, South Holland** *Also called Ae2009 Technologies Inc* ***(G-20240)***
**Ability Engineering Technology, South Holland** *Also called Bennu Group Inc* ***(G-20250)***
**Ability Fasteners Inc** ....847 593-4230
685 Fargo Ave Elk Grove Village (60007) ***(G-9256)***
**Ability Metal Company** ....847 437-7040
1355 Greenleaf Ave Elk Grove Village (60007) ***(G-9257)***
**Ability Plastics Inc** ....708 458-4480
8721 Industrial Dr Justice (60458) ***(G-12594)***
**Ability Tool Co** ....815 633-5909
9816 Norman Ave Machesney Park (61115) ***(G-14050)***
**Ability Welding Service Inc** ....630 595-3737
500 Meyer Rd Bensenville (60106) ***(G-1812)***
**Abington Argus-Sentinel** ....309 462-3189
507 N Monroe St Ste 3 Abingdon (61410) ***(G-9)***
**Abitec Corporation** ....217 465-8577
1800 S Main St Paris (61944) ***(G-17139)***
**Abitzy Inc** ....847 800-8666
2921 Hillsboro Ln Lake In The Hills (60156) ***(G-12981)***
**Abitzy Inc** ....847 659-9228
1041 N Lombard Rd Lombard (60148) ***(G-13757)***
**Abki Tech Service Inc** ....847 818-8403
764 Meadow Dr Des Plaines (60016) ***(G-8143)***
**Abkitech, Des Plaines** *Also called Abki Tech Service Inc* ***(G-8143)***
**Ablaze Welding & Fabricating** ....815 965-0046
2003 Kishwaukee St Rockford (61104) ***(G-18248)***
**Able American Plastics Inc** ....815 678-4646
9703 Us Highway 12 Frnt Unit Richmond (60071) ***(G-17956)***
**Able Barmilling & Mfg Co Inc** ....708 343-5666
1310 Main St Melrose Park (60160) ***(G-14580)***
**Able Die & Mold Inc** ....773 282-3652
4239 N Oak Park Ave # 217 Chicago (60634) ***(G-3709)***
**Able Die Casting Corporation** ....847 678-1991
3907 Wesley Ter Schiller Park (60176) ***(G-19797)***
**Able Electropolishing, Chicago** *Also called Metco Treating and Dev Co* ***(G-5702)***
**Able Electropolishing Co Inc** ....773 277-1600
2001 S Kilbourn Ave Chicago (60623) ***(G-3710)***
**Able Engravers Inc** ....847 676-3737
9521 Kedvale Ave Skokie (60076) ***(G-19945)***
**Able Metal Hose Inc** ....630 543-9620
15 W Laura Dr Addison (60101) ***(G-15)***
**Able Printing Service** ....708 788-7115
6837 Stanley Ave Berwyn (60402) ***(G-2054)***
**ABM Marking Ltd** ....618 277-3773
2799 S Belt W Belleville (62226) ***(G-1606)***
**ABM Marking Services Ltd** ....618 277-3773
2799 S Belt W Belleville (62226) ***(G-1607)***
**Abner Trucking Co Inc** ....618 676-1301
207 S 1st St Se Clay City (62824) ***(G-7261)***
**About Face Designs Inc** ....847 914-9040
1510 Old Deerfield Rd # 211 Highland Park (60035) ***(G-11821)***
**About Learning Inc** ....847 487-1800
441 W Bonner Rd Wauconda (60084) ***(G-21436)***
**Above & Beyond Black Oxiding** ....708 345-7100
1029 N 27th Ave Melrose Park (60160) ***(G-14581)***
**ABRA Enterprises Inc** ....847 866-6903
606 Sheridan Rd Apt 1e Evanston (60202) ***(G-10001)***
**Abrading Machinery Division, Broadview** *Also called AAM-Ro Corporation* ***(G-2552)***
**Abrasic 90 Inc** ....800 447-4248
7525 N Oak Park Ave Niles (60714) ***(G-15955)***
**Abrasive Rubber Wheel Co** ....847 587-0900
135 S Us Highway 12 Fox Lake (60020) ***(G-10273)***
**Abrasive Technology Inc** ....847 888-7100
1175 Bowes Rd Elgin (60123) ***(G-8931)***
**Abrasive West LLC** ....630 736-0818
1292 Humbracht Cir Ste F Bartlett (60103) ***(G-1328)***
**Abrasive-Form LLC (PA)** ....630 220-3437
454 Scott Dr Bloomingdale (60108) ***(G-2091)***
**Abraxis Bioscience LLC** ....310 437-7715
1300 Chase Ave Elk Grove Village (60007) ***(G-9258)***
**Abraxis Bioscience LLC** ....310 883-1300
2020 N Ruby St Melrose Park (60160) ***(G-14582)***
**ABS Equipment Division, Itasca** *Also called ABS Graphics Inc* ***(G-12223)***
**ABS Graphics Inc (PA)** ....630 495-2400
900 N Rohlwing Rd Itasca (60143) ***(G-12223)***
**ABS Tool & Machine Inc** ....815 968-4630
1202 20th Ave Rockford (61104) ***(G-18249)***
**Absolute Grinding and Mfg** ....815 964-1999
2400 11th St Rockford (61104) ***(G-18250)***
**Absolute Indus Fabricators, Addison** *Also called Aif Inc* ***(G-27)***
**Absolute Process Instruments (PA)** ....847 918-3510
1220 American Way Libertyville (60048) ***(G-13299)***
**Absolute Stoneworks Inc** ....708 652-7600
5738 W 26th St Cicero (60804) ***(G-7175)***
**Absolute Turn Inc** ....847 459-4629
1704 S Wolf Rd Wheeling (60090) ***(G-21997)***
**Absolute Windows Inc** ....708 599-9191
9630 S 76th Ave Oak Lawn (60457) ***(G-16594)***
**Absolutely Custom, Spring Grove** *Also called Sportdecals Sport & Spirit Pro* ***(G-20365)***
**Abundance House Treasure Nfp** ....312 788-4316
1309 S Kedzie Ave Chicago (60623) ***(G-3711)***
**Abundant Living Christian Ctr** ....708 896-6181
14540 Lincoln Ave Dolton (60419) ***(G-8362)***
**Abundant Venture Innovation AC** ....312 291-1910
111 E Wacker Dr Ste 300 Chicago (60601) ***(G-3712)***
**Abyss Salon Inc** ....312 880-0263
67 E 16th St Ste 5 Chicago (60616) ***(G-3713)***
**AC Mold, Saint Charles** *Also called A & C Mold Company Inc* ***(G-19130)***
**AC Nalco Chemical Co** ....630 305-1000
1601 W Diehl Rd Naperville (60563) ***(G-15587)***
**AC Precision Tool Inc** ....630 797-5161
6n553 Crestwood Dr Saint Charles (60175) ***(G-19131)***
**Academy Corp** ....847 359-3000
219 Avondale Dr Palatine (60067) ***(G-16995)***
**Academy of Awards II, Peoria** *Also called Academy Screenprinting Awards* ***(G-17300)***
**Academy Screenprinting Awards** ....309 686-0026
1316 E War Memorial Dr Peoria (61614) ***(G-17300)***
**Accel Corporation** ....630 579-6961
900 Douglas Rd Batavia (60510) ***(G-1402)***
**Accelerated Assemblies Inc** ....630 616-6680
725 Nicholas Blvd Elk Grove Village (60007) ***(G-9259)***
**Accelerated Pharma Inc** ....773 517-0789
15w155 81st St Burr Ridge (60527) ***(G-2819)***
**Accelrted Mch Design Engrg LLC** ....815 316-6381
3044 Eastrock Ct Rockford (61109) ***(G-18251)***
**Accent Metal Finishing Inc** ....847 678-7420
9331 Byron St Schiller Park (60176) ***(G-19798)***
**Accents By Fred** ....708 366-9850
7519 Madison St Forest Park (60130) ***(G-10234)***
**Access Assembly LLC** ....847 894-1047
1047 E High St Mundelein (60060) ***(G-15463)***
**Access Casters** ....773 881-4186
10141 S Western Ave Chicago (60643) ***(G-3714)***
**Access Flooring Co Inc** ....847 781-0100
680 Alhambra Ln Hoffman Estates (60169) ***(G-11989)***
**Access International Inc** ....312 920-9366
180 N Stetson Ave Chicago (60601) ***(G-3715)***
**Access Japan LLC** ....773 583-7183
5130 N Bernard St Chicago (60625) ***(G-3716)***
**Access Medical Supply Inc** ....847 891-6210
1672 Wright Blvd Schaumburg (60193) ***(G-19420)***
**Access Technologies, Skokie** *Also called Norfolk Medical Products Inc* ***(G-20046)***
**Accessing Your Abilities Inc** ....309 761-4016
733 S Chestnut St Kewanee (61443) ***(G-12667)***
**Acciona Windpower N Amer LLC** ....319 643-9463
333 W Wacker Dr Ste 1500 Chicago (60606) ***(G-3717)***
**Acclaim Sign Company, Saint Charles** *Also called Toms Signs* ***(G-19284)***
**Acco Brands Inc** ....847 541-9500
4 Corporate Dr Lake Zurich (60047) ***(G-13032)***
**Acco Brands Corporation (PA)** ....847 541-9500
4 Corporate Dr Lake Zurich (60047) ***(G-13033)***
**Acco Brands USA LLC (HQ)** ....800 222-6462
4 Corporate Dr Lake Zurich (60047) ***(G-13034)***
**Acco Brands USA LLC** ....708 280-4702
2171 W Executive Dr # 500 Addison (60101) ***(G-16)***
**Acco Brands USA LLC** ....847 272-3700
500 Bond St Lincolnshire (60069) ***(G-13423)***
**Accord Carton Co** ....708 272-3050
6155 W 115th St Alsip (60803) ***(G-428)***
**Accord Packaging, Alsip** *Also called Accord Carton Co* ***(G-428)***
**Accord Packaging LLC** ....708 272-3050
6155 W 115th St Alsip (60803) ***(G-429)***
**Accorn Gran Natural Stone Inc (PA)** ....312 663-5000
2727 W Madison St Chicago (60612) ***(G-3718)***
**Accr, Chicago** *Also called American Chamber of* ***(G-3854)***

ALPHABETIC

(PA)=Parent Co (HQ)=Headquarters (DH)=Div Headquarters
2017 Harris Illinois Industrial Directory
1149

**Accro Precision Grinding Inc** ....... 708 681-0520
2080 N Hawthorne Ave Melrose Park (60160) *(G-14583)*
**Accruent LLC** ....... 847 425-3600
500 Davis St Ste 1000 Evanston (60201) *(G-10002)*
**Accu Cut Inc** ....... 815 229-3525
1617 Magnolia St Rockford (61104) *(G-18252)*
**Accu-Chem Industries Inc** ....... 708 344-0900
1930 George St Ste 3 Melrose Park (60160) *(G-14584)*
**Accu-Cut Diamond Bore Sizing (HQ)** ....... 708 457-8800
4238 N Sayre Ave Norridge (60706) *(G-16094)*
**Accu-Cut Diamond Tool Company (PA)** ....... 708 457-8800
423840 N Sayre Ave Norridge (60706) *(G-16095)*
**Accu-Fab Incorporated** ....... 847 541-4230
1550 Abbott Dr Wheeling (60090) *(G-21998)*
**Accu-Grind Manufacturing Inc** ....... 847 526-2700
386 Hollow Hill Rd Wauconda (60084) *(G-21437)*
**Accu-Wright Fiberglass Inc** ....... 618 337-3318
2393 Carol St East Saint Louis (62206) *(G-8739)*
**Accubow LLC** ....... 815 250-0607
350 5th St Ste 266 Peru (61354) *(G-17498)*
**Accucast Inc** ....... 815 394-1875
5113 27th Ave Rockford (61109) *(G-18253)*
**Accudata L.L.C., Moline** *Also called Inn Partners LLC (G-14944)*
**Accuity Inc** ....... 847 676-9600
1007 Church St Ste 600 Evanston (60201) *(G-10003)*
**Acculight LLC** ....... 630 847-1000
2570 United Ln Elk Grove Village (60007) *(G-9260)*
**Accumation Inc** ....... 815 455-6250
6211 Factory Rd Crystal Lake (60014) *(G-7526)*
**Accuquest Hearing Center Inc** ....... 847 588-1895
7317 N Harlem Ave Niles (60714) *(G-15956)*
**Accurail Inc** ....... 630 365-6400
400 W Nebraska St Elburn (60119) *(G-8873)*
**Accurate Anodizing Div, Cicero** *Also called Saporito Finishing Co (G-7228)*
**Accurate Anodizing Division, Chicago** *Also called Saporito Finishing Co (G-6443)*
**Accurate Auto Manufacturing Co** ....... 618 244-0727
1804 S 8th St Mount Vernon (62864) *(G-15397)*
**Accurate Business Controls Inc** ....... 815 633-5500
7846 Burden Rd Machesney Park (61115) *(G-14051)*
**Accurate Carriers Inc** ....... 630 790-3430
500 Mitchell Rd Glendale Heights (60139) *(G-11007)*
**Accurate Carriers USA, Glendale Heights** *Also called Accurate Carriers Inc (G-11007)*
**Accurate Cnc Machine, Roscoe** *Also called Accurate CNc Machining Inc (G-18888)*
**Accurate CNc Machining Inc** ....... 815 623-6516
5365 Edith Ln Roscoe (61073) *(G-18888)*
**Accurate Cstm Sash Mllwk Corp** ....... 708 423-0423
5516 W 110th St Ste 1 Oak Lawn (60453) *(G-16595)*
**Accurate Custom Cabinets Inc** ....... 630 458-0460
115 W Fay Ave Addison (60101) *(G-17)*
**Accurate Die Cutting Inc** ....... 847 437-7215
120 Joey Dr Elk Grove Village (60007) *(G-9261)*
**Accurate Elc Mtr & Pump Co** ....... 708 448-2792
6955 W 111th St Worth (60482) *(G-22631)*
**Accurate Engine & Machine Inc** ....... 773 237-4942
5053 W Diversey Ave Chicago (60639) *(G-3719)*
**Accurate Fabricators Inc** ....... 618 451-1886
1603 Cleveland Blvd Granite City (62040) *(G-11258)*
**Accurate Fabricators Svcs Inc** ....... 618 530-7883
1603 Cleveland Blvd Granite City (62040) *(G-11259)*
**Accurate Finishers** ....... 630 543-8575
1433 W Fullerton Ave B Addison (60101) *(G-18)*
**Accurate Grinding Co Inc** ....... 708 371-1887
14003 S Harrison Ave Posen (60469) *(G-17727)*
**Accurate Industrial Supply Co** ....... 708 422-7050
6647 99th St Chicago Ridge (60415) *(G-7138)*
**Accurate Metal Components Inc** ....... 847 520-5900
7540 N Caldwell Ave Niles (60714) *(G-15957)*
**Accurate Metal Fabricating LLC** ....... 773 235-0400
1657 N Kostner Ave Chicago (60639) *(G-3720)*
**Accurate Metal Finishing Co** ....... 847 428-7705
359 Sola Dr Gilberts (60136) *(G-10911)*
**Accurate Metallizing Inc** ....... 708 424-7747
5340 W 111th St Ste 2 Oak Lawn (60453) *(G-16596)*
**Accurate Metals Illinois LLC** ....... 815 966-6320
2524 11th St Rockford (61104) *(G-18254)*
**Accurate Partitions Corp** ....... 708 442-6801
8000 Joliet Rd Mc Cook (60525) *(G-14444)*
**Accurate Parts Mfg Co** ....... 630 616-4125
1100 Industrial Dr Bensenville (60106) *(G-1813)*
**Accurate Perforating Co Inc** ....... 773 254-3232
3636 S Kedzie Ave Chicago (60632) *(G-3721)*
**Accurate Printing Inc** ....... 708 824-0058
4749 136th St Crestwood (60445) *(G-7473)*
**Accurate Products Incorporated** ....... 773 878-2200
4645 N Ravenswood Ave Chicago (60640) *(G-3722)*
**Accurate Radiation Shielding** ....... 847 639-5533
206 Cleveland St Cary (60013) *(G-3321)*
**Accurate Reliable Technology, Bridgeview** *Also called Art Cnc Machining LLC (G-2468)*
**Accurate Repro Inc** ....... 630 428-4433
2368 Corporate Ln Ste 100 Naperville (60563) *(G-15588)*
**Accurate Rivet Manufacturing** ....... 630 766-3401
343 Beinoris Dr Wood Dale (60191) *(G-22330)*
**Accurate Security & Lock Corp** ....... 815 455-0133
5533 Danbury Cir Lake In The Hills (60156) *(G-12982)*
**Accurate Spring Tech Inc** ....... 815 344-3333
5801 W Hill St McHenry (60050) *(G-14475)*
**Accurate Tool & Mfg Corp** ....... 708 652-4266
350 N La Salle Dr # 1100 Chicago (60654) *(G-3723)*
**Accurate Wire Strip Frming Inc** ....... 630 260-1000
175 Tubeway Dr Carol Stream (60188) *(G-3089)*
**Accuride Corporation** ....... 630 454-4299
950 N Raddant Rd Batavia (60510) *(G-1403)*
**Accuride Corporation** ....... 630 568-3914
201 E Ogden Ave Ste 220 Hinsdale (60521) *(G-11938)*
**Accuride Distribution Center, Batavia** *Also called Accuride Corporation (G-1403)*
**Accuro Medical Products LLC** ....... 800 669-4757
70 W Madison St Ste 3200 Chicago (60602) *(G-3724)*
**Accushim Inc (PA)** ....... 708 442-6448
4601 Lawndale Ave Lyons (60534) *(G-14029)*
**Accusol Incorporated** ....... 773 283-4686
9632 S Kildare Ave Oak Lawn (60453) *(G-16597)*
**Accutech Machining Inc** ....... 630 350-2066
381 Evergreen Ave Bensenville (60106) *(G-1814)*
**Accutone Hearing Aid Inc** ....... 773 545-3279
1580 Sherman Ave Evanston (60201) *(G-10004)*
**Accutrace Inc** ....... 847 290-9900
2425 Touhy Ave Elk Grove Village (60007) *(G-9262)*
**Accuware Incorporated** ....... 630 858-8409
799 Roosevelt Rd 3-218 Glen Ellyn (60137) *(G-10957)*
**Ace Action Elevator Services** ....... 773 708-1666
619 N Lotus Ave Chicago (60644) *(G-3725)*
**Ace Anodizing Impregnating Inc** ....... 708 547-6680
4161 Butterfield Rd Hillside (60162) *(G-11907)*
**Ace Bakeries** ....... 312 225-4973
3241 S Halsted St Chicago (60608) *(G-3726)*
**Ace Coating Enterprises Inc (PA)** ....... 708 547-6680
4161 Butterfield Rd Hillside (60162) *(G-11908)*
**Ace Custom Upholstery & Rod Sp** ....... 618 842-2913
200 W Delaware St Fairfield (62837) *(G-10135)*
**Ace Engraving & Specialties Co** ....... 815 759-2093
4204 Ponca St McHenry (60050) *(G-14476)*
**Ace Graphics Inc** ....... 630 357-2244
2052 Corporate Ln Naperville (60563) *(G-15589)*
**Ace Grease Service Inc (PA)** ....... 618 781-1207
9035 State Route 163 Millstadt (62260) *(G-14820)*
**Ace Grease Service Inc** ....... 618 337-0974
9011 State Route 163 Millstadt (62260) *(G-14821)*
**Ace Industries, Chicago** *Also called Acme Spinning Company Inc (G-3734)*
**Ace Industries, Chicago** *Also called Ace Plating Company (G-3727)*
**Ace Machine & Tool** ....... 815 793-5077
314 Wood St Dekalb (60115) *(G-8072)*
**Ace Machining of Rockford Inc** ....... 815 398-3200
3380 Forest View Rd Rockford (61109) *(G-18255)*
**Ace Metal Crafts Company** ....... 847 455-1010
484 Thomas Dr Bensenville (60106) *(G-1815)*
**Ace Metal Refinishers Inc** ....... 800 323-7147
2001 Spring Rd Oak Brook (60523) *(G-16484)*
**Ace Metal Refinishers Inc (PA)** ....... 630 778-9200
978 N Dupage Ave Lombard (60148) *(G-13758)*
**Ace Metal Spinning Inc** ....... 708 389-5635
11630 S Mayfield Ave Alsip (60803) *(G-430)*
**Ace of Diamonds, Chicago** *Also called Hakimian Gem Co (G-5033)*
**Ace Pcb Design Inc** ....... 847 674-8745
5138 Conrad St Skokie (60077) *(G-19946)*
**Ace Plastics Inc** ....... 815 635-1368
7942 N 3350 East Rd Chatsworth (60921) *(G-3626)*
**Ace Plating Company** ....... 773 376-1800
3433 W 48th Pl Chicago (60632) *(G-3727)*
**Ace Precision Tool & Mfg Co** ....... 847 690-0111
1612 Landmeier Rd Elk Grove Village (60007) *(G-9263)*
**Ace Printing Co** ....... 618 259-2711
615 E Airline Dr East Alton (62024) *(G-8598)*
**Ace Sand Blast, Chicago** *Also called Ace Sandblast Company (del) (G-3728)*
**Ace Sandblast Company (del)** ....... 773 777-6654
4601 W Roscoe St Chicago (60641) *(G-3728)*
**Ace Sign Co** ....... 217 522-8417
2540 S 1st St Springfield (62704) *(G-20384)*
**Ace Wood Products LLC** ....... 630 557-2115
3s854 Finley Rd Sugar Grove (60554) *(G-20716)*
**Aces, Chicago** *Also called Advanced Cstm Enrgy Sltons Inc (G-3768)*
**Aceva LLC** ....... 201 978-7928
624 W Glen Ave Peoria (61614) *(G-17301)*
**Ach Food Companies Inc** ....... 708 458-8690
6400 S Archer Rd Summit Argo (60501) *(G-20759)*
**Aci, Spring Valley** *Also called Aqua Control Inc (G-20374)*
**Aci Plastics Manufacturing** ....... 630 629-0400
1430 W Bernard Dr Addison (60101) *(G-19)*
**Acj Partners LLC** ....... 630 745-1335
11552 S Bell Ave Chicago (60643) *(G-3729)*

**Acl Inc**......773 285-0295
840 W 49th Pl Chicago (60609) ***(G-3730)***

**Acm Inc**......847 473-1991
2254 Commonwealth Ave North Chicago (60064) ***(G-16172)***

**Acm Publishing**......217 498-7500
5378 Possum Trot Rd Rochester (62563) ***(G-18114)***

**Acme Alliance LLC (HQ)**......847 272-9520
3610 Commercial Ave Northbrook (60062) ***(G-16196)***

**Acme Auto Electric Co**......708 754-5420
2626 Chicago Rd S Chicago Hts (60411) ***(G-19098)***

**Acme Awning Co**......847 446-0153
1500 Old Deerfield Rd # 21 Highland Park (60035) ***(G-11822)***

**Acme Awning Co Inc**......847 446-0153
325 Pebblecreek Dr Lake Zurich (60047) ***(G-13035)***

**Acme Button & Buttonhole Co**......773 907-8400
4638 N Ravenswood Ave # 2 Chicago (60640) ***(G-3731)***

**Acme Control Service Inc**......773 774-9191
6140 W Higgins Ave Chicago (60630) ***(G-3732)***

**Acme Design Inc**......847 841-7400
37 N Union St Elgin (60123) ***(G-8932)***

**Acme Die Casting LLC**......847 272-9520
3610 Commercial Ave Northbrook (60062) ***(G-16197)***

**Acme Finishing Company LLC**......847 640-7890
1595 Oakton St Elk Grove Village (60007) ***(G-9264)***

**Acme Finishing Company Inc**......847 640-7890
1595 Oakton St Elk Grove Village (60007) ***(G-9265)***

**Acme Grinding & Manufacturing**......815 323-1380
6871 Belford Indus Dr Belvidere (61008) ***(G-1726)***

**Acme Industrial Company**......847 428-3911
441 Maple Ave Carpentersville (60110) ***(G-3271)***

**Acme Industries Inc**......847 296-3346
1325 Pratt Blvd Elk Grove Village (60007) ***(G-9266)***

**Acme Marble Co Inc**......630 964-7162
1103 Belair Dr Darien (60561) ***(G-7786)***

**Acme Metallizing Co Inc**......773 767-7000
5958 S Central Ave Chicago (60638) ***(G-3733)***

**Acme Sales, Chicago** *Also called Acme Button & Buttonhole Co* ***(G-3731)***

**Acme Scale Systems, Villa Park** *Also called Florida Metrology LLC* ***(G-21252)***

**Acme Screw Co (PA)**......630 665-2200
1201 W Union Ave Wheaton (60187) ***(G-21933)***

**Acme Screw Co**......815 332-7548
125 E State St Cherry Valley (61016) ***(G-3637)***

**Acme Spinning Company Inc**......773 927-2711
3433 W 48th Pl Fl 1 Chicago (60632) ***(G-3734)***

**Acme Wire Products LLC**......708 345-4430
2915 S 18th Ave Fl 1 Broadview (60155) ***(G-2553)***

**Acmealliance, Northbrook** *Also called Acme Alliance LLC* ***(G-16196)***

**Acn Indpndent Bus Rprsentative**......618 623-4238
820 Cardiff Ct O Fallon (62269) ***(G-16460)***

**Acnc, Lisle** *Also called American Comm & Networks* ***(G-13558)***

**Aco Inc**......773 774-5200
5656 N Northwest Hwy Chicago (60646) ***(G-3735)***

**Acomtech Mold Inc**......847 741-3537
39w433 Highland Ave Ste 1 Elgin (60124) ***(G-8933)***

**ACORN BOOK, Springfield** *Also called Elliot Institute For Social SC* ***(G-20434)***

**Acorn Diversified Inc**......708 478-1051
17809 New Jersey Ct # 14 Orland Park (60467) ***(G-16837)***

**Acorn Granite & Marble, Chicago** *Also called Accorn Gran Natural Stone Inc* ***(G-3718)***

**Acorn Wire and Iron Works LLC**......312 243-6414
2035 S Racine Ave Chicago (60608) ***(G-3736)***

**Acoustic Avenue Inc**......217 544-9810
3023 E Sangamon Ave Springfield (62702) ***(G-20385)***

**Acoustic Medsystems Inc**......217 355-8888
208 Burwash Ave Savoy (61874) ***(G-19408)***

**Acoustx, Savoy** *Also called Acoustic Medsystems Inc* ***(G-19408)***

**ACP PUBLICATIONS, South Holland** *Also called American Catholic Press Inc* ***(G-20242)***

**Acp Tower Holdings LLC (PA)**......800 835-8527
311 S Wacker Dr Ste 4300 Chicago (60606) ***(G-3737)***

**Acquamed Technologies Inc**......630 728-4014
195 Kendall Point Dr # 16 Oswego (60543) ***(G-16901)***

**Acquaviva Winery LLC**......630 365-0333
47 W 614 Rr 38 Maple Park (60151) ***(G-14197)***

**Acra Electric Corporation**......847 678-8870
3801 25th Ave Schiller Park (60176) ***(G-19799)***

**Acres of Sky Communications**......815 493-2560
446 S Broad St Lanark (61046) ***(G-13149)***

**Acresso Software Inc**......408 642-3865
1000 E Wdfield Rd Ste 400 Schaumburg (60173) ***(G-19421)***

**Acro Magnetics Inc**......815 943-5018
24005 Il Route 173 Harvard (60033) ***(G-11617)***

**Acrofab**......630 350-7941
1100 Entry Dr Unit 1 Bensenville (60106) ***(G-1816)***

**Acrylic Design Works Inc**......773 843-1300
5023 W 66th St Chicago (60638) ***(G-3738)***

**Acrylic Service Inc**......630 543-0336
1060 W Republic Dr Addison (60101) ***(G-20)***

**Acrylic Ventures Inc**......847 901-4440
1857 Elmdale Ave Ste A Glenview (60026) ***(G-11094)***

**ACS, Chicago** *Also called Antares Computer Systems Inc* ***(G-3915)***

**ACS Group, Schaumburg** *Also called Sterling Products Inc* ***(G-19740)***

**ACS Susico, Skokie** *Also called Sub-Surface Sign Co Ltd* ***(G-20094)***

**Acsys Lasertechnik US Inc (HQ)**......224 699-9572
2541 Tech Dr Ste 404 Elgin (60124) ***(G-8934)***

**Acta Publications**......773 989-3036
4848 N Clark St Chicago (60640) ***(G-3739)***

**Actavis Pharma Inc**......847 377-5480
705 Tri State Pkwy Ste B Gurnee (60031) ***(G-11418)***

**Actavis Pharma Inc**......847 855-0812
605 Tri State Pkwy Gurnee (60031) ***(G-11419)***

**Actega North America Inc**......847 690-9310
1550 Carmen Dr Bldg 7 Elk Grove Village (60007) ***(G-9267)***

**Action Advertising Inc**......312 791-0660
2420 S Michigan Ave Chicago (60616) ***(G-3740)***

**Action Cabinet Sales Inc**......847 717-0011
1150 Davis Rd Ste K Elgin (60123) ***(G-8935)***

**Action Carbide Grinding Co**......847 891-9026
1118 Lunt Ave Ste B Schaumburg (60193) ***(G-19422)***

**Action Flag Co**......800 669-9639
1900 Egerton Ct Woodridge (60517) ***(G-22449)***

**Action Graphics and Signs Inc**......618 939-5755
8802 Summer Rd Columbia (62236) ***(G-7350)***

**Action Packaging, Rockford** *Also called Compak Inc* ***(G-18320)***

**Action Painting & Cleaning, Franklin Park** *Also called Production Chemical Co Inc* ***(G-10563)***

**Action Prcsion Crbide Grinding, Schaumburg** *Also called Action Carbide Grinding Co* ***(G-19422)***

**Action Pump Co**......847 516-3636
170 Chicago St Cary (60013) ***(G-3322)***

**Action Rotary Die Inc**......630 628-6830
1208 W National Ave Addison (60101) ***(G-21)***

**Action Screen Print Inc**......630 393-1990
30 W 260 Butterfield Warrenville (60555) ***(G-21340)***

**Action Tool & Mfg Inc**......815 874-5775
5573 Sandy Hollow Rd Rockford (61109) ***(G-18256)***

**Action Turbine Repair Svc Inc**......708 924-9601
5120 W Lawndale Ave Summit Argo (60501) ***(G-20760)***

**Active Automation Inc**......847 427-8100
530 Bennett Rd Elk Grove Village (60007) ***(G-9268)***

**Active Copier, Chicago** *Also called Active Office Solutions* ***(G-3741)***

**Active Graphics Inc**......708 656-8900
5500 W 31st St Cicero (60804) ***(G-7176)***

**Active Grinding & Mfg Co**......708 344-0510
1800 Parkes Dr Broadview (60155) ***(G-2554)***

**Active Office Solutions**......773 539-3333
3839 W Devon Ave Chicago (60659) ***(G-3741)***

**Active Simulations Inc**......630 747-8393
312 S Lombard Ave Oak Park (60302) ***(G-16648)***

**Active Tool and Machine Inc**......708 599-0022
8445 Beloit Ave Oak Lawn (60455) ***(G-16598)***

**Active Wireworks, Bartlett** *Also called Elite Wireworks Corporation* ***(G-1345)***

**Actown-Electrocoil Inc**......
2414 Highview St Spring Grove (60081) ***(G-20324)***

**Acument Global Techologies**......815 544-7574
830 E Menomonie St Belvidere (61008) ***(G-1727)***

**Acument Tm Global Technologies, Belvidere** *Also called Camcar LLC* ***(G-1742)***

**Acura Pharmaceuticals Inc (PA)**......847 705-7709
616 N North Ct Ste 120 Palatine (60067) ***(G-16996)***

**Ad Deluxe Sign Company Inc**......815 556-8469
23856 W Andrew Rd Ste 103 Plainfield (60585) ***(G-17576)***

**Ad Electric Sign Inc**......708 222-8000
6549 28th St Berwyn (60402) ***(G-2055)***

**AD Huesing Corporation**......309 788-5652
527 37th Ave Rock Island (61201) ***(G-18157)***

**Ad Images**......847 956-1887
2258 Landmeier Rd Ste F Elk Grove Village (60007) ***(G-9269)***

**Ad Special TZ Inc**......847 845-6767
2456 Palazzo Ct Buffalo Grove (60089) ***(G-2650)***

**Ad Works Inc**......217 342-9688
17866 N Us Highway 45 Effingham (62401) ***(G-8821)***

**Ad-Deluxe Sign Co, Plainfield** *Also called Ad Deluxe Sign Company Inc* ***(G-17576)***

**Ada Holding Company Inc (HQ)**......312 440-2897
211 E Chicago Ave B29 Chicago (60611) ***(G-3742)***

**Ada Metal Products Inc**......847 673-1190
7120 N Capitol Dr Lincolnwood (60712) ***(G-13500)***

**Adair Enterprises Inc**......847 640-7789
1499 Tonne Rd Elk Grove Village (60007) ***(G-9270)***

**Adam Tool & Mfg Co Inc**......630 530-8810
900 N Larch Ave Elmhurst (60126) ***(G-9830)***

**Adams & Masterson Memorials, Pana** *Also called Pana Monument Co* ***(G-17136)***

**Adams Apple Distributing LP**......847 832-9900
2301 Ravine Way Glenview (60025) ***(G-11095)***

**Adams Elevator Equipment Co (HQ)**......847 581-2900
100 S Wacker Dr Ste 1250 Chicago (60606) ***(G-3743)***

**Adams Machine Shop**......630 851-6060
1223 Arthur Rd Naperville (60540) ***(G-15590)***

**Adams Memorials, Charleston** *Also called Wendell Adams* ***(G-3615)***

**Adams Network, Quincy** *Also called Adams Telephone Co-Operative* ***(G-17789)***



(PA)=Parent Co (HQ)=Headquarters (DH)=Div Headquarters
2017 Harris Illinois
Industrial Directory
1151

**Adams Outdoor Advg Ltd Partnr** ........ 309 692-2482
911 Sw Adams St Peoria (61602) ***(G-17302)***
**Adams Outdoor Advg Peoria, Peoria** *Also called Adams Outdoor Advg Ltd Partnr* ***(G-17302)***
**Adams Printing Co** ........ 618 529-2396
2350 N Mcroy Dr Carbondale (62901) ***(G-3000)***
**Adams Steel Service Inc** ........ 815 385-9100
2022 S Il Route 31 Ste A McHenry (60050) ***(G-14477)***
**Adams Street Iron Inc** ........ 312 733-3229
9127 S Kedzie Ave Evergreen Park (60805) ***(G-10109)***
**Adams Telephone Co-Operative** ........ 217 224-9566
301 Oak St Quincy (62301) ***(G-17789)***
**Adapt Seals Co** ........ 309 463-2482
565 Lake Wildwood Dr Varna (61375) ***(G-21132)***
**Adaptive Insights Inc** ........ 800 303-6346
1600 Golf Rd Rolling Meadows (60008) ***(G-18707)***
**Adaptive Testing Technologies, Chicago** *Also called Psychiatric Assessments Inc* ***(G-6220)***
**Adazon Inc** ........ 847 235-2700
1485 N Western Ave Lake Forest (60045) ***(G-12874)***
**ADC, Carlinville** *Also called Area Diesel Service Inc* ***(G-3030)***
**ADC 360, Romeoville** *Also called Automated Design Corp* ***(G-18801)***
**ADC Diecasting LLC** ........ 847 541-3030
901 Chase Ave Elk Grove Village (60007) ***(G-9271)***
**ADC Diecasting LLC (PA)** ........ 847 541-3030
901 Chase Ave Elk Grove Village (60007) ***(G-9272)***
**Adco Amrcn Day Camp Outfitters, Skokie** *Also called Cloz Companies Inc* ***(G-19983)***
**Adco Global Inc (HQ)** ........ 847 282-3485
100 Tri State Intl # 135 Lincolnshire (60069) ***(G-13424)***
**Adcraft Printers Inc** ........ 815 932-6432
1355 W Jeffery St Kankakee (60901) ***(G-12601)***
**Addax Sound Company** ........ 847 412-0000
3647 Woodhead Dr Northbrook (60062) ***(G-16198)***
**Addison Business Systems Inc** ........ 708 371-5454
12555 S Menard Ave Palos Heights (60463) ***(G-17098)***
**Addison Central Pathology** ........ 847 685-9326
5645 W Addison St Chicago (60634) ***(G-3744)***
**Addison Electric Inc** ........ 800 517-4871
502 W Factory Rd Addison (60101) ***(G-22)***
**Addison Electro Polishing Div, Addison** *Also called K & P Industries Inc* ***(G-163)***
**Addison Engraving Inc** ........ 630 833-9123
204 W Ridge Rd Villa Park (60181) ***(G-21232)***
**Addison Interiors Company** ........ 630 628-1345
711 W Fullerton Ave Ste A Addison (60101) ***(G-23)***
**Addison Precision Products** ........ 815 857-4466
200 E Kellen Dr Amboy (61310) ***(G-596)***
**Addison Precision Tech LLC** ........ 773 626-4747
4343 S Oakley Ave Chicago (60609) ***(G-3745)***
**Addison Pro Plastics Inc** ........ 630 543-6770
503 S Westgate St Ste D Addison (60101) ***(G-24)***
**Addison Steel Inc** ........ 847 998-9445
1340 Bonnie Glen Ln Glenview (60025) ***(G-11096)***
**Addition Technology Inc** ........ 847 297-8419
820 Oak Creek Dr Lombard (60148) ***(G-13759)***
**Addvalue2print LLC** ........ 847 551-1570
555 Plate Dr Ste 6 East Dundee (60118) ***(G-8628)***
**Ade Inc (PA)** ........ 773 646-3400
1430 E 130th St Chicago (60633) ***(G-3746)***
**Adel Tool Co LLP** ........ 708 867-8530
4640 N Ronald St Chicago (60706) ***(G-3747)***
**Adel Woodworks (PA)** ........ 815 886-9006
15523 Weber Rd Ste 104 Romeoville (60446) ***(G-18790)***
**Adello Biologics LLC** ........ 312 235-3665
3440 S Dearborn St # 300 Chicago (60616) ***(G-3748)***
**Adermanns Welding & Mch & Co** ........ 217 342-3234
1310 Pike Ave Effingham (62401) ***(G-8822)***
**Adesso Solutions LLC** ........ 847 342-1095
3701 Algonquin Rd Ste 270 Rolling Meadows (60008) ***(G-18708)***
**Adflow Networks** ........ 866 423-3569
203 N Lasalle St Ste 2100 Chicago (60601) ***(G-3749)***
**Adhereon Corporation** ........ 312 997-5002
222 Mdse Mart Plz # 1230 Chicago (60654) ***(G-3750)***
**Adhes Tape Technology Inc** ........ 847 496-7949
3339 N Ridge Ave Arlington Heights (60004) ***(G-702)***
**Adhesves Sealants Coatings Div, Aurora** *Also called HB Fuller Company* ***(G-1024)***
**Adient US LLC** ........ 815 895-2095
1701 Bethany Rd Sycamore (60178) ***(G-20785)***
**Adjustable Clamp Company (PA)** ........ 312 666-0640
404 N Armour St Chicago (60642) ***(G-3751)***
**ADK Arms Inc** ........ 847 981-9800
2301 Estes Ave Elk Grove Village (60007) ***(G-9273)***
**Adk Products Inc** ........ 847 710-0021
2821 Old Higgins Rd Elk Grove Village (60007) ***(G-9274)***
**Adkins Energy LLC** ........ 815 369-9173
4350 W Galena Rd Lena (61048) ***(G-13272)***
**Adler Norco Inc** ........ 847 473-3600
2331 Creekwood Dr Mundelein (60060) ***(G-15464)***
**ADM, Chicago** *Also called Archer-Daniels-Midland Company* ***(G-3941)***
**ADM, Clinton** *Also called Archer-Daniels-Midland Company* ***(G-7277)***
**ADM, Decatur** *Also called Archer-Daniels-Midland Company* ***(G-7833)***
**ADM, Decatur** *Also called Archer-Daniels-Midland Company* ***(G-7834)***
**ADM, Peoria** *Also called Archer-Daniels-Midland Company* ***(G-17309)***
**ADM, Altamont** *Also called Archer-Daniels-Midland Company* ***(G-549)***
**ADM, Bushnell** *Also called Archer-Daniels-Midland Company* ***(G-2897)***
**ADM, Decatur** *Also called Archer-Daniels-Midland Company* ***(G-7836)***
**ADM, Quincy** *Also called Archer-Daniels-Midland Company* ***(G-17794)***
**ADM, Quincy** *Also called Archer-Daniels-Midland Company* ***(G-17796)***
**ADM, Decatur** *Also called Archer-Daniels-Midland Company* ***(G-7840)***
**ADM Animal Nutrition, Effingham** *Also called Archer-Daniels-Midland Company* ***(G-8824)***
**ADM Animal Nutrition, Lincoln** *Also called Archer-Daniels-Midland Company* ***(G-13404)***
**ADM Grain Company** ........ 217 424-5200
4666 E Faries Pkwy Decatur (62526) ***(G-7820)***
**ADM Holdings LLC** ........ 217 422-7281
350 N Water St Decatur (62523) ***(G-7821)***
**ADM Holdings LLC** ........ 312 634-8100
191 N Wacker Dr Ste 1500 Chicago (60606) ***(G-3752)***
**ADM Holdings LLC (HQ)** ........ 217 424-5200
4666 E Faries Pkwy Decatur (62526) ***(G-7822)***
**ADM Imaging Inc** ........ 630 834-7100
100 W Roosevelt Rd A1-200 Wheaton (60187) ***(G-21934)***
**ADM International Inc** ........ 773 774-2400
1900 Marquette St North Chicago (60064) ***(G-16173)***
**ADM Milling Co** ........ 312 666-2465
1300 W Carroll Ave Fl 2 Chicago (60607) ***(G-3753)***
**ADM Trucking Inc** ........ 217 451-4288
2100 N Jasper St Decatur (62526) ***(G-7823)***
**Admiral Graphics, Arlington Heights** *Also called Thompson & Walsh LLC* ***(G-855)***
**Admo** ........ 847 741-5777
2550 Decade Ct Ste A Elgin (60124) ***(G-8936)***
**Adnama Inc** ........ 312 922-0509
1513 S State St Chicago (60605) ***(G-3754)***
**ADP Pallet Inc** ........ 773 638-3800
7300 S Kostner Ave Chicago (60629) ***(G-3755)***
**Adrian Orgas Gheorghe** ........ 773 355-1200
1010 N Apple Tree Ct Palatine (60067) ***(G-16997)***
**ADS, Lake Forest** *Also called Amity Die and Stamping Co* ***(G-12879)***
**ADS, Peoria** *Also called Ag-Defense Systems Inc* ***(G-17303)***
**ADS LLC** ........ 256 430-3366
144 Tower Dr Burr Ridge (60527) ***(G-2820)***
**Adsensa Corporation** ........ 312 559-2881
404 S Wells St Fl 5 Chicago (60607) ***(G-3756)***
**Advanage Diversified Pdts Inc** ........ 708 331-8390
16615 Halsted St Harvey (60426) ***(G-11650)***
**Advance Adhesives, Chicago** *Also called Aabbitt Adhesives Inc* ***(G-3701)***
**Advance Adhesives, Chicago** *Also called Aabbitt Adhesives Inc* ***(G-3702)***
**Advance Automation Company** ........ 773 539-7633
3526 N Elston Ave Chicago (60618) ***(G-3757)***
**Advance Awnair Corp** ........ 708 422-2730
15418 S 70th Ct Orland Park (60462) ***(G-16838)***
**Advance Bindery Co** ........ 847 662-2418
3811 Hawthorne Ct Waukegan (60087) ***(G-21518)***
**Advance Design Inc** ........ 815 338-0843
10915 Pheasant Ln Woodstock (60098) ***(G-22534)***
**Advance Enameling Co** ........ 773 737-7356
5849 S Bishop St Chicago (60636) ***(G-3758)***
**Advance Engineering Corp** ........ 847 760-9421
440 S Mclean Blvd Elgin (60123) ***(G-8937)***
**Advance Equipment Mfg Co** ........ 773 287-8220
4615 W Chicago Ave Chicago (60651) ***(G-3759)***
**Advance Instant Printing Co** ........ 312 346-0986
5 S Wabash Ave Ste 414 Chicago (60603) ***(G-3760)***
**Advance Iron Works Inc** ........ 708 798-3540
1325 171st St East Hazel Crest (60429) ***(G-8663)***
**Advance Machining** ........ 630 521-9392
405 Evergreen Ave Bensenville (60106) ***(G-1817)***
**Advance Manufacturing** ........ 618 245-6515
204 Through St Farina (62838) ***(G-10172)***
**Advance Metalworking Company** ........ 309 853-3387
3726 Us Highway 34 Kewanee (61443) ***(G-12668)***
**Advance Pallet Incorporated** ........ 847 697-5700
600 Woodbury St South Elgin (60177) ***(G-20179)***
**Advance Plastic Corp** ........ 773 637-5922
4866 W Cortland St Chicago (60639) ***(G-3761)***
**Advance Press Sign Inc** ........ 630 833-1600
719 N Addison Rd Villa Park (60181) ***(G-21233)***
**Advance Printers Machine Shop** ........ 773 588-3169
4271 N Elston Ave Chicago (60618) ***(G-3762)***
**Advance Screw Products Inc** ........ 773 237-0034
5160 W Homer St Chicago (60639) ***(G-3763)***
**Advance Security Products, Belleville** *Also called Marbil Enterprises Inc* ***(G-1651)***
**Advance Steel Services Inc** ........ 773 619-2977
4722 W Harrison St Chicago (60644) ***(G-3764)***
**Advance Technologies Inc** ........ 815 297-1771
430 Challenge St Freeport (61032) ***(G-10644)***
**Advance Thermal Corp** ........ 630 595-5150
226 Gerry Dr Wood Dale (60191) ***(G-22331)***
**Advance Thermal Corp (HQ)** ........ 630 595-5150
226 Gerry Dr Wood Dale (60191) ***(G-22332)***

## ALPHABETIC SECTION

**Advance Tools LLC** .................................................. 855 685-0633
  2456 Saranac Ln  Glenview  (60026)  *(G-11097)*
**Advance Uniform Company** .................................... 312 922-1797
  33 E 13th St Ste 1  Chicago  (60605)  *(G-3765)*
**Advance Ureathane, West Chicago** Also called Innocor Inc *(G-21721)*
**Advance Welding & Equipment** ............................... 630 759-3334
  6688 Joliet Rd  Countryside  (60525)  *(G-7411)*
**Advance Wheel Corporation** ................................... 773 471-5734
  5335 S Western Blvd Ste H  Chicago  (60609)  *(G-3766)*
**Advance World Trade Inc (PA)** ................................ 773 777-7100
  4321 N Knox Ave  Chicago  (60641)  *(G-3767)*
**Advanced Asphalt Co (PA)** ...................................... 815 872-9911
  308 W Railroad Ave  Princeton  (61356)  *(G-17741)*
**Advanced Assembly** ................................................ 630 379-6158
  703 Blue Ridge Dr  Streamwood  (60107)  *(G-20639)*
**Advanced Audio Devices LLC** .................................. 847 604-9630
  725 N Mckinley Rd Ste 102  Lake Forest  (60045)  *(G-12875)*
**Advanced Audio Technology Inc** .............................. 630 665-3344
  200 Easy St Ste E  Carol Stream  (60188)  *(G-3090)*
**Advanced Automation Systems** ............................... 815 877-1075
  5318 Forest Hills Ct  Loves Park  (61111)  *(G-13912)*
**Advanced Battery  LLC** ............................................ 309 755-7775
  1410 11th St W  Milan  (61264)  *(G-14772)*
**Advanced Battery Systems, Milan** Also called Advanced Battery LLC *(G-14772)*
**Advanced Biological Concepts, Osco** Also called Helfter Enterprises Inc *(G-16899)*
**Advanced Bird Control, East Moline** Also called Nixalite of America Inc *(G-8689)*
**Advanced Careers Learning Ctrs, Chicago** Also called Sullivan Cgliano Training Ctrs *(G-6614)*
**Advanced Cstm Enrgy Sltons Inc** ............................. 312 428-9540
  2545 W Diversey Ave  Chicago  (60647)  *(G-3768)*
**Advanced Custom Shapes** ....................................... 618 684-2222
  550 N 19th St  Murphysboro  (62966)  *(G-15570)*
**Advanced Diamond Tech Inc** ................................... 815 293-0900
  48 E Belmont Dr  Romeoville  (60446)  *(G-18791)*
**Advanced Digital & Mold Inc** ................................... 630 595-8242
  833 Eagle Dr  Bensenville  (60106)  *(G-1818)*
**Advanced Drainage Systems Inc** ............................. 815 539-2160
  1600 Industrial Dr  Mendota  (61342)  *(G-14714)*
**Advanced Electronics  Inc** ....................................... 630 293-3300
  721 Winston St  West Chicago  (60185)  *(G-21652)*
**Advanced EMR Solutions Inc** .................................. 877 327-6160
  5 Revere Dr Ste 430  Northbrook  (60062)  *(G-16199)*
**Advanced Engneered Systems Inc** .......................... 815 624-7797
  14328 Commercial Pkwy  South Beloit  (61080)  *(G-20135)*
**Advanced Extruder Tech Inc** ................................... 847 238-9651
  2281 E Devon Ave  Elk Grove Village  (60007)  *(G-9275)*
**Advanced Fiber Products  LLC** ................................ 847 768-9001
  200 Howard Ave Ste 244  Des Plaines  (60018)  *(G-8144)*
**Advanced Finishing** ................................................. 815 964-3367
  1044 Tuneberg Pkwy  Belvidere  (61008)  *(G-1728)*
**Advanced Flexible Mtls LLC** .................................... 770 222-6000
  2 N La Salle St Ste 1200  Chicago  (60602)  *(G-3769)*
**Advanced Fltration Systems Inc (PA)** ...................... 217 351-3073
  3206 Farber Dr  Champaign  (61822)  *(G-3444)*
**Advanced Flxble Composites Inc (PA)** .................... 847 658-3938
  14 Walter Ct  Lake In The Hills  (60156)  *(G-12983)*
**Advanced Graphics Tech Inc** ................................... 817 481-8561
  8140 Cass Ave  Darien  (60561)  *(G-7787)*
**Advanced Heat Treating Inc** .................................... 815 877-8593
  980 Industrial Ct  Loves Park  (61111)  *(G-13913)*
**Advanced Lubrication  Inc (PA)** ............................... 815 932-3288
  4517 E 2000n Rd  Kankakee  (60901)  *(G-12602)*
**Advanced Machine & Engrg Co** ............................... 815 962-6076
  2500 Latham St  Rockford  (61103)  *(G-18257)*
**Advanced Machine and Engrg, Rockford** Also called Goellner Inc *(G-18400)*
**Advanced Machine Co Inc** ....................................... 773 545-9790
  4450 W Belmont Ave  Chicago  (60641)  *(G-3770)*
**Advanced Machine Products Inc** ............................. 618 254-4112
  207 S Delmar Ave  Hartford  (62048)  *(G-11609)*
**Advanced Mbility Solutions LLC** .............................. 618 658-8580
  3205 W Commercial Rd  Marion  (62959)  *(G-14247)*
**Advanced Metalcraft  Inc** ........................................ 847 451-0771
  9128 Belden Ave  Franklin Park  (60131)  *(G-10384)*
**Advanced Micro Lites Inc** ........................................ 630 365-5450
  205 Dempsey St Ste A  Elburn  (60119)  *(G-8874)*
**Advanced Microderm  Inc** ....................................... 630 980-3300
  904 S Roselle Rd 302  Schaumburg  (60193)  *(G-19423)*
**Advanced Mobility &** ............................................... 708 235-2800
  6370 W Emerald Pkwy # 107  Monee  (60449)  *(G-14991)*
**Advanced Molding Tech Inc** .................................... 815 334-3600
  1425 Lake Ave  Woodstock  (60098)  *(G-22535)*
**Advanced On-Site Concrete Inc** .............................. 773 622-7836
  5308 W Grand Ave  Chicago  (60639)  *(G-3771)*
**Advanced Ozone Tech Inc** ....................................... 630 964-1300
  2743 Curtiss St  Downers Grove  (60515)  *(G-8385)*
**Advanced Pattern Works  LLC** ................................ 618 346-9039
  305 Railroad Ave  Collinsville  (62234)  *(G-7312)*
**Advanced Plastic Corp** ............................................ 847 674-2070
  3725 W Lunt Ave  Lincolnwood  (60712)  *(G-13501)*

**Advanced Plbg & Pipe Fitting** .................................. 618 554-2677
  15498 N 1590th St  Newton  (62448)  *(G-15936)*
**Advanced Polymer Alloys LLC** ................................. 847 836-8119
  400 Maple Ave Ste A  Carpentersville  (60110)  *(G-3272)*
**Advanced Prcsion Machining Ltd** ............................ 630 860-2549
  766 Birginal Dr  Bensenville  (60106)  *(G-1819)*
**Advanced Precision Mfg Inc (PA)** ............................ 847 981-9800
  2301 Estes Ave  Elk Grove Village  (60007)  *(G-9276)*
**Advanced Prototype Molding** .................................. 847 202-4200
  263 N Woodwork Ln  Palatine  (60067)  *(G-16998)*
**Advanced Retinal Institute Inc** ............................... 617 821-5597
  1123 N Oak Park Ave  Oak Park  (60302)  *(G-16649)*
**Advanced Robotics Research** ................................. 630 544-0040
  791 Sigmund Rd  Naperville  (60563)  *(G-15591)*
**Advanced Specialty Lighting** ................................... 708 867-3140
  7227 W Wilson Ave  Harwood Heights  (60706)  *(G-11681)*
**Advanced Steel Fabrication** .................................... 847 956-6565
  181 Randall St  Elk Grove Village  (60007)  *(G-9277)*
**Advanced Strobe Products, Harwood Heights** Also called Advanced Specialty Lighting *(G-11681)*
**Advanced Strobe Products  Inc** ............................... 708 867-3100
  7227 W Wilson Ave  Chicago  (60706)  *(G-3772)*
**Advanced Technologies Inc** .................................... 847 329-9875
  310 Busse Hwy Ste 241  Park Ridge  (60068)  *(G-17178)*
**Advanced Thermal Processing** ............................... 630 595-9000
  501 Eastern Ave  Bensenville  (60106)  *(G-1820)*
**Advanced Valve Tech Inc (PA)** ................................. 847 364-3700
  800 Busse Rd  Elk Grove Village  (60007)  *(G-9278)*
**Advanced Valve Tech Inc** ........................................ 877 489-4909
  12601 Homan Ave  Blue Island  (60406)  *(G-2237)*
**Advanced Weighing Systems Inc** ............................ 630 916-6179
  1433 W Fullerton Ave H  Addison  (60101)  *(G-25)*
**Advanced Welding Ltd** ............................................ 708 205-4559
  760 W Factory Rd  Addison  (60101)  *(G-26)*
**Advanced Welding Services** ................................... 630 759-3334
  8250 School St  La Grange  (60525)  *(G-12724)*
**Advanced Window Corp** .......................................... 773 379-3500
  4935 W Le Moyne St  Chicago  (60651)  *(G-3773)*
**Advangene Consumables Inc** ................................. 847 283-9780
  21 N Skokie Hwy Ste 104  Lake Bluff  (60044)  *(G-12827)*
**Advantage Components  Inc** .................................. 815 725-8644
  2240 Oak Leaf St  Joliet  (60436)  *(G-12450)*
**Advantage Direct  Inc** ............................................. 847 427-1185
  1822 Elmhurst Rd  Elk Grove Village  (60007)  *(G-9279)*
**Advantage Machining Inc** ....................................... 630 897-1220
  601 W New York St Frnt  Aurora  (60506)  *(G-1101)*
**Advantage Manufacturing Inc** ................................. 773 626-2200
  1458 N Lamon Ave  Chicago  (60651)  *(G-3774)*
**Advantage Optics  Inc** ............................................ 630 548-9870
  1555 Bond St Ste 115  Naperville  (60563)  *(G-15592)*
**Advantage Press Inc** ............................................... 630 960-5305
  3033 Ogden Ave Ste 110  Lisle  (60532)  *(G-13553)*
**Advantage Printing  Inc** .......................................... 630 627-7468
  1920 S Highland Ave # 300  Lombard  (60148)  *(G-13760)*
**Advantage Seal  Inc** ............................................... 630 226-0200
  694 Veterans Pkwy Ste A  Bolingbrook  (60440)  *(G-2277)*
**Advantage Structures LLC** ...................................... 773 734-9305
  10554 S Muskegon Ave  Chicago  (60617)  *(G-3775)*
**Advantage Tool and Mold Inc** .................................. 847 301-9020
  1501 Kathleen Way  Elk Grove Village  (60007)  *(G-9280)*
**Advantage Unlimited, Bensenville** Also called R N I Industries Inc *(G-1974)*
**Advantage Worldwide Wholesale, Arlington Heights** Also called Mechanical Music Corp *(G-801)*
**Advantech Bb Smartworx, Ottawa** Also called B+b Smartworx Inc *(G-16949)*
**Advantech Limited** .................................................. 815 397-9133
  601 N Russell Ave  Aurora  (60506)  *(G-1102)*
**Advantech Plastics LLC** .......................................... 815 338-8383
  2500 S Eastwood Dr  Woodstock  (60098)  *(G-22536)*
**Advantex Inc** .......................................................... 618 505-0701
  326 Bargraves Blvd  Troy  (62294)  *(G-21002)*
**Advent Tool & Mfg Inc** ............................................ 847 395-9707
  710 Anita Ave  Antioch  (60002)  *(G-613)*
**Adventure Advertising, Ottawa** Also called Ottawa Publishing Co Inc *(G-16976)*
**Adventure Sports Outdoors, Tremont** Also called Red Nose Inc *(G-20985)*
**Adventures Unlimited (PA)** ..................................... 815 253-6390
  303 Main St  Kempton  (60946)  *(G-12661)*
**Advert Display Products Inc** ................................... 815 513-5432
  3727 N Division St  Morris  (60450)  *(G-15090)*
**Advertisers Bindery Inc** ......................................... 312 939-4995
  739 S Clark St Fl 3  Chicago  (60605)  *(G-3776)*
**Advertising Advice Inc (PA)** .................................... 847 272-0707
  3000 Dundee Rd Ste 108  Northbrook  (60062)  *(G-16200)*
**Advertising Age, Chicago** Also called Crain Communications Inc *(G-4494)*
**Advertising Designs, Crestwood** Also called Fanning Communications Inc *(G-7488)*
**Advertising Premiums Inc** ...................................... 888 364-9710
  800 W Central Rd Ste 162  Mount Prospect  (60056)  *(G-15308)*
**Advertising Products Inc** ....................................... 847 758-0415
  680 Fargo Ave  Elk Grove Village  (60007)  *(G-9281)*

**Advertising/Displays/Printing, Northfield** *Also called Asa Inc* ***(G-16391)***
**Advocate** .......... 815 694-2122
330 N 4th St Clifton (60927) ***(G-7272)***
**Advocate Printing, Clifton** *Also called Advocate* ***(G-7272)***
**Advocations Inc** .......... 815 568-7505
17709 Collins Rd Woodstock (60098) ***(G-22537)***
**Ae Sewer & Septics Inc** .......... 847 289-9084
241 Adams St Elgin (60123) ***(G-8938)***
**Ae2009 Technologies Inc** .......... 708 331-0025
16140 Vincennes Ave South Holland (60473) ***(G-20240)***
**AEC, Elgin** *Also called Advance Engineering Corp* ***(G-8937)***
**Aemm A Electric** .......... 708 403-6700
8448 Camelia Ln Orland Park (60462) ***(G-16839)***
**Aen Industries Inc** .......... 708 758-3000
1522 Union Ave Chicago Heights (60411) ***(G-7077)***
**AEP Inc** .......... 618 466-7668
1225 Cabin Club Dr Alton (62002) ***(G-558)***
**Aero Alehouse** .......... 815 977-5602
6164 E Riverside Blvd Loves Park (61111) ***(G-13914)***
**Aero Apmc Inc** .......... 630 766-0910
411 S County Line Rd Franklin Park (60131) ***(G-10385)***
**Aero Flash Signal, Chicago** *Also called Mellish & Murray Co* ***(G-5683)***
**Aero Industries Inc** .......... 815 943-7818
450 Commanche Cir Harvard (60033) ***(G-11618)***
**Aero Precision Machining, Franklin Park** *Also called Aero Apmc Inc* ***(G-10385)***
**Aero Products Holdings Inc** .......... 847 485-3200
1834 Walden Office Sq # 300 Schaumburg (60173) ***(G-19424)***
**Aero Products International, Schaumburg** *Also called Aero Products Holdings Inc* ***(G-19424)***
**Aero Rubber Company Inc** .......... 800 662-1009
8100 185th St Tinley Park (60487) ***(G-20886)***
**Aero Tool & Stamping, Franklin Park** *Also called S & L Tool Co Inc* ***(G-10579)***
**Aero Vac Brazing Heat Treating, Itasca** *Also called Bulaw Welding & Engineering Co* ***(G-12239)***
**Aero-Cables Corp** .......... 815 609-6600
114 Kirkland Cir Ste A Oswego (60543) ***(G-16902)***
**Aero-Tech Light Bulb Co (PA)** .......... 847 534-6580
534 Pratt Ave N Schaumburg (60193) ***(G-19425)***
**Aerodine Magazine** .......... 847 358-4355
1514 Banbury Rd Inverness (60067) ***(G-12200)***
**Aerodyne Incorporated** .......... 773 588-2905
2612 W Barry Ave Chicago (60618) ***(G-3777)***
**Aerofast Inc** .......... 630 668-6575
360 Gundersen Dr Carol Stream (60188) ***(G-3091)***
**Aeroflash Signal, Chicago** *Also called Mellish & Murray Co* ***(G-5684)***
**Aeromax Industries Inc** .......... 847 756-4085
28 W079 Industrial Ave Lake Barrington (60010) ***(G-12798)***
**Aeromotive, Chicago** *Also called Aerodyne Incorporated* ***(G-3777)***
**Aeromotive Services Inc** .......... 224 535-9220
345 Willard Ave Elgin (60120) ***(G-8939)***
**Aeronautical Electric Company, Chicago** *Also called Aco Inc* ***(G-3735)***
**Aeropharm Technology LLC** .......... 847 937-6100
100 Abbott Park Rd North Chicago (60064) ***(G-16174)***
**Aeropres Corporation** .......... 815 478-3266
100 S Park Rd Manhattan (60442) ***(G-14167)***
**Aeropulse LLC** .......... 215 245-7600
1336 Enterprise Dr Romeoville (60446) ***(G-18792)***
**Aerostar Global Logistics Inc (PA)** .......... 630 396-7890
901 Oak Creek Dr Lombard (60148) ***(G-13761)***
**Aerostar Technical Services, Lombard** *Also called Aerostar Global Logistics Inc* ***(G-13761)***
**Aerostars Inc** .......... 847 736-8171
6413 Kingsbridge Dr Cary (60013) ***(G-3323)***
**Aerotech Inc** .......... 618 942-5131
403 S Pershing St Energy (62933) ***(G-9984)***
**Aerotronic Controls Co (PA)** .......... 847 228-6504
2101 Arthur Ave Elk Grove Village (60007) ***(G-9282)***
**Aertrade LLC (PA)** .......... 630 428-4440
1585 Beverly Ct Ste 128 Aurora (60502) ***(G-954)***
**Aerus Electrolux** .......... 847 949-4222
900 N Lake St Ste 100 Mundelein (60060) ***(G-15465)***
**AES, South Beloit** *Also called Advanced Engneered Systems Inc* ***(G-20135)***
**Aesphetics Medical Ltd** .......... 630 416-1400
477 E Bttrfeld Rd Ste 408 Lombard (60148) ***(G-13762)***
**Aetna Bearing Company** .......... 630 694-0024
1081 Sesame St Franklin Park (60131) ***(G-10386)***
**Aetna Engineering Works Inc** .......... 773 785-0489
12001 S Calumet Ave Chicago (60628) ***(G-3778)***
**Aeverie Inc** .......... 844 238-3743
129 Manchester Ct Buffalo Grove (60089) ***(G-2651)***
**AF, Chicago** *Also called Art-Flo Shirt & Lettering Co* ***(G-3953)***
**AF Antronics Inc** .......... 217 328-0800
1906 N Federal Dr Urbana (61801) ***(G-21068)***
**Afam Concept Inc** .......... 773 838-1336
7401 S Pulaski Rd Ste A Chicago (60629) ***(G-3779)***
**Afar Imports & Interiors Inc (PA)** .......... 217 744-3262
3125 S Douglas Ave Springfield (62704) ***(G-20386)***
**Afc Cable Systems Inc (HQ)** .......... 508 998-1131
16100 Lathrop Ave Harvey (60426) ***(G-11651)***
**Afc Machining Division, Mundelein** *Also called Muntz Industries Inc* ***(G-15534)***
**Afco Industries Inc** .......... 618 742-6469
8161 State Highway 37 Olmsted (62970) ***(G-16757)***
**Afco Lite American Fluorescent, Waukegan** *Also called Afx Inc* ***(G-21519)***
**Afco Products Incorporated** .......... 847 299-1055
1030 Commerce Dr Lake Zurich (60047) ***(G-13036)***
**Affinnova Inc** .......... 781 464-4700
233 S Wacker Dr Ste 6225 Chicago (60606) ***(G-3780)***
**Affirmed LLC** .......... 847 550-0170
280a N Rand Rd Ste A Lake Zurich (60047) ***(G-13037)***
**Affri Inc** .......... 224 374-0931
850 Dillon Dr Wood Dale (60191) ***(G-22333)***
**Affton Fabg & Wldg Co Inc** .......... 314 781-4100
1635 Sauget Business Blvd Sauget (62206) ***(G-19381)***
**Affy Tapple LLC** .......... 773 338-1100
6300 W Gross Point Rd Niles (60714) ***(G-15958)***
**Afi Industries Inc** .......... 630 462-0400
475 Kehoe Blvd Carol Stream (60188) ***(G-3092)***
**Afm Heatsheets, Chicago** *Also called Advanced Flexible Mtls LLC* ***(G-3769)***
**African American Ctr For Hnb** .......... 618 549-3965
123 Indianwood Blvd # 1062 Park Forest (60466) ***(G-17168)***
**Afrogen Tech & Centers, Park Forest** *Also called African American Ctr For Hnb* ***(G-17168)***
**Afs Classico LLC** .......... 309 786-8833
507 34th Ave Rock Island (61201) ***(G-18158)***
**Afs Inc** .......... 847 437-2345
3232 Nordic Rd Arlington Heights (60005) ***(G-703)***
**Afshar Inc** .......... 773 645-8922
3224 W Altgeld St Chicago (60647) ***(G-3781)***
**Afterdark Outdoor Lighting** .......... 708 243-1228
15451 Nolan Ct Lockport (60491) ***(G-13702)***
**Afton Chemical Corporation** .......... 618 583-1000
501 Monsanto Ave East Saint Louis (62206) ***(G-8740)***
**Afton Chemical Corporation** .......... 708 728-1546
7201 W 65th St Bedford Park (60638) ***(G-1533)***
**Afx Inc (PA)** .......... 847 249-5970
2345 Ernie Krueger Cir Waukegan (60087) ***(G-21519)***
**AG Hohlfelder Sheet Metal, Rockford** *Also called Hohlfelder A H Shtmtl Htg Coolg* ***(G-18420)***
**AG Manufacturing - Illinois, Rochelle** *Also called A&G Manufacturing Inc* ***(G-18076)***
**AG Medical Systems Inc** .......... 847 458-3100
13 Prosper Ct Ste B Lake In The Hills (60156) ***(G-12984)***
**AG Precision Inc** .......... 847 724-7786
2443 Fontana Dr Glenview (60025) ***(G-11098)***
**AG Solutions, Paxton** *Also called Plastic Designs Inc* ***(G-17243)***
**Ag-Defense Systems Inc** .......... 309 495-7258
801 W Main St Ste A118 Peoria (61606) ***(G-17303)***
**Agate Publishing Inc** .......... 847 475-4457
1328 Greenleaf St Evanston (60202) ***(G-10005)***
**Agave Loco LLC** .......... 847 383-6052
1175 Corporate Woods Pkwy # 218 Vernon Hills (60061) ***(G-21142)***
**AGC, Addison** *Also called Amerigraphics Corp* ***(G-39)***
**AGCO Corporation** .......... 630 406-3248
1500 N Raddant Rd Batavia (60510) ***(G-1404)***
**AGCO Recycling LLC** .......... 217 224-9048
4425 Gardner Expy Quincy (62305) ***(G-17790)***
**Agena Manufacturing Co** .......... 630 668-5086
360 Gundersen Dr Carol Stream (60188) ***(G-3093)***
**Aggregate Materials Company** .......... 815 747-2430
18525 Us Highway 20 W East Dubuque (61025) ***(G-8616)***
**Aggresive Motor Sports** .......... 630 761-1550
201 Oswald Ave Batavia (60510) ***(G-1405)***
**Aggressive Motorsports Inc** .......... 847 846-7488
227 Oswald Ave Batavia (60510) ***(G-1406)***
**Agi Corp** .......... 815 708-0502
6075 Material Ave Ste 100 Loves Park (61111) ***(G-13915)***
**Agile Health Technologies Inc** .......... 630 247-5565
2728 Forgue Dr Ste 106 Naperville (60564) ***(G-15789)***
**Agilent Technologies Inc** .......... 800 227-9770
4187 Collection Center Dr Chicago (60693) ***(G-3782)***
**Agilent Technologies Inc** .......... 847 690-0431
720 W Algonquin Rd Arlington Heights (60005) ***(G-704)***
**Agmaco, Broadview** *Also called Active Grinding & Mfg Co* ***(G-2554)***
**Agnes & Chris Gulik** .......... 847 931-9641
408 W Amberside Dr Elgin (60124) ***(G-8940)***
**Agresearch Inc** .......... 815 726-0410
1 Genstar Ln Joliet (60435) ***(G-12451)***
**Agri-News Publications Inc (HQ)** .......... 815 223-2558
426 2nd St La Salle (61301) ***(G-12760)***
**Agribase International Inc** .......... 847 810-0167
1901 N Roselle Rd Ste 800 Schaumburg (60195) ***(G-19426)***
**Agriplastics LLC** .......... 847 604-8847
11 N Skokie Hwy Lake Bluff (60044) ***(G-12828)***
**Agriscience Inc** .......... 212 365-4214
5115 N Martha St Peoria (61614) ***(G-17304)***
**Agritech Worldwide Inc (PA)** .......... 847 549-6002
1011 Campus Dr Mundelein (60060) ***(G-15466)***
**Agro Chem West, Saybrook** *Also called Agro-Chem Inc* ***(G-19413)***
**Agro-Chem Inc** .......... 309 475-8311
127 S Center St Saybrook (61770) ***(G-19413)***
**Agrochem Inc** .......... 847 564-1304
3703 Pebble Beach Rd Northbrook (60062) ***(G-16201)***

**Agrowtek Inc**....847 380-3009
173 Ambrogio Dr Ste A Gurnee (60031) *(G-11420)*
**AGS Machine Co Inc**....630 766-7777
872 Eagle Dr Bensenville (60106) *(G-1821)*
**AGS Partners LLC**....630 446-7777
905 W Irving Park Rd Itasca (60143) *(G-12224)*
**AGS Technology Inc**....847 534-6600
951 Douglas Rd Batavia (60510) *(G-1407)*
**Agsco Corporation (PA)**....847 520-4455
160 W Hintz Rd Wheeling (60090) *(G-21999)*
**Agt Products, Addison** *Also called American Gasket Tech Inc (G-36)*
**Agusta Mill Works**....309 787-4616
117 17th St E Milan (61264) *(G-14773)*
**Agvision, Springfield** *Also called Brandt Consolidated Inc (G-20399)*
**Ah, Freeport** *Also called Anchor-Harvey Components LLC (G-10646)*
**Ah Tensor International LLC**....630 739-9600
10330 Argonne Woods Dr # 300 Woodridge (60517) *(G-22450)*
**Ahead LLC (PA)**....312 924-4492
401 N Michigan Ave # 3400 Chicago (60611) *(G-3783)*
**Ahlstrom Filtration LLC**....217 824-9611
1200 E Elm St Taylorville (62568) *(G-20831)*
**Ai Ind**....773 265-6640
4015 W Carroll Ave Chicago (60624) *(G-3784)*
**Ai Industries, Chicago** *Also called Ai Ind (G-3784)*
**Ai Technologies, Palatine** *Also called Amtech Industries LLC (G-17001)*
**Aic, Gurnee** *Also called American Industrial Company (G-11427)*
**Aichar, Chicago** *Also called Error Free Software LLC (G-4774)*
**Aid For Women Northern Lk Cnty**....847 249-2700
4606 Old Grand Ave Apt 2 Gurnee (60031) *(G-11421)*
**Aidar Express Inc**....773 757-3447
2814 W Arthur Ave Apt 1 Chicago (60645) *(G-3785)*
**Aif Inc**....630 495-0077
1393 W Jeffrey Dr Addison (60101) *(G-27)*
**Aiknow Inc**....312 391-9452
2243 Glouceston Ln Naperville (60564) *(G-15790)*
**Aileys 3 Welding**....815 683-2181
Rr 24 Box West Crescent City (60928) *(G-7455)*
**Aim Business Printers, Buffalo Grove** *Also called Aim Graphic Machinery Ltd (G-2652)*
**AIM Distribution Inc**....815 986-2770
510 18th Ave Rockford (61104) *(G-18258)*
**Aim Graphic Machinery Ltd**....847 215-8000
1374 Abbott Ct Buffalo Grove (60089) *(G-2652)*
**Aim Inc**....630 941-0027
586 S Rex Blvd Elmhurst (60126) *(G-9831)*
**Aim Screen Printing Supply LLC**....630 357-4293
2731 Willow Ridge Dr Naperville (60564) *(G-15791)*
**Aimtron Corporation (PA)**....630 372-7500
555 S Vermont St Palatine (60067) *(G-16999)*
**Air Land and Sea Interiors**....630 834-1717
220 E Saint Charles Rd Villa Park (60181) *(G-21234)*
**Air Caddy**....708 383-5541
310 Lake St Ste 8 Oak Park (60302) *(G-16650)*
**Air Caster LLC**....217 877-1237
2887 N Woodford St Decatur (62526) *(G-7824)*
**Air Diffusion Systems A John**....847 782-0044
3964 Grove Ave Gurnee (60031) *(G-11422)*
**Air Duct Manufacturing Inc**....630 620-9866
1515 W Fullerton Ave B Addison (60101) *(G-28)*
**Air Gage Company**....847 695-0911
516 Slade Ave Elgin (60120) *(G-8941)*
**Air International C W T US**....217 422-1896
675 W South Side Dr Decatur (62521) *(G-7825)*
**Air Mite Devices Inc**....224 338-0071
606 Long Lake Dr Round Lake (60073) *(G-19051)*
**Air Products and Chemicals Inc**....618 452-5335
2200 Monroe St Granite City (62040) *(G-11260)*
**Air Products and Chemicals Inc**....815 223-2924
Civic Rd Industrial Park La Salle (61301) *(G-12761)*
**Air Products and Chemicals Inc**....618 451-0577
35 N Gate Indus Dr Granite City (62040) *(G-11261)*
**Air Products and Chemicals Inc**....815 423-5032
25915 S Frontage Rd Channahon (60410) *(G-3564)*
**Air Stamping Inc**....217 342-1283
3 Legend Park Effingham (62401) *(G-8823)*
**Air Van Co, Chicago** *Also called Chicago Copper & Iron Works (G-4312)*
**Air Vent Inc**....309 692-6969
7700 N Harker Dr Ste B Peoria (61615) *(G-17305)*
**Air-Drive Inc**....847 625-0226
4070 Ryan Rd Gurnee (60031) *(G-11423)*
**Air-X Remanufacturing Corp**....708 598-0044
8909 Odell Ave Bridgeview (60455) *(G-2459)*
**Air802 LLC**....630 585-6383
2570 Beverly Dr Ste 140 Aurora (60502) *(G-955)*
**Air802 Corporation**....630 428-3108
2570 Beverly Dr Ste 140 Aurora (60502) *(G-956)*
**Aira Enterprise Inc**....708 458-4360
6855 W 65th St Ste 2 Bedford Park (60638) *(G-1534)*
**Airbrake Products Inc**....708 594-1110
10334 Alveston St Orland Park (60462) *(G-16840)*
**Airbus Ds Communications Inc**....708 450-1911
10330 W Roosevelt Rd # 205 Westchester (60154) *(G-21828)*
**Aircraft Gear Corporation (PA)**....815 877-7473
611 Beacon St Loves Park (61111) *(G-13916)*
**Aircraft Plywood Mfg Inc**....618 654-6740
806 Cedar St Highland (62249) *(G-11775)*
**Airdronic Test & Balance Inc**....815 561-0339
801 1st Ave Rochelle (61068) *(G-18077)*
**Aires Press Inc**....847 698-6813
227 Murphy Lake Ln Park Ridge (60068) *(G-17179)*
**Airgas Inc**....773 785-3000
12722 S Wentworth Ave Chicago (60628) *(G-3786)*
**Airgas Inc**....773 785-3000
12745 S Wentworth Ave Chicago (60628) *(G-3787)*
**Airgas Usa LLC**....815 935-7750
184 N Kinzie Ave Bradley (60915) *(G-2412)*
**Airgas USA LLC**....708 354-0813
5235 9th Ave Countryside (60525) *(G-7412)*
**Airgas USA LLC**....815 289-1928
10853 N 2nd St Machesney Park (61115) *(G-14052)*
**Airgas USA LLC**....708 482-8400
5220 East Ave Countryside (60525) *(G-7413)*
**Airgas USA LLC**....618 439-7207
12238 Petroff Rd Benton (62812) *(G-2020)*
**Airgas USA LLC**....630 231-9260
1250 W Washington St West Chicago (60185) *(G-21653)*
**Airgun Designs USA Inc**....847 520-7507
401 Florine Ct Cary (60013) *(G-3324)*
**Airmite Devices Inc Cylndrs, Round Lake** *Also called Air Mite Devices Inc (G-19051)*
**Airo Tool & Manufacturing Inc**....815 547-7588
6823 Irene Rd Belvidere (61008) *(G-1729)*
**Airport Aviation Professionals**....773 948-6631
5757 S Cicero Ave Chicago (60638) *(G-3788)*
**Airways Digital Media, Chicago** *Also called Airways Video Inc (G-3789)*
**Airways Video Inc**....773 539-8400
4055 W Peterson Ave # 204 Chicago (60646) *(G-3789)*
**Aisin Electronics Illinois LLC**....618 997-9800
11000 Redco Dr Marion (62959) *(G-14248)*
**Aisin Light Metals LLC**....618 997-7900
11000 Redco Dr Marion (62959) *(G-14249)*
**Aisin Mfg Illinois LLC**....618 998-8333
1100 Glenn Clarida Dr Marion (62959) *(G-14250)*
**Aisin Mfg Illinois LLC (HQ)**....618 998-8333
11000 Redco Dr Marion (62959) *(G-14251)*
**Aiwa, Chicago** *Also called Hale Devices Inc (G-5034)*
**Aixacct Systems Inc**....952 303-4077
715 N Wheaton Ave Wheaton (60187) *(G-21935)*
**AJ Oster LLC**....630 260-0950
180 Alexandra Way Carol Stream (60188) *(G-3094)*
**Aj Welding Services**....708 843-2701
1017 S Oak Park Ave Oak Park (60304) *(G-16651)*
**Ajax Tool Works Inc**....847 455-5420
10801 Franklin Ave Franklin Park (60131) *(G-10387)*
**Ajax Tools, Franklin Park** *Also called Ajax Tool Works Inc (G-10387)*
**Aji Custom Cabinets**....847 312-7847
5720 Wilmot Rd McHenry (60051) *(G-14478)*
**Ajinomoto Windsor Inc**....815 452-2361
301 W 3rd St Toluca (61369) *(G-20972)*
**Ajr Enterprises Inc**....630 377-8886
1200 Rukel Way Saint Charles (60174) *(G-19132)*
**Ajs Premier Printing Inc**....847 838-6350
893 Main St Antioch (60002) *(G-614)*
**AJS Publications**....847 526-5027
229 Brier Ct Island Lake (60042) *(G-12212)*
**AK Steel Corporation**....815 267-3838
24036 Nightingale Ct Plainfield (60585) *(G-17577)*
**AKD Controls Inc**....815 633-4586
10340 Product Dr Machesney Park (61115) *(G-14053)*
**Akers Packaging Service Inc**....773 731-2900
1037 E 87th St Chicago (60619) *(G-3790)*
**Akers Packaging Solutions Inc**....217 468-2396
7573 N State Route 48 Oreana (62554) *(G-16816)*
**Akers Packg Solutions Decatur, Oreana** *Also called Akers Packaging Solutions Inc (G-16816)*
**Akerue Industries LLC (PA)**....847 395-3300
90 Mcmillen Rd Antioch (60002) *(G-615)*
**Akhan Semiconductor Inc**....847 855-8400
940 Lakeside Dr Gurnee (60031) *(G-11424)*
**Akinsun Heat Co Inc**....630 289-9506
1538 Brandy Pkwy Streamwood (60107) *(G-20640)*
**Akorn Inc**....847 625-1100
5605 Centerpoint Ct Ste B Gurnee (60031) *(G-11425)*
**Akorn Inc (PA)**....847 279-6100
1925 W Field Ct Ste 300 Lake Forest (60045) *(G-12876)*
**Akorn Inc**....217 423-9715
1222 W Grand Ave Decatur (62522) *(G-7826)*
**Akorn Inc**....847 279-6166
50 Lake Pkwy Ste 110 Vernon Hills (60061) *(G-21143)*

ALPHABETIC

**Akorn Pharmaceuticals, Decatur** *Also called Akorn Inc* ***(G-7826)***
**Akrylix Inc (PA)**....773 869-9005
171 Ontario St Frankfort (60423) ***(G-10291)***
**Akshar Limited**....815 942-1433
70 Gore Rd Morris (60450) ***(G-15091)***
**Akshar Plastic Inc**....815 635-3536
1101 Bell St Bloomington (61701) ***(G-2142)***
**Aksys Ltd**....847 229-2020
2 Marriott Dr Lincolnshire (60069) ***(G-13425)***
**Akzo Nobel Aerospace Coatings, Waukegan** *Also called Akzo Nobel Coatings Inc* ***(G-21520)***
**Akzo Nobel Chemicals LLC (HQ)**....312 544-7000
525 W Van Buren St # 1600 Chicago (60607) ***(G-3791)***
**Akzo Nobel Coatings Inc**....630 792-1619
931 N Du Page Ave Lombard (60148) ***(G-13763)***
**Akzo Nobel Coatings Inc**....847 623-4200
E Water St Waukegan (60085) ***(G-21520)***
**Akzo Nobel Functional Chem LLC (HQ)**....312 544-7000
525 W Van Buren St # 1600 Chicago (60607) ***(G-3792)***
**Akzo Nobel Inc (HQ)**....312 544-7000
525 W Van Buren St Fl 16 Chicago (60607) ***(G-3793)***
**Akzo Nobel Surfc Chemistry LLC (HQ)**....312 544-7000
525 W Van Buren St Fl 16 Chicago (60607) ***(G-3794)***
**Akzonobel, Chicago** *Also called Akzo Nobel Inc* ***(G-3793)***
**Akzonobel, Chicago** *Also called Akzo Nobel Functional Chem LLC* ***(G-3792)***
**Al Bar Laboratories Inc**....847 251-1218
127 Green Bay Rd Wilmette (60091) ***(G-22241)***
**Al Bar-Wilmette Platers, Wilmette** *Also called Al Bar Laboratories Inc* ***(G-22241)***
**Al Cook Electric Motors**....309 653-2337
21845 N 850th Rd Adair (61411) ***(G-11)***
**Al Gelato Chicago LLC**....847 455-5355
9133 Belden Ave Franklin Park (60131) ***(G-10388)***
**Al Jr's Glass, Chicago** *Also called Alfred Robinson* ***(G-3804)***
**Al Mite Manufacturing Co Inc**....815 654-0720
1215 Shappert Dr Machesney Park (61115) ***(G-14054)***
**Al3 Inc**....847 441-7888
170 Linden St Winnetka (60093) ***(G-22300)***
**Alabaster Box Creations LLC**....708 473-6880
15301 Kenton Ave Oak Forest (60452) ***(G-16572)***
**Alagor Industries Incorporated (PA)**....630 766-2910
489 Thomas Dr Bensenville (60106) ***(G-1822)***
**Alali Enterprises Inc**....630 827-9231
1228 Narragansett Dr Carol Stream (60188) ***(G-3095)***
**Alamo Group (il) Inc**....217 784-4261
1020 S Sangamon Ave Gibson City (60936) ***(G-10897)***
**Alan and Assoc, Orland Park** *Also called Clear View Shade Inc* ***(G-16847)***
**Alan Manufacturing Corp**....815 568-6836
5017 Ritz Rd Marengo (60152) ***(G-14217)***
**Alan Rocca Ltd**....630 323-5800
3824 York Rd Ste B Oak Brook (60523) ***(G-16485)***
**Alan Rocca Fine Jewelery, Oak Brook** *Also called Alan Rocca Ltd* ***(G-16485)***
**Alan Stamping, Marengo** *Also called Alan Manufacturing Corp* ***(G-14217)***
**Alang Pattern Inc**....773 722-9481
3635 S 61st Ave Cicero (60804) ***(G-7177)***
**Alanson Manufacturing LLC**....773 762-2530
4408 W Cermak Rd Chicago (60623) ***(G-3795)***
**Alao Temitope**....331 454-3333
29 Brookhill Ct Collinsville (62234) ***(G-7313)***
**Alarm Press**....312 341-1290
1325 Remington Rd Ste H Schaumburg (60173) ***(G-19427)***
**Albea**....847 439-8220
1500 Midway Ct Ste W9 Elk Grove Village (60007) ***(G-9283)***
**Albert F Amling LLC (PA)**....630 333-1720
331 N York St Elmhurst (60126) ***(G-9832)***
**Albert J Wagner & Son LLC**....815 459-1287
2510 Il Route 176 Ste B Crystal Lake (60014) ***(G-7527)***
**Albert Vivo Upholstery Co Inc**....312 226-7779
836 Lakeview Ln Burr Ridge (60527) ***(G-2821)***
**Albert Whitman & Company**....847 232-2800
250 S Northwest Hwy # 320 Park Ridge (60068) ***(G-17180)***
**Alberti Enterprises Inc**....847 810-7610
825 S Waukegan Rd A8151 Lake Forest (60045) ***(G-12877)***
**Alberto Daza**....773 638-9880
4243 W Arthington St Chicago (60624) ***(G-3796)***
**Albright Enterprises Inc**....630 357-2300
426 W 5th Ave Naperville (60563) ***(G-15593)***
**Alca Industrial Instrs Svc, Franklin Park** *Also called Best Rep Company Corporation* ***(G-10411)***
**Alcast Company (PA)**....309 691-5513
8821 N University St Peoria (61615) ***(G-17306)***
**Alcast Company**....309 691-5513
8820 N Pioneer Rd Peoria (61615) ***(G-17307)***
**Alcatel-Lucent USA Inc**....630 979-0210
2000 Lucent Ln Naperville (60563) ***(G-15594)***
**Alco Spring Industries Inc**....708 755-0438
2300 Euclid Ave Chicago Heights (60411) ***(G-7078)***
**Alcon Components**....847 788-0901
716 N Arlington Hts Rd Arlington Heights (60004) ***(G-705)***
**Alcon Laboratories Inc**....312 751-6200
400 W Superior St Chicago (60654) ***(G-3797)***
**Alcon Tool & Mfg Co Inc**....773 545-8742
5266 N Elston Ave Chicago (60630) ***(G-3798)***
**Alconix Usa Inc**....847 717-7407
25 Northwest Point Blvd # 800 Elk Grove Village (60007) ***(G-9284)***
**Aldea Technologies Inc**....800 804-0635
904 S Roselle Rd 394 Schaumburg (60193) ***(G-19428)***
**Alden & Ott Printing Inks Co (HQ)**....847 956-6830
616 E Brook Dr Arlington Heights (60005) ***(G-706)***
**Alden & Ott Printing Inks Co**....847 364-6817
2050 S Carboy Rd Mount Prospect (60056) ***(G-15309)***
**Aldi Inc**....815 877-0861
1545 W Lane Rd Machesney Park (61115) ***(G-14055)***
**Aldo-Shane Corporation**....714 361-4830
105 N Rochester St Lanark (61046) ***(G-13150)***
**Aldon Co**....847 623-8800
3410 Sunset Ave Waukegan (60087) ***(G-21521)***
**Aldonex Inc**....708 547-5663
2917 Saint Charles Rd Bellwood (60104) ***(G-1693)***
**Aldrich Company, Wyoming** *Also called Aldrico Inc* ***(G-22636)***
**Aldrico Inc**....309 695-2311
341 E Williams St Wyoming (61491) ***(G-22636)***
**Aldridge Electric Inc (PA)**....847 680-5200
844 E Rockland Rd Libertyville (60048) ***(G-13300)***
**Ale Syndicate Brewers LLC**....773 340-2337
2601 W Diversey Ave Chicago (60647) ***(G-3799)***
**Ale USA Inc**....630 713-5194
1960 Nperville Wheaton Rd Naperville (60563) ***(G-15595)***
**Alecto Industries Inc**....708 344-1488
148 S 8th Ave Maywood (60153) ***(G-14414)***
**Aledo Welding Enterprises Inc**....309 582-2019
1802 Se 3rd St Aledo (61231) ***(G-367)***
**Alef Sausage Inc**....847 968-2533
1026 Campus Dr Mundelein (60060) ***(G-15467)***
**Alef Sausage & Deli, Mundelein** *Also called Ifa International Inc* ***(G-15508)***
**Alegra Printing, Elgin** *Also called Allegra Print & Imaging Inc* ***(G-8942)***
**Alegria Company**....608 726-2336
2952 N Kilbourn Ave Chicago (60641) ***(G-3800)***
**Alert Manufacturing, Elk Grove Village** *Also called All-State Industries Inc* ***(G-9286)***
**Alert Scrw Products Inc**....847 587-1360
100 Honing Rd Fox Lake (60020) ***(G-10274)***
**Alert Tubing Fabricators Inc**....815 633-5065
8019 Commercial Ave Loves Park (61111) ***(G-13917)***
**Alert Tubing Fabricators Inc**....847 253-7237
8019 Commercial Ave Schaumburg (60193) ***(G-19429)***
**Alessco Inc (PA)**....773 327-7919
2237 N Janssen Ave Chicago (60614) ***(G-3801)***
**Alex and Ani LLC**....630 574-2329
100 Oakbrook Ctr Oak Brook (60523) ***(G-16486)***
**Alex Displays & Co**....312 829-2948
401 N Leavitt St Chicago (60612) ***(G-3802)***
**Alex Smart Inc**....773 244-9275
1800 W Grace St Apt 322 Chicago (60613) ***(G-3803)***
**Alexander Brewster LLC**....618 346-8580
1401 N Bluff Rd Collinsville (62234) ***(G-7314)***
**Alexander Lumber Co**....217 429-2729
2729 N 22nd St Decatur (62526) ***(G-7827)***
**Alexander Lumber Co**....815 754-1000
164 S Loves Rd Cortland (60112) ***(G-7383)***
**Alexander Manufacturing Co**....309 728-2224
500 Lincoln St Towanda (61776) ***(G-20978)***
**Alexander Signs & Designs Inc**....815 933-3100
1511 Commerce Dr Bourbonnais (60914) ***(G-2386)***
**Alexander Technique**....847 337-7926
1830 Sherman Ave Ste 302 Evanston (60201) ***(G-10006)***
**Alexeter Technologies LLC (PA)**....847 419-1507
830 Seton Ct Ste 6 Wheeling (60090) ***(G-22000)***
**Alexi's One Stop Shop, Bridgeview** *Also called Amis Inc* ***(G-2465)***
**Alexis Fire Equipment Company**....309 482-6121
109 E Broadway Ave Alexis (61412) ***(G-375)***
**Alfa Controls Inc**....847 978-9245
311 Egidi Dr Wheeling (60090) ***(G-22001)***
**Alfa Laval Inc**....630 354-6090
321 Foster Ave Wood Dale (60191) ***(G-22334)***
**Alfa Mfg Industries Inc**....847 470-9595
7845 Merrimac Ave Morton Grove (60053) ***(G-15186)***
**ALFA TOOLS, Morton Grove** *Also called Sandtech Inc* ***(G-15234)***
**Alfa Tools, Morton Grove** *Also called Alfa Mfg Industries Inc* ***(G-15186)***
**Alfred Robinson**....773 487-5777
7525 S Evans Ave Chicago (60619) ***(G-3804)***
**Alfredos Iron Works Inc**....815 748-1177
280 W Lincoln Hwy Cortland (60112) ***(G-7384)***
**Algen Enterprises Ltd**....217 428-4888
2020 E Locust St Decatur (62521) ***(G-7828)***
**Algus Packaging Inc**....815 756-1881
1212 E Taylor St Dekalb (60115) ***(G-8073)***
**Alhencam Seal Coat Inc**....217 422-4605
1887 Sangamon Rd Decatur (62521) ***(G-7829)***
**Ali Group North America Corp (HQ)**....847 215-6565
101 Corporate Woods Pkwy Vernon Hills (60061) ***(G-21144)***

**Alicom, Naperville** *Also called National Def Intelligence Inc (G-15818)*
**Alicona Corporation**....630 372-9900
1261 Humbracht Cir Ste G Bartlett (60103) *(G-1329)*
**Alicona Manufacturing Inc**....630 736-2718
1261 Humbracht Cir Ste A Bartlett (60103) *(G-1330)*
**Align Production Systems LLC**....217 423-6001
2230 N Brush College Rd Decatur (62526) *(G-7830)*
**Alin Machining Company Inc (PA)**....708 681-1043
3131 W Soffel Ave Melrose Park (60160) *(G-14585)*
**Alin Machining Company Inc**....708 345-8600
80 Kendall Point Dr Oswego (60543) *(G-16903)*
**Aline International LLC**....708 478-2471
9100 W 191st St Ste 103 Mokena (60448) *(G-14850)*
**All American Athletics Ltd**....815 432-8326
100 Laird Ln Watseka (60970) *(G-21413)*
**All American Chemical Co Inc**....847 297-2840
1701 N 33rd Ave Melrose Park (60160) *(G-14586)*
**All American Nut & Candy Corp**....630 595-6473
930 Fairway Dr Bensenville (60106) *(G-1823)*
**All American Spring Stamping**....847 928-9468
10220 Franklin Ave Franklin Park (60131) *(G-10389)*
**All American Trophy King Inc**....708 597-2121
13811 Cicero Ave Crestwood (60445) *(G-7474)*
**All American Washer Werks Inc**....847 566-9091
912 E High St Mundelein (60060) *(G-15468)*
**All American Wood Register Co**....815 356-1000
7103 Sands Rd Crystal Lake (60014) *(G-7528)*
**All Cell Technologies LLC**....773 922-1155
2321 W 41st St Chicago (60609) *(G-3805)*
**All Cnc Solutions Inc**....847 972-1139
7617 Parkside Ave Skokie (60077) *(G-19947)*
**All Container Inc**....847 677-2100
7060 N Lawndale Ave Lincolnwood (60712) *(G-13502)*
**All Cut Inc**....630 910-6505
8195 S Lemont Rd Darien (60561) *(G-7788)*
**All Electric Mtr Repr Svc Inc (PA)**....773 925-2404
6726 S Ashland Ave Chicago (60636) *(G-3806)*
**All Foam Industries, Elmhurst** *Also called K & S Service & Rental Corp (G-9893)*
**All Foam Pdts Safety Foam Proc, Buffalo Grove** *Also called All Foam Products Co (G-2653)*
**All Foam Products Co (PA)**....847 913-9341
2546 Live Oak Ln Buffalo Grove (60089) *(G-2653)*
**All For Dogs Inc**....708 744-4113
1707 Burshire Dr Plainfield (60586) *(G-17578)*
**All Fresh Food Products (PA)**....847 864-5030
2156 Green Bay Rd Evanston (60201) *(G-10007)*
**All Gear Inc**....847 564-9016
3675 Commercial Ave Northbrook (60062) *(G-16202)*
**All In Stitches**....309 944-4084
100 E Main St Geneseo (61254) *(G-10796)*
**All Line Inc**....630 820-1800
31w310 91st St Naperville (60564) *(G-15792)*
**All Metal Machine**....815 389-0168
14305 Dorr Rd South Beloit (61080) *(G-20136)*
**All Metal Recycling Company**....847 530-4825
409 N Addison Rd Villa Park (60181) *(G-21235)*
**All Nation Line Division, Carol Stream** *Also called Scale Railroad Equipment (G-3234)*
**All Pallet Service**....618 451-7545
1459 State St Granite City (62040) *(G-11262)*
**All Precision Mfg LLC**....217 563-7070
153 N 5th St Nokomis (62075) *(G-16055)*
**All Printing & Graphics Inc**....773 553-3049
125 S Clark St Fl 3 Chicago (60603) *(G-3807)*
**All Printing & Graphics Inc (PA)**....708 450-1512
2250 S 14th Ave Broadview (60155) *(G-2555)*
**All Pro Paving Inc**....815 806-2222
27 E 36th St Steger (60475) *(G-20566)*
**All Purpose Prtg & Bus Forms**....708 389-9192
12557 S Laramie Ave 2 Alsip (60803) *(G-431)*
**All Right Sales Inc**....773 558-4800
28w240 Trieste Ln West Chicago (60185) *(G-21654)*
**All Rite Industries Inc**....847 540-0300
470 Oakwood Rd Lake Zurich (60047) *(G-13038)*
**All Saints Monument Co Inc**....847 824-1248
20 S River Rd Des Plaines (60016) *(G-8145)*
**All Seasons Co, Decatur** *Also called All Seasons Heating & AC (G-7831)*
**All Seasons Heating & AC**....217 429-2022
167 Excelsior School Rd Decatur (62521) *(G-7831)*
**All Seasons Screen Prtg & EMB, Chicago** *Also called Wellspring Investments LLC (G-6955)*
**All She Wrote**....773 529-0100
825 W Armitage Ave Chicago (60614) *(G-3808)*
**All Signs & Wonders Co**....630 232-9019
1020 W Fabyan Pkwy Geneva (60134) *(G-10807)*
**All Spun Metal Products, Lombard** *Also called Spectracrafts Ltd (G-13856)*
**All Star Custom Awards**....630 428-1515
1203 Hidden Spring Dr Naperville (60540) *(G-15596)*
**All Star Injection Molders Inc**....630 978-4046
24w959 Ramm Dr Unit 5 Naperville (60564) *(G-15793)*
**All Star Publishing**....630 428-1515
1203 Hidden Spring Dr Naperville (60540) *(G-15597)*
**All Stars -N- Stitches Inc**....618 435-5555
418 E Main St Benton (62812) *(G-2021)*
**All Stone Inc**....815 529-1754
1525 Azalea Cir Romeoville (60446) *(G-18793)*
**All Style Awning Corporation**....708 343-2323
2100 W Lake St Ste A Melrose Park (60160) *(G-14587)*
**All Suburban Generator, Willowbrook** *Also called Michael Wilton Cstm Homes Inc (G-22221)*
**All Tech Systems & Install**....815 609-0685
11952 S Spaulding Schl Dr Plainfield (60585) *(G-17579)*
**All Type Hydraulics Corp**....618 585-4844
149 S Washington St Bunker Hill (62014) *(G-2803)*
**All Weather Courts Inc**....217 364-4546
Rr Box 276 Dawson (62520) *(G-7816)*
**All Weather Products Co LLC**....847 981-0386
1500 Greenleaf Ave Elk Grove Village (60007) *(G-9285)*
**All West Plastics Inc**....847 395-8830
606 Drom Ct Antioch (60002) *(G-616)*
**All Wood or Metal Radiator Cov**....773 973-7328
2933 W Greenleaf Ave Chicago (60645) *(G-3809)*
**All-American Sign Co Inc**....708 422-2203
5501 W 109th St Ste 1 Oak Lawn (60453) *(G-16599)*
**All-Brite Anodizing Co Inc (PA)**....708 562-0502
100 W Lake St Northlake (60164) *(G-16425)*
**All-Brite Sign Co Inc**....309 829-1551
1803 Marina Dr Normal (61761) *(G-16063)*
**All-Feed Proc & Packg Inc (PA)**....309 629-0001
210 S 1st St Alpha (61413) *(G-425)*
**All-Feed Proc & Packg Inc**....309 932-3119
717 W Division St Galva (61434) *(G-10782)*
**All-Pak Manufacturing Corp**....630 851-5859
1221 Jackson St Ste A-B Aurora (60505) *(G-1103)*
**All-Right Sign Inc**....708 754-6366
3628 Union Ave Steger (60475) *(G-20567)*
**All-Rite Spring Co**....815 675-1350
2200 Spring Ridge Dr Spring Grove (60081) *(G-20325)*
**All-State Industries Inc**....847 350-0460
2651 Carl Blvd Elk Grove Village (60007) *(G-9286)*
**All-Steel Structures Inc**....708 210-1313
16301 Vincennes Ave South Holland (60473) *(G-20241)*
**All-Style Custom Tops**....708 532-6606
5555 175th St Tinley Park (60477) *(G-20887)*
**All-Vac Industries Inc**....847 675-2290
7350 Central Park Ave Skokie (60076) *(G-19948)*
**All-Ways Quick Print**....708 403-8422
14609 Birch St Orland Park (60462) *(G-16841)*
**Allan Brooks & Associates Inc**....847 537-7500
413 Park Ave Lake Villa (60046) *(G-13010)*
**Allans Welding & Machine Inc**....618 392-3708
3815 E Ilinois Hwy 250 Olney (62450) *(G-16758)*
**Allcare Inc (PA)**....630 830-7486
2580 Foxfield Rd Ste 101 Saint Charles (60174) *(G-19133)*
**Allcell, Chicago** *Also called All Cell Technologies LLC (G-3805)*
**Allcom Products Illinois LLC**....847 468-8830
695 Sundown Rd South Elgin (60177) *(G-20180)*
**Allegheny Color Corporation**....815 741-1391
1401 Mound Rd Rockdale (60436) *(G-18213)*
**Allegheny Ludlum LLC**....708 974-8801
8687 S 77th Ave Bridgeview (60455) *(G-2460)*
**Allegion Lcn & Falcon Closers, Princeton** *Also called Allegion S&S US Holding Co (G-17742)*
**Allegion S&S US Holding Co**....815 875-3311
121 W Railroad Ave Princeton (61356) *(G-17742)*
**Allegra Coal City, Bourbonnais** *Also called Tgrv LLC (G-2407)*
**Allegra Marketing Print & Mail, Elk Grove Village** *Also called Woogl Corporation (G-9816)*
**Allegra Marketing Print Mail**....630 790-0444
1945 Wright Blvd Schaumburg (60193) *(G-19430)*
**Allegra Marketing Print Web, Aurora** *Also called Bat Business Services Inc (G-1118)*
**Allegra Mktg Print Mail Inc., Naperville** *Also called Spell It With Color Inc (G-15753)*
**Allegra Network LLC**....815 877-3400
1982 Belford North Dr Belvidere (61008) *(G-1730)*
**Allegra Network LLC**....630 801-9335
987 Oak Ave Aurora (60506) *(G-1104)*
**Allegra Print & Imaging, Evanston** *Also called Evanston Graphic Imaging Inc (G-10033)*
**Allegra Print & Imaging, Alsip** *Also called Anikam Inc (G-433)*
**Allegra Print & Imaging, Rolling Meadows** *Also called M & R Printing Inc (G-18742)*
**Allegra Print & Imaging, Glendale Heights** *Also called Rightway Printing Inc (G-11064)*
**Allegra Print & Imaging, Northbrook** *Also called Officers Printing Inc (G-16323)*
**Allegra Print & Imaging, Roselle** *Also called Snegde Deep (G-18978)*
**Allegra Print & Imaging, Aurora** *Also called Allegra Network LLC (G-1104)*
**Allegra Print & Imaging**....630 963-9100
2200 Ogden Ave Ste 500a Lisle (60532) *(G-13554)*
**Allegra Print & Imaging**....815 524-3902
576 W Taylor Rd Romeoville (60446) *(G-18794)*
**Allegra Print & Imaging Inc**....847 697-1434
909 Davis Rd Elgin (60123) *(G-8942)*
**Allegro Publishing Inc**....847 565-9083
2421 N Artesian Ave Chicago (60647) *(G-3810)*
**Allen Awards, Streamwood** *Also called A 1 Trophies Awards & Engrv (G-20638)*

ALPHABETIC

# Allen Entertainment Management — ALPHABETIC SECTION

**Allen Entertainment Management**..................630 752-0903
471 Essex Pl  Carol Stream  (60188)  *(G-3096)*

**Allen Larson**..................773 454-2210
1914 N Washtenaw Ave  Chicago  (60647)  *(G-3811)*

**Allen Paper Company**..................312 454-4500
641 W Lake St Ste L101  Chicago  (60661)  *(G-3812)*

**Allen Popovich**..................815 712-7404
23215 Cooper Rd  Custer Park  (60481)  *(G-7686)*

**Allendale Gravel Co  Inc (PA)**..................618 263-3521
18306 Wabash 18 Ave  Allendale  (62410)  *(G-420)*

**Allenform Con Forming Pdts, Itasca** Also called Kodiak Concrete Forms Inc  *(G-12298)*

**Allens Farm Quality Meats**..................217 896-2532
Rr 49  Homer  (61849)  *(G-12073)*

**Allergan  Inc**..................714 246-4500
605 Tri State Pkwy  Gurnee  (60031)  *(G-11426)*

**Allerton Charter Coach**..................217 344-2600
714 S 6th St  Champaign  (61820)  *(G-3445)*

**Allerton Supply Company**..................217 896-2522
1050 N &Amp 2600 E  Homer  (61849)  *(G-12074)*

**Allform Manufacturing Co**..................847 680-0144
342 4th St  Libertyville  (60048)  *(G-13301)*

**Allfresh Food Products  Inc (HQ)**..................847 869-3100
2156 Green Bay Rd  Evanston  (60201)  *(G-10008)*

**Alliance Commodities Illinois, Oak Brook** Also called Forestree  Inc  *(G-16516)*

**Alliance Creative Group  Inc (PA)**..................847 885-1800
1066 National Pkwy  Schaumburg  (60173)  *(G-19431)*

**Alliance Display, Dekalb** Also called Rock-Tenn Company  *(G-8116)*

**Alliance Door and Hardware LLC**..................630 451-7070
9015-17 Odell Ave  Bridgeview  (60455)  *(G-2461)*

**Alliance Envelope & Print LLC**..................847 446-4079
854 Prospect Ave  Winnetka  (60093)  *(G-22301)*

**Alliance For Illinois Mfg**..................773 594-9292
8420 W Bryn Mawr Ave  Chicago  (60631)  *(G-3813)*

**Alliance Graphics**..................312 280-8000
1652 W Ogden Ave Apt 4  Chicago  (60612)  *(G-3814)*

**Alliance Investment Corp**..................847 933-0400
9150 Kenneth Ave  Skokie  (60076)  *(G-19949)*

**Alliance Laser Sales Inc (PA)**..................847 487-1945
275 Industrial Dr  Wauconda  (60084)  *(G-21438)*

**Alliance Pipeline Inc**..................815 941-5874
6155 E Us Route 6  Morris  (60450)  *(G-15092)*

**Alliance Plastics**..................888 643-1432
830 Fairway Dr Ste 104  Bensenville  (60106)  *(G-1824)*

**Alliance Service Co**..................708 746-5026
21200 S La Grange Rd  Frankfort  (60423)  *(G-10292)*

**Alliance Specialties Corp**..................847 487-1945
275 Industrial Dr  Wauconda  (60084)  *(G-21439)*

**Alliance Steel 1, LLC, Bedford Park** Also called A2 Sales  LLC  *(G-1532)*

**Alliance Steel Corporation**..................708 924-1200
6499 W 66th Pl  Bedford Park  (60638)  *(G-1535)*

**Alliance Tool & Manufacturing**..................708 345-5444
91 Wilcox St  Maywood  (60153)  *(G-14415)*

**Alliance Wheel Services LLC**..................309 444-4334
302 W Holland St  Washington  (61571)  *(G-21377)*

**Alliance Wor Processing LLC, Dahlgren** Also called Hamilton County Coal  LLC  *(G-7690)*

**Allie Woodworking**..................847 244-1919
3035 Sunset Ave  Waukegan  (60087)  *(G-21522)*

**Allied Asphalt Paving Co Inc (PA)**..................630 289-6080
1100 Brandt Dr  Elgin  (60120)  *(G-8943)*

**Allied Asphalt Paving Co Inc**..................847 824-2848
10555 Waveland Ave  Franklin Park  (60131)  *(G-10390)*

**Allied Asphalt Paving Company, Hoffman Estates** Also called Plote Construction Inc  *(G-12036)*

**Allied Die Casting Company III, Franklin Park** Also called RCM Industries  Inc  *(G-10571)*

**Allied Die Casting Corporation**..................815 385-9330
3923 W West Ave  McHenry  (60050)  *(G-14479)*

**Allied Garage Door  Inc**..................630 279-0795
310 W Gerri Ln  Addison  (60101)  *(G-29)*

**Allied Gear Co**..................773 287-8742
4901 W Arthington St  Chicago  (60644)  *(G-3815)*

**Allied Graphics Inc**..................847 419-8830
1398 Busch Pkwy  Buffalo Grove  (60089)  *(G-2654)*

**Allied Instrument Service Inc**..................708 788-1912
3136 Clarence Ave  Berwyn  (60402)  *(G-2056)*

**Allied Iron & Steel, Peoria** Also called A Miller & Co  *(G-17298)*

**Allied Machine Tool & Dye**..................708 388-7676
13430 Kolmar Ave  Crestwood  (60445)  *(G-7475)*

**Allied Metal Co (PA)**..................312 225-2800
1300 N Kostner Ave  Chicago  (60651)  *(G-3816)*

**Allied Print & Copy, Chicago** Also called Allied Printing Inc  *(G-3817)*

**Allied Printing Inc**..................773 334-5200
5640 N Broadway St  Chicago  (60660)  *(G-3817)*

**Allied Production Drilling**..................815 969-0940
4004 Auburn St  Rockford  (61101)  *(G-18259)*

**Allied Rivet  Inc**..................630 208-0120
1172 Commerce Dr  Geneva  (60134)  *(G-10808)*

**Allied Scoring Tables  Inc**..................815 654-8807
5417 Forest Hills Ct  Loves Park  (61111)  *(G-13918)*

**Allied Stone, Milan** Also called Riverstone Group  Inc  *(G-14804)*

**Allied Telesis  Inc**..................312 726-1990
123 N Wacker Dr Ste 2130  Chicago  (60606)  *(G-3818)*

**Allied Tube & Conduit Corp (HQ)**..................708 339-1610
16100 Lathrop Ave  Harvey  (60426)  *(G-11652)*

**Allied Tube and Conduit**..................708 225-2955
16100 Center Ave  Harvey  (60426)  *(G-11653)*

**Allied Welding, Chillicothe** Also called Ter-Son Corporation  *(G-7171)*

**Allied Welding  Inc**..................309 274-6227
1820 N Santa Fe Ave  Chillicothe  (61523)  *(G-7161)*

**Allied-Locke Industries Inc**..................800 435-7752
1020 Subic Rd  Dixon  (61021)  *(G-8322)*

**Alligator Rec & Artist MGT Inc**..................773 973-7736
1441 W Devon Ave  Chicago  (60660)  *(G-3819)*

**Allison's Comfort Shoes, Maryville** Also called New Step Orthotic Lab  Inc  *(G-14345)*

**Allkut Tool Incorporated**..................815 476-9656
601 Davy Ln  Wilmington  (60481)  *(G-22269)*

**Allmetal Inc (PA)**..................630 250-8090
1 Pierce Pl Ste 900  Itasca  (60143)  *(G-12225)*

**Allmetal  Inc**..................630 766-8500
636 Thomas Dr  Bensenville  (60106)  *(G-1825)*

**Allmetal  Inc**..................630 766-1407
224-230 Foster Ave  Bensenville  (60106)  *(G-1826)*

**Allmetal  Inc**..................630 350-2524
377 Balm Ct  Wood Dale  (60191)  *(G-22335)*

**Allocator Logistics, South Holland** Also called Eunice Larry  *(G-20268)*

**Alloy Chrome Inc**..................847 678-2880
9328 Bernice Ave  Schiller Park  (60176)  *(G-19800)*

**Alloy Engineering & Casting Co, Champaign** Also called Illinois Ni Cast  LLC  *(G-3500)*

**Alloy Rod Products  Inc**..................815 562-8200
601 W New York St Ste 4  Aurora  (60506)  *(G-1105)*

**Alloy Rod Products  Inc**..................815 562-8200
100 Quarry Rd  Rochelle  (61068)  *(G-18078)*

**Alloy Sling Chains  Inc (PA)**..................708 647-4900
1406 175th St  East Hazel Crest  (60429)  *(G-8664)*

**Alloy Specialties  Inc**..................815 586-4728
32028 N 1500 East Rd  Blackstone  (61313)  *(G-2087)*

**Alloy Tech**..................217 253-3939
608 E Pinzon St  Tuscola  (61953)  *(G-21014)*

**Alloy Welding Corp**..................708 345-6756
2033 Janice Ave  Melrose Park  (60160)  *(G-14588)*

**Alloyd Brands**..................843 383-7000
1500 Paramount Pkwy  Batavia  (60510)  *(G-1408)*

**Alloys Tech Inc**..................708 248-5041
3305 Butler St  S Chicago Hts  (60411)  *(G-19099)*

**Alloyweld Inspection Co  Inc**..................630 595-2145
796 Maple Ln  Bensenville  (60106)  *(G-1827)*

**Allprint Graphics Inc**..................847 519-9898
1034 National Pkwy  Schaumburg  (60173)  *(G-19432)*

**Allpro Fleet Maint Systems**..................708 430-1400
8614 Lamon Ave  Burbank  (60459)  *(G-2806)*

**Allquip Co Inc**..................309 944-6153
524 E Exchange St  Geneseo  (61254)  *(G-10797)*

**Allscripts Healthcare  LLC**..................312 506-1200
222 Merchandise Mart Plz  Chicago  (60654)  *(G-3820)*

**Allscripts Healthcare  LLC**..................800 334-8534
222 Merchandise Mart Plz  Chicago  (60654)  *(G-3821)*

**Allscrpts Hlthcare Sltions Inc (PA)**..................312 506-1200
222 Merchandise Mart Plz  Chicago  (60654)  *(G-3822)*

**Allscrpts Hlthcare Sltions Inc**..................312 506-1200
222 Merchandise Mart Plz # 2024  Chicago  (60654)  *(G-3823)*

**Allstar Dental  Inc**..................847 325-5134
204 Us Highway 45  Vernon Hills  (60061)  *(G-21145)*

**Allstar Embroidery**..................847 913-1133
240 Blackthorn Dr  Buffalo Grove  (60089)  *(G-2655)*

**Allstar Fasteners  Inc**..................847 640-7827
1550 Arthur Ave  Elk Grove Village  (60007)  *(G-9287)*

**Allstar Tool & Molds Inc**..................630 766-0162
799 Eagle Dr Ste A  Bensenville  (60106)  *(G-1828)*

**Allstate Metal Fabricators Inc**..................630 860-1500
365 Beinoris Dr  Wood Dale  (60191)  *(G-22336)*

**Allstate Printing Inc**..................847 640-4401
620 Bennett Rd  Elk Grove Village  (60007)  *(G-9288)*

**Allstates Rubber & Tool Corp**..................708 342-1030
8201 183rd St Ste M  Tinley Park  (60487)  *(G-20888)*

**Alltec Gates Inc (PA)**..................708 301-9361
15941 Harlem Ave Ste 325  Tinley Park  (60477)  *(G-20889)*

**Alltech Associates  Inc (HQ)**..................773 261-2252
415 S Kilpatrick Ave  Chicago  (60644)  *(G-3824)*

**Alltech Plastics Inc**..................847 352-2309
821 Thornton Ct Apt 2b  Schaumburg  (60193)  *(G-19433)*

**Alltemated  Inc (PA)**..................847 394-5800
3353 N Ridge Ave  Arlington Heights  (60004)  *(G-707)*

**Allured Publishing Corporation**..................630 653-2155
336 Gundersen Dr Ste A  Carol Stream  (60188)  *(G-3097)*

**Allwood Cabinet**..................773 778-1242
3343 W Columbus Ave  Chicago  (60652)  *(G-3825)*

**Ally Global Corporation**..................773 822-3373
6033 N Sheridan Rd 23d  Chicago  (60660)  *(G-3826)*

**Ally International Trading, Chicago** Also called Ally Global Corporation  *(G-3826)*

**Allyn House, The, Nauvoo** Also called Missouri Wood Craft Inc  *(G-15853)*

**Alm Distributors LLC** ........ 708 865-8000
2060 Janice Ave Melrose Park (60160) ***(G-14589)***
**Alm Materials Handling LLC** ........ 815 673-5546
200 Benchmark Indus Dr Streator (61364) ***(G-20682)***
**Alm Positioners Inc** ........ 309 787-6200
8080 Centennial Expy Rock Island (61201) ***(G-18159)***
**Almacen Inc** ........ 847 934-7955
927 Kirkwood Dr Inverness (60067) ***(G-12201)***
**Alois Box Co Inc** ........ 708 681-4090
2000 N Mannheim Rd Melrose Park (60160) ***(G-14590)***
**Alomar Inc** ........ 312 855-0714
5 S Wabash Ave Ste 316 Chicago (60603) ***(G-3827)***
**Alpha Acrylic Design** ........ 847 818-8178
3359 N Ridge Ave Ste A Arlington Heights (60004) ***(G-708)***
**Alpha AG Inc (PA)** ........ 217 546-2724
8295 Bomke Rd Pleasant Plains (62677) ***(G-17681)***
**Alpha Assembly Solutions Inc** ........ 847 426-4241
2541 Technology Dr Elgin (60124) ***(G-8944)***
**Alpha Bag Group, Rockford** *Also called ABG Bag Inc* ***(G-18247)***
**Alpha Bedding LLC** ........ 847 550-5110
1290 Ensell Rd Lake Zurich (60047) ***(G-13039)***
**Alpha Circuit Corporation** ........ 630 617-5555
730 N Oaklawn Ave Elmhurst (60126) ***(G-9833)***
**Alpha Coating Technologies LLC** ........ 630 268-8787
1735 W Cortland Ct Addison (60101) ***(G-30)***
**Alpha Industries Inc** ........ 847 945-1740
1720 Christopher Dr Deerfield (60015) ***(G-7974)***
**Alpha Industries MGT Inc** ........ 773 359-8000
1650 E 95th St Chicago (60617) ***(G-3828)***
**Alpha Laser of Chicago** ........ 708 478-0464
9632 194th Pl Mokena (60448) ***(G-14851)***
**Alpha Machine Corp** ........ 708 532-2313
1742 Ferro Dr New Lenox (60451) ***(G-15869)***
**Alpha Natural Resources Inc** ........ 618 298-2394
1000 Beall Woods Dr Keensburg (62852) ***(G-12660)***
**Alpha Omega Plastics Company** ........ 847 956-8777
1099 Touhy Ave Elk Grove Village (60007) ***(G-9289)***
**Alpha Omega Profile Extrusion** ........ 847 956-8777
1099 Touhy Ave Elk Grove Village (60007) ***(G-9290)***
**Alpha Packaging Minnesota Inc** ........ 507 454-3830
6824 Paysphere Cir Chicago (60674) ***(G-3829)***
**Alpha Pages LLC (PA)** ........ 847 733-1740
107 W Van Buren St # 203 Chicago (60605) ***(G-3830)***
**Alpha Pcb Designs Inc** ........ 773 631-5543
6815 W Higgins Ave Chicago (60656) ***(G-3831)***
**Alpha Precision Inc** ........ 630 553-7331
9750 Rte 126 Yorkville (60560) ***(G-22648)***
**Alpha Printing, Willowbrook** *Also called Zone Inc* ***(G-22240)***
**Alpha Products Inc** ........ 708 594-3883
5570 W 70th Pl Bedford Park (60638) ***(G-1536)***
**Alpha Services II Inc** ........ 618 997-9999
1806 N Court St Marion (62959) ***(G-14252)***
**Alpha Star Tool and Mold Inc** ........ 815 455-2802
11 Burdent Dr Crystal Lake (60014) ***(G-7529)***
**Alpha Swiss Industries Inc** ........ 815 455-3031
700 Tek Dr Crystal Lake (60014) ***(G-7530)***
**Alpha Tekniko, Lake Zurich** *Also called Alpha Bedding LLC* ***(G-13039)***
**Alpha Tool & Die Inc** ........ 847 622-8849
74 Lockman Cir Elgin (60123) ***(G-8945)***
**Alphabet Shop Inc** ........ 847 888-3150
300 Elgin Ave Elgin (60120) ***(G-8946)***
**Alphadigital Inc** ........ 708 482-4488
417 N La Grange Rd La Grange Park (60526) ***(G-12752)***
**Alphagage** ........ 815 391-6400
5245 27th Ave Rockford (61109) ***(G-18260)***
**AlphaGraphics, Chicago** *Also called Moran Graphics Inc* ***(G-5803)***
**AlphaGraphics, Mokena** *Also called Printers Quill Inc* ***(G-14897)***
**AlphaGraphics, Aurora** *Also called Cynlar Inc* ***(G-992)***
**AlphaGraphics, Bloomington** *Also called Grandcentral Enterprises Inc* ***(G-2171)***
**AlphaGraphics, Vernon Hills** *Also called P H C Enterprises Inc* ***(G-21186)***
**AlphaGraphics, Des Plaines** *Also called Cloverdale Corporation* ***(G-8171)***
**AlphaGraphics, Schaumburg** *Also called Cifuentes Luis & Nicole Inc* ***(G-19472)***
**AlphaGraphics, Bannockburn** *Also called Print & Design Services LLC* ***(G-1264)***
**AlphaGraphics, Saint Charles** *Also called Avid of Illinois Inc* ***(G-19140)***
**AlphaGraphics, La Grange Park** *Also called Alphadigital Inc* ***(G-12752)***
**AlphaGraphics, Elk Grove Village** *Also called Gamma Alpha Visual* ***(G-9496)***
**AlphaGraphics, Chicago** *Also called Basswood Associates Inc* ***(G-4053)***
**AlphaGraphics** ........ 630 261-1227
17w703 Butterfield Rd A Oakbrook Terrace (60181) ***(G-16694)***
**AlphaGraphics 468, Wood Dale** *Also called Bitforms Inc* ***(G-22345)***
**AlphaGraphics Printshops** ........ 630 964-9600
1997 Ohio St Ste B Lisle (60532) ***(G-13555)***
**AlphaGraphics US 590, Crystal Lake** *Also called Jamether Incorporated* ***(G-7593)***
**Alpina Manufacturing LLC** ........ 773 202-8887
6460 W Cortland St Chicago (60707) ***(G-3832)***
**Alpine Amusement Co Inc** ........ 708 233-9131
8037 Neva Ave Oak Lawn (60459) ***(G-16600)***
**Alpine Energy Systems LLC** ........ 630 581-4840
700 Commerce Dr Ste 500 Oak Brook (60523) ***(G-16487)***
**Alpine Imports, Loves Park** *Also called Craft World Inc* ***(G-13928)***
**Alpine Refrigeration, Streamwood** *Also called Kool Technologies Inc* ***(G-20662)***
**Alply Insulated Panels LLC** ........ 217 324-6700
1401 Eilerman Ave Litchfield (62056) ***(G-13680)***
**Alps Group Inc (PA)** ........ 815 469-3800
8779 W Laraway Rd Frankfort (60423) ***(G-10293)***
**Alps Group Inc** ........ 815 469-3800
55 E Monroe St Ste 3800 Chicago (60603) ***(G-3833)***
**Alps Group, The, Frankfort** *Also called Alps Group Inc* ***(G-10293)***
**Alro Group, Melrose Park** *Also called Alro Steel Corporation* ***(G-14591)***
**Alro Steel Corporation** ........ 708 202-3200
4501 James Pl Melrose Park (60160) ***(G-14591)***
**Alro Steel Corporation** ........ 708 534-5400
777 Industrial Dr Park Forest (60484) ***(G-17176)***
**Alsip Express Newspaper, Midlothian** *Also called Southwest Messenger Press Inc* ***(G-14769)***
**Alsip Mfg Inc** ........ 708 333-4446
16700 Carse Ave Harvey (60426) ***(G-11654)***
**Alsip Minimill LLC** ........ 708 272-8700
13101 S Pulaski Rd Alsip (60803) ***(G-432)***
**Alstat Wood Products** ........ 618 684-5167
456 Highway 4 Murphysboro (62966) ***(G-15571)***
**Alster Machining Corp** ........ 773 384-2370
4243 W Diversey Ave Chicago (60639) ***(G-3834)***
**Alstom Transportation Inc** ........ 630 369-2201
1001 Frontenac Rd Naperville (60563) ***(G-15598)***
**Alston Race Cars, Antioch** *Also called Glk Enterprises Inc* ***(G-636)***
**Alta Vista Graphic Corporation** ........ 773 267-2530
3435 N Kimball Ave Chicago (60618) ***(G-3835)***
**Alta Vista Solutions Inc** ........ 312 473-3050
2035 W Grand Ave Chicago (60612) ***(G-3836)***
**Altair Corporation (del) (HQ)** ........ 847 634-9540
350 Barclay Blvd Lincolnshire (60069) ***(G-13426)***
**Altak Inc** ........ 630 622-0300
250 Covington Dr Bloomingdale (60108) ***(G-2092)***
**Altamira Art Glass** ........ 708 848-3799
202 And A Half S Mrion St Oak Park (60302) ***(G-16652)***
**Altamont Co** ........ 800 626-5774
901 N Church St Thomasboro (61878) ***(G-20859)***
**Altamont News** ........ 618 483-6176
7 Do It Dr Altamont (62411) ***(G-548)***
**Altathera Pharmaceuticals LLC** ........ 312 445-8900
200 S Wacker Dr Ste 3100 Chicago (60606) ***(G-3837)***
**Altec Printing LLC** ........ 708 489-2484
4931 141st St Crestwood (60445) ***(G-7476)***
**Alter Recycling, Bartonville** *Also called Alter Trading Corporation* ***(G-1390)***
**Alter Scrap, Quincy** *Also called Alter Trading Corporation* ***(G-17791)***
**Alter Trading Corporation** ........ 217 223-0156
2834 Gardner Expy Quincy (62305) ***(G-17791)***
**Alter Trading Corporation** ........ 309 828-6084
501 E Stewart St Bloomington (61701) ***(G-2143)***
**Alter Trading Corporation** ........ 309 697-6161
7000 S Adams St Ste 2 Bartonville (61607) ***(G-1390)***
**Altera Corporation** ........ 847 240-0313
425 N Martingale Rd # 1320 Schaumburg (60173) ***(G-19434)***
**Alternative Bearings Corp** ........ 847 240-9630
870 E Higgins Rd Ste 135 Schaumburg (60173) ***(G-19435)***
**Alternative Technologies** ........ 888 858-4678
123 N 10th Ave Melrose Park (60160) ***(G-14592)***
**Alternative TS** ........ 618 257-0230
5300 N Belt W Belleville (62226) ***(G-1608)***
**Alternative Wastewater Systems** ........ 630 761-8720
1815 Phelps Dr Batavia (60510) ***(G-1409)***
**Althea Crutex Inc** ........ 630 595-7200
148 E Irving Park Rd Wood Dale (60191) ***(G-22337)***
**Altivity Packaging, Carol Stream** *Also called Graphic Packaging Holding Co* ***(G-3161)***
**Altivity Packaging, Carol Stream** *Also called Graphic Packaging Intl Inc* ***(G-3163)***
**Altman & Koehler Foundry** ........ 773 373-7737
505 W Root St Chicago (60609) ***(G-3838)***
**Altman Manufacturing Co Inc** ........ 630 963-0031
1990 Ohio St Lisle (60532) ***(G-13556)***
**Altman Pattern and Foundry Co** ........ 773 586-9100
6820 W 63rd St Chicago (60638) ***(G-3839)***
**Alto Vinyards Inc (PA)** ........ 618 893-4898
8515 Highway 127 Alto Pass (62905) ***(G-556)***
**Alton Industries Inc** ........ 708 865-2000
2700 S 21st Ave Broadview (60155) ***(G-2556)***
**Alton Sheet Metal Corp** ........ 618 462-0609
801 E Broadway Alton (62002) ***(G-559)***
**Alton Steel Inc** ........ 618 463-4490
5 Cut St Alton (62002) ***(G-560)***
**Altona Co** ........ 815 232-7819
70 E Monterey St Freeport (61032) ***(G-10645)***
**Altonat, Altamont** *Also called Better News Papers Inc* ***(G-550)***
**Altorfer Power Systems** ........ 309 697-1234
6315 W Fauber Rd Bartonville (61607) ***(G-1391)***
**Altran Corp** ........ 815 455-5650
365 E Terra Cotta Ave Crystal Lake (60014) ***(G-7531)***



(PA)=Parent Co (HQ)=Headquarters (DH)=Div Headquarters
2017 Harris Illinois
Industrial Directory
1159

# ALPHABETIC SECTION

**Alu-Bra Foundry Inc** .................................................. 630 766-3112
630 E Green St Bensenville (60106) *(G-1829)*
**Alum-I-Tank Inc** ......................................................... 815 943-6649
11317 N Us Highway 14 Harvard (60033) *(G-11619)*
**Alumafloor & More Inc** .............................................. 630 628-0226
870 S Fiene Dr Addison (60101) *(G-31)*
**Alumapro Inc** .............................................................. 224 569-3650
1 Union Special Plz Huntley (60142) *(G-12131)*
**Aluminite of Paris** ...................................................... 217 463-2233
2009 S Main St Paris (61944) *(G-17140)*
**Aluminum and Zinc Die, Schiller Park** Also called Soldy Manufacturing Inc *(G-19875)*
**Aluminum Case Co, Chicago** Also called Mfz Ventures Inc *(G-5715)*
**Aluminum Castings Corporation** .............................. 309 343-8910
340 S Kellogg St Galesburg (61401) *(G-10737)*
**Aluminum Coil Anodizing Corp (PA)** ......................... 630 837-4000
501 E Lake St Streamwood (60107) *(G-20641)*
**Aluminum Drive Line Products** ................................. 708 946-9777
746 Penfield St Beecher (60401) *(G-1596)*
**Alumitank, Harvard** Also called Alum-I-Tank Inc *(G-11619)*
**Alva/Amco Pharmacal Companies** ........................... 847 663-0700
7711 N Merrimac Ave Niles (60714) *(G-15959)*
**Alvar Inc** .................................................................... 309 248-7523
112 State Route 89 Washburn (61570) *(G-21374)*
**Alvarez & Marsal Inc** ................................................ 312 601-4220
540 W Madison St Fl 18 Chicago (60661) *(G-3840)*
**Alwan Printing Inc** .................................................... 708 598-9600
7825 S Roberts Rd Bridgeview (60455) *(G-2462)*
**Always There Express Corp** ..................................... 773 931-3744
20w538 Elizabeth Dr Downers Grove (60516) *(G-8386)*
**Alyce Designs Inc (PA)** ............................................. 847 966-6933
7901 Caldwell Ave Morton Grove (60053) *(G-15187)*
**AM Harper Products Inc** .......................................... 312 767-8283
2300 W Jarvis Ave Apt 3 Chicago (60645) *(G-3841)*
**AM Ko Oriental Foods** .............................................. 217 398-2922
101 E Springfield Ave Champaign (61820) *(G-3446)*
**AM Metal Spinning Co Inc** ........................................ 630 616-8634
756 Larson Ln Bensenville (60106) *(G-1830)*
**AM PM Printers, Cortland** Also called Michael Burza *(G-7393)*
**AM Precision Machine Inc** ....................................... 847 439-9955
170 Lively Blvd Elk Grove Village (60007) *(G-9291)*
**AM Swiss Screw Mch Pdts Inc** ................................ 847 468-9300
345 Industrial Dr South Elgin (60177) *(G-20181)*
**Am-Don Partnership** ................................................. 217 355-7750
1819 S Neil St Ste A Champaign (61820) *(G-3447)*
**Am-Ko Oriental Grocery, Champaign** Also called AM Ko Oriental Foods *(G-3446)*
**Am2pat Inc (PA)** ....................................................... 847 726-9443
3034 W Devon Ave Chicago (60659) *(G-3842)*
**AMA SUBSCRIPTIONS, Chicago** Also called American Medical Association *(G-3863)*
**Amada America Inc** .................................................. 877 262-3287
1091 W Hawthorn Dr Itasca (60143) *(G-12226)*
**Amag Manufacturing Inc** .......................................... 773 667-5184
4940 S East End Ave 11c Chicago (60615) *(G-3843)*
**Amaitis and Associates Inc (PA)** ............................. 847 428-1269
810 Lively Blvd Wood Dale (60191) *(G-22338)*
**Amani Froyo LLC** ...................................................... 941 744-1111
2005 S Meyers Rd Apt 316 Oakbrook Terrace (60181) *(G-16695)*
**Amar Plastics Inc** ..................................................... 630 627-4105
100 W Industrial Rd Addison (60101) *(G-32)*
**Amav Enterprises Ltd** ............................................... 630 761-3077
1921 W Wilson St Ste A Batavia (60510) *(G-1410)*
**Amazing Cabinets & Design Corp** ............................ 773 405-0174
2400 Delta Ln Elk Grove Village (60007) *(G-9292)*
**Ambassador Printing, Chicago** Also called Babak Inc *(G-4024)*
**Ambassador Steel Corporation** ............................... 815 876-9089
28 W Mechanic St Princeton (61356) *(G-17743)*
**Ambassador Steel Corporation** ............................... 815 929-3770
1050 Saint George Rd Bourbonnais (60914) *(G-2387)*
**Amber Engineering and Mfg Co** ............................... 847 595-6966
2400 Brickvale Dr Elk Grove Village (60007) *(G-9293)*
**Amber Soft Inc** .......................................................... 630 377-6945
28214 W Northwest Hwy Lake Barrington (60010) *(G-12799)*
**Amberaw Asphalt Materials, Lawrenceville** Also called Asphalt Products Inc *(G-13195)*
**Amberleaf Cabinetry Inc** .......................................... 773 247-8282
1400 W 37th St Chicago (60609) *(G-3844)*
**Ambi-Design Incorporated** ....................................... 815 964-7568
4654 Crested Butte Trl Rockford (61114) *(G-18261)*
**Ambient Lightning and Electric** ............................... 708 529-3434
10033 Menard Ave Oak Lawn (60453) *(G-16601)*
**Ambir Technology Inc** ............................................... 630 530-5400
820 Sivert Dr Wood Dale (60191) *(G-22339)*
**Amboy News** ............................................................. 815 857-2311
245 E Main St Amboy (61310) *(G-597)*
**Ambraw Asphalt Materials Inc** ................................. 618 943-4716
S 15th St Lawrenceville (62439) *(G-13194)*
**Ambrotos Inc** ............................................................ 815 355-8217
4219 Belson Ln Crystal Lake (60014) *(G-7532)*
**Amcast Inc** ............................................................... 630 766-7450
350 Meyer Rd Bensenville (60106) *(G-1831)*
**Amco Engineering Co, Des Plaines** Also called IMS Engineered Products LLC *(G-8211)*

**Amco Machines Division, Somonauk** Also called Precision Entps Fndry Mch Inc *(G-20129)*
**Amcol, Belvidere** Also called American Colloid Company *(G-1731)*
**Amcol, Hoffman Estates** Also called American Colloid Company *(G-11992)*
**Amcol Hlth Buty Solutions Inc (HQ)** ........................ 847 851-1300
2870 Forbs Ave Hoffman Estates (60192) *(G-11990)*
**Amcol International Corp (HQ)** ................................ 847 851-1500
2870 Forbs Ave Hoffman Estates (60192) *(G-11991)*
**Amcor Flexibles LLC (HQ)** ....................................... 224 313-7000
2150 E Lake Cook Rd Buffalo Grove (60089) *(G-2656)*
**Amcor Phrm Packg USA LLC** ................................... 847 298-5626
1731 S Mount Prospect Rd Des Plaines (60018) *(G-8146)*
**Amcor Rigid Plastics Usa LLC** ................................ 630 406-3500
1300 S River St Batavia (60510) *(G-1411)*
**Amcor Rigid Plastics Usa LLC** ................................ 630 773-3235
750 Expressway Dr Itasca (60143) *(G-12227)*
**Amcor Rigid Plastics Usa LLC** ................................ 630 406-3500
1300 S River St Batavia (60510) *(G-1412)*
**Amcraft Manufacturing Inc** ..................................... 847 439-4565
580 Lively Blvd Elk Grove Village (60007) *(G-9294)*
**AMD Industries Inc (PA)** .......................................... 708 863-8900
4620 W 19th St Cicero (60804) *(G-7178)*
**Amedico Laboratories LLC** ..................................... 347 857-7546
17w173 16th St Oakbrook Terrace (60181) *(G-16696)*
**Amelio Bros Meats** ................................................... 708 300-2920
4322 Whitehall Ln Richton Park (60471) *(G-17975)*
**Amenities Home Design** .......................................... 312 421-2450
1529 W Glenlake Ave Chicago (60660) *(G-3845)*
**Amer Needle & Novelty, Buffalo Grove** Also called American Needle Inc *(G-2657)*
**Amer Nitrogen Co** .................................................... 847 681-1068
184 Leonard Wood S # 107 Highland Park (60035) *(G-11823)*
**Amer Sports Company (HQ)** .................................... 773 714-6400
8750 W Bryn Mawr Ave Chicago (60631) *(G-3846)*
**Ameralloy Steel Corporation** .................................. 847 967-0600
7848 Merrimac Ave Morton Grove (60053) *(G-15188)*
**Amerex Corporation** ................................................ 309 382-4389
540 S Main St North Pekin (61554) *(G-16192)*
**Ameri Label Company** .............................................. 847 895-8000
2015 Pennsbury Ln Bartlett (60133) *(G-1315)*
**Ameri Rolls and Guides** ........................................... 815 588-0486
337 Clover Ridge Dr Lockport (60441) *(G-13703)*
**Ameri-Tex** ................................................................. 847 247-0777
1520 Mccormick Blvd Mundelein (60060) *(G-15469)*
**Ameribest Fasteners, Schiller Park** Also called Gayton Group Inc *(G-19833)*
**America Display Inc** ................................................. 708 430-7000
10061 S 76th Ave Bridgeview (60455) *(G-2463)*
**America International Dist, Chicago** Also called Sign America *(G-6507)*
**America Printing Inc** ................................................ 847 229-8358
716 Gregor Ln Wheeling (60090) *(G-22002)*
**American Ad Bag Company Inc** .............................. 815 338-0300
1510 Lamb Rd Woodstock (60098) *(G-22538)*
**American Advertising Assoc Inc** ............................ 773 312-5110
9101 S Lake Shore Dr Chicago (60617) *(G-3847)*
**American Aerospace Material, Franklin Park** Also called Mandel Metals Inc *(G-10521)*
**American Air Filter Co Inc** ...................................... 502 637-0011
24828 Network Pl Chicago (60673) *(G-3848)*
**American Alum Extrusion Co LLC** .......................... 877 896-2236
5253 Mccurry Rd Roscoe (61073) *(G-18889)*
**American Apparels & Promotions, Lake In The Hills** Also called Graphic Source Group Inc *(G-12995)*
**American Asp Surfc Recycl Inc** .............................. 708 448-9540
13301 Southwest Hwy Ste H Orland Park (60462) *(G-16842)*
**American Assn Endodontists** ................................. 312 266-7255
211 E Chicago Ave # 1100 Chicago (60611) *(G-3849)*
**American Assn Insur Svcs (PA)** ............................. 630 681-8347
701 Warrenville Rd # 100 Lisle (60532) *(G-13557)*
**American Assn Nurosurgeons Inc (PA)** ................. 847 378-0500
5550 Meadowbrook Dr Rolling Meadows (60008) *(G-18709)*
**American Association of Indivi (PA)** ...................... 312 280-0170
625 N Michigan Ave # 401 Chicago (60611) *(G-3850)*
**American Bakeware, Northbrook** Also called Harris Potteries LP *(G-16268)*
**American Bar Association (PA)** .............................. 312 988-5000
321 N Clark St Ste Ll2 Chicago (60654) *(G-3851)*
**American Bar Foundation** ....................................... 312 988-6500
750 N Lk Shr Dr Fl 4th Chicago (60611) *(G-3852)*
**American Bare Conductor Inc** ................................ 815 224-3422
2969 Chartres St La Salle (61301) *(G-12762)*
**American Bee Journal, The, Hamilton** Also called Dadant & Sons Inc *(G-11533)*
**American Bell Screen Prtg Co** ................................ 815 623-5522
11447 2nd St Ste 1 Roscoe (61073) *(G-18890)*
**American Binding, Elk Grove Village** Also called Phoenix Binding Corp *(G-9678)*
**American Biooptics LLC** .......................................... 847 467-0628
1801 Maple Ave Ste 4316 Evanston (60201) *(G-10009)*
**American Blending & Filling Co** .............................. 847 689-1000
3505 Birchwood Dr Waukegan (60085) *(G-21523)*
**American Blue Rbbon Hldngs LLC** .......................... 708 687-7650
16425 Kilbourne Ave Oak Forest (60452) *(G-16573)*
**American Bottling Company** ................................... 217 356-0577
815 Pioneer St Champaign (61820) *(G-3448)*

**American Bottling Company** ....708 947-5000
401 N Railroad Ave Northlake (60164) *(G-16426)*
**American Bottling Company** ....815 877-7777
5300 Forest Hills Rd Loves Park (61111) *(G-13919)*
**American Bottling Company** ....309 693-2777
7215 N Kckapoo Edwards Rd Edwards (61528) *(G-8781)*
**American Boxboard LLC** ....708 924-9810
1400 Paramount Pkwy Batavia (60510) *(G-1413)*
**American Brite Dental, Chicago** *Also called Brite Dental PC (G-4170)*
**American Broom Company, Mattoon** *Also called Luco Mop Company (G-14398)*
**American Buff Intl Inc** ....217 465-1411
219 W Court St Paris (61944) *(G-17141)*
**American Buildings Company** ....309 527-5420
2101 E Main St El Paso (61738) *(G-8865)*
**American Bullnose Co Midw** ....630 238-1300
373 Balm Ct Wood Dale (60191) *(G-22340)*
**American Calibration Inc** ....815 356-5839
4410 Il Route 176 Ste 11 Crystal Lake (60014) *(G-7533)*
**American Campaigns** ....773 261-6800
5333 W Lake St Chicago (60644) *(G-3853)*
**American Cast Products Inc** ....708 895-5152
17730 Chicago Ave Frnt Lansing (60438) *(G-13156)*
**American Cast Stone** ....630 291-0250
14563 136th St Lemont (60439) *(G-13223)*
**American Catholic Press Inc** ....708 331-5485
16565 State St South Holland (60473) *(G-20242)*
**American Chamber of** ....312 960-9400
5 S Wabash Ave Ste 1405a Chicago (60603) *(G-3854)*
**American Chemet Corporation (PA)** ....847 948-0800
740 Waukegan Rd Ste 202 Deerfield (60015) *(G-7975)*
**American Chemet Export, Deerfield** *Also called American Chemet Corporation (G-7975)*
**American Chemical & Eqp Inc** ....815 675-9199
128 W Lake St 130 Northlake (60164) *(G-16427)*
**American Church Supply** ....847 464-4140
41w699 Foxtail Cir Saint Charles (60175) *(G-19134)*
**American Chute Systems Inc** ....815 723-7632
603 E Washington St Joliet (60433) *(G-12452)*
**American Cips** ....618 393-5641
4978 N Il 130 Olney (62450) *(G-16759)*
**American Circuit Services Inc** ....847 895-0500
801 Albion Ave Ste B Schaumburg (60193) *(G-19436)*
**American Circuit Systems Inc** ....630 543-4450
712 S Westgate St Addison (60101) *(G-33)*
**American City Bus Journals Inc** ....312 873-2200
233 N Michigan Ave # 1810 Chicago (60601) *(G-3855)*
**American Classic Rebar Corp** ....708 225-1010
15810 Suntone Dr South Holland (60473) *(G-20243)*
**American Classifieds Inc** ....217 356-4804
505 E University Ave C Champaign (61820) *(G-3449)*
**American Cllege Chest Physcans (PA)** ....224 521-9800
2595 Patriot Blvd Glenview (60026) *(G-11099)*
**American Cnc Machine Co Inc** ....630 628-6490
749 W Fullerton Ave Addison (60101) *(G-34)*
**American Coal Company (HQ)** ....618 268-6311
9085 Highway 34 N Galatia (62935) *(G-10711)*
**American Colloid Company** ....618 452-8143
1601 Walnut St Granite City (62040) *(G-11263)*
**American Colloid Company** ....304 882-2123
3422 Cameron Dr Elgin (60124) *(G-8947)*
**American Colloid Company** ....815 547-5369
2786 Newburg Rd Belvidere (61008) *(G-1731)*
**American Colloid Company (HQ)** ....847 851-1700
2870 Forbs Ave Hoffman Estates (60192) *(G-11992)*
**American Colloid Minerals Co** ....800 527-9948
1500 W Shure Dr Fl 7 Arlington Heights (60004) *(G-709)*
**American Color Alticor** ....847 472-7500
1800 Landmeier Rd Ste A Elk Grove Village (60007) *(G-9295)*
**American Comm & Networks** ....630 241-2800
1958 Ohio St Lisle (60532) *(G-13558)*
**American Concorde Systems** ....773 342-9951
1548 Burgundy Pkwy Streamwood (60107) *(G-20642)*
**American Control Elec LLC** ....815 624-6950
14300 De La Tour Dr South Beloit (61080) *(G-20137)*
**American Controls & Automation** ....630 293-8841
897 Industrial Dr West Chicago (60185) *(G-21655)*
**American Convenience Inc** ....815 344-6040
2102 W Il Route 120 McHenry (60051) *(G-14480)*
**American Cooner, Sesser** *Also called C and H Publishing Co (G-19894)*
**American Cotton Products Div, Chicago** *Also called Sea-Rich Corp (G-6464)*
**American Couplings Co** ....630 323-4442
40 Chestnut Ave Westmont (60559) *(G-21875)*
**American Custom Publishing** ....847 816-8660
328 W Lincoln Ave Libertyville (60048) *(G-13302)*
**American Custom Woodworking** ....847 526-5900
1247 Karl Ct Wauconda (60084) *(G-21440)*
**American Data Centre Inc (PA)** ....847 358-7111
25 W Palatine Rd Palatine (60067) *(G-17000)*
**American Deck & Sunroom C** ....217 586-4840
2603 Appaloosa Ln Mahomet (61853) *(G-14157)*
**American Dental, Chicago** *Also called Hu-Friedy Mfg Co LLC (G-5126)*
**American Dental Products Inc** ....630 238-0275
603 Country Club Dr Ste B Bensenville (60106) *(G-1832)*
**American Die Supplies Acquisit** ....630 766-6226
618 N Edgewood Ave Wood Dale (60191) *(G-22341)*
**American Diesel Tube Corp** ....630 628-1830
1240 W Capitol Dr Addison (60101) *(G-35)*
**American Digital Corporation** ....847 637-4300
25 Northwest Point Blvd # 200 Elk Grove Village (60007) *(G-9296)*
**American Dragway Trophy Co, Chicago** *Also called American Trophy & Award Co Inc (G-3881)*
**American Drilling Inc** ....847 850-5090
625 Glenn Ave Wheeling (60090) *(G-22003)*
**American Dryer Inc** ....734 421-2400
5700 Mcdermott Dr Berkeley (60163) *(G-2043)*
**American Electronic Pdts Inc** ....630 889-9977
2001 Midwest Rd Ste 105 Oak Brook (60523) *(G-16488)*
**American EMB & Screen Prtg, Glendale Heights** *Also called American EMB & Screen Prtg LLC (G-11008)*
**American EMB & Screen Prtg LLC** ....630 766-2825
1935 Brandon Ct Ste A Glendale Heights (60139) *(G-11008)*
**American Engraving Inc** ....630 543-2525
151 Wilson Ct Bensenville (60106) *(G-1833)*
**American Enlightenment LLC** ....773 687-8996
2023 W Carroll Ave Ste 45 Chicago (60612) *(G-3856)*
**American Equipment & Mch Inc** ....618 533-3857
2400 S Wabash Ave Centralia (62801) *(G-3404)*
**American Extrusion Intl Corp (PA)** ....815 624-6616
498 Prairie Hill Rd South Beloit (61080) *(G-20138)*
**American Fas & Components** ....815 397-2698
810 20th St Rockford (61104) *(G-18262)*
**American Fastening Systems, Glendale Heights** *Also called Si Enterprises Inc (G-11069)*
**American Fixture** ....217 429-1300
3040 N Norwood Ave Decatur (62526) *(G-7832)*
**American Flange & Mfg Co Inc (HQ)** ....630 665-7900
290 Fullerton Ave Carol Stream (60188) *(G-3098)*
**American Food Distrs Corp** ....708 331-1982
374 E 167th St Harvey (60426) *(G-11655)*
**American Fuel Economy Inc** ....815 433-3226
1772 N 2753rd Rd Ottawa (61350) *(G-16946)*
**American Fur Enterprises** ....618 542-2018
413 S Greenwood Ave Du Quoin (62832) *(G-8550)*
**American Gaming & Elec Inc (HQ)** ....708 290-2100
9500 W 55th St Ste A Countryside (60525) *(G-7414)*
**American Gasket & Rubber, Schaumburg** *Also called Plastic Specialties & Tech Inc (G-19693)*
**American Gasket Tech Inc** ....630 543-1510
10 W Laura Dr Addison (60101) *(G-36)*
**American Gear Inc** ....815 537-5111
910 Swanson Dr Prophetstown (61277) *(G-17767)*
**American Graphic Systems Inc** ....708 614-7007
7650 185th St Ste A Tinley Park (60477) *(G-20890)*
**American Graphics Network Inc** ....847 729-7220
1625 Glenview Rd Unit 309 Glenview (60025) *(G-11100)*
**American Grinders Inc** ....815 943-4902
3 Lincoln St Ste 3 Harvard (60033) *(G-11620)*
**American Grinding & Machine Co (PA)** ....773 889-4343
2000 N Mango Ave Chicago (60639) *(G-3857)*
**American Hao Feng Co, Deerfield** *Also called JAm International Co Ltd (G-8016)*
**American Header Tool Tech, Rockford** *Also called Amtech Inc (G-18266)*
**American Holiday Lights Inc** ....630 769-9999
6813 Hobson Valley Dr # 102 Woodridge (60517) *(G-22451)*
**American Home Aluminium Co** ....773 925-9442
12127 S Paulina St Calumet Park (60827) *(G-2956)*
**American Home Aluminum Co, Calumet Park** *Also called American Home Aluminium Co (G-2956)*
**American Hosp Assn Svcs Del (HQ)** ....312 422-2000
155 N Wacker Dr Ste 400 Chicago (60606) *(G-3858)*
**American Imaging MGT Inc** ....708 236-8500
2 Westbrook Ct Ste 800 Westchester (60154) *(G-21829)*
**American Imaging MGT Inc** ....847 564-8500
540 Lake Cook Rd Ste 300 Deerfield (60015) *(G-7976)*
**American Inds A Div A Stucki, Jerseyville** *Also called A Stucki Company (G-12416)*
**American Industrial Company** ....847 855-9200
1080 Tri State Pkwy Gurnee (60031) *(G-11427)*
**American Industrial Direct LLC (PA)** ....800 382-1200
2545 Millennium Dr Elgin (60124) *(G-8948)*
**American Industrial Werks Inc** ....847 477-2648
904 S Roselle Rd Ste 208 Schaumburg (60193) *(G-19437)*
**American Inks and Coatings Co** ....630 226-0994
1225 Lakeside Dr 1 Romeoville (60446) *(G-18795)*
**American Kitchen Delights Inc** ....708 210-3200
15320 Cooper Ave Harvey (60426) *(G-11656)*
**American Label Company** ....630 830-4444
1678 Wright Blvd Ste D Schaumburg (60193) *(G-19438)*
**American Labelmark Company (PA)** ....773 478-0900
5724 N Pulaski Rd Chicago (60646) *(G-3859)*
**American Led Ltg Solutions LLC** ....847 931-1900
1645 Todd Farm Dr Elgin (60123) *(G-8949)*

A L P H A B E T I C

(PA)=Parent Co (HQ)=Headquarters (DH)=Div Headquarters
2017 Harris Illinois Industrial Directory
1161

**American Library Association** 312 280-5718
50 E Huron St Chicago (60611) **(G-3860)**
**American Light Bulb Mfg Inc** 843 464-0755
534 Pratt Ave N Schaumburg (60193) **(G-19439)**
**American Litho Incorporated** 630 682-0600
175 Mercedes Dr Carol Stream (60188) **(G-3099)**
**American Litho Incorporated** 630 462-1700
175 Mercedes Dr Carol Stream (60188) **(G-3100)**
**American Louver Company (PA)** 847 470-0400
7700 Austin Ave Skokie (60077) **(G-19950)**
**American Machine** 815 539-6558
215 E 12th St Mendota (61342) **(G-14715)**
**American Machine Pdts & Svcs** 708 743-9088
11863 W Josephine Dr Mokena (60448) **(G-14852)**
**American Machine Tools Inc** 773 775-6285
5864 N Northwest Hwy Chicago (60631) **(G-3861)**
**American Machining Inc** 815 498-1593
405 E Lafayette St Ste 1 Somonauk (60552) **(G-20124)**
**American Machining & Wldg Inc** 773 586-2585
6009 S New England Ave Chicago (60638) **(G-3862)**
**American Marble & Granite Inc** 815 741-1710
1930 Donmaur Dr Crest Hill (60403) **(G-7457)**
**American Marketing & Pubg LLC** 815 756-2840
915 E Lincoln Hwy Dekalb (60115) **(G-8074)**
**American Medical Association (PA)** 312 464-5000
330 N Wabash Ave # 39300 Chicago (60611) **(G-3863)**
**American Medical Association** 312 464-2555
515 N State St Fl 9 Chicago (60654) **(G-3864)**
**American Medical Industries** 847 918-9800
28915 N Herky Dr Ste 107 Lake Bluff (60044) **(G-12829)**
**American Metal Fibers Inc (PA)** 847 295-8166
13420 Rockland Rd Lake Bluff (60044) **(G-12830)**
**American Metal Installers & FA** 630 993-0812
55 W Home Ave Villa Park (60181) **(G-21236)**
**American Metal Mfg Inc** 847 651-6097
6323 N Avondale Ave # 125 Chicago (60631) **(G-3865)**
**American Metal Perforating Inc** 773 523-8884
3201 W 36th Pl Chicago (60632) **(G-3866)**
**American Metalcraft Inc** 800 333-9133
3708 River Rd Ste 800 Franklin Park (60131) **(G-10391)**
**American Milling Company** 309 347-6888
1811 American St Pekin (61554) **(G-17253)**
**American Molding Tech Inc** 847 437-6900
2350 Lunt Ave Elk Grove Village (60007) **(G-9297)**
**American Monument Co** 618 993-8968
306 S Court St Marion (62959) **(G-14253)**
**American Name Plate & Metal De** 773 376-1400
4501 S Kildare Ave Chicago (60632) **(G-3867)**
**American National Can Co** 630 406-3500
1300 S River St Batavia (60510) **(G-1414)**
**American Needle Inc (PA)** 847 215-0011
1275 Busch Pkwy Buffalo Grove (60089) **(G-2657)**
**American Nickel Works Inc** 312 942-0070
1223 W Lake St Chicago (60607) **(G-3868)**
**American NTN Bearing Mfg Corp (HQ)** 847 741-4545
1525 Holmes Rd Elgin (60123) **(G-8950)**
**American NTN Bearing Mfg Corp** 847 671-5450
9515 Winona Ave Schiller Park (60176) **(G-19801)**
**American Nurseryman Pubg Co** 847 234-5867
1696 Oak Knoll Dr Lake Forest (60045) **(G-12878)**
**American Outfitters Ltd** 847 623-3959
3700 Sunset Ave Waukegan (60087) **(G-21524)**
**American Packaging McHy Inc** 815 337-8580
2550 S Eastwood Dr Woodstock (60098) **(G-22539)**
**American Pallet Co Inc** 847 662-5525
1105 Greenfield Ave Waukegan (60085) **(G-21525)**
**American Partsmith Inc** 630 520-0432
901 Atlantic Dr West Chicago (60185) **(G-21656)**
**American Perforator Company** 815 469-4300
22803 S Mustang Rd Ste A Frankfort (60423) **(G-10294)**
**American Phrm Partners Inc** 847 969-2700
1501 E Woodfield Rd Schaumburg (60173) **(G-19440)**
**American Piping Group Inc** 815 772-7470
800 French Creek Rd Morrison (61270) **(G-15141)**
**American Piping Products Inc** 708 339-1753
15801 Van Drunen Rd South Holland (60473) **(G-20244)**
**American Plastics Technoligies, Schiller Park** *Also called RAO Design International Inc* **(G-19865)**
**American Plating & Mfg Co** 773 890-4907
3941 S Keeler Ave Chicago (60632) **(G-3869)**
**American Powder Coatings Inc** 630 762-0100
420 38th Ave Saint Charles (60174) **(G-19135)**
**American Precision Elec Inc (PA)** 630 510-8080
25w624 Saint Charles Rd Carol Stream (60188) **(G-3101)**
**American Precision Machine** 847 428-5950
845 Commerce Pkwy Carpentersville (60110) **(G-3273)**
**American Precision Machining** 847 455-1720
11135 Franklin Ave Franklin Park (60131) **(G-10392)**
**American Prgrssive Crcuits Inc** 630 495-6900
1772 W Armitage Ct Addison (60101) **(G-37)**
**American Process Systems Div, Gurnee** *Also called Eirich Machines Inc* **(G-11446)**
**American Publishing Co Inc** 815 692-2366
125 W Locust St Fairbury (61739) **(G-10121)**
**American Quality Mfg Inc** 815 226-9301
3519 Kishwaukee St Ste 1 Rockford (61109) **(G-18263)**
**American Quick Print Inc** 847 253-2700
1000 Brown St Ste 212 Wauconda (60084) **(G-21441)**
**American Quickprint, Wauconda** *Also called American Quick Print Inc* **(G-21441)**
**American Rack, Chicago** *Also called Associated Rack Corporation* **(G-3970)**
**American Rack Company** 773 763-7309
5810 N Northwest Hwy Chicago (60631) **(G-3870)**
**American Reprographics Co LLC** 847 647-1131
6328 W Gross Point Rd Niles (60714) **(G-15960)**
**American Rotors Inc** 847 263-1300
3873 Clearview Ct Gurnee (60031) **(G-11428)**
**American Science & Surplus Inc** 773 763-0313
5316w N Milwaukee Ave Chicago (60630) **(G-3871)**
**American Science and Tech Corp (PA)** 312 433-3800
1367 W Chicago Ave Chicago (60642) **(G-3872)**
**American Screw Machine Co** 847 455-4308
2833 N Comm St Franklin Park (60131) **(G-10393)**
**American Sea and Air** 773 262-5960
2600 W Peterson Ave Chicago (60659) **(G-3873)**
**American Shtmtl Fbricators Inc** 708 877-7200
525 N Williams St Thornton (60476) **(G-20867)**
**American Sign & Lighting Co** 847 258-8151
350 N La Salle Dr # 1100 Chicago (60654) **(G-3874)**
**American Slide-Chart Co (PA)** 630 665-3333
25w 550 Geneva Rd Carol Stream (60188) **(G-3102)**
**American Soc HM Inspectors Inc (PA)** 847 759-2820
932 Lee St Ste 101 Des Plaines (60016) **(G-8147)**
**American Soc Plastic Surgeons (PA)** 847 228-9900
444 E Algonquin Rd # 100 Arlington Heights (60005) **(G-710)**
**American Soda Ftn Exch Inc** 312 733-5000
455 N Oakley Blvd Chicago (60612) **(G-3875)**
**American Spcalty Advg Prtg Co** 847 272-5255
899 Skokie Blvd Ste 112 Northbrook (60062) **(G-16203)**
**American Specialty Toy** 312 222-0984
432 N Clark St Ste 305 Chicago (60654) **(G-3876)**
**American Speed Enterprises** 309 764-3601
3006 Avenue Of The Cities Moline (61265) **(G-14917)**
**American Speedy Printing, East Peoria** *Also called Selnar Inc* **(G-8733)**
**American Speedy Printing, Pekin** *Also called We-B-Print Inc* **(G-17293)**
**American Speedy Printing, Chicago** *Also called Josco Inc* **(G-5326)**
**American Speedy Printing, Galesburg** *Also called Marnic Inc* **(G-10766)**
**American Speedy Printing Ctrs** 847 806-0135
859 Oakton St Elk Grove Village (60007) **(G-9298)**
**American Stair Corporation Inc** 815 886-9600
642 Forestwood Dr Romeoville (60446) **(G-18796)**
**American Standard Circuits Inc** 630 639-5444
475 Industrial Dr West Chicago (60185) **(G-21657)**
**American Steel Carports Inc** 800 487-4010
832 N East St Kewanee (61443) **(G-12669)**
**American Steel Fabricators Inc** 847 807-4200
1985 Anson Dr Melrose Park (60160) **(G-14593)**
**American Store Fixtures, Skokie** *Also called American Louver Company* **(G-19950)**
**American Supply Association (PA)** 630 467-0000
1200 N Arlngton Hts 150 Itasca (60143) **(G-12228)**
**American Tape Measures** 312 208-0282
6717 W Foster Ave Chicago (60656) **(G-3877)**
**American Titanium Works LLC** 312 327-3178
30 N La Salle St Ste 2200 Chicago (60602) **(G-3878)**
**American Total Engine Co** 847 623-2737
27840 W Concrete Dr Ste B Ingleside (60041) **(G-12186)**
**American Trade & Coml Svc LLC** 202 910-8808
303 S Halsted St Apt 3 Chicago (60661) **(G-3879)**
**American Trade Magazines LLC** 312 497-7707
566 W Lake St Ste 420 Chicago (60661) **(G-3880)**
**American Tristar Inc (HQ)** 920 872-2181
525 Dunham Rd Saint Charles (60174) **(G-19136)**
**American Tristar Inc** 630 262-5500
2089 Pillsbury Dr Geneva (60134) **(G-10809)**
**American Trophy & Award Co Inc** 312 939-3252
1006 S Michigan Ave # 503 Chicago (60605) **(G-3881)**
**American Vacuum Co** 847 674-8383
7301 Monticello Ave Skokie (60076) **(G-19951)**
**American Vulko Tread Corp** 847 956-1300
690 Chase Ave Elk Grove Village (60007) **(G-9299)**
**American Watersource LLC** 630 778-9900
1228 Bards Ave Naperville (60564) **(G-15794)**
**American Welding & Gas Inc** 630 527-2550
3900 W North Ave Stone Park (60165) **(G-20632)**
**American Wheel Corp** 708 458-9141
5939 W 66th St Chicago (60638) **(G-3882)**
**American Wilbert Vault Corp** 773 238-2746
11118 S Rockwell St Chicago (60655) **(G-3883)**
**American Wilbert Vault Corp (PA)** 708 366-3210
7525 W 99th Pl Bridgeview (60455) **(G-2464)**

ALPHABETIC SECTION
Amplivox Sound Systems LLC (PA)

**American Wilbert Vault Corp** ....847 824-4415
165 S River Rd Des Plaines (60016) *(G-8148)*
**American Wilbert Vault Corp** ....847 741-3089
954 Bluff City Blvd Elgin (60120) *(G-8951)*
**American Woodworks** ....630 279-1629
718 Hillcrest Dr Sleepy Hollow (60118) *(G-20117)*
**American Yeast Corp Tennessee** ....630 932-1290
1417 S Jeffrey Dr Addison (60101) *(G-38)*
**American/Jebco Corporation** ....847 455-3150
11330 Melrose Ave Franklin Park (60131) *(G-10394)*
**Americana Building Pdts Inc (PA)** ....618 548-2800
2 Industrial Dr Salem (62881) *(G-19326)*
**Americaneagle.com, Des Plaines** *Also called Svanaco Inc (G-8284)*
**Americas Community Bankers** ....312 644-3100
363 W Erie St Fl 4 Chicago (60654) *(G-3884)*
**Americas Food Technologies Inc** ....708 532-1222
7700 185th St Tinley Park (60477) *(G-20891)*
**Americas Styrenics LLC** ....815 418-6403
26332 S Frontage Rd Channahon (60410) *(G-3565)*
**Americhem Systems Inc** ....630 495-9300
1740 Molitor Rd Aurora (60505) *(G-1106)*
**Americlean Inc** ....314 741-8901
23 E Ferguson Ave Wood River (62095) *(G-22440)*
**Americn Foreign Lang Newspaper** ....312 368-4815
55 E Jackson Blvd Ste 920 Chicago (60604) *(G-3885)*
**Americo Chemical Products Inc** ....630 588-0830
551 Kimberly Dr Carol Stream (60188) *(G-3103)*
**Americoats, Franklin Park** *Also called Coatings International Inc (G-10439)*
**Americor Electronics Ltd** ....847 956-6200
675 Lively Blvd Elk Grove Village (60007) *(G-9300)*
**Americut Wire Edm Inc** ....847 675-1754
8045 Ridgeway Ave Skokie (60076) *(G-19952)*
**Ameriflon Ltd (PA)** ....847 541-6000
930 Seton Ct Wheeling (60090) *(G-22004)*
**AmeriGas** ....708 544-1131
4158 Division St Hillside (60162) *(G-11909)*
**Amerigraphics Corp** ....630 543-9790
1010 W National Ave Addison (60101) *(G-39)*
**Amerigreen Pallets** ....309 698-3463
280 Fondulac Dr East Peoria (61611) *(G-8700)*
**Ameriguard Corporation** ....630 986-1900
7701 S Grant St Burr Ridge (60527) *(G-2822)*
**Ameriken Die Supply Inc** ....630 766-6226
618 N Edgewood Ave Wood Dale (60191) *(G-22342)*
**Amerikos Lietuvis Corp** ....708 924-0403
7950 W 99th St Oak Lawn (60457) *(G-16602)*
**Amerilights Inc** ....847 219-1476
146 Roundtree Ct Bloomingdale (60108) *(G-2093)*
**Amerinet of Michigan Inc** ....708 466-0110
3909 White Eagle Dr W Naperville (60564) *(G-15795)*
**Ameriplate Inc** ....815 744-8585
600 Joyce Rd Joliet (60436) *(G-12453)*
**Ameriscan Designs Inc** ....773 542-1291
4147 W Ogden Ave Chicago (60623) *(G-3886)*
**Amerisourcebergen Corporation** ....815 221-3600
1001 Taylor Rd Romeoville (60446) *(G-18797)*
**Amerisrcbergen Solutions Group** ....847 808-2600
1400 Busch Pkwy Buffalo Grove (60089) *(G-2658)*
**Amerisun Inc** ....800 791-9458
1141 W Bryn Mawr Ave Itasca (60143) *(G-12229)*
**Ameritex Industries Inc** ....217 324-4044
14 Litchfield Plz Ste 1a Litchfield (62056) *(G-13681)*
**Amerline Enterprises Co Inc** ....847 671-6554
9509 Winona Ave Schiller Park (60176) *(G-19802)*
**Ameropan Oil Corp** ....773 847-4400
3301 S California Ave Chicago (60608) *(G-3887)*
**Ames Metal Products Company** ....773 523-3230
2211 Foster Ave Wheeling (60090) *(G-22005)*
**Ametek Inc** ....847 596-7000
1450 S Lakeside Dr Waukegan (60085) *(G-21526)*
**Ametek Inc** ....630 621-3121
1725 Western Dr West Chicago (60185) *(G-21658)*
**Ametek Power Instruments, West Chicago** *Also called Ametek Inc (G-21658)*
**Ametek Powervar, Waukegan** *Also called Ametek Inc (G-21526)*
**Ametek-Ncc Holding, West Chicago** *Also called National Control Holdings (G-21748)*
**Amex Nooter LLC (HQ)** ....708 429-8300
18501 Maple Creek Dr Tinley Park (60477) *(G-20892)*
**Amfab LLC** ....630 783-2570
1385 101st St Ste A Lemont (60439) *(G-13224)*
**Amfi, Lake Bluff** *Also called American Metal Fibers Inc (G-12830)*
**Amfotek, Tinley Park** *Also called Americas Food Technologies Inc (G-20891)*
**AMG International Inc** ....847 439-1001
1480 E Devon Ave Elk Grove Village (60007) *(G-9301)*
**Amglo Kemlite Laboratories Inc (PA)** ....630 238-3031
215 Gateway Rd Bensenville (60106) *(G-1834)*
**Amiberica Inc** ....773 247-3600
3701 S Ashland Ave Chicago (60609) *(G-3888)*
**Amic Global Inc (PA)** ....847 600-3590
353 Hastings Dr Buffalo Grove (60089) *(G-2659)*

**Amigo Mobility Center** ....630 268-8670
17w620 14th St Ste 101 Oakbrook Terrace (60181) *(G-16697)*
**Amigoni Construction** ....309 923-3701
800 N State St Roanoke (61561) *(G-18047)*
**Amis Inc** ....708 598-9700
7506 W 90th St Bridgeview (60455) *(G-2465)*
**Amish Country Heirlooms LLC** ....217 253-9200
1304 Tuscola Blvd Unit 14 Tuscola (61953) *(G-21015)*
**Amitron Inc** ....847 290-9800
2001 Landmeier Rd Elk Grove Village (60007) *(G-9302)*
**Amitron Crop, Elk Grove Village** *Also called Amitron Inc (G-9302)*
**Amity Die and Stamping Co** ....847 680-6600
13870 W Polo Trail Dr Lake Forest (60045) *(G-12879)*
**Amity Hospital Services Inc** ....708 206-3970
4921 173rd St Ste 2 Country Club Hills (60478) *(G-7403)*
**Amity Packing Company Inc (PA)** ....312 942-0270
4220 S Kildare Ave Chicago (60632) *(G-3889)*
**Amj Industries Inc** ....815 654-9000
4000 Auburn St Unit 104 Rockford (61101) *(G-18264)*
**Amk Enterprises Chicago Inc** ....312 523-7212
3605 S Calumet Ave Chicago (60653) *(G-3890)*
**Amk Kitchen Bar** ....773 270-4115
1954 W Armitage Ave Chicago (60622) *(G-3891)*
**Amkine Inc** ....847 526-7088
230 Industrial Dr Wauconda (60084) *(G-21442)*
**Amkus Inc** ....630 515-1800
2700 Wisconsin Ave Downers Grove (60515) *(G-8387)*
**Amkus Rescue Systems, Downers Grove** *Also called Amkus Inc (G-8387)*
**Amling Donuts Inc** ....847 426-5327
98 N Kennedy Dr Carpentersville (60110) *(G-3274)*
**Amling's Flowerland, Elmhurst** *Also called Albert F Amling LLC (G-9832)*
**Ammentorp Tool Company Inc** ....847 671-9290
9828 Franklin Ave Franklin Park (60131) *(G-10395)*
**Ammeraal Beltech Inc (HQ)** ....847 673-6720
7501 Saint Louis Ave Skokie (60076) *(G-19953)*
**Ammeraal Beltech Inc** ....847 673-1736
7501 Saint Louis Ave Skokie (60076) *(G-19954)*
**Ammeraal Beltech Inc** ....847 673-6720
7455 Saint Louis Ave Skokie (60076) *(G-19955)*
**Amnet Systems LLC** ....217 954-0130
110 W Main St Urbana (61801) *(G-21069)*
**Amnetic LLC** ....877 877-3678
1645 S River Rd Ste 8 Des Plaines (60018) *(G-8149)*
**Amoco, Naperville** *Also called BP Products North America Inc (G-15609)*
**Amoco Technology Company (del) (HQ)** ....312 861-6000
200 E Randolph St # 2100 Chicago (60601) *(G-3892)*
**Amos Industries Inc** ....630 393-0606
30w102 Butterfield Rd Warrenville (60555) *(G-21341)*
**AMP Americas LLC (PA)** ....312 300-6700
1130 W Monroe St Ste 1 Chicago (60607) *(G-3893)*
**AMP CNG, Chicago** *Also called AMP Americas LLC (G-3893)*
**Ampac Flexibles, Cary** *Also called Ampac Flexicon LLC (G-3325)*
**Ampac Flexibles LLC** ....630 439-3160
825 Turnberry Ct Hanover Park (60133) *(G-11574)*
**Ampac Flexicon LLC** ....630 439-3160
825 Turnberry Ct Hanover Park (60133) *(G-11575)*
**Ampac Flexicon LLC (HQ)** ....847 639-3530
165 Chicago St Cary (60013) *(G-3325)*
**Ampac Holdings LLC** ....847 639-3530
165 Chicago St Cary (60013) *(G-3326)*
**Ampco Aquisition, Arlington Heights** *Also called Ampco Metal Incorporated (G-711)*
**Ampco Metal Incorporated (PA)** ....847 437-6000
1117 E Algonquin Rd Arlington Heights (60005) *(G-711)*
**Ampel Incorporated** ....847 952-1900
925 Estes Ave Elk Grove Village (60007) *(G-9303)*
**Amperite Co., Elgin** *Also called Olympic Controls Corp (G-9128)*
**Ampex Screw Mfg Inc** ....847 228-1202
2936 Malmo Dr Arlington Heights (60005) *(G-712)*
**Amphenol Antel, Rockford** *Also called Amphenol Antenna Solutions Inc (G-18265)*
**Amphenol Antenna Solutions Inc (HQ)** ....815 399-0001
1300 Capital Dr Rockford (61109) *(G-18265)*
**Amphenol Corporation** ....800 944-6446
2100 Western Ct Ste 300 Lisle (60532) *(G-13559)*
**Amphenol Corporation** ....847 478-5600
100 Tristate Intl Lincolnshire (60069) *(G-13427)*
**Amphenol Eec Inc** ....773 463-8343
4050 N Rockwell St Chicago (60618) *(G-3894)*
**Amphenol Fiber Optic Products** ....630 960-1010
2100 Western Ct Ste 300 Lisle (60532) *(G-13560)*
**Amphenol T&M Antennas Inc (HQ)** ....847 478-5600
100 Tri State Intl # 255 Lincolnshire (60069) *(G-13428)*
**Amplate, Chicago** *Also called American Plating & Mfg Co (G-3869)*
**Ample Supply Company** ....815 895-3500
1401 S Prairie Dr Sycamore (60178) *(G-20786)*
**Amplivox Prtable Sound Systems, Northbrook** *Also called Amplivox Sound Systems LLC (G-16204)*
**Amplivox Sound Systems LLC (PA)** ....800 267-5486
650 Anthony Trl Ste D Northbrook (60062) *(G-16204)*

ALPHABETIC

(PA)=Parent Co (HQ)=Headquarters (DH)=Div Headquarters
2017 Harris Illinois Industrial Directory
1163

**Amric Resources** ... 309 664-0391
2422 E Washington St # 102  Bloomington  (61704)  *(G-2144)*

**Amron Stair Works Inc (PA)** ... 847 426-4800
152 Industrial Dr  Gilberts  (60136)  *(G-10912)*

**AMS, Lake In The Hills**  Also called AG Medical Systems Inc  *(G-12984)*

**AMS LLC** ... 773 904-7740
2445 N Seminary Ave  Chicago  (60614)  *(G-3895)*

**AMS Seals Inc** ... 815 609-4977
12149 Rhea Dr  Plainfield  (60585)  *(G-17580)*

**AMS Store and Shred LLC** ... 847 458-3100
13 Prosper Ct Ste B  Lake In The Hills  (60156)  *(G-12985)*

**Amsoil Inc** ... 630 595-8385
485 Thomas Dr  Bensenville  (60106)  *(G-1835)*

**Amst, Monee**  Also called Advanced Mobility &  *(G-14991)*

**Amstadt Industries, Lombard**  Also called Line Craft Tool Company Inc  *(G-13820)*

**Amsted Industries Incorporated (PA)** ... 312 645-1700
180 N Stetson Ave  Chicago  (60601)  *(G-3896)*

**Amsted Industries Incorporated** ... 312 645-1700
2 Prudential Plaza 180  Chicago  (60601)  *(G-3897)*

**Amsted Rail Company Inc** ... 312 258-8000
10 S Riverside Plz Fl 10  Chicago  (60606)  *(G-3898)*

**Amsted Rail Company Inc** ... 618 452-2111
1700 Walnut St  Granite City  (62040)  *(G-11264)*

**Amsted Rail Company Inc (HQ)** ... 312 922-4501
311 S Wacker Dr Ste 5300  Chicago  (60606)  *(G-3899)*

**Amsted Rail Company Inc** ... 618 225-6463
1078 19th St  Granite City  (62040)  *(G-11265)*

**Amsysco Inc** ... 630 296-8383
1200 Windham Pkwy  Romeoville  (60446)  *(G-18798)*

**Amt (additive Mfg Tech Inc** ... 847 258-4475
1201 Oakton St Ste 1  Elk Grove Village  (60007)  *(G-9304)*

**Amt Corp** ... 847 459-6177
717 Juneway Ave  Deerfield  (60015)  *(G-7977)*

**Amt Kikai, Barrington**  Also called Miyanohitec Machinery Inc  *(G-1292)*

**Amtab Manufacturing Corp** ... 630 301-7600
652 N Highland Ave  Aurora  (60506)  *(G-1107)*

**Amtec Molded Products Inc** ... 815 226-0187
1355 Holmes Rd Ste A  Elgin  (60123)  *(G-8952)*

**Amtec Precision Products, Elgin**  Also called North Amercn Acquisition Corp  *(G-9124)*

**Amtec Precision Products, Elgin**  Also called North Amercn Acquisition Corp  *(G-9125)*

**Amtec Precision Products Inc (PA)** ... 847 695-8030
1875 Holmes Rd  Elgin  (60123)  *(G-8953)*

**Amtech Inc** ... 815 962-0500
1819 9th St  Rockford  (61104)  *(G-18266)*

**Amtech Industries LLC** ... 847 202-3488
666 S Vermont St  Palatine  (60067)  *(G-17001)*

**Amtex, Glendale Heights**  Also called Surya Electronics Inc  *(G-11080)*

**Amtex Chemicals LLC** ... 630 268-0085
450 E 22nd St Ste 164  Lombard  (60148)  *(G-13764)*

**Amv International Inc** ... 815 282-9990
7814 Forest Hills Rd  Loves Park  (61111)  *(G-13920)*

**Amvex, Gurnee**  Also called Ohio Medical LLC  *(G-11479)*

**Amwell** ... 630 898-6900
1740 Molitor Rd  Aurora  (60505)  *(G-1108)*

**Amy Schutt** ... 618 994-7405
420 N Thompson St  Carrier Mills  (62917)  *(G-3305)*

**Amy Wertheim (PA)** ... 309 830-4361
1865 2200th St Bldg 2  Atlanta  (61723)  *(G-946)*

**An Environmental Inks** ... 800 728-8200
450 Wegner Dr  West Chicago  (60185)  *(G-21659)*

**Anah Machine Mfg Co** ... 847 228-6450
801 Pratt Blvd  Elk Grove Village  (60007)  *(G-9305)*

**Analog Devices Inc** ... 847 519-3669
1901 N Roselle Rd Ste 100  Schaumburg  (60195)  *(G-19441)*

**Analog Outfitters Inc** ... 217 202-6134
701 Pacesetter Dr  Rantoul  (61866)  *(G-17917)*

**Anamet Electrical Inc** ... 217 234-8844
1000 Broadway Ave E  Mattoon  (61938)  *(G-14382)*

**Anamet Inc (PA)** ... 217 234-8844
799 Roosevelt Rd 4-313  Glen Ellyn  (60137)  *(G-10958)*

**Anart Inc** ... 708 447-0225
440 Repton Rd  Riverside  (60546)  *(G-18028)*

**Anash Educational Institute** ... 773 338-7704
2929 W Greenleaf Ave  Chicago  (60645)  *(G-3900)*

**Anatol Equipment Mfg Co** ... 847 367-9760
919 Sherwood Dr  Lake Bluff  (60044)  *(G-12831)*

**Anatomical Worldwide LLC** ... 312 224-4772
1630 Darrow Ave  Evanston  (60201)  *(G-10010)*

**Anatomywarehouse.com, Evanston**  Also called Anatomical Worldwide LLC  *(G-10010)*

**Anbek Inc** ... 815 672-6087
222 3rd St  La Salle  (61301)  *(G-12763)*

**Anbek Inc** ... 815 223-0734
222 3rd St  La Salle  (61301)  *(G-12764)*

**Anbek Inc (PA)** ... 815 434-7340
104 W Madison St  Ottawa  (61350)  *(G-16947)*

**Anbm, Elgin**  Also called American NTN Bearing Mfg Corp  *(G-8950)*

**Anchor Abrasives Company** ... 708 444-4300
7651 185th St  Tinley Park  (60477)  *(G-20893)*

**Anchor Brake Shoe Company LLC (HQ)** ... 630 293-1110
1920 Downs Dr  West Chicago  (60185)  *(G-21660)*

**Anchor Glass Container Corp** ... 815 672-7761
1901 N Shabbona St  Streator  (61364)  *(G-20683)*

**Anchor Products Company** ... 630 543-9124
52 W Official Rd  Addison  (60101)  *(G-40)*

**Anchor Welding & Fabrication** ... 815 937-1640
2950 N Lowe Rd  Aroma Park  (60910)  *(G-878)*

**Anchor-Harvey Components LLC** ... 815 233-3833
600 W Lamm Rd  Freeport  (61032)  *(G-10646)*

**Ancient Graffiti Inc** ... 847 726-5800
300 E Il Route 22  Lake Zurich  (60047)  *(G-13040)*

**Andee Boiler & Welding Co, Chicago**  Also called Murphy Brothers Enterprises  *(G-5836)*

**Andel Services Inc** ... 630 566-0210
1145 S Union St  Aurora  (60505)  *(G-1109)*

**Andersen Machine & Welding Inc** ... 815 232-4664
1731 Lincoln Dr  Freeport  (61032)  *(G-10647)*

**Andersen Welding, Chicago**  Also called Welding Shop  *(G-6952)*

**Anderson & Marter Cabinets** ... 630 406-9840
845 E Wilson St  Batavia  (60510)  *(G-1415)*

**Anderson & Vreeland-Illinois** ... 847 255-2110
525 W University Dr  Arlington Heights  (60004)  *(G-713)*

**Anderson - Snow Corp** ... 847 678-2084
9225 Ivanhoe St  Schiller Park  (60176)  *(G-19803)*

**Anderson Awning & Shutter** ... 815 654-1155
8414 N 2nd St  Machesney Park  (61115)  *(G-14056)*

**Anderson Casting Company Inc** ... 312 733-1185
1721 W Carroll Ave  Chicago  (60612)  *(G-3901)*

**Anderson Copper & Brass Co LLC (HQ)** ... 708 535-9030
7231 W Laraway Rd  Frankfort  (60423)  *(G-10295)*

**Anderson Copper & Brass Co LLC** ... 815 469-8201
255 Industry Ave  Frankfort  (60423)  *(G-10296)*

**Anderson Die Castings, Elk Grove Village**  Also called ADC Diecasting LLC  *(G-9272)*

**Anderson Engrg New Prague Inc** ... 630 736-0900
312 Roma Jean Pkwy  Streamwood  (60107)  *(G-20643)*

**Anderson Fittings, Frankfort**  Also called Anderson Copper & Brass Co LLC  *(G-10295)*

**Anderson Fittings, Frankfort**  Also called Anderson Copper & Brass Co LLC  *(G-10296)*

**Anderson House Foundation** ... 630 461-7254
258 Harwarden St  Glen Ellyn  (60137)  *(G-10959)*

**Anderson Limousine, Machesney Park**  Also called Anderson Awning & Shutter  *(G-14056)*

**Anderson Msnry Refr Spcalist I, Lake Zurich**  Also called Anderson Msnry Refr Spcialists  *(G-13041)*

**Anderson Msnry Refr Spcialists** ... 847 540-8885
25675 N Stoney Kirk Ct  Lake Zurich  (60047)  *(G-13041)*

**Anderson Safford Mkg Graphics** ... 847 827-8968
570 E Northwest Hwy Ste 7  Des Plaines  (60016)  *(G-8150)*

**Anderson Shumaker Company** ... 773 287-0874
824 S Central Ave  Chicago  (60644)  *(G-3902)*

**Anderson Tage Co** ... 815 397-3040
2316 7th Ave  Rockford  (61104)  *(G-18267)*

**Anderson Truss Company** ... 618 982-9228
12418 Poordo Rd  Pittsburg  (62974)  *(G-17559)*

**Anderson, Richard Shop, Sycamore**  Also called Richard A Anderson  *(G-20814)*

**Andersons Candy Shop Inc (PA)** ... 815 678-6000
10301 N Main St  Richmond  (60071)  *(G-17957)*

**Andersson Tool & Die LLP** ... 847 746-8866
1717 Kenosha Rd  Zion  (60099)  *(G-22678)*

**Andover Junction Publications** ... 815 538-3060
467 N 46th Rd  Mendota  (61342)  *(G-14716)*

**Andrea and ME and ME Too** ... 708 955-3850
22401 Thomas Dr Apt 3n  Richton Park  (60471)  *(G-17976)*

**Andrew C Arnold** ... 815 220-0282
2228 4th St  Peru  (61354)  *(G-17499)*

**Andrew Corporation** ... 779 435-6000
2700 Ellis Rd  Joliet  (60433)  *(G-12454)*

**Andrew Distribution Inc (PA)** ... 708 410-2400
1841 Gardner Rd  Broadview  (60155)  *(G-2557)*

**Andrew International Svcs Corp** ... 779 435-6000
2700 Ellis Rd  Joliet  (60433)  *(G-12455)*

**Andrew McDonald** ... 618 867-2323
100 N Ash St  De Soto  (62924)  *(G-7818)*

**Andrew New Zealand Inc** ... 708 873-3507
10500 W 153rd St  Orland Park  (60462)  *(G-16843)*

**Andrew Solutions, Joliet**  Also called Commscope Technologies LLC  *(G-12476)*

**Andrew Technologies Inc** ... 847 520-5770
305 Alderman Ave  Wheeling  (60090)  *(G-22006)*

**Andrew Toschak** ... 630 553-3434
1025 Mchugh Rd  Yorkville  (60560)  *(G-22649)*

**Andrews Automotive Company** ... 773 768-1122
10055 S Torrence Ave  Chicago  (60617)  *(G-3903)*

**Andrews Caramel LLC** ... 773 286-2224
6620 W Dakin St  Chicago  (60634)  *(G-3904)*

**Andrews Caramel Apples Inc** ... 773 286-2224
5471 River Park Dr  Libertyville  (60048)  *(G-13303)*

**Andrews Converting LLC** ... 708 352-2555
707 E 47th St  La Grange  (60525)  *(G-12725)*

**Andrews Decal & Label Company, Chicago**  Also called Gallas Label & Decal  *(G-4909)*

**Andria Lieu, Chicago**  Also called Laqueus Inc  *(G-5460)*

**Andria's Steak Sauce, O Fallon** *Also called Andrias Food Group Inc* ***(G-16461)***
**Andria's Steak Sauce, O Fallon** *Also called Andrias Food Group Inc* ***(G-16462)***
**Andrias Food Group Inc (PA)**....618 632-4866
6805 Old Collinsville Rd O Fallon (62269) ***(G-16461)***
**Andrias Food Group Inc**....618 632-3118
6813 Old Collinsville Rd O Fallon (62269) ***(G-16462)***
**Androck Hardware Corporation**....815 229-1144
711 19th St Rockford (61104) ***(G-18268)***
**Android Indstres- Blvidere LLC**....815 547-3742
1222 Crosslink Pkwy Belvidere (61008) ***(G-1732)***
**Android Industries LLC**....815 544-4165
1222 Crosslink Pkwy Belvidere (61008) ***(G-1733)***
**Andscot Co Inc**....847 455-5800
9117 Medill Ave Franklin Park (60131) ***(G-10396)***
**Andy Dallas & Co**....217 351-5974
101 E University Ave Champaign (61820) ***(G-3450)***
**Andy Wurst**....630 964-4410
17w411 N Frontage Rd Darien (60561) ***(G-7789)***
**Andys Deli and Mikolajczyk (PA)**....773 722-1000
4021 W Kinzie St Chicago (60624) ***(G-3905)***
**Andys Pet Shop, Peru** *Also called Andrew C Arnold* ***(G-17499)***
**Anees Upholstery**....312 243-2919
1500 S Western Ave Ste 3 Chicago (60608) ***(G-3906)***
**Anfinsen Plastic Moulding Inc**....630 554-4100
445b Treasure Dr Unit B Oswego (60543) ***(G-16904)***
**Angel Equipment LLC**....815 455-4320
1941 Johns Dr Glenview (60025) ***(G-11101)***
**Angel Rose Energy LLC**....618 392-3700
4368 N Holly Rd Olney (62450) ***(G-16760)***
**Angel Wind Energy Inc**....815 471-2020
113 N Pine St Onarga (60955) ***(G-16808)***
**Angela Yang Chingjui**....630 724-0596
1026 Sean Cir Darien (60561) ***(G-7790)***
**Angelo Bruni**....773 754-5422
4107 Chesapeake Dr Apt 3b Aurora (60504) ***(G-957)***
**Angels Heavenly Funeral Home**....773 239-8700
1811 W 103rd St Chicago (60643) ***(G-3907)***
**Angle Metal Manufacturing Co**....847 437-8666
1497 Tonne Rd Elk Grove Village (60007) ***(G-9306)***
**Angle Press Inc**....847 439-6388
415 E Golf Rd Ste 101 Arlington Heights (60005) ***(G-714)***
**Angle Sheet Metal, Elk Grove Village** *Also called Angle Metal Manufacturing Co* ***(G-9306)***
**Angle Tool Company**....847 593-7572
425 Crossen Ave Elk Grove Village (60007) ***(G-9307)***
**Angleboard, Kankakee** *Also called Signode Industrial Group LLC* ***(G-12650)***
**Anheuser-Busch LLC**....708 206-2881
17751 Hillcrest Dr Country Club Hills (60478) ***(G-7404)***
**Anheuser-Busch LLC**....630 512-9002
1011 Warrenville Rd # 350 Lisle (60532) ***(G-13561)***
**Anikam Inc**....708 385-0200
12549 S Holiday Dr Alsip (60803) ***(G-433)***
**Animal Center International**....217 214-0536
4124 Kochs Ln Quincy (62305) ***(G-17792)***
**Animal Health Div, Chicago Heights** *Also called Zoetis LLC* ***(G-7137)***
**Animated Advg Techniques Inc**....312 372-4694
210 S Desplaines St Chicago (60661) ***(G-3908)***
**Animated Manufacturing Company**....708 333-6688
106 W 154th St South Holland (60473) ***(G-20245)***
**Anixter Inc**....512 989-4254
2301 Patriot Blvd Glenview (60026) ***(G-11102)***
**Anixter Inc**....800 323-8167
2301 Patriot Blvd Glenview (60026) ***(G-11103)***
**Anjay Traders Inc**....847 888-8562
450 Shepard Dr Ste 17h Elgin (60123) ***(G-8954)***
**Anjel Scents LLC**....313 729-0719
6657 S Minerva Ave Chicago (60637) ***(G-3909)***
**Anju Software Inc**....630 243-9810
9018 Heritage Pkwy # 600 Woodridge (60517) ***(G-22452)***
**Anliker Custom Wood**....815 657-7510
208 W Wabash Ave Forrest (61741) ***(G-10260)***
**Ann Printing, Edwardsville** *Also called Anns Printing & Copying Co* ***(G-8788)***
**Anna Plant, Anna** *Also called Illini Ready Mix Inc* ***(G-605)***
**Anna Quarries Inc**....618 833-5121
1000 Quarry Rd Anna (62906) ***(G-600)***
**Anna-Jonesboro Motor Co Inc**....618 833-4486
100 S Green St Anna (62906) ***(G-601)***
**Annaka Enterprises**....773 768-5490
8917 S Commercial Ave Chicago (60617) ***(G-3910)***
**Annas Draperies & Associates**....773 282-1365
5908 W Montrose Ave Chicago (60634) ***(G-3911)***
**Annies Frozen Custard**....618 656-0289
245 S Buchanan St Edwardsville (62025) ***(G-8787)***
**Anns Bakery Inc**....773 384-5562
2158 W Chicago Ave Chicago (60622) ***(G-3912)***
**Anns Printing & Copying Co**....618 656-6878
219 2nd Ave Ste E Edwardsville (62025) ***(G-8788)***
**Anodizing Specialists Ltd**....847 437-9495
210 Crossen Ave Elk Grove Village (60007) ***(G-9308)***
**Another Chance Community Dev**....773 998-1641
1641 W 79th St Chicago (60620) ***(G-3913)***
**Another Vision**....847 884-7325
2133 Hitching Post Ln Schaumburg (60194) ***(G-19442)***
**Anp Inc**....309 757-0372
1515 5th Ave Ste 428 Moline (61265) ***(G-14918)***
**Anpec Industries Inc**....815 239-2303
216 Main St Pecatonica (61063) ***(G-17250)***
**ANR Pipeline Company**....309 667-2158
296 N 600th Ave New Windsor (61465) ***(G-15929)***
**Anritsu Indus Slutions USA Inc, Elk Grove Village** *Also called Anritsu Infivis Inc* ***(G-9309)***
**Anritsu Infivis Inc**....847 419-9729
1001 Cambridge Dr Elk Grove Village (60007) ***(G-9309)***
**Anscor, Schiller Park** *Also called Anderson - Snow Corp* ***(G-19803)***
**Anselmo Die and Index Co Inc**....847 397-1200
2235 Hammond Dr Ste F Schaumburg (60173) ***(G-19443)***
**Anselmo Index, Schaumburg** *Also called Anselmo Die and Index Co Inc* ***(G-19443)***
**Ansonia Copper & Brass Inc (PA)**....866 607-7066
900 N Michigan Ave # 1600 Chicago (60611) ***(G-3914)***
**Antares Computer Systems Inc**....773 783-8855
8114 S Maryland Ave # 12 Chicago (60619) ***(G-3915)***
**Antenex Inc**....847 839-6910
1751 Wilkening Ct Schaumburg (60173) ***(G-19444)***
**Anthony Collins**....847 566-5350
287 N Lake St Mundelein (60060) ***(G-15470)***
**Anthony Liftgates Inc**....815 842-3383
1037 W Howard St Pontiac (61764) ***(G-17696)***
**Anthony's, East Peoria** *Also called Chips Aleeces Pita* ***(G-8706)***
**Anthos and Co LLC**....773 744-6813
2010 Dundee Rd Inverness (60067) ***(G-12202)***
**Anti-Seize Technology, Franklin Park** *Also called AST Industries Inc* ***(G-10405)***
**Antigua Casa Sherry-Brener (PA)**....773 737-1711
3145 W 63rd St Chicago (60629) ***(G-3916)***
**Antioch Fine Arts Foundation**....847 838-2274
41380 N Il Route 83 Antioch (60002) ***(G-617)***
**Antioch Packing House**....847 838-6800
510 Main St Antioch (60002) ***(G-618)***
**Antiques & Crafts Monthly, The, Rochester** *Also called Acm Publishing* ***(G-18114)***
**Antiques Cllecting Hobbies Mag, Naperville** *Also called Lightner Publishing Corp* ***(G-15691)***
**Antler Inn Manufactory Inc**....309 799-1132
7501 50th St Milan (61264) ***(G-14774)***
**Antolak Management Co Inc**....312 464-1800
447 E Ohio St Chicago (60611) ***(G-3917)***
**Antolin Interiors Usa Inc**....618 327-4416
18355 Enterprise Ave Nashville (62263) ***(G-15833)***
**Anton-Argires Inc**....708 388-6250
12345 S Latrobe Ave Alsip (60803) ***(G-434)***
**Anvil International LLC**....708 534-1414
7979 183rd St Ste D Tinley Park (60477) ***(G-20894)***
**Any Color, Washington** *Also called Salzman Printing* ***(G-21391)***
**Anylogic N Amer Ltd Lblty Co**....312 635-3344
20 N Wacker Dr Ste 2044 Chicago (60606) ***(G-3918)***
**Anytime Blacktopping**....618 931-6958
804 E Chain Of Rocks Rd Granite City (62040) ***(G-11266)***
**Anytime Heating & AC**....630 851-6696
10s264 Schoger Dr Ste 2 Naperville (60564) ***(G-15796)***
**Anytime Window Cleaning Inc**....773 235-5677
2517 N Monticello Ave Chicago (60647) ***(G-3919)***
**Anywave Communication Tech Inc**....847 415-2258
300 Knightsbridge Pkwy Lincolnshire (60069) ***(G-13429)***
**AP, Broadview** *Also called Arrow Pneumatics Inc* ***(G-2559)***
**AP Machine Inc**....708 450-1010
1975 N 17th Ave Melrose Park (60160) ***(G-14594)***
**APAC 90 Texas Holding Inc**....312 321-2299
401 N Wabash Ave Ste 740 Chicago (60611) ***(G-3920)***
**APAC II LLC**....618 426-1338
39 Schatte Rd Campbell Hill (62916) ***(G-2974)***
**APAC Unlimited Inc**....847 441-4282
790 W Frontage Rd Ste 214 Northfield (60093) ***(G-16390)***
**Apache Supply**....708 409-1040
324 La Porte Ave Melrose Park (60164) ***(G-14595)***
**Apak Packaging Group Inc**....630 616-7275
208 Berg St Algonquin (60102) ***(G-377)***
**Apana Inc**....309 303-4007
7201 N Drake Ct Peoria (61615) ***(G-17308)***
**Apco Enterprises Inc**....708 430-7333
9901 S 76th Ave Bridgeview (60455) ***(G-2466)***
**Apco Packaging Inc**....708 430-7333
9901 S 76th Ave Bridgeview (60455) ***(G-2467)***
**Apco Valve & Primer, Schaumburg** *Also called Fkavpc Inc* ***(G-19530)***
**Apex Colors**....219 764-3301
1031 W Bryn Mawr Ave 1a Chicago (60660) ***(G-3921)***
**Apex Dental Materials Inc**....847 719-1133
330 Telser Rd Lake Zurich (60047) ***(G-13042)***
**Apex Engineering Products Corp**....630 820-8888
1241 Shoreline Dr Aurora (60504) ***(G-958)***
**Apex Manufacturing Inc**....815 728-0108
5409 Craftwell Dr Ste A Ringwood (60072) ***(G-17987)***

ALPHABETIC

**Apex Material Technologies LLC** ....815 727-3010
10 Industry Ave Joliet (60435) ***(G-12456)***
**Apex Pattern Works** ....309 346-2905
836 Brenkman Dr Pekin (61554) ***(G-17254)***
**Apex Tool Works Inc** ....847 394-5810
3200 Tollview Dr Rolling Meadows (60008) ***(G-18710)***
**Apex Wire Products Company Inc** ....847 671-1830
9030 Gage Ave Franklin Park (60131) ***(G-10397)***
**Apf US Inc** ....217 304-0027
2204 Kickapoo Dr Danville (61832) ***(G-7702)***
**Aph Custom Wood & Metal Pdts** ....708 410-1274
2801 S 25th Ave Broadview (60155) ***(G-2558)***
**Aphelion Precision Tech Corp** ....847 215-7285
1800 Greenleaf Ave Elk Grove Village (60007) ***(G-9310)***
**API, Elk Grove Village** *Also called Advertising Products Inc* ***(G-9281)***
**API Publishing Services LLC** ....312 644-6610
330 N Wabash Ave Ste 2000 Chicago (60611) ***(G-3922)***
**APL Engineered Materials Inc** ....217 367-1340
2401 Willow Rd Urbana (61802) ***(G-21070)***
**APL Logistics Americas Ltd** ....630 783-0200
2649 Internationale Pkwy Woodridge (60517) ***(G-22453)***
**APM Process Center, Dekalb** *Also called L M C Inc* ***(G-8101)***
**Apmi, Elk Grove Village** *Also called Advanced Precision Mfg Inc* ***(G-9276)***
**Apoc, Abbott Park** *Also called Abbott Point of Care Inc* ***(G-6)***
**Apolinski John** ....847 696-3156
920 Brookline Ln Park Ridge (60068) ***(G-17181)***
**Apollo Colors, Rockdale** *Also called Scientific Colors Inc* ***(G-18232)***
**Apollo Colors Mfg Plant, Rockdale** *Also called Scientific Colors Inc* ***(G-18233)***
**Apollo Computer Solutions Inc (PA)** ....312 671-3575
914 55th St 2 Downers Grove (60515) ***(G-8388)***
**Apollo Machine & Manufacturing** ....847 677-6444
7617 Parkside Ave Skokie (60077) ***(G-19956)***
**Apollo Plastics Corporation** ....773 282-9222
5333 N Elston Ave Chicago (60630) ***(G-3923)***
**Apollo Printing Inc** ....815 741-3065
2135 183rd St Homewood (60430) ***(G-12091)***
**Apostrophe Brands** ....312 832-0300
225 W Hubbard St Ste 600 Chicago (60654) ***(G-3924)***
**Apparel Works Intl LLC** ....224 235-4240
51 Sherwood Ter Ste G Lake Bluff (60044) ***(G-12832)***
**Apple Express** ....708 483-8168
1701 S 1st Ave Ste 307 Maywood (60153) ***(G-14416)***
**Apple Graphics Inc** ....630 389-2222
934 Paramount Pkwy Batavia (60510) ***(G-1416)***
**Apple Lube Center** ....217 787-7035
3316 Robbins Rd Ste A Springfield (62704) ***(G-20387)***
**Apple Press Inc** ....815 224-1451
329 N 25th Rd Peru (61354) ***(G-17500)***
**Apple Print, Itasca** *Also called George Vaggelatos* ***(G-12269)***
**Apple Printing Center** ....630 932-9494
1433 W Fullerton Ave E Addison (60101) ***(G-41)***
**Apple Rush Company** ....847 730-5324
4300 Dipaolo Ctr Glenview (60025) ***(G-11104)***
**Appleton Group, Rosemont** *Also called Appleton Grp LLC* ***(G-18989)***
**Appleton Grp LLC (HQ)** ....847 268-6000
9377 W Higgins Rd Rosemont (60018) ***(G-18989)***
**Appleton Rack & Pinions Inc** ....815 467-9583
110 Industrial Dr Unit E Minooka (60447) ***(G-14836)***
**Appliance Information and Repr** ....217 698-8858
10190 Buckhart Rd Rochester (62563) ***(G-18115)***
**Appliance Repair** ....708 456-1020
4911 N Delphia Ave Norridge (60706) ***(G-16096)***
**Applied Arts & Sciences Inc** ....407 288-8228
21432 Prestancia Dr Mokena (60448) ***(G-14853)***
**Applied Hydraulic Services** ....773 638-8500
944 N Spaulding Ave Chicago (60651) ***(G-3925)***
**Applied Hydraulics Corporation** ....773 638-8500
944 N Spaulding Ave Chicago (60651) ***(G-3926)***
**Applied Mechanical Tech LLC** ....815 472-2700
135 Industrial Dr Momence (60954) ***(G-14978)***
**Applied Polymer System Inc** ....847 301-1712
507 Estes Ave Schaumburg (60193) ***(G-19445)***
**Applied Products Inc** ....815 633-3825
12000 Product Dr Machesney Park (61115) ***(G-14057)***
**Applied Systems Inc (PA)** ....708 534-5575
200 Applied Pkwy University Park (60484) ***(G-21041)***
**Applied Tech Publications Inc** ....847 382-8100
535 Plainfield Rd Ste A Willowbrook (60527) ***(G-22199)***
**Applied Thermal Coatings** ....815 372-4305
221 Rocbaar Dr Romeoville (60446) ***(G-18799)***
**Applus Technologies Inc (PA)** ....312 661-1604
120 S La Salle St # 1450 Chicago (60603) ***(G-3927)***
**Appsanity Advisory LLC** ....847 638-1172
335 Auburn Ave Winnetka (60093) ***(G-22302)***
**Apr Graphics Inc** ....847 329-7800
4825 Main St Skokie (60077) ***(G-19957)***
**Aprimo Marketing Operations Uk, Chicago** *Also called Aprimo US LLC* ***(G-3928)***
**Aprimo US LLC** ....877 794-8556
230 W Monroe St Ste 1200 Chicago (60606) ***(G-3928)***
**Apser Laboratory Inc** ....630 543-3333
625 W Factory Rd Ste B Addison (60101) ***(G-42)***
**Apser Labs, Addison** *Also called Apser Laboratory Inc* ***(G-42)***
**APT Tool Inc** ....815 337-0051
1301 Cobblestone Way Woodstock (60098) ***(G-22540)***
**Aptargroup Inc** ....779 220-4430
265 Exchange Dr Crystal Lake (60014) ***(G-7534)***
**Aptargroup Inc (PA)** ....815 477-0424
475 W Terra Cotta Ave E Crystal Lake (60014) ***(G-7535)***
**Aptargroup Inc** ....847 462-3900
4900 Prime Pkwy McHenry (60050) ***(G-14481)***
**Aptargroup Inc** ....847 639-2124
1160 Silver Lake Rd Cary (60013) ***(G-3327)***
**Aptargroup International LLC (HQ)** ....815 477-0424
475 W Terra Cotta Ave E Crystal Lake (60014) ***(G-7536)***
**Aptean Holdings Inc** ....773 975-3100
2000 N Racine Ave Chicago (60614) ***(G-3929)***
**Aptimmune Biologics Inc** ....217 377-8866
60 Hazelwood Dr Champaign (61820) ***(G-3451)***
**APV Consolidated Inc** ....847 678-4300
5100 River Rd Fl 3 Schiller Park (60176) ***(G-19804)***
**Aqua Belle Manufacturing Co, Highland Park** *Also called J II Inc* ***(G-11845)***
**Aqua Coat Inc** ....815 209-0808
1061 Davis Rd Elgin (60123) ***(G-8955)***
**Aqua Control Inc** ....815 664-4900
6a Wolfer Industrial Park Spring Valley (61362) ***(G-20374)***
**Aqua Farm, Chicago** *Also called Direct Marketing 1 Corporation* ***(G-4608)***
**Aqua Golf Inc (PA)** ....217 824-2097
6 Manor Ct Taylorville (62568) ***(G-20832)***
**Aqua Marine Pools, Loves Park** *Also called Rockford Sewer Co Inc* ***(G-13987)***
**Aqua-Tech Co** ....847 383-7075
1875 Big Timber Rd Ste C Elgin (60123) ***(G-8956)***
**Aquadine Inc (PA)** ....800 497-3463
495 Commanche Cir Harvard (60033) ***(G-11621)***
**Aquadine Nutritional System, Harvard** *Also called Aquadine Inc* ***(G-11621)***
**Aquagreen Dispositions LLC** ....708 606-0211
25731 S Bristol Ln Monee (60449) ***(G-14992)***
**Aquarium Adventure & Pet Land, Hoffman Estates** *Also called Starfish Ventures Inc* ***(G-12059)***
**Aquarius Fluid Products Inc** ....847 289-9090
2585 Millennium Dr Ste B Elgin (60124) ***(G-8957)***
**Aquarius Metal Products Inc (PA)** ....847 659-9266
12795 Muir Dr Huntley (60142) ***(G-12132)***
**Aquatrol Inc** ....630 365-2363
600 E North St Elburn (60119) ***(G-8875)***
**Aquaviva Winery (PA)** ....815 899-4444
219 W State St Sycamore (60178) ***(G-20787)***
**Aqueous Solutions LLC** ....217 531-1206
301 N Neil St Ste 400 Champaign (61820) ***(G-3452)***
**Aquion Inc (PA)** ....847 725-3000
101 S Gary Ave Unit A Roselle (60172) ***(G-18926)***
**Aquion Partners Ltd Partnr** ....847 437-9400
2080 Lunt Ave Elk Grove Village (60007) ***(G-9311)***
**AR Concepts USA Inc** ....847 392-4608
520 N Hicks Rd Ste 120 Palatine (60067) ***(G-17002)***
**AR Industries** ....630 543-0282
1405 W Bernard Dr Ste C Addison (60101) ***(G-43)***
**AR Inet Corp** ....603 380-3903
2336 Pagosa Springs Dr Aurora (60503) ***(G-959)***
**Ar-En Party Printers Inc** ....847 673-7390
3416 Oakton St Skokie (60076) ***(G-19958)***
**Ar1510 LLC** ....309 944-6939
745 Hanford St Geneseo (61254) ***(G-10798)***
**Arachnid 360 LLC (PA)** ....815 654-0212
6212 Material Ave Loves Park (61111) ***(G-13921)***
**Aracon Drpery Vntian Blind Ltd** ....773 252-1281
3015 N Kedzie Ave Chicago (60618) ***(G-3930)***
**Aracon Venetian Blind-Drapery, Chicago** *Also called Aracon Drpery Vntian Blind Ltd* ***(G-3930)***
**Arba Retail Systems Copr, Naperville** *Also called Arba Retail Systems Corp* ***(G-15797)***
**Arba Retail Systems Corp** ....630 620-8566
2760 Forgue Dr Ste 106 Naperville (60564) ***(G-15797)***
**Arbetman & Associates** ....708 386-8586
635 S Humphrey Ave Oak Park (60304) ***(G-16653)***
**Arbor Products** ....847 653-6210
614 Wisner St Park Ridge (60068) ***(G-17182)***
**Arbortech Corporation** ....847 462-1111
3607 Chapel Hill Rd Ste M Johnsburg (60051) ***(G-12430)***
**Arby Graphic Service Inc** ....847 763-0900
6019 W Howard St Niles (60714) ***(G-15961)***
**ARC Industries Inc** ....847 303-5005
2020 Hammond Dr Schaumburg (60173) ***(G-19446)***
**ARC Mobile LLC** ....201 838-3410
3944 Johnson Ave Western Springs (60558) ***(G-21863)***
**ARC Technologies, Hinsdale** *Also called Nelson-Rose Inc* ***(G-11954)***
**ARC-Tronics Inc** ....847 437-0211
1150 Pagni Dr Elk Grove Village (60007) ***(G-9312)***
**Arcadia Press Inc** ....847 451-6390
10915 Franklin Ave Ste L Franklin Park (60131) ***(G-10398)***

**Arcam Cad To Metal Inc** ....630 357-5700
55 Shuman Blvd Ste 850 Naperville (60563) ***(G-15599)***
**Arcanum Alloy Design Inc** ....219 508-5531
3440 S Dearborn St 206s Chicago (60616) ***(G-3931)***
**Arcelor Mittal USA LLC** ....312 899-3500
1 S Dearborn St Ste 1800 Chicago (60603) ***(G-3932)***
**Arcelormittal Riverdale Inc** ....708 849-8803
13500 S Perry Ave Riverdale (60827) ***(G-18014)***
**Arcelormittal South Chicago** ....312 899-3300
1 S Dearborn St Ste 2100 Chicago (60603) ***(G-3933)***
**Arcelormittal USA LLC** ....312 899-3400
1 S Dearborn St Ste 2100 Chicago (60603) ***(G-3934)***
**Arcelormittal USA LLC (HQ)** ....312 346-0300
1 S Dearborn St Ste 1800 Chicago (60603) ***(G-3935)***
**Arcelormittal USA of Chicago, Chicago** *Also called Arcelormittal USA LLC* ***(G-3934)***
**Arch Chemicals Inc** ....630 955-0401
940 E Diehl Rd Ste 110 Naperville (60563) ***(G-15600)***
**Arch Chemicals Inc** ....630 365-1720
809 Hicks Dr Ste A Elburn (60119) ***(G-8876)***
**Arch Printing** ....630 896-6610
710 Morton Ave North Aurora (60542) ***(G-16118)***
**Arch Printing Inc** ....630 966-0235
710 Morton Ave Ste N Aurora (60506) ***(G-1110)***
**Archer Engineering Company** ....773 247-3501
3154 S Archer Ave Chicago (60608) ***(G-3936)***
**Archer General Contg & Fabg** ....708 757-7902
22498 Miller Rd Steger (60475) ***(G-20568)***
**Archer Industries & Supplies** ....773 777-2698
3452 N Knox Ave Chicago (60641) ***(G-3937)***
**Archer Manufacturing Corp** ....773 585-7181
4439 S Knox Ave Chicago (60632) ***(G-3938)***
**Archer Metal & Paper Co** ....773 585-3030
4619 S Knox Ave Chicago (60632) ***(G-3939)***
**Archer Screw Products Inc (PA)** ....847 451-1150
11341 Melrose Ave Franklin Park (60131) ***(G-10399)***
**Archer Tinning & Re-Tinning Co (PA)** ....773 927-7240
1019 W 47th St Chicago (60609) ***(G-3940)***
**Archer Wire International Corp (PA)** ....708 563-1700
7300 S Narragansett Ave Bedford Park (60638) ***(G-1537)***
**Archer-Daniels-Midland Company (PA)** ....312 634-8100
77 W Wacker Dr Ste 4600 Chicago (60601) ***(G-3941)***
**Archer-Daniels-Midland Company** ....815 362-2180
54 Stephenson St German Valley (61039) ***(G-10890)***
**Archer-Daniels-Midland Company** ....217 935-3620
714 N Grant St Clinton (61727) ***(G-7277)***
**Archer-Daniels-Midland Company** ....217 424-5882
3665 E Division Decatur (62525) ***(G-7833)***
**Archer-Daniels-Midland Company** ....217 222-7100
1000 N 30th St Quincy (62301) ***(G-17793)***
**Archer-Daniels-Midland Company** ....217 424-5236
466 Ferrys Pkwy Decatur (62525) ***(G-7834)***
**Archer-Daniels-Midland Company** ....309 673-7828
1 Edmund St Peoria (61602) ***(G-17309)***
**Archer-Daniels-Midland Company** ....618 483-6171
601 W Division St Altamont (62411) ***(G-549)***
**Archer-Daniels-Midland Company** ....309 772-2141
160 E Main St Bushnell (61422) ***(G-2897)***
**Archer-Daniels-Midland Company** ....217 424-5413
350 N Water St Decatur (62523) ***(G-7835)***
**Archer-Daniels-Midland Company** ....224 544-5980
927 N Shore Dr Lake Bluff (60044) ***(G-12833)***
**Archer-Daniels-Midland Company** ....217 424-5200
2235 N Brush College Rd Decatur (62526) ***(G-7836)***
**Archer-Daniels-Midland Company** ....217 342-3986
1 Goodlife Dr Effingham (62401) ***(G-8824)***
**Archer-Daniels-Midland Company** ....217 424-5858
3883 E Faries Pkwy Decatur (62526) ***(G-7837)***
**Archer-Daniels-Midland Company** ....217 424-5200
4666 E Faries Pkwy Ste 1 Decatur (62526) ***(G-7838)***
**Archer-Daniels-Midland Company** ....217 224-1800
2100 Gardner Expy Quincy (62305) ***(G-17794)***
**Archer-Daniels-Midland Company** ....217 732-6678
2250 5th St Lincoln (62656) ***(G-13404)***
**Archer-Daniels-Midland Company** ....217 424-5785
3615 E Faries Pkwy Decatur (62526) ***(G-7839)***
**Archer-Daniels-Midland Company** ....217 224-1800
1900 Gardner Expy Quincy (62301) ***(G-17795)***
**Archer-Daniels-Midland Company** ....618 432-7194
408 S Railroad St Patoka (62875) ***(G-17230)***
**Archer-Daniels-Midland Company** ....217 224-1875
2701 Refinery Rd Quincy (62305) ***(G-17796)***
**Archer-Daniels-Midland Company** ....217 424-5200
3700 E Division St Decatur (62526) ***(G-7840)***
**Archer-Daniels-Midland Company** ....217 424-5200
4666 E Faries Pkwy Ste 1 Decatur (62526) ***(G-7841)***
**Archi-Cepts** ....618 594-8810
1630 Franklin St Carlyle (62231) ***(G-3052)***
**Architctral Bldrs Hdwr Mfg Inc** ....630 875-9900
1222 Ardmore Ave Itasca (60143) ***(G-12230)***
**Architctural Grilles Sunshades** ....708 479-9458
9950 W 190th St Mokena (60448) ***(G-14854)***
**Architectual Woodworking** ....847 259-3331
305 Brian Ln Prospect Heights (60070) ***(G-17772)***
**Architectural Cast Ston** ....630 377-4800
2775 Norton Creek Dr West Chicago (60185) ***(G-21661)***
**Architectural Distributors** ....847 223-5800
162 Center St Grayslake (60030) ***(G-11320)***
**Architectural Fan Coil Inc** ....312 399-1203
3900 W Palmer St Chicago (60647) ***(G-3942)***
**Architectural Metal Solutions, Alsip** *Also called Doralco Inc* ***(G-458)***
**Architectural Metals LLC** ....815 654-2370
6200 Forest Hills Rd Loves Park (61111) ***(G-13922)***
**Arclar Coal, Equality** *Also called Peabody Arclar Mining LLC* ***(G-9989)***
**Arco Automobile, Oak Lawn** *Also called Arco Automotive Elec Svc Co* ***(G-16603)***
**Arco Automotive Elec Svc Co** ....708 422-2976
10707 S Cicero Ave Oak Lawn (60453) ***(G-16603)***
**Arco Brand, Lake Villa** *Also called C & F Packing Co Inc* ***(G-13012)***
**Arcoa Group Inc (PA)** ....847 693-7519
3300 Washington St Waukegan (60085) ***(G-21527)***
**Arcoa USA, Waukegan** *Also called Arcoa Group Inc* ***(G-21527)***
**Arcola Rcord Hrld-Rankin Publr, Arcola** *Also called Arcola Record Herald* ***(G-665)***
**Arcola Record Herald** ....217 268-4950
118 E Main St Arcola (61910) ***(G-665)***
**Arcon Ring and Specialty Corp** ....630 682-5252
123 Easy St Carol Stream (60188) ***(G-3104)***
**Arconic Inc** ....217 431-3800
1 Customer Pl Danville (61834) ***(G-7703)***
**Arctic Blast Co, Lake Bluff** *Also called Duroweld Company Inc* ***(G-12841)***
**Arcturus Performance Pdts LLC** ....630 204-0211
3955 Commerce Dr Saint Charles (60174) ***(G-19137)***
**Ardagh Conversion Systems Inc** ....847 438-4100
570 Telser Rd Ste B Lake Zurich (60047) ***(G-13043)***
**Ardagh Glass Inc** ....217 732-1796
1200 N Logan St Lincoln (62656) ***(G-13405)***
**Ardagh Glass Inc** ....708 849-4010
13850 Cottage Grove Ave Dolton (60419) ***(G-8363)***
**Ardagh Metal Beverage USA Inc** ....773 399-3000
8770 W Bryn Mawr Ave # 175 Chicago (60631) ***(G-3943)***
**Ardekin Precision LLC** ....815 397-1069
1321 Capital Dr Rockford (61109) ***(G-18269)***
**Ardent Mills LLC** ....618 463-4411
145 W Broadway Alton (62002) ***(G-561)***
**Ardent Mills LLC** ....618 826-2371
101 Water St Chester (62233) ***(G-3650)***
**Area Diesel Service Inc (PA)** ....217 854-2641
1300 University St Carlinville (62626) ***(G-3030)***
**Area Disposal Service Inc** ....217 935-1300
9550 Heritage Rd Clinton (61727) ***(G-7278)***
**Area Fabricators** ....217 455-3426
1735 Highway 24 Coatsburg (62325) ***(G-7300)***
**Area Marketing Inc** ....815 806-8844
10221 W Lincoln Hwy Frankfort (60423) ***(G-10297)***
**Area Rigging & Millwright Svcs, Rockford** *Also called Patrick Holdings Inc* ***(G-18531)***
**Arens Controls Company LLc** ....847 844-4700
3602 N Kennicott Ave Arlington Heights (60004) ***(G-715)***
**Argentum Medical LLC** ....888 551-0188
2571 Kaneville Ct Geneva (60134) ***(G-10810)***
**Argo Manufacturing Co** ....630 377-1750
4n944 Old Lafox Rd Wasco (60183) ***(G-21372)***
**Argon Medical, Wheeling** *Also called Manan Medical Products Inc* ***(G-22099)***
**Argus Brewery** ....773 941-4050
11314 S Front Ave Chicago (60628) ***(G-3944)***
**Argus Systems Group, Savoy** *Also called Innovative SEC Systems Inc* ***(G-19410)***
**Argyle Cut Stone Co** ....847 456-6210
1046 Woodlawn Ave Des Plaines (60016) ***(G-8151)***
**ARI Industries Inc** ....630 953-9100
381 S Ari Ct Addison (60101) ***(G-44)***
**Aria Corporation** ....847 918-9329
29471 N Northwoods Dr Libertyville (60048) ***(G-13304)***
**Ariba Inc** ....630 649-7600
3333 Warrenville Rd # 130 Lisle (60532) ***(G-13562)***
**Arid Technologies Inc** ....630 681-8500
323 S Hale St Wheaton (60187) ***(G-21936)***
**ARINC Incorporated** ....800 633-6882
8 Eagle Ctr Ste 4 O Fallon (62269) ***(G-16463)***
**Arizon Strctures Worldwide LLC** ....618 451-7250
1200 W 7th St Granite City (62040) ***(G-11267)***
**Arjay Instant Printing** ....847 438-9059
25785 N Hillview Ct Mundelein (60060) ***(G-15471)***
**Ark Technologies Inc (PA)** ....630 377-8855
3655 Ohio Ave Saint Charles (60174) ***(G-19138)***
**Arkadian Gaming LLC** ....708 377-5656
11227 Distinctive Dr Orland Park (60467) ***(G-16844)***
**Arkema Coating Resins, Alsip** *Also called Arkema Inc* ***(G-435)***
**Arkema Inc** ....708 396-3001
12840 S Pulaski Rd Alsip (60803) ***(G-435)***
**Arkema Inc** ....708 385-2188
12840 S Pulaski Rd Alsip (60803) ***(G-436)***
**Arla Graphics Inc** ....847 470-0005
875 Mountain Dr Deerfield (60015) ***(G-7978)***

A L P H A B E T I C

**Arland Clean Fuels LLC** 847 868-8580
630 Davis St Ste 300 Evanston (60201) ***(G-10011)***
**Arlen-Jacob Manufacturing Co** 815 485-4777
2 Ford Dr Ste H New Lenox (60451) ***(G-15870)***
**Arlington Plating Company** 847 359-1490
600 S Vermont St Palatine (60067) ***(G-17003)***
**Arlington Signs & Banners, Arlington Heights** *Also called Stelmont Inc* ***(G-843)***
**Arlington Specialties Inc** 847 545-9500
1515 Carmen Dr Elk Grove Village (60007) ***(G-9313)***
**Arlington Strl Stl Co Inc** 847 577-2200
1727 E Davis St Arlington Heights (60005) ***(G-716)***
**Armacell LLC** 708 596-9501
16800 S Canal St South Holland (60473) ***(G-20246)***
**Armada Nutrition LLC** 931 451-7808
285 Fullerton Ave Carol Stream (60188) ***(G-3105)***
**Armalite, Geneseo** *Also called Ar1510 LLC* ***(G-10798)***
**Armbrust Paper Tubes Inc** 773 586-3232
6255 S Harlem Ave Chicago (60638) ***(G-3945)***
**Armil/Cfs Inc** 708 339-6810
15660 La Salle St South Holland (60473) ***(G-20247)***
**Armin Industries, South Elgin** *Also called Armin Molding Corp* ***(G-20182)***
**Armin Molding Corp** 847 742-1864
1500 N La Fox St South Elgin (60177) ***(G-20182)***
**Armin Tool and Mfg Co (PA)** 847 742-1864
1500 N Lafox St South Elgin (60177) ***(G-20183)***
**Armitage Industries Inc** 847 288-9090
2550 Edgington St Ste A Franklin Park (60131) ***(G-10400)***
**Armitage Machine Co Inc** 309 697-9050
6035 Washington St Peoria (61607) ***(G-17310)***
**Armitage Welding** 773 772-1442
3212 W Armitage Ave Chicago (60647) ***(G-3946)***
**Armoloy of Illinois Inc** 815 758-6657
114 Simonds Ave Dekalb (60115) ***(G-8075)***
**Armor Coated Technology Corp** 815 636-7200
1190 Anvil Rd Machesney Park (61115) ***(G-14058)***
**Armour-Eckrich Meats LLC (HQ)** 630 281-5000
4225 Naperville Rd # 600 Lisle (60532) ***(G-13563)***
**Armstrong Aerospace Inc** 847 250-5132
1377 Industrial Dr Itasca (60143) ***(G-12231)***
**Armstrong Aerospace Inc** 630 285-0200
1437 Harmony Ct Itasca (60143) ***(G-12232)***
**Army Navy Supply Depot, Marengo** *Also called Your Supply Depot Limited* ***(G-14245)***
**Arndt Enterprise Ltd** 847 234-5736
674 Timber Ln Ste 200 Lake Forest (60045) ***(G-12880)***
**Arndt's Hallmark Shop, Newton** *Also called Arndts Stores Inc* ***(G-15937)***
**Arndts Stores Inc (PA)** 618 783-2511
106 W Washington St Newton (62448) ***(G-15937)***
**Arnel Industries Inc** 630 543-6500
57 W Interstate Rd Addison (60101) ***(G-45)***
**Arnette Pattern Co Inc** 618 451-7700
3203 Missouri Ave Granite City (62040) ***(G-11268)***
**Arnold Engineering Co (HQ)** 815 568-2000
300 N West St Marengo (60152) ***(G-14218)***
**Arnold Magnetic Tech Corp** 815 568-2000
300 N West St Marengo (60152) ***(G-14219)***
**Arnold Monument Co Inc (PA)** 217 546-2102
1621 Wabash Ave Springfield (62704) ***(G-20388)***
**Arntzen Corporation** 815 334-0788
14600 Washington St Woodstock (60098) ***(G-22541)***
**Aro Metal Stamping Company Inc** 630 351-7676
78 Congress Cir W Roselle (60172) ***(G-18927)***
**Arpac LLC (PA)** 847 678-9034
9555 Irving Park Rd Schiller Park (60176) ***(G-19805)***
**Arquilla Inc** 815 455-2470
4220 Waller St Ste 1 Crystal Lake (60012) ***(G-7537)***
**Arris Group Inc** 630 281-3000
2400 Ogden Ave Ste 180 Lisle (60532) ***(G-13564)***
**Arro Corporation** 708 352-8200
7250 Santa Fe Dr Hodgkins (60525) ***(G-11970)***
**Arro Corporation** 773 978-1251
10459 S Muskegon Ave Chicago (60617) ***(G-3947)***
**Arro Corporation** 708 352-7412
7550 Santa Fe Dr Hodgkins (60525) ***(G-11971)***
**Arro Liquid Division, Hodgkins** *Also called Arro Corporation* ***(G-11971)***
**Arro Packing, Chicago** *Also called Arro Corporation* ***(G-3947)***
**Arrow Aluminum Castings Inc** 815 338-4480
2617 S Il Route 47 Woodstock (60098) ***(G-22542)***
**Arrow Asphalt Paving (PA)** 618 277-3009
910 N 2nd St Swansea (62226) ***(G-20774)***
**Arrow Edm Inc** 217 893-4277
1120 Veterans Pkwy Rantoul (61866) ***(G-17918)***
**Arrow Engineering Inc** 815 397-0862
5191 27th Ave Rockford (61109) ***(G-18270)***
**Arrow Gear Company (PA)** 630 969-7640
2301 Curtiss St Downers Grove (60515) ***(G-8389)***
**Arrow Gear Company** 630 969-7640
5240 Belmont Rd Downers Grove (60515) ***(G-8390)***
**Arrow Group Indust, Breese** *Also called Arrow Shed LLC* ***(G-2438)***
**Arrow Group Industries, Breese** *Also called Arrow Shed LLC* ***(G-2437)***
**Arrow Pin and Products Inc** 708 755-7575
51 E 34th St S Chicago Hts (60411) ***(G-19100)***
**Arrow Pneumatics Inc** 708 343-6177
2111 W 21st St Broadview (60155) ***(G-2559)***
**Arrow Road Construction Co (PA)** 847 437-0700
3401 S Busse Rd Mount Prospect (60056) ***(G-15310)***
**Arrow Road Construction Co** 847 658-1140
10500 S Il Route 31 Algonquin (60102) ***(G-378)***
**Arrow Sales & Service Inc** 815 223-0251
3101 E 3rd Rd La Salle (61301) ***(G-12765)***
**Arrow Shed LLC (HQ)** 618 526-4546
1101 N 4th St Breese (62230) ***(G-2437)***
**Arrow Shed LLC** 618 526-4546
1101 N 4th St Breese (62230) ***(G-2438)***
**Arrow Sheet Metal Company** 815 455-2019
1032 Ascot Dr Crystal Lake (60014) ***(G-7538)***
**Arrow Signs (PA)** 618 466-0818
4545 N Alby Rd Godfrey (62035) ***(G-11222)***
**Arroweye Solutions Inc (PA)** 312 253-9400
549 W Randolph St Ste 200 Chicago (60661) ***(G-3948)***
**Arrowhead Brick Pavers Inc** 630 393-1584
30w218 Bttrfeld Rd Unit A Warrenville (60555) ***(G-21342)***
**Arrows Up Inc** 847 305-2550
3 W College Dr Rear 1 Arlington Heights (60004) ***(G-717)***
**Arrowtech Pallet & Crating** 815 547-9300
860 E Jackson St Belvidere (61008) ***(G-1734)***
**ARS Marine Inc East Location** 815 942-2600
1142 Cemetery Rd Morris (60450) ***(G-15093)***
**Arsco** 708 755-1733
1001 Washington St Chicago Heights (60411) ***(G-7079)***
**Art & Son Design, Wauconda** *Also called Art & Son Sign Inc* ***(G-21443)***
**Art & Son Sign Inc** 847 526-7205
1090 Brown St Wauconda (60084) ***(G-21443)***
**Art Bookbinders of America** 312 226-4100
451 N Claremont Ave Chicago (60612) ***(G-3949)***
**Art Casting of IL Inc** 815 732-7777
5 Madison St Oregon (61061) ***(G-16818)***
**Art Classics Ltd, Trenton** *Also called East Wisconsin LLC* ***(G-20991)***
**Art Clay World Usa Inc** 708 857-8800
4535 Southwest Hwy Oak Lawn (60453) ***(G-16604)***
**Art Cnc Machining LLC** 708 907-3090
9824 Industrial Dr Bridgeview (60455) ***(G-2468)***
**Art Crystal II Enterprises Inc** 630 739-0222
7852 47th St Lyons (60534) ***(G-14030)***
**Art In Print Review** 773 697-9478
3500 N Lake Shore Dr Chicago (60657) ***(G-3950)***
**Art Jewel Enterprises Ltd** 630 260-0400
460 Randy Rd Carol Stream (60188) ***(G-3106)***
**Art Media Resources Inc** 312 663-5351
1965 W Pershing Rd Ste 4 Chicago (60609) ***(G-3951)***
**Art Newvo Incorporated** 847 838-0304
25819 W Grail Lk Rd Ste 1 Antioch (60002) ***(G-619)***
**Art of Running, The, Glencoe** *Also called Panache Editions Ltd* ***(G-11005)***
**Art of Shaving - Fl LLC** 847 568-0881
4999 Old Orchard Ctr M14 Skokie (60077) ***(G-19959)***
**Art of Shaving - Fl LLC** 312 527-1604
520 N Michigan Ave # 122 Chicago (60611) ***(G-3952)***
**Art of Shaving - Fl LLC** 630 684-0277
100 Oakbrook Ctr Oak Brook (60523) ***(G-16489)***
**Art Wire Works Inc** 708 458-3993
6711 S Leclaire Ave Bedford Park (60638) ***(G-1538)***
**Art-Craft Printers** 847 455-2201
9108 Belden Ave Franklin Park (60131) ***(G-10401)***
**Art-Flo Shirt & Lettering Co** 708 656-5422
6939 W 59th St Chicago (60638) ***(G-3953)***
**Artemide Inc** 312 475-0100
351 W Hubbard St Ste 602 Chicago (60654) ***(G-3954)***
**Artganiks, Naperville** *Also called I T C W Inc* ***(G-15671)***
**Arthur Coyle Press** 773 465-8418
2730 W Coyle Ave Chicago (60645) ***(G-3955)***
**Arthur Custom Tank LLC** 217 543-4022
510 E Progress St Arthur (61911) ***(G-880)***
**Arthur Graphic Clarion** 217 543-2151
113 E Illinois St Arthur (61911) ***(G-881)***
**Arthur Leo Kuhl** 618 752-5473
1023 N 500th St Ingraham (62434) ***(G-12199)***
**Arthur R Baker Inc** 708 301-4828
13507 W Oakwood Ct Homer Glen (60491) ***(G-12076)***
**Artisan Handprints Inc** 773 725-1799
4234 N Pulaski Rd Chicago (60641) ***(G-3956)***
**Artisan Signs, Orland Park** *Also called Mostert & Ferguson Signs* ***(G-16876)***
**Artisan Signs & Lighting, Orland Park** *Also called Pellegrini Enterprises Inc* ***(G-16884)***
**Artistic Carton Company (PA)** 847 741-0247
1975 Big Timber Rd Elgin (60123) ***(G-8958)***
**Artistic Dental Studio Inc** 630 679-8686
470 Woodcreek Dr Bolingbrook (60440) ***(G-2278)***
**Artistic Engraving Corporation** 708 409-0149
2929 S 18th Ave Ste B Broadview (60155) ***(G-2560)***
**Artistic Framing Inc (PA)** 847 808-0200
860 Chaddick Dr Ste F Wheeling (60090) ***(G-22007)***

**Artistries By Tommy Musto Inc** 630 674-8667
159 W Lake St Ste 1 Bloomingdale (60108) *(G-2094)*
**Artistry Engraving & Embossing** 773 775-4888
6000 N Northwest Hwy Chicago (60631) *(G-3957)*
**Artline Screen Printing Inc** 815 963-8125
1309 7th St Rockford (61104) *(G-18271)*
**Artpol Printing Inc** 773 622-0498
7011 W Higgins Ave Chicago (60656) *(G-3958)*
**Arts & Letters Marshall Signs** 773 927-4442
3610 S Albany Ave Chicago (60632) *(G-3959)*
**Arts Tamales** 309 367-2850
1453 Hickory Point Rd Metamora (61548) *(G-14739)*
**Artsonia LLC** 224 538-5060
1350 Tri State Pkwy # 106 Gurnee (60031) *(G-11429)*
**Arttig Art** 847 804-8001
140 Shepard Ave Ste H Wheeling (60090) *(G-22008)*
**Artwear** 618 234-5522
1916 Lebanon Ave Belleville (62221) *(G-1609)*
**Arvens Technology Inc** 650 776-5443
801 W Main St Peoria (61606) *(G-17311)*
**Arvey Paper, Chicago** *Also called Tjmj Inc (G-6731)*
**Arway Confections, Chicago** *Also called Baldi Candy Co (G-4032)*
**Arxium Inc** 847 808-2600
1400 Busch Pkwy Buffalo Grove (60089) *(G-2660)*
**Aryzta Great Kitchens, Romeoville** *Also called Aryzta LLC (G-18800)*
**Aryzta LLC** 708 498-2300
111 Northwest Ave Northlake (60164) *(G-16428)*
**Aryzta LLC** 815 306-7171
300 Innovation Dr Romeoville (60446) *(G-18800)*
**AS Fabricating Inc** 618 242-7438
15518 N Il Highway 37 Mount Vernon (62864) *(G-15398)*
**ASA, Itasca** *Also called American Supply Association (G-12228)*
**Asa Inc** 847 446-1856
723 Happ Rd Northfield (60093) *(G-16391)*
**Asahi Kasei Bioprocess Inc** 847 834-0800
1855 Elmdale Ave Glenview (60026) *(G-11105)*
**Asai Chicago** 708 239-0133
12559 S Holiday Dr Ste C Alsip (60803) *(G-437)*
**ASAP Pallets Inc** 630 350-7689
480 Podlin Dr Franklin Park (60131) *(G-10402)*
**ASAP Pallets Inc** 630 917-0180
2711 Washington Blvd Bellwood (60104) *(G-1694)*
**ASAP Printing, Morton Grove** *Also called Printing Source Inc (G-15228)*
**ASap Specialties Inc Del** 847 223-7699
888 E Belvidere Rd # 111 Grayslake (60030) *(G-11321)*
**Asbestos Control & Envmtl Svc** 630 690-0189
31 W 780 Poss Rd Eola (60519) *(G-9988)*
**ASC Fasteners, Sycamore** *Also called Ample Supply Company (G-20786)*
**Ascent Mfg Co** 847 806-6600
123 Scott St Elk Grove Village (60007) *(G-9314)*
**Asco Power Technologies LP** 630 505-4050
3s701 West Ave Ste 300 Warrenville (60555) *(G-21343)*
**Asco Valve Inc** 630 789-2082
443 S Banbury Rd Arlington Heights (60005) *(G-718)*
**Ascon Corp** 630 482-2950
472 Ridgelawn Trl Batavia (60510) *(G-1417)*
**Ash Pallet Management Inc (PA)** 847 473-5700
61 Mcmillen Rd Antioch (60002) *(G-620)*
**Ash Pallet Management Inc** 847 473-5700
9400 King St Franklin Park (60131) *(G-10403)*
**ASHI, Des Plaines** *Also called American Soc HM Inspectors Inc (G-8147)*
**Ashland ABC Choice Inc** 773 488-7800
7903 S Ashland Ave Chicago (60620) *(G-3960)*
**Ashland Aluminum Company Inc** 773 278-6440
1925 N Mendell St Chicago (60642) *(G-3961)*
**Ashland Chemical Incorporated** 708 891-0760
14201 Paxton Ave Calumet City (60409) *(G-2935)*
**Ashland Door Solutions LLC** 773 348-5106
185 Martin Ln Elk Grove Village (60007) *(G-9315)*
**Ashland Fuel & Quick Lube** 773 434-8870
5901 S Ashland Ave Chicago (60636) *(G-3962)*
**Ashland Lock & SEC Solutions, Chicago** *Also called A Ashland Lock Company (G-3684)*
**Ashland Screening Corporation** 708 758-8800
475 E Joe Orr Rd Chicago Heights (60411) *(G-7080)*
**Ashley Lauren** 847 733-9470
636 Church St Ste 701 Evanston (60201) *(G-10012)*
**Ashley Lauren Natural Products, Evanston** *Also called Ashley Lauren (G-10012)*
**Ashley Oil Co** 217 932-2112
508 Deere Run Ln Casey (62420) *(G-3380)*
**Ashley's Cutom Stationary, Hinsdale** *Also called Ashleys Inc (G-11939)*
**Ashleys Inc** 630 794-0804
30 E 1st St Hinsdale (60521) *(G-11939)*
**Ashton Diversified Enterprises** 630 739-0981
19w442 Deerpath Ln Lemont (60439) *(G-13225)*
**Ashton Gill Publishing LLC** 847 673-8675
2906 Central St Fl 1 Evanston (60201) *(G-10013)*
**Asi, Crystal Lake** *Also called Alpha Swiss Industries Inc (G-7530)*
**Asi Sign Systems Inc** 773 478-5241
2650c W Bradley Pl Chicago (60618) *(G-3963)*
**Asico LLC** 630 986-8032
26 Plaza Dr Westmont (60559) *(G-21876)*
**Ask Products Inc** 630 896-4056
544 N Highland Ave Aurora (60506) *(G-1111)*
**Asko Inc** 773 785-4515
15600 Vincennes Ave South Holland (60473) *(G-20248)*
**Asm Sensors Inc** 630 832-3202
650 W Grand Ave Ste 205 Elmhurst (60126) *(G-9834)*
**Asmw, Mc Cook** *Also called A&S Machining & Welding Inc (G-14443)*
**Aspen API Inc (HQ)** 847 635-0985
2136 S Wolf Rd Des Plaines (60018) *(G-8152)*
**Aspen Cabinet Dist Corp** 847 381-4241
364 N Bateman Cir Barrington (60010) *(G-1268)*
**Aspen Carpet Designs** 815 483-8501
11335 Stratford Rd Mokena (60448) *(G-14855)*
**Aspen Foods, Chicago** *Also called Koch Meat Co Inc (G-5396)*
**Aspen Foods, Chicago** *Also called Jcg Industries Inc (G-5286)*
**Aspen Foods Inc** 312 829-7282
1115 W Fulton Market Chicago (60607) *(G-3964)*
**Aspen Industries Inc** 630 238-0611
480 Country Club Dr Bensenville (60106) *(G-1836)*
**Aspen Manufacturing Company** 630 495-0922
1001 W Republic Dr Ste 6 Addison (60101) *(G-46)*
**Aspen Printing Services LLC** 630 357-3203
405 S River Rd Naperville (60540) *(G-15601)*
**Aspen Shutters Inc** 847 979-0166
2235 Hammond Dr Ste F Schaumburg (60173) *(G-19447)*
**Asphalt Maint Systems Inc (PA)** 815 986-6977
238 Charles St South Beloit (61080) *(G-20139)*
**Asphalt Maintenance** 815 234-7325
8579 N River Dr Byron (61010) *(G-2911)*
**Asphalt Products Inc** 618 943-4716
6574 Akin Rd Lawrenceville (62439) *(G-13195)*
**Assa Abloy Entrance Systems US** 847 228-5600
1630 Jarvis Ave Elk Grove Village (60007) *(G-9316)*
**Assemble and Mail Group Inc** 309 473-2006
508 S Buchanan St Heyworth (61745) *(G-11764)*
**Assemblers Inc** 773 378-3000
2850 W Columbus Ave Chicago (60652) *(G-3965)*
**Assembly International Inc** 847 437-3120
775 Touhy Ave Elk Grove Village (60007) *(G-9317)*
**Assemtech Inc** 630 876-4990
245 W Roosevelt Rd Ste 8 West Chicago (60185) *(G-21662)*
**Asset Partners Inc** 312 224-8300
4403 W Lawrence Ave # 200 Chicago (60630) *(G-3966)*
**Associate Computer Systems** 618 997-3653
211 N Market St Ste A Marion (62959) *(G-14254)*
**Associate General Labs Inc** 847 678-2717
9035 Exchange Ave Franklin Park (60131) *(G-10404)*
**Associated Agri-Business Inc** 618 498-2977
100 S State St Jerseyville (62052) *(G-12417)*
**Associated Agri-Business Inc (PA)** 618 498-2977
229 Elm St Eldred (62027) *(G-8927)*
**Associated Attractions Entps** 773 376-1900
4834 S Halsted St 14 Chicago (60609) *(G-3967)*
**Associated Design Inc** 708 974-9100
11160 Southwest Hwy Ste B Palos Hills (60465) *(G-17114)*
**Associated Design Service, Palos Hills** *Also called Associated Design Inc (G-17114)*
**Associated Equipment Distrs (PA)** 630 574-0650
650 E Algonquin Rd # 305 Schaumburg (60173) *(G-19448)*
**Associated Group Holdings LLC (PA)** 312 662-5488
30 S Wacker Dr Ste 1600 Chicago (60606) *(G-3968)*
**Associated Metal Mfg, Chicago** *Also called Kcp Metal Fabrications Inc (G-5367)*
**Associated Printers Inc** 847 548-8929
43215 N Grandview Ter Antioch (60002) *(G-621)*
**Associated Professionals** 847 931-0095
665 Tollgate Rd Ste F Elgin (60123) *(G-8959)*
**Associated Publications Inc** 312 266-8680
875 N Michigan Ave # 3434 Chicago (60611) *(G-3969)*
**Associated Rack Corporation** 616 554-6004
5810 N Northwest Hwy Chicago (60631) *(G-3970)*
**Associated Research Inc** 847 367-4077
13860 W Laurel Dr Lake Forest (60045) *(G-12881)*
**Associates Engraving Company** 217 523-4565
2601 Colt Rd Springfield (62707) *(G-20389)*
**Association Management Center** 847 375-4700
8735 W Higgins Rd Ste 300 Chicago (60631) *(G-3971)*
**Assurance Clg Restoration LLC** 630 444-3600
3740 Stern Ave Saint Charles (60174) *(G-19139)*
**Assurance Technologies Inc** 630 550-5000
1251 Humbracht Cir Ste A Bartlett (60103) *(G-1331)*
**Assured Welding Service Inc** 847 671-1414
9301 Byron St Schiller Park (60176) *(G-19806)*
**AST Industries Inc** 847 455-2300
2345 17th St Franklin Park (60131) *(G-10405)*
**Asta Service Inc** 630 271-0960
5821 Iris Ln Lisle (60532) *(G-13565)*
**Astec Mobile Screens Inc** 815 626-6374
2704 W Le Fevre Rd Sterling (61081) *(G-20582)*

**Astellas Pharma Inc** ....800 695-4321
1 Astellas Way Northbrook (60062) ***(G-16205)***
**Astellas US Holding Inc (HQ)** ....224 205-8800
1 Astellas Way Northbrook (60062) ***(G-16206)***
**Astellas US LLC** ....800 888-7704
3 Parkway N Deerfield (60015) ***(G-7979)***
**Astellas US Technologies Inc** ....847 317-8800
3 Parkway N Ste 300 Deerfield (60015) ***(G-7980)***
**Asteroid Grinding & Mfg Inc** ....847 298-8109
2190 S Wolf Rd Des Plaines (60018) ***(G-8153)***
**Astoria Wire & Metal Products, Bedford Park** *Also called Astoria Wire Products Inc* ***(G-1539)***
**Astoria Wire Products Inc** ....708 496-9950
5303 W 74th Pl Bedford Park (60638) ***(G-1539)***
**Astral Power Systems Inc** ....630 518-1741
31 W Downer Pl Ste 408 Aurora (60506) ***(G-1112)***
**Astro Machine Corporation** ....847 364-6363
630 Lively Blvd Elk Grove Village (60007) ***(G-9318)***
**Astro Plastic Containers Inc** ....708 458-7100
6735 S Old Harlem Ave Bedford Park (60638) ***(G-1540)***
**Astro Tool Co Inc** ....630 876-3402
1200 Atlantic Dr West Chicago (60185) ***(G-21663)***
**Astro-Craft Inc** ....815 675-1500
7509 Spring Grove Rd Spring Grove (60081) ***(G-20326)***
**Astro-Physics Inc** ....815 282-1513
11250 Forest Hills Rd Machesney Park (61115) ***(G-14059)***
**Astron Dental Corporation** ....847 726-8787
815 Oakwood Rd Ste G Lake Zurich (60047) ***(G-13044)***
**At Home Magazine** ....217 351-5282
15 E Main St Champaign (61820) ***(G-3453)***
**AT&I Resources LLC (HQ)** ....918 925-0154
444 W Interstate Rd Addison (60101) ***(G-47)***
**AT&T Corp** ....630 693-5000
851 Oak Creek Dr Lombard (60148) ***(G-13765)***
**AT&T Corp** ....312 602-4108
1 S Wacker Dr Ste 3900 Chicago (60606) ***(G-3972)***
**AT&T Midwest, Chicago** *Also called AT&T Teleholdings Inc* ***(G-3973)***
**AT&T Teleholdings Inc (HQ)** ....800 257-0902
30 S Wacker Dr Fl 34 Chicago (60606) ***(G-3973)***
**Ata Finishing Corp** ....847 677-8560
8225 Kimball Ave Skokie (60076) ***(G-19960)***
**Ataraxia LLC** ....618 446-3219
884 Industrial St Albion (62806) ***(G-355)***
**Atch Inc (PA)** ....847 295-5055
825 S Waukegan Rd Pmb 157 Lake Forest (60045) ***(G-12882)***
**Atcs LLC, Chicago** *Also called American Trade & Coml Svc LLC* ***(G-3879)***
**Ateco Automotive, Ingleside** *Also called American Total Engine Co* ***(G-12186)***
**Athena Design Group Inc** ....312 733-2828
3500 S Morgan St 1 Chicago (60609) ***(G-3974)***
**Athena Precision Machining, Bensenville** *Also called JM Tool & Die LLC* ***(G-1929)***
**Athenex Pharmaceutical Div LLC** ....847 922-8041
10 N Martingale Rd # 230 Schaumburg (60173) ***(G-19449)***
**Athenian Foods Co** ....708 343-6700
1814 N 15th Ave Melrose Park (60160) ***(G-14596)***
**Athenian Pastries & Food, Melrose Park** *Also called Athenian Foods Co* ***(G-14596)***
**Atherton Foundry Products Inc** ....708 849-4615
13000 S Halsted St Riverdale (60827) ***(G-18015)***
**Athletic & Sports Seating** ....630 837-5566
676 Bonded Pkwy Ste L Streamwood (60107) ***(G-20644)***
**Athletic Fundraising.com, Pekin** *Also called Varsity Publications Inc* ***(G-17292)***
**Athletic Image** ....217 347-7377
510 W Jaycee Ave Ste 3 Effingham (62401) ***(G-8825)***
**Athletic Outfitters Inc** ....815 942-6696
409 Liberty St Morris (60450) ***(G-15094)***
**Athletic Sewing Mfg Co (PA)** ....773 589-0361
7449 W Irving Park Rd # 1 Chicago (60634) ***(G-3975)***
**Athletic Specialties Inc** ....847 487-7880
240 Industrial Dr Wauconda (60084) ***(G-21444)***
**Athllete LLC** ....773 829-3752
948 W Briarcliff Rd Bolingbrook (60440) ***(G-2279)***
**ATI, Chicago** *Also called Allied Telesis Inc* ***(G-3818)***
**ATI Allegheny Ludlum, Bridgeview** *Also called Allegheny Ludlum LLC* ***(G-2460)***
**ATI Oldco Inc (HQ)** ....630 860-5600
1420 Brewster Creek Blvd Bartlett (60103) ***(G-1332)***
**ATI Wah Chang, Northbrook** *Also called Tdy Industries LLC* ***(G-16376)***
**Atk Foods Inc (PA)** ....312 829-2250
1143 W Lake St Chicago (60607) ***(G-3976)***
**Atkore International Inc (HQ)** ....708 339-1610
16100 Lathrop Ave Harvey (60426) ***(G-11657)***
**Atkore International Group Inc (PA)** ....708 339-1610
16100 Lathrop Ave Harvey (60426) ***(G-11658)***
**Atkore Intl Holdings Inc (HQ)** ....708 225-2051
16100 Lathrop Ave Harvey (60426) ***(G-11659)***
**Atlantic Beverage Company Inc (PA)** ....847 412-6200
1033 Skokie Blvd Ste 600 Northbrook (60062) ***(G-16207)***
**Atlantic Engineering** ....847 782-1762
42008 N Delany Rd Zion (60099) ***(G-22679)***
**Atlantic Press Inc** ....708 496-2400
6721 W 73rd St Chicago (60638) ***(G-3977)***
**Atlantis Match Company, Frankfort** *Also called Bradley Industries Inc* ***(G-10304)***
**Atlantis Products Inc** ....630 971-9680
586 Territorial Dr Ste H Bolingbrook (60440) ***(G-2280)***
**Atlas ABC Corporation** ....773 646-4500
1855 E 122nd St Chicago (60633) ***(G-3978)***
**Atlas Boiler & Welding Company** ....815 963-3360
424 N Grove Ave Elgin (60120) ***(G-8960)***
**Atlas Building Components Inc** ....618 639-0222
5 Industrial Dr Jerseyville (62052) ***(G-12418)***
**Atlas Components Inc** ....815 332-4904
4055 S Perryville Rd Cherry Valley (61016) ***(G-3638)***
**Atlas Concrete Products Co** ....217 528-7368
2500 Peerless Mine Rd Springfield (62702) ***(G-20390)***
**Atlas Copco Compressors LLC** ....847 640-6067
2501 Landmeier Rd Ste 109 Elk Grove Village (60007) ***(G-9319)***
**Atlas Copco Compressors LLC** ....281 590-7500
75 Remittance Dr # 3009 Chicago (60675) ***(G-3979)***
**Atlas Copco Comptec Inc** ....847 726-9866
14 Rosewood Dr Hawthorn Woods (60047) ***(G-11701)***
**Atlas Die LLC** ....630 351-5140
2000 Bloomingdale Rd # 235 Glendale Heights (60139) ***(G-11009)***
**Atlas Energy Products, East Moline** *Also called Atlas Roofing Corporation* ***(G-8670)***
**Atlas Fibre Company (PA)** ....847 674-1234
3411 Woodhead Dr Northbrook (60062) ***(G-16208)***
**Atlas Holding Inc (HQ)** ....773 646-4500
1855 E 122nd St Chicago (60633) ***(G-3980)***
**Atlas Maintenance Service Inc** ....773 486-3386
2055 N Kedzie Ave Chicago (60647) ***(G-3981)***
**Atlas Manufacturing** ....773 327-3005
4114 N Ravenswood Ave Chicago (60613) ***(G-3982)***
**Atlas Manufacturing Ltd** ....815 943-1400
1001 W Roosevelt St Harvard (60033) ***(G-11622)***
**Atlas Match LLC** ....815 469-2314
5009 Lawn Ave Western Springs (60558) ***(G-21864)***
**Atlas Material Tstg Tech LLC (HQ)** ....773 327-4520
1500 Bishop Ct Mount Prospect (60056) ***(G-15311)***
**Atlas Material Tstg Tech LLC** ....773 327-4520
1800 W Belle Plaine Ave F Chicago (60613) ***(G-3983)***
**Atlas Putty Products Co** ....708 429-5858
8351 185th St Tinley Park (60487) ***(G-20895)***
**Atlas Ready Mix Inc** ....618 271-0774
2901 Missouri Ave East Saint Louis (62205) ***(G-8741)***
**Atlas Roofing Corporation** ....309 752-7121
3110 Morton Dr East Moline (61244) ***(G-8670)***
**Atlas Screen Supply Co., Schiller Park** *Also called Damy Corp* ***(G-19819)***
**Atlas Tool & Die Works Inc** ....708 442-1661
4633 Lawndale Ave Lyons (60534) ***(G-14031)***
**Atlas Tube (chicago) LLC** ....773 646-4500
1855 E 122nd St Chicago (60633) ***(G-3984)***
**Atlas Uniform Company** ....312 492-8527
1412 W Wa Blvd Fl 2 Chicago (60607) ***(G-3985)***
**Atm America Corp** ....800 298-0030
1900 N Austin Ave Ste 69 Chicago (60639) ***(G-3986)***
**Atmi Dynacore LLC (PA)** ....815 838-9492
551 S Independence Blvd Lockport (60441) ***(G-13704)***
**Atmi Plant, Aurora** *Also called Atmi Precast Inc* ***(G-1114)***
**Atmi Precast Inc (PA)** ....630 897-0577
960 Ridgeway Ave Fl 2 Aurora (60506) ***(G-1113)***
**Atmi Precast Inc** ....630 897-0577
930 Ridgeway Ave Aurora (60506) ***(G-1114)***
**Ato Systems, Lake Forest** *Also called Perfect Circle Projectiles LLC* ***(G-12942)***
**Atomic Engineering Co** ....847 228-1387
365 Kent Ave Elk Grove Village (60007) ***(G-9320)***
**Atomoweld Co** ....773 736-5577
5515 W Montrose Ave Chicago (60641) ***(G-3987)***
**Ats Acoustics, Piper City** *Also called Ats Commercial Group LLC* ***(G-17558)***
**Ats Commercial Group LLC** ....815 686-2705
15 W Main St Piper City (60959) ***(G-17558)***
**Ats Sortimat USA LLC** ....847 925-1234
5655 Meadowbrook Indus Ct Rolling Meadows (60008) ***(G-18711)***
**Atsp Innovations LLC** ....217 239-1703
60 Hazelwood Dr Champaign (61820) ***(G-3454)***
**Attic Gifts, Mundelein** *Also called In The Attic Inc* ***(G-15509)***
**Attune Medical** ....312 994-0174
3440 S Dearborn St 215-S Chicago (60616) ***(G-3988)***
**Atwood-Hamlin Mfg Co Inc** ....815 678-7291
5614 Kenosha St Richmond (60071) ***(G-17958)***
**Atwoot Herald, Mount Zion** *Also called Village of Mt Zion* ***(G-15457)***
**Aubrey Sign Co Inc** ....630 482-9901
1847 Suncast Ln Batavia (60510) ***(G-1418)***
**Auburn Iron Works Inc** ....708 422-7330
12924 S Forestview Rd Palos Heights (60463) ***(G-17099)***
**Audibel Hearing Aid Center, Mattoon** *Also called Audibel Hearing Aid Services* ***(G-14383)***
**Audibel Hearing Aid Services** ....217 234-6426
408 Country Club Rd Mattoon (61938) ***(G-14383)***
**Audibel Hearing Center** ....217 670-1183
2347 W Monroe St Springfield (62704) ***(G-20391)***
**Audio Installers Inc** ....815 969-7500
5061 Contractors Dr Loves Park (61111) ***(G-13923)***

**Audio Supply Inc** ....847 549-6086
1367 Wilhelm Rd Mundelein (60060) ***(G-15472)***
**Audio Tech Bus Bk Summaries** ....630 734-0500
1314 Kensington Rd # 4953 Oak Brook (60523) ***(G-16490)***
**Audio Video Electronics LLC** ....847 983-4761
7440 Long Ave Skokie (60077) ***(G-19961)***
**August Hill Winery** ....815 224-8199
21 N 2551st Rd Peru (61354) ***(G-17501)***
**Augusta Eagle** ....217 392-2715
600 Main St Augusta (62311) ***(G-951)***
**Augusta Label Corp** ....630 537-1961
7938 S Madison St Burr Ridge (60527) ***(G-2823)***
**Augustan, Oak Brook** *Also called NRR Corp* ***(G-16550)***
**Augusthill Winery Co** ....815 667-5211
106 Mill St Utica (61373) ***(G-21106)***
**Aunt Em's Gourmet Popcorn, Deer Creek** *Also called Marianne Strawn* ***(G-7965)***
**Auntie Anne's, Aurora** *Also called P Double Corporation* ***(G-1061)***
**Auntie Mmmms** ....217 509-6012
105 N Ohio St Camp Point (62320) ***(G-2971)***
**Aura Systems Inc** ....217 423-4100
2345 E Garfield Ave Decatur (62526) ***(G-7842)***
**Aurora Bearing Company** ....630 897-8941
901 Aucutt Rd Montgomery (60538) ***(G-15027)***
**Aurora Circuits Inc** ....630 978-3830
2250 White Oak Cir Aurora (60502) ***(G-960)***
**Aurora Circuits LLC** ....630 978-3830
2250 White Oak Cir Aurora (60502) ***(G-961)***
**Aurora Cord & Cable Company, Aurora** *Also called Elc Industries Corp* ***(G-1144)***
**Aurora Custom Machining Inc** ....630 859-2638
1038 Sill Ave Aurora (60506) ***(G-1115)***
**Aurora Fastprint Inc** ....630 896-5980
54 E Galena Blvd Aurora (60505) ***(G-1116)***
**Aurora Metals Division LLC** ....630 844-4900
1995 Greenfield Rd Montgomery (60538) ***(G-15028)***
**Aurora Narinder** ....773 275-2100
4549 N Clark St Chicago (60640) ***(G-3989)***
**Aurora Orthopedic Laboratories, North Aurora** *Also called Tuu Duc Le Inc* ***(G-16148)***
**Aurora Packing Company Inc** ....630 897-0551
125 S Grant St North Aurora (60542) ***(G-16119)***
**Aurora Pump, North Aurora** *Also called Pentair Flow Technologies LLC* ***(G-16140)***
**Aurora Sign Co** ....630 898-5900
1100 Route 34 Ste 2 Aurora (60503) ***(G-962)***
**Aurora Spclty Txtles Group Inc** ....800 864-0303
2705 N Bridge St Yorkville (60560) ***(G-22650)***
**Aurora Tent & Awning Co, Plainfield** *Also called Stritzel Awnng Svc/Aurra Tent* ***(G-17654)***
**Aurora Textile Finishing Co, Aurora** *Also called Meridian Industries Inc* ***(G-1186)***
**Austin Graphic** ....815 432-4983
105 N Jefferson St Watseka (60970) ***(G-21414)***
**Austin Tool & Die Co (PA)** ....847 509-5800
3555 Woodhead Dr Northbrook (60062) ***(G-16209)***
**Austin Voice Newspaper, Chicago** *Also called Megamedia Enterprises Inc* ***(G-5680)***
**Austin-Westran LLC (PA)** ....815 234-2811
602 E Blackhawk Dr Byron (61010) ***(G-2912)***
**Austin-Westran LLC** ....815 234-2811
420 N Main St Montgomery (60538) ***(G-15029)***
**Austins Saloon & Eatery** ....847 549-1972
481 Peterson Rd Libertyville (60048) ***(G-13305)***
**Auth-Florence Mfg** ....
591 Mitchell Rd Glendale Heights (60139) ***(G-11010)***
**Authentic Street Signs Inc** ....618 349-8878
183 Main St Saint Peter (62880) ***(G-19320)***
**Authority Screenprint & EMB** ....630 236-0289
10148 Clow Creek Rd Ste D Plainfield (60585) ***(G-17581)***
**Auto Body Tool Mart, Elgin** *Also called American Industrial Direct LLC* ***(G-8948)***
**Auto Head and Engine Exchange** ....708 448-8762
6603 W 111th St Worth (60482) ***(G-22632)***
**Auto Injury Solutions Inc** ....312 229-2704
222 Merchandise Mart Plz # 900 Chicago (60654) ***(G-3990)***
**Auto Meter Products Inc** ....815 991-2292
413 W Elm St Sycamore (60178) ***(G-20788)***
**Auto Truck, Bartlett** *Also called ATI Oldco Inc* ***(G-1332)***
**Auto Truck Group LLC (HQ)** ....630 860-5600
1420 Brewster Creek Blvd Bartlett (60103) ***(G-1333)***
**Auto Truck Grp Wyn Flt Equipme, Bartlett** *Also called Auto Truck Group LLC* ***(G-1333)***
**Auto-Owners Insurance, Mount Zion** *Also called Gibson Insurance Inc* ***(G-15451)***
**Autocut Machine Co** ....815 436-1900
23702 S Vetter Rd Elwood (60421) ***(G-9978)***
**Autogenesis LLC** ....630 851-9424
3909 75th St Aurora (60504) ***(G-963)***
**Autojet Technologies, Glendale Heights** *Also called Spraying Systems Co* ***(G-11072)***
**Automated Design Corp** ....630 783-1150
1404 Joliet Rd Ste B Romeoville (60446) ***(G-18801)***
**Automated Logic Chicago, Lisle** *Also called Automated Logic Corporation* ***(G-13566)***
**Automated Logic Corporation** ....630 852-1700
2400 Ogden Ave Ste 100 Lisle (60532) ***(G-13566)***
**Automated Mfg Solutions Inc** ....815 477-2428
6126 Factory Rd Crystal Lake (60014) ***(G-7539)***
**Automated Systems & Control Co** ....847 735-8310
11 N Skokie Hwy Ste 115 Lake Bluff (60044) ***(G-12834)***
**Automatic Anodizing Corp** ....773 478-3304
3340 W Newport Ave Chicago (60618) ***(G-3991)***
**Automatic Building Contrls LLC** ....847 296-4000
3315 Algonquin Rd Ste 550 Rolling Meadows (60008) ***(G-18712)***
**Automatic Feeder Company Inc** ....847 534-2300
921 Albion Ave Schaumburg (60193) ***(G-19450)***
**Automatic Fire Controls, Mokena** *Also called Fire Systems Holdings Inc* ***(G-14861)***
**Automatic Fire Sprinkler, Normal** *Also called Cintas Corporation* ***(G-16067)***
**Automatic Fire Sprinkler LLC** ....309 862-2724
1809 Industrial Park Dr Normal (61761) ***(G-16064)***
**Automatic Machinery Resources** ....630 543-4944
1001 W Republic Dr Ste 8 Addison (60101) ***(G-48)***
**Automatic Precision Inc** ....708 867-1116
4609 N Ronald St Chicago (60706) ***(G-3992)***
**Automatic Production Equipment** ....847 439-1448
815 Touhy Ave Elk Grove Village (60007) ***(G-9321)***
**Automatic Spring Coiling, Chicago** *Also called Matthew Warren Inc* ***(G-5656)***
**Automatic Swiss Corporation** ....630 543-3888
1130 W National Ave Ste A Addison (60101) ***(G-49)***
**Automation Design & Mfg Inc** ....630 896-4206
841 S River St Aurora (60506) ***(G-1117)***
**Automation International Inc** ....217 446-9500
1020 Bahls St Danville (61832) ***(G-7704)***
**Automation Systems Inc** ....847 671-9515
2001 N 17th Ave Melrose Park (60160) ***(G-14597)***
**Automax Corporation** ....630 972-1919
1940 Internationale Pkwy # 550 Woodridge (60517) ***(G-22454)***
**Automotion Inc** ....708 229-3700
11000 Lavergne Ave Oak Lawn (60453) ***(G-16605)***
**Automotive Engine Specialties** ....847 956-1244
173 Randall St Elk Grove Village (60007) ***(G-9322)***
**Automotive Group, Broadview** *Also called Robert Bosch LLC* ***(G-2610)***
**Automotive Metal Specialist** ....309 383-2980
417 Schmitt Ln Germantown Hills (61548) ***(G-10895)***
**Automotive Systems Group, Sycamore** *Also called Adient US LLC* ***(G-20785)***
**Automtic Lquid Packg Solutions, Arlington Heights** *Also called Diamond Machine Werks Inc* ***(G-746)***
**Automtic Lquid Pckg Sltons LLC** ....847 372-3336
2445 E Oakton St Arlington Heights (60005) ***(G-719)***
**Autonamic Corporation** ....815 675-6300
7806 Industrial Dr Spring Grove (60081) ***(G-20327)***
**Autonetics Inc** ....847 426-8525
425 Maple Ave Carpentersville (60110) ***(G-3275)***
**Autonics USA Inc** ....847 680-8160
1353 Armour Blvd Mundelein (60060) ***(G-15473)***
**Autonomic Materials Inc** ....217 863-2023
495 County Road 1300 N Champaign (61822) ***(G-3455)***
**Autonomoustuff LLC** ....314 270-2123
306 Erie Ave Morton (61550) ***(G-15153)***
**Autonomy Inc** ....312 580-9100
303 E Wacker Dr Ste 2700 Chicago (60601) ***(G-3993)***
**Autoparts Holdings Ltd** ....203 830-7800
1900 W Field Ct Lake Forest (60045) ***(G-12883)***
**Autotech Tech Ltd Partnr** ....563 359-7501
363 Saint Paul Blvd Carol Stream (60188) ***(G-3107)***
**Autotech Tech Ltd Partnr** ....563 359-7501
28617 Network Pl Chicago (60673) ***(G-3994)***
**Autotech Tech Ltd Partnr** ....630 668-8886
343 Saint Paul Blvd Carol Stream (60188) ***(G-3108)***
**Autotype Americas Incorporated** ....847 818-8262
1675 Winnetka Cir Rolling Meadows (60008) ***(G-18713)***
**Autrol America, Schaumburg** *Also called Autrol Corporation of America* ***(G-19451)***
**Autrol Corporation of America** ....847 779-5000
10 N Martingale Rd # 470 Schaumburg (60173) ***(G-19451)***
**Autumn Mill** ....217 795-3399
13014 Cemetery Rd Argenta (62501) ***(G-689)***
**Autumn Woods Ltd** ....630 868-3535
112 N Main St Wheaton (60187) ***(G-21937)***
**Autumn Woods Ltd (PA)** ....630 668-2080
375 Gundersen Dr Carol Stream (60188) ***(G-3109)***
**Aux Sable Liquid Products, Morris** *Also called Aux Sable Midstream LLC* ***(G-15096)***
**Aux Sable Liquid Products LP (PA)** ....815 941-5800
6155 E Us Route 6 Morris (60450) ***(G-15095)***
**Aux Sable Midstream LLC** ....815 941-5800
6155 E Us Route 6 Morris (60450) ***(G-15096)***
**Aux Sable Sand & Gravel, Morris** *Also called Lafarge Aux Sable LLC* ***(G-15112)***
**Auxitrol SA** ....815 874-2471
3358 N Publishers Dr Rockford (61109) ***(G-18272)***
**AV Stumpfl Usa Corp** ....630 359-0999
960 N Industrial Dr Ste 3 Elmhurst (60126) ***(G-9835)***
**Available Business Group Inc** ....773 247-4141
3944 S Morgan St Chicago (60609) ***(G-3995)***
**Available Spring and Mfg Co** ....847 520-4854
350 Holbrook Dr Wheeling (60090) ***(G-22009)***
**Avalign Technologies Inc (PA)** ....855 282-5446
2275 Half Day Rd Ste 126 Bannockburn (60015) ***(G-1253)***

**Avan Precast Concrete Pdts Inc** .......................................... 708 757-6200
  3201 211th St Lynwood (60411) *(G-14017)*
**Avan Tool & Die Co Inc** .......................................... 773 287-1670
  4612 W Maypole Ave Chicago (60644) *(G-3996)*
**Avana Electric Motors Inc** .......................................... 847 588-0400
  1445 Brummel Ave Elk Grove Village (60007) *(G-9323)*
**Avana Electrotek, Elk Grove Village** Also called Avana Electric Motors Inc *(G-9323)*
**Avani Spices LLC** .......................................... 847 532-1075
  1690 Stone Ridge Ln Algonquin (60102) *(G-379)*
**Avant Tecno USA Inc** .......................................... 847 380-9822
  3020 Malmo Dr Arlington Heights (60005) *(G-720)*
**Avanti Engineering Inc (PA)** .......................................... 630 260-1333
  200 W Lake Dr Glendale Heights (60139) *(G-11011)*
**Avanti Foods Company** .......................................... 815 379-2155
  109 Depot St Walnut (61376) *(G-21329)*
**Avanti Motor Carriers Inc** .......................................... 630 313-9160
  4440 White Ash Ln Naperville (60564) *(G-15798)*
**Avasarala Inc** .......................................... 847 969-0630
  1 E Northwest Hwy Ste 214 Palatine (60067) *(G-17004)*
**Avatar Corporation** .......................................... 708 534-5511
  500 Central Ave University Park (60484) *(G-21042)*
**Avaya Inc** .......................................... 847 885-3598
  2500 W Higgins Rd Schaumburg (60195) *(G-19452)*
**Ave Inc** .......................................... 815 727-0153
  126 S Des Plaines St Joliet (60436) *(G-12457)*
**Avec Inc** .......................................... 217 670-0439
  3027 English Row Ave # 205 Naperville (60564) *(G-15799)*
**Avectra Inc** .......................................... 312 425-9094
  10 S Wacker Dr Ste 1120 Chicago (60606) *(G-3997)*
**Aveda Corporation** .......................................... 847 413-0438
  L325 Woodfield Mall Schaumburg (60173) *(G-19453)*
**Avenir Publishing Inc** .......................................... 312 577-7200
  65 E Wacker Pl Ste 400 Chicago (60601) *(G-3998)*
**Aventine Renewable Energy (HQ)** .......................................... 309 347-9200
  1300 S 2nd St Pekin (61554) *(G-17255)*
**Aventine Rnwble Enrgy Holdings, Pekin** Also called Pacific Ethanol Pekin Inc *(G-17279)*
**Avenue Metal Manufacturing Co** .......................................... 312 243-3483
  1640 W Ogden Ave Chicago (60612) *(G-3999)*
**Avers Machine & Mfg Inc** .......................................... 847 447-3430
  3999 25th Ave Schiller Park (60176) *(G-19807)*
**Averus Usa Inc (PA)** .......................................... 800 913-7034
  2410 Vantage Dr Elgin (60124) *(G-8961)*
**Avery Dennison Corporation** .......................................... 877 214-0909
  7542 N Natchez Ave Niles (60714) *(G-15962)*
**Avery Dennison Corporation** .......................................... 847 824-7450
  902 Feehanville Dr Mount Prospect (60056) *(G-15312)*
**Avery Dnnson Ret Info Svcs LLC** .......................................... 626 304-2000
  15178 Collection Ctr Dr Chicago (60693) *(G-4000)*
**Avexis Inc** .......................................... 847 572-8280
  2275 Half Day Rd Ste 160 Bannockburn (60015) *(G-1254)*
**Avg Advanced Technologies LP** .......................................... 630 668-3900
  343 Saint Paul Blvd Carol Stream (60188) *(G-3110)*
**Avg Group of Companies (HQ)** .......................................... 630 668-8886
  363 Saint Paul Blvd Carol Stream (60188) *(G-3111)*
**Avg LTI, Carol Stream** Also called Avg Group of Companies *(G-3111)*
**AVI-Spl Employee** .......................................... 847 437-7712
  2266 Palmer Dr Schaumburg (60173) *(G-19454)*
**Avia, LLC, Chicago** Also called Abundant Venture Innovation AC *(G-3712)*
**Aviation Services Group Inc** .......................................... 708 425-4700
  10524 Major Ave Chicago Ridge (60415) *(G-7139)*
**Aviation Services Group of IL, Chicago Ridge** Also called Aviation Services Group Inc *(G-7139)*
**Avid of Illinois Inc** .......................................... 847 698-2775
  2740 E Main St Saint Charles (60174) *(G-19140)*
**Avis Commercial Anodizing, Chicago** Also called P B A Corp *(G-6039)*
**Avista Group Corporation** .......................................... 877 772-8826
  955 Pratt Blvd Elk Grove Village (60007) *(G-9324)*
**Avista USA, Elk Grove Village** Also called Avista Group Corporation *(G-9324)*
**Avlon Industries Inc** .......................................... 708 344-0709
  1999 N 15th Ave Melrose Park (60160) *(G-14598)*
**Avoca Ridge Ltd** .......................................... 815 692-4772
  310 S 7th St Ste 2 Fairbury (61739) *(G-10122)*
**Avocet Polymer Tech Inc** .......................................... 773 523-2872
  4047 W 40th St Chicago (60632) *(G-4001)*
**Avoco International LLC (PA)** .......................................... 847 795-0200
  720 Bonnie Ln Elk Grove Village (60007) *(G-9325)*
**Avsec Printing Inc** .......................................... 815 722-2961
  825 Plainfield Rd Ste 1 Joliet (60435) *(G-12458)*
**Avt Service Technologies, Blue Island** Also called Advanced Valve Tech Inc *(G-2237)*
**Avtec Inc** .......................................... 618 337-7800
  6 Industrial Park East Saint Louis (62206) *(G-8742)*
**Avtec (usa) Powertrain Corp** .......................................... 773 708-9686
  2023 N Halsted St Chicago (60614) *(G-4002)*
**Avw Equipment Company Inc** .......................................... 708 343-7738
  105 S 9th Ave Maywood (60153) *(G-14417)*
**Awa, Ottawa** Also called A Wiley & Associates *(G-16945)*
**Award Concepts Inc** .......................................... 630 513-7801
  110 S 11th Ave Saint Charles (60174) *(G-19141)*
**Award Concepts Mfg Co, Saint Charles** Also called Award Concepts Inc *(G-19141)*

**Award Designs Inc** .......................................... 815 227-1264
  1947 N Lyford Rd Ste B Rockford (61107) *(G-18273)*
**Award Emblem Mfg Co Inc** .......................................... 630 739-0800
  179 E South Frontage Rd Bolingbrook (60440) *(G-2281)*
**Award/Visionps Inc** .......................................... 331 318-7800
  208 S Jefferson St Chicago (60661) *(G-4003)*
**Awards and More Inc** .......................................... 773 581-7771
  8544 S Pulaski Rd Chicago (60652) *(G-4004)*
**Awem Corporation** .......................................... 217 670-1451
  1 W Old State Capitol Plz # 703 Springfield (62701) *(G-20392)*
**Awerkamp Machine Co (PA)** .......................................... 217 222-3480
  237 N 7th St Quincy (62301) *(G-17797)*
**Awerkamp Machine Co** .......................................... 217 222-3490
  321 Broadway St Quincy (62301) *(G-17798)*
**Awerkamp Steel, Quincy** Also called Awerkamp Machine Co *(G-17798)*
**Awesome Amusements Co., Addison** Also called Nite Lite Signs & Balloons Inc *(G-229)*
**Awesome Hand Services LLC** .......................................... 630 445-8695
  1151 Rohlwing Rd Rolling Meadows (60008) *(G-18714)*
**AWI / Titanium** .......................................... 708 263-9970
  15146 Geoffrey Rd Oak Forest (60452) *(G-16574)*
**Awnings By Zip Dee Inc** .......................................... 847 640-0460
  96 Crossen Ave Elk Grove Village (60007) *(G-9326)*
**Awnings Express** .......................................... 773 579-1437
  2415 W 24th Pl Chicago (60608) *(G-4005)*
**Awnings Over Chicagoland Inc** .......................................... 847 233-0310
  10204 Franklin Ave Franklin Park (60131) *(G-10406)*
**Awnings Unlimited Inc** .......................................... 708 485-6769
  9445 Ogden Ave Brookfield (60513) *(G-2622)*
**Aww 10 Inc** .......................................... 630 595-7600
  10 Gateway Rd Bensenville (60106) *(G-1837)*
**Axelent Inc** .......................................... 708 745-3128
  14503 S Gougar Rd # 900 Lockport (60491) *(G-13705)*
**Axios Medtech Inc** .......................................... 312 224-7856
  2167 N Camden Ln Round Lake Beach (60073) *(G-19072)*
**Axiosonic LLC** .......................................... 217 342-3412
  2600 S Raney St Effingham (62401) *(G-8826)*
**Axis Design Architectual Mllwk** .......................................... 630 466-4549
  239 State Route 47 Sugar Grove (60554) *(G-20717)*
**Axis International Marketing** .......................................... 847 297-0744
  1800 S Wolf Rd Ste 2 Des Plaines (60018) *(G-8154)*
**Axis Manufacturing Inc** .......................................... 847 350-0200
  2436 Delta Ln Elk Grove Village (60007) *(G-9327)*
**Axletech International** .......................................... 773 264-1234
  1120 W 119th St Chicago (60643) *(G-4006)*
**Axletech International LLC** .......................................... 877 547-3907
  1020 W 119th St Chicago (60643) *(G-4007)*
**Axode Corp** .......................................... 312 578-9897
  35 E Wacker Dr Ste 670 Chicago (60601) *(G-4008)*
**Axon Electric LLC** .......................................... 630 834-4090
  9114 Virginia Rd Ste 105 Lake In The Hills (60156) *(G-12986)*
**Axon Telecom LLC** .......................................... 618 278-4606
  177 Snake Rd Dorsey (62021) *(G-8380)*
**Aydin Displays, Schaumburg** Also called Sparton Aydin LLC *(G-19733)*
**Ayla Group Inc** .......................................... 630 954-9432
  1262 Dunamon Dr Bartlett (60103) *(G-1334)*
**Azcon Inc (PA)** .......................................... 312 559-3100
  820 W Jackson Blvd # 425 Chicago (60607) *(G-4009)*
**Azcon Inc.** .......................................... 815 548-7000
  101 Avenue K Sterling (61081) *(G-20583)*
**Azcon Metals, Chicago** Also called Azcon Inc *(G-4009)*
**Azilsa Inc** .......................................... 312 919-1741
  1425 W Schaumburg Rd Schaumburg (60194) *(G-19455)*
**Azimuth Cnc Inc** .......................................... 815 399-4433
  5291 28th Ave Rockford (61109) *(G-18274)*
**Aztec Corporation**
  2800 Maple Ave Apt 34a Downers Grove (60515) *(G-8391)*
**Aztec Material Service Corp (PA)** .......................................... 773 521-0909
  3624 W 26th St Fl 2 Chicago (60623) *(G-4010)*
**Aztec Plastic Company** .......................................... 312 733-0900
  1747 W Carroll Ave Chicago (60612) *(G-4011)*
**Aztec Products** .......................................... 217 726-8631
  3321 Blueberry Ln Springfield (62711) *(G-20393)*
**Azteca Foods Inc (PA)** .......................................... 708 563-6600
  5005 S Nagle Ave Chicago (60638) *(G-4012)*
**Azteca Jewelry (PA)** .......................................... 773 929-0796
  3334 N Lincoln Ave Chicago (60657) *(G-4013)*
**Aztech Engineering Inc** .......................................... 630 236-3200
  2675 White Oak Cir Ste 1 Aurora (60502) *(G-964)*
**Aztech Locknut Company, Aurora** Also called Aztech Engineering Inc *(G-964)*
**Azusa Inc** .......................................... 618 244-6591
  1406 Salem Rd Mount Vernon (62864) *(G-15399)*
**Azusa Printing, Mount Vernon** Also called Azusa Inc *(G-15399)*
**Azz Incorporated** .......................................... 815 723-5000
  625 Mills Rd Joliet (60433) *(G-12459)*
**B & B Awards and Recognition, Bloomington** Also called B&B Awards and Recognition Inc *(G-2146)*
**B & B Custom TS & Gifts** .......................................... 618 463-0443
  2714 Corner Ct Alton (62002) *(G-562)*

**B & B Equipment** ....217 562-2511
401 S Business 5 Assumption (62510) *(G-930)*
**B & B Fabrications LLC** ....217 620-3210
901 W Jefferson St Sullivan (61951) *(G-20739)*
**B & B Formica Appliers Inc** ....773 804-1015
5617 W Grand Ave Chicago (60639) *(G-4014)*
**B & B Machine Inc** ....309 786-3279
1221 2nd Ave Rock Island (61201) *(G-18160)*
**B & B Printing, Kewanee** *Also called Bailleu & Bailleu Printing Inc (G-12670)*
**B & B Printing Company** ....217 285-6072
115 E Washington St A Pittsfield (62363) *(G-17561)*
**B & B Publishing Co Inc** ....815 933-1131
500 Brown Blvd Bourbonnais (60914) *(G-2388)*
**B & B Specialty Company Inc** ....708 652-9234
5133 W 25th Pl Cicero (60804) *(G-7179)*
**B & B Tank Truck Construction (PA)** ....618 378-3337
760 Us Highway 45 Norris City (62869) *(G-16111)*
**B & B Tool Co** ....815 229-5792
5005 27th Ave Rockford (61109) *(G-18275)*
**B & D Independence Inc** ....618 262-7117
1024 Empire St Mount Carmel (62863) *(G-15260)*
**B & D Murray Manufacturing Co** ....815 568-6176
3911 N Il Route 23 Marengo (60152) *(G-14220)*
**B & G Machine Inc** ....618 262-2269
421 W 9th St Mount Carmel (62863) *(G-15261)*
**B & G Sheet Metal** ....773 265-6121
3056 W Walton St Chicago (60622) *(G-4015)*
**B & H Biotechnologies LLC** ....630 915-3227
6520 Chaucer Rd Willowbrook (60527) *(G-22200)*
**B & H Industries, Warrenville** *Also called Robal Company Inc (G-21361)*
**B & J Wet Enterprises, Rolling Meadows** *Also called Bandjwet Enterprises Inc (G-18715)*
**B & J Wire Inc** ....877 787-9473
1919 S Fairfield Ave # 1 Chicago (60608) *(G-4016)*
**B & M Automotive** ....309 637-4977
1811 S Oakwood Ave Peoria (61605) *(G-17312)*
**B & M Machine Inc** ....630 350-8950
768 Industrial Dr Bensenville (60106) *(G-1838)*
**B & M Machine Shop, Watseka** *Also called B & M Screw Machine Inc (G-21415)*
**B & M Plastic Inc** ....847 258-4437
2001 Arthur Ave Elk Grove Village (60007) *(G-9328)*
**B & M Screw Machine Inc** ....815 432-5892
900 E Cherry St Watseka (60970) *(G-21415)*
**B & R Grinding Co** ....630 595-7789
459 Podlin Dr Franklin Park (60131) *(G-10407)*
**B & S Auto Rebuilders Inc** ....773 283-3763
3513 N Cicero Ave Chicago (60641) *(G-4017)*
**B & T Polishing Co** ....847 658-6415
2433 W Fulton St Chicago (60612) *(G-4018)*
**B & W Machine Company Inc** ....847 364-4500
71 Gordon St Elk Grove Village (60007) *(G-9329)*
**B A Die Mold Inc** ....630 978-4747
3685 Prairie Lake Ct Aurora (60504) *(G-965)*
**B A I Publishers** ....847 537-1300
190 Abbott Dr Ste A Wheeling (60090) *(G-22010)*
**B A P Enterprises Inc** ....708 849-0900
14235 Cottage Grove Ave Dolton (60419) *(G-8364)*
**B Allan Graphics Inc** ....708 396-1704
11629 S Mayfield Ave Alsip (60803) *(G-438)*
**B and A Screen Printing** ....217 762-2632
350 W Burnside Rd Monticello (61856) *(G-15074)*
**B and B Amusement Illinois LLC** ....309 585-2077
1404 Mrtin Luther King Dr Bloomington (61701) *(G-2145)*
**B and K Mueller Industries** ....847 290-1108
2021 Lunt Ave Elk Grove Village (60007) *(G-9330)*
**B Andrews Inc** ....847 381-7444
200 Applebee St Ste 202 Barrington (60010) *(G-1269)*
**B B M Packing Co Inc** ....312 243-1061
874 N Milwaukee Ave Chicago (60642) *(G-4019)*
**B B Milling Co Inc** ....217 376-3131
300 North St Emden (62635) *(G-9983)*
**B C Die & Mold Inc** ....630 543-5090
1046 W Republic Dr Addison (60101) *(G-50)*
**B C I, Libertyville** *Also called BCI Acrylic Inc (G-13307)*
**B C T, Machesney Park** *Also called Business Cards Tomorrow (G-14062)*
**B C T, Machesney Park** *Also called Business Card Systems Inc (G-14061)*
**B Creative Screen Print Co** ....815 806-3037
8844 W Steger Rd Frankfort (60423) *(G-10298)*
**B D, Downers Grove** *Also called Becton Dickinson and Company (G-8396)*
**B D C Inc** ....847 741-2233
1185 Jansen Farm Ct Elgin (60123) *(G-8962)*
**B D Enterprises** ....618 462-5861
655 E Broadway Alton (62002) *(G-563)*
**B D Medical Systems-Injection, Naperville** *Also called Becton Dickinson and Company (G-15604)*
**B D Sport Photos and Trophies, Alton** *Also called B D Enterprises (G-563)*
**B E, Quincy** *Also called Broadcast Electronics Inc (G-17809)*
**B F I, Chicago** *Also called Beverage Flavors Intl LLC (G-4097)*
**B F Shaw Printing Company** ....815 875-4461
800 Ace Rd Princeton (61356) *(G-17744)*
**B F Shaw Printing Company** ....815 625-3600
3200 E Lincolnway Sterling (61081) *(G-20584)*
**B F Shaw Printing Company** ....815 732-6166
121 S 4th St Ste A Oregon (61061) *(G-16819)*
**B Gunther & Co** ....630 969-5595
4742 Main St Lisle (60532) *(G-13567)*
**B I L, Lake Forest** *Also called Brunswick International Ltd (G-12889)*
**B J Fehr Machine Co** ....309 923-8691
209 N Main St Roanoke (61561) *(G-18048)*
**B J Plastic Molding Co (PA)** ....630 766-3200
435 S County Line Rd Franklin Park (60131) *(G-10408)*
**B J Plastic Molding Co** ....630 766-8750
778 County Line Rd Bensenville (60106) *(G-1839)*
**B JS Printables** ....618 656-8625
1415 Troy Rd Edwardsville (62025) *(G-8789)*
**B L I Tool & Die Inc** ....217 434-9106
1468 Highway 24 Fowler (62338) *(G-10272)*
**B M I Inc** ....847 839-6000
1751 Wilkening Ct Schaumburg (60173) *(G-19456)*
**B M S Enterprise** ....815 730-3450
1039 Railroad St Frnt Rockdale (60436) *(G-18214)*
**B M S Tool & Equipment Co, Bridgeport** *Also called Bridgeport Air Comprsr & Tl Co (G-2450)*
**B M W Inc** ....847 439-0095
415 Bennett Rd Elk Grove Village (60007) *(G-9331)*
**B N Blance Enrgy Solutions LLC** ....847 287-7466
2019 N Wainwright Ct Palatine (60074) *(G-17005)*
**B N K Inc** ....630 231-5640
330 S Neltnor Blvd West Chicago (60185) *(G-21664)*
**B P I Printing & Duplicating (PA)** ....773 327-7300
3223 N Lakewood Ave Chicago (60657) *(G-4020)*
**B P I Printing & Duplicating** ....773 822-0111
3950 S Morgan St Chicago (60609) *(G-4021)*
**B Quad Oil Inc** ....618 656-4419
1405 Troy Rd Ste B Edwardsville (62025) *(G-8790)*
**B R I Operations, Flora** *Also called Booth Resources Inc (G-10201)*
**B Radtke and Sons Inc** ....847 546-3999
101 W Main St Ste 2 Round Lake Park (60073) *(G-19083)*
**B S Grinding Inc** ....847 787-0770
2535 United Ln Elk Grove Village (60007) *(G-9332)*
**B T Brown Manufacturing** ....815 947-3633
14871 E Airport Rd Kent (61044) *(G-12665)*
**B T M Industries Inc** ....815 338-6464
604 Washington St Woodstock (60098) *(G-22543)*
**B T Technology Inc** ....217 322-3768
320 N Railroad St Rushville (62681) *(G-19090)*
**B W M Global** ....847 785-1355
3740 Hawthorne Ct Waukegan (60087) *(G-21528)*
**B&A Livestock Feed Company LLC** ....618 245-6422
201 E Jefferson Ave Farina (62838) *(G-10173)*
**B&B Awards and Recognition Inc** ....309 828-9698
1210 Towanda Ave Ste 9 Bloomington (61701) *(G-2146)*
**B&B Machining Incorporated** ....630 898-3009
24 Gastville St Aurora (60503) *(G-966)*
**B&Bimc LLC** ....815 433-5100
707 E Dayton Rd Ottawa (61350) *(G-16948)*
**B&H Machine Inc** ....618 281-3737
251 Southwoods Ctr Ste 1 Columbia (62236) *(G-7351)*
**B&L Services Inc** ....630 257-1688
1042 Florence St Lemont (60439) *(G-13226)*
**B&W Technologies Inc** ....888 749-8878
405 Barclay Blvd Lincolnshire (60069) *(G-13430)*
**B+b Smartworx Inc (HQ)** ....815 433-5100
707 E Dayton Rd Ottawa (61350) *(G-16949)*
**B-Clean Laundromat Inc** ....678 983-5492
5419 S Halsted St Chicago (60609) *(G-4022)*
**B-O-F Corporation** ....630 585-0020
801 N Commerce St Aurora (60504) *(G-967)*
**B/E Aerospace Inc** ....561 791-5000
1220 Central Ave Hanover Park (60133) *(G-11576)*
**Ba Le Meat Processing & Whl Co** ....773 506-2499
2405 W Ardmore Ave Chicago (60659) *(G-4023)*
**Babak Inc** ....312 419-8686
1 N La Salle St Chicago (60602) *(G-4024)*
**Babbitting Service Inc** ....847 841-8008
1617 Louise Dr South Elgin (60177) *(G-20184)*
**Babcock & Wilcox Powr Generatn** ....630 719-5120
1431 Opus Pl Ste 600 Downers Grove (60515) *(G-8392)*
**Babylon Travel & Tour Service, Chicago** *Also called Ganji Klames (G-4914)*
**Bach & Associates** ....618 277-1652
120 N 36th St Belleville (62226) *(G-1610)*
**Bach Plastic Works Inc** ....847 680-4342
1711 Young Dr B Libertyville (60048) *(G-13306)*
**Bach Timber & Pallet Inc** ....815 885-3774
8858 Grove St Caledonia (61011) *(G-2930)*
**Bachi Company Div, Itasca** *Also called Jardis Industries Inc (G-12289)*
**Background Investigator, The, Morton Grove** *Also called Steven Brownstein (G-15238)*
**Bact Process Systems Inc** ....847 577-0950
3345 N Arlington Hts B Arlington Heights (60004) *(G-721)*

ALPHABETIC

(PA)=Parent Co (HQ)=Headquarters (DH)=Div Headquarters
2017 Harris Illinois Industrial Directory
1173

**Bad Boys Neons, Springfield** *Also called Shinn Enterprises* ***(G-20523)***
**Bad Girlz Enterprises Inc** 618 215-1428
414 S 39th St East Saint Louis (62207) ***(G-8743)***
**Bada Beans** 630 655-0693
215 S Monroe St Hinsdale (60521) ***(G-11940)***
**Bade Herman & Son Trucking, Villa Grove** *Also called Herman Bade & Sons* ***(G-21228)***
**Badge-A-Minit Ltd (HQ)** 815 883-8822
345 N Lewis Ave Oglesby (61348) ***(G-16746)***
**Badger Air Brush Co** 847 678-3104
9128 Belmont Ave Franklin Park (60131) ***(G-10409)***
**Badger Basket Co, Lake Zurich** *Also called Standard Container Co of Edgar* ***(G-13134)***
**Badger Molding Inc** 847 483-9005
2041 Foster Ave Wheeling (60090) ***(G-22011)***
**Badger Pallet Inc** 815 943-1147
630 W Blackman St Harvard (60033) ***(G-11623)***
**Baer Heating & Cooling Inc** 618 224-7344
11974 Old Us Highway 50 Trenton (62293) ***(G-20989)***
**Bag and Barrier Corporation** 217 849-3271
505 E Rte 121 Toledo (62468) ***(G-20961)***
**Bagcraft, Chicago** *Also called Packaging Dynamics Corporation* ***(G-6055)***
**Bagcraftpapercon I LLC (HQ)** 620 856-2800
3900 W 43rd St Chicago (60632) ***(G-4025)***
**Bagmakers Inc** 815 923-2247
6606 S Union Rd Union (60180) ***(G-21033)***
**Bahk Eye Care, Chicago** *Also called Bahk Eye Center Inc* ***(G-4026)***
**Bahk Eye Center Inc** 773 561-1199
5441 N Lincoln Ave Chicago (60625) ***(G-4026)***
**Bahr Tool & Die Co** 847 392-4447
2201 Foster Ave Wheeling (60090) ***(G-22012)***
**Baier Home Center** 815 457-2300
120 S 2nd St Cissna Park (60924) ***(G-7253)***
**Baier Publishing Company** 815 457-2245
119 W Garfield Ave Cissna Park (60924) ***(G-7254)***
**Bailey Business Group** 618 548-3566
3089 State Route 37 Salem (62881) ***(G-19327)***
**Bailey Hardwoods Inc** 217 529-6800
628 Kimble Ct Springfield (62703) ***(G-20394)***
**Baileys Fudge & Fine Gifts Inc** 217 231-3834
307 N 36th St Ste 210 Quincy (62301) ***(G-17799)***
**Bailleu & Bailleu Printing Inc** 309 852-2517
214 S Main St Ste A Kewanee (61443) ***(G-12670)***
**Baily International Inc (PA)** 618 451-8878
1122 State Route 3 National Stock Yards (62071) ***(G-15849)***
**Baird Inc** 217 526-3407
577 Illinois Route 48 Morrisonville (62546) ***(G-15150)***
**Baja Sales Inc** 708 672-9245
15 Charles Ct Crete (60417) ***(G-7508)***
**Bak Electric** 708 458-3578
7951 S Oketo Ave Bridgeview (60455) ***(G-2469)***
**Baka Vitaliy** 773 370-5522
2224 W Chicago Ave Chicago (60622) ***(G-4027)***
**Baked** 773 384-7655
2246 W North Ave Chicago (60647) ***(G-4028)***
**Baked Apple Pancake House** 630 515-9000
1224 Ogden Ave Downers Grove (60515) ***(G-8393)***
**Baked By Betsy Inc** 847 292-1434
707 Greenleaf Ave Wilmette (60091) ***(G-22242)***
**Baker & Nosh** 773 989-7393
1303 W Wilson Ave Chicago (60640) ***(G-4029)***
**Baker Atlas, Olney** *Also called Baker Hghes Olfld Oprtions Inc* ***(G-16761)***
**Baker Avenue Investments Inc (PA)** 309 427-2500
205 Eastgate Dr Washington (61571) ***(G-21378)***
**Baker Drapery Corporation** 309 691-3295
5516 N Big Hollow Rd Peoria (61615) ***(G-17313)***
**Baker Elements Inc** 630 660-8100
159 N Marion St Oak Park (60301) ***(G-16654)***
**Baker Hghes Olfld Oprtions Inc** 618 393-2919
930 S West St Olney (62450) ***(G-16761)***
**Baker La Russo** 630 788-5108
911 Joan Ct Naperville (60540) ***(G-15602)***
**Baker Manufacturing LLC** 847 362-3663
1349 Rockland Rd Lake Bluff (60044) ***(G-12835)***
**Baker's Custom Lettering, Naperville** *Also called Baker La Russo* ***(G-15602)***
**Bakery Crescent Corporation** 847 956-6470
270 E Algonquin Rd Arlington Heights (60005) ***(G-722)***
**Bakery Feeds, Seneca** *Also called Griffin Industries LLC* ***(G-19886)***
**Bala & Anula Fuels Inc** 630 766-1807
154 S York Rd Bensenville (60106) ***(G-1840)***
**Balanceuticals Group, Chicago** *Also called Health King Enterprise Inc* ***(G-5059)***
**Balancing Services, Chicago** *Also called Balanstar Corporation* ***(G-4030)***
**Balanstar Corporation (PA)** 773 261-5034
5030 W Lake St Chicago (60644) ***(G-4030)***
**Baldi Candy Co (PA)** 773 463-7600
3425 N Kimball Ave Chicago (60618) ***(G-4031)***
**Baldi Candy Co** 773 267-5770
3323 W Newport Ave Chicago (60618) ***(G-4032)***
**Baldor Electric Company** 630 296-1400
1055 Remington Blvd Ste B Bolingbrook (60440) ***(G-2282)***
**Baldwin Americas, Fairfield** *Also called Web Printing Controls Co Inc* ***(G-10161)***
**Baldwin Graphic Systems Inc** 630 261-9180
1051 N Main St Ste B Lombard (60148) ***(G-13766)***
**Baldwin OXY-Dry Corporation (HQ)** 630 595-3651
1210 N Swift Rd Addison (60101) ***(G-51)***
**Baldwin Richardson Foods Co (PA)** 815 464-9994
1 Tower Ln Oakbrook Terrace (60181) ***(G-16698)***
**Bales Mold Service Inc** 630 852-4665
2824 Hitchcock Ave Ste A Downers Grove (60515) ***(G-8394)***
**Baley Enterprises Inc** 708 681-0900
1206 N 31st Ave Melrose Park (60160) ***(G-14599)***
**Ball Corporation**
1717 Gifford Rd Elgin (60120) ***(G-8963)***
**Ball Foster Glass Container** 708 849-1500
13850 Cottage Grove Ave Dolton (60419) ***(G-8365)***
**Ball Foster Glass Container Co** 217 735-1511
1200 N Logan St Lincoln (62656) ***(G-13406)***
**Ball Plastic Container Div, Batavia** *Also called Amcor Rigid Plastics Usa LLC* ***(G-1412)***
**Ball Publishing** 630 208-9080
622 Town Rd West Chicago (60185) ***(G-21665)***
**Ballard Bros Inc** 217 374-2137
420 E Lincoln St White Hall (62092) ***(G-22183)***
**Ballard Bros Con Pdts & Excav, White Hall** *Also called Ballard Bros Inc* ***(G-22183)***
**Ballco Manufacturing Co Inc (PA)** 630 898-1600
2375 Liberty St Aurora (60502) ***(G-968)***
**Ballek Die Mold Inc** 847 885-2300
2125 Stonington Ave Hoffman Estates (60169) ***(G-11993)***
**Ballert Orthopedic of Chicago, Chicago** *Also called Gema Inc* ***(G-4924)***
**Balloon Art By Dj** 815 736-6123
231 W Joliet St Newark (60541) ***(G-15932)***
**Ballotready Inc** 301 706-0708
1626 N Honore St Chicago (60622) ***(G-4033)***
**Bally Foil Graphics Inc** 847 427-1509
1701 Elmhurst Rd Elk Grove Village (60007) ***(G-9333)***
**Balon International Corp** 773 379-7779
5410 W Roosevelt Rd 133a Chicago (60644) ***(G-4034)***
**Balsley Fast Printing, Rockton** *Also called Balsley Printing Inc* ***(G-18692)***
**Balsley Printing Inc** 815 637-8787
119 E Main St Rockton (61072) ***(G-18691)***
**Balsley Printing Inc (PA)** 815 624-7515
119 E Main St Rockton (61072) ***(G-18692)***
**Baltic Networks, Lisle** *Also called Vargyas Networks Inc* ***(G-13676)***
**Bamberger Polymers Inc** 630 773-8626
1 Pierce Pl Ste 255c Itasca (60143) ***(G-12233)***
**Bams Manufacturing Co Inc** 800 206-0613
421 Bennett Rd Elk Grove Village (60007) ***(G-9334)***
**Band of Shoppers Inc** 312 857-4250
2669 N Greenview Ave F Chicago (60614) ***(G-4035)***
**Bandage, The Div, Lanark** *Also called Hygienic Fabrics & Filters Inc* ***(G-13155)***
**Bandgrip Inc** 844 968-6322
311 S Wacker Dr Ste 650 Chicago (60606) ***(G-4036)***
**Bandjwet Enterprises Inc** 847 797-9250
3603 Edison Pl Rolling Meadows (60008) ***(G-18715)***
**Bando Usa Inc (HQ)** 630 773-6600
1149 W Bryn Mawr Ave Itasca (60143) ***(G-12234)***
**Bangert Casing Pulling Corp** 618 676-1411
1 Industrial Dr Clay City (62824) ***(G-7262)***
**Bankier Companies Inc** 847 647-6565
6151 W Gross Point Rd Niles (60714) ***(G-15963)***
**Bankmark Inc** 847 683-9834
46w299 Middleton Rd Hampshire (60140) ***(G-11542)***
**Banner Equipment Co** 815 941-9600
1370 Bungalow Rd Morris (60450) ***(G-15097)***
**Banner Medical, Carol Stream** *Also called Banner Service Corporation* ***(G-3112)***
**Banner Moulded Products** 708 452-0033
3050 River Rd River Grove (60171) ***(G-18005)***
**Banner Publications** 309 338-3294
350 N 1st St Cuba (61427) ***(G-7679)***
**Banner Sale Management Service, Cuba** *Also called Banner Publications* ***(G-7679)***
**Banner Service Corporation (PA)** 630 653-7500
494 E Lies Rd Carol Stream (60188) ***(G-3112)***
**Banner Up Signs, Sycamore** *Also called E K Kuhn Inc* ***(G-20795)***
**Bannon Enterprises Inc** 847 529-9265
2627 Lorraine Cir Geneva (60134) ***(G-10811)***
**Banta Book Group, Saint Charles** *Also called RR Donnelley & Sons Company* ***(G-19255)***
**Bantix Technologies LLC** 630 446-0886
490 Pennsylvania Ave Glen Ellyn (60137) ***(G-10960)***
**Banyan Technologies Inc** 312 967-9885
1452 E 53rd St Fl 2 Chicago (60615) ***(G-4037)***
**Baps Investors Group LLC** 847 818-8444
3940 Industrial Ave Rolling Meadows (60008) ***(G-18716)***
**Baptist General Conference (PA)** 800 323-4215
2002 S Arlington Hts Rd Arlington Heights (60005) ***(G-723)***
**Bar Code Dr Inc** 815 547-1001
4337 S Perryville Rd Cherry Valley (61016) ***(G-3639)***
**Bar Code Graphics Inc** 312 664-0700
65 E Wacker Pl Ste 1800 Chicago (60601) ***(G-4038)***
**Bar Codes Inc** 800 351-9962
200 W Monroe St Fl 10 Chicago (60606) ***(G-4039)***

**Bar List Publishing Co** ....847 498-0100
2900 Macarthur Blvd Northbrook (60062) *(G-16210)*
**Bar Processing Corporation** ....708 757-4570
1601 Wentworth Ave Ste 33 Chicago Heights (60411) *(G-7081)*
**Bar Stool Depotcom** ....815 727-7294
816 Caton Ave Joliet (60435) *(G-12460)*
**Bar-B-Que Industries Inc** ....773 227-5400
4460 W Armitage Ave Chicago (60639) *(G-4040)*
**Bar/Bri Group, Chicago** *Also called West Publishing Corporation (G-6961)*
**Barbeque Select, Chicago** *Also called New Specialty Products Inc (G-5894)*
**Barcar Manufacturing Inc** ....630 365-5200
1 N 081 Thryselius Dr Elburn (60119) *(G-8877)*
**Barclay Business Group Inc** ....847 325-5555
250 Parkway Dr Ste 150 Lincolnshire (60069) *(G-13431)*
**Barco Stamping Co (PA)** ....630 293-5155
1095 Carolina Dr West Chicago (60185) *(G-21666)*
**Barcodesource Inc (PA)** ....630 545-9590
245 W Roosevelt Rd # 109 West Chicago (60185) *(G-21667)*
**Barcodesupplies.com, West Chicago** *Also called Barcodesource Inc (G-21667)*
**Barcoding Inc** ....847 726-7777
333 E Il Route 83 Ste 201 Mundelein (60060) *(G-15474)*
**Barcor Inc** ....847 940-0750
1413 Aitken Dr Bannockburn (60015) *(G-1255)*
**Barcor Inc** ....847 831-2650
1510 Old Deerfield Rd # 206 Highland Park (60035) *(G-11824)*
**Bard Optical, Decatur** *Also called J A K Enterprises Inc (G-7897)*
**Bardash & Bukowski Inc** ....312 829-2080
329 W 18th St Ste 908 Chicago (60616) *(G-4041)*
**Bards Products Inc (PA)** ....800 323-5499
1427 Armour Blvd Mundelein (60060) *(G-15475)*
**Bare Development Inc** ....708 352-2273
5425 9th Ave Countryside (60525) *(G-7415)*
**Barilla America Inc (HQ)** ....515 956-4400
885 Sunset Ridge Rd Northbrook (60062) *(G-16211)*
**Bark Project Management Inc** ....630 964-5876
7017 Roberts Dr Woodridge (60517) *(G-22455)*
**Barkaat Foods LLC** ....773 376-8723
3810 S Halsted St Chicago (60609) *(G-4042)*
**Barker Metal Craft Inc** ....773 588-9300
2955 N California Ave Chicago (60618) *(G-4043)*
**Barks Publications Inc** ....312 321-9440
500 N Michigan Ave # 901 Chicago (60611) *(G-4044)*
**Barnaby Complete Printing Svcs, Sycamore** *Also called Barnaby Inc (G-20789)*
**Barnaby Inc** ....815 895-6555
1620 Dekalb Ave Sycamore (60178) *(G-20789)*
**Barnant, Bartlett** *Also called Thermo Fisher Scientific Inc (G-1380)*
**Barnes & Noble College** ....309 677-2320
830 N Elmwood Ave Peoria (61606) *(G-17314)*
**Barnes & Noble College** ....708 209-3173
7400 Augusta St River Forest (60305) *(G-17996)*
**Barnes Industrial Equipment** ....630 213-9240
155 Sangra Ct Streamwood (60107) *(G-20645)*
**Barnes International Inc (PA)** ....815 964-8661
814 Chestnut St Rockford (61102) *(G-18276)*
**Barnes Machine Shop LLC** ....217 774-5308
209 N Pine St Shelbyville (62565) *(G-19905)*
**Barnett Bob Redi-Mix, Harrisburg** *Also called Bob Barnett Redi-Mix Inc (G-11596)*
**Barnett Redi-Mix Inc** ....618 276-4298
11300 Highway 1 Junction (62954) *(G-12593)*
**Barnett-Bates Corporation** ....815 726-5223
500 Mills Rd Joliet (60433) *(G-12461)*
**Barneys Aluminum Specialties** ....815 723-5341
340 Ruby St Joliet (60435) *(G-12462)*
**Baron Manufacturing Co LLC** ....630 628-9110
730 Baker Dr Itasca (60143) *(G-12235)*
**Baron-Blakeslee Sfc Inc** ....847 796-0822
2900 Macarthur Blvd Northbrook (60062) *(G-16212)*
**Baroque Silversmith Inc (PA)** ....312 357-2813
55 E Washington St # 302 Chicago (60602) *(G-4045)*
**Barrel Maker Printing** ....773 490-3065
3065 N Rockwell St Ste 8 Chicago (60618) *(G-4046)*
**Barriersafe Solutions Intl Inc (HQ)** ....847 735-0163
150 N Field Dr Ste 210 Lake Forest (60045) *(G-12884)*
**Barrington Automation Ltd** ....847 458-0900
9116 Virginia Rd Lake In The Hills (60156) *(G-12987)*
**Barrington Cardinal Whse LLC** ....847 387-3676
340 W Northwest Hwy Barrington (60010) *(G-1270)*
**Barrington Clinical Partners** ....847 508-9737
25377 N Wagon Wheel Ct Barrington (60010) *(G-1271)*
**Barrington Company** ....815 933-3233
195 N Euclid Ave Bradley (60915) *(G-2413)*
**Barrington Financial Services** ....847 404-1767
3 Sunvalley Ct Lake In The Hills (60156) *(G-12988)*
**Barrington Millwork LLC** ....847 304-0791
27214 W Henry Ln Lake Barrington (60010) *(G-12800)*
**Barrington Packaging Systems** ....847 382-8063
835 Barrington Point Rd Barrington (60010) *(G-1272)*
**Barrington Packg Systems Group, Barrington** *Also called Barrington Packaging Systems (G-1272)*
**Barrington Print & Copy Inc** ....847 382-1185
200 James St Barrington (60010) *(G-1273)*
**Barron 2m Inc** ....847 219-3650
3745 Ruby St Apt 5 Schiller Park (60176) *(G-19808)*
**Barron Metal Finishing LLC** ....815 962-8053
1350 Preston St Rockford (61102) *(G-18277)*
**Barry Callebaut USA LLC** ....312 496-7300
2144 Paysphere Cir Chicago (60674) *(G-4047)*
**Barry Callebaut USA LLC (HQ)** ....312 496-7300
600 W Chicago Ave Ste 860 Chicago (60654) *(G-4048)*
**Barry Electric Div, Maywood** *Also called National Cycle Inc (G-14430)*
**Barry Schuster, Mundelein** *Also called Rkb Distributors (G-15552)*
**Barry Signs Inc** ....773 327-1183
6950 W Imlay St Chicago (60631) *(G-4049)*
**Barry-Whmller Cont Systems Inc (HQ)** ....630 759-6800
1305 Lakeview Dr Romeoville (60446) *(G-18802)*
**Barsanti Woodwork Corporation** ....773 284-6888
3838 W 51st St Chicago (60632) *(G-4050)*
**Bartec Orb Inc** ....773 927-8600
4724 S Christiana Ave Chicago (60632) *(G-4051)*
**Bartech Precision Machining Co** ....630 243-9068
16135 New Ave Ste 3 Lemont (60439) *(G-13227)*
**Bartell Corporation** ....847 854-3232
3671 Persimmon Dr Algonquin (60102) *(G-380)*
**Bartell Grinding and Mch LLC** ....708 408-1700
8312 Joliet Rd Unit 9 Mc Cook (60525) *(G-14445)*
**Barth Wind Elan Furs, Morton Grove** *Also called Elan Furs (G-15195)*
**Bartlett Farms, Dallas City** *Also called Jack Bartlett (G-7697)*
**Barton Manufacturing LLC (HQ)** ....217 428-0711
1395 S Taylorville Rd Decatur (62521) *(G-7843)*
**Barton Manufacturing LLC** ....217 428-0726
600 E Wabash Ave Decatur (62523) *(G-7844)*
**Bartonville Equipment Rental** ....309 633-0227
7301 S Adams St Bartonville (61607) *(G-1392)*
**Bas Success Express Inc** ....847 258-5550
9001 Golf Rd Apt 7h Des Plaines (60016) *(G-8155)*
**Base-Line II Inc** ....847 336-8403
2001 N Delany Rd Gurnee (60031) *(G-11430)*
**Baseball Digest, Evanston** *Also called Grandstand Publishing LLC (G-10045)*
**Baseline Graphics Inc** ....630 964-9566
5424 Webster St Downers Grove (60515) *(G-8395)*
**Basement Dewatering Systems** ....309 647-0331
3100 N Main St Canton (61520) *(G-2981)*
**Basement Flood Protector Inc** ....847 438-6770
707 Rose Rd Lake Zurich (60047) *(G-13045)*
**BASF Construction Chem LLC** ....847 249-4080
1810 Northwestern Ave Gurnee (60031) *(G-11431)*
**BASF Corporation** ....815 932-9863
2525 S Kensington Ave Kankakee (60901) *(G-12603)*
**Basic Industries, Hecker** *Also called Hottenrott Company Inc (G-11732)*
**Basin Transports** ....618 829-3323
112 E 4th St Saint Elmo (62458) *(G-19303)*
**Basnett, John, Fairfield** *Also called Basnetts Investments (G-10136)*
**Basnetts Investments** ....618 842-4040
215 Se 3rd St Ste 208 Fairfield (62837) *(G-10136)*
**Bass Brother Incorporated** ....773 638-7628
4441 W Fillmore St Chicago (60624) *(G-4052)*
**Bass-Mollett Publishers Inc** ....618 664-3141
507 Monroe St Greenville (62246) *(G-11387)*
**Basswood Associates Inc (PA)** ....312 240-9400
1017 W Washington Blvd Chicago (60607) *(G-4053)*
**Bat Business Services Inc** ....630 801-9335
987 Oak Ave Aurora (60506) *(G-1118)*
**Batavia Container Inc** ....630 879-2100
1400 Paramount Pkwy Batavia (60510) *(G-1419)*
**Batavia Foundry and Machine Co** ....630 879-1319
717 First St Batavia (60510) *(G-1420)*
**Batavia Instant Print** ....630 262-0370
33w480 Fabyan Pkwy # 104 West Chicago (60185) *(G-21668)*
**Bates Abrasive Products Inc** ....773 586-8700
6230 S Oak Park Ave Chicago (60638) *(G-4054)*
**Bath Solutions Inc** ....817 429-2318
858 W Armitage Ave Chicago (60614) *(G-4055)*
**Batteries Plus 287** ....630 279-3478
240 E Roosevelt Rd Villa Park (60181) *(G-21237)*
**Battle Balls Bubble Soccer, Chicago** *Also called Peak Healthcare Advisors LLC (G-6093)*
**Bauermeister Inc** ....901 363-0921
601 Corporate Woods Pkwy Vernon Hills (60061) *(G-21146)*
**Bauhaus Zwick Co, Quincy** *Also called West Zwick Corp (G-17903)*
**Baum Holdings Inc** ....847 488-0650
506 Sundown Rd South Elgin (60177) *(G-20185)*
**Baumbach Manufacturing** ....630 941-0505
650 W Grand Ave Elmhurst (60126) *(G-9836)*
**Baumer Financial Publishing, Chicago** *Also called Imagination Publishing LLC (G-5161)*
**Baxalta Export Corporation** ....224 948-2000
1 Baxter Pkwy Deerfield (60015) *(G-7981)*
**Baxalta Incorporated (HQ)** ....224 940-2000
1200 Lakeside Dr Bannockburn (60015) *(G-1256)*

ALPHABETIC

(PA)=Parent Co (HQ)=Headquarters (DH)=Div Headquarters
2017 Harris Illinois Industrial Directory
1175

**Baxalta US Inc** .................................................. 312 648-2244
135 S Lasalle St Ste 3425 Chicago (60603) *(G-4056)*

**Baxalta US Inc** .................................................. 847 948-2000
25212 W Il Route 120 Round Lake (60073) *(G-19052)*

**Baxalta World Trade LLC (HQ)** ...................... 224 948-2000
1 Baxter Pkwy Deerfield (60015) *(G-7982)*

**Baxalta Worldwide LLC** ................................. 224 948-2000
1 Baxter Pkwy Deerfield (60015) *(G-7983)*

**Baxter Diagnostics Inc** ................................... 201 337-1212
900 Corporate Grove Dr Buffalo Grove (60089) *(G-2661)*

**Baxter Global Holdings II Inc (HQ)** ............... 847 948-2000
1 Baxter Pkwy Deerfield (60015) *(G-7984)*

**Baxter Healthcare Corporation** ..................... 847 522-8600
400 Lakeview Pkwy Vernon Hills (60061) *(G-21147)*

**Baxter Healthcare Corporation** ..................... 800 422-9837
1 Baxter Pkwy Deerfield (60015) *(G-7985)*

**Baxter Healthcare Corporation** ..................... 847 270-4757
7621 Center Dr Wonder Lake (60097) *(G-22321)*

**Baxter Healthcare Corporation** ..................... 847 948-3206
1606 Beech St Spring Grove (60081) *(G-20328)*

**Baxter Healthcare Corporation** ..................... 847 948-4251
75 Tri State Intl Lincolnshire (60069) *(G-13432)*

**Baxter Healthcare Corporation** ..................... 224 270-6300
32360 N Wilson Rd Round Lake (60073) *(G-19053)*

**Baxter Healthcare Corporation** ..................... 847 367-2544
440 N Fairway Dr Vernon Hills (60061) *(G-21148)*

**Baxter Healthcare Corporation** ..................... 847 578-4671
2105 S Waukegan Rd Waukegan (60085) *(G-21529)*

**Baxter Healthcare Corporation** ..................... 847 948-2000
1435 Lake Cook Rd Deerfield (60015) *(G-7986)*

**Baxter Healthcare Corporation** ..................... 847 940-6599
25212 W Illinois Rte 120 Round Lake (60073) *(G-19054)*

**Baxter Healthcare Corporation** ..................... 847 948-2000
1 Baxter Pkwy Deerfield (60015) *(G-7987)*

**Baxter International Inc (PA)** ........................ 224 948-2000
1 Baxter Pkwy Deerfield (60015) *(G-7988)*

**Baxter V Mueller** .............................................. 847 774-6800
7280 N Caldwell Ave Niles (60714) *(G-15964)*

**Baxter Vineyards** ............................................. 217 453-2528
2010 Parley St Nauvoo (62354) *(G-15852)*

**Baxter World Trade Corporation (HQ)** .......... 224 948-2000
1 Baxter Pkwy Deerfield (60015) *(G-7989)*

**Bay Foods Inc** .................................................. 312 346-5757
1026 E Jackson Blvd Chicago (60607) *(G-4057)*

**Bay Plastics** ..................................................... 847 299-2045
1245 E Forest Ave Ste 8 Des Plaines (60018) *(G-8156)*

**Bay Valley Foods LLC** .................................... 815 239-2631
215 W 3rd St Pecatonica (61063) *(G-17251)*

**Bay Valley Foods LLC** .................................... 773 927-7700
4401 W 44th Pl Chicago (60632) *(G-4058)*

**Bay Valley Foods LLC** .................................... 708 409-5300
2021 Spring Rd Ste 600 Oak Brook (60523) *(G-16491)*

**Bayer Corporation** .......................................... 847 725-6320
25 Northwest Point Blvd Elk Grove Village (60007) *(G-9335)*

**Bays English Muffin Corp** .............................. 312 829-5253
1026 W Jackson Blvd Chicago (60607) *(G-4059)*

**Bays Michigan Corp** ....................................... 312 346-5757
1026 W Jackson Blvd Chicago (60607) *(G-4060)*

**Bazaar Inc** ........................................................ 708 583-1800
1900 5th Ave River Grove (60171) *(G-18006)*

**Bb Services LLC** .............................................. 630 941-8122
205 E Butterfield Rd Elmhurst (60126) *(G-9837)*

**BBC Fasteners Inc** .......................................... 708 597-9100
4210 W Shirley Ln Alsip (60803) *(G-439)*

**BBC Innovation Corporation** ......................... 847 458-2334
7900 S Illinois Rt 31 Crystal Lake (60014) *(G-7540)*

**Bbs Automation Chicago Inc** ......................... 630 351-3000
1580 Hecht Ct Bartlett (60103) *(G-1335)*

**Bc Asi Capital II Inc** ........................................ 708 534-5575
200 Applied Pkwy University Park (60484) *(G-21043)*

**Bc Enterprises** ................................................. 618 655-0784
99 Shore Dr Sw Edwardsville (62025) *(G-8791)*

**Bc International** ............................................... 847 674-7384
4909 Old Orchard Ctr Skokie (60077) *(G-19962)*

**Bc Machine** ...................................................... 815 962-7884
1704 16th Ave Rockford (61104) *(G-18278)*

**Bc Welding Inc** ................................................. 708 258-0076
308 E Crawford St Peotone (60468) *(G-17484)*

**Bc Welding Service and Repair, Peotone** Also called Bc Welding Inc *(G-17484)*

**BCI Acrylic Inc (PA)** ........................................ 847 963-8827
1800 Industrial Dr Libertyville (60048) *(G-13307)*

**Bcs Industries, Chicago** Also called Charles N Benner Inc *(G-4293)*

**Bdc Capital Enterprises LLC** ......................... 847 908-0650
1515 E Wdfield Rd Ste 110 Schaumburg (60173) *(G-19457)*

**Bdi Enterprises** ................................................ 773 354-6433
9825 W Roosevelt Rd Westchester (60154) *(G-21830)*

**Be Group Inc** .................................................... 312 436-0301
1507 E 53rd St Chicago (60615) *(G-4061)*

**Be McGonagle Inc** .......................................... 847 394-0413
858 S Arthur Ave Arlington Heights (60005) *(G-724)*

**Be Products Inc** ............................................... 312 201-9669
180 W Washington St Fl 10 Chicago (60602) *(G-4062)*

**Be Something Studio, Melrose Park** Also called Zagone Studio LLC *(G-14713)*

**Bea's Best, Chicago** Also called City Foods Inc *(G-4382)*

**Beachwaver** ...................................................... 224 513-5817
408 N Milwaukee Ave # 202 Libertyville (60048) *(G-13308)*

**Beachys Counter Tops Inc** ............................. 217 543-2143
129 E Sr 133 Arthur (61911) *(G-882)*

**Beacon Fas & Components Inc** ..................... 847 541-0404
198 Carpenter Ave Wheeling (60090) *(G-22013)*

**Beacon Inc** ....................................................... 708 544-9900
12223 S Laramie Ave Alsip (60803) *(G-440)*

**Beacon Solutions Inc** ..................................... 303 513-0469
111 E Wacker Dr Ste 3000 Chicago (60601) *(G-4063)*

**Beacon Terminal Pin, Wheeling** Also called Beacon Fas & Components Inc *(G-22013)*

**Beall Manufacturing Inc (PA)** ........................ 618 259-8154
421 N Shamrock St East Alton (62024) *(G-8599)*

**Beam Global Spirits & Wine LLC (HQ)** ........ 847 948-8888
510 Lake Cook Rd Deerfield (60015) *(G-7990)*

**Beam Suntory, Deerfield** Also called Beam Global Spirits & Wine LLC *(G-7990)*

**Beam Suntory Inc (HQ)** .................................. 847 948-8888
510 Lake Cook Rd Deerfield (60015) *(G-7991)*

**Bean and Body, Chicago** Also called Fast Forward Energy Inc *(G-4815)*

**Bean Products Inc** .......................................... 312 666-3600
1500 S Western Ave Ste 40 Chicago (60608) *(G-4064)*

**Bean Stich Inc** ................................................. 630 422-1269
237 Evergreen Ave Bensenville (60106) *(G-1841)*

**Beans Printing Inc** .......................................... 217 223-5555
3710 Broadway St Quincy (62305) *(G-17800)*

**Bear Creek Truss Inc** ...................................... 217 543-3329
615 N County Road 250 E Tuscola (61953) *(G-21016)*

**Bear Mtal Wldg Fabrication Inc** .................... 630 261-9353
948 N Ridge Ave Lombard (60148) *(G-13767)*

**Bear-Stewart Corporation (PA)** ..................... 773 276-0400
1025 N Damen Ave Chicago (60622) *(G-4065)*

**Beard Enterprises Inc** .................................... 630 357-3278
931 E Ogden Ave Ste 127 Naperville (60563) *(G-15603)*

**Beardsley & Piper L.L.C., Aurora** Also called Simpson Technologies *(G-1078)*

**Beardsley Printery Inc** .................................... 309 788-4041
1103 51st Ave Rock Island (61201) *(G-18161)*

**Beardstown Newspapers Inc** ......................... 217 323-1010
1210 Wall St Beardstown (62618) *(G-1520)*

**Beardstown Tube Plant, Beardstown** Also called Caraustar Industrial and Con *(G-1521)*

**Bearing Division, Sterling** Also called Frantz Manufacturing Company *(G-20593)*

**Bearing Headquarters Co, Elk Grove Village** Also called Headco Industries Inc *(G-9519)*

**Bearing Headquarters Co, Joliet** Also called Headco Industries Inc *(G-12509)*

**Bearing Sales Corporation (PA)** .................... 773 282-8686
4153 N Kostner Ave Chicago (60641) *(G-4066)*

**Bearings Manufacturing Company** ............... 773 583-6703
1033 N Kolmar Ave Chicago (60651) *(G-4067)*

**Bearse Manufacturing Co** .............................. 773 235-8710
3815 W Cortland St Chicago (60647) *(G-4068)*

**Bearse USA, Chicago** Also called Bearse Manufacturing Co *(G-4068)*

**Beas Bags** ........................................................ 847 486-1943
315 Cherry Ln Glenview (60025) *(G-11106)*

**Beastgrip Co** .................................................... 312 283-5283
1269 Rand Rd Des Plaines (60016) *(G-8157)*

**Beatrice Companies Inc** ................................. 602 225-2000
2 N La Salle St Chicago (60602) *(G-4069)*

**Beau-Brehm L Ranches, Mount Vernon** Also called Brehm Oil Inc *(G-15402)*

**Beauticontrol** .................................................... 217 223-0382
1702 Locust St Quincy (62301) *(G-17801)*

**Beauty Vault LLC** ............................................. 773 621-5189
3355 N Lincoln Ave Ste 14 Chicago (60657) *(G-4070)*

**Beaver Creek Enterprises Inc (PA)** ............... 815 723-9455
801 Rowell Ave Joliet (60433) *(G-12463)*

**Beaver Creek Golf Carts, Joliet** Also called Beaver Creek Enterprises Inc *(G-12463)*

**Beaver-Visitec Intl Holdings** .......................... 847 739-3219
272 E Deerpath Ste 328 Lake Forest (60045) *(G-12885)*

**Beaver-Visitec Intl Inc** .................................... 847 739-3219
272 E Deerpath Ste 328 Lake Forest (60045) *(G-12886)*

**Bechara Sim** ..................................................... 847 913-9950
121 Willow Pkwy Buffalo Grove (60089) *(G-2662)*

**Beck Shoe Products Company** ..................... 618 656-5819
203 W High St Edwardsville (62025) *(G-8792)*

**Becker Brothers Graphite Corp** ..................... 708 410-0700
39 Legion St Maywood (60153) *(G-14418)*

**Becker Jules D Wood Products** ..................... 847 526-8002
25250 W Old Rand Rd Wauconda (60084) *(G-21445)*

**Becker Specialty Corporation (HQ)** .............. 847 766-3555
2526 Delta Ln Elk Grove Village (60007) *(G-9336)*

**Beckman Coulter Inc** ...................................... 800 526-3821
1500 N Mittel Blvd Wood Dale (60191) *(G-22343)*

**Becks Light Gauge Aluminum Co** ................. 847 290-9990
1425 Tonne Rd Elk Grove Village (60007) *(G-9337)*

**Becks Medical & Indus Gases** ....................... 618 273-9019
1411 Locust St Eldorado (62930) *(G-8917)*

# ALPHABETIC SECTION — Beltone Corporation (HQ)

**Becsis LLC** .................................................... 630 400-6454
2197 Brookwood Dr  South Elgin (60177)  *(G-20186)*

**Becton  Dickinson and Company** ..................... 630 428-3499
5 E 14th Ave  Naperville (60563)  *(G-15604)*

**Becton  Dickinson and Company** ..................... 630 743-2006
1400 Opus Pl Ste 805  Downers Grove (60515)  *(G-8396)*

**Bedding Group  Inc (PA)** ................................. 309 788-0401
2350 5th St  Rock Island (61201)  *(G-18162)*

**Bedding Group, The, Rock Island** Also called Bedding Group  Inc  *(G-18162)*

**Bedford  Rakim** .............................................. 773 749-3086
3022 Bernice Ave Apt 3s  Lansing (60438)  *(G-13157)*

**Bedford  Rakim** .............................................. 773 759-3947
17125 Evans Dr  South Holland (60473)  *(G-20249)*

**Bee Boat Co Inc** ............................................ 217 379-2605
209 E Green St  Paxton (60957)  *(G-17236)*

**Bee Clean Specialties LLC** ............................. 847 451-0844
550 Albion Ave  Schaumburg (60193)  *(G-19458)*

**Bee Designs Embroidery & Scree** ................... 815 393-4593
24637 Esmond Rd  Malta (60150)  *(G-14165)*

**Bee Line Service Inc** ..................................... 815 233-1812
2291 Us Highway 20 E  Freeport (61032)  *(G-10648)*

**Bee Sales Comapny (PA)** ............................... 847 600-4400
6330 W Touhy Ave  Niles (60714)  *(G-15965)*

**Bee-Jay Industries Inc** ................................... 708 867-4431
148 Paxton Rd  Bloomingdale (60108)  *(G-2095)*

**Beechner Heat Treating Co Inc** ....................... 815 397-4314
905 Brooke Rd  Rockford (61109)  *(G-18279)*

**Beecken Petty Okeefe & Co LLC (PA)** ............. 312 435-0300
131 S Dearborn St Ste 122  Chicago (60603)  *(G-4071)*

**Beelman Ready-Mix  Inc** ................................. 618 357-6120
5780 State Route 154  Pinckneyville (62274)  *(G-17544)*

**Beelman Ready-Mix  Inc** ................................. 618 478-2044
17558 Mockingbird Rd  Nashville (62263)  *(G-15834)*

**Beelman Ready-Mix  Inc** ................................. 618 526-0260
8200 Old Us Highway 50  Breese (62230)  *(G-2439)*

**Beelman Ready-Mix  Inc (PA)** ......................... 618 646-5300
1 Racehorse Dr  East Saint Louis (62205)  *(G-8744)*

**Beelman Ready-Mix  Inc** ................................. 618 244-9600
13425 N Shiloh Dr  Mount Vernon (62864)  *(G-15400)*

**Beelman Ready-Mix  Inc** ................................. 618 247-3866
100 Cemetery Rd  Sandoval (62882)  *(G-19355)*

**Beelman Slag Sales** ...................................... 618 452-8120
2000 Edwardsville Rd  Madison (62060)  *(G-14139)*

**Beeman & Sons Inc** ....................................... 217 232-4268
5815 E Snake Trail Rd  Martinsville (62442)  *(G-14332)*

**Beer Nuts  Inc** ............................................... 309 827-8580
103 N Robinson St  Bloomington (61701)  *(G-2147)*

**Befco Manufacturing Co., Oak Lawn** Also called G & F Manufacturing Co  Inc  *(G-16621)*

**Befco Manufacturing Co Inc** ........................... 708 424-4170
5555 W 109th St  Oak Lawn (60453)  *(G-16606)*

**Begel Industries, Chicago** Also called Tmb Industries Inc  *(G-6732)*

**Behabelt USA** ................................................ 630 521-9835
860 Devon Ave  Bensenville (60106)  *(G-1842)*

**Behr Process Corporation** .............................. 630 289-6247
950 S Il Route 59  Bartlett (60103)  *(G-1336)*

**Behr Process Corporation** .............................. 708 753-0136
21701 Mark Collins Dr # 200  Chicago Heights (60411)  *(G-7082)*

**Behr Process Corporation** .............................. 708 753-1820
21399 Torrence Ave Ste 1  Lynwood (60411)  *(G-14018)*

**Behr Process Corporation** .............................. 708 757-6350
270 State St Ste 1  Chicago Heights (60411)  *(G-7083)*

**BEI Electronics LLC (HQ)** ............................... 217 224-9600
4100 N 24th St  Quincy (62305)  *(G-17802)*

**BEI Holding Corporation** ................................. 217 224-9600
4100 N 24th St  Quincy (62305)  *(G-17803)*

**Bel Brands Usa  Inc (HQ)** ............................... 312 462-1500
30 S Wacker Dr Ste 3000  Chicago (60606)  *(G-4072)*

**Bel Mar Wire Products Inc** ............................. 773 342-3800
2343 N Damen Ave  Chicago (60647)  *(G-4073)*

**Bel-Air Manufacturing  Inc** ............................. 773 276-7550
3525 W Potomac Ave  Chicago (60651)  *(G-4074)*

**Belair Hd Studios LLC** ................................... 312 254-5188
2233 S Throop St  Chicago (60608)  *(G-4075)*

**Belboz Corp** .................................................. 708 856-6099
742 Evans Ct  Dolton (60419)  *(G-8366)*

**Belcar Products  Inc** ...................................... 630 462-1950
500 Randy Rd Ste B  Carol Stream (60188)  *(G-3113)*

**Belco International Toy Co** ............................. 847 256-6818
806 Lawler Ave  Wilmette (60091)  *(G-22243)*

**Belden Energy Solutions Inc** .......................... 800 235-3361
719 S Berkley Ave  Elmhurst (60126)  *(G-9838)*

**Belden Enterprises LP** ................................... 618 829-3274
801 N Elm St  Saint Elmo (62458)  *(G-19304)*

**Belden Machine Corporation** .......................... 708 344-4600
2500 Braga Dr  Broadview (60155)  *(G-2561)*

**Belden Tools  Inc** .......................................... 708 344-4600
2500 Braga Dr  Broadview (60155)  *(G-2562)*

**Belford Electronics Inc** ................................... 630 705-3020
1460 W Jeffrey Dr  Addison (60101)  *(G-52)*

**Belgian Chocolatier Piron Inc** ......................... 847 864-5504
509 Main St Fl A  Evanston (60202)  *(G-10014)*

**Belke Manufacturing Company, Chicago** Also called American Rack Company  *(G-3870)*

**Bell & Gossett, Morton Grove** Also called Fluid Handling LLC  *(G-15198)*

**Bell Aromatics, Northbrook** Also called Bell Flavors & Fragrances Inc  *(G-16213)*

**Bell Brothers** ................................................. 618 544-2157
201 N Jefferson St  Robinson (62454)  *(G-18055)*

**Bell Cabinet & Millwork Co** ............................ 708 425-1200
9340 S Kedzie Ave  Evergreen Park (60805)  *(G-10110)*

**Bell City Battery Mfg Inc (PA)** ........................ 618 233-0437
34 Empire Dr Ste 2  Belleville (62220)  *(G-1611)*

**Bell Flavors & Fragrances Inc (PA)** ................. 847 291-8300
500 Academy Dr  Northbrook (60062)  *(G-16213)*

**Bell Litho  Inc (PA)** ....................................... 847 952-3300
370 Crossen Ave  Elk Grove Village (60007)  *(G-9338)*

**Bell Litho  Inc** .............................................. 847 290-9300
1820 Lunt Ave  Elk Grove Village (60007)  *(G-9339)*

**Bell Racing Co, Champaign** Also called Bell Racing Usa  LLC  *(G-3456)*

**Bell Racing Usa  LLC** .................................... 217 239-5355
301 Mercury Dr Ste 8  Champaign (61822)  *(G-3456)*

**Bell Sports** ................................................... 309 693-2746
909 Pacesetter Dr  Rantoul (61866)  *(G-17919)*

**Bell Sports  Inc** ............................................ 217 893-9300
1001 Innovation Rd  Rantoul (61866)  *(G-17920)*

**Bella Architectural  Products** ......................... 708 339-4782
16910 Lathrop Ave  Harvey (60426)  *(G-11660)*

**Bella Cabinet, Bridgeview** Also called Eddie Gapastione  *(G-2487)*

**Bella Casa** .................................................... 630 455-5900
322 N Adams St  Hinsdale (60521)  *(G-11941)*

**Bella Elevator  LLC** ....................................... 410 685-0344
10000 N Galena Rd  Peoria (61615)  *(G-17315)*

**Bella Pharmaceuticals Inc** ............................. 773 279-5350
3101 W Devon Ave  Chicago (60659)  *(G-4076)*

**Bella Salon, Lake Forest** Also called Cindys Nail & Hair Care  *(G-12891)*

**Bella Sign Co** ............................................... 630 539-0343
9 Presidential Dr  Roselle (60172)  *(G-18928)*

**Bella T Winery, Creal Springs** Also called Bella Terra Winery  LLC  *(G-7453)*

**Bella Terra Winery  LLC** ................................. 618 658-8882
755 Parker City Rd  Creal Springs (62922)  *(G-7453)*

**Bellaflora Foods, Chicago** Also called BF Foods  Inc  *(G-4099)*

**Bellaflora Foods Ltd** ..................................... 773 252-6113
4334 W Chicago Ave  Chicago (60651)  *(G-4077)*

**Belle-Aire Fragrances Inc (PA)** ....................... 847 816-3500
1600 Baskin Rd  Mundelein (60060)  *(G-15476)*

**Bellen Container Corporation** ......................... 847 741-5600
1460 Bowes Rd  Elgin (60123)  *(G-8964)*

**Belleville Automotive, Belleville** Also called L M C Automotive Inc  *(G-1647)*

**Belleville Boot Company, Belleville** Also called Belleville Shoe Mfg Co  *(G-1612)*

**Belleville News Democrat, Belleville** Also called McClatchy Newspapers  Inc  *(G-1655)*

**Belleville Shoe Mfg Co (PA)** ........................... 618 233-5600
100 Premier Dr  Belleville (62220)  *(G-1612)*

**Bellisario Holdings LLC** ................................. 847 867-2960
117 Elmore St  Park Ridge (60068)  *(G-17183)*

**Bellman-Melcor Holdings Inc** ......................... 708 532-5000
7575 183rd St  Tinley Park (60477)  *(G-20896)*

**Bellota Agrsltions Tls USA LLC** ...................... 309 787-2491
1421 11th St W  Milan (61264)  *(G-14775)*

**Bellows Shoppe** ............................................ 847 446-5533
1048 Gage St Ste 301  Winnetka (60093)  *(G-22303)*

**Bellwood Dunkin Donuts** ................................ 708 401-5601
502 Mannheim Rd  Bellwood (60104)  *(G-1695)*

**Bellwood Electric Motors Inc** ......................... 708 544-7223
200 25th Ave  Bellwood (60104)  *(G-1696)*

**Bellwood Industries Inc (PA)** .......................... 773 522-1002
4351 W Roosevelt Rd  Chicago (60624)  *(G-4078)*

**Belmont Electro Co Inc** .................................. 773 472-4641
8920 47th St  Brookfield (60513)  *(G-2623)*

**Belmont Plating Works  Inc (PA)** .................... 847 678-0200
9145 King St  Franklin Park (60131)  *(G-10410)*

**Belmont Sausage Company** ........................... 847 357-1515
2201 Estes Ave  Elk Grove Village (60007)  *(G-9340)*

**Belmonte Printing Co** .................................... 847 352-8841
525 W Wise Rd Ste D  Schaumburg (60193)  *(G-19459)*

**Beloit Pattern Works** ..................................... 815 389-2578
819 Ingersoll Pl  South Beloit (61080)  *(G-20140)*

**Beloved Characters  Ltd** ................................ 773 599-0073
6456 W 64th Pl Apt 3  Chicago (60638)  *(G-4079)*

**Belrich Inc**
2341 N Lister Ave  Chicago (60614)  *(G-4080)*

**Belrock Printing Inc** ...................................... 815 547-1096
915 W Perry St  Belvidere (61008)  *(G-1735)*

**Belson Outdoors  LLC (HQ)** ............................ 630 897-8489
111 N River Rd  North Aurora (60542)  *(G-16120)*

**Belson Steel Center Scrap Inc** ....................... 815 932-7416
1685 N State Route 50  Bourbonnais (60914)  *(G-2389)*

**Belt-Way Scales  Inc** ..................................... 815 625-5573
1 Beltway Rd  Rock Falls (61071)  *(G-18126)*

**Beltone Corporation (HQ)** ............................... 847 832-3300
2601 Patriot Blvd  Glenview (60026)  *(G-11107)*

---

(PA)=Parent Co  (HQ)=Headquarters  (DH)=Div Headquarters

2017 Harris Illinois Industrial Directory

**Beltoutlet.com, Plainfield** *Also called Phoenix Leather Goods LLC* ***(G-17639)***
**Belvedere Usa LLC (PA)**.....815 544-3131
1 Belvedere Blvd Belvidere (61008) ***(G-1736)***
**Belvidere Daily Republican Co**.....815 547-0084
130 S State St Ste 101 Belvidere (61008) ***(G-1737)***
**Belvin J & F Sheet Metal Co**.....312 666-5222
675 N Milwaukee Ave Chicago (60642) ***(G-4081)***
**Belzona Gateway Inc**.....888 774-2984
8124 Bunkum Rd Caseyville (62232) ***(G-3393)***
**Bem Cnc, Schaumburg** *Also called Bem Mold Inc* ***(G-19460)***
**Bem Mold Inc**.....847 805-9750
410 Remington Rd Schaumburg (60173) ***(G-19460)***
**Bem Wireless LLC**.....815 337-0541
2654 Corporate Pkwy Algonquin (60102) ***(G-381)***
**Bema Inc**.....630 279-7800
744 N Oaklawn Ave Elmhurst (60126) ***(G-9839)***
**Bemco Matress, Springfield** *Also called Bemco Mattress Inc* ***(G-20395)***
**Bemco Mattress Inc**.....217 529-0777
4952 Industrial Ave Springfield (62703) ***(G-20395)***
**Bemis Hydraulics, Galesburg** *Also called Midwest Hydra-Line Inc* ***(G-10768)***
**Bemis Packaging Inc**.....708 544-1600
5303 Saint Charles Rd Bellwood (60104) ***(G-1697)***
**Benchmarc Display Incorporated (PA)**.....847 541-2828
1001 Woodlands Pkwy Vernon Hills (60061) ***(G-21149)***
**Benchmark Cabinets & Mllwk Inc**.....309 697-5855
5913 W Plank Rd Peoria (61604) ***(G-17316)***
**Benchmark Electronics Inc**.....309 822-8587
388 Riverview Blf Metamora (61548) ***(G-14740)***
**Benchmark Properties Ltd**.....618 395-7023
5076 N Il 130 Olney (62450) ***(G-16762)***
**Bende Inc**.....847 913-0304
925 Corporate Woods Pkwy Vernon Hills (60061) ***(G-21150)***
**Bender Mat Fctry Fton Slepshop (PA)**.....217 328-1700
1206 N Cunningham Ave A Urbana (61802) ***(G-21071)***
**Benders Mat Fctry Sleep Shoppe, Urbana** *Also called Bender Mat Fctry Fton Slepshop* ***(G-21071)***
**Bending Specialists LLC**.....815 726-6281
3051 S State St Lockport (60441) ***(G-13706)***
**Bendinger Bruce Crtve Comm In**.....773 871-1179
2144 N Hudson Ave Ste 1 Chicago (60614) ***(G-4082)***
**Bendsen Signs & Graphics Inc**.....217 877-2345
1506 E Mcbride Ave Decatur (62526) ***(G-7845)***
**Beneficial Reuse Management, Chicago** *Also called Gypsoil Pelletized Pdts LLC* ***(G-5015)***
**Beneficial Reuse MGT LLC (PA)**.....312 784-0300
372 W Ontario St Ste 501 Chicago (60654) ***(G-4083)***
**Benessere Vineyard Inc (PA)**.....708 560-9840
2100 Clearwater Dr # 250 Oak Brook (60523) ***(G-16492)***
**Benetech Inc (HQ)**.....630 844-1300
2245 Sequoia Dr Ste 300 Aurora (60506) ***(G-1119)***
**Benetech (taiwan) LLC (HQ)**.....630 844-1300
2245 Sequoia Dr Ste 300 Aurora (60506) ***(G-1120)***
**Benjamin Moore & Co**.....708 343-6000
320 Fullerton Ave Ste 200 Carol Stream (60188) ***(G-3114)***
**Bennett Industries, Peotone** *Also called North America Packaging Corp* ***(G-17491)***
**Bennett Metal Products Inc**.....618 244-1911
700 Rackaway St Mount Vernon (62864) ***(G-15401)***
**Bennett Technologies Inc**.....708 389-9501
6732 173rd St Ste 9 Tinley Park (60477) ***(G-20897)***
**Bennu Group Inc**.....708 331-0025
16140 Vincennes Ave South Holland (60473) ***(G-20250)***
**Beno J Gundlach Company**.....618 233-1781
211 N 21st St Belleville (62226) ***(G-1613)***
**Bensenville Screw Products**.....630 860-5222
796 County Line Rd Bensenville (60106) ***(G-1843)***
**Bentleys Pet Stuff LLC**.....312 222-1012
509 N La Salle Dr Chicago (60654) ***(G-4084)***
**Bentleys Pet Stuff LLC**.....847 793-0500
4196 Illinois Rte 83 Long Grove (60047) ***(G-13886)***
**Bentleys Pet Stuff LLC (HQ)**.....224 567-4700
4192 Ill Rte 83 Ste C Long Grove (60047) ***(G-13887)***
**Benton Evening News Co**.....618 438-5611
111 E Church St Benton (62812) ***(G-2022)***
**Bentronics, Bensenville** *Also called General Electro Corporation* ***(G-1908)***
**Benzinger Printing**.....815 784-6560
673 Park Ave Ste 1 Genoa (60135) ***(G-10875)***
**Berens Inc**.....815 932-0913
1650 E Sheridan St Kankakee (60901) ***(G-12604)***
**Berens Inc**.....815 935-3237
1269 E 5000s Rd Saint Anne (60964) ***(G-19118)***
**Berg Industries Inc**.....815 874-1588
3455 S Mulford Rd Rockford (61109) ***(G-18280)***
**Berge Plating Works Inc (PA)**.....309 788-2831
617 25th Ave Rock Island (61201) ***(G-18163)***
**Bergeron Group Inc**.....815 741-1635
99 Republic Ave Joliet (60435) ***(G-12464)***
**Bergesch Heating & Cooling**.....618 259-4620
8116 Wolf Rd Alton (62002) ***(G-564)***
**Berghaus Pipe Organ Builders**.....708 544-4052
2151 Madison St Ste 1 Bellwood (60104) ***(G-1698)***
**Bergmann Orthotic Lab Inc**.....847 446-3616
1730 Holder Ln Northfield (60093) ***(G-16392)***
**Bergmann Orthotic Laboratory**.....847 729-7923
1864 Johns Dr Glenview (60025) ***(G-11108)***
**Bergst Engineering, Addison** *Also called Bergst Special Tools Inc* ***(G-53)***
**Bergst Special Tools Inc**.....630 543-1020
723 W Annoreno Dr Addison (60101) ***(G-53)***
**Bergstrom Climate Systems LLC (HQ)**.....815 874-7821
2390 Blackhawk Rd Rockford (61109) ***(G-18281)***
**Bergstrom Electrified Systems**.....815 874-7821
2390 Blackhawk Rd Rockford (61109) ***(G-18282)***
**Bergstrom Inc (PA)**.....815 874-7821
2390 Blackhawk Rd Rockford (61109) ***(G-18283)***
**Bergstrom Inc**.....847 394-4013
4060 Mound Rd Joliet (60436) ***(G-12465)***
**Bergstrom Parts LLC**.....815 874-7821
5910 Falcon Rd Rockford (61109) ***(G-18284)***
**Beringer Aero Usa Inc**.....708 667-7891
4118 N Nashville Ave Chicago (60634) ***(G-4085)***
**Berkshire Investments LLC**.....708 656-7900
1601 S 54th Ave Cicero (60804) ***(G-7180)***
**Berland Communications, Chicago** *Also called Berland Printing Inc* ***(G-4086)***
**Berland Printing Inc**.....773 702-1999
3950 S Morgan St Chicago (60609) ***(G-4086)***
**Bernard Cffey Vtrans Fundation**.....630 687-0033
1634 Mulligan Dr Naperville (60563) ***(G-15605)***
**Bernard Food Industries Inc (PA)**.....847 869-5222
1125 Hartrey Ave Evanston (60202) ***(G-10015)***
**Berndt & Thacker Inc**.....630 628-1934
761 W Racquet Club Dr B Addison (60101) ***(G-54)***
**Berner Food & Beverage LLC (PA)**.....815 563-4222
2034 E Factory Rd Dakota (61018) ***(G-7694)***
**Berner Food & Beverage LLC**.....815 865-5136
10010 N Rock City Rd Rock City (61070) ***(G-18124)***
**Berner Foods, Dakota** *Also called Berner Food & Beverage LLC* ***(G-7694)***
**Bernhard Woodwork Ltd**.....847 291-1040
3670 Woodhead Dr Northbrook (60062) ***(G-16214)***
**Berny Metal Products Inc**.....847 742-8500
655 Sundown Rd South Elgin (60177) ***(G-20187)***
**Berridge Manufacturing Company**.....630 231-7495
1175 Carolina Dr West Chicago (60185) ***(G-21669)***
**Berry Global Inc**.....815 334-5225
1008 Courtaulds Dr Woodstock (60098) ***(G-22544)***
**Berry Global Inc**.....847 884-1200
1228 Tower Rd Schaumburg (60173) ***(G-19461)***
**Berry Global Inc**
495 Green Bay Rd Lake Bluff (60044) ***(G-12836)***
**Berry Global Inc**.....847 541-7900
800 Corporate Grove Dr Buffalo Grove (60089) ***(G-2663)***
**Berry Global Inc**.....630 375-0358
999 Bilter Rd Aurora (60502) ***(G-969)***
**Berry Global Inc**.....708 396-1470
5750 W 118th St Alsip (60803) ***(G-441)***
**Berry Global Films LLC**.....708 239-4619
12900 S Pulaski Rd Alsip (60803) ***(G-442)***
**Bert Packing Co Inc**.....312 733-0346
170 N Green St Chicago (60607) ***(G-4087)***
**Bertco Enterprises Inc**.....618 234-9283
108 N Jackson St Belleville (62220) ***(G-1614)***
**Berteau-Lowell Pltg Works Inc**.....773 276-3135
2320 W Fullerton Ave Chicago (60647) ***(G-4088)***
**Bertram Oil Co**.....618 546-1122
604 W Locust Ln Robinson (62454) ***(G-18056)***
**Bertsche Engineering Corp**.....847 537-8757
711 Dartmouth Ln Buffalo Grove (60089) ***(G-2664)***
**Bes Designs & Associates Inc (PA)**.....217 443-4619
2412 Georgetown Rd Danville (61832) ***(G-7705)***
**Besam Entrance Solutions, Elk Grove Village** *Also called Assa Abloy Entrance Systems US* ***(G-9316)***
**Besco Awards & Embroidery**.....847 395-4862
43085 N Crawford Rd Antioch (60002) ***(G-622)***
**Besco Marketing, Antioch** *Also called Besco Awards & Embroidery* ***(G-622)***
**Besleys Accessories Inc**.....773 561-3300
4541 N Ravenswood Ave # 203 Chicago (60640) ***(G-4089)***
**Besly Cutting Tools Inc**.....815 389-2231
16200 Woodmint Ln South Beloit (61080) ***(G-20141)***
**Bessco Tube Bending Pipe Fabg**.....708 339-3977
16000 Van Drunen Rd South Holland (60473) ***(G-20251)***
**Bessler Welding Inc**.....309 699-6224
5313 N Main St East Peoria (61611) ***(G-8701)***
**Best Access Systems, Lombard** *Also called Stanley Security Solutions Inc* ***(G-13859)***
**Best Advertising Spc & Prtg**.....708 448-1110
11437 S Natoma Ave Worth (60482) ***(G-22633)***
**Best Air, Hampshire** *Also called RPS Products Inc* ***(G-11562)***
**Best Brake Die Inc**.....708 388-1896
13434 Kolmar Ave Crestwood (60445) ***(G-7477)***
**Best Bus Sales, Des Plaines** *Also called Zimmerman Enterprises Inc* ***(G-8308)***
**Best Chicago Meat Company LLC**.....773 523-8161
4649 W Armitage Ave Chicago (60639) ***(G-4090)***

**Best Croutons LLC** .......773 927-8200
1140 S Washtenaw Ave Chicago (60612) ***(G-4091)***
**Best Cutting Die Co (PA)** .......847 675-5522
8080 Mccormick Blvd Skokie (60076) ***(G-19963)***
**Best Designs Inc** .......618 985-4445
11521 Kevin Ln Carterville (62918) ***(G-3309)***
**Best Diamond Plastics LLC** .......773 336-3485
1401 E 98th St Chicago (60628) ***(G-4092)***
**Best Display Systems, Galva** *Also called John H Best & Sons Inc* ***(G-10791)***
**Best Foods Baking Group, Summit Argo** *Also called Ach Food Companies Inc* ***(G-20759)***
**Best Institutional Supply Co** .......708 216-0000
15 N 9th Ave Maywood (60153) ***(G-14419)***
**Best Kept Secrets** .......773 431-0353
2119 121st St Blue Island (60406) ***(G-2238)***
**Best Machine & Welding Co Inc** .......708 343-4455
2729 Meadowdale Ln Woodridge (60517) ***(G-22456)***
**Best Manufacturing & Wldg Inc** .......815 562-4107
231 Powers Rd 251n Rochelle (61068) ***(G-18079)***
**Best Metal Corporation** .......815 337-0420
925 Dieckman St Woodstock (60098) ***(G-22545)***
**Best Metal Extrusions Inc** .......847 981-0797
1900 E Devon Ave Elk Grove Village (60007) ***(G-9341)***
**Best Neon Sign Co Inc** .......773 586-2700
6025 S New England Ave Chicago (60638) ***(G-4093)***
**Best Newspapers In Illinois** .......217 728-7381
100 W Monroe St Sullivan (61951) ***(G-20740)***
**Best Pallet Company LLC** .......815 637-1500
1110 Widsor Rd Loves Park (61111) ***(G-13924)***
**Best Pallet Company LLC (PA)** .......312 242-4009
166 W Washington St # 300 Chicago (60602) ***(G-4094)***
**Best Rep Company Corporation** .......847 451-6644
9224 Grand Ave Ste 2 Franklin Park (60131) ***(G-10411)***
**Best Technology Systems Inc** .......815 254-9554
12024 S Aero Dr Plainfield (60585) ***(G-17582)***
**Best Way Carpet & Uphl Clg** .......618 544-8585
1401 N Johnson St Robinson (62454) ***(G-18057)***
**Best-Tronics Mfg Inc** .......708 802-9677
18500 Graphic Ct Tinley Park (60477) ***(G-20898)***
**Bestair Pro** .......847 683-3400
281 Keyes Ave Hampshire (60140) ***(G-11543)***
**Bestairpro, Hampshire** *Also called Bestair Pro* ***(G-11543)***
**Bestar Technologies Inc** .......520 439-9204
4n953 Old Lafox Rd B Saint Charles (60175) ***(G-19142)***
**Bestmetal, A Division of PSM, Woodstock** *Also called PSM Industries Inc* ***(G-22602)***
**Bestproto Inc** .......224 387-3280
3603 Edison Pl Rolling Meadows (60008) ***(G-18717)***
**Bestpysanky Inc** .......877 797-2659
6212 Madison Ct Morton Grove (60053) ***(G-15189)***
**Bestwords Org Corp** .......618 939-4324
8934 Trolley Rd Columbia (62236) ***(G-7352)***
**Beta Pak Inc** .......708 466-7844
1600 Beta Dr Sugar Grove (60554) ***(G-20718)***
**Bethany Pharmacol Co Inc** .......217 665-3395
131 Hwy 121 E Bethany (61914) ***(G-2084)***
**Bets, Chicago** *Also called Bishops Engrv & Trophy Svc Inc* ***(G-4114)***
**Bettendorf Stanford, Salem** *Also called Stanford Bettendorf Inc* ***(G-19353)***
**Better Built Buildings** .......217 267-7824
604 E Kelly Ave Westville (61883) ***(G-21928)***
**Better Earth LLC** .......844 243-6333
2444 W 16th St Ste 4r Chicago (60608) ***(G-4095)***
**Better Earth Premium Compost** .......309 697-0963
1400 S Cameron Ln Peoria (61607) ***(G-17317)***
**Better Gaskets Inc** .......847 276-7635
26218 W Ingleside Ave Ingleside (60041) ***(G-12187)***
**Better Gaskets Sealing Systems, Ingleside** *Also called Better Gaskets Inc* ***(G-12187)***
**Better Mens Wear, Chicago** *Also called BMW Sportswear Inc* ***(G-4133)***
**Better News Papers Inc (PA)** .......618 566-8282
314 E Church St Ste 1 Mascoutah (62258) ***(G-14348)***
**Better News Papers Inc** .......618 483-6176
118 N Main St Altamont (62411) ***(G-550)***
**Betty Watters** .......618 232-1150
Rr 1 Box 27 Hamburg (62045) ***(G-11526)***
**Beutel Corporation (PA)** .......309 786-8134
1800 11th St Rock Island (61201) ***(G-18164)***
**Bev Art HM Brewing Winemaking, Chicago** *Also called Beverage Art Inc* ***(G-4096)***
**Bevel Granite, Merrionette Park** *Also called Rogan Granitindustrie Inc* ***(G-14737)***
**Bevel Granite Co Inc** .......708 388-9060
11849 S Kedzie Ave Merrionette Park (60803) ***(G-14736)***
**Beverage Art Inc** .......773 881-9463
10033 S Western Ave Chicago (60643) ***(G-4096)***
**Beverage Flavors Intl LLC** .......773 248-3860
3150 N Campbell Ave Chicago (60618) ***(G-4097)***
**Beverly Clark Collections, Wauconda** *Also called Wedding Brand Investors LLC* ***(G-21513)***
**Beverly Fndry Prcsion McHining, Lansing** *Also called American Cast Products Inc* ***(G-13156)***
**Beverly Materials, Hoffman Estates** *Also called Plote Construction Inc* ***(G-12035)***
**Beverly Materials LLC** .......847 695-9300
1100 Brandt Dr Hoffman Estates (60192) ***(G-11994)***
**Beverly Review, Chicago** *Also called T R Communications Inc* ***(G-6663)***
**Beverly Shear Mfg Corporation** .......773 233-2063
3004 W 111th St Ste 1 Chicago (60655) ***(G-4098)***
**Bevolution Group, Chicago** *Also called Juice Tyme Inc* ***(G-5335)***
**Bevstream Corp** .......630 761-0060
600 Kingsland Dr Batavia (60510) ***(G-1421)***
**BF Foods Inc** .......773 252-6113
4334 W Chicago Ave Chicago (60651) ***(G-4099)***
**BF Manufacturing LLC** .......312 446-1163
3810 S Halsted St Chicago (60609) ***(G-4100)***
**Bfafv, Benton** *Also called Bio Fuels By American Farmers* ***(G-2023)***
**Bfc Forms Service Inc** .......630 879-9240
1051 N Kirk Rd Batavia (60510) ***(G-1422)***
**Bfc Print** .......630 879-9240
1051 N Kirk Rd Batavia (60510) ***(G-1423)***
**BFI Waste Systems N Amer Inc** .......847 429-7370
1330 Gasket Dr Elgin (60120) ***(G-8965)***
**Bfw Coating** .......847 639-2155
740 Industrial Dr Ste G Cary (60013) ***(G-3328)***
**Bg Die Mold Inc** .......847 961-5861
11520 Smith Dr Huntley (60142) ***(G-12133)***
**BGF Performance Systems LLC** .......773 539-7099
5454 N Bernard St Chicago (60625) ***(G-4101)***
**Bh Sports, Chicago** *Also called Bhs Media LLC* ***(G-4102)***
**Bhs Media LLC** .......312 701-0000
123 W Madison St Ste 1600 Chicago (60602) ***(G-4102)***
**Bi Audio Headsets, Northbrook** *Also called Addax Sound Company* ***(G-16198)***
**Bi Protec, Dekalb** *Also called Armoloy of Illinois Inc* ***(G-8075)***
**Bi Software Inc** .......224 622-4706
808 Linden Cir Hoffman Estates (60169) ***(G-11995)***
**Bi State Furniture Inc** .......309 662-6562
18 Currency Dr Bloomington (61704) ***(G-2148)***
**Bi State Steel Co** .......309 755-0668
503 7th St East Moline (61244) ***(G-8671)***
**Bi-Link Metal Specialties Inc (PA)** .......630 858-5900
391 Glen Ellyn Rd Bloomingdale (60108) ***(G-2096)***
**Bi-Petro Inc (PA)** .......217 535-0181
3150 Executive Park Dr Springfield (62703) ***(G-20396)***
**Bi-Phase Technologies LLC** .......952 886-6450
201 Mittel Dr Wood Dale (60191) ***(G-22344)***
**Bi-State Biking LLC** .......618 531-0432
807 Coral Dr Fairview Heights (62208) ***(G-10166)***
**Bi-State Furniture Rentl & Sls, Bloomington** *Also called Bi State Furniture Inc* ***(G-2148)***
**Bi-Torq Valve Automation, Lafox** *Also called Strahman Valves Inc* ***(G-12797)***
**Bi-Torq Valve Automation Inc** .......630 208-9343
1n046 Linlar Dr Lafox (60147) ***(G-12793)***
**Biagios Gourmet Foods Inc** .......708 867-4641
7319 W Lawrence Ave Chicago (60706) ***(G-4103)***
**Bias Power Inc** .......847 419-9180
975 Deerfield Pkwy Buffalo Grove (60089) ***(G-2665)***
**Bias Power Technology Inc** .......847 991-2427
414 S Vermont St Palatine (60067) ***(G-17006)***
**Bible Truth Publishers Inc** .......630 543-1441
59 W Industrial Rd Addison (60101) ***(G-55)***
**Bick Broadcasting Inc** .......217 223-9693
408 N 24th St Quincy (62301) ***(G-17804)***
**Biddison Autobody** .......309 673-6277
3100 W Farmington Rd A Peoria (61604) ***(G-17318)***
**Bidwells Candies, Humboldt** *Also called Bobbie Haycraft* ***(G-12128)***
**Bierdeman Box LLC** .......847 256-0302
3445 Riverside Dr Wilmette (60091) ***(G-22244)***
**Bierman Welding Inc** .......217 342-2050
1103 S Willow St Effingham (62401) ***(G-8827)***
**Biewer Fabricating Inc** .......630 530-8922
208 W Stone Rd Villa Park (60181) ***(G-21238)***
**Biewer John A Co of Seneca, Seneca** *Also called John A Biewer Lumber Company* ***(G-19887)***
**Big 3 Precision Products Inc (PA)** .......618 533-3251
2923 S Wabash Ave Centralia (62801) ***(G-3405)***
**Big Als Machines Inc** .......618 963-2619
204 Il Highway 14 Enfield (62835) ***(G-9987)***
**Big Beam Emergency Systems Inc** .......815 459-6100
290 E Prairie St Crystal Lake (60014) ***(G-7541)***
**Big Creek Forestry & Logging L** .......217 822-8282
75 Archer Ave Marshall (62441) ***(G-14318)***
**Big Dog Treestand Inc** .......309 263-6800
120 Detroit Pkwy Morton (61550) ***(G-15154)***
**Big Frontire, Paxton** *Also called Paxton Packing LLC* ***(G-17241)***
**Big Game International, Northbrook** *Also called South Bend Sporting Goods Inc* ***(G-16367)***
**Big Game Software, Elmhurst** *Also called Fantasy Coverage Inc* ***(G-9870)***
**Big Joe Forklift, Lombard** *Also called Big Lift LLC* ***(G-13768)***
**Big Joes Sealcoati** .......630 935-7032
6563 Fernwood Dr Lisle (60532) ***(G-13568)***
**Big Kser Precision Tooling Inc** .......847 228-7660
2600 Huntington Blvd Hoffman Estates (60192) ***(G-11996)***
**Big Lift LLC (PA)** .......630 916-2600
1060 N Garfield St Lombard (60148) ***(G-13768)***
**Big M Manufacturing LLC** .......217 824-9372
928 E 1090 North Rd Taylorville (62568) ***(G-20833)***

ALPHABETIC

**Big R Car Wash Inc (PA)**....217 367-4958
501 E University Ave Urbana (61802) *(G-21072)*
**Big River Prairie Gold LLC**....319 753-1100
1100 Se 2nd St Galva (61434) *(G-10783)*
**Big River Resources Galva LLC**....309 932-2033
1100 Se 2nd St Galva (61434) *(G-10784)*
**Big River Zinc Corporation**....618 274-5000
2401 Mississippi Ave Sauget (62201) *(G-19382)*
**Big Rver Rsrces W Brlngton LLC**....309 734-8423
903 S Sunny Ln Monmouth (61462) *(G-15010)*
**Big T Graphics, Sparta** *Also called Norvida USA Inc (G-20319)*
**Big Ten Network Services LLC**....312 329-3666
600 W Chicago Ave Ste 875 Chicago (60654) *(G-4104)*
**Big Time Bats, Mundelein** *Also called Hampster Industries Inc (G-15507)*
**Big Tuna, Frankfort** *Also called Woow Sushi Orland Park LLC (G-10377)*
**Bighand Inc (HQ)**....312 893-5906
125 S Wacker Dr Ste 300 Chicago (60606) *(G-4105)*
**Bigtime Fantasy Sports Inc**....630 605-7544
149 W Washington Blvd Lombard (60148) *(G-13769)*
**Bikast Graphics Inc**....847 487-8822
1000 Brown St Ste 214 Wauconda (60084) *(G-21446)*
**Biker Threads Inc**....618 993-3046
500 S Court St Marion (62959) *(G-14255)*
**Biking Life Magazine, The, Fairview Heights** *Also called Bi-State Biking LLC (G-10166)*
**Bill Chandler Farms**....618 752-7551
5182 Bucktown Ln Noble (62868) *(G-16049)*
**Bill Peterson**....815 378-8633
25007 Flat Iron Rd Harvard (60033) *(G-11624)*
**Bill Rodgers Drlg & Producing, West Salem** *Also called Rodgers Bill Oil Min Bits Svc (G-21824)*
**Bill Weeks Inc**....217 523-8735
229 N Grand Ave W Springfield (62702) *(G-20397)*
**Bill West Enterprises Inc**....217 886-2591
2170 Arcadia Rd Jacksonville (62650) *(G-12378)*
**Bill's Auto & Truck Repair, Des Plaines** *Also called Signs Plus (G-8275)*
**Biller Press & Manufacturing**....847 395-4111
966 Victoria St Antioch (60002) *(G-623)*
**Billiards Digest, Chicago** *Also called Luby Publishing Inc (G-5556)*
**Billing Office, Urbana** *Also called Mid-America Sand & Gravel (G-21094)*
**Bills Best Feeds, Emden** *Also called B B Milling Co Inc (G-9983)*
**Bills Machine & Power Transm (PA)**....618 392-2500
4678 Weinmann Dr Ste B Olney (62450) *(G-16763)*
**Bills Shade & Blind Service (PA)**....773 493-5000
765 E 69th Pl Chicago (60637) *(G-4106)*
**Billy & Rachel Poignant**....309 713-5500
237 Crossover Rd Lacon (61540) *(G-12785)*
**Billy Cash For Gold Inc**....773 905-2447
101 N 19th Ave Melrose Park (60160) *(G-14600)*
**Bilt-Rite Metal Products, Leland** *Also called Bilt-Rite Metal Products Inc (G-13218)*
**Bilt-Rite Metal Products Inc**....815 495-2211
100 E North St Leland (60531) *(G-13218)*
**Bilz Tool Company**....630 495-3996
1140 N Main St Lombard (60148) *(G-13770)*
**Bimba Manufacturing Company (PA)**....708 534-8544
25150 S Governors Hwy University Park (60484) *(G-21044)*
**Bimba Manufacturing Company**....708 534-7997
500 S Spruce St Manteno (60950) *(G-14181)*
**Bimba Manufacturing Company**....708 534-8544
9450 W Laraway Rd Frankfort (60423) *(G-10299)*
**Bimbo Bakeries Usa Inc**....773 254-3578
2503 S Blue Island Ave Chicago (60608) *(G-4107)*
**Bimbo Bakeries Usa Inc**....815 626-6797
1204 12th Ave Rock Falls (61071) *(G-18127)*
**Bimbo Bakeries Usa Inc**....309 797-4968
5205 22nd Ave Moline (61265) *(G-14919)*
**Bin Long & Electric**....309 758-5407
6240 E 2100th St Adair (61411) *(G-12)*
**Binder Tool Inc**....847 678-4222
9833 Franklin Ave Franklin Park (60131) *(G-10412)*
**Bindery & Distribution Service**....847 550-7000
9 Overbrook Rd South Barrington (60010) *(G-20131)*
**Bindery Maintenance Services**....618 945-7480
777 E State St Bridgeport (62417) *(G-2449)*
**Bing Construction Company, Frankfort** *Also called Bing Engineering Inc (G-10300)*
**Bing Engineering Inc**....708 228-8005
20240 S Pine Hill Rd Frankfort (60423) *(G-10300)*
**Bing Yeung Jewelers Inc**....708 749-4800
6916 Cermak Rd Berwyn (60402) *(G-2057)*
**Bingaman Metal Spinning, Rolling Meadows** *Also called Bingaman-Precision Metal Spini (G-18718)*
**Bingaman-Precision Metal Spini**....847 392-5620
1000 Carnegie St Rolling Meadows (60008) *(G-18718)*
**Binks Industries Inc**....630 801-1100
1997a Aucutt Rd Montgomery (60538) *(G-15030)*
**Binzel Industries LLC**....847 506-0003
3051 S State St Lockport (60441) *(G-13707)*
**Bio Fuels By American Farmers**....561 859-6251
10163 Sugar Creek Rd Benton (62812) *(G-2023)*
**Bio Green Inc**....847 740-9637
30937 N Gilmer Rd Volo (60073) *(G-21308)*
**Bio Industries Inc**....847 215-8999
540 Allendale Dr Ste B Wheeling (60090) *(G-22014)*
**Bio Packaging Films LLC**....847 566-4444
909 Tower Rd Mundelein (60060) *(G-15477)*
**Bio Services Inc**....630 808-2125
4917 Butterfield Rd Hillside (60162) *(G-11910)*
**Bio Star Films LLC**....773 254-5959
4848 S Hoyne Ave Chicago (60609) *(G-4108)*
**Bio-Bridge Science Inc**....630 328-0213
1801 S Meyers Rd Ste 220 Oakbrook Terrace (60181) *(G-16699)*
**Bio-Logic Systems, Mundelein** *Also called Natus Medical Incorporated (G-15536)*
**Bio-Logic Systems Corp**....847 949-0456
1 Bio Logic Plz Mundelein (60060) *(G-15478)*
**Bio-RAD Laboratories Inc**....847 699-2217
1400 E Touhy Ave Des Plaines (60018) *(G-8158)*
**Bioaffinity Inc**....815 988-5077
641 S Main St Rockford (61101) *(G-18285)*
**Bioblend Lubricants Intl**....630 227-1800
2439 Reeves Rd Joliet (60436) *(G-12466)*
**Biocare Labs Inc**....708 496-8657
5202 W 70th Pl Bedford Park (60638) *(G-1541)*
**Biochemical Lab**....708 447-3923
247 Addison Rd Riverside (60546) *(G-18029)*
**Bioconcepts Inc (HQ)**....630 986-0007
100 Tower Dr Ste 101 Burr Ridge (60527) *(G-2824)*
**Bioelements Inc**....773 525-3509
4043 N Ravenswood Ave # 216 Chicago (60613) *(G-4109)*
**Bioforce Nanosciences Inc**....515 233-8333
6248 N Lakewood Ave Chicago (60660) *(G-4110)*
**Biologos Inc**....630 801-4740
2235 Cornell Ave Montgomery (60538) *(G-15031)*
**Biomerieux Inc**....630 628-6055
1105 N Main St Lombard (60148) *(G-13771)*
**Bion Enterprises Ltd**....847 544-5044
455 State St Ste 100 Des Plaines (60016) *(G-8159)*
**Biospawn Lure Co**....773 458-0752
9332 Hamlin Ave Evanston (60203) *(G-10016)*
**Biosynergy Inc (PA)**....847 956-0471
1940 E Devon Ave Elk Grove Village (60007) *(G-9342)*
**Biovantage Fuels LLC**....815 544-6028
1201 Crosslink Pkwy Belvidere (61008) *(G-1738)*
**Bircher America Inc**....847 952-3730
870 Pratt Ave N Schaumburg (60193) *(G-19462)*
**Bird Dog Bay Inc**....312 631-3108
2010 W Fulton St Chicago (60612) *(G-4111)*
**Bird Dog Diversified**....847 741-0700
1670 Cambridge Dr Elgin (60123) *(G-8966)*
**Bird-X Inc**....312 226-2473
300 N Oakley Blvd Chicago (60612) *(G-4112)*
**Birdsell Machine & Orna Inc**....217 243-5849
531 W Independence Ave Jacksonville (62650) *(G-12379)*
**Birkeys Construction Equipment, Urbana** *Also called Birkeys Farm Store Inc (G-21073)*
**Birkeys Farm Store Inc**....217 337-1772
2202 S High Cross Rd Urbana (61802) *(G-21073)*
**Birnberg Machinery Inc**....847 673-5242
4828 Main St Skokie (60077) *(G-19964)*
**Birom Cabinetry LLC**....312 286-7132
1433 W Fullerton Ave L Addison (60101) *(G-56)*
**Biron Studio General Svcs Inc**....708 229-2600
7352 W 79th St Bridgeview (60455) *(G-2470)*
**Bis, Huntley** *Also called Business Identity Spc Inc (G-12134)*
**Bisco Enterprise Inc**....630 628-1831
550 Albion Ave Ste 40 Schaumburg (60193) *(G-19463)*
**Bisco Inc**....847 534-6000
1100 W Irving Park Rd Schaumburg (60193) *(G-19464)*
**Bisco Intl Inc**....708 544-6308
543 Granville Ave Hillside (60162) *(G-11911)*
**Bish Creative Display Inc**....847 438-1500
945 Telser Rd Lake Zurich (60047) *(G-13046)*
**Bishop Engineering Company (PA)**....630 305-9538
6495 Bannister Ct Lisle (60532) *(G-13569)*
**Bishop Image Group Inc**....312 735-8153
4018 W Irving Park Rd Chicago (60641) *(G-4113)*
**Bishops Engrv & Trophy Svc Inc**....773 777-5014
6708 W Belmont Ave Chicago (60634) *(G-4114)*
**Bison Gear & Engineering Corp (PA)**....630 377-0153
3850 Ohio Ave Saint Charles (60174) *(G-19143)*
**Bissell Inc**....815 423-1300
20200 Ira Morgan Dr Elwood (60421) *(G-9979)*
**Bit Brokers International Ltd**....618 435-5811
5568 Logan Rd West Frankfort (62896) *(G-21804)*
**Bitforms Inc**....630 595-6800
360 Georgetown Sq Wood Dale (60191) *(G-22345)*
**Bits of Gold Jewelry, Nashville** *Also called Marion Oelze (G-15839)*
**Bitter End Yacht Club Intl**....312 506-6205
875 N Michigan Ave # 3707 Chicago (60611) *(G-4115)*
**Bittle**....618 539-6099
713 N Kristie Lynn St Freeburg (62243) *(G-10633)*

# ALPHABETIC SECTION — Blue Island Beer Co

**Bitzer Products Company** .......................................................... 708 345-0795
  2222 Allegany Dr  Naperville  (60565)  *(G-15606)*
**Biz 3 Publicity** .......................................................................... 773 342-3331
  1321 N Milwaukee Ave  Chicago  (60622)  *(G-4116)*
**Biz Pins Inc** ............................................................................. 847 695-6212
  2111 Big Timber Rd  Elgin  (60123)  *(G-8967)*
**Bizbash Media  Inc** .................................................................. 312 436-2525
  5437 N Ashland Ave  Chicago  (60640)  *(G-4117)*
**Bizstarterscom LLC** ................................................................. 847 305-4626
  126 E Wing St Ste 321  Arlington Heights  (60004)  *(G-725)*
**BJ Mold & Die Inc** ................................................................... 630 595-1797
  780 Creel Dr Ste 1  Wood Dale  (60191)  *(G-22346)*
**Bjs Enterprises Inc** ................................................................. 815 432-5176
  834 S Hanson Dr  Watseka  (60970)  *(G-21416)*
**BJs Welding Services Etc Co** .................................................. 773 964-5836
  1521 E 83rd St  Chicago  (60619)  *(G-4118)*
**Bk Production Specialties** ...................................................... 847 526-5150
  387 Hollow Hill Rd  Wauconda  (60084)  *(G-21447)*
**Bka Inc** .................................................................................... 847 831-3535
  1999 Castlewood Rd  Highland Park  (60035)  *(G-11825)*
**Blac Inc** ................................................................................... 630 279-6400
  195 W Spangler Ave Ste A  Elmhurst  (60126)  *(G-9840)*
**Blachford Corporation** ............................................................ 815 464-2100
  401 Center Rd  Frankfort  (60423)  *(G-10301)*
**Blachford Enterprises Inc (HQ)** .............................................. 630 231-8300
  1400 Nuclear Dr  West Chicago  (60185)  *(G-21670)*
**Blachford Investments  Inc** .................................................... 630 231-8300
  1400 Nuclear Dr  West Chicago  (60185)  *(G-21671)*
**Black & Decker Corporation** .................................................. 630 521-1097
  901 S Rohlwing Rd Ste A  Addison  (60101)  *(G-57)*
**Black Bison Water Services LLC (PA)** .................................... 630 272-5935
  953 W Fulton St U 2 2 U  Chicago  (60607)  *(G-4119)*
**Black Box Corporation** ........................................................... 312 656-8807
  9365 Windsor Pkwy  Tinley Park  (60487)  *(G-20899)*
**Black Bros Co (PA)** ................................................................. 815 539-7451
  501 9th Ave  Mendota  (61342)  *(G-14717)*
**Black Enterprize Magazine, Chicago** Also called *Earl G Graves  Ltd*  *(G-4674)*
**Black Hstory Educatonal Netwrk, Chicago** Also called *Morgen Transportation Inc*  *(G-5805)*
**Black Magic Customs Inc** ....................................................... 815 786-1977
  4686 E 29th Rd  Sandwich  (60548)  *(G-19360)*
**Black Market Parts  Inc** .......................................................... 630 562-9400
  776 W Hawthorne Ln  West Chicago  (60185)  *(G-21672)*
**Black Mountain Products Inc** ................................................. 224 655-5955
  1412 Ridgeview Dr  McHenry  (60050)  *(G-14482)*
**Black Point Studios llc** ........................................................... 773 791-2377
  1937 N Winchester Ave # 1  Chicago  (60622)  *(G-4120)*
**Black Rhino Concealment** ...................................................... 847 783-6499
  24 Center Dr Ste 6  Gilberts  (60136)  *(G-10913)*
**Black Rock Milling and Pav Co** ............................................... 847 952-0700
  2400 Terminal Dr  Arlington Heights  (60005)  *(G-726)*
**Black Spectacles Blog** ............................................................ 312 884-9091
  1105 S Vine Ave  Park Ridge  (60068)  *(G-17184)*
**Black Start Labs  Inc** ............................................................... 630 444-1800
  1500 Foundry St Ste 8  Saint Charles  (60174)  *(G-19144)*
**Black Swan Manufacturing Co** ............................................... 773 227-3700
  4540 W Thomas St  Chicago  (60651)  *(G-4121)*
**Black-Jack Grout Pumps  Inc** ................................................. 815 494-2904
  4871 Hydraulic Rd  Rockford  (61109)  *(G-18286)*
**Blackberry Historical Farm, Aurora** Also called *Fox Valley Park District*  *(G-1157)*
**Blackburn Sampling Inc** ......................................................... 309 342-8429
  77 S Henderson St  Galesburg  (61401)  *(G-10738)*
**Blackhawk Biofuels  LLC** ........................................................ 217 431-6600
  210 W Spring St Ste 1  Freeport  (61032)  *(G-10649)*
**Blackhawk Corrugated LLC** ................................................... 844 270-2296
  700 Kimberly Dr  Carol Stream  (60188)  *(G-3115)*
**Blackhawk Courtyards  LLC** ................................................... 416 298-8101
  700 Kimberly Dr  Carol Stream  (60188)  *(G-3116)*
**Blackhawk Industrial Dist Inc** ................................................. 773 736-9600
  245 E Lies Rd  Carol Stream  (60188)  *(G-3117)*
**Blackhawk Molding Co Inc (PA)** ............................................ 630 628-6218
  120 W Interstate Rd  Addison  (60101)  *(G-58)*
**Blackjack Customs** ................................................................. 847 361-5225
  2920 Frontenac St  North Chicago  (60064)  *(G-16175)*
**Blackjack Lighting** .................................................................. 847 941-0588
  2961 Kingston Dr  Buffalo Grove  (60089)  *(G-2666)*
**Blackwing For Pets  Inc** .......................................................... 203 762-8620
  17618 W Edwards Rd  Antioch  (60002)  *(G-624)*
**Blair Company** ....................................................................... 847 439-3980
  225 N Arlington Heights R  Elk Grove Village  (60007)  *(G-9343)*
**Blake Awning, Rockford** Also called *Blake Co Inc*  *(G-18287)*
**Blake Co Inc** ........................................................................... 815 962-3852
  1135 Charles St  Rockford  (61104)  *(G-18287)*
**Blandings Ltd** ......................................................................... 773 478-3542
  2635 W Fletcher St  Chicago  (60618)  *(G-4122)*
**Blando G Mfg Jewelers** .......................................................... 708 387-0014
  9228 Broadway Ave  Brookfield  (60513)  *(G-2624)*
**Blando's Marry ME Jewelry, Countryside** Also called *G Blando Jewelers Inc*  *(G-7425)*
**Blanke Industries Incorporated** ............................................. 847 487-2780
  1099 Brown St Ste 103  Wauconda  (60084)  *(G-21448)*
**Blasart, Chicago** Also called *A Jule Enterprise Inc*  *(G-3689)*
**Blast Products, Madison** Also called *Damco Products  Inc*  *(G-14141)*
**Blast Products Inc** .................................................................. 618 452-4700
  224 State St  Madison  (62060)  *(G-14140)*
**Blast Zone** .............................................................................. 847 996-0100
  645 Lakeview Pkwy  Vernon Hills  (60061)  *(G-21151)*
**Blastline USA, Carol Stream** Also called *Blastline USA Inc*  *(G-3118)*
**Blastline USA Inc** ................................................................... 630 871-0147
  226 S Westgate Dr Ste B  Carol Stream  (60188)  *(G-3118)*
**Blaz Cartage, Chicago** Also called *Scott Janczak*  *(G-6460)*
**Blaz-Man Gear Inc** ................................................................. 708 599-9700
  7461 W 93rd St Ste F  Bridgeview  (60455)  *(G-2471)*
**Blazing Beads, Chicago** Also called *Afshar Inc*  *(G-3781)*
**Blazing Color Inc** ................................................................... 618 826-3001
  1007 State St  Chester  (62233)  *(G-3651)*
**Bleigh Construction Company** .............................................. 217 222-5005
  3522 S 6th St  Quincy  (62305)  *(G-17805)*
**Blending and Transfer Systems, Chicago** Also called *Emerson Electric Co*  *(G-4742)*
**Blending and Transfer Systems, Chicago** Also called *FMC Technologies  Inc*  *(G-4865)*
**Blew Chemical Company** ...................................................... 708 448-5780
  12501 S Richard Ave  Palos Heights  (60463)  *(G-17100)*
**Bley  LLC** ............................................................................... 847 290-0117
  700 Chase Ave  Elk Grove Village  (60007)  *(G-9344)*
**Bli Legacy  Inc (PA)** ............................................................... 847 428-6059
  1013 Tamarac Dr  Carpentersville  (60110)  *(G-3276)*
**Blind Connection Inc** ............................................................ 630 728-6275
  3763 Sonoma Cir  Lake In The Hills  (60156)  *(G-12989)*
**Blind Quest, Troy** Also called *Hilling Services Inc*  *(G-21008)*
**Blind Williamson & Drapery** ................................................. 309 694-7339
  230 Cracklewood Ln  East Peoria  (61611)  *(G-8702)*
**Bliss Ring Company Inc** ........................................................ 847 446-3440
  1095 Willow Rd  Winnetka  (60093)  *(G-22304)*
**Blissful Brownies Inc** ............................................................. 541 308-0226
  619 Highview Ter  Lake Forest  (60045)  *(G-12887)*
**Blistex Inc (PA)** ...................................................................... 630 571-2870
  1800 Swift Dr  Oak Brook  (60523)  *(G-16493)*
**Blistex Inc.** ............................................................................. 630 571-2870
  100 Windsor Dr  Oak Brook  (60523)  *(G-16494)*
**Blitz Lures  LLC** ..................................................................... 309 256-1574
  11919 N Windcrest Ct  Dunlap  (61525)  *(G-8566)*
**Block and Company  Inc** ....................................................... 847 537-7200
  1111 Wheeling Rd  Wheeling  (60090)  *(G-22015)*
**Block Heavy and Highway Pdts, Kankakee** Also called *Dayton Superior Corporation*  *(G-12608)*
**Block Steel Corp** .................................................................... 847 965-6700
  6101 Oakton St Ste 2  Skokie  (60077)  *(G-19965)*
**Blockmaster Electronics Inc** .................................................. 847 956-1680
  1400 Howard St  Elk Grove Village  (60007)  *(G-9345)*
**Blocksmoy  Inc** ....................................................................... 847 260-9070
  10632 Grand Ave  Franklin Park  (60131)  *(G-10413)*
**Blomberg Bros Inc** ................................................................. 618 245-6321
  Hwy 37 S  Farina  (62838)  *(G-10174)*
**Blommer Chocolate Company** .............................................. 800 621-1606
  600 W Kinzie St  Chicago  (60654)  *(G-4123)*
**Blommer Machinery Company** .............................................. 312 226-7700
  600 W Kinzie St  Chicago  (60654)  *(G-4124)*
**Bloom-Norm Printing Inc** ....................................................... 309 663-8545
  100 N University St # 242  Normal  (61761)  *(G-16065)*
**Blooming Color  Inc** .............................................................. 630 705-9200
  230 Eisenhower Ln N  Lombard  (60148)  *(G-13772)*
**Bloomington Offset Process Inc** ............................................ 309 662-3395
  1705 S Veterans Pkwy  Bloomington  (61701)  *(G-2149)*
**Bloomington Tent & Awning Inc** ............................................ 309 828-3411
  226 E Market St  Bloomington  (61701)  *(G-2150)*
**Blowers  LLC** ......................................................................... 708 594-1800
  835 N Industrial Dr  Elmhurst  (60126)  *(G-9841)*
**Bls Enterprises  Inc** ................................................................ 630 766-1300
  1120 Thorndale Ave  Bensenville  (60106)  *(G-1844)*
**Bluco Corporation** ................................................................. 630 637-1820
  3500 Thayer Ct  Aurora  (60504)  *(G-970)*
**Blue Blaze Coal Cpitl Resource** ............................................. 309 647-2000
  420 W Locust St  Canton  (61520)  *(G-2982)*
**Blue Book of Building & Cnstr, Lombard** Also called *Contractors Register  Inc*  *(G-13784)*
**Blue Brothers Coatings** ......................................................... 847 265-5400
  2415 N Quaker Hollow Ln  Round Lake Beach  (60073)  *(G-19073)*
**Blue Chip Construction Inc** ................................................... 630 208-5254
  435 Stevens St  Geneva  (60134)  *(G-10812)*
**Blue Chip Industries  Inc** ....................................................... 309 854-7100
  1134 W South St  Kewanee  (61443)  *(G-12671)*
**Blue Chip Mfg  LLC** ............................................................... 630 553-6321
  37 Stonehill Rd  Oswego  (60543)  *(G-16905)*
**Blue Comet Transport  Inc** .................................................... 773 617-9512
  4919 W Parker Ave  Chicago  (60639)  *(G-4125)*
**Blue Diamond Athletic Disp Inc** ............................................. 847 414-9971
  1933 Loomes Ave  Downers Grove  (60516)  *(G-8397)*
**Blue Gem Computers  Inc.** .................................................... 708 562-5524
  822 East St  Morris  (60450)  *(G-15098)*
**Blue Island Beer Co** ............................................................... 708 954-8085
  13357 Olde Western Ave  Blue Island  (60406)  *(G-2239)*

---

(PA)=Parent Co  (HQ)=Headquarters  (DH)=Div Headquarters

**Blue Island Newspaper Prtg Inc**......708 333-1006
262 W 147th St Harvey (60426) ***(G-11661)***
**Blue Island Sun**......708 388-9033
12607 Artesian Ave Blue Island (60406) ***(G-2240)***
**Blue Light Inc**......630 400-4539
1440 Maple Ave Ste 5b Lisle (60532) ***(G-13570)***
**Blue Linx Corporation**......708 235-4200
2101 Dralle Rd University Park (60484) ***(G-21045)***
**Blue Monkey Graphics Inc**......708 488-9501
7540 Roosevelt Rd Ste 4 Forest Park (60130) ***(G-10235)***
**Blue Nile Trucking LLC**......618 215-1077
404 N 27th St East Saint Louis (62205) ***(G-8745)***
**Blue Pearl Stone Tech LLC**......708 698-5700
333 Washington Ave La Grange (60525) ***(G-12726)***
**Blue Ribbon Fastener Company**......847 673-1248
8220 Kimball Ave Frnt Skokie (60076) ***(G-19966)***
**Blue Ridge Forge Inc**......309 274-5377
316 W Cedar St Chillicothe (61523) ***(G-7162)***
**Blue Ridge Land and Cattle**......217 762-9652
1068 E 1765 North Rd Monticello (61856) ***(G-15075)***
**Blue Sky Bio LLC**......718 376-0422
888 E Belvidere Rd # 212 Grayslake (60030) ***(G-11322)***
**Blue Sky Vineyard**......618 995-9463
3150 S Rocky Comfort Rd Makanda (62958) ***(G-14162)***
**Blue Software LLC**......773 957-1669
8430 W Bryn Mawr Ave # 1100 Chicago (60631) ***(G-4126)***
**Blueair Inc**......888 258-3247
100 N La Salle St # 1900 Chicago (60602) ***(G-4127)***
**Blueberry Woodworking Inc**......773 230-7179
2824 Birch St Franklin Park (60131) ***(G-10414)***
**Bluebird Lanes**......773 582-2828
3900 W Columbus Ave Chicago (60652) ***(G-4128)***
**Bluemastiff Group LLC**......708 704-3529
903 W 35th St Ste 562 Chicago (60609) ***(G-4129)***
**Bluescope Buildings N Amer Inc**......217 348-7676
890 W State St Charleston (61920) ***(G-3590)***
**Bluesun Hitech, Naperville** *Also called Lightfoot Technologies Inc* ***(G-15690)***
**Bluetown Skateboard Co LLC**......312 718-4786
1344 N Oakley Blvd Ste 2 Chicago (60622) ***(G-4130)***
**Bluewater Thermal Solutions, Northlake** *Also called Bwt LLC* ***(G-16432)***
**Bluewater Thermal Solutions, Rockford** *Also called Bwt LLC* ***(G-18293)***
**Bluffs Vineyard & Winery L L C**......618 763-4447
1505 Business Highway 13 Murphysboro (62966) ***(G-15572)***
**Blumthal Gas Geologist, Olney** *Also called Benchmark Properties Ltd* ***(G-16762)***
**Bluskies International, Saint Charles** *Also called Marine Canada Acquisition* ***(G-19215)***
**Blustor Pmc Inc**......312 265-3058
401 N Michigan Ave # 1200 Chicago (60611) ***(G-4131)***
**Bm Machine & Fabrication, Olney** *Also called Bills Machine & Power Transm* ***(G-16763)***
**Bm Welding, Addison** *Also called Gallon Industries Inc* ***(G-127)***
**BMC, Chicago** *Also called Bearings Manufacturing Company* ***(G-4067)***
**BMC 1092 Inc**......708 544-2200
2200 Parkes Dr Broadview (60155) ***(G-2563)***
**BMC Software Inc**......331 777-8700
1901 Butterfield Rd # 420 Downers Grove (60515) ***(G-8398)***
**Bmg Seltec, Oak Brook** *Also called Fivecubits Inc* ***(G-16513)***
**Bmi Products Northern Ill Inc**......847 395-7110
28919 W Il Route 173 Antioch (60002) ***(G-625)***
**Bms Manufacturing Company Inc**......309 787-3158
651 8th Ave W Milan (61264) ***(G-14776)***
**Bmt Prnting Crtgraph Espclists**......773 646-4700
12941 S Exchange Ave Chicago (60633) ***(G-4132)***
**BMW Sportswear Inc**......773 265-0110
3967 W Madison St Chicago (60624) ***(G-4133)***
**Bn Delfi USA Inc**......847 280-0447
530 Cumberland Trl Elgin (60123) ***(G-8968)***
**Bn National Trail**......618 783-8709
8810 Commercial Ave Newton (62448) ***(G-15938)***
**BNP Media Inc**......630 690-4200
155 N Pfingsten Rd # 205 Deerfield (60015) ***(G-7992)***
**Boaters World, Chicago** *Also called Cyn Industries Inc* ***(G-4531)***
**Boatman Signs**......618 548-6567
1700 E Main St Salem (62881) ***(G-19328)***
**Bob Barnett Redi-Mix Inc (PA)**......618 252-3581
285 Garden Heights Rd Harrisburg (62946) ***(G-11596)***
**Bob C Beverages LLC**......847 520-7582
419 Harvester Ct Wheeling (60090) ***(G-22016)***
**Bob Chinn's Premium Beverages, Wheeling** *Also called Bob C Beverages LLC* ***(G-22016)***
**Bob Evans Farms Inc**......309 932-2194
1001 Sw 2nd St Galva (61434) ***(G-10785)***
**Bob Folder Lures Co**......217 787-1116
2071 Hazlett Rd Springfield (62707) ***(G-20398)***
**Bob Ulrichs Pallets**......217 224-2568
5910 Dove Ln Quincy (62305) ***(G-17806)***
**Bobbi Screen Printing**......773 847-8200
4573 S Archer Ave Chicago (60632) ***(G-4134)***
**Bobbie Haycraft**......217 856-2194
110 Homann Ct Humboldt (61931) ***(G-12128)***
**Bobco Enterprises Inc Del**......773 722-1700
212 Garden Way Bloomingdale (60108) ***(G-2097)***
**Bobs Business Inc**......630 238-5790
730 Thomas Dr Bensenville (60106) ***(G-1845)***
**Bobs Market & Greenhouse**......217 442-8155
1118 E Voorhees St Danville (61832) ***(G-7706)***
**Bobs Tshirt Store**......618 567-1730
419 Jackson St Mascoutah (62258) ***(G-14349)***
**Boc Global Helium Inc**......630 897-1900
1998 Albright Rd Montgomery (60538) ***(G-15032)***
**Bock's Identi Co., Mattoon** *Also called Bocks Cattle-Identi Co Inc* ***(G-14384)***
**Bocks Cattle-Identi Co Inc**......217 234-6634
3101 Cedar Ave Mattoon (61938) ***(G-14384)***
**Bodacious Beads Inc**......847 699-7959
1942 S River Rd Des Plaines (60018) ***(G-8160)***
**Bodine Electric Company (PA)**......773 478-3515
201 Northfield Rd Northfield (60093) ***(G-16393)***
**BODINE ELECTRIC OF DECATUR, Decatur** *Also called Rathje Enterprises Inc* ***(G-7932)***
**Bodine Electric of Decatur, Danville** *Also called Rathje Enterprises Inc* ***(G-7763)***
**Bodines Baking Company**......217 853-7707
2136 N Dennis Ave Decatur (62526) ***(G-7846)***
**Bodycote Thermal Proc Inc**......708 236-5360
1975 N Ruby St Melrose Park (60160) ***(G-14601)***
**Boeing Aerospace - Tams Inc (HQ)**......312 544-2000
100 N Riverside Plz Chicago (60606) ***(G-4135)***
**Boeing Company (PA)**......312 544-2000
100 N Riverside Plz Chicago (60606) ***(G-4136)***
**Boeing Company**......847 240-0767
1515 E Wdfield Rd Ste 320 Schaumburg (60173) ***(G-19465)***
**Boeing Irving Company**......312 544-2000
100 N Riverside Plz Fl 35 Chicago (60606) ***(G-4137)***
**Boeing LTS Inc**......312 544-2000
100 N Riverside Plz Chicago (60606) ***(G-4138)***
**Boekeloo Heating & Sheet Metal**......708 877-6560
601 N Williams St Thornton (60476) ***(G-20868)***
**Boetje Foods Inc**......309 788-4352
2736 12th St Rock Island (61201) ***(G-18165)***
**Bofa Americas Inc**......618 205-5007
303 S Madison St Staunton (62088) ***(G-20553)***
**Bogart Industries LLC**......224 242-4578
315 E Reader St Elburn (60119) ***(G-8878)***
**Bohl Machine & Tool Company**......309 799-5122
4405 78th Ave Milan (61264) ***(G-14777)***
**Bohler**......630 883-3000
2505 Millennium Dr Elgin (60124) ***(G-8969)***
**Boiler Tube & Fabrication Div, Romeoville** *Also called Chicago Tube and Iron Company* ***(G-18810)***
**Boland Hill Media LLC**......877 658-0418
3 Golf Ctr Ste 314 Hoffman Estates (60169) ***(G-11997)***
**Bolchazy-Carducci Publishers**......847 526-4344
1570 Baskin Rd Mundelein (60060) ***(G-15479)***
**Bold Diagnostics LLC**......806 543-5743
222 Merchandise Mart Plz Chicago (60654) ***(G-4139)***
**Bold Machine Works Inc**......217 428-6644
1677 S Taylorville Rd Decatur (62521) ***(G-7847)***
**Boldt Metronics International, Schaumburg** *Also called B M I Inc* ***(G-19456)***
**Boler Company (PA)**......630 773-9111
500 Park Blvd Ste 1010 Itasca (60143) ***(G-12236)***
**Boler Company**......630 910-2800
800 S Frontage Rd Woodridge (60517) ***(G-22457)***
**Boler Ventures LLC (PA)**......630 773-9111
500 Park Blvd Ste 1010 Itasca (60143) ***(G-12237)***
**Boley Tool & Machine Works Inc**......309 694-2722
1044 Spring Bay Rd East Peoria (61611) ***(G-8703)***
**Bolhuis Woodworking Co**......708 333-5100
14250 W Joliet Rd Manhattan (60442) ***(G-14168)***
**Bolingbrook Communications Inc**......630 759-9500
1938 University Ln Ste C Lisle (60532) ***(G-13571)***
**Bolingbrook Quarry, Plainfield** *Also called Legacy Vulcan LLC* ***(G-17618)***
**Boltswitch Inc**......815 459-6900
6208 Commercial Rd Crystal Lake (60014) ***(G-7542)***
**Bolzoni Auramo Inc**......708 957-8809
17635 Hoffman Way Homewood (60430) ***(G-12092)***
**Bom Bon Corp**......773 277-8777
3748 W 26th St Chicago (60623) ***(G-4140)***
**Bombardier Learjet, Des Plaines** *Also called Learjet Inc* ***(G-8222)***
**Bombay Electronics, Skokie** *Also called Audio Video Electronics LLC* ***(G-19961)***
**Bomel Tool Manufacturing Co**......708 343-3663
2111 Roberts Dr Broadview (60155) ***(G-2564)***
**Bona Fide Corp**......847 970-8693
100 Shepard Ave Wheeling (60090) ***(G-22017)***
**Bonanno Vintners LLC**......773 477-8351
2614 N Paulina St Chicago (60614) ***(G-4141)***
**Bond & Fayette County Shopper**......618 664-4566
201 N 3rd St Ste Frnt Greenville (62246) ***(G-11388)***
**Bond Broadcasting Inc**......618 664-3300
309 W Main St Greenville (62246) ***(G-11389)***
**Bond Brothers & Co**......708 442-5510
7826 47th St Lyons (60534) ***(G-14032)***
**Bond Brothers Hardwoods**......618 272-4811
412 W Main St Ridgway (62979) ***(G-17983)***

## ALPHABETIC SECTION

**Bone & Rattle Inc** .................................................. 312 813-8830
320 W Ohio St Ste 3w  Chicago  (60654)  *(G-4142)*
**Bone A Fide Pet Grooming** .................................... 217 872-0907
1220 E Pershing Rd Ste 1  Decatur  (62526)  *(G-7848)*
**Boneco North America Corp** .................................. 630 983-3294
1801 N Mill St Ste A  Naperville  (60563)  *(G-15607)*
**Bonell Manufacturing Company** ............................ 708 849-1770
13521 S Halsted St Fl 1  Riverdale  (60827)  *(G-18016)*
**Bonnell Industries Inc** .......................................... 815 284-3819
1385 Franklin Grove Rd  Dixon  (61021)  *(G-8323)*
**Bonnie's Slick Printing, Gurnee** *Also called Proforma Quality Business Svcs (G-11492)*
**Bonsal American Inc** ............................................ 847 678-6220
10352 Franklin Ave  Franklin Park  (60131)  *(G-10415)*
**Book House For Children Div, Lake Bluff** *Also called United Educators Inc (G-12868)*
**Book Power Inc** ..................................................... 630 790-4144
253 Traver Ave  Glen Ellyn  (60137)  *(G-10961)*
**Bookends Publishing** ............................................ 312 988-1500
2001 N Halsted St Ste 201  Chicago  (60614)  *(G-4143)*
**Booklist, Chicago** *Also called American Library Association (G-3860)*
**Boom Company Inc** .............................................. 847 459-6199
161 Wheeling Rd  Wheeling  (60090)  *(G-22018)*
**Boone County Shopper Inc** ................................... 815 544-2166
112 Leonard Ct  Belvidere  (61008)  *(G-1739)*
**Booth Oil Co Inc** .................................................... 618 662-7696
Rr 2  Flora  (62839)  *(G-10200)*
**Booth Resources Inc** ............................................ 618 662-4955
7965 Old Highway 50  Flora  (62839)  *(G-10201)*
**Booths and Upholstery By Ray** ............................. 773 523-3555
1400 W 37th St  Chicago  (60609)  *(G-4144)*
**Borg Warner Automotive, Bellwood** *Also called Borgwarner Transm Systems (G-1700)*
**Borg-Warner Emissions Systems, Dixon** *Also called Borgwarner Inc (G-8324)*
**Borgwarner Emissions Systems, Dixon** *Also called Borgwarner Inc (G-8325)*
**Borgwarner Inc** ..................................................... 815 288-1462
1350 Franklin Grove Rd  Dixon  (61021)  *(G-8324)*
**Borgwarner Inc** ..................................................... 248 754-9200
700 25th Ave  Bellwood  (60104)  *(G-1699)*
**Borgwarner Inc** ..................................................... 248 754-9200
300 S Maple St  Frankfort  (60423)  *(G-10302)*
**Borgwarner Inc** ..................................................... 815 288-1462
1350 Franklin Grove Rd  Dixon  (61021)  *(G-8325)*
**Borgwarner Transm Systems** ................................ 708 547-2600
700 25th Ave  Bellwood  (60104)  *(G-1700)*
**Borgwarner Transm Systems Inc** .......................... 815 469-2721
300 S Maple St  Frankfort  (60423)  *(G-10303)*
**Borgwarner Transm Systems Inc** .......................... 815 469-7819
10807 S Fairfield Ave  Chicago  (60655)  *(G-4145)*
**Borgwarner Transm Systems Inc** .......................... 708 731-4540
2437 W North Ave  Melrose Park  (60160)  *(G-14602)*
**Boring Industries** .................................................. 815 986-1172
2219 N Central Ave  Rockford  (61101)  *(G-18288)*
**Bork Industries** ..................................................... 630 365-5517
44w508 Ic Trl  Maple Park  (60151)  *(G-14198)*
**Borns Picture Frames** ........................................... 630 876-1709
540 Bellview Ave  West Chicago  (60185)  *(G-21673)*
**Borny Enterprise Corp** .......................................... 646 662-1514
625 N Michigan Ave # 1001  Chicago  (60611)  *(G-4146)*
**Borse Industries Inc** ............................................. 630 325-1210
7409 S Quincy St  Willowbrook  (60527)  *(G-22201)*
**Bos Machine Tool Services Inc** ............................. 309 658-2223
621 Main St  Hillsdale  (61257)  *(G-11901)*
**Bosch Auto Svc Solutions Inc** .............................. 815 407-3900
1385 N Weber Rd  Romeoville  (60446)  *(G-18803)*
**Bosch Sftwr Innovations Corp** .............................. 312 368-2500
161 N Clark St Ste 3550  Chicago  (60601)  *(G-4147)*
**Bose Corporation** .................................................. 630 575-8044
65 Oakbrook Ctr  Hinsdale  (60523)  *(G-11942)*
**Bose Corporation** .................................................. 630 585-6654
1650 Premium Outlet Blvd # 1257  Aurora  (60502)  *(G-971)*
**Bose Factory Store, Aurora** *Also called Bose Corporation (G-971)*
**Bose Showcase Store, Hinsdale** *Also called Bose Corporation (G-11942)*
**Bosley Medical Institute** ....................................... 312 642-5252
676 N Michigan Ave # 3850  Chicago  (60611)  *(G-4148)*
**Boss Balloon Company Inc** ................................... 309 852-2131
1221 Page St  Kewanee  (61443)  *(G-12672)*
**Boss Holdings Inc (PA)** ......................................... 309 852-2131
1221 Page St  Kewanee  (61443)  *(G-12673)*
**Boss Manufacturing Company (HQ)** ..................... 309 852-2131
1221 Page St  Kewanee  (61443)  *(G-12674)*
**Boss Manufacturing Holdings (HQ)** ...................... 309 852-2781
1221 Page St  Kewanee  (61443)  *(G-12675)*
**Boss Manufacturing Holdings** ............................... 309 852-2131
1221 Page St  Kewanee  (61443)  *(G-12676)*
**Bost Corporation (PA)** ........................................... 708 344-7023
601 Saint Charles Rd  Maywood  (60153)  *(G-14420)*
**Bost Corporation** .................................................. 708 450-9234
2780 Thomas St  Melrose Park  (60160)  *(G-14603)*
**Bostic Publishing Company** .................................. 773 551-7065
3236 N Sacramento Ave  Chicago  (60618)  *(G-4149)*

**Boston Leather Inc** ................................................ 815 622-1635
1801 Eastwood Dr  Sterling  (61081)  *(G-20585)*
**Boston Warehouse Trading Corp** .......................... 630 992-5604
2600 Beverly Dr  Aurora  (60502)  *(G-972)*
**Botkin Lumber Company Inc** ................................ 217 287-2127
201 S Baughman Rd  Taylorville  (62568)  *(G-20834)*
**Botti Studio of Architectural (PA)** .......................... 847 869-5933
919 Grove St  Evanston  (60201)  *(G-10017)*
**Bottle-Free Water** .................................................. 630 462-6807
350 S Main Pl  Carol Stream  (60188)  *(G-3119)*
**Bottoms Up Dy-Dee Wash Dpr Svc, Waukegan** *Also called Bottoms Up Inc (G-21530)*
**Bottoms Up Inc** ..................................................... 847 336-0040
201 N Green Bay Rd  Waukegan  (60085)  *(G-21530)*
**Botts Welding and Trck Svc Inc (PA)** .................... 815 338-0594
335 N Eastwood Dr  Woodstock  (60098)  *(G-22546)*
**Boudin Bakery, Addison** *Also called Chicago Bread Company (G-73)*
**Bound + D Termined Inc** ....................................... 847 696-1501
60 S Dee Rd Apt E  Park Ridge  (60068)  *(G-17185)*
**Bourn & Bourn Inc** ................................................ 815 965-4013
2500 Kishwaukee St  Rockford  (61104)  *(G-18289)*
**Bourn & Koch Inc (PA)** .......................................... 815 965-4013
2500 Kishwaukee St  Rockford  (61104)  *(G-18290)*
**Bourrette Logging** ................................................. 815 591-3761
1012 Blackhawk B  Hanover  (61041)  *(G-11571)*
**Bow Brothers Co Inc** ............................................ 217 359-0555
3108 W Springfield Ave  Champaign  (61822)  *(G-3457)*
**Bowe Bell + Hwell Holdings Inc** ............................ 312 541-9300
760 S Wolf Rd  Wheeling  (60090)  *(G-22019)*
**Bowe Bell + Hwell Scanners LLC** .......................... 847 675-7600
760 S Wolf Rd  Wheeling  (60090)  *(G-22020)*
**Bowebellhowell, Wheeling** *Also called Bowe Bell + Hwell Holdings Inc (G-22019)*
**Bowen Guerrero & Howe LLC** ............................... 312 447-2370
825 W Chicago Ave  Chicago  (60642)  *(G-4150)*
**Bowhunting.com, Huntley** *Also called Hunting Network LLC (G-12145)*
**Bowl Doctors Inc** .................................................. 815 282-6009
7664 Hawks Rdg  Machesney Park  (61115)  *(G-14060)*
**Bowl-Tronics Enterprises Inc** ................................ 847 741-4500
1115 Sherwood Ave  Elgin  (60120)  *(G-8970)*
**Bowlmor AMF Corp** ............................................... 708 456-4100
3111 River Rd  River Grove  (60171)  *(G-18007)*
**Bowlmor AMF Corp** ............................................... 847 367-1600
316 Center Dr  Vernon Hills  (60061)  *(G-21152)*
**Bows Arts Inc** ........................................................ 847 501-3161
1944 Lehigh Ave Ste B  Glenview  (60026)  *(G-11109)*
**Bowtie Inc** ............................................................. 630 515-9493
477 E Bttrfield Rd Ste 200  Lombard  (60148)  *(G-13773)*
**Bowtree Inc** ........................................................... 217 430-8884
720 E Tolton Dr  Quincy  (62305)  *(G-17807)*
**Box Enclsres Assembly Svcs Inc (PA)** .................. 847 932-4700
14092 W Lambs Ln  Libertyville  (60048)  *(G-13309)*
**Box Form Inc** ........................................................ 773 927-8808
1334 W 43rd St  Chicago  (60609)  *(G-4151)*
**Box Manufacturing Inc** ......................................... 309 637-6228
201 Spring St  Peoria  (61603)  *(G-17319)*
**Box of Rain Ltd** ..................................................... 847 640-6996
1504 E Algonquin Rd  Arlington Heights  (60005)  *(G-727)*
**Box Office Magazine, Chicago** *Also called R L D Communications Inc (G-6267)*
**Box USA** ................................................................ 708 562-6000
401 Northwest Ave  Northlake  (60164)  *(G-16429)*
**Boyce Industries Inc** ............................................. 708 345-0455
4915 Division St  Melrose Park  (60160)  *(G-14604)*
**Boyd Sawmill** ........................................................ 618 735-2056
19775 N Boyd Ln  Dix  (62830)  *(G-8317)*
**Boyd Spotting Inc** ................................................. 217 669-2418
1310 N 300 East Rd  Cisco  (61830)  *(G-7249)*
**Boyer Corporation** ................................................ 708 352-2553
9600 W Ogden Ave  La Grange  (60525)  *(G-12727)*
**Boyleston 21st Century LLC** ................................. 708 387-2012
9118 47th St Ste 3  Brookfield  (60513)  *(G-2625)*
**Bozki Inc** ............................................................... 312 767-2122
205 W Wacker Dr Ste 1320  Chicago  (60606)  *(G-4152)*
**BP, Warrenville** *Also called Standard Oil Company (G-21362)*
**BP America Inc (HQ)** ............................................. 630 420-5111
4101 Winfield Rd Ste 200  Warrenville  (60555)  *(G-21344)*
**BP Amoco Chemical Company** ............................. 630 420-5111
150 W Warrenville Rd  Naperville  (60563)  *(G-15608)*
**BP Elc Mtrs Pump & Svc Inc** ................................. 773 539-4343
8135 Ridgeway Ave  Skokie  (60076)  *(G-19967)*
**BP Products North America Inc** ............................ 630 420-4300
150 W Warrenville Rd  Naperville  (60563)  *(G-15609)*
**BP Products North America Inc** ............................ 312 594-7689
30 S Wacker Dr Ste 900  Chicago  (60606)  *(G-4153)*
**BP Shipping** .......................................................... 630 393-1032
150 W Warrenville Rd  Naperville  (60563)  *(G-15610)*
**BP Solar International Inc** ..................................... 301 698-4200
150 W Warrenville Rd  Naperville  (60563)  *(G-15611)*
**Bpi Holdings International Inc (PA)** ...................... 815 363-9000
4400 Prime Pkwy  McHenry  (60050)  *(G-14483)*
**Bpn Chicago** ......................................................... 312 799-4100
875 N Michigan Ave # 1850  Chicago  (60611)  *(G-4154)*

**Bpo Assistant, Monticello** *Also called Track My Foreclosures LLC* ***(G-15088)***
**Bprex Healthcare Packaging Inc (HQ)**..........800 537-0178
600 Deerfield Pkwy Buffalo Grove (60089) ***(G-2667)***
**Bps Fuels Inc**..........217 452-7608
352 N Morgan St Virginia (62691) ***(G-21304)***
**BR Concepts International Inc**..........847 674-9481
7436 Kildare Ave Skokie (60076) ***(G-19968)***
**BR Machine Inc**..........815 434-0427
3312 E 2153rd Rd Ottawa (61350) ***(G-16950)***
**Braas Company, Elgin** *Also called Motion Industries Inc* ***(G-9113)***
**Braceunder, Libertyville** *Also called Therapeutic Envisions Inc* ***(G-13390)***
**Brad Foote Gear Works Inc**..........708 298-1100
47 E Chicago Ave Ste 332 Naperville (60540) ***(G-15612)***
**Braden Rock Bit**..........618 435-4519
14447 State Highway 34 Benton (62812) ***(G-2024)***
**Bradley Adhsive Applctions Inc (PA)**..........630 443-8424
410 38th Ave Saint Charles (60174) ***(G-19145)***
**Bradley Group, The, Saint Charles** *Also called Bradley Adhsive Applctions Inc* ***(G-19145)***
**Bradley Industries Inc**..........815 469-2314
524 Center Rd Frankfort (60423) ***(G-10304)***
**Bradley Machining Inc**..........630 543-2875
753 W Annoreno Dr Addison (60101) ***(G-59)***
**Bradley Smoker USA Inc**..........309 343-1124
644 Enterprise Ave Galesburg (61401) ***(G-10739)***
**Bradley University Bookstore, Peoria** *Also called Barnes & Noble College* ***(G-17314)***
**Brads Printing Inc**..........847 662-0447
925 W Glen Flora Ave Waukegan (60085) ***(G-21531)***
**Braeburn Systems LLC**..........866 268-8892
2215 Cornell Ave Montgomery (60538) ***(G-15033)***
**Braeside LLC**..........847 395-8500
945 Anita Ave Antioch (60002) ***(G-626)***
**Braeside Displays, Antioch** *Also called Braeside LLC* ***(G-626)***
**Bragi NA LLC**..........708 717-5000
20635 Abbley Woods Ste 303 Frankfort (60423) ***(G-10305)***
**Brahlers Truckers Supply Inc (HQ)**..........217 243-6471
21 Harold Cox Dr Jacksonville (62650) ***(G-12380)***
**Braindok LLC**..........847 877-1586
2104 Birchwood Ln Buffalo Grove (60089) ***(G-2668)***
**Brainerd Chemical Midwest LLC**..........918 622-1214
209 Brewer Rd Danville (61834) ***(G-7707)***
**Brainlab Inc**..........800 784-7700
5 Westbrook Corp Ctr Westchester (60154) ***(G-21831)***
**Brainstorm USA**..........773 509-1227
3525 W Peterson Ave # 107 Chicago (60659) ***(G-4155)***
**Brainware Company**..........773 250-6465
4802 N Broadway St 201a Chicago (60640) ***(G-4156)***
**Brainworx Studio**..........773 743-8200
6531 N Albany Ave Chicago (60645) ***(G-4157)***
**Brake Drum Tool Co America Div, Waukegan** *Also called Illinois Carbide Tool Co Inc* ***(G-21569)***
**Brake Parts Inc India LLC (HQ)**..........815 363-9000
4400 Prime Pkwy McHenry (60050) ***(G-14484)***
**Brake Parts Inc LLC (HQ)**..........815 363-9000
4400 Prime Pkwy McHenry (60050) ***(G-14485)***
**Brake Parts Inc LLC**..........217 324-2161
725 Mckinley Ave Litchfield (62056) ***(G-13682)***
**Brakur Custom Cabinetry Inc**..........630 355-2244
18656 S State Route 59 Shorewood (60404) ***(G-19923)***
**Bramic Industries, Addison** *Also called Lenrok Industries Inc* ***(G-179)***
**Bran-Zan Holdings LLC (PA)**..........847 342-0000
1655 N Arlington Heights Arlington Heights (60004) ***(G-728)***
**Branch Lines Ltd**..........847 256-4294
1200 N Branch Rd Wilmette (60091) ***(G-22245)***
**Branchfield Casting**..........309 932-2278
502 Se Industrial Ave Galva (61434) ***(G-10786)***
**Brand X-Ray Company**..........630 543-5331
910 S Westwood Ave Addison (60101) ***(G-60)***
**Branding Iron Holdings Inc (PA)**..........618 337-8400
1682 Sauget Business Blvd Sauget (62206) ***(G-19383)***
**Brandon Mtdba Okaeri Noodle Sp**..........847 966-0991
5432 Main St Skokie (60077) ***(G-19969)***
**Brandt Assoc**..........847 362-0556
1002 Muir Ave Lake Bluff (60044) ***(G-12837)***
**Brandt Consolidated Inc (PA)**..........217 547-5800
2935 S Koke Mill Rd Springfield (62711) ***(G-20399)***
**Brandt Consolidated Inc**..........217 626-1123
788 E 3070 North Rd Farmer City (61842) ***(G-10178)***
**Brandt Consolidated Inc**..........217 438-6158
300 W Jefferson St Auburn (62615) ***(G-948)***
**Brandt Consolidated Inc**..........309 365-7201
610 W Main St Lexington (61753) ***(G-13291)***
**Brandt Interiors**..........847 251-3543
803 Ridge Rd Wilmette (60091) ***(G-22246)***
**Brandt Printing, Morris** *Also called D G Brandt Inc* ***(G-15105)***
**Braner Usa Inc (PA)**..........847 671-6210
9301 W Bernice St Schiller Park (60176) ***(G-19809)***
**Branmark Strategy Group LLC**..........847 849-9080
2013 Burr Oak Dr W Glenview (60025) ***(G-11110)***
**Branson Ultrasonics Corp**..........847 229-0800
1585 Barclay Blvd Buffalo Grove (60089) ***(G-2669)***
**Branstiter Printing Co**..........217 245-6533
217 E Morgan St Jacksonville (62650) ***(G-12381)***
**Brasel Products Inc**..........630 879-3759
715 Hunter Dr Batavia (60510) ***(G-1424)***
**Brass Creations Inc**..........773 237-7755
5610 W Bloomingdale Ave # 4 Chicago (60639) ***(G-4158)***
**Brass Ring Entertainment, Marengo** *Also called Dan Horenberger* ***(G-14224)***
**Braun Manufacturing Co Inc**..........847 635-2050
1350 Feehanville Dr Mount Prospect (60056) ***(G-15313)***
**Brave Products Inc**..........815 672-0551
1705 N Shabbona St Streator (61364) ***(G-20684)***
**Bravilor Bonamat LLC**..........630 423-9400
1204 Bilter Rd Aurora (60502) ***(G-973)***
**Bravura Moulding Company**..........262 633-1882
28915 N Herky Dr Ste 103 Lake Bluff (60044) ***(G-12838)***
**BRC Manufacturing Co, Skokie** *Also called BR Concepts International Inc* ***(G-19968)***
**Breachers Tape, Arlington Heights** *Also called Fontana Associates Inc* ***(G-755)***
**Breaker Press Co Inc**..........773 927-1666
2421 S Western Ave Chicago (60608) ***(G-4159)***
**Breakfast Fuel LLC**..........847 251-3835
1222 Washington Ct Wilmette (60091) ***(G-22247)***
**Breakroom Brewery**..........773 564-9534
2925 W Montrose Ave Chicago (60618) ***(G-4160)***
**Breckenridge Material Company**..........618 398-4141
10 Tucker Dr Caseyville (62232) ***(G-3394)***
**Breedlove Sporting Goods Inc (PA)**..........309 852-2434
123 W 2nd St Kewanee (61443) ***(G-12677)***
**Breedlove Sporting Goods Inc**..........309 852-2434
215 W 2nd St Kewanee (61443) ***(G-12678)***
**Breedlove's, Kewanee** *Also called Breedlove Sporting Goods Inc* ***(G-12677)***
**Brees Studio Inc**..........618 687-3331
430 S 19th St Murphysboro (62966) ***(G-15573)***
**Breese Journal, Breese** *Also called Breese Publishing Co Inc* ***(G-2440)***
**Breese Publishing Co Inc (PA)**..........618 526-7211
8060 Old Us Highway 50 Breese (62230) ***(G-2440)***
**Breeze Printing Co (PA)**..........217 824-2233
212 S Main St Taylorville (62568) ***(G-20835)***
**Breeze-Courier, Taylorville** *Also called Breeze Printing Co* ***(G-20835)***
**Brehm Oil Inc (PA)**..........618 242-4620
1915 Broadway St Mount Vernon (62864) ***(G-15402)***
**Bremner-Davis Eductl Systems, Chicago** *Also called Fox International Corp* ***(G-4880)***
**Bremskerl North America Inc**..........847 289-3460
1291 Humbracht Cir Bartlett (60103) ***(G-1337)***
**Brenco Machine and Tool Inc**..........815 356-5100
6117 Factory Rd Crystal Lake (60014) ***(G-7543)***
**Brenda Miller**..........618 678-2639
130 Old Highway 50 Xenia (62899) ***(G-22643)***
**Brennan Engineering, Danville** *Also called Estad Stamping & Mfg Co* ***(G-7717)***
**Brennan Equipment and Mfg Inc**..........708 534-5500
730 Central Ave University Park (60484) ***(G-21046)***
**Brenner Tank Services LLC**..........773 468-6390
803 E 120th St Chicago (60628) ***(G-4161)***
**Brent Pumps Supply, Norris City** *Also called William R Becker* ***(G-16116)***
**Bretford Manufacturing Inc (PA)**..........847 678-2545
11000 Seymour Ave Franklin Park (60131) ***(G-10416)***
**Bretmar Steel Industry**..........847 382-5940
467 E Lake Shore Dr Barrington (60010) ***(G-1274)***
**Brevity LLC**..........312 375-3996
1750 N Clybourn Ave Chicago (60614) ***(G-4162)***
**Brewer Company**..........708 339-9000
3852 W 159th Pl Harvey (60428) ***(G-11662)***
**Brewer Utility Systems Inc**..........217 224-5975
1628 Madison St Quincy (62301) ***(G-17808)***
**Brewers Bottlers & Bev Corp**..........773 262-9711
7233 N Sheridan Rd Ste 5 Chicago (60626) ***(G-4163)***
**Brewster Cheese Company**..........815 947-3361
300 W Railroad Ave Stockton (61085) ***(G-20630)***
**Brex-Arlington Incorporated**..........847 255-6284
714 E Kensington Rd Arlington Heights (60004) ***(G-729)***
**Brg Sports Inc**..........217 893-9300
1001 Innovation Rd Rantoul (61866) ***(G-17921)***
**Brg Sports Inc (HQ)**..........831 461-7500
9801 W Higgins Rd Rosemont (60018) ***(G-18990)***
**Brg Sports Inc**..........217 819-5187
301 Mercury Dr Ste 8 Champaign (61822) ***(G-3458)***
**Brian Bequette Cabinetry**..........618 670-5427
18630 White City Rd Staunton (62088) ***(G-20554)***
**Brian Burcar**..........815 856-2271
310 Walnut St Leonore (61332) ***(G-13285)***
**Brian Hobbs**..........618 758-1303
207 E Mill St Coulterville (62237) ***(G-7398)***
**Brian Kinney**..........309 206-4219
1529 28th St Rock Island (61201) ***(G-18166)***
**Brian Lindstrom**..........309 463-2388
2412 Wenona Rd Varna (61375) ***(G-21133)***
**Brian Paul Inc**..........847 398-8677
721 Alsace Ct Buffalo Grove (60089) ***(G-2670)***

**Brian Robert Awning Co** ....847 679-1140
8152 Lawndale Ave Skokie (60076) ***(G-19970)***
**Bricks Inc (PA)** ....630 897-6926
723 S Lasalle St Aurora (60505) ***(G-1121)***
**Bricks Inc** ....773 523-5718
3425 S Kedzie Ave Ste 1 Chicago (60623) ***(G-4164)***
**Bridal Originals, Collinsville** *Also called SASI Corporation* ***(G-7340)***
**Bridge City Mechanical Inc** ....309 944-4873
777 E Culver Ct Geneseo (61254) ***(G-10799)***
**Bridge Wave Electronics, Darien** *Also called Angela Yang Chingjui* ***(G-7790)***
**Bridgeline Digital Inc** ....312 784-5720
30 N La Salle St Ste 2000 Chicago (60602) ***(G-4165)***
**Bridgeport Air Comprsr & Tl Co** ....618 945-7163
745 Monroe St Bridgeport (62417) ***(G-2450)***
**Bridgeport Pharmacy Inc** ....312 326-3200
3201 S Wallace St Chicago (60616) ***(G-4166)***
**Bridgeport Steel Sales Inc** ....312 326-4800
2730 S Hillock Ave Chicago (60608) ***(G-4167)***
**Bridgestone Americas** ....309 452-4411
1600 Fort Jesse Rd Normal (61761) ***(G-16066)***
**Bridgestone Ret Operations LLC** ....630 893-6336
2015 Bloomingdale Rd Glendale Heights (60139) ***(G-11012)***
**Bridgeview Custom Kit Cabinets** ....708 598-1221
8655 Beloit Ave Bridgeview (60455) ***(G-2472)***
**Bridgeview Machining Inc** ....708 599-4060
9009 S Thomas Ave Bridgeview (60455) ***(G-2473)***
**Bridgford Foods Corporation** ....312 733-0300
170 N Green St Chicago (60607) ***(G-4168)***
**Bridgford Marketing, Chicago** *Also called Bridgford Foods Corporation* ***(G-4168)***
**Briergate Tool & Engrg Co** ....630 766-7050
1007 Industrial Dr Bensenville (60106) ***(G-1846)***
**Bright Designs Inc** ....847 428-6012
14n690 Sleepy Hollow Rd Dundee (60118) ***(G-8559)***
**Bright Light Sign Company Inc** ....847 550-8902
310 Telser Rd Lake Zurich (60047) ***(G-13047)***
**Bright Metal Finishing Co, Chicago** *Also called Dana Anodizing Inc* ***(G-4550)***
**Bright Metals Finishing Corp** ....773 486-2312
3905 W Armitage Ave Chicago (60647) ***(G-4169)***
**Brighter Electric Inc** ....630 325-4915
5945 Bentley Ave Willowbrook (60527) ***(G-22202)***
**Brighton Cabinetry Inc** ....217 235-1978
2908 Lake Land Blvd Mattoon (61938) ***(G-14385)***
**Brighton Cabinetry Inc (PA)** ....217 895-3000
1095 Industrial Park Ave Neoga (62447) ***(G-15857)***
**Brighton Collectibles LLC** ....847 674-6719
4999 Old Orchard Ctr M17 Skokie (60077) ***(G-19971)***
**Brighton-Best Intl Inc** ....562 808-8000
940 Enterprise St Ste 100 Aurora (60504) ***(G-974)***
**Brigitflex Inc** ....847 741-1452
1725 Fleetwood Dr Elgin (60123) ***(G-8971)***
**Brijen Electronics, Rolling Meadows** *Also called Parth Consultants Inc* ***(G-18758)***
**Brilliant Color Corp** ....847 367-3300
14044 W Petronella Dr # 3 Libertyville (60048) ***(G-13310)***
**Brinkman Company Inc** ....630 595-3640
460 Evergreen Ave Bensenville (60106) ***(G-1847)***
**Briscoe Signs LLC** ....630 529-1616
119 N Bokelman St Roselle (60172) ***(G-18929)***
**Bristar** ....847 678-5000
3541 Martens St Ste 304 Franklin Park (60131) ***(G-10417)***
**Bristol Blacktop, Aurora** *Also called Andel Services Inc* ***(G-1109)***
**Bristol Hose & Fitting Inc** ....708 492-3456
1 W Lake St Northlake (60164) ***(G-16430)***
**Bristol Towing & Transport, Northlake** *Also called Bristol Transport Inc* ***(G-16431)***
**Bristol Transport Inc** ....708 343-6411
1 W Lake St Northlake (60164) ***(G-16431)***
**Brite Dental PC (PA)** ....773 735-8353
5917 S Pulaski Rd Chicago (60629) ***(G-4170)***
**Brite One Inc** ....708 481-8005
21649 Richmond Rd Matteson (60443) ***(G-14368)***
**Brite Site Supply Inc** ....773 772-7300
4616 W Fullerton Ave Chicago (60639) ***(G-4171)***
**Brite-O-Matic Mfg Inc** ....847 956-1100
527 W Algonquin Rd Arlington Heights (60005) ***(G-730)***
**Briteseed LLC** ....206 384-0311
4660 N Ravenswood Ave Chicago (60640) ***(G-4172)***
**British Cnvrtng Sltns Nrth AME** ....281 764-6651
650 W Grand Ave Ste 201 Elmhurst (60126) ***(G-9842)***
**Britt Industries Inc** ....847 640-1177
3010 Malmo Dr Arlington Heights (60005) ***(G-731)***
**Brk Brands Inc (HQ)** ....630 851-7330
3901 Liberty St Aurora (60504) ***(G-975)***
**Broad Ocean Motors LLC** ....630 908-4720
910 Pasquinelli Dr Westmont (60559) ***(G-21877)***
**Broadcast Electronics, Quincy** *Also called BEI Holding Corporation* ***(G-17803)***
**Broadcast Electronics, Quincy** *Also called BEI Electronics LLC* ***(G-17802)***
**Broadcast Electronics Inc (HQ)** ....217 224-9600
4100 N 24th St Quincy (62305) ***(G-17809)***
**Broadwind Energy Inc (PA)** ....708 780-4800
3240 S Central Ave Cicero (60804) ***(G-7181)***
**Brocade Cmmnctions Systems Inc** ....630 273-5530
20 N Martingale Rd # 290 Schaumburg (60173) ***(G-19466)***
**Brochem Industries Inc** ....708 206-2874
1229 171st St East Hazel Crest (60429) ***(G-8665)***
**Brock Equipment Company (PA)** ....815 459-4210
455 Borden St Woodstock (60098) ***(G-22547)***
**Brock Industrial Services LLC** ....815 730-3350
2210 Oak Leaf St Joliet (60436) ***(G-12467)***
**Brockway Standard Inc** ....773 893-2100
1440 S Kilbourn Ave Chicago (60623) ***(G-4173)***
**Brodie's, Galesburg** *Also called J Brodie Meat Products Inc* ***(G-10761)***
**Brohman Industries Inc** ....630 761-8160
2635 N Kildare Ave Chicago (60639) ***(G-4174)***
**Broken Earth Winery** ....847 383-5052
219 Rbert Prker Coffin Rd Long Grove (60047) ***(G-13888)***
**Broken Oar Inc** ....847 639-9468
614 Rawson Bridge Rd Port Barrington (60010) ***(G-17718)***
**Brokers Print Mail Rsource Inc** ....708 532-9900
17732 Oak Park Ave Tinley Park (60477) ***(G-20900)***
**Brolite Products Incorporated** ....630 830-0340
1900 S Park Ave Streamwood (60107) ***(G-20646)***
**Brombereks Flagstone Co Inc (PA)** ....630 257-0686
910 Singer Ave Lemont (60439) ***(G-13228)***
**Bromine Systems Inc** ....630 624-3303
1001 W Republic Dr Ste 9 Addison (60101) ***(G-61)***
**Bronson & Bratton Inc** ....630 986-1815
220 Shore Dr Burr Ridge (60527) ***(G-2825)***
**Bronson Machine Shop, Blue Island** *Also called E B Bronson & Co Inc* ***(G-2247)***
**Bronte Press** ....815 932-5192
6712 N 4180w Rd Bourbonnais (60914) ***(G-2390)***
**Bronze Memorial Inc** ....773 276-7972
1842 N Elston Ave Chicago (60642) ***(G-4175)***
**Brook Crompton Americas, South Holland** *Also called Brook Crompton Usa Inc* ***(G-20252)***
**Brook Crompton Usa Inc** ....708 893-0690
350 W Armory Dr South Holland (60473) ***(G-20252)***
**Brooke Burial Vault Co, Ottawa** *Also called Oakwood Memorial Park Inc* ***(G-16973)***
**Brooke Graphics LLC** ....847 593-1300
1331 Greenleaf Ave Elk Grove Village (60007) ***(G-9346)***
**Brookfield Farms, Chicago** *Also called Nationwide Foods Inc* ***(G-5869)***
**Brookline Shade Company, Chicago** *Also called Illinois Window Shade Co* ***(G-5159)***
**Brooks Allan, Lake Villa** *Also called Allan Brooks & Associates Inc* ***(G-13010)***
**Brookstone Resources Inc** ....618 382-2893
1615 Oak St Carmi (62821) ***(G-3062)***
**Bros Lithographing Company** ....312 666-0919
1326 W Washington Blvd Chicago (60607) ***(G-4176)***
**Brothers Decorating** ....815 648-2214
10305 Vanderkarr Rd Hebron (60034) ***(G-11715)***
**Brothers Leal LLC** ....708 385-4400
12007 S Cicero Ave Alsip (60803) ***(G-443)***
**Brown & Meyers Inc** ....618 524-3838
1400 W 10th St Metropolis (62960) ***(G-14752)***
**Brown & Miller Literary Assoc** ....312 922-3063
410 S Michigan Ave # 460 Chicago (60605) ***(G-4177)***
**Brown Line Metal Works LLC** ....312 884-7644
4001 N Ravenswood Ave 303a Chicago (60613) ***(G-4178)***
**Brown Metal Products Ltd** ....309 936-7384
513 N Spring Atkinson (61235) ***(G-943)***
**Brown Packing Company Inc (PA)** ....708 849-7990
1 Dutch Valley Dr South Holland (60473) ***(G-20253)***
**Brown Wood Products Company (PA)** ....847 673-4780
7040 N Lawndale Ave Lincolnwood (60712) ***(G-13503)***
**Brown Woodworking** ....815 477-8333
1804 Blue Island Dr Crystal Lake (60012) ***(G-7544)***
**Brownfield Sports Inc** ....217 367-8321
300 S Broadway Ave Urbana (61801) ***(G-21074)***
**Browns Global Exchange** ....708 345-0955
1928 S 21st Ave Maywood (60153) ***(G-14421)***
**Bruce Klapman Inc** ....847 657-8880
1955 Raymond Dr Ste 105 Northbrook (60062) ***(G-16215)***
**Bruce McCullough** ....217 773-3130
1161 980n Ave Mount Sterling (62353) ***(G-15390)***
**Brucher Machining Inc** ....630 876-1661
1030 Atlantic Dr West Chicago (60185) ***(G-21674)***
**Bruin Brake Cables, Fox Lake** *Also called Methods Distrs & Mfrs Inc* ***(G-10279)***
**Brumleve Canvas Products, Teutopolis** *Also called Brumleve Industries Inc* ***(G-20847)***
**Brumleve Industries Inc** ....217 857-3777
1317 W Main St Teutopolis (62467) ***(G-20847)***
**Brunet Snow Service Company** ....847 846-0037
174 Hawthorne Ave Wood Dale (60191) ***(G-22347)***
**Brunner & Lay Inc** ....847 678-3232
756 N Industrial Dr Elmhurst (60126) ***(G-9843)***
**Brunos Automotive Products** ....630 458-0043
14 W Industrial Rd Ste A Addison (60101) ***(G-62)***
**Brunswick Corporation (PA)** ....847 735-4700
1 N Field Ct Lake Forest (60045) ***(G-12888)***
**Brunswick Corporation** ....847 288-3300
10601 Belmont Ave Franklin Park (60131) ***(G-10418)***
**Brunswick Corporation** ....847 288-3300
10600 Belmont Ave Franklin Park (60131) ***(G-10419)***

ALPHABETIC

(PA)=Parent Co (HQ)=Headquarters (DH)=Div Headquarters
2017 Harris Illinois
Industrial Directory
1185

**Brunswick International Ltd (HQ)** ........ 847 735-4700
1 N Field Ct Lake Forest (60045) ***(G-12889)***
**Brunswick Zone River Grove, River Grove** *Also called Bowlmor AMF Corp* ***(G-18007)***
**Brush Creek Quarry, Mode** *Also called Iola Quarry Inc* ***(G-14849)***
**Brusic-Rose Inc** ........ 708 458-9900
7300 S Central Ave Bedford Park (60638) ***(G-1542)***
**Bruss Company** ........ 773 282-2900
3548 N Kostner Ave Chicago (60641) ***(G-4179)***
**Bryco Machine Inc** ........ 708 614-1900
8059 185th St Tinley Park (60487) ***(G-20901)***
**Brynolf Manufacturing Inc** ........ 815 873-8878
412 18th Ave Rockford (61104) ***(G-18291)***
**Bryton Technology Inc (PA)** ........ 309 995-3379
3134 State Route 78 Toulon (61483) ***(G-20976)***
**BSB International Corp** ........ 847 791-9272
225 James St Ste 4 Bensenville (60106) ***(G-1848)***
**BSC Imports Incorporated** ........ 773 844-4788
213 N Morgan St Unit 2c Chicago (60607) ***(G-4180)***
**BSI-Bath Solutions, Chicago** *Also called Bath Solutions Inc* ***(G-4055)***
**BSN Sports LLC** ........ 217 788-0914
510 E Apple Orchard Rd # 100 Springfield (62703) ***(G-20400)***
**Bssi, Lake Forest** *Also called Barriersafe Solutions Intl Inc* ***(G-12884)***
**BT & E Co** ........ 815 544-6431
6877 Belford Indus Dr Belvidere (61008) ***(G-1740)***
**BT Tech, Rushville** *Also called B T Technology Inc* ***(G-19090)***
**Btd Manufacturing Inc** ........ 309 444-1268
118 Muller Rd Washington (61571) ***(G-21379)***
**Btn, Chicago** *Also called Big Ten Network Services LLC* ***(G-4104)***
**BTR Controls Inc** ........ 847 608-9500
1570 Todd Farm Dr Elgin (60123) ***(G-8972)***
**Bubble Bubble Inc** ........ 815 455-2366
35 Berkshire Dr Ste 3 Crystal Lake (60014) ***(G-7545)***
**Bucher Hydraulics Inc** ........ 847 429-0700
2545 Northwest Pkwy Elgin (60124) ***(G-8973)***
**Bucket Mart Inc** ........ 813 390-8626
300 W Longstreet Rd Marion (62959) ***(G-14256)***
**Buckeye Terminals LLC** ........ 217 342-2336
18264 N Highway 45 Effingham (62401) ***(G-8828)***
**Buckley Powder Co** ........ 217 285-5531
1353 W Washington St Pittsfield (62363) ***(G-17562)***
**Buckner Sand Co (PA)** ........ 630 653-3700
290 S Main Pl Ste 101 Carol Stream (60188) ***(G-3120)***
**Bucktown Polymers** ........ 312 436-1460
1658 N Milwaukee Ave # 421 Chicago (60647) ***(G-4181)***
**Bucthel Metal Finishing Corp** ........ 847 427-8704
1945 Touhy Ave Elk Grove Village (60007) ***(G-9347)***
**Budapest Tool** ........ 630 250-0711
1300 Industrial Dr Ste A Itasca (60143) ***(G-12238)***
**Budd AA Inc** ........ 630 879-1740
1310 Turnberry Dr North Aurora (60542) ***(G-16121)***
**Budding Polishing & Met Finshg** ........ 708 396-1166
130 E 168th St South Holland (60473) ***(G-20254)***
**Budget Printing Center** ........ 618 655-1636
3709 Edwardsville Rd # 1 Edwardsville (62025) ***(G-8793)***
**Budget Sign** ........ 708 354-7512
930 S Kensington Ave La Grange (60525) ***(G-12728)***
**Budget Signs** ........ 618 259-4460
333 E Edwardsville Rd Wood River (62095) ***(G-22441)***
**Budget Signs Trophies Plaques, Wood River** *Also called Budget Signs* ***(G-22441)***
**Budmark Oil Company Inc** ........ 618 937-2495
106 E Oak St West Frankfort (62896) ***(G-21805)***
**Budnick Converting Inc** ........ 618 281-8090
200 Admiral Weinel Blvd Columbia (62236) ***(G-7353)***
**Buell Airhorns, Lyons** *Also called Buell Manufacturing Company* ***(G-14033)***
**Buell Manufacturing Company** ........ 708 447-6320
8125 47th St Lyons (60534) ***(G-14033)***
**Buff & Go Inc** ........ 773 719-4436
47 W Polk St Ste 100-558 Chicago (60605) ***(G-4182)***
**Buffalo Arms** ........ 630 969-1796
112 Tower Rd Downers Grove (60515) ***(G-8399)***
**Buh Hines Group LLC** ........ 847 336-1460
1547 Saint Paul Ave Gurnee (60031) ***(G-11432)***
**Buhl Press** ........ 708 449-8989
5656 Mcdermott Dr Berkeley (60163) ***(G-2044)***
**Buhlwork Design Guild** ........ 630 325-5340
320 Luthin Rd Oak Brook (60523) ***(G-16495)***
**Buhrke Industries LLC (HQ)** ........ 847 981-7550
511 W Algonquin Rd Arlington Heights (60005) ***(G-732)***
**Buhrke Industries LLC** ........ 847 981-7550
2500 Curtiss St Downers Grove (60515) ***(G-8400)***
**Builders Cabinet Supply, Chicago** *Also called Orchard Hill Cabinetry Inc* ***(G-6005)***
**Builders Chicago Corporation** ........ 224 654-2122
9820 W Foster Ave Rosemont (60018) ***(G-18991)***
**Builders Ironworks Inc** ........ 708 754-4092
3242 Louis Sherman Dr Steger (60475) ***(G-20569)***
**Builders Ironworks Inc** ........ 708 672-1047
399 Greenbriar Dr Crete (60417) ***(G-7509)***
**Builders Ready-Mix Co** ........ 847 866-6300
2525 Oakton St Evanston (60202) ***(G-10018)***
**Builders Supply Co, Galesburg** *Also called GBS Liquidating Corp* ***(G-10753)***
**Builders United Sales Co Inc** ........ 815 467-2224
713 Briarcliff Dr Minooka (60447) ***(G-14837)***
**Builders Warehouse Inc** ........ 309 672-1760
812 Sw Washington St Peoria (61602) ***(G-17320)***
**Buildex Electronics Inc** ........ 847 437-2299
1734 Elmhurst Rd Elk Grove Village (60007) ***(G-9348)***
**Building Products Corp (PA)** ........ 618 233-4427
950 Freeburg Ave Belleville (62220) ***(G-1615)***
**Bulaw Welding & Engineering Co** ........ 630 228-8300
750 N Rohlwing Rd Itasca (60143) ***(G-12239)***
**Bulk Lift International LLC** ........ 847 428-6059
1013 Tamarac Dr Carpentersville (60110) ***(G-3277)***
**Bulk Molding Compounds Inc (HQ)** ........ 630 377-1065
1600 Powis Ct West Chicago (60185) ***(G-21675)***
**Bulkley Dunton Publishing, Des Plaines** *Also called Veritiv Operating Company* ***(G-8298)***
**Bull Moose Tube Company** ........ 708 757-7700
555 E 16th St Chicago Heights (60411) ***(G-7084)***
**Bull Valley Hardwood (PA)** ........ 815 701-9400
18014 Collins Rd Woodstock (60098) ***(G-22548)***
**Bullards Bakery** ........ 618 842-6666
906 E Main St Fairfield (62837) ***(G-10137)***
**Bullen Midwest Inc (PA)** ........ 773 785-2300
900 E 103rd St Ste D Chicago (60628) ***(G-4183)***
**Bulletin** ........ 618 553-9764
103 W Main St Ste 4 Oblong (62449) ***(G-16729)***
**Bullseye Imprinting & EMB** ........ 630 834-8175
846 N York St Ste C Elmhurst (60126) ***(G-9844)***
**Bumper Scuffs** ........ 847 489-7926
37254 N Piper Ln Lake Villa (60046) ***(G-13011)***
**Bumper Works, Danville** *Also called Flex-N-Gate Corporation* ***(G-7720)***
**Bunge Milling Inc** ........ 217 442-1801
321 E North St Danville (61832) ***(G-7708)***
**Bunge North America Foundation** ........ 217 784-8261
Rts 9& 47 # 9 Gibson City (60936) ***(G-10898)***
**Bunge Oils Inc** ........ 815 523-8129
725 N Kinzie Ave Bradley (60915) ***(G-2414)***
**Bunge Oils Inc** ........ 815 939-3631
885 N Kinzie Ave Bradley (60915) ***(G-2415)***
**Bunker Hill Publication** ........ 618 585-4411
150 N Washington St Bunker Hill (62014) ***(G-2804)***
**Bunn-O-Matic Corporation** ........ 217 528-8739
825 S Airport Dr Springfield (62707) ***(G-20401)***
**Bunn-O-Matic Corporation** ........ 217 529-6601
1500 Stevenson Dr Springfield (62703) ***(G-20402)***
**Bunny Bread, Anna** *Also called Lewis Brothers Bakeries Inc* ***(G-607)***
**Bunzel, Morton Grove** *Also called Keenpac LLC* ***(G-15209)***
**Bunzl Retail LLC** ........ 847 733-1469
8338 Austin Ave Morton Grove (60053) ***(G-15190)***
**Burdeens Jewelry Ltd** ........ 847 459-8980
1151 W Lake Cook Rd Buffalo Grove (60089) ***(G-2671)***
**Burdett Burner Mfg Inc** ........ 630 617-5060
335 S Ardmore Ave Villa Park (60181) ***(G-21239)***
**Burdzy Tool & Die Co** ........ 847 671-6666
9355 Byron St Schiller Park (60176) ***(G-19810)***
**Bureau County Republican, Princeton** *Also called B F Shaw Printing Company* ***(G-17744)***
**Bureau of National Affairs** ........ 773 775-8801
6692 N Sioux Ave Chicago (60646) ***(G-4184)***
**Bureau Valley Chief** ........ 815 646-4731
108 W Main St Tiskilwa (61368) ***(G-20958)***
**Burgess Manufacturing Inc** ........ 847 680-1724
1911 Industrial Dr Libertyville (60048) ***(G-13311)***
**Burgess-Norton Mfg Co Inc (HQ)** ........ 630 232-4100
737 Peyton St Geneva (60134) ***(G-10813)***
**Burgess-Norton Mfg Co Inc** ........ 630 232-4100
500 Western Ave Geneva (60134) ***(G-10814)***
**Burghof Engineering & Mfg Co** ........ 847 634-0737
16051 W Deerfield Pkwy # 1 Lincolnshire (60069) ***(G-13433)***
**Burgopak Limited** ........ 312 255-0827
213 W Institute Pl # 301 Chicago (60610) ***(G-4185)***
**Burke R E Roofing & Shtmtl Co, Skokie** *Also called R E Burke Roofing Co Inc* ***(G-20068)***
**Burke Tool & Manufacturing Inc** ........ 618 542-6441
339 E Olive St Du Quoin (62832) ***(G-8551)***
**Burke Whistles Inc** ........ 618 534-7953
389 Wells St Murphysboro (62966) ***(G-15574)***
**Burke, Roger G Jewelers, Peoria** *Also called Roger Burke Jewelers Inc* ***(G-17445)***
**Burks Hardwood Lumber, Vernon** *Also called Burks Sawmill* ***(G-21139)***
**Burks Sawmill** ........ 618 432-5451
9411 Us Highway 51 Vernon (62892) ***(G-21139)***
**Burmac Manufacturing Inc** ........ 815 434-1660
4000 Burmac Rd Ottawa (61350) ***(G-16951)***
**Burnex Corporation** ........ 815 728-1317
5418 Business Pkwy Ringwood (60072) ***(G-17988)***
**Burning Leaf Cigars** ........ 815 267-3570
577 S 3rd St Ste 101 Geneva (60134) ***(G-10815)***
**Burns Machine Company** ........ 815 434-3131
4000 Burmac Rd Ottawa (61350) ***(G-16952)***
**Burns Machine Company (PA)** ........ 815 434-1660
4000 Burmac Rd Ottawa (61350) ***(G-16953)***

**Burr Ridge Lighting Inc**....630 323-4850
40 S Cass Ave Westmont (60559) *(G-21878)*
**Burrito Beach LLC**....312 861-1986
233 N Michigan Ave C023 Chicago (60601) *(G-4186)*
**Burry Foodservice, Saint Charles** *Also called Quality Bakeries LLC (G-19247)*
**Burstan Inc**....847 787-0380
2530 United Ln Elk Grove Village (60007) *(G-9349)*
**Burt Coyote Co**....309 358-1602
104 N Union St Yates City (61572) *(G-22646)*
**Busatis Inc**....630 844-9803
1755 Aucutt Rd Montgomery (60538) *(G-15034)*
**Bushnell Illinois Tank Co**....309 772-3106
650 W Davis St Bushnell (61422) *(G-2898)*
**Bushnell Locker Service**....309 772-2783
330 Green St Bushnell (61422) *(G-2899)*
**Bushnell Welding & Radiator**....309 772-9289
120 Charles St Bushnell (61422) *(G-2900)*
**Business Card Systems Inc**....815 877-0990
11025 Raleigh Ct Machesney Park (61115) *(G-14061)*
**Business Cards Tomorrow**....815 877-0990
11025 Raleigh Ct Machesney Park (61115) *(G-14062)*
**Business Express R & A Prtg, Chicago** *Also called Negs & Litho Inc (G-5881)*
**Business Forms Finishing Svc**....773 229-0230
5410 S Sayre Ave Chicago (60638) *(G-4187)*
**Business Graphics, Elmhurst** *Also called Stevens Group LLc (G-9945)*
**Business Identity Spc Inc**....847 669-1946
10418 Oxford Dr Huntley (60142) *(G-12134)*
**Business Insurance (PA)**....877 812-1587
150 N Michigan Ave # 1800 Chicago (60601) *(G-4188)*
**Business Magazine, Arcola** *Also called Rankin Publishing Inc (G-683)*
**Business Systems Consultants**....312 553-1253
333 N Michigan Ave # 912 Chicago (60601) *(G-4189)*
**Business Valuation Group Inc**....312 595-1900
400 N La Salle Dr # 3905 Chicago (60654) *(G-4190)*
**Businessmine LLC**....630 541-8480
784 Oak Creek Dr Lombard (60148) *(G-13774)*
**Buss Boyz Customs Inc**....815 369-2803
216 S Center St Lena (61048) *(G-13273)*
**Buster Services Inc**....773 247-2070
3301 W 47th Pl Chicago (60632) *(G-4191)*
**Buster Snow Inc**....847 673-4275
7356 N Kildare Ave Lincolnwood (60712) *(G-13504)*
**Busy Beaver Button Company**....773 645-3359
3407 W Armitage Ave Chicago (60647) *(G-4192)*
**Butcher Block Furn By Oneill**....312 666-9144
555 W 16th St Chicago (60616) *(G-4193)*
**Butera Finer Foods Inc**....708 456-5939
4411 N Cumberland Ave Norridge (60706) *(G-16097)*
**Butera Markets, Norridge** *Also called Butera Finer Foods Inc (G-16097)*
**Butler Bros Steel Rule Die Co**....815 630-4629
303 Amendodge Dr Shorewood (60404) *(G-19924)*
**Butterball LLC**....800 575-3365
2125 Rochester Rd Montgomery (60538) *(G-15035)*
**Butterfield Cleaners**....847 816-7060
1420 S Butterfield Rd Mundelein (60060) *(G-15480)*
**Butterfield Color Inc (PA)**....630 906-1980
625 W Illinois Ave Aurora (60506) *(G-1122)*
**Button Man Printing Inc**....630 549-0438
7 E Main St Saint Charles (60174) *(G-19146)*
**Buww Coverings Incorporated (PA)**....815 394-1985
4462 Boeing Dr Rockford (61109) *(G-18292)*
**Buyersvine Inc**....630 235-6804
641 S Bodin St Hinsdale (60521) *(G-11943)*
**Buzard Pipe Organ Builders LLC**....217 352-1955
112 W Hill St Champaign (61820) *(G-3459)*
**Buzard Pipe Organ Craftsmen, Champaign** *Also called Buzard Pipe Organ Builders LLC (G-3459)*
**Buzz Sales Company Inc**....815 459-1170
6110 Official Rd Crystal Lake (60014) *(G-7546)*
**Buzzfire Incorporated**....630 572-9200
2625 Bttrfeld Rd Ste 230s Oak Brook (60523) *(G-16496)*
**Buzzi Unicem USA Inc**....815 768-3660
450 Railroad St Joliet (60436) *(G-12468)*
**BV USA Enterprises**....224 619-7888
1680-1682 Carmen Dr Elk Grove Village (60007) *(G-9350)*
**Bvc Veneer, Lisle** *Also called R S Bacon Veneer Company (G-13648)*
**Bw Container Systems, Romeoville** *Also called Barry-Whmller Cont Systems Inc (G-18802)*
**Bw Dallas LLC**....847 441-1892
1 Northfield Plz Ste 521 Northfield (60093) *(G-16394)*
**Bw Exhibits**....847 697-9224
41 Prairie Pkwy Gilberts (60136) *(G-10914)*
**Bw Industries**....630 784-1020
27w230 Beecher Ave Ste 1 Winfield (60190) *(G-22283)*
**Bway Corporation**....847 956-0750
1350 Arthur Ave Elk Grove Village (60007) *(G-9351)*
**Bway Corporation**....773 254-8700
3200 S Kilbourn Ave Chicago (60623) *(G-4194)*
**Bway Parent Company Inc (HQ)**....773 890-3300
3200 S Kilbourn Ave Chicago (60623) *(G-4195)*
**Bwt LLC**....708 410-8000
75 E Lake St Northlake (60164) *(G-16432)*
**Bwt LLC**....630 210-4577
5136 27th Ave Rockford (61109) *(G-18293)*
**Bxb Intl Inc**....312 240-1966
9101 Sahler Ave Apt 1 Brookfield (60513) *(G-2626)*
**By Dozen Bakery Inc**....815 636-0668
8324 N 2nd St Machesney Park (61115) *(G-14063)*
**Bycap Inc**....773 561-4976
5505 N Wolcott Ave Chicago (60640) *(G-4196)*
**Byers Printing Company, Springfield** *Also called Springfield Printing Inc (G-20531)*
**Bypak Inc**....815 933-2870
195 N Euclid Ave Bradley (60915) *(G-2416)*
**Byrne & Schaefer Inc**....815 727-5000
1061 Caton Farm Rd Lockport (60441) *(G-13708)*
**Byron Blacktop Inc**....815 234-2225
3499 E Tower Rd Byron (61010) *(G-2913)*
**Byron Blacktop Inc (PA)**....815 234-8115
1291 Kysor Dr Byron (61010) *(G-2914)*
**Byron Ready Mix, Oregon** *Also called Rogers Ready Mix & Mtls Inc (G-16831)*
**Bystronic Inc (HQ)**....847 214-0300
200 Airport Rd Elgin (60123) *(G-8974)*
**Bytebin LLC**....312 286-0740
516 N Ogden Ave 55 Chicago (60642) *(G-4197)*
**Byttow Enterprises Inc**....708 754-4995
3205 Loverock Ave Steger (60475) *(G-20570)*
**Byus Steel Inc**....630 879-2200
1750 Hubbard Ave Batavia (60510) *(G-1425)*
**Bz Bearing & Power Inc (PA)**....877 850-3993
8731 Orchard Dr Hickory Hills (60457) *(G-11767)*
**C & B Services**....847 462-8484
6305 Lake Shore Dr Cary (60013) *(G-3329)*
**C & B Welders Inc**....773 722-0097
2645 W Monroe St Chicago (60612) *(G-4198)*
**C & C Bakery Inc**....773 276-4233
2655 W Huron St Chicago (60612) *(G-4199)*
**C & C Can Co Inc**....312 421-2372
1838 W Grand Ave Chicago (60622) *(G-4200)*
**C & C Electronics Inc**....847 550-0177
25719 N Hillview Ct Mundelein (60060) *(G-15481)*
**C & C Embroidery Inc**....815 777-6167
800 Spring St Ste 201 Galena (61036) *(G-10715)*
**C & C Printing Controls Inc**....630 810-0484
5015 Chase Ave Downers Grove (60515) *(G-8401)*
**C & C Publications**....815 723-0325
254 E Cass St Joliet (60432) *(G-12469)*
**C & C Sport Stop**....618 632-7812
115 N Lincoln Ave O Fallon (62269) *(G-16464)*
**C & C Tooling Inc (PA)**....630 543-5523
344 W Interstate Rd Addison (60101) *(G-63)*
**C & D Machining Inc**....815 778-4946
207 E Commercial St Lyndon (61261) *(G-14013)*
**C & D Rebuilders**....618 273-9862
1219 Us Highway 45 N Eldorado (62930) *(G-8918)*
**C & E Specialties Inc**....815 229-9230
2530 Laude Dr Rockford (61109) *(G-18294)*
**C & F Forge Company (PA)**....847 455-6609
9100 Parklane Ave Franklin Park (60131) *(G-10420)*
**C & F Machine Corp**....630 924-0300
176 Covington Dr Bloomingdale (60108) *(G-2098)*
**C & F Packing Co Inc**....847 245-2000
515 Park Ave Lake Villa (60046) *(G-13012)*
**C & H Gravel C Inc**....217 857-3425
14046 N 1600th St Teutopolis (62467) *(G-20848)*
**C & J Industries**....708 757-4495
21850 Sunset Ln Sauk Village (60411) *(G-19391)*
**C & J Metal Products Inc**....847 455-0766
11119 Franklin Ave Franklin Park (60131) *(G-10421)*
**C & K Custom Signs, Decatur** *Also called Cachera and Klemm Inc (G-7849)*
**C & L Manufacturing Entps**....618 465-7623
2109 Holland St Alton (62002) *(G-565)*
**C & L Printing Company**....312 235-0380
228 S Wabash Ave Ste 260 Chicago (60604) *(G-4201)*
**C & L Supreme Mfg Co, Des Plaines** *Also called Supreme Manufacturing Company (G-8283)*
**C & L Tiling Inc (PA)**....217 773-3357
196 Us24 1075n Ave Timewell (62375) *(G-20884)*
**C & L Tiling Inc**....217 773-3357
196 Us24 1075n Ave Timewell (62375) *(G-20885)*
**C & M Engineering**....815 932-3388
110 Mooney Dr Ste 8 Bourbonnais (60914) *(G-2391)*
**C & M Recycling Inc**....847 578-1066
1600 Morrow Ave North Chicago (60064) *(G-16176)*
**C & R Industries, Joliet** *Also called C & S Chemicals Inc (G-12470)*
**C & R Scrap Metal, Chicago** *Also called Archer Metal & Paper Co (G-3939)*
**C & S Chemicals Inc**....815 722-6671
1306 Mckinley St Joliet (60436) *(G-12470)*
**C & S Fabrication Services Inc**....815 363-8510
5390 Fieldstone Way Johnsburg (60051) *(G-12431)*
**C & S Steel Rule Die Co Inc**....773 254-4027
4305 S Homan Ave Chicago (60632) *(G-4202)*

ALPHABETIC

**C & V Granite Inc** ....847 966-0275
9120 Cherry Ave Morton Grove (60053) ***(G-15191)***
**C A C, Carol Stream** *Also called Cac Corporation* ***(G-3122)***
**C A Larson & Son Inc** ....847 717-6010
5n200 Wooley Rd Maple Park (60151) ***(G-14199)***
**C A S C O, Pittsfield** *Also called Complete Asphalt Service Co* ***(G-17567)***
**C and C Machine Tool Service** ....630 810-0484
5015 Chase Ave Downers Grove (60515) ***(G-8402)***
**C and H Gravel, Teutopolis** *Also called C & H Gravel C Inc* ***(G-20848)***
**C and H Publishing Co (PA)** ....618 625-2711
114 E Franklin St Sesser (62884) ***(G-19894)***
**C B & A Inc** ....815 561-0255
1040 S Main St Rochelle (61068) ***(G-18080)***
**C B E Inc** ....630 571-2610
110 Oak Brook Rd Oak Brook (60523) ***(G-16497)***
**C B Ferrari Incorporated** ....847 756-4100
22179 N Pepper Rd Lake Barrington (60010) ***(G-12801)***
**C B M Plastics Inc** ....217 543-3870
398 E St Rt 133 Arthur (61911) ***(G-883)***
**C Becky & Company Inc** ....847 818-1021
708 S Na Wa Ta Ave Mount Prospect (60056) ***(G-15314)***
**C C I, Sugar Grove** *Also called Finishes Unlimited Inc* ***(G-20724)***
**C C P Express Inc** ....773 315-0317
2630 Highland Ave Berwyn (60402) ***(G-2058)***
**C C T, Volo** *Also called Composite Cutter Tech Inc* ***(G-21311)***
**C CN Chicago Corp** ....847 671-3319
421 S Irmen Dr Ste B Addison (60101) ***(G-64)***
**C Cretors & Co (PA)** ....847 616-6900
176 Mittel Dr Wood Dale (60191) ***(G-22348)***
**C D Nelson Consulting Inc** ....847 487-4870
27421 N Darrell Rd Wauconda (60084) ***(G-21449)***
**C D S Office Technologies, Springfield** *Also called CDs Office Systems Inc* ***(G-20411)***
**C D T Manufacturing Inc** ....847 679-2361
8020 Monticello Ave Skokie (60076) ***(G-19972)***
**C D Tools Machining Inc** ....773 859-2028
33 W Fullerton Ave Addison (60101) ***(G-65)***
**C E Dienberg Printing Company** ....708 848-4406
114 Madison St Lowr 1 Oak Park (60302) ***(G-16655)***
**C E R Machining & Tooling Ltd** ....708 442-9614
8214 47th St Lyons (60534) ***(G-14034)***
**C F Anderson & Co** ....312 341-0850
701 S Lasalle St Fl 2 Chicago (60605) ***(G-4203)***
**C F C Interantional** ....708 753-0679
385 E Joe Orr Rd Chicago Heights (60411) ***(G-7085)***
**C F I, Bensenville** *Also called Complete Flashings Inc* ***(G-1864)***
**C H Hanson Company (PA)** ....630 848-2000
2000 N Aurora Rd Naperville (60563) ***(G-15613)***
**C H Hanson Company** ....630 848-2000
2000 N Aurora Rd Naperville (60563) ***(G-15614)***
**C H I Overhead Doors Inc** ....217 543-2135
1485 Sunrise Dr Arthur (61911) ***(G-884)***
**C H Millery LLC** ....773 476-7525
6430 S Ashland Ave Chicago (60636) ***(G-4204)***
**C Hofbauer Inc** ....630 920-1222
11433 Ridgewood Ln Burr Ridge (60527) ***(G-2826)***
**C I C, Mossville** *Also called Central Illinois Counter Tops* ***(G-15252)***
**C I F Industries Inc** ....618 635-2010
20988 Old Route 66 Staunton (62088) ***(G-20555)***
**C J Holdings Inc** ....309 274-3141
110 W Walnut St Chillicothe (61523) ***(G-7163)***
**C J T, Carol Stream** *Also called Cjt Koolcarb Inc* ***(G-3129)***
**C Johnson Sign Co, Franklin Park** *Also called Johnson Sign Co* ***(G-10509)***
**C K North America Inc** ....815 524-4246
1243 Naperville Dr Romeoville (60446) ***(G-18804)***
**C Keller Manufacturing Inc** ....630 833-5593
925 N Ellsworth Ave Villa Park (60181) ***(G-21240)***
**C L Graphics Inc** ....815 455-0900
134 Virginia Rd Ste A Crystal Lake (60014) ***(G-7547)***
**C L Greenslade Sales Inc (PA)** ....847 593-3450
505 E Golf Rd Ste H Arlington Heights (60005) ***(G-733)***
**C L I Laboratories, Des Plaines** *Also called Colormetric Laboratories Inc* ***(G-8172)***
**C L Vault & Safe Srv** ....708 237-0039
6754 W 89th Pl Oak Lawn (60453) ***(G-16607)***
**C Line Products Inc (PA)** ....847 827-6661
1100 E Business Center Dr Mount Prospect (60056) ***(G-15315)***
**C M C, Joliet** *Also called CMC America Corporation* ***(G-12475)***
**C M C Industries Inc** ....630 377-0530
2525 Production Dr Saint Charles (60174) ***(G-19147)***
**C M F Enterprises Inc** ....847 526-9499
950 N Rand Rd Ste 113 Wauconda (60084) ***(G-21450)***
**C M Holding Co Inc** ....847 438-2171
800 Ela Rd Lake Zurich (60047) ***(G-13048)***
**C M I Novacast Inc** ....847 699-9020
500 E Touhy Ave Ste B Des Plaines (60018) ***(G-8161)***
**C M Industries Inc** ....847 550-0033
505 Oakwood Rd Ste 120 Lake Zurich (60047) ***(G-13049)***
**C M J Associates Inc** ....708 636-2995
10745 S Kolmar Ave Oak Lawn (60453) ***(G-16608)***
**C M Products, Lake Zurich** *Also called R and R Brokerage Co* ***(G-13121)***
**C M S Publishing Inc** ....708 839-9201
8695 Archer Ave Ste 10 Willow Springs (60480) ***(G-22193)***
**C M Sell Woodwork** ....847 526-3627
28116 W Maple Ave Wauconda (60084) ***(G-21451)***
**C N C Central Inc** ....630 595-1453
177 Il Route 83 Bensenville (60106) ***(G-1849)***
**C N C HI-Tech Inc** ....847 201-8151
26575 W Commerce Dr # 611 Volo (60073) ***(G-21309)***
**C N F, Saint Charles** *Also called Strathmore Press* ***(G-19273)***
**C N Tool, Elk Grove Village** *Also called Source United LLC* ***(G-9745)***
**C P, Lake Forest** *Also called Colbert Packaging Corporation* ***(G-12892)***
**C P Contractor** ....630 235-2381
6340 Fremont Dr Hanover Park (60133) ***(G-11577)***
**C P Environmental Inc** ....630 759-8866
1336 Enterprise Dr Ste 2 Romeoville (60446) ***(G-18805)***
**C P O Inc** ....630 898-7733
1500 Dearborn Ave Ofc Aurora (60505) ***(G-1123)***
**C R Kesner Company** ....630 232-8118
2520 Kaneville Ct Geneva (60134) ***(G-10816)***
**C R L, Highland Park** *Also called Laurel Industries Inc* ***(G-11851)***
**C R Plastics Inc** ....847 541-3601
851 Seton Ct Ste 1c Wheeling (60090) ***(G-22021)***
**C R V Electronics Corp** ....815 675-6500
2249 Pierce Dr Spring Grove (60081) ***(G-20329)***
**C Rockelmann Co, Saint Charles** *Also called American Church Supply* ***(G-19134)***
**C S C Inc** ....217 925-5908
100 Zumbahlen Ave Ste C Dieterich (62424) ***(G-8312)***
**C S I, Downers Grove** *Also called Compusystems Inc* ***(G-8416)***
**C S I, Raleigh** *Also called Centrifugal Services Inc* ***(G-17908)***
**C S O Corp (PA)** ....630 365-6600
10 N Sauber Rd Virgil (60151) ***(G-21302)***
**C Streeter Enterprise** ....773 858-4388
28 E Jackson Blvd Fl 10 Chicago (60604) ***(G-4205)***
**C Tri Co** ....309 467-4715
1035 W Center St Eureka (61530) ***(G-9994)***
**C U Plastic LLC** ....888 957-9993
100 4th Ave Rochelle (61068) ***(G-18081)***
**C U Services LLC** ....847 439-2303
725 Parkview Cir Elk Grove Village (60007) ***(G-9352)***
**C W Publications Inc** ....800 554-5537
1705 37th Ave Sterling (61081) ***(G-20586)***
**C&C Sealants** ....708 717-0686
576 Covered Bridge Dr Elgin (60124) ***(G-8975)***
**C&R Directional Boring** ....630 458-0055
880 S Fiene Dr Addison (60101) ***(G-66)***
**C&R Scrap Iron & Metal** ....847 459-9815
251 E Dundee Rd Wheeling (60090) ***(G-22022)***
**C&S Services, Johnsburg** *Also called C & S Fabrication Services Inc* ***(G-12431)***
**C-E Minerals Inc** ....618 285-6558
Ferrell Rd Rosiclare (62982) ***(G-19047)***
**C-G Custom Graphics, Bloomington** *Also called Custom Graphics* ***(G-2158)***
**C-Storm Electronic LLC** ....630 406-1353
441 Horizon Dr W Saint Charles (60175) ***(G-19148)***
**C-Tech Systems Division, Elk Grove Village** *Also called Medalist Industries Inc* ***(G-9617)***
**C-V Cstom Cntrtops Cbinets Inc** ....708 388-5066
12525 Irving Ave Blue Island (60406) ***(G-2241)***
**C. R. I., Chicago** *Also called Channeled Resources Inc* ***(G-4287)***
**C.E. Printed Products, Carol Stream** *Also called Chicago Envelope Inc* ***(G-3127)***
**C/B Machine Tool Corp** ....847 288-1807
9321 Schiller Blvd Franklin Park (60131) ***(G-10422)***
**C2 Imaging LLC** ....847 439-7834
1200 Chase Ave Elk Grove Village (60007) ***(G-9353)***
**C2 Imaging LLC** ....312 238-3800
600 W Van Buren St # 604 Chicago (60607) ***(G-4206)***
**C2 Premium Paint** ....847 251-6906
101 Green Bay Rd Wilmette (60091) ***(G-22248)***
**C2 Publishing Inc** ....630 834-4994
5101 Darmstadt Rd Hillside (60162) ***(G-11912)***
**C2 Water Inc** ....312 550-1159
732 Cummings Ave Kenilworth (60043) ***(G-12662)***
**Ca Inc** ....312 201-8557
123 N Wacker Dr Ste 2125 Chicago (60606) ***(G-4207)***
**Ca Inc** ....631 342-6000
3333 Warrenville Rd # 800 Lisle (60532) ***(G-13572)***
**CA Custom Woodworking** ....630 201-6154
254 Main St Oswego (60543) ***(G-16906)***
**Cab Communications Inc** ....847 963-8740
50 N Brockway St Ste 4-11 Palatine (60067) ***(G-17007)***
**Cabanas Manufacturing Jewelers** ....312 726-0333
9 N Wabash Ave Ste 555 Chicago (60602) ***(G-4208)***
**Cabcraft, Carpentersville** *Also called Donald Kranz* ***(G-3283)***
**Cabinet Broker Ltd** ....847 352-1898
1061 Rohlwing Rd Elk Grove Village (60007) ***(G-9354)***
**Cabinet Designs** ....708 614-8603
15537 New England Ave Oak Forest (60452) ***(G-16575)***
**Cabinet Factories Outlet, Arthur** *Also called Masterbrand Cabinets Inc* ***(G-910)***

**Cabinet Gallery LLC** .....618 882-4801
205 Madison St Highland (62249) ***(G-11776)***
**Cabinets & Granite Direct LLC** .....630 588-8886
1175 N Gary Ave Carol Stream (60188) ***(G-3121)***
**Cabinets By Custom Craft Inc** .....815 637-4001
5261 Swanson Rd Roscoe (61073) ***(G-18891)***
**Cabinets Doors and More LLC** .....847 395-6334
25819 W Grass Lake Rd Antioch (60002) ***(G-627)***
**Cabinetwerks, Northfield** *Also called Orren Pickell Builders Inc* ***(G-16415)***
**Cable Company (PA)** .....847 437-5267
498 Bonnie Ln Elk Grove Village (60007) ***(G-9355)***
**Cable Electric Company Inc** .....708 458-8900
7640 Archer Rd Oak Lawn (60458) ***(G-16609)***
**Cable Management Products Inc** .....630 723-0470
1005 N Commons Dr Aurora (60504) ***(G-976)***
**Cablofil Inc** .....618 566-3230
8319 State Route 4 Mascoutah (62258) ***(G-14350)***
**Cablofil/Legrand, Mascoutah** *Also called Cablofil Inc* ***(G-14350)***
**Cabot Corporation** .....217 253-3370
700 E Us Highway 36 Tuscola (61953) ***(G-21017)***
**Cabot Corporation** .....217 253-5752
700 E Us Highway 36 Tuscola (61953) ***(G-21018)***
**Cabot McRlectronics Polsg Corp** .....630 543-6682
39 W Official Rd Addison (60101) ***(G-67)***
**Cabot Microelectronics Corp (PA)** .....630 375-6631
870 N Commons Dr Aurora (60504) ***(G-977)***
**Cabot Microelectronics Corp** .....630 375-6631
845 Enterprise St Aurora (60504) ***(G-978)***
**Cabot Microelectronics Corp** .....630 375-6631
500 N Commons Dr Aurora (60504) ***(G-979)***
**Cabworks LLC** .....773 588-1731
2701 N Pulaski Rd Chicago (60639) ***(G-4209)***
**Cac Corporation (PA)** .....630 221-5200
307 E Lies Rd Carol Stream (60188) ***(G-3122)***
**Cachera and Klemm Inc** .....217 876-7446
2271 E Hubbard Ave Decatur (62526) ***(G-7849)***
**Cacini Inc** .....847 884-1162
711 E Golf Rd Schaumburg (60173) ***(G-19467)***
**Cacique USA** .....630 766-0059
1371 N Wood Dale Rd Wood Dale (60191) ***(G-22349)***
**Cadaco Division, Chicago** *Also called Rapid Displays Inc* ***(G-6291)***
**Cadbury, Loves Park** *Also called Mondelez Global LLC* ***(G-13968)***
**Caddy, Wheeling** *Also called EJ Cady & Company* ***(G-22045)***
**Cade Communications Inc** .....773 477-7184
3018 N Sheridan Rd Apt 2s Chicago (60657) ***(G-4210)***
**Cadicam Inc** .....847 394-3610
2200 Foster Ave Wheeling (60090) ***(G-22023)***
**Cadillac Products, Broadview** *Also called Clements National Company* ***(G-2569)***
**Cadillac Products Packaging Co** .....217 463-1444
2005 S Main St Paris (61944) ***(G-17142)***
**Cadillac Tank Met Fbrctors Inc** .....630 543-2600
225 W Gerri Ln Addison (60101) ***(G-68)***
**Cadore-Miller Printing Inc** .....708 430-7091
9901 S 78th Ave Hickory Hills (60457) ***(G-11768)***
**Caduceus Communications Inc** .....773 549-4800
4043 N Ravenswood Ave # 309 Chicago (60613) ***(G-4211)***
**Cafetine Panio** .....773 697-8007
2706 W Division St Chicago (60622) ***(G-4212)***
**Caffero Tool & Mfg** .....224 293-2600
1537 Brandy Pkwy Streamwood (60107) ***(G-20647)***
**Caibros Americas LLC** .....312 593-3128
116 Deere Park Ct Highland Park (60035) ***(G-11826)***
**Caid Tronics, Naperville** *Also called Hemmerle Jr Irvin* ***(G-15670)***
**Cain Millwork Inc** .....815 561-9700
1 Cain Pkwy Rochelle (61068) ***(G-18082)***
**Cain Tubular Products Inc** .....630 584-5330
310 Kirk Rd Saint Charles (60174) ***(G-19149)***
**Cairo Diagnostic Center** .....618 734-1500
13289 Kessler Rd Cairo (62914) ***(G-2927)***
**Cairo Dry Kilns Inc** .....618 734-1039
14372 State Highway 37 Cairo (62914) ***(G-2928)***
**Cais, Elmhurst** *Also called CU Info Systems* ***(G-9861)***
**Caisson Inc (PA)** .....815 547-5925
720 Logistics Dr Belvidere (61008) ***(G-1741)***
**Caisson Industries Inc (PA)** .....815 568-6554
20020 E Grant Hwy Marengo (60152) ***(G-14221)***
**Cal-Ill Gasket Co** .....773 287-9605
4716 W Rice St Chicago (60651) ***(G-4213)***
**Cal-Tronics Systems Inc** .....630 350-0044
729 Creel Dr Wood Dale (60191) ***(G-22350)***
**Calco, Richmond** *Also called 815 Pallets Inc* ***(G-17954)***
**Calco Controls Inc** .....847 639-3858
439 S Dartmoor Dr Crystal Lake (60014) ***(G-7548)***
**Calco Cutaways, Crystal Lake** *Also called Calco Controls Inc* ***(G-7548)***
**Calco Ltd** .....630 539-1800
960 Muirfield Dr Bartlett (60133) ***(G-1316)***
**Calcon Machine Inc** .....815 495-9227
210 E Lincoln Ave Leland (60531) ***(G-13219)***
**Caldwell Letter Service Inc** .....773 847-0708
4500 S Kolin Ave Ste 1 Chicago (60632) ***(G-4214)***
**Caldwell Plumbing Co** .....630 588-8900
821 Childs St Wheaton (60187) ***(G-21938)***
**Caldwell Woodworks** .....217 566-2434
501 S Old Route 66 Williamsville (62693) ***(G-22190)***
**Calgon Carbon Corporation** .....815 741-5452
303 Mound Rd Ste A1 Rockdale (60436) ***(G-18215)***
**Calhoun Quarry Incorporated (PA)** .....618 396-2229
25 Main St Batchtown (62006) ***(G-1517)***
**Calhoun Quarry Incorporated** .....618 576-9223
Eldred Rd Hardin (62047) ***(G-11593)***
**California Muffler and Brakes** .....773 776-8990
5059 S California Ave Chicago (60632) ***(G-4215)***
**California Pure Delite Juice &, Chicago** *Also called Florida Fruit Juices Inc* ***(G-4863)***
**Calihan Pork Processors Inc** .....309 674-9175
1 South St Peoria (61602) ***(G-17321)***
**Call Potential LLC** .....877 552-2557
24047 W Lockport St Naperville (60540) ***(G-15615)***
**Callahan Industries, Lombard** *Also called Frank R Walker Company* ***(G-13802)***
**Callahan Mining Corporation** .....312 489-5800
104 S Michigan Ave # 900 Chicago (60603) ***(G-4216)***
**Callender Construction Co Inc (PA)** .....217 285-2161
928 W Washington St Pittsfield (62363) ***(G-17563)***
**Callies Cuties Inc** .....815 566-6885
24860 Madison St Plainfield (60544) ***(G-17583)***
**Callison Distributing LLC** .....618 277-4300
4 Premier Dr Belleville (62220) ***(G-1616)***
**Callpod Inc** .....312 829-2680
850 W Jackson Blvd # 400 Chicago (60607) ***(G-4217)***
**Calma Optima Foods** .....847 962-8329
10915 Franklin Ave Ste A Franklin Park (60131) ***(G-10423)***
**Calmer Corn Heads Inc** .....309 629-9000
3056 N 700th Ave Lynn Center (61262) ***(G-14015)***
**Calo Corporation** .....630 879-2202
197 Alder Dr North Aurora (60542) ***(G-16122)***
**Calport Aviation Company** .....630 588-8091
4n220 84 Ct Bartlett (60133) ***(G-1317)***
**Calser Corp** .....618 277-0329
302 N Belt E Swansea (62226) ***(G-20775)***
**Calumet Armature and Elc LLC** .....708 841-6880
1050 W 134th St Riverdale (60827) ***(G-18017)***
**Calumet Brass Foundry Inc** .....708 849-3040
14610 Lakeside Ave Dolton (60419) ***(G-8367)***
**Calumet Container Corp** .....773 646-3653
12440 S Stony Island Ave Chicago (60633) ***(G-4218)***
**Calumet Lubr Co Ltd Partnr** .....708 832-2463
14000 S Mackinaw Ave Burnham (60633) ***(G-2815)***
**Calumet Motorsports Inc** .....708 895-0398
3441 Washington St Lansing (60438) ***(G-13158)***
**Calumet Rubber Corp** .....773 536-6350
3545 S Normal Ave Ste A Chicago (60609) ***(G-4219)***
**Calumet Screw Machine Products** .....708 479-1660
19600 97th Ave Mokena (60448) ***(G-14856)***
**Calutech Inc** .....708 614-0228
15646 S 70th Ct 1 Orland Park (60462) ***(G-16845)***
**Calvert Systems** .....309 523-3262
21114 94th Ave N Port Byron (61275) ***(G-17719)***
**Calx Trading Corporation** .....630 456-6721
1245 Amaranth Dr Naperville (60564) ***(G-15800)***
**CAM Co Inc** .....630 556-3110
400 Rhodes Ave Big Rock (60511) ***(G-2086)***
**CAM Systems** .....800 208-3244
20 N Wacker Dr Ste 4015 Chicago (60606) ***(G-4220)***
**CAM Tek Lubricants Inc** .....708 477-3000
9540 W 144th Pl Ste 2a Orland Park (60462) ***(G-16846)***
**Cambrdg Printing Corp** .....630 510-2100
780 W Army Trail Rd Carol Stream (60188) ***(G-3123)***
**Cambridge Brands Mfg Inc (HQ)** .....773 838-3400
7401 S Cicero Ave Chicago (60629) ***(G-4221)***
**Cambridge Business** .....800 619-6473
777 Oakmont Ln Ste 1800 Westmont (60559) ***(G-21879)***
**Cambridge Chronicle** .....309 937-3303
119 W Exchange St Cambridge (61238) ***(G-2965)***
**Cambridge Monument Co, Rock Island** *Also called Beutel Corporation* ***(G-18164)***
**Cambridge Pattern Works** .....309 937-5370
105 E Railroad St Cambridge (61238) ***(G-2966)***
**Cambridge Sensor Limited, Plainfield** *Also called Cambridge Sensors USA LLC* ***(G-17584)***
**Cambridge Sensors USA LLC** .....877 374-4062
23866 W Industrial Dr N Plainfield (60585) ***(G-17584)***
**Cambridge-Lee Industries LLC** .....708 388-0121
12255 S Laramie Ave Alsip (60803) ***(G-444)***
**Camcar, Belvidere** *Also called Acument Global Techologies* ***(G-1727)***
**Camcar LLC** .....815 544-7574
826 E Madison St Belvidere (61008) ***(G-1742)***
**Camco Manufacturing, Crestwood** *Also called Camshop Industrial LLC* ***(G-7479)***
**Camco Manufacturing Inc** .....708 597-4288
13933 Kildare Ave Crestwood (60445) ***(G-7478)***
**Camco Screw Machine Products, Crestwood** *Also called Camco Manufacturing Inc* ***(G-7478)***

ALPHABETIC

**Camcraft Inc (PA)**...................................................630 582-6001
  1080 Muirfield Dr  Hanover Park  (60133)  *(G-11578)*
**Camel Grinding Wheels, Niles** *Also called Abrasic 90 Inc (G-15955)*
**Cameo Container Corporation**..............................773 254-1030
  1415 W 44th St  Chicago  (60609)  *(G-4222)*
**Cameo Mold & Duplicating, West Chicago** *Also called Cameo Mold Corp (G-21676)*
**Cameo Mold Corp**....................................................630 876-1340
  1125 Carolina Dr  West Chicago  (60185)  *(G-21676)*
**Camera Ready Copies Inc**......................................847 215-8611
  740 Pinecrest Dr  Prospect Heights  (60070)  *(G-17773)*
**Cameron Electric Motor Corp**...............................312 939-5770
  551 W Lexington St  Chicago  (60607)  *(G-4223)*
**Cameron Printing Inc**.............................................630 231-3301
  1275 W Roosevelt Rd # 119  West Chicago  (60185)  *(G-21677)*
**Camet, Schiller Park** *Also called Chicago Powdered Metal Pdts Co (G-19813)*
**Camfil USA Inc**.......................................................815 459-6600
  500 S Main St  Crystal Lake  (60014)  *(G-7549)*
**Camilles of Canton Inc**..........................................309 647-7403
  1400 S Avenue B  Canton  (61520)  *(G-2983)*
**Cammun LLC**...........................................................312 628-1201
  345 N Canal St Apt 1408  Chicago  (60606)  *(G-4224)*
**Camo Clad Inc**........................................................618 342-6860
  471 Camo Clad Dr  Mounds  (62964)  *(G-15258)*
**Campbell Cab, Wauconda** *Also called Campbell International Inc (G-21452)*
**Campbell Camie Inc**...............................................314 968-3222
  2651 Warrenville Rd # 300  Downers Grove  (60515)  *(G-8403)*
**Campbell Energy LLC**............................................618 382-3939
  1238 County Road 1500 N  Carmi  (62821)  *(G-3063)*
**Campbell International Inc**...................................408 661-0794
  120 Kent Ave  Wauconda  (60084)  *(G-21452)*
**Campbell Management Services**..........................847 566-9020
  1500 S Lake St Ste A  Mundelein  (60060)  *(G-15482)*
**Campbell Publishing Co Inc**..................................618 498-1234
  832 S State St  Jerseyville  (62052)  *(G-12419)*
**Campbell Publishing Co Inc**..................................217 285-2345
  115 W Jefferson St  Pittsfield  (62363)  *(G-17564)*
**Campbell Publishing Inc (PA)**...............................217 742-3313
  4 S Hill St  Winchester  (62694)  *(G-22278)*
**Campbell Science Corp**.........................................815 962-7415
  641 S Main St  Rockford  (61101)  *(G-18295)*
**Campeche Restaurant & Bar, Galena** *Also called Campeche Restaurant Inc (G-10716)*
**Campeche Restaurant Inc**.....................................815 776-9950
  230 N Commerce St  Galena  (61036)  *(G-10716)*
**Campus Cardboard**...............................................847 373-7673
  600 Waukegan Rd  Northbrook  (60062)  *(G-16216)*
**Campus Sportswear Incorporated**........................217 344-0944
  710 S 6th St Ste B  Champaign  (61820)  *(G-3460)*
**Camryn Industries LLC**.........................................815 544-1900
  3458 Morreim Dr  Belvidere  (61008)  *(G-1743)*
**Cams Inc**.................................................................773 929-3656
  1960 N Lincoln Park W # 2207  Chicago  (60614)  *(G-4225)*
**Camshop Industrial LLC**........................................708 597-4288
  13933 Kildare Ave  Crestwood  (60445)  *(G-7479)*
**Camtek Inc**.............................................................309 661-0348
  2402 E Empire St  Bloomington  (61799)  *(G-2151)*
**Canada Organization & Dev LLC (HQ)**.................630 743-2563
  3005 Highland Pkwy  Downers Grove  (60515)  *(G-8404)*
**Canadian Harvest LP**............................................309 343-7808
  701 W 6th St  Galesburg  (61401)  *(G-10740)*
**Canam Steel Corporation**......................................815 224-9588
  9 Unytite Dr  Peru  (61354)  *(G-17502)*
**Canconex Inc**..........................................................847 458-9955
  901 Armstrong St  Algonquin  (60102)  *(G-382)*
**Candle Enterprises Inc**..........................................618 526-8070
  580 N 2nd St  Breese  (62230)  *(G-2441)*
**Candle-Licious**.......................................................847 488-9982
  634 E Lincolnway  Morrison  (61270)  *(G-15142)*
**Candoc, Chicago** *Also called Cudner & OConnor Co (G-4514)*
**Candy Controls, Niles** *Also called Candy Mfg Co Inc (G-15966)*
**Candy Mfg Co Inc**..................................................847 588-2639
  5633 W Howard St  Niles  (60714)  *(G-15966)*
**Candy Tech LLC**.....................................................847 229-1011
  309 S Northwest Hwy # 2  Park Ridge  (60068)  *(G-17186)*
**Candyality (PA)**......................................................773 472-7800
  3737 N Southport Ave # 1  Chicago  (60613)  *(G-4226)*
**Cane Plus**...............................................................217 522-4035
  2225 S Whittier Ave  Springfield  (62704)  *(G-20403)*
**Canham Graphics**..................................................217 585-5085
  4524 Industrial Ave  Springfield  (62703)  *(G-20404)*
**Cannon Ball Marketing Inc**....................................630 971-2127
  701 59th St  Lisle  (60532)  *(G-13573)*
**Canny Innovative Solutions Inc**............................847 323-1271
  888 E Belvidere Rd # 208  Grayslake  (60030)  *(G-11323)*
**Canny Tool & Mold Corporation**............................847 548-1573
  888 E Belvidere Rd # 207  Grayslake  (60030)  *(G-11324)*
**Cano Container Corporation (PA)**.........................630 585-7500
  3920 Enterprise Ct  Aurora  (60504)  *(G-980)*
**Canon Solutions America Inc**................................630 351-1227
  1800 Bruning Dr W  Itasca  (60143)  *(G-12240)*

**Cantarero Pallets Inc**.............................................773 413-7017
  1900 N Austin Ave  Chicago  (60639)  *(G-4227)*
**Canton Noodle Company, Chicago** *Also called YMC Corp (G-7052)*
**Canton Redi-Mix Inc**..............................................309 668-2261
  22381 N State Highway 78  Canton  (61520)  *(G-2984)*
**Canton Redi-Mix Inc**..............................................309 647-0019
  1130 W Locust St  Canton  (61520)  *(G-2985)*
**Canvas Communication**........................................815 464-5947
  7320 W Benton Dr  Frankfort  (60423)  *(G-10306)*
**Canvas Creations Inc**............................................309 343-5082
  1565 Meadow Lark Dr  Galesburg  (61401)  *(G-10741)*
**Canyon Foods Inc**..................................................773 890-9888
  1150 W 40th St  Chicago  (60609)  *(G-4228)*
**Cap, Hillsboro** *Also called Contract Assembly Partners (G-11888)*
**Cap & Seal Co**........................................................847 741-3101
  1591 Fleetwood Dr  Elgin  (60123)  *(G-8976)*
**Cap & Seal Company, Elgin** *Also called Sealco Industries Inc (G-9173)*
**Cap Factory**...........................................................618 273-9662
  816 State St  Eldorado  (62930)  *(G-8919)*
**Cap Today**..............................................................847 832-7377
  325 Waukegan Rd  Northfield  (60093)  *(G-16395)*
**Capable Controls Inc (PA)**....................................630 860-6514
  790 Maple Ln  Bensenville  (60106)  *(G-1850)*
**Cape Prosthetics-Orthotics Inc**.............................618 457-4692
  2355 Sweets Dr Ste G  Carbondale  (62902)  *(G-3001)*
**Capers North America LLC**...................................708 995-7500
  760 Village Ctr Dr Ste 250  Burr Ridge  (60527)  *(G-2827)*
**Capital Advanced Technologies**............................630 690-1696
  309 Village Dr  Carol Stream  (60188)  *(G-3124)*
**Capital Computer Consultants, Skokie** *Also called Capital Tours & Travel Inc (G-19973)*
**Capital Engineering & Mfg Co, Barrington** *Also called Cem LLC (G-1276)*
**Capital Merchant Solutions Inc**............................309 452-5990
  3005 Gill St Ste 2  Bloomington  (61704)  *(G-2152)*
**Capital Printing & Die-Cutting, Aurora** *Also called Capital Prtg & Die Cutng Inc (G-1124)*
**Capital Prtg & Die Cutng Inc**.................................630 896-5520
  303 S Highland Ave  Aurora  (60506)  *(G-1124)*
**Capital Pttern Model Works Inc**.............................630 469-8200
  410 Windy Point Dr  Glendale Heights  (60139)  *(G-11013)*
**Capital Rubber Corporation**..................................630 595-6644
  1140 Tower Ln  Bensenville  (60106)  *(G-1851)*
**Capital Tours & Travel Inc**.....................................847 274-1138
  8820 Skokie Blvd 105  Skokie  (60077)  *(G-19973)*
**Capitol Carton Company (PA)**...............................312 563-9690
  346 N Justine St Ste 406  Chicago  (60607)  *(G-4229)*
**Capitol Carton Company**.......................................312 491-2220
  1917 W Walnut St  Chicago  (60612)  *(G-4230)*
**Capitol City Machine**.............................................217 529-0293
  2840 Adlai Stevenson Dr  Springfield  (62703)  *(G-20405)*
**Capitol City Tool & Design**....................................217 544-9250
  1330 Taylor Ave  Springfield  (62703)  *(G-20406)*
**Capitol Coil Inc**......................................................847 891-1390
  821 Albion Ave Ste B  Schaumburg  (60193)  *(G-19468)*
**Capitol Containers, Chicago** *Also called Capitol Carton Company (G-4229)*
**Capitol Impressions Inc**........................................309 633-1400
  1622 W Moss Ave  Peoria  (61606)  *(G-17322)*
**Capitol Ready-Mix Inc (PA)**..................................217 528-1100
  1900 E Mason St  Springfield  (62702)  *(G-20407)*
**Capitol Resource and Inv Co, Canton** *Also called Blue Blaze Coal Cpitl Resource (G-2982)*
**Capitol Wholesale Meats Inc**................................708 485-4800
  8751 W 50th St  Mc Cook  (60525)  *(G-14446)*
**Capitol Wood Works LLC**......................................217 522-5553
  1010 E Edwards St  Springfield  (62703)  *(G-20408)*
**Caples-El Transport Inc**........................................708 300-2727
  560 Buffalo Ave  Calumet City  (60409)  *(G-2936)*
**Capol LLC**...............................................................224 545-5095
  707 Lake Cook Rd Ste 320  Deerfield  (60015)  *(G-7993)*
**Capron Mfg Co (PA)**..............................................815 569-2301
  200 Burr Oak Rd  Capron  (61012)  *(G-2994)*
**Caps Group, The, Chicago** *Also called Group 329 LLC (G-5005)*
**Capsim MGT Simulations Inc**...............................312 477-7200
  55 E Monroe St Ste 3210  Chicago  (60603)  *(G-4231)*
**Capsonic Automotive Inc**......................................847 888-0930
  1595 Highpoint Dr  Elgin  (60123)  *(G-8977)*
**Capsonic Automotive Inc**......................................847 888-7300
  495 Renner Dr  Elgin  (60123)  *(G-8978)*
**Capsonic Automotive Inc (PA)**..............................847 888-7300
  460 2nd St  Elgin  (60123)  *(G-8979)*
**Capsonic Automotive Inc**......................................915 872-3585
  4219 Solutions Ctr  Chicago  (60677)  *(G-4232)*
**Capsonic Automotive & Arospc, Elgin** *Also called Capsonic Automotive Inc (G-8977)*
**Capsonic Group, Elgin** *Also called Capsonic Automotive Inc (G-8978)*
**Capsonic Group LLC (PA)**.....................................847 888-7264
  460 2nd St  Elgin  (60123)  *(G-8980)*
**Captain Curts Food Products**................................773 783-8400
  8206 S Cottage Grove Ave  Chicago  (60619)  *(G-4233)*
**Captain Hook Inc**...................................................309 565-7676
  5125 S Hnna Cy Glsford Rd  Hanna City  (61536)  *(G-11567)*
**Captaincurtfoods.com, Chicago** *Also called Captain Curts Food Products (G-4233)*

**Captains Emporium Inc** ....773 972-7609
1200 W 35th St Chicago (60609) ***(G-4234)***
**Captivision Inc** ....630 235-8763
263 Heritage Ct Bolingbrook (60490) ***(G-2283)***
**Car - Mon Products Inc** ....847 695-9000
1225 Davis Rd Elgin (60123) ***(G-8981)***
**Car Shop Inc** ....309 797-4188
421 12th St Moline (61265) ***(G-14920)***
**Caramel-A Bakery Ltd** ....773 227-2635
3945 W Armitage Ave Chicago (60647) ***(G-4235)***
**Caramela Bakery, Chicago** *Also called Caramel-A Bakery Ltd* ***(G-4235)***
**Caraustar Industrial and Con** ....217 323-5225
100 Forest Ln Beardstown (62618) ***(G-1521)***
**Caraustar Industries Inc** ....773 308-7622
555 N Tripp Ave Chicago (60624) ***(G-4236)***
**Caravan Ingredients Inc** ....708 849-8590
14622 Lakeside Ave Dolton (60419) ***(G-8368)***
**Carbco Manufacturing Inc** ....630 377-1410
2525 Production Dr Saint Charles (60174) ***(G-19150)***
**Carbit Corporation (PA)** ....312 280-2300
927 W Blackhawk St Chicago (60642) ***(G-4237)***
**Carbit Paint Co, Chicago** *Also called Carbit Corporation* ***(G-4237)***
**Carbon On Chicago LLC** ....312 225-3200
810 N Marshfield Ave Chicago (60622) ***(G-4238)***
**Carbon Solutions Group LLC** ....312 638-9077
1130 W Monroe St Ste 1 Chicago (60607) ***(G-4239)***
**Carbondale Night Life** ....618 549-2799
701 W Main St Carbondale (62901) ***(G-3002)***
**Carbondale Times, Carbondale** *Also called Carbondale Night Life* ***(G-3002)***
**Carbondale Trophy Co, Carbondale** *Also called Rudon Enterprises Inc* ***(G-3022)***
**Card Dynamix LLC** ....630 685-4060
1120 Windham Pkwy Romeoville (60446) ***(G-18806)***
**Card Prsnlzation Solutions LLC** ....630 543-2630
80 Internationale Blvd C Glendale Heights (60139) ***(G-11014)***
**Cardiac Imaging Inc** ....630 834-7100
2 Transam Plaza Dr # 420 Oakbrook Terrace (60181) ***(G-16700)***
**Cardinal Cattle** ....309 479-1302
9736 Modena Rd Wyoming (61491) ***(G-22637)***
**Cardinal Colorprint Prtg Corp** ....630 467-1000
1270 Ardmore Ave Itasca (60143) ***(G-12241)***
**Cardinal Construction Co** ....618 842-5553
705 S 1st St Fairfield (62837) ***(G-10138)***
**Cardinal Engineering Inc** ....309 342-7474
1640 N Kellogg St Galesburg (61401) ***(G-10742)***
**Cardinal Enterprises** ....618 994-4454
562 Ferrel Rd Stonefort (62987) ***(G-20637)***
**Cardinal Forge, Rochelle** *Also called C B & A Inc* ***(G-18080)***
**Cardinal Health Inc** ....847 578-4443
1500 S Waukegan Rd Waukegan (60085) ***(G-21532)***
**Cardinal Health 200 LLC** ....847 473-3200
1300 S Waukegan Rd 124 Waukegan (60085) ***(G-21533)***
**Cardinal Health 200 LLC** ....847 689-8410
1430 S Waukegan Rd Waukegan (60085) ***(G-21534)***
**Cardinal Hill Candles & Crafts, Rochester** *Also called Edwin Waldmire & Virginia* ***(G-18117)***
**Cardinal Medical Services, Waukegan** *Also called Cardinal Health Inc* ***(G-21532)***
**Cardinal Pallet Co** ....773 725-5387
505 W 43rd St Chicago (60609) ***(G-4240)***
**Cardinal Professional Products** ....714 761-3292
3150 N Woodford St Decatur (62526) ***(G-7850)***
**Cardon Mold Finishing Inc** ....630 543-5431
703 W Annoreno Dr Ste 4 Addison (60101) ***(G-69)***
**Cardthartic LLC** ....217 239-5895
30102 Research Rd Champaign (61822) ***(G-3461)***
**Cardwell Westinghouse Company** ....773 483-7575
8400 S Stewart Ave Chicago (60620) ***(G-4241)***
**Care Child Companies** ....630 295-6770
1 Tiffany Pt Ste 115 Bloomingdale (60108) ***(G-2099)***
**Care Creations, Skokie** *Also called Laser Reproductions Inc* ***(G-20026)***
**Care Education Group Inc** ....708 361-4110
126 Commons Dr Palos Park (60464) ***(G-17127)***
**Care Solutions Incorporated** ....815 301-4034
365 Millennium Dr Ste D Crystal Lake (60012) ***(G-7550)***
**Carefusion Corporation** ....858 617-2000
75 N Fairway Dr Vernon Hills (60061) ***(G-21153)***
**Carematix Inc** ....312 627-9300
209 W Jackson Blvd # 800 Chicago (60606) ***(G-4242)***
**Carey Color Inc** ....630 761-2605
2500 Enterprise Cir West Chicago (60185) ***(G-21678)***
**Carey Electric Co Inc** ....847 949-9294
24809 W Chardon Rd Grayslake (60030) ***(G-11325)***
**Cargill Incorporated** ....618 662-8070
6 Industrial Park Flora (62839) ***(G-10202)***
**Cargill Incorporated** ....815 942-0932
301 Griggs St Morris (60450) ***(G-15099)***
**Cargill Incorporated** ....217 872-7653
765 E Pythian Ave Decatur (62526) ***(G-7851)***
**Cargill Incorporated** ....773 375-7255
12200 S Torrence Ave Chicago (60617) ***(G-4243)***
**Cargill Incorporated** ....309 827-7100
115 S Euclid Ave Bloomington (61701) ***(G-2153)***
**Cargill Incorporated** ....630 505-7788
400 E Diehl Rd Ste 330 Naperville (60563) ***(G-15616)***
**Cargill Cocoa & Chocolate Inc** ....815 578-2000
217 Tulip Cir Island Lake (60042) ***(G-12213)***
**Cargill Dry Corn Ingrdents Inc (HQ)** ....217 465-5331
616 S Jefferson St Paris (61944) ***(G-17143)***
**Cargill Food Distribution, Woodridge** *Also called Cargill Meat Solutions Corp* ***(G-22458)***
**Cargill Meat Solutions Corp** ....630 739-1746
10420 Woodward Ave Woodridge (60517) ***(G-22458)***
**Cargo Support Industries Inc** ....
242 Willow St Inverness (60010) ***(G-12207)***
**Cargois Inc** ....847 357-1901
2700 Coyle Ave Elk Grove Village (60007) ***(G-9356)***
**Caribbean Adventures Magazine, Riverwoods** *Also called Steven Fisher* ***(G-18044)***
**Caribbean American Bkg Co Inc** ....773 761-0700
1539 W Howard St Chicago (60626) ***(G-4244)***
**Carl Buddig and Company (PA)** ....708 798-0900
950 175th St Homewood (60430) ***(G-12093)***
**Carl Gorr Printing Co (PA)** ....815 338-3191
1002 Mchenry Ave Woodstock (60098) ***(G-22549)***
**Carl Manufacturing USA Inc** ....847 884-2842
100 E Pierce Rd Ste 100 Itasca (60143) ***(G-12242)***
**Carl Stahl Decorcble Innovtns** ....312 454-2996
8080 S Madison St Burr Ridge (60527) ***(G-2828)***
**Carlberg Design Inc** ....217 341-3291
1215 E Clary St Petersburg (62675) ***(G-17534)***
**Carlin Mfg A Div Grs Holdg LLC** ....559 276-0123
131 W Jefferson Ave # 223 Naperville (60540) ***(G-15617)***
**Carline Leathers, Chicago** *Also called Loren Girovich* ***(G-5541)***
**Carlinville Waste Water Plants** ....217 854-6506
1345 Mayo St Carlinville (62626) ***(G-3031)***
**Carlson Capitol Mfg Co, Rockford** *Also called Carlson Capitol Mfg Co* ***(G-18296)***
**Carlson Capitol Mfg Co** ....815 398-3110
2319 23rd Ave Rockford (61104) ***(G-18296)***
**Carlson Scientific Inc** ....708 258-6377
514 S Third St Peotone (60468) ***(G-17485)***
**Carlson STI, Elgin** *Also called Carlson Tool & Machine Company* ***(G-8983)***
**Carlson Sti Inc** ....630 232-2460
1875 Big Timber Rd Ste A Elgin (60123) ***(G-8982)***
**Carlson Tool & Machine Company** ....630 232-2460
1875 Big Timber Rd Elgin (60123) ***(G-8983)***
**Carlyle Brewing Co** ....815 963-2739
215 E State St Rockford (61104) ***(G-18297)***
**Carlyle Sand & Gravel Ltd** ....618 594-8263
11842 State Route 127 Carlyle (62231) ***(G-3053)***
**Carmen Matthew LLC** ....630 784-7500
1225 Bowes Rd Elgin (60123) ***(G-8984)***
**Carmi Times** ....618 382-4176
323 E Main St Carmi (62821) ***(G-3064)***
**Carmona Gear Cutting** ....815 963-8236
1707 Magnolia St Rockford (61104) ***(G-18298)***
**Carnaghi Towing & Repair Inc** ....217 446-0333
2000 Georgetown Rd Tilton (61833) ***(G-20878)***
**Carnation Enterprises** ....847 804-5928
8630 N National Ave Niles (60714) ***(G-15967)***
**Carney Flow Technics LLC** ....815 277-2600
181 Ontario St Frankfort (60423) ***(G-10307)***
**Carol Andrzejewski** ....630 369-9711
2339 Kalamazoo Dr Naperville (60565) ***(G-15618)***
**Carol Douglas Company, Silvis** *Also called River City Sign Company Inc* ***(G-19940)***
**Caroline Cole Inc** ....618 233-0600
711 S Illinois St Belleville (62220) ***(G-1617)***
**Caroline Rose Inc** ....708 386-1011
741 Madison St Oak Park (60302) ***(G-16656)***
**Carols Cookies Inc** ....847 831-4500
3184 Macarthur Blvd Northbrook (60062) ***(G-16217)***
**Carousel Candies, Geneva** *Also called Silvestri Sweets Inc* ***(G-10867)***
**Carousel Checks Inc** ....708 599-8576
8906 S Harlem Ave Bridgeview (60455) ***(G-2474)***
**Carpenter Contractors Amer Inc** ....815 544-1699
2340 Newburg Rd Ste 200 Belvidere (61008) ***(G-1744)***
**Carpenter Specialty Alloys, Bolingbrook** *Also called Carpenter Technology Corp* ***(G-2284)***
**Carpenter Technology Corp** ....630 771-1020
902 Carlow Dr Bolingbrook (60490) ***(G-2284)***
**Carpenters Millwork Co** ....708 339-7707
16046 Vandustrial Ln South Holland (60473) ***(G-20255)***
**Carpenters Millwork Co (PA)** ....708 339-7707
224 W Stone Rd Villa Park (60181) ***(G-21241)***
**Carpentersville Quarry Inc** ....847 836-1550
800 Bolz Rd Carpentersville (60110) ***(G-3278)***
**Carpet One, Chicago** *Also called L & L Flooring Inc* ***(G-5418)***
**Carpets By Kuniej (PA)** ....815 232-9060
1308 S Armstrong Ave Freeport (61032) ***(G-10650)***
**Carquest Auto Parts, Decatur** *Also called Donnelly Automotive Machine* ***(G-7877)***
**Carr Machine & Tool Inc** ....847 593-8003
1301 Jarvis Ave Elk Grove Village (60007) ***(G-9357)***

ALPHABETIC

(PA)=Parent Co (HQ)=Headquarters (DH)=Div Headquarters
2017 Harris Illinois
Industrial Directory
1191

**Carrera Stone Systems of Chica**......847 566-2277
675 Tower Rd Mundelein (60060) *(G-15483)*
**Carrier Commercial Rfrgn Inc**......815 624-8333
750 N Blackhawk Blvd Rockton (61072) *(G-18693)*
**Carroll County Locker**......815 493-2370
122 E Carroll St Lanark (61046) *(G-13151)*
**Carroll County Review**......815 259-2131
809 W Main St Thomson (61285) *(G-20864)*
**Carroll Distrg & Cnstr Sup Inc**......630 892-4855
1031 W Lake St Aurora (60506) *(G-1125)*
**Carroll Distrg & Cnstr Sup Inc**......630 243-0272
13087 Main St Lemont (60439) *(G-13229)*
**Carroll Distrg & Cnstr Sup Inc**......815 941-1548
460 Briscoe Dr Morris (60450) *(G-15100)*
**Carroll Distrg & Cnstr Sup Inc**......309 449-6044
201 Ford Ave Hopedale (61747) *(G-12121)*
**Carroll Distrg & Cnstr Sup Inc**......217 223-8126
2221 N 24th St Quincy (62301) *(G-17810)*
**Carroll Distrg & Cnstr Sup Inc**......630 369-6520
1700 Quincy Ave Naperville (60540) *(G-15619)*
**Carroll Distrg & Cnstr Sup Inc**......815 464-0100
121 Industry Ave Frankfort (60423) *(G-10308)*
**Carroll Industrial Coatings, Milledgeville** *Also called Carroll Industrial Molds Inc (G-14816)*
**Carroll Industrial Molds Inc**......815 225-7250
202 N Washington St Milledgeville (61051) *(G-14816)*
**Carroll International Corp (PA)**......630 983-5979
55 N Mayflower Rd Lake Forest (60045) *(G-12890)*
**Carroll Tool & Manufacturing**......630 766-3363
827 Eagle Dr Bensenville (60106) *(G-1852)*
**Carrolls Welding & Fabrication**......217 728-8720
819 N Market St Sullivan (61951) *(G-20741)*
**Carson Printing Inc**......847 836-0900
1110 Heinz Dr Ste C East Dundee (60118) *(G-8629)*
**Carson Properties Inc (PA)**......630 832-3322
953 N Larch Ave Elmhurst (60126) *(G-9845)*
**Carstens Incorporated**......708 669-1500
7310 W Wilson Ave Chicago (60706) *(G-4245)*
**Carstin Brands Inc**......217 543-3331
520 E 2nd St Arthur (61911) *(G-885)*
**Cartec, Mount Vernon** *Also called Dennis Carnes (G-15410)*
**Cartel Holdings Inc (PA)**......815 334-0250
3 Lincoln St Ste 2a Harvard (60033) *(G-11625)*
**Carter Anna Brooks LLC**......618 382-3939
1238 County Road 1500 N Carmi (62821) *(G-3065)*
**Carter Hoffmann LLC**......847 362-5500
1551 Mccormick Blvd Mundelein (60060) *(G-15484)*
**Carter Motor Company, Warren** *Also called Stable Beginning Corporation (G-21337)*
**Carter Printing Co Inc**......217 227-4464
607 Elevator St Farmersville (62533) *(G-10183)*
**Carters Inc**......847 870-0185
12 E Randhurst Village Rd Mount Prospect (60056) *(G-15316)*
**Carters Inc**......708 345-6680
1312 Winston Plz Melrose Park (60160) *(G-14605)*
**Carters Inc**......630 690-6182
132 Danada Sq W Wheaton (60189) *(G-21939)*
**Carterville Courier**......618 985-6187
122 S Division St Carterville (62918) *(G-3310)*
**Cartoncraft Inc**......630 377-1230
2900 Dukane Dr Ste 2 Saint Charles (60174) *(G-19151)*
**Cartpac Inc**......630 283-8979
245 E North Ave Carol Stream (60188) *(G-3125)*
**Cartridge World Bloomingdale, Bloomingdale** *Also called Dauphin Enterprise Inc (G-2101)*
**Cartridge World Decatur**......217 875-0465
215 E Ash Ave Ste D Decatur (62526) *(G-7852)*
**Cartridge World Sterling**......815 625-2345
3307 E Lincolnway Ste 1 Sterling (61081) *(G-20587)*
**Carus Chemical Company, La Salle** *Also called Carus Corporation (G-12766)*
**Carus Corporation (HQ)**......815 223-1500
315 5th St Peru (61354) *(G-17503)*
**Carus Corporation**......815 223-1500
1500 8th St La Salle (61301) *(G-12766)*
**Carus Corporation**......815 223-1565
1500 8th St La Salle (61301) *(G-12767)*
**Carus Group Inc (PA)**......815 223-1500
315 5th St Peru (61354) *(G-17504)*
**Carus Publishing Company (HQ)**......603 924-7209
70 E Lake St Ste 800 Chicago (60601) *(G-4246)*
**Carus Publishing Company**......312 701-1720
70 E Lake St Ste 800 Chicago (60601) *(G-4247)*
**Carver Custom Woodworks, Milan** *Also called Agusta Mill Works (G-14773)*
**Cary Physcl Therapy Spt Rehab, Cary** *Also called Deborah Morris Gulbrandson Pt (G-3333)*
**Casa De Monte Cristo**......708 352-6668
1332 W 55th St Countryside (60525) *(G-7416)*
**Casa De Puros**......708 725-7180
7410 Madison St Forest Park (60130) *(G-10236)*
**Casa Di Castronovo Inc**......815 962-4731
722 N Main St Rockford (61103) *(G-18299)*
**Casa Nostra Bakery Co Inc**......847 455-5175
3140 Mannheim Rd Franklin Park (60131) *(G-10424)*
**Cascades Enviropac Aurora, Aurora** *Also called Cascades Plastics Inc (G-981)*
**Cascades Plastics Inc**......450 469-3389
2300 Raddant Rd Ste B Aurora (60502) *(G-981)*
**Casco Manufacturing Inc**......630 771-9555
600 Territorial Dr Ste C Bolingbrook (60440) *(G-2285)*
**Case Guys, Bedford Park** *Also called A W Enterprises Inc (G-1531)*
**Case New Holl Burr Ridge Opera, Burr Ridge** *Also called Cnh Industrial America LLC (G-2833)*
**Case Paluch & Associates Inc**......773 465-0098
1806 W Greenleaf Ave Chicago (60626) *(G-4248)*
**Casey Products, Woodridge** *Also called General Fas Acquisition Co (G-22481)*
**Casey Spring Co Inc**......708 867-8949
4630 N Ronald St Harwood Heights (60706) *(G-11682)*
**Casey Stone Co**......217 857-3425
14046 N 1600th St Teutopolis (62467) *(G-20849)*
**Cash House Music Group LLC**......847 471-7401
1320 Laci Ct Indian Creek (60061) *(G-12185)*
**Casper Ernest E Hairgoods**......773 545-2800
6033 N Cicero Ave Chicago (60646) *(G-4249)*
**CASS COUNTY STAR GAZZETTE, Beardstown** *Also called Beardstown Newspapers Inc (G-1520)*
**Cass Meats**......217 452-3072
5815 Il Route 78 Virginia (62691) *(G-21305)*
**Cassetica Software Inc**......312 546-3668
22 W Washington St # 1500 Chicago (60602) *(G-4250)*
**Cassini Cabinetry**......847 244-9755
701 Belvidere Rd Waukegan (60085) *(G-21535)*
**Cast Aluminum Solutions LLC**......630 482-5325
1310 Kingsland Dr Batavia (60510) *(G-1426)*
**Cast Films Inc**......847 808-0363
401 Chaddick Dr Wheeling (60090) *(G-22024)*
**Cast Industries Inc**......217 522-8292
580 North St Springfield (62704) *(G-20409)*
**Cast Products Inc**......708 457-1500
4200 N Nordica Ave Norridge (60706) *(G-16098)*
**Cast Rite Steel Casting Corp**......312 738-2900
2135 W Carroll Ave Chicago (60612) *(G-4251)*
**Cast Technologies Inc (PA)**......309 676-1715
1100 Sw Washington St Peoria (61602) *(G-17323)*
**Cast21 Inc**......847 772-8547
60 Hazelwood Dr Champaign (61820) *(G-3462)*
**Caster Warehouse Inc**......847 836-5712
1011 Tamarac Dr Carpentersville (60110) *(G-3279)*
**Casting House Inc**......312 782-7160
5 S Wabash Ave Ste 614 Chicago (60603) *(G-4252)*
**Casting Impregnators Inc (PA)**......847 455-1000
11150 Addison Ave Franklin Park (60131) *(G-10425)*
**Castino & Associates Inc**......847 291-7446
3065 Dundee Rd Northbrook (60062) *(G-16218)*
**Castle Craft Products Inc**......630 279-7494
1133 N Ellsworth Ave Villa Park (60181) *(G-21242)*
**Castle Metal Finishing Corp**......847 678-6041
4631 25th Ave Schiller Park (60176) *(G-19811)*
**Castle Metal Products Corp**......847 806-4540
1947 Quincy Ct Glendale Heights (60139) *(G-11015)*
**Castle-Printech Inc**......815 758-5484
121 Industrial Dr Dekalb (60115) *(G-8076)*
**Castlegate Publishers Inc**......847 382-6420
25597 W Drake Rd Barrington (60010) *(G-1275)*
**Castro Foods Wholesale Inc**......773 869-0641
1365 W 37th St Chicago (60609) *(G-4253)*
**Castrol Industrial N Amer Inc (HQ)**......877 641-1600
150 W Warrenville Rd Naperville (60563) *(G-15620)*
**Castronovo's Bridal Shop, Rockford** *Also called Casa Di Castronovo Inc (G-18299)*
**Castwell Products LLC**......847 966-9552
7800 Austin Ave Skokie (60077) *(G-19974)*
**Casward Tool Works Inc**......773 486-4900
1422 N Kilpatrick Ave Chicago (60651) *(G-4254)*
**Cat I Manufacturing Inc**......847 931-1200
865 Commerce Dr South Elgin (60177) *(G-20188)*
**Cat-I Glass Manufacturing, South Elgin** *Also called Cat I Manufacturing Inc (G-20188)*
**Catalent Pharma Solutions Inc**......815 338-9500
2210 Lake Shore Dr Woodstock (60098) *(G-22550)*
**Catalina Coating & Plas Inc**......847 806-1340
870 Greenleaf Ave Elk Grove Village (60007) *(G-9358)*
**Catalina Graphic Films, Elk Grove Village** *Also called Catalina Coating & Plas Inc (G-9358)*
**Catalina Graphics Inc**......773 973-7780
2325 W Farwell Ave Apt 3s Chicago (60645) *(G-4255)*
**Catalog Designers Inc**......847 228-0025
106 Buckingham Ct Elk Grove Village (60007) *(G-9359)*
**Catalyst Chicago**......312 427-4830
332 S Michigan Ave Ste 37 Chicago (60604) *(G-4256)*
**Catalyst Paper**......224 307-2650
960 Grove St Evanston (60201) *(G-10019)*
**Catalytic Inc**......312 927-8750
23 W Jefferson Ave Fl 2 Naperville (60540) *(G-15621)*
**Catalytic Products Intl Inc**......847 438-0334
980 Ensell Rd Lake Zurich (60047) *(G-13050)*
**Catalyze, Chicago** *Also called Mhub (G-5717)*

**Catapult Communications Corp**....847 884-0048
1821 Walden Office Sq # 120 Schaumburg (60173) ***(G-19469)***
**Catapult Global LLC**....847 364-8149
1000 Lee St Elk Grove Village (60007) ***(G-9360)***
**Catapult Marketing**....312 216-4460
233 N Michigan Ave # 810 Chicago (60601) ***(G-4257)***
**Catching Hydraulics Co Ltd**....708 344-2334
1733 N 25th Ave Melrose Park (60160) ***(G-14606)***
**Cater Chemical Co**....630 980-2300
30 Monaco Dr Roselle (60172) ***(G-18930)***
**Caterina Foods, Lake Bluff** *Also called Archer-Daniels-Midland Company* ***(G-12833)***
**Caterpilar, Carrier Mills** *Also called Caterpillar Globl Min Amer LLC* ***(G-3306)***
**Caterpillar Authorized Dealer, Morton** *Also called Spl Software Alliance LLC* ***(G-15182)***
**Caterpillar Authorized Dealer, Bartonville** *Also called Altorfer Power Systems* ***(G-1391)***
**Caterpillar Brazil LLC (HQ)**....309 675-1000
100 Ne Adams St Peoria (61629) ***(G-17324)***
**Caterpillar Gb LLC**....309 675-1000
100 Ne Adams St Peoria (61629) ***(G-17325)***
**Caterpillar Global Mining LLC**....618 378-3441
635 Il Highway 1 Norris City (62869) ***(G-16112)***
**Caterpillar Globl Min Amer LLC**....618 982-9000
9580 Highway 13 W Carrier Mills (62917) ***(G-3306)***
**Caterpillar Inc (PA)**....309 675-1000
100 Ne Adams St Peoria (61629) ***(G-17326)***
**Caterpillar Inc**....815 729-5511
540 Joyce Rd Joliet (60436) ***(G-12471)***
**Caterpillar Inc**....630 859-5000
325 S Rte 31 Montgomery (60538) ***(G-15036)***
**Caterpillar Inc**....217 475-4000
3000 N 27th St Decatur (62525) ***(G-7853)***
**Caterpillar Inc**....309 675-1000
600 W Washington St East Peoria (61611) ***(G-8704)***
**Caterpillar Inc**....815 584-4887
1200 E Mazon Ave Dwight (60420) ***(G-8588)***
**Caterpillar Inc**....309 675-5681
7022 W Middle Rd Peoria (61607) ***(G-17327)***
**Caterpillar Inc**....309 633-8788
8826 W Us Highway 24 Mapleton (61547) ***(G-14205)***
**Caterpillar Inc**....309 578-2086
28194 Caterpillar Ln Washington (61571) ***(G-21380)***
**Caterpillar Inc**....217 424-1809
2701 Pershing Rd Decatur (62526) ***(G-7854)***
**Caterpillar Inc**....815 729-5511
2200 Channahon Rd Rockdale (60436) ***(G-18216)***
**Caterpillar Inc**....309 266-4294
1900 E Old Galena Rd Mossville (61552) ***(G-15248)***
**Caterpillar Inc**....903 712-4505
14009 Old Galena Rd Mossville (61552) ***(G-15249)***
**Caterpillar Inc**....888 614-4328
501 Sw Jefferson Ave Peoria (61605) ***(G-17328)***
**Caterpillar Inc**....309 675-4408
300 Hamilton Blvd Ste 300 Peoria (61602) ***(G-17329)***
**Caterpillar Inc**....815 842-6000
1300 4h Park Rd Pontiac (61764) ***(G-17697)***
**Caterpillar Inc**....706 779-4620
8826 W Us Highway 24 Mapleton (61547) ***(G-14206)***
**Caterpillar Inc**....309 578-2473
Old Galena Rd Ste H Mossville (61552) ***(G-15250)***
**Caterpillar Inc**....309 675-1000
1335 Sw Washington St Peoria (61602) ***(G-17330)***
**Caterpillar Inc**....309 578-8250
330 Sw Washington St Peoria (61602) ***(G-17331)***
**Caterpillar Inc**....309 675-6223
Illinois Rte 29 Mossville (61552) ***(G-15251)***
**Caterpillar Inc**....309 494-0858
Rr 31 Box S Aurora (60507) ***(G-1126)***
**Caterpillar Inc**....309 675-1000
330 Sw Adams St Peoria (61602) ***(G-17332)***
**Caterpillar Inc**....309 494-0138
100 Tractor Dr East Peoria (61630) ***(G-8699)***
**Caterpillar Inc**....309 675-6590
2400 Sw Washington St Peoria (61602) ***(G-17333)***
**Caterpillar Luxembourg LLC (HQ)**....309 675-1000
100 Ne Adams St Peoria (61629) ***(G-17334)***
**Caterpillar Power Systems**....309 675-1000
100 Ne Adams St Peoria (61629) ***(G-17335)***
**Catholic Book Covers, Franklin Park** *Also called J S Printing Inc* ***(G-10503)***
**Catholic Press Assn of The US**....312 380-6789
205 W Monroe St Chicago (60606) ***(G-4258)***
**Cathys Sweet Creations**....815 886-6769
519 W Lockport Rd Plainfield (60544) ***(G-17585)***
**Catlyst Reaction LLC**....708 941-4616
16624 Marshfield Ave Markham (60428) ***(G-14301)***
**Catty Corporation**....815 943-2143
6111 White Oaks Rd Harvard (60033) ***(G-11626)***
**Caulfields Restaurant Ltd**....708 798-1599
1035 Sterling Ave Flossmoor (60422) ***(G-10223)***
**Cavanaugh Government Group LLC**....630 210-8668
8432 Beloit Ave Bridgeview (60455) ***(G-2475)***
**Cavco Printers**....618 988-8011
406 N Pershing St Energy (62933) ***(G-9985)***
**Cavco Printers Prtg & Copy Ctr, Energy** *Also called Cavco Printers* ***(G-9985)***
**Cavero Coatings Company LLC**....630 616-2868
422 County Line Rd Bensenville (60106) ***(G-1853)***
**Caviton Inc**....217 621-5746
3401 S Deer Ridge Dr Urbana (61802) ***(G-21075)***
**Caxton Club**....312 266-8825
60 W Walton St Chicago (60610) ***(G-4259)***
**CAXTON CLUB CHICAGO, THE, Chicago** *Also called Caxton Club* ***(G-4259)***
**Caysh, Chicago** *Also called Livegift Inc* ***(G-5524)***
**CB & I Water, Bourbonnais** *Also called CB&i LLC* ***(G-2392)***
**CB&i LLC**....815 936-5440
1035 E 5000n Rd Bourbonnais (60914) ***(G-2392)***
**Cbana Labs Inc (PA)**....217 819-5201
2021 S 1st St Ste 206 Champaign (61820) ***(G-3463)***
**Cbc Restaurant Corp**....773 463-0665
2711 W George St Chicago (60618) ***(G-4260)***
**CBS Broadcasting Inc**....708 206-2900
1055 175th St Ste 102 Homewood (60430) ***(G-12094)***
**Cbt, Mount Olive** *Also called Compania Brasileira De T* ***(G-15301)***
**CC Distributing Services Inc**....800 931-2668
13655 Kenton Ave Crestwood (60445) ***(G-7480)***
**CC Industries, Chicago** *Also called Henry Crown and Company* ***(G-5072)***
**Ccar Industries**....217 345-3300
200 W Locust Ave Charleston (61920) ***(G-3591)***
**CCH Incorporated (HQ)**....847 267-7000
2700 Lake Cook Rd Riverwoods (60015) ***(G-18037)***
**CCI Manufacturing IL Corp**....630 685-7534
15550 Canal Bank Rd Lemont (60439) ***(G-13230)***
**CCI Manufacturing Illinois, Lemont** *Also called CCI Manufacturing IL Corp* ***(G-13230)***
**CCI Power Supplies LLC**....847 362-6500
616 N North Ct Ste 250 Palatine (60067) ***(G-17008)***
**CCI Redi Mix**....217 342-2299
2604 N Haarmann St Effingham (62401) ***(G-8829)***
**Cck Automations Inc**....217 243-6040
500 Capitol Way Jacksonville (62650) ***(G-12382)***
**CCL Dispensing Systems LLC**....847 816-9400
901 Technology Way Libertyville (60048) ***(G-13312)***
**CCL Label (chicago) Inc**....630 406-9991
1862 Suncast Ln Batavia (60510) ***(G-1427)***
**CCMHA, Taylorville** *Also called Christian Cnty Mntal Hlth Assn* ***(G-20836)***
**Cco Holdings LLC**....618 505-3505
523 Troy Plz Troy (62294) ***(G-21003)***
**Cco Holdings LLC**....618 651-6486
2762 Troxler Way Highland (62249) ***(G-11777)***
**CCS Contractor Eqp & Sup Inc (PA)**....630 393-9020
1567 Frontenac Rd Naperville (60563) ***(G-15622)***
**Ccsi International Inc**....815 544-8385
8642 Us Highway 20 Garden Prairie (61038) ***(G-10793)***
**Ccty USA Bearing Co**....847 540-8196
1111 Rose Rd Lake Zurich (60047) ***(G-13051)***
**Cd LLC**....312 275-5747
363 W Erie St Ste 400w Chicago (60654) ***(G-4261)***
**CD Magic Inc**....708 582-3496
116 S Prospect St Roselle (60172) ***(G-18931)***
**Cda Industries Inc**....630 357-7654
1228 Jane Ave Naperville (60540) ***(G-15623)***
**Cdc Enterprises Inc**....815 790-4205
1512 River Terrace Dr Johnsburg (60051) ***(G-12432)***
**Cdc Group Inc**....847 480-8830
140 S Dearborn St Ste 420 Chicago (60603) ***(G-4262)***
**CDI Computer Dealers, Chicago** *Also called CDI Computers (us) Corp* ***(G-4263)***
**CDI Computers (us) Corp**....888 226-5727
500 N Michigan Ave # 600 Chicago (60611) ***(G-4263)***
**CDI Corp**....773 205-2960
3440 N Knox Ave Chicago (60641) ***(G-4264)***
**Cdj Technologies Inc**....321 277-7807
2737 Blackhawk Rd Wilmette (60091) ***(G-22249)***
**CDK Global Inc (PA)**....847 397-1700
1950 Hassell Rd Hoffman Estates (60169) ***(G-11998)***
**CDL Technology Inc**....630 543-5240
511 S Vista Ave Addison (60101) ***(G-70)***
**Cds Engineering, Elgin** *Also called Agnes & Chris Gulik* ***(G-8940)***
**CDs Office Systems Inc (PA)**....800 367-1508
612 S Dirksen Pkwy Springfield (62703) ***(G-20410)***
**CDs Office Systems Inc**....217 351-5046
3108 Farber Dr Ofc Champaign (61822) ***(G-3464)***
**CDs Office Systems Inc**....630 305-9034
612 S Dirksen Pkwy Springfield (62703) ***(G-20411)***
**Cds Office Technologies, Springfield** *Also called CDs Office Systems Inc* ***(G-20410)***
**Cdv, Rockford** *Also called Stuhr Manufacturing Co* ***(G-18636)***
**Cdv Corp**....815 397-3903
5085 27th Ave Rockford (61109) ***(G-18300)***
**Cdw Merchants, Morton Grove** *Also called Bunzl Retail LLC* ***(G-15190)***
**Cec Industries Ltd**....847 821-1199
599 Bond St Lincolnshire (60069) ***(G-13434)***
**Cec, The Ozone Co, Downers Grove** *Also called Advanced Ozone Tech Inc* ***(G-8385)***

ALPHABETIC

**Cecomp Electronics Inc** 847 918-3510
1220 American Way Libertyville (60048) ***(G-13313)***
**Cedar Concepts Corporation** 773 890-5790
4100 S Packers Ave Chicago (60609) ***(G-4265)***
**Cedar Creek LLC** 618 797-1220
122 E Chanin Of Rocks Rd Granite City (62040) ***(G-11269)***
**Cedar Rustic Fence Co., Joliet** *Also called Bergeron Group Inc* ***(G-12464)***
**Cedille Chicago Nfp** 773 989-2515
1205 W Balmoral Ave Chicago (60640) ***(G-4266)***
**CEDILLE RECORDS, Chicago** *Also called Cedille Chicago Nfp* ***(G-4266)***
**CEF Industries LLC (HQ)** 630 628-2299
320 S Church St Addison (60101) ***(G-71)***
**Ceg Subsidiary LLC (PA)** 618 262-8666
714 N Walnut St Mount Carmel (62863) ***(G-15262)***
**Celco Tool & Engineering Inc** 847 671-2520
9300 Bernice Ave Schiller Park (60176) ***(G-19812)***
**Celerity Pharmaceuticals LLC** 847 999-0131
9450 Bryn Mawr Ave # 640 Rosemont (60018) ***(G-18992)***
**Celgene Corporation** 908 673-9000
2045 Cornell Ave Melrose Park (60160) ***(G-14607)***
**Celinco Inc (PA)** 815 964-2256
2320 Kishwaukee St Rockford (61104) ***(G-18301)***
**Cell Parts Manufacturing Co** 847 669-9690
10675 Wolf Dr Huntley (60142) ***(G-12135)***
**Cell-Safe Life Sciences LLC** 847 674-7075
7350 Ridgeway Ave Skokie (60076) ***(G-19975)***
**Cellar LLC (PA)** 618 956-9900
326 Vermont Rd Carterville (62918) ***(G-3311)***
**Cellas Confections Inc (HQ)** 773 838-3400
7401 S Cicero Ave Chicago (60629) ***(G-4267)***
**Cellusuede Products Inc** 815 964-8619
1515 Elmwood Rd Rockford (61103) ***(G-18302)***
**Celtic Environmental** 708 442-5823
6640 99th Pl Chicago Ridge (60415) ***(G-7140)***
**Cem LLC** 708 333-3761
6000 Garlands Ln Ste 120 Barrington (60010) ***(G-1276)***
**Cemec Inc (PA)** 630 495-9696
1516 Centre Cir Downers Grove (60515) ***(G-8405)***
**Cemex Cement Inc** 773 995-5100
12101 S Doty Ave Chicago (60633) ***(G-4268)***
**Cengage Learning Inc** 630 554-0821
2651 Warrenville Rd # 550 Downers Grove (60515) ***(G-8406)***
**Centec Automation Inc** 847 791-9430
420 S Vermont St Palatine (60067) ***(G-17009)***
**Centech Plastics Inc** 847 364-4433
855 Touhy Ave Elk Grove Village (60007) ***(G-9361)***
**Center Ethanol Company LLC** 618 875-3008
231 Monsanto Ave Sauget (62201) ***(G-19384)***
**Center Tool Company Inc** 847 683-7559
250 Industrial Dr Hampshire (60140) ***(G-11544)***
**Center-111 W Burnham Wash LLC** 312 368-5320
111 W Washington St Chicago (60602) ***(G-4269)***
**Centerless Grinding Co** 847 455-7660
2330 17th St Unit B Franklin Park (60131) ***(G-10426)***
**Centor North America Inc** 630 957-1000
966 Corporate Blvd # 130 Aurora (60502) ***(G-982)***
**Central Autmtc Screw Pdts Inc** 630 766-7966
372 Meyer Rd Bensenville (60106) ***(G-1854)***
**Central Can Company Inc** 773 254-8700
3200 S Kilbourn Ave Chicago (60623) ***(G-4270)***
**Central Chemical and Service** 630 653-9200
262 Carlton Dr Carol Stream (60188) ***(G-3126)***
**Central Concrete Products (PA)** 217 523-7964
3241 Terminal Ave Springfield (62707) ***(G-20412)***
**Central Concrete Products** 217 673-6111
403 N Ladue Rd Woodson (62695) ***(G-22530)***
**Central Decal Company Inc** 630 325-9892
6901 High Grove Blvd Burr Ridge (60527) ***(G-2829)***
**Central Die Cutting, Chicago** *Also called Animated Advg Techniques Inc* ***(G-3908)***
**Central Graphics Corp** 630 759-1696
1302 Enterprise Dr Romeoville (60446) ***(G-18807)***
**Central Hauling, Champaign** *Also called Southfield Corporation* ***(G-3543)***
**Central Hydraulics Inc** 309 527-5238
513 State Route 251 El Paso (61738) ***(G-8866)***
**Central IL Business Magazine** 217 351-5281
15 E Main St Champaign (61820) ***(G-3465)***
**Central Ill Communications LLC** 217 753-2226
1240 S 6th St Springfield (62703) ***(G-20413)***
**Central Ill Fbrcation Whse Inc** 217 367-2323
510 E Main St Urbana (61802) ***(G-21076)***
**Central Illinois Bus Publs Inc** 309 683-3060
5005 N Glen Park Place Rd Peoria (61614) ***(G-17336)***
**Central Illinois Counter Tops (PA)** 309 579-3550
11001 State St Mossville (61552) ***(G-15252)***
**Central Illinois Door** 309 828-0087
1001 Morrissey Dr Bloomington (61701) ***(G-2154)***
**Central Illinois Glass &** 309 367-4242
506 W Mount Vernon St Metamora (61548) ***(G-14741)***
**Central Illinois Granite Inc** 309 263-6880
909 Detroit Ct Morton (61550) ***(G-15155)***
**Central Illinois Hardwood** 309 352-2363
15634 Toboggan Ave Green Valley (61534) ***(G-11378)***
**Central Illinois Homes Guide** 309 688-6419
7307 N Willow Lake Ct Peoria (61614) ***(G-17337)***
**Central Illinois Mfg Co** 217 762-8184
201 N Champaign St Bement (61813) ***(G-1800)***
**Central Illinois Newspapers** 217 935-3171
111 S Monroe St Clinton (61727) ***(G-7279)***
**Central Illinois Poultry Proc** 217 543-2937
119 N Cr 000 E Arthur (61911) ***(G-886)***
**Central Illinois Scale Co** 309 697-0033
6000 Washington St Ste 2 Peoria (61607) ***(G-17338)***
**Central Illinois Sign Company** 217 523-4740
3040 E Linden Ave Springfield (62702) ***(G-20414)***
**Central Illinois Steel Company (PA)** 217 854-3251
21050 Route 4 Carlinville (62626) ***(G-3032)***
**Central Illinois Truss (PA)** 309 447-6644
105 Prospect Dr Deer Creek (61733) ***(G-7961)***
**Central Industries of Indiana** 618 943-2311
Rr 4 Box 200 Lawrenceville (62439) ***(G-13196)***
**Central Ink Corporation (PA)** 630 231-6500
1100 Harvester Rd West Chicago (60185) ***(G-21679)***
**Central Ink of Wisconsin Div, West Chicago** *Also called Central Ink Corporation* ***(G-21679)***
**Central Limestone Company Inc** 815 736-6341
16805 Quarry Rd Morris (60450) ***(G-15101)***
**Central Machines Inc** 847 634-6900
645 Margate Dr Lincolnshire (60069) ***(G-13435)***
**Central Machining Inc** 217 854-6646
502 W 1st North St Carlinville (62626) ***(G-3033)***
**Central Machining Service** 217 422-7472
2057 E Olive St Decatur (62526) ***(G-7855)***
**Central Manufacturing Company** 309 387-6591
4258 Springfield Rd East Peoria (61611) ***(G-8705)***
**Central Molded Products LLC** 773 622-4000
1978 N Lockwood Ave Chicago (60639) ***(G-4271)***
**Central Mountain Coffee LLC** 309 981-0094
520 N Chambers St Galesburg (61401) ***(G-10743)***
**Central Newspaper Incorporated** 630 416-4191
40 Shuman Blvd Ste 305 Naperville (60563) ***(G-15624)***
**Central Printers & Graphics** 773 586-3711
6109 W 63rd St Bedford Park (60638) ***(G-1543)***
**Central Radiator Cabinet Co (PA)** 773 539-1700
8857 N 5 Corners Rd Lena (61048) ***(G-13274)***
**Central Rbr Extrusions Ill Inc** 618 654-1171
193 Woodcrest Dr Dre Highland (62249) ***(G-11778)***
**Central RC Hobbies** 309 686-8004
Peoria Hts Peoria (61616) ***(G-17339)***
**Central Rubber Company** 815 544-2191
844 E Jackson St Belvidere (61008) ***(G-1745)***
**Central Service Center** 217 423-3900
715 N Bright St Decatur (62522) ***(G-7856)***
**Central Sheet Metal Pdts Inc** 773 583-2424
7251 Linder Ave Skokie (60077) ***(G-19976)***
**Central Specialties, Crystal Lake** *Also called Nelson-Whittaker Ltd* ***(G-7618)***
**Central States Pallets** 217 494-2710
26 Highland Ln Chatham (62629) ***(G-3617)***
**Central Steel and Wire Company** 773 471-3800
3000 W 51st St Chicago (60632) ***(G-4272)***
**Central Steel Fabricators** 708 652-2037
2100 Parkes Dr Broadview (60155) ***(G-2565)***
**Central Stone Company (HQ)** 309 757-8250
1701 5th Ave Moline (61265) ***(G-14921)***
**Central Stone Company** 309 776-3900
5533 E 400th St Colchester (62326) ***(G-7307)***
**Central Stone Company** 217 327-4300
38084 County Highway 21 Chambersburg (62323) ***(G-3443)***
**Central Stone Company** 217 723-4410
26176 487th St Pittsfield (62363) ***(G-17565)***
**Central Stone Company** 217 224-7330
8514 Rock Quarry Rd Quincy (62305) ***(G-17811)***
**Central Tool Specialities Co** 630 543-6351
325 W Factory Rd Ste A Addison (60101) ***(G-72)***
**Central Township Road & Bridge** 618 704-5517
920 E Bowman Dr Greenville (62246) ***(G-11390)***
**Central Welding Shop, Kewanee** *Also called Fred Stollenwerk* ***(G-12685)***
**Central Wire Inc (HQ)** 815 923-2131
6509 Olson Rd Union (60180) ***(G-21034)***
**Central Wood LLC** 217 543-2662
226 E County Road 200n Arcola (61910) ***(G-666)***
**Central Wood Products Inc** 217 728-4412
1819 Cr 1300e Sullivan (61951) ***(G-20742)***
**Centralia Machine & Fab Inc** 618 533-9010
306 S Chestnut St Centralia (62801) ***(G-3406)***
**Centralia Morning Sentinel** 618 532-5601
232 E Broadway Centralia (62801) ***(G-3407)***
**Centralia Press Ltd (PA)** 618 532-5604
232 E Broadway Centralia (62801) ***(G-3408)***
**Centralia Press Ltd** 618 246-2000
1808 Broadway St Mount Vernon (62864) ***(G-15403)***
**Centralia Sentinel, Centralia** *Also called Centralia Press Ltd* ***(G-3408)***

**Centric Co Inc** ....708 728-9061
4153 W End Rd Downers Grove (60515) ***(G-8407)***
**Centric Mfg Solutions Inc** ....815 315-9258
875 N Michigan Ave # 3614 Chicago (60611) ***(G-4273)***
**Centrifugal Services Inc** ....618 268-4850
5595 Highway 34 N Raleigh (62977) ***(G-17908)***
**Centro Inc** ....309 751-9700
1001 13th St East Moline (61244) ***(G-8672)***
**Centroid and Cardinal Engrg, Galesburg** *Also called Cardinal Engineering Inc* ***(G-10742)***
**Centup Industries LLC** ....312 291-1687
1901 W Chicago Ave Apt 2 Chicago (60622) ***(G-4274)***
**Centurion N D T, Streamwood** *Also called Centurion Non Destructive Tstg* ***(G-20648)***
**Centurion Non Destructive Tstg** ....630 736-5500
1400 Yorkshire Dr Streamwood (60107) ***(G-20648)***
**Century Aluminum Company (PA)** ....312 696-3101
1 S Wacker Dr Ste 1000 Chicago (60606) ***(G-4275)***
**Century Fasteners & Mch Co Inc** ....773 463-3900
4901 Fairview Ln Ste 1 Skokie (60077) ***(G-19977)***
**Century Filter Products Inc** ....773 477-1790
2939 N Oakley Ave Chicago (60618) ***(G-4276)***
**Century Metal Spinning Co Inc** ....630 595-3900
430 Meyer Rd Bensenville (60106) ***(G-1855)***
**Century Mold & Tool Co** ....847 364-5858
855 Touhy Ave Elk Grove Village (60007) ***(G-9362)***
**Century Molded Plastics Inc** ....847 729-3455
3120 W Lake Ave Glenview (60026) ***(G-11111)***
**Century Pipe Organ Company, Aurora** *Also called C P O Inc* ***(G-1123)***
**Century Printing** ....618 632-2486
510 Pepperwood Ct O Fallon (62269) ***(G-16465)***
**Century Signs Inc** ....217 224-7419
2704 N 30th St Quincy (62305) ***(G-17812)***
**Century Spring Corporation** ....800 237-5225
4045 W Thorndale Ave Chicago (60646) ***(G-4277)***
**Cenveo Inc** ....636 240-5817
3001 N Rockwell St Chicago (60618) ***(G-4278)***
**Cenveo Inc** ....773 267-1717
3001 N Rockwell St Chicago (60618) ***(G-4279)***
**Cenveo Inc** ....773 539-0411
2950 N Campbell Ave Chicago (60618) ***(G-4280)***
**Cenveo Inc** ....217 243-4258
320 E Morton Ave Jacksonville (62650) ***(G-12383)***
**Cenveo Corporation** ....312 286-6400
5445 N Elston Ave Chicago (60630) ***(G-4281)***
**Cera Ltd** ....773 334-1042
5542 N Lakewood Ave Chicago (60640) ***(G-4282)***
**Cerro Flow Products LLC (HQ)** ....618 337-6000
3000 Mississippi Ave Sauget (62206) ***(G-19385)***
**Certified Asphalt Paving** ....847 441-5000
540 W Frontage Rd # 3175 Northfield (60093) ***(G-16396)***
**Certified Business Forms Inc** ....773 286-8194
5732 W Patterson Ave Chicago (60634) ***(G-4283)***
**Certified Heat Treating Co** ....309 693-7711
8917 N University St Peoria (61615) ***(G-17340)***
**Certified Polymers Inc** ....630 515-0007
4479 Lawn Ave Western Springs (60558) ***(G-21865)***
**Certified Power Inc** ....847 573-3800
970 Campus Dr Mundelein (60060) ***(G-15485)***
**Certified Tank & Mfg LLC** ....217 525-1433
3520 Norman St Springfield (62702) ***(G-20415)***
**Certiweld Inc** ....708 389-0148
13953 Kostner Ave Crestwood (60445) ***(G-7481)***
**Cervones Welding Service Inc** ....847 985-6865
1104 Lunt Ave Schaumburg (60193) ***(G-19470)***
**Ces, Ottawa** *Also called Clover Technologies Group LLC* ***(G-16956)***
**Ces Material Handling, Eureka** *Also called Crane Equipment & Services Inc* ***(G-9996)***
**Cetco, Hoffman Estates** *Also called Colloid Envmtl Tech Co LLC* ***(G-12002)***
**CF Gear Holdings LLC (PA)** ....847 376-8322
2064 Mannheim Rd Des Plaines (60018) ***(G-8162)***
**CF Industries Inc (HQ)** ....847 405-2400
4 Parkway N Ste 400 Deerfield (60015) ***(G-7994)***
**CF Industries Inc** ....309 654-2218
4 Miles W On Rte 84 Albany (61230) ***(G-352)***
**CF Industries Enterprises Inc** ....847 405-2400
4 Parkway N Ste 400 Deerfield (60015) ***(G-7995)***
**CF Industries Holdings Inc (PA)** ....847 405-2400
4 Parkway N Ste 400 Deerfield (60015) ***(G-7996)***
**CF Industries Nitrogen Llc (HQ)** ....847 405-2400
4 Parkway N Ste 400 Deerfield (60015) ***(G-7997)***
**CF Industries Nitrogen LLC (HQ)** ....847 405-2400
4 Parkway N Ste 400 Deerfield (60015) ***(G-7998)***
**CF Industries Sales LLC** ....847 405-2400
4 Parkway N Ste 400 Deerfield (60015) ***(G-7999)***
**Cfa Software, Addison** *Also called Computerized Fleet Analysis* ***(G-80)***
**Cfc Inc** ....847 257-8920
30 E Oakton St Des Plaines (60018) ***(G-8163)***
**CFC Applied Holographics, Chicago Heights** *Also called CFC International Corporation* ***(G-7087)***
**CFC International Inc** ....708 891-3456
500 State St Chicago Heights (60411) ***(G-7086)***
**CFC International Corporation (HQ)** ....708 323-4131
500 State St Chicago Heights (60411) ***(G-7087)***
**CFC Wire Forms Inc** ....630 879-7575
1000 Douglas Rd Batavia (60510) ***(G-1428)***
**Cfcl, Schaumburg** *Also called Chicago Freight Car Leasing Co* ***(G-19471)***
**Cfpg Ltd (HQ)** ....630 679-1420
2500 Intrntonale Pkwy Woodridge (60517) ***(G-22459)***
**CGC Corporation** ....773 838-3400
7401 S Cicero Ave Chicago (60629) ***(G-4284)***
**Cgi Automated Mfg Inc** ....815 221-5300
275 Innovation Dr Romeoville (60446) ***(G-18808)***
**Cgk Enterprises Inc** ....847 888-1362
695 Church Rd Elgin (60123) ***(G-8985)***
**Cgk Enterprises Inc** ....815 942-0080
1362 Bungalow Rd Morris (60450) ***(G-15102)***
**CGR Technologies Inc** ....847 934-7622
350 W Colfax St Palatine (60067) ***(G-17010)***
**Ch Distillery, Chicago** *Also called 773 LLC* ***(G-3675)***
**CH Machining Company** ....630 595-1050
1044 Fairway Dr Bensenville (60106) ***(G-1856)***
**Chad Mazeika** ....815 298-8118
3705 Burrmont Rd Rockford (61107) ***(G-18303)***
**Chadwick Manufacturing Ltd** ....815 684-5152
224 N Main St Chadwick (61014) ***(G-3440)***
**Chain O'Lakes Ready-Mixed Co, Bridgeview** *Also called Southfield Corporation* ***(G-2529)***
**Challenge Printers** ....773 252-0212
4354 W Armitage Ave Chicago (60639) ***(G-4285)***
**Challenge Publications L T D** ....309 421-0392
1948 Riverview Dr Macomb (61455) ***(G-14121)***
**Challenge Tool Co** ....847 640-8085
60 Joey Dr Elk Grove Village (60007) ***(G-9363)***
**Challenger Fabricators Inc** ....815 704-0077
4095 Prairie Hill Rd South Beloit (61080) ***(G-20142)***
**Challenger Lighting Co Inc** ....847 717-4700
1400 Kingsland Dr Batavia (60510) ***(G-1429)***
**Challinor Wood Products Inc** ....847 256-8828
1213 Wilmette Ave Ste 208 Wilmette (60091) ***(G-22250)***
**Chalon Wood Products Inc** ....630 243-9793
12670 111th St Lemont (60439) ***(G-13231)***
**Chamberlain Group Inc** ....630 833-0618
300 Windsor Dr Oak Brook (60523) ***(G-16498)***
**Chamberlain Group Inc (HQ)** ....630 279-3600
300 Windsor Dr Oak Brook (60523) ***(G-16499)***
**Chamberlain Manufacturing Corp (HQ)** ....630 279-3600
300 Windsor Dr Oak Brook (60523) ***(G-16500)***
**Chambers Gasket & Mfg Co** ....773 626-8800
4701 W Rice St Chicago (60651) ***(G-4286)***
**Chambers Marketing Options** ....847 584-2626
1008 Bonaventure Dr Elk Grove Village (60007) ***(G-9364)***
**Chambliss Welding, Dahlgren** *Also called Jacob Chambliss* ***(G-7691)***
**Chamfermatic Inc** ....815 636-5082
7842 Burden Rd Machesney Park (61115) ***(G-14064)***
**Champaign Cnty Tent & Awng Co** ....217 328-5749
308 E Anthony Dr Urbana (61802) ***(G-21077)***
**Champion A Gardner Denver Co, Princeton** *Also called Gardner Denver Inc* ***(G-17750)***
**Champion Chisel Works Inc** ....815 535-0647
804 E 18th St Rock Falls (61071) ***(G-18128)***
**Champion Foods LLC** ....815 648-2725
9910 Main St Hebron (60034) ***(G-11716)***
**Champion Laboratories Inc (HQ)** ....618 445-6011
200 S 4th St Albion (62806) ***(G-356)***
**Champion Laboratories Inc** ....618 445-6011
200 S 4th St Albion (62806) ***(G-357)***
**Champion Laboratories Inc** ....803 684-3205
200 S 4th St Albion (62806) ***(G-358)***
**Champion Laboratories Inc** ....618 445-6011
301 Industrial Dr Albion (62806) ***(G-359)***
**Champion Laboratories Inc** ....618 445-6011
328 Industrial Dr Albion (62806) ***(G-360)***
**Champion Medical Tech Inc** ....866 803-3720
765 Ela Rd Ste 200 Lake Zurich (60047) ***(G-13052)***
**Champion Packaging & Dist Inc** ....630 755-4220
1840 Internationale Pkwy Woodridge (60517) ***(G-22460)***
**Champion Pizza, Hebron** *Also called Champion Foods LLC* ***(G-11716)***
**Champion Silkscreen & EMB, Park Forest** *Also called Ronald J Nixon* ***(G-17175)***
**Champion Wood Pallets Inc** ....630 801-8036
105 Hankes Ave Ste 100 Aurora (60505) ***(G-1127)***
**Champs Sports, Lombard** *Also called Foot Locker Retail Inc* ***(G-13801)***
**Channeled Resources Inc (PA)** ....312 733-4200
240 N Ashland Ave Chicago (60607) ***(G-4287)***
**Char Crust Co Inc** ....773 528-0600
3017 N Lincoln Ave Chicago (60657) ***(G-4288)***
**Charger Water Conditioning Inc (HQ)** ....847 967-9558
8150 Lehigh Ave Ste A Morton Grove (60053) ***(G-15192)***
**Charles Atwater Assoc Inc** ....815 678-4813
5705 George St Richmond (60071) ***(G-17959)***
**Charles Autin Limited** ....312 432-0888
1801 S Canal St Chicago (60616) ***(G-4289)***

ALPHABETIC

# Charles C Thomas Publisher | ALPHABETIC SECTION

**Charles C Thomas Publisher**..................217 789-8980
2600 S 1st St  Springfield  (62704)  *(G-20416)*
**Charles Chauncey Wells Inc**..................708 524-0695
735 N Grove Ave  Oak Park  (60302)  *(G-16657)*
**Charles Cicero Fingerhut (PA)**..................708 652-3643
5537 W Cermak Rd  Chicago  (60804)  *(G-4290)*
**Charles Crane**..................815 258-5375
188 E 3100 North Rd  Clifton  (60927)  *(G-7273)*
**Charles E Mahoney Company**..................618 235-3355
209 Service St  Swansea  (62226)  *(G-20776)*
**Charles Electronics  LLC**..................815 244-7981
302 S East St  Mount Carroll  (61053)  *(G-15290)*
**Charles Fingerhut Bakeries, Chicago** Also called Charles Cicero Fingerhut *(G-4290)*
**Charles H Kerr Publishing Co**..................773 262-1329
1726 W Jarvis Ave  Chicago  (60626)  *(G-4291)*
**Charles H Luck Envelope Inc**..................847 451-1500
10551 Anderson Pl  Franklin Park  (60131)  *(G-10427)*
**Charles Horberg Jewelers Inc**..................312 263-4924
5 S Wabash Ave Ste 706  Chicago  (60603)  *(G-4292)*
**Charles Industries  Ltd (PA)**..................847 806-6300
5600 Apollo Dr  Rolling Meadows  (60008)  *(G-18719)*
**Charles Industries  Ltd**..................217 826-2318
16265 E National Rd  Marshall  (62441)  *(G-14319)*
**Charles Industries  Ltd**..................217 893-8335
201 Shellhouse Dr  Rantoul  (61866)  *(G-17922)*
**Charles Industries  Ltd**..................217 932-2068
400 Se 8th St  Casey  (62420)  *(G-3381)*
**Charles Industries  Ltd**..................217 932-5294
503 Ne 15th St  Casey  (62420)  *(G-3382)*
**Charles K Eichen**..................217 854-9751
20002 Claremont Rd  Carlinville  (62626)  *(G-3034)*
**Charles N Benner  Inc**..................312 829-4300
401 N Western Ave Ste 4  Chicago  (60612)  *(G-4293)*
**Charles R Frontczak**..................224 392-4151
4816 Mohawk Rd  Rockford  (61107)  *(G-18304)*
**Charles River Laboratories Inc**..................309 923-7122
117 W Husseman St  Roanoke  (61561)  *(G-18049)*
**Charles Selon Associates, Northbrook** Also called A M Lee Inc *(G-16195)*
**Charles Sheridan and Sons**..................847 903-7209
2331 Church St  Evanston  (60201)  *(G-10020)*
**Charleston Concrete Supply Co**..................217 345-6404
2417 18th St  Charleston  (61920)  *(G-3592)*
**Charleston County Market**..................217 345-7031
551 W Lincoln Ave  Charleston  (61920)  *(G-3593)*
**Charleston Farrier Contruction, Charleston** Also called Charleston Concrete Supply Co *(G-3592)*
**Charleston Graphics Inc**..................
807a 18th St  Charleston  (61920)  *(G-3594)*
**Charleston Industries  Inc**..................847 228-7150
1005 Tonne Rd  Elk Grove Village  (60007)  *(G-9365)*
**Charleston Ready Mix, Charleston** Also called Mid-Illinois Concrete  Inc *(G-3604)*
**Charleston Stone Company**..................217 345-6292
9709 N County Rd 2000 E  Ashmore  (61912)  *(G-928)*
**Charlie, Northbrook** Also called Mosaic Construction *(G-16315)*
**Charlotte Dmg Inc**..................630 227-3900
265 Spring Lake Dr  Itasca  (60143)  *(G-12243)*
**Charlotte Louise Tate**..................773 849-3236
1304 E 87th St  Chicago  (60619)  *(G-4294)*
**Charnor  Inc**..................309 787-2427
1711 1st Ave E  Milan  (61264)  *(G-14778)*
**Charter Dura-Bar  Inc (HQ)**..................815 338-3900
2100 W Lake Shore Dr  Woodstock  (60098)  *(G-22551)*
**Charter Dura-Bar  Inc**..................815 338-7800
1800 W Lake Shore Dr  Woodstock  (60098)  *(G-22552)*
**Charter Dura-Bar  Inc**..................847 854-1044
2401 Huntington Dr N  Algonquin  (60102)  *(G-383)*
**Chartnet Technologies  Inc**..................630 385-4100
220 Garden St  Yorkville  (60560)  *(G-22651)*
**Chartrand Equipement Co, Ellis Grove** Also called Chartrand Equipment Co Inc *(G-9826)*
**Chartrand Equipment Co Inc**..................618 853-2314
6760 State Route 3  Ellis Grove  (62241)  *(G-9826)*
**Chartwell Studio Inc**..................847 868-8674
824 Sheridan Rd  Evanston  (60202)  *(G-10021)*
**Charwat Food Group  Ltd**..................630 847-3473
3 Grant Sq 251  Hinsdale  (60521)  *(G-11944)*
**Chas Levy Circulating Co**..................630 353-2500
815 Ogden Ave  Lisle  (60532)  *(G-13574)*
**Chas O Larson Co**..................815 625-0503
2602 E Rock Falls Rd  Rock Falls  (61071)  *(G-18129)*
**Chase Corporation**..................630 752-3622
1800 S Naperville Rd  Wheaton  (60189)  *(G-21940)*
**Chase Corporation**..................708 385-4679
12657 S Ridgeland Ave  Palos Heights  (60463)  *(G-17101)*
**Chase Corporation**..................847 866-8500
1527 Lyons St  Evanston  (60201)  *(G-10022)*
**Chase Fasteners  Inc**..................708 345-0335
1539 N 25th Ave  Melrose Park  (60160)  *(G-14608)*
**Chase Group LLC**..................847 564-2000
305 Era Dr  Northbrook  (60062)  *(G-16219)*

**Chase Products Co**..................708 865-1000
2727 Gardner Rd  Broadview  (60155)  *(G-2566)*
**Chase Security Systems Inc**..................773 594-1919
5947 N Milwaukee Ave  Chicago  (60646)  *(G-4295)*
**Chassis Service Unlimited**..................847 336-2305
2984 N Wadsworth Rd  Waukegan  (60087)  *(G-21536)*
**Chateau Food Products  Inc**..................708 863-4207
6137 W Cermak Rd  Chicago  (60804)  *(G-4296)*
**Chatham Clarion, Auburn** Also called South County Publications *(G-949)*
**Chatham Corporation (PA)**..................847 634-5506
350 Barclay Blvd  Lincolnshire  (60069)  *(G-13436)*
**Chatham Plastics Inc**..................217 483-1481
7 Kemp Dr  Chatham  (62629)  *(G-3618)*
**Chaulsetts Painting**..................618 931-6958
804 E Chain Of Rocks Rd  Granite City  (62040)  *(G-11270)*
**Checkpoint Systems  Inc**..................630 771-4240
1140 Windham Pkwy  Romeoville  (60446)  *(G-18809)*
**Ched Markay Inc**..................847 566-3307
1065 E High St  Mundelein  (60060)  *(G-15486)*
**Cheers Food and Fuel 240**..................618 995-9153
845 S Broadway  Goreville  (62939)  *(G-11250)*
**Cheers Food Fuel**..................618 827-4836
510 Ne Front St  Dongola  (62926)  *(G-8379)*
**Cheese Cake, Chicago** Also called Jr Bakery *(G-5331)*
**Cheese Merchants America LLC**..................630 221-0580
1301 Schiferl Rd  Bartlett  (60103)  *(G-1338)*
**Chef M J Brando, Arlington Heights** Also called Bran-Zan Holdings LLC *(G-728)*
**Chef Solutions  Inc**..................800 877-1157
120 W Palatine Rd  Wheeling  (60090)  *(G-22025)*
**Chelar Tool & Die  Inc**..................618 234-6550
11 N Florida Ave  Belleville  (62221)  *(G-1618)*
**Chellino Cheese Co, Joliet** Also called Topz Dairy Products Co *(G-12583)*
**Chelsea Framing Products Inc**..................847 550-5556
333 Enterprise Pkwy  Lake Zurich  (60047)  *(G-13053)*
**Chelsea's Beads, Highland Park** Also called Smart Creations Inc *(G-11869)*
**Chem Free Solutions (PA)**..................630 541-7931
8420 Evergreen Ln  Darien  (60561)  *(G-7791)*
**Chem Processing  Inc (PA)**..................815 874-8118
3910 Linden Oaks Dr  Rockford  (61109)  *(G-18305)*
**Chem Processing  Inc**..................815 965-1037
715 N Madison St  Rockford  (61107)  *(G-18306)*
**Chem Spec Corporation**..................847 891-2133
2n900 Bowgren Dr  Elburn  (60119)  *(G-8879)*
**Chem Trade Global**..................847 675-2682
3832 Dobson St  Skokie  (60076)  *(G-19978)*
**Chem-Cast  Ltd**..................217 443-5532
1009 Lynch Rd  Danville  (61834)  *(G-7709)*
**Chem-Impex International Inc**..................630 350-5015
935 Dillon Dr  Wood Dale  (60191)  *(G-22351)*
**Chem-Plate Industries  Inc**..................708 345-3588
30 N 8th Ave  Maywood  (60153)  *(G-14422)*
**Chem-Plate Industries  Inc (PA)**..................847 640-1600
1800 Touhy Ave  Elk Grove Village  (60007)  *(G-9366)*
**Chem-Tainer Industries Inc**..................630 932-7778
2 N 225 Grace  Lombard  (60148)  *(G-13775)*
**Chemalloy Company LLC**..................
9700 W Higgins Rd # 1000  Rosemont  (60018)  *(G-18993)*
**Chemblend of America  LLC**..................630 521-1600
240 Foster Ave  Bensenville  (60106)  *(G-1857)*
**Chemi-Flex LLC**..................630 627-9650
1040 N Ridge Ave  Lombard  (60148)  *(G-13776)*
**Chemical Processing & Acc**..................847 793-2387
175 Old Hlf Day Rd 140-10  Lincolnshire  (60069)  *(G-13437)*
**Chemical Pump**..................815 464-1908
23233 S Center Rd  Frankfort  (60423)  *(G-10309)*
**Chemical Specialties Mfg Corp**..................309 697-5400
8316 W Route 24  Mapleton  (61547)  *(G-14207)*
**Chemix Corp**..................708 754-2150
330 W 194th St  Glenwood  (60425)  *(G-11215)*
**Chemprobe Inc**..................847 231-4534
888 E Belvidere Rd # 313  Grayslake  (60030)  *(G-11326)*
**Chemring Energetic Devices Inc**..................630 969-0620
2525 Curtiss St  Downers Grove  (60515)  *(G-8408)*
**Chemsci Technologies Inc**..................815 608-9135
6574 Revlon Dr  Belvidere  (61008)  *(G-1746)*
**Chemsong Inc**..................
22w471 Mccarron Rd  Glen Ellyn  (60137)  *(G-10962)*
**Chemstation Chicago LLC**..................630 279-2857
934 N Oaklawn Ave Ste 1  Elmhurst  (60126)  *(G-9846)*
**Chemtech Plastics  Inc**..................630 503-6000
765 Church Rd  Elgin  (60123)  *(G-8986)*
**Chemtech Services  Inc**..................815 838-4800
20648 Gaskin Dr  Lockport  (60446)  *(G-13709)*
**Chemtool Incorporated (HQ)**..................815 957-4140
801 W Rockton Rd  Rockton  (61072)  *(G-18694)*
**Chemtool Incorporated**..................815 459-1250
8200 Ridgefield Rd  Crystal Lake  (60012)  *(G-7551)*
**Chemtrade Chemicals US LLC**..................618 274-4363
2500 Kingshighway  East Saint Louis  (62201)  *(G-8746)*

# ALPHABETIC SECTION

**Chenoa Locker Inc** .................................................. 815 945-7323
 8 N Veto St  Chenoa  (61726)  *(G-3633)*
**Chep/Millwood, Melrose Park** *Also called Millwood Inc (G-14674)*
**Cherry Instruments, Chicago** *Also called Wrightwood Technologies Inc (G-7037)*
**Cherry Meat Packers Inc** .......................................... 773 927-1200
 4750 S California Ave  Chicago  (60632)  *(G-4297)*
**Cherry Street Printing & Award** ............................... 618 252-6814
 211 E Poplar St Ste 2  Harrisburg  (62946)  *(G-11597)*
**Cherry Valley Feed Supplies** .................................... 815 332-7665
 1595 S Bell School Rd  Cherry Valley  (61016)  *(G-3640)*
**Cheryl & Co** ............................................................. 708 386-1255
 1018 Lake St  Oak Park  (60301)  *(G-16658)*
**Cheryl's, Oak Park** *Also called Cheryl & Co (G-16658)*
**Chesley Limited** ....................................................... 847 562-9292
 3170 Macarthur Blvd  Northbrook  (60062)  *(G-16220)*
**Chester Brass and Aluminum** .................................. 618 826-2391
 600 Barron St  Chester  (62233)  *(G-3652)*
**Chester Dairy Company Inc (PA)** ............................. 618 826-2394
 1915 State St  Chester  (62233)  *(G-3653)*
**Chester Dairy Company Inc** ..................................... 618 826-2395
 1912 Swanwick St  Chester  (62233)  *(G-3654)*
**Chester Foundry, Chester** *Also called Chester Brass and Aluminum (G-3652)*
**Chester White Swine Rcord Assn** ............................ 309 691-0151
 6320 N Sheridan Rd Ste A  Peoria  (61614)  *(G-17341)*
**Chesterfield Awning Co Inc (PA)** ............................. 708 596-4434
 16999 Van Dam Rd  South Holland  (60473)  *(G-20256)*
**Chevron Commercial Inc** ......................................... 618 654-5555
 3545 George St  Highland  (62249)  *(G-11779)*
**Chewy Software LLC** .............................................. 773 935-2627
 507 W Aldine Ave Apt 1b  Chicago  (60657)  *(G-4298)*
**Chgo Daily Law Bulletin** .......................................... 217 525-6735
 401 S 2nd St  Springfield  (62701)  *(G-20417)*
**CHi Doors Holdings Inc (HQ)** .................................. 217 543-2135
 1485 Sunrise Dr  Arthur  (61911)  *(G-887)*
**CHI Home Improvement Mag Inc** ............................. 630 801-7788
 2031 Bryn Mawr Dr  Aurora  (60506)  *(G-1128)*
**CHI Montes, Cicero** *Also called Tele Guia Spanish TV Guide (G-7235)*
**CHI Overhead Doors, Arthur** *Also called CHi Doors Holdings Inc (G-887)*
**CHI-Town Printing Inc** ............................................. 773 577-2500
 6025 N Cicero Ave  Chicago  (60646)  *(G-4299)*
**Chicago Adhesive Products** ..................................... 630 978-7766
 1105 S Frontenac St  Aurora  (60504)  *(G-983)*
**Chicago Agent Magazine** ......................................... 773 296-6001
 2000 N Racine Ave  Chicago  (60614)  *(G-4300)*
**Chicago Alum Castings Co Inc** ................................ 773 762-3009
 205 W Wacker Dr Ste 1818  Chicago  (60606)  *(G-4301)*
**Chicago American Mfg LLC** .................................... 773 376-0100
 4500 W 47th St  Chicago  (60632)  *(G-4302)*
**Chicago Anodizing Company** .................................. 773 533-3737
 4112 W Lake St  Chicago  (60624)  *(G-4303)*
**Chicago Apparel Company, Chicago** *Also called Nguyen Chau (G-5909)*
**Chicago Art Center Co** ............................................ 773 817-2725
 6540 N Washtenaw Ave  Chicago  (60645)  *(G-4304)*
**Chicago Beverage Systems LLC** .............................. 773 826-4100
 441 N Kilbourn Ave  Chicago  (60624)  *(G-4305)*
**Chicago Blind Company** .......................................... 815 553-5525
 20607 Burl Ct  Joliet  (60433)  *(G-12472)*
**Chicago Block, Berwyn** *Also called Northfield Block Company (G-2069)*
**Chicago Boating Publications** .................................. 312 266-8400
 851 N La Salle Dr  Chicago  (60610)  *(G-4306)*
**Chicago Booth Mfg Inc** ............................................ 773 378-8400
 5000 W Roosevelt Rd # 202  Chicago  (60644)  *(G-4307)*
**Chicago Bottling Industries** ..................................... 847 885-8093
 2075 Stonington Ave  Hoffman Estates  (60169)  *(G-11999)*
**Chicago Bread Company (HQ)** ................................ 630 620-1849
 1405 W Fullerton Ave  Addison  (60101)  *(G-73)*
**Chicago Brick Oven LLC (PA)** .................................. 630 359-4793
 559 S Kenilworth Ave  Elmhurst  (60126)  *(G-9847)*
**Chicago Bridal Store Inc** ......................................... 773 445-4450
 2146 W 95th St  Chicago  (60643)  *(G-4308)*
**Chicago Bullet Proof System, University Park** *Also called Metaltek Fabricating Inc (G-21056)*
**Chicago Can Conveyor Corp** ................................... 708 430-0988
 8912 Moore Dr  Bridgeview  (60455)  *(G-2476)*
**Chicago Candle Company** ....................................... 773 637-5279
 2701 N Sayre Ave  Chicago  (60707)  *(G-4309)*
**Chicago Candy & Nut, Chicago** *Also called Baldi Candy Co (G-4031)*
**Chicago Car Seal Company** .................................... 773 278-9400
 594 Brookside Rd  Chicago  (60612)  *(G-4310)*
**Chicago Cardinal Communication** ........................... 708 424-1446
 10232 S Kenton Ave  Oak Lawn  (60453)  *(G-16610)*
**Chicago Carton Plant, Chicago** *Also called Caraustar Industries Inc (G-4236)*
**Chicago Catalog, Chicago** *Also called Haggin Marketing Inc (G-5031)*
**Chicago Chain and Transm Co (PA)** ........................ 630 482-9000
 650 E Plainfield Rd  Countryside  (60525)  *(G-7417)*
**Chicago Chinese Times** .......................................... 630 717-4567
 424 Fort Hill Dr Ste 100  Naperville  (60540)  *(G-15625)*

**Chicago Circuits Corporation** .................................. 847 238-1623
 2685 United Ln  Elk Grove Village  (60007)  *(G-9367)*
**Chicago Citizen Newsppr Group (PA)** ..................... 773 783-1251
 806 E 78th St  Chicago  (60619)  *(G-4311)*
**Chicago Clamp Company** ....................................... 708 343-8311
 2350 S 27th Ave  Broadview  (60155)  *(G-2567)*
**Chicago Cnc Machining Co** ..................................... 708 352-1255
 6880 River Rd Unit 2  Hodgkins  (60525)  *(G-11972)*
**Chicago Collection Magazine, Chicago** *Also called Northwest Publishing LLC (G-5941)*
**Chicago Contract Bridge Assn (PA)** ........................ 630 355-5560
 1624 Masters Ct  Naperville  (60563)  *(G-15626)*
**Chicago Conveyor, Waukegan** *Also called United Conveyor Corporation (G-21635)*
**Chicago Copper & Iron Works** ................................ 773 327-2780
 3550 N Spaulding Ave  Chicago  (60618)  *(G-4312)*
**Chicago Crate Inc** ................................................... 708 380-4716
 440 Roe Ct  Downers Grove  (60516)  *(G-8409)*
**Chicago Creative Directory, Chicago** *Also called Creative Directory Inc (G-4498)*
**Chicago Crusader News Group (PA)** ....................... 773 752-2500
 6429 S King Dr  Chicago  (60637)  *(G-4313)*
**Chicago Culinary Center, Northbrook** *Also called T Hasegawa USA Inc (G-16375)*
**Chicago Custom Packing, Chicago** *Also called Harvest Food Group Inc (G-5052)*
**Chicago Cutting Die Co** .......................................... 847 509-5800
 3555 Woodhead Dr  Northbrook  (60062)  *(G-16221)*
**Chicago Data Solutions Inc** .................................... 847 370-4609
 146 Somerset Rd  Willowbrook  (60527)  *(G-22203)*
**Chicago Defender Newspaper, Chicago** *Also called Real Times II LLC (G-6305)*
**Chicago Defender Publishing Co** ............................. 312 225-2400
 4445 S King Dr  Chicago  (60653)  *(G-4314)*
**Chicago Deportivo Group Inc** .................................. 708 387-7724
 3748 Cleveland Ave  Brookfield  (60513)  *(G-2627)*
**Chicago Dial Indicator Company** ............................. 847 827-7186
 1372 Redeker Rd  Des Plaines  (60016)  *(G-8164)*
**Chicago Die Casting Mfg Co** ................................... 847 671-5010
 9148 King St  Franklin Park  (60131)  *(G-10428)*
**Chicago Direct Mail, Oak Brook** *Also called Flyerinc Corporation (G-16515)*
**Chicago Dowel Company Inc** .................................. 773 622-2000
 4700 W Grand Ave  Chicago  (60639)  *(G-4315)*
**Chicago Drapery & Carpet, Chicago** *Also called Cdc Group Inc (G-4262)*
**Chicago Dreis & Krump, Peotone** *Also called Dreis and Krump Mfg Co (G-17488)*
**Chicago Drive Line Inc** ........................................... 708 385-1900
 11500 S Central Ave  Alsip  (60803)  *(G-445)*
**Chicago Dropcloth Tarpaulin Co** ............................. 773 588-3123
 3719 W Lawrence Ave  Chicago  (60625)  *(G-4316)*
**Chicago Dryer Company** ......................................... 773 235-4430
 2200 N Pulaski Rd  Chicago  (60639)  *(G-4317)*
**Chicago Dscovery Solutions LLC** ............................ 815 609-2071
 23561 W Main St  Plainfield  (60544)  *(G-17586)*
**Chicago Dye Works** ................................................ 847 931-7968
 18 N State St  Elgin  (60123)  *(G-8987)*
**Chicago Enclosures** ............................................... 708 344-6600
 1975 N 17th Ave  Melrose Park  (60160)  *(G-14609)*
**Chicago Envelope Inc (PA)** ..................................... 630 668-0400
 685 Kimberly Dr  Carol Stream  (60188)  *(G-3127)*
**Chicago Export Packing Co** .................................... 773 247-8911
 1501 W 38th St  Chicago  (60609)  *(G-4318)*
**Chicago Extruded Metals Co, Cicero** *Also called Berkshire Investments LLC (G-7180)*
**Chicago Fastener Inc** .............................................. 708 479-9770
 10902 Walnut Ln  Mokena  (60448)  *(G-14857)*
**Chicago Faucet Company (HQ)** .............................. 847 803-5000
 2100 Clearwater Dr  Des Plaines  (60018)  *(G-8165)*
**Chicago Faucet Federal Cr Un** ................................ 847 803-5000
 2100 Clearwater Dr  Des Plaines  (60018)  *(G-8166)*
**Chicago Film Archive Nfp** ....................................... 773 478-3799
 5746 N Drake Ave  Chicago  (60659)  *(G-4319)*
**Chicago Flameproof WD Spc Corp (PA)** .................. 630 859-0009
 1200 S Lake St  Montgomery  (60538)  *(G-15037)*
**Chicago Floral Planters Inc** .................................... 708 423-2754
 10139 S Harlem Ave  Chicago Ridge  (60415)  *(G-7141)*
**Chicago Flyhouse Incorporated** .............................. 773 533-1590
 2925 W Carroll Ave  Chicago  (60612)  *(G-4320)*
**Chicago Freight Car Leasing Co (PA)** ..................... 847 318-8000
 425 N Martingale Rd Fl 6  Schaumburg  (60173)  *(G-19471)*
**Chicago Going Out Guide, Chicago** *Also called Real Estate News Corp (G-6302)*
**Chicago Gourmet Wholesale Bky, Elk Grove Village** *Also called New Chicago Wholesale Bky Inc (G-9650)*
**Chicago Grinding & Machine Co** ............................. 708 343-4399
 1950 N 15th Ave  Melrose Park  (60160)  *(G-14610)*
**Chicago Group Acquisition LLC** .............................. 312 755-0720
 350 N Orleans St Fl 10-S  Chicago  (60654)  *(G-4321)*
**Chicago Hardware and Fix Co (PA)** ......................... 847 455-6609
 9100 Parklane Ave  Franklin Park  (60131)  *(G-10429)*
**Chicago Harley Davidson Inc** .................................. 312 274-9666
 66 E Ohio St  Chicago  (60611)  *(G-4322)*
**Chicago Heights Pallets Co** .................................... 708 757-7641
 1200 State St  Chicago Heights  (60411)  *(G-7088)*
**Chicago Heights Star Tool and** ................................ 708 758-2525
 640 217th St  Chicago Heights  (60411)  *(G-7089)*
**Chicago Heights Steel, Chicago Heights** *Also called CHS Acquisition Corp (G-7090)*

**Chicago Home Improvement Mag, Aurora** *Also called CHI Home Improvement Mag Inc* *(G-1128)*
**Chicago Honeymooners LLC** ................................................. 312 399-5699
 3341 W Sunnyside Ave # 2  Chicago  (60625)  *(G-4323)*
**Chicago Industrial Pump Co** ................................................ 847 214-8988
 822 Schneider Dr  South Elgin  (60177)  *(G-20189)*
**Chicago Ink & Research Co Inc** ........................................... 847 395-1078
 97 Ida Ave  Antioch  (60002)  *(G-628)*
**Chicago Iron Works Corporation (PA)** ................................. 312 829-1062
 439 N Western Ave  Chicago  (60612)  *(G-4324)*
**Chicago Jet Group LLC (PA)** ............................................... 630 466-3600
 43 W 522 Rr 30  Sugar Grove  (60554)  *(G-20719)*
**Chicago Jewish News** .......................................................... 847 966-0606
 5301 Dempster St Ste 100  Skokie  (60077)  *(G-19979)*
**Chicago Jewish Star, Skokie** *Also called Star Media Group* *(G-20091)*
**Chicago Kiln Service** ............................................................ 847 436-0919
 2312 Wing St  Rolling Meadows  (60008)  *(G-18720)*
**Chicago Kite** ......................................................................... 773 467-1428
 5445 N Harlem Ave  Chicago  (60656)  *(G-4325)*
**Chicago Knitting Mills** ........................................................... 773 463-1464
 3344 W Montrose Ave  Chicago  (60618)  *(G-4326)*
**Chicago Lab Products** .......................................................... 312 942-0730
 660 N Union Ave  Chicago  (60654)  *(G-4327)*
**Chicago Latex Products Inc** ................................................. 815 459-9680
 345 E Terra Cotta Ave  Crystal Lake  (60014)  *(G-7552)*
**Chicago Lifesttyle, The, Carol Stream** *Also called Allen Entertainment Management* *(G-3096)*
**Chicago Lighthouse Industries** ............................................ 312 666-1331
 1850 W Roosevelt Rd Ste 1  Chicago  (60608)  *(G-4328)*
**Chicago Local Foods  LLC** ................................................. 312 432-6575
 1427 W Willow St  Chicago  (60642)  *(G-4329)*
**Chicago Magazine, Chicago** *Also called Tribune Publishing Company LLC* *(G-6774)*
**Chicago Magnesium** ............................................................ 708 926-9531
 14050 Wood St  Dixmoor  (60426)  *(G-8319)*
**Chicago Mailing Tube Company** .......................................... 312 243-6050
 400 N Leavitt St  Chicago  (60612)  *(G-4330)*
**Chicago Materials Corporation** ............................................ 630 257-5600
 13769 Main St  Lemont  (60439)  *(G-13232)*
**Chicago Meat Authority  Inc** ................................................. 773 254-3811
 1120 W 47th Pl  Chicago  (60609)  *(G-4331)*
**Chicago Meat, The, Chicago** *Also called Cherry Meat Packers  Inc* *(G-4297)*
**Chicago Menu Co, Glenview** *Also called Greek Art Printing & Pubg Co* *(G-11133)*
**Chicago Metal Fabricators Inc** ............................................. 773 523-5755
 3724 S Rockwell St  Chicago  (60632)  *(G-4332)*
**Chicago Metal Rolled Pdts Co (PA)** ..................................... 773 523-5757
 3715 S Rockwell St  Chicago  (60632)  *(G-4333)*
**Chicago Metallic Company LLC** ........................................... 708 563-4600
 4849 S Austin Ave  Chicago  (60638)  *(G-4334)*
**Chicago Mltlingua Graphics Inc (PA)** .................................... 847 386-7187
 550 W Frontage Rd # 2700  Northfield  (60093)  *(G-16397)*
**Chicago Mold Engrg Co Inc** ................................................. 630 584-1311
 615 Stetson Ave  Saint Charles  (60174)  *(G-19152)*
**Chicago Molding Outlet** ........................................................ 773 471-6870
 5858 S Kedzie Ave Ste 1  Chicago  (60629)  *(G-4335)*
**Chicago Motorcars** ............................................................... 630 221-1800
 27w 110 North Ave  West Chicago  (60185)  *(G-21680)*
**Chicago Mtal Sup Fbrcation Inc** ........................................... 773 227-6200
 4940 W Grand Ave  Chicago  (60639)  *(G-4336)*
**Chicago News LLC**
 415 E Golf Rd Ste 106  Arlington Heights  (60005)  *(G-734)*
**Chicago Off Set, Elk Grove Village** *Also called Sung Ji USA* *(G-9760)*
**Chicago Offset, Elk Grove Village** *Also called FL 1* *(G-9479)*
**Chicago Oriental Cnstr Inc** ................................................... 312 733-9633
 1835 S Canal St 2f  Chicago  (60616)  *(G-4337)*
**Chicago Oriental Wholesale Mkt, Chicago** *Also called Chicago Oriental Cnstr Inc* *(G-4337)*
**Chicago Ornamental Iron  Inc** ............................................... 773 321-9635
 1249 W 47th St  Chicago  (60609)  *(G-4338)*
**Chicago Pallet Service  Inc** .................................................. 847 439-8330
 1305 S 1st Ave  Maywood  (60153)  *(G-14423)*
**Chicago Pallet Service  Inc (HQ)** ......................................... 847 439-8754
 1875 Greenleaf Ave  Elk Grove Village  (60007)  *(G-9368)*
**Chicago Pallet Service II Inc (PA)** ........................................ 847 439-8330
 1875 Greenleaf Ave  Elk Grove Village  (60007)  *(G-9369)*
**Chicago Panel & Truss  Inc** ................................................. 630 870-1300
 875 Aurora Ave Ste 1  Aurora  (60505)  *(G-1129)*
**Chicago Paper Tub & Can, Chicago** *Also called Multi Packaging Solutions Inc* *(G-5832)*
**Chicago Paper Tube & Can Co., Chicago** *Also called Rolled Edge  Inc* *(G-6385)*
**Chicago Parent News Magazine, Oak Park** *Also called Wednesday Journal  Inc* *(G-16691)*
**Chicago Park District** ........................................................... 708 857-2653
 10736 Lombard Ave  Chicago Ridge  (60415)  *(G-7142)*
**Chicago Pastry  Inc** .............................................................. 630 529-6161
 142 N Bloomingdale Rd  Bloomingdale  (60108)  *(G-2100)*
**Chicago Pastry  Inc** .............................................................. 630 972-0404
 556 Saint James Gate  Bolingbrook  (60440)  *(G-2286)*
**Chicago Pipe Bending & Coil Co** ......................................... 773 379-1918
 4535 W Lake St  Chicago  (60624)  *(G-4339)*
**Chicago Pixels Mulitmedia  Nfp** ........................................... 312 513-7949
 5016 N Parkside Ave Apt 2  Chicago  (60630)  *(G-4340)*

**Chicago Plastic Systems  Inc** .............................................. 815 455-4599
 440 S Dartmoor Dr  Crystal Lake  (60014)  *(G-7553)*
**Chicago Powdered Metal Pdts Co** ...................................... 847 678-2836
 9700 Waveland Ave  Schiller Park  (60131)  *(G-19813)*
**Chicago Precious Mtls Exch LLC** ........................................ 312 854-7084
 30 S Wacker Dr Fl 22  Chicago  (60606)  *(G-4341)*
**Chicago Prepress Color Inc** ................................................. 708 385-3465
 14650 Kostner Ave  Midlothian  (60445)  *(G-14765)*
**Chicago Press Corporation** ................................................. 773 276-1500
 1112 N Homan Ave  Chicago  (60651)  *(G-4342)*
**Chicago Print Partners  LLC** ............................................... 312 525-2015
 120 W Laura Dr  Addison  (60101)  *(G-74)*
**Chicago Printing and EMB Inc** ............................................. 630 628-1777
 777 W Factory Rd  Addison  (60101)  *(G-75)*
**Chicago Printing Center, Schaumburg** *Also called Wide Image Incorporated* *(G-19789)*
**Chicago Producers Inc** ........................................................ 312 226-6900
 7507 Madison St Ste D4  Forest Park  (60130)  *(G-10237)*
**Chicago Protective Apparel Inc** ........................................... 847 674-7900
 3425 Cleveland St  Skokie  (60076)  *(G-19980)*
**Chicago Prvnce of The Soc Jsus** ......................................... 773 281-1818
 3441 N Ashland Ave  Chicago  (60657)  *(G-4343)*
**Chicago Quadrill Co** ............................................................. 847 824-4196
 1840 Busse Hwy  Des Plaines  (60016)  *(G-8167)*
**Chicago Retractable Awnings, Antioch** *Also called Midwest Screens  LLC* *(G-646)*
**Chicago Review Press Inc (PA)** ........................................... 312 337-0747
 814 N Franklin St Ste 100  Chicago  (60610)  *(G-4344)*
**Chicago Rivet & Machine Co (PA)** ....................................... 630 357-8500
 901 Frontenac Rd  Naperville  (60563)  *(G-15627)*
**Chicago Roll Co  Inc** ............................................................ 630 627-8888
 970 N Lombard Rd  Lombard  (60148)  *(G-13777)*
**Chicago Sales, Naperville** *Also called Nestle Usa  Inc* *(G-15711)*
**Chicago Salt Service, Chicago** *Also called Morton Salt  Inc* *(G-5809)*
**Chicago Scenic Studios  Inc** ................................................ 312 274-9900
 1315 N North Branch St  Chicago  (60642)  *(G-4345)*
**Chicago School Woodworking LLC** ..................................... 773 275-1170
 5680 N Northwest Hwy  Chicago  (60646)  *(G-4346)*
**Chicago Sea Ray Inc** ........................................................... 815 385-2720
 31535 N Us Highway 12  Volo  (60073)  *(G-21310)*
**Chicago Sensor  Inc** ............................................................ 773 252-9660
 1736 W Pierce Ave  Chicago  (60622)  *(G-4347)*
**Chicago Shade Makers Inc** ................................................. 708 597-5590
 12617 S Kroll Dr  Alsip  (60803)  *(G-446)*
**Chicago Sheet Plant, Bedford Park** *Also called Packaging Corporation America* *(G-1570)*
**Chicago Shirt & Lettering Co** ............................................... 773 745-0222
 1751 N Harlem Ave  Chicago  (60707)  *(G-4348)*
**Chicago Show  Inc** .............................................................. 847 955-0200
 851 Asbury Dr  Buffalo Grove  (60089)  *(G-2672)*
**Chicago Sign Designs, Elk Grove Village** *Also called E B G B Inc* *(G-9441)*
**Chicago Sign Group** ............................................................ 847 899-9021
 305 Albert Dr  Vernon Hills  (60061)  *(G-21154)*
**Chicago Silk Screen Sup Co Inc** .......................................... 312 666-1213
 882 N Milwaukee Ave  Chicago  (60642)  *(G-4349)*
**Chicago Slitter, Itasca** *Also called Rdi Group  Inc* *(G-12347)*
**Chicago Soy Dairy, Lombard** *Also called We Love Soy  Inc* *(G-13881)*
**Chicago Sports Media Inc** ................................................... 847 676-1900
 7842 Lincoln Ave  Skokie  (60077)  *(G-19981)*
**Chicago Steaks, Chicago** *Also called Tomcyndi  Inc* *(G-6737)*
**Chicago Steel Container Corp** ............................................. 773 277-2244
 1846 S Kilbourn Ave  Chicago  (60623)  *(G-4350)*
**Chicago Stool and Chair Inc** ................................................ 847 289-9955
 1230 Saint Charles St  Elgin  (60120)  *(G-8988)*
**Chicago Sun-Times Features Inc (HQ)** ................................ 312 321-3000
 350 N Orleans St Ste 1000  Chicago  (60654)  *(G-4351)*
**Chicago Sun-Times Features Inc** ........................................ 312 321-2043
 350 N Orleans St Ste 1000  Chicago  (60654)  *(G-4352)*
**Chicago Switchboard Co Inc** ............................................... 630 833-2266
 470 W Wrightwood Ave  Elmhurst  (60126)  *(G-9848)*
**Chicago T-Shirt Authority, Glendale Heights** *Also called Sunburst Sportswear  Inc* *(G-11079)*
**Chicago Tag & Label  Inc** .................................................... 847 362-5100
 2501 Commerce Dr  Libertyville  (60048)  *(G-13314)*
**Chicago Tank Lining Sales** .................................................. 847 328-0500
 3603 Hillside Rd  Evanston  (60201)  *(G-10023)*
**Chicago Tank Removal  Inc** ................................................. 312 214-6144
 70 W Madison St Ste 1400a  Chicago  (60602)  *(G-4353)*
**Chicago Technical Sales Inc** ............................................... 630 889-7121
 17w755 Butterfield Rd  Oakbrook Terrace  (60181)  *(G-16701)*
**Chicago Tempered Glass  Inc** ............................................. 773 583-2300
 2945 N Mozart St  Chicago  (60618)  *(G-4354)*
**Chicago Toffee Co, Glenview** *Also called Chocolate Potpourri  Ltd* *(G-11112)*
**Chicago Transmission Parts** ................................................ 773 427-6100
 3016 N Cicero Ave  Chicago  (60641)  *(G-4355)*
**Chicago Tribune** ................................................................... 773 910-6462
 665 W Sheridan Rd  Chicago  (60613)  *(G-4356)*
**Chicago Tribune Company (HQ)** .......................................... 312 222-3232
 435 N Michigan Ave # 200  Chicago  (60611)  *(G-4357)*
**Chicago Tribune Company** .................................................. 312 222-3232
 777 W Chicago Ave  Chicago  (60654)  *(G-4358)*
**Chicago Tribune Company** .................................................. 312 222-8611
 435 N Michigan Ave # 200  Chicago  (60611)  *(G-4359)*

ALPHABETIC SECTION
Cicero Plastic Products Inc

**Chicago Tube and Iron Company** ....815 834-2500
1 Chicago Tube Dr Romeoville (60446) ***(G-18810)***
**Chicago Tube and Iron Company** ....309 787-4947
1040 11th St W Milan (61264) ***(G-14779)***
**Chicago Turnrite Co Inc** ....773 626-8404
4459 W Lake St Chicago (60624) ***(G-4360)***
**Chicago Uniforms Company** ....312 913-1006
550 W Roosevelt Rd Chicago (60607) ***(G-4361)***
**Chicago Waterjet Inc** ....847 350-1898
42 Martin Ln Elk Grove Village (60007) ***(G-9370)***
**Chicago Wedding Resouce, Northbrook** *Also called Gail McGrath & Associates Inc* ***(G-16262)***
**Chicago Weekend, Chicago** *Also called Chicago Citizen Newsppr Group* ***(G-4311)***
**Chicago Weekly** ....773 702-7718
1131 E 57th St Chicago (60637) ***(G-4362)***
**Chicago White Metal Cast Inc** ....630 595-4424
649 N Rte 83 Bensenville (60106) ***(G-1858)***
**Chicago Wicker & Trading Co** ....708 563-2890
5625 W 115th St Alsip (60803) ***(G-447)***
**Chicago Wire, Chicago** *Also called Reino Tool & Manufacturing Co* ***(G-6326)***
**Chicago Wire Design Inc** ....773 342-4220
1750 N Kimball Ave Ste 1 Chicago (60647) ***(G-4363)***
**Chicago-Wilcox Mfg Co (PA)** ....708 339-5000
16928 State St South Holland (60473) ***(G-20257)***
**Chicagoland Closets LLC** ....630 906-0000
850 Ridgeway Ave Ste A Aurora (60506) ***(G-1130)***
**Chicagoland Metal Fabricators** ....847 260-5320
10355 Franklin Ave Franklin Park (60131) ***(G-10430)***
**Chicagoland Raceway** ....708 203-8003
2255 Maple Ave Downers Grove (60515) ***(G-8410)***
**Chicagoland Tails, Chicago** *Also called Tails Inc* ***(G-6666)***
**Chicagone Developers Inc** ....773 783-2105
557 E 75th St Chicago (60619) ***(G-4364)***
**Chicagos Finest Iron Works** ....773 646-4484
3319 W Washington Blvd Chicago (60624) ***(G-4365)***
**Chicagos Finest Ironworks** ....708 895-4484
17564 Chicago Ave Lansing (60438) ***(G-13159)***
**Chicagostyle Weddings** ....847 584-2626
1008 Bonaventure Dr Elk Grove Village (60007) ***(G-9371)***
**Chicap Pipe Line Company** ....708 479-1219
18401 Wolf Rd Mokena (60448) ***(G-14858)***
**Chicap Pipeline** ....618 432-5311
1505 Dickey Pond Rd Vernon (62892) ***(G-21140)***
**Chickens & Things, Naperville** *Also called Ramona Sedivy* ***(G-15738)***
**Chicor Inc** ....630 953-6154
2021 Midwest Rd Ste 200 Oak Brook (60523) ***(G-16501)***
**Child Evngelism Fellowship Inc** ....630 983-7708
365 Du Pahze St Naperville (60565) ***(G-15628)***
**Chillin Products Inc** ....815 725-7253
1039 Railroad St Frnt Rockdale (60436) ***(G-18217)***
**Chimney King LLC** ....847 244-8860
57 Noll St Waukegan (60085) ***(G-21537)***
**China Journal Inc** ....312 326-3228
2146a S Archer Ave Chicago (60616) ***(G-4366)***
**China Ying Inc** ....630 428-2638
1567 N Aurora Rd Ste 139 Naperville (60563) ***(G-15629)***
**Chinese American News** ....312 225-5600
610 W 31st St Chicago (60616) ***(G-4367)***
**Chino Works America Inc** ....630 328-0014
121 S Wilke Rd Ste 226 Arlington Heights (60005) ***(G-735)***
**Chipita America Inc (HQ)** ....708 731-2434
1 Westbrook Corporate Ctr Westchester (60154) ***(G-21832)***
**Chips Aleeces Pita** ....309 699-8859
308 Illini Dr East Peoria (61611) ***(G-8706)***
**Chips Manufacturing Inc** ....630 682-4477
741 Winston St West Chicago (60185) ***(G-21681)***
**Chips Marine** ....217 728-2610
1068 Cr 1025n Sullivan (61951) ***(G-20743)***
**Chiquita, Princeville** *Also called Seneca Foods Corporation* ***(G-17766)***
**Chirch Global Mfg LLC** ....815 385-5600
320 Cary Point Dr Cary (60013) ***(G-3330)***
**Chisholm, Boyd & White Company, Chicago** *Also called Venturedyne Ltd* ***(G-6884)***
**Chocolat By Daniel** ....815 969-7990
211 E State St Rockford (61104) ***(G-18307)***
**Chocolate Affair, Highland** *Also called Joyce Greiner* ***(G-11799)***
**Chocolate Chocolate Chocolate, O Fallon** *Also called Eat Investments LLC* ***(G-16467)***
**Chocolate Potpourri Ltd** ....847 729-8878
3908 Kiess Dr Glenview (60026) ***(G-11112)***
**Choi Brands Inc** ....773 489-2800
3401 W Division St Chicago (60651) ***(G-4368)***
**Choice Cabinet Chicago** ....630 599-1099
2000 Bloomingdale Rd # 135 Glendale Heights (60139) ***(G-11016)***
**Choice Cap Inc** ....847 588-3443
6310 W Touhy Ave Ste 111 Niles (60714) ***(G-15968)***
**Choice Furnishings Inc** ....847 329-0004
7518 Saint Louis Ave # 1053 Skokie (60076) ***(G-19982)***
**Choice Treat Equipment Mfg** ....708 442-2004
8130 47th St Lyons (60534) ***(G-14035)***
**Choice Usa LLC** ....847 428-2252
80 Industrial Dr Unit 111 Gilberts (60136) ***(G-10915)***
**Choochs** ....847 888-0211
64 S Grove Ave Elgin (60120) ***(G-8989)***
**Chopper Mm LLC** ....309 875-3544
500 Knox Road 900 E Maquon (61458) ***(G-14215)***
**Chris Dj Mix LLC** ....312 725-3838
1408 W Fillmore St Chicago (60607) ***(G-4369)***
**Chris Industries Inc (PA)** ....847 729-9292
2810 Old Willow Rd Northbrook (60062) ***(G-16222)***
**Chris Plating Inc** ....847 729-9271
2810 Old Willow Rd Northbrook (60062) ***(G-16223)***
**Chrisman Fuel** ....217 463-3400
102 Mcmillan St Paris (61944) ***(G-17144)***
**Chrisman Leader** ....217 269-2811
140 W Madison Ave Chrisman (61924) ***(G-7173)***
**Christ Bros Products LLC** ....618 537-6174
820 S Fritz St Lebanon (62254) ***(G-13212)***
**Christensen Precision Products** ....630 543-6525
1056 W Republic Dr Addison (60101) ***(G-76)***
**Christian Century** ....312 263-7510
104 S Michigan Ave # 1100 Chicago (60603) ***(G-4370)***
**Christian Cnty Mntal Hlth Assn (PA)** ....217 824-9675
707 Mcadam Dr Taylorville (62568) ***(G-20836)***
**Christian National Womans (PA)** ....847 864-1396
1730 Chicago Ave Ste 4585 Evanston (60201) ***(G-10024)***
**Christian Specialized Services** ....217 546-7338
2312 S Wiggins Ave Springfield (62704) ***(G-20418)***
**Christian Wolf Inc** ....618 667-9522
12618 Pioneer Rd Bartelso (62218) ***(G-1314)***
**Christiana Industries Inc** ....773 465-6330
6500 N Clark St Chicago (60626) ***(G-4371)***
**Christianica Center** ....847 657-3818
1807 Prairie St Glenview (60025) ***(G-11113)***
**Christianity Today Intl** ....630 260-6200
465 Gundersen Dr Carol Stream (60188) ***(G-3128)***
**Christiansen Sawmill and Log** ....815 315-7520
20080 Grade School Rd Caledonia (61011) ***(G-2931)***
**Christina's Bakery, German Valley** *Also called La Bella Chrstnas Kitchens Inc* ***(G-10891)***
**Christopher Concrete Products** ....618 724-2951
110 N Mine Rd Buckner (62819) ***(G-2647)***
**Christopher Glass & Aluminum** ....312 256-8500
3014 W Fillmore St Chicago (60612) ***(G-4372)***
**Christopher R Cline Prtg Ltd** ....847 981-0500
931 Oakton St Elk Grove Village (60007) ***(G-9372)***
**Christopher Wagner** ....630 205-9200
563 Cardinal Ave Oswego (60543) ***(G-16907)***
**Christos Woodworking** ....708 975-5045
5865 W 124th St Alsip (60803) ***(G-448)***
**Christys Kitchen** ....815 735-6791
2203 Aplington St La Salle (61301) ***(G-12768)***
**Chromatech Printing Inc** ....847 699-0333
16 Mary St Des Plaines (60016) ***(G-8168)***
**Chrome Crankshaft Company LLC** ....815 725-9030
4166 Mound Rd Joliet (60436) ***(G-12473)***
**Chrome Shop The, Rock Island** *Also called Berge Plating Works Inc* ***(G-18163)***
**Chrometec LLC** ....630 792-8777
820 N Ridge Ave Ste I Lombard (60148) ***(G-13778)***
**Chromium Industries Inc (PA)** ....773 287-3716
4645 W Chicago Ave Chicago (60651) ***(G-4373)***
**Chromold Plating Inc** ....815 344-8644
1631 Oak Dr McHenry (60050) ***(G-14486)***
**Chronicle Newspapers Inc** ....630 845-5247
1000 Randall Rd Geneva (60134) ***(G-10817)***
**CHS Acquisition Corp** ....708 756-5648
211 E Main St Chicago Heights (60411) ***(G-7090)***
**CHS Annawan, Annawan** *Also called Patriot Renewable Fuels LLC* ***(G-611)***
**CHS Rochelle, Rochelle** *Also called Illinois River Energy LLC* ***(G-18095)***
**Chucking Machine Products Inc** ....847 678-1192
3550 Birch St Franklin Park (60131) ***(G-10431)***
**Church of Brethren Inc (PA)** ....847 742-5100
1451 Dundee Ave Elgin (60120) ***(G-8990)***
**Church Street Brewing Co LLC** ....630 438-5725
1480 Industrial Dr Ste C Itasca (60143) ***(G-12244)***
**Churchill Cabinet Company** ....708 780-0070
4616 W 19th St Cicero (60804) ***(G-7182)***
**Churchill Wilmslow Corporation** ....312 759-8911
162 N Franklin St Ste 200 Chicago (60606) ***(G-4374)***
**Churny Company Inc** ....847 646-5500
200 E Randolph St Chicago (60601) ***(G-4375)***
**Chwey Software LLC** ....773 525-6445
1246 W George St Chicago (60657) ***(G-4376)***
**Ciba Vision Inc** ....847 294-3000
333 Howard Ave Des Plaines (60018) ***(G-8169)***
**CIC North America Inc** ....847 873-0860
5410 Newport Dr Ste 40 Rolling Meadows (60008) ***(G-18721)***
**Cicero Iron Metal & Paper Inc** ....708 863-8601
5901 W Ogden Ave Ste 7 Cicero (60804) ***(G-7183)***
**Cicero Plastic Products Inc** ....815 886-9522
121 Anton Dr Romeoville (60446) ***(G-18811)***

ALPHABETIC

(PA)=Parent Co (HQ)=Headquarters (DH)=Div Headquarters
2017 Harris Illinois Industrial Directory
1199

**Cicerone Certification Program**............773 549-4800
4043 N Ravenswood Ave # 306 Chicago (60613) ***(G-4377)***
**Cider Gould & Apple**............630 365-2233
2s230 Green Rd Elburn (60119) ***(G-8880)***
**Cie Source, Chicago** *Also called IB Source Inc* ***(G-5134)***
**Cif Industries Inc**............618 635-2010
20988 Old Route 66 Staunton (62088) ***(G-20556)***
**Cifuentes Luis & Nicole Inc**............847 490-3660
636 Remington Rd Ste D Schaumburg (60173) ***(G-19472)***
**Cigar Mix & Detail Shop**............708 396-1826
12408 S Ashland Ave Calumet Park (60827) ***(G-2957)***
**Cigtechs**............847 802-4586
4069 W Algonquin Rd Algonquin (60102) ***(G-384)***
**Cigtechs (PA)**............630 855-6513
173 W Irving Park Rd Roselle (60172) ***(G-18932)***
**Cim Bar Code Technology Inc**............847 559-9776
350 Pfingsten Rd Ste 102 Northbrook (60062) ***(G-16224)***
**Cim-Tech Plastics Inc**............847 350-0900
2670 United Ln Elk Grove Village (60007) ***(G-9373)***
**Cim-Tek Filtration, Bement** *Also called Central Illinois Mfg Co* ***(G-1800)***
**Cimc Capital, Oakbrook Terrace** *Also called Cimc Leasing Usa Inc* ***(G-16702)***
**Cimc Leasing Usa Inc**............630 785-6875
2 Transam Plaza Dr # 320 Oakbrook Terrace (60181) ***(G-16702)***
**Cimentos N Votorantim Amer Inc**............708 458-0400
7601 W 79th St Bridgeview (60455) ***(G-2477)***
**Cimino Machine Corp**............773 767-7000
5958 S Central Ave Chicago (60638) ***(G-4378)***
**Cinch Cnnctivity Solutions Inc (HQ)**............847 739-0300
1700 S Finley Rd Lombard (60148) ***(G-13779)***
**Cinch Connectors Inc (HQ)**............630 705-6001
1700 S Finley Rd Lombard (60148) ***(G-13780)***
**Cinch Connectors Inc**............630 705-6001
1700 S Finley Rd Lombard (60148) ***(G-13781)***
**Cindys Nail & Hair Care**............847 234-0780
950 N Western Ave Ste G Lake Forest (60045) ***(G-12891)***
**Cindys Pocket Kitchen**............815 388-8385
23802 Chemung St Harvard (60033) ***(G-11627)***
**Cinemaquest Inc**............847 603-7649
5250 Grand Ave Ste 14 Gurnee (60031) ***(G-11433)***
**Cino Incorporated**............630 377-7242
3n264 Loretta Dr Saint Charles (60175) ***(G-19153)***
**Cintas Corporation**............309 821-1920
1809 Industrial Park Dr Normal (61761) ***(G-16067)***
**Cintas Corporation**............708 563-2626
5600 W 73rd St Chicago (60638) ***(G-4379)***
**Cintas Corporation**............708 424-4747
9525 S Cicero Ave Oak Lawn (60453) ***(G-16611)***
**Cintas Corporation No 2**............708 424-4747
9525 S Cicero Ave Oak Lawn (60453) ***(G-16612)***
**Cipher Tech Solutions, Montgomery** *Also called Cipher Technology Solution* ***(G-15038)***
**Cipher Technology Solution**............630 892-2355
1556 Crescent Lake Dr Montgomery (60538) ***(G-15038)***
**Ciprianis Pasta & Sauce Inc**............630 851-3086
1050 Northfield Dr Aurora (60505) ***(G-1131)***
**Ciprianis Spaghetti & Sauce Co**............708 755-6212
1025 W End Ave Chicago Heights (60411) ***(G-7091)***
**Circle Boring & Machine Co (PA)**............815 398-4150
3161 Forest View Rd Rockford (61109) ***(G-18308)***
**Circle Boring & Machine Co**............815 397-3040
2316 7th Ave Rockford (61104) ***(G-18309)***
**Circle Caster Engineering Co**............847 455-2206
10706 Grand Ave Ste 1 Franklin Park (60131) ***(G-10432)***
**Circle Cutting Tools Inc**............815 398-4153
3161 Forest View Rd Rockford (61109) ***(G-18310)***
**Circle Engineering Company**............847 455-2204
10706 Grand Ave Ste 1 Franklin Park (60131) ***(G-10433)***
**Circle Gear & Machine Co Inc**............708 652-1000
1501 S 55th Ct Cicero (60804) ***(G-7184)***
**Circle K Industries Inc**............847 949-0363
25563 N Gilmer Rd Mundelein (60060) ***(G-15487)***
**Circle Metal Specialties Inc**............708 597-1700
4029 W 123rd St Alsip (60803) ***(G-449)***
**Circle Studio Stained Glass**............847 432-7249
946 Central Ave Highland Park (60035) ***(G-11827)***
**Circle Studio Stained Glass**............773 588-4848
3928 N Elston Ave Chicago (60618) ***(G-4380)***
**Circle Systems Inc (PA)**............815 286-3271
479 W Lincoln Ave Hinckley (60520) ***(G-11934)***
**Circle T Mfg**............217 728-4834
1801a Cr 1300e Sullivan (61951) ***(G-20744)***
**Circom Inc**............630 595-4460
505 W Main St Bensenville (60106) ***(G-1859)***
**Circuit Assembly & Mfg, Bloomington** *Also called Camtek Inc* ***(G-2151)***
**Circuit Engineering LLC**............847 806-7777
1390 Lunt Ave Elk Grove Village (60007) ***(G-9374)***
**Circuit Works Corporation (PA)**............847 283-8600
3135 N Oak Grove Ave Waukegan (60087) ***(G-21538)***
**Circuit World Inc**............630 250-1100
751 Hilltop Dr Itasca (60143) ***(G-12245)***
**Circuitron Inc**............815 886-9010
211 Rocbaar Dr Romeoville (60446) ***(G-18812)***
**Circuitronics**............630 668-5407
201 N Gables Blvd Wheaton (60187) ***(G-21941)***
**Cirrus Products**............630 501-1881
711 W Racquet Club Dr Addison (60101) ***(G-77)***
**CIS Systems Inc**............847 827-0747
4338 Regency Dr Glenview (60025) ***(G-11114)***
**Cisco, Carlinville** *Also called Central Illinois Steel Company* ***(G-3032)***
**Cisco Heating & Cooling**............309 637-6809
3304 W Linda Ln Peoria (61605) ***(G-17342)***
**Cisco Systems Inc**............847 678-6600
9501 Tech Blvd Ste 100 Des Plaines (60018) ***(G-8170)***
**Cisco Systems Inc**............217 363-4500
2302 Fox Dr Champaign (61820) ***(G-3466)***
**Cision US Inc (PA)**............312 922-2400
130 E Randolph St Fl 7 Chicago (60601) ***(G-4381)***
**Ciske & Dresch**............630 251-9200
1125 Paramount Pkwy Ste F Batavia (60510) ***(G-1430)***
**Cislak Manufacturing Inc**............847 647-1819
7450 N Natchez Ave Niles (60714) ***(G-15969)***
**Cisne Iron Works Inc**............618 673-2188
701 S Jones St Cisne (62823) ***(G-7250)***
**Cissna Park News, Cissna Park** *Also called Baier Publishing Company* ***(G-7254)***
**Cita Technologies LLC**............847 419-9118
975 Deerfield Pkwy Buffalo Grove (60089) ***(G-2673)***
**Citation Oil & Gas Corp**............618 966-2101
Hwy 14 E Crossville (62827) ***(G-7521)***
**Citation Oil & Gas Corp**............618 548-2331
2302 Hoots Chapel Rd Odin (62870) ***(G-16739)***
**Citgo Petroleum Corporation**............847 734-7611
13500 New Ave Lemont (60439) ***(G-13233)***
**Citgo Petroleum Corporation**............847 818-1800
1201 Ogden Ave Downers Grove (60515) ***(G-8411)***
**Citgo Petroleum Corporation**............847 229-1159
775 W Dundee Rd Wheeling (60090) ***(G-22026)***
**Citgo Refinery, Lemont** *Also called Pdv Midwest Refining LLC* ***(G-13254)***
**Citizenprime LLC**............708 995-1241
8940 W 192nd St Ste I Mokena (60448) ***(G-14859)***
**Citizens Bank National Assn**............708 755-0741
101 Dixie Hwy Chicago Heights (60411) ***(G-7092)***
**Citrix Systems Inc**............847 716-4797
540 W Frontage Rd # 3100 Northfield (60093) ***(G-16398)***
**City Beverage LLC**............708 333-4360
2064 W 167th St Markham (60428) ***(G-14302)***
**City Business Journals Network, Chicago** *Also called American City Bus Journals Inc* ***(G-3855)***
**City Foods Inc**............773 523-1566
4230 S Racine Ave Chicago (60609) ***(G-4382)***
**City Iron Works, Elgin** *Also called City Ornamental Iron Works* ***(G-8991)***
**City Living Design Inc**............312 335-0711
401 E Ontario St Apt 1302 Chicago (60611) ***(G-4383)***
**City of Chicago**............312 744-0940
6441 N Ravenswood Ave # 49 Chicago (60626) ***(G-4384)***
**City of Chicago**............773 686-2254
11601 W Touhy Ave Chicago (60666) ***(G-4385)***
**City of Chicago**............773 581-8000
6500 S Pulaski Rd Fl 2 Chicago (60629) ***(G-4386)***
**City of Chicago**............312 746-6583
4830 W Chicago Ave Chicago (60651) ***(G-4387)***
**City of Danville**............217 442-1564
5 Southgate Ct Tilton (61833) ***(G-20879)***
**City of Pekin**............309 477-2325
1208 Koch St Pekin (61554) ***(G-17256)***
**City Ornamental Iron Works**............847 888-8898
1140 Morningside Dr Elgin (60123) ***(G-8991)***
**City Screen Inc (PA)**............773 588-5642
5540 N Kedzie Ave Chicago (60625) ***(G-4388)***
**City Sports & Stage Door Dance**............708 687-9950
15801 Oak Park Ave Oak Forest (60452) ***(G-16576)***
**City Subn Auto Svc Goodyear**............773 355-5550
5674 N Northwest Hwy Chicago (60646) ***(G-4389)***
**City Utility Equipment**............815 254-6673
22414 W 143rd St Plainfield (60544) ***(G-17587)***
**City Zenith, Chicago** *Also called Cityzenith LLC* ***(G-4390)***
**Cityblue Technologies LLC (PA)**............309 676-6633
404 Sw Adams St Peoria (61602) ***(G-17343)***
**Citywide Printing, Des Plaines** *Also called Jph Enterprises Inc* ***(G-8217)***
**Cityzenith LLC**............312 282-2900
220 N Green St Chicago (60607) ***(G-4390)***
**Civil Constrs Inc Illinois, Elizabeth** *Also called Civil Constructors Inc* ***(G-9241)***
**Civil Constructors Inc**............815 858-2691
1307 W Longhollow Rd Elizabeth (61028) ***(G-9241)***
**Civilian Force Arms Inc**............630 926-6982
1208b Badger St Yorkville (60560) ***(G-22652)***
**Civitas Media LLC**............217 245-6121
235 W State St Jacksonville (62650) ***(G-12384)***
**CJ Anderson & Company**............708 867-4002
4751 N Olcott Ave Harwood Heights (60706) ***(G-11683)***

## ALPHABETIC SECTION — Clements National Company (HQ)

**CJ Drilling Inc** .................................................. 847 854-3888
19n041 Galligan Rd Dundee (60118) *(G-8560)*

**CJCwood Products Inc** ......................................... 815 479-5190
95 Grant St Crystal Lake (60014) *(G-7554)*

**Cjj Industries Inc** ............................................... 708 921-9290
211 Community Dr La Grange Park (60526) *(G-12753)*

**Cjs Printing** ..................................................... 309 968-6585
118 N Broadway St Manito (61546) *(G-14172)*

**Cjt Koolcarb Inc (PA)** .......................................... 630 690-5933
494 Mission St Carol Stream (60188) *(G-3129)*

**CK Acquisition Holdings Inc** .................................. 773 646-0115
13535 S Torrence Ave Q Chicago (60633) *(G-4391)*

**Ckd, Lake Zurich** Also called Coordinated Kitchen Dev Inc *(G-13057)*

**Ckd USA Corporation (HQ)** ................................... 847 368-0539
4080 Winnetka Ave Rolling Meadows (60008) *(G-18722)*

**Clad-Rex Steel LLC** ............................................ 847 455-7373
11500 King St Franklin Park (60131) *(G-10434)*

**Claire Manufacturing, Downers Grove** Also called Claire-Sprayway Inc *(G-8412)*

**Claire-Sprayway Inc (HQ)** .................................... 630 628-3000
2651 Warrenville Rd # 300 Downers Grove (60515) *(G-8412)*

**Claire-Sprayway Inc** ........................................... 630 628-3000
2651 Warrenville Rd # 300 Downers Grove (60515) *(G-8413)*

**Clarence Hancock Sawmill Inc** .............................. 618 854-2232
1191 E White Ln Noble (62868) *(G-16050)*

**Clariant Plas Coatings USA Inc** ............................. 630 562-9700
625 Wegner Dr West Chicago (60185) *(G-21682)*

**Clarich Mold Corp** ............................................. 708 865-8120
10119 W Roosevelt Rd Westchester (60154) *(G-21833)*

**Claridge Products and Eqp Inc** ............................. 847 991-8822
923 N State St Elgin (60123) *(G-8992)*

**Clark Tashaunda** ............................................... 708 247-8274
12406 S Morgan St Calumet Park (60827) *(G-2958)*

**Clark Caster Co** ................................................ 708 366-1913
7310 Roosevelt Rd Forest Park (60130) *(G-10238)*

**Clark County Ready Mix, Martinsville** Also called Mid-Illinois Concrete Inc *(G-14338)*

**Clark Gear Works Inc** ......................................... 630 561-2320
1218 Saratoga Dr Carol Stream (60188) *(G-3130)*

**Clark Printing & Marketing** .................................. 217 363-5300
501 Mercury Dr Champaign (61822) *(G-3467)*

**Clark Wire & Cable Co Inc** ................................... 847 949-9944
408 Washington Blvd Ste A Mundelein (60060) *(G-15488)*

**Clarke Aquatic Services Inc** ................................. 630 894-2000
675 Sidwell Ct Saint Charles (60174) *(G-19154)*

**Clarke Div, Batavia** Also called Tegrant Corporation *(G-1505)*

**Clarke Equipment Company** ................................. 701 241-8700
2649 Internationale Pkwy Woodridge (60517) *(G-22461)*

**Clarke Group Inc** .............................................. 630 894-2000
675 Sidwell Ct Saint Charles (60174) *(G-19155)*

**Clarke Mosquito Ctrl Pdts Inc (PA)** ........................ 630 894-2000
675 Sidwell Ct Saint Charles (60174) *(G-19156)*

**Clarkson Soy Products LLC** ................................. 217 763-9511
320 E South St Cerro Gordo (61818) *(G-3439)*

**Clarkwestern Dietrich Building** ............................ 815 561-2360
501 S Steward Rd Rochelle (61068) *(G-18083)*

**Clarus Therapeutics Inc** ..................................... 847 562-4300
555 Skokie Blvd Ste 340 Northbrook (60062) *(G-16225)*

**Class, Palatine** Also called Complete Lawn and Snow Service *(G-17014)*

**Class A Grinding** ............................................... 815 874-2118
3704 Samuelson Rd Rockford (61109) *(G-18311)*

**Class Printing, Schaumburg** Also called Allprint Graphics Inc *(G-19432)*

**Classic Automation & Tool** .................................. 708 388-6311
4329 136th Ct Crestwood (60445) *(G-7482)*

**Classic Color Inc** .............................................. 708 484-0000
2424 S 25th Ave Broadview (60155) *(G-2568)*

**Classic Embroidery Inc** ...................................... 708 485-7034
6939 W 59th St Chicago (60638) *(G-4392)*

**Classic Fasteners LLC** ....................................... 630 605-0195
3540 Stern Ave Saint Charles (60174) *(G-19157)*

**Classic Foods, Lincolnwood** Also called Danziger Kosher Catering Inc *(G-13506)*

**Classic Group, The, Chicago** Also called Classic Vending Inc *(G-4395)*

**Classic Impressions Inc** .......................................
150 Kendall Point Dr B Oswego (60543) *(G-16908)*

**Classic Management, Hainesville** Also called Classic Printery Inc *(G-11522)*

**Classic Metal Company Inc** ................................. 815 252-0104
115 16th St Mendota (61342) *(G-14718)*

**Classic Midwest Die Mold Inc** .............................. 773 227-8000
1140 N Kostner Ave Chicago (60651) *(G-4393)*

**Classic Molding Co Inc** ...................................... 847 671-7888
3800 Wesley Ter Schiller Park (60176) *(G-19814)*

**Classic Packaging Corporation** ............................ 224 723-5157
3390 Commercial Ave Northbrook (60062) *(G-16226)*

**Classic Printery Inc** .......................................... 847 546-6555
336 W Main St Hainesville (60073) *(G-11522)*

**Classic Printing Co Inc** ...................................... 217 428-1733
529 N Martin Luther King Decatur (62523) *(G-7857)*

**Classic Products Inc** ......................................... 815 344-0051
4010 W Albany St McHenry (60050) *(G-14487)*

**Classic Prtg Thermography Inc** ............................ 630 595-7765
735 N Edgewood Ave Ste F Wood Dale (60191) *(G-22352)*

**Classic Remix** .................................................. 312 915-0521
116 W Illinois St Fl 6w-B Chicago (60654) *(G-4394)*

**Classic Roadliner Corporation** ............................. 708 769-0666
8027 Marion Dr Apt 1e Justice (60458) *(G-12595)*

**Classic Screen Printing Inc** ................................. 708 771-9355
1401 Circle Ave Ste 1n Forest Park (60130) *(G-10239)*

**Classic Sheet Metal Inc** ..................................... 630 694-0300
1065 Sesame St Franklin Park (60131) *(G-10435)*

**Classic Vending Inc** .......................................... 773 252-7000
2155 S Carpenter St Chicago (60608) *(G-4395)*

**Classic Windows Inc** ......................................... 847 362-3100
750 Liberty Dr Libertyville (60048) *(G-13315)*

**Classical Statuary & Decor** ................................. 815 462-3408
21621 S Schoolhouse Rd New Lenox (60451) *(G-15871)*

**Classified Ventures** .......................................... 847 472-2718
1905 Lunt Ave Elk Grove Village (60007) *(G-9375)*

**Classique Signs & Engrv Inc** ................................ 217 228-7446
1702 Harrison St Quincy (62301) *(G-17813)*

**Classroom Technologies LLC** .............................. 708 548-1642
9227 Gulfstream Rd Frankfort (60423) *(G-10310)*

**Claud S Gordon Company** ................................... 815 678-2211
5710 Kenosha St Richmond (60071) *(G-17960)*

**Claviers Piano Explorer, Northbrook** Also called Instrumentalists Inc *(G-16278)*

**Clay Cnty Rhbilitation Ctr Inc** .............................. 618 662-6607
1 Commercial Dr Flora (62839) *(G-10203)*

**Clay County Advocate Press** ............................... 618 662-6397
105 W North Ave Flora (62839) *(G-10204)*

**Clay County Industries, Flora** Also called Clay Cnty Rhbilitation Ctr Inc *(G-10203)*

**Clay Vollmar Products Co** .................................. 847 540-5850
124 N Buesching Rd Lake Zurich (60047) *(G-13054)*

**Clay Vollmar Products Co (PA)** ............................ 773 774-1234
5835 W Touhy Ave Chicago (60646) *(G-4396)*

**Claymount Americas Corporation** ........................ 630 271-9729
2545 Curtiss St Downers Grove (60515) *(G-8414)*

**CLC Lubricants Company (PA)** ............................ 630 232-7900
0n902 Old Kirk Rd Geneva (60134) *(G-10818)*

**Clean and Science USA Co Ltd** ............................ 847 461-9292
475 N Martingale Rd Schaumburg (60173) *(G-19473)*

**Clean Energy Renewables LLC** ............................ 309 797-4844
4709 15th Street A Moline (61265) *(G-14922)*

**Clean Harbors Wichita LLC** ................................ 815 675-1272
2500 Westward Dr Spring Grove (60081) *(G-20330)*

**Clean Motion Inc** ............................................. 607 323-1778
4444 W Chicago Ave Chicago (60651) *(G-4397)*

**Clean Shop Division, Chicago Heights** Also called Aen Industries Inc *(G-7077)*

**Clean Sweep Environmental Inc** .......................... 630 879-8750
1805 Phelps Dr Batavia (60510) *(G-1431)*

**Clear Focus Imaging Inc (PA)** .............................. 707 544-7990
9201 Belmont Ave Ste 100c Franklin Park (60131) *(G-10436)*

**Clear Lake Sand & Gravel Co** .............................. 217 725-6999
2500 Shadow Chaser Dr Springfield (62711) *(G-20419)*

**Clear Lam Packaging Inc (PA)** ............................. 847 439-8570
1950 Pratt Blvd Elk Grove Village (60007) *(G-9376)*

**Clear Lam Packaging Inc** ................................... 847 378-1200
1900 Pratt Blvd Elk Grove Village (60007) *(G-9377)*

**Clear Nda LLC** ................................................ 470 222-6320
350 S Northwest Hwy # 300 Park Ridge (60068) *(G-17187)*

**Clear Pack Company** ........................................ 847 957-6282
11610 Copenhagen Ct Franklin Park (60131) *(G-10437)*

**Clear Print Inc** ................................................ 815 795-6225
768 Adams St Ottawa (61350) *(G-16954)*

**Clear Sight Inc** ................................................ 630 323-3590
220 Rosewood Ct Westmont (60559) *(G-21880)*

**Clear Stand, Brighton** Also called Piasa Plastics Inc *(G-2544)*

**Clear View Industries Inc** .................................. 815 267-3593
2429 Von Esch Rd Unit G Plainfield (60586) *(G-17588)*

**Clear View Shade Inc** ....................................... 708 535-8631
15430 S 70th Ct 32 Orland Park (60462) *(G-16847)*

**Clearchoice Mobility Inc** ................................... 847 986-6313
839 E Rollins Rd Round Lake Beach (60073) *(G-19074)*

**Clearnda, Park Ridge** Also called Clear Nda LLC *(G-17187)*

**Cleartrial LLC** ................................................. 877 206-4846
233 S Wacker Dr Ste 4500 Chicago (60606) *(G-4398)*

**Cleary Pallet Sales Inc** ..................................... 815 784-3048
32570 Genoa Rd Genoa (60135) *(G-10876)*

**Cleats Manufacturing Company, Chicago** Also called Cleats Mfg Inc *(G-4399)*

**Cleats Mfg Inc (PA)** ......................................... 773 521-0300
1855 S Kilbourn Ave Chicago (60623) *(G-4399)*

**Cleats Mfg Inc** ................................................ 773 542-0453
1701 S Kostner Ave Chicago (60623) *(G-4400)*

**Cleavenger Associates Inc** ................................. 630 221-0007
27w474 Jewell Rd Ste 2w Winfield (60190) *(G-22284)*

**Clement Industries Inc Del** ................................ 708 458-9141
5939 W 66th St Bedford Park (60638) *(G-1544)*

**Clement Wheel, Bedford Park** Also called Clement Industries Inc Del *(G-1544)*

**Clementi Products Inc** ..................................... 773 622-0795
2832 N Narragansett Ave Chicago (60634) *(G-4401)*

**Clements National Company (HQ)** ....................... 708 594-5890
2150 Parkes Dr Broadview (60155) *(G-2569)*

**Clements National Company** 708 594-5890
2150 Parkes Dr Broadview (60155) *(G-2570)*

**Cleo Communications Inc (PA)** 815 654-8110
4949 Harrison Ave Ste 200 Rockford (61108) *(G-18312)*

**Cleveland Hdwr & Forging Co** 630 896-9850
138 Pierce St Aurora (60505) *(G-1132)*

**Cleveland Quarry, Cleveland** *Also called Riverstone Group Inc (G-7271)*

**Cleveland Steel Container Corp** 708 258-0700
117 E Lincoln St Peotone (60468) *(G-17486)*

**Click Block, Rolling Meadows** *Also called Click-Block Corporation (G-18723)*

**Click-Block Corporation** 847 749-1651
1100 Hicks Rd Rolling Meadows (60008) *(G-18723)*

**Clientloyalty LLC** 312 307-5716
220 N Green St Ste 6015 Chicago (60607) *(G-4402)*

**Clifford W Estes Co Inc** 815 433-0944
1289 W Marquette St Ottawa (61350) *(G-16955)*

**Cliffords Pub Inc** 847 259-3000
1503 N Rand Rd Palatine (60074) *(G-17011)*

**Clifton Chemical Company (PA)** 815 697-2343
160 S Locust St Chebanse (60922) *(G-3630)*

**Climate Sltion Wndows Dors Inc** 847 233-9800
10100 Pacific Ave Franklin Park (60131) *(G-10438)*

**Climco Coils Company** 815 772-3717
701 Klimstra Ct Morrison (61270) *(G-15143)*

**Clinard Ready Mix Inc** 217 773-3965
Rr 24 Box West Mount Sterling (62353) *(G-15391)*

**Cline Concrete Products** 217 283-5012
438 W Thompson Ave Hoopeston (60942) *(G-12107)*

**Clinere Products Inc** 847 837-4020
28977 N Lemon Rd Mundelein (60060) *(G-15489)*

**Clingan Steel Inc** 847 228-6200
2525 Arthur Ave Elk Grove Village (60007) *(G-9378)*

**Clinkenbeard & Associates Inc** 815 226-0291
577 Grable St Rockford (61109) *(G-18313)*

**Clintex Laboratories Inc** 773 493-9777
140 W 62nd St Chicago (60621) *(G-4403)*

**Clinton County Materials Corp** 618 533-4252
100 Rhodes St Centralia (62801) *(G-3409)*

**Clinton Daily Journal, Clinton** *Also called Central Illinois Newspapers (G-7279)*

**Clinton Oil Corp** 815 356-1124
250 N Il Route 31 176 Crystal Lake (60014) *(G-7555)*

**Clinton Topper Newspaper** 815 654-4850
11512 N 2nd St Machesney Park (61115) *(G-14065)*

**Cliqster LLC** 847 732-1457
212 Pine Point Dr Highland Park (60035) *(G-11828)*

**Clodfelter Engraving Inc** 314 968-8418
2109 Holland St Alton (62002) *(G-566)*

**Cloos Robotic Welding Inc (HQ)** 847 923-9988
911 Albion Ave Schaumburg (60193) *(G-19474)*

**Cloos Robotics De Mexico, Schaumburg** *Also called Cloos Robotic Welding Inc (G-19474)*

**Clopay Building Pdts Co Inc** 708 346-0901
10047 Virginia Ave Ste A Chicago Ridge (60415) *(G-7143)*

**Clorox Company** 510 271-7000
7201 S Adams St Willowbrook (60527) *(G-22204)*

**Clorox Hidden Valley Mfg** 847 229-5500
1197 Willis Ave Wheeling (60090) *(G-22027)*

**Clorox Products Mfg Co** 708 728-4200
5063 S Merrimac Ave Chicago (60638) *(G-4404)*

**Clorox Products Mfg Co** 708 728-4200
5064 S Merrimac Ave Chicago (60638) *(G-4405)*

**Clorox Products Mfg Co** 847 229-5500
1197 Willis Ave Wheeling (60090) *(G-22028)*

**Closet By Design, Addison** *Also called Mountain Horizions Inc (G-222)*

**Closet Concept** 217 375-4214
1881 E 300 North Rd Milford (60953) *(G-14811)*

**Closet Concpts By Shlvng Unlim, Cherry Valley** *Also called Shelving and Bath Unlimited (G-3647)*

**Closet Works Inc** 630 832-3322
953 N Larch Ave Elmhurst (60126) *(G-9849)*

**Closet Works LLC** 630 832-4422
953 N Larch Ave Elmhurst (60126) *(G-9850)*

**Closet Works Division, Elmhurst** *Also called Carson Properties Inc (G-9845)*

**Closets By Design, Aurora** *Also called Chicagoland Closets LLC (G-1130)*

**Cloud 9 Division, Inverness** *Also called Mason Engineering & Designing (G-12209)*

**Cloud In A Vault, Mount Prospect** *Also called Cyber Innovation Labs LLC (G-15325)*

**Clover Club Bottling Co Inc** 773 261-7100
356 N Kilbourn Ave Chicago (60624) *(G-4406)*

**Clover Custom Counters Inc** 708 598-8912
9220 S Octavia Ave Bridgeview (60455) *(G-2478)*

**Clover Global, Ottawa** *Also called 4l Technologies Inc (G-16944)*

**Clover Global Headquarters** 815 431-8100
2700 W Higgins Rd Ste 100 Hoffman Estates (60169) *(G-12000)*

**Clover Plastics LLC** 630 473-6488
1145 Howard Dr West Chicago (60185) *(G-21683)*

**Clover Signs** 773 588-2828
2944 W Montrose Ave Apt 1 Chicago (60618) *(G-4407)*

**Clover Technologies Group LLC** 815 431-8100
2700 W Higgins Rd Ste 100 Hoffman Estates (60169) *(G-12001)*

**Clover Technologies Group LLC (HQ)** 815 431-8100
4200 Columbus St Ottawa (61350) *(G-16956)*

**Clover Technologies Group LLC** 815 431-8100
700 E Dayton Rd Ottawa (61350) *(G-16957)*

**Clover Wireless, Hoffman Estates** *Also called Clover Global Headquarters (G-12000)*

**Cloverdale Corporation** 847 296-9225
1583 Lee St Des Plaines (60018) *(G-8171)*

**Cloverhill Bakery, Chicago** *Also called Cloverhill Pastry-Vend LLC (G-4408)*

**Cloverhill Pastry-Vend LLC** 773 745-9800
2035 N Narragansett Ave Chicago (60639) *(G-4408)*

**Cloverleaf Feed Co Inc** 217 589-5010
Rr 267 Box S Roodhouse (62082) *(G-18882)*

**Clown Global Brands LLC** 847 564-5950
3184 Doolittle Dr Northbrook (60062) *(G-16227)*

**Cloyes Gear and Products Inc** 630 420-0900
1152 Frontenac Rd Naperville (60563) *(G-15630)*

**Cloz Companies Inc (PA)** 773 247-8879
5550 Touhy Ave Ste 202 Skokie (60077) *(G-19983)*

**Club House Designs, Chicago** *Also called Orland Sports Ltd (G-6014)*

**Clugston Tibbitts Funeral Home (PA)** 309 833-2188
303 E Washington St Macomb (61455) *(G-14122)*

**Clugston-Tibbots Monument Co, Macomb** *Also called Clugston Tibbitts Funeral Home (G-14122)*

**Clutch Systems Inc** 815 282-7960
10901 N 2nd St Machesney Park (61115) *(G-14066)*

**Clybourn Metal Finishing Co** 773 525-8162
2240 N Clybourn Ave Chicago (60614) *(G-4409)*

**Clyde Printing Company** 773 847-5900
3520 S Morgan St Fl 2a Chicago (60609) *(G-4410)*

**Clyde's Delicious Donuts, Addison** *Also called Herman Seekamp Inc (G-145)*

**CM Associates, Tinley Park** *Also called Cypress Multigraphics LLC (G-20907)*

**Cma Inc** 847 848-0674
929 Kelly Ave Joliet (60435) *(G-12474)*

**Cma Inc (PA)** 630 551-3100
19 Stonehill Rd Oswego (60543) *(G-16909)*

**Cma, Flodyne, Hydradyne, Hanover Park** *Also called Flodyne Inc (G-11581)*

**Cmb Printing Inc** 630 323-1110
15w700 79th St Unit 4 Burr Ridge (60527) *(G-2830)*

**CMC America Corporation** 815 726-4337
208 S Center St Joliet (60436) *(G-12475)*

**CMC Electronics Aurora LLC** 630 556-9619
84 N Dugan Rd Sugar Grove (60554) *(G-20720)*

**CMC Granite & Marble, Aurora** *Also called Heartland Granite Inc (G-1025)*

**CMC Tool Manufacturing** 630 350-0300
229 Evergreen Ave Bensenville (60106) *(G-1860)*

**Cmd Conveyor Inc** 708 237-0996
10008 Anderson Ave Chicago Ridge (60415) *(G-7144)*

**Cmetrix Inc** 630 595-9800
165 Mittel Dr Wood Dale (60191) *(G-22353)*

**Cmg Contmid Group, Park Forest** *Also called Continental/Midland LLC (G-17169)*

**Cmg Precision Machining Co Inc** 630 759-8080
1342 Enterprise Dr Romeoville (60446) *(G-18813)*

**CMI, Elmhurst** *Also called Copy-Mor Inc (G-9856)*

**CMI, Chicago** *Also called Craftmaster Manufacturing Inc (G-4490)*

**CMI Display, Chicago** *Also called Continental Marketing Inc (G-4458)*

**CMI Foods, Chicago** *Also called Custom Menu Insights LLC (G-4524)*

**Cml Technologies Inc** 708 450-1911
10330 W Roosevelt Rd # 205 Westchester (60154) *(G-21834)*

**Cmp Anodizing, Elk Grove Village** *Also called Cmp Associates Inc (G-9379)*

**Cmp Associates Inc** 847 956-1313
1340 Howard St Elk Grove Village (60007) *(G-9379)*

**Cmp Millwork Co** 630 832-6462
601 S Il Route 83 Ste 100 Elmhurst (60126) *(G-9851)*

**Cmt, Elk Grove Village** *Also called Centech Plastics Inc (G-9361)*

**Cmt International Inc** 618 549-1829
1400 N Wood Rd Murphysboro (62966) *(G-15575)*

**Cmv Sharper Finish Inc** 773 276-4800
4500 W Augusta Blvd Chicago (60651) *(G-4411)*

**Cnc Indusitries, Elk Grove Village** *Also called X-L-Engineering Corp (G-9820)*

**Cnc Machining, Arcola** *Also called G L Doemelt (G-669)*

**Cnc Swiss Inc** 630 543-9595
761 W Racquet Club Dr A Addison (60101) *(G-78)*

**CNE Inc** 847 534-7135
1018 Lunt Ave Schaumburg (60193) *(G-19475)*

**Cnh Capital America LLC (HQ)** 630 887-2233
6900 Veterans Blvd Burr Ridge (60527) *(G-2831)*

**Cnh Case Construction, Burr Ridge** *Also called Cnh Industrial America LLC (G-2832)*

**Cnh Industrial America LLC** 847 263-5793
2450 W Air Ln Waukegan (60087) *(G-21539)*

**Cnh Industrial America LLC** 309 965-2233
1498 Us Highway 150 Goodfield (61742) *(G-11244)*

**Cnh Industrial America LLC** 706 629-5572
6900 Veterans Blvd Burr Ridge (60527) *(G-2832)*

**Cnh Industrial America LLC** 309 965-2217
600 E Peoria St Goodfield (61742) *(G-11245)*

**Cnh Industrial America LLC** 630 887-2233
6900 Veterans Blvd Burr Ridge (60527) *(G-2833)*

# ALPHABETIC SECTION — Coles Craft Corporation

**Cnlc-Stc Inc (HQ)** .................................................. 312 321-3000
  350 N Orleans St  Chicago  (60654)  *(G-4412)*
**Cnv Enterprises Inc** ............................................. 815 405-6762
  8282 Old Ridge Rd  Plainfield  (60544)  *(G-17589)*
**Co-Fair Corporation** ............................................ 847 626-1500
  7301 Saint Louis Ave  Skokie  (60076)  *(G-19984)*
**Co-Ordinated Packaging Inc** ............................... 847 559-8877
  726 Anthony Trl  Northbrook  (60062)  *(G-16228)*
**Co-Rect Bar Products, Lincolnshire** Also called Co-Rect Products Inc *(G-13438)*
**Co-Rect Products Inc (PA)** .................................. 763 542-9200
  300 Knightsbridge Pkwy # 400  Lincolnshire  (60069)  *(G-13438)*
**Coach Inc** ......................................................... 630 232-0667
  306 Commons Dr  Geneva  (60134)  *(G-10819)*
**Coach Inc** ......................................................... 708 349-1053
  432 Orland Square Dr  Orland Park  (60462)  *(G-16848)*
**Coach House Inc** .............................................. 217 543-3761
  700 E Mill St  Arthur  (61911)  *(G-888)*
**Coach House Garages, Arthur** Also called Coach House Inc *(G-888)*
**Coakley Mfg & Metrology** .................................. 847 202-9331
  1141 N Doe Rd  Palatine  (60067)  *(G-17012)*
**Coal City Courant** .............................................. 815 634-0315
  271 S Broadway St  Coal City  (60416)  *(G-7291)*
**Coal City Redi-Mix Co Inc** ................................. 815 634-4455
  640 S Mazon St  Coal City  (60416)  *(G-7292)*
**Coal Field Development Co** ................................ 630 653-3700
  290 S Main Pl Ste 101  Carol Stream  (60188)  *(G-3131)*
**Coalesse** ........................................................... 312 622-6269
  222 Merchds Mrt Plz 1032  Chicago  (60654)  *(G-4413)*
**Coast Crane Company (HQ)** ............................... 847 215-6500
  1110 W Lake Cook Rd # 220  Buffalo Grove  (60089)  *(G-2674)*
**Coated Sand Solutions, Rochelle** Also called U S Silica Company *(G-18113)*
**Coates Screen, Saint Charles** Also called Sun Chemical Corporation *(G-19274)*
**Coating & Systems Integration** ........................... 312 335-1848
  47 W Division St Pmb 124  Chicago  (60610)  *(G-4414)*
**Coating Methods Incorporated** ........................... 847 428-8800
  853 Commerce Pkwy  Carpentersville  (60110)  *(G-3280)*
**Coating Specialty Inc** ......................................... 708 754-3311
  3311 Holeman Ave Ste 7  S Chicago Hts  (60411)  *(G-19101)*
**Coatings Applications Inc** .................................. 847 238-9408
  2671 United Ln  Elk Grove Village  (60007)  *(G-9380)*
**Coatings International Inc** .................................. 847 455-1400
  3429 Runge St  Franklin Park  (60131)  *(G-10439)*
**Cobalt Tool & Manufacturing** .............................. 630 530-8898
  131 W Home Ave  Villa Park  (60181)  *(G-21243)*
**Cobatco Inc** ...................................................... 309 676-2663
  1215 Ne Adams St  Peoria  (61603)  *(G-17344)*
**Cobius Hlthcare Solutions LLC** ........................... 847 656-8700
  853 Sanders Rd Ste 313  Northbrook  (60062)  *(G-16229)*
**Cobra Coal Inc** .................................................. 630 560-1050
  3n060 Powis Rd  West Chicago  (60185)  *(G-21684)*
**Cobra Metal Works Inc** ...................................... 847 214-8400
  1140 Jansen Farm Dr  Elgin  (60123)  *(G-8993)*
**Cobraa Inc** ........................................................ 618 228-7380
  350 W 4th St  Aviston  (62216)  *(G-1243)*
**Cobraco Manufacturing Inc (PA)** ......................... 847 726-5800
  300 E Il Route 22  Lake Zurich  (60047)  *(G-13055)*
**Coca Cola** ......................................................... 630 588-8786
  775 East Dr  Carol Stream  (60188)  *(G-3132)*
**Coca Cola Fleet Service** ..................................... 847 600-2279
  7500 N Oak Park Ave  Niles  (60714)  *(G-15970)*
**Coca-Cola, Chicago** Also called Emmert John *(G-4744)*
**Coca-Cola, Niles** Also called Coca Cola Fleet Service *(G-15970)*
**Coca-Cola, Carol Stream** Also called Coca Cola *(G-3132)*
**Coca-Cola Bottling Co Cnsld** .............................. 217 223-5183
  3321 Cannonball Rd  Quincy  (62305)  *(G-17814)*
**Coca-Cola Btlg Wisconsin Del** ............................ 847 647-0200
  7400 N Oak Park Ave  Niles  (60714)  *(G-15971)*
**Coca-Cola Company** .......................................... 847 647-0200
  7400 N Oak Park Ave  Niles  (60714)  *(G-15972)*
**Coca-Cola Refreshments USA Inc** ...................... 630 513-5247
  105 Industrial Dr  Saint Charles  (60174)  *(G-19158)*
**Coca-Cola Refreshments USA Inc** ...................... 217 348-1001
  1321 Loxa Rd  Charleston  (61920)  *(G-3595)*
**Coca-Cola Refreshments USA Inc** ...................... 708 597-6700
  5321 W 122nd St  Alsip  (60803)  *(G-450)*
**Coca-Cola Refreshments USA Inc** ...................... 815 636-7300
  10400 N 2nd St  Machesney Park  (61115)  *(G-14067)*
**Coca-Cola Refreshments USA Inc** ...................... 847 647-0200
  7425 N Oak Park Ave  Niles  (60714)  *(G-15973)*
**Coca-Cola Refreshments USA Inc** ...................... 309 787-1700
  4415 85th Ave W  Rock Island  (61201)  *(G-18167)*
**Coca-Cola Refreshments USA Inc** ...................... 708 597-4700
  12200 S Laramie Ave  Chicago  (60803)  *(G-4415)*
**Coca-Cola Refreshments USA Inc** ...................... 815 933-2653
  1220 Harvard Dr  Kankakee  (60901)  *(G-12605)*
**Coca-Cola Refreshments USA Inc** ...................... 217 544-4892
  3495 E Sangamon Ave  Springfield  (62707)  *(G-20420)*
**Coca-Cola Refreshments USA Inc** ...................... 217 367-1761
  2809 N Lincoln Ave  Urbana  (61802)  *(G-21078)*
**Coca-Cola Refreshments USA Inc** ...................... 618 542-2101
  Hwy 51 S  Du Quoin  (62832)  *(G-8552)*
**Cocacola Bottling Co** ......................................... 815 220-3100
  3808 Progress Blvd  Peru  (61354)  *(G-17505)*
**Cocajo Blades & Leather** .................................... 217 370-6634
  481 Oxley Rd  Franklin  (62638)  *(G-10378)*
**Code Sixfour LLC** .............................................. 312 429-4802
  111 W Illinois St  Chicago  (60654)  *(G-4416)*
**Coding Solutions Inc** .......................................... 630 377-5825
  394 38th Ave  Saint Charles  (60174)  *(G-19159)*
**Coding Solutions Inc** .......................................... 630 443-9602
  394 38th Ave  Saint Charles  (60174)  *(G-19160)*
**Cody Metal Finishing Inc** ................................... 773 252-2026
  1620 N Throop St  Chicago  (60642)  *(G-4417)*
**Coe Equipment Inc** ............................................ 217 498-7200
  5953 Cherry St  Rochester  (62563)  *(G-18116)*
**Coeur Inc** .......................................................... 815 648-1093
  11411 Price Rd  Hebron  (60034)  *(G-11717)*
**Coeur Capital Inc** ............................................... 312 489-5800
  104 S Michigan Ave  Chicago  (60603)  *(G-4418)*
**Coeur Mining Inc (PA)** ....................................... 312 489-5800
  104 S Michigan Ave # 900  Chicago  (60603)  *(G-4419)*
**Coeur Rochester Inc** .......................................... 312 661-2436
  104 S Michigan Ave  Chicago  (60603)  *(G-4420)*
**Cofair Products Inc** ............................................ 847 626-1500
  7301 Saint Louis Ave  Skokie  (60076)  *(G-19985)*
**Coffee Brewmasters Usa LLC** ............................. 773 294-9665
  351 Hastings Dr  Buffalo Grove  (60089)  *(G-2675)*
**Coffee News of Dupage County, Carol Stream** Also called Alali Enterprises Inc *(G-3095)*
**Cognex Corporation** .......................................... 630 505-9990
  800 E Diehl Rd Ste 125  Naperville  (60563)  *(G-15631)*
**Cognizant Tech Solutions Corp** .......................... 630 955-0617
  3333 Warrenville Rd # 350  Lisle  (60532)  *(G-13575)*
**Coi Company, Chicago** Also called Chicago Ornamental Iron Inc *(G-4338)*
**Coil It, Elk Grove Village** Also called Majestic Spring Inc *(G-9609)*
**Coil Sales and Manufacturing, Marshall** Also called Charles Industries Ltd *(G-14319)*
**Coilcraft Incorporated** ........................................ 815 879-4408
  1837 N Euclid Ave  Princeton  (61356)  *(G-17745)*
**Coilcraft Incorporated** ........................................ 815 732-6834
  9 Clay St  Oregon  (61061)  *(G-16820)*
**Coilcraft Incorporated** ........................................ 815 288-7051
  924 Jaybee Ave  Dixon  (61021)  *(G-8326)*
**Coilform Company (PA)** ..................................... 630 232-8000
  2571 Kaneville Ct  Geneva  (60134)  *(G-10820)*
**Coiltechnic Inc** .................................................. 815 675-9260
  2402 Spring Ridge Dr C  Spring Grove  (60081)  *(G-20331)*
**Coin Macke Laundry** .......................................... 847 459-1109
  124b Messner Dr  Wheeling  (60090)  *(G-22029)*
**Coinstar Procurement LLC** ................................. 630 424-4788
  1 Tower Ln Ste 900  Oakbrook Terrace  (60181)  *(G-16703)*
**Cokel D J Wldg Stl Fabricators, Princeville** Also called Cokel Dj Welding Bay & Muffler *(G-17763)*
**Cokel Dj Welding Bay & Muffler** ......................... 309 385-4567
  224 E Evans St  Princeville  (61559)  *(G-17763)*
**Cokel Jim Prtble Wldg Sp Servi, Monmouth** Also called Jim Cokel Welding *(G-15015)*
**Cokel Welding Shop** .......................................... 217 357-3312
  117 S Madison St  Carthage  (62321)  *(G-3312)*
**Cokel's Welding, Aledo** Also called Aledo Welding Enterprises Inc *(G-367)*
**Coki Foods LLC** ................................................. 708 261-5758
  110 N Willow Rd Apt 4  Elmhurst  (60126)  *(G-9852)*
**Colbert Packaging Corporation (PA)** ................... 847 367-5990
  28355 N Bradley Rd  Lake Forest  (60045)  *(G-12892)*
**Colberts Custom Framing** .................................. 630 717-1448
  1283 S Naper Blvd  Naperville  (60540)  *(G-15632)*
**Colborne Acquisition Co LLC** ............................. 847 371-0101
  28495 N Ballard Dr  Lake Forest  (60045)  *(G-12893)*
**Cold Headers Inc (PA)** ....................................... 773 775-7900
  5514 N Elston Ave 14  Chicago  (60630)  *(G-4421)*
**Cold Stone Creamery 488** .................................
  324 Randall Rd  South Elgin  (60177)  *(G-20190)*
**Coldstone, Joliet** Also called Huddlestun Creamery Inc *(G-12512)*
**Cole Pallet Services Corp** .................................. 815 758-3226
  1300 Oak St  Dekalb  (60115)  *(G-8077)*
**Cole-Parmer Instrument Co LLC** ........................ 847 381-7050
  28092 W Commercial Ave  Lake Barrington  (60010)  *(G-12802)*
**Coleman Cable LLC** .......................................... 847 672-2508
  1530 S Shields Dr  Waukegan  (60085)  *(G-21540)*
**Coleman Cable LLC** .......................................... 847 672-2300
  1530 S Shields Dr  Waukegan  (60085)  *(G-21541)*
**Coleman Cable LLC (HQ)** ................................... 847 672-2300
  1530 S Shields Dr  Waukegan  (60085)  *(G-21542)*
**Coleman Cable LLC** .......................................... 847 672-2300
  1530 S Shields Dr  Waukegan  (60085)  *(G-21543)*
**Coleman Lawn Equipment Inc** ............................ 618 529-0181
  210 E Walnut St  Carbondale  (62901)  *(G-3003)*
**Coles Appliance & Furn Co** ................................ 773 525-1797
  4026 N Lincoln Ave  Chicago  (60618)  *(G-4422)*
**Coles Craft Corporation** ..................................... 630 858-8171
  868 Baker Ct  Glen Ellyn  (60137)  *(G-10963)*

**Colfax Welding & Fabricating** ... 847 359-4433
605 W Colfax St  Palatine  (60067)  *(G-17013)*
**Collagen Usa Inc** ... 708 716-0251
3048 N Milwaukee Ave  Chicago  (60618)  *(G-4423)*
**Collapsible Core Inc** ... 630 408-1693
631 Superior Dr  Romeoville  (60446)  *(G-18814)*
**Colleagues of Beer Inc** ... 847 727-3318
520 Laurie Ct  Grayslake  (60030)  *(G-11327)*
**Colleens Confection** ... 630 653-2231
190 Easy St Ste I  Carol Stream  (60188)  *(G-3133)*
**College Bound Publications** ... 773 262-5810
7658 N Rogers Ave  Chicago  (60626)  *(G-4424)*
**Colley Elevator Company** ... 630 766-7230
226 William St  Bensenville  (60106)  *(G-1861)*
**Collins Bros, Mount Vernon** *Also called Collins Brothers Oil Corp* *(G-15404)*
**Collins Brothers Oil Corp (PA)** ... 618 244-1093
218 N 9th St  Mount Vernon  (62864)  *(G-15404)*
**Collinson Stone Co (PA)** ... 309 787-7983
225 1st St E  Milan  (61264)  *(G-14780)*
**Collinsville Custom Kitchens** ... 618 288-2000
6 Schiber Ct  Maryville  (62062)  *(G-14340)*
**Collinsville Herald Journal, Collinsville** *Also called Madison County Publications* *(G-7333)*
**Collinsville Ice & Fuel Co** ... 618 344-3272
800 N Bluff Rd  Collinsville  (62234)  *(G-7315)*
**Collinsville Sports Store** ... 618 345-5588
2211 Vandalia St  Collinsville  (62234)  *(G-7316)*
**Colloid Envmtl Tech Co LLC (HQ)** ... 847 851-1500
2870 Forbs Ave  Hoffman Estates  (60192)  *(G-12002)*
**Colnago America Inc** ... 312 239-6666
1528 W Adams St Ste 4b  Chicago  (60607)  *(G-4425)*
**Colonade Interiors II, Burr Ridge** *Also called Ameriguard Corporation* *(G-2822)*
**Colonial Bag Corporation** ... 630 690-3999
205 Fullerton Ave  Carol Stream  (60188)  *(G-3134)*
**Colony Inc (PA)** ... 847 426-5300
2531 Tech Dr Ste 314  Elgin  (60124)  *(G-8994)*
**Colony Display, Elgin** *Also called Colony Inc* *(G-8994)*
**Color Communications Inc (PA)** ... 773 638-1400
4000 W Fillmore St  Chicago  (60624)  *(G-4426)*
**Color Corporation of America** ... 815 987-3700
200 Sayre St  Rockford  (61104)  *(G-18314)*
**Color Signs** ... 847 368-0101
3110 N Arlington Hts Rd  Arlington Heights  (60004)  *(G-736)*
**Color Smiths Inc** ... 708 562-0061
747 N Church Rd Ste E6  Elmhurst  (60126)  *(G-9853)*
**Color Tone Printing** ... 708 385-1442
2619 Orchard St  Blue Island  (60406)  *(G-2242)*
**Color Works Graphics Inc** ... 847 383-5270
451 N Racine Ave  Chicago  (60642)  *(G-4427)*
**Color4** ... 847 996-6880
28100 N Ashley Cir Ste 10  Libertyville  (60048)  *(G-13316)*
**Colorex Chemical Co Inc** ... 630 238-3124
834 Foster Ave  Bensenville  (60106)  *(G-1862)*
**Colorforms, Clinton** *Also called RR Donnelley & Sons Company* *(G-7288)*
**Colorjar LLC** ... 312 489-8510
435 N La Salle Dr Ste 201  Chicago  (60654)  *(G-4428)*
**Colorkraft Roll Products Inc (PA)** ... 217 382-4967
1 Harry Glynn Dr  Martinsville  (62442)  *(G-14333)*
**Colorlab Cosmetics Inc (PA)** ... 815 965-0026
1112 5th Ave  Rockford  (61104)  *(G-18315)*
**Colormetric Laboratories Inc** ... 847 803-3737
1261 Rand Rd Ste A  Des Plaines  (60016)  *(G-8172)*
**Colors Chicago Inc** ... 312 265-1642
420 W Huron St Fl 1  Chicago  (60654)  *(G-4429)*
**Colors For Plastics Inc** ... 847 437-0033
2239 Pratt Blvd  Elk Grove Village  (60007)  *(G-9381)*
**Colors For Plastics Inc (PA)** ... 847 437-0033
2245 Pratt Blvd  Elk Grove Village  (60007)  *(G-9382)*
**Colorwave Graphics LLC** ... 815 397-4293
2024 Windsor Rd  Loves Park  (61111)  *(G-13925)*
**Colson Group Holdings LLC (PA)** ... 630 613-2941
1815 S Meyers Rd Ste 750  Oakbrook Terrace  (60181)  *(G-16704)*
**Colson Publications, Mount Sterling** *Also called Democrat Message* *(G-15392)*
**Colt Technology Services LLC** ... 312 465-2484
141 W Jackson Blvd # 2808  Chicago  (60604)  *(G-4430)*
**Columbia Aluminum Recycl Ltd** ... 708 758-8888
400 E Lincoln Hwy  Chicago Heights  (60411)  *(G-7093)*
**Columbia Metal Spinning Co, Chicago** *Also called Craft Metal Spinning Co* *(G-4489)*
**Columbia Metal Spinning Co** ... 773 685-2800
4351 N Normandy Ave  Chicago  (60634)  *(G-4431)*
**Columbia Quarry Company (PA)** ... 618 281-7631
210 State Route 158  Columbia  (62236)  *(G-7354)*
**Columbia Quarry Company** ... 618 939-8833
5440 Quarry Dr  Waterloo  (62298)  *(G-21400)*
**Columbia Sportswear Company** ... 312 649-3758
830 N Michigan Ave Ste 3  Chicago  (60611)  *(G-4432)*
**Columbia Tool & Gage Co., Niles** *Also called Accurate Metal Components Inc* *(G-15957)*
**Columbian Rope Company** ... 888 593-7999
12010 S Paulina St  Calumet Park  (60827)  *(G-2959)*
**Columbus Foods Company, Des Plaines** *Also called Cfc Inc* *(G-8163)*

**Columbus Industries Inc** ... 309 245-1010
17383 E State Route 116  Fairview  (61432)  *(G-10165)*
**Columbus McKinnon Corporation** ... 800 548-2930
801 W Center St  Eureka  (61530)  *(G-9995)*
**Columbus McKinnon Corporation** ... 630 783-2188
2143 Internationale Pkwy  Woodridge  (60517)  *(G-22462)*
**Columbus McKinnon Corporation** ... 630 783-1195
10321 Werch Dr Ste 100  Woodridge  (60517)  *(G-22463)*
**Columbus Meats Inc** ... 312 829-2480
906 W Randolph St Fl 1  Chicago  (60607)  *(G-4433)*
**Colvin Printing** ... 708 331-4580
12958 Ashland Ave  Blue Island  (60406)  *(G-2243)*
**Com-Graphics Inc** ... 312 226-0900
329 W 18th St Fl 10  Chicago  (60616)  *(G-4434)*
**Com-Pac International Inc** ... 618 529-2421
800 W Industrial Park Rd  Carbondale  (62901)  *(G-3004)*
**Combe Laboratories Inc** ... 217 893-4490
200 Shellhouse Dr  Rantoul  (61866)  *(G-17923)*
**Combined Metals Chicago LLC** ... 847 683-0500
1 Hauk Rd  Hampshire  (60140)  *(G-11545)*
**Combined Metals Holding Inc** ... 708 547-8800
2401 Grant Ave  Bellwood  (60104)  *(G-1701)*
**Combined Technologies Inc (PA)** ... 847 968-4855
732 Florsheim Dr Ste 14  Libertyville  (60048)  *(G-13317)*
**Combo Color, Melrose Park** *Also called Saltzman Printers Inc* *(G-14690)*
**Comcast Corporation** ... 217 498-3274
2930 State St  Quincy  (62301)  *(G-17815)*
**Comers Welding Service Inc** ... 630 892-0168
1105 S Lake St  Montgomery  (60538)  *(G-15039)*
**Comet Conection Inc** ... 312 243-5400
5040 W 127th St  Alsip  (60803)  *(G-451)*
**Comet Die & Engraving Company** ... 630 833-5600
909 N Larch Ave  Elmhurst  (60126)  *(G-9854)*
**Comet Fabricating & Welding Co** ... 815 229-0468
5620 Falcon Rd  Rockford  (61109)  *(G-18316)*
**Comet Neon** ... 630 668-6366
1120 N Ridge Ave  Lombard  (60148)  *(G-13782)*
**Comet Press, Alsip** *Also called Comet Conection Inc* *(G-451)*
**Comet Roll & Machine Company** ... 630 268-1407
405 Stone Dr  Saint Charles  (60174)  *(G-19161)*
**Comet Supply Inc** ... 309 444-2712
312 Muller Rd  Washington  (61571)  *(G-21381)*
**Comet Tool Inc** ... 847 956-0126
880 Nicholas Blvd  Elk Grove Village  (60007)  *(G-9383)*
**Comforts Home Services Inc** ... 847 856-8002
1551 Aucutt Rd  Montgomery  (60538)  *(G-15040)*
**Comlink Technologies Inc** ... 630 279-5445
320 Meyer Rd  Bensenville  (60106)  *(G-1863)*
**Commax Inc** ... 847 995-0994
1171 Tower Rd  Schaumburg  (60173)  *(G-19476)*
**Commercial Copy Printing Ctr** ... 847 981-8590
520 Bennett Rd  Elk Grove Village  (60007)  *(G-9384)*
**Commercial Dynamics Inc** ... 847 439-5300
2025 S Arlington Hts Rd  Arlington Heights  (60005)  *(G-737)*
**Commercial Fabricators Inc (PA)** ... 708 594-1199
7247 S 78th Ave Ste 1  Bridgeview  (60455)  *(G-2479)*
**Commercial Fast Print** ... 815 673-1196
318 E Main St  Streator  (61364)  *(G-20685)*
**Commercial Finishes Co Ltd** ... 847 981-9222
540 Lively Blvd  Elk Grove Village  (60007)  *(G-9385)*
**Commercial Machine Services** ... 847 806-1901
1099 Touhy Ave  Elk Grove Village  (60007)  *(G-9386)*
**Commercial Metals Company** ... 815 928-9600
780 Eastgate Indus Pkwy  Kankakee  (60901)  *(G-12606)*
**Commercial Pallet Inc** ... 312 226-6699
2029 W Hubbard St  Chicago  (60612)  *(G-4435)*
**Commercial Plastics Company (PA)** ... 847 566-1700
800 Allanson Rd  Mundelein  (60060)  *(G-15490)*
**Commercial Printers, Chicago** *Also called Breaker Press Co Inc* *(G-4159)*
**Commercial Product Group, Moline** *Also called Harrington Signal Inc* *(G-14942)*
**Commercial Prtg Graphics Arts, Villa Park** *Also called Printed Impressions Inc* *(G-21279)*
**Commercial Prtg of Rockford** ... 815 965-4759
1120 2nd Ave  Rockford  (61104)  *(G-18317)*
**Commercial Rfrgn Centl III Inc** ... 217 235-5016
2020 Prairie Ave  Mattoon  (61938)  *(G-14386)*
**Commercial Stainless Services** ... 847 349-1560
1201 Busse Rd  Elk Grove Village  (60007)  *(G-9387)*
**Common Goal Systems Inc** ... 630 592-4200
188 W Industrial Dr # 240  Elmhurst  (60126)  *(G-9855)*
**Common Ground Publishing LLC** ... 217 328-0405
2001 S 1st St Ste 202  Champaign  (61820)  *(G-3468)*
**Common Scents Mom** ... 309 389-3216
10812 W Timber Rd  Mapleton  (61547)  *(G-14208)*
**Commscope Technologies LLC (HQ)** ... 708 236-6600
4 Westbrook Corporate Ctr  Westchester  (60154)  *(G-21835)*
**Commscope Technologies LLC** ... 779 435-6000
2700 Ellis Rd  Joliet  (60433)  *(G-12476)*
**Communication Coil Inc** ... 847 671-1333
9601 Soreng Ave  Schiller Park  (60176)  *(G-19815)*

ALPHABETIC SECTION Concrete & Marble Polishing &

**Communication Technologies Inc**....630 384-0900
188 Internationale Blvd Glendale Heights (60139) *(G-11017)*
**Community Advantage Network (PA)**....847 376-8943
1163 Lee St Des Plaines (60016) *(G-8173)*
**Community Cllabration Acquatio**....815 316-6390
303 N Main St Ste 803 Rockford (61101) *(G-18318)*
**Community Collaboration Inc**....815 316-4660
303 N Main St Ste 800 Rockford (61101) *(G-18319)*
**Community Gospel Center**....773 486-7661
2880 N Milwaukee Ave Chicago (60618) *(G-4436)*
**Community Magazine Group**....312 880-0370
1550 S Indiana Ave Chicago (60605) *(G-4437)*
**Community Newsppr Holdings Inc**....217 774-2161
100 W Main St Shelbyville (62565) *(G-19906)*
**Community Optical Service, Chicago** *Also called Community Gospel Center (G-4436)*
**Community Rady Mix of Pttsfeld**....217 285-5548
1503 Kamar Dr Pittsfield (62363) *(G-17566)*
**Community Ready Mix Pittsfield, Pittsfield** *Also called Community Rady Mix of Pttsfeld (G-17566)*
**Community Readymix Inc**....217 245-6668
710 Brooklyn Ave Jacksonville (62650) *(G-12385)*
**Community Support Systems (PA)**....217 705-4300
618 W Main St Teutopolis (62467) *(G-20850)*
**Compak Inc**....815 399-2699
1139 Alton Ave Rockford (61109) *(G-18320)*
**Compania Brasileira De T**....319 550-6440
21218 Sunset St Mount Olive (62069) *(G-15301)*
**Compass Minerals Intl Inc**....773 978-7258
9200 S Ewing Ave Chicago (60617) *(G-4438)*
**Competition Electronics Inc**....815 874-8001
3469 Precision Dr Rockford (61109) *(G-18321)*
**Competitive Edge Opportunities**....815 322-2164
426 Scotland Rd Unit A Lakemoor (60051) *(G-13143)*
**Complete Asphalt Service Co**....217 285-6099
1601 Kaymar Dr Pittsfield (62363) *(G-17567)*
**Complete Custom Woodworks**....309 644-1911
3 Crestview Dr Coal Valley (61240) *(G-7294)*
**Complete Flashings Inc**....630 595-9725
211 Beeline Dr Ste 2 Bensenville (60106) *(G-1864)*
**Complete Lawn and Snow Service**....847 776-7287
544 W Colfax St Ste 5 Palatine (60067) *(G-17014)*
**Complete Mold Polishing Inc**....630 406-7668
1219 Paramount Pkwy Batavia (60510) *(G-1432)*
**Complete Woman, Chicago** *Also called Associated Publications Inc (G-3969)*
**Completely Nuts Inc**....847 394-4312
600 E Grand Ave Chicago (60611) *(G-4439)*
**Compliancesigns Inc**....800 578-1245
56 S Main St Chadwick (61014) *(G-3441)*
**Compliancesigns.com, Chadwick** *Also called Compliancesigns Inc (G-3441)*
**Component Hardware Inc**....847 458-8181
120 Center Dr Gilberts (60136) *(G-10916)*
**Component Parts Company**....815 477-2323
7301 Foxfire Dr Crystal Lake (60012) *(G-7556)*
**Component Plastics Inc**....847 695-9200
700 Tollgate Rd Elgin (60123) *(G-8995)*
**Component Precast Supply Inc**....630 483-2900
4n325 Powis Rd West Chicago (60185) *(G-21685)*
**Component Products Inc**....847 301-1000
521 Morse Ave Schaumburg (60193) *(G-19477)*
**Component Sales Incorporated**....630 543-9666
130 S Fairbank St Addison (60101) *(G-79)*
**Component Specialty Inc (HQ)**....847 742-4400
412 N State St Elgin (60123) *(G-8996)*
**Component Tool & Mfg Co**....708 672-5505
25416 S Dixie Hwy Ste 1 Crete (60417) *(G-7510)*
**Componenta USA LLC**....309 691-7000
8515 N University St Peoria (61615) *(G-17345)*
**Components Express Inc**....630 257-0605
10330 Argonne Woods Dr # 100 Woodridge (60517) *(G-22464)*
**Composing Room Inc**....708 795-7523
1851 Kenilworth Ave 1 Berwyn (60402) *(G-2059)*
**Composite Bearings Mfg**....630 595-8334
720 N Edgewood Ave Wood Dale (60191) *(G-22354)*
**Composite Cutter Tech Inc**....847 740-6875
31632 N Ellis Dr Unit 210 Volo (60073) *(G-21311)*
**Composition One Inc**....630 588-1900
400 Lake St Ste 110b Roselle (60172) *(G-18933)*
**Compound Bow Rifle Sight Inc**....618 526-4427
1004 S Walnut St Breese (62230) *(G-2442)*
**Comprehensive Convgnt Solut**....847 558-1401
830 W Il Route 22 Ste 51 Lake Zurich (60047) *(G-13056)*
**Compressed Air Advisors Inc**....877 247-2381
11038 Martindale Dr Westchester (60154) *(G-21836)*
**Compressor Services, Johnsburg** *Also called On-Line Compressor Inc (G-12440)*
**Comprhnsive Prsthtics Orthtics (PA)**....708 387-9700
8400 Brookfield Ave Ste 1 Brookfield (60513) *(G-2628)*
**Compsoft Tech Sltons Group Inc**....847 517-9608
1701 E Wdfield Rd Ste 211 Schaumburg (60173) *(G-19478)*
**Comptia Learning LLC**....630 678-8490
3500 Lacey Rd Ste 100 Downers Grove (60515) *(G-8415)*
**Comptons Encyclopedia, Chicago** *Also called Success Publishing Group Inc (G-6611)*
**Compu Doc Inc**....630 554-5800
105 Theodore Dr Ste A Oswego (60543) *(G-16910)*
**Compu-Tap Inc**....708 594-5773
6257 S Archer Rd Ste A Summit Argo (60501) *(G-20761)*
**Compusystems Inc (PA)**....708 344-9070
2651 Warrenville Rd # 400 Downers Grove (60515) *(G-8416)*
**Computaforms, Waukegan** *Also called Medical Records Co (G-21588)*
**Computer Business Forms Co**....773 775-0155
6525 N Olmsted Ave Chicago (60631) *(G-4440)*
**Computer Industry Almanac Inc**....847 758-1926
1013 S Belmont Ave Arlington Heights (60005) *(G-738)*
**Computer Pwr Solutions Ill Ltd**....618 281-8898
235 Southwoods Ctr Columbia (62236) *(G-7355)*
**Computer Svcs & Consulting Inc**....855 827-8328
1613 S Michigan Ave Chicago (60616) *(G-4441)*
**Computerized Fleet Analysis**....630 543-1410
1020 W Fullerton Ave A Addison (60101) *(G-80)*
**Computerprox**....847 516-8560
163 E Chicago St Fl 2 Elgin (60120) *(G-8997)*
**Computers At Work Inc**....815 776-9470
10890 E Golf View Dr Galena (61036) *(G-10717)*
**Computhink Inc**....630 705-9050
151 E 22nd St Lombard (60148) *(G-13783)*
**Computing Integrity Inc**....217 355-4469
3102 Valleybrook Dr Champaign (61822) *(G-3469)*
**Compx Fort, Grayslake** *Also called Fort Lock Corporation (G-11338)*
**Compx International Inc**....847 543-4583
715 Center St Grayslake (60030) *(G-11328)*
**Compx Security Products Inc**....847 234-1864
715 Center St Grayslake (60030) *(G-11329)*
**Compx Timberline, Grayslake** *Also called Compx Security Products Inc (G-11329)*
**Comtec Industries Ltd**....630 759-9000
10210 Werch Dr Ste 204 Woodridge (60517) *(G-22465)*
**Comtelco Industries, Glendale Heights** *Also called Whisco Component Engrg Inc (G-11092)*
**Comvigo Inc**....240 255-4093
410 Woodgate Ct Willowbrook (60527) *(G-22205)*
**Con Mold**....708 442-6002
4164 May St Hillside (60162) *(G-11913)*
**Con-Tech, Northbrook** *Also called Conservation Technology Ltd (G-16232)*
**Con-Temp Cabinets Inc**....630 892-7300
201 Poplar Pl North Aurora (60542) *(G-16123)*
**Con-Trol-Cure Inc**....773 248-0099
1229 W Cortland St Chicago (60614) *(G-4442)*
**Cona LLC**....773 750-7485
3827 N Kenneth Ave Chicago (60641) *(G-4443)*
**Conagra, Chester** *Also called Ardent Mills LLC (G-3650)*
**Conagra Brands Inc (PA)**....312 549-5000
222 Merchandise Mart Plz Chicago (60654) *(G-4444)*
**Conagra Brands Inc**....630 455-5200
3250 Lacey Rd Ste 600 Downers Grove (60515) *(G-8417)*
**Conagra Brands Inc**....630 857-1000
750 E Diehl Rd Ste 111 Naperville (60563) *(G-15633)*
**Conagra Dairy Foods Company (HQ)**....630 848-0975
222 Merchandise Mart Plz # 1300 Chicago (60654) *(G-4445)*
**Conagra Fods Fd Ingrdients Inc**....630 682-5600
193 Alexandra Way Carol Stream (60188) *(G-3135)*
**Conagra Foods, Chicago** *Also called Conagra Brands Inc (G-4444)*
**Conair Corporation**....203 351-9000
205 Shellhouse Dr Rantoul (61866) *(G-17924)*
**Concentric Itasca Inc**....630 268-1528
800 Hollywood Ave Itasca (60143) *(G-12246)*
**Concentric Rockford Inc**....815 398-4400
2222 15th St Rockford (61104) *(G-18322)*
**Concep Machine Co Inc**....847 498-9740
1800 Holste Rd Northbrook (60062) *(G-16230)*
**Concept and Design Services**....847 259-1675
807 S Golfview Pl Mount Prospect (60056) *(G-15317)*
**Concept Cleaning Service, Cahokia** *Also called Ronald Allen (G-2925)*
**Concept Industries Inc**....847 258-3545
199 Gaylord St Elk Grove Village (60007) *(G-9388)*
**Concept Laboratories Inc**....773 395-7300
1400 W Wabansia Ave Chicago (60642) *(G-4446)*
**Concepts and Controls Inc**....847 478-9296
2530 Apple Hill Ct N Buffalo Grove (60089) *(G-2676)*
**Concepts Magnet**....847 253-3351
515 S Edward St Mount Prospect (60056) *(G-15318)*
**Concord Cabinets Inc (PA)**....217 894-6507
1276 E 2575th St Clayton (62324) *(G-7269)*
**Concord Oil & Gas Corporation**....618 393-2124
1712 S Whittle Ave Olney (62450) *(G-16764)*
**Concord Well Service Inc**....618 395-4405
1102 N East St Olney (62450) *(G-16765)*
**Concorde Laboratories Inc**....630 717-5300
4504 Concorde Pl Lisle (60532) *(G-13576)*
**Concorde Mfg & Fabrication Inc**....815 344-3788
1620 S Schroeder Ln McHenry (60050) *(G-14488)*
**Concrete & Marble Polishing &**....773 968-6897
718 E Old Willow Rd Prospect Heights (60070) *(G-17774)*

A L P H A B E T I C

(PA)=Parent Co (HQ)=Headquarters (DH)=Div Headquarters
2017 Harris Illinois Industrial Directory
1205

**Concrete 1 Inc**....630 357-1329
429 E 8th Ave Naperville (60563) *(G-15634)*
**Concrete Countertop Supply, Crystal Lake** *Also called Fishstone Studio Inc (G-7579)*
**Concrete Products**....815 339-6395
304 E Harper Ave Granville (61326) *(G-11317)*
**Concrete Products Ziano, Granville** *Also called Concrete Products (G-11317)*
**Concrete Specialities Co Inc**....847 608-1200
1375 Gifford Rd Elgin (60120) *(G-8998)*
**Concrete Specialties Co (PA)**....847 608-1200
1375 Gifford Rd Elgin (60120) *(G-8999)*
**Concrete Supply LLC**....618 646-5300
1 Racehorse Dr East Saint Louis (62205) *(G-8747)*
**Concrete Supply of Illinois, East Saint Louis** *Also called Concrete Supply LLC (G-8747)*
**Concrete Supply Tolono Inc**....217 485-3100
1466 County Road 1100 N Urbana (61802) *(G-21079)*
**Concrete Unit Step Co Inc**....618 344-7256
8915 Collinsville Rd Collinsville (62234) *(G-7317)*
**Condominiums Northbrook Cort 1**....847 498-1640
830 Audubon Way Apt 217 Lincolnshire (60069) *(G-13439)*
**Condominiums Northbrook Court, Lincolnshire** *Also called Condominiums Northbrook Cort 1 (G-13439)*
**Condor Granites Intl Inc**....847 635-7214
1605 Dundee Ave Ste H Elgin (60120) *(G-9000)*
**Condor Labels Inc**....708 429-0707
7613 185th St Tinley Park (60477) *(G-20902)*
**Condor Machine Tool**....773 767-5985
5315 W 63rd St Chicago (60638) *(G-4447)*
**Condor Tool & Manufacturing**....630 628-8200
321 W Gerri Ln Addison (60101) *(G-81)*
**Conectec International, Lincolnshire** *Also called Sentral Assemblies LLC (G-13477)*
**Conex Cable LLC**....800 877-8089
1007 E Locust St Dekalb (60115) *(G-8078)*
**Confab Systems Inc**....708 388-4103
14831 S Mckinley Ave Posen (60469) *(G-17728)*
**Conferences I/O, Chicago** *Also called Goeducation LLC (G-4969)*
**Conform Industries Inc**....630 285-0272
561 Estes Ave Schaumburg (60193) *(G-19479)*
**Congress Printing Company**....312 733-6599
2136 S Peoria St Chicago (60608) *(G-4448)*
**Conley Precision Engines Inc**....630 858-3160
825 Duane St Glen Ellyn (60137) *(G-10964)*
**Conmat Inc (HQ)**....815 235-2200
2283 Us Highway 20 E Freeport (61032) *(G-10651)*
**Connecteriors LLC**....773 549-3333
3100 N Clybourn Ave Chicago (60618) *(G-4449)*
**Connections Company, Naperville** *Also called Dalco Marketing Services (G-15641)*
**Connectmedia Ventures LLC**....773 327-3188
2538 N Marshfield Ave Chicago (60614) *(G-4450)*
**Connector Concepts Inc**....847 541-4020
1530 Mccormick Blvd Mundelein (60060) *(G-15491)*
**Connell Mc Machine & Welding**....815 868-2275
8934 N Korth Rd Mc Connell (61050) *(G-14442)*
**Connelly & Associates**....847 372-5001
892 E Glencoe St Palatine (60074) *(G-17015)*
**Connelly-Gpm Inc**....773 247-7231
3154 S California Ave Chicago (60608) *(G-4451)*
**Connie's Naturals,, Carol Stream** *Also called Mjs-Cn LLC (G-3200)*
**Connomac, La Grange** *Also called French Corporation (G-12732)*
**Connomac Corporation**....708 482-3434
340 Washington Ave La Grange (60525) *(G-12729)*
**Connor Electric Services Inc**....630 823-8230
649 Estes Ave Schaumburg (60193) *(G-19480)*
**Connor Sports Flooring LLC (HQ)**....847 290-9020
1830 Howard St Ste F Elk Grove Village (60007) *(G-9389)*
**Connor Voice and Data Tech, Schaumburg** *Also called Connor Electric Services Inc (G-19480)*
**Connor-Winfield Corp (PA)**....630 851-4722
2111 Comprehensive Dr Aurora (60505) *(G-1133)*
**Conopco Inc**....773 916-4400
2816 S Kilbourn Ave Chicago (60623) *(G-4452)*
**Conopco Inc**....847 520-8002
491 Arborgate Ln Buffalo Grove (60089) *(G-2677)*
**Conrad Press Ltd**....
120 N Main St Stop 1 Columbia (62236) *(G-7356)*
**Conscisys Corp**....630 810-4444
1125 Mistwood Pl Downers Grove (60515) *(G-8418)*
**Conservation Tech III LLC**....847 559-5500
725 Landwehr Rd Northbrook (60062) *(G-16231)*
**Conservation Technology Ltd**....847 559-5500
725 Landwehr Rd Northbrook (60062) *(G-16232)*
**Consolidated Carqueville Prtg**....630 246-6451
1536 Bourbon Pkwy Streamwood (60107) *(G-20649)*
**Consolidated Container Co LLC**....815 943-7828
875 W Diggins St Harvard (60033) *(G-11628)*
**Consolidated Container Co LLC**....630 231-7150
1300 Northwest Ave West Chicago (60185) *(G-21686)*
**Consolidated Displays Co Inc**....630 851-8666
1210 Us Highway 34 Oswego (60543) *(G-16911)*
**Consolidated Elec Wire & Cable**....847 455-8830
11044 King St Franklin Park (60131) *(G-10440)*
**Consolidated Foam Inc**....847 850-5011
1670 Barclay Blvd Buffalo Grove (60089) *(G-2678)*
**Consolidated Materials Inc (PA)**....815 568-1538
8920 S Rt 23 Marengo (60152) *(G-14222)*
**Consolidated Mill Supply Inc (PA)**....847 706-6715
1530 E Dundee Rd Ste 200 Palatine (60074) *(G-17016)*
**Consolidated Paving Inc**....309 693-3505
6918 N Galena Rd Peoria (61614) *(G-17346)*
**Consolidated Printing Co Inc**....773 631-2800
5942 N Northwest Hwy Chicago (60631) *(G-4453)*
**Consource LLC**....847 382-8100
535 Plainfield Rd Ste A Willowbrook (60527) *(G-22206)*
**Construction Bus Media LLC**....847 359-6493
579 N 1st Bank Dr Ste 220 Palatine (60067) *(G-17017)*
**Construction Equipment**....618 345-0799
34 Empire Dr Ste 1 Belleville (62220) *(G-1619)*
**Construction Solutions LLC**....630 834-1929
222 W Stone Rd Villa Park (60181) *(G-21244)*
**Consulate General Lithuania**....312 397-0382
455 N Ctyfrnt Plz Dr # 800 Chicago (60611) *(G-4454)*
**Consumer Guide, Morton Grove** *Also called Publications International Ltd (G-15229)*
**Consumer Vinegar and Spice**....708 354-1144
745 S Ashland Ave La Grange (60525) *(G-12730)*
**Consumerbase LLC**....312 600-8000
33 N Dearborn St Ste 200 Chicago (60602) *(G-4455)*
**Consumers Dgest Cmmnctions LLC**....847 607-3000
520 Lake Cook Rd Ste 500 Deerfield (60015) *(G-8000)*
**Consumers Packing Co Inc**....708 344-0047
1301 Carson Dr Melrose Park (60160) *(G-14611)*
**Container Graphics Corp**....847 584-0299
492 Lunt Ave Schaumburg (60193) *(G-19481)*
**Container Hdlg Systems Corp**....708 482-9900
621 E Plainfield Rd Countryside (60525) *(G-7418)*
**Container Service Group Inc**....815 744-8693
2132 Gould Ct Unit A Rockdale (60436) *(G-18218)*
**Container Specialties Inc**....708 615-1400
10800 Belmont Ave Ste 200 Franklin Park (60131) *(G-10441)*
**Contech Engnered Solutions LLC**....217 529-5461
1110 Stevenson Dr Springfield (62703) *(G-20421)*
**Contech Engnered Solutions LLC**....630 573-1110
1200 Harger Rd Ste 707 Oak Brook (60523) *(G-16502)*
**Contech Lighting, Northbrook** *Also called Conservation Tech III LLC (G-16231)*
**Contempo Autographic & Signs**....708 371-5499
13866 Cicero Ave Crestwood (60445) *(G-7483)*
**Contempo Industries Inc**....815 337-6267
455 Borden St Woodstock (60098) *(G-22553)*
**Contempo Marble & Granite Inc**....312 455-0022
411 N Paulina St Chicago (60622) *(G-4456)*
**Contemporary Ctrl Systems Inc (PA)**....630 963-1993
2431 Curtiss St Downers Grove (60515) *(G-8419)*
**Contemporary Marble Inc**....618 281-6200
8533 Hanover Indus Dr Columbia (62236) *(G-7357)*
**Contemprary Enrgy Slutions LLC**....630 768-3743
2951 Beth Ln Naperville (60564) *(G-15801)*
**Contempri Homes, Pinckneyville** *Also called Contempri Industries Inc (G-17545)*
**Contempri Industries Inc**....618 357-5361
1000 W Water St Pinckneyville (62274) *(G-17545)*
**Content That Works, Chicago** *Also called F M Aquisition Corp (G-4806)*
**Continent Corp**....773 733-1584
227 Tiger St Bolingbrook (60490) *(G-2287)*
**Continental Assembly Inc**....773 472-8004
4317 N Ravenswood Ave Chicago (60613) *(G-4457)*
**Continental Auto Systems Inc**....847 862-5000
21440 W Lake Cook Rd Deer Park (60010) *(G-7969)*
**Continental Automation Inc**....630 584-5100
303 N 4th St Saint Charles (60174) *(G-19162)*
**Continental Automotive Inc**....847 862-6300
21440 W Lake Cook Rd Deer Park (60010) *(G-7970)*
**Continental Bindery Corp**....847 439-6811
700 Fargo Ave Elk Grove Village (60007) *(G-9390)*
**Continental Carbonic Pdts Inc**....217 428-2080
2550 N Brush College Rd Decatur (62526) *(G-7858)*
**Continental Carbonic Pdts Inc**....309 346-7515
140 Distillery Rd Pekin (61554) *(G-17257)*
**Continental Carbonic Pdts Inc (HQ)**....217 428-2068
3985 E Harrison Ave Decatur (62526) *(G-7859)*
**Continental Chicago, Park Ridge** *Also called Continental Usa Inc (G-17188)*
**Continental Concepts, Cicero** *Also called Royal Box Group LLC (G-7226)*
**Continental Cutoff Machine, Addison** *Also called Kiene Diesel Accessories Inc (G-167)*
**Continental Datalabel Inc (PA)**....847 742-1600
1855 Fox Ln Elgin (60123) *(G-9001)*
**Continental General Tire, Mount Vernon** *Also called Continental Tire Americas LLC (G-15406)*
**Continental Marketing Inc**....773 467-8300
5696 N Milwaukee Ave Chicago (60646) *(G-4458)*
**Continental Materials Corp (PA)**....312 541-7200
440 S La Salle St # 3100 Chicago (60605) *(G-4459)*

**Continental Midland** ....... 708 441-1000
1340 W 127th St Calumet Park (60827) *(G-2960)*
**Continental Mills Inc** ....... 217 540-4000
1200 Stevens Ave Effingham (62401) *(G-8830)*
**Continental Resources III Inc (PA)** ....... 618 242-1717
830 Il Highway 15 E Mount Vernon (62864) *(G-15405)*
**Continental Sales Inc** ....... 847 381-6530
213 W Main St Barrington (60010) *(G-1277)*
**Continental Screws Mch Pdts** ....... 847 459-7766
160 Abbott Dr Wheeling (60090) *(G-22030)*
**Continental Studios Inc** ....... 773 542-0309
1300 S Kostner Ave Chicago (60623) *(G-4460)*
**Continental Supply Co** ....... 708 448-2728
21 Carriage Trl Palos Heights (60463) *(G-17102)*
**Continental Tire Americas LLC** ....... 618 246-2466
11525 N Il Highway 142 Mount Vernon (62864) *(G-15406)*
**Continental Tire Americas LLC** ....... 618 242-7100
Hwy 142 S Mount Vernon (62864) *(G-15407)*
**Continental Tire Americas LLC** ....... 618 246-2585
10075 Progress Pkwy Mascoutah (62258) *(G-14351)*
**Continental Usa Inc** ....... 847 823-0958
1100 N Cumberland Ave Park Ridge (60068) *(G-17188)*
**Continental Web Press Inc (PA)** ....... 630 773-1903
1430 Industrial Dr Itasca (60143) *(G-12247)*
**Continental Web Press KY Inc** ....... 630 773-1903
1430 Industrial Dr Itasca (60143) *(G-12248)*
**Continental Web Press KY Inc (PA)** ....... 859 485-1500
1430 Industrial Dr Itasca (60143) *(G-12249)*
**Continental Window and GL Corp** ....... 773 794-1600
4311 W Belmont Ave Chicago (60641) *(G-4461)*
**Continental Window South Inc** ....... 773 767-1300
4600 S Kolmar Ave Chicago (60632) *(G-4462)*
**Continental/Midland LLC (HQ)** ....... 708 747-1200
24000 S Western Ave Park Forest (60466) *(G-17169)*
**Contmid Inc** ....... 708 747-1200
24000 S Western Ave Park Forest (60466) *(G-17170)*
**Contour Machining Inc** ....... 847 364-0111
640 Fargo Ave Elk Grove Village (60007) *(G-9391)*
**Contour Saws Inc** ....... 800 259-6834
900 Graceland Ave Des Plaines (60016) *(G-8174)*
**Contour Screw Products Inc** ....... 847 357-1190
3014 Malmo Dr Arlington Heights (60005) *(G-739)*
**Contour Tool Works Inc** ....... 847 947-4700
1712 N Lee Ct Palatine (60074) *(G-17018)*
**Contract Assembly Partners** ....... 217 960-3352
679 Washboard Trl Hillsboro (62049) *(G-11888)*
**Contract Industries Inc** ....... 708 458-8150
6641 S Narragansett Ave Bedford Park (60638) *(G-1545)*
**Contract Packaging Plus Inc** ....... 708 356-1100
1239 Spruce Ave Bensenville (60106) *(G-1865)*
**Contract Transportation Sys Co** ....... 217 342-5757
711 W Wabash Ave Effingham (62401) *(G-8831)*
**Contractor Advisors, Chicago** *Also called Be Group Inc* *(G-4061)*
**Contractors Ready-Mix Inc** ....... 217 482-5530
210 E Elm St Mason City (62664) *(G-14362)*
**Contractors Ready-Mix Inc (PA)** ....... 217 735-2565
601 S Kickapoo St Lincoln (62656) *(G-13407)*
**Contractors Register Inc** ....... 630 519-3480
555 Waters Edge Ste 150 Lombard (60148) *(G-13784)*
**Control Designs Inc** ....... 847 918-9347
4006 Grove Ave Gurnee (60031) *(G-11434)*
**Control Equipment Company Inc** ....... 847 891-7500
1115 Morse Ave Schaumburg (60193) *(G-19482)*
**Control Masters Inc** ....... 630 968-2390
5235 Katrine Ave Downers Grove (60515) *(G-8420)*
**Control Panels Inc** ....... 815 654-6000
1350 Harder Ct Rockford (61103) *(G-18323)*
**Control Research Inc** ....... 847 352-4920
908 Albion Ave Schaumburg (60193) *(G-19483)*
**Control Solutions LLC** ....... 630 806-7062
2520 Diehl Rd Aurora (60502) *(G-984)*
**Control Systems Inc** ....... 847 438-6228
3603 Crestview Dr Long Grove (60047) *(G-13889)*
**Control Weigh** ....... 847 540-8260
100 Lake Blvd Apt 677 Buffalo Grove (60089) *(G-2679)*
**Control Works Inc** ....... 630 444-1942
2701 Dukane Dr Ste B Saint Charles (60174) *(G-19163)*
**Controlled Thermal Processing (PA)** ....... 847 651-5511
1521 Bourbon Pkwy Streamwood (60107) *(G-20650)*
**Controllink Incorporated** ....... 847 622-1100
1650 Cambridge Dr Elgin (60123) *(G-9002)*
**Convergent Advisors** ....... 312 971-2602
22 W Washington St # 1500 Chicago (60602) *(G-4463)*
**Convergent Bill Ete Ort T** ....... 847 387-4059
2000 W Att Center Dr Rm 4 Hoffman Estates (60192) *(G-12003)*
**Convergent Group LLC** ....... 847 274-6336
521 Deerpath Ct Deerfield (60015) *(G-8001)*
**Conversion Energy Systems Inc** ....... 312 489-8875
200 W Monroe St Ste 1700 Chicago (60606) *(G-4464)*
**Converting Systems Inc** ....... 847 519-0232
1045 Remington Rd Schaumburg (60173) *(G-19484)*
**Converting Technology Inc** ....... 847 290-0590
1557 Carmen Dr Elk Grove Village (60007) *(G-9392)*
**Conveyor Installations Inc** ....... 630 859-8900
1723 E Wilson St Batavia (60510) *(G-1433)*
**Conveyors Plus Inc** ....... 708 361-1512
13301 Southwest Hwy Ste J Orland Park (60462) *(G-16849)*
**Conwed Plastics** ....... 630 293-3737
390 Wegner Dr Ste B West Chicago (60185) *(G-21687)*
**Conxall Corporation** ....... 630 834-7504
601 E Wildwood Ave Villa Park (60181) *(G-21245)*
**Cook Merritt** ....... 630 980-3070
800 Lake St Ste 118 Roselle (60172) *(G-18934)*
**Cook Chocolate Company, Chicago** *Also called Worlds Finest Chocolate Inc* *(G-7033)*
**Cook Communications Minis** ....... 847 741-5168
850 N Grove Ave Elgin (60120) *(G-9003)*
**Cook Communications Ministries** ....... 847 741-0800
850 N Grove Ave Elgin (60120) *(G-9004)*
**Cook Fabrication Signs Graphic** ....... 309 360-3805
325 N Deer Crk Deer Creek (61733) *(G-7962)*
**Cook JV Printing** ....... 708 799-0007
4061 183rd St Country Club Hills (60478) *(G-7405)*
**Cook Portable Warehouses, Cobden** *Also called Cook Sales Inc* *(G-7301)*
**Cook Printing Co Inc** ....... 217 345-2514
921 S 19th St Mattoon (61938) *(G-14387)*
**Cook Sales Inc (PA)** ....... 618 893-2114
3455 Old Highway 51 N Cobden (62920) *(G-7301)*
**Cook's Sports, Roselle** *Also called Cook Merritt* *(G-18934)*
**Cook, David C, Elgin** *Also called Cook Communications Ministries* *(G-9004)*
**Cookie Dough Creations Co** ....... 630 369-4833
22 W Chicago Ave Ste H Naperville (60540) *(G-15635)*
**Cookie Kingdom Inc** ....... 815 883-3331
1201 E Walnut St Oglesby (61348) *(G-16747)*
**Cool Fluidics Inc** ....... 815 861-4063
123 S Eastwood Dr Ste 145 Woodstock (60098) *(G-22554)*
**Cooler Concepts Inc** ....... 815 462-3866
21753 S Center Ave New Lenox (60451) *(G-15872)*
**Cooley Wire Products Mfg Co** ....... 847 678-8585
5025 River Rd Schiller Park (60176) *(G-19816)*
**Coon Run Drainage & Levee Dst** ....... 217 248-5511
826 Arenzville Rd Arenzville (62611) *(G-688)*
**Cooper B-Line Inc (HQ)** ....... 618 654-2184
509 W Monroe St Highland (62249) *(G-11780)*
**Cooper B-Line Inc** ....... 618 667-6779
816 Lions Dr Troy (62294) *(G-21004)*
**Cooper B-Line Inc** ....... 618 357-5353
3764 Longspur Rd Pinckneyville (62274) *(G-17546)*
**Cooper Equipment Company Inc** ....... 708 367-1291
763 W Old Monee Rd Crete (60417) *(G-7511)*
**Cooper Lake Millworks Inc** ....... 217 847-2681
1202 N State Highway 96 Hamilton (62341) *(G-11530)*
**Cooper Lighting LLC** ....... 312 595-2770
2550 United Ln Elk Grove Village (60007) *(G-9393)*
**Cooper Lighting LLC** ....... 847 956-8400
400 Busse Rd Elk Grove Village (60007) *(G-9394)*
**Cooper Oil Co** ....... 708 349-2893
9500 W 159th St Orland Park (60467) *(G-16850)*
**Cooper Smith International Inc** ....... 847 595-7572
2701 Busse Rd Elk Grove Village (60007) *(G-9395)*
**Coopers Hawk Production LLC** ....... 708 839-2920
430 E Plainfield Rd Countryside (60525) *(G-7419)*
**Coopers Hawk Winery & Rest, Countryside** *Also called Coopers Hwk Intermedte Holdng* *(G-7420)*
**Coopers Hwk Intermedte Holdng (PA)** ....... 708 839-2920
5325 9th Ave Countryside (60525) *(G-7420)*
**Coopers Hwk Intermedte Holdng** ....... 708 215-5674
430 E Plainfield Rd Countryside (60525) *(G-7421)*
**Coordinate Machine Company** ....... 630 894-9880
59 Congress Cir W Roselle (60172) *(G-18935)*
**Coordinated Kitchen Dev Inc** ....... 847 847-7692
1525 Coral Reef Way Lake Zurich (60047) *(G-13057)*
**Coordinated Packaging, Northbrook** *Also called Co-Ordinated Packaging Inc* *(G-16228)*
**Coorens Communications Inc** ....... 773 235-8688
2134 W Pierce Ave Chicago (60622) *(G-4465)*
**Copar Corporation** ....... 708 496-1859
5744 W 77th St Burbank (60459) *(G-2807)*
**Copar International, Burbank** *Also called Copar Corporation* *(G-2807)*
**Cope & Sons Asphalt** ....... 618 462-2207
3510 Thomas Ave Alton (62002) *(G-567)*
**Cope Plastics Inc (PA)** ....... 618 466-0221
4441 Indl Dr Alton (62002) *(G-568)*
**Cope Plastics Inc** ....... 630 226-1664
4 Territorial Ct Bolingbrook (60440) *(G-2288)*
**Cope Plastics Inc** ....... 309 787-4465
8110 42nd St W Rock Island (61201) *(G-18168)*
**Copies Overnight Inc (PA)** ....... 630 690-2000
262 Commonwealth Dr Carol Stream (60188) *(G-3136)*
**Copley Press Inc** ....... 217 732-2101
2201 Woodlawn Rd Lincoln (62656) *(G-13408)*
**Coppolinos Itln BF Grill & Bar, Chicago** *Also called Joseph Coppolino* *(G-5328)*

ALPHABETIC

(PA)=Parent Co (HQ)=Headquarters (DH)=Div Headquarters
2017 Harris Illinois
Industrial Directory
1207

**Copresco, Carol Stream** *Also called Copies Overnight Inc* ***(G-3136)***
**Copy Express Inc** ....815 338-7161
301 E Calhoun St Ste 2 Woodstock (60098) ***(G-22555)***
**Copy Mat Printing**....309 452-1392
1103 Martin Luther King D Bloomington (61701) ***(G-2155)***
**Copy Service Inc**....815 758-1151
1005 W Lincoln Hwy Dekalb (60115) ***(G-8079)***
**COPY WORKS, Oak Forest** *Also called In-Print Graphics Inc* ***(G-16584)***
**Copy Workshop, The, Chicago** *Also called Bendinger Bruce Crtve Comm In* ***(G-4082)***
**Copy-Mor Inc**....312 666-4000
767 N Industrial Dr Elmhurst (60126) ***(G-9856)***
**Copyco Printing Inc**....847 824-4400
95 Bradrock Dr Des Plaines (60018) ***(G-8175)***
**Copyline**....773 375-8127
9026 S Cregier Ave Chicago (60617) ***(G-4466)***
**Copyset Shop Inc**....847 768-2679
1801 E Oakton St Des Plaines (60018) ***(G-8176)***
**Cora Lee Candies Inc**....847 724-2754
1844 Waukegan Rd Glenview (60025) ***(G-11115)***
**Coral Chemical Company**....847 246-6666
1915 Industrial Ave Zion (60099) ***(G-22680)***
**Coral Lake, Marengo** *Also called Consolidated Materials Inc* ***(G-14222)***
**Coralite Dental Products Inc**....847 679-3400
7227 Hamlin Ave Skokie (60076) ***(G-19986)***
**Coras Trailer Manufacturing, Streator** *Also called Coras Welding Shop Inc* ***(G-20686)***
**Coras Welding Shop Inc**....815 672-7950
410 W Broadway St Streator (61364) ***(G-20686)***
**Corbett Accel Healthcare Grp C**....312 475-2505
225 N Michigan Ave # 1420 Chicago (60601) ***(G-4467)***
**Corcom, Mundelein** *Also called Te Connectivity Corporation* ***(G-15563)***
**Core Components Inc**....630 690-0520
154 Easy St Carol Stream (60188) ***(G-3137)***
**Core Finishing Inc**....630 521-9635
717 Thomas Dr Bensenville (60106) ***(G-1866)***
**Core Integrated Marketing, Chicago Heights** *Also called Poll Enterprises Inc* ***(G-7117)***
**Core Pipe, Carol Stream** *Also called Gerlin Inc* ***(G-3157)***
**Core Pipe Products Inc**....630 690-7000
170 Tubeway Dr Carol Stream (60188) ***(G-3138)***
**Core-Mark International Inc**....847 593-1800
405 Lively Blvd Elk Grove Village (60007) ***(G-9396)***
**Corefx Ingredients LLC (HQ)**....773 271-2663
4725 W North Ave Ste 240 Chicago (60639) ***(G-4468)***
**Corefx Ingredients LLC**....773 271-2663
12495 N Pleasant Hill Rd Orangeville (61060) ***(G-16814)***
**Coregistics, Wheeling** *Also called Iam Acquisition LLC* ***(G-22073)***
**Cores For You Inc**....217 847-3233
160 Industrial Park Hamilton (62341) ***(G-11531)***
**Coretechs Corp**....847 295-3720
245 Butler Dr Lake Forest (60045) ***(G-12894)***
**Corey Steel Company**....800 323-2750
2800 S 61st Ct Cicero (60804) ***(G-7185)***
**Coriant Operations Inc (PA)**....847 382-8817
1415 W Diehl Rd Naperville (60563) ***(G-15636)***
**Corken Inc (HQ)**....405 946-5576
105 Albrecht Dr Lake Bluff (60044) ***(G-12839)***
**Corless Equipment Co**....773 776-8383
7155 S Fairfield Ave Chicago (60629) ***(G-4469)***
**Corn Products International, Chicago** *Also called Ingredion Incorporated* ***(G-5193)***
**Cornelius Inc (HQ)**....630 539-6850
101 Regency Dr Glendale Heights (60139) ***(G-11018)***
**Cornell Forge Company**....708 458-1582
6666 W 66th St Chicago (60638) ***(G-4470)***
**Corner Bakery Cafe, Chicago** *Also called Cbc Restaurant Corp* ***(G-4260)***
**Corner Stone, Chicago** *Also called Cornerstone Communications* ***(G-4471)***
**Cornerstone Building Products**....217 543-2829
226 E Cr 600 N Arthur (61911) ***(G-889)***
**Cornerstone Communications**....773 989-2087
920 W Wilson Ave Chicago (60640) ***(G-4471)***
**Cornerstone Community Outreach**....773 506-4904
4615 N Clifton Ave Chicago (60640) ***(G-4472)***
**Cornerstone Media**....779 529-0108
450 S Spruce St Unit H Manteno (60950) ***(G-14182)***
**Cornerstone Polishing Company**....618 777-2754
85 Zach Ln Ozark (62972) ***(G-16993)***
**Cornerstones Publishing I**....847 998-4746
3054 Crestwood Ln Glenview (60025) ***(G-11116)***
**Cornfields LLC**....847 263-7000
3830 Sunset Ave Waukegan (60087) ***(G-21544)***
**Coronado Conservation Inc**....301 512-4671
5807 S Woodlawn Ave Chicago (60637) ***(G-4473)***
**Corpak Medsystems Inc (HQ)**....847 537-4601
1001 Asbury Dr Buffalo Grove (60089) ***(G-2680)***
**Corporate Business Card Ltd**....847 455-5760
9611 Franklin Ave Franklin Park (60131) ***(G-10442)***
**Corporate Disk Company (PA)**....800 634-3475
4610 Prime Pkwy McHenry (60050) ***(G-14489)***
**Corporate Electric Inc**....847 963-2800
926 Estes Ct Schaumburg (60193) ***(G-19485)***
**Corporate Graphics Inc**....630 762-9000
3710 Illinois Ave Saint Charles (60174) ***(G-19164)***
**Corporate Graphics America Inc**....773 481-2100
5312 N Elston Ave Chicago (60630) ***(G-4474)***
**Corporate Identification Solut**....773 763-9600
5563 N Elston Ave Chicago (60630) ***(G-4475)***
**Corporate Promotions Inc**....630 964-5000
4712 Main St Ste 202 Lisle (60532) ***(G-13577)***
**Corporate Sign Systems Inc**....847 882-6100
920 Central Ave Roselle (60172) ***(G-18936)***
**Corporate Textiles Inc**....847 433-4111
6529 N Lincoln Ave 5 Lincolnwood (60712) ***(G-13505)***
**Corporation Supply Co Inc (PA)**....312 726-3375
205 W Randolph St Ste 610 Chicago (60606) ***(G-4476)***
**Corpro Screen Tech Inc**....815 633-1201
5129 Forest Hills Ct Loves Park (61111) ***(G-13926)***
**Corr-Pak Corporation**....708 442-7806
8000 Joliet Rd Ste 100 Mc Cook (60525) ***(G-14447)***
**Correct Tool Inc**....630 595-6055
869 Fairway Dr Bensenville (60106) ***(G-1867)***
**Correctional Technologies Inc**....630 455-0811
7530 Plaza Ct Willowbrook (60527) ***(G-22207)***
**Corrective Asphalt Mtls LLC**....618 254-3855
300 Daniel Boone Trl South Roxana (62087) ***(G-20312)***
**Corrflow, Aurora** *Also called Infopro Inc* ***(G-1029)***
**Corrigan Corporation America**....800 462-6478
104 Ambrogio Dr Gurnee (60031) ***(G-11435)***
**Corrigan Manufacturing Co (PA)**....815 399-9326
1818 Christina St Rockford (61104) ***(G-18324)***
**Corro-Shield International Inc**....847 298-7770
2575 United Ln Elk Grove Village (60007) ***(G-9397)***
**Corrpak Inc**....618 758-2755
1231 State Route 13 Coulterville (62237) ***(G-7399)***
**Corrugated Converting Eqp**....618 532-2138
306 S Chestnut St Centralia (62801) ***(G-3410)***
**Corrugated Metals Inc**....815 323-1310
6550 Revlon Dr Belvidere (61008) ***(G-1747)***
**Corrugated Supplies Co LLC (PA)**....708 458-5525
5043 W 67th St Bedford Park (60638) ***(G-1546)***
**Corsaw Hardwood Lumber Inc**....309 293-2055
26015 N County Highway 2 Smithfield (61477) ***(G-20119)***
**Corsetti Structural Steel Inc**....815 726-0186
2515 New Lenox Rd Joliet (60433) ***(G-12477)***
**Corsicana Bedding LLC**....630 264-0032
970 S Lake St Aurora (60506) ***(G-1134)***
**Cortech USA, Willowbrook** *Also called Correctional Technologies Inc* ***(G-22207)***
**Cortek Endoscopy Inc**....847 526-2266
206 Jamie Ln Wauconda (60084) ***(G-21453)***
**Cortelyou Excavating**....309 772-2922
494 W Davis St Bushnell (61422) ***(G-2901)***
**Cortelyou Machine & Welding**....618 592-3961
511 E Main St Oblong (62449) ***(G-16730)***
**Cortes Enterprise Inc**....779 777-1061
255 W Lincoln Hwy Cortland (60112) ***(G-7385)***
**Cortina Companies Inc**....847 455-2800
10706 Grand Ave Ste 1 Franklin Park (60131) ***(G-10443)***
**Cortina Safety Products, Franklin Park** *Also called Cortina Tool & Molding Co* ***(G-10444)***
**Cortina Tool & Molding Co**....847 455-2800
10706 Grand Ave Ste 1 Franklin Park (60131) ***(G-10444)***
**Cortube Products Co**....708 429-6700
18500 Spring Creek Dr Tinley Park (60477) ***(G-20903)***
**Corus America Inc**....847 585-2599
475 N Martingale Rd # 400 Schaumburg (60173) ***(G-19486)***
**Corwin Printing**....618 263-3936
1004 Landes St Mount Carmel (62863) ***(G-15263)***
**Corydon Converting Company Inc**....630 898-9896
1350 Shore Rd Ste 120 Naperville (60563) ***(G-15637)***
**Corydon Converting Company Inc (PA)**....630 983-1900
1350 Shore Rd Ste 120 Naperville (60563) ***(G-15638)***
**Cosas Inc**....312 492-6100
2170 S Canalport Ave Chicago (60608) ***(G-4477)***
**Cosmedent Inc**....312 644-9388
401 N Michigan Ave # 2500 Chicago (60611) ***(G-4478)***
**Cosmo Films Inc (HQ)**....630 458-5200
775 W Belden Ave Ste D Addison (60101) ***(G-82)***
**Cosmopolitan Foot Care**....312 984-5111
1 S Wacker Dr Fl 11 Chicago (60606) ***(G-4479)***
**Cosmopolitan Machine Rebuilder**....630 595-8141
346 Evergreen Ave Bensenville (60106) ***(G-1868)***
**Cosmos Chicago, Wood Dale** *Also called Cosmos Granite & Marble Corp* ***(G-22355)***
**Cosmos Granite & Marble Corp**....630 595-8025
811 Lively Blvd Wood Dale (60191) ***(G-22355)***
**Cosmos Manufacturing Inc**....708 756-1400
111 E 34th St S Chicago Hts (60411) ***(G-19102)***
**Cosmos Plastics Company**....847 451-1307
3630 Wolf Rd Franklin Park (60131) ***(G-10445)***
**Coster Company**....312 541-7200
200 S Wacker Dr Ste 4000 Chicago (60606) ***(G-4480)***
**Cosveyor Inc**....630 859-8900
1723 E Wilson St Batavia (60510) ***(G-1434)***

**Cottage Collage** ....847 541-7205
449 White Pine Rd Buffalo Grove (60089) *(G-2681)*
**Cottage Door Press LLC** ....224 228-6000
218 James St Barrington (60010) *(G-1278)*
**Cotton Goods Manufacturing Co** ....773 265-0088
259 N California Ave Chicago (60612) *(G-4481)*
**Cougar Industries Inc** ....815 224-1200
3600 Cougar Dr Peru (61354) *(G-17506)*
**Coulson Publications, Pittsfield** *Also called Pike County Express (G-17574)*
**Counter** ....312 666-5335
666 W Diversey Pkwy Chicago (60614) *(G-4482)*
**Counter Cft Svc Systems & Pdts** ....630 629-7336
720 Concord Ln Lombard (60148) *(G-13785)*
**Counter Craft Inc** ....847 336-8205
2113 Northwestern Ave Waukegan (60087) *(G-21545)*
**Counter Creations LLC** ....815 568-1000
22521 W Grant Hwy Marengo (60152) *(G-14223)*
**Counter-Intelligence** ....708 974-3326
8150 W 107th St Palos Hills (60465) *(G-17115)*
**Countertop Creations** ....618 736-2700
6th St And Hwy 142 Dahlgren (62828) *(G-7689)*
**Counting House, Martinsville** *Also called Pap-R Products Company (G-14339)*
**Country Cast Products** ....815 777-1070
7650 W Us Highway 20 Galena (61036) *(G-10718)*
**Country Donut, Schaumburg** *Also called Joshi Brothers Inc (G-19590)*
**Country Donuts, Carpentersville** *Also called Amling Donuts Inc (G-3274)*
**Country Heritage Crafts, Arthur** *Also called Okaw Valley Woodworking LLC (G-916)*
**Country Home Magazine, Chicago** *Also called Meredith Corp (G-5689)*
**Country Journal Publishing Co** ....217 877-9660
3065 Pershing Ct Decatur (62526) *(G-7860)*
**Country Side Woodworking** ....217 543-4190
550 N Cr 240 E Arthur (61911) *(G-890)*
**Country Stone Inc (PA)** ....309 787-1744
6300 75th Ave Ste A Milan (61264) *(G-14781)*
**Country Village Meats** ....815 849-5532
401 N Pennsylvania St Sublette (61367) *(G-20714)*
**Country Workshop** ....217 543-4094
651 N Cr 125 E Arthur (61911) *(G-891)*
**Countryside Pure Water Solutio** ....847 255-5524
3 W College Dr Rear 1 Arlington Heights (60004) *(G-740)*
**County Asphalt Inc** ....618 224-9033
427 S Madison St Trenton (62293) *(G-20990)*
**County Journal, Percy** *Also called Willis Publishing (G-17496)*
**County Line Inc** ....217 268-5056
750 N Cr 250 E Arthur (61911) *(G-892)*
**County Line Tool, East Peoria** *Also called Tag Tool Services Incorporated (G-8736)*
**County Market, Quincy** *Also called Niemann Foods Foundation (G-17862)*
**County Materials Corp** ....217 352-4181
702 N Edwin St Champaign (61821) *(G-3470)*
**County Materials Corp** ....217 544-4607
2917 N Dirksen Pkwy Springfield (62702) *(G-20422)*
**County of Piatt** ....217 762-7009
101 W Washington St # 214 Monticello (61856) *(G-15076)*
**County Packaging Inc** ....708 597-1100
13600 Kildare Ave Crestwood (60445) *(G-7484)*
**County Tool & Die** ....217 324-6527
1400 W Hudson Dr Litchfield (62056) *(G-13683)*
**Couplings Company Inc** ....847 634-8990
570 Bond St Lincolnshire (60069) *(G-13440)*
**Coupon Magazine, Elgin** *Also called Progressive Publications Inc (G-9150)*
**Cour Pharmaceuticals Dev** ....773 621-3241
2215 Sanders Rd Ste 428 Northbrook (60062) *(G-16233)*
**Courier Publishing Co, Washington** *Also called Washington Courier (G-21394)*
**Coursons Coring & Drilling** ....618 349-8765
Nr Hwy 185 Saint Peter (62880) *(G-19321)*
**Court & Slope Inc** ....847 697-3600
780 Church Rd Elgin (60123) *(G-9005)*
**Courtesy Metal Polishing** ....630 832-1862
735 N Addison Rd Ste B Villa Park (60181) *(G-21246)*
**Cousins Packaging Inc** ....708 258-0063
312 E Corning Ave Peotone (60468) *(G-17487)*
**Coutland Components, Cortland** *Also called Alexander Lumber Co (G-7383)*
**Covachem LLC** ....815 714-8421
6260 E Riverside Blvd Loves Park (61111) *(G-13927)*
**Covalence Plastics, Lake Bluff** *Also called Berry Global Inc (G-12836)*
**Cover Connection, Wauconda** *Also called C M F Enterprises Inc (G-21450)*
**Coveris, Chicago** *Also called Cpg Finance Inc (G-4487)*
**Coveris Holding Corp (HQ)** ....773 877-3300
8600 W Bryn Mawr Ave Chicago (60631) *(G-4483)*
**Covey Machine Inc** ....773 650-1530
3604 S Morgan St Chicago (60609) *(G-4484)*
**Covidien LP** ....815 444-2500
815 Tek Dr Crystal Lake (60014) *(G-7557)*
**Covidien LP** ....815 744-3766
3901 Rock Creek Blvd Joliet (60431) *(G-12478)*
**Covington Service Installation** ....309 376-4921
1907 County Road 275 N Carlock (61725) *(G-3049)*
**Cowtan and Tout Inc** ....312 644-0717
222 Merchds Mart Plz 638 Chicago (60654) *(G-4485)*
**Cox Electric Motor Service** ....217 344-2458
1409 Triumph Dr Urbana (61802) *(G-21080)*
**Cox Metal Processing, Chicago** *Also called National Material LP (G-5864)*
**Coy Oil Inc** ....618 966-2126
503 S State St Crossville (62827) *(G-7522)*
**Coyle Print Group Inc** ....847 784-1080
5115 Suffield Ter Skokie (60077) *(G-19987)*
**Coyote Transportation Inc** ....630 204-5729
600 Thomas Dr Bensenville (60106) *(G-1869)*
**Cozent LLC** ....630 781-2822
2135 City Gate Ln Ste 300 Naperville (60563) *(G-15639)*
**Cozzini LLC** ....773 478-9700
4300 W Bryn Mawr Ave Chicago (60646) *(G-4486)*
**CP Moyen Co** ....847 673-6866
8157 Monticello Ave Skokie (60076) *(G-19988)*
**CP Screw Machine Products** ....630 766-2313
211 Beeline Dr Ste 3 Bensenville (60106) *(G-1870)*
**CPA Systems Incorporated** ....630 858-3057
369 Birchbrook Ct Glen Ellyn (60137) *(G-10965)*
**CPC Aeroscience Inc (PA)** ....954 974-5440
2651 Warrenville Rd # 300 Downers Grove (60515) *(G-8421)*
**Cpg Finance Inc** ....773 877-3300
8600 W Bryn Mawr Ave Chicago (60631) *(G-4487)*
**Cpg Printing & Graphics** ....309 820-1392
1103 Martin Luther King D Bloomington (61701) *(G-2156)*
**CPI, Norridge** *Also called Cast Products Inc (G-16098)*
**CPI, Rockford** *Also called Chem Processing Inc (G-18305)*
**CPI Satcom Division- Lisle, Lisle** *Also called Bolingbrook Communications Inc (G-13571)*
**Cpiprint, East Dundee** *Also called Carson Printing Inc (G-8629)*
**CPM Co Inc** ....815 385-7700
1805 Dot St McHenry (60050) *(G-14490)*
**Cpp, Edelstein** *Also called Custom Power Products Inc (G-8779)*
**Cppc, Paris Plant, Paris** *Also called Cadillac Products Packaging Co (G-17142)*
**Cpr Printing Inc (PA)** ....630 377-8420
321 Stevens St Ste E Geneva (60134) *(G-10821)*
**Cpsi, Columbia** *Also called Computer Pwr Solutions Ill Ltd (G-7355)*
**Cq Industries Inc** ....630 530-0177
477 W Fullerton Ave Elmhurst (60126) *(G-9857)*
**CR Laurence Co Inc** ....773 242-2871
5501 W Ogden Ave Cicero (60804) *(G-7186)*
**Crabtree & Evelyn Ltd** ....630 898-3478
1650 Premium Outlet Blvd # 1151 Aurora (60502) *(G-985)*
**Craft Beer Institute, Chicago** *Also called Caduceus Communications Inc (G-4211)*
**Craft Die Casting Corporation** ....773 237-9710
1831 N Lorel Ave Chicago (60639) *(G-4488)*
**Craft Metal Spinning Co** ....773 685-4700
4351 N Normandy Ave Chicago (60634) *(G-4489)*
**Craft Pallet Inc** ....618 437-5382
1620 N Benton Ln INA (62846) *(G-12184)*
**Craft World Inc** ....800 654-6114
6836 Forest Hills Rd Loves Park (61111) *(G-13928)*
**Craftmaster Manufacturing Inc (HQ)** ....800 405-2233
500 W Monroe St Ste 2010 Chicago (60661) *(G-4490)*
**Crafts Technology, Elk Grove Village** *Also called Craftstech Inc (G-9398)*
**Craftsman Custom Metals LLC** ....847 655-0040
3838 River Rd Schiller Park (60176) *(G-19817)*
**Craftsman Pltg & Tinning Corp (PA)** ....773 477-1040
1250 W Melrose St Chicago (60657) *(G-4491)*
**Craftsman Tool & Mold Co** ....630 851-8700
2750 Church Rd Aurora (60502) *(G-986)*
**Craftsmen Printing** ....217 283-9574
217 Bank St Hoopeston (60942) *(G-12108)*
**Craftstech Inc** ....847 758-3100
91 Joey Dr Elk Grove Village (60007) *(G-9398)*
**Craftwood Inc** ....630 758-1740
889 N Larch Ave Ste 100 Elmhurst (60126) *(G-9858)*
**Craig Alan Salon, Naperville** *Also called Second Chance Inc (G-15826)*
**Craig Industries Inc** ....217 228-2421
401 Delaware St Quincy (62301) *(G-17816)*
**Crain Communications Inc (PA)** ....312 649-5200
150 N Michigan Ave # 1800 Chicago (60601) *(G-4492)*
**Crain Communications Inc** ....312 649-5411
150 N Michigan Ave # 1800 Chicago (60601) *(G-4493)*
**Crain Communications Inc** ....312 649-5200
150 E Michigan Ave Chicago (60601) *(G-4494)*
**Crain Enterprises Inc** ....618 748-9227
100 Ohio Ave Mound City (62963) *(G-15256)*
**Crain's Chicago Business, Chicago** *Also called Crain Communications Inc (G-4493)*
**Crandall Stats and Sensors Inc** ....815 979-3340
1354 Clifford Ave Loves Park (61111) *(G-13929)*
**Crane Composites Inc (HQ)** ....815 467-8600
23525 W Eames St Channahon (60410) *(G-3566)*
**Crane Composites Inc** ....630 378-9580
594 Territorial Dr Ste D Bolingbrook (60440) *(G-2289)*
**Crane Composites Inc** ....815 467-1437
23525 W Eames St Channahon (60410) *(G-3567)*

A L P H A B E T I C

**Crane Dorray Corporation** ....630 893-7553
320 S Lombard Rd Addison (60101) ***(G-83)***
**Crane Equipment, Clifton** *Also called Charles Crane* ***(G-7273)***
**Crane Equipment & Services Inc (HQ)** ....309 467-6262
801 W Center St Eureka (61530) ***(G-9996)***
**Crane Nuclear Inc** ....630 226-4900
860 Remington Blvd Bolingbrook (60440) ***(G-2290)***
**Crane Valve Services, Bolingbrook** *Also called Crane Nuclear Inc* ***(G-2290)***
**Crash Candles, Mount Prospect** *Also called C Becky & Company Inc* ***(G-15314)***
**Crate & Barrel, Northbrook** *Also called Euromarket Designs Inc* ***(G-16252)***
**Crawford Company, Rock Island** *Also called Crawford Heating & Cooling Co* ***(G-18169)***
**Crawford County Oil LLC** ....618 544-3493
7005 E 1050th Ave Robinson (62454) ***(G-18058)***
**Crawford Heating & Cooling Co** ....309 788-4573
1306 Mill St Rock Island (61201) ***(G-18169)***
**Crawford Sausage Co Inc** ....773 277-3095
2310 S Pulaski Rd Chicago (60623) ***(G-4495)***
**Crazy Horse Concrete Inc** ....217 523-4420
1600 E Clear Lake Ave Springfield (62703) ***(G-20423)***
**Crazy Quilt Patch Factory, Elmhurst** *Also called Cq Industries Inc* ***(G-9857)***
**Crd Enterprises Inc** ....847 438-4299
549 Capital Dr Lake Zurich (60047) ***(G-13058)***
**Crea and Crea** ....630 292-5625
1115 Struckman Blvd Bartlett (60103) ***(G-1339)***
**Cream Team Logistics LLC** ....708 541-9128
15348 9th Ave Phoenix (60426) ***(G-17540)***
**Creapan USA Corp** ....312 836-3704
401 N Michigan Ave # 1200 Chicago (60611) ***(G-4496)***
**Creasey Construction III Inc** ....217 546-1277
3540 S Park Ave Springfield (62704) ***(G-20424)***
**Creasey Printing Services Inc** ....217 787-1055
1905 Morning Sun Ln Springfield (62711) ***(G-20425)***
**Create USA Modem Eight** ....630 519-3403
1801 S Meyers Rd Oakbrook Terrace (60181) ***(G-16705)***
**Creative Bedding Technologies** ....815 444-9088
300 Exchange Dr Crystal Lake (60014) ***(G-7558)***
**Creative Cabinetry Inc** ....708 460-2900
9632 W 143rd St Orland Park (60462) ***(G-16851)***
**Creative Cabinets Countertops** ....217 446-6406
3817 N Vermilion St Danville (61832) ***(G-7710)***
**Creative Cakes LLC** ....708 614-9755
16649 Oak Park Ave Ste F Tinley Park (60477) ***(G-20904)***
**Creative Clothing Created 4 U** ....847 543-0051
488 Wood Duck Ct Grayslake (60030) ***(G-11330)***
**Creative Concepts Fabrication** ....630 940-0500
3725 Stern Ave Saint Charles (60174) ***(G-19165)***
**Creative Confections Inc** ....847 724-0990
1955 Johns Dr Glenview (60025) ***(G-11117)***
**Creative Contract Packg LLC** ....630 851-6226
3777 Exchange Ave Aurora (60504) ***(G-987)***
**Creative Controls Systems Inc** ....815 629-2358
15929 Hauley Rd Rockton (61072) ***(G-18695)***
**Creative Conveniences By K&E** ....847 975-8526
55 N Buesching Rd Apt 312 Lake Zurich (60047) ***(G-13059)***
**Creative Covers Inc** ....708 233-6880
7508 W 90th St Bridgeview (60455) ***(G-2480)***
**Creative Curricula Inc** ....815 363-9419
1621 Park St McHenry (60050) ***(G-14491)***
**Creative Design, Somonauk** *Also called Weakley Enterprises Inc* ***(G-20130)***
**Creative Design Builders, Chicago** *Also called Creative Designs Kitc* ***(G-4497)***
**Creative Designs Kitc** ....773 327-8400
4355 N Ravenswood Ave Chicago (60613) ***(G-4497)***
**Creative Directory Inc** ....773 427-7777
5219 W Belle Plaine Ave Chicago (60641) ***(G-4498)***
**Creative Graphic Arts Inc** ....847 498-2678
3690 Oak Ave Northbrook (60062) ***(G-16234)***
**Creative Hi-Tech Ltd** ....224 653-4000
710 Cooper Ct Schaumburg (60173) ***(G-19487)***
**Creative Ideas Inc** ....217 245-1378
4 Sunnydale Ave Jacksonville (62650) ***(G-12386)***
**Creative Inds Terrazzo Pdts** ....773 235-9088
1753 N Spaulding Ave Chicago (60647) ***(G-4499)***
**Creative Iron Solutions, Naperville** *Also called Electrostatic Concepts Inc* ***(G-15804)***
**Creative Label Inc (PA)** ....847 981-3800
2450 Estes Ave Elk Grove Village (60007) ***(G-9399)***
**Creative Lithocraft Inc (PA)** ....847 352-7002
1730 Wright Blvd Schaumburg (60193) ***(G-19488)***
**Creative Lithocraft Inc** ....847 352-7002
1730 Wright Blvd Schaumburg (60193) ***(G-19489)***
**Creative Machining Tech LLC** ....309 755-7700
1949 Saint Johns Ave # 200 Highland Park (60035) ***(G-11829)***
**Creative Marble Inc** ....217 359-7271
4002 Kearns Dr Champaign (61822) ***(G-3471)***
**Creative Menu's Plus, Burr Ridge** *Also called Rick Styfer* ***(G-2877)***
**Creative Merchandising Systems** ....847 955-9990
425 Village Grn Unit 307 Lincolnshire (60069) ***(G-13441)***
**Creative Metal Products** ....773 638-3200
1101 S Kilbourn Ave Chicago (60624) ***(G-4500)***
**Creative Perky Cuisine LLC** ....312 870-0282
6601 Martin France Cir Tinley Park (60477) ***(G-20905)***
**Creative Printing, Dixon** *Also called Tlm Enterprises Inc* ***(G-8356)***
**Creative Prtg & Smart Ideas** ....773 481-6522
3406 N Cicero Ave Chicago (60641) ***(G-4501)***
**Creative Science Activities** ....847 870-1746
2 E Clarendon St Prospect Heights (60070) ***(G-17775)***
**Creative Steel Fabricators** ....847 803-2090
1024 North Ave Des Plaines (60016) ***(G-8177)***
**Creative Steel Rule Dies Inc** ....630 307-8880
1935 Brandon Ct Ste D Glendale Heights (60139) ***(G-11019)***
**Creative Werks LLC** ....630 860-2222
1350 Munger Rd Bartlett (60103) ***(G-1340)***
**Creative Werks LLC (PA)** ....630 860-2222
222 Sievert Ct Bensenville (60106) ***(G-1871)***
**Creative Wood Concepts Inc** ....773 384-9960
1680 N Ada St Chicago (60642) ***(G-4502)***
**Credit & Management Systems** ....618 654-3500
13648 Alpine Way Highland (62249) ***(G-11781)***
**Credit Card Systems Inc** ....847 459-8320
180 Shepard Ave Wheeling (60090) ***(G-22031)***
**Creekside Printing, Elgin** *Also called Taykit Inc* ***(G-9202)***
**Crescend Technologies LLC (PA)** ....847 908-5400
140 E State Pkwy Schaumburg (60173) ***(G-19490)***
**Crescent Cardboard Co, Wheeling** *Also called Potomac Corporation* ***(G-22126)***
**Crescent Cardboard Company LLC** ....888 293-3956
100 W Willow Rd Wheeling (60090) ***(G-22032)***
**CRESCENT FOODS, Chicago** *Also called 2000plus Groups Inc* ***(G-3663)***
**Crest Chemical Industries Ltd** ....815 485-2138
1066 Industry Rd Ste A New Lenox (60451) ***(G-15873)***
**Crest Greetings Inc** ....708 210-0800
444 W 31st St Chicago (60616) ***(G-4503)***
**Crest Industries, New Lenox** *Also called Crest Chemical Industries Ltd* ***(G-15873)***
**Crest Metal Craft Inc** ....773 978-0950
2900 E 95th St Chicago (60617) ***(G-4504)***
**Crestwood Associates LLC** ....847 394-8820
240 E Lincoln St Mount Prospect (60056) ***(G-15319)***
**Crestwood Custom Cabinets** ....708 385-3167
13960 Kildare Ave Crestwood (60445) ***(G-7485)***
**Crestwood Industries Inc** ....847 680-9088
1345 Wilhelm Rd Mundelein (60060) ***(G-15492)***
**Creswell Woodworking CA** ....847 381-9222
911 Rail Dr Unit C Woodstock (60098) ***(G-22556)***
**Creta Farms Usa LLC** ....630 282-5964
654 Cochise Cir Bolingbrook (60440) ***(G-2291)***
**Crete Rod, The, Schaumburg** *Also called Material Haulers Inc* ***(G-19636)***
**Crete Twp** ....708 672-3111
26730 S Stoney Island Ave Crete (60417) ***(G-7512)***
**Crew Beacon LLC** ....888 966-4455
1635 W Belmont Ave # 703 Chicago (60657) ***(G-4505)***
**Cricket Magazine Group, Chicago** *Also called Carus Publishing Company* ***(G-4246)***
**Cricket Publishing, Chicago** *Also called Carus Publishing Company* ***(G-4247)***
**Crisp Container Corporation** ....618 998-0400
700 Skyline Dr Marion (62959) ***(G-14257)***
**Criss Cross Express Illinois, Rantoul** *Also called Jancorp LLC* ***(G-17929)***
**Cristaux Inc** ....773 775-6020
1343 Brummel Ave Elk Grove Village (60007) ***(G-9400)***
**Cristaux International, Elk Grove Village** *Also called Cristaux Inc* ***(G-9400)***
**Crl Glass Machinery, Cicero** *Also called CR Laurence Co Inc* ***(G-7186)***
**Crl Industries Inc (HQ)** ....847 940-3550
500 Lake Cook Rd Ste 430 Deerfield (60015) ***(G-8002)***
**Crm North America LLC** ....708 603-3475
2308 17th St Franklin Park (60131) ***(G-10446)***
**Crocs Inc** ....630 820-3572
1650 Premium Outlet Blvd # 931 Aurora (60502) ***(G-988)***
**Cronkhite Industries Inc** ....217 443-3700
2212 Kickapoo Dr Danville (61832) ***(G-7711)***
**Cronus Technologies Inc** ....847 839-0088
424 E State Pkwy Schaumburg (60173) ***(G-19491)***
**Crooked Creek Outdoors** ....309 837-3000
1025 W Grant St Macomb (61455) ***(G-14123)***
**Crooked Trails Sawmill** ....618 244-1547
18058 E Il Highway 142 Opdyke (62872) ***(G-16810)***
**Crop Production Services Inc** ....815 853-4078
795 County Road 3100 E Wenona (61377) ***(G-21647)***
**Crop Production Services Inc** ....217 427-2181
12895 E Lyons Rd Catlin (61817) ***(G-3401)***
**Crop Production Services Inc** ....217 466-5430
3240 Il Highway 16 Kansas (61933) ***(G-12659)***
**Crosby Group LLC** ....708 333-3005
16868 Lathrop Ave Harvey (60426) ***(G-11663)***
**Cross Container Corporation** ....847 844-3200
400 Maple Ave Ste B Carpentersville (60110) ***(G-3281)***
**Cross Express Company** ....847 439-7457
153 Crest Ave Elk Grove Village (60007) ***(G-9401)***
**Cross Oil & Well Service Inc** ....618 592-4609
104 E Missouri St Oblong (62449) ***(G-16731)***
**Cross Tread Industries Inc** ....630 850-7100
12021 91st St Willow Springs (60480) ***(G-22194)***

**Crosscom Inc**...630 871-5500
528 W Roosevelt Rd Lla Wheaton (60187) *(G-21942)*
**Crosslink Coatings Corporation**...815 467-7970
24115 S Municipal Dr Channahon (60410) *(G-3568)*
**Crossmark Printing Inc (PA)**...708 532-8263
18400 76th Ave Ste A Tinley Park (60477) *(G-20906)*
**Crossmark Printing Inc**...708 754-4000
410 Ashland Ave Ste 300 Chicago Heights (60411) *(G-7094)*
**Crossroad Crating & Pallet**...815 657-8409
27700 E 700 North Rd Forrest (61741) *(G-10261)*
**Crosstech Communications Inc**...312 382-0111
111 N Jefferson St Chicago (60661) *(G-4506)*
**Crosstree Inc**...773 227-1234
1906 N Milwaukee Ave Chicago (60647) *(G-4507)*
**Crossway Bibles, Nfp, Wheaton** *Also called Good News Publishers (G-21951)*
**Crosswind Printing**...847 356-1009
588 Crosswind Ln Lindenhurst (60046) *(G-13546)*
**Crosswords Club, The, Naperville** *Also called MTS Publishing Co (G-15701)*
**Crowdmatrix Fx LLC**...312 329-1170
333 W Hubbard St Apt 901 Chicago (60654) *(G-4508)*
**Crowdsource Solutions Inc (PA)**...855 276-9376
33 Bronze Pointe Blvd Swansea (62226) *(G-20777)*
**Crowe, Therese Design, Chicago** *Also called Therese Crowe Design Ltd (G-6711)*
**Crowley-Sheppard Asphalt Inc**...708 499-2900
6525 99th Pl Chicago Ridge (60415) *(G-7145)*
**Crowleys Yacht Yard Lakeside**...773 221-9990
3434 E 95th St Chicago (60617) *(G-4509)*
**Crown Battery Manufacturing Co**...630 530-8060
1199 N Ellsworth Ave Villa Park (60181) *(G-21247)*
**Crown Battery Manufacturing Co**...708 946-2535
27456 S Hickory St Beecher (60401) *(G-1597)*
**Crown Coatings Company**...630 365-9925
215 W Nebraska St Elburn (60119) *(G-8881)*
**Crown Concepts Corporation**...815 941-1081
7080 Lisbon Rd Morris (60450) *(G-15103)*
**Crown Cork & Seal Usa Inc**...708 239-5555
5555 W 115th St Alsip (60803) *(G-452)*
**Crown Cork & Seal Usa Inc**...815 933-9351
1035 E North St Bradley (60915) *(G-2417)*
**Crown Cork & Seal Usa Inc**...708 239-5000
11535 S Central Ave Alsip (60803) *(G-453)*
**Crown Cork & Seal Usa Inc**...217 672-3533
970 W North St Warrensburg (62573) *(G-21338)*
**Crown Cork & Seal Usa Inc**...217 872-6100
255 W Pershing Rd Decatur (62526) *(G-7861)*
**Crown Cork & Seal Usa Inc**...630 851-7774
3737 Exchange Ave Aurora (60504) *(G-989)*
**Crown Coverings Inc**...630 546-2959
814 Central Ave Roselle (60172) *(G-18937)*
**Crown Custom Cabinetry Inc**...815 942-0432
1110 E Washington St Morris (60450) *(G-15104)*
**Crown Equipment Corporation**...847 397-1900
2055 Hammond Dr Schaumburg (60173) *(G-19492)*
**Crown Equipment Corporation**...815 773-0022
4100 Olympic Blvd Joliet (60431) *(G-12479)*
**Crown Equipment Corporation**...309 663-9200
1714 E Hamilton Rd Bloomington (61704) *(G-2157)*
**Crown Gym Mats Inc**...847 381-8282
27929 W Industrial Ave Lake Barrington (60010) *(G-12803)*
**Crown Kandy Enterprise Ltd**...708 580-6494
1127 S Mannheim Rd # 313 Westchester (60154) *(G-21837)*
**Crown Kandy Publishing, Westchester** *Also called Crown Kandy Enterprise Ltd (G-21837)*
**Crown Lift Trucks, Schaumburg** *Also called Crown Equipment Corporation (G-19492)*
**Crown Lift Trucks, Joliet** *Also called Crown Equipment Corporation (G-12479)*
**Crown Lift Trucks, Bloomington** *Also called Crown Equipment Corporation (G-2157)*
**Crown Machine, Addison** *Also called CDL Technology Inc (G-70)*
**Crown Machine Inc**...815 877-7700
2707 N Main St Rockford (61103) *(G-18325)*
**Crown Metal Manufacturing Co (PA)**...630 279-9800
765 S Il Route 83 Elmhurst (60126) *(G-9859)*
**Crown Premiums Inc (PA)**...815 469-8789
22774 Citation Rd Unit A Frankfort (60423) *(G-10311)*
**Crown Tool Company Inc**...630 766-3050
681 Country Club Dr Bensenville (60106) *(G-1872)*
**Crown Trophy**...309 699-1766
235 E Washington St Ste C East Peoria (61611) *(G-8707)*
**Crownline Boats, West Frankfort** *Also called Leisure Properties LLC (G-21811)*
**Cruise Boiler and Repr Co Inc**...630 279-7111
824 N Addison Ave Elmhurst (60126) *(G-9860)*
**Crusade Enterprises Inc**...618 662-4461
200 E North Ave Flora (62839) *(G-10205)*
**Crush Stone, Quincy** *Also called Central Stone Company (G-17811)*
**Crushed Grapes Ltd**...618 659-3530
10 Greenfield Dr Millstadt (62260) *(G-14822)*
**CRUSHERS CLUB, Chicago** *Also called Restoring Path (G-6338)*
**Crutcher Mfg**...309 725-3545
202 N Jeffrey St Cooksville (61730) *(G-7372)*
**Crutcher Mfg**...309 724-8206
102 S West St Ellsworth (61737) *(G-9827)*

**Crv Industries Inc**...630 595-3777
777 Maple Ln Bensenville (60106) *(G-1873)*
**Crv Lancaster Cams & Indexers, Bensenville** *Also called Crv Industries Inc (G-1873)*
**Crw Finishing Inc (PA)**...630 495-4994
1470 W Jeffrey Dr Addison (60101) *(G-84)*
**Cryogenic Systems Equipment**...708 385-4216
2363 136th St Blue Island (60406) *(G-2244)*
**Crystal Cave**...847 251-1160
1946 Lehigh Ave Ste E Glenview (60026) *(G-11118)*
**Crystal Die and Mold Inc**...847 658-6535
5521 Meadowbrook Indus Ct Rolling Meadows (60008) *(G-18724)*
**Crystal Edge, Chicago** *Also called Slee Corporation (G-6527)*
**Crystal Lake Beer Company**...779 220-9288
150 N Main St Crystal Lake (60014) *(G-7559)*
**Crystal Lake Brewing, Crystal Lake** *Also called Crystal Lake Beer Company (G-7559)*
**Crystal Nails McHenry**...815 363-5498
2030 N Richmond Rd McHenry (60051) *(G-14492)*
**Crystal Partners Inc**...847 882-0467
838 Prince Charles Ct Schaumburg (60195) *(G-19493)*
**Crystal Precision Drilling**...815 633-5460
5122 Torque Rd Loves Park (61111) *(G-13930)*
**Crystal Productions Co**...847 657-8144
3701 Coml Ave Ste 10 Northbrook (60062) *(G-16235)*
**Crystal Win & Door Systems Ltd**...773 376-6688
1300 W 35th St Chicago (60609) *(G-4510)*
**Crystatech Inc**...847 768-0500
1700 S Mount Prospect Rd Des Plaines (60018) *(G-8178)*
**Cs Magazine Front Desk Chicago, Chicago** *Also called Modern Luxury Media LLC (G-5783)*
**CSC Learning, Chicago** *Also called Computer Svcs & Consulting Inc (G-4441)*
**Csd, Dorsey** *Also called Axon Telecom LLC (G-8380)*
**Csi Chicago Inc**...773 665-2226
2216 W Winnemac Ave Chicago (60625) *(G-4511)*
**CSI Cutting Specialist Inc**...731 352-5351
421 N Shamrock St East Alton (62024) *(G-8600)*
**Csi Manufacturing Inc**...309 937-2653
Hwy 81 E Cambridge (61238) *(G-2967)*
**Csi of Tolono, Urbana** *Also called Concrete Supply Tolono Inc (G-21079)*
**Csi2d Inc**...312 282-7407
4907 Turnberry Dr Hoffman Estates (60010) *(G-12071)*
**Csiteq LLC**...312 265-1509
437 W Division St Apt 316 Chicago (60610) *(G-4512)*
**Csl Behring LLC**...815 932-6773
1201 N Kinzie Ave Bradley (60915) *(G-2418)*
**Csl Plasma Inc**...708 343-8845
1977 N Mannheim Rd Melrose Park (60160) *(G-14612)*
**CSM Fastener Products Co**...630 350-8282
1133 Bryn Mawr Ave Bensenville (60106) *(G-1874)*
**CSM Products Inc (HQ)**...815 444-1671
545 Dakota St Ste A Crystal Lake (60012) *(G-7560)*
**CSP Information Group Inc**...630 574-5075
1100 Jorie Blvd Ste 260 Oak Brook (60523) *(G-16503)*
**CSP Magazine, Oak Brook** *Also called CSP Information Group Inc (G-16503)*
**CST Industries Inc**...815 756-1551
345 Harvestore Dr Dekalb (60115) *(G-8080)*
**Ctc Machine Service Inc**...630 876-5120
756 W Hawthorne Ln West Chicago (60185) *(G-21688)*
**Ctg Advanced Materials LLC**...630 226-9080
479 Quadrangle Dr Ste E Bolingbrook (60440) *(G-2292)*
**CTI, Libertyville** *Also called Combined Technologies Inc (G-13317)*
**CTI, Elk Grove Village** *Also called Converting Technology Inc (G-9392)*
**CTI Industries Corporation (PA)**...847 382-1000
22160 N Pepper Rd Lake Barrington (60010) *(G-12804)*
**CTI Industries Corporation**...800 284-5605
800 Church St Lake Zurich (60047) *(G-13060)*
**CTS Advanced Materials LLC**...630 226-9080
479 Quadrangle Dr Ste E Bolingbrook (60440) *(G-2293)*
**CTS Automotive LLC (HQ)**...630 614-7201
2375 Cabot Dr Lisle (60532) *(G-13578)*
**CTS Automotive LLC**...815 385-9480
5213 Prime Pkwy McHenry (60050) *(G-14493)*
**CTS Corporation (PA)**...630 577-8800
2375 Cabot Dr Lisle (60532) *(G-13579)*
**CTS Electronic Components Inc (HQ)**...630 577-8800
2375 Cabot Dr Lisle (60532) *(G-13580)*
**CU Info Systems**...630 607-0300
100 N Addison Ave Elmhurst (60126) *(G-9861)*
**Cub Foods Inc**...309 689-0140
5001 N Big Hollow Rd # 5 Peoria (61615) *(G-17347)*
**Cub Foods 83, Springfield** *Also called Niemann Foods Foundation (G-20487)*
**Cubby Hole of Carlinville Inc (PA)**...217 854-8511
12472 Route 108 Carlinville (62626) *(G-3035)*
**Cubby Hole, The, Carlinville** *Also called Cubby Hole of Carlinville Inc (G-3035)*
**Cube Tomato Inc**...224 653-2655
636 Remington Rd Ste B Schaumburg (60173) *(G-19494)*
**Cubic Trnsp Systems Inc**...312 257-3242
221 N La Salle St Ste 500 Chicago (60601) *(G-4513)*
**Cudner & OConnor Co**...773 826-0200
4035 W Kinzie St Chicago (60624) *(G-4514)*

ALPHABETIC

(PA)=Parent Co (HQ)=Headquarters (DH)=Div Headquarters 2017 Harris Illinois Industrial Directory 1211

**Culen Tool & Manufacturing Co** ....... 708 387-1580
9128 47th St Ste 1 Brookfield (60513) ***(G-2629)***
**Culinary Co-Pack Inc** ....... 847 451-1551
9140 Belden Ave Franklin Park (60131) ***(G-10447)***
**Culinary Co-Pack Incorporated** ....... 847 451-1551
2300 N 17th Ave Franklin Park (60131) ***(G-10448)***
**Culligan International Company (HQ)** ....... 847 430-2800
9399 W Higgins Rd # 1100 Rosemont (60018) ***(G-18994)***
**Culligan International Company** ....... 847 430-1338
1520 Harris Rd Libertyville (60048) ***(G-13318)***
**Cullinan & Sons Inc (PA)** ....... 309 925-2711
121 W Park St Tremont (61568) ***(G-20981)***
**Culmac Inc** ....... 309 944-5197
720 Hanford St Ste 2 Geneseo (61254) ***(G-10800)***
**Cultivated Energy Group Inc** ....... 312 203-8833
10702 Seaman Rd Hebron (60034) ***(G-11718)***
**Culture Studio LLC** ....... 312 243-8304
1151 W 40th St Chicago (60609) ***(G-4515)***
**Cummins - Allison Corp (PA)** ....... 847 759-6403
852 Feehanville Dr Mount Prospect (60056) ***(G-15320)***
**Cummins - Allison Corp** ....... 847 299-9550
891 Feehanville Dr Mount Prospect (60056) ***(G-15321)***
**Cummins - Allison Corp** ....... 847 299-9550
851 Feehanville Dr Mount Prospect (60056) ***(G-15322)***
**Cummins - Allison Corp** ....... 630 833-2285
851 N Addison Ave Elmhurst (60126) ***(G-9862)***
**Cummins Crosspoint LLC** ....... 309 452-4454
450 W Northtown Rd Normal (61761) ***(G-16068)***
**Cummins Diesel Sales, Hodgkins** *Also called Cummins Npower LLC* ***(G-11973)***
**Cummins Dist Holdco Inc** ....... 309 787-4300
7820 42nd St W Rock Island (61201) ***(G-18170)***
**Cummins Filtration Inc** ....... 931 526-9551
3011 Illinois Rte 176 Crystal Lake (60014) ***(G-7561)***
**Cummins Great Plains Diesel, Rock Island** *Also called Cummins Dist Holdco Inc* ***(G-18170)***
**Cummins Inc** ....... 309 787-4300
7820 42nd St W Rock Island (61201) ***(G-18171)***
**Cummins Npower LLC** ....... 708 579-9222
7145 Santa Fe Dr Hodgkins (60525) ***(G-11973)***
**Cummins-American Corp** ....... 847 299-9550
852 Feehanville Dr Mount Prospect (60056) ***(G-15323)***
**Cunningham Electronics Corp** ....... 618 833-7775
120 N Main St Anna (62906) ***(G-602)***
**Cupcake Counter LLC** ....... 312 422-0800
229 W Madison St Chicago (60606) ***(G-4516)***
**Cupcake Holdings LLC** ....... 800 794-5866
2240 75th St Woodridge (60517) ***(G-22466)***
**Cupcakeologist LLC** ....... 630 656-2272
751 E Boughton Rd Bolingbrook (60440) ***(G-2294)***
**CURATE SNACKS, Abbott Park** *Also called Abbott Laboratories* ***(G-1)***
**Curatek Pharmaceuticals Ltd** ....... 847 806-7674
1965 Pratt Blvd Elk Grove Village (60007) ***(G-9402)***
**Curbside Splendor** ....... 224 515-6512
2816 N Kedzie Ave Chicago (60618) ***(G-4517)***
**Curlee Mfg** ....... 847 268-6517
9377 W Higgins Rd Rosemont (60018) ***(G-18995)***
**Curran Contracting Company** ....... 815 758-8113
2220 County Farm Rd Dekalb (60115) ***(G-8081)***
**Curran Contracting Company (HQ)** ....... 815 455-5100
286 Memorial Ct Crystal Lake (60014) ***(G-7562)***
**Curran Group Inc (PA)** ....... 815 455-5100
286 Memorial Ct Crystal Lake (60014) ***(G-7563)***
**Current Plus Electric LLC** ....... 618 394-4827
8265 W State Route 161 Belleville (62223) ***(G-1620)***
**Current Works Inc** ....... 847 497-9650
1395 Horizon Dr Johnsburg (60051) ***(G-12433)***
**Curry Ready Mix of Mason City, Mason City** *Also called Contractors Ready-Mix Inc* ***(G-14362)***
**Curry Ready Mix of Petersburg** ....... 217 632-2516
1106 N 7th St Petersburg (62675) ***(G-17535)***
**Curry Ready-Mix of Decatur** ....... 217 428-7177
2200 N Woodford St Decatur (62526) ***(G-7862)***
**Curt Herrmann Construction Inc** ....... 815 748-0531
512 Maplewood Ave Dekalb (60115) ***(G-8082)***
**Curt Smith Sporting Goods Inc (PA)** ....... 618 233-5177
213 E Main St Belleville (62220) ***(G-1621)***
**Curtis Metal Finishing Company** ....... 815 282-1433
10911 N 2nd St Machesney Park (61115) ***(G-14068)***
**Curtis Metal Finishing Company** ....... 815 633-6693
9917 N Alpine Rd Machesney Park (61115) ***(G-14069)***
**Curtis Thermal Processing, Machesney Park** *Also called Curtis Metal Finishing Company* ***(G-14068)***
**Curtis Woodworking Inc** ....... 815 544-3543
4820 Newburg Rd Belvidere (61008) ***(G-1748)***
**Curto-Ligonier Foundries Co** ....... 708 345-2250
1215 N 31st Ave Melrose Park (60160) ***(G-14613)***
**Cushing and Company (PA)** ....... 312 266-8228
420 W Huron St Chicago (60654) ***(G-4518)***
**Cushioneer Inc** ....... 815 748-5505
1651 Pleasant St Dekalb (60115) ***(G-8083)***

**Custom & Hard To Find Wigs** ....... 773 777-0222
4065 N Milwaukee Ave Chicago (60641) ***(G-4519)***
**Custom Accents, Elk Grove Village** *Also called Custom Plastics Inc* ***(G-9404)***
**Custom Aluminum Products Inc** ....... 847 717-5000
312 Eureka St Genoa (60135) ***(G-10877)***
**Custom Aluminum Products Inc (PA)** ....... 847 717-5000
414 Division St South Elgin (60177) ***(G-20191)***
**Custom AP & Promotions Inc** ....... 815 398-9823
4602 E State St Ste 1 Rockford (61108) ***(G-18326)***
**Custom Assembly LLC** ....... 630 595-4855
555 Pond Dr Wood Dale (60191) ***(G-22356)***
**Custom Assembly Solutions Inc** ....... 847 224-5800
101 E State Pkwy Schaumburg (60173) ***(G-19495)***
**Custom Bindery Services, Addison** *Also called Hopkins Printing & Envelope Co* ***(G-148)***
**Custom Blades & Tools Inc** ....... 630 860-7650
1084 Fairway Dr Bensenville (60106) ***(G-1875)***
**Custom Blending & Pckaging of** ....... 618 286-1140
108 Coulter Rd Dupo (62239) ***(G-8569)***
**Custom Blow Molding** ....... 630 820-9700
2560 White Oak Cir # 140 Aurora (60502) ***(G-990)***
**Custom Boxes Inc** ....... 630 364-3944
681 W Briarcliff Rd Bolingbrook (60440) ***(G-2295)***
**Custom By Lamar Inc** ....... 312 738-2160
1332 W Madison St Chicago (60607) ***(G-4520)***
**Custom Cabinet Man Inc** ....... 847 249-0007
3816 Grandview Ave Ste B Gurnee (60031) ***(G-11436)***
**Custom Cabinet Refacers Inc** ....... 847 695-8800
2482 Technology Dr Elgin (60124) ***(G-9006)***
**Custom Calendar Corp** ....... 708 547-6191
875 E 22nd St Apt 202 Lombard (60148) ***(G-13786)***
**Custom Calender, Lombard** *Also called Custom Calendar Corp* ***(G-13786)***
**Custom Canvas LLC** ....... 847 587-0225
26463 W Grand Ave Ingleside (60041) ***(G-12188)***
**Custom Case Co Inc** ....... 773 585-1164
6045 S Knox Ave Chicago (60629) ***(G-4521)***
**Custom Chemical Engineering, Springfield** *Also called Custom Chemical Inc* ***(G-20426)***
**Custom Chemical Inc** ....... 217 529-0878
4524 Industrial Ave Springfield (62703) ***(G-20426)***
**Custom Chrome & Polishing** ....... 618 885-9499
18416 Stagecoach Rd Jerseyville (62052) ***(G-12420)***
**Custom Coating Innovations Inc** ....... 618 808-0500
30 Commerce Dr Lebanon (62254) ***(G-13213)***
**Custom Countertop Creations** ....... 847 695-8800
330 Randall Rd South Elgin (60177) ***(G-20192)***
**Custom Craft Cabinetry** ....... 630 897-2334
605 N Broadway Ste 1 Aurora (60505) ***(G-1135)***
**Custom Crafted Door Inc** ....... 309 527-5075
2810 County Road 520 N El Paso (61738) ***(G-8867)***
**Custom Culinary Inc (HQ)** ....... 630 928-4898
2505 S Finley Rd Ste 100 Lombard (60148) ***(G-13787)***
**Custom Culinary Inc** ....... 630 299-0500
2100 Wiesbrook Rd Oswego (60543) ***(G-16912)***
**Custom Cut EDM Inc** ....... 847 647-9500
5423 Fargo Ave Skokie (60077) ***(G-19989)***
**Custom Cut Stencil Company Inc** ....... 618 277-5077
132 Iowa Ave Belleville (62220) ***(G-1622)***
**Custom Cutting Tools Inc** ....... 815 986-0320
5405 Forest Hills Ct Loves Park (61111) ***(G-13931)***
**Custom Cuttingedge Tool Inc** ....... 847 622-0457
1217 Paramount Pkwy Batavia (60510) ***(G-1435)***
**Custom Cylinder Inc** ....... 847 516-6467
700 Industrial Dr Ste I Cary (60013) ***(G-3331)***
**Custom Design Services & Assoc** ....... 815 226-9747
220 E State St Rockford (61104) ***(G-18327)***
**Custom Designs By Georgio** ....... 847 233-0410
9955 Pacific Ave Franklin Park (60131) ***(G-10449)***
**Custom Direct Inc** ....... 630 529-1936
715 E Irving Park Rd Roselle (60172) ***(G-18938)***
**Custom Enclsrs Div Cstm Lnear, Wheeling** *Also called Custom Linear Grille Inc* ***(G-22033)***
**Custom Enterprises** ....... 618 439-6626
131 Industrial Park Rd Benton (62812) ***(G-2025)***
**Custom Fabricating Htg & Coolg** ....... 815 726-0477
1120 Manhattan Rd Joliet (60433) ***(G-12480)***
**Custom Fabrications Inc** ....... 847 531-5912
1625 Weld Rd Ste B Elgin (60123) ***(G-9007)***
**Custom Fbrication Coatings Inc** ....... 618 452-9540
1107 22nd St Granite City (62040) ***(G-11271)***
**Custom Feeder Co of Rockford** ....... 815 654-2444
6207 Material Ave Ste 1 Loves Park (61111) ***(G-13932)***
**Custom Fiberglass of Illinois** ....... 309 344-7727
875 Enterprise Ave Galesburg (61401) ***(G-10744)***
**Custom Films Inc** ....... 217 826-2326
1400 Archer Ave Marshall (62441) ***(G-14320)***
**Custom Filter LLC** ....... 630 906-2100
2300 Raddant Rd Ste A Aurora (60502) ***(G-991)***
**Custom Fit Architectural Mtls, Chicago** *Also called Custom Fit Shtmetal Roofg Corp* ***(G-4522)***
**Custom Fit Shtmetal Roofg Corp** ....... 773 227-9019
222 N Maplewood Ave Chicago (60612) ***(G-4522)***

**Custom Flooring Insets, East Dundee** *Also called Grads Inc* ***(G-8641)***
**Custom Foam Works Inc** 618 920-2810
31 Sequoia Dr Troy (62294) ***(G-21005)***
**Custom Food Products, Oswego** *Also called Custom Culinary Inc* ***(G-16912)***
**Custom Golf By Tanis** 708 481-4433
21750 Main St Unit 17 Matteson (60443) ***(G-14369)***
**Custom Grain Systems LLC** 812 881-8175
15733 Gollyville Rd Lawrenceville (62439) ***(G-13197)***
**Custom Graphics** 309 828-0717
1212 Towanda Ave Lowr Bloomington (61701) ***(G-2158)***
**Custom Graphics Inc (PA)** 309 633-0850
4100 Ricketts Ave Bartonville (61607) ***(G-1393)***
**Custom Hard Chrome Service Co** 847 759-1420
7083 Barry St Rosemont (60018) ***(G-18996)***
**Custom Innovation LLC** 847 847-7100
4634 Twin Lakes Ln Long Grove (60047) ***(G-13890)***
**Custom Linear Grille Inc** 847 520-5511
500 Harvester Ct Ste 3 Wheeling (60090) ***(G-22033)***
**Custom Lumbermill Works** 309 875-3534
221 E St Maquon (61458) ***(G-14216)***
**Custom Machine Inc** 815 284-3820
895 Shop Rd Dixon (61021) ***(G-8327)***
**Custom Machinery Inc** 847 678-3033
3910 Wesley Ter Schiller Park (60176) ***(G-19818)***
**Custom Machining & Design LLC** 847 364-2601
1510 Midway Ct Ste E5 Elk Grove Village (60007) ***(G-9403)***
**Custom Machining Company** 630 766-2600
401 Evergreen Ave Bensenville (60106) ***(G-1876)***
**Custom Magnetics Inc** 773 463-6500
4050 N Rockwell St Chicago (60618) ***(G-4523)***
**Custom Menu Insights LLC** 312 237-3860
20 N Wacker Dr Ste 3705 Chicago (60606) ***(G-4524)***
**Custom Metal Products Corp** 815 397-3306
1827 Broadway Rockford (61104) ***(G-18328)***
**Custom Metal Products Div, Rockford** *Also called Custom Metal Products Corp* ***(G-18328)***
**Custom Millers Supply Inc** 309 734-6312
511 S 3rd St Monmouth (61462) ***(G-15011)***
**Custom Mold Services** 847 364-6589
1605 W Algonquin Rd Mount Prospect (60056) ***(G-15324)***
**Custom Monogramming** 815 625-9044
206 Dixon Ave Ste D Rock Falls (61071) ***(G-18130)***
**Custom Plastics Inc** 847 439-6770
1940 Lunt Ave Elk Grove Village (60007) ***(G-9404)***
**Custom Plastics Inc** 847 640-4723
1890 Lunt Ave Elk Grove Village (60007) ***(G-9405)***
**Custom Plastics of Peoria** 309 697-2888
4623 Enterprise Dr Bartonville (61607) ***(G-1394)***
**Custom Power Products Inc** 309 249-2704
19727 N State Route 40 Edelstein (61526) ***(G-8779)***
**Custom Product Innovations** 618 628-0111
40 Commerce Dr Lebanon (62254) ***(G-13214)***
**Custom Railz & Stairs Inc** 773 592-7210
7808 La Crosse Ave Oak Lawn (60459) ***(G-16613)***
**Custom Railz & Stairz Inc** 773 592-7210
6740 S Belt Circle Dr Chicago (60638) ***(G-4525)***
**Custom Rods By Grandt Ltd** 847 577-0848
203 S Highland Ave Arlington Heights (60005) ***(G-741)***
**Custom Screen Printing** 217 543-3691
111 N Vine St Arthur (61911) ***(G-893)***
**Custom Seal & Rubber Products** 888 356-2966
112 E Hitt St Mount Morris (61054) ***(G-15295)***
**Custom Sign Consultants Inc** 312 533-2302
1928 W Fulton St Chicago (60612) ***(G-4526)***
**Custom Signs On Metal LLC** 217 443-5347
301 Mayfield St Tilton (61833) ***(G-20880)***
**Custom Stainless Steel Inc (PA)** 618 435-2605
350 Industrial Park Dr Benton (62812) ***(G-2026)***
**Custom Stone Wrks Acqstion Inc** 630 669-1119
165 W Stephenie Dr Cortland (60112) ***(G-7386)***
**Custom Superfinishing Grinding** 847 699-9710
7083 Barry St Rosemont (60018) ***(G-18997)***
**Custom Systems Inc** 314 355-4575
3660 State Route 111 Granite City (62040) ***(G-11272)***
**Custom Telephone Printing Inc** 815 338-0000
1002 Mchenry Ave Woodstock (60098) ***(G-22557)***
**Custom Tool & Gage Co Inc** 847 671-5306
10109 Franklin Ave Franklin Park (60131) ***(G-10450)***
**Custom Tool Inc** 217 465-8538
926 N Central Ave Paris (61944) ***(G-17145)***
**Custom Towels Inc** 618 539-5005
6410 Hilgard Memorial Dr Freeburg (62243) ***(G-10634)***
**Custom Trophies** 217 422-3353
947 N Water St Decatur (62523) ***(G-7863)***
**Custom Window Accents** 815 943-7651
900 W Diggins St Harvard (60033) ***(G-11629)***
**Custom Wood & Laminate Ltd** 815 727-4168
1102 Davison St Joliet (60433) ***(G-12481)***
**Custom Wood Creations** 618 346-2208
776 Timberlane Dr Collinsville (62234) ***(G-7318)***
**Custom Wood Designs Inc** 708 799-3439
14237 Kilbourne Ave Crestwood (60445) ***(G-7486)***
**Custom Woodwork & Interiors (PA)** 217 546-0006
3208 S Douglas Ave Springfield (62704) ***(G-20427)***
**Custom Woodworking Inc** 630 584-7106
125 N 11th Ave Saint Charles (60174) ***(G-19166)***
**Customergauge USA LLC** 773 669-5915
401 N Michigan Ave # 1200 Chicago (60611) ***(G-4527)***
**Customeyes, Rock Island** *Also called Essilor Laboratories Amer Inc* ***(G-18176)***
**Customwood Stairs Inc** 630 739-5252
1424 Sherman Rd Romeoville (60446) ***(G-18815)***
**Cut - To - Size Technology Inc** 630 543-8328
345 S Fairbank St Addison (60101) ***(G-85)***
**Cut Rate Printers, Chicago** *Also called Swift Impressions Inc* ***(G-6650)***
**Cut Rite Die Co** 847 394-0492
732 N Dryden Ave Arlington Heights (60004) ***(G-742)***
**Cutco Abrasive Co, Saint Charles** *Also called C M C Industries Inc* ***(G-19147)***
**Cutshaw Instls Inc** 847 426-9208
216 Dundee Ave East Dundee (60118) ***(G-8630)***
**Cutting Edge Communications** 815 788-9419
764 Grandview Dr Crystal Lake (60014) ***(G-7564)***
**Cutting Edge Industries Inc** 847 678-1777
9015 Exchange Ave Franklin Park (60131) ***(G-10451)***
**Cutting Edge Machining Inc** 847 427-1392
105 Randall St Ste B Elk Grove Village (60007) ***(G-9406)***
**Cutting Tool Innovations Inc** 630 766-4839
759 Industrial Dr Bensenville (60106) ***(G-1877)***
**Cvp Systems Inc** 630 852-1190
2518 Wisconsin Ave Downers Grove (60515) ***(G-8422)***
**Cwi** 618 443-2030
8384 Valley Steel Rd Sparta (62286) ***(G-20316)***
**CWI Displays Corp** 773 277-0040
4041 W Ogden Ave Chicago (60623) ***(G-4528)***
**Cws Cabinets** 847 258-4468
225 Stanley St Elk Grove Village (60007) ***(G-9407)***
**Cy Laser LLC** 630 208-1931
65 N River Ln Ste 209 Geneva (60134) ***(G-10822)***
**Cy-Tec Inc** 815 756-8416
221 Industrial Dr Dekalb (60115) ***(G-8084)***
**Cyber Innovation Labs LLC** 847 804-4724
1221 E Business Center Dr Mount Prospect (60056) ***(G-15325)***
**Cyberbond LLC** 630 761-0341
401 N Raddant Rd Batavia (60510) ***(G-1436)***
**Cyborg Systems Inc (HQ)** 312 279-7000
233 S Wacker Dr Ste 3640 Chicago (60606) ***(G-4529)***
**Cyclone Energy Shot, New Lenox** *Also called Dynamic Nutritionals Inc* ***(G-15878)***
**Cyclops Industrial Inc** 815 962-1984
126 Monroe St Rockford (61101) ***(G-18329)***
**Cyclops Welding Co** 815 223-0685
11 Joliet St La Salle (61301) ***(G-12769)***
**Cygnet Midwest, Naperville** *Also called Media Unlimited Inc* ***(G-15816)***
**Cygnus Corp Packaging Div, Chicago** *Also called Cygnus Corporation* ***(G-4530)***
**Cygnus Corporation** 773 785-2845
340 E 138th St Chicago (60827) ***(G-4530)***
**Cygnus D/B/A Marietta Chicago, Chicago** *Also called Marietta Corporation* ***(G-5619)***
**Cylinder Maintenance & Sup Inc** 708 754-5040
3305 Butler Ave Steger (60475) ***(G-20571)***
**Cylinder Services Inc** 630 466-9820
629 N Heartland Dr Sugar Grove (60554) ***(G-20721)***
**Cymatics Inc** 630 420-7117
31w280 Diehl Rd Ste 104 Naperville (60563) ***(G-15640)***
**Cyn Industries Inc** 773 895-4324
1661 N Elston Ave Chicago (60642) ***(G-4531)***
**Cynlar Inc** 630 820-2200
1585 Beverly Ct Ste 125 Aurora (60502) ***(G-992)***
**Cynthia Espy, Chicago** *Also called Amenities Home Design* ***(G-3845)***
**Cypress Multigraphics LLC (PA)** 708 633-1166
8500 185th St Ste A Tinley Park (60487) ***(G-20907)***
**Cyrulik Inc** 217 935-6969
1100 E Johnson St Clinton (61727) ***(G-7280)***
**Cyrus Shank Company** 630 618-4732
575 Exchange Ct Aurora (60504) ***(G-993)***
**Cyrus Shank Company (HQ)** 708 652-2700
4645 W Roosevelt Rd Cicero (60804) ***(G-7187)***
**Czarnik Memorials Inc** 708 458-4443
7300 Archer Rd Justice (60458) ***(G-12596)***
**Czarnik Precision Grinding Mch** 708 229-9639
5530 W 110th St Ste 8 Oak Lawn (60453) ***(G-16614)***
**Czech American TV Herald** 708 813-0028
124 Sunset Ridge Rd Willowbrook (60527) ***(G-22208)***
**D & B Fabricators & Distrs** 630 325-3811
16w065 Jeans Rd Lemont (60439) ***(G-13234)***
**D & D Business Inc** 630 935-3522
10s428 Carrington Cir Willowbrook (60527) ***(G-22209)***
**D & D Construction Co LLC** 217 852-6631
220 Cherry St Dallas City (62330) ***(G-7695)***
**D & D Counter Tops Co Inc**
9710 Forest Hills Rd Machesney Park (61115) ***(G-14070)***



(PA)=Parent Co (HQ)=Headquarters (DH)=Div Headquarters
2017 Harris Illinois Industrial Directory
1213

**D & D Embroidery** ............................................. 309 266-7092
140 S Main St  Morton  (61550)  *(G-15156)*

**D & D Jewelers, Sycamore**  Also called D & D Sukach Inc  *(G-20790)*

**D & D Manufacturing** ........................................ 815 339-9100
6th St Rr 26  Hennepin  (61327)  *(G-11733)*

**D & D Manufacturing Inc** ................................. 888 300-6869
500 Territorial Dr  Bolingbrook  (60440)  *(G-2296)*

**D & D Manufacturing Entps, Bolingbrook**  Also called D & D Tooling and Mfg Inc  *(G-2297)*

**D & D Printing Inc** ............................................. 708 425-2080
9737 Southwest Hwy  Oak Lawn  (60453)  *(G-16615)*

**D & D Sukach Inc** .............................................. 815 895-3377
303 W State St  Sycamore  (60178)  *(G-20790)*

**D & D Tooling and Mfg Inc (PA)** ..................... 888 300-6869
500 Territorial Dr  Bolingbrook  (60440)  *(G-2297)*

**D & D Tooling Inc** ............................................. 630 759-0015
500 Territorial Dr  Bolingbrook  (60440)  *(G-2298)*

**D & E Pallet Inc** ................................................ 708 891-4307
14358 Martha St  Chicago  (60633)  *(G-4532)*

**D & G Welding Supply Company** .................. 815 675-9890
7705 Industrial Dr Ste E  Spring Grove  (60081)  *(G-20332)*

**D & H Granite and Marble Sup** ...................... 773 869-9988
1520 W Pershing Rd  Chicago  (60609)  *(G-4533)*

**D & H Precision Tooling Co** ............................ 815 653-9611
7522 Barnard Mill Rd  Wonder Lake  (60097)  *(G-22322)*

**D & J International Inc** .................................... 847 966-9260
7793 N Caldwell Ave  Niles  (60714)  *(G-15974)*

**D & J Machine Shop Inc** ................................. 815 472-6057
2120 N 11250e Rd  Momence  (60954)  *(G-14979)*

**D & J Metalcraft Company Inc** ...................... 773 878-6446
4451 N Ravenswood Ave  Chicago  (60640)  *(G-4534)*

**D & J Plastics Inc** ............................................ 847 534-0601
735 Morse Ave  Schaumburg  (60193)  *(G-19496)*

**D & K Custom Machine Design** ..................... 847 956-4757
1795 Commerce Dr  Elk Grove Village  (60007)  *(G-9408)*

**D & K Group Inc (PA)** ...................................... 847 956-0160
1795 Commerce Dr  Elk Grove Village  (60007)  *(G-9409)*

**D & K International Inc (HQ)** .......................... 847 439-3423
1795 Commerce Dr  Elk Grove Village  (60007)  *(G-9410)*

**D & K Machine and Tool Inc** .......................... 847 439-8691
1080 Howard St  Elk Grove Village  (60007)  *(G-9411)*

**D & M Custom Injection M** ............................. 847 683-2054
150 French Rd  Burlington  (60109)  *(G-2811)*

**D & M Pattern Co** ............................................ 217 877-0064
987 Montgomery Ct  Decatur  (62526)  *(G-7864)*

**D & M Plastics, Burlington**  Also called D & M Custom Injection M  *(G-2811)*

**D & M Tool Llc** ................................................. 847 731-3600
2013 Horizon Ct  Zion  (60099)  *(G-22681)*

**D & M Welding Inc** .......................................... 708 233-6080
8314 S 77th Ave  Bridgeview  (60455)  *(G-2481)*

**D & N Deburring Co Inc** .................................. 847 451-7702
2919 Birch St  Franklin Park  (60131)  *(G-10452)*

**D & P Construction Co Inc (PA)** ..................... 773 714-9330
5521 N Cmderland Ste 1106  Chicago  (60656)  *(G-4535)*

**D & R Autochuck Inc** ...................................... 815 398-9131
5248 27th Ave  Rockford  (61109)  *(G-18330)*

**D & R Ekstrom Carlson Co** ............................. 815 394-1744
5248 27th Ave  Rockford  (61109)  *(G-18331)*

**D & R Machine Company Inc (LA)** ................. 618 465-5611
4131 Alby St  Alton  (62002)  *(G-569)*

**D & R Press** ...................................................... 708 452-0500
7959 W Grand Ave  Elmwood Park  (60707)  *(G-9966)*

**D & S Communications Inc (PA)** .................... 847 468-8082
1355 N Mclean Blvd  Elgin  (60123)  *(G-9008)*

**D & S Manufacturing Inc** ................................ 815 637-8889
5604 Pike Rd  Loves Park  (61111)  *(G-13933)*

**D & S Wire Inc** ................................................. 847 766-5520
2531 E Devon Ave  Elk Grove Village  (60007)  *(G-9412)*

**D & W Mfg Co Inc** ............................................ 773 533-1542
3237 W Lake St  Chicago  (60624)  *(G-4536)*

**D & Z Exploration Inc** ..................................... 618 829-3274
901 N Elm St  Saint Elmo  (62458)  *(G-19305)*

**D A Matot Inc** ................................................... 708 547-1888
2501 Van Buren St  Bellwood  (60104)  *(G-1702)*

**D and D Pallets** ................................................ 630 800-1102
725 S Broadway  Aurora  (60505)  *(G-1136)*

**D and I Analyst Inc (PA)** ................................. 217 636-7500
13343 Fitschen Rd  Athens  (62613)  *(G-937)*

**D and K Plastics** .............................................. 712 723-5372
2127 State Route 47  Yorkville  (60560)  *(G-22653)*

**D and R Tech** ................................................... 224 353-6693
1118 Lunt Ave Ste F  Schaumburg  (60193)  *(G-19497)*

**D and S Molding & Dctg Inc** .......................... 815 399-2734
2816 Kishwaukee St  Rockford  (61109)  *(G-18332)*

**D B M Services Corp** ....................................... 630 964-5678
1996 University Ln  Lisle  (60532)  *(G-13581)*

**D C Cooper Corporation** ................................. 309 924-1941
Junction 116 & 94  Stronghurst  (61480)  *(G-20712)*

**D C Estate Winery** ........................................... 815 218-0573
8925 Stateline Rd  South Beloit  (61080)  *(G-20143)*

**D C Grove Electric Inc** .................................... 847 587-0864
155 Sayton Rd Ste A  Fox Lake  (60020)  *(G-10275)*

**D C T/Precision LLC** ........................................ 217 475-0141
1260 E North St  Decatur  (62521)  *(G-7865)*

**D Castris, Rockford**  Also called Midwest Stitch  *(G-18507)*

**D D G Inc (PA)** .................................................. 847 412-0277
1955 Shermer Rd Ste 300  Northbrook  (60062)  *(G-16236)*

**D D Sales Inc** ................................................... 217 857-3196
1608 W Main St  Teutopolis  (62467)  *(G-20851)*

**D E Asbury Inc (PA)** ........................................ 217 222-0617
1479 Keokuk St  Hamilton  (62341)  *(G-11532)*

**D E Signs & Storage LLC** ................................ 618 939-8050
6167 State Route 3  Waterloo  (62298)  *(G-21401)*

**D E Specialty Tool & Mfg Inc** ........................ 847 678-0004
9865 Franklin Ave  Franklin Park  (60131)  *(G-10453)*

**D F I, Aurora**  Also called Detroit Forming Inc  *(G-994)*

**D G Brandt Inc** ................................................. 815 942-4064
901 Liberty St  Morris  (60450)  *(G-15105)*

**D G Printing Inc** .............................................. 847 397-7779
2246 Palmer Dr Ste 106  Schaumburg  (60173)  *(G-19498)*

**D J Peters Orthopedics Ltd** .......................... 309 664-6930
908 N Hershey Rd Ste 1  Bloomington  (61704)  *(G-2159)*

**D Kersey Construction Co** ............................. 847 919-4980
4130 Timberlane Dr  Northbrook  (60062)  *(G-16237)*

**D L Austin Steel Supply Corp (PA)** ............... 618 345-7200
500 Camelot Dr  Collinsville  (62234)  *(G-7319)*

**D L S, Roselle**  Also called RR Donnelley Logistics SE  *(G-18970)*

**D L S, Itasca**  Also called Diversfied Lbling Slutions Inc  *(G-12252)*

**D L Sheet Metal** .............................................. 708 599-5538
8717 W 98th Pl  Palos Hills  (60465)  *(G-17116)*

**D L V Printing Service Inc** ............................. 773 626-1661
5825 W Corcoran Pl  Chicago  (60644)  *(G-4537)*

**D Little Drilling** ............................................... 618 943-3721
4734 Country Club Rd  Saint Francisville  (62460)  *(G-19312)*

**D M C Mold & Tool Corp** ................................ 847 639-3098
740 Industrial Dr Ste H  Cary  (60013)  *(G-3332)*

**D M L, Schaumburg**  Also called Dml Distribution Inc  *(G-19507)*

**D M Manufacturing 2 Inc** ................................ 618 455-3550
490 S Main St  Sainte Marie  (62459)  *(G-19323)*

**D M O Inc** ......................................................... 815 756-3638
195 W Stephenie Dr  Cortland  (60112)  *(G-7387)*

**D Machine Inc** ................................................. 815 877-5991
921 River Ln  Loves Park  (61111)  *(G-13934)*

**D ME To ME** ..................................................... 815 485-3632
14001 W Illinois Hwy  New Lenox  (60451)  *(G-15874)*

**D N D Coating** .................................................. 309 379-3021
313 W Main St  Stanford  (61774)  *(G-20551)*

**D N M Sealcoating Inc** .................................... 630 365-1816
300 Railroad St  Elburn  (60119)  *(G-8882)*

**D N Welding & Fabricating Inc** ...................... 847 244-6410
3627 Washington St Bldg 5  Waukegan  (60085)  *(G-21546)*

**D R Sperry & Co** .............................................. 630 892-4361
623 Rathbone Ave  Aurora  (60506)  *(G-1137)*

**D R Walters** ..................................................... 618 926-6337
65 County Road 300 N  Norris City  (62869)  *(G-16113)*

**D S A, Lake Barrington**  Also called D S Arms Incorporated  *(G-12805)*

**D S Arms Incorporated** ................................... 847 277-7258
27 W 990 Indl Ave  Lake Barrington  (60010)  *(G-12805)*

**D S Precision Tool Company** ......................... 630 627-0696
1420 Brook Dr  Downers Grove  (60515)  *(G-8423)*

**D W Machine Products Inc** ............................ 618 654-2161
1111 6th St  Highland  (62249)  *(G-11782)*

**D W Packaging Solutions, Elk Grove Village**  Also called D&W Fine Pack LLC  *(G-9414)*

**D W Ram Manufacturing Co** ........................... 708 633-7900
18530 Spring Creek Dr # 1  Tinley Park  (60477)  *(G-20908)*

**D W Terry Welding Company** ......................... 618 433-9722
1860 E Broadway  Alton  (62002)  *(G-570)*

**D&J Arlington Heights Inc** ............................. 847 577-8200
1814 N Arlington Hts Rd  Arlington Heights  (60004)  *(G-743)*

**D&M Perlman Fine Jwly Gift LLC** ................... 847 426-8881
740 S 8th St  West Dundee  (60118)  *(G-21795)*

**D&M Plastics, Burlington**  Also called Owen Plastics LLC  *(G-2813)*

**D&W Fine Pack Holdings LLC (HQ)** ............... 847 378-1200
1900 Pratt Blvd  Elk Grove Village  (60007)  *(G-9413)*

**D&W Fine Pack LLC** ........................................ 800 323-0422
800 Ela Rd  Lake Zurich  (60047)  *(G-13061)*

**D&W Fine Pack LLC (HQ)** ............................... 847 378-1200
1900 Pratt Blvd  Elk Grove Village  (60007)  *(G-9414)*

**D-M-S Holdings Inc (HQ)** ................................ 847 680-6811
1931 Norman Dr  Waukegan  (60085)  *(G-21547)*

**D-Orum Corporation** ........................................ 773 567-2064
325 W 103rd St  Chicago  (60628)  *(G-4538)*

**D.P. Filters, Peoria**  Also called Dust Patrol Inc  *(G-17351)*

**D/C Export & Domestic Pkg Inc (PA)** ............ 847 593-4200
1300 E Devon Ave  Elk Grove Village  (60007)  *(G-9415)*

**D/C Group The, Elk Grove Village**  Also called D/C Export & Domestic Pkg Inc  *(G-9415)*

**D/C Industries LLC** ......................................... 630 876-1100
1215 Atlantic Dr  West Chicago  (60185)  *(G-21689)*

## ALPHABETIC SECTION — Dangios

**D2 Lighting LLC** .......... 708 243-9059
5718 Harvey Ave  La Grange Highlands  (60525)  *(G-12749)*

**D5 Design Met Fabrication LLC** .......... 773 770-4705
441 N Campbell Ave  Chicago  (60612)  *(G-4539)*

**Da Closet** .......... 708 206-1414
4139 167th St  Country Club Hills  (60478)  *(G-7406)*

**Dabecca Natural Foods Inc** .......... 773 291-1428
700 E 107th St  Chicago  (60628)  *(G-4540)*

**Dabel Incorporated** .......... 217 398-3389
602 E Green St  Champaign  (61820)  *(G-3472)*

**Dabir Surfaces Inc (HQ)** .......... 708 867-6777
7447 W Wilson Ave  Chicago  (60706)  *(G-4541)*

**Dabrico Inc** .......... 815 939-0580
1555 Commerce Dr  Bourbonnais  (60914)  *(G-2393)*

**Dach Fence Co, Rockford** Also called William Dach  *(G-18683)*

**Daco Incorporated (PA)** .......... 630 897-8797
609 Airport Rd  North Aurora  (60542)  *(G-16124)*

**Daco Products LLC** .......... 630 373-2245
609 Airport Rd  North Aurora  (60542)  *(G-16125)*

**Dadant & Sons Inc (PA)** .......... 217 847-3324
51 S 2nd St Ste 2  Hamilton  (62341)  *(G-11533)*

**Dadant & Sons Inc** .......... 217 852-3324
Hwy 9 S  Dallas City  (62330)  *(G-7696)*

**Dado Lighting LLC** .......... 877 323-6584
4700 Gilbert Ave 47-217  Western Springs  (60558)  *(G-21866)*

**Dadum Die & Design, Buffalo Grove** Also called Dadum Inc  *(G-2682)*

**Dadum Inc** .......... 847 541-7851
950 Beechwood Rd  Buffalo Grove  (60089)  *(G-2682)*

**Daesam Corporation** .......... 917 653-2000
888 E Belvidere Rd # 306  Grayslake  (60030)  *(G-11331)*

**Dagger Tool Co Inc** .......... 630 279-5050
501 W Interstate Rd  Addison  (60101)  *(G-86)*

**Daigger Scientific Inc** .......... 800 621-7193
620 Lakeview Pkwy  Vernon Hills  (60061)  *(G-21155)*

**Daily American, The, West Frankfort** Also called Gatehouse Media LLC  *(G-21809)*

**Daily Dollar Savings LLC** .......... 860 883-0351
9448 Skokie Blvd  Morton Grove  (60053)  *(G-15193)*

**Daily Egyptian Siu Newspaper** .......... 618 536-3311
1100 Lincoln Dr Rm 1259  Carbondale  (62901)  *(G-3005)*

**Daily General LLC** .......... 217 273-0719
2757 W Le Moyne St Ste 2  Chicago  (60622)  *(G-4542)*

**Daily Herald, Arlington Heights** Also called Paddock Publications Inc  *(G-815)*

**Daily Herald, Schaumburg** Also called Paddock Publications Inc  *(G-19680)*

**Daily Herald, Libertyville** Also called Paddock Publications Inc  *(G-13365)*

**Daily Herald, Lisle** Also called Paddock Publications Inc  *(G-13638)*

**Daily Highway Express, Winthrop Harbor** Also called Rd Daily Enterprises  *(G-22320)*

**Daily Journal The, Kankakee** Also called Small Newspaper Group  *(G-12651)*

**Daily Journal, The, Kankakee** Also called Kankakee Daily Journal Co LLC  *(G-12632)*

**Daily Kratom** .......... 815 768-7104
4010 Brenton Dr  Joliet  (60431)  *(G-12482)*

**Daily Lawrenceville Record** .......... 618 943-2331
1209 State St  Lawrenceville  (62439)  *(G-13198)*

**Daily Lawrenceville Record (PA)** .......... 618 544-2101
302 S Cross St  Robinson  (62454)  *(G-18059)*

**Daily Leader Newspaper, Pontiac** Also called Gatehouse Media LLC  *(G-17701)*

**Daily Money Matters LLC** .......... 847 729-8393
2200 Goldenrod Ln  Glenview  (60026)  *(G-11119)*

**Daily News Condominium Assn** .......... 312 492-8526
222 S Racine Ave  Chicago  (60607)  *(G-4543)*

**Daily News Tribune Inc (PA)** .......... 815 223-2558
426 2nd St  La Salle  (61301)  *(G-12770)*

**Daily News Tribune Inc** .......... 815 539-5200
900 Washington St  Mendota  (61342)  *(G-14719)*

**Daily News/Daily Record, Robinson** Also called Daily Lawrenceville Record  *(G-18059)*

**DAILY NORTHWESTERN NEWSPAPER, Evanston** Also called Students Publishing Company In  *(G-10097)*

**Daily Projects** .......... 224 209-8636
124 S Randall Rd  Algonquin  (60102)  *(G-385)*

**Daily Register, Harrisburg** Also called Gatehouse Media LLC  *(G-11600)*

**Daily Republican Register, Mount Carmel** Also called Mt Carmel Register Co Inc  *(G-15276)*

**Daily Robinson News Inc** .......... 618 544-2101
302 S Cross St  Robinson  (62454)  *(G-18060)*

**Daily Times, The, Ottawa** Also called Ottawa Publishing Co Inc  *(G-16975)*

**Daily Whale** .......... 312 787-5204
222 W Ontario St  Chicago  (60654)  *(G-4544)*

**Dainichi Machinery Inc** .......... 630 681-1572
745 Kimberly Dr  Carol Stream  (60188)  *(G-3139)*

**Dairy Dynamics LLC** .......... 847 758-7300
17820 Washington St  Elk Grove Village  (60007)  *(G-9416)*

**Daito Pharmaceuticals Amer Inc** .......... 847 205-0800
633 Skokie Blvd Ste 210  Northbrook  (60062)  *(G-16238)*

**Dakkota Integrated Systems LLC** .......... 517 694-6500
12525 S Carondolet Ave  Chicago  (60633)  *(G-4545)*

**Dal Acres West Kennel** .......... 217 793-3647
2508 W Jefferson St  Springfield  (62702)  *(G-20428)*

**Dalco Marketing Services** .......... 630 961-3366
216 Durham Ct  Naperville  (60540)  *(G-15641)*

**Dale K Brown** .......... 815 338-0222
130 Wshngton St Unit Rear  Woodstock  (60098)  *(G-22558)*

**Dale Schawitsch** .......... 217 224-5161
234 N 4th St  Quincy  (62301)  *(G-17817)*

**Dale's Diesel Service, Teutopolis** Also called D D Sales Inc  *(G-20851)*

**Dalec Controls Inc** .......... 847 671-7676
16140 Vincennes Ave  South Holland  (60473)  *(G-20258)*

**Dalec Electronics Inc** .......... 847 671-7676
16140 Vincennes Ave  South Holland  (60473)  *(G-20259)*

**Daley Automation LLC (PA)** .......... 630 384-9900
1111 S Washington St  Naperville  (60540)  *(G-15642)*

**Dalkey Archive Press** .......... 217 244-5700
University Of Illinois 6  Champaign  (61820)  *(G-3473)*

**Dalkey Archive Press, The, Champaign** Also called Dalkey Archive Press  *(G-3473)*

**Dallas & Co Costumes & Magic, Champaign** Also called Andy Dallas & Co  *(G-3450)*

**Dallas Corporation** .......... 630 322-8000
4340 Cross St  Downers Grove  (60515)  *(G-8424)*

**Dallas Scrub** .......... 312 651-6012
212 W Superior St  Chicago  (60654)  *(G-4546)*

**Dalmatian Fire Equipment Ltd** .......... 708 201-1730
531 Monroe St  Dolton  (60419)  *(G-8369)*

**Daly Engineered Filtration Inc** .......... 708 355-1550
942 E Hillside Rd  Naperville  (60540)  *(G-15643)*

**Dalzell & Company** .......... 815 477-8816
41 N Williams St  Crystal Lake  (60014)  *(G-7565)*

**DAmatos Bakery** .......... 312 733-5456
1125 W Grand Ave  Chicago  (60642)  *(G-4547)*

**DAmatos Bakery Inc** .......... 312 733-6219
1332 W Grand Ave  Chicago  (60642)  *(G-4548)*

**Damco Products Inc** .......... 618 452-4700
224 State St  Madison  (62060)  *(G-14141)*

**Damen Carbide Tool Company Inc** .......... 630 766-7875
344 Beinoris Dr  Wood Dale  (60191)  *(G-22357)*

**DAmico Associates Inc** .......... 847 291-7446
3065 Dundee Rd  Northbrook  (60062)  *(G-16239)*

**Damien Corporation** .......... 630 369-3549
6s204 Cohasset Rd  Naperville  (60540)  *(G-15644)*

**Damron Corporation** .......... 773 265-2724
4433 W Ohio St  Chicago  (60624)  *(G-4549)*

**Damron Tea, Chicago** Also called Damron Corporation  *(G-4549)*

**Dams Inc** .......... 708 385-3092
5919 W 118th St  Alsip  (60803)  *(G-454)*

**Damy Corp** .......... 847 233-0515
9353 Seymour Ave  Schiller Park  (60176)  *(G-19819)*

**Dan De Tash Knits** .......... 708 970-6238
1118 S 2nd Ave  Maywood  (60153)  *(G-14424)*

**Dan Horenberger** .......... 818 394-0028
1004 N Taylor St  Marengo  (60152)  *(G-14224)*

**Dana Anodizing Inc** .......... 773 486-2312
3905 W Armitage Ave  Chicago  (60647)  *(G-4550)*

**Dana Auto Systems Group LLC** .......... 630 960-4200
1945 Ohio St  Lisle  (60532)  *(G-13582)*

**Dana Corp Power Tech Group, Robinson** Also called Dana Sealing Manufacturing LLC  *(G-18061)*

**Dana Driveshaft Mfg LLC** .......... 815 626-6700
2001 Eastwood Dr  Sterling  (61081)  *(G-20588)*

**Dana Driveshaft Products, Sterling** Also called Dana Driveshaft Mfg LLC  *(G-20588)*

**Dana Molded** .......... 847 783-1800
810 Commerce Pkwy  Carpentersville  (60110)  *(G-3282)*

**Dana Plastic Container Corp (HQ)** .......... 847 670-0650
6 N Hickory Ave  Arlington Heights  (60004)  *(G-744)*

**Dana Plastic Container Corp** .......... 630 529-7878
200 W Central Rd  Roselle  (60172)  *(G-18939)*

**Dana Sealing Manufacturing LLC** .......... 618 544-8651
1201 E Victor Dana Rd  Robinson  (62454)  *(G-18061)*

**Danaher Corporation** .......... 815 568-8001
1300 N State St  Marengo  (60152)  *(G-14225)*

**Danaher Corporation** .......... 800 866-6659
1675 N Delany Rd  Gurnee  (60031)  *(G-11437)*

**Danaher Indus Sensors Contrls, Gurnee** Also called Dynapar Corporation  *(G-11443)*

**Danco Converting** .......... 847 718-0448
455 E North Ave Ave  Chicago  (60610)  *(G-4551)*

**Dancyn Recovery Systems** .......... 309 829-5450
707 N East St  Bloomington  (61701)  *(G-2160)*

**Dandelion Distributors Inc** .......... 815 675-9800
888 E Belvidere Rd # 114  Grayslake  (60030)  *(G-11332)*

**Dandurand Custom Woodworking** .......... 708 489-6440
2606 W Walter Zimny Dr  Posen  (60469)  *(G-17729)*

**Dane Industries LLC** .......... 815 234-2811
602 E Blackhawk Dr  Byron  (61010)  *(G-2915)*

**Danfoss Inc** .......... 815 639-8600
7500 Beverage Blvd  Loves Park  (61111)  *(G-13935)*

**Danfoss LLC** .......... 888 326-3677
4401 N Bell School Rd  Loves Park  (61111)  *(G-13936)*

**Danfoss Power Electronics, Loves Park** Also called Danfoss LLC  *(G-13936)*

**Danfoss Power Solutions US Co** .......... 815 233-4200
580 N Henderson Rd  Freeport  (61032)  *(G-10652)*

**Dangios** .......... 773 533-3000
3050 W Taylor St  Chicago  (60612)  *(G-4552)*

**Daniel & Sons Mech Contrs Inc** ....618 997-2822
105 Hilltop Ln Marion (62959) **(G-14258)**
**Daniel Bruce LLC** ....917 583-1538
2365 N Irene Dr Palatine (60074) **(G-17019)**
**Daniel J Nickel & Assocs PC** ....312 345-1850
3052 N Haussen Ct Chicago (60618) **(G-4553)**
**Daniel M Powers & Assoc Ltd** ....630 685-8400
575 W Crossroads Pkwy B Bolingbrook (60440) **(G-2299)**
**Daniel Mfg Inc** ....309 963-4227
273 County Road 1850 E Carlock (61725) **(G-3050)**
**Daniels Health, Chicago** *Also called Daniels Sharpsmart Inc* **(G-4554)**
**Daniels Jewelry & Mfg Co** ....847 998-5222
1436 Waukegan Rd Glenview (60025) **(G-11120)**
**Daniels Printing & Office Sup, Oak Forest** *Also called Dans Printing & Off Sups Inc* **(G-16577)**
**Daniels Sharpsmart Inc (HQ)** ....312 546-8900
111 W Jackson Blvd # 720 Chicago (60604) **(G-4554)**
**Danielson Food Products Inc** ....773 285-2111
215 W Root St Chicago (60609) **(G-4555)**
**Danisco Sweeteners, Thomson** *Also called E I Du Pont De Nemours & Co* **(G-20865)**
**Danish Maid Butter Company** ....773 731-8787
8512 S Commercial Ave Chicago (60617) **(G-4556)**
**Danko Industries** ....630 882-6070
181 Wolf St Unit C Yorkville (60560) **(G-22654)**
**Danlee Wood Products Inc** ....815 938-9016
207 S Chestnut St Forreston (61030) **(G-10268)**
**Dans Dirt and Gravel** ....630 479-6622
1212 5th St Aurora (60505) **(G-1138)**
**Dans Printing & Off Sups Inc** ....708 687-3055
14800 Cicero Ave Ste 101 Oak Forest (60452) **(G-16577)**
**Dans Rubber Stamp & Signs** ....815 964-5603
1704 Burton St Rockford (61103) **(G-18333)**
**Danville Brass and Aluminum, Danville** *Also called Marble Machine Inc* **(G-7752)**
**Danville Metal Stamping Co Inc (PA)** ....217 446-0647
20 Oakwood Ave Danville (61832) **(G-7712)**
**Danville Metal Stamping Co Inc** ....217 446-0647
17 Oakwood Ave Danville (61832) **(G-7713)**
**Danville Metal Stamping Co Inc** ....217 446-0647
1100 Martin St Danville (61832) **(G-7714)**
**Danze Inc** ....630 754-0277
2500 Internationale Pkwy Woodridge (60517) **(G-22467)**
**Danziger Kosher Catering Inc** ....847 982-1818
3910 W Devon Ave Lincolnwood (60712) **(G-13506)**
**Daprato Rigali Inc** ....773 763-5511
6030 N Northwest Hwy Chicago (60631) **(G-4557)**
**Dar Enterprises Inc** ....815 961-8748
217 7th St Rockford (61104) **(G-18334)**
**Darbe Products Company Inc** ....630 985-0769
2936 Two Paths Dr Woodridge (60517) **(G-22468)**
**Dard Products Inc** ....847 328-5000
912 Custer Ave Evanston (60202) **(G-10025)**
**Darda Enterprises Inc** ....847 270-0410
301 N Dean Dr Palatine (60074) **(G-17020)**
**Darios Pallets Corp** ....312 421-3413
339 N California Ave Chicago (60612) **(G-4558)**
**Dark Matter Printing** ....217 791-4059
7 Ridge Dr Decatur (62521) **(G-7866)**
**Dark Speed Works** ....312 772-3275
122 N Wheaton Ave # 551 Wheaton (60187) **(G-21943)**
**Darling Ingredients Inc** ....773 376-5550
3443 S Lawndale Ave Chicago (60623) **(G-4559)**
**Darling Ingredients Inc** ....618 271-8190
2 Exchange Ave National Stock Yards (62071) **(G-15850)**
**Darling Ingredients Inc** ....217 482-3261
1000 S Main St Mason City (62664) **(G-14363)**
**Darling Ingredients Inc** ....309 476-8111
202 Bengston St Lynn Center (61262) **(G-14016)**
**Darling International Inc** ....708 388-3223
3000 Wireton Rd Blue Island (60406) **(G-2245)**
**Darlington Climate Control, Collinsville** *Also called J D Refrigeration* **(G-7328)**
**Darnall Printing** ....309 827-7212
801 W Chestnut St Ste B Bloomington (61701) **(G-2161)**
**Darnell Welding** ....618 945-9538
9210 Lanterman Rd Bridgeport (62417) **(G-2451)**
**Darrell Fickas Sawmill** ....618 676-1200
940 S 1st St Se Clay City (62824) **(G-7263)**
**Dart Castings Inc** ....708 388-4914
12400 S Lombard Ln Alsip (60803) **(G-455)**
**Dart Clearview Film Products, Chicago** *Also called Dart Container Michigan LLC* **(G-4560)**
**Dart Container Corp Illinois (PA)** ....630 896-4631
310 Evergreen Dr North Aurora (60542) **(G-16126)**
**Dart Container Corp Illinois** ....630 896-4631
310 Evergreen Dr North Aurora (60542) **(G-16127)**
**Dart Container Michigan LLC** ....312 221-1245
1650 E 95th St Chicago (60617) **(G-4560)**
**Dart Technology Inc** ....847 534-0357
801 Lunt Ave Schaumburg (60193) **(G-19499)**
**Darwill Inc** ....708 449-7770
11900 Roosevelt Rd Hillside (60162) **(G-11914)**
**Daryl Keylor** ....217 452-3035
201 N Pitt St Virginia (62691) **(G-21306)**
**Das Foods LLC (PA)** ....224 715-9289
2041 W Carroll Ave C222 Chicago (60612) **(G-4561)**
**Dasco Pro Inc** ....815 962-3727
340 Blackhawk Park Ave Rockford (61104) **(G-18335)**
**Dasher Dependable Reindeer LLC** ....630 513-7737
3010 Royal Queens Ct Saint Charles (60174) **(G-19167)**
**Dashire Inc** ....847 236-0776
150 Doral Ct Deerfield (60015) **(G-8003)**
**Dat Metal Fabricating, Fairmount** *Also called Decatur Aeration and Temp* **(G-10162)**
**Data Accessories Inc** ....847 669-3640
40w735 Powers Rd Huntley (60142) **(G-12136)**
**Data Cable Technologies Inc** ....630 226-5600
1306 Enterprise Dr Ste E Romeoville (60446) **(G-18816)**
**Data Com PLD Inc** ....708 839-9620
153 Santa Fe Ln Willow Springs (60480) **(G-22195)**
**Data Comm For Business Inc (PA)** ....217 897-1741
2949 County Road 1000 E Dewey (61840) **(G-8310)**
**Data Link Communications** ....815 405-2856
21153 Kildare Ave Matteson (60443) **(G-14370)**
**Data Management Center, Glendale Heights** *Also called Communication Technologies Inc* **(G-11017)**
**Datafordummies** ....618 421-2323
32 N 1550th St Flat Rock (62427) **(G-10195)**
**Datair Employee Beneft Systems** ....630 325-2600
735 N Cass Ave Westmont (60559) **(G-21881)**
**Datamax Oneil Printer Supplies, Robinson** *Also called Pioneer Labels Inc* **(G-18068)**
**Datasis Corporation** ....847 427-0909
1687 Elmhurst Rd Elk Grove Village (60007) **(G-9417)**
**Datix (usa) Inc** ....312 724-7776
155 N Wacker Dr Ste 1930 Chicago (60606) **(G-4562)**
**Datum Machine Works Inc** ....815 877-8502
2219 N Central Ave Rockford (61101) **(G-18336)**
**Datum Tool and Mfg Inc** ....847 742-4092
200 Kane St South Elgin (60177) **(G-20193)**
**Dauber Company Inc** ....815 442-3569
577 N 18th Rd Tth Tonica (61370) **(G-20973)**
**Daubert Cromwell LLC (PA)** ....708 293-7750
12701 S Ridgeway Ave Alsip (60803) **(G-456)**
**Daubert Industries Inc (PA)** ....630 203-6800
700 S Central Ave Burr Ridge (60527) **(G-2834)**
**Daubert Vci Inc (HQ)** ....630 203-6800
1333 Burr Ridge Pkwy # 200 Burr Ridge (60527) **(G-2835)**
**Dauphin Enterprise Inc** ....630 893-6300
358 W Army Trail Rd # 150 Bloomingdale (60108) **(G-2101)**
**Dave White** ....618 898-1130
1269 Conty Rod 970 E Cisne (62823) **(G-7251)**
**Davenport Dryer L L C** ....309 786-1500
600 River Dr Moline (61265) **(G-14923)**
**Davenport Tractor Inc** ....309 781-8305
11115 Knoxville Rd Milan (61264) **(G-14782)**
**Daves Auto Repiar** ....630 682-4411
211 E Saint Charles Rd Carol Stream (60188) **(G-3140)**
**Daves Electronic Service** ....217 283-5010
105 E Penn St Hoopeston (60942) **(G-12109)**
**Daves Welding Service Inc** ....630 655-3224
7201 Leonard Dr Darien (60561) **(G-7792)**
**David Architectural Metals Inc** ....773 376-3200
3100 S Kilbourn Ave Chicago (60623) **(G-4563)**
**David H Pool** ....847 695-5007
1405 Timber Dr Ste B Elgin (60123) **(G-9009)**
**David H Vander Ploeg** ....708 331-7700
534 W 162nd St South Holland (60473) **(G-20260)**
**David Hall** ....309 797-9721
1529 46th Ave Moline (61265) **(G-14924)**
**David Hayes** ....815 238-7690
1935 Locust Rd Steward (60553) **(G-20623)**
**David Jeskey** ....630 659-6337
1523 Banbury Ave Saint Charles (60174) **(G-19168)**
**David L Knoche** ....618 466-7120
611 Armsway Blvd Godfrey (62035) **(G-11223)**
**David Linderholm** ....847 336-3755
2210 Grand Ave Unit 2 Waukegan (60085) **(G-21548)**
**David Martin** ....217 564-2440
504 E 4th St Ivesdale (61851) **(G-12377)**
**David Michael Productions** ....630 972-9640
1340 Internationale Pkwy # 100 Woodridge (60517) **(G-22469)**
**David Nelson Exquisite Jewelry** ....815 741-4702
1312 W Jefferson St Ste 2 Joliet (60435) **(G-12483)**
**David Schutte** ....217 223-5464
1226 N 14th St Quincy (62301) **(G-17818)**
**David Taylor** ....217 222-6480
2201 N 24th St Quincy (62301) **(G-17819)**
**David Teplica M D** ....773 296-9900
803 W Hutchinson St Chicago (60613) **(G-4564)**
**David V Michals** ....847 671-6767
9505 Winona Ave Schiller Park (60176) **(G-19820)**
**David Yates** ....618 656-7879
6407 Sworm Ln Edwardsville (62025) **(G-8794)**

ALPHABETIC SECTION Decore-Ative Specialties

**Davidson Farms of Creston, Creston** *Also called Davidson Grain Incorporated* ***(G-7471)***

**Davidson Grain Incorporated** 815 384-3208
5960 S Woodlawn Rd Creston (60113) ***(G-7471)***

**Davidson Redi-Mix Concrete, Oak Forest** *Also called T H Davidson & Co Inc* ***(G-16591)***

**Davies Mfg, Fulton** *Also called Fulton Corporation* ***(G-10701)***

**Davies Molding LLC** 630 510-8188
350 Kehoe Blvd Carol Stream (60188) ***(G-3141)***

**Davis Athletic Equipment Co** 708 563-9006
5021 W 66th St Bedford Park (60638) ***(G-1547)***

**Davis Machine Company Inc** 815 723-9121
312 Henderson Ave Joliet (60432) ***(G-12484)***

**Davis Welding, Milford** *Also called Robert Davis & Son Inc* ***(G-14814)***

**Davis Welding & Manfctg Inc** 217 784-5480
511 W 8th St Gibson City (60936) ***(G-10899)***

**Davison Co Ltd** 815 966-2905
1812 Harlem Blvd Rockford (61103) ***(G-18337)***

**Davitz Mold Co Inc** 847 426-4848
570 Rock Road Dr Ste D East Dundee (60118) ***(G-8631)***

**Dawe's Laboratories, Arlington Heights** *Also called Dawes LLC* ***(G-745)***

**Dawes LLC (PA)** 847 577-2020
3355 N Arlington Hts Rd Arlington Heights (60004) ***(G-745)***

**Dawn Equipment Company Inc** 815 899-8000
370 N Cross St Sycamore (60178) ***(G-20791)***

**Dawn Food Products Inc** 815 933-0600
785 N Kinzie Ave Bradley (60915) ***(G-2419)***

**Dax Steel Rule Dies Inc** 708 448-4436
13250 Jean Creek Dr Orland Park (60462) ***(G-16852)***

**Day International, Batavia** *Also called Varn International Inc* ***(G-1516)***

**Day International Group Inc** 630 406-6501
1333 N Kirk Rd Batavia (60510) ***(G-1437)***

**Dayton Richmond, Oregon** *Also called Dayton Superior Corporation* ***(G-16821)***

**Dayton Superior Corporation** 847 391-4700
2400 Arthur Ave Elk Grove Village (60007) ***(G-9418)***

**Dayton Superior Corporation** 219 476-4106
2150b S Us Highway 45 52 Kankakee (60901) ***(G-12607)***

**Dayton Superior Corporation** 815 732-3136
402 S 1st St Oregon (61061) ***(G-16821)***

**Dayton Superior Corporation** 219 476-4106
2150b S Us Highway 45 52 Kankakee (60901) ***(G-12608)***

**Dayton Superior Corporation** 815 936-3300
2150 W Jeffery St Kankakee (60901) ***(G-12609)***

**Db Professionals, Rolling Meadows** *Also called Global Tech & Resources Inc* ***(G-18732)***

**Dbm Tubecutting Service, Lisle** *Also called D B M Services Corp* ***(G-13581)***

**Dbp Communications** 312 263-1569
656 W Randolph St Ste 4w Chicago (60661) ***(G-4565)***

**Dbp Communications Inc** 312 263-1569
4849 N Milwaukee Ave # 502 Chicago (60630) ***(G-4566)***

**DC Works Inc** 847 464-4280
10n421 Burlington Rd Hampshire (60140) ***(G-11546)***

**DCS, Melrose Park** *Also called Diversified Cnstr Svcs LLC* ***(G-14620)***

**DCS Mechanical, Aurora** *Also called Tin Man Heating & Cooling Inc* ***(G-1225)***

**Dct, Decatur** *Also called D C T/Precision LLC* ***(G-7865)***

**Dct Mount Vernon, Mount Vernon** *Also called Decatur Custom Tool Inc* ***(G-15408)***

**Dcx-Chol Enterprises Inc** 309 353-4455
225 Enterprise Dr Pekin (61554) ***(G-17258)***

**Ddazzledistributors, Calumet Park** *Also called Clark Tashaunda* ***(G-2958)***

**Ddc Journal, Chicago** *Also called Avenir Publishing Inc* ***(G-3998)***

**Ddi Printing, Willowbrook** *Also called D & D Business Inc* ***(G-22209)***

**Ddk Scientific Corporation** 618 235-2849
1 11th Fairway Ct Belleville (62220) ***(G-1623)***

**DDN Industries Inc** 847 885-8595
2155 Stnngton Ave Ste 221 Hoffman Estates (60169) ***(G-12004)***

**Ddu Magnetics Inc** 708 325-6587
20152 Cypress Ave Lynwood (60411) ***(G-14019)***

**De Amertek Corporation Inc (PA)** 630 572-0800
2000 S Finley Rd Lombard (60148) ***(G-13788)***

**DE Asbury Inc** 217 222-0617
2615 Ellington Rd Quincy (62305) ***(G-17820)***

**De Boer & Associates** 630 972-1600
736 Dorchester Dr Bolingbrook (60440) ***(G-2300)***

**De Enterprises Inc** 708 345-8088
1945 Gardner Rd Broadview (60155) ***(G-2571)***

**De Kalb Plating Co Inc** 815 756-6112
221 Grove St Dekalb (60115) ***(G-8085)***

**De Luca Visual Solutions Inc** 847 884-6300
1084 National Pkwy Schaumburg (60173) ***(G-19500)***

**De Vine Distributors LLC** 773 248-7005
3034 W Devon Ave Ste 104 Chicago (60659) ***(G-4567)***

**De Vries International Inc** 773 248-6695
3139 N Lincoln Ave Chicago (60657) ***(G-4568)***

**De-Sta-Co Camco Products, Wheeling** *Also called Industrial Motion Control LLC* ***(G-22076)***

**Deadline Prtg Clor Copying LLC** 847 437-9000
2289 E Devon Ave Elk Grove Village (60007) ***(G-9419)***

**Deady Brian Rfg Inc** 708 479-8249
10457 Venice Ln Orland Park (60467) ***(G-16853)***

**Deagostini Publishing USA Inc** 212 432-4070
121 E Calhoun St Ste E Woodstock (60098) ***(G-22559)***

**Dealer Tire LLC** 847 671-0683
3708 River Rd Ste 600 Franklin Park (60131) ***(G-10454)***

**Dealers Edge, Waterloo** *Also called D E Signs & Storage LLC* ***(G-21401)***

**Dealers Transmission Exchange, Roselle** *Also called TKT Enterprises Inc* ***(G-18983)***

**Dean B Scott** 630 960-4455
1319 Butterfield Rd # 524 Downers Grove (60515) ***(G-8425)***

**Dean Food Products Company** 847 678-1680
3600 River Rd Franklin Park (60131) ***(G-10455)***

**Dean Foods Company**
1126 Kilburn Ave Rockford (61101) ***(G-18338)***

**Dean Foods Company** 847 669-5123
11713 Mill St Huntley (60142) ***(G-12137)***

**Dean Foods Company** 815 943-7375
6303 Maxon Rd Harvard (60033) ***(G-11630)***

**Dean Foods Company** 217 428-6726
965 S Wyckles Rd Decatur (62522) ***(G-7867)***

**Dean P & O Services, Evanston** *Also called Dean Prsthtic Orthtic Svcs Ltd* ***(G-10026)***

**Dean Patterson** 708 430-0477
9208 S Oketo Ave Unit B Bridgeview (60455) ***(G-2482)***

**Dean Printing Systems** 847 526-9545
4358 Shooting Star Dr Island Lake (60042) ***(G-12214)***

**Dean Prsthtic Orthtic Svcs Ltd** 847 475-7080
2530 Crawford Ave Ste 218 Evanston (60201) ***(G-10026)***

**Dearborn Tool & Mfg Inc** 630 655-1260
7749 S Grant St Burr Ridge (60527) ***(G-2836)***

**Deatak Inc** 815 322-2013
4004 W Dayton St McHenry (60050) ***(G-14494)***

**Debbie Harshman** 217 335-2112
725 Bainbridge St Barry (62312) ***(G-1311)***

**Debcor Inc** 708 333-2191
513 W Taft Dr South Holland (60473) ***(G-20261)***

**Deborah Morris Gulbrandson Pt** 847 639-4140
2615 3 Oaks Rd Ste 1a Cary (60013) ***(G-3333)***

**Debourg Corp** 815 338-7852
10004 Bull Valley Rd Bull Valley (60098) ***(G-2798)***

**Dec Art Designs Inc** 312 329-0553
2970 Maria Ave Ste 226 Northbrook (60062) ***(G-16240)***

**Dec Tool Corp** 630 513-9883
2651 Dukane Dr Saint Charles (60174) ***(G-19169)***

**Decal Works LLC** 815 784-4000
2021 Johnson Ct Kingston (60145) ***(G-12706)***

**Decams Cabinets Inc** 847 360-4970
23431 N Elm Rd Lincolnshire (60069) ***(G-13442)***

**Decardy Diecasting, Chicago** *Also called Vogel/Hill Corporation* ***(G-6912)***

**Decatur Aeration and Temp** 217 733-2800
101 N Main St Fairmount (61841) ***(G-10162)***

**Decatur Aeration Inc** 217 422-6828
101 Main St Decatur (62523) ***(G-7868)***

**Decatur Blue Print Company** 217 423-7589
230 W Wood St Decatur (62523) ***(G-7869)***

**Decatur Bottling Co** 217 429-5415
2112 N Brush College Rd Decatur (62526) ***(G-7870)***

**Decatur Counter Top, Decatur** *Also called Alexander Lumber Co* ***(G-7827)***

**Decatur Custom Tool Inc** 618 244-4078
5101 Lake Ter Ne Mount Vernon (62864) ***(G-15408)***

**Decatur Foundry Inc** 217 429-5261
1745 N Illinois St Decatur (62526) ***(G-7871)***

**Decatur Industrial Elc Inc (PA)** 217 428-6621
1650 E Garfield Ave Decatur (62526) ***(G-7872)***

**Decatur Industrial Elc Inc** 618 244-1066
1313 Harlan Rd Mount Vernon (62864) ***(G-15409)***

**Decatur Machine & Tool Co, Decatur** *Also called Algen Enterprises Ltd* ***(G-7828)***

**Decatur Plating & Mfg Co** 217 422-8514
1147 E Garfield Ave Decatur (62526) ***(G-7873)***

**Decatur Tribune, Decatur** *Also called Osborne Publications Inc* ***(G-7924)***

**Decatur Wood Products LLC** 217 424-2602
800 E Garfield Ave Decatur (62526) ***(G-7874)***

**Decibel Audio Inc** 773 862-6700
1429 N Milwaukee Ave Chicago (60622) ***(G-4569)***

**Decision Systems Company** 815 885-3000
8937 Sheringham Dr Roscoe (61073) ***(G-18892)***

**Deco Adhesive Pdts 1985 Ltd** 847 472-2100
500 Thorndale Ave Ste H Elk Grove Village (60007) ***(G-9420)***

**Deco Labels & Tags, Elk Grove Village** *Also called Deco Adhesive Pdts 1985 Ltd* ***(G-9420)***

**Deco Labels & Tags Ltd** 847 472-2100
500 E Thorndale Ave Ste H Wood Dale (60191) ***(G-22358)***

**Deco Manufacturing Company** 217 872-6450
5054 Cundiff Ct Decatur (62526) ***(G-7875)***

**Decoplate, Northbrook** *Also called Hookset Enterprises LLC* ***(G-16271)***

**Decor Rv Locks, Franklin Park** *Also called Suburban Metalcraft Inc* ***(G-10598)***

**Decorative Industries Inc** 773 229-0015
6935 W 62nd St Chicago (60638) ***(G-4570)***

**Decorators Supply Corporation** 773 847-6300
3610 S Morgan St Ste 2 Chicago (60609) ***(G-4571)***

**Decorators Vault, Mokena** *Also called Tanya Shipley* ***(G-14910)***

**Decore Tool & Mfg Inc** 630 681-9760
159 Easy St Carol Stream (60188) ***(G-3142)***

**Decore-Ative Specialties** 630 947-6294
387 Oakmont Dr Cary (60013) ***(G-3334)***

ALPHABETIC

**Dedica Energy Corporation** ......... 217 235-9191
104 N 11th St  Mattoon  (61938)  *(G-14388)*
**Dedicated Tcs  LLC** ......... 815 467-9560
23330 S Frontage Rd W  Channahon  (60410)  *(G-3569)*
**Deductly  LLC** ......... 312 945-8265
917 W Washington Blvd  Chicago  (60607)  *(G-4572)*
**Dee Concrete Accessories** ......... 708 452-0250
7350 W Montrose Ave  Norridge  (60706)  *(G-16099)*
**Dee Drilling Co (PA)** ......... 618 262-4136
431 N Market St  Mount Carmel  (62863)  *(G-15264)*
**Dee Erectors Inc** ......... 630 327-1185
8314 Old Fence Ct  Downers Grove  (60517)  *(G-8426)*
**Deedrick Machine Inc** ......... 217 598-2366
105 E Market St  Sadorus  (61872)  *(G-19117)*
**Deelone Distributing Inc** ......... 309 788-1444
1419 9th St  Rock Island  (61201)  *(G-18172)*
**Deem Woodworks** ......... 217 832-9614
22 N Deer Lk  Villa Grove  (61956)  *(G-21227)*
**Deep Coat  LLC** ......... 630 466-1505
550 N Heartland Dr  Sugar Grove  (60554)  *(G-20722)*
**Deep Rock Energy Corporation** ......... 618 548-2779
631 S Broadway Ave  Salem  (62881)  *(G-19329)*
**Deep Rock Energy Corporation** ......... 618 548-2779
7601 Oleary Rd  Kinmundy  (62854)  *(G-12709)*
**Deep Value  Inc** ......... 312 239-0143
10 S Riverside Plz # 1800  Chicago  (60606)  *(G-4573)*
**Deephole Drilling Service, Rockford** Also called Pgi Mfg LLC *(G-18533)*
**Deer Creek Flange Pipe Co Inc** ......... 309 447-6981
300 N Logan St  Deer Creek  (61733)  *(G-7963)*
**Deer Processing** ......... 309 799-5994
11928 Niabi Zoo Rd  Coal Valley  (61240)  *(G-7295)*
**Deere & Company (PA)** ......... 309 765-8000
1 John Deere Pl  Moline  (61265)  *(G-14925)*
**Deere & Company** ......... 309 765-8000
1100 13th Ave  East Moline  (61244)  *(G-8673)*
**Deere & Company** ......... 309 748-0580
3800 Avenue Of The Cities # 108  Moline  (61265)  *(G-14926)*
**Deere & Company** ......... 309 765-3177
400 19th St  Moline  (61265)  *(G-14927)*
**Deere & Company** ......... 309 765-8000
15 S 80th St  Moline  (61266)  *(G-14928)*
**Deere & Company** ......... 800 765-9588
1100 13th Ave  East Moline  (61244)  *(G-8674)*
**Deere & Company** ......... 309 765-8000
1515 5th St  East Moline  (61244)  *(G-8675)*
**Deere & Company** ......... 309 765-8275
3400 80th St  Moline  (61265)  *(G-14929)*
**Deere & Company** ......... 309 765-8000
909 River Dr  Moline  (61265)  *(G-14930)*
**Deere & Company** ......... 309 748-8260
3400 80th St Swob  Moline  (61265)  *(G-14931)*
**Deere & Company** ......... 309 765-8000
3400 80th St  Moline  (61265)  *(G-14932)*
**Deere & Company** ......... 309 765-2960
1 John Deere Pl  Moline  (61265)  *(G-14933)*
**Deere & Company** ......... 309 765-8277
1 John Deere Pl  Moline  (61265)  *(G-14934)*
**Deere & Company** ......... 309 765-7310
501 River Dr  Moline  (61265)  *(G-14935)*
**Deerfield Bakery** ......... 847 520-0068
201 N Buffalo Grove Rd  Buffalo Grove  (60089)  *(G-2683)*
**Deerland Dairy, Freeport** Also called Douglas Graybill *(G-10653)*
**Deerpath Publishing Co Inc** ......... 847 234-3385
692 Linden Ave  Lake Forest  (60045)  *(G-12895)*
**Defender Steel Door & Window (PA)** ......... 708 780-7320
6119 W 35th St  Cicero  (60804)  *(G-7188)*
**Deif  Inc** ......... 970 530-2261
185 Hansen Ct Ste 125  Wood Dale  (60191)  *(G-22359)*
**Deines-Nitz Solutions  LLC** ......... 309 658-9985
721 Chase Rd  Erie  (61250)  *(G-9991)*
**Deja Investments  Inc (PA)** ......... 630 408-9222
279 Marquette Dr  Bolingbrook  (60440)  *(G-2301)*
**Dekalb Confectionary  Inc (PA)** ......... 815 758-5990
149 N 2nd St  Dekalb  (60115)  *(G-8086)*
**Dekalb Feeds  Inc (PA)** ......... 815 625-4546
105 Dixon Ave  Rock Falls  (61071)  *(G-18131)*
**Dekalb Forge Company (PA)** ......... 815 756-3538
1832 Pleasant St  Dekalb  (60115)  *(G-8087)*
**Deks North America Inc** ......... 312 219-2110
2700 W Roosevelt Rd  Chicago  (60608)  *(G-4574)*
**Del Great Frame Up Systems Inc (PA)** ......... 847 808-1955
9335 Belmont Ave Ste 100  Franklin Park  (60131)  *(G-10456)*
**Del Medical  Inc** ......... 800 800-6006
241 Covington Dr  Bloomingdale  (60108)  *(G-2102)*
**Del Medical Systems Group, Bloomingdale** Also called Del Medical  Inc *(G-2102)*
**Del Monte Foods  Inc** ......... 309 968-7033
812 S Adams St  Manito  (61546)  *(G-14173)*
**Del Monte Foods  Inc** ......... 815 562-1359
600 N 15th St  Rochelle  (61068)  *(G-18084)*

**Del Monte Foods  Inc** ......... 630 836-8131
451 Willis Ave  Rochelle  (61068)  *(G-18085)*
**Del Storm Products  Inc** ......... 217 446-3377
2003 E Voorhees St  Danville  (61834)  *(G-7715)*
**Del-Co-West Inc** ......... 309 799-7543
7507 50th St  Milan  (61264)  *(G-14783)*
**Delair Publishing Company Inc** ......... 708 345-7000
2085 Cornell Ave  Melrose Park  (60160)  *(G-14614)*
**Delaney Sheet Metal Co** ......... 847 991-9579
116 N Benton St  Palatine  (60067)  *(G-17021)*
**Delaney Sheetmetal, Palatine** Also called Delaney Sheet Metal Co *(G-17021)*
**Delante Group Inc** ......... 312 493-4371
35 E Wacker Dr Ste 900  Chicago  (60601)  *(G-4575)*
**Delaval Manufacturing** ......... 847 298-5505
1855 S Mount Prospect Rd  Des Plaines  (60018)  *(G-8179)*
**Delavan Times** ......... 309 244-7111
314 S Locust St  Delavan  (61734)  *(G-8133)*
**Deli Star Ventures  Inc** ......... 618 233-0400
3 Amann Ct  Belleville  (62220)  *(G-1624)*
**Delicias Brianna** ......... 773 409-4394
4911 N Western Ave  Chicago  (60625)  *(G-4576)*
**Dell Cove Spice Co** ......... 312 339-8389
4900 N Hermitage Ave 3  Chicago  (60640)  *(G-4577)*
**Dell Software  Inc** ......... 630 836-0503
975 Weiland Rd Unit 200  Buffalo Grove  (60089)  *(G-2684)*
**Delleman Associates & Corp** ......... 708 345-9520
8 N 6th Ave  Maywood  (60153)  *(G-14425)*
**Dells Raceway Park Inc** ......... 815 494-0074
13750 Metric Rd  Roscoe  (61073)  *(G-18893)*
**Delmark Records, Chicago** Also called Robert Koester *(G-6368)*
**Delobian Foods** ......... 773 564-0913
7424 N Western Ave  Chicago  (60645)  *(G-4578)*
**Delphi Automotive Systems  LLC** ......... 847 391-2000
25 E Algonquin Rd  Des Plaines  (60016)  *(G-8180)*
**Dels Metal Co** ......... 309 788-1993
1605 1st St  Rock Island  (61201)  *(G-18173)*
**Delta Circuits Inc** ......... 630 876-0691
730 W Hawthorne Ln  West Chicago  (60185)  *(G-21690)*
**Delta Design  Inc (PA)** ......... 708 424-9400
3140 W 92nd St  Evergreen Park  (60805)  *(G-10111)*
**Delta Design  Inc** ......... 708 424-9400
3140 W 92nd St  Evergreen Park  (60805)  *(G-10112)*
**Delta Erectors  Inc** ......... 708 267-9721
18w178 Buckingham Ln  Villa Park  (60181)  *(G-21248)*
**Delta Golf, Chicago** Also called Golfco  Inc *(G-4976)*
**Delta Label Inc** ......... 618 233-8984
920 Scheel St  Belleville  (62221)  *(G-1625)*
**Delta Laboratories  Inc** ......... 630 351-1798
2690 Delta Ln  Elk Grove Village  (60007)  *(G-9421)*
**Delta Metal Products Co** ......... 773 745-9220
1953 N Latrobe Ave  Chicago  (60639)  *(G-4579)*
**Delta Molding LLC** ......... 847 414-7773
421 Thompson Blvd  Buffalo Grove  (60089)  *(G-2685)*
**Delta Power Company (PA)** ......... 815 397-6628
4484 Boeing Dr  Rockford  (61109)  *(G-18339)*
**Delta Precision Circuits  Inc** ......... 847 758-8000
1370 Lively Blvd  Elk Grove Village  (60007)  *(G-9422)*
**Delta Press  Inc** ......... 847 671-3200
756 W Kimball Ave  Palatine  (60067)  *(G-17022)*
**Delta Products Group Inc** ......... 630 357-5544
1655 Eastwood Dr  Aurora  (60506)  *(G-1139)*
**Delta Sales, Geneseo** Also called Culmac Inc *(G-10800)*
**Delta Secondary  Inc** ......... 630 766-1180
1000 Industrial Dr Ste 3d  Bensenville  (60106)  *(G-1878)*
**Delta Steel Boilers Div, Elmhurst** Also called Cruise Boiler and Repr Co Inc *(G-9860)*
**Delta Structures  Inc** ......... 630 694-8700
18w675 18th St  Lombard  (60148)  *(G-13789)*
**Delta Waseca, Naperville** Also called Newf  LLC *(G-15714)*
**Delta-Ha, Inc., Westmont** Also called Ha-Usa  Inc *(G-21889)*
**Delta-Therm Corporation** ......... 847 526-2407
6711 Sands Rd Ste A  Crystal Lake  (60014)  *(G-7566)*
**Delta-Unibus Corp** ......... 708 409-1200
515 N Railroad Ave  Northlake  (60164)  *(G-16433)*
**Deltar Body Interior, Frankfort** Also called Illinois Tool Works Inc *(G-10334)*
**Deltrol Corp** ......... 708 547-0500
3001 Grant Ave  Bellwood  (60104)  *(G-1703)*
**Deltrol Fluid Products, Bellwood** Also called Deltrol Corp *(G-1703)*
**Deluxe Check Printers, Des Plaines** Also called Deluxe Corporation *(G-8181)*
**Deluxe Corporation** ......... 847 635-7200
1600 E Touhy Ave  Des Plaines  (60018)  *(G-8181)*
**Deluxe Express** ......... 847 756-0429
25026 Michele Dr  Plainfield  (60544)  *(G-17590)*
**Deluxe Fixture, Franklin Park** Also called Deluxe Stitcher Company Inc *(G-10457)*
**Deluxe Johnson (HQ)** ......... 847 635-7200
1600 E Touhy Ave  Des Plaines  (60018)  *(G-8182)*
**Deluxe Printing** ......... 312 225-0061
2816 S Wentworth Ave # 1  Chicago  (60616)  *(G-4580)*
**Deluxe Stitcher Company  Inc** ......... 847 455-4400
3747 Acorn Ln  Franklin Park  (60131)  *(G-10457)*

# ALPHABETIC SECTION

**Demand One, Aurora** *Also called Kelvyn Press Inc* *(G-1040)*
**Demarco Industrial Vacuum Corp** .......... 815 344-2222
 1030 Lutter Dr Crystal Lake (60014) *(G-7567)*
**Dematic Corp** .......... 630 852-9200
 750 Warrenville Rd # 101 Lisle (60532) *(G-13583)*
**Demco Inc** .......... 708 345-4822
 2975 W Soffel Ave Melrose Park (60160) *(G-14615)*
**Demco Products Inc** .......... 708 636-6240
 4644 W 92nd St Oak Lawn (60453) *(G-16616)*
**Demeter Millwork LLC** .......... 312 224-4440
 2324 W Fulton St Chicago (60612) *(G-4581)*
**Demetrios Tailor Inc** .......... 708 974-0304
 8444 S 88th Ave Justice (60458) *(G-12597)*
**Demis Printing Inc** .......... 773 282-9128
 1601 Oakton St Park Ridge (60068) *(G-17189)*
**Democrat Company Corp** .......... 217 357-2149
 31 N Washington St Carthage (62321) *(G-3313)*
**Democrat Message** .......... 217 773-3371
 123 W Main St Mount Sterling (62353) *(G-15392)*
**Demond Signs Inc** .......... 618 624-7260
 93 Betty Ln O Fallon (62269) *(G-16466)*
**Demoulin Brothers & Company (PA)** .......... 618 664-2000
 1025 S 4th St Greenville (62246) *(G-11391)*
**Demoulin Brothers & Company** .......... 618 533-3810
 302 Swan Ave Centralia (62801) *(G-3411)*
**Dempsey Tool Inc** .......... 815 210-4896
 735 Lunt Ave Schaumburg (60193) *(G-19501)*
**Den Graphix Inc** .......... 309 962-2000
 111 S Chestnut St Le Roy (61752) *(G-13207)*
**Denbur Inc (PA)** .......... 630 986-9667
 650 Blackhawk Dr Westmont (60559) *(G-21882)*
**Dendick Engineering and Mch Co** .......... 815 464-6100
 6040 W 129th Pl Palos Heights (60463) *(G-17103)*
**Dendick Wire EDM Specialist, Palos Heights** *Also called Dendick Engineering and Mch Co* *(G-17103)*
**Denise Allen Robinson Inc** .......... 773 275-8080
 4510 N Ravenswood Ave Chicago (60640) *(G-4582)*
**Dennco Inc (PA)** .......... 708 862-0070
 14350 S Saginaw Ave Burnham (60633) *(G-2816)*
**Dennis Carnes** .......... 618 244-1770
 2118 Brownsville Rd Mount Vernon (62864) *(G-15410)*
**Dennis Wright** .......... 847 816-6110
 229 Augusta Dr Vernon Hills (60061) *(G-21156)*
**Denoninational Headquarters, Elgin** *Also called Church of Brethren Inc* *(G-8990)*
**Denor Graphics Inc** .......... 847 364-1130
 665 Lunt Ave Elk Grove Village (60007) *(G-9423)*
**Denoyer - Geppert Science Co** .......... 800 621-1014
 7514 Saint Louis Ave Skokie (60076) *(G-19990)*
**Dental Arts Laboratories Inc** .......... 309 342-3117
 1172 Monroe St Ste 5 Galesburg (61401) *(G-10745)*
**Dental Crafts Lab Inc** .......... 815 872-3221
 211 S 5th St Princeton (61356) *(G-17746)*
**Dental Laboratory Inc** .......... 630 262-3700
 37w391 Keslinger Rd Geneva (60134) *(G-10823)*
**Dental Sealants & More** .......... 309 692-6435
 214 W Wolf Rd Peoria (61614) *(G-17348)*
**Dental Technologies Inc** .......... 847 677-5500
 6901 N Hamlin Ave Lincolnwood (60712) *(G-13507)*
**Dental USA Inc** .......... 815 363-8003
 5005 Mccullom Lake Rd McHenry (60050) *(G-14495)*
**Dentalez Alabama Inc** .......... 773 624-4330
 5000 S Halsted St Chicago (60609) *(G-4583)*
**Dentsply Sirona Inc** .......... 847 640-4800
 901 W Oakton St Des Plaines (60018) *(G-8183)*
**Deny Machine Shop, Lansing** *Also called DMS Industries Inc* *(G-13160)*
**Department Aviation Sign Shop, Chicago** *Also called City of Chicago* *(G-4385)*
**Department Streets Sanitation, Chicago** *Also called City of Chicago* *(G-4384)*
**Dependable Electric** .......... 618 592-3314
 728 E State Hwy 33 Oblong (62449) *(G-16732)*
**Dependable Graphics & Services** .......... 630 231-2746
 911 Industrial Dr West Chicago (60185) *(G-21691)*
**Dept 28 Inc** .......... 847 285-1343
 1169 Tower Rd Schaumburg (60173) *(G-19502)*
**Depth Action Marketing Group** .......... 847 475-7122
 2512 Lawndale Ave Evanston (60201) *(G-10027)*
**Depue Mechanical Inc (PA)** .......... 815 447-2267
 216 W 4th S Depue (61322) *(G-8134)*
**Deputante Inc** .......... 773 545-9531
 4113 W Newport Ave Chicago (60641) *(G-4584)*
**Der Holtzmacher Ltd** .......... 815 895-4887
 1649 Afton Rd Sycamore (60178) *(G-20792)*
**Der-Holtzmacher, Sycamore** *Also called Der Holtzmacher Ltd* *(G-20792)*
**Derby Industries LLC** .......... 309 344-0547
 1033 Enterprise Ave Galesburg (61401) *(G-10746)*
**Derby Supply Chain Solutions, Galesburg** *Also called Derby Industries LLC* *(G-10746)*
**Derbytech Inc** .......... 309 755-2662
 700 16th Ave East Moline (61244) *(G-8676)*
**Derbyteescom** .......... 309 264-1033
 622 Gateway Dr Henry (61537) *(G-11739)*
**Deringer-Ney Inc (PA)** .......... 847 566-4100
 616 Atrium Dr Ste 100 Vernon Hills (60061) *(G-21157)*
**Dermatique Laser & Skin** .......... 630 262-2515
 407 S 3rd St Ste 240 Geneva (60134) *(G-10824)*
**Derse Inc** .......... 847 473-2149
 3696 Bur Wood Dr Waukegan (60085) *(G-21549)*
**Des Moines Stamp Mfg Co, Moline** *Also called A 1 Marking Products* *(G-14916)*
**Des Plaines Journal Inc** .......... 847 299-5511
 622 Graceland Ave Des Plaines (60016) *(G-8184)*
**Des Plaines Printing Inc** .......... 847 465-3300
 999 Commerce Ct Buffalo Grove (60089) *(G-2686)*
**Des Plaines Valley News, Summit Argo** *Also called Heritage Media Svcs Co of Ill* *(G-20763)*
**Desco Dryers, Elk Grove Village** *Also called Desco Inc* *(G-9424)*
**Desco Inc** .......... 847 439-2130
 1240 Howard St Elk Grove Village (60007) *(G-9424)*
**Desert Southwest Fitness Inc** .......... 520 292-0011
 1607 N Market St Champaign (61820) *(G-3474)*
**Deshamusic Inc** .......... 818 257-2716
 1645 W Ogden Ave Unit 713 Chicago (60612) *(G-4585)*
**Design and Woodworks, Fairbury** *Also called Avoca Ridge Ltd* *(G-10122)*
**Design Business Printing, Chicago** *Also called Dbp Communications* *(G-4565)*
**Design Enhanced Mfg Co** .......... 815 946-3562
 9796 W Il Route 64 Polo (61064) *(G-17687)*
**Design Graphics Inc** .......... 815 462-3323
 1309 S Schoolhouse Rd # 3 New Lenox (60451) *(G-15875)*
**Design Group Signage Corp** .......... 847 390-0350
 2135 Frontage Rd Des Plaines (60018) *(G-8185)*
**Design Lab, Chicago** *Also called Interesting Products Inc* *(G-5211)*
**Design Loft Imaging Inc** .......... 847 439-2486
 393 Bianco Dr Elk Grove Village (60007) *(G-9425)*
**Design Manufacturing & Eqp Co** .......... 217 824-9219
 400 S Baughman Rd Taylorville (62568) *(G-20837)*
**Design Merchants** .......... 630 208-1850
 125 S 7th St Geneva (60134) *(G-10825)*
**Design Metals Fabrication Inc** .......... 630 752-9060
 361 Randy Rd Ste 106 Carol Stream (60188) *(G-3143)*
**Design Packaging Company Inc** .......... 847 835-3327
 100 Hazel Ave Glencoe (60022) *(G-10998)*
**Design Phase Inc** .......... 847 473-0077
 1771 S Lakeside Dr Waukegan (60085) *(G-21550)*
**Design Plus Industries Inc (PA)** .......... 309 697-9778
 6311 W Development Dr Peoria (61604) *(G-17349)*
**Design Scientific Inc** .......... 616 582-5225
 1189 Wilmette Ave Wilmette (60091) *(G-22251)*
**Design Systems Inc** .......... 309 263-7706
 361 Erie Ave Morton (61550) *(G-15157)*
**Design Technology Inc** .......... 630 920-1300
 768 Burr Oak Dr Westmont (60559) *(G-21883)*
**Design Woodworks** .......... 847 566-6603
 27266 N Owens Rd Mundelein (60060) *(G-15493)*
**Designa Access Corporation** .......... 630 891-3105
 777 Oakmont Ln Ste 2000 Westmont (60559) *(G-21884)*
**Designation Inc** .......... 847 367-9100
 1352 Armour Blvd Ste A Mundelein (60060) *(G-15494)*
**Designed For Just For You** .......... 309 221-2667
 106 Pam Ln Macomb (61455) *(G-14124)*
**Designed Plastics Inc** .......... 630 694-7300
 1133 Bryn Mawr Ave Bensenville (60106) *(G-1879)*
**Designed Stairs Inc (PA)** .......... 815 786-2021
 1480 E 6th St Sandwich (60548) *(G-19361)*
**Designer Blinds, Naperville** *Also called Carol Andrzejewski* *(G-15618)*
**Designer Decks By Mj Inc** .......... 815 744-7914
 270 E Minooka Rd Morris (60450) *(G-15106)*
**Designovations Inc** .......... 815 645-8598
 7339 E Wildwood Rd Stillman Valley (61084) *(G-20625)*
**Designs & Signs By Anderson, Ottawa** *Also called Anbek Inc* *(G-16947)*
**Designs and Signs By Anderson, La Salle** *Also called Anbek Inc* *(G-12764)*
**Designs Unlimited** .......... 618 357-6728
 1242 S Main St Pinckneyville (62274) *(G-17547)*
**Desitalk Chicago LLC** .......... 773 856-0545
 2652 W Devon Ave Ste B Chicago (60659) *(G-4586)*
**Desk & Door Nameplate Company** .......... 815 806-8670
 9310 Gulfstream Rd Frankfort (60423) *(G-10312)*
**Deslauriers Inc (PA)** .......... 708 544-4455
 1245 Barnsdale Rd La Grange Park (60526) *(G-12754)*
**Dessertwerks Inc (PA)** .......... 847 487-8239
 1421 Allyson Ct Libertyville (60048) *(G-13319)*
**Detail Master, Prospect Heights** *Also called Leisure Time Products Inc* *(G-17782)*
**Details Etc** .......... 708 932-5543
 19256 85th Ct Mokena (60448) *(G-14860)*
**Detonics Defense Technologies, Millstadt** *Also called Double Nickel LLC* *(G-14823)*
**Detrex Corporation** .......... 708 345-3806
 2537 W Le Moyne St Melrose Park (60160) *(G-14616)*
**Detroit Forming Inc** .......... 630 820-0500
 2700 Church Rd Aurora (60502) *(G-994)*
**Deublin Company (PA)** .......... 847 689-8600
 2050 Norman Dr Waukegan (60085) *(G-21551)*
**Devansoy Inc** .......... 712 792-9665
 10010 N Rock City Rd Rock City (61070) *(G-18125)*

# Devco Casting — ALPHABETIC SECTION

**Devco Casting** .................................................. 312 456-0076
  5 S Wabash Ave Ste 407  Chicago  (60603)  *(G-4587)*
**Device Technologies Inc** ................................... 630 553-7178
  1211 Badger St Ste H  Yorkville  (60560)  *(G-22655)*
**Devil Dog Arms  Inc** ......................................... 847 790-4004
  650 Telser Rd  Lake Zurich  (60047)  *(G-13062)*
**Devils Due Publishing** ...................................... 773 412-6427
  3021 W Diversey Ave Apt 2  Chicago  (60647)  *(G-4588)*
**Devon Discount Pharmacy, Chicago**  Also called Power Partners  LLC  *(G-6158)*
**Devon Precision Machine Pdts** ........................ 847 233-9700
  10140 Pacific Ave  Franklin Park  (60131)  *(G-10458)*
**Dewrich Inc** ...................................................... 847 249-7445
  1379 Saint Paul Ave  Gurnee  (60031)  *(G-11438)*
**Dex Media  Inc** ................................................ 312 240-6000
  200 E Randolph St Fl 70  Chicago  (60601)  *(G-4589)*
**Dexton Enterprises** ......................................... 309 788-1881
  1324 2nd St  Rock Island  (61201)  *(G-18174)*
**Deyco  Inc** ....................................................... 630 553-5666
  102 Beaver St  Yorkville  (60560)  *(G-22656)*
**Dezign Sewing Inc** .......................................... 773 549-4336
  4001 N Rvnswd Ave 505  Chicago  (60613)  *(G-4590)*
**Dezurik  Inc** ..................................................... 847 985-5580
  1420 Wright Blvd  Schaumburg  (60193)  *(G-19503)*
**Dezurik Apco Hilton, Schaumburg**  Also called Dezurik  Inc  *(G-19503)*
**Df Fan Services Inc** ........................................ 630 876-1495
  495 Wegner Dr  West Chicago  (60185)  *(G-21692)*
**Df Goldsmith, Evanston**  Also called Dfg Mercury Corp  *(G-10028)*
**Dfg Confectionary LLC (PA)** ........................... 847 412-1961
  60 Revere Dr Ste 750  Northbrook  (60062)  *(G-16241)*
**Dfg Mercury Corp** ........................................... 847 869-7800
  909 Pitner Ave  Evanston  (60202)  *(G-10028)*
**Dfk America Inc** .............................................. 630 324-6793
  2215 Curtiss St  Downers Grove  (60515)  *(G-8427)*
**DFT Inc** ........................................................... 630 628-8352
  423 W Interstate Rd  Addison  (60101)  *(G-87)*
**Dg Digital Printing** .......................................... 815 961-0000
  214 N Rockton Ave  Rockford  (61103)  *(G-18340)*
**Dg Wood Processing** ...................................... 217 543-2128
  120 E Cr 200 N  Arthur  (61911)  *(G-894)*
**Dgm Electronics Inc** ........................................ 815 389-2040
  13654 Metric Rd  Roscoe  (61073)  *(G-18894)*
**Dgs Import  Inc** ............................................... 847 595-7016
  5513 N Cumberland Ave  Chicago  (60656)  *(G-4591)*
**Dh2 Studio, Palatine**  Also called Techline Studio  *(G-17080)*
**Dhaliwal Labs Illinois  LLC** .............................. 312 690-7734
  5202 W 70th Pl  Bedford Park  (60638)  *(G-1548)*
**Di Cicco Concrete Products** ............................ 708 754-5691
  128 E 14th St  Chicago Heights  (60411)  *(G-7095)*
**Di-Carr Printing Company** ............................... 708 863-0069
  1630 S Cicero Ave  Cicero  (60804)  *(G-7189)*
**Dia Packaging, Marengo**  Also called Caisson Industries  Inc  *(G-14221)*
**Diablo Furnaces  LLC** ..................................... 815 636-7502
  7723 Burden Rd  Machesney Park  (61115)  *(G-14071)*
**Diageo North America Inc** ............................... 815 267-4400
  24440 W 143rd St  Plainfield  (60544)  *(G-17591)*
**Diager USA Inc** ................................................ 630 762-8443
  1820 Wallace Ave Ste 122  Saint Charles  (60174)  *(G-19170)*
**Diagnostic Photonics  Inc** ............................... 312 320-5478
  222 Merchandise Mart Plz # 1230  Chicago  (60654)  *(G-4592)*
**Diagraph MSP & ITW Company, Marion**  Also called Illinois Tool Works Inc  *(G-14269)*
**Diagrind Inc** ..................................................... 708 460-4333
  10491 164th Pl  Orland Park  (60467)  *(G-16854)*
**Dial Corporation** .............................................. 630 892-4381
  2000 Aucutt Rd  Montgomery  (60538)  *(G-15041)*
**Dial Industries Inc** ........................................... 815 397-7994
  2902 Eastrock Dr  Rockford  (61109)  *(G-18341)*
**Dial Machine  Inc** ............................................ 815 397-6660
  2902 Eastrock Dr  Rockford  (61109)  *(G-18342)*
**Dial Tool Industries  Inc** .................................. 630 543-3600
  201 S Church St  Addison  (60101)  *(G-88)*
**Diamant Toys Unlimited, Batavia**  Also called Amav Enterprises Ltd  *(G-1410)*
**Diamond Bag & Print Co, Northbrook**  Also called Diamond Cellophane Pdts Inc  *(G-16242)*
**Diamond Blast Corporation** ............................ 708 681-2640
  1741 N 30th Ave  Melrose Park  (60160)  *(G-14617)*
**Diamond Cellophane Pdts Inc** ........................ 847 418-3000
  2855 Shermer Rd  Northbrook  (60062)  *(G-16242)*
**Diamond Coat, Batavia**  Also called Aggressive Motorsports Inc  *(G-1406)*
**Diamond Die & Bevel Cutng LLC** ................... 224 387-3200
  2087 Foster Ave  Wheeling  (60090)  *(G-22034)*
**Diamond Dogs** ................................................. 773 267-0069
  3800 W Montrose Ave  Chicago  (60618)  *(G-4593)*
**Diamond Edge Manufacturing** ........................ 630 458-1630
  644 W Winthrop Ave  Addison  (60101)  *(G-89)*
**Diamond Envelope Corporation (PA)** ............. 630 499-2800
  2270 White Oak Cir  Aurora  (60502)  *(G-995)*
**Diamond Graphics of Berwyn** ......................... 708 749-2500
  6625 26th St Ste 1  Berwyn  (60402)  *(G-2060)*
**Diamond Heat Treat  Inc** ................................. 815 873-1348
  3691 Publishers Dr  Rockford  (61109)  *(G-18343)*

**Diamond Icic Corporation** ............................... 309 269-8652
  916 21st St  Rock Island  (61201)  *(G-18175)*
**Diamond Industrial Sales Ltd** ......................... 630 858-3687
  175 Cortland Ct  Glen Ellyn  (60137)  *(G-10966)*
**Diamond J Glass** ............................................. 847 973-2741
  498 S Us Highway 12 Ste A  Fox Lake  (60020)  *(G-10276)*
**Diamond Machine Werks  Inc** ........................ 847 437-0665
  2445 E Oakton St  Arlington Heights  (60005)  *(G-746)*
**Diamond Marketing Solutions, Carol Stream**  Also called National Data Svcs Chicago Inc  *(G-3204)*
**Diamond Plating Company Inc** ....................... 618 451-7740
  5 Caine Dr  Madison  (62060)  *(G-14142)*
**Diamond Quality Manufacturing** ..................... 815 521-4184
  24109 S Northern Ill Dr  Channahon  (60410)  *(G-3570)*
**Diamond Ready Mix Inc** .................................. 630 355-5414
  27w742 North Ln  Naperville  (60540)  *(G-15645)*
**Diamond Screen Process Inc** ......................... 847 439-6200
  321 Bond St  Elk Grove Village  (60007)  *(G-9426)*
**Diamond Spray Painting Inc** ........................... 630 513-5600
  1840 Production Dr  Saint Charles  (60174)  *(G-19171)*
**Diamond Tool & Mold  Inc** .............................. 630 543-7011
  1212 W National Ave  Addison  (60101)  *(G-90)*
**Diamond Web Printing LLC** ............................ 630 663-0350
  2820 Hitchcock Ave  Downers Grove  (60515)  *(G-8428)*
**Diamond Wholesale Group  Inc** ..................... 708 529-7495
  7325 W 87th St  Bridgeview  (60455)  *(G-2483)*
**Diamondaire Corp** ........................................... 630 355-7464
  117 W Main St Ste 110  Saint Charles  (60174)  *(G-19172)*
**Dianas Bananas Inc** ........................................ 773 638-6800
  2733 W Harrison St  Chicago  (60612)  *(G-4594)*
**Diaz Pallets** ...................................................... 630 340-3736
  760 Prairie St  Aurora  (60506)  *(G-1140)*
**Diaz Printing** .................................................... 773 887-3366
  4725 W Grand Ave  Chicago  (60639)  *(G-4595)*
**Dibi Accessories, Palatine**  Also called Daniel Bruce LLC  *(G-17019)*
**Dice Mold & Engineering Inc** .......................... 630 773-3595
  75 N Prospect Ave  Itasca  (60143)  *(G-12250)*
**Dicianni Graphics Incorporated** ...................... 630 833-5100
  421 S Addison Rd  Addison  (60101)  *(G-91)*
**Dick Blick Company** ........................................ 309 343-6181
  695 Us Highway 150 E  Galesburg  (61401)  *(G-10747)*
**Dicke Safety Products, Downers Grove**  Also called Dicke Tool Company  *(G-8429)*
**Dicke Tool Company (PA)** .............................. 630 969-0050
  1201 Warren Ave  Downers Grove  (60515)  *(G-8429)*
**Dickey Sign Co** ................................................ 618 797-1262
  116 Springfield Dr  Granite City  (62040)  *(G-11273)*
**Dicks Custom Cabinet Shop** ........................... 815 358-2663
  202 W Main St  Cornell  (61319)  *(G-7381)*
**Dickson Company, The, Addison**  Also called Dickson/Unigage Inc  *(G-92)*
**Dickson/Unigage Inc** ....................................... 630 543-3747
  930 S Westwood Ave  Addison  (60101)  *(G-92)*
**Dicom Transportation Group LP (PA)** ............ 312 255-4800
  676 N Michigan Ave # 3700  Chicago  (60611)  *(G-4596)*
**Diddy Dogs Inc** ................................................ 815 517-0451
  1180 W Lincoln Hwy  Dekalb  (60115)  *(G-8088)*
**Die Cast Machinery  LLC** ................................ 847 360-9170
  3246 W Monroe St  Waukegan  (60085)  *(G-21552)*
**Die Craft Metal Products** ................................ 847 593-1433
  1001 Nicholas Blvd Ste H  Elk Grove Village  (60007)  *(G-9427)*
**Die Cut Group Inc** ........................................... 630 629-9211
  850 N Du Page Ave Ste 5  Lombard  (60148)  *(G-13790)*
**Die Cut Plates, Dolton**  Also called T A U Inc  *(G-8377)*
**Die Darrell** ....................................................... 309 282-9112
  106 W Burton Ave  Eureka  (61530)  *(G-9997)*
**Die Mold Jig Grinding & Mfg** .......................... 847 228-1444
  1485 Landmeier Rd Ste M  Elk Grove Village  (60007)  *(G-9428)*
**Die Pros Inc** .................................................... 630 543-2025
  1233 W Capitol Dr Ste B  Addison  (60101)  *(G-93)*
**Die Specialty Co** ............................................. 312 303-5738
  1510 Cleveland Ave  La Grange Park  (60526)  *(G-12755)*
**Die World Steel Rule Dies** .............................. 815 399-8675
  2519 15th Ave  Rockford  (61108)  *(G-18344)*
**Diebold Incorporated** ...................................... 847 598-3300
  900 National Pkwy Ste 420  Schaumburg  (60173)  *(G-19504)*
**Diebolds Cabinet Shop** ................................... 773 772-3076
  1938 N Springfield Ave  Chicago  (60647)  *(G-4597)*
**Diecasm  LLC** .................................................. 877 343-2276
  540 Hawthorne Rd  Buffalo Grove  (60089)  *(G-2687)*
**Diecrafters  Inc** ................................................ 708 656-3336
  1349 S 55th Ct  Cicero  (60804)  *(G-7190)*
**Diehl Controls North Amer Inc** ....................... 630 955-9055
  1813 N Mill St Ste A  Naperville  (60563)  *(G-15646)*
**Diemasters Manufacturing Inc** ....................... 847 640-9900
  2100 Touhy Ave  Elk Grove Village  (60007)  *(G-9429)*
**Diequa Corporation (PA)** ................................ 630 980-1133
  180 Covington Dr  Bloomingdale  (60108)  *(G-2103)*
**Dierzen Trailer Co** ........................................... 815 695-5291
  101 N Fayette St  Newark  (60541)  *(G-15933)*
**Dierzen-Kewanee Heavy Inds** ........................ 309 853-2316
  101 Franklin St  Kewanee  (61443)  *(G-12679)*

# ALPHABETIC SECTION — Dixmor Division, Chicago Heights

**Dies Plus Inc** .................................................. 630 285-1065
  1425 Industrial Dr  Itasca  (60143)  *(G-12251)*
**Diesel Mining Equipment, Raleigh** *Also called Wallace Auto Parts & Svcs Inc (G-17912)*
**Diesel Radiator Co (PA)** ................................... 708 345-2839
  1990 Janice Ave  Melrose Park  (60160)  *(G-14618)*
**Diesel Radiator Co** ........................................... 708 865-7299
  3030 W Hirsch St  Melrose Park  (60160)  *(G-14619)*
**Dieter Construction Inc** ................................... 630 960-9662
  6817 Hobson Valley Dr # 120  Woodridge  (60517)  *(G-22470)*
**Dietrich Industries Inc** .................................... 815 207-0110
  3901 Olympic Blvd  Joliet  (60431)  *(G-12485)*
**Dietzgen Corporation** ...................................... 217 348-8111
  1555 N 5th St  Charleston  (61920)  *(G-3596)*
**Digi Cell Communications** .............................. 847 808-7900
  98 E Dundee Rd  Wheeling  (60090)  *(G-22035)*
**Digi Trax Corporation** ...................................... 847 613-2100
  650 Heathrow Dr  Lincolnshire  (60069)  *(G-13443)*
**Digistitch Embroidery & Design** ....................... 773 229-8630
  6535 W Archer Ave  Chicago  (60638)  *(G-4598)*
**Digital Artz LLC** ................................................ 618 651-1500
  188 Woodcrest Dr  Highland  (62249)  *(G-11783)*
**Digital Check Corp (PA)** .................................. 847 446-2285
  630 Dundee Rd Ste 210  Northbrook  (60062)  *(G-16243)*
**Digital Check Technologies, Northbrook** *Also called Digital Check Corp (G-16243)*
**Digital Edge Signs Inc** .................................... 847 838-4760
  248 W Depot St A  Antioch  (60002)  *(G-629)*
**Digital Factory Inc (PA)** .................................. 708 320-9879
  917 E 78th St Apt 203w  Chicago  (60619)  *(G-4599)*
**Digital Greensigns Inc** .................................... 312 624-8550
  1606 W Grace St  Chicago  (60613)  *(G-4600)*
**Digital H2o Inc** ................................................. 847 456-8424
  18 S Michigan Ave Fl 12  Chicago  (60603)  *(G-4601)*
**Digital Homes Technologies, Palatine** *Also called J P Goldenne Incorporated (G-17045)*
**Digital Hub LLC** ............................................... 312 943-6161
  1040 N Halsted St  Chicago  (60642)  *(G-4602)*
**Digital Ignite LLC (HQ)** .................................... 630 317-7904
  101 W 22nd St Ste 104  Lombard  (60148)  *(G-13791)*
**Digital Imports, Evanston** *Also called Loop Limited (G-10066)*
**Digital Living Inc** ............................................. 708 434-1197
  410 Madison St  Oak Park  (60302)  *(G-16659)*
**Digital Minds Inc** ............................................. 847 430-3390
  9501 W Devon Ave Ste 603  Rosemont  (60018)  *(G-18998)*
**Digital Optics Tech Inc** .................................... 847 358-2592
  1645 Hicks Rd Ste H  Rolling Meadows  (60008)  *(G-18725)*
**Digital Palace, Mount Prospect** *Also called Ideal/Mikron Inc (G-15336)*
**Digital Prtg & Total Graphics** .......................... 630 627-7400
  123 Eisenhower Ln N  Lombard  (60148)  *(G-13792)*
**Digital Publishing Group, Chicago** *Also called A To Z Type & Graphic Inc (G-3692)*
**Digital Realty Inc** ............................................. 630 428-7979
  303 N Mill St  Naperville  (60540)  *(G-15647)*
**Digitaldrive Tech** .............................................. 630 510-1580
  1601 E Prairie Ave  Wheaton  (60187)  *(G-21944)*
**Digitone, Schaumburg** *Also called Precision Language & Graphics (G-19700)*
**Dike-O-Seal Incorporated** ............................... 773 254-3224
  3965 S Keeler Ave  Chicago  (60632)  *(G-4603)*
**Dilaberto Co Inc** .............................................. 630 892-8448
  417 Cleveland Ave  Aurora  (60506)  *(G-1141)*
**Dilars Embroidery & Monograms** ................... 815 338-6066
  1320 Zimmerman Rd  Woodstock  (60098)  *(G-22560)*
**Dill Brothers Inc** .............................................. 847 746-8323
  3401 20th St  Zion  (60099)  *(G-22682)*
**Dimend Scaasi Ltd** ......................................... 312 857-1700
  5 S Wabash Ave Ste 1734  Chicago  (60603)  *(G-4604)*
**Dimension Data North Amer Inc** ..................... 847 278-6413
  1700 E Golf Rd Ste 1100  Schaumburg  (60173)  *(G-19505)*
**Dimension Molding Corporation** ..................... 630 628-0777
  777 W Annoreno Dr  Addison  (60101)  *(G-94)*
**Dimples Donuts** .............................................. 630 406-0303
  328 E Wilson St  Batavia  (60510)  *(G-1438)*
**Dinamica Generale Us Inc** ............................. 815 751-9916
  2300 Galvin Dr  Elgin  (60124)  *(G-9010)*
**Dines Machine & Manufacturing, Danville** *Also called G P Cole Inc (G-7725)*
**Dingo Inc** ......................................................... 217 868-5615
  14480 N 1025th St  Effingham  (62401)  *(G-8832)*
**Dinkels Bakery Inc** .......................................... 773 281-7300
  3329 N Lincoln Ave  Chicago  (60657)  *(G-4605)*
**Dino Design Incorporated** .............................. 773 763-4223
  6538 N Milwaukee Ave  Chicago  (60631)  *(G-4606)*
**Dino Publishing LLC** ....................................... 312 822-9266
  350 W Hubbard St Ste 400  Chicago  (60654)  *(G-4607)*
**Dionex Corporation** ......................................... 847 295-7500
  3000 Lakeside Dr Ste 116n  Bannockburn  (60015)  *(G-1257)*
**Dip Seal Plastics Inc** ...................................... 815 398-3533
  2311 23rd Ave  Rockford  (61104)  *(G-18345)*
**Dippit Inc** ......................................................... 630 762-6500
  1879 N Neltnor Blvd 326  West Chicago  (60185)  *(G-21693)*
**Direct Automation Inc** ..................................... 815 675-0588
  7800 Winn Rd  Spring Grove  (60081)  *(G-20333)*

**Direct Dimension Inc (PA)** .............................. 815 479-1936
  8195 Pyott Rd  Algonquin  (60156)  *(G-386)*
**Direct Envelope, Wheeling** *Also called Managed Marketing Inc (G-22098)*
**Direct Mail Equipment Services** ..................... 815 485-7010
  14460 W Edison Dr Ste D  New Lenox  (60451)  *(G-15876)*
**Direct Marketing 1 Corporation** ...................... 773 234-9122
  9701 S Lowe Ave  Chicago  (60628)  *(G-4608)*
**Direct Selling Strategies** ................................. 847 993-3188
  5600 N River Rd Ste 800  Rosemont  (60018)  *(G-18999)*
**Directions Magazine, Glencoe** *Also called Elliott Jsj & Associates Inc (G-10999)*
**Dirk Vander Noot** ............................................ 224 558-1878
  811 Andover Ct  Prospect Heights  (60070)  *(G-17776)*
**Dirtt Envmtl Solutions Inc** ............................... 312 245-2870
  325 N Wells St Ste 1000  Chicago  (60654)  *(G-4609)*
**Disa Holding Corp (HQ)** ................................. 630 820-3000
  80 Kendall Point Dr  Oswego  (60543)  *(G-16913)*
**Disco Machine & Mfg Inc** .............................. 708 456-0835
  7327 W Agatite Ave  Norridge  (60706)  *(G-16100)*
**Discount Battery Sales, Quincy** *Also called Dale Schawitsch (G-17817)*
**Discount Computer Supply Inc** ...................... 847 883-8743
  871 Shambliss Ln  Buffalo Grove  (60089)  *(G-2688)*
**Discount Eyewear, Rock Falls** *Also called Scuba Optics Inc (G-18151)*
**Discount Video Warehouse, Chicago** *Also called Roscor Corporation (G-6394)*
**Discuss Music Education Co** ........................ 773 561-2796
  2720 W Winnemac Ave Apt 1  Chicago  (60625)  *(G-4610)*
**Disk.com, McHenry** *Also called Corporate Disk Company (G-14489)*
**Diskin Systems Inc** ........................................ 815 276-7288
  9550 S Il Route 31  Algonquin  (60102)  *(G-387)*
**Dispense-Rite, Northbrook** *Also called Diversified Metal Products Inc (G-16244)*
**Display Graphics Systems LLC** ..................... 800 706-9670
  4900 S Rockwell St  Chicago  (60632)  *(G-4611)*
**Display Link Inc** .............................................. 815 968-0778
  311 S Main St  Rockford  (61101)  *(G-18346)*
**Display Plan Lpdg** .......................................... 773 525-3787
  1901 N Clybourn Ave # 400  Chicago  (60614)  *(G-4612)*
**Display Worldwide LLC** .................................. 815 439-2695
  2202 Portside Lakes Ct  Plainfield  (60586)  *(G-17592)*
**Displayplan US, Chicago** *Also called Display Plan Lpdg (G-4612)*
**Distillery Wine & Allied** ................................... 309 347-1444
  300 Mclean St  Pekin  (61554)  *(G-17259)*
**Distinctive Cabinets, Aurora** *Also called Dilaberto Co Inc (G-1141)*
**Distinctive Foods LLC (PA)** ............................ 847 459-3600
  654 Wheeling Rd  Wheeling  (60090)  *(G-22036)*
**Distinctive Foods LLC** .................................... 847 459-3600
  450 Evergreen Ave  Bensenville  (60106)  *(G-1880)*
**Distinctive SIGns& The Neon Ex** ................... 847 245-7159
  1868 E Belvidere Rd A  Grayslake  (60030)  *(G-11333)*
**Distribution Enterprises Inc** ............................ 847 582-9276
  28457 N Ballard Dr Ste A1  Lake Forest  (60045)  *(G-12896)*
**Diversatech Metalfab LLC** .............................. 309 747-4159
  108 S Center St  Gridley  (61744)  *(G-11404)*
**Diversey Inc** .................................................... 262 631-4001
  1564 Old Barn Rd Fl 5  Bartlett  (60103)  *(G-1341)*
**Diversfied Ill Green Works LLC** ...................... 773 544-7777
  2419 W Byron St  Chicago  (60618)  *(G-4613)*
**Diversfied Lbling Slutions Inc (PA)** ................ 630 625-1225
  1285 Hamilton Pkwy  Itasca  (60143)  *(G-12252)*
**Diversified Adtee Inc** ...................................... 309 454-2555
  1200 Fort Jesse Rd  Normal  (61761)  *(G-16069)*
**Diversified Cnstr Svcs LLC** ............................. 708 344-4900
  2001 Cornell Ave  Melrose Park  (60160)  *(G-14620)*
**Diversified CPC Intl Inc (HQ)** ......................... 815 423-5991
  24338 W Durkee Rd  Channahon  (60410)  *(G-3571)*
**Diversified Fleet MGT Inc** ............................... 815 578-1051
  776 Ridgeview Dr  McHenry  (60050)  *(G-14496)*
**Diversified Machining Inc** ............................... 815 316-8561
  6151 Montague Rd  Rockford  (61102)  *(G-18347)*
**Diversified Metal Products Inc** ....................... 847 753-9595
  2205 Carlson Dr  Northbrook  (60062)  *(G-16244)*
**Diversified Print Group** ................................... 630 893-8920
  358 W Army Trail Rd # 140  Bloomingdale  (60108)  *(G-2104)*
**Diversifoam Products, Mendota** *Also called Minnesota Diversified Pdts Inc (G-14728)*
**Divino, Grayslake** *Also called Joint Asia Dev Group LLC (G-11349)*
**Division 5 Metals Inc** ...................................... 815 901-5001
  2314 Old State Rd  Kirkland  (60146)  *(G-12711)*
**Division C, Chicago** *Also called ZF Chassis Systems Chicago LLC (G-7066)*
**Division Sonoco Products Co, Franklin Park** *Also called Clear Pack Company (G-10437)*
**Dix McGuire Commodities LLC** ..................... 847 496-5320
  201 E Dundee Rd Ste 2  Palatine  (60074)  *(G-17023)*
**Dixie Carbonic Inc** .......................................... 217 428-2068
  3985 E Harrison Ave  Decatur  (62526)  *(G-7876)*
**Dixie Cream Donut Shop** ............................... 618 937-4866
  510 W Main St  West Frankfort  (62896)  *(G-21806)*
**Dixline Corporation (PA)** ................................ 309 932-2011
  136 Exchange St  Galva  (61434)  *(G-10787)*
**Dixline Corporation** ......................................... 309 932-2011
  26 Sw 4th Ave  Galva  (61434)  *(G-10788)*
**Dixmor Division, Chicago Heights** *Also called Ptc Group Holdings Corp (G-7118)*

(PA)=Parent Co  (HQ)=Headquarters  (DH)=Div Headquarters

**Dixon Brass**......630 323-3716
40 Chestnut Ave Westmont (60559) ***(G-21885)***
**Dixon Direct LLC**......815 284-2211
1226 W 7th St Dixon (61021) ***(G-8328)***
**Dixon Pallet Service**......773 238-9569
10340 S Lowe Ave Chicago (60628) ***(G-4614)***
**Dixon-Marquette Cement, Dixon** *Also called Southfield Corporation* ***(G-8352)***
**Diy Cabinet Warehouse, Arthur** *Also called Masterbrand Cabinets Inc* ***(G-911)***
**Dj Illinois River Valley Calls**......309 348-2112
7949 State Rte 78 Pekin (61554) ***(G-17260)***
**Dj Liquors Inc**......815 645-1145
5657 N Junction Way Davis Junction (61020) ***(G-7810)***
**DJB Corporation**......815 469-7533
9527 Corsair Rd Ste 2w Frankfort (60423) ***(G-10313)***
**Djh Industries Inc**......309 246-8456
400 N Commercial St Lacon (61540) ***(G-12786)***
**Djr Inc**......773 581-5204
5900 W 65th St Chicago (60638) ***(G-4615)***
**Djw Machining Inc**......847 956-5330
2912 Malmo Dr Arlington Heights (60005) ***(G-747)***
**DK Knutsen**......815 626-4388
609 W 3rd St Sterling (61081) ***(G-20589)***
**DK Precision Inc**......847 985-8008
614 Lunt Ave Schaumburg (60193) ***(G-19506)***
**DK Surface Hardening Inc**......708 233-9095
7424 W 90th St Bridgeview (60455) ***(G-2484)***
**Dkb Industries LLC**......630 450-4151
3940 White Eagle Dr Naperville (60564) ***(G-15802)***
**Dla Document Services**......618 256-4686
901 South Dr Bldg 700e Scott Air Force Base (62225) ***(G-19885)***
**Dlc Inc**......224 567-8656
3 S 080 Talbot Ave Park Ridge (60068) ***(G-17190)***
**DLM Manufacturing Inc**......815 964-3800
919 Taylor St Rockford (61101) ***(G-18348)***
**DLP Coatings Inc**......847 350-0113
2301 Eastern Ave Elk Grove Village (60007) ***(G-9430)***
**DLS Custom Embroidery Inc**......847 593-5957
1665 Tonne Rd Elk Grove Village (60007) ***(G-9431)***
**DLS Printing & Promotions, Elk Grove Village** *Also called DLS Custom Embroidery Inc* ***(G-9431)***
**Dlt Electric LLC**......630 552-4115
202 W Main St Plano (60545) ***(G-17663)***
**DMarv Design Specialty Prtrs**......708 389-4420
13010 Western Ave Blue Island (60406) ***(G-2246)***
**Dmg Charlotte LLC (HQ)**......704 583-1193
2400 Huntington Blvd Hoffman Estates (60192) ***(G-12005)***
**Dmg Mori Seiki U.S.a, Hoffman Estates** *Also called Dmg Mori Usa Inc* ***(G-12006)***
**Dmg Mori Usa Inc (HQ)**......847 593-5400
2400 Huntington Blvd Hoffman Estates (60192) ***(G-12006)***
**Dmi Information Process Center**......773 378-2644
5090 W Harrison St Chicago (60644) ***(G-4616)***
**DMJ Group Inc**......847 322-7533
2413 W Algonquin Rd # 227 Algonquin (60102) ***(G-388)***
**Dml Distribution Inc**......630 839-9041
1814 W Weathersfield Way Schaumburg (60193) ***(G-19507)***
**Dml LLC**......630 231-8873
419 Colford Ave West Chicago (60185) ***(G-21694)***
**Dmr International Inc**......815 704-5678
720 S Eastwood Dr Ste 243 Woodstock (60098) ***(G-22561)***
**Dms Inc**......847 726-2828
1120 Ensell Rd Lake Zurich (60047) ***(G-13063)***
**DMS Industries Inc (PA)**......708 895-8000
1925 177th St Lansing (60438) ***(G-13160)***
**Dmtg North America LLC**......815 637-8500
1301 Eddy Ave Rockford (61103) ***(G-18349)***
**Dnepr Techologies Inc**......773 603-3360
3304 N Broadway St # 163 Chicago (60657) ***(G-4617)***
**Dnow LP**......618 842-9176
2210 W Delaware St Fairfield (62837) ***(G-10139)***
**DNp Enterprises Inc (PA)**......630 628-7210
1213 W Capitol Dr Addison (60101) ***(G-95)***
**Do It Best, Monee** *Also called Wille Bros Co* ***(G-15008)***
**Do It Best, Chicago** *Also called Dumore Supplies Inc* ***(G-4649)***
**Do You See Entertainment, Chicago** *Also called Do You See What I See Entertai* ***(G-4618)***
**Do You See What I See Entertai**......773 612-1269
2544 W North Ave Apt 3d Chicago (60647) ***(G-4618)***
**Do-Rite Die & Engineering Co**......708 754-4355
3344 Butler St S Chicago Hts (60411) ***(G-19103)***
**Do-Rite Donuts**......312 422-0150
50 W Randolph St Chicago (60601) ***(G-4619)***
**Dobake Bakeries Inc**......630 620-1849
1405 W Fullerton Ave Addison (60101) ***(G-96)***
**Dober Chemical Corp (PA)**......630 410-7300
11230 Katherines Crossin Ste 100 Woodridge (60517) ***(G-22471)***
**Dober Group, Woodridge** *Also called Dober Chemical Corp* ***(G-22471)***
**Dobinski Marketing**......773 248-5880
3843 N Fremont St Chicago (60613) ***(G-4620)***
**Dobratz Sales Company Inc**......224 569-3081
5945 Lucerne Ln Lake In The Hills (60156) ***(G-12990)***

**Doctors Choice Inc**......312 666-1111
600 W Cermak Rd Ste 1a Chicago (60616) ***(G-4621)***
**Doctors Interior Plantscaping**......708 333-3323
255 W Taft Dr South Holland (60473) ***(G-20262)***
**Document Capture Technologies, Wood Dale** *Also called Ambir Technology Inc* ***(G-22339)***
**Document Centre, Roselle** *Also called Composition One Inc* ***(G-18933)***
**Document Publishing Group**......847 783-0670
2511 Tech Dr Ste 102 Elgin (60124) ***(G-9011)***
**Document Services, Champaign** *Also called University of Illinois* ***(G-3552)***
**DOD Technologies Inc**......815 788-5200
675 Industrial Dr Cary (60013) ***(G-3335)***
**Dodge Machine Tool**......815 544-0967
204 S Main St Belvidere (61008) ***(G-1749)***
**Doerock Inc**......217 543-2101
901 E Columbia St Arthur (61911) ***(G-895)***
**Doga USA Corporation**......847 669-8529
12060 Raymond Ct Huntley (60142) ***(G-12138)***
**Doings Newspaper, Hinsdale** *Also called Pioneer Newspapers Inc* ***(G-11958)***
**Dolche Truckload Corp**......800 719-4921
473 W Northwest Hwy 2e Palatine (60067) ***(G-17024)***
**Doll Furniture Co Inc**......309 452-2606
400 N Beech St Normal (61761) ***(G-16070)***
**Dollar Express**......815 399-9719
4225 Charles St Rockford (61108) ***(G-18350)***
**Dollar Mix**......773 582-7110
3744 W 63rd St Chicago (60629) ***(G-4622)***
**Dolls Lettering Inc**......815 467-8000
110 Industrial Dr Unit A Minooka (60447) ***(G-14838)***
**Dolores Shingleur Advertising, Northbrook** *Also called American Spcalty Advg Prtg Co* ***(G-16203)***
**Dom Plastic Div, Saint Anne** *Also called Eastern Illinois Clay Company* ***(G-19120)***
**Dom Plastics, Saint Anne** *Also called Eastern Illinois Clay Company* ***(G-19121)***
**Domeny Tool & Stamping Company**......847 526-5700
354 Hollow Hill Rd Wauconda (60084) ***(G-21454)***
**Dominicks Finer Foods Inc**......630 584-1750
2063 Lincoln Hwy Saint Charles (60174) ***(G-19173)***
**Dominique Graves**......773 368-5289
6800 S Cornell Ave 1c Chicago (60649) ***(G-4623)***
**Domino Amjet Inc**......847 662-3148
4321 Lee Ave Gurnee (60031) ***(G-11439)***
**Domino Amjet Inc (HQ)**......847 244-2501
1290 Lakeside Dr Gurnee (60031) ***(G-11440)***
**Domino Engineering Corp**......217 824-9441
208 S Spresser St Taylorville (62568) ***(G-20838)***
**Domino Foods Inc**......773 254-8282
2905 S Western Ave Chicago (60608) ***(G-4624)***
**Domino Foods Inc**......773 646-2203
2400 E 130th St Chicago (60633) ***(G-4625)***
**Domino Holdings Inc (HQ)**......847 244-2501
1290 Lakeside Dr Gurnee (60031) ***(G-11441)***
**Domino Lasers Inc**......847 855-1364
1290 Lakeside Dr Gurnee (60031) ***(G-11442)***
**Domino Sugar, Chicago** *Also called Domino Foods Inc* ***(G-4624)***
**Domino Sugar, Chicago** *Also called Domino Foods Inc* ***(G-4625)***
**Domino's Pastry Shop, Hickory Hills** *Also called Dominos Pastries Inc* ***(G-11769)***
**Dominos Pastries Inc**......773 889-3549
7731 W 98th St Ste E Hickory Hills (60457) ***(G-11769)***
**Dominos Pizza LLC**......630 783-0738
10410 Woodward Ave # 100 Woodridge (60517) ***(G-22472)***
**Doms Incorporated**......847 838-6723
940 Anita Ave Antioch (60002) ***(G-630)***
**Don Anderson Co**......618 495-2511
101 S Hickory St Hoffman (62250) ***(G-11988)***
**Don Churro, Chicago** *Also called El Moro De Letran Churros & Ba* ***(G-4708)***
**Don Johns Inc (PA)**......630 326-9650
701 N Raddant Rd Batavia (60510) ***(G-1439)***
**Don Leventhal Group LLC**......618 783-4424
1508 W Jourdan St Newton (62448) ***(G-15939)***
**Don Poore Saw Mill Inc**......618 757-2240
15694 Blairsville Rd Springerton (62887) ***(G-20382)***
**Don's Custom Draperies, McHenry** *Also called Dons Drapery Service* ***(G-14497)***
**Donald Kranz**......847 428-1616
10 W Main St Fl 1 Carpentersville (60110) ***(G-3283)***
**Donaldson & Associates Inc**......708 633-1090
12141 W 159th St Ste A Lockport (60491) ***(G-13710)***
**Donaldson Company Inc**......309 667-2885
3230 65th Ave New Windsor (61465) ***(G-15930)***
**Donaldson Company Inc**......815 288-3374
815 W Progress Dr Dixon (61021) ***(G-8329)***
**Donath Aircraft Service**......217 528-6667
1733 S Glenwood Ave Springfield (62704) ***(G-20429)***
**Doncasters, Paris** *Also called Iet-Meco* ***(G-17150)***
**Doncasters Inc**......217 465-6500
2121 S Main St Paris (61944) ***(G-17146)***
**Done Rite Sealcoating Inc**......630 830-5310
412 E North Ave Streamwood (60107) ***(G-20651)***
**Donermen LLC**......773 430-2828
2849 W Belmont Ave A Chicago (60618) ***(G-4626)***

**Donghia Showrooms Inc** ........ 312 822-0766
631 Merchandise Mart 63 Chicago (60654) ***(G-4627)***
**Donkey Brands LLC** ........ 630 251-2007
281 Carlton Dr Carol Stream (60188) ***(G-3144)***
**Donkey Chips, Carol Stream** *Also called Donkey Brands LLC* ***(G-3144)***
**Donna Karan Company LLC** ........ 630 236-8900
1650 Premium Outlet Blvd # 313 Aurora (60502) ***(G-996)***
**Donnas House of Type Inc** ........ 217 522-5050
23267 Railsplitter Ln Athens (62613) ***(G-938)***
**Donnelley and Sons Co R R** ........ 708 924-6200
5858 W 73rd St Chicago (60638) ***(G-4628)***
**Donnelley Financial LLC** ........ 312 326-8000
111 S Wacker Dr Ste 3500 Chicago (60606) ***(G-4629)***
**Donnells Printing & Off Pdts** ........ 815 842-6541
708 W Howard St Pontiac (61764) ***(G-17698)***
**Donnelly Automotive Machine** ........ 217 428-7414
1298 E Eldorado St Decatur (62521) ***(G-7877)***
**Donr Co** ........ 773 895-3359
61 W 15th St Apt 401 Chicago (60605) ***(G-4630)***
**Dons Drapery Service** ........ 815 385-4759
2210 Orchard Beach Rd McHenry (60050) ***(G-14497)***
**Dons Meat Market** ........ 309 968-6026
203 W Market St Manito (61546) ***(G-14174)***
**Dons Welding** ........ 847 526-1177
552 S Rand Rd Wauconda (60084) ***(G-21455)***
**Donson Machine** ........ 708 468-8392
15440 S 70th Ct Orland Park (60462) ***(G-16855)***
**Donson Machine Company** ........ 708 388-0880
12416 S Kedvale Ave Alsip (60803) ***(G-457)***
**Dontech Industries Inc** ........ 847 428-8222
76 Center Dr Gilberts (60136) ***(G-10917)***
**Dontrell Percy** ........ 773 418-4900
11257 S Bishop St Chicago (60643) ***(G-4631)***
**Donut Palace** ........ 618 692-0532
443 S Buchanan St Edwardsville (62025) ***(G-8795)***
**Doody Enterprises Inc** ........ 312 239-6226
1100 Lake St Ste LI25 Oak Park (60301) ***(G-16660)***
**Dooley Brothers Plumbing & Htg** ........ 309 852-2720
306 N Tremont St Kewanee (61443) ***(G-12680)***
**Dooling Machine Products Inc (PA)** ........ 618 254-0724
107 N Delmar Ave Hartford (62048) ***(G-11610)***
**Doosan, Crestwood** *Also called County Packaging Inc* ***(G-7484)***
**Doosan Infracore America Corp** ........ 847 437-1010
1701 Howard St Ste F Elk Grove Village (60007) ***(G-9432)***
**Doosan Infrcre Amrca Midw Tech, Elk Grove Village** *Also called Doosan Infracore America Corp* ***(G-9432)***
**Doral Inc** ........ 630 543-5523
344 W Interstate Rd Addison (60101) ***(G-97)***
**Doralco Inc** ........ 708 388-9324
5919 W 118th St Alsip (60803) ***(G-458)***
**Doran Scales Inc** ........ 630 879-1200
1315 Paramount Pkwy Batavia (60510) ***(G-1440)***
**Doras Spinning Wheel Inc** ........ 618 466-1900
96 Northport Dr Alton (62002) ***(G-571)***
**Dorbin Metal Strip Mfg Co Inc** ........ 708 656-2333
2404 S Cicero Ave Cicero (60804) ***(G-7191)***
**Dordan Manufacturing Company** ........ 815 334-0087
2025 Castle Rd Woodstock (60098) ***(G-22562)***
**Doreen's Gourmet Frozen Pizza, Calumet City** *Also called Doreens Pizza Inc* ***(G-2937)***
**Doreens Pizza Inc (PA)** ........ 708 862-7499
130 State St Calumet City (60409) ***(G-2937)***
**Dorenfest Group Ltd** ........ 312 464-3000
444 N Michigan Ave # 1200 Chicago (60611) ***(G-4632)***
**Doric Products Inc (PA)** ........ 217 826-6302
201 W Us Highway 40 Marshall (62441) ***(G-14321)***
**Doris Bridal Boutique** ........ 847 433-2575
448 Sheridan Rd Ste 1 Highwood (60040) ***(G-11884)***
**Doris Company** ........ 224 302-5605
1541 S Shields Dr Waukegan (60085) ***(G-21553)***
**Dorma Architectural Hardware, Steeleville** *Also called Dorma Usa Inc* ***(G-20560)***
**Dorma Usa Inc** ........ 847 295-2700
924 Sherwood Dr Lake Bluff (60044) ***(G-12840)***
**Dorma Usa Inc** ........ 717 336-3881
1003 W Broadway Steeleville (62288) ***(G-20560)***
**Dos Bro Corp** ........ 773 334-1919
6116 N Broadway St Chicago (60660) ***(G-4633)***
**Dosimetry Medicine Group, Schaumburg** *Also called Siemens Med Solutions USA Inc* ***(G-19727)***
**DOT Black Group** ........ 312 204-8000
329 W 18th St Ste 800 Chicago (60616) ***(G-4634)***
**DOT Press LLC** ........ 312 421-0293
1941 W Fulton St Chicago (60612) ***(G-4635)***
**DOT Sharper Printing Inc** ........ 847 581-9033
8120 River Dr Ste 1 Morton Grove (60053) ***(G-15194)***
**Dots UT Inc** ........ 217 390-3286
2716 W Clark Rd Ste E Champaign (61822) ***(G-3475)***
**Doty & Sons Concrete Products** ........ 815 895-2884
1275 E State St Sycamore (60178) ***(G-20793)***
**Doubet Window & Door, Peoria** *Also called Sheraton Road Lumber* ***(G-17455)***

**Double D Printing Inc** ........ 630 406-8666
103 S Lincoln St Batavia (60510) ***(G-1441)***
**Double Good LLC** ........ 630 568-5544
16w030 83rd St Burr Ridge (60527) ***(G-2837)***
**Double Image Press Inc** ........ 630 893-6777
151 N Brandon Dr Glendale Heights (60139) ***(G-11020)***
**Double M Machine Inc** ........ 815 692-4676
614 W Pine St Fairbury (61739) ***(G-10123)***
**Double Nickel LLC** ........ 618 476-3200
609 S Breese St Ste 101 Millstadt (62260) ***(G-14823)***
**Double Nickel Holdings LLC** ........ 618 476-3200
609 S Breese St Ste 101 Millstadt (62260) ***(G-14824)***
**Double R Manufacturing Co, Leonore** *Also called Brian Burcar* ***(G-13285)***
**Double-Disc Grinding Corp** ........ 708 410-1770
2041 Janice Ave Melrose Park (60160) ***(G-14621)***
**Doubletake Marketing Inc** ........ 845 598-3175
54 Williamsburg Rd Evanston (60203) ***(G-10029)***
**Dougherty E J Oil & Stone Sup** ........ 618 271-4414
1501 Lincoln Ave East Saint Louis (62204) ***(G-8748)***
**Doughman Don & Assoc** ........ 312 321-1011
222 Merchandise Mart Plz # 947 Chicago (60654) ***(G-4636)***
**Doughnut Boy** ........ 773 463-6328
250 Parkway Dr Ste 270 Lincolnshire (60069) ***(G-13444)***
**Douglas County Mil Moldings** ........ 217 268-4689
326 E County Road 100n Arcola (61910) ***(G-667)***
**Douglas County Molding, Arcola** *Also called Douglas County Mil Moldings* ***(G-667)***
**Douglas County Wood Products** ........ 217 543-2888
491 N Cr 100 E Arthur (61911) ***(G-896)***
**Douglas Graybill** ........ 815 218-1749
3693 N Dakota Rd Freeport (61032) ***(G-10653)***
**Douglas Knty Kreative Kitchens, Arthur** *Also called County Line Inc* ***(G-892)***
**Douglas Net Company** ........ 815 427-6350
200 Eastern Illinois St Saint Anne (60964) ***(G-19119)***
**Douglas Press Inc** ........ 800 323-0705
2810 Madison St Bellwood (60104) ***(G-1704)***
**Doumak Inc (PA)** ........ 800 323-0318
1004 Fairway Dr Bensenville (60106) ***(G-1881)***
**Doumak Inc** ........ 630 594-5400
1004 Fairway Dr Bensenville (60106) ***(G-1882)***
**Doumak Inc** ........ 847 981-2180
2491 Estes Ave Elk Grove Village (60007) ***(G-9433)***
**Dove Dental Studio** ........ 847 679-2434
6201 W Howard St Ste 202 Niles (60714) ***(G-15975)***
**Dove Foundation** ........ 312 217-3683
5056 N Marine Dr Apt C4 Chicago (60640) ***(G-4637)***
**Dove Industries Inc** ........ 618 234-4509
229 Taft St Belleville (62220) ***(G-1626)***
**Dove Products Inc** ........ 815 727-4683
3357 S State St Lockport (60441) ***(G-13711)***
**Dove Steel Inc** ........ 815 588-3772
16035 W Red Cloud Dr Lockport (60441) ***(G-13712)***
**Dovee Manufacturing Inc** ........ 847 437-8122
640 Church Rd Elgin (60123) ***(G-9012)***
**Dover Artificial Lift Intl LLC (HQ)** ........ 630 743-2563
3005 Highland Pkwy Downers Grove (60515) ***(G-8430)***
**Dover Corporation (PA)** ........ 630 541-1540
3005 Highland Pkwy # 200 Downers Grove (60515) ***(G-8431)***
**Dover Energy Automation LLC (PA)** ........ 630 541-1540
3005 Highland Pkwy Downers Grove (60515) ***(G-8432)***
**Dover Europe Inc (HQ)** ........ 630 541-1540
3005 Highland Pkwy # 200 Downers Grove (60515) ***(G-8433)***
**Dover Industrial Chrome Inc** ........ 773 478-2022
2929 N Campbell Ave Chicago (60618) ***(G-4638)***
**Dover Prtg Identification Inc (HQ)** ........ 630 541-1540
3005 Highland Pkwy # 200 Downers Grove (60515) ***(G-8434)***
**Dovin Machine Shop** ........ 815 672-5247
521 Lundy St Streator (61364) ***(G-20687)***
**Dow Agrosciences LLC** ........ 630 428-8494
1323 Dunrobin Rd Naperville (60540) ***(G-15648)***
**Dow Agrosciences LLC** ........ 815 844-3128
18078 N 1500 East Rd Pontiac (61764) ***(G-17699)***
**Dow Chemical, Kankakee** *Also called Rohm and Haas Company* ***(G-12646)***
**Dow Chemical Company** ........ 217 784-2093
454 E 300n Rd Gibson City (60936) ***(G-10900)***
**Dow Chemical Company** ........ 847 439-2240
2401 Pratt Blvd Elk Grove Village (60007) ***(G-9434)***
**Dow Chemical Company** ........ 815 423-5921
26332 S Frontage Rd Channahon (60410) ***(G-3572)***
**Dow Chemical Company** ........ 815 653-2411
5005 Barnard Mill Rd Ringwood (60072) ***(G-17989)***
**Dow Chemical Company** ........ 815 476-9688
901 E Kankakee River Dr # 1 Wilmington (60481) ***(G-22270)***
**Dow Chemical Company** ........ 815 933-8900
1400 Harvard Dr Kankakee (60901) ***(G-12610)***
**Dow Chemical Company** ........ 815 933-5514
550 N Hobbie Ave Kankakee (60901) ***(G-12611)***
**Dow Jones & Company Inc** ........ 618 651-2300
915 Hemlock St Highland (62249) ***(G-11784)***
**Dow Jones & Company Inc** ........ 312 580-1023
1 S Wacker Dr Ste 2100 Chicago (60606) ***(G-4639)***

ALPHABETIC

**Dowell Lynnea** .... 309 543-3854
18937 E Cr 1800n Havana (62644) ***(G-11694)***
**Down River, Blue Island** *Also called Signode Industrial Group LLC* ***(G-2270)***
**Downen Enterprises, Shawneetown** *Also called Jader Fuel Co Inc* ***(G-19904)***
**Downey Investments Inc** .... 708 345-8000
2125 Gardner Rd Broadview (60155) ***(G-2572)***
**Downtown Sports** .... 815 284-2255
1202 S Galena Ave Dixon (61021) ***(G-8330)***
**Doyle Equipment Mfg Co** .... 217 222-1592
4001 Broadway St Quincy (62305) ***(G-17821)***
**Doyle Signs Inc (PA)** .... 630 543-9490
232 W Interstate Rd Addison (60101) ***(G-98)***
**Dpcac LLC** .... 630 741-7900
1345 Norwood Ave Itasca (60143) ***(G-12253)***
**Dpe Incorporated** .... 773 306-0105
7647 S Kedzie Ave Chicago (60652) ***(G-4640)***
**DPM Solutions LLC** .... 630 285-1170
1521 Industrial Dr Itasca (60143) ***(G-12254)***
**Dps Digital Print Svc** .... 847 836-7734
555 Plate Dr Ste 4 East Dundee (60118) ***(G-8632)***
**Dqm, Oswego** *Also called Sealtec* ***(G-16932)***
**Dqm Inc** .... 630 692-0633
120 Kendall Point Dr Oswego (60543) ***(G-16914)***
**Dr Earles LLC** .... 312 225-7200
2930 S Michigan Ave # 100 Chicago (60616) ***(G-4641)***
**Dr Pepper Snapple Group Inc** .... 708 947-5000
401 N Railroad Ave Northlake (60164) ***(G-16434)***
**Dr Pepper/7 Up Bottling Group** .... 217 585-1496
4600 Industrial Ave Springfield (62703) ***(G-20430)***
**Drag City** .... 312 455-1015
2921 N Cicero Ave Chicago (60641) ***(G-4642)***
**Dragon Die Mold Inc** .... 630 836-0699
30w250 Butterfield Rd # 311 Warrenville (60555) ***(G-21345)***
**Drake Envelope Printing Co** .... 217 374-2772
207 White St White Hall (62092) ***(G-22184)***
**Dramatic Publishing Company** .... 815 338-7170
311 Washington St Woodstock (60098) ***(G-22563)***
**Drapery House Inc** .... 847 318-1161
1420 Oakton St Park Ridge (60068) ***(G-17191)***
**Drapery Room Inc** .... 708 301-3374
15757 Annico Dr Ste 5 Homer Glen (60491) ***(G-12077)***
**Draperyland Inc** .... 630 521-1000
368 Georgetown Sq Wood Dale (60191) ***(G-22360)***
**DRAUGAS PUBLISHING, Chicago** *Also called Lithuanian Catholic Press* ***(G-5519)***
**Draves Archery, Effingham** *Also called Draves Investment Inc* ***(G-8833)***
**Draves Investment Inc** .... 888 678-0251
1707w Ave Of Mid America Effingham (62401) ***(G-8833)***
**Drawing Technology Inc** .... 815 877-5133
1550 Elmwood Rd Rockford (61103) ***(G-18351)***
**Dreamland** .... 847 524-6060
1415 W Schaumburg Rd Schaumburg (60194) ***(G-19508)***
**Dreamworld Golf** .... 847 803-4757
353 N River Rd Des Plaines (60016) ***(G-8186)***
**Dreamwrks Grphic Cmmnctons LLC** .... 847 679-6710
2323 Ravine Way Glenview (60025) ***(G-11121)***
**Dreher Orthopedic Industries (PA)** .... 708 848-4646
214 Chicago Ave Ste 1 Oak Park (60302) ***(G-16661)***
**Drehobl Art Glass Company** .... 773 286-2566
5108 W Irving Park Rd Chicago (60641) ***(G-4643)***
**Dreis and Krump Mfg Co** .... 708 258-1200
481 S Governors Hwy 2 Peotone (60468) ***(G-17488)***
**Dreisilker Electric Motors Inc (PA)** .... 630 469-7510
352 Roosevelt Rd Glen Ellyn (60137) ***(G-10967)***
**Dresbach Distributing Co** .... 815 223-0116
102 Pike St Peru (61354) ***(G-17507)***
**Dresser Inc** .... 847 437-5940
1550 Greenleaf Ave Elk Grove Village (60007) ***(G-9435)***
**Drewrys Brewing Company** .... 815 385-9115
5402 Brittany Dr McHenry (60050) ***(G-14498)***
**Drexel House of Drapes Inc** .... 618 624-5415
3721 Lebanon Ave Belleville (62221) ***(G-1627)***
**Drexel Vinisitian and Blind, Belleville** *Also called Drexel House of Drapes Inc* ***(G-1627)***
**Dreymiller & Kray Inc** .... 847 683-2271
140 S State St Hampshire (60140) ***(G-11547)***
**DRG Molding & Pad Printing Inc** .... 847 223-3398
1631 Wood St D Round Lake Beach (60073) ***(G-19075)***
**Drieselman Manufacturing Co** .... 217 222-1986
2028 Quintron Way Quincy (62305) ***(G-17822)***
**Drig Corporation** .... 312 265-1509
437 W Division St Apt 316 Chicago (60610) ***(G-4644)***
**Driv-Lok Inc (PA)** .... 815 895-8161
1140 Park Ave Sycamore (60178) ***(G-20794)***
**Drive Shaft Unlimited Inc** .... 708 447-2211
4323 Joliet Rd Lyons (60534) ***(G-14036)***
**Driver Services** .... 505 267-8686
120 George St Apt 517 Bensenville (60106) ***(G-1883)***
**Drives & Motion Division, Waukegan** *Also called Yaskawa America Inc* ***(G-21642)***
**Drivetrain Svc & Components, Bensenville** *Also called P & A Driveline & Machine Inc* ***(G-1962)***
**Drivnn LLC** .... 815 222-4447
6355 Commonwealth Dr Loves Park (61111) ***(G-13937)***
**Drr Construction, McHenry** *Also called Reliable Sand and Gravel Co* ***(G-14551)***
**Drug Source Company LLC** .... 708 236-1768
1 Westbrook Corporate Ctr Westchester (60154) ***(G-21838)***
**Drug Testing Suppliers Inc** .... 618 208-3810
421 Saint John Dr Godfrey (62035) ***(G-11224)***
**Drum Manufacturing** .... 217 923-5625
804 E York Rd Greenup (62428) ***(G-11381)***
**Drumbeaters of America Inc** .... 630 365-5527
215 W Nebraska St Elburn (60119) ***(G-8883)***
**Drumheller Bag Corporation** .... 309 676-1006
1114 Sw Adams St Peoria (61602) ***(G-17350)***
**Drummond Industries Inc** .... 773 637-1264
639 Thomas Dr Bensenville (60106) ***(G-1884)***
**Dry Systems Technologies LLC (HQ)** .... 630 427-2051
10420 Rising Ct Woodridge (60517) ***(G-22473)***
**Dry Systems Technologies LLC** .... 618 658-3000
1430 Us Highway 45 N Vienna (62995) ***(G-21222)***
**Drywear Apparel LLC** .... 847 687-8540
21231 W Brandon Rd Kildeer (60047) ***(G-12699)***
**Ds Containers Inc** .... 630 406-9600
1789 Hubbard Ave Batavia (60510) ***(G-1442)***
**DS Polishing & Metal Finshg** .... 309 755-0544
1201 7th St East Moline (61244) ***(G-8677)***
**Ds Production LLC** .... 708 873-3142
16101 108th Ave Orland Park (60467) ***(G-16856)***
**Ds Services of America Inc** .... 773 586-8600
6055 S Harlem Ave Chicago (60638) ***(G-4645)***
**Ds Services of America Inc** .... 800 322-6272
2425 Laude Dr Rockford (61109) ***(G-18352)***
**Ds Services of America Inc** .... 815 469-7100
9409 Gulfstream Rd Frankfort (60423) ***(G-10314)***
**Ds2 Tech, Elizabeth** *Also called Jeanblanc International Inc* ***(G-9242)***
**Dsi Inc** .... 309 965-5110
401 State Route 117 Goodfield (61742) ***(G-11246)***
**DSI Spaceframes Inc** .... 630 607-0045
509 S Westgate St Addison (60101) ***(G-99)***
**Dsign In Plastics Inc** .... 847 288-8085
10915 Franklin Ave Ste J Franklin Park (60131) ***(G-10459)***
**DSM Desotech Inc (HQ)** .... 847 697-0400
1122 Saint Charles St Elgin (60120) ***(G-9013)***
**DSM Functional Materials, Elgin** *Also called DSM Desotech Inc* ***(G-9013)***
**Dspc Company (PA)** .... 815 997-1116
3939 S Central Ave Rockford (61102) ***(G-18353)***
**Dsr Screenprinting** .... 630 855-2790
676 Bonded Pkwy Ste L Streamwood (60107) ***(G-20652)***
**Dss Rapak Inc** .... 630 296-2000
1201 Windham Pkwy Ste D Romeoville (60446) ***(G-18817)***
**Dswfitness, Champaign** *Also called Desert Southwest Fitness Inc* ***(G-3474)***
**Dt Metronic Inc** .... 847 593-0945
1860 S Elmhurst Rd Mount Prospect (60056) ***(G-15326)***
**Dtc Products Inc** .... 630 513-3323
2651 Dukane Dr Saint Charles (60174) ***(G-19174)***
**Dti, Rockford** *Also called Drawing Technology Inc* ***(G-18351)***
**Dti Molding Technologies Inc** .... 630 543-3600
201 S Church St Addison (60101) ***(G-100)***
**Dtk Construction Inc** .... 312 296-2762
200 Sumac Rd Ste A Wheeling (60090) ***(G-22037)***
**Dtk Stone Works, Wheeling** *Also called Dtk Construction Inc* ***(G-22037)***
**Dtmf, Gridley** *Also called Diversatech Metalfab LLC* ***(G-11404)***
**Dtrs Enterprises Inc** .... 630 296-6890
1317 Rosemary Dr Bolingbrook (60490) ***(G-2302)***
**DTS America Inc** .... 847 783-0401
427 E 4th St East Dundee (60118) ***(G-8633)***
**Dtv Innovations LLC (PA)** .... 847 919-3550
2402 Millennium Dr Elgin (60124) ***(G-9014)***
**Du Bro Products Inc** .... 847 526-2136
480 W Bonner Rd Wauconda (60084) ***(G-21456)***
**Du Page Precision Products Co (PA)** .... 630 849-2940
3695 Darlene Ct Ste 101 Aurora (60504) ***(G-997)***
**Du Page Precision Products Co** .... 630 849-2940
811 Shoreline Dr Aurora (60504) ***(G-998)***
**Du Pont Delaware Inc** .... 630 285-2700
500 Park Blvd Ste 545 Itasca (60143) ***(G-12255)***
**Du Quoin, IL Plant, Du Quoin** *Also called General Cable Industries Inc* ***(G-8556)***
**Du-Call Miller Plastics Inc** .... 630 964-6020
901 N Batavia Ave Ste 3 Batavia (60510) ***(G-1443)***
**Du-Kane Asphalt Co** .... 630 953-1500
600 S Lombard Rd Addison (60101) ***(G-101)***
**Dual Mfg Co Inc** .... 773 267-4457
3522 Martens St Franklin Park (60131) ***(G-10460)***
**Dual Voltage Distributors** .... 847 519-1201
1252 Remington Rd Ste A Schaumburg (60173) ***(G-19509)***
**Dubois Chemicals Group Inc** .... 708 458-2000
7025 W 66th Pl Chicago (60638) ***(G-4646)***
**Duchossois Industries Inc Non** .... 630 279-3600
300 Windsor Dr Oak Brook (60523) ***(G-16504)***

**Duckys Formal Wear Inc** 309 342-5914
244 E Main St Galesburg (61401) *(G-10748)*
**Dude Products Inc** 773 661-1126
1744 W Beach Ave U2 Chicago (60622) *(G-4647)*
**Dudek & Bock Spring Mfg Co (PA)** 773 379-4100
5100 W Roosevelt Rd Chicago (60644) *(G-4648)*
**Duhack Lehn & Associates Inc** 815 777-3460
1228 N Blackjack Rd Galena (61036) *(G-10719)*
**Dukane Corporation (PA)** 630 797-4900
2900 Dukane Dr Saint Charles (60174) *(G-19175)*
**Dukane Ias LLC** 630 797-4900
2900 Dukane Dr Saint Charles (60174) *(G-19176)*
**Dulce Vida Juice Bar LLC** 224 236-5045
2003 Irving Park Rd Hanover Park (60133) *(G-11579)*
**Dumore Supplies Inc** 312 949-6260
2525 S Wabash Ave Chicago (60616) *(G-4649)*
**Dun-Rite Tool & Machine Co** 815 758-5464
55 W Lincoln Hwy Cortland (60112) *(G-7388)*
**Dun-Rite Tooling, Cortland** *Also called Dun-Rite Tool & Machine Co (G-7388)*
**Dun-Wel Lithograph Co Inc** 773 327-8811
3338 N Ravenswood Ave Chicago (60657) *(G-4650)*
**Dunajec Bakery & Deli** 773 585-9611
8339 S Harlem Ave Bridgeview (60455) *(G-2485)*
**Dunamis International** 773 504-5733
1239 W Madison St Chicago (60607) *(G-4651)*
**Duncan Oil Company Inc** 618 548-2923
300 S Washington St Salem (62881) *(G-19330)*
**Dundee Design LLC** 847 494-2360
570 Rock Road Dr Ste P East Dundee (60118) *(G-8634)*
**Dundee Truck & Trlr Works LLC** 224 484-8182
407 Christina Dr East Dundee (60118) *(G-8635)*
**Dundee Truck Repair & Wash, East Dundee** *Also called Dundee Truck & Trlr Works LLC (G-8635)*
**Dundick Corporation** 708 656-6363
4616 W 20th St Cicero (60804) *(G-7192)*
**Dune Manufacturing Company** 708 681-2905
1800 N 15th Ave Melrose Park (60160) *(G-14622)*
**Dunham Designs Inc** 815 462-0100
1024 S Cedar Rd New Lenox (60451) *(G-15877)*
**Dunhill Corp** 815 806-8600
9218 Corsair Rd Unit 1 Frankfort (60423) *(G-10315)*
**Dunigan Custom Woodworking** 708 351-5213
1426 Ridge Rd Homewood (60430) *(G-12095)*
**Dunkin Donuts** 708 460-3088
14461 S La Grange Rd Orland Park (60462) *(G-16857)*
**Dunkin' Donuts, Chicago** *Also called Union Foods Inc (G-6814)*
**Dunkin' Donuts, Bellwood** *Also called Bellwood Dunkin Donuts (G-1695)*
**Dunkin' Donuts, West Chicago** *Also called B N K Inc (G-21664)*
**Dunkin' Donuts, Palos Heights** *Also called Walter & Kathy Anczerewicz (G-17113)*
**Dunkin' Donuts, Wheaton** *Also called Express Donuts Enterprise Inc (G-21947)*
**Dunkin' Donuts, Lake Zurich** *Also called Jay Elka (G-13091)*
**Dunlee Corporation** 630 585-2100
555 N Commerce St Aurora (60504) *(G-999)*
**Dunlee Division, Aurora** *Also called Philips Medical Systems Clevel (G-1065)*
**Dunteman and Co** 309 772-2166
115 E Twyman St Bushnell (61422) *(G-2902)*
**Duo Display, Chicago** *Also called Duo Usa Incorporated (G-4653)*
**Duo Graphics** 847 228-7080
1612 Landmeier Rd Ste C Elk Grove Village (60007) *(G-9436)*
**Duo North America** 312 421-7755
329 W 18th St Ste 607 Chicago (60616) *(G-4652)*
**Duo Plex Glass Ltd (PA)** 708 532-4422
15626 S 70th Ct Orland Park (60462) *(G-16858)*
**Duo Usa Incorporated** 312 421-7755
329 W 18th St Ste 714 Chicago (60616) *(G-4653)*
**Duo-Fast Corporation (HQ)** 847 944-2288
155 Harlem Ave Glenview (60025) *(G-11122)*
**Dupage Chropractic Centre Ltd** 630 858-9780
45 S Park Blvd Ste 155 Glen Ellyn (60137) *(G-10968)*
**Dupage Mechanical** 630 620-1122
270 Larkin Dr Ste D Wheeling (60090) *(G-22038)*
**Dupage Products Group** 630 969-7200
2250 Curtiss St Downers Grove (60515) *(G-8435)*
**Dupli Group Inc** 773 549-5285
3628 N Lincoln Ave Chicago (60613) *(G-4654)*
**Dupont, Itasca** *Also called Du Pont Delaware Inc (G-12255)*
**Dupont, El Paso** *Also called E I Du Pont De Nemours & Co (G-8868)*
**Duquoin Dental Associates** 618 542-8832
1266 S Washington St Du Quoin (62832) *(G-8553)*
**Dura Bar Division, Woodstock** *Also called Charter Dura-Bar Inc (G-22552)*
**Dura Feed Inc** 815 395-1115
7542 Forest Hills Rd Loves Park (61111) *(G-13938)*
**Dura Operating LLC** 815 947-3333
301 S Simmons St Stockton (61085) *(G-20631)*
**Dura Products Corporation** 815 939-1399
2 E Bradford Dr Bradley (60915) *(G-2420)*
**Dura Wax Company** 815 385-5000
4101 W Albany St McHenry (60050) *(G-14499)*
**Dura-Bar Div, Woodstock** *Also called Charter Dura-Bar Inc (G-22551)*
**Dura-Crafts Corp** 815 464-3561
9408 Gulfstream Rd Frankfort (60423) *(G-10316)*
**Durabilt Division, Bradley** *Also called Dura Products Corporation (G-2420)*
**Durabilt Dyvex Inc** 708 397-4673
2545 S 25th Ave Broadview (60155) *(G-2573)*
**Durabilt Manufacturing, Broadview** *Also called Durabilt Dyvex Inc (G-2573)*
**Durable Design Products Inc** 708 707-1147
1520 Franklin Ave River Forest (60305) *(G-17997)*
**Durable Engravers Inc** 630 766-6420
521 S County Line Rd Franklin Park (60131) *(G-10461)*
**Durable Inc (PA)** 847 541-4400
750 Northgate Pkwy Wheeling (60090) *(G-22039)*
**Durable Manufacturing Company** 630 766-0398
232 Evergreen Ave Unit B Bensenville (60106) *(G-1885)*
**Durable Office Products Corp** 847 787-0100
2475 S Wolf Rd Des Plaines (60018) *(G-8187)*
**Durable Packaging Intl, Wheeling** *Also called Durable Inc (G-22039)*
**Durabuilt Die Corp** 847 437-2086
619 Woodview Ave Elk Grove Village (60007) *(G-9437)*
**Duracell Company** 203 796-4000
181 W Madison St Fl 44 Chicago (60602) *(G-4655)*
**Duraclean International Inc** 847 704-7100
220 W Campus Dr Ste A Arlington Heights (60004) *(G-748)*
**Duracrest Fabrics** 847 350-0030
2474 Delta Ln Elk Grove Village (60007) *(G-9438)*
**Duradek, Mundelein** *Also called Duval Group Ltd (G-15495)*
**Duraflex Inc** 847 462-1007
765 Industrial Dr Cary (60013) *(G-3336)*
**Duratech Corporation** 618 533-8891
2520 S Wabash Ave Centralia (62801) *(G-3412)*
**Duratrack Inc** 847 806-0202
950 Morse Ave Elk Grove Village (60007) *(G-9439)*
**Duravant (PA)** 630 635-3910
3500 Lacey Rd Ste 290 Downers Grove (60515) *(G-8436)*
**Duravant LLC (HQ)** 630 635-3910
3500 Lacey Rd Ste 290 Downers Grove (60515) *(G-8437)*
**Durex Industries, Cary** *Also called Durex International Corp (G-3338)*
**Durex Industries Inc** 847 462-2706
305 Cary Point Dr Cary (60013) *(G-3337)*
**Durex International Corp** 847 639-5600
190 Detroit St Cary (60013) *(G-3338)*
**Durite Screw Corporation** 773 622-3410
1815 N Long Ave 35 Chicago (60639) *(G-4656)*
**Duro Art Industries Inc (PA)** 773 743-3430
1832 W Juneway Ter Chicago (60626) *(G-4657)*
**Duro Cast Inc** 815 498-2317
145 E Market St Somonauk (60552) *(G-20125)*
**Duro Decal Co, Chicago** *Also called Duro Art Industries Inc (G-4657)*
**Duro Hilex Poly LLC** 708 385-8674
12245 S Central Ave Alsip (60803) *(G-459)*
**Duro-Chrome Industries Inc** 847 487-2900
275 Indl Dr Wauconda (60084) *(G-21457)*
**Duroweld Company Inc** 847 680-3064
1565 Rockland Rd Lake Bluff (60044) *(G-12841)*
**Durr - All Corporation** 815 943-1032
1001 W Diggins St Ste 2 Harvard (60033) *(G-11631)*
**Dust Logging LLC** 217 844-2305
16666 E 2050th Ave Effingham (62401) *(G-8834)*
**Dust Patrol Inc** 309 676-1161
2706 Sw Washington St Peoria (61602) *(G-17351)*
**Dusty Lane Wood Products** 618 426-9045
295 Dusty Ln Campbell Hill (62916) *(G-2975)*
**Dutch Prairie Conveyors** 618 349-6177
844 N 1625 St Shobonier (62885) *(G-19921)*
**Dutch Valley Meats Inc** 217 543-3354
376 E Sr 133 Arthur (61911) *(G-897)*
**Dutch Valley Partners LLC** 815 937-8812
4067 E 4000n Rd Bourbonnais (60914) *(G-2394)*
**Dutch Valley Veal, South Holland** *Also called Brown Packing Company Inc (G-20253)*
**Duval Group Ltd** 847 949-7001
452 Morris Ave Mundelein (60060) *(G-15495)*
**Duvas USA Limited** 312 266-1420
676 N Michigan Ave # 2800 Chicago (60611) *(G-4658)*
**Dva Mayday Corporation** 847 848-7555
8108 Redtail Dr Village of Lakewood (60014) *(G-21290)*
**Dva Metal Fabrication Inc** 224 577-8217
1427 Tonne Rd Elk Grove Village (60007) *(G-9440)*
**Dva Metal Fabrication Inc** 224 577-8217
1656 Brighton Dr Mundelein (60060) *(G-15496)*
**Dvcc Inc** 630 323-3105
40 Chestnut Ave Westmont (60559) *(G-21886)*
**Dvd Overseas Electronics, Schaumburg** *Also called Dual Voltage Distributors (G-19509)*
**Dvoraks Creations Inc** 815 838-2214
1521 Daviess Ave Lockport (60441) *(G-13713)*
**Dwyer Products & Services, Itasca** *Also called Dpcac LLC (G-12253)*
**Dyco-TEC Products Ltd (PA)** 630 837-6410
29w600 Schick Rd Bartlett (60103) *(G-1342)*
**Dyer's Superchargers, Summit Argo** *Also called Dyers Machine Service Inc (G-20762)*

A
L
P
H
A
B
E
T
I
C

**Dyers Machine Service Inc** 708 496-8100
7665 W 63rd St Summit Argo (60501) ***(G-20762)***
**Dyna Comp Inc** 815 455-5570
6215 Factory Rd Ste C Crystal Lake (60014) ***(G-7568)***
**Dyna Cut Industries, Carol Stream** *Also called Dynacut Industries Inc* ***(G-3145)***
**Dyna-Burr Chicago Inc** 708 250-6744
65 E Lake St Northlake (60164) ***(G-16435)***
**Dyna-Tone Litho Inc** 630 595-1073
168 Henderson St Bensenville (60106) ***(G-1886)***
**Dynacast Inc** 847 608-2200
195 Corporate Dr Elgin (60123) ***(G-9015)***
**Dynachem Inc** 217 662-2136
15662 E 980 North Rd Westville (61883) ***(G-21929)***
**Dynaco Door, Mundelein** *Also called Dynaco Usa Inc* ***(G-15497)***
**Dynaco Usa Inc (HQ)** 847 562-4910
935 Campus Dr Mundelein (60060) ***(G-15497)***
**Dynacoil Inc** 847 731-3300
2000 Lewis Ave Zion (60099) ***(G-22683)***
**Dynacron** 773 378-0736
1017 N Cicero Ave Chicago (60651) ***(G-4659)***
**Dynacut Industries Inc** 630 462-1900
500 Randy Rd Ste A Carol Stream (60188) ***(G-3145)***
**Dynagraphics Incorporated** 217 876-9950
3220 N Woodford St Decatur (62526) ***(G-7878)***
**Dynamac Inc** 630 543-0033
1229 W Capitol Dr Addison (60101) ***(G-102)***
**Dynamesh Inc** 630 293-5454
512 Kingsland Dr Batavia (60510) ***(G-1444)***
**Dynami Solutions LLC** 618 363-2771
2 Loggers Trl Edwardsville (62025) ***(G-8796)***
**Dynamic Automation Inc** 312 782-8555
3445 W Arthur Ave Lincolnwood (60712) ***(G-13508)***
**Dynamic Door Service Inc** 847 885-4751
1165 Deep Woods Dr Elgin (60120) ***(G-9016)***
**Dynamic Indus Solution Solvers, New Lenox** *Also called Melissa A Miller* ***(G-15893)***
**Dynamic Iron Inc** 708 672-7617
24001 S Western Ave Park Forest (60466) ***(G-17171)***
**Dynamic Machining Inc** 815 675-3330
2304 Spring Ridge Dr C Spring Grove (60081) ***(G-20334)***
**Dynamic Manufacturing Inc (PA)** 708 343-8753
1930 N Mannheim Rd Melrose Park (60160) ***(G-14623)***
**Dynamic Manufacturing Inc** 708 681-0682
1800 N 30th Ave Ste 1 Melrose Park (60160) ***(G-14624)***
**Dynamic Manufacturing Inc** 708 547-7081
4300 Madison St Hillside (60162) ***(G-11915)***
**Dynamic Manufacturing Inc** 708 343-8753
1930 N Mannheim Rd Melrose Park (60160) ***(G-14625)***
**Dynamic Manufacturing Inc** 708 547-9011
4211 Madison St Hillside (60162) ***(G-11916)***
**Dynamic Manufacturing Inc** 708 343-8753
1801 N 32nd Ave Melrose Park (60160) ***(G-14626)***
**Dynamic Mfg Torque Converters, Melrose Park** *Also called Dynamic Manufacturing Inc* ***(G-14625)***
**Dynamic Nutritionals Inc** 815 545-9171
1014 S Cooper Rd New Lenox (60451) ***(G-15878)***
**Dynamic Precision Products** 847 526-2054
1280 Kyle Ct Wauconda (60084) ***(G-21458)***
**Dynamicsignals LLC (PA)** 815 838-0005
900 N State St Lockport (60441) ***(G-13714)***
**Dynapar Corporation (HQ)** 847 662-2666
1675 N Delany Rd Gurnee (60031) ***(G-11443)***
**Dynasty Mold Builders, Wauconda** *Also called Illinois Mold Builders Inc* ***(G-21471)***
**Dynawave Corporation** 630 232-4945
2520 Kaneville Ct Geneva (60134) ***(G-10826)***
**Dyne Inc** 815 521-1111
7280 E Us Highway 6 Minooka (60447) ***(G-14839)***
**Dyneer Corporation** 217 228-6011
2701 Spruce St Quincy (62301) ***(G-17823)***
**Dyno Manufacturing Inc** 618 451-6609
2 Fox Industrial Dr Madison (62060) ***(G-14143)***
**Dyno Nobel Inc** 217 285-5621
31879 State Highway 106 Barry (62312) ***(G-1312)***
**Dyno Nobel Inc** 217 285-5531
1353 W Washington St Detroit (62363) ***(G-8309)***
**Dynomax Inc** 224 542-1031
640 Heathrow Dr Lincolnshire (60069) ***(G-13445)***
**Dynomax Inc (PA)** 847 680-8833
1535 Abbott Dr Wheeling (60090) ***(G-22040)***
**Dyson Inc (HQ)** 312 469-5950
600 W Chicago Ave Ste 275 Chicago (60654) ***(G-4660)***
**Dyson B2b Inc** 312 469-5950
600 W Chicago Ave Ste 275 Chicago (60654) ***(G-4661)***
**Dytec Midwest Inc (PA)** 847 255-3200
1855 Rohlwing Rd Ste C Rolling Meadows (60008) ***(G-18726)***
**Dzro-Bans International Inc** 779 324-2740
3011 183rd St Homewood (60430) ***(G-12096)***
**E A M & J Inc** 847 622-9200
1620 Cambridge Dr Elgin (60123) ***(G-9017)***
**E & D Web Inc** 815 562-5800
1100a S Main St Rochelle (61068) ***(G-18086)***
**E & E Machine & Engineering Co** 708 841-5208
14016 S Indiana Ave Riverdale (60827) ***(G-18018)***
**E & E Pattern Works Inc** 847 689-1088
1209 Morrow Ave North Chicago (60064) ***(G-16177)***
**E & F Tool Company Inc** 815 729-1305
213 Amendodge Dr Joliet (60404) ***(G-12486)***
**E & H Graphic Service** 708 748-5656
21750 Main St Unit 21 Matteson (60443) ***(G-14371)***
**E & H Tubing Inc (PA)** 773 522-3100
4401 W Roosevelt Rd Chicago (60624) ***(G-4662)***
**E & J Gallo Winery** 630 505-4000
4225 Naperville Rd # 330 Lisle (60532) ***(G-13584)***
**E & J Precision Machining Inc** 815 363-2522
4215 W Orleans St McHenry (60050) ***(G-14500)***
**E & L Communication** 773 890-1656
2644 W 47th St Chicago (60632) ***(G-4663)***
**E & R Powder Coatings Inc** 773 523-9510
3729 W 49th St Chicago (60632) ***(G-4664)***
**E & T Plastic Mfg Co Inc** 630 628-9048
140 S Fairbank St Addison (60101) ***(G-103)***
**E & T Plastics of Illinois, Addison** *Also called E & T Plastic Mfg Co Inc* ***(G-103)***
**E A, Alsip** *Also called Engineered Abrasives Inc* ***(G-462)***
**E A A Enterprises Inc** 630 279-0150
250 E Saint Charles Rd Villa Park (60181) ***(G-21249)***
**E B Bronson & Co Inc** 708 385-3600
12826 Irving Ave Blue Island (60406) ***(G-2247)***
**E B G B Inc** 847 228-9333
220 Lively Blvd Elk Grove Village (60007) ***(G-9441)***
**E B Inc** 815 758-6646
116 E State St De Kalb (60115) ***(G-7817)***
**E C Machining Inc** 708 496-0116
8267 S 86th Ct Justice (60458) ***(G-12598)***
**E C S, Broadview** *Also called Elevator Cable & Supply Co* ***(G-2574)***
**E C Schultz & Co Inc** 847 640-1190
333 Crossen Ave Elk Grove Village (60007) ***(G-9442)***
**E Casper Hairpieces, Chicago** *Also called Casper Ernest E Hairgoods* ***(G-4249)***
**E D M, Lake Zurich** *Also called Electronic Design & Mfg Inc* ***(G-13066)***
**E F I, Centralia** *Also called Engineered Fluid Inc* ***(G-3413)***
**E Formella & Sons Inc** 708 598-0909
411 E Plainfield Rd Countryside (60525) ***(G-7422)***
**E Gornell & Sons Inc** 773 489-2330
2241 N Knox Ave Chicago (60639) ***(G-4665)***
**E H Baare Corporation** 618 546-1575
500 S Heath Toffee Ave Robinson (62454) ***(G-18062)***
**E H Wachs** 815 943-4785
600 Knightsbridge Pkwy Lincolnshire (60069) ***(G-13446)***
**E H Wachs Company, Lincolnshire** *Also called 1883 Properties Inc* ***(G-13422)***
**E I Du Pont De Nemours & Co** 309 527-5115
2830 Us Highway 24 El Paso (61738) ***(G-8868)***
**E I Du Pont De Nemours & Co** 815 259-3311
10994 Three Mile Rd Thomson (61285) ***(G-20865)***
**E I P Inc (PA)** 847 885-3615
2200 W Higgins Rd Ste 355 Hoffman Estates (60169) ***(G-12007)***
**E I T Inc** 630 359-3543
2593 Arcadia Cir Naperville (60540) ***(G-15649)***
**E J Basler Co** 847 678-8880
9511 Ainslie St Schiller Park (60176) ***(G-19821)***
**E J Kupjack & Associates Inc** 847 823-6661
2233 S Throop St Apt 319 Chicago (60608) ***(G-4666)***
**E J Self Furniture (PA)** 847 394-0899
516 E Northwest Hwy Mount Prospect (60056) ***(G-15327)***
**E J Somerville, Melrose Park** *Also called Ej Somerville Plating Co* ***(G-14631)***
**E J Welch Co Inc** 847 238-0100
2601 Lively Blvd Elk Grove Village (60007) ***(G-9443)***
**E K Kuhn Inc** 815 899-9211
1170 E State St Sycamore (60178) ***(G-20795)***
**E M C Industry** 217 543-2894
441 E Cr 400 N Arthur (61911) ***(G-898)***
**E M F Y & Associates, Rockford** *Also called Charles R Frontczak* ***(G-18304)***
**E M Glabus Co Inc** 630 766-3027
420 County Line Rd Bensenville (60106) ***(G-1887)***
**E M S, Lake In The Hills** *Also called Emissions Systems Incorporated* ***(G-12991)***
**E Mc** 217 228-1280
906 Vermont St Quincy (62301) ***(G-17824)***
**E N M Company** 773 775-8400
5617 N Northwest Hwy Chicago (60646) ***(G-4667)***
**E N M Digital Counters, Chicago** *Also called E N M Company* ***(G-4667)***
**E N P Inc (PA)** 800 255-4906
603 14th St Mendota (61342) ***(G-14720)***
**E N P Inc** 815 539-7471
2001 E Main St Mendota (61342) ***(G-14721)***
**E O Schweitzer Manufacturing, Lake Zurich** *Also called Schweitzer Engrg Labs Inc* ***(G-13127)***
**E P Computer, Champaign** *Also called Ep Technology Corporation USA* ***(G-3482)***
**E P M Sales Co Inc** 630 761-2051
280 Belleview Ln Batavia (60510) ***(G-1445)***
**E Pharm Nutrition, Seymour** *Also called Savind Inc* ***(G-19898)***

**E R Wagner Manufacturing Co** ... 708 485-3400
8822 47th St Brookfield (60513) *(G-2630)*
**E Rowe Foundry & Machine Co** ... 217 382-4135
147 W Cumberland St Martinsville (62442) *(G-14334)*
**E S I, Itasca** *Also called Environmental Specialties Inc (G-12259)*
**E S I Steel Fabrication, Salem** *Also called Esi Steel & Fabrication (G-19331)*
**E Solutions Business** ... 855 324-3339
300 N La Salle Dr # 4925 Chicago (60654) *(G-4668)*
**E W Enterprises Inc** ... 618 345-2244
1 Meadow Heights Prof Par Collinsville (62234) *(G-7320)*
**E W I, Rantoul** *Also called Eagle Wings Industries Inc (G-17925)*
**E Z Lube** ... 815 439-3980
1984 Essington Rd Joliet (60435) *(G-12487)*
**E Z Sign Co Inc** ... 815 469-4080
15347 Cicero Ave Rear Oak Forest (60452) *(G-16578)*
**E Z Trail Inc (PA)** ... 217 543-3471
1050 E Columbia St Arthur (61911) *(G-899)*
**E&D Printing Services Inc** ... 815 609-8222
15857 Spanglers Farm Dr Plainfield (60544) *(G-17593)*
**E+e Elektronik Corporation** ... 508 530-3068
333 E State Pkwy Schaumburg (60173) *(G-19510)*
**E-J Industries Inc** ... 312 226-5023
1275 S Campbell Ave Chicago (60608) *(G-4669)*
**E-Jay Plastics Co** ... 630 543-4000
115 W Laura Dr Addison (60101) *(G-104)*
**E-Lite Tool & Mfg Co** ... 618 236-1580
122 Industrial Dr Belleville (62220) *(G-1628)*
**E-M Metal Fabricator** ... 847 593-9970
145 Joey Dr Elk Grove Village (60007) *(G-9444)*
**E-Quip Manufacturing Co** ... 815 464-0053
230 Industry Ave Frankfort (60423) *(G-10317)*
**E-T-A Circuit Breakers, Mount Prospect** *Also called Oakland Industries Ltd (G-15358)*
**E-Z Cuff Inc** ... 847 549-1550
1840 Industrial Dr # 260 Libertyville (60048) *(G-13320)*
**E-Z Products Inc** ... 847 551-9199
92 E End Dr Gilberts (60136) *(G-10918)*
**E-Z Rotational Molder Inc** ... 847 806-1327
1001 Nicholas Blvd Ste F Elk Grove Village (60007) *(G-9445)*
**E-Z Tree Recycling Inc** ... 773 493-8600
7050 S Dorchester Ave Chicago (60637) *(G-4670)*
**E2 Manufacturing Group LLC** ... 224 399-9608
3776 Hawthorne Ct Waukegan (60087) *(G-21554)*
**E2s LLC** ... 708 629-0714
5120 W 125th Pl Unit A Alsip (60803) *(G-460)*
**E3 Artisan Inc** ... 815 575-9315
113 S Benton St Woodstock (60098) *(G-22564)*
**Ea Mackay Enterprises Inc** ... 630 627-7010
104 N West Rd Lombard (60148) *(G-13793)*
**Eagle Burial Vault** ... 815 722-8660
9535 W Steger Rd Frankfort (60423) *(G-10318)*
**Eagle Cabinet Inc** ... 847 289-9992
1625 Dundee Ave Elgin (60120) *(G-9018)*
**Eagle Carpet Services Ltd** ... 956 971-8560
135 S Fairbank St Addison (60101) *(G-105)*
**Eagle Chassis Inc** ... 217 525-1941
2877 N Dirksen Pkwy Springfield (62702) *(G-20431)*
**Eagle Companies Inc** ... 309 686-9054
4214 E Rome Rd Chillicothe (61523) *(G-7164)*
**Eagle Connector Corporation** ... 847 593-8737
401 Crossen Ave Elk Grove Village (60007) *(G-9446)*
**Eagle Electronics Inc** ... 847 891-5800
1735 Mitchell Blvd Schaumburg (60193) *(G-19511)*
**Eagle Enterprises Inc** ... 618 643-2588
Hc 14 Box E Mc Leansboro (62859) *(G-14464)*
**Eagle Express Mail LLC** ... 618 377-6245
333 W Bethalto Dr Ste C Bethalto (62010) *(G-2081)*
**Eagle Forum (PA)** ... 618 462-5415
322 State St Ste 301 Alton (62002) *(G-572)*
**Eagle Freight Inc** ... 708 202-0651
3710 River Rd Ste 200 Franklin Park (60131) *(G-10462)*
**Eagle Gear & Manufacturing Co** ... 630 628-6100
740 W Racquet Club Dr Addison (60101) *(G-106)*
**Eagle Grips, Carol Stream** *Also called Art Jewel Enterprises Ltd (G-3106)*
**Eagle High Mast Ltg Co Inc** ... 847 473-3800
1070a S Northpoint Blvd Waukegan (60085) *(G-21555)*
**Eagle Machine Company** ... 312 243-7407
1725 W Walnut St Chicago (60612) *(G-4671)*
**Eagle Medical Concepts Inc** ... 618 475-3671
6001 Old Collinsville Rd 4c Fairview Heights (62208) *(G-10167)*
**Eagle Panel System Inc** ... 618 326-7132
127 N Maple St Mulberry Grove (62262) *(G-15459)*
**Eagle Plastics & Supply Inc** ... 708 331-6232
15446 Wentworth Ave South Holland (60473) *(G-20263)*
**Eagle Press, Crystal Lake** *Also called LAC Enterprises Inc (G-7601)*
**Eagle Printing Company** ... 309 762-0771
2957 12th Ave Moline (61265) *(G-14936)*
**Eagle Publications** ... 309 462-5758
507 N Monroe St Ste 3 Abingdon (61410) *(G-10)*
**Eagle Publications Inc** ... 618 345-5400
2 Eastport Plaza Dr # 100 Collinsville (62234) *(G-7321)*

**Eagle Screen Print Inds Inc** ... 708 579-0454
5326 East Ave Countryside (60525) *(G-7423)*
**Eagle Seal, Mc Leansboro** *Also called Eagle Enterprises Inc (G-14464)*
**Eagle Stone and Brick Inc** ... 618 282-6722
450 N Main St Red Bud (62278) *(G-17940)*
**Eagle Test Systems Inc (HQ)** ... 847 367-8282
2200 Millbrook Dr Buffalo Grove (60089) *(G-2689)*
**Eagle Tool Ram Shop, Crystal Lake** *Also called Eagle Tool Us LLC (G-7569)*
**Eagle Tool Us LLC** ... 815 459-4177
4014 Northwest Hwy Ste 1a Crystal Lake (60014) *(G-7569)*
**Eagle Tubular Products Inc** ... 618 463-1702
105 Chessen Ln Alton (62002) *(G-573)*
**Eagle Wings Industries Inc** ... 217 892-4322
400 Shellhouse Dr Rantoul (61866) *(G-17925)*
**Eaglestone Inc** ... 630 587-1115
3705 Swenson Ave Saint Charles (60174) *(G-19177)*
**Eakas Corporation** ... 815 223-8811
6251 State Route 251 Peru (61354) *(G-17508)*
**Eam Pallets** ... 708 333-0596
15224 Dixie Hwy Ste A Harvey (60426) *(G-11664)*
**Ear Hustle 411 LLC** ... 773 616-3598
123 W Madison St Ste 806 Chicago (60602) *(G-4672)*
**Earl Ad Inc** ... 312 666-7106
2201 S Union Ave Ste 2 Chicago (60616) *(G-4673)*
**Earl G Graves Ltd** ... 312 664-8667
625 N Michigan Ave # 422 Chicago (60611) *(G-4674)*
**Earl G Graves Pubg Co Inc** ... 312 274-0682
625 N Michigan Ave # 401 Chicago (60611) *(G-4675)*
**Earl Mich, Wood Dale** *Also called Mich Enterprises Inc (G-22399)*
**Earlville Cold Stor Lckr LLC** ... 815 246-9469
101 N East St Earlville (60518) *(G-8593)*
**Early Bird Advertising Inc** ... 847 253-1423
502 Grego Ct Prospect Heights (60070) *(G-17777)*
**Early Edition** ... 312 345-0786
69 W Washington St Ll10 Chicago (60602) *(G-4676)*
**Earshot Inc** ... 773 383-1798
560 W Washington Blvd # 240 Chicago (60661) *(G-4677)*
**Earth Friendly Products, Addison** *Also called Venus Laboratories Inc (G-339)*
**Earth Stone Products III Inc** ... 847 671-3000
4535 25th Ave Schiller Park (60176) *(G-19822)*
**Earthcomber LLC** ... 708 366-1600
110 N Marion St Oak Park (60301) *(G-16662)*
**Earthgrains** ... 630 859-8782
321 Airport Rd North Aurora (60542) *(G-16128)*
**Earthgrains Refrigertd Dough P** ... 630 455-5200
3250 Lacey Rd Ste 600 Downers Grove (60515) *(G-8438)*
**Earths Healing Cafe LLC** ... 773 728-0598
1942 W Montrose Ave Ste 1 Chicago (60613) *(G-4678)*
**Earthsafe Systems Inc (PA)** ... 312 226-7600
2041 W Carroll Ave Chicago (60612) *(G-4679)*
**Earthwise Environmental Inc** ... 630 475-3070
777 N Edgewood Ave Wood Dale (60191) *(G-22361)*
**Earthwise Recycled Pallet** ... 618 286-6015
336 Mcbride Ave Dupo (62239) *(G-8570)*
**East Balt Bakeries, Chicago** *Also called East Balt Commissary LLC (G-4681)*
**East Balt Bakery of Florida** ... 407 933-2222
1801 W 31st Pl Chicago (60608) *(G-4680)*
**East Balt Commissary LLC** ... 773 376-4444
1801 W 31st Pl Chicago (60608) *(G-4681)*
**East Bank Neon Inc** ... 618 345-9517
8146 Gass Ln Collinsville (62234) *(G-7322)*
**East Central Communications Co** ... 217 892-9613
1332 Harmon Dr Rantoul (61866) *(G-17926)*
**East Coast Signs Advertising** ... 215 458-9042
1418 Elmhurst Rd Elk Grove Village (60007) *(G-9447)*
**East Dbque Ntrgn Frtlizers LLC** ... 815 747-3101
16675 Us Highway 20 W East Dubuque (61025) *(G-8617)*
**East End Express Lube Inc** ... 618 257-1049
928 Carlyle Ave Belleville (62221) *(G-1629)*
**East Moline Herald Print Inc** ... 309 755-5224
824 15th Ave East Moline (61244) *(G-8678)*
**East Savanna Welding** ... 815 273-7371
525 3rd St Apt 215 Savanna (61074) *(G-19396)*
**East Savanna Welding & Repairs, Savanna** *Also called East Savanna Welding (G-19396)*
**East Side Cafe, Warrenville** *Also called Preziosio Ltd (G-21359)*
**East Side Jersey Dairy Inc (HQ)** ... 217 854-2547
1100 Broadway Carlinville (62626) *(G-3036)*
**East Side Tool & Die Co Inc** ... 618 397-1633
2762 N 89th St Caseyville (62232) *(G-3395)*
**East St Louis Monitor Pubg Co, East Saint Louis** *Also called Monitor Newspaper Inc (G-8761)*
**East St Louis Trml & Stor Co** ... 618 271-2185
1501 Lincoln Ave East Saint Louis (62204) *(G-8749)*
**East West Intergrated Therapys** ... 815 788-0574
2719 Red Barn Rd Crystal Lake (60012) *(G-7570)*
**East West Martial Arts Sups** ... 773 878-7711
5544 N Western Ave Chicago (60625) *(G-4682)*
**East Wisconsin LLC** ... 618 224-9133
11 E Wisconsin St Trenton (62293) *(G-20991)*

ALPHABETIC

(PA)=Parent Co (HQ)=Headquarters (DH)=Div Headquarters
2017 Harris Illinois Industrial Directory
1227

**Eastco Inc** .................................................. 708 499-1701
   5500 W 111th St  Oak Lawn  (60453)  *(G-16617)*
**Eastern Accents  Inc** .................................... 773 604-7300
   4201 W Belmont Ave  Chicago  (60641)  *(G-4683)*
**Eastern Company** ........................................ 847 537-1800
   301 W Hintz Rd  Wheeling  (60090)  *(G-22041)*
**Eastern Illinois Clay Company (PA)** ............. 815 427-8144
   460 S Elm Ave  Saint Anne  (60964)  *(G-19120)*
**Eastern Illinois Clay Company** .................... 815 427-8106
   498 S Oak St  Saint Anne  (60964)  *(G-19121)*
**Eastern Kitchen & Bath** .............................. 312 492-7248
   401 N Western Ave Ste 1  Chicago  (60612)  *(G-4684)*
**Eastern Services, Norris City**  Also called B & B Tank Truck Construction  *(G-16111)*
**Eastgate Cleaners** ....................................... 630 627-9494
   837 Westmore-Myers Rd A10  Lombard  (60148)  *(G-13794)*
**Eastland Fabrication LLC** ........................... 815 493-8399
   14273 Il Route 73  Lanark  (61046)  *(G-13152)*
**Eastrich Printing & Sales** ............................ 815 232-4216
   2252 W Galena Ave  Freeport  (61032)  *(G-10654)*
**Eastview Manufacturing Inc** ........................ 847 741-2514
   970 Elizabeth St  Elgin  (60120)  *(G-9019)*
**Eastwood Enterprises Inc** ........................... 847 940-4008
   1020 Chapel Ct  Deerfield  (60015)  *(G-8004)*
**Easy Heat  Inc** ............................................ 847 268-6000
   9377 W Higgins Rd  Rosemont  (60018)  *(G-19000)*
**Easy Pay & Data Inc** .................................... 217 398-9729
   902 N Country Fair Dr # 6  Champaign  (61821)  *(G-3476)*
**Easy Trac Gps  Inc** ...................................... 630 359-5804
   4234 Ridgeland Ave  Berwyn  (60402)  *(G-2061)*
**Easyshow LLC** ............................................ 847 480-7177
   450 Skokie Blvd Ste 1200  Northbrook  (60062)  *(G-16245)*
**Eat Investments  LLC** ................................. 618 624-5350
   3960 Green Mt  O Fallon  (62269)  *(G-16467)*
**Eaton, Highland**  Also called Cooper B-Line  Inc  *(G-11780)*
**Eaton Cor Actuator & Sensor Di, Rochelle**  Also called Eaton Corporation  *(G-18087)*
**Eaton Corporation** ...................................... 217 732-3131
   1725 1200th Ave  Lincoln  (62656)  *(G-13409)*
**Eaton Corporation** ...................................... 815 562-2107
   200 E Avenue G  Rochelle  (61068)  *(G-18087)*
**Eaton Corporation** ...................................... 815 398-6585
   2477 Eastrock Dr Ste B  Rockford  (61108)  *(G-18354)*
**Eaton Hydraulics LLC** ................................. 618 667-2553
   816 Lions Dr  Troy  (62294)  *(G-21006)*
**Eaton Inflatable LLC** ................................... 312 664-7867
   821 W Eastman St  Chicago  (60642)  *(G-4685)*
**Eaton Tool & Machine Inc** ........................... 815 874-6664
   4677 Stenstrom Rd  Rockford  (61109)  *(G-18355)*
**Eazypower Corporation** .............................. 773 278-5000
   2321 N Keystone Ave  Chicago  (60639)  *(G-4686)*
**Eazypower Corporation (PA)** ...................... 773 278-5000
   60639 W Belden St Ste 10  Chicago  (60639)  *(G-4687)*
**Ebe Industrial  LLC** ..................................... 815 379-2400
   507 W North St  Walnut  (61376)  *(G-21330)*
**Eberhart Sign & Lighting Co (PA)** ............... 618 656-7256
   104 1st Ave  Edwardsville  (62025)  *(G-8797)*
**Eberle Manufacturing Company** .................. 847 215-0100
   230 Larkin Dr  Wheeling  (60090)  *(G-22042)*
**Ebers Drilling Co** ........................................ 618 826-5398
   4318 State Route 150  Chester  (62233)  *(G-3655)*
**Eberspaecher North America Inc** ................ 815 544-1421
   725 Logistics Dr  Belvidere  (61008)  *(G-1750)*
**Ebk Containers, Lake In The Hills**  Also called Jodi Maurer  *(G-12996)*
**Ebling Electric Company** ............................ 312 455-1885
   2222 W Hubbard St  Chicago  (60612)  *(G-4688)*
**Ebonyenergy Publishing Inc Nfp** ................. 773 851-5159
   10960 S Prospect Ave  Chicago  (60643)  *(G-4689)*
**Ebooks2go** ................................................. 847 598-1145
   1111 N Plaza Dr Ste 652  Schaumburg  (60173)  *(G-19512)*
**Ebro Foods  Inc** .......................................... 773 696-0150
   1330 W 43rd St  Chicago  (60609)  *(G-4690)*
**Ebro Packing Company, Chicago**  Also called Ebro Foods  Inc  *(G-4690)*
**Ebsco Industries  Inc** ................................. 800 245-7224
   555 W Taft Dr  South Holland  (60473)  *(G-20264)*
**Ebsco Industries  Inc** ................................. 847 244-1800
   2245 N Delany Rd  Waukegan  (60087)  *(G-21556)*
**Ebway Industries Inc** .................................. 630 860-5959
   1201 Ardmore Ave  Itasca  (60143)  *(G-12256)*
**EC Harms Met Fabricators Inc** .................... 309 385-2132
   1017 N Santa Fe Ave  Princeville  (61559)  *(G-17764)*
**Eccofab, Rockford**  Also called Ekstrom Carlson Fabricating Co  *(G-18360)*
**Ecd-Network LLC** ....................................... 917 670-0821
   320 W Ohio St Ste 3w  Chicago  (60654)  *(G-4691)*
**Ecf Holdings  LLC** ...................................... 224 723-5524
   3550 Woodhead Dr  Northbrook  (60062)  *(G-16246)*
**Echo  Incorporated (HQ)** ............................ 847 540-8400
   400 Oakwood Rd  Lake Zurich  (60047)  *(G-13064)*
**Echo  Incorporated** .................................... 847 540-3500
   1000 Rose Rd  Lake Zurich  (60047)  *(G-13065)*
**Echo Prophetstown** .................................... 815 537-5107
   342 Washington St  Prophetstown  (61277)  *(G-17768)*
**Eckert Orchards Inc (PA)** ............................ 618 233-0513
   951 S Green Mount Rd  Belleville  (62220)  *(G-1630)*
**Ecli Products  LLC (HQ)** ............................. 630 449-5000
   3851 Exchange Ave  Aurora  (60504)  *(G-1000)*
**Eclipse  Inc (HQ)** ....................................... 815 877-3031
   1665 Elmwood Rd  Rockford  (61103)  *(G-18356)*
**Eclipse Awnings Inc** ................................... 708 636-3160
   3609 W 95th St  Evergreen Park  (60805)  *(G-10113)*
**Eclipse Combustion Inc (HQ)** ..................... 815 877-3031
   1665 Elmwood Rd  Rockford  (61103)  *(G-18357)*
**Eclipse Lighting  Inc (PA)** ........................... 847 260-0333
   9245 Ivanhoe St  Schiller Park  (60176)  *(G-19823)*
**Eclipse Usa Inc** .......................................... 773 816-0886
   2231 N 75th Ct  Elmwood Park  (60707)  *(G-9967)*
**Eco Green Analytics LLC** ............................ 847 691-1148
   735 Castlewood Ln  Deerfield  (60015)  *(G-8005)*
**Eco Print Mail Consultants, Chicago**  Also called Grace Enterprises  Inc  *(G-4983)*
**Eco-Light, Mount Prospect**  Also called Good Earth Lighting  Inc  *(G-15333)*
**Eco-Pur Solutions  LLC** .............................. 630 917-8789
   694 Veterans Pkwy Ste F  Chicago  (60606)  *(G-4692)*
**Eco-Pur Solutions  LLC** .............................. 630 226-2300
   1245 Naperville Dr  Romeoville  (60446)  *(G-18818)*
**Eco-Tech Plastics LLC** ................................ 262 539-3811
   1519 Woodlark Dr  Northbrook  (60062)  *(G-16247)*
**Ecoco  Inc** ................................................. 773 745-7700
   1830 N Lamon Ave  Chicago  (60639)  *(G-4693)*
**Ecodyne Water Treatment LLC** ................... 630 961-5043
   1270 Frontenac Rd  Naperville  (60563)  *(G-15650)*
**Ecolab, Naperville**  Also called Nalco Company LLC  *(G-15704)*
**Ecolab Ff Aperion Care St** .......................... 618 829-5581
   221 E Cumberland Rd  Saint Elmo  (62458)  *(G-19306)*
**Ecolab Inc** ................................................. 815 389-8132
   5151 E Rockton Rd  Roscoe  (61073)  *(G-18895)*
**Ecolab Inc** ................................................. 815 729-7334
   3001 Channahon Rd  Joliet  (60436)  *(G-12488)*
**Ecolab Inc** ................................................. 847 350-2229
   1060 Thorndale Ave  Elk Grove Village  (60007)  *(G-9448)*
**Ecolab Inc** ................................................. 815 389-4063
   5151 E Rockton Rd  South Beloit  (61080)  *(G-20144)*
**Ecolo-Mid West, Naperville**  Also called Nu-Recycling Technology Inc  *(G-15820)*
**Ecolocap Solutions Inc** .............................. 866 479-7041
   1250 S Grove Ave Ste 308  Barrington  (60010)  *(G-1279)*
**Ecologic  LLC (PA)** ..................................... 630 869-0495
   18w140 Butterfield Rd # 1180  Oakbrook Terrace  (60181)  *(G-16706)*
**Ecologic Industries  LLC** ............................ 847 234-5855
   1472 Saint Paul Ave  Gurnee  (60031)  *(G-11444)*
**Ecology Tech, Aurora**  Also called S & S Metal Recyclers  Inc  *(G-1213)*
**Ecolotech Asl  Inc** ..................................... 630 859-0485
   611 Phoenix Ct  Aurora  (60505)  *(G-1142)*
**Ecomed Solutions  LLC** .............................. 866 817-7114
   214 Terrace Dr  Mundelein  (60060)  *(G-15498)*
**Econodome Kits, Sullivan**  Also called Faze Change Produx  *(G-20746)*
**Economic Coating, Melrose Park**  Also called Economic Plastic Coating Inc  *(G-14627)*
**Economic Plastic Coating Inc** .................... 708 343-2216
   1829 Gardner Rd  Melrose Park  (60160)  *(G-14627)*
**Economy Iron Inc** ...................................... 708 343-1777
   3132 W Hirsch St  Melrose Park  (60160)  *(G-14628)*
**Econopin** .................................................. 708 599-5002
   8540 S Thomas Ave  Bridgeview  (60455)  *(G-2486)*
**Ecool LLC** ................................................. 309 966-3701
   350 N Walnut St  Champaign  (61820)  *(G-3477)*
**Ecothermics Corporation** ........................... 217 621-2402
   3880 N Main St Ste D  Peoria  (61611)  *(G-17483)*
**Ecoturf Midwest Inc** ................................... 630 350-9500
   789 Golf Ln  Bensenville  (60106)  *(G-1888)*
**Ecp Incorporated** ....................................... 630 754-4200
   11210 Katherines Xing # 100  Woodridge  (60517)  *(G-22474)*
**Ecsi, Springfield**  Also called Envirnmntal Ctrl Solutions Inc  *(G-20435)*
**Ed Co** ....................................................... 708 614-0695
   8304 Lilac Ln  Tinley Park  (60477)  *(G-20909)*
**ED Etnyre & Co** .......................................... 815 732-2116
   1333 S Daysville Rd  Oregon  (61061)  *(G-16822)*
**Ed Garvey and Company (PA)** ..................... 847 647-1900
   7400 N Lehigh Ave  Niles  (60714)  *(G-15976)*
**Ed Hartwig Trucking & Excvtg** .................... 309 364-3672
   312 Jefferson St  Henry  (61537)  *(G-11740)*
**Ed Hill S Custom Canvas** ........................... 815 476-5042
   8655 E Mallard Ln  Wilmington  (60481)  *(G-22271)*
**Ed Kabrick Beef Inc** .................................... 217 656-3263
   218 E Main St  Plainville  (62365)  *(G-17662)*
**Ed Stan Fabricating Co** ............................... 708 863-7668
   4859 W Ogden Ave  Chicago  (60804)  *(G-4694)*
**Ed Weitekamp Inc** ..................................... 217 229-4239
   5046 N 23rd Ave  Raymond  (62560)  *(G-17938)*
**Eddie Gapastione** ...................................... 708 430-3881
   8927 S Octavia Ave  Bridgeview  (60455)  *(G-2487)*
**Eddie Z'S, La Grange**  Also called EZ Blinds and Drapery  Inc  *(G-12731)*
**Eddies Cousin Inc** ..................................... 217 679-5777
   1951 W Monroe St  Springfield  (62704)  *(G-20432)*

**Eden Fuels LLC** .......... 847 676-9470
5025 Old Orchard Rd  Skokie  (60077)  *(G-19991)*

**Eden Park Illumination Inc** .......... 217 403-1866
903 N Country Fair Dr  Champaign  (61821)  *(G-3478)*

**Eden's and Old Orchard's Shell, Skokie** Also called Eden Fuels LLC *(G-19991)*

**Edgar A Weber & Company** .......... 847 215-1980
549 Palwaukee Dr  Wheeling  (60090)  *(G-22043)*

**Edgar A Weber & Company** .......... 847 215-1980
549 Palwaukee Dr  Wheeling  (60090)  *(G-22044)*

**Edgar County Locker Service** .......... 217 466-5000
116 E Steidl Rd  Paris  (61944)  *(G-17147)*

**Edgar H Fey Jewelers Inc (PA)** .......... 708 352-4115
833 N Washington St  Naperville  (60563)  *(G-15651)*

**Edgar Pallets** .......... 773 454-8919
4122 W Ogden Ave  Chicago  (60623)  *(G-4695)*

**Edgars Custom Cabinets** .......... 847 928-0922
3315 Dora St  Franklin Park  (60131)  *(G-10463)*

**Edge Communication** .......... 708 749-7818
3825 Kenilworth Ave  Berwyn  (60402)  *(G-2062)*

**Edge Electronics, Kirkland** Also called RB Manufacturing & Electronics *(G-12717)*

**Edge Mold Corporation** .......... 630 616-8108
885 Fairway Dr  Bensenville  (60106)  *(G-1889)*

**Edgebrook Eyecare** .......... 815 397-5959
1603 N Alpine Rd Ste 121  Rockford  (61107)  *(G-18358)*

**Edgetool Industrial Supplies, Waukegan** Also called David Linderholm *(G-21548)*

**Edgewater Products Company Inc** .......... 708 345-9200
3315 W North Ave  Melrose Park  (60160)  *(G-14629)*

**Edgewell Per Care Brands LLC** .......... 708 544-5550
5000 Proviso Dr  Melrose Park  (60163)  *(G-14630)*

**Edgo Technical Sales Inc** .......... 630 961-8398
9s131 Skylane Dr  Naperville  (60564)  *(G-15803)*

**Edison Electric** .......... 815 464-1006
21851 Blue Bird Ln  Frankfort  (60423)  *(G-10319)*

**Edison Graphics, Des Plaines** Also called Wyka LLC *(G-8306)*

**Edison Pallet & Wood Products** .......... 630 653-3416
371 County Farm Rd  Winfield  (60190)  *(G-22285)*

**Edk Construction Inc** .......... 630 853-3484
1325 Chapman Dr  Darien  (60561)  *(G-7793)*

**Edlong Corporation (PA)** .......... 847 439-9230
225 Scott St  Elk Grove Village  (60007)  *(G-9449)*

**Edlong Flavors, Elk Grove Village** Also called Edlong Corporation *(G-9449)*

**EDM Department, Bartlett** Also called EDM Dept Inc *(G-1343)*

**EDM Dept Inc** .......... 630 736-0531
1261 Humbracht Cir Ste A  Bartlett  (60103)  *(G-1343)*

**EDM Scorpio Inc** .......... 847 931-5164
84 Joslyn Dr  Elgin  (60120)  *(G-9020)*

**Edmark Visual Identification** .......... 800 923-8333
4552 N Kilbourn Ave  Chicago  (60630)  *(G-4696)*

**Edmik Inc** .......... 847 263-0460
3850 Grove Ave  Gurnee  (60031)  *(G-11445)*

**Edmik Plastics, Gurnee** Also called Edmik Inc *(G-11445)*

**Edmpartscom Inc** .......... 630 427-1603
8197 S Lemont Rd  Darien  (60561)  *(G-7794)*

**Edmund D Schmelzie & Sons** .......... 312 782-7230
29 E Madison St Ste 1214  Chicago  (60602)  *(G-4697)*

**Edoc Communications, Mount Prospect** Also called PHI Group Inc *(G-15364)*

**Edovo, Chicago** Also called Jail Education Solutions Inc *(G-5272)*

**Edqu Media LLC** .......... 773 803-9793
9158 S Michigan Ave  Chicago  (60619)  *(G-4698)*

**EDR ELECTRONICS INC., Arlington Heights** Also called Box of Rain Ltd *(G-727)*

**Edrington Group Usa LLC** .......... 630 701-9202
1600 16th St  Oak Brook  (60523)  *(G-16505)*

**Eds Pallet Service** .......... 618 248-5386
409 N Commercial St  Albers  (62215)  *(G-353)*

**Edsal Manufacturing Co Inc (PA)** .......... 773 475-3020
4400 S Packers Ave  Chicago  (60609)  *(G-4699)*

**Edsal Manufacturing Co Inc** .......... 773 475-3013
1555 W 44th St  Chicago  (60609)  *(G-4700)*

**Education Partners Project Ltd** .......... 773 675-6643
4800 S Chicago Beach Dr 1901s  Chicago  (60615)  *(G-4701)*

**Educational Directories Inc** .......... 847 891-1250
1025 W Wise Rd Ste 101  Schaumburg  (60193)  *(G-19513)*

**Educational Insights Inc** .......... 847 573-8400
380 N Fairway Dr  Vernon Hills  (60061)  *(G-21158)*

**Educational Resources, Hoffman Estates** Also called HMS Teach Inc *(G-12016)*

**Edventure Promotions Inc** .......... 312 440-1800
770 N La Salle Dr Ste 500  Chicago  (60654)  *(G-4702)*

**Edward F Data** .......... 708 597-0158
12625 S Kroll Dr  Alsip  (60803)  *(G-461)*

**Edward Fields Incorporated** .......... 312 644-0400
222 Merchandise Mart Plz # 635  Chicago  (60654)  *(G-4703)*

**Edward Hull Cabinet Shop** .......... 217 864-3011
1310 N State Highway 121  Mount Zion  (62549)  *(G-15450)*

**Edward J Warren Jr** .......... 630 882-8817
2921 Alden Ave  Yorkville  (60560)  *(G-22657)*

**Edwards County Concrete LLC** .......... 618 445-2711
327 Industrial Dr  Albion  (62806)  *(G-361)*

**Edwards Creative Services LLC** .......... 309 756-0199
435 1st St E  Milan  (61264)  *(G-14784)*

**Edwardsville Intelligencer, Edwardsville** Also called Edwardsville Publishing Co *(G-8799)*

**Edwardsville Mch & Wldg Co Inc** .......... 618 656-5145
1509 Troy Rd  Edwardsville  (62025)  *(G-8798)*

**Edwardsville Publishing Co** .......... 618 656-4700
117 N 2nd St  Edwardsville  (62025)  *(G-8799)*

**Edwardsville Water Treatment** .......... 618 692-7053
3735 Wanda Rd  Edwardsville  (62025)  *(G-8800)*

**Edwin Waldmire & Virginia** .......... 217 498-9375
Hc 2  Rochester  (62563)  *(G-18117)*

**Eenigenburg Mfg Inc** .......... 708 474-0850
19530 Burnham Ave  Lansing  (60438)  *(G-13161)*

**Ees Inc** .......... 708 343-1800
4300 W North Ave  Stone Park  (60165)  *(G-20633)*

**Efco Corporation** .......... 630 378-4720
595 Territorial Dr Ste A  Bolingbrook  (60440)  *(G-2303)*

**Effective Energy Assoc LLC** .......... 815 248-9280
1979 Sunline Dr  Davis  (61019)  *(G-7805)*

**Effici Inc** .......... 401 584-2266
939 N Plum Grove Rd  Schaumburg  (60173)  *(G-19514)*

**Efficient Energy Lighting Inc** .......... 630 272-9388
530 Hopkins Ln  Sycamore  (60178)  *(G-20796)*

**Effimax Solar** .......... 217 550-2422
60 Hazelwood Dr  Champaign  (61820)  *(G-3479)*

**Effingham Daily News, Effingham** Also called Newspaper Holding Inc *(G-8850)*

**Effingham Equity Inc** .......... 217 268-5128
912 E County Road 600n  Arcola  (61910)  *(G-668)*

**Effingham Monument Co Inc** .......... 217 857-6085
Rr 33 Box E  Effingham  (62401)  *(G-8835)*

**Effingham Printing Company, Effingham** Also called Rusty & Angela Buzzard *(G-8857)*

**Effingham Signs & Graphics** .......... 217 347-8711
1009 S Oak St  Effingham  (62401)  *(G-8836)*

**Eg Group Inc** .......... 309 692-0968
8703 N University St F  Peoria  (61615)  *(G-17352)*

**Egan Visual/West Inc** .......... 800 266-2387
222 W Merchandise Mart Pl Ste 1079  Chicago  (60654)  *(G-4704)*

**Egan Wagner Corporation** .......... 630 985-8007
2929 Two Paths Dr  Woodridge  (60517)  *(G-22475)*

**Egd Manufacturing Inc** .......... 815 964-2900
2320 Kishwaukee St  Rockford  (61104)  *(G-18359)*

**Egg Cream America Inc (PA)** .......... 847 559-2700
633 Skokie Blvd Ste 200  Northbrook  (60062)  *(G-16248)*

**Egp, Chicago** Also called Engineered Glass Products LLC *(G-4754)*

**Ehrhardt Tool & Machine LLC** .......... 314 436-6900
25 Central Industrial Dr  Granite City  (62040)  *(G-11274)*

**Ehs Solutions LLC** .......... 309 282-9121
1530 W Altorfer Dr  Peoria  (61615)  *(G-17353)*

**Eichen Lumber Co Inc** .......... 217 854-9751
20002 Claremont Rd  Carlinville  (62626)  *(G-3037)*

**Eichen's Saw Mill, Carlinville** Also called Charles K Eichen *(G-3034)*

**Eickmans Processing Co Inc** .......... 815 247-8451
3226 S Pecatonica Rd  Seward  (61077)  *(G-19896)*

**Eiesland Builders Inc** .......... 847 998-1731
2041 Johns Dr  Glenview  (60025)  *(G-11123)*

**Eiesland Woodwork, Glenview** Also called Eiesland Builders Inc *(G-11123)*

**Eifeler Coatings Tech Inc** .......... 630 587-1220
3800 Commerce Dr  Saint Charles  (60174)  *(G-19178)*

**Eifeler-Lafer Inc., Saint Charles** Also called Eifeler Coatings Tech Inc *(G-19178)*

**Eighty Nine Robotics LLC** .......... 512 573-9091
965 W Chicago Ave  Chicago  (60642)  *(G-4705)*

**Eikenberry Sheet Metal Works** .......... 815 625-0955
412 E 3rd St  Sterling  (61081)  *(G-20590)*

**Einstein Crest** .......... 847 965-7791
9347 N Milwaukee Ave  Niles  (60714)  *(G-15977)*

**Eirich Machines Inc** .......... 847 336-2444
4033 Ryan Rd  Gurnee  (60031)  *(G-11446)*

**Eis** .......... 630 530-7500
752 N Larch Ave  Elmhurst  (60126)  *(G-9863)*

**Eisendrath Inc** .......... 847 432-3899
716 Central Ave Apt B  Highland Park  (60035)  *(G-11830)*

**Eisenhower High School - Blue** .......... 708 385-6815
12700 Sacramento Ave  Blue Island  (60406)  *(G-2248)*

**EJ Cady & Company** .......... 847 537-2239
135 Wheeling Rd  Wheeling  (60090)  *(G-22045)*

**Ej Somerville Plating Co** .......... 708 345-5100
1305 N 31st Ave  Melrose Park  (60160)  *(G-14631)*

**Ej Usa Inc** .......... 815 740-1640
310 Garnet Dr  New Lenox  (60451)  *(G-15879)*

**EJL Custom Golf Clubs Inc (PA)** .......... 630 654-8887
825 75th St Ste F  Willowbrook  (60527)  *(G-22210)*

**Ek Success Brands, Woodridge** Also called Wilton Brands LLC *(G-22526)*

**Eklind Tool Co** .......... 847 994-8550
11040 King St  Franklin Park  (60131)  *(G-10464)*

**Eklund Metal Treating Inc** .......... 815 877-7436
721 Beacon St  Loves Park  (61111)  *(G-13939)*

**Eklunds Typesetting & Prtg LLC** .......... 630 924-0057
11 W Irving Park Rd  Roselle  (60172)  *(G-18940)*

**Eks Fiber Optics LP** .......... 312 291-4482
150 N Michigan Ave  Chicago  (60601)  *(G-4706)*

# ALPHABETIC SECTION

**Ekstrom Carlson Fabricating Co** ..................................... 815 226-1511
1204 Milford Ave  Rockford  (61109)  *(G-18360)*
**El Campeon Food Products, Chicago** *Also called Sparrer Sausage Company Inc (G-6551)*
**El Dia Newspaper** ..................................... 708 956-7282
6331 26th St Apt 1  Berwyn  (60402)  *(G-2063)*
**El Encanto Products  Inc** ..................................... 773 940-1807
4041 W Ogden Ave Ste 12  Chicago  (60623)  *(G-4707)*
**El Giloy Specialty Metals, Hampshire** *Also called Combined Metals Chicago LLC (G-11545)*
**El Greg Pizza, Chicago** *Also called Greg El- Inc (G-5001)*
**El Moro De Letran Churros & Ba** ..................................... 312 733-3173
1626 S Blue Island Ave  Chicago  (60608)  *(G-4708)*
**El Paso Journal** ..................................... 309 527-8595
51 W Front St  El Paso  (61738)  *(G-8869)*
**El Popocatapetl Industries Inc** ..................................... 773 843-0888
4246 W 47th St  Chicago  (60632)  *(G-4709)*
**El Popocatapetl Industries Inc (PA)** ..................................... 312 421-6143
1854 W 21st St  Chicago  (60608)  *(G-4710)*
**El Sol Dechicago Newspaper** ..................................... 773 235-7655
4217 W Fullerton Ave  Chicago  (60639)  *(G-4711)*
**El Tradicional** ..................................... 773 925-0335
7647 S Kedzie Ave  Chicago  (60652)  *(G-4712)*
**El-Milagro  Inc (PA)** ..................................... 773 579-6120
3050 W 26th St  Chicago  (60623)  *(G-4713)*
**El-Milagro  Inc** ..................................... 773 650-1614
2919 S Western Ave Fl 1  Chicago  (60608)  *(G-4714)*
**El-Ranchero Food Products** ..................................... 773 843-0430
4457 S Kildare Ave  Chicago  (60632)  *(G-4715)*
**El-Ranchero Food Products (PA)** ..................................... 773 847-9167
2547 S Kedzie Ave  Chicago  (60623)  *(G-4716)*
**Elan Express  Inc** ..................................... 815 713-1190
3815 N Mulford Rd Ste 4  Rockford  (61114)  *(G-18361)*
**Elan Furs** ..................................... 317 255-6100
3841 E 82nd St  Morton Grove  (60053)  *(G-15195)*
**Elan Industries  Inc** ..................................... 630 679-2000
650 S Schmidt Rd Ard  Bolingbrook  (60440)  *(G-2304)*
**Elanza Technologies Inc** ..................................... 312 396-4187
500 N Michigan Ave # 600  Chicago  (60611)  *(G-4717)*
**Elas Tek Molding Inc** ..................................... 815 675-9012
7517 Meyer Rd Ste 1  Spring Grove  (60081)  *(G-20335)*
**Elastec  Inc (PA)** ..................................... 618 382-2525
1309 W Main St  Carmi  (62821)  *(G-3066)*
**Elastec / American Marine, Carmi** *Also called Elastec  Inc (G-3066)*
**Elastek Molding, Spring Grove** *Also called Elas Tek Molding Inc (G-20335)*
**Elastocon Tpe Technologies Inc** ..................................... 217 498-8500
3105 E Dotmar Dr  Springfield  (62703)  *(G-20433)*
**Elba Tool Co Inc** ..................................... 847 895-4100
220 Covington Dr  Bloomingdale  (60108)  *(G-2105)*
**Elburn Herald, Saint Charles** *Also called Kaneland Publications Inc (G-19203)*
**Elburn Market Inc** ..................................... 630 365-6461
250 S Main St  Elburn  (60119)  *(G-8884)*
**Elburn Metal Stamping  Inc** ..................................... 630 365-2500
44w210 Keslinger Rd  Elburn  (60119)  *(G-8885)*
**Elc Industries Corp** ..................................... 630 851-1616
325 S Union St  Aurora  (60505)  *(G-1143)*
**Elc Industries Corp** ..................................... 630 851-1616
401 Hankes Ave  Aurora  (60505)  *(G-1144)*
**Elcast Lighting, Addison** *Also called Elcast Manufacturing Inc (G-107)*
**Elcast Manufacturing Inc** ..................................... 630 628-1992
815 S Kay Ave Ste B  Addison  (60101)  *(G-107)*
**Elco Laboratories  Inc (PA)** ..................................... 708 534-3000
2450 W Horner Ave  University Park  (60484)  *(G-21047)*
**Elcon Inc (PA)** ..................................... 815 467-9500
600 Twin Rail Dr  Minooka  (60447)  *(G-14840)*
**Eldest Daughter LLC** ..................................... 949 677-7385
1305 N Damen Ave  Chicago  (60622)  *(G-4718)*
**Eldorado Daily Journal, Eldorado** *Also called Sun-Times Media Group  Inc (G-8923)*
**Elec Easel** ..................................... 815 444-9700
2600 Behan Rd  Crystal Lake  (60014)  *(G-7571)*
**Election Services Division, Rockford** *Also called Election Systems & Sftwr LLC (G-18362)*
**Election Systems & Sftwr LLC** ..................................... 815 397-8144
929 S Alpine Rd Ste 301  Rockford  (61108)  *(G-18362)*
**Electri-Flex Company (del)** ..................................... 630 307-1095
222 Central Ave  Roselle  (60172)  *(G-18941)*
**Electric Conduit Cnstr Co** ..................................... 630 293-4474
816 Hicks Dr  Elburn  (60119)  *(G-8886)*
**Electric Conduit Construction** ..................................... 630 859-9310
601 E North St  Elburn  (60119)  *(G-8887)*
**Electric Grand** ..................................... 630 363-8893
2252 Cornell Ave  Montgomery  (60538)  *(G-15042)*
**Electric Motor Corp** ..................................... 773 725-1050
3865 N Milwaukee Ave  Chicago  (60641)  *(G-4719)*
**Electric Supply Direct, Burr Ridge** *Also called Etcon Corp (G-2840)*
**Electric Vehicle Technologies** ..................................... 847 673-8330
7320 Linder Ave  Skokie  (60077)  *(G-19992)*
**Electrical Equipment Corp, Chicago** *Also called Amphenol Eec  Inc (G-3894)*
**Electrical Safety Testing Eqp, Lake Forest** *Also called Ikonix Group  Inc (G-12916)*
**Electrmchnical Bench Reference, Chicago** *Also called Barks Publications Inc (G-4044)*
**Electro Freeze, East Moline** *Also called HC Duke & Son LLC (G-8681)*

**Electro Motive Diesel, Mc Cook** *Also called Progress Rail Locomotive Inc (G-14456)*
**Electro-Circuits  Inc** ..................................... 630 339-3389
1651 Mitchell Blvd  Schaumburg  (60193)  *(G-19515)*
**Electro-Glo Distribution Inc** ..................................... 815 224-4030
316 Raccuglia Dr  La Salle  (61301)  *(G-12771)*
**Electro-Matic Products Co** ..................................... 773 235-4010
2235 N Knox Ave  Chicago  (60639)  *(G-4720)*
**Electro-Max  Inc** ..................................... 847 683-4100
105 Rowell Rd Ste D  Hampshire  (60140)  *(G-11548)*
**Electro-Technic Products  Inc** ..................................... 773 561-2349
4642 N Ravenswood Ave  Chicago  (60640)  *(G-4721)*
**Electroform Company (PA)** ..................................... 815 633-1113
11070 Raleigh Ct  Machesney Park  (61115)  *(G-14072)*
**Electrohone Technologies Inc** ..................................... 815 363-5536
4615 Prime Pkwy  McHenry  (60050)  *(G-14501)*
**Electrolizing Inc (HQ)** ..................................... 815 758-6657
114 Simonds Ave  Dekalb  (60115)  *(G-8089)*
**Electron Beam Technologies Inc** ..................................... 815 935-2211
1275 Harvard Dr  Kankakee  (60901)  *(G-12612)*
**Electronic Assembly Corp** ..................................... 847 793-4400
2400 Millbrook Dr  Buffalo Grove  (60089)  *(G-2690)*
**Electronic Design & Mfg Inc** ..................................... 847 550-1912
1225 Flex Ct  Lake Zurich  (60047)  *(G-13066)*
**Electronic Displays  Inc** ..................................... 630 628-0658
135 S Church St  Addison  (60101)  *(G-108)*
**Electronic Equipment Exchange, Danville** *Also called Vermilion Steel Fabrication (G-7778)*
**Electronic Interconnect Corp** ..................................... 847 364-4848
2375 Estes Ave  Elk Grove Village  (60007)  *(G-9450)*
**Electronic Plating Co** ..................................... 708 652-8100
1821 S 54th Ave  Cicero  (60804)  *(G-7193)*
**Electronic Resources Corp** ..................................... 630 620-0725
920 N Ridge Ave Ste A8  Lombard  (60148)  *(G-13795)*
**Electronic System Design Inc** ..................................... 847 358-8212
225 Foster Ave  Bensenville  (60106)  *(G-1890)*
**Electronic Technology Group, South Holland** *Also called Techno - Grphics Trnsltons Inc (G-20308)*
**Electronica Aviation LLC** ..................................... 407 498-1092
150 S Wacker Dr Ste 2403  Chicago  (60606)  *(G-4722)*
**Electronics Boutique Amer Inc** ..................................... 618 465-3125
128 Alton Sq  Alton  (62002)  *(G-574)*
**Electrostatic Concepts  Inc** ..................................... 630 585-5080
31w335 Schoger Dr  Naperville  (60564)  *(G-15804)*
**Electrowire, Schaumburg** *Also called Hamalot  Inc (G-19547)*
**Elegance In Awards & Gifts, Chicago** *Also called R S Owens & Co  Inc (G-6273)*
**Elegant Acquisition LLC** ..................................... 708 652-3400
5253 W Roosevelt Rd  Cicero  (60804)  *(G-7194)*
**Elegant Concepts Ltd** ..................................... 708 456-9590
7444 W Grand Ave  Elmwood Park  (60707)  *(G-9968)*
**Elegant Embroidery  Inc** ..................................... 847 540-8003
100 Oakwood Rd Ste C  Lake Zurich  (60047)  *(G-13067)*
**Elegant Packaging, Cicero** *Also called Elegant Acquisition LLC (G-7194)*
**Elektron N Magnesium Amer Inc (HQ)** ..................................... 618 452-5190
1001 College St  Madison  (62060)  *(G-14144)*
**Elematec USA Corporation** ..................................... 847 466-1451
500 Park Blvd Ste 760  Itasca  (60143)  *(G-12257)*
**Elemech  Inc** ..................................... 630 417-2845
2275 White Oak Cir Aurora  Aurora  (60502)  *(G-1001)*
**Element Bars  Inc** ..................................... 888 411-3536
5001 W Belmont Ave  Chicago  (60641)  *(G-4723)*
**Element Collection** ..................................... 217 898-5175
2731 County Road 100 N  Allerton  (61810)  *(G-421)*
**Element14 Inc** ..................................... 773 784-5100
300 S Riverside Plz # 2200  Chicago  (60606)  *(G-4724)*
**Elemental Art Jewelry** ..................................... 773 844-4812
5917 N Broadway St  Chicago  (60660)  *(G-4725)*
**Elementbars.com, Chicago** *Also called Element Bars  Inc (G-4723)*
**Elements Group** ..................................... 312 664-2252
2033 N Larrabee St  Chicago  (60614)  *(G-4726)*
**Elenco Electronics  Inc** ..................................... 847 541-3800
150 Carpenter Ave  Wheeling  (60090)  *(G-22046)*
**Elevance Rnewable Sciences Inc (PA)** ..................................... 630 296-8880
2501 Davey Rd  Woodridge  (60517)  *(G-22476)*
**Elevator Cable & Supply Co** ..................................... 708 338-9700
2741 S 21st Ave  Broadview  (60155)  *(G-2574)*
**Elevators USA Incorporated** ..................................... 847 847-1856
932 Donata Ct  Lake Zurich  (60047)  *(G-13068)*
**Elexa Commercial Products, Deerfield** *Also called Elexa Consumer Products  Inc (G-8006)*
**Elexa Consumer Products  Inc** ..................................... 773 794-1300
2275 Half Day Rd Ste 333  Deerfield  (60015)  *(G-8006)*
**Elfi  LLC** ..................................... 815 439-1833
6001 S Knox Ave  Chicago  (60629)  *(G-4727)*
**Elfi Wall Systems, Chicago** *Also called Elfi LLC (G-4727)*
**Elfring Fonts Inc** ..................................... 630 377-3520
2020 Dean St Ste N  Saint Charles  (60174)  *(G-19179)*
**Elg Metals  Inc** ..................................... 773 374-1500
103rd St The Calumet Riv  Chicago  (60617)  *(G-4728)*
**Elgalabwater  LLC** ..................................... 630 343-5251
5 Earl Ct Ste 100  Woodridge  (60517)  *(G-22477)*

**Elgiloy Specialty Metals**...847 683-0500
1 Hauk Rd Hampshire (60140) *(G-11549)*
**Elgin CAM Co**...847 741-1757
425 Shepard Dr Elgin (60123) *(G-9021)*
**Elgin Center Pharmacy Inc**...847 697-1600
1554 Todd Farm Dr Elgin (60123) *(G-9022)*
**Elgin Die Mold Co**...847 464-0140
14n002 Prairie St Pingree Grove (60140) *(G-17555)*
**Elgin Engineering Center, Elgin** *Also called Nidec Motor Corporation (G-9123)*
**Elgin Equipment Group LLC (HQ)**...630 434-7200
2001 Bttrfeld Rd Ste 1020 Downers Grove (60515) *(G-8439)*
**Elgin Granite Works, Saint Charles** *Also called St Charles Memorial Works Inc (G-19268)*
**Elgin Industries Inc (PA)**...847 742-1720
1100 Jansen Farm Dr Elgin (60123) *(G-9023)*
**Elgin Instant Print**...847 931-9006
293 S Aldine St Elgin (60123) *(G-9024)*
**Elgin Molded Plastics Inc (PA)**...847 931-2455
909 Grace St Elgin (60120) *(G-9025)*
**Elgin National Industries Inc (PA)**...630 434-7200
2001 Bttrfeld Rd Ste 1020 Downers Grove (60515) *(G-8440)*
**Elgin Sheet Metal Co**...847 742-3486
695 Schneider Dr Ste 1 South Elgin (60177) *(G-20194)*
**Elgin Sweeper Company**...847 741-5370
1300 W Bartlett Rd Elgin (60120) *(G-9026)*
**Elginex Corporation**...815 786-8406
1002 E 3rd St Sandwich (60548) *(G-19362)*
**Elgo Electronic Inc**...630 626-1639
1261 Hardt Cir Bartlett (60103) *(G-1344)*
**Eli Morris Group LLC**...773 314-7173
4335 W 21st St Chicago (60623) *(G-4729)*
**Elia Day Spa**...708 535-1450
5251 147th St Ste 3 Oak Forest (60452) *(G-16579)*
**Elim Pdtric Phrmaceuticals Inc**...412 266-5968
Corp Ctr 1600 Glf Rd 12 Rolling Meadows (60008) *(G-18727)*
**Elimparcial Newspaper, Cicero** *Also called Teleguia Inc (G-7237)*
**Elis Cheesecake Company**...773 205-3800
6701 W Forest Preserve Dr Chicago (60634) *(G-4730)*
**Elise S Allen**...309 673-2613
1600 Mrtn Lthr Kng Jr Dr Peoria (61605) *(G-17354)*
**Elite Access Systems Inc**...800 528-5880
845 N Larch Ave Elmhurst (60126) *(G-9864)*
**Elite Custom Woodworking**...630 888-4322
219 S Water St Batavia (60510) *(G-1446)*
**Elite Die & Finishing Inc**...708 389-4848
358 W Armory Dr South Holland (60473) *(G-20265)*
**Elite Extrusion Technology Inc**...630 485-2020
3620 Ohio Ave Saint Charles (60174) *(G-19180)*
**Elite Fabrication Inc**...773 274-4474
1524 W Jarvis Ave Chicago (60626) *(G-4731)*
**Elite Fasteners Inc**...815 397-8848
2005 15th St Rockford (61104) *(G-18363)*
**Elite Fiber Optics LLC**...630 225-9454
616 Enterprise Dr Ste 102 Oak Brook (60523) *(G-16506)*
**Elite Imaging**...618 632-2900
317 Salem Pl Ste 130 East Saint Louis (62208) *(G-8750)*
**Elite Impressions & Graphics**...847 695-3730
645 Stevenson Rd South Elgin (60177) *(G-20195)*
**Elite Industries**...224 433-6988
5710 Des Plaines Ct Gurnee (60031) *(G-11447)*
**Elite Kids**...815 451-9600
825 Munshaw Ln Crystal Lake (60014) *(G-7572)*
**Elite Machining Co**...708 308-0947
8435 S 77th Ct Bridgeview (60455) *(G-2488)*
**Elite Manufacturer LLC**...779 777-3857
1402 Laurel Oaks Dr Streamwood (60107) *(G-20653)*
**Elite Manufacturing Tech Inc**...630 351-5757
333 Munroe Dr Bloomingdale (60108) *(G-2106)*
**Elite McHning of Chicago Ridge**...708 423-0767
6655 99th St Chicago Ridge (60415) *(G-7146)*
**Elite Monument Co**...217 532-6080
1119 School St Hillsboro (62049) *(G-11889)*
**Elite Power Boats Inc**...618 654-6292
3645 George St Highland (62249) *(G-11785)*
**Elite Precious Metals Inc**...312 929-3055
1440 W Taylor St Ste 315 Chicago (60607) *(G-4732)*
**Elite Publishing and Design**...888 237-8119
616 Abington St Peoria (61603) *(G-17355)*
**Elite Wireworks Corporation**...630 837-9100
1239 Humbracht Cir Bartlett (60103) *(G-1345)*
**Elitegen Corp**...630 637-6917
1112 Sheldon Ct Naperville (60540) *(G-15652)*
**Elk Grove Corrugated Plant, Elk Grove Village** *Also called Weyerhaeuser Company (G-9811)*
**Elk Grove Custom Sheet Metal**...847 352-2845
106 N Lively Blvd Elk Grove Village (60007) *(G-9451)*
**Elk Grove Recycle, Elk Grove Village** *Also called Legacy Vulcan LLC (G-9593)*
**Elk Grove Rubber & Plastic Co**...630 543-5656
99 W Commercial Ave Addison (60101) *(G-109)*
**Elk Grove Signs Inc**...847 427-0005
1670 Greenleaf Ave Elk Grove Village (60007) *(G-9452)*
**Elk Heating & Sheet Metal Inc**...618 251-4747
473 N Wood River Ave Wood River (62095) *(G-22442)*
**Elkay Manufacturing Company**...815 493-8850
105 N Rochester St Lanark (61046) *(G-13153)*
**Elkay Manufacturing Company**...708 681-1880
2700 S 17th Ave Broadview (60155) *(G-2575)*
**Elkay Manufacturing Company**...815 273-7001
6400 Penn Ave Savanna (61074) *(G-19397)*
**Elkay Manufacturing Company**...630 574-8484
2700 S 17th Ave Broadview (60155) *(G-2576)*
**Elkay Plumbing Products Co (HQ)**...630 574-8484
2222 Camden Ct Oak Brook (60523) *(G-16507)*
**Elkay Vrgnia Dcrative Surfaces**...630 574-8484
2222 Camden Ct Oak Brook (60523) *(G-16508)*
**Ella Engineering Incorporated**...847 354-4767
800 Morse Ave Elk Grove Village (60007) *(G-9453)*
**Elle Magazine, Chicago** *Also called Hearst Corporation (G-5065)*
**Ellers Custom Cabinets Inc**...309 633-0101
17956 Springfield Rd Groveland (61535) *(G-11415)*
**Elliot Institute For Social SC**...217 525-8202
524 E Lawrence Ave Springfield (62703) *(G-20434)*
**Elliott Aviation Arcft Sls Inc**...309 799-3183
6601 74th Ave Milan (61264) *(G-14785)*
**Elliott Jsj & Associates Inc**...847 242-0412
194 Green Bay Rd Glencoe (60022) *(G-10999)*
**Elliott Machine & Tool Corp**...630 543-6755
511 W Interstate Rd Addison (60101) *(G-110)*
**Elliott Publishing Inc**...217 645-3033
103 E Hannibal St Liberty (62347) *(G-13295)*
**Elliott Publishing Inc**...217 593-6515
202 E State St Camp Point (62320) *(G-2972)*
**Ellis Corporation (PA)**...630 250-9222
1400 W Bryn Mawr Ave Itasca (60143) *(G-12258)*
**Ellners Welding and Machine Sp**...618 282-4302
8421 Nathan Ln Prairie Du Rocher (62277) *(G-17739)*
**Ellwood Group Inc**...815 725-9030
4166 Mound Rd Joliet (60436) *(G-12489)*
**Elm Products Corp**...847 336-0020
2233 Northwestern Ave F Waukegan (60087) *(G-21557)*
**Elm Street Design Inc**...815 455-3622
3916 Overland Rd Crystal Lake (60012) *(G-7573)*
**Elm Street Industries Inc**...309 854-7000
206 W 4th St Kewanee (61443) *(G-12681)*
**Elm Tool and Manufacturing Co**...847 455-6805
10257 Dickens Ave Melrose Park (60164) *(G-14632)*
**Elmed Incorporated**...630 543-2792
35 N Brandon Dr Glendale Heights (60139) *(G-11021)*
**Elmer L Larson L C (PA)**...815 895-4837
21218 Airport Rd Sycamore (60178) *(G-20797)*
**Elmhurst Enterprise Group Inc**...847 228-5945
11 E Golf Rd Arlington Heights (60005) *(G-749)*
**Elmhurst-Chicago Stone Company (PA)**...630 832-4000
400 W 1st St Elmhurst (60126) *(G-9865)*
**Elmhurst-Chicago Stone Company**...630 557-2446
45 W 371 Main Kaneville (60144) *(G-12599)*
**Elmhurst-Chicago Stone Company**...630 983-6410
351 Royce Rd Bolingbrook (60440) *(G-2305)*
**Elmos Tombstone Service**...773 643-0200
6023 S State St Chicago (60621) *(G-4733)*
**Elmot Inc**...773 791-7039
4923 W Fullerton Ave Chicago (60639) *(G-4734)*
**Elmwood Locker Service, Elmwood** *Also called Powers John (G-9965)*
**Eln Group LLC**...847 477-1496
39 Longmeadow Rd Winnetka (60093) *(G-22305)*
**Elona Biotechnologies Inc**...317 865-4770
55 E Monroe St Ste 3800 Chicago (60603) *(G-4735)*
**Elongated Plastics Inc**...224 456-0559
677 Alice Dr Northbrook (60062) *(G-16249)*
**Elorac Inc (PA)**...847 362-8200
100 N Fairway Dr Ste 134 Vernon Hills (60061) *(G-21159)*
**Elpac Components, Westchester** *Also called Elpac Electronics Inc (G-21839)*
**Elpac Electronics Inc**...708 316-4407
4 Westbrook Corporate Ctr # 900 Westchester (60154) *(G-21839)*
**Els Electronic Lighting Spc**...708 453-3666
2715 N 77th Ave Elmwood Park (60707) *(G-9969)*
**Elster Thermal Solutions, Rockford** *Also called Eclipse Inc (G-18356)*
**Elston Materials LLC**...773 235-3100
1420 N Elston Ave Chicago (60642) *(G-4736)*
**EM Smith & Co**...309 691-6812
826 W Detweiller Dr Peoria (61615) *(G-17356)*
**Emac Inc**...618 529-4525
2390 Emac Ln Carbondale (62902) *(G-3006)*
**Emack & Bolios**...309 682-3530
4534 N Prospect Rd Peoria (61616) *(G-17357)*
**Embassy Security Group Inc**...800 627-1325
11535 183rd Pl Ste 107 Orland Park (60467) *(G-16859)*
**Embeddedkits**...847 401-7488
1025 Oakland Dr Streamwood (60107) *(G-20654)*
**Embedor Technologies Inc**...202 681-0359
60 Hazelwood Dr Champaign (61820) *(G-3480)*

ALPHABETIC

**Emberglo Div of Midco Intl, Chicago** *Also called Midco International Inc* ***(G-5733)***
**Embodied Labs Inc**...336 971-5886
222 Merchandise Mart Plz Chicago (60654) ***(G-4737)***
**Embossed Graphics Inc**...630 236-4000
1175 S Frontenac St Aurora (60504) ***(G-1002)***
**Embroid ME, Peoria** *Also called Sew Wright Embroidery Inc* ***(G-17452)***
**Embroid ME**...815 485-4155
2399 E Joliet Hwy New Lenox (60451) ***(G-15880)***
**Embroidery Choices**...708 597-9093
2633 New St Blue Island (60406) ***(G-2249)***
**Embroidery Experts Inc**...847 403-0200
595 Lakeview Pkwy Vernon Hills (60061) ***(G-21160)***
**Embroidery Express Inc**...630 365-9393
217 Dempsey St Ste C Elburn (60119) ***(G-8888)***
**Embroidery House, Peoria** *Also called Senn Enterprises Inc* ***(G-17451)***
**Embroidery Services Inc**...847 588-2660
6287 W Howard St Niles (60714) ***(G-15978)***
**EMC**...480 225-5498
22824 W Winchester Dr Channahon (60410) ***(G-3573)***
**EMC Corporation**...630 505-3273
4225 Naperville Rd # 500 Lisle (60532) ***(G-13585)***
**EMC Innovations Inc**...815 741-2546
1252 Woodland Ct Joliet (60436) ***(G-12490)***
**EMC Machining Inc**...630 860-7076
905 Fairway Dr Bensenville (60106) ***(G-1891)***
**Emco Chemical Distributors Inc**...262 427-0400
2100 Commonwealth Ave North Chicago (60064) ***(G-16178)***
**Emco Gears Inc (PA)**...847 220-4327
160 King St Elk Grove Village (60007) ***(G-9454)***
**Emco Metalworks Co**...708 222-1011
1505 S Laramie Ave Cicero (60804) ***(G-7195)***
**Emco Wheaton Usa Inc (HQ)**...281 856-1300
1800 Gardner Expy Quincy (62305) ***(G-17825)***
**EMD, Mc Cook** *Also called Progress Rail Locomotive Inc* ***(G-14457)***
**EMD Millipore Corporation**...815 937-8270
195 W Birch St Kankakee (60901) ***(G-12613)***
**EMD Millipore Corporation**...815 932-9017
2407 Eastgate Pkwy Kankakee (60901) ***(G-12614)***
**Emecole Inc**...815 372-2493
50 Montrose Romeoville (60446) ***(G-18819)***
**Emeelys Socks and More**...847 529-3026
2415 1/2 W 63rd St Chicago (60629) ***(G-4738)***
**Emerald Biofuels LLC (PA)**...847 420-0898
300 N La Salle Dr # 4925 Chicago (60654) ***(G-4739)***
**Emerald City Jewelers, Quincy** *Also called Emerald City Jewelry Inc* ***(G-17826)***
**Emerald City Jewelry Inc**...217 222-8896
3236 Broadway St Quincy (62301) ***(G-17826)***
**Emerald Machine Inc**...773 924-3659
4641 S Halsted St Chicago (60609) ***(G-4740)***
**Emerald One LLC**...601 529-6793
300 N La Salle Dr # 4925 Chicago (60654) ***(G-4741)***
**Emerald Performance Mtls LLC**...309 364-2311
1550 County Road 1450 N Henry (61537) ***(G-11741)***
**Emerald Polymer Additives LLC**...309 364-2311
1550 County Road 1450 N Henry (61537) ***(G-11742)***
**Emerald Printing & Promotions**...815 344-3303
1009 Bay Rd Lot 8 McHenry (60051) ***(G-14502)***
**Emerge Technology Group LLC**...800 613-1501
1000 N Rand Rd Ste 111 Wauconda (60084) ***(G-21459)***
**Emerson, Oak Forest** *Also called Instrument & Valve Services Co* ***(G-16585)***
**Emerson Electric Co**...847 585-8300
1901 South St Elgin (60123) ***(G-9027)***
**Emerson Electric Co**...312 803-4321
222 W Adams St Ste 400 Chicago (60606) ***(G-4742)***
**Emerson Industries LLC (PA)**...630 279-0920
721 N Yale Ave Villa Park (60181) ***(G-21250)***
**Emerson Press, Divernon** *Also called Leonard Emerson* ***(G-8316)***
**Emerson Process Management**...708 535-5120
4320 166th St Oak Forest (60452) ***(G-16580)***
**Emhart Teknologies LLC**...877 364-2781
12337 Collections Ctr Dr Chicago (60693) ***(G-4743)***
**EMI, Grayslake** *Also called Engineered Mills Inc* ***(G-11335)***
**EMI Division, Rockford** *Also called Gunite EMI Corporation* ***(G-18409)***
**Eminent Technologies LLC**...630 416-2311
215 Shuman Blvd Ste 403 Naperville (60563) ***(G-15653)***
**Emissions Systems Incorporated**...847 669-8044
480 Wright Dr Lake In The Hills (60156) ***(G-12991)***
**Emlin Cosmetics Inc (PA)**...630 860-5773
290 Beeline Dr Bensenville (60106) ***(G-1892)***
**Emmel Inc**...847 254-5178
13 Baldwin Ct Lake In The Hills (60156) ***(G-12992)***
**Emmert John**...773 292-6580
1401 N Cicero Ave Chicago (60651) ***(G-4744)***
**Emmett's Ale House, Wheaton** *Also called Emmetts Tavern & Brewing Co* ***(G-21945)***
**Emmett's Ale House, Palatine** *Also called Emmetts Tavern & Brewing Co* ***(G-17025)***
**Emmetts Tavern & Brewing Co**...630 434-8500
5200 Main St Downers Grove (60515) ***(G-8441)***
**Emmetts Tavern & Brewing Co**...630 480-7181
121 W Front St Wheaton (60187) ***(G-21945)***
**Emmetts Tavern & Brewing Co**...847 359-1533
110 N Brockway St Palatine (60067) ***(G-17025)***
**Emmetts Tavern & Brewing Co (PA)**...847 428-4500
128 W Main St West Dundee (60118) ***(G-21796)***
**EMPCO-LITE DIV, Elgin** *Also called Elgin Molded Plastics Inc* ***(G-9025)***
**Empcor, Chicago** *Also called Expanded Metal Products Corp* ***(G-4795)***
**Empire Acoustical Systems Inc**...815 261-0072
1111 Ace Rd Princeton (61356) ***(G-17747)***
**Empire Bronze Corp**...630 916-9722
1130 N Ridge Ave Lombard (60148) ***(G-13796)***
**Empire Comfort Systems Inc**...618 233-7420
918 Freeburg Ave Belleville (62220) ***(G-1631)***
**Empire Crankshafts**...847 640-8101
742 Lively Blvd Elk Grove Village (60007) ***(G-9455)***
**Empire Hard Chrome Inc (PA)**...773 762-3156
1615 S Kostner Ave Chicago (60623) ***(G-4745)***
**Empire Hard Chrome Inc**...312 226-7548
1537 S Wood St Chicago (60608) ***(G-4746)***
**Empire Screw Manufacturing Co**...630 833-7060
747 N Yale Ave Villa Park (60181) ***(G-21251)***
**Empowered Press LLC**...630 400-3127
139 Pineridge Dr S Oswego (60543) ***(G-16915)***
**EMR Manufacturing Inc**...630 766-3366
617 N Central Ave Wood Dale (60191) ***(G-22362)***
**Ems Acrylics & Silk Screener (PA)**...773 777-5656
4840 W Diversey Ave Chicago (60639) ***(G-4747)***
**Ems Industrial and Service Co**...815 678-2700
10800 N Main St Richmond (60071) ***(G-17961)***
**Emsur USA LLC (HQ)**...847 274-9450
2800 Carl Blvd Elk Grove Village (60007) ***(G-9456)***
**Emt, Rockford** *Also called Ewikon Molding Tech Inc* ***(G-18373)***
**Emt, Bloomingdale** *Also called Elite Manufacturing Tech Inc* ***(G-2106)***
**Emt International Inc**...630 655-4145
760 Pasquinelli Dr # 300 Westmont (60559) ***(G-21887)***
**Emtech Machining & Grinding**...815 338-1580
911 Rail Dr Woodstock (60098) ***(G-22565)***
**Emulsicoat Inc**...217 344-7775
705 E University Ave Urbana (61802) ***(G-21081)***
**Emulsions Inc**...618 943-2615
1105 Adams St Lawrenceville (62439) ***(G-13199)***
**Emv Welding Inc**...630 853-3199
850 Hearthstone Ct Aurora (60506) ***(G-1145)***
**En Es Cee Technology, Elk Grove Village** *Also called North Shore Consultants Inc* ***(G-9655)***
**En Pointe Cabinetry**...847 787-0777
950 Thorndale Ave Elk Grove Village (60007) ***(G-9457)***
**En-Chro Plating Inc**...708 450-1250
2755 W Lake St Melrose Park (60160) ***(G-14633)***
**Enameled Steel and Sign Co**...773 481-2270
4568 W Addison St Chicago (60641) ***(G-4748)***
**Enbarr LLC**...630 217-2101
431 Ford Ln Bartlett (60103) ***(G-1346)***
**Encap Technologies Inc (PA)**...510 337-2700
707 S Vermont St Palatine (60067) ***(G-17026)***
**Encap Technologies Inc**...510 337-2700
640 S Vermont St Palatine (60067) ***(G-17027)***
**Enchanted Signs of Rockford (PA)**...815 874-5100
4626 Shropshire Dr Rockford (61109) ***(G-18364)***
**Enclosures Inc (HQ)**...847 678-2020
9200 Ivanhoe St Schiller Park (60176) ***(G-19824)***
**Encompass Group LLC**...847 680-3388
955 Campus Dr Mundelein (60060) ***(G-15499)***
**Encon Environmental Concepts**...630 543-1583
643 W Winthrop Ave Addison (60101) ***(G-111)***
**Encore Fastners, Northbrook** *Also called Ecf Holdings LLC* ***(G-16246)***
**Encyclopaedia Britannica Inc (HQ)**...847 777-2241
325 N Lasalle St Ste 200 Chicago (60654) ***(G-4749)***
**Endeavor Technologies Inc**...630 562-0300
417 Stone Dr Saint Charles (60174) ***(G-19181)***
**Endepth Vision Systems LLC**...630 329-7909
2497 Sun Valley Rd Lisle (60532) ***(G-13586)***
**Enders Engineering, Glendale Heights** *Also called Enders Process Equipment Corp* ***(G-11022)***
**Enders Process Equipment Corp**...630 469-3787
746 Armitage Ave Glendale Heights (60139) ***(G-11022)***
**Endofix Ltd**...708 715-3472
9118 Ogden Ave Ste 1 Brookfield (60513) ***(G-2631)***
**Endoplus, Mundelein** *Also called J Stone Inc* ***(G-15513)***
**Endotronix Inc**...630 504-2861
1005 Intrnle Pkwy Ste 104 Woodridge (60517) ***(G-22478)***
**Endpoint Graphics, Alsip** *Also called Om Printing Corporation* ***(G-503)***
**Endure Holdings Inc**...224 558-1828
24317 W 143rd St Ste 103 Plainfield (60544) ***(G-17594)***
**Enercon Engineering Inc (PA)**...800 218-8831
201 Altorfer Ln East Peoria (61611) ***(G-8708)***
**Enercon Engineering Inc**...309 694-1418
301 Altorfer Ln East Peoria (61611) ***(G-8709)***
**Energex Tube, Chicago** *Also called Zekelman Industries Inc* ***(G-7061)***
**Energy Absorption Systems Inc (HQ)**...312 467-6750
70 W Madison St Ste 2350 Chicago (60602) ***(G-4750)***

**Energy Culvert Co Inc**.......618 942-7381
501 E College St Energy (62933) *(G-9986)*
**Energy Group Inc (PA)**.......847 836-2000
14 N 679 Isle Rr 25 Dundee (60118) *(G-8561)*
**Energy Parts Solutions Inc**.......224 653-9412
820 Estes Ave Schaumburg (60193) *(G-19516)*
**Energy Solutions Inc**.......618 465-5404
1520 Worden Ave Alton (62002) *(G-575)*
**Energy Tees**.......708 771-0000
1401 Circle Ave Ste 1n Forest Park (60130) *(G-10240)*
**Energy Vault LLC**.......847 722-1128
363 W Erie St Chicago (60654) *(G-4751)*
**Energy-Glazed Systems Inc**.......847 223-4500
350 Center St Grayslake (60030) *(G-11334)*
**Enerstar Inc**.......847 350-3400
742 Foster Ave Bensenville (60106) *(G-1893)*
**Enersys**.......630 455-4872
801 Warrenville Rd # 250 Lisle (60532) *(G-13587)*
**Enertech Global LLC (HQ)**.......618 664-9010
2506 S Elm St Greenville (62246) *(G-11392)*
**Engelhardt Enterprises Inc**.......847 277-7070
710 Bradwell Rd Inverness (60010) *(G-12208)*
**Engelhardt Gear Co**.......847 766-7070
2526 American Ln Elk Grove Village (60007) *(G-9458)*
**Engelhardt-Link Inc**.......847 593-5850
185 King St Elk Grove Village (60007) *(G-9459)*
**Engert Co Inc**.......847 673-1633
8103 Monticello Ave Skokie (60076) *(G-19993)*
**Enghouse Interactive Inc**.......630 472-9669
700 Commerce Dr Ste 100 Oak Brook (60523) *(G-16509)*
**Engility Corporation**.......847 583-1216
5600 Old Orchard Rd Bsmt Skokie (60077) *(G-19994)*
**Engility Corporation**.......708 596-8245
16501 Kedzie Ave Ph Rm245 Harvey (60428) *(G-11665)*
**Engine Efficiency Systems LLC**.......630 590-5241
6125 S Madison St Burr Ridge (60527) *(G-2838)*
**Engine Rebuilders & Supply**.......708 338-1113
4010 W North Ave Stone Park (60165) *(G-20634)*
**Engine Solutions Inc**.......815 979-2312
1928 12th St Rockford (61104) *(G-18365)*
**Engineered Abrasives Inc**.......662 582-4143
11631 S Austin Ave Alsip (60803) *(G-462)*
**Engineered Components Co (PA)**.......847 985-8000
1100 Davis Rd Ste A Elgin (60123) *(G-9028)*
**Engineered Finishing Systems, Elmhurst** *Also called Engineering Finshg Systems LLC* *(G-9866)*
**Engineered Fluid Inc (PA)**.......618 533-1351
1308 N Maple St Centralia (62801) *(G-3413)*
**Engineered Fluid Inc**.......618 533-1351
1308 N Maple St Centralia (62801) *(G-3414)*
**Engineered Fluid Pwr Con Cons**.......815 332-3344
3637 Cutty Sark Rd Cherry Valley (61016) *(G-3641)*
**Engineered Foam Solutions Inc**.......708 769-4130
16000 Van Drunen Rd # 600 South Holland (60473) *(G-20266)*
**Engineered Glass Products LLC (HQ)**.......312 326-4710
2857 S Halsted St Chicago (60608) *(G-4752)*
**Engineered Glass Products LLC**.......773 843-1964
929 W Exchange Ave Chicago (60609) *(G-4753)*
**Engineered Glass Products LLC (PA)**.......312 326-4710
2857 S Halsted St Chicago (60608) *(G-4754)*
**Engineered Materials Inc (PA)**.......847 821-8280
89 Chestnut Ter Buffalo Grove (60089) *(G-2691)*
**Engineered Mills Inc**.......847 548-0044
888 E Belvidere Rd Grayslake (60030) *(G-11335)*
**Engineered Plastic Components**.......217 892-2026
300 Shellhouse Dr Rantoul (61866) *(G-17927)*
**Engineered Plastic Pdts Corp**.......847 952-8400
2542 Pratt Blvd Elk Grove Village (60007) *(G-9460)*
**Engineered Plastic Systems LLC**.......800 480-2327
885 Church Rd Elgin (60123) *(G-9029)*
**Engineered Plumbing Spc LLC**.......630 682-1555
2312 Oak Leaf St Joliet (60436) *(G-12491)*
**Engineered Polymer Systems Div, Elgin** *Also called Parker-Hannifin Corporation* *(G-9135)*
**Engineered Security & Sound**.......630 876-8853
1275 W Roosevelt Rd # 110 West Chicago (60185) *(G-21695)*
**Engineering Design & Dev, Morton** *Also called Engineering Design & Dev Inc* *(G-15158)*
**Engineering Design & Dev Inc**.......309 266-6298
1001 W Jefferson St Morton (61550) *(G-15158)*
**Engineering Finshg Systems LLC (PA)**.......815 893-6090
202 E Bttrfield Rd Ste 20 Elmhurst (60126) *(G-9866)*
**Engineering Products Company**.......815 436-9055
15125 S Meadow Ln Plainfield (60544) *(G-17595)*
**Engineering Prototype Inc**.......708 447-3155
2537 S 6th Ave Riverside (60546) *(G-18030)*
**Engineering Resources, Vernon Hills** *Also called Steamgard LLC* *(G-21204)*
**Engineered Polymr Solutions Inc**.......815 987-3700
1215 Nelson Blvd Rockford (61104) *(G-18366)*
**Engineered Polymr Solutions Inc (HQ)**.......815 568-4205
1400 N State St Marengo (60152) *(G-14226)*
**Enginred Molding Solutions Inc**.......815 363-9600
4913 Prime Pkwy McHenry (60050) *(G-14503)*
**Enginuity Communications Corp**.......630 444-0778
3545 Stern Ave Saint Charles (60174) *(G-19182)*
**Engis Corporation (PA)**.......847 808-9400
105 W Hintz Rd Wheeling (60090) *(G-22047)*
**Engle Manufacturing Co**.......815 738-2282
214 Main St Leaf River (61047) *(G-13210)*
**Englewood Co Op**.......773 873-1201
900 W 63rd Pkwy Chicago (60621) *(G-4755)*
**Enhanced Plasmonics LLC**.......904 238-9270
820 Davis St Ste 216 Evanston (60201) *(G-10030)*
**Enjoy Life Foods, Chicago** *Also called Enjoy Life Natural Brands LLC* *(G-4756)*
**Enjoy Life Natural Brands LLC (HQ)**.......773 632-2163
8770 W Bryn Mawr Ave Chicago (60631) *(G-4756)*
**Enjoylife Inc**.......847 966-3377
8244 Lehigh Ave Morton Grove (60053) *(G-15196)*
**Ennis Inc**.......815 875-2000
200 W Railroad Ave Princeton (61356) *(G-17748)*
**ENR General Machining Co**.......773 523-2944
3725 W 49th St Chicago (60632) *(G-4757)*
**Enrico Formella, Countryside** *Also called E Formella & Sons Inc* *(G-7422)*
**Enrollment Rx LLC**.......847 233-0088
9511 River St Ste 100 Schiller Park (60176) *(G-19825)*
**Ensembles Inc**.......630 527-0004
2320 Flambeau Dr Naperville (60564) *(G-15805)*
**Ensign Emblem Ltd**.......217 877-8224
2435 E Federal Dr Decatur (62526) *(G-7879)*
**Ensource Inc**.......312 912-1048
2826 S Union Ave Chicago (60616) *(G-4758)*
**Entappia LLC**.......630 546-4531
1052 Sundew Ct Aurora (60504) *(G-1003)*
**Enterprise AC & Htg Co**.......708 430-2212
6112 111th St Chicago Ridge (60415) *(G-7147)*
**Enterprise Oil Co**.......312 487-2025
3200 S Western Ave Chicago (60608) *(G-4759)*
**Enterprise Pallet Inc**.......815 928-8546
1166 E 6000n Rd Bourbonnais (60914) *(G-2395)*
**Enterprise Printing, Downers Grove** *Also called Perryco Inc* *(G-8501)*
**Enterprise Products Company**.......708 534-6266
23313 S Ridgeland Ave Monee (60449) *(G-14993)*
**Enterprise Service Corporation**.......773 589-2727
5400 Milton Pkwy Des Plaines (60018) *(G-8188)*
**Enterprise Signs Inc**.......773 614-8324
10447 S Hale Ave Apt 1 Chicago (60643) *(G-4760)*
**Enterprises One Stop**.......773 924-5506
48 E Garfield Blvd Chicago (60615) *(G-4761)*
**Entience**.......217 649-2590
305 W Michigan Ave Urbana (61801) *(G-21082)*
**Entrac Systems, Mount Vernon** *Also called Km Enterprises Inc* *(G-15420)*
**Entrepreneur Media Inc**.......312 923-0818
205 W Wacker Dr Ste 1820 Chicago (60606) *(G-4762)*
**Entrigue Designs**.......708 647-6159
825 Maple Ave Homewood (60430) *(G-12097)*
**Entropy International Inc USA**.......630 834-3872
918 N Oaklawn Ave Elmhurst (60126) *(G-9867)*
**Entrust Services LLC (PA)**.......630 699-9132
608 S Washington St Naperville (60540) *(G-15654)*
**Envelope Division, Danville** *Also called Westrock Mwv LLC* *(G-7784)*
**Envelopes Only Inc**.......630 213-2500
2000 S Park Ave Streamwood (60107) *(G-20655)*
**Envestnet Inc (PA)**.......312 827-2800
35 E Wacker Dr Ste 2400 Chicago (60601) *(G-4763)*
**Envestnet Rtrment Slutions LLC (HQ)**.......312 827-7957
35 E Wacker Dr Chicago (60601) *(G-4764)*
**Envirnmntal Ctrl Solutions Inc (PA)**.......217 793-8966
2020 Timberbrook Dr Springfield (62702) *(G-20435)*
**Enviro Tech International Inc**.......708 343-6641
1800 N 25th Ave Melrose Park (60160) *(G-14634)*
**Enviro-Buildings, Quincy** *Also called Craig Industries Inc* *(G-17816)*
**Enviro-Chem Inc**.......847 549-7797
228 Alexandria Dr Vernon Hills (60061) *(G-21161)*
**Enviro-Safe Refrigerants Inc**.......309 346-1110
400 Margaret St Ste 1 Pekin (61554) *(G-17261)*
**Envirocoat Inc**.......847 673-3649
7440 Saint Louis Ave Skokie (60076) *(G-19995)*
**Environetics Inc**.......815 838-8331
1201 Commerce St Lockport (60441) *(G-13715)*
**Environmental Inks & Coatings, West Chicago** *Also called An Environmental Inks* *(G-21659)*
**Environmental Inks & Coding (PA)**.......630 231-7313
450 Wegner Dr West Chicago (60185) *(G-21696)*
**Environmental Products Co Div, Batavia** *Also called Material Control Inc* *(G-1467)*
**Environmental Solutions Intl, Batavia** *Also called Producers Envmtl Pdts LLC* *(G-1487)*
**Environmental Specialties Inc**.......630 860-7070
1600 Glenlake Ave Itasca (60143) *(G-12259)*
**Environmental Systems Res Inst**.......312 609-0966
221 N La Salle St Ste 863 Chicago (60601) *(G-4765)*
**Envirox LLC**.......217 442-8596
1938 E Fairchild St Danville (61832) *(G-7716)*

ALPHABETIC

**Envision 3, Bloomingdale** *Also called Envision Graphics LLC* ***(G-2107)***
**Envision Graphics LLC**.....630 825-1200
225 Madsen Dr Bloomingdale (60108) ***(G-2107)***
**Envision Inc**.....847 735-0789
40 N Ahwahnee Rd Lake Forest (60045) ***(G-12897)***
**Envision Unlimited**.....773 651-1100
8562 S Vincennes Ave Chicago (60620) ***(G-4766)***
**Enz (usa) Inc**.....630 692-7880
1585 Beverly Ct Ste 115 Aurora (60502) ***(G-1004)***
**Enzymes Incorporated**.....847 487-5401
1099 Brown St Ste 102 Wauconda (60084) ***(G-21460)***
**Eoe Inc**.....847 550-1665
590 Telser Rd Ste A Lake Zurich (60047) ***(G-13069)***
**Ep Purification Inc**.....217 693-7950
2105 W Park Ct Champaign (61821) ***(G-3481)***
**Ep Technology Corporation USA**.....217 351-7888
1401 Interstate Dr Champaign (61822) ***(G-3482)***
**Epazz Inc (PA)**.....312 955-8161
325 N Milwaukee Ave Ste G Wheeling (60090) ***(G-22048)***
**EPC Rantoul, Rantoul** *Also called Engineered Plastic Components* ***(G-17927)***
**Epco, Plainfield** *Also called Engineering Products Company* ***(G-17595)***
**Epcor Industrial Inc**.....847 545-9212
1325 Louis Ave Elk Grove Village (60007) ***(G-9461)***
**Epe Industries Usa Inc**.....800 315-0336
1109 Kirk St Elk Grove Village (60007) ***(G-9462)***
**Epe Industries USA Chicago, Elk Grove Village** *Also called Epe Industries Usa Inc* ***(G-9462)***
**Epic Eye**.....309 210-6212
1869 E 19th Rd Grand Ridge (61325) ***(G-11257)***
**Epic Metals Corporation**.....847 803-6411
2400 E Devon Ave Ste 205 Des Plaines (60018) ***(G-8189)***
**Epir Inc**.....630 842-0893
590 Territorial Dr Ste B Bolingbrook (60440) ***(G-2306)***
**Epir Technologies Inc**.....630 771-0203
590 Territorial Dr Ste B Bolingbrook (60440) ***(G-2307)***
**Epiworks Inc**.....217 373-1590
1606 Rion Dr Champaign (61822) ***(G-3483)***
**Epix Inc**.....847 465-1818
381 Lexington Dr Buffalo Grove (60089) ***(G-2692)***
**Epix Tube Co Inc**.....630 844-0960
500 N Broadway Aurora (60505) ***(G-1146)***
**Eplan Software & Svcs N Ameri**.....517 762-5800
425 N Martingale Rd # 470 Schaumburg (60173) ***(G-19517)***
**Epoxy Chemicals, Kirkland** *Also called The Euclid Chemical Company* ***(G-12720)***
**EPS Solutions Incorporated**.....815 206-0868
1525 W Lake Shore Dr Woodstock (60098) ***(G-22566)***
**Epscca**.....815 568-3020
1400 N State St Marengo (60152) ***(G-14227)***
**Epublishing Inc**.....312 768-6800
720 N Franklin St Chicago (60654) ***(G-4767)***
**Eqes Inc**.....630 858-6161
799 Roosevelt Rd 6-208 Glen Ellyn (60137) ***(G-10969)***
**Equa Star Chemical Corp**.....815 942-7011
8805 Tabler Rd Morris (60450) ***(G-15107)***
**Equi-Chem International Inc**.....630 784-0432
510 Tower Blvd Carol Stream (60188) ***(G-3146)***
**Equilibrium Contact Center Inc**.....888 708-1405
1410 Auburn St Rockford (61103) ***(G-18367)***
**Equilon Enterprises LLC**.....312 733-1849
1001 W Jackson Blvd Chicago (60607) ***(G-4768)***
**Equinox Group Inc**.....312 226-7002
329 W 18th St Ste 1000 Chicago (60616) ***(G-4769)***
**Equipment Engineering & Sales, Glen Ellyn** *Also called Eqes Inc* ***(G-10969)***
**Equipment Monitor & Control, Carbondale** *Also called Emac Inc* ***(G-3006)***
**Equipment Rent and Royalty, Northbrook** *Also called ER&r Inc* ***(G-16250)***
**Equipmentbag.com, Wheaton** *Also called Wyckoff Advertising Inc* ***(G-21990)***
**Equipto Electronics Corp (PA)**.....630 897-4691
351 Woodlawn Ave Aurora (60506) ***(G-1147)***
**Equisoft Inc**.....815 629-2789
8176 W Oliver Rd Winnebago (61088) ***(G-22295)***
**Equistar, Morris** *Also called Lyondell Chemical Company* ***(G-15114)***
**Equistar Chemicals LP**.....217 253-3311
625 E Us Highway 36 Tuscola (61953) ***(G-21019)***
**Equitrade Group**.....312 499-9500
225 W Washington St # 2200 Chicago (60606) ***(G-4770)***
**Equity Concepts Co Inc (PA)**.....815 226-1300
5758 Elaine Dr Rockford (61108) ***(G-18368)***
**Equity Lifestyle Prpts Inc**.....815 857-3333
970 Green Wing Rd Amboy (61310) ***(G-598)***
**Equus Power I LP**.....847 908-2878
1900 E Golf Rd Ste 1030 Schaumburg (60173) ***(G-19518)***
**Equustock LLC**.....866 962-4686
8179 Starwood Dr Ste 1 Loves Park (61111) ***(G-13940)***
**ER&r Inc**.....847 791-5671
800 Midway Rd Apt 2n Northbrook (60062) ***(G-16250)***
**ERA Development Group Inc**.....708 252-6979
2224 Greenview Rd Northbrook (60062) ***(G-16251)***
**ERA Industries Inc**.....847 357-1320
1800 Greenleaf Ave Elk Grove Village (60007) ***(G-9463)***
**ERA Tool and Manufacturing Co**.....847 298-6333
3200 16th St Zion (60099) ***(G-22684)***
**Erasermitt Incorporated**.....312 842-2855
2001 S Michigan Ave 18q Chicago (60616) ***(G-4771)***
**Erbeck One Chem & Lab Sup Inc**.....312 203-0078
15607 W Waterford Ln Manhattan (60442) ***(G-14169)***
**Erbes Electric**.....815 849-5508
409 W Main St Sublette (61367) ***(G-20715)***
**Erdco Engineering Corporation**.....847 328-0550
721 Custer Ave Evanston (60202) ***(G-10031)***
**Erect - O -Veyor Corporation**.....630 766-1200
421 S County Line Rd Franklin Park (60131) ***(G-10465)***
**Erect-A-Tube Inc**.....815 943-4091
701 W Park St Harvard (60033) ***(G-11632)***
**Erell Manufacturing Company**.....847 427-3000
2678 Coyle Ave Elk Grove Village (60007) ***(G-9464)***
**Ergo Automatics, Arlington Heights** *Also called Ergo Help Inc* ***(G-750)***
**Ergo Help Inc**.....847 593-0722
2466 E Oakton St Arlington Heights (60005) ***(G-750)***
**Ergo-Tech Incorporated**.....630 773-2222
217 Catalpa Ave Itasca (60143) ***(G-12260)***
**Ergonomic Office Chairs, Lake Forest** *Also called The United Group Inc* ***(G-12970)***
**Ergoseal Inc (PA)**.....630 462-9600
346 Commerce Dr Carol Stream (60188) ***(G-3147)***
**Eri America Inc**.....847 550-9710
353 Enterprise Pkwy Lake Zurich (60047) ***(G-13070)***
**Eric Harr**.....618 538-7889
7508 Triple Lakes Rd East Carondelet (62240) ***(G-8613)***
**Erickson Tool & Machine Co**.....815 397-2653
1903 20th Ave Rockford (61104) ***(G-18369)***
**Ericson S Log & Lumber Co (PA)**.....309 667-2147
11 State Highway 17 New Windsor (61465) ***(G-15931)***
**Ericson Textile Co, Saint Anne** *Also called Douglas Net Company* ***(G-19119)***
**Erie Group International Inc**.....309 659-2233
1201 S Main St Rochelle (61068) ***(G-18088)***
**Erie Vehicle Company**.....773 536-6300
60 E 51st St Chicago (60615) ***(G-4772)***
**Erin Rope Corporation**.....708 377-1084
2661 139th St Blue Island (60406) ***(G-2250)***
**Ermak Usa Inc**.....847 640-7765
2860 S River Rd Ste 145 Des Plaines (60018) ***(G-8190)***
**Erowa Technology Inc**.....847 290-0295
2535 S Clearbrook Dr Arlington Heights (60005) ***(G-751)***
**Erq Systems Inc**.....815 469-1072
10439 S Maplewood Ave Chicago (60655) ***(G-4773)***
**Error Free Software LLC**.....312 461-0300
200 S Wacker Dr Ste 2400 Chicago (60606) ***(G-4774)***
**Erva Tool & Die Company**.....773 533-7806
3100 W Grand Ave Chicago (60622) ***(G-4775)***
**Ervin Equipments (HQ)**.....217 849-3125
608 N Ohio St Toledo (62468) ***(G-20962)***
**ES Investments Inc**.....618 345-6151
1997 Lemontree Ln Collinsville (62234) ***(G-7323)***
**Escalade Sports, Olney** *Also called U S Weight Inc* ***(G-16799)***
**Esco Lighting Inc**.....773 427-7000
3254 N Kilbourn Ave Chicago (60641) ***(G-4776)***
**Esd, Prospect Heights** *Also called Creative Science Activities* ***(G-17775)***
**Esi Fuel & Energy Group LLC**.....716 465-4289
1997 Lemontree Ln Collinsville (62234) ***(G-7324)***
**Esi Steel & Fabrication**.....618 548-3017
1645 N Broadway Ave Salem (62881) ***(G-19331)***
**Esma Inc**.....708 331-0456
450 Taft Dr Ste 101 South Holland (60473) ***(G-20267)***
**Esmark, Hinsdale** *Also called Severstal US Holdings II Inc* ***(G-11964)***
**ESP T-Shirt Co Inc**.....630 393-1033
2s130 Roxbury Ct Warrenville (60555) ***(G-21346)***
**Espe Manufacturing Co**.....847 678-8950
9220 Ivanhoe St Schiller Park (60176) ***(G-19826)***
**Espee**.....224 256-9570
1701 E Wdfeld Rd Ste 636 Schaumburg (60173) ***(G-19519)***
**Espee Biopharma & Finechem LLC**.....888 851-6667
1701 E Woodfield Rd # 636 Schaumburg (60173) ***(G-19520)***
**Esquify Inc**.....917 553-3741
805 W Buckingham Pl 2w Chicago (60657) ***(G-4777)***
**Esri, Chicago** *Also called Environmental Systems Res Inst* ***(G-4765)***
**Essannay Show It Inc**.....312 733-5511
451 W Grand Ave Chicago (60642) ***(G-4778)***
**Essen Nutrition Corporation**.....630 739-6700
1414 Sherman Rd Romeoville (60446) ***(G-18820)***
**Essential Creations**.....773 238-1700
2112 W 95th St Chicago (60643) ***(G-4779)***
**Essential Elmnts Therapeutic M**.....815 623-6810
5516 Clayton Cir Roscoe (61073) ***(G-18896)***
**Essential Flooring Inc**.....630 788-3121
566 Lincoln Station Dr Oswego (60543) ***(G-16916)***
**Essentra Components Inc**.....815 943-6487
7400 Industrial Dr Forest Park (60130) ***(G-10241)***
**Essentra Components-Richco, Forest Park** *Also called Essentra Components Inc* ***(G-10241)***

**Essentra International LLC (HQ)** ....866 800-0775
2 Westbrook Corp Ctr # 200 Westchester (60154) ***(G-21840)***
**Essentra Packaging US Inc (HQ)** ....704 418-8692
2 Westbrook Corp Ctr Westchester (60154) ***(G-21841)***
**Essentra Specialty Tapes Inc** ....708 488-1025
7400 Industrial Dr Forest Park (60130) ***(G-10242)***
**Essex Electro Engineers Inc** ....847 891-4444
2015 Mitchell Blvd Schaumburg (60193) ***(G-19521)***
**Essex Group Inc** ....630 628-7841
758 W Racquet Club Dr Addison (60101) ***(G-112)***
**Essilor Laboratories Amer Inc** ....309 787-2727
4470 48th Avenue Ct Rock Island (61201) ***(G-18176)***
**Essroc Cement Corp** ....708 388-0797
1400 W 134th St Riverdale (60827) ***(G-18019)***
**Est Lighting Inc** ....847 612-1705
10305 Covell St Richmond (60071) ***(G-17962)***
**Estad Stamping & Mfg Co** ....217 442-4600
1005 Griggs St Danville (61832) ***(G-7717)***
**Estee Bedding Company** ....800 521-7378
945 E 93rd St Chicago (60619) ***(G-4780)***
**Estes Laser & Mfg Inc** ....847 301-8231
930 Lunt Ave Schaumburg (60193) ***(G-19522)***
**Estima, Evanston** *Also called Thomas A Doan* ***(G-10102)***
**Estructuras Inc** ....773 522-2200
2232 S Pulaski Rd Chicago (60623) ***(G-4781)***
**Estwing Manufacturing Co Inc** ....815 397-9521
2647 8th St Rockford (61109) ***(G-18370)***
**ET Products LLC** ....800 325-5746
8128 S Madison St Burr Ridge (60527) ***(G-2839)***
**ET Simonds Materials Company** ....618 457-8191
1500 N Oakland Ave Carbondale (62901) ***(G-3007)***
**Etch-Tech Inc** ....630 833-4234
494 W Wrightwood Ave Elmhurst (60126) ***(G-9868)***
**Etcon Corp** ....630 325-6100
7750 S Grant St Burr Ridge (60527) ***(G-2840)***
**Etel Inc** ....847 519-3380
333 E State Pkwy Schaumburg (60173) ***(G-19523)***
**Ethan Company Incorporated** ....815 715-2283
306 Harvard Ct Shorewood (60404) ***(G-19925)***
**Ethereal Confections, Woodstock** *Also called E3 Artisan Inc* ***(G-22564)***
**Ethnic Media LLC** ....224 676-0778
704 S Milwaukee Ave Wheeling (60090) ***(G-22049)***
**Ethyl Corp** ....618 583-1292
501 Monsanto Ave East Saint Louis (62206) ***(G-8751)***
**Eti Solid State Lighting Inc** ....855 384-7754
720 Corporate Woods Pkwy Vernon Hills (60061) ***(G-21162)***
**Etnyre International Ltd (PA)** ....815 732-2116
1333 S Daysville Rd Oregon (61061) ***(G-16823)***
**Eton Machine Co Ltd** ....847 426-3380
1485 Davis Rd Ste B Elgin (60123) ***(G-9030)***
**Ets Lindgren, Wood Dale** *Also called Ets-Lindgren Inc* ***(G-22363)***
**Ets-Lindgren Inc (HQ)** ....630 307-7200
1360 N Wood Dale Rd Ste G Wood Dale (60191) ***(G-22363)***
**Etti, Wauconda** *Also called Extrusion Tooling Technology* ***(G-21461)***
**Etymotic Research Inc** ....847 228-0006
61 Martin Ln Elk Grove Village (60007) ***(G-9465)***
**Eugene Ewbank** ....630 705-0400
118 Kirkland Cir Ste B Oswego (60543) ***(G-16917)***
**Eunice Larry** ....708 339-5678
22 W 154th St South Holland (60473) ***(G-20268)***
**Euphoria Catering and Events** ....630 301-4369
611 Pennsylvania Ave Aurora (60506) ***(G-1148)***
**Eureka Chemical Labs Inc** ....773 847-9672
4701 S Whipple St Chicago (60632) ***(G-4782)***
**Eureka Locker Inc** ....309 467-2731
110 4h Park Rd Eureka (61530) ***(G-9998)***
**Eureka Printing & Stationery, Eureka** *Also called Paul D Burton* ***(G-10000)***
**Euro Marble & Granite Inc** ....847 233-0700
4552 Ruby St Schiller Park (60176) ***(G-19827)***
**Euro Marble Supply Ltd** ....847 233-0700
4552 Ruby St Schiller Park (60176) ***(G-19828)***
**Euro West Decorative Surfaces, Chicago** *Also called Stonepeak Ceramics Inc* ***(G-6599)***
**Euro-Tech Cabinetry Rmdlg Corp** ....815 254-3876
12515 Rhea Dr Plainfield (60585) ***(G-17596)***
**Euromarket Designs Inc (HQ)** ....847 272-2888
1250 Techny Rd Northbrook (60062) ***(G-16252)***
**European American Industries, Lake Bluff** *Also called American Medical Industries* ***(G-12829)***
**European Classic Bakery** ....773 774-8755
5930 N Elston Ave Chicago (60646) ***(G-4783)***
**European Ornamental Iron Works** ....630 705-9300
1786 W Armitage Ct Addison (60101) ***(G-113)***
**European Wood Works Inc** ....773 662-6607
1151 Woodlake Dr Carol Stream (60188) ***(G-3148)***
**Euroview Enterprises LLC** ....630 227-3300
420 W Wrightwood Ave Elmhurst (60126) ***(G-9869)***
**Eva's Bridal, Orland Park** *Also called Halanick Enterprises Inc* ***(G-16864)***
**Evac Environmental Solutions, Cherry Valley** *Also called Evac North America Inc* ***(G-3642)***
**Evac North America Inc (HQ)** ....815 654-8300
1445 Huntwood Dr Cherry Valley (61016) ***(G-3642)***
**Evac Systems Fire & Rescue** ....309 764-7812
400 24th St Moline (61265) ***(G-14937)***
**Evan Lewis Inc** ....773 539-0402
3368 N Elston Ave Chicago (60618) ***(G-4784)***
**Evang Lthn Ch Dr Mrtn Luth KG** ....773 380-2540
8765 W Higgins Rd Ste 600 Chicago (60631) ***(G-4785)***
**Evangelical Missions Info Svc** ....630 752-7158
500 College Ave Wheaton (60187) ***(G-21946)***
**Evangelical Missions Quarterly, Wheaton** *Also called Evangelical Missions Info Svc* ***(G-21946)***
**Evangers Dog and Cat Fd Co Inc** ....847 537-0102
221 Wheeling Rd Wheeling (60090) ***(G-22050)***
**Evans Food Group Ltd (HQ)** ....773 254-7400
4118 S Halsted St Chicago (60609) ***(G-4786)***
**Evans Foods Inc (HQ)** ....773 254-7400
4118 S Halsted St Chicago (60609) ***(G-4787)***
**Evans Heating and Air Inc** ....217 483-8440
6172 Lick Rd Chatham (62629) ***(G-3619)***
**Evans Manufacturing, Rock Island** *Also called Premium Manufacturing Inc* ***(G-18192)***
**Evans Talaiha** ....618 327-8200
550 W Saint Louis St Nashville (62263) ***(G-15835)***
**Evans Tool & Manufacturing** ....630 897-8656
6s252 Hankes Rd Aurora (60506) ***(G-1149)***
**Evanston Awning Company** ....847 864-4520
2801 Central St Evanston (60201) ***(G-10032)***
**Evanston Graphic Imaging Inc** ....847 869-7446
1255 Hartrey Ave Evanston (60202) ***(G-10033)***
**Evanston Sentinel Corporation** ....847 492-0177
1229 Emerson St Ste 2w Evanston (60201) ***(G-10034)***
**Evapco Inc** ....410 756-2600
62140 Collection Ctr Chicago (60693) ***(G-4788)***
**Evapco Inc** ....217 923-3431
1723 E York Rd Greenup (62428) ***(G-11382)***
**Evapco Midwest, Greenup** *Also called Evapco Inc* ***(G-11382)***
**Eve J Alfille Gallery & Studio, Evanston** *Also called Eve J Alfille Ltd* ***(G-10035)***
**Eve J Alfille Ltd** ....847 869-7920
623 Grove St Evanston (60201) ***(G-10035)***
**Evenson Explosives LLC** ....815 942-5800
2019 Dunn Rd Morris (60450) ***(G-15108)***
**Event Catering Group** ....708 534-3100
325 W Glengate Ave Chicago Heights (60411) ***(G-7096)***
**Event Equipment Sales LLC** ....708 352-0662
7515 Santa Fe Dr Hodgkins (60525) ***(G-11974)***
**Evention LLC** ....773 733-4256
121 W Wacker Dr Ste 3200 Chicago (60601) ***(G-4789)***
**Ever Ready Pin & Manufacturing** ....815 874-4949
5560 International Dr Rockford (61109) ***(G-18371)***
**Ever-Redi Printing Inc** ....708 352-4378
331 Justina St Hinsdale (60521) ***(G-11945)***
**Everblast Inc** ....815 788-8660
820 Mcardle Dr Ste C Crystal Lake (60014) ***(G-7574)***
**Eveready Welding Service Inc** ....708 532-2432
18111 Harlem Ave Tinley Park (60477) ***(G-20910)***
**Evergreen Drive Systems, Morton Grove** *Also called Howland Technology Inc* ***(G-15200)***
**Evergreen Energy LLC** ....618 384-9295
645 W Illinois Hwy 14 Carmi (62821) ***(G-3067)***
**Evergreen Fs Inc** ....815 934-5422
19484 N 3000 East Rd Cullom (60929) ***(G-7681)***
**Evergreen Manufacturing Inc** ....217 382-5108
1 Harry Glynn Dr Martinsville (62442) ***(G-14335)***
**Evergreen Marathon** ....708 636-5700
2755 W 87th St Evergreen Park (60805) ***(G-10114)***
**Evergreen Pool & Spa Center, Sandoval** *Also called Evergreen Pool & Spa LLC* ***(G-19356)***
**Evergreen Pool & Spa LLC** ....618 247-3555
Us Hwys 50 & 51 Sandoval (62882) ***(G-19356)***
**Evergreen Printing** ....708 499-0688
9420 S Trumbull Ave Evergreen Park (60805) ***(G-10115)***
**Evergreen Resource Inc** ....630 428-9077
3404 Frankstowne Dr 5 Naperville (60565) ***(G-15655)***
**Evergreen Scale Models Inc** ....224 567-8099
65 Bradrock Dr Des Plaines (60018) ***(G-8191)***
**Everlast Portable Buildings** ....217 543-4080
1565 Cr 1800n Sullivan (61951) ***(G-20745)***
**Everlights Inc** ....773 734-9873
8027 Lawndale Ave Skokie (60076) ***(G-19996)***
**Everpure, Hanover Park** *Also called Pentair Fltrtion Solutions LLC* ***(G-11589)***
**Everpurse Inc** ....650 204-3212
212 W Superior St Chicago (60654) ***(G-4790)***
**Eversharp Pen Company** ....847 366-5030
9240 Belmont Ave Unit A Franklin Park (60131) ***(G-10466)***
**Everwill Inc** ....847 357-0446
1400 E Devon Ave Elk Grove Village (60007) ***(G-9466)***
**Everything Xclusive** ....309 370-7450
4010 N Brandywine Dr Peoria (61614) ***(G-17358)***
**Evo Exhibits LLC** ....630 520-0710
399 Wegner Dr West Chicago (60185) ***(G-21697)***

ALPHABETIC

**Evolution Sorbent Products LLC** 630 293-8055
1270 Nuclear Dr West Chicago (60185) *(G-21698)*
**Evolution Sorbent Products LLC (PA)** 630 293-8055
1149 Howard Dr West Chicago (60185) *(G-21699)*
**Evonik Corporation** 309 697-6220
8300 W Route 24 Mapleton (61547) *(G-14209)*
**Evonik Corporation** 630 230-0176
7420 S County Line Rd Burr Ridge (60527) *(G-2841)*
**Evoqua Water Technologies LLC** 815 921-8325
4669 Shepherd Trl Rockford (61103) *(G-18372)*
**Evoqua Water Technologies LLC** 618 451-1205
3202 W 20th St Granite City (62040) *(G-11275)*
**Evoys Corp** 773 736-4200
4142 W Lawrence Ave Chicago (60630) *(G-4791)*
**Evraz Inc NA (HQ)** 312 533-3621
200 E Randolph St # 7800 Chicago (60601) *(G-4792)*
**Evraz Oregon Steel, Chicago** *Also called Evraz Inc NA (G-4792)*
**Evsco Inc** 847 362-7068
2309 N Ringwood Rd Ste M McHenry (60050) *(G-14504)*
**EW Bredemeier and Co** 773 237-1600
6625 W Diversey Ave Chicago (60707) *(G-4793)*
**Ewab Engineering Inc** 847 247-0015
1971 Kelley Ct Libertyville (60048) *(G-13321)*
**Ewert, Alsip** *Also called Midwest Group Dist & Svcs Inc (G-492)*
**Ewikon Molding Tech Inc** 815 874-7270
5652 International Dr Rockford (61109) *(G-18373)*
**Eww Enterprise Inc** 815 463-9607
1311 S Schoolhouse Rd # 2 New Lenox (60451) *(G-15881)*
**Ex-Cell Kaiser LLC** 847 451-0451
11240 Melrose Ave Franklin Park (60131) *(G-10467)*
**Exact Data, Chicago** *Also called Consumerbase LLC (G-4455)*
**Exact Machine Company Inc** 815 963-7905
2502 Preston St Rockford (61102) *(G-18374)*
**Exact Tool Company Inc** 847 632-1140
2123 Foster Ave Wheeling (60090) *(G-22051)*
**Examiner Publications Inc** 630 830-4145
4n781 Gerber Rd Bartlett (60103) *(G-1347)*
**Examiner, The, Bartlett** *Also called Examiner Publications Inc (G-1347)*
**Excarb Inc** 217 493-8477
4404 Ironwood Ln Champaign (61822) *(G-3484)*
**Excel Ltd Inc** 847 543-9138
888 E Belvidere Rd # 105 Grayslake (60030) *(G-11336)*
**Excel Bottling Co** 618 526-7159
488 S Broadway Breese (62230) *(G-2443)*
**Excel Color Corporation** 847 734-1270
110 Martin Ln Elk Grove Village (60007) *(G-9467)*
**Excel Displays & Packaging, Aurora** *Also called Georg-Pcific Corrugated IV LLC (G-1014)*
**Excel Electro Assembly Inc** 847 621-2500
1595 Brummel Ave Elk Grove Village (60007) *(G-9468)*
**Excel Forms Inc** 630 801-1936
44 1/2 W Downer Pl Ste 46 Aurora (60506) *(G-1150)*
**Excel Gear Inc** 815 623-3414
11865 Main St Roscoe (61073) *(G-18897)*
**Excel Glass Inc** 847 801-5200
10507 Delta Pkwy Schiller Park (60176) *(G-19829)*
**Excel Group Holdings Inc (PA)** 630 773-1815
800 Baker Dr Itasca (60143) *(G-12261)*
**Excel Machine & Tool** 815 467-1177
24050 S Northern Ill Dr Channahon (60410) *(G-3574)*
**Excel Machining Inc** 773 585-6666
5654 W 65th St Chicago (60638) *(G-4794)*
**Excel Screen Prtg & EMB Inc** 847 801-5200
10507 Delta Pkwy Schiller Park (60176) *(G-19830)*
**Excel Specialty Corp** 773 262-7575
28101 N Ballard Dr Ste A Lake Forest (60045) *(G-12898)*
**Excelitas Technologies Corp** 847 537-4277
160 E Marquardt Dr Wheeling (60090) *(G-22052)*
**Excell Electronics Corporation** 847 766-7455
2425 American Ln Elk Grove Village (60007) *(G-9469)*
**Excell Fastener Solutions Inc** 630 424-3360
920 N Ridge Ave Ste A7 Lombard (60148) *(G-13797)*
**Excelled Sheepskin & Lea Coat** 309 852-3341
1700 Burlington Ave Kewanee (61443) *(G-12682)*
**Excelled Sheepskin & Lea Coat** 309 852-3341
1700 Burlington Ave Kewanee (61443) *(G-12683)*
**Excellent Bindery Inc** 630 766-9050
500 Eastern Ave Bensenville (60106) *(G-1894)*
**Excelsior Inc** 815 987-2900
4982 27th Ave Rockford (61109) *(G-18375)*
**Excelsior Inc** 815 987-2900
4982 27th Ave Rockford (61109) *(G-18376)*
**Excitingwindows By Susan Day** 217 652-2821
47 Fairview Ln Springfield (62711) *(G-20436)*
**Exclusive Boarding, Elburn** *Also called Harry Otto Printing Company (G-8889)*
**Exclusive Pro Sports Ltd** 815 877-8585
5035 28th Ave Rockford (61109) *(G-18377)*
**Exclusive Publications Inc** 847 963-0400
3830 Bordeaux Dr Hoffman Estates (60192) *(G-12008)*
**Exclusive Stone** 847 593-6963
1361 Jarvis Ave Elk Grove Village (60007) *(G-9470)*
**Exclusive Wood Group, Northbrook** *Also called ERA Development Group Inc (G-16251)*
**Exclusively Expo (PA)** 630 378-4600
1225 Naperville Dr Romeoville (60446) *(G-18821)*
**Exclusively Expo** 630 378-4600
1201 Naperville Dr Romeoville (60446) *(G-18822)*
**Executive Performance Fuel LLC** 847 364-1933
1060 Talbots Ln Elk Grove Village (60007) *(G-9471)*
**Exelon Corporation** 815 357-6761
2602 N 21st Rd Marseilles (61341) *(G-14308)*
**Exex Holding Corporation** 815 703-7295
1201 Naperville Dr Romeoville (60446) *(G-18823)*
**Exide Technologies** 630 862-2200
3950 Sussex Ave Aurora (60504) *(G-1005)*
**Exide Technologies** 678 566-9000
829 Parkview Blvd Lombard (60148) *(G-13798)*
**Exo Fabrication Inc** 630 501-1136
1140 W Fullerton Ave Addison (60101) *(G-114)*
**Exopack Holding, Chicago** *Also called Coveris Holding Corp (G-4483)*
**Expandable Habitats** 815 624-6784
11022 N Main St Rockton (61072) *(G-18696)*
**Expanded Metal Products Corp** 773 735-4500
4633 S Knox Ave Chicago (60632) *(G-4795)*
**Expercolor Inc** 773 465-3400
3737 Chase Ave Skokie (60076) *(G-19997)*
**Experimental Aircraft Examiner** 847 226-0777
69 Mohawk St Cary (60013) *(G-3339)*
**Experior Transport, Alsip** *Also called Polmax LLC (G-511)*
**Expert Locksmith Inc** 917 751-9267
100 W Randolph St Chicago (60601) *(G-4796)*
**Expert Manufacturing Systems, Deerfield** *Also called High Tech Research Inc (G-8012)*
**Expert Metal Finishing Inc** 708 583-2550
2120 West St River Grove (60171) *(G-18008)*
**Expo Engineered Inc** 708 780-7155
1824 S Cicero Ave Cicero (60804) *(G-7196)*
**Export Packaging Co Inc (PA)** 309 756-4288
525 10th Ave E Milan (61264) *(G-14786)*
**Express Care** 815 521-2185
24361 W Eames St Channahon (60410) *(G-3575)*
**Express Donuts Enterprise Inc** 630 510-9310
15 Danada Sq E Wheaton (60189) *(G-21947)*
**Express Grinding Inc** 847 434-5827
119 Joey Dr Elk Grove Village (60007) *(G-9472)*
**Express LLC** 708 453-0566
4122 N Harlem Ave Norridge (60706) *(G-16101)*
**Express Machining & Molds** 630 350-8480
456 Dominic Ct Franklin Park (60131) *(G-10468)*
**Express Print Champaign LLC** 217 693-7079
510 N Cunningham Ave # 10 Urbana (61802) *(G-21083)*
**Express Printing, Wheeling** *Also called Link-Letters Ltd (G-22094)*
**Express Printing Ctr of Libert** 847 675-0659
5125 Sherwin Ave Skokie (60077) *(G-19998)*
**Express Prtg & Promotions Inc** 847 498-9640
1537 Windy Hill Dr Northbrook (60062) *(G-16253)*
**Express Publishing Inc** 773 725-6218
6121 W Belmont Ave Chicago (60634) *(G-4797)*
**Express Signs & Lighting Maint** 815 725-9080
212 Amendodge Dr Shorewood (60404) *(G-19926)*
**Expression Wear Inc** 815 732-1556
2781 W Mud Creek Rd Mount Morris (61054) *(G-15296)*
**Expressions By Christine Inc** 217 223-2750
711 Maine St Quincy (62301) *(G-17827)*
**Expri Publishing & Printing** 773 274-5955
2328 W Touhy Ave Chicago (60645) *(G-4798)*
**Exress Motor and Lift Parts** 630 327-2000
1018 Lambrecht Dr Frankfort (60423) *(G-10320)*
**Extentel Wrless Communications** 847 809-3131
90 Dirleton Ln Inverness (60067) *(G-12203)*
**Exterior Services** 773 660-1457
327 E 115th St Chicago (60628) *(G-4799)*
**Extol Hydro Technologies Inc** 708 717-4371
13020 Ridgewood Dr Palos Park (60464) *(G-17128)*
**Exton Corp** 847 391-8100
1 Innovation Dr Des Plaines (60016) *(G-8192)*
**Exton Corporation, Des Plaines** *Also called Exton Corp (G-8192)*
**Extractor Corporation** 847 742-3532
685 Martin Dr South Elgin (60177) *(G-20196)*
**Extreme Force Valve Inc** 618 494-5795
515 Mound St Jerseyville (62052) *(G-12421)*
**Extreme Glass, Melrose Park** *Also called Glass Dimensions Inc (G-14647)*
**Extreme Manufacturing Inc** 630 350-8566
735 N Edgewood Ave Wood Dale (60191) *(G-22364)*
**Extreme Tools Inc** 630 202-8324
740 Frontenac Rd Naperville (60563) *(G-15656)*
**Extreme Welding & Machine Serv** 618 272-7237
529 S Jarrell St Ridgway (62979) *(G-17984)*
**Extreme Woodworking Inc** 224 338-8179
24650 W Luther Ave Apt B Round Lake (60073) *(G-19055)*
**Extrude Hone LLC** 847 669-5355
10663 Wolf Dr Huntley (60142) *(G-12139)*

ALPHABETIC SECTION Faiths Jewelry Designs, Chicago

**Extruded Solutions Inc** ...630 871-6450
322 Saint Paul Blvd Carol Stream (60188) *(G-3149)*
**Extrusion Science, Savanna** *Also called Metform LLC (G-19400)*
**Extrusion Tooling Technology** ...847 526-1606
1000 N Rand Rd Ste 210 Wauconda (60084) *(G-21461)*
**Exxon Mobil Corporation** ...217 854-3291
14491 Brushy Mound Rd Carlinville (62626) *(G-3038)*
**Exxonmobil Pipeline Company** ...815 423-5571
Interstate 55 & Smth Brg Elwood (60421) *(G-9980)*
**Eye Candy Optics Corporation** ...773 697-7370
2121 W Division St Ste 1e Chicago (60622) *(G-4800)*
**Eye Surgeons of Libertyville** ...847 362-3811
1880 W Winchester Rd # 105 Libertyville (60048) *(G-13322)*
**Eyeball Music, Chicago** *Also called Alligator Rec & Artist MGT Inc (G-3819)*
**Eyelation LLC** ...888 308-4703
18501 Maple Creek Dr # 400 Tinley Park (60477) *(G-20911)*
**Eyewearplanet Com Inc** ...847 513-6203
3150 Commercial Ave Northbrook (60062) *(G-16254)*
**EZ Blinds and Drapery Inc (PA)** ...708 246-6600
1 Raquel Way La Grange (60525) *(G-12731)*
**EZ Comfort Heating & AC** ...630 289-2020
1290 Evergreen Ln Elgin (60123) *(G-9031)*
**Ezee Roll Manufacturing Co** ...217 339-2279
20 N 3000 East Rd Hoopeston (60942) *(G-12110)*
**Eztech Manufacturing Inc** ...630 293-0010
1200 Howard Dr West Chicago (60185) *(G-21700)*
**F & A Industries Company LLC** ...630 504-9839
9204 S Pulaski Rd Apt 2e Oak Lawn (60453) *(G-16618)*
**F & F Publishing Inc** ...847 480-0330
144 Sheridan Rd Highland Park (60035) *(G-11831)*
**F & L Drapery Inc** ...815 932-8997
6279 Warren St Saint Anne (60964) *(G-19122)*
**F & L Electronics LLC** ...217 586-2132
103 N Prairieview Rd Mahomet (61853) *(G-14158)*
**F & R Plastics Inc** ...847 336-1330
642 Westmoreland Ave Waukegan (60085) *(G-21558)*
**F & S Engraving Inc** ...847 870-8400
1620 W Central Rd Mount Prospect (60056) *(G-15328)*
**F & Y Enterprises Inc** ...847 526-0620
1205 Karl Ct Ste 115 Wauconda (60084) *(G-21462)*
**F and F Screw Products** ...815 968-7330
2136 12th St Rockford (61104) *(G-18378)*
**F and L Pallets Inc** ...773 364-0798
3018 S Spaulding Ave Fl 1 Chicago (60623) *(G-4801)*
**F and S Enterprises Plainfield** ...815 439-9655
2035 Havenhill Dr Plainfield (60586) *(G-17597)*
**F B Williams Co** ...773 233-4255
10017 S Claremont Ave Chicago (60643) *(G-4802)*
**F C D Inc** ...847 498-3711
1925 Holste Rd Northbrook (60062) *(G-16255)*
**F C L Graphics Inc** ...708 867-5500
4600 N Olcott Ave Harwood Heights (60706) *(G-11684)*
**F G Lighting Inc** ...847 295-0445
1111 Foster Ave Lake Bluff (60044) *(G-12842)*
**F H Leinweber Co Inc (PA)** ...708 424-7000
9812 S Cicero Ave Oak Lawn (60453) *(G-16619)*
**F H Leinweber Co Inc** ...773 568-7722
346 W 107th Pl Chicago (60628) *(G-4803)*
**F Hyman & Co** ...312 664-3810
1329 N Clybourn Ave Fl 1 Chicago (60610) *(G-4804)*
**F J Murphy & Son Inc** ...217 787-3477
1800 Factory St Springfield (62702) *(G-20437)*
**F K Pattern & Foundry Company** ...847 578-5260
1400 Morrow Ave North Chicago (60064) *(G-16179)*
**F Kreutzer & Co** ...773 826-5767
2646 W Madison St Chicago (60612) *(G-4805)*
**F L Beard Service Corp** ...618 262-5193
800 Stokes St Mount Carmel (62863) *(G-15265)*
**F L C, Sugar Grove** *Also called Falex Corporation (G-20723)*
**F L T, Wood Dale** *Also called Finish Line Transmission Inc (G-22367)*
**F Lee Charles & Sons Inc** ...815 547-7141
1473 Flora Church Rd Kirkland (60146) *(G-12712)*
**F M Aquisition Corp** ...773 728-8351
3750 N Lake Shore Dr 8d Chicago (60613) *(G-4806)*
**F M I, Chicago** *Also called Flexan LLC (G-4860)*
**F N Smith Corporation** ...815 732-2171
1200 S 2nd St Oregon (61061) *(G-16824)*
**F P M Heat Treating, Elk Grove Village** *Also called F P M LLC (G-9473)*
**F P M LLC (PA)** ...847 228-2525
1501 Lively Blvd Elk Grove Village (60007) *(G-9473)*
**F P M LLC** ...815 332-4961
648 Bypass Us Hwy 20 Cherry Valley (61016) *(G-3643)*
**F S Gateway Inc** ...618 458-6588
3145 Maeystown Rd Fults (62244) *(G-10709)*
**F T I Inc** ...312 943-4015
416 W Erie St Chicago (60654) *(G-4807)*
**F V M, Plano** *Also called Fox Valley Molding Inc (G-17665)*
**F Vogelmann and Company** ...815 469-2285
440 Center Rd Frankfort (60423) *(G-10321)*
**F Weber Printing Co Inc** ...815 468-6152
450 N Locust St Manteno (60950) *(G-14183)*
**F-C Enterprises Inc** ...815 254-7295
12249 Rhea Dr Ste 3 Plainfield (60585) *(G-17598)*
**Fab Con Industries Inc** ...618 969-9040
101 E Deyoung Eldorado (62930) *(G-8920)*
**Fab Werks Inc** ...815 724-0317
911 Brian Dr Crest Hill (60403) *(G-7458)*
**Fab-Rite Sheet Metal** ...847 228-0300
74 Bradrock Dr Des Plaines (60018) *(G-8193)*
**Fabbri Sausage Manufacturing** ...312 829-6363
166 N Aberdeen St Chicago (60607) *(G-4808)*
**Fabco Enterprises Inc** ...708 333-4644
16812 Lathrop Ave Harvey (60426) *(G-11666)*
**Fabcorr, Coulterville** *Also called Corrpak Inc (G-7399)*
**Faber Builders Discount, Sterling** *Also called Ronnie P Faber (G-20610)*
**Fabick Mining LLC** ...618 982-9000
635 Illinois Highway 1 Norris City (62869) *(G-16114)*
**Fabmax Inc** ...630 766-0370
501 N Edgewood Ave Wood Dale (60191) *(G-22365)*
**Fabracraft Manufacturing, Elk Grove Village** *Also called Amcraft Manufacturing Inc (G-9294)*
**Fabric Images Inc** ...847 488-9877
325 Corporate Dr Elgin (60123) *(G-9032)*
**Fabricated Metal Systems Inc** ...815 886-6200
646 Forestwood Dr Ste C Romeoville (60446) *(G-18824)*
**Fabricated Metals Co** ...847 718-1300
2121 Landmeier Rd Elk Grove Village (60007) *(G-9474)*
**Fabricated Products Co Inc** ...630 898-6460
1875 Plain Ave Aurora (60502) *(G-1006)*
**Fabricating & Welding Corp** ...773 928-2050
12246 S Halsted St Chicago (60628) *(G-4809)*
**Fabricating Machinery & Eqp, Wood Dale** *Also called Fabricating Machinery Sales (G-22366)*
**Fabricating Machinery Sales** ...630 350-2266
640 Pond Dr Ste A Wood Dale (60191) *(G-22366)*
**Fabricators & Mfrs Assn Intl (PA)** ...815 399-8700
2135 Point Blvd Elgin (60123) *(G-9033)*
**Fabricators and Mfrs Assn, Elgin** *Also called Tube & Pipe Association Intl (G-9217)*
**Fabricators Unlimited Inc** ...847 223-7986
55 S Barron Blvd Grayslake (60030) *(G-11337)*
**Fabrick Molded Plastic Div, McHenry** *Also called CTS Automotive LLC (G-14493)*
**Fabrik Industries Inc** ...815 385-9480
5213 Prime Pkwy McHenry (60050) *(G-14505)*
**Fabrik Molded Plastics, McHenry** *Also called Fabrik Industries Inc (G-14505)*
**Fabtec Manufacturing Inc** ...847 671-4888
9896 Franklin Ave Franklin Park (60131) *(G-10469)*
**Fabtek Aero Ltd** ...630 552-3622
432 E South St Plano (60545) *(G-17664)*
**Fac Enterprises Inc** ...847 844-4000
2755 Spectrum Dr Elgin (60124) *(G-9034)*
**Facemakers Inc (PA)** ...815 273-3944
140 N 5th St Savanna (61074) *(G-19398)*
**Facemakers Inc** ...815 273-3944
800 Chicago Ave Savanna (61074) *(G-19399)*
**Factory Direct Worldwide LLC** ...847 272-6464
230 Messner Dr Wheeling (60090) *(G-22053)*
**Factory Location, Carol Stream** *Also called Scale-Tronix Inc (G-3235)*
**Factory Plaza Inc** ...630 616-9999
429 Evergreen Ave Bensenville (60106) *(G-1895)*
**Fahrner Asphalt Sealers LLC** ...815 986-1180
129 Phelps Ave Ste 215 Rockford (61108) *(G-18379)*
**Fairbanks Morse Pump Corp (PA)** ...630 859-7000
800 Airport Rd North Aurora (60542) *(G-16129)*
**Fairbanks Wire Corporation** ...847 683-2600
260 Industrial Dr Ste B Hampshire (60140) *(G-11550)*
**Fairbury Division, Fairbury** *Also called Ptc Tubular Products LLC (G-10131)*
**FAIRBURY FAIR ASSOCIATION, Fairbury** *Also called John Joda Post 54 (G-10128)*
**Fairchild Industries Inc** ...847 550-9580
475 Capital Dr Lake Zurich (60047) *(G-13071)*
**Fairfield Acid and Frac Co** ...618 842-9186
Hwy 15 W Fairfield (62837) *(G-10140)*
**Fairfield Processing Corp** ...618 452-8404
1201 W 1st St Granite City (62040) *(G-11276)*
**Fairfield Ready Mix Inc** ...618 842-9462
County Rte 45 N Fairfield (62837) *(G-10141)*
**Fairmount Redi-Mix, Fairmount** *Also called Ferber George & Sons (G-10163)*
**Fairmount Santrol Inc** ...815 433-2449
4115 Progress Dr Ottawa (61350) *(G-16958)*
**Fairmount Santrol Inc** ...815 587-4410
776 Centennial Dr Ottawa (61350) *(G-16959)*
**Fairmount Santrol Inc** ...815 538-2645
300 Vermillion St Troy Grove (61372) *(G-21012)*
**Fairview Heights Tribune, Mascoutah** *Also called Herald Publications (G-14353)*
**Faith Printing** ...217 675-2191
824 Bills Rd Franklin (62638) *(G-10379)*
**Faiths Designs** ...773 768-5804
7916 S Kingston Ave Chicago (60617) *(G-4810)*
**Faiths Jewelry Designs, Chicago** *Also called Faiths Designs (G-4810)*

ALPHABETIC

**Falcon Press Inc** ............................................. 815 455-9099
   341 E Crystal Lake Ave  Crystal Lake  (60014)  *(G-7575)*
**Falex Corporation** ............................................ 630 556-3679
   1020 Airpark Dr  Sugar Grove  (60554)  *(G-20723)*
**Fall Protection Systems Inc (PA)** .................... 618 452-7000
   2901 Old Nickel Plate Rd  Madison  (62060)  *(G-14145)*
**Falling Springs Quarry, Dupo**  Also called Stolle Casper Quar & Contg Co  *(G-8579)*
**Famaco Corp** .................................................... 217 442-4412
   110 Atwood St  Tilton  (61833)  *(G-20881)*
**Famar Flavor LLC** ............................................. 708 926-2951
   4711 137th St  Crestwood  (60445)  *(G-7487)*
**Family Eye Care** ............................................... 708 614-2311
   17730 Oak Park Ave Ste B  Tinley Park  (60477)  *(G-20912)*
**Family Gard/Brk, Aurora**  Also called Brk Brands Inc  *(G-975)*
**Family Health Foods, Arthur**  Also called Helmuth Custom Kitchens LLC  *(G-904)*
**Family Record, Palos Heights**  Also called Graphic Communicators Inc  *(G-17106)*
**Family Time Computing Inc** ............................. 309 664-1742
   4 Yount Dr  Bloomington  (61704)  *(G-2162)*
**Family Time Magazine, Frankfort**  Also called Area Marketing Inc  *(G-10297)*
**Famous Fossil Vinyard & Winery** ..................... 815 563-4665
   395 W Cedarville Rd  Freeport  (61032)  *(G-10655)*
**Famous Lubricants Inc** ..................................... 773 268-2555
   124 W 47th St  Chicago  (60609)  *(G-4811)*
**Fanboys Games & Movies LLC** ......................... 847 894-6448
   400 Ascot Dr  Park Ridge  (60068)  *(G-17192)*
**Fancher Printers, South Holland**  Also called Little Doloras  *(G-20286)*
**Fanfest Corporation** ......................................... 847 658-2000
   3604 Oak Knoll Rd  Crystal Lake  (60012)  *(G-7576)*
**Fanmar Inc** ....................................................... 708 563-0505
   901 Greenleaf Ave  Elk Grove Village  (60007)  *(G-9475)*
**Fannie May Cnfctons Brands Inc (HQ)** ............ 773 693-9100
   2457 W North Ave  Melrose Park  (60160)  *(G-14635)*
**Fannie May Fine Chocolate, Melrose Park**  Also called Fannie May Cnfctons Brands Inc  *(G-14635)*
**Fanning Communications Inc** .......................... 708 293-1430
   4701 Midlothian Tpke # 4  Crestwood  (60445)  *(G-7488)*
**Fanplastic Molding Co** ..................................... 815 923-6950
   10704 Harmony Hill Rd  Marengo  (60152)  *(G-14228)*
**Fantastic Lettering Inc** ..................................... 773 685-7650
   5644 W Lawrence Ave  Chicago  (60630)  *(G-4812)*
**Fantasy Coverage Inc** ...................................... 630 592-8082
   261 N York St Ste 202  Elmhurst  (60126)  *(G-9870)*
**Fantasy Festival Costume Magic, Crystal Lake**  Also called Fanfest Corporation  *(G-7576)*
**Fantus Paper Products, Chicago**  Also called P S Greetings Inc  *(G-6040)*
**Fanuc America Corporation** ............................. 847 898-5000
   1800 Lakewood Blvd  Hoffman Estates  (60192)  *(G-12009)*
**Far East Food Inc** ............................................ 312 733-1688
   1836 S Canal St  Chicago  (60616)  *(G-4813)*
**Far East Trading Co, Chicago**  Also called Far East Food Inc  *(G-4813)*
**Far West Print Solutions LLC** ........................... 630 879-9500
   714 Fairfield Way  North Aurora  (60542)  *(G-16130)*
**Farina Locker Service** ...................................... 618 245-6491
   23 7 Madison St  Farina  (62838)  *(G-10175)*
**Farina News** ..................................................... 618 245-6216
   109 N Walnut St  Farina  (62838)  *(G-10176)*
**Fariss John** ...................................................... 815 433-3803
   3700 N Shore Dr  Moline  (61265)  *(G-14938)*
**Fariss Step & Railing Co, Moline**  Also called Fariss John  *(G-14938)*
**Farm Fresh Str D&M Dar Stores, Chester**  Also called Chester Dairy Company Inc  *(G-3653)*
**Farm Progress Companies Inc (HQ)** ............... 630 690-5600
   255 38th Ave Ste P  Saint Charles  (60174)  *(G-19183)*
**Farm Week** ....................................................... 309 557-3140
   1701 Towanda Ave  Bloomington  (61701)  *(G-2163)*
**Farmer Bros Co** ................................................ 217 787-7565
   3430c Constitution Dr  Springfield  (62711)  *(G-20438)*
**Farmer's Fridge, Chicago**  Also called Romaine Empire LLC  *(G-6387)*
**Farmercityjournal.com, Bloomington**  Also called Pantagraph Publishing Co  *(G-2209)*
**Farmers Brothers Coffee, Springfield**  Also called Farmer Bros Co  *(G-20438)*
**Farmers Mill Inc** .............................................. 618 445-2114
   438 County Road 1500 N  Albion  (62806)  *(G-362)*
**Farmers Packing Inc** ........................................ 618 445-3822
   657 Illinois Route 15  Albion  (62806)  *(G-363)*
**Farmington Crematory, Farmington**  Also called Farmington Wilbert Vault Corp  *(G-10186)*
**Farmington Foods Inc (PA)** ............................. 708 771-3600
   7419 Franklin St  Forest Park  (60130)  *(G-10243)*
**Farmington Locker/Ice Plant Co** ..................... 309 245-4621
   101 W Fort St  Farmington  (61531)  *(G-10185)*
**Farmington Wilbert Vault Corp (PA)** ............... 309 245-2133
   22413 E State Route 116  Farmington  (61531)  *(G-10186)*
**Farmweld Inc** ................................................... 217 857-6423
   18413 E Us Highway 40  Teutopolis  (62467)  *(G-20852)*
**Farrow Lumber Co** .......................................... 618 734-0255
   Hwy 37 N  Cairo  (62914)  *(G-2929)*
**Fas-Trak Industries Inc** .................................... 708 570-0650
   4654 W Crocus Ave  Monee  (60449)  *(G-14994)*
**Fashahnn Corporation** ..................................... 773 994-3132
   8016 S Cottage Grove Ave  Chicago  (60619)  *(G-4814)*
**Fashion Craft Corporation** ............................... 847 998-0092
   1421 Old Deerfield Rd  Highland Park  (60035)  *(G-11832)*
**Fashion Fair Cosmetics Div, Chicago**  Also called Johnson Publishing Company LLC  *(G-5320)*
**Fashionaire, Oak Park**  Also called Unitex Industries Inc  *(G-16690)*
**Fasprint of Central Illinois, Monticello**  Also called H2o Ltd  *(G-15077)*
**Faspro Technologies Inc** .................................. 847 364-9999
   165 King St  Elk Grove Village  (60007)  *(G-9476)*
**Faspro Technologies Inc (PA)** .......................... 847 392-9500
   500 W Campus Dr  Arlington Heights  (60004)  *(G-752)*
**Fast Color, North Aurora**  Also called Janssen Avenue Boys Inc  *(G-16136)*
**Fast Forward Energy Inc** .................................. 312 860-0978
   2023 W Carroll Ave  Chicago  (60612)  *(G-4815)*
**Fast Forward Welding Inc** ................................ 815 254-1901
   23840 W Andrew Rd Ste 4  Plainfield  (60585)  *(G-17599)*
**Fast Heat Inc (PA)** ........................................... 630 359-6300
   776 N Oaklawn Ave  Elmhurst  (60126)  *(G-9871)*
**Fast Heat International, Elmhurst**  Also called Fast Heat Inc  *(G-9871)*
**Fast Impressions, Decatur**  Also called Dynagraphics Incorporated  *(G-7878)*
**Fast Lane Applications LLC** ............................. 815 245-2145
   219 Fox St  Cary  (60013)  *(G-3340)*
**Fast Lane Threads Custom EMB** ..................... 815 544-9898
   1467 Mckinley Ave Ste A  Belvidere  (61008)  *(G-1751)*
**Fast Pipe Lining Inc** ......................................... 815 712-8646
   320 Raccuglia Dr  La Salle  (61301)  *(G-12772)*
**Fast Print Shop** ................................................ 618 997-1976
   501 W Deyoung St Ste 7  Marion  (62959)  *(G-14259)*
**Fast Printing of Joliet Inc** ................................. 815 723-0080
   842 Plainfield Rd  Joliet  (60435)  *(G-12492)*
**Fast Signs** ........................................................ 773 698-8115
   1101 W Belmont Ave  Chicago  (60657)  *(G-4816)*
**Fast Signs** ........................................................ 815 730-7828
   1920 Plainfield Rd  Joliet  (60403)  *(G-12493)*
**Fast Signs 590** ................................................. 815 937-1855
   601a N 5th Ave  Kankakee  (60901)  *(G-12615)*
**Fast Track Printing Inc** ..................................... 773 761-9400
   2715 W Touhy Ave  Chicago  (60645)  *(G-4817)*
**Fasteners For Retail Inc** ................................... 847 296-5511
   1600 Birchwood Ave  Des Plaines  (60018)  *(G-8194)*
**Fastrack Stairs & Rails Ltd** .............................. 847 531-6252
   303 N 11th St  Dekalb  (60115)  *(G-8090)*
**Fastron Co** ....................................................... 630 766-5000
   2040 Janice Ave  Melrose Park  (60160)  *(G-14636)*
**Fastsigns, Chicago**  Also called Fast Signs  *(G-4816)*
**Fastsigns, Gurnee**  Also called Holmes Associates Inc  *(G-11460)*
**Fastsigns, Kankakee**  Also called Fast Signs 590  *(G-12615)*
**Fastsigns, Northbrook**  Also called Castino & Associates Inc  *(G-16218)*
**Fastsigns, Arlington Heights**  Also called D&J Arlington Heights Inc  *(G-743)*
**Fastsigns, Champaign**  Also called Mbm Business Assistance Inc  *(G-3512)*
**Fastsigns, Chicago**  Also called Antolak Management Co Inc  *(G-3917)*
**Fastsigns, Bloomington**  Also called Heron Bay Inc  *(G-2178)*
**Fastsigns, Naperville**  Also called Beard Enterprises Inc  *(G-15603)*
**Fastsigns, Northbrook**  Also called DAmico Associates Inc  *(G-16239)*
**Fastsigns, Joliet**  Also called Fast Signs  *(G-12493)*
**Fastsigns, Schaumburg**  Also called M & R Media Inc  *(G-19628)*
**Fastsigns, Peoria**  Also called Geebees Inc  *(G-17369)*
**Fastsigns** ......................................................... 312 344-1765
   118 N Halsted St  Chicago  (60661)  *(G-4818)*
**Fastsigns** ......................................................... 847 981-1965
   1701 Howard St Ste C  Elk Grove Village  (60007)  *(G-9477)*
**Fastsigns** ......................................................... 312 332-7446
   180 N Wacker Dr Ste 100  Chicago  (60606)  *(G-4819)*
**Fastsigns** ......................................................... 847 675-1600
   3450 W Devon Ave  Lincolnwood  (60712)  *(G-13509)*
**Fastsigns** ......................................................... 847 680-7446
   1350 S Milwaukee Ave  Libertyville  (60048)  *(G-13323)*
**Fastsigns 100201, Schaumburg**  Also called De Luca Visual Solutions Inc  *(G-19500)*
**Fastsigns International** .................................... 847 967-7222
   7911 Golf Rd  Morton Grove  (60053)  *(G-15197)*
**Fastway Printing Inc** ........................................ 847 882-0950
   14 E Schaumburg Rd Ste 3  Schaumburg  (60194)  *(G-19524)*
**Fastway Printing Service, Schaumburg**  Also called Fastway Printing Inc  *(G-19524)*
**Father & Daughters Printing** ............................ 708 749-8286
   6426 Cermak Rd  Berwyn  (60402)  *(G-2064)*
**Father Marcellos & Son** ................................... 312 654-2565
   645 W North Ave  Chicago  (60610)  *(G-4820)*
**Faulstich Printing Company Inc** ...................... 217 442-4994
   2001 E Voorhees St  Danville  (61834)  *(G-7718)*
**Fausto's Bread Bakery, Arlington Heights**  Also called Faustos Bakery  *(G-753)*
**Faustos Bakery** ................................................ 847 255-9049
   16 S Evergreen Ave  Arlington Heights  (60005)  *(G-753)*
**Favorite Foods** ................................................. 847 401-7126
   4226 Yorkshire Ln  Northbrook  (60062)  *(G-16256)*
**Faxitron X-Ray LLC** .......................................... 847 465-9729
   575 Bond St  Lincolnshire  (60069)  *(G-13447)*
**Fay Electric Wire, Elmhurst**  Also called Taycorp Inc  *(G-9948)*

ALPHABETIC SECTION Fernwood Printers Ltd

**Fayco Enterprises Inc (PA)**....618 283-0638
1313 Sunset Dr Vandalia (62471) *(G-21113)*
**Faye Jewellery Chez**....815 477-1818
6314 Tilgee Rd Crystal Lake (60012) *(G-7577)*
**Faze Change Produx**....217 728-2184
1331 Cr 1470e Sullivan (61951) *(G-20746)*
**FBC Industries Inc (PA)**....847 241-6143
1933 N Meacham Rd Ste 550 Schaumburg (60173) *(G-19525)*
**FBC Industries Inc**....847 839-0880
110 E Avenue H Rochelle (61068) *(G-18089)*
**Fbm Galaxy Inc**....847 362-0925
1301 Laura Ln Lake Bluff (60044) *(G-12843)*
**Fbs Group Inc**....773 229-8675
6513 W 64th St Chicago (60638) *(G-4821)*
**Fbsa LLC**....773 524-2440
4545 W Augusta Blvd Chicago (60651) *(G-4822)*
**Fc Lighting, Saint Charles** *Also called Lighting Innovations Inc (G-19211)*
**Fca LLC**....309 949-3999
2212 Us Highway 6 Coal Valley (61240) *(G-7296)*
**Fca LLC**....309 385-2588
610 S Walnut St Princeville (61559) *(G-17765)*
**Fca LLC (PA)**....309 792-3444
7601 John Deere Pkwy Moline (61265) *(G-14939)*
**FCA Packaging, Moline** *Also called Fca LLC (G-14939)*
**FCA US LLC**....630 724-2321
901 Warrenville Rd # 550 Lisle (60532) *(G-13588)*
**FCA US LLC**....630 637-3000
1980 High Grove Ln Naperville (60540) *(G-15657)*
**Fcm Mills, Lombard** *Also called Sturtevant Inc (G-13861)*
**Fdf Armature Inc**....630 458-0452
220 W Gerri Ln Addison (60101) *(G-115)*
**Feathersound, Chicago** *Also called Eastern Accents Inc (G-4683)*
**Federal Envelope Company**....630 595-2000
608 Country Club Dr Bensenville (60106) *(G-1896)*
**Federal Equipment & Svcs Inc**....847 731-9002
3200 16th St Zion (60099) *(G-22685)*
**Federal Heath Sign Company LLC**....630 887-6800
7501 S Quincy St Ste 175 Willowbrook (60527) *(G-22211)*
**Federal Mogul Driveline Pdts, Berwyn** *Also called Federal-Mogul Corporation (G-2065)*
**Federal Prison Industries**....618 664-6361
Us Rt 40 4th St Greenville (62246) *(G-11393)*
**Federal Prison Industries**....309 346-8588
2600 S 2nd St Pekin (61554) *(G-17262)*
**Federal Screw Products, Gurnee** *Also called Fsp LLC (G-11450)*
**Federal Sign, Willowbrook** *Also called Federal Heath Sign Company LLC (G-22211)*
**Federal Signal Corporation**....708 534-4756
2645 Federal Signal Dr University Park (60484) *(G-21048)*
**Federal Signal Corporation (PA)**....630 954-2000
1415 W 22nd St Ste 1100 Oak Brook (60523) *(G-16510)*
**Federal Signal Corporation**....708 534-3400
2645 Federal Signal Dr University Park (60484) *(G-21049)*
**Federal Signal Corporation**....708 534-3400
2645 Federal Signal Dr University Park (60484) *(G-21050)*
**Federal Signal Credit Corp**....630 954-2000
1415 W 22nd St Ste 1100 Oak Brook (60523) *(G-16511)*
**Federal Signal-Codespear, University Park** *Also called Federal Signal Corporation (G-21048)*
**Federal Uniform LLC**....847 658-5470
4015 W Carroll Ave Chicago (60624) *(G-4823)*
**Federal-Mogul Corporation**....847 674-7700
7450 Mccormick Blvd Skokie (60076) *(G-19999)*
**Federal-Mogul Corporation**....815 271-9600
4500 Prime Pkwy McHenry (60050) *(G-14506)*
**Federal-Mogul Corporation**....248 354-7700
4929 S Mason Berwyn (60402) *(G-2065)*
**Federal-Mogul Motorparts, McHenry** *Also called Federal-Mogul Corporation (G-14506)*
**Federated Paint Mfg Co (PA)**....708 345-4848
5812 S Homan Ave Chicago (60629) *(G-4824)*
**Fedex Corporation**....847 918-7730
281 W Townline Rd Ste 100 Vernon Hills (60061) *(G-21163)*
**Fedex Ground Package Sys Inc**....800 463-3339
115 W Lake Dr Ste 100 Glendale Heights (60139) *(G-11023)*
**Fedex Office & Print Svcs Inc**....708 345-0984
2509 W North Ave Melrose Park (60160) *(G-14637)*
**Fedex Office & Print Svcs Inc**....312 492-8355
1 S Sangamon St Chicago (60607) *(G-4825)*
**Fedex Office & Print Svcs Inc**....630 469-2677
714 Roosevelt Rd Glen Ellyn (60137) *(G-10970)*
**Fedex Office & Print Svcs Inc**....773 472-3066
744 W Fullerton Ave Chicago (60614) *(G-4826)*
**Fedex Office & Print Svcs Inc**....312 341-9644
71 E Jackson Blvd Chicago (60604) *(G-4827)*
**Fedex Office & Print Svcs Inc**....847 475-8650
2518 Green Bay Rd Evanston (60201) *(G-10036)*
**Fedex Office & Print Svcs Inc**....312 755-0325
540 N Michigan Ave Chicago (60611) *(G-4828)*
**Fedex Office & Print Svcs Inc**....815 229-0033
6240 Mulford Village Dr Rockford (61107) *(G-18380)*
**Fedex Office & Print Svcs Inc**....312 595-0768
505 N Michigan Ave Chicago (60611) *(G-4829)*
**Fedex Office & Print Svcs Inc**....847 329-9464
6829 N Lincoln Ave Lincolnwood (60712) *(G-13510)*
**Fedex Office & Print Svcs Inc**....217 355-3400
505 S Mattis Ave Champaign (61821) *(G-3485)*
**Fedex Office & Print Svcs Inc**....847 729-3030
1623 Waukegan Rd Glenview (60025) *(G-11124)*
**Fedex Office & Print Svcs Inc**....309 685-4093
3465 N University St Peoria (61604) *(G-17359)*
**Fedex Office & Print Svcs Inc**....630 759-5784
251 S Weber Rd Bolingbrook (60490) *(G-2308)*
**Fedex Office & Print Svcs Inc**....847 459-8008
76 W Dundee Rd Buffalo Grove (60089) *(G-2693)*
**Fedex Office & Print Svcs Inc**....708 452-0149
1720 N Harlem Ave Elmwood Park (60707) *(G-9970)*
**Fedex Office & Print Svcs Inc**....847 823-9360
678 N Northwest Hwy Park Ridge (60068) *(G-17193)*
**Fedex Office & Print Svcs Inc**....312 663-1149
720 S Michigan Ave Chicago (60605) *(G-4830)*
**Fedex Office & Print Svcs Inc**....847 670-7283
1 W Rand Rd Ste F Mount Prospect (60056) *(G-15329)*
**Fedex Office & Print Svcs Inc**....847 292-7176
9300 Bryn Mawr Ave Rosemont (60018) *(G-19001)*
**Fedex Office & Print Svcs Inc**....708 799-5323
17952 Halsted St Homewood (60430) *(G-12098)*
**Fedex Office & Print Svcs Inc**....630 894-1800
369 W Army Trail Rd Bloomingdale (60108) *(G-2108)*
**Fedex Office & Print Svcs Inc**....847 670-4100
205 W Rand Rd Arlington Heights (60004) *(G-754)*
**Fedex Office & Print Svcs Inc**....312 670-4460
444 N Wells St Fl 1 Chicago (60654) *(G-4831)*
**Fedex Office Print & Ship Ctr, Rosemont** *Also called Fedex Office & Print Svcs Inc (G-19001)*
**Feeder Corporation of America**....708 343-4900
4429 James Pl Melrose Park (60160) *(G-14638)*
**Feedstffs Intrnet Subscription, Saint Charles** *Also called Farm Progress Companies Inc (G-19183)*
**Feelsure Health Corparation**....847 823-0137
120 Columbia Ave Park Ridge (60068) *(G-17194)*
**Feelsure Health Corporation**....847 446-7881
503 Orchard Ln Winnetka (60093) *(G-22306)*
**Fehr Cab Interiors**....815 692-3355
10116 N 1900 East Rd Fairbury (61739) *(G-10124)*
**Fehrenbacher Ready-Mix Inc**....618 395-2306
1401 S Whittle Ave Olney (62450) *(G-16766)*
**Fehring Ornamental Iron Works**....217 483-6727
10128 Gilreath Rd Chatham (62629) *(G-3620)*
**Felco, Melrose Park** *Also called Forest Electric Company (G-14639)*
**Felde Tool & Machine Co Inc**....309 692-5870
2324 W Altorfer Dr Peoria (61615) *(G-17360)*
**Felice Hosiery Co Inc (PA)**....312 922-3710
632 W Roosevelt Rd Chicago (60607) *(G-4832)*
**Felice Hosiery Company Inc**....312 922-3710
632 W Roosevelt Rd Chicago (60607) *(G-4833)*
**Felix Partners LLC**....847 648-8449
1845 Hicks Rd Ste C Rolling Meadows (60008) *(G-18728)*
**Feller Oilfield Service Inc**....618 267-5650
Hwy 40 W Saint Elmo (62458) *(G-19307)*
**Fellowes Trading Company**....630 893-1600
1789 Norwood Ave Itasca (60143) *(G-12262)*
**Fellowship Black Light**....773 826-7790
2859 W Wilcox St Chicago (60612) *(G-4834)*
**Felste Co Inc**....217 283-4884
217 N 9th Ave Hoopeston (60942) *(G-12111)*
**Fema L & L Food Services Inc**....217 835-2018
103 N 2nd St Benld (62009) *(G-1805)*
**Fema's, Benld** *Also called Fema L & L Food Services Inc (G-1805)*
**Female Health Company (PA)**....312 595-9123
150 N Michigan Ave # 1580 Chicago (60601) *(G-4835)*
**Femina Sport Inc**....630 271-1876
5100 Walnut Ave Downers Grove (60515) *(G-8442)*
**Femsa, Frankfort** *Also called Paratech Incorporated (G-10348)*
**Fenix Manufacturing LLC**....815 208-0755
2001 9th St Fulton (61252) *(G-10700)*
**Fenwal Inc (HQ)**....847 550-2300
3 Corporate Dr Ste 300 Lake Zurich (60047) *(G-13072)*
**Fenwal Holdings Inc (HQ)**....847 550-2300
3 Corporate Dr Ste 300 Lake Zurich (60047) *(G-13073)*
**Feralloy Corporation (HQ)**....503 286-8869
8755 W Higgins Rd Ste 970 Chicago (60631) *(G-4836)*
**Ferber George & Sons**....217 733-2184
102 S Pine St Fairmount (61841) *(G-10163)*
**Ferguson Enterprises Inc**....217 425-7262
1226 E Garfield Ave Decatur (62526) *(G-7880)*
**Ferguson Enterprises Inc**....217 425-7262
500 W Eldorado St Decatur (62522) *(G-7881)*
**Fern Manufacturing Company**....630 260-9350
333 Kimberly Dr Carol Stream (60188) *(G-3150)*
**Fernandez Windows Corp**....773 762-2365
2535 S Ridgeway Ave Chicago (60623) *(G-4837)*
**Fernwood Printers Ltd**....630 964-9449
14955 Mission Ave Oak Forest (60452) *(G-16581)*

ALPHABETIC

(PA)=Parent Co (HQ)=Headquarters (DH)=Div Headquarters
2017 Harris Illinois Industrial Directory
1239

**Ferrara Candy Company (PA)**............708 366-0500
1 Tower Ln Ste 2700 Oakbrook Terrace (60181) ***(G-16707)***
**Ferrara Candy Company**............630 366-0500
7301 Harrison St Forest Park (60130) ***(G-10244)***
**Ferrara Candy Company**............630 378-4197
901 Carlow Dr Bolingbrook (60490) ***(G-2309)***
**Ferrara Candy Company**............708 432-4407
3000 Washington Blvd Bellwood (60104) ***(G-1705)***
**Ferrara Candy Company**............708 488-1892
7525 Industrial Dr Forest Park (60130) ***(G-10245)***
**Ferrara Pan Candy Co, Forest Park** *Also called Ferrara Candy Company* ***(G-10244)***
**Ferrellgas LP**............815 877-7333
10522 N 2nd St Machesney Park (61115) ***(G-14073)***
**Ferrellgas LP**............815 599-8967
10522 N 2nd St Machesney Park (61115) ***(G-14074)***
**Ferrite International Company**............847 249-4900
39105 Magnetics Blvd Wadsworth (60083) ***(G-21322)***
**Ferro Asphalt Company**............815 744-6633
2111 Moen Ave Rockdale (60436) ***(G-18219)***
**Ferro Corporation**............847 623-0370
1219 Glen Rock Ave Waukegan (60085) ***(G-21559)***
**Fertilizer Inc**............708 458-8615
5820 W 66th St Chicago (60638) ***(G-4838)***
**Fertilizer Inc**............708 458-8615
5820 W 66th St Bedford Park (60638) ***(G-1549)***
**Fetco, Lake Zurich** *Also called Food Equipment Technologies Co* ***(G-13075)***
**Fetzer Surgical LLC**............630 635-2520
1019 W Wise Rd Ste 201 Schaumburg (60193) ***(G-19526)***
**Fey & Company, Naperville** *Also called Edgar H Fey Jewelers Inc* ***(G-15651)***
**Ffg Restoration Inc**............708 240-4873
2737 S 12th Ave Broadview (60155) ***(G-2577)***
**Ffr Merchandising, Des Plaines** *Also called Fasteners For Retail Inc* ***(G-8194)***
**Fgc Plasma Solutions LLC**............954 591-1429
9700 S Case Ave Bldg 203 Lemont (60439) ***(G-13235)***
**Fgfi LLC**............708 598-0909
411 E Plainfield Rd Countryside (60525) ***(G-7424)***
**Fgs, Broadview** *Also called Financial Graphic Services Inc* ***(G-2580)***
**Fgs Inc**............312 421-3060
815 W Van Buren St # 302 Chicago (60607) ***(G-4839)***
**Fgs-IL LLC**............630 375-8500
780 Mcclure Rd Aurora (60502) ***(G-1007)***
**FH Ayer Manufacturing Co**............708 755-0550
2015 S Halsted St Chicago Heights (60411) ***(G-7097)***
**FHB Lighting Inc**............888 364-8802
800 E Northwest Hwy # 700 Palatine (60074) ***(G-17028)***
**FHP Inc**............708 452-4100
505 N Railroad Ave Northlake (60164) ***(G-16436)***
**FHP-Berner USA LP**............630 270-1400
2188a Diehl Rd Aurora (60502) ***(G-1008)***
**Fiber Options Div, Chicago** *Also called Buster Services Inc* ***(G-4191)***
**Fiber Winders Inc**............618 548-6388
1111 S Broadway Ave Salem (62881) ***(G-19332)***
**Fiberbasin Inc**............630 978-0705
1500 Dearborn Ave Ste 13 Aurora (60505) ***(G-1151)***
**Fiberforge Corporation**............970 945-9377
70 W Madison St Ste 2300 Chicago (60602) ***(G-4840)***
**Fibergel Technologies Inc**............847 549-6002
1011 Campus Dr Mundelein (60060) ***(G-15500)***
**Fiberglass Innovations LLC**............815 962-9338
2219 Kishwaukee St Rockford (61104) ***(G-18381)***
**Fiberglass International, Aroma Park** *Also called New Dimension Models* ***(G-879)***
**Fiberglass Solutions Corp**............630 458-0756
436 W Belden Ave Addison (60101) ***(G-116)***
**Fiberlink LLC**............312 951-8500
230 E Ohio St Ste 212 Chicago (60611) ***(G-4841)***
**Fiberteq LLC**............217 431-2111
3650 Southgate Dr Danville (61834) ***(G-7719)***
**Fibertex Nonwovens LLC**............815 349-3200
27981 W Concrete Dr Ingleside (60041) ***(G-12189)***
**Fibre Drum Company**............815 933-3222
1650 E Sheridan St Kankakee (60901) ***(G-12616)***
**Fibre-TEC Partitions LLC**............773 436-4028
5301 S Western Blvd Ste 1 Chicago (60609) ***(G-4842)***
**Fibro Inc (HQ)**............815 229-1300
139 Harrison Ave Rockford (61104) ***(G-18382)***
**Fibromanta, Rockford** *Also called Fibro Inc* ***(G-18382)***
**FIC America Corp (HQ)**............630 871-7609
485 E Lies Rd Carol Stream (60188) ***(G-3151)***
**Fidelity Bindery Company**............708 343-6833
2829 S 18th Ave Broadview (60155) ***(G-2578)***
**Fidelity Print Cmmncations LLC**............708 343-6833
2829 S 18th Ave 33 Broadview (60155) ***(G-2579)***
**Fidelity Tool & Mold Ltd (PA)**............630 879-2300
1885 Suncast Ln Batavia (60510) ***(G-1447)***
**Field Holdings LLC (PA)**............847 509-2250
400 Skokie Blvd Ste 860 Northbrook (60062) ***(G-16257)***
**Field Manufacturing Corp**............815 455-5596
1661 Brompton Ln Ste B Crystal Lake (60014) ***(G-7578)***
**Field Outfitting Co., The, Chicago** *Also called Tfo Group LLC* ***(G-6709)***
**Field Ventures LLC**............847 509-2250
400 Skokie Blvd Ste 860 Northbrook (60062) ***(G-16258)***
**Field Works Inc**............847 658-8200
1220 Armstrong St Algonquin (60102) ***(G-389)***
**Fielders Choice**............618 937-2294
708 S Logan St West Frankfort (62896) ***(G-21807)***
**Fifth Ave Provision, Westchester** *Also called Lorenzo Frozen Foods Ltd* ***(G-21848)***
**Fifth Quarter**............618 346-6659
1770 Triad Rd Saint Jacob (62281) ***(G-19315)***
**File System Labs LLC**............617 431-4313
3387 Commercial Ave Northbrook (60062) ***(G-16259)***
**Fillo's Frijoles, South Elgin** *Also called Sofrito Foods LLC* ***(G-20226)***
**Filmfax Magazine Inc**............847 866-7155
1320 Oakton St Evanston (60202) ***(G-10037)***
**Filter Friend Z Inc**............847 824-4049
2280 Magnolia St Des Plaines (60018) ***(G-8195)***
**Filter Kleen Inc**............708 447-4666
8432 44th Pl Lyons (60534) ***(G-14037)***
**Filter Monkey LLC**............630 773-4402
424 S Lombard Rd Itasca (60143) ***(G-12263)***
**Filter Renew Tecnologies**............815 344-2200
3205 Lakeside Ct McCullom Lake (60050) ***(G-14471)***
**Filter Technology Inc**............773 523-7200
7200 S Leamington Ave Bedford Park (60638) ***(G-1550)***
**Filters To You**............815 939-0700
183 E North St Bradley (60915) ***(G-2421)***
**Filtertek Inc (HQ)**............815 648-2410
11411 Price Rd Hebron (60034) ***(G-11719)***
**Filtran Holdings LLC (PA)**............847 635-6670
875 Seegers Rd Des Plaines (60016) ***(G-8196)***
**Filtran LLC (HQ)**............847 635-6670
875 Seegers Rd Des Plaines (60016) ***(G-8197)***
**Filtration Group Corporation (PA)**............815 726-4600
912 E Washington St Ste 1 Joliet (60433) ***(G-12494)***
**Filtration Group LLC**............630 968-1563
600 W 22nd St Ste 300 Oak Brook (60523) ***(G-16512)***
**Filtration Group LLC**............815 726-4600
912 E Washington St Ste 1 Joliet (60433) ***(G-12495)***
**Fim Engineering LLC**............773 880-8841
2199 E 1120 North Rd Milford (60953) ***(G-14812)***
**Final Call Inc (PA)**............773 602-1230
734 W 79th St Chicago (60620) ***(G-4843)***
**Final Call Newspaper, The, Chicago** *Also called Final Call Inc* ***(G-4843)***
**Final Finish Boat Works**............847 603-1345
811 Pickard Ave Antioch (60002) ***(G-631)***
**Financial and Professional Reg**............217 782-2127
325 W Adams St Lbby Springfield (62704) ***(G-20439)***
**Financial Graphic Service, Broadview** *Also called Kelvyn Press Inc* ***(G-2591)***
**Financial Graphic Services Inc (PA)**............708 343-0448
2910 S 18th Ave Broadview (60155) ***(G-2580)***
**Finchs Beer Company LLC**............773 919-8012
1800 W Walnut St Chicago (60612) ***(G-4844)***
**Fine Arts Engraving Co**............800 688-4400
311 S Wacker Dr Ste 300 Chicago (60606) ***(G-4845)***
**Fine Gold Mfg Jewelers**............630 323-9600
777 N York Rd Ste 27 Hinsdale (60521) ***(G-11946)***
**Fine Line Printing**............773 582-9709
5181 S Archer Ave Chicago (60632) ***(G-4846)***
**Finer Line Inc**............847 884-1611
1306 N Plum Grove Rd Schaumburg (60173) ***(G-19527)***
**Finer Line Engraving, Schaumburg** *Also called Finer Line Inc* ***(G-19527)***
**Fingers, Chicago** *Also called Gregory Lamar & Assoc Inc* ***(G-5002)***
**Finish Line Horse Products Inc**............630 694-0000
115 Gateway Rd Bensenville (60106) ***(G-1897)***
**Finish Line Transmission Inc**............630 350-7776
801 N Central Ave Wood Dale (60191) ***(G-22367)***
**Finish Line USA Inc**............847 608-7800
1750 Todd Farm Dr Ste A Elgin (60123) ***(G-9035)***
**Finished Metals Incorporated**............773 229-1600
6146 S New England Ave Chicago (60638) ***(G-4847)***
**Finishers Exchange**............847 462-0533
744 Northwest Hwy Fox River Grove (60021) ***(G-10286)***
**Finishes Unlimited Inc**............630 466-4881
482 Wheeler Rd Sugar Grove (60554) ***(G-20724)***
**Finishing Company**............630 521-9635
717 Thomas Dr Bensenville (60106) ***(G-1898)***
**Finishing Company**............630 559-0808
136 W Commercial Ave Addison (60101) ***(G-117)***
**Finishing Group**............847 884-4890
1300 Basswood Rd Ste 200r Schaumburg (60173) ***(G-19528)***
**Finishing Touch**............309 789-6444
15383 E Cheyenne Dr Cuba (61427) ***(G-7680)***
**Finishing Touch Inc**............773 774-7349
5580 N Northwest Hwy Chicago (60630) ***(G-4848)***
**Finite Resources Ltd**............618 252-3733
520 S Mckinley St Harrisburg (62946) ***(G-11598)***
**Finkl Steel - Chicago, Chicago** *Also called A Finkl & Sons Co* ***(G-3687)***
**Finks Oil Co Inc**............618 548-5757
519 W Boone St Salem (62881) ***(G-19333)***

**Finoric LLC** ....773 829-5811
1263 Chalet Rd Apt 211n Naperville (60563) ***(G-15658)***
**Finzer Holding LLC (PA)** ....847 390-6200
129 Rawls Rd Des Plaines (60018) ***(G-8198)***
**Finzer Roller Inc (PA)** ....847 390-6200
129 Rawls Rd Des Plaines (60018) ***(G-8199)***
**Finzer Roller Pennsylvania, Des Plaines** *Also called Finzer Holding LLC* ***(G-8198)***
**Fire CAM LLC** ....618 416-8390
321 Clearwater Dr Belleville (62220) ***(G-1632)***
**Fire Chariot LLC** ....815 561-3688
770 Wiscold Dr Rochelle (61068) ***(G-18090)***
**Fire Place By Ignite, Downers Grove** *Also called Tagitsold Inc* ***(G-8529)***
**Fire Sentry Corporation** ....714 694-0823
405 Barclay Blvd Lincolnshire (60069) ***(G-13448)***
**Fire Systems Holdings Inc** ....708 333-4130
8940 W 192nd St Ste M Mokena (60448) ***(G-14861)***
**Firefly International Enrgy Co (PA)** ....781 937-0619
6533 N Galena Rd Peoria (61614) ***(G-17361)***
**Firefly Mobile Inc** ....305 538-2777
1325 Remington Rd Ste H Schaumburg (60173) ***(G-19529)***
**Firepenny, Mokena** *Also called Citizenprime LLC* ***(G-14859)***
**Fireplace & Chimney Authority** ....630 279-8500
120 E Lake St Elmhurst (60126) ***(G-9872)***
**Firestone, Glendale Heights** *Also called Bridgestone Ret Operations LLC* ***(G-11012)***
**Firestone, Normal** *Also called Bridgestone Americas* ***(G-16066)***
**Firm of John Dickinson (PA)** ....847 680-1000
2000 Hollister Dr Libertyville (60048) ***(G-13324)***
**First & Main Inc** ....630 587-1000
2400 E Main St Saint Charles (60174) ***(G-19184)***
**First Alert Inc (HQ)** ....630 499-3295
3901 Liberty St Aurora (60504) ***(G-1009)***
**First Amrcn Plstic Mlding Entp** ....815 624-8538
810 Progressive Ln South Beloit (61080) ***(G-20145)***
**First Ayd Corporation** ....847 622-0001
1325 Gateway Dr Elgin (60124) ***(G-9036)***
**First Choice Building Pdts Inc** ....630 350-2770
740 N Edgewood Ave Wood Dale (60191) ***(G-22368)***
**First Electric Motor Shop Inc** ....217 698-0672
1130 W Reynolds St Springfield (62702) ***(G-20440)***
**First Header Die Inc** ....815 282-5161
1313 Anvil Rd Machesney Park (61115) ***(G-14075)***
**First Impression** ....815 883-3357
211 S Columbia Ave Oglesby (61348) ***(G-16748)***
**First Impression of Chicago** ....773 224-3434
218 E 79th St Chicago (60619) ***(G-4849)***
**First Light Inc** ....630 520-0017
245 W Roosevelt Rd Ste 3 West Chicago (60185) ***(G-21701)***
**First Mate Yacht Detailing** ....847 249-7654
35 E Madison St Waukegan (60085) ***(G-21560)***
**First Priority Inc (PA)** ....847 531-1215
1590 Todd Farm Dr Elgin (60123) ***(G-9037)***
**First Stage Fabrication Inc** ....618 282-8320
340 Kennedy Dr Red Bud (62278) ***(G-17941)***
**First State Bank** ....217 239-3000
101 E Windsor Rd Champaign (61820) ***(G-3486)***
**First Step Womens Center** ....217 523-0100
104 E North Grand Ave A Springfield (62702) ***(G-20441)***
**First String Enterprises Inc (PA)** ....708 614-1200
18650 Graphic Ct Tinley Park (60477) ***(G-20913)***
**First-Light Usa LLC** ....217 687-4048
205 S Main St Seymour (61875) ***(G-19897)***
**Fisa North America Inc** ....847 593-2080
260 Stanley St Elk Grove Village (60007) ***(G-9478)***
**Fischbein LLC, Downers Grove** *Also called Duravant LLC* ***(G-8437)***
**FISCHER NUT COMPANY, Elgin** *Also called John B Sanfilippo & Son Inc* ***(G-9083)***
**Fischer Paper Products Inc (PA)** ....847 395-6060
179 Ida Ave Antioch (60002) ***(G-632)***
**Fischer Stone & Materials LLC** ....815 233-3232
1567 N Heine Rd Freeport (61032) ***(G-10656)***
**Fish King Inc** ....773 736-4974
5228 W Giddings St Chicago (60630) ***(G-4850)***
**Fish Oven and Equipment Corp** ....847 526-8686
120 Kent Ave Wauconda (60084) ***(G-21463)***
**Fish Window Cleaning, Oswego** *Also called James A Freund LLC* ***(G-16923)***
**Fisher & Ludlow Inc** ....217 324-6106
1501 Eilerman Ave Ste 400 Litchfield (62056) ***(G-13684)***
**Fisher & Ludlow Inc** ....217 324-6106
1501 Eilerman Ave Litchfield (62056) ***(G-13685)***
**Fisher & Ludlow Inc** ....815 932-1200
1115 E 5000n Rd Bourbonnais (60914) ***(G-2396)***
**Fisher Container Corp, Buffalo Grove** *Also called Fisher Container Corp* ***(G-2694)***
**Fisher Container Corp** ....847 541-0000
1111 Busch Pkwy Buffalo Grove (60089) ***(G-2694)***
**Fisher Container Holdings LLC (PA)** ....847 541-0000
1111 Busch Pkwy Buffalo Grove (60089) ***(G-2695)***
**Fisher Controls Intl LLC** ....847 956-8020
1124 Tower Rd Chicago (60673) ***(G-4851)***
**Fisher Printing Inc (PA)** ....708 598-1500
8640 S Oketo Ave Bridgeview (60455) ***(G-2489)***
**Fisher Printing Inc** ....708 598-9266
8645 S Thomas Ave Bridgeview (60455) ***(G-2490)***
**Fisher Safety, Hanover Park** *Also called Fisher Scientific Company LLC* ***(G-11580)***
**Fisher Scientific Company LLC** ....412 490-8300
4500 Turnberry Dr Hanover Park (60133) ***(G-11580)***
**Fishermans Quarters** ....217 791-5104
2886 S Mount Zion Rd Decatur (62521) ***(G-7882)***
**Fisheye Grahphics, Chicago** *Also called Fisheye Services Incorporated* ***(G-4852)***
**Fisheye Services Incorporated** ....773 942-6314
5443 N Broadway St Chicago (60640) ***(G-4852)***
**Fishing Facts, Burr Ridge** *Also called Midwest Outdoors Ltd* ***(G-2867)***
**Fishstone Studio Inc** ....815 276-0299
110 East St Crystal Lake (60014) ***(G-7579)***
**Fiskars Brands Inc** ....800 635-7668
1 Sprinkler Ln Peoria (61615) ***(G-17362)***
**Fiskars Brands Inc** ....309 690-2200
1 Sprinkler Ln Peoria (61615) ***(G-17363)***
**Fitness Wear Inc** ....847 486-1704
1940 Lehigh Ave Ste B Glenview (60026) ***(G-11125)***
**Fitpac Co Ltd** ....630 428-9077
14 N Center St 22 Bensenville (60106) ***(G-1899)***
**Fitz Chem Corporation** ....630 467-8383
450 E Devon Ave Ste 175 Itasca (60143) ***(G-12264)***
**Fitzpatrick Company, The, Elmhurst** *Also called Idex Mpt Inc* ***(G-9884)***
**Five Brother Inc** ....309 663-6323
2905 Gill St Ste B Bloomington (61704) ***(G-2164)***
**Five P Drilling Inc** ....618 943-9771
10585 Cabin Hill Dr Bridgeport (62417) ***(G-2452)***
**Five Star Desserts and Foods** ....773 375-5100
8559 S Constance Ave Chicago (60617) ***(G-4853)***
**Five Star Industries Inc (PA)** ....618 542-4880
1308 Wells Street Rd Du Quoin (62832) ***(G-8554)***
**Five Star Printing Inc** ....217 965-3355
169 W Jackson St Virden (62690) ***(G-21296)***
**Fivecubits Inc (HQ)** ....630 749-4182
1315 W 22nd St Ste 300 Oak Brook (60523) ***(G-16513)***
**Fivecubits Inc** ....925 273-1862
1315 W 22nd St Ste 300 Oak Brook (60523) ***(G-16514)***
**Fives Landis Corp** ....815 389-2251
481 Gardner St South Beloit (61080) ***(G-20146)***
**Fix It Fast Ltd** ....708 401-8320
14922 Lawndale Ave Midlothian (60445) ***(G-14766)***
**Fixture Company** ....847 214-3100
8770 W Bryn Mawr Ave Chicago (60631) ***(G-4854)***
**Fixture Hardware Co (PA)** ....773 777-6100
4711 N Lamon Ave Chicago (60630) ***(G-4855)***
**Fjcj LLC** ....618 785-2217
11000 Baldwin Rd Baldwin (62217) ***(G-1250)***
**Fjw Optical Systems Inc** ....847 358-2500
322 N Woodwork Ln Palatine (60067) ***(G-17029)***
**Fkavpc Inc** ....847 524-9000
1420 Wright Blvd Schaumburg (60193) ***(G-19530)***
**Fkm Usa LLC** ....815 469-2473
21950 S La Grange Rd A Frankfort (60423) ***(G-10322)***
**FL 1** ....847 956-9400
128 N Lively Blvd Fl 1 Elk Grove Village (60007) ***(G-9479)***
**FL West Corporation** ....708 342-0500
7610 162nd Pl Tinley Park (60477) ***(G-20914)***
**Flagsource, Batavia** *Also called J C Schultz Enterprises Inc* ***(G-1459)***
**Flaherty Incorporated** ....773 472-8456
9047 Terminal Ave Skokie (60077) ***(G-20000)***
**Flame Guard Usa LLC** ....815 219-4074
4 Hillview Dr Units A&B Lake Barrington (60010) ***(G-12806)***
**Flamingos Icecream** ....708 749-4287
6733 Cermak Rd Berwyn (60402) ***(G-2066)***
**Flanders Corporation** ....815 472-4230
11360 E State Rte 114 Momence (60954) ***(G-14980)***
**Flanders Precisionaire, Momence** *Also called Flanders Corporation* ***(G-14980)***
**Flash Printing Inc** ....847 288-9101
9224 Grand Ave Ste 1 Franklin Park (60131) ***(G-10470)***
**Flashcut Cnc, Deerfield** *Also called Worth-Pfaff Innovations Inc* ***(G-8068)***
**Flashtric, Chicago** *Also called Turk Electric Sign Co* ***(G-6793)***
**Flatland Forge & Design, De Soto** *Also called Andrew McDonald* ***(G-7818)***
**Flatout Gaskets, Mundelein** *Also called Flatout Group Llc* ***(G-15501)***
**Flatout Group Llc** ....847 837-9200
668 Tower Rd Mundelein (60060) ***(G-15501)***
**Flavorchem Corporation (PA)** ....630 932-8100
1525 Brook Dr Downers Grove (60515) ***(G-8443)***
**Flavorfocus LLC** ....630 520-9060
1210 N Swift Rd Addison (60101) ***(G-118)***
**Fleet Management Solutions Inc (HQ)** ....805 787-0508
2700 Patriot Blvd Ste 200 Glenview (60026) ***(G-11126)***
**Fleetchem LLC (PA)** ....708 957-5311
1222 Brassie Ave Ste 19 Flossmoor (60422) ***(G-10224)***
**Fleetpride Inc** ....630 455-6881
7630 S Madison St Willowbrook (60527) ***(G-22212)***
**Fleetpride Inc** ....708 430-2081
7400 W 87th St Bridgeview (60455) ***(G-2491)***

ALPHABETIC

**Fleetwood Press Inc**............708 485-6811
9321 Ogden Ave Brookfield (60513) ***(G-2632)***
**Fleischmanns Vinegar Co Inc**............773 523-2817
4801 S Oakley Ave Chicago (60609) ***(G-4856)***
**Fleming Music Technology Ctr**............708 316-8662
408 W Elm St Wheaton (60189) ***(G-21948)***
**Flender, Elgin** *Also called Siemens Industry Inc* ***(G-9177)***
**Flex Court Electronic, Kewanee** *Also called Flex Court International Inc* ***(G-12684)***
**Flex Court International Inc**............309 852-0899
4328 Us Highway 34 Kewanee (61443) ***(G-12684)***
**Flex Lighting II LLC**............312 929-3488
25 E Washington St # 510 Chicago (60602) ***(G-4857)***
**Flex N Gate Plastics, Danville** *Also called Flex-N-Gate Corporation* ***(G-7721)***
**Flex-N-Gate Chicago LLC**............217 255-5098
502 E Anthony Dr Urbana (61802) ***(G-21084)***
**Flex-N-Gate Corporation**............217 442-4018
3403 Lynch Creek Dr Danville (61834) ***(G-7720)***
**Flex-N-Gate Corporation (PA)**............217 384-6600
1306 E University Ave Urbana (61802) ***(G-21085)***
**Flex-N-Gate Corporation**............217 384-6600
1306 E University Ave Urbana (61802) ***(G-21086)***
**Flex-N-Gate Corporation**............217 255-5025
502 E Anthony Dr Urbana (61802) ***(G-21087)***
**Flex-N-Gate Corporation**............217 442-4018
3403 Lynch Creek Dr Danville (61834) ***(G-7721)***
**Flex-N-Gate Corporation**............217 278-2400
601 Guardian Way Urbana (61802) ***(G-21088)***
**Flex-N-Gate Plant, Urbana** *Also called Flex-N-Gate Corporation* ***(G-21086)***
**Flex-O-Glass Inc (PA)**............773 261-5200
4647 W Augusta Blvd Ste 1 Chicago (60651) ***(G-4858)***
**Flex-O-Glass Inc**............773 379-7878
1100 N Cicero Ave Ste 1 Chicago (60651) ***(G-4859)***
**Flex-O-Glass Inc**............815 288-1424
1200 Warp Rd Dixon (61021) ***(G-8331)***
**Flex-Pak Packaging Products**............630 761-3335
651 N Raddant Rd Batavia (60510) ***(G-1448)***
**Flex-Weld Inc**............815 334-3662
1425 Lake Ave Woodstock (60098) ***(G-22567)***
**Flexan LLC (PA)**............773 685-6446
6626 W Dakin St Chicago (60634) ***(G-4860)***
**Flexera Holdings LP**............847 466-4000
300 Park Blvd Ste 500 Itasca (60143) ***(G-12265)***
**Flexera Software LLC (PA)**............800 374-4353
300 Park Blvd Ste 500 Itasca (60143) ***(G-12266)***
**Flexible Safety Zoning Co, Romeoville** *Also called Nafisco Inc* ***(G-18851)***
**Flexicore Slab, East Saint Louis** *Also called St Louis Flexicore Inc* ***(G-8770)***
**Flexicraft Industries Inc (PA)**............312 738-3588
2315 W Hubbard St Chicago (60612) ***(G-4861)***
**Flexisnake, Chillicothe** *Also called Imagination Products Corp* ***(G-7167)***
**Flexitech Inc (HQ)**............309 664-7828
1719 E Hamilton Rd Bloomington (61704) ***(G-2165)***
**Flexo Prepress Solutions, Oswego** *Also called Eugene Ewbank* ***(G-16917)***
**Flexografix Inc**............630 350-0100
27 W 136 St Charles Carol Stream (60188) ***(G-3152)***
**Flextron Inc**............630 543-5995
130 W Fay Ave Addison (60101) ***(G-119)***
**Flextron Circuit Assembly, Wood Dale** *Also called S & M Group Inc* ***(G-22418)***
**Flextronics Intl USA Inc**............847 383-1529
700 Corporate Grove Dr Buffalo Grove (60089) ***(G-2696)***
**Flexxsonic Corporation**............847 452-7226
1516 N Elmhurst Rd Mount Prospect (60056) ***(G-15330)***
**Fli Products, West Chicago** *Also called First Light Inc* ***(G-21701)***
**Fli Products LLC**............630 520-0017
245 W Roosevelt Rd Ste 20 West Chicago (60185) ***(G-21702)***
**Flink Company (PA)**............815 673-4321
502 N Vermillion St Streator (61364) ***(G-20688)***
**Flinn & Dreffein Engrg Co**............847 272-6374
4025 Michelline Ln Northbrook (60062) ***(G-16260)***
**Flinn Scientific Inc**............800 452-1261
770 N Raddant Rd Batavia (60510) ***(G-1449)***
**Flint Group US LLC**............630 526-9903
1333 N Kirk Rd Batavia (60510) ***(G-1450)***
**Flint Group US LLC**............618 349-8384
619 N 2200 St Saint Peter (62880) ***(G-19322)***
**Flint Hills Resources LP**............815 224-1525
501 Brunner St Peru (61354) ***(G-17509)***
**Flint Hlls Rsources Joliet LLC**............815 224-5232
501 Brunner St Peru (61354) ***(G-17510)***
**Flip Flop Puzzle Mats, Chicago** *Also called Alessco Inc* ***(G-3801)***
**Fliptabs Inc**............815 701-2584
7213 Loras Ln Wonder Lake (60097) ***(G-22323)***
**Flirty Cupcakes LLC**............312 545-1096
1101 W Lake St Ste 303 Chicago (60607) ***(G-4862)***
**Flix Candy, Niles** *Also called Imaginings 3 Inc* ***(G-15987)***
**Flock It Ltd**............815 247-8775
13142 Murphy Rd Winnebago (61088) ***(G-22296)***
**Flocon Inc**............815 943-5893
714 W Park St Harvard (60033) ***(G-11633)***
**Flocon Inc (PA)**............815 444-1500
339 Cary Point Dr Cary (60013) ***(G-3341)***
**Floden Enterprises**............847 566-7898
674 E Hawley St Mundelein (60060) ***(G-15502)***
**Flodyne Inc**............630 563-3600
1000 Muirfield Dr Hanover Park (60133) ***(G-11581)***
**Floline Archtctral Systems LLC**............815 733-5044
16108 S Rte 59 Ste 108 Plainfield (60586) ***(G-17600)***
**Flolo Corporation (PA)**............630 595-1010
1400 Harvester Rd West Chicago (60185) ***(G-21703)***
**Flolo Corporation**............847 249-0880
1401 N Delany Rd Gurnee (60031) ***(G-11448)***
**Floor-Chem Inc**............630 789-2152
1313 Enterprise Dr Ste D Romeoville (60446) ***(G-18825)***
**Flooring Warehouse Direct Inc**............815 730-6767
14126 Camdan Rd Homer Glen (60491) ***(G-12078)***
**Flora Bowl**............618 662-4561
927 W North Ave Flora (62839) ***(G-10206)***
**Flora Ready Mix Inc**............618 662-4818
11170 Old Highway 50 Flora (62839) ***(G-10207)***
**Floralstar Enterprises**............847 726-0124
68 Tournament Dr N Hawthorn Woods (60047) ***(G-11702)***
**Flores Precision Products**............630 264-2222
413 Cleveland Ave Aurora (60506) ***(G-1152)***
**Florida Favorite Fertilizer, Northbrook** *Also called Wedgworths Inc* ***(G-16385)***
**Florida Fruit Juices Inc**............773 586-6200
7001 W 62nd St Chicago (60638) ***(G-4863)***
**Florida Metrology LLC**............630 833-3800
1100 N Villa Ave Villa Park (60181) ***(G-21252)***
**Florists Transworld Dlvry Inc**............630 719-7800
3113 Woodcreek Dr Downers Grove (60515) ***(G-8444)***
**Florock, Chicago** *Also called Tennant Company* ***(G-6701)***
**Flossmoor Station Brewing Co, Flossmoor** *Also called Caulfields Restaurant Ltd* ***(G-10223)***
**Flotek Inc**............815 943-6816
339 Cary Point Dr Cary (60013) ***(G-3342)***
**Flow Control US Holding Corp**............630 307-3000
1040 Muirfield Dr Hanover Park (60133) ***(G-11582)***
**Flow Pro Products Inc**............815 836-1900
1000 W Crssrds Pkwy 1 Bolingbrook (60490) ***(G-2310)***
**Flow Valves International LLC**............847 866-1188
500 Davis St Ste 600 Evanston (60201) ***(G-10038)***
**Flow-Eze Company**............815 965-1062
3209 Auburn St Rockford (61101) ***(G-18383)***
**Flowers Distributing Inc**............618 255-1021
4605 Hedge Rd East Alton (62024) ***(G-8601)***
**Flowserve Corporation**............630 762-4100
1400 Powis Ct West Chicago (60185) ***(G-21704)***
**Flowserve Corporation**............630 543-4240
409 S Vista Ave Addison (60101) ***(G-120)***
**Flowserve Corporation**............630 762-4100
1400 Powis Ct West Chicago (60185) ***(G-21705)***
**Flowserve Corporation**............630 435-9596
10 Eisenhower Ln N Lombard (60148) ***(G-13799)***
**Flowserve Corporation**............630 260-1310
1311 Santa Rosa Ave Wheaton (60187) ***(G-21949)***
**Flowserve Fsd Corporation**............630 783-1468
1020 Davey Rd Ste 100 Woodridge (60517) ***(G-22479)***
**Flowserve US Inc**............630 655-5700
161 Tower Dr Ste D Burr Ridge (60527) ***(G-2842)***
**Floyd Steel Erectors Inc**............630 238-8383
310 Richert Rd Wood Dale (60191) ***(G-22369)***
**Floyds Welding Service**............618 395-2414
3519 N Union Dr Olney (62450) ***(G-16767)***
**Floydware LLC**............630 469-1078
1020 Parkview Blvd Lombard (60148) ***(G-13800)***
**Flp Industries LLC**............847 215-8650
500 Harvester Ct Ste 2 Wheeling (60090) ***(G-22054)***
**FLS Pekin, Pekin** *Also called Flsmidth Pekin LLC* ***(G-17263)***
**Flsmidth Pekin LLC (HQ)**............309 347-3031
14425 Wagonseller Rd Pekin (61554) ***(G-17263)***
**Fluid Air, Aurora** *Also called Spraying Systems Co* ***(G-1082)***
**Fluid Handling LLC**............773 267-1600
8200 Austin Ave Morton Grove (60053) ***(G-15198)***
**Fluid Logic Inc**............847 459-2202
1001 Commerce Ct Buffalo Grove (60089) ***(G-2697)***
**Fluid Management Inc (HQ)**............847 537-0880
1023 Wheeling Rd Wheeling (60090) ***(G-22055)***
**Fluid Manufacturing Services**............800 458-5262
105 Albrecht Dr Lake Bluff (60044) ***(G-12844)***
**Fluid Mnagement Operations LLC (HQ)**............847 537-0880
1023 Wheeling Rd Wheeling (60090) ***(G-22056)***
**Fluid Power Concrete Lifting, Cherry Valley** *Also called Engineered Fluid Pwr Con Cons* ***(G-3641)***
**Fluid Pump Service Inc**............847 228-0750
435 Bennett Rd Elk Grove Village (60007) ***(G-9480)***
**Fluid Pump Systems, Elk Grove Village** *Also called Fluid Pump Service Inc* ***(G-9480)***
**Fluid-Aire Dynamics Inc**............847 678-8388
530 Albion Ave Schaumburg (60193) ***(G-19531)***

## ALPHABETIC SECTION — Forge Resources Group LLC (PA)

**Flurida Group Inc** .................................................. 310 513-0888
 2439 Haider Ave  Naperville  (60564)  *(G-15806)*
**Flurry Industries Inc** ............................................. 630 882-8361
 2002 Prairie Rose Ln  Yorkville  (60560)  *(G-22658)*
**Flyerinc Corporation** ............................................ 630 655-3400
 700 Commerce Dr Ste 500  Oak Brook  (60523)  *(G-16515)*
**Flying S, Palestine** Also called S Flying Inc  *(G-17095)*
**Flynn Guitars & Music, Wilmette** Also called Flynn Guitars Inc  *(G-22252)*
**Flynn Guitars Inc** ................................................ 800 585-9555
 165 Green Bay Rd Ste B  Wilmette  (60091)  *(G-22252)*
**FM, Wheeling** Also called Fluid Management Inc  *(G-22055)*
**FM Graphic Impressions Inc** ................................. 630 897-8788
 84 S Lasalle St  Aurora  (60505)  *(G-1153)*
**FM Woodworking** ................................................ 847 533-1545
 325 Red Bridge Rd  Lake Zurich  (60047)  *(G-13074)*
**Fma, Elgin** Also called Fabricators & Mfrs Assn Intl  *(G-9033)*
**Fma Communicatons Inc** ..................................... 815 227-8284
 2135 Point Blvd  Elgin  (60123)  *(G-9038)*
**FMC Corporation** ................................................ 309 695-2571
 Hwy 17 E  Wyoming  (61491)  *(G-22638)*
**FMC Corporation** ................................................ 815 824-2153
 100 E Lee Rd  Lee  (60530)  *(G-13217)*
**FMC Subsea Service Inc** ..................................... 312 861-6174
 200 E Randolph St Fl 66  Chicago  (60601)  *(G-4864)*
**FMC Technologies Inc** ......................................... 312 803-4321
 222 W Adams St Ste 400  Chicago  (60606)  *(G-4865)*
**Fmi Inc** ............................................................... 847 350-1535
 2382 United Ln  Elk Grove Village  (60007)  *(G-9481)*
**Fms, Trivoli** Also called Frame Material Supply Inc  *(G-20999)*
**Fms of Wisconsin Div, Mokena** Also called Frank Miller & Sons Inc  *(G-14863)*
**Fms USA Inc** ...................................................... 847 519-4400
 2155 Stnngton Ave Ste 119  Hoffman Estates  (60169)  *(G-12010)*
**Fna Ip Holdings Inc** ............................................. 847 348-1500
 1825 Greenleaf Ave  Elk Grove Village  (60007)  *(G-9482)*
**Fnh Ready Mix Inc** .............................................. 815 235-1400
 751 Il Route 26 N  Freeport  (61032)  *(G-10657)*
**Focal Point Lighting, Chicago** Also called Focal Point LLC  *(G-4867)*
**Focal Point Lighting Inc** ...................................... 773 247-9494
 4201 S Pulaski Rd  Chicago  (60632)  *(G-4866)*
**Focal Point LLC (PA)** .......................................... 773 247-9494
 4141 S Pulaski Rd  Chicago  (60632)  *(G-4867)*
**Focus Marketing Group Inc** .................................. 815 363-2525
 3320 Rocky Beach Rd  Johnsburg  (60051)  *(G-12434)*
**Focus Mfg** .......................................................... 815 877-6043
 1833 Madron Rd  Rockford  (61107)  *(G-18384)*
**Focus Poly** ......................................................... 847 981-6890
 801 Chase Ave  Elk Grove Village  (60007)  *(G-9483)*
**Fodeo, Western Springs** Also called Reel Life Dvd LLC  *(G-21872)*
**Fola Community Action Services** .......................... 773 487-4310
 8014 S Ashland Ave  Chicago  (60620)  *(G-4868)*
**Folding Guard, Bedford Park** Also called L & P Guarding LLC  *(G-1560)*
**Folk Race Cars** .................................................. 815 629-2418
 9027 Freeport Rd  Durand  (61024)  *(G-8585)*
**Folkerts Manufacturing Inc** .................................. 815 968-7426
 2229 23rd Ave  Rockford  (61104)  *(G-18385)*
**Follett School Solutions Inc** ................................. 815 759-1700
 1340 Ridgeview Dr  McHenry  (60050)  *(G-14507)*
**Folsoms Bakery Inc** ............................................ 815 622-7870
 319 1st Ave  Rock Falls  (61071)  *(G-18132)*
**Foltz Welding Ltd** ............................................... 618 432-7777
 501 E Clinton Ave  Patoka  (62875)  *(G-17231)*
**Fona** .................................................................. 630 462-1414
 525 Randy Rd  Carol Stream  (60188)  *(G-3153)*
**Fona Distribution Center, Saint Charles** Also called Fona International Inc  *(G-19185)*
**Fona International, Geneva** Also called Interntnal Ingredient Mall LLC  *(G-10839)*
**Fona International Inc** ......................................... 630 578-8600
 3940 Swenson Ave  Saint Charles  (60174)  *(G-19185)*
**Fona International Inc (PA)** ................................. 630 578-8600
 1900 Averill Rd  Geneva  (60134)  *(G-10827)*
**Fona Uk Ltd** ....................................................... 331 442-5779
 1900 Averill Rd  Geneva  (60134)  *(G-10828)*
**Fontana Associates Inc** ....................................... 888 707-8273
 2605 S Clearbrook Dr  Arlington Heights  (60005)  *(G-755)*
**Fontanini Itln Meats Sausages, Mc Cook** Also called Capitol Wholesale Meats Inc  *(G-14446)*
**Fontela Electric Incorporated (PA)** ...................... 630 932-1600
 1406 W Jeffrey Dr  Addison  (60101)  *(G-121)*
**Fonterra (usa) Inc (HQ)** ...................................... 847 928-1600
 9525 Bryn Mawr Ave # 700  Rosemont  (60018)  *(G-19002)*
**Food Bikes, Chicago** Also called Wrench  *(G-7036)*
**Food Equipment Technologies Co (PA)** ............... 847 719-3000
 600 Rose Rd  Lake Zurich  (60047)  *(G-13075)*
**Food Evolution, Schiller Park** Also called Rt Wholesale  *(G-19869)*
**Food Group, Alton** Also called Ardent Mills LLC  *(G-561)*
**Food Industry News, Des Plaines** Also called Food Service Publishing Co  *(G-8200)*
**Food Processing Magazine, Schaumburg** Also called Putman Media Inc  *(G-19705)*
**Food Purveyors Logistics** .................................... 630 229-6168
 760 Inland Cir Apt 101  Naperville  (60563)  *(G-15659)*

**Food Service** ...................................................... 815 933-0725
 1501 E Maple St  Kankakee  (60901)  *(G-12617)*
**Food Service Publishing Co** ................................. 847 699-3300
 3166 S River Rd Ste 40  Des Plaines  (60018)  *(G-8200)*
**Food Service Publishing Co** ................................. 847 699-3300
 1440 Renaissance Dr # 210  Park Ridge  (60068)  *(G-17195)*
**Fooda Inc** .......................................................... 312 752-4352
 363 W Erie St Ste 500e  Chicago  (60654)  *(G-4869)*
**Foodhandler Inc** ................................................. 866 931-3613
 2301 Lunt Ave  Elk Grove Village  (60007)  *(G-9484)*
**Foods & Things Inc** ............................................ 618 526-4478
 604 N 1st St  Breese  (62230)  *(G-2444)*
**Foodservice Database Co Inc** .............................. 773 745-9400
 5724 W Diversey Ave  Chicago  (60639)  *(G-4870)*
**Foodservice Equipment Reports, Evanston** Also called Ashton Gill Publishing LLC  *(G-10013)*
**Foot Locker Retail Inc** ........................................ 630 678-0155
 112 Yorktown Ctr  Lombard  (60148)  *(G-13801)*
**Forbidden Root A Benefit LLC** ............................. 312 464-7910
 444 N Michigan Ave  Chicago  (60611)  *(G-4871)*
**Forbidden Sweets Inc** ......................................... 847 838-9692
 471 Main St Ste 4  Antioch  (60002)  *(G-633)*
**Forbo Siegling LLC** ............................................ 630 595-4031
 918 N Central Ave  Wood Dale  (60191)  *(G-22370)*
**Force America Inc** .............................................. 815 730-3600
 500 Brookforest Ave  Joliet  (60404)  *(G-12496)*
**Force Enterprises, Tinley Park** Also called First String Enterprises Inc  *(G-20913)*
**Force Manufacturing Inc** ..................................... 847 265-6500
 266 Park Ave  Lake Villa  (60046)  *(G-13013)*
**Forcerl** ............................................................... 847 432-7588
 1350 Forest Ave  Highland Park  (60035)  *(G-11833)*
**Ford Gum & Machine Company Inc** ..................... 847 955-0003
 1615 Barclay Blvd  Buffalo Grove  (60089)  *(G-2698)*
**Ford Motor Company** ......................................... 708 757-5700
 1000 E Lincoln Hwy  Ford Heights  (60411)  *(G-10233)*
**Ford Tool & Machining Inc (PA)** .......................... 815 633-5727
 2205 Range Rd  Loves Park  (61111)  *(G-13941)*
**Ford-Tool, Loves Park** Also called Triwire Inc  *(G-14004)*
**Fordoc Incorporated** ........................................... 708 452-8400
 2636 Haymond Ave  River Grove  (60171)  *(G-18009)*
**Forecast, Rosemont** Also called Philips Lighting N Amer Corp  *(G-19022)*
**Forecast Five** ..................................................... 630 657-6400
 2135 City Gate Ln  Naperville  (60563)  *(G-15660)*
**Foreclosure Report, Lake Barrington** Also called John C Grafft  *(G-12811)*
**Foreman Tool & Mold Corp (PA)** ......................... 630 377-6389
 3850 Swenson Ave  Saint Charles  (60174)  *(G-19186)*
**Foremost Electric & Transm Inc (PA)** .................. 309 699-2200
 6518 W Plank Rd  Peoria  (61604)  *(G-17364)*
**Foremost Industrial Tech, Peoria** Also called Foremost Electric & Transm Inc  *(G-17364)*
**Foremost Plastic Pdts Co Inc** .............................. 708 452-5300
 7834 W Grand Ave  Elmwood Park  (60707)  *(G-9971)*
**Foremost Plastics, Elmwood Park** Also called Foremost Plastic Pdts Co Inc  *(G-9971)*
**Forest Awards & Engraving** ................................. 630 595-2242
 336 E Irving Park Rd  Wood Dale  (60191)  *(G-22371)*
**Forest City Auto Electric Co** ................................ 815 963-4350
 1255 23rd Ave  Rockford  (61104)  *(G-18386)*
**Forest City Counter Tops Inc** .............................. 815 633-8602
 6050 Broadcast Pkwy  Loves Park  (61111)  *(G-13942)*
**Forest City Diagnostic Imaging** ........................... 815 398-1300
 735 N Perryville Rd Ste 2  Rockford  (61107)  *(G-18387)*
**Forest City Grinding Inc** ..................................... 815 874-2424
 4844 Stenstrom Rd  Rockford  (61109)  *(G-18388)*
**Forest City Industry Inc** ..................................... 815 877-4084
 6100 Material Ave  Loves Park  (61111)  *(G-13943)*
**Forest City Satellite** ........................................... 815 639-0500
 432 Heartland Dr  Davis Junction  (61020)  *(G-7811)*
**Forest City Technologies Inc** ............................... 815 965-5880
 892 Southrock Dr  Rockford  (61102)  *(G-18389)*
**Forest Electric Company** .................................... 708 681-0180
 1301 Armitage Ave Ste B  Melrose Park  (60160)  *(G-14639)*
**Forest Envelope Company** .................................. 630 515-1200
 309 E Crossroads Pkwy  Bolingbrook  (60440)  *(G-2311)*
**Forest Lee LLC** .................................................. 312 379-0032
 440 N Wells St Ste 530  Chicago  (60654)  *(G-4872)*
**Forest Packaging Corporation** ............................. 847 981-7000
 1955 Estes Ave  Elk Grove Village  (60007)  *(G-9485)*
**Forest Plating Co** ............................................... 708 366-2071
 930 Des Plaines Ave  Forest Park  (60130)  *(G-10246)*
**Forest Printing Co** .............................................. 708 366-5100
 7214 Madison St Ste 1  Forest Park  (60130)  *(G-10247)*
**Forestech Wood Products** ................................... 217 279-3659
 204 W Washington St  West Union  (62477)  *(G-21826)*
**Forestree** ........................................................... 708 598-8789
 2021 Midwest Rd Ste 200  Oak Brook  (60523)  *(G-16516)*
**Forever Fly LLC** ................................................. 312 981-9161
 934 N Waller Ave  Chicago  (60651)  *(G-4873)*
**Forge Resources Group, Dekalb** Also called Dekalb Forge Company  *(G-8087)*
**Forge Resources Group LLC (PA)** ....................... 815 758-6400
 1832 Pleasant St  Dekalb  (60115)  *(G-8091)*

## Forge Resources Group LLC — ALPHABETIC SECTION

Forge Resources Group LLC .......... 815 758-6400
  1801 Pleasant St  Dekalb  (60115)  *(G-8092)*
Forge Resources Group LLC (PA) .......... 815 758-6400
  1832 Pleasant St  Dekalb  (60115)  *(G-8093)*
Forgings & Stampings Inc (PA) .......... 815 962-5597
  1025 23rd Ave  Rockford  (61104)  *(G-18390)*
Fork Standards, Lombard  Also called FSI Technologies Inc  *(G-13803)*
Forking By Frank, Evanston  Also called Franks Maintenance & Engrg  *(G-10040)*
Form Plastics Company .......... 630 443-1400
  3825 Stern Ave  Saint Charles  (60174)  *(G-19187)*
Form Relief Tool Co Inc .......... 815 393-4263
  14499 E Il Route 72  Davis Junction  (61020)  *(G-7812)*
Form Walern Grinding Inc .......... 815 874-7000
  4717 Colt Rd  Rockford  (61109)  *(G-18391)*
Form-All Spring Stamping Inc .......... 630 595-8833
  380 Meyer Rd  Bensenville  (60106)  *(G-1900)*
Forman Co Inc .......... 309 734-3413
  609 W Broadway  Monmouth  (61462)  *(G-15012)*
Formar Inc .......... 630 543-1151
  1049 W Republic Dr  Addison  (60101)  *(G-122)*
Formax Inc .......... 708 479-3000
  9150 W 191st St  Mokena  (60448)  *(G-14862)*
Formco Metal Products Inc .......... 630 766-4441
  556 Clayton Ct  Wood Dale  (60191)  *(G-22372)*
Formco Plastics Inc .......... 630 860-7998
  904 Fairway Dr  Bensenville  (60106)  *(G-1901)*
Formcraft Tool Company .......... 773 476-8727
  6453 S Bell Ave  Chicago  (60636)  *(G-4874)*
Formed Fastener Mfg Inc .......... 708 496-1219
  7247 S 78th Ave Ste 1  Bridgeview  (60455)  *(G-2492)*
Formel Industries Inc .......... 847 928-5100
  2355 25th Ave  Franklin Park  (60131)  *(G-10471)*
Forming America Ltd (PA) .......... 888 993-1304
  1200 N Prince Crossing Rd  West Chicago  (60185)  *(G-21706)*
Forms Design Plus Coleman Prtg .......... 309 685-6000
  1105 E War Memorial Dr # 1  Peoria  (61616)  *(G-17365)*
Forms Etc By Marty Walsh .......... 708 499-6767
  9205 S Keating Ave Ste 3  Oak Lawn  (60453)  *(G-16620)*
Forms Specialist Inc .......... 847 298-2868
  131 Camden Ct  Lincolnshire  (60069)  *(G-13449)*
Formtec Inc .......... 630 752-9700
  180 W Lake Dr  Glendale Heights  (60139)  *(G-11024)*
Formtek Inc (HQ) .......... 630 285-1500
  711 Ogden Ave  Lisle  (60532)  *(G-13589)*
Formula Systems North America .......... 847 350-0655
  2300 Eastern Ave  Elk Grove Village  (60007)  *(G-9486)*
Formulations Inc .......... 847 674-9141
  8050 Ridgeway Ave  Skokie  (60076)  *(G-20001)*
Forno Palese Baking Company .......... 630 595-5502
  1235 Humbracht Cir Ste 1  Bartlett  (60103)  *(G-1348)*
Forrest Consulting .......... 630 730-9619
  479 N Main St Ste 220  Glen Ellyn  (60137)  *(G-10971)*
Forrest Pallet Service, Poplar Grove  Also called Steve Forrest  *(G-17717)*
Forrest Press Inc .......... 847 381-1621
  1010 W Northwest Hwy  Barrington  (60010)  *(G-1280)*
Forrest Press Printing, Barrington  Also called Forrest Press Inc  *(G-1280)*
Forrest Redi-Mix Inc .......... 815 657-8241
  321 W Krack St  Forrest  (61741)  *(G-10262)*
Forreston Tool Inc .......... 815 938-3626
  400 E Avon St  Forreston  (61030)  *(G-10269)*
Forster Products Inc .......... 815 493-6360
  310 Se Lanark Ave  Lanark  (61046)  *(G-13154)*
Forster Tool & Mfg Co Inc .......... 630 616-8177
  1135 Industrial Dr  Bensenville  (60106)  *(G-1902)*
Forsyth Brothers Concrete Pdts .......... 217 548-2770
  104 E North Sherman St  Fithian  (61844)  *(G-10193)*
Fort Dearborn Company .......... 847 357-2300
  1530 Morse Ave  Elk Grove Village  (60007)  *(G-9487)*
Fort Dearborn Company .......... 773 774-4321
  6035 W Gross Point Rd  Niles  (60714)  *(G-15979)*
Fort Lock Corporation (HQ) .......... 708 456-1100
  715 Center St  Grayslake  (60030)  *(G-11338)*
Forte Automation Systems Inc .......... 815 316-6247
  8155 Burden Rd  Machesney Park  (61115)  *(G-14076)*
Forte Incorporated .......... 815 224-8300
  601 2nd St Ste 3  La Salle  (61301)  *(G-12773)*
Forte Print Corporation .......... 773 391-0105
  3139 W Chicago Ave  Chicago  (60622)  *(G-4875)*
Fortella Company Inc .......... 312 567-9000
  214 W 26th St  Chicago  (60616)  *(G-4876)*
Fortella Forture Cookies, Chicago  Also called Fortella Company Inc  *(G-4876)*
Forterra Pressure Pipe Inc (PA) .......... 815 389-4800
  4416 Prairie Hill Rd  South Beloit  (61080)  *(G-20147)*
Forterra Pressure Pipe Inc .......... 815 389-4800
  4416 Prairie Hill Rd  South Beloit  (61080)  *(G-20148)*
Fortitud Inc .......... 312 919-4938
  8 Benton Ct  Algonquin  (60102)  *(G-390)*
Fortman & Associates Ltd .......... 847 524-0741
  472 Potomac Ln  Elk Grove Village  (60007)  *(G-9488)*

Fortuna Baking Company .......... 630 681-3000
  149 Easy St  Carol Stream  (60188)  *(G-3154)*
Fortune Brands Home & SEC Inc (PA) .......... 847 484-4400
  520 Lake Cook Rd  Deerfield  (60015)  *(G-8007)*
Fortune International Tech LLC .......... 847 429-9791
  5883 Chatham Dr  Hoffman Estates  (60192)  *(G-12011)*
Fortune Metal Midwest LLC .......... 630 778-7776
  1212 E 6th St  Sandwich  (60548)  *(G-19363)*
Forza Customs .......... 708 474-6625
  17809 Torrence Ave  Lansing  (60438)  *(G-13162)*
Fosbinder Fabrication Inc .......... 309 764-0913
  130 35th St  Moline  (61265)  *(G-14940)*
Foseco, Champaign  Also called Vesuvius U S A Corporation  *(G-3556)*
Foster Electric (usa) Inc (HQ) .......... 847 310-8200
  1000 E State Pkwy Ste G  Schaumburg  (60173)  *(G-19532)*
Foster Electric America, Schaumburg  Also called Foster Electric (usa) Inc  *(G-19532)*
Foster Learning LLC .......... 618 656-6836
  900 Timberlake Dr  Edwardsville  (62025)  *(G-8801)*
Fotofab LLC .......... 773 463-6211
  3758 W Belmont Ave  Chicago  (60618)  *(G-4877)*
Fotofabrication, Chicago  Also called Fotofab LLC  *(G-4877)*
Fotofabrication Corp .......... 773 463-6211
  3758 W Belmont Ave  Chicago  (60618)  *(G-4878)*
Foulds Inc .......... 414 964-1428
  520 E Church St  Libertyville  (60048)  *(G-13325)*
Foulk Electric Inc .......... 309 435-7006
  200 E Alder Rd  Canton  (61520)  *(G-2986)*
Foundation Lithuanian Minor .......... 630 969-1316
  908 Rob Roy Pl  Downers Grove  (60516)  *(G-8445)*
Fountain Products Inc .......... 630 991-7237
  2769 Cascade Falls Cir  Elgin  (60124)  *(G-9039)*
Fountain Technologies Ltd .......... 847 537-3677
  423 Denniston Ct  Wheeling  (60090)  *(G-22057)*
Four Acre Wood Products .......... 217 543-2971
  553 N Cr 240 E  Arthur  (61911)  *(G-900)*
Four Seasons Ace Hardware .......... 618 439-2101
  11230 State Highway 37  Benton  (62812)  *(G-2027)*
Four Seasons Gutter Prote .......... 309 694-4565
  1815 Meadow Ave  East Peoria  (61611)  *(G-8710)*
Four Star Tool Inc .......... 224 735-2419
  5521 Meadowbrook Ct  Rolling Meadows  (60008)  *(G-18729)*
Four White Socks LLC .......... 312 257-6456
  270 E Pearson St Apt 1502  Chicago  (60611)  *(G-4879)*
Four Winds Music Pubg LLC .......... 618 699-1356
  1226 N 5th St  Vandalia  (62471)  *(G-21114)*
Four-Tech Industries Co .......... 708 444-8230
  18545 West Creek Dr  Tinley Park  (60477)  *(G-20915)*
Fourell Corp .......... 217 742-3186
  410 E Jefferson St  Winchester  (62694)  *(G-22279)*
Fourier Systems Inc .......... 708 478-5333
  12610 W Hank Ct E  Homer Glen  (60491)  *(G-12079)*
Fournie Farms Inc .......... 618 344-8527
  925 Mcdonough Lake Rd  Collinsville  (62234)  *(G-7325)*
Fourth Quarter Holdings Inc .......... 847 249-7445
  1379 Saint Paul Ave  Gurnee  (60031)  *(G-11449)*
Fox Controls Inc .......... 847 464-5096
  11n26 Rippburger Rd  Elgin  (60123)  *(G-9040)*
Fox Creek Vineyards .......... 618 395-3325
  5502 N Fox Rd  Olney  (62450)  *(G-16768)*
Fox Enterprises Inc .......... 630 513-9010
  50 N 17th St  Saint Charles  (60174)  *(G-19188)*
Fox International Corp .......... 773 465-3634
  7366 N Greenview Ave  Chicago  (60626)  *(G-4880)*
Fox Machine & Tool Inc .......... 847 357-1845
  985 Lively Blvd  Elk Grove Village  (60007)  *(G-9489)*
Fox Metal Services Inc .......... 847 439-9696
  1064 Baybrook Ln  Carol Stream  (60188)  *(G-3155)*
Fox Meter Inc .......... 630 968-3635
  5403 Patton Dr Ste 218  Lisle  (60532)  *(G-13590)*
Fox Redi-Mix Inc .......... 217 774-2110
  1300 W South 5th St  Shelbyville  (62565)  *(G-19907)*
Fox Ridge Stone Co .......... 630 554-9101
  6275 State Route 71  Oswego  (60543)  *(G-16918)*
Fox Tool & Manufacturing Inc (PA) .......... 815 338-3046
  900 Dieckman St  Woodstock  (60098)  *(G-22568)*
Fox Valley Chemical Company .......... 815 653-2660
  5201 Mann Dr  Ringwood  (60072)  *(G-17990)*
Fox Valley Home Brew & Winery .......... 630 892-0742
  14 W Downer Pl  Aurora  (60506)  *(G-1154)*
Fox Valley Iron & Metal Corp .......... 630 897-5907
  637 N Broadway  Aurora  (60505)  *(G-1155)*
Fox Valley Labor News Inc .......... 630 897-4022
  726 N Edgelawn Dr  Aurora  (60506)  *(G-1156)*
Fox Valley Machining Co Inc .......... 630 859-0700
  198 Poplar Pl  North Aurora  (60542)  *(G-16131)*
Fox Valley Molding Inc (PA) .......... 630 552-3176
  113 S Center St  Plano  (60545)  *(G-17665)*
Fox Valley Park District .......... 630 892-1550
  100 S Barnes Rd  Aurora  (60506)  *(G-1157)*

**Fox Valley Pregnancy Center (PA)**.......847 697-0200
101 E State St South Elgin (60177) ***(G-20197)***
**Fox Valley Printing Co Inc**.......419 232-3348
1810 Fox Mead Cir Montgomery (60538) ***(G-15043)***
**Fox Valley Sandblasting Inc**.......630 553-6050
1211 Badger St Yorkville (60560) ***(G-22659)***
**Fox Valley Signs Inc**.......630 896-3113
219 W Galena Blvd Aurora (60506) ***(G-1158)***
**Fox Valley Stamping Company**.......847 741-2277
385 Production Dr South Elgin (60177) ***(G-20198)***
**Fox Valley Winery Inc**.......630 554-0404
5600 Us Highway 34 Oswego (60543) ***(G-16919)***
**FP International, Thornton** *Also called Free-Flow Packaging Intl Inc* ***(G-20869)***
**Fpm Heat Treating**.......815 332-4961
648 Us Highway 20 Cherry Valley (61016) ***(G-3644)***
**Fpm Heat Treatment**.......847 274-7269
1349 W Bryn Mawr Ave Itasca (60143) ***(G-12267)***
**Fra No 3800 W Division**.......708 338-0690
3800 Division St Stone Park (60165) ***(G-20635)***
**Fra-Milco Cabinets Co Inc**.......
386 Nevada A Ct Frankfort (60423) ***(G-10323)***
**Fracar Sheet Metal Mfg Co Inc**.......847 678-1600
9521 Ainslie St Schiller Park (60176) ***(G-19831)***
**Fragrance Island**.......773 488-2700
641 E 79th St Chicago (60619) ***(G-4881)***
**Fragrance Master, Saint Charles** *Also called Odorite International Inc* ***(G-19227)***
**Frahtex Inc**.......773 796-7914
2650 W Belden Ave Apt 214 Chicago (60647) ***(G-4882)***
**Frain Group, Carol Stream** *Also called Cartpac Inc* ***(G-3125)***
**Fram Filtration, Albion** *Also called Champion Laboratories Inc* ***(G-360)***
**Fram Group Limited, Lake Forest** *Also called Fram Group Operations LLC* ***(G-12899)***
**Fram Group Operations LLC (HQ)**.......800 890-2075
1900 W Field Ct Lake Forest (60045) ***(G-12899)***
**Framarx Corporation**.......708 755-3530
3224 Butler Ave Steger (60475) ***(G-20572)***
**Framarx Waxstar, Steger** *Also called Framarx Corporation* ***(G-20572)***
**Frame Game**.......573 754-2385
119 E Quincy St Pleasant Hill (62366) ***(G-17680)***
**Frame House Inc**.......708 383-1616
163 S Oak Park Ave Oak Park (60302) ***(G-16663)***
**Frame House Passport Photos, Oak Park** *Also called Frame House Inc* ***(G-16663)***
**Frame Mart Inc**.......309 452-0658
1211 Silver Oak Cir Normal (61761) ***(G-16071)***
**Frame Material Supply Inc**.......309 362-2323
520 N Trivoli Rd Trivoli (61569) ***(G-20999)***
**Frame World, Lake In The Hills** *Also called Barrington Automation Ltd* ***(G-12987)***
**Framery**.......618 656-5749
216 E Park St Edwardsville (62025) ***(G-8802)***
**Franch & Sons Trnsp Inc**.......630 392-3307
329 N Mill Rd Unit 108 Addison (60101) ***(G-123)***
**Francis L Morris**.......618 676-1724
1377 Angling Rd Clay City (62824) ***(G-7264)***
**Francis Screw Products Co Inc**.......847 647-9462
7400 N Milwaukee Ave Niles (60714) ***(G-15980)***
**Frank A Edmunds & Co Inc (PA)**.......773 586-2772
6111 S Sayre Ave Chicago (60638) ***(G-4883)***
**Frank Bender Jewels, Northfield** *Also called Frank S Bender Inc* ***(G-16399)***
**Frank E Galloway**.......618 948-2578
4808 Moffett Ln Sumner (62466) ***(G-20770)***
**Frank Miller & Sons Inc (PA)**.......708 201-7200
10002 W 190th Pl Mokena (60448) ***(G-14863)***
**Frank O Carlson & Co Inc**.......773 847-6900
3622 S Morgan St Ste 2r Chicago (60609) ***(G-4884)***
**Frank R Walker Company**.......630 613-9312
700 Springer Dr Lombard (60148) ***(G-13802)***
**Frank S Bender Inc**.......847 441-7370
316 Happ Rd Northfield (60093) ***(G-16399)***
**Frank S Johnson & Company**.......847 492-1660
1718 Sherman Ave Ste 211 Evanston (60201) ***(G-10039)***
**Frankenstitch Promotions LLC**.......847 459-4840
460 W Hintz Rd Wheeling (60090) ***(G-22058)***
**Frankfort Machine & Tools Inc**.......815 469-9902
285 Industry Ave Frankfort (60423) ***(G-10324)***
**Franklin Automation Inc**.......630 466-1900
1981 Bucktail Ln Sugar Grove (60554) ***(G-20725)***
**Franklin Display Group Inc (PA)**.......815 544-6676
910 E Lincoln Ave Belvidere (61008) ***(G-1752)***
**Franklin Fueling Systems Inc**.......207 283-0156
21054 Network Pl Chicago (60673) ***(G-4885)***
**Franklin Maintenance**.......815 284-6806
1597 Nachusa Rd Dixon (61021) ***(G-8332)***
**Franklin Park Building Mtls**.......847 455-3985
9400 Chestnut Ave Franklin Park (60131) ***(G-10472)***
**Franklin Screw Products Inc**.......815 784-8500
600 S Sycamore St Unit 1 Genoa (60135) ***(G-10878)***
**Franklin Well Services Inc**.......812 494-2800
10483 May Chapel Rd Lawrenceville (62439) ***(G-13200)***
**Franklin Wire Works Inc**.......815 544-6676
2519 Business Route 20 Belvidere (61008) ***(G-1753)***

**Franks Auto Insurance A Div BR, Evanston** *Also called Frank S Johnson & Company* ***(G-10039)***
**Franks Dgtal Prtg Off Sups Inc**.......630 892-2511
723 Aurora Ave Aurora (60505) ***(G-1159)***
**Franks Maintenance & Engrg**.......847 475-1003
945 Pitner Ave Evanston (60202) ***(G-10040)***
**Franmar Chemical**.......309 829-5952
11 Mary Ellen Way Bloomington (61701) ***(G-2166)***
**Frantz Bearing Division, Sterling** *Also called Frantz Manufacturing Company* ***(G-20591)***
**Frantz Manufacturing Company (PA)**.......815 625-3333
3201 W Lefevre Rd Sterling (61081) ***(G-20591)***
**Frantz Manufacturing Company**.......815 625-7063
3809 W Lincoln Hwy Sterling (61081) ***(G-20592)***
**Frantz Manufacturing Company**.......815 564-0991
3201 W Le Fevre Rd Sterling (61081) ***(G-20593)***
**Franz Discount Office Products, Lake Barrington** *Also called Franz Stationery Company Inc* ***(G-12807)***
**Franz Stationery Company Inc**.......847 593-0060
81 Vista Ln Lake Barrington (60010) ***(G-12807)***
**Frasca Air Services, Urbana** *Also called Frasca International Inc* ***(G-21089)***
**Frasca International Inc (PA)**.......217 344-9200
906 Airport Rd Urbana (61802) ***(G-21089)***
**Fraser Millwork Inc**.......708 447-3262
8109 Ogden Ave Lyons (60534) ***(G-14038)***
**Fratelli Coffee Company**.......847 671-7300
4936 River Rd Schiller Park (60176) ***(G-19832)***
**Frazer Manufacturing Corp**.......815 625-5411
903 Industrial Park Rd Rock Falls (61071) ***(G-18133)***
**Fred Hutson Mineral Products**.......618 994-4383
805 S Ledford St Harrisburg (62946) ***(G-11599)***
**Fred Kennerly**.......815 398-6861
1619 Arden Ave Rockford (61107) ***(G-18392)***
**Fred Pigg Dental Lab**.......618 439-6829
405 E Park St Ste 3 Benton (62812) ***(G-2028)***
**Fred Stollenwerk**.......309 852-3794
801 Elmwood Ave Kewanee (61443) ***(G-12685)***
**Freda Custom Foods Inc**.......847 412-5900
2900 Shermer Rd Northbrook (60062) ***(G-16261)***
**Freddie Bear Sports**.......708 532-4133
17250 Oak Park Ave Tinley Park (60477) ***(G-20916)***
**Freddie Bear Sports.com, Tinley Park** *Also called Freddie Bear Sports* ***(G-20916)***
**Frederick P Schall, McHenry** *Also called Deatak Inc* ***(G-14494)***
**Frederics Frame Studio Inc**.......312 243-2950
1230 W Jackson Blvd Chicago (60607) ***(G-4886)***
**Frederking Construction Co**.......618 483-5031
8595 N 300th St Altamont (62411) ***(G-551)***
**Fredette Racing Products, Beecher** *Also called W L & J Enterprises Inc* ***(G-1604)***
**Fredman Bros Furniture Co Inc**.......309 674-2011
908 Sw Washington St Peoria (61602) ***(G-17366)***
**Fredrick Hoy**.......309 691-4410
5405 N Knoxville Ave Fl 1 Peoria (61614) ***(G-17367)***
**Free Press Advocate, Wilmington** *Also called Free Press Newspapers* ***(G-22272)***
**Free Press Newspapers, Coal City** *Also called Coal City Courant* ***(G-7291)***
**Free Press Newspapers**.......815 476-7966
111 S Water St Wilmington (60481) ***(G-22272)***
**Free Press Progress Inc**.......217 563-2115
112 W State St Nokomis (62075) ***(G-16056)***
**Free-Flow Packaging Intl Inc**.......708 589-6500
16850 Canal St Thornton (60476) ***(G-20869)***
**Freeburg Printing & Publishing**.......618 539-3320
820 S State St Freeburg (62243) ***(G-10635)***
**Freedman Seating Company (PA)**.......773 524-2440
4545 W Augusta Blvd Chicago (60651) ***(G-4887)***
**Freedom Air Filtration Inc**.......815 744-8999
1712 Arden Pl Joliet (60435) ***(G-12497)***
**Freedom Communications Inc**.......217 245-6121
235 W State St Jacksonville (62650) ***(G-12387)***
**Freedom Design & Decals Inc**.......815 806-8172
18811 90th Ave Ste G Mokena (60448) ***(G-14864)***
**Freedom Fastener Inc (PA)**.......847 891-3686
869 E Schaumburg Rd # 149 Schaumburg (60194) ***(G-19533)***
**Freedom Fuel & Food Inc**.......773 233-5350
8950 S Ashland Ave Chicago (60620) ***(G-4888)***
**Freedom Graphic Systems, Aurora** *Also called Fgs-IL LLC* ***(G-1007)***
**Freedom Material Resources Inc**.......618 937-6415
1186 State Highway 37 West Frankfort (62896) ***(G-21808)***
**Freedom Pines, Skokie** *Also called Lanzatech Inc* ***(G-20025)***
**Freedom Sausage Inc**.......815 792-8276
4155 E 1650th Rd Earlville (60518) ***(G-8594)***
**Freeman Energy Corporation (HQ)**.......217 698-3949
3008 Happy Landing Dr Springfield (62711) ***(G-20442)***
**Freeman Products Inc**.......847 439-1000
1225 Arthur Ave Elk Grove Village (60007) ***(G-9490)***
**Freeman Products Worldwide, Elk Grove Village** *Also called AMG International Inc* ***(G-9301)***
**Freeman United Coal Mining Co**.......217 627-2161
22393 Crown Two Mine Rd 2 Mine Girard (62640) ***(G-10945)***
**Freeman United Coal Mining Co (HQ)**.......217 698-3300
4440 Ash Grove Dr Ste A Springfield (62711) ***(G-20443)***

**Freemans Sports Inc** ........ 630 553-0515
129 E Hydraulic St Yorkville (60560) ***(G-22660)***
**Freeport Journal Standard, Freeport** *Also called Journal Standard* ***(G-10670)***
**Freeport Press Inc** ........ 815 232-1181
1031 W Empire St Freeport (61032) ***(G-10658)***
**Freesen Inc** ........ 309 827-4554
1523 Cottage Ave Bloomington (61701) ***(G-2167)***
**Freeshopper Ad Paper Inc** ........ 847 675-2783
7301 N Lincoln Ave # 185 Lincolnwood (60712) ***(G-13511)***
**Freeway-Rockford Inc** ........ 815 397-6425
4701 Boeing Dr Rockford (61109) ***(G-18393)***
**Freight Car Services Inc** ........ 217 443-4106
2313 Cannon St Ste 2 Danville (61832) ***(G-7722)***
**Freight House Kit & Bath Str, Dixon** *Also called Scheffler Custom Woodworking* ***(G-8348)***
**Freightcar America Inc (PA)** ........ 800 458-2235
2 N Rverside Plz Ste 1300 Chicago (60606) ***(G-4889)***
**Freightcar America Inc** ........ 217 443-4106
2313 Cannon St Danville (61832) ***(G-7723)***
**Freitas P Sabah** ........ 708 386-8934
6105 1/2 North Ave Oak Park (60302) ***(G-16664)***
**French Corporation** ........ 708 354-9000
340 Washington Ave La Grange (60525) ***(G-12732)***
**French Qrter Prof Off Bldg LLC** ........ 815 972-0681
21625 S Mattox Ln Joliet (60404) ***(G-12498)***
**French Studio Ltd** ........ 618 942-5328
821 S Park Ave Stop 1 Herrin (62948) ***(G-11748)***
**Frequency Devices Inc** ........ 815 434-7800
1784 Chessie Ln Unit 1 Ottawa (61350) ***(G-16960)***
**Fresco Plaster Finishes Inc** ........ 847 277-1484
228 James St Ste 2 Barrington (60010) ***(G-1281)***
**Fresenius Kabi Usa Inc** ........ 708 450-7500
2020 N Ruby St Melrose Park (60160) ***(G-14640)***
**Fresenius Kabi Usa Inc** ........ 708 410-4761
2020 N Ruby St Melrose Park (60160) ***(G-14641)***
**Fresenius Kabi Usa Inc (HQ)** ........ 847 969-2700
3 Corporate Dr Ste 300 Lake Zurich (60047) ***(G-13076)***
**Fresenius Kabi Usa Inc** ........ 708 450-7509
2020 N Ruby St Melrose Park (60160) ***(G-14642)***
**Fresenius Kabi Usa Inc** ........ 708 345-6170
2020 N Ruby St Melrose Park (60160) ***(G-14643)***
**Fresenius Kabi Usa LLC (HQ)** ........ 847 550-2300
3 Corporate Dr Ste 300 Lake Zurich (60047) ***(G-13077)***
**Fresenius Kabi Usa LLC** ........ 847 983-7100
The Illinois Scienc Skokie (60077) ***(G-20002)***
**Fresenius Kabi USA LLC** ........ 847 550-2300
3 Corporate Dr Ste 300 Lake Zurich (60047) ***(G-13078)***
**Fresenius Kabi USA LLC** ........ 708 343-6100
2045 Cornell Ave Melrose Park (60160) ***(G-14644)***
**Fresenius Usa Inc** ........ 773 262-7147
2277 W Howard St Chicago (60645) ***(G-4890)***
**Fresh Concept Enterprises Inc** ........ 815 254-7295
12249 Rhea Dr Plainfield (60585) ***(G-17601)***
**Fresh Express Incorporated** ........ 630 736-3900
1109 E Lake St Streamwood (60107) ***(G-20656)***
**Fresh Facs** ........ 618 357-9697
612 County Rd Pinckneyville (62274) ***(G-17548)***
**Fresh Look & Sons** ........ 815 325-9692
406 E Main St Morris (60450) ***(G-15109)***
**Fresh Solutions For Your Home, University Park** *Also called Elco Laboratories Inc* ***(G-21047)***
**Freudenberg & Co, Aurora** *Also called Freudenberg Household Pdts LP* ***(G-1010)***
**Freudenberg Household Pdts LP** ........ 630 270-1400
2188 Diehl Rd Aurora (60502) ***(G-1010)***
**Frey Wiss Prcsion McHining Inc** ........ 630 595-9073
384 Beinoris Dr Wood Dale (60191) ***(G-22373)***
**Fri Jado Inc** ........ 630 633-7944
1401 Davey Rd Ste 100 Woodridge (60517) ***(G-22480)***
**Fricke Dental Manufacturing Co** ........ 630 540-1900
165 Roma Jean Pkwy Streamwood (60107) ***(G-20657)***
**Fricke International Inc** ........ 630 833-2627
208 W Ridge Rd Villa Park (60181) ***(G-21253)***
**Fricker Machine Shop & Salvage** ........ 618 285-3271
Rr 1 Elizabethtown (62931) ***(G-9245)***
**Friedrich Klatt and Associates** ........ 773 753-1806
5240 S Hyde Park Blvd Chicago (60615) ***(G-4891)***
**Friend Oil Co** ........ 618 842-9161
Enterprise Rd Rr 3 Fairfield (62837) ***(G-10142)***
**Friendly Remedies, Woodridge** *Also called Symbria Rx Services LLC* ***(G-22520)***
**Friendly Signs Inc** ........ 815 933-7070
1281 N Schuyler Ave Kankakee (60901) ***(G-12618)***
**Friends Fuel** ........ 773 434-9387
8200 S Kedzie Ave Chicago (60652) ***(G-4892)***
**Frigel North America Inc** ........ 847 540-0160
150 Prairie Lake Rd Ste A East Dundee (60118) ***(G-8636)***
**Frigid Coil/Frick Inc** ........ 630 562-4602
1800 W Hawthorne Ln E2 West Chicago (60185) ***(G-21707)***
**Frigid Fluid Company** ........ 708 836-1215
11631 W Grand Ave Melrose Park (60164) ***(G-14645)***
**Frings America Inc** ........ 630 851-5826
3015 E New York St A2-143 Aurora (60504) ***(G-1011)***
**Frito-Lay North America Inc** ........ 217 532-5040
1400 E Tremont St Hillsboro (62049) ***(G-11890)***
**Frito-Lay North America Inc** ........ 217 776-2320
1050 County Road 2300 E Sidney (61877) ***(G-19936)***
**Frito-Lay North America Inc** ........ 815 468-3940
450 N Grove St Manteno (60950) ***(G-14184)***
**Frito-Lay North America Inc** ........ 708 331-7200
4170 166th St Oak Forest (60452) ***(G-16582)***
**Frito-Lay North America Inc** ........ 618 997-2865
5309 Meadowland Pkwy Marion (62959) ***(G-14260)***
**Fromm Airpad Inc** ........ 630 393-9790
3s320 Rockwell St Warrenville (60555) ***(G-21347)***
**Frontida Biopharm Inc** ........ 215 620-3527
2500 Molitor Rd Aurora (60502) ***(G-1012)***
**Frontier Signs & Lighting** ........ 309 694-7300
15419 N 7th St Chillicothe (61523) ***(G-7165)***
**Frontier Soups, Gurnee** *Also called K M J Enterprises Inc* ***(G-11465)***
**Frost A Glato Shpp-Highland Pk, Highland Park** *Also called Gelato Enterprises LLC* ***(G-11835)***
**Frost A Glato Shpp-Highland Pk, Naperville** *Also called Gelato Enterprises LLC* ***(G-15663)***
**Frye-Williamson Press Inc** ........ 217 522-7744
901 N Macarthur Blvd Springfield (62702) ***(G-20444)***
**Fryer To Fuel Inc** ........ 309 654-2875
26700 171st Ave N Cordova (61242) ***(G-7375)***
**Fryman Electric** ........ 309 387-6540
3801 Sheridan Rd Pekin (61554) ***(G-17264)***
**Fs Depot Inc** ........ 847 468-2350
2645 Federal Signal Dr University Park (60484) ***(G-21051)***
**Fsg Crest LLC** ........ 708 210-0800
770 Parc Ct Lake In The Hills (60156) ***(G-12993)***
**FSI Print, Lincolnshire** *Also called Forms Specialist Inc* ***(G-13449)***
**FSI Technologies Inc** ........ 630 932-9380
668 E Western Ave Lombard (60148) ***(G-13803)***
**Fsp LLC** ........ 773 992-2600
245 Ambrogio Dr Gurnee (60031) ***(G-11450)***
**Ft Motors Inc** ........ 773 737-5581
5929 S Ashland Ave Apt 29 Chicago (60636) ***(G-4893)***
**FTC Family of Companies, Bloomington** *Also called Family Time Computing Inc* ***(G-2162)***
**Fuchs Corporation (HQ)** ........ 800 323-7755
17050 Lathrop Ave Harvey (60426) ***(G-11667)***
**Fuchs Lubricants Co, Harvey** *Also called Fuchs Corporation* ***(G-11667)***
**Fuel Fitness** ........ 708 367-0707
1379 Main St Crete (60417) ***(G-7513)***
**Fuel Research & Instrument Co** ........ 630 953-2459
1919 S Highland Ave Lombard (60148) ***(G-13804)***
**Fuel Tech Inc (PA)** ........ 630 845-4500
27601 Bella Vista Pkwy Warrenville (60555) ***(G-21348)***
**Fugate Inc** ........ 309 472-6830
204 Loren St Washington (61571) ***(G-21382)***
**Fugiel Railroad Supply Corp** ........ 847 516-6862
700 Industrial Dr Ste E Cary (60013) ***(G-3343)***
**Fuji Hunt, Rolling Meadows** *Also called Fujifilm Hunt Chem USA Inc* ***(G-18730)***
**Fuji Impulse American Corp** ........ 847 236-9190
1735 Lisa Marie Ct Deerfield (60015) ***(G-8008)***
**Fujifilm Hunt Chem USA Inc** ........ 847 259-8800
900 Carnegie St Rolling Meadows (60008) ***(G-18730)***
**Fulfillment Center, The, Downers Grove** *Also called MPS Chicago Inc* ***(G-8492)***
**Full Court Press Inc** ........ 773 779-1135
9146 S Pleasant Ave Chicago (60643) ***(G-4894)***
**Full Line Printing Inc** ........ 312 642-8080
361 W Chicago Ave Chicago (60654) ***(G-4895)***
**Full-Fill Industries LLC** ........ 217 286-3532
400 N Main St Henning (61848) ***(G-11737)***
**Fuller Asphalt & Landscape** ........ 618 797-1169
4353 Lake Dr Granite City (62040) ***(G-11277)***
**Fuller Brothers Ready Mix** ........ 217 532-2422
935 Ash St Hillsboro (62049) ***(G-11891)***
**Fulling Motor USA Inc** ........ 847 894-6238
1601 Park Ridge Pt Park Ridge (60068) ***(G-17196)***
**Fulton Corporation (PA)** ........ 815 589-3211
303 8th Ave Fulton (61252) ***(G-10701)***
**Fulton County Democrat, Canton** *Also called Martin Publishing Co* ***(G-2989)***
**Fulton County Rehabilitation (PA)** ........ 309 647-6510
500 N Main St Canton (61520) ***(G-2987)***
**Fulton Metal Works Inc** ........ 217 476-8223
1763 Ashland Rd Ashland (62612) ***(G-926)***
**Fulton Street Brewery LLC** ........ 312 915-0071
1800 W Fulton St Chicago (60612) ***(G-4896)***
**Fun Incorporated** ........ 773 745-3837
333 Alice St Wheeling (60090) ***(G-22059)***
**Fun Industries Inc** ........ 309 755-5021
627 15th Ave East Moline (61244) ***(G-8679)***
**Funeral Register Books Inc** ........ 217 627-3235
499 Rachel Rd Girard (62640) ***(G-10946)***
**Funk Linko Group Inc** ........ 708 757-7421
26815 S Winfield Rd Monee (60449) ***(G-14995)***
**Funquilts Inc** ........ 708 445-9871
719 Iowa St Oak Park (60302) ***(G-16665)***

**Furnel Inc (PA)** ....630 543-0885
350 S Stewart Ave Addison (60101) ***(G-124)***
**Furniture Services Inc** ....847 520-9490
410 Mercantile Ct Wheeling (60090) ***(G-22060)***
**Furry Inc** ....217 446-0084
2005 E Voorhees St Danville (61834) ***(G-7724)***
**Furst-Mcness Company (PA)** ....800 435-5100
120 E Clark St Freeport (61032) ***(G-10659)***
**Fuse LLC** ....708 449-8989
5656 Mcdermott Dr Berkeley (60163) ***(G-2045)***
**Fuseco** ....847 749-4158
2255 Lois Dr Rolling Meadows (60008) ***(G-18731)***
**Fusibond Piping Systems Inc** ....630 969-4488
2615 Curtiss St Downers Grove (60515) ***(G-8446)***
**Fusion Chemical Corporation** ....847 656-5285
350 S Northwest Hwy # 300 Park Ridge (60068) ***(G-17197)***
**Fusion OEM, Burr Ridge** *Also called Fusion Systems Incorporated* ***(G-2843)***
**Fusion Systems Incorporated** ....630 323-4115
6951 High Grove Blvd Burr Ridge (60527) ***(G-2843)***
**Fusion Tech Integrated Inc (PA)** ....309 774-4275
218 20th Ave Roseville (61473) ***(G-19045)***
**Futaba Corporation of America (HQ)** ....847 884-1444
711 E State Pkwy Schaumburg (60173) ***(G-19534)***
**Future Environmental Inc (PA)** ....708 479-6900
19701 97th Ave Mokena (60448) ***(G-14865)***
**Future Tool Inc** ....815 395-0012
2029 23rd Ave Rockford (61104) ***(G-18394)***
**Futures Magazine Inc** ....312 846-4600
107 W Van Buren St # 203 Chicago (60605) ***(G-4897)***
**Futuro Foods Inc** ....773 418-2720
3848 N Pioneer Ave Chicago (60634) ***(G-4898)***
**Fuyao Glass Illinois Inc** ....217 864-2392
2768 E Elwin Rd Decatur (62521) ***(G-7883)***
**G & C Enterprises Inc** ....618 747-2272
18837 County Line Rd Jonesboro (62952) ***(G-12591)***
**G & E Automatic** ....815 654-7766
10462 Product Dr Ste B Machesney Park (61115) ***(G-14077)***
**G & F Manufacturing Co Inc** ....708 424-4170
5555 W 109th St Oak Lawn (60453) ***(G-16621)***
**G & G Printing, Bradley** *Also called G & G Studios /Broadway Prtg* ***(G-2422)***
**G & G Studios /Broadway Prtg** ....815 933-8181
345 W Broadway St Bradley (60915) ***(G-2422)***
**G & H Balancer Service** ....773 509-1988
2212 Strawberry Ln Glenview (60026) ***(G-11127)***
**G & J Associates Inc** ....847 255-0123
1315 E Davis St Arlington Heights (60005) ***(G-756)***
**G & K Baking LLC** ....630 415-8687
16 Olympia Ct Oak Brook (60523) ***(G-16517)***
**G & L Counter Tops Corporation** ....815 786-2244
1010 E 3rd St Ste C Sandwich (60548) ***(G-19364)***
**G & M Die Casting Company Inc** ....630 595-2340
284 Richert Rd Wood Dale (60191) ***(G-22374)***
**G & M Fabricating Inc** ....815 282-1744
9014 Swanson Dr Roscoe (61073) ***(G-18898)***
**G & M Industries Inc** ....618 344-6655
208 Yorktown Dr Collinsville (62234) ***(G-7326)***
**G & M Manufacturing Corp** ....815 455-1900
111 S Main St Crystal Lake (60014) ***(G-7580)***
**G & M Metal Fabricators Inc** ....847 678-6501
9120 Gage Ave Franklin Park (60131) ***(G-10473)***
**G & M Steel Fabricating, Granite City** *Also called Accurate Fabricators Inc* ***(G-11258)***
**G & M Woodworking Inc** ....708 425-4013
5656 W 88th Pl Oak Lawn (60453) ***(G-16622)***
**G & P Products Inc** ....708 442-9667
4215 Lawndale Ave Lyons (60534) ***(G-14039)***
**G & R Stained Glass** ....847 455-7026
2919 Emerson St Franklin Park (60131) ***(G-10474)***
**G & S Asphalt Inc** ....217 826-2421
16870 N Quality Lime Rd Marshall (62441) ***(G-14322)***
**G & S Manufacturing Inc** ....847 674-7666
2345 Waukegan Rd Ste 155 Bannockburn (60015) ***(G-1258)***
**G & S Pallets** ....630 574-2741
66 Windsor Dr Oak Brook (60523) ***(G-16518)***
**G & W Electric Company** ....708 389-8307
3450 127th St Blue Island (60406) ***(G-2251)***
**G & W Technical Corporation** ....847 487-0990
578 E Burnett Rd Island Lake (60042) ***(G-12215)***
**G & Z Industries Inc** ....847 215-2300
541 Chaddick Dr Wheeling (60090) ***(G-22061)***
**G A I M Engineering, Bensenville** *Also called G A I M Plastics Incorporated* ***(G-1903)***
**G A I M Engineering, Bensenville** *Also called GAim Plastics Incorporated* ***(G-1904)***
**G A I M Plastics Incorporated** ....630 350-9500
789 Golf Ln Bensenville (60106) ***(G-1903)***
**G and D Enterprises Inc** ....847 981-8661
1425 E Algonquin Rd Arlington Heights (60005) ***(G-757)***
**G B C Velobind, Addison** *Also called Acco Brands USA LLC* ***(G-16)***
**G B Holdings Inc** ....773 265-3000
600 N Kilbourn Ave Chicago (60624) ***(G-4899)***
**G Blando Jewelers Inc** ....630 627-7963
3 Countryside Plz Countryside (60525) ***(G-7425)***
**G Branch Corp** ....630 458-1909
409 S Vista Ave Unit B Addison (60101) ***(G-125)***
**G D S Professional Bus Display** ....309 829-3298
1103 Martin Luther King D Bloomington (61701) ***(G-2168)***
**G E I, Roanoke** *Also called Gingrich Enterprises Inc* ***(G-18050)***
**G E Mathis Company** ....773 586-3800
6100 S Oak Park Ave Chicago (60638) ***(G-4900)***
**G F Ltd** ....708 333-8300
16255 Vincennes Ave South Holland (60473) ***(G-20269)***
**G F Printing** ....618 797-0576
2439 Hemlock Ave Granite City (62040) ***(G-11278)***
**G G Premier Precision Inc** ....708 588-1234
500 Shawmut Ave La Grange Park (60526) ***(G-12756)***
**G H Meiser & Co** ....708 388-7867
2407 W 140th Pl Posen (60469) ***(G-17730)***
**G I A Publications Inc (PA)** ....708 496-3800
7404 S Mason Ave Chicago (60638) ***(G-4901)***
**G I C, Chicago** *Also called Graphic Image Corporation* ***(G-4989)***
**G I W, Aurora** *Also called Garbe Iron Works Inc* ***(G-1160)***
**G J Nikolas & Co Inc** ....708 544-0320
2800 Washington Blvd Bellwood (60104) ***(G-1706)***
**G K Enterprises Inc (PA)** ....708 587-2150
26000 S Whiting Way Ste 2 Monee (60449) ***(G-14996)***
**G K L Corporation** ....815 886-5900
5 Greenwood Ave Romeoville (60446) ***(G-18826)***
**G L Beaumont Lumber Company (PA)** ....618 423-2323
Rr 51 Box S Ramsey (62080) ***(G-17913)***
**G L Doemelt** ....217 268-4243
299 Egyptian Trl Arcola (61910) ***(G-669)***
**G L Tool and Manufacturing Co** ....630 628-1992
815 S Kay Ave Ste A Addison (60101) ***(G-126)***
**G M Sign Inc** ....847 546-0424
704 Sunset Dr Round Lake (60073) ***(G-19056)***
**G Messmore Company** ....708 343-8114
2000 S 25th Ave Broadview (60155) ***(G-2581)***
**G N F, Oak Lawn** *Also called Befco Manufacturing Co Inc* ***(G-16606)***
**G P Albums, Chicago** *Also called General Products* ***(G-4932)***
**G P Cole Inc** ....217 431-3029
1120 Industrial St Danville (61832) ***(G-7725)***
**G P Concrete & Iron Works** ....815 842-2270
Rr 1 Pontiac (61764) ***(G-17700)***
**G P I, Lake In The Hills** *Also called General Products Intl Ltd* ***(G-12994)***
**G P International, Island Lake** *Also called Vulcan Ladder Usa LLC* ***(G-12220)***
**G R Leonard & Co Inc (PA)** ....847 797-8101
115 E University Dr Arlington Heights (60004) ***(G-758)***
**G T C Industries Inc** ....708 369-9815
609 Sara Ln Naperville (60565) ***(G-15661)***
**G T Express Ltd** ....708 338-0303
165 W Lake St Northlake (60164) ***(G-16437)***
**G T I Spindle, Bloomington** *Also called Gti Spindle Technology Inc* ***(G-2175)***
**G T L Technologies Inc** ....630 469-9818
413 2nd Pl Ste 100 Glendale Heights (60139) ***(G-11025)***
**G T Laboratories Inc** ....847 998-4776
3333 Warrenville Rd # 200 Lisle (60532) ***(G-13591)***
**G T Motoring Inc** ....847 466-7463
860 Greenleaf Ave Elk Grove Village (60007) ***(G-9491)***
**G T Services of Illionois Inc** ....309 925-5111
22387 State Route 9 Tremont (61568) ***(G-20982)***
**G Y Industries LLC** ....708 210-1300
70 W Madison St Ste 2300 Chicago (60602) ***(G-4902)***
**G&D Integrated Services Inc** ....309 284-6700
50 Commerce Dr Morton (61550) ***(G-15159)***
**G&D Intgrted Mfg Logistics Inc** ....309 284-6700
50 Commerce Dr Morton (61550) ***(G-15160)***
**G&E Transportation Inc (HQ)** ....404 350-6497
500 W Monroe St Chicago (60661) ***(G-4903)***
**G&G Kraft Build** ....773 744-6522
218 Fishing Ln Wood Dale (60191) ***(G-22375)***
**G&G Machine Shop Inc** ....217 892-9696
1580 E Grove Ave Ste 2 Rantoul (61866) ***(G-17928)***
**G&M Metal** ....630 616-1126
1970 Estes Ave Elk Grove Village (60007) ***(G-9492)***
**G&R Machining Inc** ....847 526-7364
3205 Poplar Dr Island Lake (60042) ***(G-12216)***
**G-Fast Distribution Inc** ....847 926-0722
1954 1st St 228 Highland Park (60035) ***(G-11834)***
**G-M Services** ....618 532-2324
309 Country Club Rd Centralia (62801) ***(G-3415)***
**G-P Manufacturing Co Inc** ....847 473-9001
1535 S Lakeside Dr Waukegan (60085) ***(G-21561)***
**G-W Communications Inc** ....815 476-7966
111 S Water St Wilmington (60481) ***(G-22273)***
**G.T.L. International, Glendale Heights** *Also called G T L Technologies Inc* ***(G-11025)***
**G1 Industries Co, Joy** *Also called Robin L Barnhouse* ***(G-12592)***
**G2 Crowd Inc** ....847 748-7559
20 N Wacker Dr Ste 1800 Chicago (60606) ***(G-4904)***
**G2 Labs, Chicago** *Also called G2 Crowd Inc* ***(G-4904)***
**Gabel & Schubert Bronze** ....773 878-6800
4500 N Ravenswood Ave Chicago (60640) ***(G-4905)***

ALPHABETIC

**Gabriel Enterprises** ....773 342-8705
1734 W North Ave Chicago (60622) ***(G-4906)***
**Gadge Signs Inc** ....815 462-4490
215 E Otto Dr Ste A New Lenox (60451) ***(G-15882)***
**Gadgetworld Enterprises Inc** ....773 703-0796
10956 S Western Ave Chicago (60643) ***(G-4907)***
**Gaertner Scientific Corp** ....847 673-5006
3650 Jarvis Ave Skokie (60076) ***(G-20003)***
**Gafco, Melrose Park** *Also called Graphic Arts Finishing Company* ***(G-14648)***
**Gage Applied Technologies LLC** ....815 838-0005
900 N State St Lockport (60441) ***(G-13716)***
**Gage Assembly Co** ....847 679-5180
3771 W Morse Ave Lincolnwood (60712) ***(G-13512)***
**Gage Food Products, Bensenville** *Also called Windy Acquisition LLC* ***(G-2015)***
**Gage Grinding Company Inc (PA)** ....847 639-3888
40 Detroit St Unit D Cary (60013) ***(G-3344)***
**Gage Manufacturing Inc** ....847 228-7300
820 Touhy Ave Elk Grove Village (60007) ***(G-9493)***
**Gage Tool & Manufacturing Inc** ....847 640-1069
1025 Pauly Dr Elk Grove Village (60007) ***(G-9494)***
**Gail E Stephens** ....618 372-0140
110 Ransom St Brighton (62012) ***(G-2540)***
**Gail Glasser Brickman, Skokie** *Also called Century Fasteners & Mch Co Inc* ***(G-19977)***
**Gail McGrath & Associates Inc** ....847 770-4620
3453 Commercial Ave Northbrook (60062) ***(G-16262)***
**GAim Plastics Incorporated (PA)** ....630 350-9500
789 Golf Ln Bensenville (60106) ***(G-1904)***
**Gaither Tool Co** ....217 245-0545
21 Harold Cox Dr Jacksonville (62650) ***(G-12388)***
**Galactic Clothing, Chicago** *Also called Allen Larson* ***(G-3811)***
**Galactic Tool Co** ....815 962-3420
1402 18th Ave Rockford (61104) ***(G-18395)***
**Galaxy Circuits Inc** ....630 462-1010
383 Randy Rd Carol Stream (60188) ***(G-3156)***
**Galaxy Embroidery Inc** ....312 243-8991
1211 S Western Ave Chicago (60608) ***(G-4908)***
**Galaxy Industries Inc** ....847 639-8580
231 Jandus Rd Cary (60013) ***(G-3345)***
**Galaxy Precision Mfg Inc** ....847 238-9066
2636 United Ln Elk Grove Village (60007) ***(G-9495)***
**Galaxy Sourcing Inc** ....630 532-5003
744 N Michigan Ave Villa Park (60181) ***(G-21254)***
**Galena Cellars Winery (PA)** ....815 777-3330
515 S Main St Galena (61036) ***(G-10720)***
**Galena Cellars Winery** ....815 777-3429
4746 N Ford Rd Galena (61036) ***(G-10721)***
**Galena Garlic Co** ....331 248-0342
318 W State St Geneva (60134) ***(G-10829)***
**Galena Manufacturing Co Inc** ....815 777-2078
100 Monroe St Galena (61036) ***(G-10722)***
**Galena Mine Division, Chicago** *Also called Callahan Mining Corporation* ***(G-4216)***
**Galena Road Gravel Inc** ....309 274-6388
5129 E Truitt Rd Chillicothe (61523) ***(G-7166)***
**Galenas Kandy Kitchen** ....815 777-0241
100 N Main St Galena (61036) ***(G-10723)***
**Galeria De Graphics, Galesburg** *Also called Go Van Goghs Tee Shirt* ***(G-10755)***
**Galesburg Builders Supply, Galesburg** *Also called Gunther Construction Co* ***(G-10756)***
**Galesburg Castings Inc** ....309 343-6178
940 Avenue C St Galesburg (61401) ***(G-10749)***
**Galesburg Manufacturing Co (PA)** ....309 342-3173
1835 Lacon Dr Galesburg (61401) ***(G-10750)***
**Galesburg Register Mail, Galesburg** *Also called Register-Mail* ***(G-10773)***
**Galesburg Sign & Lighting** ....309 342-9798
1518 S Henderson St Galesburg (61401) ***(G-10751)***
**Gall Machine Co** ....708 352-2800
9640 Joliet Rd Countryside (60525) ***(G-7426)***
**Gallagher Corporation** ....847 249-3440
3908 Morrison Dr Gurnee (60031) ***(G-11451)***
**Gallas Label & Decal** ....773 775-1000
6559 N Avondale Ave Chicago (60631) ***(G-4909)***
**Gallasi Cut Stone & Marble LLC** ....708 479-9494
10001 191st St Mokena (60448) ***(G-14866)***
**Galleon Industries Inc** ....708 478-5444
16714 Cherry Creek Ct Joliet (60433) ***(G-12499)***
**Galleon Printing Co, Joliet** *Also called Galleon Industries Inc* ***(G-12499)***
**Galleria Retail Tech Solutions** ....312 822-3437
401 N Michigan Ave Chicago (60611) ***(G-4910)***
**Gallery Office Pdts & Prtrs** ....708 798-2220
18031 Dixie Hwy Homewood (60430) ***(G-12099)***
**Gallimore Industries Inc** ....847 356-3331
200 Park Ave Ste B Lake Villa (60046) ***(G-13014)***
**Gallon Industries Inc** ....630 628-1020
341 W Factory Rd Addison (60101) ***(G-127)***
**Galloway Como Processing** ....815 626-0305
24578 Stone St Sterling (61081) ***(G-20594)***
**Galloway Logging, Sumner** *Also called Frank E Galloway* ***(G-20770)***
**Galloway Meats & Poultry, Sterling** *Also called Galloway Como Processing* ***(G-20594)***
**Galloy and Van Etten Inc (PA)** ....773 928-4800
11756 S Halsted St Chicago (60628) ***(G-4911)***
**Galmar Enterprises Inc** ....815 463-9826
14408 W Edison Dr Ste F New Lenox (60451) ***(G-15883)***
**Galva Iron and Metal Co Inc** ....309 932-3450
625 Se Industrial Ave Galva (61434) ***(G-10789)***
**Galvanize Labs Inc** ....630 258-1476
6728 W Highland Dr Palos Heights (60463) ***(G-17104)***
**Galvanized Stairs, East Lynn** *Also called Greene Welding & Hardware Inc* ***(G-8668)***
**Gam Enterprises Inc** ....847 649-2500
901 E Business Center Dr Mount Prospect (60056) ***(G-15331)***
**Gam Gear, Mount Prospect** *Also called Gam Enterprises Inc* ***(G-15331)***
**Gama Electronics Inc** ....815 356-9600
1240 Cobblestone Way Woodstock (60098) ***(G-22569)***
**Gamenamics Inc** ....847 844-7688
2541 Tech Dr Ste 406 Elgin (60124) ***(G-9041)***
**Gameplan Inc** ....877 284-9180
5 Revere Dr Ste 103 Northbrook (60062) ***(G-16263)***
**Gamestop Inc** ....773 568-0457
800 N Kedzie Ave Chicago (60651) ***(G-4912)***
**Gamestop Corp** ....773 545-9602
3951 N Broadway St Chicago (60613) ***(G-4913)***
**Gamestop Corp** ....618 258-8611
662 Wesley Dr Wood River (62095) ***(G-22443)***
**Gametime Screen Printing** ....815 297-5263
311 E South St Freeport (61032) ***(G-10660)***
**Gamma Alpha Visual** ....847 956-0633
86 Biesterfield Rd Elk Grove Village (60007) ***(G-9496)***
**Gamma Products Inc** ....708 974-4100
7730 W 114th Pl Ste 1 Palos Hills (60465) ***(G-17117)***
**Gamma Quality, Norridge** *Also called Joseph Ringelstein* ***(G-16103)***
**Gammerler US Corp** ....941 465-4400
431 Lakeview Ct Ste B Mount Prospect (60056) ***(G-15332)***
**Gammon Group Inc** ....815 722-6400
1009 Geneva St Shorewood (60404) ***(G-19927)***
**Ganji Klames** ....773 478-9000
3418 W Bryn Mawr Ave Chicago (60659) ***(G-4914)***
**Gannett Health Care Group, Hoffman Estates** *Also called Gannett Stllite Info Ntwrk Inc* ***(G-12012)***
**Gannett Satellite Info Netwrk** ....312 216-1407
225 N Michigan Ave # 1600 Chicago (60601) ***(G-4915)***
**Gannett Stllite Info Ntwrk Inc** ....847 839-1700
1721 Moon Lake Blvd # 540 Hoffman Estates (60169) ***(G-12012)***
**Gannett Stllite Info Ntwrk LLC** ....630 629-1280
495 N Commons Dr Ste 102 Aurora (60504) ***(G-1013)***
**Gannon Graphics, Schaumburg** *Also called Marty Gannon* ***(G-19632)***
**Gannon Graphics** ....847 895-1043
1015 Morse Ave Schaumburg (60193) ***(G-19535)***
**Gano Welding Supplies Inc** ....217 345-3777
320 Railroad Ave Charleston (61920) ***(G-3597)***
**Garbe Iron Works Inc** ....630 897-5100
456 N Broadway Aurora (60505) ***(G-1160)***
**Garcoa Inc** ....708 905-5118
8838 Brookfield Ave Brookfield (60513) ***(G-2633)***
**Gard Rogard Inc** ....847 836-7700
250 Williams St Carpentersville (60110) ***(G-3284)***
**Gard, Ron, Chicago** *Also called Guess Whackit & Hope Inc* ***(G-5010)***
**Garden Impression, Geneva** *Also called Design Merchants* ***(G-10825)***
**Garden Prairie Organics LLC** ....815 597-1318
11887 Us Rt 20 Garden Prairie (61038) ***(G-10794)***
**Garden Prrie Pool Spa Enclsres, Garden Prairie** *Also called Ccsi International Inc* ***(G-10793)***
**Garden Watering, Mount Prospect** *Also called Robert Bosch Tool Corporation* ***(G-15369)***
**Gardien, Buffalo Grove** *Also called Consolidated Foam Inc* ***(G-2678)***
**Gardner Abrasive Products, South Beloit** *Also called Fives Landis Corp* ***(G-20146)***
**Gardner Denver Inc** ....209 823-0356
1301 N Euclid Ave Princeton (61356) ***(G-17749)***
**Gardner Denver Inc** ....217 222-5400
1800 Gardner Expy Quincy (62305) ***(G-17828)***
**Gardner Denver Inc** ....815 875-3321
1301 N Euclid Ave Princeton (61356) ***(G-17750)***
**Gardner Denver Inc** ....847 676-8800
5621 W Howard St Niles (60714) ***(G-15981)***
**Gardner Products Inc** ....815 562-6011
224 4th Ave Rochelle (61068) ***(G-18091)***
**Garen Eaton Farms LLC** ....217 228-0324
630 Sunset Dr Quincy (62305) ***(G-17829)***
**Garfilds Bev Whse - Barrington, Barrington** *Also called Barrington Cardinal Whse LLC* ***(G-1270)***
**Garman Trucking, Fairfield** *Also called Fairfield Ready Mix Inc* ***(G-10141)***
**Garratt-Callahan Company** ....630 543-4411
340 S La Londe Ave Addison (60101) ***(G-128)***
**Garrelts & Sons Inc** ....815 385-3821
2309 N Ringwood Rd Ste A McHenry (60050) ***(G-14508)***
**Garrelts & Sons Water Trtmnt, McHenry** *Also called Garrelts & Sons Inc* ***(G-14508)***
**Garren Sawmill & Farm, Dix** *Also called Boyd Sawmill* ***(G-8317)***
**Gartech Manufacturing Co** ....217 324-6527
1400 W Hudson Dr Litchfield (62056) ***(G-13686)***
**Garver Feeds (PA)** ....217 422-2201
222 E Wabash Ave Decatur (62523) ***(G-7884)***

**Garver Inc**...217 932-2441
10234 N 230th St Casey (62420) ***(G-3383)***
**Garvey Group, The, Niles** *Also called Ed Garvey and Company* ***(G-15976)***
**Garvin Electrical Manufacturer, Franklin Park** *Also called Garvin Industries Inc* ***(G-10475)***
**Garvin Industries Inc**...847 455-0188
3700 Sandra St Franklin Park (60131) ***(G-10475)***
**Gary & Larry Brown Trucking (PA)**...618 268-6377
5525 Highway 34 N Raleigh (62977) ***(G-17909)***
**Gary Bryan Kitchens & Bath, Springfield** *Also called Custom Woodwork & Interiors* ***(G-20427)***
**Gary Galassi and Sons Inc**...815 886-3906
44 Devonwood Ave Romeoville (60446) ***(G-18827)***
**Gary Galassi Stone & Steel, Romeoville** *Also called Gary Galassi and Sons Inc* ***(G-18827)***
**Gary Grimm & Associates Inc**...217 357-3401
1204 Buchanan St Carthage (62321) ***(G-3314)***
**Gary Poppins LLC**...847 455-2200
10929 Franklin Ave Ste N Franklin Park (60131) ***(G-10476)***
**Gary Quarries, Hamilton** *Also called Gray Quarries Inc* ***(G-11534)***
**Gary W Berger**...708 588-0200
25 Birch St Countryside (60525) ***(G-7427)***
**Gasket & Seal Fabricators Inc**...314 241-3673
1640 Sauget Indl Pkwy East Saint Louis (62206) ***(G-8752)***
**Gast Monuments Inc (PA)**...773 262-2400
1900 W Peterson Ave Chicago (60660) ***(G-4916)***
**Gate Systems Corporation**...847 731-6700
690 Chandler Rd Apt 401 Gurnee (60031) ***(G-11452)***
**Gatehouse Media LLC**...309 852-2181
105 E Central Blvd Kewanee (61443) ***(G-12686)***
**Gatehouse Media LLC**...618 783-2324
700 W Washington St Newton (62448) ***(G-15940)***
**Gatehouse Media LLC**...217 788-1300
1 Copley Plz Springfield (62701) ***(G-20445)***
**Gatehouse Media LLC**...618 393-2931
206 S Whittle Ave Olney (62450) ***(G-16769)***
**Gatehouse Media LLC**...618 937-2850
111 S Emma St West Frankfort (62896) ***(G-21809)***
**Gatehouse Media LLC**...585 598-0030
18w140 Butterfield Rd # 450 Oakbrook Terrace (60181) ***(G-16708)***
**Gatehouse Media LLC**...815 842-1153
318 N Main St Pontiac (61764) ***(G-17701)***
**Gatehouse Media LLC**...618 253-7146
35 S Vine St Harrisburg (62946) ***(G-11600)***
**Gatehouse Media LLC**...309 734-3164
400 S Main St Monmouth (61462) ***(G-15013)***
**Gatehouse Media III Holdings**...585 598-0030
1 News Plz Peoria (61643) ***(G-17368)***
**Gatehouse Media Illinois Ho**...217 788-1300
1 Copley Plz Springfield (62701) ***(G-20446)***
**Gates Corporation**...309 343-7171
630 Us Highway 150 E Galesburg (61401) ***(G-10752)***
**Gates Inc**...217 335-2378
134 Smith St Barry (62312) ***(G-1313)***
**Gates Repair & Machine, Barry** *Also called Gates Inc* ***(G-1313)***
**Gates Rubber Co, The, Galesburg** *Also called Gates Corporation* ***(G-10752)***
**Gatesair Inc**...217 222-8200
3200 Wisman Ln Quincy (62301) ***(G-17830)***
**Gateway Cable Inc (PA)**...630 766-7969
1998 Ohio St Ste 100 Lisle (60532) ***(G-13592)***
**Gateway Cable Inc**...630 766-7969
11 Gateway Rd Bensenville (60106) ***(G-1905)***
**Gateway Construction Company**...708 868-2926
2723 E Hammond Ave Chicago (60633) ***(G-4917)***
**Gateway Crushing & Screening**...618 337-1954
3936 Mississippi Ave East Saint Louis (62206) ***(G-8753)***
**Gateway Erectors, Chicago** *Also called Gateway Construction Company* ***(G-4917)***
**GATEWAY F. S. INC, Fults** *Also called F S Gateway Inc* ***(G-10709)***
**Gateway Fabricators Inc**...618 271-5700
633 Collinsville Ave East Saint Louis (62201) ***(G-8754)***
**Gateway Fs Inc**...618 824-6631
18 N Mill Rd Venedy (62214) ***(G-21136)***
**Gateway Fuels Inc**...618 248-5000
5260 State Route 161 Albers (62215) ***(G-354)***
**Gateway Industrial Power Inc (PA)**...888 865-8675
921 Fournie Ln Collinsville (62234) ***(G-7327)***
**Gateway Industrial Power Inc**...309 821-1035
13958 Roberto Rd Ste 2 Bloomington (61705) ***(G-2169)***
**Gateway Mine, Coulterville** *Also called Peabody Coal Company* ***(G-7402)***
**Gateway Packaging Co Gran Cy, Granite City** *Also called Gateway Packaging Company LLC* ***(G-11280)***
**Gateway Packaging Company (PA)**...618 451-0010
20 Central Industrial Dr Granite City (62040) ***(G-11279)***
**Gateway Packaging Company LLC (HQ)**...618 415-0010
20 Central Industrial Dr Granite City (62040) ***(G-11280)***
**Gateway Printing, Huntley** *Also called Rohrer Corporation* ***(G-12174)***
**Gateway Propane LLC**...618 286-3005
237 Coulter Rd East Carondelet (62240) ***(G-8614)***
**Gateway Rail Services Inc**...618 451-0100
1980 3rd St Madison (62060) ***(G-14146)***
**Gateway Screw & Rivet Inc**...630 539-2232
301 High Grove Blvd Glendale Heights (60139) ***(G-11026)***
**Gateway Seed Company Inc (PA)**...618 327-8000
5517 Van Buren Rd Nashville (62263) ***(G-15836)***
**Gateway Truck and Rfrgn, Collinsville** *Also called Gateway Industrial Power Inc* ***(G-7327)***
**Gatlin Chapel, Blue Island** *Also called Gatling Printing Inc* ***(G-2252)***
**Gatling Printing Inc**...708 388-4746
2946 Wireton Rd Blue Island (60406) ***(G-2252)***
**Gator Die Supplies, Rockford** *Also called Rockform Tooling & Machinery* ***(G-18592)***
**Gator Products Inc**...847 836-0581
80 Industrial Dr Unit 105 Gilberts (60136) ***(G-10919)***
**Gatorade Company (HQ)**...312 821-1000
555 W Monroe St Fl 1 Chicago (60661) ***(G-4918)***
**Gatto Industrial Platers Inc**...773 287-0100
4620 W Roosevelt Rd Chicago (60644) ***(G-4919)***
**Gaunt Industries Inc**...847 671-0776
9828 Franklin Ave Franklin Park (60131) ***(G-10477)***
**Gavel Company Div, The, Lincolnwood** *Also called Brown Wood Products Company* ***(G-13503)***
**Gavin Machine & Manufacturing, Sandwich** *Also called Gavin Woodworking Inc* ***(G-19365)***
**Gavin Woodworking Inc**...815 786-2242
16119 Chicago Rd Sandwich (60548) ***(G-19365)***
**Gavina Graphics**...217 345-9228
1920 18th St Charleston (61920) ***(G-3598)***
**Gaw-Ohara Envelope Co (PA)**...773 638-1200
500 N Sacramento Blvd Chicago (60612) ***(G-4920)***
**Gayety Candy Co Inc (PA)**...708 418-0062
3306 Ridge Rd Lansing (60438) ***(G-13163)***
**Gayetys Chocolates & Ice Cream, Lansing** *Also called Gayety Candy Co Inc* ***(G-13163)***
**Gaytan Signs & Co Inc**...815 726-2975
317 Mcdonough St Joliet (60436) ***(G-12500)***
**Gayton Enterprises LLC**...847 462-4030
2823 Waterfront Ave Algonquin (60102) ***(G-391)***
**Gayton Group Inc**...847 233-0509
9353 Seymour Ave Schiller Park (60176) ***(G-19833)***
**Gazette (PA)**...815 777-0105
716 S Bench St Galena (61036) ***(G-10724)***
**Gazette Democrat**...618 833-2150
108 Lafayette St 112 Anna (62906) ***(G-603)***
**Gazette News Office, Bunker Hill** *Also called Bunker Hill Publication* ***(G-2804)***
**Gazette Newspapers, Machesney Park** *Also called Rock Valley Publishing LLC* ***(G-14103)***
**Gazette Printing Co**...309 389-2811
508 W Main St Glasford (61533) ***(G-10951)***
**Gazette-Democrat**...618 833-2158
112 Lafayette St Anna (62906) ***(G-604)***
**Gb Marketing Inc**...847 367-0101
200 N Fairway Dr Ste 202 Vernon Hills (60061) ***(G-21164)***
**GBA Systems Integrators LLC**...913 492-0400
1701 River Dr Ste 100 Moline (61265) ***(G-14941)***
**Gbc Metals LLC**...618 258-2350
305 Lewis And Clark Blvd East Alton (62024) ***(G-8602)***
**Gbc Metals LLC (HQ)**...618 258-2350
427 N Shamrock St East Alton (62024) ***(G-8603)***
**Gbj I LLC**...815 877-4041
1590 Northrock Ct Rockford (61103) ***(G-18396)***
**Gbn Nails LLC**...773 881-8880
1822 W 95th St Chicago (60643) ***(G-4921)***
**GBS Document Solutions, Princeton** *Also called Ennis Inc* ***(G-17748)***
**GBS Liquidating Corp**...309 342-4155
2530 Grand Ave Galesburg (61401) ***(G-10753)***
**Gc America Inc (HQ)**...708 597-0900
3737 W 127th St Alsip (60803) ***(G-463)***
**Gc Dies LLC (PA)**...630 758-4100
877 N Larch Ave Elmhurst (60126) ***(G-9873)***
**Gc Manufacturing America LLC**...708 597-0900
3737 W 127th St Alsip (60803) ***(G-464)***
**Gc Packaging LLC (PA)**...630 758-4100
877 N Larch Ave Elmhurst (60126) ***(G-9874)***
**Gcg Corp**...847 298-2285
4344 Regency Dr Glenview (60025) ***(G-11128)***
**GCI, Bolingbrook** *Also called General Converting Inc* ***(G-2312)***
**Gcm, Chicago** *Also called Global Contract Mfg Inc* ***(G-4957)***
**Gcm Chicago, Schiller Park** *Also called Hi-Tech Manufacturing LLC* ***(G-19836)***
**Gcom Inc**...217 351-4241
1201 Fieldstone Dr Savoy (61874) ***(G-19409)***
**Gcp Applied Technologies**...410 531-4000
2051 Waukegan Rd Bannockburn (60015) ***(G-1259)***
**Gcs Steel Installers Inc**...630 487-6736
2256 Margaret Dr Montgomery (60538) ***(G-15044)***
**Gds, Bloomington** *Also called G D S Professional Bus Display* ***(G-2168)***
**Gds Enterprises**...217 543-3681
399 E Progress St Arthur (61911) ***(G-901)***
**GE Betz Inc**...630 543-8480
333 S Lombard Rd Addison (60101) ***(G-129)***
**GE Fairchild Mining Equipment**...618 559-3216
707 N Hickory St Du Quoin (62832) ***(G-8555)***
**GE Healthcare Holdings Inc**...847 398-8400
3350 N Ridge Ave Arlington Heights (60004) ***(G-759)***



ALPHABETIC

**GE Healthcare Inc** 312 243-0787
161 Tower Dr Ste A Burr Ridge (60527) ***(G-2844)***
**GE Healthcare Inc** 630 595-6642
945 N Edgewood Ave Ste A1 Wood Dale (60191) ***(G-22376)***
**GE Intelligent Platforms Inc** 630 829-4000
901 Warrenville Rd # 300 Lisle (60532) ***(G-13593)***
**GE Motors, Chicago** *Also called Motormakers De Kalb Credit Un* ***(G-5814)***
**GE Polymers LLC** 312 674-7434
109 Symonds Dr Unit 15 Hinsdale (60522) ***(G-11947)***
**GE Transportation, Chicago** *Also called G&E Transportation Inc* ***(G-4903)***
**Gea Farm Technologies Inc (HQ)** 630 548-8200
1880 Country Farm Dr Naperville (60563) ***(G-15662)***
**Gea Farm Technologies Inc** 630 759-1063
1354 Enterprise Dr Romeoville (60446) ***(G-18828)***
**Gear & Repair** 708 387-0144
9100 Plainfield Rd Ste 13 Brookfield (60513) ***(G-2634)***
**Gear Products & Mfg Inc** 708 344-0875
9007 S Thomas Ave Bridgeview (60455) ***(G-2493)***
**Gear Shop, The, Harwood Heights** *Also called Gears Gears Gears Inc* ***(G-11685)***
**Gear Technology, Elk Grove Village** *Also called Randall Publishing Inc* ***(G-9709)***
**Gearon Company, The, Chicago** *Also called Metomic Corporation* ***(G-5705)***
**Gears Gears Gears Inc** 708 366-6555
4615 N Ronald St Harwood Heights (60706) ***(G-11685)***
**Gebco Machine Inc** 618 452-6120
2900 Emzee Ave Granite City (62040) ***(G-11281)***
**Geebees Inc** 309 682-5300
3024 N University St Peoria (61604) ***(G-17369)***
**Gehl Company, Belvidere** *Also called Manitou Americas Inc* ***(G-1769)***
**Gehrke Technology Group Inc (PA)** 847 498-7320
1050 N Rand Rd Wauconda (60084) ***(G-21464)***
**Geib Industries Inc** 847 455-4550
901 E Jefferson St Bensenville (60106) ***(G-1906)***
**Geismar** 847 697-7510
1415 Davis Rd Elgin (60123) ***(G-9042)***
**Geitek Automation Inc** 815 385-3500
4615 Prime Pkwy McHenry (60050) ***(G-14509)***
**Geka Manufacturing Corporation** 224 238-5080
1690 Cambridge Dr Elgin (60123) ***(G-9043)***
**Gelato Enterprises LLC** 847 432-2233
617 Central Ave Highland Park (60035) ***(G-11835)***
**Gelato Enterprises LLC** 630 210-8457
50 S Main St Ste 138 Naperville (60540) ***(G-15663)***
**Gelita USA Chicago** 708 891-8400
10 Wentworth Ave Calumet City (60409) ***(G-2938)***
**Gelnex, Chicago** *Also called In3gredients Inc* ***(G-5171)***
**Gelscrubs** 312 243-4612
1100 W Cermak Rd Ste B501 Chicago (60608) ***(G-4922)***
**Gem Acquisition Company Inc** 773 735-3300
5942 S Central Ave Chicago (60638) ***(G-4923)***
**Gem Business Forms, Chicago** *Also called Gem Acquisition Company Inc* ***(G-4923)***
**Gem Electric Motor Repair** 815 756-5317
1400 E Lincoln Hwy Dekalb (60115) ***(G-8094)***
**Gem Manufacturing Corporation** 630 458-0014
367 S Rohlwing Rd Ste Q Addison (60101) ***(G-130)***
**Gema Inc (PA)** 773 508-6690
2434 W Peterson Ave Chicago (60659) ***(G-4924)***
**Gemco (PA)** 217 446-7900
1019 Griggs St Danville (61832) ***(G-7726)***
**Gemcom Inc** 800 871-6840
200 N Pearl St Willow Springs (60480) ***(G-22196)***
**Gemini Digital Inc** 630 894-9430
860 Lake St Ste 606 Roselle (60172) ***(G-18942)***
**Gemini Industries Inc** 618 251-3352
1 Gemini Industrial Dr Roxana (62084) ***(G-19084)***
**Gemini Steel Inc (PA)** 815 472-4462
1450 N 11250e Rd Momence (60954) ***(G-14981)***
**Gemini Tool & Manufacturing** 847 678-5000
3541 Martens St Franklin Park (60131) ***(G-10478)***
**Gemtar Inc** 618 548-1353
138 Woodland Dr Salem (62881) ***(G-19334)***
**Gemworld International Inc** 847 657-0555
2640 Patriot Blvd Ste 240 Northbrook (60062) ***(G-16264)***
**Genacc LLC** 309 253-9034
60 State St Ste 101 Peoria (61602) ***(G-17370)***
**General Air Compressor Inc** 630 860-1717
1078 Fairway Dr Bensenville (60106) ***(G-1907)***
**General Assembly & Mfg Corp** 847 516-6462
750 Industrial Dr Ste B Cary (60013) ***(G-3346)***
**General Bandages Inc** 847 966-8383
717 N Washington Ave Park Ridge (60068) ***(G-17198)***
**General Cable Industries Inc** 618 542-4761
1453 S Washington St Du Quoin (62832) ***(G-8556)***
**General Contractor Inc** 618 533-5213
190 Industrial Park Dr Sandoval (62882) ***(G-19357)***
**General Converting Inc** 630 378-9800
250 W Crossroads Pkwy Bolingbrook (60440) ***(G-2312)***
**General Cutng Tl Svc & Mfg Inc** 847 677-8770
6440 N Ridgeway Ave Lincolnwood (60712) ***(G-13513)***
**General Design Jewelers Inc** 312 201-9047
5 S Wabash Ave Ste 217 Chicago (60603) ***(G-4925)***
**General Dynamics Adv Inf Sys** 703 876-3000
50 S La Salle St Chicago (60603) ***(G-4926)***
**General Dynamics Ordnance** 618 985-8211
6658 Route 148 Marion (62959) ***(G-14261)***
**General Electric Company** 217 235-4081
1501 S 19th St Mattoon (61938) ***(G-14389)***
**General Electric Company** 309 664-1513
1601 General Electric Rd Bloomington (61704) ***(G-2170)***
**General Electric Company** 708 780-2600
1543 S 54th Ave Cicero (60804) ***(G-7197)***
**General Electric Company** 630 334-0054
2015 Spring Rd Ste 400 Oak Brook (60523) ***(G-16519)***
**General Electric Company** 847 304-7400
2501 Barrington Rd Hoffman Estates (60192) ***(G-12013)***
**General Electric Company** 708 924-5055
7337 S Mason Ave Bedford Park (60638) ***(G-1551)***
**General Electro Corporation** 630 595-8989
1069 Bryn Mawr Ave Bensenville (60106) ***(G-1908)***
**General Engineering Works** 630 543-8000
1515 W Wrightwood Ct Addison (60101) ***(G-131)***
**General Exhibits and Displays** 847 934-1943
1425 Appleby Rd Inverness (60067) ***(G-12204)***
**General Fas Acquisition Co** 630 960-3360
11230 Katherines Xing Woodridge (60517) ***(G-22481)***
**General Foam Plastics Corp** 847 851-9995
1051 E Main St East Dundee (60118) ***(G-8637)***
**General Forging Die Co Inc** 815 874-4224
4635 Hydraulic Rd Rockford (61109) ***(G-18397)***
**General Grind & Machine Inc** 309 582-5959
2103 Se 5th St Aledo (61231) ***(G-368)***
**General Grinding Co** 630 543-9088
1514 W Wrightwood Ct Addison (60101) ***(G-132)***
**General Laminating Company** 847 639-8770
179 Northwest Hwy Ste 3 Cary (60013) ***(G-3347)***
**General Loose Leaf Bindery Inc** 847 244-9700
3811 Hawthorne Ct Waukegan (60087) ***(G-21562)***
**General Lrng Communications, Northbrook** *Also called M I T Financial Group Inc* ***(G-16303)***
**General Machine Inc** 618 234-1919
6038 Schiermeier Rd Freeburg (62243) ***(G-10636)***
**General Machine & Tl Works Inc** 312 337-2177
313 W Chestnut St Chicago (60610) ***(G-4927)***
**General Machine and Tool Inc (PA)** 815 727-4342
348 Caton Farm Rd Lockport (60441) ***(G-13717)***
**General Machinery & Mfg Co** 773 235-3700
2634 N Keeler Ave Chicago (60639) ***(G-4928)***
**General Machining Service Inc** 708 636-4848
5521 W 110th St Ste 6 Oak Lawn (60453) ***(G-16623)***
**General Manufacturing LLC** 708 345-8600
1725 N 33rd Ave Melrose Park (60160) ***(G-14646)***
**General Methods Co, Morton** *Also called Morton Automatic Electric Co* ***(G-15166)***
**General Mills Inc** 630 844-1125
1370 Orchard Rd Montgomery (60538) ***(G-15045)***
**General Mills Inc** 630 231-1140
1600 Huntington Dr Calumet City (60409) ***(G-2939)***
**General Mills Inc** 309 342-9165
1557 S Henderson St Galesburg (61401) ***(G-10754)***
**General Mills Inc** 815 544-7399
915 E Pleasant St Belvidere (61008) ***(G-1754)***
**General Mills Inc** 630 577-3800
2441 Warrenville Rd # 610 Lisle (60532) ***(G-13594)***
**General Mills Green Giant** 815 547-5311
725 Landmark Dr Belvidere (61008) ***(G-1755)***
**General Motor Sign** 847 546-0424
704 Sunset Dr Round Lake (60073) ***(G-19057)***
**General Motors LLC** 815 733-0668
1355 Remington Blvd Bolingbrook (60490) ***(G-2313)***
**General Packaging Products Inc** 312 226-5611
1700 S Canal St Chicago (60616) ***(G-4929)***
**General Pallet** 773 660-8550
13513 S Calumet Ave Chicago (60827) ***(G-4930)***
**General Plating Co Inc** 630 543-0088
303 W Fay Ave Addison (60101) ***(G-133)***
**General Precision Mfg LLC** 847 624-4969
2670 Greenleaf Ave Elk Grove Village (60007) ***(G-9497)***
**General Press Colors Ltd** 630 543-7878
53 W Jackson Blvd # 1115 Chicago (60604) ***(G-4931)***
**General Products** 773 463-2424
4045 N Rockwell St Chicago (60618) ***(G-4932)***
**General Products Intl Ltd** 847 458-6357
9245 S Il Route 31 Lake In The Hills (60156) ***(G-12994)***
**General RV Center Inc** 847 669-5570
14000 Automall Dr Huntley (60142) ***(G-12140)***
**General Sand & Gravel, Rock Island** *Also called Riverstone Group Inc* ***(G-18201)***
**General Steel & Materials, Mattoon** *Also called Mervis Industries Inc* ***(G-14402)***
**General Surface Hardening (PA)** 312 226-5472
2108 W Fulton St Chicago (60612) ***(G-4933)***
**Generation Copy Inc** 847 866-0469
960 Grove St Evanston (60201) ***(G-10041)***

**Geneseo Publication, Cambridge** *Also called Liberty Group Publishing* ***(G-2968)***
**Geneseo Republic, The, Geneseo** *Also called Liberty Group Publishing* ***(G-10802)***
**Genesis Comics Group** 312 544-7473
2631 S Ind Ave Apt 1410 Chicago (60616) ***(G-4934)***
**Genesis Electric & Tech Inc** 847 258-5218
356 Lively Blvd Elk Grove Village (60007) ***(G-9498)***
**Genesis III Inc** 815 537-7900
5575 Lyndon Rd Prophetstown (61277) ***(G-17769)***
**Genesis Inc (PA)** 630 351-4400
980 Central Ave Roselle (60172) ***(G-18943)***
**Genesis Mold Corp** 847 573-9431
854 Liberty Dr Ste C Libertyville (60048) ***(G-13326)***
**Genesis Press Inc** 630 467-1000
1270 Ardmore Ave Itasca (60143) ***(G-12268)***
**Genesis Print & Copy Svcs Inc** 773 374-1020
8319 S Stony Island Ave Chicago (60617) ***(G-4935)***
**Genetics Development Corp** 847 283-9780
21 N Skokie Hwy Ste 104 Lake Bluff (60044) ***(G-12845)***
**Geneva Construction Company** 630 892-6536
216 Butterfield Rd North Aurora (60542) ***(G-16132)***
**Geneva Glass Works, Geneva** *Also called Geneva Glassworks Inc* ***(G-10830)***
**Geneva Glassworks Inc** 630 232-1200
560 Lark St Bldg C Geneva (60134) ***(G-10830)***
**Geneva Manufacturing Co** 847 697-1161
900 Schneider Dr South Elgin (60177) ***(G-20199)***
**Geneva Running Outfitters LLC** 331 248-0221
221 W State St Geneva (60134) ***(G-10831)***
**Geneva Wood Fuels LLC** 773 296-0700
2550 N Lakeview Ave S2206 Chicago (60614) ***(G-4936)***
**Gengler-Lowney Laser Works** 630 801-4840
899 Sullivan Rd Aurora (60506) ***(G-1161)***
**Genie Pro Sales Center, Itasca** *Also called Overhead Door Corporation* ***(G-12338)***
**Genisys Decision Corporation** 708 524-5100
1150 S Taylor Ave Ste 200 Oak Park (60304) ***(G-16666)***
**Gennco International Inc** 847 541-3333
200 Larkin Dr Ste F Wheeling (60090) ***(G-22062)***
**Genoa Business Forms Inc** 815 895-2800
445 Park Ave Sycamore (60178) ***(G-20798)***
**Genoa Kingston Kirkland News, Sycamore** *Also called Kane County Cronicle* ***(G-20805)***
**Genoa Manufacturing Center, Genoa** *Also called Greenlee Textron Inc* ***(G-10879)***
**Gensler Gardens Inc (PA)** 815 874-9634
8631 11th St Davis Junction (61020) ***(G-7813)***
**Gentner Fabrication Inc** 773 523-2505
2847 W 47th Pl Chicago (60632) ***(G-4937)***
**Gentry Small Engine Repair** 217 849-3378
124 Court House Sq Toledo (62468) ***(G-20963)***
**Genuine Parts Company** 630 293-1300
1225 W Roosevelt Rd Chicago (60608) ***(G-4938)***
**Genuine Scooters LLC** 773 271-8514
2700 W Grand Ave Chicago (60612) ***(G-4939)***
**Genwoods Holdco LLC** 815 732-2141
2606 S Il Route 2 Oregon (61061) ***(G-16825)***
**Geo B Carpenter Co Division, Elmhurst** *Also called Tri Vantage LLC* ***(G-9952)***
**Geo J Rothan Co** 309 674-5189
1200 W Johnson St Peoria (61605) ***(G-17371)***
**Geo Lauterer, Chicago** *Also called George Lauterer Corporation* ***(G-4943)***
**Geo N Mitchell Drlg Co Inc** 618 382-2343
1239 County Road 1500 N Carmi (62821) ***(G-3068)***
**Geo T Schmidt Inc (PA)** 847 647-7117
6151 W Howard St Niles (60714) ***(G-15982)***
**Geocap Financial Solutions, Burr Ridge** *Also called Cnh Capital America LLC* ***(G-2831)***
**Geokat Granite** 773 265-1423
4460 W Lexington St Chicago (60624) ***(G-4940)***
**Geomentum Inc (HQ)** 630 729-7500
3025 Highland Pkwy # 700 Downers Grove (60515) ***(G-8447)***
**Geomentum Inc** 630 729-7500
3025 Highland Pkwy Downers Grove (60515) ***(G-8448)***
**Geomentum Solutions, Downers Grove** *Also called Geomentum Inc* ***(G-8447)***
**Georg Jensen Inc** 312 642-9160
959 N Michigan Ave Chicago (60611) ***(G-4941)***
**Georg-Pcific Corrugated IV LLC** 630 896-3610
4390 Liberty St Aurora (60504) ***(G-1014)***
**George Drowne Cabinet Sand** 847 234-1487
517 Lincoln Ave Lake Bluff (60044) ***(G-12846)***
**George Electronics Inc** 708 331-1983
11625 Hidden Valley Cv Orland Park (60467) ***(G-16860)***
**George Erckman Jewelers** 312 263-7380
55 E Washington St # 807 Chicago (60602) ***(G-4942)***
**George Hansen & Co Inc** 630 628-8700
50 W Laura Dr Addison (60101) ***(G-134)***
**George Lauterer Corporation** 312 913-1881
310 S Racine Ave Chicago (60607) ***(G-4943)***
**George Nottoli & Sons Inc** 773 589-1010
7652 W Belmont Ave Chicago (60634) ***(G-4944)***
**George Pagels Company** 708 478-7036
9910 W 190th St Ste H Mokena (60448) ***(G-14867)***
**George Press Inc** 217 324-2242
905 N Old Route 66 Litchfield (62056) ***(G-13687)***
**George S Music Room** 773 767-4676
5700 S Cicero Ave Ste 59 Chicago (60638) ***(G-4945)***
**George Vaggelatos** 847 361-3880
400 W Center St Itasca (60143) ***(G-12269)***
**George W Pierson Company** 815 726-3351
2121 Maple Rd Joliet (60432) ***(G-12501)***
**George Wilson** 847 342-1111
477 Greystone Ln Prospect Heights (60070) ***(G-17778)***
**George's Farm Supply, West Salem** *Also called West Salem Knox County Htchy* ***(G-21825)***
**Georges Printwear, Lake Zurich** *Also called JLJ Corp* ***(G-13092)***
**Georgetown Spice Company, Elk Grove Village** *Also called Arlington Specialties Inc* ***(G-9313)***
**Georgetown Waste Water** 217 662-2525
208 S Walnut St Georgetown (61846) ***(G-10886)***
**Georgetown Wood and Pallet Co** 217 662-2563
5781 State Route 1 Georgetown (61846) ***(G-10887)***
**Georgia-Pacific LLC** 847 885-3920
895 Hillcrest Blvd Hoffman Estates (60169) ***(G-12014)***
**Georgia-Pacific LLC** 217 999-2511
900 S Old Route 66 Mount Olive (62069) ***(G-15302)***
**Georgia-Pacific Bldg Pdts LLC** 630 449-7200
2540 Prospect Ct Aurora (60502) ***(G-1015)***
**Georgia-Pacific LLC** 815 423-9990
21837 W Mississippi Ave Elwood (60421) ***(G-9981)***
**Georgies Greek Tasty Food Inc** 773 987-1298
2527 W Carmen Ave Chicago (60625) ***(G-4946)***
**Geotest Instrument Corp (PA)** 847 869-7645
241 S Frontage Rd Ste 38 Burr Ridge (60527) ***(G-2845)***
**Gepco International Inc (HQ)** 847 795-9555
1770 Birchwood Ave Des Plaines (60018) ***(G-8201)***
**Gerald Graff** 312 343-2612
6818 N Kildare Ave Lincolnwood (60712) ***(G-13514)***
**Gerald R Page Corporation (PA)** 847 398-5575
309 E Kenilworth Ave Prospect Heights (60070) ***(G-17779)***
**Gerali Custom Design Inc** 847 760-0500
1482 Sheldon Dr Elgin (60120) ***(G-9044)***
**Gerard Printing Company** 847 437-6442
710 Bonnie Ln Elk Grove Village (60007) ***(G-9499)***
**Gerardo and Quintana Auto Elc** 773 424-0634
4034 W 63rd St Chicago (60629) ***(G-4947)***
**Gerb Vibration Control Systems** 630 724-1660
1950 Ohio St Lisle (60532) ***(G-13595)***
**Gerber Manufacturing (gm) LLC** 708 478-0100
9830 W 190th St Ste F Mokena (60448) ***(G-14868)***
**Gerber Plumbing Fixtures, Woodridge** *Also called Cfpg Ltd* ***(G-22459)***
**Gerber Plumbing Fixtures LLC** 630 679-1420
2500 Intrntonale Pkwy Woodridge (60517) ***(G-22482)***
**Gerdau Ameristeel US Inc** 815 544-9651
2595 Tripp Rd Belvidere (61008) ***(G-1756)***
**Gerdau Ameristeel US Inc** 815 547-0400
2595 Tripp Rd Belvidere (61008) ***(G-1757)***
**Gerhard Designing & Mfg Inc** 708 599-4664
8540 S Thomas Ave Ste A Bridgeview (60455) ***(G-2494)***
**Gerlin Inc** 630 653-5232
170 Tubeway Dr Carol Stream (60188) ***(G-3157)***
**Germain Saint Press Inc** 847 882-7400
1120 Stonehedge Dr Schaumburg (60194) ***(G-19536)***
**German American Nat Congress (PA)** 773 561-9181
4740 N Western Ave Fl 2 Chicago (60625) ***(G-4948)***
**Germann Instruments Inc** 847 329-9999
8845 Forestview Rd Evanston (60203) ***(G-10042)***
**Gerresheimer Glass Inc** 708 757-6853
1131 Arnold St Chicago Heights (60411) ***(G-7098)***
**Gesell Oil Well Service LLC** 618 547-7114
101 S Adams St Kinmundy (62854) ***(G-12710)***
**Gesells Pump Sales & Service** 618 439-7354
Hwy 37 S Whittington (62897) ***(G-22186)***
**Geske & Sons, Crystal Lake** *Also called Geske and Sons Inc* ***(G-7582)***
**Geske and Sons Inc (PA)** 815 459-2407
400 E Terra Cotta Ave Crystal Lake (60014) ***(G-7581)***
**Geske and Sons Inc** 815 459-2407
400 E Terra Cotta Ave Crystal Lake (60014) ***(G-7582)***
**Getex Corporation** 630 993-1300
311 Woodview Ct Hinsdale (60523) ***(G-11948)***
**Gett Industries Ltd** 309 799-5131
7307 50th St Milan (61264) ***(G-14787)***
**Getz Fire Equipment Co** 309 637-1440
1440 Sw Jefferson Ave Peoria (61605) ***(G-17372)***
**Getz Industrial, Peoria** *Also called Getz Fire Equipment Co* ***(G-17372)***
**GF Parent LLC (PA)** 312 255-4800
676 N Michigan Ave Chicago (60611) ***(G-4949)***
**Gfc, Pittsfield** *Also called God Family Country LLC* ***(G-17568)***
**Gfi Innovations LLC** 847 263-9000
861 Anita Ave Antioch (60002) ***(G-634)***
**Gfi Metal Treating, Rockford** *Also called Golfers Family Corporation* ***(G-18401)***
**Gfx Dynamic** 847 543-4600
32088 N Pine Ave Grayslake (60030) ***(G-11339)***
**Gfx International Inc (PA)** 847 543-7179
333 Barron Blvd Grayslake (60030) ***(G-11340)***

A L P H A B E T I C

**Ggb Chicago, Waukegan** *Also called Ggb North America LLC* ***(G-21563)***
**Ggb North America LLC**....847 775-1859
2300 Norman Dr Waukegan (60085) ***(G-21563)***
**Ggc Corp**....847 671-6500
4300 United Pkwy Schiller Park (60176) ***(G-19834)***
**Gh Cranes Corporation**....815 277-5328
9134 Gulfstream Rd Frankfort (60423) ***(G-10325)***
**Gh Printing Co Inc (PA)**....630 960-4115
5207 Walnut Ave Downers Grove (60515) ***(G-8449)***
**Ghetzler Aero-Power Corp**....224 513-5636
26 Manchester Ln Vernon Hills (60061) ***(G-21165)***
**Gholson Pump & Repairs Co**....618 382-4730
725 County Road 1450 N Carmi (62821) ***(G-3069)***
**Ghp Group Inc (PA)**....847 324-5900
6440 W Howard St Niles (60714) ***(G-15983)***
**Gianni Incorporated**....708 863-6696
4615 W Roosevelt Rd Cicero (60804) ***(G-7198)***
**Giant Globes Inc**....773 772-2917
4433 W Montana St Chicago (60639) ***(G-4950)***
**Giba Electric**....773 685-4420
4054 W Warwick Ave Chicago (60641) ***(G-4951)***
**Gibbon America Inc**....847 931-1255
801 N State St Ste A Elgin (60123) ***(G-9045)***
**Gibbon America II Corp**....847 931-1255
801 N State St Ste A Elgin (60123) ***(G-9046)***
**Gibbon Printing Inks, Elgin** *Also called Gibbon America II Corp* ***(G-9046)***
**Gibbs Machine Corp**....815 336-9000
411 S Main Coleta (61081) ***(G-7310)***
**Gibraltar Chemical Works Inc**....708 333-0600
114 E 168th St South Holland (60473) ***(G-20270)***
**Gibson Insurance Inc**....217 864-4877
300 N State Highway 121 Mount Zion (62549) ***(G-15451)***
**Gier Radio & Television Inc**....815 722-8514
201 E Cail St Ste 1 Joliet (60432) ***(G-12502)***
**Gift Chech Graphics, Schaumburg** *Also called Creative Lithocraft Inc* ***(G-19489)***
**Gift Check Program 2013 Inc**....630 986-5081
1400 Opus Pl Ste 810 Downers Grove (60515) ***(G-8450)***
**Gift Wraping Center, Skokie** *Also called Wrap & Send Services* ***(G-20115)***
**Gifts For You, Burr Ridge** *Also called Techny Advisors LLC* ***(G-2883)***
**Giftware News, Chicago** *Also called Talcott Communications Corp* ***(G-6668)***
**Gig Karasek LLC**....630 549-0394
3955 Commerce Dr Saint Charles (60174) ***(G-19189)***
**Gil Instruments Co**....815 459-8764
500 Oxford Ln Crystal Lake (60014) ***(G-7583)***
**Gilbert Electric**....618 458-7235
3585 Kaskaskia Rd Fults (62244) ***(G-10710)***
**Gilbert Spring Corporation**....773 486-6030
2301 N Knox Ave Chicago (60639) ***(G-4952)***
**Gilberts Craft Sausages LLC**....630 923-8969
207a W Front St Wheaton (60187) ***(G-21950)***
**Gilco Real Estate Company**....847 298-1717
515 Jarvis Ave Des Plaines (60018) ***(G-8202)***
**Gilday Service Company, Antioch** *Also called Gilday Services* ***(G-635)***
**Gilday Services**....847 395-0853
25870 W Hermann Ave Antioch (60002) ***(G-635)***
**Gill Athletics, Champaign** *Also called Litania Sports Group Inc* ***(G-3510)***
**Gill Athletics**....800 637-3090
2808 Gemini Ct Champaign (61822) ***(G-3487)***
**Gillespie City Water**....217 839-3279
400 Pear St Gillespie (62033) ***(G-10941)***
**Gillette Company**....847 689-3111
3500 16th St North Chicago (60064) ***(G-16180)***
**Gilman Star Inc**....815 265-7332
203 N Central St 7 Gilman (60938) ***(G-10942)***
**Gilmore Marketing Concepts, Elgin** *Also called Kim Gilmore* ***(G-9089)***
**Gilster-Mary Lee, Chester** *Also called Mary Lee Packaging Corporation* ***(G-3659)***
**Gilster-Mary Lee Corporation**....618 826-3102
111 Industrial Dr Chester (62233) ***(G-3656)***
**Gilster-Mary Lee Corporation (HQ)**....618 826-2361
1037 State St Chester (62233) ***(G-3657)***
**Gilster-Mary Lee Corporation**....618 272-3261
606 W Main St Ridgway (62979) ***(G-17985)***
**Ginger Bliss Juice LLC**....773 456-0181
15 Spinning Wheel Rd Hinsdale (60521) ***(G-11949)***
**Gingerich Custom Woodworking**....217 578-3491
750 N Cr 250 E Arthur (61911) ***(G-902)***
**Gingrich Enterprises Inc**....309 923-7312
1503 W Front St Roanoke (61561) ***(G-18050)***
**Gino's Pizza, Walnut** *Also called Avanti Foods Company* ***(G-21329)***
**Giovanini Metals Corp**....815 842-0500
1320 N Main St Pontiac (61764) ***(G-17702)***
**Giovanni Rana, Oak Brook** *Also called Rana Meal Solutions LLC* ***(G-16558)***
**Girard Chemical Company**....630 293-5886
605 Country Club Dr Ste F Bensenville (60106) ***(G-1909)***
**Girl's Gear, Alton** *Also called Langa Resource Group Inc* ***(G-581)***
**Girls In The Garage, Carrier Mills** *Also called Amy Schutt* ***(G-3305)***
**Girls In White Satin**....217 245-5400
300 E State St Jacksonville (62650) ***(G-12389)***
**Girlygirl**....708 633-7290
17037 Odell Ave Tinley Park (60477) ***(G-20917)***
**Gisco Inc**....630 910-3000
8193 S Lemont Rd Darien (60561) ***(G-7795)***
**Givaudan Flavors Corporation**....630 682-5600
195 Alexandra Way Carol Stream (60188) ***(G-3158)***
**Givaudan Flavors Corporation**....630 773-8484
880 W Thorndale Ave Itasca (60143) ***(G-12270)***
**Givaudan Flavors Corporation**....847 608-6200
580 Tollgate Rd Ste A Elgin (60123) ***(G-9047)***
**Givaudan Fragrances Corp**....847 735-0221
1720 N Waukegan Rd Lake Forest (60045) ***(G-12900)***
**Gki Cutting Tools, Rockford** *Also called Gki Incorporated* ***(G-18398)***
**Gki Incorporated**....815 459-2330
1639 N Alpine Rd Ste 401 Rockford (61107) ***(G-18398)***
**GKN Aerospace Inc**....630 737-1456
550 Warrenville Rd # 400 Lisle (60532) ***(G-13596)***
**GKN America Corp (HQ)**....630 972-9300
2715 Davey Rd Ste 300 Woodridge (60517) ***(G-22483)***
**GKN North America Services Inc (HQ)**....630 972-9300
2715 Davey Rd Ste 300 Woodridge (60517) ***(G-22484)***
**GKN Rockford Inc**....815 633-7460
1200 Windsor Rd Loves Park (61111) ***(G-13944)***
**GKN Stromag Inc**....937 433-3882
2715 Davey Rd Ste 100 Woodridge (60517) ***(G-22485)***
**GKN Walterscheid Inc**....630 972-9300
2715 Davey Rd Woodridge (60517) ***(G-22486)***
**GL Downs Inc**....618 993-9777
1805 Wolff Dr Marion (62959) ***(G-14262)***
**GL Led LLC**....312 600-9363
501 W 18th St Chicago (60616) ***(G-4953)***
**GL Precision Tube, Aurora** *Also called Great Lakes Precision Tube Inc* ***(G-1164)***
**Glamox Aqua Signal Corporation (HQ)**....847 639-6412
1125 Alexander Ct Cary (60013) ***(G-3348)***
**Glanbia Performance Ntrtn Inc**....630 256-7445
948 Meridian Lake Dr Aurora (60504) ***(G-1016)***
**Glanbia Performance Ntrtn Inc**....630 236-3126
600 N Commerce St Aurora (60504) ***(G-1017)***
**Glanbia Performance Ntrtn Inc (HQ)**....630 236-0097
3500 Lacey Rd Downers Grove (60515) ***(G-8451)***
**Glancer Magazine**....630 428-4387
248 Belle Vue Ln Sugar Grove (60554) ***(G-20726)***
**Glaser USA Inc**....847 362-7878
14181 W Hawthorne Ave Lake Forest (60045) ***(G-12901)***
**Glasford Gazette, Glasford** *Also called Gazette Printing Co* ***(G-10951)***
**Glass America Midwest Inc (PA)**....877 743-7237
977 N Oaklawn Ave Ste 200 Elmhurst (60126) ***(G-9875)***
**Glass America Midwest Inc**....203 932-0248
977 N Oaklawn Ave Ste 200 Elmhurst (60126) ***(G-9876)***
**Glass Artistry**....847 998-5800
1908 Janke Dr Northbrook (60062) ***(G-16265)***
**Glass Cleaner, Elgin** *Also called A J Funk & Co* ***(G-8929)***
**Glass Concepts LLC**....773 650-0520
1956 W 17th St Chicago (60608) ***(G-4954)***
**Glass Dimensions Inc**....708 410-2305
1942 N 15th Ave Melrose Park (60160) ***(G-14647)***
**Glass Fx**....217 359-0048
202 S 1st St Champaign (61820) ***(G-3488)***
**Glass Haus**....815 459-5849
2412 S Justen Rd McHenry (60050) ***(G-14510)***
**Glasstek Inc**....630 978-9897
10s059 Schoger Dr Unit 40 Naperville (60564) ***(G-15807)***
**Glazed Structures Inc**....847 223-4560
350 Center St Grayslake (60030) ***(G-11341)***
**Glazers Stoller Distrg LLC**....847 350-3200
2881 Busse Rd Franklin Park (60131) ***(G-10479)***
**GLC Engineering, Addison** *Also called GLC Industries Inc* ***(G-135)***
**GLC Industries Inc**....630 628-5870
326 W Gerri Ln Addison (60101) ***(G-135)***
**Gld Industries Inc**....217 390-9594
4411 Southford Trace Dr Champaign (61822) ***(G-3489)***
**Glen Lake Inc**....630 668-3492
285 Fullerton Ave Carol Stream (60188) ***(G-3159)***
**Glen Oak Foods, Aurora** *Also called OSI International Foods Ltd* ***(G-1060)***
**Glen Products**....847 998-1361
927 Harms Rd Glenview (60025) ***(G-11129)***
**Glen-Gery Corporation**....815 795-6911
1401 Broadway St Marseilles (61341) ***(G-14309)***
**Glenair Inc**....847 679-8833
7000 N Lawndale Ave Lincolnwood (60712) ***(G-13515)***
**Glendale Incorporated**....630 770-1965
322 Ste B W St Charles Rd Villa Park (60181) ***(G-21255)***
**Glendale Pharma, Villa Park** *Also called Glendale Incorporated* ***(G-21255)***
**Glendale Woodworking**....630 545-1520
641 E North Ave Glendale Heights (60139) ***(G-11027)***
**Glenmark Burgers, Chicago** *Also called Best Chicago Meat Company LLC* ***(G-4090)***
**Glenmark Industries Ltd**....773 927-4800
4545 S Racine Ave Ste 1 Chicago (60609) ***(G-4955)***

## ALPHABETIC SECTION

**Glenraven Inc** .................................................. 847 515-1321
40w260 Apache Ln  Huntley  (60142)  *(G-12141)*

**Glenview Custom Cabinets Inc** ........................ 847 345-5754
1921 Pickwick Ln  Glenview  (60026)  *(G-11130)*

**Glenview Grind** ................................................ 847 729-0111
1837 Glenview Rd  Glenview  (60025)  *(G-11131)*

**Glenview Health Systems, Glenview** *Also called Glenview Systems  Inc  (G-11132)*

**Glenview Pharma Inc** ...................................... 773 856-3205
6404 N Fairfield Ave  Chicago  (60645)  *(G-4956)*

**Glenview Systems  Inc** .................................... 847 724-2691
3048 N Lake Ter  Glenview  (60026)  *(G-11132)*

**Glenwood Tool & Mold Inc** ............................... 630 289-3400
1251 Humbracht Cir Ste D  Bartlett  (60103)  *(G-1349)*

**Glidden Professional Paint Ctr, Meredosia** *Also called PPG Architectural Finishes Inc (G-14734)*

**Glidden Professional Paint Ctr, Chicago** *Also called PPG Architectural Finishes Inc (G-6161)*

**Glidden Professional Paint Ctr, Gurnee** *Also called PPG Architectural Finishes Inc (G-11487)*

**Glidden Professional Paint Ctr, Itasca** *Also called PPG Architectural Finishes Inc (G-12344)*

**Glidden Professional Paint Ctr, Aurora** *Also called PPG Architectural Finishes Inc (G-1067)*

**Glidden Professional Paint Ctr, Peoria** *Also called PPG Architectural Finishes Inc (G-17432)*

**Glidden Professional Paint Ctr, Des Plaines** *Also called PPG Architectural Finishes Inc (G-8259)*

**Glideaway Bed Carriage Mf, Peoria** *Also called Fredman Bros Furniture Co Inc (G-17366)*

**Glidera  Inc** ...................................................... 773 350-4000
188 W Industrial Dr # 240  Elmhurst  (60126)  *(G-9877)*

**Glitech Inc** ....................................................... 708 753-1220
330 E Joe Orr Rd Unit 1  Chicago Heights  (60411)  *(G-7099)*

**Glitter Your Pallet** ........................................... 708 516-8494
14350 S Saddle Brook Ln  Homer Glen  (60491)  *(G-12080)*

**Glk Enterprises Inc** ......................................... 847 395-7368
248 E Depot St Unit 2  Antioch  (60002)  *(G-636)*

**Glo Document Solutions, Elk Grove Village** *Also called Bell Litho  Inc (G-9338)*

**Glo-Mold Inc** .................................................... 847 671-1762
3800 Wesley Ter  Schiller Park  (60176)  *(G-19835)*

**Global Abrasive Products  Inc** .......................... 630 543-9466
39 W Factory Rd  Addison  (60101)  *(G-136)*

**Global Brass and Copper  Inc (HQ)** .................. 502 873-3000
305 Lewis And Clark Blvd  East Alton  (62024)  *(G-8604)*

**Global Brass and Copper  Inc** .......................... 618 258-5330
1901 N Roselle Rd  East Alton  (62024)  *(G-8605)*

**Global Brass Cop Holdings Inc (PA)** ................ 847 240-4700
475 N Marti Rd  Schaumburg  (60173)  *(G-19537)*

**Global Cmpnent Tech Amrcas Inc** ................... 815 568-4507
19720 E Grant Hwy  Marengo  (60152)  *(G-14229)*

**Global Contract Mfg Inc** .................................. 312 432-6200
156 N Jefferson St # 300  Chicago  (60661)  *(G-4957)*

**Global Cosmetics Industry, Carol Stream** *Also called Allured Publishing Corporation (G-3097)*

**Global Decor  Inc** ............................................. 847 437-9600
1501 Nicholas Blvd  Elk Grove Village  (60007)  *(G-9500)*

**Global Development, Streator** *Also called Shredderhotlinecom Company (G-20701)*

**Global Display Solutions  Inc** .......................... 815 282-2328
5217 28th Ave  Rockford  (61109)  *(G-18399)*

**Global Endoscopy  Inc** ..................................... 847 910-5836
878 Cass Ln  Elk Grove Village  (60007)  *(G-9501)*

**Global Fastener Engrg Inc** ............................... 847 929-9563
31632 N Ellis Dr Unit 302  Volo  (60073)  *(G-21312)*

**Global Field Services Intl Inc** .......................... 847 931-8930
1875 Fox Ln  Elgin  (60123)  *(G-9048)*

**Global Fire Control  Inc** ................................... 309 314-0919
1201 7th St Ste 103  East Moline  (61244)  *(G-8680)*

**Global Gear & Machining LLC** ......................... 630 969-9400
2500 Curtiss St  Downers Grove  (60515)  *(G-8452)*

**Global General Contractors LLC** ..................... 708 663-0476
9018 Walnut Ln  Tinley Park  (60487)  *(G-20918)*

**Global Green Products LLC (PA)** ..................... 708 341-3670
8617 Golfview Dr  Orland Park  (60462)  *(G-16861)*

**Global Industries  Inc** ...................................... 630 681-2818
1879 Internationale Blvd  Glendale Heights  (60139)  *(G-11028)*

**Global Maintenance  LLC** ................................ 270 933-1281
654 Kennedy Dr  Metropolis  (62960)  *(G-14753)*

**Global Manufacturing** ..................................... 630 908-7633
324 Central Ave  Willowbrook  (60527)  *(G-22213)*

**Global Material Tech Inc (PA)** .......................... 847 495-4700
750 W Lake Cook Rd # 480  Buffalo Grove  (60089)  *(G-2699)*

**Global Material Tech Inc** ................................. 773 247-6000
2825 W 31st St  Chicago  (60623)  *(G-4958)*

**Global Medical Services LLC (PA)** .................. 847 460-8086
12904 Rockfish Ln  Plainfield  (60585)  *(G-17602)*

**Global Pharma Device Solutions** .................... 708 212-5801
6454 W 74th St  Chicago  (60638)  *(G-4959)*

**Global Stone  Inc** ............................................. 847 718-1418
51 Joey Dr  Elk Grove Village  (60007)  *(G-9502)*

**Global Tech & Resources  Inc** ......................... 630 364-4260
3601 Algonquin Rd Ste 650  Rolling Meadows  (60008)  *(G-18732)*

**Global Technologies I  LLC (PA)** ..................... 312 255-8350
980 N Michigan Ave # 1400  Chicago  (60611)  *(G-4960)*

**Global Telephony Magazine** ............................ 312 840-8405
330 N Wabash Ave Ste 2300  Chicago  (60611)  *(G-4961)*

**Global Tool & Die Inc** ...................................... 847 956-1200
1355 Tonne Rd  Elk Grove Village  (60007)  *(G-9503)*

**Global Track Property USA Inc** ........................ 630 213-6863
31w300 W Bartlett Rd  Bartlett  (60103)  *(G-1350)*

**Global Track Warehouse USA, Bartlett** *Also called Global Track Property USA Inc (G-1350)*

**Global Turnings  Inc** ........................................ 630 562-0946
1092 Carolina Dr Ste 4  West Chicago  (60185)  *(G-21708)*

**Global Water Technology  Inc** ......................... 708 349-9991
14604 John Humphrey Dr  Orland Park  (60462)  *(G-16862)*

**Global Web Systems  Inc** ................................ 630 782-9690
742 Cutter Ln  Elk Grove Village  (60007)  *(G-9504)*

**Globaltech International LLC (PA)** .................. 630 327-6909
3909 75th St Ste 105  Aurora  (60504)  *(G-1018)*

**Globe Lift  LLC** ................................................ 630 844-4247
101 W Illinois Ave  Aurora  (60506)  *(G-1162)*

**Globe Precision Machining Inc** ....................... 815 389-4586
1317 Railtree Ave  South Beloit  (61080)  *(G-20149)*

**Globe Telecom, Bensenville** *Also called Driver Services (G-1883)*

**Globe Ticket** .................................................... 847 258-1000
350 Randy Rd Ste 1  Carol Stream  (60188)  *(G-3160)*

**Globe Union Group Inc (HQ)** ........................... 630 679-1420
2500 Internationale Pkwy  Woodridge  (60517)  *(G-22487)*

**Globepharm  Inc** ............................................. 847 914-0922
313 Pine St  Deerfield  (60015)  *(G-8009)*

**Glober Manufacturing Company** .................... 847 829-4883
625 Spruce Tree Dr  Cary  (60013)  *(G-3349)*

**Globetec Midwest Partners  LLC** .................... 847 608-9300
403 Joseph Dr  South Elgin  (60177)  *(G-20200)*

**Globus Food Products LLC** ............................ 847 378-8221
2258 Landmeier Rd Ste A  Elk Grove Village  (60007)  *(G-9505)*

**Glorius Renditions** .......................................... 815 315-0177
508 E Third St  Leaf River  (61047)  *(G-13211)*

**Glover Oil Field Service Inc** ............................ 618 395-3624
4993 N Il 130  Olney  (62450)  *(G-16770)*

**Glucosentient  Inc** .......................................... 217 487-4087
60 Hazelwood Dr  Champaign  (61820)  *(G-3490)*

**Glue  Inc** ......................................................... 312 451-4018
5701 N Sheridan Rd Apt 4m  Chicago  (60660)  *(G-4962)*

**Gluetech  Inc** .................................................. 847 455-2707
701 Creel Dr  Wood Dale  (60191)  *(G-22377)*

**Glunz Cellars, Grayslake** *Also called Glunz Fmly Winery Cellars Inc (G-11342)*

**Glunz Fmly Winery Cellars Inc (PA)** ................ 847 548-9463
888 E Belvidere Rd # 107  Grayslake  (60030)  *(G-11342)*

**Gluten Free Bakery, Chicago** *Also called Mybread  LLC (G-5843)*

**GM Casting House  Inc** ................................... 312 782-7160
5 S Wabash Ave Ste 614  Chicago  (60603)  *(G-4963)*

**GM Laminating & Mounting Corp** .................... 630 941-7979
1041 S Il Route 83  Elmhurst  (60126)  *(G-9878)*

**GM Lighting, Mokena** *Also called Gerber Manufacturing (gm) LLC (G-14868)*

**GM Mounting and Laminating, Elmhurst** *Also called Tree Towns Reprographics  Inc (G-9951)*

**GM Partners** ................................................... 847 895-7627
219 Lundy Ln  Schaumburg  (60193)  *(G-19538)*

**GM Scrap Metals** ............................................ 618 259-8570
220 Franklin Ave  Cottage Hills  (62018)  *(G-7397)*

**Gma Inc** .......................................................... 630 595-1255
756 Birginal Dr  Bensenville  (60106)  *(G-1910)*

**GMC Technologies Inc** .................................... 847 426-8618
215 Prairie Lake Rd Ste A  East Dundee  (60118)  *(G-8638)*

**Gmd Mobile Pressure Wshg Svcs** ................... 773 826-1903
539 N Saint Louis Ave  Chicago  (60624)  *(G-4964)*

**Gmh Metal Fabrication  Inc** ............................. 309 253-6429
136 Fleur De Lis Dr  East Peoria  (61611)  *(G-8711)*

**GMI Packaging Co** .......................................... 734 972-7389
1600 E 122nd St  Chicago  (60633)  *(G-4965)*

**Gmk Finishing** ................................................. 630 837-0568
1967 Southfield Dr  Bartlett  (60103)  *(G-1351)*

**Gmm Holdings LLC** ......................................... 312 255-9830
175 E Delaware Pl Unit 6  Chicago  (60611)  *(G-4966)*

**Gmmco, Chicago** *Also called General Machinery & Mfg Co (G-4928)*

**Gmp Metal Products, Oakbrook Terrace** *Also called Wozniak Industries  Inc (G-16723)*

**Gmt, Buffalo Grove** *Also called Global Material Tech Inc (G-2699)*

**Gmt  Inc** .......................................................... 847 697-8161
180 S Melrose Ave  Elgin  (60123)  *(G-9049)*

**GNB Industrial Global Business, Lombard** *Also called Exide Technologies (G-13798)*

**Go Calendars** .................................................. 847 816-1563
106 Hawthorn Ctr  Vernon Hills  (60061)  *(G-21166)*

**Go Getter Racing Clutches, Hartford** *Also called Advanced Machine Products  Inc (G-11609)*

**Go Jo Pallets & Supplies Inc** .......................... 815 254-1631
22538 Bass Lake Rd  Plainfield  (60544)  *(G-17603)*

**Go Packaging, Lombard** *Also called Welch Packaging  LLC (G-13882)*

**Go Steady  LLC** ............................................... 630 293-3243
505 Wegner Dr  West Chicago  (60185)  *(G-21709)*

**Go Van Goghs Tee Shirt** .................................. 309 342-1112
237 E Tompkins St  Galesburg  (61401)  *(G-10755)*

**Go2 Partners, Des Plaines** *Also called Print Management Partners Inc (G-8265)*

**Goalgetters Inc** .................................................. 708 579-9800
639 S La Grange Rd Fl 2  La Grange  (60525)  *(G-12733)*
**Goble Manufacturing Inc** ..................................... 217 932-5615
704 W Main St  Casey  (62420)  *(G-3384)*
**God Family Country LLC** .................................... 217 285-6487
34273 210th Ave  Pittsfield  (62363)  *(G-17568)*
**Godbey Industries** ................................................ 773 769-4391
4417 N Hermitage Ave  Chicago  (60640)  *(G-4967)*
**Goding Electric Company** .................................... 630 858-7700
686 E Fullerton Ave  Glendale Heights  (60139)  *(G-11029)*
**Godiva Chocolatier Inc** ........................................ 630 820-5842
1650 Premium Outlet Blvd # 1213  Aurora  (60502)  *(G-1019)*
**Godiva Chocolatier Inc** ........................................ 847 329-8620
27 Old Orchard Rd Ste D25  Skokie  (60077)  *(G-20004)*
**Godiva Chocolatier Inc** ........................................ 312 280-1133
845 N Michigan Ave Fl 4  Chicago  (60611)  *(G-4968)*
**Godiva Chocolatier Inc** ........................................ 847 918-0124
116 Hawthorn Ctr Ste 116  Vernon Hills  (60061)  *(G-21167)*
**Goeducation LLC** ................................................. 312 800-1838
321 N Clark St Ste 2550  Chicago  (60654)  *(G-4969)*
**Goelitz Confectionery Company** ........................ 847 689-2225
1501 Morrow Ave  North Chicago  (60064)  *(G-16181)*
**Goellner Inc (PA)** ................................................ 815 962-6076
2500 Latham St  Rockford  (61103)  *(G-18400)*
**Gogo Intermediate Holdings LLC (HQ)** ............ 630 647-1400
1250 N Arlington Rd  Itasca  (60143)  *(G-12271)*
**Gogo LLC (HQ)** .................................................. 630 647-1400
111 N Canal St Fl 15  Chicago  (60606)  *(G-4970)*
**Gogo LLC** ............................................................. 630 647-1400
814 Thorndale Ave  Bensenville  (60106)  *(G-1911)*
**Gohear LLC** ......................................................... 847 574-7829
100 Saunders Rd  Lake Forest  (60045)  *(G-12902)*
**Going Vertical Inc** ................................................ 847 669-3377
11175 Dundee Rd  Huntley  (60142)  *(G-12142)*
**Gold Coast Baking Co** ......................................... 630 620-1849
1405 W Fullerton Ave  Addison  (60101)  *(G-137)*
**Gold Leaf, Albion**  Also called Ataraxia LLC  *(G-355)*
**Gold Market Publications, Virden**  Also called Five Star Printing Inc  *(G-21296)*
**Gold Nugget Publications Inc (PA)** .................... 217 965-3355
169 W Jackson St  Virden  (62690)  *(G-21297)*
**Gold Seal Cabinets Countertops** ........................ 630 906-0366
1750 Eastwood Dr  Aurora  (60506)  *(G-1163)*
**Gold Standard Baking Inc (PA)** ......................... 773 523-2333
3700 S Kedzie Ave  Chicago  (60632)  *(G-4971)*
**Gold Star Fs Inc** ................................................... 309 659-2801
9087 Moline Rd  Erie  (61250)  *(G-9992)*
**Gold-Slvr-Bronze Medal Mus Inc** ...................... 847 272-6854
1442 Garnet Ct  Gurnee  (60031)  *(G-11453)*
**Golda House** ......................................................... 773 927-0140
3128 W 41st St  Chicago  (60632)  *(G-4972)*
**Golda Inc** .............................................................. 217 895-3602
100 Trowbridge Rd  Neoga  (62447)  *(G-15858)*
**Golden Bag, East Dundee**  Also called Golden Plastics LLC  *(G-8640)*
**Golden Bag Company Inc** ................................... 847 836-7766
290 Illinois St  East Dundee  (60118)  *(G-8639)*
**Golden Dragon Fortune Cookies** ....................... 312 842-8199
2323 S Archer Ave  Chicago  (60616)  *(G-4973)*
**Golden Eagle Distributing LLC (PA)** ................ 618 993-8900
2713 Merchant St  Marion  (62959)  *(G-14263)*
**Golden Grain Company** ...................................... 708 458-7020
7700 W 71st St  Bridgeview  (60455)  *(G-2495)*
**Golden Grape Estate, Naperville**  Also called Prp Wine International Inc  *(G-15734)*
**Golden Health Products Inc** ............................... 217 223-3209
1701 Springmeier Dr  Quincy  (62305)  *(G-17831)*
**Golden Hill Ingredients LLC** .............................. 773 406-3409
851 W Grand Ave  Chicago  (60642)  *(G-4974)*
**Golden Hydraulic & Machine** ............................. 708 597-4265
2966 Wireton Rd  Blue Island  (60406)  *(G-2253)*
**Golden Locker Inc (PA)** ..................................... 217 696-4456
1880 E 2400th St  Camp Point  (62320)  *(G-2973)*
**Golden Plastics LLC** ............................................ 847 836-7766
290 Illinois St  East Dundee  (60118)  *(G-8640)*
**Golden Prairie News** ............................................ 217 226-3721
301 S Chestnut St  Assumption  (62510)  *(G-931)*
**Golden Road Productions** ................................... 217 335-2606
27652 County Highway 13  New Canton  (62356)  *(G-15868)*
**Golden State Foods Corp** .................................... 618 537-6121
720 W Mc Allister St  Lebanon  (62254)  *(G-13215)*
**Golden Trophy Steaks, Chicago**  Also called Bruss Company  *(G-4179)*
**Golden Valley Hardscapes LLC** .......................... 309 654-2261
18715 Route 84 N  Cordova  (61242)  *(G-7376)*
**Goldfish Swim Schl Roskow Vlg, Chicago**  Also called Goldfish Swim School Lincoln  *(G-4975)*
**Goldfish Swim School Lincoln** ........................... 773 588-7946
2630 W Bradley Pl  Chicago  (60618)  *(G-4975)*
**Goldies Baking Inc** .............................................. 224 757-0820
31632 N Ellis Dr Unit 306  Volo  (60073)  *(G-21313)*
**Goldman Dental, Wauconda**  Also called Goldman Products Inc  *(G-21465)*

**Goldman Products Inc** ......................................... 847 526-1166
379 Hollow Hill Rd  Wauconda  (60084)  *(G-21465)*
**Goldsmith, The, Aledo**  Also called Rodger Murphy  *(G-372)*
**Goldy Metals Trading, Naperville**  Also called Avec Inc  *(G-15799)*
**Golf Gazette** ......................................................... 815 838-0184
428 S Washington St  Lockport  (60441)  *(G-13718)*
**Golf Trucks, Countryside**  Also called Bare Development Inc  *(G-7415)*
**Golfcar Utility Systems, Quincy**  Also called Brewer Utility Systems Inc  *(G-17808)*
**Golfco Inc** ............................................................. 773 777-7877
4727 W Montrose Ave  Chicago  (60641)  *(G-4976)*
**Golfers Family Corporation** ............................... 815 968-0094
1531 Preston St  Rockford  (61102)  *(G-18401)*
**Golosinas El Canto** ............................................... 847 625-5103
1115 Washington St  Waukegan  (60085)  *(G-21564)*
**Gone For Good** .................................................... 217 753-0414
1411 E Jefferson St  Springfield  (62703)  *(G-20447)*
**Gonnella Baking Co (PA)** ................................... 312 733-2020
1117 Wiley Rd  Schaumburg  (60173)  *(G-19539)*
**Gonnella Baking Co** ............................................. 312 733-2020
1117 Wiley Rd  Schaumburg  (60173)  *(G-19540)*
**Gonnella Baking Co** ............................................. 630 820-3433
2435 Church Rd  Aurora  (60502)  *(G-1020)*
**Gonnella Baking Co** ............................................. 847 884-8829
2361 Palmer Dr  Schaumburg  (60173)  *(G-19541)*
**Gonnella Frozen Products LLC (HQ)** ............... 847 884-8829
1117 Wiley Rd  Schaumburg  (60173)  *(G-19542)*
**Gooch & Associates Printing, Springfield**  Also called J Gooch & Associates Inc  *(G-20461)*
**Good Earth Lighting Inc** ..................................... 847 808-1133
1400 E Business Center Dr # 104  Mount Prospect  (60056)  *(G-15333)*
**Good Impressions Inc** ......................................... 847 831-4317
3150 Skokie Valley Rd # 24  Highland Park  (60035)  *(G-11836)*
**Good Lite Co (PA)** ............................................... 847 841-1145
1155 Jansen Farm Dr  Elgin  (60123)  *(G-9050)*
**Good News Printing** ............................................ 708 389-1127
5535 W 131st St  Palos Heights  (60463)  *(G-17105)*
**Good News Publishers (PA)** ............................... 630 868-6025
1300 Crescent St  Wheaton  (60187)  *(G-21951)*
**Good Sam Enterprises LLC (HQ)** ..................... 847 229-6720
250 Parkway Dr Ste 270  Lincolnshire  (60069)  *(G-13450)*
**Good Times Roll** ................................................. 217 285-4885
1241 W Washington St  Pittsfield  (62363)  *(G-17569)*
**Good World Noodle Inc** ..................................... 312 326-0441
2522 S Halsted St  Chicago  (60608)  *(G-4977)*
**Goodco Products LLC** ......................................... 630 258-6384
6688 Joliet Rd Ste 185  Countryside  (60525)  *(G-7428)*
**Gooder-Henrichsen Company Inc (PA)** ............ 708 757-5030
2900 State St  Chicago Heights  (60411)  *(G-7100)*
**Goodheart Wilcox Publisher, Tinley Park**  Also called Goodheart-Willcox Company Inc  *(G-20919)*
**Goodheart-Willcox Company Inc (PA)** ............. 708 687-0315
18604 West Creek Dr  Tinley Park  (60477)  *(G-20919)*
**Goodhome Foods Inc** .......................................... 847 816-6832
100 Saunders Rd  Lake Forest  (60045)  *(G-12903)*
**Goodman Distribution Inc** .................................. 773 376-8214
815 W Pershing Rd Ste C  Chicago  (60609)  *(G-4978)*
**Goodman Packaging Equipment, Waukegan**  Also called Prototype Equipment Corp  *(G-21609)*
**Goodman Sawmill** ................................................ 309 547-3597
114 N Broadway St  Lewistown  (61542)  *(G-13289)*
**Goodrich Corporation** ......................................... 815 226-6000
4747 Harrison Ave  Rockford  (61108)  *(G-18402)*
**Goodrich Corporation** ......................................... 815 226-6000
4747 Harrison Ave  Rockford  (61108)  *(G-18403)*
**Goodrich Sensor Systems** ................................... 847 546-5749
34232 N Bluestem Rd  Round Lake  (60073)  *(G-19058)*
**Goose Holdings Inc** ............................................. 312 226-1119
1800 W Fulton St  Chicago  (60612)  *(G-4979)*
**Goose Island Beer Company, Chicago**  Also called Fulton Street Brewery LLC  *(G-4896)*
**Goose Island Brew Pub, Chicago**  Also called Lincoln Park Brewery Inc  *(G-5507)*
**Goose Island Brewer, Chicago**  Also called Goose Holdings Inc  *(G-4979)*
**Goose Island Mfg & Supply Corp** ...................... 708 343-4225
17725 Volbrecht Rd Ste 1  Lansing  (60438)  *(G-13164)*
**Goose Printing Co** ............................................... 847 673-1414
8833 Ewing Ave  Evanston  (60203)  *(G-10043)*
**Gord Industrial Plastics Inc** ................................ 815 786-9494
1310 E 6th St  Sandwich  (60548)  *(G-19366)*
**Gordon Burke John Publisher** ............................ 847 866-8625
1032 Cleveland St  Evanston  (60202)  *(G-10044)*
**Gordon Caplan Inc** ............................................... 773 489-3300
2040 W North Ave  Chicago  (60647)  *(G-4980)*
**Gordon Hann** ........................................................ 630 761-1835
154 W Wilson St  Batavia  (60510)  *(G-1451)*
**Gordys Machine and Tool Inc** ............................ 618 842-9331
1101 Sw 3rd St  Fairfield  (62837)  *(G-10143)*
**Goreville Auto Parts & Mch Sp** .......................... 618 995-2375
Rr 37  Goreville  (62939)  *(G-11251)*
**Goreville Concrete Inc** ........................................ 618 995-2670
301 N Hubbard Ave  Goreville  (62939)  *(G-11252)*

Goreville Gazette .................................................. 618 995-9445
  205 S Broadway  Goreville  (62939)  *(G-11253)*
Gorman & Associates .............................................. 309 691-9087
  7501 N University St # 122  Peoria  (61614)  *(G-17373)*
Gorman Brothers Ready Mix Inc ................................. 618 498-2173
  721 S State St  Jerseyville  (62052)  *(G-12422)*
Gorman Ready Mix, Jerseyville  Also called Gorman Brothers Ready Mix Inc  *(G-12422)*
Gorr Communication Products, Woodstock  Also called Carl Gorr Printing Co  *(G-22549)*
Gosia Cartage  Ltd ................................................. 312 613-8735
  6400 River Rd  Hodgkins  (60525)  *(G-11975)*
Gospel Synergy Magazine Inc ................................... 708 272-6640
  12649 S Ashland Ave  Calumet Park  (60827)  *(G-2961)*
Goss International Corporation, Woodridge  Also called Goss International LLC  *(G-22488)*
Goss International LLC (HQ) .................................... 630 796-7560
  9018 Heritage Pkwy # 1200  Woodridge  (60517)  *(G-22488)*
Gossett Printing Inc ............................................... 618 548-2583
  2100 Old Texas Ln  Salem  (62881)  *(G-19335)*
Got 2b Scrappin ................................................... 217 347-3600
  1901 S 4th St Ste 11  Effingham  (62401)  *(G-8837)*
Goudie Tool & Engineering, Lake Zurich  Also called Goudie Tool and Engrg Del  *(G-13079)*
Goudie Tool and Engrg Del ..................................... 847 438-5597
  480 Telser Rd  Lake Zurich  (60047)  *(G-13079)*
Gourmet Frog Pastry Shop ...................................... 847 433-7038
  316 Green Bay Rd  Highland Park  (60035)  *(G-11837)*
Gourmet Gorilla  Inc (PA) ........................................ 877 219-3663
  1200 W Cermak Rd  Chicago  (60608)  *(G-4981)*
Govqa Inc .......................................................... 630 985-1300
  900 S Frontage Rd Ste 110  Woodridge  (60517)  *(G-22489)*
GP, Zion  Also called Graphic Partners Inc  *(G-22686)*
GP Liquidation Inc ................................................ 630 784-9736
  1427 W Jeffrey Dr  Addison  (60101)  *(G-138)*
Gpa  Inc ............................................................ 773 650-2020
  8740 W 50th St  Mc Cook  (60525)  *(G-14448)*
GPA Media Inc .................................................... 773 968-3728
  228 157th St  Calumet City  (60409)  *(G-2940)*
Gpe Controls  Inc (HQ) .......................................... 708 236-6000
  5911 Butterfield Rd  Hillside  (60162)  *(G-11917)*
Gpi Manufacturing  Inc .......................................... 847 615-8900
  940 W North Shore Dr  Lake Bluff  (60044)  *(G-12847)*
Gpi Prototype & Mfg Svcs, Lake Bluff  Also called Gpi Manufacturing Inc  *(G-12847)*
GPI Industries Incorporated .................................... 708 877-8200
  395 Armory Dr  Thornton  (60476)  *(G-20870)*
GPM Mfg  Inc ..................................................... 847 550-8200
  1199 Flex Ct  Lake Zurich  (60047)  *(G-13080)*
Gpo Reference Standards, North Chicago  Also called Abbott Laboratories  *(G-16163)*
Grab Brothers Ir Works Co Corp ............................... 847 288-1055
  2302 17th St  Franklin Park  (60131)  *(G-10480)*
Graber Concrete Pipe Company ............................... 630 894-5950
  24w121 Army Trail Rd  Bloomingdale  (60108)  *(G-2109)*
Grace & Truth Inc ................................................ 217 442-1120
  210 Chestnut St  Danville  (61832)  *(G-7727)*
Grace Auto Body Frame ......................................... 847 963-1234
  320 W Colfax St  Palatine  (60067)  *(G-17030)*
Grace Davison, Chicago  Also called W R Grace & Co  *(G-6921)*
Grace Dvson Discovery Sciences, Chicago  Also called Alltech Associates Inc  *(G-3824)*
Grace Enterprises  Inc .......................................... 773 465-5300
  2050 W Devon Ave Ste 2  Chicago  (60659)  *(G-4982)*
Grace Enterprises  Inc (PA) .................................... 773 465-5300
  2050 W Devon Ave Ste 2  Chicago  (60659)  *(G-4983)*
Grace Printing and Mailing ..................................... 847 423-2100
  8130 Saint Louis Ave  Skokie  (60076)  *(G-20005)*
Graceland Custom Products Inc ............................... 630 616-4143
  1017 Graceland Ave  Bensenville  (60106)  *(G-1912)*
Grads Inc .......................................................... 847 426-3904
  205 Prairie Lake Rd Ste C  East Dundee  (60118)  *(G-8641)*
Graf Ink Printing  Inc ............................................ 618 273-4231
  24 W Church St  Harrisburg  (62946)  *(G-11601)*
Grafcor Packaging  Inc ......................................... 815 639-2380
  1030 River Ln  Loves Park  (61111)  *(G-13945)*
Grafcor Packaging  Inc (PA) ................................... 815 963-1300
  121 Loomis St  Rockford  (61101)  *(G-18404)*
Graffs Tooling Center Inc ....................................... 618 357-5005
  801 S Main St  Pinckneyville  (62274)  *(G-17549)*
Graham Packaging Co Europe LLC ............................ 630 293-8616
  1760 W Hawthorne Ln  West Chicago  (60185)  *(G-21710)*
Graham Packaging Co Europe LLC ............................ 630 562-5912
  1445 Northwest Ave  West Chicago  (60185)  *(G-21711)*
Graham Packaging Co Europe LLC ............................ 630 231-0850
  1275 Nuclear Dr  West Chicago  (60185)  *(G-21712)*
Graham Packaging Company  LP .............................. 630 739-9150
  2400 Internationale Pkwy # 1  Woodridge  (60517)  *(G-22490)*
Graham Welding Inc ............................................. 217 422-1423
  813 E North St  Decatur  (62521)  *(G-7885)*
Grain Journal, Decatur  Also called Country Journal Publishing Co  *(G-7860)*
Grain Systems, Vandalia  Also called Gsi Group  LLC  *(G-21115)*
Grain Systems, Paris  Also called Gsi Group  LLC  *(G-17148)*
Gram Colossal Inc ............................................... 847 223-5757
  888 E Belvidere Rd # 113  Grayslake  (60030)  *(G-11343)*

Granadino Food Services Corp ................................ 708 717-2930
  260 Cortland Ave Ste 11  Lombard  (60148)  *(G-13805)*
Grand Forms & Systems Inc ................................... 847 259-4600
  204 N Kennicott Ave  Arlington Heights  (60005)  *(G-760)*
Grand Printing & Graphics Inc ................................. 312 218-6780
  105 W Madison St Ste 1100  Chicago  (60602)  *(G-4984)*
Grand Products  Inc (PA) ....................................... 800 621-6101
  1718 Hampshire Dr  Elk Grove Village  (60007)  *(G-9506)*
Grand Specialties Co ............................................ 630 629-8000
  110 Oakbrook Ctr  Oak Brook  (60523)  *(G-16520)*
Grand Trunk, Skokie  Also called Travel Hammock Inc  *(G-20102)*
Grandcentral Enterprises  Inc .................................. 309 287-5362
  716 E Empire St Ste B  Bloomington  (61701)  *(G-2171)*
Grande Diva Hair Salon ......................................... 217 383-0023
  1711 W John St Apt 6  Champaign  (61821)  *(G-3491)*
Grandstand Publishing LLC .................................... 847 491-6440
  990 Grove St Ste 400  Evanston  (60201)  *(G-10045)*
Grandt's Custom Fishing Rods, Arlington Heights  Also called Custom Rods By Grandt Ltd  *(G-741)*
Grangrit, Baldwin  Also called Fjcj LLC  *(G-1250)*
Granite City Journals, Collinsville  Also called Madison County Publications  *(G-7332)*
Granite City Works, Granite City  Also called United States Steel Corp  *(G-11310)*
Granite Designs of Illinois ...................................... 773 772-5300
  945 N California Ave  Chicago  (60622)  *(G-4985)*
Granite Gallery  Inc .............................................. 773 279-9200
  3430 W Henderson St  Chicago  (60618)  *(G-4986)*
Granite Mountain  Inc ........................................... 708 774-1442
  538 E Illinois Hwy Ste A  New Lenox  (60451)  *(G-15884)*
Granite Works LLC ............................................... 847 837-1688
  1150 Allanson Rd  Mundelein  (60060)  *(G-15503)*
Granite Xperts Inc ............................................... 847 364-1900
  1091 E Green St  Franklin Park  (60131)  *(G-10481)*
Graniteworks ..................................................... 815 288-3350
  1220 S Galena Ave  Dixon  (61021)  *(G-8333)*
Granitex  Corp (PA) ............................................. 630 888-1838
  704 N Larch Ave  Elmhurst  (60126)  *(G-9879)*
Granja & Sons Printing .......................................... 773 762-3840
  2707 S Pulaski Rd  Chicago  (60623)  *(G-4987)*
Grant J Grapperhaus ............................................ 618 410-4428
  470 Pike Dr E  Highland  (62249)  *(G-11786)*
Grant Park Packing Company Inc .............................. 312 421-4096
  3434 Runge St  Franklin Park  (60131)  *(G-10482)*
Grant Wood Works ............................................... 847 328-4349
  2204 Green Bay Rd  Evanston  (60201)  *(G-10046)*
Grante Foods International LLC ................................ 773 751-9551
  780 Arthur Ave  Elk Grove Village  (60007)  *(G-9507)*
Granville Ready Mix, Granville  Also called J W Ossola Company Inc  *(G-11318)*
Granville Ready Mix, Granville  Also called JW Ossola Co Inc  *(G-11319)*
Graph-Pak, Franklin Park  Also called Graphic Packaging Corporation  *(G-10483)*
Graphbury Machines  LLC ...................................... 754 779-4285
  5800 N Western Ave  Chicago  (60659)  *(G-4988)*
Graphic Arts Bindery LLC ....................................... 708 416-4290
  1020 S Main St  Rochelle  (61068)  *(G-18092)*
Graphic Arts Finishing Company ............................... 708 345-8484
  1990 N Mannheim Rd  Melrose Park  (60160)  *(G-14648)*
Graphic Arts Services  Inc (PA) ................................ 630 629-7770
  333 W Saint Charles Rd  Villa Park  (60181)  *(G-21256)*
Graphic Arts Studio  Inc (PA) ................................... 847 381-1105
  28 W 111 Coml Ave  Commercial  Barrington  (60010)  *(G-1282)*
Graphic Chemical & Ink Co ..................................... 630 832-6004
  728 N Yale Ave  Villa Park  (60181)  *(G-21257)*
Graphic Communicators  Inc ................................... 708 385-7550
  12500 S Meade Ave  Palos Heights  (60463)  *(G-17106)*
Graphic Converting  Inc ........................................ 630 758-4100
  877 N Larch Ave  Elmhurst  (60126)  *(G-9880)*
Graphic Engravers  Inc ......................................... 630 595-0400
  691 Country Club Dr  Bensenville  (60106)  *(G-1913)*
Graphic Image Corporation ..................................... 312 829-7800
  2035 W Grand Ave  Chicago  (60612)  *(G-4989)*
Graphic Industries  Inc ......................................... 847 357-9870
  645 Stevenson Rd  South Elgin  (60177)  *(G-20201)*
Graphic Innovators  Inc ......................................... 847 718-1516
  855 Morse Ave  Elk Grove Village  (60007)  *(G-9508)*
Graphic Marking Systems, Lake Forest  Also called Distribution Enterprises Inc  *(G-12896)*
Graphic Packaging Corporation ................................ 847 451-7400
  11250 Addison Ave  Franklin Park  (60131)  *(G-10483)*
Graphic Packaging Holding Co ................................. 630 260-6500
  400 E North Ave  Carol Stream  (60188)  *(G-3161)*
Graphic Packaging Intl Inc ..................................... 630 260-6500
  400 E North Ave  Carol Stream  (60188)  *(G-3162)*
Graphic Packaging Intl Inc ..................................... 618 533-2721
  2333 S Wabash Ave  Centralia  (62801)  *(G-3416)*
Graphic Packaging Intl Inc ..................................... 630 260-6500
  400 E North Ave  Carol Stream  (60188)  *(G-3163)*
Graphic Packaging Intl Inc ..................................... 847 437-1700
  1500 Nicholas Blvd  Elk Grove Village  (60007)  *(G-9509)*
Graphic Packaging Intl Inc ..................................... 847 354-3554
  1500 Nicholas Blvd  Elk Grove Village  (60007)  *(G-9510)*

Graphic Pallet & Transport ALPHABETIC SECTION

**Graphic Pallet & Transport** ....630 904-4951
10225 Bode St Plainfield (60585) *(G-17604)*
**Graphic Partners Inc** ....847 872-9445
4300 Il Route 173 Zion (60099) *(G-22686)*
**Graphic Parts Intl Inc** ....773 725-4900
4321 N Knox Ave Chicago (60641) *(G-4990)*
**Graphic Photo Engravers, Bensenville** *Also called Graphic Engravers Inc (G-1913)*
**Graphic Press** ....312 909-6100
545 N Dearborn St # 3002 Chicago (60654) *(G-4991)*
**Graphic Press Inc** ....847 272-6000
6511 Oakton St Morton Grove (60053) *(G-15199)*
**Graphic Promotions Inc** ....815 726-3288
405 Earl Rd Shorewood (60404) *(G-19928)*
**Graphic Sciences Inc** ....630 226-0994
582 Territorial Dr Ste A Bolingbrook (60440) *(G-2314)*
**Graphic Score Book Co Inc** ....847 823-7382
306 Busse Hwy Park Ridge (60068) *(G-17199)*
**Graphic Screen Printing Inc** ....708 429-3330
15640 S 70th Ct Orland Park (60462) *(G-16863)*
**Graphic Source Group Inc** ....847 854-2670
1119 W Algonquin Rd Ste B Lake In The Hills (60156) *(G-12995)*
**Graphic Tool Corp** ....630 250-9800
1211 Norwood Ave Itasca (60143) *(G-12272)*
**Graphics & Technical Systems** ....708 974-3806
11137 Northwest Rd Apt E Palos Hills (60465) *(G-17118)*
**Graphics Group LLC** ....708 867-5500
4600 N Olcott Ave Chicago (60706) *(G-4992)*
**Graphics Plus Inc** ....630 968-9073
1808 Ogden Ave Lisle (60532) *(G-13597)*
**Graphtek LLC (PA)** ....847 279-1925
600 Academy Dr Ste 100 Northbrook (60062) *(G-16266)*
**Grass Valley Usa LLC** ....847 803-8060
10600 W Higgins Rd Rosemont (60018) *(G-19003)*
**Grasso Graphics Inc** ....708 489-2060
5156 W 125th Pl Alsip (60803) *(G-465)*
**Grate Signs Inc** ....815 729-9700
4044 Mcdonough St Joliet (60431) *(G-12503)*
**Gravure Ink, Franklin Park** *Also called Patrick Industries Inc (G-10548)*
**Gray Machine & Welding Inc** ....309 788-2501
710 30th Ave Rock Island (61201) *(G-18177)*
**Gray Quarries Inc** ....217 847-2712
750 E County Road 1220 Hamilton (62341) *(G-11534)*
**Gray Wolf Graphics Inc** ....815 356-0895
457 S Dartmoor Dr Crystal Lake (60014) *(G-7584)*
**Grayhill Inc (PA)** ....708 354-1040
561 W Hillgrove Ave La Grange (60525) *(G-12734)*
**Grayhill Inc** ....847 428-6990
459 Maple Ave Carpentersville (60110) *(G-3285)*
**Graymills Corporation** ....773 477-4100
2601 S 25th Ave Broadview (60155) *(G-2582)*
**Graymon Graphics Inc** ....773 737-0176
4934 S Rockwell St Chicago (60632) *(G-4993)*
**Grays Cabinet Co** ....618 948-2211
Rr 1 Saint Francisville (62460) *(G-19313)*
**Grayslake Feed Sales Inc** ....847 223-4855
81 E Belvidere Rd Grayslake (60030) *(G-11344)*
**Grayslake Yard, Grayslake** *Also called Legacy Vulcan LLC (G-11350)*
**Great American Popcorn Company** ....815 777-4116
110 S Main St Galena (61036) *(G-10725)*
**Great Books Foundation** ....312 332-5870
233 N Michigan Ave # 420 Chicago (60601) *(G-4994)*
**Great Dane Limited Partnership** ....309 854-0407
324 N Main St Kewanee (61443) *(G-12687)*
**Great Dane Limited Partnership** ....309 854-0407
2006 Kentville Rd Kewanee (61443) *(G-12688)*
**Great Dane Limited Partnership** ....773 254-5533
2006 Kentville Rd Kewanee (61443) *(G-12689)*
**Great Dane Limited Partnership (HQ)** ....773 254-5533
222 N Lasalle St Ste 920 Chicago (60601) *(G-4995)*
**Great Dane Trailers, Chicago** *Also called Great Dane Limited Partnership (G-4995)*
**Great Dane Trlrs-Kewanee Plant, Kewanee** *Also called Great Dane Limited Partnership (G-12688)*
**Great Display Company Llc** ....309 821-1037
704 S Mclean St Bloomington (61701) *(G-2172)*
**Great Holloween Stores, Elgin** *Also called Orr Marketing Corp (G-9130)*
**Great Impressions Inc** ....847 367-6725
19071 W Casey Rd Libertyville (60048) *(G-13327)*
**Great Lakes Art Foundry Inc** ....847 213-0800
7336 Ridgeway Ave Skokie (60076) *(G-20006)*
**Great Lakes Bag & Vinyl, Highland Park** *Also called Morton Group Ltd (G-11857)*
**Great Lakes Boating Magazine, Chicago** *Also called Chicago Boating Publications (G-4306)*
**Great Lakes Clay & Supply Inc** ....224 535-8127
927 N State St Elgin (60123) *(G-9051)*
**Great Lakes Coca-Cola Dist LLC** ....847 227-6500
6250 N River Rd Ste 9000 Rosemont (60018) *(G-19004)*
**Great Lakes Envmtl Mar Del** ....312 332-3377
39 S La Salle St Ste 308 Chicago (60603) *(G-4996)*
**Great Lakes Finishing Eqp Inc** ....708 345-5300
842 Schneider Dr South Elgin (60177) *(G-20202)*
**Great Lakes Forge Company** ....773 277-2800
2141 S Spaulding Ave Chicago (60623) *(G-4997)*
**Great Lakes GL & Mirror Corp** ....847 647-1036
6261 W Howard St Niles (60714) *(G-15984)*
**Great Lakes Lifting** ....815 931-4825
4910 Wilshire Blvd Country Club Hills (60478) *(G-7407)*
**Great Lakes Lumber and Pallet** ....773 243-6839
2137 N Home Ave Park Ridge (60068) *(G-17200)*
**Great Lakes Mech Svcs Inc** ....708 672-5900
100 Tri State Intl Lincolnshire (60069) *(G-13451)*
**Great Lakes Metal Works, Skokie** *Also called Great Lakes Art Foundry Inc (G-20006)*
**Great Lakes Packing Co Intl** ....773 927-6660
1535 W 43rd St Chicago (60609) *(G-4998)*
**Great Lakes Pallet, Chicago** *Also called Best Pallet Company LLC (G-4094)*
**Great Lakes Pallet Company, Loves Park** *Also called Best Pallet Company LLC (G-13924)*
**Great Lakes Precision Tube Inc** ....630 859-8940
237 S Highland Ave Aurora (60506) *(G-1164)*
**Great Lakes Region, Itasca** *Also called Subaru of America Inc (G-12361)*
**Great Lakes Service Center, Romeoville** *Also called Tdw Services Inc (G-18873)*
**Great Lakes Service Chicago** ....630 627-4022
52 Eisenhower Ln N Lombard (60148) *(G-13806)*
**Great Lakes Stair & Steel Inc** ....708 430-2323
10130 Virginia Ave Chicago Ridge (60415) *(G-7148)*
**Great Lakes Tool & Mold Inc** ....630 964-7121
6817 Hobson Valley Dr # 116 Woodridge (60517) *(G-22491)*
**Great Lakes Washer Company** ....630 887-7447
127 Tower Dr Burr Ridge (60527) *(G-2846)*
**Great Midwest Packaging LLC** ....847 395-4500
3828 Hawthorne Ct Waukegan (60087) *(G-21565)*
**Great Northern Lumber Inc** ....708 388-1818
2200 Burr Oak Ave Blue Island (60406) *(G-2254)*
**Great Planes Model Mfg Inc** ....217 367-2707
706 W Bradley Ave Urbana (61801) *(G-21090)*
**Great Plins Model Maufacturing, Urbana** *Also called Hobbico Inc (G-21091)*
**Great River Printing, Hamilton** *Also called D E Asbury Inc (G-11532)*
**Great River Ready Mix Inc** ....217 847-3515
750 E County Road 1220 Hamilton (62341) *(G-11535)*
**Great Software Laboratory Inc** ....630 655-8905
60 E Monroe St Unit 4301 Chicago (60603) *(G-4999)*
**Great Spirit Hardwoods LLC** ....224 801-1969
7 Jackson St East Dundee (60118) *(G-8642)*
**Greater Than, Highland Park** *Also called Team Sider Inc (G-11877)*
**Greatlakes Architectural Millw** ....312 829-7110
2135 W Fulton St Chicago (60612) *(G-5000)*
**Grebner Machine & Tool Inc** ....309 248-7768
1866 County Road 00 N Washburn (61570) *(G-21375)*
**Grecian Delight Foods Inc (PA)** ....847 364-1010
1201 Tonne Rd Elk Grove Village (60007) *(G-9511)*
**Grecian Delight Foods, Inc Del, Elk Grove Village** *Also called Grecian Delight Foods Inc (G-9511)*
**Greek Art Printing & Pubg Co** ....847 724-8860
2921 Covert Rd Glenview (60025) *(G-11133)*
**Green Book Lenders Guide, The, Elgin** *Also called Reid Communications Inc (G-9163)*
**Green Box America Inc** ....630 616-5400
1900 E Golf Rd Ste 950 Schaumburg (60173) *(G-19543)*
**Green Earth Technologies Inc** ....847 991-0436
617 S Middleton Ave Palatine (60067) *(G-17031)*
**Green Energy Solutions Inc** ....708 672-1900
30 Cornwall Dr Crete (60417) *(G-7514)*
**Green Field Operation, Chicago** *Also called BF Manufacturing LLC (G-4100)*
**Green Gables Country Store** ....309 897-7160
201 Bonita Ave Bradford (61421) *(G-2411)*
**Green Giant** ....815 544-0438
915 E Pleasant St Belvidere (61008) *(G-1758)*
**Green Investment Group Inc** ....618 465-7277
601 E 3rd St Ste 215 Alton (62002) *(G-576)*
**Green Ladder Technologies LLC** ....630 457-1872
1540 Louis Bork Dr Batavia (60510) *(G-1452)*
**Green Mountain Flavors Inc** ....630 554-9530
442 Treasure Dr Oswego (60543) *(G-16920)*
**Green Organics Inc** ....630 871-0108
290 S Main Pl Ste 103 Carol Stream (60188) *(G-3164)*
**Green Plains Madison LLC** ....618 451-8195
395 Bissell St Madison (62060) *(G-14147)*
**Green Plains Partners LP** ....618 451-4420
395 Bissell St Madison (62060) *(G-14148)*
**Green Planet Bottling LLC** ....312 962-4444
105 W Townline Rd Ste 125 Vernon Hills (60061) *(G-21168)*
**Green Products LLC** ....815 407-0900
221 Rocbaar Dr Romeoville (60446) *(G-18829)*
**Green Roof Solutions Inc** ....847 297-7936
4336 Regency Dr Glenview (60025) *(G-11134)*
**Green Valley Mfg Ill Inc** ....217 864-4125
100 Green Valley Dr Mount Zion (62549) *(G-15452)*
**Greenberg Casework Company Inc** ....815 624-0288
592 Quality Ln South Beloit (61080) *(G-20150)*
**Greenbrier Castings, Peoria** *Also called Gunderson Rail Services LLC (G-17375)*

ALPHABETIC SECTION Grower Equipment & Supply Co

**Greenbrier Companies Inc** 847 838-1435
23858 W Sarah Ct Antioch (60002) *(G-637)*
**Greencast Services Inc** 630 723-8000
3 Grant Sq Ste 200 Hinsdale (60521) *(G-11950)*
**Greencycle of Indiana Inc (HQ)** 847 441-6606
400 Central Ave Ste 115 Northfield (60093) *(G-16400)*
**Greene Jersey Shoppers (PA)** 217 942-3626
428 N Main St Carrollton (62016) *(G-3307)*
**Greene Welding & Hardware Inc** 217 375-4244
41774 N Main St East Lynn (60932) *(G-8668)*
**Greenfield Products LLC (PA)** 708 596-5200
3111 167th St Hazel Crest (60429) *(G-11707)*
**Greenlee Diamond Tool Co** 866 451-3316
2375 Touhy Ave Elk Grove Village (60007) *(G-9512)*
**Greenlee Textron Inc** 815 784-5127
702 W Main St Genoa (60135) *(G-10879)*
**Greenlee Textron Inc (HQ)** 815 397-7070
4455 Boeing Dr Rockford (61109) *(G-18405)*
**Greenlees Filter LLC** 708 366-3256
350 Corporate Woods Pkwy Vernon Hills (60061) *(G-21169)*
**Greenridge Farm Inc** 847 434-1803
2355 Greenleaf Ave Elk Grove Village (60007) *(G-9513)*
**Greens Machine Shop** 618 532-4631
315 E Kell St Centralia (62801) *(G-3417)*
**Greenslade Fastener Svcs LLC** 815 398-4073
129 Phelps Ave Ste 800 Rockford (61108) *(G-18406)*
**Greenup Press Inc** 217 923-3704
104 E Cumberland St Greenup (62428) *(G-11383)*
**Greenville Advocate Inc** 618 664-3144
305 S 2nd St Greenville (62246) *(G-11394)*
**Greenville Ready Mix, Greenville** *Also called Mid-Illinois Concrete Inc (G-11399)*
**Greenwood Inc (PA)** 800 798-4900
1126 N Kimball St Danville (61832) *(G-7728)*
**Greenwood Inc** 217 431-6034
1126 N Kimball St Danville (61832) *(G-7729)*
**Greenwood Associates Inc** 847 579-5500
6280 W Howard St Niles (60714) *(G-15985)*
**Greenwood Plastics, Danville** *Also called Greenwood Inc (G-7728)*
**Greenwood Plastics Industries, Danville** *Also called Greenwood Inc (G-7729)*
**Greg El- Inc** 773 478-9050
6024 N Keystone Ave Chicago (60646) *(G-5001)*
**Greg Lambert Construction** 815 468-7361
5485 N 5000e Rd Bourbonnais (60914) *(G-2397)*
**Greg Screw Machine Products** 630 694-8875
647 N Central Ave Ste 103 Wood Dale (60191) *(G-22378)*
**Greg Signs** 815 726-5655
1201 N Broadway St Joliet (60435) *(G-12504)*
**Greg Waters** 618 798-9758
3477 Nameoki Rd Granite City (62040) *(G-11282)*
**Gregor Jonsson Associates Inc** 847 247-4200
13822 W Laurel Dr Lake Forest (60045) *(G-12904)*
**Gregory Lamar & Assoc Inc** 312 595-1545
345 N La Salle Dr # 2103 Chicago (60654) *(G-5002)*
**Gregory Martin** 815 265-4527
325 E Park Ct Gilman (60938) *(G-10943)*
**Gregs Frozen Custard Company** 847 837-4175
1490 S Lake St Mundelein (60060) *(G-15504)*
**Greif Inc** 815 838-7210
1225 Daviess Ave Lockport (60441) *(G-13719)*
**Greif Inc** 708 371-4777
4300 W 130th St Alsip (60803) *(G-466)*
**Greif Inc** 815 935-7575
150 E North St Bradley (60915) *(G-2423)*
**Greif Inc** 217 468-2396
7573 N Rte 48 Oreana (62554) *(G-16817)*
**Greif Inc** 630 961-9786
5s220 Frontenac Rd Naperville (60563) *(G-15664)*
**Greif Inc** 630 961-1842
5 S 220 Frontenace Rd Naperville (60540) *(G-15665)*
**Grem Machining Division, Lemont** *Also called Machining Technology Inc (G-13240)*
**Gremp Steel Co** 708 389-7393
14100 S Western Ave Posen (60469) *(G-17731)*
**Gridley Division, Gridley** *Also called Jbs United Inc (G-11407)*
**Gridley Meats Inc** 309 747-2120
205 E 3rd St Gridley (61744) *(G-11405)*
**Gridley Welding Inc** 309 747-2325
116 E 3rd St Gridley (61744) *(G-11406)*
**Gridley Welding Shop, Gridley** *Also called Gridley Welding Inc (G-11406)*
**Grier Abrasive Co Inc** 708 333-6445
123 W Taft Dr South Holland (60473) *(G-20271)*
**Grieve Corporation** 847 546-8225
500 Hart Rd Round Lake (60073) *(G-19059)*
**Griffard & Associates LLC** 217 316-1732
1022 Kochs Ln Quincy (62305) *(G-17832)*
**Griffin John** 708 301-2316
15751 Annico Dr Ste 2 Lockport (60491) *(G-13720)*
**Griffin Industries LLC** 815 357-8200
410 Shipyard Rd Seneca (61360) *(G-19886)*
**Griffin Machining Inc** 847 360-0098
2233 Northwestern Ave D Waukegan (60087) *(G-21566)*
**Griffin Plating Co Inc** 773 342-5181
1636 W Armitage Ave Chicago (60622) *(G-5003)*
**Griffith Company** 847 524-4173
1102 Helene Ln Schaumburg (60193) *(G-19544)*
**Griffith Foods Group Inc (PA)** 708 371-0900
1 Griffith Ctr Alsip (60803) *(G-467)*
**Griffith Foods Inc (HQ)** 708 371-0900
12200 S Central Ave Alsip (60803) *(G-468)*
**Griffith Foods Worldwide Inc (HQ)** 708 371-0900
12200 S Central Ave Alsip (60803) *(G-469)*
**Griffith Laboratories, Alsip** *Also called Griffith Foods Worldwide Inc (G-469)*
**Griffith Laboratories USA Inc** 773 523-7509
1437 W 37th St Chicago (60609) *(G-5004)*
**Griffith Solutions Inc** 847 384-1810
529 Warren Ave Park Ridge (60068) *(G-17201)*
**Grifols Shared Svcs N Amer Inc** 309 827-3031
511 W Washington St Bloomington (61701) *(G-2173)*
**Grigalanz Software Enterprises, Jerseyville** *Also called Phillip Grigalanz (G-12425)*
**Grimm Metal Fabricators Inc** 630 792-1710
1121 N Garfield St Lombard (60148) *(G-13807)*
**Grind Lap Services Inc** 630 458-1111
1045 W National Ave Addison (60101) *(G-139)*
**Grindal Company** 630 250-8950
1551 Industrial Dr Itasca (60143) *(G-12273)*
**Grinding Specialty Co Inc** 847 724-6493
1879 N Neltnor Blvd West Chicago (60185) *(G-21713)*
**Griswold Feed Inc** 815 432-2811
890 E Walnut St Watseka (60970) *(G-21417)*
**Griswold Machine Co (PA)** 708 333-4258
241 W Taft Dr South Holland (60473) *(G-20272)*
**Gro Alliance LLC** 217 792-3355
247 1500th Ave Mount Pulaski (62548) *(G-15388)*
**Gro Products Inc** 815 308-5423
1010 Trakk Ln Ste D Woodstock (60098) *(G-22570)*
**Gro-Mar Industries Inc** 708 343-5901
2725 Thomas St Melrose Park (60160) *(G-14649)*
**Groen Process Equipment Div, Elk Grove Village** *Also called Lee Industries Inc (G-9590)*
**Groff Testing Corporation** 815 939-1153
1410 Stanford Dr Kankakee (60901) *(G-12619)*
**Grohe America Inc (HQ)** 630 582-7711
200 N Gary Ave Ste G Roselle (60172) *(G-18944)*
**Grohne Concrete Products Co** 217 877-4197
2594 N Water St Decatur (62526) *(G-7886)*
**Grommes Precision, Gurnee** *Also called Precision Electronics Inc (G-11490)*
**Groomsmart Inc** 847 836-6007
4672 W Main St Dundee (60118) *(G-8562)*
**Groovy Logistics Inc** 847 946-1491
1120 Manhattan Rd Joliet (60433) *(G-12505)*
**Grosch Irrigation Company** 217 482-5479
13590 Sr 29 Mason City (62664) *(G-14364)*
**Grosch Well Drilling, Mason City** *Also called Grosch Irrigation Company (G-14364)*
**GROsse&sons Htg &SHeet Met Inc** 708 447-8397
4236 Elm Ave Lyons (60534) *(G-14040)*
**Groth Manufacturing** 847 428-5950
845 Commerce Pkwy Carpentersville (60110) *(G-3286)*
**Ground Cover Marketing, Kewanee** *Also called Rhino Tool Company (G-12694)*
**Group 3 Envelope F & S Type** 630 766-1230
237 Evergreen Ave Ste B Bensenville (60106) *(G-1914)*
**Group 329 LLC (PA)** 312 828-0200
329 W 18th St Ste 800 Chicago (60616) *(G-5005)*
**Group II Communications, Oak Brook** *Also called Integrated Mdsg Systems LLC (G-16525)*
**Group Industries Inc** 708 877-6200
459 N Williams St Thornton (60476) *(G-20871)*
**Group O Inc** 309 736-8660
7300 50th St Milan (61264) *(G-14788)*
**Group O Inc** 309 736-8311
120 4th Ave E Milan (61264) *(G-14789)*
**Group O Inc** 309 736-8100
4905 77th Ave E Milan (61264) *(G-14790)*
**Group O Supply Chain Solution, Milan** *Also called Group O Inc (G-14788)*
**Groupe Lacasse LLC (PA)** 312 670-9100
222 Merchandise Mart Plz Chicago (60654) *(G-5006)*
**Grovak Instant Printing Co** 847 675-2414
701 S Meier Rd Mount Prospect (60056) *(G-15334)*
**Grove Communications, Crystal Lake** *Also called Grove Design & Advertising Inc (G-7585)*
**Grove Design & Advertising Inc** 815 459-4552
3918 Valley View Rd Crystal Lake (60012) *(G-7585)*
**Grove Industrial** 815 385-4800
3915 Spring Grove Rd Johnsburg (60051) *(G-12435)*
**Grove Plastic Inc** 847 678-8244
10352 Front Ave Franklin Park (60131) *(G-10484)*
**Grove Plating Company Inc** 847 639-7651
400 Algonquin Rd Fox River Grove (60021) *(G-10287)*
**Grover Welding Company** 847 966-3119
9120 Terminal Ave Skokie (60077) *(G-20007)*
**Grow Masters** 224 399-9877
4641 Old Grand Ave Gurnee (60031) *(G-11454)*
**Grower Equipment & Supply Co** 847 223-3100
294 E Belvidere Rd Hainesville (60030) *(G-11523)*

ALPHABETIC

**Growmark Energy LLC**...309 557-6000
1701 Towanda Ave Bloomington (61701) **(G-2174)**
**Grphic Richards Communications**...708 547-6000
2700 Van Buren St Bellwood (60104) **(G-1707)**
**Grs Holding LLC (PA)**...630 355-1660
131 W Jefferson Ave # 223 Naperville (60540) **(G-15666)**
**Grumen Manufacturing Inc**...847 473-2233
4081 Ryan Rd Ste 101 Gurnee (60031) **(G-11455)**
**Grundfos Water Utility Inc**...630 236-5500
3905 Enterprise Ct Aurora (60504) **(G-1021)**
**Grupo Antolin Illinois Inc**...815 544-8020
642 Crystal Pkwy Belvidere (61008) **(G-1759)**
**Gs Custom Works Inc**...815 233-4724
2110 Park Crest Dr Freeport (61032) **(G-10661)**
**Gs Metals Corp**...618 357-5353
3764 Longspur Rd Pinckneyville (62274) **(G-17550)**
**Gsb Medal Music, Gurnee** *Also called Gold-Slvr-Bronze Medal Mus Inc* **(G-11453)**
**GSE, Lincolnshire** *Also called Good Sam Enterprises LLC* **(G-13450)**
**Gsf St. Louis, Lebanon** *Also called Golden State Foods Corp* **(G-13215)**
**Gsg Industries**...618 544-7976
1708 W Main St Robinson (62454) **(G-18063)**
**Gsi Group LLC**...618 283-9792
110 S Coles St Vandalia (62471) **(G-21115)**
**Gsi Group LLC**...217 463-1612
13217 Illinois Hwy 133 W Paris (61944) **(G-17148)**
**Gsi Group LLC**...217 463-8016
13217 Il Highway 133 Paris (61944) **(G-17149)**
**Gsi Group LLC**...217 226-4401
1004 E Illinois St Assumption (62510) **(G-932)**
**Gsi Group LLC**...217 287-6244
2400 S Spresser St Taylorville (62568) **(G-20839)**
**Gsi Holdings Corp (HQ)**...217 226-4421
1004 E Illinois St Assumption (62510) **(G-933)**
**Gsi Technologies LLC**...630 325-8181
311 Shore Dr Burr Ridge (60527) **(G-2847)**
**Gt Business Services, Tremont** *Also called G T Services of Illionois Inc* **(G-20982)**
**Gt Flow Technology Inc**...815 636-9982
5364 Mainsail Dr Roscoe (61073) **(G-18899)**
**Gti Spindle Technology Inc**...309 820-7887
14015 Carole Dr Ste 2 Bloomington (61705) **(G-2175)**
**Gtx Inc**...847 699-7421
300 E Touhy Ave Des Plaines (60018) **(G-8203)**
**Gtx Surgery Inc**...847 920-8489
848 Dodge Ave Unit 384 Evanston (60202) **(G-10047)**
**Guardian Angel Outreach**...815 672-4567
405 S Illinois St Streator (61364) **(G-20689)**
**Guardian Consolidated Tech Inc (HQ)**...815 334-3600
1425 Lake Ave Woodstock (60098) **(G-22571)**
**Guardian Construction Pdts Inc**...630 820-8899
10s359 Normantown Rd Naperville (60564) **(G-15808)**
**Guardian Electric Mfg Co (HQ)**...815 334-3600
1425 Lake Ave Woodstock (60098) **(G-22572)**
**Guardian Energy Tech Inc**...800 516-0949
2033 Milwaukee Ave # 136 Riverwoods (60015) **(G-18038)**
**Guardian Equipment Inc**...312 447-8100
1140 N North Branch St Chicago (60642) **(G-5007)**
**Guardian Horse Bedding, Loves Park** *Also called Equustock LLC* **(G-13940)**
**Guardian Rollform LLC**...847 382-8074
27951 W Industrial Ave Lake Barrington (60010) **(G-12808)**
**Guardian West, Urbana** *Also called Flex-N-Gate Corporation* **(G-21088)**
**Guero Pallets**...312 593-4276
2525 S Rockwell St Chicago (60608) **(G-5008)**
**Guess Inc**...312 440-9592
605 N Michigan Ave # 200 Chicago (60611) **(G-5009)**
**Guess Whackit & Hope Inc**...773 342-4273
1883 N Milwaukee Ave Chicago (60647) **(G-5010)**
**Guide Line Industries Inc**...815 777-3722
1453 W Schapville Rd Scales Mound (61075) **(G-19415)**
**Guildhall Publishers Ltd**...309 693-9232
931 W Loire Ct Apt 1306 Peoria (61614) **(G-17374)**
**Gulf Coast Exploration Inc**...847 226-4654
983 Harvard Ct Highland Park (60035) **(G-11838)**
**Gulf Coast Switching Co LLC**...312 324-7353
224 S Michigan Ave # 600 Chicago (60604) **(G-5011)**
**Gulf Petroleum LLC**...312 803-0373
71 W Hubbard St Apt 4701 Chicago (60654) **(G-5012)**
**Gulfstream Aerospace Corp**...630 470-9146
472 Quail Dr Naperville (60565) **(G-15667)**
**Gunderson Rail Services LLC**...309 676-1597
15 Leland St Peoria (61602) **(G-17375)**
**Gunderson Rail Services LLC**...866 858-3919
1545 State St Chicago Heights (60411) **(G-7101)**
**Gundlach Equipment Corporation**...618 233-7208
1 Freedom Dr Belleville (62226) **(G-1633)**
**Gunite Corporation (HQ)**...815 490-6260
302 Peoples Ave Rockford (61104) **(G-18407)**
**Gunite Corporation**...815 964-3301
302 Peoples Ave Rockford (61104) **(G-18408)**
**Gunite EMI Corporation**...815 964-7124
302 Peoples Ave Rockford (61104) **(G-18409)**
**Gunther Construction Co (HQ)**...309 343-1032
816 N Henderson St Galesburg (61401) **(G-10756)**
**Guntner US (HQ)**...847 781-0900
110 W Hillcrest Blvd # 105 Schaumburg (60195) **(G-19545)**
**Gurman Food Co**...847 837-1100
906 Tower Rd Mundelein (60060) **(G-15505)**
**Gurtler Chemicals Inc (PA)**...708 331-2550
15475 La Salle St South Holland (60473) **(G-20273)**
**Gurtler Industries, South Holland** *Also called Gurtler Chemicals Inc* **(G-20273)**
**Gus Berthold Electric Company (PA)**...312 243-5767
1900 W Carroll Ave Chicago (60612) **(G-5013)**
**Gusco Silicone Rbr & Svcs LLC**...773 770-5008
1500 Dearborn Ave Aurora (60505) **(G-1165)**
**Gust-John Foods & Pdts Corp**...630 879-8700
1350 Paramount Pkwy Batavia (60510) **(G-1453)**
**Gutter Masters**...309 686-1234
2117 E Cornell St Peoria (61614) **(G-17376)**
**Guys Hi-Def Inc**...708 261-7487
1948 Essington Rd Ste C Joliet (60435) **(G-12506)**
**Guzzler Manufacturing Inc**...815 672-3171
1621 S Illinois St Streator (61364) **(G-20690)**
**Gvw Group LLC (PA)**...847 681-8417
625 Roger Williams Ave Highland Park (60035) **(G-11839)**
**Gvw Holdings, Highland Park** *Also called Gvw Group LLC* **(G-11839)**
**Gy Packaging LLC**...847 272-8803
3215 Commercial Ave Northbrook (60062) **(G-16267)**
**Gycor International Ltd**...630 754-8070
10216 Werch Dr Ste 108 Woodridge (60517) **(G-22492)**
**Gymtek Incorporated**...815 547-0771
6853 Indy Dr Belvidere (61008) **(G-1760)**
**Gyood**...773 360-8810
2048 W Belmont Ave Chicago (60618) **(G-5014)**
**Gypsoil Pelletized Pdts LLC**...312 784-0300
372 W Ontario St Ste 501 Chicago (60654) **(G-5015)**
**Gyro Processing Inc**...800 491-0733
3338 N Ashland Ave Chicago (60657) **(G-5016)**
**H & B Hams**...618 372-8690
202 W Plum St Brighton (62012) **(G-2541)**
**H & B Machine Corporation**...312 829-4850
1943 W Walnut St Chicago (60612) **(G-5017)**
**H & B Quality Tooling Inc**...217 223-2387
924 Jersey St Quincy (62301) **(G-17833)**
**H & D Motor Service**...217 342-3262
901 W Cumberland Rd Altamont (62411) **(G-552)**
**H & H Custom Countertops, Bourbonnais** *Also called H & H Custom Woodworking Inc* **(G-2398)**
**H & H Custom Woodworking Inc**...815 932-6820
1858 N State Route 50 # 5 Bourbonnais (60914) **(G-2398)**
**H & H Drilling Co**...618 529-3697
59 Pineview Rd Carbondale (62901) **(G-3008)**
**H & H Fabric Cutters**...773 772-1904
4431 W Rice St Chicago (60651) **(G-5018)**
**H & H Graphics Illinois Inc**...847 383-6285
450 Corporate Woods Pkwy Vernon Hills (60061) **(G-21170)**
**H & H Machining**...309 365-7010
500 S Spencer St Lexington (61753) **(G-13292)**
**H & H Motor Service Inc**...708 652-6100
5130 W 16th St Cicero (60804) **(G-7199)**
**H & H Printing**...847 866-9520
1800 Dempster St Evanston (60202) **(G-10048)**
**H & H Services Inc**...618 633-2837
391 N Old Route 66 Hamel (62046) **(G-11528)**
**H & M Thread Rolling Co Inc**...847 451-1570
9212 Grand Ave Franklin Park (60131) **(G-10485)**
**H & M Woodworks**...608 289-3141
1610 N County Road 1200 Hamilton (62341) **(G-11536)**
**H & R Block, Chicago** *Also called H&R Block Inc* **(G-5025)**
**H & R Block Inc**...847 566-5557
1527 S Lake St Mundelein (60060) **(G-15506)**
**H & R Tool & Machine Co**...618 344-7683
19 W Scates St Caseyville (62232) **(G-3396)**
**H & S Publications Inc**...309 344-1333
2310 Us Highway 150 N Wataga (61488) **(G-21398)**
**H A Framburg & Company (PA)**...708 547-5757
941 Cernan Dr Bellwood (60104) **(G-1708)**
**H A Friend & Company Inc (PA)**...847 746-1248
1535 Lewis Ave Zion (60099) **(G-22687)**
**H A Gartenberg & Company**...847 821-7590
260 Blackthorn Dr Buffalo Grove (60089) **(G-2700)**
**H A Phillips & Co (PA)**...630 377-0050
770 Enterprise Ave Dekalb (60115) **(G-8095)**
**H and D Distribution Inc**...847 247-2011
28045 N Ashley Cir Unit 1 Libertyville (60048) **(G-13328)**
**H B H Print Co**...847 662-2233
1400 Saint Paul Ave Gurnee (60031) **(G-11456)**
**H B Products Incorporated**...773 735-0936
4625 W 63rd St Chicago (60629) **(G-5019)**
**H B Taylor Co**...773 254-4805
4830 S Christiana Ave Chicago (60632) **(G-5020)**

**H Borre & Sons Inc**...847 524-8890
617 Cortland Dr Lake Zurich (60047) *(G-13081)*
**H C Schau & Son Inc**...630 783-1000
10350 Argonne Dr Ste 400 Woodridge (60517) *(G-22493)*
**H D A Fans Inc**...630 627-2087
1455 Brummel Ave 300 Elk Grove Village (60007) *(G-9514)*
**H D C, Burr Ridge** *Also called Medtext Inc (G-2866)*
**H E Associates Inc**...630 553-6382
201 Beaver St Yorkville (60560) *(G-22661)*
**H E Wisdom & Sons Inc (HQ)**...847 841-7002
1575 Executive Dr Elgin (60123) *(G-9052)*
**H E Wisdom & Sons Inc**...847 841-7002
1500 Scottsdale Ct Elgin (60123) *(G-9053)*
**H F I, West Chicago** *Also called Howler Fabrication & Wldg Inc (G-21716)*
**H F K, Cary** *Also called Chirch Global Mfg LLC (G-3330)*
**H Field & Sons Inc**...847 434-0970
2605 S Clearbrook Dr Arlington Heights (60005) *(G-761)*
**H G & N Fertilizer, Clinton** *Also called Harbach Gillan & Nixon Inc (G-7282)*
**H G Acquisition Corp (PA)**...630 382-1000
7020 High Grove Blvd Burr Ridge (60527) *(G-2848)*
**H H Interantional Inc**...847 697-7805
1010 Douglas Rd Elgin (60120) *(G-9054)*
**H Hal Kramer Co**...773 539-9648
4318 N Western Ave Chicago (60618) *(G-5021)*
**H Hal Kramer Co (PA)**...847 441-0213
1865 Old Willow Rd # 231 Northfield (60093) *(G-16401)*
**H J M P Corp (HQ)**...708 345-5370
1930 George St Ste 2 Melrose Park (60160) *(G-14650)*
**H J Mohr & Sons Company**...708 366-0338
915 S Maple Ave Oak Park (60304) *(G-16667)*
**H K Tellabs Limited**...630 445-5333
1415 W Diehl Rd Naperville (60563) *(G-15668)*
**H Kramer & Co**...312 226-6600
1345 W 21st St Chicago (60608) *(G-5022)*
**H L Clausing Inc**...847 676-0330
8038 Monticello Ave Skokie (60076) *(G-20008)*
**H L M Sales Inc**...815 455-6922
618 S Northwest Hwy Barrington (60010) *(G-1283)*
**H M C Products Inc**...815 885-1900
7165 Greenlee Dr Caledonia (61011) *(G-2932)*
**H M I, Hudson** *Also called Hamilton-Maurer Intl Inc (G-12123)*
**H N C Products Inc**...217 935-9100
8631 Sunset Rd Clinton (61727) *(G-7281)*
**H P, Lincoln** *Also called Heritage Packaging LLC (G-13410)*
**H R Larke Corp**...847 204-2776
999 Saddle Creek Ln Crystal Lake (60014) *(G-7586)*
**H R Slater Co Inc**...312 666-1855
2050 W 18th St Chicago (60608) *(G-5023)*
**H S Crocker Company Inc (PA)**...847 669-3600
12100 Smith Dr Huntley (60142) *(G-12143)*
**H S I Fire and Safety Group (PA)**...847 427-8340
107 Garlisch Dr Elk Grove Village (60007) *(G-9515)*
**H V Manufacturing Vanguar**...847 229-5502
1197 Willis Ave Wheeling (60090) *(G-22063)*
**H W Hostetler & Sons**...815 438-7816
27445 Hurd Rd Deer Grove (61243) *(G-7967)*
**H Watson Jewelry Co**...312 236-1104
29 E Madison St Ste 1007 Chicago (60602) *(G-5024)*
**H&H Crushing Inc**...309 275-0643
2401 W Rhodora Ave West Peoria (61604) *(G-21822)*
**H&H Die Manufacturing Inc**...708 479-6267
22772 Challenger Rd A Frankfort (60423) *(G-10326)*
**H&R Block Inc**...773 582-3444
8065 S Ccero Ave Unit 30b Chicago (60652) *(G-5025)*
**H&S Machine & Tools Inc**...618 451-0164
35 Central Industrial Dr Granite City (62040) *(G-11283)*
**H&Z Fuel & Food Inc**...815 399-9108
3420 E State St Rockford (61108) *(G-18410)*
**H-O-H Water Technology Inc (PA)**...847 358-7400
500 S Vermont St Palatine (60067) *(G-17032)*
**H.B. Fuller Construction Pdts, Aurora** *Also called HB Fuller Cnstr Pdts Inc (G-1023)*
**H2o, East Dundee** *Also called Humidity 2 Optimization LLC (G-8644)*
**H2o Ltd (PA)**...217 762-7441
119 E Washington St Ste 1 Monticello (61856) *(G-15077)*
**H2o Filter Inc**...630 963-3303
4407 Chelsea Ave Lisle (60532) *(G-13598)*
**H2o Mobil, Tiskilwa** *Also called Hydrotec Systems Company Inc (G-20959)*
**H2o Pod Inc**...630 240-1769
490 Pennsylvania Ave Glen Ellyn (60137) *(G-10972)*
**H3 Group LLC**...309 222-6027
900 Sw Adams St Peoria (61602) *(G-17377)*
**H3 Life Science Corporation**...708 705-1299
1 Westbrook Corporate Ctr Westchester (60154) *(G-21842)*
**Ha International, Westmont** *Also called Ha-International LLC (G-21888)*
**Ha-International LLC (HQ)**...630 575-5700
630 Oakmont Ln Westmont (60559) *(G-21888)*
**Ha-International LLC**...815 732-3898
1449 W Devils Backbone Rd Oregon (61061) *(G-16826)*
**Ha-Usa Inc (HQ)**...630 575-5700
630 Oakmont Ln Westmont (60559) *(G-21889)*
**Haaker Mold Co Inc**...847 253-8103
628 N Salem Ave Arlington Heights (60004) *(G-762)*
**Haakes Awning**...618 529-4808
2525 Edgewood Ln Carbondale (62901) *(G-3009)*
**Haapanen Brothers Inc**...847 662-2233
1400 Saint Paul Ave Gurnee (60031) *(G-11457)*
**Habegger Corporation**...309 793-7172
520 2nd St Rock Island (61201) *(G-18178)*
**Hach Company**...800 227-4224
2207 Collection Center Dr Chicago (60693) *(G-5026)*
**Hackett Precision Company Inc**...615 227-3136
70 W Madison St Ste 2300 Chicago (60602) *(G-5027)*
**Hadady Corporation (PA)**...219 322-7417
510 W 172nd St South Holland (60473) *(G-20274)*
**Hadady Machining Company Inc (PA)**...708 474-8620
16730 Chicago Ave Lansing (60438) *(G-13165)*
**Hadco Tool Co LLC**...847 677-6263
8105 Monticello Ave Skokie (60076) *(G-20009)*
**Haddock Tool & Manufacturing**...815 786-2739
917 E Railroad St Sandwich (60548) *(G-19367)*
**Hadley Gear Manufacturing Co**...773 722-1030
4444 W Roosevelt Rd Chicago (60624) *(G-5028)*
**Haeger Industries Inc (PA)**...847 426-3441
510 Market Loop Ste 104 West Dundee (60118) *(G-21797)*
**Haeger Potteries Div, West Dundee** *Also called Haeger Industries Inc (G-21797)*
**Hafner Duplicating Company**...312 362-0120
601 S La Salle St Chicago (60605) *(G-5029)*
**Hafner Printing Co Inc**...312 362-0120
601 S La Salle St Ste 150 Chicago (60605) *(G-5030)*
**Hagen Manufacturing Inc**...224 735-2099
318 Holbrook Dr Wheeling (60090) *(G-22064)*
**Haggard Well Services Inc**...618 262-5060
1309 Poplar St Mount Carmel (62863) *(G-15266)*
**Haggerty Corporation**...309 793-4328
520 2nd St Rock Island (61201) *(G-18179)*
**Haggin Marketing Inc**...312 343-2611
343 W Erie St Ste 600 Chicago (60654) *(G-5031)*
**Hahn Industries**...815 689-2133
300 S Walnut St Cullom (60929) *(G-7682)*
**Hahn Ready-Mix Company**...309 582-2436
1600 Se 6th St Aledo (61231) *(G-369)*
**Haimer Usa LLC**...630 833-1500
134 E Hill St Villa Park (60181) *(G-21258)*
**Hairline Creations Inc (PA)**...773 282-5454
5850 W Montrose Ave 54 Chicago (60634) *(G-5032)*
**Hajoca Corporation**...309 663-7524
2047 Ireland Grove Rd B Bloomington (61704) *(G-2176)*
**Hakimian Gem Co**...312 236-6969
5 S Wabash Ave Ste 1212 Chicago (60603) *(G-5033)*
**Hako Minuteman Inc**...630 627-6900
111 S Rohlwing Rd Addison (60101) *(G-140)*
**Hakwood**...630 219-3388
55 S Main St Ste 355 Naperville (60540) *(G-15669)*
**Hal Mather & Sons Incorporated**...815 338-4000
11803 Highway 120 Woodstock (60098) *(G-22573)*
**Halanick Enterprises Inc**...708 403-3334
14428 John Humphrey Dr Orland Park (60462) *(G-16864)*
**Halas Vocational Center, Chicago** *Also called Envision Unlimited (G-4766)*
**Hale Devices Inc (PA)**...305 394-4119
965 W Chicago Ave Chicago (60642) *(G-5034)*
**Half Acre Beer Company**...773 248-4038
4257 N Lincoln Ave Chicago (60618) *(G-5035)*
**Half Price Bks Rec Mgzines Inc**...847 588-2286
5605 W Touhy Ave Niles (60714) *(G-15986)*
**Hall Fabrication Inc**...217 322-2212
429 W Clinton St Rushville (62681) *(G-19091)*
**Hall Shrpning Stnes A Rh Pryda, Chicago** *Also called Rh Preyda Company (G-6348)*
**Hallen Burial Vault Inc**...815 544-6138
3690 Newburg Rd Belvidere (61008) *(G-1761)*
**Hallmark Cabinet Company**...708 757-7807
3225 Rennie Smith Dr Chicago Heights (60411) *(G-7102)*
**Hallmark Industries Inc**...847 301-8050
624 Estes Ave Schaumburg (60193) *(G-19546)*
**Hallmark Surfaces, Chicago Heights** *Also called Hallmark Cabinet Company (G-7102)*
**Hallstar Company (PA)**...312 554-7400
120 S Riverside Plz # 1620 Chicago (60606) *(G-5036)*
**Hallstar Company**...708 594-5947
5851 W 73rd St Bedford Park (60638) *(G-1552)*
**Hallstar Services Corp**...312 554-7400
120 S Riverside Plz # 1620 Chicago (60606) *(G-5037)*
**Halper Publishing Company**...847 542-9793
913 Forest Ave Apt 2s Evanston (60202) *(G-10049)*
**Halsted Packing House Co**...312 421-5147
445 N Halsted St Chicago (60642) *(G-5038)*
**Halter Machine Shop Inc**...618 943-2224
9452 Peachtree Rd Lawrenceville (62439) *(G-13201)*
**Hamalot Inc (PA)**...847 944-1500
933 Remington Rd Schaumburg (60173) *(G-19547)*

ALPHABETIC

(PA)=Parent Co (HQ)=Headquarters (DH)=Div Headquarters
2017 Harris Illinois Industrial Directory
1259

**Hamel Tire and Concrete Pdts** .......... 618 633-2405
200 Hamel Ave Hamel (62046) ***(G-11529)***
**Hamel Tire Service, Hamel** *Also called Hamel Tire and Concrete Pdts* ***(G-11529)***
**Hamilton Beach Brands Inc** .......... 847 252-7036
3100 W Higgins Rd Ste 155 Hoffman Estates (60169) ***(G-12015)***
**Hamilton Concrete Products Co** .......... 217 847-3118
400 Windy Woods Dr Hamilton (62341) ***(G-11537)***
**Hamilton Construction Co, Hamilton** *Also called Hamilton Concrete Products Co* ***(G-11537)***
**Hamilton County Coal LLC** .......... 618 648-2603
18033 County Road 500 E Dahlgren (62828) ***(G-7690)***
**Hamilton County Concrete Co** .......... 618 643-4333
Ollie St Mc Leansboro (62859) ***(G-14465)***
**Hamilton Sundstrand Corp** .......... 815 226-6000
4747 Harrison Ave Rockford (61108) ***(G-18411)***
**Hamilton-Maurer Intl Inc** .......... 713 468-6805
14391 E 2400 North Rd Hudson (61748) ***(G-12123)***
**Hammer Enterprises Inc** .......... 217 662-8225
5781 State Route 1 Georgetown (61846) ***(G-10888)***
**Hammer Source, The, Naperville** *Also called Ironwood Mfg Inc* ***(G-15679)***
**Hammond Printing** .......... 847 724-1539
1622 Pickwick Ln Glenview (60026) ***(G-11135)***
**Hammond Suzuki Usa Inc** .......... 630 543-0277
733 W Annoreno Dr Addison (60101) ***(G-141)***
**Hampden Corporation** .......... 312 583-3000
1550 W Carroll Ave # 207 Chicago (60607) ***(G-5039)***
**Hampster Industries Inc** .......... 866 280-2287
26400 N Pheasant Run Mundelein (60060) ***(G-15507)***
**Hamsher Lakeside Funerals** .......... 847 587-2100
12 N Pistakee Lake Rd Fox Lake (60020) ***(G-10277)***
**Han-Win Products Inc** .......... 630 897-1591
726 S Broadway Aurora (60505) ***(G-1166)***
**Hanco, Chicago** *Also called M Handelsman & Co* ***(G-5581)***
**Hancock County Journal-Pilot, Carthage** *Also called Democrat Company Corp* ***(G-3313)***
**Hancock County Shopper** .......... 217 847-6628
1830 Keokuk St Hamilton (62341) ***(G-11538)***
**Hand Tool America** .......... 847 947-2866
45 Buckingham Ln Buffalo Grove (60089) ***(G-2701)***
**Handcut Foods LLC** .......... 312 239-0381
1441 W Willow St Chicago (60642) ***(G-5040)***
**Handi Products Inc** .......... 847 816-7525
510 North Ave Libertyville (60048) ***(G-13329)***
**Handi-Foil Corp (PA)** .......... 847 520-1000
135 E Hintz Rd Wheeling (60090) ***(G-22065)***
**Handi-Foil Corp** .......... 847 520-5742
1234 Peterson Dr Wheeling (60090) ***(G-22066)***
**Handi-Ramp, Libertyville** *Also called Handi Products Inc* ***(G-13329)***
**Handling Systems Inc** .......... 708 352-1213
408 E Cossitt Ave La Grange (60525) ***(G-12735)***
**Hands of Many LLC** .......... 917 841-9969
1301 Braeburn Ave Flossmoor (60422) ***(G-10225)***
**Hands To Work Railroading** .......... 708 489-9776
12217 S Cicero Ave Alsip (60803) ***(G-470)***
**Handy Button Machine Co (PA)** .......... 847 459-0900
29 E Hintz Rd Wheeling (60090) ***(G-22067)***
**Handy Helper Fencing, Coulterville** *Also called Brian Hobbs* ***(G-7398)***
**Handy Kenlin Group, The, Wheeling** *Also called Handy Button Machine Co* ***(G-22067)***
**Hangables Inc** .......... 847 673-9770
7237 Saint Louis Ave Skokie (60076) ***(G-20010)***
**Hanger Inc** .......... 847 695-6955
649 Ridgeview Dr McHenry (60050) ***(G-14511)***
**Hanger Inc** .......... 708 679-1006
4525 Lincoln Hwy Matteson (60443) ***(G-14372)***
**Hanger Clinic, Decatur** *Also called Hanger Prosthetics &* ***(G-7887)***
**Hanger Clinic, Oak Lawn** *Also called Hanger Prosthetics &* ***(G-16624)***
**Hanger Clinic, Herrin** *Also called Hanger Prosthetics &* ***(G-11749)***
**Hanger Clinic, Gurnee** *Also called Hanger Prosthetics &* ***(G-11458)***
**Hanger Clinic, Lincolnshire** *Also called Hanger Prosthetics &* ***(G-13452)***
**Hanger Clinic, Aurora** *Also called Hanger Prosthetics &* ***(G-1022)***
**Hanger Clinic, McHenry** *Also called Hanger Prosthetics &* ***(G-14512)***
**Hanger Clinic, Joliet** *Also called Hanger Prosthetics &* ***(G-12507)***
**Hanger Prosthetics &** .......... 217 429-6656
1910 S Mount Zion Rd D Decatur (62521) ***(G-7887)***
**Hanger Prosthetics &** .......... 708 371-9999
10837 S Cicero Aveste 100 Oak Lawn (60453) ***(G-16624)***
**Hanger Prosthetics &** .......... 618 997-1451
404 Rushing Dr Herrin (62948) ***(G-11749)***
**Hanger Prosthetics &** .......... 847 623-6080
35 Tower Ct Ste C Gurnee (60031) ***(G-11458)***
**Hanger Prosthetics &** .......... 847 478-8154
300 Village Grn Ste 205 Lincolnshire (60069) ***(G-13452)***
**Hanger Prosthetics &** .......... 630 820-5656
4255 Westbrook Dr Ste 215 Aurora (60504) ***(G-1022)***
**Hanger Prosthetics &** .......... 815 344-3070
649 Ridgeview Dr McHenry (60050) ***(G-14512)***
**Hanger Prosthetics &** .......... 815 937-0241
694 Essington Rd Unit B Joliet (60435) ***(G-12507)***
**Hanger Prosthetics & Orthotics** .......... 618 288-8920
2118 Vadalabene Dr Maryville (62062) ***(G-14341)***
**Hanger Prsthetcs & Ortho Inc** .......... 708 957-0240
17530 Kedzie Ave Hazel Crest (60429) ***(G-11708)***
**Hanger Prsthetcs & Ortho Inc** .......... 815 937-0241
450 N Kennedy Dr Ste 2 Kankakee (60901) ***(G-12620)***
**Hanger Prsthetcs & Ortho Inc** .......... 815 744-9944
694 Essington Rd Unit B Joliet (60435) ***(G-12508)***
**Hangerjack, Mokena** *Also called Applied Arts & Sciences Inc* ***(G-14853)***
**Hanigs Footwear Inc** .......... 773 248-1977
1515 Sheridan Rd Ste 2 Wilmette (60091) ***(G-22253)***
**Hanjitech Inc** .......... 847 707-5611
5750 W Bloomingdale Ave Chicago (60639) ***(G-5041)***
**Hankwang U S A Incorporated, Lombard** *Also called HK America Inc* ***(G-13809)***
**Hanley Design Inc** .......... 309 682-9665
2519 N Rockwood Dr Peoria (61604) ***(G-17378)***
**Hanley Industries Inc** .......... 618 465-8892
3640 Seminary St Alton (62002) ***(G-577)***
**Hanlon Group Ltd** .......... 773 525-3666
1872 N Clybourn Ave # 504 Chicago (60614) ***(G-5042)***
**Hanna Hopper Trlr Sls & Rv Ctr** .......... 217 243-3374
298 Moeller Rd Jacksonville (62650) ***(G-12390)***
**Hanna Steel Corporation** .......... 309 478-3800
220 Hanna Dr Pekin (61554) ***(G-17265)***
**Hanover Displays Inc** .......... 773 334-9934
1601 Tonne Rd Elk Grove Village (60007) ***(G-9516)***
**Hansel Walter J & Assoc Inc (PA)** .......... 815 678-6065
4311 Hill Rd Richmond (60071) ***(G-17963)***
**Hansels Custom Tech Inc** .......... 815 496-2345
405 E Si Johnson Ave Sheridan (60551) ***(G-19918)***
**Hansen Custom Cabinet Inc** .......... 847 356-1100
23418 W Apollo Ct Lake Villa (60046) ***(G-13015)***
**Hansen Lumber Company, Galesburg** *Also called Western Illinois Enterprises* ***(G-10779)***
**Hansen Packing Co** .......... 618 498-3714
807 State Highway 16 Jerseyville (62052) ***(G-12423)***
**Hansen Plastics Corp** .......... 847 741-4510
2758 Alft Ln Elgin (60124) ***(G-9055)***
**Hansen Plastics Corp** .......... 847 741-4510
1300 Abbott Dr Elgin (60123) ***(G-9056)***
**Hansen Printing Co Inc** .......... 708 599-1500
9745 Industrial Dr Ste 10 Bridgeview (60455) ***(G-2496)***
**Hansen Technologies Corp (HQ)** .......... 706 335-5551
681 Commerce St Burr Ridge (60527) ***(G-2849)***
**Hansens Mfrs Win Coverings (PA)** .......... 815 935-0010
200 N Washington Ave Bradley (60915) ***(G-2424)***
**Hanson Aggregates East LLC** .......... 815 398-2300
5011 E State St Rockford (61108) ***(G-18412)***
**Hanson Material Service, Romeoville** *Also called Material Service Corporation* ***(G-18842)***
**Hanson Material Service, Westchester** *Also called Material Service Corporation* ***(G-21850)***
**Hanson Metal Finishing Inc** .......... 847 520-1463
1057 Kenilworth Dr Wheeling (60090) ***(G-22068)***
**Hansvedt, Rantoul** *Also called Arrow Edm Inc* ***(G-17918)***
**Hantemp Controls, Westmont** *Also called Hantemp Corporation* ***(G-21890)***
**Hantemp Corporation** .......... 630 537-1049
33 Chestnut Ave Westmont (60559) ***(G-21890)***
**Happy Dog Barkery** .......... 630 512-0822
5118 Main St Ste A Downers Grove (60515) ***(G-8453)***
**Haran Technologies, Champaign** *Also called Haran Ventures LLC* ***(G-3493)***
**Haran Technologies LLC** .......... 217 239-1628
1804 Vale St Champaign (61822) ***(G-3492)***
**Haran Ventures LLC** .......... 217 239-1628
1804 Vale St Champaign (61822) ***(G-3493)***
**Harbach Gillan & Nixon Inc (PA)** .......... 217 935-8378
618 W Van Buren St Clinton (61727) ***(G-7282)***
**Harbach Gillan & Nixon Inc** .......... 217 794-5117
40 Ag Rd Maroa (61756) ***(G-14305)***
**Harbach Nixon & Willson Inc (HQ)** .......... 217 935-8378
618 W Van Buren St Clinton (61727) ***(G-7283)***
**Harbison Corporation** .......... 815 224-2633
4444 Hollerich Dr Peru (61354) ***(G-17511)***
**Harbison Fischer Sales Co, Grayville** *Also called Harbison-Fischer Inc* ***(G-11369)***
**Harbison-Fischer Inc** .......... 618 375-3841
1421 N Court St Grayville (62844) ***(G-11369)***
**Harbisonwalker Intl Inc** .......... 708 474-5350
1400 Huntington Dr Calumet City (60409) ***(G-2941)***
**Harbor Manufacturing Inc** .......... 708 614-6400
8300 185th St Tinley Park (60487) ***(G-20920)***
**Harbor Village LLC** .......... 773 338-2222
2241 W Howard St Chicago (60645) ***(G-5043)***
**Harcros Chemicals Inc** .......... 815 740-9971
17031 Canal St Thornton (60476) ***(G-20872)***
**Hardball Chemical Co, Lincoln** *Also called Vernon Micheal* ***(G-13421)***
**Harder Signs Inc** .......... 815 874-7777
4695 Stenstrom Rd Rockford (61109) ***(G-18413)***
**Hardin County Independent** .......... 618 287-2361
2527 W 1st St Elizabethtown (62931) ***(G-9246)***
**Hardin Industries LLC** .......... 309 246-8456
400 N Commercial St Lacon (61540) ***(G-12787)***
**Hardin Signs Inc** .......... 309 688-4111
3116 N Biltmore Ave Peoria (61604) ***(G-17379)***

ALPHABETIC SECTION Havoline Xpress Lube LLC

**Hardt Electric** ....312 822-0869
415 E North Water St Chicago (60611) ***(G-5044)***
**Hardware Representatives, Bridgeview** *Also called Formed Fastener Mfg Inc* ***(G-2492)***
**Hardwood Line Manufacturing Co** ....773 463-2600
4045 N Elston Ave Chicago (60618) ***(G-5045)***
**Hardwood Lumber Products Co** ....309 538-4411
21046 E Cr 800n Kilbourne (62655) ***(G-12697)***
**Hardy Company, The, Evanston** *Also called John Hardy Co* ***(G-10059)***
**Hardy Radiator Repair** ....217 223-8320
1710 N 12th St Quincy (62301) ***(G-17834)***
**Hardy's Auto Sales, Quincy** *Also called Hardy Radiator Repair* ***(G-17834)***
**Harger Inc (PA)** ....847 548-8700
301 Ziegler Dr Grayslake (60030) ***(G-11345)***
**Harger Lightning & Grounding, Grayslake** *Also called Harger Inc* ***(G-11345)***
**Harig Manufacturing Corp** ....847 647-9500
5423 Fargo Ave Skokie (60077) ***(G-20011)***
**Harig Products Inc** ....847 695-1000
1875 Big Timber Rd Elgin (60123) ***(G-9057)***
**Harlan Vance Company** ....309 888-4804
1741 Hovey Ave Normal (61761) ***(G-16072)***
**Harmon Inc** ....630 759-8060
100 E Crssrads Pkwy Ste B Bolingbrook (60440) ***(G-2315)***
**Harmon Inc** ....312 726-5050
4161 S Morgan St Chicago (60609) ***(G-5046)***
**Harmony House, Morton Grove** *Also called Success Journal Corp* ***(G-15240)***
**Harmony Metal Fabrication Inc** ....847 426-8900
148 Industrial Dr Gilberts (60136) ***(G-10920)***
**Harners Bakery Restaurant** ....630 892-5545
10 W State St North Aurora (60542) ***(G-16133)***
**Harold L Ray Truck & Trctr Svc** ....618 673-2701
Hwy 45 N Cisne (62823) ***(G-7252)***
**Harold Prefinished Wood Inc** ....618 548-1414
5318 State Route 37 Salem (62881) ***(G-19336)***
**Harrier Interior Products** ....847 934-1310
319 W Colfax St Palatine (60067) ***(G-17033)***
**Harrington King Prforating Inc** ....773 626-1800
5655 W Fillmore St Chicago (60644) ***(G-5047)***
**Harrington Signal Inc** ....309 762-0731
2519 4th Ave Moline (61265) ***(G-14942)***
**Harris and Discount Supplies** ....847 726-3800
450 E Il Route 22 Lake Zurich (60047) ***(G-13082)***
**Harris Bmo Bank National Assn** ....815 886-1900
630 N Independence Blvd Romeoville (60446) ***(G-18830)***
**Harris Bookbinding LLC** ....773 287-9414
5375 Walnut Ave Downers Grove (60515) ***(G-8454)***
**Harris Clothing & Uniforms Inc** ....309 671-4543
1025 N Sheridan Rd Peoria (61606) ***(G-17380)***
**Harris Companies Inc** ....217 578-2231
521 N Illinois St Atwood (61913) ***(G-947)***
**Harris Equipment Corporation** ....708 343-0866
2040 N Hawthorne Ave Melrose Park (60160) ***(G-14651)***
**Harris Lubricants** ....708 849-1935
14335 Dorchester Ave Dolton (60419) ***(G-8370)***
**Harris Metals & Recycling** ....217 235-1808
1213 N 11th St Mattoon (61938) ***(G-14390)***
**Harris Potteries LP (PA)** ....847 564-5544
707 Skokie Blvd Ste 220 Northbrook (60062) ***(G-16268)***
**Harris Precision Tools Inc** ....708 422-5808
10081 Anderson Ave Chicago Ridge (60415) ***(G-7149)***
**Harris Skokie** ....847 675-6300
9731 Skokie Blvd Skokie (60077) ***(G-20012)***
**Harris Steel Company (PA)** ....708 656-5500
1223 S 55th Ct Cicero (60804) ***(G-7200)***
**Harris William & Company Inc (PA)** ....312 621-0590
191 N Wacker Dr Ste 1500 Chicago (60606) ***(G-5048)***
**Harrison Harmonicas LLC** ....312 379-9427
4541 N Ravenswood Ave # 203 Chicago (60640) ***(G-5049)***
**Harrison Martha Print Studio** ....949 290-8630
3222 Carrington Dr Crystal Lake (60014) ***(G-7587)***
**Harry J Bosworth Company (PA)** ....847 679-3400
820 Davis St Ste 216 Evanston (60201) ***(G-10050)***
**Harry J Trainor** ....630 493-1163
2113 Oxnard Dr Downers Grove (60516) ***(G-8455)***
**Harry Otto Printing Company** ....630 365-6111
707 E North St Ste A Elburn (60119) ***(G-8889)***
**Harsco Corporation** ....309 347-1962
13090 E Manito Rd Pekin (61554) ***(G-17266)***
**Harsco Corporation** ....217 237-4335
226 E 1640 Rd Pawnee (62558) ***(G-17234)***
**Hart & Cooley Inc** ....630 665-5549
815 Kimberly Dr Carol Stream (60188) ***(G-3165)***
**Hart - Clayton Inc** ....217 525-1610
2000 E Cornell Ave Ste 2 Springfield (62703) ***(G-20448)***
**Hart Electric LLC** ....815 368-3341
102 S Main St Lostant (61334) ***(G-13906)***
**Hart Schaffner & Marx, Des Plaines** *Also called W Diamond Group Corporation* ***(G-8301)***
**Hartford Lubricant Complex, Hartford** *Also called Phillips 66* ***(G-11614)***
**Harting Elektronik, Elgin** *Also called Harting Inc of North America* ***(G-9058)***
**Harting Inc of North America** ....847 741-2700
1375 Crispin Dr Elgin (60123) ***(G-9058)***
**Harting Inc of North America (HQ)** ....847 741-1500
1370 Bowes Rd Elgin (60123) ***(G-9059)***
**Hartland Cutting Tools Inc** ....847 639-9400
240 Jandus Rd Cary (60013) ***(G-3350)***
**Hartman Publishing Group Ltd** ....312 822-0202
1006 S Michigan Ave # 200 Chicago (60605) ***(G-5050)***
**Hartmann** ....618 684-6814
29 Steven Dr Murphysboro (62966) ***(G-15576)***
**Hartmarx Corporation** ....312 357-5325
101 N Wacker Dr Chicago (60606) ***(G-5051)***
**Hartrich Meats Inc** ....618 455-3172
326 W Embarras St Sainte Marie (62459) ***(G-19324)***
**Harts Top and Cabinet Shop** ....708 957-4666
4941 173rd St Ste 1 Country Club Hills (60478) ***(G-7408)***
**Harts Top Shop, Country Club Hills** *Also called Harts Top and Cabinet Shop* ***(G-7408)***
**Hartwig Roll Off Containers, Henry** *Also called Ed Hartwig Trucking & Excvtg* ***(G-11740)***
**Hartz Mountain Corporation** ....847 517-2596
1100 E Woodfield Rd Schaumburg (60173) ***(G-19548)***
**Harvard Building Products, Harvard** *Also called A-Ok Inc* ***(G-11616)***
**Harvard Factory Automation Inc** ....815 943-1195
490 Commanche Cir Harvard (60033) ***(G-11634)***
**Harvard State Bank** ....815 943-4400
35 N Ayer St Harvard (60033) ***(G-11635)***
**Harvest Food Group Inc** ....773 847-3313
4412 W 44th St Chicago (60632) ***(G-5052)***
**Harvest Publications Div, Arlington Heights** *Also called Baptist General Conference* ***(G-723)***
**Harvest Valley Bakery Inc** ....815 224-9030
348 Civic Rd La Salle (61301) ***(G-12774)***
**Harvey Bros Inc** ....309 342-3137
2181 Grand Ave Galesburg (61401) ***(G-10757)***
**Harvey Cement Products Inc** ....708 333-1900
16030 Park Ave Harvey (60426) ***(G-11668)***
**Harvey Fuels** ....708 339-0777
2 E 159th St Harvey (60426) ***(G-11669)***
**Harvey Pallets Inc** ....708 293-1831
2200 138th St Blue Island (60406) ***(G-2255)***
**Haskris Co** ....847 956-6420
100 Kelly St Elk Grove Village (60007) ***(G-9517)***
**Hass and Associates, Northbrook** *Also called Sport Electronics Inc* ***(G-16369)***
**Hassebrock Asphalt Sealing** ....618 566-7214
111 W Poplar St Mascoutah (62258) ***(G-14352)***
**Hastie Mining & Trucking (PA)** ....618 289-4536
Hwy 146 Cave In Rock (62919) ***(G-3402)***
**Hastie Mining & Trucking** ....618 285-3600
68 Bohn St Rosiclare (62982) ***(G-19048)***
**Hastings Manufacturing Inc** ....800 338-8688
3708 Thorne Briar Ct Millstadt (62260) ***(G-14825)***
**Hastings Printing** ....217 253-5086
111 Sale St Tuscola (61953) ***(G-21020)***
**Hatcher Associates Inc** ....773 252-2171
1612 N Throop St Chicago (60642) ***(G-5053)***
**Hats For You** ....773 481-1611
7509 W Belmont Ave Chicago (60634) ***(G-5054)***
**Hattan Tool Company** ....708 597-9308
4909 W 128th Pl Alsip (60803) ***(G-471)***
**Hatzer Ready Mix, Streator** *Also called Joe Hatzer & Son Inc* ***(G-20692)***
**Hatzer Ready Mix, Streator** *Also called Joe Hatzer & Son Inc* ***(G-20693)***
**Hauhinco LP** ....618 993-5399
810 Skyline Dr Marion (62959) ***(G-14264)***
**Haumiller Engineering Company** ....847 695-9111
445 Renner Dr Elgin (60123) ***(G-9060)***
**Haus Sign Incorporated** ....708 598-8740
8907 Moore Dr Bridgeview (60455) ***(G-2497)***
**Hausermann Abrading Process Co** ....630 543-6688
300 W Laura Dr Addison (60101) ***(G-142)***
**Hausermann Controls Co** ....630 543-6688
300 W Laura Dr Addison (60101) ***(G-143)***
**Hausermann Die & Machine, Addison** *Also called Hausermann Controls Co* ***(G-143)***
**Hausermann Die & Machine Co** ....630 543-6688
300 W Laura Dr Addison (60101) ***(G-144)***
**Hausner Hard - Chrome Inc (PA)** ....847 439-6010
670 Greenleaf Ave Elk Grove Village (60007) ***(G-9518)***
**Haussermann Usa LLC** ....847 272-9850
425 Huehl Rd Bldg 10 Northbrook (60062) ***(G-16269)***
**Haute Noir Magzine, Chicago** *Also called Haute Noir Media Group Inc* ***(G-5055)***
**Haute Noir Media Group Inc** ....312 869-4526
220 N Green St Chicago (60607) ***(G-5055)***
**Havana Metal Culverts Division, Havana** *Also called Metal Culverts Inc* ***(G-11699)***
**Havana Printing & Mailing** ....309 543-2000
217 W Market St Havana (62644) ***(G-11695)***
**Havanah Fuel** ....309 543-2211
520 E Laurel Ave Havana (62644) ***(G-11696)***
**Having A Good Time** ....847 330-8460
1710 E Woodfield Rd Schaumburg (60173) ***(G-19549)***
**Havoline Xpress Lube LLC** ....847 221-5724
1402 N Rand Rd Palatine (60074) ***(G-17034)***

ALPHABETIC

**Havoline Xpress Lube LLC (PA)** .................. 224 757-5628
  810 Sunset Dr  Round Lake  (60073)  *(G-19060)*
**Hawk Fastener Services** .................. 708 489-2000
  12324 S Laramie Ave  Alsip  (60803)  *(G-472)*
**Hawk Molding Inc** .................. 224 523-2888
  435 Andrea Ct  Harvard  (60033)  *(G-11636)*
**Hawk Technology, Rock Island**  Also called JC Automation Inc  *(G-18185)*
**Hawkins  Inc** .................. 708 258-3797
  32040 S Route 45  Peotone  (60468)  *(G-17489)*
**Hawthorne Press** .................. 708 652-9000
  5615 W Roosevelt Rd  Cicero  (60804)  *(G-7201)*
**Hawthorne Press Inc** .................. 847 587-0582
  208 Chateau Dr  Spring Grove  (60081)  *(G-20336)*
**Hayden Mills Inc** .................. 618 962-3136
  119 Washington Ave  Omaha  (62871)  *(G-16807)*
**Hayes Abrasives  Inc** .................. 217 532-6850
  Smith Rd 120  Hillsboro  (62049)  *(G-11892)*
**Hayes Cabinets, Steward**  Also called David Hayes  *(G-20623)*
**Haymarket Brewing Company  LLC** .................. 312 638-0700
  737 W Randolph St  Chicago  (60661)  *(G-5056)*
**Haymarket Pub & Brewery, Chicago**  Also called Haymarket Brewing Company  LLC  *(G-5056)*
**Haynes Express  Inc** .................. 309 793-6080
  2000 5th St  Rock Island  (61201)  *(G-18180)*
**Haynes Motor Express, Rock Island**  Also called Haynes Express  Inc  *(G-18180)*
**Haynes-Bent  Inc** .................. 630 845-3316
  35179 S Old Chicago Rd  Wilmington  (60481)  *(G-22274)*
**Hazen Display Corporation (PA)** .................. 815 248-2925
  537 Baintree Rd  Davis  (61019)  *(G-7806)*
**HB Coatings  LLC** .................. 618 215-8161
  932 Fairway Park Dr  Madison  (62060)  *(G-14149)*
**HB Fuller Adhesives  LLC** .................. 815 357-6726
  7440 W Dupont Rd  Morris  (60450)  *(G-15110)*
**HB Fuller Cnstr Pdts Inc (HQ)** .................. 630 978-7766
  1105 S Frontenac St  Aurora  (60504)  *(G-1023)*
**HB Fuller Cnstr Pdts Inc** .................. 847 776-4375
  315 S Hicks Rd  Palatine  (60067)  *(G-17035)*
**HB Fuller Company** .................. 847 358-9555
  1105 S Frontenac St  Aurora  (60504)  *(G-1024)*
**HB Plastics, Freeport**  Also called Hbp  Inc  *(G-10662)*
**Hbm Somat, Champaign**  Also called Hottinger Bldwin Msrements Inc  *(G-3495)*
**Hbp  Inc** .................. 815 235-3000
  107 N Henderson Rd  Freeport  (61032)  *(G-10662)*
**HC Duke & Son LLC** .................. 309 755-4553
  2116 8th Ave  East Moline  (61244)  *(G-8681)*
**Hc Materials, Bolingbrook**  Also called Ctg Advanced Materials  LLC  *(G-2292)*
**Hcc  Inc** .................. 815 539-9371
  1501 1st Ave  Mendota  (61342)  *(G-14722)*
**Hci Cabinetry and Design Inc** .................. 630 584-0266
  3755 E Main St  Saint Charles  (60174)  *(G-19190)*
**Hcs Hahn Calibration Service** .................. 847 567-2500
  20575 N William Ave  Lincolnshire  (60069)  *(G-13453)*
**Hd Electric Company** .................. 847 473-4980
  1475 S Lakeside Dr  Waukegan  (60085)  *(G-21567)*
**HD Hudson Manufacturing Co (PA)** .................. 312 644-2830
  500 N Michigan Ave Fl 23  Chicago  (60611)  *(G-5057)*
**Head Manufacturing, South Elgin**  Also called Uca Group  Inc  *(G-20231)*
**Headball Inc** .................. 618 628-2656
  41 Acorn Lake Dr  Belleville  (62221)  *(G-1634)*
**Headco Industries  Inc** .................. 847 640-6490
  109 N Lively Blvd  Elk Grove Village  (60007)  *(G-9519)*
**Headco Industries  Inc** .................. 815 729-4016
  2104 Oak Leaf St Unit D  Joliet  (60436)  *(G-12509)*
**Header Die and Tool  Inc** .................. 815 397-0123
  3022 Eastrock Ct  Rockford  (61109)  *(G-18414)*
**Headhunter2000 Inc** .................. 708 533-3769
  328 Major Dr  Northlake  (60164)  *(G-16438)*
**Headly Manufacturing Co (PA)** .................. 708 338-0800
  2700 23rd St  Broadview  (60155)  *(G-2583)*
**Headly Manufacturing Co** .................. 708 338-0800
  2111 Roberts Dr  Broadview  (60155)  *(G-2584)*
**Headly Mfg, Broadview**  Also called Headly Manufacturing Co  *(G-2584)*
**Heafner Contracting  Inc** .................. 618 466-3678
  27457 Heafner Dr  Godfrey (62035)  *(G-11225)*
**Healing Scents** .................. 815 874-0924
  1986 Will James Rd  Rockford  (61109)  *(G-18415)*
**Health Administration Press** .................. 312 424-2800
  1 N Franklin St Ste 1600  Chicago  (60606)  *(G-5058)*
**Health King Enterprise  Inc** .................. 312 567-9978
  238 W 31st St Ste 1  Chicago  (60616)  *(G-5059)*
**Health O Meter Professional, Countryside**  Also called Pelstar LLC  *(G-7440)*
**Healthcare Labels Inc** .................. 847 382-3993
  245 Honey Lake Ct  North Barrington  (60010)  *(G-16151)*
**Healthcare Research  LLC** .................. 773 592-3508
  744 N Wells St Fl 3  Chicago  (60654)  *(G-5060)*
**Healthcom  Inc** .................. 217 728-8331
  1600 W Jackson St  Sullivan  (61951)  *(G-20747)*
**Healthdentl  LLC** .................. 800 845-5172
  10052 Bode St Ste E  Plainfield  (60585)  *(G-17605)*
**Healthengine** .................. 312 340-8555
  875 N Michigan Ave # 3100  Chicago  (60611)  *(G-5061)*
**Healthful Habits LLC** .................. 224 489-4256
  245 W Roosevelt Rd  West Chicago  (60185)  *(G-21714)*
**Healthleaders Inc** .................. 312 932-0848
  1404 N Cleveland Ave  Chicago  (60610)  *(G-5062)*
**Healthlight LLC** .................. 224 231-0342
  920 E State Pkwy Unit B  Schaumburg  (60173)  *(G-19550)*
**Healthsmart International, Waukegan**  Also called D-M-S Holdings  Inc  *(G-21547)*
**Healthware Systems, Elgin**  Also called Document Publishing Group  *(G-9011)*
**Healthware Systems Inc** .................. 847 783-0670
  2511 Tech Dr Ste 102  Elgin  (60124)  *(G-9061)*
**Healthwise Gourmet Coffees (PA)** .................. 847 382-3230
  76 Woodberry Rd  Deer Park  (60010)  *(G-7971)*
**Healthy Life Nutraceutics Inc** .................. 201 253-9053
  500 Lake Cook Rd Ste 350  Deerfield  (60015)  *(G-8010)*
**Healthy-Txt  LLC** .................. 630 945-1787
  950 W Monroe St Unit 813  Chicago  (60607)  *(G-5063)*
**Hearing Aid Warehouse Inc** .................. 217 431-4700
  1005 N Gilbert St  Danville  (61832)  *(G-7730)*
**Hearing Associates PC** .................. 847 662-9300
  35 Tower Ct Ste A  Gurnee  (60031)  *(G-11459)*
**Hearing Screening Assoc LLC** .................. 855 550-9427
  3333 N Kennicott Ave  Arlington Heights  (60004)  *(G-763)*
**Hearst Communications  Inc** .................. 309 829-9000
  301 W Washington St  Bloomington  (61701)  *(G-2177)*
**Hearst Corporation** .................. 312 984-5166
  333 W Wacker Dr Ste 950  Chicago  (60606)  *(G-5064)*
**Hearst Corporation** .................. 312 984-5100
  333 W Wacker Dr Ste 950  Chicago  (60606)  *(G-5065)*
**Heart & Soul Memories Inc** .................. 847 478-1931
  1938 Sheridan Rd  Buffalo Grove  (60089)  *(G-2702)*
**Heart 4 Heart Inc (PA)** .................. 217 544-2699
  2924 N Dirksen Pkwy  Springfield  (62702)  *(G-20449)*
**Heart Printing & Form Service, Arlington Heights**  Also called Heart Printing Inc  *(G-764)*
**Heart Printing Inc** .................. 847 259-2100
  1624 W Northwest Hwy  Arlington Heights  (60004)  *(G-764)*
**Heartfelt Framing Gallery, Kewanee**  Also called Heartfelt Gifts Inc  *(G-12690)*
**Heartfelt Gifts Inc** .................. 309 852-2296
  224 N Main St  Kewanee  (61443)  *(G-12690)*
**Hearthside Food Solutions LLC** .................. 217 784-4238
  310 W 10th St  Gibson City  (60936)  *(G-10901)*
**Hearthside Food Solutions  LLC** .................. 815 853-4348
  775 State Route 251  Wenona  (61377)  *(G-21648)*
**Hearthside Food Solutions  LLC (PA)** .................. 630 967-3600
  3250 Lacey Rd Ste 200  Downers Grove  (60515)  *(G-8456)*
**Heartland Bench and Pew, Sandwich**  Also called Designed Stairs  Inc  *(G-19361)*
**Heartland Candle Co** .................. 815 698-2200
  2739 N 700 East Rd  Ashkum  (60911)  *(G-925)*
**Heartland Classics Inc** .................. 618 783-4444
  1705 W Jourdan St  Newton  (62448)  *(G-15941)*
**Heartland Granite  Inc** .................. 630 499-8000
  701 N Commerce St  Aurora  (60504)  *(G-1025)*
**Heartland Hardwoods Inc** .................. 217 844-3312
  20871 N 1600th St  Effingham  (62401)  *(G-8838)*
**Heartland Harvest  Inc** .................. 815 932-2100
  2401 Eastgate Indus Pkwy  Kankakee  (60901)  *(G-12621)*
**Heartland House Designs** .................. 708 383-2278
  741 N Oak Park Ave  Oak Park  (60302)  *(G-16668)*
**Heartland Inspection Company** .................. 630 788-3607
  510 Nathan Lattin Ln  Sycamore  (60178)  *(G-20799)*
**Heartland Labels  Inc** .................. 217 826-8324
  17135 N Quality Lime Rd  Marshall  (62441)  *(G-14323)*
**Heartland Machine and Sup LLC** .................. 217 543-2678
  337 E Sr 133  Arthur  (61911)  *(G-903)*
**Heartland Publications Inc** .................. 217 529-9506
  7900 Olde Carriage Way  Springfield  (62712)  *(G-20450)*
**Hearwell** .................. 217 824-5210
  1221 W Spresser St  Taylorville  (62568)  *(G-20840)*
**Heat and Control  Inc** .................. 309 342-5518
  1721 Us Highway 164  Galesburg  (61401)  *(G-10758)*
**Heat Armor  LLC** .................. 773 938-1030
  4400 W 45th St Ste B  Chicago  (60632)  *(G-5066)*
**Heat Seal Tooling Corporation** .................. 815 626-6009
  300 Avenue A  Rock Falls  (61071)  *(G-18134)*
**Heat Transfer Laboratories** .................. 708 715-4300
  2 Mid America Plz Ste 800  Oakbrook Terrace  (60181)  *(G-16709)*
**Heat Treat, Chicago**  Also called Axletech International  *(G-4006)*
**Heatcraft Refrigeration Pdts, Danville**  Also called Heatcraft Rfrgn Pdts LLC  *(G-7731)*
**Heatcraft Rfrgn Pdts LLC** .................. 217 446-3710
  1001 E Voorhees St Ste B  Danville  (61832)  *(G-7731)*
**Heathrow Scientific LLC** .................. 847 816-5070
  620 Lakeview Pkwy  Vernon Hills  (60061)  *(G-21171)*
**Heavenly Enterprises** .................. 773 783-2981
  8401 S 85th Ct  Hickory Hills  (60457)  *(G-11770)*
**Heavy Equipment Products** .................. 630 377-3005
  11 S 2nd Ave Ste 3  Saint Charles  (60174)  *(G-19191)*

**Heavy Hitters LLC**......630 258-2991
304 153rd Pl Calumet City (60409) ***(G-2942)***
**Heavy Metal Industries LLC**......309 966-3007
6718 W Plank Rd Ste 4 Peoria (61604) ***(G-17381)***
**Heavy Quip Incorporated**......312 368-7997
55 W Wacker Dr Ste 1120 Chicago (60601) ***(G-5067)***
**Heckmann Building Products Inc**......708 865-2403
1501 N 31st Ave Melrose Park (60160) ***(G-14652)***
**Hedricks Welding & Fabrication**......217 846-3230
201 Main St Foosland (61845) ***(G-10232)***
**HEF Corporation**......708 343-0866
2010 N Ruby St Melrose Park (60160) ***(G-14653)***
**Hefke Machines & Machining**......630 896-6617
1060 Johnston Dr Aurora (60506) ***(G-1167)***
**Heico Companies LLC (PA)**......312 419-8220
70 W Madison St Ste 5600 Chicago (60602) ***(G-5068)***
**Heico Ohmite LLC**......847 258-0300
1600 Golf Rd Ste 850 Rolling Meadows (60008) ***(G-18733)***
**Heidelberg USA Inc**......847 550-0915
21805 W Feld Pkwy Ste 180 Barrington (60010) ***(G-1284)***
**Heidenhain Corporation (HQ)**......847 490-1191
333 E State Pkwy Schaumburg (60173) ***(G-19551)***
**Heidenhain Holding Inc (HQ)**......716 661-1700
333 E State Pkwy Schaumburg (60173) ***(G-19552)***
**Heidolph NA LLC**......224 265-9600
1241 Jarvis Ave Elk Grove Village (60007) ***(G-9520)***
**Heidolph North America, Elk Grove Village** *Also called Heidolph NA LLC* ***(G-9520)***
**Heidt's Hot Rod Shop, Lake Zurich** *Also called Heidts Automotive LLC* ***(G-13083)***
**Heidtman Steel Products Inc**......618 451-0052
10 Northgate Indus Dr Granite City (62040) ***(G-11284)***
**Heidtman Steel Products Inc**......618 451-0052
10 Northgate Indus Dr Granite City (62040) ***(G-11285)***
**Heidts Automotive LLC**......847 487-0150
800 Oakwood Rd Lake Zurich (60047) ***(G-13083)***
**Heil Sound Ltd**......618 257-3000
5800 N Illinois St Fairview Heights (62208) ***(G-10168)***
**Heim Group**......708 496-7403
7201 S Narragansett Ave Chicago (60638) ***(G-5069)***
**Heiman Sign Studio**......815 397-6909
6909 Canter Ct Rockford (61108) ***(G-18416)***
**Heimburger House Pubg Co Inc**......708 366-1973
7236 Madison St Forest Park (60130) ***(G-10248)***
**Heimlich Jones, Markham** *Also called Ken Don LLC* ***(G-14303)***
**Heinkels Packing Company Inc**......217 428-4401
2005 N 22nd St Decatur (62526) ***(G-7888)***
**Heise Industries Inc**......847 223-2410
123 Hawley St Grayslake (60030) ***(G-11346)***
**Heisler Stone Co Inc**......815 244-2685
18463 Cyclone Ridge Rd Mount Carroll (61053) ***(G-15291)***
**Heiss Welding Inc**......815 434-1838
260 W Marquette St Ottawa (61350) ***(G-16961)***
**Helander Metal Spinning Co**......630 268-9292
931 N Ridge Ave Lombard (60148) ***(G-13808)***
**Helena Chemical Company**......217 234-2726
3559 E County Road 1000n Mattoon (61938) ***(G-14391)***
**Helena Chemical Company**......217 382-4241
9666 E Angling Rd Martinsville (62442) ***(G-14336)***
**Helene Printing Inc**......630 482-3300
24 S Addison St Apt 805 Bensenville (60106) ***(G-1915)***
**Helfter Enterprises Inc**......309 522-5505
301 Main St Osco (61274) ***(G-16899)***
**Heligear Acquisition Co (PA)**......708 728-2000
6006 W 73rd St Bedford Park (60638) ***(G-1553)***
**Heligear Acquisition Co**......708 728-2055
1000 Burr Ridge Pkwy Burr Ridge (60527) ***(G-2850)***
**Helio Precision Products Inc (PA)**......847 473-1300
601 N Skokie Hwy Ste B Lake Bluff (60044) ***(G-12848)***
**Helivalues**......847 487-8258
1001 N Old Rand Rd # 101 Wauconda (60084) ***(G-21466)***
**Helix International Inc (PA)**......847 709-0666
2150 Lively Blvd Elk Grove Village (60007) ***(G-9521)***
**Helix International Mch Div, Elk Grove Village** *Also called Helix International Inc* ***(G-9521)***
**Hella Corporate Center USA Inc**......734 414-0900
50 Industrial Park Flora (62839) ***(G-10208)***
**Hella Corporate Center USA Inc**......618 662-4402
1101 Vincennes Ave Flora (62839) ***(G-10209)***
**Hella Electronics, Flora** *Also called Hella Corporate Center USA Inc* ***(G-10208)***
**Hella Electronics Corporation**......618 662-5186
1101 Vincennes Ave Flora (62839) ***(G-10210)***
**Helle Sawmills, Farmington** *Also called Sawmill Hydraulics* ***(G-10188)***
**Helm Tool Company Incorporated**......847 952-9528
1290 Brummel Ave Elk Grove Village (60007) ***(G-9522)***
**Helmuth Custom Kitchens LLC**......217 543-3588
2004 Cr 1800e Arthur (61911) ***(G-904)***
**Hemingway Chimney Inc**......708 333-0355
16940 Vincennes Ave South Holland (60473) ***(G-20275)***
**Hemmerle Jr Irvin**......630 334-4392
1526 Treeline Ct Naperville (60565) ***(G-15670)***
**Hempel Group Inc**......630 389-2222
934 Paramount Pkwy Batavia (60510) ***(G-1454)***
**Henderson Co Inc**......773 628-7216
6020 N Keating Ave Chicago (60646) ***(G-5070)***
**Henderson County Quill, Stronghurst** *Also called Henderson Hancock Quill Inc* ***(G-20713)***
**Henderson Engineering Co Inc (PA)**......815 786-9471
95 N Main St Sandwich (60548) ***(G-19368)***
**Henderson Eye Center**......217 698-9477
3330 Ginger Creek Dr C Springfield (62711) ***(G-20451)***
**Henderson Family**......309 236-6783
208 N College Ave Aledo (61231) ***(G-370)***
**Henderson Hancock Quill Inc**......309 924-1871
102 N Broadway St Stronghurst (61480) ***(G-20713)***
**Henderson Products Inc**......847 836-4996
124 Industrial Dr Gilberts (60136) ***(G-10921)***
**Henderson Products Inc**......847 515-3482
11921 Smith Dr Huntley (60142) ***(G-12144)***
**Henderson Truck Equipment, Gilberts** *Also called Henderson Products Inc* ***(G-10921)***
**Henderson Water District**......618 498-6418
1004 State Highway 16 Jerseyville (62052) ***(G-12424)***
**Hendrick Metal Products LLC**......847 742-7002
1320 Gateway Dr Elgin (60124) ***(G-9062)***
**Hendrickson, Woodridge** *Also called Boler Company* ***(G-22457)***
**Hendrickson International Corp**......815 727-4031
501 Caton Farm Rd Joliet (60434) ***(G-12510)***
**Hendrickson Usa LLC (HQ)**......630 874-9700
500 Park Blvd Ste 450 Itasca (60143) ***(G-12274)***
**Hendrix Industrial Gastrux Inc**......847 526-1700
1301 N Old Rand Rd Wauconda (60084) ***(G-21467)***
**Henes Usa Inc**......312 448-6130
125 Milwaukee Ave Ste 301 Glenview (60025) ***(G-11136)***
**Heng Tuo Usa Inc (PA)**......630 705-1898
1 Transam Plaza Dr # 545 Oakbrook Terrace (60181) ***(G-16710)***
**Henkel Consumer Goods Inc**......847 426-4552
2175 Point Blvd Ste 180 Elgin (60123) ***(G-9063)***
**Henkel Corporation**......847 468-9200
1345 Gasket Dr Elgin (60120) ***(G-9064)***
**Henkelman Inc**......331 979-2013
493 W Fullerton Ave Elmhurst (60126) ***(G-9881)***
**Hennessy Sheet Metal**......708 754-6342
3256 Butler St S Chicago Hts (60411) ***(G-19104)***
**Hennig Gasket & Seals Inc**......312 243-8270
2350 W Cullerton St Chicago (60608) ***(G-5071)***
**Hennig Inc (HQ)**......815 636-9900
9900 N Alpine Rd Machesney Park (61115) ***(G-14078)***
**Henning Machine & Die Works**......217 286-3393
4 N Main St Henning (61848) ***(G-11738)***
**Henry A Engelhart**......217 563-2176
1626 E 27nd Rd Nokomis (62075) ***(G-16057)***
**Henry Baron Enterprises Inc**......847 681-2755
940 Augusta Way Apt 105 Highland Park (60035) ***(G-11840)***
**Henry Crown and Company (PA)**......312 236-6300
222 N La Salle St # 2000 Chicago (60601) ***(G-5072)***
**Henry J'S Famous Foods, Chicago** *Also called Bar-B-Que Industries Inc* ***(G-4040)***
**Henry News Republican**......309 364-3250
709 3rd St Henry (61537) ***(G-11743)***
**Henry Pratt Company LLC (HQ)**......630 844-4000
401 S Highland Ave Aurora (60506) ***(G-1168)***
**Henry Printing Inc**......618 529-3040
975 Charles Rd Carbondale (62901) ***(G-3010)***
**Henry Tech Inc Intl Sls Co, Chatham** *Also called Henry Technologies Inc* ***(G-3621)***
**Henry Technologies Inc (HQ)**......217 483-2406
701 S Main St Chatham (62629) ***(G-3621)***
**Henry Technologies Inc**......217 483-2406
701 S Main St Chatham (62629) ***(G-3622)***
**Henry Tool & Die Co (PA)**......847 671-1361
10012 Pacific Ave Franklin Park (60131) ***(G-10486)***
**Henry-Lee & Company LLC**......312 648-1575
549 W Randolph St Ste 500 Chicago (60661) ***(G-5073)***
**Hensaal Management Group Inc**......312 624-8133
4632 W Monroe St Chicago (60644) ***(G-5074)***
**Hentzen Coatings Inc**......414 353-4200
1500 Lathem St Batavia (60510) ***(G-1455)***
**Hepalink USA Inc (PA)**......630 206-1788
233 S Wacker Dr Ste 9300 Chicago (60606) ***(G-5075)***
**Hera Cnsltng Interntnl Opratn**......630 515-8819
4307 Westerhoff Dr Lisle (60532) ***(G-13599)***
**Herald & Review, Decatur** *Also called Lee Enterprises Incorporated* ***(G-7906)***
**Herald Country Market, The, Bourbonnais** *Also called B & B Publishing Co Inc* ***(G-2388)***
**Herald Mount Olive**......217 999-3941
102 E Main St Mount Olive (62069) ***(G-15303)***
**Herald Newspapers Inc**......773 643-8533
1525 E 53rd St Ste 920 Chicago (60615) ***(G-5076)***
**Herald Printing, East Moline** *Also called East Moline Herald Print Inc* ***(G-8678)***
**Herald Publications (PA)**......618 566-8282
314 E Church St Ste 1 Mascoutah (62258) ***(G-14353)***
**Herald Whig Quincy**......217 222-7600
130 N 5th St Quincy (62301) ***(G-17835)***
**Herbaland Inc (PA)**......773 267-7225
3127 N Milwaukee Ave Chicago (60618) ***(G-5077)***

ALPHABETIC

Herbs Bakery Inc

ALPHABETIC SECTION

**Herbs Bakery Inc** ....847 741-0249
1020 Larkin Ave Elgin (60123) *(G-9065)*
**Herbs License Service, Collinsville** *Also called Precision Service (G-7337)*
**Hercules Industrial Division, Addison** *Also called GE Betz Inc (G-129)*
**Hercules Iron Works Inc** ....312 226-2405
846 W Superior St Chicago (60642) *(G-5078)*
**Herff Jones LLC** ....217 268-4543
901 Bob King Dr Arcola (61910) *(G-670)*
**Herff Jones LLC** ....815 756-4743
901 N 1st St Ste 7 Dekalb (60115) *(G-8096)*
**Herff Jones LLC** ....773 463-1144
3333 N Elston Ave Chicago (60618) *(G-5079)*
**Herff Jones LLC** ....217 351-9500
1000 N Market St Champaign (61820) *(G-3494)*
**Herff Jones LLC** ....708 425-0130
6305 W 95th St Ste 1w Oak Lawn (60453) *(G-16625)*
**Herff Jones LLC** ....317 612-3705
125 Fencl Ln Hillside (60162) *(G-11918)*
**Heritage Custom Trailers, Benton** *Also called Knight Bros Inc (G-2033)*
**Heritage Media Svcs Co of Ill** ....708 594-9340
7676 W 63rd St Summit Argo (60501) *(G-20763)*
**Heritage Mold Incorporated** ....815 397-1117
3170 Forest View Rd Rockford (61109) *(G-18417)*
**Heritage Packaging LLC** ....217 735-4406
2350 5th St Lincoln (62656) *(G-13410)*
**Heritage Press Inc** ....847 362-9699
312 Peterson Rd Libertyville (60048) *(G-13330)*
**Heritage Printing (PA)** ....815 537-2372
219 Washington St Prophetstown (61277) *(G-17770)*
**Heritage Products Corporation** ....847 419-8835
1398 Busch Pkwy Buffalo Grove (60089) *(G-2703)*
**Heritage Rstoration Design Inc** ....309 637-5404
207 Voris St Peoria (61603) *(G-17382)*
**Heritage Sheet Metal Inc** ....847 724-8449
2049 Johns Dr Glenview (60025) *(G-11137)*
**Heritage Signs Ltd** ....847 549-1942
1840 Industrial Dr # 240 Libertyville (60048) *(G-13331)*
**Herman Bade & Sons** ....217 832-9444
608 N Henson Rd Villa Grove (61956) *(G-21228)*
**Herman L Loeb LLC** ....618 943-2227
600 Country Club Rd Lawrenceville (62439) *(G-13202)*
**Herman Seekamp Inc** ....630 628-6555
1120 W Fullerton Ave Addison (60101) *(G-145)*
**Herman's World of Embroidery, Rock Island** *Also called Hermans Inc (G-18181)*
**Hermanitas Cupcakes** ....708 620-9396
1067 Stewart Ave Calumet City (60409) *(G-2943)*
**Hermann Gene Signs & Service** ....618 244-3681
12436 E Lakewood Dr Mount Vernon (62864) *(G-15411)*
**Hermans Inc** ....309 206-4892
2820 46th Ave Rock Island (61201) *(G-18181)*
**Hermitage Group Inc** ....773 561-3773
5151 N Ravenswood Ave Chicago (60640) *(G-5080)*
**Herner-Geissler Wdwkg Corp** ....312 226-3400
400 N Hermitage Ave Chicago (60622) *(G-5081)*
**Heron Bay Inc** ....309 661-1300
1605 General Elc Rd Ste 1 Bloomington (61704) *(G-2178)*
**Herr Display Vans Inc** ....708 755-7926
3328 Louis Sherman Dr Steger (60475) *(G-20573)*
**Herrin News Litho, Herrin** *Also called French Studio Ltd (G-11748)*
**Herris Group LLC** ....630 908-7393
7780 S Quincy St Willowbrook (60527) *(G-22214)*
**Herrmann Signs & Service** ....618 246-6537
12436 E Lakewood Dr Mount Vernon (62864) *(G-15412)*
**Herrmann Ultrasonics Inc** ....630 626-1626
1261 Hardt Cir Bartlett (60103) *(G-1352)*
**Herschberger Window Mfg** ....217 543-2106
623 N County Road 250 E Tuscola (61953) *(G-21021)*
**Herschberger Wood Working** ....217 543-4075
145 E Cr 300 N Arthur (61911) *(G-905)*
**Hershey Company** ....800 468-1714
1751 Lake Cook Rd Deerfield (60015) *(G-8011)*
**Hershey Company** ....618 544-3111
1401 W Main St Robinson (62454) *(G-18064)*
**Hershey Creamery Company** ....708 339-4656
601 W 167th St South Holland (60473) *(G-20276)*
**Hersheys Metal Meister, Claremont** *Also called Hersheys Metal Meister LLC (G-7256)*
**Hersheys Metal Meister LLC** ....217 234-4700
7405 E Mount Pleasant Ln Claremont (62421) *(G-7256)*
**Hertz Corporation** ....630 897-0956
1375 Bohr Ave Montgomery (60538) *(G-15046)*
**Hertzberg Ernst & Sons** ....773 525-3518
1751 W Belmont Ave Chicago (60657) *(G-5082)*
**Hess Machine Inc** ....618 887-4444
10724 Pocahontas Rd Marine (62061) *(G-14246)*
**Hester Cabinets & Millwork** ....815 634-4555
655 S Marguerite St Coal City (60416) *(G-7293)*
**Heuft Usa Inc** ....630 395-9521
2820 Thatcher Rd Downers Grove (60515) *(G-8457)*
**Hevco Industries** ....708 344-1342
1500 Dearborn Ave Ste 10 Aurora (60505) *(G-1169)*
**Hexacomb Corporation (HQ)** ....847 955-7984
1296 Barclay Blvd Buffalo Grove (60089) *(G-2704)*
**Hexagon Marketing, Chicago** *Also called Hexagon Metrology Inc (G-5083)*
**Hexagon Metrology Inc** ....312 624-8786
440 N Wells St Chicago (60654) *(G-5083)*
**Hexion Inc** ....708 728-8834
8600 W 71st St Bedford Park (60501) *(G-1554)*
**Hfa Inc** ....847 520-1000
135 E Hintz Rd Wheeling (60090) *(G-22069)*
**Hfd Graphics Equipment, Waukegan** *Also called Hfd Manufacturing Inc (G-21568)*
**Hfd Manufacturing Inc** ....847 263-5050
1813 W Glen Flora Ave Waukegan (60085) *(G-21568)*
**Hfo Chicago LLC** ....847 258-2850
555 Busse Rd Elk Grove Village (60007) *(G-9523)*
**Hfr Precision Machining Inc** ....630 556-4325
1015 Airpark Dr Sugar Grove (60554) *(G-20727)*
**Hg-Farley Laserlab USA Inc** ....815 874-1400
4635 Colt Rd Rockford (61109) *(G-18418)*
**Hgh Products, Godfrey** *Also called David L Knoche (G-11223)*
**HH Backer Associates Inc** ....312 578-1818
18 S Michigan Ave # 1100 Chicago (60603) *(G-5084)*
**HI Prcision TI Makers McHy Inc** ....630 694-0200
774 Foster Ave Bensenville (60106) *(G-1916)*
**HI Tech** ....708 957-4210
1551 187th St Homewood (60430) *(G-12100)*
**HI Tech Colorants** ....630 762-0368
5n634 Lostview Ln Saint Charles (60175) *(G-19192)*
**HI Tech Machining & Welding** ....708 331-3608
16120 Vincennes Ave South Holland (60473) *(G-20277)*
**HI Tek Tool & Machining Inc** ....847 836-6422
2413 W Algonquin Rd Algonquin (60102) *(G-392)*
**Hi-Cone Div, Charleston** *Also called Illinois Tool Works Inc (G-3599)*
**Hi-Cone Division, Itasca** *Also called Illinois Tool Works Inc (G-12282)*
**Hi-Def Communications** ....217 258-6679
3116 Pine Ave Mattoon (61938) *(G-14392)*
**Hi-Five Sportswear Inc** ....815 637-6044
7836 N 2nd St Machesney Park (61115) *(G-14079)*
**Hi-Grade Egg Producers, Loda** *Also called Midwest Poultry Services LP (G-13753)*
**Hi-Grade Welding & Mfg, Schaumburg** *Also called Hi-Grade Welding and Mfg LLC (G-19553)*
**Hi-Grade Welding and Mfg LLC** ....847 640-8172
140 Commerce Dr Schaumburg (60173) *(G-19553)*
**Hi-Perfrmnce Fastening Systems, Bensenville** *Also called Matthew Warren Inc (G-1946)*
**Hi-Tech Builidng Systems** ....847 526-5310
28613 N Jackson Ave Wauconda (60084) *(G-21468)*
**Hi-Tech Elctronic Pdts Mfg Inc** ....815 220-1543
25 Hi Tech Dr Oglesby (61348) *(G-16749)*
**Hi-Tech Manufacturing LLC (PA)** ....847 678-1616
9815 Leland Ave Schiller Park (60176) *(G-19836)*
**Hi-Tech Plastics Inc** ....847 577-1805
2074 Foster Ave 78 Wheeling (60090) *(G-22070)*
**Hi-Tech Polymers Inc** ....815 282-2272
7967 Crest Hills Dr Loves Park (61111) *(G-13946)*
**Hi-Tech Towers Inc** ....217 784-5212
496 N 600e Rd Gibson City (60936) *(G-10902)*
**Hi-Tech Welding Services Inc** ....630 595-8160
233 William St Bensenville (60106) *(G-1917)*
**Hiatt Brothers, De Kalb** *Also called E B Inc (G-7817)*
**Hickman Williams & Company** ....708 656-8818
1410 S 55th Ct Cicero (60804) *(G-7202)*
**Hickman Williams & Co, Cicero** *Also called Hickman Williams & Company (G-7202)*
**Hickman Williams & Company** ....630 574-2150
2015 Spring Rd Ste 715 Oak Brook (60523) *(G-16521)*
**Hickory Street Cabinets** ....618 667-9676
208 S Hickory St Troy (62294) *(G-21007)*
**Hicx Solutions Inc** ....630 560-3640
1 Tower Ln Ste 1700 Oakbrook Terrace (60181) *(G-16711)*
**Hidalgo Fine Cabinetry** ....630 753-9323
8952 Hanslik Ct Ste 22 Naperville (60564) *(G-15809)*
**Hidden Hollow Stables Inc** ....309 243-7979
9222 Brimfield Jubilee Rd Dunlap (61525) *(G-8567)*
**Hidden Lake Winery Ltd** ....618 228-9111
10580 Wellen Rd Aviston (62216) *(G-1244)*
**Hidrostal LLC** ....630 240-6271
2225 White Oak Cir Aurora (60502) *(G-1026)*
**Hidrostal Pumps, Aurora** *Also called Hidrostal LLC (G-1026)*
**HIG Chemicals Holdings** ....773 376-9000
4650 S Racine Ave Chicago (60609) *(G-5085)*
**Higgins Bros Inc** ....773 523-0124
1428 W 37th St Chicago (60609) *(G-5086)*
**Higgins Forms & Systems, Des Plaines** *Also called Higgins Quick Print (G-8204)*
**Higgins Glass Studio LLC** ....708 447-2787
33 E Quincy St Ste A Riverside (60546) *(G-18031)*
**Higgins Handcrafted Glass, Riverside** *Also called Higgins Glass Studio LLC (G-18031)*
**Higgins Quick Print** ....847 635-7700
2410 S River Rd Des Plaines (60018) *(G-8204)*
**Higgs Welding LLC** ....217 925-5999
101 Zumbahlen Ave Dieterich (62424) *(G-8313)*

ALPHABETIC SECTION
Hodgson Mill Inc

**High Impact Fabricating LLC**....708 235-8912
1149 Central Ave University Park (60484) ***(G-21052)***
**High Performance Entp Inc**....773 283-1778
3500 N Kostner Ave Chicago (60641) ***(G-5087)***
**High Performance Lubr LLC**....815 468-3535
500 S Spruce St Manteno (60950) ***(G-14185)***
**High Performance Packaging, Lakemoor** *Also called Competitive Edge Opportunities* ***(G-13143)***
**High Performance Uniforms, Chicago** *Also called High Performance Entp Inc* ***(G-5087)***
**High Point Recovery Company**....217 821-7777
603 County Road 500 E Toledo (62468) ***(G-20964)***
**High Speed Welding Inc**....630 971-8929
728 Vandustrial Dr Ste 5 Westmont (60559) ***(G-21891)***
**High Standard Fabricating Inc**....815 965-6517
3336 Seward Ave Rockford (61108) ***(G-18419)***
**High Tech Research Inc (PA)**....847 215-9797
1020 Milwaukee Ave # 330 Deerfield (60015) ***(G-8012)***
**High-5 Printwear Inc**....847 818-0081
3311 N Ridge Ave Arlington Heights (60004) ***(G-765)***
**High-Life Products Inc**....847 991-9449
615 W Colfax St Palatine (60067) ***(G-17036)***
**Highland Baking Company Inc**....847 677-2789
2301 Shermer Rd Northbrook (60062) ***(G-16270)***
**Highland Journal Printing Inc (PA)**....618 654-4131
1014 Laurel St Highland (62249) ***(G-11787)***
**Highland Mch & Screw Pdts Co**....618 654-2103
700 5th St Highland (62249) ***(G-11788)***
**Highland Metal Inc**....708 544-6641
541 Hyde Park Ave Hillside (60162) ***(G-11919)***
**Highland Mfg & Sls Co (PA)**....618 654-2161
1111 6th St Highland (62249) ***(G-11789)***
**Highland News Leader**....618 654-2366
1 Woodcrest Prof Park Highland (62249) ***(G-11790)***
**Highland Printers**....618 654-5880
907 Main St Stop 4 Highland (62249) ***(G-11791)***
**Highland Southern Wire Inc (PA)**....618 654-2161
1111 6th St Highland (62249) ***(G-11792)***
**Highland Spring & Specialty**....618 654-3831
150 Matter Dr Highland (62249) ***(G-11793)***
**Highland Supply, Highland** *Also called Highland Mfg & Sls Co* ***(G-11789)***
**Highland Supply, Highland** *Also called Highland Southern Wire Inc* ***(G-11792)***
**Highland Supply Corporation (PA)**....618 654-2161
1111 6th St Highland (62249) ***(G-11794)***
**Highland Wire Inc (PA)**....618 654-2161
1111 6th St Highland (62249) ***(G-11795)***
**Highlandnews Leader, Highland** *Also called McClatchy Newspapers Inc* ***(G-11802)***
**Higman LLC**....618 785-2545
609 W Myrtle St Baldwin (62217) ***(G-1251)***
**Hilander 00805, Rockford** *Also called Kroger Co* ***(G-18457)***
**Hildebrant J Boyd & Co Inc**....847 839-0850
1305 Remington Rd Schaumburg (60173) ***(G-19554)***
**Hill Design, McHenry** *Also called Accurate Spring Tech Inc* ***(G-14475)***
**Hill Design Products Inc**....815 344-3333
5801 W Hill St McHenry (60050) ***(G-14513)***
**Hill Engineering Inc**....630 315-5070
373 Randy Rd Carol Stream (60188) ***(G-3166)***
**Hill Holdings Inc**....815 625-6600
1602 Mcneil Rd Rock Falls (61071) ***(G-18135)***
**Hill Printing and Office Sup, Marion** *Also called Sigley Printing & Off Sup Co* ***(G-14287)***
**Hill Top Pallet**....618 426-9810
612 Bollman Rd Ava (62907) ***(G-1237)***
**Hill-Rom Holdings Inc (PA)**....312 819-7200
2 Prudential Plz Ste 4100 Chicago (60601) ***(G-5088)***
**Hillers Sheet Metal Works**....217 532-2595
150 N Oak St Hillsboro (62049) ***(G-11893)***
**Hilling Services Inc**....618 667-2005
546 Troy Ofallon Rd Troy (62294) ***(G-21008)***
**Hills Electric Motor Service**....815 625-0305
305 1st Ave Rock Falls (61071) ***(G-18136)***
**Hillsboro Energy LLC**....217 532-3983
925 S Main St Ste 2 Hillsboro (62049) ***(G-11894)***
**Hillsboro Journal Inc**....217 532-3933
431 S Main St Hillsboro (62049) ***(G-11895)***
**Hillshire Brands Company (HQ)**....312 614-6000
400 S Jefferson St Fl 1 Chicago (60607) ***(G-5089)***
**Hillshire Brands Company**....800 727-2533
600 Wiscold Dr Rochelle (61068) ***(G-18093)***
**Hillshire Brands Company**....847 956-7575
1325 Chase Ave Elk Grove Village (60007) ***(G-9524)***
**Hillshire Brands Company**....312 614-6000
400 S Jefferson St Fl 1 Chicago (60607) ***(G-5090)***
**Hillshire Brands Company**....847 310-9400
1355 Remington Rd Ste U Schaumburg (60173) ***(G-19555)***
**Hillshire Brands Company**....630 991-5100
3131 Woodcreek Dr Downers Grove (60515) ***(G-8458)***
**Hillside Industries Inc**....708 498-1100
1 Mth Plz Hillside (60162) ***(G-11920)***
**Hilltop Group Home, Dixon** *Also called Kreider Services Incorporated* ***(G-8336)***
**Hillyer Inc**....309 837-6434
1420 E Carroll St Macomb (61455) ***(G-14125)***
**Hillyer's U-Store-It, Macomb** *Also called Hillyer Inc* ***(G-14125)***
**Hilscher North America Inc**....630 505-5301
2525 Cabot Dr Ste 200 Lisle (60532) ***(G-13600)***
**Hilti Inc**....847 364-9818
135 W Diversey Ave Elmhurst (60126) ***(G-9882)***
**Hinckley & Schmitt Inc**....773 586-8600
6055 S Harlem Ave Chicago (60638) ***(G-5091)***
**Hinckley Concrete Products Co**....815 286-3235
540 W Lincoln Ave Hinckley (60520) ***(G-11935)***
**Hinckley Spring, Rockford** *Also called Ds Services of America Inc* ***(G-18352)***
**Hinckley Springs, Chicago** *Also called Hinckley & Schmitt Inc* ***(G-5091)***
**Hinckley Springs, Chicago** *Also called Ds Services of America Inc* ***(G-4645)***
**Hinckley Springs, Frankfort** *Also called Ds Services of America Inc* ***(G-10314)***
**Hinman Specialty Fuels**....847 868-6026
825 Elmwood Ave Evanston (60202) ***(G-10051)***
**Hinsdale Hospital, Westmont** *Also called Westmont Mri Center* ***(G-21927)***
**Hipro Manufacturing Inc**....815 432-5271
1909 E 1800 N Rd Watseka (60970) ***(G-21418)***
**Hipskind Tech Sltons Group Inc**....630 920-0960
17w220 22nd St Ste 450 Oakbrook Terrace (60181) ***(G-16712)***
**Hire-Nelson Company Inc**....630 543-9400
325 W Factory Rd Ste B Addison (60101) ***(G-146)***
**Hirise Promotions & Marketing, Chicago** *Also called Information Usa Inc* ***(G-5189)***
**Hirose Electric (usa) Inc (HQ)**....630 282-6700
2300 Warrenville Rd # 150 Downers Grove (60515) ***(G-8459)***
**His Company Inc**....847 885-2922
1601 Wilkening Rd Schaumburg (60173) ***(G-19556)***
**Hisco, Schaumburg** *Also called His Company Inc* ***(G-19556)***
**Historcal Genealogical Soc Mou, Sullivan** *Also called Moultri Cnty Hstrcl/Gnlgcl Sct* ***(G-20754)***
**Historic Timber & Plank Inc**....618 372-4546
16092 Lageman Ln Brighton (62012) ***(G-2542)***
**Hitachi Metals America LLC**....847 364-7200
85 W Algonquin Rd Ste 400 Arlington Heights (60005) ***(G-766)***
**Hites Hardwood Lumber Inc**....618 723-2136
364 E Il 250 Noble (62868) ***(G-16051)***
**Hiwood USA, Lake Zurich** *Also called Seshin USA Inc* ***(G-13130)***
**Hixsters Upper Deck**....815 745-2700
162 E Main St Warren (61087) ***(G-21335)***
**HK America Inc**....630 916-0200
1120 N Garfield St Lombard (60148) ***(G-13809)***
**HK Woodwork**....773 964-2468
925 Seton Ct Ste 7 Wheeling (60090) ***(G-22071)***
**Hl Metals LLC**....312 590-3360
910 Spruce St Winnetka (60093) ***(G-22307)***
**Hlh Associates**....773 646-5900
1701 E 122nd St Chicago (60633) ***(G-5092)***
**HM Manufacturing Inc**....847 487-8700
1200 Henri Dr Wauconda (60084) ***(G-21469)***
**HM Witt & Co**....773 250-5000
3313 W Newport Ave Chicago (60618) ***(G-5093)***
**HMC, Sugar Grove** *Also called Hy-Tek Manufacturing Co Inc* ***(G-20728)***
**HMC Holdings LLC (PA)**....847 541-5070
720 Dartmouth Ln Buffalo Grove (60089) ***(G-2705)***
**Hmg, Bolingbrook** *Also called 7000 Inc* ***(G-2275)***
**Hmh, Itasca** *Also called Houghton Mifflin Harcourt Co* ***(G-12275)***
**HMK Mattress Holdings LLC**....773 472-7390
3216 N Broadway St Chicago (60657) ***(G-5094)***
**HMK Mattress Holdings LLC**....847 798-8023
180 Barrington Rd Schaumburg (60194) ***(G-19557)***
**HMK Mattress Holdings LLC**....708 429-0704
15840 S Harlem Ave Orland Park (60462) ***(G-16865)***
**HMM Pallets Inc**....773 927-3448
3344 S Lawndale Ave Chicago (60623) ***(G-5095)***
**HMS Elevators, Downers Grove** *Also called Home Mobility Solutions Inc* ***(G-8461)***
**HMS Teach Inc**....800 624-2926
3150 W Higgins Rd Ste 140 Hoffman Estates (60169) ***(G-12016)***
**Hmshost Corporation**....847 678-2098
10201 Belle Plaine Ave Schiller Park (60176) ***(G-19837)***
**Hmt Manufacturing Inc**....847 473-2310
2323 Commonwealth Ave North Chicago (60064) ***(G-16182)***
**Hn Precision, Lake Bluff** *Also called Helio Precision Products Inc* ***(G-12848)***
**Hnrc Dissolution Co**....618 758-4501
12626 Sarah Rd Coulterville (62237) ***(G-7400)***
**HO-KA TURKEY FARM, Waterman** *Also called Kauffman Poultry Farms Inc* ***(G-21407)***
**Hobbico Inc**....217 367-2707
706 W Bradley Ave Urbana (61801) ***(G-21091)***
**Hobsource**....847 229-9120
834 E Rand Rd Ste 2 Mount Prospect (60056) ***(G-15335)***
**Hockey Warehouse, Alsip** *Also called Jerrys Pro Shop Inc* ***(G-476)***
**Hocking Oil Company Inc**....618 263-3258
123 W 4th St Ste 103 Mount Carmel (62863) ***(G-15267)***
**Hodgson Mill Inc**....217 347-0105
1100 Stevens Ave Effingham (62401) ***(G-8839)***

ALPHABETIC

**Hoeing Die & Mold Engraving** ..................................... 630 543-0006
   441 W Interstate Rd  Addison  (60101)  *(G-147)*
**Hoerbiger-Origa Corporation** ..................................... 800 283-1377
   100 W Lake Dr  Glendale Heights  (60139)  *(G-11030)*
**Hoerr Racing Products, Edwards** *Also called R/A Hoerr  Inc  (G-8784)*
**Hoffer Plastics Corporation** ..................................... 847 741-5740
   500 N Collins St  South Elgin  (60177)  *(G-20203)*
**Hoffman J&M Farm Holdings Inc** ..................................... 847 671-6280
   3999 25th Ave  Schiller Park  (60176)  *(G-19838)*
**Hoffman Nuclear Medicine Group, Hoffman Estates** *Also called Siemens Med Solutions USA Inc  (G-12053)*
**Hoffman Tool  Inc** ..................................... 815 692-4643
   1301 W Oak St  Fairbury  (61739)  *(G-10125)*
**Hoffman Tool & Die  Inc** ..................................... 815 692-2628
   1303 W Oak St  Fairbury  (61739)  *(G-10126)*
**Hofhaus, Chicago** *Also called John Hofmeister & Son  Inc  (G-5314)*
**Hofmeister Wldg & Fabrication** ..................................... 217 833-2451
   402 N Wall St  Griggsville  (62340)  *(G-11412)*
**Hogan Woodwork Inc** ..................................... 708 354-4525
   5328 East Ave  Countryside  (60525)  *(G-7429)*
**Hogback Hardwoods, Orangeville** *Also called Hogback Haven Maple Farm  (G-16815)*
**Hogback Haven Maple Farm** ..................................... 815 291-9440
   13800 N Hogback Rd  Orangeville  (61060)  *(G-16815)*
**Hogg Hollow Winery LLC** ..................................... 618 695-9463
   48 E Glendale Rd  Golconda  (62938)  *(G-11239)*
**Hogg Welding Inc** ..................................... 708 339-0033
   16201 Clinton St  Harvey  (60426)  *(G-11670)*
**Hohlfder A H Shtmtl Htg Coolg** ..................................... 815 965-9134
   2911 Prairie Rd  Rockford  (61102)  *(G-18420)*
**Hohmann & Barnard Illinois LLC** ..................................... 773 586-6700
   9999 Virginia Ave  Chicago Ridge  (60415)  *(G-7150)*
**Hoist Liftruck Mfg  Inc (PA)** ..................................... 708 458-2200
   6499 W 65th St  Bedford Park  (60638)  *(G-1555)*
**Hoku Solar Power I  LLC** ..................................... 312 803-4972
   125 S Clark St Fl 17  Chicago  (60603)  *(G-5096)*
**Holbrook Mfg  Inc** ..................................... 847 229-1999
   288 Holbrook Dr  Wheeling  (60090)  *(G-22072)*
**Holcim (us)  Inc** ..................................... 773 721-8352
   3221 E 95th St  Chicago  (60617)  *(G-5097)*
**Holcim (us) Inc** ..................................... 773 731-1320
   3020 E 103rd St  Chicago  (60617)  *(G-5098)*
**Holden Industries  Inc (PA)** ..................................... 847 940-1500
   500 Lake Cook Rd Ste 400  Deerfield  (60015)  *(G-8013)*
**Holder Publishing Corporation** ..................................... 309 828-7533
   25 Monarch Dr  Bloomington  (61704)  *(G-2179)*
**Hole In The Wall Screen Arts** ..................................... 217 243-9100
   112 Park St  Jacksonville  (62650)  *(G-12391)*
**Holiday Bright Lights  Inc (PA)** ..................................... 312 226-8281
   954 W Wa Blvd Ste 705  Chicago  (60607)  *(G-5099)*
**Holiday Gift Check Program, Downers Grove** *Also called Gift Check Program 2013 Inc  (G-8450)*
**Holidynamics, Chicago** *Also called Holiday Bright Lights  Inc  (G-5099)*
**Holland  LP (HQ)** ..................................... 708 672-2300
   1000 Holland Dr  Crete  (60417)  *(G-7515)*
**Holland Applied Technologies (HQ)** ..................................... 630 325-5130
   7050 High Grove Blvd  Burr Ridge  (60527)  *(G-2851)*
**Holland Design Group Inc** ..................................... 847 526-8848
   1090 Brown St  Wauconda  (60084)  *(G-21470)*
**Holland Laboratories, Peoria** *Also called Holland Specialty Co  (G-17383)*
**Holland Manufacturing Corp** ..................................... 708 849-1000
   13901 Indiana Ave  Dolton  (60419)  *(G-8371)*
**Holland Printing Inc** ..................................... 708 596-9000
   922 E 162nd St  South Holland  (60473)  *(G-20278)*
**Holland Safety Equipment  Inc** ..................................... 847 680-9930
   726 Mckinley Ave  Libertyville  (60048)  *(G-13332)*
**Holland Specialty Co** ..................................... 309 697-9262
   4611 W Middle Rd  Peoria  (61605)  *(G-17383)*
**Holland Specialty Vehicles, Crete** *Also called Holland  LP  (G-7515)*
**Hollingsworth & Vose Company** ..................................... 847 222-9228
   4256 N Arlington Hts Rd  Arlington Heights  (60004)  *(G-767)*
**Hollingworth Candies Inc** ..................................... 815 838-2275
   926 N State St  Lockport  (60441)  *(G-13721)*
**Hollister Incorporated (PA)** ..................................... 847 680-1000
   2000 Hollister Dr  Libertyville  (60048)  *(G-13333)*
**Hollister Wound Care LLC** ..................................... 847 996-6000
   1580 S Milwaukee Ave # 405  Libertyville  (60048)  *(G-13334)*
**Hollister-Whitney Elev Corp** ..................................... 217 222-0466
   2603 N 24th St  Quincy  (62305)  *(G-17836)*
**Holly Press, The, Grayslake** *Also called Dandelion Distributors Inc  (G-11332)*
**Hollymatic Corporation** ..................................... 708 579-3700
   600 E Plainfield Rd  Countryside  (60525)  *(G-7430)*
**Hollywood International Co** ..................................... 708 926-9437
   13636 Western Ave  Blue Island  (60406)  *(G-2256)*
**Hollywood Tools  LLC** ..................................... 773 793-3119
   1455 Marshview Ct Ste 8  West Chicago  (60185)  *(G-21715)*
**Holm Industries** ..................................... 309 343-3332
   611 S Linwood Rd  Galesburg  (61401)  *(G-10759)*
**Holmes Associates Inc** ..................................... 847 336-4515
   4949 Grand Ave Ste 2  Gurnee  (60031)  *(G-11460)*
**Holmes Bros  Inc** ..................................... 217 442-1430
   510 Junction St  Danville  (61832)  *(G-7732)*
**Hologram, Chicago** *Also called Konekt Inc  (G-5403)*
**Holshouser Machine & Tool Inc** ..................................... 618 451-0164
   35 Central Industrial Dr  Granite City  (62040)  *(G-11286)*
**Holsolutions Inc** ..................................... 888 847-5467
   21200 S La Grange Rd # 119  Frankfort  (60423)  *(G-10327)*
**Holstein Garage Inc** ..................................... 630 668-0328
   309 W Front St  Wheaton  (60187)  *(G-21952)*
**Holt Building, Newton** *Also called Jesse B Holt  Inc  (G-15942)*
**Holt Publications Inc** ..................................... 618 654-6206
   12047 Travis Ln  Highland  (62249)  *(G-11796)*
**Holten Meat  Inc** ..................................... 618 337-8400
   1682 Sauget Business Blvd  Sauget  (62206)  *(G-19386)*
**Holton Food Products Company** ..................................... 708 352-5599
   500 W Burlington Ave  La Grange  (60525)  *(G-12736)*
**Holy Cow Sports Incorporated** ..................................... 630 852-9001
   5004 Chase Ave  Downers Grove  (60515)  *(G-8460)*
**Holy Hill Gourmet, Chicago** *Also called Chicago Candle Company  (G-4309)*
**Homan Bindery** ..................................... 773 276-1500
   1112 N Homan Ave  Chicago  (60651)  *(G-5100)*
**Home & Leisure Lifestyles LLC** ..................................... 618 651-0358
   907 Washington St  Highland  (62249)  *(G-11797)*
**Home City Ice (PA)** ..................................... 773 622-9400
   2248 N Natchez Ave  Chicago  (60707)  *(G-5101)*
**Home City Ice Company** ..................................... 217 877-7733
   2304 N Martn Lthr Kng Jr  Decatur  (62526)  *(G-7889)*
**Home Cut Donuts Inc** ..................................... 815 726-2132
   1317 E Washington St  Joliet  (60433)  *(G-12511)*
**Home Design Alternatives  Inc (PA)** ..................................... 314 731-1427
   1325 Remington Rd Ste H  Schaumburg  (60173)  *(G-19558)*
**Home Fires Inc** ..................................... 815 967-4100
   1100 11th St  Rockford  (61104)  *(G-18421)*
**Home For All Heros Nfp** ..................................... 309 808-2789
   101 Mapehill Dr  Bloomington  (61701)  *(G-2180)*
**Home Ice, Decatur** *Also called Home City Ice Company  (G-7889)*
**Home Juice Co of Memphis, Melrose Park** *Also called H J M P Corp  (G-14650)*
**Home Juice Corp** ..................................... 708 681-2678
   1930 George St Ste 2  Melrose Park  (60160)  *(G-14654)*
**Home Mobility Solutions Inc** ..................................... 630 800-7800
   5239 Thatcher Rd  Downers Grove  (60515)  *(G-8461)*
**Home Owners Bargain Outlet, Waukegan** *Also called Oak Creek Distribution LLC  (G-21596)*
**Home Pages, Dekalb** *Also called American Marketing & Pubg LLC  (G-8074)*
**Home Pdts Intl - N Amer Inc (HQ)** ..................................... 773 890-1010
   4501 W 47th St  Chicago  (60632)  *(G-5102)*
**Home Run Inn Frozen Foods Corp** ..................................... 630 783-9696
   1300 Internationale Pkwy  Woodridge  (60517)  *(G-22494)*
**Home School Enrichment  Inc** ..................................... 309 347-1392
   124 Thrush Ave  Pekin  (61554)  *(G-17267)*
**Home Shopper Publishing** ..................................... 309 742-2521
   208 E Hawthorne St Unit A  Elmwood  (61529)  *(G-9963)*
**Home Specialty Connection Inc** ..................................... 815 363-1934
   4955 N Damen Ave Apt 1r  Chicago  (60625)  *(G-5103)*
**Home Style** ..................................... 847 455-5000
   11125 Franklin Ave  Franklin Park  (60131)  *(G-10487)*
**Home Water Products, Peru** *Also called William N Pasulka  (G-17532)*
**Home World Business, Lincolnshire** *Also called Icd Publications Inc  (G-13456)*
**Homecontrolplus Incorporated** ..................................... 847 823-8414
   1884 Fenton Ln  Park Ridge  (60068)  *(G-17202)*
**Homefire Hearth Inc** ..................................... 815 997-1123
   3815 Marsh Ave  Rockford  (61114)  *(G-18422)*
**Homeland** ..................................... 708 415-4555
   13910 S Mormann Ln  Homer Glen  (60491)  *(G-12081)*
**Homer Township Vision Center, Lockport** *Also called Reding Optics Inc  (G-13741)*
**Homer Vintage Bakery** ..................................... 217 896-2538
   111 S Main St  Homer  (61849)  *(G-12075)*
**Homers Ice Cream  Inc** ..................................... 847 251-0477
   1237 Green Bay Rd  Wilmette  (60091)  *(G-22254)*
**Homers Rest & Ice Cream Parlor, Wilmette** *Also called Homers Ice Cream  Inc  (G-22254)*
**Hometown Hangout LLC** ..................................... 309 639-2108
   106 S State Route 180  Williamsfield  (61489)  *(G-22189)*
**Hometown News Group LP** ..................................... 815 246-4600
   107 W Railroad St  Earlville  (60518)  *(G-8595)*
**Hometown Phone Book, Collinsville** *Also called Eagle Publications Inc  (G-7321)*
**Homeway Homes  Inc** ..................................... 309 965-2312
   100 Homeway Ct  Deer Creek  (61733)  *(G-7964)*
**Homewerks Worldwide  LLC** ..................................... 877 319-3757
   55 Albrecht Dr  Lake Bluff  (60044)  *(G-12849)*
**Homewood-Flossmoor Chronicle** ..................................... 630 728-2661
   1361 Olive Rd  Homewood  (60430)  *(G-12101)*
**Homnay Magazine** ..................................... 773 334-6655
   1114 W Argyle St  Chicago  (60640)  *(G-5104)*
**Honey Bear Ham** ..................................... 312 942-1160
   1160 W Grand Ave Ste 1  Chicago  (60642)  *(G-5105)*
**Honey Fluff Doughnuts** ..................................... 708 579-1826
   6566 Joliet Rd  Countryside  (60525)  *(G-7431)*
**Honey Foods  Inc** ..................................... 847 928-9300
   4028 Tugwell St  Franklin Park  (60131)  *(G-10488)*

**Honeywell, Alsip** *Also called Prestone Products Corporation* ***(G-513)***
**Honeywell** ....815 235-5500
315 E Stephenson St Freeport (61032) ***(G-10663)***
**Honeywell Analytics Inc (HQ)** ....847 955-8200
405 Barclay Blvd Lincolnshire (60069) ***(G-13454)***
**Honeywell International Inc** ....815 235-5500
315 E Stephenson St Freeport (61032) ***(G-10664)***
**Honeywell International Inc** ....618 524-2111
2768 N Us Hwy 45 N Metropolis (62960) ***(G-14754)***
**Honeywell International Inc** ....630 960-5282
7714 Baker Ct Darien (60561) ***(G-7796)***
**Honeywell International Inc** ....630 922-0138
4412 Buttermilk Ct Naperville (60564) ***(G-15810)***
**Honeywell International Inc** ....630 554-5342
637 Salem Cir Oswego (60543) ***(G-16921)***
**Honeywell International Inc** ....847 797-4000
1460 1500 W Dundee Rd Arlington Heights (60004) ***(G-768)***
**Honeywell International Inc** ....815 235-5500
315 E Stephenson St Freeport (61032) ***(G-10665)***
**Honeywell International Inc** ....618 940-0401
704 E 5th St Metropolis (62960) ***(G-14755)***
**Honeywell International Inc** ....480 353-3020
1 Bank One Plz Chicago (60670) ***(G-5106)***
**Honeywell International Inc** ....847 701-3038
407 N Quentin Rd Palatine (60067) ***(G-17037)***
**Honeywell International Inc** ....847 391-2000
25 E Algonquin Rd Des Plaines (60016) ***(G-8205)***
**Honeywell International Inc** ....815 777-2780
11309 W Chetlain Ln Galena (61036) ***(G-10726)***
**Honeywell International Inc** ....630 377-6580
3825 Ohio Ave Saint Charles (60174) ***(G-19193)***
**Honeywell International Inc** ....973 455-2000
24004 Network Pl Chicago (60673) ***(G-5107)***
**Honeywell International Inc** ....309 383-4045
539 Justa Rd Metamora (61548) ***(G-14742)***
**Honeywell International Inc** ....
209 Brewer Rd Danville (61834) ***(G-7733)***
**Honeywell International Inc** ....217 431-3710
3401 Lynch Creek Dr Danville (61834) ***(G-7734)***
**Honeywell Safety Pdts USA Inc** ....309 786-7741
101 13th Ave Rock Island (61201) ***(G-18182)***
**Honeywell UOP, Des Plaines** *Also called UOP LLC* ***(G-8292)***
**Hong Kong Market, Chicago** *Also called Hop Kee Incorporated* ***(G-5109)***
**Hong Kong Market Chicago Inc** ....312 791-9111
2425 S Wallace St Chicago (60616) ***(G-5108)***
**Honor Med Maskiner Corp** ....847 741-9400
600 Church Rd Elgin (60123) ***(G-9066)***
**Hontech International Corp** ....847 364-9800
1000 Lee St Elk Grove Village (60007) ***(G-9525)***
**Hoogwegt US Inc** ....847 918-8787
100 Saunders Rd Ste 200 Lake Forest (60045) ***(G-12905)***
**Hooker Custom Harness Inc** ....815 233-5478
324 E Stephenson St Freeport (61032) ***(G-10666)***
**Hooker Harness, Freeport** *Also called Hooker Custom Harness Inc* ***(G-10666)***
**Hookset Enterprises LLC** ....224 374-1936
710 Landwehr Rd Ste B Northbrook (60062) ***(G-16271)***
**Hoopeston Foods, Hoopeston** *Also called Teasdale Foods Inc* ***(G-12118)***
**Hooray Puree Inc** ....312 515-0266
310 Busse Hwy Ste 322 Park Ridge (60068) ***(G-17203)***
**Hoosier Precast LLC** ....815 459-4545
2220 Il Route 176 Crystal Lake (60014) ***(G-7588)***
**Hoosier Stamping & Mfg Corp** ....812 426-2778
399 Industrial Park Dr Grayville (62844) ***(G-11370)***
**Hoosier Stamping & Mfg Corp** ....618 375-2057
832 W Spring St Grayville (62844) ***(G-11371)***
**Hop Kee Incorporated (PA)** ....312 791-9111
2425 S Wallace St Chicago (60616) ***(G-5109)***
**Hopcroft Electric Inc** ....618 288-7302
606 Glen Crossing Rd Glen Carbon (62034) ***(G-10952)***
**Hope Pallet Inc** ....815 412-4606
936 Moen Ave Ste 16 Rockdale (60436) ***(G-18220)***
**Hope Publishing Company** ....630 665-3200
380 S Main Pl Carol Stream (60188) ***(G-3167)***
**Hopkins Grease Company, Lake In The Hills** *Also called MW Hopkins & Sons Inc* ***(G-13000)***
**Hopkins Machine Corporation** ....773 772-2800
4243 W Diversey Ave Chicago (60639) ***(G-5110)***
**Hopkins Printing & Envelope Co** ....630 543-8227
120 W Laura Dr Addison (60101) ***(G-148)***
**Hopkins Saws & Cart, Belle Rive** *Also called Hopkins Saws & Karts Inc* ***(G-1605)***
**Hopkins Saws & Karts Inc** ....618 756-2778
9398 N Markham Ln Belle Rive (62810) ***(G-1605)***
**Hopper Graphics Inc** ....708 489-0459
6106 W 127th St Palos Heights (60463) ***(G-17107)***
**Hopper Trailer Sales & Service, Jacksonville** *Also called Hanna Hopper Trlr Sls & Rv Ctr* ***(G-12390)***
**Hopperstad Customs** ....815 547-7534
6860 Imron Dr Belvidere (61008) ***(G-1762)***
**Horan Glass Block Inc** ....773 586-4808
6742 W Archer Ave Chicago (60638) ***(G-5111)***
**Horizon Die Company Inc** ....847 426-8558
160 Windsor Dr East Dundee (60118) ***(G-8643)***
**Horizon Displays, LLC, Dekalb** *Also called Horizon Downing LLC* ***(G-8097)***
**Horizon Downing LLC** ....815 758-6867
1115 E Locust St Dekalb (60115) ***(G-8097)***
**Horizon Fuel Cell Americas** ....312 316-8050
18 S Michigan Ave # 1200 Chicago (60603) ***(G-5112)***
**Horizon Graphics** ....309 699-4287
222 Meadow Ave East Peoria (61611) ***(G-8712)***
**Horizon Metals, Chicago** *Also called Monett Metals Inc* ***(G-5794)***
**Horizon Metals Inc** ....773 478-8888
3925 N Pulaski Rd Chicago (60641) ***(G-5113)***
**Horizon Pharma Inc (HQ)** ....224 383-3000
150 Saunders Rd Ste 400 Lake Forest (60045) ***(G-12906)***
**Horizon Publications Inc (PA)** ....618 993-1711
1120 N Carbon St Ste 100 Marion (62959) ***(G-14265)***
**Horizon Publications (2003) (PA)** ....618 993-1711
1120 N Carbon St Ste 100 Marion (62959) ***(G-14266)***
**Horizon Sperfinishing Grinding, Rosemont** *Also called Custom Superfinishing Grinding* ***(G-18997)***
**Horizon Steel Treating Inc** ....847 639-4030
231 Jandus Rd Cary (60013) ***(G-3351)***
**Horizon Therapeutics Inc** ....224 383-3000
150 Saunders Rd Ste 150 Lake Forest (60045) ***(G-12907)***
**Horizon, The, Marion** *Also called Review* ***(G-14285)***
**Horizontal Systems Inc** ....217 932-6218
14305 N State Highway 49 Casey (62420) ***(G-3385)***
**Hormann LLC (HQ)** ....877 654-6762
5050 Baseline Rd Montgomery (60538) ***(G-15047)***
**Hormann LLC** ....630 859-3000
5050 Baseline Rd Montgomery (60538) ***(G-15048)***
**Horse Creek Outfitters** ....217 544-2740
600 S Dirksen Pkwy 600a Springfield (62703) ***(G-20452)***
**Horsehead Corporation** ....773 933-9260
2701 E 114th St Chicago (60617) ***(G-5114)***
**Horween Leather Company** ....773 772-2026
2015 N Elston Ave Ste 1 Chicago (60614) ***(G-5115)***
**Hospira Inc (HQ)** ....224 212-2000
275 N Field Dr Lake Forest (60045) ***(G-12908)***
**Hospira Inc** ....224 212-6244
375 N Field Dr Bldg H3 Lake Forest (60045) ***(G-12909)***
**Hospira Worldwide LLC (HQ)** ....224 212-2000
275 N Field Dr Lake Forest (60045) ***(G-12910)***
**Hospital & Physician Pubg** ....618 997-9375
6116 N Chamnesstown Rd Marion (62959) ***(G-14267)***
**Hospital Hlth Care Systems Inc (PA)** ....708 863-3400
7830 47th St Ste 1 Lyons (60534) ***(G-14041)***
**Hospital Labels Co Div, Chicago** *Also called Labels Unlimited Incorporated* ***(G-5430)***
**Hospital Physician, Marion** *Also called Hospital & Physician Pubg* ***(G-14267)***
**Hospital Therapy Products Inc** ....630 766-7101
757 N Central Ave Wood Dale (60191) ***(G-22379)***
**Hospitology Products LLC** ....630 359-5075
131 S Lombard Rd Addison (60101) ***(G-149)***
**Hostforweb Incorporated** ....312 343-4678
7061 N Kedzie Ave Ste 302 Chicago (60645) ***(G-5116)***
**Hostmann Steinberg Inc (HQ)** ....502 968-5961
2850 Festival Dr Kankakee (60901) ***(G-12622)***
**Hostmann Steinberg Inc** ....815 401-5493
4 Windsor Ct Bourbonnais (60914) ***(G-2399)***
**Hot Food Boxes Inc** ....773 533-5912
4109 W Lake St Chicago (60624) ***(G-5117)***
**Hot Mexican Peppers Inc** ....773 843-9774
2215 W 47th St Chicago (60609) ***(G-5118)***
**Hot Rod Chassis & Cycle Inc** ....630 458-0808
59 W Factory Rd Addison (60101) ***(G-150)***
**Hot Shots Nm LLC** ....815 484-0500
4330 Charles St Rockford (61108) ***(G-18423)***
**Hotel Amerika** ....219 508-9418
434 W Briar Pl Apt 4 Chicago (60657) ***(G-5119)***
**Hottenrott Company Inc** ....618 473-2531
351 S Main St Hecker (62248) ***(G-11732)***
**Hottinger Bldwin Msrements Inc** ....217 328-5359
1806 Fox Dr Ste A Champaign (61820) ***(G-3495)***
**Hotvapes Ltd** ....775 468-8273
7240 N Milwaukee Ave Chicago (60647) ***(G-5120)***
**Hough General Homes, Hillsboro** *Also called Elite Monument Co* ***(G-11889)***
**Houghton International Inc** ....610 666-4000
6600 S Nashville Ave Chicago (60638) ***(G-5121)***
**Houghton Mifflin Harcourt** ....928 467-9599
1900 S Batavia Ave Geneva (60134) ***(G-10832)***
**Houghton Mifflin Harcourt Co** ....630 467-6049
761 District Dr Itasca (60143) ***(G-12275)***
**Houghton Mifflin Harcourt Pubg** ....630 208-5704
1900 S Batavia Ave Geneva (60134) ***(G-10833)***
**Houghton Mifflin Harcourt Pubg** ....630 467-6095
425 Spring Lake Dr Itasca (60143) ***(G-12276)***
**Houghton Mifflin Harcourt Pubg** ....847 869-2300
909 Davis St Ste 300 Evanston (60201) ***(G-10052)***

ALPHABETIC

**Houghton Mifflin Harcourt Pubg**...708 869-2300
1560 Sherman Ave Evanston (60201) **(G-10053)**
**Houpt Revolving Cutters Inc**...618 395-1913
516 W Butler St Olney (62450) **(G-16771)**
**House Granite & Marble Corp**...847 928-1111
5136 Pearl St Schiller Park (60176) **(G-19839)**
**House of Atlas LLC**...847 491-1800
1578 Sherman Ave Fl 2 Evanston (60201) **(G-10054)**
**House of Color**...708 352-3222
9912 W 55th St Countryside (60525) **(G-7432)**
**House of Doolittle Ltd (PA)**...847 593-3417
3001 Malmo Dr Arlington Heights (60005) **(G-769)**
**House of Graphics**...630 682-0810
370 Randy Rd Carol Stream (60188) **(G-3168)**
**House of Rattan Inc (PA)**...630 627-8160
18w375 Roosevelt Rd Lombard (60148) **(G-13810)**
**House On The Hill Inc**...630 279-4455
2206 N Main St Wheaton (60187) **(G-21953)**
**Houser Meats**...217 322-4994
14320 Scotts Mill Rd Rushville (62681) **(G-19092)**
**Hovi Industries Incorporated (PA)**...815 512-7500
380 Veterans Pkwy Ste 110 Bolingbrook (60440) **(G-2316)**
**Howard Displays Inc**...
844 Auburn Ct Highland Park (60035) **(G-11841)**
**Howard Energy Corporation**...618 263-3000
519 W 3rd St Mount Carmel (62863) **(G-15268)**
**Howard Medical Company**...773 278-1440
1690 N Elston Ave Chicago (60642) **(G-5122)**
**Howard Pet Products Inc**...973 398-3038
425 38th Ave Saint Charles (60174) **(G-19194)**
**Howard Press Printing Inc**...708 345-7437
303 E North Ave Lowr 100 Northlake (60164) **(G-16439)**
**Howard Sportswear Graphics**...847 695-8195
1421 Holmes Rd 1433 Elgin (60123) **(G-9067)**
**Howe Corporation**...773 235-0200
1650 N Elston Ave Chicago (60642) **(G-5123)**
**Howell Asphalt Company (PA)**...217 234-8877
1020 N 13th St Mattoon (61938) **(G-14393)**
**Howell Paving, Mattoon** *Also called Howell Asphalt Company* **(G-14393)**
**Howell Welding Corporation**...630 616-1100
1071 Waveland Ave Franklin Park (60131) **(G-10489)**
**Howland Technology Inc**...847 965-9808
8129 Austin Ave Morton Grove (60053) **(G-15200)**
**Howler Fabrication & Wldg Inc**...630 293-9300
1100 Carolina Dr West Chicago (60185) **(G-21716)**
**Howmedica Osteonics Corp**...309 663-6414
7 Westport Ct Bloomington (61704) **(G-2181)**
**Howw Manufacturing Company Inc**...847 382-4380
28020 W Commercial Ave Lake Barrington (60010) **(G-12809)**
**Hoya Corporation**...618 281-3344
301 Vision Dr Columbia (62236) **(G-7358)**
**Hoya Lens of Chicago Inc**...847 678-4700
3531 Martens St Franklin Park (60131) **(G-10490)**
**Hoya Vision Care, Franklin Park** *Also called Hoya Lens of Chicago Inc* **(G-10490)**
**Hoya Vision Care, Columbia** *Also called Hoya Corporation* **(G-7358)**
**HP Inc**...847 342-2000
25 Northwest Point Blvd Elk Grove Village (60007) **(G-9526)**
**HP Inc**...847 207-9118
1935 S Plum Grove Rd # 199 Palatine (60067) **(G-17038)**
**HP Interactive Inc**...773 681-4440
2461 W Balmoral Ave Chicago (60625) **(G-5124)**
**HP2000 APU, Marion** *Also called Parks Industries LLC* **(G-14276)**
**Hpc Automation, Chicago** *Also called Hackett Precision Company Inc* **(G-5027)**
**Hpc of Pennsylvania Inc**...618 993-1711
1120 N Carbon St Ste 100 Marion (62959) **(G-14268)**
**Hpd LLC**...815 436-3013
23563 W Main St Plainfield (60544) **(G-17606)**
**HPD Evporation Crystallization, Plainfield** *Also called Hpd LLC* **(G-17606)**
**Hpfs, Bensenville** *Also called Lre Products Inc* **(G-1942)**
**Hpl Stampings Inc (PA)**...847 540-1400
425 Enterprise Pkwy Lake Zurich (60047) **(G-13084)**
**HPp Precision Machine Co Inc**...815 469-2608
22829 S Mustang Rd Frankfort (60423) **(G-10328)**
**Hq Printers Inc**...312 782-2020
200 N La Salle St Lbby 2 Chicago (60601) **(G-5125)**
**Hqf Manufacturing, East Dundee** *Also called Peter Fox* **(G-8652)**
**HRB America Corporation**...630 513-1800
3485 Swenson Ave Saint Charles (60174) **(G-19195)**
**Hs Technology Inc**...630 572-7650
900 Jorie Blvd Ste 195 Oak Brook (60523) **(G-16522)**
**Hsa, Arlington Heights** *Also called Hearing Screening Assoc LLC* **(G-763)**
**Hsa Chicago Office, Schaumburg** *Also called Sk Hynix America Inc* **(G-19729)**
**Hst Materials Inc**...847 640-1803
1631 Brummel Ave Elk Grove Village (60007) **(G-9527)**
**Hts Chicago Inc**...630 352-3690
107 W Willow Ave Wheaton (60187) **(G-21954)**
**Hts Hancock Transcriptions Svc (PA)**...217 379-9241
136 S Market St Paxton (60957) **(G-17237)**
**Hu-Friedy Mfg Co LLC (PA)**...773 975-3975
3232 N Rockwell St Chicago (60618) **(G-5126)**
**Hu-Friedy Mfg Co LLC**...847 257-4500
1666 E Touhy Ave Des Plaines (60018) **(G-8206)**
**Hub Manufacturing Company Inc**...773 252-1373
1212 N Central Park Ave Chicago (60651) **(G-5127)**
**Hub Printing & Office Supplies, Rochelle** *Also called Hub Printing Company Inc* **(G-18094)**
**Hub Printing Company Inc**...815 562-7057
101 Maple Ave Rochelle (61068) **(G-18094)**
**Hub Stamping & Mfg Co, Chicago** *Also called Hub Manufacturing Company Inc* **(G-5127)**
**Hubbard One, Chicago** *Also called Thomson Reuters (legal) Inc* **(G-6718)**
**Hubbell Incorporated**...972 756-1184
1455 Sequoia Dr Ste 113 Aurora (60506) **(G-1170)**
**Hubbell Power Systems Inc**...618 797-5000
131 Enterprise Dr Edwardsville (62025) **(G-8803)**
**Hubbell Power Systems Inc**...618 797-5000
131 Enterprise Dr Edwardsville (62025) **(G-8804)**
**Hubbell Wiegmann Inc**...618 539-3542
501 W Apple St Freeburg (62243) **(G-10637)**
**Huber Carbonates LLC**...217 224-8737
3150 Gardner Expy Quincy (62305) **(G-17837)**
**Hubergroup Usa Inc (HQ)**...815 929-9293
2850 Festival Dr Kankakee (60901) **(G-12623)**
**Hucks Food Fuel**...618 286-5111
110 S Main St Dupo (62239) **(G-8571)**
**Hudapack Mtal Treating Ill Inc**...630 793-1916
550 Mitchell Rd Glendale Heights (60139) **(G-11031)**
**Huddlestun Creamery Inc**...815 609-1893
1153 Brookforest Ave Joliet (60404) **(G-12512)**
**Hudson Boiler & Tank Company**...312 666-4780
3101 S State St Lockport (60441) **(G-13722)**
**Hudson Color Concentrates, Niles** *Also called Midwest Color* **(G-16007)**
**Hudson Technologies Inc**...217 373-1414
3402 N Mattis Ave Champaign (61822) **(G-3496)**
**Hudson Tool & Die Co**...847 678-8710
3845 Carnation St Franklin Park (60131) **(G-10491)**
**Hue Circle Inc**...224 567-8116
4315 Regency Dr Glenview (60025) **(G-11138)**
**Hueber LLC (PA)**...815 393-4879
110 S Main St Creston (60113) **(G-7472)**
**Huels Oil Company**...877 338-6277
16320 Old Us Highway 50 Carlyle (62231) **(G-3054)**
**Huestis Medical, Gilberts** *Also called Huestis Pro-Tronics Inc* **(G-10922)**
**Huestis Pro-Tronics Inc**...847 426-1055
106 Industrial Dr Gilberts (60136) **(G-10922)**
**Huetone Imprints Inc**...630 694-9610
90 N Lively Blvd Elk Grove Village (60007) **(G-9528)**
**Huff & Puff Industries Ltd**...847 381-8255
125 Arrowhead Ln North Barrington (60010) **(G-16152)**
**Hugh Courtright & Co Ltd**...708 534-8400
26749 S Governors Hwy Monee (60449) **(G-14997)**
**Hughes & Son Inc**...815 459-1887
652 W Terra Cotta Ave Crystal Lake (60014) **(G-7589)**
**Hughes Sign Co, Crystal Lake** *Also called Hughes & Son Inc* **(G-7589)**
**Hugo Boss Usa Inc**...847 517-1461
5 Woodfield Mall Schaumburg (60173) **(G-19559)**
**Hulse Excavating**...815 796-4106
20289 N 400 East Rd Flanagan (61740) **(G-10194)**
**Humaginarium LLC**...312 788-7719
325 S Grove Ave Oak Park (60302) **(G-16669)**
**Human Factor RES Group Inc**...618 476-3200
609 Suth Brese St Ste 101 Millstadt (62260) **(G-14826)**
**Human Svc Ctr Southern Metro E (PA)**...618 282-6233
10257 State Route 3 Red Bud (62278) **(G-17942)**
**Humboldt Broom Company**...217 268-3718
901 E County Road 300n Arcola (61910) **(G-671)**
**Humboldt Mfg Co (PA)**...708 456-6300
875 Tollgate Rd Elgin (60123) **(G-9068)**
**Humid-A-Mist, New Lenox** *Also called Galmar Enterprises Inc* **(G-15883)**
**Humidity 2 Optimization LLC**...847 991-7488
105 Prairie Lake Rd Ste D East Dundee (60118) **(G-8644)**
**Huml Industries Inc**...847 426-8061
78 E End Dr Gilberts (60136) **(G-10923)**
**Humpsman, Peru** *Also called Nova Chemicals Inc* **(G-17523)**
**Hunt Enterprises Inc**...708 354-8464
5542 S La Grange Rd Countryside (60525) **(G-7433)**
**Hunt Foods Company, Naperville** *Also called Conagra Brands Inc* **(G-15633)**
**Hunt Printing & Graphics, Countryside** *Also called Hunt Enterprises Inc* **(G-7433)**
**Hunter Foundry Machinery Corp**...847 397-5110
2222 Hammond Dr Schaumburg (60196) **(G-19560)**
**Hunter Manufacturing Group Inc**...859 254-7573
227 Northgate St Ste 3 Lake Forest (60045) **(G-12911)**
**Hunter Marketing Inc**...630 541-8480
6523 Royal Glen Ct Lisle (60532) **(G-13601)**
**Hunter Mfg LLP (PA)**...859 254-7573
227 Northgate St Ste 3 Lake Forest (60045) **(G-12912)**
**Hunter Panels LLC**...847 671-2516
9201 Belmont Ave Ste 100b Franklin Park (60131) **(G-10492)**

## ALPHABETIC SECTION — I T W Deltar/Diamed Corp

Hunter-Nusport Inc .................................................. 815 254-7520
   24317 W 143rd St  Plainfield  (60544)  *(G-17607)*
Hunter-Stevens Company Inc ................................. 847 671-5014
   4003 Fleetwood Dr  Franklin Park  (60131)  *(G-10493)*
Hunting Network LLC .............................................. 847 659-8200
   11964 Oak Creek Pkwy  Huntley  (60142)  *(G-12145)*
Huntley & Associates Inc ........................................ 224 381-8500
   47 Carolyn Ct  Lake Zurich  (60047)  *(G-13085)*
Huntsman Expndable Polymers Lc .......................... 815 224-5463
   501 Brunner St  Peru  (61354)  *(G-17512)*
Huntsman International LLC ................................... 815 653-1500
   5015 Barnard Mill Rd  Ringwood  (60072)  *(G-17991)*
Huntsman P&A Americas LLC ................................. 618 646-2119
   2051 Lynch Ave  East Saint Louis  (62204)  *(G-8755)*
Hunzinger Williams Inc ........................................... 847 381-1878
   27w982 Commercial Ave  Lake Barrington  (60010)  *(G-12810)*
Hurletron Incorporated ............................................ 847 680-7022
   1820 Tempel Dr  Libertyville  (60048)  *(G-13335)*
Hurley Chicago Company Inc ................................. 815 472-0087
   601 Hill St  Momence  (60954)  *(G-14982)*
Hurst Chemical Company ...................................... 815 964-0451
   2020 Cunningham Rd  Rockford  (61102)  *(G-18424)*
Hurst Enterprises Inc ............................................. 708 344-9291
   1771 English Dr  Glendale Heights  (60139)  *(G-11032)*
Hurst Manufacturing Co ......................................... 309 756-9960
   823 9th St W  Milan  (61264)  *(G-14791)*
Husar Picture Frame, Chicago *Also called J R Husar Inc* *(G-5263)*
Husky Injection Molding ......................................... 708 479-9049
   8845 W 192nd St Ste B  Mokena  (60448)  *(G-14869)*
Hussain Shaheen ................................................... 630 405-8009
   1900 Danube Way  Bolingbrook  (60490)  *(G-2317)*
Hustedt Manufacturing Jewelers ............................. 217 784-8462
   113 N Sangamon Ave  Gibson City  (60936)  *(G-10903)*
Huston Patterson Printers, Decatur *Also called Huston-Patterson Corporation* *(G-7890)*
Huston-Patterson Corporation (PA) ......................... 217 429-5161
   123 W North St Fl 4  Decatur  (62522)  *(G-7890)*
Hutchens-Bit Service Inc ........................................ 618 439-9485
   11898 Commerce Ln  Benton  (62812)  *(G-2029)*
Hutton Welding Service Inc .................................... 217 932-5585
   11995 N 180th St  Casey  (62420)  *(G-3386)*
Huyear Trucking Inc ............................................... 217 854-3551
   708 Sumner St  Carlinville  (62626)  *(G-3039)*
Huygen Corporation (PA) ........................................ 815 455-2200
   1025 Lutter Dr  Crystal Lake  (60014)  *(G-7590)*
Hw Holdco LLC ...................................................... 773 824-2400
   5600 N River Rd Ste 250  Rosemont  (60018)  *(G-19005)*
HWI, Ottawa *Also called Heiss Welding Inc* *(G-16961)*
Hy Spreckman & Sons Inc ...................................... 312 236-2173
   9725 Woods Dr Unit 1302  Skokie  (60077)  *(G-20013)*
Hy Tech Cnc Machining Inc
   600 Morse Ave Ste D  Schaumburg  (60193)  *(G-19561)*
Hy-Dac Rubber Mfg Co, Smithton *Also called Hydac Rubber Manufacturing* *(G-20120)*
Hy-Tek Manufacturing Co Inc ................................. 630 466-7664
   1998 Bucktail Ln  Sugar Grove  (60554)  *(G-20728)*
Hybris (us) Corporation (HQ) .................................. 312 265-5010
   20 N Wacker Dr Ste 2900  Chicago  (60606)  *(G-5128)*
Hydac Rubber Manufacturing ................................. 618 233-2129
   301 S Main St  Smithton  (62285)  *(G-20120)*
Hyde Park Herald, Chicago *Also called Herald Newspapers Inc* *(G-5076)*
Hydra Fold Auger Inc .............................................. 217 379-2614
   931 N 1600e Rd  Loda  (60948)  *(G-13751)*
Hydra-Stop, Burr Ridge *Also called ADS LLC* *(G-2820)*
Hydra-Stop LLC ...................................................... 708 389-5111
   144 Tower Dr Ste A  Burr Ridge  (60527)  *(G-2852)*
Hydraforce Inc (PA) ................................................ 847 793-2300
   500 Barclay Blvd  Lincolnshire  (60069)  *(G-13455)*
Hydralic Cartridge Systems Div, Lincolnshire *Also called Parker-Hannifin Corporation* *(G-13472)*
Hydraulic Accumulator, Machesney Park *Also called Parker-Hannifin Corporation* *(G-14095)*
Hydraulic Hoses & Fittings, Northlake *Also called Bristol Hose & Fitting Inc* *(G-16430)*
Hydraulic Net, Addison *Also called Hydraulicnet LLC* *(G-151)*
Hydraulicnet LLC .................................................... 630 543-7630
   719 W Fullerton Ave A  Addison  (60101)  *(G-151)*
Hydrive Sales ......................................................... 708 478-8194
   8808 Clare Ave  Mokena  (60448)  *(G-14870)*
Hydro Ink Corp ....................................................... 847 674-0057
   7331 Monticello Ave  Skokie  (60076)  *(G-20014)*
Hydro-Gear Inc (HQ) .............................................. 217 728-2581
   1411 S Hamilton St  Sullivan  (61951)  *(G-20748)*
Hydrophi Tech Group Inc ....................................... 630 981-0098
   1000 Jorie Blvd Ste 250  Oak Brook  (60523)  *(G-16523)*
Hydrosil International Ltd ....................................... 847 741-1600
   125 Prairie Lake Rd  East Dundee  (60118)  *(G-8645)*
Hydrotec Systems Company Inc (PA) ..................... 815 624-6644
   145 E Main St  Tiskilwa  (61368)  *(G-20959)*
Hydrox Chemical Company Inc .............................. 847 468-9400
   825 Tollgate Rd Ste B  Elgin  (60123)  *(G-9069)*
Hydrox Laboratories, Elgin *Also called Hydrox Chemical Company Inc* *(G-9069)*

Hygeia Industries Inc ............................................. 847 380-2030
   1855 Elmdale Ave  Glenview  (60026)  *(G-11139)*
Hygienic Fabrics & Filters Inc (PA) ......................... 815 493-2502
   118 S Broad St  Lanark  (61046)  *(G-13155)*
Hylan Design Ltd .................................................... 312 243-7341
   329 W 18th St Ste 700  Chicago  (60616)  *(G-5129)*
Hyperera Inc .......................................................... 312 842-2288
   2316 S Wentworth Ave Fl 1  Chicago  (60616)  *(G-5130)*
Hypermax Engineering Inc ..................................... 847 428-5655
   255 Higgins Rd  Gilberts  (60136)  *(G-10924)*
Hyperstitch ............................................................ 815 568-0590
   117 W Prairie St  Marengo  (60152)  *(G-14230)*
Hyponex Corporation .............................................. 815 772-2167
   9349 Garden Plain Rd  Morrison  (61270)  *(G-15144)*
Hyspan Precision Products Inc ............................... 773 277-0700
   17111 Wallace St  South Holland  (60473)  *(G-20279)*
Hyster Co ............................................................... 217 443-7000
   1010 E Fairchild St  Danville  (61832)  *(G-7735)*
Hyster-Yale Group Inc ............................................ 217 443-7416
   1010 E Fairchild St  Danville  (61832)  *(G-7736)*
Hytel Group Inc (PA) .............................................. 847 683-9800
   290 Industrial Dr  Hampshire  (60140)  *(G-11551)*
Hyundai Wia Machine Amer Corp ........................... 201 636-5600
   265 Spring Lake Dr  Itasca  (60143)  *(G-12277)*
Hznp Usa Inc ......................................................... 224 383-3000
   150 Saunders Rd Ste 200  Lake Forest  (60045)  *(G-12913)*
I A E Inc ................................................................. 219 882-2400
   837 N Harlem Ave Apt 1n  Oak Park  (60302)  *(G-16670)*
I AM A Print Shoppe, Chicago *Also called Klein Printing Inc* *(G-5387)*
I B P, Goodfield *Also called Tyson Fresh Meats Inc* *(G-11249)*
I C Dynamics Inc .................................................... 708 922-0501
   23716 Springs Ct Unit 111  Plainfield  (60585)  *(G-17608)*
I C G, Chicago *Also called Interntional Casings Group Inc* *(G-5225)*
I C Innovations Inc ................................................. 847 279-7888
   1101 Golf Ave  Highland Park  (60035)  *(G-11842)*
I C S, Roselle *Also called Instrmntation Ctrl Systems Inc* *(G-18947)*
I C S, Decatur *Also called International Control Svcs Inc* *(G-7896)*
I C T W Ink (PA) ..................................................... 630 893-4658
   968 Lake St Ste A  Roselle  (60172)  *(G-18945)*
I C Universal Inc .................................................... 630 766-1169
   1040 Fairway Dr  Bensenville  (60106)  *(G-1918)*
I D Rockford Shop Inc ............................................ 815 335-1150
   105 N Pecatonica St  Winnebago  (61088)  *(G-22297)*
I D T, Elgin *Also called Tri-Dim Filter Corporation* *(G-9213)*
I D Togs ................................................................. 618 235-1538
   67 Cheshire Dr  Belleville  (62223)  *(G-1635)*
I D Tool Specialty Company .................................... 815 432-2007
   819 N Jefferson St  Watseka  (60970)  *(G-21419)*
I E C, Aurora *Also called Industrial Enclosure Corp* *(G-1171)*
I E Press & Graphics, Belvidere *Also called Ink Enterprises Inc* *(G-1764)*
I F & G Metal Craft Co ............................................ 847 488-0630
   405 Industrial Dr  South Elgin  (60177)  *(G-20204)*
I F I, Melrose Park *Also called Industrial Fiberglass Inc* *(G-14657)*
I F S, Potomac *Also called Illini Fs Inc* *(G-17738)*
I F S C O Industries, Chicago *Also called Illinois Fibre Specialty Co* *(G-5157)*
I Forge Company LLC ............................................ 815 535-0600
   2900 E Rock Falls Rd  Rock Falls  (61071)  *(G-18137)*
I Hardware Direct Inc ............................................. 708 325-0000
   642 Blackhawk Dr  Westmont  (60559)  *(G-21892)*
I Kustom Cabinets Inc ............................................ 773 343-6858
   220 Oakridge Ave  Highwood  (60040)  *(G-11885)*
I M M Inc ............................................................... 773 767-3700
   5262 S Kolmar Ave  Chicago  (60632)  *(G-5131)*
I P C Automation Inc .............................................. 815 759-3934
   4615 Prime Pkwy  McHenry  (60050)  *(G-14514)*
I P G, South Elgin *Also called Integrated Print Graphics Inc* *(G-20206)*
I P G Warehouse Ltd .............................................. 773 722-5527
   600 N Pulaski Rd  Chicago  (60624)  *(G-5132)*
I P R, Bartlett *Also called Industrial Phrm Resources Inc* *(G-1357)*
I P S, Rockford *Also called Ingersoll Prod Systems LLC* *(G-18434)*
I Pulloma Paints ..................................................... 847 426-4140
   1 Day Ln  Carpentersville  (60110)  *(G-3287)*
I Q Infinity LLC ...................................................... 773 651-2556
   7624 S Wood St  Chicago  (60620)  *(G-5133)*
I S C America Inc (PA) ........................................... 630 616-1331
   750 Creel Dr  Wood Dale  (60191)  *(G-22380)*
I S C O, Morton Grove *Also called International Spring Company* *(G-15203)*
I T Audit Search, Wheaton *Also called Nano Technologies Inc* *(G-21970)*
I T C W Inc ............................................................ 630 305-8849
   584 Beaconsfield Ave  Naperville  (60565)  *(G-15671)*
I T R Inc ................................................................ 217 245-4478
   21 Harold Cox Dr  Jacksonville  (62650)  *(G-12392)*
I T W Affrdbl Hsing Invstments, Glenview *Also called ITW International Holdings LLC* *(G-11153)*
I T W Chronotherm, Elmhurst *Also called Illinois Tool Works Inc* *(G-9885)*
I T W Deltar/Diamed Corp ....................................... 847 593-8811
   830 Lee St  Elk Grove Village  (60007)  *(G-9529)*

I T W Inc ALPHABETIC SECTION

**I T W Inc**..........847 657-6171
155 Harlem Ave Glenview (60025) ***(G-11140)***
**I T W Shakeproof Indus Pdts, Machesney Park** *Also called Illinois Tool Works Inc* ***(G-14080)***
**I Tech, Rolling Meadows** *Also called Northern Information Tech* ***(G-18752)***
**I TW Deltar Insert Molded Pdts**..........847 593-8811
830 Lee St Elk Grove Village (60007) ***(G-9530)***
**I W M Corporation**..........847 695-0700
399 Hammond Ave Elgin (60120) ***(G-9070)***
**I-N-I Machining Inc**..........309 496-1002
17128 Route 2 & 92 East Moline (61244) ***(G-8682)***
**I2c LLC**..........630 281-2330
1708 Chepstow Ct Naperville (60540) ***(G-15672)***
**I80 Equipment LLC**..........309 949-3701
20490 E 550th St Colona (61241) ***(G-7343)***
**I94 Rv LLC**..........847 395-9500
16125 Russel Rd Russell (60075) ***(G-19097)***
**IAC Belvidere, Belvidere** *Also called International Automotive* ***(G-1765)***
**Iam Acquisition LLC**..........847 259-7800
230 W Palatine Rd Wheeling (60090) ***(G-22073)***
**IB Source Inc**..........312 698-7062
516 N Ogden Ave Ste 111 Chicago (60642) ***(G-5134)***
**Ibanum Manufacturing LLC**..........815 262-5373
5963 Cambridge Chase Rockford (61107) ***(G-18425)***
**Ibarra Group LLC**..........773 650-0503
3100 S Homan Ave Chicago (60623) ***(G-5135)***
**Ibbotson Heating Co**..........847 253-0866
514 S Arthur Ave Arlington Heights (60005) ***(G-770)***
**Ibbysscrubs, Chicago** *Also called Olivia R Aguilar-Camacho* ***(G-5984)***
**Ibi, Cary** *Also called Illinois Blower Inc* ***(G-3352)***
**IBM, Schaumburg** *Also called International Bus Mchs Corp* ***(G-19572)***
**IBM, Chicago** *Also called International Bus Mchs Corp* ***(G-5219)***
**Ibs Conversions Inc**..........630 571-9100
2625 Bttrfeld Rd Ste 114w Oak Brook (60523) ***(G-16524)***
**Ibt Inc**..........618 244-5353
601 S 10th St Mount Vernon (62864) ***(G-15413)***
**Icanvasart, Morton Grove** *Also called Kroto Inc* ***(G-15210)***
**ICC Intrntonal Celsius Concept**..........773 993-4405
2385 S 59th Ct Cicero (60804) ***(G-7203)***
**Iccn Holdings, Woodridge** *Also called Inventus Power Holdings Inc* ***(G-22498)***
**Icd Publications Inc**..........847 913-8295
175 Old Hlf Day Rd # 240 Lincolnshire (60069) ***(G-13456)***
**Iceberg Enterprises LLC (PA)**..........847 685-9500
2700 S River Rd Ste 303 Des Plaines (60018) ***(G-8207)***
**Icg Illinois**..........217 947-2332
781 600th St Elkhart (62634) ***(G-9825)***
**Icg Illinois LLC (HQ)**..........217 566-3000
5945 Lester Rd Williamsville (62693) ***(G-22191)***
**ICI, Glendale Heights** *Also called Inventive Concepts Intl LLC* ***(G-11035)***
**ICI Fiberite**..........708 403-3788
14342 Beacon Ave Orland Park (60462) ***(G-16866)***
**Icnet Systems Inc**..........630 836-8073
1 Baxter Pkwy Deerfield (60015) ***(G-8014)***
**Icon Acquisition Holdings LP (PA)**..........312 751-8000
680 N Lake Shore Dr Chicago (60611) ***(G-5136)***
**Icon Co**..........630 545-2345
1s640 Sunnybrook Rd Glen Ellyn (60137) ***(G-10973)***
**Icon Identity Solutions Inc (PA)**..........847 364-2250
1418 Elmhurst Rd Elk Grove Village (60007) ***(G-9531)***
**Icon Identity Solutions Inc**..........847 364-2250
1418 Elmhurst Rd Elk Grove Village (60007) ***(G-9532)***
**Icon Mech Cnstr & Engrg LLC**..........618 452-0035
1616 Cleveland Blvd Granite City (62040) ***(G-11287)***
**Icon Metalcraft Inc**..........630 766-5600
940 Dillon Dr Wood Dale (60191) ***(G-22381)***
**Icon Power Roller Inc**..........630 545-2345
2882 E 24th Rd Marseilles (61341) ***(G-14310)***
**Iconn Systems LLC**..........630 827-6000
1110 N Garfield St Lombard (60148) ***(G-13811)***
**ICP Industrial Inc (PA)**..........630 227-1692
1600 Glenlake Ave Itasca (60143) ***(G-12278)***
**Icream Group LLC**..........773 342-2834
1537 N Milwaukee Ave # 1 Chicago (60622) ***(G-5137)***
**Ics Saint Louis, Venice** *Also called Sho Pak LLC* ***(G-21137)***
**ID Additives Inc**..........708 588-0081
512 W Burlington Ave # 208 La Grange (60525) ***(G-12737)***
**ID Label Inc (PA)**..........847 265-1200
425 Park Ave Lake Villa (60046) ***(G-13016)***
**Id3 Inc**..........847 734-9781
768 W Algonquin Rd Arlington Heights (60005) ***(G-771)***
**Idaho Timber, Rochelle** *Also called Southeast Wood Treating Inc* ***(G-18110)***
**Iddc, Long Grove** *Also called International Drug Dev Cons* ***(G-13892)***
**Idea Media Services LLC**..........312 226-2900
600 W Chicago Ave Ste 1 Chicago (60654) ***(G-5138)***
**Idea Tool & Manufacturing Co**..........312 476-1080
5615 S Claremont Ave Chicago (60636) ***(G-5139)***
**Ideal Advertising & Printing (PA)**..........815 965-1713
116 N Winnebago St Rockford (61101) ***(G-18426)***
**Ideal Box Co (PA)**..........708 594-3100
4800 S Austin Ave Chicago (60638) ***(G-5140)***
**Ideal Cabinet Solutions Inc**..........618 514-7087
1105 W Main St Alhambra (62001) ***(G-418)***
**Ideal Fabricators Inc**..........217 999-7017
621 S Main St Mount Olive (62069) ***(G-15304)***
**Ideal Gerit Drum Ring Mfg, Chicago** *Also called Meyer Steel Drum Inc* ***(G-5713)***
**Ideal Industries Inc (PA)**..........815 895-5181
1375 Park Ave Sycamore (60178) ***(G-20800)***
**Ideal Industries Inc**..........815 758-2656
1330 E Lincoln Hwy Dekalb (60115) ***(G-8098)***
**Ideal Industries Inc**..........815 895-1108
434 Borden Ave Dock14 Sycamore (60178) ***(G-20801)***
**Ideal Industries Inc**..........815 895-5181
1000 Park Ave Sycamore (60178) ***(G-20802)***
**Ideal Media LLC (PA)**..........312 456-2822
200 E Randolph St # 7000 Chicago (60601) ***(G-5141)***
**Ideal Roller, Chicago** *Also called Rotation Dynamics Corporation* ***(G-6399)***
**Ideal Sign Solutions LLC**..........847 695-9091
1275 Hunters Rdg W # 200 Hoffman Estates (60192) ***(G-12017)***
**Ideal Stitcher & Manufacturing, Chicago** *Also called W R Pabich Manufacturing Co* ***(G-6925)***
**Ideal Supply Inc (PA)**..........847 961-5900
11400 Kreutzer Rd Huntley (60142) ***(G-12146)***
**Ideal Turf Inc**..........309 691-3362
614 W Ravinwoods Rd Peoria (61615) ***(G-17384)***
**Ideal/Mikron Inc**..........847 873-0254
130 S Waverly Pl Mount Prospect (60056) ***(G-15336)***
**Ideas, Elk Grove Village** *Also called Lemoy International Inc* ***(G-9594)***
**Ideas Inc (PA)**..........630 620-2010
625 S Main St Lombard (60148) ***(G-13812)***
**Ideas Inc**..........708 596-1055
16131 Clinton St Harvey (60426) ***(G-11671)***
**Idek Graphics LLC**..........630 530-1232
926 S Prospect Ave Elmhurst (60126) ***(G-9883)***
**Identatronics Inc**..........847 437-2654
2510 Il Route 176 Ste E Crystal Lake (60014) ***(G-7591)***
**Identco International Corp (PA)**..........815 385-0011
28164 W Concrete Dr Ingleside (60041) ***(G-12190)***
**Identco West LLC**..........815 385-0011
28164 W Concrete Dr Ingleside (60041) ***(G-12191)***
**Identcorp Industries**..........708 896-6407
14209 Maryland Ave Dolton (60419) ***(G-8372)***
**Identi-Graphics Inc**..........630 801-4845
101 Knell St Montgomery (60538) ***(G-15049)***
**Identification Products Mfg Co (PA)**..........847 367-6452
13777 W Laurel Dr Lake Forest (60045) ***(G-12914)***
**Identiti Resources Ltd**..........847 301-0510
1201 Wiley Rd Ste 150 Schaumburg (60173) ***(G-19562)***
**Identity Optical Lab**..........309 807-3160
2221 W College Ave Normal (61761) ***(G-16073)***
**Idevconcepts Inc**..........312 351-1615
100 E 14th St Apt 904 Chicago (60605) ***(G-5142)***
**Idex Corporation (PA)**..........847 498-7070
1925 W Field Ct Ste 200 Lake Forest (60045) ***(G-12915)***
**Idex Mpt Inc (HQ)**..........630 530-3333
832 Indul Dr Elmhurst (60126) ***(G-9884)***
**IDI Fabrication Inc**..........630 783-2246
1385 101st St Lemont (60439) ***(G-13236)***
**Idot North Side Sign Shop**..........847 705-4033
201 Center Ct Schaumburg (60196) ***(G-19563)***
**Idrc, Rushville** *Also called Innovative Design and RES Inc* ***(G-19093)***
**IDS Lift-Net, Cicero** *Also called Integrated Display Systems* ***(G-7206)***
**Idx Chicago, Chicago** *Also called Idx Corporation* ***(G-5143)***
**Idx Corporation**..........312 600-9783
224-230 W Huron St Chicago (60654) ***(G-5143)***
**Ieg LLC**..........312 944-1727
350 N Orleans St Ste 1200 Chicago (60654) ***(G-5144)***
**Iei, Bolingbrook** *Also called Institutional Equipment Inc* ***(G-2321)***
**IEM, Vernon Hills** *Also called Independent Eyewear Mfg LLC* ***(G-21175)***
**Iemco Corporation**..........773 728-4400
4530 N Ravenswood Ave Chicago (60640) ***(G-5145)***
**Iep Quality Inc**..........217 840-0570
2705 N Salisbury Ct Champaign (61821) ***(G-3497)***
**Iepa Printing, Springfield** *Also called State Attorney Appellate* ***(G-20536)***
**Ies, Oak Brook** *Also called Interntional Eqp Solutions LLC* ***(G-16526)***
**Iesco Inc**..........708 594-1250
5235 W 65th St Unit B Chicago (60638) ***(G-5146)***
**Iet-Meco**..........217 465-6575
2121 S Main St Paris (61944) ***(G-17150)***
**If Walls Could Talk**..........847 219-5527
323 W Harvard Cir South Elgin (60177) ***(G-20205)***
**Ifa International Inc**..........847 566-0008
354356 Townline Rd Mundelein (60060) ***(G-15508)***
**Ifastgroupe Usa LLC**..........450 658-7148
2626 Warrenville Rd # 400 Downers Grove (60515) ***(G-8462)***
**Ifco**..........630 226-0650
400 W Crssrads Pkwy Ste A Bolingbrook (60440) ***(G-2318)***
**Ifh Group Inc (PA)**..........800 435-7003
3300 E Rock Falls Rd Rock Falls (61071) ***(G-18138)***

**Ifh Group Inc** ... 815 380-2367
5505 Anne St Galt (61037) *(G-10781)*
**Ifm, Litchfield** *Also called International Filter Mfg Corp (G-13688)*
**Ifpra Inc** ... 708 410-0100
1127 S Mannheim Rd # 203 Westchester (60154) *(G-21843)*
**Ifs North America Inc (HQ)** ... 888 437-4968
300 Park Blvd Ste 555 Itasca (60143) *(G-12279)*
**Igar Bridal Inc** ... 224 318-2337
723 E Dundee Rd Arlington Heights (60004) *(G-772)*
**Iggys Auto Parts** ... 708 452-9790
7230 W Montrose Ave Norridge (60706) *(G-16102)*
**Igm Solutions Inc** ... 847 918-1790
1900 Enterprise Ct Libertyville (60048) *(G-13336)*
**Ignite Design, Chicago** *Also called Ignite Usa LLC (G-5147)*
**Ignite Usa LLC** ... 312 432-6223
180 N La Salle St Ste 700 Chicago (60601) *(G-5147)*
**Igt Testing Systems Inc** ... 847 952-2448
543 W Golf Rd Arlington Heights (60005) *(G-773)*
**Iguanamed LLC** ... 312 546-4182
363 W Erie St Ste 200e Chicago (60654) *(G-5148)*
**Iheartcommunications Inc** ... 312 255-5100
875 N Michigan Ave # 3100 Chicago (60611) *(G-5149)*
**Ihi Turbo America Co (HQ)** ... 217 774-9571
1598 State Highway 16 Shelbyville (62565) *(G-19908)*
**Iht, Crystal Lake** *Also called Induction Heat Treating Corp (G-7592)*
**Iic Acquisitions II LLC (PA)** ... 217 224-9600
4100 N 24th St Quincy (62305) *(G-17838)*
**Iicle, Springfield** *Also called Illinois Inst Cntng Legl Ed (G-20454)*
**Iindigenous Railroad Svcs LLC** ... 630 517-8207
205 S Lorraine Rd Wheaton (60187) *(G-21955)*
**Ikan Creations LLC** ... 312 204-7333
2010 S Wabash Ave Ste H Chicago (60616) *(G-5150)*
**Iko Midwest Inc** ... 815 936-9600
235 W South Tec Dr Kankakee (60901) *(G-12624)*
**Ikonix Group Inc (PA)** ... 847 367-4671
28105 N Keith Dr Lake Forest (60045) *(G-12916)*
**IL Green Pastures Fiber Co-Op** ... 815 751-0887
28668 Bell Rd Kirkland (60146) *(G-12713)*
**IL International LLC (PA)** ... 773 276-0070
1720 N Elston Ave Chicago (60642) *(G-5151)*
**Ileesh Products LLC** ... 847 383-6695
100 N Fairway Dr Ste 114 Vernon Hills (60061) *(G-21172)*
**Ilf Technologies LLC** ... 630 789-9770
7001 S Adams St Willowbrook (60527) *(G-22215)*
**Ilf Technologies LLC** ... 630 759-1776
1215 S Laramie Ave Cicero (60804) *(G-7204)*
**Ilight Technologies Inc (PA)** ... 312 876-8630
118 S Clinton St Ste 370 Chicago (60661) *(G-5152)*
**Ilikecrochet.com, Northbrook** *Also called Prime Publishing LLC (G-16343)*
**Ill Battery Spxcialists L** ... 773 478-8600
4120 W Belmont Ave Chicago (60641) *(G-5153)*
**Ill Dept Natural Resources** ... 217 498-9208
9898 Cascade Rd Rochester (62563) *(G-18118)*
**Ill Dept Natural Resources** ... 217 782-4970
1 Natural Resources Way # 100 Springfield (62702) *(G-20453)*
**Illco Inc** ... 815 725-9100
2106 Mcdonough St Joliet (60436) *(G-12513)*
**Illiana Cores Inc** ... 618 586-9800
10156 N 1725th St Palestine (62451) *(G-17093)*
**Illiana Machine & Mfg Corp** ... 708 479-1333
19700 97th Ave Mokena (60448) *(G-14871)*
**Illiana Orthopedics Inc** ... 708 532-0061
17378 Overhill Ave Tinley Park (60477) *(G-20921)*
**Illiana Real Log Homes Inc** ... 815 471-4004
107 N Fritz Dr Milford (60953) *(G-14813)*
**Illini Aerofab Inc** ... 217 425-2971
4455 W Main St Decatur (62522) *(G-7891)*
**Illini Castings LLC** ... 217 446-6365
1940 E Fairchild St Danville (61832) *(G-7737)*
**Illini Concrete Inc (PA)** ... 618 235-4141
1300 E A St Belleville (62221) *(G-1636)*
**Illini Concrete Inc** ... 618 398-4141
10 Tucker Dr Caseyville (62232) *(G-3397)*
**Illini Coolant Management Corp (PA)** ... 847 966-1079
8011 Parkside Ave Morton Grove (60053) *(G-15201)*
**Illini Digital Printing Co** ... 618 271-6622
680 N 20th St East Saint Louis (62205) *(G-8756)*
**Illini Foundry Co Inc** ... 309 697-3142
6523 N Galena Rd Peoria (61614) *(G-17385)*
**Illini Fs Inc** ... 217 442-4737
6637 E 3050 North Rd Potomac (61865) *(G-17738)*
**Illini Hi-Reach Inc** ... 847 428-3311
15n320 Route 25 Unit A East Dundee (60118) *(G-8646)*
**Illini Mattress Company Inc** ... 217 359-0156
514 S Country Fair Dr Champaign (61821) *(G-3498)*
**Illini Media Co (PA)** ... 217 337-8300
512 E Green St Fl 3 Champaign (61820) *(G-3499)*
**Illini Precast LLC** ... 708 562-7700
2255 Entp Dr Ste 5501 Westchester (60154) *(G-21844)*
**Illini Precision Machining Inc** ... 217 425-5780
750 E Prairie Ave Decatur (62523) *(G-7892)*
**Illini Ready Mix Inc** ... 618 833-7321
300 Mckinley St Anna (62906) *(G-605)*
**Illini Ready Mix Inc (PA)** ... 618 734-0287
801 W Industrial Park Rd Carbondale (62901) *(G-3011)*
**Illini Ready Mix Inc** ... 618 529-1626
801 W Industrial Park Rd Carbondale (62901) *(G-3012)*
**Illini Tech Services, Carlinville** *Also called Integrated Media Inc (G-3040)*
**Illini/Altco Inc** ... 847 549-0321
450 Bunker Ct Vernon Hills (60061) *(G-21173)*
**Illinoi Eye Surgns/Quantm Visn** ... 618 315-6560
3000 Broadway St Mount Vernon (62864) *(G-15414)*
**Illinois Agricultural Assn, Bloomington** *Also called Farm Week (G-2163)*
**Illinois Agrinews Inc** ... 815 223-7448
426 2nd St La Salle (61301) *(G-12775)*
**Illinois Baking** ... 773 995-7200
10839 S Langley Ave Chicago (60628) *(G-5154)*
**Illinois Block and Tackle Inc** ... 618 451-8696
1635 W 1st St Ste 312 Granite City (62040) *(G-11288)*
**Illinois Blower Inc** ... 847 639-5500
750 Industrial Dr Ste E Cary (60013) *(G-3352)*
**Illinois Bottle Mfg Co** ... 847 595-9000
701 E Devon Ave Elk Grove Village (60007) *(G-9533)*
**Illinois Box & Pallet, Taylorville** *Also called Botkin Lumber Company Inc (G-20834)*
**Illinois Broaching Co (PA)** ... 847 678-3080
4200 Grace St Schiller Park (60176) *(G-19840)*
**Illinois Carbide Tool Co Inc (PA)** ... 847 244-1110
1322 Belvidere Rd Waukegan (60085) *(G-21569)*
**Illinois Casket Company** ... 773 483-4500
6747 S Halsted St Chicago (60621) *(G-5155)*
**Illinois Cast Stone** ... 815 943-6050
343 S Division St Ste 1 Harvard (60033) *(G-11637)*
**Illinois Cement Company LLC (HQ)** ... 815 224-2112
1601 Rockwell Rd La Salle (61301) *(G-12776)*
**Illinois Central Gulf Car Shop** ... 618 533-8281
600 Gilmore St Centralia (62801) *(G-3418)*
**Illinois Corn Processing LLC** ... 309 353-3990
1301 S Front St Pekin (61554) *(G-17268)*
**Illinois Dermatological Center, Elk Grove Village** *Also called Michael A Greenberg MD Ltd (G-9625)*
**Illinois Electro Deburring Co (PA)** ... 847 678-5010
2915 Birch St Franklin Park (60131) *(G-10494)*
**Illinois Embroidery Service** ... 618 526-8006
580 N 2nd St Breese (62230) *(G-2445)*
**Illinois Engineered Pdts Inc** ... 312 850-3710
2035 S Racine Ave Chicago (60608) *(G-5156)*
**Illinois Engraving & Mfg Co, Chicago** *Also called Iemco Corporation (G-5145)*
**Illinois Fibre Specialty Co (PA)** ... 773 376-1122
4301 S Western Blvd Chicago (60609) *(G-5157)*
**Illinois Forge Company, Rock Falls** *Also called I Forge Company LLC (G-18137)*
**Illinois Foundation Seeds Inc** ... 217 485-6420
1178 County Road 900 N Tolono (61880) *(G-20971)*
**Illinois Fuel Company LLC** ... 618 275-4486
920 Gape Hollow Rd Herod (62947) *(G-11747)*
**Illinois Glove Company** ... 800 342-5458
650 Anthony Trl Ste A Northbrook (60062) *(G-16272)*
**Illinois Hand & Upper Extremit** ... 847 956-0099
515 W Algonquin Rd Arlington Heights (60005) *(G-774)*
**Illinois Inst Cntng Legl Ed** ... 217 787-2080
2395 W Jefferson St Springfield (62702) *(G-20454)*
**Illinois Instruments Inc** ... 815 344-6212
2401 Hiller Rdg Ste A Johnsburg (60051) *(G-12436)*
**Illinois Lift Equipment Inc** ... 888 745-0577
1201 W Hawthorne Ln West Chicago (60185) *(G-21717)*
**Illinois Meter Inc** ... 618 438-6039
1500 W Webster St Benton (62812) *(G-2030)*
**Illinois Mold Builders Inc** ... 847 526-0400
250 Jamie Ln Wauconda (60084) *(G-21471)*
**Illinois Newspaper In Educatn** ... 847 427-4388
1 Copley Plz Springfield (62701) *(G-20455)*
**Illinois Ni Cast LLC** ... 217 398-3200
1700 W Washington St Champaign (61821) *(G-3500)*
**Illinois Office Sup Elect Prtg** ... 815 434-0186
1119 La Salle St Ottawa (61350) *(G-16962)*
**Illinois Oil Marketing Eqp Inc (PA)** ... 309 347-1819
850 Brenkman Dr Pekin (61554) *(G-17269)*
**Illinois Oil Marketing Eqp Inc** ... 217 935-5107
601 E Leander St Clinton (61727) *(G-7284)*
**Illinois Oil Products Inc** ... 309 788-1896
2715 36th St Rock Island (61201) *(G-18183)*
**Illinois Pallets Inc** ... 773 640-9228
8075 Tec Air Ave Willow Springs (60480) *(G-22197)*
**Illinois Pneumatic Inc** ... 815 654-9301
9325 Starboard Dr Ste B Roscoe (61073) *(G-18900)*
**Illinois Pneumatic Tool Co, Addison** *Also called Ivan Schwenker (G-156)*
**Illinois Printing Services Inc** ... 217 728-2786
800 S Patterson Rd Sullivan (61951) *(G-20749)*

A
L
P
H
A
B
E
T
I
C

**Illinois Pro-Turn Inc** **ALPHABETIC SECTION**

**Illinois Pro-Turn Inc**....847 462-1870
309 Cary Point Dr Ste F Cary (60013) ***(G-3353)***
**Illinois Rack Enterprises Inc**....815 385-5750
480 Scotland Rd Ste A Lakemoor (60051) ***(G-13144)***
**Illinois Radio Network, Springfield** *Also called Saga Communications Inc* ***(G-20517)***
**Illinois Recovery Group I**....815 230-7920
2390 S Broadway Rd Braceville (60407) ***(G-2410)***
**Illinois Retina Institute SC**....309 589-1880
4505 N Rockwood Dr 1 Peoria (61615) ***(G-17386)***
**Illinois River Energy LLC**....815 561-0650
4000 N Division Rochelle (61068) ***(G-18095)***
**Illinois River Winery Inc**....815 691-8031
16w420 Timberlake Dr Willowbrook (60527) ***(G-22216)***
**Illinois Road Contractors Inc (PA)**....217 245-6181
520 N Webster Ave Jacksonville (62650) ***(G-12393)***
**Illinois Soc For Rsprtory Care**....815 742-9367
6110 Thorncrest Dr Rockford (61109) ***(G-18427)***
**Illinois Sports News, Chicago** *Also called Wabash Publishing Co Inc* ***(G-6930)***
**Illinois State Usbc Wba**....309 827-6355
402 W Hamilton Rd Bloomington (61704) ***(G-2182)***
**Illinois Steel Service Inc (PA)**....312 926-7440
1127 S Washtenaw Ave Chicago (60612) ***(G-5158)***
**Illinois Sterling Ltd**....847 526-5151
540 S Rand Rd Wauconda (60084) ***(G-21472)***
**Illinois Switchboard Corp**....630 543-0910
125 W Laura Dr Addison (60101) ***(G-152)***
**Illinois Tag Co**....773 626-0542
287 Commonwealth Dr Carol Stream (60188) ***(G-3169)***
**Illinois Times, Springfield** *Also called Central Ill Communications LLC* ***(G-20413)***
**Illinois Tool Works**....815 648-2416
11411 Price Rd Hebron (60034) ***(G-11720)***
**Illinois Tool Works Inc**....630 825-7900
700 High Grove Blvd Glendale Heights (60139) ***(G-11033)***
**Illinois Tool Works Inc (PA)**....847 724-7500
155 Harlem Ave Glenview (60025) ***(G-11141)***
**Illinois Tool Works Inc**....708 325-2300
7201 S 78th St Bridgeview (60455) ***(G-2498)***
**Illinois Tool Works Inc**....630 372-2150
1452 Brewster Creek Blvd Bartlett (60103) ***(G-1353)***
**Illinois Tool Works Inc**....847 876-9400
195 E Algonquin Rd Des Plaines (60016) ***(G-8208)***
**Illinois Tool Works Inc**....708 681-3891
2550 S 27th Ave Broadview (60155) ***(G-2585)***
**Illinois Tool Works Inc**....630 773-9300
1140 W Bryn Mawr Ave Itasca (60143) ***(G-12280)***
**Illinois Tool Works Inc**....708 720-0300
250 Industry Ave Frankfort (60423) ***(G-10329)***
**Illinois Tool Works Inc**....847 657-4639
3640 W Lake Ave Glenview (60026) ***(G-11142)***
**Illinois Tool Works Inc**....630 595-3500
1349 W Bryn Mawr Ave Itasca (60143) ***(G-12281)***
**Illinois Tool Works Inc**....708 720-0300
21601 S Harlem Ave Frankfort (60423) ***(G-10330)***
**Illinois Tool Works Inc**....630 752-4000
475 N Gary Ave Carol Stream (60188) ***(G-3170)***
**Illinois Tool Works Inc**....630 595-3500
86 Chancellor Dr Roselle (60172) ***(G-18946)***
**Illinois Tool Works Inc**....708 720-2600
21555 S Harlem Ave Frankfort (60423) ***(G-10331)***
**Illinois Tool Works Inc**....630 773-9301
1140 W Bryn Mawr Ave Itasca (60143) ***(G-12282)***
**Illinois Tool Works Inc**....217 345-2166
1155 N 5th St Charleston (61920) ***(G-3599)***
**Illinois Tool Works Inc**....630 787-3298
950 Pratt Blvd Elk Grove Village (60007) ***(G-9534)***
**Illinois Tool Works Inc**....630 315-2150
425 N Gary Ave Carol Stream (60188) ***(G-3171)***
**Illinois Tool Works Inc**....708 720-7070
21701 S Harlem Ave Frankfort (60423) ***(G-10332)***
**Illinois Tool Works Inc**....847 593-8811
830 Lee St Elk Grove Village (60007) ***(G-9535)***
**Illinois Tool Works Inc**....847 350-0193
2471 Brickvale Dr Elk Grove Village (60007) ***(G-9536)***
**Illinois Tool Works Inc**....847 741-7900
1201 Saint Charles St Elgin (60120) ***(G-9071)***
**Illinois Tool Works Inc**....847 918-6473
14050 W Lambs Ln Unit 1 Libertyville (60048) ***(G-13337)***
**Illinois Tool Works Inc**....708 342-6000
9629 197th St Mokena (60448) ***(G-14872)***
**Illinois Tool Works Inc**....708 720-7800
22501 Bohlmann Pkwy Richton Park (60471) ***(G-17977)***
**Illinois Tool Works Inc**....847 821-2170
888 Forest Edge Dr Vernon Hills (60061) ***(G-21174)***
**Illinois Tool Works Inc**....847 299-2222
195 E Algonquin Rd Des Plaines (60016) ***(G-8209)***
**Illinois Tool Works Inc**....708 343-0728
2550 S 27th Ave Broadview (60155) ***(G-2586)***
**Illinois Tool Works Inc**....618 997-1716
5307 Meadowland Pkwy Marion (62959) ***(G-14269)***
**Illinois Tool Works Inc**....708 720-0300
250 Industry Ave Frankfort (60423) ***(G-10333)***
**Illinois Tool Works Inc**....847 657-5300
155 Harlem Ave Glenview (60025) ***(G-11143)***
**Illinois Tool Works Inc**....708 479-7200
9629 197th St Mokena (60448) ***(G-14873)***
**Illinois Tool Works Inc**....815 654-1510
10818 N 2nd St Machesney Park (61115) ***(G-14080)***
**Illinois Tool Works Inc**....847 215-8925
180 Hastings Dr Buffalo Grove (60089) ***(G-2706)***
**Illinois Tool Works Inc**....847 724-6100
3650 W Lake Ave Glenview (60026) ***(G-11144)***
**Illinois Tool Works Inc**....847 783-5500
2501 Galvin Dr Elgin (60124) ***(G-9072)***
**Illinois Tool Works Inc**....815 654-1510
10818 N 2nd St Machesney Park (61115) ***(G-14081)***
**Illinois Tool Works Inc**....815 448-7300
804 Commercial Dr Mazon (60444) ***(G-14438)***
**Illinois Tool Works Inc**....708 458-7320
7701 W 71st St Bridgeview (60455) ***(G-2499)***
**Illinois Tool Works Inc**....847 766-9000
2700 York Rd Elk Grove Village (60007) ***(G-9537)***
**Illinois Tool Works Inc**....847 537-8800
600 Knightsbridge Pkwy Lincolnshire (60069) ***(G-13457)***
**Illinois Tool Works Inc**....630 993-9990
935 N Oaklawn Ave Elmhurst (60126) ***(G-9885)***
**Illinois Tool Works Inc**....847 295-6500
41 Waukegan Rd Lake Bluff (60044) ***(G-12850)***
**Illinois Tool Works Inc**....708 720-3541
21701 S Harlem Ave Frankfort (60423) ***(G-10334)***
**Illinois Tool Works Inc**....847 724-7500
2550 Millbrook Dr Buffalo Grove (60089) ***(G-2707)***
**Illinois Tool Works Inc**....708 479-7200
8402 183rd St Ste D Tinley Park (60487) ***(G-20922)***
**Illinois Tool Works Inc**....847 657-4022
3660 W Lake Ave Glenview (60026) ***(G-11145)***
**Illinois Transit Assembly Corp**....618 451-0100
1980 3rd St Madison (62060) ***(G-14150)***
**Illinois Valley Container Inc**....815 223-7200
2 Terminal Rd Peru (61354) ***(G-17513)***
**Illinois Valley Glass & Mirror**....309 682-6603
3300 Ne Adams St Ste A Peoria (61603) ***(G-17387)***
**Illinois Valley Gutters Inc**....309 698-8140
157 Thunderbird Ln East Peoria (61611) ***(G-8713)***
**Illinois Valley Machine Sp Inc**....815 586-4511
108 N Lincoln St Ransom (60470) ***(G-17916)***
**Illinois Valley Minerals LLC**....815 442-8402
575 N 18th Rd Tonica (61370) ***(G-20974)***
**Illinois Valley Paving Co**....217 422-1010
Rr 51 Box S Elwin (62532) ***(G-9977)***
**Illinois Valley Plastics, Washington** *Also called Iplastics LLC* ***(G-21383)***
**Illinois Valley Press East**....217 586-2512
303 E Main St Ste D Mahomet (61853) ***(G-14159)***
**Illinois Valley Printing Inc**....309 674-4942
619 Spring St Peoria (61603) ***(G-17388)***
**Illinois Water Tech Inc**....815 636-8884
5443 Swanson Ct Roscoe (61073) ***(G-18901)***
**Illinois Weld & Machine Inc**....309 565-0533
123 S 2nd St Hanna City (61536) ***(G-11568)***
**Illinois Weld & Machine Inc (PA)**....309 565-0533
101 S 2nd St Hanna City (61536) ***(G-11569)***
**Illinois Window Shade Co**....773 743-6025
6250 N Broadway St Chicago (60660) ***(G-5159)***
**Illinois Wood Fiber Products**....847 836-6176
99 Day Ln Carpentersville (60110) ***(G-3288)***
**Illmo R/X Service**....217 877-1192
3373 N Woodford St Decatur (62526) ***(G-7893)***
**Illmo R/X Services, Decatur** *Also called Illmo R/X Service* ***(G-7893)***
**Illuminight Lighting LLC**....312 685-4448
1954 1st St 394 Highland Park (60035) ***(G-11843)***
**Illumivation Studios LLC**....312 261-5561
2415 W 19th St Unit 3 Chicago (60608) ***(G-5160)***
**ILmachine Company Inc**....847 243-9900
421 Harvester Ct Wheeling (60090) ***(G-22074)***
**Ilmo Products Company (PA)**....217 245-2183
7 Eastgate Dr Jacksonville (62650) ***(G-12394)***
**Ilpea Industries Inc**....309 343-3332
611 S Linwood Rd Galesburg (61401) ***(G-10760)***
**Imac Motion Control Corp**....847 741-4622
1301 Bowes Rd Ste A Elgin (60123) ***(G-9073)***
**Imada Inc**....847 562-0834
3100 Dundee Rd Ste 707 Northbrook (60062) ***(G-16273)***
**Image 360 - Mokena, Mokena** *Also called Store 409 Inc* ***(G-14905)***
**Image Circuit Inc**....847 622-3300
925 Estes Ave Elk Grove Village (60007) ***(G-9538)***
**Image Custom Drapery**....630 837-0107
137 Amherst Dr Bartlett (60103) ***(G-1354)***
**Image Industries Inc (PA)**....847 659-0100
11220 Main St Huntley (60142) ***(G-12147)***

# ALPHABETIC SECTION

Independence Inc

Image Pact Printing .................................................. 708 460-6070
  18650 Graphic Ct  Tinley Park  (60477)  *(G-20923)*
Image Plus Inc .......................................................... 630 852-4920
  4248 Belle Aire Ln Ste 1  Downers Grove  (60515)  *(G-8463)*
Image Print Inc (PA) ................................................ 815 672-1068
  810 W Bridge St  Streator  (61364)  *(G-20691)*
Image Signs Inc ....................................................... 815 282-4141
  7323 N Alpine Rd  Loves Park  (61111)  *(G-13947)*
Image Systems Bus Slutions LLC ........................ 847 378-8249
  1776 Commerce Dr  Elk Grove Village  (60007)  *(G-9539)*
Image Technology Inc ............................................ 847 622-3300
  937 Davis Rd  Elgin  (60123)  *(G-9074)*
Imagecare Maintenance Svcs LLC ...................... 847 631-3306
  1418 Elmhurst Rd  Elk Grove Village  (60007)  *(G-9540)*
Images Alive Ltd ..................................................... 847 498-5550
  638 Anthony Trl  Northbrook  (60062)  *(G-16274)*
Imageworks Creative Group, Highland  Also called Digital Artz LLC  *(G-11783)*
Imageworks Manufacturing Inc ............................ 708 503-1122
  49 South St  Park Forest  (60466)  *(G-17172)*
Imagination Products Corp .................................... 309 274-6223
  227 W Cedar St  Chillicothe  (61523)  *(G-7167)*
Imagination Publishing LLC ................................... 312 887-1000
  600 W Fulton St Ste 600  Chicago  (60661)  *(G-5161)*
Imagine That Candle Co ......................................... 708 481-6370
  4107 Applewood Ln  Matteson  (60443)  *(G-14373)*
Imagineering Inc ....................................................... 847 806-0003
  2425 Touhy Ave  Elk Grove Village  (60007)  *(G-9541)*
Imaging Equipment Sales, Highland Park  Also called Bka Inc  *(G-11825)*
Imaging Systems  Inc (PA) ..................................... 630 875-1100
  1009 W Hawthorn Dr  Itasca  (60143)  *(G-12283)*
Imaginings 3  Inc ....................................................... 847 647-1370
  6401 W Gross Point Rd  Niles  (60714)  *(G-15987)*
Imanage LLC (PA) ..................................................... 312 667-7000
  540 W Madison St Ste 2400  Chicago  (60661)  *(G-5162)*
Imanis Original Bean Pies & F ............................... 773 716-7007
  3931 S Leavitt St  Chicago  (60609)  *(G-5163)*
Imap, Grayslake  Also called International Mold & Prod LLC  *(G-11347)*
Imbert Construction Inds Inc ................................. 847 588-3170
  7030 N Austin Ave  Niles  (60714)  *(G-15988)*
Imco, Benton  Also called Illinois Meter Inc  *(G-2030)*
Imco Precast LLC ..................................................... 217 742-5300
  730 State Route 106  Winchester  (62694)  *(G-22280)*
Imcopex ..................................................................... 630 980-1015
  1271 Humbracht Cir  Bartlett  (60103)  *(G-1355)*
Imcp Inc ..................................................................... 630 477-8600
  900 N Arlington  Itasca  (60143)  *(G-12284)*
Imds, Geneva  Also called Innovative Molecular Diagnosti  *(G-10838)*
Imed Glenview ......................................................... 847 298-2200
  1247 Milwaukee Ave  Glenview  (60025)  *(G-11146)*
Imedia Network  Inc ................................................ 847 331-1774
  3414 N Milwaukee Ave 2n  Chicago  (60641)  *(G-5164)*
IMI Manufacturing Inc ............................................. 630 771-0003
  694 Veterans Pkwy Ste B  Bolingbrook  (60440)  *(G-2319)*
IMI McR  Inc ............................................................. 309 734-6282
  1301 N Main St Ste 3  Monmouth  (61462)  *(G-15014)*
Imp, Skokie  Also called Industrial Market Place  *(G-20015)*
Impac Group Inc ...................................................... 708 344-9100
  1950 N Ruby St  Melrose Park  (60160)  *(G-14655)*
Impac Products, Chicago  Also called J B Watts Company Inc  *(G-5256)*
Impact Bronze Plaques, La Grange  Also called Impact Signs & Graphics  Inc  *(G-12738)*
Impact Polymer  LLC ............................................... 847 441-2394
  790 W Frontage Rd  Northfield  (60093)  *(G-16402)*
Impact Prtrs & Lithographers ............................... 847 981-9676
  1370 E Higgins Rd  Elk Grove Village  (60007)  *(G-9542)*
Impact Signs & Graphics  Inc ............................... 708 469-7178
  26 E Burlington Ave  La Grange  (60525)  *(G-12738)*
Impact Technologies Inc ........................................ 708 246-5041
  4521 Grand Ave  Western Springs  (60558)  *(G-21867)*
Imperial Fabricators Co .......................................... 773 463-5522
  9119 Medill Ave  Franklin Park  (60131)  *(G-10495)*
Imperial Glass Structures Co ................................ 847 253-6150
  2120 Foster Ave  Wheeling  (60090)  *(G-22075)*
Imperial Group Mfg Inc .......................................... 615 325-9224
  311 W Superior St Ste 510  Chicago  (60654)  *(G-5165)*
Imperial Kitchens & Bath Inc ................................ 708 485-0020
  8918 Ogden Ave  Brookfield  (60513)  *(G-2635)*
Imperial Marble Corp .............................................. 815 498-2303
  327 E Lasalle St  Somonauk  (60552)  *(G-20126)*
Imperial Metals Group, Chicago  Also called Imperial Zinc Corp  *(G-5169)*
Imperial Mfg Group Inc .......................................... 618 465-3133
  1450 Discovery Pkwy  Alton  (62002)  *(G-578)*
Imperial Oil  Inc ....................................................... 773 866-1235
  4346 N Western Ave  Chicago  (60618)  *(G-5166)*
Imperial Packaging Corporation ........................... 847 486-0800
  640 Executive Dr  Willowbrook  (60527)  *(G-22217)*
Imperial Pizza, Streamwood  Also called Randolph Packing Co  *(G-20670)*
Imperial Plating Company III ................................ 773 586-3500
  7030 W 60th St  Chicago  (60638)  *(G-5167)*
Imperial Punch & Manufacturing .......................... 815 226-8200
  2016 23rd Ave  Rockford  (61104)  *(G-18428)*
Imperial Rivets & Fasteners Co ............................ 630 964-0208
  7201 Walden Ln  Darien  (60561)  *(G-7797)*
Imperial Stone Collection ...................................... 847 640-8817
  460 Lively Blvd Ste 1  Elk Grove Village  (60007)  *(G-9543)*
Imperial Store Fixtures Inc .................................... 773 348-1137
  3768 N Clark St  Chicago  (60613)  *(G-5168)*
Imperial Technical Services .................................. 708 403-1564
  14001 Thomas Dr  Orland Park  (60462)  *(G-16867)*
Imperial Trailer Mfg Inc ......................................... 618 395-2414
  3519 N Union Dr  Olney  (62450)  *(G-16772)*
Imperial Woodworking Company (PA) ................. 847 221-2107
  310 N Woodwork Ln  Palatine  (60067)  *(G-17039)*
Imperial Woodworking Entps Inc ......................... 847 358-6920
  310 N Woodwork Ln  Palatine  (60067)  *(G-17040)*
Imperial Zinc Corp (PA) .......................................... 773 264-5900
  1031 E 103rd St  Chicago  (60628)  *(G-5169)*
Impossible Objects LLC .......................................... 847 400-9582
  3455 Commercial Ave  Northbrook  (60062)  *(G-16275)*
Impress Printing ...................................................... 630 933-8966
  210 N Hale St  Wheaton  (60187)  *(G-21956)*
Impress Printing & Design Inc .............................. 815 730-9440
  1325 W Jefferson St  Joliet  (60435)  *(G-12514)*
Impression Printing ................................................. 708 614-8660
  4901 Lorin Ln  Oak Forest  (60452)  *(G-16583)*
Impressive Impressions .......................................... 312 432-0501
  329 W 18th St Ste 306  Chicago  (60616)  *(G-5170)*
Imprex International  Inc ....................................... 847 364-4930
  2916 Malmo Dr  Arlington Heights  (60005)  *(G-775)*
Impro Graphics, Arlington Heights  Also called Impro International Inc  *(G-776)*
Impro Industries Usa  Inc ...................................... 630 759-0280
  375 Sw Frontage Rd Ste D  Bolingbrook  (60440)  *(G-2320)*
Impro International Inc ........................................... 847 398-3870
  3110 N Arlington Hts Rd  Arlington Heights  (60004)  *(G-776)*
IMS, Bourbonnais  Also called Tms International LLC  *(G-2408)*
IMS Buhrke-Olson, Arlington Heights  Also called Olson Metal Products  LLC  *(G-812)*
IMS Buhrke-Olson, Arlington Heights  Also called Buhrke Industries  LLC  *(G-732)*
IMS Buhrke-Olson, Downers Grove  Also called Buhrke Industries LLC  *(G-8400)*
IMS Companies  LLC (PA) ...................................... 847 391-8100
  1 Innovation Dr  Des Plaines  (60016)  *(G-8210)*
IMS Engineered Products  LLC ............................. 847 391-8100
  1 Innovation Dr  Des Plaines  (60016)  *(G-8211)*
IMS Olson  LLC ........................................................ 630 969-9400
  2500 Curtiss St  Downers Grove  (60515)  *(G-8464)*
Imtran Industries Inc .............................................. 630 752-4000
  475 N Gary Ave  Carol Stream  (60188)  *(G-3172)*
In A Bind Assembly Fulfillment ............................ 815 568-6952
  4104 Millstream Rd  Marengo  (60152)  *(G-14231)*
In Aaw Hair Emporium LLC .................................... 779 227-1450
  423 Buell Ave 1  Joliet  (60435)  *(G-12515)*
In Color Graphics Coml Prtg .................................. 847 697-0003
  1855 Fox Ln  Elgin  (60123)  *(G-9075)*
In Focus Restaurant & Bar Sup, Joliet  Also called Bar Stool Depotcom  *(G-12460)*
In Midwest Service Enterprises ............................ 217 224-1932
  2221 N 24th St  Quincy  (62301)  *(G-17839)*
In The Attic Inc ........................................................ 847 949-5077
  1955 Buckingham Rd  Mundelein  (60060)  *(G-15509)*
In These Times, Chicago  Also called Institute For Public Affairs  *(G-5207)*
In-Place Machining Co Inc .................................... 847 669-3006
  11414 Smith Dr Unit D  Huntley  (60142)  *(G-12148)*
In-Print Graphics  Inc (PA) .................................... 708 396-1010
  4201 166th St  Oak Forest  (60452)  *(G-16584)*
In3gredients Inc ...................................................... 312 577-4275
  30 N Michigan Ave Ste 505  Chicago  (60602)  *(G-5171)*
Inc 1105 Media ........................................................ 847 358-7272
  800 E Northwest Hwy # 306  Palatine  (60074)  *(G-17041)*
Inc Midwest Die Mold ............................................ 224 353-6417
  624 Lunt Ave  Schaumburg  (60193)  *(G-19564)*
Inc., Dix McGuire Intl, Palatine  Also called Dix McGuire Commodities LLC  *(G-17023)*
Incline Construction  Inc ....................................... 815 577-8881
  131 Airport Dr Unit H  Joliet  (60431)  *(G-12516)*
Incline Welding & Construction, Joliet  Also called Incline Construction  Inc  *(G-12516)*
Inclusion Solutions  LLC ........................................ 847 869-2500
  2000 Greenleaf St Ste 3  Evanston  (60202)  *(G-10055)*
Incobrasa Industries  Ltd ....................................... 815 265-4803
  540 E Us Highway 24  Gilman  (60938)  *(G-10944)*
Incon Industries Inc ................................................ 630 728-4014
  3955 Commerce Dr  Saint Charles  (60174)  *(G-19196)*
Incon Processing  LLC (HQ) .................................. 630 305-8556
  970 Douglas Rd  Batavia  (60510)  *(G-1456)*
Indar Ventures LLC ................................................. 708 343-4900
  4429 James Pl  Melrose Park  (60160)  *(G-14656)*
Inde Enterprises Inc ................................................ 815 338-8844
  671 E Calhoun St  Woodstock  (60098)  *(G-22574)*
Indecor ....................................................................... 773 561-7670
  8222 Lehigh Ave  Morton Grove  (60053)  *(G-15202)*
Independence  Inc ................................................... 312 675-2105
  47 E Oak St Ste 2w  Chicago  (60611)  *(G-5172)*

**Independence Tube Corporation (HQ)** 708 496-0380
6226 W 74th St Chicago (60638) ***(G-5173)***
**Independence Tube Corporation** 815 795-4400
1201 Broadway St Marseilles (61341) ***(G-14311)***
**Independent Antique RAD Mfg** 847 458-7400
200 Berg St Algonquin (60102) ***(G-393)***
**Independent Awning Co, South Holland** *Also called Chesterfield Awning Co Inc* ***(G-20256)***
**Independent Eyewear Mfg LLC** 847 537-0008
255 Corp Woods Pkwy Vernon Hills (60061) ***(G-21175)***
**Independent Network Tv LLC** 312 953-8508
1525 Circle Ave Ste 3 Forest Park (60130) ***(G-10249)***
**Independent News** 217 662-6001
2202 Kickapoo Dr Danville (61832) ***(G-7738)***
**Independent News, The, Danville** *Also called Independent News* ***(G-7738)***
**Independent Outdoor Ltd** 630 960-2460
5009 Chase Ave Downers Grove (60515) ***(G-8465)***
**Independent Publishers Group, Chicago** *Also called I P G Warehouse Ltd* ***(G-5132)***
**Independent Publishers Group, Chicago** *Also called Chicago Review Press Inc* ***(G-4344)***
**Indepth Graphics & Printing, Woodstock** *Also called Inde Enterprises Inc* ***(G-22574)***
**Indesco Oven Products Inc** 217 622-6345
15935 Whisper Ln Petersburg (62675) ***(G-17536)***
**Indev Gauging Systems Inc** 815 282-4463
5235 26th Ave Rockford (61109) ***(G-18429)***
**Indev Gauging Systems Inc** 815 282-4463
6830 Forest Hills Rd Loves Park (61111) ***(G-13948)***
**India Tribune Ltd (PA)** 773 588-5077
3304 W Peterson Ave Chicago (60659) ***(G-5174)***
**Indian Point Oil & Gas, Salem** *Also called Jerry D Graham Oil* ***(G-19337)***
**Indiana Agri-News Inc** 317 726-5391
420 2nd St La Salle (61301) ***(G-12777)***
**Indiana Precision Inc** 765 361-0247
130 N Jackson St Danville (61832) ***(G-7739)***
**Indiana Steel & Tube, Chicago** *Also called E & H Tubing Inc* ***(G-4662)***
**Indigo Cigar Factory** 217 348-1514
503 7th St Charleston (61920) ***(G-3600)***
**Indigo Digital Printing LLC** 312 753-3025
900 S Wabash Ave Side Chicago (60605) ***(G-5175)***
**Indigo Time** 847 255-4818
800 W Central Rd Ste 162 Mount Prospect (60056) ***(G-15337)***
**Indilab Inc** 847 928-1050
10367 Franklin Ave Franklin Park (60131) ***(G-10496)***
**Indium Corporation of America** 847 439-9134
80 Scott St Elk Grove Village (60007) ***(G-9544)***
**Indorama Ventures Oxide & Glyl (HQ)** 800 365-0794
2610 Lake Cook Rd Ste 133 Riverwoods (60015) ***(G-18039)***
**Induction Heat Treating Corp** 815 477-7788
775 Tek Dr Crystal Lake (60014) ***(G-7592)***
**Induction Innovations Inc** 847 836-6933
1175 Jansen Farm Ct Elgin (60123) ***(G-9076)***
**Induspac Rtp Inc** 919 484-9484
8100 77th Ave Bridgeview (60455) ***(G-2500)***
**Industec, Dupo** *Also called Interstate Industrial Tech* ***(G-8572)***
**Industra Sharp Inc** 708 877-1200
107 E Juliette St Ste 1 Thornton (60476) ***(G-20873)***
**Industrial Controls Inc** 630 752-8100
1183 Pierson Dr Ste 105 Batavia (60510) ***(G-1457)***
**Industrial Cstm Powdr Coating, Decatur** *Also called Industrial Cstm Pwdr Cting Inc* ***(G-7894)***
**Industrial Cstm Pwdr Cting Inc** 217 423-4272
661 E Wood St Decatur (62523) ***(G-7894)***
**Industrial Diamond Products** 847 272-7840
3045 Macarthur Blvd Northbrook (60062) ***(G-16276)***
**Industrial Electric Svc Inc (PA)** 708 997-2090
1055 Martingale Dr Bartlett (60103) ***(G-1356)***
**Industrial Enclosure Corp** 630 898-7499
619 N Loucks St Ste A Aurora (60505) ***(G-1171)***
**Industrial Fence Inc (PA)** 773 521-9900
1300 S Kilbourn Ave Chicago (60623) ***(G-5176)***
**Industrial Fiberglass Inc** 708 681-2707
1100 Main St Melrose Park (60160) ***(G-14657)***
**Industrial Filter Pump Mfg Co** 708 656-7800
4915 W 67th St Bedford Park (60638) ***(G-1556)***
**Industrial Filter Pump Mfg Co** 708 656-7800
5900 W Ogden Ave Cicero (60804) ***(G-7205)***
**Industrial Finance Systems** 847 592-0200
300 Park Blvd Itasca (60143) ***(G-12285)***
**Industrial Finishing Inc** 847 451-4230
2337 17th St Franklin Park (60131) ***(G-10497)***
**Industrial Gas Products Inc** 618 337-1030
2350 Falling Springs Rd East Saint Louis (62206) ***(G-8757)***
**Industrial Graphite Products** 630 350-0155
429 S County Line Rd Franklin Park (60131) ***(G-10498)***
**Industrial Graphite Sales LLC** 815 943-5502
450 Commanche Cir Harvard (60033) ***(G-11638)***
**Industrial Hard Chrome Ltd** 630 208-7000
501 Fluid Power Dr Geneva (60134) ***(G-10834)***
**Industrial Instrument Svc Corp** 773 581-3355
5643 W 63rd Pl Chicago (60638) ***(G-5177)***
**Industrial Kinetics Inc (PA)** 630 655-0300
2535 Curtiss St Downers Grove (60515) ***(G-8466)***
**Industrial Maintenance & McHy** 815 726-0030
9618 194th Pl Mokena (60448) ***(G-14874)***
**Industrial Market Place** 847 676-1900
7842 Lincoln Ave Ste 100 Skokie (60077) ***(G-20015)***
**Industrial Measurement Systems** 630 236-5901
2760 Beverly Dr Ste 4 Aurora (60502) ***(G-1027)***
**Industrial Mint Wldg Machining** 773 376-6526
1431 W Pershing Rd Chicago (60609) ***(G-5178)***
**Industrial Modern Pattern** 847 296-4930
7115 Barry St Rosemont (60018) ***(G-19006)***
**Industrial Molded Products** 847 358-2160
800 Allanson Rd Mundelein (60060) ***(G-15510)***
**Industrial Molds Inc (PA)** 815 397-2971
5175 27th Ave Rockford (61109) ***(G-18430)***
**Industrial Motion Control LLC (HQ)** 847 459-5200
1444 S Wolf Rd Wheeling (60090) ***(G-22076)***
**Industrial Packaging Division, Chicago** *Also called Flex-O-Glass Inc* ***(G-4859)***
**Industrial Pallets LLC** 708 351-8783
1462 Glen Ellyn Rd Glendale Heights (60139) ***(G-11034)***
**Industrial Park Machine & Tool** 708 754-7080
3326 Butler St S Chicago Hts (60411) ***(G-19105)***
**Industrial Phrm Resources Inc (PA)** 630 823-4700
1241 Hardt Cir Bartlett (60103) ***(G-1357)***
**Industrial Pipe and Supply Co** 708 652-7511
5100 W 16th St Chicago (60804) ***(G-5179)***
**Industrial Proccess and Sensor, Alton** *Also called C & L Manufacturing Entps* ***(G-565)***
**Industrial Roller Co (PA)** 618 234-0740
218 N Main St Smithton (62285) ***(G-20121)***
**Industrial Roller Co** 618 234-0740
211 N Smith St Smithton (62285) ***(G-20122)***
**Industrial Rubber & Sup Entp** 217 429-3747
2670 E Garfield Ave Decatur (62526) ***(G-7895)***
**Industrial Service Pallet Inc** 708 655-4963
1505 Hawk Ave Melrose Park (60160) ***(G-14658)***
**Industrial Service Solutions (PA)** 917 609-6979
875 N Michigan Ave Chicago (60611) ***(G-5180)***
**Industrial Solutions, Elgin** *Also called Wagner Systems Inc* ***(G-9226)***
**Industrial Specialty Chem Inc (HQ)** 708 339-1313
410 W 169th St South Holland (60473) ***(G-20280)***
**Industrial Steel Cnstr Inc (PA)** 630 232-7473
413 Old Kirk Rd Geneva (60134) ***(G-10835)***
**Industrial Steel Cnstr Inc** 219 885-7600
6120 River Rd Hodgkins (60525) ***(G-11976)***
**Industrial Technology, Chicago** *Also called Tower Oil & Technology Co* ***(G-6752)***
**Industrial Titanium Corp** 847 272-2730
3045 Commercial Ave Northbrook (60062) ***(G-16277)***
**Industrial Tool and Repair** 309 633-0939
218 S Starr Ln Ste A Peoria (61604) ***(G-17389)***
**Industrial Vacuum** 630 357-7700
21694 Oak Ln Maple Park (60151) ***(G-14200)***
**Industrial Waste Elimination** 312 498-0880
115 N Martha St Peoria (61614) ***(G-17390)***
**Industrial Water Management, Elgin** *Also called I W M Corporation* ***(G-9070)***
**Industrial Water Trtmnt Soltns (HQ)** 708 339-1313
16880 Lathrop Ave Harvey (60426) ***(G-11672)***
**Industrial Welder Rebuilders** 708 371-5688
11700 S Mayfield Ave Alsip (60803) ***(G-473)***
**Industrial Welding Inc** 815 535-9300
805 Antec Rd Rock Falls (61071) ***(G-18139)***
**Industrial Wire & Cable Corp** 847 726-8910
66 N Buesching Rd Lake Zurich (60047) ***(G-13086)***
**Industrial Wire Cable II Corp** 847 726-8910
66 N Buesching Rd Lake Zurich (60047) ***(G-13087)***
**Industrialexport.net, Northbrook** *Also called USA Industrial Export Corp* ***(G-16381)***
**Industries Publication Inc** 630 357-5269
4412 Black Partridge Ln Lisle (60532) ***(G-13602)***
**Industryreadycom Inc** 773 575-7001
2950 W Carroll Ave Ste 3 Chicago (60612) ***(G-5181)***
**Inelco, Chicago** *Also called Inglot Electronics Corp* ***(G-5192)***
**Ineos Americas LLC** 630 857-7463
150 W Warrenville Rd Naperville (60563) ***(G-15673)***
**Ineos Americas LLC** 630 857-7000
3030 Warrenville Rd # 650 Lisle (60532) ***(G-13603)***
**Ineos Bio Americas, Lisle** *Also called Ineos Bio USA LLC* ***(G-13604)***
**Ineos Bio USA LLC (HQ)** 630 857-7000
3030 Warrenville Rd # 650 Lisle (60532) ***(G-13604)***
**Ineos New Planet Bioenergy LLC** 630 857-7143
3030 Warrenville Rd # 650 Lisle (60532) ***(G-13605)***
**Ineos Silicas Americas LLC** 815 727-3651
111 Ingalls Ave Joliet (60435) ***(G-12517)***
**Ineos Styrolution America LLC** 815 423-5541
25846 S Frontage Rd Channahon (60410) ***(G-3576)***
**Ineos Styrolution America LLC (HQ)** 630 820-9500
4245 Meridian Pkwy # 151 Aurora (60504) ***(G-1028)***
**Ineos Technologies, Lisle** *Also called Ineos Americas LLC* ***(G-13603)***
**Inertia Machine Corporation** 815 233-1619
730 S Hancock Ave Ste A Freeport (61032) ***(G-10667)***
**Infamous Industries Inc** 708 789-2326
9253 S 89th Ct Hickory Hills (60457) ***(G-11771)***

## ALPHABETIC SECTION

Infiniscene Inc .......................................................... 630 567-0452
  25 W Hubbard St Fl 5  Chicago  (60654)  *(G-5182)*
Infinite Cnvrgnce Slutions Inc (PA) ........................ 224 764-3400
  3231 N Wilke Rd  Arlington Heights  (60004)  *(G-777)*
Infiniti Golf ............................................................... 630 520-0626
  245 W Roosevelt Rd Ste 9  West Chicago  (60185)  *(G-21718)*
Infinity Cmmncations Group Ltd ............................ 708 352-1086
  5350 East Ave  Countryside  (60525)  *(G-7434)*
Infinity Metal Spinning Inc .................................... 773 731-4467
  10247 S Avenue O  Chicago  (60617)  *(G-5183)*
Infinity Signs, Countryside  Also called Infinity Cmmncations Group Ltd  *(G-7434)*
Infinity Tool Mfg LLC ............................................ 618 439-4042
  11648 Skylane Dr  Benton  (62812)  *(G-2031)*
Infinitybox Inc ........................................................ 847 232-1991
  1410 Brummel Ave  Elk Grove Village  (60007)  *(G-9545)*
Inflight Entertainment Pdts, Carpentersville  Also called Video Refurbishing Svcs Inc  *(G-3304)*
Info Corner Materials Inc ....................................... 217 566-3561
  4300 Bachmann Dr  Springfield  (62707)  *(G-20456)*
Infocomm Div, Freeport  Also called Wagner Printing Co  *(G-10698)*
Infogix Inc (PA) ...................................................... 630 505-1800
  1240 E Diehl Rd Ste 400  Naperville  (60563)  *(G-15674)*
Infopro Inc ............................................................. 630 978-9231
  2920 Norwalk Ct  Aurora  (60502)  *(G-1029)*
Infor (us) Inc ......................................................... 312 279-1245
  8725 W Higgins Rd  Chicago  (60631)  *(G-5184)*
Infor (us) Inc ......................................................... 312 258-6000
  500 W Madison St Fl 22  Chicago  (60661)  *(G-5185)*
Information Builders Inc ........................................ 630 971-6700
  20 N Martingale Rd # 430  Schaumburg  (60173)  *(G-19565)*
Information Resources Inc .................................... 312 474-3380
  150 N Clinton St  Chicago  (60661)  *(G-5186)*
Information Resources Inc (PA) ............................ 312 726-1221
  150 N Clinton St  Chicago  (60661)  *(G-5187)*
Information Resources Inc .................................... 312 474-3154
  1201 Nashua Ln  Bartlett  (60133)  *(G-1318)*
Information Resources Inc .................................... 312 474-8900
  550 W Washington Blvd # 6  Chicago  (60661)  *(G-5188)*
Information Usa Inc .............................................. 312 943-6288
  1555 N Dearborn Pkwy Ofc  Chicago  (60610)  *(G-5189)*
Informative Systems Inc ....................................... 217 523-8422
  5119 Old Route 36  Springfield  (62707)  *(G-20457)*
Infoscan, Chicago  Also called Information Resources Inc  *(G-5187)*
Infosys Limited ...................................................... 630 482-5000
  2300 Cabot Dr Ste 250  Lisle  (60532)  *(G-13606)*
Infrastructure Def Tech LLC .................................. 800 379-1822
  6550 Revlon Dr  Belvidere  (61008)  *(G-1763)*
Infratrol LLC .......................................................... 779 475-3098
  602 E Blackhawk Dr  Byron  (61010)  *(G-2916)*
Ing Bank Fsb ......................................................... 312 981-1236
  21 E Chestnut St  Chicago  (60611)  *(G-5190)*
Ingenious Concepts Inc ......................................... 630 539-8059
  22w313 Temple Dr  Medinah  (60157)  *(G-14576)*
Ingenium Aerospace LLC ...................................... 815 525-2000
  5389 International Dr  Rockford  (61109)  *(G-18431)*
Ingersoll Cutting Tool Company (HQ) .................... 815 387-6600
  845 S Lyford Rd  Rockford  (61108)  *(G-18432)*
Ingersoll Machine Tools Inc (HQ) .......................... 815 987-6000
  707 Fulton Ave  Rockford  (61103)  *(G-18433)*
Ingersoll Prod Systems LLC (HQ) ......................... 815 637-8500
  1301 Eddy Ave  Rockford  (61103)  *(G-18434)*
Ingersoll-Rand Company ....................................... 630 530-3800
  131 W Diversey Ave  Elmhurst  (60126)  *(G-9886)*
Ingersoll-Rand Company ....................................... 704 655-4000
  15768 Collection Ctr Dr  Chicago  (60693)  *(G-5191)*
Inglese Box Co Ltd ............................................... 847 669-1700
  13851 Prime Point Rd  Huntley  (60142)  *(G-12149)*
Inglot Electronics Corp .......................................... 773 286-5881
  4878 N Elston Ave  Chicago  (60630)  *(G-5192)*
Ingram, Rockford  Also called Celinco Inc  *(G-18301)*
Ingram Soil Testing Centre, Athens  Also called D and I Analyst Inc  *(G-937)*
Ingram Vault Co, Jerseyville  Also called Unique Concrete Concepts Inc  *(G-12427)*
Ingredients Inc ...................................................... 847 419-9595
  1130 W Lake Cook Rd # 320  Buffalo Grove  (60089)  *(G-2708)*
Ingredion Incorporated (PA) .................................. 708 551-2600
  5 Westbrook Corporate Ctr # 500  Westchester  (60154)  *(G-21845)*
Ingredion Incorporated .......................................... 309 550-9136
  8310 W Rte 24  Mapleton  (61547)  *(G-14210)*
Ingredion Incorporated .......................................... 708 551-2600
  141 W Jackson Blvd # 340  Chicago  (60604)  *(G-5193)*
Ingredion Incorporated .......................................... 708 728-3535
  6400 S Archer Rd  Summit Argo  (60501)  *(G-20764)*
Ingredion Incorporated .......................................... 708 563-2400
  6400 S Archer Rd Bldg 90  Argo  (60501)  *(G-693)*
Inhance Technologies LLC .................................... 630 231-7515
  829 W Hawthorne Ln  West Chicago  (60185)  *(G-21719)*
Initial Choice ......................................................... 847 234-5884
  226 E Westminster  Lake Forest  (60045)  *(G-12917)*

Initial Impressions Inc ........................................... 630 208-9399
  405 Stevens St  Geneva  (60134)  *(G-10836)*
Initially Ewe .......................................................... 708 246-7777
  1058 Hillgrove Ave  Western Springs  (60558)  *(G-21868)*
Ink Enterprises Inc ................................................ 815 547-5515
  1982 Belford North Dr  Belvidere  (61008)  *(G-1764)*
Ink Smart Inc ........................................................ 708 349-9555
  9979 W 151st St  Orland Park  (60462)  *(G-16868)*
Ink Solution, Flossmoor  Also called Springbox Inc  *(G-10229)*
Ink Solutions LLC (PA) ......................................... 847 593-5200
  800 Estes Ave  Elk Grove Village  (60007)  *(G-9546)*
Ink Spot Printing ................................................... 773 528-0288
  2 N Riverside Plz Ste 365  Chicago  (60606)  *(G-5194)*
Ink Spot Silk Screen .............................................. 847 724-6234
  84 Park Dr  Glenview  (60025)  *(G-11147)*
Ink Spots Prtg & Meida Design .............................. 708 754-1300
  1131 175th St Ste B  Homewood  (60430)  *(G-12102)*
Ink Spots Prtg Mdia Design Inc ............................. 708 754-1300
  18300 S Halsted St  Glenwood  (60425)  *(G-11216)*
Ink Stop Inc .......................................................... 847 478-0631
  330 Foxford Dr  Buffalo Grove  (60089)  *(G-2709)*
Ink Systems Inc .................................................... 847 427-2200
  800 Estes Ave  Elk Grove Village  (60007)  *(G-9547)*
Ink Well, Chicago  Also called Jans Graphics Inc  *(G-5278)*
Ink Well ................................................................. 618 398-1427
  10603 Lincoln Trl  Fairview Heights  (62208)  *(G-10169)*
Ink Well Printing ................................................... 815 224-1366
  24 W Us Highway 6  Peru  (61354)  *(G-17514)*
Ink Well Printing & Design Ltd .............................. 847 923-8060
  604 Albion Ave  Schaumburg  (60193)  *(G-19566)*
Ink2image, Glenview  Also called CIS Systems Inc  *(G-11114)*
Inkdot LLC ............................................................ 630 768-6415
  2032 W Fulton St 263a  Chicago  (60612)  *(G-5195)*
Inkling ................................................................... 312 376-8129
  6723 N Greenview Ave  Chicago  (60626)  *(G-5196)*
Inkn Tees ............................................................... 847 244-2266
  2901 N Delany Rd Ste 105  Waukegan  (60087)  *(G-21570)*
Inkpartners Corporation ........................................ 773 843-1786
  3662 S Hermitage Ave  Chicago  (60609)  *(G-5197)*
Inky Printers (PA) .................................................. 815 235-3700
  122 N Van Buren Ave  Freeport  (61032)  *(G-10668)*
Inlaid Woodcraft Co .............................................. 815 784-6386
  12814 Ellen Dr  Genoa  (60135)  *(G-10880)*
Inland Broaching & Tool Co, Elgin  Also called J M Resources Inc  *(G-9080)*
Inland Broaching and TI Co LLC ........................... 847 233-0033
  1441 Timber Dr  Elgin  (60123)  *(G-9077)*
Inland Fastener Inc ............................................... 630 293-3800
  770 W Hawthorne Ln  West Chicago  (60185)  *(G-21720)*
Inland Midwest Corporation (HQ) .......................... 773 775-2111
  612 W Lamont Rd  Elmhurst  (60126)  *(G-9887)*
Inland Plastics Inc ................................................. 815 933-3500
  1310 E Birch St  Kankakee  (60901)  *(G-12625)*
Inland Tech Holdings LLC ..................................... 618 476-7678
  609 S Breese St  Millstadt  (62260)  *(G-14827)*
Inland Tool Company ............................................ 217 792-3206
  727 N Topper Dr  Mount Pulaski  (62548)  *(G-15389)*
Inlet & Pipe Protection Inc .................................... 630 355-3288
  24137 111th St Ste A  Naperville  (60564)  *(G-15811)*
Inman Electric Motors Inc ..................................... 815 223-2288
  314 Civic Rd  La Salle  (61301)  *(G-12778)*
Inn Intl Newspaper Network .................................. 309 764-5314
  1521 47th Ave  Moline  (61265)  *(G-14943)*
Inn Partners LLC ................................................... 309 743-0800
  1510 47th Ave  Moline  (61265)  *(G-14944)*
Innerweld Cover Co .............................................. 847 497-3009
  21227 W Coml Dr Ste E  Mundelein  (60060)  *(G-15511)*
Innerworkings Inc (PA) ......................................... 312 642-3700
  600 W Chicago Ave Ste 850  Chicago  (60654)  *(G-5198)*
Innocor Inc ............................................................ 630 231-0622
  1700 Downs Dr Ste 200  West Chicago  (60185)  *(G-21721)*
Innocor Foam Tech W Chcago LLC ...................... 732 945-6222
  1750 Downs Dr  West Chicago  (60185)  *(G-21722)*
Innocor Foam Technologies LLC ........................... 630 293-0780
  1750 Downs Dr  West Chicago  (60185)  *(G-21723)*
Innolux Technology USA Inc (HQ) ........................ 847 490-5315
  2300 Barrington Rd # 400  Hoffman Estates  (60169)  *(G-12018)*
Innophos Inc ......................................................... 708 757-6111
  1101 Arnold St  Chicago Heights  (60411)  *(G-7103)*
Innophos Inc ......................................................... 773 468-2300
  512 E 138th St  Chicago  (60803)  *(G-5199)*
Innoquest Inc ........................................................ 815 337-8555
  910 Hobe Rd  Woodstock  (60098)  *(G-22575)*
Innotech Manufacturing LLC ................................. 618 244-6261
  915 S 13th St  Mount Vernon  (62864)  *(G-15415)*
Innova Global LLC ................................................ 630 568-5609
  16w235 83rd St Ste A  Burr Ridge  (60527)  *(G-2853)*
Innova Print Fulfillment Inc ................................... 630 845-3215
  2000 Batavia Ave # 310  Geneva  (60134)  *(G-10837)*
Innova Systems Inc ............................................... 630 920-8880
  8330 S Madison St Ste 60  Burr Ridge  (60527)  *(G-2854)*

**Innova Uev, Burr Ridge** *Also called Innova Global LLC* ***(G-2853)***
**Innova Uev LLC** ....630 568-5609
16w235 83rd St Ste A Burr Ridge (60527) ***(G-2855)***
**Innovalink, Chicago** *Also called Asset Partners Inc* ***(G-3966)***
**Innovate Technologies Inc** ....630 587-4220
761 N 17th St Saint Charles (60174) ***(G-19197)***
**Innovation Center, Ottawa** *Also called Fairmount Santrol Inc* ***(G-16958)***
**Innovation Plus Power Systems** ....630 457-1105
3960 Commerce Dr Saint Charles (60174) ***(G-19198)***
**Innovation Specialists Inc** ....815 372-9001
2328 E Lincoln Hwy # 356 New Lenox (60451) ***(G-15885)***
**Innovations For Learning Inc** ....800 975-3452
518 Davis St Evanston (60201) ***(G-10056)***
**Innovative Automation** ....708 418-8720
3116 192nd St Lansing (60438) ***(G-13166)***
**Innovative Components Inc** ....847 885-9050
1050 National Pkwy Schaumburg (60173) ***(G-19567)***
**Innovative Custom Software Inc** ....630 892-5022
1323 Bond St Ste 103 Naperville (60563) ***(G-15675)***
**Innovative Design & Graphics, Evanston** *Also called Innovtive Design Graphics Corp* ***(G-10057)***
**Innovative Design and RES Inc** ....217 322-3907
338 W Lafayette St Rushville (62681) ***(G-19093)***
**Innovative Fix Solutions LLC** ....815 395-8500
1122 Milford Ave Rockford (61109) ***(G-18435)***
**Innovative Fix Solutions LLC** ....815 395-8500
1122 Milford Ave Rockford (61109) ***(G-18436)***
**Innovative Gringing Inc** ....630 766-4567
690 County Line Rd Bensenville (60106) ***(G-1919)***
**Innovative Hess Products LLC** ....847 676-3260
2605 S Clearbrook Dr Arlington Heights (60005) ***(G-778)***
**Innovative Industrial Svcs LLC** ....309 527-2035
700 S Fayette St El Paso (61738) ***(G-8870)***
**Innovative Machine Inc** ....309 945-9445
925 Dilenbeck Dr Geneseo (61254) ***(G-10801)***
**Innovative Mag Drive LLC** ....630 543-4240
6911 W 59th St Chicago (60638) ***(G-5200)***
**Innovative Mag-Drive LLC** ....630 543-4240
409 S Vista Ave Addison (60101) ***(G-153)***
**Innovative Mktg Solutions Inc** ....630 227-4300
1320 N Plum Grove Rd Schaumburg (60173) ***(G-19568)***
**Innovative Mobile Marketing** ....815 929-1029
1511 Commerce Dr Bourbonnais (60914) ***(G-2400)***
**Innovative Molecular Diagnosti** ....630 845-8246
1436 Fargo Blvd Geneva (60134) ***(G-10838)***
**Innovative Plastech Inc** ....630 232-1808
1260 Kingsland Dr Batavia (60510) ***(G-1458)***
**Innovative Plastic A Teraco Co, Roselle** *Also called Teraco-II Inc* ***(G-18981)***
**Innovative Projects Lab Inc** ....847 605-2125
150 N Martingale Rd # 838 Schaumburg (60173) ***(G-19569)***
**Innovative Rack & Gear Company** ....630 766-2652
365 Balm Ct Wood Dale (60191) ***(G-22382)***
**Innovative SEC Systems Inc** ....217 355-6308
1809 Woodfield Dr Savoy (61874) ***(G-19410)***
**Innovative Sports Training Inc** ....773 244-6470
3711 N Ravenswood Ave # 150 Chicago (60613) ***(G-5201)***
**Innovative Swab Technologies, Waukegan** *Also called Great Midwest Packaging LLC* ***(G-21565)***
**Innovo Corp** ....847 616-0063
2385 United Ln Elk Grove Village (60007) ***(G-9548)***
**Innovtive Design Graphics Corp** ....847 475-7772
1327 Greenleaf St 1 Evanston (60202) ***(G-10057)***
**Innovtive Design Solutions LLC** ....708 547-1942
2501 Van Buren St Bellwood (60104) ***(G-1709)***
**Innoware Plastic Inc** ....678 690-5100
150 Saunders Rd Ste 150 Lake Forest (60045) ***(G-12918)***
**Inoprints** ....312 994-2351
700 N Green St Ste 503 Chicago (60642) ***(G-5202)***
**Inpharmco Inc** ....708 596-9262
1028 E 168th St South Holland (60473) ***(G-20281)***
**Inplex Custom Extruders LLC** ....847 827-7046
1657 Frontenac Rd Naperville (60563) ***(G-15676)***
**Inpro/Seal LLC** ....309 787-8940
4221 81st Ave W Rock Island (61201) ***(G-18184)***
**Inrule Technology Inc** ....312 648-1800
651 W Washington Blvd # 500 Chicago (60661) ***(G-5203)***
**Inscerco Mfg Inc** ....708 597-8777
4621 138th St Crestwood (60445) ***(G-7489)***
**Insertech LLC (PA)** ....847 516-6184
711 Indl Dr Cary (60013) ***(G-3354)***
**Insertech International Inc** ....847 416-6184
711 Industrial Dr Cary (60013) ***(G-3355)***
**Inside Beverages** ....847 438-1338
635 Oakwood Rd Lake Zurich (60047) ***(G-13088)***
**Inside Council** ....312 654-3500
222 S Riverside Plz # 620 Chicago (60606) ***(G-5204)***
**Inside Track Trading** ....630 585-9218
2905 Lahinch Ct Aurora (60503) ***(G-1030)***
**Insight Advertising Inc** ....847 647-0004
6954 W Touhy Ave Ste 101 Niles (60714) ***(G-15989)***
**Insight Beverages Inc** ....847 438-1598
750 Oakwood Rd Lake Zurich (60047) ***(G-13089)***
**Insight Beverages Inc (HQ)** ....847 438-1598
750 Oakwood Rd Lake Zurich (60047) ***(G-13090)***
**Insignia Design Ltd** ....301 254-9221
2118 Plum Grove Rd 191 Rolling Meadows (60008) ***(G-18734)***
**Insignia Stone** ....815 463-9802
1901 Howell Dr Ste 1 New Lenox (60451) ***(G-15886)***
**Inspira Industries Inc** ....630 907-2123
1455 Carlson Ct North Aurora (60542) ***(G-16134)***
**Instant Collating Service Inc** ....312 243-4703
2443 W 16th St Chicago (60608) ***(G-5205)***
**Instantwhip-Chicago Inc** ....773 235-5588
1535 N Cicero Ave Chicago (60651) ***(G-5206)***
**Instar Auto Carriers LLC** ....708 428-6318
15255 S 94th Ave Ste 500 Orland Park (60462) ***(G-16869)***
**Institute For Public Affairs** ....773 772-0100
2040 N Milwaukee Ave Fl 2 Chicago (60647) ***(G-5207)***
**Institutional Equipment Inc (PA)** ....630 771-0990
704 Veterans Pkwy Ste B Bolingbrook (60440) ***(G-2321)***
**Institutional Foods Packing Co** ....847 904-5250
2350 Ravine Way Ste 200 Glenview (60025) ***(G-11148)***
**Instrmntation Ctrl Systems Inc** ....630 543-6200
360 Heritage Dr Roselle (60172) ***(G-18947)***
**Instrument & Valve Services Co** ....708 535-5120
4320 166th St Oak Forest (60452) ***(G-16585)***
**Instrument Laboratories Div, Wheeling** *Also called International Electro Magnetic* ***(G-22077)***
**Instrument Services Inc** ....815 623-2993
4075 Steele Dr Machesney Park (61115) ***(G-14082)***
**Instrumentalists Inc** ....847 446-5000
1838 Techny Ct Northbrook (60062) ***(G-16278)***
**Instrumentics, Rosemont** *Also called Lifewatch Technologies Inc* ***(G-19014)***
**Insty Prints Palatine Inc** ....847 963-0000
453 S Vermont St Ste A Palatine (60067) ***(G-17042)***
**Insty-Prints, Waukegan** *Also called Instyprints of Waukegan Inc* ***(G-21571)***
**Insty-Prints, Elk Grove Village** *Also called Valee Inc* ***(G-9804)***
**Insty-Prints, Palatine** *Also called Insty Prints Palatine Inc* ***(G-17042)***
**Insty-Prints of Champaign Inc** ....217 356-6166
1822 Glenn Park Dr Champaign (61821) ***(G-3501)***
**Instyprints of Waukegan Inc** ....847 336-5599
1711 Grand Ave Ste 1 Waukegan (60085) ***(G-21571)***
**Insulated Transport Products, Glenview** *Also called Signode Industrial Group LLC* ***(G-11198)***
**Insulation Solutions Inc** ....309 698-0062
401 Truck Haven Rd East Peoria (61611) ***(G-8714)***
**Insulators Supply Inc** ....847 394-2836
741 Pinecrest Dr Prospect Heights (60070) ***(G-17780)***
**Insulco Inc** ....309 353-6145
825 S 2nd St Pekin (61554) ***(G-17270)***
**Insync Manufacturing LLC** ....815 304-6300
601a N 5th Ave Kankakee (60901) ***(G-12626)***
**Intec-Mexico LLC** ....847 358-0088
666 S Vermont St Palatine (60067) ***(G-17043)***
**Intech Industries Inc** ....847 487-5599
1101 Brown St Wauconda (60084) ***(G-21473)***
**Integra Graphics and Forms Inc** ....708 385-0950
4749 136th St Crestwood (60445) ***(G-7490)***
**Integral Automation Inc** ....630 654-4300
16 W 171 Shore Ct Burr Ridge (60527) ***(G-2856)***
**Integratech, Elgin** *Also called Integrity Technologies LLC* ***(G-9078)***
**Integrated Circuits Research** ....630 830-9024
6600 Appletree St Hanover Park (60133) ***(G-11583)***
**Integrated Display Systems (PA)** ....708 298-9661
5130 W 16th St Cicero (60804) ***(G-7206)***
**Integrated Dna Tech Modem** ....847 745-1700
8930 Gross Point Rd Skokie (60077) ***(G-20016)***
**Integrated Document Tech, Itasca** *Also called Imaging Systems Inc* ***(G-12283)***
**Integrated Industries Inc** ....773 299-1970
4201 W 36th St Ste 1 Chicago (60632) ***(G-5208)***
**Integrated Label Corporation** ....815 874-2500
3407 Pyramid Dr Rockford (61109) ***(G-18437)***
**Integrated Lighting Tech Inc (PA)** ....630 750-3786
1317 Rosemary Dr Bolingbrook (60490) ***(G-2322)***
**Integrated Mdsg Systems LLC** ....630 571-2020
1111 W 22nd St Ste 600 Oak Brook (60523) ***(G-16525)***
**Integrated Measurement Systems** ....847 956-1940
600 Bonnie Ln Elk Grove Village (60007) ***(G-9549)***
**Integrated Media Inc** ....217 854-6260
909 Broadway Ste B Carlinville (62626) ***(G-3040)***
**Integrated Medical Tech Inc (PA)** ....309 662-3614
2422 E Washington St # 103 Bloomington (61704) ***(G-2183)***
**Integrated Mfg Tech LLC** ....618 282-8306
401 Randolph St Red Bud (62278) ***(G-17943)***
**Integrated Packg & Fastener** ....847 439-5730
1678 Carmen Dr Elk Grove Village (60007) ***(G-9550)***
**Integrated Power Services LLC** ....708 877-5310
17001 Vincennes Rd Thornton (60476) ***(G-20874)***

**Integrated Print Graphics Inc (PA)**.....847 695-6777
645 Stevenson Rd South Elgin (60177) *(G-20206)*
**Integrated Print Graphics Inc**.....847 888-2880
635 Stevenson Rd South Elgin (60177) *(G-20207)*
**Integrating Green Technologies, Bolingbrook** *Also called Integrated Lighting Tech Inc (G-2322)*
**Integrity Manufacturing Inc**.....815 514-8230
612 Schoolgate Ct New Lenox (60451) *(G-15887)*
**Integrity Material Hdlg Svcs**.....847 669-6233
11932 Oak Creek Pkwy R Huntley (60142) *(G-12150)*
**Integrity Prtg McHy Svcs LLC**.....847 834-9484
1650 Glen Lake Rd Hoffman Estates (60169) *(G-12019)*
**Integrity Sign Company**.....708 532-5038
18770 88th Ave Unit A Mokena (60448) *(G-14875)*
**Integrity Technologies LLC**.....850 240-6089
1140 Peachtree Ln Unit B Elgin (60120) *(G-9078)*
**Intek Strength, Herrin** *Also called Orthotech Sports - Med Eqp Inc (G-11752)*
**Intel Americas Inc**.....847 706-5779
425 N Matingale 1500 Schaumburg (60173) *(G-19570)*
**Intel Corp**.....847 602-1170
1 Corporate Dr Ste 310 Long Grove (60047) *(G-13891)*
**Intel Corporation**.....408 765-8080
21003 Network Pl Chicago (60673) *(G-5209)*
**Intel East**.....312 725-2014
660 W Pickwick Ct Apt 1w Mount Prospect (60056) *(G-15338)*
**Intel Printing Inc**.....708 343-1144
1805 Beach St Broadview (60155) *(G-2587)*
**Intelex Usa LLC**.....847 496-1727
105 Prairie Lake Rd East Dundee (60118) *(G-8647)*
**Intellgent Prcsses Automtn Inc**.....630 656-1215
111 S Lombard Rd Ste 7 Addison (60101) *(G-154)*
**Intellidrain Inc**.....312 725-4332
600 Davis St Fl 3 Evanston (60201) *(G-10058)*
**Intelligent Designs LLC**.....630 235-7965
1640 Raleigh Ct Wheaton (60189) *(G-21957)*
**Intelligent Instrument Sy**.....630 323-3911
16w251 S Frontage Rd # 23 Burr Ridge (60527) *(G-2857)*
**Intelliginix Consulting Svcs, Chicago** *Also called Turner Agward (G-6794)*
**Intelligrated Systems Inc**.....630 985-4350
9014 Heritage Pkwy # 308 Woodridge (60517) *(G-22495)*
**Intelliwheels Inc**.....630 341-1942
60 Hazelwood Dr Champaign (61820) *(G-3502)*
**Inter Swiss Ltd**.....773 379-0400
5410 W Roosevelt Rd # 242 Chicago (60644) *(G-5210)*
**Inter-Continental Trdg USA Inc**.....847 640-1777
1601 W Algonquin Rd Mount Prospect (60056) *(G-15339)*
**Inter-Market Inc**.....847 729-5330
1946 Lehigh Ave Ste A Glenview (60026) *(G-11149)*
**Inter-State Studio & Pubg Co**.....815 874-0342
3446 Colony Bay Dr Rockford (61109) *(G-18438)*
**Inter-Trade Global LLC**.....618 954-6119
107 W Main St Belleville (62220) *(G-1637)*
**Interactive Bldg Solutions LLC**.....815 724-0525
1919 Cherry Hill Rd Joliet (60433) *(G-12518)*
**Interactive Data Technologies, Athens** *Also called Donnas House of Type Inc (G-938)*
**Interactive Inks Coatings Corp**.....847 289-8710
1610 Shanahan Dr South Elgin (60177) *(G-20208)*
**Interesting Products Inc**.....773 265-1100
328 N Albany Ave Chicago (60612) *(G-5211)*
**Interexpo Ltd**.....847 489-7056
22438 N Clayton Ct Kildeer (60047) *(G-12700)*
**Interface Protein Tech Inc**.....630 963-8809
5401 Patton Dr Ste 110 Lisle (60532) *(G-13607)*
**Interfaceflor LLC**.....312 775-6307
600 W Van Buren St # 800 Chicago (60607) *(G-5212)*
**Interfaceflor LLC**.....312 836-3389
440 N Wells St Ste 200 Chicago (60654) *(G-5213)*
**Interfaceflor LLC**.....312 822-9640
222 Merchandise Mart Plz # 130 Chicago (60654) *(G-5214)*
**Interflo Industries Inc**.....847 228-0606
695 Lunt Ave Elk Grove Village (60007) *(G-9551)*
**Intergrted Thrmforming Systems**.....630 906-6895
305 Hankes Ave Aurora (60505) *(G-1172)*
**Interior Fashions Contract**.....847 358-6050
120 S Northwest Hwy Palatine (60074) *(G-17044)*
**Interior Tectonics LLC**.....312 515-7779
1716 N Cleveland Ave Chicago (60614) *(G-5215)*
**Interlake Mecalux Inc (HQ)**.....708 344-9999
1600 N 25th Ave Melrose Park (60160) *(G-14659)*
**Interlake Mecalux Inc**.....815 844-7191
701 N Interlake Dr Pontiac (61764) *(G-17703)*
**Intermail Direct Marketing**.....630 274-6333
151 Eastern Ave Bensenville (60106) *(G-1920)*
**Intermatic Incorporated (PA)**.....815 675-2321
7777 Winn Rd Spring Grove (60081) *(G-20337)*
**Intermec Technologies Corp**.....312 475-0106
375 W Erie St Apt 314 Chicago (60654) *(G-5216)*
**Intermerican Clinical Svcs Inc**.....773 252-1147
2651 W Division St Chicago (60622) *(G-5217)*
**Intermet Metals Services Inc**.....847 605-1300
1375 E Wdfield Rd Ste 520 Schaumburg (60173) *(G-19571)*
**Interminal Services**.....773 978-8129
2040 E 106th St Chicago (60617) *(G-5218)*
**Intermodal Live, Western Springs** *Also called Impact Technologies Inc (G-21867)*
**Intermolding Technology LLC**.....847 376-8517
85 Bradrock Dr Des Plaines (60018) *(G-8212)*
**Intermountain Electronics Inc**.....618 339-6743
400 Swan Ave Centralia (62801) *(G-3419)*
**International Automotive**.....815 544-2102
1236 Crosslink Pkwy Belvidere (61008) *(G-1765)*
**International Bus Mchs Corp**.....847 706-3461
425 N Martingale Rd Schaumburg (60173) *(G-19572)*
**International Bus Mchs Corp**.....312 423-6640
222 S Riverside Plz # 1 Chicago (60606) *(G-5219)*
**International College Surgeons (PA)**.....312 642-6502
1516 N Lake Shore Dr Fl 3 Chicago (60610) *(G-5220)*
**International Control Svcs Inc**.....217 422-6700
606 W Imboden Dr Decatur (62521) *(G-7896)*
**International Cutting Die Inc**.....708 343-3333
2030 Janice Ave Melrose Park (60160) *(G-14660)*
**International Drug Dev Cons**.....847 634-9586
1549 Rfd Long Grove (60047) *(G-13892)*
**International Electro Magnetic**.....847 358-4622
1033 Noel Ave Wheeling (60090) *(G-22077)*
**International Filter Mfg Corp**.....217 324-2303
713 W Columbian Blvd S Litchfield (62056) *(G-13688)*
**International Golden Foods Inc**.....630 860-5552
819 Industrial Dr Bensenville (60106) *(G-1921)*
**International Graphics & Assoc**.....630 584-2248
38w598 Clubhouse Dr Saint Charles (60175) *(G-19199)*
**International Ice Bagging Syst**.....312 633-4000
234 Dennis Ln Glencoe (60022) *(G-11000)*
**International Locksmith, Glencoe** *Also called International Silver Plating (G-11001)*
**International Marketing & Mfg, Chicago** *Also called I M M Inc (G-5131)*
**International Mold & Prod LLC**.....313 617-5251
1397 Mayfair Ln Grayslake (60030) *(G-11347)*
**International Molding Mch Co**.....708 354-1380
1201 Barnsdale Rd Ste 1 La Grange Park (60526) *(G-12757)*
**International News**.....773 283-8323
4917 N Milwaukee Ave 14 Chicago (60630) *(G-5221)*
**International Paint LLC**.....847 623-4200
1 E Water St Waukegan (60085) *(G-21572)*
**International Paper Company**.....708 728-8200
5300 W 73rd St Chicago (60638) *(G-5222)*
**International Paper Company**.....618 233-5460
3001 Otto St Belleville (62226) *(G-1638)*
**International Paper Company**.....630 896-2061
1001 Knell St Montgomery (60538) *(G-15050)*
**International Paper Company**.....815 398-2100
2100 23rd Ave Rockford (61104) *(G-18439)*
**International Paper Company**.....708 562-6000
401 Northwest Ave Northlake (60164) *(G-16440)*
**International Paper Company**.....
1300 Bowes Rd Elgin (60123) *(G-9079)*
**International Paper Company**.....217 735-1221
1601 5th St Lincoln (62656) *(G-13411)*
**International Paper Company**.....630 449-7200
2540 Prospect Ct Aurora (60502) *(G-1031)*
**International Paper Company**.....630 585-3300
4140 Campus Dr Aurora (60504) *(G-1032)*
**International Paper Company**.....630 653-3500
139 Fullerton Ave Carol Stream (60188) *(G-3173)*
**International Paper Company**.....847 390-1300
100 E Oakton St Des Plaines (60018) *(G-8213)*
**International Paper Company**.....217 774-2176
500 W Dacey Dr Shelbyville (62565) *(G-19909)*
**International Paper Company**.....847 228-7227
25 Northwest Point Blvd # 300 Elk Grove Village (60007) *(G-9552)*
**International Paper Company**.....708 728-1000
7333 S Lockwood Ave Bedford Park (60638) *(G-1557)*
**International Paper Company**.....630 585-3400
4160 Campus Dr Aurora (60504) *(G-1033)*
**International Paper Company**.....630 250-1300
1225 W Bryn Mawr Ave Itasca (60143) *(G-12286)*
**International Polymers, Kewanee** *Also called Blue Chip Industries Inc (G-12671)*
**International Proc Co Amer**.....847 437-8400
1485 Lively Blvd Elk Grove Village (60007) *(G-9553)*
**International Services, Chicago** *Also called Success Vending Mfg Co LLC (G-6612)*
**International Silver Plating**.....847 835-0705
364 Park Ave Glencoe (60022) *(G-11001)*
**International Source Solutions**.....847 251-8265
3229 Wilmette Ave Wilmette (60091) *(G-22255)*
**International Spring Company**.....847 470-8170
7901 Nagle Ave Morton Grove (60053) *(G-15203)*
**International Supply Co**.....309 249-6211
2717 W North St Edelstein (61526) *(G-8780)*
**International Tactical Trainin**.....872 221-4886
915 N Racine Ave Apt 2se Chicago (60642) *(G-5223)*

ALPHABETIC

(PA)=Parent Co (HQ)=Headquarters (DH)=Div Headquarters
2017 Harris Illinois Industrial Directory
1277

**International Technologies Inc**...847 301-9005
627 Estes Ave Schaumburg (60193) ***(G-19573)***
**International Titanium Powder**...815 834-2112
20634 Gaskin Dr Lockport (60446) ***(G-13723)***
**International Toner Corp (PA)**...847 276-2700
1081 Johnson Dr Buffalo Grove (60089) ***(G-2710)***
**International Traffic Corp**...815 675-1430
2402 Spring Ridge Dr E Spring Grove (60081) ***(G-20338)***
**International Water Werks Inc**...847 669-1902
11470 Kreutzer Rd Huntley (60142) ***(G-12151)***
**International Wood Design Inc**...773 227-9270
941 N California Ave Chicago (60622) ***(G-5224)***
**International Wood Products**...630 530-6164
2812 Stuart Kaplan Ct Aurora (60503) ***(G-1034)***
**Internet Industry Almanac, Arlington Heights** *Also called Computer Industry Almanac Inc* ***(G-738)***
**Internet Retailer, Chicago** *Also called Vertical Web Media LLC* ***(G-6888)***
**Interntional Casings Group Inc (PA)**...773 376-9200
4420 S Wolcott Ave Chicago (60609) ***(G-5225)***
**Interntional Chem Formulations, Broadview** *Also called De Enterprises Inc* ***(G-2571)***
**Interntional Cmpt Concepts Inc**...847 808-7789
300 Wainwright Dr Northbrook (60062) ***(G-16279)***
**Interntional Eqp Solutions LLC (HQ)**...630 570-6880
2211 York Rd Ste 320 Oak Brook (60523) ***(G-16526)***
**Interntional Metal Finshg Svcs**...815 234-5254
8692 Glacier Dr Byron (61010) ***(G-2917)***
**Interntnal Awkening Ministries**...630 653-8616
123 N Washington St Wheaton (60187) ***(G-21958)***
**Interntnal Ingredient Mall LLC**...630 462-1414
1900 Averill Rd Geneva (60134) ***(G-10839)***
**Interntnal Mscal Suppliers Inc**...847 774-2938
364 Pennsylvania Ave Glen Ellyn (60137) ***(G-10974)***
**Interntnal Mseum Srgcal Scence, Chicago** *Also called International College Surgeons* ***(G-5220)***
**Interntonal Creative RES Group, Chicago** *Also called Baka Vitaliy* ***(G-4027)***
**Interntonal Hair Solutions LLC**...404 474-3547
120 W Golf Rd Schaumburg (60195) ***(G-19574)***
**Interoptic, Naperville** *Also called Advantage Optics Inc* ***(G-15592)***
**Interplex Daystar Inc**...847 455-2424
11130 King St 1 Franklin Park (60131) ***(G-10499)***
**Interra Global Corporation**...847 292-8600
800 Busse Hwy Ste 101 Park Ridge (60068) ***(G-17204)***
**Interscience International, Bolingbrook** *Also called Interscience Technologies Inc* ***(G-2323)***
**Interscience Technologies Inc**...630 759-4444
205 Sunshine Dr Bldg 100 Bolingbrook (60490) ***(G-2323)***
**Intersect Healthcare Systems**...847 457-2159
230 Northgate St Unit 145 Lake Forest (60045) ***(G-12919)***
**Interserve, Belvidere** *Also called Caisson Inc* ***(G-1741)***
**Intersol Industries Inc**...630 238-0385
241 James St Bensenville (60106) ***(G-1922)***
**Intersports Screen Printing**...773 489-7383
2407 N Central Park Ave Chicago (60647) ***(G-5226)***
**Interstate All Battery Center**...217 214-1069
101 N 48th St Quincy (62305) ***(G-17840)***
**Interstate Battery System Intl**...708 424-2288
10336 S Cicero Ave Oak Lawn (60453) ***(G-16626)***
**Interstate Cargo Inc**...630 701-7744
380 Internationale Dr A Bolingbrook (60440) ***(G-2324)***
**Interstate Graphics Inc**...815 877-6777
7817 Burden Rd Machesney Park (61115) ***(G-14083)***
**Interstate Industrial Tech**...618 286-4900
510 N Main St Dupo (62239) ***(G-8572)***
**Interstate Mechanical Inc**...312 961-9291
1882 S Normal Ave 1 Chicago (60616) ***(G-5227)***
**Interstate Power Systemd, Carol Stream** *Also called Interstate Power Systems Inc* ***(G-3174)***
**Interstate Power Systems Inc**...630 871-1111
210 Alexandra Way Carol Stream (60188) ***(G-3174)***
**Interstate Power Systems Inc**...952 854-2044
3736 11th St Rockford (61109) ***(G-18440)***
**Intertape Polymer Corp**...618 549-2131
2200 N Mcroy Dr Carbondale (62901) ***(G-3013)***
**Intertape Polymer Group, Carbondale** *Also called Intertape Polymer Corp* ***(G-3013)***
**Intertech Development Company**...847 679-3377
7401 Linder Ave Skokie (60077) ***(G-20017)***
**Intervarsity Press, Westmont** *Also called Intervrsity Chrstn Fllwshp/Usa* ***(G-21893)***
**Intervrsity Chrstn Fllwshp/Usa**...630 734-4000
430 Plaza Dr Frnt Westmont (60559) ***(G-21893)***
**Intex Lighting LLC**...847 380-2027
1300 E Wdfield Rd Ste 400 Schaumburg (60173) ***(G-19575)***
**Intex Systems Corp**...630 636-6594
22 Crestview Dr Oswego (60543) ***(G-16922)***
**Intown Electric**...847 305-4816
900 E Euclid Ave Arlington Heights (60004) ***(G-779)***
**Intra Action Corp**...708 547-6644
3719 Warren Ave Bellwood (60104) ***(G-1710)***
**Intra-Cut Die Cutting Inc**...773 775-6228
5559 N Northwest Hwy Chicago (60630) ***(G-5228)***
**Intratek Inc**...847 640-0007
54 N Lively Blvd Elk Grove Village (60007) ***(G-9554)***
**Intratherm LLC**...630 333-5419
1212 S Naper Blvd 119-221 Naperville (60540) ***(G-15677)***
**Intravation Inc (PA)**...847 299-6423
1113 Hewitt Dr Des Plaines (60016) ***(G-8214)***
**Intrepid Molding Inc**...847 526-9477
285 Industrial Dr Wauconda (60084) ***(G-21474)***
**Intrepid Tool Industries LLC**...773 467-4200
5296 N Northwest Hwy Chicago (60630) ***(G-5229)***
**Invektek Llc**...312 343-0600
2039 N Lincoln Ave Unit P Chicago (60614) ***(G-5230)***
**Invenergy**...815 795-4964
2192 E 25th Rd Marseilles (61341) ***(G-14312)***
**Invenergy Wind Fin Co III LLC**...312 224-1400
1 S Wacker Dr Ste 1900 Chicago (60606) ***(G-5231)***
**Invensys Controls, Hanover** *Also called Robertshaw Controls Company* ***(G-11573)***
**Invensys Environmental Contrls, Rockford** *Also called Schneider Elc Buildings LLC* ***(G-18608)***
**Inventex Medical, Niles** *Also called Inventive Display Group LLC* ***(G-15990)***
**Inventive Concepts Intl LLC**...847 350-6102
500 Wall St Glendale Heights (60139) ***(G-11035)***
**Inventive Display Group LLC**...847 588-1100
7415 N Melvina Ave Niles (60714) ***(G-15990)***
**Inventive Mfg Inc**...847 647-9500
5423 Fargo Ave Skokie (60077) ***(G-20018)***
**Inventus Power Inc (PA)**...630 410-7900
1200 Internationale Pkwy Woodridge (60517) ***(G-22496)***
**Inventus Power (illinois) LLC**...630 410-7900
1200 Internationale Pkwy Woodridge (60517) ***(G-22497)***
**Inventus Power Holdings Inc**...630 410-7900
1200 Internationale Pkwy Woodridge (60517) ***(G-22498)***
**Inverom Corporation**...630 568-5609
16w235 83rd St Ste A Burr Ridge (60527) ***(G-2858)***
**Investment Information Svcs**...312 669-1650
300 S Wacker Dr Ste 2880 Chicago (60606) ***(G-5232)***
**Invisible Fencing of Quad City**...309 797-1688
5202 38th Ave Ste 2 Moline (61265) ***(G-14945)***
**Invisible Institute**...415 669-4691
6100 S Blackstone Ave Chicago (60637) ***(G-5233)***
**Invisio Communications Inc**...412 327-6578
150 N Michigan Ave # 1950 Chicago (60601) ***(G-5234)***
**Invision Software Inc**...312 474-7767
3333 Warrenville Rd # 200 Lisle (60532) ***(G-13608)***
**Invision Software AG, Lisle** *Also called Invision Software Inc* ***(G-13608)***
**Invitation Creations Inc**...847 432-4441
580 Roger Williams Ave # 24 Highland Park (60035) ***(G-11844)***
**INX Digital International Co**...630 382-1800
150 N Martingale Rd # 700 Schaumburg (60173) ***(G-19576)***
**INX Group Ltd**...708 799-1993
1000 Maple Rd Homewood (60430) ***(G-12103)***
**INX Group Ltd (HQ)**...630 382-1800
150 N Martingale Rd # 700 Schaumburg (60173) ***(G-19577)***
**INX International Ink Co (HQ)**...630 382-1800
150 N Martingale Rd # 700 Schaumburg (60173) ***(G-19578)***
**INX International Ink Co**...630 681-7200
1860 Western Dr West Chicago (60185) ***(G-21724)***
**INX International Ink Co**...708 496-3600
5001 S Mason Ave Chicago (60638) ***(G-5235)***
**INX International Ink Co**...800 233-4657
150 N Martingale Rd # 700 Schaumburg (60173) ***(G-19579)***
**INX International Ink Co**...630 382-1800
150 N Martingale Rd # 700 Schaumburg (60173) ***(G-19580)***
**INX International Ink Co**...630 382-1800
150 N Martingale Rd # 700 Schaumburg (60173) ***(G-19581)***
**INX International Ink Co**...630 681-7100
1760 Western Dr West Chicago (60185) ***(G-21725)***
**Io Lighting LLC**...847 735-7000
370 Corporate Woods Pkwy Vernon Hills (60061) ***(G-21176)***
**Iodon Inc**...708 799-4062
18610 John Ave Country Club Hills (60478) ***(G-7409)***
**Iola Quarry Inc**...217 682-3865
2671 County Hwy 6 Mode (62444) ***(G-14849)***
**Ionit Technologies Inc**...847 205-9651
2311 Dorina Dr Northfield (60093) ***(G-16403)***
**Iosso Products Co, Elk Grove Village** *Also called International Proc Co Amer* ***(G-9553)***
**Ip Automation, Addison** *Also called Intellgent Prcsses Automtn Inc* ***(G-154)***
**Ip Media Holdings**...847 714-1177
55 E Hintz Rd Wheeling (60090) ***(G-22078)***
**Iplastics LLC (PA)**...309 444-8884
300 N Cummings Ln Washington (61571) ***(G-21383)***
**Ipr Group, Carol Stream** *Also called Stand Fast Group LLC* ***(G-3246)***
**Ipr Systems Inc**...708 385-7500
11651 S Mayfield Ave Alsip (60803) ***(G-474)***
**Ips & Luggage Co Inc**...630 894-2414
685 Washington Ct Roselle (60172) ***(G-18948)***
**Ipsen Inc**...815 239-2385
325 John St Pecatonica (61063) ***(G-17252)***

**Ipsen Inc (HQ)** ....815 332-4941
984 Ipsen Rd Cherry Valley (61016) *(G-3645)*
**Ipt, Lisle** *Also called Interface Protein Tech Inc (G-13607)*
**Ipurse Inc** ....312 344-3449
70 W Madison St Chicago (60602) *(G-5236)*
**Iq7 Technology Inc** ....917 670-1715
161 E Chicago Ave Chicago (60611) *(G-5237)*
**Ireco LLC** ....630 741-0155
577 W Lamont Rd Elmhurst (60126) *(G-9888)*
**Irene Quary, Belvidere** *Also called William Charles Cnstr Co LLC (G-1797)*
**Iretired LLC** ....630 285-9500
700 District Dr Itasca (60143) *(G-12287)*
**Irish Dancing Magazine** ....630 279-7521
110 E Schiller St Ste 206 Elmhurst (60126) *(G-9889)*
**Irmko Tool Works Inc** ....630 350-7550
205 Park St Bensenville (60106) *(G-1923)*
**Iron Castle Inc** ....773 890-0575
3847 S Kedzie Ave Chicago (60632) *(G-5238)*
**Iron-A-Way LLC** ....309 266-7232
220 W Jackson St Morton (61550) *(G-15161)*
**Ironform Holdings Co (PA)** ....312 374-4810
311 W Superior St Ste 510 Chicago (60654) *(G-5239)*
**Ironsafe LLC** ....877 297-1833
1807 W Diehl Rd Naperville (60563) *(G-15678)*
**Ironwood Industries Inc** ....847 362-8681
115 S Bradley Rd Libertyville (60048) *(G-13338)*
**Ironwood Mfg Inc** ....630 778-8963
24w260 Hemlock Ln Naperville (60540) *(G-15679)*
**Irving Press Inc** ....847 595-6650
2530 United Ln Elk Grove Village (60007) *(G-9555)*
**Irwin Industrial Tool Company** ....815 235-4171
29 E Stephenson St Freeport (61032) *(G-10669)*
**Irwin Seating Company** ....618 483-6157
610 E Cumberland Rd Altamont (62411) *(G-553)*
**ISA Chicago** ....630 317-7169
470 Mission St Unit 7 Carol Stream (60188) *(G-3175)*
**ISachs Sons Inc** ....312 733-2815
4500 S Kolin Ave Ste 1a Chicago (60632) *(G-5240)*
**Isates Inc** ....309 691-8822
2251 W Altorfer Dr Peoria (61615) *(G-17391)*
**Isbs, Elk Grove Village** *Also called Image Systems Bus Slutions LLC (G-9539)*
**ISC Water Solutions, South Holland** *Also called Industrial Specialty Chem Inc (G-20280)*
**Isco International Inc (PA)** ....630 283-3100
444 E State Pkwy Ste 123 Schaumburg (60173) *(G-19582)*
**Isco International LLC** ....847 391-9400
444 E State Pkwy Ste 123 Schaumburg (60173) *(G-19583)*
**Ise Inc** ....703 319-0390
222 Merchandise Mart Plz Chicago (60654) *(G-5241)*
**Isenberg Bath Corporation** ....972 510-5916
1325 W Irving Park Rd Bensenville (60106) *(G-1924)*
**Isewa LLC** ....847 877-1586
2104 Birchwood Ln Buffalo Grove (60089) *(G-2711)*
**Isewan USA Inc** ....630 561-2807
10 N Martingale Rd # 400 Schaumburg (60173) *(G-19584)*
**Ishot Products Inc** ....312 497-4190
558 Payton Ln Bolingbrook (60440) *(G-2325)*
**ISI Printing, Springfield** *Also called Informative Systems Inc (G-20457)*
**Isis3d LLC** ....516 426-5410
1210 E 54th St Chicago (60615) *(G-5242)*
**Isky North America Inc (PA)** ....937 641-1368
47 W Polk St Ste 208 Chicago (60605) *(G-5243)*
**Ism Machinery Incorporated** ....847 231-8002
1915 Enterprise Ct Libertyville (60048) *(G-13339)*
**Isoflex Packaging, Chicago** *Also called Alpha Industries MGT Inc (G-3828)*
**Isoprime Corporation** ....630 737-0963
505 Warrenville Rd # 104 Lisle (60532) *(G-13609)*
**Isovac Products LLC** ....630 679-1740
1306 Enterprise Dr Ste A Romeoville (60446) *(G-18831)*
**Isp, Homewood** *Also called Ink Spots Prtg & Meida Design (G-12102)*
**Israel Levy Diamnd Cutters Inc** ....312 368-8540
29 E Madison St Ste 700 Chicago (60602) *(G-5244)*
**ISS Medical Inc** ....217 359-8681
1602 Newton Dr Champaign (61822) *(G-3503)*
**It Transportation Company** ....773 383-5073
5156 W Winnemac Ave Chicago (60630) *(G-5245)*
**Italia Foods Inc** ....847 397-4479
2127 Hammond Dr Schaumburg (60173) *(G-19585)*
**Italian Trade Agency, Chicago** *Also called Publishing Task Force (G-6224)*
**Italvibras Usa Inc** ....815 872-1350
1940 Vans Way Princeton (61356) *(G-17751)*
**Itasca Plastics Inc** ....630 443-4446
3750 Ohio Ave Saint Charles (60174) *(G-19200)*
**Iten Industries Inc** ....630 543-2820
1545 W Wrightwood Ct Addison (60101) *(G-155)*
**Iterative Therapeutics Inc** ....773 455-7203
2201 W Campbell Park Dr Chicago (60612) *(G-5246)*
**Iterna LLC** ....630 585-7400
2600 Beverly Dr Ste 107 Aurora (60502) *(G-1035)*
**Iterum Therapeutics US Limited** ....312 763-3975
200 W Monroe St Ste 1575 Chicago (60606) *(G-5247)*
**Itg Brands LLC** ....217 529-5746
900 Christopher Ln Ste 7 Springfield (62712) *(G-20458)*
**Ithaca Education, Chicago** *Also called Thinkcercacom Inc (G-6714)*
**Itron Corporation Del (PA)** ....708 222-5320
3131 S Austin Blvd Cicero (60804) *(G-7207)*
**Its A Girl Thing** ....630 232-2778
618 W State St Geneva (60134) *(G-10840)*
**Its Easy With Jesus Printing, Franklin** *Also called Faith Printing (G-10379)*
**Its Solar LLC** ....618 476-7678
609 S Breese St Millstadt (62260) *(G-14828)*
**ITT Bell & Gossett** ....847 966-3700
8200 Austin Ave Morton Grove (60053) *(G-15204)*
**ITT Water & Wastewater USA Inc** ....847 966-3700
8200 Austin Ave Morton Grove (60053) *(G-15205)*
**ITT Water & Wastewater USA Inc** ....708 342-0484
8402 W 183 Th Ste A Tinley Park (60477) *(G-20924)*
**Itus Corporation LLC** ....888 537-5661
2130 S Goebbert Rd # 104 Arlington Heights (60005) *(G-780)*
**ITW, Glenview** *Also called Ransburg Corporation (G-11190)*
**ITW, Tinley Park** *Also called Illinois Tool Works Inc (G-20922)*
**ITW Bldg Components Group (HQ)** ....847 634-1900
155 Harlem Ave Glenview (60025) *(G-11150)*
**ITW Blding Cmponents Group Inc** ....217 324-0303
7 Skyview Dr Litchfield (62056) *(G-13689)*
**ITW Brands, Bartlett** *Also called Illinois Tool Works Inc (G-1353)*
**ITW Buildex, Roselle** *Also called Illinois Tool Works Inc (G-18946)*
**ITW Delpro, Frankfort** *Also called Illinois Tool Works Inc (G-10330)*
**ITW Deltar Bdy Intr Richton Pk, Richton Park** *Also called Illinois Tool Works Inc (G-17977)*
**ITW Deltar Ipac, Frankfort** *Also called Illinois Tool Works Inc (G-10332)*
**ITW Deltar Seat Component** ....630 993-9990
935 N Oaklawn Ave Elmhurst (60126) *(G-9890)*
**ITW Dynatec** ....847 657-4830
3600 W Lake Ave Glenview (60026) *(G-11151)*
**ITW Engineered Components, Mokena** *Also called Illinois Tool Works Inc (G-14872)*
**ITW Fastex, Hebron** *Also called Illinois Tool Works (G-11720)*
**ITW Filtration, Elk Grove Village** *Also called Illinois Tool Works Inc (G-9535)*
**ITW Flter Pdts Trnsm Fltration, Hebron** *Also called Filtertek Inc (G-11719)*
**ITW Global Investments Inc (HQ)** ....847 724-7500
155 Harlem Ave Glenview (60025) *(G-11152)*
**ITW International Holdings LLC (HQ)** ....847 724-7500
3600 W Lake Ave Glenview (60026) *(G-11153)*
**ITW Minigrip/Zip-Pak, Ottawa** *Also called Minigrip Inc (G-16969)*
**ITW Motion** ....708 720-0300
21601 S Harlem Ave Frankfort (60423) *(G-10335)*
**ITW Paslode, Glenview** *Also called ITW Bldg Components Group (G-11150)*
**ITW Paslode, Elgin** *Also called Illinois Tool Works Inc (G-9072)*
**ITW Ramset Red Head, Elk Grove Village** *Also called Illinois Tool Works Inc (G-9536)*
**ITW Shake Proof Auto Division, Machesney Park** *Also called Illinois Tool Works Inc (G-14081)*
**ITW Shakeproof Group, Broadview** *Also called Illinois Tool Works Inc (G-2585)*
**ITW Shakeproof-Elk Grove, Elk Grove Village** *Also called Illinois Tool Works Inc (G-9537)*
**ITW Switches, Des Plaines** *Also called Illinois Tool Works Inc (G-8208)*
**IV & Respiratory Care Services** ....618 398-2720
65 S 65th St Ste 1 Belleville (62223) *(G-1639)*
**Ivan Carlson Associates Inc** ....312 829-4616
2224 W Fulton St Chicago (60612) *(G-5248)*
**Ivan Schwenker** ....630 543-7798
1480 W Bernard Dr Ste A Addison (60101) *(G-156)*
**Ivanhoe Industries Inc (PA)** ....847 566-7170
26267 N Hickory Rd Mundelein (60060) *(G-15512)*
**Ivanhoe Industries Inc** ....847 872-3311
3333 20th St Zion (60099) *(G-22688)*
**Ivans Insurance Solutions, University Park** *Also called Applied Systems Inc (G-21041)*
**Ives-Way Products Inc** ....847 740-0658
2030 N Nicole Ln Round Lake Beach (60073) *(G-19076)*
**Ixmation North America, Bartlett** *Also called Bbs Automation Chicago Inc (G-1335)*
**Ixtapa Foods** ....773 788-9701
6135 S Nottingham Ave Chicago (60638) *(G-5249)*
**Iya Foods LLC** ....630 854-7107
348 Smoketree Bsn Dr North Aurora (60542) *(G-16135)*
**J & A Sheet Metal Shop Inc** ....773 276-3739
1800 N Campbell Ave Chicago (60647) *(G-5250)*
**J & B Truck Services Ltd** ....708 430-8760
9012 S Oketo Ave Bridgeview (60455) *(G-2501)*
**J & C Premier Concepts Inc** ....309 523-2344
1506 N High St Port Byron (61275) *(G-17720)*
**J & D Instant Signs** ....847 965-2800
5614 Dempster St Morton Grove (60053) *(G-15206)*
**J & E Seating LLC** ....847 956-1700
950 Pratt Blvd Elk Grove Village (60007) *(G-9556)*
**J & F Engineering, Addison** *Also called Doral Inc (G-97)*
**J & G Fabricating Inc** ....708 385-9147
12653 Irving Ave Blue Island (60406) *(G-2257)*

ALPHABETIC

(PA)=Parent Co (HQ)=Headquarters (DH)=Div Headquarters
2017 Harris Illinois Industrial Directory
1279

**J & I Son Tool Company Inc** ....847 455-4200
9219 Parklane Ave Franklin Park (60131) **(G-10500)**
**J & J Carbide & Tool Inc** ....708 489-0300
5656 W 120th St Alsip (60803) **(G-475)**
**J & J Electric Motor Repair Sp** ....217 529-0015
2800 S 11th St Springfield (62703) **(G-20459)**
**J & J Equipment Inc** ....309 449-5442
260 4th Ave Hopedale (61747) **(G-12122)**
**J & J Express Envelopes Inc** ....847 253-7146
645 Stevenson Rd South Elgin (60177) **(G-20209)**
**J & J Fish, Rockford** *Also called Dar Enterprises Inc* **(G-18334)**
**J & J Industries Inc** ....630 595-8878
107 Gateway Rd Bensenville (60106) **(G-1925)**
**J & J Manufacturing, Chillicothe** *Also called C J Holdings Inc* **(G-7163)**
**J & J Mr Quick Print Inc** ....773 767-7776
5729 S Archer Ave Chicago (60638) **(G-5251)**
**J & J Powder Coating, Zion** *Also called Joseph Kristan* **(G-22689)**
**J & J Printing, Chicago** *Also called J & J Mr Quick Print Inc* **(G-5251)**
**J & J Quality Pallets Inc** ....618 262-6426
226 W 11th St Mount Carmel (62863) **(G-15269)**
**J & J Silk Screening** ....773 838-9000
5316 S Monitor Ave Chicago (60638) **(G-5252)**
**J & J Woodwork Furniture Inc** ....708 563-9581
7001 W 66th Pl Chicago (60638) **(G-5253)**
**J & L Engineering, Rockford** *Also called Uhlar Inc* **(G-18659)**
**J & L Gear Incorporated** ....630 832-1880
726 N Princeton Ave Ste C Villa Park (60181) **(G-21259)**
**J & L Thread Grinding Inc** ....815 389-4644
816 Dearborn Ave South Beloit (61080) **(G-20151)**
**J & M Fab Metals Inc** ....815 758-0354
6710 S Grant Hwy Marengo (60152) **(G-14232)**
**J & M Plating Inc** ....815 964-4975
4500 Kishwaukee St Rockford (61109) **(G-18441)**
**J & M Representatives Inc** ....217 268-4504
401 E County Road 200n Arcola (61910) **(G-672)**
**J & S Machine Works Inc** ....708 344-2101
1733 N 25th Ave Melrose Park (60160) **(G-14661)**
**J & S Tool Inc** ....
4142 W Lake St Chicago (60624) **(G-5254)**
**J & W Counter Tops Inc (PA)** ....217 544-0876
600 North St Springfield (62704) **(G-20460)**
**J A K Enterprises Inc** ....217 422-3881
288 N Park St Decatur (62523) **(G-7897)**
**J and D Installers Inc** ....847 288-0783
9330 Franklin Ave Franklin Park (60131) **(G-10501)**
**J and J Prfmce Powdr Coating** ....309 376-4340
410 E Washington St Carlock (61725) **(G-3051)**
**J and K Molding** ....224 276-3355
31632 N Ellis Dr Unit 201 Volo (60073) **(G-21314)**
**J and K Printing** ....708 229-9558
5629 W 84th Pl Oak Lawn (60459) **(G-16627)**
**J B Burling Group Ltd** ....773 327-5362
540 W Aldine Ave Ste 6 Chicago (60657) **(G-5255)**
**J B Metal Works Inc** ....847 824-4253
1325 Lee St Des Plaines (60018) **(G-8215)**
**J B Oil Field Cnstr & Sup** ....618 936-2350
218 E Sycamore St Sumner (62466) **(G-20771)**
**J B Watts Company Inc** ....773 643-1855
6224 S Vernon Ave Chicago (60637) **(G-5256)**
**J Brodie Meat Products Inc** ....309 342-1500
605 W 6th St Galesburg (61401) **(G-10761)**
**J C Communications Company** ....312 236-5122
318 W Adams St Ste 1406 Chicago (60606) **(G-5257)**
**J C Decaux New York Inc** ....312 456-2999
3959 S Morgan St Chicago (60609) **(G-5258)**
**J C Embroidery & Screen Print** ....630 595-4670
406 Industrial Dr Bensenville (60106) **(G-1926)**
**J C Hose & Tube Inc** ....630 543-4747
236 S La Londe Ave Ste C Addison (60101) **(G-157)**
**J C Products Inc** ....847 208-9616
1961 Tunbridge Ct Algonquin (60102) **(G-394)**
**J C Schultz Enterprises Inc** ....800 323-9127
951 Swanson Dr Batavia (60510) **(G-1459)**
**J D Graphic Co Inc** ....847 364-4000
1101 Arthur Ave Elk Grove Village (60007) **(G-9557)**
**J D M Coatings Inc** ....708 755-6300
3300 Louis Sherman Dr Steger (60475) **(G-20574)**
**J D Machining** ....847 428-8690
57 Center Dr Ste B Gilberts (60136) **(G-10925)**
**J D Plating Works Inc** ....847 662-6484
1424 12th St Waukegan (60085) **(G-21573)**
**J D Refrigeration** ....618 345-0041
6849 Fedder Ln Collinsville (62234) **(G-7328)**
**J Design Works Inc** ....847 812-0891
210 Ironbark Way Bolingbrook (60440) **(G-2326)**
**J E Tomes & Associates Inc** ....708 653-5100
2513 140th Pl Blue Island (60406) **(G-2258)**
**J F Schroeder Company Inc** ....847 357-8600
2616 S Clearbrook Dr Arlington Heights (60005) **(G-781)**
**J F Wagner Printing Co** ....847 564-0017
3004 Commercial Ave Northbrook (60062) **(G-16280)**
**J Francis & Assoc** ....309 697-5931
4603 Carol Ct Bartonville (61607) **(G-1395)**
**J G B Uniforms & Career AP, Chicago** *Also called J G Uniforms Inc* **(G-5259)**
**J G Uniforms Inc** ....773 545-4644
5949 W Irving Park Rd Chicago (60634) **(G-5259)**
**J Garvin Industries** ....708 819-1148
9628 S Harding Ave Evergreen Park (60805) **(G-10116)**
**J Gayleen Hammond, Rushville** *Also called Stitchables Embroidery* **(G-19096)**
**J Gooch & Associates Inc** ....217 522-7575
140 W Lenox Ave Springfield (62704) **(G-20461)**
**J H Benedict Co Inc** ....309 694-3111
3211 N Main St East Peoria (61611) **(G-8715)**
**J H Botts LLC** ....815 726-5885
253 Bruce St Joliet (60432) **(G-12519)**
**J H H of Illinois Inc** ....630 293-0739
1331 Howard Dr West Chicago (60185) **(G-21726)**
**J H Robison & Associates Ltd (PA)** ....847 559-9662
905 Voltz Rd Northbrook (60062) **(G-16281)**
**J II Inc** ....847 432-8979
1292 Old Skokie Rd Highland Park (60035) **(G-11845)**
**J J Collins Sons Inc (PA)** ....630 960-2525
7125 Janes Ave Ste 200 Woodridge (60517) **(G-22499)**
**J J Collins Sons Inc** ....309 664-5404
24 Chiswick Cir Bloomington (61704) **(G-2184)**
**J J Collins Sons Inc** ....217 345-7606
2351 Madison Ave Charleston (61920) **(G-3601)**
**J J Mata Inc** ....773 750-0643
2524 W Devon Ave Chicago (60659) **(G-5260)**
**J K Creative Printers, Quincy** *Also called Jost & Kiefer Printing Company* **(G-17842)**
**J K Custom Countertops** ....630 495-2324
820 N Ridge Ave Ste A Lombard (60148) **(G-13813)**
**J K Manufacturing Co** ....708 563-2500
7301 W 66th St Bedford Park (60638) **(G-1558)**
**J K Printing & Mailing Inc** ....847 432-7717
2090 Green Bay Rd Highland Park (60035) **(G-11846)**
**J L Lawrence & Co** ....217 235-3622
1921 Richmond Ave Mattoon (61938) **(G-14394)**
**J L M Plastics Corporation** ....815 722-0066
1012 Collins St Joliet (60432) **(G-12520)**
**J M Fabricating Inc** ....815 359-2024
214 S 1st St Harmon (61042) **(G-11595)**
**J M Lustig Custom Cabinets Co** ....217 342-6661
921 E Fayette Ave Effingham (62401) **(G-8840)**
**J M Office Products, Crest Hill** *Also called J M Printers Inc* **(G-7459)**
**J M Printers Inc (PA)** ....815 727-1579
510 Pasadena Ave Crest Hill (60403) **(G-7459)**
**J M Resources Inc** ....630 690-7337
1441 Timber Dr Elgin (60123) **(G-9080)**
**J M Signs** ....847 945-7446
1664 Garand Dr Deerfield (60015) **(G-8015)**
**J Mac Metals Inc** ....309 822-2023
330 Se Industrial Ave Galva (61434) **(G-10790)**
**J N Machinery Corp** ....224 699-9161
1081 Rock Road Ln East Dundee (60118) **(G-8648)**
**J N P, Blue Island** *Also called Color Tone Printing* **(G-2242)**
**J N R Custo-Matic Screw Inc** ....630 260-1333
200 W Lake Dr Glendale Heights (60139) **(G-11036)**
**J Oshana & Son Printing** ....773 283-8311
4021 W Irving Park Rd Chicago (60641) **(G-5261)**
**J P Goldenne Incorporated** ....847 776-5063
346 N Northwest Hwy Palatine (60067) **(G-17045)**
**J P Printing Inc** ....773 626-5222
5639 W Division St Chicago (60651) **(G-5262)**
**J P Vincent & Sons Inc** ....815 777-2365
11340 W Us Highway 20 Galena (61036) **(G-10727)**
**J R Finishers Inc** ....847 301-2556
616 Albion Ave Schaumburg (60193) **(G-19586)**
**J R Fridrich Inc** ....847 439-1554
1830 Lunt Ave Elk Grove Village (60007) **(G-9558)**
**J R G Oil Co Inc** ....618 842-9131
306 Petroleum Blvd Te A Fairfield (62837) **(G-10144)**
**J R Husar Inc** ....312 243-7888
1631 W Carroll Ave Chicago (60612) **(G-5263)**
**J R Mold Inc** ....630 289-2192
65 Sangra Ct Streamwood (60107) **(G-20658)**
**J R Short Milling Company (PA)** ....815 937-2635
1580 Grinnell Rd Kankakee (60901) **(G-12627)**
**J R Short Milling Company** ....815 937-2633
1580 Grinnell Rd Kankakee (60901) **(G-12628)**
**J Ream Manufacturing** ....630 983-6945
31w280 Diehl Rd Ste 101 Naperville (60563) **(G-15680)**
**J S, West Chicago** *Also called Jel Sert Co* **(G-21727)**
**J S Paluch Co Inc (PA)** ....847 678-9300
3708 River Rd Ste 400 Franklin Park (60131) **(G-10502)**
**J S Printing Inc** ....847 678-6300
9832 Franklin Ave Franklin Park (60131) **(G-10503)**
**J Schneerberger Corp** ....847 888-3498
1380 Gateway Dr Ste 8 Elgin (60124) **(G-9081)**

**J Stewart & Co** ....847 419-9595
1130 W Lake Cook Rd # 320 Buffalo Grove (60089) *(G-2712)*
**J Stilling Enterprises Inc** ....630 584-5050
330 S 2nd St Ste A Saint Charles (60174) *(G-19201)*
**J Stone Inc** ....847 325-5660
750 Tower Rd Ste A Mundelein (60060) *(G-15513)*
**J T C Inc** ....773 292-9262
4710 W North Ave Chicago (60639) *(G-5264)*
**J T Fennell Co Inc (PA)** ....309 274-2145
1104 N Front St Chillicothe (61523) *(G-7168)*
**J Toor Menswear, Chicago** *Also called Jtoor LLC (G-5334)*
**J W Ossola Company Inc** ....815 339-6112
502 E Harper Ave Granville (61326) *(G-11318)*
**J W Reynolds Monument Co Inc** ....618 833-6014
517 E Vienna St Ste A Anna (62906) *(G-606)*
**J W Rudy Co Inc** ....618 676-1616
506 S 1st St Se Clay City (62824) *(G-7265)*
**J W Todd Co** ....630 406-5715
709 Morton Ave Aurora (60506) *(G-1173)*
**J Wallace & Associates Inc** ....630 960-4221
1409 Centre Cir Downers Grove (60515) *(G-8467)*
**J&A Mtchell Stl Fbricators Inc** ....815 939-2144
2524 S 8000w Rd Kankakee (60901) *(G-12629)*
**J&A Pallets Service Inc** ....708 333-6601
1225 Arnold St Chicago Heights (60411) *(G-7104)*
**J&E Storm Services Inc** ....630 401-3793
17807 65th Ct Tinley Park (60477) *(G-20925)*
**J&I Tool Company, Franklin Park** *Also called J & I Son Tool Company Inc (G-10500)*
**J&J Ready Mix Inc** ....309 676-0579
100 Cass St East Peoria (61611) *(G-8716)*
**J&M Food Products Company, Chicago** *Also called My Own Meals Inc (G-5841)*
**J-Industries Inc** ....815 654-0055
5129 Forest Hills Ct Loves Park (61111) *(G-13949)*
**J-Marcs Corporation** ....815 786-2293
1074 W Church St Sandwich (60548) *(G-19369)*
**J-Soft Tech, Chicago** *Also called Jones Software Corp (G-5322)*
**J-TEC Metal Products Inc** ....630 875-1300
1320 Ardmore Ave Itasca (60143) *(G-12288)*
**J. J. Collins Printers, Woodridge** *Also called J J Collins Sons Inc (G-22499)*
**J. L. Clark, Inc., Rockford** *Also called JL Clark LLC (G-18447)*
**J. P. Bell Fabricating, Inc., Wood Dale** *Also called EMR Manufacturing Inc (G-22362)*
**J.H. Botts, Joliet** *Also called J H Botts LLC (G-12519)*
**J/B Industries Inc** ....630 851-9444
601 N Farnsworth Ave Aurora (60505) *(G-1174)*
**J2sys LLC** ....630 542-1342
102 Naperville Rd Clarendon Hills (60514) *(G-7257)*
**J2sys Robot, Clarendon Hills** *Also called J2sys LLC (G-7257)*
**J6 Polymers LLC** ....815 517-1179
633 Enterprise Ave Ste 3 Dekalb (60115) *(G-8099)*
**Jaali Bean Inc** ....312 730-5095
1941 Wesy Oakdale Ave Chicago (60657) *(G-5265)*
**Jab Distributors LLC** ....847 998-6901
1500 S Wolf Rd Wheeling (60090) *(G-22079)*
**Jabat Inc** ....618 392-3010
715 N West St Olney (62450) *(G-16773)*
**Jabber Labs Inc** ....607 227-6353
175 N Harbor Dr Apt 2902 Chicago (60601) *(G-5266)*
**Jac US Inc** ....312 421-2268
2444 W 16th St Ste 4 Chicago (60608) *(G-5267)*
**Jack & Lidias Resort Inc** ....847 356-1389
3610 N Edgewood St Lake Villa (60046) *(G-13017)*
**Jack Bartlett** ....217 659-3575
2745 N County Road 2150 Dallas City (62330) *(G-7697)*
**Jack Beall Vertical Service In** ....847 426-7958
2085 Orchard Ln Carpentersville (60110) *(G-3289)*
**Jack R Phillips** ....618 242-8411
2015 Broadway St Mount Vernon (62864) *(G-15416)*
**Jack Ruch Archtctral Mouldings, Bloomington** *Also called Jack Ruch Quality Homes Inc (G-2185)*
**Jack Ruch Quality Homes Inc** ....309 663-6595
2908 Gill St Ste 2 Bloomington (61704) *(G-2185)*
**Jack Shepard Logging** ....618 845-3496
14225 Shepard Ln Ullin (62992) *(G-21031)*
**Jack Walters & Sons Corp** ....618 842-2642
204 E Main St Fairfield (62837) *(G-10145)*
**Jackhammer** ....773 743-5772
6406 N Clark St Chicago (60626) *(G-5268)*
**Jackson County Sand & Grav Co** ....618 763-4711
1 Sickler Rd Gorham (62940) *(G-11254)*
**Jackson Marking Products Co** ....618 242-7901
9105 N Rainbow Ln Mount Vernon (62864) *(G-15417)*
**Jackson Oil Corporation** ....618 263-6521
809 W 9th St Mount Carmel (62863) *(G-15270)*
**Jackson Spring & Mfg Co** ....847 952-8850
299 Bond St Elk Grove Village (60007) *(G-9559)*
**Jacksonville Art Glass Inc** ....217 245-0500
54 N Central Park Plz Jacksonville (62650) *(G-12395)*
**Jacksonville Journal-Courier, Jacksonville** *Also called Civitas Media LLC (G-12384)*
**Jacksonville Machine Inc** ....217 243-1119
2265 W Morton Ave Jacksonville (62650) *(G-12396)*
**Jacksonville Monument Co** ....217 245-2514
330 E State St Jacksonville (62650) *(G-12397)*
**Jacob Chambliss** ....618 731-6632
127 County Road 600 E Dahlgren (62828) *(G-7691)*
**Jacob Hay Co** ....847 215-8880
509 N Wolf Rd Wheeling (60090) *(G-22080)*
**Jacobs Boiler & Mech Inds Inc** ....773 385-9900
6632 W Diversey Ave Chicago (60707) *(G-5269)*
**Jacobs Reproduction** ....618 374-2198
25116 Beltrees Rd Elsah (62028) *(G-9976)*
**Jacobs Trucking** ....618 687-3578
3191 W Harrison Rd Murphysboro (62966) *(G-15577)*
**Jacobsen Lenticu, Itasca** *Also called Lens Lenticlear Lenticular (G-12303)*
**Jacobson Acqstion Holdings LLC** ....847 623-1414
1414 Jacobson Dr Waukegan (60085) *(G-21574)*
**JAD Group Inc** ....847 223-1804
888 E Belvidere Rd # 213 Grayslake (60030) *(G-11348)*
**Jada Specialties Inc** ....847 272-7799
3834 Normandy Ln Northbrook (60062) *(G-16282)*
**Jaday Industries** ....847 928-1033
10002 Pacific Ave Franklin Park (60131) *(G-10504)*
**Jade Screen Printing** ....618 463-2325
220 Main St Alton (62002) *(G-579)*
**Jader Fuel Co Inc** ....618 269-3101
117 S Edison St Shawneetown (62984) *(G-19904)*
**Jaeger Saw & Cutter Works, Rockford** *Also called Jaeger Saw and Cutter Inc (G-18442)*
**Jaeger Saw and Cutter Inc** ....815 963-0313
81005 5th Ave Rockford (61104) *(G-18442)*
**Jaffee Investment Partnr LP** ....312 321-1515
410 N Michigan Ave # 400 Chicago (60611) *(G-5270)*
**Jagjita Corp** ....217 374-6016
654 N Main St White Hall (62092) *(G-22185)*
**Jagoli** ....312 563-0583
401 N Western Ave Ste 2 Chicago (60612) *(G-5271)*
**Jahns Structure Jacking System** ....630 365-2455
15 S 1st St Elburn (60119) *(G-8890)*
**Jai-S Record Label** ....708 351-4279
22011 Central Park Ave Park Forest (60466) *(G-17173)*
**Jail Education Solutions Inc** ....773 263-0718
215 W Superior St Ste 600 Chicago (60654) *(G-5272)*
**Jaix Leasing Company** ....312 928-0850
2 N Riverside Plz Chicago (60606) *(G-5273)*
**Jakes McHning Rbilding Svc Inc** ....630 892-3291
131 2nd St Aurora (60506) *(G-1175)*
**Jakes World Design** ....217 348-3043
2736 N County Road 1100e Lerna (62440) *(G-13287)*
**Jalaa Fiberglass Inc** ....217 923-3433
1654 County Road 350n Greenup (62428) *(G-11384)*
**Jalor Company** ....847 202-1172
545 Tollgate Rd Ste E Elgin (60123) *(G-9082)*
**JAm International Co Ltd** ....847 827-6391
500 Lake Cook Rd Ste 350 Deerfield (60015) *(G-8016)*
**Jamaica Pyrotechnics (PA)** ....217 649-2902
212 Franks Dr Philo (61864) *(G-17539)*
**Jamali Kopy Kat Printing Inc** ....708 544-6164
2501 Saint Charles Rd Bellwood (60104) *(G-1711)*
**Jamar Packaging, West Chicago** *Also called J H H of Illinois Inc (G-21726)*
**Jamco Products Inc (HQ)** ....815 624-0400
1 Jamco Ct South Beloit (61080) *(G-20152)*
**Jamco Tool & Cams Inc** ....847 678-0280
10151 Franklin Ave Franklin Park (60131) *(G-10505)*
**Jame Roll Form Products Inc** ....847 455-0496
2401 Rose St Franklin Park (60131) *(G-10506)*
**James A Freund LLC** ....630 664-7692
26 Longford Ct Oswego (60543) *(G-16923)*
**James B Beam Import, Deerfield** *Also called Jim Beam Brands Co (G-8019)*
**James Coleman Company** ....847 963-8100
1500 Hicks Rd Rolling Meadows (60008) *(G-18735)*
**James Electronics Div, Chicago** *Also called Custom Magnetics Inc (G-4523)*
**James G Carter** ....309 543-2634
15907 Sr 97 Havana (62644) *(G-11697)*
**James Howard Co** ....815 497-2831
623 W Chestnut St Compton (61318) *(G-7366)*
**James Injection Molding Co** ....847 564-3820
300 Pfingsten Rd Northbrook (60062) *(G-16283)*
**James J Sandoval** ....734 717-7555
333 N Grace St Lombard (60148) *(G-13814)*
**James L Tracey Co** ....630 907-8999
1480 Sequoia Dr Ste A2 Aurora (60506) *(G-1176)*
**James Precious Metals Plating** ....773 774-8700
5700 N Northwest Hwy Chicago (60646) *(G-5274)*
**James R Wilbat Glass Studio** ....847 940-0015
924 Woodward Ave Deerfield (60015) *(G-8017)*
**James Randall** ....309 444-8765
201 Monroe St Washington (61571) *(G-21384)*
**James Ray Monroe Corporation (PA)** ....618 532-4575
308 W Noleman St Centralia (62801) *(G-3420)*

ALPHABETIC

**James Street Dental P C** ....630 232-9535
22 James St Ste 3 Geneva (60134) ***(G-10841)***
**James W Smith Printing Company** ....847 244-6486
1573 Saint Paul Ave Gurnee (60031) ***(G-11461)***
**James Walker Mfg Co** ....708 754-4020
511 W 195th St Glenwood (60425) ***(G-11217)***
**Jameson Books Inc** ....815 434-7905
722 Columbus St Ottawa (61350) ***(G-16963)***
**Jameson Steel Fabrication Inc** ....217 354-2205
19965 Newtown Rd Oakwood (61858) ***(G-16725)***
**Jamesons Asphalt Service** ....630 830-7266
123 W Green Meadows Blvd Streamwood (60107) ***(G-20659)***
**Jamether Incorporated** ....815 444-9971
6294 Northwest Hwy Crystal Lake (60014) ***(G-7593)***
**Jamex Jewelry Inc** ....312 726-7867
5 S Wabash Ave Ste 404 Chicago (60603) ***(G-5275)***
**Jamiel Inc** ....217 423-1000
151 N Jasper St Decatur (62521) ***(G-7898)***
**Jan-Air Inc** ....815 678-4516
10815 Commercial St Richmond (60071) ***(G-17964)***
**Janco Process Controls Inc** ....847 526-0800
368 W Liberty St Wauconda (60084) ***(G-21475)***
**Jancorp LLC (PA)** ....217 892-4830
608 Kopman St Rantoul (61866) ***(G-17929)***
**Jane Stodden Bridals** ....815 223-2091
955 Marquette St La Salle (61301) ***(G-12779)***
**Janelle Publications Inc** ....815 756-2300
116 Twombly Rd Dekalb (60115) ***(G-8100)***
**Janes Lettering Service Inc** ....309 243-7669
12200 N Brentfield Dr # 13 Dunlap (61525) ***(G-8568)***
**Janik Custom Millwork Inc** ....708 482-4844
6017 Lenzi Ave Ste 1 Hodgkins (60525) ***(G-11977)***
**Janin Group Inc** ....630 554-8906
43 Crestview Dr Oswego (60543) ***(G-16924)***
**Janis Plastics Inc** ....847 838-5500
330 North Ave Antioch (60002) ***(G-638)***
**Janitor Ltd** ....773 936-3389
218 N Jefferson St # 202 Chicago (60661) ***(G-5276)***
**Janler Corporation** ....773 774-0166
6545 N Avondale Ave Chicago (60631) ***(G-5277)***
**Jans** ....815 722-9360
321 Richards St Joliet (60433) ***(G-12521)***
**Jans Graphics Inc** ....312 644-4700
2 N Riverside Plz Ste 365 Chicago (60606) ***(G-5278)***
**Janssen Avenue Boys Inc** ....630 627-0202
200 Alder Dr A North Aurora (60542) ***(G-16136)***
**Janssen Machine Inc** ....815 877-9901
985 Industrial Ct Loves Park (61111) ***(G-13950)***
**Janssen Pharmaceutica Inc** ....312 750-0507
20 N Wacker Dr Ste 1442 Chicago (60606) ***(G-5279)***
**Janssen, Ron, Loves Park** *Also called Janssen Machine Inc* ***(G-13950)***
**Japan Economic Journal, Chicago** *Also called Nikkei America Holdings Inc* ***(G-5919)***
**Jarco, Salem** *Also called Polar Corporation* ***(G-19343)***
**Jarden Corporation** ....201 836-7070
3901 Liberty St Aurora (60504) ***(G-1036)***
**Jardis Industries Inc (PA)** ....630 860-5959
1201 Ardmore Ave Itasca (60143) ***(G-12289)***
**Jardis Industries Inc** ....630 773-5600
1201 Ardmore Ave Itasca (60143) ***(G-12290)***
**Jarr Printing Co** ....815 363-5435
5435 Bull Valley Rd # 300 McHenry (60050) ***(G-14515)***
**Jarries Shoe Bags** ....773 379-4044
107 S Parkside Ave Chicago (60644) ***(G-5280)***
**Jarvis Bros & Marcell Inc (PA)** ....217 422-3120
1210 S Jasper St Decatur (62521) ***(G-7899)***
**Jarvis Corp** ....800 363-1075
1950 Estes Ave Elk Grove Village (60007) ***(G-9560)***
**Jarvis Drilling Co (PA)** ....217 422-3120
132 S Water St Ste 331 Decatur (62523) ***(G-7900)***
**Jarvis Electric** ....618 806-2767
1017 Hartman Ln O Fallon (62269) ***(G-16468)***
**Jarvis Lighting, Elk Grove Village** *Also called Jarvis Corp* ***(G-9560)***
**Jarvis Welding Co** ....309 647-0033
124 E Pine St Canton (61520) ***(G-2988)***
**JAS Dahern Signs** ....773 254-0717
3257 S Harding Ave Chicago (60623) ***(G-5281)***
**JAS Express Inc** ....847 836-7984
8307 Seeman Rd Union (60180) ***(G-21035)***
**Jasiek Motor Rebuilding Inc** ....815 883-3678
451 E State Route 71 Oglesby (61348) ***(G-16750)***
**Jason Incorporated** ....630 627-7000
201 S Swift Rd Addison (60101) ***(G-158)***
**Jason Incorporated** ....847 362-8300
1530 Artaius Pkwy Libertyville (60048) ***(G-13340)***
**Jason Industrial, Carol Stream** *Also called Jason of Illinois Inc* ***(G-3176)***
**Jason Lau Jewelry** ....312 750-1028
29 E Madison St Ste 1107 Chicago (60602) ***(G-5282)***
**Jason of Illinois Inc** ....630 752-0600
221 S Westgate Dr Ste N2 Carol Stream (60188) ***(G-3176)***

**Jav Machine Craft Inc** ....708 867-8608
4624 N Oketo Ave Chicago (60706) ***(G-5283)***
**Java Express** ....217 525-2430
1827 N Peoria Rd Springfield (62702) ***(G-20462)***
**Javamania Coffee Roastery Inc** ....815 885-3654
8179 Starwood Dr Ste 4 Loves Park (61111) ***(G-13951)***
**Jax Amusements** ....618 887-4761
11109 Fruit Rd Alhambra (62001) ***(G-419)***
**Jax Asphalt Company Inc** ....618 244-0500
1800 Waterworks Rd Mount Vernon (62864) ***(G-15418)***
**Jay A Morris (PA)** ....815 432-6440
2238 E Township Road 165 Watseka (60970) ***(G-21420)***
**Jay Cee Plastic Fabricators** ....773 276-1920
2133 W Mclean Ave Chicago (60647) ***(G-5284)***
**Jay Elka** ....847 540-7776
1180 Heather Dr Lake Zurich (60047) ***(G-13091)***
**Jay Morris Trucking, Watseka** *Also called Jay A Morris* ***(G-21420)***
**Jay Printing** ....847 934-6103
553 N Hicks Rd Palatine (60067) ***(G-17046)***
**Jay R Steel and Welding, Mundelein** *Also called Jay RS Steel & Welding Inc* ***(G-15514)***
**Jay RS Steel & Welding Inc** ....847 949-9353
840 Tower Rd Mundelein (60060) ***(G-15514)***
**Jays Import and Wholesale, Chicago** *Also called Sarj Kalidas LLC* ***(G-6446)***
**JB & S Machining** ....815 258-4007
1675 Enterprise Way Bourbonnais (60914) ***(G-2401)***
**JB Enterprises II Inc (PA)** ....630 372-8300
375 Roma Jean Pkwy Streamwood (60107) ***(G-20660)***
**JB Mfg & Screw Machine** ....630 850-6978
16w154 Hillside Ln Burr Ridge (60527) ***(G-2859)***
**JB Mfg & Screw Machine PR** ....847 451-0892
9243 Parklane Ave Franklin Park (60131) ***(G-10507)***
**Jbc Holding Co (PA)** ....217 347-7701
3601 S Banker St Effingham (62401) ***(G-8841)***
**Jbl - Alton** ....618 466-0411
2345 State St Alton (62002) ***(G-580)***
**Jbl Marketing Inc** ....847 266-1080
1473 Chantilly Ct Highland Park (60035) ***(G-11847)***
**Jbs United Inc** ....217 285-2121
502 N Madison St Pittsfield (62363) ***(G-17570)***
**Jbs United Inc** ....309 747-2196
116 W 2nd St Gridley (61744) ***(G-11407)***
**Jbs Usa LLC** ....217 323-3774
8295 Arenzville Rd Beardstown (62618) ***(G-1522)***
**Jbsmwg Corp** ....847 675-1865
7170 N Ridgeway Ave Lincolnwood (60712) ***(G-13516)***
**JBT, Chicago** *Also called John Bean Technologies Corp* ***(G-5310)***
**Jbw Machining Inc** ....847 451-0276
2826 Birch St Franklin Park (60131) ***(G-10508)***
**JC Automation Inc** ....309 270-7000
8072 Centennial Expy Rock Island (61201) ***(G-18185)***
**JC Metalcrafters Inc** ....815 942-9891
1360 East St Morris (60450) ***(G-15111)***
**JC Penney Optical, Vernon Hills** *Also called US Vision Inc* ***(G-21214)***
**JC Tool and Mold Inc** ....630 483-2203
1529 Burgundy Pkwy Streamwood (60107) ***(G-20661)***
**Jca International, Park Ridge** *Also called Apolinski John* ***(G-17181)***
**Jcb Inc** ....912 704-2995
800 Bilter Rd Ste A Aurora (60502) ***(G-1037)***
**Jcdecaux Chicago LLC** ....312 456-2999
3959 S Morgan St Chicago (60609) ***(G-5285)***
**Jcg Industries Inc** ....312 829-7282
1115 W Fulton Market Chicago (60607) ***(G-5286)***
**Jcl Specialty Products Inc** ....815 806-2202
19106 S Blackhawk Pkwy Mokena (60448) ***(G-14876)***
**Jcw Investments Inc** ....708 478-7323
11415 183rd Pl Ste E Orland Park (60467) ***(G-16870)***
**JD Norman Industries Inc (PA)** ....630 458-3700
787 W Belden Ave Addison (60101) ***(G-159)***
**JD Pro Productions Inc** ....708 485-2126
4123 Maple Ave Brookfield (60513) ***(G-2636)***
**Jda Aqua Cutting Inc** ....815 485-8028
22037 Howell Dr Ste B New Lenox (60451) ***(G-15888)***
**Jdb Machining Inc** ....708 749-9596
4635 S Harlem Ave Forest View (60402) ***(G-10258)***
**Jdb Manufacturing Company** ....708 749-9596
4635 S Harlem Ave Forest View (60402) ***(G-10259)***
**Jdi Mold and Tool LLC** ....815 759-5646
2510 Hiller Rdg Johnsburg (60051) ***(G-12437)***
**Jdl Graphics Inc** ....815 694-2979
3043 N 1600 East Rd Clifton (60927) ***(G-7274)***
**Jds Labs Inc** ....618 366-0475
909 N Bluff Rd Collinsville (62234) ***(G-7329)***
**Jds Printing Inc** ....630 208-1195
1709 President St Glendale Heights (60139) ***(G-11037)***
**Jeanblanc International Inc** ....815 598-3400
6686 S Derinda Rd Elizabeth (61028) ***(G-9242)***
**Jebco" Screw" and Speciality, Franklin Park** *Also called American/Jebco Corporation* ***(G-10394)***
**Jeco Equipment Company, Schaumburg** *Also called Jeffrey Elevator Co Inc* ***(G-19587)***

## ALPHABETIC SECTION — Jhelsa Metal Polsg Fabrication

**Jedi Corporation**..................................................815 344-5334
4450 Bull Valley Rd Ste 2  Mchenry  (60050)  *(G-14516)*

**Jefco Screw Machine Products**..........................815 282-2000
6203 Material Ave  Loves Park  (61111)  *(G-13952)*

**Jeff's Soda, Northbrook**  *Also called Egg Cream America Inc*  *(G-16248)*

**Jefferies Orchard Sawmill**.................................217 487-7582
1016 Jefferies Rd  Springfield  (62707)  *(G-20463)*

**Jefferson County Ready Mix, Mount Vernon**  *Also called Quad-County Ready Mix Corp*  *(G-15442)*

**Jefferson Ice, Chicago**  *Also called Home City Ice*  *(G-5101)*

**Jeffrey Elevator Co Inc**.....................................847 524-2400
570 Estes Ave  Schaumburg  (60193)  *(G-19587)*

**Jeffrey Jae Inc (PA)**..........................................847 394-1313
907 E Brookwood Dr  Arlington Heights  (60004)  *(G-782)*

**Jeffrey Jae Inc**.................................................847 808-2002
1125 Wheeling Rd  Wheeling  (60090)  *(G-22081)*

**Jeffs Small Engine Inc**......................................630 904-6840
12438 S Route 59  Plainfield  (60585)  *(G-17609)*

**Jel Sert Co**.......................................................630 231-7590
Conde St Rr 59  West Chicago  (60185)  *(G-21727)*

**Jelco Inc**..........................................................847 459-5207
450 Wheeling Rd  Wheeling  (60090)  *(G-22082)*

**Jeld-Wen Inc**....................................................312 544-5041
500 W Monroe St Ste 2010  Chicago  (60661)  *(G-5287)*

**Jeld-Wen Inc**....................................................217 893-4444
201 Evans Rd  Rantoul  (61866)  *(G-17930)*

**Jeld-Wen Windows, Rantoul**  *Also called Jeld-Wen Inc*  *(G-17930)*

**Jeleniz**.............................................................217 235-6789
1414 Broadway Ave  Mattoon  (61938)  *(G-14395)*

**Jelinek & Sons Inc**...........................................630 355-3474
25400 W Hafenrichter Rd  Plainfield  (60585)  *(G-17610)*

**Jelly Belly Candy Company**..............................847 689-2225
1501 Morrow Ave  North Chicago  (60064)  *(G-16183)*

**Jellyvision Inc**.................................................312 266-0606
848 W Eastman St Ste 104  Chicago  (60642)  *(G-5288)*

**Jem Associates Ltd (PA)**..................................847 808-8377
5206 N Meade Ave  Chicago  (60630)  *(G-5289)*

**Jem Tool & Manufacturing Co**..........................630 595-1686
797 Industrial Dr  Bensenville  (60106)  *(G-1927)*

**Jemison Elc Box Swtchboard Inc**.....................815 459-4060
371 E Prairie St Unit H  Crystal Lake  (60014)  *(G-7594)*

**Jen-Sko-Vec Machining & Engrg**.....................773 776-7400
5335 S Western Blvd  Chicago  (60609)  *(G-5290)*

**Jenco Metal Products Inc**................................847 956-0550
1690 W Imperial Ct  Mount Prospect  (60056)  *(G-15340)*

**Jenkins Displays Co**........................................618 335-3874
107 S Railroad St  Patoka  (62875)  *(G-17232)*

**Jenkins Truck & Farm, Patoka**  *Also called Jenkins Displays Co*  *(G-17232)*

**Jenner Precision Inc**........................................815 692-6655
8735 N 2000 East Rd  Fairbury  (61739)  *(G-10127)*

**Jenny Capp Co**................................................773 217-0057
6605 S Harvard Ave  Chicago  (60621)  *(G-5291)*

**Jensen and Son Inc**.........................................815 895-3855
353 N Maple St  Sycamore  (60178)  *(G-20803)*

**Jensen Plating Works Inc (PA)**.........................773 252-7733
183844 N Western Ave  Chicago  (60647)  *(G-5292)*

**Jensen Plating Works Inc**................................773 252-7733
1842 N Western Ave  Chicago  (60647)  *(G-5293)*

**Jeremiah Fleming Music Sites, Wheaton**  *Also called Fleming Music Technology Ctr*  *(G-21948)*

**Jerhen Industries Inc**.......................................815 397-0400
5052 28th Ave  Rockford  (61109)  *(G-18443)*

**Jernberg Industries LLC (HQ)**.........................773 268-3004
328 W 40th Pl  Chicago  (60609)  *(G-5294)*

**Jernberg Industries LLC**.................................630 972-7000
455 Gibraltar Dr  Bolingbrook  (60440)  *(G-2327)*

**Jernberg of Bolingbrook, Bolingbrook**  *Also called Jernberg Industries LLC*  *(G-2327)*

**Jero Medical Eqp & Sups Inc**..........................773 305-4193
4444 W Chicago Ave  Chicago  (60651)  *(G-5295)*

**Jerome Remien Corporation**............................847 806-0888
409 Busse Rd  Elk Grove Village  (60007)  *(G-9561)*

**Jeron Electronic Systems Inc**..........................773 275-1900
7501 N Natchez Ave  Niles  (60714)  *(G-15991)*

**Jerry Berry Contracting Co**..............................618 594-3339
1691 Kane St  Carlyle  (62231)  *(G-3055)*

**Jerry D Graham Oil**..........................................618 548-5540
1213 S Broadway Ave  Salem  (62881)  *(G-19337)*

**Jerry H Simpson**..............................................618 654-3235
604 12th St  Highland  (62249)  *(G-11798)*

**Jerry's Tackle Shop, Highland**  *Also called Jerry H Simpson*  *(G-11798)*

**Jerrys Pro Shop Inc**.........................................708 597-1144
12609 S Kroll Dr  Alsip  (60803)  *(G-476)*

**Jersey County Journal, Jerseyville**  *Also called Campbell Publishing Co Inc*  *(G-12419)*

**Jescorp Inc**.....................................................847 378-1200
1900 Pratt Blvd  Elk Grove Village  (60007)  *(G-9562)*

**Jess Electric**....................................................217 243-7946
2360 Mound Rd  Jacksonville  (62650)  *(G-12398)*

**Jesse B Holt Inc**..............................................618 783-3075
13 Hillcrest Dr  Newton  (62448)  *(G-15942)*

**Jessie White Drvrs Svcs Fclty, Chicago**  *Also called Secretary of State Illinois*  *(G-6469)*

**Jessis Hideout**.................................................618 343-4346
421 S Main St  Caseyville  (62232)  *(G-3398)*

**Jessup Manufacturing Company (PA)**.............815 385-6650
2815 W Rte 120  Mchenry  (60051)  *(G-14517)*

**Jessup Manufacturing Company**.....................847 362-0961
1701 Rockland Rd  Lake Bluff  (60044)  *(G-12851)*

**Jesus People USA Full Gos**............................773 989-2083
5242 N Elston Ave  Chicago  (60630)  *(G-5296)*

**Jesus People USA Full Gospel M, Chicago**  *Also called Lakefront Roofing Supply*  *(G-5443)*

**Jet Aviation St Louis Inc (HQ)**.........................618 646-8000
6400 Curtiss Steinberg Dr  Cahokia  (62206)  *(G-2923)*

**Jet Finishers Inc**..............................................847 718-0501
136 W Commercial Ave  Addison  (60101)  *(G-160)*

**Jet Grinding & Manufacturing**..........................847 956-8646
2309 E Oakton St Ste A  Arlington Heights  (60005)  *(G-783)*

**Jet Industries Inc**.............................................773 586-8900
6025 S Oak Park Ave  Chicago  (60638)  *(G-5297)*

**Jet Rack Corp**..................................................773 586-2150
6200 S New England Ave  Chicago  (60638)  *(G-5298)*

**Jetin Systems Inc**............................................815 726-4686
800 Railroad St  Joliet  (60436)  *(G-12522)*

**Jetpower LLC**..................................................847 856-8359
905 Lakeside Dr Ste 2  Gurnee  (60031)  *(G-11462)*

**Jets Computing Inc**.........................................618 585-6676
200 S Brighton St  Bunker Hill  (62014)  *(G-2805)*

**Jewel - Osco 3316, Hoffman Estates**  *Also called Jewel Osco Inc*  *(G-12020)*

**Jewel Machine Inc**...........................................815 765-3636
302 Kingsbury Dr Se  Poplar Grove  (61065)  *(G-17713)*

**Jewel Osco Inc (HQ)**.......................................630 948-6000
150 E Pierce Rd Ste 200  Itasca  (60143)  *(G-12291)*

**Jewel Osco Inc**................................................630 355-2172
1759 W Ogden Ave Ste A  Naperville  (60540)  *(G-15681)*

**Jewel Osco Inc**................................................847 882-6477
1071 N Roselle Rd  Hoffman Estates  (60169)  *(G-12020)*

**Jewel Osco Inc**................................................630 226-1892
1200 W Boughton Rd  Bolingbrook  (60440)  *(G-2328)*

**Jewel Osco Inc**................................................773 728-7730
5516 N Clark St  Chicago  (60640)  *(G-5299)*

**Jewel Osco Inc**................................................773 784-1922
5343 N Broadway St  Chicago  (60640)  *(G-5300)*

**Jewel Osco Inc**................................................847 677-3331
9449 Skokie Blvd  Skokie  (60077)  *(G-20019)*

**Jewel Osco Inc**................................................708 352-0120
5545 S Brainard Ave  Countryside  (60525)  *(G-7435)*

**Jewel Osco Inc**................................................630 584-4594
2073 Prairie St  Saint Charles  (60174)  *(G-19202)*

**Jewel Osco Inc**................................................630 859-1212
1952 W Galena Blvd  Aurora  (60506)  *(G-1177)*

**Jewel Osco Inc**................................................815 464-5352
21164 N Lagrange Rd  Frankfort  (60423)  *(G-10336)*

**Jewel Osco Inc**................................................847 428-3547
1250 W Main St  West Dundee  (60118)  *(G-21798)*

**Jewel Osco Inc**................................................847 854-2692
103 S Randall Rd  Algonquin  (60102)  *(G-395)*

**Jewel-Osco 3013, Bolingbrook**  *Also called Jewel Osco Inc*  *(G-2328)*

**Jewel-Osco 3052, Frankfort**  *Also called Jewel Osco Inc*  *(G-10336)*

**Jewel-Osco 3059, Naperville**  *Also called Jewel Osco Inc*  *(G-15681)*

**Jewel-Osco 3154, Countryside**  *Also called Jewel Osco Inc*  *(G-7435)*

**Jewel-Osco 3252, Aurora**  *Also called Jewel Osco Inc*  *(G-1177)*

**Jewel-Osco 3256, Algonquin**  *Also called Jewel Osco Inc*  *(G-395)*

**Jewel-Osco 3331, Saint Charles**  *Also called Jewel Osco Inc*  *(G-19202)*

**Jewel-Osco 3407, Chicago**  *Also called Jewel Osco Inc*  *(G-5299)*

**Jewel-Osco 3425, Des Plaines**  *Also called Jewel-Osco Inc*  *(G-8216)*

**Jewel-Osco 3443, Chicago**  *Also called Jewel Osco Inc*  *(G-5300)*

**Jewel-Osco 3465, Skokie**  *Also called Jewel Osco Inc*  *(G-20019)*

**Jewel-Osco Inc**................................................847 296-7786
1500 Lee St  Des Plaines  (60018)  *(G-8216)*

**Jewell Resources Corporation (HQ)**...............276 935-8810
1011 Warrenville Rd # 600  Lisle  (60532)  *(G-13610)*

**Jewerly and Beyond**........................................312 833-6785
608 Newbury Ln B  Schaumburg  (60173)  *(G-19588)*

**Jf Industries Inc**..............................................773 775-8840
7751 W Rosedale Ave  Chicago  (60631)  *(G-5301)*

**Jf Labs, Chicago**  *Also called Afam Concept Inc*  *(G-3779)*

**Jfb Hart Coatings Inc**......................................949 724-9737
10200 S Mandel St Ste C  Plainfield  (60585)  *(G-17611)*

**Jfb Hart Coatings Inc (PA)**..............................630 783-1917
10200 S Mandel St Ste C  Plainfield  (60585)  *(G-17612)*

**Jgc United Publishing Corps**...........................815 968-6601
1710 N Main St Fl 1  Rockford  (61103)  *(G-18444)*

**Jgr Commercial Solutions Inc**.........................847 669-7010
11414 Smith Dr Unit G  Huntley  (60142)  *(G-12152)*

**Jh Choppers LLC**............................................618 420-2500
3 Hungate Ln  Maryville  (62062)  *(G-14342)*

**Jhelsa Metal Polsg Fabrication**.......................773 385-6628
1900 N Austin Ave Ste 71  Chicago  (60639)  *(G-5302)*

**Jht Robertson Lumber Inc** ....618 842-2004
408 Airport Rd Fairfield (62837) *(G-10146)*
**Jiffy Metal Products Inc** ....773 626-8090
5025 W Lake St Chicago (60644) *(G-5303)*
**Jigsaw Solutions Inc** ....630 926-1948
1296 Lakeview Dr Romeoville (60446) *(G-18832)*
**Jii Holdings LLC** ....847 945-5591
1751 Lake Cook Rd Ste 550 Deerfield (60015) *(G-8018)*
**Jim Beam Brands Co (HQ)** ....847 948-8903
510 Lake Cook Rd Ste 200 Deerfield (60015) *(G-8019)*
**Jim Cokel Welding** ....309 734-5063
204 E 6th Ave Monmouth (61462) *(G-15015)*
**Jim Haley Oil Production Co** ....618 382-7338
1415 W Main St Carmi (62821) *(G-3070)*
**Jim Jolly Sales Inc** ....847 669-7570
11225 Giordano Ct Huntley (60142) *(G-12153)*
**Jim Maui Inc** ....888 666-5905
1 Aloha Ln Peoria (61615) *(G-17392)*
**Jim Noodle & Rice** ....773 935-5923
2819 N Lincoln Ave Chicago (60657) *(G-5304)*
**Jim Sterner Machines** ....815 962-8983
2500 N Main St Ste 25 Rockford (61103) *(G-18445)*
**Jim's Plumbing, Streamwood** *Also called Caffero Tool & Mfg* *(G-20647)*
**Jiminee's Doll Clothes, Roselle** *Also called Jiminees Inc* *(G-18949)*
**Jiminees Inc** ....630 295-8002
359 W Irving Park Rd D Roselle (60172) *(G-18949)*
**Jimmy Diesel Inc** ....708 482-4500
2s401 Burning Trl Wheaton (60189) *(G-21959)*
**Jimmy's Healthy Foods, Chicago** *Also called Jimmybars* *(G-5305)*
**Jimmybars** ....888 676-7971
2558 W 16th St Fl 5th Chicago (60608) *(G-5305)*
**Jindilli Beverages LLC** ....630 581-5697
8100 S Madison St Burr Ridge (60527) *(G-2860)*
**Jing MEI Industrial USA Inc (PA)** ....847 671-0800
10275 W Higgins Rd # 470 Rosemont (60018) *(G-19007)*
**Jinhap US Corporation (HQ)** ....630 833-2880
900 N Church Rd Elmhurst (60126) *(G-9891)*
**Jinny Corp** ....773 588-7200
3505 N Kimball Ave Chicago (60618) *(G-5306)*
**Jj Wood Working** ....708 426-6854
9016 Odell Ave Bridgeview (60455) *(G-2502)*
**Jjc Epoxy Inc** ....630 231-5600
1105 Carolina Dr West Chicago (60185) *(G-21728)*
**Jjj Brass and Aluminum Foundry** ....608 363-9225
413 Clark St South Beloit (61080) *(G-20153)*
**Jjm Printing Inc** ....815 499-3067
311 1st Ave Sterling (61081) *(G-20595)*
**Jjm Products LLC** ....630 319-9325
1052 Zygmunt Cir Westmont (60559) *(G-21894)*
**Jjs Global Ventures Inc** ....847 999-4313
1900 E Golf Rd Ste 950 Schaumburg (60173) *(G-19589)*
**Jjs High TEC Machining Inc** ....618 775-8840
103 N Everett St Odin (62870) *(G-16740)*
**Jk Audio Inc** ....815 786-2929
1311 E 6th St Sandwich (60548) *(G-19370)*
**Jk Installs, Greenville** *Also called Jklein Enterprises Inc* *(G-11395)*
**JK Williams Distilling LLC** ....309 839-0591
526 High Point Ln East Peoria (61611) *(G-8717)*
**Jklein Enterprises Inc** ....618 664-4554
505a W South Ave Greenville (62246) *(G-11395)*
**JKS Ventures Inc (PA)** ....708 345-9344
2035 Indian Boundry Dr Melrose Park (60160) *(G-14662)*
**JKS Ventures Inc** ....708 338-3408
3800 W Lake St Melrose Park (60160) *(G-14663)*
**JL Clark LLC** ....815 961-5677
2300 S 6th St Rockford (61104) *(G-18446)*
**JL Clark LLC (HQ)** ....815 961-5609
923 23rd Ave Rockford (61104) *(G-18447)*
**JLJ Corp** ....847 726-9795
250 Telser Rd Ste D Lake Zurich (60047) *(G-13092)*
**Jlm Woodworking** ....309 275-8259
500 Orlando Ave Normal (61761) *(G-16074)*
**Jlo Metal Products Co A Corp** ....773 889-6242
5841 W Dickens Ave Chicago (60639) *(G-5307)*
**JM Circle Enterprise Inc** ....708 946-3333
28255 S Cottage Grove Ave Beecher (60401) *(G-1598)*
**JM Die Tooling Co** ....630 616-7776
466 Meyer Rd Bensenville (60106) *(G-1928)*
**JM Huber Corporation** ....217 224-1100
3150 Gardner Expy Quincy (62305) *(G-17841)*
**JM Industries LLC** ....708 849-4700
1000 W 142nd St Riverdale (60827) *(G-18020)*
**JM Tool & Die LLC** ....630 595-1274
299 Beeline Dr Bensenville (60106) *(G-1929)*
**Jmd Screw Products** ....815 505-9113
2873 E Fairfield Trl Belvidere (61008) *(G-1766)*
**Jme Technologies Inc** ....815 477-8800
2520 Route 176 Bldg 3 Crystal Lake (60014) *(G-7595)*
**Jmi Crafted Coml Mllwk Inc** ....708 331-6331
3032 W 167th St Harvey (60428) *(G-11673)*
**Jmk Computerized Tdis Inc** ....217 384-8891
703 S Glover Ave Urbana (61802) *(G-21092)*
**JMr Precision Machining Inc** ....847 279-3982
630 S Wheeling Rd Mundelein (60060) *(G-15515)*
**JMS Auto Electric, Lombard** *Also called James J Sandoval* *(G-13814)*
**JMS Metals Inc** ....618 443-1000
1255 W Broadway St Sparta (62286) *(G-20317)*
**Jn Pump Holdings Inc (PA)** ....708 754-2940
1249 Center Ave Chicago Heights (60411) *(G-7105)*
**Jns Glass Coating, Yorkville** *Also called Strausberger Assoc Sls & Mktg* *(G-22671)*
**Jo Davies County Transit, Galena** *Also called Workshop* *(G-10736)*
**Jo Go Pallet & Supplies** ....815 254-1631
22538 Bass Lake Rd Plainfield (60544) *(G-17613)*
**Jo MO Enterprises Inc** ....708 599-8098
7825 W 87th Pl Bridgeview (60455) *(G-2503)*
**Jo Snow Inc** ....773 732-3045
2852 W Lyndale St Chicago (60647) *(G-5308)*
**Jo-Ann Fabrics & Crafts, Arlington Heights** *Also called Jo-Ann Stores LLC* *(G-784)*
**Jo-Ann Stores LLC** ....847 394-9742
373 E Palatine Rd Arlington Heights (60004) *(G-784)*
**Joans Trophy & Plaque Co** ....309 674-6500
508 Ne Jefferson Ave Peoria (61603) *(G-17393)*
**Jodaat Inc** ....630 916-7776
18w333 Roosevelt Rd Ste 1 Lombard (60148) *(G-13815)*
**Jodi Maurer** ....847 961-5347
5001 Princeton Ln Lake In The Hills (60156) *(G-12996)*
**Joe Anthony & Associates** ....708 935-0804
5151 Sauk Trl Richton Park (60471) *(G-17978)*
**Joe Chicken & Fish, Richton Park** *Also called Joe Anthony & Associates* *(G-17978)*
**Joe Hatzer & Son Inc (PA)** ....815 673-5571
602 Lundy St Streator (61364) *(G-20692)*
**Joe Hatzer & Son Inc** ....815 672-2161
2515 1/2 N Bloomington St Streator (61364) *(G-20693)*
**Joe Hunt** ....618 392-2000
1911 E Main St Olney (62450) *(G-16774)*
**Joe Zsido Sales & Design Inc** ....618 435-2605
350 Industrial Park Rd Benton (62812) *(G-2032)*
**Joes Automotive Inc** ....815 937-9281
560 S Washington Ave Kankakee (60901) *(G-12630)*
**Joes Printing** ....773 545-6063
6025 N Cicero Ave Chicago (60646) *(G-5309)*
**Jofas Print Corporation** ....815 534-5725
22856 Lkview Estates Blvd Frankfort (60423) *(G-10337)*
**John & Helen Inc** ....815 654-1070
988 Industrial Ct Loves Park (61111) *(G-13953)*
**John A Biewer Lumber Company** ....815 357-6792
524 E Union St Seneca (61360) *(G-19887)*
**John B Sanfilippo & Son Inc (PA)** ....847 289-1800
1703 N Randall Rd Elgin (60123) *(G-9083)*
**John B Sanfilippo & Son Inc** ....847 690-8432
2350 Fox Ln Elgin (60123) *(G-9084)*
**John Bean Technologies Corp (PA)** ....312 861-5900
70 W Madison St Ste 4400 Chicago (60602) *(G-5310)*
**John Beyer Race Cars** ....773 779-5313
10718 S Homan Ave Chicago (60655) *(G-5311)*
**John Buechner Inc** ....312 263-2226
8 S Michigan Ave Ste 607 Chicago (60603) *(G-5312)*
**John C Grafft (PA)** ....847 842-9200
28045 Roberts Rd Lake Barrington (60010) *(G-12811)*
**John Crane Inc (HQ)** ....312 605-7800
227 W Monroe St Ste 1800 Chicago (60606) *(G-5313)*
**John Crane Inc** ....815 459-0420
29-31 Burdent Dr Crystal Lake (60014) *(G-7596)*
**John Crane Inc** ....847 967-2400
6400 Oakton St Morton Grove (60053) *(G-15207)*
**John Dagys Media LLC** ....708 373-0180
8011 W 125th St Palos Park (60464) *(G-17129)*
**John Deere, Moline** *Also called Deere & Company* *(G-14927)*
**John Deere, Moline** *Also called Deere & Company* *(G-14930)*
**John Deere Accounts Payble, Moline** *Also called Deere & Company* *(G-14929)*
**John Deere AG Holdings Inc** ....309 765-8000
1 John Deere Pl Moline (61265) *(G-14946)*
**John Deere Authorized Dealer, South Roxana** *Also called Mikes Inc* *(G-20314)*
**John Deere Authorized Dealer, Rockford** *Also called West Side Tractor Sales Co* *(G-18678)*
**John Deere Authorized Dealer, Anna** *Also called Anna-Jonesboro Motor Co Inc* *(G-601)*
**John Deere Cnstr & For Co** ....309 765-8000
1515 5th Ave Ste 200 Moline (61265) *(G-14947)*
**John Deere Harvester, East Moline** *Also called Deere & Company* *(G-8673)*
**John Deere Seeding Group, Moline** *Also called Deere & Company* *(G-14935)*
**John Deere Waterloo Works, Moline** *Also called Deere & Company* *(G-14932)*
**John F Mate Co** ....847 381-8131
27930 W Industrial Ave # 5 Lake Barrington (60010) *(G-12812)*
**John Gile, Rockford** *Also called Jgc United Publishing Corps* *(G-18444)*
**John Gillen Company, Cicero** *Also called Tvo Acquisition Corporation* *(G-7239)*
**John H Best & Sons Inc** ....309 932-2124
1 Burlington Rd Galva (61434) *(G-10791)*
**John Hardy Co** ....847 864-8060
1728 Brummel St Evanston (60202) *(G-10059)*

**John Harland Company** ....815 293-4350
1003 Birch Ln Romeoville (60446) ***(G-18833)***
**John Hauter Dremel** ....800 437-3635
1800 W Central Rd Mount Prospect (60056) ***(G-15341)***
**John Hofmeister & Son Inc** ....773 847-0700
2386 S Blue Island Ave Chicago (60608) ***(G-5314)***
**John J Moesle Wholesale Meats** ....773 847-4900
4725 S Talman Ave Chicago (60632) ***(G-5315)***
**John J Monaco Products Co Inc** ....708 344-3333
3120 W Lake St Melrose Park (60160) ***(G-14664)***
**John J Rickhoff Shtmtl Co Inc** ....708 331-2970
320 E 152nd St Phoenix (60426) ***(G-17541)***
**John Joda Post 54** ....815 692-3222
600 S 3rd St Fairbury (61739) ***(G-10128)***
**John Killough Dpm Cws (PA)** ....217 348-3339
1301 Deerpath Charleston (61920) ***(G-3602)***
**John King Usa Inc** ....309 698-9250
200 Catherine St Unit 7b East Peoria (61611) ***(G-8718)***
**John Maneely Company** ....773 254-0617
4435 S Western Blvd Chicago (60609) ***(G-5316)***
**John Morrell & Co** ....630 993-8763
771 W Crssrads Pkwy Ste A Bolingbrook (60490) ***(G-2329)***
**John Parker Advertising Co** ....217 892-4118
520 E Grove Ave Rantoul (61866) ***(G-17931)***
**John R Nalbach Engineering Co** ....708 579-9100
621 E Plainfield Rd Countryside (60525) ***(G-7436)***
**John S Swift Company Inc (PA)** ....847 465-3300
999 Commerce Ct Buffalo Grove (60089) ***(G-2713)***
**John S Swift of Des Plaines, Buffalo Grove** *Also called Des Plaines Printing LLC* ***(G-2686)***
**John Thomas Inc** ....815 288-2343
1560 Lovett Dr Dixon (61021) ***(G-8334)***
**John Thomas Company, Dixon** *Also called John Thomas Inc* ***(G-8334)***
**John Tobin Millwork Co (PA)** ....630 832-3780
231 W North Ave Villa Park (60181) ***(G-21260)***
**Johnny Rckets Firewrks Display** ....847 501-1270
4410 N Hamilton Ave Chicago (60625) ***(G-5317)***
**Johnny Vans Smokehouse** ....773 750-1589
924 W Gordon Ter Apt 3 Chicago (60613) ***(G-5318)***
**Johnnys Little LLC** ....217 243-2570
1848 Mound Rd Jacksonville (62650) ***(G-12399)***
**Johnos Inc (PA)** ....630 897-6929
1804 E New York St Aurora (60505) ***(G-1178)***
**Johns Manville Corporation** ....815 744-1545
2151 Channahon Rd Rockdale (60436) ***(G-18221)***
**Johns-Byrne Company (PA)** ....847 583-3100
6701 W Oakton St Niles (60714) ***(G-15992)***
**Johnsbyrne, Niles** *Also called Johns-Byrne Company* ***(G-15992)***
**Johnsbyrne Graphic Tech Corp** ....847 583-3100
6701 W Oakton St Niles (60714) ***(G-15993)***
**Johnson & Johnson** ....847 640-5400
1350 Estes Ave Elk Grove Village (60007) ***(G-9563)***
**Johnson & Johnson** ....815 282-5671
5500 Forest Hills Rd Loves Park (61111) ***(G-13954)***
**Johnson Bag Co Inc** ....847 438-2424
1166 Flex Ct Lake Zurich (60047) ***(G-13093)***
**Johnson Contrls Authorized Dlr, Joliet** *Also called Ecolab Inc* ***(G-12488)***
**Johnson Contrls Authorized Dlr, Joliet** *Also called Illco Inc* ***(G-12513)***
**Johnson Contrls Authorized Dlr, Elk Grove Village** *Also called Ecolab Inc* ***(G-9448)***
**Johnson Contrls Btry Group Inc** ....630 232-4270
300 S Glengarry Dr Geneva (60134) ***(G-10842)***
**Johnson Controls Inc** ....815 288-3859
629 N Galena Ave Ste 210 Dixon (61021) ***(G-8335)***
**Johnson Controls Inc** ....309 427-2800
3850 N Main St East Peoria (61611) ***(G-8719)***
**Johnson Controls Inc** ....630 573-0897
78 Oakbrook Ctr Oak Brook (60523) ***(G-16527)***
**Johnson Controls Inc** ....815 397-5147
7316 Argus Dr 1 Rockford (61107) ***(G-18448)***
**Johnson Controls Inc** ....331 212-3800
3600 Thayer Ct Ste 300 Aurora (60504) ***(G-1038)***
**Johnson Controls Inc** ....847 364-1500
3007 Malmo Dr Arlington Heights (60005) ***(G-785)***
**Johnson Controls Inc** ....217 793-8858
4231 Westgate Dr Springfield (62711) ***(G-20464)***
**Johnson Controls Inc** ....630 279-0050
450 W Wrightwood Ave Elmhurst (60126) ***(G-9892)***
**Johnson Controls Inc** ....630 351-9407
153 Stratford Square Mall Bloomingdale (60108) ***(G-2110)***
**Johnson Controls Inc** ....312 829-5956
850 W Jackson Blvd # 420 Chicago (60607) ***(G-5319)***
**Johnson Custom Cabinets** ....815 675-9690
7609 Blivin St Spring Grove (60081) ***(G-20339)***
**Johnson Diaries** ....708 478-2882
9850 W 190th St Ste E Mokena (60448) ***(G-14877)***
**Johnson Editorial Limited, Mokena** *Also called Johnson Diaries* ***(G-14877)***
**Johnson Group, Des Plaines** *Also called Deluxe Johnson* ***(G-8182)***
**Johnson Oil Company, Wheaton** *Also called R H Johnson Oil Co Inc* ***(G-21974)***
**Johnson Pattern & Mch Works** ....815 433-2775
350 W Marquette St Ottawa (61350) ***(G-16964)***
**Johnson Power Ltd (PA)** ....708 345-4300
2530 Braga Dr Broadview (60155) ***(G-2588)***
**Johnson Press America Inc** ....815 844-5161
800 N Court St Pontiac (61764) ***(G-17704)***
**Johnson Printing** ....630 595-8815
729 Il Route 83 Ste 323 Bensenville (60106) ***(G-1930)***
**Johnson Publishing Company LLC (PA)** ....312 322-9200
200 S Michigan Ave Fl 21 Chicago (60604) ***(G-5320)***
**Johnson Pumps America Inc** ....847 671-7867
5885 11th St Rockford (61109) ***(G-18449)***
**Johnson Rolan Co Inc** ....309 674-9671
718 Sw Adams St Peoria (61602) ***(G-17394)***
**Johnson Seat & Canvas Shop** ....815 756-2037
25 S Somonauk Rd Cortland (60112) ***(G-7389)***
**Johnson Sign Co** ....847 678-2092
9615 Waveland Ave Franklin Park (60131) ***(G-10509)***
**Johnson Steel Rule Die Co** ....773 921-4334
5410 W Roosevelt Rd # 228 Chicago (60644) ***(G-5321)***
**Johnson Tool Company** ....708 453-8600
11528 Smith Dr 3 Huntley (60142) ***(G-12154)***
**Johnsons Processing Plant** ....815 684-5183
201 Il Route 40 E Chadwick (61014) ***(G-3442)***
**Johnsons Screen Printing** ....630 262-8210
419 Stevens St Ste C Geneva (60134) ***(G-10843)***
**Johnston & Jennings Inc** ....708 757-5375
1200 State St Ste 1 Chicago Heights (60411) ***(G-7106)***
**Joiner Sheet Metal & Roofing** ....618 664-9488
817 E Harris Ave Greenville (62246) ***(G-11396)***
**Joint Asia Dev Group LLC** ....847 223-1804
888 E Belvidere Rd # 213 Grayslake (60030) ***(G-11349)***
**Joliet Cabinet Company Inc** ....815 727-4096
405 Caton Farm Rd Lockport (60441) ***(G-13724)***
**Joliet Herald Newspaper** ....815 280-4100
2175 Oneida St Joliet (60435) ***(G-12523)***
**Joliet Orthotics** ....708 798-1767
2119 Vardon Ln Flossmoor (60422) ***(G-10226)***
**Joliet Pallets** ....
111 Bissel St Joliet (60432) ***(G-12524)***
**Joliet Pattern Works Inc** ....815 726-5373
508 Pasadena Ave Crest Hill (60403) ***(G-7460)***
**Joliet Refinery, Elwood** *Also called Exxonmobil Pipeline Company* ***(G-9980)***
**Joliet Sand and Gravel Company** ....815 741-2090
2509 Mound Rd Rockdale (60436) ***(G-18222)***
**Joliet Technologies LLC** ....815 725-9696
1724 Tomich Ct Crest Hill (60403) ***(G-7461)***
**Joliet Times Weekly, Joliet** *Also called C & C Publications* ***(G-12469)***
**Jomar Electric Coil Mfg Inc** ....630 279-1494
218 W Stone Rd Villa Park (60181) ***(G-21261)***
**Jonem Grp Inc DBA Sign A Rama** ....224 848-4620
28039 W Coml Ave Ste 9 Lake Barrington (60010) ***(G-12813)***
**Jones and Coontz, Rock Falls** *Also called Dekalb Feeds Inc* ***(G-18131)***
**Jones Brothers Mch & Wldg Inc** ....618 945-4609
145 E Olive St Bridgeport (62417) ***(G-2453)***
**Jones Design Group Ltd** ....630 462-9340
27w230 Beecher Ave Ste 1 Winfield (60190) ***(G-22286)***
**Jones Garrison Sons Mch Works** ....618 847-2161
Hwy 15 W Fairfield (62837) ***(G-10147)***
**Jones Medical Instrument Co** ....630 571-1980
200 Windsor Dr Ste A Oak Brook (60523) ***(G-16528)***
**Jones Packing Co** ....815 943-4488
22701 Oak Grove Rd Harvard (60033) ***(G-11639)***
**Jones Products Co, Woodstock** *Also called Shannon Industries Inc* ***(G-22610)***
**Jones Software Corp** ....312 952-0011
531 S Plymouth Ct Ste 104 Chicago (60605) ***(G-5322)***
**Jones Watch and Jewelry Repair, Springfield** *Also called Michael P Jones* ***(G-20481)***
**Jones Wood Products** ....618 826-2682
11801 Ebenezer Rd Rockwood (62280) ***(G-18704)***
**Joong-Ang Daily News** ....847 228-7200
790 Busse Rd Elk Grove Village (60007) ***(G-9564)***
**Jopac Companies, The, Bloomington** *Also called Moran Auto Parts and Mch Sp* ***(G-2203)***
**Jordan Gold Inc** ....708 430-7008
8741 Ridgeland Ave Oak Lawn (60453) ***(G-16628)***
**Jordan Industrial Controls Inc** ....217 864-4444
215 Casa Park Dr Mount Zion (62549) ***(G-15453)***
**Jordan Industries Inc (PA)** ....847 945-5591
1751 Lake Cook Rd Ste 550 Deerfield (60015) ***(G-8020)***
**Jordan Paper Box Company** ....773 287-5362
5045 W Lake St Chicago (60644) ***(G-5323)***
**Jordan Services** ....630 416-6701
2100 Scarlet Oak Ln Lisle (60532) ***(G-13611)***
**Jordan Specialty Plastics Inc (HQ)** ....847 945-5591
1751 Lake Cook Rd Ste 550 Deerfield (60015) ***(G-8021)***
**Jorge A Cruz** ....773 722-2828
240 N Harding Ave Chicago (60624) ***(G-5324)***
**Jorh Frame & Moulding Co Inc** ....708 747-3440
21750 Main St Ste 14&15 Matteson (60443) ***(G-14374)***
**Joriki LLC** ....312 848-1136
1220 W Wrightwood Ave Chicago (60614) ***(G-5325)***
**Josco Inc** ....708 867-7189
4830 N Harlem Ave Chicago (60706) ***(G-5326)***

ALPHABETIC

(PA)=Parent Co (HQ)=Headquarters (DH)=Div Headquarters
2017 Harris Illinois Industrial Directory
1285

**Joseph B Krisher** .................................................. 618 677-2016
9950 Drum Hill Rd  Mascoutah  (62258)  *(G-14354)*
**Joseph B Pigato MD Ltd** .......................................... 815 937-2122
375 N Wall St Ste P630  Kankakee  (60901)  *(G-12631)*
**Joseph C Rakers** .................................................. 618 670-6995
209 Pocahontas St  Pocahontas  (62275)  *(G-17683)*
**Joseph C Wolf** ..................................................... 312 332-3135
5 S Wabash Ave Ste 1018  Chicago  (60603)  *(G-5327)*
**Joseph Coppolino** ................................................. 773 735-8647
4455 W 55th St  Chicago  (60632)  *(G-5328)*
**Joseph D Smithies** ................................................ 618 632-6141
7409 N Illinois St  Caseyville  (62232)  *(G-3399)*
**Joseph Kristan** .................................................... 847 731-3131
2805 Ebenezer Ave  Zion  (60099)  *(G-22689)*
**Joseph Ringelstein** ................................................ 708 955-7467
4110 1/2 N Octavia Ave  Norridge  (60706)  *(G-16103)*
**Joseph Taylor Inc** ................................................. 309 762-5323
708 18th Avenue A  Moline  (61265)  *(G-14948)*
**Joseph Woodworking Corporation** ................................ 847 233-9766
4226 Grace St  Schiller Park  (60176)  *(G-19841)*
**Josephs Food Products Co Inc** .................................. 708 338-4090
2759 S 25th Ave  Broadview  (60155)  *(G-2589)*
**Josephs Printing Service** ....................................... 847 724-4429
1739 Chestnut Ave Ste 107  Glenview  (60025)  *(G-11154)*
**Joshi Brothers Inc** ............................................... 847 895-0200
1218 S Roselle Rd  Schaumburg  (60193)  *(G-19590)*
**Jost & Kiefer Printing Company** ............................... 217 222-5145
2029 Hllster Whitney Pkwy  Quincy  (62305)  *(G-17842)*
**Jostens Inc** ........................................................ 630 963-3500
5980 State Route 53 Ste A  Lisle  (60532)  *(G-13612)*
**Jostens Inc** ........................................................ 217 483-8989
114 W Walnut St  Chatham  (62629)  *(G-3623)*
**Journal, Kankakee** Also called Small Newspaper Group  *(G-12652)*
**Journal & Topics Newspapers, Des Plaines** Also called Des Plaines Journal Inc  *(G-8184)*
**Journal Fabrication, Mount Olive** Also called Herald Mount Olive  *(G-15303)*
**Journal News** ..................................................... 217 532-3933
425 S Main St  Hillsboro  (62049)  *(G-11896)*
**Journal News** ..................................................... 217 324-6604
510 N State St  Litchfield  (62056)  *(G-13690)*
**Journal of Banking and Fin** .................................... 618 203-9074
4 Oxford Ln  Glen Carbon  (62034)  *(G-10953)*
**Journal Standard** ................................................. 815 232-1171
50 W Douglas St Ste 900  Freeport  (61032)  *(G-10670)*
**Journal Star-Peoria** ............................................. 309 833-2449
1432 E Jackson St  Macomb  (61455)  *(G-14126)*
**Journal-Courier, Jacksonville** Also called Freedom Communications Inc  *(G-12387)*
**Journey Circuits Inc** ............................................ 630 283-0604
830 E Higgins Rd Ste 111h  Schaumburg  (60173)  *(G-19591)*
**Joy Technologies Inc** ............................................ 618 242-3650
4111 N Water Tower Pl B  Mount Vernon  (62864)  *(G-15419)*
**Joyce Greiner** ..................................................... 618 654-9340
801 9th St  Highland  (62249)  *(G-11799)*
**JP Leatherworks Inc** ............................................ 847 317-9804
1038 Somerset Ave  Deerfield  (60015)  *(G-8022)*
**JP O'Callaghan, Chicago** Also called Regent Window Fashions LLC  *(G-6324)*
**JP Orthotics** ...................................................... 217 885-3047
9234 Broadway St  Quincy  (62305)  *(G-17843)*
**Jph Enterprises Inc** ............................................. 847 390-0900
420 Lee St  Des Plaines  (60016)  *(G-8217)*
**Jpi, Philo** Also called Jamaica Pyrotechnics  *(G-17539)*
**Jpmorgan Chase & Co** ........................................... 773 978-3408
9138 S Commercial Ave  Chicago  (60617)  *(G-5329)*
**Jpmorgan Chase Bank Nat Assn** ............................... 630 653-1270
411 S Schmale Rd  Carol Stream  (60188)  *(G-3177)*
**Jpmorgan Chase Bank Nat Assn** ............................... 847 392-1600
2 E Euclid Ave  Prospect Heights  (60070)  *(G-17781)*
**Jpmorgan Chase Bank Nat Assn** ............................... 708 868-1274
1783 River Oaks Dr  Calumet City  (60409)  *(G-2944)*
**Jpmorgan Chase Bank Nat Assn** ............................... 815 462-2800
500 W Maple St Ste 2  New Lenox  (60451)  *(G-15889)*
**Jpmorgan Chase Bank Nat Assn** ............................... 847 726-4000
1289 S Rand Rd  Lake Zurich  (60047)  *(G-13094)*
**Jpmorgan Chase Bank Nat Assn** ............................... 847 663-1235
7007 W Dempster St  Niles  (60714)  *(G-15994)*
**Jpmorgan Chase Bank Nat Assn** ............................... 217 353-4234
201 W University Ave # 1  Champaign  (61820)  *(G-3504)*
**Jpmorgan Chase Bank Nat Assn** ............................... 773 994-2490
353 W 83rd St  Chicago  (60620)  *(G-5330)*
**Jpmorgan Chase Bank Nat Assn** ............................... 847 685-0490
500 Busse Hwy  Park Ridge  (60068)  *(G-17205)*
**Jql Electronics Inc (PA)** ....................................... 630 873-2020
3501 Algonquin Rd Ste 230  Rolling Meadows  (60008)  *(G-18736)*
**Jr Bakery** ......................................................... 773 465-6733
2841 W Howard St  Chicago  (60645)  *(G-5331)*
**Jr Industries LLC** ............................................... 773 908-5317
4218 N California Ave  Chicago  (60618)  *(G-5332)*
**Jr Lighting Design Inc** ......................................... 708 460-6319
18464 West Creek Dr  Tinley Park  (60477)  *(G-20926)*
**Jr Plastics LLC** .................................................. 773 523-5454
2850 W Columbus Ave  Chicago  (60652)  *(G-5333)*
**Jr Royals Athletics** ............................................. 224 659-2906
1073 Compass Pt  Elgin  (60123)  *(G-9085)*
**Jr Sons Welding, Alsip** Also called Edward F Data  *(G-461)*
**Jr Tech Inc** ....................................................... 847 214-8860
1600 Todd Farm Dr Ste A  Elgin  (60123)  *(G-9086)*
**Jrb Attachments LLC** ........................................... 319 378-3696
2211 York Rd Ste 320  Oak Brook  (60523)  *(G-16529)*
**Jrd Labs LLC** .................................................... 847 818-1076
2613 Greenleaf Ave  Elk Grove Village  (60007)  *(G-9565)*
**Jrm International Inc** .......................................... 815 282-9330
5701 Industrial Ave  Loves Park  (61111)  *(G-13955)*
**Jsa Tool & Engineering, Northbrook** Also called Strategic Mfg Partner LLC  *(G-16372)*
**Jsc Products Inc** ................................................ 847 290-9520
2270 Elmhurst Rd  Elk Grove Village  (60007)  *(G-9566)*
**Jsjs, Elburn** Also called Jahns Structure Jacking System  *(G-8890)*
**Jsn Inc** ............................................................ 708 410-1800
611 Saint Charles Rd  Maywood  (60153)  *(G-14426)*
**Jsn Printing Inc** ................................................. 815 582-4014
1400 Essington Rd  Joliet  (60435)  *(G-12525)*
**Jsolo Corp** ........................................................ 847 964-9188
607 Carriage Way  Deerfield  (60015)  *(G-8023)*
**Jsp Mold** .......................................................... 815 225-7110
404 E 4th St  Milledgeville  (61051)  *(G-14817)*
**Jsq Inc** ............................................................ 847 731-8800
13950 W Adams Rd  Wadsworth  (60083)  *(G-21323)*
**JT Cullen Co Inc** ................................................ 815 589-2412
901 31st Ave  Fulton  (61252)  *(G-10702)*
**Jt Products Co** .................................................. 773 378-4550
1515 N 25th Ave  Melrose Park  (60160)  *(G-14665)*
**Jtec Industries Inc** ............................................. 309 698-9301
201 Carver Ln  East Peoria  (61611)  *(G-8720)*
**Jtekt Toyoda Americas Corp (HQ)** ............................ 847 253-0340
316 W University Dr  Arlington Heights  (60004)  *(G-786)*
**Jth Enterprises Inc** ............................................. 847 394-3355
311 W University Dr  Arlington Heights  (60004)  *(G-787)*
**Jtoor LLC** ......................................................... 312 291-8249
900 N Michigan Ave 308a  Chicago  (60611)  *(G-5334)*
**Juice Tyme Inc (PA)** ........................................... 773 579-1291
4401 S Oakley Ave  Chicago  (60609)  *(G-5335)*
**Julian Elec Svc & Engrg Inc** .................................. 630 920-8950
701 Blackhawk Dr  Westmont  (60559)  *(G-21895)*
**July 25th Corporation** ......................................... 309 664-6444
1708 E Hamilton Rd Ste B  Bloomington  (61704)  *(G-2186)*
**Junker Inc** ........................................................ 630 231-3770
391 Wegner Dr Ste A  West Chicago  (60185)  *(G-21729)*
**Jupiter Industries Inc (PA)** ................................... 847 925-5120
1821 Walden Office Sq # 400  Schaumburg  (60173)  *(G-19592)*
**Jury Verdict Reporter** .......................................... 312 644-7800
415 N State St Ste 1  Chicago  (60654)  *(G-5336)*
**Juskie Printing Corp** ........................................... 630 663-8833
2820 Hitchcock Ave Ste E  Downers Grove  (60515)  *(G-8468)*
**Just Another Button** ............................................ 618 667-8531
116 W Market St  Troy  (62294)  *(G-21009)*
**Just Ice Inc** ...................................................... 773 301-7323
1400 W 46th St  Chicago  (60609)  *(G-5337)*
**Just Manufacturing Company (PA)** ............................ 847 678-5151
9233 King St  Franklin Park  (60131)  *(G-10510)*
**Just Parts Inc (PA)** ............................................ 815 756-2184
121 W Elm Ave  Cortland  (60112)  *(G-7390)*
**Just Rite Rental, Naperville** Also called CCS Contractor Eqp & Sup Inc  *(G-15622)*
**Just Sashes** ...................................................... 773 205-1429
5952 W Addison St  Chicago  (60634)  *(G-5338)*
**Just Turkey** ...................................................... 708 957-2222
4353 S Cottage Grove Ave  Chicago  (60653)  *(G-5339)*
**Just Your Type Inc** ............................................. 847 864-8890
1800 Dempster St  Evanston  (60202)  *(G-10060)*
**Justrite Manufacturing Co LLC** ............................... 217 234-7486
3921 Dewitt Ave  Mattoon  (61938)  *(G-14396)*
**Justrite Mfg, Mattoon** Also called Justrite Manufacturing Co LLC  *(G-14396)*
**Juvenesse By Elaine Gayle Inc** ............................... 312 944-1211
680 N Lake Shore Dr # 1007  Chicago  (60611)  *(G-5340)*
**Jvc Advanced Media USA Inc** .................................. 630 237-2439
10 N Martingale Rd # 575  Schaumburg  (60173)  *(G-19593)*
**Jvi Inc** ............................................................ 847 675-1560
7131 N Ridgeway Ave  Lincolnwood  (60712)  *(G-13517)*
**Jvk Precision Hard Chrome Inc** ............................... 630 628-0810
29 W Commercial Ave  Addison  (60101)  *(G-161)*
**JW Express** ....................................................... 630 697-1037
440 Lively Blvd  Elk Grove Village  (60007)  *(G-9567)*
**JW Fasteners Inc** ................................................ 815 963-2658
1311 Preston St  Rockford  (61102)  *(G-18450)*
**JW Ossola Co Inc** ................................................ 815 339-6113
And Elm St Rr 71  Granville  (61326)  *(G-11319)*
**JW Sealants Inc** .................................................. 630 398-1010
1478 Beaumont Cir  Bartlett  (60103)  *(G-1358)*
**JW Welding** ....................................................... 618 228-7213
11 S Clement Dr  Aviston  (62216)  *(G-1245)*

## ALPHABETIC SECTION — Kahuna LLC

JWT Farms Inc ................................................... 618 664-3429
 1072 Il Route 143  Pocahontas  (62275)  *(G-17684)*
Jx Nippon Oil & Energy Lubrica ........................ 847 413-2188
 20 N Martingale Rd # 300  Schaumburg  (60173)  *(G-19594)*
K & A Bread LLC ................................................ 708 757-7750
 401 E Joe Orr Rd  Chicago Heights  (60411)  *(G-7107)*
K & A Precision Machine Inc ............................ 847 998-1933
 2500 Ravine Way  Glenview  (60025)  *(G-11155)*
K & B Machining ................................................ 847 663-9534
 6206 Madison Ct  Morton Grove  (60053)  *(G-15208)*
K & D Counter Tops  Inc (PA) ........................... 618 224-9630
 102 N Lincoln St  Trenton  (62293)  *(G-20992)*
K & G Men's Superstore, Orland Park Also called K&G Mens Company Inc  *(G-16871)*
K & H Tool Co ..................................................... 630 766-4588
 164 Devon Ave  Bensenville  (60106)  *(G-1931)*
K & J Phillips Corporation ................................. 630 355-0660
 526 W 5th Ave  Naperville  (60563)  *(G-15682)*
K & J Synthetic Lubricants ................................ 630 628-1011
 405 W Myrick Ave  Addison  (60101)  *(G-162)*
K & K Abrasives & Supplies .............................. 773 582-9500
 5161 S Millard Ave  Chicago  (60632)  *(G-5341)*
K & K Buildings, Ewing Also called K & K Storage Barns  LLC  *(G-10120)*
K & K Iron Works  LLC (PA) .............................. 708 924-0000
 5100 Lawndale Ave Ste 7  Mc Cook  (60525)  *(G-14449)*
K & K Metal Works Inc ...................................... 618 271-4680
 2034 Saint Clair Ave  East Saint Louis  (62205)  *(G-8758)*
K & K Storage Barns  LLC ................................. 618 927-0533
 19867 Ketterman Ln  Ewing  (62836)  *(G-10120)*
K & K Tool & Die Inc .......................................... 309 829-4479
 915 E Oakland Ave  Bloomington  (61701)  *(G-2187)*
K & L Looseleaf Products  Inc .......................... 847 357-9733
 425 Bonnie Ln  Elk Grove Village  (60007)  *(G-9568)*
K & M Printing Company  Inc ............................ 847 884-1100
 1410 N Meacham Rd Frnt  Schaumburg  (60173)  *(G-19595)*
K & N Laboratories Inc ...................................... 708 482-3240
 633 S La Grange Rd  La Grange  (60525)  *(G-12739)*
K & P Industries Inc .......................................... 630 628-6676
 1120 W Republic Dr Ste H  Addison  (60101)  *(G-163)*
K & P Welding .................................................... 217 536-5245
 12374 E 550th Ave  Watson  (62473)  *(G-21433)*
K & S Engineering, Chicago Also called Midwest Model Aircraft Co  *(G-5747)*
K & S Manufacturing Co Inc ............................. 815 232-7519
 24 S Hooker Ave  Freeport  (61032)  *(G-10671)*
K & S Printing Services ..................................... 815 899-2923
 510 N Main St Ste 1  Sycamore  (60178)  *(G-20804)*
K & S Service & Rental Corp (PA) .................... 630 279-4292
 471 W Monroe St  Elmhurst  (60126)  *(G-9893)*
K & W Auto Electric ........................................... 217 857-1717
 103 N Automotive Dr  Teutopolis  (62467)  *(G-20853)*
K 9 Tag Company Inc (PA) ................................ 847 304-8247
 2116 Grand Ave  Waukegan  (60085)  *(G-21575)*
K A & F Group  LLC .......................................... 847 780-4600
 2680 Greenwood Ave  Highland Park  (60035)  *(G-11848)*
K and A Graphics Inc ........................................ 847 244-2345
 4090 Ryan Rd Ste A  Gurnee  (60031)  *(G-11463)*
K B K Truck and Trlr Repr Co ........................... 630 422-7265
 810 N Central Ave  Wood Dale  (60191)  *(G-22383)*
K B Metal Company ........................................... 309 248-7355
 1172 County Road 2100 N  Washburn  (61570)  *(G-21376)*
K B Sales & Service, Geneva Also called O Brien Bill  *(G-10854)*
K B Tool Inc ........................................................ 630 595-4340
 211 Beeline Dr Ste 7  Bensenville  (60106)  *(G-1932)*
K C Audio ........................................................... 708 636-4928
 4824 W 129th St  Alsip  (60803)  *(G-477)*
K C Printing Services Inc .................................. 847 382-8822
 22292 N Pepper Rd Ste A  Lake Barrington  (60010)  *(G-12814)*
K Chae Corp ....................................................... 847 763-0077
 3630 W Pratt Ave  Lincolnwood  (60712)  *(G-13518)*
K D Custom Sawing Logging ........................... 309 231-4805
 6570 Illinois Route 29  Green Valley  (61534)  *(G-11379)*
K D Industries Illinois  Inc ................................. 309 854-7100
 1134 W South St  Kewanee  (61443)  *(G-12691)*
K D Iron Works ................................................... 847 991-3039
 542 W Colfax St Ste 5  Palatine  (60067)  *(G-17047)*
K D L Machining Inc .......................................... 309 477-3036
 1917 S 2nd St  Pekin  (61554)  *(G-17271)*
K D R Productions, Hoffman Estates Also called Ken Young Construction Co  *(G-12021)*
K D Welding Inc ................................................. 815 591-3545
 2 River Bend Dr  Hanover  (61041)  *(G-11572)*
K Fleye Designs ................................................. 773 531-0716
 532 N Long Ave  Chicago  (60644)  *(G-5342)*
K H M Plastics Inc ............................................. 847 249-4910
 4090 Ryan Rd Ste B  Gurnee  (60031)  *(G-11464)*
K H Steuernagel Technical Ltg ......................... 773 327-4520
 4114 N Ravenswood Ave # 1  Chicago  (60613)  *(G-5343)*
K K Gourmet LLC ............................................... 847 727-5858
 9817 N Hunters Ln  Spring Grove  (60081)  *(G-20340)*
K K O Inc ............................................................. 815 569-2324
 100 E Grove St  Capron  (61012)  *(G-2995)*
K M I International Corp ................................... 630 627-6300
 1411 W Jeffrey Dr  Addison  (60101)  *(G-164)*
K M J Enterprises Inc ........................................ 847 688-1200
 2001 Swanson Ct  Gurnee  (60031)  *(G-11465)*
K M K, Trenton Also called Kmk Metal Fabricators  Inc  *(G-20993)*
K O G Mfg & Bindery Corp ................................ 847 263-5050
 1813 W Glen Flora Ave  Waukegan  (60085)  *(G-21576)*
K P Enterprises Inc ........................................... 630 509-2174
 792 County Line Rd Ste A  Bensenville  (60106)  *(G-1933)*
K R J Inc ............................................................. 309 925-5123
 101 S West St  Tremont  (61568)  *(G-20983)*
K R Komarek Inc (PA) ........................................ 847 956-0060
 548 Clayton Ct  Wood Dale  (60191)  *(G-22384)*
K R N Machine & Laser Center, Herrin Also called K R N Machine and Laser Center  *(G-11750)*
K R N Machine and Laser Center ..................... 618 942-6064
 516 N Park Ave  Herrin  (62948)  *(G-11750)*
K R O Enterprises  Ltd ...................................... 309 797-2213
 1806 15th Street Pl  Moline  (61265)  *(G-14949)*
K Systems Corporation ..................................... 708 449-0400
 4931 Butterfield Rd  Hillside  (60162)  *(G-11921)*
K Three Welding Service Inc ............................ 708 563-2911
 814 W 120th St  Chicago  (60643)  *(G-5344)*
K Trox Sales Inc ................................................ 815 568-1521
 6807 Paulson Dr  Marengo  (60152)  *(G-14233)*
K V F Company (PA) .......................................... 847 437-5100
 950 Lively Blvd  Elk Grove Village  (60007)  *(G-9569)*
K V F Company .................................................. 847 437-5019
 1325 Landmeier Rd  Elk Grove Village  (60007)  *(G-9570)*
K&G Mens Company Inc ................................... 708 349-2579
 180 Orland Park Pl  Orland Park  (60462)  *(G-16871)*
K&H Fuel ............................................................. 815 405-4364
 22193 Clove Dr  Frankfort  (60423)  *(G-10338)*
K&I Light Kandi Led Inc .................................... 773 745-1533
 2600 N Cicero Ave  Chicago  (60639)  *(G-5345)*
K&J Finishing  Inc ............................................. 815 965-9655
 716 Cedar St  Rockford  (61102)  *(G-18451)*
K&R Enterprises I  Inc ...................................... 847 502-3371
 28128 Gray Barn Ln  Lake Barrington  (60010)  *(G-12815)*
K&S International  Inc ....................................... 847 229-0202
 901 Deerfield Pkwy  Buffalo Grove  (60089)  *(G-2714)*
K+s Montana Holdings  LLC (HQ) .................... 312 807-2000
 123 N Wacker Dr  Chicago  (60606)  *(G-5346)*
K+s Salt LLC (HQ) ............................................. 844 789-3991
 123 N Wacker Dr Fl 6  Chicago  (60606)  *(G-5347)*
K-B-K Tool and Mfg Inc .................................... 847 674-3636
 7309 Monticello Ave  Skokie  (60076)  *(G-20020)*
K-C Tool Co ........................................................ 630 983-5960
 552 S Washington St  Naperville  (60540)  *(G-15683)*
K-Display Corp ................................................... 773 586-2042
 6150 S Oak Park Ave  Chicago  (60638)  *(G-5348)*
K-G Spray-Pak Inc ............................................. 630 543-7600
 2651 Warrenville Rd # 300  Downers Grove  (60515)  *(G-8469)*
K-Log  Inc .......................................................... 847 872-6611
 1224 27th St Zion  Zion  (60099)  *(G-22690)*
K-Met Industries  Inc ......................................... 708 534-3300
 25911 S Ridgeland Ave  Monee  (60449)  *(G-14998)*
K-Metal Products  Incorporated ....................... 773 476-2700
 2310 W 78th St  Chicago  (60620)  *(G-5349)*
K-Tron Inc .......................................................... 708 460-2128
 9704 Hummingbird Hill Dr  Orland Park  (60467)  *(G-16872)*
K1 Speed Buffalo Grove, Buffalo Grove Also called K1 Speed-Illinois  Inc  *(G-2715)*
K1 Speed-Illinois  Inc ........................................ 847 941-9400
 301 Hastings Dr  Buffalo Grove  (60089)  *(G-2715)*
K2 Tables, Crystal Lake Also called 20 20 Medical Systems  Inc  *(G-7524)*
Kaas Industries Inc ........................................... 847 298-9106
 7035 Barry St  Rosemont  (60018)  *(G-19008)*
Kabert Industries Inc (PA) ................................. 630 833-2115
 321 W Saint Charles Rd  Villa Park  (60181)  *(G-21262)*
Kabinet Kraft ...................................................... 618 395-1047
 536 E Cherry St  Olney  (62450)  *(G-16775)*
Kackert Enterprises Inc .................................... 630 898-9339
 824 2nd Ave  Aurora  (60505)  *(G-1179)*
Kaco Signs, Centralia Also called Michael Reggis Clark  *(G-3422)*
Kadon Precision Machining Inc ....................... 815 874-5850
 3744 Publishers Dr  Rockford  (61109)  *(G-18452)*
Kae Dj Publishing .............................................. 773 233-2609
 12003 S Pulaski Rd # 202  Chicago  (60803)  *(G-5350)*
Kaelco Entrmt Holdings Inc ............................. 217 600-7815
 3 Henson Pl Ste 1  Champaign  (61820)  *(G-3505)*
Kaeppler Machining, Elk Grove Village Also called Ulrich Kaeppler  *(G-9795)*
Kafka Manufacturing Inc .................................. 708 771-0970
 7600 Industrial Dr  Forest Park  (60130)  *(G-10250)*
Kafko International  Ltd ................................... 847 763-0333
 3555 Howard St  Skokie  (60076)  *(G-20021)*
Kagan Industries, Chicago Also called Creative Metal Products  *(G-4500)*
Kahuna Atm, Bloomington Also called Kahuna LLC  *(G-2188)*
Kahuna LLC ........................................................ 888 357-8472
 807 Arcadia Dr Ste B  Bloomington  (61704)  *(G-2188)*

(PA)=Parent Co  (HQ)=Headquarters  (DH)=Div Headquarters

**Kai Lee Couture Inc** 773 426-1668
5612 S King Dr Chicago (60637) *(G-5351)*
**Kaiser Manufacturing Co** 773 235-4705
1440 N Pulaski Rd Chicago (60651) *(G-5352)*
**Kalamazoo Outdoor Gourmet LLC (HQ)** 312 423-8770
810 W Washington Blvd Chicago (60607) *(G-5353)*
**Kalena LLC** 773 598-0033
1937 N Mohawk St Chicago (60614) *(G-5354)*
**Kalle USA Inc** 847 775-0781
5750 Centerpoint Ct Ste B Gurnee (60031) *(G-11466)*
**Kaltband North America Inc** 773 248-6684
3750 N Lake Shore Dr 16a Chicago (60613) *(G-5355)*
**Kam Group Inc** 630 679-9668
486 W North Frontage Rd Bolingbrook (60440) *(G-2330)*
**Kam Tool and Mold** 815 338-8360
1300 Cobblestone Way Woodstock (60098) *(G-22576)*
**Kama Enterprises Inc** 773 551-9642
4925 N Newcastle Ave Chicago (60656) *(G-5356)*
**Kaman Automation Inc** 847 273-9050
1261 Wiley Rd Ste A Schaumburg (60173) *(G-19596)*
**Kaman Industrial Tech Corp** 317 248-8355
827 N Central Ave Wood Dale (60191) *(G-22385)*
**Kaman Tool Corporation** 708 652-9023
3147 S Austin Blvd Cicero (60804) *(G-7208)*
**Kamco Representatives Inc** 630 516-0417
504 W Wrightwood Ave Elmhurst (60126) *(G-9894)*
**Kamflex Conveyor Corporation** 630 682-1555
2312 Oak Leaf St Joliet (60436) *(G-12526)*
**Kamflex, LLC, Joliet** *Also called Engineered Plumbing Spc LLC (G-12491)*
**Kamstra Door Service Inc** 708 895-9990
2007 Thornton Lansing Rd Lansing (60438) *(G-13167)*
**Kan-Du Manufacturing Co Inc** 708 681-0370
1776 Clendenin Ln Riverwoods (60015) *(G-18040)*
**Kana Software Inc** 312 447-5600
30 S Wacker Dr Ste 1300 Chicago (60606) *(G-5357)*
**Kanaflex Corporation Illinois (HQ)** 847 634-6100
800 Woodlands Pkwy Vernon Hills (60061) *(G-21177)*
**Kanan Fashions Inc (PA)** 630 240-1234
1010 Jorie Blvd Ste 324 Oak Brook (60523) *(G-16530)*
**Kanbo International (us) Inc** 630 873-6320
2 Mid America Plz Ste 800 Oakbrook Terrace (60181) *(G-16713)*
**Kane County Chronicle, Crystal Lake** *Also called Shaw Suburban Media Group Inc (G-7649)*
**Kane County Cronicle** 815 895-7033
513 W State St Sycamore (60178) *(G-20805)*
**Kane Graphical Corporation** 773 384-1200
2255 W Logan Blvd Chicago (60647) *(G-5358)*
**Kanebridge Corporation**
1125 Gateway Dr Elgin (60124) *(G-9087)*
**Kaneland Publications Inc** 630 365-6446
333 N Randall Rd Ste 111 Saint Charles (60174) *(G-19203)*
**Kanetic Inc** 847 382-9922
22102 N Pepper Rd Ste 107 Lake Barrington (60010) *(G-12816)*
**Kaney Group LLC (PA)** 815 986-4359
1321 Capital Dr Rockford (61109) *(G-18453)*
**Kankakee Alignment, Kankakee** *Also called Kankakee Spring and Alignment (G-12633)*
**Kankakee Daily Journal Co LLC (HQ)** 815 937-3300
8 Dearborn Sq Kankakee (60901) *(G-12632)*
**Kankakee Industrial Tech** 815 933-6683
359 S Kinzie Ave Bradley (60915) *(G-2425)*
**Kankakee Industrial Technology, Decatur** *Also called Decatur Industrial Elc Inc (G-7872)*
**Kankakee Spring and Alignment** 815 932-6718
88 W Issert Dr Kankakee (60901) *(G-12633)*
**Kankakee Tent & Awning Co** 815 932-8000
679b W 2000s Rd Kankakee (60901) *(G-12634)*
**Kanneberg Custom Kitchens Inc** 815 654-1110
1242 Shappert Dr Machesney Park (61115) *(G-14084)*
**Kap Holdings LLC** 708 948-0226
137 N Oak Park Ave # 214 Oak Park (60301) *(G-16671)*
**Kapak Company LLC** 952 541-0730
825 Turnberry Ct Hanover Park (60133) *(G-11584)*
**Kaplan Inc** 312 263-4344
205 W Randolph St Chicago (60606) *(G-5359)*
**Kaplan Educational Center, Chicago** *Also called Kaplan Inc (G-5359)*
**Kapp Company LLC** 618 676-1000
3600 E White Ln Olney (62450) *(G-16776)*
**Kapstone Kraft Paper Corp (HQ)** 252 533-6000
1101 Skokie Blvd Ste 300 Northbrook (60062) *(G-16284)*
**Kapstone Paper and Packg Corp (PA)** 847 239-8800
1101 Skokie Blvd Ste 300 Northbrook (60062) *(G-16285)*
**Kara Graphics Inc** 630 964-8122
6823 Hobson Valley Dr # 201 Woodridge (60517) *(G-22500)*
**Karen Young** 312 202-0142
10 W Elm St Apt 900 Chicago (60610) *(G-5360)*
**Karens Krafts** 217 466-8100
8057 Il Hwy 16 Paris (61944) *(G-17151)*
**Karimi Saifuddin** 630 379-9344
14017 S Lakeridge Dr Plainfield (60544) *(G-17614)*
**Karl Lambrecht Corp** 773 472-5442
4204 N Lincoln Ave Chicago (60618) *(G-5361)*
**Karlin Foods Corp** 847 441-8330
1845 Oak St Ste 19 Northfield (60093) *(G-16404)*
**Karly Iron Works Inc** 815 477-3430
4014 Northwest Hwy Ste 4c Crystal Lake (60014) *(G-7597)*
**Karma Yacht Sales LLC (PA)** 773 254-0200
3231 S Halsted St Apt 3s Chicago (60608) *(G-5362)*
**Karnak Midwest LLC** 708 338-3388
2601 Gardner Rd Broadview (60155) *(G-2590)*
**Kaser Power Equipment Inc** 309 289-2176
480 Henderson Rd Knoxville (61448) *(G-12721)*
**Kasha Industries Inc** 618 375-2511
1 Plastic Ln Grayville (62844) *(G-11372)*
**Kasha Industries Inc** 618 375-2511
1 Plastics Ln Grayville (62844) *(G-11373)*
**Kasias Deli Inc (PA)** 312 666-2900
440 N Oakley Blvd Chicago (60612) *(G-5363)*
**Kaskaskia Mechanical Insul Co** 618 768-4526
6606 State Route 15 Mascoutah (62258) *(G-14355)*
**Kaskaskia Tool and Machine Inc** 618 475-3301
107 S Benton St New Athens (62264) *(G-15860)*
**Kaskey Kids Inc** 847 441-3092
1485 Scott Ave Winnetka (60093) *(G-22308)*
**Kasper, Aurora** *Also called Nine West Holdings Inc (G-1057)*
**Kastalon Inc** 708 389-2210
4100 W 124th Pl Alsip (60803) *(G-478)*
**Kastalon Polyurethane Products, Alsip** *Also called Kastalon Inc (G-478)*
**Kastelic Canvas Inc** 815 436-8160
15940 S Lincoln Hwy Plainfield (60586) *(G-17615)*
**Kastle Therapeutics LLC** 312 883-5695
181 W Madison St Ste 3745 Chicago (60602) *(G-5364)*
**Katco Enterprises LLC** 217 429-5855
2243 Highland Rd Decatur (62521) *(G-7901)*
**Kathy's Kitchen, Virginia** *Also called Daryl Keylor (G-21306)*
**Kats Meow** 815 747-2113
288 Sinsinawa Ave East Dubuque (61025) *(G-8618)*
**Katy's Goodness, Oak Park** *Also called Katys LLC (G-16672)*
**Katys LLC (PA)** 708 522-9814
1040 S Maple Ave Oak Park (60304) *(G-16672)*
**Kauffman Poultry Farms Inc** 815 264-3470
8519 Leland Rd Waterman (60556) *(G-21407)*
**Kaufman Woodworking** 217 543-3607
29 E Cr 100 N Arthur (61911) *(G-906)*
**Kaufman-Worthen Machinery Inc** 847 360-9170
2326 W Wadsworth Rd Waukegan (60087) *(G-21577)*
**Kaufmans Custom Cabinets** 217 268-4330
363 E County Road 200n Arcola (61910) *(G-673)*
**Kautzmann Machine Works Inc** 847 455-9105
9105 Belden Ave Franklin Park (60131) *(G-10511)*
**Kavalierglass North Amer Inc** 847 364-7303
1301 Brummel Ave Elk Grove Village (60007) *(G-9571)*
**Kavanaugh Electric Inc** 708 503-1310
9511 Corsair Rd Ste B Frankfort (60423) *(G-10339)*
**Kawneer Company Inc** 815 224-2708
2528 7th St Peru (61354) *(G-17515)*
**Kay & Cee** 773 425-9169
1204 W 127th St Calumet Park (60827) *(G-2962)*
**Kay Home Products, Antioch** *Also called Akerue Industries LLC (G-615)*
**Kay Manufacturing Company** 708 862-6800
602 State St Calumet City (60409) *(G-2945)*
**Kayacht, Tinley Park** *Also called P W C Sports (G-20936)*
**Kaybee Engineering Company Inc** 630 968-7100
100 E Quincy St Westmont (60559) *(G-21896)*
**Kaybee Engnrng, Westmont** *Also called Kaybee Engineering Company Inc (G-21896)*
**Kaydon Acquisition Xii Inc** 217 443-3592
130 N Jackson St Danville (61832) *(G-7740)*
**Kaye Lee & Company Inc** 312 236-9686
5 S Wabash Ave Ste 200 Chicago (60603) *(G-5365)*
**Kaylen Industries Inc** 847 671-6767
9505 Winona Ave Schiller Park (60176) *(G-19842)*
**Kayser Lure Corp** 217 964-2110
107 Junction St Ursa (62376) *(G-21105)*
**Kazmier Tooling Inc** 773 586-0300
6001 S Oak Park Ave Chicago (60638) *(G-5366)*
**KB Publishing Inc (PA)** 708 331-6352
924 E 162nd St South Holland (60473) *(G-20282)*
**KB Publishing Inc** 708 331-6352
930 E 162nd St South Holland (60473) *(G-20283)*
**Kccdd Inc** 309 344-2030
1200 Monmouth Blvd Galesburg (61401) *(G-10762)*
**Kci Chemical, Matteson** *Also called Konzen Chemicals Inc (G-14375)*
**Kci Satellite** 800 664-2602
101 N Industrial Park Dr Pittsfield (62363) *(G-17571)*
**Kcp Metal Fabrications Inc** 773 775-0318
5475 N Northwest Hwy Chicago (60630) *(G-5367)*
**Kcura LLC (PA)** 312 263-1177
231 S Lasalle St Fl 8 Chicago (60604) *(G-5368)*
**Kd Steel Inc** 630 201-1619
4243 Chicago Ave Westmont (60559) *(G-21897)*

# ALPHABETIC SECTION — Kerrigan Corporation Inc

**Kdk Upset Forging Co** ............................................... 708 388-8770
2645 139th St Blue Island (60406) *(G-2259)*

**Kdm Enterprises LLC** .............................................. 877 591-9768
820 Commerce Pkwy Carpentersville (60110) *(G-3290)*

**Keane Gillette Publishing LLC** ............................... 630 279-7521
110 E Schiller St Ste 206 Elmhurst (60126) *(G-9895)*

**Keating of Chicago Inc** ........................................... 815 569-2324
100 E Grove St Capron (61012) *(G-2996)*

**Keats Manufacturing Co** ........................................ 847 520-1133
350 Holbrook Dr Wheeling (60090) *(G-22083)*

**Keckley Manufacturing Company** ......................... 847 674-8422
3400 Cleveland St Skokie (60076) *(G-20022)*

**Keebler Company** .................................................. 630 820-9457
2707 N Eola Rd Ste A Aurora (60502) *(G-1039)*

**Keebler Foods Company (HQ)** .............................. 630 833-2900
677 N Larch Ave Elmhurst (60126) *(G-9896)*

**Keene Technology Inc** ........................................... 815 624-8988
698 Quality Ln South Beloit (61080) *(G-20154)*

**Keene Technology Inc (PA)** ................................... 815 624-8989
14357 Commercial Pkwy South Beloit (61080) *(G-20155)*

**Keenpac LLC (HQ)** ................................................ 845 291-8680
8338 Austin Ave Morton Grove (60053) *(G-15209)*

**Keeper Corp** ........................................................... 630 773-9393
1345 Industrial Dr Itasca (60143) *(G-12292)*

**Keeper Thermal Bag Co Inc** .................................. 630 213-0125
1006 Poplar Ln Bartlett (60103) *(G-1359)*

**Keepes Funeral Home Inc** ..................................... 618 262-5200
1500 N Cherry St Mount Carmel (62863) *(G-15271)*

**Keflex, Woodstock** Also called Flex-Weld Inc *(G-22567)*

**Kegley Machine Co** ................................................ 309 346-8914
615 Main St Pekin (61554) *(G-17272)*

**Keil-Forness Comfort Systems** ............................. 618 233-3039
301 N Illinois St Belleville (62220) *(G-1640)*

**Kelch, Bob Floors, Peoria** Also called T J P Investments Inc *(G-17465)*

**Kelco Industries Inc (PA)** ...................................... 815 334-3600
1425 Lake Ave Woodstock (60098) *(G-22577)*

**Keleen Leathers Inc** ............................................... 630 590-5300
1010 Executive Dr Ste 400 Westmont (60559) *(G-21898)*

**Keller Grain & Livestock Inc** .................................. 618 455-3634
7031 N 1900th St Willow Hill (62480) *(G-22192)*

**Keller Group Inc (PA)** ............................................ 847 446-7550
1 Northfield Plz Ste 510 Northfield (60093) *(G-16405)*

**Keller Orthotics Inc (PA)** ........................................ 773 929-4700
2451 N Lincoln Ave Chicago (60614) *(G-5369)*

**Keller United Elc & Mch Co** .................................. 217 382-4521
12 S York St Martinsville (62442) *(G-14337)*

**Kellermann Manufacturing Co, Wauconda** Also called Kellermann Manufacturing Inc *(G-21476)*

**Kellermann Manufacturing Inc** ............................. 847 526-7266
1000 N Rand Rd Ste 224 Wauconda (60084) *(G-21476)*

**Kelley Construction Inc** ........................................ 217 422-1800
2454 N 27th St Decatur (62526) *(G-7902)*

**Kelley Crematory, Champaign** Also called Kelley Vault Co Inc *(G-3506)*

**Kelley Iron Works, East Peoria** Also called Kelley Ornamental Iron LLC *(G-8721)*

**Kelley Ornamental Iron LLC (PA)** ......................... 309 697-9870
4303 N Main St East Peoria (61611) *(G-8721)*

**Kelley Ornamental Iron LLC** ................................. 309 820-7540
1206 Towanda Ave Ste 1 Bloomington (61701) *(G-2189)*

**Kelley Vault Co Inc** ................................................ 217 355-5551
1901 W Springer Dr Champaign (61821) *(G-3506)*

**Kellogg Company** .................................................. 773 254-0900
2945 W 31st St Chicago (60623) *(G-5370)*

**Kellogg Company** .................................................. 630 941-0300
545 W Lamont Rd Elmhurst (60126) *(G-9897)*

**Kellogg Company** .................................................. 217 258-3251
3801 Dewitt Ave Mattoon (61938) *(G-14397)*

**Kellogg Company** .................................................. 630 820-9457
700 Commerce Dr Ste 400 Oak Brook (60523) *(G-16531)*

**Kellogg Company** .................................................. 773 995-7200
750 E 110th St Chicago (60628) *(G-5371)*

**Kellogg Printing Co** ............................................... 309 734-8388
95 Public Sq Monmouth (61462) *(G-15016)*

**Kellogg's, Elmhurst** Also called Kellogg Company *(G-9897)*

**Kelly & Son Forestry & Log LLC** ........................... 815 275-6877
1783 Ashford Ln Crystal Lake (60014) *(G-7598)*

**Kelly Corned Beef Co Chicago** ............................. 773 588-2882
3531 N Elston Ave Chicago (60618) *(G-5372)*

**Kelly Eisenberg, Chicago** Also called Kelly Corned Beef Co Chicago *(G-5372)*

**Kelly Flour Company** ............................................. 312 933-3104
260 E Chestnut St # 4406 Chicago (60611) *(G-5373)*

**Kelly Printing Co Inc** ............................................. 217 443-1792
205 Oregon Ave Danville (61832) *(G-7741)*

**Kelly Systems Inc (PA)** ......................................... 312 733-3224
422 N Western Ave Chicago (60612) *(G-5374)*

**Kellyjo Makes Scents** ............................................ 618 281-4241
3050 Steppig Rd Columbia (62236) *(G-7359)*

**Kellys Sign Shop** ................................................... 217 477-0167
1004 N Vermilion St Danville (61832) *(G-7742)*

**Kelmscott Communications, Berkeley** Also called Voris Communication Co Inc *(G-2051)*

**Kelvyn Press Inc (HQ)** ........................................... 708 343-0448
2910 S 18th Ave Broadview (60155) *(G-2591)*

**Kelvyn Press Inc** .................................................... 630 585-8160
880 Enterprise St Ste F Aurora (60504) *(G-1040)*

**Kemell Enterprises LLC** ........................................ 618 671-1513
612 Ganim Dr Belleville (62221) *(G-1641)*

**Kemis Kollections** ................................................. 773 431-2037
6007 S Wood St Apt 2 Chicago (60636) *(G-5375)*

**Kemlite Sequentia Products, Channahon** Also called Crane Composites Inc *(G-3567)*

**Kemp Manufacturing Company (PA)** ................... 309 682-7292
4310 N Voss St Peoria (61616) *(G-17395)*

**Kempco Window Treatments Inc** ......................... 708 754-4484
74 E 23rd St Chicago Heights (60411) *(G-7108)*

**Kemper Industries** ................................................ 217 826-5712
1017 Clarksville Rd Marshall (62441) *(G-14324)*

**Kempner Company Inc** ......................................... 312 733-1606
629 W Cermak Rd Ste 201 Chicago (60616) *(G-5376)*

**Ken Don LLC** .......................................................... 708 596-4910
2222 W 162nd St Markham (60428) *(G-14303)*

**Ken Elliott Co Inc** .................................................. 618 466-8200
3704 Riehl Ln Godfrey (62035) *(G-11226)*

**Ken Matthews & Associates Inc** ........................... 630 628-6470
415 W Belden Ave Ste H Addison (60101) *(G-165)*

**Ken Young Construction Co** ................................. 847 358-3026
1185 Ash Rd Hoffman Estates (60169) *(G-12021)*

**Kencor Stairs & Woodworking** ............................. 630 279-8980
311 W Stone Rd Villa Park (60181) *(G-21263)*

**Kendall County Concrete Inc** ............................... 630 851-9197
695 Route 34 Aurora (60503) *(G-1041)*

**Kendall County Record (PA)** ................................ 630 553-7034
109 W Veterans Pkwy Yorkville (60560) *(G-22662)*

**Kendall Printing Co** .............................................. 630 553-9200
948 N Bridge St Yorkville (60560) *(G-22663)*

**Kendel Witte Die & Mold, Freeport** Also called Witte Kendel Die & Mold *(G-10699)*

**Keneal Graphic Solutions, Romeoville** Also called Keneal Industries Inc *(G-18834)*

**Keneal Industries Inc** ............................................ 815 886-1300
679 Parkwood Ave Romeoville (60446) *(G-18834)*

**Kenent Screw Machine Products** ......................... 815 624-7216
4843 Yale Bridge Rd Rockton (61072) *(G-18697)*

**Kenilworth Press Incorporated** ............................ 847 256-5210
1223 Green Bay Rd Wilmette (60091) *(G-22256)*

**Kenmode Tool and Engrg Inc** ............................... 847 658-5041
820 W Algonquin Rd Algonquin (60102) *(G-396)*

**Kennametal Inc** ..................................................... 309 578-1888
Olglena Rd Mossville (61552) *(G-15253)*

**Kennametal Inc** ..................................................... 630 963-2910
2150 Western Ct Ste 300 Lisle (60532) *(G-13613)*

**Kennametal Inc** ..................................................... 815 226-0650
21 Airport Dr Rockford (61109) *(G-18454)*

**Kennamtal Tricon Mtls Svcs Inc** ........................... 708 235-0563
2605 Federal Signal Dr University Park (60484) *(G-21053)*

**Kennedy's Creative Awards, Waukegan** Also called K 9 Tag Company Inc *(G-21575)*

**Kenneth W Templeman** ........................................ 847 912-2740
382 Minuet Cir Volo (60073) *(G-21315)*

**Kens Quick Print Inc** ............................................. 847 831-4410
1500 Old Deerfield Rd # 5 Highland Park (60035) *(G-11849)*

**Kens Street Rod Repair** ........................................ 815 874-1811
5521 International Dr Rockford (61109) *(G-18455)*

**Kensen Tool & Die Inc** .......................................... 847 455-0150
9200 Parklane Ave Franklin Park (60131) *(G-10512)*

**Kent H Landsberg Co, Sycamore** Also called Sycamore Containers Inc *(G-20818)*

**Kent Nutrition Group Inc** ..................................... 815 874-2411
1612 S Bend Rd Rockford (61109) *(G-18456)*

**Kent Nutrition Group Inc** ..................................... 217 323-1216
8679 Kent Feed Rd Beardstown (62618) *(G-1523)*

**Kent Precision Foods Group Inc** .......................... 630 226-0071
1000 Dalton Ln Ste A Bolingbrook (60490) *(G-2331)*

**Kent Precision Foods Group Inc** .......................... 630 226-0498
1000 Dalton Ln Ste A Bolingbrook (60490) *(G-2332)*

**Kenwood Electrical Systems, Machesney Park** Also called Unlimited Svcs Wisconsin Inc *(G-14117)*

**Keonix Corporation** .............................................. 847 259-9430
922 N Chicago Ave Arlington Heights (60004) *(G-788)*

**Kep Woodworking** ................................................ 847 480-9545
3240 Techny Rd Northbrook (60062) *(G-16286)*

**Kepner Products Company** .................................. 630 279-1550
995 N Ellsworth Ave Villa Park (60181) *(G-21264)*

**Kerala Express Newspaper** .................................. 773 465-5359
2050 W Devon Ave Apt 1w Chicago (60659) *(G-5377)*

**Kerins Industries Inc** ............................................. 630 515-9111
8408 Wilmette Ave Ste A Darien (60561) *(G-7798)*

**Kern Precision** ...................................................... 331 979-0954
1010 W Fullerton Ave E Addison (60101) *(G-166)*

**Kernel Kutter Inc** .................................................. 815 877-1515
10509 Tartan Ct Machesney Park (61115) *(G-14085)*

**Kerogen Resources Inc** ........................................ 618 382-3114
645 Il Highway 14 Carmi (62821) *(G-3071)*

**Kerrigan Corporation Inc** ..................................... 847 251-8994
811 Ridge Rd Wilmette (60091) *(G-22257)*

**Kerry Holding Co** ....309 747-3534
320 W Gridley Rd Gridley (61744) *(G-11408)*
**Kerry Inc** ....847 595-1003
1301 Mark St Elk Grove Village (60007) *(G-9572)*
**Kerry Inc** ....309 747-3534
320 W Gridley Rd Gridley (61744) *(G-11409)*
**Kerry Inc** ....708 450-3260
3141 W North Ave Melrose Park (60160) *(G-14666)*
**Kerry Ingredients, Melrose Park** *Also called Kerry Inc (G-14666)*
**Kerry Ingredients & Flavours** ....847 595-1003
1301 Mark St Elk Grove Village (60007) *(G-9573)*
**Kerry Ingredients and Flavours, Elk Grove Village** *Also called Kerry Inc (G-9572)*
**Kesher Stam** ....773 973-7826
2817 W Touhy Ave Chicago (60645) *(G-5378)*
**Keson Industries Inc** ....630 820-4200
810 N Commerce St Aurora (60504) *(G-1042)*
**Kessmann General Construction, Highland** *Also called Kessmanns Cabinet Shop & Cnstr (G-11800)*
**Kessmanns Cabinet Shop & Cnstr** ....618 654-2538
2679 Vulliet Rd Highland (62249) *(G-11800)*
**Kester Inc** ....630 616-6882
940 W Thorndale Ave Itasca (60143) *(G-12293)*
**Kester Inc (HQ)** ....630 616-4000
800 W Thorndale Ave Itasca (60143) *(G-12294)*
**Kestler Digital Printing Inc** ....773 581-5918
2845 W 48th Pl Chicago (60632) *(G-5379)*
**Kettler Casting Co Inc** ....618 234-5303
2640 Old Freeburg Rd Belleville (62220) *(G-1642)*
**Kevin Kewney** ....217 228-7444
410 S 10th St Quincy (62301) *(G-17844)*
**Kevron Printing & Design Inc** ....708 229-7725
9831 S 78th Ave Ste F Hickory Hills (60457) *(G-11772)*
**Kevs Kans Inc** ....309 303-3999
1501 W Front St Roanoke (61561) *(G-18051)*
**Kewanee Star Courier, Kewanee** *Also called Gatehouse Media LLC (G-12686)*
**Kewanee Triangle Concrete, Kewanee** *Also called Triangle Concrete Co Inc (G-12695)*
**Kewaunee Scientific Corp** ....847 675-7744
3150 Skokie Valley Rd # 8 Highland Park (60035) *(G-11850)*
**Key Car Stereo** ....217 446-4556
12078 Us Route 150 Oakwood (61858) *(G-16726)*
**Key Colony Inc** ....630 783-8572
16300 103rd St Lemont (60439) *(G-13237)*
**Key Magazine, Chicago** *Also called This Week In Chicago Inc (G-6716)*
**Key One Graphics Services Inc** ....
89 W Main St Ste 102 West Dundee (60118) *(G-21799)*
**Key Outdoor Inc** ....815 224-4742
2968 Saint Vincent Ave La Salle (61301) *(G-12780)*
**Key Printing** ....815 933-1800
111 E Court St Kankakee (60901) *(G-12635)*
**Key Source, Peoria** *Also called Need To Know Inc (G-17415)*
**Key West Metal Industries Inc** ....708 371-1470
13831 Kostner Ave Crestwood (60445) *(G-7491)*
**Keyesport Manufacturing Inc** ....618 749-5510
1610 Mulberry St Keyesport (62253) *(G-12696)*
**Keyrock Energy LLC** ....618 982-9710
20227 Thorn Rd Thompsonville (62890) *(G-20862)*
**Keys Manufacturing Company Inc** ....217 465-4001
13338 N 1900th St Paris (61944) *(G-17152)*
**Keystone Aniline, Chicago** *Also called Milliken & Company (G-5764)*
**Keystone Bakery Holdings LLC (HQ)** ....603 792-3113
520 Lake Cook Rd Deerfield (60015) *(G-8024)*
**Keystone Consolidated Inds Inc** ....309 697-7020
7000 S Adams St Peoria (61641) *(G-17396)*
**Keystone Consolidated Inds Inc** ....708 753-1200
317 E 11th St Chicago Heights (60411) *(G-7109)*
**Keystone Display Inc** ....815 648-2456
11916 Maple Ave Hebron (60034) *(G-11721)*
**Keystone Printing & Publishing** ....815 678-2591
5512 May Ave Richmond (60071) *(G-17965)*
**Keystone Printing Service, Richmond** *Also called Keystone Printing & Publishing (G-17965)*
**Keystone Printing Services** ....773 622-7210
2451 N Harlem Ave Chicago (60707) *(G-5380)*
**Keystone-Calumet Inc** ....708 753-1200
317 E 11th St Chicago Heights (60411) *(G-7110)*
**Keystroke Graphics, Oswego** *Also called Silent W Communications Inc (G-16934)*
**Kfi, Rolling Meadows** *Also called Komatsu Forklift USA LLC (G-18738)*
**Khaki Army, Glen Ellyn** *Also called Naked Army USA LLC (G-10982)*
**Khc Corporation** ....815 337-7630
333 E Judd St Woodstock (60098) *(G-22578)*
**Khm, Gurnee** *Also called K H M Plastics Inc (G-11464)*
**Ki, Chicago** *Also called Krueger International Inc (G-5413)*
**Ki Industries Inc** ....708 449-1990
5540 Mcdermott Dr Berkeley (60163) *(G-2046)*
**Kickapoo Creek Winery** ....309 495-9463
6605 N Smith Rd Edwards (61528) *(G-8782)*
**Kidde Fire Triner Holdings LLC (PA)** ....312 219-7900
155 N Wacker Dr Ste 4150 Chicago (60606) *(G-5381)*
**Kidsbooks LLC (PA)** ....773 509-0707
3535 W Peterson Ave Chicago (60659) *(G-5382)*
**Kieffer Holding Co (PA)** ....877 543-3337
585 Bond St Lincolnshire (60069) *(G-13458)*
**Kieft Bros Inc** ....630 832-8090
837 S Riverside Dr Elmhurst (60126) *(G-9898)*
**Kiel Machine Products** ....
877 Arthur Dr Elgin (60120) *(G-9088)*
**Kiene Diesel Accessories Inc** ....630 543-7170
325 S Fairbank St Addison (60101) *(G-167)*
**Kienstra Pipe & Precast LLC** ....618 482-3283
1072 Eagle Park Rd Madison (62060) *(G-14151)*
**Kier Mfg Co** ....630 953-9500
1450 W Jeffrey Dr Addison (60101) *(G-168)*
**Kik Custom Products Inc (HQ)** ....217 442-1400
1 W Hegeler Ln Danville (61832) *(G-7743)*
**Kik Danville, Danville** *Also called Kik Custom Products Inc (G-7743)*
**Kik International Inc** ....905 660-0444
780 W Army Trail Rd 209 Carol Stream (60188) *(G-3178)*
**Kile Machine & Tool Inc** ....217 446-8616
3231 Illini Rd Danville (61834) *(G-7744)*
**Kilgus Farmstead Inc** ....815 692-6080
21471 E 670 North Rd Fairbury (61739) *(G-10129)*
**Killeen Confectionery LLC (PA)** ....312 804-0009
600 20th St Wilmette (60091) *(G-22258)*
**Kilt of Schaumburg** ....847 413-2000
1140 E Higgins Rd Schaumburg (60173) *(G-19597)*
**Kim & Sctts Grmet Pretzels Inc** ....800 578-9478
2107 W Carroll Ave Chicago (60612) *(G-5383)*
**Kim Gilmore** ....847 931-1511
2250 Point Blvd Ste 321 Elgin (60123) *(G-9089)*
**Kim Gough** ....309 734-3511
1201 N Main St Ste 2 Monmouth (61462) *(G-15017)*
**Kim Laboratories Inc** ....217 337-6666
601 S Century Blvd # 1203 Rantoul (61866) *(G-17932)*
**Kim Tiffani Institute LLC** ....312 260-9000
3926 W Touhy Ave 310 Lincolnwood (60712) *(G-13519)*
**Kimball Office Inc** ....800 349-9827
325 N Wells St Ste 100 Chicago (60654) *(G-5384)*
**Kimberly-Clark Corporation** ....312 371-5166
2275 Half Day Rd Ste 350 Deerfield (60015) *(G-8025)*
**Kimberly-Clark Corporation** ....815 886-7872
740 Pro Logis Pkwy Romeoville (60446) *(G-18835)*
**Kimberly-Clark Corporation** ....708 409-8500
505 Northwest Ave Ste C Northlake (60164) *(G-16441)*
**Kimco U S A, Marshall** *Also called Kimco USA Inc (G-14325)*
**Kimco USA Inc** ....800 788-1133
118 E Trefz Dr Marshall (62441) *(G-14325)*
**Kimmaterials Inc** ....618 466-0352
9434 Godfrey Rd Godfrey (62035) *(G-11227)*
**Kimmy Compost Inc** ....847 372-9201
807 Oakton St Evanston (60202) *(G-10061)*
**Kims Menswear Ltd** ....773 373-2237
326 E 47th St Chicago (60653) *(G-5385)*
**Kinast Inc** ....217 852-3525
549 Oak St Dallas City (62330) *(G-7698)*
**Kindlon Enterprises Inc (PA)** ....708 367-4000
2300 Raddant Rd Ste B Aurora (60502) *(G-1043)*
**Kinea Touch, Chicago** *Also called Tanvas Inc (G-6674)*
**Kinetic BEI LLC** ....847 888-8060
2197 Brookwood Dr South Elgin (60177) *(G-20210)*
**Kinetic Fit Works Inc** ....630 340-5168
34 Lake Ridge Rd Galena (61036) *(G-10728)*
**Kinetic Orthotic Inc** ....708 246-9266
3958 Rose Ave Western Springs (60558) *(G-21869)*
**King & Sons Monuments** ....815 786-6321
131 E Center St Ste 1 Sandwich (60548) *(G-19371)*
**King Circuit** ....630 629-7300
1651 Mitchell Blvd Schaumburg (60193) *(G-19598)*
**King Metal Co** ....708 388-3845
4200 W 122nd St Alsip (60803) *(G-479)*
**King Midas Seafood Entps Inc** ....847 566-2192
309 N Lake St Ste 200 Mundelein (60060) *(G-15516)*
**King of Software Inc** ....847 354-8745
1232 Willow Ave Des Plaines (60016) *(G-8218)*
**King S Court Exterior** ....630 904-4305
2328 Skylane Dr Naperville (60564) *(G-15812)*
**King Systems Inc (PA)** ....309 879-2668
1130 Lakeview Rd S Dahinda (61428) *(G-7688)*
**King Tool and Die Inc** ....630 787-0799
210 Gateway Rd Bensenville (60106) *(G-1934)*
**King's Food Products, Belleville** *Also called Deli Star Ventures Inc (G-1624)*
**Kingery Printing Company (PA)** ....217 347-5151
3012 S Banker St Effingham (62401) *(G-8842)*
**Kingery Steel Fabricators Inc** ....708 474-6665
16895 Chicago Ave Lansing (60438) *(G-13168)*
**Kingport Industries LLC** ....847 480-5745
1912 Shermer Rd Northbrook (60062) *(G-16287)*
**Kingsbury Enterprises Inc** ....708 535-7590
15007 Moorings Ln Oak Forest (60452) *(G-16586)*

**Kinney Electrical Mfg Co** 847 742-9600
678 Buckeye St Elgin (60123) *(G-9090)*
**Kinoco Inc** 618 378-3802
230 County Road 500 E Norris City (62869) *(G-16115)*
**Kinser Woodworks** 618 549-4540
120 Old Lower Cobden Rd Makanda (62958) *(G-14163)*
**Kinsman Enterprises Inc** 618 932-3838
10804 Mark Twain Rd West Frankfort (62896) *(G-21810)*
**Kipp Manufacturing Company Inc** 630 768-9051
375 Hollow Hill Rd Wauconda (60084) *(G-21477)*
**Kirby Lester LLC (HQ)** 847 984-3377
13700 W Irma Lee Ct Lake Forest (60045) *(G-12920)*
**Kirby Sheet Metal Works Inc** 773 247-6477
4209 S Western Blvd Chicago (60609) *(G-5386)*
**Kirk Wood Products Inc** 309 829-6661
10424 E 1400 North Rd Bloomington (61705) *(G-2190)*
**Kirkland Sawmill Inc** 815 522-6150
606 W Main St Kirkland (60146) *(G-12714)*
**Kirkman Composites** 309 734-5606
1201 N Main St Ste 2 Monmouth (61462) *(G-15018)*
**Kishknows Inc** 708 252-3648
3831 Janis Dr Richton Park (60471) *(G-17979)*
**Kishwaukee Forge Company** 815 758-4451
520 E N Ave Cortland (60112) *(G-7391)*
**Kishwood, Genoa** *Also called Inlaid Woodcraft Co* *(G-10880)*
**Kitagawa Usa Inc** 847 310-8198
301 Commerce Dr Schaumburg (60173) *(G-19599)*
**Kitagawa-Northtech Inc** 847 310-8787
301 Commerce Dr Schaumburg (60173) *(G-19600)*
**Kitamura Machinery USA Inc (HQ)** 847 520-7755
78 Century Dr Wheeling (60090) *(G-22084)*
**Kitbuilders Magazine LLC** 618 588-5232
1117 Harvey Ln New Baden (62265) *(G-15862)*
**Kitchen & Bath Gallery** 217 214-0310
615 Jersey St Quincy (62301) *(G-17845)*
**Kitchen Cooked Inc (PA)** 309 245-2191
632 N Main St Farmington (61531) *(G-10187)*
**Kitchen Cooked Inc** 309 772-2798
110 Industrial Park Rd Bushnell (61422) *(G-2903)*
**Kitchen Design Studio, Addison** *Also called Mica Furniture Mfg Inc* *(G-205)*
**Kitchen Krafters Inc** 815 675-6061
7801 Industrial Dr Ste D Spring Grove (60081) *(G-20341)*
**Kitchen Transformation Inc** 847 758-1905
1410 Jarvis Ave Elk Grove Village (60007) *(G-9574)*
**Kitchens To Go Built By Carlin, Naperville** *Also called Grs Holding LLC* *(G-15666)*
**Kitchens.com, Chicago** *Also called White Picket Media Inc* *(G-6973)*
**Kitchy Koo Gourmet Co** 708 499-5236
7845 Lamon Ave Oak Lawn (60459) *(G-16629)*
**Kite Woodworking Co** 217 728-4346
1124 W Harrison St Sullivan (61951) *(G-20750)*
**Kitty Pallets, Bellwood** *Also called R K J Pallets Inc* *(G-1717)*
**Kiwi Coders Corp** 847 541-4511
265 Messner Dr Wheeling (60090) *(G-22085)*
**Kjellberg Printing** 630 653-2244
805 W Liberty Dr Wheaton (60187) *(G-21960)*
**KJK Corp** 815 389-0566
7306 Barngate Dr South Beloit (61080) *(G-20156)*
**KK Stevens Publishing Co** 309 329-2151
100 N Pearl St Astoria (61501) *(G-934)*
**Kkj Industries LLC** 630 202-9160
49 E Van Buren St Villa Park (60181) *(G-21265)*
**Kksp Precision Machining LLC (PA)** 630 260-1735
1688 Glen Ellyn Rd Glendale Heights (60139) *(G-11038)*
**Kkt Chillers Inc** 847 734-1600
1280 Landmeier Rd Elk Grove Village (60007) *(G-9575)*
**Kl Watch Service Inc** 847 368-8780
800 W Central Rd Ste 103 Mount Prospect (60056) *(G-15342)*
**Klai-Co Idntification Pdts Inc** 847 573-0375
13777 W Laurel Dr Lake Forest (60045) *(G-12921)*
**Klaman Hardwood** 217 972-7888
4351 N Macarthur Rd Decatur (62526) *(G-7903)*
**Klass Electric Company Inc** 847 437-5555
101 Kelly St Ste C Elk Grove Village (60007) *(G-9576)*
**Klean-Ko Inc** 630 620-1860
960 N Lombard Rd Ste A Lombard (60148) *(G-13816)*
**Kleen Cut Tool Inc** 630 447-7020
30w250 Butterfield Rd # 309 Warrenville (60555) *(G-21349)*
**Kleer Pak Mfg Co Inc** 630 543-0208
320 S La Londe Ave Addison (60101) *(G-169)*
**Klehm Family Winery LLC** 847 609-9997
44w637 Il Route 72 Hampshire (60140) *(G-11552)*
**Klein Plastics Company LLC** 616 863-9900
450 Bond St Lincolnshire (60069) *(G-13459)*
**Klein Printing Inc** 773 235-2121
3035 W Fullerton Ave Chicago (60647) *(G-5387)*
**Klein Tools Inc (PA)** 847 821-5500
450 Bond St Lincolnshire (60069) *(G-13460)*
**Klein Tools Inc** 815 282-0530
9929 N Alpine Rd Machesney Park (61115) *(G-14086)*
**Klein Tools Inc** 847 228-6999
2300 E Devon Ave Elk Grove Village (60007) *(G-9577)*
**Klein Tools Inc** 847 821-5500
450 Bond St Lincolnshire (60069) *(G-13461)*
**Kleinhoffer Manufacturing Inc** 815 725-3638
1852 Terry Dr Joliet (60436) *(G-12527)*
**Klh Printing Corp** 847 459-0115
664 Wheeling Rd Wheeling (60090) *(G-22086)*
**Klimko Ink Inc** 815 459-5066
125 S Virginia St Crystal Lake (60014) *(G-7599)*
**Klimp Industries Inc** 630 682-0752
175 Tubeway Dr Carol Stream (60188) *(G-3179)*
**Klimp Industries Inc** 630 790-0600
175 Tubeway Dr Carol Stream (60188) *(G-3180)*
**Klm Commercial Sweeping Inc** 618 978-9276
320 Saint Sabre Dr Belleville (62226) *(G-1643)*
**KLM Tool Company** 630 458-1700
930 S Stiles Dr Addison (60101) *(G-170)*
**Kloeckner Metals Corporation** 773 646-6363
13535 S Torrence Ave # 10 Chicago (60633) *(G-5388)*
**Km Enterprises Inc** 618 204-0888
320 S 11th St Ste 2 Mount Vernon (62864) *(G-15420)*
**Km Press Incorporated** 618 277-1222
120 Iowa Ave Belleville (62220) *(G-1644)*
**Km4 Manufacturing** 708 924-5150
7420 S Meade Ave Bedford Park (60638) *(G-1559)*
**Kmf Enterprises Inc** 630 858-2210
20 Danada Sq W Wheaton (60189) *(G-21961)*
**Kmk Metal Fabricators Inc** 618 224-2000
408 E Broadway Trenton (62293) *(G-20993)*
**Kmp Products LLC** 630 956-0438
1060 Zygmunt Cir Westmont (60559) *(G-21899)*
**Kmp Tool Grinding Inc** 847 205-9640
1808 Janke Dr Ste J Northbrook (60062) *(G-16288)*
**Kms Industries LLC** 331 225-2671
923 W National Ave Addison (60101) *(G-171)*
**Knaack LLC** 815 459-6020
420 E Terra Cotta Ave Crystal Lake (60014) *(G-7600)*
**Knaack Manufacturing, Crystal Lake** *Also called Knaack LLC* *(G-7600)*
**Knapheide Manufacturing Co** 217 222-7134
436 S 6th St Quincy (62301) *(G-17846)*
**Knapheide Manufacturing Co** 217 223-1848
1848 Westphalia Strasse Quincy (62305) *(G-17847)*
**Knapheide Mfg Co** 217 223-1848
3109 N 30th St Quincy (62305) *(G-17848)*
**Knapp Industrial Wood** 815 657-8854
820 N Center St Forrest (61741) *(G-10263)*
**Knauer Industries Ltd** 815 725-0246
19505 Ne Frontage Rd Joliet (60404) *(G-12528)*
**Kniffen Brothers Sawmill** 618 629-2437
16794 Buxton Rd Whittington (62897) *(G-22187)*
**Knight Bros Inc** 618 439-9626
10764 Industrial Park Rd Benton (62812) *(G-2033)*
**Knight Hawk Coal LLC (PA)** 618 426-3662
500 Cutler Trico Rd Percy (62272) *(G-17495)*
**Knight Hawk Coal LLC** 618 497-2768
7290 County Line Rd Cutler (62238) *(G-7687)*
**Knight Packaging Group, Chicago** *Also called Knight Paper Box Company* *(G-5390)*
**Knight Packaging Group Inc** 773 585-2035
4651 W 72nd St Chicago (60629) *(G-5389)*
**Knight Paper Box Company (PA)** 773 585-2035
4651 W 72nd St Chicago (60629) *(G-5390)*
**Knight Plastics LLC** 815 334-1240
1008 Courtaulds Dr Woodstock (60098) *(G-22579)*
**Knight Printing and Litho Svcs, Island Lake** *Also called Knight Prtg & Litho Svc Ltd* *(G-12217)*
**Knight Prtg & Litho Svc Ltd** 847 487-7700
706 E Burnett Rd Island Lake (60042) *(G-12217)*
**Knight Tool Works Inc** 847 678-1237
1200 Abbott Dr Ste C Elgin (60123) *(G-9091)*
**Knighthouse Media Inc** 312 676-1100
150 N Michigan Ave # 900 Chicago (60601) *(G-5391)*
**Knighthouse Publishing, Chicago** *Also called Knighthouse Media Inc* *(G-5391)*
**Knights of Immaculata, Libertyville** *Also called Marytown* *(G-13347)*
**Knipex Tools LP** 847 398-8520
2035 S Arlington Heights Arlington Heights (60005) *(G-789)*
**Knock On Metal Inc (PA)** 312 372-4569
221 N La Salle St # 3315 Chicago (60601) *(G-5392)*
**Knoll Steel Inc** 815 675-9400
2851 N Us Highway 12 Spring Grove (60081) *(G-20342)*
**Knott So Shabby** 618 281-6002
117 W Locust St Columbia (62236) *(G-7360)*
**Knowledgeshift Inc** 630 221-8759
26w245 Grand Ave Ste 200 Wheaton (60187) *(G-21962)*
**Knowles Corporation (PA)** 630 250-5100
1151 Maplewood Dr Itasca (60143) *(G-12295)*
**Knowles Elec Holdings Inc** 630 250-5100
1151 Maplewood Dr Itasca (60143) *(G-12296)*
**Knowles Electronics LLC (HQ)** 630 250-5100
1151 Maplewood Dr Itasca (60143) *(G-12297)*

Knox Capital Holdings LLC ALPHABETIC SECTION

**Knox Capital Holdings LLC**.......312 402-1425
212 W Kinzie St Chicago (60654) ***(G-5393)***
**Kns Companies Inc**.......630 665-9010
475 Randy Rd Carol Stream (60188) ***(G-3181)***
**Koala Cabinets**.......630 818-1289
333 Charles Ct West Chicago (60185) ***(G-21730)***
**Kobac**.......847 520-6000
1007 Commerce Ct Buffalo Grove (60089) ***(G-2716)***
**Kobawala Poly-Pack Inc**.......312 664-3810
800 W 5th Ave Ste 212 Naperville (60563) ***(G-15684)***
**Kobelco Advnced Cting Amer Inc**.......847 520-6000
1007 Commerce Ct Buffalo Grove (60089) ***(G-2717)***
**Koch Industries Inc**.......312 867-1295
9 E Superior St Chicago (60611) ***(G-5394)***
**Koch Industries Inc**.......773 375-3700
3259 E 100th St Chicago (60617) ***(G-5395)***
**Koch Meat Co Inc**.......847 384-5940
4404 W Berteau Ave Chicago (60641) ***(G-5396)***
**Kocisis Brothers Machine, Alsip** *Also called Kocsis Technologies Inc* ***(G-482)***
**Kocour Co**.......773 847-1111
4800 S Saint Louis Ave Chicago (60632) ***(G-5397)***
**Kocsis Brothers Machine Co (PA)**.......708 597-8110
11755 S Austin Ave Alsip (60803) ***(G-480)***
**Kocsis Technologies Inc (PA)**.......708 597-4177
11755 S Austin Ave Alsip (60803) ***(G-481)***
**Kocsis Technologies Inc**.......708 597-4177
11755 S Austin Ave Alsip (60803) ***(G-482)***
**Koderhandt Inc**.......618 233-4808
1651 N Charles St Belleville (62221) ***(G-1645)***
**Kodiak LLC**.......248 545-7520
4320 S Knox Ave Chicago (60632) ***(G-5398)***
**Kodiak Concrete Forms Inc**.......630 773-9339
1320 Industrial Dr Ste C Itasca (60143) ***(G-12298)***
**Kodiak LLC**.......773 284-9975
4320 S Knox Ave Chicago (60632) ***(G-5399)***
**Koebers Prosthetic Orthpd Lab (PA)**.......309 676-2276
3834 W Irving Park Rd # 1 Chicago (60618) ***(G-5400)***
**Koehler Bindery Inc**.......773 539-7979
3802 W Montrose Ave Chicago (60618) ***(G-5401)***
**Koehler Enterprises Inc**.......847 451-4966
2960 Hart Ct Franklin Park (60131) ***(G-10513)***
**Koenemann Sausage Co**.......815 385-6260
27090 Volo Village Rd Volo (60073) ***(G-21316)***
**Koenig Body & Equipment Inc**.......309 673-7435
2428 W Farmington Rd West Peoria (61604) ***(G-21823)***
**Koenig Machine & Welding Inc**.......217 228-6538
2707 N 24th St Quincy (62305) ***(G-17849)***
**Koerner Aviation Inc**.......815 932-4222
1520 S State Route 115 Kankakee (60901) ***(G-12636)***
**Koflo Corporation**.......847 516-3700
309 Cary Point Dr Ste A Cary (60013) ***(G-3356)***
**Kohler Co**.......847 734-1777
11449 Morning Glory Ln Huntley (60142) ***(G-12155)***
**Kohler Co**.......630 323-7674
775 Village Center Dr Burr Ridge (60527) ***(G-2861)***
**Kohler Co**.......847 635-8071
1180 Milwaukee Ave Glenview (60025) ***(G-11156)***
**Kohler K&B Store, Glenview** *Also called Kohler Co* ***(G-11156)***
**Kohlert Manufacturing Corp**.......630 584-0013
2851 Dukane Dr Saint Charles (60174) ***(G-19204)***
**Kohnens Concrete Products Inc**.......618 277-2120
503 Green St Germantown (62245) ***(G-10892)***
**Kohns Electric**.......309 463-2331
1555 Key Ct S Varna (61375) ***(G-21134)***
**Kohout Woodwork Inc**.......630 628-6257
759 W Factory Rd Addison (60101) ***(G-172)***
**Koi Computers Inc**.......630 627-8811
200 W North Ave Lombard (60148) ***(G-13817)***
**Kokes Kid Zone**.......217 483-4615
1033 Jason Pl Chatham (62629) ***(G-3624)***
**Kokoku Rubber Inc (HQ)**.......847 517-6770
1375 E Wdfield Rd Ste 560 Schaumburg (60173) ***(G-19601)***
**Kolb-Lena Inc**.......815 369-4577
3990 N Sunnyside Rd Lena (61048) ***(G-13275)***
**Kolb-Lena Bresse Bleu, Inc., Lena** *Also called Kolb-Lena Inc* ***(G-13275)***
**Kolbi Pipe Marker Co, Arlington Heights** *Also called R L Kolbi Company* ***(G-826)***
**Kolcraft Enterprises Inc (PA)**.......312 361-6315
1100 W Monroe St Ste 200 Chicago (60607) ***(G-5402)***
**Kold-Ban International Ltd**.......847 658-8561
8390 Pingree Rd Lake In The Hills (60156) ***(G-12997)***
**Kolorcure Corporation**.......630 879-9050
1180 Lyon Rd Batavia (60510) ***(G-1460)***
**Komar Screw Corp (PA)**.......847 965-9090
7790 N Merrimac Ave Niles (60714) ***(G-15995)***
**Komatsu America Corp**.......309 672-7000
2300 Ne Adams St Peoria (61639) ***(G-17397)***
**Komatsu America Corp (HQ)**.......847 437-5800
1701 Golf Rd Ste 1-100 Rolling Meadows (60008) ***(G-18737)***
**Komatsu Forklift USA LLC (HQ)**.......847 437-5800
1701 Golf Rd Ste 1 Rolling Meadows (60008) ***(G-18738)***
**Komax Corporation (HQ)**.......847 537-6640
1100 E Corp Grove Dr Buffalo Grove (60089) ***(G-2718)***
**Komax Systems Rockford Inc**.......815 885-8800
4608 Interstate Blvd Loves Park (61111) ***(G-13956)***
**Komet, Schaumburg** *Also called Martin Tool Works Inc* ***(G-19631)***
**Komet America Holding Inc (HQ)**.......847 923-8400
2050 Mitchell Blvd Schaumburg (60193) ***(G-19602)***
**Komet of America Inc**.......847 923-8400
2050 Mitchell Blvd Schaumburg (60193) ***(G-19603)***
**Komori America Corporation (HQ)**.......847 806-9000
5520 Meadowbrook Indus Ct Rolling Meadows (60008) ***(G-18739)***
**Kon Printing Inc**.......630 879-2211
316 E Wilson St Batavia (60510) ***(G-1461)***
**Kona Blackbird Inc**.......815 792-8750
3624 E 2351st Rd Serena (60549) ***(G-19892)***
**Kone Elevator (HQ)**.......309 764-6771
1 Kone Ct Moline (61265) ***(G-14950)***
**Kone Escalator Div, Coal Valley** *Also called Kone Inc* ***(G-7297)***
**Kone Inc (HQ)**.......630 577-1650
4225 Naperville Rd # 400 Lisle (60532) ***(G-13614)***
**Kone Inc**.......309 945-4961
2266 Us Highway 6 Coal Valley (61240) ***(G-7297)***
**Konekt Inc**.......773 733-0471
111 W Illinois St Chicago (60654) ***(G-5403)***
**Kongskilde Industries Inc**.......309 452-3300
19500 N 1425 East Rd Hudson (61748) ***(G-12124)***
**Konica Minolta**.......630 893-8238
1000 Stevenson Ct Ste 109 Roselle (60172) ***(G-18950)***
**Konica Minolta Business Soluti**.......309 671-1360
401 Sw Water St Peoria (61602) ***(G-17398)***
**Konveau Inc**.......312 476-9385
805 E Drexel Sq Chicago (60615) ***(G-5404)***
**Konzen Chemicals Inc**.......708 878-7636
4248 Oakwood Ln Matteson (60443) ***(G-14375)***
**Kool Technologies Inc**.......630 483-2256
714 Bonded Pkwy Ste A Streamwood (60107) ***(G-20662)***
**Koontz Services**.......618 375-7613
1598 County Road 1100 E Carmi (62821) ***(G-3072)***
**Kop-Coat Inc**.......847 272-2278
1608 Barclay Blvd Buffalo Grove (60089) ***(G-2719)***
**Kopis Machine Co Inc**.......630 543-4138
330 W Interstate Rd Addison (60101) ***(G-173)***
**Kopp Welding Inc**.......847 593-2070
991 Oakton St Elk Grove Village (60007) ***(G-9578)***
**Koppers Industries Inc**.......309 343-5157
Rr 41 Box S Galesburg (61402) ***(G-10763)***
**Koppers Industries Inc**.......708 656-5900
3900 S Laramie Ave Cicero (60804) ***(G-7209)***
**Korea Daily News**.......847 545-1767
790 Busse Rd Elk Grove Village (60007) ***(G-9579)***
**Korea Times**.......847 626-0388
615 Milwaukee Ave Ste 12 Glenview (60025) ***(G-11157)***
**Korea Times Chicago Inc**.......847 626-0388
615 Milwaukee Ave Ste 12 Glenview (60025) ***(G-11158)***
**Korea Tribune Inc**.......847 956-9101
1699 Wall St Ste 201 Mount Prospect (60056) ***(G-15343)***
**Korean Air**.......773 686-2730
5600 Mannheim Rd Chicago (60666) ***(G-5405)***
**Korean Media Group LLC**.......847 391-4112
3520 Milwaukee Ave Fl 2 Northbrook (60062) ***(G-16289)***
**Korex Chicago LLC**.......708 458-4890
6200 W 51st St Ste 7 Chicago (60638) ***(G-5406)***
**Korex Corporation**.......708 458-4890
6200 W 51st St Ste 6 Chicago (60638) ***(G-5407)***
**Korhumel Inc**.......847 330-0335
230 Parktrail Ct Schaumburg (60173) ***(G-19604)***
**Korinek & Co Inc**.......708 652-2870
4828 W 25th St Cicero (60804) ***(G-7210)***
**Kormex Metal Craft Inc**.......630 953-8856
961 Dupage Ave Lombard (60148) ***(G-13818)***
**Kornick Enterprises LLC**.......847 884-1162
711 E Golf Rd Schaumburg (60173) ***(G-19605)***
**Korpack Inc**.......630 213-3600
290 Madsen Dr Bldg 100 Bloomingdale (60108) ***(G-2111)***
**Korte Meat Processing Inc**.......618 654-3813
810 Deal St Highland (62249) ***(G-11801)***
**Kory Farm Equipment Division, Schaumburg** *Also called Korhumel Inc* ***(G-19604)***
**Kosmos Tool Inc**.......815 675-2200
2727 Rt 12 Spring Grove (60081) ***(G-20343)***
**Koson Tool Inc**.......815 277-2107
9235 Corsair Rd Ste B Frankfort (60423) ***(G-10340)***
**Kostelac Grease Service Inc**.......314 436-7166
8105 Pecan Tree Ln Belleville (62223) ***(G-1646)***
**Kosto Food Products Company**.......847 487-2600
1325 N Old Rand Rd Wauconda (60084) ***(G-21478)***
**Koswell Pattern Works Inc**.......708 757-5225
3149 Glenwood Dyer Rd H Lynwood (60411) ***(G-14020)***
**Kotter Ready Mix, Metropolis** *Also called Metropolis Ready Mix Inc* ***(G-14758)***
**Koval Inc**.......773 944-0089
5121 N Ravenswood Ave Grw Chicago (60640) ***(G-5408)***

**Kowal Custom Cabinet & Furn**......708 597-3367
2900 Wireton Rd Blue Island (60406) *(G-2260)*
**Kowalik Brothers, Chicago** *Also called United States Audio Corp (G-6827)*
**Kowalski Memorials Inc**......630 462-7226
195 Kehoe Blvd Ste 1 Carol Stream (60188) *(G-3182)*
**Koza**......773 646-0958
13548 S Burley Ave Chicago (60633) *(G-5409)*
**Kozin Woodwork US**......815 568-8918
3911 N Il Route 23 Marengo (60152) *(G-14234)*
**Kp Performance Inc**......780 809-1908
5000 Proviso Dr Ste 2 Melrose Park (60163) *(G-14667)*
**Kps Capital Partners LP**......630 972-7000
455 Gibraltar Dr Bolingbrook (60440) *(G-2333)*
**Kr Machine**......815 248-2250
15322 Eicks Rd Durand (61024) *(G-8586)*
**Kr Strikeforce Bowling, Broadview** *Also called Strikeforce Bowling LLC (G-2615)*
**Krack Corporation**......630 250-0187
890 Remington Blvd Ste A Bolingbrook (60440) *(G-2334)*
**Kraft Custom Design Inc**......815 485-5506
22032 Howell Dr New Lenox (60451) *(G-15890)*
**Kraft Fods Ltin Amer Holdg LLC (PA)**......847 646-2000
3 Lakes Dr Northfield (60093) *(G-16406)*
**Kraft Food Ingredients Corp (HQ)**......901 381-6500
801 Waukegan Rd Glenview (60025) *(G-11159)*
**Kraft Foods, Glenview** *Also called Kraft Pizza Company Inc (G-11163)*
**Kraft Foods, Glenview** *Also called Kraft Food Ingredients Corp (G-11159)*
**Kraft Foods, Naperville** *Also called Mondelez Global LLC (G-15699)*
**Kraft Foods Asia PCF Svcs LLC (HQ)**......847 943-4000
3 Parkway N Ste 300 Deerfield (60015) *(G-8026)*
**Kraft Heinz Company (PA)**......412 456-5700
200 E Randolph St # 7300 Chicago (60601) *(G-5410)*
**Kraft Heinz Company**......847 646-2000
801 Waukegan Rd Glenview (60025) *(G-11160)*
**Kraft Heinz Foods Company**......847 291-3900
2301 Shermer Rd Northbrook (60062) *(G-16290)*
**Kraft Heinz Foods Company**......815 338-7000
1300 Claussen Dr Woodstock (60098) *(G-22580)*
**Kraft Heinz Foods Company**......847 646-3690
801 Waukegan Rd Glenview (60025) *(G-11161)*
**Kraft Heinz Foods Company**......630 505-0170
3030 Warrenville Rd # 200 Lisle (60532) *(G-13615)*
**Kraft Heinz Foods Company**......847 646-2000
801 Waukegan Rd Glenview (60025) *(G-11162)*
**Kraft Heinz Foods Company**......618 451-4820
2901 Missouri Ave Granite City (62040) *(G-11289)*
**Kraft Heinz Foods Company**......847 646-2000
3 Lakes Dr 2b Northfield (60093) *(G-16407)*
**Kraft Heinz Foods Company**......618 512-9100
2901 Missouri Ave Granite City (62040) *(G-11290)*
**Kraft Heinz Foods Company**......630 227-1474
367 Haynes Dr Wood Dale (60191) *(G-22386)*
**Kraft Heinz Foods Company**......217 378-1900
1701 W Bradley Ave Champaign (61821) *(G-3507)*
**Kraft Pizza Company Inc (HQ)**......847 646-2000
1 Kraft Ct Glenview (60025) *(G-11163)*
**Kraft Services**......309 662-6178
209 S Prospect Rd Bloomington (61704) *(G-2191)*
**Krafty Kabinets**......815 369-5250
106 W Provost St Lena (61048) *(G-13276)*
**Kraig Corporation**......847 928-0630
10253 Franklin Ave Franklin Park (60131) *(G-10514)*
**Kraly Tire Repair Materials**......708 863-5981
5936 W 35th St Cicero (60804) *(G-7211)*
**Kram Digital Solutions Inc (PA)**......312 222-0431
1717 Chestnut Ave Glenview (60025) *(G-11164)*
**Kramer Window Co**......708 343-4780
1219 Orchard Ave Maywood (60153) *(G-14427)*
**Kranos Corporation (PA)**......217 324-3978
710 Industrial Dr Litchfield (62056) *(G-13691)*
**Kraus & Naimer Inc**......847 298-2450
200 Howard Ave Ste 270 Des Plaines (60018) *(G-8219)*
**Kravet Inc**......847 870-1414
3441 N Ridge Ave Arlington Heights (60004) *(G-790)*
**Kreg Medical Inc**......312 829-8904
1940 Janice Ave Melrose Park (60160) *(G-14668)*
**Kreider Services Incorporated (PA)**......815 288-6691
500 Anchor Rd Dixon (61021) *(G-8336)*
**Kreis Tool & Mfg Co Inc**......847 289-3700
1615 Cambridge Dr Elgin (60123) *(G-9092)*
**Kreischer Optics Ltd**......815 344-4220
1729 Oak Dr McHenry (60050) *(G-14518)*
**Krel Laboratories Inc**......773 826-4487
388 N Avers Ave Chicago (60624) *(G-5411)*
**Kremer Precision Machine Inc**......217 868-2627
10748 E 1850th Ave Shumway (62461) *(G-19932)*
**Kress Corporation (PA)**......309 446-3395
227 W Illinois St Brimfield (61517) *(G-2547)*
**Kresser Precision Inds Inc**......815 899-2202
433 N California St # 2 Sycamore (60178) *(G-20806)*

**Krick Enterprises Inc**......630 515-1085
1548 Ogden Ave Downers Grove (60515) *(G-8470)*
**Kriese Mfg**......815 748-2683
231 N Juniper St Cortland (60112) *(G-7392)*
**Kris Dee and Associates Inc**......630 503-4093
755 Schneider Dr South Elgin (60177) *(G-20211)*
**Krisdee, South Elgin** *Also called Kris Dee and Associates Inc (G-20211)*
**Kristel Displays, Saint Charles** *Also called Kristel Limited Partnership (G-19205)*
**Kristel Limited Partnership**......630 443-1290
555 Kirk Rd Saint Charles (60174) *(G-19205)*
**Kristine Van Stockum's Hand PA, Deerfield** *Also called Van Stockum Kristine (G-8064)*
**Kroger Co**......815 332-7267
2206 Barnes Blvd Rockford (61112) *(G-18457)*
**Kroger Co**......309 694-6298
201 S Main St East Peoria (61611) *(G-8722)*
**Kroh-Wagner Inc**......773 252-2031
2331 N Pulaski Rd Chicago (60639) *(G-5412)*
**Kromray Hydraulic McHy Inc**......630 257-8655
870 Kromray Rd Lemont (60439) *(G-13238)*
**Kronos Foods Corp (PA)**......773 847-2250
1 Kronos Glendale Heights (60139) *(G-11039)*
**Kronos Incorporated**......847 969-6501
475 N Martingale Rd # 870 Schaumburg (60173) *(G-19606)*
**Kropp Forge, Chicago** *Also called Park-Hio Frged McHned Pdts LLC (G-6084)*
**Kroto Inc**......800 980-1089
8280 Austin Ave Morton Grove (60053) *(G-15210)*
**Krueger and Company**......630 833-5650
900 N Industrial Dr Elmhurst (60126) *(G-9899)*
**Krueger International Inc**......312 467-6850
1181 Merchandise Mart Chicago (60654) *(G-5413)*
**Krueger Steel & Wire, Elmhurst** *Also called Krueger and Company (G-9899)*
**Krug-Northwest Electric Motors, Grayslake** *Also called Heise Industries Inc (G-11346)*
**Kruger North America Inc**......708 851-3670
1033 South Blvd Ste 200 Oak Park (60302) *(G-16673)*
**Krum Kreations**......815 772-8296
22585 Carroll Rd Morrison (61270) *(G-15145)*
**Krygier Design Inc**......620 766-1001
635 Wheat Ln Wood Dale (60191) *(G-22387)*
**Krygier Machine Company Inc**......708 331-5255
15938 Suntone Dr South Holland (60473) *(G-20284)*
**Ksem Inc**......618 656-5388
6471 Miller Dr Edwardsville (62025) *(G-8805)*
**Ksi Conveyor Inc**......815 457-2403
454 N State Route 49 Cissna Park (60924) *(G-7255)*
**Kso Metalfab Inc**......630 372-1200
250 Roma Jean Pkwy Streamwood (60107) *(G-20663)*
**Ksr Software LLC**......847 705-0100
388 N Chalary Ct Palatine (60067) *(G-17048)*
**Ktm Industries Inc**......217 224-5861
2701 Weiss Ln Quincy (62305) *(G-17850)*
**Ktm Lab Service Co Inc**......708 351-6780
716 Morse Ave Schaumburg (60193) *(G-19607)*
**Kturbo USA Inc**......630 406-1473
1183 Pierson Dr Ste 118 Batavia (60510) *(G-1462)*
**Kubota Authorized Dealer, Metropolis** *Also called Michaels Equipment Co (G-14759)*
**Kuchar Combine Performance**......217 854-9838
300 Route 4 Carlinville (62626) *(G-3041)*
**Kuchar High Perfomance Parts, Carlinville** *Also called Kuchar Combine Performance (G-3041)*
**Kuester Tool & Die Inc**......217 223-1955
1400 N 30th St Quincy (62301) *(G-17851)*
**Kuhl's Trailer Sales, Ingraham** *Also called Arthur Leo Kuhl (G-12199)*
**Kult of Athena, Elgin** *Also called Proton Multimedia Inc (G-9152)*
**Kuna Corp**......815 675-0140
1512 Spring Ct Spring Grove (60081) *(G-20344)*
**Kunde Woodwork Inc**......847 669-2030
11901 Smith Dr Huntley (60142) *(G-12156)*
**Kuntry Kettle**......618 426-1600
178 Gordon Rd Ava (62907) *(G-1238)*
**Kunverji Enterprise Corp**......847 683-2954
395 S Main St Burlington (60109) *(G-2812)*
**Kunz Carpentry (PA)**......618 224-7892
16 E Broadway Trenton (62293) *(G-20994)*
**Kunz Engineering Inc**......815 539-6954
2100 Welland Rd Mendota (61342) *(G-14723)*
**Kunz Glove Co Inc**......312 733-8780
1532 W Fulton St Chicago (60607) *(G-5414)*
**Kunz Industries Inc**......708 596-7717
15800 Suntone Dr South Holland (60473) *(G-20285)*
**Kuriyama of America Inc (HQ)**......847 755-0360
360 E State Pkwy Schaumburg (60173) *(G-19608)*
**Kurland Steel Company, Urbana** *Also called Central Ill Fbrcation Whse Inc (G-21076)*
**Kurts Carstar Collision Ctr**......618 345-4519
1 Mueller Dr Maryville (62062) *(G-14343)*
**Kurtzon Lighting, Chicago** *Also called Morris Kurtzon Incorporated (G-5806)*
**Kurz Transfer Products LP**......847 228-0001
220 Martin Ln Elk Grove Village (60007) *(G-9580)*

ALPHABETIC

Kusmierek Industries Inc ALPHABETIC SECTION

**Kusmierek Industries Inc**.......708 258-3100
6434 W North Peotone Rd Peotone (60468) **(G-17490)**
**Kut-Rite Tool Co., Streamwood** *Also called Retondo Enterprises Inc* **(G-20671)**
**Kut-Rite Tool Company**.......630 837-8130
1539 Brandy Pkwy Streamwood (60107) **(G-20664)**
**Kuusakoski Philadelphia LLC**.......215 533-8323
13543 S Route 30 Plainfield (60544) **(G-17616)**
**Kvd Enterprises LLC**.......618 726-5114
1392 Frontage Rd Ste 10 O Fallon (62269) **(G-16469)**
**Kvd Sewer, O Fallon** *Also called Kvd Enterprises LLC* **(G-16469)**
**Kvf-Quad Corporation**.......563 529-1916
808 13th St East Moline (61244) **(G-8683)**
**Kvh Industries Inc**.......708 444-2800
8412 185th St Tinley Park (60487) **(G-20927)**
**Kvk Foundry Inc**.......815 695-5212
302 Vine St Millington (60537) **(G-14819)**
**Kw Container, Chicago** *Also called Kw Plastics* **(G-5415)**
**Kw Plastics**.......708 757-5140
270 S State St Chicago (60604) **(G-5415)**
**Kw Precast LLC**.......708 562-7700
2255 Entp Dr Ste 1510 Westchester (60154) **(G-21846)**
**Kwalyti Tling McHy Rblding Inc**.......630 761-8040
1690 E Fabyan Pkwy Batavia (60510) **(G-1463)**
**Kwik Kopy Printing, Alsip** *Also called Grasso Graphics Inc* **(G-465)**
**Kwik Kopy Printing, Saint Charles** *Also called West Vly Graphics & Print Inc* **(G-19293)**
**Kwik Kopy Printing, Peoria** *Also called Ro-Web Inc* **(G-17444)**
**Kwik Kopy Printing, Chicago** *Also called Wolfam Holdings Corporation* **(G-7020)**
**Kwik Kopy Printing, Arlington Heights** *Also called Elmhurst Enterprise Group Inc* **(G-749)**
**Kwik Kopy Printing, Crystal Lake** *Also called Klimko Ink Inc* **(G-7599)**
**Kwik Mark Inc**.......815 363-8268
4071 W Albany St McHenry (60050) **(G-14519)**
**Kwik Print Inc**.......630 773-3225
206 W Irving Park Rd Itasca (60143) **(G-12299)**
**Kwik-Wall Company, Springfield** *Also called Capitol Wood Works LLC* **(G-20408)**
**Kwikset Corporation**.......630 577-0500
4225 Naperville Rd # 340 Lisle (60532) **(G-13616)**
**Kwm Gutterman Inc**.......815 725-9205
795 S Larkin Ave Rockdale (60436) **(G-18223)**
**Kwok's Food Service, Chicago** *Also called Charles Autin Limited* **(G-4289)**
**Kws Cereals Usa LLC**.......815 200-2666
4101 Colleen Dr Champaign (61822) **(G-3508)**
**Kyjen Company LLC**.......847 504-4010
333 Skokie Blvd Ste 104 Northbrook (60062) **(G-16291)**
**Kylon Midwest**.......773 699-3640
238 E 108th St Apt 2w Chicago (60628) **(G-5416)**
**Kyowa Industrial Co Ltd USA**.......847 459-3500
711 Glenn Ave Wheeling (60090) **(G-22087)**
**L & B Global Power LLC**.......847 323-0770
5231 W Cullom Ave Chicago (60641) **(G-5417)**
**L & C Imaging Inc**.......309 829-1802
908 White Oak Rd Bloomington (61701) **(G-2192)**
**L & D Group Inc**.......630 892-8941
420 N Main St Montgomery (60538) **(G-15051)**
**L & H Company Inc (PA)**.......630 571-7200
2215 York Rd Ste 304 Oak Brook (60523) **(G-16532)**
**L & J Engineering Inc (HQ)**.......708 236-6000
5911 Butterfield Rd Hillside (60162) **(G-11922)**
**L & J Holding Company Ltd (PA)**.......708 236-6000
5911 Butterfield Rd Hillside (60162) **(G-11923)**
**L & J Industrial Staples Inc**.......815 864-3337
15 W Market St Shannon (61078) **(G-19899)**
**L & J Producers Inc**.......217 932-5639
3795 E 700th Rd Casey (62420) **(G-3387)**
**L & J Technologies, Hillside** *Also called L & J Engineering Inc* **(G-11922)**
**L & J Technologies, Hillside** *Also called L & J Holding Company Ltd* **(G-11923)**
**L & L Flooring Inc**.......773 935-9314
3071 N Lincoln Ave Chicago (60657) **(G-5418)**
**L & M Greenhouses, Saint Charles** *Also called Michael Clesen* **(G-19220)**
**L & M Hardware Ltd**.......312 805-2752
2600 Warrenville Rd # 202 Downers Grove (60515) **(G-8471)**
**L & M Manufacturing Inc**.......309 734-3009
101 Franklin St Kewanee (61443) **(G-12692)**
**L & M Screw Machine Products**.......630 801-0455
321 Webster St Montgomery (60538) **(G-15052)**
**L & M Steel Services Inc**.......309 755-3713
3660 Morton Dr East Moline (61244) **(G-8684)**
**L & M Tool & Die Co Inc**.......847 364-9760
1570 Louis Ave Elk Grove Village (60007) **(G-9581)**
**L & M Tool & Die Works**.......815 625-3256
803 Avenue C Rock Falls (61071) **(G-18140)**
**L & M Welding Inc**.......773 237-8500
4619 W Armitage Ave Chicago (60639) **(G-5419)**
**L & N Structures Inc (PA)**.......815 426-2164
104 S Park Rd Herscher (60941) **(G-11759)**
**L & P Guarding LLC**.......708 325-0400
5858 W 73rd St Bedford Park (60638) **(G-1560)**
**L & S Label Printing Inc**.......815 964-6753
4337 S Perryville Rd # 102 Cherry Valley (61016) **(G-3646)**
**L & T Services Inc**.......815 397-6260
1004 Samuelson Rd Rockford (61109) **(G-18458)**
**L & W Bedding Inc**.......309 762-6019
1211 16th Ave Moline (61265) **(G-14951)**
**L & W Fuels**.......815 848-8360
5484 N 2100 East Rd Fairbury (61739) **(G-10130)**
**L & W Tool & Screw Mch Pdts**.......847 238-1212
1447 Ardmore Ave Itasca (60143) **(G-12300)**
**L A Bedding Corp**.......773 715-9641
3421 W 48th Pl Chicago (60632) **(G-5420)**
**L A D Specialties**.......708 430-1588
9010 Beloit Ave Ste F Oak Lawn (60455) **(G-16630)**
**L A M Inc De**.......630 860-9700
620 Wheat Ln Ste B Wood Dale (60191) **(G-22388)**
**L A Motors Incorporated**.......773 736-7305
4034 N Tripp Ave Chicago (60641) **(G-5421)**
**L A T Enterprise Inc**.......630 543-5533
423 W Interstate Rd Addison (60101) **(G-174)**
**L C Mold Inc**.......847 593-5004
3640 Edison Pl Rolling Meadows (60008) **(G-18740)**
**L C Neelydrilling Inc**.......618 544-2726
702 N Jackson St Robinson (62454) **(G-18065)**
**L D Redmer Screw Pdts Inc**.......630 787-0504
515 Thomas Dr Bensenville (60106) **(G-1935)**
**L D Redmer Screw Products**.......630 787-0507
448 Du Pahze St Naperville (60565) **(G-15685)**
**L E D Tool & Die Inc**.......708 597-2505
12625 S Kroll Dr Chicago (60803) **(G-5422)**
**L F I, Northbrook** *Also called Library Furniture Intl* **(G-16295)**
**L I K Inc**.......630 213-1282
304 Roma Jean Pkwy Streamwood (60107) **(G-20665)**
**L J Iron Works, Morton Grove** *Also called Lichtnwald - Johnston Ir Works* **(G-15212)**
**L K Beutel Machining Co Inc**.......847 895-5310
536 Morse Ave Schaumburg (60193) **(G-19609)**
**L L Bean Inc**.......847 568-3600
4999 Old Orchard Ctr F18 Skokie (60077) **(G-20023)**
**L Land Hardwoods**.......708 496-9000
6247 W 74th St Bedford Park (60638) **(G-1561)**
**L M C Inc**.......815 758-3514
1142 Glidden Ave Dekalb (60115) **(G-8101)**
**L M C Automotive Inc**.......618 235-5242
1200 W Main St Belleville (62220) **(G-1647)**
**L M J Tooling & Manufacturing, Woodstock** *Also called Serien Manufacturing Inc* **(G-22608)**
**L M K Fabrication Inc**.......815 433-1530
1779 Chessie Ln Ottawa (61350) **(G-16965)**
**L M Machine Shop Inc**.......815 625-3256
803 Avenue C Rock Falls (61071) **(G-18141)**
**L M Sheet Metal Inc**.......815 654-1837
6727 Elm Ave Loves Park (61111) **(G-13957)**
**L P M Inc**.......847 866-9777
1553 Sherman Ave Evanston (60201) **(G-10062)**
**L P S Express Inc**.......217 636-7683
1620 S 5th St Ste A Springfield (62703) **(G-20465)**
**L P T, Lake Zurich** *Also called Loch Precision Technologies* **(G-13096)**
**L R Gregory and Son Inc**.......847 247-0216
1233 Rockland Rd Lake Bluff (60044) **(G-12852)**
**L S Diesel Repair Inc**.......217 283-5537
220 N 10th Ave Hoopeston (60942) **(G-12112)**
**L S Starrett Co**.......847 816-9999
50 Lakeview Pkwy Ste 107 Vernon Hills (60061) **(G-21178)**
**L Surges Custom Woodwork**.......815 774-9663
225 Maple St Joliet (60432) **(G-12529)**
**L T D Industries Inc**.......309 547-3251
14310 E Back Rd Lewistown (61542) **(G-13290)**
**L T L Co**.......815 874-0913
4801 American Rd Rockford (61109) **(G-18459)**
**L T P LLC**.......815 723-9400
490 Mills Rd Joliet (60433) **(G-12530)**
**L T Properties Inc (PA)**.......217 423-8772
1395 S Taylorville Rd Decatur (62521) **(G-7904)**
**L V Barnhouse & Sons**.......309 586-5404
49 N Prairie St Ste D Galesburg (61401) **(G-10764)**
**L W Schneider Inc**.......815 875-3835
1180 N 6th St Princeton (61356) **(G-17752)**
**L-Data Corporation**.......312 552-7855
203 N La Salle St # 2169 Chicago (60601) **(G-5423)**
**L-V Industries Inc**.......630 595-9251
508 Meyer Rd Bensenville (60106) **(G-1936)**
**L/J Fabricators Inc**.......815 397-9099
944 Research Pkwy Rockford (61109) **(G-18460)**
**L3 Technologies Inc**.......212 697-1111
1200 Hicks Rd Rolling Meadows (60008) **(G-18741)**
**La Autentica Michoacana Never**.......630 516-1888
507 S Addison Rd Addison (60101) **(G-175)**
**La Bella Chrstnas Kitchens Inc**.......815 801-1600
25 Church St German Valley (61039) **(G-10891)**
**La Boost Inc**.......630 444-1755
3n555 17th St Saint Charles (60174) **(G-19206)**
**La Casa Del Tequila Corp**.......708 652-3640
6144 W 26th St Cicero (60804) **(G-7212)**

**La Chicanita Bakery (PA)** ....630 499-8845
700 E New York St Ste 110 Aurora (60505) *(G-1180)*
**La Conchita Bakery** ....847 623-4094
1703 Washington St Waukegan (60085) *(G-21578)*
**La Criolla Inc** ....312 243-8882
907 W Randolph St Chicago (60607) *(G-5424)*
**La Dolce Bella Cupcakes** ....847 987-3738
1228 Newbridge Ave Lockport (60441) *(G-13725)*
**La Force Inc** ....630 325-1950
7501 S Quincy St Willowbrook (60527) *(G-22218)*
**La Force Inc** ....847 415-5107
280 Corporate Woods Pkwy Vernon Hills (60061) *(G-21179)*
**La Hispamex Food Products Inc** ....708 780-1808
1859 S 55th Ave Cicero (60804) *(G-7213)*
**La Luc Bakery Inc** ....847 740-0303
246 N Cedar Lake Rd Frnt Round Lake (60073) *(G-19061)*
**La Marche Mfg Co (PA)** ....847 299-1188
106 Bradrock Dr Des Plaines (60018) *(G-8220)*
**La Mexicana Tortilleria Inc** ....773 247-5443
2703 S Kedzie Ave Chicago (60623) *(G-5425)*
**La Nueva Michoacana** ....815 722-3720
30 Ohio St Joliet (60432) *(G-12531)*
**La Quinta Gas Pipeline Company** ....217 430-6781
1416 Donlee St Quincy (62305) *(G-17852)*
**La Raza Chicago Inc** ....312 870-7000
200 S Michigan Ave # 1600 Chicago (60604) *(G-5426)*
**La Raza Newspaper, Chicago** *Also called La Raza Chicago Inc* *(G-5426)*
**La Ron Jewelers** ....312 263-3898
5 S Wabash Ave Ste 806 Chicago (60603) *(G-5427)*
**La Salle Co Esda** ....815 433-5622
711 E Etna Rd Ottawa (61350) *(G-16966)*
**La Salle Mfg & Mch Co, Rockford** *Also called Pgi Mfg LLC* *(G-18534)*
**La Sweet Inc** ....252 340-0390
4433 W Touhy Ave Ste 207 Lincolnwood (60712) *(G-13520)*
**La-Co Industries Inc (PA)** ....847 427-3220
1201 Pratt Blvd Elk Grove Village (60007) *(G-9582)*
**La-Z-Boy Incorporated** ....773 384-4440
2647 N Elston Ave Chicago (60647) *(G-5428)*
**LAB Equipment Inc (PA)** ....630 595-4288
1549 Ardmore Ave Itasca (60143) *(G-12301)*
**Lab Software Inc** ....815 521-9116
2021 Holt Rd Minooka (60447) *(G-14841)*
**Lab TEC Cosmt By Marzena Inc** ....630 396-3970
1470 W Bernard Dr Addison (60101) *(G-176)*
**Lab Ten LLC** ....815 877-1410
5029 Willow Creek Rd Machesney Park (61115) *(G-14087)*
**Labaquette Kedzie Inc** ....773 925-0455
5859 S Kedzie Ave Chicago (60629) *(G-5429)*
**Label Graphics Co Inc** ....815 648-2478
12024 3rd Ave Hebron (60034) *(G-11722)*
**Label Printers LP** ....630 897-6970
1710 Landmark Rd Aurora (60506) *(G-1181)*
**Label Tek Inc** ....630 820-8499
3505 Thayer Ct Ste 200 Aurora (60504) *(G-1044)*
**Labelmaster Division, Chicago** *Also called American Labelmark Company* *(G-3859)*
**Labelquest Inc** ....630 833-9400
493 W Fullerton Ave Elmhurst (60126) *(G-9900)*
**Labels Unlimited Incorporated** ....773 523-7500
3400 W 48th Pl Chicago (60632) *(G-5430)*
**Laboratory Builders Inc** ....630 598-0216
166 Shore Dr Burr Ridge (60527) *(G-2862)*
**Laboratory Media Corporation** ....630 897-8000
1731 Commerce Dr Montgomery (60538) *(G-15053)*
**Labriola, Alsip** *Also called Rjl Inc* *(G-521)*
**Labriola Baking Company LLC** ....708 377-0400
3701 W 128th Pl Alsip (60803) *(G-483)*
**Labthermics Technologies** ....217 351-7722
701 Devonshire Dr Ste B5 Champaign (61820) *(G-3509)*
**LAC Enterprises Inc** ....815 455-5044
2530 Il Route 176 Ste 9 Crystal Lake (60014) *(G-7601)*
**Lacava** ....773 637-9600
1100 W Cermak Rd Ste B403 Chicago (60608) *(G-5431)*
**Lacava LLC** ....773 637-9600
6630 W Wrightwood Ave Chicago (60707) *(G-5432)*
**Lacava Design, Chicago** *Also called Lacava LLC* *(G-5432)*
**Lace Technologies Inc** ....630 762-3865
315 S Fairbank St Addison (60101) *(G-177)*
**Lacertus Branding LLC** ....224 523-5100
1569 Barclay Blvd Buffalo Grove (60089) *(G-2720)*
**Lacey-Bauer, Pearl** *Also called Martha Lacey* *(G-17247)*
**Lachata Design Ltd** ....708 946-2757
3006 E Indiana Ave Beecher (60401) *(G-1599)*
**Lacy Enterprises Inc** ....773 264-2557
724 E 104th St Chicago (60628) *(G-5433)*
**Ladder Industries Inc (HQ)** ....800 360-6789
500 Lake Cook Rd Ste 400 Deerfield (60015) *(G-8027)*
**Lafarge Aggregates Ill Inc (HQ)** ....847 742-6060
7n394 S Mclean Blvd South Elgin (60177) *(G-20212)*
**Lafarge Aux Sable LLC** ....815 941-1423
4225 Dellos Rd Morris (60450) *(G-15112)*
**Lafarge Building Materials Inc (HQ)** ....678 746-2000
8700 W Bryn Mawr Ave 300n Chicago (60631) *(G-5434)*
**Lafarge North America Inc** ....630 892-1616
105 Conco St North Aurora (60542) *(G-16137)*
**Lafarge North America Inc (HQ)** ....703 480-3600
8700 W Bryn Mawr Ave Ll Chicago (60631) *(G-5435)*
**Lafarge North America Inc** ....847 742-6060
1310 Rt 31 South Elgin (60177) *(G-20213)*
**Lafarge North America Inc** ....815 741-2090
2509 Mound Rd Rockdale (60436) *(G-18224)*
**Lafarge North America Inc** ....618 289-3404
Rr 1 Cave In Rock (62919) *(G-3403)*
**Lafarge North America Inc** ....773 372-1000
Rr 1 Box 128 Golconda (62938) *(G-11240)*
**Lafarge North America Inc** ....618 543-7541
2500 Portland Rd Grand Chain (62941) *(G-11256)*
**Lafarge North America Inc** ....847 599-0391
315 E Sea Horse Dr Waukegan (60085) *(G-21579)*
**Lafarge North America Inc** ....773 372-1000
8700 W Bryn Mawr Ave Ll Chicago (60631) *(G-5436)*
**Lafarge North America Inc** ....773 646-5228
2150 E 130th St Chicago (60633) *(G-5437)*
**Lafox Manufacturing Corp** ....630 232-0266
1 N 278 Lafox Rd Lafox (60147) *(G-12794)*
**Lafox Screw Products Inc** ....847 695-1732
440 N Gilbert St South Elgin (60177) *(G-20214)*
**Lafrancaise Bakery, Wheeling** *Also called Chef Solutions Inc* *(G-22025)*
**Lagunitas Brewing Company** ....773 522-1308
2607 W 17th St Chicago (60608) *(G-5438)*
**Lah Inc** ....815 282-4939
6309 Material Ave Ste 2 Loves Park (61111) *(G-13958)*
**Lahood Construction Inc** ....309 699-5080
3305 N Main St East Peoria (61611) *(G-8723)*
**Laird Technologies Inc** ....847 839-6900
1751 Wilkening Ct Schaumburg (60173) *(G-19610)*
**Lake Area Disposal Service Inc** ....217 522-9271
2742 S 6th St Springfield (62703) *(G-20466)*
**Lake Area Recycling Services, Springfield** *Also called Lake Area Disposal Service Inc* *(G-20466)*
**Lake Book Manufacturing Inc** ....708 345-7000
2085 Cornell Ave Melrose Park (60160) *(G-14669)*
**Lake Cable LLC** ....888 518-8086
529 Thomas Dr Bensenville (60106) *(G-1937)*
**Lake Consumer Products** ....847 793-0230
730 Corporate Woods Pkwy Vernon Hills (60061) *(G-21180)*
**Lake Cook C V, Wheeling** *Also called Lake County C V Joints Inc* *(G-22088)*
**Lake Country Storage, Varna** *Also called Adapt Seals Co* *(G-21132)*
**Lake County C V Joints Inc** ....847 537-7588
133 Wheeling Rd Wheeling (60090) *(G-22088)*
**Lake County Grading Co LLC (PA)** ....847 362-2590
32901 N Milwaukee Ave Libertyville (60048) *(G-13341)*
**Lake County Machining, Waukegan** *Also called Steve Green* *(G-21619)*
**Lake County Press Inc (PA)** ....847 336-4333
98 Noll St Waukegan (60085) *(G-21580)*
**Lake County Technologies Inc** ....847 658-1330
28w080 Coml Ave Unit 7 Barrington (60010) *(G-1285)*
**Lake County Tool Works North** ....847 662-4542
15986 Hwy 173 Wadsworth (60083) *(G-21324)*
**Lake Electronics Inc** ....847 201-1270
31632 N Ellis Dr Unit 203 Volo (60073) *(G-21317)*
**Lake Fabrication Inc** ....217 832-2761
4 S Sycamore St Villa Grove (61956) *(G-21229)*
**Lake Media Services Inc** ....312 739-0423
333 N Michigan Ave # 1831 Chicago (60601) *(G-5439)*
**Lake Pacific Partners LLC** ....312 578-1110
120 S La Salle St # 1510 Chicago (60603) *(G-5440)*
**Lake Process Systems Inc** ....847 381-7663
27930 W Commercial Ave Lake Barrington (60010) *(G-12817)*
**Lake Sara Properties LLC** ....708 267-1187
8100 163rd St Tinley Park (60477) *(G-20928)*
**Lake Shore Printing** ....847 679-4110
4124 Oakton St Apt C Skokie (60076) *(G-20024)*
**Lake Shore Stair Co Inc (PA)** ....815 363-7777
28090 W Concrete Dr Ingleside (60041) *(G-12192)*
**Lake Street Pallets** ....773 889-2266
4600 W Armitage Ave Chicago (60639) *(G-5441)*
**Lakefront Roofing Supply** ....312 275-0270
977 W Cermak Rd Chicago (60608) *(G-5442)*
**Lakefront Roofing Supply (HQ)** ....773 509-0400
2950 N Western Ave Chicago (60618) *(G-5443)*
**Lakefront Sculpture Exhibit** ....312 719-0207
1807 N Orleans St Ste 1s Chicago (60614) *(G-5444)*
**Lakefront Supply, Chicago** *Also called Jesus People USA Full Gos* *(G-5296)*
**Lakeland Boating Magazine** ....312 276-0610
630 Davis St Ste 301 Evanston (60201) *(G-10063)*
**Lakeland Pallets Inc** ....616 949-9515
2080 Gary Ln Ste 3 Geneva (60134) *(G-10844)*
**Lakeland Plastics Inc** ....847 680-1550
1550 Mccormick Blvd Mundelein (60060) *(G-15517)*

ALPHABETIC

**Lakenburges Motor Co** .......... 618 523-4231
806 Walnut St Germantown (62245) ***(G-10893)***
**Lakes Reg Prtg & Graphics LLC** .......... 847 838-5838
25325 W Hickory St Antioch (60002) ***(G-639)***
**Lakeshore Lacrosse LLC** .......... 773 350-4356
20 Danada Sq W Ste 289 Wheaton (60189) ***(G-21963)***
**Lakeshore Lighting LLC** .......... 847 989-5843
25741 N Hillview Ct Mundelein (60060) ***(G-15518)***
**Lakeside Lithography LLC** .......... 312 243-3001
1600 S Laflin St Chicago (60608) ***(G-5445)***
**Lakeside Publishing Co LLC** .......... 847 491-6440
990 Grove St Ste 400 Evanston (60201) ***(G-10064)***
**Lakeside Screw Products Inc** .......... 630 495-1606
1395 W Jeffrey Dr Addison (60101) ***(G-178)***
**Lakeview Energy LLC (PA)** .......... 312 386-5897
300 W Adams St Ste 830 Chicago (60606) ***(G-5446)***
**Lakeview Equipment Co** .......... 847 548-7705
1327 W Wash Blvf U 5f Round Lake (60073) ***(G-19062)***
**Lakeview Metals Inc (PA)** .......... 847 838-9800
905 Anita Ave Antioch (60002) ***(G-640)***
**Lakeview Oral and Maxillofacia** .......... 773 327-9500
1628 W Belmont Ave Chicago (60657) ***(G-5447)***
**Lakeview Prcsion Machining Inc** .......... 847 742-7170
751 Schneider Dr South Elgin (60177) ***(G-20215)***
**Lakewood Countertop, Bloomingdale** *Also called Pearl Design Group LLC* ***(G-2128)***
**Lakin General, Montgomery** *Also called A Lakin & Sons Inc* ***(G-15026)***
**Lakin General Corporation** .......... 773 871-6360
2001 Greenfield Rd Montgomery (60538) ***(G-15054)***
**Lakone Company** .......... 630 892-4251
1003 Aucutt Rd Montgomery (60538) ***(G-15055)***
**Lamar Owings** .......... 630 232-0564
730 Forrest Ave Geneva (60134) ***(G-10845)***
**Lambda Publications Inc** .......... 773 871-7610
5443 N Broadway St # 101 Chicago (60640) ***(G-5448)***
**Lambert Bridge & Iron, Bourbonnais** *Also called Greg Lambert Construction* ***(G-2397)***
**Lamboo Inc** .......... 866 966-2999
311 W Edwards St Litchfield (62056) ***(G-13692)***
**Lamboo Technologies LLC** .......... 866 966-2999
311 W Edwards St Litchfield (62056) ***(G-13693)***
**Lambright Distributors** .......... 217 543-2083
35 E Cr 200 N Arthur (61911) ***(G-907)***
**Lamco Advertising Specialties, Chicago** *Also called Laminet Cover Company* ***(G-5451)***
**Lamco Slings & Rigging Inc** .......... 309 764-7400
4960 41st Street Ct Moline (61265) ***(G-14952)***
**Laminarp** .......... 847 884-9298
1670 Basswood Rd Schaumburg (60173) ***(G-19611)***
**Laminart Inc** .......... 800 323-7624
1670 Basswood Rd Schaumburg (60173) ***(G-19612)***
**Laminate Craft, Lincolnwood** *Also called Yazdan Essie* ***(G-13544)***
**Laminated Components Inc** .......... 815 648-4811
12204 Hansen Rd Hebron (60034) ***(G-11723)***
**Laminated Designs Countertops** .......... 815 877-7222
9731 N 2nd St Machesney Park (61115) ***(G-14088)***
**Lamination Specialties Corp (PA)** .......... 312 243-2181
235 N Artesian Ave Chicago (60612) ***(G-5449)***
**Lamination Specialties Corp** .......... 773 254-7500
4444 S Kildare Ave Chicago (60632) ***(G-5450)***
**Laminet Cover Company** .......... 773 622-6700
4900 W Bloomingdale Ave Chicago (60639) ***(G-5451)***
**Laminting Bnding Solutions Inc** .......... 847 573-0375
27885 Irma Lee Cir Lake Forest (60045) ***(G-12922)***
**Lamonica Ornamental Iron Works** .......... 773 638-6633
3311 W Chicago Ave Chicago (60651) ***(G-5452)***
**Lamons Gasket Company** .......... 815 744-3902
3305 Corporate Dr Joliet (60431) ***(G-12532)***
**Lamp Co of America Inc** .......... 630 584-4001
214 S 13th Ave Saint Charles (60174) ***(G-19207)***
**Lampe Publications** .......... 309 741-9790
401 W Main St Elmwood (61529) ***(G-9964)***
**Lampholders Assemblies Inc** .......... 773 205-0005
4106 N Nashville Ave Chicago (60634) ***(G-5453)***
**Lampley Oil Inc** .......... 618 439-6288
720 W Main St Benton (62812) ***(G-2034)***
**Lampshade Inc** .......... 773 522-2300
4041 W Ogden Ave Ste 1 Chicago (60623) ***(G-5454)***
**Lamson Oil Company (HQ)** .......... 815 226-8090
2217 20th Ave Rockford (61104) ***(G-18461)***
**Lana Jewelry, Lake Forest** *Also called Lana Unlimited Co* ***(G-12923)***
**Lana Unlimited Co (PA)** .......... 312 226-7050
736 N Western Ave Ste 308 Lake Forest (60045) ***(G-12923)***
**Lancer Manufacturing Inc (PA)** .......... 630 595-1150
301 Beinoris Dr Wood Dale (60191) ***(G-22389)***
**Lanco International Inc (PA)** .......... 708 596-5200
3111 167th St Hazel Crest (60429) ***(G-11709)***
**Land of Nod, The, Chicago** *Also called Meadowbrook LLC* ***(G-5672)***
**Land OFrost Inc (PA)** .......... 708 474-7100
16850 Chicago Ave Lansing (60438) ***(G-13169)***
**Land-O-Tackle, Bensenville** *Also called Plastech Inc* ***(G-1964)***
**Landairsea Systems Inc** .......... 847 462-8100
2040 Dillard Ct Woodstock (60098) ***(G-22581)***
**Landau Real Estate Svcs LLC** .......... 312 379-9146
9936 S Green St Chicago (60643) ***(G-5455)***
**Landau RES, Chicago** *Also called Landau Real Estate Svcs LLC* ***(G-5455)***
**Landauer Inc (PA)** .......... 708 755-7000
2 Science Rd Glenwood (60425) ***(G-11218)***
**Landcraft Auto & Marine Inc** .......... 708 385-0717
13626 Cicero Ave Crestwood (60445) ***(G-7492)***
**Landcraft Marine, Crestwood** *Also called Landcraft Auto & Marine Inc* ***(G-7492)***
**Landis Plastics, Alsip** *Also called Berry Global Inc* ***(G-441)***
**Landman Dental** .......... 312 266-6480
625 N Michigan Ave # 1020 Chicago (60611) ***(G-5456)***
**Landmarx Screen Printing** .......... 217 223-4601
3902 Payson Rd Quincy (62305) ***(G-17853)***
**Landquist & Son Inc** .......... 847 674-6600
9850 W 190th St Ste L Mokena (60448) ***(G-14878)***
**Landsberg Chicago, Lombard** *Also called Orora North America* ***(G-13839)***
**Lane Construction Corporation** .......... 815 846-4466
611 W Jefferson St 201aa Shorewood (60404) ***(G-19929)***
**Lane Industries Inc (PA)** .......... 847 498-6650
1200 Shermer Rd Ste 400 Northbrook (60062) ***(G-16292)***
**Lane Technical Sales Inc** .......... 773 775-1613
6465 N Avondale Ave Chicago (60631) ***(G-5457)***
**Lane Tool & Mfg Co Inc** .......... 847 622-1506
655 Sundown Rd South Elgin (60177) ***(G-20216)***
**Lang Dental Mfg Co Inc** .......... 847 215-6622
175 Messner Dr Wheeling (60090) ***(G-22089)***
**Lang Exterior Inc (PA)** .......... 773 737-4500
2323 W 59th St Chicago (60636) ***(G-5458)***
**Lang Exterior Mfg Co, Chicago** *Also called Lang Exterior Inc* ***(G-5458)***
**Langa Resource Group Inc** .......... 618 462-1899
705 Belle St Alton (62002) ***(G-581)***
**Lange Electric Inc** .......... 217 347-7626
912 E Fayette Ave Effingham (62401) ***(G-8843)***
**Lange Sign Group** .......... 815 747-2448
1780 Il Route 35 N East Dubuque (61025) ***(G-8619)***
**Langham Engineering** .......... 815 223-5250
1414 Shooting Park Rd Peru (61354) ***(G-17516)***
**Langheim Ready Mix Inc** .......... 217 625-2351
110 E Jefferson St Girard (62640) ***(G-10947)***
**Langston Bag of Peoria LLC** .......... 309 676-1006
1114 Sw Adams St Peoria (61602) ***(G-17399)***
**Lanigan Holdings LLC (PA)** .......... 708 596-5200
3111 167th St Hazel Crest (60429) ***(G-11710)***
**Laninver USA Inc (PA)** .......... 847 367-8787
2800 Carl Bulevard Elk Grove Village (60007) ***(G-9583)***
**Lanmar Inc** .......... 800 233-5520
3160 Doolittle Dr Northbrook (60062) ***(G-16293)***
**Lans Printing Inc** .......... 708 895-6226
2581 Glenwd Lansing Rd A Lynwood (60411) ***(G-14021)***
**Lansa Inc** .......... 630 874-7042
2001 Butterfield Rd # 102 Downers Grove (60515) ***(G-8472)***
**Lansing Cut Stone Co** .......... 708 474-7515
3125 Glenwood Lansing Rd Lansing (60438) ***(G-13170)***
**Lansing Wings Inc** .......... 708 895-3300
3720 Ridge Rd Lansing (60438) ***(G-13171)***
**Lantech Logistics, Hazel Crest** *Also called Lanco International Inc* ***(G-11709)***
**Lanterna Medical Tech USA** .......... 847 446-9995
821 Foxdale Ave Winnetka (60093) ***(G-22309)***
**Lanxess Corporation** .......... 630 789-8440
7330 S Madison St Willowbrook (60527) ***(G-22219)***
**Lanxess Solutions US Inc** .......... 309 633-9480
8220 W Route 24 Mapleton (61547) ***(G-14211)***
**Lanzatech Inc (HQ)** .......... 630 439-3050
8045 Lamon Ave Ste 400 Skokie (60077) ***(G-20025)***
**Lapham-Hickey Steel Corp (PA)** .......... 708 496-6111
5500 W 73rd St Chicago (60638) ***(G-5459)***
**Laqueus Inc** .......... 773 508-1993
7435 N Western Ave Chicago (60645) ***(G-5460)***
**Larckers Recycling Svcs Inc** .......... 630 922-0759
3119 Reflection Dr Naperville (60564) ***(G-15813)***
**Laredo Foods Inc** .......... 773 762-1500
3401 W Cermak Rd Chicago (60623) ***(G-5461)***
**Laredo Spices & Herbs, Chicago** *Also called Laredo Foods Inc* ***(G-5461)***
**Larentia Led LLC** .......... 312 291-9111
2010 W Fulton St Chicago (60612) ***(G-5462)***
**Lares Technologies LLC** .......... 630 408-4368
748 Charismatic Dr Oswego (60543) ***(G-16925)***
**Laron Oil Corporation** .......... 847 836-2000
14 N 679 Rr 25 Dundee (60118) ***(G-8563)***
**Larry Musgrave Logging** .......... 618 842-6386
414 Nw 6th St Fairfield (62837) ***(G-10148)***
**Larry Pontnack** .......... 815 732-7751
6309 E Brick Rd Oregon (61061) ***(G-16827)***
**Larry Ragan** .......... 618 698-1041
3809 Rolling Meadows Dr Belleville (62221) ***(G-1648)***
**Larrys Better Built Battery** .......... 618 758-2011
9321 Deer Run Ln Coulterville (62237) ***(G-7401)***

**Larrys Garage & Machine Shop** ....815 968-8416
101 Vista Ter Rockford (61102) *(G-18462)*
**Larsen & Toubro Infotech Ltd** ....847 303-3900
1821 Walden Office Sq # 400 Schaumburg (60173) *(G-19613)*
**Larsen Envelope Co Inc** ....847 952-9020
165 Gaylord St Elk Grove Village (60007) *(G-9584)*
**Larsen Manufacturing LLC (PA)** ....847 970-9600
1201 Allanson Rd Mundelein (60060) *(G-15519)*
**Larson Hardware Manufacturing, Rock Falls** *Also called Chas O Larson Co (G-18129)*
**Larson-Juhl US LLC** ....630 307-9700
550 Congress Cir N Roselle (60172) *(G-18951)*
**Las Systems Inc** ....847 462-8100
2040 Dillard Ct Woodstock (60098) *(G-22582)*
**Lasalle Chemical & Supply Co** ....847 470-1234
6108 Madison Ct Morton Grove (60053) *(G-15211)*
**Lasalle Chemical Co., Morton Grove** *Also called Lasalle Chemical & Supply Co (G-15211)*
**Laser Art Studio, Chicago** *Also called Presentation Studios Intl LLC (G-6180)*
**Laser Center Corporation** ....630 422-1975
401 Eastern Ave Bensenville (60106) *(G-1938)*
**Laser Creations, South Beloit** *Also called Walnut Creek Hardwood (G-20173)*
**Laser Energy Systems** ....815 282-8200
4924 Torque Rd Loves Park (61111) *(G-13959)*
**Laser Expressions Ltd** ....847 419-9600
165 N Arlngton Hgts Rd Buffalo Grove (60089) *(G-2721)*
**Laser Images, Quincy** *Also called Kevin Kewney (G-17844)*
**Laser Innovations Inc** ....217 522-8580
2276 North Grand Ave E Springfield (62702) *(G-20467)*
**Laser Plus Technologies LLC** ....847 787-9017
2450 American Ln Elk Grove Village (60007) *(G-9585)*
**Laser Pro** ....847 742-1055
978 N Mclean Blvd Elgin (60123) *(G-9093)*
**Laser Products Industries Inc** ....877 679-1300
1344 Enterprise Dr Romeoville (60446) *(G-18836)*
**Laser Reproductions Inc** ....847 410-0397
8228 Mccormick Blvd Skokie (60076) *(G-20026)*
**Laser Technologies Inc** ....630 761-1200
1120 Frontenac Rd Naperville (60563) *(G-15686)*
**Laser Technology Group Inc** ....847 524-4088
1029 Charlela Ln Apt 407 Elk Grove Village (60007) *(G-9586)*
**Laser Tek Industries, Spring Grove** *Also called Tonerhead Inc (G-20369)*
**Laserage, Waukegan** *Also called Ltc Holdings Inc (G-21585)*
**Lasersketch Ltd** ....630 243-6360
1319 Enterprise Dr Romeoville (60446) *(G-18837)*
**Lashcon Inc** ....217 742-3186
540 Coultas Rd Winchester (62694) *(G-22281)*
**Lasner Beauty Supply, Chicago** *Also called Lasner Bros Inc (G-5463)*
**Lasner Bros Inc** ....773 935-7383
3649 N Ashland Ave Chicago (60613) *(G-5463)*
**Lason Inc** ....217 893-1515
1000 S Perimeter Rd Rantoul (61866) *(G-17933)*
**Lasons Label Co** ....773 775-2606
5666 N Northwest Hwy Chicago (60646) *(G-5464)*
**Last Minute Copy Shop, Tinley Park** *Also called Last Minute Prtg & Copy Ctr (G-20929)*
**Last Minute Gourmet, Chicago** *Also called Taylor Farms Illinois Inc (G-6680)*
**Last Minute Prtg & Copy Ctr** ....888 788-2965
8201 183rd St Ste C Tinley Park (60487) *(G-20929)*
**Lathom Pin - Div, Loves Park** *Also called Ford Tool & Machining Inc (G-13941)*
**Latino Arts & Communications** ....773 501-0029
3514 W Diversey Ave 212 Chicago (60647) *(G-5465)*
**Lattice Energy LLC** ....312 861-0115
175 N Harbor Dr Apt 3205 Chicago (60601) *(G-5466)*
**Lattice Incorporated** ....630 949-3250
1751 S Nprvlle Rd Ste 100 Wheaton (60189) *(G-21964)*
**Lau Nae Winery Inc** ....618 282-9463
1522 State Route 3 Red Bud (62278) *(G-17944)*
**Lauber Tool Co Inc** ....847 228-5969
170 Seegers Ave Elk Grove Village (60007) *(G-9587)*
**Laughing Dog Graphics** ....309 392-3330
207 N Main Ave Minier (61759) *(G-14833)*
**Laundry Services Company** ....630 327-9329
4805 Pershing Ave Downers Grove (60515) *(G-8473)*
**Laundryworld, Chicago** *Also called Lloyd M Hughes Enterprises Inc (G-5527)*
**Laurel Industries Inc** ....847 432-8204
280 Laurel Ave Highland Park (60035) *(G-11851)*
**Laurel Manufacturing LLC** ....773 961-8545
5700 N Lincoln Ave # 203 Chicago (60659) *(G-5467)*
**Laurel Metal Products Inc** ....847 674-0064
3500 W Touhy Ave Skokie (60076) *(G-20027)*
**Lauren Lein Ltd** ....312 527-1714
208 W Kinzie St Ste 3 Chicago (60654) *(G-5468)*
**Laurenceleste Inc** ....708 383-3432
230 Clinton Ave Oak Park (60302) *(G-16674)*
**Laux Grafix Inc** ....618 337-4558
3709 Mississippi Ave East Saint Louis (62206) *(G-8759)*
**Lavell General Handyman Svcs** ....773 691-3101
8150 S Anthony Ave Chicago (60617) *(G-5469)*
**Lavender Crest Winery** ....309 949-2565
5401 Us Highway 6 Colona (61241) *(G-7344)*
**Laverns Wood Items** ....217 268-4544
421 E County Road 200n Arcola (61910) *(G-674)*
**Lavezzi Precision Inc** ....630 582-1230
250 Madsen Dr Bloomingdale (60108) *(G-2112)*
**Law Bulletin Publishing Co (PA)** ....312 416-1860
415 N State St Ste 1 Chicago (60654) *(G-5470)*
**Law Bulletin Publishing Co** ....847 883-9100
1360 Abbott Ct Buffalo Grove (60089) *(G-2722)*
**Lawlor Family Winery, Galena** *Also called Galena Cellars Winery (G-10720)*
**Lawlor Family Winery, Galena** *Also called Galena Cellars Winery (G-10721)*
**Lawlor Marketing** ....847 357-1080
2035 S Arlington Hts Rd Arlington Heights (60005) *(G-791)*
**Lawndale Forging & Tool Works** ....773 277-2800
2141 S Spaulding Ave Chicago (60623) *(G-5471)*
**Lawndale News, Cicero** *Also called Lawndale Press Inc (G-7214)*
**Lawndale Press Inc (PA)** ....708 656-6900
5533 W 25th St Cicero (60804) *(G-7214)*
**Lawrence Allen** ....618 786-3794
21031 State Highway 3 Grafton (62037) *(G-11255)*
**Lawrence Foods Inc** ....847 437-2400
2200 Lunt Ave Elk Grove Village (60007) *(G-9588)*
**Lawrence J L & Co Dental Labs, Mattoon** *Also called J L Lawrence & Co (G-14394)*
**Lawrence Maddock** ....847 394-1698
500 S Arthur Ave Arlington Heights (60005) *(G-792)*
**Lawrence Oil Company Inc** ....618 262-4138
801 W 9th St Rm 208 Mount Carmel (62863) *(G-15272)*
**Lawrence Packaging Intl** ....630 682-2600
1761 S Nprvlle Rd Ste 201 Wheaton (60189) *(G-21965)*
**Lawrence Rgan Cmmnications Inc (PA)** ....312 960-4100
316 N Michigan Ave # 400 Chicago (60601) *(G-5472)*
**Lawrence Screw Products Inc (PA)** ....708 867-5150
7230 W Wilson Ave Harwood Heights (60706) *(G-11686)*
**Lawrence Screw Products Inc** ....217 735-1230
437 8th St Lincoln (62656) *(G-13412)*
**Lawter Inc (HQ)** ....312 662-5700
200 N La Salle St # 2600 Chicago (60601) *(G-5473)*
**Layco, Marshall** *Also called Yargus Manufacturing Inc (G-14331)*
**Lays Mining Service Inc** ....618 244-6570
1121 S 10th St Mount Vernon (62864) *(G-15421)*
**Laystrom Manufacturing Co** ....773 342-4800
3900 W Palmer St Chicago (60647) *(G-5474)*
**Lazare Printing Co Inc** ....773 871-2500
709 W Wrightwood Ave # 1 Chicago (60614) *(G-5475)*
**Lb Staley Elmwood, Canton** *Also called Canton Redi-Mix Inc (G-2984)*
**Lbe Ltd** ....847 907-4959
21038 N Andover Rd Kildeer (60047) *(G-12701)*
**Lbl Lighting LLC (PA)** ....708 755-2100
7400 Linder Ave Skokie (60077) *(G-20028)*
**Lbp Manufacturing LLC (PA)** ....800 545-6200
1325 S Cicero Ave Cicero (60804) *(G-7215)*
**Lbs Marketing Ltd** ....815 965-5234
1525 Kilburn Ave Rockford (61101) *(G-18463)*
**Lc Holdings of Delaware Inc (PA)** ....847 940-3550
500 Lake Cook Rd Ste 430 Deerfield (60015) *(G-8028)*
**LC Industries Inc** ....312 455-0500
2781 Katherine Way Elk Grove Village (60007) *(G-9589)*
**Lcg Sales Inc** ....773 378-7455
5410 W Roosevelt Rd # 231 Chicago (60644) *(G-5476)*
**Lcr Hallcrest Llc (PA)** ....847 998-8580
1911 Pickwick Ln Glenview (60026) *(G-11165)*
**Lcv Company** ....309 738-6452
919 15th Ave East Moline (61244) *(G-8685)*
**LDI Industries Inc** ....847 669-7510
12901 Jim Dhamer Dr Huntley (60142) *(G-12157)*
**LDR Global Industries LLC** ....773 265-3000
600 N Kilbourn Ave Chicago (60624) *(G-5477)*
**Le Claire Investment Inc (HQ)** ....309 757-8250
1701 5th Ave Moline (61265) *(G-14953)*
**Le Petit Pain Holdings LLC (PA)** ....312 981-3770
676 N Michigan Ave Chicago (60611) *(G-5478)*
**Le Print Express, Dekalb** *Also called Nancy J Perkins (G-8107)*
**Lea & Sachs Inc (PA)** ....847 296-8000
1267 Rand Rd Des Plaines (60016) *(G-8221)*
**Lead n Glass Tm** ....847 255-2074
2039 Foster Ave Ste A Wheeling (60090) *(G-22090)*
**Leader** ....217 469-0045
429 E Warren St Saint Joseph (61873) *(G-19316)*
**Leader Accessories LLC** ....877 662-9808
14225 Hansberry Rd Rockton (61072) *(G-18698)*
**Leader Union Publishing, Fairbury** *Also called American Publishing Co Inc (G-10121)*
**Leading Edge Group Inc (PA)** ....815 316-3500
1800 16th Ave Rockford (61104) *(G-18464)*
**Leading Edge Hydraulics, Rockford** *Also called Leading Edge Group Inc (G-18464)*
**Leading Energy Designs Ltd** ....815 382-8852
440 Lawndale Ave Woodstock (60098) *(G-22583)*
**Leading Lady Company, Neoga** *Also called Golda Inc (G-15858)*
**Leaffilter North LLC** ....630 595-9605
587 N Edgewood Ave Wood Dale (60191) *(G-22390)*
**Leahy-Ifp Company, Glenview** *Also called Institutional Foods Packing Co (G-11148)*

ALPHABETIC

**Lean Protein Team LLC**...440 525-1532
235 W Van Buren St Chicago (60607) *(G-5479)*
**Leanoptima LLC**...847 648-1592
1311 N Deer Ave Palatine (60067) *(G-17049)*
**Leapfrog Product Dev LLC**...312 229-0089
159 N Racine Ave Ste 3e Chicago (60607) *(G-5480)*
**Learjet Inc**...847 553-0172
251 Wille Rd Ste A Des Plaines (60018) *(G-8222)*
**Learning Curve International (HQ)**...630 573-7200
1111 W 22nd St Ste 320 Oak Brook (60523) *(G-16533)*
**Learning Resources Inc (PA)**...847 573-9471
380 N Fairway Dr Vernon Hills (60061) *(G-21181)*
**Learning Seed LLC**...847 540-8855
208 S Jefferson St # 402 Chicago (60661) *(G-5481)*
**Leas Baking Company LLC**...708 710-3404
14660 Pebble Creek Ct Homer Glen (60491) *(G-12082)*
**Leasing Dynamics, Saint Charles** *Also called Water Dynamics Inc (G-19292)*
**Leatherneck Hardware Inc**...217 431-3096
1017 Bahls St Danville (61832) *(G-7745)*
**Lebanon Chemical, Danville** *Also called Lebanon Seaboard Corporation (G-7746)*
**Lebanon Seaboard Corporation**...217 446-0983
508 W Ross Ln Danville (61834) *(G-7746)*
**Lebolt Print Service Inc**...847 681-1210
802 Stables Ct E Highwood (60040) *(G-11886)*
**Lechler Inc**...630 377-6611
445 Kautz Rd Saint Charles (60174) *(G-19208)*
**Lecip Inc**...312 626-2525
881 Il Route 83 Bensenville (60106) *(G-1939)*
**Lectro Graphics Inc**...847 537-3592
851 Seton Ct Ste 1b Wheeling (60090) *(G-22091)*
**Lectro Stik Corp**...630 894-1355
1957 Quincy Ct Glendale Heights (60139) *(G-11040)*
**Led Business Solutions LLC**...844 464-5337
433 Maple Ave Downers Grove (60515) *(G-8474)*
**Led Industries Inc**...888 700-7815
3001 N Us Highway 12 Spring Grove (60081) *(G-20345)*
**Led Lighting Inc**...847 412-4880
1555 Barclay Blvd Buffalo Grove (60089) *(G-2723)*
**LED Rite LLC**...847 683-8000
120 Rowell Rd Hampshire (60140) *(G-11553)*
**Led Signs Led Lighting, Chicago** *Also called GL Led LLC (G-4953)*
**Ledcor Construction Inc**...630 916-1200
18w140 Butterfield Rd Oakbrook Terrace (60181) *(G-16714)*
**Ledretrofitting Inc**...815 347-5047
2n138 Bernice Ave Glen Ellyn (60137) *(G-10975)*
**Lee Allison Company Inc**...773 276-7172
1820 W Webster Ave # 301 Chicago (60614) *(G-5482)*
**Lee Armand & Co Ltd**...312 455-1200
840 N Milwaukee Ave Chicago (60642) *(G-5483)*
**Lee Brothers Welding Inc**...309 342-6017
575 Lincoln St Galesburg (61401) *(G-10765)*
**Lee Electric**...618 244-6810
11689 E Il Highway 148 Mount Vernon (62864) *(G-15422)*
**Lee Enterprises Incorporated**...309 829-9000
301 W Washington St Bloomington (61701) *(G-2193)*
**Lee Enterprises Incorporated**...217 421-8955
1605 N Brant Ct Decatur (62521) *(G-7905)*
**Lee Enterprises Incorporated**...309 743-0800
1521 47th Ave Moline (61265) *(G-14954)*
**Lee Enterprises Incorporated**...618 998-8499
3000 W Deyoung St Ste 336 Marion (62959) *(G-14270)*
**Lee Enterprises Incorporated**...217 421-6920
601 E William St Decatur (62523) *(G-7906)*
**Lee Enterprises Incorporated**...618 529-5454
710 N Illinois Ave Carbondale (62901) *(G-3014)*
**Lee Enterprises Incorporated**...217 421-8940
604 E William St Decatur (62523) *(G-7907)*
**Lee Foss Electric Motor Svc**...708 681-5335
3418 W North Ave Melrose Park (60165) *(G-14670)*
**Lee Gilster-Mary Corporation**...618 826-2361
981 State St Chester (62233) *(G-3658)*
**Lee Gilster-Mary Corporation**...618 965-3426
705 N Sparta St Steeleville (62288) *(G-20561)*
**Lee Gilster-Mary Corporation**...618 443-5676
403 E 4th St Sparta (62286) *(G-20318)*
**Lee Gilster-Mary Corporation**...618 533-4808
100 W Calumet St Centralia (62801) *(G-3421)*
**Lee Gilster-Mary Corporation**...815 472-6456
305 E Washington St Momence (60954) *(G-14983)*
**Lee Gilster-Mary Corporation**...618 965-3449
10 Industrial Park Steeleville (62288) *(G-20562)*
**Lee Industries Inc**...847 462-1865
1900 Pratt Blvd Elk Grove Village (60007) *(G-9590)*
**Lee Jensen Sales Co Inc (PA)**...815 459-0929
101 W Terra Cotta Ave Crystal Lake (60014) *(G-7602)*
**Lee Quigley Company**...708 563-1600
5301 W 65th St Ste D Chicago (60638) *(G-5484)*
**Lee Sauzek**...618 539-5815
316 Silverthorne Dr Freeburg (62243) *(G-10638)*
**Lee Weitzman Furniture Inc**...312 243-3009
1500 S Western Ave Ste 4 Chicago (60608) *(G-5485)*
**Lee-Wel Printing Corporation**...630 682-0935
1554 S County Farm Rd Wheaton (60189) *(G-21966)*
**Leeco Steel Products**...630 427-2100
1011 Warrenville Rd # 500 Lisle (60532) *(G-13617)*
**Leesons Cakes Inc**...708 429-1330
6713 163rd Pl Tinley Park (60477) *(G-20930)*
**Leg Up LLC**...312 282-2725
639 W Diversey Pkwy # 205 Chicago (60614) *(G-5486)*
**Legacy 3d LLC**...815 727-5454
2020 N Raynor Ave Crest Hill (60403) *(G-7462)*
**Legacy Audio, Springfield** *Also called Acoustic Avenue Inc (G-20385)*
**Legacy Foods Mfg LLC**...224 639-5297
498 Franklin Ln Elk Grove Village (60007) *(G-9591)*
**Legacy Foods Mfg LLC**...847 595-9106
2775 Katherine Way Elk Grove Village (60007) *(G-9592)*
**Legacy International Assoc LLC**...847 823-1602
1420 Park Ridge Blvd Park Ridge (60068) *(G-17206)*
**Legacy Plastics Inc**...815 226-3013
5040 27th Ave Rockford (61109) *(G-18465)*
**Legacy Prints**...815 946-9112
607 S Division Ave Polo (61064) *(G-17688)*
**Legacy Vulcan LLC**...630 955-8500
1000 E Warrenville Rd Naperville (60563) *(G-15687)*
**Legacy Vulcan LLC**...815 468-8141
6141 N Rte 50 Manteno (60950) *(G-14186)*
**Legacy Vulcan LLC**...847 437-4181
1520 Midway Ct Elk Grove Village (60007) *(G-9593)*
**Legacy Vulcan LLC**...217 932-2611
9129 N 230th St Casey (62420) *(G-3388)*
**Legacy Vulcan LLC**...815 726-6900
595 W Laraway Rd Joliet (60436) *(G-12533)*
**Legacy Vulcan LLC**...773 890-2360
3910 S Racine Ave Chicago (60609) *(G-5487)*
**Legacy Vulcan LLC**...217 963-2196
2855 S Lincoln Memorial P Decatur (62522) *(G-7908)*
**Legacy Vulcan LLC**...630 739-0182
1361 Joliet Rd Romeoville (60446) *(G-18838)*
**Legacy Vulcan LLC**...217 498-7263
1200 Jostes Rd Rochester (62563) *(G-18119)*
**Legacy Vulcan LLC**...708 485-6602
5500 Joliet Rd Mc Cook (60525) *(G-14450)*
**Legacy Vulcan LLC**...815 895-6501
12502 Lloyd Rd Sycamore (60178) *(G-20807)*
**Legacy Vulcan LLC**...217 963-2196
2855 Lincoln Pkwy Harristown (62537) *(G-11607)*
**Legacy Vulcan LLC**...815 436-3535
Rr 126 Plainfield (60544) *(G-17617)*
**Legacy Vulcan LLC**...847 578-9622
29821 N Skokie Hwy Lake Bluff (60044) *(G-12853)*
**Legacy Vulcan LLC**...847 548-4623
875 S State Route 83 Grayslake (60030) *(G-11350)*
**Legacy Vulcan LLC**...630 904-1110
22933 W Hassert Blvd Plainfield (60585) *(G-17618)*
**Legacy Vulcan Corp**...815 937-7928
1277 S 7000w Rd Kankakee (60901) *(G-12637)*
**Legacy Woodwork Inc**...847 451-7602
9137 Cherry Ave Franklin Park (60131) *(G-10515)*
**Legal Files Software Inc**...217 726-6000
801 S Durkin Dr Ste A Springfield (62704) *(G-20468)*
**Legend Creative Group, Lake Zurich** *Also called Legend Promotions (G-13095)*
**Legend Dynamix Inc**...847 789-7007
77 Mcmillen Rd Ste 106 Antioch (60002) *(G-641)*
**Legend Engraving Company, Antioch** *Also called Legend Dynamix Inc (G-641)*
**Legend Promotions**...847 438-3528
815 Oakwood Rd Ste B Lake Zurich (60047) *(G-13095)*
**Legend Racing Enterprises Inc**...847 923-8979
616 Morse Ave Schaumburg (60193) *(G-19614)*
**Legendary Baking, Oak Forest** *Also called American Blue Rbbon Hldngs LLC (G-16573)*
**Leggero Foods**...815 871-9640
2625 N Mulford Rd 134 Rockford (61114) *(G-18466)*
**Leggett & Platt Incorporated**...
13535 S Torrence Ave Chicago (60633) *(G-5488)*
**Leggett & Platt Incorporated**...708 458-1800
205 W Wacker Dr Ste 922 Chicago (60606) *(G-5489)*
**Leggett & Platt Incorporated**...847 768-6139
1798 Sherwin Ave Des Plaines (60018) *(G-8223)*
**Leggett & Platt Incorporated**...815 233-0022
1555 Il Route 75 E Ste 2 Freeport (61032) *(G-10672)*
**Leggett & Platt 0338, Chicago** *Also called Leggett & Platt Incorporated (G-5490)*
**Leggett & Platt 0351, Freeport** *Also called Leggett & Platt Incorporated (G-10672)*
**Leggett & Platt 0n09, North Aurora** *Also called Leggett & Platt Incorporated (G-16138)*
**Leggett & Platt Incorporated**...708 458-1800
6755 W 65th St Chicago (60638) *(G-5490)*
**Leggett & Platt Incorporated**...630 801-0609
241 Airport Rd North Aurora (60542) *(G-16138)*
**Leggs Manufacturing**...618 842-9847
900 W Delaware St Fairfield (62837) *(G-10149)*

**Legible Signs Group Corp** ....815 654-0100
2221 Nimtz Rd Loves Park (61111) ***(G-13960)***
**Legislative Printing** ....217 782-7312
401 S Spring St Springfield (62706) ***(G-20469)***
**Legistek LLC** ....312 399-4891
211 W Wacker Dr 201 Chicago (60606) ***(G-5491)***
**Legna Iron Works Inc** ....630 894-8056
80 Central Ave Roselle (60172) ***(G-18952)***
**Lehigh Consumer Products LLC (HQ)** ....630 851-7330
3901 Liberty St Aurora (60504) ***(G-1045)***
**Lehigh Group, The, Aurora** *Also called Lehigh Consumer Products LLC* ***(G-1045)***
**Lehman Fast Tech** ....847 742-5202
37w468 Elmer Ct Elgin (60124) ***(G-9094)***
**Lei Graphics, Alsip** *Also called Luttrell Engraving Inc* ***(G-485)***
**Leica McRosystems Holdings Inc** ....800 248-0123
1700 Leider Ln Buffalo Grove (60089) ***(G-2724)***
**Leica Microsystems Inc** ....847 405-0123
1700 Leider Ln Buffalo Grove (60089) ***(G-2725)***
**Leica Microsystems Inc (HQ)** ....847 405-0123
1700 Leider Ln Buffalo Grove (60089) ***(G-2726)***
**Leisure Properties LLC** ....618 937-6426
11884 Country Club Rd West Frankfort (62896) ***(G-21811)***
**Leisure Time Products Inc** ....847 287-2863
101 Patricia Ln Prospect Heights (60070) ***(G-17782)***
**LELAND HOUSE, Chicago** *Also called Cornerstone Community Outreach* ***(G-4472)***
**Lemaitre Vascular Inc** ....847 462-2191
912 Northwest Hwy Ste 106 Fox River Grove (60021) ***(G-10288)***
**Lemanski Heating & AC** ....815 232-4519
1398 S Armstrong Ave Freeport (61032) ***(G-10673)***
**Lemfco Inc** ....815 777-0242
100 S Comm St Galena (61036) ***(G-10729)***
**Lemke Machine Products Inc** ....815 338-1560
629 W Kimball Ave Woodstock (60098) ***(G-22584)***
**Lemko Corporation** ....630 948-3025
1 Pierce Pl Ste 700w Itasca (60143) ***(G-12302)***
**Lemont Scrap Processing** ....630 257-6532
16229 New Ave Lemont (60439) ***(G-13239)***
**Lemoy International Inc (PA)** ....847 427-0840
95 King St Elk Grove Village (60007) ***(G-9594)***
**Lena AJS Maid Meats** ....815 369-4522
500 W Main St Lena (61048) ***(G-13277)***
**Lena Mercantile** ....815 369-9955
101 W Railroad St Lena (61048) ***(G-13278)***
**Lena Sign Shop** ....815 369-9090
109 W Railroad St Lena (61048) ***(G-13279)***
**Lenco Electronics Inc** ....815 344-2900
1330 S Belden St McHenry (60050) ***(G-14520)***
**Lenhardt Tool and Die Company** ....618 462-1075
3400 Bloomer Dr Alton (62002) ***(G-582)***
**Lennox Industries Inc** ....630 378-7054
860 W Crossroads Pkwy Romeoville (60446) ***(G-18839)***
**Lenova Inc (PA)** ....312 733-1098
4580 Roosevelt Rd Hillside (60162) ***(G-11924)***
**Lenrok Industries Inc** ....630 628-1946
542 W Winthrop Ave Addison (60101) ***(G-179)***
**Lens Lenticlear Lenticular** ....630 467-0900
19w030 Marino Ct Itasca (60143) ***(G-12303)***
**Lenscrafters Crafters** ....618 632-2312
271 Saint Clair Sq Fairview Heights (62208) ***(G-10170)***
**Leo A Bachrach Jewelers Inc** ....312 263-3111
55 E Washington St # 801 Chicago (60602) ***(G-5492)***
**Leo Bachrach and Son, Chicago** *Also called Leo A Bachrach Jewelers Inc* ***(G-5492)***
**Leo Burnett Company Inc (HQ)** ....312 220-5959
35 W Wacker Dr Fl 21 Chicago (60601) ***(G-5493)***
**Leonard A Unes Printing Co** ....309 674-4942
619 Spring St Peoria (61603) ***(G-17400)***
**Leonard Associates Inc** ....815 226-9609
6733 Hedgewood Rd Rockford (61108) ***(G-18467)***
**Leonard Emerson** ....217 628-3441
103 W Dodds St Divernon (62530) ***(G-8316)***
**Leonard Publishing Co** ....773 486-2737
7508 W Belle Plaine Ave Norridge (60706) ***(G-16104)***
**Leonard's Guide, Arlington Heights** *Also called G R Leonard & Co Inc* ***(G-758)***
**Leonards Bakery** ....847 564-4977
2776 Dundee Rd Northbrook (60062) ***(G-16294)***
**Leonards Unit Step Co** ....815 744-1263
1515 Channahon Rd Rockdale (60436) ***(G-18225)***
**Leonards Unit Step of Moline** ....309 792-9641
24415 Ridge Rd Colona (61241) ***(G-7345)***
**Leos Dancewear Inc** ....773 889-7700
7601 North Ave River Forest (60305) ***(G-17998)***
**Leos Sign** ....773 227-2460
1334 N Kostner Ave Chicago (60651) ***(G-5494)***
**Leppala Machining Inc** ....847 625-0270
12726d W Wadsworth Rd Beach Park (60087) ***(G-1518)***
**Lerner New York, Geneva** *Also called New York & Company Inc* ***(G-10853)***
**Leroys Plastic Co Inc** ....630 898-7006
1650 Mountain St Aurora (60505) ***(G-1182)***
**Leroys Welding & Fabg Inc** ....847 215-6151
363 Alice St Wheeling (60090) ***(G-22092)***
**Les Wilson Inc** ....618 382-4667
205 Industrial Ave Carmi (62821) ***(G-3073)***
**Lesker Company Inc** ....708 343-2277
528 N York Rd Bensenville (60106) ***(G-1940)***
**Lessabah Arts Center, Oak Park** *Also called Freitas P Sabah* ***(G-16664)***
**Lessy Messy LLC** ....708 790-7589
3143 Aviara Ct Naperville (60564) ***(G-15814)***
**Lester Building Systems LLC** ....217 348-7676
890 W State St Charleston (61920) ***(G-3603)***
**Lester L Brossard Co** ....815 338-7825
930 Dieckman St Woodstock (60098) ***(G-22585)***
**Lester Lampert Inc** ....312 944-6888
57 E Oak St Chicago (60611) ***(G-5495)***
**Lester Manufacturing Inc** ....815 986-1172
2219 N Central Ave Rockford (61101) ***(G-18468)***
**Letellier Material Hdlg Eqp, South Holland** *Also called Peerless Chain Company* ***(G-20297)***
**Letraw Manufacturing Co** ....815 987-9670
200 Quaker Rd Ste 2 Rockford (61104) ***(G-18469)***
**Letter-Rite Express LLC** ....847 678-1100
1660 Wind Song Ln Aurora (60504) ***(G-1046)***
**Lettering Specialists Inc** ....847 674-3414
8020 Lawndale Ave Skokie (60076) ***(G-20029)***
**Lettermen Signage Inc** ....708 479-5161
19912 Wolf Rd Mokena (60448) ***(G-14879)***
**Letters Unlimited Inc** ....847 891-7811
1010 Morse Ave Ste E Schaumburg (60193) ***(G-19615)***
**Levi Strauss & Co** ....773 486-3900
1552 N Milwaukee Ave Chicago (60622) ***(G-5496)***
**Levi Strauss & Co** ....847 619-0655
5 Woodfeld Shopg Ctr 11 # 114 Schaumburg (60173) ***(G-19616)***
**Leviton Manufacturing Co Inc** ....630 539-0249
471 Fox Ct Bloomingdale (60108) ***(G-2113)***
**Leviton Manufacturing Co Inc** ....630 443-0500
3837 E Main St Ste 331 Saint Charles (60174) ***(G-19209)***
**Leviton Manufacturing Co Inc** ....630 350-2656
700 Golf Ln Bensenville (60106) ***(G-1941)***
**Levolor Window Furnishings Inc** ....800 346-3278
2707 Butterfield Rd Oak Brook (60523) ***(G-16534)***
**Lew Electric Fittings Co** ....630 665-2075
371 Randy Rd Carol Stream (60188) ***(G-3183)***
**Lew-El Tool & Manufacturing Co** ....773 804-1133
1935 N Leclaire Ave Chicago (60639) ***(G-5497)***
**Lewa Acquisition Corp** ....847 940-3535
500 Lake Cook Rd Ste 430 Deerfield (60015) ***(G-8029)***
**Lewis Acquisition Corp** ....773 486-5660
712 W Winthrop Ave Addison (60101) ***(G-180)***
**Lewis Brothers Bakeries Inc** ....618 833-5185
101 Springfield Ave Ste I Anna (62906) ***(G-607)***
**Lewis Machine & Tool Co** ....309 787-7151
1305 11th St W Milan (61264) ***(G-14792)***
**Lewis N Clark Travel ACC, Elk Grove Village** *Also called LC Industries Inc* ***(G-9589)***
**Lewis Paper Place Inc** ....847 808-1343
220 E Marquardt Dr Wheeling (60090) ***(G-22093)***
**Lewis Plastics, Addison** *Also called Lewis Acquisition Corp* ***(G-180)***
**Lewis Process Systems Inc** ....630 510-8200
294 Commonwealth Dr Carol Stream (60188) ***(G-3184)***
**Lewis Spring and Mfg Company (PA)** ....847 588-7030
7500 N Natchez Ave Niles (60714) ***(G-15996)***
**Lex Holding Co** ....708 594-9200
1400 16th St Ste 250 Oak Brook (60523) ***(G-16535)***
**Lexcentral Steel, Oak Brook** *Also called Lexington Steel Corporation* ***(G-16536)***
**Lexi Group Inc** ....866 675-1683
3023 N Clark St Ste 778 Chicago (60657) ***(G-5498)***
**Lexington Leather Goods Co** ....773 287-5500
5414 W Roosevelt Rd Chicago (60644) ***(G-5499)***
**Lexington Steel Corporation** ....708 594-9200
1400 16th St Ste 250 Oak Brook (60523) ***(G-16536)***
**Lexmark International Inc** ....847 318-5700
9700 W Higgins Rd Ste 930 Rosemont (60018) ***(G-19009)***
**Lexpress Inc** ....773 517-7095
1176 Cove Dr Prospect Heights (60070) ***(G-17783)***
**Lexray LLC** ....630 664-6740
3041 Woodcreek Dr Ste 102 Downers Grove (60515) ***(G-8475)***
**Leybold USA Inc** ....724 327-5700
25968 Network Pl Chicago (60673) ***(G-5500)***
**Leyden Lawn Sprinklers** ....630 665-5520
23w274 North Ave Glen Ellyn (60137) ***(G-10976)***
**Lezza Spumoni and Desserts Inc** ....708 547-5969
4009 Saint Charles Rd Bellwood (60104) ***(G-1712)***
**LFA Industries Inc** ....630 762-7391
1820 Wallace Ave Ste 122 Saint Charles (60174) ***(G-19210)***
**Lg Innotek USA Inc** ....847 941-8713
2000 Millbrook Dr Lincolnshire (60069) ***(G-13462)***
**Lgb Industries** ....847 639-1691
91 Fairfield Ln Cary (60013) ***(G-3357)***
**Lhs Inc** ....630 832-3875
188 W Industrial Dr # 26 Elmhurst (60126) ***(G-9901)***
**Ll Gear Inc** ....630 226-1688
1292 Lakeview Dr Romeoville (60446) ***(G-18840)***

ALPHABETIC

Liaison Home Automation LLC
ALPHABETIC SECTION

**Liaison Home Automation LLC**....888 279-1235
111 E Ashland Ave Mount Zion (62549) ***(G-15454)***
**Liam Brex**....630 848-0222
222 S Main St Naperville (60540) ***(G-15688)***
**Libation Container Inc**....312 287-4524
4519 N Mozart St Chicago (60625) ***(G-5501)***
**Libbey Inc**....630 818-3400
1850 Blackhawk Dr West Chicago (60185) ***(G-21731)***
**Libco Industries Inc**....815 623-7677
10567 Main St Roscoe (61073) ***(G-18902)***
**Liberty Bee, Liberty** *Also called Elliott Publishing Inc* ***(G-13295)***
**Liberty Classics Inc**....847 367-1288
1860 W Winchester Rd # 103 Libertyville (60048) ***(G-13342)***
**Liberty Coach Inc**....847 578-4600
1400 Morrow Ave North Chicago (60064) ***(G-16184)***
**Liberty Diversified Intl Inc**....217 935-8361
10670 State Highway 10 Clinton (61727) ***(G-7285)***
**Liberty Diversified Intl Inc**....309 787-6161
3402 78th Ave W Rock Island (61201) ***(G-18186)***
**Liberty Engineering Company, Roscoe** *Also called Libco Industries Inc* ***(G-18902)***
**Liberty Feed Mill**....217 645-3441
203 Richfield Rd Liberty (62347) ***(G-13296)***
**Liberty Flags, Waukegan** *Also called Seasonal Designs Inc* ***(G-21613)***
**Liberty Graphics, Tinley Park** *Also called Liberty Lithographers Inc* ***(G-20931)***
**Liberty Group Pubg III Hldings, Flora** *Also called Clay County Advocate Press* ***(G-10204)***
**Liberty Group Publishing (PA)**....309 944-1779
108 W 1st St Geneseo (61254) ***(G-10802)***
**Liberty Group Publishing**....309 937-3303
119 W Exchange St Cambridge (61238) ***(G-2968)***
**Liberty Group Publishing**....618 937-2850
111 S Emma St West Frankfort (62896) ***(G-21812)***
**Liberty Grove Software Inc**....630 858-7388
189 Newton Ave Ste B Glen Ellyn (60137) ***(G-10977)***
**Liberty Limestone Inc**....815 385-5011
430 W Wegner Rd McHenry (60051) ***(G-14521)***
**Liberty Lithographers Inc**....708 633-7450
18625 West Creek Dr Tinley Park (60477) ***(G-20931)***
**Liberty Machinery Company**....847 276-2761
111 Schelter Rd Lincolnshire (60069) ***(G-13463)***
**Liberty Subn Chcago Newspapers, Downers Grove** *Also called Suburban Life Publication* ***(G-8528)***
**Liberty Tire Recycling LLC**....773 871-6360
2044 N Dominick St Chicago (60614) ***(G-5502)***
**Libertyville Brewing Company**....847 362-6688
345 N Milwaukee Ave Libertyville (60048) ***(G-13343)***
**Libman Company**....217 268-4200
220 N Sheldon St Arcola (61910) ***(G-675)***
**Liborio Baking Co Inc**....708 452-7222
8212 Grand Ave River Grove (60171) ***(G-18010)***
**Library Furniture Intl**....847 564-9497
1945 Techny Rd Ste 10 Northbrook (60062) ***(G-16295)***
**Lice B Gone, Belleville** *Also called Safe Effective Alternatives* ***(G-1675)***
**Lichtnwald - Johnston Ir Works**....847 966-1100
7840 Lehigh Ave Morton Grove (60053) ***(G-15212)***
**Lickenbrock & Sons Inc**....618 632-4977
328 W State St O Fallon (62269) ***(G-16470)***
**Licon Inc**....618 485-2222
23297 County Highway 7 Ashley (62808) ***(G-927)***
**Lids Corporation**....708 873-9606
416 Orland Square Dr Orland Park (60462) ***(G-16873)***
**Liese Lumber Co Inc**....618 234-0105
2215 S Belt W Belleville (62226) ***(G-1649)***
**Life Fitness Inc (HQ)**....847 288-3300
9525 Bryn Mawr Ave Fl 6 Rosemont (60018) ***(G-19010)***
**Life Fitness Inc**....847 288-3300
10601 Belmont Ave Franklin Park (60131) ***(G-10516)***
**Life Fitness Inc**....800 494-6344
9525 Bryn Mawr Ave Rosemont (60018) ***(G-19011)***
**Life Fitness Mfg Fcilty, Franklin Park** *Also called Brunswick Corporation* ***(G-10418)***
**Life Fitness US, Franklin Park** *Also called Brunswick Corporation* ***(G-10419)***
**Life Spine Inc**....847 884-6117
13951 Quality Dr Huntley (60142) ***(G-12158)***
**Life Tronics International, Chicago** *Also called Litetronics Technologies Inc* ***(G-5518)***
**Lifeline Scientific Inc (PA)**....847 294-0300
1 Pierce Pl Ste 475w Itasca (60143) ***(G-12304)***
**Lifesafety Power Inc**....224 324-4240
750 Tower Rd Unit B Mundelein (60060) ***(G-15520)***
**Lifespan Brands LLC**....630 315-3300
1200 Thorndale Ave Elk Grove Village (60007) ***(G-9595)***
**Lifetime Creations**....708 895-2770
17838 Chappel Ave Lansing (60438) ***(G-13172)***
**Lifetime Roof Tile, Naperville** *Also called Lifetime Rooftile Company* ***(G-15689)***
**Lifetime Rooftile Company (PA)**....630 355-7922
1805 High Grove Ln Naperville (60540) ***(G-15689)***
**Lifetouch Services Inc**....815 633-3881
5126 Forest Hills Ct Loves Park (61111) ***(G-13961)***
**Lifewatch Corp (HQ)**....847 720-2100
10255 W Higgins Rd # 100 Rosemont (60018) ***(G-19012)***
**Lifewatch Services Inc (HQ)**....847 720-2100
10255 W Higgins Rd # 100 Rosemont (60018) ***(G-19013)***
**Lifewatch Technologies Inc**....800 633-3361
10255 W Higgins Rd # 100 Rosemont (60018) ***(G-19014)***
**Lifeway Foods Inc (PA)**....847 967-1010
6431 Oakton St Morton Grove (60053) ***(G-15213)***
**Lift Systems Inc (PA)**....309 764-9842
1505 7th St East Moline (61244) ***(G-8686)***
**Lift-All Company Inc**....630 534-6860
1620 Fullerton Ct Ste 400 Glendale Heights (60139) ***(G-11041)***
**Liftex Corporation**....847 782-0572
4155 Grove Ave Gurnee (60031) ***(G-11467)***
**Lifting & Components Parts LLC**....224 315-5294
1900 E Golf Rd Ste 950a Schaumburg (60173) ***(G-19617)***
**Liftmaster, Oak Brook** *Also called Chamberlain Group Inc* ***(G-16499)***
**Lifts of Illinois Inc**....309 923-7450
415 W Front St Roanoke (61561) ***(G-18052)***
**Liftseat Corporation**....630 424-2840
2001 Midwest Rd Ste 204 Oak Brook (60523) ***(G-16537)***
**Light Efficient Design, Cary** *Also called Tadd LLC* ***(G-3375)***
**Light Matrix Inc**....847 590-0856
339 S Valor Ct Palatine (60074) ***(G-17050)***
**Light of Mine LLC**....312 840-8570
401 N Michigan Ave # 1200 Chicago (60611) ***(G-5503)***
**Light The Lamp Brewery, Grayslake** *Also called Colleagues of Beer Inc* ***(G-11327)***
**Light To Form LLC**....847 498-5832
2905 Macarthur Blvd Northbrook (60062) ***(G-16296)***
**Light Waves LLC**....847 251-1622
1000 Skokie Blvd Wilmette (60091) ***(G-22259)***
**Lightfoot Technologies Inc**....331 302-1297
2135 City Gate Ln Ste 300 Naperville (60563) ***(G-15690)***
**Lighthouse Marketing Services**....630 482-9900
115 Flinn St Batavia (60510) ***(G-1464)***
**Lighthouse Printing Inc**....708 479-7776
21754 S Center Ave New Lenox (60451) ***(G-15891)***
**Lighting Control Systems, West Chicago** *Also called Microlite Corporation* ***(G-21742)***
**Lighting Design By Michael Ant**....708 289-4783
9840 Forestview Dr Mokena (60448) ***(G-14880)***
**Lighting Innovations Inc**....630 889-8100
3609 Swenson Ave Saint Charles (60174) ***(G-19211)***
**Lightitech LLC**....847 910-4177
200 W Superior St Ste 400 Chicago (60654) ***(G-5504)***
**Lightner Publishing Corp (PA)**....312 939-4767
1849 Syracuse Rd Naperville (60565) ***(G-15691)***
**Lightning Graphic**....815 623-1937
10444 Rock Ln Roscoe (61073) ***(G-18903)***
**Lightolier Genlyte Inc**....847 364-8250
951 Busse Rd Elk Grove Village (60007) ***(G-9596)***
**Lights On Service, Byron** *Also called Interntional Metal Finshg Svcs* ***(G-2917)***
**Lights Prosthetic Eyes Inc**....309 676-3663
1318 W Candletree Dr # 3 Peoria (61614) ***(G-17401)***
**Lightscape Inc**....847 247-8800
342 4th St Libertyville (60048) ***(G-13344)***
**Lightworks Communcation Inc**....847 966-1110
5632 Carol Ave Morton Grove (60053) ***(G-15214)***
**Ligo Products Inc**....708 478-1800
9100 W 191st St Ste 101 Mokena (60448) ***(G-14881)***
**Lilly Air Systems Co Inc**....630 773-2225
217 Catalpa Ave Itasca (60143) ***(G-12305)***
**Lilly Industries Inc**....630 773-2222
427 W Irving Park Rd Itasca (60143) ***(G-12306)***
**Lilly Steam Trap, Itasca** *Also called Lilly Industries Inc* ***(G-12306)***
**Lily-Canada Holding Corp (PA)**....847 831-4800
1700 Old Deerfield Rd Highland Park (60035) ***(G-11852)***
**Limitless Coffee LLC**....630 779-3778
316 N Elizabeth St Chicago (60607) ***(G-5505)***
**Limitless Coffee & Tea, Chicago** *Also called Limitless Coffee LLC* ***(G-5505)***
**Limitless Innovations Inc**....855 843-4828
4800 Metalmaster Dr McHenry (60050) ***(G-14522)***
**Lincoln Advanced Tech LLC**....815 286-3500
161 Maple St Hinckley (60520) ***(G-11936)***
**Lincoln Bark LLC**....800 428-4027
858 W Armitage Ave 240 Chicago (60614) ***(G-5506)***
**Lincoln Electric Company**....630 783-3600
115 E Crlroads Pkwy Ste A Bolingbrook (60440) ***(G-2335)***
**Lincoln Green Mazda Inc**....217 391-2400
3760 6th Street Frontage Springfield (62703) ***(G-20470)***
**Lincoln Heritage Winery LLC**....618 833-3783
772 Kaolin Rd Cobden (62920) ***(G-7302)***
**Lincoln Land Enterprises, Posen** *Also called Parts Specialists Inc* ***(G-17734)***
**Lincoln Office, Washington** *Also called Baker Avenue Investments Inc* ***(G-21378)***
**Lincoln Office LLC (HQ)**....309 427-2500
205 Eastgate Dr Washington (61571) ***(G-21385)***
**Lincoln Park Brewery Inc**....312 915-0071
1800 N Clybourn Ave Ste B Chicago (60614) ***(G-5507)***
**Lincoln Printers Inc**....217 732-3121
711 Broadway St Lincoln (62656) ***(G-13413)***
**Lincoln Square Printing**....773 334-9030
4607 N Western Ave Fl 1 Chicago (60625) ***(G-5508)***

**Lincoln State Steel Div, Rockford** *Also called Mc Chemical Company* ***(G-18487)***
**Lincolndailynewscom**...217 732-7443
601 Keokuk St Lincoln (62656) ***(G-13414)***
**Lincolnland Agri-Energy LLC**...618 586-2321
10406 N 1725th St Palestine (62451) ***(G-17094)***
**Lincolnland Archtctral Grphics**...217 629-9009
12 Covered Bridge Acres Glenarm (62536) ***(G-10996)***
**Lincolnland Graphics, Glenarm** *Also called Lincolnland Archtctral Grphics* ***(G-10996)***
**Lincolnshire Printing Inc**...815 578-0740
4004 W Dayton St McHenry (60050) ***(G-14523)***
**Lind-Remsen Printing Co Inc**...815 969-0610
3918 S Central Ave Rockford (61102) ***(G-18470)***
**Linda Levinson Designs Inc**...312 951-6943
111 E Oak St 3 Chicago (60611) ***(G-5509)***
**Linde Gas North America LLC**...630 857-6460
2000 S 25th Ave Ste S Broadview (60155) ***(G-2592)***
**Linde Gas North America LLC**...708 345-0894
2000 S 25th Ave Ste S Broadview (60155) ***(G-2593)***
**Linde LLC**...630 690-3010
640 Kimberly Dr Carol Stream (60188) ***(G-3185)***
**Linde LLC**...630 515-2576
1751 W Diehl Rd Ste 300 Naperville (60563) ***(G-15692)***
**Linde LLC**...618 251-5217
1200 S Delmar Ave Hartford (62048) ***(G-11611)***
**Linde North America Inc**...309 353-9717
125 Distillery Rd Pekin (61554) ***(G-17273)***
**Linde North America Inc**...630 257-3612
810 E Romeo Rd Lockport (60441) ***(G-13726)***
**Lindemann Chimney Co, Lake Bluff** *Also called Lindemann Chimney Service Inc* ***(G-12854)***
**Lindemann Chimney Service Inc (PA)**...847 918-7994
110 Albrecht Dr Lake Bluff (60044) ***(G-12854)***
**Lindsay Metal Madness Inc**...815 568-4560
711 W Grant Hwy Marengo (60152) ***(G-14235)***
**Lindstrand Balloons USA, Galena** *Also called A R B C Inc* ***(G-10714)***
**Lindstrom Farm, Varna** *Also called Brian Lindstrom* ***(G-21133)***
**Lindy Manufacturing Company**...630 963-4126
5200 Katrine Ave Downers Grove (60515) ***(G-8476)***
**Line Craft Inc**...630 932-1182
10 W North Ave Lombard (60148) ***(G-13819)***
**Line Craft Tool Company Inc**...630 932-1182
10 W North Ave Lombard (60148) ***(G-13820)***
**Line Group Inc (PA)**...847 593-6810
539 W Algonquin Rd Arlington Heights (60005) ***(G-793)***
**Line of Advance Nfp**...312 768-0043
2126 W Armitage Ave Apt 3 Chicago (60647) ***(G-5510)***
**Line Tool & Stamping Co, Arlington Heights** *Also called Line Group Inc* ***(G-793)***
**Linear Dimensions Inc**...312 321-1810
445 E Ohio St Ste 350 Chicago (60611) ***(G-5511)***
**Linear Industries Inc**...847 428-5793
2531 Tech Dr Ste 310 Elgin (60124) ***(G-9095)***
**Linear Kinetics Inc**...630 365-0075
48 W 989 Rr 64 Maple Park (60151) ***(G-14201)***
**Liners Direct, Roselle** *Also called Rht Inc* ***(G-18967)***
**Lingle Design Group Inc**...815 369-9155
158 W Main St Lena (61048) ***(G-13280)***
**Link Tools Intl (usa) Inc**...773 549-3000
2440 N Lakeview Ave Chicago (60614) ***(G-5512)***
**Link-Letters Ltd**...847 459-1199
309 N Wolf Rd Wheeling (60090) ***(G-22094)***
**Linkedhealth Solutions**...312 600-6684
700 N Green St Chicago (60642) ***(G-5513)***
**Linkhouse LLC**...312 671-2225
274 Northbury Ct Unit B1 Schaumburg (60193) ***(G-19618)***
**Linmore Publishing Co**...847 382-7606
409 South St Barrington (60010) ***(G-1286)***
**Linn West Paper Company**...773 561-3839
4649 N Magnolia Ave Chicago (60640) ***(G-5514)***
**Linne Machine Company Inc**...217 446-5746
209 Avenue C Danville (61832) ***(G-7747)***
**Linpac Ropak Packaging Central, Elk Grove Village** *Also called Ropak Central Inc* ***(G-9718)***
**Lintec of America Inc**...847 229-0547
935 National Pkwy # 93553 Schaumburg (60173) ***(G-19619)***
**Linwood LLC**...217 446-1110
917 N Walnut St Ste 101 Danville (61832) ***(G-7748)***
**Linx**...847 910-5303
1807 W Sunnyside Ave 2c Chicago (60640) ***(G-5515)***
**Linx Enterprises LLC**...224 409-2206
5051 S Forrestville Ave Chicago (60615) ***(G-5516)***
**Lion Ornamental Concrete Pdts**...630 892-7304
111 N Railroad St Montgomery (60538) ***(G-15056)***
**Lion Productions LLC**...630 845-1610
619 Campbell St Geneva (60134) ***(G-10846)***
**Lion Tool & Die Co**...847 658-8898
910 W Algonquin Rd Algonquin (60102) ***(G-397)***
**Lion Welding Service Inc**...630 543-5230
729 W Fullerton Ave 4d Addison (60101) ***(G-181)***
**Lionheart Critical Pow**...847 291-1413
13151 Executive Ct Huntley (60142) ***(G-12159)***
**Lipscomb Engineering Inc**...630 231-3833
1215 W Washington St West Chicago (60185) ***(G-21732)***
**Lipsner Smith Co**...847 677-3000
4700 W Chase Ave Lincolnwood (60712) ***(G-13521)***
**Liqua Fit Inc (PA)**...630 965-8067
100 N Atkinson Rd Ste 102 Grayslake (60030) ***(G-11351)***
**Liquid Container Inc**...630 562-5812
1760 W Hawthorne Ln West Chicago (60185) ***(G-21733)***
**Liquid Controls LLC (HQ)**...847 295-1050
105 Albrecht Dr Lake Bluff (60044) ***(G-12855)***
**Liquid Lf Sprators Systems Div, Aurora** *Also called Thomas Pump Company* ***(G-1085)***
**Liquid Resin International**...618 392-3590
4295 N Holly Rd Olney (62450) ***(G-16777)***
**Liquidfire**...312 376-7448
8554 W Rascher Ave Apt 2n Chicago (60656) ***(G-5517)***
**Liquitech Inc**...630 693-0500
421 Eisenhower Ln S Lombard (60148) ***(G-13821)***
**Lisa's Clarinet Shop, Glen Ellyn** *Also called Interntnal Mscal Suppliers Inc* ***(G-10974)***
**Lists & Letters**...847 520-5207
480 W Hintz Rd Wheeling (60090) ***(G-22095)***
**Litania Sports Group Inc**...217 367-8438
601 Mercury Dr Champaign (61822) ***(G-3510)***
**Litchfield News Herald Inc**...217 324-2121
112 E Ryder St Litchfield (62056) ***(G-13694)***
**Litestage Lighting Systems, Bensenville** *Also called Formco Plastics Inc* ***(G-1901)***
**Litetronics Technologies Inc**...708 333-6707
6969 W 73rd St Chicago (60638) ***(G-5518)***
**Lith Liqure**...847 458-5180
461 N Randall Rd Lake In The Hills (60156) ***(G-12998)***
**Litho Research Incorporated**...630 860-7070
1600 Glenlake Ave Itasca (60143) ***(G-12307)***
**Litho Type LLC**...708 895-3720
16710 Chicago Ave Lansing (60438) ***(G-13173)***
**Lithographic Industries Inc**...773 921-7955
2445 Gardner Rd Broadview (60155) ***(G-2594)***
**Lithographics Services, Westmont** *Also called Lithoprint Inc* ***(G-21900)***
**Lithoprint Inc**...630 964-9200
111 E Chicago Ave Westmont (60559) ***(G-21900)***
**Lithotype Company Inc**...630 771-1920
594 Territorial Dr Ste G Bolingbrook (60440) ***(G-2336)***
**Lithuanian Catholic Press**...773 585-9500
4545 W 63rd St Chicago (60629) ***(G-5519)***
**Lithuanian Press Inc**...773 776-3399
2711 W 71st St Chicago (60629) ***(G-5520)***
**Litt Aluminium & Shtmtl Co**...708 366-4720
9825 W Roosevelt Rd Westchester (60154) ***(G-21847)***
**Littelfuse Inc (PA)**...773 628-1000
8755 W Higgins Rd Ste 500 Chicago (60631) ***(G-5521)***
**Littelfuse Inc**...217 531-3100
2110 S Oak St Champaign (61820) ***(G-3511)***
**Littelfuse Inc**...773 628-1000
8755 W Higgins Rd Ste 300 Chicago (60631) ***(G-5522)***
**Littell LLC**...630 916-6662
1211 Tower Rd Schaumburg (60173) ***(G-19620)***
**Littell International Inc**...630 622-4950
1211 Tower Rd Schaumburg (60173) ***(G-19621)***
**Little Creek Woodworking**...217 543-2815
1473 Cr 1675e Arthur (61911) ***(G-908)***
**Little Doloras**...708 331-1330
130 W 168th St South Holland (60473) ***(G-20286)***
**Little Egypt Gas A & Wldg Sups**...618 937-2271
10603 Bencie Ln West Frankfort (62896) ***(G-21813)***
**Little Giant, University Park** *Also called Brennan Equipment and Mfg Inc* ***(G-21046)***
**Little Journeys Limited**...847 677-0350
7914 Kildare Ave Skokie (60076) ***(G-20030)***
**Little Lady Foods Inc (PA)**...847 806-1440
2323 Pratt Blvd Elk Grove Village (60007) ***(G-9597)***
**Little Miss Muffin, Lincolnshire** *Also called Doughnut Boy* ***(G-13444)***
**Little Shop of Papers Ltd**...847 382-7733
740 W Northwest Hwy Barrington (60010) ***(G-1287)***
**Little Village Printing Inc**...708 749-4414
3210 Grove Ave Apt 2w Berwyn (60402) ***(G-2067)***
**Littleson Inc (PA)**...815 968-8349
124 N Water St Ste 204 Rockford (61107) ***(G-18471)***
**Litwiller Machine and Supply, Tremont** *Also called K R J Inc* ***(G-20983)***
**Live Daily LLC**...312 286-6706
2627 W Lunt Ave Chicago (60645) ***(G-5523)***
**Live Love Hair**...530 554-2471
17734 Commercial Ave Lansing (60438) ***(G-13174)***
**Live Wire & Cable Co**...847 577-5483
409 W University Dr Arlington Heights (60004) ***(G-794)***
**Livegift Inc**...312 725-4514
222 Merchandise Mart Plz Chicago (60654) ***(G-5524)***
**Liveone Inc**...312 282-2320
333 N Michigan Ave # 2800 Chicago (60601) ***(G-5525)***
**Living Royal**...312 906-7600
500 Quail Hollow Dr Wheeling (60090) ***(G-22096)***
**Livingston Innovations LLC**...847 808-0900
1377 Barclay Blvd Buffalo Grove (60089) ***(G-2727)***

ALPHABETIC

**Livingston Products Inc**....847 808-0900
3242 W Monroe St Waukegan (60085) *(G-21581)*
**Livingstone Corporation**....630 871-1212
205 N Washington St Wheaton (60187) *(G-21967)*
**Livorsi Marine Inc**....847 548-5900
715 Center St Grayslake (60030) *(G-11352)*
**Lixi Inc**....630 620-4646
1438 Brook Dr Downers Grove (60515) *(G-8477)*
**Lizotte Sheet Metal Inc**....618 656-3066
632 W Schwarz St Edwardsville (62025) *(G-8806)*
**Lj Fabricators, Rockford** *Also called L/J Fabricators Inc (G-18460)*
**Ljm Equipment Co**....847 291-0162
205 Huehl Rd Northbrook (60062) *(G-16297)*
**Lkq Broadway Auto Parts Inc**....312 621-1950
500 W Madison St Ste 2800 Chicago (60661) *(G-5526)*
**LL Display Group Ltd**....847 982-0231
7085 N Ridgeway Ave Lincolnwood (60712) *(G-13522)*
**LL Electronics**....217 586-6477
103 S Prairieview Rd Mahomet (61853) *(G-14160)*
**Lla Exploration Inc**....217 623-4096
1747 N 800 East Rd Taylorville (62568) *(G-20841)*
**LLC Ethersonic Techno**....708 441-4730
4203 Oakwood Ln Matteson (60443) *(G-14376)*
**LLC Urban Farmer**....815 468-7200
655 Mulberry St Manteno (60950) *(G-14187)*
**Lloyd American Corporation (PA)**....815 964-4191
4435 Manchester Dr Rockford (61109) *(G-18472)*
**Lloyd Hearing Aid, Rockford** *Also called Lloyd American Corporation (G-18472)*
**Lloyd M Hughes Enterprises Inc**....773 363-6331
6331 S Martin L King Dr Chicago (60637) *(G-5527)*
**Lloyd Midwest Graphics**....815 282-8828
7103 N 2nd St Machesney Park (61115) *(G-14089)*
**Lmk Technologies LLC**....815 433-1530
1779 Chessie Ln Ottawa (61350) *(G-16967)*
**Lmpl Management Corporation**....708 636-2443
5757 W 95th St Ste 3 Oak Lawn (60453) *(G-16631)*
**LMS Innovations Inc**....312 613-2345
2734 W Leland Ave Apt 3 Chicago (60625) *(G-5528)*
**Lmsys, Chicago** *Also called World Class Technologies Inc (G-7029)*
**Lmt Inc**....309 932-3311
1105 Se 2nd St Galva (61434) *(G-10792)*
**Lmt Onsrud LP**....847 362-1560
1081 S Northpoint Blvd Waukegan (60085) *(G-21582)*
**Lmt Usa Inc**....630 969-5412
1081 S Northpoint Blvd Waukegan (60085) *(G-21583)*
**Lo Riser Trailers, Kewanee** *Also called Advance Metalworking Company (G-12668)*
**Lo-Ko Performance Coatings**....708 424-7863
5340 W 111th St Ste 1 Oak Lawn (60453) *(G-16632)*
**Load Redi Inc**....217 784-4200
1124 S Sangamon Ave Gibson City (60936) *(G-10904)*
**Loadsense Technologies LLC**....312 239-0146
1658 N Milwaukee Ave # 512 Chicago (60647) *(G-5529)*
**Loberg Excavating Inc**....815 443-2874
12268 W Sabin Church Rd Pearl City (61062) *(G-17248)*
**Local 46 Training Program Tr**....217 528-4041
2888 E Cook St Springfield (62703) *(G-20471)*
**Local Wine Tours, Lake Bluff** *Also called Terlato Wine Group Ltd (G-12867)*
**Localfix Solutions LLC**....312 569-0619
26w194 Prestwick Ln Winfield (60190) *(G-22287)*
**Loch Precision Technologies**....847 438-1400
1215 Berkley Rd Lake Zurich (60047) *(G-13096)*
**Lochman Ref Silk Screen Co**....847 475-6266
2405 Oakton St Evanston (60202) *(G-10065)*
**Lock & Roll Trailer Hitch, Chicago** *Also called Great Lakes Forge Company (G-4997)*
**Locker Room Screen Printing**....630 759-2533
253 S Schmidt Rd Bolingbrook (60440) *(G-2337)*
**Locknut Technology Inc**....630 628-5330
351 S Lombard Rd Addison (60101) *(G-182)*
**Lockport Fish Pantry**....815 588-3543
604 E 9th St Lockport (60441) *(G-13727)*
**Lockport Steel Fabricators LLC**....815 726-6281
3051 S State St Lockport (60441) *(G-13728)*
**Loda Electronics Co**....217 386-2554
307 S Elm St Loda (60948) *(G-13752)*
**Lodaat LLC (PA)**....630 248-2380
2 Mid America Plz Ste 800 Oakbrook Terrace (60181) *(G-16715)*
**Lodaat LLC**....630 852-7544
410 40th St Downers Grove (60515) *(G-8478)*
**Lodan Electronics Inc**....847 398-5311
3311 N Kennicott Ave Arlington Heights (60004) *(G-795)*
**Loders Croklaan BV**....815 730-5200
24708 W Durkee Rd Channahon (60410) *(G-3577)*
**Loders Croklaan Usa LLC**....815 730-5200
24708 W Durkee Rd Channahon (60410) *(G-3578)*
**Lodolce Meat Co Inc**....708 863-4655
5238 W 24th Pl Cicero (60804) *(G-7216)*
**Loeb Oil, Lawrenceville** *Also called Herman L Loeb LLC (G-13202)*
**Lofthouse Bakery Products Inc**....630 455-5229
3250 Lacey Rd Ste 600 Downers Grove (60515) *(G-8479)*
**Logan Actuator Co**....815 943-9500
550 Chippewa Rd Harvard (60033) *(G-11640)*
**Logan Graphic Products Inc**....847 526-5515
1100 Brown St Wauconda (60084) *(G-21479)*
**Logan Mason Rehabilitation, Lincoln** *Also called Mental Health Ctrs Centl Ill (G-13415)*
**Logan Square Aluminum Sup Inc (PA)**....773 235-2500
2500 N Pulaski Rd Chicago (60639) *(G-5530)*
**Logan Square Aluminum Sup Inc**....847 985-1700
1450 Mitchell Blvd Schaumburg (60193) *(G-19622)*
**Logan Square Aluminum Sup Inc**....847 676-4767
4767 W Touhy Ave Lincolnwood (60712) *(G-13523)*
**Logan Square Aluminum Sup Inc**....773 846-8300
204 W 83rd St Chicago (60620) *(G-5531)*
**Logan Square Aluminum Sup Inc**....773 278-3600
2622 N Pulaski Rd Chicago (60639) *(G-5532)*
**Logic Printing, Downers Grove** *Also called S G S Inc (G-8517)*
**Logical Design Solutions Inc**....630 786-5999
562 Asbury Drive Aurora Aurora (60502) *(G-1047)*
**Logicgate Inc**....312 279-2775
214 W Ohio St Fl 1 Chicago (60654) *(G-5533)*
**Logistic Department, Lisle** *Also called Molex LLC (G-13626)*
**Logo Wear Unlimited Inc**....309 367-2333
104 S Menard St Metamora (61548) *(G-14743)*
**Logo Works**....815 942-4700
824 Liberty St Morris (60450) *(G-15113)*
**Logo's & More, Breese** *Also called Illinois Embroidery Service (G-2445)*
**Logoplaste Chicago LLC**....815 230-6961
14420 N Van Dyke Rd Plainfield (60544) *(G-17619)*
**Logoplaste Fort Worth LLC**....815 230-6961
14420 N Van Dyke Rd Plainfield (60544) *(G-17620)*
**Logoplaste Racine LLC**....815 230-6961
14420 N Van Dyke Rd Plainfield (60544) *(G-17621)*
**Logoplaste Usa Inc (HQ)**....815 230-6961
14420 N Van Dyke Rd Plainfield (60544) *(G-17622)*
**Lohr Quarry, Godfrey** *Also called Kimmaterials Inc (G-11227)*
**Lohrberg Lumber**....618 473-2061
5662 L Rd Waterloo (62298) *(G-21402)*
**Lokman Enterprises Inc**....773 654-0525
7240 N Ridge Blvd Apt 102 Chicago (60645) *(G-5534)*
**Lom, Chicago** *Also called Light of Mine LLC (G-5503)*
**Loma International Inc**....630 588-0900
550 Kehoe Blvd Carol Stream (60188) *(G-3186)*
**Loma Systems, Carol Stream** *Also called Loma International Inc (G-3186)*
**Lombard Archtctral Prcast Pdts**....708 389-1060
4245 W 123rd St Chicago (60803) *(G-5535)*
**Lombard Investment Company (PA)**....708 389-1060
4245 W 123rd St Alsip (60803) *(G-484)*
**Lombard Swiss Screw Company**....630 576-5096
420 S Rohlwing Rd Addison (60101) *(G-183)*
**London Shoe Shop & Western Wr**....618 345-9570
125 W Main St Collinsville (62234) *(G-7330)*
**Lone Star Industries Inc**....815 883-3173
490 Portland Ave Oglesby (61348) *(G-16751)*
**Lone Wolf Portable Treestand, Brimfield** *Also called Oak Leaf Outdoors Inc (G-2548)*
**Lonelino Sign Company Inc**....217 243-2444
2122 E Morton Ave Jacksonville (62650) *(G-12400)*
**Lonelybrand LLC (PA)**....312 880-7506
118 W Kinzie St Chicago (60654) *(G-5536)*
**Loneoak Timber & Veneere Co**....618 426-3065
45 Longhorn Trl Ava (62907) *(G-1239)*
**Long Construction Services**....217 443-2876
617 1/2 E Voorhees St Danville (61832) *(G-7749)*
**Long Elevator and Mch Co Inc (HQ)**....217 629-9648
2908 Old Rochester Rd Springfield (62703) *(G-20472)*
**Long Grove Apple Haus, Long Grove** *Also called Mangel and Co (G-13894)*
**Long Grove Confectionery Co (PA)**....847 459-3100
333 Lexington Dr Buffalo Grove (60089) *(G-2728)*
**Long Screw, Loves Park** *Also called Lsl Precision Machining Inc (G-13962)*
**Long View Publishing Co Inc**....773 446-9920
3339 S Halsted St Ste 4 Chicago (60608) *(G-5537)*
**Lonnie Hickam**....618 893-4223
2726 Sadler Rd Pomona (62975) *(G-17693)*
**Lonnies Stonecrafters Inc**....815 316-6565
3291 S Alpine Rd Rockford (61109) *(G-18473)*
**Lonza Inc**....309 697-7200
8316 W Rte 24 Mapleton (61547) *(G-14212)*
**Loomcraft Textile & Supply Co**....847 680-0000
647 Lakeview Pkwy Vernon Hills (60061) *(G-21182)*
**Loop Attachment Co**....847 922-0642
1509 N Hudson Ave Apt 3 Chicago (60610) *(G-5538)*
**Loop Automotive LLC**....847 912-9090
303 W Ohio St Apt 2609 Chicago (60654) *(G-5539)*
**Loop Belt Industries Inc**....630 469-1300
21w171 Hill Ave Glen Ellyn (60137) *(G-10978)*
**Loop Limited**....312 612-1010
825 Chicago Ave Ste C2 Evanston (60202) *(G-10066)*
**Loose Petals, Chicago** *Also called Karen Young (G-5360)*

**Lopez Plumbing Systems Inc**......773 424-8225
5816 S Claremont Ave Chicago (60636) *(G-5540)*
**Loraes Drapery Workroom Inc**......847 358-7999
1204 W Colfax St Palatine (60067) *(G-17051)*
**Lorbern Mfg Inc**......847 301-8600
708 Morse Ave Schaumburg (60193) *(G-19623)*
**Lordahl Engineering, Long Grove** *Also called Lordahl Manufacturing Co (G-13893)*
**Lordahl Engineering Co, Waukegan** *Also called Lordahl Manufacturing Co (G-21584)*
**Lordahl Manufacturing Co (PA)**......847 244-0448
1001 S Lewis Ave Waukegan (60085) *(G-21584)*
**Lordahl Manufacturing Co**......847 244-0448
1571 Rfd Long Grove (60047) *(G-13893)*
**Loren Girovich**......773 334-1444
5328 N Wayne Ave Chicago (60640) *(G-5541)*
**Loren Tool & Manufacturing Co**......630 595-0100
430 Podlin Dr Franklin Park (60131) *(G-10517)*
**Lorenzo Frozen Foods Ltd**......708 343-7670
9940 W Roosevelt Rd Westchester (60154) *(G-21848)*
**Lorenzos Delectable LLC**......773 791-3327
4552 S Lamon Ave Chicago (60638) *(G-5542)*
**Lorette Dies Inc**......630 279-9682
246 E 2nd St Elmhurst (60126) *(G-9902)*
**Lorton Group LLC**......844 352-5089
419 Vine St Wilmette (60091) *(G-22260)*
**Los Gamas Inc**......872 829-3514
3333 W Armitage Ave Chicago (60647) *(G-5543)*
**Los Mangos**......773 542-1522
3058 S Avers Ave Chicago (60623) *(G-5544)*
**Los Mangos I, Chicago** *Also called Los Mangos (G-5544)*
**Los Primos Pallets Inc**......773 418-3584
2013 W Ferdinand St Chicago (60612) *(G-5545)*
**Losangeles Features Syndicate**......847 446-4082
650 Winnetka Mews Apt 110 Winnetka (60093) *(G-22310)*
**Loso Trucking Inc**......312 601-2231
55 E Monroe St Ste 3800 Chicago (60603) *(G-5546)*
**Lothson Guitars**......815 756-2031
10580 Keslinger Rd Dekalb (60115) *(G-8102)*
**Lotton Art Glass Co**......708 672-1400
24760 S Country Ln Crete (60417) *(G-7516)*
**Lottus Inc**......847 691-9464
3216 Ronald Rd Glenview (60025) *(G-11166)*
**Lotus Creative Innovations LLC**......815 440-8999
970 Melugins Grove Rd Compton (61318) *(G-7367)*
**Lou Plucinski**......815 758-7888
110 Industrial Dr Dekalb (60115) *(G-8103)*
**Lou's Spring & Welding, Peru** *Also called Lous Spring and Welding Shop (G-17517)*
**Louis Marsch Inc**......217 526-3723
601 Carlin St Morrisonville (62546) *(G-15151)*
**Louis Meskan Brass Foundry Inc**......773 237-7662
2007 N Major Ave 13 Chicago (60639) *(G-5547)*
**Louisville Ladder Inc**......309 692-1895
7921 N Hale Ave Peoria (61615) *(G-17402)*
**Lous Spring and Welding Shop**......815 223-4282
2850 May Rd Peru (61354) *(G-17517)*
**Louvers International Inc**......630 782-9977
851 N Church Ct Elmhurst (60126) *(G-9903)*
**Lovatt & Radcliffe Ltd**......815 568-9797
9635 Keystone Ave Skokie (60076) *(G-20031)*
**Love Journey Inc**......773 447-5591
8121 S Colfax Ave Chicago (60617) *(G-5548)*
**Love Joy Technology, Downers Grove** *Also called Powdered Metal Tech LLC (G-8507)*
**Love ME Tenders LLC**......847 564-2533
2863 Woodmere Dr Northbrook (60062) *(G-16298)*
**Lovejoy Inc (HQ)**......630 852-0500
2655 Wisconsin Ave Downers Grove (60515) *(G-8480)*
**Lovejoy Industries Inc (PA)**......859 873-6828
3610 Commercial Ave Northbrook (60062) *(G-16299)*
**Lowrey Organ Company, Wood Dale** *Also called Midi Music Center Inc (G-22400)*
**Loyal Casket Co**......773 722-4065
134 S California Ave Chicago (60612) *(G-5549)*
**Loyalty Publishing Inc**......309 693-0840
4414 Entec Dr Bartonville (61607) *(G-1396)*
**Loyola Paper Company**......847 956-7770
951 Lunt Ave Elk Grove Village (60007) *(G-9598)*
**LPI Worldwide Inc**......773 826-8600
4821 S Aberdeen St Chicago (60609) *(G-5550)*
**Lpz Inc**......773 579-6120
2919 S Western Ave Chicago (60608) *(G-5551)*
**Lre, Schaumburg** *Also called Legend Racing Enterprises Inc (G-19614)*
**Lre Products Inc**......630 238-8321
733 Maple Ln Bensenville (60106) *(G-1942)*
**Lrm Grinding Co Inc**......708 458-7878
7333 S 76th Ave Bridgeview (60455) *(G-2504)*
**Lrwmotivequest, Evanston** *Also called Motivequest LLC (G-10075)*
**Lsa United Inc**......773 476-7439
1020 E Emerson Ave Lombard (60148) *(G-13822)*
**Lsc Communications Inc (PA)**......773 272-9200
191 N Wacker Dr Ste 1400 Chicago (60606) *(G-5552)*
**Lsc Communications Us LLC (HQ)**......844 572-5720
191 N Wacker Dr Ste 1400 Chicago (60606) *(G-5553)*
**Lsc Communications Us LLC**......815 844-5181
1600 N Main St Pontiac (61764) *(G-17705)*
**LSI STEEL PROCESSING DIVISION, Chicago** *Also called Lamination Specialties Corp (G-5449)*
**LSI Steel Processing Division, Chicago** *Also called Lamination Specialties Corp (G-5450)*
**Lsk Import**......847 342-8447
100 S Wacker Dr Ste 700 Chicago (60606) *(G-5554)*
**Lsl Health Care, Chicago** *Also called Lsl Industries Inc (G-5555)*
**Lsl Industries Inc**......773 878-1100
5535 N Wolcott Ave Chicago (60640) *(G-5555)*
**Lsl Precision Machining Inc**......815 633-4701
2210 Nimtz Rd Loves Park (61111) *(G-13962)*
**Lsp Industries Inc (PA)**......815 226-8090
5060 27th Ave Rockford (61109) *(G-18474)*
**Lssp Corporation**......630 428-0099
109 S Stauffer Dr Naperville (60540) *(G-15693)*
**Ltb Graphics Inc**......630 238-1754
749 N Edgewood Ave Wood Dale (60191) *(G-22391)*
**Ltc Holdings Inc (HQ)**......847 249-5900
3021 N Delany Rd Waukegan (60087) *(G-21585)*
**Ltf, Northbrook** *Also called Light To Form LLC (G-16296)*
**LTI, Aurora** *Also called Ecli Products LLC (G-1000)*
**LTI, Carol Stream** *Also called Autotech Tech Ltd Partnr (G-3108)*
**Lub-Tek Petroleum Products (PA)**......815 741-0414
2439 Reeves Rd Joliet (60436) *(G-12534)*
**Lube Rite**......217 267-7766
802 S State St Westville (61883) *(G-21930)*
**Lubeq Corporation**......847 931-1020
1380 Gateway Dr Ste 6 Elgin (60124) *(G-9096)*
**Lubrication Enterprises LLC**......800 537-7683
12924 Tipperary Ln Plainfield (60585) *(G-17623)*
**Lubrication Technology Inc**......740 574-5150
3851 Exchange Ave Aurora (60504) *(G-1048)*
**Lubrizol Corporation**......630 355-3605
40 Shuman Blvd Ste 264 Naperville (60563) *(G-15694)*
**Luby Publishing Inc**......312 341-1110
55 E Jackson Blvd Ste 401 Chicago (60604) *(G-5556)*
**Lucas Coatings, Alsip** *Also called RM Lucas Co (G-522)*
**Luck E Strike Corporation**......630 313-2408
2100 Enterprise Ave Geneva (60134) *(G-10847)*
**Luck E Strike USA, Geneva** *Also called Luck E Strike Corporation (G-10847)*
**Lucksfood**......773 878-7778
1109 W Argyle St Chicago (60640) *(G-5557)*
**Lucky Brand Dungarees LLC**......847 550-1647
20530 N Rand Rd Ste 418 Deer Park (60010) *(G-7972)*
**Lucky Games Inc (PA)**......773 549-9051
574 Alice Dr Northbrook (60062) *(G-16300)*
**Lucky Games Inc**......773 549-9051
574 Alice Dr Northbrook (60062) *(G-16301)*
**Lucky Yuppy Puppy Co Inc**......847 437-7879
533 W Golf Rd Arlington Heights (60005) *(G-796)*
**Luckyprints, Chicago** *Also called American Enlightenment LLC (G-3856)*
**Luco Mop Company**......217 235-1992
1200 Moultrie Ave Mattoon (61938) *(G-14398)*
**Lucta U S A Inc**......847 996-3400
950 Technology Way # 110 Libertyville (60048) *(G-13345)*
**Ludis Foods Adams Inc**......312 939-2877
23 E Adams St Chicago (60603) *(G-5558)*
**Ludwig Dairy Products Inc (PA)**......847 860-8646
1270 Mark St Elk Grove Village (60007) *(G-9599)*
**Ludwig Medical Inc**......217 342-6570
1010 N Parkview St Effingham (62401) *(G-8844)*
**Luebbers Welding & Mfg Inc**......618 594-2489
2420 Old State Rd Carlyle (62231) *(G-3056)*
**Luke Graphics Inc**......773 775-6733
6000 N Northwest Hwy Chicago (60631) *(G-5559)*
**Lululemon USA Inc**......773 227-1869
1627 N Damen Ave Chicago (60647) *(G-5560)*
**Lulus**......773 865-8978
2401 S Ridgeway Ave Chicago (60623) *(G-5561)*
**Lulus Real Froyo**......630 299-3854
1147 N Eola Rd Aurora (60502) *(G-1049)*
**Lumber Specialists Inc**......217 351-5311
300 W Main St Urbana (61801) *(G-21093)*
**Lumber Specialists Inc**......217 762-2511
118 E Washington St Monticello (61856) *(G-15078)*
**Lumber Specialists Inc**......217 443-8484
137 N Walnut St Danville (61832) *(G-7750)*
**Lumberyard Suppliers Inc**......618 931-0315
4200 Horseshoe Lake Rd Granite City (62040) *(G-11291)*
**Lumberyard Suppliers Inc**......217 965-4911
700 S Springfield St Virden (62690) *(G-21298)*
**Lumec Control Products Inc**......309 691-4747
1711 W Detweiller Dr Peoria (61615) *(G-17403)*
**Lumenart Ltd**......773 254-0744
3333 W 47th St Chicago (60632) *(G-5562)*

**Lumenart Ltd** ....773 254-0744
320 N Damen Ave Ste D300 Chicago (60612) ***(G-5563)***
**Lumenergi Inc** ....866 921-4652
70 W Madison St Ste 2300 Chicago (60602) ***(G-5564)***
**Lumenite Control Technology** ....847 455-1450
2331 17th St Franklin Park (60131) ***(G-10518)***
**Lumenite Electronic, Franklin Park** *Also called Lumenite Control Technology* ***(G-10518)***
**Lumina Inc** ....312 829-8970
512 N Racine Ave Chicago (60642) ***(G-5565)***
**Luminescence Media Group Nfp** ....312 602-3302
3740 N Lake Shore Dr Chicago (60613) ***(G-5566)***
**Lumisource LLC** ....847 699-8988
2950 Old Higgins Rd Elk Grove Village (60007) ***(G-9600)***
**Luna Azul Communications Inc** ....773 616-0007
1340 Hackberry Rd Deerfield (60015) ***(G-8030)***
**Luna It Services** ....213 537-2764
1658 N Milwaukee Ave # 222 Chicago (60647) ***(G-5567)***
**Luna Mattress Transport Inc** ....773 847-1812
3357 W 47th Pl Chicago (60632) ***(G-5568)***
**Lund Industries Inc** ....847 459-1460
3175 Macarthur Blvd Northbrook (60062) ***(G-16302)***
**Lundbeck LLC (HQ)** ....847 282-1000
6 Parkway N Ste 400 Deerfield (60015) ***(G-8031)***
**Lundbeck Pharmaceuticals LLC** ....847 282-1000
6 Parkway N Ste 400 Deerfield (60015) ***(G-8032)***
**Lundmark Inc** ....630 628-1199
350 S La Londe Ave Addison (60101) ***(G-184)***
**Lundmark Wax Co, Addison** *Also called Lundmark Inc* ***(G-184)***
**Lunquist Manufacturing Corp** ....815 874-2437
5681 11th St Rockford (61109) ***(G-18475)***
**Luon Energy LLC** ....217 419-2678
605 Buttercup Dr Savoy (61874) ***(G-19411)***
**Lure Group LLC** ....630 222-6515
5 Privett Ct Bolingbrook (60490) ***(G-2338)***
**Luren Precision Chicago Co Ltd** ....847 882-1388
707 Remington Rd Ste 1 Schaumburg (60173) ***(G-19624)***
**Luse Thermal Technologies LLC** ....630 862-2600
3990 Enterprise Ct Aurora (60504) ***(G-1050)***
**Luster Leaf Products Inc (PA)** ....815 337-5560
2220 Tech Ct Woodstock (60098) ***(G-22586)***
**Luster Products Inc (PA)** ....773 579-1800
1104 W 43rd St Chicago (60609) ***(G-5569)***
**Lutamar Electrical Assemblies** ....847 679-5400
8030 Ridgeway Ave Skokie (60076) ***(G-20032)***
**Lutheran General Printing Svcs** ....847 298-8040
799 Biermann Ct Ste 130 Mount Prospect (60056) ***(G-15344)***
**Lutheran Magazine, Chicago** *Also called Evang Lthn Ch Dr Mrtn Luth KG* ***(G-4785)***
**Luthers Form Grinding Company, Loves Park** *Also called Lah Inc* ***(G-13958)***
**Luttrell Engraving Inc** ....708 489-3800
5000 W 128th Pl Alsip (60803) ***(G-485)***
**Lutz Corp** ....800 203-7740
208 N Parkside Rd Normal (61761) ***(G-16075)***
**Lutz Sales Company, Schaumburg** *Also called Trellborg Sling Sltions US Inc* ***(G-19769)***
**Luvo Usa LLC (PA)** ....847 485-8595
2095 Hammond Dr Schaumburg (60173) ***(G-19625)***
**Luvo Usa LLC** ....847 485-8595
2095 Hammond Dr Schaumburg (60173) ***(G-19626)***
**Luxis International Inc** ....800 240-1473
1292 S 7th St Dekalb (60115) ***(G-8104)***
**Luxon Printing Inc** ....630 293-7710
375 Wegner Dr West Chicago (60185) ***(G-21734)***
**Luxurious Lathers Ltd** ....844 877-7627
15 Spinning Wheel Rd Hinsdale (60521) ***(G-11951)***
**Luxury Bath Liners Inc** ....630 295-9084
1958 Brandon Ct Glendale Heights (60139) ***(G-11042)***
**Luxury Bath Systems, Streator** *Also called Murray Cabinetry & Tops Inc* ***(G-20696)***
**Luxury Living Inc** ....847 845-3863
5 Tamarack Ct Cary (60013) ***(G-3358)***
**Luxury MBL & Gran Design Inc** ....773 656-2125
3206 N Kilpatrick Ave Chicago (60641) ***(G-5570)***
**Lv Ventures Inc (PA)** ....312 993-1800
233 S Wacker Dr Ste 2150 Chicago (60606) ***(G-5571)***
**Lv Ventures Inc** ....312 993-1758
233 S Wacker Dr Ste 2150 Chicago (60606) ***(G-5572)***
**Lyko Woodworking & Cnstr** ....773 583-4561
4157 N Elston Ave Chicago (60618) ***(G-5573)***
**Lynda Hervas** ....847 985-1690
800 Morse Ave Schaumburg (60193) ***(G-19627)***
**Lynfred Winery Inc (PA)** ....630 529-9463
15 S Roselle Rd Roselle (60172) ***(G-18953)***
**Lynns Printing Co** ....618 465-7701
3050 Homer M Adams Pkwy Alton (62002) ***(G-583)***
**Lyon LLC (HQ)** ....630 892-8941
420 N Main St Montgomery (60538) ***(G-15057)***
**Lyon LLC** ....815 432-4595
475 N Veterans Pkwy Watseka (60970) ***(G-21421)***
**Lyon & Dittrich Holding Co, Montgomery** *Also called L & D Group Inc* ***(G-15051)***
**Lyon & Healy Harps Inc** ....312 786-1881
168 N Ogden Ave Chicago (60607) ***(G-5574)***
**Lyon & Healy Holding Corp (HQ)** ....312 786-1881
168 N Ogden Ave Chicago (60607) ***(G-5575)***
**Lyon Workspace Products Inc** ....630 892-8941
420 N Main St Montgomery (60538) ***(G-15058)***
**Lyondell Chemical Company** ....815 942-7011
8805 Tabler Rd Morris (60450) ***(G-15114)***
**M & A Grocery** ....708 749-9786
6719 Pershing Rd Stickney (60402) ***(G-20624)***
**M & B Services Ltd Inc** ....217 463-2162
213 E Union St Paris (61944) ***(G-17153)***
**M & B Supply Inc** ....309 944-3206
208 W 1st St Geneseo (61254) ***(G-10803)***
**M & D Printing Div, Effingham** *Also called Kingery Printing Company* ***(G-8842)***
**M & D Supplies, Gilman** *Also called Gregory Martin* ***(G-10943)***
**M & F Fabrication & Welding** ....217 457-2221
2243 Mud Creek Rd Concord (62631) ***(G-7368)***
**M & G Graphics Inc** ....773 247-1596
3500 W 38th St Chicago (60632) ***(G-5576)***
**M & G Simplicitees** ....224 372-7426
39420 N Il Route 59 # 4 Lake Villa (60046) ***(G-13018)***
**M & I Acid Company Inc** ....618 676-1638
1107 S Main St Clay City (62824) ***(G-7266)***
**M & I Heating and Cooling Inc** ....773 743-7073
6405 N Campbell Ave Chicago (60645) ***(G-5577)***
**M & J Manufacturing Co Inc** ....847 364-6066
1450 Jarvis Ave Elk Grove Village (60007) ***(G-9601)***
**M & L Well Service Inc** ....618 393-7144
3648 N Illinois 130 Olney (62450) ***(G-16778)***
**M & L Well Service Inc** ....618 395-4538
800 E Main St Olney (62450) ***(G-16779)***
**M & M Exposed Aggregate Co** ....847 551-1818
155 S Washington St Carpentersville (60110) ***(G-3291)***
**M & M Paltech Inc** ....630 350-7890
860 E Jackson St Belvidere (61008) ***(G-1767)***
**M & M Patio Stone Company, Carpentersville** *Also called M & M Exposed Aggregate Co* ***(G-3291)***
**M & M Pump Co** ....217 935-2517
404 S Portland Pl Apt 2 Clinton (61727) ***(G-7286)***
**M & M Tooling Inc** ....630 595-8834
395 E Potter St Wood Dale (60191) ***(G-22392)***
**M & M Welding Inc** ....815 895-3955
410 N Main St Sycamore (60178) ***(G-20808)***
**M & N Dental** ....815 678-0036
9716 Ill Route 12 Richmond (60071) ***(G-17966)***
**M & P Talking Tees Inc** ....262 495-4000
960 W Rollins Rd Round Lake Beach (60073) ***(G-19077)***
**M & R Custom Millwork** ....815 547-8549
1979 Belford North Dr Belvidere (61008) ***(G-1768)***
**M & R Graphics Inc** ....708 534-6621
2401 Bond St University Park (60484) ***(G-21054)***
**M & R Media Inc** ....847 884-6300
1084 National Pkwy Schaumburg (60173) ***(G-19628)***
**M & R Precision Machining Inc** ....847 364-1050
680 Lively Blvd Elk Grove Village (60007) ***(G-9602)***
**M & R Printing Inc** ....847 398-2500
5100 Newport Dr Ste 4 Rolling Meadows (60008) ***(G-18742)***
**M & R Printing Equipment Inc (HQ)** ....800 736-6431
440 Medinah Rd Roselle (60172) ***(G-18954)***
**M & R Sales and Service, Roselle** *Also called M & R Printing Equipment Inc* ***(G-18954)***
**M & S Industrial Co Inc** ....773 252-1616
4334 W Division St Chicago (60651) ***(G-5578)***
**M & S Oil Well Cementing Co (PA)** ....618 262-7962
Hwy 1 N Mount Carmel (62863) ***(G-15273)***
**M & S Technologies Inc** ....847 763-0500
5715 W Howard St Niles (60714) ***(G-15997)***
**M & W Curios, Xenia** *Also called Brenda Miller* ***(G-22643)***
**M & W Feed Service** ....815 858-2412
201 S Ash St Elizabeth (61028) ***(G-9243)***
**M & W Gear Company, Gibson City** *Also called Alamo Group (il) Inc* ***(G-10897)***
**M & W Grinding of Rockford** ....815 874-9481
4697 Hydraulic Rd Rockford (61109) ***(G-18476)***
**M A C, Gurnee** *Also called Marantec America Corporation* ***(G-11469)***
**M A I, Carol Stream** *Also called Media Associates Intl Inc* ***(G-3192)***
**M and M Pallet Inc** ....708 272-4447
2810 Vermont St Blue Island (60406) ***(G-2261)***
**M B E, Gilberts** *Also called R & I Ornamental Iron Inc* ***(G-10933)***
**M B Jewelers Inc** ....312 853-3490
29 E Madison St Ste 1835 Chicago (60602) ***(G-5579)***
**M Buckman & Son Co** ....815 663-9411
200 S Greenwood St Spring Valley (61362) ***(G-20375)***
**M C F Printing Company** ....630 279-0301
118 S York St Ste 212 Elmhurst (60126) ***(G-9904)***
**M C Steel Inc** ....847 350-9618
43160 N Crawford Rd Antioch (60002) ***(G-642)***
**M CA Chicago** ....312 384-1220
7065 Veterans Blvd Burr Ridge (60527) ***(G-2863)***
**M Cor Inc** ....630 860-1150
227 James St Ste 6 Bensenville (60106) ***(G-1943)***

# ALPHABETIC SECTION — Machinex Technologies Inc

M D Harmon Inc (PA) .......... 618 662-8925
  752 Jupiter Dr  Xenia  (62899)  *(G-22644)*
M E Barber Co Inc .......... 217 428-4591
  1660 S Taylorville Rd  Decatur  (62521)  *(G-7909)*
M E F Corp .......... 815 965-8604
  1614 Christina St  Rockford  (61104)  *(G-18477)*
M F K Enterprises Inc .......... 630 516-1230
  717 N Yale Ave  Villa Park  (60181)  *(G-21266)*
M G A, Gurnee  *Also called Metropolitan Graphic Arts Inc (G-11471)*
M G M Displays Inc .......... 708 594-3699
  4956 S Monitor Ave  Chicago  (60638)  *(G-5580)*
M H Detrick Company .......... 708 479-5085
  9400 Bormet Dr Ste 10  Mokena  (60448)  *(G-14882)*
M H Electric Motor & Ctrl Corp .......... 630 393-3736
  30w250 Calumet Ave W  Warrenville  (60555)  *(G-21350)*
M Handelsman & Co .......... 312 427-0784
  6124 N Saint Louis Ave  Chicago  (60659)  *(G-5581)*
M I E America Inc .......... 847 981-6100
  420 Bennett Rd  Elk Grove Village  (60007)  *(G-9603)*
M I L, Elk Grove Village  *Also called Magnetic Inspection Lab Inc (G-9606)*
M I T Financial Group  Inc .......... 847 205-3000
  900 Skokie Blvd Ste 200  Northbrook  (60062)  *(G-16303)*
M Inc .......... 312 853-0512
  205 W Wacker Dr Ste 307  Chicago  (60606)  *(G-5582)*
M J Burton Engraving Co .......... 217 223-7273
  300 N 12th St  Quincy  (62301)  *(G-17854)*
M J Celco Inc (PA) .......... 847 671-1900
  3900 Wesley Ter  Schiller Park  (60176)  *(G-19843)*
M J Kull LLC .......... 217 246-5952
  1911 3rd St  Lerna  (62440)  *(G-13288)*
M J Molding, Hebron  *Also called Sherwood Tool  Inc (G-11726)*
M K Advantage Inc .......... 773 902-5272
  1055 W Bryn Mawr Ave F216  Chicago  (60660)  *(G-5583)*
M L Products, Dixon  *Also called Zuma Corporation (G-8361)*
M L Rongo  Inc .......... 630 540-1120
  1281 Humbracht Cir Ste A  Bartlett  (60103)  *(G-1360)*
M L S Printing Co Inc .......... 847 948-8902
  537 Hermitage Dr  Deerfield  (60015)  *(G-8033)*
M Lizen Manufacturing Co .......... 708 755-7213
  2625 Federal Signal Dr  University Park  (60484)  *(G-21055)*
M M Marketing .......... 815 459-7968
  4501 Il Route 176 Ste B  Crystal Lake  (60014)  *(G-7603)*
M Martinez Inc .......... 847 740-6364
  828 Warrior St  Round Lake Heights  (60073)  *(G-19081)*
M Mauritzon & Company  Inc .......... 773 235-6000
  3939 W Belden Ave  Chicago  (60647)  *(G-5584)*
M O W Printing  Inc .......... 618 345-5525
  526 Vandalia St  Collinsville  (62234)  *(G-7331)*
M P I Labels Systems, University Park  *Also called Miller Products  Inc (G-21058)*
M P V  Inc .......... 847 234-3960
  214 Fairway Rd  Lake Zurich  (60047)  *(G-13097)*
M Putterman & Co LLC (HQ) .......... 773 927-4120
  4834 S Oakley Ave  Chicago  (60609)  *(G-5585)*
M Putterman & Co LLC .......... 773 734-1000
  1581 E 98th St  Chicago  (60628)  *(G-5586)*
M R C, Oak Brook  *Also called Michaels Ross and Cole Inc (G-16543)*
M R C, Joliet  *Also called MRC Global (us) Inc (G-12544)*
M R Glenn Electric  Inc .......... 708 479-9200
  200 W 6th St  Lockport  (60441)  *(G-13729)*
M R O Solutions LLC .......... 847 588-2480
  5645 W Howard St  Niles  (60714)  *(G-15998)*
M S —action Machining Corp .......... 815 344-3770
  4061 W Dayton St  McHenry  (60050)  *(G-14524)*
M S A Printing Co .......... 847 593-5699
  850 Touhy Ave  Elk Grove Village  (60007)  *(G-9604)*
M S Tool & Engineering .......... 630 876-3437
  1200 Atlantic Dr  West Chicago  (60185)  *(G-21735)*
M SM, Sterling  *Also called Westwood Machine & Tool Co (G-20622)*
M Squared Industries LLC .......... 708 606-2603
  828 W Grace St  Chicago  (60613)  *(G-5587)*
M T E Hydraulics, Rockford  *Also called Mechanical Tool & Engrg Co (G-18490)*
M T H Industries, Hillside  *Also called Hillside Industries Inc (G-11920)*
M T I Industries, Volo  *Also called Marine Technologies Inc (G-21318)*
M T M Assn For Standards & RES .......... 847 299-1111
  1111 E Touhy Ave Ste 280  Des Plaines  (60018)  *(G-8224)*
M T S, Saint Charles  *Also called Metal Technology Solutions (G-19219)*
M Ward Manufacturing Co Inc .......... 847 864-4786
  2222-2230 Main St  Evanston  (60202)  *(G-10067)*
M Wells Printing Co .......... 312 455-0400
  329 W 18th St Ste 502  Chicago  (60616)  *(G-5588)*
M& L Noodle .......... 773 878-3333
  1130 W Argyle St  Chicago  (60640)  *(G-5589)*
M&J Hauling Inc .......... 312 342-6596
  2048 W Hubbard St  Chicago  (60612)  *(G-5590)*
M&M Embroidery Corp .......... 847 209-1086
  1188 E Cunningham Dr  Palatine  (60074)  *(G-17052)*
M&M Mars, Chicago  *Also called Mars Chocolate North Amer LLC (G-5630)*
M&R Custom Mill Work, Belvidere  *Also called M & R Custom Millwork (G-1768)*

M&R Holdings  Inc (PA) .......... 630 858-6101
  440 Medinah Rd  Roselle  (60172)  *(G-18955)*
M&R Printing, Roselle  *Also called M&R Holdings  Inc (G-18955)*
M-1 Tool Works Inc .......... 815 344-1275
  1419 S Belden St  McHenry  (60050)  *(G-14525)*
M-Wave International  LLC .......... 630 562-5550
  100 High Grove Blvd  Glendale Heights  (60139)  *(G-11043)*
M. Bauer & Associates, Bannockburn  *Also called Marshall Bauer (G-1260)*
M.S.i, Broadview  *Also called Multi Swatch Corporation (G-2600)*
M.S.I., Addison  *Also called Mexacali Silkscreen Inc (G-203)*
M13 Graphics, Schaumburg  *Also called M13 Inc (G-19629)*
M13 Inc .......... 847 310-1913
  1300 Basswood Rd Ste 100  Schaumburg  (60173)  *(G-19629)*
M2m Enterprises  LLC .......... 847 899-7565
  930 Ascot Dr  Elgin  (60123)  *(G-9097)*
Maac Machinery Co  Inc .......... 630 665-1700
  590 Tower Blvd  Carol Stream  (60188)  *(G-3187)*
Maaldar Pukhtoon Group  LLC .......... 630 696-1723
  339 E Army Trail Rd  Glendale Heights  (60139)  *(G-11044)*
Maasdam Pow'r-Pull, Schaumburg  *Also called Pullr Holding Company  LLC (G-19704)*
Maass Midwest Mfg Inc (PA) .......... 847 669-5135
  11283 Dundee Rd  Huntley  (60142)  *(G-12160)*
Maasscorp  Inc .......... 763 383-1400
  1400 Eddy Ave  Rockford  (61103)  *(G-18478)*
Mab Pharmacy Inc .......... 773 342-5878
  2643 W Division St Ste 1  Chicago  (60622)  *(G-5591)*
Mac American Corporation .......... 847 277-9450
  530 Fox Glen Ct  Barrington  (60010)  *(G-1288)*
Mac Graphics Group Inc .......... 630 620-7200
  17w703 Butterfield Rd D  Oakbrook Terrace  (60181)  *(G-16716)*
Mac Lean-Fogg Company (PA) .......... 847 566-0010
  1000 Allanson Rd  Mundelein  (60060)  *(G-15521)*
Mac Lean-Fogg Company .......... 847 288-2534
  11411 Addison Ave  Franklin Park  (60131)  *(G-10519)*
Mac Medical Inc .......... 618 719-6757
  325 W Main St  Belleville  (62220)  *(G-1650)*
Mac's Snacks, Chicago  *Also called Evans Foods  Inc (G-4787)*
Mac-Ster  Inc .......... 847 830-7013
  1420 W Bernard Dr  Addison  (60101)  *(G-185)*
Mac-Weld Inc .......... 618 529-1828
  612 San Diego Rd  Carbondale  (62901)  *(G-3015)*
Mac-Weld Partnership, Carbondale  *Also called Mac-Weld Inc (G-3015)*
Macari Appliance Center, Shelbyville  *Also called Macari Service Center Inc (G-19910)*
Macari Service Center Inc (PA) .......... 217 774-4214
  N Rte 128  Shelbyville  (62565)  *(G-19910)*
Maccarb Inc .......... 877 427-2499
  2430 Millennium Dr  Elgin  (60124)  *(G-9098)*
Macdermid Enthone Inc .......... 708 598-3210
  9809 Industrial Dr  Bridgeview  (60455)  *(G-2505)*
Mace Iron Works  Inc (PA) .......... 708 479-2456
  221 Industry Ave  Frankfort  (60423)  *(G-10341)*
Mach Mechanical Group  LLC .......... 630 674-6224
  28w016 Country View Dr  Naperville  (60564)  *(G-15815)*
Mach Mining  LLC .......... 618 983-3020
  16468 Liberty School Rd  Marion  (62959)  *(G-14271)*
Machine & Design .......... 630 858-6416
  767 Willis St  Glen Ellyn  (60137)  *(G-10979)*
Machine Control Systems Inc (PA) .......... 708 389-2160
  12424 S Austin Ave  Palos Heights  (60463)  *(G-17108)*
Machine Control Systems Inc .......... 708 597-1200
  12549 S Laramie Ave  Alsip  (60803)  *(G-486)*
Machine Job Shop, Milan  *Also called Gett Industries Ltd (G-14787)*
Machine Medics LLC .......... 309 633-5454
  5726 W Plank Rd  Peoria  (61604)  *(G-17404)*
Machine Solution Providers Inc .......... 630 717-7040
  2659 Wisconsin Ave  Downers Grove  (60515)  *(G-8481)*
Machine Tech Services, Marseilles  *Also called Machine Technology Inc (G-14313)*
Machine Technology Inc .......... 815 444-4837
  221 Erick St  Crystal Lake  (60014)  *(G-7604)*
Machine Technology Inc (PA) .......... 815 795-6818
  1020 Broadway St  Marseilles  (61341)  *(G-14313)*
Machine Tool Acc & Mfg Co .......... 773 489-0903
  1915 W Fullerton Ave  Chicago  (60614)  *(G-5592)*
Machine Tools Div., Addison  *Also called Mitsubishi Heavy Inds Amer Inc (G-217)*
Machine Works  Inc .......... 708 597-1665
  5621 W 120th St  Alsip  (60803)  *(G-487)*
Machine Works of Decatur Inc .......... 217 428-3896
  2035 E Garfield Ave  Decatur  (62526)  *(G-7910)*
Machined Concepts  LLC .......... 847 708-4923
  1760 Britannia Dr Ste 8  Elgin  (60124)  *(G-9099)*
Machined Metals Manufacturing .......... 847 364-6116
  1450 Jarvis Ave  Elk Grove Village  (60007)  *(G-9605)*
Machined Products, Elk Grove Village  *Also called Fabricated Metals Co (G-9474)*
Machinex Manufacturing Co Inc .......... 630 766-4210
  225 James St Ste 4  Bensenville  (60106)  *(G-1944)*
Machinex Technologies Inc .......... 773 867-8801
  8770 W Bryn Mawr Ave # 1300  Chicago  (60631)  *(G-5593)*

**Machining Systems Corporation** .......................... 708 385-7903
14003 Kostner Ave  Crestwood  (60445)  *(G-7493)*
**Machining Technology Inc** .................................... 815 469-0400
418 Keepataw Dr  Lemont  (60439)  *(G-13240)*
**Macholl Metal Fabrication** .................................... 815 597-1908
6934 Garden Prairie Rd  Garden Prairie  (61038)  *(G-10795)*
**Mackay Mitchell Envelope Co** .............................. 847 418-3866
707 Skokie Blvd Ste 600  Northbrook  (60062)  *(G-16304)*
**Mackenzie Johnson** .............................................. 630 244-2367
1826 S 10th Ave  Maywood  (60153)  *(G-14428)*
**Mackin Group LLC** ................................................ 847 245-4201
447 Red Cedar Rd  Lake Villa  (60046)  *(G-13019)*
**Macklin Inc (PA)** ................................................... 815 562-4803
6089 Dement Rd  Rochelle  (61068)  *(G-18096)*
**Macks Wood Working** .......................................... 630 953-2559
544 S Highland Ave  Lombard  (60148)  *(G-13823)*
**Maclean Fastener Services LLC** .......................... 847 353-8402
355 W Dundee Rd Ste 105  Buffalo Grove  (60089)  *(G-2729)*
**Maclean Fasteners, Mundelein**  Also called Mac Lean-Fogg Company  *(G-15521)*
**Maclean Senior Industries LLC** ............................ 630 350-1600
610 Pond Dr  Wood Dale  (60191)  *(G-22393)*
**Maclee Chemical Company Inc** ............................ 847 480-0953
1316 Edgewood Ln  Northbrook  (60062)  *(G-16305)*
**Macneal Hospital** .................................................. 773 581-2199
4009 W 59th St  Chicago  (60629)  *(G-5594)*
**Maco Antennas, Mount Carroll**  Also called Charles Electronics LLC  *(G-15290)*
**Maco Business Forms, Peoria**  Also called Proform  *(G-17437)*
**Maco-Sys LLC** ...................................................... 779 888-3260
4317 Maray Dr  Rockford  (61107)  *(G-18479)*
**Macomb Concrete Products Inc** .......................... 309 772-3826
11 Hillcrest Dr  Bushnell  (61422)  *(G-2904)*
**Macon Metal Products Co** ................................... 217 824-7205
803 W Calvert St  Taylorville  (62568)  *(G-20842)*
**Macon Sand & Gravel, Decatur**  Also called Legacy Vulcan LLC  *(G-7908)*
**Macoupin County Enquirer Inc** ............................ 217 854-2534
125 E Main St  Carlinville  (62626)  *(G-3042)*
**Macoupin Energy LLC** .......................................... 217 854-3291
14300 Brushy Mound Rd  Carlinville  (62626)  *(G-3043)*
**Macoupin Energy LLC** .......................................... 217 854-3291
14300 Brushy Mound Rd  Carlinville  (62626)  *(G-3044)*
**Madden Communications Inc (PA)** ...................... 630 787-2200
901 Mittel Dr  Wood Dale  (60191)  *(G-22394)*
**Madden Communications Inc** .............................. 630 784-4325
355 Longview Dr  Bloomingdale  (60108)  *(G-2114)*
**Madden Ventures Inc** ........................................... 847 487-0644
1045 Campus Dr Ste A  Mundelein  (60060)  *(G-15522)*
**Made As Intended Inc** .......................................... 630 789-3494
3423 Spring Rd  Oak Brook  (60523)  *(G-16538)*
**Made By Hands Inc** .............................................. 773 761-4200
3501 N Southport Ave # 352  Chicago  (60657)  *(G-5595)*
**Made Rite Bedding Company** .............................. 847 349-5886
11221 Melrose Ave  Franklin Park  (60131)  *(G-10520)*
**Mademoiselle Inc** ................................................. 773 394-4555
4200 W Schubert Ave  Chicago  (60639)  *(G-5596)*
**Madison Capital Partners Corp (PA)** ................... 312 277-0323
500 W Madison St Ste 3890  Chicago  (60661)  *(G-5597)*
**Madison County Publications** .............................. 618 344-0265
2 Executive Dr  Collinsville  (62234)  *(G-7332)*
**Madison County Publications (HQ)** ..................... 618 344-0264
113 E Clay St  Collinsville  (62234)  *(G-7333)*
**Madison Farms Butter Company (PA)** ................ 217 854-2547
1100 Broadway  Carlinville  (62626)  *(G-3045)*
**Madison Inds Holdings LLC (PA)** ........................ 312 277-0156
500 W Madison St Ste 3890  Chicago  (60661)  *(G-5598)*
**Madmaxmar Group Inc** ........................................ 630 320-3700
1 Pierce Pl Ste 510w  Itasca  (60143)  *(G-12308)*
**Mafomsic Incorporated** ........................................ 630 279-2005
756 N Industrial Dr  Elmhurst  (60126)  *(G-9905)*
**Mag Daddy LLC** ................................................... 847 719-5600
1155 Rose Rd  Lake Zurich  (60047)  *(G-13098)*
**Mag Tag** ............................................................... 847 647-6255
7113 N Austin Ave  Niles  (60714)  *(G-15999)*
**Mag-Drive LLC** ..................................................... 847 690-0871
2225 E Oakton St  Arlington Heights  (60005)  *(G-797)*
**Magazine Advertising Dept, Chicago**  Also called Hearst Corporation  *(G-5064)*
**Magazine Plus** ...................................................... 773 281-4106
2445 N Clark St  Chicago  (60614)  *(G-5599)*
**Magenta LLC (PA)** ............................................... 773 777-5050
15160 New Ave  Lockport  (60441)  *(G-13730)*
**Magic Mist, The, Lincolnshire**  Also called Paralleldirect LLC  *(G-13471)*
**Magic Mold Removal** ............................................ 630 486-0912
689 Wood St  Aurora  (60505)  *(G-1183)*
**Magic Sleep Mattress Co Inc** ............................... 815 795-6942
220 Commercial St  Marseilles  (61341)  *(G-14314)*
**Magic Solutions Inc** ............................................. 312 647-8688
5455 N Sheridan Rd # 3809  Chicago  (60640)  *(G-5600)*
**Magid Glove Safety Mfg Co LLC (PA)** ................. 773 384-2070
1300 Naperville Dr  Romeoville  (60446)  *(G-18841)*
**Magid Glove Safety Mfg Co LLC** ......................... 773 384-2070
1805 N Hamlin Ave  Chicago  (60647)  *(G-5601)*

**Magiglide, Mokena**  Also called Landquist & Son Inc  *(G-14878)*
**Magna Exteriors America Inc** ............................... 618 327-4381
18310 Enterprise Ave  Nashville  (62263)  *(G-15837)*
**Magna Extrors Intrors Amer Inc** .......................... 847 548-9170
414 Flanders Ln  Grayslake  (60030)  *(G-11353)*
**Magna Extrors Intrors Amer Inc** .......................... 618 327-2136
18355 Enterprise Ave  Nashville  (62263)  *(G-15838)*
**Magna-Flux International** ..................................... 815 623-7634
11898 Burnside Ln  Roscoe  (61073)  *(G-18904)*
**Magna-Lock Acquisition, Rockford**  Also called Magna-Lock Usa Inc  *(G-18480)*
**Magna-Lock Usa Inc** ............................................ 815 962-8700
2730 Eastrock Dr  Rockford  (61109)  *(G-18480)*
**Magnalock, Rockford**  Also called Tri-Cam Inc  *(G-18656)*
**Magneco Inc (HQ)** ................................................ 630 543-6660
223 W Interstate Rd  Addison  (60101)  *(G-186)*
**Magneco Inc** ......................................................... 630 543-6660
206 W Factory Rd  Addison  (60101)  *(G-187)*
**Magneco/Metrel Inc (PA)** ..................................... 630 543-6660
223 W Interstate Rd  Addison  (60101)  *(G-188)*
**Magnecraft, Schaumburg**  Also called SE Relays LLC  *(G-19724)*
**Magnet-Schultz Amer Holdg LLC (PA)** ................ 630 789-0600
401 Plaza Dr  Westmont  (60559)  *(G-21901)*
**Magnet-Schultz America Inc** ................................ 630 789-0600
401 Plaza Dr  Westmont  (60559)  *(G-21902)*
**Magnetic Coil Manufacturing Co** ......................... 630 787-1948
325 Beinoris Dr Ste A  Wood Dale  (60191)  *(G-22395)*
**Magnetic Components, Schiller Park**  Also called Marvel Electric Corporation  *(G-19846)*
**Magnetic Devices Inc** ........................................... 815 459-0077
150 Virginia Rd Ste 5  Crystal Lake  (60014)  *(G-7605)*
**Magnetic Inspection Lab Inc** ............................... 847 437-4488
1401 Greenleaf Ave  Elk Grove Village  (60007)  *(G-9606)*
**Magnetic Occasions & More Inc** ......................... 815 462-4141
21605 S Schoolhouse Rd  New Lenox  (60451)  *(G-15892)*
**Magnetic Signs** .................................................... 773 476-6551
4922 S Western Ave  Chicago  (60609)  *(G-5602)*
**Magnetrol International Inc (PA)** ......................... 630 723-6600
705 Enterprise St  Aurora  (60504)  *(G-1051)*
**Magnetstreet, Carol Stream**  Also called Master Marketing Intl Inc  *(G-3189)*
**Magnetstreet, Carol Stream**  Also called Master Marketing Intl Inc  *(G-3190)*
**Magnify Peace, Chicago**  Also called Dove Foundation  *(G-4637)*
**Magnum International Inc** .................................... 708 889-9999
1965 Bernice Rd Ste 2se  Lansing  (60438)  *(G-13175)*
**Magnum Machining LLC** ...................................... 815 678-6800
11427 Coml Ave Unit 19  Richmond  (60071)  *(G-17967)*
**Magnum Steel Works Inc** .................................... 618 244-5190
200 Shiloh Dr  Mount Vernon  (62864)  *(G-15423)*
**Magnus Screw Products Co** ................................ 773 889-2344
1818 N Latrobe Ave  Chicago  (60639)  *(G-5603)*
**Magnuson Group Inc** ............................................ 630 783-8100
1400 Internationale Pkwy  Woodridge  (60517)  *(G-22501)*
**Magrabar LLC** ....................................................... 847 965-7550
6100 Madison Ct  Morton Grove  (60053)  *(G-15215)*
**Magros Processing** .............................................. 217 438-2880
3150 Stanton St  Springfield  (62703)  *(G-20473)*
**Mah Machine Company** ....................................... 708 656-1826
3301 S Central Ave  Cicero  (60804)  *(G-7217)*
**Mahans Fiberglass** .............................................. 309 562-7349
106 E Main St  Easton  (62633)  *(G-8777)*
**Maher Publications Inc** ........................................ 630 941-2030
102 N Haven Rd  Elmhurst  (60126)  *(G-9906)*
**Mahoney Asphalt, Swansea**  Also called Charles E Mahoney Company  *(G-20776)*
**Mahoney Environmental Inc (PA)** ........................ 815 730-2087
712 Essington Rd  Joliet  (60435)  *(G-12535)*
**Mahoney Foundries Inc** ....................................... 309 784-2311
29 N Main St  Vermont  (61484)  *(G-21138)*
**Mahoney Publishing Inc** ...................................... 815 369-5384
707 Maple St  Lena  (61048)  *(G-13281)*
**MAI Apparel, Oak Brook**  Also called Made As Intended Inc  *(G-16538)*
**Maid O Mist LLC** .................................................. 773 685-7300
3217 N Pulaski Rd  Chicago  (60641)  *(G-5604)*
**Maidenform LLC** .................................................. 630 898-8419
1650 Premium Outlet Blvd # 233  Aurora  (60502)  *(G-1052)*
**Maiers Bakery** ...................................................... 847 967-8042
9328 Waukegan Rd  Morton Grove  (60053)  *(G-15216)*
**Mail Box Store, The, Bethalto**  Also called Eagle Express Mail LLC  *(G-2081)*
**Mail-Well, Chicago**  Also called Cenveo Corporation  *(G-4281)*
**Mail-Well, Chicago**  Also called Cenveo Inc  *(G-4279)*
**Mail-Well, Chicago**  Also called Cenveo Inc  *(G-4280)*
**Mailbox International Inc** ..................................... 847 541-8466
220 Messner Dr  Wheeling  (60090)  *(G-22097)*
**Mailbox Plus** ........................................................ 847 577-1737
1516 N Elmhurst Rd  Mount Prospect  (60056)  *(G-15345)*
**Mailcrafters, Crestwood**  Also called Inscerco Mfg Inc  *(G-7489)*
**Mailers Company, Elk Grove Village**  Also called Pulver Inc  *(G-9701)*
**Maimin Technology Group Inc** ............................. 847 263-8200
227 Ambrogio Dr Ste B  Gurnee  (60031)  *(G-11468)*
**Main Office, Ramsey**  Also called G L Beaumont Lumber Company  *(G-17913)*

**Main Source Machining** ....815 962-8770
2411 Latham St Rockford (61103) *(G-18481)*
**Main Steel LLC (PA)** ....847 916-1220
2200 Pratt Blvd Elk Grove Village (60007) *(G-9607)*
**Main Steel - Corporate 6001, Elk Grove Village** *Also called Main Steel Polishing Co Inc (G-9608)*
**Main Steel Polishing Co Inc (PA)** ....847 916-1220
2200 Pratt Blvd Elk Grove Village (60007) *(G-9608)*
**Main Street Market Roscoe Inc** ....815 623-6328
9515 N 2nd St Roscoe (61073) *(G-18905)*
**Main Street Meat Co, Roscoe** *Also called Main Street Market Roscoe Inc (G-18905)*
**Main Street Records** ....618 244-2737
313 S 10th St Mount Vernon (62864) *(G-15424)*
**Main Street Visuals Inc** ....847 869-7446
8340 Callie Ave Unit 110 Morton Grove (60053) *(G-15217)*
**Main Surplus Store, Aurora** *Also called Johnos Inc (G-1178)*
**Maintenance Tech Training, Willowbrook** *Also called Applied Tech Publications Inc (G-22199)*
**Majestic Archtctural Wdwrk Inc** ....708 240-8484
2150 Madison St Bellwood (60104) *(G-1713)*
**Majestic Spring Inc** ....847 593-8887
1390 Jarvis Ave Elk Grove Village (60007) *(G-9609)*
**Majesty Cases Inc** ....847 546-2558
34550 N Wilson Rd Ingleside (60041) *(G-12193)*
**Major Die & Engineering Co** ....630 773-3444
1352 Industrial Dr Itasca (60143) *(G-12309)*
**Major Prime Plastics Inc** ....630 953-4111
300 S Mitchell Ct Addison (60101) *(G-189)*
**Major Wire Incorporated** ....708 457-0121
7014 W Cullom Ave Norridge (60706) *(G-16105)*
**Major-Prime Plastics Inc** ....630 834-9400
649 N Ardmore Ave Villa Park (60181) *(G-21267)*
**Mak-System Corp** ....847 803-4863
2720 S River Rd Ste 225 Des Plaines (60018) *(G-8225)*
**Make It Better LLC** ....847 256-4642
1150 Wilmette Ave Ste I Wilmette (60091) *(G-22261)*
**Make It Better.net, Wilmette** *Also called Make It Better LLC (G-22261)*
**Makerite Mfg Co Inc** ....815 389-3902
13571 Metric Rd Roscoe (61073) *(G-18906)*
**Maki Sushi & Noodle Shop** ....847 318-1920
12 S Northwest Hwy Park Ridge (60068) *(G-17207)*
**Makkah Printing** ....630 980-2315
1979 Bloomingdale Rd Glendale Heights (60139) *(G-11045)*
**Mako Mold Corporation** ....630 377-9010
3820 Ohio Ave Ste 7 Saint Charles (60174) *(G-19212)*
**Mako Networks, Elgin** *Also called D & S Communications Inc (G-9008)*
**Makowskis Real Sausage Co** ....312 842-5330
2710 S Poplar Ave Chicago (60608) *(G-5605)*
**Makray Manufacturing Company (PA)** ....708 456-7100
4400 N Harlem Ave Norridge (60706) *(G-16106)*
**Makray Manufacturing Company** ....847 260-5408
9515 Seymour Ave Schiller Park (60176) *(G-19844)*
**Malca-Amit North America Inc** ....312 346-1507
5 S Wabash Ave Ste 1414 Chicago (60603) *(G-5606)*
**Malcolite Corporation (PA)** ....847 562-1350
1161 Lake Cook Rd Ste I Deerfield (60015) *(G-8034)*
**Mall Graphic Inc** ....847 668-7600
12693 Cold Springs Dr Huntley (60142) *(G-12161)*
**Mall Publishing, Huntley** *Also called Mall Graphic Inc (G-12161)*
**Mallard Handling Solutions LLC (PA)** ....815 625-9491
101 Mallard Rd Sterling (61081) *(G-20596)*
**Mallard Manufacturing, Sterling** *Also called Mallard Handling Solutions LLC (G-20596)*
**Mallinckrodt LLC** ....618 664-2111
100 Louis Latzer Dr Greenville (62246) *(G-11397)*
**Mallof Abruzino Nash Mktg Inc** ....630 929-5200
765 Kimberly Dr Carol Stream (60188) *(G-3188)*
**Malthandlingcom LLC** ....773 888-7718
800 N Winthrop Ave S 2 Chicago (60660) *(G-5607)*
**Malvaes Solutions Incorporated** ....773 823-1034
4243 W Ogden Ave Chicago (60623) *(G-5608)*
**Mama Bosso Pizza, Rock Island** *Also called Afs Classico LLC (G-18158)*
**Mamata Enterprises Inc (HQ)** ....941 205-0227
2275 Cornell Ave Montgomery (60538) *(G-15059)*
**Man Marketing, Carol Stream** *Also called Mallof Abruzino Nash Mktg Inc (G-3188)*
**Managed Marketing Inc** ....847 279-8260
2232 Foster Ave Wheeling (60090) *(G-22098)*
**Manan Medical Products Inc (HQ)** ....847 637-3333
241 W Palatine Rd Wheeling (60090) *(G-22099)*
**Manan Tool & Manufacturing** ....847 637-3333
241 W Palatine Rd Wheeling (60090) *(G-22100)*
**Mancillas International Ltd (PA)** ....847 441-7748
47 Longmeadow Rd Winnetka (60093) *(G-22311)*
**Mancillas Intl, Winnetka** *Also called Mancillas International Ltd (G-22311)*
**Mancuso Cheese Company** ....815 722-2475
612 Mills Rd Ste 1 Joliet (60433) *(G-12536)*
**Mandel Metals Inc (PA)** ....847 455-6606
11400 Addison Ave Franklin Park (60131) *(G-10521)*
**Mandel Metals Inc** ....847 455-7446
11400 W Addison St Franklin Park (60131) *(G-10522)*
**Mandis Dental Laboratory** ....618 345-3777
607 Vandalia St Ste 300 Collinsville (62234) *(G-7334)*
**Mandus Group Ltd** ....309 786-1507
2408 4th Ave Rock Island (61201) *(G-18187)*
**Mandys Kitchen & Grill** ....630 348-2264
431u N Bolingbrook Dr Bolingbrook (60440) *(G-2339)*
**Mangel & Co, Buffalo Grove** *Also called Long Grove Confectionery Co (G-2728)*
**Mangel and Co (PA)** ....847 459-3100
333 Lexington Dr Buffalo Grove (60089) *(G-2730)*
**Mangel and Co** ....847 634-0730
230 Rbert Prker Coffin Rd Long Grove (60047) *(G-13894)*
**Mangelsdorf Seed Co, Teutopolis** *Also called Siemer Enterprises Inc (G-20855)*
**Mangold Networks** ....224 402-0068
514 S 1st St West Dundee (60118) *(G-21800)*
**Manhattan Eyelash EXT Sew On** ....847 818-8774
8 S Dunton Ave Arlington Heights (60005) *(G-798)*
**Manitex International Inc (PA)** ....708 430-7500
9725 Industrial Dr Bridgeview (60455) *(G-2506)*
**Manitex Material Handling Div, Bridgeview** *Also called Schaeff Lift Truck Inc (G-2527)*
**Manitou Americas Inc** ....262 334-9461
888 Landmark Dr Belvidere (61008) *(G-1769)*
**Manitowoc Lifts and Mfg LLC** ....815 748-9500
155 Harvestore Dr Dekalb (60115) *(G-8105)*
**Mann+hummel Filtration Tech** ....800 407-9263
4500 Prime Pkwy McHenry (60050) *(G-14526)*
**Mann+hummel Filtration Technol** ....815 759-7744
1380 Corporate Dr McHenry (60050) *(G-14527)*
**Manna Organics LLC** ....630 795-0500
4650 Western Ave Lisle (60532) *(G-13618)*
**Manner Plating Inc** ....815 877-7791
926 River Ln Loves Park (61111) *(G-13963)*
**Manning Material Services Inc** ....847 669-5750
11804 S Il Route 47 Huntley (60142) *(G-12162)*
**Manor Tool and Mfg Co (PA)** ....847 678-2020
9200 Ivanhoe St Schiller Park (60176) *(G-19845)*
**Manpasand Restaurant, Arlington Heights** *Also called Swagath Group Inc (G-849)*
**Manroland Inc (HQ)** ....630 920-2000
800 E Oakhill Dr Westmont (60559) *(G-21903)*
**Manroland Web Systems Inc** ....630 920-5850
2150 Western Ct Ste 420 Lisle (60532) *(G-13619)*
**Manroland Websystems, Westmont** *Also called Manroland Inc (G-21903)*
**Manscore LLC** ....630 297-7502
1239 Gilbert Ave Downers Grove (60515) *(G-8482)*
**Manteno Quarry, Manteno** *Also called Legacy Vulcan LLC (G-14186)*
**Manu Industries Inc** ....847 891-6412
977 Lunt Ave Schaumburg (60193) *(G-19630)*
**Manu-TEC of Illinois LLC** ....630 543-3022
415 W Belden Ave Ste E Addison (60101) *(G-190)*
**Manufactured Specialties Inc** ....630 444-1992
3575 Stern Ave Saint Charles (60174) *(G-19213)*
**Manufacturers Alliance Corp** ....847 696-1600
320 W Saint Charles Rd Villa Park (60181) *(G-21268)*
**Manufacturers Inv Group LLC** ....630 285-0800
690 Hilltop Dr Itasca (60143) *(G-12310)*
**Manufacturers News Inc** ....847 864-7000
1633 Central St Evanston (60201) *(G-10068)*
**Manufacturing / Woodworking** ....847 730-4823
1054 S River Rd Des Plaines (60016) *(G-8226)*
**Manufacturing Tech Group Inc** ....815 966-2300
3520 N Main St Rockford (61103) *(G-18482)*
**Manufasteners House Iq Inc** ....847 705-6538
427 S Middleton Ave Palatine (60067) *(G-17053)*
**Manufctrers Claring Hse of Ill (PA)** ....773 545-6300
4875 N Elston Ave Chicago (60630) *(G-5609)*
**Manufctrng-Resourcing Intl Inc** ....217 821-3733
5265 E 1800th Ave Shumway (62461) *(G-19933)*
**Manufcture Dsign Innvation Inc** ....773 526-7773
1760 Metoyer Ct Unit F West Chicago (60185) *(G-21736)*
**Map Oil Co Inc** ....618 375-7616
139 County Road 990 E Grayville (62844) *(G-11374)*
**Map Systems, Elk Grove Village** *Also called Clear Lam Packaging Inc (G-9377)*
**Mapei Corporation** ....630 293-5800
530 Industrial Dr West Chicago (60185) *(G-21737)*
**Mapes & Sprowl Steel LLC** ....800 777-1025
1100 E Devon Ave Elk Grove Village (60007) *(G-9610)*
**Maple Park Landscape Supplies, Maple Park** *Also called Maple Park Trucking Inc (G-14202)*
**Maple Park Trucking Inc** ....815 899-1958
50w 363 Isle Rr 64 Maple Park (60151) *(G-14202)*
**Maplehurst Bakeries LLC** ....773 826-1245
3220 W Grand Ave Chicago (60651) *(G-5610)*
**Maplehurst Farms Inc (PA)** ....815 562-8723
936 S Moore Rd Rochelle (61068) *(G-18097)*
**Mar Cor Purification Inc** ....630 435-1017
2850 Hitchcock Ave Downers Grove (60515) *(G-8483)*
**Mar Graphics** ....618 935-2111
523 S Meyer Ave Valmeyer (62295) *(G-21112)*
**Mar-Don Corporation** ....847 823-4958
115 Columbia Ave Park Ridge (60068) *(G-17208)*

ALPHABETIC

**Mar-Fre Manufacturing Co** 630 377-1022
2541 Dukane Dr Saint Charles (60174) ***(G-19214)***
**Mar-TEC Research Inc** 630 879-1200
1315 Paramount Pkwy Batavia (60510) ***(G-1465)***
**Maranatha Christian Revival Ch, Chicago** *Also called Marantha Wrld Rvval Ministries* ***(G-5611)***
**Marantec America Corporation (HQ)** 847 596-6400
5705 Centerpoint Ct Gurnee (60031) ***(G-11469)***
**Marantha Wrld Rvval Ministries (PA)** 773 384-7717
4301 W Diversey Ave Chicago (60639) ***(G-5611)***
**Marathon Cutting Die Inc** 847 398-5165
2340 Foster Ave Wheeling (60090) ***(G-22101)***
**Marathon Gas, Rolling Meadows** *Also called 4200 Kirchoff Corp* ***(G-18705)***
**Marathon Manufacturing Inc** 630 543-6262
110 W Laura Dr Addison (60101) ***(G-191)***
**Marathon One Stop Shop, Newton** *Also called Petron Oil Production Inc* ***(G-15946)***
**Marathon Petroleum Company LP** 618 544-2121
400 S Marathon Ave Robinson (62454) ***(G-18066)***
**Marathon Petroleum Company LP** 618 829-3288
200 E 4th St Saint Elmo (62458) ***(G-19308)***
**Marathon Sportswear Inc** 708 389-5390
12757 Homan Ave Blue Island (60406) ***(G-2262)***
**Marathon Technologies Inc** 847 378-8572
800 Nicholas Blvd Elk Grove Village (60007) ***(G-9611)***
**Marbil Enterprises Inc** 618 257-1810
129 Wild Rose Dr Belleville (62221) ***(G-1651)***
**Marble Emporium Inc** 847 205-4000
2200 Carlson Dr Northbrook (60062) ***(G-16306)***
**Marble Machine Inc (PA)** 217 431-3014
21204 Rileysburg Rd Danville (61834) ***(G-7751)***
**Marble Machine Inc** 217 442-0746
205 Oakwood Ave Danville (61832) ***(G-7752)***
**Marble Works, South Elgin** *Also called Wienmar Inc* ***(G-20235)***
**Marc Business Forms Inc** 847 568-9200
6416 N Ridgeway Ave Lincolnwood (60712) ***(G-13524)***
**Marca Industries Inc** 773 884-4500
5901 W 79th St 400 Burbank (60459) ***(G-2808)***
**Marcal Rope & Rigging Inc (PA)** 618 462-0172
1862 E Broadway Alton (62002) ***(G-584)***
**Marcal Rope & Rigging Inc** 618 462-0172
5357 Industrial Park Dr Metropolis (62960) ***(G-14756)***
**Marcells Pallet Inc (PA)** 773 265-1200
4221 W Ferdinand St Chicago (60624) ***(G-5612)***
**March Manufacturing Inc (PA)** 847 729-5300
1819 Pickwick Ln Glenview (60026) ***(G-11167)***
**March Pumps, Glenview** *Also called March Manufacturing Inc* ***(G-11167)***
**Marcmetals** 847 905-0018
2114 Central St Apt B Evanston (60201) ***(G-10069)***
**Marco Lighting Components Inc (PA)** 312 829-6900
457 N Leavitt St Chicago (60612) ***(G-5613)***
**Marconi, Des Plaines** *Also called V Formusa Co* ***(G-8296)***
**Marconi Bakery Company** 708 757-6315
212 E 16th St Chicago Heights (60411) ***(G-7111)***
**Marcoot Jersey Creamery LLC** 618 664-1110
526 Dudleyville Rd Greenville (62246) ***(G-11398)***
**Marcor, Downers Grove** *Also called Mar Cor Purification Inc* ***(G-8483)***
**Marcres Manufacturing Inc** 847 439-1808
600 W Carboy Rd Mount Prospect (60056) ***(G-15346)***
**Marcres Metal Works, Mount Prospect** *Also called Marcres Manufacturing Inc* ***(G-15346)***
**Marcus Press** 630 351-1857
168 Constitution Dr Bloomingdale (60108) ***(G-2115)***
**Marcy Enterprises Inc** 708 352-7220
250 Kings Ct La Grange Park (60526) ***(G-12758)***
**Marcy Laboratories Inc** 630 377-6655
4n215 Powis Rd West Chicago (60185) ***(G-21738)***
**Maren Engineering Corporation** 708 333-6250
111 W Taft Dr South Holland (60473) ***(G-20287)***
**Marena Marena Two Inc** 773 327-0619
665 W Sheridan Rd Chicago (60613) ***(G-5614)***
**Marengo Tool & Die Works Inc** 815 568-7411
201 E Railroad St Marengo (60152) ***(G-14236)***
**Marengo Union Times** 815 568-5400
709 Lura Ln Marengo (60152) ***(G-14237)***
**Mares Service Inc** 708 656-1660
4611 W 34th St Cicero (60804) ***(G-7218)***
**Mareta Ravioli & Noodle, Leonore** *Also called Mareta Ravioli Inc* ***(G-13286)***
**Mareta Ravioli Inc** 815 856-2621
303 Gary St Leonore (61332) ***(G-13286)***
**Marges Aunt Potato Salad** 708 612-2300
3938 Arthur Ave Brookfield (60513) ***(G-2637)***
**Margies Brands Inc** 773 643-1417
6122 S Dorchester Ave Chicago (60637) ***(G-5615)***
**Maria Salazar Rivas, Oak Forest** *Also called We Clean* ***(G-16593)***
**Mariah Media Inc** 312 222-1100
444 N Michigan Ave # 3350 Chicago (60611) ***(G-5616)***
**Marianne Strawn** 309 447-6612
405 E 1st Ave Deer Creek (61733) ***(G-7965)***
**Marias Chicken ATI Atihan** 847 699-3113
9054 W Golf Rd Niles (60714) ***(G-16000)***
**Marie Gere Corporation** 847 540-1154
1275 Ensell Rd Lake Zurich (60047) ***(G-13099)***
**Marie's Salad Dressings, Thornton** *Also called Ventura Foods LLC* ***(G-20876)***
**Mariegold Bake Shoppe** 773 561-1978
5752 N California Ave Chicago (60659) ***(G-5617)***
**Maries Custom Made Choir Robes** 773 826-1214
3838 W Madison St Chicago (60624) ***(G-5618)***
**Marietta Corporation** 773 816-5137
340 E 138th St Chicago (60827) ***(G-5619)***
**Marin Software Incorporated** 312 267-2083
140 S Dearborn St 300a Chicago (60603) ***(G-5620)***
**Marine Canada Acquisition** 630 513-5809
3491 Swenson Ave Saint Charles (60174) ***(G-19215)***
**Marine Engine and Drive S** 630 606-6124
1330 W Washington St West Chicago (60185) ***(G-21739)***
**Marine Technologies Inc** 847 546-9001
31632 N Ellis Dr Unit 301 Volo (60073) ***(G-21318)***
**Mario Escobar** 773 202-8497
4608 W Diversey Ave Ste 1 Chicago (60639) ***(G-5621)***
**Marion Fire Sprnklr Alarm Inc** 618 889-9106
1820 N Court St Marion (62959) ***(G-14272)***
**Marion Oelze (PA)** 618 327-9224
11872 County Highway 27 # 3 Nashville (62263) ***(G-15839)***
**Marion Tool & Die Inc** 309 266-6551
701 Flint Ave Morton (61550) ***(G-15162)***
**Marjan Hot Tinning, Montgomery** *Also called Marjan Inc* ***(G-15060)***
**Marjan Inc** 630 906-0053
1801 Albright Rd Montgomery (60538) ***(G-15060)***
**Marjo Graphics Inc** 847 367-1305
1510 Bull Creek Dr Libertyville (60048) ***(G-13346)***
**Mark Bst-Pro Inc (HQ)** 630 833-9900
655 W Grand Ave Ste 220 Elmhurst (60126) ***(G-9907)***
**Mark Collins** 847 324-5500
4443 Oakton St Skokie (60076) ***(G-20033)***
**Mark Development Corporation** 815 339-2226
Mennie Dr Rr 71 Mark (61340) ***(G-14298)***
**Mark Industries** 847 487-8670
535 N Legion Ct Wauconda (60084) ***(G-21480)***
**Mark Lahey** 217 243-4433
107 S Johnson St Jacksonville (62650) ***(G-12401)***
**Mark Power International** 815 877-5984
7897 Burden Rd Machesney Park (61115) ***(G-14090)***
**Mark Promotions, Naperville** *Also called E I T Inc* ***(G-15649)***
**Mark Radtke Co Division, Chicago** *Also called Kirby Sheet Metal Works Inc* ***(G-5386)***
**Mark S Machine Shop Inc** 815 895-3955
416 N Main St Sycamore (60178) ***(G-20809)***
**Mark Twain Press Inc** 847 255-2700
3312 Sheridan Ln Mundelein (60060) ***(G-15523)***
**Mark Your Space Inc** 630 289-7082
1235 Humbracht Cir Ste 9 Bartlett (60103) ***(G-1361)***
**Mark-It Company, Batavia** *Also called P & L Mark-It Inc* ***(G-1478)***
**Markal Company, Elk Grove Village** *Also called La-Co Industries Inc* ***(G-9582)***
**Market Connect Inc** 847 726-6788
21616 Cambridge Dr Kildeer (60047) ***(G-12702)***
**Market Ready Inc** 847 689-1000
3505 Birchwood Dr Waukegan (60085) ***(G-21586)***
**Market Square Food Company** 847 599-6070
475 Keller Dr Park City (60085) ***(G-17166)***
**Marketing & Technology Group** 312 266-3311
1415 N Dayton St Ste 115 Chicago (60642) ***(G-5622)***
**Marketing Analytics Inc** 847 733-8459
1603 Orrington Ave A Evanston (60201) ***(G-10070)***
**Marketing Card Technology LLC** 630 985-7900
8245 Lemont Rd Darien (60561) ***(G-7799)***
**Markham Cabinet Works Inc** 708 687-3074
4235 151st St Midlothian (60445) ***(G-14767)***
**Markham Division 9 Inc** 708 503-0657
2213 W Wolpers Rd Park Forest (60466) ***(G-17174)***
**Markham Industry Inc** 815 338-0116
1013 E Kimball Ave Woodstock (60098) ***(G-22587)***
**Marking Specialists Group, Buffalo Grove** *Also called Marking Specialists/Poly* ***(G-2731)***
**Marking Specialists/Poly** 847 793-8100
1000 Asbury Dr Ste 2 Buffalo Grove (60089) ***(G-2731)***
**Markman Peat Corp** 815 772-4014
13161 Fenton Rd Morrison (61270) ***(G-15146)***
**Marks Custom Seating** 630 980-8270
816 Central Ave Roselle (60172) ***(G-18956)***
**Markus Cabinet Manufacturing (PA)** 618 228-7376
601 S Clinton St Aviston (62216) ***(G-1246)***
**Marland Clutch** 800 216-3515
449 Gardner St South Beloit (61080) ***(G-20157)***
**Marlboro Wire Ltd** 217 224-7989
2403 N 24th St Quincy (62305) ***(G-17855)***
**Marley Candles** 815 485-6604
12525 187th St Mokena (60448) ***(G-14883)***
**Marlow Hill Drilling Inc** 618 867-2978
107 Old Kimmel Bridge Rd Murphysboro (62966) ***(G-15578)***
**Marmon Engineered Components (HQ)** 312 372-9500
181 W Madison St Fl 26 Chicago (60602) ***(G-5623)***

# ALPHABETIC SECTION — Master Engraving

**Marmon Group LLC (HQ)** ... 312 372-9500
181 W Madison St Ste 2600  Chicago  (60602)  *(G-5624)*

**Marmon Holdings Inc (HQ)** ... 312 372-9500
181 W Madison St Ste 2600  Chicago  (60602)  *(G-5625)*

**Marmon Industrial LLC (HQ)** ... 312 372-9500
181 W Madison St Fl 26  Chicago  (60602)  *(G-5626)*

**Marmon Industries LLC (HQ)** ... 312 372-9500
181 W Madison St Ste 2600  Chicago  (60602)  *(G-5627)*

**Marmon Ret & End User Tech Inc (HQ)** ... 312 372-9500
181 W Madison St Fl 26  Chicago  (60602)  *(G-5628)*

**Marmon Retail Services Inc (HQ)** ... 312 332-0317
181 W Madison St  Chicago  (60602)  *(G-5629)*

**Marnic Inc (PA)** ... 309 343-1418
439 N Henderson St  Galesburg  (61401)  *(G-10766)*

**Maro Carton Inc** ... 708 649-9982
333 31st Ave  Bellwood  (60104)  *(G-1714)*

**Maroa AG, Maroa** Also called Harbach Gillan & Nixon Inc  *(G-14305)*

**Marquardt Printing Company** ... 630 887-8500
7530 S Madison St Ste 3  Willowbrook  (60527)  *(G-22220)*

**Marquette Enterprises LLC** ... 877 689-0001
3505 Birchwood Dr  Waukegan  (60085)  *(G-21587)*

**Marquis Energy LLC** ... 815 925-7300
11953 Prairie Indus Pkwy  Hennepin  (61327)  *(G-11734)*

**Marqutte Stl Sup Fbrcation Inc** ... 815 433-0178
800 W Marquette St  Ottawa  (61350)  *(G-16968)*

**Marr-Sales Factory Outlet, Marseilles** Also called Magic Sleep Mattress Co Inc  *(G-14314)*

**Mars Incorporated** ... 630 878-8877
418 N Washington St  Wheaton  (60187)  *(G-21968)*

**Mars Chocolate North Amer LLC** ... 662 335-8000
2019 N Oak Park Ave  Chicago  (60707)  *(G-5630)*

**Mars Chocolate North Amer LLC** ... 630 850-9898
15w660 79th St  Burr Ridge  (60527)  *(G-2864)*

**Marsh Products, Batavia** Also called Spectrum Cos International  *(G-1497)*

**Marsh Shipping Supply Co LLC (PA)** ... 618 343-1006
926 Mcdonough Lake Rd E  Collinsville  (62234)  *(G-7335)*

**Marsha Lega Gallery 28, Joliet** Also called Marsha Lega Studio Inc  *(G-12537)*

**Marsha Lega Studio Inc**
28 W Crowley Ave  Joliet  (60432)  *(G-12537)*

**Marshall Advocate, Marshall** Also called Strohm Newspapers Inc  *(G-14329)*

**Marshall Bauer** ... 847 236-1847
2000 Meadow Ln  Bannockburn  (60015)  *(G-1260)*

**Marshall Electric Inc** ... 618 382-3932
1707 Oak St Ste B  Carmi  (62821)  *(G-3074)*

**Marshall Furniture Inc** ... 847 395-9350
999 Anita Ave  Antioch  (60002)  *(G-643)*

**Marshall Manufacturing LLC** ... 312 914-7288
2300 N Lincoln Park W  Chicago  (60614)  *(G-5631)*

**Marshall Middleby Inc (HQ)** ... 847 289-0204
1400 Toastmaster Dr  Elgin  (60120)  *(G-9100)*

**Marshall Mold & Engineering, Glendale Heights** Also called Marshall Mold Inc  *(G-11046)*

**Marshall Mold Inc** ... 630 582-1800
1934 Bentley Ct Ste A  Glendale Heights  (60139)  *(G-11046)*

**Marshall Pubg & Promotions** ... 224 238-3530
123 S Hough St  Barrington  (60010)  *(G-1289)*

**Marshall Sign Co, Chicago** Also called Arts & Letters Marshall Signs  *(G-3959)*

**Marshall Wolf Automation Inc (PA)** ... 847 658-8130
923 S Main St  Algonquin  (60102)  *(G-398)*

**Martha Lacey** ... 217 723-4380
47424 212th Ave  Pearl  (62361)  *(G-17247)*

**Martin Automatic Inc** ... 815 654-4800
1661 Northrock Ct  Rockford  (61103)  *(G-18483)*

**Martin Dental Laboratory Inc** ... 708 597-8880
411 New Ave Unit 2  Lockport  (60441)  *(G-13731)*

**Martin Engineering Company (PA)** ... 309 852-2384
1 Martin Pl  Neponset  (61345)  *(G-15859)*

**Martin Exploration Mgt Co (PA)** ... 708 385-6500
4501 W 127th St  Alsip  (60803)  *(G-488)*

**Martin Glass Company (PA)** ... 618 277-1946
25 Center Plz  Belleville  (62220)  *(G-1652)*

**Martin Machine Co, Ivesdale** Also called David Martin  *(G-12377)*

**Martin Marietta Materials Inc** ... 618 285-6267
Missouri Portland Rd  Golconda  (62938)  *(G-11241)*

**Martin Oil, Alsip** Also called Martin Exploration Mgt Co  *(G-488)*

**Martin Peter Associates Inc** ... 773 478-2400
2650 W Montrose Ave Ste 1  Chicago  (60618)  *(G-5632)*

**Martin Publishing Co** ... 309 647-9501
31 S Main St  Canton  (61520)  *(G-2989)*

**Martin Publishing Co (PA)** ... 309 543-2000
217 W Market St  Havana  (62644)  *(G-11698)*

**Martin Publishing Co** ... 309 647-9501
31 S Main St  Canton  (61520)  *(G-2990)*

**Martin Publishing Company, Canton** Also called Martin Publishing Co  *(G-2990)*

**Martin Publishing Company, Havana** Also called Havana Printing & Mailing  *(G-11695)*

**Martin Sprocket & Gear (PA)** ... 847 298-8844
1505 Birchwood Ave  Des Plaines  (60018)  *(G-8227)*

**Martin Tool Works Inc** ... 847 923-8400
2050 Mitchell Blvd  Schaumburg  (60193)  *(G-19631)*

**Martinez Management Inc** ... 847 822-7202
2413 W Algonquin Rd  Algonquin  (60102)  *(G-399)*

**Martinez Printing LLC** ... 773 732-8108
2714 N Mulligan Ave  Chicago  (60639)  *(G-5633)*

**Marty Gannon** ... 847 895-1059
1025 Morse Ave  Schaumburg  (60193)  *(G-19632)*

**Marty Lundeen** ... 630 250-8917
311 Willow St  Itasca  (60143)  *(G-12311)*

**Marucco Stddard Frenbach Walsh** ... 217 698-3535
3445 Liberty Dr  Springfield  (62704)  *(G-20474)*

**Maruichi Leavitt Pipe Tube LLC** ... 800 532-8488
3655 Solutions Ctr  Chicago  (60677)  *(G-5634)*

**Maruichi Leavitt Pipe Tube LLC** ... 773 239-7700
1717 W 115th St  Chicago  (60643)  *(G-5635)*

**Marv's Scooters, Belleville** Also called Pruett Enterprises Inc  *(G-1667)*

**Marv-O-Lus Manufacturing Co (PA)** ... 773 826-1717
220 N Washtenaw Ave  Chicago  (60612)  *(G-5636)*

**Marvco Tool & Manufacturing** ... 847 437-4900
775 Lively Blvd  Elk Grove Village  (60007)  *(G-9612)*

**Marvel Abrasive Products, Chicago** Also called Bates Abrasive Products Inc  *(G-4054)*

**Marvel Abrasives Products LLC** ... 800 621-0673
6230 S Oak Park Ave  Chicago  (60638)  *(G-5637)*

**Marvel Electric Corporation (PA)** ... 773 327-2644
3425 N Ashland Ave  Chicago  (60657)  *(G-5638)*

**Marvel Electric Corporation** ... 847 671-0632
9520 Ainslie St  Schiller Park  (60176)  *(G-19846)*

**Marvel Group Inc** ... 773 523-4804
3800 W 44th St  Chicago  (60632)  *(G-5639)*

**Marvel Group Inc (PA)** ... 773 523-4804
3843 W 43rd St  Chicago  (60632)  *(G-5640)*

**Marvel Group Inc** ... 773 523-4804
4417 S Springfield Ave  Chicago  (60632)  *(G-5641)*

**Marvel Industries Incorporated (PA)** ... 847 325-2930
700 Dartmouth Ln  Buffalo Grove  (60089)  *(G-2732)*

**Marvel Machining Co Inc** ... 630 350-0075
231 Evergreen Ave  Bensenville  (60106)  *(G-1945)*

**Marvin Feig & Associates Inc** ... 773 384-5228
5707 W Howard St  Niles  (60714)  *(G-16001)*

**Marvin Schumaker Plbg Inc** ... 815 626-8130
25457 Front St  Sterling  (61081)  *(G-20597)*

**Marvin Suckow** ... 618 483-5570
5267 N 700th St  Mason  (62443)  *(G-14361)*

**Mary A. Metcalf, Chicago** Also called Tunnel Vision Consulting Group  *(G-6791)*

**Mary E Fisher** ... 618 964-1528
5679 Wards Mill Rd  Marion  (62959)  *(G-14273)*

**Mary Hill Memorials, Chicago** Also called Venetian Monument Company  *(G-6880)*

**Mary Lee Packaging Corporation (PA)** ... 618 826-2361
1037 State St  Chester  (62233)  *(G-3659)*

**Mary McHelle Winery Vinyrd LLC** ... 217 942-6250
Rr 2 Box 7a  Carrollton  (62016)  *(G-3308)*

**Marytown** ... 847 367-7800
1600 W Park Ave  Libertyville  (60048)  *(G-13347)*

**Marzeya Bakery Inc** ... 773 374-7855
8908 S Commercial Ave  Chicago  (60617)  *(G-5642)*

**Masa Uno Inc** ... 708 749-4866
6311 Cermak Rd Ste 2  Berwyn  (60402)  *(G-2068)*

**Masco Corporation** ... 847 303-3088
1821 Walden Office Sq # 400  Schaumburg  (60173)  *(G-19633)*

**Mascoutah Herald, Mascoutah** Also called Better News Papers Inc  *(G-14348)*

**Mashburn Well Drilling** ... 217 794-3728
214 N Pine St  Maroa  (61756)  *(G-14306)*

**Mason Chemical Company (HQ)** ... 847 290-1621
721 W Algonquin Rd Ste A  Arlington Heights  (60005)  *(G-799)*

**Mason City Banner Times** ... 217 482-3276
126 N Tonica St  Mason City  (62664)  *(G-14365)*

**Mason County Democrat, Havana** Also called Martin Publishing Co  *(G-11698)*

**Mason Engineering & Designing** ... 630 595-5000
505 W Lancaster Ct  Inverness  (60010)  *(G-12209)*

**Mason Welding Inc** ... 708 755-0621
3321 Holeman Ave  S Chicago Hts  (60411)  *(G-19106)*

**Mason Well Servicing Inc** ... 618 375-4411
111 S Court St  Grayville  (62844)  *(G-11375)*

**Masonite Corporation** ... 630 584-6330
1955 Powis Rd  West Chicago  (60185)  *(G-21740)*

**Massage Chair Deals, Burbank** Also called Tifb Media Group Inc  *(G-2810)*

**Massey Grafix** ... 815 644-4620
1637 E 1900 North Rd  Watseka  (60970)  *(G-21422)*

**Mast Harness Shop** ... 217 543-3463
488 Post Oak Rd  Campbell Hill  (62916)  *(G-2976)*

**Master Builders, Gurnee** Also called BASF Construction Chem LLC  *(G-11431)*

**Master Cabinets** ... 847 639-1323
209 Cleveland St Ste D  Cary  (60013)  *(G-3359)*

**Master Chemical Co, Chicago** Also called Master Well Comb Co Inc  *(G-5646)*

**Master Containers Inc** ... 863 425-5571
1900 W Field Ct  Lake Forest  (60045)  *(G-12924)*

**Master Control Systems Inc (PA)** ... 847 295-1010
910 N Shore Dr  Lake Bluff  (60044)  *(G-12856)*

**Master Cut E D M Inc** ... 847 534-0343
1025 Lunt Ave Ste C  Schaumburg  (60193)  *(G-19634)*

**Master Engraving** ... 217 965-5885
246 E Dean St  Virden  (62690)  *(G-21299)*

Master Engraving Inc ALPHABETIC SECTION

**Master Engraving Inc** ....217 627-3279
499 Rachel Rd Girard (62640) *(G-10948)*
**Master Fog LLC** ....773 918-9080
23852 W Industrial Dr N Plainfield (60585) *(G-17624)*
**Master Foundry Inc** ....217 223-7396
4808 Ellington Rd Quincy (62305) *(G-17856)*
**Master Graphics LLC** ....815 562-5800
1100 S Main St Rochelle (61068) *(G-18098)*
**Master Guard Security Co** ....618 398-7749
6125 State St East Saint Louis (62203) *(G-8760)*
**Master Hydraulics & Machining** ....847 895-5578
540 Morse Ave Schaumburg (60193) *(G-19635)*
**Master Machine Craft Inc** ....815 874-3078
6401 Falcon Rd Rockford (61109) *(G-18484)*
**Master Machine Group** ....847 472-9940
1515 Commerce Dr Elgin (60123) *(G-9101)*
**Master Manufacturing Co** ....630 833-7060
747 N Yale Ave Villa Park (60181) *(G-21269)*
**Master Marketing Intl Inc** ....630 909-1846
280 Gerzevske Ln Carol Stream (60188) *(G-3189)*
**Master Marketing Intl Inc (PA)** ....630 653-5525
280 Gerzevske Ln Carol Stream (60188) *(G-3190)*
**Master Mechanic Mfg Inc** ....847 573-3812
970 Campus Dr Mundelein (60060) *(G-15524)*
**Master Molded Products LLC** ....847 695-9700
1000 Davis Rd Elgin (60123) *(G-9102)*
**Master Paper Box Company Inc** ....773 927-0252
3641 S Iron St Chicago (60609) *(G-5643)*
**Master Polishing & Buffing** ....773 731-3883
10247 S Avenue O Chicago (60617) *(G-5644)*
**Master Print** ....708 499-4037
5533 W 109th St Ste 220 Oak Lawn (60453) *(G-16633)*
**Master Spring & Wire Form Co** ....708 453-2570
1340 Ardmore Ave Itasca (60143) *(G-12312)*
**Master Tape Printers Inc** ....773 283-8273
4517 N Elston Ave Chicago (60630) *(G-5645)*
**Master Tech Tool Inc** ....815 363-4001
4539 Prime Pkwy McHenry (60050) *(G-14528)*
**Master Well Comb Co Inc** ....847 540-8300
1830 N Lamon Ave Chicago (60639) *(G-5646)*
**Master-Cast Inc** ....630 879-3866
155 E Saint Charles Rd B Carol Stream (60188) *(G-3191)*
**Master-Halco Inc** ....618 395-4365
4633 E Radio Tower Ln Olney (62450) *(G-16780)*
**Master-Halco Inc** ....630 293-5560
1261 Atlantic Dr West Chicago (60185) *(G-21741)*
**Masterblend International LLC** ....815 423-5551
4673 Weitz Rd Morris (60450) *(G-15115)*
**Masterbrand Cabinets Inc** ....217 543-3311
501 W Progress St Arthur (61911) *(G-909)*
**Masterbrand Cabinets Inc** ....217 543-3466
N Arthur Atwood Rd Arthur (61911) *(G-910)*
**Masterbrand Cabinets Inc** ....503 241-4964
100 N Vine St Arthur (61911) *(G-911)*
**Mastercoil Spring, McHenry** *Also called Classic Products Inc* *(G-14487)*
**Mastercraft Furn Rfinishing Inc** ....773 722-5730
3140 W Chicago Ave Chicago (60622) *(G-5647)*
**Mastercraft Rug Design** ....630 655-3393
838 Chestnut St Hinsdale (60521) *(G-11952)*
**Masterfeed Corporation** ....630 879-1133
1326 Hollister Dr Batavia (60510) *(G-1466)*
**Masterite Tool & Mfg** ....630 653-2028
825 James Ct Wheaton (60189) *(G-21969)*
**Mastermolding Inc** ....815 741-1230
1715 Terry Dr Joliet (60436) *(G-12538)*
**Masterpiece Framing** ....630 893-4390
109 S Bloomingdale Rd Bloomingdale (60108) *(G-2116)*
**Masters & Alloy LLC** ....312 582-1880
12841 S Pulaski Rd Alsip (60803) *(G-489)*
**Masters & Yates Machine, Rockford** *Also called Masters Yates Inc* *(G-18486)*
**Masters Billiard Chalk, Chicago** *Also called Tweeten Fibre Co* *(G-6795)*
**Masters Co Inc** ....630 238-9292
890 Lively Blvd Wood Dale (60191) *(G-22396)*
**Masters Plating Co Inc** ....815 226-8846
2228 20th Ave Rockford (61104) *(G-18485)*
**Masters Shop** ....217 643-7826
1621 County Road 2500 N Thomasboro (61878) *(G-20860)*
**Masters Yates Inc** ....815 227-9585
2430 20th St Rockford (61104) *(G-18486)*
**Mastertrak, Wood Dale** *Also called Xisync LLC* *(G-22439)*
**Masud Jewelers Inc** ....312 236-0547
17 N Wabash Ave Ste 430 Chicago (60602) *(G-5648)*
**Mat Capital LLC (PA)** ....847 821-9630
6700 Wildlife Way Long Grove (60047) *(G-13895)*
**Mat Engine Technologies LLC (HQ)** ....847 821-9630
6700 Wildlife Way Long Grove (60047) *(G-13896)*
**Mat Holdings Inc (PA)** ....847 821-9630
6700 Wildlife Way Long Grove (60047) *(G-13897)*
**Mat Industries LLC (HQ)** ....847 821-9630
6700 Wildlife Way Long Grove (60047) *(G-13898)*
**MAT-AUTOMOTIVE, Long Grove** *Also called Tiger Accessory Group LLC* *(G-13902)*
**MAT-AUTOMOTIVE, Long Grove** *Also called Mat Holdings Inc* *(G-13897)*
**Matchless Metal Polish Company (PA)** ....773 924-1515
840 W 49th Pl Chicago (60609) *(G-5649)*
**Matchless Parisian Novelty Inc (PA)** ....773 924-1515
840 W 49th Pl Chicago (60609) *(G-5650)*
**Matcon, Port Byron** *Also called Material Control Systems Inc* *(G-17721)*
**Matcon 2, Cordova** *Also called Material Control Systems Inc* *(G-7378)*
**Matcon Manufacturing Inc** ....309 755-1020
15509 Route 84 N Cordova (61242) *(G-7377)*
**Matcon Usa Inc** ....856 256-1330
832 N Industrial Dr Elmhurst (60126) *(G-9908)*
**Matcor Metal Fabrication Group, Morton** *Also called Matcor Mtal Fbrication Ill Inc* *(G-15163)*
**Matcor Mtal Fbrication Ill Inc (HQ)** ....309 263-1707
1021 W Birchwood St Morton (61550) *(G-15163)*
**Mate Technologies Inc** ....847 289-1010
1695 Todd Farm Dr Elgin (60123) *(G-9103)*
**Material Control Inc** ....630 892-4274
525 N River St Ste 100 Batavia (60510) *(G-1467)*
**Material Control Systems Inc (PA)** ....309 523-3774
201 N Main St Port Byron (61275) *(G-17721)*
**Material Control Systems Inc** ....309 654-9031
15509 Route 84 N Cordova (61242) *(G-7378)*
**Material Haulers Inc** ....815 857-4336
655 Lunt Ave Schaumburg (60193) *(G-19636)*
**Material Sciences Corporation** ....847 439-2210
2250 Pratt Blvd Elk Grove Village (60007) *(G-9613)*
**Material Service Corporation** ....815 838-2400
681 S Material Rd Romeoville (60446) *(G-18842)*
**Material Service Corporation** ....847 658-4559
Rr 31 Algonquin (60102) *(G-400)*
**Material Service Corporation** ....708 877-6540
620 W 183rd St Thornton (60476) *(G-20875)*
**Material Service Corporation** ....708 447-1100
2235 Entp Dr Ste 3504 Westchester (60154) *(G-21849)*
**Material Service Corporation (HQ)** ....708 731-2600
2235 Entp Dr Ste 3504 Westchester (60154) *(G-21850)*
**Material Service Corporation** ....217 563-2531
22283 Taylorville Rd Nokomis (62075) *(G-16058)*
**Material Service Corporation** ....815 942-1830
125 N Independence Blvd Romeoville (60446) *(G-18843)*
**Material Service Corporation** ....217 732-2117
25142 Quarry Ave Athens (62613) *(G-939)*
**Material Service Corporation** ....708 485-8211
9101 W 47th St Mc Cook (60525) *(G-14451)*
**Material Service Corporation** ....815 838-3420
125 N Independence Blvd Romeoville (60446) *(G-18844)*
**Material Service Resources (HQ)** ....630 325-7736
222 N La Salle St # 1200 Chicago (60601) *(G-5651)*
**Material Service Yard 12, Nokomis** *Also called Material Service Corporation* *(G-16058)*
**Material Svc Yard 67, Romeoville** *Also called Material Service Corporation* *(G-18844)*
**Material Testing Tech Inc** ....847 215-1211
420 Harvester Ct Wheeling (60090) *(G-22102)*
**Materion Brush Inc** ....630 832-9650
606 W Lamont Rd Elmhurst (60126) *(G-9909)*
**Mather Dataforms, Woodstock** *Also called Hal Mather & Sons Incorporated* *(G-22573)*
**Matheson Tri-Gas Inc** ....309 697-1933
7700 W Wheeler Rd Mapleton (61547) *(G-14213)*
**Matheson Tri-Gas Inc** ....815 727-2202
200 Alessio Dr Joliet (60433) *(G-12539)*
**Matheu Tool Works Inc** ....773 327-9274
2426 N Clybourn Ave Fl 1 Chicago (60614) *(G-5652)*
**Mathew Equipment Company, Crystal Lake** *Also called Mathews Company* *(G-7606)*
**Mathews Company** ....815 459-2210
500 Industrial Rd Crystal Lake (60012) *(G-7606)*
**Mathews Fan Company, Libertyville** *Also called Matthewsgerbar Ltd* *(G-13349)*
**Mathis Energy LLC** ....309 925-3177
701 E Pearl St Tremont (61568) *(G-20984)*
**Matiss Inc** ....773 418-1895
2101 S Carpenter St Ste 2 Chicago (60608) *(G-5653)*
**Matrex Exhibits Inc** ....630 628-2233
301 S Church St Addison (60101) *(G-192)*
**Matrix Circuits LLC (PA)** ....319 367-5000
37575 N Il Route 59 Lake Villa (60046) *(G-13020)*
**Matrix Design LLC** ....847 841-8260
1627 Louise Dr South Elgin (60177) *(G-20217)*
**Matrix Design Automation, South Elgin** *Also called Matrix Design LLC* *(G-20217)*
**Matrix International Ltd** ....815 389-3771
449 Gardner St South Beloit (61080) *(G-20158)*
**Matrix IV Inc** ....815 338-4500
610 E Judd St Woodstock (60098) *(G-22588)*
**Matrix Machine & Tool Mfg** ....708 452-8707
8044 Grand Ave River Grove (60171) *(G-18011)*
**Matrix Nac, Chicago** *Also called Matrix North Amercn Cnstr Inc* *(G-5654)*
**Matrix North Amercn Cnstr Inc (HQ)** ....312 754-6605
1 E Wacker Dr Ste 1110 Chicago (60601) *(G-5654)*
**Matrix Packaging Inc** ....630 458-1942
1035 W Republic Dr Addison (60101) *(G-193)*

**Matrix Plastic Products, Wood Dale** *Also called Matrix Tooling Inc* ***(G-22397)***
**Matrix Precision Corporation** .......... 773 283-1739
6154 W Belmont Ave Chicago (60634) ***(G-5655)***
**Matrix Press** .......... 847 885-7076
1258 Remington Rd Ste A Schaumburg (60173) ***(G-19637)***
**Matrix Service Inc** .......... 618 466-4862
3403 E Broadway Alton (62002) ***(G-585)***
**Matrix Tooling Inc** .......... 630 595-6144
949 Aec Dr Wood Dale (60191) ***(G-22397)***
**Matt Pak Inc** .......... 847 451-4018
2910 Commerce St Franklin Park (60131) ***(G-10523)***
**Matt Snell and Sons** .......... 618 695-3555
4530 Mount Shelter Rd Vienna (62995) ***(G-21223)***
**Mattaliano Furniture, Chicago** *Also called M Inc* ***(G-5582)***
**Mattarusky Inc** .......... 630 469-4125
1n272 Pleasant Ave Glen Ellyn (60137) ***(G-10980)***
**Matthew Christopher Inc** .......... 212 938-6820
904 Lusted Ln Batavia (60510) ***(G-1468)***
**Matthew Warren Inc** .......... 847 364-5000
989 Pauly Dr Elk Grove Village (60007) ***(G-9614)***
**Matthew Warren Inc** .......... 630 860-7766
733 Maple Ln Bensenville (60106) ***(G-1946)***
**Matthew Warren Inc** .......... 847 671-6767
9505 Winona Ave Schiller Park (60176) ***(G-19847)***
**Matthew Warren Inc (HQ)** .......... 847 349-5760
9501 Tech Blvd Ste 401 Rosemont (60018) ***(G-19015)***
**Matthew Warren Inc** .......... 773 539-5600
4045 W Thorndale Ave Chicago (60646) ***(G-5656)***
**Matthews Fan Company, Libertyville** *Also called Matthews-Gerbar Ltd* ***(G-13348)***
**Matthews-Gerbar Ltd (PA)** .......... 847 680-9043
1881 Industrial Dr Libertyville (60048) ***(G-13348)***
**Matthewsgerbar Ltd** .......... 847 680-9043
1881 Industrial Dr Libertyville (60048) ***(G-13349)***
**Mattoon Precision Mfg** .......... 217 235-6000
2408 S 14th St Mattoon (61938) ***(G-14399)***
**Mattoon Printing Center** .......... 217 234-3100
212 N 20th St Mattoon (61938) ***(G-14400)***
**Mattoon-Charleston Ready Mix, Mattoon** *Also called Mid-Illinois Concrete Inc* ***(G-14404)***
**Matts Cookie Company** .......... 847 537-3888
482 N Milwaukee Ave Wheeling (60090) ***(G-22103)***
**Mattsn/Witt Precision Pdts Inc** .......... 847 382-7810
28005 W Industrial Ave Lake Barrington (60010) ***(G-12818)***
**Mattson Lamp Plant** .......... 217 258-9390
1501 S 19th St Mattoon (61938) ***(G-14401)***
**Maul Asphalt Sealcoating Inc** .......... 630 420-8765
1111 Carmel Ct Naperville (60540) ***(G-15695)***
**Maurey Instrument Corp** .......... 708 388-9898
5959 W 115th St Alsip (60803) ***(G-490)***
**Mauser Usa LLC** .......... 773 261-2332
903 N Kilpatrick Ave Chicago (60651) ***(G-5657)***
**Mautino Distributing Co Inc** .......... 815 664-4311
501 W 1st St Spring Valley (61362) ***(G-20376)***
**Mavea LLC** .......... 905 712-2045

1707 N Randall Rd Ste 200 Elgin (60123) ***(G-9104)***
**Maverick Tool Company Inc** .......... 630 766-2313
211 Beeline Dr Ste 5 Bensenville (60106) ***(G-1947)***
**Max Fire Box, Godfrey** *Also called Max Fire Training Inc* ***(G-11228)***
**Max Fire Training Inc** .......... 618 210-2079
901 Hampton Ct Godfrey (62035) ***(G-11228)***
**Max Miller** .......... 708 758-7760
3000 State St S Chicago Hts (60411) ***(G-19107)***
**Max Resources Inc** .......... 708 478-5656
9951 W 190th St Ste G Mokena (60448) ***(G-14884)***
**Maxant Technologies, Niles** *Also called 7 Mile Solutions Inc* ***(G-15952)***
**Maxco Ready Mix, Washington** *Also called Maxheimer Construction Inc* ***(G-21386)***
**Maxheimer Construction Inc** .......... 309 444-4200
25130 Schuck Rd Washington (61571) ***(G-21386)***
**Maxi-Mix Inc** .......... 773 489-6747
1416 W Willow St Chicago (60642) ***(G-5658)***
**Maxi-Vac Inc** .......... 224 699-9760
367 S Rohlwing Rd Ste F Addison (60101) ***(G-194)***
**Maxi-Vac Inc** .......... 630 620-6669
120 Prairie Lake Rd Ste C East Dundee (60118) ***(G-8649)***
**Maxim Inc** .......... 217 544-7015
2709 E Ash St Springfield (62703) ***(G-20475)***
**Maximum Prtg & Graphics Inc** .......... 630 737-0270
911 Burlington Ave Downers Grove (60515) ***(G-8484)***
**Maxit, Antioch** *Also called Bmi Products Northern Ill Inc* ***(G-625)***
**Maxon Plastics Inc** .......... 630 761-3667
1069 Kingsland Dr Batavia (60510) ***(G-1469)***
**Maxon Shooters Supplies Inc** .......... 847 298-4867
75 Bradrock Dr Des Plaines (60018) ***(G-8228)***
**Maxon Shters Sups Indoor Range, Des Plaines** *Also called Maxon Shooters Supplies Inc* ***(G-8228)***
**Maxs One Stop** .......... 618 235-4005
1319 N 17th St Belleville (62226) ***(G-1653)***
**Maxs Screen Machine Inc (PA)** .......... 773 878-4949
6125 N Nrthwst Hwy Frnt 1 Chicago (60631) ***(G-5659)***
**Maxwell Counters Inc** .......... 309 928-2848
324 S Plum St Farmer City (61842) ***(G-10179)***
**Maxxsonics Usa Inc** .......... 847 540-7700
851 E Park Ave Libertyville (60048) ***(G-13350)***
**May Sand and Gravel Inc** .......... 815 338-4761
3013 Thompson Rd Wonder Lake (60097) ***(G-22324)***
**May Wood Industries Inc** .......... 708 489-1515
12636 S Springfield Ave Chicago (60803) ***(G-5660)***
**Maya Romanoff Corporation (PA)** .......... 773 465-6909
3435 Madison St Skokie (60076) ***(G-20034)***
**Mayatech Corporation** .......... 847 297-0930
1000 Graceland Ave Des Plaines (60016) ***(G-8229)***
**Mayco Manufacturing LLC** .......... 618 451-4400
1200 16th St Granite City (62040) ***(G-11292)***
**Mayco-Granite City Inc** .......... 618 451-4400
1200 16th St Granite City (62040) ***(G-11293)***
**Mayekawa USA Inc (HQ)** .......... 773 516-5070
1850 Jarvis Ave Elk Grove Village (60007) ***(G-9615)***
**Mayfair Games Inc (PA)** .......... 847 677-6655
8060 Saint Louis Ave Skokie (60076) ***(G-20035)***
**Mayfair Metal Spinning Co Inc** .......... 847 358-7450
538 S Vermont St Palatine (60067) ***(G-17054)***
**Maylan Skincare, Oakbrook Terrace** *Also called Amedico Laboratories LLC* ***(G-16696)***
**Mayline Investments Inc (PA)** .......... 847 948-9340
555 Skokie Blvd Northbrook (60062) ***(G-16307)***
**Maynard Inc** .......... 773 235-5225
2341 N Milwaukee Ave Chicago (60647) ***(G-5661)***
**Mayne Pharma USA Inc** .......... 224 212-2660
275 N Field Dr Lake Forest (60045) ***(G-12925)***
**Maytec Inc** .......... 847 429-0321
901 Wesemann Dr Dundee (60118) ***(G-8564)***
**Maze Nails Div, Peru** *Also called W H Maze Company* ***(G-17530)***
**Mazel & Co Inc (PA)** .......... 773 533-1600
4300 W Ferdinand St Chicago (60624) ***(G-5662)***
**MB Box Inc** .......... 815 589-3043
1201 4th St Fulton (61252) ***(G-10703)***
**MB Corp & Associates** .......... 847 214-8843
860 Commerce Dr South Elgin (60177) ***(G-20218)***
**MB Machine Inc** .......... 815 864-3555
10214 N Mount Vernon Rd Shannon (61078) ***(G-19900)***
**MB Quart Entertainment, Libertyville** *Also called Maxxsonics Usa Inc* ***(G-13350)***
**MB Steel Company Inc** .......... 618 877-7000
9 Fox Industrial Dr Madison (62060) ***(G-14152)***
**MBA Manufacturing Inc** .......... 847 566-2555
1248 Allanson Rd Mundelein (60060) ***(G-15525)***
**MBA Marketing Inc** .......... 847 566-2555
1248 Allanson Rd Mundelein (60060) ***(G-15526)***
**MBC Cmpsite Bring Mnfactioring, Wood Dale** *Also called Composite Bearings Mfg* ***(G-22354)***
**Mbc-Aerosol, South Elgin** *Also called MB Corp & Associates* ***(G-20218)***
**Mbexpress, Bloomingdale** *Also called Madden Communications Inc* ***(G-2114)***
**Mbh Promotions Inc** .......... 847 634-2411
1108 Gail Dr Buffalo Grove (60089) ***(G-2733)***
**MBI Tools LLC** .......... 815 844-0937
15116 E 2100 North Rd Pontiac (61764) ***(G-17706)***
**MBL Bion, Des Plaines** *Also called Bion Enterprises Ltd* ***(G-8159)***
**Mbm Business Assistance Inc** .......... 217 398-6600
313 N Mattis Ave Ste 114 Champaign (61821) ***(G-3512)***
**MBR Tool Inc** .......... 847 671-4491
5118 Pearl St Schiller Park (60176) ***(G-19848)***
**Mbs Manufacturing** .......... 630 227-0300
1100 E Green St Franklin Park (60131) ***(G-10524)***
**Mburger II (PA)** .......... 312 428-3548
5 W Ontario St Chicago (60654) ***(G-5663)***
**Mc Adams Multigraphics Inc** .......... 630 990-1707
900 Jorie Blvd Ste 26 Oak Brook (60523) ***(G-16539)***
**Mc Brady Engineering Inc** .......... 815 744-8900
1251 S Larkin Ave Rockdale (60436) ***(G-18226)***
**Mc Brady Exports, Rockdale** *Also called Mc Brady Engineering Inc* ***(G-18226)***
**Mc Chemical Company** .......... 618 965-3668
1208 N Cherry St Steeleville (62288) ***(G-20563)***
**Mc Chemical Company (PA)** .......... 815 964-7687
720 South St Rockford (61102) ***(G-18487)***
**Mc Cleary Equipment Inc** .......... 815 389-3053
239 Oak Grove Ave South Beloit (61080) ***(G-20159)***
**Mc Cook Manufacturing Plant, Mc Cook** *Also called UOP LLC* ***(G-14460)***
**Mc Dist & Mfg Co** .......... 630 628-5180
310 W Gerri Ln Addison (60101) ***(G-195)***
**Mc Gowen Rifle Barrels, Saint Anne** *Also called McGowen Rifle Barrels* ***(G-19123)***
**Mc Henry Machine Co Inc** .......... 815 875-1953
1309 Il Highway 26 Princeton (61356) ***(G-17753)***
**Mc Henry Screw Products Inc** .......... 815 344-4638
4515 Prime Pkwy McHenry (60050) ***(G-14529)***
**Mc Kinney Steel & Sales Inc** .......... 847 746-3344
813 29th St Zion (60099) ***(G-22691)***
**Mc Laminated Cabinets** .......... 773 301-0393
3115 Dora St Franklin Park (60131) ***(G-10525)***
**Mc Lean County Concrete Co, Bloomington** *Also called McLean County Asphalt Co* ***(G-2194)***

ALPHABETIC

**Mc Mechanical Contractors Inc**.......708 460-0075
15774 S La Grange Rd # 245 Orland Park (60462) *(G-16874)*
**Mc Metals & Fabricating Inc**.......847 961-5242
10683 Wolf Dr Huntley (60142) *(G-12163)*
**McAllister Equipment Co**.......217 789-0351
100 Tri State Intl # 215 Lincolnshire (60069) *(G-13464)*
**McArthur Machining Inc**.......847 838-6998
303 Main St Ste 100a Antioch (60002) *(G-644)*
**McAteer's Landscape Lighting, Belleville** *Also called McAteers Wholesale (G-1654)*
**McAteers Wholesale**.......618 233-3400
3101 S Belt W Belleville (62226) *(G-1654)*
**McBride & Shoff Inc**.......309 367-4193
723 N Wiedman St Metamora (61548) *(G-14744)*
**McC Technology Inc**.......630 377-7200
2422 W Main St Unit 4d Saint Charles (60175) *(G-19216)*
**McCain Foods Usa Inc (HQ)**.......630 955-0400
2275 Cabot Dr Lisle (60532) *(G-13620)*
**McCain Usa Inc (HQ)**.......800 938-7799
2275 Cabot Dr Lisle (60532) *(G-13621)*
**McCann Concrete Products Inc**.......618 377-3888
8709 N State Route 159 Dorsey (62021) *(G-8381)*
**McCarren Group, The, Rockford** *Also called Flow-Eze Company (G-18383)*
**McCarthy Enterprises Inc**.......847 367-5718
15060 W Clover Ln Libertyville (60048) *(G-13351)*
**McCarty's Contemporary Marble, Columbia** *Also called Contemporary Marble Inc (G-7357)*
**McClatchy Newspapers Inc**.......618 239-2624
120 S Illinois St Belleville (62220) *(G-1655)*
**McClatchy Newspapers Inc**.......618 654-2366
1 Woodcrest Prof Park Highland (62249) *(G-11802)*
**McCleary Inc (PA)**.......815 389-3053
239 Oak Grove Ave South Beloit (61080) *(G-20160)*
**McClendon Holdings Affiliates, Chicago** *Also called McClendon Holdings LLC (G-5664)*
**McClendon Holdings LLC**.......773 251-2314
7200 S Exchange Ave Ste A Chicago (60649) *(G-5664)*
**McCloskey Eyman Mlone Mfg Svcs**.......309 647-4000
37 S 1st Ave Canton (61520) *(G-2991)*
**McConnell Chase Software Works**.......312 540-1508
360 E Randolph St # 3202 Chicago (60601) *(G-5665)*
**McCook Cold Storage Corp**.......708 387-2585
8801 W 50th St Mc Cook (60525) *(G-14452)*
**McCormicks Enterprises Inc**.......847 398-8680
216 W Campus Dr Ste 101 Arlington Heights (60004) *(G-800)*
**McCracken Label Co**.......773 581-8860
5303 S Keeler Ave Chicago (60632) *(G-5666)*
**McCrone Associates Inc**.......630 887-7100
850 Pasquinelli Dr Westmont (60559) *(G-21904)*
**McCurdy Tool & Machining Co**.......815 765-2117
1912 Krupke Rd Caledonia (61011) *(G-2933)*
**McDonald Supply Div, Bloomington** *Also called Hajoca Corporation (G-2176)*
**McDonnell Components Inc**.......815 547-9555
828 Landmark Dr Belvidere (61008) *(G-1770)*
**McDonough Democrat Inc**.......309 772-2129
358 E Main St Bushnell (61422) *(G-2905)*
**McDowell Inc**.......309 467-2335
809 W Center St Eureka (61530) *(G-9999)*
**McElroy Metal Mill Inc**.......217 935-9421
10940 State Hwy 10 Clinton (61727) *(G-7287)*
**McEnglevan Indus Frnc Mfg Inc**.......217 446-0941
708 Griggs St Danville (61832) *(G-7753)*
**McFarland Welding and Machine**.......618 627-2838
4066 N Thompsonville Rd Thompsonville (62890) *(G-20863)*
**McGill, Woodstock** *Also called Sws Industries Inc (G-22616)*
**McGill Asphalt Construction Co**.......708 924-1755
4956 S Monitor Ave Chicago (60638) *(G-5667)*
**McGinley Kawasaki, Highland** *Also called Motor Sport Marketing Group (G-11803)*
**McGowen Rifle Barrels**.......815 937-9816
5961 Spruce Ln Saint Anne (60964) *(G-19123)*
**McGrath Press Inc**.......815 356-5246
740 Duffy Dr Crystal Lake (60014) *(G-7607)*
**McGrath Printing Custom Ap Inc., Crystal Lake** *Also called McGrath Press Inc (G-7607)*
**MCI Service Parts Inc**.......419 994-4141
200 E Oakton St Des Plaines (60018) *(G-8230)*
**Mcli, Des Plaines** *Also called Motor Coach Inds Intl Inc (G-8235)*
**McIlvaine Co**.......847 784-0012
191 Waukegan Rd Ste 208 Northfield (60093) *(G-16408)*
**McIntyre & Associates**.......847 639-8050
41 Nippersink Rd Apt 3 Fox Lake (60020) *(G-10278)*
**McKean Pallet Co**.......309 246-7543
1046 State Route 26 Lacon (61540) *(G-12788)*
**McKernin Exhibits Inc**.......708 333-4500
570 W Armory Dr South Holland (60473) *(G-20288)*
**McKillip Industries Inc (PA)**.......815 439-1050
207 Beaver St Yorkville (60560) *(G-22664)*
**McKlein Company LLC**.......773 235-0600
4447 W Cortland St Ste A Chicago (60639) *(G-5668)*
**McKlein USA, Chicago** *Also called McKlein Company LLC (G-5668)*
**McKnight's Assisted Living, Northbrook** *Also called McKnights Long Term Care News (G-16308)*
**McKnights Long Term Care News**.......847 559-2884
900 Skokie Blvd Ste 114 Northbrook (60062) *(G-16308)*
**McLaughlin Body Co (PA)**.......309 762-7755
2430 River Dr Moline (61265) *(G-14955)*
**McLaughlin Body Co**.......309 736-6105
1400 5th St East Moline (61244) *(G-8687)*
**McLean County Asphalt Co (PA)**.......309 827-6115
1100 W Market St Bloomington (61701) *(G-2194)*
**McLean Machine Tools, Lake Barrington** *Also called McLean Manufacturing Company (G-12819)*
**McLean Manufacturing Company**.......847 277-9912
28040 W Industrial Ave Lake Barrington (60010) *(G-12819)*
**McLean Subsurface Utility**.......336 988-2520
237 E Stuart Ave Decatur (62526) *(G-7911)*
**McNdt Pipeline Ltd (PA)**.......815 467-5200
24154 S Northern Ill Dr Channahon (60410) *(G-3579)*
**McNish Corporation (PA)**.......630 892-7921
840 N Russell Ave Aurora (60506) *(G-1184)*
**MCS Booths, Roselle** *Also called Marks Custom Seating (G-18956)*
**MCS Management Corp (PA)**.......847 680-3707
5 Keuka Ct Hawthorn Woods (60047) *(G-11703)*
**MCS Midwest LLC**.......630 393-7402
85 Hankes Ave Aurora (60505) *(G-1185)*
**McShares Inc**.......217 762-2561
226 W Livingston St Monticello (61856) *(G-15079)*
**McShares Inc (PA)**.......217 762-2561
1835 E N St Monticello (61856) *(G-15080)*
**McX Press**.......630 784-4325
355 Longview Dr Bloomingdale (60108) *(G-2117)*
**MD Labs, Brookfield** *Also called Comprhnsive Prsthtics Orthtics (G-2628)*
**MD Technologies Inc**.......815 598-3143
6965 S Pleasant Hill Rd Elizabeth (61028) *(G-9244)*
**Mdhearingaid, Chicago** *Also called SC Industries Inc (G-6449)*
**Mdi-Co, West Chicago** *Also called Manufcture Dsign Innvation Inc (G-21736)*
**Mdm Communications Inc**.......708 582-9667
8737 Central Park Ave Skokie (60076) *(G-20036)*
**Mdm Construction Supply LLC**.......815 847-7340
815 N Church St Ste 3 Rockford (61103) *(G-18488)*
**ME and Gia Inc**.......708 583-1111
7434 W North Ave Elmwood Park (60707) *(G-9972)*
**MEA Inc**.......847 766-9040
2600 American Ln Elk Grove Village (60007) *(G-9616)*
**Mead Fluid Dynamics Inc**.......773 685-6800
4114 N Knox Ave Chicago (60641) *(G-5669)*
**Mead Johnson & Company LLC**.......847 832-2420
225 N Canal St Chicago (60606) *(G-5670)*
**Mead Johnson Nutrition, Chicago** *Also called Mead Johnson & Company LLC (G-5670)*
**Mead Johnson Nutrition Company (PA)**.......312 466-5800
225 N Canal St 25 Chicago (60606) *(G-5671)*
**Mead Products LLC**.......847 541-9500
4 Corporate Dr Lake Zurich (60047) *(G-13100)*
**Meade Electric Co, Oak Brook** *Also called L & H Company Inc (G-16532)*
**Meaden Precision Machined Pdts**.......630 655-0888
16w210 83rd St Burr Ridge (60527) *(G-2865)*
**Meaden Screw Products Company, Burr Ridge** *Also called Meaden Precision Machined Pdts (G-2865)*
**Meador Industries Inc**.......847 671-5042
10031 Franklin Ave Franklin Park (60131) *(G-10526)*
**Meadowbrook LLC**.......312 475-9903
900 W North Ave Chicago (60642) *(G-5672)*
**Meadoweld Machine Inc**.......815 623-3939
530 Eastern Ave South Beloit (61080) *(G-20161)*
**Meadoworks LLC**.......847 640-8580
935 National Pkwy # 93510 Schaumburg (60173) *(G-19638)*
**Meadowvale Inc**.......630 553-0202
109 Beaver St Yorkville (60560) *(G-22665)*
**Meagher Sign & Graphics Inc**.......618 662-7446
225 Hagen Dr Flora (62839) *(G-10211)*
**Mealplot Inc**.......217 419-2681
60 Hazelwood Dr Champaign (61820) *(G-3513)*
**Measured Plastics Gleason, Bourbonnais** *Also called Measured Plastics Inc (G-2402)*
**Measured Plastics Inc**.......815 939-4408
861 E 6000n Rd Bourbonnais (60914) *(G-2402)*
**Meatball Vault Original**.......312 285-2090
131 N Clinton St Ste 21 Chicago (60661) *(G-5673)*
**Meats By Linz Inc (PA)**.......708 862-0830
414 State St Calumet City (60409) *(G-2946)*
**Meau, Vernon Hills** *Also called Mitsubishi Elc Automtn Inc (G-21183)*
**Mecanica En General Santoyo**.......708 652-2217
5222 W 26th St Cicero (60804) *(G-7219)*
**Mecc Alte Inc**.......815 344-0530
1229 Adams Dr McHenry (60051) *(G-14530)*
**Mech-Tronics Corporation (PA)**.......708 344-9823
1635 N 25th Ave Melrose Park (60160) *(G-14671)*
**Mech-Tronics Corporation**.......708 344-0202
1701 N 25th Ave Melrose Park (60160) *(G-14672)*
**Mech-Tronics Nucleaur Div, Melrose Park** *Also called Mech-Tronics Corporation (G-14672)*

**Mechanical Devices Company** 309 663-2843
2005 General Electric Rd Bloomington (61704) *(G-2195)*
**Mechanical Engineering Pdts** 312 421-3375
1319 W Lake St Chicago (60607) *(G-5674)*
**Mechanical Indus Stl Svcs Inc (PA)** 815 521-1725
24226 S Northern Ill Dr Channahon (60410) *(G-3580)*
**Mechanical Music Corp** 847 398-5444
3319 N Ridge Ave Arlington Heights (60004) *(G-801)*
**Mechanical Power Inc** 847 487-0070
135 Kerry Ln Wauconda (60084) *(G-21481)*
**Mechanical Products Corp** 630 543-4842
330 W Gerri Ln Addison (60101) *(G-196)*
**Mechanical Tool & Engrg Co (PA)** 815 397-4701
4701 Kishwaukee St Rockford (61109) *(G-18489)*
**Mechanical Tool & Engrg Co** 815 397-4701
4700 Boeing Dr Rockford (61109) *(G-18490)*
**Mechanics Planing Mill Inc** 618 288-3000
1 Cottonwood Indus Park Glen Carbon (62034) *(G-10954)*
**Mechanovent, Effingham** *Also called New York Blower Company (G-8849)*
**Meco Doncasters, Paris** *Also called Doncasters Inc (G-17146)*
**Meda Pharmaceuticals Inc** 217 424-8400
705 E Eldorado St Decatur (62523) *(G-7912)*
**Medacta Usa Inc** 312 878-2381
1556 W Carroll Ave Chicago (60607) *(G-5675)*
**Medalist Industries Inc** 847 766-9000
2700 Elmhurst Rd Elk Grove Village (60007) *(G-9617)*
**Medallion Media Group, Aurora** *Also called Medallion Press Inc (G-1053)*
**Medallion Press Inc** 630 513-8316
4222 Meridian Pkwy # 110 Aurora (60504) *(G-1053)*
**Medaowview Ventures II Inc (PA)** 847 965-1700
8350 Lehigh Ave Morton Grove (60053) *(G-15218)*
**Medcal Sales LLC** 847 837-2771
1 Medline Pl Mundelein (60060) *(G-15527)*
**Medco Inc** 847 296-3021
55 Bradrock Dr Des Plaines (60018) *(G-8231)*
**Medcore International LLC** 630 645-9900
900 Jorie Blvd Ste 220 Oak Brook (60523) *(G-16540)*
**Medela LLC (HQ)** 800 435-8316
1101 Corporate Dr McHenry (60050) *(G-14531)*
**Mederer Group** 630 860-4587
745 Birginal Dr Ste B Bensenville (60106) *(G-1948)*
**Medford Aero Arms LLC** 773 961-7686
4541 N Ravenswood Ave Chicago (60640) *(G-5676)*
**Medgyn Products Inc** 630 627-4105
100 W Industrial Rd Addison (60101) *(G-197)*
**Media Associates Intl Inc** 630 260-9063
351 S Main Pl Ste 230 Carol Stream (60188) *(G-3192)*
**Media Unlimited Inc** 630 527-0900
5024 Ace Ln Ste 112 Naperville (60564) *(G-15816)*
**Mediafly Inc** 312 281-5175
150 N Michigan Ave # 2000 Chicago (60601) *(G-5677)*
**Mediarecall Holdings LLC** 847 513-6710
3363 Commercial Ave Northbrook (60062) *(G-16309)*
**Mediatec Publishing Inc (PA)** 312 676-9900
111 E Wacker Dr Ste 1200 Chicago (60601) *(G-5678)*
**Mediatec Publishing Inc** 510 834-0100
111 E Wacker Dr Ste 1200 Chicago (60601) *(G-5679)*
**Medical Adherence Tech Inc** 847 525-6300
825 Heather Ln Winnetka (60093) *(G-22312)*
**Medical Cmmnctions Systems Inc (PA)** 708 895-4500
17595 Paxton Ave Lansing (60438) *(G-13176)*
**Medical ID Fashions Company** 847 404-6789
408 Swan Blvd Deerfield (60015) *(G-8035)*
**Medical Liability Monitor Inc** 312 944-7900
7234 W North Ave Ste 101 Elmwood Park (60707) *(G-9973)*
**Medical Memories LLC** 847 478-0078
2274 Avalon Dr Buffalo Grove (60089) *(G-2734)*
**Medical Murray, North Barrington** *Also called Murray Inc (G-16153)*
**Medical Radiation Concepts** 630 289-1515
857 Marina Ter W Bartlett (60103) *(G-1362)*
**Medical Records Co** 847 662-6373
317 Stewart Ave Waukegan (60085) *(G-21588)*
**Medical Resource Inc** 847 249-0854
140 Ambrogio Dr Gurnee (60031) *(G-11470)*
**Medical Screening Labs Inc** 847 647-7911
5727 W Howard St Niles (60714) *(G-16002)*
**Medical Specialties Distrs LLC** 630 307-6200
1549 Hunter Rd Hanover Park (60133) *(G-11585)*
**Medical Supplies, Joliet** *Also called Covidien LP (G-12478)*
**Medieval Builders LLC** 331 245-7791
508 Lunt Ave Schaumburg (60193) *(G-19639)*
**Medifix Inc** 847 965-1898
8727 Narragansett Ave Morton Grove (60053) *(G-15219)*
**Medigroup Inc** 630 554-5533
14a Stonehill Rd Oswego (60543) *(G-16926)*
**Medimmune LLC** 847 356-3274
839 Colony Ct Lindenhurst (60046) *(G-13547)*
**Medimmune LLC** 618 235-8730
1668 Golf Course Dr Belleville (62220) *(G-1656)*
**Medline Industries Inc** 847 557-2400
1501 Harris Rd Libertyville (60048) *(G-13352)*
**Medline Industries Inc (PA)** 847 949-5500
3 Lakes Dr Northfield (60093) *(G-16409)*
**Medline Industries Inc** 847 949-2056
1200 Townline Rd Mundelein (60060) *(G-15528)*
**Medline Industries Inc** 847 949-5500
1170 S Northpoint Blvd Waukegan (60085) *(G-21589)*
**Medline Industries Inc** 847 949-5500
1 Medline Pl Mundelein (60060) *(G-15529)*
**Medplast Group Inc** 630 706-5500
1520 Kensington Rd # 313 Oak Brook (60523) *(G-16541)*
**Medselect, Buffalo Grove** *Also called Amerisrcbergen Solutions Group (G-2658)*
**Medtec Applications Inc** 224 353-6752
35 N Brandon Dr Ste A Glendale Heights (60139) *(G-11047)*
**Medtex Health Services Inc** 630 789-0330
554 Willowcreek Ct Clarendon Hills (60514) *(G-7258)*
**Medtext Inc** 630 325-3277
15w560 89th St Burr Ridge (60527) *(G-2866)*
**Medtorque, Elmhurst** *Also called Inland Midwest Corporation (G-9887)*
**Medtronic Inc** 815 444-2500
815 Tek Dr Crystal Lake (60014) *(G-7608)*
**Medtronic Inc** 630 627-6677
1 E 22nd St Ste 407 Lombard (60148) *(G-13824)*
**Mef Construction Inc** 847 741-8601
707 Mariner Ct Elgin (60120) *(G-9105)*
**Mega Corporation** 847 985-1900
516 Morse Ave Schaumburg (60193) *(G-19640)*
**Mega Circuit Inc** 630 543-8460
1040 S Westgate St Addison (60101) *(G-198)*
**Mega International Ltd** 309 764-5310
506 16th St Moline (61265) *(G-14956)*
**Megamedia Enterprises Inc** 773 889-0880
5236 W North Ave Chicago (60639) *(G-5680)*
**MEI, Buffalo Grove** *Also called Bechara Sim (G-2662)*
**MEI, La Grange Park** *Also called Marcy Enterprises Inc (G-12758)*
**MEI LLC** 630 285-1505
315 N Linden St Itasca (60143) *(G-12313)*
**MEI Realty Ltd** 847 358-5000
1601 W Colonial Pkwy Inverness (60067) *(G-12205)*
**Meier Granite Company** 847 678-7300
9966 Pacific Ave Franklin Park (60131) *(G-10527)*
**Meilahn Manufacturing Company, Chicago** *Also called Djr Inc (G-4615)*
**Meinhardt Diamond Tool Co** 773 267-3260
3800 W Belmont Ave Chicago (60618) *(G-5681)*
**Meinhart Grain Farm Inc** 217 683-2692
3546 E 1900th Ave Montrose (62445) *(G-15089)*
**Meister Industries Inc** 815 623-8919
6608 Saladino Dr Roscoe (61073) *(G-18907)*
**Meitheal Pharmaceuticals Inc** 773 951-6542
2340 S River Rd Ste 208 Des Plaines (60018) *(G-8232)*
**Mekanism Inc** 415 908-4000
950 W Washington Blvd Chicago (60607) *(G-5682)*
**Mektronix Technology Inc** 847 680-3300
530 N Milwaukee Ave Ste B Libertyville (60048) *(G-13353)*
**Mel Price Company Inc (PA)** 217 442-9092
16395 Lewis Rd Danville (61834) *(G-7754)*
**Mel Price Containers, Danville** *Also called Mel Price Company Inc (G-7754)*
**Mel-O-Cream Donuts (PA)** 217 544-4644
217 E Laurel St Springfield (62704) *(G-20476)*
**Mel-O-Cream Donuts** 217 528-2303
525 North Grand Ave E Springfield (62702) *(G-20477)*
**Mel-O-Cream Donuts Intl Inc** 217 483-1825
5456 International Pkwy Springfield (62711) *(G-20478)*
**Melco Insulation, Marion** *Also called Mary E Fisher (G-14273)*
**Melinda I Rhodes (PA)** 815 569-2789
15423 Capron Rd Capron (61012) *(G-2997)*
**Melissa A Miller** 708 529-7786
13957 W Illinois Hwy # 4 New Lenox (60451) *(G-15893)*
**Mellish & Murray Co (PA)** 312 733-3513
1700 W Fulton St Chicago (60612) *(G-5683)*
**Mellish & Murray Co** 312 379-0335
1700 W Fulton St Chicago (60612) *(G-5684)*
**Melon Ink Screen Print** 847 726-0003
100 Oakwood Rd Ste B Lake Zurich (60047) *(G-13101)*
**Melt Design Inc** 630 443-4000
3803 Illinois Ave Saint Charles (60174) *(G-19217)*
**Melters and More** 815 419-2043
512 N Division St Chenoa (61726) *(G-3634)*
**Melton Electric Co** 309 697-1422
5900 Washington St Peoria (61607) *(G-17405)*
**Melvin Wolf and Associates Inc** 847 433-9098
956 Deerfield Rd Highland Park (60035) *(G-11853)*
**Melyx Inc (PA)** 309 654-2551
18715 Route 84 N Cordova (61242) *(G-7379)*
**Memdem Inc** 571 205-8778
449 S Kenilworth Ave Elmhurst (60126) *(G-9910)*
**Meminger Metal Finishing Inc (PA)** 309 582-3363
2107 Se 8th St Aledo (61231) *(G-371)*

**Memorable Inc** ....847 272-8207
3336 Commercial Ave Northbrook (60062) ***(G-16310)***
**Memorial Breast Diagnstc Svcs** ....217 788-4042
747 N Rutledge St Springfield (62702) ***(G-20479)***
**Menard Inc** ....815 474-6767
2611 Eldamain Rd Plano (60545) ***(G-17666)***
**Menard Inc** ....708 346-9144
9100 S Western Ave Evergreen Park (60805) ***(G-10117)***
**Menard Inc** ....715 876-5911
2619 Eldamain Rd Bldg 220 Plano (60545) ***(G-17667)***
**Menard Inc** ....708 780-0260
2333 S Cicero Ave Cicero (60804) ***(G-7220)***
**Menasha Packaging Company LLC** ....773 227-6000
4545 W Palmer St Chicago (60639) ***(G-5685)***
**Menasha Packaging Company LLC** ....312 880-4620
350 N Clark St Ste 300 Chicago (60654) ***(G-5686)***
**Menasha Packaging Company LLC** ....618 931-7805
21 W Gtwy Commerce Ctr Dr Edwardsville (62025) ***(G-8807)***
**Menasha Packaging Company LLC** ....708 728-0372
7770 W 71st St Bridgeview (60455) ***(G-2507)***
**Menasha Packaging Company LLC** ....618 501-6040
9 Gatway Cmmerce Ctr Dr E Edwardsville (62025) ***(G-8808)***
**Menasha Packaging Company LLC** ....815 639-0144
800 S Weber Rd Ste A Bolingbrook (60490) ***(G-2340)***
**Menasha Packaging Company LLC** ....309 787-1747
7800 14th St W Rock Island (61201) ***(G-18188)***
**Mencarini Enterprises Inc** ....815 398-9565
4911 26th Ave Rockford (61109) ***(G-18491)***
**Mendota Agri-Products Inc (PA)** ....815 539-5633
448 N 3973rd Rd Mendota (61342) ***(G-14724)***
**Mendota Monument Co** ....815 539-7276
606 Main St Mendota (61342) ***(G-14725)***
**Mendota Reporter** ....815 539-9396
703 Illinois Ave Mendota (61342) ***(G-14726)***
**Mendota Welding & Mfg** ....815 539-6944
1605 One Half 13th Ave Mendota (61342) ***(G-14727)***
**Menges Roller Co Inc** ....847 487-8877
260 Industrial Dr Wauconda (60084) ***(G-21482)***
**Menk Usa LLC** ....815 626-9730
2207 Enterprise Dr Sterling (61081) ***(G-20598)***
**Menne's Finishing Touch, Cuba** *Also called Finishing Touch* ***(G-7680)***
**Mennel Milling Co** ....217 999-2161
415 E Main St Mount Olive (62069) ***(G-15305)***
**Mennies Machine Company (PA)** ....815 339-2226
Mennie Dr Rr 71 Mark (61340) ***(G-14299)***
**Mennon Rubber & Safety Pdts** ....847 678-8250
4932 River Rd Schiller Park (60176) ***(G-19849)***
**Meno Stone Co Inc** ....630 257-9220
10800 Route 83 Lemont (60439) ***(G-13241)***
**Menoni & Mocogni Inc** ....847 432-0850
2160 Skokie Valley Rd Highland Park (60035) ***(G-11854)***
**Mental Health Ctrs Centl Ill** ....217 735-1413
760 S Postville Dr Lincoln (62656) ***(G-13415)***
**Menus To Go** ....630 483-0848
676 Bonded Pkwy Ste A Streamwood (60107) ***(G-20666)***
**Mer-Pla Inc** ....847 530-9798
4535 W Fullerton Ave Chicago (60639) ***(G-5687)***
**Mercedes Fabrication** ....708 709-9240
57 E 24th St Chicago Heights (60411) ***(G-7112)***
**Merchants Metals LLC** ....847 249-4086
2800 Northwestern Ave Waukegan (60087) ***(G-21590)***
**Mercury Plastics Inc** ....888 884-1864
4535 W Fullerton Ave Chicago (60639) ***(G-5688)***
**Mercury Products Corp (PA)** ....847 524-4400
1201 Mercury Dr Schaumburg (60193) ***(G-19641)***
**Mercury Products Corp** ....847 524-4400
1201 Mercury Dr Schaumburg (60193) ***(G-19642)***
**Mercurys Green LLC** ....708 865-9134
9201 King St Franklin Park (60131) ***(G-10528)***
**Mercy Home For Boys and Girls, Chicago** *Also called Mission of Our Lady of Mercy* ***(G-5771)***
**Meredith Corp** ....312 580-1623
333 N Michigan Ave # 1500 Chicago (60601) ***(G-5689)***
**Merge Healthcare Incorporated (HQ)** ....312 565-6868
71 S Wacker Dr Ste 2 Chicago (60606) ***(G-5690)***
**Merichem Chem Rfinery Svcs LLC** ....847 285-3850
650 E Algonquin Rd Schaumburg (60173) ***(G-19643)***
**Meridian** ....815 885-4646
8173 Starwood Dr Loves Park (61111) ***(G-13964)***
**Meridian Healthcare** ....815 633-5326
1718 Northrock Ct Rockford (61103) ***(G-18492)***
**Meridian Industries Inc** ....630 892-7651
911 N Lake St Aurora (60506) ***(G-1186)***
**Meridian Laboratories Inc** ....847 808-0081
1130 W Lake Cook Rd # 202 Buffalo Grove (60089) ***(G-2735)***
**Meridian Parts Inc** ....630 718-1995
445 Jackson Ave Ste 202 Naperville (60540) ***(G-15696)***
**Merisant Company (HQ)** ....312 840-6000
125 S Wacker Dr Ste 3150 Chicago (60606) ***(G-5691)***
**Merisant Foreign Holdings I (HQ)** ....312 840-6000
33 N Dearborn St Ste 200 Chicago (60602) ***(G-5692)***
**Merisant Us Inc (HQ)** ....312 840-6000
125 S Wacker Dr Ste 3150 Chicago (60606) ***(G-5693)***
**Merisant Us Inc** ....815 929-2700
1551 N Boudreau Rd Manteno (60950) ***(G-14188)***
**Merit Emplyment Assssment Svcs** ....815 320-3680
342 Alana Dr New Lenox (60451) ***(G-15894)***
**Merit Tool Engineering Co Inc** ....773 283-1114
4827 W Wilson Ave Chicago (60630) ***(G-5694)***
**Merix Pharmaceutical Corp** ....847 277-1111
18 E Dundee Rd Bldg 3 Barrington (60010) ***(G-1290)***
**Merkel Woodworking Inc** ....630 458-0700
300 S Stewart Ave Addison (60101) ***(G-199)***
**Merlin Technologies Inc** ....630 232-9223
2724 Country Club Ter Rockford (61103) ***(G-18493)***
**Merrill Corporation** ....312 263-3524
311 S Wacker Dr Ste 1800 Chicago (60606) ***(G-5695)***
**Merrill Corporation** ....312 386-2200
200 W Jackson Blvd Fl 11 Chicago (60606) ***(G-5696)***
**Merrill Fine Arts Engrv Inc (HQ)** ....312 786-6300
311 S Wacker Dr Ste 300 Chicago (60606) ***(G-5697)***
**Merrimac Lab, Geneva** *Also called Dental Laboratory Inc* ***(G-10823)***
**Merritt & Edwards Corporation** ....309 828-4741
302 E Washington St Bloomington (61701) ***(G-2196)***
**Merritt Farm Equipment Inc** ....217 746-5331
1875 E County Road 2000 N Carthage (62321) ***(G-3315)***
**Merritt Rv, Carthage** *Also called Merritt Farm Equipment Inc* ***(G-3315)***
**Merry Walker Corporation** ....847 837-9580
21350 W Sylvan Dr S Mundelein (60060) ***(G-15530)***
**Mertel Gravel Company Inc** ....815 223-0468
2400 Water St Peru (61354) ***(G-17518)***
**Mervis Industries Inc** ....217 235-5575
612 N Logan St Mattoon (61938) ***(G-14402)***
**Mervis Industries Inc** ....217 753-1492
1100 S 9th St Springfield (62703) ***(G-20480)***
**Mervis Recycling, Springfield** *Also called Mervis Industries Inc* ***(G-20480)***
**Meryll 200000 Mile Check, Yorkville** *Also called Deyco Inc* ***(G-22656)***
**Merz Air Conditioning and Htg** ....217 342-2323
509 S Willow St Effingham (62401) ***(G-8845)***
**Merz Vault Company Inc** ....618 548-2859
2918 State Route 37 Salem (62881) ***(G-19338)***
**Mesh Company, Naperville** *Also called Cloyes Gear and Products Inc* ***(G-15630)***
**Meskan Foundry, Chicago** *Also called Louis Meskan Brass Foundry Inc* ***(G-5547)***
**Message Mediums LLC** ....877 450-0075
222 Merchandise Mart Plz # 1818 Chicago (60654) ***(G-5698)***
**Messenger** ....618 235-9601
2620 Lebanon Ave Unit 2 Belleville (62221) ***(G-1657)***
**Messer Machine** ....815 398-6248
2327 20th Ave Rockford (61104) ***(G-18494)***
**Met Co Industries Inc** ....630 584-5100
303 N 4th St Saint Charles (60174) ***(G-19218)***
**Met Plastics, Elk Grove Village** *Also called Met2plastic LLC* ***(G-9619)***
**Met Plastics** ....847 228-5070
333 King St Elk Grove Village (60007) ***(G-9618)***
**Met-L-Flo Inc** ....630 409-9860
720 N Heartland Dr Ste S Sugar Grove (60554) ***(G-20729)***
**Met-Pro Technologies LLC** ....630 775-0707
905 Sivert Dr Wood Dale (60191) ***(G-22398)***
**Met2plastic LLC** ....847 228-5070
701 Lee St Elk Grove Village (60007) ***(G-9619)***
**Meta TEC Development Inc (PA)** ....309 246-2960
125 N Commercial St Lacon (61540) ***(G-12789)***
**Meta TEC of Illinois Inc** ....309 246-2960
125 N Commercial St Lacon (61540) ***(G-12790)***
**Meta-Meg Tool Corporation** ....847 742-3600
1434 Davis Rd Elgin (60123) ***(G-9106)***
**Metal Acesories, Elk Grove Village** *Also called Dayton Superior Corporation* ***(G-9418)***
**Metal Arts Finishing Inc** ....630 892-6744
1001 S Lake St Aurora (60506) ***(G-1187)***
**Metal Box International Inc** ....847 455-8500
11600 King St Franklin Park (60131) ***(G-10529)***
**Metal Briquetters, Rosemont** *Also called Chemalloy Company LLC* ***(G-18993)***
**Metal Center News** ....630 571-1067
1100 Jorie Blvd Ste 207 Oak Brook (60523) ***(G-16542)***
**Metal Ceramics Inc** ....847 678-2293
9306 Belmont Ave Franklin Park (60131) ***(G-10530)***
**Metal Component Machining** ....815 643-2207
1900 N County Rd Malden (61337) ***(G-14164)***
**Metal Construction News, Skokie** *Also called Modern Trade Communications* ***(G-20041)***
**Metal Crafters, Monmouth** *Also called Kim Gough* ***(G-15017)***
**Metal Culverts Inc** ....309 543-2271
15732 Rte 97 S Havana (62644) ***(G-11699)***
**Metal Cutting Tools Corp** ....815 226-0650
21 Airport Dr Rockford (61109) ***(G-18495)***
**Metal Decor, Springfield** *Also called Associates Engraving Company* ***(G-20389)***
**Metal Edge Inc** ....708 756-4696
47 E 34th St S Chicago Hts (60411) ***(G-19108)***
**Metal Finishers, Arlington Heights** *Also called Britt Industries Inc* ***(G-731)***

**Metal Finishing Pros Corp** ....630 883-8339
41 N Union St Elgin (60123) ***(G-9107)***
**Metal Finishing Research Corp** ....773 373-0800
4025 S Princeton Ave Chicago (60609) ***(G-5699)***
**Metal Images Inc** ....847 488-9877
325 Corporate Dr Elgin (60123) ***(G-9108)***
**Metal Impact LLC** ....847 718-0192
1501 Oakton St Elk Grove Village (60007) ***(G-9620)***
**Metal Impact South LLC** ....847 718-9300
1501 Oakton St Elk Grove Village (60007) ***(G-9621)***
**Metal Impregnating Corp** ....630 543-3443
121 W Official Rd Addison (60101) ***(G-200)***
**Metal Improvement Company LLC** ....630 543-4950
678 W Winthrop Ave Addison (60101) ***(G-201)***
**Metal Improvement Company LLC** ....630 620-6808
129 Eisenhower Ln S Lombard (60148) ***(G-13825)***
**Metal Management Inc** ....773 721-1100
9331 S Ewing Ave Chicago (60617) ***(G-5700)***
**Metal Management Inc** ....773 489-1800
1509 W Cortland St Chicago (60642) ***(G-5701)***
**Metal Mfg LLC** ....815 432-4595
475 N Veterans Pkwy Watseka (60970) ***(G-21423)***
**Metal Prep Services Inc** ....815 874-7631
5434 International Dr Rockford (61109) ***(G-18496)***
**Metal Products Sales Corp** ....708 301-6844
15700 S Parker Rd Lockport (60491) ***(G-13732)***
**Metal Resources Inc (PA)** ....630 616-1850
15 Salt Creek Ln Ste 312 Hinsdale (60521) ***(G-11953)***
**Metal Resources Intl LLC** ....847 806-7200
1965 Pratt Blvd Elk Grove Village (60007) ***(G-9622)***
**Metal Sales Manufacturing Corp** ....309 787-1200
8111 29th St W Rock Island (61201) ***(G-18189)***
**Metal Spinners Inc** ....815 625-0390
802 E 11th St Rock Falls (61071) ***(G-18142)***
**Metal Sprmarkets Chicago Niles** ....847 647-2423
6285 W Howard St Niles (60714) ***(G-16003)***
**Metal Strip Buiding Products** ....847 742-8500
1345 Norwood Ave Itasca (60143) ***(G-12314)***
**Metal Substrates, Carpentersville** *Also called Performance Industries Inc* ***(G-3294)***
**Metal Tech Inc** ....630 529-7400
80 Monaco Dr Roselle (60172) ***(G-18957)***
**Metal Technology Solutions** ....630 587-1450
36w797 Red Gate Ct Saint Charles (60175) ***(G-19219)***
**Metal Works, Northbrook** *Also called We Innovex Inc* ***(G-16384)***
**Metal Works Machine Inc** ....217 868-5111
11100 E 1850th Ave Shumway (62461) ***(G-19934)***
**Metal-Matic Inc** ....708 594-7553
7200 S Narragansett Ave Bedford Park (60638) ***(G-1562)***
**Metal-Rite Inc** ....708 656-3832
3140 S 61st Ave Cicero (60804) ***(G-7221)***
**Metalcote, Rockton** *Also called Chemtool Incorporated* ***(G-18694)***
**Metalex Corporation (HQ)** ....847 362-8300
1530 Artaius Pkwy Libertyville (60048) ***(G-13354)***
**Metalex Corporation** ....847 362-5400
700 Liberty Dr Libertyville (60048) ***(G-13355)***
**Metalock Corporation (PA)** ....815 666-1560
2021 N Raynor Ave Crest Hill (60403) ***(G-7463)***
**Metals & Metals LLC** ....630 866-4200
999 Remington Blvd Ste C Bolingbrook (60440) ***(G-2341)***
**Metals and Services Inc** ....630 627-2900
145 N Swift Rd Addison (60101) ***(G-202)***
**Metals Technology Corporation** ....630 221-2500
120 N Schmale Rd Carol Stream (60188) ***(G-3193)***
**Metals USA Rockford** ....815 874-8536
4902 Hydraulic Rd Rockford (61109) ***(G-18497)***
**Metalstamp Inc** ....815 467-7800
6800 E Minooka Rd Minooka (60447) ***(G-14842)***
**Metalsupermarkets LLC, Bolingbrook** *Also called Metals & Metals LLC* ***(G-2341)***
**Metaltek Fabricating Inc** ....708 534-9102
2595 Bond St University Park (60484) ***(G-21056)***
**Metamation Inc (PA)** ....775 826-1717
3501 Algonquin Rd Ste 680 Rolling Meadows (60008) ***(G-18743)***
**Metamora Industries LLC** ....309 367-2368
723 N Wiedman St Metamora (61548) ***(G-14745)***
**Metco Treating and Dev Co** ....773 277-1600
2001 S Kilbourn Ave Chicago (60623) ***(G-5702)***
**Metcut, Rockford** *Also called Metal Cutting Tools Corp* ***(G-18495)***
**Meteer Inc** ....217 636-7280
16592 Kincaid St Athens (62613) ***(G-940)***
**Meteer Manufacturing Co** ....217 636-8109
25904 Meteer Ln Athens (62613) ***(G-941)***
**Metform LLC** ....815 273-2201
2551 Wacker Rd Savanna (61074) ***(G-19400)***
**Metform LLC** ....815 273-0230
7034 Rte 84 S Savanna (61074) ***(G-19401)***
**Metform LLC (HQ)** ....847 566-0010
1000 Allanson Rd Mundelein (60060) ***(G-15531)***
**Method Molds Inc** ....815 877-0191
5085 Contractors Dr Loves Park (61111) ***(G-13965)***
**Methode Development Co** ....708 867-6777
7401 W Wilson Ave Chicago (60706) ***(G-5703)***
**Methode Electronics Inc (PA)** ....708 867-6777
7401 W Wilson Ave Chicago (60706) ***(G-5704)***
**Methode Electronics Inc** ....847 577-9545
1700 Hicks Rd Rolling Meadows (60008) ***(G-18744)***
**Methode Electronics Inc** ....217 357-3941
111 W Buchanan St Carthage (62321) ***(G-3316)***
**Methods Distrs & Mfrs Inc** ....847 973-1449
104 Sayton Rd Fox Lake (60020) ***(G-10279)***
**Meto-Grafics Inc** ....847 639-0044
111 Erick St Ste 116 Crystal Lake (60014) ***(G-7609)***
**Metokote Corporation** ....815 223-1190
5750 State Route 251 Peru (61354) ***(G-17519)***
**Metomic Corporation** ....773 247-4716
2944 W 26th St Chicago (60623) ***(G-5705)***
**Metraflex Company** ....312 738-3800
2323 W Hubbard St Chicago (60612) ***(G-5706)***
**Metrasens Inc** ....603 541-6509
2150 Western Ct Ste 360 Lisle (60532) ***(G-13622)***
**Metric Felt Co** ....708 479-7979
10201 191st St Bldg 3 Mokena (60448) ***(G-14885)***
**Metric Machine Shop Inc** ....847 439-9891
101 Kelly St Ste D Elk Grove Village (60007) ***(G-9623)***
**Metrie** ....815 717-2660
2200 W Haven Ave New Lenox (60451) ***(G-15895)***
**Metritrack Inc** ....708 498-3578
4415 Harrison St Ste 230 Hillside (60162) ***(G-11925)***
**Metro Cabinet Refinishers** ....217 498-7174
7032 Ramblewood Dr Rochester (62563) ***(G-18120)***
**Metro East Fiberglass Repair** ....618 235-9217
1166 Heneral Ave Belleville (62220) ***(G-1658)***
**Metro East Manufacturing** ....618 233-0182
1120 N Illinois St Swansea (62226) ***(G-20778)***
**Metro Paint Supplies** ....708 385-7701
14032 Kostner Ave Unit G Crestwood (60445) ***(G-7494)***
**Metro Printing & Pubg Inc** ....618 476-9587
109 W Washington St Millstadt (62260) ***(G-14829)***
**Metro Service Center** ....618 524-8583
103 W 10th St Ste Ba Metropolis (62960) ***(G-14757)***
**Metro Tool Company** ....847 673-6790
3650 Oakton St Skokie (60076) ***(G-20037)***
**Metroeast Motorsports Inc** ....618 628-2466
1714 Frontage Rd O Fallon (62269) ***(G-16471)***
**Metrology Resource Group Inc** ....815 703-3141
3503 20th St Rockford (61109) ***(G-18498)***
**Metrom LLC (not Llc)** ....847 847-7233
904 Donata Ct Lake Zurich (60047) ***(G-13102)***
**Metrom Rail LLC** ....847 874-7233
1125 Mitchell Ct Crystal Lake (60014) ***(G-7610)***
**Metropolis Ready Mix Inc (PA)** ....618 524-8221
1200 E 2nd St Metropolis (62960) ***(G-14758)***
**Metropolitan Brewing LLC** ....773 474-6893
5121 N Ravenswood Ave Chicago (60640) ***(G-5707)***
**Metropolitan Graphic Arts Inc** ....847 566-9502
3818 Grandville Ave Gurnee (60031) ***(G-11471)***
**Metropolitan Industries Inc** ....815 886-9200
37 Forestwood Dr Romeoville (60446) ***(G-18845)***
**Metropolitan Newspapers, The, Oakbrook Terrace** *Also called Gatehouse Media LLC* ***(G-16708)***
**Metropolitan Printers** ....309 694-1114
109 E Washington St East Peoria (61611) ***(G-8724)***
**Metropolitan Pump Company, Romeoville** *Also called Metropolitan Industries Inc* ***(G-18845)***
**Mettler-Toledo LLC** ....630 790-3355
2640 White Oak Cir Ste A Aurora (60502) ***(G-1054)***
**Metzger Welding & Machine, Mattoon** *Also called Metzger Welding Service* ***(G-14403)***
**Metzger Welding Service** ....217 234-2851
2900 Marshall Ave Mattoon (61938) ***(G-14403)***
**Metzka Inc** ....815 932-6363
431 S Washington Ave Kankakee (60901) ***(G-12638)***
**Mexacali Silkscreen Inc** ....630 628-9313
931 W National Ave Addison (60101) ***(G-203)***
**Mexicali Hard Chrome Corp** ....630 543-0646
502 W Winthrop Ave Addison (60101) ***(G-204)***
**Mexicandy Distributor Inc** ....773 847-0024
2332 S Blue Island Ave Chicago (60608) ***(G-5708)***
**Mexichem Specialty Resins Inc** ....309 364-2154
1546 County Road 1450 N Henry (61537) ***(G-11744)***
**Mexico Distributor Inc** ....
2286 S Blue Island Ave Chicago (60608) ***(G-5709)***
**Mexico Enterprise Corporation** ....920 568-8900
6859 W 64th Pl Chicago (60638) ***(G-5710)***
**Mexifeast Foods Inc** ....773 356-6386
8414 S Brandon Ave 2 Chicago (60617) ***(G-5711)***
**Mexinox USA Inc** ....224 533-6700
2275 Half Day Rd Ste 300 Bannockburn (60015) ***(G-1261)***
**Mextell Inc** ....630 595-4146
459 S Cottage Hill Ave Elmhurst (60126) ***(G-9911)***
**Meyer E M S, Normal** *Also called Meyer Electronic Mfg Svcs Inc* ***(G-16076)***

**Meyer Electronic Mfg Svcs Inc** ....309 808-4100
440 Wylie Dr Normal (61761) *(G-16076)*
**Meyer Engineering Co** ....847 746-1500
1139 Lewis Ave Winthrop Harbor (60096) *(G-22319)*
**Meyer Enterprises LLC (PA)** ....309 698-0062
401 Truck Haven Rd East Peoria (61611) *(G-8725)*
**Meyer Glass Design Inc** ....847 675-7219
9237 Springfield Ave Evanston (60203) *(G-10071)*
**Meyer Machine & Equipment Inc (PA)** ....847 395-2970
351 Main St Antioch (60002) *(G-645)*
**Meyer Material Co Merger Corp** ....847 658-7811
1s194 Il Route 47 Elburn (60119) *(G-8891)*
**Meyer Material Co Merger Corp** ....847 824-4111
1s194 Il Route 47 Elburn (60119) *(G-8892)*
**Meyer Material Co Merger Corp** ....815 943-2605
20806 Mcguire Rd Harvard (60033) *(G-11641)*
**Meyer Material Co Merger Corp** ....815 568-6119
1s194 Il Route 47 Elburn (60119) *(G-8893)*
**Meyer Material Co Merger Corp** ....815 385-4920
1s194 Il Route 47 Elburn (60119) *(G-8894)*
**Meyer Material Co Merger Corp** ....847 689-9200
30288 N Skokie Hwy Lake Bluff (60044) *(G-12857)*
**Meyer Material Co Merger Corp** ....815 568-7205
1s194 Il Route 47 Elburn (60119) *(G-8895)*
**Meyer Material Handling** ....414 768-1631
1s194 Il Route 47 Elburn (60119) *(G-8896)*
**Meyer Metal Systems Inc** ....847 468-0500
1111 Davis Rd Elgin (60123) *(G-9109)*
**Meyer Steel Drum Inc** ....773 522-3030
2000 S Kilbourn Ave Chicago (60623) *(G-5712)*
**Meyer Steel Drum Inc (PA)** ....773 376-8376
3201 S Millard Ave Chicago (60623) *(G-5713)*
**Meyer Systems** ....815 436-7077
25035 W Black Rd Joliet (60404) *(G-12540)*
**Meyer Tool & Manufacturing Inc** ....708 425-9080
4601 Southwest Hwy Oak Lawn (60453) *(G-16634)*
**Meyercord Revenue Inc** ....630 682-6200
475 Village Dr Carol Stream (60188) *(G-3194)*
**MFC, Peoria** *Also called Midwest Hydra-Line Inc* ***(G-17407)***
**Mfi Industries Inc** ....708 841-0727
14000 S Stewart Ave Riverdale (60827) *(G-18021)*
**Mfp Holding Co (HQ)** ....312 666-3366
1414 S Western Ave Chicago (60608) *(G-5714)*
**Mfrontiers LLC** ....224 513-5312
1631 Northwind Blvd Libertyville (60048) *(G-13356)*
**Mfs Holdings LLC** ....815 385-7700
1805 Dot St McHenry (60050) *(G-14532)*
**Mfw Services Inc** ....708 522-5879
215 W 155th St South Holland (60473) *(G-20289)*
**Mfz Ventures Inc** ....773 247-4611
3333 W 48th Pl Chicago (60632) *(G-5715)*
**Mgb Engineering Company (PA)** ....847 956-7444
1099 Touhy Ave Elk Grove Village (60007) *(G-9624)*
**Mgi Services, Aurora** *Also called Mid-America Underground LLC* ***(G-1188)***
**Mgn Tool & Mfg Co Inc** ....630 849-3575
373 Randy Rd Carol Stream (60188) *(G-3195)*
**Mgp Holding Corp** ....847 967-5600
6451 Main St Morton Grove (60053) *(G-15220)*
**Mgp Ingredients Illinois Inc** ....309 353-3990
1301 S Front St Pekin (61554) *(G-17274)*
**Mgpi Processing Inc** ....309 353-3990
1301 S Front St Pekin (61554) *(G-17275)*
**Mgr Imports, Lincolnwood** *Also called Quay Corporation Inc* ***(G-13531)***
**Mgs Group North America Inc** ....847 371-1158
14050 W Lambs Ln Ste 4 Libertyville (60048) *(G-13357)*
**Mgs Manufacturing Group, Antioch** *Also called All West Plastics Inc* ***(G-616)***
**Mgs Mfg Group Inc** ....847 968-4335
14050 Lands Ln Ste 2 Libertyville (60048) *(G-13358)*
**Mgsolutions Inc** ....630 530-2005
451 N York St Elmhurst (60126) *(G-9912)*
**Mh Equipment Company** ....217 443-7210
1010 E Fairchild St Danville (61832) *(G-7755)*
**Mh/1993/Foods Inc** ....708 331-7453
16117 La Salle St South Holland (60473) *(G-20290)*
**MHS Ltd** ....773 736-3333
6616 W Irving Park Rd Chicago (60634) *(G-5716)*
**Mhub** ....773 580-1485
965 W Chicago Ave Chicago (60642) *(G-5717)*
**Mhwp** ....618 228-7600
307 W Harrison St Aviston (62216) *(G-1247)*
**Mi-Jack Products Inc (HQ)** ....708 596-5200
3111 167th St Hazel Crest (60429) *(G-11711)*
**Mi-Jack Systems & Tech LLC** ....708 596-3780
3111 167th St Hazel Crest (60429) *(G-11712)*
**Mi-Te Fast Printers Inc** ....312 236-3278
311 Park Ave Glencoe (60022) *(G-11002)*
**Mi-Te Fast Printers Inc (PA)** ....312 236-8352
180 W Washington St Fl 2 Chicago (60602) *(G-5718)*
**Mi-Te Printing & Graphics, Glencoe** *Also called Mi-Te Fast Printers Inc* ***(G-11002)***
**Mi-Te Printing & Graphics, Chicago** *Also called Mi-Te Fast Printers Inc* ***(G-5718)***
**Mia Bossi, Chicago** *Also called Jac US Inc* ***(G-5267)***
**Mic Quality Service Inc** ....847 778-5676
3500 S Morgan St Chicago (60609) *(G-5719)*
**Mica Furniture Mfg Inc** ....708 430-1150
1130 W Fullerton Ave Addison (60101) *(G-205)*
**Mich Enterprises Inc** ....630 616-9000
720 Creel Dr Wood Dale (60191) *(G-22399)*
**Michael A Greenberg MD Ltd** ....847 364-4717
800 Biesterfield Rd # 3002 Elk Grove Village (60007) *(G-9625)*
**Michael Burza** ....815 909-0233
122 E Meadow Dr Cortland (60112) *(G-7393)*
**Michael Christopher Ltd** ....815 308-5018
1007 Trakk Ln Woodstock (60098) *(G-22589)*
**Michael Clesen** ....630 377-3075
4n932 Clesen Dr Saint Charles (60175) *(G-19220)*
**Michael Goss Custom Cabinets** ....217 864-4600
11760 Cemetery Rd Argenta (62501) *(G-690)*
**Michael Lewis Company (HQ)** ....708 688-2200
8900 W 50th St Mc Cook (60525) *(G-14453)*
**Michael P Jones** ....217 787-7457
3124 Montvale Dr Ste C Springfield (62704) *(G-20481)*
**Michael Reggis Clark** ....618 533-3841
1308 N Elm St Centralia (62801) *(G-3422)*
**Michael Scott Inc** ....847 965-8700
111 Deer Lake Rd Ste 130 Deerfield (60015) *(G-8036)*
**Michael Wilton Cstm Homes Inc** ....630 508-1200
6458 Cambridge Rd Willowbrook (60527) *(G-22221)*
**Michael Zimmerman** ....847 272-5560
3364 Commercial Ave Northbrook (60062) *(G-16311)*
**Michaelangelo Foods LLC** ....773 425-3498
1800 N Pulaski Rd Chicago (60639) *(G-5720)*
**Michaels Ross and Cole Inc (PA)** ....630 916-0662
2001 Midwest Rd Ste 310 Oak Brook (60523) *(G-16543)*
**Michaels Dawg House LLC** ....847 485-7600
809 N Quentin Rd Palatine (60067) *(G-17055)*
**Michaels Equipment Co** ....618 524-8560
5481 Illinois 145 Rd Metropolis (62960) *(G-14759)*
**Michals Accessory Mart Inc** ....312 263-0066
55 E Washington St # 601 Chicago (60602) *(G-5721)*
**Michals-Kagan & Associates, Chicago** *Also called Michals Accessory Mart Inc* ***(G-5721)***
**Michel Fertilizer & Equipment** ....618 242-6000
1313 Shawnee St Mount Vernon (62864) *(G-15425)*
**Michel's Frame Shop & Gallery, Niles** *Also called Michels Frame Shop* ***(G-16004)***
**Michelangelo & Donata Burdi** ....773 427-1437
6411 W Addison St Chicago (60634) *(G-5722)*
**Michele Foods, South Holland** *Also called Mh/1993/Foods Inc* ***(G-20290)***
**Michele Terrell** ....312 305-0876
230c Dodge Ave Evanston (60202) *(G-10072)*
**Michelmann Steel Cnstr Co** ....217 222-0555
137 N 2nd St Quincy (62301) *(G-17857)*
**Michels Frame Shop** ....847 647-7366
7120 W Touhy Ave Niles (60714) *(G-16004)*
**Michigan Renewable Carbon, Chicago** *Also called Rnfl Acquisition LLC* ***(G-6366)***
**Mickey Finns Brewery, Libertyville** *Also called Libertyville Brewing Company* ***(G-13343)***
**Mickey Truck Bodies Inc** ....309 827-8227
14661 Old Colonial Rd Bloomington (61705) *(G-2197)*
**Mickhali Local Distributors, Chicago** *Also called Charlotte Louise Tate* ***(G-4294)***
**Micro Circuit Inc** ....630 628-5760
1225 W National Ave Addison (60101) *(G-206)*
**Micro Craft Manufacturing Co** ....847 679-2022
7248 Saint Louis Ave Skokie (60076) *(G-20038)*
**Micro Industries Inc** ....815 625-8000
200 W 2nd St Rock Falls (61071) *(G-18143)*
**Micro Lapping & Grinding Co** ....847 455-5446
2330 17th St Unit B Franklin Park (60131) *(G-10531)*
**Micro Machines Intl LLC** ....815 985-3652
605 Fulton Ave Rockford (61103) *(G-18499)*
**Micro Mold Corporation** ....630 628-0777
777 W Annoreno Dr Addison (60101) *(G-207)*
**Micro Punch & Die Co** ....815 874-5544
5536 International Dr Rockford (61109) *(G-18500)*
**Micro Screw Machine Co Inc** ....815 397-2115
2115 15th St Rockford (61104) *(G-18501)*
**Micro Surface Corporation** ....815 942-4221
465 Briscoe Dr Morris (60450) *(G-15116)*
**Micro Tech Components, Chicago** *Also called Micro Thread Corporation* ***(G-5723)***
**Micro Thread Corporation** ....773 775-1200
6260 N Northwest Hwy Chicago (60631) *(G-5723)*
**Micro West Ltd** ....630 766-7160
326 Evergreen Ave Bensenville (60106) *(G-1949)*
**Microchip Technology Inc** ....630 285-0071
333 W Pierce Rd Ste 180 Itasca (60143) *(G-12315)*
**Microcut Engineering, Gilberts** *Also called Gator Products Inc* ***(G-10919)***
**Microdynamics Corporation (PA)** ....630 276-0527
1400 Shore Rd Naperville (60563) *(G-15697)*
**Microdynamics Group, Naperville** *Also called Microdynamics Corporation* ***(G-15697)***
**Micrograms Inc** ....815 877-4455
5615 Jensen Dr Loves Park (61111) *(G-13966)*
**Micrograms Software, Loves Park** *Also called Micrograms Inc* ***(G-13966)***

**Microguide Inc** ....630 964-3335
1635 Plum Ct Downers Grove (60515) *(G-8485)*
**Microlink Devices Inc** ....847 588-3001
6457 W Howard St Niles (60714) *(G-16005)*
**Microlite, Batavia** *Also called Musco Sports Lighting LLC (G-1473)*
**Microlite Corporation (HQ)** ....630 876-0500
1150 Powis Rd Ste 8 West Chicago (60185) *(G-21742)*
**Microlution Inc** ....773 282-6495
6635 W Irving Park Rd Chicago (60634) *(G-5724)*
**Micromatic Spring Stamping Inc (PA)** ....630 607-0141
45 N Church St Addison (60101) *(G-208)*
**Micron Engineering Co** ....815 455-2888
2125 E Dean Woodstock Crystal Lake (60039) *(G-7611)*
**Micron Industries Corporation (PA)** ....630 516-1222
1211 W 22nd St Ste 200 Oak Brook (60523) *(G-16544)*
**Micron Industries Corporation** ....815 380-2222
1801 Westwood Dr Ste 2 Sterling (61081) *(G-20599)*
**Micron Metal Finishing LLC** ....708 599-0055
8585 S 77th Ave Bridgeview (60455) *(G-2508)*
**Micron Mold & Mfg Inc** ....630 871-9531
1085 Idaho St Carol Stream (60188) *(G-3196)*
**Micron Power, Oak Brook** *Also called Micron Industries Corporation (G-16544)*
**Micron Power, Sterling** *Also called Micron Industries Corporation (G-20599)*
**Micronics Engineered Filtrtion, Romeoville** *Also called C P Environmental Inc (G-18805)*
**Microprint Inc** ....630 969-1710
1294 Lakeview Dr Romeoville (60446) *(G-18846)*
**Micros Systems Inc** ....443 285-6000
2 Pierce Pl Ste 1700 Itasca (60143) *(G-12316)*
**Microsoft Corporation** ....630 725-4000
3025 Highland Pkwy # 300 Downers Grove (60515) *(G-8486)*
**Microsoft Corporation** ....309 665-0113
2203 E Empire St Ste J Bloomington (61704) *(G-2198)*
**Microsoft Corporation** ....708 409-4759
601 Northwest Ave Northlake (60164) *(G-16442)*
**Microstrategy Incorporated** ....703 589-0734
475 N Martingale Rd # 770 Schaumburg (60173) *(G-19644)*
**Microsun Electronics Corp** ....630 410-7900
1200 Internationale Pkwy # 101 Woodridge (60517) *(G-22502)*
**Microtech Machine Inc** ....847 870-0707
222 Camp Mcdonald Rd Wheeling (60090) *(G-22104)*
**Microtek Pattern Inc** ....217 428-0433
2035 N Jasper St Decatur (62526) *(G-7913)*
**Microthincom Inc** ....630 543-0501
661 Frontier Way Bensenville (60106) *(G-1950)*
**Microware Inc** ....847 943-9113
2418 Swainwood Dr Glenview (60025) *(G-11168)*
**Microwave RES & Applications** ....630 480-7456
190 Easy St Ste A Carol Stream (60188) *(G-3197)*
**Microway Systems Div Glenair, Lincolnwood** *Also called Glenair Inc (G-13515)*
**Microway Systems Inc** ....847 679-8833
7000 N Lawndale Ave Lincolnwood (60712) *(G-13525)*
**Microweb** ....309 426-2385
550 N Main St Roseville (61473) *(G-19046)*
**Mid America Chemical, Glenview** *Also called Mid America Intl Inc (G-11169)*
**Mid America Ems Industries** ....630 916-8203
818 Dighton Ln Schaumburg (60173) *(G-19645)*
**Mid America Intl Inc** ....847 635-8303
1245 Milwaukee Ave # 202 Glenview (60025) *(G-11169)*
**Mid America Recycling, Mahomet** *Also called Mid-America Sand & Gravel (G-14161)*
**Mid America Web Solutions, Belleville** *Also called Headball Inc (G-1634)*
**Mid American Elevator, Chicago** *Also called Spacesaver Parking Company (G-6549)*
**Mid Central Printing & Mailing** ....847 251-4040
1211 Wilmette Ave Wilmette (60091) *(G-22262)*
**Mid City Printing Service** ....773 777-5400
5566 N Northwest Hwy Chicago (60630) *(G-5725)*
**Mid City Truck Bdy & Equipment** ....630 628-9080
1404 Fullerton 14th Ave Unit B 14th Addison (60101) *(G-209)*
**Mid Country Malt Supply** ....708 339-7005
330 W Armory Dr South Holland (60473) *(G-20291)*
**Mid Illinois Quarry Company** ....217 932-2611
9129 N 230th St Casey (62420) *(G-3389)*
**Mid Oaks Investments LLC (PA)** ....847 215-3475
750 W Lake Cook Rd # 460 Buffalo Grove (60089) *(G-2736)*
**Mid Pack** ....773 626-3500
4610 W West End Ave Chicago (60644) *(G-5726)*
**Mid River Minerals Inc** ....815 941-7524
4675 Weitz Rd Morris (60450) *(G-15117)*
**Mid State Graphics (PA)** ....309 772-3843
496 W Harris Ave Bushnell (61422) *(G-2906)*
**Mid States Corporation** ....708 754-1760
3245 Holeman Ave S Chicago Hts (60411) *(G-19109)*
**Mid States Distributing, Fairfield** *Also called Mid States Salvage (G-10150)*
**Mid States Salvage** ....618 842-6741
6 Petroleum Blvd Fairfield (62837) *(G-10150)*
**Mid States Tool & Cutter, Bensenville** *Also called Midstates Cutting Tools Inc (G-1951)*
**Mid West Investors Solutions, Geneva** *Also called R & R Creative Graphics Inc (G-10861)*
**Mid-America Carbonates LLC** ....217 222-3500
520 N 30th St Quincy (62301) *(G-17858)*
**Mid-America Government Supply, Glendale Heights** *Also called Mid-America Taping Reeling Inc (G-11048)*
**Mid-America Plastic Company** ....815 938-3110
500 E Avon St Forreston (61030) *(G-10270)*
**Mid-America Sand & Gravel (PA)** ....217 586-4536
250 County Rd 2050 N Mahomet (61853) *(G-14161)*
**Mid-America Sand & Gravel** ....217 355-1307
2906 N Oak St Urbana (61802) *(G-21094)*
**Mid-America Taping Reeling Inc (PA)** ....630 629-6646
121 Exchange Blvd Glendale Heights (60139) *(G-11048)*
**Mid-America Truck Corporation** ....815 672-3211
1807 N Bloomington St Streator (61364) *(G-20694)*
**Mid-America Underground LLC** ....630 443-9999
901 Ridgeway Ave Aurora (60506) *(G-1188)*
**Mid-American Elevator Co Inc (PA)** ....773 486-6900
820 N Wolcott Ave Chicago (60622) *(G-5727)*
**Mid-American Elevator Co Inc** ....815 740-1204
1000 Sak Dr Unit A Joliet (60403) *(G-12541)*
**Mid-American Elevator Eqp Co** ....773 486-6900
820 N Wolcott Ave Chicago (60622) *(G-5728)*
**Mid-Amrica Prtctive Ctings Inc** ....630 628-4501
85 W Industrial Rd Addison (60101) *(G-210)*
**Mid-Central Business Forms** ....309 692-9090
1413 W Sunnyview Dr Peoria (61614) *(G-17406)*
**Mid-City Die & Mold Corp** ....773 278-4844
1743 N Keating Ave Chicago (60639) *(G-5729)*
**Mid-Continent Fastener Inc** ....815 625-1081
1104 E 17th St Rock Falls (61071) *(G-18144)*
**Mid-Illinois Caliper Co Inc** ....
2803 N Dirksen Pkwy Springfield (62702) *(G-20482)*
**Mid-Illinois Concrete Inc** ....217 235-5858
1413 Dewitt Ave E Mattoon (61938) *(G-14404)*
**Mid-Illinois Concrete Inc** ....217 382-6650
1001 N Ridgelawn Rd Martinsville (62442) *(G-14338)*
**Mid-Illinois Concrete Inc** ....618 664-1340
1311 S 4th St Greenville (62246) *(G-11399)*
**Mid-Illinois Concrete Inc** ....618 283-1600
1021 Janette Dr Vandalia (62471) *(G-21116)*
**Mid-Illinois Concrete Inc** ....217 345-6404
2417 18th St Charleston (61920) *(G-3604)*
**Mid-Oak Distillery Inc** ....708 925-9318
4330 Midlothian Tpke # 2 Crestwood (60445) *(G-7495)*
**Mid-State Industries Oper Inc (PA)** ....217 268-3900
908 Bob King Dr Arcola (61910) *(G-676)*
**Mid-State Tank Co Inc** ....217 728-8383
1357 Johnson Creek Rd Sullivan (61951) *(G-20751)*
**Mid-State Timber & Veneer Co** ....618 423-2619
Rr Box 61 Ramsey (62080) *(G-17914)*
**Mid-States Concrete Inds LLC** ....815 389-2277
500 S Park Ave 550 South Beloit (61080) *(G-20162)*
**Mid-States Door and Hardware, Quincy** *Also called Michelmann Steel Cnstr Co (G-17857)*
**Mid-States Forging Die-Tool** ....815 226-2313
2844 Eastrock Dr Rockford (61109) *(G-18502)*
**Mid-States Industrial Inc** ....815 357-1663
519 Shipyard Rd Seneca (61360) *(G-19888)*
**Mid-States Screw Corporation** ....815 397-2440
1817 18th Ave Rockford (61104) *(G-18503)*
**Mid-States Services LLC** ....618 842-4726
6 Petroleum Blvd Fairfield (62837) *(G-10151)*
**Mid-States Wire Proc Corp** ....773 379-3775
4642 W Maypole Ave Chicago (60644) *(G-5730)*
**Mid-West Feeder Inc** ....815 544-2994
601 E Pleasant St Belvidere (61008) *(G-1771)*
**Mid-West Millwork Wholesale** ....618 407-5940
9 W Green St Mascoutah (62258) *(G-14356)*
**Mid-West Screw Products Inc (PA)** ....773 283-6032
3523 N Kenton Ave Chicago (60641) *(G-5731)*
**Mid-West Spring & Stamping Inc (HQ)** ....630 739-3800
1404 Joliet Rd Ste C Romeoville (60446) *(G-18847)*
**Mid-West Spring & Stamping Inc** ....630 739-3800
1404 Joliet Rd Ste C Romeoville (60446) *(G-18848)*
**Mid-West Spring and Stamping, Romeoville** *Also called Mid-West Spring Mfg Co (G-18849)*
**Mid-West Spring Mfg Co, Romeoville** *Also called Mid-West Spring & Stamping Inc (G-18848)*
**Mid-West Spring Mfg Co (PA)** ....630 739-3800
1404 Joliet Rd Ste C Romeoville (60446) *(G-18849)*
**Midaco Corporation** ....847 593-8420
2000 Touhy Ave Elk Grove Village (60007) *(G-9626)*
**Midamerica Industries Inc** ....309 787-5119
1519 1st Ave E Milan (61264) *(G-14793)*
**MidAmerican Prtg Systems Inc** ....312 663-4720
1716 W Grand Ave Chicago (60622) *(G-5732)*
**MidAmerican Technology Inc** ....815 496-2400
3708 E 25th Rd Serena (60549) *(G-19893)*
**Midas Muffler, Springfield** *Also called Pack 2000 Inc (G-20496)*
**Midco Exploration Inc** ....630 655-2198
414 Plaza Dr Ste 204 Westmont (60559) *(G-21905)*
**Midco International Inc** ....773 604-8700
4140 W Victoria St Chicago (60646) *(G-5733)*
**Midco Petroleum Inc** ....630 655-2198
336 S Cass Ave Westmont (60559) *(G-21906)*

ALPHABETIC

**Midco Production Co Inc (PA)** ....630 655-2198
414 Plaza Dr Ste 204 Westmont (60559) **(G-21907)**
**Middleby Cooking Systems Group, Elgin** *Also called Marshall Middleby Inc* **(G-9100)**
**Middleby Corporation (PA)** ....847 741-3300
1400 Toastmaster Dr Elgin (60120) **(G-9110)**
**Middleby Corporation** ....847 741-3300
1400 Toastmaster Dr Elgin (60120) **(G-9111)**
**Middleby Worldwide Inc (HQ)** ....847 741-3300
1400 Toastmaster Dr Elgin (60120) **(G-9112)**
**Middletons Mouldings Inc** ....517 278-6610
1325 Remington Rd Ste H Schaumburg (60173) **(G-19646)**
**Middletown Coke Company LLC** ....630 284-1755
1011 Warrenville Rd # 600 Lisle (60532) **(G-13623)**
**Midi Music Center Inc** ....708 352-3388
989 Aec Dr Wood Dale (60191) **(G-22400)**
**Midland Coal Company** ....309 362-2795
2203 N Trivoli Rd Trivoli (61569) **(G-21000)**
**Midland Davis Corporation (PA)** ....309 637-4491
3301 4th Ave Moline (61265) **(G-14957)**
**Midland Industrial Plastics, Machesney Park** *Also called Midland Plastics Inc* **(G-14091)**
**Midland Industries Inc** ....312 664-7300
1424 N Halsted St Chicago (60642) **(G-5734)**
**Midland Manufacturing Corp** ....847 677-0333
7733 Gross Point Rd Skokie (60077) **(G-20039)**
**Midland Metal Products Co** ....773 927-5700
1200 W 37th St Chicago (60609) **(G-5735)**
**MIDLAND PAPER & PRODUCTS, Moline** *Also called Midland Davis Corporation* **(G-14957)**
**Midland Plastics Inc** ....262 938-7000
295 W Walnut St Roselle (60172) **(G-18958)**
**Midland Plastics Inc** ....815 282-4079
7861 Burden Rd Machesney Park (61115) **(G-14091)**
**Midland Printing, Skokie** *Also called Alliance Investment Corp* **(G-19949)**
**Midland Product LLC** ....708 444-8200
18600 Graphic Ct Tinley Park (60477) **(G-20932)**
**Midland Railway Supply Inc (PA)** ....618 467-6305
1815 W Delmar Ave Godfrey (62035) **(G-11229)**
**Midland Stamping and** ....847 678-7573
9521 Ainslie St Schiller Park (60176) **(G-19850)**
**Midland Stamping and Fabg Corp (PA)** ....847 678-7573
9521 Ainslie St Schiller Park (60176) **(G-19851)**
**Midmark Corporation** ....847 415-9800
675 Heathrow Dr Lincolnshire (60069) **(G-13465)**
**Midnight Marble, Palatine** *Also called Wasowski Jacek* **(G-17087)**
**Midpoint Packaging LLC** ....630 613-9922
5157 Thatcher Rd Downers Grove (60515) **(G-8487)**
**Midstate Core Co** ....217 429-2673
777 E William St Decatur (62521) **(G-7914)**
**Midstate Industries** ....217 268-3900
809 S Hamilton St Sullivan (61951) **(G-20752)**
**Midstate Iron & Metals, Taylorville** *Also called Midstate Salvage Corp* **(G-20843)**
**Midstate Manufacturing Company** ....309 342-9555
750 W 3rd St Galesburg (61401) **(G-10767)**
**Midstate Salvage Corp** ....217 824-6047
1402 W South St Taylorville (62568) **(G-20843)**
**Midstates Cutting Tools Inc** ....630 595-0700
304 Meyer Rd Bensenville (60106) **(G-1951)**
**Midtown Fuels** ....217 347-7191
503 W Jefferson Ave Effingham (62401) **(G-8846)**
**Midtronics Inc (PA)** ....630 323-2800
7000 Monroe St Willowbrook (60527) **(G-22222)**
**Midway Cap Company** ....773 384-0911
1239 W Madison St Ste 3 Chicago (60607) **(G-5736)**
**Midway Cap Company** ....773 384-0911
4513 W Armitage Ave Chicago (60639) **(G-5737)**
**Midway Displays Inc** ....708 563-2323
6554 S Austin Ave Bedford Park (60638) **(G-1563)**
**Midway Food LLC** ....773 294-0730
3937 S Lowe Ave Chicago (60609) **(G-5738)**
**Midway Games Inc (HQ)** ....773 961-2222
2704 W Roscoe St Chicago (60618) **(G-5739)**
**Midway Grinding Inc** ....847 439-7424
1451 Lunt Ave Elk Grove Village (60007) **(G-9627)**
**Midway Industries Inc** ....708 594-2600
6750 S Belt Circle Dr Chicago (60638) **(G-5740)**
**Midway Machine & Tool Co Inc** ....708 385-3450
5828 W 117th Pl Alsip (60803) **(G-491)**
**Midway Machine Products & Svcs** ....847 860-8180
2690 American Ln Elk Grove Village (60007) **(G-9628)**
**Midway Stone Co, Hillsdale** *Also called Riverstone Group Inc* **(G-11903)**
**Midway Windows and Doors, Chicago** *Also called Midway Industries Inc* **(G-5740)**
**Midwesco Filter Resources Inc** ....540 773-4780
309 Braddock St Niles (60714) **(G-16006)**
**Midwest Aero Support Inc** ....815 398-9202
1303 Turret Dr Machesney Park (61115) **(G-14092)**
**Midwest Air Pro Inc** ....773 622-4566
2054 N New England Ave Chicago (60707) **(G-5741)**
**Midwest Assembly & Packg Inc** ....
1000 Brown St Ste 209 Wauconda (60084) **(G-21483)**
**Midwest Awnings Inc** ....309 762-3339
2201 155th St Cameron (61423) **(G-2970)**
**Midwest Bio Fuel Inc** ....309 965-2612
125 W Fisk St Goodfield (61742) **(G-11247)**
**Midwest Bio Manufacturing Div** ....815 542-6417
310 2650 N Ave Tampico (61283) **(G-20828)**
**Midwest Bio-Systems Inc** ....815 438-7200
28933 35 E St Tampico (61283) **(G-20829)**
**Midwest Biodiesel Products LLC** ....618 254-2920
7350 State Route 111 South Roxana (62087) **(G-20313)**
**Midwest Biofluids Inc** ....630 790-9708
22w080 Glen Valley Dr Glen Ellyn (60137) **(G-10981)**
**Midwest Blow Molding LLC** ....618 283-9223
1111 Imco Dr Vandalia (62471) **(G-21117)**
**Midwest Brass Forging Co** ....847 678-7023
10015 Franklin Ave 21 Franklin Park (60131) **(G-10532)**
**Midwest Business Center, Lisle** *Also called FCA US LLC* **(G-13588)**
**Midwest Cad Design Inc** ....847 397-0220
2385 Hammond Dr Ste 14 Schaumburg (60173) **(G-19647)**
**Midwest Cage Company** ....815 806-0005
9217 Gulfstream Rd # 101 Frankfort (60423) **(G-10342)**
**Midwest Can Company (PA)** ....708 615-1400
1950 N Mannheim Rd Melrose Park (60160) **(G-14673)**
**Midwest Canvas Corp (PA)** ....773 287-4400
4635 W Lake St Chicago (60644) **(G-5742)**
**Midwest Carpet Recycling Inc** ....855 406-8600
38334 N Munn Rd Lake Villa (60046) **(G-13021)**
**Midwest Cement Products Inc** ....815 284-2342
809 Central St Woosung (61091) **(G-22630)**
**Midwest Cnstr Svcs Inc Peoria (PA)** ....309 697-1000
4200 Ricketts Ave Bartonville (61607) **(G-1397)**
**Midwest Coach Builders Inc** ....630 690-1420
200 Easy St Ste I Carol Stream (60188) **(G-3198)**
**Midwest Coatings Inc** ....815 717-8914
21765 S Center Ave New Lenox (60451) **(G-15896)**
**Midwest Color** ....847 647-1364
6240 W Gross Point Rd Niles (60714) **(G-16007)**
**Midwest Control, Wauconda** *Also called Intech Industries Inc* **(G-21473)**
**Midwest Control Corp** ....708 599-1331
9063 S Octavia Ave Bridgeview (60455) **(G-2509)**
**Midwest Converters Inc** ....815 229-9808
5112 28th Ave Rockford (61109) **(G-18504)**
**Midwest Converting Inc** ....708 924-1510
6634 W 68th St Bedford Park (60638) **(G-1564)**
**Midwest Cortland Inc** ....847 671-0376
235 W Laura Dr Addison (60101) **(G-211)**
**Midwest Custom Case Inc (PA)** ....708 672-2900
425 Crossing Dr Unit A University Park (60484) **(G-21057)**
**Midwest Design & Automtn Inc** ....618 392-2892
302 N Walnut St Olney (62450) **(G-16781)**
**Midwest Detention Systems Inc** ....815 521-4580
105 Industrial Dr Minooka (60447) **(G-14843)**
**Midwest Display & Mfg Inc** ....815 962-2199
127 N Wyman St Apt 4 Rockford (61101) **(G-18505)**
**Midwest Driveshaft Inc** ....630 513-9292
3712 Illinois Ave Saint Charles (60174) **(G-19221)**
**Midwest EDM Specialties Inc** ....815 521-2130
24108 S Northern Ill Dr Channahon (60410) **(G-3581)**
**Midwest Elc Mtr Inc Danville** ....217 442-5656
819 N Bowman Ave Danville (61832) **(G-7756)**
**Midwest Electronics Recycling** ....847 249-7011
3300 Washington St Waukegan (60085) **(G-21591)**
**Midwest Energy Management Inc** ....630 759-6007
10 E 22nd St Ste 111 Lombard (60148) **(G-13826)**
**Midwest Exchange Entps Inc** ....847 599-9595
4012 Morrison Dr Gurnee (60031) **(G-11472)**
**Midwest Fabrication-Countertop** ....217 528-0571
2863 Singer Ave Springfield (62703) **(G-20483)**
**Midwest Feeder, Belvidere** *Also called Mid-West Feeder Inc* **(G-1771)**
**Midwest Fiber Inc Decatur** ....217 424-9460
1902 N Water St Decatur (62526) **(G-7915)**
**Midwest Fiber Solutions** ....217 971-7400
1600 Hunter Ridge Dr Springfield (62704) **(G-20484)**
**Midwest Fibre Products Inc** ....309 596-2955
2819 95th Ave Viola (61486) **(G-21292)**
**Midwest Finishers Pwdrctng** ....217 536-9098
10235 N 800th St Effingham (62401) **(G-8847)**
**Midwest Foods Mfg Inc** ....847 455-4636
11359 Franklin Ave Franklin Park (60131) **(G-10533)**
**Midwest Foundry Products, Palatine** *Also called Darda Enterprises Inc* **(G-17020)**
**Midwest Fuel Injction Svc Corp** ....847 991-7867
543 S Vermont St Ste A Palatine (60067) **(G-17056)**
**Midwest Galvanizing Inc** ....773 434-2682
7400 S Damen Ave Chicago (60636) **(G-5743)**
**Midwest Glass Co, Hillside** *Also called Shoreline Glass Co Inc* **(G-11933)**
**Midwest Gold Stampers Inc** ....773 775-5253
5707 N Northwest Hwy Chicago (60646) **(G-5744)**
**Midwest Grain Products, Pekin** *Also called Mgpi Processing Inc* **(G-17275)**
**Midwest Graphic Industries** ....630 509-2972
605 Country Club Dr Ste A Bensenville (60106) **(G-1952)**

**Midwest Graphics, Bensenville** *Also called Midwest Graphic Industries* **(G-1952)**
**Midwest Ground Effects** ....708 516-5874
1713 Fox Ridge Dr Plainfield (60586) **(G-17625)**
**Midwest Group Dist & Svcs Inc** ....708 597-0059
5801 W 117th Pl Alsip (60803) **(G-492)**
**Midwest Hardfacing LLC** ....815 622-9420
2505 E 4th St Rock Falls (61071) **(G-18145)**
**Midwest Hot Rods Inc** ....815 254-7637
23533 W Main St Plainfield (60544) **(G-17626)**
**Midwest Hydra-Line Inc** ....309 674-6570
817 Ne Adams St Peoria (61603) **(G-17407)**
**Midwest Hydra-Line Inc (HQ)** ....309 342-6171
698 Us Highway 150 E Galesburg (61401) **(G-10768)**
**Midwest Ice Cream Company LLC** ....630 879-0800
1253 Kingsland Dr Batavia (60510) **(G-1470)**
**Midwest Ice Cream Company LLC (HQ)** ....815 544-2105
630 Meadow St Belvidere (61008) **(G-1772)**
**Midwest Imperial Steel** ....815 469-1072
5555 W 109th St Oak Lawn (60453) **(G-16635)**
**Midwest Index Inc** ....847 995-8425
2121 W Army Trail Rd # 105 Addison (60101) **(G-212)**
**Midwest Ink Co** ....708 345-7177
2701 S 12th Ave Broadview (60155) **(G-2595)**
**Midwest Innovations Inc** ....815 578-1401
4137 W Orleans St McHenry (60050) **(G-14533)**
**Midwest Innovative Pdts LLC** ....888 945-4545
9370 W Laraway Rd Ste E Frankfort (60423) **(G-10343)**
**Midwest Insert Composite Mold, Rolling Meadows** *Also called Baps Investors Group LLC* **(G-18716)**
**Midwest Intgrted Companies LLC** ....847 426-6354
275 Sola Dr Gilberts (60136) **(G-10926)**
**Midwest Keyless Inc** ....815 675-0404
2414 Highview St Spring Grove (60081) **(G-20346)**
**Midwest Label Resorces, Addison** *Also called AT&I Resources LLC* **(G-47)**
**Midwest Labels & Decals Inc** ....630 543-7556
1001 W Republic Dr Ste 11 Addison (60101) **(G-213)**
**Midwest Labs, Chicago** *Also called Midwest Uncuts Inc* **(G-5752)**
**Midwest Laser Incorporated** ....708 974-0084
10639 S 82nd Ct Palos Hills (60465) **(G-17119)**
**Midwest Law Printing Co Inc** ....312 431-0185
226 S Wabash Ave Fl 4 Chicago (60604) **(G-5745)**
**Midwest Lifting Products Inc** ....214 356-7102
1635 W 1st St Ste 312 Granite City (62040) **(G-11294)**
**Midwest Lminating Coatings Inc** ....708 653-9500
12650 S Laramie Ave Alsip (60803) **(G-493)**
**Midwest Machine Company Ltd** ....630 628-0485
1001 W Republic Dr Ste 13 Addison (60101) **(G-214)**
**Midwest Machine Service Inc** ....708 229-1122
5632 Pleasant Blvd Alsip (60803) **(G-494)**
**Midwest Machine Tool Inc** ....815 427-8665
485 S Oak St Saint Anne (60964) **(G-19124)**
**Midwest Machining & Fabg, Granite City** *Also called Arnette Pattern Co Inc* **(G-11268)**
**Midwest Manufacturing & Distrg** ....773 866-1010
6025 N Keystone Ave Chicago (60646) **(G-5746)**
**Midwest Marine Div, Chicago** *Also called ONeill Products Inc* **(G-5991)**
**Midwest Marketing Distrs Inc** ....309 663-6972
904 S Eldorado Rd Bloomington (61704) **(G-2199)**
**Midwest Marketing Distrs Inc (PA)** ....309 688-8858
2000 E War Memorial Dr # 2 Peoria (61614) **(G-17408)**
**Midwest Material Management, Gilberts** *Also called Midwest Intgrted Companies LLC* **(G-10926)**
**Midwest Metal Coatings LLC** ....618 451-2971
9 Konzen Ct Granite City (62040) **(G-11295)**
**Midwest Metals Inc** ....618 295-3444
1296 Green Diamond Rd Marissa (62257) **(G-14296)**
**Midwest Mixing Inc** ....708 422-8100
5630 Pleasant Blvd Chicago Ridge (60415) **(G-7151)**
**Midwest Mktg/Pdctn Mfg Co** ....217 256-3414
521 Main St Warsaw (62379) **(G-21370)**
**Midwest Mobile Canning LLC** ....815 861-4515
1228 Westport Rdg Crystal Lake (60014) **(G-7612)**
**Midwest Model Aircraft Co** ....773 229-0740
6917 W 59th St Chicago (60638) **(G-5747)**
**Midwest Molding Inc** ....224 208-1110
1560 Hecht Ct Bartlett (60103) **(G-1363)**
**Midwest Molding Solutions** ....309 663-7374
3001 Gill St Bloomington (61704) **(G-2200)**
**Midwest Motor Specialists Inc** ....815 942-0083
421 W Illinois Ave Morris (60450) **(G-15118)**
**Midwest Nameplate Corp** ....708 614-0606
15127 S 73rd Ave Ste H Orland Park (60462) **(G-16875)**
**Midwest Nonwovens LLC** ....618 337-9662
1642 Sauget Business Blvd Sauget (62206) **(G-19387)**
**Midwest Oil LLC** ....309 456-3663
135 S Chestnut St Good Hope (61438) **(G-11243)**
**Midwest Orthotic Services LLC** ....773 930-3770
5521 N Cumberland Ave Chicago (60656) **(G-5748)**
**Midwest Outdoors Ltd** ....630 887-7722
111 Shore Dr Burr Ridge (60527) **(G-2867)**
**Midwest Packaging & Cont Inc** ....815 633-6800
9718 Forest Hills Rd Machesney Park (61115) **(G-14093)**
**Midwest Patterns Inc** ....217 228-6900
4901 N 12th St Quincy (62305) **(G-17859)**
**Midwest Perma-Column Inc** ....309 589-7949
7407 N Kckapoo Edwards Rd Edwards (61528) **(G-8783)**
**Midwest Pipe Supports Inc** ....630 665-6400
2171 Newport Cir Bartlett (60133) **(G-1319)**
**Midwest Poultry Services LP** ....217 386-2313
Hwy 45 N Ste 2 Loda (60948) **(G-13753)**
**Midwest Powder Coatings Inc** ....630 587-2918
3865 Swenson Ave Saint Charles (60174) **(G-19222)**
**Midwest Press Brake Dies Inc** ....708 598-3860
7520 W 100th Pl Bridgeview (60455) **(G-2510)**
**Midwest Processing Company** ....217 424-5200
4666 E Faries Pkwy Decatur (62526) **(G-7916)**
**Midwest Promotional Group Co** ....708 563-0600
16w 211 S Frontage Rd Burr Ridge (60527) **(G-2868)**
**Midwest Pub Safety Outfitters** ....866 985-0013
414 Redman Way Sw Poplar Grove (61065) **(G-17714)**
**Midwest Radiant Oil and Gas** ....618 476-1303
3668 Lake Ln Millstadt (62260) **(G-14830)**
**Midwest Rail Junction** ....815 963-0200
1907 Cumberland St Rockford (61103) **(G-18506)**
**Midwest Railcar Corporation (HQ)** ....618 288-2233
4949 Autumn Oaks Dr Ste B Maryville (62062) **(G-14344)**
**Midwest Reconditioning Div, Bloomington** *Also called Mickey Truck Bodies Inc* **(G-2197)**
**Midwest Recumbent Bicycles** ....618 343-1885
109 W George St Mascoutah (62258) **(G-14357)**
**Midwest Recycling Co** ....815 744-4922
2324 Mound Rd Rockdale (60436) **(G-18227)**
**Midwest Remanufacturing LLC** ....708 496-9100
5836 W 66th St Fl 2 Bedford Park (60638) **(G-1565)**
**Midwest Research Labs LLC (PA)** ....847 283-9176
476 Oakwood Ave Lake Forest (60045) **(G-12926)**
**Midwest Saw Inc** ....630 293-4252
850 Meadowview Xing Ste 4 West Chicago (60185) **(G-21743)**
**Midwest Screens LLC** ....847 557-5015
303 Main St Ste 111 Antioch (60002) **(G-646)**
**Midwest Sealing Products Inc** ....847 459-2202
1001 Commerce Ct Buffalo Grove (60089) **(G-2737)**
**Midwest Sign & Lighting Inc** ....708 365-5555
4910 Wilshire Blvd Country Club Hills (60478) **(G-7410)**
**Midwest Signs & Structures Inc (PA)** ....847 249-8398
4215 Grove Ave Gurnee (60031) **(G-11473)**
**Midwest Signworks** ....815 942-3517
307 Bedford Rd Morris (60450) **(G-15119)**
**Midwest Silkscreening Inc** ....217 892-9596
104 N Century Blvd Rantoul (61866) **(G-17934)**
**Midwest Skylite Company Inc** ....847 214-9505
1505 Gilpen Ave South Elgin (60177) **(G-20219)**
**Midwest Skylite Service Inc** ....847 214-9505
907 Lunt Ave Schaumburg (60193) **(G-19648)**
**Midwest Socks LLC** ....773 283-3952
4120 N Leamington Ave Chicago (60641) **(G-5749)**
**Midwest Sport Turf Systems LLC** ....630 923-8342
10138 Bode St Ste E Plainfield (60585) **(G-17627)**
**Midwest Stair Parts** ....630 723-3991
31w335 Schoger Dr Naperville (60564) **(G-15817)**
**Midwest Stitch** ....815 394-1516
6767 Charles St Rockford (61108) **(G-18507)**
**Midwest Stone Sales Inc (PA)** ....815 254-6600
11926 S Aero Dr Plainfield (60585) **(G-17628)**
**Midwest Store Fixtures, University Park** *Also called Midwest Custom Case Inc* **(G-21057)**
**Midwest Stucco-Eifs Dist, Addison** *Also called Ken Matthews & Associates Inc* **(G-165)**
**Midwest Suburban Publishing (HQ)** ....708 633-6880
6901 159th St Unit 2 Tinley Park (60477) **(G-20933)**
**Midwest Sun-Ray Lighting & Sig** ....618 656-2884
4762 E Chain Of Rocks Rd Granite City (62040) **(G-11296)**
**Midwest Sun-Ray Ltg & Sign, Granite City** *Also called Midwest Sun-Ray Lighting & Sig* **(G-11296)**
**Midwest Swiss Embroideries Co** ....773 631-7120
5590 N Northwest Hwy Chicago (60630) **(G-5750)**
**Midwest Testing Services Inc** ....815 223-6696
3705 Progress Blvd Ste 2 Peru (61354) **(G-17520)**
**Midwest Tool & Manufacturing** ....815 282-6754
7864 Burden Rd Machesney Park (61115) **(G-14094)**
**Midwest Tool Inc** ....773 588-1313
4055 W Peterson Ave # 205 Chicago (60646) **(G-5751)**
**Midwest Tool Technology** ....630 207-6076
44w720 Main Street Rd Elburn (60119) **(G-8897)**
**Midwest Trailer Mfg LLC** ....309 897-8216
2000 Kentville Rd Kewanee (61443) **(G-12693)**
**Midwest Treasure Detectors** ....217 223-4769
2408 Cherry St Ste 1 Quincy (62301) **(G-17860)**
**Midwest Tropical Entps Inc** ....847 679-6666
3420 W Touhy Ave Skokie (60076) **(G-20040)**
**Midwest Tungsten Service Inc** ....630 325-1001
540 Executive Dr Willowbrook (60527) **(G-22223)**

ALPHABETIC

**Midwest Turned Products LLC**....847 551-4482
80 Prairie Pkwy Gilberts (60136) *(G-10927)*
**Midwest Ultrasonics Inc**....630 434-9458
2000 Harper Rd Darien (60561) *(G-7800)*
**Midwest Uncuts Inc**....312 664-3131
5585 N Lynch Ave Chicago (60630) *(G-5752)*
**Midwest Utility, Burr Ridge** *Also called STI Holdings Inc (G-2882)*
**Midwest Water Group Inc**....866 526-6558
4410 S Hi Point Rd McHenry (60050) *(G-14534)*
**Midwest Wheel Covers Inc**....847 609-9980
27175 W Flynn Creek Dr Barrington (60010) *(G-1291)*
**Midwest Wire Works (PA)**....815 874-1701
4657 Stenstrom Rd Rockford (61109) *(G-18508)*
**Midwest Wood Inc**....815 273-3333
2727 Wacker Rd Savanna (61074) *(G-19402)*
**Midwest Woodcrafters Inc**....630 665-0901
26w415 Saint Charles Rd Carol Stream (60188) *(G-3199)*
**Midwest-Design Inc**....708 615-1572
2350 S 27th Ave Broadview (60155) *(G-2596)*
**Midwestern Contractors, Elburn** *Also called Electric Conduit Construction (G-8887)*
**Midwestern Family Magazine LLC**....309 303-7309
3823 N Harmon Ave Peoria (61614) *(G-17409)*
**Midwestern Mch Hydraulics Inc**....618 246-9440
17265 N Timberline Ln Mount Vernon (62864) *(G-15426)*
**Midwestern Pet Foods Inc**....309 734-3121
617 S D St Monmouth (61462) *(G-15019)*
**Midwestern Rust Proof Inc**....773 725-6636
3636 N Kilbourn Ave Chicago (60641) *(G-5753)*
**Mifab Inc (PA)**....773 341-3030
1321 W 119th St Chicago (60643) *(G-5754)*
**Mifco, Danville** *Also called McEnglevan Indus Frnc Mfg Inc (G-7753)*
**Migala Report**....312 948-0260
566 W Adams St Ste 404 Chicago (60661) *(G-5755)*
**Migatron Corporation**....815 338-5800
935 Dieckman St Ste A Woodstock (60098) *(G-22590)*
**Mighty Hook Inc**....773 378-1909
1017 N Cicero Ave Chicago (60651) *(G-5756)*
**Mighty Mites Awards and Sons**....847 297-0035
1297 Rand Rd Des Plaines (60016) *(G-8233)*
**Mihalis Marine**....773 445-6220
1224 W 91st St Chicago (60620) *(G-5757)*
**Mii Inc**....630 879-3000
1380 Nagel Blvd Batavia (60510) *(G-1471)*
**Mik Tool & Die Co Inc**....847 487-4311
1000 Brown St Ste 304 Wauconda (60084) *(G-21484)*
**Mikari, Dekalb** *Also called Southmoor Estates Inc (G-8121)*
**Mike Meier & Sons Fence Mfg**....847 587-1111
7501 Meyer Rd Ste 1 Spring Grove (60081) *(G-20347)*
**Mike Simon Trucking LLC**....618 659-8755
3114 Sand Rd Edwardsville (62025) *(G-8809)*
**Mikes Inc (PA)**....618 254-4491
109 Velma Ave South Roxana (62087) *(G-20314)*
**Mikes Anodizing Co**....773 722-5778
859 N Spaulding Ave Chicago (60651) *(G-5758)*
**Mikes Machinery Rebuilders**....630 543-6400
125 W Factory Rd Addison (60101) *(G-215)*
**Mikron Designs Inc**....847 726-3990
705 Rose Rd Lake Zurich (60047) *(G-13103)*
**Mikus Elc & Generators Inc**....224 757-5534
31632 N Ellis Dr Unit 109 Volo (60073) *(G-21319)*
**Milan Stone Quarry, Milan** *Also called Collinson Stone Co (G-14780)*
**Milan, Wilbert Vault Co, Milan** *Also called Wilbert Vault Company (G-14809)*
**Milano Bakery Inc**....815 727-2253
433 S Chicago St Joliet (60436) *(G-12542)*
**Milano Direct**....847 566-1387
823 E Orchard St Mundelein (60060) *(G-15532)*
**Milano Metals & Recyling, Mount Vernon** *Also called Shapiro Bros of Illinois Inc (G-15445)*
**Milano Railcar Services LLC**....618 242-4004
510 S 6th St Mount Vernon (62864) *(G-15427)*
**Milans Machining & Mfg Co Inc**....708 780-6600
1301 S Laramie Ave Cicero (60804) *(G-7222)*
**Milco Precision Machining Inc**....630 628-5730
730 W Annoreno Dr Addison (60101) *(G-216)*
**Milcon, Wood Dale** *Also called Custom Assembly LLC (G-22356)*
**Miles Bros**....618 937-4115
1000 S Jefferson St West Frankfort (62896) *(G-21814)*
**Miles Technologies, Mundelein** *Also called Barcoding Inc (G-15474)*
**Military Medical News**....312 368-4860
55 E Jackson Blvd # 1820 Chicago (60604) *(G-5759)*
**Milk Design Company**....312 563-6455
14150 S Western Ave Posen (60469) *(G-17732)*
**Milk Products Holdings N Amer (HQ)**....847 928-1600
9525 Bryn Mawr Ave Rosemont (60018) *(G-19016)*
**Milkhouse Diner, Viola** *Also called Viola Ice Cream Shoppe (G-21295)*
**Mill Carb, Aurora** *Also called Miller Carbonic Inc (G-1189)*
**Mill Creek Mining Inc**....309 787-1414
700 4th St W Milan (61264) *(G-14794)*
**Mill Products Division, Crystal Lake** *Also called Tc Industries Inc (G-7660)*
**Mill Tek Metals, Itasca** *Also called Millenia Products Group Inc (G-12318)*
**Millcraft**....618 426-9819
2116 Trico Rd Campbell Hill (62916) *(G-2977)*
**Millenia Metals LLC**....630 458-0401
1345 Norwood Ave Itasca (60143) *(G-12317)*
**Millenia Products Group Inc (PA)**....630 458-0401
1345 Norwood Ave Itasca (60143) *(G-12318)*
**Millenia Specialty Metals LLC**....630 458-0401
1345 Norwood Ave Itasca (60143) *(G-12319)*
**Millenia Trucking LLC**....630 458-0401
1345 Norwood Ave Itasca (60143) *(G-12320)*
**Millennium Electronics Inc**....815 479-9755
300 Millennium Dr Crystal Lake (60012) *(G-7613)*
**Millennium Marking Company (HQ)**....847 806-1750
2600 Greenleaf Ave Elk Grove Village (60007) *(G-9629)*
**Millennium Mold & Tool**....847 438-5600
1194 Heather Dr Lake Zurich (60047) *(G-13104)*
**Millennium Mold Design Inc**....815 344-9790
3513 W Elm St McHenry (60050) *(G-14535)*
**Millennium Printing Inc**....847 590-8182
434 S Reuter Dr Arlington Heights (60005) *(G-802)*
**Miller and Company LLC (HQ)**....847 696-2400
9700 W Higgins Rd # 1000 Rosemont (60018) *(G-19017)*
**Miller Carbonic Inc**....773 624-5651
1691 Landmark Rd Aurora (60506) *(G-1189)*
**Miller Container, Rock Island** *Also called Liberty Diversified Intl Inc (G-18186)*
**Miller Enterprises, Champaign** *Also called Miller Roger Weston (G-3514)*
**Miller Ervin B, Arthur** *Also called Country Workshop (G-891)*
**Miller Fertilizer Inc (PA)**....217 382-4241
601 W Main St Casey (62420) *(G-3390)*
**Miller Formers Co, McHenry** *Also called Mfs Holdings LLC (G-14532)*
**Miller Group Multiplex Div, Dupo** *Also called Multiplex Display Fixture Co (G-8574)*
**Miller Manufacturing Co Inc**....636 343-5700
1610 Design Way Dupo (62239) *(G-8573)*
**Miller Midwestern Die Co**....815 338-6686
1076 Lake Ave Woodstock (60098) *(G-22591)*
**Miller Pallet**....217 589-4411
Rr 1 Box 34a Roodhouse (62082) *(G-18883)*
**Miller Products Inc**....708 534-5111
825 Central Ave University Park (60484) *(G-21058)*
**Miller Purcell Co Inc**....815 485-2142
244 W 3rd Ave New Lenox (60451) *(G-15897)*
**Miller Roger Weston**....217 352-0476
2611 W Cardinal Rd Champaign (61822) *(G-3514)*
**Miller Testing Service**....618 262-5911
1125 W 3rd St Mount Carmel (62863) *(G-15274)*
**Miller Tiling Co Inc**....217 971-4709
17951 Nine Mile Rd Virden (62690) *(G-21300)*
**Miller Whiteside Wood Working**....309 827-6470
3645 N 400 East Rd Mc Lean (61754) *(G-14463)*
**Miller's Ready Mix, S Chicago Hts** *Also called Max Miller (G-19107)*
**Miller-Whiteside Woodworking, Mc Lean** *Also called Miller Whiteside Wood Working (G-14463)*
**Millercoors LLC (HQ)**....312 496-2700
250 S Wacker Dr Ste 800 Chicago (60606) *(G-5760)*
**Millercoors LLC**....312 496-2700
150 S Wacker Dr Ste 2520 Chicago (60606) *(G-5761)*
**Millers Country Crafts Inc**....618 426-3108
150 Millers Country Ln Ava (62907) *(G-1240)*
**Millers Eureka Inc**....312 666-9383
2121 W Hubbard St Chicago (60612) *(G-5762)*
**Millers Fertilizer & Feed**....217 783-6321
300 E Cedar St Cowden (62422) *(G-7452)*
**Millfab, Crystal Lake** *Also called CJCwood Products Inc (G-7554)*
**Milliken & Company**....800 241-4826
222 Merchandise Mart Plz # 1149 Chicago (60654) *(G-5763)*
**Milliken & Company**....312 666-2015
2501 W Fulton St Chicago (60612) *(G-5764)*
**Milliken Valve LLC (HQ)**....610 861-8803
401 S Highland Ave Aurora (60506) *(G-1190)*
**Milliken Valve Co Inc**....217 425-7410
500 W Eldorado St Decatur (62522) *(G-7917)*
**Milliken Valve Company, Aurora** *Also called Milliken Valve LLC (G-1190)*
**Mills Machine Inc**....815 273-4707
2416 Jackson St Savanna (61074) *(G-19403)*
**Mills Machining**....815 933-9193
295 Stebbings Ct Ste 4 Bradley (60915) *(G-2426)*
**Mills Pallet**....773 533-6458
4500 W Roosevelt Rd Chicago (60624) *(G-5765)*
**Millsdale Plant, Elwood** *Also called Stepan Company (G-9982)*
**Millstadt Rendering Company**....618 538-5312
3151 Clover Leaf Schl Rd Belleville (62223) *(G-1659)*
**Millstadt Township**....618 476-3592
18 E Harrison St Millstadt (62260) *(G-14831)*
**Millusions, Elk Grove Village** *Also called AM Precision Machine Inc (G-9291)*
**Millwood Inc**....708 343-7341
5000 Proviso Dr Ste 1 Melrose Park (60163) *(G-14674)*
**Milmour Products, Arlington Heights** *Also called Innovative Hess Products LLC (G-778)*

ALPHABETIC SECTION
Mix Kitchen

**Milplex Circuits Inc** ....630 250-1580
1301 Ardmore Ave Itasca (60143) ***(G-12321)***
**Milton Division, Elmhurst** *Also called Nsa (chi) Liquidating Corp* ***(G-9916)***
**Milvia** ....312 527-3403
222 Merchandise Mart Plz 1427a Chicago (60654) ***(G-5766)***
**Milwaukee Electric Tool Corp** ....847 588-3356
6310 W Gross Point Rd Niles (60714) ***(G-16008)***
**Mimosa Acoustics Inc** ....217 359-9740
335 N Fremont St Champaign (61820) ***(G-3515)***
**Minarik Drives, South Beloit** *Also called American Control Elec LLC* ***(G-20137)***
**Minasian Rug Corporation** ....847 864-1010
1244 Chicago Ave Evanston (60202) ***(G-10073)***
**Mince Master, Chicago** *Also called 2 M Tool Company Inc* ***(G-3662)***
**Mincon Inc** ....618 435-3404
107 Industrial Park Rd Benton (62812) ***(G-2035)***
**Mincon Rockdrills USA, Benton** *Also called Mincon Inc* ***(G-2035)***
**Mindful Mix** ....847 284-4404
15 Maple Ave Lake Zurich (60047) ***(G-13105)***
**Minelab Americas Inc** ....630 401-8150
1938 University Ln Ste A Lisle (60532) ***(G-13624)***
**Miner Elastomer Products Corp** ....630 232-3000
1200 E State St Geneva (60134) ***(G-10848)***
**Miner Enterprises Inc (PA)** ....630 232-3000
1200 E State St Geneva (60134) ***(G-10849)***
**Mineral Masters Corporation** ....630 293-7727
130 W Grand Lake Blvd West Chicago (60185) ***(G-21744)***
**Mineral Products Inc** ....618 433-3150
1170 Telephone Rd Galatia (62935) ***(G-10712)***
**Minerallac Company (PA)** ....630 543-7080
100 Gast Rd Hampshire (60140) ***(G-11554)***
**Minerals Technologies Inc** ....847 851-1500
2870 Forbs Ave Hoffman Estates (60192) ***(G-12022)***
**Minerva Sportswear Inc** ....309 661-2387
608 Iaa Dr Bloomington (61701) ***(G-2201)***
**Ming Trading LLC** ....773 442-2221
2845 W 48th Pl Chicago (60632) ***(G-5767)***
**Miniature Injection Molding, Burlington** *Also called Veejay Plastics Inc* ***(G-2814)***
**Minic Precision Inc** ....815 675-0451
7706 Industrial Dr Ste K Spring Grove (60081) ***(G-20348)***
**Minigrip Inc** ....845 680-2710
1510 Warehouse Dr Ottawa (61350) ***(G-16969)***
**Minimill Technologies Inc** ....315 857-7107
505 N Lake Shore Dr # 5407 Chicago (60611) ***(G-5768)***
**Mining International LLC** ....630 232-4246
719 Shady Ave Geneva (60134) ***(G-10850)***
**Mining International LLC** ....815 722-0900
1955 Patterson Rd Joliet (60436) ***(G-12543)***
**Minnesota Diversified Pdts Inc** ....815 539-3106
1101 Lori Ln Mendota (61342) ***(G-14728)***
**Minnesota Office Technology** ....312 236-0400
4 Territorial Ct Ste S Bolingbrook (60440) ***(G-2342)***
**Minor League Inc** ....618 548-8040
905 E Main St Salem (62881) ***(G-19339)***
**Minority Auto Hdlg Specialists (HQ)** ....708 757-8758
22401 Sauk Pointe Dr Chicago Heights (60411) ***(G-7113)***
**Minova USA Inc** ....618 993-2611
809 Skyline Dr Marion (62959) ***(G-14274)***
**Mint Masters Inc** ....847 451-1133
9136 Belden Ave Franklin Park (60131) ***(G-10534)***
**Minute Man Press** ....847 839-9600
1037 W Golf Rd Hoffman Estates (60169) ***(G-12023)***
**Minute Men Inc** ....630 692-1583
1725 N Frnswrth Ave Ste A Aurora (60505) ***(G-1191)***
**Minuteman International Inc (HQ)** ....630 627-6900
14n845 Us Highway 20 Pingree Grove (60140) ***(G-17556)***
**Minuteman International Inc** ....847 683-5210
14n845 Us Highway 20 Hampshire (60140) ***(G-11555)***
**Minuteman Press, Hoffman Estates** *Also called Minute Man Press* ***(G-12023)***
**Minuteman Press, Champaign** *Also called Mmpcu Limited* ***(G-3516)***
**Minuteman Press, Naperville** *Also called T C W F Inc* ***(G-15759)***
**Minuteman Press, Wood Dale** *Also called Althea Crutex Inc* ***(G-22337)***
**Minuteman Press, Saint Charles** *Also called T F N W Inc* ***(G-19277)***
**Minuteman Press, McHenry** *Also called Schommer Inc* ***(G-14554)***
**Minuteman Press, Evanston** *Also called L P M Inc* ***(G-10062)***
**Minuteman Press, Mundelein** *Also called Floden Enterprises* ***(G-15502)***
**Minuteman Press, Joliet** *Also called Jsn Printing Inc* ***(G-12525)***
**Minuteman Press, Westchester** *Also called P P Graphics Inc* ***(G-21852)***
**Minuteman Press, Chicago** *Also called R T P Inc* ***(G-6274)***
**Minuteman Press, Warrenville** *Also called Weimer Design & Print Ltd Inc* ***(G-21368)***
**Minuteman Press, Deerfield** *Also called Jsolo Corp* ***(G-8023)***
**Minuteman Press, Wheeling** *Also called Rodin Enterprises Inc* ***(G-22142)***
**Minuteman Press, Elmhurst** *Also called W R S Inc* ***(G-9959)***
**Minuteman Press, Lyons** *Also called Steve Bortman* ***(G-14046)***
**Minuteman Press** ....708 524-4940
6949 North Ave Oak Park (60302) ***(G-16675)***
**Minuteman Press** ....708 598-4915
8330 W 95th St Apt 1 Hickory Hills (60457) ***(G-11773)***
**Minuteman Press** ....630 541-9122
6670 S Brainard Ave # 203 Countryside (60525) ***(G-7437)***
**Minuteman Press** ....630 584-7383
1574 E Main St Saint Charles (60174) ***(G-19223)***
**Minuteman Press** ....630 279-0438
347 W Eugenia St Lombard (60148) ***(G-13827)***
**Minuteman Press Inc** ....847 577-2411
1324 W Algonquin Rd Arlington Heights (60005) ***(G-803)***
**Minuteman Press Intl Inc** ....630 574-0090
1301 W 22nd St Ste 709 Oak Brook (60523) ***(G-16545)***
**Minuteman Press Morton Grove** ....847 470-0212
6038 Dempster St Morton Grove (60053) ***(G-15221)***
**Minuteman Press of Countryside** ....708 354-2190
6566 Joliet Rd Countryside (60525) ***(G-7438)***
**Minuteman Press of Lansing** ....708 895-0505
17930 Torrence Ave Ste A Lansing (60438) ***(G-13177)***
**Minuteman Press of Rockford** ....815 633-2992
5128 N 2nd St Loves Park (61111) ***(G-13967)***
**Minuteman Press of Waukegan** ....847 244-6288
3701 Grand Ave Ste A Gurnee (60031) ***(G-11474)***
**Mio Med Orthopedics Inc** ....773 477-8991
2502 N Clark St 212 Chicago (60614) ***(G-5769)***
**Miracle Press Company** ....773 722-6176
2951 W Carroll Ave Chicago (60612) ***(G-5770)***
**Mirek Cabinets** ....630 350-8336
1086 Waveland Ave Franklin Park (60131) ***(G-10535)***
**Mirror-Democrat** ....815 244-2411
308 N Main St Mount Carroll (61053) ***(G-15292)***
**Mirus Research** ....309 828-3100
618 E Lincoln St Normal (61761) ***(G-16077)***
**Mislich Bros, Pontiac** *Also called MBI Tools LLC* ***(G-17706)***
**Miss Joans Cupcakes** ....630 881-5707
1899 Marne Rd Bolingbrook (60490) ***(G-2343)***
**Misselhorn Welding & Machines** ....618 426-3714
310 S Main St Campbell Hill (62916) ***(G-2978)***
**Mission Control Systems Inc** ....847 956-7650
700 Oakton St Elk Grove Village (60007) ***(G-9630)***
**Mission of Our Lady of Mercy (PA)** ....312 738-7568
1140 W Jackson Blvd Ste 1 Chicago (60607) ***(G-5771)***
**Mission Popcorn, Chicago** *Also called Revolution Companies Inc* ***(G-6341)***
**Mission Press Inc** ....312 455-9501
600 W Cermak Rd Ste 1a Chicago (60616) ***(G-5772)***
**Mission Signs Inc** ....630 243-6731
1415 Chestnut Xing Lemont (60439) ***(G-13242)***
**Missouri Wood Craft Inc** ....217 453-2204
1400 Mulholland St Nauvoo (62354) ***(G-15853)***
**Mistic Metal Mover Inc** ....815 875-1371
1160 N 6th St Princeton (61356) ***(G-17754)***
**Mitchco Farms LLC** ....618 382-5032
1239 County Road 1500 N Carmi (62821) ***(G-3075)***
**Mitchel Home** ....773 205-9902
3652 N Tripp Ave Chicago (60641) ***(G-5773)***
**Mitchell Aircraft Products** ....815 331-8609
2309 N Ringwood Rd Ste U McHenry (60050) ***(G-14536)***
**Mitchell Arcft Expendables LLC** ....847 516-3773
1160 Alexander Ct Cary (60013) ***(G-3360)***
**Mitchell Optics Inc** ....217 688-2219
2072 County Road 1100 N Sidney (61877) ***(G-19937)***
**Mitchell Printing, Centralia** *Also called James Ray Monroe Corporation* ***(G-3420)***
**Mitchlls Cndies Ice Creams Inc** ....708 799-3835
18211 Dixie Hwy Homewood (60430) ***(G-12104)***
**Mitek Corporation** ....608 328-5560
1 Mitek Plz Winslow (61089) ***(G-22317)***
**Mitek Corporation** ....815 367-3000
1 Mitek Plz Winslow (61089) ***(G-22318)***
**Mitel Networks Inc** ....312 479-9000
70 W Madison St Ste 1600 Chicago (60602) ***(G-5774)***
**Mitsubishi Elc Automtn Inc (HQ)** ....847 478-2100
500 Corporate Woods Pkwy Vernon Hills (60061) ***(G-21183)***
**Mitsubishi Electric Us Inc** ....708 354-2900
5218 Dansher Rd Countryside (60525) ***(G-7439)***
**Mitsubishi Heavy Inds Amer Inc** ....630 693-4700
1225 N Greenbriar Dr B Addison (60101) ***(G-217)***
**Mitsubishi Materials USA Corp** ....847 519-1601
1314 N Plum Grove Rd Schaumburg (60173) ***(G-19649)***
**Mitsuboshi Chem. Corporation, Lombard** *Also called Molds & Tooling* ***(G-13828)***
**Mitsubshi Elevators Escalators, Countryside** *Also called Mitsubishi Electric Us Inc* ***(G-7439)***
**Mitsutoyo-Kiko USA Inc** ....847 981-5200
1600 Golf Rd Ste 1200 Rolling Meadows (60008) ***(G-18745)***
**Mittal Steel USA Inc** ....312 899-3440
1 S Dearborn St Ste 1800 Chicago (60603) ***(G-5775)***
**Mity Inc (PA)** ....630 365-5030
700 E North St Ste B Elburn (60119) ***(G-8898)***
**Miwon NA** ....630 568-5850
669 Executive Dr Willowbrook (60527) ***(G-22224)***
**Mix Foods LLC** ....224 338-0377
25635 W Venetian Dr Ingleside (60041) ***(G-12194)***
**Mix Kitchen** ....312 649-0330
610 N Fairbanks Ct Ste 3a Chicago (60611) ***(G-5776)***

ALPHABETIC

**Mix Match LLC** ... 708 201-0009
14725 Drexel Ave Dolton (60419) ***(G-8373)***
**Mix N Mingle** ... 815 308-5170
124 Cass St Ste 2 Woodstock (60098) ***(G-22592)***
**Mixing Division, Carmi** *Also called Vibracoustic Usa Inc* ***(G-3081)***
**Miyano Machinery USA Inc (HQ)** ... 630 766-4141
2316 Touhy Ave Elk Grove Village (60007) ***(G-9631)***
**Miyanohitec Machinery Inc** ... 847 382-2794
50 Dundee Ln Barrington (60010) ***(G-1292)***
**Mizkan America Inc (HQ)** ... 847 590-0059
1661 Feehanville Dr # 200 Mount Prospect (60056) ***(G-15347)***
**Mizkan America Holdings Inc (HQ)** ... 847 590-0059
1661 Feehanville Dr # 300 Mount Prospect (60056) ***(G-15348)***
**Mizrahi Grill** ... 847 831-1400
215 Skokie Valley Rd Highland Park (60035) ***(G-11855)***
**Mj Burton Gifts & Engraving, Quincy** *Also called M J Burton Engraving Co* ***(G-17854)***
**Mj Celco International LLC** ... 847 671-1900
3900 Wesley Ter Schiller Park (60176) ***(G-19852)***
**Mj Snyder Ironworks Inc** ... 217 826-6440
15640 E National Rd Marshall (62441) ***(G-14326)***
**Mj Works Hose & Fitting LLC (PA)** ... 708 995-5723
11122 W 189th Pl Bldg C1 Mokena (60448) ***(G-14886)***
**Mjf Woodworking** ... 815 679-6700
5250 W Flanders Rd McHenry (60050) ***(G-14537)***
**MJM Graphics** ... 847 234-1802
433 Greenwood Ave Lake Forest (60045) ***(G-12927)***
**Mjmc Inc** ... 708 596-5200
3111 167th St Hazel Crest (60429) ***(G-11713)***
**Mjs-Cn LLC** ... 630 580-7200
191 S Gary Ave Ste 180 Carol Stream (60188) ***(G-3200)***
**Mjsrf Inc** ... 888 677-6175
1864 S Elmhurst Rd Mount Prospect (60056) ***(G-15349)***
**Mjt Design and Prtg Entps Inc** ... 708 240-4323
4219 Butterfield Rd 1a Hillside (60162) ***(G-11926)***
**Mk Environmental Inc (PA)** ... 630 848-0585
7150 S Madison St Ste 2 Willowbrook (60527) ***(G-22225)***
**Mk Signs Inc** ... 773 545-4444
4900 N Elston Ave Ste M Chicago (60630) ***(G-5777)***
**Mk Systems Incorporated (PA)** ... 847 709-6180
1455 Brummel Ave Elk Grove Village (60007) ***(G-9632)***
**Mk Test Systems Americas Inc** ... 773 569-3778
22102 N Pepper Rd Ste 116 Lake Barrington (60010) ***(G-12820)***
**MK Tile Ink** ... 773 964-8905
5851 S Neenah Ave Chicago (60638) ***(G-5778)***
**Mkc Electric** ... 630 844-9700
1791 Commerce Dr Montgomery (60538) ***(G-15061)***
**ML Content** ... 847 212-8824
25566 W Ivanhoe Rd Wauconda (60084) ***(G-21485)***
**Mla Franklin Park Inc** ... 847 451-0279
2925 Lucy Ln Franklin Park (60131) ***(G-10536)***
**Mlevel Inc** ... 888 564-5395
205 W Wacker Dr Ste 820 Chicago (60606) ***(G-5779)***
**Mlp Seating, Elk Grove Village** *Also called J & E Seating LLC* ***(G-9556)***
**Mlp Seating Corp** ... 847 956-1700
950 Pratt Blvd Elk Grove Village (60007) ***(G-9633)***
**MMC Armory, Mark** *Also called Mennies Machine Company* ***(G-14299)***
**MMC Precision Holdings Corp (PA)** ... 309 266-7176
1021 W Birchwood St Morton (61550) ***(G-15164)***
**Mmf Pos, Wheeling** *Also called Block and Company Inc* ***(G-22015)***
**Mmma** ... 309 888-8765
2601 W College Ave Ste A Normal (61761) ***(G-16078)***
**Mmp, Des Plaines** *Also called Montana Metal Products LLC* ***(G-8234)***
**Mmp Company, Taylorville** *Also called Macon Metal Products Co* ***(G-20842)***
**Mmpcu Limited** ... 217 355-0500
905 S Neil St Ste B Champaign (61820) ***(G-3516)***
**Mmt, Chicago** *Also called Marketing & Technology Group* ***(G-5622)***
**Mni, Evanston** *Also called Manufacturers News Inc* ***(G-10068)***
**MNP Precision Parts LLC (HQ)** ... 815 391-5256
1111 Samuelson Rd Rockford (61109) ***(G-18509)***
**Mo-Par City, Oregon** *Also called Larry Pontnack* ***(G-16827)***
**Mobell Muscle, Chicago** *Also called Xmt Solutions LLC* ***(G-7046)***
**Mobil Trailer Transport Inc** ... 630 993-1200
223 E Adele Ct Villa Park (60181) ***(G-21270)***
**Mobile Air Inc** ... 847 755-0586
380 Windy Point Dr Glendale Heights (60139) ***(G-11049)***
**Mobile Endoscopix LLC** ... 847 380-8992
3330 Dundee Rd Ste C1 Northbrook (60062) ***(G-16312)***
**Mobile Mini Inc** ... 708 297-2004
12658 S Winchester Ave # 2 Calumet Park (60827) ***(G-2963)***
**Mobile Pallet Service Inc** ... 630 231-6597
1300 W Roosevelt Rd West Chicago (60185) ***(G-21745)***
**Mobile Systems, Elk Grove Village** *Also called Parker-Hannifin Corporation* ***(G-9670)***
**Mobilehop Technology LLC** ... 312 504-3773
838 W 31st St Unit 3g Chicago (60608) ***(G-5780)***
**Mobileskin Imaging, Kildeer** *Also called Interexpo Ltd* ***(G-12700)***
**Mobilia Inc** ... 708 865-0700
1023 Cernan Dr Bellwood (60104) ***(G-1715)***
**Mobility Center of Chicago, Oakbrook Terrace** *Also called Amigo Mobility Center* ***(G-16697)***
**Mobility Connection Inc** ... 815 965-8090
4100 E State St Rockford (61108) ***(G-18510)***
**Mobility Masters, Carol Stream** *Also called Midwest Coach Builders Inc* ***(G-3198)***
**Mobiloc LLC** ... 773 742-1329
5800 W 117th Pl Alsip (60803) ***(G-495)***
**Mobilty Works** ... 815 254-2000
23855 W Andrew Rd Ste 3 Plainfield (60585) ***(G-17629)***
**Modagrafics Inc** ... 800 860-3169
5300 Newport Dr Rolling Meadows (60008) ***(G-18746)***
**Modahl & Scott, Bloomington** *Also called Southfield Corporation* ***(G-2225)***
**Model Printers, Moline** *Also called Van Lancker Steven* ***(G-14975)***
**Models Plus Inc** ... 847 231-4300
888 E Belvidere Rd # 110 Grayslake (60030) ***(G-11354)***
**Modern Abrasive Corp** ... 815 675-2352
2855 N Us Highway 12 Spring Grove (60081) ***(G-20349)***
**Modern Aids Inc** ... 847 437-8600
201 Bond St Elk Grove Village (60007) ***(G-9634)***
**Modern Card Co, Lincolnwood** *Also called K Chae Corp* ***(G-13518)***
**Modern Fluid Technology Inc** ... 815 356-0001
93 Berkshire Dr Ste F Crystal Lake (60014) ***(G-7614)***
**Modern Food Concepts Inc** ... 815 534-5747
22813 Challenger Rd C Frankfort (60423) ***(G-10344)***
**Modern Gear & Machine Inc** ... 630 350-9173
406 Evergreen Ave Bensenville (60106) ***(G-1953)***
**Modern Graphic Systems Inc** ... 773 476-6898
4922 S Western Ave Chicago (60609) ***(G-5781)***
**Modern Home Products Corp (PA)** ... 847 395-6556
150 S Ram Rd Antioch (60002) ***(G-647)***
**Modern Lighting Tech LLC** ... 312 624-9267
1751 W Grand Ave Chicago (60622) ***(G-5782)***
**Modern Luxury Media LLC** ... 312 274-2500
33 W Monroe St Ste 2100 Chicago (60603) ***(G-5783)***
**Modern Metal Products, Chicago** *Also called Trend Publishing Inc* ***(G-6767)***
**Modern Methods Creative Inc** ... 309 263-4100
2613 N Knoxville Ave Peoria (61604) ***(G-17410)***
**Modern Methods LLC** ... 309 263-4100
408 N Nebraska Ave Morton (61550) ***(G-15165)***
**Modern Pattern Works Inc** ... 309 676-2157
1100 Sw Washington St Peoria (61602) ***(G-17411)***
**Modern Plating Corporation** ... 815 235-1790
701 S Hancock Ave Freeport (61032) ***(G-10674)***
**Modern Pltg Coatings Finishes, Freeport** *Also called Modern Plating Corporation* ***(G-10674)***
**Modern Printing Colors Inc** ... 708 681-5678
1951 W 21st St Broadview (60155) ***(G-2597)***
**Modern Printing of Quincy** ... 217 223-1063
2615 Ellington Rd Quincy (62305) ***(G-17861)***
**Modern Process Equipment Inc** ... 773 254-3929
3125 S Kolin Ave Chicago (60623) ***(G-5784)***
**Modern Silicone Tech Inc (PA)** ... 727 507-9800
2345 Waukegan Rd Ste 155 Bannockburn (60015) ***(G-1262)***
**Modern Specialties Company** ... 312 648-5800
661 W Lake St Chicago (60661) ***(G-5785)***
**Modern Sprout LLC** ... 312 342-2114
1451 N Ashland Ave Chicago (60622) ***(G-5786)***
**Modern Trade Communications (PA)** ... 847 674-2200
8833 Gross Point Rd # 308 Skokie (60077) ***(G-20041)***
**Modern Tube LLC (PA)** ... 877 848-3300
193 Rosedale Ct Bloomingdale (60108) ***(G-2118)***
**Modernfold Doors of Chicago** ... 630 654-4560
648 Blackhawk Dr Westmont (60559) ***(G-21908)***
**Moduslink Corporation** ... 708 496-7800
6112 W 73rd St Bedford Park (60638) ***(G-1566)***
**Moeller Ready Mix Inc** ... 217 243-7471
Rr 67 Box S Jacksonville (62650) ***(G-12402)***
**Moes River North LLC** ... 312 245-2000
155 W Kinzie St Chicago (60654) ***(G-5787)***
**Moesle Meat Company, Chicago** *Also called John J Moesle Wholesale Meats* ***(G-5315)***
**Moffat Wire & Display Inc** ... 630 458-8560
324 S La Londe Ave Addison (60101) ***(G-218)***
**Moffitt Co** ... 847 678-5450
9347 Seymour Ave Schiller Park (60176) ***(G-19853)***
**Mohawk Industries Inc** ... 630 972-8000
969 Veterans Pkwy Ste B Bolingbrook (60490) ***(G-2344)***
**Mohawk Spring, Schiller Park** *Also called Matthew Warren Inc* ***(G-19847)***
**Mohican Petroleum Inc** ... 312 782-6385
21 S Clark St Ste 3980 Chicago (60603) ***(G-5788)***
**Moisture Detection Inc** ... 847 426-0464
2200 Stonington Ave Hoffman Estates (60169) ***(G-12024)***
**Mold Express Inc** ... 773 766-0874
8142 W Frest Preserve Ave Chicago (60634) ***(G-5789)***
**Mold Repair and Manufacturing** ... 815 477-1332
2520 Il Route 176 Ste 5 Crystal Lake (60014) ***(G-7615)***
**Mold Seekers** ... 847 650-8025
319 Fairfax Ln Grayslake (60030) ***(G-11355)***
**Mold Shields Inc** ... 708 983-5931
230 N 2nd Ave Villa Park (60181) ***(G-21271)***
**Mold-Rite Plastics LLC (HQ)** ... 518 561-1812
30 N La Salle St Ste 2425 Chicago (60602) ***(G-5790)***
**Mold-Tech Midwest, Carol Stream** *Also called Standex International Corp* ***(G-3249)***

**Molded Displays** ....773 892-4098
739 Old Trail Rd Highland Park (60035) ***(G-11856)***
**Molding Services Group Inc** ....847 931-1491
2051 N La Fox St Lowr 1 South Elgin (60177) ***(G-20220)***
**Molding Services Illinois Inc** ....618 395-3888
126 N West St Olney (62450) ***(G-16782)***
**Molds & Tooling** ....630 627-9650
1040 N Ridge Ave Lombard (60148) ***(G-13828)***
**Moldtronics Inc** ....630 968-7000
703 Rogers St Downers Grove (60515) ***(G-8488)***
**Moldworks Inc** ....815 520-8819
11052 Jasmine Dr Roscoe (61073) ***(G-18908)***
**Molex LLC (HQ)** ....630 969-4550
2222 Wellington Ct Lisle (60532) ***(G-13625)***
**Molex LLC** ....847 353-2500
333 Knightsbridge Pkwy # 200 Lincolnshire (60069) ***(G-13466)***
**Molex LLC** ....630 527-4357
2200 Wellington Ct Lisle (60532) ***(G-13626)***
**Molex LLC** ....630 527-4363
575 Veterans Pkwy Ste A Bolingbrook (60440) ***(G-2345)***
**Molex LLC** ....630 969-4747
575 Veterans Pkwy Ste A Bolingbrook (60440) ***(G-2346)***
**Molex LLC** ....630 512-8787
5224 Katrine Ave Downers Grove (60515) ***(G-8489)***
**Molex Inc. Switch Division, Naperville** *Also called Molex Incorporated* ***(G-15698)***
**Molex Incorporated** ....630 969-4550
1750 Country Farm Dr Naperville (60563) ***(G-15698)***
**Molex International Inc (HQ)** ....630 969-4550
2222 Wellington Ct Lisle (60532) ***(G-13627)***
**Molex Premise Networks Inc** ....866 733-6659
2222 Wellington Ct Lisle (60532) ***(G-13628)***
**Moline Consumers Co** ....309 757-8289
200 23rd Ave Moline (61265) ***(G-14958)***
**Moline Dispatch Publishing Co (HQ)** ....309 764-4344
1720 5th Ave Moline (61265) ***(G-14959)***
**Moline Forge Inc** ....309 762-5506
4101 4th Ave Moline (61265) ***(G-14960)***
**Moline Semicon LLC** ....309 755-0433
605 17th Ave East Moline (61244) ***(G-8688)***
**Moline Welding Inc (PA)** ....309 756-0643
3603 78th Ave Milan (61264) ***(G-14795)***
**Moline Welding Inc** ....309 756-0643
3603 78th Ave Milan (61264) ***(G-14796)***
**Molor Products Company** ....630 375-5999
110 Kirkland Cir Ste K Oswego (60543) ***(G-16927)***
**Mom Dad & ME (PA)** ....773 735-9606
7601 S Ccero Ave Ste 1970 Chicago (60652) ***(G-5791)***
**Momence Packing Co** ....815 472-6485
334 W North St Momence (60954) ***(G-14984)***
**Momence Pallet Corporation** ....815 472-6451
11414 E State Route 114 Momence (60954) ***(G-14985)***
**Monahan Filaments LLC (HQ)** ....217 268-4957
215 Egyptian Trl Arcola (61910) ***(G-677)***
**Monahan Partners Inc** ....217 268-5758
200 N Oak St Arcola (61910) ***(G-678)***
**Monarch Manufacturing** ....630 519-4580
118 E Goebel Dr Lombard (60148) ***(G-13829)***
**Monarch Mfg Corp Amer** ....217 728-2552
Hc 32 Box S Sullivan (61951) ***(G-20753)***
**Monarch Tool & Die Co** ....630 530-8886
862 N Industrial Dr Elmhurst (60126) ***(G-9913)***
**Monastery Hill Bindery, Chicago** *Also called Hertzberg Ernst & Sons* ***(G-5082)***
**Monco Fabricators Inc** ....630 293-0063
645 Joliet St West Chicago (60185) ***(G-21746)***
**Monda Window & Door Corp** ....773 254-8888
4101 W 42nd Pl Chicago (60632) ***(G-5792)***
**Mondays Pub, Anna** *Also called Gazette-Democrat* ***(G-604)***
**Mondelez Global LLC** ....773 925-4300
7300 S Kedzie Ave Chicago (60629) ***(G-5793)***
**Mondelez Global LLC** ....815 877-8081
5500 Forest Hills Rd Loves Park (61111) ***(G-13968)***
**Mondelez Global LLC (HQ)** ....847 943-4000
3 Parkway N Ste 300 Deerfield (60015) ***(G-8037)***
**Mondelez Global LLC** ....630 369-1909
1555 W Ogden Ave Naperville (60540) ***(G-15699)***
**Mondelez International Inc (PA)** ....847 943-4000
3 Parkway N Ste 300 Deerfield (60015) ***(G-8038)***
**Mondelez Intl Holdings LLC (HQ)** ....800 572-3847
3 Parkway N Ste 300 Deerfield (60015) ***(G-8039)***
**Mondi Romeoville Inc** ....630 378-9886
1140 Arbor Dr Romeoville (60446) ***(G-18850)***
**Monett Metals Inc** ....773 478-8888
3925 N Pulaski Rd Chicago (60641) ***(G-5794)***
**Money Stretcher, Peoria** *Also called Gatehouse Media Ill Holdings* ***(G-17368)***
**Monitor Newspaper Inc** ....618 271-0468
1501 State St East Saint Louis (62205) ***(G-8761)***
**Monitor Publishing Inc** ....773 205-0303
6304 N Nagle Ave Ste B Chicago (60646) ***(G-5795)***
**Monitor Sign Co** ....217 234-2412
316 N Division St Mattoon (61938) ***(G-14405)***
**Monitor Technologies LLC** ....630 365-9403
44w320 Keslinger Rd Elburn (60119) ***(G-8899)***
**Monmouth Grain & Dryer, Monmouth** *Also called Big Rver Rsrces W Brlngton LLC* ***(G-15010)***
**Monmouth Metal Culvert Co** ....309 734-7723
706 W 3rd Ave Ste 708 Monmouth (61462) ***(G-15020)***
**Monmouth Ready Mix Corp** ....309 734-3211
620 S 2nd St Monmouth (61462) ***(G-15021)***
**Monmouth Stone Co (PA)** ....309 734-7951
1420 N Main St Monmouth (61462) ***(G-15022)***
**Monnex International Inc (PA)** ....847 850-5263
330 Hastings Dr Buffalo Grove (60089) ***(G-2738)***
**Monogen Inc** ....847 573-6700
140 S Dearborn St Ste 420 Chicago (60603) ***(G-5796)***
**Monogram Creative Group Inc** ....312 802-1433
1723 Wildberry Dr Unit C Glenview (60025) ***(G-11170)***
**Monogram Etched Crystal, Evanston** *Also called Monogram of Evanston Inc* ***(G-10074)***
**Monogram of Evanston Inc** ....847 864-8100
2108 Jackson Ave Evanston (60201) ***(G-10074)***
**Monograms & More** ....630 789-8424
7926 S Madison St Burr Ridge (60527) ***(G-2869)***
**Monolithic Industries Inc** ....630 985-6009
7613 Woodridge Dr Woodridge (60517) ***(G-22503)***
**Monona Holdings LLC (HQ)** ....630 946-0630
1952 Mc Dowell Rd Ste 207 Naperville (60563) ***(G-15700)***
**Monotype Imaging Inc** ....847 718-0400
985 Busse Rd Elk Grove Village (60007) ***(G-9635)***
**Monotype Imaging Inc** ....847 718-0400
1699 Wall St Ste 420 Mount Prospect (60056) ***(G-15350)***
**Monoxivent Systems Inc** ....309 764-9605
1306 Mill St Rock Island (61201) ***(G-18190)***
**Monroe Associates Inc** ....217 665-3898
1545 Cr 375e Bethany (61914) ***(G-2085)***
**Monroe County Clarion, Collinsville** *Also called Suburban Newspapers of Greater* ***(G-7342)***
**Monsanto Company** ....309 829-6640
14018 Carole Dr Bloomington (61705) ***(G-2202)***
**Monsanto Company** ....815 264-8153
460 E Adams St Waterman (60556) ***(G-21408)***
**Mont Eagle Products Inc (PA)** ....618 455-3344
219 S Main St Sainte Marie (62459) ***(G-19325)***
**Montana Metal Products LLC (HQ)** ....847 803-6600
25 Howard Ave Des Plaines (60018) ***(G-8234)***
**Montana Minerals Dev Co** ....800 426-5564
1500 W Shure Dr Arlington Heights (60004) ***(G-804)***
**Montauk Chicago Inc** ....312 951-5688
401 N Wells St Ste 108a Chicago (60654) ***(G-5797)***
**Montclare Scientific Glass** ....847 255-6870
25 N Hickory Ave Arlington Heights (60004) ***(G-805)***
**Montefusco Heating & Shtmtl Co** ....309 691-7400
2200 W Altorfer Dr Ste D Peoria (61615) ***(G-17412)***
**Montefusco Htg Shtmtl & A Con, Peoria** *Also called Montefusco Heating & Shtmtl Co* ***(G-17412)***
**Monterey Mushrooms Inc** ....815 875-4436
27268 Us Highway 6 Princeton (61356) ***(G-17755)***
**Monthly Aspectarian, The, Morton Grove** *Also called Lightworks Communcation Inc* ***(G-15214)***
**Monticello Design & Mfg** ....217 762-8551
822 Old Route 47 Monticello (61856) ***(G-15081)***
**Montrose Glass & Mirror Corp** ....773 478-6433
3916 W Montrose Ave Fl 1 Chicago (60618) ***(G-5798)***
**Monty Burcenski** ....815 838-0934
1213 S Lincoln St Lockport (60441) ***(G-13733)***
**Monument Company, Beardstown** *Also called Riverside Memorial Co* ***(G-1527)***
**Monumental Art Works** ....708 389-3038
2152 Vermont St Ste A2 Blue Island (60406) ***(G-2263)***
**Monumental Manufacturing Co** ....708 544-0916
4300 Roosevelt Rd Hillside (60162) ***(G-11927)***
**Moody Bible Inst of Chicago (PA)** ....312 329-4000
820 N La Salle Dr Chicago (60610) ***(G-5799)***
**Moody Bible Inst of Chicago** ....312 329-2102
210 W Chestnut St Chicago (60610) ***(G-5800)***
**Moody Press A Division of MBI, Chicago** *Also called Moody Bible Inst of Chicago* ***(G-5800)***
**Moog Inc** ....770 987-7550
3650 Woodhead Dr Northbrook (60062) ***(G-16313)***
**Moog Inc** ....847 498-0700
3650 Woodhead Dr Northbrook (60062) ***(G-16314)***
**Moog Quickset, Northbrook** *Also called Quickset International Inc* ***(G-16350)***
**Moon Guy Hong Food Inc** ....773 927-3233
3823 S Halsted St Chicago (60609) ***(G-5801)***
**Moon Jump Inc** ....630 983-0953
1750 W Armitage Ct Addison (60101) ***(G-219)***
**Moonbeam Babies** ....847 245-7371
259 Thrush Cir Lindenhurst (60046) ***(G-13548)***
**Moonlight Woodworking** ....815 728-9121
5409 Craftwell Dr Ringwood (60072) ***(G-17992)***
**Moons Industries America Inc** ....630 833-5940
1113 N Prospect Ave Itasca (60143) ***(G-12322)***
**Moore Machine Works** ....815 625-0536
706 Gregden Shores Dr Sterling (61081) ***(G-20600)***

ALPHABETIC

**Moore Memorials** 708 636-6532
5960 111th St Chicago Ridge (60415) ***(G-7152)***
**Moore North America Fin Inc** 847 607-6000
111 S Wacker Dr Ste 3600 Chicago (60606) ***(G-5802)***
**Moore-Addison Co** 630 543-6744
518 W Factory Rd Addison (60101) ***(G-220)***
**Moran Cristobalian** 630 506-4777
549 Peebles Ct Batavia (60510) ***(G-1472)***
**Moran Auto Parts and Mch Sp** 309 663-6449
1001 Croxton Ave Bldg 1 Bloomington (61701) ***(G-2203)***
**Moran Graphics Inc** 312 226-3900
1017 W Wa Blvd Unit 101 Chicago (60607) ***(G-5803)***
**Moran Properties Inc** 312 440-1962
1407 N Dearborn St Chicago (60610) ***(G-5804)***
**Mordern Flow Equipment, Villa Grove** *Also called Pauls Machine & Welding Corp* ***(G-21230)***
**Moreno and Sons Inc** 815 725-8600
2366 Plainfield Rd Crest Hill (60403) ***(G-7464)***
**Morey Industries Inc** 708 343-3220
2000 Beach St Broadview (60155) ***(G-2598)***
**Morgan Bronze Products Inc** 847 526-6000
340 E Il Route 22 Lake Zurich (60047) ***(G-13106)***
**Morgan Li LLC** 708 758-5300
383 E 16th St Chicago Heights (60411) ***(G-7114)***
**Morgan Ohare Inc** 630 543-6780
701 W Factory Rd Addison (60101) ***(G-221)***
**Morgan Robt Inc** 217 466-4777
1914 S Central Ave Paris (61944) ***(G-17154)***
**Morgen Transportation Inc** 773 405-1250
8 S Michigan Ave Ste 1600 Chicago (60603) ***(G-5805)***
**Moriteq Rubber Co** 847 734-0970
710 W Algonquin Rd Arlington Heights (60005) ***(G-806)***
**Moriteq USA Contacts, Arlington Heights** *Also called Moriteq Rubber Co* ***(G-806)***
**Morkes Chocolates, Palatine** *Also called Morkes Inc* ***(G-17057)***
**Morkes Inc** 847 359-3511
1890 N Rand Rd Palatine (60074) ***(G-17057)***
**Morningfields** 847 309-8460
800 Devon Ave Ste 7 Park Ridge (60068) ***(G-17209)***
**Morningside Woodcraft** 217 268-4313
545 E County Road 200n Arcola (61910) ***(G-679)***
**Morrell Incorporated** 630 858-4600
340 Windy Point Dr Glendale Heights (60139) ***(G-11050)***
**Morris Cody & Assoc** 847 945-8050
400 Lake Cook Rd Ste 207 Deerfield (60015) ***(G-8040)***
**Morris Construction Inc** 618 544-8504
Marathon Ave Robinson (62454) ***(G-18067)***
**Morris Daily Herald Publisher, Morris** *Also called Morris Publishing Company* ***(G-15120)***
**Morris Industries Inc** 630 739-1502
11237 Joliet Rd Lemont (60439) ***(G-13243)***
**Morris Kurtzon Incorporated** 773 277-2121
1420 S Talman Ave Chicago (60608) ***(G-5806)***
**Morris Magnetics Inc** 847 487-0829
1220 N Old Rand Rd Wauconda (60084) ***(G-21486)***
**Morris Meat Packing Co Inc** 708 865-8566
1406 S 5th Ave Maywood (60153) ***(G-14429)***
**Morris Packaging LLC (PA)** 309 663-9100
211 N Williamsburg Dr A Bloomington (61704) ***(G-2204)***
**Morris Pallet Skids Inc** 618 786-2241
15133 Newbern Rd Dow (62022) ***(G-8382)***
**Morris Publishing Company** 815 942-3221
1802 N Div St Ste 314 Morris (60450) ***(G-15120)***
**MORris&wade, Chicago** *Also called Eli Morris Group LLC* ***(G-4729)***
**Morrison Cont Hdlg Solutions, Glenwood** *Also called Morrison Timing Screw Company* ***(G-11219)***
**Morrison Timing Screw Company** 708 331-6600
335 W 194th St Glenwood (60425) ***(G-11219)***
**Morrison Weighing Systems Inc** 309 799-7311
7605 50th St Milan (61264) ***(G-14797)***
**Morrow Shoe and Boot Inc** 217 342-6833
320 W Jefferson Ave Effingham (62401) ***(G-8848)***
**Morse Automotive Corporation (PA)** 773 843-9000
750 W Lake Cook Rd # 480 Buffalo Grove (60089) ***(G-2739)***
**Morse Heavy Duty, Buffalo Grove** *Also called Morse Automotive Corporation* ***(G-2739)***
**Mortgage Market Info Svcs** 630 834-7555
53 E Saint Charles Rd Villa Park (60181) ***(G-21272)***
**Morton Automatic Electric Co** 309 263-7577
641 W David St Morton (61550) ***(G-15166)***
**Morton Buildings Inc** 217 357-3713
1825 E Us Highway 136 Carthage (62321) ***(G-3317)***
**Morton Buildings Inc** 630 904-1122
1519 N Il Route 23 Streator (61364) ***(G-20695)***
**Morton Buildings Inc** 309 936-7282
605 E Henry St Atkinson (61235) ***(G-944)***
**Morton Group Ltd** 847 831-2766
1510 Old Deerfield Rd Highland Park (60035) ***(G-11857)***
**Morton Grove Auto Electric, Arlington Heights** *Also called Lawrence Maddock* ***(G-792)***
**Morton Grove Med Imaging LLC (PA)** 847 213-2700
9000 Waukegan Rd Ste 110 Morton Grove (60053) ***(G-15222)***
**Morton Grove Phrmceuticals Inc** 847 967-5600
6451 Main St Morton Grove (60053) ***(G-15223)***
**Morton Industrial Group Inc (HQ)** 309 266-7176
1021 W Birchwood St Morton (61550) ***(G-15167)***
**Morton Industries LLC** 309 263-2590
70 Commerce Dr Morton (61550) ***(G-15168)***
**Morton International LLC (HQ)** 312 807-2696
123 N Wacker Dr Ste 2400 Chicago (60606) ***(G-5807)***
**Morton International LLC** 773 235-2341
1357 N Elston Ave Chicago (60642) ***(G-5808)***
**Morton Intl Inc Adhsves Spclty** 815 653-2042
5005 Barnard Mill Rd Ringwood (60072) ***(G-17993)***
**Morton Machining, Morton** *Also called Marion Tool & Die Inc* ***(G-15162)***
**Morton Metalcraft Co PA** 309 266-7176
1021 W Birchwood St Morton (61550) ***(G-15169)***
**Morton Nippon Coatings** 708 868-7403
2701 E 170th St Lansing (60438) ***(G-13178)***
**Morton Ready Mix Concrete, Morton** *Also called Southfield Corporation* ***(G-15181)***
**Morton Salt, Chicago** *Also called Morton International LLC* ***(G-5807)***
**Morton Salt Inc (HQ)** 312 807-2000
444 W Lake St Ste 3000 Chicago (60606) ***(G-5809)***
**Morton Suggestion Company LLC** 847 255-4770
800 W Central Rd Ste 101 Mount Prospect (60056) ***(G-15351)***
**Morton Yokohama Inc** 312 807-2000
123 N Wacker Dr Fl 27 Chicago (60606) ***(G-5810)***
**Mosaic Construction** 847 504-0177
425 Huehl Rd Bldg 15b Northbrook (60062) ***(G-16315)***
**Mosaicos Inc** 773 777-8453
4948 N Pulaski Rd Chicago (60630) ***(G-5811)***
**Mosedale Manufacturing, Franklin Park** *Also called Reliance Tool & Mfg Co* ***(G-10573)***
**Moss Holding Company (HQ)** 847 238-4200
2600 Elmhurst Rd Elk Grove Village (60007) ***(G-9636)***
**Moss Inc** 800 341-1557
2600 Elmhurst Rd Elk Grove Village (60007) ***(G-9637)***
**Mossan Inc** 857 247-4122
28 Ashburn Ct Unit Z1 Schaumburg (60193) ***(G-19650)***
**Mostardi Platt, Hoffman Estates** *Also called Platt G Mostardi* ***(G-12034)***
**Mostert & Ferguson Signs** 815 485-1212
15617 S 71st Ct Orland Park (60462) ***(G-16876)***
**Motamed Medical Publishing Co** 773 761-6667
7141 N Kedzie Ave # 1504 Chicago (60645) ***(G-5812)***
**Motec Inc** 630 241-9595
555 Rogers St Ste 5 Downers Grove (60515) ***(G-8490)***
**Motion Access LLC** 847 357-8832
775 Nicholas Blvd Elk Grove Village (60007) ***(G-9638)***
**Motion Industries Inc** 847 760-6630
440 Airport Rd Ste J Elgin (60123) ***(G-9113)***
**Motivequest LLC (HQ)** 847 905-6100
723 Chicago Ave Evanston (60202) ***(G-10075)***
**Motor Capacitors Inc** 773 774-6666
335 Beinoris Dr Wood Dale (60191) ***(G-22401)***
**Motor Coach Inds Intl Inc (HQ)** 847 285-2000
200 E Oakton St Des Plaines (60018) ***(G-8235)***
**Motor Coach Industries** 847 285-2000
200 E Oakton St Des Plaines (60018) ***(G-8236)***
**Motor Oil Inc** 847 956-7550
2250 Arthur Ave Elk Grove Village (60007) ***(G-9639)***
**Motor Row Development Corp** 773 525-3311
2303 S Mich Ave Ste Assoc Chicago (60616) ***(G-5813)***
**Motor Sport Marketing Group** 618 654-6750
7 Shamrock Blvd Highland (62249) ***(G-11803)***
**Motormakers De Kalb Credit Un** 815 756-6331
3726 N Wayne Ave Chicago (60613) ***(G-5814)***
**Motorola International Capital** 847 576-5000
1303 E Algonquin Rd Schaumburg (60196) ***(G-19651)***
**Motorola Mobility Holdings LLC (HQ)** 847 523-5000
222 Merchandise Mart Plz # 1600 Chicago (60654) ***(G-5815)***
**Motorola Mobility LLC** 847 523-5000
222 Merchandise Mart Plz Chicago (60654) ***(G-5816)***
**Motorola Mobility LLC (HQ)** 800 668-6765
222 Merchandise Mart Plz Chicago (60654) ***(G-5817)***
**Motorola Solutions Inc (PA)** 847 576-5000
500 W Monroe St Ste 4400 Chicago (60661) ***(G-5818)***
**Motorola Solutions Inc** 847 538-6959
2835 Farmington Rd Northbrook (60062) ***(G-16316)***
**Motorola Solutions Inc** 847 341-3485
2301 W 22nd St Ste 102 Oak Brook (60523) ***(G-16546)***
**Motorola Solutions Inc** 630 308-9394
1299 E Algonquin Rd Hoffman Estates (60196) ***(G-12025)***
**Motorola Solutions Inc** 630 353-8000
1411 Opus Pl Ste 350 Downers Grove (60515) ***(G-8491)***
**Motorola Solutions Inc** 847 576-8600
1295 E Algonquin Rd Schaumburg (60196) ***(G-19652)***
**Motorola Solutions Inc** 847 523-5000
622 N Us Highway 45 Libertyville (60048) ***(G-13359)***
**Motorola Solutions Inc** 847 540-8815
1155 W Dundee Rd Arlington Heights (60004) ***(G-807)***
**Motorola Solutions Inc** 847 523-5000
1200 Technology Way Libertyville (60048) ***(G-13360)***
**Motorola Solutions Inc** 847 541-1014
2700 International Dr West Chicago (60185) ***(G-21747)***

## ALPHABETIC SECTION — Mueller Mfg Corp (PA)

Motorola Solutions Inc .................................................. 708 476-8226
  1100 E Woodfield Rd # 535 Schaumburg (60173) *(G-19653)*
Motorola Solutions Inc .................................................. 800 331-6456
  1303 E Algonquin Rd Schaumburg (60196) *(G-19654)*
Motorola Solutions Inc .................................................. 847 576-5000
  2520 Galvin Dr Elgin (60124) *(G-9114)*
Motr Grafx LLC .......................................................... 847 600-5656
  7430 N Lehigh Ave Niles (60714) *(G-16009)*
Motus Digital Llc ........................................................ 972 943-0008
  131 Cornell Ave Des Plaines (60016) *(G-8237)*
Moulder's Friend, The, Dallas City Also called Kinast Inc *(G-7698)*
Moultri Cnty Hstrcl/Gnlgcl Sct ........................................ 217 728-4085
  117 E Harrison St Sullivan (61951) *(G-20754)*
Moultrie County Hardwoods LLC
  Rr 1 Box 170-F Arthur (61911) *(G-912)*
Moultrie County Redi-Mix Co ......................................... 217 728-2334
  622 S Worth St Sullivan (61951) *(G-20755)*
MOUNT CARMEL STABILIZATION, Mount Carmel Also called Omni Materials Inc *(G-15279)*
Mount Vernon Iron Works LLC ....................................... 618 244-2313
  10950 N Cactus Ln Mount Vernon (62864) *(G-15428)*
Mount Vernon Mills ..................................................... 618 882-6300
  1001 Main St Highland (62249) *(G-11804)*
Mount Vernon Neon Sign Co ......................................... 618 242-0645
  1 Neon Dr Mount Vernon (62864) *(G-15429)*
Mount Vernon Zone, Mount Vernon Also called Centralia Press Ltd *(G-15403)*
Mountain Horizons Inc ................................................. 630 501-0190
  150 S Church St Addison (60101) *(G-222)*
Mountain Valley Spring Co LLC ..................................... 618 242-4963
  423 S 8th St Mount Vernon (62864) *(G-15430)*
Mountaineer Newspapers Inc (HQ) ................................. 815 562-2061
  211 E Il Route 38 Rochelle (61068) *(G-18099)*
Movie Facts Inc (PA) .................................................... 847 299-9700
  1870 Busse Hwy Ste 200 Des Plaines (60016) *(G-8238)*
Moving Up Garage Door Company, Mchenry Also called Worth Door Company *(G-14572)*
Moweaqua Packing Plant .............................................. 217 768-4714
  601 N Main St Moweaqua (62550) *(G-15458)*
Moxie Apparel LLC ..................................................... 312 243-9040
  222 S Morgan St Ste 3c Chicago (60607) *(G-5819)*
Mp Manufacturing Inc .................................................. 815 334-1112
  13802 Washington St Ste B Woodstock (60098) *(G-22593)*
Mp Mold Inc .............................................................. 630 613-8086
  1480 W Bernard Dr Addison (60101) *(G-223)*
Mp Steel Chicago LLC ................................................. 773 242-0853
  5757 W Ogden Ave Ste 4 Chicago (60804) *(G-5820)*
Mp Technologies LLC .................................................. 847 491-4253
  1801 Maple Ave Ste 5 Evanston (60201) *(G-10076)*
Mpc Containment Intl LLC ............................................ 773 927-4120
  4834 S Oakley Ave Chicago (60609) *(G-5821)*
Mpc Containment Systems LLC (HQ) ............................. 773 927-4121
  4834 S Oakley Ave Chicago (60609) *(G-5822)*
Mpc Containment Systems LLC .................................... 773 734-1000
  4834 S Oakley Ave Chicago (60609) *(G-5823)*
Mpc Group LLC (PA) ................................................... 773 927-4120
  4834 S Oakley Ave Chicago (60609) *(G-5824)*
Mpc Products Corporation (HQ) .................................... 847 673-8300
  6300 W Howard St Niles (60714) *(G-16010)*
Mpc Products Corporation ........................................... 847 673-8300
  5600 W Jarvis Ave Niles (60714) *(G-16011)*
Mpc Products Corporation ........................................... 847 673-8300
  6300 W Howard St Niles (60714) *(G-16012)*
MPD Inc ................................................................... 847 489-7705
  13795 W Polo Trail Dr A Lake Forest (60045) *(G-12928)*
Mpd Medical Systems Inc ............................................ 815 477-0707
  2530 Il Route 176 Ste 3 Crystal Lake (60014) *(G-7616)*
MPE Business Forms Inc ............................................. 815 748-3676
  1120 Oak St Dekalb (60115) *(G-8106)*
Mpm Industries, Glen Carbon Also called Mechanics Planing Mill Inc *(G-10954)*
Mpp Sycamore Div 6063, Sycamore Also called Orora Packaging Solutions *(G-20812)*
Mpr Plastics Inc ......................................................... 847 468-9950
  1551 Scottsdale Ct # 100 Elgin (60123) *(G-9115)*
MPS Chicago Inc (HQ) ................................................. 630 932-9000
  1500 Centre Cir Downers Grove (60515) *(G-8492)*
MPS Chicago Inc ........................................................ 630 932-5583
  315 Eisenhower Ln S Bolingbrook (60440) *(G-2347)*
Mr Auto Electric ......................................................... 217 523-3659
  2649 E Cook St Springfield (62703) *(G-20485)*
Mr Cake, Chicago Also called Mario Escobar *(G-5621)*
Mr Dvr Llc ................................................................. 708 827-5030
  6723 W 111th St Worth (60482) *(G-22634)*
Mr T Shirt and Dollar Plus ............................................ 708 596-9150
  75 W 159th St Harvey (60426) *(G-11674)*
Mr. Pak's, Chicago Also called Wisepak Foods LLC *(G-7006)*
Mr. Rooter Plumbing, Joliet Also called Ave Inc *(G-12457)*
MRC Global (us) Inc ................................................... 314 231-3400
  3672 State Route 111 Granite City (62040) *(G-11297)*
MRC Global (us) Inc ................................................... 815 729-7742
  4026 Mound Rd Joliet (60436) *(G-12544)*
MRC Polymers Inc (PA) ............................................... 773 890-9000
  3307 S Lawndale Ave Chicago (60623) *(G-5825)*

Mrgfastman, Highland Park Also called G-Fast Distribution Inc *(G-11834)*
Mrk Industries Inc ...................................................... 847 362-8720
  1821 Industrial Dr Libertyville (60048) *(G-13361)*
Mrl Industries, Itasca Also called Manufacturers Inv Group LLC *(G-12310)*
Mrs Fishers Inc ......................................................... 815 964-9114
  1231 Fulton Ave Rockford (61103) *(G-18511)*
Mrs Mike's Potato Chips, Freeport Also called Altona Co *(G-10645)*
Mrs Weavers Salads, Franklin Park Also called Dean Food Products Company *(G-10455)*
Mrs. Fisher's Chips, Rockford Also called Mrs Fishers Inc *(G-18511)*
Mrt Sureway Inc (PA) .................................................. 847 801-3010
  2959 Hart Ct Franklin Park (60131) *(G-10537)*
Ms, Addison Also called Metals and Services Inc *(G-202)*
Ms Astral Tool, West Chicago Also called M S Tool & Engineering *(G-21735)*
Ms. Bossy Boots, Crystal Lake Also called Shoelace Inc *(G-7650)*
MSA, Westmont Also called Magnet-Schultz America Inc *(G-21902)*
MSC Pre Finish Metals Egv Inc (HQ) .............................. 847 439-2210
  2250 Pratt Blvd Elk Grove Village (60007) *(G-9640)*
Mseed Group LLC ...................................................... 847 226-1147
  535 W Taft Dr South Holland (60473) *(G-20292)*
Msf Graphics Inc ........................................................ 847 446-6900
  959 Lee St Des Plaines (60016) *(G-8239)*
MSF&w, Springfield Also called Marucco Stddard Frenbach Walsh *(G-20474)*
MSI, Saint Charles Also called Manufactured Specialties Inc *(G-19213)*
MSI Green Inc ........................................................... 312 421-6550
  1958 W Grand Ave Chicago (60622) *(G-5826)*
MSI Southland, Lincolnwood Also called Rutgers Enterprises Inc *(G-13535)*
Msm Promotions, Chicago Also called Maxs Screen Machine Inc *(G-5659)*
MSP, Downers Grove Also called Machine Solution Providers Inc *(G-8481)*
Mssc, Collinsville Also called Marsh Shipping Supply Co LLC *(G-7335)*
Mssc LLC .................................................................. 618 343-1006
  926 Mcdonough Lake Rd E Collinsville (62234) *(G-7336)*
MST Div, Bolingbrook Also called Kps Capital Partners LP *(G-2333)*
Msystems Group LLC .................................................. 630 567-3930
  38w426 Mallard Lake Rd Saint Charles (60175) *(G-19224)*
Mt Carmel Machine Shop Inc ........................................ 618 262-4591
  10011 N 1250th Blvd Mount Carmel (62863) *(G-15275)*
Mt Carmel Register Co Inc ........................................... 618 262-5144
  117 E 4th St Mount Carmel (62863) *(G-15276)*
MT Case Company ..................................................... 630 227-1019
  569 N Edgewood Ave Wood Dale (60191) *(G-22402)*
Mt Crmel Stblzation Group Inc (PA) ............................... 618 262-5118
  1611 College Dr Mount Carmel (62863) *(G-15277)*
Mt Greenwood Embroidery ........................................... 773 779-5798
  3136 W 111th St Chicago (60655) *(G-5827)*
Mt Tool and Manufacturing Inc ...................................... 847 985-6211
  1118 Lunt Ave Ste E Schaumburg (60193) *(G-19655)*
Mt Vernon Electric, Mount Vernon Also called Decatur Industrial Elc Inc *(G-15409)*
Mt Vernon Mold Works Inc ........................................... 618 242-6040
  15 Industrial Dr Mount Vernon (62864) *(G-15431)*
Mt. Vernon Register News, Mount Vernon Also called Newspaper Holding Inc *(G-15434)*
MTA USA Corp ........................................................... 847 847-5503
  710 E State Pkwy Ste B Schaumburg (60173) *(G-19656)*
Mte Hydraulics, Rockford Also called Mechanical Tool & Engrg Co *(G-18489)*
Mtech Cnc Machining Inc ............................................ 224 848-0818
  1154 Rose Rd Lake Zurich (60047) *(G-13107)*
Mth Enterprises LLC .................................................. 708 498-1100
  1 Mth Plz Hillside (60162) *(G-11928)*
MTI, Elk Grove Village Also called Marathon Technologies Inc *(G-9611)*
MTM ASSOCIATION, Des Plaines Also called M T M Assn For Standards & RES *(G-8224)*
Mtm Jostens Inc ........................................................ 815 875-1111
  615 S 6th St Princeton (61356) *(G-17756)*
Mtm Recognition Corporation ....................................... 815 875-1111
  615 S 6th St Princeton (61356) *(G-17757)*
MTS Publishing Co .................................................... 630 955-9750
  800 W 5th Ave Ste 204a Naperville (60563) *(G-15701)*
Mtx, Winslow Also called Mitek Corporation *(G-22318)*
Mtx/Oaktron, Winslow Also called Mitek Corporation *(G-22317)*
Mu Dai LLC ............................................................... 312 982-0040
  35 E Wacker Dr Fl 14 Chicago (60601) *(G-5828)*
Mucci Kirkpatrick Sheet Metal ...................................... 815 433-3350
  1908 Ottawa Ave Ottawa (61350) *(G-16970)*
Mudlark Papers Inc .................................................... 630 717-7616
  1031 Shimer Ct Naperville (60565) *(G-15702)*
Mueller Co LLC .......................................................... 217 423-4471
  500 W Eldorado St Decatur (62522) *(G-7918)*
Mueller Company Plant 4 ............................................. 217 425-7424
  1226 E Garfield Ave Decatur (62526) *(G-7919)*
Mueller Custom Cabinetry Inc ...................................... 815 448-5448
  4730 S Old Mazon Rd Mazon (60444) *(G-14439)*
Mueller Door Company ............................................... 815 385-8550
  27100 N Darrell Rd Wauconda (60084) *(G-21487)*
Mueller Industries Inc ................................................. 847 290-1108
  2021 Lunt Ave Elk Grove Village (60007) *(G-9641)*
Mueller Metal Products, Elk Grove Village Also called Mueller Mfg Corp *(G-9642)*
Mueller Mfg Corp (PA) ................................................ 847 640-1666
  300 Lively Blvd Elk Grove Village (60007) *(G-9642)*

**Mueller Orna Ir Works Inc** ....847 758-9941
655 Lively Blvd Elk Grove Village (60007) ***(G-9643)***
**Muffler** ....217 344-1676
102 W University Ave Urbana (61801) ***(G-21095)***
**Muffys Inc** ....815 433-6839
423 W Madison St Ottawa (61350) ***(G-16971)***
**Muhammad Sotavia** ....708 966-2262
9601 165th St Orland Park (60467) ***(G-16877)***
**Muhammed Citizens, Mahomet** *Also called Illinois Valley Press East* ***(G-14159)***
**Muhs Cabinet Creation, Noble** *Also called Muhs Funiture Manufacturing* ***(G-16052)***
**Muhs Funiture Manufacturing** ....618 723-2590
4808 N Passport Rd Noble (62868) ***(G-16052)***
**Muir Omni Graphics Inc (PA)** ....309 673-7034
908 W Main St Peoria (61606) ***(G-17413)***
**Mulch Center LLC** ....847 459-7200
21457 Milwaukee Ave Deerfield (60015) ***(G-8041)***
**Mulch It Inc** ....847 566-9372
19738 W Martin Dr Mundelein (60060) ***(G-15533)***
**Mullen Circle Brand Inc** ....847 676-1880
3514 W Touhy Ave Skokie (60076) ***(G-20042)***
**Mullen Foods LLC** ....773 716-9001
6740 N Edgebrook Ter Chicago (60646) ***(G-5829)***
**Muller Quaker Dairy LLC** ....312 821-1000
555 W Monroe St Fl 7 Chicago (60661) ***(G-5830)***
**Muller Roofing & Construction, Chicago** *Also called Ted Muller* ***(G-6686)***
**Muller-Pinehurst Dairy Inc** ....815 968-0441
2110 Ogilby Rd Rockford (61102) ***(G-18512)***
**Mullins Food Products Inc** ....708 344-3224
2200 S 25th Ave Broadview (60155) ***(G-2599)***
**Multax Corporation** ....309 266-9765
424 W Edgewood Ct Morton (61550) ***(G-15170)***
**Multi Art Press** ....773 775-0515
7560 N Milwaukee Ave Chicago (60631) ***(G-5831)***
**Multi Packaging Solutions Inc** ....773 283-9500
4221 N Normandy Ave Chicago (60634) ***(G-5832)***
**Multi Swatch Corporation** ....708 344-9440
2600 S 25th Ave Ste Y Broadview (60155) ***(G-2600)***
**Multi-Ad Services, Peoria** *Also called SGS International LLC* ***(G-17453)***
**Multi-Lngua Communications, Northfield** *Also called Chicago Mltlingua Graphics Inc* ***(G-16397)***
**Multi-Pack Chicago, Mount Prospect** *Also called Multi-Pack Solutions LLC* ***(G-15352)***
**Multi-Pack Solutions LLC (PA)** ....847 635-6772
1804 W Central Rd Mount Prospect (60056) ***(G-15352)***
**Multi-Plastics Inc** ....630 226-0580
606 Territorial Dr Ste C Bolingbrook (60440) ***(G-2348)***
**Multicopy Corp** ....847 446-7015
1739 Harding Rd Northfield (60093) ***(G-16410)***
**Multifilm Packaging Corp** ....847 695-7600
1040 N Mclean Blvd Elgin (60123) ***(G-9116)***
**Multifoil Packaging, Elgin** *Also called Multifilm Packaging Corp* ***(G-9116)***
**Multimail Solutions** ....847 516-9977
700 Industrial Dr Cary (60013) ***(G-3361)***
**Multimetal Products Corp** ....847 662-9110
3965 Grove Ave Gurnee (60031) ***(G-11475)***
**Multiple Metal Production** ....847 679-1510
8030 Lawndale Ave Skokie (60076) ***(G-20043)***
**Multiplex Display Fixture Co** ....800 325-3350
1610 Design Way Dupo (62239) ***(G-8574)***
**Multiplex Industries Inc** ....630 906-9780
1650 Se River Rd Montgomery (60538) ***(G-15062)***
**Multitech Cold Forming LLC** ....630 949-8200
250 Kehoe Blvd Carol Stream (60188) ***(G-3201)***
**Multitech Industries** ....815 206-0015
10603 Arabian Trl Woodstock (60098) ***(G-22594)***
**Multitech Industries Inc (PA)** ....630 784-9200
350 Village Dr Carol Stream (60188) ***(G-3202)***
**Multitech McHned Cmponents LLC** ....630 949-8200
250 Kehoe Blvd Carol Stream (60188) ***(G-3203)***
**Mulvain Woodworks** ....815 248-2305
14578 Center Rd Durand (61024) ***(G-8587)***
**Municipal Electronics Inc** ....217 877-8601
2267 E Hubbard Ave Decatur (62526) ***(G-7920)***
**Munoz Flour Tortilleria Inc** ....773 523-1837
1707 W 47th St Chicago (60609) ***(G-5833)***
**Muntons Malted Ingredients Inc** ....630 812-1600
2505 S Finley Rd Ste 130 Lombard (60148) ***(G-13830)***
**Muntz Industries Inc** ....847 949-8280
710 Tower Rd Mundelein (60060) ***(G-15534)***
**Murata Electronics N Amer Inc** ....847 330-9200
425 N Martingale Rd # 1540 Schaumburg (60173) ***(G-19657)***
**Murdock Company Inc** ....847 566-0050
936 Turret Ct Mundelein (60060) ***(G-15535)***
**Murff Enterprises LLC** ....203 685-5556
9331 S Clyde Ave Chicago (60617) ***(G-5834)***
**Murnane Packaging Corporation** ....708 449-1200
607 Northwest Ave Northlake (60164) ***(G-16443)***
**Murnane Specialties Inc (PA)** ....708 449-1200
607 Northwest Ave Northlake (60164) ***(G-16444)***
**Muro Pallets Corp** ....773 640-8606
5208 S Mozart St Chicago (60632) ***(G-5835)***
**Murpack, Northlake** *Also called Murnane Packaging Corporation* ***(G-16443)***
**Murphy Brothers Enterprises** ....773 874-9020
7649 S State St Chicago (60619) ***(G-5836)***
**Murphy Oil Usa Inc** ....217 442-7882
4105 N Vermilion St Danville (61834) ***(G-7757)***
**Murphy USA** ....815 578-9053
2901 N Richmond Rd Johnsburg (60051) ***(G-12438)***
**Murphy USA 6511, Danville** *Also called Murphy Oil Usa Inc* ***(G-7757)***
**Murphy USA Inc** ....815 337-2440
1265 Lake Ave Woodstock (60098) ***(G-22595)***
**Murphy USA Inc** ....630 801-4950
1927 Us Route 30 Montgomery (60538) ***(G-15063)***
**Murphy USA Inc** ....815 936-6144
503 Riverstone Pkwy Kankakee (60901) ***(G-12639)***
**Murphys Pub** ....847 526-1431
110 Slocum Lake Rd Wauconda (60084) ***(G-21488)***
**Murray Inc (PA)** ....847 620-7990
400 N Rand Rd North Barrington (60010) ***(G-16153)***
**Murray Cabinetry & Tops Inc** ....815 672-6992
407 N Bloomington St Streator (61364) ***(G-20696)***
**Murray Printing Service Inc** ....847 310-8959
635 Remington Rd Ste F Schaumburg (60173) ***(G-19658)***
**Murrays Disc Auto Stores Inc** ....847 458-7179
108 N Randall Rd Lake In The Hills (60156) ***(G-12999)***
**Murrays Disc Auto Stores Inc** ....847 882-4384
38 E Golf Rd Ste C Schaumburg (60173) ***(G-19659)***
**Murrays Disc Auto Stores Inc** ....708 430-8155
7100 W 87th St Bridgeview (60455) ***(G-2511)***
**Murrihy Pallet Co** ....615 370-7000
1919 W 74th St Chicago (60636) ***(G-5837)***
**Murvin & Meier Oil Co** ....847 277-8380
1531 S Grove Ave Unit 203 Barrington (60010) ***(G-1293)***
**Murvin & Meir Oil Co** ....618 395-4405
1102 N East St Olney (62450) ***(G-16783)***
**Murvin Oil Company** ....618 393-2124
1712 S Whittle Ave Olney (62450) ***(G-16784)***
**Musco Sports Lighting LLC** ....630 876-0500
902 Paramount Pkwy Ste A Batavia (60510) ***(G-1473)***
**Mushro Machine & Tool Co** ....815 672-5848
819 E Bridge St Streator (61364) ***(G-20697)***
**Music Connection Inc** ....708 364-7590
10751 165th St Ste 104 Orland Park (60467) ***(G-16878)***
**Music Evolution, Tinley Park** *Also called Nueva Vida Productions Inc* ***(G-20935)***
**Music Inc. Magazine, Elmhurst** *Also called Maher Publications Inc* ***(G-9906)***
**Music Solutions** ....630 759-3033
490 Woodcreek Dr Ste D Bolingbrook (60440) ***(G-2349)***
**Mutual Steel, Highland Park** *Also called Mutual Svcs Highland Pk Inc* ***(G-11858)***
**Mutual Svcs Highland Pk Inc** ....847 432-3815
2760 Skokie Valley Rd Highland Park (60035) ***(G-11858)***
**Mvs Molding Inc** ....847 740-7700
701 Long Lake Dr Round Lake (60073) ***(G-19063)***
**MW Hopkins & Sons Inc** ....847 458-1010
9150 Pyott Rd Lake In The Hills (60156) ***(G-13000)***
**Mw Industries, Rosemont** *Also called Matthew Warren Inc* ***(G-19015)***
**Mwrbents, Mascoutah** *Also called Midwest Recumbent Bicycles* ***(G-14357)***
**Mwsts, Plainfield** *Also called Midwest Sport Turf Systems LLC* ***(G-17627)***
**Mww Food Processing USA LLC** ....800 582-1574
4300 W Bryn Mawr Ave Chicago (60646) ***(G-5838)***
**Mx Tech Inc** ....815 936-6277
450 S Schuyler Ave Bradley (60915) ***(G-2427)***
**My Bed Inc** ....800 326-9233
14040 S Shoshoni Dr Lockport (60491) ***(G-13734)***
**My Eye Doctor** ....847 325-4440
158 Mchenry Rd Buffalo Grove (60089) ***(G-2740)***
**My Eye Doctor (PA)** ....312 782-4208
29 E Madison St Ste 808 Chicago (60602) ***(G-5839)***
**My Finished Book, Chicago** *Also called Beloved Characters Ltd* ***(G-4079)***
**My Konjac Sponge Inc** ....630 345-3653
300 Lake View Pl North Barrington (60010) ***(G-16154)***
**My Local Beacon Llc** ....888 482-6691
73 W Monroe St Ste 323 Chicago (60603) ***(G-5840)***
**My Own Meals Inc** ....773 378-6505
5410 W Roosevelt Rd # 301 Chicago (60644) ***(G-5841)***
**My Own Meals Inc (PA)** ....847 948-1118
400 Lake Cook Rd Ste 107 Deerfield (60015) ***(G-8042)***
**My Sports Warehouse, Vernon Hills** *Also called Wagner International LLC* ***(G-21216)***
**My-Lin Manufacturing Co Inc** ....630 897-4100
820 N Russell Ave Aurora (60506) ***(G-1192)***
**My-Signguycom Inc** ....888 223-9703
5570 N Lynch Ave Chicago (60630) ***(G-5842)***
**Mybread LLC** ....312 600-9633
2000 W Fulton St Chicago (60612) ***(G-5843)***
**Myco Inc** ....815 395-8500
1122 Milford Ave Rockford (61109) ***(G-18513)***
**Mycogen Seeds, Pontiac** *Also called Dow Agrosciences LLC* ***(G-17699)***
**Myeccho LLC** ....224 639-3068
550 Graceland Ave Apt 11 Des Plaines (60016) ***(G-8240)***

**Myers Concrete & Construction**....815 732-2591
1100 Bennett Dr Oregon (61061) *(G-16828)*
**Myers Inc**....309 725-3710
99999 Route 1 S Varna (61375) *(G-21135)*
**Myerson LLC (PA)**....312 432-8200
5106 N Ravenswood Ave Chicago (60640) *(G-5844)*
**Myhomeeq LLC**....773 328-7034
1741 N Western Ave Chicago (60647) *(G-5845)*
**Mypowr, Evanston** *Also called Stryde Technologies Inc (G-10096)*
**Mystic Pizza Food Company, Elk Grove Village** *Also called Globus Food Products LLC (G-9505)*
**Mzm Manufacturing Inc**....815 624-8666
5409 Swanson Ct Roscoe (61073) *(G-18909)*
**N & M Type & Design**....630 834-3696
562 S Rex Blvd Elmhurst (60126) *(G-9914)*
**N & S Pattern Co**....815 874-6166
4911 Hydraulic Rd Rockford (61109) *(G-18514)*
**N A L, Flora** *Also called North American Lighting Inc (G-10212)*
**N Bujarski Inc**....847 884-1600
725 E Golf Rd Schaumburg (60173) *(G-19660)*
**N Contour Concepts Inc**....708 599-9571
7415 W 90th St Bridgeview (60455) *(G-2512)*
**N E S Traffic Safety**....312 603-7444
8770 W Bryn Mawr Ave Chicago (60631) *(G-5846)*
**N Fly Cycle Inc**....815 562-4620
2439 Gurler Rd Ashton (61006) *(G-929)*
**N G K Spark Plugs, Wood Dale** *Also called NGK Spark Plugs (usa) Inc (G-22406)*
**N Henry & Son Inc**....847 870-0797
900 N Rohlwing Rd Itasca (60143) *(G-12323)*
**N J Tech Inc**....847 428-1001
160 Industrial Dr Ste 5 Gilberts (60136) *(G-10928)*
**N K C Inc**....630 628-9159
751 W Winthrop Ave Addison (60101) *(G-224)*
**N P D Inc**....708 424-6788
4720 W 103rd St Oak Lawn (60453) *(G-16636)*
**N W Horizontal Boring**....618 566-9117
8100 Summerfield South Rd Mascoutah (62258) *(G-14358)*
**N'Digo, Chicago** *Also called Hartman Publishing Group Ltd (G-5050)*
**Nabisco, Chicago** *Also called Mondelez Global LLC (G-5793)*
**Nablus Sweets Inc**....708 205-6534
4800 N Kedzie Ave Chicago (60625) *(G-5847)*
**Nablus Sweets Inc (PA)**....708 529-3911
8320 S Harlem Ave Bridgeview (60455) *(G-2513)*
**Nacme Steel Processing LLC**....847 806-7226
1965 Pratt Blvd Elk Grove Village (60007) *(G-9644)*
**Nacme Steel Processing LLC**....773 468-3309
429 W 127th St Chicago (60628) *(G-5848)*
**Naco Printing Co Inc**....618 664-0423
202 S 2nd St Greenville (62246) *(G-11400)*
**Nadig Newspapers Inc**....773 286-6100
4937 N Milwaukee Ave Chicago (60630) *(G-5849)*
**Naegele Inc**....708 388-7766
5661 W 120th St Alsip (60803) *(G-496)*
**Nafisco Inc**....815 372-3300
808 Forestwood Dr Romeoville (60446) *(G-18851)*
**Nagano International Corp**....847 537-0011
999 Deerfield Pkwy Buffalo Grove (60089) *(G-2741)*
**Nagle Pumps, Chicago Heights** *Also called Jn Pump Holdings Inc (G-7105)*
**Nagle Pumps, Chicago Heights** *Also called Ruthman Pump and Engineering (G-7124)*
**Naija Foods, North Aurora** *Also called Iya Foods LLC (G-16135)*
**Nail Superstore, Franklin Park** *Also called Skyline Beauty Supply Inc (G-10589)*
**Nak Won Korean Bakery**....773 588-8769
3746 W Lawrence Ave Chicago (60625) *(G-5850)*
**Nakano Foods, Mount Prospect** *Also called Mizkan America Inc (G-15347)*
**Nakano Foods, Mount Prospect** *Also called Mizkan America Holdings Inc (G-15348)*
**Naked Army USA LLC**....630 456-8738
582 Hillside Ave Glen Ellyn (60137) *(G-10982)*
**Nal Worldwide Holdings Inc**....630 261-3100
1200 N Greenbriar Dr A Addison (60101) *(G-225)*
**Nal.syncreon Addison, Addison** *Also called Nal Worldwide Holdings Inc (G-225)*
**Nalco Champion - An Ecolab Co, Naperville** *Also called Nalco Company LLC (G-15703)*
**Nalco Company LLC (HQ)**....630 305-1000
1601 W Diehl Rd Naperville (60563) *(G-15703)*
**Nalco Company LLC**....
1601 W Diehl Rd Naperville (60563) *(G-15704)*
**Nalco Company LLC**....630 305-2451
1 Nalco Ctr Naperville (60563) *(G-15705)*
**Nalco Holding Company (HQ)**....630 305-1000
1601 W Diehl Rd Naperville (60563) *(G-15706)*
**Nalco Holdings LLC (HQ)**....630 305-1000
1601 W Diehl Rd Naperville (60563) *(G-15707)*
**Nali Inc**....708 442-8710
266 S Prospect Ave Clarendon Hills (60514) *(G-7259)*
**Nama Graphics E LLC**....262 966-3853
15751 Annico Dr Ste 2 Homer Glen (60491) *(G-12083)*
**Namaste Laboratories LLC (HQ)**....708 824-1393
310 S Racine Ave Fl 8 Chicago (60607) *(G-5851)*
**Namco America Inc**....847 264-5610
951 Cambridge Dr Elk Grove Village (60007) *(G-9645)*
**Nameplate & Panel Technology, Carol Stream** *Also called Photo Techniques Corp (G-3213)*
**Nameplate Robinson & Precision**....847 678-2255
10129 Pacific Ave Franklin Park (60131) *(G-10538)*
**Nampac, Oak Brook** *Also called North America Packaging Corp (G-16547)*
**Nanas Kitchen Inc**....815 363-8500
1313 Old Bay Rd Johnsburg (60051) *(G-12439)*
**Nanco Sales Co Inc**....630 892-9820
320 N Highland Ave Aurora (60506) *(G-1193)*
**Nancy J Perkins**....815 748-7121
1950 Dekalb Ave Ste D Dekalb (60115) *(G-8107)*
**Nancys Lettering Shop**....217 345-6007
1115 Lincoln Ave Charleston (61920) *(G-3605)*
**Nanex LLC**....847 501-4787
818 Elm St Uppr 2 Winnetka (60093) *(G-22313)*
**Nano Gas Technologies Inc**....586 229-2656
506 Cambridge Cir Deerfield (60015) *(G-8043)*
**Nano Technologies Inc**....630 517-8824
1765 Mustang Ct Wheaton (60189) *(G-21970)*
**Nanochem Solutions Inc (PA)**....708 563-9200
1701 Quincy Ave Ste 10 Naperville (60540) *(G-15708)*
**Nanochem Solutions Inc**....815 224-8480
5350 Donlar Ave Peru (61354) *(G-17521)*
**Nanocor LLC (HQ)**....847 851-1900
2870 Forbs Ave Hoffman Estates (60192) *(G-12026)*
**Nanocytomics LLC**....847 467-2868
1801 Maple Ave Ste 19 Evanston (60201) *(G-10077)*
**Nanofast Inc**....312 943-4223
416 W Erie St Chicago (60654) *(G-5852)*
**Nanolube Inc**....630 706-1250
9 N Main St Ste 2 Lombard (60148) *(G-13831)*
**Nanophase Technologies Corp**....630 771-6747
453 Commerce St Burr Ridge (60527) *(G-2870)*
**Nanophase Technologies Corp (PA)**....630 771-6708
1319 Marquette Dr Romeoville (60446) *(G-18852)*
**Nantpharma LLC**....847 243-1200
1701 Golf Rd Ste 3-1007 Rolling Meadows (60008) *(G-18747)*
**Nantsound Inc**....847 939-6101
960 N Northwest Hwy Park Ridge (60068) *(G-17210)*
**NAPA Auto Parts, Chicago** *Also called Genuine Parts Company (G-4938)*
**NAPA Auto Parts, Goreville** *Also called Goreville Auto Parts & Mch Sp (G-11251)*
**Napco Inc**....630 406-1100
1141 N Raddant Rd Batavia (60510) *(G-1474)*
**Naper Dental**....630 369-6818
300 E 5th Ave Ste 400 Naperville (60563) *(G-15709)*
**Napersoft Inc**....630 420-1515
40 Shuman Blvd Ste 293 Naperville (60563) *(G-15710)*
**Napier Machine & Welding Inc**....217 525-8740
2519 South Grand Ave E Springfield (62703) *(G-20486)*
**Nara Dips Inc**....773 837-0601
122 E Lincoln Hwy Dekalb (60115) *(G-8108)*
**Narda Inc**....312 648-2300
222 S Riverside Plz Chicago (60606) *(G-5853)*
**Narima Inc**....847 818-9620
3350 Kirchoff Rd Rolling Meadows (60008) *(G-18748)*
**Narita Manufacturing Inc**....248 345-1777
828 Landmark Dr Belvidere (61008) *(G-1773)*
**Narrative Health Network Inc**....312 600-9154
1201 S Prrie Ave Apt 4103 Chicago (60605) *(G-5854)*
**Narvick Bros Construction, Morris** *Also called Narvick Bros Lumber Co Inc (G-15121)*
**Narvick Bros Lumber Co Inc (PA)**....815 942-1173
1037 Armstrong St Morris (60450) *(G-15121)*
**Narvick Bros Lumber Co Inc**....815 521-1173
801 Rail Way Ct Minooka (60447) *(G-14844)*
**Narvick Bros Ready Mix, Minooka** *Also called Narvick Bros Lumber Co Inc (G-14844)*
**Nas Media Group Inc (PA)**....312 371-7499
424 Brookwood Ter 2 Olympia Fields (60461) *(G-16803)*
**Nas Media Group Inc**....773 824-0242
6324 S Kimbark Ave # 400 Chicago (60637) *(G-5855)*
**Nasaba Magazine, Chicago** *Also called W Whorton & Co (G-6927)*
**Nascar Car Wash**....630 236-3400
3068 E New York St Aurora (60502) *(G-1055)*
**Nascote Industries Inc**....419 324-3392
675 Corporate Pkwy Belvidere (61008) *(G-1774)*
**Nascote Industries Inc (HQ)**....618 327-3286
18310 Enterprise Ave Nashville (62263) *(G-15840)*
**Nascote Industries Inc**....618 478-2092
17582 Mockingbird Rd Nashville (62263) *(G-15841)*
**Nascote Industries Inc**....618 327-3286
18355 Enterprise Ave Nashville (62263) *(G-15842)*
**Nashua Corporation**....847 692-9130
250 S Northwest Hwy # 203 Park Ridge (60068) *(G-17211)*
**Nashville Interior Systems Div, Nashville** *Also called Antolin Interiors Usa Inc (G-15833)*
**Nashville Memorial Co**....618 327-8492
542 E Saint Louis St Nashville (62263) *(G-15843)*
**Nashville News**....618 327-3411
211 W Saint Louis St Nashville (62263) *(G-15844)*
**Nashville News, The, Nashville** *Also called Nashville News (G-15844)*

ALPHABETIC

(PA)=Parent Co (HQ)=Headquarters (DH)=Div Headquarters
2017 Harris Illinois Industrial Directory
1327

**Nass Fresco Finishes, Barrington** *Also called Fresco Plaster Finishes Inc* ***(G-1281)***
**Nataz Specialty Coatings Inc**............773 247-7030
3300 W 31st St Chicago (60623) ***(G-5856)***
**Nathan Winston Service Inc**............815 758-4545
132 N 3rd St Dekalb (60115) ***(G-8109)***
**Nation Inc**............847 844-7300
400 Maple Ave Ste B Carpentersville (60110) ***(G-3292)***
**Nation Pizza and Foods, Schaumburg** *Also called Nation Pizza Products LP* ***(G-19661)***
**Nation Pizza Products LP**............847 397-3320
601 E Algonquin Rd Schaumburg (60173) ***(G-19661)***
**National Aerospace Corp**............847 566-5834
28 Sequoia Rd Hawthorn Woods (60047) ***(G-11704)***
**National Associates Realtors, Chicago** *Also called Realtor Magazine* ***(G-6308)***
**National Association Realtors (PA)**............800 874-6500
430 N Michigan Ave Lowr 2 Chicago (60611) ***(G-5857)***
**National Association Realtors**............800 874-6500
430 N Michigan Ave Lowr 2 Chicago (60611) ***(G-5858)***
**National Bathing Products, Romeoville** *Also called G K L Corporation* ***(G-18826)***
**National Bedding Company LLC**............847 645-0200
2600 4th Ave Hoffman Estates (60192) ***(G-12027)***
**National Bedding Company LLC (HQ)**............847 645-0200
2600 Forbs Ave Hoffman Estates (60192) ***(G-12028)***
**National Beef Packing Co LLC**............312 332-6166
30 N Michigan Ave # 1702 Chicago (60602) ***(G-5859)***
**National Beef Packing Intl, Chicago** *Also called National Beef Packing Co LLC* ***(G-5859)***
**National Binding Sups Eqp Inc**............630 801-7600
39w254 Sheldon Ct Geneva (60134) ***(G-10851)***
**National Biscuit Company**............773 925-0654
7300 S Kedzie Ave Chicago (60629) ***(G-5860)***
**National Bolt & Nut Corp**............630 307-8800
144 Covington Dr Bloomingdale (60108) ***(G-2119)***
**National Bus Trader Inc**............815 946-2341
9698 W Judson Rd Polo (61064) ***(G-17689)***
**National Bus Trader Magazine, Polo** *Also called National Bus Trader Inc* ***(G-17689)***
**National Bushing & Mfg**............847 847-1553
505 Oakwood Rd Ste 240 Lake Zurich (60047) ***(G-13108)***
**National Cap and Set Screw Co**............815 675-2363
2991 N Us Highway 12 Spring Grove (60081) ***(G-20350)***
**National Casein Company (PA)**............773 846-7300
601 W 80th St Chicago (60620) ***(G-5861)***
**National Casein New Jersey Inc (PA)**............773 846-7300
601 W 80th St Chicago (60620) ***(G-5862)***
**National Casein of California (PA)**............773 846-7300
601 W 80th St Chicago (60620) ***(G-5863)***
**National Coatings Inc (PA)**............309 342-4184
604 Us Highway 150 E Galesburg (61401) ***(G-10769)***
**National Component Sales Inc**............847 439-0333
1229 E Algonquin Rd Jk Arlington Heights (60005) ***(G-808)***
**National Concrete Pipe Co (PA)**............630 766-3600
11825 Franklin Ave Franklin Park (60131) ***(G-10539)***
**National Control Holdings**............630 231-5900
1725 Western Dr West Chicago (60185) ***(G-21748)***
**National Cycle Inc**............708 343-0400
2200 S Maywood Dr Maywood (60153) ***(G-14430)***
**National Data Svcs Chicago Inc (HQ)**............630 597-9100
900 Kimberly Dr Carol Stream (60188) ***(G-3204)***
**National Data-Label Corp**............630 616-9595
301 Arthur Ct Bensenville (60106) ***(G-1954)***
**National Def Intelligence Inc**............630 757-4007
2863 95th St 143-380 Naperville (60564) ***(G-15818)***
**National Detroit, Rockford** *Also called Gbj I LLC* ***(G-18396)***
**National Detroit Inc**............815 877-4041
1590 Northrock Ct Rockford (61103) ***(G-18515)***
**National Direct Lighting**............708 371-4950
4101 W 123rd St Alsip (60803) ***(G-497)***
**National Emergency Med ID Inc**............847 366-1267
100 Lincolnwood Ct Spring Grove (60081) ***(G-20351)***
**National Excelsior Company, Lansing** *Also called Goose Island Mfg & Supply Corp* ***(G-13164)***
**National Gift Card Corp**............815 477-4288
300 Millennium Dr Crystal Lake (60012) ***(G-7617)***
**National Grinding Wheel, Salem** *Also called Radiac Abrasives Inc* ***(G-19347)***
**National Header Die Corp**............815 636-7201
1190 Anvil Rd Rockford (61115) ***(G-18516)***
**National Industrial Coatings, Itasca** *Also called ICP Industrial Inc* ***(G-12278)***
**National Interchem LLC**............708 597-7777
13750 Chatham St Blue Island (60406) ***(G-2264)***
**National Jewelers Co., Chicago** *Also called Victor Levy Jewelry Co Inc* ***(G-6894)***
**National Liquid Fertilizer, Chicago** *Also called Fertilizer Inc* ***(G-4838)***
**National Liquid Fertilizer, Bedford Park** *Also called Fertilizer Inc* ***(G-1549)***
**National Locksmith Magazine, Streamwood** *Also called National Publishing Company* ***(G-20667)***
**National Lumber, Aurora** *Also called Silvacor Inc* ***(G-1218)***
**National Machine Repair Inc**............708 672-7711
115 W Burville Rd Crete (60417) ***(G-7517)***
**National Maint & Repr Inc (HQ)**............618 254-7451
401 S Hawthorne St Hartford (62048) ***(G-11612)***
**National Material Company LLC (PA)**............847 806-7200
1965 Pratt Blvd Elk Grove Village (60007) ***(G-9646)***
**National Material LP**............773 646-6300
12100 S Stony Island Ave Chicago (60633) ***(G-5864)***
**National Metal Fabricators LLC**............847 439-5321
2395 Greenleaf Ave Elk Grove Village (60007) ***(G-9647)***
**National Metal Works Inc**............815 282-5533
916 River Ln Loves Park (61111) ***(G-13969)***
**National Metalwares LP (PA)**............630 892-9000
900 N Russell Ave Aurora (60506) ***(G-1194)***
**National Micro Systems Inc**............312 566-0414
2 E 8th St Ste 100 Chicago (60605) ***(G-5865)***
**National Multi Products Co, Lake Forest** *Also called Excel Specialty Corp* ***(G-12898)***
**National Oilwell, Fairfield** *Also called Dnow LP* ***(G-10139)***
**National Peace Officers' Press, Troy** *Also called R L Allen Industries* ***(G-21011)***
**National Porges Radiator Corp**............773 224-3000
320 W 83rd St Chicago (60620) ***(G-5866)***
**National Power Corp**............773 685-2662
4330 W Belmont Ave Chicago (60641) ***(G-5867)***
**National Printing Resources, Chicago** *Also called Bardash & Bukowski Inc* ***(G-4041)***
**National Processing Co-Plant 1, Chicago** *Also called Nacme Steel Processing LLC* ***(G-5848)***
**National Publishing Company**............630 837-2044
1533 Burgundy Pkwy Streamwood (60107) ***(G-20667)***
**National Railway Equipment Co**............618 242-6590
1100 Shawnee St Mount Vernon (62864) ***(G-15432)***
**National Railway Equipment Co**............618 241-9270
908 Shawnee St Mount Vernon (62864) ***(G-15433)***
**National Railway Equipment Co**............309 755-6800
300 9th St N Silvis (61282) ***(G-19939)***
**National Rubber Stamp Co Inc**............773 281-6522
5320 N Lowell Ave Apt 311 Chicago (60630) ***(G-5868)***
**National Safety Council (PA)**............630 285-1121
1121 Spring Lake Dr Itasca (60143) ***(G-12324)***
**National School Services Inc**............847 438-3859
3254 Mayflower Ln Long Grove (60047) ***(G-13899)***
**National Sign, Addison** *Also called Nsi Signs Inc* ***(G-230)***
**National Sporting Goods Assn**............847 296-6742
1601 Feehanville Dr # 300 Mount Prospect (60056) ***(G-15353)***
**National Technical Systems Inc**............815 315-9250
3761 S Central Ave Rockford (61102) ***(G-18517)***
**National Technology Inc**............847 506-1300
1101 Carnegie St Rolling Meadows (60008) ***(G-18749)***
**National Temp-Trol Products**............630 920-1919
667 Executive Dr Willowbrook (60527) ***(G-22226)***
**National Tool & Machine Co**............618 271-6445
1235 Piggott Ave East Saint Louis (62201) ***(G-8762)***
**National Tool & Mfg Co**............847 806-9800
581 Wheeling Rd Wheeling (60090) ***(G-22105)***
**National Trackwork Inc**............630 250-0600
1500 Industrial Dr Itasca (60143) ***(G-12325)***
**National Tractor Parts Inc**............630 552-4235
12127a Galena Rd Plano (60545) ***(G-17668)***
**National Vinegar Co**............618 395-1011
203 W South Ave Olney (62450) ***(G-16785)***
**National Window Shade Co, Willowbrook** *Also called National Temp-Trol Products* ***(G-22226)***
**Nationwide Foods Inc**............773 787-4900
700 E 107th St Chicago (60628) ***(G-5869)***
**Nationwide Glove Co Inc (PA)**............618 252-7192
925 Bauman Ln Harrisburg (62946) ***(G-11602)***
**Nationwide News Monitor**............312 424-4224
9239 Kilpatrick Ave Skokie (60076) ***(G-20044)***
**Natl Senior Hlth & Fitnes Day, Libertyville** *Also called American Custom Publishing* ***(G-13302)***
**Natural Beginnings**............773 457-0509
15904 S Selfridge Cir Plainfield (60586) ***(G-17630)***
**Natural Cedar Products Inc**............815 416-0223
1600 Edgewater Dr Morris (60450) ***(G-15122)***
**Natural Choice Corporation**............815 874-4444
5677 Sockness Dr Rockford (61109) ***(G-18518)***
**Natural Distribution Company**............630 350-1700
550 Clayton Ct Wood Dale (60191) ***(G-22403)***
**Natural Fiber Welding Inc**............309 685-3591
801 W Main St Lab B206 Peoria (61606) ***(G-17414)***
**Natural Formulations, Skokie** *Also called Formulations Inc* ***(G-20001)***
**Natural Gas Pipeline Amer LLC**............618 495-2211
7501 Huey Rd Centralia (62801) ***(G-3423)***
**Natural Gas Pipeline Amer LLC**............815 426-2151
5611 S 12000w Rd Herscher (60941) ***(G-11760)***
**Natural Gas Pipeline Amer LLC**............618 829-3224
6 Miles N On Elm St Saint Elmo (62458) ***(G-19309)***
**Natural Packaging Inc**............708 246-3420
550 Hillgrove Ave Ste 518 La Grange (60525) ***(G-12740)***
**Natural Polymers LLC**............888 563-3111
4n325 Powis Rd West Chicago (60185) ***(G-21749)***
**Natural Products Inc**............847 509-5835
3555 Woodhead Dr Northbrook (60062) ***(G-16317)***
**Natural Resources Ill Dept**............618 439-4320
503 E Main St Benton (62812) ***(G-2036)***

## ALPHABETIC SECTION — Nelson Stud Welding Inc

**Natural Stone Inc** .................................................. 847 735-1129
611 Rockland Rd Ste 208  Lake Bluff  (60044)  *(G-12858)*
**Naturally Clean, Darien** Also called Chem Free Solutions  *(G-7791)*
**Nature House Inc** .................................................. 217 833-2393
30494 State Highway 107  Griggsville  (62340)  *(G-11413)*
**Nature S American Co** ........................................... 630 246-4776
665 W North Ave Ste 105  Lombard  (60148)  *(G-13832)*
**Nature's Touch, Northbrook** Also called Agrochem Inc  *(G-16201)*
**Natures American Co** ............................................ 630 246-4274
3105 N Ashland Ave  Chicago  (60657)  *(G-5870)*
**Natures Appeal Mfg Corp** ...................................... 630 880-6222
1788 W Whispering Ct  Addison  (60101)  *(G-226)*
**Natures Best Christmas Trees** ............................... 815 765-2960
13001 Il Route 76  Poplar Grove  (61065)  *(G-17715)*
**Natures Best Inc (PA)** ........................................... 631 232-3355
3500 Lacey Rd Ste 1200  Downers Grove  (60515)  *(G-8493)*
**Natures Healing Remedies Inc** ............................... 773 589-9996
7742 W Addison St  Chicago  (60634)  *(G-5871)*
**Natures Sources LLC** ............................................ 847 663-9168
5665 W Howard St  Niles  (60714)  *(G-16013)*
**Natus Medical Incorporated** ................................... 847 949-5200
1 Bio Logic Plz  Mundelein  (60060)  *(G-15536)*
**Naurex Inc** ........................................................... 847 871-0377
1801 Maple Ave Ste 70  Evanston  (60201)  *(G-10078)*
**Nautic Global Group LLC** ....................................... 574 457-5731
333 W Wacker Dr Ste 600  Chicago  (60606)  *(G-5872)*
**Nautilus Medical** ................................................... 866 520-6477
1300 S Grove Ave Ste 200  Barrington  (60010)  *(G-1294)*
**Nauvoo Mill & Bakery** ........................................... 217 453-6734
1530 Mulholland St  Nauvoo  (62354)  *(G-15854)*
**Nauvoo Products Inc** ............................................ 217 453-2817
1420 Mulholland St  Nauvoo  (62354)  *(G-15855)*
**Navatek Resources Inc** ......................................... 847 301-0174
1505 Wright Blvd  Schaumburg  (60193)  *(G-19662)*
**Navigator & Journal Register, Grayville** Also called S & R Media LLC  *(G-11376)*
**Navigo Technologies LLC** ..................................... 312 560-9257
1770 S Randall Rd Ste 161  Geneva  (60134)  *(G-10852)*
**Navigon Inc** ......................................................... 312 268-1500
200 W Madison St Ste 650  Chicago  (60606)  *(G-5873)*
**Navillus Woodworks LLC** ...................................... 312 375-2680
2100 N Major Ave  Chicago  (60639)  *(G-5874)*
**Navipoint Genomics LLC** ...................................... 630 464-8013
2515 Dewes Ln  Naperville  (60564)  *(G-15819)*
**Navis Industries Inc** ............................................ 224 293-2000
2500 Tech Dr Ste 100  Elgin  (60123)  *(G-9117)*
**Navistar Inc (HQ)** ................................................ 331 332-5000
2701 Navistar Dr  Lisle  (60532)  *(G-13629)*
**Navistar Inc** ........................................................
10400 W North Ave  Melrose Park  (60160)  *(G-14675)*
**Navistar Inc** ........................................................ 630 963-0769
3333 Finley Rd  Downers Grove  (60515)  *(G-8494)*
**Navistar Inc** ........................................................ 331 332-5000
2701 Navistar Dr  Lisle  (60532)  *(G-13630)*
**Navistar Inc** ........................................................ 331 332-5000
2700 Haven Ave  Joliet  (60433)  *(G-12545)*
**Navistar Inc** ........................................................ 317 352-4500
10400 W North Ave  Melrose Park  (60160)  *(G-14676)*
**Navistar Inc** ........................................................ 662 494-3421
2701 Navistar Dr  Lisle  (60532)  *(G-13631)*
**Navistar Inc** ........................................................ 815 230-0060
23815 W Lockport St  Plainfield  (60544)  *(G-17631)*
**Navistar Defense LLC (HQ)** ................................... 331 332-3500
2701 Navistar Dr  Lisle  (60532)  *(G-13632)*
**Navistar International Corp (PA)** ........................... 331 332-5000
2701 Navistar Dr  Lisle  (60532)  *(G-13633)*
**Navitas Electronics Corp** ...................................... 702 293-4670
1200 Internationale Pkwy # 125  Woodridge  (60517)  *(G-22504)*
**Navitor Inc** .......................................................... 800 323-0253
7220 W Wilson Ave  Harwood Heights  (60706)  *(G-11687)*
**Navman Wireless Holdings LP (HQ)** ...................... 866 527-9896
2701 Patriot Blvd Ste 200  Glenview  (60026)  *(G-11171)*
**Navman Wireless North Amer Ltd** ......................... 866 527-9896
2700 Patriot Blvd Ste 200  Glenview  (60026)  *(G-11172)*
**Navran Advncd Nanoprdcts Dev** ............................ 847 331-0809
2055 Kettering Rd Ste 101  Hoffman Estates  (60169)  *(G-12029)*
**Naylor Automotive Engrg Co Inc** ........................... 773 582-6900
4645 S Knox Ave  Chicago  (60632)  *(G-5875)*
**Naylor Pipe Company (PA)** .................................... 773 721-9400
1230 E 92nd St  Chicago  (60619)  *(G-5876)*
**Nb Coatings Inc (HQ)** .......................................... 800 323-3224
2701 E 170th St  Lansing  (60438)  *(G-13179)*
**Nb Corporation of America (HQ)** .......................... 630 295-8880
930 Muirfield Dr  Hanover Park  (60133)  *(G-11586)*
**Nb Finishing Inc** ................................................. 847 364-7500
3131 W Soffel Ave  Melrose Park  (60160)  *(G-14677)*
**Nbs Corporation** ................................................. 847 860-8856
1501 Tonne Rd  Elk Grove Village  (60007)  *(G-9648)*
**Nbs Systems Inc (PA)** .......................................... 217 999-3472
1000 S Old Route 66  Mount Olive  (62069)  *(G-15306)*

**Ncab Group Usa Inc** ............................................. 630 562-5550
1300 Norwood Ave  Itasca  (60143)  *(G-12326)*
**Ncc, Chicago** Also called J T C Inc  *(G-5264)*
**Nci Group Inc** ..................................................... 309 527-3095
21 E Front St  El Paso  (61738)  *(G-8871)*
**Nci Technology, Oakbrook Terrace** Also called Heng Tuo Usa Inc  *(G-16710)*
**Ncp Commercial, Paxton** Also called Nexstep Commercial Pdts LLC  *(G-17238)*
**ND Industries Inc** ............................................... 847 498-3600
1840 Raymond Dr  Northbrook  (60062)  *(G-16318)*
**ND Manifold** ....................................................... 815 923-4305
6614 S Union Rd  Union  (60180)  *(G-21036)*
**Nduja Artisans Co** .............................................. 312 550-6991
2817 N Harlem Ave  Chicago  (60707)  *(G-5877)*
**Ndy Manufacturing Inc** ....................................... 815 426-2330
4590 N 11000w Rd  Bonfield  (60913)  *(G-2385)*
**Nea Agora Packing Co** ........................................ 312 421-5130
1056 W Taylor St  Chicago  (60607)  *(G-5878)*
**Neal-Schuman Publishers Inc** .............................. 312 944-6780
50 E Huron St  Chicago  (60611)  *(G-5879)*
**Neals Trailer Sales** .............................................. 217 792-5136
1670 1100th St  Lincoln  (62656)  *(G-13416)*
**Neat-OH International LLC** .................................. 847 441-4290
790 W Frontage Rd Ste 303  Northfield  (60093)  *(G-16411)*
**Nebraska Plastics Incorporated** ........................... 217 423-9007
354 S Glencoe Ave  Decatur  (62522)  *(G-7921)*
**Nec Display Solutions Amer Inc** .......................... 630 467-5000
500 Park Blvd Ste 1100  Itasca  (60143)  *(G-12327)*
**Nec Display Solutions Amer Inc (HQ)** .................. 630 467-3000
500 Park Blvd Ste 1100  Itasca  (60143)  *(G-12328)*
**Necta Sweet Inc** ................................................. 847 215-9955
1554 Barclay Blvd  Buffalo Grove  (60089)  *(G-2742)*
**Nedras Printing Inc** ............................................ 618 846-3853
897 E 900 Ave  Shobonier  (62885)  *(G-19922)*
**Need, Bolingbrook** Also called Hussain Shaheen  *(G-2317)*
**Need To Know Inc** .............................................. 309 691-3877
1723 W Detweiller Dr  Peoria  (61615)  *(G-17415)*
**Needham Shop Inc** ............................................. 630 557-9019
46 W 840 Main  Kaneville  (60144)  *(G-12600)*
**Neenah Foundry Co** ............................................ 800 558-5075
925 Lambrecht Dr  Frankfort  (60423)  *(G-10345)*
**Neesh By Dar, Chicago** Also called Denise Allen Robinson Inc  *(G-4582)*
**Nefab Inc** ........................................................... 705 748-4888
3105 N Ashland Ave 394  Chicago  (60657)  *(G-5880)*
**Nefab Packaging N Centl LLC** ..............................
850 Mark St  Elk Grove Village  (60007)  *(G-9649)*
**Nega, Schaumburg** Also called Nippon Electric Glass Amer Inc  *(G-19665)*
**Negative, McHenry** Also called Super Mix Inc  *(G-14562)*
**Negs & Litho Inc** ................................................ 847 647-7770
6501 N Avondale Ave  Chicago  (60631)  *(G-5881)*
**Nehring Electrical Works Co** ............................... 815 756-2741
1005 E Locust St  Dekalb  (60115)  *(G-8110)*
**Neil Enterprises Inc** ........................................... 847 549-0321
450 Bunker Ct  Vernon Hills  (60061)  *(G-21184)*
**Neil International Inc (PA)** .................................. 847 549-7627
450 Bunker Ct  Vernon Hills  (60061)  *(G-21185)*
**Neiland Custom Products** ................................... 815 825-2233
400 Il Route 38  Malta  (60150)  *(G-14166)*
**Neiman Bros Co Inc** ........................................... 773 463-3000
3322 W Newport Ave  Chicago  (60618)  *(G-5882)*
**Neiman Brothers Co, Chicago** Also called Neiman Bros Co Inc  *(G-5882)*
**Neisewander Enterprises Inc (PA)** ....................... 815 288-1431
1101 E River Rd  Dixon  (61021)  *(G-8337)*
**Neiweem Industries Inc (PA)** .............................. 847 487-1239
21 Greenview Rd  Oakwood Hills  (60013)  *(G-16727)*
**Nekg Holdings Inc** ............................................. 815 383-1379
26709 S Kimberly Ln  Channahon  (60410)  *(G-3582)*
**Nelco Coil Supply Company** ................................ 847 259-7517
1500 E Ironwood Dr  Mount Prospect  (60056)  *(G-15354)*
**Nelsen Steel and Wire LP** .................................... 847 671-9700
9400 Belmont Ave  Franklin Park  (60131)  *(G-10540)*
**Nelsen Steel Company, Franklin Park** Also called Nelsen Steel and Wire LP  *(G-10540)*
**Nelson & Lavold Manufacturing** .......................... 312 943-6300
1530 N Halsted St 34  Chicago  (60642)  *(G-5883)*
**Nelson - Harkins Inds Inc** ................................... 773 478-6243
5301 N Kedzie Ave  Chicago  (60625)  *(G-5884)*
**Nelson C D Mfg & Sup Co, Wauconda** Also called C D Nelson Consulting Inc  *(G-21449)*
**Nelson Door Co** .................................................. 217 543-3489
2245 Cr 1500e  Arthur  (61911)  *(G-913)*
**Nelson Enterprises Inc** ....................................... 815 633-1100
5447 Mainsail Dr  Roscoe  (61073)  *(G-18910)*
**Nelson Global Products Inc** ................................ 309 263-8914
231 Detroit Ave  Morton  (61550)  *(G-15171)*
**Nelson Manufacturing Co Inc** .............................. 815 229-0161
2516 20th St  Rockford  (61104)  *(G-18519)*
**Nelson Sash Systems Inc** ................................... 708 385-5815
4650 W 120th St  Alsip  (60803)  *(G-498)*
**Nelson Stud Welding Inc** .................................... 708 430-3770
18601 Graphic Ct  Tinley Park  (60477)  *(G-20934)*

**Nelson-Rose Inc** — 760 744-7400
120 E Ogden Ave Ste 130  Hinsdale  (60521)  *(G-11954)*

**Nelson-Whittaker Ltd** — 815 459-6000
220 Exchange Dr Ste D  Crystal Lake  (60014)  *(G-7618)*

**Nemera Buffalo Grove LLC (HQ)** — 847 541-7900
600 Deerfield Pkwy  Buffalo Grove  (60089)  *(G-2743)*

**Nemera Buffalo Grove LLC** — 847 325-3629
800 Corporate Grove Dr  Buffalo Grove  (60089)  *(G-2744)*

**Nemera Buffalo Grove LLC** — 847 325-3628
800 Corporate Grove Dr  Buffalo Grove  (60089)  *(G-2745)*

**Nemera US Holding Inc (HQ)** — 847 325-3620
600 Deerfield Pkwy  Buffalo Grove  (60089)  *(G-2746)*

**Nemeth Tool Inc (PA)** — 630 595-0409
143 Murray Dr  Wood Dale  (60191)  *(G-22404)*

**Neo Orthotics Inc** — 309 699-0354
100 Park Pl  East Peoria  (61611)  *(G-8726)*

**Neolight Labs LLC** — 312 242-1773
34768 N Elm St  Ingleside  (60041)  *(G-12195)*

**Neolight Technologies LLC** — 773 561-1410
34768 N Elm St  Ingleside  (60041)  *(G-12196)*

**Neomek Incorporated** — 630 879-5400
241 Oswald Ave  Batavia  (60510)  *(G-1475)*

**Neomek Engineering, Batavia**  Also called Neomek Incorporated  *(G-1475)*

**Neon Art** — 773 588-5883
4752 N Avers Ave  Chicago  (60625)  *(G-5885)*

**Neon Design Inc** — 773 880-5020
3722 N Ashland Ave  Chicago  (60613)  *(G-5886)*

**Neon Express Signs** — 773 463-7335
5026 N Broadway St  Chicago  (60640)  *(G-5887)*

**Neon Moon Ltd** — 847 849-3200
14 Walbridge Ct  Algonquin  (60102)  *(G-401)*

**Neon Nights Dj Svc** — 309 820-9000
2902 Essington St  Bloomington  (61705)  *(G-2205)*

**Neon Prism Electric Sign Co** — 630 879-1010
1213 Paramount Pkwy  Batavia  (60510)  *(G-1476)*

**Neon Shop Inc** — 773 227-0303
2247 N Western Ave  Chicago  (60647)  *(G-5888)*

**Neon Works of St Louis, East Alton**  Also called Staar Bales Lestarge Inc  *(G-8611)*

**Neopost R Meadows** — 630 467-0604
1200 N Arlington Hts Rd  Itasca  (60143)  *(G-12329)*

**Neovision Usa Inc** — 847 533-0541
21720 W Long Grove Rd C33  Deer Park  (60010)  *(G-7973)*

**Nep Electronics Inc (PA)** — 630 595-8500
805 Mittel Dr  Wood Dale  (60191)  *(G-22405)*

**Neptun Light Inc** — 847 735-8330
13950 W Bus Ctr Dr  Lake Forest  (60045)  *(G-12929)*

**Neptune USA Inc** — 847 987-3804
1022 Howard Dr  Schaumburg  (60193)  *(G-19663)*

**Nerd Island Studios LLC** — 224 619-5361
1347 Ferndale Ave  Highland Park  (60035)  *(G-11859)*

**Nesterowicz & Associates Inc** — 815 522-4469
313 W Main St  Kirkland  (60146)  *(G-12715)*

**Nestle Beverage Division, Jacksonville**  Also called Nestle Usa Inc  *(G-12403)*

**Nestle Clinical Nutrition, Buffalo Grove**  Also called Nestle Usa Inc  *(G-2747)*

**Nestle Confections, Franklin Park**  Also called Nestle Usa Inc  *(G-10541)*

**Nestle Confections Factory, Bloomington**  Also called Nestle Usa Inc  *(G-2206)*

**Nestle Prepared Foods Company** — 630 671-3721
601 Wall St  Glendale Heights  (60139)  *(G-11051)*

**Nestle Usa Inc** — 847 808-5404
2150 E Lake Cook Rd # 800  Buffalo Grove  (60089)  *(G-2747)*

**Nestle Usa Inc** — 309 263-2651
216 N Morton Ave  Morton  (61550)  *(G-15172)*

**Nestle Usa Inc** — 217 243-9175
1111 Carnation Dr  Jacksonville  (62650)  *(G-12403)*

**Nestle Usa Inc** — 630 773-2090
1445 Norwood Ave  Itasca  (60143)  *(G-12330)*

**Nestle Usa Inc** — 630 505-5387
650 E Diehl Rd Ste 100  Naperville  (60563)  *(G-15711)*

**Nestle Usa Inc** — 847 957-7850
3401 Mount Prospect Rd  Franklin Park  (60131)  *(G-10541)*

**Nestle Usa Inc** — 309 829-1031
2501 Beich Rd  Bloomington  (61705)  *(G-2206)*

**Nestle Usa Inc** — 847 808-5300
2150 E Lake Cook Rd # 800  Buffalo Grove  (60089)  *(G-2748)*

**Nestle Waters North Amer Inc** — 630 271-7300
10335 Argonne Woods Dr  Woodridge  (60517)  *(G-22505)*

**Nestles Nutrition, Buffalo Grove**  Also called Nestle Usa Inc  *(G-2748)*

**Nestus American Wind Tech, Tiskilwa**  Also called Vestas-American Wind Tech Inc  *(G-20960)*

**Netcom Inc** — 847 537-6300
599 Wheeling Rd  Wheeling  (60090)  *(G-22106)*

**Netgain Motors Inc** — 630 243-9100
800 S State St Ste 4  Lockport  (60441)  *(G-13735)*

**Netgear Inc** — 630 955-0080
1000 E Warrenville Rd  Naperville  (60563)  *(G-15712)*

**Netnotes, Spring Grove**  Also called Kuna Corp  *(G-20344)*

**Netranix Enterprise**
336 Pinto Dr  Bolingbrook  (60440)  *(G-2350)*

**Network Harbor Inc** — 309 633-9118
5607 Washington St  Peoria  (61607)  *(G-17416)*

**Network Merchants LLC** — 847 352-4850
201 Main St  Roselle  (60172)  *(G-18959)*

**Network Printing Inc** — 847 566-4146
109 Alexandra Ct  Mundelein  (60060)  *(G-15537)*

**Networked Robotics Corporation** — 847 424-8019
825 Chicago Ave  Evanston  (60202)  *(G-10079)*

**Neuero Corporation** — 630 231-9020
1201 W Hawthorne Ln  West Chicago  (60185)  *(G-21750)*

**Neuman Bakery Specialties Inc** — 630 916-8909
1405 W Jeffrey Dr  Addison  (60101)  *(G-227)*

**Neurotherapeutics Pharma Inc** — 773 444-4180
8750 W Bryn Mawr Ave # 440  Chicago  (60631)  *(G-5889)*

**Neuses Tools, Rolling Meadows**  Also called P K Neuses Incorporated  *(G-18756)*

**Nevco Inc (PA)** — 618 664-0360
301 E Harris Ave  Greenville  (62246)  *(G-11401)*

**Neveria Michoacana LLC** — 630 783-3518
132 N Bolingbrook Dr  Bolingbrook  (60440)  *(G-2351)*

**Neverstrip LLC** — 708 588-9707
111 S Hinsdale  Hinsdale  (60521)  *(G-11955)*

**Nevin Labs, Chicago**  Also called Dentalez Alabama Inc  *(G-4583)*

**New Age Surfaces LLC** — 630 226-0011
1237 Naperville Dr  Romeoville  (60446)  *(G-18853)*

**New Alliance Production LLC** — 309 928-3123
1701 N John St  Farmer City  (61842)  *(G-10180)*

**New Archery Products LLC** — 708 488-2500
7500 Industrial Dr  Forest Park  (60130)  *(G-10251)*

**New Avon LLC** — 847 966-0200
6901 Golf Rd  Morton Grove  (60053)  *(G-15224)*

**New C F & I Inc** — 312 533-3555
200 E Randolph St # 7800  Chicago  (60601)  *(G-5890)*

**New Century Performance Inc** — 618 466-6383
3704 Riehl Ln  Godfrey  (62035)  *(G-11230)*

**New Chicago Wholesale Bky Inc** — 847 981-1600
795 Touhy Ave  Elk Grove Village  (60007)  *(G-9650)*

**New Cie Inc** — 815 224-1485
85 Chartres St  La Salle  (61301)  *(G-12781)*

**New Cie Inc** — 815 224-1511
3349 Becker Dr  Peru  (61354)  *(G-17522)*

**New City Communications** — 312 243-8786
770 N Halsted St Ste 183  Chicago  (60642)  *(G-5891)*

**New City News, Chicago**  Also called New City Communications  *(G-5891)*

**New Dimension Models** — 815 935-1001
105 W Front St  Aroma Park  (60910)  *(G-879)*

**New Dimensions Precision Mac** — 815 923-8300
6614 S Union Rd  Union  (60180)  *(G-21037)*

**New Herald News LLC** — 217 651-8064
727 Galena St  Lincoln  (62656)  *(G-13417)*

**New Image Upholstery** — 630 542-5560
21 Cedar Ct  South Elgin  (60177)  *(G-20221)*

**New Lenox Machine Co Inc** — 815 584-4866
1200 E Mazon Ave Ste B  Dwight  (60420)  *(G-8589)*

**New Life Printing & Publishing** — 847 658-4111
1508 S Main St  Algonquin  (60102)  *(G-402)*

**New Life Screen Printing, Orland Park**  Also called Spirit Warrior Inc  *(G-16895)*

**New Line Hardwoods Inc** — 309 657-7621
8727 Arenzville Rd  Beardstown  (62618)  *(G-1524)*

**New Metal Crafts Inc** — 312 787-6991
6453 N Kilpatrick Ave  Lincolnwood  (60712)  *(G-13526)*

**New Metal Fabrication Corp** — 618 532-9000
931 S Brookside St  Centralia  (62801)  *(G-3424)*

**New Millenium Directories (PA)** — 815 626-5737
324 1st Ave  Sterling  (61081)  *(G-20601)*

**New Millennium Investment** — 708 358-1512
1100 Rossell Ave  Oak Park  (60302)  *(G-16676)*

**New Ngc Inc** — 847 623-8100
515 E Sea Horse Dr  Waukegan  (60085)  *(G-21592)*

**New Packing Company** — 312 666-1314
1249 W Lake St  Chicago  (60607)  *(G-5892)*

**New Panel Brick Company of Ill** — 847 696-1686
4345 Di Paolo Ctr  Glenview  (60025)  *(G-11173)*

**New Process Steel LP** — 708 389-3482
5761 W 118th St  Alsip  (60803)  *(G-499)*

**New SBL Inc** — 773 376-8280
1001 W 45th St Ste B  Chicago  (60609)  *(G-5893)*

**New Specialty Products Inc** — 773 847-0230
1421 W 47th St  Chicago  (60609)  *(G-5894)*

**New Spin Cycle** — 773 952-7490
1400 E 47th St Ste A  Chicago  (60653)  *(G-5895)*

**New Star Custom Lighting Co** — 773 254-7827
4000 S Bell Ave  Chicago  (60609)  *(G-5896)*

**New Step Orthotic Lab Inc** — 618 208-4444
14 Schiber Ct  Maryville  (62062)  *(G-14345)*

**New Taste Good Noodle Inc** — 312 842-8980
2559 S Archer Ave  Chicago  (60608)  *(G-5897)*

**New Tech Marketing Inc** — 630 378-4300
1312 Marquette Dr Ste H  Romeoville  (60446)  *(G-18854)*

**New Triangle Oil Company** — 618 262-4131
600 Chestnut St  Mount Carmel  (62863)  *(G-15278)*

**New Vision Print & Marketing** — 630 406-0509
31w280 Diehl Rd Ste 104  Naperville  (60563)  *(G-15713)*

**New Vision Software Inc**.....847 382-1532
130 Kainer Ave Barrington (60010) *(G-1295)*
**New Wave Express Inc**.....630 238-3129
842 Foster Ave Bensenville (60106) *(G-1955)*
**New World Products Inc**.....630 690-5625
494 Mission St Carol Stream (60188) *(G-3205)*
**New World Trnsp Systems**.....773 509-5931
5895 N Rogers Ave Chicago (60646) *(G-5898)*
**New York & Company Inc**.....630 232-7693
410 Commons Dr Geneva (60134) *(G-10853)*
**New York & Company Inc**.....630 783-2910
639 E Boughton Rd Ste 135 Bolingbrook (60440) *(G-2352)*
**New York Blower Company**.....217 347-3233
1304 W Jaycee Ave Effingham (62401) *(G-8849)*
**New-Indy IVEX LLC**.....309 686-3830
1 Sloan St Peoria (61603) *(G-17417)*
**Newark Element 14, Chicago** *Also called Element14 Inc (G-4724)*
**Newater International Inc**.....630 894-5000
122 E Lake St Bloomingdale (60108) *(G-2120)*
**Newby Oil Company Inc**.....815 756-7688
2270 Oakland Dr Sycamore (60178) *(G-20810)*
**Newby, Wayne Nsp, Sycamore** *Also called Newby Oil Company Inc (G-20810)*
**Newell, Oak Brook** *Also called Levolor Window Furnishings Inc (G-16534)*
**Newell & Haney Inc**.....618 277-3660
6601 W Main St Belleville (62223) *(G-1660)*
**Newell Operating Company (HQ)**.....815 235-4171
29 E Stephenson St Freeport (61032) *(G-10675)*
**Newera Software Inc**.....815 784-3345
9505 Wolf Rd Kingston (60145) *(G-12707)*
**Newf LLC (PA)**.....630 330-5462
608 Driftwood Ct Naperville (60540) *(G-15714)*
**Newhaven Display Intl Inc**.....847 844-8795
2661 Galvin Ct Elgin (60124) *(G-9118)*
**Newhealth Solutions LLC**.....803 627-8378
3935 Sunnyside Ave Brookfield (60513) *(G-2638)*
**Newko Proto Type, Palatine** *Also called Newko Tool & Engineering Co (G-17058)*
**Newko Tool & Engineering Co**.....847 359-1670
720 S Vermont St Palatine (60067) *(G-17058)*
**Newly Weds Foods Inc (PA)**.....773 489-7000
4140 W Fullerton Ave Chicago (60639) *(G-5899)*
**Newly Weds Foods Inc**.....773 628-6900
4849 N Milwaukee Ave # 700 Chicago (60630) *(G-5900)*
**Newman Welding & Machine Shop**.....618 435-5591
400 W Bond St Benton (62812) *(G-2037)*
**Newman-Green Inc**.....630 543-6500
57 W Interstate Rd Addison (60101) *(G-228)*
**Newmax, Elk Grove Village** *Also called Fortman & Associates Ltd (G-9488)*
**Newmedical Technology Inc**.....847 412-1000
310 Era Dr Northbrook (60062) *(G-16319)*
**Newovo Plastics LLC**.....224 535-8183
345 Willard Ave Elgin (60120) *(G-9119)*
**Newport Coffee House, Deerfield** *Also called Nuri Corp (G-8044)*
**Newport Pallet**.....217 662-6577
310 S Main St Georgetown (61846) *(G-10889)*
**Newport Printing Services Inc**.....847 632-1000
1250 Remington Rd Schaumburg (60173) *(G-19664)*
**News & Letters**.....312 663-0839
59 E Van Buren St Chicago (60605) *(G-5901)*
**News Gazette, Urbana** *Also called Lumber Specialists Inc (G-21093)*
**News Gazette, Champaign** *Also called News-Gazette Inc (G-3519)*
**News Gazette Inc**.....217 351-5252
15 E Main St Champaign (61820) *(G-3517)*
**News Marketer, Tinley Park** *Also called Midwest Suburban Publishing (G-20933)*
**News Media Corporation (PA)**.....815 562-2061
211 E Il Route 38 Rochelle (61068) *(G-18100)*
**News Metropolis**.....618 524-2141
111 E 5th St Metropolis (62960) *(G-14760)*
**News Progress, Sullivan** *Also called Best Newspapers In Illinois (G-20740)*
**News-Gazette Inc**.....217 351-8128
810 Hamilton Dr Champaign (61820) *(G-3518)*
**News-Gazette Inc (PA)**.....217 351-5252
15 E Main St Champaign (61820) *(G-3519)*
**News-Tribune, Mendota** *Also called Daily News Tribune Inc (G-14719)*
**Newspaper 7 Days (PA)**.....847 272-2212
704 S Milwaukee Ave Wheeling (60090) *(G-22107)*
**Newspaper Holding Inc**.....618 242-0113
911 Broadway St Mount Vernon (62864) *(G-15434)*
**Newspaper Holding Inc**.....618 643-2387
200 S Washinton St Ste 1 Mc Leansboro (62859) *(G-14466)*
**Newspaper Holding Inc**.....217 446-1000
17 W North St Danville (61832) *(G-7758)*
**Newspaper Holding Inc**.....217 347-7151
201 N Banker St Effingham (62401) *(G-8850)*
**Newspaper National Network**.....312 644-1142
500 N Michigan Ave # 2210 Chicago (60611) *(G-5902)*
**Newspaper Solutions Inc**.....773 930-3404
4968 N Milwaukee Ave 1n Chicago (60630) *(G-5903)*
**Newsprint Ink Inc**.....618 667-3111
201 E Market St Stop 6 Troy (62294) *(G-21010)*
**Newssor Manufacturing Inc**.....618 259-1174
302 Dry St East Alton (62024) *(G-8606)*
**Newsweb Corporation (PA)**.....773 975-5727
1645 W Fullerton Ave Chicago (60614) *(G-5904)*
**Newtec Window & Door Inc**.....773 869-9888
3159 W 36th St Chicago (60632) *(G-5905)*
**Newton Broom & Brush Co, Newton** *Also called Don Leventhal Group LLC (G-15939)*
**Newton Implement Partnership**.....618 783-8716
9460 E State Highway 33 Newton (62448) *(G-15943)*
**Newton Press Mentor, Newton** *Also called Gatehouse Media LLC (G-15940)*
**Newton Ready Mix Inc**.....618 783-8611
8560 N State Highway 130 Newton (62448) *(G-15944)*
**Nex Gen Manufacturing Inc**.....847 487-7077
1055 N Old Rand Rd Wauconda (60084) *(G-21489)*
**Nexergy Tauber LLC**.....708 316-4407
4 Westbrook Corp Ctr 90 Westchester (60154) *(G-21851)*
**Nexhand Inc**.....619 820-2988
2500 N Lakeview Ave Chicago (60614) *(G-5906)*
**Nexpump Inc**.....630 365-4639
820 Stover Dr Unit B Elburn (60119) *(G-8900)*
**Nexstep Commercial Pdts LLC**.....217 379-2377
1450 W Ottawa Rd Paxton (60957) *(G-17238)*
**Next Day Toner Supplies Inc**.....708 478-1000
11411 183rd St Ste A Orland Park (60467) *(G-16879)*
**Next Gen Manufacturing Inc**.....847 289-8444
1330 Crispin Dr Ste 205 Elgin (60123) *(G-9120)*
**Next Generation Inc**.....312 953-7514
13304 Skyline Dr Plainfield (60585) *(G-17632)*
**Next Gerneration**.....630 261-1477
1052 N Du Page Ave Lombard (60148) *(G-13833)*
**Nextpoint Inc**.....773 929-4000
4043 N Ravenswood Ave Chicago (60613) *(G-5907)*
**Nextstep Commercial Products**.....217 379-2377
1450 W Ottawa Rd Paxton (60957) *(G-17239)*
**Nexus Office Systems Inc**.....847 836-1095
2250 Point Blvd Ste 125 Elgin (60123) *(G-9121)*
**Nexus Supply Consortium Inc**.....630 649-2868
13g Fernwood Dr Bolingbrook (60440) *(G-2353)*
**Nexx Business Solutions Inc**.....708 252-1958
17w727 Butterfield Rd Oakbrook Terrace (60181) *(G-16717)*
**NFC Company Inc**.....773 472-6468
2944 N Leavitt St Chicago (60618) *(G-5908)*
**NFC Suburban, Chicago** *Also called NFC Company Inc (G-5908)*
**NGK Spark Plugs (usa) Inc**.....630 595-7894
850 Aec Dr Wood Dale (60191) *(G-22406)*
**Ngp, Morton** *Also called Peoria Tube Forming Corp (G-15176)*
**NGS Printing Inc**.....847 741-4411
1400 Crispin Dr Elgin (60123) *(G-9122)*
**Nguyen Chau**.....773 506-1066
2311 W Howard St Chicago (60645) *(G-5909)*
**Nhanced Semiconductors Inc**.....408 759-4060
1415 Bond St Ste 155 Naperville (60563) *(G-15715)*
**Niagara Lasalle Corporation**.....708 596-2700
16655 S Canal St South Holland (60473) *(G-20293)*
**Nice Card Company**.....773 467-8450
803 S Aldine Ave Park Ridge (60068) *(G-17212)*
**Nicholas Machine & Tool Inc**.....847 298-2035
7027 Barry St Rosemont (60018) *(G-19018)*
**Nichols Aluminum LLC**.....847 634-3150
200 Schelter Rd Lincolnshire (60069) *(G-13467)*
**Nichols Net & Twine Inc**.....618 797-0211
2200 State Route 111 Granite City (62040) *(G-11298)*
**Nickel Composite Coatings Inc**.....708 563-2780
6454 W 74th St Chicago (60638) *(G-5910)*
**Nickel Putter**.....312 337-7888
1229 N North Branch St Chicago (60642) *(G-5911)*
**Nickelodeon Jr Mag Chicago, Chicago** *Also called Nickelodeon Magazines Inc (G-5912)*
**Nickelodeon Magazines Inc**.....312 836-0668
401 N Michigan Ave # 2200 Chicago (60611) *(G-5912)*
**Nickels Electric**.....309 676-1350
1208 W Smith St Peoria (61605) *(G-17418)*
**Nickels Quarters LLC**.....630 514-5779
1651 Bolson Dr Downers Grove (60516) *(G-8495)*
**Nicks Metal Fabg & Sons**.....708 485-1170
9132 47th St Brookfield (60513) *(G-2639)*
**Nicor Gas, Kankakee** *Also called Northern Illinois Gas Company (G-12640)*
**Nicor Gas, Carthage** *Also called Northern Illinois Gas Company (G-3318)*
**Nicor Gas, Crystal Lake** *Also called Northern Illinois Gas Company (G-7620)*
**Nicor Gas, Ottawa** *Also called Northern Illinois Gas Company (G-16972)*
**Nicor Gas, Joliet** *Also called Northern Illinois Gas Company (G-12546)*
**Nicor Gas, Mendota** *Also called Northern Illinois Gas Company (G-14729)*
**Nicor Products, Joliet** *Also called American Chute Systems Inc (G-12452)*
**Nidec Motor Corporation**.....847 439-3760
25 Northwest Point Blvd # 900 Elk Grove Village (60007) *(G-9651)*
**Nidec Motor Corporation**.....847 585-8430
1901 South St Elgin (60123) *(G-9123)*
**Nidec Motor Corporation**.....847 439-3760
1905 S Mount Prospect Rd Des Plaines (60018) *(G-8241)*

ALPHABETIC

**Nidec-Shimpo America Corp (HQ)** ....630 924-7138
1701 Glenlake Ave Itasca (60143) ***(G-12331)***
**Niedermaier Inc (PA)** ....312 492-9400
1700 N Throop St Chicago (60642) ***(G-5913)***
**Niedermaier Furniture, Chicago** *Also called Niedermaier Inc* ***(G-5913)***
**Nielsen & Bainbridge LLC** ....708 546-2135
7830 W 71st St Ste 1 Bridgeview (60455) ***(G-2514)***
**Nieman & Considine Inc** ....312 326-1053
2323 S Michigan Ave Chicago (60616) ***(G-5914)***
**Niemann Foods Foundation** ....217 222-0190
520 N 24th St Quincy (62301) ***(G-17862)***
**Niemann Foods Foundation** ....217 793-4091
3001 S Veterans Pkwy Springfield (62704) ***(G-20487)***
**Niese Walter Machine Mfg Co** ....773 774-7337
6551 N Olmsted Ave Chicago (60631) ***(G-5915)***
**Night Vision Corporation** ....847 677-7611
4324 W Chase Ave Lincolnwood (60712) ***(G-13527)***
**Nightingale Corp** ....800 363-8954
222 Merchandise Mart Plz # 1078 Chicago (60654) ***(G-5916)***
**Nijhuis Water Technology Inc** ....312 466-9900
560 W Washington Blvd # 320 Chicago (60661) ***(G-5917)***
**Nike Inc** ....773 846-5460
8510 S Cottage Grove Ave Chicago (60619) ***(G-5918)***
**Nike Inc** ....630 585-9568
1650 Prem Outlet Blvd # 601 Aurora (60502) ***(G-1056)***
**Nikkei America Holdings Inc** ....312 263-8877
125 S Wacker Dr Ste 1080 Chicago (60606) ***(G-5919)***
**Nikkin Flux Corp** ....618 656-2125
512 Phillipena St Edwardsville (62025) ***(G-8810)***
**Nikli Fuels Inc** ....309 363-2425
801 S 2nd St Pekin (61554) ***(G-17276)***
**Nikro Industries Inc** ....630 530-0558
1115 N Ellsworth Ave Villa Park (60181) ***(G-21273)***
**Nikwood Products Inc** ....309 658-2341
32111 Highway 2 N Hillsdale (61257) ***(G-11902)***
**Nilan/Primarc Tool & Mold, Hoffman Estates** *Also called Nilan/Primarc Tool & Mold Inc* ***(G-12030)***
**Nilan/Primarc Tool & Mold Inc** ....847 885-2300
2125 Stonington Ave Hoffman Estates (60169) ***(G-12030)***
**Niles Auto Parts** ....847 215-2549
20734 N Elizabeth Ave Lincolnshire (60069) ***(G-13468)***
**Nimco Corporation** ....815 459-4200
1000 Nimco Dr Crystal Lake (60014) ***(G-7619)***
**Nimlok, Des Plaines** *Also called Orbus LLC* ***(G-8247)***
**Nimlok Company (PA)** ....847 647-1012
111 Rawls Rd Des Plaines (60018) ***(G-8242)***
**Nine West Holdings Inc** ....630 236-9258
1640 Premium Outlet Blvd Aurora (60502) ***(G-1057)***
**Nippon Electric Glass Amer Inc (HQ)** ....630 285-8323
1515 E Wdfield Rd Ste 720 Schaumburg (60173) ***(G-19665)***
**Nippon Sharyo Mfg LLC** ....815 562-8600
1600 Ritchie Ct Rochelle (61068) ***(G-18101)***
**Nippon Yakin America Inc** ....847 685-6644
2800 S River Rd Des Plaines (60018) ***(G-8243)***
**Nique Soul Catering, Chicago** *Also called Dominique Graves* ***(G-4623)***
**Nissan Forklift, Marengo** *Also called Unicarriers Americas Corp* ***(G-14244)***
**Nissan Forklift, Marengo** *Also called Global Cmpnent Tech Amrcas Inc* ***(G-14229)***
**Nissei America Inc** ....847 228-5000
721 Landmeier Rd Elk Grove Village (60007) ***(G-9652)***
**Nissha Usa Inc (HQ)** ....847 413-2665
1051 Perimeter Dr Ste 600 Schaumburg (60173) ***(G-19666)***
**Nisshin Holding Inc** ....847 290-5100
1701 Golf Rd Ste 3-1004 Rolling Meadows (60008) ***(G-18750)***
**Nisshin Steel USA, Rolling Meadows** *Also called Nisshin Holding Inc* ***(G-18750)***
**Nite Lite Signs & Balloons Inc** ....630 953-2866
506 S Westgate St Addison (60101) ***(G-229)***
**Nite Owl Prints LLC** ....630 541-6273
1323 Butterfield Rd # 102 Downers Grove (60515) ***(G-8496)***
**Nitek International LLC** ....847 259-8900
5410 Newport Dr Ste 24 Rolling Meadows (60008) ***(G-18751)***
**Nitrex Inc** ....630 851-5880
1900 Plain Ave Aurora (60502) ***(G-1058)***
**Nitrogen Labs Inc** ....312 504-8134
618 W Hill St Champaign (61820) ***(G-3520)***
**Nixalite of America Inc (PA)** ....309 755-8771
1025 16th Ave East Moline (61244) ***(G-8689)***
**Njc Machine Co** ....708 442-6004
8338 47th St Lyons (60534) ***(G-14042)***
**Nls Analytics LLC** ....312 593-0293
375 Dundee Rd Glencoe (60022) ***(G-11003)***
**Nnm Manufacturing LLC** ....815 436-9201
24133 W 143rd St Plainfield (60544) ***(G-17633)***
**NNt Enterprises Incorporated** ....630 875-9600
1320 Norwood Ave Itasca (60143) ***(G-12332)***
**No Surrender Inc (PA)** ....773 929-7920
1056 W Belmont Ave Chicago (60657) ***(G-5920)***
**Nobert Plating Co** ....312 421-4040
340 N Ashland Ave Chicago (60607) ***(G-5921)***
**Nobility Corporation** ....847 677-3204
5404 Touhy Ave Skokie (60077) ***(G-20045)***
**Nobleson and Associates, Rockford** *Also called Forest City Grinding Inc* ***(G-18388)***
**Nobu Nutritional Baking Co Inc** ....847 344-7336
13 Quindel Ave Schaumburg (60193) ***(G-19667)***
**Nogi Brands LLC** ....312 371-7974
2106 W Erie St Chicago (60612) ***(G-5922)***
**Noise Barriers LLC** ....847 843-0500
2001 Kelley Ct Libertyville (60048) ***(G-13362)***
**Nokia Networks, Naperville** *Also called Nokia Slutions Networks US LLC* ***(G-15716)***
**Nokia Slutions Networks US LLC** ....224 248-8204
1455 W Shure Dr Arlington Heights (60004) ***(G-809)***
**Nokia Slutions Networks US LLC** ....630 979-9572
2000 Lucent Ln Naperville (60563) ***(G-15716)***
**Nokomis Quarry Company** ....217 563-2011
23311 Taylorville Rd Nokomis (62075) ***(G-16059)***
**Nolan Fire Pump System Testing, Elgin** *Also called Aquarius Fluid Products Inc* ***(G-8957)***
**Nolan Sealants Inc** ....630 774-5713
1 Bloomingdale Pl Apt 104 Bloomingdale (60108) ***(G-2121)***
**Nolte & Tyson Inc** ....847 551-3313
24 Center Dr Ste 1 Gilberts (60136) ***(G-10929)***
**Non Violent Toys Inc** ....847 835-9066
1179 Hohlfelder Rd Glencoe (60022) ***(G-11004)***
**Non-For Profit Nat Trade Assn, Schaumburg** *Also called Associated Equipment Distrs* ***(G-19448)***
**Non-Metals Inc** ....630 378-9866
486 W North Frontage Rd Bolingbrook (60440) ***(G-2354)***
**None, Warrenville** *Also called Plymouth Tube Company* ***(G-21355)***
**Noodle Party** ....773 205-0505
4205 W Lawrence Ave Chicago (60630) ***(G-5923)***
**Noon Hour Food Products Inc (PA)** ....312 382-1177
215 N Desplaines St Fl 1 Chicago (60661) ***(G-5924)***
**Noor International Inc** ....847 985-2300
2015 Pennsbury Ln Bartlett (60133) ***(G-1320)***
**Nopalina, Waukegan** *Also called Salud Natural Entrepreneur Inc* ***(G-21612)***
**Nor Service Inc** ....815 232-8379
215 S State Ave Freeport (61032) ***(G-10676)***
**Norchem Inc** ....708 478-4777
8910 W 192nd St Ste O Mokena (60448) ***(G-14887)***
**Norchem Industries, A Division, Mokena** *Also called Norchem Inc* ***(G-14887)***
**Nordco, Spring Grove** *Also called Northern Ordinance Corporation* ***(G-20352)***
**Nordent Manufacturing Inc** ....847 437-4780
610 Bonnie Ln Elk Grove Village (60007) ***(G-9653)***
**Nordex Usa Inc (HQ)** ....208 383-6500
300 S Wacker Dr Ste 1500 Chicago (60606) ***(G-5925)***
**Nordmeyer Graphics** ....815 697-2634
100 Dieter Rd Chebanse (60922) ***(G-3631)***
**Nordson Asymtek Inc** ....760 431-1919
25033 Network Pl Chicago (60673) ***(G-5926)***
**Nordson Corporation** ....815 784-5025
416 Holly Ct Genoa (60135) ***(G-10881)***
**Norfolk Medical Products Inc** ....847 674-7075
7350 Ridgeway Ave Skokie (60076) ***(G-20046)***
**Norfolk Southern Corporation** ....773 933-5698
2543 W Columbus Ave Chicago (60629) ***(G-5927)***
**Norforge and Machining Inc** ....309 772-3124
195 N Dean St Bushnell (61422) ***(G-2907)***
**Noridge Die & Mold, Bensenville** *Also called Quality Plastic Products Inc* ***(G-1972)***
**Norix Group Inc** ....630 231-1331
1800 W Hawthorne Ln Ste N West Chicago (60185) ***(G-21751)***
**Norkin Jewelry Co Inc** ....312 782-7311
55 E Washington St # 203 Chicago (60602) ***(G-5928)***
**Norkol Inc** ....708 531-1000
11650 W Grand Ave Northlake (60164) ***(G-16445)***
**Norkol Converting Corporation (PA)** ....708 531-1000
11650 W Grand Ave Melrose Park (60164) ***(G-14678)***
**Norlux, Elgin** *Also called Carmen Matthew LLC* ***(G-8984)***
**Norm Gordon & Associates Inc** ....847 564-7022
3911 Kiess Dr Glenview (60026) ***(G-11174)***
**Normal Cornbelters** ....309 451-3432
1000 W Raab Rd Normal (61761) ***(G-16079)***
**Normalite Newspaper** ....309 454-5476
1702 W College Ave Ste G Normal (61761) ***(G-16080)***
**Norman Filter Company LLC** ....708 233-5521
9850 Industrial Dr Bridgeview (60455) ***(G-2515)***
**Norman P Moeller** ....847 991-3933
372 Rolling Wood Ln Apt D Lake Barrington (60010) ***(G-12821)***
**Norman Technology, Carol Stream** *Also called Ergoseal Inc* ***(G-3147)***
**Norridge Jewelry** ....312 984-1036
29 E Madison St Ste 1202 Chicago (60602) ***(G-5929)***
**Norris Production Solutions, Downers Grove** *Also called Dover Artificial Lift Intl LLC* ***(G-8430)***
**Norskobok Press** ....847 516-0085
7001 Owl Way Cary (60013) ***(G-3362)***
**Nortech, Schaumburg** *Also called Custom Assembly Solutions Inc* ***(G-19495)***
**Nortech Packaging LLC** ....847 884-1805
101 E State Pkwy Schaumburg (60173) ***(G-19668)***

ALPHABETIC SECTION Northwest Premier Printing

**North Amercn Acquisition Corp**..........847 695-8030
1355 Holmes Rd Elgin (60123) *(G-9124)*
**North Amercn Acquisition Corp (HQ)**..........847 695-8030
1875 Holmes Rd Elgin (60123) *(G-9125)*
**North Amercn Ret Dealers Assn, Chicago** *Also called Narda Inc (G-5853)*
**North America O M C G Inc**..........630 860-1016
857 Industrial Dr Ste 1 Bensenville (60106) *(G-1956)*
**North America Packaging Corp**..........630 845-8726
515 N First St Peotone (60468) *(G-17491)*
**North America Packaging Corp (HQ)**..........630 203-4100
1515 W 22nd St Ste 550 Oak Brook (60523) *(G-16547)*
**North American Adhesives, West Chicago** *Also called Mapei Corporation (G-21737)*
**North American Bear Co Inc (PA)**..........773 376-3457
1200 W 35th St Chicago (60609) *(G-5930)*
**North American Die Castng Assn**..........773 202-1000
5439 W Lawrence Ave Chicago (60630) *(G-5931)*
**North American EN Inc**..........847 952-3680
776 Lunt Ave Elk Grove Village (60007) *(G-9654)*
**North American Fund III LP (PA)**..........312 332-4950
135 S La Salle St # 3225 Chicago (60603) *(G-5932)*
**North American Gear and Axel, Chicago** *Also called United States Gear Corporation (G-6828)*
**North American Jewelers Inc**..........312 425-9000
5 S Wabash Ave Ste 1512 Chicago (60603) *(G-5933)*
**North American Lighting Inc (HQ)**..........217 465-6600
2275 S Main St Paris (61944) *(G-17155)*
**North American Lighting Inc**..........618 548-6249
1875 W Main St Salem (62881) *(G-19340)*
**North American Lighting Inc**..........618 662-4483
20 Industrial Park Flora (62839) *(G-10212)*
**North American Press Inc**..........847 515-3882
12203 Spring Creek Dr Huntley (60142) *(G-12164)*
**North American Refining Co**..........708 762-5117
7601 W 47th St Mc Cook (60525) *(G-14454)*
**North American Safety Products**..........815 469-1144
8910 W 192nd St Ste C Mokena (60448) *(G-14888)*
**North American Signal Co**..........847 537-8888
605 Wheeling Rd Wheeling (60090) *(G-22108)*
**North Amrcn Herb Spice Ltd LLC**..........847 367-6070
13900 W Polo Trail Dr Lake Forest (60045) *(G-12930)*
**North Chicago Iron Works Inc**..........847 689-2000
1305 Morrow Ave North Chicago (60064) *(G-16185)*
**North County News Inc**..........618 282-3803
124 S Main St Red Bud (62278) *(G-17945)*
**North Halsted Dental Spa**..........773 296-0325
3710 N Halsted St Chicago (60613) *(G-5934)*
**North Okaw Woodworking**..........217 856-2178
2409 E County Road 1700n Humboldt (61931) *(G-12129)*
**North Point Investments Inc (PA)**..........312 977-4386
70 W Madison St Ste 3500 Chicago (60602) *(G-5935)*
**North Sails Group LLC**..........773 489-1308
1665 N Elston Ave Chicago (60642) *(G-5936)*
**North Shore Consultants Inc**..........847 290-1599
613 Thorndale Ave Elk Grove Village (60007) *(G-9655)*
**North Shore Distillery LLC**..........847 574-2499
13990 W Rockland Rd Libertyville (60048) *(G-13363)*
**North Shore Paving Inc**..........847 201-1710
24752 W Orchard Pl Round Lake Heights (60073) *(G-19082)*
**North Shore Printers Inc**..........847 623-0037
535 S Sheridan Rd Waukegan (60085) *(G-21593)*
**North Shore Sign Company**..........847 816-7020
1925 Industrial Dr Libertyville (60048) *(G-13364)*
**North Shore Stairs**..........847 295-7906
100 N Skokie Hwy Ste D Lake Bluff (60044) *(G-12859)*
**North Shore Truck & Equipment**..........847 887-0200
29800 N Skokie Hwy Ste B Lake Bluff (60044) *(G-12860)*
**North Shore Wtr Rclamation Dst**..........847 623-6060
Dahringer Rd Waukegan (60085) *(G-21594)*
**North Star Lighting LLC**..........708 681-4330
835 N Industrial Dr Elmhurst (60126) *(G-9915)*
**North Star Pickle LLC**..........847 970-5555
968 Donata Ct Lake Zurich (60047) *(G-13109)*
**North Star Stamping & Tool Inc**..........847 658-9400
1264 Industrial Dr Lake In The Hills (60156) *(G-13001)*
**North-West Drapery Service**..........773 282-7117
4507 N Milwaukee Ave Chicago (60630) *(G-5937)*
**Northcape International, Alsip** *Also called Chicago Wicker & Trading Co (G-447)*
**Northeast Illinois Regional**..........708 246-0304
914 Burlington Ave Western Springs (60558) *(G-21870)*
**Northern Division, Crystal Lake** *Also called Triumph Twist Drill Co Inc (G-7670)*
**Northern Ill Blood Bnk Inc (PA)**..........815 965-8751
419 N 6th St Rockford (61107) *(G-18520)*
**Northern Ill Wilbert Vlt Co, Belvidere** *Also called Northern Illinois Wilbert Vlt (G-1775)*
**Northern Illi Electrcl Jnt App**..........815 969-8484
619 Southrock Dr Rockford (61102) *(G-18521)*
**Northern Illinois Gas Company**..........630 983-8676
2704 Festival Dr Kankakee (60901) *(G-12640)*
**Northern Illinois Gas Company**..........217 357-3105
1375 Buchanan St Carthage (62321) *(G-3318)*
**Northern Illinois Gas Company**..........630 983-8676
300 W Terra Cotta Ave Crystal Lake (60014) *(G-7620)*
**Northern Illinois Gas Company**..........815 433-3850
1629 Champlain St Ottawa (61350) *(G-16972)*
**Northern Illinois Gas Company**..........815 693-3907
3000 E Cass St Joliet (60432) *(G-12546)*
**Northern Illinois Gas Company**..........815 223-8097
169 N 36th Rd Mendota (61342) *(G-14729)*
**Northern Illinois Lumber Spc**..........630 859-3226
1200 S Lake St Montgomery (60538) *(G-15064)*
**Northern Illinois Metal Finshg, Rockford** *Also called K&J Finishing Inc (G-18451)*
**Northern Illinois Mold Corp**..........847 669-2100
17n520 Adams Dr Dundee (60118) *(G-8565)*
**Northern Illinois Pallet Inc**..........815 236-9242
1285 Wentworth Dr Fox Lake (60020) *(G-10280)*
**Northern Illinois Real Estate**..........630 257-2480
1244 State St Ste 351 Lemont (60439) *(G-13244)*
**Northern Illinois Wilbert Vlt**..........815 544-3355
845 E Jackson St Belvidere (61008) *(G-1775)*
**Northern Information Tech**..........800 528-4343
5410 Newport Dr Ste 24 Rolling Meadows (60008) *(G-18752)*
**Northern Lighting & Power Inc**..........708 383-9926
1138 Woodbine Ave Oak Park (60302) *(G-16677)*
**Northern Ordinance Corporation**..........815 675-6400
7806 Industrial Dr Spring Grove (60081) *(G-20352)*
**Northern Orgle County Temple, Byron** *Also called Rock Valley Publishing LLC (G-2919)*
**Northern Pallet and Supply Co (PA)**..........847 716-1400
464 Central Ave Ste 18 Northfield (60093) *(G-16412)*
**Northern Precision Plas Inc**..........815 544-8099
6553 Revlon Dr Belvidere (61008) *(G-1776)*
**Northern Prints, Wheeling** *Also called RCM Industries Inc (G-22133)*
**Northern Products Company**..........708 597-8501
11536 S Central Ave Alsip (60803) *(G-500)*
**Northern Prosthetics**..........815 226-0444
2629 Charles St Rockford (61108) *(G-18522)*
**Northern Star Plating Division, Loves Park** *Also called Superior Metal Finishing (G-13995)*
**Northern Technologies Inc**..........440 246-6999
4350 Weaver Pkwy Warrenville (60555) *(G-21351)*
**Northfield Block Company (HQ)**..........847 816-9000
1 Hunt Ct Mundelein (60060) *(G-15538)*
**Northfield Block Company**..........815 941-4100
3400 Bungalow Rd Morris (60450) *(G-15123)*
**Northfield Block Company**..........847 949-3600
1455 Leighton Tower Rd Mundelein (60060) *(G-15539)*
**Northfield Block Company**..........708 458-8130
5400 W Canal Bank Rd Berwyn (60402) *(G-2069)*
**Northfield Holdings LLC**..........847 755-0700
700 Wiley Farm Ct Schaumburg (60173) *(G-19669)*
**Northgate Technologies Inc**..........847 608-8900
1591 Scottsdale Ct Elgin (60123) *(G-9126)*
**Northpoint Heating & Air Cond**..........847 731-1067
1101 Shiloh Blvd Rear 2 Zion (60099) *(G-22692)*
**Northrop Grmmn Spce & Mssn Sys**..........630 773-6900
1131 W Bryn Mawr Ave Itasca (60143) *(G-12333)*
**Northrop Grumman Systems Corp**..........847 259-9600
600 Hicks Rd Rolling Meadows (60008) *(G-18753)*
**Northrop Grumman Technical**..........847 259-2396
600 Hicks Rd Rolling Meadows (60008) *(G-18754)*
**Northstar Aerospace (usa) Inc**..........708 728-2000
6006 W 73rd St Bedford Park (60638) *(G-1567)*
**Northstar Aerospace Chicago, Bedford Park** *Also called Heligear Acquisition Co (G-1553)*
**Northstar Custom Cabinetry**..........708 597-2099
14825 S Mckinley Ave Posen (60469) *(G-17733)*
**Northstar Group Inc**..........847 726-0880
577 Capital Dr Lake Zurich (60047) *(G-13110)*
**Northstar Industries Inc**..........630 446-7800
591 Mitchell Rd Glendale Heights (60139) *(G-11052)*
**Northstar Metal Products, Glendale Heights** *Also called Northstar Industries Inc (G-11052)*
**Northstar Trading LLC**..........224 422-6050
1411 Enterprise Dr Romeoville (60446) *(G-18855)*
**Northtech Power, Crystal Lake** *Also called Ntpwind Power Inc (G-7621)*
**Northtech Work Holding, Schaumburg** *Also called Kitagawa-Northtech Inc (G-19600)*
**Northwest Dental Prosthetics**..........773 505-9191
6124 N Milwaukee Ave # 16 Chicago (60646) *(G-5938)*
**Northwest Donut, Palatine** *Also called Spunky Dunker Donuts (G-17076)*
**Northwest Frame Company Inc**..........847 359-0987
252 N Cady Dr Palatine (60074) *(G-17059)*
**Northwest Instrumentation Inc**..........847 825-0699
310 Busse Hwy 259 Park Ridge (60068) *(G-17213)*
**Northwest Marble Products (PA)**..........630 860-2288
1229 Silver Pine Dr Hoffman Estates (60010) *(G-12072)*
**Northwest Mold & Machine Corp**..........847 690-1501
131 Martin Ln Elk Grove Village (60007) *(G-9656)*
**Northwest Pallet Supply Co**..........815 544-6001
3648 Morreim Dr Belvidere (61008) *(G-1777)*
**Northwest Pipe Company**..........312 587-8702
1050 N State St Fl Mezz7 Chicago (60610) *(G-5939)*
**Northwest Premier Printing**..........773 736-1882
5421 W Addison St Chicago (60641) *(G-5940)*

ALPHABETIC

**Northwest Printing Inc** .......815 943-7977
20 N Ayer St Harvard (60033) ***(G-11642)***
**Northwest Publishing LLC** .......312 329-0600
500 N Dearborn St # 1014 Chicago (60654) ***(G-5941)***
**Northwest Side Press, Chicago** *Also called Nadig Newspapers Inc* ***(G-5849)***
**Northwest Snow Timber Svc Ltd** .......847 778-4998
328 Washington St Glenview (60025) ***(G-11175)***
**Northwest Tool Co Inc** .......630 350-4770
342 Evergreen Ave Bensenville (60106) ***(G-1957)***
**Northwestern Corporation** .......815 942-1300
922 Armstrong St Morris (60450) ***(G-15124)***
**Northwestern Cup & Logo Inc** .......773 874-8000
41 W 84th St Fl 1 Chicago (60620) ***(G-5942)***
**Northwestern Flavors LLC** .......630 231-6111
120 N Aurora St West Chicago (60185) ***(G-21752)***
**Northwestern Illinois Farmer** .......815 369-2811
119 W Railroad St Lena (61048) ***(G-13282)***
**Northwoods Wreaths Company** .......847 615-9491
450 W Deerpath Lake Forest (60045) ***(G-12931)***
**Northwstern Globl Hlth Fndtion** .......214 207-9485
2707 N Lincoln Ave Apt B Chicago (60614) ***(G-5943)***
**Norton Machine Co** .......217 748-6115
711 S Chicago St Rossville (60963) ***(G-19050)***
**Norvida USA Inc** .......618 282-2992
310 S Vine St Sparta (62286) ***(G-20319)***
**Norwalk Tank Co, Joliet** *Also called George W Pierson Company* ***(G-12501)***
**Norway Press Inc** .......773 846-9422
400 W 76th St Ste 1105 Chicago (60620) ***(G-5944)***
**Norwood House Press Inc** .......866 565-2900
6150 N Milwaukee Ave # 2 Chicago (60646) ***(G-5945)***
**Norwood Industries Inc** .......773 788-1508
7001 W 60th St Chicago (60638) ***(G-5946)***
**Norwood Marketing Systems, Frankfort** *Also called Illinois Tool Works Inc* ***(G-10329)***
**Norwood Paper, Chicago** *Also called Norwood Industries Inc* ***(G-5946)***
**Nosco Gurnee Mfg Site, Gurnee** *Also called Nosco Inc* ***(G-11476)***
**Nosco Inc (HQ)** .......847 336-4200
651 S MI King Jr Ave Waukegan (60085) ***(G-21595)***
**Nosco Inc** .......847 336-4200
2199 N Delany Rd Gurnee (60031) ***(G-11476)***
**Nosko Manufacturing Inc** .......847 678-0813
3901 25th Ave Schiller Park (60176) ***(G-19854)***
**Nostalgia Fireworks, Osco** *Also called Nostalgia Pyrotechnics Inc* ***(G-16900)***
**Nostalgia Pyrotechnics Inc** .......309 522-5136
119 South St Osco (61274) ***(G-16900)***
**Nova Chemicals Inc** .......815 224-1525
501 Brunner St Peru (61354) ***(G-17523)***
**Nova Metals Inc** .......630 690-4300
279 Commonwealth Dr Carol Stream (60188) ***(G-3206)***
**Nova Printing and Litho Co** .......773 486-8500
1621 E Dogwood Ln Mount Prospect (60056) ***(G-15355)***
**Nova Solutions Inc (PA)** .......217 342-7070
421 Industrial Ave Effingham (62401) ***(G-8851)***
**Nova Systems Ltd** .......630 879-2296
2111 Comprehensive Dr Aurora (60505) ***(G-1195)***
**Nova The Right Solution, Effingham** *Also called Nova Solutions Inc* ***(G-8851)***
**Nova Tronics Inc** .......630 455-1034
7701 S Grant St Ste C Burr Ridge (60527) ***(G-2871)***
**Nova Wildcat Amerock LLC** .......815 266-6416
1750 Lincoln Dr Freeport (61032) ***(G-10677)***
**Nova-Chrome Inc** .......847 455-8200
3200 Wolf Rd Franklin Park (60131) ***(G-10542)***
**Novacare Prosthetics Orthotics, Carbondale** *Also called Cape Prosthetics-Orthotics Inc* ***(G-3001)***
**Novak Business Forms Inc** .......630 932-9850
20 Eisenhower Ln N Lombard (60148) ***(G-13834)***
**Novalex Therapeutics Inc** .......630 750-9334
2242 W Harrison St # 201 Chicago (60612) ***(G-5947)***
**Novanta Inc** .......781 266-5700
106 Marshall Dr Newton (62448) ***(G-15945)***
**Novapack, Paris** *Also called Pvc Container Corporation* ***(G-17159)***
**Novaspect Inc (PA)** .......847 956-8020
1124 Tower Rd Schaumburg (60173) ***(G-19670)***
**Novation Industries, McHenry** *Also called W M Plastics Inc* ***(G-14570)***
**Novatronix Inc** .......630 860-4300
600 Wheat Ln Wood Dale (60191) ***(G-22407)***
**Novel Electronic Designs Inc** .......309 224-9945
143 N 3rd St Chillicothe (61523) ***(G-7169)***
**Novel Products Inc** .......815 624-4888
3266 Yale Bridge Rd Rockton (61072) ***(G-18699)***
**Novian Health Inc** .......312 266-7200
430 W Erie St Ste 500 Chicago (60654) ***(G-5948)***
**Novilase Chicago, Chicago** *Also called Novian Health Inc* ***(G-5948)***
**Novipax LLC (HQ)** .......630 686-2735
2215 York Rd Ste 504 Oak Brook (60523) ***(G-16548)***
**Novo Card Publishers Inc** .......847 947-8090
5410 W Roosevelt Rd # 302 Chicago (60644) ***(G-5949)***
**Novo Surgical Inc** .......877 860-6686
700 Comme Dr Ste 500 No 1 Oak Brook (60523) ***(G-16549)***
**Novomatic Americas Sales LLC** .......224 802-2974
1050 E Business Center Dr Mount Prospect (60056) ***(G-15356)***
**Novum Pharma LLC** .......877 404-4724
640 N La Salle Dr Ste 670 Chicago (60654) ***(G-5950)***
**Now Foods, Bloomingdale** *Also called Now Health Group Inc* ***(G-2123)***
**Now Health Group Inc (PA)** .......630 545-9098
244 Knollwood Dr Ste 300 Bloomingdale (60108) ***(G-2122)***
**Now Health Group Inc** .......888 669-3663
395 Glen Ellyn Rd Bloomingdale (60108) ***(G-2123)***
**Now Natural Foods, Bloomingdale** *Also called Now Health Group Inc* ***(G-2122)***
**Nowfab** .......815 675-2916
6413 Johnsburg Rd Spring Grove (60081) ***(G-20353)***
**Npc Sealants, Maywood** *Also called Nu-Puttie Corporation* ***(G-14433)***
**Npc Sealants** .......708 681-1040
1208 S 8th Ave Maywood (60153) ***(G-14431)***
**Npi Holding Corp (HQ)** .......217 391-1229
1500 Taylor Ave Springfield (62703) ***(G-20488)***
**Npn360** .......847 215-7300
1400 S Wolf Rd Wheeling (60090) ***(G-22109)***
**Npt Automotive Machine Shop** .......618 233-1344
308 N 44th St Belleville (62226) ***(G-1661)***
**NRR Corp** .......630 915-8388
705 Deer Trail Ln Oak Brook (60523) ***(G-16550)***
**Nrtx LLC** .......224 717-0465
1454 W Melrose St Ste 2 Chicago (60657) ***(G-5951)***
**NS Precision Lathe Inc** .......708 867-5023
519 Lake St Maywood (60153) ***(G-14432)***
**Nsa (chi) Liquidating Corp** .......708 728-2000
205 E Bttrfeld Rd Ste 238 Elmhurst (60126) ***(G-9916)***
**Nsc, Itasca** *Also called National Safety Council* ***(G-12324)***
**Nsga Retail Focus, Mount Prospect** *Also called National Sporting Goods Assn* ***(G-15353)***
**Nsi, Buffalo Grove** *Also called Necta Sweet Inc* ***(G-2742)***
**Nsi Signs Inc** .......630 433-3525
100-110 W Fay Ave Addison (60101) ***(G-230)***
**Nsk-America Corporation** .......847 843-7664
1800 Global Pkwy Hoffman Estates (60192) ***(G-12031)***
**Nss Exteriors, Alsip** *Also called Nelson Sash Systems Inc* ***(G-498)***
**Nta Precision Axle Corporation** .......630 690-6300
795 Kimberly Dr Carol Stream (60188) ***(G-3207)***
**Ntm, Wheeling** *Also called National Tool & Mfg Co* ***(G-22105)***
**NTN Bearing Corporation** .......847 298-7500
1805 E University Dr Macomb (61455) ***(G-14127)***
**NTN USA Corporation (HQ)** .......847 298-4652
1600 Bishop Ct Mount Prospect (60056) ***(G-15357)***
**NTN Warehouse, Macomb** *Also called NTN Bearing Corporation* ***(G-14127)***
**NTN-Bower Corporation (HQ)** .......309 837-0440
711 Bower Rd Macomb (61455) ***(G-14128)***
**NTN-Bower Corporation** .......309 837-0322
711 Bower Rd Macomb (61455) ***(G-14129)***
**Ntpwind Power Inc** .......815 345-1931
4702 Rte 176 Crystal Lake (60014) ***(G-7621)***
**NTS Technical Systems, Rockford** *Also called National Technical Systems Inc* ***(G-18517)***
**Nu Again** .......630 564-5590
494 E Thornwood Dr Bartlett (60103) ***(G-1364)***
**Nu Glo Sign Company** .......847 223-6160
18880 W Gages Lake Rd Grayslake (60030) ***(G-11356)***
**Nu Mill Inc** .......630 458-8950
1001 W Republic Dr Ste 7 Addison (60101) ***(G-231)***
**Nu Vision Media Inc** .......773 495-5254
1327 W Wa Blvd Ste 102b Chicago (60607) ***(G-5952)***
**Nu-Art Printing** .......618 533-9971
614 W Broadway Centralia (62801) ***(G-3425)***
**Nu-Dell Manufacturing Co Inc (PA)** .......847 803-4500
400 E Randolph St Chicago (60601) ***(G-5953)***
**Nu-Dell Plastics, Chicago** *Also called Nu-Dell Manufacturing Co Inc* ***(G-5953)***
**Nu-Life Inc of Illinois** .......618 943-4500
Hwy 1 S Lawrenceville (62439) ***(G-13203)***
**Nu-Metal Products Inc** .......815 459-2075
260 E Prairie St Crystal Lake (60014) ***(G-7622)***
**Nu-Puttie Corporation** .......708 681-1040
1208 S 8th Ave Maywood (60153) ***(G-14433)***
**Nu-Recycling Technology Inc** .......630 904-5237
10364 Book Rd Naperville (60564) ***(G-15820)***
**Nu-Way Electronics Inc** .......847 437-7120
165 Martin Ln Elk Grove Village (60007) ***(G-9657)***
**Nu-Way Industries Inc** .......847 298-7710
555 Howard Ave Des Plaines (60018) ***(G-8244)***
**Nu-Way Signs Inc** .......847 243-0164
2320 Foster Ave Wheeling (60090) ***(G-22110)***
**Nu-World Amaranth Inc (PA)** .......630 369-6819
552 S Washington St # 120 Naperville (60540) ***(G-15717)***
**Nu-World Foods, Naperville** *Also called Nu-World Amaranth Inc* ***(G-15717)***
**Nuair Filter Company LLC (HQ)** .......309 888-4331
2219 W College Ave Normal (61761) ***(G-16081)***
**Nuance Solutions, Chicago** *Also called Bullen Midwest Inc* ***(G-4183)***
**Nuarc Company Inc (HQ)** .......847 967-4400
440 Medinah Rd Roselle (60172) ***(G-18960)***

**Nuclear Power Outfitters LLC** ....630 963-0320
1955 University Ln Lisle (60532) *(G-13634)*
**Nuclin Diagnostics Inc** ....847 498-5210
3322 Commercial Ave Northbrook (60062) *(G-16320)*
**Nucor Steel Kankakee Inc** ....815 937-3131
1 Nucor Way Bourbonnais (60914) *(G-2403)*
**Nucurrent Inc** ....312 575-0388
641 W Lake St Ste 304 Chicago (60661) *(G-5954)*
**Nudo Products Inc** ....217 528-5636
2508 South Grand Ave E Springfield (62703) *(G-20489)*
**Nudo Products Inc (HQ)** ....217 528-5636
1500 Taylor Ave Springfield (62703) *(G-20490)*
**Nuestro Mundo Newspaper (PA)** ....773 446-9920
3339 S Halsted St Chicago (60608) *(G-5955)*
**Nuestro Queso LLC** ....815 443-2100
752 N Kent Rd Kent (61044) *(G-12666)*
**Nuestro Queso LLC (PA)** ....224 366-4320
9500 Bryn Mawr Ave Rosemont (60018) *(G-19019)*
**Nueva Vida Productions Inc** ....708 444-8474
17531 70th Ct Tinley Park (60477) *(G-20935)*
**Nuevos Semana Newspaper** ....847 991-3939
1180 E Dundee Rd Palatine (60074) *(G-17060)*
**Nufarm Americas Inc (HQ)** ....708 377-1330
11901 S Austin Ave Ste A Alsip (60803) *(G-501)*
**Nufarm Americas Inc** ....708 756-2010
220 E 17th St Fl 2 Chicago Heights (60411) *(G-7115)*
**Nufarm North American Office, Alsip** *Also called Nufarm Americas Inc (G-501)*
**Numalliance - North Amer Inc** ....847 439-4500
1361 Howard St Elk Grove Village (60007) *(G-9658)*
**Numat Technologies Inc** ....301 233-5329
8025 Lamon Ave Ste 43 Skokie (60077) *(G-20047)*
**Number One, Chicago** *Also called Aurora Narinder (G-3989)*
**Numerical Control Incorporated** ....708 389-8140
12325 S Keeler Ave Alsip (60803) *(G-502)*
**Numeridex Incorporated** ....847 541-8840
632 Wheeling Rd Wheeling (60090) *(G-22111)*
**Nuri Corp** ....847 940-7134
1121 Half Day Rd Deerfield (60015) *(G-8044)*
**Nusource Inc** ....847 201-8934
26575 W Cmmrc Dr 505 Round Lake (60073) *(G-19064)*
**Nutec Manufacturing, New Lenox** *Also called TEC Systems Inc (G-15917)*
**Nutheme Sign Company** ....847 230-0067
2659 Wisconsin Ave Downers Grove (60515) *(G-8497)*
**Nutherm International Inc** ....618 244-6000
501 S 11th St Mount Vernon (62864) *(G-15435)*
**Nutraceuticals and Pharma Tls, Oakbrook Terrace** *Also called Lodaat LLC (G-16715)*
**Nutrasweet Company (HQ)** ....312 873-5000
222 Merchandise Mart Plz # 936 Chicago (60654) *(G-5956)*
**Nutriad Inc** ....847 214-4860
201 Flannigan Rd Hampshire (60140) *(G-11556)*
**Nutritional Institute LLC** ....847 223-7699
100 S Atkinson Rd Ste 116 Grayslake (60030) *(G-11357)*
**Nutrivo LLC (PA)** ....630 270-1700
1785 N Edgelawn Dr Aurora (60506) *(G-1196)*
**Nuvixa, Urbana** *Also called Personify (G-21097)*
**Nuway Distributors, Chicago** *Also called Doctors Choice Inc (G-4621)*
**Nuway Electronics, Elk Grove Village** *Also called Nu-Way Electronics Inc (G-9657)*
**Nuyen Awning Co** ....630 892-3995
850 Ridgeway Ave Ste C Aurora (60506) *(G-1197)*
**NV Business Publishers Corp** ....847 441-5645
540 W Frontage Rd # 3124 Northfield (60093) *(G-16413)*
**Nxp Usa Inc** ....847 843-6824
2800 W Higgins Rd Ste 600 Hoffman Estates (60169) *(G-12032)*
**Nyclo Screw Machine Pdts Inc** ....815 229-7900
3610 Mansfield St Rockford (61109) *(G-18523)*
**Nycor Products Inc** ....815 727-9883
603 E Washington St Joliet (60433) *(G-12547)*
**Nylok Chicago, Lincolnwood** *Also called Nylok Fastener Corporation (G-13528)*
**Nylok Fastener Corporation** ....847 674-9680
6465 W Proesel Ave Lincolnwood (60712) *(G-13528)*
**Nypro Hanover Park, Hanover Park** *Also called Nypro Inc (G-11588)*
**Nypro Hanover Park** ....630 868-3517
401 S Gary Ave Roselle (60172) *(G-18961)*
**Nypro Inc** ....630 773-3341
6325 Muirfield Dr Hanover Park (60133) *(G-11587)*
**Nypro Inc** ....630 671-2000
6325 Muirfield Dr Hanover Park (60133) *(G-11588)*
**Nypromold Inc** ....847 855-2200
955 Tri State Pkwy Gurnee (60031) *(G-11477)*
**Nystrom, Chicago** *Also called Herff Jones LLC (G-5079)*
**O & G Spring & Wire, Chicago** *Also called Will Don Corp (G-6980)*
**O & I Woodworking** ....217 543-3155
125 E County Rd 50 E Arthur (61911) *(G-914)*
**O & K American Corp (HQ)** ....773 767-2500
4630 W 55th St Chicago (60632) *(G-5957)*
**O & L Machine Inc** ....815 963-6600
1115 18th Ave Rockford (61104) *(G-18524)*
**O & P Kinetic** ....815 401-7260
453 S Main St Bourbonnais (60914) *(G-2404)*
**O & W Wire Co Inc** ....773 776-5919
7816 S Oakley Ave Chicago (60620) *(G-5958)*
**O Adjust Matic Pump Company** ....630 766-1490
429 E Potter St Wood Dale (60191) *(G-22408)*
**O Brien Bill** ....630 980-5571
0n175 Alexander Dr Geneva (60134) *(G-10854)*
**O C Keckley Company (PA)** ....847 674-8422
3400 Cleveland St Skokie (60076) *(G-20048)*
**O Chilli Frozen Foods Inc** ....847 562-1991
1251 Shermer Rd Northbrook (60062) *(G-16321)*
**O E I, Hoffman Estates** *Also called Omron Electronics LLC (G-12033)*
**O E M Marketing Inc (PA)** ....847 985-9490
1015 Lunt Ave Schaumburg (60193) *(G-19671)*
**O K Jobbers Inc** ....217 728-7378
215 S Hamilton St Sullivan (61951) *(G-20756)*
**O R Lasertechnology Inc** ....847 593-5711
1420 Howard St Elk Grove Village (60007) *(G-9659)*
**O S P, Bloomington** *Also called Original Smith Printing Inc (G-2207)*
**O Signs Inc** ....312 888-3386
325 N Hoyne Ave Chicago (60612) *(G-5959)*
**O'Meara/Brown Publications, Evanston** *Also called Lakeland Boating Magazine (G-10063)*
**O'Neill Products, Chicago** *Also called Butcher Block Furn By Oneill (G-4193)*
**O-Cedar Commercial** ....217 379-2377
131 N Railroad Ave Paxton (60957) *(G-17240)*
**O.k Jobbers, Sullivan** *Also called O K Jobbers Inc (G-20756)*
**O2cool LLC** ....312 951-6700
168 N Clinton St Ste 500 Chicago (60661) *(G-5960)*
**O2m Technologies LLC** ....773 910-8533
2242 W Harrison St Ste 20 Chicago (60612) *(G-5961)*
**Oag Aviation Worldwide LLC (HQ)** ....630 515-5300
801 Warrenville Rd # 555 Lisle (60532) *(G-13635)*
**Oak Court Creations** ....815 467-7676
202 Oak Ct Minooka (60447) *(G-14845)*
**Oak Creek Distribution LLC (PA)** ....800 244-5263
2650 Belvidere Rd Waukegan (60085) *(G-21596)*
**Oak Foundation, Geneva** *Also called Oasis International Limited (G-10855)*
**Oak Leaf Outdoors Inc** ....309 691-9653
10216 W Civil Defense Rd Brimfield (61517) *(G-2548)*
**Oak Ridge Molded Products, McHenry** *Also called Oakridge Products LLC (G-14538)*
**Oak State, Wenona** *Also called Hearthside Food Solutions LLC (G-21648)*
**Oak Technical LLC (PA)** ....931 455-7011
600 Holiday Plaza Dr # 130 Matteson (60443) *(G-14377)*
**Oakland Enterprises Inc** ....630 377-1121
310 N 5th St Saint Charles (60174) *(G-19225)*
**Oakland Industries Ltd** ....847 827-7600
1551 Bishop Ct Mount Prospect (60056) *(G-15358)*
**Oakland Noodle Company** ....217 346-2322
10 W Main St Oakland (61943) *(G-16724)*
**Oakley Inc** ....312 787-2545
835 N Michigan Ave # 7000 Chicago (60611) *(G-5962)*
**Oakley Industrial McHy Inc** ....847 966-0052
1601 Lunt Ave Elk Grove Village (60007) *(G-9660)*
**Oakley Signs & Graphics Inc** ....224 612-5045
471 N 3rd Ave Des Plaines (60016) *(G-8245)*
**Oakridge Corporation** ....630 435-5900
15800 New Ave Lemont (60439) *(G-13245)*
**Oakridge Hobbies, Lemont** *Also called Oakridge Corporation (G-13245)*
**Oakridge Products LLC** ....815 363-4700
4612 Century Ct McHenry (60050) *(G-14538)*
**Oakwood Memorial Park Inc** ....815 433-0313
2405 Champlain St Ottawa (61350) *(G-16973)*
**Oandg Spring and Wire, Chicago** *Also called Willdon Corp (G-6981)*
**Oas Software Corp** ....630 513-2990
2801 Majestic Oaks Ln Saint Charles (60174) *(G-19226)*
**Oasis Audio LLC** ....630 668-5367
289 S Main Pl Carol Stream (60188) *(G-3208)*
**Oasis International Limited** ....630 326-0045
1770 S Randall Rd Ste A Geneva (60134) *(G-10855)*
**Oban Composites LLC** ....866 607-0284
1300 W Belmont Ave # 311 Chicago (60657) *(G-5963)*
**OBerry Enterprises Inc (PA)** ....815 728-9480
5306 Bsineil Pkwy Ste 110 Ringwood (60072) *(G-17994)*
**Oberthur Tech Amer Corp** ....630 551-0792
2764 Golfview Rd Naperville (60563) *(G-15718)*
**Oberweis Dairy Inc** ....847 368-9060
9 E Dundee Rd Arlington Heights (60004) *(G-810)*
**Oberweis Dairy Inc** ....630 906-6455
2274 Us Highway 30 Oswego (60543) *(G-16928)*
**Oberweis Dairy Inc** ....708 660-1350
124 N Oak Park Ave Oak Park (60301) *(G-16678)*
**Oberweis Dairy Inc** ....630 782-0141
1018 S York St Elmhurst (60126) *(G-9917)*
**Oberweis Dairy Inc** ....847 290-9222
1735 Algonquin Rd Rolling Meadows (60008) *(G-18755)*
**Oberweis Dairy Inc** ....630 474-0284
651 E Roosevelt St Glen Ellyn (60137) *(G-10983)*
**Oberweis Ice Cream and Dar Str, Arlington Heights** *Also called Oberweis Dairy Inc (G-810)*
**Obies Tackle Co Inc** ....618 234-5638
124 Cardinal Dr Belleville (62221) *(G-1662)*

ALPHABETIC

**Obiter Research LLC**..........217 359-1626
2809 Gemini Ct Champaign (61822) *(G-3521)*
**OBrien Architectural Mtls Inc**..........773 868-1065
858 W Armitage Ave # 205 Chicago (60614) *(G-5964)*
**OBrien Scntfic GL Blowing LLC**..........217 762-3636
750 W Railroad St Monticello (61856) *(G-15082)*
**OBrothers Bakery Inc**..........847 249-0091
2820 Belvidere Rd Waukegan (60085) *(G-21597)*
**Occidental Chemical Corp**..........773 284-0079
4201 W 69th St Chicago (60629) *(G-5965)*
**Occidental Chemical Corp**..........618 482-6346
520 Monsanto Ave Sauget (62206) *(G-19388)*
**Occly LLC**..........773 969-5080
2835 N Sheffield Ave Chicago (60657) *(G-5966)*
**Oce Bruning, Charleston** *Also called Oce-Van Der Grinten NV (G-3606)*
**Oce-Van Der Grinten NV**..........217 348-8111
815 Reasor Dr Charleston (61920) *(G-3606)*
**Ocean Cliff Corporation (PA)**..........847 729-9074
3419 Ralmark Ln Glenview (60026) *(G-11176)*
**Oceanaire Inc**..........847 583-0311
6228 Oakton St Morton Grove (60053) *(G-15225)*
**Oceancomm Incorporated**..........800 757-3266
60 Hazelwood Dr Champaign (61820) *(G-3522)*
**Oceanic Food Express Inc**..........847 480-7217
1715 Longvalley Dr Northbrook (60062) *(G-16322)*
**Ochem Inc (PA)**..........847 403-7044
9044 Buckingham Park Dr Des Plaines (60016) *(G-8246)*
**Ochem Inc**..........847 403-7044
2201 W Campbell Park Dr Chicago (60612) *(G-5967)*
**Oci Manufacturing Company, Oregon** *Also called ED Etnyre & Co (G-16822)*
**Ockerlund Industries Inc**..........630 620-1269
1555 W Wrightwood Ct Addison (60101) *(G-232)*
**Ockerlund Wood Products Co**..........630 620-1269
1555 W Wrightwood Ct Addison (60101) *(G-233)*
**Ocm Inc**..........847 462-4258
1215 Henri Dr Wauconda (60084) *(G-21490)*
**Ocs America Inc**..........630 595-0111
945 Dillon Dr Wood Dale (60191) *(G-22409)*
**Octane Motorsports LLC**..........224 419-5460
3056 Washington St 2b Waukegan (60085) *(G-21598)*
**Octapharma Plasma Inc**..........708 409-0900
17 W North Ave Northlake (60164) *(G-16446)*
**Octapharma Plasma Inc**..........630 375-0028
418 Hill Ave Aurora (60505) *(G-1198)*
**Octapharma Plasma Inc**..........217 546-8605
1770 Wabash Ave Springfield (62704) *(G-20491)*
**Octavia Tool & Gage Company**..........847 913-9233
135 Kelly St Elk Grove Village (60007) *(G-9661)*
**Octura Models Inc**..........847 674-7351
7351 Hamlin Ave Skokie (60076) *(G-20049)*
**Ocularis Pharma**..........708 712-6263
2436 S 6th Ave Riverside (60546) *(G-18032)*
**ODaniel Trucking Co**..........618 382-5371
1249 County Road 1500 N Carmi (62821) *(G-3076)*
**Odin Fire Protection District**..........618 775-8292
100 Perkins St Odin (62870) *(G-16741)*
**Odin Foam, Itasca** *Also called W S Darley & Co (G-12372)*
**Odin Industries Inc**..........630 365-2475
740 Hicks Dr Elburn (60119) *(G-8901)*
**Odl Inc (PA)**..........815 434-0655
1304 Starfire Dr Ottawa (61350) *(G-16974)*
**Odm Tool & Mfg Co Inc**..........708 485-6130
9550 Joliet Rd Hodgkins (60525) *(G-11978)*
**Odom Tool and Technology Inc**..........815 895-8545
216 W Page St Sycamore (60178) *(G-20811)*
**Odorite International Inc**..........816 920-5000
320 37th Ave Saint Charles (60174) *(G-19227)*
**Odra Inc**..........847 249-2910
4310 Lee Ave Gurnee (60031) *(G-11478)*
**Odum Concrete Products Inc**..........618 942-4572
201 Rushing Dr Herrin (62948) *(G-11751)*
**Odum Concrete Products Inc (PA)**..........618 993-6211
1800 N Court St Marion (62959) *(G-14275)*
**Odwalla Inc**..........773 687-8667
2837 N Cambridge Ave Chicago (60657) *(G-5968)*
**Odx Media LLC**..........847 868-0548
848 Dodge Ave Evanston (60202) *(G-10080)*
**Oec Graphics-Chicago LLC**..........630 455-6700
7630 S Quincy St Willowbrook (60527) *(G-22227)*
**Oei Products, Saint Charles** *Also called Oakland Enterprises Inc (G-19225)*
**Oelze Equipment Company LLC**..........618 327-9111
11800 County Highway 27 Nashville (62263) *(G-15845)*
**OEM Solutions Inc**..........708 574-8893
700 Commerce Dr Ste 500 Oak Brook (60523) *(G-16551)*
**Oems, Oak Brook** *Also called OEM Solutions Inc (G-16551)*
**Oerlikon**..........847 619-5541
1475 E Wdfield Rd Ste 201 Schaumburg (60173) *(G-19672)*
**Oerlikon Blzers Cating USA Inc (HQ)**..........847 619-5541
1475 E Wdfield Rd Ste 201 Schaumburg (60173) *(G-19673)*
**Oerlikon Blzers Cating USA Inc**..........847 695-5200
1181 Jansen Farm Ct Elgin (60123) *(G-9127)*
**OFallon Pressure Cast Co**..........618 632-8694
1418 Frontage Rd O Fallon (62269) *(G-16472)*
**Off The Press**..........815 436-9612
16041 S Lincoln Hwy # 103 Plainfield (60586) *(G-17634)*
**Offical Helicopter Blue Book, Wauconda** *Also called Helivalues (G-21466)*
**Office & Commercial RE Mag, Schaumburg** *Also called Bdc Capital Enterprises LLC (G-19457)*
**Office Assistants Inc**..........708 346-0505
9722 S Cicero Ave Oak Lawn (60453) *(G-16637)*
**Office of Mines & Minerals, Benton** *Also called Natural Resources Ill Dept (G-2036)*
**Office of Spcial Dputy Rceiver, Chicago** *Also called State of Illinois (G-6578)*
**Office Snax Inc**..........630 789-1783
125 Windsor Dr Ste 105 Oak Brook (60523) *(G-16552)*
**OfficeMax Incorporated**..........877 969-6629
800 W Bryn Mawr Ave Itasca (60143) *(G-12334)*
**OfficeMax North America Inc**..........815 748-3007
2350 Sycamore Rd Ste E Dekalb (60115) *(G-8111)*
**Officers Printing Inc**..........847 480-4663
710 Landwehr Rd Ste B Northbrook (60062) *(G-16323)*
**Official Issue Inc**..........847 795-1066
4640 N Oketo Ave Harwood Heights (60706) *(G-11688)*
**Offko Tool Inc**..........815 933-9474
1995 S Kensington Ave Kankakee (60901) *(G-12641)*
**Offsprings Inc**..........773 525-1800
1451 W Webster Ave Chicago (60614) *(G-5969)*
**Offworld Designs**..........815 786-7080
624 W Center St Sandwich (60548) *(G-19372)*
**Ofgd Inc**..........708 283-7101
2401 Lincoln Hwy Olympia Fields (60461) *(G-16804)*
**Ogden Foods LLC (PA)**..........773 277-8207
4320 W Ogden Ave Chicago (60623) *(G-5970)*
**Ogden Foods LLC**..........773 801-0125
4325 W Ogden Ave Chicago (60623) *(G-5971)*
**Ogden Metalworks Inc**..........217 582-2552
301 N Marilyn St Ogden (61859) *(G-16743)*
**Ogden Minuteman Inc**..........773 542-6917
3939 W Ogden Ave Chicago (60623) *(G-5972)*
**Ogden Offset Printers Inc**..........773 284-7797
6150 S Archer Ave Chicago (60638) *(G-5973)*
**Ogden Top & Trim Shop Inc**..........708 484-5422
6609 Ogden Ave Berwyn (60402) *(G-2070)*
**Ogle County Life**..........815 732-2156
311 Washington St Oregon (61061) *(G-16829)*
**Ogle County Newspaper, Oregon** *Also called B F Shaw Printing Company (G-16819)*
**Oglesby & Oglesby Gunmakers**..........217 487-7100
744 W Andrew Rd Springfield (62707) *(G-20492)*
**OGorman Son Carpentry Contrs**..........815 485-8997
1930 Airway Ct New Lenox (60451) *(G-15898)*
**OHara Autoglass Inc**..........217 323-2300
7339 Drainage Rd Beardstown (62618) *(G-1525)*
**OHare Precision Metals LLC**..........847 640-6050
2404 Hamilton Rd Arlington Heights (60005) *(G-811)*
**OHare Shell Partners Inc**..........847 678-1900
4111 Mannheim Rd Schiller Park (60176) *(G-19855)*
**OHare Spring Company Inc**..........847 298-1360
930 Lee St Elk Grove Village (60007) *(G-9662)*
**Ohio Medical, Gurnee** *Also called Omc Investors LLC (G-11480)*
**Ohio Medical LLC (HQ)**..........847 855-0500
1111 Lakeside Dr Gurnee (60031) *(G-11479)*
**Ohio Pulp Mills Inc (PA)**..........312 337-7822
737 N Michigan Ave # 1450 Chicago (60611) *(G-5974)*
**Ohmite Holding LLC (HQ)**..........847 258-0300
27501 Bella Vista Pkwy Warrenville (60555) *(G-21352)*
**Ohmite Manufacturing, Warrenville** *Also called Ohmite Holding LLC (G-21352)*
**Ohmx Corporation**..........847 491-8500
1801 Maple Ave Ste 18 Evanston (60201) *(G-10081)*
**Oi Glass Containers Oi G9**..........815 672-1548
901 N Shabbona St Streator (61364) *(G-20698)*
**Oil Filter Recyclers Inc**..........309 329-2131
Rr 1 Astoria (61501) *(G-935)*
**Oil-Dri Corporation America (PA)**..........312 321-1515
410 N Michigan Ave # 400 Chicago (60611) *(G-5975)*
**Oil-Dri Corporation America**..........618 745-6881
700 Industrial Park Rd Mounds (62964) *(G-15259)*
**Oil-Dri Corporation America**..........312 321-1516
410 N Michigan Aveste 400 Chicago (60611) *(G-5976)*
**Ojedas Welding Co**..........708 595-3799
312 S 3rd Ave Maywood (60153) *(G-14434)*
**Okamura Corp**..........312 645-0115
222 Merchandise Mart Plz 11-124 Chicago (60654) *(G-5977)*
**Okaw Truss Inc**..........217 543-3371
368 E Sr 133 Arthur (61911) *(G-915)*
**Okaw Valley Woodworking LLC**..........217 543-5180
432 E Sr 133 Arthur (61911) *(G-916)*
**Okawville Times**..........618 243-5563
109 E Walnut St Okawville (62271) *(G-16754)*

# ALPHABETIC SECTION

**Omni Products Inc (PA)**

**Olcott Plastics Inc** .................................................. 630 584-0555
  95 N 17th St  Saint Charles  (60174)  *(G-19228)*
**Old Blue Construction, Knoxville**  Also called Old Blue Illinois Inc *(G-12722)*
**Old Blue Illinois Inc** ................................................ 309 289-7921
  1277 Knox Road 1600 N  Knoxville  (61448)  *(G-12722)*
**Old Capitol Monument Works Inc (PA)** ................. 217 324-5673
  627 S 6th St  Vandalia  (62471)  *(G-21118)*
**Old Colony Baking Company Inc** .......................... 847 498-5434
  29699 Il Highway 29  Spring Valley  (61362)  *(G-20377)*
**Old Fashioned Meat Co Inc** ................................. 312 421-4555
  920 W Fulton Market  Chicago  (60607)  *(G-5978)*
**Old Gary Inc (HQ)** ................................................ 219 648-3000
  350 N Orleans St Fl 10  Chicago  (60654)  *(G-5979)*
**Old Heritage Creamery LLC** ................................. 217 268-4355
  222 N County Road 575e  Arcola  (61910)  *(G-680)*
**Old Mill Vineyard LLC** ........................................ 309 258-9954
  700 Coon Creek Rd  Metamora  (61548)  *(G-14746)*
**Old Style Iron Works Inc** ..................................... 773 265-5787
  7843 S Claremont Ave  Chicago  (60620)  *(G-5980)*
**Old Town Oil Evanston** ........................................ 312 787-9595
  1924 Central St  Evanston  (60201)  *(G-10082)*
**Old World Global LLC** ........................................ 800 323-5440
  4065 Commercial Ave  Northbrook  (60062)  *(G-16324)*
**Old World Inds Holdings LLC** ............................. 800 323-5440
  4065 Commercial Ave  Northbrook  (60062)  *(G-16325)*
**Old World Millworks, Maple Park**  Also called C A Larson & Son Inc *(G-14199)*
**Oldcastle Buildingenvelope Inc** ........................... 773 523-8400
  4161 S Morgan St  Chicago  (60609)  *(G-5981)*
**Oldcastle Buildingenvelope Inc** ........................... 630 250-7270
  2901 Lively Blvd  Elk Grove Village  (60007)  *(G-9663)*
**Oldcastle Lawn & Garden Inc** .............................. 618 274-1222
  1130 Queeny Ave  East Saint Louis  (62206)  *(G-8763)*
**Oldcastle Lawn & Grdn Midwest, East Saint Louis**  Also called Oldcastle Lawn & Garden Inc *(G-8763)*
**Oldcastle Precast Inc** ........................................... 309 661-4608
  1204 Aurora Way  Normal  (61761)  *(G-16082)*
**Olde Print Shoppe Inc** .......................................... 618 395-3833
  1314 E Main St  Olney  (62450)  *(G-16786)*
**Oldendorf Machining & Fabg** ............................... 708 946-2498
  3041 E Offner Rd  Beecher  (60401)  *(G-1600)*
**Ole Mexican Foods Inc** ........................................ 708 458-3296
  5140 W 73rd St Unit A  Bedford Park  (60638)  *(G-1568)*
**Ole Saltys of Rockford Inc** ................................... 815 637-2447
  3131 Summerdale Ave  Rockford  (61101)  *(G-18525)*
**Ole Saltys of Rockford Inc (PA)** ........................... 815 637-2447
  1920 E Riverside Blvd  Loves Park  (61111)  *(G-13970)*
**Olin Brass, East Alton**  Also called Gbc Metals LLC *(G-8603)*
**Olin Corporation** ................................................. 618 258-5668
  250 Olin Industrial Dr  East Alton  (62024)  *(G-8607)*
**Olin Corporation** ................................................. 618 258-2000
  600 Powder Mill Rd  East Alton  (62024)  *(G-8608)*
**Olin Corporation** ................................................. 618 258-2245
  15025 State Highway 111  Brighton  (62012)  *(G-2543)*
**Olin Engineered Systems Inc** .............................. 618 258-2874
  427 N Shamrock St  East Alton  (62024)  *(G-8609)*
**Olin Fabricated Products, East Alton**  Also called Olin Corporation *(G-8607)*
**Olive and Vinnies** ................................................ 630 534-6457
  449 N Main St  Glen Ellyn  (60137)  *(G-10984)*
**Olive Leclaire Oil Co** ............................................ 888 255-1867
  1524 Coral Dr  Yorkville  (60560)  *(G-22666)*
**Olive Mill, The, Geneva**  Also called Olive Oil Store Inc *(G-10856)*
**Olive Mount Mart** ................................................ 773 476-4964
  3536 W 63rd St  Chicago  (60629)  *(G-5982)*
**Olive Oil Market Place** ........................................ 618 304-3769
  1018 Richard Dr  Godfrey  (62035)  *(G-11231)*
**Olive Oil Marketplace Inc (PA)** ............................. 618 304-3769
  108 W 3rd St  Alton  (62002)  *(G-586)*
**Olive Oil Store Inc (PA)** ....................................... 630 262-0210
  315 James St  Geneva  (60134)  *(G-10856)*
**Olive Oils & More LLC** ......................................... 618 656-4645
  1990 Troy Rd Ste A  Edwardsville  (62025)  *(G-8811)*
**Olive Spartathlon Oil & Gre** ................................. 312 782-9855
  6301 N Tripp Ave  Chicago  (60646)  *(G-5983)*
**Olive Tree Foods Inc** ........................................... 847 872-2762
  2439 Galilee Ave  Zion  (60099)  *(G-22693)*
**Olivers Helicopters Inc** ....................................... 847 697-7346
  726 Tipperary St  Gilberts  (60136)  *(G-10930)*
**Olivet Woodworking** ........................................... 773 505-5225
  316 Hickory Rd  Lake Zurich  (60047)  *(G-13111)*
**Olivia R Aguilar-Camacho** ................................... 773 600-6864
  5757 N Sheridan Rd  Chicago  (60660)  *(G-5984)*
**Olney Daily Mail** .................................................. 618 393-2931
  206 S Whittle Ave  Olney  (62450)  *(G-16787)*
**Olney Daily Reporter, Olney**  Also called Gatehouse Media LLC *(G-16769)*
**Olney Machine & Design Inc** .............................. 618 392-6634
  4632 E Radio T  Olney  (62450)  *(G-16788)*
**Olon Decoratives, Geneva**  Also called Olon Industries Inc (us) *(G-10857)*
**Olon Industries Inc (us) (HQ)** .............................. 630 232-4705
  411 Union St  Geneva  (60134)  *(G-10857)*
**Olon Industries Inc (us)** ...................................... 630 232-4705
  411 Union St  Geneva  (60134)  *(G-10858)*
**Olshaws Interior Services** ................................... 312 421-3131
  407 S Peoria St  Chicago  (60607)  *(G-5985)*
**Olson Aluminum Castings Ltd** ............................ 815 229-3292
  2135 15th St  Rockford  (61104)  *(G-18526)*
**Olson Machining Inc** ........................................... 815 675-2900
  1804 Holian Dr  Spring Grove  (60081)  *(G-20354)*
**Olson Metal Products LLC (HQ)** ......................... 847 981-7550
  511 W Algonquin Rd  Arlington Heights  (60005)  *(G-812)*
**Olsun Electrics Corporation** ................................ 815 678-2421
  10901 Commercial St  Richmond  (60071)  *(G-17968)*
**Oltenia Inc** .......................................................... 773 987-2888
  4905 N Opal Ave  Norridge  (60706)  *(G-16107)*
**Oltman & Sons Inc** .............................................. 309 364-2849
  1526 County Rd 1500 E  Henry  (61537)  *(G-11745)*
**Oltman Ready Mix, Henry**  Also called Oltman & Sons Inc *(G-11745)*
**Oly Ola Edging Inc** .............................................. 630 833-3033
  124 E Saint Charles Rd  Villa Park  (60181)  *(G-21274)*
**Olympia Gyros Co, Chicago**  Also called Original Greek Specialties *(G-6012)*
**Olympia Manufacturing Inc** ................................. 309 387-2633
  101 Annie Ln  East Peoria  (61611)  *(G-8727)*
**Olympia Meat Packers Inc** .................................. 312 666-2222
  810 W Randolph St  Chicago  (60607)  *(G-5986)*
**Olympic Bindery Inc** ............................................ 847 577-8132
  1105 N Chestnut Ave  Arlington Heights  (60004)  *(G-813)*
**Olympic Controls Corp** ........................................ 847 742-3566
  1250 Crispin Dr  Elgin  (60123)  *(G-9128)*
**Olympic Meat Packing, Chicago**  Also called Olympia Meat Packers Inc *(G-5986)*
**Olympic Petroleum Corporation** .......................... 847 995-0996
  1171 Tower Rd  Schaumburg  (60173)  *(G-19674)*
**Olympic Petroleum Corporation (PA)** ................. 708 876-7900
  5000 W 41st St  Cicero  (60804)  *(G-7223)*
**Olympic Signs Inc** ............................................... 630 424-6100
  1130 N Garfield St  Lombard  (60148)  *(G-13835)*
**Olympic Steel Inc** ................................................ 847 584-4000
  1901 Mitchell Blvd  Schaumburg  (60193)  *(G-19675)*
**Olympic Trophy and Awards Co** ......................... 773 631-9500
  5860 N Northwest Hwy  Chicago  (60631)  *(G-5987)*
**Olympus America Inc** .......................................... 630 953-2080
  1900 Springer Dr  Lombard  (60148)  *(G-13836)*
**Olyola Etching, Villa Park**  Also called Oly Ola Edging Inc *(G-21274)*
**Om Printing Corporation** ..................................... 708 482-4750
  12250 S Cicero Ave Ste 110  Alsip  (60803)  *(G-503)*
**Omaha Grain & Fertilizer, Omaha**  Also called Hayden Mills Inc *(G-16807)*
**OMalley Welding and Fabg** ................................. 630 553-1604
  1209 Badger St  Yorkville  (60560)  *(G-22667)*
**Omar Medical Supplies Inc (PA)** ......................... 708 922-4377
  345 E Wacker Dr Unit 4601  Chicago  (60601)  *(G-5988)*
**OMAR SUPPLIES, Chicago**  Also called Omar Medical Supplies Inc *(G-5988)*
**Omc Investors LLC (HQ)** ..................................... 847 855-6220
  1111 Lakeside Dr  Gurnee  (60031)  *(G-11480)*
**Omcg North America, Bensenville**  Also called North America O M C G Inc *(G-1956)*
**Omega Door Frame Products** ............................. 630 773-9900
  1222 Ardmore Ave  Itasca  (60143)  *(G-12335)*
**Omega Moulding North Amer Inc** ....................... 630 509-2397
  1420 Thorndale Ave  Elk Grove Village  (60007)  *(G-9664)*
**Omega Partners** .................................................. 618 254-0603
  1402 S Delmar Ave  Hartford  (62048)  *(G-11613)*
**Omega Plating Inc** ............................................... 708 389-5410
  4704 137th St  Crestwood  (60445)  *(G-7496)*
**Omega Printing Inc** .............................................. 630 595-6344
  201 William St  Bensenville  (60106)  *(G-1958)*
**Omega Products Inc** ............................................ 618 939-3445
  502 Walnut St  Waterloo  (62298)  *(G-21403)*
**Omega Publishing Services Inc** .......................... 630 968-0440
  1137 Mistwood Pl  Downers Grove  (60515)  *(G-8498)*
**Omega Royal Graphics Inc** ................................. 847 952-8000
  1621 Brummel Ave  Elk Grove Village  (60007)  *(G-9665)*
**Omega Sign & Lighting Inc** ................................. 630 237-4397
  100 W Fay Ave  Addison  (60101)  *(G-234)*
**Omex Technologies Inc** ....................................... 847 850-5858
  300 E Marquardt Dr # 107  Wheeling  (60090)  *(G-22112)*
**Omg Inc** .............................................................. 630 228-8377
  300 S Mitchell Ct  Addison  (60101)  *(G-235)*
**Omg Handbags LLC** ........................................... 847 337-9499
  2045 W Grand Ave Ste 202  Chicago  (60612)  *(G-5989)*
**Omiotek Coil Spring Co (PA)** ............................... 630 495-4056
  833 N Ridge Ave  Lombard  (60148)  *(G-13837)*
**Omni Containment Systems LLC** ........................ 847 468-1772
  1501 Commerce Drive Elgin  Elgin  (60123)  *(G-9129)*
**Omni Craft Inc** ..................................................... 815 838-1285
  411 New Ave Unit 1  Lockport  (60441)  *(G-13736)*
**Omni Gear and Machine Corp** ............................. 815 723-4327
  90 Bissel St  Joliet  (60432)  *(G-12548)*
**Omni Materials Inc** .............................................. 618 262-5118
  1611 College Dr  Mount Carmel  (62863)  *(G-15279)*
**Omni Products Inc (PA)** ....................................... 815 344-3100
  3911 W Dayton St  McHenry  (60050)  *(G-14539)*

**Omni Publishing Co** — 847 483-9668
45 Versailles Ct  Wheeling (60090)  *(G-22113)*
**Omni Pump Repairs  Inc** — 847 451-0000
9224 Chestnut Ave  Franklin Park (60131)  *(G-10543)*
**Omni Vision Inc** — 630 893-1720
2000 Bloomingdale Rd # 245  Glendale Heights (60139)  *(G-11053)*
**Omni-Tech Systems Inc** — 309 962-2281
7 Demma Dr  Le Roy (61752)  *(G-13208)*
**Omnicare Group  Inc** — 708 949-8802
13557 Parkland Ct  Homer Glen (60491)  *(G-12084)*
**Omnimax International  Inc** — 309 747-2937
17904 E 3100 North Rd  Gridley (61744)  *(G-11410)*
**Omnimax International  Inc** — 770 449-7066
6235 W 73rd St  Bedford Park (60638)  *(G-1569)*
**Omnitronix Corporation** — 630 837-1400
349 Roma Jean Pkwy  Streamwood (60107)  *(G-20668)*
**Omron Automotive Elec Inc (HQ)** — 630 443-6800
3709 Ohio Ave  Saint Charles (60174)  *(G-19229)*
**Omron Electronics LLC (HQ)** — 847 843-7900
2895 Greenspt Pkwy 200  Hoffman Estates (60169)  *(G-12033)*
**Omron Global, Saint Charles** Also called Omron Automotive Elec Inc  *(G-19229)*
**Omron Healthcare  Inc (HQ)** — 847 680-6200
1925 W Field Ct  Lake Forest (60045)  *(G-12932)*
**On Cor, Aurora** Also called On-Cor Frozen Foods  LLC  *(G-1199)*
**On Paint It Company** — 219 765-5639
140 Tygert Ln  Dekalb (60115)  *(G-8112)*
**On Target Grinding and Mfg** — 708 418-3905
2250 199th St Ste 3  Lynwood (60411)  *(G-14022)*
**On Time Circuits Inc** — 630 955-1110
3121 Ridgeland Ave  Lisle (60532)  *(G-13636)*
**On Time Decorations Inc** — 708 357-6072
1411 S Laramie Ave  Cicero (60804)  *(G-7224)*
**On Time Envelopes & Printing** — 630 682-0466
615 Kimberly Dr  Carol Stream (60188)  *(G-3209)*
**On Time Printing and Finishing** — 708 544-4500
4206 Warren Ave  Hillside (60162)  *(G-11929)*
**On-Cor Frozen Foods  LLC (HQ)** — 630 692-2283
1225 Corp Blvd Ste 300  Aurora (60505)  *(G-1199)*
**On-Cor Frozen Foods  LLC** — 630 692-2283
1225 Corp Blvd Ste 300  Aurora (60505)  *(G-1200)*
**On-Line Compressor Inc** — 847 497-9750
5723 Weatherstone Way  Johnsburg (60051)  *(G-12440)*
**On-Target Sports Marketing** — 847 458-9360
9117 Trinity Dr  Lake In The Hills (60156)  *(G-13002)*
**Oncourse Learning, Hoffman Estates** Also called Tegna Inc  *(G-12064)*
**Oncquest** — 847 682-4703
43323 N Oak Crest Ln  Zion (60099)  *(G-22694)*
**Oncquest Pharma, Zion** Also called Oncquest  *(G-22694)*
**One Accord Unity  Nfp** — 630 649-0793
1886 Marne Rd  Bolingbrook (60490)  *(G-2355)*
**One Earth Energy  LLC** — 217 784-5321
202 Jordan Dr  Gibson City (60936)  *(G-10905)*
**One Love** — 708 832-1740
96 River Oaks Ctr Ste T13  Calumet City (60409)  *(G-2947)*
**One Plus Corp** — 847 498-0955
3182 Macarthur Blvd  Northbrook (60062)  *(G-16326)*
**One Shot LLC** — 773 646-5900
1701 E 122nd St  Chicago (60633)  *(G-5990)*
**One Way Safety  LLC** — 708 579-0229
418 Shawmut Ave Ste B  La Grange (60525)  *(G-12741)*
**One Way Solutions LLC** — 847 446-0872
400 Central Ave Ste 320  Northfield (60093)  *(G-16414)*
**Onefire Media Group  Inc** — 309 740-0345
214 Pecan St Ste 100  Peoria (61602)  *(G-17419)*
**ONeill Products Inc** — 312 243-3413
555 W 16th St  Chicago (60616)  *(G-5991)*
**Oneims Printing  LLC** — 773 297-2050
8833 Groil Pt Rd Ste 202  Skokie (60077)  *(G-20050)*
**Onion Company, The, Chicago** Also called Onion Inc  *(G-5993)*
**Onion Inc** — 312 751-0503
730 N Franklin St Ste 701  Chicago (60654)  *(G-5992)*
**Onion Inc (PA)** — 312 751-0503
730 N Franklin St Ste 701  Chicago (60654)  *(G-5993)*
**Onkens Incorporated** — 309 562-7477
320 E Main St  Easton (62633)  *(G-8778)*
**Online Bus Applications, Woodridge** Also called Anju Software  Inc  *(G-22452)*
**Online Eei, Romeoville** Also called Exex Holding Corporation  *(G-18823)*
**Online Electronics Inc** — 847 871-1700
1261 Jarvis Ave  Elk Grove Village (60007)  *(G-9666)*
**Online Inc** — 815 363-8008
4071 W Albany St  McHenry (60050)  *(G-14540)*
**Online Merchant Systems LLC** — 847 973-2337
35453 N Indian Ln  Ingleside (60041)  *(G-12197)*
**Only Child Brewing Company LLC** — 847 877-9822
1350 Tri State Pkwy # 124  Gurnee (60031)  *(G-11481)*
**Only For One Printers** — 847 947-4119
540 Allendale Dr Ste K  Wheeling (60090)  *(G-22114)*
**Onsite Woodwork Corporation (PA)** — 815 633-6400
4100 Rock Valley Pkwy  Loves Park (61111)  *(G-13971)*

**Onsrud Cutter LP, Waukegan** Also called Lmt Onsrud LP  *(G-21582)*
**Onsrud Machine Corp** — 847 520-5300
3926 Russett Ln  Northbrook (60062)  *(G-16327)*
**Ontario Die USA** — 630 761-6562
950 Paramount Pkwy Ste 3  Batavia (60510)  *(G-1477)*
**Onx USA LLC** — 630 343-8940
1001 Warrenville Rd  Lisle (60532)  *(G-13637)*
**Onyx Environmental Svcs LLC (HQ)** — 630 218-1500
700 E Bttrfield Rd Ste 201  Lombard (60148)  *(G-13838)*
**Oostman Fabricating & Wldg Inc** — 630 241-1315
45 E Chicago Ave  Westmont (60559)  *(G-21909)*
**Open Advanced Mri Crystl** — 815 444-1330
820 E Terra Cotta Ave # 102  Crystal Lake (60014)  *(G-7623)*
**Open Kitchens Inc (PA)** — 312 666-5334
1161 W 21st St  Chicago (60608)  *(G-5994)*
**Open Kitchens  Inc** — 312 666-5334
2141 S Racine Ave  Chicago (60608)  *(G-5995)*
**Open Point Solutions, Chicago** Also called Productive Edge LLC  *(G-6207)*
**Open Waters Seafood Company** — 847 329-8585
5010 Howard St  Skokie (60077)  *(G-20051)*
**Opportunity  Inc** — 847 831-9400
1200 Old Skokie Rd  Highland Park (60035)  *(G-11860)*
**Opsdirt  LLC** — 773 412-1179
948 N Winchester Ave # 3  Chicago (60622)  *(G-5996)*
**Optech Ortho & Prosth Svcs** — 708 364-9700
18016 Wolf Rd  Orland Park (60467)  *(G-16880)*
**Optech Ortho & Prosth Svcs (PA)** — 815 932-8564
119 E Court St Ste 100  Kankakee (60901)  *(G-12642)*
**Optek, Batavia** Also called Aggressive Motor Sports  *(G-1405)*
**Opti-Sand Incorporated** — 630 293-1245
31 W 037 North Ave  West Chicago (60185)  *(G-21753)*
**Opti-Vue Inc** — 630 274-6121
224 James St  Bensenville (60106)  *(G-1959)*
**Optical Systems, Arlington Heights** Also called Vibgyor Optics Inc  *(G-864)*
**Opticent  Inc** — 410 829-7384
600 Davis St Fl 3  Evanston (60201)  *(G-10083)*
**Opticote  Inc** — 847 678-8900
10455 Seymour Ave  Franklin Park (60131)  *(G-10544)*
**Optimal Automatics Co** — 847 439-9110
120 Stanley St  Elk Grove Village (60007)  *(G-9667)*
**Optimal Construction Svcs Inc** — 630 365-5050
843 Shepherd Ln  Elburn (60119)  *(G-8902)*
**Optimal Energy LLC** —
507 W Golf Rd  Arlington Heights (60005)  *(G-814)*
**Optimum Granite & Marble  Inc** — 800 920-6033
735 Schneider Dr Ste 4  South Elgin (60177)  *(G-20222)*
**Optimum Nutrition, Downers Grove** Also called Glanbia Performance Ntrtn Inc  *(G-8451)*
**Optimus Advantage LLC** — 847 905-1000
10 S Lasalle  Chicago (60606)  *(G-5997)*
**Optiva Signs, Chicago** Also called Ilight Technologies  Inc  *(G-5152)*
**Opw Fuel MGT Systems Inc (HQ)** — 708 352-9617
6900 Santa Fe Dr  Hodgkins (60525)  *(G-11979)*
**Opw Fueling Components Inc** — 708 485-4200
6900 Santa Fe Dr  Hodgkins (60525)  *(G-11980)*
**Opw Fueling Management Systems, Hodgkins** Also called Opw Fueling Components Inc  *(G-11980)*
**Oquawka Boats and Fabrications** — 309 867-2213
1312 E State Highway 164  Oquawka (61469)  *(G-16812)*
**Oquawka Cross Current Newsppr, Monmouth** Also called Gatehouse Media  LLC  *(G-15013)*
**Ora Holdings, Waukegan** Also called Rock-Tred 2 LLC  *(G-21610)*
**Oracle Corporation** — 773 404-9300
980 N Michigan Ave # 1400  Chicago (60611)  *(G-5998)*
**Oracle Corporation** — 312 692-5270
330 N Wabash Ave Ste 2400  Chicago (60611)  *(G-5999)*
**Oracle Corporation** — 630 931-6400
17th Fl 2 Pierce Pl  Itasca (60143)  *(G-12336)*
**Oracle Corporation** — 262 957-3000
233 S Wacker Dr Ste 4500  Chicago (60606)  *(G-6000)*
**Oracle Hcm User Group Inc** — 312 222-9350
330 N Wabash Ave Ste 2000  Chicago (60611)  *(G-6001)*
**Oracle Systems Corporation** — 312 245-1580
401 N Michigan Ave # 2200  Chicago (60611)  *(G-6002)*
**Orange Crush  LLC** — 847 537-7900
231 Wheeling Rd  Wheeling (60090)  *(G-22115)*
**Orange Crush  LLC (PA)** — 708 544-9440
321 Center St  Hillside (60162)  *(G-11930)*
**Orange Crush  LLC** — 847 428-6176
507 Rock Road Dr  East Dundee (60118)  *(G-8650)*
**Orange Crush  LLC** — 630 739-5560
1001 N Independence Blvd  Romeoville (60446)  *(G-18856)*
**Orat Inc** — 630 567-6728
761 N 17th St Ste 4  Saint Charles (60174)  *(G-19230)*
**Oratech Inc** — 217 793-2735
4777 Alex Blvd  Springfield (62711)  *(G-20493)*
**Orbis Rpm  LLC** — 217 876-8655
1781 Hubbard Ave  Decatur (62526)  *(G-7922)*
**Orbis Rpm  LLC** — 630 844-9255
261 Airport Rd  North Aurora (60542)  *(G-16139)*

**Orbis Rpm LLC** 309 697-1549
4428 Ricketts Ave Bartonville (61607) *(G-1398)*
**Orbis Rpm LLC** 773 376-9775
4400 W 45th St Chicago (60632) *(G-6003)*
**Orbit Enterprises Inc** 630 469-3405
3525 S Cass Ct Unit T3n Oak Brook (60523) *(G-16553)*
**Orbit Machining Company** 847 678-1050
9440 Ainslie St Schiller Park (60176) *(G-19856)*
**Orbit Room** 773 588-8540
2959 N California Ave Chicago (60618) *(G-6004)*
**Orbus Exhibit & Display Group, Woodridge** *Also called Orbus LLC (G-22506)*
**Orbus LLC (PA)** 630 226-1155
9033 Murphy Rd Woodridge (60517) *(G-22506)*
**Orbus LLC** 847 647-1012
111 Rawls Rd Des Plaines (60018) *(G-8247)*
**Orca Graphic House, Chicago** *Also called Case Paluch & Associates Inc (G-4248)*
**Orchard Hill Cabinetry Inc (PA)** 312 829-4300
401 N Western Ave Ste 3 Chicago (60612) *(G-6005)*
**Orchard Products Inc** 847 818-6760
500 W Huntington Commons Mount Prospect (60056) *(G-15359)*
**Orchard View Winery** 618 547-9911
307 2nd St Alma (62807) *(G-422)*
**Orchid Labs, Downers Grove** *Also called Flavorchem Corporation (G-8443)*
**Ordner Well Service Inc** 618 676-1950
946 Sunset Rd Sw Clay City (62824) *(G-7267)*
**Orecx** 312 895-5292
1 N La Salle St Ste 1375 Chicago (60602) *(G-6006)*
**Oregon Fire Protection Dst** 815 732-7214
106 S 1st St Oregon (61061) *(G-16830)*
**Oreillys Auto Parts Store** 847 360-0012
2507 Grand Ave Waukegan (60085) *(G-21599)*
**Organ Recovery Systems Inc** 847 824-2600
1 Pierce Pl Ste 475w Itasca (60143) *(G-12337)*
**Organized Home** 217 698-6460
2601 Chuckwagon Dr Springfield (62711) *(G-20494)*
**Organized Noise Inc** 630 820-9855
231 Raintree Ct Aurora (60504) *(G-1059)*
**Organnica Inc** 312 925-7272
3437 Maple Ave Berwyn (60402) *(G-2071)*
**Organon API, Des Plaines** *Also called Aspen API Inc (G-8152)*
**Orica Nitrogen, Morris** *Also called Orica USA Inc (G-15125)*
**Orica USA Inc** 815 357-8711
7700 W Dupont Rd Morris (60450) *(G-15125)*
**Orient Machining & Welding Inc** 708 371-3500
14501 Wood St Ste A Dixmoor (60426) *(G-8320)*
**Oriental Kitchen Corporation (PA)** 312 738-2850
223 N Justine St Chicago (60607) *(G-6007)*
**Oriental Kitchen Corporation** 312 738-2850
223 N Justine St Chicago (60607) *(G-6008)*
**Oriental Noodle** 773 279-1595
3808 W Lawrence Ave Chicago (60625) *(G-6009)*
**Origami Risk LLC (PA)** 312 546-6515
222 Merchandise Mart Plz # 2300 Chicago (60654) *(G-6010)*
**Original Ferrara Bakery, Chicago** *Also called Original Ferrara Inc (G-6011)*
**Original Ferrara Inc** 312 666-2200
2210 W Taylor St Chicago (60612) *(G-6011)*
**Original Greek Specialties** 773 735-2250
5757 W 59th St Chicago (60638) *(G-6012)*
**Original Notolli & Sons, Chicago** *Also called George Nottoli & Sons Inc (G-4944)*
**Original Shutter Man** 773 966-7160
1231 W 74th Pl Chicago (60636) *(G-6013)*
**Original Smith Printing Inc (HQ)** 309 663-0325
2 Hardman Dr Bloomington (61701) *(G-2207)*
**Original Systems** 847 945-7660
2590 Chianti Trl Riverwoods (60015) *(G-18041)*
**Orinoco Systems LLC (PA)** 630 510-0775
300 S Carlton Ave Ste 100 Wheaton (60187) *(G-21971)*
**Orion Enterprises, Monmouth** *Also called Forman Co Inc (G-15012)*
**Orion Media Logistics Inc** 847 866-6215
1619 Florence Ave Evanston (60201) *(G-10084)*
**Orion Metals Co** 847 412-9532
3318 Maple Leaf Dr Glenview (60026) *(G-11177)*
**Orion Offset, Palatine** *Also called Orion Star Corp (G-17061)*
**Orion Petro Corporation (PA)** 618 244-2370
125 N 11th St Rear Mount Vernon (62864) *(G-15436)*
**Orion Star Corp** 847 776-2300
236 E Northwest Hwy Ste A Palatine (60067) *(G-17061)*
**Orion Tool Die & Machine Co** 309 526-3303
1400 16th St Orion (61273) *(G-16835)*
**Orland Park Bakery Ltd** 708 349-8516
14850 S La Grange Rd Orland Park (60462) *(G-16881)*
**Orland Sports Ltd** 773 685-3711
5610 W Bloomingdale Ave # 1 Chicago (60639) *(G-6014)*
**Orlandi Statuary Company** 773 489-0303
1801 N Central Park Ave Chicago (60647) *(G-6015)*
**Orli Diamonds, Chicago** *Also called Steinmetz R (us) Ltd (G-6586)*
**Ormco, Decatur** *Also called Ornamental Metalworks Inc (G-7923)*
**Ornamental Iron Shop** 618 281-6072
148 Hill Castle Dr Columbia (62236) *(G-7361)*
**Ornamental Metalworks Inc** 217 424-2326
2136 N Woodford St # 100 Decatur (62526) *(G-7923)*
**Orochem Technologies Inc** 630 210-8300
340 Shuman Blvd Naperville (60563) *(G-15719)*
**Orora North America** 630 613-2600
100 E Progress Rd Lombard (60148) *(G-13839)*
**Orora Packaging Solutions** 815 895-2343
215 Fair St Sycamore (60178) *(G-20812)*
**Orora Visual TX LLC** 847 647-1900
7400 N Lehigh Ave Niles (60714) *(G-16014)*
**Orr Marketing Corp** 847 401-5171
784 Scott Dr Elgin (60123) *(G-9130)*
**Orren Pickell Builders Inc** 847 572-5200
550 W Frontage Rd # 3800 Northfield (60093) *(G-16415)*
**Orsolinis Welding & Fabg** 773 722-9855
3040 W Carroll Ave Chicago (60612) *(G-6016)*
**Orstrom Woodworking Ltd** 847 697-1163
1502 Sawgrass Ct Elgin (60123) *(G-9131)*
**Ortho Molecular Products Inc (PA)** 815 337-0089
1991 Duncan Pl Woodstock (60098) *(G-22596)*
**Ortho Seating LLC** 773 276-3539
4444 W Ohio St Chicago (60624) *(G-6017)*
**Ortho-Clinical Diagnostics Inc** 618 281-3882
8 Briarhill Ln Columbia (62236) *(G-7362)*
**Orthotech Sports - Med Eqp Inc (PA)** 618 942-6611
1211 Weaver Rd Herrin (62948) *(G-11752)*
**Orthotic & Prosthetic Assoc** 217 789-1450
355 W Carpenter St Ste B Springfield (62702) *(G-20495)*
**Ortman Fluid Power Inc** 217 277-0321
1400 N 30th St Ste 20 Quincy (62301) *(G-17863)*
**Ortman-Mccain Co** 312 666-2244
2303 W 18th St Chicago (60608) *(G-6018)*
**Orvis Company Inc** 312 440-0662
142 E Ontario St Ste 1 Chicago (60611) *(G-6019)*
**Os Farr, Crystal Lake** *Also called Camfil USA Inc (G-7549)*
**Osbon Lithographers** 847 825-7727
1218 S Crescent Ave Park Ridge (60068) *(G-17214)*
**Osborne Publications Inc** 217 422-9702
132 S Water St Ste 424 Decatur (62523) *(G-7924)*
**Osbornes Mch Weld Fabrication** 217 795-4716
8269 Dunbar Rd Argenta (62501) *(G-691)*
**Oscars Foods Inc (PA)** 773 622-6822
6125 W Belmont Ave Chicago (60634) *(G-6020)*
**OSG Power Tools Inc** 630 561-4008
759 Industrial Dr Bensenville (60106) *(G-1960)*
**OSG Usa Inc (HQ)** 630 790-1400
676 E Fullerton Ave Glendale Heights (60139) *(G-11054)*
**OSG Usa Inc** 630 274-2100
759 Industrial Dr Bensenville (60106) *(G-1961)*
**OSI Group, West Chicago** *Also called OSI Industries LLC (G-21754)*
**OSI Group LLC (PA)** 630 851-6600
1225 Corp Blvd Ste 300 Aurora (60505) *(G-1201)*
**OSI Industries LLC** 630 231-9090
711 Industrial Dr West Chicago (60185) *(G-21754)*
**OSI Industries LLC (HQ)** 630 851-6600
1225 Corp Blvd Ste 105 Aurora (60505) *(G-1202)*
**OSI Industries LLC** 773 847-2000
4545 S Racine Ave Chicago (60609) *(G-6021)*
**OSI International Foods Ltd** 630 851-6600
1225 Corp Blvd Ste 300 Aurora (60504) *(G-1060)*
**Osmer Woodworking Inc** 815 973-5809
406 E Bradshaw St Dixon (61021) *(G-8338)*
**Oso Technologies Inc** 844 777-2575
722 W Killarney St Urbana (61801) *(G-21096)*
**Osorio Iron Works** 773 772-4060
4515 W Thomas St Chicago (60651) *(G-6022)*
**Ostrom & Co Inc** 503 281-6469
28w600 Roosevelt Rd Winfield (60190) *(G-22288)*
**Ostrom Glass & Metal Works, Winfield** *Also called Ostrom & Co Inc (G-22288)*
**Ot Systems Limited** 630 554-9178
18 W Main St Plano (60545) *(G-17669)*
**Otak International Inc** 630 373-9229
2080 N 16th Ave Melrose Park (60160) *(G-14679)*
**Otis Elevator Company** 312 454-1616
651 W Washington Blvd 1n Chicago (60661) *(G-6023)*
**Otis Elevator Company** 618 529-3411
201 W Kennicott St Carbondale (62901) *(G-3016)*
**Otr Wheel Engineering Inc (HQ)** 217 223-7705
4400 Kochs Ln Quincy (62305) *(G-17864)*
**Ottawa Publishing Co Inc (HQ)** 815 433-2000
110 W Jefferson St Ottawa (61350) *(G-16975)*
**Ottawa Publishing Co Inc** 815 434-3330
300 W Joliet St Ottawa (61350) *(G-16976)*
**Otten Construction Co Inc** 618 768-4310
786 Old Saint Louis Rd Addieville (62214) *(G-13)*
**Otter Creek Sand & Gravel** 309 759-4293
4125 N Stoneyard Rd Havana (62644) *(G-11700)*
**Otto & Sons Div, Aurora** *Also called OSI Industries LLC (G-1202)*
**Ottos Canvas Shop** 217 543-3307
1749b State Highway 133 Arthur (61911) *(G-917)*

ALPHABETIC

**Ottos Drapery Service Inc**...773 777-7755
5219 W Cullom Ave Chicago (60641) *(G-6024)*
**Otus LLC**...312 229-7648
900 N Michigan Ave # 1600 Chicago (60611) *(G-6025)*
**Outback USA Inc**...863 699-2220
5n825 Prairie Springs Dr Saint Charles (60175) *(G-19231)*
**Outbreak Designs**...217 370-5418
1458 S Main St South Jacksonville (62650) *(G-20311)*
**Outdoor Advertising, Rock Falls** *Also called Turnroth Sign Company Inc (G-18156)*
**Outdoor Environments LLC**...847 325-5000
288 S Buffalo Grove Rd Buffalo Grove (60089) *(G-2749)*
**Outdoor Notebook Publishing**...630 257-6534
14805 131st St Lemont (60439) *(G-13246)*
**Outdoor Power Inc**...217 228-9890
2703 Broadway St Quincy (62301) *(G-17865)*
**Outdoor Solutions Team Inc**...312 446-4220
1315 Southwind Dr Northbrook (60062) *(G-16328)*
**Outdoor Space LLC**...773 857-5296
3120 N Sheffield Ave # 1 Chicago (60657) *(G-6026)*
**Outdoors Synergy Products Tech**...630 552-3111
431 E South St Plano (60545) *(G-17670)*
**Outlaw Tees**...217 453-2359
85 N Iowa St Nauvoo (62354) *(G-15856)*
**Outokmpu High Prfmce Stainless, Bannockburn** *Also called Outokumpu Stainless Usa LLC (G-1263)*
**Outokumpu Stainless Usa LLC**...847 405-6604
2275 Half Day Rd Ste 300 Deerfield (60015) *(G-8045)*
**Outokumpu Stainless Usa LLC**...847 317-1400
2275 Half Day Rd Ste 300 Bannockburn (60015) *(G-1263)*
**Output Medical Inc**...630 430-8024
4660 N Ravenswood Ave Chicago (60640) *(G-6027)*
**Outre', Evanston** *Also called Filmfax Magazine Inc (G-10037)*
**Outside Plant Magazine, Schaumburg** *Also called Practical Communications Inc (G-19699)*
**Outward Houndraise The Woof, Northbrook** *Also called Kyjen Company LLC (G-16291)*
**Oval Brand Fire Products, Glendale Heights** *Also called Oval Fire Products Corporation (G-11055)*
**Oval Fire Products Corporation**...630 635-5000
115 W Lake Dr Ste 300 Glendale Heights (60139) *(G-11055)*
**Overgrad Inc**...312 324-4952
2545 W Diversey Ave # 215 Chicago (60647) *(G-6028)*
**Overhead Door Corporation**...630 775-9118
295 S Prospect Ave Itasca (60143) *(G-12338)*
**Overhead Door Solutions Inc**...847 359-3667
920 W Kenilworth Ave Palatine (60067) *(G-17062)*
**Overnite Protos, Elk Grove Village** *Also called Online Electronics Inc (G-9666)*
**Overt Press Inc**...773 284-0909
4625 W 53rd St Chicago (60632) *(G-6029)*
**Overton Chicago Gear Corp**...773 638-0508
2823 W Fulton St Chicago (60612) *(G-6030)*
**Ovis Loader Attachments Inc**...618 203-2757
1555 S Wall St Carbondale (62901) *(G-3017)*
**Owanza Corporation**...312 281-2900
300 N La Salle Dr # 4295 Chicago (60654) *(G-6031)*
**Owen Plastics LLC**...847 683-2054
150 French Rd Burlington (60109) *(G-2813)*
**Owen Walker**...217 285-4012
837 W Adams St Pittsfield (62363) *(G-17572)*
**Owens Corning Sales LLC**...815 226-4627
2710 Laude Dr Rockford (61109) *(G-18527)*
**Owens Corning Sales LLC**...708 594-6911
5824 S Archer Rd Argo (60501) *(G-694)*
**Owens Corning Sales LLC**...708 594-6935
7800 W 59th St Argo (60501) *(G-695)*
**Owens Welding & Fabricating**...773 265-9900
548 N Sacramento Blvd Chicago (60612) *(G-6032)*
**Owens-Brockway Glass Cont Inc**...815 672-3141
901 N Shabbona St Streator (61364) *(G-20699)*
**Owens-Corning Fiberglass Tech**...708 563-9091
7734 W 59th St Argo (60501) *(G-696)*
**Own The Night App**...773 216-0245
1735 N Paulina St Apt 305 Chicago (60622) *(G-6033)*
**Ox Paperboard LLC**...309 346-4118
1525 S 2nd St Pekin (61554) *(G-17277)*
**Oxbow Carbon LLC**...630 257-7751
12308 New Ave Lemont (60439) *(G-13247)*
**Oxbow Midwest, Lemont** *Also called Oxbow Carbon LLC (G-13247)*
**Oxbow Midwest Calcining LLC**...630 257-7751
12308 New Ave Lemont (60439) *(G-13248)*
**Oxxford Clothes Xx Inc (HQ)**...312 829-3600
1220 W Van Buren St Fl 7 Chicago (60607) *(G-6034)*
**OXY Chem, Sauget** *Also called Occidental Chemical Corp (G-19388)*
**Oxytech Systems Inc**...847 888-8611
852 Commerce Pkwy Carpentersville (60110) *(G-3293)*
**Ozinga Bros Inc (PA)**...708 326-4200
19001 Old Lagrange Rd # 30 Mokena (60448) *(G-14889)*
**Ozinga Bros Inc**...708 326-4200
1750 State St Chicago Heights (60411) *(G-7116)*
**Ozinga Chicago Ready Mix Con**...708 479-9050
12660 S Laramie Ave Alsip (60803) *(G-504)*
**Ozinga Chicago Ready Mix Con**...312 432-5700
1818 E 103rd St Chicago (60617) *(G-6035)*
**Ozinga Chicago Ready Mix Con**...773 862-2817
2001 N Mendell St Chicago (60614) *(G-6036)*
**Ozinga Chicago Ready Mix Con (HQ)**...847 447-0353
2255 S Lumber St Chicago (60616) *(G-6037)*
**Ozinga Chicago Ready Mix Con**...312 432-5700
2255 S Lumber St Chicago (60616) *(G-6038)*
**Ozinga Concrete Products Inc**...847 426-0920
2521 Tech Dr Ste 212 Elgin (60124) *(G-9132)*
**Ozinga Concrete Products Inc**...708 479-9050
401 Brier Hill Rd Hampshire (60140) *(G-11557)*
**Ozinga Indiana Rdymx Con Inc**...708 479-9050
19001 Old Lagrange Rd Mokena (60448) *(G-14890)*
**Ozinga Materials Inc**...309 364-3401
19001 Old Lagrange Rd Mokena (60448) *(G-14891)*
**Ozinga Ready Mix Concrete Inc**...708 326-4200
19001 Old Lagrange Rd # 300 Mokena (60448) *(G-14892)*
**Ozinga S Subn Rdymx Con Inc**...708 479-3080
18825 Old Lagrange Rd Mokena (60448) *(G-14893)*
**Ozinga S Subn Rdymx Con Inc (HQ)**...708 326-4201
19001 Old Lagrange Rd # 300 Mokena (60448) *(G-14894)*
**Ozinga South Suburban RMC, Mokena** *Also called Ozinga S Subn Rdymx Con Inc (G-14894)*
**Ozko Sign & Lighting Company**...224 653-8531
1119 Lunt Ave Schaumburg (60193) *(G-19676)*
**Ozonology Inc**...847 998-8808
1515 Paddock Dr Northbrook (60062) *(G-16329)*
**P & A Driveline & Machine Inc**...630 860-7474
292 Devon Ave Ste 18 Bensenville (60106) *(G-1962)*
**P & D Center, Chicago** *Also called Americas Community Bankers (G-3884)*
**P & G Keene Elec Rbldrs LLC**...708 430-5770
8432 Beloit Ave Bridgeview (60455) *(G-2516)*
**P & G Machine & Tool Inc**...618 283-0273
1910 Illini Ave Vandalia (62471) *(G-21119)*
**P & G Machine Shop, Vandalia** *Also called P & G Machine & Tool Inc (G-21119)*
**P & H Manufacturing Co**...217 774-2123
604 S Lodge St Shelbyville (62565) *(G-19911)*
**P & H Pattern Inc**...815 795-2449
225 Lincoln St Marseilles (61341) *(G-14315)*
**P & J Technologies**...847 995-1108
1356 Saint Claire Pl Schaumburg (60173) *(G-19677)*
**P & L Mark-It Inc (PA)**...630 879-7590
291 Oswald Ave Batavia (60510) *(G-1478)*
**P & L Tool & Manufacturing Co**...708 754-4777
3624 Union Ave Steger (60475) *(G-20575)*
**P & M Ornamental Ir Works Inc**...708 267-2868
1200 N 31st Ave Melrose Park (60160) *(G-14680)*
**P & P Artec Handrail Div, Wood Dale** *Also called P & P Artec Inc (G-22410)*
**P & P Artec Inc (HQ)**...630 860-2990
700 Creel Dr Wood Dale (60191) *(G-22410)*
**P & P Industries Inc (PA)**...815 623-3297
2100 Enterprise Dr Sterling (61081) *(G-20602)*
**P & P Press Inc**...309 691-8511
6513 N Galena Rd Peoria (61614) *(G-17420)*
**P & S Cochran Printers Inc (PA)**...309 691-6668
8325 N Allen Rd Peoria (61615) *(G-17421)*
**P B A Corp**...312 666-7370
522 N Western Ave Chicago (60612) *(G-6039)*
**P B R W Enterprises Inc**...815 337-5519
12201 Baker Ter Woodstock (60098) *(G-22597)*
**P Double Corporation**...630 585-7160
1100 Fox Valley Ctr Aurora (60504) *(G-1061)*
**P E R, Plainfield** *Also called Precision Engine Rebuilders (G-17642)*
**P F Pettibone & Co**...815 344-7811
2220 Il Route 176 A Crystal Lake (60014) *(G-7624)*
**P H C Enterprises Inc**...847 816-7373
222 Hawthorn Vlg Cmns Vernon Hills (60061) *(G-21186)*
**P I P, Normal** *Also called Bloom-Norm Printing Inc (G-16065)*
**P I W Corporation**...708 301-5100
15765 Annico Dr Homer Glen (60491) *(G-12085)*
**P J Repair Service Inc**...618 548-5690
108 S Missouri Ave Salem (62881) *(G-19341)*
**P K B, Westmont** *Also called Pet King Brands Inc (G-21911)*
**P K Neuses Incorporated**...847 253-6555
1401 Rohlwing Rd Rolling Meadows (60008) *(G-18756)*
**P L R Sales Inc**...217 733-2245
14187 N 850 E Rd Fairmount (61841) *(G-10164)*
**P M Armor Inc**...847 797-9940
237 E Prospect Ave Mount Prospect (60056) *(G-15360)*
**P M C, Romeoville** *Also called Precision McHned Cmponents Inc (G-18860)*
**P M C, Spring Grove** *Also called Precision Molded Concepts (G-20358)*
**P M Mfg Services Inc**...630 553-6924
9626 Lisbon Rd Yorkville (60560) *(G-22668)*
**P M Mold Company (PA)**...847 923-5400
800 Estes Ave Schaumburg (60193) *(G-19678)*
**P M Mold Company**...847 923-5400
800 Estes Ave Schaumburg (60193) *(G-19679)*
**P M P, Addison** *Also called Precision Metal Products Inc (G-252)*

# ALPHABETIC SECTION

P M S Consolidated .................................................847 364-0011
  2400 E Devon Ave  Elk Grove Village  (60007)  *(G-9668)*
P N K Ventures Inc .................................................630 527-0500
  1701 Quincy Ave Ste 24  Naperville  (60540)  *(G-15720)*
P P Graphics Inc .....................................................708 343-2530
  1939 S Mannheim Rd  Westchester  (60154)  *(G-21852)*
P P S, Saint Charles  *Also called Packaging Prtg Specialists Inc (G-19232)*
P R Manufacturing Co ...........................................309 596-2986
  2650 85th Ave  Viola  (61486)  *(G-21293)*
P R S, Jacksonville  *Also called Pallet Repair Systems  Inc (G-12406)*
P S A, Wauconda  *Also called Professional Sales Associates (G-21493)*
P S G, Franklin Park  *Also called Prairie State Impressions LLC (G-10557)*
P S Greetings  Inc (PA) ..........................................708 831-5340
  5730 N Tripp Ave  Chicago  (60646)  *(G-6040)*
P S Greetings  Inc ..................................................847 673-7255
  4901 Main St  Skokie  (60077)  *(G-20052)*
P T I, Aurora  *Also called Processing Tech Intl LLC (G-1070)*
P T L Manufacturing  Inc .......................................618 277-6789
  101 Industrial Dr  Belleville  (62220)  *(G-1663)*
P V S Manufacturing Div, Woodstock  *Also called Wheeling Service & Supply (G-22624)*
P W C E, Goodfield  *Also called Paul Wever Construction Eqp Co (G-11248)*
P W C Sports .........................................................708 516-6183
  8200 185th St  Tinley Park  (60487)  *(G-20936)*
P&L Group Ltd ........................................................773 660-1930
  24 E 107th St  Chicago  (60628)  *(G-6041)*
P-Americas LLC .....................................................773 893-2300
  1400 W 35th St  Chicago  (60609)  *(G-6042)*
P-Americas LLC .....................................................309 266-2400
  801 W Birchwood St  Morton  (61550)  *(G-15173)*
P-Americas LLC .....................................................773 451-4499
  4931 S Union Ave  Chicago  (60609)  *(G-6043)*
P-Americas LLC .....................................................312 821-2266
  555 W Monroe St Ste 1  Chicago  (60661)  *(G-6044)*
P-Americas LLC .....................................................773 624-8013
  650 W 51st St  Chicago  (60609)  *(G-6045)*
P-K Tool & Mfg Co (PA) .......................................773 235-4700
  4700 W Le Moyne St  Chicago  (60651)  *(G-6046)*
P.F., Crystal Lake  *Also called P F Pettibone & Co (G-7624)*
Paani Foods Inc .....................................................312 420-4624
  6167 N Broadway St # 300  Chicago  (60660)  *(G-6047)*
Paap Printing .........................................................217 345-6878
  507 Jackson Ave  Charleston  (61920)  *(G-3607)*
Paasche Airbrush Co .............................................773 867-9191
  4311 N Normandy Ave  Chicago  (60634)  *(G-6048)*
Pac Team US Productions  LLC ...........................773 360-8960
  4447 W Armitage Ave  Chicago  (60639)  *(G-6049)*
Pac-Clad Metal Roofing, Elk Grove Village  *Also called Petersen Aluminum Corporation (G-9676)*
Pacap LLC .............................................................773 754-7089
  4753 N Broadway St # 1034  Chicago  (60640)  *(G-6050)*
Pace Foundation ....................................................309 691-3553
  3528 W Chartwell Rd  Peoria  (61614)  *(G-17422)*
Pace Industries  Inc (PA) .......................................312 226-5500
  2545 W Polk St  Chicago  (60612)  *(G-6051)*
Pace Machinery Group  Inc ..................................630 377-1750
  4n944 Old Lafox Rd  Wasco  (60183)  *(G-21373)*
Pace Print Plus ......................................................847 381-1720
  1010 W Northwest Hwy  Barrington  (60010)  *(G-1296)*
Pacific Bearing Corp (PA) .....................................815 389-5600
  6402 E Rockton Rd  Roscoe  (61073)  *(G-18911)*
Pacific Coast Feather Company ..........................847 827-1210
  414 E Golf Rd  Des Plaines  (60016)  *(G-8248)*
Pacific Cycle Inc ....................................................618 393-2508
  4730 E Radio Tower Ln  Olney  (62450)  *(G-16789)*
Pacific Electronics Corp .......................................815 206-5450
  10200 Us Highway 14  Woodstock  (60098)  *(G-22598)*
Pacific Ethanol Canton  LLC ................................309 347-9200
  1300 S 2nd St  Pekin  (61554)  *(G-17278)*
Pacific Ethanol Pekin  Inc ....................................309 347-9200
  1300 S 2nd St  Pekin  (61554)  *(G-17279)*
Pacific Granites Inc ..............................................312 835-7777
  5 S Wabash Ave Ste 511  Chicago  (60603)  *(G-6052)*
Pacific Industries Intl, Woodstock  *Also called Pacific Electronics Corp (G-22598)*
Pacific Press, Mount Carmel  *Also called Ppt Industrial Machines Inc (G-15281)*
Pacific Press Technologies, Mount Carmel  *Also called Ceg Subsidiary LLC (G-15262)*
Pacific Press Technologies LP .............................618 262-8666
  714 N Walnut St  Mount Carmel  (62863)  *(G-15280)*
Pack 2000 Inc ........................................................217 529-4408
  2109 Stevenson Dr  Springfield  (62703)  *(G-20496)*
Packaging AM Inc .................................................630 568-9506
  537 Eth Burr Ridge  (60527)  *(G-2872)*
Packaging By Design, Elgin  *Also called Bellen Container Corporation (G-8964)*
Packaging Corporation America ..........................847 388-6000
  250 S Shaddle Ave  Mundelein  (60060)  *(G-15540)*
Packaging Corporation America (PA) ..................847 482-3000
  1955 W Field Ct  Lake Forest  (60045)  *(G-12933)*
Packaging Corporation America ..........................618 934-3100
  11620 Old Us Highway 50  Trenton  (62293)  *(G-20995)*
Packaging Corporation America ..........................708 821-1600
  5445 W 73rd St  Chicago  (60638)  *(G-6053)*
Packaging Corporation America ..........................773 378-8700
  5230 W Roosevelt Rd  Chicago  (60644)  *(G-6054)*
Packaging Corporation America ..........................708 594-5260
  5555 W 73rd St  Bedford Park  (60638)  *(G-1570)*
Packaging Corporation America ..........................618 662-6700
  32 Industrial Park  Flora  (62839)  *(G-10213)*
Packaging Design Corporation .............................630 323-1354
  101 Shore Dr  Burr Ridge  (60527)  *(G-2873)*
Packaging Dynamics, Chicago  *Also called Bagcraftpapercon I LLC (G-4025)*
Packaging Dynamics Corporation (HQ) ...............773 254-8000
  3900 W 43rd St  Chicago  (60632)  *(G-6055)*
Packaging Dynamics Oper Co ..............................773 843-8000
  3900 W 43rd St  Chicago  (60632)  *(G-6056)*
Packaging Personified  Inc (PA) ...........................630 653-1655
  246 Kehoe Blvd  Carol Stream  (60188)  *(G-3210)*
Packaging Prtg Specialists Inc ............................630 513-8060
  3915 Stern Ave  Saint Charles  (60174)  *(G-19232)*
Packaging Systems, Romeoville  *Also called Rapak LLC (G-18862)*
Packers By Products Inc ......................................618 271-0660
  1087 Rte 3 N  National Stock Yards  (62071)  *(G-15851)*
Packers Supplies & Eqp LLC ................................630 543-5810
  341 W Factory Rd  Addison  (60101)  *(G-236)*
Packet, Chicago  *Also called Paket Corporation (G-6057)*
Packpors, Chicago  *Also called Kodiak LLC (G-5399)*
Paco Corporation ..................................................708 430-2424
  9945 Industrial Dr  Bridgeview  (60455)  *(G-2517)*
PAcrimson Fire Risk Svcs Inc ..............................630 424-3400
  920 N Ridge Ave Ste C7  Lombard  (60148)  *(G-13840)*
Pactiv Intl Holdings Inc (HQ) ...............................847 482-2000
  1900 W Field Ct  Lake Forest  (60045)  *(G-12934)*
Pactiv LLC (HQ) .....................................................847 482-2000
  1900 W Field Ct  Lake Forest  (60045)  *(G-12935)*
Pactiv LLC ..............................................................219 924-4120
  1900 W Field Ct  Lake Forest  (60045)  *(G-12936)*
Pactiv LLC ..............................................................847 482-2000
  1900 W Field Ct  Lake Forest  (60045)  *(G-12937)*
Pactiv LLC ..............................................................
  605 Heathrow Dr  Lincolnshire  (60069)  *(G-13469)*
Pactiv LLC ..............................................................317 390-5306
  304 Ne Main St  Grant Park  (60940)  *(G-11312)*
Pactiv LLC ..............................................................715 723-4181
  1900 W Field Ct  Lake Forest  (60045)  *(G-12938)*
Pactiv LLC ..............................................................708 924-2402
  7701 W 79th St  Bridgeview  (60455)  *(G-2518)*
Pactiv LLC ..............................................................618 934-4311
  11620 Hwy 50  Trenton  (62293)  *(G-20996)*
Pactiv LLC ..............................................................815 469-2112
  437 Center Rd  Frankfort  (60423)  *(G-10346)*
Pactiv LLC ..............................................................630 262-6335
  315 Kirk Rd  Saint Charles  (60174)  *(G-19233)*
Pactiv LLC ..............................................................217 479-1144
  2230 E Morton Ave  Jacksonville  (62650)  *(G-12404)*
Pactiv LLC ..............................................................847 459-8049
  777 Wheeling Rd  Wheeling  (60090)  *(G-22116)*
Pactiv LLC ..............................................................708 496-2900
  7207 S Mason Ave  Bedford Park  (60638)  *(G-1571)*
Pactiv LLC ..............................................................847 451-1480
  2607 Rose St  Franklin Park  (60131)  *(G-10545)*
Pactiv LLC ..............................................................217 243-3311
  500 E Superior Ave  Jacksonville  (62650)  *(G-12405)*
Pactiv LLC ..............................................................708 534-6595
  1175 Central Ave Ste 1  University Park  (60484)  *(G-21059)*
Pactiv Molded Products, Lake Forest  *Also called Pactiv LLC (G-12936)*
Pactra Corp ............................................................847 281-0308
  2112 Beaver Creek Dr  Vernon Hills  (60061)  *(G-21187)*
Paddlewheel The, Havana  *Also called James G Carter (G-11697)*
Paddock Industries Inc ........................................618 277-1580
  306 N Main St  Smithton  (62285)  *(G-20123)*
Paddock Publications  Inc (PA) ............................847 427-4300
  155 E Algonquin Rd  Arlington Heights  (60005)  *(G-815)*
Paddock Publications  Inc ....................................847 608-2700
  385 Airport Rd Ste A  Elgin  (60123)  *(G-9133)*
Paddock Publications  Inc ....................................847 427-5545
  1000 Albion Ave  Schaumburg  (60193)  *(G-19680)*
Paddock Publications  Inc ....................................847 680-5800
  1795 N Butterfield Rd # 100  Libertyville  (60048)  *(G-13365)*
Paddock Publications  Inc ....................................630 955-3500
  4300 Commerce Ct Ste 100  Lisle  (60532)  *(G-13638)*
Padma's Plantation, Batavia  *Also called Urban Home Furniture & ACC Inc (G-1514)*
Pagepath Technologies Inc ..................................630 689-4111
  13 E Main St  Plano  (60545)  *(G-17671)*
Paginatio, Chicago  *Also called Chicago Tribune Company (G-4359)*
Paint Glider, Chicago  *Also called White Eagle Brands Inc (G-6971)*
Painted Quarter Ridge ..........................................618 534-9734
  948 Possom Rd  Ava  (62907)  *(G-1241)*
Pak Source Inc .......................................................309 786-7374
  690 Mill St  Rock Island  (61201)  *(G-18191)*

**Paket Corporation** .................................................. 773 221-7300
  9165 S Lake Shore Dr  Chicago  (60617)  *(G-6057)*
**Pakistan News** ...................................................... 773 271-6400
  6033 N Sheridan Rd  Chicago  (60660)  *(G-6058)*
**Pal Health Technologies  Inc (PA)** ..................... 309 347-8785
  1805 Riverway Dr  Pekin  (61554)  *(G-17280)*
**Pal Midwest Ltd (PA)** ........................................... 815 965-2981
  1030 S Main St  Rockford  (61101)  *(G-18528)*
**Paladin, Oak Brook** Also called Jrb Attachments LLC  *(G-16529)*
**Paladin Brands International H** .......................... 319 378-3696
  2211 York Rd Ste 320  Oak Brook  (60523)  *(G-16554)*
**Palaestra, Macomb** Also called Challenge Publications L T D  *(G-14121)*
**Palapa Coatings  Inc** ........................................... 847 628-6360
  325 Corporate Dr  Elgin  (60123)  *(G-9134)*
**Palatine Welding Company** ................................ 847 358-1075
  3848 Berdnick St  Rolling Meadows  (60008)  *(G-18757)*
**Paldo Sign and Display Company** ..................... 708 456-1711
  8110 Grand Ave  River Grove  (60171)  *(G-18012)*
**Paleo Prime LLC** .................................................. 312 659-6596
  1106 W Newport Ave Apt 3  Chicago  (60657)  *(G-6059)*
**Paleteria Azteca 2, Chicago** Also called Paleteria Azteca Inc  *(G-6060)*
**Paleteria Azteca Inc** ............................................ 773 277-1423
  3119 W Cermak Rd  Chicago  (60623)  *(G-6060)*
**Paleteria El Sabor** ............................................... 312 243-2308
  1639 W 18th St  Chicago  (60608)  *(G-6061)*
**Paleteria El Sabor De Michoacn** ........................ 773 376-3880
  2456 W 47th St  Chicago  (60632)  *(G-6062)*
**Palladium Energy Group  Inc (HQ)** ..................... 630 410-7900
  1200 Internationale Pkwy # 101  Woodridge  (60517)  *(G-22507)*
**Pallet Base LLC** ................................................... 312 316-6137
  1000 W Wa Blvd Unit 229  Chicago  (60607)  *(G-6063)*
**Pallet Recyclers  Inc** ........................................... 815 432-4022
  106 E Jefferson Ave  Watseka  (60970)  *(G-21424)*
**Pallet Repair Systems  Inc** ................................. 217 291-0009
  2 Eastgate Dr  Jacksonville  (62650)  *(G-12406)*
**Pallet Solution** .................................................... 773 837-8677
  205 S Bartlett Rd  Streamwood  (60107)  *(G-20669)*
**Pallet Solution  Inc** ............................................. 618 445-2316
  Hwy 130 N  Albion  (62806)  *(G-364)*
**Pallet Wrapz** ........................................................ 847 729-5850
  2009 Johns Dr  Glenview  (60025)  *(G-11178)*
**Pallet Wrapz  Inc** ................................................. 847 729-5850
  2009 Johns Dr  Glenview  (60025)  *(G-11179)*
**Palletmaxx  Inc** .................................................... 708 385-9595
  4818 137th St Ste 1  Crestwood  (60445)  *(G-7497)*
**Pallets International Holding** ............................. 773 391-7223
  500 W Armory Dr  South Holland  (60473)  *(G-20294)*
**Pallets Plus Inc** .................................................... 847 318-1853
  1000 Cedar St  Park Ridge  (60068)  *(G-17215)*
**Pallets Shop** ........................................................ 618 920-6875
  5312 Deerwood Lk  Springfield  (62703)  *(G-20497)*
**Pallett  Wilson** ..................................................... 217 543-3555
  1858 Cr 1300e  Sullivan  (61951)  *(G-20757)*
**Palm International Inc (PA)** ................................ 630 357-1437
  1159 Palmetto Ct Ste B  Naperville  (60540)  *(G-15721)*
**Palm Labs Adhesives LLC** .................................. 773 799-8470
  2550 N Lakeview Ave  Chicago  (60614)  *(G-6064)*
**Palmer Printing Inc** ............................................. 312 427-7150
  739 S Clark St Fl 1  Chicago  (60605)  *(G-6065)*
**Palmgren Steel Products  Inc** ............................ 773 265-5700
  4444 W Ohio St  Chicago  (60624)  *(G-6066)*
**Palmyra Modesto Water Comm** ......................... 217 436-2519
  9934 Water Plant Rd  Palmyra  (62674)  *(G-17097)*
**Palo Verde Suspension Inc** ................................ 815 939-2196
  4136 W 6940n Rd  Bourbonnais  (60914)  *(G-2405)*
**Paltech Enterprises Illinois, Belvidere** Also called M & M Paltech Inc  *(G-1767)*
**Palwaukee Printing Company** ............................ 847 459-0240
  1684 S Wolf Rd  Wheeling  (60090)  *(G-22117)*
**Pam Printers and Publs Inc (PA)** ....................... 217 222-4030
  1012 Vermont St  Quincy  (62301)  *(G-17866)*
**Pamacheyon Publishing Inc** .............................. 815 395-0101
  305 Saint Louis Ave  Rockford  (61104)  *(G-18529)*
**Pamarco Global Graphics  Inc** ........................... 630 879-7300
  125 Flinn St  Batavia  (60510)  *(G-1479)*
**Pamarco Global Graphics  Inc** ........................... 847 459-6000
  171 E Marquardt Dr  Wheeling  (60090)  *(G-22118)*
**Pamco Printed Tape Label Inc (HQ)** .................. 847 803-2200
  2200 S Wolf Rd  Des Plaines  (60018)  *(G-8249)*
**Pan America Environmental Inc** ........................ 847 487-9166
  2309 N Ringwood Rd Ste G  McHenry  (60050)  *(G-14541)*
**Pan American Screw Div, Chicago** Also called Marmon Group LLC  *(G-5624)*
**Pan Pac International Inc** .................................. 847 222-9077
  3456 N Ridge Ave Ste 300  Arlington Heights  (60004)  *(G-816)*
**Pan-O-Graphics Inc** ............................................. 630 834-7123
  408 S Washington St  Elmhurst  (60126)  *(G-9918)*
**Pana Limestone Company** .................................. 217 562-4231
  325 N 1600 East Rd  Pana  (62557)  *(G-17135)*
**Pana Monument Co (PA)** ..................................... 217 562-5121
  2 N Poplar St  Pana  (62557)  *(G-17136)*

**Pana News Inc (PA)** ............................................. 217 562-2111
  205 S Locust St  Pana  (62557)  *(G-17137)*
**Pana News Palladium, Pana** Also called Pana News Inc  *(G-17137)*
**Panache Editions Ltd** ......................................... 847 921-8574
  234 Dennis Ln  Glencoe  (60022)  *(G-11005)*
**Panasonic Corp North America** ......................... 630 801-0359
  800 Bilter Rd  Aurora  (60502)  *(G-1062)*
**Panasonic Corp North America** ......................... 847 637-9700
  1000 Asbury Dr  Buffalo Grove  (60089)  *(G-2750)*
**Panasonic Fctry Solutions Amer, Buffalo Grove** Also called Panasonic Corp North America  *(G-2750)*
**Panatech Computer Management** .................... 847 678-8848
  9950 Lawrence Ave Ste 318  Schiller Park  (60176)  *(G-19857)*
**Panatrol Corporation** ......................................... 630 655-4700
  161 Tower Dr Ste D  Burr Ridge  (60527)  *(G-2874)*
**Panchos Ice Cream** ............................................ 773 254-3141
  4055 W 31st St  Chicago  (60623)  *(G-6067)*
**Pancon Illinois LLC** ............................................ 630 972-6400
  440 Quadrangle Dr Ste A  Bolingbrook  (60440)  *(G-2356)*
**Panda Graphics Inc** ........................................... 312 666-7642
  451 N Racine Ave Fl 1  Chicago  (60642)  *(G-6068)*
**Pandaderia El Acambaro** ................................... 312 666-6316
  1720 W 18th St  Chicago  (60608)  *(G-6069)*
**Panduit Corp (PA)** ............................................... 708 532-1800
  18900 Panduit Dr  Tinley Park  (60487)  *(G-20937)*
**Panduit Corp** ....................................................... 708 460-1800
  10500 W 167th St  Orland Park  (60467)  *(G-16882)*
**Panduit Corp** ....................................................... 815 836-1800
  16530 W 163rd St  Lockport  (60441)  *(G-13737)*
**Panek Precision Products Co** ........................... 847 291-9755
  455 Academy Dr  Northbrook  (60062)  *(G-16330)*
**Panel Authority  Inc** ............................................ 815 838-0488
  411 New Ave Unit 1  Lockport  (60441)  *(G-13738)*
**Panel Window Co Inc** ......................................... 708 485-0310
  9509 Ogden Ave  Brookfield  (60513)  *(G-2640)*
**Panelshopnet Inc** ............................................... 630 692-0214
  3460 Ohara Ter  Naperville  (60564)  *(G-15821)*
**Panhandle Eastrn Pipe Line LP** ......................... 217 753-1108
  1801 Business Park Dr  Springfield  (62703)  *(G-20498)*
**Pannon Mord Polishing** ...................................... 630 893-9252
  210 Freeport Dr  Bloomingdale  (60108)  *(G-2124)*
**Pantagraph Printing and Sty Co (PA)** ............... 309 829-1071
  217 W Jefferson St  Bloomington  (61701)  *(G-2208)*
**Pantagraph Publishing Co (PA)** ........................ 309 829-9000
  301 W Washington St  Bloomington  (61701)  *(G-2209)*
**Panther Products** ............................................... 618 664-1071
  102 W Main St  Greenville  (62246)  *(G-11402)*
**Panthervision, West Dundee** Also called Waters Industries  Inc  *(G-21803)*
**Panzer Tool Corp** ................................................ 630 519-5214
  920 N Ridge Ave Ste A2  Lombard  (60148)  *(G-13841)*
**Paoli Inc** .............................................................. 312 644-5509
  222 Merchandise Mart Plz # 380  Chicago  (60654)  *(G-6070)*
**Paoli, Stephen International, Rockford** Also called Stephen Paoli Mfg Corp  *(G-18634)*
**Pap-R Products Company (PA)** .......................... 775 828-4141
  1 Harry Glynn Dr  Martinsville  (62442)  *(G-14339)*
**Papa Charlies  Inc** .............................................. 773 522-7900
  1800 S Kostner Ave  Chicago  (60623)  *(G-6071)*
**Papanicholas Coffee Company, Batavia** Also called Napco  Inc  *(G-1474)*
**Papendik Inc** ....................................................... 708 492-6230
  8711 Robinhood Dr  Orland Park  (60462)  *(G-16883)*
**Paper** ................................................................... 815 584-1901
  204 E Chippewa St  Dwight  (60420)  *(G-8590)*
**Paper Benders Supply Inc (PA)** ......................... 815 577-7583
  12024 S Aero Dr Ste 10  Plainfield  (60585)  *(G-17635)*
**Paper Graphics Inc** ............................................ 847 276-2727
  612 Heathrow Dr  Lincolnshire  (60069)  *(G-13470)*
**Paper Machine Services  Inc** ............................. 608 365-8095
  7283 Barngate Dr  South Beloit  (61080)  *(G-20163)*
**Paper Moon Recycling Inc** ................................. 847 548-8875
  123 Bluff Ave  Grayslake  (60030)  *(G-11358)*
**Paper Spot** .......................................................... 815 464-8533
  11 S White St Ste 201  Frankfort  (60423)  *(G-10347)*
**Paper Tube  LLC** ................................................. 847 477-0563
  971 N Milwaukee Ave # 22  Wheeling  (60090)  *(G-22119)*
**Paper, The, Barry** Also called Debbie Harshman  *(G-1311)*
**Paperchine  Inc (HQ)** .......................................... 815 389-8200
  1155 Prairie Hill Rd  Rockton  (61072)  *(G-18700)*
**Paperworks** .......................................................... 630 969-3218
  904 62nd St  Downers Grove  (60516)  *(G-8499)*
**Papiros Graphics** ................................................ 773 581-3000
  4557 W 59th St  Chicago  (60629)  *(G-6072)*
**Papmpered Pups** ................................................ 815 782-8383
  2011 Essington Rd  Joliet  (60435)  *(G-12549)*
**Pappas & Pappas Enterprises, Saint Charles** Also called Form Plastics Company  *(G-19187)*
**Pappone Inc** ........................................................ 630 234-4738
  2041 W Carroll Ave C214  Chicago  (60612)  *(G-6073)*
**Papyrus Press Inc** .............................................. 773 342-0700
  3441 W Grand Ave  Chicago  (60651)  *(G-6074)*

**Papys Foods Inc** ....815 385-3313
4131 W Albany St McHenry (60050) *(G-14542)*
**Par Fabricating Co, Blue Island** *Also called J & G Fabricating Inc (G-2257)*
**Par Golf Supply Inc** ....847 891-1222
550 Pratt Ave N Schaumburg (60193) *(G-19681)*
**Para Tech Systems Company, Rockford** *Also called Merlin Technologies Inc (G-18493)*
**Parade Publications Inc** ....312 661-1620
500 N Michigan Ave # 910 Chicago (60611) *(G-6075)*
**Paradigm Bioaviation LLC** ....309 663-2303
2933 E Empire St Bloomington (61704) *(G-2210)*
**Paradigm Coatings LLC** ....847 961-6466
11259 Kiley Dr Huntley (60142) *(G-12165)*
**Paradigm Development Group Inc** ....847 545-9600
27 W 230 Becher Ave Ste 2 Winfield (60190) *(G-22289)*
**Paragon Automation Inc** ....847 593-0434
1410 Brummel Ave Elk Grove Village (60007) *(G-9669)*
**Paragon Group Inc** ....847 526-1800
274 Jamie Ln Wauconda (60084) *(G-21491)*
**Paragon International Inc** ....847 240-2981
1901 N Roselle Rd Ste 711 Schaumburg (60195) *(G-19682)*
**Paragon Manufacturing Inc** ....708 345-1717
2001 N 15th Ave Melrose Park (60160) *(G-14681)*
**Paragon Print & Mail Prod Inc** ....630 671-2222
109 Fairfield Way Ste 202 Bloomingdale (60108) *(G-2125)*
**Paragon Spring Company** ....773 489-6300
4435 W Rice St Ste 45 Chicago (60651) *(G-6076)*
**Paragon Valuation Group, Schaumburg** *Also called Paragon International Inc (G-19682)*
**Parallel Machine Products Inc** ....847 359-1012
255 N Woodwork Ln Palatine (60067) *(G-17063)*
**Parallel Solutions LLC** ....847 708-9227
1251 N Plum Grove Rd # 160 Schaumburg (60173) *(G-19683)*
**Paralleldirect LLC** ....847 748-2025
103 Schelter Rd Ste 20 Lincolnshire (60069) *(G-13471)*
**Paramount Laminates Inc** ....630 594-1840
907 N Central Ave Wood Dale (60191) *(G-22411)*
**Paramount Plastics Inc** ....815 834-4100
140 S Dearborn St Ste 420 Chicago (60603) *(G-6077)*
**Paramount Plastics LLC** ....815 834-4100
140 S Dearborn St Ste 420 Chicago (60603) *(G-6078)*
**Paramount Sintered Pdts LLP** ....847 746-8866
1717 Kenosha Rd Zion (60099) *(G-22695)*
**Paramount Truck Body Co Inc** ....312 666-6441
2107 W Fulton St Chicago (60612) *(G-6079)*
**Paramount Wire Specialties** ....773 252-5636
4106 W Chicago Ave 10 Chicago (60651) *(G-6080)*
**Paratech Incorporated (PA)** ....815 469-3911
1025 Lambrecht Dr Frankfort (60423) *(G-10348)*
**Parenteau Studios** ....312 337-8015
3401 N Knox Ave Chicago (60641) *(G-6081)*
**Parenti & Raffaelli Ltd** ....847 253-5550
215 E Prospect Ave Mount Prospect (60056) *(G-15361)*
**Paris Beacon News** ....217 465-6424
218 N Main St Paris (61944) *(G-17156)*
**Paris Frozen Foods Inc** ....217 532-3822
305 Springfield Rd Hillsboro (62049) *(G-11897)*
**Paris Frozen Foods Locker, Hillsboro** *Also called Paris Frozen Foods Inc (G-11897)*
**Paris Metal Products LLC** ....217 465-6321
13571 Il Highway 133 Paris (61944) *(G-17157)*
**Pariso Inc** ....773 889-4383
1836 N Lockwood Ave Chicago (60639) *(G-6082)*
**Park Electric Motor Service** ....217 442-1977
1204 N Collett St Danville (61832) *(G-7759)*
**Park Engineering Inc** ....847 455-1424
9227 Parklane Ave Franklin Park (60131) *(G-10546)*
**Park Industries, Melrose Park** *Also called Park Manufacturing Corp Inc (G-14682)*
**Park It Bike Racks Company, Batavia** *Also called Treetop Marketing Inc (G-1510)*
**Park Lawn Association Inc** ....708 425-7377
5040 W 111th St Oak Lawn (60453) *(G-16638)*
**Park License Service Inc** ....815 633-5511
6402 N 2nd St Loves Park (61111) *(G-13972)*
**Park Manufacturing Corp Inc** ....708 345-6090
1819 N 30th Ave Melrose Park (60160) *(G-14682)*
**Park Packing Company Inc** ....773 254-0100
4107 S Ashland Ave Chicago (60609) *(G-6083)*
**Park Press, South Holland** *Also called KB Publishing Inc (G-20282)*
**Park Press Inc** ....708 331-6352
930 E 162nd St South Holland (60473) *(G-20295)*
**Park Printing Inc (PA)** ....708 430-4878
9903 S Roberts Rd Palos Hills (60465) *(G-17120)*
**Park Products Inc** ....630 543-2474
409 W Kay Ave Addison (60101) *(G-237)*
**Park Tool & Machine Co Inc** ....630 530-5110
111 W Home Ave Villa Park (60181) *(G-21275)*
**Park View Manufacturing Corp** ....618 548-9054
2510 S Broadway Ave Salem (62881) *(G-19342)*
**Park-Hio Frged McHned Pdts LLC** ....708 652-6691
5301 W Roosevelt Rd Chicago (60804) *(G-6084)*
**Park-Ohio Industries Inc** ....708 652-6691
5301 W Roosevelt Rd Chicago (60804) *(G-6085)*
**Parke & Son Inc** ....217 875-0572
3523 Rupp Pkwy Decatur (62526) *(G-7925)*
**Parker Fabrication Inc (PA)** ....309 266-8413
501 E Courtland St Morton (61550) *(G-15174)*
**Parker Hnnfin Elctrnic Contrls, Morton** *Also called Parker-Hannifin Corporation (G-15175)*
**Parker House Sausage Company (PA)** ....773 538-1112
4605 S State St Chicago (60609) *(G-6086)*
**Parker International Pdts Inc** ....815 524-5831
650 Forest Edge Dr Vernon Hills (60061) *(G-21188)*
**Parker Metal, Vernon Hills** *Also called Parker International Pdts Inc (G-21188)*
**Parker Tool & Die Co** ....847 566-2229
20844 W Park Ave Mundelein (60060) *(G-15541)*
**Parker-Hannifin Corporation** ....847 258-6200
850 Arthur Ave Elk Grove Village (60007) *(G-9670)*
**Parker-Hannifin Corporation** ....847 836-6859
2565 Northwest Pkwy Elgin (60124) *(G-9135)*
**Parker-Hannifin Corporation** ....708 681-6300
2445 S 25th Ave Broadview (60155) *(G-2601)*
**Parker-Hannifin Corporation** ....815 636-4100
10711 N 2nd St Machesney Park (61115) *(G-14095)*
**Parker-Hannifin Corporation** ....847 955-5000
595 Schelter Rd Ste 100 Lincolnshire (60069) *(G-13472)*
**Parker-Hannifin Corporation** ....847 298-2400
500 S Wolf Rd Des Plaines (60016) *(G-8250)*
**Parker-Hannifin Corporation** ....630 427-2020
10625 Beaudin Blvd Woodridge (60517) *(G-22508)*
**Parker-Hannifin Corporation** ....309 266-2200
1651 N Main St Morton (61550) *(G-15175)*
**Parking Systems Inc** ....847 891-3819
911 Estes Ct Schaumburg (60193) *(G-19684)*
**Parks Industries LLC** ....618 997-9608
15460 Crabtree School Rd Marion (62959) *(G-14276)*
**Parkson Corporation** ....847 816-3700
562 Bunker Ct Vernon Hills (60061) *(G-21189)*
**Parkview Orthopaedic Group** ....815 727-3030
688 Cedar Crossings Dr New Lenox (60451) *(G-15899)*
**Parkview Sand & Gravel Inc (PA)** ....262 534-4347
41 Walter Ct Lake In The Hills (60156) *(G-13003)*
**Parkway Metal Products Inc** ....847 789-4000
130 Rawls Rd Des Plaines (60018) *(G-8251)*
**Parkway Printers** ....217 525-2485
3755 N Dirksen Pkwy Springfield (62707) *(G-20499)*
**Parr Instrument Company (PA)** ....309 762-7716
211 53rd St Moline (61265) *(G-14961)*
**Parrot Press** ....773 376-6333
4484 S Archer Ave Chicago (60632) *(G-6087)*
**Parrott and Assoc Formerly, Bloomington** *Also called Five Brother Inc (G-2164)*
**Parsons Company Inc** ....309 467-9100
1386 State Route 117 Roanoke (61561) *(G-18053)*
**Part Stop Inc** ....618 377-5238
5120 State Route 140 Bethalto (62010) *(G-2082)*
**Partec Inc** ....847 678-9520
9301 Belmont Ave Franklin Park (60131) *(G-10547)*
**Partex Marking Systems Inc** ....630 516-0400
1155 N Main St Lombard (60148) *(G-13842)*
**Parth Consultants Inc** ....847 758-1400
5005 Newport Dr Ste 204 Rolling Meadows (60008) *(G-18758)*
**Parting Line Tool Inc** ....847 669-0331
11915 Smith Ct Huntley (60142) *(G-12166)*
**Partner, Plainfield** *Also called Display Worldwide LLC (G-17592)*
**Partner Health LLC** ....847 208-6074
736 Nw Ave Ste 326 Lake Forest (60045) *(G-12939)*
**Partners Manufacturing Inc** ....847 352-1080
625 Lunt Ave Schaumburg (60193) *(G-19685)*
**Partners Resource Inc** ....630 620-9161
831 Woodland Dr Glen Ellyn (60137) *(G-10985)*
**Parts Specialists Inc** ....708 371-2444
14639 S Short St Posen (60469) *(G-17734)*
**Partscription, Oak Park** *Also called Kap Holdings LLC (G-16671)*
**Party Fantasy** ....847 837-0010
390 Townline Rd Ste 7150 Mundelein (60060) *(G-15542)*
**Party Plate LLC** ....708 268-4571
5 Martin Ct Lemont (60439) *(G-13249)*
**Partylite Inc** ....630 845-6025
603 Kingsland Dr Batavia (60510) *(G-1480)*
**Parvin-Clauss Sign Co Inc** ....866 490-2877
165 Tubeway Dr Carol Stream (60188) *(G-3211)*
**Paslode Corp** ....641 672-2515
155 Harlem Ave Glenview (60025) *(G-11180)*
**Pass, Elburn** *Also called Perimeter Access Sys Svcs Inc (G-8903)*
**Passco Parts & Electronics, Lansing** *Also called Bedford Rakim (G-13157)*
**Passion Fruit Drink Inc** ....708 769-4749
17335 Sterling Ct South Holland (60473) *(G-20296)*
**Pasta Pappone, Chicago** *Also called Pappone Inc (G-6073)*
**Pastafresh Co** ....773 745-5888
3418 N Harlem Ave Chicago (60634) *(G-6088)*
**Pastafresh Homemade Pasta, Chicago** *Also called Pastafresh Co (G-6088)*
**Pastificio Inc** ....847 432-5459
122 Highwood Ave Ste 1r Highwood (60040) *(G-11887)*

ALPHABETIC

**Pastorelli Food Products Inc**...312 455-1006
901 W Lake St Chicago (60607) ***(G-6089)***
**Pat 24 Inc**...708 336-8671
7107 W 79th St Burbank (60459) ***(G-2809)***
**Pate Company Inc**...630 705-1920
245 Eisenhower Ln S Lombard (60148) ***(G-13843)***
**Patientbond LLC**...312 445-8751
126 N York St Ste 2 Elmhurst (60126) ***(G-9919)***
**Patio Plus**...815 433-2399
1624 W Main St Ottawa (61350) ***(G-16977)***
**Patko Tool & Manufacturing**...630 616-8802
767 Gasoline Aly Bensenville (60106) ***(G-1963)***
**Patkus Machine Co**...815 398-7818
2607 Marshall St Rockford (61109) ***(G-18530)***
**Patlin Enterprises Inc**...815 675-6606
2907 N Us Highway 12 Spring Grove (60081) ***(G-20355)***
**Patricia Locke Ltd**...847 949-2303
817 E Orchard St Mundelein (60060) ***(G-15543)***
**Patrick Cabinetry Inc**...630 307-9333
192 Ring Neck Ln Bloomingdale (60108) ***(G-2126)***
**Patrick Holdings Inc (PA)**...815 874-5300
5894 Sandy Hollow Rd Rockford (61109) ***(G-18531)***
**Patrick Impressions LLC**...630 257-9336
16135 New Ave Ste 1a Lemont (60439) ***(G-13250)***
**Patrick Industries Inc**...630 595-0595
1077 Sesame St Franklin Park (60131) ***(G-10548)***
**Patrick Manufacturing Inc**...847 697-5920
667 N State St Elgin (60123) ***(G-9136)***
**Patrin Pharma Inc**...800 936-3088
7817 Babb Ave Skokie (60077) ***(G-20053)***
**Patriot Fuels Biodiesel LLC**...309 935-5700
101 Patriot Way Annawan (61234) ***(G-610)***
**Patriot Fuels LLC**...847 551-5946
10219 Vine St East Dundee (60118) ***(G-8651)***
**Patriot Home Improvement Inc (PA)**...630 800-1901
2150 Jericho Rd Aurora (60506) ***(G-1203)***
**Patriot Materials LLC**...630 501-0260
750 N Industrial Dr Elmhurst (60126) ***(G-9920)***
**Patriot Renewable Fuels LLC**...309 935-5700
101 Patriot Way Annawan (61234) ***(G-611)***
**Patrone Ready Mix, Melrose Park** *Also called Southfield Corporation* ***(G-14694)***
**Patt Supply Corporation**...708 442-3901
8111 47th St Lyons (60534) ***(G-14043)***
**Patterson Avenue Tool Company**...847 949-8100
6515 High Meadow Ct Long Grove (60047) ***(G-13900)***
**Patterson Medical Products Inc (HQ)**...630 393-6671
28100 Torch Pkwy Warrenville (60555) ***(G-21353)***
**Patterson Printing & Signs, Bridgeview** *Also called Dean Patterson* ***(G-2482)***
**Patterson Products**...618 723-2688
580 E Antioch Ln Noble (62868) ***(G-16053)***
**Patti Group Incorporated (PA)**...630 243-6320
12301 New Ave Ste A Lemont (60439) ***(G-13251)***
**Patton Printing and Graphics**...217 347-0220
902 W Wabash Ave B Effingham (62401) ***(G-8852)***
**Patty Style Shop**...618 654-2015
621 Broadway Apt 1 Highland (62249) ***(G-11805)***
**Patty's Style Shop, Highland** *Also called Patty Style Shop* ***(G-11805)***
**Paul & Ron Manufacturing Inc**...309 596-2986
2650 85th Ave Viola (61486) ***(G-21294)***
**Paul Bjekich, President, Joliet** *Also called Relay Systems America Inc* ***(G-12565)***
**Paul D Burton**...309 467-2613
124 N Main St Eureka (61530) ***(G-10000)***
**Paul D Metal Products Inc**...773 847-1400
2225 W Pershing Rd Chicago (60609) ***(G-6090)***
**Paul D Stark & Associates (PA)**...630 964-7111
509 Blackburn Ct Downers Grove (60516) ***(G-8500)***
**Paul O Abbe Division, Bensenville** *Also called Aaron Engnered Process Eqp Inc* ***(G-1809)***
**Paul Sisti**...773 472-5615
3520 N Lake Shore Dr Chicago (60657) ***(G-6091)***
**Paul Sisti Studio, Chicago** *Also called Paul Sisti* ***(G-6091)***
**Paul Wever Construction Eqp Co**...309 965-2005
401 W Martin Dr Goodfield (61742) ***(G-11248)***
**Paulmar Industries Inc**...847 395-2520
39804 N Stonebridge Ct Antioch (60002) ***(G-648)***
**Pauls Machine & Welding Corp (PA)**...217 832-2541
650 N Sycamore St Villa Grove (61956) ***(G-21230)***
**Pauls Mc Culloch Sales**...217 323-2159
11136 Il Route 125 Beardstown (62618) ***(G-1526)***
**Paulson Press Inc**...847 290-0080
904 Cambridge Dr Elk Grove Village (60007) ***(G-9671)***
**Paulson's Litho, Elk Grove Village** *Also called Paulson Press Inc* ***(G-9671)***
**Paveloc Industries Inc**...815 568-4700
8302 S Il Route 23 Marengo (60152) ***(G-14238)***
**Paver Protector Inc**...630 488-0069
57 Railroad St 171 Gilberts (60136) ***(G-10931)***
**Paw Office Machines Inc**...815 363-9780
816 Madison Ave McHenry (60050) ***(G-14543)***
**Paw Paw Co-Operative Grain**...815 627-2071
243 Flagg St Paw Paw (61353) ***(G-17233)***
**Pawnee Oil Corporation**...217 522-5440
1204 N 5th St Springfield (62702) ***(G-20500)***
**Pawz & Klawz**...630 257-0245
447 Talcott Ave Lemont (60439) ***(G-13252)***
**Paxton Packing LLC**...623 707-5604
145 W State St Paxton (60957) ***(G-17241)***
**Paxton Ready Mix Inc**...217 379-2303
745 N Market St Paxton (60957) ***(G-17242)***
**Payless For Granite, Elk Grove Village** *Also called Kitchen Transformation Inc* ***(G-9574)***
**Paylocity Holding Corporation (PA)**...847 463-3200
3850 N Wilke Rd Arlington Heights (60004) ***(G-817)***
**Paylocity Holding Corporation**...331 701-7975
27w675 South Ln Naperville (60540) ***(G-15722)***
**Payment Pathways Inc**...312 346-9400
8745 W Higgins Rd Ste 240 Chicago (60631) ***(G-6092)***
**Payne Chauna**...618 580-2584
6600 W Main St Ste 8 Belleville (62223) ***(G-1664)***
**Payson Casters Inc (PA)**...847 336-6200
2323 N Delany Rd Gurnee (60031) ***(G-11482)***
**Payson Casters Inc**...847 336-5033
2335 N Delany Rd Gurnee (60031) ***(G-11483)***
**Pbc Linear, Roscoe** *Also called Pacific Bearing Corp* ***(G-18911)***
**Pbi Redi Mix & Trucking**...217 562-3717
2 N Walnut St Pana (62557) ***(G-17138)***
**PC Aquisition, Lemont** *Also called PC Successor Inc* ***(G-13253)***
**PC Concepts**...847 223-6490
2388 N Fox Chase Dr Round Lake Beach (60073) ***(G-19078)***
**PC Marble Inc**...708 385-3360
5859 W 117th Pl Alsip (60803) ***(G-505)***
**PC Successor Inc**...630 783-2400
1005 101st St Ste A Lemont (60439) ***(G-13253)***
**Pc-Tel Inc (PA)**...630 372-6800
471 Brighton Ct Bloomingdale (60108) ***(G-2127)***
**PCA, Lake Forest** *Also called Packaging Corporation America* ***(G-12933)***
**PCA, Chicago** *Also called Packaging Corporation America* ***(G-6054)***
**PCA, Flora** *Also called Packaging Corporation America* ***(G-10213)***
**PCA Chicago Container, Chicago** *Also called Packaging Corporation America* ***(G-6053)***
**PCA Corrugated and Display LLC**...847 482-3000
1955 W Field Ct Lake Forest (60045) ***(G-12940)***
**PCA International Inc (HQ)**...847 482-3000
1955 W Field Ct Lake Forest (60045) ***(G-12941)***
**PCA Tech Center, Mundelein** *Also called Packaging Corporation America* ***(G-15540)***
**Pcb Express Inc**...847 952-8896
600 E Higgins Rd Ste 2c Elk Grove Village (60007) ***(G-9672)***
**Pcb Services, Glendale Heights** *Also called Precision Technologies Inc* ***(G-11058)***
**Pcbl Retail Holdings LLC**...610 761-4838
5 Revere Dr Ste 206 Northbrook (60062) ***(G-16331)***
**PCC, Urbana** *Also called Plastic Container Corporation* ***(G-21098)***
**PCI, Elburn** *Also called Quikrete Chicago* ***(G-8906)***
**Pcr Machining, Broadview** *Also called Precision Cnncting Rod Svc Inc* ***(G-2602)***
**Pcs Nitrogen Inc (HQ)**...847 849-4200
1101 Skokie Blvd Ste 400 Northbrook (60062) ***(G-16332)***
**Pcs Nitrogen Fertilizer LP**...847 849-4200
1101 Skokie Blvd Ste 400 Northbrook (60062) ***(G-16333)***
**Pcs Nitrogen Trinidad Corp**...847 849-4200
1101 Skokie Blvd Ste 400 Northbrook (60062) ***(G-16334)***
**Pcs Ntrgen Frtlzer Oprtons Inc (HQ)**...847 849-4200
1101 Skokie Blvd Ste 400 Northbrook (60062) ***(G-16335)***
**Pcs Phosphate Company Inc (HQ)**...847 849-4200
1101 Skokie Blvd Ste 400 Northbrook (60062) ***(G-16336)***
**Pcs Phosphate Company Inc**...815 795-5111
2660 E Us Highway 6 Marseilles (61341) ***(G-14316)***
**Pcs Sales, Northbrook** *Also called Pcs Phosphate Company Inc* ***(G-16336)***
**Pdi, Lake Zurich** *Also called Performance Design Inc* ***(G-13113)***
**PDQ Machine Inc**...815 282-7575
7909b Burden Rd Machesney Park (61115) ***(G-14096)***
**PDQ Tool & Stamping Co**...708 841-3000
14901 Greenwood Rd Dolton (60419) ***(G-8374)***
**Pdss Construction**...847 980-6090
7516 Davis St Morton Grove (60053) ***(G-15226)***
**Pdv Midwest Refining LLC**...630 257-7761
135th St New Ave Lemont (60439) ***(G-13254)***
**Peabody Arclar Mining LLC**...618 273-4314
420 Long Lane Rd Equality (62934) ***(G-9989)***
**Peabody Coal Company**...618 758-2395
13101 Zeigler 11 Rd Coulterville (62237) ***(G-7402)***
**Peabody Midwest Mining LLC**...618 276-5006
12250 Mclain Rd Equality (62934) ***(G-9990)***
**Peacock Printing & Silk Screen, Mount Vernon** *Also called Peacock Printing Inc* ***(G-15437)***
**Peacock Printing Inc**...618 242-3157
1112 Jordan St Mount Vernon (62864) ***(G-15437)***
**Peak Computer Systems Inc**...618 398-5612
6400 W Main St Ste 1a Belleville (62223) ***(G-1665)***
**Peak Healthcare Advisors LLC**...646 479-0005
4043 N Ravenswood Ave # 225 Chicago (60613) ***(G-6093)***
**Peanut Butter Partners LLC**...847 489-5322
564 Crescent Blvd Glen Ellyn (60137) ***(G-10986)***

**Pearl Design Group LLC**....630 295-8401
170 Covington Dr Bloomingdale (60108) ***(G-2128)***
**Pearl Perfect Inc**....847 679-6251
8220 Austin Ave Morton Grove (60053) ***(G-15227)***
**Pearl Valley Organix Inc**....815 443-2170
968 S Kent Rd Pearl City (61062) ***(G-17249)***
**Pearson Fastener Corporation**....815 397-4460
1400 Samuelson Rd Rockford (61109) ***(G-18532)***
**Pearson Industries Inc**....847 963-9633
5420 Newport Dr Ste 56 Rolling Meadows (60008) ***(G-18759)***
**Pease Plastics, Glenview** *Also called Acrylic Ventures Inc* ***(G-11094)***
**Pease's Candy Shops, Springfield** *Also called Peases Inc* ***(G-20501)***
**Peases Inc (PA)**....217 523-3721
1701 S State St Springfield (62704) ***(G-20501)***
**Peases Inc**....217 529-2912
4753 Jeffory St Springfield (62703) ***(G-20502)***
**Pebblefork Partners Inc**....708 449-8989
5656 Mcdermott Dr Berkeley (60163) ***(G-2047)***
**Pechiney Cast Plate**....847 299-0220
8770 W Bryn Mawr Ave Fl 9 Chicago (60631) ***(G-6094)***
**Pecora Tool & Die Co Inc**....847 524-1275
520 Morse Ave Schaumburg (60193) ***(G-19686)***
**Pecora Tool Service Inc**....847 524-1275
520 Morse Ave Schaumburg (60193) ***(G-19687)***
**Pecson Distributors LLC**....815 342-7977
27543 S Forest View Ln Beecher (60401) ***(G-1601)***
**Pedco, Villa Park** *Also called Precision Engineering & Dev Co* ***(G-21278)***
**Peddinghaus Corporation (PA)**....815 937-3800
300 N Washington Ave Bradley (60915) ***(G-2428)***
**Peddinghause, Bradley** *Also called Structural Steel Systems Limi* ***(G-2434)***
**Pedigree Ovens Inc**....815 943-8144
495 Commanche Cir Harvard (60033) ***(G-11643)***
**Peelmaster Medical Packaging, Niles** *Also called Peelmaster Packaging Corp* ***(G-16015)***
**Peelmaster Packaging Corp**....847 966-6161
6153 W Mulford St Niles (60714) ***(G-16015)***
**Peep Eliminator, Breese** *Also called Compound Bow Rifle Sight Inc* ***(G-2442)***
**Peeps Inc**....708 935-4201
8945 W 103rd St Palos Hills (60465) ***(G-17121)***
**Peer Bearing Company (HQ)**....877 600-7337
2200 Norman Dr Waukegan (60085) ***(G-21600)***
**Peer Foods Inc (HQ)**....773 927-1440
1200 W 35th St Fl 3 Chicago (60609) ***(G-6095)***
**Peerless**....773 294-2667
4855 S Racine Ave Chicago (60609) ***(G-6096)***
**Peerless America Incorporated**....217 342-0400
1201 W Wabash Ave Effingham (62401) ***(G-8853)***
**Peerless Chain Company**....708 339-0545
16650 State St South Holland (60473) ***(G-20297)***
**Peerless Confection Company (PA)**....773 281-6100
7383 N Lincoln Ave # 100 Lincolnwood (60712) ***(G-13529)***
**Peerless Industries Inc (PA)**....630 375-5100
2300 White Oak Cir Aurora (60502) ***(G-1063)***
**Peerless-Av, Aurora** *Also called Peerless Industries Inc* ***(G-1063)***
**Peerless-Premier Appliance Co (PA)**....618 233-0475
119 S 14th St Belleville (62220) ***(G-1666)***
**Peg N Reds**....618 586-2015
212 S Main St New Lenox (60451) ***(G-15900)***
**Pegas Window Inc**....773 394-6466
4100 W Grand Ave Ste 1 Chicago (60651) ***(G-6097)***
**Pegasus Mfg Inc**....309 342-9337
1382 Enterprise Ave Galesburg (61401) ***(G-10770)***
**Pei/Genesis Inc**....215 673-0400
3701 Algonquin Rd Ste 710 Rolling Meadows (60008) ***(G-18760)***
**Pekay Machine & Engrg Co Inc**....312 829-5530
2520 W Lake St Chicago (60612) ***(G-6098)***
**Pekin Hardwood Lumber Co., Pekin** *Also called Woodworkers Shop Inc* ***(G-17296)***
**Pekin Mill, Pekin** *Also called Ox Paperboard LLC* ***(G-17277)***
**Pekin Paperboard Company LP**....309 346-4118
1525 S 2nd St Pekin (61554) ***(G-17281)***
**Pekin Sand and Gravel LLC**....309 347-8917
13018 E Manito Rd Pekin (61554) ***(G-17282)***
**Pekin Weldors Inc**....309 382-3627
1525 Edgewater Dr North Pekin (61554) ***(G-16193)***
**Pelbo Americas Inc**....630 395-7788
1701 Quincy Ave Ste 12 Naperville (60540) ***(G-15723)***
**Pelco Tool & Mold Inc**....630 871-1010
181 Exchange Blvd Glendale Heights (60139) ***(G-11056)***
**Pelegan Inc**....708 442-9797
277 Northwood Rd Riverside (60546) ***(G-18033)***
**Pella Corporation**....309 663-7132
1407 N Veterans Pkwy B3 Bloomington (61704) ***(G-2211)***
**Pella Corporation**....309 663-7132
1407 N Veterans Pkwy B3 Bloomington (61704) ***(G-2212)***
**Pella Corporation**....309 663-7132
1407 N Veterans Pkwy B3 Bloomington (61704) ***(G-2213)***
**Pella Corporation**....309 663-7132
1407 N Veterans Pkwy B3 Bloomington (61704) ***(G-2214)***
**Pella Window Door, Bloomington** *Also called Pella Corporation* ***(G-2211)***
**Pella Window Door, Bloomington** *Also called Pella Corporation* ***(G-2212)***
**Pella Window Door, Bloomington** *Also called Pella Corporation* ***(G-2213)***
**Pella Window Door, Bloomington** *Also called Pella Corporation* ***(G-2214)***
**Pellegrini Enterprises Inc**....815 717-6408
15617 S 71st Ct Orland Park (60462) ***(G-16884)***
**Pelron Corporation**....708 442-9100
7847 W 47th St Mc Cook (60525) ***(G-14455)***
**Pelstar LLC**....708 377-0600
9500 W 55th St Ste C Countryside (60525) ***(G-7440)***
**Pen At Hand**....847 498-9174
4120 Terri Lyn Ln Northbrook (60062) ***(G-16337)***
**Penco Electric**....847 423-2159
7153 N Austin Ave Niles (60714) ***(G-16016)***
**Pendragon Software Corporation**....847 816-9660
118 S Clinton St Ste 570 Chicago (60661) ***(G-6099)***
**Pengo Products Company, Chicago** *Also called City Screen Inc* ***(G-4388)***
**Penguin Foods, Rockford** *Also called M E F Corp* ***(G-18477)***
**Penn Aluminum Intl LLC (HQ)**....618 684-2146
1117 N 2nd St Murphysboro (62966) ***(G-15579)***
**Pennant Foods**....708 752-8730
11746 S Austin Ave Alsip (60803) ***(G-506)***
**Pennsylvania Carbon Products, Northbrook** *Also called Graphtek LLC* ***(G-16266)***
**Penray Companies Inc (PA)**....800 323-6329
440 Denniston Ct Wheeling (60090) ***(G-22120)***
**Penstock Construction Services**....630 816-2456
2508 Ruth Fitzgerald Dr Plainfield (60586) ***(G-17636)***
**Pentair Flow Technologies LLC**....630 859-7000
800 Airport Rd North Aurora (60542) ***(G-16140)***
**Pentair Fltrtion Solutions LLC (HQ)**....630 307-3000
1040 Muirfield Dr Hanover Park (60133) ***(G-11589)***
**Pentair Fltrtion Solutions LLC**....630 307-3000
1040 Muirfield Dr Bartlett (60133) ***(G-1321)***
**Pentegra Systems LLC**....630 941-6000
780 W Belden Ave Ste A Addison (60101) ***(G-238)***
**Penton Media Inc**....212 204-4200
24652 Network Pl Chicago (60673) ***(G-6100)***
**Penton Media - Aviation Week, Chicago** *Also called Penton Media Inc* ***(G-6100)***
**People & Places Newspaper**....847 804-6985
4303 Atlantic Ave Schiller Park (60176) ***(G-19858)***
**People Against Dirty Mfg Pbc**....415 568-4600
720 E 111th St Chicago (60628) ***(G-6101)***
**People's Weekly World, Chicago** *Also called Long View Publishing Co Inc* ***(G-5537)***
**Peopleadmin Inc**....877 637-5800
4611 N Ravenswood Ave # 201 Chicago (60640) ***(G-6102)***
**Peoples Cmplete Buiding Centre, Watseka** *Also called Peoples Coal and Lumber Co* ***(G-21425)***
**Peoples Coal and Lumber Co (PA)**....815 432-2456
121 S 3rd St Watseka (60970) ***(G-21425)***
**Peoples Tribune**....773 486-3551
2421 W Pratt Blvd Chicago (60645) ***(G-6103)***
**Peoria Journal Star Inc**....585 598-0030
1 News Plz Peoria (61643) ***(G-17423)***
**Peoria Manufacturing Co Inc**....708 429-4200
17620 Duvan Dr Tinley Park (60477) ***(G-20938)***
**Peoria Midwest Equipment Inc**....309 454-6800
2150 W College Ave Normal (61761) ***(G-16083)***
**Peoria Neuroinnovations LLC**....217 899-0443
801 W Main St Peoria (61606) ***(G-17424)***
**Peoria Open M R I**....309 692-7674
6708 N Knoxville Ave # 2 Peoria (61614) ***(G-17425)***
**Peoria Packing Ltd (PA)**....312 226-2600
1307 W Lake St Chicago (60607) ***(G-6104)***
**Peoria Packing Ltd**....815 465-9824
8372 N 12000e Rd Grant Park (60940) ***(G-11313)***
**Peoria Post Inc**....309 688-3628
834 E Glen Ave Peoria (61616) ***(G-17426)***
**Peoria Tube Forming Corp**....309 822-0274
231 Detroit Ave Morton (61550) ***(G-15176)***
**Peoria Wilbert Vault Co Inc**....309 383-2882
510 Townhall Rd Metamora (61548) ***(G-14747)***
**Peotone Vidette, Peotone** *Also called Russell Publications Inc* ***(G-17492)***
**Pep Drilling Co (PA)**....618 242-2205
123 S 10th St Ste 210 Mount Vernon (62864) ***(G-15438)***
**Pep Industries Inc**....630 833-0404
725 N Wisconsin Ave Villa Park (60181) ***(G-21276)***
**Pep Wauconda, Elgin** *Also called Wauconda Tool & Engineering Co* ***(G-9231)***
**Pepperball, Lake Forest** *Also called United Tactical Systems LLC* ***(G-12978)***
**Pepsi Cola Btlg Co Rock Island, Rock Island** *Also called AD Huesing Corporation* ***(G-18157)***
**Pepsi Cola Gen Bttlers of Lima (HQ)**....847 253-1000
3501 Algonquin Rd Ste 700 Rolling Meadows (60008) ***(G-18761)***
**Pepsi Mid America**....217 826-8118
202 Vine St Marshall (62441) ***(G-14327)***
**Pepsi Midamerica, Marion** *Also called Crisp Container Corporation* ***(G-14257)***
**Pepsi Midamerica**....618 242-6285
205 N Davidson St Mount Vernon (62864) ***(G-15439)***
**Pepsi Midamerica Co (PA)**....618 997-1377
2605 W Main St Marion (62959) ***(G-14277)***
**Pepsi-Cola Chmpign Urbana Btlr**....217 352-4126
1306 W Anthony Dr Champaign (61821) ***(G-3523)***

ALPHABETIC

**Pepsi-Cola Gen Bottlers Inc (HQ)** 847 598-3000
1475 E Wdfeld Rd Ste 1300 Schaumburg (60173) ***(G-19688)***
**Pepsi-Cola General Bottlers VA** 847 253-1000
3501 Algonquin Rd Rolling Meadows (60008) ***(G-18762)***
**Pepsico, Champaign** *Also called Pepsi-Cola Chmpign Urbana Btlr* ***(G-3523)***
**Pepsico, Schaumburg** *Also called Pepsi-Cola Gen Bottlers Inc* ***(G-19688)***
**Pepsico, Springfield** *Also called Springfield Pepsi Cola Btlg Co* ***(G-20530)***
**Pepsico, Decatur** *Also called Decatur Bottling Co* ***(G-7870)***
**Pepsico, Chicago** *Also called P-Americas LLC* ***(G-6042)***
**Pepsico, Morton** *Also called P-Americas LLC* ***(G-15173)***
**Pepsico, Quincy** *Also called Refreshment Services Inc* ***(G-17886)***
**Pepsico, Chicago** *Also called P-Americas LLC* ***(G-6043)***
**Pepsico, Springfield** *Also called Refreshment Services Inc* ***(G-20511)***
**Pepsico, Rolling Meadows** *Also called Pepsi Cola Gen Bttlers of Lima* ***(G-18761)***
**Pepsico, Chicago** *Also called P-Americas LLC* ***(G-6044)***
**Pepsico, Decatur** *Also called Refreshment Services Inc* ***(G-7933)***
**Pepsico, Chicago** *Also called P-Americas LLC* ***(G-6045)***
**Pepsico Inc** 312 821-1000
555 W Monroe St Fl 1 Chicago (60661) ***(G-6105)***
**Peradata Technology Corp** 631 588-2216
4324 N Damen Ave Chicago (60618) ***(G-6106)***
**Perez Health Incorporated** 708 788-0101
2215 Oak Park Ave Berwyn (60402) ***(G-2072)***
**Perfect Circle Projectiles LLC** 847 367-8960
28101 N Ballard Dr Ste C Lake Forest (60045) ***(G-12942)***
**Perfect Clean, Niles** *Also called Umf Corporation* ***(G-16045)***
**Perfect Pasta Inc** 630 543-8300
31 S Fairbank St Ste B Addison (60101) ***(G-239)***
**Perfect Pipe & Supply Corp** 630 628-6728
440 S Mclean Blvd Elgin (60123) ***(G-9137)***
**Perfect Plastic Printing Corp** 630 584-1600
311 Kautz Rd Ste 1 Saint Charles (60174) ***(G-19234)***
**Perfect Powder Coating** 847 322-6666
16571 W Applewood Ct Gurnee (60031) ***(G-11484)***
**Perfect Shutters Inc** 815 648-2401
12213 Il Route 173 Hebron (60034) ***(G-11724)***
**Perfect Smiles (PA)** 708 687-6100
6056 159th St Oak Forest (60452) ***(G-16587)***
**Perfectclean, Skokie** *Also called Umf Corporation* ***(G-20104)***
**Perfection Custom Closets & Co** 847 647-6461
7183 N Austin Ave Niles (60714) ***(G-16017)***
**Perfection Equipment Inc** 847 244-7200
4259 Lee Ave Gurnee (60031) ***(G-11485)***
**Perfection Plating Inc** 847 593-6506
775 Morse Ave Elk Grove Village (60007) ***(G-9673)***
**Perfection Probes Inc** 847 726-8868
24241 W Rose Ave Lake Zurich (60047) ***(G-13112)***
**Perfection Signs & Graphics** 708 795-0611
6737 Cermak Rd Berwyn (60402) ***(G-2073)***
**Perfection Spring Stmping Corp** 847 437-3900
1449 E Algonquin Rd Mount Prospect (60056) ***(G-15362)***
**Perfection Vault Co Inc** 217 673-6111
403 N Ladue Rd Woodson (62695) ***(G-22531)***
**Perfectvision Mfg Inc** 630 226-9890
1 Gateway Ct Ste Aa Bolingbrook (60440) ***(G-2357)***
**Performance Auto Salon Inc** 815 468-6882
17 E Sixth St Manteno (60950) ***(G-14189)***
**Performance Automotive** 618 377-0020
475 S Prairie St Bethalto (62010) ***(G-2083)***
**Performance Battery Group Inc** 630 293-5505
870 W Hawthorne Ln A West Chicago (60185) ***(G-21755)***
**Performance Design Inc** 847 719-1535
238 Telser Rd Lake Zurich (60047) ***(G-13113)***
**Performance Diesel Service** 217 375-4429
7586 E 4200 North Rd Hoopeston (60942) ***(G-12113)***
**Performance Gear Systems Inc** 630 739-6666
14309 S Route 59 Plainfield (60544) ***(G-17637)***
**Performance Industries Inc** 972 393-6881
20 Lake Marian Rd Carpentersville (60110) ***(G-3294)***
**Performance Lawn & Power** 217 857-3717
1311 W Main St Teutopolis (62467) ***(G-20854)***
**Performance Mailing & Prtg Inc** 847 549-0500
777 N Milwaukee Ave Libertyville (60048) ***(G-13366)***
**Performance Manufacturing** 630 231-8099
782 W Hawthorne Ln West Chicago (60185) ***(G-21756)***
**Performance Material Division, Itasca** *Also called Shima American Corporation* ***(G-12353)***
**Performance Military Group Inc** 847 325-4450
300 Knightsbridge Pkwy # 116 Lincolnshire (60069) ***(G-13473)***
**Performance Pattern & Mch Inc** 309 676-0907
2421 Sw Adams St Peoria (61602) ***(G-17427)***
**Performance Pro Plumbing Inc** 630 566-5207
3915 Liberty Blvd Westmont (60559) ***(G-21910)***
**Performance Stamping Co Inc** 847 426-2233
20 Lake Marian Rd Carpentersville (60110) ***(G-3295)***
**Performance Welding LLC** 217 412-5722
10333 W Washington St Rd Maroa (61756) ***(G-14307)***
**Perftech Inc** 630 554-0010
251 Airport Rd North Aurora (60542) ***(G-16141)***

**Perimeter Access Sys Svcs Inc** 630 556-4283
116 Paul St Elburn (60119) ***(G-8903)***
**Peritus Plastics LLC** 815 448-2005
804 Commercial Dr Mazon (60444) ***(G-14440)***
**Perkins Construction** 815 233-9655
4872 W Lily Creek Rd Freeport (61032) ***(G-10678)***
**Perkins Engines Inc (HQ)** 309 578-7364
N4 Ac6160 # 6160 Mossville (61552) ***(G-15254)***
**Perkins Enterprise Inc** 708 560-3837
15518 S Park Ave South Holland (60473) ***(G-20298)***
**Perkins Manfacturing, Bolingbrook** *Also called Hovi Industries Incorporated* ***(G-2316)***
**Perkins Manufacturing Co** 708 482-9500
380 Veterans Pkwy Ste 110 Bolingbrook (60440) ***(G-2358)***
**Perkins Products Inc** 708 458-2000
7025 W 66th Pl Bedford Park (60638) ***(G-1572)***
**Perle & Sons Jewelers Inc** 630 357-3357
8 W Jefferson Ave Naperville (60540) ***(G-15724)***
**Perma Graphics Printers** 815 485-6955
216 N Marley Rd New Lenox (60451) ***(G-15901)***
**Perma-Pipe Inc (HQ)** 847 966-2190
7720 N Lehigh Ave Niles (60714) ***(G-16018)***
**Perma-Pipe Intl Holdings Inc (PA)** 847 966-1000
6410 W Howard St Niles (60714) ***(G-16019)***
**Perma-Treat of Illinois Inc** 618 997-5646
1800 Permatreat Dr Marion (62959) ***(G-14278)***
**Permabilt of Illinois, Le Roy** *Also called Omni-Tech Systems Inc* ***(G-13208)***
**Permacor Inc** 708 422-3353
9540 Tulley Ave Oak Lawn (60453) ***(G-16639)***
**Permalert E S P, Niles** *Also called Perma-Pipe Inc* ***(G-16018)***
**Permatreat Lumber, Marion** *Also called Perma-Treat of Illinois Inc* ***(G-14278)***
**Permatron Corporation** 847 434-1421
2020 Touhy Ave Elk Grove Village (60007) ***(G-9674)***
**Permissions Group Inc** 847 635-6550
1247 Milwaukee Ave # 303 Glenview (60025) ***(G-11181)***
**Permobil Inc** 847 568-0001
7515 Linder Ave Skokie (60077) ***(G-20054)***
**Perq/Hci LLC (HQ)** 847 375-5000
5600 N River Rd Ste 900 Rosemont (60018) ***(G-19020)***
**Perritt Capital Mangement, Chicago** *Also called Investment Information Svcs* ***(G-5232)***
**Perry Adult Living Inc** 618 542-5421
1308 Wells Street Rd Du Quoin (62832) ***(G-8557)***
**Perry Johnson Inc** 847 635-0010
10255 W Higgins Rd # 140 Rosemont (60018) ***(G-19021)***
**Perry Johnson Consulting, Rosemont** *Also called Perry Johnson Inc* ***(G-19021)***
**Perryco Inc (PA)** 303 652-8282
6920 Webster St Downers Grove (60516) ***(G-8501)***
**Perryco Inc** 815 436-2431
15507 S Route 59 Plainfield (60544) ***(G-17638)***
**Perryco Inc** 217 322-3321
110 E Lafayette St Rushville (62681) ***(G-19094)***
**Pershing Road Recycle, Chicago** *Also called Legacy Vulcan LLC* ***(G-5487)***
**Personal Battery Caddy, Saint Charles** *Also called Tools Aviation LLC* ***(G-19285)***
**Personalitee's, Prospect Heights** *Also called Woolenwear Co* ***(G-17786)***
**Personalized Pillows Co** 847 226-7393
16783 W Old Orchard Dr Wadsworth (60083) ***(G-21325)***
**Personalized Threads** 815 431-1815
2655 E 1559th Rd Ottawa (61350) ***(G-16978)***
**Personify** 217 840-2638
208a W Main St Urbana (61801) ***(G-21097)***
**Perspecto Map Company Inc** 815 356-1288
367 Cumberland Ln Village of Lakewood (60014) ***(G-21291)***
**Perten Instruments Inc** 217 585-9440
6444 6th Street Frontage A Springfield (62712) ***(G-20503)***
**Pervasive Health Inc** 312 257-2967
1 N La Salle St Ste 1825 Chicago (60602) ***(G-6107)***
**Pet AG, Hampshire** *Also called Pet-Ag Inc* ***(G-11558)***
**Pet Age Magazine, Chicago** *Also called HH Backer Associates Inc* ***(G-5084)***
**Pet Celebrations Inc** 630 832-6549
269 N Highland Ave Elmhurst (60126) ***(G-9921)***
**Pet Factory Inc** 847 281-8054
845 E High St Mundelein (60060) ***(G-15544)***
**Pet Groom Products Div, Melrose Park** *Also called Veeco Manufacturing Inc* ***(G-14705)***
**Pet King Brands Inc** 630 241-3905
710 Vandustrial Dr Westmont (60559) ***(G-21911)***
**Pet OFallon LLC** 618 628-3300
610 E State St O Fallon (62269) ***(G-16473)***
**Pet-Ag Inc** 847 683-2288
255 Keyes Ave Hampshire (60140) ***(G-11558)***
**Petainer Manufacturing USA Inc** 630 326-9921
515 N River St Ste 206 Batavia (60510) ***(G-1481)***
**Petco, Lake Forest** *Also called Polyurthane Engrg Tchnques Inc* ***(G-12947)***
**Petco Petroleum Corporation** 618 242-8718
123 S 10th St Ste 505 Mount Vernon (62864) ***(G-15440)***
**Petco Petroleum Corporation (PA)** 630 654-1740
108 E Ogden Ave Ste 100 Hinsdale (60521) ***(G-11956)***
**Pete Frcano Sons Cstm HM Bldrs** 847 258-4626
1225 Howard St Elk Grove Village (60007) ***(G-9675)***

**Petego Egr LLC**....312 726-1341
8 S Michigan Ave Ste 1601 Chicago (60603) ***(G-6108)***
**Peter Baker & Son Co (PA)**....847 362-3663
1349 Rockland Rd Lake Bluff (60044) ***(G-12861)***
**Peter Baker & Son Co**....815 344-1640
914 W Illinois Rte 120 Mc Henry (60050) ***(G-14462)***
**Peter Built**....618 337-4000
2350 Sauget Indus Pkwy East Saint Louis (62206) ***(G-8764)***
**Peter Fox**....847 428-2249
578 Rock Road Dr Ste 4 East Dundee (60118) ***(G-8652)***
**Peter Lehman Inc**....847 395-7997
40126 N Il Route 83 Antioch (60002) ***(G-649)***
**Peter Perella & Co**....815 727-4526
600 N Scott St Joliet (60432) ***(G-12550)***
**Peter Troost Monument, Hillside** *Also called Monumental Manufacturing Co* ***(G-11927)***
**Peter Troost Monument Co**....773 585-0242
6605 S Pulaski Rd Chicago (60629) ***(G-6109)***
**Peters Body Shop & Towing Inc**....217 223-5250
823 N 54th St Quincy (62305) ***(G-17867)***
**Peters Construction**....773 489-5555
3441 W Grand Ave Chicago (60651) ***(G-6110)***
**Peters Machine Inc**....217 875-2578
3765 N Westlawn Ave Decatur (62526) ***(G-7926)***
**Peters Machine Works Inc**....708 496-3005
8277 S 86th Ct Oak Lawn (60458) ***(G-16640)***
**Petersburg Observer Co Inc**....217 632-2236
235 E Sangamon Ave Petersburg (62675) ***(G-17537)***
**Petersburg Painting & Pwr Wshg, Springfield** *Also called Petersburg Power Washing Inc* ***(G-20504)***
**Petersburg Power Washing Inc**....217 415-9013
829 S 11th St Springfield (62703) ***(G-20504)***
**Petersen Aluminum Corporation (PA)**....847 228-7150
1005 Tonne Rd Elk Grove Village (60007) ***(G-9676)***
**Petersen Finishing Corporation (PA)**....847 228-7150
1005 Tonne Rd Elk Grove Village (60007) ***(G-9677)***
**Petersen Sand & Gravel Inc**....815 344-1060
914 Rand Rd Ste A Lakemoor (60051) ***(G-13145)***
**Petersen/Tru-Cut Automotive, Watseka** *Also called T & S Business Group LLC* ***(G-21429)***
**Peterson Alumminum, Elk Grove Village** *Also called Charleston Industries Inc* ***(G-9365)***
**Peterson Brothers Plastics**....773 286-5666
2929 N Pulaski Rd Chicago (60641) ***(G-6111)***
**Peterson Dermond Design LLC**....414 383-5029
900 Grove St Ste 10 Evanston (60201) ***(G-10085)***
**Peterson Elc Panl Mfg Co Inc**....708 449-2270
5550 Mcdermott Dr Berkeley (60163) ***(G-2048)***
**Peterson Elctr-Msical Pdts Inc**....708 388-3311
11601 S Mayfield Ave Alsip (60803) ***(G-507)***
**Peterson Farms, Harvard** *Also called Bill Peterson* ***(G-11624)***
**Peterson Intl Entp Ltd**....847 541-3700
504 Glenn Ave Wheeling (60090) ***(G-22121)***
**Peterson Manufacturing Company, Plainfield** *Also called Nnm Manufacturing LLC* ***(G-17633)***
**Peterson Publication Services**....630 469-6732
887 Hill Ave Glen Ellyn (60137) ***(G-10987)***
**Petnet Solutions Inc**....847 297-3721
200 Howard Ave Ste 240 Des Plaines (60018) ***(G-8252)***
**Petote LLC**....312 455-0873
2444 W 16th St Ste 4 Chicago (60608) ***(G-6112)***
**Petra Companies The, East Saint Louis** *Also called Petra Industries Inc* ***(G-8765)***
**Petra Industries Inc**....618 271-0022
6400 Collinsville Rd East Saint Louis (62201) ***(G-8765)***
**Petra Manufacturing Co**....773 622-1475
6600 W Armitage Ave Chicago (60707) ***(G-6113)***
**Petrak Industries Incorporated**....815 483-2290
17250 New Lenox Rd Joliet (60433) ***(G-12551)***
**Petri Welding & Prop Repr Inc**....217 243-1748
2253 W Morton Ave Jacksonville (62650) ***(G-12407)***
**Petro Chem Echer Erhardt LLC**....773 847-7535
2628 S Sacramento Ave Chicago (60623) ***(G-6114)***
**Petro Enterprises Inc**....708 425-1551
10242 Ridgeland Ave Chicago Ridge (60415) ***(G-7153)***
**Petro Prop Inc**....630 910-4738
7948 Highland Ave Downers Grove (60516) ***(G-8502)***
**Petro-Chem Industries Div, Chicago** *Also called Petro Chem Echer Erhardt LLC* ***(G-6114)***
**Petrochem Inc**....630 513-6350
6n999 Whispering Trl Saint Charles (60175) ***(G-19235)***
**Petron Oil Production Inc (PA)**....618 783-4486
405 E Jourdan St Apt 3 Newton (62448) ***(G-15946)***
**Petronics Inc**....608 630-6527
60 Hazelwood Dr Rm 216 Champaign (61820) ***(G-3524)***
**Pets Stop, Melrose Park** *Also called Sunscape Time Inc* ***(G-14698)***
**Pexco LLC (HQ)**....847 296-5511
1600 Birchwood Ave Des Plaines (60018) ***(G-8253)***
**Pfanstiehl Inc**....847 623-0370
1219 Glen Rock Ave Waukegan (60085) ***(G-21601)***
**PFC, Romeoville** *Also called Plastic Film Corp America Inc* ***(G-18857)***
**Pfeifer Industries LLC**....630 596-9000
2180 Corp Ln Unit 104 Naperville (60563) ***(G-15725)***
**Pfingsten Partners LLC (PA)**....312 222-8707
300 N Lasalle St 5400 Chicago (60654) ***(G-6115)***
**Pfingsten Partners Fund IV LP**....312 222-8707
300 N La Salle Dr Chicago (60654) ***(G-6116)***
**Pfizer Inc**....847 506-8895
700 E Business Center Dr Mount Prospect (60056) ***(G-15363)***
**Pfizer Inc**....847 639-3020
2323 Grove Ln Cary (60013) ***(G-3363)***
**Pg Display, Rockford** *Also called Process Graphics Corp* ***(G-18542)***
**Pgi Mfg LLC**....815 398-0313
614 Grable St Rockford (61109) ***(G-18533)***
**Pgi Mfg LLC**....800 821-3475
614 Grable St Rockford (61109) ***(G-18534)***
**PH Tool Manufacturing**....847 952-9441
1200 Andrea Ln Des Plaines (60018) ***(G-8254)***
**Phalanx Training Inc**....847 859-9156
617 Grove St Ste A Evanston (60201) ***(G-10086)***
**Pharma Logistics**....847 388-3104
1050 E High St Mundelein (60060) ***(G-15545)***
**Pharmaceutical Labs and Cons I**....630 359-3831
1010 W Fullerton Ave Addison (60101) ***(G-240)***
**Pharmacy Services of Rockford, Rockford** *Also called Hot Shots Nm LLC* ***(G-18423)***
**Pharmacy Store, Kankakee** *Also called Riverside Medi-Center Inc* ***(G-12645)***
**Pharmanutrients Inc**....847 234-2334
37 Sherwood Ter Ste 109 Lake Bluff (60044) ***(G-12862)***
**Pharmasyn Inc**....847 752-8405
1840 Industrial Dr # 140 Libertyville (60048) ***(G-13367)***
**Pharmdium Hlthcare Hldings Inc**....800 523-7749
2 Conway Prk 150 N Lake Forest (60045) ***(G-12943)***
**Pharmedium Healthcare Corp (PA)**....847 457-2300
150 N Field Dr Ste 350 Lake Forest (60045) ***(G-12944)***
**Pheasant Hollow Winery Inc**....618 629-2302
14931 State Highway 37 Whittington (62897) ***(G-22188)***
**Phelps Farms**....815 624-7263
4639 W Rockton Rd Rockton (61072) ***(G-18701)***
**Phelps Industries LLC**....815 397-0236
5213 26th Ave Rockford (61109) ***(G-18535)***
**Phenome Technologies Inc**....847 962-1273
23220 N Indian Creek Rd Lincolnshire (60069) ***(G-13474)***
**PHI Group Inc**....847 824-5610
555 E Business Center Dr Mount Prospect (60056) ***(G-15364)***
**Phibro Animal Health, Quincy** *Also called Prince Agri Products Inc* ***(G-17872)***
**Philadelphia Gear, Mokena** *Also called Timken Gears & Services Inc* ***(G-14911)***
**Philip Morris USA Inc**....847 605-9595
300 N Martingale Rd # 700 Schaumburg (60173) ***(G-19689)***
**Philip Reinisch Company**....312 644-6776
1555 Naperville Wheaton R Naperville (60563) ***(G-15726)***
**Philip W Weiss Monument Works, Belleville** *Also called Weiss Monument Works Inc* ***(G-1690)***
**Philips Elec N Amer Corp**....630 585-2000
555 N Commerce St Aurora (60504) ***(G-1064)***
**Philips Lighting N Amer Corp**....800 825-5844
10275 W Higgins Rd # 800 Rosemont (60018) ***(G-19022)***
**Philips Lighting N Amer Corp**....708 307-3000
440 Medinah Rd Roselle (60172) ***(G-18962)***
**Philips Medical Systems Clevel**....630 585-2000
555 N Commerce St Aurora (60504) ***(G-1065)***
**Phillip C Cowen**....630 208-1848
106 7th Pl Geneva (60134) ***(G-10859)***
**Phillip Grigalanz**....219 628-6706
114 N Washington St Jerseyville (62052) ***(G-12425)***
**Phillip Rodgers**....815 877-5461
5366 Forest Hills Ct Loves Park (61111) ***(G-13973)***
**Phillips & Johnston Inc**....815 778-3355
900 E Commercial St Lyndon (61261) ***(G-14014)***
**Phillips 66**....618 251-2800
2300 S Delmar Ave Hartford (62048) ***(G-11614)***
**Phillips Granite Industries, Mount Vernon** *Also called Jack R Phillips* ***(G-15416)***
**Phillips Pharmaceuticals Inc**....630 328-0016
710 E Ogden Ave Ste 207 Naperville (60563) ***(G-15727)***
**Philly Fasteners Corp**....847 584-9408
224 W Beech Dr Schaumburg (60193) ***(G-19690)***
**Philos Technologies Inc**....630 945-2933
1011 Commerce Ct Buffalo Grove (60089) ***(G-2751)***
**Phils Auto Body**....773 847-7156
833 W 35th St Chicago (60609) ***(G-6117)***
**Phoebe & Frances**....847 446-5480
566 Chestnut St Winnetka (60093) ***(G-22314)***
**Phoenix Art Woodworks**....847 279-1576
500 Harvester Ct Ste 7 Wheeling (60090) ***(G-22122)***
**Phoenix Binding Corp**....847 981-1111
1100 Pratt Blvd Elk Grove Village (60007) ***(G-9678)***
**Phoenix Business Solutions LLC**....708 388-1330
12543 S Laramie Ave Alsip (60803) ***(G-508)***
**Phoenix Converting LLC**....630 285-1500
1251 Ardmore Ave Itasca (60143) ***(G-12339)***
**Phoenix Electric Mfg Co**....773 477-8855
3625 N Halsted St Chicago (60613) ***(G-6118)***

ALPHABETIC

(PA)=Parent Co (HQ)=Headquarters (DH)=Div Headquarters

# ALPHABETIC SECTION

**Phoenix Fabrication & Sup Inc**...............................708 754-5901
3215 Butler St  S Chicago Hts  (60411)  *(G-19110)*
**Phoenix Graphics Inc**............................................847 699-9520
2375 Magnolia St  Des Plaines  (60018)  *(G-8255)*
**Phoenix Graphix**...................................................618 531-3664
4513 Swanwick Rice Rd  Pinckneyville  (62274)  *(G-17551)*
**Phoenix Industries, Galesburg** *Also called Kccdd Inc (G-10762)*
**Phoenix Industries Inc**..........................................708 478-5474
10601 Saint John Dr  Mokena  (60448)  *(G-14895)*
**Phoenix Inks and Coatings  LLC**..........................630 972-2500
20w267 101st St  Lemont  (60439)  *(G-13255)*
**Phoenix Intl Publications Inc**..............................312 739-4400
8501 W Higgins Rd Ste 300  Chicago  (60631)  *(G-6119)*
**Phoenix Leather Goods LLC**................................815 267-3926
23824 W Andrew Rd Ste 102  Plainfield  (60585)  *(G-17639)*
**Phoenix Marketing Services**................................630 616-8000
104 Terrace Dr  Mundelein  (60060)  *(G-15546)*
**Phoenix Modular Elevator Inc**.............................618 244-2314
4800 Phoenix Dr  Mount Vernon  (62864)  *(G-15441)*
**Phoenix Paper Products Inc**................................815 368-3343
1652 N Us Highway 251  Lostant  (61334)  *(G-13907)*
**Phoenix Press Inc**................................................630 833-2281
140 E Hill St  Villa Park  (60181)  *(G-21277)*
**Phoenix Services  LLC**.........................................708 849-3527
13500 S Perry Ave  Riverdale  (60827)  *(G-18022)*
**Phoenix Tool Corp**...............................................847 956-1886
700 Lunt Ave  Elk Grove Village  (60007)  *(G-9679)*
**Phoenix Trading Chicago  Inc**.............................847 304-5181
26809 W Lakeridge Dr  Lake Barrington  (60010)  *(G-12822)*
**Phoenix Tree Publishing Inc**................................773 251-0309
5660 N Jersey Ave  Chicago  (60659)  *(G-6120)*
**Phoenix Unlimited Ltd**.........................................847 515-1263
11514 Smith Dr Unit D  Huntley  (60142)  *(G-12167)*
**Phoenix Welding Co  Inc**.....................................630 616-1700
9220 Parklane Ave  Franklin Park  (60131)  *(G-10549)*
**Phoenix Woodworking Corp**................................815 338-9338
2000 Duncan Pl  Woodstock  (60098)  *(G-22599)*
**Phonak  LLC (HQ)**.................................................630 821-5000
4520 Weaver Pkwy Ste 1  Warrenville  (60555)  *(G-21354)*
**Phosphate Resource Ptrs**....................................847 739-1200
100 Saunders Rd Ste 300  Lake Forest  (60045)  *(G-12945)*
**Photex, Chicago** *Also called Midwest Law Printing Co Inc (G-5745)*
**Photo Copy Service, Cherry Valley** *Also called L & S Label Printing Inc (G-3646)*
**Photo Graphic Design Service**.............................815 672-4417
124 N Bloomington St  Streator  (61364)  *(G-20700)*
**Photo Techniques Corp**.......................................630 690-9360
399 Gundersen Dr  Carol Stream  (60188)  *(G-3212)*
**Photo Techniques Corp (PA)**...............................630 690-9360
387 Gundersen Dr  Carol Stream  (60188)  *(G-3213)*
**Photonicare  Inc**..................................................405 880-7209
60 Hazelwood Dr  Champaign  (61820)  *(G-3525)*
**Photosteel, Tilton** *Also called Custom Signs On Metal  LLC (G-20880)*
**Php Racengines Inc**.............................................847 526-9393
950 N Rand Rd Ste 107  Wauconda  (60084)  *(G-21492)*
**Phylrich International, Lanark** *Also called Aldo-Shane Corporation (G-13150)*
**Physician Software Systems LLC**........................630 717-8192
3333 Warrenville Rd # 200  Lisle  (60532)  *(G-13639)*
**Physicians Record Co Inc**....................................800 323-9268
3000 Ridgeland Ave  Berwyn  (60402)  *(G-2074)*
**Piasa Plastics Inc**................................................618 372-7516
615 N Main St  Brighton  (62012)  *(G-2544)*
**Piatt County Clerk Recorder, Monticello** *Also called County of Piatt (G-15076)*
**Piatt County Journal Repub, Monticello** *Also called Lumber Specialists  Inc (G-15078)*
**Piatt County Service Co**......................................217 489-2411
1070 Old Us 150  Mansfield  (61854)  *(G-14178)*
**Piatt County Service Co**......................................217 678-5511
878 State Highway 105  Bement  (61813)  *(G-1801)*
**Piccolino Inc**........................................................708 259-2072
802 S Clay St  Hinsdale  (60521)  *(G-11957)*
**Picis Clinical Solutions  Inc**................................847 993-2200
9500 W Higgins Rd # 1100  Rosemont  (60018)  *(G-19023)*
**Pickard Incorporated**...........................................847 395-3800
782 Pickard Ave  Antioch  (60002)  *(G-650)*
**Picket Fence Florist, Paxton** *Also called Hts Hancock Transcriptions Svc (G-17237)*
**Pickles Sorrel  Inc**...............................................773 379-4748
5610 W Taylor St  Chicago  (60644)  *(G-6121)*
**Pickling Steel, Waterman** *Also called Vision Pickling and Proc Inc (G-21410)*
**Picnic Tables  Inc**................................................630 482-6200
222 State St  Batavia  (60510)  *(G-1482)*
**Picture Frame Factory, Franklin Park** *Also called Sarj USA Inc (G-10582)*
**Picture Frame Factory, Franklin Park** *Also called Mercurys Green LLC (G-10528)*
**Picture Frame Fulfillment LLC**............................847 260-5071
9201 King St  Franklin Park  (60131)  *(G-10550)*
**Picture Perfect Puzzles LLC**................................847 838-0848
39721 N Beck Rd  Lake Villa  (60046)  *(G-13022)*
**Picture Stone Inc**.................................................773 875-5021
108 N Kenilworth Ave  Mount Prospect  (60056)  *(G-15365)*
**Pie Piper, Bensenville** *Also called Distinctive Foods LLC (G-1880)*

**Pie Piper Products, Wheeling** *Also called Distinctive Foods LLC (G-22036)*
**Piece, Chicago** *Also called Resco 8 LLC (G-6336)*
**Piece Works Specialists Inc**.................................309 266-7016
300 W Adams St  Morton  (61550)  *(G-15177)*
**Pieces of Learning  Inc**........................................618 964-9426
1112 N Carbon St Unit A  Marion  (62959)  *(G-14279)*
**Piedmont Hardware Brands, Freeport** *Also called Nova Wildcat Amerock  LLC (G-10677)*
**Piemonte Bakery Company Inc**...........................815 962-4833
1122 Rock St  Rockford  (61101)  *(G-18536)*
**Pierce & Stevens Chemical**..................................630 653-3800
245 Kehoe Blvd  Carol Stream  (60188)  *(G-3214)*
**Pierce Box & Paper Corporation**..........................815 547-0117
4133 Newburg Rd  Belvidere  (61008)  *(G-1778)*
**Pierce Crandell & Co Inc**......................................847 549-6015
14047 W Petronella Dr # 103  Libertyville  (60048)  *(G-13368)*
**Pierce Distribution Svcs Co, Loves Park** *Also called Pierce Packaging Co (G-13974)*
**Pierce Packaging Co (PA)**....................................815 636-5650
2028 E Riverside Blvd  Loves Park  (61111)  *(G-13974)*
**Pierce Packaging Co**............................................815 636-5656
2130 W Townline Rd  Peoria  (61615)  *(G-17428)*
**Pierce Packaging Co**............................................815 636-5656
1200 Windsor Rd  Loves Park  (61111)  *(G-13975)*
**Piersons Mattress & Furn Co, Peoria** *Also called Piersons Mattress Inc (G-17429)*
**Piersons Mattress Inc**..........................................309 637-8455
1034 S Western Ave  Peoria  (61605)  *(G-17429)*
**Pike County Concrete Inc**....................................217 285-5548
1503 Kamar Dr  Pittsfield  (62363)  *(G-17573)*
**Pike County Express**............................................217 285-5415
129 N Madison St  Pittsfield  (62363)  *(G-17574)*
**Pike Press, Pittsfield** *Also called Campbell Publishing Co Inc (G-17564)*
**Pikids, Chicago** *Also called Phoenix Intl Publications Inc (G-6119)*
**Pilkington North America  Inc**..............................630 545-0063
500 Windy Point Dr  Glendale Heights  (60139)  *(G-11057)*
**Pilkington North America  Inc**..............................815 433-0932
300 Center 20th St  Ottawa  (61350)  *(G-16979)*
**Pilla Exec Inc**........................................................312 882-8263
2447 W 80th St  Chicago  (60652)  *(G-6122)*
**Pillar Enterprises Inc**...........................................630 966-2566
121 S Lincolnway Ste 103  North Aurora  (60542)  *(G-16142)*
**Pillarhouse USA Inc**.............................................847 593-9080
201 Lively Blvd  Elk Grove Village  (60007)  *(G-9680)*
**Pillow Factory  Inc (HQ)**.......................................847 680-3388
900 Busch Pkwy  Buffalo Grove  (60089)  *(G-2752)*
**Pillsbury Company  LLC**......................................847 541-8888
135 N Arlington Heghts  Buffalo Grove  (60089)  *(G-2753)*
**Pilot Corporation of America**..............................773 792-1111
1300 Higgins Rd Ste 214  Park Ridge  (60068)  *(G-17216)*
**Pilot Township Road District**...............................815 426-6221
300 E Kankakee Ave  Herscher  (60941)  *(G-11761)*
**Pilz Automtn Safety Ltd Partnr**............................734 354-0272
7021 Solutions Ctr  Chicago  (60677)  *(G-6123)*
**Pimco Plastics Inc**...............................................815 675-6464
7517 Meyer Rd  Spring Grove  (60081)  *(G-20356)*
**Pin Hsiao & Associates LLC**................................206 818-0155
1040 Sterling Ave  Flossmoor  (60422)  *(G-10227)*
**Pin Up Tattoo**........................................................815 477-7515
424 W Virginia St  Crystal Lake  (60014)  *(G-7625)*
**Pine Environmental Svcs LLC**.............................847 718-1246
1450 Elmhurst Rd  Elk Grove Village  (60007)  *(G-9681)*
**Pine Ridge Archery, Wauconda** *Also called Du Bro Products Inc (G-21456)*
**Pinehurst Bus Solutions Corp**.............................630 842-6155
26w362 Pinehurst Dr  Winfield  (60190)  *(G-22290)*
**Pines Trailer, Kewanee** *Also called Great Dane Limited Partnership (G-12689)*
**Pineview Woodworking, Arthur** *Also called Richard Schrock (G-920)*
**Pingotopia  Inc**.....................................................847 503-9333
3334 Commercial Ave  Northbrook  (60062)  *(G-16338)*
**Pingoworld, Northbrook** *Also called Pingotopia  Inc (G-16338)*
**Pinnacle, Chicago** *Also called Myerson LLC (G-5844)*
**Pinnacle Exploration Corp**...................................618 395-8100
510 E Lafayette St  Olney  (62450)  *(G-16790)*
**Pinnacle Foods Group LLC**..................................618 829-3275
1000 Brewbaker Dr  Saint Elmo  (62458)  *(G-19310)*
**Pinnacle Foods Group LLC**..................................217 235-3181
3801 Dewitt Ave  Mattoon  (61938)  *(G-14406)*
**Pinnacle Foods Group LLC**..................................731 343-4995
100 W Calumet St  Centralia  (62801)  *(G-3426)*
**Pinnacle Metals  Inc**............................................815 232-1600
611 W Lamm Rd  Freeport  (61032)  *(G-10679)*
**Pinnacle Publishing Inc**.......................................218 444-2180
316 N Michigan Ave Cl20  Chicago  (60601)  *(G-6124)*
**Pinnacle Real Estate Inv, Freeport** *Also called Pinnacle Metals  Inc (G-10679)*
**Pinnacle Wood Products  Inc**...............................815 385-0792
1703 S Schroeder Ln  McHenry  (60050)  *(G-14544)*
**Pinnakle Technologies Inc**..................................630 352-0070
75 Executive Dr Ste 353  Aurora  (60504)  *(G-1066)*
**Pinney Printing Company (PA)**............................815 626-2727
1991 Industrial Dr  Sterling  (61081)  *(G-20603)*

**Pinney Printing Company** 815 626-2727
1991 Industrial Dr Sterling (61081) ***(G-20604)***
**Pinoy Monthly** 847 329-1073
5323 Wright Ter Skokie (60077) ***(G-20055)***
**Pins & Needles Consignment** 217 299-7365
7580 N Pawnee Rd Pawnee (62558) ***(G-17235)***
**Pintas Cultured Marble** 708 385-3360
5859 W 117th Pl Alsip (60803) ***(G-509)***
**Pinter Sheet Metal Work, Chicago** *Also called Delta Metal Products Co* ***(G-4579)***
**Pinto Noodle & Rice** 847 328-8881
1931 Central St Evanston (60201) ***(G-10087)***
**Pintsch Tiefenbach Us Inc** 618 993-8513
810 Skyline Dr Marion (62959) ***(G-14280)***
**Pio Woodworking Inc** 630 628-6900
1130 W Fullerton Ave Addison (60101) ***(G-241)***
**Pioneer Container McHy Inc** 618 533-7833
1674 Woods Ln Centralia (62801) ***(G-3427)***
**Pioneer Express** 217 236-3022
404 W Highway St Perry (62362) ***(G-17497)***
**Pioneer Forms Inc** 773 539-8587
3921 N Elston Ave Chicago (60618) ***(G-6125)***
**Pioneer Grinding & Mfg Co** 847 678-6565
10011 Franklin Ave Franklin Park (60131) ***(G-10551)***
**Pioneer Hi-Bred Intl Inc** 309 962-2931
28857 E 200 North Rd Le Roy (61752) ***(G-13209)***
**Pioneer Industries Intl Inc (PA)** 630 543-7676
500 Park Blvd Ste 250 Itasca (60143) ***(G-12340)***
**Pioneer Labels Inc** 618 546-5418
7656 E 700th Ave Robinson (62454) ***(G-18068)***
**Pioneer Newspapers Inc (HQ)** 847 486-0600
350 N Orleans St Fl 10 Chicago (60654) ***(G-6126)***
**Pioneer Newspapers Inc** 708 383-3200
1010 Lake St Ste 104 Oak Park (60301) ***(G-16679)***
**Pioneer Newspapers Inc** 630 887-0600
440 E Ogden Ave Ste 2 Hinsdale (60521) ***(G-11958)***
**Pioneer Pavers Inc** 847 833-9866
4910 Pioneer Rd McHenry (60051) ***(G-14545)***
**Pioneer Powder Coatings LLC** 847 671-1100
9240 Belmont Ave Unit B Franklin Park (60131) ***(G-10552)***
**Pioneer Press, Chicago** *Also called Pioneer Newspapers Inc* ***(G-6126)***
**Pioneer Press, Chicago** *Also called Schaumburg Review* ***(G-6450)***
**Pioneer Printing Service Inc** 312 337-4283
1340 N Astor St Chicago (60610) ***(G-6127)***
**Pioneer Pump and Packing Inc** 217 791-5293
1501 N 22nd St Decatur (62526) ***(G-7927)***
**Pioneer Service Inc** 630 628-0249
542 W Factory Rd Addison (60101) ***(G-242)***
**PIP Printing, Peoria** *Also called P & S Cochran Printers Inc* ***(G-17421)***
**PIP Printing, Northbrook** *Also called Michael Zimmerman* ***(G-16311)***
**PIP Printing, Rockford** *Also called Mencarini Enterprises Inc* ***(G-18491)***
**PIP Printing** 847 998-6330
1220 Waukegan Rd Glenview (60025) ***(G-11182)***
**PIP Printing Inc** 815 464-0075
9218 Corsair Rd Unit 3 Frankfort (60423) ***(G-10349)***
**Pipe Scraper Div, Macomb** *Also called Richardson Enterprises* ***(G-14131)***
**Pipeline Trading Systems LLC** 312 212-4288
1 S Dearborn St Ste 2100 Chicago (60603) ***(G-6128)***
**Piper Plastics Inc (PA)** 847 367-0110
1840 Enterprise Ct Libertyville (60048) ***(G-13369)***
**Pipestone Passages** 773 735-2488
5407 S Avers Ave Chicago (60632) ***(G-6129)***
**Pistoleercom LLC** 618 288-4649
12 Schiber Ct Maryville (62062) ***(G-14346)***
**Piston Automotive LLC** 313 541-8789
3458 Morreim Dr Belvidere (61008) ***(G-1779)***
**Pit Pal Product, Zion** *Also called S & D Development & Prototype* ***(G-22696)***
**Pita Pan Old World Bakery, Chicago Heights** *Also called K & A Bread LLC* ***(G-7107)***
**Pitchfork Media Inc** 773 395-5937
3317 W Fullerton Ave Chicago (60647) ***(G-6130)***
**Pitney Bowes Inc** 312 209-2216
2330 Hammond Dr Ste G Schaumburg (60173) ***(G-19691)***
**Pitney Bowes Inc** 773 755-5808
3640 N Bosworth Ave 3s Chicago (60613) ***(G-6131)***
**Pitney Bowes Inc** 312 419-7114
230 W Monroe St Ste 1150 Chicago (60606) ***(G-6132)***
**Pitney Bowes Inc** 630 435-7476
2200 Western Ct Ste 100 Lisle (60532) ***(G-13640)***
**Pitney Bowes Inc** 630 435-7500
750 Warrenville Rd # 300 Lisle (60532) ***(G-13641)***
**Pitney Bowes Inc** 800 784-4224
1025 Hilltop Dr Itasca (60143) ***(G-12341)***
**Pittco Architectural Mtls Inc** 800 992-7488
1530 Landmeier Rd Elk Grove Village (60007) ***(G-9682)***
**Pittsburgh Glass Works LLC** 630 879-5100
1020 Olympic Dr Batavia (60510) ***(G-1483)***
**Pittsfield Mch Tl & Wldg Co** 217 656-4000
306 W State St Payson (62360) ***(G-17246)***
**Pivot Point Beauty School, Chicago** *Also called Pivot Point Usa Inc* ***(G-6133)***
**Pivot Point Usa Inc (PA)** 800 886-4247
8725 W Higgins Rd Ste 700 Chicago (60631) ***(G-6133)***
**Pivotal Production LLC** 773 726-7706
356 E Sutherland St Chicago (60619) ***(G-6134)***
**Pix North America Inc** 217 516-8348
1222 E Voorhees St Danville (61834) ***(G-7760)***
**Pix2doc LLC** 312 925-4010
1968 Pleasant Hill Ln Lisle (60532) ***(G-13642)***
**Pixel Pushers Incorporated** 847 550-6560
1050 Ensell Rd Ste 108 Lake Zurich (60047) ***(G-13114)***
**Pixie Sparkle, Glenview** *Also called Teitelbaum Brothers Inc* ***(G-11208)***
**Pjla Music** 847 382-3212
22n159 Pepper Rd Barrington (60010) ***(G-1297)***
**Pk Corporation** 847 879-1070
527 Newberry Dr Elk Grove Village (60007) ***(G-9683)***
**Plainfield Signs Inc** 815 439-1063
219 W Main St Plainfield (60544) ***(G-17640)***
**Planet Earth Antifreeze Inc** 815 282-2463
6307 Material Ave Loves Park (61111) ***(G-13976)***
**Planks Apple Butter** 217 268-4933
175 N County Road 525e Arcola (61910) ***(G-681)***
**Planks Cabinet Shop Inc** 217 543-2687
1620 State Highway 133 Arthur (61911) ***(G-918)***
**Plano Metal Specialties Inc** 630 552-8510
320 W State Rte 34 Plano (60545) ***(G-17672)***
**Plano Molding Company LLC (HQ)** 630 552-3111
431 E South St Plano (60545) ***(G-17673)***
**Plano Molding Company LLC** 630 552-9557
510 Duvick Ave Sandwich (60548) ***(G-19373)***
**Plano Molding Company LLC** 815 538-3111
1800 Hume Dr Mendota (61342) ***(G-14730)***
**Plano Molding Company LLC** 815 786-3331
500 Duvick Ave Sandwich (60548) ***(G-19374)***
**Plano Synergy Holding Inc (PA)** 630 552-3111
431 E South St Plano (60545) ***(G-17674)***
**Plant 06, Nashville** *Also called Beelman Ready-Mix Inc* ***(G-15834)***
**Plant 2, Hillside** *Also called Dynamic Manufacturing Inc* ***(G-11916)***
**Plant 4, West Chicago** *Also called Graham Packaging Co Europe LLC* ***(G-21711)***
**Plant 6, Mc Henry** *Also called Peter Baker & Son Co* ***(G-14462)***
**Planter Inc** 773 637-7777
1820 N Major Ave Chicago (60639) ***(G-6135)***
**Plantlink, Urbana** *Also called Oso Technologies Inc* ***(G-21096)***
**Plas-Co Inc** 618 476-1761
1475 B And H Indus Ct Millstadt (62260) ***(G-14832)***
**Plasma Technology Systems, Elgin** *Also called Plasmatreat USA Inc* ***(G-9138)***
**Plasmag Pump Div, Mundelein** *Also called Murdock Company Inc* ***(G-15535)***
**Plasmatreat USA Inc (PA)** 847 783-0622
2541 Tech Dr Ste 407 Elgin (60124) ***(G-9138)***
**Plaspros Inc (PA)** 815 430-2300
1143 Ridgeview Dr McHenry (60050) ***(G-14546)***
**Plaspros Inc** 847 639-6492
511 Cove Dr Cary (60013) ***(G-3364)***
**Plastak Inc** 630 466-4100
44w40 Scott Rd Sugar Grove (60554) ***(G-20730)***
**Plastech Inc** 630 595-7222
873 Fairway Dr Bensenville (60106) ***(G-1964)***
**Plastech Molding Inc** 847 398-0355
2222 Foster Ave Wheeling (60090) ***(G-22123)***
**Plastic Art, Lombard** *Also called Specialized Woodwork Inc* ***(G-13854)***
**Plastic Bag Manufacturer, East Dundee** *Also called Golden Bag Company Inc* ***(G-8639)***
**Plastic Binding Laminating Inc** 847 573-0375
27885 Irma Lee Cir # 105 Lake Forest (60045) ***(G-12946)***
**Plastic Container Corporation (PA)** 217 352-2722
2508 N Oak St Urbana (61802) ***(G-21098)***
**Plastic Designs Inc** 217 379-9214
1330 S Vermillion St Paxton (60957) ***(G-17243)***
**Plastic Film Corp America Inc (PA)** 630 887-0800
1287 Naperville Dr Ste A Romeoville (60446) ***(G-18857)***
**Plastic Laminate Speciality Co, Millstadt** *Also called Plas-Co Inc* ***(G-14832)***
**Plastic Letter & Signs Inc** 847 251-3719
3223 Lake Ave Ste 15c Wilmette (60091) ***(G-22263)***
**Plastic Packaging Systems, Kankakee** *Also called Signode Industrial Group LLC* ***(G-12649)***
**Plastic Parts Intl Inc** 815 637-9222
1248 Shappert Dr Machesney Park (61115) ***(G-14097)***
**Plastic Power Corporation** 847 233-9601
4046 Tugwell St Franklin Park (60131) ***(G-10553)***
**Plastic Power Extrusions Corp** 847 233-9901
3860 River Rd Schiller Park (60176) ***(G-19859)***
**Plastic Powerdrive Pdts LLC** 847 637-5233
1589 Highpoint Dr Elgin (60123) ***(G-9139)***
**Plastic Products Company Inc** 309 762-6532
4610 44th St Moline (61265) ***(G-14962)***
**Plastic Products Inc** 847 874-3440
1515 E Wdfield Rd Ste 860 Schaumburg (60173) ***(G-19692)***
**Plastic Services and Products** 708 868-3800
14201 Paxton Ave Calumet City (60409) ***(G-2948)***
**Plastic Services Group** 847 368-1444
115 S Wilke Rd Ste 206e Arlington Heights (60005) ***(G-818)***

ALPHABETIC

**Plastic Specialists America** ... 847 406-7547
4225 Tiger Lily Ln # 308 Gurnee (60031) ***(G-11486)***
**Plastic Specialties & Tech Inc** ... 847 781-2414
119 Commerce Dr Schaumburg (60173) ***(G-19693)***
**Plastic Technologies Inc** ... 847 841-8610
1200 Abbott Dr Elgin (60123) ***(G-9140)***
**Plasticrest Products Inc** ... 773 826-2163
4519 W Harrison St Chicago (60624) ***(G-6136)***
**Plastics** ... 847 931-9391
39w446 Capulet Cir Elgin (60124) ***(G-9141)***
**Plastics Color & Compounding** ... 708 868-3800
14201 Paxton Ave Calumet City (60409) ***(G-2949)***
**Plastics Color Corp Illinois** ... 708 868-3800
14201 Paxton Ave Calumet City (60409) ***(G-2950)***
**Plastics Color Corporation (HQ)** ... 708 868-3800
14201 Paxton Ave Calumet City (60409) ***(G-2951)***
**Plastics Color-Chip, Calumet City** *Also called Plastic Services and Products* ***(G-2948)***
**Plastics D-E-F** ... 312 226-4337
3065 W Armitage Ave Chicago (60647) ***(G-6137)***
**Plastics Printing Group Inc** ... 312 421-7980
5414 W Roosevelt Rd Chicago (60644) ***(G-6138)***
**Plastipak Packaging Inc** ... 630 231-7650
1700 Western Dr West Chicago (60185) ***(G-21757)***
**Plastipak Packaging Inc** ... 217 398-1832
3310 W Springfield Ave Champaign (61822) ***(G-3526)***
**Plastipak Packaging Inc** ... 708 385-0721
12325 S Laramie Ave Alsip (60803) ***(G-510)***
**Plastisol Products Inc** ... 630 543-1770
1002 W Republic Dr Addison (60101) ***(G-243)***
**Plastival Inc** ... 847 931-4771
1685 Holmes Rd Elgin (60123) ***(G-9142)***
**Plaston, Naperville** *Also called Boneco North America Corp* ***(G-15607)***
**Plate and Pre-Press Management** ... 847 352-0462
431 Westover Ln Schaumburg (60193) ***(G-19694)***
**Plating International Inc** ... 847 451-2101
11142 Addison Ave Franklin Park (60131) ***(G-10554)***
**Platinum Aquatech Ltd** ... 847 537-3800
300 Industrial Ln Wheeling (60090) ***(G-22124)***
**Platinum Touch Industries LLC** ... 773 775-9988
471 N 3rd Ave Des Plaines (60016) ***(G-8256)***
**Platit Inc** ... 847 680-5270
1840 Industrial Dr # 220 Libertyville (60048) ***(G-13370)***
**Platt Cases, Chicago** *Also called Platt Luggage Inc* ***(G-6139)***
**Platt County Service, Bement** *Also called Piatt County Service Co* ***(G-1801)***
**Platt G Mostardi** ... 630 993-2100
5595 Trillium Blvd Hoffman Estates (60192) ***(G-12034)***
**Platt Industrial Control Inc** ... 630 833-4388
3n301 Ellsworth Ave Addison (60101) ***(G-244)***
**Platt Luggage Inc** ... 773 838-2000
4051 W 51st St Chicago (60632) ***(G-6139)***
**Play It Again Sports 11417, Sycamore** *Also called Heartland Inspection Company* ***(G-20799)***
**Player Sports Ltd** ... 773 764-4111
2956 W Peterson Ave Chicago (60659) ***(G-6140)***
**Playground Pointers** ... 952 200-4168
109 S Quincy St Hinsdale (60521) ***(G-11959)***
**Playing With Fusion Inc** ... 309 258-7259
31201 State Route 9 Mackinaw (61755) ***(G-14118)***
**Plaza Tool & Mold Co** ... 847 537-2320
53 Century Dr Wheeling (60090) ***(G-22125)***
**Plaze Inc (HQ)** ... 630 628-4240
2651 Warrenville Rd # 300 Downers Grove (60515) ***(G-8503)***
**PLC Corp** ... 847 247-1900
220 Baker Rd Lake Bluff (60044) ***(G-12863)***
**Pledgemine, Lombard** *Also called Businessmine LLC* ***(G-13774)***
**Plews Inc (PA)** ... 815 288-3344
1550 Franklin Grove Rd Dixon (61021) ***(G-8339)***
**Plews Edelmann, Dixon** *Also called Plews Inc* ***(G-8339)***
**Plexus Corp** ... 630 250-1074
1550 W Bryn Mawr Ave Itasca (60143) ***(G-12342)***
**Plexus Corp** ... 847 793-4400
2400 Millbrook Dr Buffalo Grove (60089) ***(G-2754)***
**Plexus Manufacturing Solutions, Buffalo Grove** *Also called Plexus Corp* ***(G-2754)***
**Pliant LLC** ... 812 424-2904
1701 Golf Rd Ste 2-900 Rolling Meadows (60008) ***(G-18763)***
**Pliant Corp International** ... 847 969-3300
1701 Golf Rd Ste 2-900 Rolling Meadows (60008) ***(G-18764)***
**Pliant Corporation of Canada** ... 847 969-3300
1475 E Woodfield Rd # 700 Schaumburg (60173) ***(G-19695)***
**Pliant Investment Inc** ... 847 969-3300
1475 E Wdfield Rd Ste 600 Schaumburg (60173) ***(G-19696)***
**Pliant Solutions Corporation** ... 847 969-3300
1475 E Wdfield Rd Ste 600 Schaumburg (60173) ***(G-19697)***
**Plitek** ... 847 827-6680
69 Rawls Rd Des Plaines (60018) ***(G-8257)***
**Plochman Inc** ... 815 468-3434
1333 N Boudreau Rd Manteno (60950) ***(G-14190)***
**Plote Construction Inc** ... 847 695-0422
1100 Brandt Dr Hoffman Estates (60192) ***(G-12035)***
**Plote Construction Inc (PA)** ... 847 695-9300
1100 Brandt Dr Hoffman Estates (60192) ***(G-12036)***
**Plote Inc** ... 847 695-9467
1100 Brandt Dr Hoffman Estates (60192) ***(G-12037)***
**Pluesters Quality Meat Co** ... 618 396-2224
Batchtown Rd Hardin (62047) ***(G-11594)***
**Plug-In Electric Charge Inc** ... 224 856-5229
1660 Nicholson Dr Hoffman Estates (60192) ***(G-12038)***
**Plum Grove Printers Inc** ... 847 882-4020
2160 Stonington Ave Hoffman Estates (60169) ***(G-12039)***
**Plumbers Supply Co St Louis** ... 618 624-5151
6700 Old Collinsville Rd O Fallon (62269) ***(G-16474)***
**Plumbing Engineer Magazine, Niles** *Also called Tmb Publishing Inc* ***(G-16043)***
**Plumrose Usa Inc (HQ)** ... 732 257-6600
1901 Butterfield Rd # 305 Downers Grove (60515) ***(G-8504)***
**Pluribus Games LLC** ... 630 770-2043
725 Morton Ave Aurora (60506) ***(G-1204)***
**Plus Signs & Banners Inc** ... 630 236-6917
10s187 Schoger Dr Ste 51 Naperville (60564) ***(G-15822)***
**Plustech Inc** ... 847 490-8130
735 Remington Rd Schaumburg (60173) ***(G-19698)***
**Plymouth Tube Company (PA)** ... 630 393-3550
29w 150 Warrenville Rd Warrenville (60555) ***(G-21355)***
**Plymouth Tube Company** ... 773 489-0226
4555 W Armitage Ave Chicago (60639) ***(G-6141)***
**Plymouth Tube Company** ... 262 642-8201
29w150 Warrenville Rd Warrenville (60555) ***(G-21356)***
**Plz Aeroscience, Downers Grove** *Also called Plaze Inc* ***(G-8503)***
**Plz Aeroscience Corporation (PA)** ... 630 628-3000
2651 Warrenville Rd # 300 Downers Grove (60515) ***(G-8505)***
**PM Machine Shop** ... 217 854-3504
706 N Broad St Carlinville (62626) ***(G-3046)***
**PM Woodwind Repair Inc** ... 847 869-7049
822 Custer Ave Evanston (60202) ***(G-10088)***
**Pma Friction Products Inc** ... 630 406-9119
880 Kingsland Dr Batavia (60510) ***(G-1484)***
**Pmb Industries Inc** ... 708 442-4515
8072 53rd St La Grange (60525) ***(G-12742)***
**PMC Converting Corp** ... 773 481-2269
5080 N Kimberly Ave # 107 Chicago (60630) ***(G-6142)***
**PMI Cartoning Inc** ... 847 437-1427
850 Pratt Blvd Elk Grove Village (60007) ***(G-9684)***
**Pmp Fermentation Products Inc** ... 309 637-0400
900 Ne Adams St Peoria (61603) ***(G-17430)***
**Pmt, Frankfort** *Also called Prime Market Targeting Inc* ***(G-10353)***
**Pnc Inc (PA)** ... 815 946-2328
117 E Mason St Polo (61064) ***(G-17690)***
**PNC Financial Svcs Group Inc** ... 630 420-8400
1308 S Naper Blvd Naperville (60540) ***(G-15728)***
**Pne Wind Usa Inc** ... 773 329-3705
150 N Michigan Ave # 1500 Chicago (60601) ***(G-6143)***
**Pneu Fast Inc** ... 847 866-8787
2200 Greenleaf St Evanston (60202) ***(G-10089)***
**Pneu-Fast, Evanston** *Also called Pneu Fast Inc* ***(G-10089)***
**Pneutech Products, Schaumburg** *Also called Fluid-Aire Dynamics Inc* ***(G-19531)***
**Png Transport LLC** ... 312 218-8116
3543 S Parnell Ave Apt B Chicago (60609) ***(G-6144)***
**PO Food Specialists Ltd** ... 847 517-8315
1800 Huntington Blvd # 610 Hoffman Estates (60169) ***(G-12040)***
**Podhalanska LLC** ... 630 247-9256
1304 Oakmont Dr Unit 10 Lemont (60439) ***(G-13256)***
**Podiatry Arts Lab, Pekin** *Also called Pal Health Technologies Inc* ***(G-17280)***
**Poem Lighting Company** ... 847 395-1768
144 Oakwood Dr Antioch (60002) ***(G-651)***
**Poersch Metal Manufacturing Co** ... 773 722-0890
4027 W Kinzie St Chicago (60624) ***(G-6145)***
**Poetry Foundation** ... 312 787-7070
61 W Superior St Chicago (60654) ***(G-6146)***
**Poetry Magazine, Chicago** *Also called Poetry Foundation* ***(G-6146)***
**Poets Study Inc** ... 773 286-1355
4366 N Elston Ave Chicago (60641) ***(G-6147)***
**Poggenpohl LLC (PA)** ... 217 229-3411
31 Sparks St Raymond (62560) ***(G-17939)***
**Poggenpohl LLC** ... 217 824-2020
105 N Baughman Rd Taylorville (62568) ***(G-20844)***
**Poggenpohl Construction & Mtls, Raymond** *Also called Poggenpohl LLC* ***(G-17939)***
**Poignant Logging** ... 309 246-5647
857 State Route 26 Lacon (61540) ***(G-12791)***
**Point Five Packaging LLC** ... 847 678-5016
9555 Irving Park Rd Schiller Park (60176) ***(G-19860)***
**Point Ready Mix LLC (PA)** ... 815 578-9100
5435 Bull Valley Rd # 130 McHenry (60050) ***(G-14547)***
**Pointe International Company** ... 847 550-7001
234 Oakwood Rd Lake Zurich (60047) ***(G-13115)***
**Pokorney Manufacturing Co** ... 630 458-0406
45 N Church St Addison (60101) ***(G-245)***
**Pola Company** ... 847 470-1182
8901 N Milwaukee Ave A Niles (60714) ***(G-16020)***

**Polamer Inc** ....773 774-3600
6401 N Milwaukee Ave Chicago (60646) *(G-6148)*
**Polamer & Parcel Travel Svc, Chicago** *Also called Polamer Inc (G-6148)*
**Polancics Meats & Tenderloins** ....815 433-0324
412 W Norris Dr Ottawa (61350) *(G-16980)*
**Polar Container Corp Inc** ....847 299-5030
7123 Barry St Rosemont (60018) *(G-19024)*
**Polar Corporation** ....618 548-3660
1414 S Broadway Ave Salem (62881) *(G-19343)*
**Polar Paint Systems, Moline** *Also called Sentry Pool & Chemical Supply (G-14970)*
**Polar Tech Industries Inc (PA)** ....815 784-9000
415 E Railroad Ave Genoa (60135) *(G-10882)*
**Polaris Laser Laminations LLC** ....630 444-0760
2725 Norton Creek Dr B2 West Chicago (60185) *(G-21758)*
**Polaris Technology Group, Plainfield** *Also called Endure Holdings Inc (G-17594)*
**Polaroid Store, Northbrook** *Also called Pcbl Retail Holdings LLC (G-16331)*
**Polartech Additives Inc** ....708 458-8450
7201 W 65th St Bedford Park (60638) *(G-1573)*
**Pole Express Publishing, Chicago** *Also called Express Publishing Inc (G-4797)*
**Poli-Film America Inc (HQ)** ....847 453-8104
1 Elgiloy Dr Hampshire (60140) *(G-11559)*
**Politech Inc** ....847 516-2717
108 Turkey Run Rd Trout Valley (60013) *(G-21001)*
**Poll Enterprises Inc** ....708 756-1120
209 Glenwood Rd Chicago Heights (60411) *(G-7117)*
**Pollack Manufacturing Co LLC** ....815 520-8415
9418 Butternut Dr Crystal Lake (60014) *(G-7626)*
**Pollack Service** ....773 528-8096
3701 N Ravenswood Ave Chicago (60613) *(G-6149)*
**Pollard Bros Mfg Co** ....773 763-6868
5504 N Northwest Hwy Chicago (60630) *(G-6150)*
**Pollmann North America Inc** ....815 834-1122
950 Chicago Tube Dr Romeoville (60446) *(G-18858)*
**Polmax LLC** ....708 843-8300
12161 S Central Ave Alsip (60803) *(G-511)*
**Polonia Book Store Inc** ....773 481-6968
4738 N Milwaukee Ave Chicago (60630) *(G-6151)*
**Polpress Inc** ....773 792-1200
5566 N Northwest Hwy Chicago (60630) *(G-6152)*
**Polpress Priniting, Chicago** *Also called Polpress Inc (G-6152)*
**Poly Compounding LLC** ....847 488-0683
1390 Gateway Dr Ste 6 Elgin (60124) *(G-9143)*
**Poly Films Inc** ....708 547-7963
4101 Washington Blvd Hillside (60162) *(G-11931)*
**Poly Plastics Films Corp** ....815 636-0821
334 Northway Park Rd # 3 Machesney Park (61115) *(G-14098)*
**Poly-Clip Systems, Mundelein** *Also called Precitec Corporation (G-15547)*
**Poly-Resyn Inc** ....847 428-4031
518 Market Loop Ste A West Dundee (60118) *(G-21801)*
**Polyair Inter Pack Inc** ....773 995-1818
808 E 113th St Chicago (60628) *(G-6153)*
**Polybilt Body Company LLC (PA)** ....708 345-8050
325 Spring Lake Dr Itasca (60143) *(G-12343)*
**Polycast** ....815 648-4438
10103 Main St B Hebron (60034) *(G-11725)*
**Polyconversions Inc** ....217 893-3330
505 E Condit Dr Rantoul (61866) *(G-17935)*
**Polycorp Illinois Inc (PA)** ....773 847-7575
3620 W 38th St Chicago (60632) *(G-6154)*
**Polydesigns Ltd** ....847 433-9920
731 Orleans Dr Highland Park (60035) *(G-11861)*
**Polyenviro Labs Inc** ....708 489-0195
9960 191st St Ste K Mokena (60448) *(G-14896)*
**Polyera Corporation** ....847 677-7517
8025 Lamon Ave Ste 43 Skokie (60077) *(G-20056)*
**Polyform Products Company** ....847 427-0020
1901 Estes Ave Elk Grove Village (60007) *(G-9685)*
**Polygem, West Chicago** *Also called Jjc Epoxy Inc (G-21728)*
**Polygroup Limited, East Dundee** *Also called Polygroup Services NA Inc (G-8653)*
**Polygroup Services NA Inc (PA)** ....847 851-9995
1051 E Main St Ste 218 East Dundee (60118) *(G-8653)*
**Polymax Thermoplastic** ....847 316-9900
3210 N Oak Grove Ave Waukegan (60087) *(G-21602)*
**Polymax Tpe, Waukegan** *Also called Polymax Thermoplastic (G-21602)*
**Polymer Nation LLC (PA)** ....847 972-2157
405 N Oakwood Ave Waukegan (60085) *(G-21603)*
**Polymer Plnfeld Hldings US Inc (PA)** ....815 436-5671
24035 W Riverwalk Ct Plainfield (60544) *(G-17641)*
**Polynt Composites USA Inc (HQ)** ....847 428-2657
99 E Cottage Ave Carpentersville (60110) *(G-3296)*
**Polyone Corporation** ....815 385-8500
833 Ridgeview Dr McHenry (60050) *(G-14548)*
**Polyone Corporation** ....847 364-0011
2400 E Devon Ave Elk Grove Village (60007) *(G-9686)*
**Polyone Corporation** ....309 364-2154
1546 County Road 1450 N Henry (61537) *(G-11746)*
**Polyone Corporation** ....630 972-0505
1275 Windham Pkwy Romeoville (60446) *(G-18859)*
**Polyonics Rubber Co** ....815 765-2033
100 E Park St Poplar Grove (61065) *(G-17716)*
**Polyscience, Niles** *Also called Preston Industries Inc (G-16022)*
**Polyscience Inc** ....847 647-0611
5709 W Howard St Niles (60714) *(G-16021)*
**Polysystems Inc (PA)** ....312 332-2114
30 N La Salle St Ste 3600 Chicago (60602) *(G-6155)*
**Polytec Plastics Inc** ....630 584-8282
3730 Stern Ave Saint Charles (60174) *(G-19236)*
**Polytech Industries Inc** ....630 443-6030
1755 Wallace Ave Saint Charles (60174) *(G-19237)*
**Polyurethane Products Corp** ....630 543-6700
31 W Industrial Rd Addison (60101) *(G-246)*
**Polyurthane Engrg Tchnques Inc (PA)** ....847 362-1820
28041 N Bradley Rd Lake Forest (60045) *(G-12947)*
**Polyvinyl Record Co** ....217 403-1752
717 S Neil St Champaign (61820) *(G-3527)*
**Pomona Winery** ....618 893-2623
2865 Hickory Ridge Rd Pomona (62975) *(G-17694)*
**Pond Alliance Inc** ....877 377-8131
2764 Golfview Rd Naperville (60563) *(G-15729)*
**Pontiac Engraving** ....630 834-4424
586 Meyer Rd Bensenville (60106) *(G-1965)*
**Pontiac Granite Company Inc** ....815 842-1384
906 W North St Pontiac (61764) *(G-17707)*
**Pontiac Recyclers Inc** ....815 844-6419
15355 E 1830 North Rd Pontiac (61764) *(G-17708)*
**Pony Tools, Chicago** *Also called Adjustable Clamp Company (G-3751)*
**Pool & Pool Oil Productions** ....618 544-7590
1724 W Main St Robinson (62454) *(G-18069)*
**Pool Center Inc** ....217 698-7665
3740 Wabash Ave Ste C Springfield (62711) *(G-20505)*
**Pools Welding Inc** ....309 787-2083
816 10th Ave W Milan (61264) *(G-14798)*
**Pop Box LLC** ....630 509-2281
1700 W Irving Park Rd # 302 Chicago (60613) *(G-6156)*
**Popcorn Palace, Burr Ridge** *Also called Double Good LLC (G-2837)*
**Popular Ridge Machine Met Cft** ....618 687-1656
134 S Jungle Rd Murphysboro (62966) *(G-15580)*
**Porcelain Enamel Finishers** ....312 808-1560
1530 S State St Apt 1018 Chicago (60605) *(G-6157)*
**Porch Electric LLC** ....815 368-3230
205 N Main St Lostant (61334) *(G-13908)*
**Porche Pharmaceutical Staffing** ....312 259-3982
350 S Northwest Hwy # 300 Park Ridge (60068) *(G-17217)*
**Pork King Packing Inc** ....815 568-8024
8808 S Il Route 23 Marengo (60152) *(G-14239)*
**Port Arthur News, Chicago** *Also called APAC 90 Texas Holding Inc (G-3920)*
**Port Byron Machine Inc** ....309 523-9111
11420 228th St N Port Byron (61275) *(G-17722)*
**Portable Cmmnctons Spclsts** ....630 458-1800
901 W Lake St Addison (60101) *(G-247)*
**Portable Mvg Stor Cntl Ill Inc** ....309 693-7637
10000 N Galena Rd Peoria (61615) *(G-17431)*
**Porterville Recorder Inc** ....559 784-5000
1120 N Carbon St Ste 100 Marion (62959) *(G-14281)*
**Portillos Food Service Inc (PA)** ....630 620-0460
380 S Rohlwing Rd Addison (60101) *(G-248)*
**Portola Packaging LLC** ....630 515-8383
1140 31st St Downers Grove (60515) *(G-8506)*
**Pos Plus LLC** ....618 993-7587
1001 W Central St Marion (62959) *(G-14282)*
**Positive Impressions** ....618 438-7030
14190 State Highway 34 Benton (62812) *(G-2038)*
**Positive Packaging Inc** ....847 392-4405
1100 Hicks Rd Rolling Meadows (60008) *(G-18765)*
**Positive Packaging & Graphics, Rolling Meadows** *Also called Positive Packaging Inc (G-18765)*
**Positron Corporation (PA)** ....317 576-0183
550 Oakmont Ln Westmont (60559) *(G-21912)*
**Possehl Connector Svcs SC Inc** ....803 366-8316
1521 Morse Ave Elk Grove Village (60007) *(G-9687)*
**Post Press Production Inc (PA)** ....630 860-9833
2601 Lively Blvd Elk Grove Village (60007) *(G-9688)*
**Post-Tribune, Chicago** *Also called Old Gary Inc (G-5979)*
**Potash Corp Ssktchewan Fla Inc (HQ)** ....847 849-4200
1101 Skokie Blvd Ste 400 Northbrook (60062) *(G-16339)*
**Potash Corp Ssktchewan Fla Inc** ....847 849-4200
1101 Skokie Blvd Ste 400 Northbrook (60062) *(G-16340)*
**Potash Holding Company Inc** ....847 849-4200
1101 Skokie Blvd Ste 400 Northbrook (60062) *(G-16341)*
**Potentia, Chicago** *Also called Corbett Accel Healthcare Grp C (G-4467)*
**Pothole Pros** ....847 815-5789
3074 Chalkstone Ave Elgin (60124) *(G-9144)*
**Potomac Corporation (PA)** ....847 259-0546
2063 Foster Ave Wheeling (60090) *(G-22126)*
**Potter Rendering Co** ....580 924-2414
750 W Lake Cook Rd # 485 Buffalo Grove (60089) *(G-2755)*

ALPHABETIC

**Potter Sausage, Buffalo Grove** *Also called Potter Rendering Co* ***(G-2755)***
**Pound Bakery, Harvard** *Also called Pedigree Ovens Inc* ***(G-11643)***
**Pour It Again Sam Inc**....708 474-1744
2200 198th Pl Lynwood (60411) ***(G-14023)***
**Powbab Inc**....630 481-6140
1314 Kensington Rd # 3205 Oak Brook (60523) ***(G-16555)***
**Powder Coat Plus**....217 228-0081
4126 Kochs Ln Quincy (62305) ***(G-17868)***
**Powdered Metal Tech LLC**....630 852-0500
2655 Wisconsin Ave Downers Grove (60515) ***(G-8507)***
**Powell Electrical Systems Inc**....708 409-1200
515 N Railroad Ave Northlake (60164) ***(G-16447)***
**Powell Electrical Systems Inc**....708 409-1200
515 N Railroad Ave Northlake (60164) ***(G-16448)***
**Powell Industries Inc**....708 409-1200
515 N Railroad Ave Northlake (60164) ***(G-16449)***
**Powell Tree Care Inc**....847 364-1181
212 E Devon Ave Elk Grove Village (60007) ***(G-9689)***
**Power Dental U.S.A., McHenry** *Also called Dental USA Inc* ***(G-14495)***
**Power Distribution Eqp Co Inc**....847 455-2500
3010 Willow St Franklin Park (60131) ***(G-10555)***
**Power Electronics Intl Inc**....847 836-2071
561 Plate Dr Ste 8 East Dundee (60118) ***(G-8654)***
**Power Enclosures Inc (PA)**....309 274-9000
100 S 4th St Chillicothe (61523) ***(G-7170)***
**Power Equipment Company**....815 754-4090
211 W Stephenie Dr Cortland (60112) ***(G-7394)***
**Power Graphics & Print Inc**....847 568-1808
7345 Monticello Ave Skokie (60076) ***(G-20057)***
**Power House Tool Inc**....815 727-6301
626 Nicholson St Joliet (60435) ***(G-12552)***
**Power Industries Inc**....630 443-0671
3102 Greenwood Ln Saint Charles (60175) ***(G-19238)***
**Power Lube LLC**....847 806-7022
1461 Busse Rd Elk Grove Village (60007) ***(G-9690)***
**Power Partners LLC**....773 465-8688
1542 W Devon Ave Chicago (60660) ***(G-6158)***
**Power Parts Sign Co, Chicago** *Also called Ri-Del Mfg Inc* ***(G-6349)***
**Power Plant Repair Services, Oswego** *Also called Alin Machining Company Inc* ***(G-16903)***
**Power Plant Services, Melrose Park** *Also called Alin Machining Company Inc* ***(G-14585)***
**Power Planter Inc**....217 379-2614
931 N 1600e Rd Loda (60948) ***(G-13754)***
**Power Plus Products Inc**....773 788-9794
6410 W 74th St Ste A Bedford Park (60638) ***(G-1574)***
**Power Port Products Inc**....630 628-9102
301 W Interstate Rd Addison (60101) ***(G-249)***
**Power-Io Inc**....630 717-7335
537 Braemar Ave Naperville (60563) ***(G-15730)***
**Power-Sonic Corporation**....309 752-7750
1300 19th St Ste 200 East Moline (61244) ***(G-8690)***
**Power-Volt Inc**....630 628-9999
300 W Factory Rd Addison (60101) ***(G-250)***
**Powerboss Inc**....910 944-2105
14n845 Us Highway 20 Hampshire (60140) ***(G-11560)***
**Powercoco LLC**....614 323-5890
1658 N Milwaukee Ave # 546 Chicago (60647) ***(G-6159)***
**Powerlab Inc**....815 273-7718
9741 Powerlab Rd Savanna (61074) ***(G-19404)***
**Powermaster**....630 957-4019
1833 Downs Dr West Chicago (60185) ***(G-21759)***
**Powermaster Motorsports, West Chicago** *Also called Powermaster* ***(G-21759)***
**Powernail Company**....800 323-1653
1300 Rose Rd Lake Zurich (60047) ***(G-13116)***
**Powerone Corp**....630 443-6500
2325 Dean St Ste 200 Saint Charles (60175) ***(G-19239)***
**Powerone Environmental, Saint Charles** *Also called Powerone Corp* ***(G-19239)***
**Powerpath Microproducts Inc**....847 827-6330
200 Howard Ave Ste 238 Des Plaines (60018) ***(G-8258)***
**Powers John**....309 742-8929
214 S Magnolia St Elmwood (61529) ***(G-9965)***
**Powers Paint Shop Inc**....815 338-3619
1065 Dieckman St Woodstock (60098) ***(G-22600)***
**Powers Woodworking**....630 663-9644
6804 Hobson Valley Dr # 117 Woodridge (60517) ***(G-22509)***
**Powerschool Group LLC**....610 867-9200
2290 Collection Center Dr Chicago (60693) ***(G-6160)***
**Powersource Generator Rentals**....847 587-3991
119 Christopher Way Fox Lake (60020) ***(G-10281)***
**Powertrain Technology Inc**....847 458-2323
355 Point Ct Algonquin (60102) ***(G-403)***
**Powertronics Surgitech USA Inc**....630 305-4261
2240 Pontiac Cir Naperville (60565) ***(G-15731)***
**Powervar Inc (HQ)**....847 596-7000
1450 S Lakeside Dr Waukegan (60085) ***(G-21604)***
**Powervar Holdings LLC**....800 369-7179
1450 S Lakeside Dr Waukegan (60085) ***(G-21605)***
**Poynting Products Inc**....708 386-2139
1011 Madison St Oak Park (60302) ***(G-16680)***
**Pp3, Elk Grove Village** *Also called Post Press Production Inc* ***(G-9688)***
**PPG, Elgin** *Also called Sims Family Holdings LLC* ***(G-9183)***
**PPG 4611, O Fallon** *Also called PPG Industries Inc* ***(G-16475)***
**PPG 4612, Springfield** *Also called PPG Industries Inc* ***(G-20506)***
**PPG 5524, Alsip** *Also called PPG Industries Inc* ***(G-512)***
**PPG 5526, Stone Park** *Also called PPG Industries Inc* ***(G-20636)***
**PPG 5527, Chicago** *Also called PPG Industries Inc* ***(G-6164)***
**PPG 5532, Rolling Meadows** *Also called PPG Industries Inc* ***(G-18766)***
**PPG 5534, Elgin** *Also called PPG Industries Inc* ***(G-9145)***
**PPG 9449, Westmont** *Also called PPG Industries Inc* ***(G-21913)***
**PPG Aerospace, Chicago** *Also called Hlh Associates* ***(G-5092)***
**PPG Architectural Finishes Inc**....217 584-1323
S Washington St Meredosia (62665) ***(G-14734)***
**PPG Architectural Finishes Inc**....773 523-6333
3641 S Washtenaw Ave Chicago (60632) ***(G-6161)***
**PPG Architectural Finishes Inc**....847 336-2355
3590 Grand Ave Gurnee (60031) ***(G-11487)***
**PPG Architectural Finishes Inc**....630 773-8484
880 W Thorndale Ave Itasca (60143) ***(G-12344)***
**PPG Architectural Finishes Inc**....630 820-8692
473 S Route 59 Aurora (60504) ***(G-1067)***
**PPG Architectural Finishes Inc**....309 673-3761
404 Sw Adams St Peoria (61602) ***(G-17432)***
**PPG Architectural Finishes Inc**....847 699-8400
2200 E Devon Ave 111 Des Plaines (60018) ***(G-8259)***
**PPG Industries, Decatur** *Also called Fuyao Glass Illinois Inc* ***(G-7883)***
**PPG Industries Inc**....773 646-5900
1701 E 122nd St Chicago (60633) ***(G-6162)***
**PPG Industries Inc**....630 879-5100
1020 Olympic Dr Batavia (60510) ***(G-1485)***
**PPG Industries Inc**....773 646-5900
1701 E 122nd St Chicago (60633) ***(G-6163)***
**PPG Industries Inc**....708 597-7044
5151 W 122nd St Alsip (60803) ***(G-512)***
**PPG Industries Inc**....847 742-3340
266 Kimball St Elgin (60120) ***(G-9145)***
**PPG Industries Inc**....618 206-2250
1333 Central Park Dr # 135 O Fallon (62269) ***(G-16475)***
**PPG Industries Inc**....312 666-2277
345 N Morgan St Chicago (60607) ***(G-6164)***
**PPG Industries Inc**....847 991-0620
2180 Plum Grove Rd Rolling Meadows (60008) ***(G-18766)***
**PPG Industries Inc**....217 757-9080
3040 S 6th St Springfield (62703) ***(G-20506)***
**PPG Industries Inc**....708 345-1515
3500 W North Ave Stone Park (60165) ***(G-20636)***
**PPG Industries Inc**....630 960-3600
6136 S Cass Ave Westmont (60559) ***(G-21913)***
**Ppm, Peoria** *Also called Performance Pattern & Mch Inc* ***(G-17427)***
**Ppt Industrial Machines Inc**....800 851-3586
714 N Walnut St Mount Carmel (62863) ***(G-15281)***
**PQ Corporation**....815 667-4241
340 E Grove St Utica (61373) ***(G-21107)***
**PQ Corporation**....847 662-8566
1945 N Delany Rd Gurnee (60031) ***(G-11488)***
**PQ Ovens, Byron** *Also called Dane Industries LLC* ***(G-2915)***
**Practechal Marketing**....847 486-8600
1867 Waukegan Rd Glenview (60025) ***(G-11183)***
**Practical Baker Equipment**....815 943-8730
600 Chippewa Rd Harvard (60033) ***(G-11644)***
**Practical Communications Inc**....773 754-3250
1320 Tower Rd Schaumburg (60173) ***(G-19699)***
**Practice Law Management Mag**....312 988-6114
321 N Clark St Chicago (60654) ***(G-6165)***
**Practice Management Info Corp**....800 633-7467
2001 Butterfield Rd # 310 Downers Grove (60515) ***(G-8508)***
**Prager Associates**....309 691-1565
4035 W Tangleoaks Ct Peoria (61615) ***(G-17433)***
**Praire State Floor Covering**....309 253-5982
333 South St Pekin (61554) ***(G-17283)***
**Prairie Advocate Newspaper, Lanark** *Also called Acres of Sky Communications* ***(G-13149)***
**Prairie Area Library System (PA)**....309 799-3155
220 W 23rd Ave Coal Valley (61240) ***(G-7298)***
**Prairie Central, Decatur** *Also called Southfield Corporation* ***(G-7941)***
**Prairie Central Ready Mix**....217 877-5210
800 E Mckinley Ave Decatur (62526) ***(G-7928)***
**Prairie Construction Material, Peoria** *Also called Southfield Corporation* ***(G-17459)***
**Prairie Display Chicago Inc**....630 834-8773
758 N Industrial Dr Elmhurst (60126) ***(G-9922)***
**Prairie Farms Dairy, Rockford** *Also called Muller-Pinehurst Dairy Inc* ***(G-18512)***
**Prairie Farms Dairy Inc**....217 223-5530
415 N 24th St Quincy (62301) ***(G-17869)***
**Prairie Farms Dairy Inc**....618 393-2128
217 W Main St Olney (62450) ***(G-16791)***
**Prairie Farms Dairy Inc (PA)**....217 854-2547
1100 Broadway Carlinville (62626) ***(G-3047)***
**Prairie Farms Dairy Inc**....618 451-5600
1800 Adams St Granite City (62040) ***(G-11299)***

ALPHABETIC SECTION
Precision Machine Products

**Prairie Farms Dairy Inc** ....618 632-3632
400 W Highway 50 O Fallon (62269) ***(G-16476)***
**Prairie Farms Dairy Inc** ....618 457-4167
742 N Illinois Ave Carbondale (62901) ***(G-3018)***
**Prairie Farms Dairy Inc** ....309 686-2400
2004 N University St Peoria (61604) ***(G-17434)***
**Prairie Farms Dairy Inc** ....217 423-3459
757 N Morgan St Decatur (62521) ***(G-7929)***
**Prairie Farms Dairy Inc** ....217 245-4413
1105 W Walnut St Jacksonville (62650) ***(G-12408)***
**Prairie Fire Glass Inc** ....217 762-3332
217 W Washington St Monticello (61856) ***(G-15083)***
**Prairie Glen Imaging Ctr LLC** ....847 296-5366
9680 Golf Rd Des Plaines (60016) ***(G-8260)***
**Prairie Group Management LLC** ....708 458-0400
7601 W 79th St Ste 1 Bridgeview (60455) ***(G-2519)***
**Prairie Land Mllwrght Svcs Inc** ....815 538-3085
617 E Us Highway 34 Mendota (61342) ***(G-14731)***
**Prairie Manufacturing Inc** ....815 498-1593
405 E Lafayette St Ste 1 Somonauk (60552) ***(G-20127)***
**Prairie Material, Bridgeview** *Also called Vcna Prairie Indiana Inc* ***(G-2537)***
**Prairie Material, Bridgeview** *Also called Cimentos N Votorantim Amer Inc* ***(G-2477)***
**Prairie Materials Group** ....815 207-6750
19515 Ne Frontage Rd Shorewood (60404) ***(G-19930)***
**Prairie North Central Mtls, Manteno** *Also called Southfield Corporation* ***(G-14194)***
**Prairie Orthodontics PC** ....847 249-8800
1475 N Dilleys Rd Ste 1 Gurnee (60031) ***(G-11489)***
**Prairie Packaging Inc (HQ)** ....708 496-1172
7200 S Mason Ave Bedford Park (60638) ***(G-1575)***
**Prairie Packaging Inc** ....708 496-2900
7200 S Mason Ave Chicago (60638) ***(G-6166)***
**Prairie Packaging Inc** ....708 563-8670
7701 W 79th St Bridgeview (60455) ***(G-2520)***
**Prairie Profile** ....618 846-2116
1437 E 1050 Ave Vandalia (62471) ***(G-21120)***
**Prairie Pure Bottled Water** ....217 774-7873
603 W North 4th St Shelbyville (62565) ***(G-19912)***
**Prairie Pure Cheese** ....815 568-5000
1405 N State St Marengo (60152) ***(G-14240)***
**Prairie Seating, Skokie** *Also called Permobil Inc* ***(G-20054)***
**Prairie Shopper/Business Jurnl, Decatur** *Also called Lee Enterprises Incorporated* ***(G-7907)***
**Prairie Signs Inc** ....309 452-0463
1215 Warriner St Normal (61761) ***(G-16084)***
**Prairie State Graphics Inc** ....847 801-3100
11100 Addison Ave Franklin Park (60131) ***(G-10556)***
**Prairie State Impressions LLC** ....847 801-3100
11100 Addison Ave Franklin Park (60131) ***(G-10557)***
**Prairie State Industries Inc** ....847 428-3641
1009 Tamarac Dr Carpentersville (60110) ***(G-3297)***
**Prairie State Machine LLC** ....217 543-3768
71 E Cr 100 N Arthur (61911) ***(G-919)***
**Prairie State Screw & Bolt Co** ....847 858-9551
4219 Kayla Ln Northbrook (60062) ***(G-16342)***
**Prairie View Farms, Deer Grove** *Also called H W Hostetler & Sons* ***(G-7967)***
**Prairie Wi-FI Systems** ....515 988-3260
935 W Chestnut St Ste 530 Chicago (60642) ***(G-6167)***
**Prairie Woodworks Inc** ....309 378-2418
311 S Lincoln St Downs (61736) ***(G-8547)***
**Prairieland Fs Inc** ....309 329-2162
2452 N Bader Rd Astoria (61501) ***(G-936)***
**Prairieland Inv Property, Wauconda** *Also called Menges Roller Co Inc* ***(G-21482)***
**Prairieland Printing** ....309 647-5425
1237 Peoria St Washington (61571) ***(G-21387)***
**Prarie Material Sales Inc** ....847 733-8809
828 Davis St Evanston (60201) ***(G-10090)***
**Prarieland Printing Spp, Washington** *Also called Prairieland Printing* ***(G-21387)***
**Prater Industries Inc (HQ)** ....630 679-3200
2 Sammons Ct Bolingbrook (60440) ***(G-2359)***
**Prater-Sterling, Bolingbrook** *Also called Prater Industries Inc* ***(G-2359)***
**Prater-Sterling, Sterling** *Also called Sterling Systems & Controls* ***(G-20615)***
**Pratt Industries** ....630 254-0271
21700 Mark Collins Dr Sauk Village (60411) ***(G-19392)***
**Pratt-Read Tools LLC** ....815 895-1121
1375 Park Ave Sycamore (60178) ***(G-20813)***
**Praxair Inc** ....847 428-3405
330 Arrowhead Dr Gilberts (60136) ***(G-10932)***
**Praxair Distribution Inc** ....314 664-7900
9 Judith Ln Cahokia (62206) ***(G-2924)***
**Praxair Distribution Inc** ....309 346-3164
2100 N 8th St Pekin (61554) ***(G-17284)***
**Praxsym Inc** ....217 897-1744
120 S 3rd St Fisher (61843) ***(G-10191)***
**Pre Fnish Mtals Mrrisville Inc** ....847 439-2211
2250 Pratt Blvd Elk Grove Village (60007) ***(G-9691)***
**Pre Pack Machinery Inc** ....217 352-1010
520 S Country Fair Dr Champaign (61821) ***(G-3528)***
**Precious Metal Ref Svcs Inc** ....847 756-2700
1531 S Grove Ave Unit 104 Barrington (60010) ***(G-1298)***
**Precise Finishing Co Inc** ....847 451-2077
2842 Birch St Franklin Park (60131) ***(G-10558)***
**Precise Lapping Grinding Corp** ....708 615-0240
2041 Janice Ave Melrose Park (60160) ***(G-14683)***
**Precise Products Inc** ....630 393-9698
3s286 Talbot Ave Warrenville (60555) ***(G-21357)***
**Precise Punch Products Co, Rockford** *Also called Cdv Corp* ***(G-18300)***
**Precise Rotary Die Inc** ....847 678-0001
9250 Ivanhoe St Schiller Park (60176) ***(G-19861)***
**Precise Stamping Inc** ....630 897-6477
202 Poplar Pl North Aurora (60542) ***(G-16143)***
**Precise Tool & Manufacturing, Loves Park** *Also called Phillip Rodgers* ***(G-13973)***
**Precision Brand Products Inc** ....630 969-7200
2250 Curtiss St Downers Grove (60515) ***(G-8509)***
**Precision Chrome Inc** ....847 587-1515
105 Precision Rd Fox Lake (60020) ***(G-10282)***
**Precision Circuits Inc** ....630 515-9100
2538 Wisconsin Ave Downers Grove (60515) ***(G-8510)***
**Precision Cnncting Rod Svc Inc** ....708 345-3700
2600 W Cermak Rd Broadview (60155) ***(G-2602)***
**Precision Components Inc** ....630 462-9110
1020 Cedar Ave Ste 215 Saint Charles (60174) ***(G-19240)***
**Precision Computer Methods** ....630 208-8000
801 Drover St Elburn (60119) ***(G-8904)***
**Precision Container Inc** ....618 548-2830
1370 W Main St Salem (62881) ***(G-19344)***
**Precision Control Systems** ....630 521-0234
1980 University Ln Lisle (60532) ***(G-13643)***
**Precision Conveyor and Erct Co** ....779 324-5269
9511 Corsair Rd Ste E Frankfort (60423) ***(G-10350)***
**Precision Custom Molders Inc** ....815 675-1370
1802 Holian Dr Spring Grove (60081) ***(G-20357)***
**Precision Dialogue Direct Inc (PA)** ....773 237-2264
5501 W Grand Ave Chicago (60639) ***(G-6168)***
**Precision Die Cutting & Finish** ....773 252-5625
4027 W Le Moyne St Chicago (60651) ***(G-6169)***
**Precision Dormer LLC** ....800 877-3745
2511 Tech Dr Ste 113 Elgin (60124) ***(G-9146)***
**Precision Drive & Control Inc** ....815 235-7595
1650 S Galena Ave Freeport (61032) ***(G-10680)***
**Precision Dynamics Inc** ....815 877-1592
5029 Willow Creek Rd Machesney Park (61115) ***(G-14099)***
**Precision Electronics Inc** ....847 599-1799
1331 Estes St Gurnee (60031) ***(G-11490)***
**Precision Engine Rebuilders** ....815 254-2333
23807 W Andrew Rd Unit A Plainfield (60585) ***(G-17642)***
**Precision Engineering & Dev Co** ....630 834-5956
701 N Iowa Ave Villa Park (60181) ***(G-21278)***
**Precision Entps Fndry Mch Inc (PA)** ....815 797-1000
1000 E Precision Dr Somonauk (60552) ***(G-20128)***
**Precision Entps Fndry Mch Inc** ....815 498-2317
900 E Precision Dr Somonauk (60552) ***(G-20129)***
**Precision Finishing Systems In** ....847 907-4266
682 Chaddick Dr Wheeling (60090) ***(G-22127)***
**Precision Forming Stamping Co** ....773 489-6868
2419 W George St Chicago (60618) ***(G-6170)***
**Precision Foundry Tooling Ltd** ....217 847-3233
160 Hamilton Indus Park Hamilton (62341) ***(G-11539)***
**Precision Gage Company** ....630 655-2121
100 Shore Dr Burr Ridge (60527) ***(G-2875)***
**Precision Governors LLC** ....815 229-5300
1715 Northrock Ct Rockford (61103) ***(G-18537)***
**Precision Grinding and Mch Inc** ....
16664 Cherry Creek Ct Joliet (60433) ***(G-12553)***
**Precision Grinding Inc** ....847 238-1000
2375 American Ln Elk Grove Village (60007) ***(G-9692)***
**Precision Ground** ....815 578-2613
548 Herbert Rd Ste 2 Lakemoor (60051) ***(G-13146)***
**Precision Header Tooling Inc** ....815 874-9116
3441 Precision Dr Rockford (61109) ***(G-18538)***
**Precision Ibc Inc** ....708 396-0750
13612 Lawler Ave Crestwood (60445) ***(G-7498)***
**Precision Inc** ....847 593-2947
2210 Elmhurst Rd Elk Grove Village (60007) ***(G-9693)***
**Precision Industrial Knife** ....630 350-7898
850 Dillon Dr Wood Dale (60191) ***(G-22412)***
**Precision Ink Corporation** ....847 952-1500
151 Stanley St Elk Grove Village (60007) ***(G-9694)***
**Precision Instruments Inc** ....847 824-4194
1846 Miner St Des Plaines (60016) ***(G-8261)***
**Precision Laboratories LLC** ....800 323-6280
1429 S Shields Dr Waukegan (60085) ***(G-21606)***
**Precision Language & Graphics** ....847 413-1688
800 E Woodfield Rd # 107 Schaumburg (60173) ***(G-19700)***
**Precision Laser Marking Inc** ....630 628-8575
900 S Kay Ave Addison (60101) ***(G-251)***
**Precision Machine and** ....618 997-8795
410 N Pentecost Dr Marion (62959) ***(G-14283)***
**Precision Machine Products** ....630 860-0861
655 N Central Ave Ste G Wood Dale (60191) ***(G-22413)***

(PA)=Parent Co (HQ)=Headquarters (DH)=Div Headquarters
2017 Harris Illinois
Industrial Directory
1353

ALPHABETIC

**Precision Machining & Tool Co** ....847 674-7111
7341 Monticello Ave Skokie (60076) *(G-20058)*
**Precision Masters** ....815 397-3894
2801 Eastrock Dr Rockford (61109) *(G-18539)*
**Precision McHned Cmponents Inc** ....630 759-5555
1348 Enterprise Dr Romeoville (60446) *(G-18860)*
**Precision Metal Crafters Inc** ....847 816-3244
1840 Industrial Dr # 340 Libertyville (60048) *(G-13371)*
**Precision Metal Crafts Inc** ....815 254-2306
12201 Rhea Dr Plainfield (60585) *(G-17643)*
**Precision Metal Products Inc** ....630 458-0100
1209 W Capitol Dr Addison (60101) *(G-252)*
**Precision Metal Spinning Corp** ....847 392-5672
1000 Carnegie St Rolling Meadows (60008) *(G-18767)*
**Precision Metal Technologies** ....847 228-6630
2255 Lois Dr Ste 2 Rolling Meadows (60008) *(G-18768)*
**Precision Molded Concepts** ....815 675-0060
2402 Spring Ridge Dr C Spring Grove (60081) *(G-20358)*
**Precision Neon Glasswork** ....847 428-1200
1324 Knollwood Cir Crystal Lake (60014) *(G-7627)*
**Precision Oil Field Cnstr, Mount Sterling** *Also called Bruce McCullough (G-15390)*
**Precision Paper Tube Company (PA)** ....847 537-4250
1033 Noel Ave Wheeling (60090) *(G-22128)*
**Precision Plastic Ball Co** ....847 678-2255
10129 Pacific Ave Franklin Park (60131) *(G-10559)*
**Precision Plastic Products** ....217 784-4920
111 E 8th St Gibson City (60936) *(G-10906)*
**Precision Plating of Quincy** ....217 223-6590
2611 Locust St Quincy (62301) *(G-17870)*
**Precision Plugging and Sls Inc** ....618 395-8510
108 Linn St Olney (62450) *(G-16792)*
**Precision Plus Products Inc** ....815 459-1351
990 Lutter Dr Ste B Crystal Lake (60014) *(G-7628)*
**Precision Printing, Crest Hill** *Also called Temper Enterprises Inc (G-7469)*
**Precision Printing Inc** ....630 737-0075
230 Eisenhower Ln N Lombard (60148) *(G-13844)*
**Precision Prismatic Inc** ....708 424-0905
10247 Ridgeland Ave Ste 1 Chicago Ridge (60415) *(G-7154)*
**Precision Process Corp** ....847 640-9820
1401 Brummel Ave Elk Grove Village (60007) *(G-9695)*
**Precision Products Inc** ....217 735-1590
316 Limit St Lincoln (62656) *(G-13418)*
**Precision Products Mfg Intl** ....847 299-8500
1400 E Touhy Ave Ste 402 Des Plaines (60018) *(G-8262)*
**Precision Pump & Valve Service, Salem** *Also called Duncan Oil Company Inc (G-19330)*
**Precision Quincy Ovens LLC** ....302 602-8738
483 Gardner St South Beloit (61080) *(G-20164)*
**Precision Remanufacturing Inc** ....773 489-7225
4520 W Fullerton Ave Chicago (60639) *(G-6171)*
**Precision Reproductions Inc** ....847 724-0182
4316 Regency Dr Glenview (60025) *(G-11184)*
**Precision Resource Inc** ....847 383-1300
700 Hickory Hill Dr Vernon Hills (60061) *(G-21190)*
**Precision Resource III Div, Vernon Hills** *Also called Precision Resource Inc (G-21190)*
**Precision Screen Specialties** ....630 762-9548
3905 Commerce Dr Saint Charles (60174) *(G-19241)*
**Precision Screw Machining Co** ....773 205-4280
3511 N Kenton Ave Chicago (60641) *(G-6172)*
**Precision Service** ....618 345-2047
407 W Main St Collinsville (62234) *(G-7337)*
**Precision Service Mtr Inc** ....630 628-9900
121 W Fullerton Ave Addison (60101) *(G-253)*
**Precision Software Limited** ....312 239-1630
1011 Warrenville Rd # 210 Lisle (60532) *(G-13644)*
**Precision Stamping Pdts Inc** ....847 678-0800
4848 River Rd Schiller Park (60176) *(G-19862)*
**Precision Steel Warehouse Inc (HQ)** ....800 323-0740
3500 Wolf Rd Franklin Park (60131) *(G-10560)*
**Precision Tank & Equipment Co (PA)** ....217 452-7228
3503 Conover Rd Virginia (62691) *(G-21307)*
**Precision Tank & Equipment Co** ....217 636-7023
25203 Quarry Ave Athens (62613) *(G-942)*
**Precision Technologies Inc** ....847 439-5447
2200 Gladstone Ct Ste H Glendale Heights (60139) *(G-11058)*
**Precision Tool** ....815 464-2428
21200 S La Grange Rd Frankfort (60423) *(G-10351)*
**Precision Tool & Die Company** ....217 864-3371
445 W Main St Mount Zion (62549) *(G-15455)*
**Precision Tool Welding** ....630 285-9844
1300 Industrial Dr Ste B Itasca (60143) *(G-12345)*
**Precision Truck Products Inc** ....618 548-9011
2625 S Broadway Ave Salem (62881) *(G-19345)*
**Precision Vision Inc** ....815 223-2022
1725 Kilkenny Ct Woodstock (60098) *(G-22601)*
**Precision-Tek Mfg, Arlington Heights** *Also called Precision-Tek Mfg Inc (G-819)*
**Precision-Tek Mfg Inc** ....847 364-7800
3206 Nordic Rd Arlington Heights (60005) *(G-819)*
**Precitec Corporation** ....847 949-2800
1000 Tower Rd Mundelein (60060) *(G-15547)*
**Precoat Metals** ....618 451-0909
25 Northgate Indus Dr Granite City (62040) *(G-11300)*
**Preferred Bus Publications Inc** ....815 717-6399
1938 E Lincoln Hwy # 216 New Lenox (60451) *(G-15902)*
**Preferred Fasteners Inc** ....630 510-0200
250 S Westgate Dr Carol Stream (60188) *(G-3215)*
**Preferred Foods Products Inc** ....773 847-0230
1421 W 47th St Chicago (60609) *(G-6173)*
**Preferred Freezer Services of** ....773 254-9500
4500 W 42nd Pl Chicago (60632) *(G-6174)*
**Preferred Press Inc** ....630 980-9799
1934 Bentley Ct Ste D Glendale Heights (60139) *(G-11059)*
**Preferred Printing & Graphics** ....708 547-6880
5815 Saint Charles Rd Berkeley (60163) *(G-2049)*
**Preferred Printing Service** ....312 421-2343
2343 W Roosevelt Rd Chicago (60608) *(G-6175)*
**Preflight LLC** ....312 935-2804
200 N Lasalle Ste 1400 Chicago (60601) *(G-6176)*
**Preformance Signs** ....815 544-5044
6940 Imron Dr Belvidere (61008) *(G-1780)*
**Pregis Holding I Corporation (PA)** ....847 597-2200
1650 Lake Cook Rd Ste 400 Deerfield (60015) *(G-8046)*
**Pregis Innovative Packg LLC** ....847 597-2200
1650 Lake Cook Rd Ste 400 Deerfield (60015) *(G-8047)*
**Pregis LLC** ....331 425-6264
515 Enterprise St Aurora (60504) *(G-1068)*
**Pregis LLC (HQ)** ....847 597-9330
1650 Lake Cook Rd Ste 400 Deerfield (60015) *(G-8048)*
**Pregis LLC** ....847 597-2200
1650 Lake Cook Rd Ste 400 Deerfield (60015) *(G-8049)*
**Pregis LLC** ....618 934-4311
11620 Old Us Highway 50 Trenton (62293) *(G-20997)*
**Prella Technologies Inc** ....630 400-0626
11408 Kiley Dr Huntley (60142) *(G-12168)*
**Premier Beverage Solutions LLC** ....309 369-7117
805 Oakwood Rd East Peoria (61611) *(G-8728)*
**Premier Fabrication LLC** ....309 448-2338
303 County Highway 8 Congerville (61729) *(G-7369)*
**Premier Health Concepts LLC** ....630 575-1059
780 W Army Trail Rd Carol Stream (60188) *(G-3216)*
**Premier International Entps** ....312 857-2200
221 N La Salle St Ste 900 Chicago (60601) *(G-6177)*
**Premier Laundry Technologies, Joliet** *Also called L T P LLC (G-12530)*
**Premier Manufacturing Corp** ....847 640-6644
35 W Laura Dr Addison (60101) *(G-254)*
**Premier Metal Works Inc** ....312 226-7414
1616 S Clinton St Chicago (60616) *(G-6178)*
**Premier Packaging Corp** ....815 469-7951
9424 Gulfstream Rd Frankfort (60423) *(G-10352)*
**Premier Packaging Systems Inc** ....847 996-6860
304 Terrace Dr Mundelein (60060) *(G-15548)*
**Premier Print Group, Champaign** *Also called Premier Printing Illinois Inc (G-3529)*
**Premier Printing & Promotions** ....815 282-3890
1338 Turret Dr Ste B Machesney Park (61115) *(G-14100)*
**Premier Printing and Packaging** ....847 970-9434
1881 Hicks Rd Ste B Rolling Meadows (60008) *(G-18769)*
**Premier Printing Illinois Inc** ....217 359-2219
3104 Farber Dr Champaign (61822) *(G-3529)*
**Premier Signs Creations Inc** ....309 637-6890
710 Fayette St Peoria (61603) *(G-17435)*
**Premier Tool & Machine Inc** ....618 445-9066
330 Industrial Dr Albion (62806) *(G-365)*
**Premier Tool Works, Burr Ridge** *Also called Integral Automation Inc (G-2856)*
**Premier Travel Media** ....630 794-0696
621 Plainfield Rd Ste 406 Willowbrook (60527) *(G-22228)*
**Premiere America, Wauconda** *Also called Paragon Group Inc (G-21491)*
**Premiere Auto Service** ....773 275-8785
727 S Jefferson St Chicago (60607) *(G-6179)*
**Premiere Distribution, Evanston** *Also called Michele Terrell (G-10072)*
**Premiere Motorsports LLC** ....708 634-0007
16300 S Lincoln Hwy 1 Plainfield (60586) *(G-17644)*
**Premium Components** ....630 521-1700
1090 Bryn Mawr Ave Bensenville (60106) *(G-1966)*
**Premium Manufacturing Inc** ....309 787-3882
4608 78th Ave W Rock Island (61201) *(G-18192)*
**Premium Oil Company** ....815 963-3800
923 Fairview Ct Rockford (61101) *(G-18540)*
**Premium Pallets** ....217 974-0155
2877 N Dirksen Pkwy Springfield (62702) *(G-20507)*
**Premium Products Inc** ....630 553-6160
207 Wolf St Yorkville (60560) *(G-22669)*
**Premium Test Equipment Corp** ....630 400-2681
30 W 270 Butterfield Warrenville (60555) *(G-21358)*
**Premium Waters Inc** ....217 222-0213
1811 N 30th St Stop 1 Quincy (62301) *(G-17871)*
**Premium Wood Products Inc** ....815 787-3669
436 E Locust St Dekalb (60115) *(G-8113)*
**Prenosis Inc** ....949 246-3113
210 Hazelwood Dr Ste 103 Champaign (61822) *(G-3530)*

**Pres-On Corporation** ....630 628-2255
2600 E 107th St Bolingbrook (60440) *(G-2360)*
**Pres-On Tape & Gasket, Bolingbrook** *Also called Pres-On Corporation (G-2360)*
**Prescott's TV & Appliance, Sterling** *Also called Prescotts Inc (G-20605)*
**Prescotts Inc** ....815 626-2996
3610 E Lincolnway Sterling (61081) *(G-20605)*
**Prescription Plus Ltd (PA)** ....618 537-6202
753 True Value Dr Lebanon (62254) *(G-13216)*
**Presentation Studios Intl LLC** ....312 733-8160
1435 W Fulton St Chicago (60607) *(G-6180)*
**Press A Light Corporation** ....630 231-6566
300 Industrial Dr West Chicago (60185) *(G-21760)*
**Press America Inc** ....847 228-0333
661 Fargo Ave Elk Grove Village (60007) *(G-9696)*
**Press Brakes** ....630 916-1494
260 Cortland Ave Ste 6 Lombard (60148) *(G-13845)*
**Press Dough Inc** ....630 243-6900
22 Longwood Way Lemont (60439) *(G-13257)*
**Press Express, Lisle** *Also called Cannon Ball Marketing Inc (G-13573)*
**Press On Inc** ....630 628-1630
53 S Evergreen Ave Addison (60101) *(G-255)*
**Press Proof Printing** ....847 466-7156
180 S Western Ave Carpentersville (60110) *(G-3298)*
**Press Syndication Group LLC** ....646 325-3221
2850 N Pulaski Rd Unit 9 Chicago (60641) *(G-6181)*
**Press Tech Inc** ....847 824-4485
959 Lee St Des Plaines (60016) *(G-8263)*
**Pressure Specialist Inc** ....815 477-0007
186 Virginia Rd Crystal Lake (60014) *(G-7629)*
**Pressure Vessel Service Inc** ....773 913-7700
12260 S Carondolet Ave Chicago (60633) *(G-6182)*
**Prestige Motor Works Inc** ....630 780-6439
11258 S Route 59 1 Naperville (60564) *(G-15823)*
**Prestige Threaded Products Co, Burr Ridge** *Also called Great Lakes Washer Company (G-2846)*
**Prestige Wedding Decoration** ....847 845-0901
3405 N Ridge Ave Arlington Heights (60004) *(G-820)*
**Preston Industries Inc** ....847 647-2900
6600 W Touhy Ave Niles (60714) *(G-16022)*
**Prestone Products Corporation** ....708 371-3000
13160 S Pulaski Rd Alsip (60803) *(G-513)*
**Prestone Products Corporation** ....203 731-8185
1900 W Field Ct Lake Forest (60045) *(G-12948)*
**Prestone Products Corporation (HQ)** ....847 482-2045
1900 W Field Ct Lake Forest (60045) *(G-12949)*
**Prestress Engineering Company** ....815 586-4239
15606 E 3200 North Rd Blackstone (61313) *(G-2088)*
**Prestress Engineering Company (PA)** ....815 459-4545
2220 Il Route 176 Crystal Lake (60014) *(G-7630)*
**Prestressed Products Company, Blackstone** *Also called Prestress Engineering Company (G-2088)*
**Prestressed Products Company, Crystal Lake** *Also called Prestress Engineering Company (G-7630)*
**Pretium Packaging, Peru** *Also called Harbison Corporation (G-17511)*
**Prevention Health Sciences Inc** ....618 252-6922
5110 Highway 34 N Raleigh (62977) *(G-17910)*
**Prevue Hendyrx, Chicago** *Also called Prevue Pet Products Inc (G-6183)*
**Prevue Pet Products Inc (PA)** ....773 722-1052
224 N Maplewood Ave Chicago (60612) *(G-6183)*
**Preziosio Ltd** ....630 393-0920
30 W 270 Butterfield Rd D Warrenville (60555) *(G-21359)*
**Price Brothers Co** ....815 389-4800
4416 Prairie Hill Rd South Beloit (61080) *(G-20165)*
**Price Circuits LLC** ....847 742-4700
1300 Holmes Rd Elgin (60123) *(G-9147)*
**Price Machine Inc** ....217 892-8958
1021 County Road 2850 N Dewey (61840) *(G-8311)*
**Price Tech Group Illinois LLC (PA)** ....815 521-4667
25210-B W Reed St Channahon (60410) *(G-3583)*
**Pride In Graphics Inc** ....312 427-2000
739 S Clark St Fl 2 Chicago (60605) *(G-6184)*
**Pride Machine & Tool Co Inc** ....708 343-7190
1821 N 30th Ave Melrose Park (60160) *(G-14684)*
**Pride Manufacturing, Chicago** *Also called Cintas Corporation (G-4379)*
**Pride Metal, Watseka** *Also called Lyon LLC (G-21421)*
**Pride Metal Products, Watseka** *Also called Metal Mfg LLC (G-21423)*
**Pride Packaging LLC** ....309 663-9100
211 N Williamsburg Dr A Bloomington (61704) *(G-2215)*
**Prikos & Becker LLC** ....847 675-3910
8109 Lawndale Ave Skokie (60076) *(G-20059)*
**Prima Donna Salon, Belleville** *Also called Payne Chauna (G-1664)*
**Prime Dental Manufacturing** ....773 283-2914
4555 W Addison St Chicago (60641) *(G-6185)*
**Prime Devices Corporation** ....847 729-2550
11450 German Church Rd Willow Springs (60480) *(G-22198)*
**Prime Group Inc** ....312 922-3883
122 S Michigan Ave # 2040 Chicago (60603) *(G-6186)*
**Prime Group Realty Trust, Chicago** *Also called Prime Group Inc (G-6186)*
**Prime Industries Inc** ....630 833-6821
4611 Main St Ste A Lisle (60532) *(G-13645)*
**Prime Label & Packaging LLC** ....630 227-1300
501 N Central Ave Wood Dale (60191) *(G-22414)*
**Prime Label Group LLC** ....773 630-8793
1380 Nagel Blvd Batavia (60510) *(G-1486)*
**Prime Market Targeting Inc** ....815 469-4555
7777 W Lincoln Hwy Ste A Frankfort (60423) *(G-10353)*
**Prime Printing Inc** ....847 299-9960
967 Graceland Ave Ste 5 Des Plaines (60016) *(G-8264)*
**Prime Publishing LLC** ....847 205-9375
3400 Dundee Rd Ste 220 Northbrook (60062) *(G-16343)*
**Prime Stainless Products LLC** ....847 678-0800
4848 River Rd Schiller Park (60176) *(G-19863)*
**Prime Systems Inc** ....630 681-2100
416 Mission St Carol Stream (60188) *(G-3217)*
**Prime Time Computer Services** ....815 553-0300
2249 Highland Park Dr Joliet (60432) *(G-12554)*
**Prime Time Sports LLC** ....847 637-3500
220 W Campus Dr Ste C Arlington Heights (60004) *(G-821)*
**Prime Uv, Carol Stream** *Also called Prime Systems Inc (G-3217)*
**Primeco EDS, Greenville** *Also called Signco (G-11403)*
**Primedge Inc (PA)** ....224 265-6600
1281 Arthur Ave Elk Grove Village (60007) *(G-9697)*
**Primedia Source LLC** ....630 553-8451
627 White Oak Way Yorkville (60560) *(G-22670)*
**Primerro Frozen Foods, Elk Grove Village** *Also called Little Lady Foods Inc (G-9597)*
**Primo Granito LLC** ....773 282-6391
4527 N Mobile Ave Chicago (60630) *(G-6187)*
**Primrose Candy Co** ....800 268-9522
4111 W Parker Ave Chicago (60639) *(G-6188)*
**Prince Agri Products Inc** ....217 222-8854
229 Radio Rd Quincy (62305) *(G-17872)*
**Prince Castle LLC (HQ)** ....630 462-8800
355 Kehoe Blvd Carol Stream (60188) *(G-3218)*
**Prince Fabricators Inc** ....630 588-0088
745 N Gary Ave Carol Stream (60188) *(G-3219)*
**Prince Fabricators Division, Carol Stream** *Also called Prince Fabricators Inc (G-3219)*
**Prince Industries Inc (PA)** ....630 588-0088
745 N Gary Ave Carol Stream (60188) *(G-3220)*
**Prince Industries Shanghai, Carol Stream** *Also called Prince Industries Inc (G-3220)*
**Prince Meat Co** ....815 729-2333
8418 Gleneyre Rd Darien (60561) *(G-7801)*
**Prince Minerals Inc** ....618 285-6558
Ferrell St Rosiclare (62982) *(G-19049)*
**Prince Minerals LLC** ....646 747-4222
223 Hampshire St Quincy (62301) *(G-17873)*
**Prince Minerals LLC** ....646 747-4200
401 N Prince Plz Quincy (62305) *(G-17874)*
**Prince Race Car Engineering** ....815 625-8116
1880 Eastwood Dr Sterling (61081) *(G-20606)*
**Princess Foods Inc** ....847 933-1820
8100 Central Park Ave Skokie (60076) *(G-20060)*
**Princeton Chemicals Inc** ....847 975-6210
988 Princeton Ave Highland Park (60035) *(G-11862)*
**Princeton Fast Stop** ....815 872-0706
720 N Main St Princeton (61356) *(G-17758)*
**Princeton Industrial Products** ....847 839-8500
2119 Stonington Ave Hoffman Estates (60169) *(G-12041)*
**Princeton Ready-Mix Inc** ....815 875-3359
533 E Railroad Ave Princeton (61356) *(G-17759)*
**Princeton Sealing Wax Co** ....815 875-1943
106 W Long St Princeton (61356) *(G-17760)*
**Principal Instruments Inc** ....815 469-8159
845 Basswood Ln Frankfort (60423) *(G-10354)*
**Principal Manufacturing Corp** ....708 865-7500
2800 S 19th Ave Broadview (60155) *(G-2603)*
**Prinova Solutions LLC** ....630 868-0359
285 Fullerton Ave Carol Stream (60188) *(G-3221)*
**Prinsco Inc** ....815 635-3131
111 E Pine St Chatsworth (60921) *(G-3627)*
**Print & Design Services LLC** ....847 317-9001
2561 Waukegan Rd Bannockburn (60015) *(G-1264)*
**Print & Mailing Solutions LLC (PA)** ....708 544-9400
1053 N Schmidt Rd Romeoville (60446) *(G-18861)*
**Print and Mktg Solutions Group** ....847 498-9640
1537 Windy Hill Dr Northbrook (60062) *(G-16344)*
**Print Butler Inc** ....312 296-2804
674 Indian Path Rd Grayslake (60030) *(G-11359)*
**Print Express, Chicago** *Also called Shree Mahavir Inc (G-6501)*
**Print Graphics** ....847 249-1007
37984 N Metropolitan Ave Beach Park (60087) *(G-1519)*
**Print King Inc** ....708 499-3777
7818 S Cicero Ave Oak Lawn (60459) *(G-16641)*
**Print Loop, Elgin** *Also called David H Pool (G-9009)*
**Print Management Partners Inc (PA)** ....847 699-2999
701 Lee St Ste 1050 Des Plaines (60016) *(G-8265)*
**Print Rite Inc** ....773 625-0792
7748 W Addison St Chicago (60634) *(G-6189)*

ALPHABETIC

**Print Service & Dist Assn Psda** 312 321-5120
401 N Michigan Ave Chicago (60611) ***(G-6190)***
**Print Shop** 815 786-8278
17 E Center St Sandwich (60548) ***(G-19375)***
**Print Shop of Morris** 815 710-5030
1836 Unit B N Division St Morris (60450) ***(G-15126)***
**Print Shoppe Inc The Olde, Olney** *Also called Olde Print Shoppe Inc* ***(G-16786)***
**Print Source For Business Inc** 847 356-0190
38966 N Deep Lake Rd Lake Villa (60046) ***(G-13023)***
**Print Tech Inc** 847 949-5400
407 Wshington Blvd Unit C Mundelein (60060) ***(G-15549)***
**Print Turnaround Inc** 847 228-1762
3025 Malmo Dr Arlington Heights (60005) ***(G-822)***
**Print Xpress** 847 677-5555
8058 Lincoln Ave Skokie (60077) ***(G-20061)***
**Print-O-Tape Inc** 847 362-6433
755 Tower Rd Mundelein (60060) ***(G-15550)***
**Printco Printing, Charleston** *Also called Stearns Printing of Charleston* ***(G-3613)***
**Printech of Illinois Inc** 815 356-1195
975 Nimco Dr Ste E Crystal Lake (60014) ***(G-7631)***
**Printed Blog Inc** 312 924-1040
216 S Jefferson St Ll1 Chicago (60661) ***(G-6191)***
**Printed Impressions Inc** 773 604-8585
1640 S Ardmore Ave Villa Park (60181) ***(G-21279)***
**Printed Word Inc** 847 328-1511
1807 Central St Evanston (60201) ***(G-10091)***
**Printer Connection** 217 268-3252
319 S Elm St Arcola (61910) ***(G-682)***
**Printers Ink of Paris Inc** 217 463-2552
124 W Court St Paris (61944) ***(G-17158)***
**Printers Mark** 309 732-1174
1512 4th Ave Rock Island (61201) ***(G-18193)***
**Printers Parts Inc** 847 288-9000
2706 Edgington St Unit A Franklin Park (60131) ***(G-10561)***
**Printers Parts Store, Franklin Park** *Also called Printers Repair Parts Inc* ***(G-10562)***
**Printers Quill Inc** 708 429-3636
19135 S Blackhawk Pkwy Mokena (60448) ***(G-14897)***
**Printers Repair Parts Inc** 847 288-9000
2706 Edgington St Unit A Franklin Park (60131) ***(G-10562)***
**Printers Row LLC** 312 435-0411
500 S Dearborn St Chicago (60605) ***(G-6192)***
**Printers Row Loft** 312 431-1019
732 S Fincl Pl Ste Mgmt Chicago (60605) ***(G-6193)***
**Printers Square Condo Assn** 312 765-8794
680 S Federal St Chicago (60605) ***(G-6194)***
**Printers The, Paris** *Also called Printers Ink of Paris Inc* ***(G-17158)***
**Printforce Inc** 618 395-7746
1409 E Main St Olney (62450) ***(G-16793)***
**Printing & Duplicating, Carbondale** *Also called Southern Illinois University* ***(G-3024)***
**Printing Arts, Broadview** *Also called Ripa LLC* ***(G-2609)***
**Printing Arts Cmmnications LLC** 708 938-1600
2001 W 21st St Broadview (60155) ***(G-2604)***
**Printing By Joseph** 708 479-2669
19640 S La Grange Rd Mokena (60448) ***(G-14898)***
**Printing Circuit Boards** 630 543-3453
447 S Vista Ave Addison (60101) ***(G-256)***
**Printing Craftsmen of Joliet** 815 254-3982
2101 New Port Dr Joliet (60431) ***(G-12555)***
**Printing Craftsmen of Pontiac** 815 844-7118
509 W Howard St Pontiac (61764) ***(G-17709)***
**Printing Dimensions** 847 439-7521
1515 S Highland Ave Arlington Heights (60005) ***(G-823)***
**Printing Etc Inc** 815 562-6151
1135 Lincoln Hwy Rochelle (61068) ***(G-18102)***
**Printing Factory, The, Mundelein** *Also called Print Tech Inc* ***(G-15549)***
**Printing Impression Direc** 815 385-6688
31704 N Clearwater Dr Lakemoor (60051) ***(G-13147)***
**Printing In Remebrance Inc** 773 874-8700
8248 S Cottage Grove Ave Chicago (60619) ***(G-6195)***
**Printing On Ashland Inc** 773 488-4707
8227 S Ashland Ave Ste 1 Chicago (60620) ***(G-6196)***
**Printing Plant** 618 529-3115
606 S Illinois Ave Ste 1 Carbondale (62901) ***(G-3019)***
**Printing Plus** 708 301-3900
15751 Annico Dr Ste 5 Lockport (60491) ***(G-13739)***
**Printing Plus of Roselle Inc** 630 893-0410
205 E Irving Park Rd Roselle (60172) ***(G-18963)***
**Printing Press of Joliet Inc** 815 725-0018
1920 Donmaur Dr Joliet (60403) ***(G-12556)***
**Printing Press The, Milan** *Also called Whipples Printing Press Inc* ***(G-14808)***
**Printing Source Inc** 773 588-2930
8120 River Dr Ste 2 Morton Grove (60053) ***(G-15228)***
**Printing Store Inc** 708 383-3638
621 Madison St Oak Park (60302) ***(G-16681)***
**Printing System** 630 339-5900
1935 Brandon Ct Ste A Glendale Heights (60139) ***(G-11060)***
**Printing Unlimited, Moline** *Also called K R O Enterprises Ltd* ***(G-14949)***
**Printing Works Inc** 847 860-1920
2485 E Devon Ave Elk Grove Village (60007) ***(G-9698)***
**Printing You Can Trust** 224 676-0482
707 Mallard Ln Deerfield (60015) ***(G-8050)***
**Printing/Typesetting, Rolling Meadows** *Also called Tri-Tower Printing Inc* ***(G-18785)***
**Printjet Corporation** 815 877-7511
7816 Burden Rd Machesney Park (61115) ***(G-14101)***
**Printlink Enterprises Inc** 847 753-9800
3636 Torrey Pines Pkwy Northbrook (60062) ***(G-16345)***
**Printmart, Oak Lawn** *Also called N P D Inc* ***(G-16636)***
**Printmeisters Inc** 708 474-8400
3240 Ridge Rd Lansing (60438) ***(G-13180)***
**Printovate Technologies Inc** 847 962-3106
1931 N Meryls Ter Palatine (60074) ***(G-17064)***
**Printpack Inc** 847 888-7150
1400 Abbott Dr Elgin (60123) ***(G-9148)***
**Prints Chicago Inc** 312 243-6481
1230 W Jackson Blvd Chicago (60607) ***(G-6197)***
**Printsmart Printing & Graphics** 630 434-2000
3024 Hobson Rd Woodridge (60517) ***(G-22510)***
**Printsource Plus Inc** 708 389-6252
12128 Western Ave Blue Island (60406) ***(G-2265)***
**Printwise Inc** 630 833-2845
1670 Monticello Ct Unit E Wheaton (60189) ***(G-21972)***
**Printworld** 815 544-1000
319 S State St Belvidere (61008) ***(G-1781)***
**Prinzings of Rockford** 815 874-9654
2046 Schell Dr Rockford (61109) ***(G-18541)***
**Priority Care, Elgin** *Also called First Priority Inc* ***(G-9037)***
**Priority One Prtg & Mailing, Quincy** *Also called Timothy Helgoth* ***(G-17894)***
**Priority Print** 708 485-7080
9433 Ogden Ave Brookfield (60513) ***(G-2641)***
**Priority Printing** 773 889-6021
6942 W Diversey Ave Chicago (60707) ***(G-6198)***
**Priority Promotions, Sycamore** *Also called Visual Persuasion Inc* ***(G-20823)***
**Prism Commercial Printing Ctrs (PA)** 630 834-4443
6957 W Archer Ave Chicago (60638) ***(G-6199)***
**Prism Commercial Printing Ctrs** 773 229-2620
6901 W 59th St Chicago (60638) ***(G-6200)***
**Prism Commercial Printing Ctrs** 773 735-5400
6130 S Pulaski Rd Chicago (60629) ***(G-6201)***
**Prism Commercial Printing Ctrs** 630 834-4443
49 E Fullerton Ave Addison (60101) ***(G-257)***
**Prism Esolutions Dv Andy Frain** 630 820-3820
761 Shoreline Dr Aurora (60504) ***(G-1069)***
**Prismatec Inc** 847 562-9022
1964 Raymond Dr Northbrook (60062) ***(G-16346)***
**Prismier LLC** 630 592-4515
10216 Werch Dr Ste 118 Woodridge (60517) ***(G-22511)***
**Pristine Water Solutions Inc** 847 689-1100
1570 S Lakeside Dr Waukegan (60085) ***(G-21607)***
**Private Studios** 217 367-3530
705 Western Ave Urbana (61801) ***(G-21099)***
**Pro Access Systems Inc (PA)** 630 426-0022
116 Paul St Elburn (60119) ***(G-8905)***
**Pro Ag Inc** 815 365-2353
18500 W 3000s Rd Reddick (60961) ***(G-17952)***
**Pro Arc Inc** 815 877-1804
7440 Forest Hills Rd Loves Park (61111) ***(G-13977)***
**Pro Built Tool & Mold Inc** 815 436-9088
23839 W Andrew Rd # 103 Plainfield (60585) ***(G-17645)***
**Pro Cabinets Inc** 618 993-0008
11123 Skyline Dr Marion (62959) ***(G-14284)***
**Pro Circle Golf Centers Inc** 815 675-2747
1810 N Us Highway 12 Spring Grove (60081) ***(G-20359)***
**Pro Circle Golf Driving Range, Spring Grove** *Also called Pro Circle Golf Centers Inc* ***(G-20359)***
**Pro Form Industries Inc** 815 923-2555
17714 Jefferson St Union (60180) ***(G-21038)***
**Pro Fuel Nine Inc** 309 867-3375
101 S 8th St Oquawka (61469) ***(G-16813)***
**Pro Glass Corporation** 630 553-3141
9318 Corneils Rd Bristol (60512) ***(G-2549)***
**Pro Graphics Ink** 309 647-2526
322 N 15th Ave Canton (61520) ***(G-2992)***
**Pro Image** 708 422-7471
670 Chicago Ridge Mall Chicago Ridge (60415) ***(G-7155)***
**Pro Image Promotions Inc** 773 292-1111
2006 W Chicago Ave Chicago (60622) ***(G-6202)***
**Pro Intercom LLC (PA)** 224 406-7108
1117 Saint Andrews Ct Algonquin (60102) ***(G-404)***
**Pro Machining Inc** 815 633-4140
2131 Harlem Rd Loves Park (61111) ***(G-13978)***
**Pro Mold & Die, Roselle** *Also called Pro-Mold Incorporated* ***(G-18964)***
**Pro Patch Systems Inc** 847 356-8100
25704 W Lehmann Blvd Lake Villa (60046) ***(G-13024)***
**Pro Rep Sale IL** 847 382-1592
25560 N Countryside Dr Barrington (60010) ***(G-1299)***
**Pro TEC Metal Finishing Corp** 773 384-7853
1428 N Kilpatrick Ave Chicago (60651) ***(G-6203)***

**Pro Tech Engineering**...309 475-2502
129 W Lincoln St Saybrook (61770) *(G-19414)*
**Pro Techmation Inc**...815 459-5909
370 E Prairie St Ste 5 Crystal Lake (60014) *(G-7632)*
**Pro Tools & Equipment Inc**...847 838-6666
23529 Eagles Nest Rd Antioch (60002) *(G-652)*
**Pro Tuff Decal Inc**...815 356-9160
7505 Eastgate Aly Crystal Lake (60014) *(G-7633)*
**Pro Woodworking**...708 508-5948
6554 S Menard Ave Bedford Park (60638) *(G-1576)*
**Pro-Air Service, Co., Antioch** *Also called Meyer Machine & Equipment Inc (G-645)*
**Pro-Beam USA, Aurora** *Also called Globaltech International LLC (G-1018)*
**Pro-Bilt Buildings LLC**...217 532-9331
9181 Illinois Route 127 Hillsboro (62049) *(G-11898)*
**Pro-Fab Inc**...309 263-8454
1050 W Jefferson St Ste A Morton (61550) *(G-15178)*
**Pro-Fab Metals Inc**...618 283-2986
10949 Us 40 Vandalia (62471) *(G-21121)*
**Pro-Line Safety Products, West Chicago** *Also called Pro-Pak Industries Inc (G-21761)*
**Pro-Line Winning Ways & Penlan**...309 745-8530
2095 Washington Rd Washington (61571) *(G-21388)*
**Pro-Mold Incorporated**...630 893-3594
55 Chancellor Dr Roselle (60172) *(G-18964)*
**Pro-Orthotics Inc**...708 326-1554
11508 183rd Pl Orland Park (60467) *(G-16885)*
**Pro-Pak Industries Inc**...630 876-1050
1099 Atlantic Dr Ste 1 West Chicago (60185) *(G-21761)*
**Pro-Qua Inc**...630 543-5644
305 W Laura Dr Addison (60101) *(G-258)*
**Pro-Quip Incorporated**...708 352-5732
418 Shawmut Ave Ste A La Grange Park (60526) *(G-12759)*
**Pro-Tech Metal Specialties Inc**...630 279-7094
233 W Diversey Ave Elmhurst (60126) *(G-9923)*
**Pro-Tek, Saint Charles** *Also called Protek Inc (G-19243)*
**Pro-Tek Products Inc**...630 293-5100
1755 S Nprvlle Rd Ste 100 Wheaton (60189) *(G-21973)*
**Pro-Tran Inc**...217 348-9353
1671 Olive Ave Charleston (61920) *(G-3608)*
**Pro-Type Printing Inc (PA)**...217 379-4715
130 N Market St Paxton (60957) *(G-17244)*
**ProAm Sports Products**...708 841-4200
435 Adams St Dolton (60419) *(G-8375)*
**Problend-Eurogerm LLC**...847 221-5004
1801 Hicks Rd Ste H Rolling Meadows (60008) *(G-18770)*
**Probotix**...309 691-2643
8800b N Industrial Rd Peoria (61615) *(G-17436)*
**Proceq USA Inc**...847 623-9570
4217 Grove Ave Gurnee (60031) *(G-11491)*
**Process and Control Systems**...708 293-0557
5836 W 117th Pl Alsip (60803) *(G-514)*
**Process Engineering Corp (PA)**...815 459-1734
7426 Virginia Rd Crystal Lake (60014) *(G-7634)*
**Process Gear, Des Plaines** *Also called CF Gear Holdings LLC (G-8162)*
**Process Graphics Corp**...815 637-2500
4801 Shepherd Trl Rockford (61103) *(G-18542)*
**Process Mechanical Inc**...630 416-7021
2208 Pontiac Cir Naperville (60565) *(G-15732)*
**Process Piping Inc**...708 717-0513
18005 Semmler Dr Tinley Park (60487) *(G-20939)*
**Process Screw Products Inc**...815 864-2220
10 N Shannon Rte Shannon (61078) *(G-19901)*
**Process Systems Inc**...217 563-2872
316 E State St Nokomis (62075) *(G-16060)*
**Process Technologies Group**...630 393-4777
30w106 Butterfield Rd Warrenville (60555) *(G-21360)*
**Processed Steel Company**...815 459-2400
3703 S Il Route 31 Crystal Lake (60012) *(G-7635)*
**Processing Tech Intl LLC**...630 585-5800
2655 White Oak Cir Aurora (60502) *(G-1070)*
**Procomm Inc Hoopeston Illinois**...815 268-4303
209 W Grant Ave Onarga (60955) *(G-16809)*
**Procon Pacific LLC**...630 575-0551
1200 Jorie Blvd Ste 235 Oak Brook (60523) *(G-16556)*
**Procraft Engraving Inc**...847 673-1500
8241 Christiana Ave Skokie (60076) *(G-20062)*
**Procura LLC**...801 265-4571
900 Oakmont Ln Ste 308 Westmont (60559) *(G-21914)*
**Prodico Technologies LLC**...312 498-5152
6508 S Dorchester Ave Chicago (60637) *(G-6204)*
**Producepro Inc (PA)**...630 395-9700
9014 Heritage Pkwy # 304 Woodridge (60517) *(G-22512)*
**Producers Chemical Company**...630 466-4584
1960 Bucktail Ln Sugar Grove (60554) *(G-20731)*
**Producers Envmtl Pdts LLC**...630 482-5995
1261 N Raddant Rd Batavia (60510) *(G-1487)*
**Product Emphasis, Chicago** *Also called Fixture Hardware Co (G-4855)*
**Product Feeding Solutions Inc**...630 709-9546
5632 Pleasant Blvd Chicago Ridge (60415) *(G-7156)*
**Product Service Craft Inc**...630 964-5160
5407 Walnut Ave Downers Grove (60515) *(G-8511)*
**Productigear Inc**...773 847-4505
1900 W 34th St Chicago (60608) *(G-6205)*
**Production Chemical Co Inc**...847 455-8450
9381 Schiller Blvd Franklin Park (60131) *(G-10563)*
**Production Cutting Services**...815 264-3505
9341 State Route 23 Waterman (60556) *(G-21409)*
**Production Engineering, Warsaw** *Also called Production Manufacturing (G-21371)*
**Production Fabg & Stamping Inc**...708 755-5468
3311 Butler St S Chicago Hts (60411) *(G-19111)*
**Production Facility, Aurora** *Also called On-Cor Frozen Foods LLC (G-1200)*
**Production Manufacturing**...217 256-4211
305 Main St Warsaw (62379) *(G-21371)*
**Production Press, Jacksonville** *Also called Cenveo Inc (G-12383)*
**Production Press Inc (PA)**...217 243-3353
307 E Morgan St Jacksonville (62650) *(G-12409)*
**Production Stampings Inc**...815 495-2800
1864 N 4253rd Rd Leland (60531) *(G-13220)*
**Production Tool Companies LLC (PA)**...773 288-4400
1229 E 74th St Chicago (60619) *(G-6206)*
**Production Tooling & Automtn, Hoopeston** *Also called Production Tooling and Automtn (G-12114)*
**Production Tooling and Automtn**...217 283-7373
342 N Dixie Hwy Hoopeston (60942) *(G-12114)*
**Productionpro, Villa Park** *Also called Manufacturers Alliance Corp (G-21268)*
**Productive Displays, Addison** *Also called Productive Portable Disp Inc (G-259)*
**Productive Edge LLC (PA)**...312 561-9000
11 E Illinois St Fl 2 Chicago (60611) *(G-6207)*
**Productive Portable Disp Inc**...630 458-9100
1460 W Bernard Dr Ste A Addison (60101) *(G-259)*
**Products In Motion Inc**...815 213-7251
804 Industrial Park Rd Rock Falls (61071) *(G-18146)*
**Productworks LLC**...224 406-8810
610 Academy Dr Northbrook (60062) *(G-16347)*
**Proell Inc**...630 587-2300
2751 Dukane Dr Saint Charles (60174) *(G-19242)*
**Professional Freezing Svcs LLC**...773 847-7500
7035 W 65th St Chicago (60638) *(G-6208)*
**Professional Gem Sciences Inc**...312 920-1541
5 S Wabash Ave Ste 315 Chicago (60603) *(G-6209)*
**Professional Metal Company**...630 983-9777
951 Frontenac Rd Naperville (60563) *(G-15733)*
**Professional Metal Works LLC**...618 539-2214
9 Industrial Dr Freeburg (62243) *(G-10639)*
**Professional Meters Inc**...815 942-7000
3605 N State Route 47 D Morris (60450) *(G-15127)*
**Professional Packaging Corp (PA)**...630 896-0574
208 E Benton St Aurora (60505) *(G-1205)*
**Professional Printers**...630 739-7761
349 Marian Ct Bolingbrook (60440) *(G-2361)*
**Professional Sales Associates**...847 487-1900
1000 Brown St Ste 303 Wauconda (60084) *(G-21493)*
**Professnal Mling Prtg Svcs Inc**...630 510-1000
269 Commonwealth Dr Carol Stream (60188) *(G-3222)*
**Profile Network Inc**...847 673-0592
4709 Golf Rd Ste 807 Skokie (60076) *(G-20063)*
**Profile Plastics Inc**...847 256-1623
65 Waukegan Rd Lake Bluff (60044) *(G-12864)*
**Profile Products LLC (HQ)**...847 215-1144
750 W Lake Cook Rd # 440 Buffalo Grove (60089) *(G-2756)*
**Proform**...309 676-2535
708 Fayette St Peoria (61603) *(G-17437)*
**Proforma Awards Print & Promot**...630 897-9848
15 Ridgefield Rd Montgomery (60538) *(G-15065)*
**Proforma Coml Print Group, Naperville** *Also called Sprinter Coml Print Label Corp (G-15828)*
**Proforma Quality Business Svcs**...847 356-1959
18582 W Judy Dr Gurnee (60031) *(G-11492)*
**Proforma-Ppg Inc**...847 429-9349
158 Dawson Dr Elgin (60120) *(G-9149)*
**Prograf LLC**...815 234-4848
119 W Home Ave Villa Park (60181) *(G-21280)*
**Progress Dusters Division, Chicago** *Also called Modern Specialties Company (G-5785)*
**Progress Printing Corporation**...773 927-0123
3324 S Halsted St Ste 1 Chicago (60608) *(G-6210)*
**Progress Rail Locomotive Inc (HQ)**...800 255-5355
9301 W 55th St Mc Cook (60525) *(G-14456)*
**Progress Rail Locomotive Inc**...708 387-5510
9301 W 55th St Mc Cook (60525) *(G-14457)*
**Progress Rail Services Corp**...309 343-6176
618 Us Highway 150 E Galesburg (61401) *(G-10771)*
**Progress Rail Services Corp**...309 963-4425
5704 E 1700 North Rd Danvers (61732) *(G-7701)*
**Progress Reporter Inc**...815 472-2000
110 W River St Momence (60954) *(G-14986)*
**Progress Reporter Press, Momence** *Also called Progress Reporter Inc (G-14986)*
**Progressive Bronze Works Inc**...773 463-5500
3550 N Spaulding Ave Chicago (60618) *(G-6211)*
**Progressive Coating, Chicago** *Also called SKW Industries LLC (G-6523)*
**Progressive Coating Corp**...773 261-8900
900 S Cicero Ave Chicago (60644) *(G-6212)*

ALPHABETIC

(PA)=Parent Co (HQ)=Headquarters (DH)=Div Headquarters
2017 Harris Illinois Industrial Directory
1357

**Progressive Electronics** — 217 672-8434
266 Hwy 121 Ste 3  Warrensburg  (62573)  (G-21339)

**Progressive Environmental Svcs, Barrington** Also called Precious Metal Ref Svcs Inc  (G-1298)

**Progressive Model Design, Romeoville** Also called Circuitron Inc  (G-18812)

**Progressive Publications Inc** — 847 697-9181
85 Market St Ste 105  Elgin  (60123)  (G-9150)

**Progressive Recovery Inc** — 618 286-5000
700 Industrial Dr  Dupo  (62239)  (G-8575)

**Progressive Recycling Systems** — 217 291-0009
2 Eastgate Dr  Jacksonville  (62650)  (G-12410)

**Progressive Sheet Metal Inc** — 773 376-1155
2850 S Tripp Ave  Chicago  (60623)  (G-6213)

**Progressive Solutions Corp** — 847 639-7272
2848 Corporate Pkwy  Algonquin  (60102)  (G-405)

**Progressive Steel Treating Inc** — 815 877-2571
922 Lawn Dr  Loves Park  (61111)  (G-13979)

**Progressive Systems Netwrk Inc** — 312 382-8383
329 W 18th St Ste 605  Chicago  (60616)  (G-6214)

**Progressive Turnings Inc** — 630 898-3072
1680 Mountain St  Aurora  (60505)  (G-1206)

**Progroup Instrument Inc** — 618 466-2815
26582 Lockhaven Hl  Godfrey  (62035)  (G-11232)

**Progrssive Cmponents Intl Corp (PA)** — 847 487-1000
235 Industrial Dr  Wauconda  (60084)  (G-21494)

**Progrssive Imprssions Intl Inc (HQ)** — 309 664-0444
1 Hardman Dr  Bloomington  (61701)  (G-2216)

**Prointegration Tech LLC** — 618 409-3233
13348 Koch Rd  Highland  (62249)  (G-11806)

**Project T C, Urbana** Also called Project Te Inc  (G-21100)

**Project Te Inc** — 217 344-9833
2209 E University Ave B  Urbana  (61802)  (G-21100)

**Prolong Tool, West Chicago** Also called Dippit Inc  (G-21693)

**Promark Advertising Specialtie** — 618 483-6025
4 N Frontage Rd  Altamont  (62411)  (G-554)

**Promark Associates** — 847 676-1894
3856 Oakton St Ste 250  Skokie  (60076)  (G-20064)

**Promark International Inc (PA)** — 630 830-2500
1268 Humbracht Cir  Bartlett  (60103)  (G-1365)

**Prometco, Naperville** Also called Professional Metal Company  (G-15733)

**Promier Products Inc** — 815 223-3393
350 5th St Ste 266  Peru  (61354)  (G-17524)

**Prommar Plastics Inc** — 815 770-0555
1001 W Diggins St  Harvard  (60033)  (G-11645)

**Promoframes LLC** — 866 566-7224
1113 Tower Rd  Schaumburg  (60173)  (G-19701)

**Promotional Co of Illinois** — 847 382-0239
2222 Shetland Rd  Inverness  (60010)  (G-12210)

**Promotional TS** — 312 243-8991
1211 S Western Ave  Chicago  (60608)  (G-6215)

**Promotions Plus, Frankfort** Also called Sandra E Greene  (G-10361)

**Promoversity, Crystal Lake** Also called Rfq LLC  (G-7640)

**Prompt Motor Rewinding Service** — 847 675-7155
7509 Keystone Ave  Skokie  (60076)  (G-20065)

**Prompt Usa Inc** — 309 660-0222
1502 Red Top Ln  Minooka  (60447)  (G-14846)

**Promus Equity Partners LLC (PA)** — 312 784-3990
30 S Wacker Dr Ste 1600  Chicago  (60606)  (G-6216)

**Pronto Signs and Engraving** — 847 249-7874
2114 Grand Ave  Waukegan  (60085)  (G-21608)

**Propeller Hr Solutions Inc** — 312 342-7355
5350 Wolf Rd  Western Springs  (60558)  (G-21871)

**Prophet Gear Co** — 815 537-2002
46 Grove St  Prophetstown  (61277)  (G-17771)

**Proppant Frac Sand LLC** — 815 942-2467
130 W Illinois Ave  Morris  (60450)  (G-15128)

**Proquis Inc** — 847 278-3230
423 Walnut Ave  Elgin  (60123)  (G-9151)

**Prosco Inc** — 847 336-1323
3901 Grove Ave  Gurnee  (60031)  (G-11493)

**Proship Inc** — 312 332-7447
29 N Wacker Dr Ste 700  Chicago  (60606)  (G-6217)

**Prospan Manufacturing** — 847 815-0191
10013 Norwood St  Rosemont  (60018)  (G-19025)

**Prospan Manufacturing Co** — 630 860-1930
540 Meyer Rd  Bensenville  (60106)  (G-1967)

**Prospect Grinding Incorporated** — 847 229-9240
925 Seton Ct Ste 11  Wheeling  (60090)  (G-22129)

**Prospect Tool Company LLC** — 630 766-2200
9233 King St  Franklin Park  (60131)  (G-10564)

**Prosser Construction Co** — 217 774-5032
1410 N 1500 East Rd  Shelbyville  (62565)  (G-19913)

**Prost Heating & Cooling LLC** — 618 344-3749
6964 Lebanon Rd  Collinsville  (62234)  (G-7338)

**Prostat Corporation** — 630 238-8883
1072 Tower Ln  Bensenville  (60106)  (G-1968)

**Prosthetic Orthotic Specialist (PA)** — 309 454-8733
303 Landmark Dr Ste 5a  Normal  (61761)  (G-16085)

**Prosthetics Orthotics Han** — 847 695-6955
620 S Il Route 31 Ste 7  McHenry  (60050)  (G-14549)

**Protactic Golf Enterprises** — 708 209-1120
504 River Oaks Dr  River Forest  (60305)  (G-17999)

**Protec Equipment Resources Inc** — 847 434-5808
1501 Wright Blvd  Schaumburg  (60193)  (G-19702)

**Protech Design & Manufacturing** — 815 398-7520
1848 18th Ave  Rockford  (61104)  (G-18543)

**Protect Assoc** — 847 446-8664
2165 Shermer Rd Ste C  Northbrook  (60062)  (G-16348)

**Protect-A-Bed, Wheeling** Also called Jab Distributors LLC  (G-22079)

**Protection Controls Inc** — 773 763-3110
7317 Lawndale Ave  Skokie  (60076)  (G-20066)

**Protective Coatings & Waterpro** — 708 403-7650
9320 136th St  Orland Park  (60462)  (G-16886)

**Protective Products Intl** — 847 526-1180
140 Kerry Ln  Wauconda  (60084)  (G-21495)

**Protectofire, Skokie** Also called Protection Controls Inc  (G-20066)

**Protector, The, Woodridge** Also called Ecp Incorporated  (G-22474)

**Protectoseal Company (PA)** — 630 595-0800
225 Foster Ave  Bensenville  (60106)  (G-1969)

**Protek** — 815 773-2280
315 Airport Dr  Joliet  (60431)  (G-12557)

**Protek Inc** — 888 536-5466
209 S 3rd St  Saint Charles  (60174)  (G-19243)

**Protepo Ltd (PA)** — 847 466-1023
906 Mayfair Ct  Elk Grove Village  (60007)  (G-9699)

**Protide Pharmaceuticals Inc** — 847 726-3100
220 Telser Rd  Lake Zurich  (60047)  (G-13117)

**Proto Productions Inc** — 630 628-6626
840 S Fiene Dr  Addison  (60101)  (G-260)

**Proto-Cutter Inc** — 815 232-2300
101 S Liberty Ave Ste 1  Freeport  (61032)  (G-10681)

**Proton Multimedia Inc** — 847 531-8664
1485 Davis Rd Ste A  Elgin  (60123)  (G-9152)

**Prototech Industries Inc** — 847 223-9808
1479 Almaden Ln  Gurnee  (60031)  (G-11494)

**Prototek Tool & Mold Inc** — 847 487-2708
375 Hollow Hill Rd  Wauconda  (60084)  (G-21496)

**Prototype & Production Co** — 847 419-1553
546 Quail Hollow Dr  Wheeling  (60090)  (G-22130)

**Prototype Equipment Corp** — 847 596-9000
1081 S Northpoint Blvd  Waukegan  (60085)  (G-21609)

**Protus Construction** — 773 405-9999
1429 N Oakley Blvd  Chicago  (60622)  (G-6218)

**Provena Enterprises Inc (HQ)** — 708 478-3230
555 W Court St Ste 414  Kankakee  (60901)  (G-12643)

**Provena Randalwood Open Mri** — 630 587-9917
110 James St  Geneva  (60134)  (G-10860)

**Providence Press, Carol Stream** Also called Hope Publishing Company  (G-3167)

**Provisur Technologies** — 312 284-4698
222 N La Salle St  Chicago  (60601)  (G-6219)

**Prp Wine International Inc** — 630 995-4500
1323 Bond St Ste 179  Naperville  (60563)  (G-15734)

**Prs Inc** — 630 620-7259
434 S Ahrens Ave  Lombard  (60148)  (G-13846)

**Pru Dent Mfg Inc** — 847 301-1170
1929 Wright Blvd  Schaumburg  (60193)  (G-19703)

**Pruett Enterprises Inc** — 618 235-6184
10 E Cleveland Ave  Belleville  (62220)  (G-1667)

**Pry-Bar Company** — 815 436-3383
18542 Nw Frontage Rd  Joliet  (60404)  (G-12558)

**Pryco Inc (PA)** — 217 364-4467
3rd And Garvey  Mechanicsburg  (62545)  (G-14574)

**Pryde Graphics Plus** — 630 882-5103
306 Hubbard Cir  Plano  (60545)  (G-17675)

**PS Tobacco Inc** — 630 793-9823
434 Roosevelt Rd  Glen Ellyn  (60137)  (G-10988)

**Psa Equity LLC (PA)** — 847 478-6000
485 E Half Day Rd Ste 500  Buffalo Grove  (60089)  (G-2757)

**PSI Systems North America Inc** — 630 830-9435
1243 Humbracht Cir  Bartlett  (60103)  (G-1366)

**PSM Industries Inc** — 815 337-8800
925 Dieckman St  Woodstock  (60098)  (G-22602)

**Psychiatric Assessments Inc** — 312 878-6490
217 N Jefferson St # 601  Chicago  (60661)  (G-6220)

**Psylotech Inc** — 847 328-7100
1616 Payne St  Evanston  (60201)  (G-10092)

**Psyonic Inc** — 773 888-3252
60 Hazelwood Dr  Champaign  (61820)  (G-3531)

**Psytec Inc** — 815 758-1415
520 Linden Pl  Dekalb  (60115)  (G-8114)

**Psytronics Inc** — 847 719-1371
545 Capital Dr  Lake Zurich  (60047)  (G-13118)

**Pt Holdings Inc (PA)** — 217 691-1793
2 White Oak Rd  Springfield  (62711)  (G-20508)

**Ptc Group Holdings Corp** — 708 757-4747
475 E 16th St  Chicago Heights  (60411)  (G-7118)

**Ptc Inc** — 630 827-4900
1815 S Meyers Rd Ste 220  Oakbrook Terrace  (60181)  (G-16718)

ALPHABETIC SECTION Quad Inc (PA)

**Ptc Tubular Products LLC** ....815 692-4900
23041 E 800 North Rd Fairbury (61739) ***(G-10131)***
**PTG Impax, Warrenville** *Also called Process Technologies Group* ***(G-21360)***
**Ptm Biolabs Inc** ....312 802-6843
2201 W Campbell Park Dr Chicago (60612) ***(G-6221)***
**Public Good Software Inc** ....877 941-2747
20 N Wacker Dr Ste 3405 Chicago (60606) ***(G-6222)***
**Publications International Ltd (PA)** ....847 676-3470
8140 Lehigh Ave Morton Grove (60053) ***(G-15229)***
**Publishers Graphics LLC (PA)** ....630 221-1850
140 Della Ct Carol Stream (60188) ***(G-3223)***
**Publishers Row** ....847 568-0593
9001 Keating Ave Skokie (60076) ***(G-20067)***
**Publishing Properties LLC (HQ)** ....312 321-2299
350 N Orleans St Fl 10 Chicago (60654) ***(G-6223)***
**Publishing Task Force** ....312 670-4360
401 N Michigan Ave # 1720 Chicago (60611) ***(G-6224)***
**Pubpal LLC** ....309 222-5062
25130 Schuck Rd Washington (61571) ***(G-21389)***
**Puckered Pickle, Chicago** *Also called Pickles Sorrel Inc* ***(G-6121)***
**Pull X Machines Inc 933** ....847 952-9977
782 Church Rd Elgin (60123) ***(G-9153)***
**Pullman Innovations, Chicago** *Also called A-F Acquisition LLC* ***(G-3695)***
**Pullman Sugar LLC** ....773 260-9180
700 E 107th St Chicago (60628) ***(G-6225)***
**Pullr Holding Company LLC** ....224 366-2500
415 E State Pkwy Schaumburg (60173) ***(G-19704)***
**Pulpulp, Chicago** *Also called Thrilled LLC* ***(G-6723)***
**Puls LP** ....630 587-9780
2560 Foxfield Rd Ste 260 Saint Charles (60174) ***(G-19244)***
**Pulsarlube USA Inc** ....847 593-5300
1480 Howard St Elk Grove Village (60007) ***(G-9700)***
**Pulver Inc** ....847 734-9000
575 Bennett Rd Elk Grove Village (60007) ***(G-9701)***
**Pump House** ....618 216-2404
1523 E Edwardsville Rd Wood River (62095) ***(G-22444)***
**Pump It Up Chicago, Chicago** *Also called Eaton Inflatable LLC* ***(G-4685)***
**Pump Solutions Group (HQ)** ....630 487-2240
1815 S Meyers Rd Ste 670 Oakbrook Terrace (60181) ***(G-16719)***
**Punch Products Manufacturing** ....773 533-2800
500 S Kolmar Ave Chicago (60624) ***(G-6226)***
**Punch Skin Care Inc** ....702 333-2510
2155 W Belmont Ave Ste 34 Chicago (60618) ***(G-6227)***
**Purchasing Services Ltd Inc** ....618 566-8100
602 Industrial St Mascoutah (62258) ***(G-14359)***
**Purdy Products Company** ....847 526-5505
1255 Karl Ct Wauconda (60084) ***(G-21497)***
**Pure 111** ....618 558-7888
923 Far Oaks Dr Caseyville (62232) ***(G-3400)***
**Pure Alphalt, Chicago** *Also called Pure Asphalt Company* ***(G-6228)***
**Pure Asphalt Company** ....773 247-7030
3455 W 31st Pl Chicago (60623) ***(G-6228)***
**Pure Element** ....309 269-7823
915 33rd Ave Moline (61265) ***(G-14963)***
**Pure Essential Supply Inc** ....
1835 Wallace Ave Saint Charles (60174) ***(G-19245)***
**Pure Flo Bottling Inc** ....815 963-4797
2430 N Main St Rockford (61103) ***(G-18544)***
**Pure Lighting LLC** ....773 770-1130
1718 W Fullerton Ave Chicago (60614) ***(G-6229)***
**Pure N Natural Systems Inc** ....630 372-9681
5836 Lincoln Ave Ste 100 Morton Grove (60053) ***(G-15230)***
**Pure Skin LLC** ....217 679-6267
4000 Westgate Dr Springfield (62711) ***(G-20509)***
**Pure Valley, Chicago** *Also called Concept Laboratories Inc* ***(G-4446)***
**Purecircle USA Inc** ....866 960-8242
915 Harger Rd Ste 250 Oak Brook (60523) ***(G-16557)***
**Pureline Treatment Systems LLC** ....847 963-8465
1241 N Ellis St Bensenville (60106) ***(G-1970)***
**Pures Food Specialties LLC** ....708 344-8884
2929 S 25th Ave Broadview (60155) ***(G-2605)***
**Purified Lubricants Inc** ....708 478-3500
9629 194th St Mokena (60448) ***(G-14899)***
**Purina Mills LLC** ....618 283-2291
1500 Veterans Ave Vandalia (62471) ***(G-21122)***
**Purity Select Inc** ....847 275-3821
125 Revere Dr Northbrook (60062) ***(G-16349)***
**Puro Futbol Newspaper** ....847 858-7493
4248 Lake Park Ave Gurnee (60031) ***(G-11495)***
**Purple Clay Pottery, Chicago** *Also called BSC Imports Incorporated* ***(G-4180)***
**Pursuit Beverage Company LLC** ....888 606-3353
500 E Il Route 22 Lake Zurich (60047) ***(G-13119)***
**Puskar Precision Machining Co** ....847 888-2929
1610 Cambridge Dr Elgin (60123) ***(G-9154)***
**Putman Media Inc (PA)** ....630 467-1301
1501 E Wdfeld Rd Ste 400n Schaumburg (60173) ***(G-19705)***
**Putnam Co Records, Tonica** *Also called Tonica News* ***(G-20975)***
**Putt and Times, Okawville** *Also called Okawville Times* ***(G-16754)***

**Puzzles Bus Off Solutions Inc** ....773 891-7688
47 W Polk St Chicago (60605) ***(G-6230)***
**Pvc Container Corporation** ....217 463-6600
2015 S Main St Paris (61944) ***(G-17159)***
**Pvh Corp** ....217 253-3398
1011 E Southline Rd Tuscola (61953) ***(G-21022)***
**Pvh Corp** ....630 898-7718
1650 Premium Outlet Blvd Aurora (60502) ***(G-1071)***
**PVS Chemical Solutions Inc** ....773 933-8800
12260 S Carondolet Ave Chicago (60633) ***(G-6231)***
**PW Masonry Inc** ....847 573-0510
1230 Hunters Ln Libertyville (60048) ***(G-13372)***
**Pwf** ....815 967-0218
8123 Harrison Rd Rockford (61101) ***(G-18545)***
**Pyar & Company LLC** ....312 451-5073
1749 N Cleveland Ave Chicago (60614) ***(G-6232)***
**Pylon Plastics Inc** ....630 968-6374
2111 Ogden Ave Lisle (60532) ***(G-13646)***
**Pyramid** ....708 468-8140
9013 178th St Tinley Park (60487) ***(G-20940)***
**Pyramid Manufacturing Corp** ....630 443-0141
3815 Illinois Ave Saint Charles (60174) ***(G-19246)***
**Pyramid Sciences Inc** ....630 974-6110
9425 S Madison St Burr Ridge (60527) ***(G-2876)***
**Pyrophase Inc** ....773 324-8645
5000 S Cornell Ave 18c Chicago (60615) ***(G-6233)***
**Q and A Media Service, Chicago** *Also called Qaprintscom* ***(G-6236)***
**Q B F Graphic Group** ....708 781-9580
18650 Graphic Ct Tinley Park (60477) ***(G-20941)***
**Q C H Incorporated** ....630 820-5550
230 Kendall Point Dr Oswego (60543) ***(G-16929)***
**Q Lotus Holdings Inc** ....312 379-1800
520 N Kingsbury St # 1810 Chicago (60654) ***(G-6234)***
**Q N S, Sullivan** *Also called Quality Network Solutions Inc* ***(G-20758)***
**Q Products and Services, Hazel Crest** *Also called Q Sales Llc* ***(G-11714)***
**Q S F, Alsip** *Also called Quality Snack Foods Inc* ***(G-515)***
**Q S T, Chicago** *Also called Qst Industries Inc* ***(G-6237)***
**Q Sales Llc** ....708 271-9842
16720 Mozart Ave Ste A Hazel Crest (60429) ***(G-11714)***
**Q SC Design** ....815 933-6777
230 E Broadway St Bradley (60915) ***(G-2429)***
**Q-Matic Technologies Inc** ....847 263-7324
355 Kehoe Blvd Carol Stream (60188) ***(G-3224)***
**Q4, Schaumburg** *Also called Quadrant 4 System Corporation* ***(G-19706)***
**Qaboss Partners** ....312 203-4290
27 N Wacker Dr Ste 155 Chicago (60606) ***(G-6235)***
**Qad Inc** ....630 964-4030
1011 Warrenville Rd # 210 Lisle (60532) ***(G-13647)***
**Qaprintscom** ....312 404-2130
2721 S Halsted St Chicago (60608) ***(G-6236)***
**Qc Components & Sales Inc** ....630 268-0644
260 Cortland Ave Ste 9 Lombard (60148) ***(G-13847)***
**Qc Finishers Inc** ....847 678-2660
10244 Franklin Ave Franklin Park (60131) ***(G-10565)***
**Qc Powder Inc** ....630 832-0606
226 E Sidney Ct Villa Park (60181) ***(G-21281)***
**Qc Service Associates Inc** ....309 755-6785
1300 90th St Ste 110 East Moline (61244) ***(G-8691)***
**Qcc LLC (PA)** ....708 867-5400
7315 W Wilson Ave Harwood Heights (60706) ***(G-11689)***
**Qcfec LLC** ....309 517-1158
4401 44th Ave Moline (61265) ***(G-14964)***
**Qcircuits Inc (PA)** ....847 797-6678
2775 Algonquin Rd Ste 300 Rolling Meadows (60008) ***(G-18771)***
**Qcircuits Inc** ....618 662-8365
1 Industrial Park Flora (62839) ***(G-10214)***
**Qg LLC** ....217 347-7721
420 Industrial Ave Effingham (62401) ***(G-8854)***
**Qg LLC** ....217 347-7721
1200 W Niccum Ave Effingham (62401) ***(G-8855)***
**Qh Inc** ....708 534-7801
2412 Bond St University Park (60484) ***(G-21060)***
**Qmi Roll Shutter Supply, Itasca** *Also called Qualitas Manufacturing Inc* ***(G-12346)***
**QS Luxurious Hair & Shoes Inc** ....773 556-6092
305 47th Ave Bellwood (60104) ***(G-1716)***
**Qse Inc (PA)** ....815 432-5281
316 W Hickory St Watseka (60970) ***(G-21426)***
**Qsimaginationstation** ....708 928-9622
14641 Dante Ave Dolton (60419) ***(G-8376)***
**Qst Industries Inc (PA)** ....312 930-9400
550 W Adams St Ste 200 Chicago (60661) ***(G-6237)***
**Qst Industries Inc** ....312 930-9400
550 W Adams St Ste 200 Chicago (60661) ***(G-6238)***
**Qt Info Systems Inc** ....800 240-8761
141 W Jackson Blvd 1255a Chicago (60604) ***(G-6239)***
**Qt9 Software, Naperville** *Also called Innovative Custom Software Inc* ***(G-15675)***
**Qti, Elgin** *Also called Quality Technology Intl Inc* ***(G-9158)***
**Quad Inc (PA)** ....815 624-8538
810 Progressive Ln South Beloit (61080) ***(G-20166)***

ALPHABETIC

(PA)=Parent Co (HQ)=Headquarters (DH)=Div Headquarters
2017 Harris Illinois
Industrial Directory
1359

**Quad Cities Concrete Pdts LLC** .................................. 309 787-4919
 636 10th Ave W  Milan  (61264)  *(G-14799)*
**Quad Cities Directional Boring** .................................. 309 792-3070
 24190 N High St  Colona  (61241)  *(G-7346)*
**Quad Cities Plant, Milan**  Also called Chicago Tube and Iron Company  *(G-14779)*
**Quad City Engineering Company** .................................. 309 755-9762
 3650 Morton Dr  East Moline  (61244)  *(G-8692)*
**Quad City Hose** .................................. 563 386-8936
 9707 86th Street Ct W  Taylor Ridge  (61284)  *(G-20830)*
**Quad City Press** .................................. 309 764-8142
 1325 15th St  Moline  (61265)  *(G-14965)*
**Quad City Prosthetics Inc (PA)** .................................. 309 676-2276
 4730 44th St Ste 1  Rock Island  (61201)  *(G-18194)*
**Quad City Ultralight Aircraft** .................................. 309 764-3515
 3810 34th St  Moline  (61265)  *(G-14966)*
**Quad County Fire Equipment** .................................. 815 832-4475
 37 Main St  Saunemin  (61769)  *(G-19395)*
**Quad County Rdymx New Baden, New Baden**  Also called Quad-County Ready Mix Corp  *(G-15863)*
**Quad County Ready Mix Swansea** .................................. 618 257-9530
 300 Old Fullerton Rd  Swansea  (62226)  *(G-20779)*
**Quad Cy Prsthetic-Orthotic Lab, Rock Island**  Also called Quad City Prosthetics Inc  *(G-18194)*
**Quad Plus LLC (PA)** .................................. 815 740-0860
 1921 Cherry Hill Rd  Joliet  (60433)  *(G-12559)*
**Quad-County Rdymx Centralia, Centralia**  Also called Clinton County Materials Corp  *(G-3409)*
**Quad-County Ready Mix Corp (PA)** .................................. 618 243-6430
 300 W 12th St  Okawville  (62271)  *(G-16755)*
**Quad-County Ready Mix Corp** .................................. 618 588-4656
 7415 State Route 160  New Baden  (62265)  *(G-15863)*
**Quad-County Ready Mix Corp** .................................. 618 526-7130
 11 S Plum St  Breese  (62230)  *(G-2446)*
**Quad-County Ready Mix Corp** .................................. 618 244-6973
 9240 Sahara Rd  Mount Vernon  (62864)  *(G-15442)*
**Quad-County Ready Mix Corp** .................................. 618 327-3748
 1050 N Washington St  Nashville  (62263)  *(G-15846)*
**Quad-County Ready Mix Corp** .................................. 618 594-2732
 2090 Washington St  Carlyle  (62231)  *(G-3057)*
**Quad-County Ready Mix Corp** .................................. 618 295-3000
 655 Wshngton Cnty Line Rd  Marissa  (62257)  *(G-14297)*
**Quad-County Ready Mix Corp** .................................. 618 548-2477
 3782 Hotze Rd  Salem  (62881)  *(G-19346)*
**Quad-Illinois Inc (PA)** .................................. 847 836-1115
 2760 Spectrum Dr  Elgin  (60124)  *(G-9155)*
**Quad-Metal Inc** .................................. 630 953-0907
 1345 W Fullerton Ave  Addison  (60101)  *(G-261)*
**Quad/Graphics Inc** .................................. 815 734-4121
 404 N Wesley Ave  Mount Morris  (61054)  *(G-15297)*
**Quad/Graphics Inc** .................................. 630 343-4400
 1000 Remington Blvd # 300  Bolingbrook  (60440)  *(G-2362)*
**Quadramed Corporation** .................................. 312 396-0700
 440 N Wells St Ste 505  Chicago  (60654)  *(G-6240)*
**Quadrant 4 System Corporation (PA)** .................................. 855 995-7367
 1501 E Woodfield Rd 250s  Schaumburg  (60173)  *(G-19706)*
**Quadrant Tool and Mfg Co** .................................. 847 352-6977
 1720 W Irving Park Rd  Schaumburg  (60193)  *(G-19707)*
**Quaker Manufacturing LLC** .................................. 312 222-7111
 321 N Clark St  Chicago  (60654)  *(G-6241)*
**Quaker Oats Company (HQ)** .................................. 312 821-1000
 555 W Monroe St Fl 1  Chicago  (60661)  *(G-6242)*
**Quaker Oats Company** .................................. 217 443-4995
 1703 E Voorhees St  Danville  (61834)  *(G-7761)*
**Quaker Oats Company** .................................. 708 458-7090
 7700 W 71st St  Bridgeview  (60455)  *(G-2521)*
**Quaker Oats Europe Inc (HQ)** .................................. 312 821-1000
 555 W Monroe St Fl 1  Chicago  (60661)  *(G-6243)*
**Qualified Innovation Inc** .................................. 630 556-4136
 1016 Airpark Dr Ste B  Sugar Grove  (60554)  *(G-20732)*
**Qualifresh LLC** .................................. 847 337-1483
 7301 N Lincoln Ave # 180  Lincolnwood  (60712)  *(G-13530)*
**Qualiseal Technology, Harwood Heights**  Also called Technetics Group LLC  *(G-11691)*
**Qualiseal Technology LLC** .................................. 708 887-6080
 7319 W Wilson Ave  Harwood Heights  (60706)  *(G-11690)*
**Qualitas Manufacturing Inc (PA)** .................................. 630 529-7111
 1661 Glenlake Ave  Itasca  (60143)  *(G-12346)*
**Qualitek International Inc** .................................. 630 628-8083
 315 S Fairbank St  Addison  (60101)  *(G-262)*
**Qualitek Manufacturing Inc** .................................. 847 336-7570
 4240 Grove Ave  Gurnee  (60031)  *(G-11496)*
**Qualitex Company** .................................. 773 506-8112
 4248 N Elston Ave  Chicago  (60618)  *(G-6244)*
**Quality Armature Inc** .................................. 773 622-3951
 5259 W Grand Ave  Chicago  (60639)  *(G-6245)*
**Quality Bags Inc** .................................. 630 543-9800
 575 S Vista Ave  Addison  (60101)  *(G-263)*
**Quality Bakeries LLC** .................................. 630 553-7377
 1750 E Main St Ste 260  Saint Charles  (60174)  *(G-19247)*
**Quality Blue & Offset Printing** .................................. 630 759-8035
 7 Sunshine Ct  Bolingbrook  (60490)  *(G-2363)*

**Quality Cable & Components Inc** .................................. 309 695-3435
 109 N Madison Ave  Wyoming  (61491)  *(G-22639)*
**Quality Circle Machine Inc** .................................. 708 474-1160
 2250 199th St Ste 3  Lynwood  (60411)  *(G-14024)*
**Quality Cleaning Fluids Inc** .................................. 847 451-1190
 9216 Grand Ave  Franklin Park  (60131)  *(G-10566)*
**Quality Cnc Incorporated** .................................. 630 406-0101
 801 N Raddant Rd  Batavia  (60510)  *(G-1488)*
**Quality Coating Co** .................................. 815 875-3228
 2955 N Main St  Princeton  (61356)  *(G-17761)*
**Quality Converting Inc** .................................. 847 669-9094
 10611 Wolf Dr  Huntley  (60142)  *(G-12169)*
**Quality Cove** .................................. 618 684-5900
 1 Apple City Ctr  Murphysboro  (62966)  *(G-15581)*
**Quality Croutons Inc** .................................. 773 927-8200
 1155 W 40th St  Chicago  (60609)  *(G-6246)*
**Quality Custom Closets** .................................. 773 307-1105
 4304 Di Paolo Ctr  Glenview  (60025)  *(G-11185)*
**Quality Die Casting Co** .................................. 847 214-8840
 1760 Britannia Dr Ste 5  Elgin  (60124)  *(G-9156)*
**Quality Drilling Service LLP (PA)** .................................. 937 663-4715
 1715 Liberty St  Alton  (62002)  *(G-587)*
**Quality Elevator Products Inc** .................................. 847 581-0085
 7760 N Merrimac Ave  Niles  (60714)  *(G-16023)*
**Quality Fabricators Inc (PA)** .................................. 630 543-0540
 1035 W Fullerton Ave  Addison  (60101)  *(G-264)*
**Quality Fastener Products Inc** .................................. 224 330-3162
 1430 Davis Rd  Elgin  (60123)  *(G-9157)*
**Quality Filter Services** .................................. 618 654-3716
 14446 Baumann Rd  Highland  (62249)  *(G-11807)*
**Quality Glass and Mirror Inc** .................................. 847 290-1707
 601 W Carboy Rd  Mount Prospect  (60056)  *(G-15366)*
**Quality Glass Block, Morris**  Also called Tuminello Enterprizes Inc  *(G-15138)*
**Quality Glass Block & Win Co, Morris**  Also called Tuminello Enterprizes Inc  *(G-15137)*
**Quality Hnge A Div Spreme Hnge** .................................. 708 534-7801
 2412 Bond St  University Park  (60484)  *(G-21061)*
**Quality Intgrted Solutions Inc** .................................. 815 464-4772
 18521 Spring Creek Dr  Tinley Park  (60477)  *(G-20942)*
**Quality Iron Works Inc** .................................. 630 766-0885
 449 Evergreen Ave  Bensenville  (60106)  *(G-1971)*
**Quality Lime Company** .................................. 217 826-2343
 14915 N Quality Lime Rd  Marshall  (62441)  *(G-14328)*
**Quality Line, Marshall**  Also called Quality Lime Company  *(G-14328)*
**Quality Liquid Feeds Inc** .................................. 815 224-1553
 75 Creve Coeur St  La Salle  (61301)  *(G-12782)*
**Quality Logo Products Inc** .................................. 630 896-1627
 724 N Highland Ave  Aurora  (60506)  *(G-1207)*
**Quality Machine** .................................. 708 499-0021
 5530 W 110th St Ste 8  Oak Lawn  (60453)  *(G-16642)*
**Quality Machine Tool Services** .................................. 847 776-0073
 2385 Hammond Dr Ste 12  Schaumburg  (60173)  *(G-19708)*
**Quality Metal Finishing Co** .................................. 815 234-2711
 421 N Walnut St  Byron  (61010)  *(G-2918)*
**Quality Metal Products Inc** .................................. 309 692-8014
 7006 N Galena Rd  Peoria  (61614)  *(G-17438)*
**Quality Metal Works Inc** .................................. 309 379-5311
 200 School St  Stanford  (61774)  *(G-20552)*
**Quality Millwork and Trim, Morris**  Also called Torblo Inc  *(G-15135)*
**Quality Molding Products LLC** .................................. 224 308-4167
 281 Frances Dr  Grayslake  (60030)  *(G-11360)*
**Quality Msrement Solutions Inc** .................................. 630 406-1618
 1600 Shore Rd Ste I  Naperville  (60563)  *(G-15735)*
**Quality Neon Service** .................................. 847 299-2969
 1350 Oakwood Ave Ste A  Des Plaines  (60016)  *(G-8266)*
**Quality Network Solutions Inc** .................................. 217 728-3155
 111 E Jefferson St  Sullivan  (61951)  *(G-20758)*
**Quality Optical Inc** .................................. 773 561-0870
 4610 N Lincoln Ave  Chicago  (60625)  *(G-6247)*
**Quality Pallets Inc** .................................. 217 459-2655
 601 Kentucky Ave  Windsor  (61957)  *(G-22282)*
**Quality Paper Inc** .................................. 847 258-3999
 1855 Greenleaf Ave  Elk Grove Village  (60007)  *(G-9702)*
**Quality Plastic Products Inc** .................................. 630 766-7593
 830 Maple Ln  Bensenville  (60106)  *(G-1972)*
**Quality Plating** .................................. 815 626-5223
 406 Oak Ave  Sterling  (61081)  *(G-20607)*
**Quality Plating Works, Belleville**  Also called Koderhandt Inc  *(G-1645)*
**Quality Plus** .................................. 618 779-4931
 901 S Old Route 66  Litchfield  (62056)  *(G-13695)*
**Quality Quickprint Inc** .................................. 815 439-3430
 2405 Caton Farm Rd  Joliet  (60403)  *(G-12560)*
**Quality Quickprint Inc (PA)** .................................. 815 723-0941
 1258 Cronin Ct  Lemont  (60439)  *(G-13258)*
**Quality Quickprint Inc** .................................. 815 838-1784
 909 E 9th St  Lockport  (60441)  *(G-13740)*
**Quality Ready Mix Concrete Co** .................................. 815 589-2013
 1415 14th Ave  Fulton  (61252)  *(G-10704)*
**Quality Ready Mix Concrete Co (PA)** .................................. 815 772-7181
 14849 Lyndon Rd  Morrison  (61270)  *(G-15147)*

ALPHABETIC SECTION
Quipp Systems Inc (HQ)

**Quality Ready Mix Concrete Co** ....815 625-0750
13134 Galt Rd Sterling (61081) *(G-20608)*
**Quality Ready Mix Concrete Co** ....815 288-6416
1569 Franklin Grove Rd Dixon (61021) *(G-8340)*
**Quality Sand Company Inc** ....618 346-1070
1327 N Bluff Rd Collinsville (62234) *(G-7339)*
**Quality Service & Installation** ....847 352-4000
923 Sharon Ln Schaumburg (60193) *(G-19709)*
**Quality Sleep Shop Inc (PA)** ....708 246-2224
1519 W 55th St La Grange Highlands (60525) *(G-12750)*
**Quality Snack Foods Inc** ....708 377-7120
3750 W 131st St Alsip (60803) *(G-515)*
**Quality Sport Nets Inc** ....618 533-0700
2330 E Calumet St Centralia (62801) *(G-3428)*
**Quality Spraying Screen Prtg** ....630 584-8324
3815 Illinois Ave Saint Charles (60174) *(G-19248)*
**Quality Surface Mount Inc** ....630 350-8556
965 Dillon Dr Wood Dale (60191) *(G-22415)*
**Quality Targets** ....618 245-6515
204 Through St Farina (62838) *(G-10177)*
**Quality Tech Tool Inc** ....847 690-9643
759 Industrial Dr Bensenville (60106) *(G-1973)*
**Quality Technology Intl Inc** ....847 649-9300
1707 N Randall Rd Ste 300 Elgin (60123) *(G-9158)*
**Quality Tool & Machine Inc** ....773 721-8655
8050 S Constance Ave Chicago (60617) *(G-6248)*
**Quality Tool Inc** ....847 288-9330
9239 Parklane Ave Franklin Park (60131) *(G-10567)*
**Quality Trailer Sales Inc** ....630 739-2495
1701 N Main St Morton (61550) *(G-15179)*
**Quality Transport & Recycling, Cortland** *Also called Cortes Enterprise Inc (G-7385)*
**Quam-Nichols Company** ....773 488-5800
234 E Marquette Rd Ste 1 Chicago (60637) *(G-6249)*
**Quanex Homeshield LLC** ....815 635-3171
32140 E 830 North Rd Chatsworth (60921) *(G-3628)*
**Quanex Homeshield LLC** ....815 635-3171
32140 E 830 North Rd Chatsworth (60921) *(G-3629)*
**Quanex Screens LLC** ....217 463-2233
13323 Illinois Hwy 133 Paris (61944) *(G-17160)*
**Quantum Color Graphics LLC** ....847 967-3600
6511 Oakton St Morton Grove (60053) *(G-15231)*
**Quantum Corporation** ....312 372-2857
1 S Wacker Dr Chicago (60606) *(G-6250)*
**Quantum Design Inc (PA)** ....815 885-1300
8400 E Riverside Blvd Loves Park (61111) *(G-13980)*
**Quantum Engineering Inc** ....847 640-1340
801 Chase Ave Ste G Elk Grove Village (60007) *(G-9703)*
**Quantum Healing** ....217 414-2412
809 Timber Ridge Rd Mechanicsburg (62545) *(G-14575)*
**Quantum Legal LLC** ....847 433-4500
513 Central Ave Highland Park (60035) *(G-11863)*
**Quantum Marketing LLC** ....630 257-7012
12305 New Ave Ste H Lemont (60439) *(G-13259)*
**Quantum Mechanical LLC** ....773 480-8200
11182 Victoria Ln Huntley (60142) *(G-12170)*
**Quantum Meruit LLC** ....630 283-3555
399 Wall St Glendale Heights (60139) *(G-11061)*
**Quantum Nova Technologies** ....773 386-6816
2207 E 70th Pl Chicago (60649) *(G-6251)*
**Quantum Partners LLC** ....312 725-4668
2035 W Evergreen Ave Chicago (60622) *(G-6252)*
**Quantum Precision Inc** ....630 692-1545
385 Wegner Dr West Chicago (60185) *(G-21762)*
**Quantum Services Inc** ....815 230-5893
8115 Bluestem Ave Joliet (60431) *(G-12561)*
**Quantum Sign Corporation** ....630 466-0372
693 N Heartland Dr Sugar Grove (60554) *(G-20733)*
**Quantum Storage Systems** ....630 274-6610
2600 United Ln Elk Grove Village (60007) *(G-9704)*
**Quantum Technical Services Inc** ....815 464-1540
9524 Gulfstream Rd Frankfort (60423) *(G-10355)*
**Quantum Topping Systems, Frankfort** *Also called Quantum Technical Services Inc (G-10355)*
**Quantum Vision Centers** ....618 656-7774
3990 N Illinois St Swansea (62226) *(G-20780)*
**Quantum9 Inc** ....888 716-0404
303 W Erie St Ste L101 Chicago (60654) *(G-6253)*
**Quarasan Group Inc** ....312 981-2540
1 E Wacker Dr Ste 1900 Chicago (60601) *(G-6254)*
**Quarter Master Industries Inc** ....847 540-8999
510 Telser Rd Lake Zurich (60047) *(G-13120)*
**Quarters Concessions Inc** ....847 343-4864
4064 Stratford Ln Carpentersville (60110) *(G-3299)*
**Quartix Inc** ....855 913-6663
500 N Michigan Ave # 1607 Chicago (60611) *(G-6255)*
**Quatum Structure and Design** ....815 741-0733
2145 Moen Ave Unit 2 Rockdale (60436) *(G-18228)*
**Quay Corporation Inc (PA)** ....847 676-4233
7101 N Capitol Dr Lincolnwood (60712) *(G-13531)*
**Quebecor Wrld Mt Morris II LLC** ....815 734-4121
404 N Wesley Ave Mount Morris (61054) *(G-15298)*
**Quen-Tel Communication Svc Inc** ....815 463-1800
2759 Meadow Path New Lenox (60451) *(G-15903)*
**Quesse Moving & Storage Inc** ....815 223-0253
4438 Hollerich Dr Peru (61354) *(G-17525)*
**Questek Manufacturing Corp** ....847 428-0300
2570 Technology Dr Elgin (60124) *(G-9159)*
**Questily LLC (PA)** ....312 636-6657
3619 N Claremont Ave Chicago (60618) *(G-6256)*
**Questily LLC** ....312 636-6657
2 N La Salle St Fl 14 Chicago (60602) *(G-6257)*
**Quick Building Systems Inc** ....708 598-6733
9748 S Cambridge Ct Palos Hills (60465) *(G-17122)*
**Quick Lube, Danville** *Also called William Ingram (G-7785)*
**Quick Nic Juice LLC** ....815 315-8523
122 Indian Springs Dr # 5 Sandwich (60548) *(G-19376)*
**Quick Print, Lemont** *Also called Quality Quickprint Inc (G-13258)*
**Quick Print Shoppe** ....309 694-1204
500 Fondulac Dr East Peoria (61611) *(G-8729)*
**Quick Quality Printing Inc** ....708 895-5885
17332 Torrence Ave Lansing (60438) *(G-13181)*
**Quick Signs** ....618 549-0747
1260 N Reed Station Rd Carbondale (62902) *(G-3020)*
**Quick Signs Inc** ....630 554-7370
424 Treasure Dr Oswego (60543) *(G-16930)*
**Quick Start Pdts & Solutions** ....815 562-5414
770 Wiscold Dr Rochelle (61068) *(G-18103)*
**Quick Tabs Inc** ....630 969-7737
81 W 61st St Westmont (60559) *(G-21915)*
**Quicker Engineering** ....815 675-6516
7516 Buena Vis Spring Grove (60081) *(G-20360)*
**Quicker Printers, Chicago** *Also called Dos Bro Corp (G-4633)*
**Quickprinters** ....309 833-5250
1120 E Jackson St Macomb (61455) *(G-14130)*
**Quickset International Inc (HQ)** ....847 498-0700
3650 Woodhead Dr Northbrook (60062) *(G-16350)*
**Quicksilver Mechanical Inc** ....847 577-1564
3361 N Ridge Ave Arlington Heights (60004) *(G-824)*
**Quiet Graphics, Schaumburg** *Also called N Bujarski Inc (G-19660)*
**Quik Impressions Group Inc** ....630 495-7845
1385 W Jeffrey Dr Addison (60101) *(G-265)*
**Quikfletch, Forest Park** *Also called New Archery Products LLC (G-10251)*
**Quikrete Chicago** ....630 557-8252
1s950 Lorang Rd Elburn (60119) *(G-8906)*
**Quikrete Companies Inc** ....309 346-1184
11150 Garman Rd Pekin (61554) *(G-17285)*
**Quikrete of Peoria, Pekin** *Also called Quikrete Companies Inc (G-17285)*
**Quiller Outboard Sls Svcs LLC** ....618 232-1218
Rr 1 Box 130 Hamburg (62045) *(G-11527)*
**Quillers Outboard Kawasaki Sls, Hamburg** *Also called Quiller Outboard Sls Svcs LLC (G-11527)*
**Quilt Merchant** ....630 480-3000
27w209 Geneva Rd Winfield (60190) *(G-22291)*
**Quiltmaster Inc** ....847 426-6741
1 S Wisconsin St Carpentersville (60110) *(G-3300)*
**Quinceaneraboutiquecom Inc** ....779 324-5468
7624 W Saint Francis Rd Frankfort (60423) *(G-10356)*
**Quincy Brdcast Print Intrctive, Quincy** *Also called Quincy Media Inc (G-17879)*
**Quincy Compressor LLC** ....217 222-7700
3501 Wisman Ln Quincy (62301) *(G-17875)*
**Quincy Electric & Sign Company** ....217 223-8404
1324 Spring Lake Cors Quincy (62305) *(G-17876)*
**Quincy Foundry & Pattern Co** ....217 222-0718
435 S Front St Quincy (62301) *(G-17877)*
**Quincy Herald-Whig LLC** ....217 223-5100
130 S 5th St Quincy (62301) *(G-17878)*
**Quincy Lab Inc** ....773 622-2428
1928 N Leamington Ave Chicago (60639) *(G-6258)*
**Quincy Media Inc (PA)** ....217 223-5100
130 S 5th St Quincy (62301) *(G-17879)*
**Quincy Ready Mix Co, Quincy** *Also called Bleigh Construction Company (G-17805)*
**Quincy Socks House** ....217 506-6106
112 N 6th St Quincy (62301) *(G-17880)*
**Quincy Specialties Company** ....217 222-4057
2828 Scotia Trl Quincy (62301) *(G-17881)*
**Quincy Torque Converter Inc** ....217 228-0852
2220 Glenayre Way Quincy (62305) *(G-17882)*
**Quinn Broom Works Inc** ....217 923-3181
1527 Il Route 121 Greenup (62428) *(G-11385)*
**Quinn Print Inc** ....847 823-9100
508 Higgins Rd Park Ridge (60068) *(G-17218)*
**Quintum Technologies Inc** ....847 348-7730
1821 Walden Office Sq # 200 Schaumburg (60173) *(G-19710)*
**Quipp Inc (HQ)** ....305 623-8700
3700 W Lake Ave Glenview (60026) *(G-11186)*
**Quipp Systems Inc** ....305 304-1985
3650 W Lake Ave Glenview (60026) *(G-11187)*
**Quipp Systems Inc (HQ)** ....305 623-8700
3700 W Lake Ave Glenview (60026) *(G-11188)*

ALPHABETIC

Quixote Corporation (HQ) ALPHABETIC SECTION

**Quixote Corporation (HQ)**....312 705-8400
70 W Madison St Ste 2350 Chicago (60602) ***(G-6259)***
**Quixote Transportation Safety**....312 467-6750
70 W Madison St Ste 2350 Chicago (60602) ***(G-6260)***
**Quizworks Company, The, Johnsburg** *Also called Current Works Inc* ***(G-12433)***
**Quorum Labs LLC**....618 525-5600
895 Grayson Rd Eldorado (62930) ***(G-8921)***
**Qwik-Tip Inc**....847 640-7387
2415 E Higgins Rd Elk Grove Village (60007) ***(G-9705)***
**R & B Metal Products Inc**....815 338-1890
801 Mchenry Ave Woodstock (60098) ***(G-22603)***
**R & B Powder Coatings Inc**....773 247-8300
4000 S Bell Ave Chicago (60609) ***(G-6261)***
**R & C Auto Supply Corp**....815 625-4414
2526 E Lincolnway Sterling (61081) ***(G-20609)***
**R & C Castings, South Holland** *Also called R & C Pattern Works Inc* ***(G-20299)***
**R & C Pattern Works Inc**....708 331-1882
146 W 154th St South Holland (60473) ***(G-20299)***
**R & D Clark Ltd**....847 749-2061
1918 N Eastwood Dr Arlington Heights (60004) ***(G-825)***
**R & D Concrete Products Inc**....309 787-0264
8002 31st St W Rock Island (61201) ***(G-18195)***
**R & D Electronics Inc**....847 583-9080
7948 W Oakton St Niles (60714) ***(G-16024)***
**R & D Machine LLC**....618 282-6262
126 Jackson St Red Bud (62278) ***(G-17946)***
**R & D Oil Producers**....217 773-9299
709 N Capitol Ave Mount Sterling (62353) ***(G-15393)***
**R & D Thiel, Belvidere** *Also called Carpenter Contractors Amer Inc* ***(G-1744)***
**R & E Quality Mfg Co**....773 286-6846
7005 W School St Chicago (60634) ***(G-6262)***
**R & G Machine Shop Inc**....217 342-6622
1303 Parker Ave Effingham (62401) ***(G-8856)***
**R & G Spring Co Inc**....847 228-5640
1451 Landmeier Rd Ste L Elk Grove Village (60007) ***(G-9706)***
**R & H Products Inc**....815 744-4110
800 Moen Ave Unit 7 Rockdale (60436) ***(G-18229)***
**R & I Ornamental Iron Inc**....847 836-6934
96 Center Dr Gilberts (60136) ***(G-10933)***
**R & J Ready Mix, Naperville** *Also called Concrete 1 Inc* ***(G-15634)***
**R & J Systems Inc**....630 289-3010
1580 Birch Ave Bartlett (60133) ***(G-1322)***
**R & J Trucking and Recycl Inc**....708 563-2600
6650 S Oak Park Ave Chicago (60638) ***(G-6263)***
**R & L Business Forms Inc**....618 939-6535
8603 Gilmore Lake Rd Waterloo (62298) ***(G-21404)***
**R & L Ready Mix Inc**....618 544-7514
602 N Steel St Robinson (62454) ***(G-18070)***
**R & L Signs Inc**....708 233-0112
7430 W 90th St Bridgeview (60455) ***(G-2522)***
**R & L Truck Service Inc**....847 489-7135
39935 N Prairie View Dr Wadsworth (60083) ***(G-21326)***
**R & N Components Co**....217 543-3495
261 E County Road 600 N Tuscola (61953) ***(G-21023)***
**R & N Machine Co**....708 841-5555
14020 S Stewart Ave Riverdale (60827) ***(G-18023)***
**R & O Specialties Incorporated (HQ)**....309 736-8660
120 4th Ave E Milan (61264) ***(G-14800)***
**R & P Fuels**....630 855-2358
798 Barrington Rd Hoffman Estates (60169) ***(G-12042)***
**R & R Bindery Service Inc**....217 627-2143
499 Rachel Rd Girard (62640) ***(G-10949)***
**R & R Creative Graphics Inc**....630 208-4724
111 N Northampton Dr Geneva (60134) ***(G-10861)***
**R & R Custom Cabinet Making**....847 358-6188
515 S Vermont St Ste B Palatine (60067) ***(G-17065)***
**R & R Engines and Parts Inc**....630 628-1545
1244 W Capitol Dr Ste 4 Addison (60101) ***(G-266)***
**R & R Lithography, River Grove** *Also called R N R Photographers Inc* ***(G-18013)***
**R & R Machining Inc**....217 835-4579
125 Route 138 Benld (62009) ***(G-1806)***
**R & R Newkirk, Willow Springs** *Also called C M S Publishing Inc* ***(G-22193)***
**R & R Printnserve Inc**....630 654-4044
7585 S Madison St Hinsdale (60521) ***(G-11960)***
**R & R Services Illinois Inc**....217 424-2602
800 E Garfield Ave Decatur (62526) ***(G-7930)***
**R & S Cutterhead Mfg Co**....815 678-2611
11401 Commercial St Ste A Richmond (60071) ***(G-17969)***
**R & S Screen Printing Inc**....815 337-3935
739 Mchenry Ave Woodstock (60098) ***(G-22604)***
**R & S Steel Corporation**....309 448-2645
301 W Washington St Congerville (61729) ***(G-7370)***
**R & T Enterprises, Kewanee** *Also called Elm Street Industries Inc* ***(G-12681)***
**R & W Machine, Bedford Park** *Also called Warner Industries Inc* ***(G-1590)***
**R & W Oil Company**....618 686-3084
6166 Bible Grove Ln Louisville (62858) ***(G-13909)***
**R A E Tool and Manufacturing**....815 485-2506
1910 Clearing Ct Ste 2 New Lenox (60451) ***(G-15904)***
**R A Kerley Ink Engineers Inc (PA)**....708 344-1295
2700 S 12th Ave Broadview (60155) ***(G-2606)***
**R A R Machine & Manufacturing**....630 260-9591
5750 N Melvina Ave Chicago (60646) ***(G-6264)***
**R and B Distributors Inc**....815 433-6843
1217 Saint Clair St Ottawa (61350) ***(G-16981)***
**R and R Brokerage Co (PA)**....847 438-4600
800 Ela Rd Lake Zurich (60047) ***(G-13121)***
**R B Engineering, Bartlett** *Also called Robert Brysiewicz Incorporated* ***(G-1369)***
**R B Evans Co**....630 365-3554
808 Hicks Dr Elburn (60119) ***(G-8907)***
**R B Hayward Company**....847 671-0400
9556 River St Schiller Park (60176) ***(G-19864)***
**R B Manufacturing Inc**....815 522-3100
140 North St Kirkland (60146) ***(G-12716)***
**R B White Inc**....309 452-5816
2011 Eagle Rd Normal (61761) ***(G-16086)***
**R C Castings Inc**....708 331-1882
146 W 154th St South Holland (60473) ***(G-20300)***
**R C Coil Spring Mfg Co Inc**....630 790-3500
490 Mitchell Rd Glendale Heights (60139) ***(G-11062)***
**R C Industrial Inc**....309 756-3724
255 5th Ave W Milan (61264) ***(G-14801)***
**R C Industries Inc**....773 378-1118
1420 N Lamon Ave Chicago (60651) ***(G-6265)***
**R C Sales & Manufacturing Inc**....815 645-8898
5999 N Cox Rd Stillman Valley (61084) ***(G-20626)***
**R D Niven & Associates Ltd**....630 580-6000
955 Kimberly Dr Carol Stream (60188) ***(G-3225)***
**R D S Co**....630 893-2990
158 Covington Dr Bloomingdale (60108) ***(G-2129)***
**R E Burke Roofing Co Inc**....847 675-5010
7667 Gross Point Rd Skokie (60077) ***(G-20068)***
**R E I, Richmond** *Also called Rodifer Enterprises Inc* ***(G-17970)***
**R E Z Packaging Inc**....773 247-0800
3735 S Racine Ave Chicago (60609) ***(G-6266)***
**R Energy LLC**....618 382-7313
1001 E Main St Carmi (62821) ***(G-3077)***
**R G Controls Inc**....847 438-3981
512 Rue Chamonix Barrington (60010) ***(G-1300)***
**R G Hanson Company Inc (PA)**....309 661-9200
211 S Prospect Rd Ste 4 Bloomington (61704) ***(G-2217)***
**R H Johnson Oil Co Inc (PA)**....630 668-3649
1017 Delles Rd Wheaton (60189) ***(G-21974)***
**R Hansel & Son Inc**....815 784-5500
221 N Sycamore St Genoa (60135) ***(G-10883)***
**R I Plastics, Tower Hill** *Also called Realt Images Inc* ***(G-20980)***
**R J Graham Oil Company, Salem** *Also called Ronnie Joe Graham* ***(G-19348)***
**R J S Silk Screening Co**....708 974-3009
10708 S Roberts Rd Palos Hills (60465) ***(G-17123)***
**R J Van Drunen & Sons Inc (PA)**....815 472-3100
300 W 6th St Momence (60954) ***(G-14987)***
**R J Van Drunen & Sons Inc**....830 422-2167
214 Mechanic St Momence (60954) ***(G-14988)***
**R J Van Drunen & Sons Inc**....815 472-3211
3878 N Vincennes Trl Momence (60954) ***(G-14989)***
**R K J Pallets Inc**....708 493-0701
1003 Cernan Dr Bellwood (60104) ***(G-1717)***
**R K Precision Machine Inc**....574 293-0231
12512 S Springfield Ave Alsip (60803) ***(G-516)***
**R K Products Inc**....309 792-1927
3802 Jean St East Moline (61244) ***(G-8693)***
**R L Allen Industries**....618 667-2544
120 Collinsville Rd Ofc Troy (62294) ***(G-21011)***
**R L D Communications Inc (PA)**....312 338-7007
725 S Wells St Fl 4 Chicago (60607) ***(G-6267)***
**R L Hoener Co**....217 223-2190
2923 Gardner Expy Quincy (62305) ***(G-17883)***
**R L Kolbi Company**....847 506-1440
416 W Campus Dr Arlington Heights (60004) ***(G-826)***
**R L Lewis Industries Inc (PA)**....309 353-7670
14215 Towerline Rd Pekin (61554) ***(G-17286)***
**R L ONeal & Sons Inc**....309 458-3350
819 N County Road 3050 Plymouth (62367) ***(G-17682)***
**R M Armstrong & Son Inc**....847 669-3988
11006 Bakley St Huntley (60142) ***(G-12171)***
**R M J Distributing, Belleville** *Also called ABM Marking Ltd* ***(G-1606)***
**R M Tool & Manufacturing Co**....847 888-0433
368 Bluff City Blvd Ste 6 Elgin (60120) ***(G-9160)***
**R Machining Inc**....217 532-2174
705 Elm St Butler (62015) ***(G-2910)***
**R Maderite Inc**....847 785-0875
2306 Commonwealth Ave North Chicago (60064) ***(G-16186)***
**R Maderite Inc**....773 235-1515
1616 N Washtenaw Ave Chicago (60647) ***(G-6268)***
**R N I Industries Inc**....630 860-9147
236 William St Bensenville (60106) ***(G-1974)***
**R N R Photographers Inc**....708 453-1868
8115 Grand Ave River Grove (60171) ***(G-18013)***
**R O I, Elgin** *Also called Rieke Office Interiors Inc* ***(G-9165)***

**R P Grollman Co Inc** .................................................. 847 607-0294
1811 Lawrence Ln  Highland Park  (60035)  *(G-11864)*
**R Popernik Co Inc** .................................................... 773 434-4300
2313 W 59th St  Chicago  (60636)  *(G-6269)*
**R R Donnelley, Mattoon** *Also called RR Donnelley & Sons Company (G-14407)*
**R R Donnelley, Chicago** *Also called RR Donnelley Printing Co LP (G-6405)*
**R R Donnelley, Pontiac** *Also called R R Donnelley & Sons Company (G-17710)*
**R R Donnelley, Elgin** *Also called RR Donnelley & Sons Company (G-9169)*
**R R Donnelley, Lisle** *Also called RR Donnelley & Sons Company (G-13653)*
**R R Donnelley & Sons Company (PA)** ................. 312 326-8000
35 W Wacker Dr Ste 3650  Chicago  (60601)  *(G-6270)*
**R R Donnelley & Sons Company** ........................ 847 393-3000
850 Technology Way  Libertyville  (60048)  *(G-13373)*
**R R Donnelley & Sons Company** ........................ 815 584-2770
801 N Union St  Dwight  (60420)  *(G-8591)*
**R R Donnelley & Sons Company** ........................ 815 844-5181
1600 N Main St  Pontiac  (61764)  *(G-17710)*
**R R Sausage Factory, Chicago** *Also called Oriental Kitchen Corporation (G-6007)*
**R R Street & Co Inc** ................................................ 773 247-1190
4600 S Tripp Ave  Chicago  (60632)  *(G-6271)*
**R R Street & Co Inc (PA)** ....................................... 630 416-4244
215 Shuman Blvd Ste 403  Naperville  (60563)  *(G-15736)*
**R R Street & Co Inc** ................................................ 773 254-1277
2353 S Blue Island Ave  Chicago  (60608)  *(G-6272)*
**R S Bacon Veneer Company (PA)** ....................... 630 323-1414
770 Front St  Lisle  (60532)  *(G-13648)*
**R S Bacon Veneer Company** ................................ 331 777-4762
770 Front St  Lisle  (60532)  *(G-13649)*
**R S Corcoran Co** .................................................... 815 485-2156
500 N Vine St  New Lenox  (60451)  *(G-15905)*
**R S Cryo Equipment Inc** ....................................... 815 468-6115
629 N Grove St  Manteno  (60950)  *(G-14191)*
**R S Owens & Co Inc** .............................................. 773 282-6000
5535 N Lynch Ave  Chicago  (60630)  *(G-6273)*
**R T Beverage, Chicago** *Also called Balon International Corp (G-4034)*
**R T I, Lincolnwood** *Also called Research Technology Intl Co (G-13532)*
**R T M Precision Machining Inc** ............................ 630 595-0946
739 Kimberly Dr  Carol Stream  (60188)  *(G-3226)*
**R T P Company** ...................................................... 618 286-6100
1610 Design Way Ste B  Dupo  (62239)  *(G-8576)*
**R T P Inc** .................................................................. 312 664-6150
1249 N Clybourn Ave  Chicago  (60610)  *(G-6274)*
**R V Designer Collections, Wheeling** *Also called Shapco Inc (G-22149)*
**R W Bradley Supply, Springfield** *Also called R W Bradley Supply Company (G-20510)*
**R W Bradley Supply Company** ............................ 217 528-8438
403 N 4th St  Springfield  (62702)  *(G-20510)*
**R W G Manufacturing Inc** ..................................... 708 755-8035
3309 Holeman Ave Ste 7  S Chicago Hts  (60411)  *(G-19112)*
**R W Wilson Printing Company** ............................ 630 584-4100
220 N 4th St  Saint Charles  (60174)  *(G-19249)*
**R Z Tool Inc** ............................................................. 847 647-2350
5691 W Howard St  Niles  (60714)  *(G-16025)*
**R&B Foods Inc (HQ)** ............................................... 847 590-0059
1661 Feehanville Dr # 200  Mount Prospect  (60056)  *(G-15367)*
**R&D, Batavia** *Also called Partylite Inc (G-1480)*
**R&R Engineering, Addison** *Also called R & R Engines and Parts Inc (G-266)*
**R&R Equipment Plus1 Inc** .................................... 708 529-3931
9923 Ridgeland Ave  Chicago Ridge  (60415)  *(G-7157)*
**R&R Flight Service** ................................................ 815 538-2599
Rr 2  Earlville  (60518)  *(G-8596)*
**R&R Meat Co** .......................................................... 270 898-6296
5156 Old Marion Rd  Metropolis  (62960)  *(G-14761)*
**R&R Racing of Palm Beach Inc** ........................... 618 937-6767
15942 Mine 25 Rd Ste 28  West Frankfort  (62896)  *(G-21815)*
**R&R Research Co** .................................................. 847 345-5051
300 N Prospect Manor Ave  Mount Prospect  (60056)  *(G-15368)*
**R&R Rf Inc** ............................................................... 847 669-3720
1104 E 17th St  Rock Falls  (61071)  *(G-18147)*
**R+d Custom Automation Inc** ............................... 847 395-3330
23411 W Wall St  Lake Villa  (60046)  *(G-13025)*
**R-B Industries Inc** .................................................. 847 647-4020
6366 W Gross Point Rd  Niles  (60714)  *(G-16026)*
**R-K Press Brake Dies Inc** ..................................... 708 371-1756
12512 S Springfield Ave  Chicago  (60803)  *(G-6275)*
**R-M Industries Inc** ................................................. 630 543-3071
38 W Interstate Rd  Addison  (60101)  *(G-267)*
**R-Signs Service and Design Inc** ......................... 815 722-0283
720 Collins St Ste D  Joliet  (60432)  *(G-12562)*
**R-Squared Construction Inc** ................................ 815 232-7433
35 N Commercial Ave  Freeport  (61032)  *(G-10682)*
**R-Tech Feeders Inc** ............................................... 815 874-2990
5292 American Rd  Rockford  (61109)  *(G-18546)*
**R.E.F. Silk Screen Productions, Evanston** *Also called Lochman Ref Silk Screen Co (G-10065)*
**R.L. Ringwood, Bedford Park** *Also called Ringwood Company (G-1579)*
**R.ryvette, Chicago** *Also called Bone & Rattle Inc (G-4142)*
**R/A Hoerr Inc** .......................................................... 309 691-8789
9804 W Primrose  Edwards  (61528)  *(G-8784)*

**R/K Industries Inc** .................................................. 847 526-2222
375 Hollow Hill Rd  Wauconda  (60084)  *(G-21498)*
**Ra-Ujamaa Inc** ....................................................... 773 373-8585
622 E 47th St  Chicago  (60653)  *(G-6276)*
**Raajrtna Stinless Wire USA Inc** ........................... 847 923-8000
1015 W Wise Rd Ste 201  Schaumburg  (60193)  *(G-19711)*
**Rabbit Tool USA Inc (PA)** ..................................... 309 793-4375
105 9th St  Rock Island  (61201)  *(G-18196)*
**Raber Packing Company** ..................................... 309 673-0721
1413 N Raber Rd  Peoria  (61604)  *(G-17439)*
**Rabine Paving, Byron** *Also called Byron Blacktop Inc (G-2913)*
**Racconto, Melrose Park** *Also called Alm Distributors LLC (G-14589)*
**Raceway Electric Company Inc** .......................... 630 501-1180
270 W Saint Charles Rd  Elmhurst  (60126)  *(G-9924)*
**Rachel Switall Mag Group Nfp** ............................ 773 344-7123
1441b W Wrightwood Ave  Chicago  (60614)  *(G-6277)*
**Racine Paper Box Manufacturing** ....................... 773 227-3900
3522 W Potomac Ave  Chicago  (60651)  *(G-6278)*
**Rack Builders Inc (PA)** ......................................... 217 214-9482
3809 Dye Rd  Quincy  (62305)  *(G-17884)*
**Rackow Polymers Corporation** ............................ 630 766-3982
475 Thomas Dr  Bensenville  (60106)  *(G-1975)*
**Raco Steel Company** ............................................ 708 339-2958
2100 W 163rd Pl  Markham  (60428)  *(G-14304)*
**Radco Industries Inc** ............................................. 630 232-7966
39w 930 Midan Dr  Elburn  (60119)  *(G-8908)*
**Radco Industries Inc (PA)** .................................... 630 232-7966
700 Kingsland Dr  Batavia  (60510)  *(G-1489)*
**Radiac Abrasives Inc (HQ)** ................................... 618 548-4200
1015 S College St  Salem  (62881)  *(G-19347)*
**Radiac Abrasives Inc** ............................................ 630 898-0315
101 Kendall Point Dr  Oswego  (60543)  *(G-16931)*
**Radiad Manufacturing** ........................................... 847 678-5808
3543 Martens St  Franklin Park  (60131)  *(G-10568)*
**Radio Controlled Models Inc** ............................... 847 740-8726
229 E Rollins Rd  Round Lake Beach  (60073)  *(G-19079)*
**Radio Flyer Inc** ....................................................... 773 637-7100
6515 W Grand Ave  Chicago  (60707)  *(G-6279)*
**Radio Frequency Systems Inc** ............................ 800 321-4700
2000 Nperville Wheaton Rd  Naperville  (60563)  *(G-15737)*
**RADIO FREQUENCY SYSTEMS,INC, Naperville** *Also called Radio Frequency Systems Inc (G-15737)*
**Radiofx Inc** .............................................................. 773 255-8069
1953 N Clybourn Ave  Chicago  (60614)  *(G-6280)*
**Radionic Hi-Tech Inc** ............................................. 773 804-0100
6625 W Diversey Ave  Chicago  (60707)  *(G-6281)*
**Radionic Industries Inc** ......................................... 773 804-0100
6625 W Diversey Ave  Chicago  (60707)  *(G-6282)*
**Radius Machine & Tool Inc** .................................. 847 662-7690
4290 Lee Ave  Gurnee  (60031)  *(G-11497)*
**Radius Solutions Incorporated** ........................... 312 648-0800
150 N Michigan Ave # 300  Chicago  (60601)  *(G-6283)*
**Radovent Illinois LLC (PA)** ................................... 847 637-0297
766 W Algonquin Rd  Arlington Heights  (60005)  *(G-827)*
**Rae Products and Chem Corp (PA)** .................... 708 396-1984
11638 S Mayfield Ave  Alsip  (60803)  *(G-517)*
**Rae Supply, Harvey** *Also called Brewer Company (G-11662)*
**Ragan Kettle Corn, Belleville** *Also called Larry Ragan (G-1648)*
**Rah Enterprises Inc** ............................................... 217 223-1970
2630 S Commercial Dr  Quincy  (62305)  *(G-17885)*
**Rahco Rubber Inc** .................................................. 847 298-4200
1633 Birchwood Ave  Des Plaines  (60018)  *(G-8267)*
**Rahmanims Imports Inc (PA)** .............................. 312 236-2200
5 S Wabash Ave Ste 1211  Chicago  (60603)  *(G-6284)*
**Rahn Equipment Company** .................................. 217 431-1232
2400 Georgetown Rd  Danville  (61832)  *(G-7762)*
**Rahn USA Corp** ...................................................... 630 851-4220
1005 N Commons Dr  Aurora  (60504)  *(G-1072)*
**Rail Exchange Inc** .................................................. 708 757-3317
1150 State St  Chicago Heights  (60411)  *(G-7119)*
**Rail Forge** ................................................................ 630 561-4989
2001 W Wabansia Ave # 101  Chicago  (60647)  *(G-6285)*
**Railcraft Nexim Design** ......................................... 309 937-2360
12615 N 850th Ave  Cambridge  (61238)  *(G-2969)*
**Raildecks Intermodal** ............................................. 630 442-7676
1311 Palmer St  Downers Grove  (60516)  *(G-8512)*
**Railroad Electronics, Schiller Park** *Also called Rex Morioka (G-19867)*
**Railshop Inc** ............................................................ 847 816-0925
902 Wexford Ct  Libertyville  (60048)  *(G-13374)*
**Railway & Industrial Spc, Crest Hill** *Also called Railway & Industrial Svcs Inc (G-7465)*
**Railway & Industrial Svcs Inc** .............................. 815 726-4224
2201 N Center St  Crest Hill  (60403)  *(G-7465)*
**Railway Program Services Inc** ............................ 708 552-4000
6235 S Oak Park Ave  Chicago  (60638)  *(G-6286)*
**Raimonde Drilling Corp** ........................................ 630 458-0590
770 W Factory Rd Ste A  Addison  (60101)  *(G-268)*
**Rain Cii Carbon LLC** ............................................. 618 544-2193
12187 E 950th Ave  Robinson  (62454)  *(G-18071)*

**Rain Creek Baking Corp** ....559 347-9960
1 Sexton Dr Glendale Heights (60139) ***(G-11063)***
**Rain Publication Inc** ....312 284-2444
65 E Wacker Pl Ste 930 Chicago (60601) ***(G-6287)***
**Rainbo Sports LLC** ....847 784-9857
790 W Frontage Rd Ste 705 Northfield (60093) ***(G-16416)***
**Rainbo Sports LLC (PA)** ....847 998-1000
1440 Paddock Dr Northbrook (60062) ***(G-16351)***
**Rainbow Art Inc** ....312 421-5600
2224 W Grand Ave Chicago (60612) ***(G-6288)***
**Rainbow Cleaners** ....630 789-6989
836 E Ogden Ave Westmont (60559) ***(G-21916)***
**Rainbow Colors Inc** ....847 640-7700
935 Lee St Elk Grove Village (60007) ***(G-9707)***
**Rainbow Dusters International** ....770 627-3575
135 E Saint Charles Rd F2 Carol Stream (60188) ***(G-3227)***
**Rainbow Fabrics Inc** ....312 356-9979
620 W Roosevelt Rd Chicago (60607) ***(G-6289)***
**Rainbow Farms Enterprises Inc** ....708 534-1070
25715 S Ridgeland Ave Monee (60449) ***(G-14999)***
**Rainbow Graphics, Inc., Mundelein** *Also called Rainbow Manufacturing Inc* ***(G-15551)***
**Rainbow Lighting** ....847 480-1136
3545 Commercial Ave Northbrook (60062) ***(G-16352)***
**Rainbow Manufacturing Inc** ....847 824-9600
933 Tower Rd Mundelein (60060) ***(G-15551)***
**Rainbow Midwest Inc** ....847 955-9300
300 Corporate Woods Pkwy Vernon Hills (60061) ***(G-21191)***
**Rainbow Play Systems Illinois, Vernon Hills** *Also called Rainbow Midwest Inc* ***(G-21191)***
**Rainbow Printing, Lemont** *Also called Patrick Impressions LLC* ***(G-13250)***
**Rainbow Pure Water Inc** ....618 985-4670
610 Sneed Rd Carbondale (62902) ***(G-3021)***
**Rainbow Signs** ....815 675-6750
2404 Spring Ridge Dr A Spring Grove (60081) ***(G-20361)***
**Rainmaker** ....847 998-0838
1539 Palmgren Dr Glenview (60025) ***(G-11189)***
**Rainmaker Brands, Quincy** *Also called Griffard & Associates LLC* ***(G-17832)***
**Raised Expectations, Alsip** *Also called B Allan Graphics Inc* ***(G-438)***
**Rajner Quality Machine Works** ....847 394-8999
2092 Foster Ave Wheeling (60090) ***(G-22131)***
**Raleigh Ready Mix, Raleigh** *Also called Gary & Larry Brown Trucking* ***(G-17909)***
**Ralph Cody Gravrok** ....630 628-9570
729 W Fullerton Ave 6f Addison (60101) ***(G-269)***
**Ram Plastic Corp** ....847 669-8003
11414 Smith Dr Unit B Huntley (60142) ***(G-12172)***
**Ram R-C Models, Round Lake Beach** *Also called Radio Controlled Models Inc* ***(G-19079)***
**Ram Systems & Communication** ....847 487-7575
950 N Rand Rd Ste 202 Wauconda (60084) ***(G-21499)***
**Ramallah Jewelry, Oak Lawn** *Also called Jordan Gold Inc* ***(G-16628)***
**Ramar Industries Inc** ....847 451-0445
9211 Parklane Ave Franklin Park (60131) ***(G-10569)***
**Ramcel Engineering Co** ....847 272-6980
2926 Macarthur Blvd Northbrook (60062) ***(G-16353)***
**Ramco Group LLC** ....847 639-9899
764 Tek Dr Crystal Lake (60014) ***(G-7636)***
**Ramco Tool, Crystal Lake** *Also called Ramco Group LLC* ***(G-7636)***
**Ramco Tool & Manufacturing** ....847 639-9899
760 Industrial Dr Ste I Cary (60013) ***(G-3365)***
**Ramona Sedivy** ....630 983-1902
1840 Auburn Ave Naperville (60565) ***(G-15738)***
**Rampart LLC** ....847 367-8960
28101 N Ballard Dr Ste C Lake Forest (60045) ***(G-12950)***
**Rampro Facilities Svcs Corp** ....224 639-6378
4198 Russell Ave Gurnee (60031) ***(G-11498)***
**Ramsey News Journal** ....618 423-2411
217 S Superior St Ramsey (62080) ***(G-17915)***
**Ramsey Welding Inc** ....618 483-6248
5360 E 900th Ave Altamont (62411) ***(G-555)***
**Ramseys Machine Co** ....217 824-2320
1333 N Webster St Taylorville (62568) ***(G-20845)***
**Ramseys News Agency, New Lenox** *Also called Peg N Reds* ***(G-15900)***
**Ramsplitter Log Splitters Inc** ....815 398-4726
1936 11th St Rockford (61104) ***(G-18547)***
**Rana Meal Solutions LLC** ....630 581-4100
550 S Spitzer Rd Bartlett (60103) ***(G-1367)***
**Rana Meal Solutions LLC (HQ)** ....630 581-4100
1400 16th St Ste 275 Oak Brook (60523) ***(G-16558)***
**Rancilio North America Inc** ....630 427-1703
1340 Internationale Pkwy Woodridge (60517) ***(G-22513)***
**Rand Diversified Midwest, Edwardsville** *Also called Sjd Direct Midwest LLC* ***(G-8814)***
**Rand Jig Boring Inc** ....847 678-7416
10009 Franklin Ave Ste 1 Franklin Park (60131) ***(G-10570)***
**Rand Manufacturing Network Inc** ....847 299-8884
840 Tanglewood Dr Wheeling (60090) ***(G-22132)***
**Rand McNally, Skokie** *Also called Rm Acquisition LLC* ***(G-20077)***
**Rand McNally & Company** ....847 329-8100
9855 Woods Dr Skokie (60077) ***(G-20069)***
**Rand McNally International Co** ....847 329-8100
9855 Woods Dr Skokie (60077) ***(G-20070)***

**Randa Accessories Lea Gds LLC (PA)** ....847 292-8300
5600 N River Rd Ste 500 Rosemont (60018) ***(G-19026)***
**Randal Retail Group, Batavia** *Also called Randal Wood Displays Inc* ***(G-1490)***
**Randal Wood Displays Inc** ....630 761-0400
507 N Raddant Rd Batavia (60510) ***(G-1490)***
**Randall Manufacturing LLC** ....630 782-0001
722 N Church Rd Elmhurst (60126) ***(G-9925)***
**Randall Publications (PA)** ....847 437-6604
1840 Jarvis Ave Elk Grove Village (60007) ***(G-9708)***
**Randall Publishing Inc** ....847 437-6604
1425 Lunt Ave Elk Grove Village (60007) ***(G-9709)***
**Randolph Agricultural Services** ....309 473-3256
15125 E 625 North Rd Heyworth (61745) ***(G-11765)***
**Randolph County Herald Tribune** ....618 826-2385
1205 Swanwick St Chester (62233) ***(G-3660)***
**Randolph Dairy, Chicago** *Also called A New Dairy Company* ***(G-3690)***
**Randolph Packing Co** ....630 830-3100
275 Roma Jean Pkwy Streamwood (60107) ***(G-20670)***
**Randy Wright & Son Cnstr** ....217 478-4171
901 E Old 36 Alexander (62601) ***(G-374)***
**Randys Exper-Clean** ....217 423-1975
4925 W Main St Decatur (62522) ***(G-7931)***
**Ranger Redi-Mix & Mtls Inc** ....815 337-2662
1100 Borden Ln Woodstock (60098) ***(G-22605)***
**Rankin Publishing Inc** ....217 268-4959
204 E Main St Arcola (61910) ***(G-683)***
**Ransburg Corporation** ....847 724-7500
155 Harlem Ave Glenview (60025) ***(G-11190)***
**Rantoul Foods LLC** ....217 892-4178
205 Turner Dr Rantoul (61866) ***(G-17936)***
**RAO Design International Inc** ....847 671-6182
9451 Ainslie St Schiller Park (60176) ***(G-19865)***
**Rapak LLC (HQ)** ....630 296-2000
1201 Windham Pkwy Ste D Romeoville (60446) ***(G-18862)***
**Rapco Building Pdts & Sup Co, Richview** *Also called Rapco Ltd* ***(G-17981)***
**Rapco Ltd** ....618 249-6614
405 E 1st South St Richview (62877) ***(G-17981)***
**Rapid Air** ....815 397-2578
2812 22nd St Rockford (61109) ***(G-18548)***
**Rapid Circular Press Inc** ....312 421-5611
526 N Western Ave Chicago (60612) ***(G-6290)***
**Rapid Copy & Duplicating Co** ....312 733-3353
7959 W Grand Ave Elmwood Park (60707) ***(G-9974)***
**Rapid Displays Inc (PA)** ....773 927-5000
4300 W 47th St Chicago (60632) ***(G-6291)***
**Rapid Displays Inc** ....773 927-1500
4300 W 47th St Chicago (60632) ***(G-6292)***
**Rapid Electroplating Process** ....708 344-2504
2901 W Soffel Ave Melrose Park (60160) ***(G-14685)***
**Rapid Execution Services LLC** ....312 789-4358
141 W Jackson Blvd 300a Chicago (60604) ***(G-6293)***
**Rapid Foods Inc** ....708 366-0321
1007 Geneva St Shorewood (60404) ***(G-19931)***
**Rapid Line Industries Inc** ....815 727-4362
455 N Ottawa St Ste 1 Joliet (60432) ***(G-12563)***
**Rapid Manufacturing Inc** ....847 458-0888
1320 Chase St Ste 4 Algonquin (60102) ***(G-406)***
**Rapid Print** ....309 673-0826
934 N Bourland Ave Peoria (61606) ***(G-17440)***
**Rapid Printing Service, South Holland** *Also called David H Vander Ploeg* ***(G-20260)***
**Rapid Wire Forms Inc** ....773 586-6600
6932 W 62nd St Chicago (60638) ***(G-6294)***
**Rapp Cabinets & Woodworks Inc** ....618 736-2955
501 E Illinois Hwy 142 Dahlgren (62828) ***(G-7692)***
**Rare Birds Inc** ....847 259-7286
321 E Rand Rd Arlington Heights (60004) ***(G-828)***
**Rasmussen Press Inc** ....
606 E Green St Bensenville (60106) ***(G-1976)***
**Rasoi Resturaunt** ....847 455-8888
15 Clair Ct Roselle (60172) ***(G-18965)***
**Rathje Enterprises Inc (PA)** ....217 423-2593
1845 N 22nd St Decatur (62526) ***(G-7932)***
**Rathje Enterprises Inc** ....217 443-0022
19 Withner St Danville (61832) ***(G-7763)***
**Rational Cooking Systems Inc** ....224 366-3500
1701 Golf Rd Ste C-LI Rolling Meadows (60008) ***(G-18772)***
**Rauckman High Voltage Sales** ....618 239-0399
37 Ednick Dr Swansea (62226) ***(G-20781)***
**Rauckman Utility Products LLC** ....618 234-0001
33 Empire Dr Belleville (62220) ***(G-1668)***
**Ravco Incorporated** ....815 725-9095
1313 Colorado Ave Joliet (60435) ***(G-12564)***
**Raven Energy LLC** ....217 532-3983
925 S Main St Ste 2 Hillsboro (62049) ***(G-11899)***
**Raven Tree Press LLC** ....800 323-8270
6213 Factory Rd Ste B Crystal Lake (60014) ***(G-7637)***
**Ravens Wood Pharmacy** ....708 667-0525
4211 N Cicero Ave Chicago (60641) ***(G-6295)***
**Ravenscroft Inc** ....630 513-9911
473 Dunham Rd Ste 209 Saint Charles (60174) ***(G-19250)***

**Ravicti, Lake Forest** *Also called Horizon Therapeutics Inc* ***(G-12907)***
**Ravinia Metals, Itasca** *Also called Millenia Metals LLC* ***(G-12317)***
**Raw Thrills Inc** ....847 679-8373
5441 Fargo Ave Skokie (60077) ***(G-20071)***
**Rawnature5 LLC** ....312 800-3239
3026 W Carroll Ave Chicago (60612) ***(G-6296)***
**Ray Tool & Engineering Inc** ....630 587-0000
2440 Production Dr Saint Charles (60174) ***(G-19251)***
**Ray's Booths, Chicago** *Also called Booths and Upholstery By Ray* ***(G-4144)***
**Rayalco Inc** ....847 692-7422
712 S Fairview Ave Park Ridge (60068) ***(G-17219)***
**Rayalco Software, Park Ridge** *Also called Rayalco Inc* ***(G-17219)***
**Raycar Gear & Machine Company** ....815 874-3948
6125 11th St Rockford (61109) ***(G-18549)***
**Raydyot US, Franklin Park** *Also called Koehler Enterprises Inc* ***(G-10513)***
**Rayes Boiler & Welding Ltd** ....847 675-6655
8252 Christiana Ave Skokie (60076) ***(G-20072)***
**Raymond Earl Fine Woodworking** ....309 565-7661
201 S Main St Hanna City (61536) ***(G-11570)***
**Raymond Alstom** ....630 369-3700
2151 Fisher Dr Naperville (60563) ***(G-15739)***
**Raymond Brothers Inc** ....847 928-9300
3919 Wesley Ter Schiller Park (60176) ***(G-19866)***
**Raymond D Wright** ....618 783-2206
35 Homestead Dr Newton (62448) ***(G-15947)***
**Raynor Garage Door, Dixon** *Also called Neisewander Enterprises Inc* ***(G-8337)***
**Raynor Garage Doors, Dixon** *Also called Raynor Mfg Co* ***(G-8341)***
**Raynor Garage Doors, Dixon** *Also called Raynor Mfg Co* ***(G-8342)***
**Raynor Mfg Co (HQ)** ....815 288-1431
1101 E River Rd Dixon (61021) ***(G-8341)***
**Raynor Mfg Co** ....815 288-1431
1101 E River Rd Dixon (61021) ***(G-8342)***
**Rays Countertop Shop Inc** ....217 483-2514
125 Robb St Glenarm (62536) ***(G-10997)***
**Rays Electrical Service LLC** ....847 214-2944
37w904 Us Highway 20 Elgin (60124) ***(G-9161)***
**Rays Machine & Mfg Co Inc** ....309 699-2121
419 Truck Haven Rd East Peoria (61611) ***(G-8730)***
**Rays Power Wshg Svc Peggy Ray** ....618 939-6306
318 Bradford Ln Waterloo (62298) ***(G-21405)***
**Raytech Machining Fabrication** ....618 932-2511
10925 Mainline Rd West Frankfort (62896) ***(G-21816)***
**Raytheon Company** ....630 295-6394
4110 Winnetka Ave Rolling Meadows (60008) ***(G-18773)***
**Raytrans Distribution Svcs Inc (HQ)** ....708 503-9940
600 W Chicago Ave Ste 725 Chicago (60654) ***(G-6297)***
**Raze Vapor** ....415 596-2697
329 W Evergreen Ave Chicago (60610) ***(G-6298)***
**Razny Jewelers Ltd (PA)** ....630 932-4900
1501 W Lake St Ste 1 Addison (60101) ***(G-270)***
**RB Manufacturing & Electronics** ....815 522-3100
140 North St Kirkland (60146) ***(G-12717)***
**Rbc Services, Aurora** *Also called McNish Corporation* ***(G-1184)***
**Rbj Inc** ....309 344-5066
796 S Pearl St Galesburg (61401) ***(G-10772)***
**Rci, Milan** *Also called R C Industrial Inc* ***(G-14801)***
**Rcl Electronics** ....630 834-0156
826 S Iowa Ave Addison (60101) ***(G-271)***
**RCM Industries Inc (PA)** ....847 455-1950
3021 Cullerton St Franklin Park (60131) ***(G-10571)***
**RCM Industries Inc** ....847 455-1950
161 Carpenter Ave Wheeling (60090) ***(G-22133)***
**RCM Smith Inc** ....309 786-8833
507 34th Ave Rock Island (61201) ***(G-18197)***
**RCP Publications Inc** ....773 227-4066
3449 N Sheffield Ave Chicago (60657) ***(G-6299)***
**Rd Daily Enterprises** ....847 872-7632
911 Fulton Ave Winthrop Harbor (60096) ***(G-22320)***
**Rda Inc** ....815 427-8444
400 N 3rd Ave Saint Anne (60964) ***(G-19125)***
**Rdc Linear Enterprises LLC** ....815 547-1106
6593 Revlon Dr Dr1 Belvidere (61008) ***(G-1782)***
**RDF Inc** ....618 273-4141
2909 Richardson St Eldorado (62930) ***(G-8922)***
**Rdh Inc of Rockford** ....815 874-9421
3445 Lonergan Dr Rockford (61109) ***(G-18550)***
**Rdi Group Inc** ....630 773-4900
1025 W Thorndale Ave Itasca (60143) ***(G-12347)***
**Rdn Manufacturing Company Inc** ....630 893-4500
160 Covington Dr Bloomingdale (60108) ***(G-2130)***
**RDS Digital, Chicago** *Also called Rightsource Digital Svcs Inc* ***(G-6357)***
**RE Met Corp** ....312 733-6700
2246 W Hubbard St Chicago (60612) ***(G-6300)***
**RE-Do-It Corp** ....708 343-7125
1950 Beach St Broadview (60155) ***(G-2607)***
**Re-Maid Incorporated** ....815 315-0500
1440 Sylvan Ct Freeport (61032) ***(G-10683)***
**Re-Source Building Products, Elgin** *Also called Plastival Inc* ***(G-9142)***
**Reach Chicago LLC** ....312 923-1028
350 N Orleans St Fl 10-S Chicago (60654) ***(G-6301)***
**React Computer Services Inc** ....630 323-6200
7654 Plaza Ct Willowbrook (60527) ***(G-22229)***
**Ready Access Inc** ....800 621-5045
1815 Arthur Dr West Chicago (60185) ***(G-21763)***
**Ready Inc** ....630 501-1352
231 E Fremont Ave Apt 209 Elmhurst (60126) ***(G-9926)***
**Ready Mix Concrete, Monee** *Also called Wille Bros Co* ***(G-15009)***
**Ready Press** ....847 358-8655
340 W Colfax St Palatine (60067) ***(G-17066)***
**Reagent Chemical & RES Inc** ....618 271-8140
1700 S 20th St East Saint Louis (62207) ***(G-8766)***
**Real Alloy Recycling Inc** ....708 758-8888
400 E Lincoln Hwy Chicago Heights (60411) ***(G-7120)***
**Real Estate Communications, Chicago** *Also called Law Bulletin Publishing Co* ***(G-5470)***
**Real Estate News Corp** ....773 866-9900
3525 W Peterson Ave T10 Chicago (60659) ***(G-6302)***
**Real Neon Inc** ....630 543-0995
113 W Official Rd Addison (60101) ***(G-272)***
**Real Taste Noodles Mfg Inc** ....312 738-1893
1838 S Canal St Chicago (60616) ***(G-6303)***
**Real Times Inc of Illinois** ....312 225-2400
200 S Michigan Ave # 1700 Chicago (60604) ***(G-6304)***
**Real Times II LLC (PA)** ....312 225-2400
4445 S Dr Mrtn Lther King Martin Luther King Chicago (60653) ***(G-6305)***
**Realclearpolitics (PA)** ....773 255-5846
6160 N Cicero Ave Ste 410 Chicago (60646) ***(G-6306)***
**Realize Inc** ....312 566-8759
1803 W 95th St 509 Chicago (60643) ***(G-6307)***
**Realize.ai, Chicago** *Also called Realize Inc* ***(G-6307)***
**Really Useful Boxes Inc** ....847 238-0444
2791 Katherine Way Elk Grove Village (60007) ***(G-9710)***
**Realt Images Inc** ....217 567-3487
172 Williamsburg Hl A Tower Hill (62571) ***(G-20980)***
**REALTOR MAGAZINE, Chicago** *Also called National Association Realtors* ***(G-5857)***
**Realtor Magazine** ....312 329-1928
430 N Michigan Ave Fl 9 Chicago (60611) ***(G-6308)***
**Realty World, Warsaw** *Also called Midwest Mktg/Pdctn Mfg Co* ***(G-21370)***
**Realwheels Corporation** ....847 662-7722
3940 Tannahill Dr Gurnee (60031) ***(G-11499)***
**Ream's Meat Market, Elburn** *Also called Elburn Market Inc* ***(G-8884)***
**Reason's Locker, Buffalo Prairie** *Also called Reasons Inc* ***(G-2797)***
**Reasons Inc** ....309 537-3424
18510 206th Sw Buffalo Prairie (61237) ***(G-2797)***
**REB Steel Equipment Corp (PA)** ....773 252-0400
4556 W Grand Ave Chicago (60639) ***(G-6309)***
**REB Storage Systems Intl, Chicago** *Also called REB Steel Equipment Corp* ***(G-6309)***
**Reba Machine Corp** ....630 595-1272
767 N Edgewood Ave Wood Dale (60191) ***(G-22416)***
**Rebco Machine Specialties Inc** ....630 852-3419
138 E Quincy St Westmont (60559) ***(G-21917)***
**Rebechini Studio Inc (PA)** ....847 364-8600
680 Fargo Ave Elk Grove Village (60007) ***(G-9711)***
**Rebel Brands LLC** ....312 804-0009
600 20th St Wilmette (60091) ***(G-22264)***
**Rebel Screeners Inc** ....312 525-2670
820 W Jackson Blvd # 400 Chicago (60607) ***(G-6310)***
**Reber Welding Service** ....217 774-3441
142 S Washington St Shelbyville (62565) ***(G-19914)***
**Rebuilders Enterprises Inc** ....708 430-0030
9004 S Octavia Ave Bridgeview (60455) ***(G-2523)***
**Receiving D84v K2 Complex, North Chicago** *Also called Abbott Laboratories* ***(G-16160)***
**Reclamation LLC** ....510 441-2305
1720 N Elston Ave Chicago (60642) ***(G-6311)***
**Reco, Roodhouse** *Also called Roodhouse Envelope Co* ***(G-18884)***
**Reco of IL Inc** ....630 898-2010
1669 Dearborn Ave Aurora (60505) ***(G-1208)***
**Recognitions, Aviston** *Also called Mhwp* ***(G-1247)***
**Reconserve of Illinois Inc** ....708 354-4641
6160 River Rd Hodgkins (60525) ***(G-11981)***
**Recora Company, North Aurora** *Also called Calo Corporation* ***(G-16122)***
**Record Inc** ....312 985-7270
207 E Ohio St Ste 164 Chicago (60611) ***(G-6312)***
**Record Printing & Publishing, Millstadt** *Also called Metro Printing & Pubg Inc* ***(G-14829)***
**Recreation Management, Palatine** *Also called Cab Communications Inc* ***(G-17007)***
**Recsolu Inc** ....312 517-3200
55 E Monroe St Ste 3600 Chicago (60603) ***(G-6313)***
**Recycled Paper Greetings Inc** ....773 348-6410
111 N Canal St Ste 700 Chicago (60606) ***(G-6314)***
**Red Arrow Sales, McHenry** *Also called Midwest Water Group Inc* ***(G-14534)***
**Red Bud Industries, Red Bud** *Also called Red Bud Industries Inc* ***(G-17947)***
**Red Bud Industries Inc** ....618 282-3801
200 B And E Industrial Dr Red Bud (62278) ***(G-17947)***
**Red Center, Northbrook** *Also called Regional Emrgncy Dispatch Ctr* ***(G-16354)***
**Red Devil Manufacturing Co** ....847 215-1377
422 Mercantile Ct Wheeling (60090) ***(G-22134)***

**Red Hen Bread, Elmhurst** *Also called Red Hen Corporation* ***(G-9928)***
**Red Hen Bread Inc** 773 342-6823
745 N Larch Ave Elmhurst (60126) ***(G-9927)***
**Red Hen Corporation (PA)** 312 433-0436
745 N Larch Ave Elmhurst (60126) ***(G-9928)***
**Red Hill Lava Products Inc (PA)** 800 528-2765
8002 31st St W Rock Island (61201) ***(G-18198)***
**Red Mango Rockford** 815 282-1020
6876 Spring Creek Rd # 118 Rockford (61114) ***(G-18551)***
**Red Nose Inc** 309 925-7313
1408 Downing Ct Tremont (61568) ***(G-20985)***
**Red Parrot Juices, Lemont** *Also called Key Colony Inc* ***(G-13237)***
**Red Streak Holdings Company** 312 321-3000
350 N Orleans St Fl 10-S Chicago (60654) ***(G-6315)***
**Red Wing Brands America Inc** 815 394-1328
845 S Perryvil Rd Unit 1 Rockford (61108) ***(G-18552)***
**Red Wings Shoe Store 276, Rockford** *Also called Red Wing Brands America Inc* ***(G-18552)***
**Red's Muffler Shop, Urbana** *Also called Muffler* ***(G-21095)***
**Red-E-Mix LLC** 618 654-2166
405 Main St Highland (62249) ***(G-11808)***
**Red-E-Mix Transportation LLC** 618 654-2166
405 Main St Highland (62249) ***(G-11809)***
**Redbox Workshop Ltd** 773 478-7077
3121 N Rockwell St Chicago (60618) ***(G-6316)***
**Redd Remedies Inc** 815 614-2083
211 S Quincy Ave Bradley (60915) ***(G-2430)***
**Reddi-Pac Inc (HQ)** 847 657-5222
3700 W Lake Ave Glenview (60026) ***(G-11191)***
**Redeen Engraving Inc** 847 593-6500
670 Chase Ave Elk Grove Village (60007) ***(G-9712)***
**Redi-Strip Company** 630 529-2442
100 Central Ave Roselle (60172) ***(G-18966)***
**Redi-Weld & Mfg Co Inc** 815 455-4460
8711 Pyott Rd Lake In The Hills (60156) ***(G-13004)***
**Redin Parts Inc** 815 398-1010
1922 7th St Ste 4d Rockford (61104) ***(G-18553)***
**Redin Production Machine, Rockford** *Also called Redin Parts Inc* ***(G-18553)***
**Reding Optics Inc** 708 301-2020
13231 W 143rd St Ste 101 Lockport (60491) ***(G-13741)***
**Rediscover Music, Downers Grove** *Also called Aztec Corporation* ***(G-8391)***
**Redline Press** 630 690-9828
1613 Ogden Ave Lisle (60532) ***(G-13650)***
**Redshelf Inc** 312 878-8586
500 N Dearborn St # 1200 Chicago (60654) ***(G-6317)***
**Redshelf/Virdocs, Chicago** *Also called Redshelf Inc* ***(G-6317)***
**Reed-Union Corporation (PA)** 312 644-3200
875 N Michigan Ave # 3718 Chicago (60611) ***(G-6318)***
**Reedy Industries Inc (PA)** 847 729-9450
2440 Ravine Way Ste 200 Glenview (60025) ***(G-11192)***
**Reef Development Inc** 618 842-7711
Rr 3 Fairfield (62837) ***(G-10152)***
**Reel Life Dvd LLC** 708 579-1360
5233 Clausen Ave Western Springs (60558) ***(G-21872)***
**Reel Mate Mfg Co** 708 423-8005
10113 Buell Ct Oak Lawn (60453) ***(G-16643)***
**Reeves Lure Co** 217 864-3493
4165 Shaw Rd Lovington (61937) ***(G-14012)***
**Refined Haystack LLC** 773 627-3534
230 W Superior St 2f Chicago (60654) ***(G-6319)***
**Refiners House** 708 922-0772
20227 Overland Trl Olympia Fields (60461) ***(G-16805)***
**Reflection Software Inc** 630 585-2300
900 S Frontenac St # 100 Aurora (60504) ***(G-1073)***
**Reflections In Glass, Lake Barrington** *Also called T J M & Associates Inc* ***(G-12825)***
**Reflejos Publications LLC** 847 806-1111
155 E Algonquin Rd Arlington Heights (60005) ***(G-829)***
**Reflex Fitness Products Inc** 309 756-1050
1130 15th Ave W Milan (61264) ***(G-14802)***
**Refreshment Services Inc (PA)** 217 223-8600
1121 Locust St Quincy (62301) ***(G-17886)***
**Refreshment Services Inc** 217 522-8841
1337 E Cook St Springfield (62703) ***(G-20511)***
**Refreshment Services Inc** 217 429-5415
2112 N Brush College Rd Decatur (62526) ***(G-7933)***
**Refrigerated Dough Division, Downers Grove** *Also called Earthgrains Refrigertd Dough P* ***(G-8438)***
**Reg Seneca LLC** 888 734-8686
614 Shipyard Rd Seneca (61360) ***(G-19889)***
**Regal Converting Co Inc** 630 257-3581
14503 S Gougar Rd Unit 1 Lockport (60491) ***(G-13742)***
**Regal Cut Stone LLC** 773 826-8796
4213 W Chicago Ave Chicago (60651) ***(G-6320)***
**Regal Cutting Tools Inc** 815 389-3461
5330 E Rockton Rd Roscoe (61073) ***(G-18912)***
**Regal Health Foods Intl Inc** 773 252-1044
3705 W Grand Ave Chicago (60651) ***(G-6321)***
**Regal Johnson Co** 630 885-0688
229 Christine Way Bolingbrook (60440) ***(G-2364)***
**Regal Linen, Highland** *Also called Mount Vernon Mills* ***(G-11804)***
**Regal Manufacturing Co** 630 628-6867
844 S Kay Ave Addison (60101) ***(G-273)***
**Regal Seating Company, Addison** *Also called Regal Manufacturing Co* ***(G-273)***
**Regal Steel Erectors LLC** 847 888-3500
850 Tollgate Rd Elgin (60123) ***(G-9162)***
**Regency Crystal, Wauconda** *Also called Amkine Inc* ***(G-21442)***
**Regency Custom Woodworking** 815 689-2117
215 E Van Alstyne St Cullom (60929) ***(G-7683)***
**Regency Hand Laundry** 773 871-3950
2739 N Racine Ave Chicago (60614) ***(G-6322)***
**Regenex Corp** 815 663-2003
1 Wolfer Industrial Park Spring Valley (61362) ***(G-20378)***
**Regent Automotive Engineering** 773 889-5744
2107 N Cicero Ave Chicago (60639) ***(G-6323)***
**Regent Window Fashions LLC** 773 871-6400
917 W Irving Park Rd Chicago (60613) ***(G-6324)***
**Reggios Pizza Inc (PA)** 773 488-1411
340 W 83rd St Chicago (60620) ***(G-6325)***
**Regional Emrgncy Dispatch Ctr** 847 498-5748
1842 Shermer Rd Northbrook (60062) ***(G-16354)***
**Regional Ready Mix LLC** 815 562-1901
15051 E Lind Rd Rochelle (61068) ***(G-18104)***
**Regis Chemical Company, Morton Grove** *Also called Regis Technologies Inc* ***(G-15232)***
**Regis Technologies Inc** 847 967-6000
8210 Austin Ave Morton Grove (60053) ***(G-15232)***
**Register Publishing Co** 618 253-7146
35 S Vine St Harrisburg (62946) ***(G-11603)***
**Register-Mail (HQ)** 309 343-7181
140 S Prairie St Galesburg (61401) ***(G-10773)***
**Regunathan & Assoc Inc** 630 653-0387
1490 Jasper Dr Wheaton (60189) ***(G-21975)***
**Rehabilitation and Vocational** 618 833-5344
214 W Davie St Anna (62906) ***(G-608)***
**Rehkemper & Sons Inc (PA)** 618 526-2269
17817 Saint Rose Rd Breese (62230) ***(G-2447)***
**Rehling & Associates Inc** 630 941-3560
1010 S Swain Ave Elmhurst (60126) ***(G-9929)***
**Rehobot Inc** 815 385-7777
3980 W Albany St Ste 1 McHenry (60050) ***(G-14550)***
**Reichel Hardware Company Inc** 630 762-7394
1820 Wallace Ave Ste 122 Saint Charles (60174) ***(G-19252)***
**Reid Communications Inc** 847 741-9700
450 Shepard Dr Ste 11 Elgin (60123) ***(G-9163)***
**Reign Print Solutions Inc** 847 590-7091
550 W Campus Dr Arlington Heights (60004) ***(G-830)***
**Reilly Communication Group** 630 756-1225
3030 W Salt Creek Ln # 201 Arlington Heights (60005) ***(G-831)***
**Reilly Foam Corp** 630 392-2680
920 Frontenac Rd Naperville (60563) ***(G-15740)***
**Rein Electric** 224 433-6936
700 E Park Ave Libertyville (60048) ***(G-13375)***
**Reina Imaging, Crystal Lake** *Also called X-Ray Cassette Repair Co Inc* ***(G-7678)***
**Reino Tool & Manufacturing Co** 773 588-5800
3668 N Elston Ave Chicago (60618) ***(G-6326)***
**Reklama, Northbrook** *Also called Advertising Advice Inc* ***(G-16200)***
**Relay Services Mfg Corp** 773 252-2700
1300 N Pulaski Rd Ste 12 Chicago (60651) ***(G-6327)***
**Relay Systems America Inc** 815 730-0100
3225 Corporate Dr Joliet (60431) ***(G-12565)***
**Relco Locomotives Inc (PA)** 630 968-0670
1001 Warrenville Rd # 201 Lisle (60532) ***(G-13651)***
**Reliable Appliance and Ref** 847 581-9520
7443 Emerson St Morton Grove (60053) ***(G-15233)***
**Reliable Asphalt Corporation (PA)** 773 254-1121
3741 S Pulaski Rd Chicago (60623) ***(G-6328)***
**Reliable Asphalt Corporation** 630 497-8700
2252 Southwind Blvd Bartlett (60103) ***(G-1368)***
**Reliable Autotech Usa LLC** 815 945-7838
600 N Division St Chenoa (61726) ***(G-3635)***
**Reliable Container Inc** 630 543-6131
210 S Addison Rd Addison (60101) ***(G-274)***
**Reliable Delivery Solutions, O Fallon** *Also called Acn Indpndent Bus Rprsentative* ***(G-16460)***
**Reliable Die Service Inc** 708 458-5155
6700 W 74th St Bedford Park (60638) ***(G-1577)***
**Reliable Galvanizing Company (PA)** 773 651-2500
819 W 88th St Chicago (60620) ***(G-6329)***
**Reliable Machine Company** 815 968-8803
1327 10th Ave Rockford (61104) ***(G-18554)***
**Reliable Mail Services Inc** 847 677-6245
5116 Grove St Skokie (60077) ***(G-20073)***
**Reliable Metal Stamping Co Inc** 773 625-1177
9244 Parklane Ave Franklin Park (60131) ***(G-10572)***
**Reliable Plating Corporation** 312 421-4747
1538 W Lake St Chicago (60607) ***(G-6330)***
**Reliable Sand and Gravel Co** 815 385-5020
2121 S River Rd Ste B McHenry (60051) ***(G-14551)***
**Reliance Dental Mfg Co** 708 597-6694
5805 W 117th Pl Alsip (60803) ***(G-518)***
**Reliance Gear Corporation** 630 543-6640
205 W Factory Rd Addison (60101) ***(G-275)***

**Reliance Specialty Pdts Inc** ....847 640-8923
855 Morse Ave Elk Grove Village (60007) *(G-9713)*
**Reliance Tool & Mfg Co (PA)** ....847 695-1235
900 N State St Ste 101 Elgin (60123) *(G-9164)*
**Reliance Tool & Mfg Co** ....847 455-4350
11333 W Melrose St Franklin Park (60131) *(G-10573)*
**Reliance Tool Inc** ....815 636-2770
946 River Ln Loves Park (61111) *(G-13981)*
**Reliefwatch Inc** ....646 678-2336
1425 E 53rd St Fl 2 Chicago (60615) *(G-6331)*
**Reload Sales Inc** ....618 588-2866
418 Plum Ln New Baden (62265) *(G-15864)*
**Relx Inc** ....309 689-1000
8512 N Allen Rd Peoria (61615) *(G-17441)*
**Remco Technology Inc** ....847 329-8090
7441 Channel Rd Skokie (60076) *(G-20074)*
**Remet Corporation** ....480 766-3464
1540 E Dundee Rd Ste 170 Palatine (60074) *(G-17067)*
**Remin Kart A Bag, Joliet** *Also called Remin Laboratories Inc (G-12566)*
**Remin Laboratories Inc** ....815 723-1940
510 Manhattan Rd Joliet (60433) *(G-12566)*
**Remington Industries Inc** ....815 385-1987
3521 Chapel Hill Rd Johnsburg (60051) *(G-12441)*
**Remke Industries Inc (PA)** ....847 541-3780
310 Chaddick Dr Wheeling (60090) *(G-22135)*
**Remke Industries Inc** ....847 325-7835
310 Chaddick Dr Wheeling (60090) *(G-22136)*
**Remke Printing Inc** ....847 520-7300
1678 S Wolf Rd Wheeling (60090) *(G-22137)*
**Remmers Welding and Machine** ....815 689-2765
17809 N 3500 East Rd Cullom (60929) *(G-7684)*
**Remmert Studios Inc** ....815 933-4867
8834 W 140th St Unit 1b Orland Park (60462) *(G-16887)*
**Remodeler's Supply Center, Chicago** *Also called Logan Square Aluminum Sup Inc (G-5532)*
**Remodelers Supply Center, Chicago** *Also called Logan Square Aluminum Sup Inc (G-5530)*
**Remuriate LLC (PA)** ....815 220-5050
654 1st St Ste 200 La Salle (61301) *(G-12783)*
**Remuriate Technologies, La Salle** *Also called Remuriate LLC (G-12783)*
**Renaissance SSP Holdings Inc (HQ)** ....210 476-8194
272 E Deerpath Ste 350 Lake Forest (60045) *(G-12951)*
**Rend Lake Carbide Inc** ....618 438-0160
11601 Skylane Dr Benton (62812) *(G-2039)*
**Renegade Steel** ....716 903-2506
1458 S Canal St Chicago (60607) *(G-6332)*
**Renew Packaging LLC** ....312 421-6699
2444 W 16th St Ste 4r Chicago (60608) *(G-6333)*
**Renner & Co** ....847 639-4900
160 Chicago St Cary (60013) *(G-3366)*
**Renner Quarries Ltd (PA)** ....815 288-6699
1700 S Galena Ave Ste 116 Dixon (61021) *(G-8343)*
**Rensel-Chicago Inc (PA)** ....773 235-2100
2300 N Kilbourn Ave Chicago (60639) *(G-6334)*
**Rent-A-Center Inc** ....773 376-8883
3145 S Ashland Ave # 103 Chicago (60608) *(G-6335)*
**Rentech Development Corp** ....815 747-3101
16675 Us Highway 20 W East Dubuque (61025) *(G-8620)*
**Renu Electronics Private Ltd** ....630 879-8412
336 Mckee St Batavia (60510) *(G-1491)*
**Replace Air, Glendale Heights** *Also called Schubert Environmental Eqp Inc (G-11067)*
**Replacement Arts Inc** ....708 922-0580
14836 S Mckinley Ave Posen (60469) *(G-17735)*
**Replacement Services LLC** ....618 398-9880
15 N 1st St Belleville (62220) *(G-1669)*
**Replay S Disc Cook-Kankaee LLC** ....312 371-5018
25526 S Devonshire Ln Monee (60449) *(G-15000)*
**Replogle Globe Partners, Hillside** *Also called Herff Jones LLC (G-11918)*
**Reporter Inc (PA)** ....217 932-5211
216 S Central Ave Casey (62420) *(G-3391)*
**Reporter Money Saver, Mendota** *Also called Mendota Reporter (G-14726)*
**Repperts Warehouse Office Furn, Anna** *Also called Gazette Democrat (G-603)*
**Repro-Graphics Inc** ....847 439-1775
1900 Arthur Ave Elk Grove Village (60007) *(G-9714)*
**Reprographics (PA)** ....815 477-1018
26 Crystal Lake Plz Crystal Lake (60014) *(G-7638)*
**Republic Drill** ....708 865-7666
2058 N 15th Ave Melrose Park (60160) *(G-14686)*
**Republic Group Inc (PA)** ....800 288-8888
2301 Ravine Way Glenview (60025) *(G-11193)*
**Republic Oil Co Inc** ....618 842-7591
1508 W Delaware St Fairfield (62837) *(G-10153)*
**Republic Times LLC** ....618 939-3814
205 W Mill St Waterloo (62298) *(G-21406)*
**Republic Tobacco, Glenview** *Also called Top Tobacco LP (G-11210)*
**Request Electric** ....217 629-7789
8290 E State Route 54 # 1 Riverton (62561) *(G-18034)*
**Rescar Co, Downers Grove** *Also called Rescar Industries Inc (G-8513)*
**Rescar Industries Inc** ....618 875-3234
501 Monsanto Ave East Saint Louis (62206) *(G-8767)*
**Rescar Industries Inc (PA)** ....630 963-1114
1101 31st St Ste 250 Downers Grove (60515) *(G-8513)*
**Resco 8 LLC** ....773 772-4422
1927 W North Ave Chicago (60622) *(G-6336)*
**Resco Products Co** ....847 455-3776
9101 Belden Ave Franklin Park (60131) *(G-10574)*
**Research & Technology Center, Libertyville** *Also called USG Corporation (G-13396)*
**Research and Testing Worx Inc** ....815 734-7346
112 E Hitt St Mount Morris (61054) *(G-15299)*
**Research Flour Service Pdts Co, Monticello** *Also called McShares Inc (G-15080)*
**Research In Motion Rf Inc** ....815 444-1095
500 Coventry Ln Ste 260 Crystal Lake (60014) *(G-7639)*
**Research Mannikins Inc** ....618 426-3456
143 Lupine Ln Ava (62907) *(G-1242)*
**Research Press Company** ....217 352-3273
2612 N Mattis Ave Champaign (61822) *(G-3532)*
**Research Technology Intl Co (PA)** ....847 677-3000
4700 W Chase Ave Lincolnwood (60712) *(G-13532)*
**Residntial Stl Fabricators Inc** ....847 695-3400
1555 Gilpen Ave South Elgin (60177) *(G-20223)*
**Resin Exchange Inc** ....630 628-7266
851 S Westgate St Addison (60101) *(G-276)*
**Resinite Corporation** ....847 537-4250
1033 Noel Ave Wheeling (60090) *(G-22138)*
**Resins Inc** ....847 884-0025
2200 W Higgins Rd Ste 204 Hoffman Estates (60169) *(G-12043)*
**Resist-A-Line Industries Inc** ....815 650-3177
214 Elm St Joliet (60433) *(G-12567)*
**Resolute Industrial LLC** ....800 537-9675
298 Messner Dr Wheeling (60090) *(G-22139)*
**Resolution Systems Inc** ....616 392-8001
1189 Wilmette Ave Wilmette (60091) *(G-22265)*
**Resonance Medical LLC** ....229 292-2094
222 Merchandise Mart Plz Chicago (60654) *(G-6337)*
**Resource Plastics Inc** ....708 389-3558
5623 W 115th St Alsip (60803) *(G-519)*
**Respa Pharmaceuticals Inc** ....630 543-3333
625 W Factory Rd Addison (60101) *(G-277)*
**Respect Incorporated** ....815 806-1907
15555 Tyndall Ct Manhattan (60442) *(G-14170)*
**Respironics Inc** ....708 923-6200
12515 S 82nd Ave Palos Park (60464) *(G-17130)*
**Restorations Unlimited II Inc** ....847 639-5818
304 Jandus Rd Cary (60013) *(G-3367)*
**Restoring Path** ....773 424-7023
1406 W 64th St Chicago (60636) *(G-6338)*
**Retail Window Treatments, Park Ridge** *Also called Drapery House Inc (G-17191)*
**Retailer Watch Newsletter, Evanston** *Also called S R Bastien Co (G-10093)*
**Retailout Inc** ....312 786-4312
719 S State St Chicago (60605) *(G-6339)*
**Retmap Inc** ....312 224-8938
34435 N Bobolink Trl Grayslake (60030) *(G-11361)*
**Retondo Enterprises Inc** ....630 837-8130
1539 Brandy Pkwy Streamwood (60107) *(G-20671)*
**Rettick Enterprises Inc** ....309 275-4967
13958 Roberto Rd Ste 1 Bloomington (61705) *(G-2218)*
**Reum Corporation** ....847 625-7386
140 S Dearborn St Ste 420 Chicago (60603) *(G-6340)*
**Revcor Inc (PA)** ....847 428-4411
251 Edwards Ave Carpentersville (60110) *(G-3301)*
**Revcor Inc** ....847 428-4411
250 Illinois St Carpentersville (60110) *(G-3302)*
**Revelle Resources Inc** ....217 875-7336
275 Hickory Point Ct Forsyth (62535) *(G-10271)*
**Revere Metals LLC** ....708 945-3992
21200 S La Grange Rd # 260 Frankfort (60423) *(G-10357)*
**Review** ....309 659-2761
910 Albany St Erie (61250) *(G-9993)*
**Review** ....618 997-2222
1120 N Carbon St Ste 100 Marion (62959) *(G-14285)*
**Review Graphics Inc** ....815 623-2570
10760 Main St Roscoe (61073) *(G-18913)*
**Review Printing Co Inc** ....309 788-7094
1326 40th St Rock Island (61201) *(G-18199)*
**Review, The, Morrison** *Also called Wns Publications Inc (G-15149)*
**Reviss Services Inc** ....847 680-4522
175 E Hawthorn Pkwy # 142 Vernon Hills (60061) *(G-21192)*
**Revolution Brands LLC** ....847 902-3320
12327 Bartelt Ct Huntley (60142) *(G-12173)*
**Revolution Companies Inc** ....800 826-4083
332 S Michigan Ave # 1032 Chicago (60604) *(G-6341)*
**Rex Carton Company Inc** ....773 581-4115
4528 W 51st St Chicago (60632) *(G-6342)*
**Rex Energy Corporation** ....618 943-8700
Rr 1 Box 197 Bridgeport (62417) *(G-2454)*
**Rex Gauge Division, Buffalo Grove** *Also called Schultes Precision Mfg Inc (G-2763)*
**Rex Morioka** ....847 651-9400
4257 Wesley Ter Schiller Park (60176) *(G-19867)*
**Rex Radiator and Welding Co (PA)** ....312 421-1531
1440 W 38th St Chicago (60609) *(G-6343)*

**Rex Radiator and Welding Co** ........ 630 595-4664
367 Evergreen Ave Bensenville (60106) ***(G-1977)***
**Rex Radiator and Welding Co** ........ 815 725-6655
14 Meadow Ave Unit 1 Rockdale (60436) ***(G-18230)***
**Rex Radiator and Welding Co** ........ 847 428-1112
578 Rock Road Dr Ste 5 East Dundee (60118) ***(G-8655)***
**Rex Radiator Sales & Dist, Bensenville** *Also called Rex Radiator and Welding Co* ***(G-1977)***
**Rex Vault Co** ........ 618 783-2416
E Rte 33 Newton (62448) ***(G-15948)***
**Rexam, Buffalo Grove** *Also called Bprex Healthcare Packaging Inc* ***(G-2667)***
**Rexam Beverage Can Company (HQ)** ........ 773 399-3000
8770 W Bryn Mawr Ave Fl 8 Chicago (60631) ***(G-6344)***
**Rexam Beverage Can Company** ........ 773 247-4646
1101 W 43rd St Chicago (60609) ***(G-6345)***
**Rexam Beverage Can Company** ........ 847 238-3200
2520 Lively Blvd Elk Grove Village (60007) ***(G-9715)***
**Rexam Devices LLC** ........ 847 325-3629
800 Corporate Grove Dr Buffalo Grove (60089) ***(G-2758)***
**Rexnord Industries LLC** ........ 847 520-1428
2400 Curtiss St Downers Grove (60515) ***(G-8514)***
**Rexnord Industries LLC** ........ 630 969-1770
2400 Curtiss St Downers Grove (60515) ***(G-8515)***
**Rexnord Industries LLC** ........ 630 719-2345
2324 Curtiss St Downers Grove (60515) ***(G-8516)***
**Reyco Precision Welding Inc (PA)** ........ 847 593-2947
320 E Il Route 22 Lake Zurich (60047) ***(G-13122)***
**Reynolds Consumer Products Co, Lake Forest** *Also called Reynolds Consumer Products LLC* ***(G-12952)***
**Reynolds Consumer Products LLC** ........ 217 479-1126
500 E Superior Ave Jacksonville (62650) ***(G-12411)***
**Reynolds Consumer Products LLC** ........ 217 479-1466
2226 E Morton Ave Jacksonville (62650) ***(G-12412)***
**Reynolds Consumer Products LLC (HQ)** ........ 847 482-3500
1900 W Field Ct Lake Forest (60045) ***(G-12952)***
**Reynolds Food Packaging** ........ 815 465-2115
304 Ne Main St Grant Park (60940) ***(G-11314)***
**Reynolds Food Packaging LLC** ........ 847 482-3500
1900 W Field Ct Lake Forest (60045) ***(G-12953)***
**Reynolds Holdings Inc** ........ 630 739-0110
684 S Phillips Unit 2 Romeoville (60446) ***(G-18863)***
**Reynolds J W Rock Ages Mmrials, Vienna** *Also called Reynolds Rock of Ages* ***(G-21224)***
**Reynolds Manufacturing Company** ........ 309 787-8600
630 4th St W Milan (61264) ***(G-14803)***
**Reynolds Packaging Kama Inc** ........ 815 468-8300
1050 W Sycamore Rd Manteno (60950) ***(G-14192)***
**Reynolds Rock of Ages (PA)** ........ 618 658-2911
103 S 5th St Vienna (62995) ***(G-21224)***
**Reznik Instrument Co** ........ 847 673-3444
7337 Lawndale Ave Skokie (60076) ***(G-20075)***
**Rf Communications Inc** ........ 630 420-8882
424 Fort Hill Dr Ste 142 Naperville (60540) ***(G-15741)***
**Rf Ideas Inc (HQ)** ........ 847 870-1723
4020 Winnetka Ave Rolling Meadows (60008) ***(G-18774)***
**RF Mau Co** ........ 847 329-9731
7140 N Lawndale Ave Lincolnwood (60712) ***(G-13533)***
**Rf Plastics Co** ........ 630 628-6033
406 W Belden Ave Addison (60101) ***(G-278)***
**RF Technologies Inc (PA)** ........ 618 377-2654
330 Lexington Dr Buffalo Grove (60089) ***(G-2759)***
**Rfq LLC** ........ 815 893-6656
6213 Factory Rd Ste A Crystal Lake (60014) ***(G-7640)***
**Rgb Lights Inc** ........ 312 421-6080
6045 N Keystone Ave Chicago (60646) ***(G-6346)***
**RGI Group, Lincolnwood** *Also called Lipsner Smith Co* ***(G-13521)***
**Rgw Candy Company, Atlanta** *Also called Amy Wertheim* ***(G-946)***
**Rh Development** ........ 773 331-3772
9431 S Claremont Ave Chicago (60643) ***(G-6347)***
**Rh Preyda Company (PA)** ........ 212 880-1477
333 N Michigan Ave # 3000 Chicago (60601) ***(G-6348)***
**Rhino Pros** ........ 815 235-7767
4223 Autumn Ln Freeport (61032) ***(G-10684)***
**Rhino Tool Company** ........ 309 853-5555
620 Andrews Ave Kewanee (61443) ***(G-12694)***
**RHO Chemical Company Inc** ........ 815 727-4791
30 Industry Ave Joliet (60435) ***(G-12568)***
**Rhodes Publications, Riverton** *Also called Riverton Register* ***(G-18035)***
**Rhodes/American, Chicago** *Also called Global Material Tech Inc* ***(G-4958)***
**Rhone-Poulenc Basic Chem Co** ........ 708 757-6111
1101 Arnold St Chicago Heights (60411) ***(G-7121)***
**Rhopac Fabricated Products LLC** ........ 847 362-3300
1819 Industrial Dr Libertyville (60048) ***(G-13376)***
**Rht Inc** ........ 630 227-1737
401 S Gary Ave Unit A Roselle (60172) ***(G-18967)***
**Rhyme or Reason Woodworking** ........ 217 678-8301
280 W Moultrie St Bement (61813) ***(G-1802)***
**Rl Diamonds, Chicago** *Also called Rahmanims Imports Inc* ***(G-6284)***
**Ri-Del Mfg Inc (PA)** ........ 312 829-8720
1754 W Walnut St Chicago (60612) ***(G-6349)***
**Riah Hair, Niles** *Also called Bee Sales Comapny* ***(G-15965)***
**Ribbon Print Company** ........ 847 421-8208
508 Central Ave Ste 208 Highland Park (60035) ***(G-11865)***
**Ribbon Print USA, Highland Park** *Also called Ribbon Print Company* ***(G-11865)***
**Ribbon Supply Comp** ........ 773 237-7979
5448 W Fullerton Ave Chicago (60639) ***(G-6350)***
**Ribbon Webbing Corporation** ........ 773 287-1221
4711 W Division St Chicago (60651) ***(G-6351)***
**Riber Construction Inc** ........ 815 584-3337
405 S Old Route 66 Dwight (60420) ***(G-8592)***
**Ricar Industries Inc** ........ 847 914-9083
2468 Greenview Rd Northbrook (60062) ***(G-16355)***
**Rice Chem, Saint Charles** *Also called J Stilling Enterprises Inc* ***(G-19201)***
**Rice Precision Machining** ........ 630 543-7220
475 W Interstate Rd Addison (60101) ***(G-279)***
**Rich Industries Inc** ........ 630 766-9150
489 Thomas Dr Bensenville (60106) ***(G-1978)***
**Rich Products Corporation** ........ 815 729-4509
21511 Division St Crest Hill (60403) ***(G-7466)***
**Rich Products Corporation** ........ 847 581-1749
6200 W Mulford St Niles (60714) ***(G-16027)***
**Rich Products Corporation** ........ 309 886-2465
1902 Cobblestone Washington (61571) ***(G-21390)***
**Rich Products Corporation** ........ 847 459-5400
624 Wheeling Rd Wheeling (60090) ***(G-22140)***
**Rich-Law, Olney** *Also called Wabash Valley Service Co* ***(G-16800)***
**Richard A Anderson** ........ 815 895-5627
1653 W Motel Rd Sycamore (60178) ***(G-20814)***
**Richard King and Sons** ........ 815 654-0226
6735 Elm Ave Loves Park (61111) ***(G-13982)***
**Richard Ochwat Specialty Entp** ........ 630 682-0800
385 S Schmale Rd Carol Stream (60188) ***(G-3228)***
**Richard Schrock** ........ 217 543-3111
41 E Cr 200 N Arthur (61911) ***(G-920)***
**Richard Tindall** ........ 618 433-8107
1026 Lexington Estates Dr Godfrey (62035) ***(G-11233)***
**Richard Wolf Med Instrs Corp** ........ 847 913-1113
353 Corporate Woods Pkwy Vernon Hills (60061) ***(G-21193)***
**Richards Brick Company (PA)** ........ 618 656-0230
234 Springer Ave Edwardsville (62025) ***(G-8812)***
**Richards Company II Inc** ........ 708 385-6633
3555 W 123rd St Alsip (60803) ***(G-520)***
**Richards Electric Motor Co (PA)** ........ 217 222-7154
426 State St Quincy (62301) ***(G-17887)***
**Richards Fine Jewelry & Design** ........ 847 697-4053
321 Randall Rd South Elgin (60177) ***(G-20224)***
**Richards Sthman Rbr Stamps LLC** ........ 217 522-6801
317 E Monroe St Springfield (62701) ***(G-20512)***
**Richards-Wilcox, Aurora** *Also called Rwi Manufacturing Inc* ***(G-1212)***
**Richardson & Edwards Inc** ........ 630 543-1818
303 Hambletonian Dr Oak Brook (60523) ***(G-16559)***
**Richardson Electronics Ltd** ........ 630 208-2278
40 W 267 Keslinger Rd Lafox (60147) ***(G-12795)***
**Richardson Electronics Ltd (PA)** ........ 630 208-2200
40w267 Keslinger Rd Lafox (60147) ***(G-12796)***
**Richardson Enterprises** ........ 309 833-5395
830 W Jackson St Macomb (61455) ***(G-14131)***
**Richardson Ironworks LLC** ........ 217 359-3333
313 N Mattis Ave Ste 208 Champaign (61821) ***(G-3533)***
**Richardson Manufacturing Co** ........ 217 546-2249
2209 Old Jacksonville Rd Springfield (62704) ***(G-20513)***
**Richardson Rfpd Inc (HQ)** ........ 630 262-6800
1950 S Batavia Ave # 100 Geneva (60134) ***(G-10862)***
**Richardson Seating Corporation** ........ 312 829-4040
2545 W Arthington St Chicago (60612) ***(G-6352)***
**Richars's, South Elgin** *Also called Richards Fine Jewelry & Design* ***(G-20224)***
**Richco Graphics Inc** ........ 847 367-7277
1500 Skokie Blvd Ste 204 Northbrook (60062) ***(G-16356)***
**Rick Styfer** ........ 630 734-3244
200 Lakewood Cir Burr Ridge (60527) ***(G-2877)***
**Rickard Bindery, Chicago** *Also called Rickard Circular Folding Co* ***(G-6353)***
**Rickard Circular Folding Co** ........ 312 243-6300
325 N Ashland Ave Chicago (60607) ***(G-6353)***
**Rickard Publishing** ........ 217 482-3276
126 N Tonica St Mason City (62664) ***(G-14366)***
**Rickard Publishing** ........ 309 968-6705
106 N Broadway St Manito (61546) ***(G-14175)***
**Rico Computers Enterprises Inc** ........ 708 594-7426
7022 W 73rd Pl Chicago (60638) ***(G-6354)***
**Rico Industries Inc (PA)** ........ 312 427-0313
7000 N Austin Ave Niles (60714) ***(G-16028)***
**Rico Industries Tag Express, Niles** *Also called Rico Industries Inc* ***(G-16028)***
**Ricon Colors Inc** ........ 630 562-9000
675 Wegner Dr West Chicago (60185) ***(G-21764)***
**Ricter Corporation** ........ 708 344-3300
2600 Lexington St Broadview (60155) ***(G-2608)***
**Riddell Inc (HQ)** ........ 847 292-1472
9801 W Higgins Rd Ste 800 Rosemont (60018) ***(G-19027)***
**Riddell Sports, Rosemont** *Also called Riddell Inc* ***(G-19027)***

**Riddle McIntyre Inc** ....312 782-3317
175 N Franklin St Frnt 1 Chicago (60606) ***(G-6355)***
**Rider Dickerson Inc** ....312 427-2926
815 25th Ave Bellwood (60104) ***(G-1718)***
**Ridgefield Industries Co LLC** ....800 569-0316
8420 Railroad St Crystal Lake (60012) ***(G-7641)***
**Rieco-Titan Products Inc** ....815 464-7400
965 Lambrecht Dr Frankfort (60423) ***(G-10358)***
**Rieger Printing Inc** ....773 229-2095
5959 S Harlem Ave Bedford Park (60638) ***(G-1578)***
**Rieke Office Interiors Inc (PA)** ....847 622-9711
2000 Fox Ln Elgin (60123) ***(G-9165)***
**Rietschle Inc** ....410 712-4100
1800 Gardner Expy Quincy (62305) ***(G-17888)***
**Riggs Brothers Auto Interiors, Villa Park** *Also called Air Land and Sea Interiors* ***(G-21234)***
**Right Angle Tool Division, Bloomington** *Also called Rettick Enterprises Inc* ***(G-2218)***
**Right Bag On Time, The, Carpentersville** *Also called Bulk Lift International LLC* ***(G-3277)***
**Right/Pointe Company** ....815 754-5700
234 Harvestore Dr Dekalb (60115) ***(G-8115)***
**Righthand Technologies Inc** ....773 774-7600
7450 W Wilson Ave Chicago (60706) ***(G-6356)***
**Rightsource Digital Svcs Inc** ....888 774-2201
2242 W Harrison St # 201 Chicago (60612) ***(G-6357)***
**Rightway Printing Inc** ....630 790-0444
460 Windy Point Dr Glendale Heights (60139) ***(G-11064)***
**Rijon Awning, Blue Island** *Also called Rijon Manufacturing Company* ***(G-2266)***
**Rijon Manufacturing Company** ....708 388-2295
13733 Chatham St Blue Island (60406) ***(G-2266)***
**Riken Corporation of America** ....847 673-1400
4709 Golf Rd Ste 807 Skokie (60076) ***(G-20076)***
**Rilco Fluid Care** ....309 788-1854
1320 1st St Rock Island (61201) ***(G-18200)***
**Rinalli Boat Co Inc** ....618 467-8850
3406 W Delmar Ave Godfrey (62035) ***(G-11234)***
**Rinda Technologies Inc** ....773 736-6633
4563 N Elston Ave Fl 1 Chicago (60630) ***(G-6358)***
**Rinella Orthotics Inc** ....815 717-8970
1890 Silver Cross Blvd # 445 New Lenox (60451) ***(G-15906)***
**Ring Can, Kankakee** *Also called Ringwood Containers LP* ***(G-12644)***
**Ring Can of Illinois, Rockford** *Also called Ring Container Tech LLC* ***(G-18555)***
**Ring Container Tech LLC** ....217 875-5084
2454 E Hubbard Ave Decatur (62526) ***(G-7934)***
**Ring Container Tech LLC** ....815 229-9110
4689 Assembly Dr Rockford (61109) ***(G-18555)***
**Ring Sheet Metal Heating & AC** ....309 289-4213
213 Grove St Knoxville (61448) ***(G-12723)***
**Ring-O-Bliss, Winnetka** *Also called Bliss Ring Company Inc* ***(G-22304)***
**Ringmaster Mfg** ....815 675-4230
8001 Winn Rd Spring Grove (60081) ***(G-20362)***
**Ringspann Corporation** ....847 678-3581
10550 Anderson Pl Franklin Park (60131) ***(G-10575)***
**Ringwood, Decatur** *Also called Ring Container Tech LLC* ***(G-7934)***
**Ringwood Company** ....708 458-6000
6715 W 73rd St Bedford Park (60638) ***(G-1579)***
**Ringwood Containers LP** ....815 939-7270
1825 American Way Kankakee (60901) ***(G-12644)***
**Rinker Boat Company** ....574 457-5731
333 W Wacker Dr Ste 600 Chicago (60606) ***(G-6359)***
**Ripa LLC** ....708 938-1600
2001 W 21st St Broadview (60155) ***(G-2609)***
**Riser Machine Corp** ....708 532-2313
1744 Ferro Dr New Lenox (60451) ***(G-15907)***
**Risk Never Die Inc** ....708 240-4194
1001 W 15th St Unit 222 Chicago (60608) ***(G-6360)***
**RITA Corporation (PA)** ....815 337-2500
850 S Route 31 Crystal Lake (60014) ***(G-7642)***
**Rite Systems East Inc (HQ)** ....630 293-9174
625 Wegner Dr West Chicago (60185) ***(G-21765)***
**Rite-TEC Communications** ....815 459-7712
5812 Marietta Dr Crystal Lake (60014) ***(G-7643)***
**Riteway Brake Dies Inc** ....708 430-0795
7440 W 100th Pl Bridgeview (60455) ***(G-2524)***
**Rittal Corp (HQ)** ....847 240-4600
425 N Martingale Rd # 400 Schaumburg (60173) ***(G-19712)***
**Rivalfly National Network LLC** ....847 867-8660
320 W Ohio St Chicago (60654) ***(G-6361)***
**Rivalus, Aurora** *Also called Nutrivo LLC* ***(G-1196)***
**River Bank Laboratories Inc** ....630 232-2207
18 S 8th St Geneva (60134) ***(G-10863)***
**River Bend Printing** ....217 324-6056
60 Flat School Ln Litchfield (62056) ***(G-13696)***
**River Bend Wild Game & Sausage** ....217 688-3337
1161 County Road 2400 E Saint Joseph (61873) ***(G-19317)***
**River City Cupcake LLC** ....309 613-1312
1900 Saint Clair Dr Pekin (61554) ***(G-17287)***
**River City Enterprises, Peoria** *Also called Staffco Inc* ***(G-17460)***
**River City Millwork Inc** ....800 892-9297
200 Quaker Rd Ste 3 Rockford (61104) ***(G-18556)***
**River City Oil LLC** ....309 693-2249
3310 W Chartwell Rd Peoria (61614) ***(G-17442)***
**River City Sign Company Inc** ....309 796-3606
915 1st Ave Silvis (61282) ***(G-19940)***
**River North Hand** ....312 335-9669
356 W Superior St Chicago (60654) ***(G-6362)***
**River North Industries Inc** ....773 600-4960
1905 Spring Ct Spring Grove (60081) ***(G-20363)***
**River Redi Mix Inc** ....815 795-2025
2195 E Bluff St Marseilles (61341) ***(G-14317)***
**River Valley Mechanical Inc** ....309 364-3776
1532 County Road 1500 E Putnam (61560) ***(G-17788)***
**River View Motor Sports Inc** ....309 467-4569
1792 Hillside Rd Congerville (61729) ***(G-7371)***
**River West Radiation Center L** ....630 264-8580
1221 N Highland Ave Aurora (60506) ***(G-1209)***
**Rivercrest Sewing Center** ....708 385-2516
13310 Cicero Ave Crestwood (60445) ***(G-7499)***
**Riverdale Pltg Heat Trting LLC** ....708 849-2050
680 W 134th St Riverdale (60827) ***(G-18024)***
**Riverfront Machine Inc** ....815 663-5000
6 Wolfer Industrial Park Spring Valley (61362) ***(G-20379)***
**Rivershore Press** ....847 516-8105
24762 N River Shore Dr Cary (60013) ***(G-3368)***
**Riverside Bake Shop** ....815 385-0044
1309 N Riverside Dr McHenry (60050) ***(G-14552)***
**Riverside Chocolate Factory, McHenry** *Also called American Convenience Inc* ***(G-14480)***
**Riverside Custom Woodworking** ....815 589-3608
1225 22nd Ave Fulton (61252) ***(G-10705)***
**Riverside Graphics Corporation** ....312 372-3766
2 N Riverside Plz Ste 365 Chicago (60606) ***(G-6363)***
**Riverside Medi-Center Inc** ....815 932-6632
400 N Wall St Ste 1 Kankakee (60901) ***(G-12645)***
**Riverside Memorial Co** ....217 323-1280
216 W 2nd St Beardstown (62618) ***(G-1527)***
**Riverside Publishing, Itasca** *Also called Houghton Mifflin Harcourt Pubg* ***(G-12276)***
**Riverside Spring Company** ....815 963-3334
2136 12th St Ste 121 Rockford (61104) ***(G-18557)***
**Riverside Tool & Die Co** ....309 689-0104
1616 W Chanute Rd Ste A Peoria (61615) ***(G-17443)***
**Riverstone Group Inc** ....309 787-3141
601 Us Route 67 N Milan (61264) ***(G-14804)***
**Riverstone Group Inc** ....309 523-3159
2721 248th St N Hillsdale (61257) ***(G-11903)***
**Riverstone Group Inc** ....309 787-1415
Junction Of 280amp Rock Island (61201) ***(G-18201)***
**Riverstone Group Inc** ....309 933-1123
1001 N Broadway St Cleveland (61241) ***(G-7271)***
**Riverstone Group Inc** ....309 757-8297
200 23rd Ave Moline (61265) ***(G-14967)***
**Riverstone Group Inc** ....309 788-9543
1603 Mill St Rock Island (61201) ***(G-18202)***
**Riverton Cabinet Company** ....815 462-5300
22000 S Schoolhouse Rd New Lenox (60451) ***(G-15908)***
**Riverton Register** ....217 629-9247
100 N 6th St Riverton (62561) ***(G-18035)***
**Rivertoncabinets, New Lenox** *Also called Riverton Cabinet Company* ***(G-15908)***
**Riverview Mfg House SA** ....815 625-1459
901 Regan Rd Rock Falls (61071) ***(G-18148)***
**Riverview Printing Inc** ....815 987-1425
99 E State St Rockford (61104) ***(G-18558)***
**Riviera Tan Products, Godfrey** *Also called Riviera Tan Spa (del)* ***(G-11235)***
**Riviera Tan Spa (del)** ....618 466-1012
5114 Stiritz Ln Godfrey (62035) ***(G-11235)***
**Rix Enterprise Inc** ....618 996-8237
5891 Saraville Rd Creal Springs (62922) ***(G-7454)***
**Rj Cnc Works Inc** ....847 671-9120
10134 Pacific Ave Franklin Park (60131) ***(G-10576)***
**RJ Distributing Co** ....309 685-2794
410 High Point Ln East Peoria (61611) ***(G-8731)***
**Rj Link, Rockford** *Also called Rj Link International Inc* ***(G-18559)***
**Rj Link International Inc** ....815 874-8110
3741 Publishers Dr Rockford (61109) ***(G-18559)***
**Rj Race Cars Inc** ....309 343-7575
300 N Linwood Rd Galesburg (61401) ***(G-10774)***
**Rj Stuckel Co Inc** ....800 789-7220
94 Garlisch Dr Elk Grove Village (60007) ***(G-9716)***
**Rj45s.com, Saint Charles** *Also called David Jeskey* ***(G-19168)***
**Rjg Enterprises Ltd** ....847 752-2065
888 E Belvidere Rd # 222 Grayslake (60030) ***(G-11362)***
**Rjl Inc** ....708 385-4884
3701 W 128th Pl Alsip (60803) ***(G-521)***
**Rjs Silk Screening, Palos Hills** *Also called R J S Silk Screening Co* ***(G-17123)***
**Rjt Wood Services** ....815 858-2081
1653 S Tippett Rd Galena (61036) ***(G-10730)***
**Rkb Distributors** ....847 970-6880
216 Terrace Dr Mundelein (60060) ***(G-15552)***
**Rkc Cleaner I Corp** ....630 904-0477
4071 S Route 59 Naperville (60564) ***(G-15824)***

ALPHABETIC

(PA)=Parent Co (HQ)=Headquarters (DH)=Div Headquarters

**Rkf Enterprises**...773 723-7038
7331 S Michigan Ave Ste 1 Chicago (60619) ***(G-6364)***
**Rkfdcnc, Rockford** *Also called Chad Mazeika* ***(G-18303)***
**Rkm Enterprises**...217 348-5437
1003 Madison Ave Charleston (61920) ***(G-3609)***
**Rko Saw, Cullom** *Also called Techniks LLC* ***(G-7685)***
**RLC Industries Inc**...708 837-7300
715 S 10th Ave La Grange (60525) ***(G-12743)***
**Rlw Inc**...309 352-2499
132 Geraldine St Green Valley (61534) ***(G-11380)***
**Rm Acquisition LLC (PA)**...847 329-8100
9855 Woods Dr Skokie (60077) ***(G-20077)***
**RM Lucas Co (PA)**...773 523-4300
12400 S Laramie Ave Alsip (60803) ***(G-522)***
**RM Lucas Co**...773 523-4300
3211 S Wood St Chicago (60608) ***(G-6365)***
**Rmb Engineered Products Inc**...847 382-0100
18-1 E Dundee Rd Ste 220 Barrington (60010) ***(G-1301)***
**RMC Imaging Inc**...815 885-4521
780 Creek Bluff Ln Rockford (61114) ***(G-18560)***
**Rmcis Corporation**...630 955-1310
4300 Commerce Ct Ste 320 Lisle (60532) ***(G-13652)***
**Rmf Products Inc**...630 879-0020
1275 Paramount Pkwy Batavia (60510) ***(G-1492)***
**RMH Enterprises**...630 525-5552
611 Cadillac Dr Wheaton (60187) ***(G-21976)***
**Rmi Inc**...708 756-5640
211 E Main St Chicago Heights (60411) ***(G-7122)***
**Rmic, Bensenville** *Also called Snyder Industries Inc* ***(G-1993)***
**Rmj Distributing, Belleville** *Also called ABM Marking Services Ltd* ***(G-1607)***
**Rmts, Romeoville** *Also called Roll McHning Tech Slutions Inc* ***(G-18864)***
**Rna Corporation (PA)**...708 597-7777
13750 Chatham St Blue Island (60406) ***(G-2267)***
**Rnfl Acquisition LLC**...651 442-6011
70 W Madison St Ste 2300 Chicago (60602) ***(G-6366)***
**Rnw Machining Co Inc**...847 635-6560
7101 Barry St Rosemont (60018) ***(G-19028)***
**Ro Pal Grinding Inc**...815 964-5894
1916 20th Ave Rockford (61104) ***(G-18561)***
**Ro-Web Inc**...309 688-2155
4440 N Prospect Rd Ste C Peoria (61616) ***(G-17444)***
**Road District, Millstadt** *Also called Millstadt Township* ***(G-14831)***
**Road Ready Signs (PA)**...309 828-1007
1231 N Mason St Bloomington (61701) ***(G-2219)***
**Road Runner Sports Inc**...847 719-8941
20291 N Rand Rd Ste 105 Palatine (60074) ***(G-17068)***
**Roadex Carriers Inc**...773 454-8772
446 Irvine Ct Wheeling (60090) ***(G-22141)***
**Roadsafe Traffic Systems Inc**...217 629-7139
104 Douglas St Riverton (62561) ***(G-18036)***
**Roanoke Companies Group Inc**...630 499-5870
2560 White Oak Cir Aurora (60502) ***(G-1074)***
**Roanoke Companies Group Inc (HQ)**...630 375-0324
1105 S Frontenac St Aurora (60504) ***(G-1075)***
**Roanoke Concrete Products Co**...309 698-7882
1275 Spring Bay Rd East Peoria (61611) ***(G-8732)***
**Roanoke Milling Co**...309 923-5731
211 W Husseman St Roanoke (61561) ***(G-18054)***
**Roark Oil Field Services Inc**...618 382-4703
1036 County Road 1575 N Carmi (62821) ***(G-3078)***
**Robal Company Inc**...630 393-0777
30 W 250th Butterfield304 Warrenville (60555) ***(G-21361)***
**Robbi Joy Eklow**...847 223-0460
4 Galleon Ct Third Lake (60030) ***(G-20858)***
**Robbins Hdd LLC**...847 955-0050
1221 Flex Ct Lake Zurich (60047) ***(G-13123)***
**Robbins Pallets, Galesburg** *Also called Rbj Inc* ***(G-10772)***
**Robert B Scott Ocularists Ltd (PA)**...312 782-3558
111 N Wabash Ave Ste 1620 Chicago (60602) ***(G-6367)***
**Robert Bosch LLC (HQ)**...248 876-1000
2800 S 25th Ave Broadview (60155) ***(G-2610)***
**Robert Bosch Tool Corporation (HQ)**...224 232-2000
1800 W Central Rd Mount Prospect (60056) ***(G-15369)***
**Robert Brysiewicz Incorporated**...630 289-0903
956 S Bartlett Rd Ste 261 Bartlett (60103) ***(G-1369)***
**Robert C Weisheit Co Inc**...630 766-1213
999 Regency Dr Glendale Heights (60139) ***(G-11065)***
**Robert C Weisheit Company, Glendale Heights** *Also called Robert C Weisheit Co Inc* ***(G-11065)***
**Robert Daskal Group, Chicago** *Also called Besleys Accessories Inc* ***(G-4089)***
**Robert Davis & Son Inc**...815 889-4168
832 N State Route 1 Milford (60953) ***(G-14814)***
**Robert E Bolton**...815 725-7120
3021 Theodore St Unit E Joliet (60435) ***(G-12569)***
**Robert Higgins**...217 337-0734
405 E Pennsylvania Ave Urbana (61801) ***(G-21101)***
**Robert Kellerman & Co**...847 526-7266
1000 N Rand Rd Ste 224 Wauconda (60084) ***(G-21500)***
**Robert Koester (PA)**...773 539-5001
4121 N Rockwell St Chicago (60618) ***(G-6368)***
**Robert L Murphy**...708 424-0277
9545 S Hamlin Ave Evergreen Park (60805) ***(G-10118)***
**Robert McCormick Tribune Lbrry**...847 619-7980
1400 N Roosevelt Blvd Schaumburg (60173) ***(G-19713)***
**Robert Stern Industries Inc**...630 983-9765
2330 University Ct Naperville (60565) ***(G-15742)***
**Robert Swaar**...217 968-2232
25903 Levee St Greenview (62642) ***(G-11386)***
**Robert-Leslie Publishing LLC**...773 935-8358
4147 N Ravenswood Ave # 301 Chicago (60613) ***(G-6369)***
**Roberts and Downey Chapel Eqp**...217 795-2391
101 S North St Argenta (62501) ***(G-692)***
**Roberts Colonial House Inc**...708 331-6233
15960 Suntone Dr South Holland (60473) ***(G-20301)***
**Roberts Displays, South Holland** *Also called Roberts Colonial House Inc* ***(G-20301)***
**Roberts Draperies Center Inc**...847 255-4040
504 E Northwest Hwy Mount Prospect (60056) ***(G-15370)***
**Roberts Sheet Metal Works Inc**...773 626-3811
4447 W Kinzie St Chicago (60624) ***(G-6370)***
**Roberts Swiss Inc**...630 467-9100
1387 Ardmore Ave Itasca (60143) ***(G-12348)***
**Robertshaw Controls Company**...815 591-2417
107 N Washington St Hanover (61041) ***(G-11573)***
**Robertshaw Controls Company (HQ)**...630 260-3400
1222 Hamilton Pkwy Itasca (60143) ***(G-12349)***
**Robertson Repair**...618 895-2593
Hwy 15 Sims (62886) ***(G-19941)***
**Robertson Transformer Co**...708 388-2315
4700 137th St Ste A Crestwood (60445) ***(G-7500)***
**Robertson Worldwide, Crestwood** *Also called Robertson Transformer Co* ***(G-7500)***
**Robey Packaging Eqp & Svc**...708 758-8250
3236 Rennie Smith Dr Chicago Heights (60411) ***(G-7123)***
**Robin Hood Mat & Quilting Corp (PA)**...312 953-2960
4800 S Richmond St Chicago (60632) ***(G-6371)***
**Robin L Barnhouse**...309 737-5431
1106 120th Ave Joy (61260) ***(G-12592)***
**Robinson Daily News, Robinson** *Also called Daily Robinson News Inc* ***(G-18060)***
**Robinson Name Plate, Franklin Park** *Also called Precision Plastic Ball Co* ***(G-10559)***
**Robinson Production Inc**...618 842-6111
108 Ne 7th St Fairfield (62837) ***(G-10154)***
**Robinsport LLC**...630 724-9280
2613 York Ct Woodridge (60517) ***(G-22514)***
**Robis Elections Inc**...630 752-0220
1751 S Nprvlle Rd Ste 104 Wheaton (60189) ***(G-21977)***
**Robit Inc (HQ)**...708 667-7892
639 W Diversey Pkwy # 217 Chicago (60614) ***(G-6372)***
**Robko Flock Coating Company**...847 272-6202
1935 Stanley St Northbrook (60062) ***(G-16357)***
**Robotics Technologies Inc**...815 722-7650
20655 Burl Ct Joliet (60433) ***(G-12570)***
**Robs Aquatics**...708 444-7627
17135 Harlem Ave Tinley Park (60477) ***(G-20943)***
**Robuschi Usa Inc**...704 424-1018
1800 Gardner Expy Quincy (62305) ***(G-17889)***
**ROC Industries Inc**...618 277-6044
1218 W A St Belleville (62220) ***(G-1670)***
**Rochelle Foods LLC**...815 562-4141
1001 S Main St Rochelle (61068) ***(G-18105)***
**Rochelle News Leader, Rochelle** *Also called Rochelle Newspapers Inc* ***(G-18106)***
**Rochelle News Leader, Rochelle** *Also called Rochelle Newspapers Inc* ***(G-18107)***
**Rochelle Newspapers Inc (HQ)**...815 562-2061
211 E Il Route 38 Rochelle (61068) ***(G-18106)***
**Rochelle Newspapers Inc**...815 562-4171
211 E State Route 38 Rochelle (61068) ***(G-18107)***
**Rochelle Vault Co**...815 562-6484
2119 S Il Route 251 Rochelle (61068) ***(G-18108)***
**Rochester Midland Corporation**...630 896-8543
2200 Rochester Rd Montgomery (60538) ***(G-15066)***
**Rochester Sand & Gravel, Rochester** *Also called Legacy Vulcan LLC* ***(G-18119)***
**Rock Bottom Chicago, Chicago** *Also called Rock Bottom Minneapolis Inc* ***(G-6373)***
**Rock Bottom Minneapolis Inc**...312 755-9339
1 W Grand Ave Chicago (60654) ***(G-6373)***
**Rock Falls Div, Rock Falls** *Also called Metal Spinners Inc* ***(G-18142)***
**Rock Island Argus, Moline** *Also called Moline Dispatch Publishing Co* ***(G-14959)***
**Rock Island Cannon Company**...309 786-1507
2408 4th Ave Rock Island (61201) ***(G-18203)***
**Rock Island Ready Mixed, Rock Island** *Also called Riverstone Group Inc* ***(G-18202)***
**Rock River Arms Inc**...309 792-5780
1042 Cleveland Rd Colona (61241) ***(G-7347)***
**Rock River Blending**...815 968-7860
1515 Cunningham St Rockford (61102) ***(G-18562)***
**Rock River Fabrication, Lyndon** *Also called Phillips & Johnston Inc* ***(G-14014)***
**Rock River Ready Mix Inc (PA)**...815 288-2260
2320 S Galena Ave Dixon (61021) ***(G-8344)***
**Rock River Ready Mix Inc**...815 438-2510
24261 Prophet Rd Rock Falls (61071) ***(G-18149)***

ALPHABETIC SECTION Rogers Loose Leaf Co

**Rock River Ready Mix Inc** ....815 625-1139
1905 Mound Hill Rd Dixon (61021) *(G-8345)*
**Rock River Ready-Mix** ....815 288-2269
2320 S Galena Ave Dixon (61021) *(G-8346)*
**Rock River Sand & Gravel, Rock Falls** *Also called Rock River Ready Mix Inc (G-18149)*
**Rock River Times** ....815 964-9767
128 N Church St Rockford (61101) *(G-18563)*
**ROCK RIVER VALLEY BLOOD CENTER, Rockford** *Also called Northern Ill Blood Bnk Inc (G-18520)*
**Rock Road Companies Inc** ....815 874-2441
801 Beale Ct Rockford (61109) *(G-18564)*
**Rock Solid Imports LLC** ....331 472-4522
1004 Creekside Cir Naperville (60563) *(G-15743)*
**Rock Tops Inc** ....708 672-1450
295 W Burville Rd Crete (60417) *(G-7518)*
**Rock Valley Antique Auto Parts** ....815 645-2272
5800 N Rothwell Stillman Valley (61084) *(G-20627)*
**Rock Valley Die Sinking Inc** ....815 874-5511
2457 Baxter Rd Rockford (61109) *(G-18565)*
**Rock Valley Oil & Chemical Co (PA)** ....815 654-2400
1911 Windsor Rd Loves Park (61111) *(G-13983)*
**Rock Valley Pallet Company** ....815 654-4850
3511 Mildred Ct Machesney Park (61115) *(G-14102)*
**Rock Valley Publishing LLC (PA)** ....815 467-6397
11512 N 2nd St Machesney Park (61115) *(G-14103)*
**Rock Valley Publishing LLC** ....815 234-4821
418 W Blackhawk Dr Byron (61010) *(G-2919)*
**Rock-Tenn Company** ....815 756-8913
800 Nestle Ct Dekalb (60115) *(G-8116)*
**Rock-Tred 2 LLC (PA)** ....888 762-5873
405 N Oakwood Ave Waukegan (60085) *(G-21610)*
**Rockberry Publishing, Machesney Park** *Also called Clinton Topper Newspaper (G-14065)*
**Rockbridge Casting Inc** ....618 753-3188
25 State St Rockbridge (62081) *(G-18212)*
**Rockdale Controls Co Inc** ....815 436-6181
2419 Von Esch Rd Plainfield (60586) *(G-17646)*
**Rocket Fuel Inc** ....207 520-9075
205 N Michigan Ave # 2900 Chicago (60601) *(G-6374)*
**Rockey Mountain Steel Mills, Chicago** *Also called New C F & I Inc (G-5890)*
**Rockfon, Chicago** *Also called Chicago Metallic Company LLC (G-4334)*
**Rockford Acromatic Products, Loves Park** *Also called Aircraft Gear Corporation (G-13916)*
**Rockford Air Devices Inc** ....815 654-3330
1201 Turret Dr Machesney Park (61115) *(G-14104)*
**Rockford Ball Screw Company** ....815 961-7700
940 Southrock Dr Rockford (61102) *(G-18566)*
**Rockford Bolt & Steel Co** ....815 968-0514
126 Mill St Rockford (61101) *(G-18567)*
**Rockford Broach Inc** ....815 484-0409
4993 27th Ave Rockford (61109) *(G-18568)*
**Rockford Burrall Mch Co Inc** ....815 877-7428
4520 Shepherd Trl Rockford (61103) *(G-18569)*
**Rockford Carbide Die & Tool** ....815 394-0645
1920 20th Ave Rockford (61104) *(G-18570)*
**Rockford Cement Products Co** ....815 965-0537
315 Peoples Ave Rockford (61104) *(G-18571)*
**Rockford Chemical Co** ....815 544-3476
915 W Perry St Belvidere (61008) *(G-1783)*
**Rockford Commercial Whse Inc** ....815 623-8400
8105 Burden Rd Machesney Park (61115) *(G-14105)*
**Rockford Drop Forge Company** ....815 963-9611
2011 10th St Rockford (61104) *(G-18572)*
**Rockford Electric Equipment Co** ....815 398-4096
2010 Harrison Ave Rockford (61104) *(G-18573)*
**Rockford Foundries Inc** ....815 965-7243
212 Mill St Rockford (61101) *(G-18574)*
**Rockford Heat Treaters Inc** ....815 874-0089
4704 American Rd Rockford (61109) *(G-18575)*
**Rockford Jobbing Service Inc** ....815 398-8661
4955 28th Ave Rockford (61109) *(G-18576)*
**Rockford Linear Actuation** ....815 986-4400
2111 23rd Ave Rockford (61104) *(G-18577)*
**Rockford Linear Motion LLC** ....815 961-7900
940 Southrock Dr Rockford (61102) *(G-18578)*
**Rockford Map Publishers Inc** ....815 708-6324
124 N Water St Ste 10 Rockford (61107) *(G-18579)*
**Rockford Metal Polishing Co** ....815 282-4448
5700 Industrial Ave Loves Park (61111) *(G-13984)*
**Rockford Molded Products Inc** ....815 637-0585
5600 Pike Rd Loves Park (61111) *(G-13985)*
**Rockford Newspapers Inc** ....815 987-1200
99 E State St Rockford (61104) *(G-18580)*
**Rockford Ornamental Iron Inc** ....815 633-1162
1817 Michigan Ave Rockford (61102) *(G-18581)*
**Rockford Precision Machine** ....815 873-1018
4729 Hydraulic Rd Rockford (61109) *(G-18582)*
**Rockford Process Control Inc (PA)** ....815 966-2000
2020 7th St Rockford (61104) *(G-18583)*
**Rockford Quality Grinding Inc** ....815 227-9001
3160 Forest View Rd Rockford (61109) *(G-18584)*
**Rockford Rams Products Inc** ....815 226-0016
2902 Eastrock Dr Rockford (61109) *(G-18585)*
**Rockford Register Star, Rockford** *Also called Rockford Newspapers Inc (G-18580)*
**Rockford Register Star, Rockford** *Also called USA Today Inc (G-18665)*
**Rockford Rigging Inc (PA)** ....309 263-0566
5401 Mainsail Dr Roscoe (61073) *(G-18914)*
**Rockford Rigging Inc** ....309 263-0566
1480 S Main St Ste A Morton (61550) *(G-15180)*
**Rockford Sand & Gravel Co (HQ)** ....815 654-4700
5290 Nimtz Rd Loves Park (61111) *(G-13986)*
**Rockford Secondary Co** ....815 398-0401
2424 Laude Dr Rockford (61109) *(G-18586)*
**Rockford Separators, Rockford** *Also called Tomermo Inc (G-18653)*
**Rockford Sewer Co Inc** ....815 877-9060
6204 Forest Hills Rd Loves Park (61111) *(G-13987)*
**Rockford Systems LLC** ....815 874-7891
4620 Hydraulic Rd Rockford (61109) *(G-18587)*
**Rockford Tool and Mfg Co** ....815 398-5876
3023 Eastrock Ct Rockford (61109) *(G-18588)*
**Rockford Toolcraft Inc (PA)** ....815 398-5507
766 Research Pkwy Rockford (61109) *(G-18589)*
**Rockford Wellness & Diagnostic** ....815 708-0125
223 W State St Rockford (61101) *(G-18590)*
**Rockform Tooling & Machinery (PA)** ....770 345-4624
2974 Eastrock Dr Rockford (61109) *(G-18591)*
**Rockform Tooling & Machinery** ....815 398-7650
2974 Eastrock Dr Rockford (61109) *(G-18592)*
**Rocking Horse** ....773 486-0011
2535 N Milwaukee Ave Chicago (60647) *(G-6375)*
**Rocktenn** ....773 254-1030
1415 W 44th St Chicago (60609) *(G-6376)*
**Rocktenn Cp LLC** ....630 587-9429
417 37th Ave Saint Charles (60174) *(G-19253)*
**Rockwell Automation Inc** ....217 373-0800
2802 W Bloomington Rd Champaign (61822) *(G-3534)*
**Rockwell Automation Inc** ....414 382-3662
180 Harvester Dr Ste 190 Burr Ridge (60527) *(G-2878)*
**Rockwell Metal Products Inc** ....773 762-7030
3232 W Cermak Rd Chicago (60623) *(G-6377)*
**Rockwind Venture Partners LLC (PA)** ....630 881-6664
8500 E State St Rockford (61108) *(G-18593)*
**Rocky Lane Woodworking, Arthur** *Also called Willard R Schorck (G-924)*
**Rocky's Advanced Printing, Harrisburg** *Also called Graf Ink Printing Inc (G-11601)*
**Rockys Beverages LLC** ....312 561-3182
1813 Elmdale Ave Glenview (60026) *(G-11194)*
**Rodale Inc** ....312 726-0365
65 E Wacker Pl Ste 1101 Chicago (60601) *(G-6378)*
**Rodger Murphy** ....309 582-2202
103 W Main St Aledo (61231) *(G-372)*
**Rodgers Bill Oil Min Bits Svc** ....618 299-7771
20226 Wabash 20 Ave West Salem (62476) *(G-21824)*
**Rodifer Enterprises Inc** ....815 678-0100
5700 Walnut St Richmond (60071) *(G-17970)*
**Rodin Enterprises Inc** ....847 412-1370
544b W Dundee Rd Wheeling (60090) *(G-22142)*
**Rodney Tite Welding** ....618 845-9072
391 N Locust St Ullin (62992) *(G-21032)*
**Roe Machine Inc** ....618 983-5524
12725 Union Rd West Frankfort (62896) *(G-21817)*
**Roeda Signs Inc** ....708 333-3021
16931 State St South Holland (60473) *(G-20302)*
**Roentgen Industrial, Bartlett** *Also called Assurance Technologies Inc (G-1331)*
**Roentgen USA LLC** ....847 787-0135
3725 25th Ave Schiller Park (60176) *(G-19868)*
**Roesers Bakery** ....773 489-6900
3216 W North Ave Chicago (60647) *(G-6379)*
**Roevolution 226 LLC (PA)** ....773 658-4022
2610 Lake Cook Rd Riverwoods (60015) *(G-18042)*
**Rogan Granitindustrie Inc** ....708 758-0050
11849 S Kedzie Ave Merrionette Park (60803) *(G-14737)*
**Rogan Granitindustrie Inc (HQ)** ....708 758-0050
21550 E Lincoln Hwy Lynwood (60411) *(G-14025)*
**Rogan Group Inc (PA)** ....708 371-4191
11849 S Kedzie Ave Merrionette Park (60803) *(G-14738)*
**Roger Burke Jewelers Inc** ....309 692-0210
4700 N University St 6 Peoria (61614) *(G-17445)*
**Roger Cantu & Assocs** ....630 573-9215
1100 Jorie Blvd Ste 215 Oak Brook (60523) *(G-16560)*
**Roger Fritz & Associates Inc** ....630 355-2614
1113 N Loomis St Naperville (60563) *(G-15744)*
**Roger Jolly Skateboards** ....618 277-7113
305 N Illinois St Belleville (62220) *(G-1671)*
**Rogers Brothers Co** ....815 965-5132
1925 Kishwaukee St Rockford (61104) *(G-18594)*
**Rogers Brothers Galvanizing, Rockford** *Also called Rogers Brothers Co (G-18594)*
**Rogers Custom Trims Inc** ....773 745-6577
2101 N Monitor Ave Chicago (60639) *(G-6380)*
**Rogers Loose Leaf Co** ....312 226-1947
1555 W Fulton St Chicago (60607) *(G-6381)*

ALPHABETIC

**Rogers Metal Services Inc (PA)**...847 679-4642
7330 Monticello Ave Skokie (60076) **(G-20078)**
**Rogers Metal Services Inc**...847 679-4642
7330 Monticello Ave Skokie (60076) **(G-20079)**
**Rogers Precision Machining**...815 233-0065
5816 Us Highway 20 W Freeport (61032) **(G-10685)**
**Rogers Ready Mix & Mtls Inc (PA)**...815 234-8212
8128 N Walnut St Byron (61010) **(G-2920)**
**Rogers Ready Mix & Mtls Inc**...815 234-8044
201 E Washington St Oregon (61061) **(G-16831)**
**Rogers Ready Mix & Mtls Inc**...815 874-6626
5510 S Mulford Rd Rockford (61109) **(G-18595)**
**Rogers Ready Mix & Mtls Inc**...815 389-2223
14615 N 2nd St Roscoe (61073) **(G-18915)**
**Rogers Redi-Mix Inc (PA)**...618 282-3844
55 E Mill St Ruma (62278) **(G-19088)**
**Rogus Tool Inc**...847 824-5939
354 N East River Rd Des Plaines (60016) **(G-8268)**
**Rohbi Enterprises Inc**...708 343-2004
3020 S 25th Ave Broadview (60155) **(G-2611)**
**Rohm and Haas Company**...847 426-3245
2531 Tech Dr Ste 301 Elgin (60124) **(G-9166)**
**Rohm and Haas Company**...815 935-7725
1400 Harvard Dr Kankakee (60901) **(G-12646)**
**Rohn Products LLC (PA)**...309 697-4400
1 Fairholm Ave Peoria (61603) **(G-17446)**
**Rohn Products LLC**...309 566-3000
6718 W Plank Rd Ste 2 Peoria (61604) **(G-17447)**
**Rohner Engraving Inc**...773 244-8343
1112 N Homan Ave Chicago (60651) **(G-6382)**
**Rohner Letterpress Inc**...773 248-0800
1112 N Homan Ave Chicago (60651) **(G-6383)**
**Rohner Press, Chicago** *Also called Rohner Letterpress Inc* **(G-6383)**
**Roho Inc (HQ)**...618 277-9173
100 N Florida Ave Belleville (62221) **(G-1672)**
**Roho Inc**...618 234-4899
1501 S 74th St Belleville (62223) **(G-1673)**
**Rohrer Corporation**...847 961-5920
13701 George Bush Ct Huntley (60142) **(G-12174)**
**Rohrer Graphic Arts Inc**...630 832-3434
491 W Fullerton Ave Elmhurst (60126) **(G-9930)**
**Rohrer Litho Inc**...630 833-6610
487 W Fullerton Ave Elmhurst (60126) **(G-9931)**
**Rolfs Patisserie Inc**...847 675-6565
4343 W Touhy Ave Lincolnwood (60712) **(G-13534)**
**Roll McHning Tech Slutions Inc**...815 372-9100
641 Forestwood Dr Romeoville (60446) **(G-18864)**
**Roll Rite Inc**...815 645-8600
6549 N Junction Rd Davis Junction (61020) **(G-7814)**
**Roll Roll Met Fabricators Inc**...773 434-1315
2310 W 58th St Chicago (60636) **(G-6384)**
**Roll Source Paper**...630 875-0308
900 N Arlington Heights R Itasca (60143) **(G-12350)**
**Roll-A-Way Conveyors Inc**...847 336-5033
2335 N Delany Rd Gurnee (60031) **(G-11500)**
**Roll-Kraft Northern Inc**...815 469-0205
9324 Gulfstream Rd Ste 1e Frankfort (60423) **(G-10359)**
**Roll-O-Sheets, Schaumburg** *Also called Pliant Corporation of Canada* **(G-19695)**
**Roll-O-Sheets, Rolling Meadows** *Also called Pliant LLC* **(G-18763)**
**Rolled Edge Inc**...773 283-9500
4221 N Normandy Ave Chicago (60634) **(G-6385)**
**Rollex Corporation (PA)**...847 437-3000
800 Chase Ave Elk Grove Village (60007) **(G-9717)**
**Rolling Meadows Brewery LLC**...217 725-2492
1660 W Leland Ave Springfield (62704) **(G-20514)**
**Rolling Stone Magazine, Chicago** *Also called Wenner Media LLC* **(G-6957)**
**Rollstock Inc**...708 579-3700
600 E Plainfield Rd Countryside (60525) **(G-7441)**
**Rollys Convenient Foods Inc**...630 766-4070
923 Dolores Dr Bensenville (60106) **(G-1979)**
**Roma Bakeries Inc**...815 964-6737
523 Marchesano Dr Rockford (61102) **(G-18596)**
**Roma Packing Co**...773 927-7371
2354 S Leavitt St Chicago (60608) **(G-6386)**
**Romaine Empire LLC**...312 229-0099
155 N Wacker Dr Ste 4250 Chicago (60606) **(G-6387)**
**Roman Decorating Products LLC**...708 891-0770
824 State St Calumet City (60409) **(G-2952)**
**Roman Electric**...773 777-9246
6054 W Giddings St Chicago (60630) **(G-6388)**
**Roman Holdings Corporation**...708 891-0770
824 State St Calumet City (60409) **(G-2953)**
**Roman Signs**...847 381-3425
819 W Northwest Hwy Barrington (60010) **(G-1302)**
**Romar Cabinet & Top Co Inc**...815 467-4452
23949 S Northern Ill Dr Channahon (60410) **(G-3584)**
**Rome Industries Inc (PA)**...309 691-7120
1703 W Detweiller Dr Peoria (61615) **(G-17448)**
**Rome Metal Mfg Inc**...773 287-1755
4612 W Ohio St Chicago (60644) **(G-6389)**
**Romed Industries Corporation**...847 362-3900
320 E Il Route 22 Lake Zurich (60047) **(G-13124)**
**Romel Press Inc**...708 343-6090
1747 N 20th Ave Melrose Park (60160) **(G-14687)**
**Romero Steel Company Inc**...708 216-0001
1300 Main St Melrose Park (60160) **(G-14688)**
**Romtech Machining Inc**...630 543-7039
755 W Factory Rd Addison (60101) **(G-280)**
**Romus Incorporated**...414 350-6233
932 Central Ave Roselle (60172) **(G-18968)**
**Ron & Pats Pizza Shack**...847 395-5005
40338 N Deep Lake Rd Antioch (60002) **(G-653)**
**Ron Absher**...618 382-4646
1500 Oak St Ste C Carmi (62821) **(G-3079)**
**Ron Absher Auto Center, Carmi** *Also called Ron Absher* **(G-3079)**
**Ron Shew Welding & Fabricating, Marion** *Also called Shew Brothers Inc* **(G-14286)**
**Ron's Automotive Machine Shop, Sterling** *Also called R & C Auto Supply Corp* **(G-20609)**
**Ronald Allen**...314 568-1446
1920 Marseilles Dr Cahokia (62206) **(G-2925)**
**Ronald J Nixon**...708 748-8130
56 South St Park Forest (60466) **(G-17175)**
**Ronald S Lefors Bs Cpo**...618 259-1969
214 W Saint Louis Ave East Alton (62024) **(G-8610)**
**Roncin Custom Design**...847 669-0260
11514 Smith Dr Unit B Huntley (60142) **(G-12175)**
**Rondex Products Incorporated**...815 226-0452
324 N Gardiner Ave Rockford (61107) **(G-18597)**
**Rondout Iron & Metal Co Inc**...847 362-2750
1501 Rockland Rd Lake Bluff (60044) **(G-12865)**
**Roney Machine Works Inc**...618 462-4113
412 Pearl St Alton (62002) **(G-588)**
**Ronk Electrical Industries Inc (PA)**...217 563-8333
106 E State St Nokomis (62075) **(G-16061)**
**Ronk Electrical Industries Inc**...217 563-8333
106 E State St Nokomis (62075) **(G-16062)**
**Ronken Industries Inc**...815 664-5306
9 Wolfer Industrial Park Spring Valley (61362) **(G-20380)**
**Ronnie Joe Graham**...618 548-5544
420 W Schwartz St Salem (62881) **(G-19348)**
**Ronnie P Faber**...815 626-4561
2901 Polo Rd Sterling (61081) **(G-20610)**
**Roodhouse Envelope Co**...217 589-4321
414 S State St Roodhouse (62082) **(G-18884)**
**Roodhouse Fire Protection Dst**...217 589-5134
1140 S State St Roodhouse (62082) **(G-18885)**
**Roof Structures, New Baden** *Also called Reload Sales Inc* **(G-15864)**
**Rookie LLC**...708 278-1628
545 S Scolville Ave Oak Park (60304) **(G-16682)**
**Room Dividers Now LLC**...847 224-7900
38 Otis Rd Barrington (60010) **(G-1303)**
**Room Place, The, Lombard** *Also called Trp Acquisition Corp* **(G-13873)**
**Rooms Redux Chicago Inc**...312 835-1192
6033 N Sheridan Rd 25d Chicago (60660) **(G-6390)**
**Roosevelt Mobile**...630 293-7630
60 W Roosevelt Rd West Chicago (60185) **(G-21766)**
**Roosevelt Paper Company**...708 653-5121
5100 W 123rd St Alsip (60803) **(G-523)**
**Roosevelt Torch**...312 281-3242
18 S Michigan Ave Rm 515 Chicago (60603) **(G-6391)**
**Ropak Central Inc**...847 956-0750
1350 Arthur Ave Elk Grove Village (60007) **(G-9718)**
**Roper Whitney, Rockford** *Also called Whitney Roper LLC* **(G-18681)**
**Roq Innovation LLC**...917 770-2403
3201 S Talumet Ave Chicago (60616) **(G-6392)**
**Roquette America Inc**...847 360-0886
1550 Northwestern Ave Gurnee (60031) **(G-11501)**
**Roquette America Inc**...630 232-2157
2211 Innovation Dr Geneva (60134) **(G-10864)**
**Rorke & Riley Specialty B**...773 929-2522
3712 N Broadway St # 252 Chicago (60613) **(G-6393)**
**Roscoe Glass Co**...815 623-6268
11212 Main St Roscoe (61073) **(G-18916)**
**Roscoe Ready-Mix Inc**...815 389-0888
4896 Mccurry Rd Roscoe (61073) **(G-18917)**
**Roscoe Tool & Manufacturing**...815 633-8808
5339 Stern Dr Roscoe (61073) **(G-18918)**
**Roscor Corporation (PA)**...847 299-8080
140 S Dearborn St Ste 420 Chicago (60603) **(G-6394)**
**Rose Business Forms & Printing**...618 533-3032
125 N Walnut St Centralia (62801) **(G-3429)**
**Rose Custom Builders, Mundelein** *Also called Rose Custom Cabinets Inc* **(G-15553)**
**Rose Custom Cabinets Inc**...847 816-4800
408 Washington Blvd Ste C Mundelein (60060) **(G-15553)**
**Rose Laboratories Inc**...815 740-1121
660 Collins St Unit 2 Joliet (60432) **(G-12571)**
**Rose Limited International, Carol Stream** *Also called Richard Ochwat Specialty Entp* **(G-3228)**
**Rose Packing Company Inc**...708 458-9300
4900 S Major Ave Chicago (60638) **(G-6395)**

# ALPHABETIC SECTION
## RR Donnelley & Sons Company

Rose Pallet LLC .................................................. 708 333-3000
  7647 W 100th Pl Ste D  Bridgeview  (60455)  *(G-2525)*
Roseland II LLC .................................................. 708 479-5010
  18410 115th Ave  Orland Park  (60467)  *(G-16888)*
Roselle Custom Woodwork LLC .................................... 630 980-5655
  57 N Garden Ave  Roselle  (60172)  *(G-18969)*
Roselynn Fashions .................................................. 847 741-6000
  900 Elizabeth St  Elgin  (60120)  *(G-9167)*
Rosemount Inc ..................................................... 217 877-5278
  2241 E Hubbard Ave  Decatur  (62526)  *(G-7935)*
Rosen Printing Services, Chicago  Also called Roshan Ag Inc  *(G-6397)*
Rosengard Sue Jwly Design Ltd .................................... 312 733-1133
  2210 S Halsted St  Chicago  (60608)  *(G-6396)*
Rosenthal Manufacturing Co Inc .................................... 847 714-0404
  1840 Janke Dr  Northbrook  (60062)  *(G-16358)*
Roseri Business Forms Inc .......................................... 847 381-8012
  2236 Harrow Gate Dr  Inverness  (60010)  *(G-12211)*
Roses Moulding By Design Inc ..................................... 847 549-9200
  408 Washington Blvd Ste C  Mundelein  (60060)  *(G-15554)*
Rosette Printing LLC ................................................ 630 295-8500
  517 Widgeon Ln  Bloomingdale  (60108)  *(G-2131)*
Rosewood Software Inc ............................................ 847 438-2185
  1531 N Haven Dr  Palatine  (60074)  *(G-17069)*
Roshan Ag Inc ..................................................... 773 267-1635
  3525 W Peterson Ave # 120  Chicago  (60659)  *(G-6397)*
Rosiclare Quarry, Golconda  Also called Martin Marietta Materials Inc  *(G-11241)*
Roskuszka & Sons Inc .............................................. 630 851-3400
  969 N Farnsworth Ave  Aurora  (60505)  *(G-1210)*
Ross and White Company ........................................... 847 516-3900
  1090 Alexander Ct  Cary  (60013)  *(G-3369)*
Ross Designs Ltd .................................................. 847 831-7669
  210 Skokie Valley Rd # 5  Highland Park  (60035)  *(G-11866)*
Ross Oil Co Inc .................................................. 618 592-3808
  11172 N 450th St  Oblong  (62449)  *(G-16733)*
Ross-Gage Inc ..................................................... 708 347-3659
  2346 Alexander Ter  Homewood  (60430)  *(G-12105)*
Rotadyne Precision Mch Roller, Chicago  Also called Rotation Dynamics Corporation  *(G-6398)*
Rotadyne-Decorative Tech GP, Darien  Also called Advanced Graphics Tech Inc  *(G-7787)*
Rotadyne-Roll Group, Romeoville  Also called Rotation Dynamics Corporation  *(G-18865)*
Rotary Airlock LLC ................................................ 800 883-8955
  707 E 17th St  Rock Falls  (61071)  *(G-18150)*
Rotary Dryer Parts Inc .............................................. 217 877-2787
  2590 E Federal Dr Ste 508  Decatur  (62526)  *(G-7936)*
Rotary Forms and Systems Inc ..................................... 847 843-8585
  2500 W Higgins Rd # 1280  Hoffman Estates  (60169)  *(G-12044)*
Rotary Paper Manifold ............................................ 847 758-7800
  2300 Arthur Ave  Elk Grove Village  (60007)  *(G-9719)*
Rotary Ram Inc ................................................... 618 466-2651
  3704 Riehl Ln  Godfrey  (62035)  *(G-11236)*
Rotation Dynamics Corporation ..................................... 630 769-9700
  6120 S New England Ave  Chicago  (60638)  *(G-6398)*
Rotation Dynamics Corporation ..................................... 773 247-5600
  2512 W 24th St  Chicago  (60608)  *(G-6399)*
Rotation Dynamics Corporation ..................................... 630 679-7053
  1101 Windham Pkwy  Romeoville  (60446)  *(G-18865)*
Rotec Industries Inc (PA) ........................................... 630 279-3300
  270 Industrial Dr  Hampshire  (60140)  *(G-11561)*
Roth Neon Sign Company Inc ...................................... 618 942-6378
  1100 N 13th St  Herrin  (62948)  *(G-11753)*
Roth Sign Company, Herrin  Also called Roth Neon Sign Company Inc  *(G-11753)*
Roth's Pump Co., Milan  Also called Roy E Roth Company  *(G-14805)*
Rothenberger Usa Inc ............................................. 815 397-7617
  7130 Clinton Rd  Loves Park  (61111)  *(G-13988)*
Rothenberger USA LLC ............................................ 815 397-7617
  4455 Boeing Dr  Rockford  (61109)  *(G-18598)*
Roto Die Company, Lombard  Also called Roto-Die Company Inc  *(G-13848)*
Roto Spray Manufacturing, Mokena  Also called Rotospray Mfg Inc  *(G-14900)*
Roto-Die Company Inc ............................................ 630 932-8605
  1054 N Du Page Ave  Lombard  (60148)  *(G-13848)*
Rotospray Mfg Inc ................................................ 708 478-3307
  10315 Aileen Ave  Mokena  (60448)  *(G-14900)*
Round Lake Pallets Inc ............................................ 847 637-6162
  740 Sunset Dr  Round Lake  (60073)  *(G-19065)*
Roundtble Hlthcare Partners LP (PA) ................................ 847 482-9275
  272 E Deerpath Ste 350  Lake Forest  (60045)  *(G-12954)*
Roundup Food Equipment Div, Carol Stream  Also called A J Antunes & Co  *(G-3087)*
Rout A Bout Shop Inc ............................................. 309 829-0674
  619 W Olive St  Bloomington  (61701)  *(G-2220)*
Rout-A-Bout, Bloomington  Also called Rout A Bout Shop Inc  *(G-2220)*
Route 40 Media LLC .............................................. 309 370-5809
  4408 N Rockwood Dr # 240  Peoria  (61615)  *(G-17449)*
Route 45 Wayside ................................................ 217 867-2000
  101 S Chestnut St  Pesotum  (61863)  *(G-17533)*
Route 66 Asphalt Company ........................................ 630 739-6633
  13769 Main St  Lemont  (60439)  *(G-13260)*
Rovanco Piping Systems Inc ....................................... 815 741-6700
  20535 Se Frontage Rd  Joliet  (60431)  *(G-12572)*
ROW Window Company ........................................... 815 725-5491
  13404 Wood Duck Dr  Plainfield  (60585)  *(G-17647)*
Rowald Refrigeration Systems ..................................... 815 397-7733
  515 Grable St  Rockford  (61109)  *(G-18599)*
Rowboat Creative LLC ............................................ 773 675-2628
  2649 N Kildare Dock 1 On  Chicago  (60639)  *(G-6400)*
Rowdy Star Custom Creations ..................................... 217 497-1789
  1936 Delong St  Danville  (61832)  *(G-7764)*
Rowe Construction Div, Tremont  Also called Cullinan & Sons Inc  *(G-20981)*
Rowell Pure Water, Herrin  Also called Samuel Rowell  *(G-11754)*
Rowlar Tool & Die Div, Franklin Park  Also called Associate General Labs Inc  *(G-10404)*
Roy E Roth Company (PA) ......................................... 309 787-1791
  6th Ave And 4th St  Milan  (61264)  *(G-14805)*
Roy Winnett ..................................................... 309 367-4867
  303 W Pine St  Metamora  (61548)  *(G-14748)*
Royal Bedding Company Inc (PA) .................................. 847 645-0200
  2600 Forbs Ave  Hoffman Estates  (60192)  *(G-12045)*
Royal Box Group LLC (HQ) ........................................ 708 656-2020
  1301 S 47th Ave  Cicero  (60804)  *(G-7225)*
Royal Box Group LLC ............................................. 630 543-4464
  654 W Factory Rd  Addison  (60101)  *(G-281)*
Royal Box Group LLC ............................................. 708 222-4650
  4600 W 12th Pl  Cicero  (60804)  *(G-7226)*
Royal Brass Inc .................................................. 618 439-6341
  1202 Route 14 W  Benton  (62812)  *(G-2040)*
Royal Casting, Chicago  Also called M B Jewelers Inc  *(G-5579)*
Royal Continental Box Company, Cicero  Also called Royal Box Group LLC  *(G-7225)*
Royal Corinthian Inc .............................................. 630 876-8899
  603 Fenton Ln  West Chicago  (60185)  *(G-21767)*
Royal Die & Stamping Co Inc (HQ) ................................ 630 766-2685
  125 Mercedes Dr  Carol Stream  (60188)  *(G-3229)*
Royal Drilling & Producing ......................................... 618 966-2221
  Hwy 14  Crossville  (62827)  *(G-7523)*
Royal Drilling & Production, Crossville  Also called Royal Drilling & Producing  *(G-7523)*
Royal Envelope Corporation ....................................... 773 376-1212
  4114 S Peoria St  Chicago  (60609)  *(G-6401)*
Royal Fabricators Inc ............................................. 847 775-7466
  38360 N Cashmore Rd  Wadsworth  (60083)  *(G-21327)*
Royal Fiberglass Pools Inc ......................................... 618 266-7089
  312 Duncan Ln  Dix  (62830)  *(G-8318)*
Royal Foods & Flavors Inc ......................................... 847 595-9166
  2456 American Ln  Elk Grove Village  (60007)  *(G-9720)*
Royal Haeger Lamp Co ........................................... 309 837-9966
  1300 W Piper St  Macomb  (61455)  *(G-14132)*
Royal Kitchen & Bathroom Cabin (PA) .............................. 847 588-0011
  7727 N Milwaukee Ave  Niles  (60714)  *(G-16029)*
Royal Machine Works Inc ......................................... 815 465-6879
  204 N Stanley St  Grant Park  (60940)  *(G-11315)*
Royal Machining Corporation ...................................... 708 338-3387
  1617 N 31st Ave  Melrose Park  (60160)  *(G-14689)*
Royal Oak Farm Inc .............................................. 815 648-4141
  15908 Hebron Rd  Harvard  (60033)  *(G-11646)*
Royal Printing Co, Quincy  Also called DE Asbury Inc  *(G-17820)*
Royal Publishing Inc ............................................. 309 343-4007
  311 E Main St Ste 220  Galesburg  (61401)  *(G-10775)*
Royal Publishing Inc ............................................. 815 220-0400
  4375 Venture Dr  Peru  (61354)  *(G-17526)*
Royal Publishing Co, Galesburg  Also called Royal Publishing Inc  *(G-10775)*
Royal Smoke Shop ............................................... 815 539-3499
  1001 Main St  Mendota  (61342)  *(G-14732)*
Royal Stairs Co ................................................... 630 860-2223
  300 E Ave  Bensenville  (60106)  *(G-1980)*
Royal Stairs Co ................................................... 847 685-9448
  98 East Ave  Park Ridge  (60068)  *(G-17220)*
Royal Touch Carwash ............................................ 847 808-8600
  1701 Weiland Rd  Buffalo Grove  (60089)  *(G-2760)*
Royale Innovation Group Ltd ...................................... 312 339-1406
  794 Willow Ct  Itasca  (60143)  *(G-12351)*
Royell Communications, Virden  Also called Royer Systems Inc  *(G-21301)*
Royer Systems Inc ............................................... 217 965-3699
  427 W Dean St  Virden  (62690)  *(G-21301)*
RPI Extrusion Co ................................................. 708 389-2584
  5623 W 115th St  Alsip  (60803)  *(G-524)*
Rpk Technologies Inc ............................................ 630 595-0911
  272 Judson St  Bensenville  (60106)  *(G-1981)*
RPS Engineering Inc ............................................. 847 931-1950
  1300 Crispin Dr  Elgin  (60123)  *(G-9168)*
RPS Products Inc (PA) ............................................ 847 683-3400
  281 Keyes Ave  Hampshire  (60140)  *(G-11562)*
Rpsi, Chicago  Also called Railway Program Services Inc  *(G-6286)*
Rpt Toner LLC ................................................... 630 694-0400
  475 Supreme Dr  Bensenville  (60106)  *(G-1982)*
RR Defense Systems Inc ......................................... 312 446-9167
  341 Lively Blvd  Elk Grove Village  (60007)  *(G-9721)*
RR Donnelley, Chicago  Also called R R Donnelley & Sons Company  *(G-6270)*
RR Donnelley, Saint Charles  Also called RR Donnelley & Sons Company  *(G-19256)*
RR Donnelley & Sons Company .................................... 217 258-2675
  6821 E County Road 1100n  Mattoon  (61938)  *(G-14407)*

**RR Donnelley & Sons Company** 630 377-2586
1750 Wallace Ave Saint Charles (60174) ***(G-19254)***
**RR Donnelley & Sons Company** 217 935-2113
900 S Cain St Clinton (61727) ***(G-7288)***
**RR Donnelley & Sons Company** 312 332-4345
230 W Monroe St Ste 2500 Chicago (60606) ***(G-6402)***
**RR Donnelley & Sons Company** 847 622-1026
168 E Highland Ave Ste 2 Elgin (60120) ***(G-9169)***
**RR Donnelley & Sons Company** 630 513-4681
609 Kirk Rd Saint Charles (60174) ***(G-19255)***
**RR Donnelley & Sons Company** 630 588-5000
750 Warrenville Rd Lisle (60532) ***(G-13653)***
**RR Donnelley & Sons Company** 312 326-8000
35 W Wacker Dr Ste 3650 Chicago (60601) ***(G-6403)***
**RR Donnelley & Sons Company** 630 762-7600
609 Kirk Rd Saint Charles (60174) ***(G-19256)***
**RR Donnelley & Sons Company** 312 236-8000
111 S Wacker Dr Fl 36 Chicago (60606) ***(G-6404)***
**RR Donnelley Logistics SE** 630 672-2500
200 N Gary Ave Roselle (60172) ***(G-18970)***
**RR Donnelley Printing Co LP** 217 235-0561
6821 E County Road 1100n Mattoon (61938) ***(G-14408)***
**RR Donnelley Printing Co LP (HQ)** 312 326-8000
111 S Wacker Dr Ste 3500 Chicago (60606) ***(G-6405)***
**Rrb Fabrication Inc** 815 977-5603
5430 Forest Hills Ct Loves Park (61111) ***(G-13989)***
**Rrd Netherlands LLC** 312 326-8000
111 S Wacker Dr Chicago (60606) ***(G-6406)***
**Rrp Enterprises Inc** 847 455-5674
9510 Fullerton Ave Franklin Park (60131) ***(G-10577)***
**Rrr Graphics & Film Corp** 708 478-4573
19759 Westminster Dr Mokena (60448) ***(G-14901)***
**Rs Ductless Technical Support** 815 223-7949
227 Bucklin St La Salle (61301) ***(G-12784)***
**RS Owens Div St Regis LLC** 773 282-6000
5535 N Lynch Ave Chicago (60630) ***(G-6407)***
**Rs Used Oil Services Inc** 618 781-1717
4559 Wagon Wheel Rd Roxana (62084) ***(G-19085)***
**Rs Woodworking** 815 476-1818
119 N Water St Wilmington (60481) ***(G-22275)***
**Rsb Fuels Inc** 217 999-4409
701 W Main St Mount Olive (62069) ***(G-15307)***
**Rsf Electronics Inc (HQ)** 847 490-0351
333 E State Pkwy Schaumburg (60173) ***(G-19714)***
**RSM International** 312 634-4762
1 S Wacker Dr Chicago (60606) ***(G-6408)***
**Rt Associates Inc** 847 577-0700
385 Gilman Ave Wheeling (60090) ***(G-22143)***
**RT Blackhawk Mch Pdts Inc** 815 389-3632
956 Gardner St South Beloit (61080) ***(G-20167)***
**Rt Enterprises Inc** 847 675-1444
7540 Linder Ave Skokie (60077) ***(G-20080)***
**Rt Properties & Cnstr Corp** 708 913-7607
14227 S Parnell Ave Riverdale (60827) ***(G-18025)***
**Rt Wholesale (PA)** 847 678-3663
4260 Old River Rd Schiller Park (60176) ***(G-19869)***
**RTC Industries Inc (PA)** 847 640-2400
2800 Golf Rd Rolling Meadows (60008) ***(G-18775)***
**RTC Industries Inc** 847 640-2400
3101 S Kedzie Ave Apt S Chicago (60623) ***(G-6409)***
**RTC USA World Headquarters, Rolling Meadows** *Also called RTC Industries Inc* ***(G-18775)***
**Rte, Saint Charles** *Also called Ray Tool & Engineering Inc* ***(G-19251)***
**Rtenergy LLC** 773 975-2598
2100 N Southport Ave Chicago (60614) ***(G-6410)***
**Rtm Trend, Elgin** *Also called Reliance Tool & Mfg Co* ***(G-9164)***
**Rtm Trend Industries Inc** 847 455-4350
11333 Melrose Ave Franklin Park (60131) ***(G-10578)***
**RTS Packaging LLC** 708 338-2800
250 N Mannheim Rd Hillside (60162) ***(G-11932)***
**RTS Sentry Inc** 618 257-7100
4401 N Belt W Belleville (62226) ***(G-1674)***
**Rubber Stamp Man, Des Plaines** *Also called Anderson Safford Mkg Graphics* ***(G-8150)***
**Rubicon Technology Inc (PA)** 847 295-7000
900 E Green St Bensenville (60106) ***(G-1983)***
**Rubin Brothers Inc** 312 942-1111
2241 S Halsted St Chicago (60608) ***(G-6411)***
**Rubin Manufacturing Inc** 312 942-1111
2241 S Halsted St Chicago (60608) ***(G-6412)***
**Rubschlager Baking Corporation** 773 826-1245
3220 W Grand Ave Ste 1 Chicago (60651) ***(G-6413)***
**Ruckers Mkin Batch Candies Inc** 618 945-7778
777 Rucker St Bridgeport (62417) ***(G-2455)***
**Ruco USA Inc** 866 373-7912
915 N Central Ave Wood Dale (60191) ***(G-22417)***
**Rudd Container Corporation** 773 847-7600
4600 S Kolin Ave Chicago (60632) ***(G-6414)***
**Rudin Printing Company Inc** 217 528-5111
927 E Jackson St Springfield (62701) ***(G-20515)***
**Rudon Enterprises Inc** 618 457-0441
118 N Illinois Ave Carbondale (62901) ***(G-3022)***
**Ruff Quality Components** 309 662-0425
1707 E Hamilton Rd Bloomington (61704) ***(G-2221)***
**Rugby America, Petersburg** *Also called Carlberg Design Inc* ***(G-17534)***
**Rumco, Elk Grove Village** *Also called Matthew Warren Inc* ***(G-9614)***
**Rumshine Distilling LLC** 217 446-6960
8 Hodge St Tilton (61832) ***(G-20882)***
**Runge Enterprises Inc** 630 365-2000
1 N 020 Thryselius Dr Elburn (60119) ***(G-8909)***
**Runyon Oil Production Inc** 618 395-8510
208 Linn St Olney (62450) ***(G-16794)***
**Runyon Oil Tools Inc** 618 395-5045
331 Herman Dr Olney (62450) ***(G-16795)***
**Rursch Specialties Inc** 309 795-1502
16420 132nd St W Reynolds (61279) ***(G-17953)***
**Rusco Manufacturing Inc** 815 654-3930
1304 Anvil Rd Machesney Park (61115) ***(G-14106)***
**Ruscorr LLC** 708 458-5525
5043 W 67th St Bedford Park (60638) ***(G-1580)***
**Rush Impressions Inc** 847 671-0622
3941 25th Ave Schiller Park (60176) ***(G-19870)***
**Rush Printing On Oak** 815 344-8880
1627 Oak Dr McHenry (60050) ***(G-14553)***
**Rushville Times, Rushville** *Also called Perryco Inc* ***(G-19094)***
**Russell Brands LLC** 309 454-6737
2015 Eagle Rd Normal (61761) ***(G-16087)***
**Russell Doot Inc** 312 527-1437
11 E Hubbard St Ste 301 Chicago (60611) ***(G-6415)***
**Russell Enterprises Inc (PA)** 847 692-6050
865 Busse Hwy Park Ridge (60068) ***(G-17221)***
**Russell Ferrell** 217 847-3954
951 E County Road 1450 Hamilton (62341) ***(G-11540)***
**Russell Publications Inc** 708 258-3473
120 W North St Peotone (60468) ***(G-17492)***
**Russo Wholesale Meat Inc** 708 385-0500
12306 S Cicero Ave Alsip (60803) ***(G-525)***
**Rust-Oleum (canada) Ltd** 847 367-7700
11 E Hawthorn Pkwy Vernon Hills (60061) ***(G-21194)***
**Rust-Oleum Corporation (HQ)** 847 367-7700
11 E Hawthorn Pkwy Vernon Hills (60061) ***(G-21195)***
**Rust-Oleum Corporation** 815 967-4258
440 Blackhawk Park Ave Rockford (61104) ***(G-18600)***
**Rustic Woodcrafts** 618 584-3912
10510 E 350th Ave Flat Rock (62427) ***(G-10196)***
**Rustle Hill Winery LLC** 618 893-2700
8595 Us Highway 51 N Cobden (62920) ***(G-7303)***
**Rusty & Angela Buzzard** 217 342-9841
205 N 4th St Effingham (62401) ***(G-8857)***
**Rutgers Enterprises Inc (PA)** 847 674-7666
6511 W Proesel Ave Lincolnwood (60712) ***(G-13535)***
**Rutherford & Associates** 630 365-5263
42w465 Foxfield Dr Saint Charles (60175) ***(G-19257)***
**Ruthman Pump and Engineering** 708 754-2940
1249 Center Ave Chicago Heights (60411) ***(G-7124)***
**Rutke Signs and Safety, Westchester** *Also called Rutke Signs Inc* ***(G-21853)***
**Rutke Signs Inc** 708 841-6464
1 Westbrook Corporate Ctr # 300 Westchester (60154) ***(G-21853)***
**Rutland Inc** 217 245-7810
7 Crabtree Rd Jacksonville (62650) ***(G-12413)***
**Rutland Products, Jacksonville** *Also called Rutland Inc* ***(G-12413)***
**Rutledge Printing Co** 708 479-8282
11415 183rd Pl Ste C Orland Park (60467) ***(G-16889)***
**Ruyle Incorporated** 309 674-6644
1325 Ne Bond St Springfield (62703) ***(G-20516)***
**Rv Enterprises Ltd** 847 509-8710
8926 N Greenwood Ave Niles (60714) ***(G-16030)***
**Rv6 Performance** 630 346-7998
26w148 Waterbury Ct Wheaton (60187) ***(G-21978)***
**Rw Acquisition, Rockford** *Also called Whitney Roper Rockford Inc* ***(G-18682)***
**Rw Technologies US LLC** 815 444-6887
387 E Congress Pkwy A1 Crystal Lake (60014) ***(G-7644)***
**Rw Welding Inc** 847 541-5508
1511 S Princeton Ave Arlington Heights (60005) ***(G-832)***
**Rway Plastics Ltd** 815 476-5252
30650 S State Route 53 Wilmington (60481) ***(G-22276)***
**Rwi Holdings Inc (PA)** 630 897-6951
600 S Lake St Aurora (60506) ***(G-1211)***
**Rwi Manufacturing Inc** 800 277-1699
600 S Lake St Aurora (60506) ***(G-1212)***
**RWS Design and Controls Inc** 815 654-6000
13979 Willowbrook Rd Roscoe (61073) ***(G-18919)***
**Ryan Industries** 708 479-7600
9515 191st St Mokena (60448) ***(G-14902)***
**Ryan Manufacturing Inc** 815 695-5310
11610 N La Salle Rd Newark (60541) ***(G-15934)***
**Ryan Meat Company** 773 783-3840
6719 S State St Chicago (60637) ***(G-6416)***
**Ryan Metal Products Inc** 815 936-0700
880 N Washington Ave Kankakee (60901) ***(G-12647)***
**Ryan Products Inc** 847 670-9071
319 S Burton Pl Arlington Heights (60005) ***(G-833)***

**Ryano Resins Inc** 630 621-5677
3808 Baybrook Dr Aurora (60504) *(G-1076)*
**Ryans Glass & Metal Inc (PA)** 708 430-7790
7549 W 99th Pl Bridgeview (60455) *(G-2526)*
**Rycoline Products LLC** 773 775-6755
5540 N Northwest Hwy Chicago (60630) *(G-6417)*
**Ryeson Corporation (HQ)** 847 455-8677
555 Kimberly Dr Carol Stream (60188) *(G-3230)*
**Rylin Media LLC** 708 246-7599
5028 Lawn Ave Western Springs (60558) *(G-21873)*
**S & B Finishing Co Inc** 773 533-0033
3005 W Franklin Blvd Chicago (60612) *(G-6418)*
**S & B Jig Grinding** 815 654-7907
6820 Forest Hills Rd Loves Park (61111) *(G-13990)*
**S & C Electric Company (PA)** 773 338-1000
6601 N Ridge Blvd Chicago (60626) *(G-6419)*
**S & D Development & Prototype** 847 872-7257
2009 Horizon Ct Zion (60099) *(G-22696)*
**S & D Products Inc** 630 372-2325
1390 Schiferl Rd Bartlett (60103) *(G-1370)*
**S & G Iron Works**
2173 Galilee Ave Zion (60099) *(G-22697)*
**S & G Step Tool Inc** 773 992-0808
5203 N Rose St Chicago (60656) *(G-6420)*
**S & J Industrial Supply Corp** 708 339-1708
16060 Suntone Dr South Holland (60473) *(G-20303)*
**S & J Machine Inc** 815 297-1594
2171 E Yellow Creek Rd Freeport (61032) *(G-10686)*
**S & J Woodproducts** 815 973-1970
5305 Forest Hills Rd Rockford (61114) *(G-18601)*
**S & K Boring Inc** 815 227-4394
3360 Forest View Rd Rockford (61109) *(G-18602)*
**S & K Label Co** 630 307-2577
147 Covington Dr Bloomingdale (60108) *(G-2132)*
**S & L Tool Co Inc** 847 455-5550
2324 17th St Franklin Park (60131) *(G-10579)*
**S & M Basements** 618 533-1939
1633 Walnut Hill Rd Centralia (62801) *(G-3430)*
**S & M Group Inc** 630 766-1000
300 Bauman Ct Wood Dale (60191) *(G-22418)*
**S & M Products, Oswego** *Also called Aero-Cables Corp (G-16902)*
**S & N Manufacturing Inc** 630 232-0275
455 Stevens St Geneva (60134) *(G-10865)*
**S & P Farms** 309 772-3936
19485 N 1700th Rd Bushnell (61422) *(G-2908)*
**S & R Media LLC** 618 375-7502
113 N Middle St Grayville (62844) *(G-11376)*
**S & R Monogramming Inc** 630 369-5468
28w600 Roosevelt Rd Winfield (60190) *(G-22292)*
**S & S Electric Service** 708 366-5800
447 Hannah Ave Forest Park (60130) *(G-10252)*
**S & S Heating & Sheet Metal** 815 933-1993
222 N Industrial Dr Bradley (60915) *(G-2431)*
**S & S Hinge Company** 630 582-9500
210 Covington Dr Bloomingdale (60108) *(G-2133)*
**S & S International Inc Ill** 847 304-1890
27996 W Industrial Ave # 8 Lake Barrington (60010) *(G-12823)*
**S & S Keytax Inc** 708 656-9221
4608 W 20th St Chicago (60804) *(G-6421)*
**S & S Machining Services Inc** 708 758-8300
3151 Glenwood Dyer Rd 1c Lynwood (60411) *(G-14026)*
**S & S Maintenance** 815 725-9263
1305 Widows Rd Wilmington (60481) *(G-22277)*
**S & S Metal Recyclers Inc** 630 844-3344
336 E Sullivan Rd Aurora (60505) *(G-1213)*
**S & S Mfg Solutions LLC** 815 838-1960
15509 Weber Rd # 3 Lockport (60446) *(G-13743)*
**S & S Mold Corporation** 815 385-0818
14431 Trinity Ct Woodstock (60098) *(G-22606)*
**S & S Pallet Corp** 618 219-3218
1459 State St Granite City (62040) *(G-11301)*
**S & S Tool Company** 847 891-0780
1107 Lunt Ave Ste 1 Schaumburg (60193) *(G-19715)*
**S & S Welding & Fabrication** 847 742-7344
31w377 Spaulding Rd Elgin (60120) *(G-9170)*
**S & W Machine Works Inc** 708 597-6043
12623 S Kroll Dr Alsip (60803) *(G-526)*
**S & W Manufacturing Co Inc** 630 595-5044
216 Evergreen Ave Bensenville (60106) *(G-1984)*
**S 4 Global Inc** 708 325-1236
7300 S Narragansett Ave Bedford Park (60638) *(G-1581)*
**S A, Bensenville** *Also called Spytek Aerospace Corporation (G-1997)*
**S A Gear Company Inc** 708 496-0395
7252 W 66th St Bedford Park (60638) *(G-1582)*
**S A W Co** 630 678-5400
376 E Saint Charles Rd # 5 Lombard (60148) *(G-13849)*
**S and K Packaging Incorporated** 563 582-8895
120 N Frentress Lake Rd East Dubuque (61025) *(G-8621)*
**S and S Associates Inc** 847 584-0033
1016 Bonaventure Dr Elk Grove Village (60007) *(G-9722)*
**S B Liquidating Company** 847 758-9500
1100 Touhy Ave Elk Grove Village (60007) *(G-9723)*
**S C C Pumps Inc** 847 593-8495
708 W Algonquin Rd Arlington Heights (60005) *(G-834)*
**S D Custom Machining** 618 544-7007
9094 E 1050th Ave Robinson (62454) *(G-18072)*
**S Flying Inc** 618 586-9999
17583 E 500th Ave Palestine (62451) *(G-17095)*
**S G Acquisition Inc** 815 624-6501
14392 De La Tour Dr South Beloit (61080) *(G-20168)*
**S G C, Arlington Heights** *Also called Scranton Glltte Cmmnctions Inc (G-836)*
**S G C, Arlington Heights** *Also called SGC Horizon LLC (G-839)*
**S G C M Corp** 630 953-2428
1s171 Summit Ave Oakbrook Terrace (60181) *(G-16720)*
**S G Nelson & Co** 630 668-7900
209 N Hale St Ste 1 Wheaton (60187) *(G-21979)*
**S G S Inc** 708 544-6061
900 Ogden Ave Ste 190 Downers Grove (60515) *(G-8517)*
**S Harris Uniforms, Peoria** *Also called Harris Clothing & Uniforms Inc (G-17380)*
**S Himmelstein and Company** 847 843-3300
2490 Pembroke Ave Hoffman Estates (60169) *(G-12046)*
**S I A Electronics, Tilden** *Also called Southern Ill Auto Elec Inc (G-20877)*
**S I A Inc (PA)** 708 361-3100
11743 Southwest Hwy Palos Heights (60463) *(G-17109)*
**S L Fixtures Inc** 217 423-9907
2222 E Logan St Decatur (62526) *(G-7937)*
**S M C Graphics** 708 754-8973
1024 Lowe Ave Chicago Heights (60411) *(G-7125)*
**S P Industries Inc** 847 228-2851
1455 Elmhurst Rd Elk Grove Village (60007) *(G-9724)*
**S P M, Wheeling** *Also called Swiss Precision Machining Inc (G-22162)*
**S R Bastien Co** 847 858-1175
600 Davis St Rear Evanston (60201) *(G-10093)*
**S R Door Inc** 815 227-1148
5960 Falcon Rd Rockford (61109) *(G-18603)*
**S R P, Elk Grove Village** *Also called Standard Rubber Products Co (G-9751)*
**S S I, Romeoville** *Also called Supreme Screw Inc (G-18872)*
**S V C Printing Co** 773 286-2219
3008 N Laramie Ave Chicago (60641) *(G-6422)*
**S Vs Industries Inc** 630 408-1083
646 Wainsford Dr Hoffman Estates (60169) *(G-12047)*
**S&J Food Management Corp** 630 323-9296
435 E 4th St Hinsdale (60521) *(G-11961)*
**S&K Machine, Rockford** *Also called Spencer and Krahn Mch Tl Sls (G-18627)*
**S&R Precision Machine LLC** 815 469-6544
9305 Corsair Rd Ste A Frankfort (60423) *(G-10360)*
**S&S Recovery** 217 538-2206
227 Baldknob Trl Fillmore (62032) *(G-10189)*
**S+s Inspection Inc** 770 493-9332
1234 Hardt Cir Bartlett (60103) *(G-1371)*
**S-P Products Inc** 847 593-8595
730 Pratt Blvd Elk Grove Village (60007) *(G-9725)*
**S-P-D Incorporated** 847 882-9820
678 S Middleton Ave Palatine (60067) *(G-17070)*
**S. I. Jacobson Mfg. Company, Waukegan** *Also called Jacobson Acqstion Holdings LLC (G-21574)*
**S.E. P. I., Glendale Heights** *Also called Sound Enhancement Products Inc (G-11070)*
**S4 Industries Inc** 224 699-9674
140 Prairie Lake Rd East Dundee (60118) *(G-8656)*
**SA Industries Inc** 847 730-4823
1054 S River Rd Des Plaines (60016) *(G-8269)*
**SA Industries 2 Inc** 815 381-6200
999 Sandy Hollow Rd Rockford (61109) *(G-18604)*
**SA Nat Industrial Cnstr Co Inc** 618 246-9402
103 E Perkins Ave Mount Vernon (62864) *(G-15443)*
**Saachi Inc** 630 775-1700
364 Jennifer Ln Roselle (60172) *(G-18971)*
**Saasoom LLC** 630 561-7300
7n063 Plymouth Ct Saint Charles (60175) *(G-19258)*
**Saati Americas Corporation** 847 296-5090
901 E Business Center Dr Mount Prospect (60056) *(G-15371)*
**Saatiprint Div, Mount Prospect** *Also called Saati Americas Corporation (G-15371)*
**Sab Tool Supply Co (PA)** 847 634-3700
730 Corporate Woods Pkwy Vernon Hills (60061) *(G-21196)*
**Sabic Innovative Plas US LLC** 815 434-7000
2148 N 2753rd Rd Ottawa (61350) *(G-16982)*
**Sabinas Food Products Inc** 312 738-2412
1509 W 18th St Chicago (60608) *(G-6423)*
**Sacco-Camex Inc** 630 595-8090
460 Dominic Ct Franklin Park (60131) *(G-10580)*
**Saco Dps/Morris Wax** 815 462-0939
441 Degroate Rd New Lenox (60451) *(G-15909)*
**Saco USA (il)inc** 815 877-8832
3391 Sage Dr Rockford (61114) *(G-18605)*
**Sadannah Group LLC** 630 357-2300
426 W 5th Ave Naperville (60563) *(G-15745)*
**Sadelco USA Corp** 847 781-8844
1120 Warwick Cir N Hoffman Estates (60169) *(G-12048)*

ALPHABETIC

**SAE Customs Inc** .................................................. 855 723-2878
  27764 Volo Village Rd F  Round Lake  (60073)  *(G-19066)*
**Saf-T-Eze, Lombard**  Also called Saf-T-Lok International Corp  *(G-13850)*
**Saf-T-Lok International Corp** ................................. 630 495-2001
  300 Eisenhower Ln N  Lombard  (60148)  *(G-13850)*
**Safco LLC** ............................................................. 847 677-3204
  7631 Austin Ave  Skokie  (60077)  *(G-20081)*
**Safe Effective Alternatives** ................................... 618 236-2727
  6218 Old Saint Louis Rd  Belleville  (62223)  *(G-1675)*
**Safe Fair Food Company LLC** ............................... 904 930-4277
  318 W Adams St Ste 700c  Chicago  (60606)  *(G-6424)*
**Safe Pet Products, Westmont**  Also called Kmp Products  LLC  *(G-21899)*
**Safe Sheds  Inc** .................................................... 888 556-1531
  7029 Parrill Rd  Alma  (62807)  *(G-423)*
**Safe Traffic System Inc** ........................................ 847 233-0365
  6600 N Lincoln Ave  Lincolnwood  (60712)  *(G-13536)*
**Safe Water Technologies Inc** ................................ 847 888-6900
  996 Bluff City Blvd  Elgin  (60120)  *(G-9171)*
**Safe-Air of Illinois  Inc** ......................................... 708 652-9100
  1855 S 54th Ave  Cicero  (60804)  *(G-7227)*
**Safe-T-Quip Corporation** ..................................... 773 235-2100
  2300 N Kilbourn Ave  Chicago  (60639)  *(G-6425)*
**Safecharge LLC** .................................................. 248 866-9428
  2506 N Clark St Ste 176  Chicago  (60614)  *(G-6426)*
**Safeguard 201 Corp** ........................................... 630 241-0370
  1129 Fairview Ave  Westmont  (60559)  *(G-21918)*
**Safeguard Print & Promo, Westmont**  Also called Safeguard 201 Corp  *(G-21918)*
**Safeguard Scientifics  Inc** .................................... 312 234-9828
  3400 N Kildare Ave Apt 1r  Chicago  (60641)  *(G-6427)*
**Safelite Autoglass, Crest Hill**  Also called Safelite Glass Corp  *(G-7467)*
**Safelite Glass Corp** ............................................. 815 436-6333
  2406 Plainfield Rd  Crest Hill  (60403)  *(G-7467)*
**Safelite Glass Corp** ............................................. 877 800-2727
  1303 N Main St  Decatur  (62526)  *(G-7938)*
**Safelite Glass Corp** ............................................. 877 800-2727
  719 S Neil St  Champaign  (61820)  *(G-3535)*
**Safelite Group, Decatur**  Also called Safelite Glass Corp  *(G-7938)*
**Safemobile Inc** .................................................... 847 818-1649
  3601 Algonquin Rd Ste 320  Rolling Meadows  (60008)  *(G-18776)*
**Safeplug, Gurnee**  Also called 2d2c  Inc  *(G-11416)*
**Safersonic Us  Inc** ............................................... 847 274-1534
  2873 Arlington Ave # 110  Highland Park  (60035)  *(G-11867)*
**Safety Compound Corporation** ........................... 630 953-1515
  300 Eisenhower Ln N  Lombard  (60148)  *(G-13851)*
**Safety Security Products Co, Lake Bluff**  Also called Profile Plastics  Inc  *(G-12864)*
**Safety Socket LLC** .............................................. 224 484-6222
  49 Prairie Pkwy  Gilberts  (60136)  *(G-10934)*
**Safety Storage Inc** .............................................. 217 345-4422
  855 N 5th St  Charleston  (61920)  *(G-3610)*
**Safety-Kleen Systems  Inc** ................................... 618 875-8050
  3000 Missouri Ave  East Saint Louis  (62205)  *(G-8768)*
**Safeway Products  Inc** ........................................ 815 226-8322
  1810 15th Ave  Rockford  (61104)  *(G-18606)*
**Safeway Services Rockford Inc** ............................ 815 986-1504
  1310 Samuelson Rd  Rockford  (61109)  *(G-18607)*
**Saffire Grill Co., Rockford**  Also called Home Fires Inc  *(G-18421)*
**Safigel, Chicago**  Also called Two Tower Frames  Inc  *(G-6798)*
**Saftey Glass, Lombard**  Also called Safety Compound Corporation  *(G-13851)*
**Saga Communications  Inc** ................................. 248 631-8099
  3501 E Sangamon Ave  Springfield  (62707)  *(G-20517)*
**Sagamore Publishing LLC** .................................. 217 359-5940
  1807 N Federal Dr  Urbana  (61801)  *(G-21102)*
**Sage Clover** ....................................................... 630 220-9600
  26w400 Torrey Pines Ct  Winfield  (60190)  *(G-22293)*
**Sage Products  LLC** ........................................... 815 455-4700
  815 Tek Dr  Crystal Lake  (60014)  *(G-7645)*
**Sage Products  LLC (HQ)** ................................... 815 455-4700
  3909 3 Oaks Rd  Cary  (60013)  *(G-3370)*
**Sage Vertical Grdn Systems LLC** ......................... 312 234-9655
  730 W Randolph St Ste 300  Chicago  (60661)  *(G-6428)*
**Sagent Logistics  LP** ........................................... 847 908-1600
  1901 N Roselle Rd Ste 450  Schaumburg  (60195)  *(G-19716)*
**Sagent Pharmaceuticals Inc (HQ)** ...................... 847 908-1600
  1901 N Roselle Rd Ste 700  Schaumburg  (60195)  *(G-19717)*
**Sahara Air Dryers, Sandwich**  Also called Henderson Engineering Co Inc  *(G-19368)*
**SAI, Lake Villa**  Also called Strategic Applications Inc  *(G-13027)*
**SAI Advanced Pwr Solutions Inc (PA)** ................. 708 450-0990
  618 W Lamont Rd  Elmhurst  (60126)  *(G-9932)*
**SAI Info USA** ...................................................... 630 773-3335
  183 Bay Dr  Itasca  (60143)  *(G-12352)*
**Saicor Inc** ........................................................... 630 530-0350
  708 N Princeton Ave  Villa Park  (60181)  *(G-21282)*
**Saint Clair Tennis Club, O Fallon**  Also called St Clair Tennis Club LLC  *(G-16480)*
**Saint Mary Fuel Company** .................................. 773 918-1681
  6700 S Ashland Ave  Chicago  (60636)  *(G-6429)*
**Saint Pierre Oil, Newton**  Also called St Pierre Oil Company Inc  *(G-15949)*
**Saint Technologies Inc** ........................................ 815 864-3035
  10 N Locust St  Shannon  (61078)  *(G-19902)*

**Saint-Gobain Abrasives  Inc** ................................ 630 238-3300
  200 Fullerton Ave  Carol Stream  (60188)  *(G-3231)*
**Saint-Gobain Abrasives  Inc** ................................ 630 868-8060
  200 Fullerton Ave  Carol Stream  (60188)  *(G-3232)*
**Saints Volo & Olha Uk Cath Par** .......................... 312 829-5209
  2245 W Superior St  Chicago  (60612)  *(G-6430)*
**Sakamoto Kanagata Usa Inc** ............................... 224 856-2008
  433 Joseph Dr  South Elgin  (60177)  *(G-20225)*
**Salamander Studios Chicago Inc** ........................ 773 379-2211
  5410 W Roosevelt Rd # 306  Chicago  (60644)  *(G-6431)*
**Salco Products Inc (PA)** ...................................... 630 783-2570
  1385 101st St Ste A  Lemont  (60439)  *(G-13261)*
**Salem Business Center, Salem**  Also called Shetley Management Inc  *(G-19351)*
**Salem Times-Commoner Pubg Co (HQ)** ............... 618 548-3330
  120 S Broadway Ave  Salem  (62881)  *(G-19349)*
**Sales & Marketing Resources** ............................. 847 910-9169
  21 Ashcroft Ct  Fox River Grove  (60021)  *(G-10289)*
**Sales Midwest Prtg & Packg Inc** ......................... 309 764-5544
  426 37th St  Moline  (61265)  *(G-14968)*
**Sales Specialty Metal** ......................................... 217 864-1496
  355 Secretariat Pl  Mount Zion  (62549)  *(G-15456)*
**Sales Stretcher Enterprises** ................................ 815 223-9681
  4920 E 103rd Rd  Peru  (61354)  *(G-17527)*
**Salesforcecom  Inc** ............................................. 312 361-3555
  205 W Wacker Dr Fl 22  Chicago  (60606)  *(G-6432)*
**Salesforcecom  Inc** ............................................. 312 288-3600
  111 W Illinois St  Chicago  (60654)  *(G-6433)*
**Saliba Industries  Inc** .......................................... 847 680-2266
  13885 W Laurel Dr  Lake Forest  (60045)  *(G-12955)*
**Salient Hct, Chicago**  Also called Am2pat Inc  *(G-3842)*
**Salisbury By Honeywell, Bolingbrook**  Also called Salisbury Elec Safety LLC  *(G-2365)*
**Salisbury Elec Safety LLC** ................................... 877 406-4501
  101 E Crssrads Pkwy Ste A  Bolingbrook  (60440)  *(G-2365)*
**Salman Metal** ..................................................... 630 359-5110
  552 W Fay Ave  Elmhurst  (60126)  *(G-9933)*
**Salmons and Brown** ........................................... 312 929-6756
  44 E Superior St 1  Chicago  (60611)  *(G-6434)*
**Salsedo Press Inc** .............................................. 773 533-9900
  3139 W Chicago Ave  Chicago  (60622)  *(G-6435)*
**Salt Creek Alpacas Inc** ....................................... 309 530-7904
  3605 N 3300 East Rd  Farmer City  (61842)  *(G-10181)*
**Salt Creek Rural Park District** ............................. 847 259-6890
  530 S Williams Ave  Palatine  (60074)  *(G-17071)*
**Salter Labs** ......................................................... 661 854-3166
  272 E Deerpath Ste 302  Lake Forest  (60045)  *(G-12956)*
**Salter Labs (HQ)** ................................................ 847 739-3224
  272 E Deerpath Ste 302  Lake Forest  (60045)  *(G-12957)*
**Saltzman Printers Inc** ......................................... 708 344-4500
  2150 N 15th Ave Ste C  Melrose Park  (60160)  *(G-14690)*
**Salud Natural Entrepreneur Inc** .......................... 224 789-7400
  1120 Glen Rock Ave  Waukegan  (60085)  *(G-21611)*
**Salud Natural Entrepreneur Inc (PA)** .................. 224 789-7400
  1120 Glen Rock Ave  Waukegan  (60085)  *(G-21612)*
**Salud Natural Entrepreneurs, Waukegan**  Also called Salud Natural Entrepreneur Inc  *(G-21611)*
**Salzgitter International** ...................................... 847 692-6312
  9701 W Higgins Rd Ste 380  Rosemont  (60018)  *(G-19029)*
**Salzman Printing** ............................................... 309 745-3016
  105 Grant St  Washington  (61571)  *(G-21391)*
**Sam Solutions Inc** .............................................. 708 594-0480
  5120 S Lawndale Ave  Summit Argo  (60501)  *(G-20765)*
**Samecwei Inc** .................................................... 630 897-7888
  205 N Lake St Ste 103  Aurora  (60506)  *(G-1214)*
**Samel Botros** ..................................................... 847 466-5905
  1 Tiffany Pt Ste G1  Bloomingdale  (60108)  *(G-2134)*
**Sammons Preston, Warrenville**  Also called Patterson Medical Products Inc  *(G-21353)*
**Sammy USA Corp** ............................................... 847 364-9787
  800 Arthur Ave  Elk Grove Village  (60007)  *(G-9726)*
**Sams Pharmacy, O Fallon**  Also called Sams West  Inc  *(G-16477)*
**Sams West  Inc** .................................................. 618 622-0507
  1350 W Highway 50  O Fallon  (62269)  *(G-16477)*
**Samsung Sign Corp** ........................................... 847 816-1374
  1840 Industrial Dr # 230  Libertyville  (60048)  *(G-13377)*
**Samtek International  Inc** ................................... 314 954-4005
  10 Emerald Ter Ste C  Swansea  (62226)  *(G-20782)*
**Samuel Rowell** .................................................... 618 942-6970
  2817 S Park Ave  Herrin  (62948)  *(G-11754)*
**Samuel Strapping Systems  Inc (HQ)** ................. 630 783-8900
  1401 Davey Rd Ste 300  Woodridge  (60517)  *(G-22515)*
**San Mateo  Inc** ................................................... 630 860-6991
  1180 Industrial Dr  Bensenville  (60106)  *(G-1985)*
**San Telmo Ltd** .................................................... 847 842-9115
  330 E Main St Fl 2  Barrington  (60010)  *(G-1304)*
**Sanchem  Inc** ..................................................... 312 733-6100
  1600 S Canal St  Chicago  (60616)  *(G-6436)*
**Sanco Industries  Inc** .......................................... 847 243-8675
  21800 N Andover Rd  Kildeer  (60047)  *(G-12703)*
**Sand & Gravel Service** ....................................... 309 648-4585
  305 Murphy Ln  Metamora  (61548)  *(G-14749)*

ALPHABETIC SECTION Sb Acquisition, Elmhurst

**Sand Sculpture Co** ....815 334-9101
327 S Jefferson St Woodstock (60098) *(G-22607)*
**Sand Valley Sand & Gravel Inc** ....217 446-4210
16395 Lewis Rd Danville (61834) *(G-7765)*
**Sand-Rite Manufacturing Co** ....312 997-2200
3080 W Soffel Ave Melrose Park (60160) *(G-14691)*
**Sandbagger LLC** ....630 876-2400
765 S State Route 83 Elmhurst (60126) *(G-9934)*
**Sandbagger Corp** ....630 876-2400
765 S Il Route 83 Elmhurst (60126) *(G-9935)*
**Sandee Manufacturing Co (PA)** ....847 671-1335
10520 Waveland Ave Franklin Park (60131) *(G-10581)*
**Sandeno Inc** ....815 730-9415
2115 Moen Ave Rockdale (60436) *(G-18231)*
**Sanders Inc** ....815 634-4611
2250 Wahoo Dr Morris (60450) *(G-15129)*
**Sanderson and Associates** ....312 829-4350
400 N Racine Ave Apt 211 Chicago (60642) *(G-6437)*
**Sandes Quynetta** ....815 275-4876
752 W American St Apt 5 Freeport (61032) *(G-10687)*
**Sandlock Sandbox LLC** ....630 963-9422
1069 Zygmunt Cir Westmont (60559) *(G-21919)*
**Sandmancom Inc** ....630 980-7710
219 E Irving Park Rd Roselle (60172) *(G-18972)*
**Sandner Electric Co Inc** ....618 932-2179
903 E Saint Louis St West Frankfort (62896) *(G-21818)*
**Sandoval Fences Company, Chicago** *Also called Sandoval Fences Corp (G-6438)*
**Sandoval Fences Corp** ....773 287-0279
855 N Cicero Ave Chicago (60651) *(G-6438)*
**Sandoval Machine Works Inc** ....618 247-3588
4379 Pope Rd Sandoval (62882) *(G-19358)*
**Sandra E Greene** ....815 469-0092
228 N Locust St Frankfort (60423) *(G-10361)*
**Sandstrom Products Company (PA)** ....309 523-2121
224 S Main St Port Byron (61275) *(G-17723)*
**Sandstrom Products Company** ....309 523-2121
224 S Main St Port Byron (61275) *(G-17724)*
**Sandtech Inc** ....847 470-9595
7845 Merrimac Ave Morton Grove (60053) *(G-15234)*
**Sandvik Inc** ....847 519-1737
1665 N Penny Ln Schaumburg (60173) *(G-19718)*
**Sandvik Crmant Prductivity Ctr, Schaumburg** *Also called Sandvik Inc (G-19718)*
**Sandwich Casting & Machine, Sandwich** *Also called Trio Foundry Inc (G-19379)*
**Sandwich Casting & Machine Div, Montgomery** *Also called Trio Foundry Inc (G-15068)*
**Sandwich Millworks Inc** ....815 786-2700
700 W Center St Sandwich (60548) *(G-19377)*
**Sanford LP (HQ)** ....770 418-7000
3500 Lacey Rd Downers Grove (60515) *(G-8518)*
**Sanford Brands, Downers Grove** *Also called Sanford LP (G-8518)*
**Sanford Chemical Co Inc** ....847 437-3530
1945 Touhy Ave Elk Grove Village (60007) *(G-9727)*
**Sangam, Skokie** *Also called Princess Foods Inc (G-20060)*
**Sangamon Valley Sand & Gravel** ....217 498-7189
102 Maple Ln Rochester (62563) *(G-18121)*
**Sangchris Lake State Park, Rochester** *Also called Ill Dept Natural Resources (G-18118)*
**Sango Embroidery** ....773 582-4354
5220 S Pulaski Rd Chicago (60632) *(G-6439)*
**Sanitary Stainless Services** ....618 659-8567
703 Vassar Dr Edwardsville (62025) *(G-8813)*
**Sanks Machining Inc** ....618 635-8279
22991 Ruschaupt Rd Staunton (62088) *(G-20557)*
**Sansabelt** ....312 357-5119
101 N Wacker Dr Chicago (60606) *(G-6440)*
**Sansui America Inc** ....618 392-7000
3471 N Union Dr Olney (62450) *(G-16796)*
**Santana & Daughter Inc** ....773 237-1818
5959 W Dickens Ave Chicago (60639) *(G-6441)*
**Santas Best (PA)** ....847 459-3301
3750 Deerfield Rd # 1000 Riverwoods (60015) *(G-18043)*
**Santec Systems Inc** ....847 215-8884
2924 Malmo Dr Arlington Heights (60005) *(G-835)*
**Santelli Custom Cabinetry** ....708 771-3884
1531 Forest Ave Apt 3 River Forest (60305) *(G-18000)*
**Santucci Enterprises** ....773 286-5629
6345 W Warwick Ave Chicago (60634) *(G-6442)*
**Sanyo Seiki America Corp** ....630 876-8270
333 Charles Ct Ste 105 West Chicago (60185) *(G-21768)*
**Sap Acquisition Co LLC** ....847 229-1600
1200 Barclay Blvd Buffalo Grove (60089) *(G-2761)*
**Sapa Extrusions Inc** ....847 233-9105
6250 N River Rd Ste 5000 Rosemont (60018) *(G-19030)*
**Sapa Extrusions Inc (HQ)** ....877 710-7272
6250 N River Rd Ste 5000 Rosemont (60018) *(G-19031)*
**Sapa Extrusions North Amer LLC** ....877 922-7272
6250 N River Rd Ste 5000 Rosemont (60018) *(G-19032)*
**Saporito Finishing Co (PA)** ....708 222-5300
3119 S Austin Blvd Cicero (60804) *(G-7228)*
**Saporito Finishing Co** ....708 222-5300
3130 S Austin Blvd Chicago (60804) *(G-6443)*
**Saputo Cheese USA Inc** ....847 267-1100
1 Overlook Pt Ste 300 Lincolnshire (60069) *(G-13475)*
**Saputo Cheese USA Inc (HQ)** ....847 267-1100
1 Overlook Pt Ste 300 Lincolnshire (60069) *(G-13476)*
**Sara Lee Baking Group** ....217 585-3462
6100 S 2nd St Springfield (62711) *(G-20518)*
**Sara Lee Food & Beverage, Chicago** *Also called Hillshire Brands Company (G-5089)*
**Saratoga Food Specialties, Bolingbrook** *Also called John Morrell & Co (G-2329)*
**Sarco Hydraulics Inc (PA)** ....217 324-6577
216 N Old Route 66 Litchfield (62056) *(G-13697)*
**Sarco Putty Company** ....773 735-5577
5959 S Knox Ave Chicago (60629) *(G-6444)*
**Sarcol** ....773 533-3000
3050 W Taylor St Chicago (60612) *(G-6445)*
**Sardee Industries Inc (PA)** ....630 824-4200
5100 Academy Dr Ste 400 Lisle (60532) *(G-13654)*
**Sarj Kalidas LLC** ....708 865-9134
1344 N Western Ave Chicago (60622) *(G-6446)*
**Sarj USA Inc** ....708 865-9134
9201 King St Franklin Park (60131) *(G-10582)*
**Sas Industrial Machinery Inc** ....847 455-5526
9212 Cherry Ave Franklin Park (60131) *(G-10583)*
**SASI Corporation** ....314 922-7432
1700 Saint Louis Rd Collinsville (62234) *(G-7340)*
**Sass-N-Class Inc** ....630 655-2420
19 W 1st St Ste A Hinsdale (60521) *(G-11962)*
**Sassy Primitives Ltd** ....815 385-9302
3202 Lakeside Ct Unit 2 McCullom Lake (60050) *(G-14472)*
**Satellink Inc** ....618 983-5555
724 W 15th St Johnston City (62951) *(G-12445)*
**Satellite Certified Inc** ....815 230-3877
216 Jessie St Joliet (60433) *(G-12573)*
**Sato Lbling Solutions Amer Inc (PA)** ....630 771-4200
1140 Windham Pkwy Romeoville (60446) *(G-18866)*
**Saturn Electrical Services Inc** ....630 980-0300
380 Monaco Dr Roselle (60172) *(G-18973)*
**Saturn Manufacturing Company** ....630 860-8474
233 Park St Bensenville (60106) *(G-1986)*
**Saturn Sign** ....847 520-9009
240 Industrial Ln Ste 1 Wheeling (60090) *(G-22144)*
**Sauber Manufacturing Company** ....630 365-6600
10 N Sauber Rd Virgil (60151) *(G-21303)*
**Sauber Mfg. Co., Virgil** *Also called C S O Corp (G-21302)*
**Sauk Valley Container Corp** ....815 626-9657
1980 Eastwood Dr Sterling (61081) *(G-20611)*
**Sauk Valley Newspaper, Sterling** *Also called B F Shaw Printing Company (G-20584)*
**Sauk Valley Newspaper, Sterling** *Also called Sauk Valley Shopper Inc (G-20612)*
**Sauk Valley Printing** ....815 284-2222
113 S Peoria Ave Ste 1 Dixon (61021) *(G-8347)*
**Sauk Valley Shopper Inc** ....815 625-6700
3200 E Lincolnway Sterling (61081) *(G-20612)*
**Sausages By Amy, Chicago** *Also called Atk Foods Inc (G-3976)*
**Savage Bros Company** ....847 981-3000
1825 Greenleaf Ave Elk Grove Village (60007) *(G-9728)*
**Savanna Gas and Welding Sups, Savanna** *Also called Mills Machine Inc (G-19403)*
**Savanna Quarry Inc** ....815 273-4208
9859 Scenic Bluff Rd Savanna (61074) *(G-19405)*
**Savanna Times Journal** ....815 273-2277
121 Main St Savanna (61074) *(G-19406)*
**Savanna Times-Journal, Mount Carroll** *Also called Mirror-Democrat (G-15292)*
**Save On Printing Inc** ....847 922-7855
1451 Landmeier Rd Elk Grove Village (60007) *(G-9729)*
**Savencia Cheese USA LLC** ....815 369-4577
3990 N Sunnyside Rd Lena (61048) *(G-13283)*
**Savex Manufacturing Company** ....630 668-7219
170 Easy St Carol Stream (60188) *(G-3233)*
**Savile Rumtini, Bolingbrook** *Also called Dtrs Enterprises Inc (G-2302)*
**Savind Inc** ....217 687-2710
205 S Main St Ste B Seymour (61875) *(G-19898)*
**Savino Displays Inc** ....630 574-0777
28 Bradford Ln Hinsdale (60523) *(G-11963)*
**Savino Enterprises** ....708 385-5277
12453 Gregory St Blue Island (60406) *(G-2268)*
**Savo Group Ltd** ....312 276-7700
155 N Wacker Dr Ste 1000 Chicago (60606) *(G-6447)*
**Savo Headquarters, Chicago** *Also called Savo Group Ltd (G-6447)*
**Sawier** ....630 297-8588
7517 Florence Ave Downers Grove (60516) *(G-8519)*
**Sawmill Construction Inc** ....815 937-0037
5265 E 4000n Rd Bourbonnais (60914) *(G-2406)*
**Sawmill Hydraulics** ....309 245-2448
23522 W Farmington Rd Farmington (61531) *(G-10188)*
**Saws Unlimited Inc** ....847 640-7450
494 Bonnie Ln Elk Grove Village (60007) *(G-9730)*
**Say Cheese Cake** ....618 532-6001
421 W Noleman St Centralia (62801) *(G-3431)*
**Sazerac North America Inc (HQ)** ....502 423-5225
75 Remittance Dr # 3312 Chicago (60675) *(G-6448)*
**Sb Acquisition, Elmhurst** *Also called Sandbagger LLC (G-9934)*

ALPHABETIC

(PA)=Parent Co (HQ)=Headquarters (DH)=Div Headquarters

**Sb Boron, Bellwood** *Also called SB Boron Corporation* ***(G-1719)***
**SB Boron Corporation**..........708 547-9002
20 Davis Dr Bellwood (60104) ***(G-1719)***
**SBA, La Grange** *Also called Sergio Barajas* ***(G-12744)***
**SBA Wireless Inc**..........847 215-8720
1287 Barclay Blvd Ste 200 Buffalo Grove (60089) ***(G-2762)***
**SBC, Champaign** *Also called Am-Don Partnership* ***(G-3447)***
**Sbic America Inc**..........847 303-5430
205 Travis Ct Apt 304 Schaumburg (60195) ***(G-19719)***
**SBS Steel Belt Systems USA Inc**..........847 841-3300
59 Prairie Pkwy Gilberts (60136) ***(G-10935)***
**SC Aviation Inc**..........800 416-4176
1433 Lancaster Ave Saint Charles (60174) ***(G-19259)***
**SC Industries Inc (PA)**..........312 366-3899
917 W Wa Blvd Ste 202 Chicago (60607) ***(G-6449)***
**SC Lighting**..........630 849-3384
607 W Wise Rd Schaumburg (60193) ***(G-19720)***
**Sca, River Forest** *Also called Scientific Cmpt Assoc Corp* ***(G-18001)***
**Sca Thermosafe, Arlington Heights** *Also called Sonoco Prtective Solutions Inc* ***(G-842)***
**Scadaware Inc**..........309 665-0135
2023 Eagle Rd Normal (61761) ***(G-16088)***
**Scale Railroad Equipment**..........630 682-9170
23w546 Saint Charles Rd Carol Stream (60188) ***(G-3234)***
**Scale-Tronix Inc**..........630 653-3377
288 Carlton Dr Carol Stream (60188) ***(G-3235)***
**Scaletta Moloney Armoring (PA)**..........708 924-0099
6755 S Belt Circle Dr Bedford Park (60638) ***(G-1583)***
**Scanlab America Inc**..........630 797-2044
100 Illinois St Ste 200 Saint Charles (60174) ***(G-19260)***
**Scars Publications**..........847 281-9070
829 Brian Ct Gurnee (60031) ***(G-11502)***
**Scarzone Printing Services**..........630 595-2690
601 W Montrose Ave Wood Dale (60191) ***(G-22419)***
**SCC Holding Company LLC (PA)**..........847 444-5000
150 Saunders Rd Ste 150 Lake Forest (60045) ***(G-12958)***
**Scenery Unlimited, Forest Park** *Also called Heimburger House Pubg Co Inc* ***(G-10248)***
**Scf Services LLC**..........314 436-7559
8 Pitzman Ave Sauget (62201) ***(G-19389)***
**Schaefer Technologies LLC**..........630 406-9377
751 N Raddant Rd Batavia (60510) ***(G-1493)***
**Schaeff Lift Truck Inc**..........708 430-5301
9725 Industrial Dr Bridgeview (60455) ***(G-2527)***
**Schaeffer Electric Co (PA)**..........618 592-3231
400 S Taylor St Oblong (62449) ***(G-16734)***
**Schafer Gear Works Roscoe LLC**..........815 874-4327
5466 E Rockton Rd Roscoe (61073) ***(G-18920)***
**Schafer Gear Wrks Rockford LLC, Roscoe** *Also called Schafer Gear Works Roscoe LLC* ***(G-18920)***
**Schaff International LLC**..........847 438-4560
451 Oakwood Rd Lake Zurich (60047) ***(G-13125)***
**Schaff Piano Supply, Lake Zurich** *Also called Schaff International LLC* ***(G-13125)***
**Schaffer Tool & Design Inc**..........630 876-3800
1320 W Washington St West Chicago (60185) ***(G-21769)***
**Schantz Mfg Inc**..........618 654-1523
13480 Us Highway 40 Highland (62249) ***(G-11810)***
**Schau Southeast Sushi Inc**..........630 783-1000
10350 Argonne Dr Ste 400 Woodridge (60517) ***(G-22516)***
**Schaumburg Review**..........847 998-3400
350 N Orleans St Fl 10 Chicago (60654) ***(G-6450)***
**Schaumburg Specialties Co**..........847 451-0070
550 Albion Ave Ste 30 Schaumburg (60193) ***(G-19721)***
**Scheck & Siress**..........708 383-2257
401 Harrison St Oak Park (60304) ***(G-16683)***
**Scheck Siress Prosthetics Inc**..........630 424-0392
401 Harrison St Oak Park (60304) ***(G-16684)***
**Scheffler Custom Woodworking**..........815 284-6564
925 Depot Ave Dixon (61021) ***(G-8348)***
**Scheiwes Print and Christn Sup, Crescent City** *Also called Scheiwes Print Shop* ***(G-7456)***
**Scheiwes Print Shop**..........815 683-2398
407 Main St Crescent City (60928) ***(G-7456)***
**Schellerer Corporation Inc**..........630 980-4567
110 Ridge Ave Bloomingdale (60108) ***(G-2135)***
**Schellhorn Photo Techniques**..........773 267-5141
3916 N Elston Ave Ste 1 Chicago (60618) ***(G-6451)***
**Schepel Signs Inc**..........708 758-1441
3149 Glenwood Dyer Rd I Lynwood (60411) ***(G-14027)***
**Schiele Graphics Inc**..........847 434-5455
1880 Busse Rd Elk Grove Village (60007) ***(G-9731)***
**Schiele Group, Elk Grove Village** *Also called Schiele Graphics Inc* ***(G-9731)***
**Schilke Music Products Inc**..........708 343-8858
4520 James Pl Melrose Park (60160) ***(G-14692)***
**Schindler Logistics Center, Chicago** *Also called Adams Elevator Equipment Co* ***(G-3743)***
**Schlesinger Machinery Inc**..........630 766-4074
820 Maple Ln Bensenville (60106) ***(G-1987)***
**Schmalz Precast Concrete Mfg**..........815 747-3939
18363 Us Highway 20 W East Dubuque (61025) ***(G-8622)***
**Schmid Tool & Engineering Corp**..........630 333-1733
930 N Villa Ave Villa Park (60181) ***(G-21283)***
**Schmidt Marking Systems, Niles** *Also called Geo T Schmidt Inc* ***(G-15982)***
**Schmidt Printing, Woodstock** *Also called Dale K Brown* ***(G-22558)***
**Schmit Laboratories Inc**..........773 476-0072
500 Wall St Glendale Heights (60139) ***(G-11066)***
**Schmolz Bckenbach USA Holdings**..........630 682-3900
365 Village Dr Carol Stream (60188) ***(G-3236)***
**Schneider Elc Buildings LLC (HQ)**..........815 381-5000
839 N Perryville Rd Rockford (61107) ***(G-18608)***
**Schneider Elc Buildings LLC**..........815 227-4000
4104 Charles St Rockford (61108) ***(G-18609)***
**Schneider Elc Holdings Inc (HQ)**..........717 944-5460
200 N Martingale Rd # 100 Schaumburg (60173) ***(G-19722)***
**Schneider Electric Usa Inc**..........630 428-3849
9522 Winona Ave Schiller Park (60176) ***(G-19871)***
**Schneider Electric Usa Inc**..........312 697-4770
311 S Wacker Dr Ste 4550 Chicago (60606) ***(G-6452)***
**Schneider Electric Usa Inc**..........847 925-7773
3050 Finley Rd Ste 301 Downers Grove (60515) ***(G-8520)***
**Schneider Electric Usa Inc**..........847 441-2526
200 N Martingale Rd # 100 Schaumburg (60173) ***(G-19723)***
**Schneider Graphics Inc**..........847 550-4310
885 Telser Rd Lake Zurich (60047) ***(G-13126)***
**Schneider Pipe Organs Inc**..........217 871-4807
104 S Johnston St Kenney (61749) ***(G-12664)***
**Schnuck Markets Inc**..........618 466-0825
2712 Godfrey Rd Godfrey (62035) ***(G-11237)***
**Schnucks Pharmacy, Godfrey** *Also called Schnuck Markets Inc* ***(G-11237)***
**Scholarship Solutions LLC**..........847 859-5629
318 W Adams St Ste 1600 Chicago (60606) ***(G-6453)***
**Scholastic Inc**..........630 443-8197
2315 Dean St Ste 600 Saint Charles (60175) ***(G-19261)***
**Scholastic Inc**..........630 671-0601
301 S Gary Ave Roselle (60172) ***(G-18974)***
**Scholastic Testing Service**..........630 766-7150
480 Meyer Rd Bensenville (60106) ***(G-1988)***
**Schold Machine Corporation**..........708 458-3788
7201 W 64th Pl Chicago (60638) ***(G-6454)***
**Scholl Communications Inc**..........847 945-1891
56 Birchwood Ave Deerfield (60015) ***(G-8051)***
**Scholle Ipn Corporation (PA)**..........708 562-7290
200 W North Ave Northlake (60164) ***(G-16450)***
**Scholle Ipn Packaging Inc (HQ)**..........708 562-7290
200 W North Ave Northlake (60164) ***(G-16451)***
**Scholle Packaging, Northlake** *Also called Scholle Ipn Corporation* ***(G-16450)***
**Scholle Packaging, Northlake** *Also called Scholle Ipn Packaging Inc* ***(G-16451)***
**Scholle Packaging Inc**..........708 273-3792
120 N Railroad Ave Northlake (60164) ***(G-16452)***
**Schommer Inc**..........815 344-1404
3410 W Elm St McHenry (60050) ***(G-14554)***
**School Town LLC**..........847 943-9115
1340 Shermer Rd Ste 245 Northbrook (60062) ***(G-16359)***
**Schools Processing Service, Bensenville** *Also called Scholastic Testing Service* ***(G-1988)***
**Schrader-Bridgeport Intl Inc**..........815 288-3344
1550 Franklin Grove Rd Dixon (61021) ***(G-8349)***
**Schram Enterprises Inc**..........708 345-2252
5017 W Lake St Melrose Park (60160) ***(G-14693)***
**Schreder Lighting LLC**..........847 621-5130
2105 W Corporate Dr Addison (60101) ***(G-282)***
**Schrock Custom Woodworking**..........217 849-3375
705 Industrial Dr Toledo (62468) ***(G-20965)***
**Schrocks Sawmill**..........217 268-3632
59 N County Road 450e Arcola (61910) ***(G-684)***
**Schrocks Wood Shop**..........217 773-3842
356 650n Ave Mount Sterling (62353) ***(G-15394)***
**Schrocks Woodworking**..........217 578-3259
135 E Cr 800 N Arthur (61911) ***(G-921)***
**Schroeders Pallet Service**..........708 371-9046
13601 Western Ave Blue Island (60406) ***(G-2269)***
**Schubert Controls Corporation**..........847 526-8200
1099 Brown St Ste 109 Wauconda (60084) ***(G-21501)***
**Schubert Environmental Eqp Inc**..........630 307-9400
2000 Bloomingdale Rd # 115 Glendale Heights (60139) ***(G-11067)***
**Schuld-Bushnell, Bushnell** *Also called Bushnell Illinois Tank Co* ***(G-2898)***
**Schulhof Company**..........773 348-1123
5801 Ami Dr Richmond (60071) ***(G-17971)***
**Schultes Precision Mfg Inc**..........847 465-0300
1250 Busch Pkwy Buffalo Grove (60089) ***(G-2763)***
**Schultz Brothers Inc**..........630 458-1437
1001 W Republic Dr Ste 11 Addison (60101) ***(G-283)***
**Schultz Crematories, Streator** *Also called Wilbert Shultz Vault Co Inc* ***(G-20711)***
**Schulze & Schulze Inc**..........618 687-1106
3198 Town Creek Rd Murphysboro (62966) ***(G-15582)***
**Schulze and Burch Biscuit Co (PA)**..........773 927-6622
1133 W 35th St Chicago (60609) ***(G-6455)***
**Schumacher Electric Corp (PA)**..........847 385-1600
801 E Business Center Dr Mount Prospect (60056) ***(G-15372)***
**Schumacher Electric Corp**..........217 283-5551
1025 E Thompson Ave Hoopeston (60942) ***(G-12115)***

**Schumaker Publications Inc**....309 365-7105
Rr 2 Box 72a Lexington (61753) *(G-13293)*
**Schutt Sports, Litchfield** *Also called Kranos Corporation (G-13691)*
**Schwab Paper Products Company**....815 372-2233
636 Schwab Cir Romeoville (60446) *(G-18867)*
**Schwak, Chicago** *Also called Blue Software LLC (G-4126)*
**Schwanog LLC**....847 289-1055
1630 Todd Farm Dr Elgin (60123) *(G-9172)*
**Schwartz Oilfield Services (PA)**....618 532-0232
501 Schwartz Rd Walnut Hill (62893) *(G-21334)*
**Schwartz Pickle, Chicago** *Also called Bay Valley Foods LLC (G-4058)*
**Schwartzkopf Printing Inc**....618 463-0747
4121 Humbert Rd Alton (62002) *(G-589)*
**Schwarz Bros Manufacturing Co**....309 342-5814
584 E Brooks St Galesburg (61401) *(G-10776)*
**Schwarz Paper Company LLC (HQ)**....847 966-2550
8338 Austin Ave Morton Grove (60053) *(G-15235)*
**Schweitzer Engrg Labs Inc**....847 540-3037
450 Enterprise Pkwy Lake Zurich (60047) *(G-13127)*
**Schweitzer Engrg Labs Inc**....847 362-8304
450 Enterprise Pkwy Lake Zurich (60047) *(G-13128)*
**Schweppe Inc**....630 627-3550
800 S Rohlwing Rd Ste D Addison (60101) *(G-284)*
**SCI, Morris** *Also called Sponge-Cushion Inc (G-15131)*
**SCI, Rockford** *Also called Spider Company Inc (G-18628)*
**SCI, Elk Grove Village** *Also called Cooper Smith International Inc (G-9395)*
**SCI Box LLC**....618 244-7244
515 S 1st St Mount Vernon (62864) *(G-15444)*
**Sciaky Inc**....708 594-3841
4915 W 67th St Chicago (60638) *(G-6456)*
**Scibor Upholstering & Gallery**....708 671-9700
12210 S Harlem Ave Chicago (60643) *(G-6457)*
**Science Solutions LLC (PA)**....773 261-1197
5000 W Roosevelt Rd Dock29 Chicago (60644) *(G-6458)*
**Science Supply Solutions**....847 981-5500
605 Country Club Dr Ste E Bensenville (60106) *(G-1989)*
**Scientific Cmpt Assoc Corp (PA)**....708 771-4567
212 Lathrop Ave River Forest (60305) *(G-18001)*
**Scientific Colors Inc (PA)**....815 741-1391
1401 Mound Rd Rockdale (60436) *(G-18232)*
**Scientific Colors Inc**....815 744-5650
1550 Mound Rd Rockdale (60436) *(G-18233)*
**Scientific Instruments Inc**....847 679-1242
8236 Mccormick Blvd Skokie (60076) *(G-20082)*
**Scientific Manufacturing Inc**....847 414-5658
209 Hilltop Ln Sleepy Hollow (60118) *(G-20118)*
**Scientific Metal Treating Co**....630 582-0071
106 Chancellor Dr Roselle (60172) *(G-18975)*
**Scimatco Office**....630 879-1306
770 N Raddant Rd Batavia (60510) *(G-1494)*
**Scimitar Prototyping Inc**....630 483-3875
1529 Bourbon Pkwy Streamwood (60107) *(G-20672)*
**Scis Air Security Corporation**....847 671-9502
4321 United Pkwy Schiller Park (60176) *(G-19872)*
**Scope, The, Lena** *Also called Shoppers Guide (G-13284)*
**Scorpio Elec Dschrge Machining, Elgin** *Also called EDM Scorpio Inc (G-9020)*
**Scorpion Graphics Inc**....773 927-3203
3221 W 36th St Chicago (60632) *(G-6459)*
**Scot Electrical Products, Aurora** *Also called Win Technologies Incorporated (G-1099)*
**Scot Forge Company (PA)**....815 675-1000
8001 Winn Rd Spring Grove (60081) *(G-20364)*
**Scot Forge Company**....847 678-6000
9394 Belmont Ave Franklin Park (60131) *(G-10584)*
**Scot Industries Inc**....630 466-7591
1961 W Us Highway 30 Sugar Grove (60554) *(G-20734)*
**Scotsman Group Inc (HQ)**....847 215-4500
101 Corporate Woods Pkwy Vernon Hills (60061) *(G-21197)*
**Scotsman Ice Systems**....847 215-4500
101 Corporate Woods Pkwy Vernon Hills (60061) *(G-21198)*
**Scotsman Ice Systems Division, Vernon Hills** *Also called Scotsman Group Inc (G-21197)*
**Scotsman Industries Inc (HQ)**....847 215-4501
101 Corporate Woods Pkwy Vernon Hills (60061) *(G-21199)*
**Scotsman of Los Angeles, Vernon Hills** *Also called Scotsman Industries Inc (G-21199)*
**Scott County Times, Winchester** *Also called Campbell Publishing Inc (G-22278)*
**Scott Industrial Blower Co**....847 426-8800
15 W End Dr Gilberts (60136) *(G-10936)*
**Scott Janczak**....773 545-7233
6285 N Knox Ave Chicago (60646) *(G-6460)*
**Scott Lind Owner**....847 323-9140
9182 Trinity Dr Lake In The Hills (60156) *(G-13005)*
**Scott Oil, Newton** *Also called Trojan Oil Inc (G-15951)*
**Scott Petersen & Company, Lombard** *Also called Specialty Foods Holdings Inc (G-13855)*
**Scottish Modern Enterprises, Summit Argo** *Also called Compu-Tap Inc (G-20761)*
**Scotts Company LLC**....630 343-4070
1030 Internationale Pkwy Woodridge (60517) *(G-22517)*
**Scotts Company LLC**....815 467-1605
23580 W Bluff Rd Channahon (60410) *(G-3585)*
**Scotts Company LLC**....847 777-0700
700 Eastwood Ln Buffalo Grove (60089) *(G-2764)*
**Scranton Glltte Cmmnctions Inc (PA)**....847 391-1000
3030 W Salt Creek Ln # 201 Arlington Heights (60005) *(G-836)*
**Screen Graphics**....309 699-8513
840 Kennedy Dr Pekin (61554) *(G-17288)*
**Screen Machine Incorporated**....847 439-2233
1025 Criss Cir Elk Grove Village (60007) *(G-9732)*
**Screen North Amer Holdings Inc (HQ)**....847 870-7400
5110 Tollview Dr Rolling Meadows (60008) *(G-18777)*
**Screen Print Plus Inc**....630 236-0260
8815 Ramm Dr Ste A Naperville (60564) *(G-15825)*
**Screenprint Products, Chicago** *Also called Petra Manufacturing Co (G-6113)*
**Screentech, South Holland** *Also called Roeda Signs Inc (G-20302)*
**Screw Machine Engrg Co Inc**....773 631-7600
6425 N Avondale Ave Chicago (60631) *(G-6461)*
**Screws Industries Inc**....630 539-9200
301 High Grove Blvd Glendale Heights (60139) *(G-11068)*
**Scribe International Division, Bensenville** *Also called Singer Data Products Inc (G-1991)*
**Scribes Inc**....630 654-3800
7725 S Grant St Ste 1 Burr Ridge (60527) *(G-2879)*
**Scrn LLC**....847 513-4082
1132 W Fulton Market Chicago (60607) *(G-6462)*
**Scrollex Corporation**....630 887-8817
7888 S Quincy St Willowbrook (60527) *(G-22230)*
**Scrubair Systems Inc**....847 550-8061
1200 Ensell Rd Lake Zurich (60047) *(G-13129)*
**Scs Company**....708 203-4955
13633 Crestview Ct Crestwood (60445) *(G-7501)*
**Sct Alternative Inc**....847 215-7488
1655 Barclay Blvd Buffalo Grove (60089) *(G-2765)*
**Scuba Optics Inc**....815 625-7272
1405 8th Ave Rock Falls (61071) *(G-18151)*
**Scuba Sports Inc**....217 787-3483
1609 S Macarthur Blvd Springfield (62704) *(G-20519)*
**Scuva Optics Inc**....815 625-6195
1405 8th Ave Rock Falls (61071) *(G-18152)*
**Sdr Corp**....773 638-1800
4350 W Ohio St Chicago (60624) *(G-6463)*
**SE Relays LLC (HQ)**....847 827-9880
200 N Martingale Rd Schaumburg (60173) *(G-19724)*
**SE Steel Inc (PA)**....847 350-9618
43160 N Crawford Rd Antioch (60002) *(G-654)*
**Sea Converting Inc**....630 694-9178
895 Sivert Dr Wood Dale (60191) *(G-22420)*
**Sea Horse Blinds, Chicago** *Also called 21st Century Us-Sino Services (G-3664)*
**Sea-Rich Corp**....773 261-6633
5000 W Roosevelt Rd # 104 Chicago (60644) *(G-6464)*
**Seabee Supply Co**....630 860-1293
390 E Irving Park Rd Wood Dale (60191) *(G-22421)*
**Seaco Data Systems Inc**....630 876-2169
1360 Rolling Oaks Dr Carol Stream (60188) *(G-3237)*
**Seadog**....773 235-8100
1500 W Division St Chicago (60642) *(G-6465)*
**Seaga Manufacturing Inc**....815 297-9500
700 Seaga Dr Freeport (61032) *(G-10688)*
**Seagon Inc**....630 541-5460
1960 Ohio St Lisle (60532) *(G-13655)*
**Seal Jet Unlimited, Lansing** *Also called Seals & Components Inc (G-13182)*
**Seal Operation S L**....847 537-8100
634 Glenn Ave Wheeling (60090) *(G-22145)*
**Seal Tech Services**....847 776-0043
510 S Bennett Ave Palatine (60067) *(G-17072)*
**Seal-Rite Door, Rockford** *Also called S R Door Inc (G-18603)*
**Sealco Industries Inc (PA)**....847 741-3101
1591 Fleetwood Dr Elgin (60123) *(G-9173)*
**Sealed Air Corporation**....708 352-8700
7110 Santa Fe Dr Hodgkins (60525) *(G-11982)*
**Sealmaster, Rockford** *Also called Thorworks Industries Inc (G-18650)*
**Sealmaster Inc**....847 480-7325
425 Huehl Rd Bldg 11b Northbrook (60062) *(G-16360)*
**Sealmaster Industries, Streamwood** *Also called JB Enterprises II Inc (G-20660)*
**Sealmaster/Alsip**....708 489-0900
5844 W 117th Pl Alsip (60803) *(G-527)*
**Seals & Components Inc**....708 895-5222
17955 Chappel Ave Lansing (60438) *(G-13182)*
**Sealtec**....630 692-0633
120 Kendall Point Dr Oswego (60543) *(G-16932)*
**Sealtech, Oswego** *Also called Dqm Inc (G-16914)*
**Sealtronix Inc**....800 878-9864
11150 Addison Ave Franklin Park (60131) *(G-10585)*
**Sealy Inc**....630 879-8011
1030 E Fabyan Pkwy Batavia (60510) *(G-1495)*
**Seamans Water Technology, Granite City** *Also called Siemens Industry Inc (G-11303)*
**Seamcraft International LLC**....773 417-4002
5610 W Bloomingdale Ave # 4 Chicago (60639) *(G-6466)*
**Seamless Gutter Corp**....630 495-9800
601 E Saint Charles Rd Lombard (60148) *(G-13852)*

**Sean Matthew Innovations Inc** ....815 455-4525
314 Lorraine Dr Crystal Lake (60012) ***(G-7646)***
**Seasonal Designs Inc (PA)** ....847 688-0280
1595 S Shields Dr Waukegan (60085) ***(G-21613)***
**Seasonal Magnets** ....708 499-3235
3133 W 102nd St Evergreen Park (60805) ***(G-10119)***
**Seat Trans Inc** ....224 522-1007
620 Joseph St Lake In The Hills (60156) ***(G-13006)***
**Seats & Stools Inc** ....773 348-7900
2711 N Bosworth Ave Chicago (60614) ***(G-6467)***
**Seavivor Boats** ....847 297-5953
576 Arlington Ave Des Plaines (60016) ***(G-8270)***
**Seaway Supply Co, Maywood** *Also called Best Institutional Supply Co* ***(G-14419)***
**Seba Signs and Printing, Bridgeview** *Also called Biron Studio General Svcs Inc* ***(G-2470)***
**Sebens Backhoe Service Inc** ....217 762-7365
903 Madison St Monticello (61856) ***(G-15084)***
**Sebens Concrete Products Inc** ....217 864-2824
7000 E Us Route 36 Decatur (62521) ***(G-7939)***
**Sebis Direct Inc (PA)** ....312 243-9300
6516 W 74th St Bedford Park (60638) ***(G-1584)***
**SEC Design Technologies Inc** ....847 680-0439
1800 Tempel Dr Libertyville (60048) ***(G-13378)***
**Seco** ....618 748-9227
100 Ohio Ave Mound City (62963) ***(G-15257)***
**Secon Rubber and Plastics Inc (PA)** ....618 282-7700
240 Kaskaskia Dr Red Bud (62278) ***(G-17948)***
**Second Chance Inc** ....630 904-5955
5320 Switch Grass Ln Naperville (60564) ***(G-15826)***
**Second Child** ....773 883-0880
954 W Armitage Ave Fl 1 Chicago (60614) ***(G-6468)***
**Secretary of State Illinois** ....217 466-5220
714 Grandview St Paris (61944) ***(G-17161)***
**Secretary of State Illinois** ....217 782-4850
316 N Klein St Springfield (62702) ***(G-20520)***
**Secretary of State Illinois** ....708 388-9199
14434 Pulaski Rd Midlothian (60445) ***(G-14768)***
**Secretary of State Illinois** ....217 243-4327
901 E Morton Ave Jacksonville (62650) ***(G-12414)***
**Secretary of State Illinois** ....773 660-4963
9901 S King Dr Chicago (60628) ***(G-6469)***
**Sectional Snow Plow** ....815 932-7569
101 N Euclid Ave Bradley (60915) ***(G-2432)***
**Secure Data Inc** ....618 726-5225
640 Pierce Blvd Ste 200 O Fallon (62269) ***(G-16478)***
**Securecom Inc** ....219 314-4537
3338 E 170th St Lansing (60438) ***(G-13183)***
**Secureslice Inc** ....800 984-0494
6300 N Rockwell St Chicago (60659) ***(G-6470)***
**Security Lighting Systems Inc** ....800 544-4848
2100 Golf Rd Ste 460 Rolling Meadows (60008) ***(G-18778)***
**Security Locknut LLC** ....847 970-4050
999 Forest Edge Dr Vernon Hills (60061) ***(G-21200)***
**Security Metal Products Inc** ....815 933-3307
101 Lawn St Bradley (60915) ***(G-2433)***
**Security Molding Inc** ....630 543-8607
255 W Factory Rd Addison (60101) ***(G-285)***
**Security Systems Group, University Park** *Also called Federal Signal Corporation* ***(G-21050)***
**Sedecal Usa Inc (HQ)** ....847 394-6960
3190 N Kennicott Ave Arlington Heights (60004) ***(G-837)***
**Sedia Systems Inc (PA)** ....312 212-8010
1820 W Hubbard St Ste 300 Chicago (60622) ***(G-6471)***
**Sedona Inc (HQ)** ....309 736-4104
612 Valley View Dr Moline (61265) ***(G-14969)***
**Sedona Group, The, Moline** *Also called Sedona Inc* ***(G-14969)***
**See All Industries Inc (PA)** ....773 927-3232
3623 S Laflin Pl Chicago (60609) ***(G-6472)***
**See What You Send Inc** ....781 780-1483
2300 N Lincoln Park W Chicago (60614) ***(G-6473)***
**Seec Trasportation Corp** ....800 215-4003
190 S Lasalle Ste 2100 Chicago (60603) ***(G-6474)***
**Seedburo Equipment Company Inc** ....312 738-3700
2293 S Mount Prospect Rd Des Plaines (60018) ***(G-8271)***
**Segerdahl Corp (PA)** ....847 541-1080
1351 Wheeling Rd Wheeling (60090) ***(G-22146)***
**Segerdahl Corp** ....847 850-8811
385 Gilman Ave Wheeling (60090) ***(G-22147)***
**Segerdahl Graphics Inc** ....847 541-1080
1351 Wheeling Rd Wheeling (60090) ***(G-22148)***
**Seginus Inc** ....630 800-2795
114 Kirkland Cir Ste B Oswego (60543) ***(G-16933)***
**SEI, Bartlett** *Also called Senior Holdings Inc* ***(G-1373)***
**Seifferts Locker & Meat Proc** ....618 594-3921
1370 Fairfax St Carlyle (62231) ***(G-3058)***
**Seifferts Meat Proc & Lckr, Carlyle** *Also called Seifferts Locker & Meat Proc* ***(G-3058)***
**Seigles Cabinet Center LLC (PA)** ....224 535-7034
1331 Davis Rd Elgin (60123) ***(G-9174)***
**Seip Service & Supply Inc** ....618 532-1923
221 E Broadway Ste 101 Centralia (62801) ***(G-3432)***
**Sek Corporation (PA)** ....630 762-0606
3925 Stern Ave Saint Charles (60174) ***(G-19262)***
**Selah USA Inc** ....847 758-0702
1501 Jarvis Ave Elk Grove Village (60007) ***(G-9733)***
**Selby Implement Company, Quincy** *Also called David Taylor* ***(G-17819)***
**Selco Industries** ....708 499-1060
6655 Kitty Ave Chicago Ridge (60415) ***(G-7158)***
**Select Screen Prints & EMB** ....309 829-6511
112 Southgate Dr Bloomington (61704) ***(G-2222)***
**Select Snacks Company Inc** ....773 933-2167
825 E 99th St Chicago (60628) ***(G-6475)***
**Select Tool & Die Inc** ....630 372-0300
1261 Humbracht Cir Ste F Bartlett (60103) ***(G-1372)***
**Select Tool & Die Inc** ....630 980-8458
324 Pinecroft Dr Roselle (60172) ***(G-18976)***
**Selected Beauty Products, Waukegan** *Also called Selected Chemical Products Co* ***(G-21614)***
**Selected Chemical Products Co** ....847 623-2224
2649 N Delany Rd Waukegan (60087) ***(G-21614)***
**Selective Label & Tabs Inc** ....630 466-0091
1962 Us Rte 30 Sugar Grove (60554) ***(G-20735)***
**Selective Label & Tabs Inc** ....630 466-0091
1962 W Us Highway 30 Sugar Grove (60554) ***(G-20736)***
**Selective Plating Inc** ....630 543-1380
240 S Lombard Rd Addison (60101) ***(G-286)***
**Selee Corporation** ....847 428-4455
24 W End Dr Gilberts (60136) ***(G-10937)***
**Self-Cleaning Strainer Co, Elburn** *Also called Mity Inc* ***(G-8898)***
**Selig S LLC** ....815 785-2100
342 E Wabash Ave Forrest (61741) ***(G-10264)***
**Selig Sealing Holdings Inc (HQ)** ....815 785-2100
342 E Wabash Ave Forrest (61741) ***(G-10265)***
**Selig Sealing Products Inc (HQ)** ....815 785-2100
342 E Wabash Ave Forrest (61741) ***(G-10266)***
**Sellers Commerce LLC** ....858 345-1212
633 Skokie Blvd Ste 490 Northbrook (60062) ***(G-16361)***
**Sellstrom Manufacturing Co (HQ)** ....800 323-7402
300 Coporate Dr Elgin (60123) ***(G-9175)***
**Sellstrom Safeguards, Elgin** *Also called Sellstrom Manufacturing Co* ***(G-9175)***
**Selnar Inc (PA)** ....309 699-3977
2460 E Washington St East Peoria (61611) ***(G-8733)***
**Selrok Inc** ....630 876-8322
1151 Atlantic Dr Ste 2 West Chicago (60185) ***(G-21770)***
**Selvaggio Orna & Strl Stl Inc** ....217 528-4077
1119 W Dorlan Ave Springfield (62702) ***(G-20521)***
**Sem Minerals LP** ....217 224-8766
3806 Gardner Expy Quincy (62305) ***(G-17890)***
**Semblex Corporation (HQ)** ....630 833-2880
900 N Church Rd Elmhurst (60126) ***(G-9936)***
**Semblex Corporation** ....630 833-2880
370 W Carol Ln Elmhurst (60126) ***(G-9937)***
**Semler Industries Inc** ....847 671-5650
3800 Carnation St Franklin Park (60131) ***(G-10586)***
**Semper FI Printing LLC** ....847 640-7737
2420 E Oakton St Ste Q Arlington Heights (60005) ***(G-838)***
**Semper Paper Company, Bloomingdale** *Also called Semper/Exeter Paper Co LLC* ***(G-2136)***
**Semper/Exeter, Morton Grove** *Also called Schwarz Paper Company LLC* ***(G-15235)***
**Semper/Exeter Paper Co LLC** ....630 775-9500
1 Tiffany Pt Ste 300 Bloomingdale (60108) ***(G-2136)***
**Senario LLC** ....847 882-0677
1325 Remington Rd Ste H Schaumburg (60173) ***(G-19725)***
**Senate Democrat Leader Office** ....708 687-9696
301 S 2nd St Springfield (62706) ***(G-20522)***
**Sendele Wireless Solutions** ....815 227-4212
1475 Temple Cir Rockford (61108) ***(G-18610)***
**Sendra Service Corp** ....815 462-0061
309 Garnet Dr New Lenox (60451) ***(G-15910)***
**Seneca Custom Cabinetry** ....815 357-1322
2957 Us Highway 6 Seneca (61360) ***(G-19890)***
**Seneca Foods Corporation** ....309 385-4301
606 S Tremont St Princeville (61559) ***(G-17766)***
**Seneca Foods Corporation** ....309 545-2233
7757 Airport Rd Manito (61546) ***(G-14176)***
**Seneca Petroleum Co Inc (PA)** ....708 396-1100
13301 Cicero Ave Crestwood (60445) ***(G-7502)***
**Seneca Petroleum Co Inc** ....630 257-2268
12460 New Ave Lemont (60439) ***(G-13262)***
**Seneca Rebuild LLC** ....618 435-9445
11550 N Thompsonville Rd Macedonia (62860) ***(G-14047)***
**Seneca Sand & Gravel LLC** ....630 746-9183
2962 N 2553rd Rd Seneca (61360) ***(G-19891)***
**Senformatics LLC** ....217 419-2571
601 W Green St Champaign (61820) ***(G-3536)***
**Senior Automotive, Bartlett** *Also called Senior PLC* ***(G-1376)***
**Senior Care Pharmacy LLC** ....847 579-0093
1630 Old Deerfield Rd # 202 Highland Park (60035) ***(G-11868)***
**Senior Flexonics, Bartlett** *Also called Senior Operations LLC* ***(G-1375)***
**Senior Holdings Inc (HQ)** ....630 837-1811
300 E Devon Ave Bartlett (60103) ***(G-1373)***
**Senior Operations LLC** ....630 837-1811
300 E Devon Ave Bartlett (60103) ***(G-1374)***

ALPHABETIC SECTION Sg360, Wheeling

**Senior Operations LLC (HQ)**....630 837-1811
300 E Devon Ave Bartlett (60103) **(G-1375)**
**Senior PLC**....630 372-3511
300 E Devon Ave Bartlett (60103) **(G-1376)**
**Senju Comtek Corp**....847 549-5690
1322 Armour Blvd Mundelein (60060) **(G-15555)**
**Senn Enterprises Inc (PA)**....309 637-1147
1309 W Main St Peoria (61606) **(G-17450)**
**Senn Enterprises Inc**....309 673-4384
1829 W Main St Peoria (61606) **(G-17451)**
**Senna Design LLC**....847 821-7877
100 Corporate Woods Pkwy Vernon Hills (60061) **(G-21201)**
**Senoplast USA**....630 898-0731
75 Executive Dr Ste 129 Aurora (60504) **(G-1077)**
**Sensaphonics Inc**....312 432-1714
660 N Milwaukee Ave Ste 1 Chicago (60642) **(G-6476)**
**Sensible Designs Online Inc**....708 267-8924
10556 Great Egret Dr Orland Park (60467) **(G-16890)**
**Sensible Products Inc**....773 774-7400
7290 W Devon Ave Chicago (60631) **(G-6477)**
**Sensient Flavors**....847 645-7002
5115 Sedge Blvd Hoffman Estates (60192) **(G-12049)**
**Sensient Flavors LLC (HQ)**....317 243-3521
2800 W Higgins Rd Ste 900 Hoffman Estates (60169) **(G-12050)**
**Sensient Flavors LLC**....815 857-3691
25 E Main St Amboy (61310) **(G-599)**
**Sensient Technologies Corp**....708 481-0910
810 Carnation Ln Matteson (60443) **(G-14378)**
**Sensio America LLC (PA)**....877 501-5337
270 Tubeway Dr Carol Stream (60188) **(G-3238)**
**Sensor 21 Inc**....847 561-6233
19541 W University Dr Mundelein (60060) **(G-15556)**
**Sensor Synergy**....847 353-8200
200 N Fairway Dr Ste 198 Vernon Hills (60061) **(G-21202)**
**Sensory Essence Inc**....847 526-3645
209 Brier Ct Island Lake (60042) **(G-12218)**
**Sentinel Emrgncy Solutions LLC (PA)**....618 539-3863
502 S Richland St Freeburg (62243) **(G-10640)**
**Sentral Assemblies LLC (HQ)**....847 478-9720
595 Bond St Lincolnshire (60069) **(G-13477)**
**Sentral Group LLC (PA)**....847 478-9720
595 Bond St Lincolnshire (60069) **(G-13478)**
**Sentro Printing Equip N Movers**....779 423-0255
332 Harwich Pl Rockton (61072) **(G-18702)**
**Sentry Pool & Chemical Supply**....309 797-9721
1529 46th Ave Ste 1 Moline (61265) **(G-14970)**
**Sentry Seasonings Inc**....630 530-5370
928 N Church Rd Elmhurst (60126) **(G-9938)**
**Sentry Spring & Mfg Co**....847 584-9391
184 Inverness Ct Elk Grove Village (60007) **(G-9734)**
**Seoclarity**....773 831-4500
2800 S River Rd Ste 290 Des Plaines (60018) **(G-8272)**
**Seoco Inc**....815 874-9565
3384 N Publs Dr Ste F Rockford (61109) **(G-18611)**
**Septic Solutions Inc**....217 925-5992
314 W Center St Dieterich (62424) **(G-8314)**
**Serac Inc (HQ)**....630 510-9343
160 E Elk Trl Carol Stream (60188) **(G-3239)**
**Seraph Industries LLC**....815 222-9686
1175 Krupke Rd Caledonia (61011) **(G-2934)**
**Serbian Yellow Pages Inc**....847 588-0555
7400 N Waukegan Rd # 210 Niles (60714) **(G-16031)**
**Sereen Boats, Rockford** *Also called Sereen LLC* **(G-18612)**
**Sereen LLC**....386 527-4876
4543 Sable Ln Rockford (61109) **(G-18612)**
**Sergio Barajas**....708 238-7614
205 Washington Ave La Grange (60525) **(G-12744)**
**Serien Manufacturing Inc**....815 337-1447
900 S Eastwood Dr Woodstock (60098) **(G-22608)**
**Serionix**....651 503-3930
60 Hazelwood Dr Champaign (61820) **(G-3537)**
**Serious Energy Inc**....312 515-4606
1333 N Hickory Ave Chicago (60642) **(G-6478)**
**Seritex Inc**....201 755-3002
1052 W Republic Dr Addison (60101) **(G-287)**
**Serlin Iron & Metal Co Inc**....773 227-3826
1810 N Kilbourn Ave Chicago (60639) **(G-6479)**
**Serola Biomechanics Inc**....815 636-2780
5406 Forest Hills Ct Loves Park (61111) **(G-13991)**
**Serra Laser Precision LLC**....847 367-0282
2400 Commerce Dr Libertyville (60048) **(G-13379)**
**Serta Inc (HQ)**....847 645-0200
2600 Forbs Ave Hoffman Estates (60192) **(G-12051)**
**Serta International, Hoffman Estates** *Also called Serta Inc* **(G-12051)**
**Serta Mattress Co, Hoffman Estates** *Also called Royal Bedding Company Inc* **(G-12045)**
**Serta Mattress Company, Hoffman Estates** *Also called National Bedding Company LLC* **(G-12027)**
**Serta Mattress Company, Hoffman Estates** *Also called National Bedding Company LLC* **(G-12028)**
**Sertech, Batavia** *Also called CCL Label (chicago) Inc* **(G-1427)**
**Serv-All Die & Tool Company**....815 459-2900
110 Erick St Crystal Lake (60014) **(G-7647)**
**Servetech Water Solutions Inc**....630 784-9050
112 W Liberty Dr Wheaton (60187) **(G-21980)**
**Servi-Sure Corporation**....773 271-5900
2020 W Rascher Ave Chicago (60625) **(G-6480)**
**Service & Manufacturing Corp**....773 287-5500
5414c W Roosevelt Rd C Chicago (60644) **(G-6481)**
**Service Auto Supply**....309 444-9704
101 N Wood St Washington (61571) **(G-21392)**
**Service Center, Alsip** *Also called Uesco Industries Inc* **(G-536)**
**Service Cutting & Welding**....773 622-8366
2911 N Moody Ave Chicago (60634) **(G-6482)**
**Service Envelope Corporation**....847 559-0004
1925 Holste Rd Northbrook (60062) **(G-16362)**
**Service Industries, LLC, Rolling Meadows** *Also called Thomas Packaging LLC* **(G-18782)**
**Service King Plbg Htg Colg Elc**....847 458-8900
720 White Pine Ct Lake In The Hills (60156) **(G-13007)**
**Service Machine Company Inc**....815 654-2310
6205 Material Ave Loves Park (61111) **(G-13992)**
**Service Machine Jobs**....815 986-3033
1308 Barnes St Rockford (61104) **(G-18613)**
**Service Metal Enterprises**....630 628-1444
915 W National Ave Addison (60101) **(G-288)**
**Service Packaging Design Inc**....847 966-6592
6238 Lincoln Ave Morton Grove (60053) **(G-15236)**
**Service Printing Corporation**....847 669-9620
11960 Oak Creek Pkwy Huntley (60142) **(G-12176)**
**Service Pro Electric Mtr Repr**....630 766-1215
690 Industrial Dr Bensenville (60106) **(G-1990)**
**Service Provider, Itasca** *Also called SAI Info USA* **(G-12352)**
**Service Sheet Metal Works Inc**....773 229-0031
5000 W 73rd St Chicago (60638) **(G-6483)**
**Service Stampings of IL Inc**....630 894-7880
251 Central Ave Roselle (60172) **(G-18977)**
**Service Steel Division, East Moline** *Also called Van Pelt Corporation* **(G-8697)**
**Servicenow Inc**....630 963-4608
2001 Butterfield Rd # 240 Downers Grove (60515) **(G-8521)**
**SERVPRO La Grnge Prk/N Rvrside, Broadview** *Also called Ffg Restoration Inc* **(G-2577)**
**Sesame Solutions LLC**....630 427-3400
279 Beaudin Blvd Bolingbrook (60440) **(G-2366)**
**Seshin USA Inc**....847 550-5556
333 Enterprise Pkwy Lake Zurich (60047) **(G-13130)**
**Sesser Concrete Products Co**....618 625-2811
910 S Cockrum St Sesser (62884) **(G-19895)**
**Set Enterprises of Mi Inc**....708 758-1111
21905 Cottage Grove Ave Sauk Village (60411) **(G-19393)**
**Set Screw & Mfg Co**....847 717-3700
1210 Saint Charles St Elgin (60120) **(G-9176)**
**Sethness Caramel Color, Skokie** *Also called Sethness Products Company* **(G-20083)**
**Sethness Products Company (PA)**....847 329-2080
3422 W Touhy Ave Ste 1 Skokie (60076) **(G-20083)**
**Settima Usa Inc**....630 812-1433
1759 S Linneman Rd Mount Prospect (60056) **(G-15373)**
**Sev-Rend Corporation**....618 301-4130
5301 Horseshoe Lake Rd Collinsville (62234) **(G-7341)**
**Seven Mfg Inc**....815 356-8102
3513 Deep Wood Dr Crystal Lake (60012) **(G-7648)**
**Severstal US Holdings II Inc (HQ)**....708 756-0400
907 N Elm St Ste 100 Hinsdale (60521) **(G-11964)**
**Sew Wright Embroidery Inc**....309 691-5780
7810 N University St Peoria (61614) **(G-17452)**
**Seward Screw Acquisition LLC**....312 498-9933
1835 W Warner Ave Chicago (60613) **(G-6484)**
**Seward Screw Operating LLC**....312 498-9933
1835 W Warner Ave Chicago (60613) **(G-6485)**
**Sewer Equipment Co America**....815 835-5566
1590 Dutch Rd Dixon (61021) **(G-8350)**
**Sewer Equipment of Canada, Dixon** *Also called Sewer Equipment Co America* **(G-8350)**
**Sewing Salon**....217 345-3886
718 Jackson Ave Charleston (61920) **(G-3611)**
**Sextant Company**....847 680-6550
433 Inverness Dr Gurnee (60031) **(G-11503)**
**Sexton Wind Power LLC**....224 212-1250
49 Sherwood Ter Ste A Lake Bluff (60044) **(G-12866)**
**Seymour of Sycamore Inc (PA)**....815 895-9101
917 Crosby Ave Sycamore (60178) **(G-20815)**
**SF Contracting LLC**....618 926-1477
1030 Hamburg Rd Raleigh (62977) **(G-17911)**
**SF Holdings Group Inc (HQ)**....847 831-4800
300 Tr State Intl Ste 200 Lincolnshire (60069) **(G-13479)**
**Sfc Chemicals Ltd**....847 221-2152
1031 W Bryn Mawr Ave 1a Chicago (60660) **(G-6486)**
**Sfc of Illinois Inc**....815 745-2100
400 S Railroad St Warren (61087) **(G-21336)**
**Sg2**....847 779-5500
5250 Old Orchard Rd # 700 Skokie (60077) **(G-20084)**
**Sg360, Wheeling** *Also called Segerdahl Corp* **(G-22146)**

ALPHABETIC

**Sg360, Wheeling** *Also called Segerdahl Corp* ***(G-22147)***
**SGC Horizon LLC** ....847 391-1000
3030 W Salt Creek Ln Arlington Heights (60005) ***(G-839)***
**Sge Group, The, Chicago** *Also called Deshamusic Inc* ***(G-4585)***
**SGS International LLC** ....309 690-5231
1720 W Detweiller Dr Peoria (61615) ***(G-17453)***
**SGS Refrigeration Inc** ....815 284-2700
827 W Progress Dr Dixon (61021) ***(G-8351)***
**Shaars International Inc** ....815 315-0717
129 Phelps Ave Ste 901a Rockford (61108) ***(G-18614)***
**Shade Aire Company** ....815 623-7597
7511 Grace Dr Roscoe (61073) ***(G-18921)***
**Shade Aire Decorating, Roscoe** *Also called Shade Aire Company* ***(G-18921)***
**Shade Brookline Co** ....773 274-5513
6246 N Broadway St Chicago (60660) ***(G-6487)***
**Shademaker Products Corp** ....773 955-0998
7300 S Kimbark Ave Chicago (60619) ***(G-6488)***
**Shading Solutions Group Inc** ....630 444-2102
1770 S Randall Rd A172 Geneva (60134) ***(G-10866)***
**Shadow Manufacturing, Havana** *Also called Dowell Lynnea* ***(G-11694)***
**Shadowtech Labs Inc** ....630 413-4478
760 N Frontage Rd Ste 102 Willowbrook (60527) ***(G-22231)***
**Shady Creek Vineyard Inc** ....847 275-7979
1238 N Wellington Dr Palatine (60067) ***(G-17073)***
**Shakthi Solar Inc** ....630 842-0893
590 Territorial Dr Ste B Bolingbrook (60440) ***(G-2367)***
**Shale Lake LLC** ....618 637-2470
1499 Washington Ave Staunton (62088) ***(G-20558)***
**Shamrock Manufacturing Co Inc** ....708 331-7776
15920 Suntone Dr South Holland (60473) ***(G-20304)***
**Shamrock Plastics Inc** ....309 243-7723
2615 Alta Ln Peoria (61615) ***(G-17454)***
**Shamrock Scientific** ....800 323-0249
34 Davis Dr Bellwood (60104) ***(G-1720)***
**Shamrock Specialty Packaging, Elgin** *Also called Quad-Illinois Inc* ***(G-9155)***
**Shand & Jurs, Hillside** *Also called Gpe Controls Inc* ***(G-11917)***
**Shanin Company** ....847 676-1200
6454 N Kimball Ave Lincolnwood (60712) ***(G-13537)***
**Shank Precision Machine Co, Cicero** *Also called Cyrus Shank Company* ***(G-7187)***
**Shanks Veterinary Equipment** ....815 225-7700
505 E Old Mill St Milledgeville (61051) ***(G-14818)***
**Shannon & Sons Welding** ....630 898-7778
1218 E New York St Aurora (60505) ***(G-1215)***
**Shannon & Sons Welding Shop, Aurora** *Also called Shannon & Sons Welding* ***(G-1215)***
**Shannon Industrial Corporation (PA)** ....815 337-2349
2041 Dillard Ct Woodstock (60098) ***(G-22609)***
**Shannon Industries Inc** ....815 338-8960
114 S Shannon Dr Woodstock (60098) ***(G-22610)***
**Shapco Inc** ....847 229-1439
602 Wheeling Rd Wheeling (60090) ***(G-22149)***
**Shape Master Inc** ....217 582-2638
108 E Main St Ogden (61859) ***(G-16744)***
**Shape Master Inc** ....217 469-7027
704 E Lincoln St Saint Joseph (61873) ***(G-19318)***
**Shape-Master Tool Co** ....815 522-6186
801 W Main St Kirkland (60146) ***(G-12718)***
**Shapiro Bros of Illinois Inc** ....618 244-3168
510 S 6th St Mount Vernon (62864) ***(G-15445)***
**Share Machine Inc** ....630 906-1810
2175 Rochester Dr Ste C Aurora (60506) ***(G-1216)***
**Shared Services Center, Decatur** *Also called Archer-Daniels-Midland Company* ***(G-7835)***
**Sharin Toy Company** ....847 676-1200
6460 N Lincoln Ave Lincolnwood (60712) ***(G-13538)***
**Sharlen Electric Co (PA)** ....773 721-0700
9101 S Baltimore Ave Chicago (60617) ***(G-6489)***
**Sharn Enterprises Inc** ....815 464-9715
22749 Citation Rd Frankfort (60423) ***(G-10362)***
**Sharp Bullet Resistant Pdts** ....815 726-2626
1933 Cherry Hill Rd Joliet (60433) ***(G-12574)***
**Sharp Graphics Inc** ....847 966-7000
9144 Terminal Ave Unit B Skokie (60077) ***(G-20085)***
**Sharp Metal Products** ....847 439-5393
140 Joey Dr Elk Grove Village (60007) ***(G-9735)***
**Sharp Trading, Niles** *Also called D & J International Inc* ***(G-15974)***
**Sharpedge Solutions Inc** ....630 792-9639
2728 Forgue Dr Ste 106 Naperville (60564) ***(G-15827)***
**Sharprint Promotional Apparel, Chicago** *Also called Sharprint Slkscrn & Grphcs* ***(G-6490)***
**Sharprint Slkscrn & Grphcs** ....877 649-2554
4200 W Wrightwood Ave Chicago (60639) ***(G-6490)***
**Shartega Systems, Chicago** *Also called Synergy Technology Group Inc* ***(G-6657)***
**Shattuc Cord Specialties Inc** ....847 360-9500
2340 Ernie Krueger Cir Waukegan (60087) ***(G-21615)***
**Shaw Contract Group, Chicago** *Also called Shaw Industries Group Inc* ***(G-6491)***
**Shaw Industries Group Inc** ....312 467-1331
222 Merchandise Mart Plz # 10 Chicago (60654) ***(G-6491)***
**Shaw Media, Joliet** *Also called Joliet Herald Newspaper* ***(G-12523)***
**Shaw Suburban Media Group Inc** ....815 459-4040
7717 S Il Route 31 Crystal Lake (60014) ***(G-7649)***
**Shawcraft Sign Co** ....815 282-4105
7727 Burden Rd Machesney Park (61115) ***(G-14107)***
**Shawnee Exploration Partners** ....618 382-3223
115 Smith St Carmi (62821) ***(G-3080)***
**Shawnee Grapevines LLC** ....618 893-9463
5100 Wing Hill Rd Cobden (62920) ***(G-7304)***
**Shawnee Stone LLC (PA)** ....618 548-1585
202 W Main St Salem (62881) ***(G-19350)***
**Shawnee Winery** ....618 658-8400
200 Commercial St Vienna (62995) ***(G-21225)***
**Shawnimals LLC** ....312 235-2625
2023 W Carroll Ave C301 Chicago (60612) ***(G-6492)***
**Shaws Shack** ....618 669-2220
214 Main St Pocahontas (62275) ***(G-17685)***
**Shawver Press Inc (PA)** ....815 772-4700
120 E Lincolnway Morrison (61270) ***(G-15148)***
**Shay Mine No. 1, Carlinville** *Also called Macoupin Energy LLC* ***(G-3044)***
**Shazak Productions** ....773 406-9880
6415 N Sacramento Ave Chicago (60645) ***(G-6493)***
**Sheas Iron Works Inc** ....847 356-2922
735 N Milwaukee Ave A Lake Villa (60046) ***(G-13026)***
**Shedrain Corporation** ....708 848-5212
715 Lake St Ste 269 Oak Park (60301) ***(G-16685)***
**Sheer Graphics Inc** ....630 654-4422
47 Chestnut Ave Westmont (60559) ***(G-21920)***
**Sheet Metal Connectors Inc** ....815 874-4600
5601 Sandy Hollow Rd Rockford (61109) ***(G-18615)***
**Sheet Metal Supply Ltd** ....847 478-8500
262 S Shaddle Ave Mundelein (60060) ***(G-15557)***
**Sheet Metal Werks Inc (PA)** ....847 827-4700
455 E Algonquin Rd Arlington Heights (60005) ***(G-840)***
**Sheet Wise Printing** ....815 664-3025
208 E Saint Paul St Spring Valley (61362) ***(G-20381)***
**Sheets & Cylinder Welding Inc** ....800 442-2200
4147 W Ogden Ave Chicago (60623) ***(G-6494)***
**Shelby Tool & Die Inc** ....217 774-2189
1804 W South 2nd St Shelbyville (62565) ***(G-19915)***
**Shelbyville Daily Union, Shelbyville** *Also called Community Newsppr Holdings Inc* ***(G-19906)***
**Shell Oil Company** ....618 254-7371
200 E Lorena Ave Wood River (62095) ***(G-22445)***
**Shell Oil Products U S, Chicago** *Also called Equilon Enterprises LLC* ***(G-4768)***
**Shelter Systems** ....773 281-9270
3729 N Ravenswood Ave Chicago (60613) ***(G-6495)***
**Shelving and Bath Unlimited** ....815 378-3328
4337 S Perryville Rd # 103 Cherry Valley (61016) ***(G-3647)***
**Shenglong Intl Group Corp** ....312 388-2345
1939 Waukegan Rd Ste 205 Glenview (60025) ***(G-11195)***
**Sheraton Road Lumber** ....309 691-0858
6600 N Sheridan Rd Peoria (61614) ***(G-17455)***
**Sheri Law Art Glass Ltd** ....708 301-2800
12551 W 159th St Homer Glen (60491) ***(G-12086)***
**Sheri Lyn Kraft** ....847 724-4718
827 Wagner Rd Glenview (60025) ***(G-11196)***
**Sherman Media Company Inc** ....312 335-1962
222 E Wisconsin Ave Ste 7 Lake Forest (60045) ***(G-12959)***
**Sherman Plastics Corp (PA)** ....630 369-6170
1650 Shore Rd Naperville (60563) ***(G-15746)***
**Shermar Industries LLC** ....847 378-8073
1245 S Leslie Ln Des Plaines (60018) ***(G-8273)***
**Sherwin Industries Inc** ....815 234-8007
149 S Fox Run Ln Byron (61010) ***(G-2921)***
**Sherwin Williams, Long Grove** *Also called Sherwin-Williams Company* ***(G-13901)***
**Sherwin Williams Paint Store, Kenilworth** *Also called Sherwin-Williams Company* ***(G-12663)***
**Sherwin-Williams Company** ....847 251-6115
614 Green Bay Rd Kenilworth (60043) ***(G-12663)***
**Sherwin-Williams Company** ....847 573-0240
1618 S Milwaukee Ave Libertyville (60048) ***(G-13380)***
**Sherwin-Williams Company** ....618 662-4415
14 Industrial Park Flora (62839) ***(G-10215)***
**Sherwin-Williams Company** ....815 337-0942
631 S Eastwood Dr Woodstock (60098) ***(G-22611)***
**Sherwin-Williams Company** ....847 478-0677
4194 Il Route 83 Long Grove (60047) ***(G-13901)***
**Sherwin-Williams Company** ....708 409-4728
10551 W Cermak Rd Westchester (60154) ***(G-21854)***
**Sherwin-Williams Company** ....815 254-3559
664 S Weber Rd Romeoville (60446) ***(G-18868)***
**Sherwood Industries Inc** ....847 626-0300
7800 N Merrimac Ave Niles (60714) ***(G-16032)***
**Sherwood Tool Inc** ....815 648-1463
12120 Il Route 173 Hebron (60034) ***(G-11726)***
**Shetley Management Inc** ....618 548-1556
112 W Main St Salem (62881) ***(G-19351)***
**Shevick Sales Corp** ....312 487-2865
5620 W Jarvis Ave Niles (60714) ***(G-16033)***
**Shew Brothers Inc** ....618 997-4414
812 W Longstreet Rd Marion (62959) ***(G-14286)***
**Shews Custom Woodworking** ....217 737-5543
1441 1200th St Lincoln (62656) ***(G-13419)***

**Shield Electronics LLC** ....815 467-4134
512 Twin Rail Dr Ste 220 Minooka (60447) ***(G-14847)***
**Shiftgig Inc** ....312 763-3003
225 W Hubbard St Ste 302 Chicago (60654) ***(G-6496)***
**Shiir Rugs LLC** ....312 828-0400
208 W Kinzie St Ste 5 Chicago (60654) ***(G-6497)***
**Shima American Corporation** ....630 760-4330
500 Park Blvd Ste 725 Itasca (60143) ***(G-12353)***
**Shinetoo Lighting America LLC** ....877 957-7317
1311 Rand Rd Des Plaines (60016) ***(G-8274)***
**Shinn Enterprises** ....217 698-3344
3310 W Jefferson St Springfield (62707) ***(G-20523)***
**Shinwa Measuring Tools Corp** ....847 598-3701
1320 Tower Rd Schaumburg (60173) ***(G-19726)***
**Shipbikes.com, Oak Park** *Also called Air Caddy* ***(G-16650)***
**Shipshapes Brands, Park Forest** *Also called Imageworks Manufacturing Inc* ***(G-17172)***
**Shirt Tales** ....618 662-4572
134 W North Ave Flora (62839) ***(G-10216)***
**Sho Pak LLC** ....618 876-1597
1226 Bissell St Venice (62090) ***(G-21137)***
**Shockwaves Promotional Apparel, Arlington Heights** *Also called G and D Enterprises Inc* ***(G-757)***
**Shockyave Customs** ....815 469-9141
9565 W Lincoln Hwy Ste A Frankfort (60423) ***(G-10363)***
**Shoelace Inc** ....847 854-2500
20505 Rand Rd Ste 218 Kildeer (60047) ***(G-12704)***
**Shoelace Inc (PA)** ....847 854-2500
23 N Williams St Crystal Lake (60014) ***(G-7650)***
**Shoppe De Lee Inc** ....847 350-0580
2625 American Ln Ste A Elk Grove Village (60007) ***(G-9736)***
**Shopper Weekly Publishings, Centralia** *Also called Shoppers Weekly Inc* ***(G-3433)***
**Shoppers Guide** ....815 369-4112
213 S Center St Lena (61048) ***(G-13284)***
**Shoppers Review** ....618 654-4459
1200 12th St Highland (62249) ***(G-11811)***
**Shoppers Weekly Inc** ....618 533-7283
301 E Broadway Centralia (62801) ***(G-3433)***
**Shoppertrak Rct Corporation (HQ)** ....312 529-5300
233 S Wacker Dr Fl 41 Chicago (60606) ***(G-6498)***
**Shore Capital Partners LLC (PA)** ....312 348-7580
1 E Wacker Dr Ste 400 Chicago (60601) ***(G-6499)***
**Shoreline Glass Co Inc** ....312 829-9500
1 Mth Plz Hillside (60162) ***(G-11933)***
**Shoreline Graphics Inc** ....847 587-4804
415 Washington St Ingleside (60041) ***(G-12198)***
**Shoup Manufacturing Co Inc** ....815 933-4439
3 Stuart Dr Kankakee (60901) ***(G-12648)***
**Show Off, Roselle** *Also called Trim Suits By Show-Off Inc* ***(G-18984)***
**Showcase Corporation (PA)** ....312 651-3000
233 S Wacker Dr Ste 5150 Chicago (60606) ***(G-6500)***
**Shredderhotlinecom Company** ....815 674-5802
1215 N Bloomington St Streator (61364) ***(G-20701)***
**Shree Mahavir Inc** ....312 408-1080
311 S Wacker Dr Ste 4550 Chicago (60606) ***(G-6501)***
**Shree Printing Corp** ....773 267-9500
3011 W Irving Park Rd Chicago (60618) ***(G-6502)***
**Shrine Memorial Mausoleum Co** ....618 283-0153
627 S 6th St Vandalia (62471) ***(G-21123)***
**Shrine Memorial Vault Co, Vandalia** *Also called Shrine Memorial Mausoleum Co* ***(G-21123)***
**Shuffle Tech International LLC** ....312 787-7780
1440 N Kingsbury St # 218 Chicago (60642) ***(G-6503)***
**Shulman Brothers Inc** ....618 283-3253
101 S 4th St Vandalia (62471) ***(G-21124)***
**Shunk Corp** ....217 398-2636
47 E Kenyon Rd Champaign (61820) ***(G-3538)***
**Shup Tool & Machine Co** ....618 931-2596
4158 State Route 162 Granite City (62040) ***(G-11302)***
**Shur Co of Illinois** ....217 877-8277
4350 E Boyd Rd Decatur (62521) ***(G-7940)***
**Shure Elec of Ill Div Shure, Wheeling** *Also called Shure Incorporated* ***(G-22150)***
**Shure Incorporated** ....847 520-4404
995 Chaddick Dr Wheeling (60090) ***(G-22150)***
**Shure Products Inc** ....773 227-1001
954 W Wa Blvd Ste 515 Chicago (60607) ***(G-6504)***
**Si Enterprises Inc** ....630 539-9200
301 High Grove Blvd Glendale Heights (60139) ***(G-11069)***
**Sibor Express Ltd** ....773 499-8707
1030 S La Grange Rd # 24 La Grange (60525) ***(G-12745)***
**Sicame Corp** ....630 238-6680
544 N Highland Ave Aurora (60506) ***(G-1217)***
**Sids Well Service** ....618 375-5411
1007 N Ct Grayville (62844) ***(G-11377)***
**Sieb's Die Cutting Specialties, Lincoln** *Also called Siebs Die Cutting Specialty Co* ***(G-13420)***
**Sieber Tool Engineering LP** ....630 462-9370
344 Commerce Dr Carol Stream (60188) ***(G-3240)***
**Siebs Die Cutting Specialty Co** ....217 735-1432
912 Clinton St Lincoln (62656) ***(G-13420)***
**Sieden Sticker USA Ltd** ....312 280-7711
1506 W Grand Ave Apt 3e Chicago (60642) ***(G-6505)***
**Siegling America, Wood Dale** *Also called Forbo Siegling LLC* ***(G-22370)***
**Siemens AG** ....708 345-7290
12841 W Tanglewood Cir Palos Park (60464) ***(G-17131)***
**Siemens Corporation** ....630 850-6973
601 Oakmont Ln Ste 180 Westmont (60559) ***(G-21921)***
**Siemens Energy Inc** ....618 357-6360
4646 White Walnut Rd Pinckneyville (62274) ***(G-17552)***
**Siemens Hlthcare Dgnostics Inc** ....847 267-5300
1717 Deerfield Rd Deerfield (60015) ***(G-8052)***
**Siemens Industry Inc** ....815 672-2653
810 W Grant St Streator (61364) ***(G-20702)***
**Siemens Industry Inc** ....847 520-9084
740 Weidner Rd Apt 203 Buffalo Grove (60089) ***(G-2766)***
**Siemens Industry Inc (HQ)** ....847 215-1000
1000 Deerfield Pkwy Buffalo Grove (60089) ***(G-2767)***
**Siemens Industry Inc** ....
1500 Harvester Rd West Chicago (60185) ***(G-21771)***
**Siemens Industry Inc** ....309 664-2460
14 Currency Dr Bloomington (61704) ***(G-2223)***
**Siemens Industry Inc** ....618 451-1205
3202 W 20th St Granite City (62040) ***(G-11303)***
**Siemens Industry Inc** ....847 931-1990
1401 Madeline Ln Elgin (60124) ***(G-9177)***
**Siemens Industry Inc** ....847 215-1000
887 Deerfield Pkwy Buffalo Grove (60089) ***(G-2768)***
**Siemens Industry Inc** ....815 877-3041
4669 Shepherd Trl Rockford (61103) ***(G-18616)***
**Siemens Industry Inc** ....301 419-2600
2501 Barrington Rd Hoffman Estates (60192) ***(G-12052)***
**Siemens Manufacturing Co Inc (PA)** ....618 539-3000
410 W Washington St Freeburg (62243) ***(G-10641)***
**Siemens Manufacturing Co Inc** ....618 475-3325
500 N Johnson St New Athens (62264) ***(G-15861)***
**Siemens Med Solutions USA Inc** ....847 304-7700
2501 N Barrington Rd Schaumburg (60195) ***(G-19727)***
**Siemens Med Solutions USA Inc** ....847 304-7700
2501 Barrington Rd Hoffman Estates (60192) ***(G-12053)***
**Siemens Med Solutions USA Inc** ....847 793-4429
2500 Millbrook Dr Ste B Buffalo Grove (60089) ***(G-2769)***
**Siemens PLM Software, Downers Grove** *Also called Siemens Product Life Mgmt Sftw* ***(G-8522)***
**Siemens Product Life Mgmt Sftw** ....630 437-6700
2001 Butterfield Rd # 630 Downers Grove (60515) ***(G-8522)***
**Siemer Enterprises Inc (PA)** ....217 857-3171
515 W Main St Teutopolis (62467) ***(G-20855)***
**Sierra International LLC (PA)** ....217 324-9400
1 Sierra Pl Litchfield (62056) ***(G-13698)***
**Sierra Manufacturing Corp** ....630 458-8830
47 W Commercial Ave Addison (60101) ***(G-289)***
**Sierra Pacific Engrg & Pdts, Bolingbrook** *Also called SPEP Acquisition Corp* ***(G-2375)***
**Sievert Electric Svc & Sls Co** ....708 771-1600
1230 Hannah Ave Forest Park (60130) ***(G-10253)***
**Sigan America LLC** ....815 431-9830
1111 W Mckinley Rd Ottawa (61350) ***(G-16983)***
**Sigel Welding** ....217 844-2412
103 S Main St Sigel (62462) ***(G-19938)***
**Sigenics Inc (PA)** ....312 448-8000
3440 S Dearborn St 126s Chicago (60616) ***(G-6506)***
**Siggs Rigs** ....847 456-4012
3810 S Oak Knoll Rd Crystal Lake (60012) ***(G-7651)***
**Sigley Printing & Off Sup Co** ....618 997-5304
110 N Print Ave Marion (62959) ***(G-14287)***
**Sigma Bio Medics Industries** ....847 419-0669
1607 Barclay Blvd Buffalo Grove (60089) ***(G-2770)***
**Sigma Coachair Group (us) Inc** ....847 541-4446
1019 Ferndale Ct Wheeling (60090) ***(G-22151)***
**Sigma Coachair Group N.A., Wheeling** *Also called Sigma Coachair Group (us) Inc* ***(G-22151)***
**Sigma Coatings Inc** ....630 628-5305
150 S Church St Ste D Addison (60101) ***(G-290)***
**Sigma Digital Xray, Buffalo Grove** *Also called Sigma Bio Medics Industries* ***(G-2770)***
**Sigma Graphics Inc** ....815 433-1000
4001 Baker Rd Ottawa (61350) ***(G-16984)***
**Sigma Tool & Machining** ....815 874-0500
2324 23rd Ave Rockford (61104) ***(G-18617)***
**Sigmatron International Inc** ....847 586-5200
1901 South St Elgin (60123) ***(G-9178)***
**Sigmatron International Inc (PA)** ....847 956-8000
2201 Landmeier Rd Elk Grove Village (60007) ***(G-9737)***
**Sign** ....630 351-8400
369 W Army Trail Rd # 24 Bloomingdale (60108) ***(G-2137)***
**Sign & Banner Express** ....630 783-9700
540 E Boughton Rd Bolingbrook (60440) ***(G-2368)***
**Sign A Rama** ....630 293-7300
946 N Neltnor Blvd # 114 West Chicago (60185) ***(G-21772)***
**Sign A Rama Inc** ....630 359-5125
100 E Roosevelt Rd Ste 34 Villa Park (60181) ***(G-21284)***
**Sign America** ....773 262-7800
2748 W Devon Ave Chicago (60659) ***(G-6507)***
**Sign Appeal, Charleston** *Also called Rkm Enterprises* ***(G-3609)***

ALPHABETIC

**Sign Appeal Inc**...847 587-4300
20 E Grand Ave Fox Lake (60020) *(G-10283)*
**Sign Authority**...630 462-9850
901 W Liberty Dr A Wheaton (60187) *(G-21981)*
**Sign Central**...847 543-7600
34039 N Hainesville Rd Round Lake (60073) *(G-19067)*
**Sign Contractors**...708 795-1761
16w143 Hillside Ln Burr Ridge (60527) *(G-2880)*
**Sign Express Inc**...708 524-8811
900 S Oak Park Ave Ste 1 Oak Park (60304) *(G-16686)*
**Sign Girls Inc**...847 336-4002
3608 Grand Ave Ste C Gurnee (60031) *(G-11504)*
**Sign Holders Supply, Chicago** *Also called Marv-O-Lus Manufacturing Co (G-5636)*
**Sign Identity Inc**...630 942-1400
415 Taft Ave Ste 1b Glen Ellyn (60137) *(G-10989)*
**Sign Max, Schaumburg** *Also called CNE Inc (G-19475)*
**Sign O Rama**...815 744-8702
1107 Essington Rd Joliet (60435) *(G-12575)*
**Sign One, Morton Grove** *Also called Main Street Visuals Inc (G-15217)*
**Sign Outlet Inc**...708 824-2222
5516 W Cal Sag Rd Alsip (60803) *(G-528)*
**Sign Palace Inc**...847 228-7446
68 N Lively Blvd Elk Grove Village (60007) *(G-9738)*
**Sign Pro, Quincy** *Also called Bick Broadcasting Inc (G-17804)*
**Sign Shop The, Dekalb** *Also called Lou Plucinski (G-8103)*
**Sign Solutions**...618 443-6565
1255 W Broadway St Sparta (62286) *(G-20320)*
**Sign Team Inc**...309 302-0017
5417 180th St N East Moline (61244) *(G-8694)*
**Sign-A-Rama, West Chicago** *Also called Sign A Rama (G-21772)*
**Sign-A-Rama, Gurnee** *Also called Sign Girls Inc (G-11504)*
**Sign-A-Rama, Grayslake** *Also called Signarama (G-11363)*
**Sign-A-Rama, Belleville** *Also called Swansea Sign A Rama Inc (G-1677)*
**Sign-A-Rama, Naperville** *Also called P N K Ventures Inc (G-15720)*
**Sign-A-Rama, Romeoville** *Also called Zainab Enterprises Inc (G-18881)*
**Sign-A-Rama, Bloomingdale** *Also called Sign (G-2137)*
**Sign-A-Rama, Skokie** *Also called Mark Collins (G-20033)*
**Sign-A-Rama, Schaumburg** *Also called Cacini Inc (G-19467)*
**Sign-A-Rama, Countryside** *Also called Vinyl Graphics Inc (G-7450)*
**Sign-A-Rama, Lansing** *Also called Quick Quality Printing Inc (G-13181)*
**Sign-A-Rama, Villa Park** *Also called Sign A Rama Inc (G-21284)*
**Sign-A-Rama**...312 922-0509
1513 S State St Chicago (60605) *(G-6508)*
**Sign-A-Rama of Buffalo Grove**...847 215-1535
352 Lexington Dr Buffalo Grove (60089) *(G-2771)*
**Signa Development Group Inc (PA)**...773 418-4506
4641 N Oriole Ave Norridge (60706) *(G-16108)*
**Signa Group Inc (PA)**...847 386-7639
540 W Frontage Rd # 2105 Northfield (60093) *(G-16417)*
**Signage Plus Ltd**...815 485-0300
17908 S Parker Rd Lockport (60491) *(G-13744)*
**Signal, Chicago** *Also called Message Mediums LLC (G-5698)*
**Signal Digital Inc (PA)**...312 685-1911
111 N Canal St Ste 455 Chicago (60606) *(G-6509)*
**Signal Graphics Printing, Mundelein** *Also called Sphere Inc (G-15560)*
**Signal Lighting Operations, Salem** *Also called North American Lighting Inc (G-19340)*
**SIGNAL PRESS DIVISION, Evanston** *Also called Christian National Womans (G-10024)*
**Signalmasters Inc**...708 534-3330
26120 S Governors Hwy Monee (60449) *(G-15001)*
**Signarama**...847 543-4870
1868 E Belvidere Rd A Grayslake (60030) *(G-11363)*
**Signarama Bolingbrook, Romeoville** *Also called Reynolds Holdings Inc (G-18863)*
**Signature Business Systems Inc**...847 459-8500
500 Lake Cook Rd Fl 3 Deerfield (60015) *(G-8053)*
**Signature Design & Tailoring**...773 375-4915
8027 S Stony Island Ave Chicago (60617) *(G-6510)*
**Signature Innovations LLC**...847 758-9600
1171 Landmeier Rd Elk Grove Village (60007) *(G-9739)*
**Signature Label of Illinois**...618 283-5145
2025 N 8th St Vandalia (62471) *(G-21125)*
**Signature Nail Systems LLC**...888 445-2786
1304 S 30th St Quincy (62301) *(G-17891)*
**Signature of Chicago Inc**...630 271-1876
8428 Brookridge Rd Downers Grove (60516) *(G-8523)*
**Signco**...402 474-6646
301 E Harris Ave Greenville (62246) *(G-11403)*
**Signcraft Screenprint Inc**...815 777-3030
100 A J Harle Dr Galena (61036) *(G-10731)*
**Signcrafters Enterprises Inc**...815 648-4484
10714 Il Route 47 Hebron (60034) *(G-11727)*
**Signet Sign Company**...630 830-8242
608 White Oak Ln Bartlett (60103) *(G-1377)*
**Signkraft Co**...217 787-7105
1215 W Miller St Springfield (62702) *(G-20524)*
**Signode, Bridgeview** *Also called Illinois Tool Works Inc (G-2498)*
**Signode, Buffalo Grove** *Also called Illinois Tool Works Inc (G-2706)*
**Signode Consumable Plastics, Glenview** *Also called Signode Industrial Group LLC (G-11200)*
**Signode Corporation**...800 527-1499
3600 W Lake Ave Glenview (60026) *(G-11197)*
**Signode Industrial Group LLC (HQ)**...847 724-7500
3650 W Lake Ave Glenview (60026) *(G-11198)*
**Signode Industrial Group LLC**...815 939-6192
2150 S Us Highway 45 52 Kankakee (60901) *(G-12649)*
**Signode Industrial Group LLC**...847 483-1490
3644 W Lake Ave Glenview (60026) *(G-11199)*
**Signode Industrial Group LLC**...815 939-0033
2150m S Us Highway 45 52 Kankakee (60901) *(G-12650)*
**Signode Industrial Group LLC**...847 724-6100
3680 W Lake Ave Glenview (60026) *(G-11200)*
**Signode Industrial Group LLC**...708 371-9050
14153 Western Ave Blue Island (60406) *(G-2270)*
**Signode Industrial Group LLC**...630 268-9999
3624 W Lake Ave Glenview (60026) *(G-11201)*
**Signode Intl Holdings LLC (HQ)**...800 648-8864
3700 W Lake Ave Glenview (60026) *(G-11202)*
**Signode Ips, Glenview** *Also called Signode Corporation (G-11197)*
**Signode Packaging Systems Corp**...800 323-2464
3650 W Lake Ave Glenview (60026) *(G-11203)*
**Signode Packing Systems, Glenview** *Also called Signode Packaging Systems Corp (G-11203)*
**Signode Supply Corporation**...708 458-7320
7701 W 71st St Bridgeview (60455) *(G-2528)*
**Signs & Wonders Unlimited LLC**...847 816-9734
28318 N Oak Ln Libertyville (60048) *(G-13381)*
**Signs By Custom Cutting Inc**...630 759-2734
300 Dean Cir Bolingbrook (60440) *(G-2369)*
**Signs By Design, Crestwood** *Also called Contempo Autographic & Signs (G-7483)*
**Signs By Design**...708 599-9970
10330 S Harlem Ave Palos Hills (60465) *(G-17124)*
**Signs By Tomorrow, Arlington Heights** *Also called G & J Associates Inc (G-756)*
**Signs By Tomorrow, Elgin** *Also called Signs In Dundee Inc (G-9179)*
**Signs By Tomorrow, Bloomingdale** *Also called Schellerer Corporation Inc (G-2135)*
**Signs By Tomorrow**...815 436-0880
16200 S Lincoln Hwy # 100 Plainfield (60586) *(G-17648)*
**Signs Express, Macomb** *Also called Quickprinters (G-14130)*
**Signs For Success Inc**...847 800-4870
1538 Madison Dr Buffalo Grove (60089) *(G-2772)*
**Signs In Dundee Inc**...847 742-9530
1028 Dundee Ave Elgin (60120) *(G-9179)*
**Signs N Such, Caseyville** *Also called Joseph D Smithies (G-3399)*
**Signs Now, Gurnee** *Also called Dewrich Inc (G-11438)*
**Signs Now, Gurnee** *Also called Fourth Quarter Holdings Inc (G-11449)*
**Signs Now, Elk Grove Village** *Also called Elk Grove Signs Inc (G-9452)*
**Signs Now, Rockford** *Also called Timothy Anderson Corporation (G-18651)*
**Signs Now, Peoria** *Also called Isates Inc (G-17391)*
**Signs Now, Highland Park** *Also called Eisendrath Inc (G-11830)*
**Signs Now, Mundelein** *Also called Campbell Management Services (G-15482)*
**Signs Now, Chicago** *Also called Churchill Wilmslow Corporation (G-4374)*
**Signs Now, Lombard** *Also called Jodaat Inc (G-13815)*
**Signs Now, Downers Grove** *Also called Krick Enterprises Inc (G-8470)*
**Signs Now, Naperville** *Also called Albright Enterprises Inc (G-15593)*
**Signs Now**...847 427-0005
1670 Greenleaf Ave Elk Grove Village (60007) *(G-9740)*
**Signs Now**...800 356-3373
2525 W Hutchinson St Chicago (60618) *(G-6511)*
**Signs Now Naperville, Naperville** *Also called Sadannah Group LLC (G-15745)*
**Signs of Distinction Inc**...847 520-0787
149 Wheeling Rd Wheeling (60090) *(G-22152)*
**Signs of The Times, Hebron** *Also called Signcrafters Enterprises Inc (G-11727)*
**Signs Plus**...847 489-9009
1216 Rand Rd Des Plaines (60016) *(G-8275)*
**Signs To You**...708 429-6783
17121 Olcott Ave Tinley Park (60477) *(G-20944)*
**Signs Today Inc**...847 934-9777
342 W Colfax St Palatine (60067) *(G-17074)*
**Signscapes Inc**...847 719-2610
884 S Rand Rd Ste D Lake Zurich (60047) *(G-13131)*
**Signsdirect Inc**...309 820-1070
410 E Lafayette St Ste 1 Bloomington (61701) *(G-2224)*
**Signtastic Inc**...708 598-4749
10352 S Aspen Dr Palos Hills (60465) *(G-17125)*
**Signwise Inc**...630 932-3204
208 W North Ave Lombard (60148) *(G-13853)*
**Signworx Sign & Lighting Co**...217 413-2532
1048 Francella Ct Springfield (62702) *(G-20525)*
**Signx Co Inc**...847 639-7917
508 Cary Algonquin Rd Cary (60013) *(G-3371)*
**Sika Corporation**...815 431-1080
1515 Titanium Dr Ottawa (61350) *(G-16985)*
**Sikora Automation Incorporated**...630 833-0298
845 S Westgate St Addison (60101) *(G-291)*

**Sikora Precision Inc** ....847 468-0900
140 Will Scarlett Ln Elgin (60120) ***(G-9180)***
**Silbrico Corporation** ....708 354-3350
6300 River Rd Hodgkins (60525) ***(G-11983)***
**Silent W Communications Inc** ....630 978-2050
2758 Us Highway 34 Oswego (60543) ***(G-16934)***
**Silesia Flavors Inc** ....847 645-0270
5250 Prairie Stone Pkwy Hoffman Estates (60192) ***(G-12054)***
**Silgan Containers LLC** ....815 562-1250
400 N 15th St Rochelle (61068) ***(G-18109)***
**Silgan Containers Mfg Corp** ....217 283-5501
324 W Main St Hoopeston (60942) ***(G-12116)***
**Silgan Containers Mfg Corp** ....847 336-0552
1301 W Dugdale Rd Waukegan (60085) ***(G-21616)***
**Silgan Equipment Company** ....847 336-0552
1301 W Dugdale Rd Waukegan (60085) ***(G-21617)***
**Silgan Holdings Inc, Champaign** *Also called Silgan White Cap Corporation* ***(G-3539)***
**Silgan Plastics LLC** ....618 662-4471
2 Industrial Park Flora (62839) ***(G-10217)***
**Silgan Plastics LLC** ....815 334-1200
1005 Courtaulds Dr Woodstock (60098) ***(G-22612)***
**Silgan White Cap Americas LLC** ....630 515-8383
1140 31st St Downers Grove (60515) ***(G-8524)***
**Silgan White Cap Corporation** ....217 398-1600
3209 Farber Dr Champaign (61822) ***(G-3539)***
**Silicon Control Inc (PA)** ....847 215-7947
155 N Pfingsten Rd # 360 Deerfield (60015) ***(G-8054)***
**Silk 21 Screen Printing and Em** ....630 972-4250
505 N Pinecrest Rd Bolingbrook (60440) ***(G-2370)***
**Silk Screen Express Inc** ....708 845-5600
7611 185th St Tinley Park (60477) ***(G-20945)***
**Silk Screening By Selep** ....847 593-7050
767 W Millers Rd Des Plaines (60016) ***(G-8276)***
**Silkworm Inc** ....618 687-4077
102 S Sezmore Dr Murphysboro (62966) ***(G-15583)***
**Silkworm Screen Printing, Murphysboro** *Also called Silkworm Inc* ***(G-15583)***
**Silvacor Inc (PA)** ....630 897-9211
2111 Plum St Ste 274 Aurora (60506) ***(G-1218)***
**Silver Bros Inc** ....217 283-7751
105 E Washington St Hoopeston (60942) ***(G-12117)***
**Silver Line** ....708 832-9100
1550 Huntington Dr Calumet City (60409) ***(G-2954)***
**Silver Line Building Pdts LLC** ....708 474-9100
16801 Exchange Ave Ste 2 Lansing (60438) ***(G-13184)***
**Silver Machine Shop Inc** ....217 359-5717
713 N Market St Champaign (61820) ***(G-3540)***
**Silverline Windows, Lansing** *Also called Silver Line Building Pdts LLC* ***(G-13184)***
**Silvestri Sweets Inc** ....630 232-2500
2248 Gary Ln Geneva (60134) ***(G-10867)***
**Sim Partners Inc (PA)** ....800 260-3380
30 N La Salle St Ste 3400 Chicago (60602) ***(G-6512)***
**Sim Products, Shumway** *Also called Southern Illinois McHy Co Inc* ***(G-19935)***
**Simco Formalwear, Clarendon Hills** *Also called Nali Inc* ***(G-7259)***
**Simfax Agri-Services, Jerseyville** *Also called Associated Agri-Business Inc* ***(G-12417)***
**Simfax Agri-Services, Eldred** *Also called Associated Agri-Business Inc* ***(G-8927)***
**Simformotion LLC (PA)** ....309 263-7595
316 Sw Washington St # 300 Peoria (61602) ***(G-17456)***
**Simion Fabrication Inc** ....618 724-7331
901 W Egyptian Ave Christopher (62822) ***(G-7174)***
**Simko Grinding, Posen** *Also called Wotkun Group Inc* ***(G-17737)***
**Simmons Lightning Protection** ....217 746-3971
2094 E County Road 2115 Burnside (62330) ***(G-2817)***
**Simon Box Mfg Co** ....815 722-6661
355 Caton Farm Rd Lockport (60441) ***(G-13745)***
**Simon Global Services LLC** ....773 334-7794
5655 N Clark St Ste 5 Chicago (60660) ***(G-6513)***
**Simon Products Co, Mc Cook** *Also called Michael Lewis Company* ***(G-14453)***
**Simon Zelikman** ....847 338-8031
106 Meadow Ln Oakwood Hills (60013) ***(G-16728)***
**Simonton Building Products Inc** ....217 466-2851
13263 Il Highway 133 Paris (61944) ***(G-17162)***
**Simonton Hardwood Lumber LLC** ....618 594-2132
16515 Post Oak Rd Carlyle (62231) ***(G-3059)***
**Simonton Holdings Inc (HQ)** ....304 428-8261
520 Lake Cook Rd Deerfield (60015) ***(G-8055)***
**Simonton Windows, Paris** *Also called Simonton Building Products Inc* ***(G-17162)***
**Simonton Windows Inc** ....217 466-2851
13263 Il Highway 133 Paris (61944) ***(G-17163)***
**Simonton Windows & Doors, Paris** *Also called Simonton Windows Inc* ***(G-17163)***
**Simpex Medical Inc** ....847 757-9928
401 E Prospect Ave Mount Prospect (60056) ***(G-15374)***
**Simple Assemblies Inc** ....708 212-7494
22542 S Fernview New Lenox (60451) ***(G-15911)***
**Simple Circuits Inc** ....708 671-9600
12756 S 80th Ave Palos Park (60464) ***(G-17132)***
**Simple Mills LLC** ....312 600-6196
444 N Wells St Ste 203 Chicago (60654) ***(G-6514)***
**Simple Solutions** ....618 932-6177
110 E Main St West Frankfort (62896) ***(G-21819)***
**Simplement Inc (PA)** ....702 560-5332
1 Northfield Plz Ste 300 Northfield (60093) ***(G-16418)***
**Simplex Inc** ....217 483-1600
5300 Rising Moon Rd Springfield (62711) ***(G-20526)***
**Simplexgrinnell LP** ....630 268-1863
91 N Mitchell Ct Addison (60101) ***(G-292)***
**Simplexgrinnell LP** ....309 694-8000
686 High Point Ln East Peoria (61611) ***(G-8734)***
**Simplomatic Manufacturing Co** ....773 342-7757
1616 Berkley St Ste 100 Elgin (60123) ***(G-9181)***
**Simply Amish, Arcola** *Also called J & M Representatives Inc* ***(G-672)***
**Simply Computer Software Inc** ....815 231-0063
6085 Strathmoor Dr Ste 2b Rockford (61107) ***(G-18618)***
**Simply Salsa LLC** ....815 514-3993
12630 W 159th St Homer Glen (60491) ***(G-12087)***
**Simply Signs** ....309 849-9016
1001 W Mount Vernon St D Metamora (61548) ***(G-14750)***
**Simpson Anchor Systems, Addison** *Also called Simpson Strong-Tie Company Inc* ***(G-293)***
**Simpson Electric Company** ....847 697-2260
853 Dundee Ave Elgin (60120) ***(G-9182)***
**Simpson Strong-Tie Company Inc** ....630 293-2800
2505 Enterprise Cir West Chicago (60185) ***(G-21773)***
**Simpson Strong-Tie Company Inc** ....630 613-5100
136 W Official Rd Addison (60101) ***(G-293)***
**Simpson Technologies** ....630 978-2700
751 Shoreline Dr Aurora (60504) ***(G-1078)***
**Simpson Technologies Corp (PA)** ....630 978-2700
751 Shoreline Dr Aurora (60504) ***(G-1079)***
**Simpson Well & Pump Company** ....708 301-0826
14823 W North Creek Ct Lockport (60491) ***(G-13746)***
**Sims Company Inc** ....618 665-3901
1431 Panther Creek Ln Louisville (62858) ***(G-13910)***
**Sims Family Holdings LLC (PA)** ....847 488-1230
1111 Bowes Rd Elgin (60123) ***(G-9183)***
**Sims Rcycl Sltons Holdings Inc** ....847 455-8800
3700 Runge St Franklin Park (60131) ***(G-10587)***
**Sims Recycling Solutions Inc** ....847 455-8800
3700 Runge St Franklin Park (60131) ***(G-10588)***
**Simu Ltd (PA)** ....630 350-1060
201 Mittel Dr Wood Dale (60191) ***(G-22422)***
**Simulation Technology LLC** ....630 365-3400
747 Herra St Unit B Elburn (60119) ***(G-8910)***
**Sing S Noodle** ....312 225-2882
2171 S China Pl Chicago (60616) ***(G-6515)***
**Singer Data Products Inc (PA)** ....630 860-6500
790 Maple Ln Bensenville (60106) ***(G-1991)***
**Singer Medical Products Inc** ....630 860-6500
790 Maple Ln Bensenville (60106) ***(G-1992)***
**Singer Safety Company** ....773 235-2100
2300 N Kilbourn Ave Chicago (60639) ***(G-6516)***
**Singer, Ralph Co, Chicago** *Also called Blandings Ltd* ***(G-4122)***
**Singles Plus Printing, South Elgin** *Also called T & C Graphics Inc* ***(G-20227)***
**Singleton Pallets Co** ....708 687-7006
15603 Waverly Ave Oak Forest (60452) ***(G-16588)***
**Sipi Metals Corp (PA)** ....773 276-0070
1720 N Elston Ave Chicago (60642) ***(G-6517)***
**Sir Cooper Inc** ....630 279-0162
203 W Saint Charles Rd Villa Park (60181) ***(G-21285)***
**Sir Speedy, Aurora** *Also called Samecwei Inc* ***(G-1214)***
**Sir Speedy, Evanston** *Also called William Holloway Ltd* ***(G-10106)***
**Sir Speedy, Skokie** *Also called Lake Shore Printing* ***(G-20024)***
**Sir Speedy, Naperville** *Also called K & J Phillips Corporation* ***(G-15682)***
**Sir Speedy, Chicago** *Also called Two JS Copies Now Inc* ***(G-6797)***
**Sir Speedy Print Signs Mktg, Villa Park** *Also called E A A Enterprises Inc* ***(G-21249)***
**Sir Speedy Printing** ....312 337-0774
1711 N Clybourn Ave Chicago (60614) ***(G-6518)***
**Sir Speedy Printing Cntr 6129** ....708 349-7789
9412 W 143rd St Orland Park (60462) ***(G-16891)***
**Sir Speedy Printing Ctr 6080** ....708 351-8841
525 W Wise Rd Ste D Schaumburg (60193) ***(G-19728)***
**Sirius Automation Inc** ....847 607-9378
1558 Barclay Blvd Buffalo Grove (60089) ***(G-2773)***
**Sirius Business Software** ....708 361-5538
42 Birchwood Dr Palos Park (60464) ***(G-17133)***
**Sisco Corporation (PA)** ....618 327-3066
1520 S Mill St Nashville (62263) ***(G-15847)***
**Sisler Dairy Products Company** ....815 376-2913
102 S Grove St Ohio (61349) ***(G-16753)***
**Sisler's Ice & Ice Cream Co, Ohio** *Also called Sisler Dairy Products Company* ***(G-16753)***
**Sislers Ice Inc** ....815 756-6903
274 Harvestore Dr Dekalb (60115) ***(G-8117)***
**Site 933, Elgin** *Also called BFI Waste Systems N Amer Inc* ***(G-8965)***
**SITech Inc** ....630 761-3640
1101 N Raddant Rd Batavia (60510) ***(G-1496)***
**Sitexpedite LLC** ....847 245-2185
430 N Crooked Lake Ln Lindenhurst (60046) ***(G-13549)***
**Sivco Welding Company** ....309 944-5171
624 E Prospect St Geneseo (61254) ***(G-10804)***

ALPHABETIC

**Six Color Print LLC (PA)** ....847 336-3287
3786 Hawthorne Ct Waukegan (60087) *(G-21618)*
**Six Oaks Company** ....312 343-4037
2033 W 108th Pl Chicago (60643) *(G-6519)*
**Sj Converting LLC** ....630 262-6640
1000 Atlantic Dr West Chicago (60185) *(G-21774)*
**Sjd Direct Midwest LLC (PA)** ....618 931-2151
21 Gtewy Cmrc Ctr Dr W Edwardsville (62025) *(G-8814)*
**SJS Packaging Inc** ....630 855-4755
46 Mckinley Ln Streamwood (60107) *(G-20673)*
**Sjti, Machesney Park** *Also called Superior Joining Tech Inc* *(G-14109)*
**Sk Express Inc** ....815 748-4388
310 Dietz Ave Dekalb (60115) *(G-8118)*
**Sk Hand Tool LLC** ....815 895-7701
1600 S Prairie Dr Sycamore (60178) *(G-20816)*
**Sk Hynix America Inc** ....847 925-0196
1920 Thoreau Dr N Schaumburg (60173) *(G-19729)*
**Skach Manufacturing Co Inc** ....847 395-3560
950 Anita Ave Antioch (60002) *(G-655)*
**Skandia Inc** ....815 393-4600
5000 N Il Route 251 Davis Junction (61020) *(G-7815)*
**Skelcher Concrete Products** ....618 457-2930
490 San Diego Rd Carbondale (62901) *(G-3023)*
**SKF Arspace Sling Slutions Div, Elgin** *Also called SKF USA Inc* *(G-9184)*
**SKF Automotive Division, Elgin** *Also called SKF USA Inc* *(G-9185)*
**SKF USA Inc** ....847 742-0700
900 N State St Elgin (60123) *(G-9184)*
**SKF USA Inc** ....847 742-0700
890 N State St Ste 200 Elgin (60123) *(G-9185)*
**SKF USA Inc** ....847 742-0700
900 N State St Elgin (60123) *(G-9186)*
**Ski Seal Coating Inc** ....708 246-5656
7100 Pleasantdale Dr Countryside (60525) *(G-7442)*
**Skild Manufacturing Inc** ....847 437-1717
160 Bond St Fl 1 Elk Grove Village (60007) *(G-9741)*
**Skill-Di Inc** ....708 544-6080
2655 Harrison St Bellwood (60104) *(G-1721)*
**Skilled Plating Corp** ....773 227-0262
151618 N Kilpatrick Ave Chicago (60651) *(G-6520)*
**Skiman Sales Inc** ....847 888-8200
850 Villa St Elgin (60120) *(G-9187)*
**Skin and Laser Aesheptics, Lombard** *Also called Aespheptics Medical Ltd* *(G-13762)*
**Skin Care Systems** ....312 644-9067
119 W Hubbard St Lowr Chicago (60654) *(G-6521)*
**Skokie House** ....847 679-4570
7887 Lincoln Ave Skokie (60077) *(G-20086)*
**Skokie Millwork Inc** ....847 673-7868
8108 Lawndale Ave Skokie (60076) *(G-20087)*
**Skol Mfg Co** ....773 878-5959
4444 N Ravenswood Ave Chicago (60640) *(G-6522)*
**SKW Industries LLC** ....773 261-8900
900 S Cicero Ave Chicago (60644) *(G-6523)*
**Skyjack Equipment Inc (HQ)** ....630 797-3299
3451 Swenson Ave Saint Charles (60174) *(G-19263)*
**Skyjack Inc** ....630 262-0005
3451 Swenson Ave Saint Charles (60174) *(G-19264)*
**Skyjack Parts & Svc Skyjack, Saint Charles** *Also called Skyjack Inc* *(G-19264)*
**Skyline** ....312 300-4700
9200 W 55th St Mc Cook (60525) *(G-14458)*
**Skyline Beauty Supply Inc** ....773 275-6003
3804 Carnation St Franklin Park (60131) *(G-10589)*
**Skyline Design Inc** ....773 278-4660
1240 N Homan Ave Ste 1 Chicago (60651) *(G-6524)*
**Skyline Foods, Harvey** *Also called American Food Distrs Corp* *(G-11655)*
**Skyline International Inc** ....847 357-9077
1400 Centre Cir Downers Grove (60515) *(G-8525)*
**Skyline Printing Sales** ....847 412-1931
3004 Commercial Ave Northbrook (60062) *(G-16363)*
**Skyline Publishing, Bartonville** *Also called Loyalty Publishing Inc* *(G-1396)*
**Skyward Promotions Inc** ....815 969-0909
1140 Charles St Rockford (61104) *(G-18619)*
**Skyway Cement Company LLC** ....800 643-1808
3020 E 103rd St Chicago (60617) *(G-6525)*
**Skyway Facility, Chicago** *Also called Holcim (us) Inc* *(G-5098)*
**Skywide PS, Aurora** *Also called Skywide Publicity Solutions* *(G-1219)*
**Skywide Publicity Solutions** ....331 425-0341
1006 E Galena Blvd Aurora (60505) *(G-1219)*
**Slack Publications** ....217 268-4950
736 Dogwood Dr Arcola (61910) *(G-685)*
**Slagel Drapery Service** ....815 692-3834
302 S 8th St Fairbury (61739) *(G-10132)*
**Slagel Manufacturing Inc** ....815 688-3318
2911 N 2700 East Rd Forrest (61741) *(G-10267)*
**Slam Door Co, Wheeling** *Also called Boom Company Inc* *(G-22018)*
**Slaughter Company Inc** ....847 932-3662
28105 N Keith Dr Lake Forest (60045) *(G-12960)*
**Slavish Inc** ....309 754-8233
309 1st St Matherville (61263) *(G-14367)*
**Slayer Barbell, Port Byron** *Also called J & C Premier Concepts Inc* *(G-17720)*
**Slaymaker Fine Art Ltd** ....773 348-1450
833 W Aldine Ave Chicago (60657) *(G-6526)*
**Slaymaker Galleries, Chicago** *Also called Slaymaker Fine Art Ltd* *(G-6526)*
**Slee Corporation** ....773 777-2444
4125 N Kostner Ave Chicago (60641) *(G-6527)*
**Sleep On Latex, Niles** *Also called Shevick Sales Corp* *(G-16033)*
**Sleep6 LLC** ....844 375-3376
1332 N Halsted St Chicago (60642) *(G-6528)*
**Sleepeck Printing Company** ....708 544-8900
70 W Madison St Ste 2300 Chicago (60602) *(G-6529)*
**Sleeping Bear Inc** ....630 541-7220
5401 Patton Dr Ste 115 Lisle (60532) *(G-13656)*
**Slick Locks LLC** ....815 838-3557
15959 W 143rd St Homer Glen (60491) *(G-12088)*
**Slick Sugar Inc** ....815 782-7101
24935 Heritage Oaks Dr Plainfield (60585) *(G-17649)*
**Slicksugar.com, Plainfield** *Also called Slick Sugar Inc* *(G-17649)*
**Slide Products Inc** ....847 541-7220
430 Wheeling Rd Wheeling (60090) *(G-22153)*
**Slidecraft Inc** ....630 628-1218
532 W Winthrop Ave Addison (60101) *(G-294)*
**Slidematic Industries Inc** ....815 986-0500
1303 Samuelson Rd Rockford (61109) *(G-18620)*
**Slidematic Products Co** ....773 545-4213
4520 W Addison St Chicago (60641) *(G-6530)*
**Slidemtic Prcsion Cmpnents Inc** ....815 986-0500
1303 Samuelson Rd Rockford (61109) *(G-18621)*
**Slipchip Corporation** ....312 550-5600
118 N Clinton St Ste 205 Chicago (60661) *(G-6531)*
**Slipmate Co** ....847 289-9200
1693 Todd Farm Dr Elgin (60123) *(G-9188)*
**Sloan Industries Inc** ....630 350-1614
1550 N Michael Dr Wood Dale (60191) *(G-22423)*
**Sloan Valve Company (PA)** ....847 671-4300
10500 Seymour Ave Franklin Park (60131) *(G-10590)*
**Slsb LLC** ....618 219-4115
2000 Access Rd Madison (62060) *(G-14153)*
**Small Newspaper Group** ....708 258-3410
8 Dearborn Sq Kankakee (60901) *(G-12651)*
**Small Newspaper Group (PA)** ....815 937-3300
8 Dearborn Sq Kankakee (60901) *(G-12652)*
**Small Tools Div, Stillman Valley** *Also called Toolmasters LLC* *(G-20629)*
**Smallcakes Cupcakery of South** ....773 433-0059
100 W Higgins Rd Unit H65 South Barrington (60010) *(G-20132)*
**Smalley Steel Ring Co (PA)** ....847 537-7600
555 Oakwood Rd Lake Zurich (60047) *(G-13132)*
**Smart Choice Mobile Inc** ....708 933-6851
1856 Sibley Blvd Calumet City (60409) *(G-2955)*
**Smart Choice Mobile Inc (PA)** ....708 581-4904
7667 W 95th St Ste 300 Hickory Hills (60457) *(G-11774)*
**Smart Controls LLC** ....618 394-0300
10000 Saint Clair Ave Fairview Heights (62208) *(G-10171)*
**Smart Creations Inc** ....847 433-3451
1799 Saint Johns Ave Highland Park (60035) *(G-11869)*
**Smart Inc** ....847 464-4160
41w584 Us Highway 20 Hampshire (60140) *(G-11563)*
**Smart Living Home & Garden, Libertyville** *Also called Smart Solar Inc* *(G-13382)*
**Smart Medical Technology Inc** ....630 964-1689
8404 Wilmette Ave Ste B Darien (60561) *(G-7802)*
**Smart Motion Robotics Inc** ....815 895-8550
805 Thornwood Dr Sycamore (60178) *(G-20817)*
**Smart Office Services Inc** ....773 227-1121
3720 W Chicago Ave Chicago (60651) *(G-6532)*
**Smart Pixel Inc** ....630 771-0206
590 Territorial Dr Ste B Bolingbrook (60440) *(G-2371)*
**Smart Scan Mri LLC** ....847 623-4000
350 S Greenleaf St # 401 Gurnee (60031) *(G-11505)*
**Smart Solar Inc** ....813 343-5770
1203 Loyola Dr Libertyville (60048) *(G-13382)*
**Smart Solutions Inc** ....630 775-1517
211 Catalpa Ave Itasca (60143) *(G-12354)*
**Smart Surveillance Inc** ....630 968-5075
6444 Coach House Rd Lisle (60532) *(G-13657)*
**Smart Systems Inc** ....630 343-3333
554 Territorial Dr Bolingbrook (60440) *(G-2372)*
**Smart-Slitters, Northbrook** *Also called Rosenthal Manufacturing Co Inc* *(G-16358)*
**Smartbyte Solutions Inc** ....847 925-1870
712 W Slippery Rock Dr Palatine (60067) *(G-17075)*
**Smartsignal, Lisle** *Also called GE Intelligent Platforms Inc* *(G-13593)*
**Smartsignal Corporation** ....630 829-4000
901 Warrenville Rd # 300 Lisle (60532) *(G-13658)*
**Smb Toolroom Inc** ....309 353-7396
206 Derby St Pekin (61554) *(G-17289)*
**SMC Corporation of America** ....630 449-0600
858 Meridian Lake Dr F Aurora (60504) *(G-1080)*
**Smf Inc (PA)** ....309 432-2586
1550 N Industrial Park Rd Minonk (61760) *(G-14834)*
**Smh2 Manufacturing LLC** ....773 793-6643
2041 W Carroll Ave Chicago (60612) *(G-6533)*

ALPHABETIC SECTION Solo Cup Company LLC (PA)

**Smid Heating & Air** ....815 467-0362
23864 W Sussex Dr Channahon (60410) ***(G-3586)***
**Smile Aromatics Inc** ....847 759-0350
2454 E Dempster St # 422 Des Plaines (60016) ***(G-8277)***
**Smile Lee Faces** ....773 376-9999
4197 S Archer Ave Chicago (60632) ***(G-6534)***
**Smile of Brookfield** ....708 485-7754
9144 Broadway Ave Brookfield (60513) ***(G-2642)***
**Smith & Richardson Mfg Co** ....630 232-2581
727 May St Geneva (60134) ***(G-10868)***
**Smith and Son Machine Shop** ....217 260-3257
454 County Road 2400 E Broadlands (61816) ***(G-2550)***
**Smith Bros Engineering, Jerseyville** *Also called Smith Brothers Fabricating* ***(G-12426)***
**Smith Brothers Company, Chicago** *Also called Universal Holdings I LLC* ***(G-6832)***
**Smith Brothers Converters, Crestwood** *Also called CC Distributing Services Inc* ***(G-7480)***
**Smith Brothers Fabricating** ....618 498-5612
406 Maple Ave Jerseyville (62052) ***(G-12426)***
**Smith Bucklin & Associates, Chicago** *Also called API Publishing Services LLC* ***(G-3922)***
**Smith Filter Corporation** ....309 764-8324
5000 41st Street Ct Moline (61265) ***(G-14971)***
**Smith Greenhouse & Supplies, Mendota** *Also called E N P Inc* ***(G-14720)***
**Smith Industrial Rubber & Plas** ....815 874-5364
5463 International Dr Rockford (61109) ***(G-18622)***
**Smith Power Transmission Co** ....773 526-5512
5335 S Western Blvd Ste C Chicago (60609) ***(G-6535)***
**Smith Welding LLC** ....618 829-5414
2238 N 2225 St Saint Elmo (62458) ***(G-19311)***
**Smith, John Crane, Crystal Lake** *Also called John Crane Inc* ***(G-7596)***
**Smith-Victor, Bartlett** *Also called Promark International Inc* ***(G-1365)***
**Smithco Fabricators Inc** ....847 678-1619
9555 Ainslie St Schiller Park (60176) ***(G-19873)***
**Smithereen Company** ....800 340-1888
7400 N Melvina Ave Niles (60714) ***(G-16034)***
**Smithereen Company Del (PA)** ....847 675-0010
7400 N Melvina Ave Niles (60714) ***(G-16035)***
**Smithereen Exterminating Co, Niles** *Also called Smithereen Company Del* ***(G-16035)***
**Smithereen Pest Management, Niles** *Also called Smithereen Company* ***(G-16034)***
**Smithfield Farmland Corp** ....815 747-8809
18531 Us Highway 20 W East Dubuque (61025) ***(G-8623)***
**Smithfield Farmland Corp** ....309 734-5353
1220 N 6th St Monmouth (61462) ***(G-15023)***
**Smithfield Food, East Dubuque** *Also called Smithfield Farmland Corp* ***(G-8623)***
**Smithfield Foods Inc** ....312 577-5650
303 E Wacker Dr Ste 1100 Chicago (60601) ***(G-6536)***
**Smithfield Global Products Inc (HQ)** ....630 281-5000
4225 Naperville Rd # 600 Lisle (60532) ***(G-13659)***
**Smoco Inc** ....618 662-6458
832 W North Ave Ste A1 Flora (62839) ***(G-10218)***
**Smolich Bros** ....815 727-2144
760 Theodore St Joliet (60403) ***(G-12576)***
**Smooches Ice Cream** ....708 370-0282
3559 W Arlington St Chicago (60624) ***(G-6537)***
**Smoothie King, Glendale Heights** *Also called Maaldar Pukhtoon Group LLC* ***(G-11044)***
**SMR Components, Mundelein** *Also called Stuart Moore Racing Ltd* ***(G-15561)***
**SMS Technical Services LLC** ....708 479-1333
19700 97th Ave Mokena (60448) ***(G-14903)***
**Smt LLC** ....630 961-3000
2768 Golfview Rd Naperville (60563) ***(G-15747)***
**Smt Molding, Naperville** *Also called Smt LLC* ***(G-15747)***
**Smurfit - Stone Flexible Packg, Schaumburg** *Also called Berry Global Inc* ***(G-19461)***
**Smurfit-Stone Container, Galesburg** *Also called Westrock Cp LLC* ***(G-10780)***
**Snagamon Valley Log Builders** ....217 632-7609
21500 Old Farm Ave Petersburg (62675) ***(G-17538)***
**Snaglet LLC** ....404 449-6394
2101 Crabtree Ln Northbrook (60062) ***(G-16364)***
**Snaidero USA** ....312 644-6662
222 Mrchnds Mrt Pl 140 Chicago (60654) ***(G-6538)***
**Snak-King Corp** ....815 232-6700
3133 Industrial Dr Freeport (61032) ***(G-10689)***
**Snap Diagnostics LLC** ....847 777-0000
5210 Capitol Dr Wheeling (60090) ***(G-22154)***
**Snap Edge, Saint Charles** *Also called Sek Corporation* ***(G-19262)***
**Snap-A-Pleat Drapery System, Peoria** *Also called Baker Drapery Corporation* ***(G-17313)***
**Snap-On Tools, West Chicago** *Also called Hollywood Tools LLC* ***(G-21715)***
**Snegde Deep** ....630 351-7111
994 Woodside Dr Roselle (60172) ***(G-18978)***
**Sno Gem Inc** ....888 766-4367
4800 Metalmaster Dr McHenry (60050) ***(G-14555)***
**Sno Gem Snow Guards, McHenry** *Also called Sno Gem Inc* ***(G-14555)***
**Sno-Belt Industries, Woodstock** *Also called Markham Industry Inc* ***(G-22587)***
**Snook Equipment Crane Inc** ....815 223-0003
2139 Maxim Dr Joliet (60436) ***(G-12577)***
**Snow & Graham LLC** ....773 665-9000
4021 N Ravenswood Ave Chicago (60613) ***(G-6539)***
**Snow Command Incorporated** ....708 991-7004
1607 Tina Ln Flossmoor (60422) ***(G-10228)***
**Snow Control Inc** ....708 670-6269
7245 W 151st St Orland Park (60462) ***(G-16892)***
**Snow Printing LLC** ....618 233-0712
6428 Old Saint Louis Rd Belleville (62223) ***(G-1676)***
**Snowball Industries** ....773 316-0051
3404 N Harding Ave Chicago (60618) ***(G-6540)***
**Snyder Industries Inc** ....630 773-9510
736 Birginal Dr Bensenville (60106) ***(G-1993)***
**Sobot Tool & Manufacturing Co** ....847 480-0560
3975 Commercial Ave Northbrook (60062) ***(G-16365)***
**Soccer House** ....847 998-0088
999 Waukegan Rd Ste A Glenview (60025) ***(G-11204)***
**Social Qnect LLC** ....847 997-0077
666 Dundee Rd Ste 1904 Northbrook (60062) ***(G-16366)***
**Socialcloak Inc** ....650 549-4412
399 Sinsinawa Ave East Dubuque (61025) ***(G-8624)***
**Socius Ingredients LLC** ....847 440-0156
1033 University Pl # 110 Evanston (60201) ***(G-10094)***
**Sofiflex LLC** ....847 261-4849
4432 Grace St Schiller Park (60176) ***(G-19874)***
**Sofrito Foods LLC** ....630 302-8615
771 Reserve Ct South Elgin (60177) ***(G-20226)***
**Soft O Soft Inc** ....630 741-4414
1701 E Wdfield Rd Ste 215 Schaumburg (60173) ***(G-19730)***
**Softhaus Ltd** ....618 463-1140
518 Beacon St Alton (62002) ***(G-590)***
**Softlabz Corporation (PA)** ....847 780-7076
1180 Saint Johns Ave Highland Park (60035) ***(G-11870)***
**Software Farm, The, Earlville** *Also called Tsf Net Inc* ***(G-8597)***
**SOFTWARE FOR SUCCESS, Evanston** *Also called Innovations For Learning Inc* ***(G-10056)***
**Software Maniacs, Woodstock** *Also called P B R W Enterprises Inc* ***(G-22597)***
**Software Support Systems Inc** ....630 587-2999
803 S 5th Ave Saint Charles (60174) ***(G-19265)***
**Soho, Glenview** *Also called Century Molded Plastics Inc* ***(G-11111)***
**Soil-Biotics, Reddick** *Also called Pro Ag Inc* ***(G-17952)***
**Sojuz Ent** ....847 215-9400
464 Country Club Dr Bensenville (60106) ***(G-1994)***
**Sokol and Company** ....708 482-8250
5315 Dansher Rd Countryside (60525) ***(G-7443)***
**Solab Inc** ....708 544-2200
2715 Grant Ave Bellwood (60104) ***(G-1722)***
**Solae** ....217 784-8261
115 Jordan Dr Gibson City (60936) ***(G-10907)***
**Solae** ....217 784-2085
509 W 1st St Gibson City (60936) ***(G-10908)***
**Solae LLC** ....219 261-2124
124 N Rte 47 Gibson City (60936) ***(G-10909)***
**Solar Spring & Wire Forms, Elk Grove Village** *Also called Solar Spring Company* ***(G-9742)***
**Solar Spring Company** ....847 437-7838
345 Criss Cir Elk Grove Village (60007) ***(G-9742)***
**Solar Traffic Systems Inc** ....331 318-8500
16135 New Ave Ste 2 Lemont (60439) ***(G-13263)***
**Solar Turbines Incorporated** ....630 527-1700
40 Shuman Blvd Ste 350 Naperville (60563) ***(G-15748)***
**Solari and Huntington, Park Ridge** *Also called Solari R Mfg Jewelers* ***(G-17222)***
**Solari R Mfg Jewelers** ....847 823-4354
100 1/2 Main St Park Ridge (60068) ***(G-17222)***
**Solarscope LLC** ....847 579-0024
1360 Old Skokie Rd Ste 2n Highland Park (60035) ***(G-11871)***
**Solazyme** ....309 258-5695
910 Ne Adams St Peoria (61603) ***(G-17457)***
**Solberg International Ltd (PA)** ....630 616-4400
1151 Ardmore Ave Itasca (60143) ***(G-12355)***
**Solberg Mfg Inc (PA)** ....630 616-4400
1151 Ardmore Ave Itasca (60143) ***(G-12356)***
**Solberg Mfg Inc** ....630 773-1363
680 Baker Dr Itasca (60143) ***(G-12357)***
**Soldy Manufacturing Inc** ....847 671-3396
9370 Byron St Schiller Park (60176) ***(G-19875)***
**Sole Unique, Aurora** *Also called Organized Noise Inc* ***(G-1059)***
**Soleil Systems Inc** ....847 427-0428
1325 Remington Rd Ste H Schaumburg (60173) ***(G-19731)***
**Solid Impressions Inc** ....630 543-7300
26w455 Saint Charles Rd Carol Stream (60188) ***(G-3241)***
**Solid Sound Inc** ....847 490-2101
2400 Hassell Rd Ste 430 Hoffman Estates (60169) ***(G-12055)***
**Solid State Luminaires LLC** ....877 775-4733
3609 Swenson Ave Saint Charles (60174) ***(G-19266)***
**Solidyne Corporation** ....847 394-3333
4731 Woodland Ct Rolling Meadows (60008) ***(G-18779)***
**Solidyne Corporation** ....847 394-3333
2155 Stonington Ave # 105 Hoffman Estates (60169) ***(G-12056)***
**Sollami Company** ....618 988-1521
1200 Weaver Rd Herrin (62948) ***(G-11755)***
**Solo Cup, Lincolnshire** *Also called SF Holdings Group Inc* ***(G-13479)***
**Solo Cup Company (HQ)** ....847 831-4800
300 Tri State Intl # 200 Lincolnshire (60069) ***(G-13480)***
**Solo Cup Company LLC (PA)** ....847 444-5000
300 Tri State Intl # 200 Lincolnshire (60069) ***(G-13481)***

ALPHABETIC

**Solo Cup Investment Corp (HQ)**....847 831-4800
1700 Old Deerfield Rd Highland Park (60035) ***(G-11872)***
**Solo Cup Operating Corporation (HQ)**....847 444-5000
300 Tr State Intl Ste 200 Lincolnshire (60069) ***(G-13482)***
**Solo Cup Operating Corporation**....847 444-5000
7575 S Kostner Ave Ste 3 Chicago (60652) ***(G-6541)***
**Solo Foods**....800 328-7656
5315 Dansher Rd Countryside (60525) ***(G-7444)***
**Solo Laboratories, Broadview** *Also called BMC 1092 Inc* ***(G-2563)***
**Solomon Colors Inc (PA)**....217 522-3112
4050 Color Plant Rd Springfield (62702) ***(G-20527)***
**Solomon Plumbing**....847 498-6388
3706 Winnetka Rd Glenview (60026) ***(G-11205)***
**Solublend Technologies LLC**....815 534-5778
11487 Amhearst Ct Frankfort (60423) ***(G-10364)***
**Solutia Inc**....618 482-6536
500 Monsanto Ave Sauget (62206) ***(G-19390)***
**Solution 3 Graphics Inc**....773 233-3600
10547 S Western Ave Chicago (60643) ***(G-6542)***
**Solution Designs Inc**....847 680-7788
2042 Laurel Valley Dr Vernon Hills (60061) ***(G-21203)***
**Solution Printing & Signs, Springfield** *Also called Solution Printing Inc* ***(G-20528)***
**Solution Printing Inc**....217 529-9700
3135 S 14th St Springfield (62703) ***(G-20528)***
**Solutions Manufacturing Inc**....847 310-4506
2109 Stonington Ave Hoffman Estates (60169) ***(G-12057)***
**Solvair LLC**....630 416-4244
215 Shuman Blvd Ste 403 Naperville (60563) ***(G-15749)***
**Solvay Chemicals Inc**....618 274-0755
3500 Missouri Ave East Saint Louis (62205) ***(G-8769)***
**Solvay USA Inc**....708 441-6041
1020 State St Chicago Heights (60411) ***(G-7126)***
**Solvay USA Inc**....708 371-2000
14000 Seeley Ave Blue Island (60406) ***(G-2271)***
**Solvay USA Inc**....708 235-7200
24601 Governors Hwy University Park (60484) ***(G-21062)***
**Somat Corporation (PA)**....800 578-4260
2202 Fox Dr Ste A Champaign (61820) ***(G-3541)***
**Somebody's Pub & Grille, Arlington Heights** *Also called Be McGonagle Inc* ***(G-724)***
**Something Old, Something New, Chicago** *Also called No Surrender Inc* ***(G-5920)***
**Somic America Inc**....630 274-4423
1080 Tower Ln Bensenville (60106) ***(G-1995)***
**Sommer Products Company Inc**....309 697-1216
6523 N Galena Rd Peoria (61614) ***(G-17458)***
**Sommers & Fahrenbach Inc**....773 478-3033
3301 W Belmont Ave Chicago (60618) ***(G-6543)***
**Sommers Fare LLC**....877 377-9797
1301 Allanson Rd Mundelein (60060) ***(G-15558)***
**Songear Holding Company LLC**....630 699-1119
226 N West Ave Elmhurst (60126) ***(G-9939)***
**Sonic Low Voltage**....815 790-4400
3218 N Richmond Rd Unit 3 Johnsburg (60051) ***(G-12442)***
**Sonic Manufacturing Corp**....847 228-0015
950 Lee St Elk Grove Village (60007) ***(G-9743)***
**Sonic Tool Mfg, Elk Grove Village** *Also called Sonic Manufacturing Corp* ***(G-9743)***
**Sonistic**....217 377-9698
60 Hazelwood Dr Ste 230g Champaign (61820) ***(G-3542)***
**Sonne Industries LLC**....630 235-6734
5s528 Arlington Ave Naperville (60540) ***(G-15750)***
**Sono Italiano Corporation**....817 472-8903
655 Mulberry St Manteno (60950) ***(G-14193)***
**Sonoco Alloyd, Dekalb** *Also called Tegrant Alloyd Brands Inc* ***(G-8124)***
**Sonoco Corrflex, Bolingbrook** *Also called Sonoco Display & Packaging LLC* ***(G-2373)***
**Sonoco Display & Packaging LLC**....630 972-1990
101 E Crossroads Pkwy Bolingbrook (60440) ***(G-2373)***
**Sonoco Display & Packaging LLC**....630 789-1111
1111 Pasquinelli Dr # 600 Westmont (60559) ***(G-21922)***
**Sonoco Plastics Inc**....630 628-5859
1035 W Republic Dr Addison (60101) ***(G-295)***
**Sonoco Products Company**....630 231-1489
1500 Powis Rd West Chicago (60185) ***(G-21775)***
**Sonoco Products Company**....847 957-6282
11608 Copenhagen Ct Franklin Park (60131) ***(G-10591)***
**Sonoco Protective Solution, Dekalb** *Also called Tegrant Corporation* ***(G-8125)***
**Sonoco Protective Solutions**....847 398-0110
3930 N Ventura Dr Ste 450 Arlington Heights (60004) ***(G-841)***
**Sonoco Prtective Solutions Inc**....847 398-0110
3930 N Ventura Dr Ste 450 Arlington Heights (60004) ***(G-842)***
**Sonoco Prtective Solutions Inc**....815 787-5244
1401 Pleasant St Dekalb (60115) ***(G-8119)***
**Sonoco Prtective Solutions Inc**....708 946-3244
30553 S Dixie Hwy Beecher (60401) ***(G-1602)***
**Sonoma Orthopedic Products Inc**....847 807-4378
1388 Busch Pkwy Buffalo Grove (60089) ***(G-2774)***
**Sonoscan Inc (PA)**....847 437-6400
2149 Pratt Blvd Elk Grove Village (60007) ***(G-9744)***
**Sons Enterprises**....847 677-4444
4826 Main St Skokie (60077) ***(G-20088)***

**Sony Electronics Inc**....630 773-7500
1064 Idaho St Carol Stream (60188) ***(G-3242)***
**Sony/Atv Music Publishing LLC**....630 739-8129
351 Internationale Dr Bolingbrook (60440) ***(G-2374)***
**Sopher Design & Manufacturing**....309 699-6419
3312 Meadow Ave East Peoria (61611) ***(G-8735)***
**Sorento News, Raymond News, Hillsboro** *Also called Hillsboro Journal Inc* ***(G-11895)***
**Soring Ring, Chicago** *Also called Sorini Manufacturing Corp* ***(G-6544)***
**Sorini Manufacturing Corp**....773 247-5858
2524 S Blue Island Ave Chicago (60608) ***(G-6544)***
**Sortimat Technology LP**....847 925-1234
5655 Meadowbrook Indus Ct Rolling Meadows (60008) ***(G-18780)***
**Sortimat Techonology, Rolling Meadows** *Also called Ats Sortimat USA LLC* ***(G-18711)***
**Sota Service Ctr By Bodinets**....608 538-3500
436 E Locust St Dekalb (60115) ***(G-8120)***
**Sota Turntable, Dekalb** *Also called Sota Service Ctr By Bodinets* ***(G-8120)***
**Sotiros Foods Inc**....708 371-0002
12560 S Holiday Dr Ste B Alsip (60803) ***(G-529)***
**Sotish Ltd**....708 476-2017
23 S La Grange Rd Ste 1 La Grange (60525) ***(G-12746)***
**Sotos Pallets Inc**....815 338-7750
1150 N Rose Farm Rd Woodstock (60098) ***(G-22613)***
**Soudan Metals Company Inc (PA)**....773 548-7600
319 W 40th Pl Chicago (60609) ***(G-6545)***
**Sound Design Inc**....630 548-7000
10104 S Mandel St Ste 1 Plainfield (60585) ***(G-17650)***
**Sound Enhancement Products Inc**....847 639-4646
100 High Grove Blvd Glendale Heights (60139) ***(G-11070)***
**Sound Master & Calvert Systems, Port Byron** *Also called Calvert Systems* ***(G-17719)***
**Sound Seal Inc**....630 844-1999
401 Airport Rd North Aurora (60542) ***(G-16144)***
**Sound World Solutions, Park Ridge** *Also called Nantsound Inc* ***(G-17210)***
**Source 4-Integrated Business, Chicago** *Also called Available Business Group Inc* ***(G-3995)***
**Source Software Inc (PA)**....815 922-7717
16525 W 159th St 200 Lockport (60441) ***(G-13747)***
**Source Technology**....281 894-6171
2150 Parkes Dr Broadview (60155) ***(G-2612)***
**Source United LLC**....847 956-1459
689 Chase Ave Elk Grove Village (60007) ***(G-9745)***
**Sourcebooks Inc (PA)**....630 961-3900
1935 Brookdale Rd Ste 139 Naperville (60563) ***(G-15751)***
**Sourcennex International Co**....847 251-5500
825 Green Bay Rd Ste 240 Wilmette (60091) ***(G-22266)***
**Sourcing Solutions, Naperville** *Also called Lessy Messy LLC* ***(G-15814)***
**South Bend Sporting Goods Inc (PA)**....847 715-1400
1910 Techny Rd Northbrook (60062) ***(G-16367)***
**South Central Fs Inc**....618 283-1557
10 Interstate Dr Vandalia (62471) ***(G-21126)***
**South Central Fs Inc**....217 849-2242
403 E Madison St Toledo (62468) ***(G-20966)***
**South Chicago Packing LLC (PA)**....708 589-2400
16250 Vincennes Ave South Holland (60473) ***(G-20305)***
**South Chicago Packing LLC**....708 589-2400
945 W 38th St Chicago (60609) ***(G-6546)***
**South County Publications (PA)**....217 438-6155
110 N 5th St Auburn (62615) ***(G-949)***
**South Florida Test Service Div, Mount Prospect** *Also called Atlas Material Tstg Tech LLC* ***(G-15311)***
**South Holland Met Finshg Inc**....708 235-0842
26100 S Whiting Way Monee (60449) ***(G-15002)***
**South Midwest Division, Kankakee** *Also called Legacy Vulcan Corp* ***(G-12637)***
**South Paw Donuts, Metropolis** *Also called Brown & Meyers Inc* ***(G-14752)***
**South Shore Iron Works Inc**....773 264-2267
407 W 109th St Chicago (60628) ***(G-6547)***
**South Side Bler Wldg Works Inc**....708 478-1714
10811 Minnesota Ct Orland Park (60467) ***(G-16893)***
**South Side Boiler & Wldg Work, Orland Park** *Also called South Side Bler Wldg Works Inc* ***(G-16893)***
**South Side HM Kit Emporium Inc**....217 322-3708
110 W Lafayette St Rushville (62681) ***(G-19095)***
**South Subn Logistics Sups Corp**....312 804-3401
16610 Finch Ave Harvey (60426) ***(G-11675)***
**South Subn Wldg & Fabg Co Inc**....708 385-7160
14022 S Western Ave Posen (60469) ***(G-17736)***
**South Water Signs LLC**....630 333-4900
934 N Church Rd Ste B Elmhurst (60126) ***(G-9940)***
**South West Oil Inc**....815 416-0400
7080 Highland Dr Morris (60450) ***(G-15130)***
**Southeast Wood Treating Inc**....815 562-5007
300 E Avenue G Rochelle (61068) ***(G-18110)***
**Southeastern Container Inc**....217 342-9600
1200 Mcgrath Ave Effingham (62401) ***(G-8858)***
**Southern Blooms LLC**....618 565-1111
550 E Industrial Park Rd # 17 Murphysboro (62966) ***(G-15584)***
**Southern Glass Co**....618 532-4281
1005 Beacham Ave Centralia (62801) ***(G-3434)***
**Southern Graphic Systems LLC**....847 695-9515
150 Corporate Dr Elgin (60123) ***(G-9189)***

## ALPHABETIC SECTION — Special Tool Engineering Co

**Southern IL Crankshaft Inc** ............................................. 618 282-4100
225 Kaskaskia Dr  Red Bud  (62278)  *(G-17949)*

**Southern IL Precision** ................................................... 618 643-3340
310 W Randolph St  Mc Leansboro  (62859)  *(G-14467)*

**Southern IL Raceway** .................................................... 618 201-0500
11682 Macie Dr  Marion  (62959)  *(G-14288)*

**Southern Ill Auto Elec Inc** ............................................. 618 587-3308
730 N Minnie Ave  Tilden  (62292)  *(G-20877)*

**Southern Ill Wilbert Vlt Co** ........................................... 618 942-5845
2221 N Park Ave  Herrin  (62948)  *(G-11756)*

**Southern Ill Wine Trail Nfp** ........................................... 618 695-9463
48 E Glendale Rd  Golconda  (62938)  *(G-11242)*

**Southern Illinois Crankshafts** ....................................... 618 282-4100
225 Kaskaskia St  Ruma  (62278)  *(G-19089)*

**Southern Illinois Material, Buncombe** *Also called Southern Illinois Power Coop* *(G-2799)*

**Southern Illinois McHy Co Inc** ...................................... 217 868-5431
6903 E 1600th Ave  Shumway  (62461)  *(G-19935)*

**Southern Illinois Miners** ............................................... 618 969-8506
1000 Miners Dr  Marion  (62959)  *(G-14289)*

**Southern Illinois Power Coop** ....................................... 618 995-2371
Rr 37 Box N  Buncombe  (62912)  *(G-2799)*

**Southern Illinois Redimix Inc (PA)** ................................ 618 993-3600
11039 Skyline Dr  Marion  (62959)  *(G-14290)*

**Southern Illinois Scale Servc** ........................................ 618 723-2303
430 W South Ave  Noble  (62868)  *(G-16054)*

**Southern Illinois State Cont, Nashville** *Also called Sisco Corporation* *(G-15847)*

**Southern Illinois Stone Co (HQ)** ................................... 573 334-5261
4800 State Rt 37 N  Buncombe  (62912)  *(G-2800)*

**Southern Illinois Stone Co** ............................................ 618 995-2392
4800 Hwy 37 N  Buncombe  (62912)  *(G-2801)*

**Southern Illinois University** .......................................... 618 453-2268
210 Physical Plant Dr  Carbondale  (62901)  *(G-3024)*

**Southern Illinois Vault Co Inc** ...................................... 270 554-4436
2221 N Park Ave  Herrin  (62948)  *(G-11757)*

**Southern Illinoisan, Marion** *Also called Lee Enterprises Incorporated* *(G-14270)*

**Southern Illinoisan, Carbondale** *Also called Lee Enterprises Incorporated* *(G-3014)*

**Southern Imperial Inc (PA)** .......................................... 815 877-7041
1400 Eddy Ave  Rockford  (61103)  *(G-18623)*

**Southern Imperial Inc** .................................................. 815 877-7041
7135 Clinton Rd  Loves Park  (61111)  *(G-13993)*

**Southern Mold Finishing Inc** ........................................ 618 983-5049
500 Follis Ave  Johnston City  (62951)  *(G-12446)*

**Southern Plating Inc** .................................................... 618 983-6350
500 Follis Ave  Johnston City  (62951)  *(G-12447)*

**Southern Steel and Wire Inc (HQ)** ................................ 618 654-2161
1111 6th St  Highland  (62249)  *(G-11812)*

**Southern Triangle Oil Co, Mount Carmel** *Also called New Triangle Oil Company* *(G-15278)*

**Southern Triangle Oil Company** ................................... 618 262-4131
600 Chestnut St  Mount Carmel  (62863)  *(G-15282)*

**Southern Truss Inc** ...................................................... 618 252-8144
5510 Highway 13 W  Harrisburg  (62946)  *(G-11604)*

**Southfield Corporation** ................................................ 217 875-5455
705 E Mckinley Ave  Decatur  (62526)  *(G-7941)*

**Southfield Corporation** ................................................ 708 345-0030
5300 W Lake St  Melrose Park  (60160)  *(G-14694)*

**Southfield Corporation** ................................................ 708 563-4056
799 S Route 53  Addison  (60101)  *(G-296)*

**Southfield Corporation** ................................................ 309 676-6121
775 W Birchwood St  Morton  (61550)  *(G-15181)*

**Southfield Corporation** ................................................ 708 362-2520
7601 W 79th St  Bridgeview  (60455)  *(G-2529)*

**Southfield Corporation** ................................................ 815 284-3357
1914 White Oak Ln  Dixon  (61021)  *(G-8352)*

**Southfield Corporation** ................................................ 217 877-5210
800 E Mckinley Ave  Decatur  (62526)  *(G-7942)*

**Southfield Corporation** ................................................ 217 398-4300
3200 W Springfield Ave  Champaign  (61822)  *(G-3543)*

**Southfield Corporation** ................................................ 708 458-0400
7601 W 79th St  Oak Lawn  (60455)  *(G-16644)*

**Southfield Corporation** ................................................ 708 458-0400
7601 W 79th St  Bridgeview  (60455)  *(G-2530)*

**Southfield Corporation** ................................................ 217 379-3606
100 N 2280e Rd  Paxton  (60957)  *(G-17245)*

**Southfield Corporation** ................................................ 815 842-2333
15887 E 1200 North Rd  Pontiac  (61764)  *(G-17711)*

**Southfield Corporation** ................................................ 309 829-1087
917 E Grove St  Bloomington  (61701)  *(G-2225)*

**Southfield Corporation** ................................................ 309 676-0576
100 W Cass St  Peoria  (61602)  *(G-17459)*

**Southfield Corporation** ................................................ 815 468-8700
8215c N Us Highway 45 52  Manteno  (60950)  *(G-14194)*

**Southland Industries Inc** .............................................. 757 543-5701
2345 Waukegan Rd Ste 155  Bannockburn  (60015)  *(G-1265)*

**Southland Voice** .......................................................... 708 214-8582
1712 S Dixie Hwy Trlr 133  Crete  (60417)  *(G-7519)*

**Southmoor Estates Inc** ................................................. 815 756-1299
1032 S 7th St  Dekalb  (60115)  *(G-8121)*

**Southport Records, Chicago** *Also called Sparrow Sound Design* *(G-6552)*

**Southtown Star Newspapers** ....................................... 708 633-4800
18312 West Creek Dr  Tinley Park  (60477)  *(G-20946)*

**Southwest Denture Center, Oak Lawn** *Also called Lmpl Management Corporation* *(G-16631)*

**Southwest Messenger Press Inc** ................................... 708 388-2425
3840 147th St  Midlothian  (60445)  *(G-14769)*

**Southwest Printing Co** ................................................. 708 389-0800
12003 S Pulaski Rd  Alsip  (60803)  *(G-530)*

**Southwest Senior, Summit Argo** *Also called Vondrak Publishing Co Inc* *(G-20768)*

**Southwest Tool & Machine** .......................................... 708 349-4441
15600 116th Ct  Orland Park  (60467)  *(G-16894)*

**Southwick Machine & Design Co** ................................ 309 949-2868
21300 Briar Bluff Rd  Colona  (61241)  *(G-7348)*

**Southwire, Waukegan** *Also called Coleman Cable LLC* *(G-21542)*

**Southwire Company LLC** ............................................. 618 662-8341
Eash Rd  Flora  (62839)  *(G-10219)*

**Soy City Sock Co Inc** .................................................... 217 762-2157
1086 S Market St  Monticello  (61856)  *(G-15085)*

**Sp Industries, Elk Grove Village** *Also called S P Industries Inc* *(G-9724)*

**Space Organization Ltd** ............................................... 312 654-1400
4720 W Walton St  Chicago  (60651)  *(G-6548)*

**Spacesaver Parking Company** ..................................... 773 486-6900
820 N Wolcott Ave  Chicago  (60622)  *(G-6549)*

**Spacil Construction Co** ............................................... 708 448-3809
6018 W 123rd St  Palos Heights  (60463)  *(G-17110)*

**Spaeth Welding Inc** ..................................................... 618 588-3596
321 W Missouri St  New Baden  (62265)  *(G-15865)*

**Spanish Amercn Languag Newspap** .............................. 312 368-4840
55 E Jackson Blvd # 1820  Chicago  (60604)  *(G-6550)*

**Spannagel Tool & Die** .................................................. 630 969-7575
2732 Wisconsin Ave  Downers Grove  (60515)  *(G-8526)*

**Spannuth Boiler Co** ..................................................... 708 386-1882
264 Madison St  Oak Park  (60302)  *(G-16687)*

**Spare Part Solutions Inc** .............................................. 815 637-1490
3374 Precision Dr  Rockford  (61109)  *(G-18624)*

**Sparkle Express** ........................................................... 630 375-9801
1545 Us Highway 34  Oswego  (60543)  *(G-16935)*

**Sparks Fiberglass Inc** ................................................... 309 848-0077
5415 227th Street Ct N  Port Byron  (61275)  *(G-17725)*

**Sparrer Sausage Company Inc** ..................................... 773 762-3334
4325 W Ogden Ave  Chicago  (60623)  *(G-6551)*

**Sparrow Coffee Roastery** ............................................. 321 648-6415
10330 W Roosevelt Rd # 200  Westchester  (60154)  *(G-21855)*

**Sparrow Sound Design** ................................................ 773 281-8510
3501 N Southport Ave  Chicago  (60657)  *(G-6552)*

**Spartaclean, Machesney Park** *Also called Spartacus Group Inc* *(G-14108)*

**Spartacus Group Inc** ................................................... 815 637-1574
925 Colonial Dr  Machesney Park  (61115)  *(G-14108)*

**Spartan Adhesives Coatings Co** ................................... 815 459-8500
345 E Terra Cotta Ave  Crystal Lake  (60014)  *(G-7652)*

**Spartan Energy, Loves Park** *Also called Drivnn LLC* *(G-13937)*

**Spartan Flame Retardants Inc** ..................................... 815 459-8500
345 E Terra Cotta Ave  Crystal Lake  (60014)  *(G-7653)*

**Spartan Light Metal Pdts Inc (PA)** ............................... 618 443-4346
510 E Mcclurken Ave  Sparta  (62286)  *(G-20321)*

**Spartan Light Metal Pdts Inc** ....................................... 618 443-4346
405 E 4th St  Sparta  (62286)  *(G-20322)*

**Spartan Petroleum Company** ...................................... 618 262-4197
328 N Market St  Mount Carmel  (62863)  *(G-15283)*

**Spartan Sheet Metal Inc** .............................................. 773 895-7266
3006 W Bryn Mawr Ave  Chicago  (60659)  *(G-6553)*

**Spartan Tool LLC (HQ)** ................................................ 815 539-7411
1506 Division St  Mendota  (61342)  *(G-14733)*

**Spartanics Ltd** ............................................................. 847 394-5700
3605 Edison Pl  Rolling Meadows  (60008)  *(G-18781)*

**Sparton Aubrey LLC** .................................................... 386 740-5381
425 N Martingale Rd Ste 2  Schaumburg  (60173)  *(G-19732)*

**Sparton Aydin LLC** ...................................................... 800 772-7866
425 N Martingale Rd  Schaumburg  (60173)  *(G-19733)*

**Sparton Corporation (PA)** ........................................... 847 762-5800
425 N Martingale Rd  Schaumburg  (60173)  *(G-19734)*

**Sparton Design Services LLC (HQ)** .............................. 847 762-5800
425 N Martingale Rd # 2050  Schaumburg  (60173)  *(G-19735)*

**Sparton Emt LLC (HQ)** ................................................ 800 772-7866
425 N Martingale Rd Ste 2  Schaumburg  (60173)  *(G-19736)*

**Sparton Ied LLC** .......................................................... 847 762-5800
425 N Martingale Rd  Schaumburg  (60173)  *(G-19737)*

**Sparx EDM Inc** ............................................................. 847 722-7577
65 Sangra Ct  Streamwood  (60107)  *(G-20674)*

**Speak Out, Lombard** *Also called Ea Mackay Enterprises Inc* *(G-13793)*

**Spec Check LLC** ........................................................... 773 270-0003
910 Raleigh Rd  Mundelein  (60060)  *(G-15559)*

**Special Fastener Operations** ....................................... 815 544-6449
1993 Belford North Dr # 102  Belvidere  (61008)  *(G-1784)*

**Special Mine Services Inc (PA)** .................................... 618 932-2151
11782 Country Club Rd  West Frankfort  (62896)  *(G-21820)*

**Special Products Company, Oregon** *Also called Speeco Incorporated* *(G-16832)*

**Special Products Division, La Salle** *Also called New Cie Inc* *(G-12781)*

**Special Scents Inc** ........................................................ 708 596-9370
14815 Artesian Ave  Harvey  (60426)  *(G-11676)*

**Special Tool Engineering Co** ....................................... 773 767-6690
4539 S Knox Ave  Chicago  (60632)  *(G-6554)*

(PA)=Parent Co  (HQ)=Headquarters  (DH)=Div Headquarters

**Specialized Liftruck Svcs LLC** 708 552-2705
6650 S Narragansett Ave Bedford Park (60638) *(G-1585)*
**Specialized Separators Inc** 815 316-0626
1800 16th Ave Rockford (61104) *(G-18625)*
**Specialized Woodwork Inc** 630 627-0450
74 Eisenhower Ln N Lombard (60148) *(G-13854)*
**Specialty Box Corp** 630 897-7278
366 Smoketree Bsn Dr Pa North Aurora (60542) *(G-16145)*
**Specialty Building Resources, Deerfield** *Also called Simonton Holdings Inc (G-8055)*
**Specialty Cnstr Brands Inc (HQ)** 630 851-0782
1105 S Frontenac St Aurora (60504) *(G-1081)*
**Specialty Crate Factory (PA)** 708 756-2100
3320 Louis Sherman Dr Steger (60475) *(G-20576)*
**Specialty Enterprises Inc** 630 595-7808
1075 Waveland Ave Franklin Park (60131) *(G-10592)*
**Specialty Filaments, Arcola** *Also called Monahan Filaments LLC (G-677)*
**Specialty Foods Holdings Inc** 630 599-5900
477 E Bttrfeld Rd Ste 410 Lombard (60148) *(G-13855)*
**Specialty Graphics Supply Inc** 630 584-8202
3875 Commerce Dr Saint Charles (60174) *(G-19267)*
**Specialty Nut & Bky Sup Co Inc** 630 268-8500
1417 W Jeffrey Dr Addison (60101) *(G-297)*
**Specialty Pntg Soda Blastg Inc** 815 577-0006
24031 W Winners Circle Ct Plainfield (60585) *(G-17651)*
**Specialty Precision Tool, Chicago** *Also called Walt Ltd (G-6936)*
**Specialty Printing Company, Niles** *Also called Specialty Promotions Inc (G-16036)*
**Specialty Printing Midwest** 618 799-8472
1 Gemini Industrial Dr Roxana (62084) *(G-19086)*
**Specialty Promotions Inc (PA)** 847 588-2580
6019 W Howard St Niles (60714) *(G-16036)*
**Specialty Publishing Company** 630 933-0844
135 E Saint Charles Rd D Carol Stream (60188) *(G-3243)*
**Specialty Screw Corporation** 815 969-4100
2801 Huffman Blvd Rockford (61103) *(G-18626)*
**Specialty Tape & Label Co Inc** 708 863-3800
7830 47th St Lyons (60534) *(G-14044)*
**Specific Press Brake Dies Inc** 708 478-1776
9439 Enterprise Dr Mokena (60448) *(G-14904)*
**Specified Plating Co** 773 826-4501
320 N Harding Ave Chicago (60624) *(G-6555)*
**Speco Inc** 847 678-4240
3946 Willow St Schiller Park (60176) *(G-19876)*
**Spectacle Zoom LLC** 504 352-7237
8671 Josephine St Apt A Des Plaines (60016) *(G-8278)*
**Spectape of Midwest Inc** 630 682-8600
75 Tanglewood Dr Glen Ellyn (60137) *(G-10990)*
**Spectra Jet** 847 669-9094
10611 Wolf Dr Huntley (60142) *(G-12177)*
**Spectracrafts Ltd** 847 824-4117
931 N Ridge Ave Lombard (60148) *(G-13856)*
**Spectragen Incorporated** 847 982-0481
1005 Royal Blackheath Ct Naperville (60563) *(G-15752)*
**Spectris Holdings Inc** 847 680-3709
732 Florsheim Dr Ste 11 Libertyville (60048) *(G-13383)*
**Spectroclick Inc** 217 356-4829
904 Mayfair Rd Champaign (61821) *(G-3544)*
**Spectron Manufacturing** 720 879-7605
328 Georgetown Ct Unit C Bloomingdale (60108) *(G-2138)*
**Spectrum Brands Inc** 815 285-6500
200 E Corporate Dr Dixon (61021) *(G-8353)*
**Spectrum Cos International** 630 879-8008
336 Mckee St Batavia (60510) *(G-1497)*
**Spectrum Graphic Services Inc** 630 766-7673
398 W Wrightwood Ave Elmhurst (60126) *(G-9941)*
**Spectrum Machining Co** 630 562-9400
776 W Hawthorne Ln West Chicago (60185) *(G-21776)*
**Spectrum Media Inc** 217 234-2044
921 S 19th St Mattoon (61938) *(G-14409)*
**Spectrum Preferred Meats Inc** 815 946-3816
6194 W Pines Rd Mount Morris (61054) *(G-15300)*
**Spectrum Technologies Intl Ltd** 630 961-5244
6368 Greene Rd Woodridge (60517) *(G-22518)*
**Speeco Incorporated** 303 279-5544
2606 S Illinois Route 2 Oregon (61061) *(G-16832)*
**Speed Bleeder Products Co** 815 736-6296
13140 Apakesha Rd Newark (60541) *(G-15935)*
**Speed Ink Printing** 773 539-9700
3547 W Peterson Ave Chicago (60659) *(G-6556)*
**Speed Tech Technology Inc** 847 516-2001
314 Cary Point Dr Cary (60013) *(G-3372)*
**Speedco Inc** 618 931-1575
1201 Denham Dr Granite City (62040) *(G-11304)*
**Speedotron Corporation** 630 246-5001
1268 Humbracht Cir Bartlett (60103) *(G-1378)*
**Speedpro Imaging** 847 856-8220
1350 Tri State Pkwy Gurnee (60031) *(G-11506)*
**Speedpro North Shore** 847 983-0095
8246 Kimball Ave Skokie (60076) *(G-20089)*
**Speedpro of Dupage** 630 812-5080
441 Eisenhower Ln S Lombard (60148) *(G-13857)*
**Speedway** 815 463-0840
570 E Laraway Rd New Lenox (60451) *(G-15912)*
**Speedy Redi Mix LLC** 773 487-2000
6445 S State St Chicago (60637) *(G-6557)*
**Speedys Quick Print** 217 431-0510
44 N Vermilion St Danville (61832) *(G-7766)*
**Speidel Applicators, Stanford** *Also called Quality Metal Works Inc (G-20552)*
**Spell It With Color Inc** 630 961-5617
1644 Swallow St Naperville (60565) *(G-15753)*
**Spence Monuments Co** 217 348-5992
525 W State St Charleston (61920) *(G-3612)*
**Spencer and Krahn Mch Tl Sls (PA)** 815 282-3300
2621 Springdale Dr Rockford (61114) *(G-18627)*
**Spencer Welding Service Inc** 847 272-0580
3215 Doolittle Dr Northbrook (60062) *(G-16368)*
**Spend Radar LLC** 312 265-0764
311 S Wacker Dr Ste 2270 Chicago (60606) *(G-6558)*
**SPEP Acquisition Corp** 310 608-0693
1 Gateway Ct Ste E Bolingbrook (60440) *(G-2375)*
**Spf Supplies Inc** 847 454-9081
300 Scott St Elk Grove Village (60007) *(G-9746)*
**Spg International LLC** 815 233-0022
1555 Il Route 75 E Ste 2 Freeport (61032) *(G-10690)*
**Spg Usa Inc** 847 439-4949
501 Lively Blvd Elk Grove Village (60007) *(G-9747)*
**Sphere Inc** 847 566-4800
316 Washington Blvd Mundelein (60060) *(G-15560)*
**Spherotech Inc** 847 680-8922
27845 Irma Lee Cir # 101 Lake Forest (60045) *(G-12961)*
**Sphinx Panel and Door Inc** 618 351-9266
317 Locust St Cobden (62920) *(G-7305)*
**Spicetec, Carol Stream** *Also called Conagra Fods Fd Ingrdients Inc (G-3135)*
**Spicetec Flavors & Seasonings, Carol Stream** *Also called Givaudan Flavors Corporation (G-3158)*
**Spicy Mix Asian and American** 773 295-5765
5952 W Roosevelt Rd Chicago (60644) *(G-6559)*
**Spider Company Inc (PA)** 815 961-8200
2340 11th St Rockford (61104) *(G-18628)*
**Spider Company Inc** 815 961-8200
2340 11th St Rockford (61104) *(G-18629)*
**Spie Tool Co** 847 891-6556
1350 Wright Blvd Schaumburg (60193) *(G-19738)*
**Spike Nanotech Inc** 847 504-6273
1008 Donnington Dr Matteson (60443) *(G-14379)*
**Spinco Tool & Fabe** 815 578-8600
2518 Walnut Dr Wonder Lake (60097) *(G-22325)*
**Spinecraft LLC** 630 920-7300
777 Oakmont Ln Ste 200 Westmont (60559) *(G-21923)*
**Spinner Medical Products Inc** 312 944-8700
900 N Lake Shore Dr Ste 1 Chicago (60611) *(G-6560)*
**Spintex Inc** 847 608-5411
1331 Gateway Dr Elgin (60124) *(G-9190)*
**Spiral Binding of Illinois, Elk Grove Village** *Also called S B Liquidating Company (G-9723)*
**Spiral-Helix Inc** 224 659-7870
500 Industrial Dr Bensenville (60106) *(G-1996)*
**Spiraltech Superior Dental Imp** 312 440-7777
875 N Michigan Ave # 3106 Chicago (60611) *(G-6561)*
**Spirax Sarco Inc** 630 493-4525
1500 Eisenhower Ln # 600 Lisle (60532) *(G-13660)*
**Spirit Brands/ Zoo Piks, Lake Forest** *Also called Spirit Foodservice Inc (G-12962)*
**Spirit Concepts Inc** 708 388-4500
4365 136th Ct Crestwood (60445) *(G-7503)*
**Spirit Foodservice Inc** 214 634-1393
1900 W Field Ct Lake Forest (60045) *(G-12962)*
**Spirit Industries Inc** 217 285-4500
39920 274th Ln Griggsville (62340) *(G-11414)*
**Spirit Warrior Inc** 708 614-0020
15519 S 70th Ct Orland Park (60462) *(G-16895)*
**Spirolox Inc** 847 719-5900
555 Oakwood Rd Lake Zurich (60047) *(G-13133)*
**Spirotherm Inc** 630 307-2662
25 N Brandon Dr Glendale Heights (60139) *(G-11071)*
**Spitfire Controls, Elgin** *Also called Sigmatron International Inc (G-9178)*
**Spl Software Alliance LLC** 309 266-0304
500 N Morton Ave Morton (61550) *(G-15182)*
**Spl-Usa LLC** 312 807-2000
123 N Wacker Dr Chicago (60606) *(G-6562)*
**Splash Dog Therapy Inc** 847 296-4007
42 N Broadway St Des Plaines (60016) *(G-8279)*
**Splash Graphics Inc** 630 230-5775
7001 S Adams St Willowbrook (60527) *(G-22232)*
**Sponge-Cushion Inc** 815 942-2300
902 Armstrong St Morris (60450) *(G-15131)*
**Spooky Cool Labs LLC** 773 577-5555
5515 N Cumberland Ave # 810 Chicago (60656) *(G-6563)*
**Spoon River F S, Wataga** *Also called West Central Fs Inc (G-21399)*
**Sport Connection** 630 980-1787
741 E Nerge Rd Roselle (60172) *(G-18979)*

# ALPHABETIC SECTION

Sport Electronics Inc .................................................. 847 564-5575
  4121 Rutgers Ln  Northbrook  (60062)  *(G-16369)*
Sport Incentives Inc .................................................. 847 427-8650
  1050 Pauly Dr  Elk Grove Village  (60007)  *(G-9748)*
Sport Redi-Mix  LLC (PA) ........................................... 217 355-4222
  401 Wilbur Ave  Champaign  (61822)  *(G-3545)*
Sport Redi-Mix  LLC ................................................... 217 892-4222
  527 S Tanner St  Rantoul  (61866)  *(G-17937)*
Sport Redi-Mix  LLC ................................................... 217 582-2555
  401 Wilburn Ave  Ogden  (61859)  *(G-16745)*
Sportdecals Sport & Spirit Pro ................................... 800 435-6110
  2504 Spring Ridge Dr  Spring Grove  (60081)  *(G-20365)*
Sportland, Bloomington  Also called T G Enterprises Inc  *(G-2229)*
Sports All Sorts AP & Design ..................................... 815 756-9910
  147 N 2nd St Ste 2  Dekalb  (60115)  *(G-8122)*
Sports Awards, Chicago  Also called Stellar Recognition  Inc  *(G-6588)*
Sports Corner & Creations, Peoria  Also called Waldos Sports Corner Inc  *(G-17477)*
Sports Designs & Graphics ....................................... 217 342-2777
  807 S Maple St  Effingham  (62401)  *(G-8859)*
Sports Profiles Plus, Skokie  Also called Profile Network Inc  *(G-20063)*
Sportscar365, Palos Park  Also called John Dagys Media  LLC  *(G-17129)*
Spot Printing & Office Sups, Oakbrook Terrace  Also called S G C M Corp  *(G-16720)*
Spotlight Graphics, Schaumburg  Also called K & M Printing Company  Inc  *(G-19595)*
Spotlight Youth Theater ............................................. 847 516-2298
  755 Industrial Dr  Cary  (60013)  *(G-3373)*
Spouts of Water Inc (PA) ............................................ 303 570-5104
  9416 Margail Ave  Des Plaines  (60016)  *(G-8280)*
Spray Foam Direct, Riverwoods  Also called Guardian Energy Tech Inc  *(G-18038)*
Spraying Systems Co, Glendale Heights  Also called Spraying Systems Midwest Inc  *(G-11073)*
Spraying Systems Co (PA) ......................................... 630 665-5000
  200 W North Ave  Glendale Heights  (60139)  *(G-11072)*
Spraying Systems Co .................................................. 630 665-5001
  2580 Diehl Rd Ste E  Aurora  (60502)  *(G-1082)*
Spraying Systems Midwest Inc ................................. 630 665-5000
  N Ave And Schmale Rd  Glendale Heights  (60139)  *(G-11073)*
Spreader Inc ................................................................ 217 568-7219
  2296 County Road 3000 N  Gifford  (61847)  *(G-10910)*
Spectra Graphics Inc ................................................. 618 624-6776
  115 N Lincoln Ave  O Fallon  (62269)  *(G-16479)*
Spring (usa) Corporation ............................................ 630 527-8600
  127 Ambassador Dr Ste 147  Naperville  (60540)  *(G-15754)*
Spring Brook Nature Center ...................................... 630 773-5572
  411 N Prospect Ave  Itasca  (60143)  *(G-12358)*
Spring R-R Corporation .............................................. 630 543-7445
  100 W Laura Dr  Addison  (60101)  *(G-298)*
Spring Specialist Corporation ................................... 815 562-7991
  14400 E Dutch Rd  Kings  (61068)  *(G-12705)*
Springbox Inc ............................................................. 708 921-9944
  2842 Scott Cres  Flossmoor  (60422)  *(G-10229)*
Springfield Inc ............................................................ 309 944-5631
  420 W Main St  Geneseo  (61254)  *(G-10805)*
Springfield Armory, Geneseo  Also called Springfield  Inc  *(G-10805)*
Springfield Auto Ctr Stor Pool, Springfield  Also called Springfield Welding & Auto Bdy  *(G-20534)*
Springfield Business Journal, Springfield  Also called Springfield Publishers Inc  *(G-20532)*
Springfield Iron & Metal Co ....................................... 217 544-7131
  930 N Wolfe St  Springfield  (62702)  *(G-20529)*
Springfield Pepsi Cola Btlg Co (PA) ........................... 217 522-8841
  2900 Singer Ave  Springfield  (62703)  *(G-20530)*
Springfield Plastics  Inc ............................................. 217 438-6167
  7300 W State Route 104  Auburn  (62615)  *(G-950)*
Springfield Printing Inc ............................................. 217 787-3500
  3500 Constitution Dr  Springfield  (62711)  *(G-20531)*
Springfield Publishers Inc ........................................ 217 726-6600
  1118 W Laurel St  Springfield  (62704)  *(G-20532)*
Springfield Sales Assoc Inc ....................................... 217 529-6987
  3513 Tamarak Dr  Springfield  (62712)  *(G-20533)*
Springfield Welding & Auto Bdy ................................ 217 523-5365
  2720 Holmes Ave  Springfield  (62704)  *(G-20534)*
Springfield Woodworks .............................................. 217 483-7234
  6651 Wesley Chapel Rd  Chatham  (62629)  *(G-3625)*
Springsoft International, Bloomingdale  Also called Newater International Inc  *(G-2120)*
Sprinter Coml Print Label Corp ................................. 630 460-3492
  4820 Fesseneva Ln  Naperville  (60564)  *(G-15828)*
Spudnik Press Cooperative ....................................... 312 563-0302
  1821 W Hubbard St Ste 302  Chicago  (60622)  *(G-6564)*
Spunky Dunker Donuts (PA) ...................................... 847 358-7935
  20 S Northwest Hwy  Palatine  (60074)  *(G-17076)*
Spurt  Inc ..................................................................... 847 571-6497
  4033 Dana Ct  Northbrook  (60062)  *(G-16370)*
SPX Cooling Technologies  Inc ................................. 815 873-3767
  5885 11th St  Rockford  (61109)  *(G-18630)*
SPX Corporation ......................................................... 815 407-3915
  1385 N Weber Rd  Romeoville  (60446)  *(G-18869)*
SPX Corporation ......................................................... 847 593-8855
  800 Arthur Ave  Elk Grove Village  (60007)  *(G-9749)*
SPX Corporation ......................................................... 815 874-5556
  5885 11th St  Rockford  (61109)  *(G-18631)*
SPX Flow US LLC ........................................................ 815 874-5556
  5885 11th St  Rockford  (61109)  *(G-18632)*
SPX Haydraulic Technologies, Rockford  Also called SPX Cooling Technologies Inc  *(G-18630)*
Spyco Industries Inc .................................................. 630 655-5900
  7029 High Grove Blvd  Burr Ridge  (60527)  *(G-2881)*
Spyco Tool Co, Burr Ridge  Also called Spyco Industries  Inc  *(G-2881)*
Spytek Aerospace Corporation .................................. 847 318-7515
  450 Frontier Way Ste D  Bensenville  (60106)  *(G-1997)*
Square 1 Precision Ltg Inc ......................................... 708 343-1500
  4300 W North Ave  Melrose Park  (60165)  *(G-14695)*
Squeegee Brothers Inc (PA) ....................................... 630 510-9152
  398 E Saint Charles Rd  Carol Stream  (60188)  *(G-3244)*
Squibb Tank Company ............................................... 618 548-0141
  1001 S Broadway Ave  Salem  (62881)  *(G-19352)*
Sram  LLC (PA) ........................................................... 312 664-8800
  1000 W Fulton Market # 400  Chicago  (60607)  *(G-6565)*
SRC Electric LLC ......................................................... 224 404-6103
  360 Bennett Rd  Elk Grove Village  (60007)  *(G-9750)*
Srds, Rosemont  Also called Perq/Hci  LLC  *(G-19020)*
Srh Holdings Inc ......................................................... 847 583-2295
  6100 W Howard St  Niles  (60714)  *(G-16037)*
Srm, Centreville  Also called Steel Rebar Manufacturing LLC  *(G-3438)*
Srm Industries Inc (PA) .............................................. 847 735-0077
  1009 S Green Bay Rd  Lake Forest  (60045)  *(G-12963)*
Srmd Solutions  LLC .................................................. 217 925-5773
  202 W Center St  Dieterich  (62424)  *(G-8315)*
Srt Prosthetics Orthotics LLC ................................... 847 855-0030
  6475 Washington St # 100  Gurnee  (60031)  *(G-11507)*
Srv Professional Publications ................................... 847 330-1260
  235 Monson Ct  Schaumburg  (60173)  *(G-19739)*
Ssa, Chicago  Also called System Software Associates Del  *(G-6660)*
Ssa Global, Chicago  Also called Infor (us)  Inc  *(G-5184)*
Ssa Global Technologies, Inc, Chicago  Also called Infor (us)  *(G-5185)*
Ssab Enterprises  LLC (HQ) ........................................ 630 810-4800
  801 Warrenville Rd # 800  Lisle  (60532)  *(G-13661)*
Ssab US Holding  Inc (HQ) ......................................... 630 810-4800
  801 Warrenville Rd # 800  Lisle  (60532)  *(G-13662)*
Ssh Environmental Inds Inc (PA) ............................... 312 573-6413
  875 N Michigan Ave # 4020  Chicago  (60611)  *(G-6566)*
Ssi, Newton  Also called Newton Ready Mix Inc  *(G-15944)*
Ssn  LLC ...................................................................... 815 978-8729
  4875 E Nordic Woods Dr  Byron  (61010)  *(G-2922)*
Sst Forming Roll Inc .................................................. 847 215-6812
  1318 Busch Pkwy  Buffalo Grove  (60089)  *(G-2775)*
St Charles Memorial Works Inc (PA) ......................... 630 584-0183
  1640 W Main St  Saint Charles  (60174)  *(G-19268)*
St Charles Screw Products Inc ................................. 815 943-8060
  404 E Park St  Harvard  (60033)  *(G-11647)*
St Charles Stamping Inc ............................................ 630 584-2029
  318 N 4th St  Saint Charles  (60174)  *(G-19269)*
St Clair Tennis Club LLC ........................................... 618 632-1400
  733 Hartman Ln  O Fallon  (62269)  *(G-16480)*
St Imaging Inc ............................................................. 847 501-3344
  630 Dundee Rd Ste 210  Northbrook  (60062)  *(G-16371)*
St John S United Church of, Evanston  Also called St Johns United Church Christ  *(G-10095)*
St Johns United Church Christ ................................. 847 491-6686
  1136 Wesley Ave  Evanston  (60202)  *(G-10095)*
St Louis Flexicore Inc ................................................ 618 531-8691
  6351 Collinsville Rd  East Saint Louis  (62201)  *(G-8770)*
St Louis Scrap Trading  LLC ..................................... 618 307-9002
  5 Sunset Hills Blvd N  Edwardsville  (62025)  *(G-8815)*
St Louis Screw & Bolt, Madison  Also called Slsb LLC  *(G-14153)*
St Marys Cement ........................................................ 773 995-5100
  12101 S Doty Ave  Chicago  (60633)  *(G-6567)*
St Marys Cement Inc (us) .......................................... 313 842-4600
  1914 White Oak Ln  Dixon  (61021)  *(G-8354)*
St Nicholas Brewing Co ............................................. 618 318-3556
  12 S Oak St  Du Quoin  (62832)  *(G-8558)*
St Pierre Oil Company Inc ......................................... 618 783-4441
  102 N Van Buren St  Newton  (62448)  *(G-15949)*
St. Louis Packaging, Schaumburg  Also called Alliance Creative Group  Inc  *(G-19431)*
STA-Rite Ginnie Lou Inc ............................................ 217 774-3921
  245 E South 1st St  Shelbyville  (62565)  *(G-19916)*
Staar Bales Lestarge Inc ............................................ 618 259-6366
  450 W Saint Louis Ave  East Alton  (62024)  *(G-8611)*
Stabiloc  LLC .............................................................. 586 412-1147
  545 Kimberly Dr  Carol Stream  (60188)  *(G-3245)*
Stable Beginning Corporation ................................... 815 745-2100
  400 S Railroad St  Warren  (61087)  *(G-21337)*
Stack On Products Company, Wauconda  Also called Stack-On Products Co  *(G-21502)*
Stack-On Products Co (PA) ....................................... 847 526-1611
  1360 N Old Rand Rd  Wauconda  (60084)  *(G-21502)*
Staffco  Inc ................................................................. 309 688-3223
  3806 N Northwood Ave  Peoria  (61614)  *(G-17460)*

**Stages Construction Inc** ....773 619-2977
4722 W Harrison St Chicago (60644) *(G-6568)*
**Staging By Tish** ....630 852-9595
345 2nd St Downers Grove (60515) *(G-8527)*
**Stagnito Media, Deerfield** *Also called Stagnito Partners LLC (G-8056)*
**Stagnito Partners LLC (HQ)** ....224 632-8200
570 Lake Cook Rd Ste 310 Deerfield (60015) *(G-8056)*
**Stahl Lumber Company (PA)** ....309 695-4331
11719 S Galena Ave Wyoming (61491) *(G-22640)*
**Stahl Lumber Company** ....309 385-2552
117 S Galena Ave Wyoming (61491) *(G-22641)*
**Stahl Ready Concrete, Wyoming** *Also called Stahl Lumber Company (G-22641)*
**Stahl Ready Mix Concrete, Wyoming** *Also called Stahl Lumber Company (G-22640)*
**Stained Glass of Peoria** ....309 674-7929
512 Spring St Peoria (61603) *(G-17461)*
**Stainless Specialties Inc** ....618 654-7723
329 Il Route 143 Pocahontas (62275) *(G-17686)*
**Stainless Steel Prod, Deer Grove** *Also called Sterling Gear Inc (G-7968)*
**Stairs & Rales Inc** ....708 216-0078
1200 Main St Melrose Park (60160) *(G-14696)*
**Stairsland** ....708 853-9593
8001 47th St Fl 4 Lyons (60534) *(G-14045)*
**Stalex Inc** ....630 627-9401
1051 N Main St Ste A Lombard (60148) *(G-13858)*
**Staley Concrete Co** ....217 356-9533
4106 Kearns Dr Champaign (61822) *(G-3546)*
**Stampede Meat Inc (PA)** ....773 376-4300
7351 S 78th Ave Bridgeview (60455) *(G-2531)*
**Stan-Ed Metal Mfg Co, Chicago** *Also called Ed Stan Fabricating Co (G-4694)*
**Stancy Woodworking Co Inc** ....847 526-0252
301 Fern Dr Island Lake (60042) *(G-12219)*
**Stand Fast Group LLC** ....630 600-0900
710 Kimberly Dr Carol Stream (60188) *(G-3246)*
**Stand Fast Packaging Pdts Inc (PA)** ....630 600-0900
710 Kimberly Dr Carol Stream (60188) *(G-3247)*
**Standard Boiler Tank & Testing, Riverdale** *Also called JM Industries LLC (G-18020)*
**Standard Car Truck Company (HQ)** ....847 692-6050
6400 Shafer Ct Ste 450 Rosemont (60018) *(G-19033)*
**Standard Car Truck Company** ....630 860-5511
701 Maple Ln Bensenville (60106) *(G-1998)*
**Standard Condenser Corporation** ....847 965-2722
5412 Keeney St Morton Grove (60053) *(G-15237)*
**Standard Container Co of Edgar (PA)** ....847 438-1510
717 N Old Rand Rd Lake Zurich (60047) *(G-13134)*
**Standard Heat Treating LLC** ....773 242-0853
5757 W Ogden Ave Cicero (60804) *(G-7229)*
**Standard Heat Treating Co Inc** ....708 447-7504
5757 W Ogden Ave Chicago (60804) *(G-6569)*
**Standard Indus & Auto Eqp Inc** ....630 289-9500
6211 Church Rd Hanover Park (60133) *(G-11590)*
**Standard Laboratories Inc** ....618 539-5836
8451 River King Dr Freeburg (62243) *(G-10642)*
**Standard Laboratory, Freeburg** *Also called Standard Laboratories Inc (G-10642)*
**Standard Lifts & Equipment Inc** ....414 444-1000
6211 Church Rd Hanover Park (60133) *(G-11591)*
**Standard Machine & Tool Corp** ....309 762-6431
206 43rd St Moline (61265) *(G-14972)*
**Standard Marble & Granite** ....773 533-0450
4551 W 5th Ave Chicago (60624) *(G-6570)*
**Standard Oil Company (HQ)** ....630 836-5000
4101 Winfield Rd Ste 100 Warrenville (60555) *(G-21362)*
**Standard Perforating & Mfg, Chicago** *Also called Accurate Perforating Co Inc (G-3721)*
**Standard Precision Grinding Co** ....708 474-1211
2800 Bernice Rd Ste 1 Lansing (60438) *(G-13185)*
**Standard Provision Co, Shorewood** *Also called Rapid Foods Inc (G-19931)*
**Standard Register Inc** ....309 693-3700
1100 W Glen Ave Ste 300 Peoria (61614) *(G-17462)*
**Standard Register Inc** ....815 432-4203
112 E Walnut St Ste B Watseka (60970) *(G-21427)*
**Standard Register Inc** ....630 784-6833
20 N Wacker Dr Ste 1475 Chicago (60606) *(G-6571)*
**Standard Register Inc** ....217 793-1900
450 S Durkin Dr Ste C Springfield (62704) *(G-20535)*
**Standard Register Inc** ....847 783-1040
2768 Spectrum Dr Elgin (60124) *(G-9191)*
**Standard Register Inc** ....708 560-7600
4849 167th St Ste 201 Oak Forest (60452) *(G-16589)*
**Standard Register Inc** ....630 368-0336
900 Jorie Blvd Ste 238 Oak Brook (60523) *(G-16561)*
**Standard Register Inc** ....815 439-1050
24121 W Riverwalk Ct Plainfield (60544) *(G-17652)*
**Standard Register Inc** ....630 467-8300
1 Pierce Pl Ste 270c Itasca (60143) *(G-12359)*
**Standard Register Inc** ....630 784-6810
150 E Saint Charles Rd A Carol Stream (60188) *(G-3248)*
**Standard Rubber Products Co** ....847 593-5630
120 Seegers Ave Elk Grove Village (60007) *(G-9751)*
**Standard Safety Equipment Co** ....815 363-8565
1407 Ridgeview Dr McHenry (60050) *(G-14556)*
**Standard Sheet Metal Works Inc** ....309 633-2300
220 N Commerce Pl Peoria (61604) *(G-17463)*
**Standard Truck Parts Inc (PA)** ....815 726-4486
566 N Chicago St Joliet (60432) *(G-12578)*
**Standard Wire & Steel Works, South Holland** *Also called G F Ltd (G-20269)*
**Standex International Corp** ....630 588-0400
279 E Lies Rd Carol Stream (60188) *(G-3249)*
**Standing Water Solutions Inc** ....847 469-8876
950 N Rand Rd Ste 121 Wauconda (60084) *(G-21503)*
**Stanford Bettendorf Inc** ....618 548-3555
1370 W Main St Salem (62881) *(G-19353)*
**Stanford Products LLC (HQ)** ....618 548-2600
1139 S Broadway Ave Salem (62881) *(G-19354)*
**Stange Industrial Group** ....847 640-8470
494 Bonnie Ln Elk Grove Village (60007) *(G-9752)*
**Stanger Tool & Mold Inc** ....847 426-5826
2713 Winfield Ln Belvidere (61008) *(G-1785)*
**Stanick Tool Manufacturing Co** ....847 726-7090
1190 Heather Dr Lake Zurich (60047) *(G-13135)*
**Stanley Hartco Co** ....847 967-1122
7707 Austin Ave Skokie (60077) *(G-20090)*
**Stanley Machining & Tool Corp (PA)** ....847 426-4560
425 Maple Ave Carpentersville (60110) *(G-3303)*
**Stanley Security Solutions Inc** ....877 476-4968
840 Oak Creek Dr Lombard (60148) *(G-13859)*
**Stanley Security Solutions Inc** ....630 724-3600
2150 Western Ct Ste 300 Lisle (60532) *(G-13663)*
**Stanley Spring & Stamping Corp** ....773 777-2600
5050 W Foster Ave Chicago (60630) *(G-6572)*
**Stanron Corporation (PA)** ....773 777-2600
5050 W Foster Ave Chicago (60630) *(G-6573)*
**Stanron Steel Specialties Div, Chicago** *Also called Stanron Corporation (G-6573)*
**Stans Sportsworld Inc** ....217 359-8474
47 E Green St Champaign (61820) *(G-3547)*
**Stanton Wind Energy LLC** ....312 224-1400
1 S Wacker Dr Ste 1900 Chicago (60606) *(G-6574)*
**Star Acquisition Inc** ....847 439-0605
825 Pratt Blvd Elk Grove Village (60007) *(G-9753)*
**Star Cabinetry** ....773 725-4651
4440 W Belmont Ave Chicago (60641) *(G-6575)*
**Star Cushion Products Inc** ....618 539-7070
5 Commerce Dr Freeburg (62243) *(G-10643)*
**Star Cutter Co** ....231 264-5661
5200 Prairie Stone Pkwy Hoffman Estates (60192) *(G-12058)*
**Star Die Molding Inc** ....847 766-7952
2741 Katherine Way Elk Grove Village (60007) *(G-9754)*
**Star Electronics Corp** ....847 439-0605
825 Pratt Blvd Elk Grove Village (60007) *(G-9755)*
**Star Energy Corp Inc** ....618 584-3631
1675 N 1200 Rd Flat Rock (62427) *(G-10197)*
**Star Forge Inc** ....815 235-7750
1801 S Ihm Blvd Freeport (61032) *(G-10691)*
**Star Industries Inc** ....708 240-4862
2210 Skokie Valley Rd Highland Park (60035) *(G-11873)*
**Star Industries Intl Div, Highland Park** *Also called Star Industries Inc (G-11873)*
**Star Lite Mfg** ....630 595-8338
735 N Edgewood Ave Ste C Wood Dale (60191) *(G-22424)*
**Star Manufacturing Company, Freeport** *Also called Star Forge Inc (G-10691)*
**Star Media Group** ....847 674-7827
8200 Niles Center Rd Skokie (60077) *(G-20091)*
**Star Moulding & Trim Company** ....708 458-1040
6606 W 74th St Bedford Park (60638) *(G-1586)*
**Star Plastics, Broadview** *Also called Star Thermoplastic Alloys and (G-2614)*
**Star Silkscreen Design Inc** ....217 877-0804
2281 E Hubbard Ave Decatur (62526) *(G-7943)*
**Star Sleigh** ....630 858-2576
716 Crescent Blvd Glen Ellyn (60137) *(G-10991)*
**Star Test Dynamometer Inc** ....309 452-0371
712 Thistlewood Cc Ct Normal (61761) *(G-16089)*
**Star Thermoplastic Alloys and (PA)** ....708 343-1100
2121 W 21st St Broadview (60155) *(G-2613)*
**Star Thermoplastic Alloys and** ....708 343-1100
2121 W 21st St Broadview (60155) *(G-2614)*
**Star Thermoplastics, Broadview** *Also called Star Thermoplastic Alloys and (G-2613)*
**Star-Times Publishing Co Inc** ....618 635-2000
108 W Main St Staunton (62088) *(G-20559)*
**Starex Inc** ....847 918-5555
1880 W Winchester Rd # 206 Libertyville (60048) *(G-13384)*
**Starfire Industries LLC** ....217 721-4165
2109 S Oak St Ste 100 Champaign (61820) *(G-3548)*
**Starfish Ventures Inc** ....847 490-9334
11a Golf Ctr Hoffman Estates (60169) *(G-12059)*
**Starfruit LLC** ....312 527-3674
222 Merchandise Mart Plz # 238 Chicago (60654) *(G-6576)*
**Starhouse Inc** ....630 679-0979
1312 Enterprise Dr Lockport (60446) *(G-13748)*
**Stark Aire Fluid Bed Dryers, Downers Grove** *Also called Paul D Stark & Associates (G-8500)*
**Stark County Communications** ....309 286-4444
101 W Main St Toulon (61483) *(G-20977)*

**Stark Materials Inc** ....309 828-8520
9359 E 1000 North Rd Shirley (61772) ***(G-19920)***
**Stark Printing Company** ....847 234-8430
208 W Olmsted Ln Round Lake (60073) ***(G-19068)***
**Stark Standard Co** ....847 916-2636
4028 Tugwell St Franklin Park (60131) ***(G-10593)***
**Stark Tools and Supply Inc** ....847 772-8974
1001 Fargo Ave Ste 105 Elk Grove Village (60007) ***(G-9756)***
**Starlight Software System Inc** ....309 454-7349
25130 Arrowhead Ln Hudson (61748) ***(G-12125)***
**Starline Communications, Rockford** *Also called Fred Kennerly* ***(G-18392)***
**Starline Designs** ....773 683-7506
750 E 43rd St Chicago (60653) ***(G-6577)***
**Starmont Manufacturing Co** ....815 939-1041
655 S Harrison Ave Kankakee (60901) ***(G-12653)***
**Starmont Manufacturing Inc** ....708 758-2525
640 217th St Chicago Heights (60411) ***(G-7127)***
**Starnet Digital Publishing, Bloomington** *Also called July 25th Corporation* ***(G-2186)***
**Starro Precision P&E, Elgin** *Also called Honor Med Maskiner Corp* ***(G-9066)***
**Starro Precision Products Inc** ....847 741-9400
1730 Todd Farm Dr Elgin (60123) ***(G-9192)***
**Stars Online, Chicago** *Also called Scholarship Solutions LLC* ***(G-6453)***
**Start Magazine, Carol Stream** *Also called Specialty Publishing Company* ***(G-3243)***
**Starview Vineyard, Cobden** *Also called Shawnee Grapevines LLC* ***(G-7304)***
**State Attorney Appellate** ....217 782-3397
1021 E North Grand Ave Springfield (62702) ***(G-20536)***
**State Comptroller Print Shop, Springfield** *Also called Financial and Professional Reg* ***(G-20439)***
**State Journal Register, The, Springfield** *Also called Gatehouse Media Illinois Ho* ***(G-20446)***
**State Line Foundries Inc** ....815 389-3921
13227 N 2nd St Roscoe (61073) ***(G-18922)***
**State Line International Inc** ....708 251-5772
18107 Torrence Ave Lansing (60438) ***(G-13186)***
**State of Illinois** ....312 836-9500
222 Merchandise Mart Plz # 1450 Chicago (60654) ***(G-6578)***
**Stateline Renewable Fuels LLC** ....608 931-4634
6 Regent Ct W Buffalo Grove (60089) ***(G-2776)***
**Stationary Studio LLC (PA)** ....847 541-2499
460 Newtown Dr Buffalo Grove (60089) ***(G-2777)***
**Staunton Star Times, Staunton** *Also called Star-Times Publishing Co Inc* ***(G-20559)***
**Stay Straight Manufacturing** ....312 226-2137
4145 W Kinzie St Chicago (60624) ***(G-6579)***
**STC Inc** ....618 643-2555
1201 W Randolph St Mc Leansboro (62859) ***(G-14468)***
**STC International, Machesney Park** *Also called Rockford Commercial Whse Inc* ***(G-14105)***
**Steakhouse Premium, Mount Prospect** *Also called Advertising Premiums Inc* ***(G-15308)***
**Steam Plant, Chicago** *Also called University of Chicago* ***(G-6838)***
**Steamgard LLC** ....847 913-8400
730 Forest Edge Dr Vernon Hills (60061) ***(G-21204)***
**Stearns Printing of Charleston** ....217 345-7518
304 8th St Charleston (61920) ***(G-3613)***
**Stecker Graphics Inc** ....309 786-4973
2215 4th Ave Rock Island (61201) ***(G-18204)***
**Steel Construction Svcs Inc** ....815 678-7509
9618 Keystone Rd Richmond (60071) ***(G-17972)***
**Steel Fab, Woodridge** *Also called Samuel Strapping Systems Inc* ***(G-22515)***
**Steel Fab & Finish, Chicago** *Also called Soudan Metals Company Inc* ***(G-6545)***
**Steel Fabricating Inc** ....815 977-5355
2806 22nd St Rockford (61109) ***(G-18633)***
**Steel Fabrication and Welding** ....773 343-0731
3200 S 61st Ave Cicero (60804) ***(G-7230)***
**Steel Guard Inc** ....773 342-6265
4707 W North Ave Chicago (60639) ***(G-6580)***
**Steel Guard Safety, South Holland** *Also called Terre Haute Tent & Awning Inc* ***(G-20309)***
**Steel Management Inc** ....630 397-5083
716 Natwill Sq Geneva (60134) ***(G-10869)***
**Steel Rebar Manufacturing LLC** ....618 920-2748
4926 Church Rd Centreville (62207) ***(G-3438)***
**Steel Services Enterprises** ....708 259-1181
17500 Paxton Ave Lansing (60438) ***(G-13187)***
**Steel Solutions USA** ....815 432-4938
602 E Walnut St Watseka (60970) ***(G-21428)***
**Steel Span Inc** ....815 943-9071
630 W Blackman St Harvard (60033) ***(G-11648)***
**Steel Whse Quad Cities LLC** ....309 756-1089
4305 81st Ave W Rock Island (61201) ***(G-18205)***
**Steel-Guard Safety Corp** ....708 589-4588
16520 Vincennes Ave South Holland (60473) ***(G-20306)***
**Steelcase Inc** ....312 321-3720
222 Merchandise Mart Plz # 1032 Chicago (60654) ***(G-6581)***
**Steele & Loeber Lumber (HQ)** ....708 544-8383
801 Mannheim Rd Bellwood (60104) ***(G-1723)***
**Steelfab Inc** ....815 935-6540
2045 S Kensington Ave Kankakee (60901) ***(G-12654)***
**Steelweld Division, Galesburg** *Also called Midstate Manufacturing Company* ***(G-10767)***
**Steelwerks of Chicago LLC** ....312 792-9593
4257 W Drummond Pl Unit E Chicago (60639) ***(G-6582)***

**Steibel License Service** ....618 233-7555
2704 N Illinois St Ste D Swansea (62226) ***(G-20783)***
**Stein Inc** ....815 626-9355
610 Wallace St Sterling (61081) ***(G-20613)***
**Stein Inc** ....618 452-0836
2201 Edwardsville Rd Granite City (62040) ***(G-11305)***
**Stein Steel Mini Services, Sterling** *Also called Stein Inc* ***(G-20613)***
**Stein Still Mills, Granite City** *Also called Stein Inc* ***(G-11305)***
**Steinbach Provision Company** ....773 538-1511
741 W 47th St Chicago (60609) ***(G-6583)***
**Steiner Electric Company** ....312 421-7220
2225 W Hubbard St Chicago (60612) ***(G-6584)***
**Steiner Impressions Inc** ....815 633-4135
5596 E Riverside Blvd # 2 Loves Park (61111) ***(G-13994)***
**Steiner Industries Inc** ....773 588-3444
5801 N Tripp Ave Chicago (60646) ***(G-6585)***
**Steinmetz R (us) Ltd** ....312 332-0990
67 E Madison St Ste 1606 Chicago (60603) ***(G-6586)***
**Stelfast Inc** ....847 783-0161
2780 Spectrum Dr Elgin (60124) ***(G-9193)***
**Stellar Blending & Packaging** ....314 520-7318
1556 Decoma Dr Dupo (62239) ***(G-8577)***
**Stellar Manufacturing Company** ....618 823-3761
1647 Sauget Business Blvd Cahokia (62206) ***(G-2926)***
**Stellar Performance Mfg LLC (PA)** ....312 951-2311
640 N La Salle Dr Ste 540 Chicago (60654) ***(G-6587)***
**Stellar Plastics Corporation** ....630 443-1200
3627 Stern Ave Saint Charles (60174) ***(G-19270)***
**Stellar Recognition Inc** ....773 282-8060
5544 W Armstrong Ave Chicago (60646) ***(G-6588)***
**Stellato Printing Inc (PA)** ....815 725-1057
1801 Jared Dr Crest Hill (60403) ***(G-7468)***
**Stelmont Inc** ....847 870-0200
818 W Northwest Hwy Arlington Heights (60004) ***(G-843)***
**Steloc Fastener Co** ....847 459-6200
160 Abbott Dr Wheeling (60090) ***(G-22155)***
**Stenograph LLC (HQ)** ....630 532-5100
596 W Lamont Rd Elmhurst (60126) ***(G-9942)***
**Stenograph LLC** ....630 532-5100
596 W Lamont Rd Elmhurst (60126) ***(G-9943)***
**Stentech Inc** ....630 833-4747
853 N Industrial Dr Elmhurst (60126) ***(G-9944)***
**Stentech-Chicago, Elmhurst** *Also called Stentech Inc* ***(G-9944)***
**Step One Stairworks Inc** ....815 286-7464
201 Somonauk Rd Hinckley (60520) ***(G-11937)***
**Stepac USA Corporation (HQ)** ....630 296-2000
1201 Windham Pkwy Romeoville (60446) ***(G-18870)***
**Stepan Company (PA)** ....847 446-7500
22 W Frontage Rd Northfield (60093) ***(G-16419)***
**Stepan Company** ....815 727-4944
22500 Stepan Rd Elwood (60421) ***(G-9982)***
**Stepan Specialty Products LLC** ....847 446-7500
22 W Frontage Rd Northfield (60093) ***(G-16420)***
**Stephen Fossler Company** ....847 635-7200
1600 E Touhy Ave Des Plaines (60018) ***(G-8281)***
**Stephen Paoli Mfg Corp** ....815 965-0621
2531 11th St Rockford (61104) ***(G-18634)***
**Stephens Pipe & Steel LLC** ....800 451-2612
603 Oak Crest Dr North Aurora (60542) ***(G-16146)***
**Stepping Stones Gps LLC** ....217 529-6697
2860 Stanton St Springfield (62703) ***(G-20537)***
**Stera-Sheen, Wauconda** *Also called Purdy Products Company* ***(G-21497)***
**Stereo Optical Company Inc** ....773 867-0380
8600 W Catalpa Ave Chicago (60656) ***(G-6589)***
**Stergo Roofing** ....312 640-9008
172 W Golf Rd Ste 299 Mount Prospect (60056) ***(G-15375)***
**Sterigenics US LLC** ....847 855-0727
1003 Lakeside Dr Gurnee (60031) ***(G-11508)***
**Sterigenics US LLC** ....630 285-9121
1500 W Thorndale Ave Itasca (60143) ***(G-12360)***
**Sterigenics US LLC** ....
7775 S Quincy St Willowbrook (60527) ***(G-22233)***
**Steripro Laboratories, Itasca** *Also called Sterigenics US LLC* ***(G-12360)***
**Steris Corporation** ....847 455-2881
11457 Melrose Ave Ste B Franklin Park (60131) ***(G-10594)***
**Sterline Bridge, Bensenville** *Also called Pureline Treatment Systems LLC* ***(G-1970)***
**Sterline Manufacturing Corp** ....847 244-1234
4000 Porett Dr Ste B Gurnee (60031) ***(G-11509)***
**Sterling Books Limited** ....630 325-3853
735 S Oak St Hinsdale (60521) ***(G-11965)***
**Sterling Brands LLC** ....847 229-1600
555 Allendale Dr Wheeling (60090) ***(G-22156)***
**Sterling Die Inc** ....216 267-1300
676 E Fullerton Ave Glendale Heights (60139) ***(G-11074)***
**Sterling Extract Company Inc** ....847 451-9728
10929 Franklin Ave Ste V Franklin Park (60131) ***(G-10595)***
**Sterling Gear Inc** ....815 438-4327
1582 Hoover Rd Deer Grove (61243) ***(G-7968)***
**Sterling Lumber Company (PA)** ....708 388-2223
501 E 151st St Phoenix (60426) ***(G-17542)***

ALPHABETIC

**Sterling Mattress Factory, Herrin** *Also called Wicoff Inc* ***(G-11758)***
**Sterling Metal Craft Inc** ........ 708 652-4590
1817 S 55th Ave Ste 3 Cicero (60804) ***(G-7231)***
**Sterling Phrm Svcs LLC** ........ 618 286-4116
102 Coulter Rd East Carondelet (62240) ***(G-8615)***
**Sterling Phrm Svcs LLC (PA)** ........ 618 286-6060
109 S 2nd St Dupo (62239) ***(G-8578)***
**Sterling Plating Inc** ........ 708 867-6587
4629 N Ronald St Chicago (60706) ***(G-6590)***
**Sterling Products Inc (HQ)** ........ 847 273-7700
1100 E Woodfield Rd # 550 Schaumburg (60173) ***(G-19740)***
**Sterling RE & Investments, Fox River Grove** *Also called Sales & Marketing Resources* ***(G-10289)***
**Sterling Spring LLC (PA)** ........ 773 582-6464
5432 W 54th St Chicago (60638) ***(G-6591)***
**Sterling Spring LLC** ........ 773 777-4647
7171 W 65th St Bedford Park (60638) ***(G-1587)***
**Sterling Spring LLC** ........ 773 772-9331
7171 W 65th St Chicago (60638) ***(G-6592)***
**Sterling Steel 0530, Sterling** *Also called Sterling Steel Company LLC* ***(G-20614)***
**Sterling Steel Ball, Sterling** *Also called Frantz Manufacturing Company* ***(G-20592)***
**Sterling Steel Company LLC** ........ 815 548-7000
101 Avenue K Sterling (61081) ***(G-20614)***
**Sterling Systems & Controls** ........ 815 625-0852
24711 Emerson Rd Sterling (61081) ***(G-20615)***
**Sterling Systems Sales Corp** ........ 630 584-3580
3745 Stern Ave Saint Charles (60174) ***(G-19271)***
**Sterling Tool & Manufacturing** ........ 847 304-1800
28080 W Coml Ave Ste 8 Barrington (60010) ***(G-1305)***
**Sterling Vault Company** ........ 815 625-0077
2411 W Lincolnway Sterling (61081) ***(G-20616)***
**Sterling Wire Products Inc** ........ 815 625-3015
804 E 10th St Rock Falls (61071) ***(G-18153)***
**Sterling-Rock Falls Ready Mix** ........ 815 288-3135
1905 Mound Hill Rd Dixon (61021) ***(G-8355)***
**Stern Pinball Inc** ........ 708 345-7700
2001 Lunt Ave Elk Grove Village (60007) ***(G-9757)***
**Sternberg Lanterns Inc (PA)** ........ 847 588-3400
555 Lawrence Ave Roselle (60172) ***(G-18980)***
**Sternberg Lighting, Roselle** *Also called Sternberg Lanterns Inc* ***(G-18980)***
**Sterner Screw Machine, Rockford** *Also called Jim Sterner Machines* ***(G-18445)***
**Steroids Ltd** ........ 312 996-2364
1255 N State Pkwy Chicago (60610) ***(G-6593)***
**Steuben Township** ........ 309 208-7073
374 County Road 850 E Sparland (61565) ***(G-20315)***
**Steve Bortman** ........ 708 442-1669
7937 Ogden Ave Lyons (60534) ***(G-14046)***
**Steve Forrest** ........ 815 765-9040
290 E Park St Poplar Grove (61065) ***(G-17717)***
**Steve Green** ........ 847 623-6327
2233 Northwestern Ave B Waukegan (60087) ***(G-21619)***
**Steve O Inc** ........ 847 473-4466
1550 Green Bay Rd North Chicago (60064) ***(G-16187)***
**Steve Olson Printing & Design, North Chicago** *Also called Steve O Inc* ***(G-16187)***
**Steven A Zanetis** ........ 618 393-2176
1060 W Main St Olney (62450) ***(G-16797)***
**Steven Brownstein** ........ 847 909-6677
5830 Lincoln Ave Unit A Morton Grove (60053) ***(G-15238)***
**Steven E Wasko & Associates** ........ 773 693-2330
1580 N Northwest Hwy # 212 Park Ridge (60068) ***(G-17223)***
**Steven Fisher** ........ 847 317-1128
610 Thornmeadow Rd Riverwoods (60015) ***(G-18044)***
**Steven Madden Ltd** ........ 773 276-5486
1553 N Milwaukee Ave Chicago (60622) ***(G-6594)***
**Stevens Cabinets Inc (PA)** ........ 217 857-7100
704 W Main St Teutopolis (62467) ***(G-20856)***
**Stevens Exhibits & Displays** ........ 773 523-3900
3900 S Union Ave Chicago (60609) ***(G-6595)***
**Stevens Group LLc** ........ 331 209-2100
188 W Indl Dr Ste 428 Elmhurst (60126) ***(G-9945)***
**Stevens Instrument Company** ........ 847 336-9375
111 W Greenwood Ave Waukegan (60087) ***(G-21620)***
**Stevens Plastic Inc** ........ 847 885-2378
2125 Stonington Ave Hoffman Estates (60169) ***(G-12060)***
**Stevens Sign Co Inc** ........ 708 562-4888
57 E Fullerton Ave Northlake (60164) ***(G-16453)***
**Stevens Tot-Mate, Teutopolis** *Also called Stevens Cabinets Inc* ***(G-20856)***
**Stevenson Fabrication Svcs Inc** ........ 815 468-7941
680 Mulberry St Manteno (60950) ***(G-14195)***
**Stevenson Paper Co Inc** ........ 630 879-5000
1775 Hubbard Ave Batavia (60510) ***(G-1498)***
**Stevenson Sales & Service LLC** ........ 630 972-0330
410 Stevenson Dr Bolingbrook (60440) ***(G-2376)***
**Stevenson's Mel-O-Cream Donuts, Springfield** *Also called Mel-O-Cream Donuts* ***(G-20476)***
**Stevensons Mel-O-Cream Donuts, Springfield** *Also called Mel-O-Cream Donuts* ***(G-20477)***
**Steves Cigarettes** ........ 630 827-0820
1247 S Main St Lombard (60148) ***(G-13860)***
**Stevie S Italian Foods Inc (PA)** ........ 217 793-9693
1909 Grist Mill Dr Springfield (62711) ***(G-20538)***
**Stewart Brothers Packing Co** ........ 217 422-7741
1004 N Country Club Rd Decatur (62521) ***(G-7944)***
**Stewart Ingrdients Systems Inc** ........ 312 254-3539
1843 W Fulton St Chicago (60612) ***(G-6596)***
**Stewart Producers Inc (PA)** ........ 618 244-3754
301 N 27th St Mount Vernon (62864) ***(G-15446)***
**Stewart S Pritikin Associates, Bartlett** *Also called Vision Sales Incorporated* ***(G-1385)***
**Stewart Well Service, Mount Vernon** *Also called Stewart Producers Inc* ***(G-15446)***
**Stewarts Prvate Blend Fods Inc (PA)** ........ 773 489-2500
301 Carlton Dr Carol Stream (60188) ***(G-3250)***
**STI Holdings Inc** ........ 630 789-2713
15w700 N Frontage Rd # 140 Burr Ridge (60527) ***(G-2882)***
**Stickon Adhesive Inds Inc** ........ 847 593-5959
2605 S Clearbrook Dr Arlington Heights (60005) ***(G-844)***
**Stickon Packaging Systems, Arlington Heights** *Also called Stickon Adhesive Inds Inc* ***(G-844)***
**Stiglmeier Sausage Co Inc** ........ 847 537-9988
619 Chaddick Dr Wheeling (60090) ***(G-22157)***
**Stikkiworks Co, Glendale Heights** *Also called Lectro Stik Corp* ***(G-11040)***
**Stine Woodworking LLC** ........ 618 885-2229
16376 Bartlett Rd Dow (62022) ***(G-8383)***
**Stitch By Stitch Incorporated** ........ 847 541-2543
65 E Palatine Rd Ste 217 Prospect Heights (60070) ***(G-17784)***
**Stitch Magic Usa Inc** ........ 847 836-5000
785 S 8th St West Dundee (60118) ***(G-21802)***
**Stitch Plus, Prospect Heights** *Also called Stitch By Stitch Incorporated* ***(G-17784)***
**Stitch TEC Co Inc (PA)** ........ 618 327-8054
887 N Washington St Nashville (62263) ***(G-15848)***
**Stitchables Embroidery** ........ 217 322-3000
416 Silverleaf St Rushville (62681) ***(G-19096)***
**Stitchin Image** ........ 815 578-9890
9203 Glacier Rdg Richmond (60071) ***(G-17973)***
**Stitchmine Custom Embroidery, Glenview** *Also called Gcg Corp* ***(G-11128)***
**Stix Envelope & Mfg Co** ........ 217 589-5122
1086 S Morse St Roodhouse (62082) ***(G-18886)***
**Stock Gears Inc** ........ 224 653-9489
1801 Vermont Dr Elk Grove Village (60007) ***(G-9758)***
**Stock Manufacturing Co LLC** ........ 773 265-6640
316 N Michigan Ave Frnt 2 Chicago (60601) ***(G-6597)***
**Stockdale Block Systems LLC** ........ 815 416-1030
4675 Weitz Rd Morris (60450) ***(G-15132)***
**Stocker Hinge Mfg Co, Brookfield** *Also called E R Wagner Manufacturing Co* ***(G-2630)***
**Stockwell Greetings, Chicago** *Also called Salamander Studios Chicago Inc* ***(G-6431)***
**Stokes Sand & Gravel Inc** ........ 815 489-0680
35w160 Butterfield Rd Batavia (60510) ***(G-1499)***
**Stolle Casper Quar & Contg Co** ........ 618 337-5212
2901 Stolle Rd Dupo (62239) ***(G-8579)***
**Stolp Gore Company** ........ 630 904-5180
10101 Bode St Ste A Plainfield (60585) ***(G-17653)***
**Stone Center Inc** ........ 630 971-2060
2127 Ogden Ave Lisle (60532) ***(G-13664)***
**Stone Design Inc** ........ 630 790-5715
598 Mitchell Rd Glendale Heights (60139) ***(G-11075)***
**Stone Design Inc (PA)** ........ 630 790-5715
551 598 Mitchell Rd Glendale Heights (60139) ***(G-11076)***
**Stone Fabricators Company** ........ 847 788-8296
1604 N Clarence Ave Arlington Heights (60004) ***(G-845)***
**Stone Installation & Maint Inc** ........ 630 545-2326
598 Mitchell Rd Glendale Heights (60139) ***(G-11077)***
**Stone Lighting LLC** ........ 312 240-0400
2630 Flossmoor Rd Ste 102 Flossmoor (60422) ***(G-10230)***
**Stone Quarry, Mount Carroll** *Also called Heisler Stone Co Inc* ***(G-15291)***
**Stone Usa Inc** ........ 312 356-0988
1234 S Michigan Ave Ste D Chicago (60605) ***(G-6598)***
**Stonecasters LLC** ........ 847 526-5200
1250 Henri Dr Wauconda (60084) ***(G-21504)***
**Stonecraft Cast Stone LLC** ........ 708 653-1477
3025 Louis Sherman Dr Steger (60475) ***(G-20577)***
**Stonecrafters Inc** ........ 815 363-8730
430 W Wegner Rd Lakemoor (60051) ***(G-13148)***
**Stonepeak Ceramics Inc (HQ)** ........ 312 335-0321
314 W Superior St Ste 201 Chicago (60654) ***(G-6599)***
**Stonetree Fabrication Inc** ........ 618 332-1700
9 Production Pkwy East Saint Louis (62206) ***(G-8771)***
**Stop & Go International Inc** ........ 815 455-9080
3610 Thunderbird Ln Crystal Lake (60012) ***(G-7654)***
**Stor-Loc, Kankakee** *Also called Ryan Metal Products Inc* ***(G-12647)***
**Storage Battery Systems LLC** ........ 630 221-1700
179 Easy St Carol Stream (60188) ***(G-3251)***
**Storage Dem Envmtl Consulting, Eola** *Also called Asbestos Control & Envmtl Svc* ***(G-9988)***
**Store 409 Inc** ........ 708 478-5751
9981 W 190th St Ste K Mokena (60448) ***(G-14905)***
**Storiant Inc** ........ 617 431-8000
70 W Madison St Ste 2300 Chicago (60602) ***(G-6600)***
**Storms Industries Inc** ........ 312 243-7480
1500 S Western Ave Ste 5 Chicago (60608) ***(G-6601)***
**Stovers Fine Woodworking Inc** ........ 630 557-0072
474 Harter Rd Maple Park (60151) ***(G-14203)***

**Strahman Valves Inc**...630 208-9343
1n046 Linlar Dr Lafox (60147) *(G-12797)*
**Straightline AG Inc**...217 963-1270
8990 W Us 36 Harristown (62537) *(G-11608)*
**Straightline Erectors Inc**...708 430-5426
7812 W 91st St Oak Lawn (60457) *(G-16645)*
**Strait-O-Flex**...815 965-2625
7372 Kishwaukee Rd Stillman Valley (61084) *(G-20628)*
**Strange Engineering Inc**...847 663-1701
8300 Austin Ave Morton Grove (60053) *(G-15239)*
**Strat-O-Span Buildings Inc (PA)**...618 526-4566
7980 Old Us Highway 50 Breese (62230) *(G-2448)*
**Strata Exploration Inc**...618 842-2610
201 Ne 7th St Fairfield (62837) *(G-10155)*
**Strata-Tac Inc**...630 879-9388
3980 Swenson Ave Saint Charles (60174) *(G-19272)*
**Stratas Foods LLC**...217 424-5660
3601 E Division St Decatur (62526) *(G-7945)*
**Strateg Telekom, Chicago** *Also called Global Technologies I LLC (G-4960)*
**Strategic Applications Inc**...847 680-9385
278 Park Ave Lake Villa (60046) *(G-13027)*
**Strategic Materials Inc**...773 523-2200
10330 S Woodlawn Ave Chicago (60628) *(G-6602)*
**Strategic Mfg Partner LLC (PA)**...262 878-5213
3145 Elder Ct Northbrook (60062) *(G-16372)*
**Strathmore Company**...630 232-9677
2000 Gary Ln Geneva (60134) *(G-10870)*
**Strathmore Press**...513 483-3600
2400 E Main St Saint Charles (60174) *(G-19273)*
**Strausberger Assoc Sls & Mktg**...630 553-3447
621 White Oak Way Yorkville (60560) *(G-22671)*
**Strauss Facter Assoc Inc**...847 759-1100
1440 Renaissance Dr Park Ridge (60068) *(G-17224)*
**Streamlined Baking Co**...773 227-2635
3945 W Armitage Ave Chicago (60647) *(G-6603)*
**Streamlinx LLC**...630 864-3043
40 Shuman Blvd Ste 140 Naperville (60563) *(G-15755)*
**Streamwood Plastics Ltd**...847 895-9190
979 Lunt Ave Schaumburg (60193) *(G-19741)*
**Streamwood Plating Co**...630 830-6363
1545 Brandy Pkwy Streamwood (60107) *(G-20675)*
**Streator Asphalt Inc (HQ)**...815 426-2164
104 S Park Rd Herscher (60941) *(G-11762)*
**Streator Asphalt Inc**...815 672-8683
1019 E Livingston Rd Streator (61364) *(G-20703)*
**Streator Dependable Mfg, Streator** *Also called Streator Industrial Hdlg Inc (G-20704)*
**Streator Industrial Hdlg Inc (PA)**...815 672-0551
1705 N Shabbona St Streator (61364) *(G-20704)*
**Streator Machine Company**...815 672-2436
504 E Larue St Streator (61364) *(G-20705)*
**Streator Machine Mfg Co, Streator** *Also called Streator Machine Company (G-20705)*
**Strebor Specialties LLC**...618 286-1140
108 Coulter Rd Dupo (62239) *(G-8580)*
**Streem & Cleo Communications, Rockford** *Also called Cleo Communications Inc (G-18312)*
**Street Comedy Records, Chicago** *Also called Tony Patterson (G-6740)*
**Street Dept, Pekin** *Also called City of Pekin (G-17256)*
**Street's, Naperville** *Also called R R Street & Co Inc (G-15736)*
**Streets and Sanitation, Dept, Chicago** *Also called City of Chicago (G-4387)*
**Streetwise**...773 334-6600
4554 N Broadway St # 350 Chicago (60640) *(G-6604)*
**Stress Free Cookies Inc**...312 856-7686
605 N Ridgeway Ave Chicago (60624) *(G-6605)*
**Stretch CHI**...773 420-9355
4765 N Lincoln Ave # 207 Chicago (60625) *(G-6606)*
**Strictly Dentures**...815 969-0531
3920 E State St Ste 2 Rockford (61108) *(G-18635)*
**Strictly Neon Inc**...708 597-1616
4608 137th St Ste D Crestwood (60445) *(G-7504)*
**Strictly Signs, Crestwood** *Also called Strictly Neon Inc (G-7504)*
**Strictly Stainless Inc**...847 885-2890
2108 Stonington Ave Hoffman Estates (60169) *(G-12061)*
**Strikeforce Bowling LLC**...800 297-8555
2001 Parkes Dr Broadview (60155) *(G-2615)*
**Stripmasters Illinois Inc**...618 452-1060
1107 22nd St Granite City (62040) *(G-11306)*
**Stritzel Awnng Svc/Aurra Tent**...630 420-2000
10206 Clow Creek Rd Ste A Plainfield (60585) *(G-17654)*
**Strive Converting Corporation**...773 227-6000
4545 W Palmer St Chicago (60639) *(G-6607)*
**Strohm Newspapers Inc**...217 826-3600
610 Archer Ave Marshall (62441) *(G-14329)*
**Stromberg Allen and Company**...773 847-7131
18504 West Creek Dr Tinley Park (60477) *(G-20947)*
**Structural Design Corp**...847 816-3816
1133 Claridge Dr Libertyville (60048) *(G-13385)*
**Structural Steel Systems Limi**...815 937-3800
300 N Washington Ave Bradley (60915) *(G-2434)*
**Structurepoint LLC**...847 966-4357
5420 Old Orchard Rd Skokie (60077) *(G-20092)*
**Strut & Supply Inc**...847 756-4337
28005 W Commercial Ave Lake Barrington (60010) *(G-12824)*
**Stryco Industries, Peoria** *Also called Sommer Products Company Inc (G-17458)*
**Stryde Technologies Inc**...510 786-8890
600 Davis St Fl 3w Evanston (60201) *(G-10096)*
**Stryker Corporation**...312 386-9780
350 N Orleans St Chicago (60654) *(G-6608)*
**Strytech Adhesives**...847 509-7566
707 Skokie Blvd Ste 600 Northbrook (60062) *(G-16373)*
**Stuart Hale Company, Chicago** *Also called Sdr Corp (G-6463)*
**Stuart Moore Racing Ltd**...847 949-9100
831 E Orchard St Mundelein (60060) *(G-15561)*
**Stucchi Usa Inc**...847 956-9720
1105 Windham Pkwy Romeoville (60446) *(G-18871)*
**Students Publishing Company In**...847 491-7206
1999 Sheridan Rd Evanston (60201) *(G-10097)*
**Studio 41, Schaumburg** *Also called Logan Square Aluminum Sup Inc (G-19622)*
**Studio 41, Lincolnwood** *Also called Logan Square Aluminum Sup Inc (G-13523)*
**Studio 41, Chicago** *Also called Logan Square Aluminum Sup Inc (G-5531)*
**Studio Color Inc**...630 766-3333
1140 Industrial Dr Bensenville (60106) *(G-1999)*
**Studio Moulding**...217 523-2101
2650 Colt Rd Springfield (62707) *(G-20539)*
**Studio Out West, Forest Park** *Also called Chicago Producers Inc (G-10237)*
**Studio Technologies Inc**...847 676-9177
7440 Frontage Rd Skokie (60077) *(G-20093)*
**Studley Products Inc (PA)**...309 663-2313
903 Morrissey Dr Bloomington (61701) *(G-2226)*
**Stuecklen Manufacturing Co**...847 678-5130
10022 Pacific Ave Franklin Park (60131) *(G-10596)*
**Stuhlman Engrg Manfacturin Co, Plainfield** *Also called Stuhlman Family LLC (G-17655)*
**Stuhlman Family LLC**...815 436-2432
12435 S Industrial Dr E Plainfield (60585) *(G-17655)*
**Stuhr Manufacturing Co**...815 398-2460
5085 27th Ave Rockford (61109) *(G-18636)*
**Stumpfoll Tool & Mfg**...312 733-2632
1713 W Hubbard St Chicago (60622) *(G-6609)*
**Sturdee Metal Products Inc**...773 523-3074
1060 Grand Mesa Ave New Lenox (60451) *(G-15913)*
**Sturdi Iron Inc**...815 464-1173
22405 S Center Rd Frankfort (60423) *(G-10365)*
**Sturtevant Inc**...630 613-8968
959 N Garfield St Lombard (60148) *(G-13861)*
**Sturtvant Richmont Torque Pdts, Carol Stream** *Also called Ryeson Corporation (G-3230)*
**Stutz Company**...773 287-1068
4450 W Carroll Ave Chicago (60624) *(G-6610)*
**Style Rite Restaurant Eqp Co**...630 628-0940
578 S Vista Ave Addison (60101) *(G-299)*
**Stylemaster, Chicago** *Also called Jr Plastics LLC (G-5333)*
**Stylenquaza LLC**...847 981-0191
750 Pratt Blvd Elk Grove Village (60007) *(G-9759)*
**Su Enterprise Inc**...847 394-1656
403 N Reuter Dr Arlington Heights (60005) *(G-846)*
**Sub of Deif A/S, Denmark, Wood Dale** *Also called Deif Inc (G-22359)*
**Sub Source Inc**...815 968-7800
600 18th Ave Rockford (61104) *(G-18637)*
**Sub-Sem Inc**...815 459-4139
473 S Dartmoor Dr Crystal Lake (60014) *(G-7655)*
**Sub-Surface Sign Co Ltd**...847 675-6530
7410 Niles Center Rd Skokie (60077) *(G-20094)*
**Subaru of America Inc**...630 250-4740
500 Park Blvd Ste 255c Itasca (60143) *(G-12361)*
**Substrate Technology Inc**...815 941-4800
1384 Bungalow Rd Morris (60450) *(G-15133)*
**Suburban Chicago Newspapers**...847 336-7000
1500 W Ogden Ave Naperville (60540) *(G-15756)*
**Suburban Drive Line, Villa Park** *Also called Suburban Driveline Inc (G-21286)*
**Suburban Driveline Inc**...630 941-7101
747 W North Ave Villa Park (60181) *(G-21286)*
**Suburban Fabricators Inc**...847 729-0866
1119 Depot St Glenview (60025) *(G-11206)*
**Suburban Fix & Installation**...847 823-4047
420 S Fairview Ave Park Ridge (60068) *(G-17225)*
**Suburban Indus Tl & Mfg Co**...708 597-7788
11606 S Mayfield Ave Alsip (60803) *(G-531)*
**Suburban Industries Inc**...630 766-3773
1090 E Green St Franklin Park (60131) *(G-10597)*
**Suburban Laminating Inc**...708 389-6106
908 W Lake St Melrose Park (60160) *(G-14697)*
**Suburban Life Publication**...630 368-1100
1101 31st St Ste 260 Downers Grove (60515) *(G-8528)*
**Suburban Machine & Tool**...815 469-2221
8119 189th St Mokena (60448) *(G-14906)*
**Suburban Machine Corporation**...847 808-9095
512 Northgate Pkwy Wheeling (60090) *(G-22158)*
**Suburban Map Store, Elmhurst** *Also called GM Laminating & Mounting Corp (G-9878)*
**Suburban Metalcraft Inc**...847 678-7550
9045 Exchange Ave Franklin Park (60131) *(G-10598)*

ALPHABETIC

**Suburban Newspapers of Greater** ....618 281-7691
2 Executive Dr Collinsville (62234) ***(G-7342)***
**Suburban Plastics Co (PA)** ....847 741-4900
340 Renner Dr Elgin (60123) ***(G-9194)***
**Suburban Press Inc** ....847 255-2240
3650 N Wilke Rd Arlington Heights (60004) ***(G-847)***
**Suburban Screw Machine Pdts** ....815 337-0434
16210 Us Highway 14 Woodstock (60098) ***(G-22614)***
**Suburban Surgical Co** ....847 537-9320
275 12th St Ste A Wheeling (60090) ***(G-22159)***
**Suburban Welding & Steel LLC** ....847 678-1264
9820 Franklin Ave Franklin Park (60131) ***(G-10599)***
**Subway 25858, Chicago** *Also called Sunny Enterprises Inc* ***(G-6627)***
**Success Journal Corp** ....847 583-9000
7848 Foster St Morton Grove (60053) ***(G-15240)***
**Success Publishing Group Inc** ....708 565-2681
310 S Michigan Ave Fl 9 Chicago (60604) ***(G-6611)***
**Success Vending Mfg Co LLC** ....773 262-1685
5128 W Irving Park Rd Chicago (60641) ***(G-6612)***
**Sudden Impact Sports, Minier** *Also called Laughing Dog Graphics* ***(G-14833)***
**Sudholt Sheet Metal Inc** ....618 228-7351
350 W 4th St Aviston (62216) ***(G-1248)***
**Sue P Knits, Glenview** *Also called Sue Peterson* ***(G-11207)***
**Sue Peterson** ....847 730-3035
1100 Raleigh Rd Glenview (60025) ***(G-11207)***
**Suffolk Business Group Inc** ....847 404-2486
132 N Prospect Ave Bartlett (60103) ***(G-1379)***
**Sugar Factory Rosemont LLC** ....847 349-9161
5445 Park Pl Rosemont (60018) ***(G-19034)***
**Sugar Monkey Cupcakes Inc** ....630 527-1869
2728 Wild Timothy Rd Naperville (60564) ***(G-15829)***
**Sugar River Machine Shop** ....815 624-0214
667 Progressive Ln South Beloit (61080) ***(G-20169)***
**Sugar/Spice Extraordinry Treat** ....847 864-7800
1205 Hartrey Ave Evanston (60202) ***(G-10098)***
**Sugarcreek Woodworking** ....618 584-3817
1501 N 1300th St Flat Rock (62427) ***(G-10198)***
**Suit Plus More, Hillside** *Also called Mjt Design and Prtg Entps Inc* ***(G-11926)***
**Sukgyung At Inc** ....847 298-6570
2400 E Devon Ave Ste 283 Des Plaines (60018) ***(G-8282)***
**Sukie Group Inc** ....773 521-1800
4115 W Ogden Ave Ste 1 Chicago (60623) ***(G-6613)***
**Sullivan Cgliano Training Ctrs (PA)** ....312 422-0009
203 N La Salle St Fl M18 Chicago (60601) ***(G-6614)***
**Sullivan Home Health Products** ....217 532-6366
311 Berry St Hillsboro (62049) ***(G-11900)***
**Sullivan Press, Park Ridge** *Also called Griffith Solutions Inc* ***(G-17201)***
**Sullivan Tool and Repair Inc** ....224 856-5867
370 Brook St Unit 3 Elgin (60120) ***(G-9195)***
**Sullivans Inc** ....815 331-8347
5508 W Chasefield Cir McHenry (60050) ***(G-14557)***
**Sultry Satchels** ....773 873-5718
8111 S Morgan St Chicago (60620) ***(G-6615)***
**Sultry Satchels Inc** ....312 810-1081
8159 S Troy St Chicago (60652) ***(G-6616)***
**Sulzer Midwest Service Center, Joliet** *Also called Sulzer Pump Services (us) Inc* ***(G-12579)***
**Sulzer Pump Services (us) Inc** ....815 600-7355
2600 Citys Edge Dr Joliet (60436) ***(G-12579)***
**Suma America Inc** ....847 427-7880
855 N Wood Dale Rd Unit A Wood Dale (60191) ***(G-22425)***
**Sumida America Components Inc (HQ)** ....847 545-6700
1251 N Plum Grove Rd # 150 Schaumburg (60173) ***(G-19742)***
**Sumida America Inc** ....847 545-6700
1251 N Plum Grove Rd # 150 Schaumburg (60173) ***(G-19743)***
**Sumitomo Machinery Corp Amer** ....630 752-0200
175 W Lake Dr Glendale Heights (60139) ***(G-11078)***
**Summervlle Consulting Svcs LLC** ....618 547-7142
8655 Garrett Rd Alma (62807) ***(G-424)***
**Summit Design Solutions Inc** ....847 836-8183
402 Fallbrook Dr East Dundee (60118) ***(G-8657)***
**Summit Graphics Inc** ....309 799-5100
6810 34th Street Ct Moline (61265) ***(G-14973)***
**Summit Industries LLC** ....773 353-4000
7555 N Caldwell Ave Niles (60714) ***(G-16038)***
**Summit Laboratories Inc** ....708 333-2995
17010 Halsted St Harvey (60426) ***(G-11677)***
**Summit Metal Products Inc** ....630 879-7008
1351 Nagel Blvd Batavia (60510) ***(G-1500)***
**Summit Mold Inc** ....815 865-5809
10400 E Stanton Rd Davis (61019) ***(G-7807)***
**Summit Plastics Inc** ....815 578-8700
1207 Adams Dr McHenry (60051) ***(G-14558)***
**Summit Precision Machining, Davis** *Also called Summit Mold Inc* ***(G-7807)***
**Summit Sheet Metal Specialists** ....708 458-8622
7325 W 59th St Summit Argo (60501) ***(G-20766)***
**Summit Signworks Inc** ....847 870-0937
2265 E Ashbury Ct Arlington Heights (60004) ***(G-848)***
**Summit Stinless Stl Holdg Corp** ....732 297-9500
6133 N River Rd Ste 700 Rosemont (60018) ***(G-19035)***
**Summit Tank & Equipment Co** ....708 594-3040
7801 W 47th St Mc Cook (60525) ***(G-14459)***
**Summit Tooling Inc** ....815 385-7500
1207 Adams Dr McHenry (60051) ***(G-14559)***
**Summit Window Co Inc** ....708 594-3200
7719 W 60th Pl Ste 6 Summit Argo (60501) ***(G-20767)***
**Summitt Media Group Inc** ....312 222-1010
330 N Wabash Ave Ste 2401 Chicago (60611) ***(G-6617)***
**Sumner Press** ....618 936-2212
216 S Christy Ave Sumner (62466) ***(G-20772)***
**Sun Ag Inc** ....309 726-1331
108 N Shiner St Hudson (61748) ***(G-12126)***
**Sun America, Elk Grove Village** *Also called Bell Litho Inc* ***(G-9339)***
**Sun Chemical Corporation** ....708 562-0550
135 W Lake St Ste 2 Northlake (60164) ***(G-16454)***
**Sun Chemical Corporation** ....815 939-0136
3200 Festival Dr Kankakee (60901) ***(G-12655)***
**Sun Chemical Corporation** ....630 513-5348
2445 Production Dr Saint Charles (60174) ***(G-19274)***
**Sun Coke Energy, Lisle** *Also called Sun Coke International Inc* ***(G-13665)***
**Sun Coke International Inc (HQ)** ....630 824-1000
1011 Warrenville Rd # 600 Lisle (60532) ***(G-13665)***
**Sun Dome Inc** ....773 890-5350
3641 S Washtenaw Ave Chicago (60632) ***(G-6618)***
**Sun Gard Window Fashions, Peoria** *Also called Midwest Marketing Distrs Inc* ***(G-17408)***
**Sun Graphic Inc (HQ)** ....773 775-6755
5540 N Northwest Hwy Chicago (60630) ***(G-6619)***
**Sun Ovens International Inc** ....630 208-7273
39w835 Midan Dr Unit F Elburn (60119) ***(G-8911)***
**Sun Pattern & Model Inc** ....630 293-3366
505 Wegner Dr West Chicago (60185) ***(G-21777)***
**Sun Process Converting Inc** ....847 593-5656
1660 W Kenneth Dr Mount Prospect (60056) ***(G-15376)***
**Sun Times News Agency** ....815 672-1260
56 Sunset Dr Streator (61364) ***(G-20706)***
**Sun Transformer, Mc Leansboro** *Also called STC Inc* ***(G-14468)***
**Sun- Tmes Mdia Productions LLC** ....312 321-2299
350 N Orleans St Ste 10s Chicago (60654) ***(G-6620)***
**Sun-Times Media LLC** ....312 321-3000
350 N Orleans St Ste 1000 Chicago (60654) ***(G-6621)***
**Sun-Times Media LLC** ....312 321-2299
350 N Orleans St Ste 1000 Chicago (60654) ***(G-6622)***
**Sun-Times Media Group Inc** ....618 273-3379
1200 Locust St Eldorado (62930) ***(G-8923)***
**Sun-Times Media Group Inc (HQ)** ....312 321-2299
350 N Orleans St Fl 10 Chicago (60654) ***(G-6623)***
**Sun-Times Media Holdings LLC (HQ)** ....312 321-2299
350 N Orleans St Ste 1000 Chicago (60654) ***(G-6624)***
**Sun-Times Media Operations LLC** ....312 321-2299
350 N Orleans St Fl 10 Chicago (60654) ***(G-6625)***
**Sunbelt Plastic Extrusions, Rockford** *Also called Southern Imperial Inc* ***(G-18623)***
**Sunbird Solar LLC** ....847 509-8888
3140 Whisperwoods Ct Northbrook (60062) ***(G-16374)***
**Sunburst Shutters Illinois** ....847 697-4000
700 Church Rd Elgin (60123) ***(G-9196)***
**Sunburst Sportswear Inc (PA)** ....630 717-8680
95 N Brandon Dr Glendale Heights (60139) ***(G-11079)***
**Sunburst Technology Corp (HQ)** ....800 321-7511
1550 Executive Dr Elgin (60123) ***(G-9197)***
**Suncast Corporation (PA)** ....630 879-2050
701 N Kirk Rd Batavia (60510) ***(G-1501)***
**Suncoke Energy Inc (PA)** ....630 824-1000
1011 Warrenville Rd # 600 Lisle (60532) ***(G-13666)***
**Suncoke Energy Partners LP (HQ)** ....630 824-1000
1011 Warrenville Rd # 600 Lisle (60532) ***(G-13667)***
**Suncoke Technology and Dev LLC** ....630 824-1000
1011 Warrenville Rd Fl 6 Lisle (60532) ***(G-13668)***
**Suncraft Technologies Inc (PA)** ....630 369-7900
1301 Frontenac Rd Naperville (60563) ***(G-15757)***
**Sunday Missal Service, Quincy** *Also called Pam Printers and Publs Inc* ***(G-17866)***
**Sundstrom Pressed Steel Co** ....773 721-2237
8030 S South Chicago Ave Chicago (60617) ***(G-6626)***
**Sunemco Technologies Inc** ....630 369-8947
500 Braemar Ave Naperville (60563) ***(G-15758)***
**Sung Ji USA** ....847 956-9400
128 N Lively Blvd Elk Grove Village (60007) ***(G-9760)***
**Sungard, Chicago** *Also called Powerschool Group LLC* ***(G-6160)***
**Sunny Brook Farm, Campbell Hill** *Also called Mast Harness Shop* ***(G-2976)***
**Sunny Day Distributing Inc** ....630 779-8466
76 E Meadow Dr Cortland (60112) ***(G-7395)***
**Sunny Direct LLC (PA)** ....630 795-0800
3540 Seven Bridges Dr # 160 Woodridge (60517) ***(G-22519)***
**Sunny Enterprises Inc** ....847 219-1045
2811 S Kedzie Ave Chicago (60623) ***(G-6627)***
**Sunnywood Incorporated** ....815 675-9777
2503 Spring Ridge Dr H Spring Grove (60081) ***(G-20366)***
**Sunrise AG Service Company** ....309 538-4287
Rr 1 Kilbourne (62655) ***(G-12698)***
**Sunrise Digital, Chicago** *Also called Sunrise Hitek Service Inc* ***(G-6630)***

**Sunrise Distributors Inc (PA)**...630 400-8786
2411 United Ln Elk Grove Village (60007) ***(G-9761)***
**Sunrise Electronics Inc**...847 357-0500
130 Martin Ln Elk Grove Village (60007) ***(G-9762)***
**Sunrise Foods, Elk Grove Village** *Also called Sunrise Distributors Inc* ***(G-9761)***
**Sunrise Futures LLC**...312 612-1041
30 S Wacker Dr Ste 1706 Chicago (60606) ***(G-6628)***
**Sunrise Hardware & Supplies, Plainfield** *Also called Karimi Saifuddin* ***(G-17614)***
**Sunrise Hitek Group LLC**...773 792-8880
5915 N Northwest Hwy Chicago (60631) ***(G-6629)***
**Sunrise Hitek Service Inc**...773 792-8880
5915 N Northwest Hwy Chicago (60631) ***(G-6630)***
**Sunrise Printing Inc**...847 928-1800
9701 Cary Ave Schiller Park (60176) ***(G-19877)***
**Sunscape Time Inc**...708 345-8791
2001 Janice Ave Melrose Park (60160) ***(G-14698)***
**Sunset Food Mart Inc**...847 234-0854
825 S Waukegan Rd Ste A8 Lake Forest (60045) ***(G-12964)***
**Sunset Halthcare Solutions Inc**...877 578-6738
180 N Michigan Ave # 2000 Chicago (60601) ***(G-6631)***
**Sunshine Products, Maywood** *Also called Mackenzie Johnson* ***(G-14428)***
**Sunsource Holdings Inc**...630 317-2700
2301 W Windsor Ct Addison (60101) ***(G-300)***
**Sunstar Americas Inc (HQ)**...773 777-4000
301 E Central Rd Schaumburg (60195) ***(G-19744)***
**Sunstar Pharmaceutical Inc**...773 777-4000
1300 Abbott Dr Elgin (60123) ***(G-9198)***
**Suntimez Entertainment**...630 747-0712
5811 W Roosevelt Rd Cicero (60804) ***(G-7232)***
**Suparossa Pizza, Chicago** *Also called Biagios Gourmet Foods Inc* ***(G-4103)***
**Super Aggregates Inc (HQ)**...815 385-8000
5435 Bull Valley Rd # 330 McHenry (60050) ***(G-14560)***
**Super Life, Chicago** *Also called Unicut Corporation* ***(G-6813)***
**Super Mix, McHenry** *Also called Super Aggregates Inc* ***(G-14560)***
**Super Mix Inc**...815 544-9100
5435 Bull Valley Rd # 130 McHenry (60050) ***(G-14561)***
**Super Mix Inc (PA)**...815 578-9100
5435 Bull Valley Rd # 130 McHenry (60050) ***(G-14562)***
**Super Mix Concrete LLC**...262 742-2892
5435 Bull Valley Rd # 130 McHenry (60050) ***(G-14563)***
**Super Mix of Wisconsin Inc**...262 859-9000
5435 Bull Valley Rd # 130 McHenry (60050) ***(G-14564)***
**Super Mix of Wisconsin Inc**...815 578-9100
5435 Bull Valley Rd # 130 McHenry (60050) ***(G-14565)***
**Super Phone Store, Urbana** *Also called Robert Higgins* ***(G-21101)***
**Super Press Instant Prtg Co, Mount Prospect** *Also called Grovak Instant Printing Co* ***(G-15334)***
**Super Sign Service**...309 829-9241
621 W Olive St Bloomington (61701) ***(G-2227)***
**Super-Cut Abrasives, Carol Stream** *Also called Saint-Gobain Abrasives Inc* ***(G-3232)***
**Super-Dri Corp**...708 599-8700
9707 S 76th Ave Bridgeview (60455) ***(G-2532)***
**Superabrasives, Carol Stream** *Also called Saint-Gobain Abrasives Inc* ***(G-3231)***
**Superb Packaging Inc**...847 579-1870
659 Ridge Rd Highland Park (60035) ***(G-11874)***
**Superheat Fgh, New Lenox** *Also called Supertech Holdings Inc* ***(G-15916)***
**Superheat Fgh Services Inc**...618 251-9450
313 Garnet Dr New Lenox (60451) ***(G-15914)***
**Superheat Fgh Services Inc (HQ)**...708 478-0205
313 Garnet Dr New Lenox (60451) ***(G-15915)***
**Superior American Plastics Co**...847 229-1600
1200 Barclay Blvd Buffalo Grove (60089) ***(G-2778)***
**Superior Baking Stone Inc**...815 726-4610
926 Plainfield Rd Joliet (60435) ***(G-12580)***
**Superior Biologics II Inc**...847 469-2400
2050 E Algonquin Rd # 606 Schaumburg (60173) ***(G-19745)***
**Superior Bumpers Inc**...630 932-4910
920 N Ridge Ave Ste C3 Lombard (60148) ***(G-13862)***
**Superior Business Solutions**...815 787-1333
308 Laurel Ln Dekalb (60115) ***(G-8123)***
**Superior Coating Corporation**...815 544-3340
6860 Indy Dr Belvidere (61008) ***(G-1786)***
**Superior Fabrication & Machine**...217 762-5512
1144 E 1600 North Rd Monticello (61856) ***(G-15086)***
**Superior Findings, Chicago** *Also called Masud Jewelers Inc* ***(G-5648)***
**Superior Graphite Co (PA)**...312 559-2999
10 S Riverside Plz # 1470 Chicago (60606) ***(G-6632)***
**Superior Graphite Co**...708 458-0006
6540 S Laramie Ave Chicago (60638) ***(G-6633)***
**Superior Graphite Co**...773 890-4100
4201 W 36th St Bldg Rear Chicago (60632) ***(G-6634)***
**Superior Health Linens LLC**...630 593-5091
1160 Pierson Dr Ste 104 Batavia (60510) ***(G-1502)***
**Superior Home Products Inc**...217 726-9300
3000 Great Northern Springfield (62711) ***(G-20540)***
**Superior Industries Inc**...309 346-1742
14425 Wagonseller Rd Pekin (61554) ***(G-17290)***
**Superior Joining Tech Inc**...815 282-7581
1260 Turret Dr Machesney Park (61115) ***(G-14109)***
**Superior Knife Inc**...847 982-2280
8120 Central Park Ave Skokie (60076) ***(G-20095)***
**Superior Metal Finishing**...815 282-8888
962 Industrial Ct Loves Park (61111) ***(G-13995)***
**Superior Metal Products Inc**...630 466-1150
1993 Bucktail Ln Sugar Grove (60554) ***(G-20737)***
**Superior Metalcraft Inc**...708 418-8940
17655 Chappel Ave Lansing (60438) ***(G-13188)***
**Superior Mfg Group - Europe (PA)**...708 458-4600
5655 W 73rd St Bestle Par Chicago (60638) ***(G-6635)***
**Superior Mobile Home Service**...708 672-7799
3421 E Reichert Dr Crete (60417) ***(G-7520)***
**Superior One Electric Inc**...630 655-3300
1212 Gardner Rd Westchester (60154) ***(G-21856)***
**Superior Piling Inc**...708 496-1196
7247 S 78th Ave Ste 2 Bridgeview (60455) ***(G-2533)***
**Superior Pipe Standards Inc**...708 656-0208
3128 S 61st Ave Cicero (60804) ***(G-7233)***
**Superior Print Services Inc**...630 257-7012
12305 New Ave Ste H Lemont (60439) ***(G-13264)***
**Superior Surgical Instrumen TS**...630 628-8437
602 W Lake Park Dr Addison (60101) ***(G-301)***
**Superior Table Pad Co**...773 248-7232
3010 N Oakley Ave Chicago (60618) ***(G-6636)***
**Superior Truck Dock Services**...630 978-1697
2431 Angela Ln Aurora (60502) ***(G-1083)***
**Superior Water Services Inc**...309 691-9287
5831 N Knoxville Ave Peoria (61614) ***(G-17464)***
**Superior Water Systems, Peoria** *Also called Superior Water Services Inc* ***(G-17464)***
**Superior Welding Inc**...618 544-8822
9172 E 1050th Ave Robinson (62454) ***(G-18073)***
**Superior X Ray Tube Company**...815 338-4424
1220 Claussen Dr Woodstock (60098) ***(G-22615)***
**Superon Drug, Deerfield** *Also called Dashire Inc* ***(G-8003)***
**Supertech Holdings Inc (PA)**...708 478-0205
313 Garnet Dr New Lenox (60451) ***(G-15916)***
**Supertek Scientific LLC**...630 345-3450
744 N Michigan Ave Villa Park (60181) ***(G-21287)***
**Supertuf, East Alton** *Also called Beall Manufacturing Inc* ***(G-8599)***
**Supply Solutions Network, Byron** *Also called Ssn LLC* ***(G-2922)***
**Supply Vision Inc**...847 388-0064
220 N Green St Chicago (60607) ***(G-6637)***
**Support Central Inc**...702 202-3500
8820 Skokie Blvd Ste 320 Skokie (60077) ***(G-20096)***
**Supportstoreus, Litchfield** *Also called Quality Plus* ***(G-13695)***
**Supreme Felt & Abrasives Inc**...708 344-0134
1633 S 55th Ave Cicero (60804) ***(G-7234)***
**Supreme Frame & Moulding Co**...312 930-9056
652 W Randolph St Chicago (60661) ***(G-6638)***
**Supreme Hinge, University Park** *Also called Qh Inc* ***(G-21060)***
**Supreme Hinge Inc (PA)**...708 534-7801
2412 Bond St University Park (60484) ***(G-21063)***
**Supreme Juice Co**...773 277-5800
1307 S Pulaski Rd Chicago (60623) ***(G-6639)***
**Supreme Manufacturing Company**...847 297-8212
1755 Birchwood Ave Des Plaines (60018) ***(G-8283)***
**Supreme Saw & Service Co**...708 396-1125
1480 S Wolf Rd Wheeling (60090) ***(G-22160)***
**Supreme Screw Inc**...630 226-9000
1224 N Independence Blvd Romeoville (60446) ***(G-18872)***
**Supreme Screw Products**...708 579-3500
5227 Dansher Rd Countryside (60525) ***(G-7445)***
**Supreme Tamale Co**...773 622-3777
1495 Brummel Ave Elk Grove Village (60007) ***(G-9763)***
**Sur-Fit Corporation**...815 301-5815
110 Erick St Crystal Lake (60014) ***(G-7656)***
**Surcom Industries Inc**...773 378-0736
1017 N Cicero Ave Chicago (60651) ***(G-6640)***
**Sure Plus Manufacturing Co**...708 756-3100
185 E 12th St Chicago Heights (60411) ***(G-7128)***
**Sure Shine Polishing**...217 853-4888
1455 N Main St Decatur (62526) ***(G-7946)***
**Sure-Way Die Designs Inc (PA)**...630 323-0370
407 Plaza Dr Westmont (60559) ***(G-21924)***
**Sure-Way Products, Westmont** *Also called Sure-Way Die Designs Inc* ***(G-21924)***
**Surebond Inc**...630 762-0606
3925 Stern Ave Saint Charles (60174) ***(G-19275)***
**Surebonder Adhesives Inc**...847 487-4583
355 Hollow Hill Rd Wauconda (60084) ***(G-21505)***
**Suretint Technologies LLC**...847 509-3625
411 E Bus Ctr Dr Ste 104 Mount Prospect (60056) ***(G-15377)***
**Sureway Tool & Engineering Co, Franklin Park** *Also called Mrt Sureway Inc* ***(G-10537)***
**Surface Guard Inc**...630 236-8250
515 Enterprise St Aurora (60504) ***(G-1084)***
**Surface Manufacturing Company**...815 569-2362
135 S 4th St Capron (61012) ***(G-2998)***

ALPHABETIC

**Surface Mining Reclamation Off**....618 463-6460
501 Belle St Ste 216 Alton (62002) ***(G-591)***
**Surface Shields Inc (PA)**....708 226-9810
10457 163rd Pl Orland Park (60467) ***(G-16896)***
**Surface Solutions Group LLC**....773 427-2084
5492 N Northwest Hwy Chicago (60630) ***(G-6641)***
**Surface Solutions Illinois Inc**....708 571-3449
9615 194th Pl Mokena (60448) ***(G-14907)***
**Surfacetec Corp**....630 521-0001
471 Podlin Dr Franklin Park (60131) ***(G-10600)***
**Surge Clutch & Drive Line Co**....708 331-1352
16145 Thornton Blue Is South Holland (60473) ***(G-20307)***
**Surplus Record LLC**....312 372-9077
20 N Wacker Dr Ste 2400 Chicago (60606) ***(G-6642)***
**Surrey Books Inc**....847 475-4457
1501 Madison St Evanston (60202) ***(G-10099)***
**Surtreat Construction Svcs LLC**....630 986-0780
854 E Algonquin Rd # 110 Schaumburg (60173) ***(G-19746)***
**Suruga USA Corp**....630 628-0989
1717 N Penny Ln Ste 200 Schaumburg (60173) ***(G-19747)***
**Survyvn Ltd**....847 977-8665
4613 Glacial Trl Ringwood (60072) ***(G-17995)***
**Surya Electronics Inc**....630 858-8000
600 Windy Point Dr Glendale Heights (60139) ***(G-11080)***
**Sustainable Holding Inc**....773 324-0407
7122 S Oglesby Ave Chicago (60649) ***(G-6643)***
**Sustainable Solutions Amer Led, Chicago** *Also called Sustanble Sltions Amer Led LLC* ***(G-6644)***
**Sustainable Sourcing LLC**....815 714-8055
19633 S La Grange Rd Mokena (60448) ***(G-14908)***
**Sustanable Infrastructures Inc**....815 341-1447
20632 Abbey Dr Frankfort (60423) ***(G-10366)***
**Sustanble Sltions Amer Led LLC**....866 323-3494
910 W Van Buren St Ste 6a Chicago (60607) ***(G-6644)***
**Suzlon Wind Energy Corporation**....773 328-5077
2583 Technology Dr Elgin (60124) ***(G-9199)***
**Suzlon Wind Energy Corporation (HQ)**....773 328-5077
8750 W Bryn Mawr Ave # 300 Chicago (60631) ***(G-6645)***
**Suzy Cabinet Company Inc**....708 705-1259
2740 Washington Blvd A Bellwood (60104) ***(G-1724)***
**Suzys Swirl LLC**....847 855-9987
6310 Grand Ave Ste 300 Gurnee (60031) ***(G-11510)***
**Svanaco Inc (PA)**....847 699-0300
2600 S River Rd Des Plaines (60018) ***(G-8284)***
**Swaby Manufacturing Company (PA)**....773 626-1400
5420 W Roosevelt Rd 300b Chicago (60644) ***(G-6646)***
**Swagath Group Inc**....847 640-6446
644 E Golf Rd Arlington Heights (60005) ***(G-849)***
**Swager & Associates, Bridgeport** *Also called Team Energy LLC* ***(G-2456)***
**Swagger Foods Corporation**....847 913-1200
900 Corporate Woods Pkwy Vernon Hills (60061) ***(G-21205)***
**Swan Analytical Usa Inc**....847 229-1290
225 Larkin Dr Ste 4 Wheeling (60090) ***(G-22161)***
**Swan Manufacturing Co**....309 441-6985
62 Crestview Cir Geneseo (61254) ***(G-10806)***
**Swan Surfaces LLC**....618 532-5673
200 Swan Ave Centralia (62801) ***(G-3435)***
**Swansea Building Products Inc**....618 874-6282
494 N 33rd St East Saint Louis (62205) ***(G-8772)***
**Swansea Sign A Rama Inc**....618 234-7446
216 Frank Scott Pkwy E # 3 Belleville (62226) ***(G-1677)***
**Swanson Water Treatment Inc (PA)**....847 680-1113
509 E Park Ave Ste 101 Libertyville (60048) ***(G-13386)***
**Swarovski North America Ltd**....847 680-5150
116 Hawthorne Shopg Ctr Vernon Hills (60061) ***(G-21206)***
**Swarovski US Holding Limited**....847 679-8670
4999 Old Orchard Ctr B22 Skokie (60077) ***(G-20097)***
**Swath International Limited**....815 654-4800
1661 Northrock Ct Rockford (61103) ***(G-18638)***
**SWB Inc**....847 438-1800
529 Capital Dr Lake Zurich (60047) ***(G-13136)***
**Swd Inc**....630 543-3003
910 S Stiles Dr Addison (60101) ***(G-302)***
**Swebco Mfg Inc**....815 636-7160
7909 Burden Rd Machesney Park (61115) ***(G-14110)***
**Swedish Food Products, Chicago** *Also called Noon Hour Food Products Inc* ***(G-5924)***
**Sweet Annies Bakery Inc**....708 297-7066
19710 Governors Hwy Ste 6 Flossmoor (60422) ***(G-10231)***
**Sweet Baby Ray's, Schiller Park** *Also called Raymond Brothers Inc* ***(G-19866)***
**Sweet Beginnings LLC**....773 638-7058
3726 W Flournoy St Chicago (60624) ***(G-6647)***
**Sweet Company**....815 462-4586
18707 Hickory St Mokena (60448) ***(G-14909)***
**Sweet Creation By Sheila**....708 754-7938
803 N Rainbow Dr Glenwood (60425) ***(G-11220)***
**Sweet Endeavors Inc**....224 653-2700
1101 Tower Rd Schaumburg (60173) ***(G-19748)***
**Sweet Manufacturing Corp**....847 546-5575
111 E Chestnut St Apt 36k Chicago (60611) ***(G-6648)***
**Sweet Pops By Cindy**....630 294-0640
120 Bridge St Ste 100 Wheaton (60187) ***(G-21982)***
**Sweet Specialty Solutions LLC**....630 739-9151
1005 101st St Ste B Lemont (60439) ***(G-13265)***
**Sweet Temptations Cupcake**....309 212-2637
2303 E Washington St 5b Bloomington (61704) ***(G-2228)***
**Sweet Thyme Soaps**....708 848-0234
808 S Elmwood Ave Oak Park (60304) ***(G-16688)***
**Sweet TS LLC**....618 943-5729
12061 Indian Creek Blvd Lawrenceville (62439) ***(G-13204)***
**Sweetener Supply Corporation**....708 484-3455
2905 Ridgeland Ave Berwyn (60402) ***(G-2075)***
**Swensen's, Monee** *Also called Swenson Technology Inc* ***(G-15003)***
**Swensen's, Lindenwood** *Also called Swenson Spreader LLC* ***(G-13551)***
**Swenson Spreader LLC**....815 393-4455
127 S Walnut St Lindenwood (61049) ***(G-13551)***
**Swenson Technology Inc**....708 587-2300
26000 S Whiting Way Monee (60449) ***(G-15003)***
**Swi Energy LLC**....618 465-7277
601 E 3rd St Ste 302 Alton (62002) ***(G-592)***
**Swiatek Electric**....331 225-3052
730 N Industrial Dr Elmhurst (60126) ***(G-9946)***
**Swift Education Systems Inc**....312 257-3751
332 S Michigan Ave # 1032 Chicago (60604) ***(G-6649)***
**Swift Impressions Inc**....312 263-3800
70 E Lake St Ste 1000 Chicago (60601) ***(G-6650)***
**Swift Technologies Inc**....815 568-8402
8601 S Hill Rd Marengo (60152) ***(G-14241)***
**Swifty Print**....630 584-9063
210 W Main St Saint Charles (60174) ***(G-19276)***
**Swingmaster Corporation**....847 451-1224
11415 Melrose Ave Franklin Park (60131) ***(G-10601)***
**Swirlcup**....847 229-2200
255 Parkway Dr Ste B Lincolnshire (60069) ***(G-13483)***
**Swiss Automation Inc**....847 381-4405
1020 W Northwest Hwy Barrington (60010) ***(G-1306)***
**Swiss E D M Wirecut Inc**....847 459-4310
743 Pinecrest Dr Prospect Heights (60070) ***(G-17785)***
**Swiss Precision Machining Inc**....847 647-7111
634 Glenn Ave Wheeling (60090) ***(G-22162)***
**Swiss Products LP**....773 394-6480
4333 W Division St Chicago (60651) ***(G-6651)***
**Swisslog Consulting, Rolling Meadows** *Also called Translogic Corporation* ***(G-18784)***
**Swissport Fueling Incorpo**....773 203-5419
5000 W 63rd St Chicago (60638) ***(G-6652)***
**Swisstronics Corp**....708 403-8877
16308 107th Ave Ste 8 Orland Park (60467) ***(G-16897)***
**Switchboard Apparatus, Elmhurst** *Also called SAI Advanced Pwr Solutions Inc* ***(G-9932)***
**Switchcraft Inc (HQ)**....773 792-2700
5555 N Elston Ave Chicago (60630) ***(G-6653)***
**Switchcraft Holdco Inc (HQ)**....773 792-2700
5555 N Elston Ave Chicago (60630) ***(G-6654)***
**Switched Source LLC**....708 207-1479
18 S Michigan Ave Fl 12 Chicago (60603) ***(G-6655)***
**Switchee Bandz Usa LLC**....312 415-1100
804 Kimballwood Ln Highland Park (60035) ***(G-11875)***
**Switchee USA, Highland Park** *Also called Switchee Bandz Usa LLC* ***(G-11875)***
**Swiveloc, Carol Stream** *Also called Stabiloc LLC* ***(G-3245)***
**Sws**....815 267-7378
15720 S Route 59 Plainfield (60544) ***(G-17656)***
**Sws Industries Inc**....904 482-0091
280 Prairie Ridge Dr Woodstock (60098) ***(G-22616)***
**Sycamore Containers Inc**....815 895-2343
215 Fair St Sycamore (60178) ***(G-20818)***
**Sycamore Precision**....815 784-5151
334 E 1st St Ste 1 Genoa (60135) ***(G-10884)***
**Sycamore Welding & Fabg Co**....815 784-2557
675 Park Ave Genoa (60135) ***(G-10885)***
**Symantec Corporation**....630 706-4700
2015 Spring Rd Ste 400 Oak Brook (60523) ***(G-16562)***
**Symbol Tool Inc**....847 674-1080
8106 Ridgeway Ave Skokie (60076) ***(G-20098)***
**Symbria Rx Services LLC**....630 981-8000
7125 Janes Ave Ste 300 Woodridge (60517) ***(G-22520)***
**Symfact Inc**....847 380-4174
55 W Monroe St Ste 2900 Chicago (60603) ***(G-6656)***
**Syn-Tech Ltd**....630 628-3044
1550 W Fullerton Ave Addison (60101) ***(G-303)***
**Synax Inc**....224 352-2927
1374 Abbott Ct Buffalo Grove (60089) ***(G-2779)***
**Synchem Inc**....847 298-2436
1400 Chase Ave Elk Grove Village (60007) ***(G-9764)***
**Synergetic Industries**....309 321-8145
1484 S Main St Morton (61550) ***(G-15183)***
**Synergistic Tech Solutions Inc**....224 360-6165
750 Tower Rd Unit B Mundelein (60060) ***(G-15562)***
**Synergy Flavors Inc (HQ)**....847 487-1011
1500 Synergy Dr Wauconda (60084) ***(G-21506)***
**Synergy Flavors NY Company LLC (HQ)**....585 232-6648
1500 Synergy Dr Wauconda (60084) ***(G-21507)***

**Synergy Mech Solutions Inc**...847 437-4500
55 N Lively Blvd Elk Grove Village (60007) *(G-9765)*
**Synergy Mechanical Inc**...708 410-1004
9835 Derby Ln Westchester (60154) *(G-21857)*
**Synergy Power Group LLC**...618 247-3200
610 E Illinois Ave Sandoval (62882) *(G-19359)*
**Synergy Technology Group Inc**...773 305-3500
1250 W Augusta Blvd # 201 Chicago (60642) *(G-6657)*
**Syngenta Seeds Inc**...217 253-5646
1200 E Southline Rd Tuscola (61953) *(G-21024)*
**Synlawn of Chicago, Chicago** *Also called Outdoor Space LLC (G-6026)*
**Synopsys Inc**...847 706-2000
475 N Martingale Rd # 250 Schaumburg (60173) *(G-19749)*
**Synsel Energy Inc**...630 516-1284
445 W Fullerton Ave Elmhurst (60126) *(G-9947)*
**Syr Tech Perforating, Glendale Heights** *Also called United Steel Perforating/ARC (G-11087)*
**Syr-Tech Perforating Co**...630 942-7300
325 Windy Point Dr Glendale Heights (60139) *(G-11081)*
**Syracuse Guage, Dixon** *Also called Schrader-Bridgeport Intl Inc (G-8349)*
**Sysmex America Inc (HQ)**...847 996-4500
577 Aptakisic Rd Lincolnshire (60069) *(G-13484)*
**Systat Software Inc (HQ)**...408 876-4508
225 N Wash St Ste 425 Chicago (60606) *(G-6658)*
**System Science Corporation**...708 214-2264
1408 W Taylor St Apt 301 Chicago (60607) *(G-6659)*
**System Software Associates Del (PA)**...312 258-6000
500 W Madison St Ste 1600 Chicago (60661) *(G-6660)*
**Systematics Screen Printing**...630 521-1123
1625 Norwood Ave Itasca (60143) *(G-12362)*
**Systems & Electronics Inc**...847 228-0985
190 Gordon St Elk Grove Village (60007) *(G-9766)*
**Systems Al Snow**...312 846-6026
801 S Wells St Chicago (60607) *(G-6661)*
**Systems By Lar Inc**...815 694-3141
841 E 3000 North Rd Clifton (60927) *(G-7275)*
**Systems Equipment Services**...708 535-1273
4314 166th St Oak Forest (60452) *(G-16590)*
**Systems Intel**...847 842-0120
113 Brinker Rd Barrington (60010) *(G-1307)*
**Systems Live Ltd**...815 455-3383
6917 Red Barn Rd Crystal Lake (60012) *(G-7657)*
**Systems Piping**...847 948-1373
1625 Half Day Rd Deerfield (60015) *(G-8057)*
**Systems Service & Supply**...815 725-1836
10 Fairlane Dr Joliet (60435) *(G-12581)*
**Systems Unlimited Inc**...630 285-0010
1350 W Bryn Mawr Ave Itasca (60143) *(G-12363)*
**Systemslogix LLC**...630 784-3113
140 W Lake Dr Glendale Heights (60139) *(G-11082)*
**Sytek Audio Systems Corp**...847 345-6971
350 N Eric Dr Ste B Palatine (60067) *(G-17077)*
**T & C Graphics Inc**...630 532-5050
645 Stevenson Rd South Elgin (60177) *(G-20227)*
**T & C Metal Co**...815 459-4445
378 E Prairie St Crystal Lake (60014) *(G-7658)*
**T & E Auto Haulers, Herscher** *Also called T & E Enterprises Herscher Inc (G-11763)*
**T & E Enterprises Herscher Inc**...815 426-2761
80 Tobey Dr Herscher (60941) *(G-11763)*
**T & H Lemont Inc**...708 482-1800
5118 Dansher Rd Countryside (60525) *(G-7446)*
**T & J Meatpacking Inc**...708 757-6930
635 Glenwood Dyer Rd Chicago Heights (60411) *(G-7129)*
**T & K Precision Grinding**...708 450-0565
1301 Armitage Ave Ste C Melrose Park (60160) *(G-14699)*
**T & K Tool & Manufacturing Co**...815 338-0954
2250 S Eastwood Dr Woodstock (60098) *(G-22617)*
**T & L Mfg Corporation**...630 898-7100
1665 Dearborn Ave Aurora (60505) *(G-1220)*
**T & L Sheet Metal Inc**...630 628-7960
555 S Vista Ave Addison (60101) *(G-304)*
**T & S Business Group LLC**...815 432-7084
602 E Walnut St Watseka (60970) *(G-21429)*
**T & T Carbide**...618 439-7253
17409 Lowry Ave Logan (62856) *(G-13755)*
**T & T Distribution Inc**...815 223-0715
304 5th St Peru (61354) *(G-17528)*
**T & T Machine Shop**...847 244-2020
4406 Lee Ave Gurnee (60031) *(G-11511)*
**T & T Machinery Inc**...708 366-8747
604 Ashland Ave River Forest (60305) *(G-18002)*
**T 26 Inc**...773 862-1201
1110 N Milwaukee Ave Chicago (60642) *(G-6662)*
**T A E Signals Division, East Hazel Crest** *Also called Tool Automation Enterprises (G-8666)*
**T A U Inc**...708 841-5757
14075 Lincoln Ave Dolton (60419) *(G-8377)*
**T and D Metal Products LLC (PA)**...815 432-4938
602 E Walnut St Watseka (60970) *(G-21430)*
**T and T Cabinet Co**...815 245-6322
5505 W Chasefield Cir McHenry (60050) *(G-14566)*
**T C, Schaumburg** *Also called Thiessen Communications Inc (G-19761)*
**T C I Vacuum Forming Company**...847 622-9100
1620 Cambridge Dr Elgin (60123) *(G-9200)*
**T C W F Inc**...630 369-1360
1577 Nperville Wheaton Rd Naperville (60563) *(G-15759)*
**T C4 Inc**...618 335-3486
1207 N Carlisle Rd Vandalia (62471) *(G-21127)*
**T Cat Enterprise Inc**...630 330-6800
9300 Franklin Ave Franklin Park (60131) *(G-10602)*
**T D C Inc**...815 229-7064
2517 Pelham Rd Rockford (61107) *(G-18639)*
**T D J Group Inc**...847 639-1113
760 Industrial Dr Ste A Cary (60013) *(G-3374)*
**T E A M, Elk Grove Village** *Also called Team Impressions Inc (G-9769)*
**T E C A, Chicago** *Also called Thermoelectric Coolg Amer Corp (G-6713)*
**T E Q, Huntley** *Also called Thermform Engineered Qulty LLC (G-12179)*
**T F N W Inc**...630 584-7383
1574 E Main St Saint Charles (60174) *(G-19277)*
**T G Automotive**...630 916-7818
901 N Ridge Ave Ste 1 Lombard (60148) *(G-13863)*
**T G Enterprises Inc**...309 662-0508
2045 Ireland Grove Rd Bloomington (61704) *(G-2229)*
**T Graphics**...618 592-4145
701 S Range St Oblong (62449) *(G-16735)*
**T H Davidson & Co Inc (PA)**...815 464-2000
4243 166th St Oak Forest (60452) *(G-16591)*
**T H Davidson & Co Inc**...815 941-0280
1350 Bungalow Rd Morris (60450) *(G-15134)*
**T H K Holdings of America LLC (HQ)**...847 310-1111
200 Commerce Dr Schaumburg (60173) *(G-19750)*
**T Ham Sign Inc (PA)**...618 242-2010
7699 N Goshen Ln Opdyke (62872) *(G-16811)*
**T Hasegawa USA Inc**...847 559-6060
3100 Dundee Rd Ste 701 Northbrook (60062) *(G-16375)*
**T J Assemblies Inc**...847 671-0060
10349 Franklin Ave Franklin Park (60131) *(G-10603)*
**T J Brooks Co**...847 680-0350
804 E Park Ave Ste 104 Libertyville (60048) *(G-13387)*
**T J Kellogg Inc**...815 969-0524
4949 Safford Rd Rockford (61101) *(G-18640)*
**T J M & Associates Inc**...847 382-1993
22292 N Pepper Rd Ste D Lake Barrington (60010) *(G-12825)*
**T J Marche Ltd**...618 445-2314
11 N 5th St Albion (62806) *(G-366)*
**T J Martin & Co Division, Orland Park** *Also called Diagrind Inc (G-16854)*
**T J Metal Co**...708 388-6191
4631 W 120th St Alsip (60803) *(G-532)*
**T J P Investments Inc**...309 673-8383
2522 W War Memorial Dr Peoria (61615) *(G-17465)*
**T J S Equipment Inc**...618 656-8046
1514 Weber Dr Edwardsville (62025) *(G-8816)*
**T J Van Der Bosch & Associates**...815 344-3210
430 W Wegner Rd McHenry (60051) *(G-14567)*
**T K O Quality Offset Printing**...847 709-0455
4141 N Yale Ave Arlington Heights (60004) *(G-850)*
**T K O Waterproof Coating LLP**...815 338-2006
427 E Judd St Woodstock (60098) *(G-22618)*
**T L Swint Industries Inc**...847 358-3834
2211 Banbury Rd Inverness (60067) *(G-12206)*
**T M I S, Wauconda** *Also called Tent Maker Industrial Sup Inc (G-21509)*
**T M J, Crystal Lake** *Also called TMJ Architectural LLC (G-7666)*
**T M T Industries Inc**...815 562-0111
770 Wiscold Dr Rochelle (61068) *(G-18111)*
**T Mac Cylinders Inc**...815 877-7090
9014 Swanson Dr Roscoe (61073) *(G-18923)*
**T N T Industries Inc**...630 879-1522
1169 Lyon Rd Batavia (60510) *(G-1503)*
**T P I Inc**...847 888-0232
1172 Price Dr Elgin (60120) *(G-9201)*
**T P R Resources Inc**...630 443-9060
3604 Greenwood Ln Saint Charles (60175) *(G-19278)*
**T R Communications Inc**...773 238-3366
10546 S Western Ave Chicago (60643) *(G-6663)*
**T R Jones Machine Co Inc**...815 356-5000
3040 Hamlin Dr Machesney Park (61115) *(G-14111)*
**T R Machine Inc**...815 865-5711
103 Il Route 75 E Ste 100 Davis (61019) *(G-7808)*
**T R Z Motorsports Inc**...815 806-0838
25045 S Center Rd Frankfort (60423) *(G-10367)*
**T Renee Productions, Flora** *Also called Crusade Enterprises Inc (G-10205)*
**T S I, Galena** *Also called Technical Sealants Inc (G-10732)*
**T T T Inc**...630 860-7499
387 Crestwood Rd Wood Dale (60191) *(G-22426)*
**T&D Trucking, Watseka** *Also called T and D Metal Products LLC (G-21430)*
**T&J Turning Inc**...309 738-8762
4 Goembel Dr Colona (61241) *(G-7349)*
**T&L International Mfg/Dist Inc**...309 830-7238
25833 Hillcrest Dr Farmer City (61842) *(G-10182)*
**T&T Hydraulics, Peru** *Also called T & T Distribution Inc (G-17528)*
**T-G Ad Service, Chicago** *Also called Mer-Pla Inc (G-5687)*

ALPHABETIC

**T-Mobile, Hickory Hills** *Also called Smart Choice Mobile Inc* ***(G-11774)***
**T-Mobile Usa Inc** ....847 289-9988
416 Randall Rd South Elgin (60177) ***(G-20228)***
**T-P Electric & Manufacturing, Lawrenceville** *Also called Tracy Electric Inc* ***(G-13206)***
**T-Rex Excavating Inc** ....815 547-9955
1217 American House Dr Belvidere (61008) ***(G-1787)***
**T.S. Shure, Chicago** *Also called Shure Products Inc* ***(G-6504)***
**T/CCI Manufacturing LLC (PA)** ....217 423-0066
2120 N 22nd St Decatur (62526) ***(G-7947)***
**T/J Fabricators Inc** ....630 543-2293
2150 W Executive Dr Addison (60101) ***(G-305)***
**T2 Cabinets Inc** ....312 593-1507
1400 W 37th St Chicago (60609) ***(G-6664)***
**T2 Site Amenities Incorporated** ....847 579-9003
1805 Spruce St Highland Park (60035) ***(G-11876)***
**T9 Group LLC** ....847 912-8862
25635 N Stoney Kirk Ct Hawthorn Woods (60047) ***(G-11705)***
**Ta Oil Field Service Inc** ....618 249-9001
27573 State Route 177 Richview (62877) ***(G-17982)***
**Taap Corp** ....224 676-0653
300 Holbrook Dr Wheeling (60090) ***(G-22163)***
**Tabbies, Itasca** *Also called Xertrex International Inc* ***(G-12375)***
**Tablecraft Products Co Inc (PA)** ....847 855-9000
801 Lakeside Dr Gurnee (60031) ***(G-11512)***
**Tables Inc** ....630 365-0741
835 Drover St Elburn (60119) ***(G-8912)***
**Tacknologies** ....630 729-9900
10720 Beaudin Blvd Ste A Woodridge (60517) ***(G-22521)***
**Tacmina USA Corporation** ....312 810-8128
105 W Central Rd Schaumburg (60195) ***(G-19751)***
**Tacom Hq Inc** ....630 251-8919
3908 E 2599th Rd Sheridan (60551) ***(G-19919)***
**Tactical Lighting Systems Inc** ....800 705-0518
901 S Rohlwing Rd Ste J Addison (60101) ***(G-306)***
**Tadd LLC** ....847 380-3540
188 Northwest Hwy Ste 301 Cary (60013) ***(G-3375)***
**Tads** ....815 654-3500
10 E Riverside Blvd Loves Park (61111) ***(G-13996)***
**Taft Street Company Inc** ....217 544-3471
2300 N 16th St Springfield (62702) ***(G-20541)***
**Tag Diamond & Label** ....630 844-9395
100 Hankes Ave Aurora (60505) ***(G-1221)***
**Tag Master Line, Evanston** *Also called Dard Products Inc* ***(G-10025)***
**Tag Sales Co Inc** ....630 990-3434
1000 Jorie Blvd Ste 26 Hinsdale (60523) ***(G-11966)***
**Tag Tool Services Incorporated** ....309 694-2400
3303 N Main St Ste A East Peoria (61611) ***(G-8736)***
**Tag's Bakery & Pastry Shop, Evanston** *Also called Tags Bakery Inc* ***(G-10100)***
**Tag-Barton LLC (PA)** ....217 428-0711
1395 S Taylorville Rd Decatur (62521) ***(G-7948)***
**Tagitsold Inc** ....630 724-1800
740 Ogden Ave Downers Grove (60515) ***(G-8529)***
**Tagobi LLC** ....331 444-2951
303 S Main St Wheaton (60187) ***(G-21983)***
**Tagore Technology Inc** ....847 790-3799
5 E College Dr Ste 200 Arlington Heights (60004) ***(G-851)***
**Tags Bakery Inc** ....847 328-1200
2010 Central St Evanston (60201) ***(G-10100)***
**Tai, Orland Park** *Also called Tindall Associates Inc* ***(G-16898)***
**Taico Design Products Inc** ....773 871-9086
333 N Canal St Apt 3701 Chicago (60606) ***(G-6665)***
**Tailored Inc** ....708 387-9854
9520 47th St Ste 2 Brookfield (60513) ***(G-2643)***
**Tailored Printing Inc** ....217 522-6287
4855 Sage Rd Rochester (62563) ***(G-18122)***
**Tails Inc** ....773 564-9300
4410 N Ravenswood Ave # 1 Chicago (60640) ***(G-6666)***
**Tailwind Furniture, Cortland** *Also called D M O Inc* ***(G-7387)***
**Taisei Lamick USA Inc** ....847 258-3283
1801 Howard St Elk Grove Village (60007) ***(G-9767)***
**Tait Machine Tool Inc** ....815 932-2011
417 S Schuyler Ave Kankakee (60901) ***(G-12656)***
**Taitt Burial Garments** ....773 483-7424
6649 S Wabash Ave Chicago (60637) ***(G-6667)***
**Takasago Intl Corp USA** ....815 479-5030
300 Memorial Dr Ste 100 Crystal Lake (60014) ***(G-7659)***
**Take Your Mark Sports LLC** ....708 655-0525
1010 Longmeadow Ln Western Springs (60558) ***(G-21874)***
**Takeda Dev Ctr Americas Inc** ....224 554-6500
1 Takeda Pkwy Deerfield (60015) ***(G-8058)***
**Takeda Pharmaceuticals NA** ....972 819-5353
1 Takeda Pkwy Deerfield (60015) ***(G-8059)***
**Takeda Pharmaceuticals USA Inc (HQ)** ....224 554-6500
1 Takeda Pkwy Deerfield (60015) ***(G-8060)***
**Takeda Phrmaceuticals Amer Inc** ....224 554-6500
1 Takeda Pkwy Deerfield (60015) ***(G-8061)***
**Tal Mar Custom Met Fabricators** ....708 371-0333
4632 138th St Crestwood (60445) ***(G-7505)***
**Talaris Inc (HQ)** ....630 577-1000
3333 Warrenville Rd # 310 Lisle (60532) ***(G-13669)***
**Talcott Communications Corp (PA)** ....312 849-2220
704 N Wells St Fl 2 Chicago (60654) ***(G-6668)***
**Talk-A-Phone Co** ....773 539-1100
7530 N Natchez Ave Niles (60714) ***(G-16039)***
**Tall Trees Farm, Crystal Lake** *Also called Ridgefield Industries Co LLC* ***(G-7641)***
**Tallwood** ....815 786-8186
15751 Burr Oak Rd Plano (60545) ***(G-17676)***
**Taloc Usa Inc** ....847 665-8222
1915 Enterprise Ct Libertyville (60048) ***(G-13388)***
**Tam Tav Bakery Inc** ....773 764-8877
2944 W Devon Ave Chicago (60659) ***(G-6669)***
**Tamarack Products Inc** ....847 526-9333
1071 N Old Rand Rd Wauconda (60084) ***(G-21508)***
**Tamms Industries Inc** ....815 522-3394
3835 Il Route 72 Kirkland (60146) ***(G-12719)***
**Tammy Smith** ....618 372-8410
14 Willow Way Brighton (62012) ***(G-2545)***
**Tampico Beverages Inc** ....773 296-0190
2425 W Barry Ave Chicago (60618) ***(G-6670)***
**Tampico Beverages Inc (HQ)** ....773 296-0190
3106 N Campbell Ave Chicago (60618) ***(G-6671)***
**Tampico Press** ....312 243-5448
1919 S Blue Island Ave Chicago (60608) ***(G-6672)***
**Tampotech Decorating Inc** ....847 515-2968
10901 Union Special Plz Huntley (60142) ***(G-12178)***
**Tanaka Dental Enterprises Inc** ....847 679-1610
8001 Lincoln Ave Ste 201 Skokie (60077) ***(G-20099)***
**Tanaka Dental Products Div, Skokie** *Also called Tanaka Dental Enterprises Inc* ***(G-20099)***
**Tanaka Kikinzoku International, Schaumburg** *Also called Tanaka Kknzoku Intrnational Kk* ***(G-19753)***
**Tanaka Kikinzoku Intl Amer Inc** ....224 653-8309
475 N Martingale Rd # 150 Schaumburg (60173) ***(G-19752)***
**Tanaka Kknzoku Intrnational Kk** ....224 653-8309
475 N Martingale Rd # 150 Schaumburg (60173) ***(G-19753)***
**Tancher Corp** ....847 668-8765
1493 Vernon Ave Park Ridge (60068) ***(G-17226)***
**Tandem Industries Inc** ....630 761-6615
3820 Ohio Ave Ste 16 Saint Charles (60174) ***(G-19279)***
**Tane Corporation** ....847 705-7125
1122 W Partridge Dr Palatine (60067) ***(G-17078)***
**Tangent Systems Inc** ....847 882-3833
2155 Stnngton Ave Ste 107 Hoffman Estates (60169) ***(G-12062)***
**Tangent Technologies LLC** ....630 264-1110
1001 Sullivan Rd Aurora (60506) ***(G-1222)***
**Tangler Wrangler, Hoffman Estates** *Also called Stevens Plastic Inc* ***(G-12060)***
**Tanic Rubber Plate Co** ....630 896-2122
1013 Sill Ave Aurora (60506) ***(G-1223)***
**Tanis Custom Golf, Matteson** *Also called Custom Golf By Tanis* ***(G-14369)***
**Tanklink Corporation** ....312 379-8397
200 S Wacker Dr Ste 1800 Chicago (60606) ***(G-6673)***
**Tanko Bros Screw Mch Pdts Corp** ....708 755-8823
3361 Holeman Ave S Chicago Hts (60411) ***(G-19113)***
**Tanko Screw Products, Bensenville** *Also called L D Redmer Screw Pdts Inc* ***(G-1935)***
**Tanko Scrw Prd Corp** ....708 418-0300
19830 Stoney Island Ave Chicago Heights (60411) ***(G-7130)***
**Tanvas Inc** ....773 295-6220
600 W Van Buren St # 710 Chicago (60607) ***(G-6674)***
**Tanya Shipley** ....708 476-0433
11344 Abbey Rd Mokena (60448) ***(G-14910)***
**Tao Trading Corporation** ....773 764-6542
1420 W Howard St Apt 201 Chicago (60626) ***(G-6675)***
**Tapco Cutting Tools Inc** ....815 877-4039
5605 Pike Rd Loves Park (61111) ***(G-13997)***
**Tapco USA Inc** ....815 877-4039
5605 Pike Rd Loves Park (61111) ***(G-13998)***
**Tape Case Ltd** ....847 299-7880
150 Gaylord St Elk Grove Village (60007) ***(G-9768)***
**Tar-B Precision Machining Corp** ....630 521-9771
605 Country Club Dr Ste D Bensenville (60106) ***(G-2000)***
**Tara International LP** ....708 354-7050
9100 67th St Hodgkins (60525) ***(G-11984)***
**Taranda Specialties Inc** ....815 469-3041
8746 W Manhattan Monee Rd Frankfort (60423) ***(G-10368)***
**Tarco Printing Inc** ....630 467-1000
1270 Ardmore Ave Itasca (60143) ***(G-12364)***
**Target, Rantoul** *Also called East Central Communications Co* ***(G-17926)***
**Target Laser & Machining Inc** ....815 963-6706
2433 Fremont St Rockford (61103) ***(G-18641)***
**Target Market News Inc** ....312 408-1881
228 S Wabash Ave Ste 210 Chicago (60604) ***(G-6676)***
**Target Plastics Tech Corp** ....630 545-1776
400 Windy Point Dr Glendale Heights (60139) ***(G-11083)***
**Targin Sign Systems Inc** ....630 766-7667
160 W Irving Park Rd Wood Dale (60191) ***(G-22427)***
**Tarney Inc** ....773 235-0331
4520 W North Ave Chicago (60639) ***(G-6677)***

**Tarnow Logistics Inc** ....773 844-3203
1001 N 16th Ave Melrose Park (60160) *(G-14700)*
**Tarps Manufacturing Inc** ....217 584-1900
1000 State Highway 104 Meredosia (62665) *(G-14735)*
**Tarte Cupcakery Company** ....312 898-2103
18509 School St Lansing (60438) *(G-13189)*
**Tassos Metal Inc** ....630 953-1333
950 N Lombard Rd Lombard (60148) *(G-13864)*
**Tasty Breads International Inc** ....847 451-4000
9445 Fullerton Ave Franklin Park (60131) *(G-10604)*
**Tate & Lyle Americas LLC** ....847 396-7500
5450 Prairie Stone Pkwy # 170 Hoffman Estates (60192) *(G-12063)*
**Tate & Lyle Americas LLC (HQ)** ....217 421-2964
2200 E Eldorado St Decatur (62521) *(G-7949)*
**Tate & Lyle Citric Acid, Decatur** *Also called Tate Lyle Ingrdnts Amricas LLC (G-7950)*
**Tate and Lyle, Heyworth** *Also called Tate Lyle Ingrdnts Amricas LLC (G-11766)*
**Tate Lyle Ingrdnts Amricas LLC (HQ)** ....217 423-4411
2200 E Eldorado St Decatur (62521) *(G-7950)*
**Tate Lyle Ingrdnts Amricas LLC** ....309 473-2721
702 S Vine St Heyworth (61745) *(G-11766)*
**Tatine** ....312 733-0173
4200 W Diversey Ave Chicago (60639) *(G-6678)*
**Taubensee Steel & Wire Company (PA)** ....847 459-5100
600 Diens Dr Wheeling (60090) *(G-22164)*
**Tauber Brothers Tool & Die Co** ....708 867-9100
4701 N Olcott Ave Chicago (60706) *(G-6679)*
**Taurus Cycle** ....309 454-1565
1 Lafayette Ct Bloomington (61701) *(G-2230)*
**Taurus Die Casting LLC** ....815 316-6160
5196 27th Ave Rockford (61109) *(G-18642)*
**Taurus Safety Products Inc** ....630 620-7940
39 S Glenview Ave Lombard (60148) *(G-13865)*
**Tavern On Prospect Ltd** ....309 693-8677
5901 N Prospect Rd Ste 10 Peoria (61614) *(G-17466)*
**Taw Enterprises LLC** ....618 466-0134
5100 Seminole Ct Godfrey (62035) *(G-11238)*
**Tax Collector, Melrose Park** *Also called Bost Corporation (G-14603)*
**Taycorp Inc (PA)** ....708 629-0921
5700 W 120th St Alsip (60803) *(G-533)*
**Taycorp Inc** ....630 530-7500
752 N Larch Ave Elmhurst (60126) *(G-9948)*
**Taykit Inc** ....847 888-1150
1175 Davis Rd Elgin (60123) *(G-9202)*
**Taylor Design Inc** ....815 389-3991
5375 E Rockton Rd Roscoe (61073) *(G-18924)*
**Taylor Enterprises Inc** ....847 367-1032
5510 Fairmont Rd Ste A Libertyville (60048) *(G-13389)*
**Taylor Farms Illinois Inc** ....312 226-3328
200 N Artesian Ave Chicago (60612) *(G-6680)*
**Taylor Made Machining Inc** ....815 339-6267
W Mark Indus Park Rr 71 Mark (61340) *(G-14300)*
**Taylor Off Road Racing** ....815 544-4500
6925 Imron Dr Belvidere (61008) *(G-1788)*
**Taylor Precision Products Inc (HQ)** ....630 954-1250
2311 W 22nd St Ste 200 Oak Brook (60523) *(G-16563)*
**Taylor Spring Mfg. Co., Alsip** *Also called Taycorp Inc (G-533)*
**Taylors Candy Inc** ....708 371-0332
4855 W 115th St Alsip (60803) *(G-534)*
**Tazewell Floor Covering Inc** ....309 266-6371
419 W Jefferson St Morton (61550) *(G-15184)*
**Tazewell Machine Works Inc** ....309 347-3181
2015 S 2nd St Pekin (61554) *(G-17291)*
**Tb Cardworks Llc** ....847 229-9990
344 S Whitehall Dr Palatine (60067) *(G-17079)*
**Tbc Corporation** ....630 428-2233
915 E Ogden Ave Naperville (60563) *(G-15760)*
**Tbw Machining Inc** ....847 524-1501
1030 Morse Ave Schaumburg (60193) *(G-19754)*
**Tc Electric Controls LLC** ....847 598-3508
1320 Tower Rd Schaumburg (60173) *(G-19755)*
**Tc Industries Inc (HQ)** ....815 459-2401
3703 S Il Route 31 Crystal Lake (60012) *(G-7660)*
**Tc Printers, Salem** *Also called Salem Times-Commoner Pubg Co (G-19349)*
**Tcc, Inc, Addison** *Also called Transparent Container Co Inc (G-321)*
**TCI Manufacturing & Eqp Sls, Walnut** *Also called Tricon Inds Mfg & Eqp Sls (G-21331)*
**Tcr Systems LLC** ....217 877-5622
4900 N Brush College Rd Decatur (62526) *(G-7951)*
**Tdm Systems Inc** ....847 605-1269
1901 N Roselle Rd Ste 800 Schaumburg (60195) *(G-19756)*
**Tdr Express Inc** ....224 805-0070
5231 N Oakview St Apt 3e Chicago (60656) *(G-6681)*
**Tdr Transport, Yorkville** *Also called Edward J Warren Jr (G-22657)*
**TDS Machining Inc** ....630 964-0004
8402 Wilmette Ave Ste B Darien (60561) *(G-7803)*
**Tdw Services Inc** ....815 407-0675
565 Anderson Dr Ste A Romeoville (60446) *(G-18873)*
**Tdy Industries LLC** ....847 564-0700
700 Landwehr Rd Northbrook (60062) *(G-16376)*

**Te Connectivity Corporation** ....847 680-7400
620 S Butterfield Rd Mundelein (60060) *(G-15563)*
**Te Shurt Shop Inc** ....217 344-1226
711 S Wright St Champaign (61820) *(G-3549)*
**Team Cast Inc** ....312 263-0033
111 W Washington St # 1865 Chicago (60602) *(G-6682)*
**Team Cnc Inc** ....630 377-2723
761 N 17th St Ste 22 Saint Charles (60174) *(G-19280)*
**Team Cncept Prtg Thrmgrphy Inc** ....630 653-8326
540 Tower Blvd Carol Stream (60188) *(G-3252)*
**Team Energy LLC (PA)** ....618 943-1010
Rr 1 Box 197 Bridgeport (62417) *(G-2456)*
**Team Fenex, Sandoval** *Also called Synergy Power Group LLC (G-19359)*
**Team Impressions Inc** ....847 357-9270
360 Scott St Elk Grove Village (60007) *(G-9769)*
**Team Play Inc** ....847 952-7533
201 Crossen Ave Elk Grove Village (60007) *(G-9770)*
**Team Products Inc** ....815 244-6100
636 S East St Mount Carroll (61053) *(G-15293)*
**Team Sider Inc** ....847 767-0107
158 Hastings Ave Highland Park (60035) *(G-11877)*
**Team Technologies Inc** ....630 937-0380
1300 Nagel Blvd Batavia (60510) *(G-1504)*
**Team Works By Holzhauer Inc** ....309 745-9924
2168 Washington Rd Washington (61571) *(G-21393)*
**Teamdance Illinois** ....815 463-9044
215 Fulton St Geneva (60134) *(G-10871)*
**Teasdale Foods Inc** ....217 283-7771
215 W Washington St Hoopeston (60942) *(G-12118)*
**Tease** ....630 960-4950
4717 Seeley Ave Downers Grove (60515) *(G-8530)*
**TEC Foods Inc** ....800 315-8002
4300 W Ohio St Chicago (60624) *(G-6683)*
**TEC Rep Corporation** ....630 627-9110
1919 S Highland Ave 330a Lombard (60148) *(G-13866)*
**TEC Systems Inc** ....815 722-2800
908 Garnet Ct New Lenox (60451) *(G-15917)*
**Tech Global Inc** ....847 532-4882
2759 Pinnacle Dr Elgin (60124) *(G-9203)*
**Tech Global Inc** ....224 623-2000
2521 Tech Dr Ste 206 Elgin (60124) *(G-9204)*
**Tech Oasis International Inc** ....847 302-1590
5652 Chapel Hl Gurnee (60031) *(G-11513)*
**Tech Star Design and Mfg** ....847 290-8676
116 N Lively Blvd Elk Grove Village (60007) *(G-9771)*
**Tech Upgraders** ....877 324-8940
2007 S 9th Ave Maywood (60153) *(G-14435)*
**Tech-Mate Inc** ....847 352-9690
1671 Virginia Dr Elk Grove Village (60007) *(G-9772)*
**Tech-Max Machine Inc** ....630 875-0054
1170 Ardmore Ave Itasca (60143) *(G-12365)*
**Tech-Weld Inc** ....630 365-3000
801 E North St Elburn (60119) *(G-8913)*
**Techdrive Inc** ....312 567-3910
3255 S Dearborn St # 320 Chicago (60616) *(G-6684)*
**Techgraphic Solutions Inc** ....309 693-9400
8824 N Industrial Rd Peoria (61615) *(G-17467)*
**Techline Studio** ....212 674-1813
1463 W Winnetka St Palatine (60067) *(G-17080)*
**Technatool Inc** ....847 398-0355
2222 Foster Ave Wheeling (60090) *(G-22165)*
**Technetics Group LLC** ....708 887-6080
7319 W Wilson Ave Harwood Heights (60706) *(G-11691)*
**Technic Inc** ....773 262-2662
3265 N Ridge Ave Arlington Heights (60004) *(G-852)*
**Technical Coatings Co** ....708 343-6000
2525 W North Ave Melrose Park (60160) *(G-14701)*
**Technical Metals Inc** ....815 692-4643
1301 W Oak St Fairbury (61739) *(G-10133)*
**Technical Ordnance Inc** ....630 969-0620
2525 Curtiss St Downers Grove (60515) *(G-8531)*
**Technical Power Systems Inc** ....630 719-1471
4642 Western Ave Lisle (60532) *(G-13670)*
**Technical Sales Midwest Inc** ....847 855-2457
36149 N Edgewater Ct Gurnee (60031) *(G-11514)*
**Technical Sealants Inc** ....815 777-9797
11476 Technnical Dr Galena (61036) *(G-10732)*
**Technical Tool Enterprise** ....630 893-3390
1550 W Fullerton Ave D Addison (60101) *(G-307)*
**Technicraft Display Graphics, Peoria** *Also called Technicraft Supply Co (G-17468)*
**Technicraft Supply Co (PA)** ....309 495-5245
419 Elm St Peoria (61605) *(G-17468)*
**Technics Inc** ....630 215-3742
1000 W Crossroads Pkwy J Bolingbrook (60490) *(G-2377)*
**Technigraph, Chicago** *Also called Alpha Packaging Minnesota Inc (G-3829)*
**Techniks LLC** ....815 689-2748
424 E Jackson St Cullom (60929) *(G-7685)*
**Technimold Tool Corporation** ....847 639-4226
500 Cary Algonquin Rd # 1 Cary (60013) *(G-3376)*

ALPHABETIC

**Technipaq Inc** .................................................. 815 477-1800
975 Lutter Dr  Crystal Lake  (60014)  *(G-7661)*

**Technique Eng Inc** ............................................. 847 816-1870
968 S Northpoint Blvd  Waukegan  (60085)  *(G-21621)*

**Technique Engineering Inc** ................................. 847 816-1870
968 S Northpoint Blvd  Waukegan  (60085)  *(G-21622)*

**Technisand, Troy Grove**  Also called Fairmount Santrol Inc  *(G-21012)*

**Techno - Grphics Trnsltons Inc** .......................... 708 331-3333
1451 E 168th St  South Holland  (60473)  *(G-20308)*

**Technocure, Antioch**  Also called Pro Tools & Equipment Inc  *(G-652)*

**Technologies Dvlpmnt** ....................................... 815 943-9922
3517 Braberry Ln  Crystal Lake  (60012)  *(G-7662)*

**Technology One Welding Inc** .............................. 630 871-1296
210 Easy St Ste D  Carol Stream  (60188)  *(G-3253)*

**Technotrans America Inc (HQ)** ........................... 847 227-9200
1441 E Business Center Dr  Mount Prospect  (60056)  *(G-15378)*

**Technoweld, Chicago**  Also called Alberto Daza  *(G-3796)*

**Technox Machine & Mfg Inc** ............................... 773 745-6800
2619 N Normandy Ave  Chicago  (60707)  *(G-6685)*

**Techny Advisors LLC** ......................................... 630 771-0095
109 Shore Dr  Burr Ridge  (60527)  *(G-2883)*

**Techny Plastics Corp** ......................................... 847 498-2212
1919 Techny Rd  Northbrook  (60062)  *(G-16377)*

**Techny Precision Mfg Inc** ................................... 630 543-7065
818 S Westwood Ave Ste C  Addison  (60101)  *(G-308)*

**Technymon Technology USA Inc** ........................ 630 787-0501
730 N Edgewood Ave  Wood Dale  (60191)  *(G-22428)*

**Techpack Inc** ..................................................... 847 439-8220
1500 Midway Ct Ste W9  Elk Grove Village  (60007)  *(G-9773)*

**Techpol Automation Inc** ..................................... 847 347-4765
2083 Maple St  Des Plaines  (60018)  *(G-8285)*

**Techprint Inc** ..................................................... 847 616-0109
2330 Eastern Ave  Elk Grove Village  (60007)  *(G-9774)*

**Tecnova Electronics Inc** .................................... 847 336-6160
2383 N Delany Rd  Waukegan  (60087)  *(G-21623)*

**Tecstar Mfg Company III Div, Libertyville**  Also called Mgs Mfg Group Inc  *(G-13358)*

**Ted Holum & Associates Inc** .............................. 630 543-9355
1216 W Capitol Dr Ste C  Addison  (60101)  *(G-309)*

**Ted Muller** ......................................................... 312 435-0978
910 S Michigan Ave # 1612  Chicago  (60605)  *(G-6686)*

**Tedds Cstm Installations Inc** ............................. 815 485-6800
21719 S Center Ave Ste A  New Lenox  (60451)  *(G-15918)*

**Tedds Custom Installations, New Lenox**  Also called Tedds Cstm Installations Inc  *(G-15918)*

**Teds Custom Cabinets Inc** ................................. 773 581-4455
5946 S Pulaski Rd  Chicago  (60629)  *(G-6687)*

**Teds Shirt Shack Inc** ......................................... 217 224-9705
2811 Bluff Ridge Dr  Quincy  (62305)  *(G-17892)*

**Tee Group Films Inc** .......................................... 815 894-2331
605 N Mn Ave  Ladd  (61329)  *(G-12792)*

**Tee Lee Popcorn Inc** ......................................... 815 864-2363
101 W Badger St  Shannon  (61078)  *(G-19903)*

**Teeatude Inc** ..................................................... 312 324-3554
1016 W Jackson Blvd  Chicago  (60607)  *(G-6688)*

**Teejet Technologies LLC (HQ)** ........................... 630 665-5002
1801 Business Park Dr  Springfield  (62703)  *(G-20542)*

**Teenfitnation LLC** .............................................. 847 322-2953
12 Westlake Dr  South Barrington  (60010)  *(G-20133)*

**Teepak Usa LLC** ................................................ 217 446-6460
915 N Michigan Ave  Danville  (61834)  *(G-7767)*

**Tees Ink** ............................................................ 815 462-7300
1215 Revere Ct  New Lenox  (60451)  *(G-15919)*

**Tegna Inc** .......................................................... 847 490-6657
1721 Moon Lake Blvd # 540  Hoffman Estates  (60169)  *(G-12064)*

**Tegrant Alloyd Brands Inc (HQ)** ......................... 815 756-8451
1401 Pleasant St  Dekalb  (60115)  *(G-8124)*

**Tegrant Corporation (HQ)** .................................. 815 756-8451
1401 Pleasant St  Dekalb  (60115)  *(G-8125)*

**Tegrant Corporation** .......................................... 630 879-0121
1500 Paramount Pkwy  Batavia  (60510)  *(G-1505)*

**Tegrant Holding Corp** ........................................ 815 756-8451
1401 Pleasant St  Dekalb  (60115)  *(G-8126)*

**Tegratecs Development Corp** ............................. 847 397-0088
1320 Tower Rd  Schaumburg  (60173)  *(G-19757)*

**Tegrity Inc** ......................................................... 800 411-0579
1333 Burr Ridge Pkwy # 250  Burr Ridge  (60527)  *(G-2884)*

**Teitelbaum Brothers Inc** .................................... 847 729-3490
1944 Lehigh Ave Ste D  Glenview  (60026)  *(G-11208)*

**Tek Pak Inc (PA)** ............................................... 630 406-0560
1336 Paramount Pkwy  Batavia  (60510)  *(G-1506)*

**Tek-Cast Inc** ...................................................... 630 422-1458
195 Corporate Dr  Elgin  (60123)  *(G-9205)*

**Tekky Toys, Orland Park**  Also called Jcw Investments Inc  *(G-16870)*

**Tekni-Plex Inc** ................................................... 217 935-8311
10610 State Highway 10  Clinton  (61727)  *(G-7289)*

**Tekno Industries Inc (PA)** .................................. 630 766-6960
1250 Shore Rd  Naperville  (60563)  *(G-15761)*

**Tekvend, Park Ridge**  Also called Advanced Technologies Inc  *(G-17178)*

**Tel Aviv Kosher Bakery, Chicago**  Also called Tam Tav Bakery Inc  *(G-6669)*

**Telco Machine & Manufacturing (PA)** ................. 773 725-4441
3957 N Normandy Ave  Chicago  (60634)  *(G-6689)*

**Telco Machine & Manufacturing** ........................ 773 725-4441
6610 W Dakin St  Chicago  (60634)  *(G-6690)*

**Telcom Innovations Group LLC** ......................... 630 350-0700
125 N Prospect Ave  Itasca  (60143)  *(G-12366)*

**Tele Guia De Chicago, Cicero**  Also called Tele-Guia Inc  *(G-7236)*

**Tele Guia Spanish TV Guide** .............................. 708 656-9800
3116 S Austin Blvd  Cicero  (60804)  *(G-7235)*

**Tele Print** .......................................................... 630 941-7877
494 E Atwood Ct  Elmhurst  (60126)  *(G-9949)*

**Tele-Guia Inc** ..................................................... 708 656-9800
3116 S Austin Blvd  Cicero  (60804)  *(G-7236)*

**Telecom Audio, Sandwich**  Also called Jk Audio Inc  *(G-19370)*

**Teledyne Lecroy Inc** .......................................... 847 888-0450
2111 Big Timber Rd Ste A  Elgin  (60123)  *(G-9206)*

**Teledyne Monitor Labs Inc** ................................ 303 792-3300
12497 Collection Ctr Dr  Chicago  (60693)  *(G-6691)*

**Teledyne Reynolds Inc** ...................................... 630 754-3300
10221 Werch Dr  Woodridge  (60517)  *(G-22522)*

**Teledyne Storm Microwave, Woodridge**  Also called Teledyne Reynolds Inc  *(G-22522)*

**Teleflex Incorporated** ........................................ 847 259-7400
900 W University Dr  Arlington Heights  (60004)  *(G-853)*

**Teleflex Marine, Litchfield**  Also called Sierra International LLC  *(G-13698)*

**Telefonix Incorporated** ...................................... 847 244-4500
2340 Ernie Krueger Cir  Waukegan  (60087)  *(G-21624)*

**Telegartner Inc** .................................................. 630 616-7600
411 Dominic Ct  Franklin Park  (60131)  *(G-10605)*

**Telegraph Hill Inc** .............................................. 415 252-9097
100 N Fairway Dr Ste 106  Vernon Hills  (60061)  *(G-21207)*

**Teleguia Inc** ...................................................... 708 656-6675
3116 S Austin Blvd  Cicero  (60804)  *(G-7237)*

**Telehealth Sensors LLC** .................................... 630 879-3101
197 Alder Dr  North Aurora  (60542)  *(G-16147)*

**Telemedicine Solutions LLC** .............................. 847 519-3500
425 N Martingale Rd # 1250  Schaumburg  (60173)  *(G-19758)*

**Teleweld Inc** ...................................................... 815 672-4561
502 N Vermillion St  Streator  (61364)  *(G-20707)*

**Telguard, Chicago**  Also called Telular Corporation  *(G-6692)*

**Tella Technology Div, Lombard**  Also called Tella Tool & Mfg Co  *(G-13867)*

**Tella Tool & Mfg Co (PA)** ................................... 630 495-0545
1015 N Ridge Ave Ste 1  Lombard  (60148)  *(G-13867)*

**Tellabs Inc (HQ)** ................................................ 630 798-8800
1415 W Diehl Rd  Naperville  (60563)  *(G-15762)*

**Tellabs Mexico Inc (HQ)** .................................... 630 445-5333
1415 W Diehl Rd  Naperville  (60563)  *(G-15763)*

**Tellenar Inc** ....................................................... 815 356-8044
727 Tek Dr  Crystal Lake  (60014)  *(G-7663)*

**Tellurian Technologies Inc** ................................. 847 934-4141
3455 W Salt Creek Ln # 500  Arlington Heights  (60005)  *(G-854)*

**Telular Corporation (HQ)** ................................... 800 835-8527
200 S Wacker Dr Ste 1800  Chicago  (60606)  *(G-6692)*

**Telza Welding Co, Chicago**  Also called Telza Welding Inc  *(G-6693)*

**Telza Welding Inc** .............................................. 773 777-4467
1624 N Kilbourn Ave  Chicago  (60639)  *(G-6693)*

**Temco Communications, South Barrington**  Also called Temco Japan Co Ltd  *(G-20134)*

**Temco Grinding Inc** ........................................... 815 282-9405
1002 River Ln  Loves Park  (61111)  *(G-13999)*

**Temco Japan Co Ltd** ......................................... 847 359-3277
13 Chipping Campden Dr  South Barrington  (60010)  *(G-20134)*

**Temp Excel Properties LLC** ............................... 847 844-3845
2520 Vantage Dr  Elgin  (60124)  *(G-9207)*

**Temp-Air Inc** ...................................................... 847 931-7700
39 W 107 Highland Ave  Elgin  (60123)  *(G-9208)*

**Temp-Tech Industries Inc** .................................. 773 586-2800
6166 S Sayre Ave  Chicago  (60638)  *(G-6694)*

**Tempco Electric Heater Corp (PA)** ..................... 630 350-2252
607 N Central Ave  Wood Dale  (60191)  *(G-22429)*

**Tempco Products Co** ......................................... 618 544-3175
301 E Tempco Ave  Robinson  (62454)  *(G-18074)*

**Tempel Farms, Old Mill Creek**  Also called Tempel Steel Company  *(G-16756)*

**Tempel Holdings Inc** ......................................... 773 250-8000
5500 N Wolcott Ave  Chicago  (60640)  *(G-6695)*

**Tempel Steel Company (PA)** .............................. 773 250-8000
5500 N Wolcott Ave  Chicago  (60640)  *(G-6696)*

**Tempel Steel Company** ..................................... 773 250-8000
5454 N Wolcott Ave  Chicago  (60640)  *(G-6697)*

**Tempel Steel Company** ..................................... 773 250-8000
5500 N Wolcott Ave  Chicago  (60640)  *(G-6698)*

**Tempel Steel Company** ..................................... 847 244-5330
17000 W Wadsworth Rd  Old Mill Creek  (60083)  *(G-16756)*

**Temper Enterprises Inc** ..................................... 815 553-0374
2218 Plainfield Rd Ste B  Crest Hill  (60403)  *(G-7469)*

**Temperance Beer Company LLC** ....................... 847 864-1000
2000 Dempster St  Evanston  (60202)  *(G-10101)*

**Temperature Equipment Corp** ........................... 847 429-0818
1313 Timber Dr  Elgin  (60123)  *(G-9209)*

**Temperature Equipment Corp** ........................... 815 229-2935
1818 18th Ave  Rockford  (61104)  *(G-18643)*

# ALPHABETIC SECTION      The Label and Packaging Co, Northbrook

**Tempil Inc (HQ)** ............................................. 908 757-8300
  1201 Pratt Blvd  Elk Grove Village  (60007)  *(G-9775)*
**Temple Display Ltd** ...................................... 630 851-3331
  114 Kirkland Cir Ste C  Oswego  (60543)  *(G-16936)*
**Templegate Publishers** ............................... 217 522-3353
  302 E Adams St  Springfield  (62701)  *(G-20543)*
**Tempo Components, Marengo**  Also called Tempo Wood Products Inc  *(G-14242)*
**Tempo Graphics, Carol Stream**  Also called Tempo Holdings Inc  *(G-3254)*
**Tempo Holdings Inc (PA)** ............................ 630 462-8200
  455 E North Ave  Carol Stream  (60188)  *(G-3254)*
**Tempo Wood Products Inc** ........................ 815 568-7315
  641 W Washington St  Marengo  (60152)  *(G-14242)*
**Temprite Company** ...................................... 630 293-5910
  1555 W Hawthorne Ln 1e  West Chicago  (60185)  *(G-21778)*
**Tempro International Corp** ......................... 847 677-5370
  8343 Niles Center Rd  Skokie  (60077)  *(G-20100)*
**Tempus Health Inc** ...................................... 312 784-4400
  600 W Chicago Ave Ste 775  Chicago  (60654)  *(G-6699)*
**Tenco Hydro Inc of Illinois** ........................ 708 387-0700
  4620 Forest Ave  Brookfield  (60513)  *(G-2644)*
**Tender Loving Care Inds Inc** .................... 847 891-0230
  815 Lunt Ave  Schaumburg  (60193)  *(G-19759)*
**Tenex Corporation** ....................................... 847 504-0400
  1282 Barclay Blvd  Buffalo Grove  (60089)  *(G-2780)*
**Tenexco Inc** .................................................. 708 771-7870
  414 Clinton Pl Ste 106  River Forest  (60305)  *(G-18003)*
**Tenggren-Mehl Co Inc** ................................ 773 763-3290
  7019 W Higgins Ave  Chicago  (60656)  *(G-6700)*
**Tennant Company** ....................................... 773 376-7132
  1120 W Exchange Ave  Chicago  (60609)  *(G-6701)*
**Tenneco Automotive Oper Co Inc (HQ)** ... 847 482-5000
  500 N Field Dr  Lake Forest  (60045)  *(G-12965)*
**Tenneco Automotive Oper Co Inc** ........... 847 821-0757
  605 Heathrow Dr  Lincolnshire  (60069)  *(G-13485)*
**Tenneco Global Holdings Inc (HQ)** ......... 847 482-5000
  500 N Field Dr  Lake Forest  (60045)  *(G-12966)*
**Tenneco Inc (PA)** .......................................... 847 482-5000
  500 N Field Dr  Lake Forest  (60045)  *(G-12967)*
**Tenneco Intl Holdg Corp (HQ)** .................. 847 482-5000
  500 N Field Dr  Lake Forest  (60045)  *(G-12968)*
**Tenneco Packaging** .................................... 847 482-2000
  1900 W Field Ct  Lake Forest  (60045)  *(G-12969)*
**Tent Maker Industrial Sup Inc** .................. 847 469-6070
  531 Brown St  Wauconda  (60084)  *(G-21509)*
**Tenth and Blake Beer Company (HQ)** .... 312 496-2759
  250 S Wacker Dr Ste 800  Chicago  (60606)  *(G-6702)*
**Tepromark International Inc** ..................... 847 329-7881
  140 S Dearborn St Ste 420  Chicago  (60603)  *(G-6703)*
**Ter-Son Corporation** ................................... 309 274-6227
  1801 N Logan St  Chillicothe  (61523)  *(G-7171)*
**Teraco-II Inc** ................................................. 630 539-4400
  910 Lake St Ste 116  Roselle  (60172)  *(G-18981)*
**Terand Industries, Downers Grove**  Also called CPC Aeroscience Inc  *(G-8421)*
**Terco Inc** ....................................................... 630 894-8828
  459 Camden Dr  Bloomingdale  (60108)  *(G-2139)*
**Teresa Foods Inc** ........................................ 708 258-6200
  116 Main St  Peotone  (60468)  *(G-17493)*
**Teresa Frozen Pizzas, Peotone**  Also called Teresa Foods Inc  *(G-17493)*
**Terex Services, Addison**  Also called Terex Utilities Inc  *(G-310)*
**Terex Utilities Inc** ....................................... 847 515-7030
  1461 W Bernard Dr  Addison  (60101)  *(G-310)*
**Terlato Wine Group Ltd (PA)** ..................... 847 604-8900
  900 Armour Dr  Lake Bluff  (60044)  *(G-12867)*
**Termax Corporation (PA)** ............................ 847 519-1500
  1155 Rose Rd Ste A  Lake Zurich  (60047)  *(G-13137)*
**Ternkirst Tl & Die & Mch Works** .............. 847 437-8360
  355 Lively Blvd  Elk Grove Village  (60007)  *(G-9776)*
**Terra Cotta Holdings Co (PA)** .................. 815 459-2400
  3703 S Il Route 31  Crystal Lake  (60012)  *(G-7664)*
**Terra Nitrogen Company LP (PA)** ............ 847 405-2400
  4 Parkway N Ste 400  Deerfield  (60015)  *(G-8062)*
**Terrace Holding Company** ........................ 708 652-5600
  1325 S Cicero Ave  Cicero  (60804)  *(G-7238)*
**Terramac LLC** ............................................... 630 365-4800
  724 Hicks Dr  Elburn  (60119)  *(G-8914)*
**Terraneo Merchants Inc** ............................. 312 753-9134
  6525 W Proesel Ave  Lincolnwood  (60712)  *(G-13539)*
**Terrapin Xpress Inc** .................................... 866 823-7323
  7801 W 123rd Pl  Palos Heights  (60463)  *(G-17111)*
**Terrasource Global Corporation** ............. 618 641-6985
  1 Freedom Dr  Belleville  (62226)  *(G-1678)*
**Terre Haute Tent & Awning Inc** ................ 812 235-6068
  16520 Vincennes Ave  South Holland  (60473)  *(G-20309)*
**Terrell Materials Corporation** ................... 312 376-0105
  10600 W Higgins Rd # 300  Rosemont  (60018)  *(G-19036)*
**Terri Lynn Inc (PA)** ...................................... 847 741-1900
  1450 Bowes Rd  Elgin  (60123)  *(G-9210)*
**Terry Terri Mulgrew** .................................... 815 747-6248
  521 Montgomery Ave  East Dubuque  (61025)  *(G-8625)*

**Terry Tool & Machining Corp** .................... 847 289-1054
  563 Commonwealth Dr # 1300  East Dundee  (60118)  *(G-8658)*
**Teshurt, Champaign**  Also called Te Shurt Shop Inc  *(G-3549)*
**Tesko Enterprises, Norridge**  Also called Tesko Welding & Mfg Co  *(G-16109)*
**Tesko Welding & Mfg Co** ........................... 708 452-0045
  7350 W Montrose Ave  Norridge  (60706)  *(G-16109)*
**Tesla Motors Inc** ......................................... 312 733-9780
  1053 W Grand Ave  Chicago  (60642)  *(G-6704)*
**Testa Steel Constructors Inc** ................... 815 729-4777
  22449 Thomas Dilon Dr  Channahon  (60410)  *(G-3587)*
**Testor Corporation** ..................................... 815 962-6654
  615 Buckbee St  Rockford  (61104)  *(G-18644)*
**Tetra Medical Supply Corp** ....................... 847 647-0590
  6364 W Gross Point Rd  Niles  (60714)  *(G-16040)*
**Tetra Pak Inc** ................................................ 815 873-1222
  5691 International Dr  Rockford  (61109)  *(G-18645)*
**Tetra Pak Inc** ................................................ 847 955-6000
  600 Bunker Ct  Vernon Hills  (60061)  *(G-21208)*
**Tetra Pak Materials LP (HQ)** ..................... 847 955-6000
  101 Corporate Woods Pkwy  Vernon Hills  (60061)  *(G-21209)*
**Tetra Pak US Holdings Inc (HQ)** .............. 940 565-8800
  101 Corporate Woods Pkwy  Vernon Hills  (60061)  *(G-21210)*
**Tewell Bros Machine Inc** ........................... 217 253-6303
  300 N Parke St  Tuscola  (61953)  *(G-21025)*
**Tex Tana Inc (PA)** ........................................ 773 561-9270
  2243 W Belmont Ave Ste 1  Chicago  (60618)  *(G-6705)*
**Tex Trend Inc** ............................................... 847 215-6796
  767 Kristy Ln  Wheeling  (60090)  *(G-22166)*
**Texas Brand, Wauconda**  Also called F & Y Enterprises Inc  *(G-21462)*
**Texas Instruments Incorporated** ............. 630 836-2827
  27715 Diehl Rd  Warrenville  (60555)  *(G-21363)*
**Texmac Inc** ................................................... 630 244-4702
  224 Terrace Dr  Mundelein  (60060)  *(G-15564)*
**Textile Industries Inc** ................................. 312 829-3112
  2414 W Cullerton St Fl 3  Chicago  (60608)  *(G-6706)*
**Textron Aviation Inc** ................................... 630 443-5080
  2700 Intl Dr Ste 304  West Chicago  (60185)  *(G-21779)*
**Textron Inc** ................................................... 815 961-5293
  510 18th Ave  Rockford  (61104)  *(G-18646)*
**Textura Corporation (HQ)** .......................... 866 839-8872
  1405 Lake Cook Rd  Deerfield  (60015)  *(G-8063)*
**Teys (usa) Inc** .............................................. 312 492-7163
  770 N Halsted St Ste 202  Chicago  (60642)  *(G-6707)*
**Tfa Signs** ....................................................... 773 267-6007
  5500 N Kedzie Ave  Chicago  (60625)  *(G-6708)*
**TFC Group LLC** ........................................... 630 559-0808
  136 W Commercial Ave  Addison  (60101)  *(G-311)*
**Tfo Group LLC** ............................................. 608 469-7519
  2140 W Fulton St Ste F  Chicago  (60612)  *(G-6709)*
**Tft Inc** ............................................................ 309 531-2012
  31784 E 1400 North Rd  Colfax  (61728)  *(G-7311)*
**Tgm Fabricating Inc** ................................... 708 533-0857
  57 E 24th St  Chicago Heights  (60411)  *(G-7131)*
**Tgrv LLC (HQ)** .............................................. 815 634-2102
  1032 Margaux Rd  Bourbonnais  (60914)  *(G-2407)*
**Th Foods Inc** ................................................ 702 565-2816
  2154 Harlem Rd  Loves Park  (61111)  *(G-14000)*
**Th Foods Inc (HQ)** ...................................... 800 896-2396
  2134 Harlem Rd  Loves Park  (61111)  *(G-14001)*
**Thai Noodle** .................................................. 217 235-5584
  1418 Broadway Ave  Mattoon  (61938)  *(G-14410)*
**Thales Visionix Inc** .................................... 630 375-2008
  1444 N Farnsworth Ave # 604  Aurora  (60505)  *(G-1224)*
**Thatcher Oaks Inc** ...................................... 630 833-5700
  718 N Industrial Dr  Elmhurst  (60126)  *(G-9950)*
**Thatcher Retractbles, Elmhurst**  Also called Thatcher Oaks Inc  *(G-9950)*
**Thats So Sweet** ........................................... 903 331-7221
  429 W Main St  Lexington  (61753)  *(G-13294)*
**The Amateur Athlete Magazine, Skokie**  Also called Chicago Sports Media Inc  *(G-19981)*
**The Athletic Equipment Source** ............... 630 587-9333
  1820 Wallace Ave Ste 124  Saint Charles  (60174)  *(G-19281)*
**The Calumet Carton Company (PA)** ........ 708 331-7910
  16920 State St  South Holland  (60473)  *(G-20310)*
**The Chronicle, Hoopeston**  Also called Times Republic  *(G-12119)*
**The Curry Companies, Decatur**  Also called Curry Ready-Mix of Decatur  *(G-7862)*
**The Daily Record, Lawrenceville**  Also called Daily Lawrenceville Record  *(G-13198)*
**The Euclid Chemical Company** ............... 815 522-2308
  3835 State Route 72  Kirkland  (60146)  *(G-12720)*
**The Evanston Sentinel Newsppr, Evanston**  Also called Evanston Sentinel Corporation  *(G-10034)*
**The Gem Group, Chicago**  Also called Ebonyenergy Publishing Inc Nfp  *(G-4689)*
**The Intec Group Inc (PA)** ........................... 847 358-0088
  666 S Vermont St  Palatine  (60067)  *(G-17081)*
**The Intelligent Office, Lincolnshire**  Also called Barclay Business Group Inc  *(G-13431)*
**The Korea Centl Daily Chicago, Elk Grove Village**  Also called Joong-Ang Daily News  *(G-9564)*
**The Label and Packaging Co, Northbrook**  Also called F C D Inc  *(G-16255)*

---
(PA)=Parent Co  (HQ)=Headquarters  (DH)=Div Headquarters     2017 Harris Illinois Industrial Directory

**The Lifeguard Store Inc** ... 630 548-5500
1212 S Naper Blvd Ste 109 Naperville (60540) ***(G-15764)***
**The Master's Shop, Thomasboro** *Also called Masters Shop* ***(G-20860)***
**The Pantagraph, Bloomington** *Also called Hearst Communications Inc* ***(G-2177)***
**The Parts House** ... 309 343-0146
343 S Kellogg St Galesburg (61401) ***(G-10777)***
**The Pool Center, Dix** *Also called Royal Fiberglass Pools Inc* ***(G-8318)***
**The Syntek Group Inc** ... 773 279-0131
3415 N Pulaski Rd 23 Chicago (60641) ***(G-6710)***
**The Times** ... 815 433-2000
110 W Jefferson St Ottawa (61350) ***(G-16986)***
**The United Group Inc** ... 847 816-7100
13700 W Polo Trail Dr Lake Forest (60045) ***(G-12970)***
**Theatre In The Park, Jacksonville** *Also called Creative Ideas Inc* ***(G-12386)***
**Thelen Sand & Gravel Inc (PA)** ... 847 838-8800
28955 W Il Route 173 # 1 Antioch (60002) ***(G-656)***
**Thelen Sand & Gravel Inc** ... 847 662-0760
1020 Elizabeth St Waukegan (60085) ***(G-21625)***
**THEOSOPHICAL PUBLISHING HOUSE, Wheaton** *Also called Theosophical Society In Amer* ***(G-21984)***
**Theosophical Society In Amer (PA)** ... 630 665-0130
1926 N Main St Wheaton (60187) ***(G-21984)***
**Theosophical Society In Amer** ... 630 665-0123
306 W Geneva Rd Wheaton (60187) ***(G-21985)***
**Theosphcal Pubg Hs/Quest Bk Sp, Wheaton** *Also called Theosophical Society In Amer* ***(G-21985)***
**Ther A Pedic Midwest Inc** ... 309 788-0401
2350 5th St Rock Island (61201) ***(G-18206)***
**Therafin Corporation** ... 708 479-7300
9450 W Laraway Rd Frankfort (60423) ***(G-10369)***
**Therapeutic Envisions Inc** ... 720 323-7032
151 Blueberry Rd Libertyville (60048) ***(G-13390)***
**Therapeutic Skin Care** ... 630 244-1833
21w221 Hemstead Rd Lombard (60148) ***(G-13868)***
**Therese Crowe Design Ltd** ... 312 269-0039
29 E Madison St Ste 1401 Chicago (60602) ***(G-6711)***
**Therm-O-Web Inc** ... 847 520-5200
770 Glenn Ave Wheeling (60090) ***(G-22167)***
**Therma-Kleen Inc** ... 630 718-0212
10212 S Mandel St Ste A Plainfield (60585) ***(G-17657)***
**Thermal Bags By Ingrid Inc** ... 847 836-4400
131 Sola Dr Gilberts (60136) ***(G-10938)***
**Thermal Care Inc** ... 847 966-2260
5680 W Jarvis Ave Niles (60714) ***(G-16041)***
**Thermal Care Inc** ... 847 929-1207
6125 W Mulford St Niles (60714) ***(G-16042)***
**Thermal Ceramics Inc** ... 217 627-2101
1st & Mound St Girard (62640) ***(G-10950)***
**Thermal Industries Inc** ... 800 237-0560
830 Sivert Dr Wood Dale (60191) ***(G-22430)***
**Thermal Safe Brands, Arlington Heights** *Also called Sonoco Protective Solutions* ***(G-841)***
**Thermal Solutions Inc** ... 217 352-7019
1706 Lyndhurst Dr Savoy (61874) ***(G-19412)***
**Thermal-Chem, Franklin Park** *Also called Armitage Industries Inc* ***(G-10400)***
**Thermal-Tech Systems Inc** ... 630 639-5115
1215 Atlantic Dr West Chicago (60185) ***(G-21780)***
**Thermatome Corporation** ... 312 772-2201
2242 W Harrison St # 201 Chicago (60612) ***(G-6712)***
**Thermform Engineered Qulty LLC (HQ)** ... 847 669-5291
11320 Main St Huntley (60142) ***(G-12179)***
**Thermionics Corp (PA)** ... 800 800-5728
1214 Bunn Ave Ste 5 Springfield (62703) ***(G-20544)***
**Thermo Fisher Scientific Inc** ...
3000 Lakeside Dr Ste 116n Bannockburn (60015) ***(G-1266)***
**Thermo Fisher Scientific Inc** ... 847 381-7050
1230 Hardt Cir Bartlett (60103) ***(G-1380)***
**Thermo Mattson, Bannockburn** *Also called Thermo Fisher Scientific Inc* ***(G-1266)***
**Thermo Techniques LLC** ... 217 446-1407
20 Oakwood Ave Danville (61832) ***(G-7768)***
**Thermo-Craft Inc** ... 618 281-7055
528 S Main St Columbia (62236) ***(G-7363)***
**Thermo-Graphic LLC** ... 630 350-2226
301 Arthur Ct Bensenville (60106) ***(G-2001)***
**Thermo-Pak Co** ... 630 860-1303
360 Balm Ct Wood Dale (60191) ***(G-22431)***
**Thermocraft, Columbia** *Also called Thermo-Craft Inc* ***(G-7363)***
**Thermoelectric Coolg Amer Corp** ... 773 342-4900
4048 W Schubert Ave Chicago (60639) ***(G-6713)***
**Thermoflex Corp (PA)** ... 847 473-9001
1535 S Lakeside Dr Waukegan (60085) ***(G-21626)***
**Thermoflex Corp** ... 847 473-9001
1817-1855 S Waukegan Rd Waukegan (60085) ***(G-21627)***
**Thermohelp Inc** ... 847 821-7130
12 River Oaks Cir W Buffalo Grove (60089) ***(G-2781)***
**Thermoplastec Inc** ... 815 873-9288
4755 Colt Rd Rockford (61109) ***(G-18647)***
**Thermopol Inc** ... 815 422-0400
150 W Grant St Saint Anne (60964) ***(G-19126)***
**Thermos LLC (PA)** ... 847 439-7821
475 N Martingale Rd # 1100 Schaumburg (60173) ***(G-19760)***
**Thermosafe, Beecher** *Also called Sonoco Prtective Solutions Inc* ***(G-1602)***
**Thermosoft International Corp** ... 847 279-3800
701 Corporate Woods Pkwy Vernon Hills (60061) ***(G-21211)***
**Thia & Co** ... 630 510-9770
519 W Front St Wheaton (60187) ***(G-21986)***
**Thiessen Communications Inc** ... 847 884-0980
1300 Basswood Rd Schaumburg (60173) ***(G-19761)***
**Think Ink Inc** ... 815 459-4565
890 Cog Cir Crystal Lake (60014) ***(G-7665)***
**Thinkcercacom Inc** ... 224 412-3722
440 N Wells St Ste 720 Chicago (60654) ***(G-6714)***
**Third Day Oil & Gas LLC** ... 618 553-5538
210 S Range St Oblong (62449) ***(G-16736)***
**Third Wrld Press Fundation Inc** ... 773 651-0700
7822 S Dobson Ave Chicago (60619) ***(G-6715)***
**Thirteen Rf Inc** ... 618 687-1313
10 Alliance Ave Murphysboro (62966) ***(G-15585)***
**This Week In Chicago Inc** ... 312 943-0838
226 E Ontario St Fl 3 Chicago (60611) ***(G-6716)***
**Thk America Inc (HQ)** ... 847 310-1111
200 Commerce Dr Schaumburg (60173) ***(G-19762)***
**Tholeo Design Inc** ... 630 325-3792
418 Ridge Ave Clarendon Hills (60514) ***(G-7260)***
**Thomas & Betts Corp** ... 630 444-2151
2580 Foxfield Rd Ste 306 Saint Charles (60174) ***(G-19282)***
**Thomas A Doan** ... 847 864-8772
1560 Sherman Ave Ste 1029 Evanston (60201) ***(G-10102)***
**Thomas Electronics Inc** ... 315 923-2051
330 S La Londe Ave Addison (60101) ***(G-312)***
**Thomas Engineering Inc (PA)** ... 847 358-5800
575 W Central Rd Hoffman Estates (60192) ***(G-12065)***
**Thomas Engineering Inc** ... 815 398-0280
2500 Harrison Ave Rockford (61108) ***(G-18648)***
**Thomas Fine Stairs Inc** ... 708 387-9506
9110 47th St Brookfield (60513) ***(G-2645)***
**Thomas Gardner Denver Inc** ... 217 222-5400
1800 Gardner Expy Quincy (62305) ***(G-17893)***
**Thomas Monahan Company (PA)** ... 217 268-5771
202 N Oak St Arcola (61910) ***(G-686)***
**Thomas Packaging LLC** ... 847 392-1652
3885 Industrial Ave Rolling Meadows (60008) ***(G-18782)***
**Thomas Printing & Sty Co** ... 618 435-2801
301 S Du Quoin St Benton (62812) ***(G-2041)***
**Thomas Proestler** ... 630 971-0185
5400 Patton Dr Ste 2c Lisle (60532) ***(G-13671)***
**Thomas Publishing Printing Div** ... 618 351-6655
701 W Main St Carbondale (62901) ***(G-3025)***
**Thomas Pump Company** ... 630 851-9393
2301 Liberty St Aurora (60502) ***(G-1085)***
**Thomas Research Products LLC** ... 224 654-8626
1215 Bowes Rd Ste 1225 Elgin (60123) ***(G-9211)***
**Thomas Tees Inc** ... 217 488-2288
210 S Oak St New Berlin (62670) ***(G-15866)***
**Thomas-Zientz Group Inc** ... 847 395-2363
925 Carney Ct Antioch (60002) ***(G-657)***
**Thomason Machine Works Inc (PA)** ... 815 874-8217
5459 11th St Rockford (61109) ***(G-18649)***
**Thompson & Walsh LLC** ... 847 734-1770
547 W Golf Rd Arlington Heights (60005) ***(G-855)***
**Thompson Industries Inc** ... 815 899-6670
1018 Crosby Ave Sycamore (60178) ***(G-20819)***
**Thomson Casual Furniture Co, Galva** *Also called Dixline Corporation* ***(G-10787)***
**Thomson Linear LLC** ... 815 568-8001
1300 N State St Marengo (60152) ***(G-14243)***
**Thomson Quantitative Analytics** ... 847 610-0574
230 S La Salle St Ste 688 Chicago (60604) ***(G-6717)***
**Thomson Reuters (legal) Inc** ... 312 873-6800
1 N Dearborn St Fl 5 Chicago (60602) ***(G-6718)***
**Thomson Reuters (markets) LLC** ... 847 705-7929
651 N Williams Dr Palatine (60074) ***(G-17082)***
**Thomson Reuters Corporation** ... 312 288-4654
1 N Dearborn St Ste 1400 Chicago (60602) ***(G-6719)***
**Thomson Steel Polishing Corp** ... 773 586-2345
6150 S New England Ave Chicago (60638) ***(G-6720)***
**Thor Defense Inc** ... 630 541-5106
6121 Plymouth St Downers Grove (60516) ***(G-8532)***
**Thornton Welding Service Inc** ... 217 877-0610
4350 N Route 48 Decatur (62526) ***(G-7952)***
**Thorworks Industries Inc** ... 815 969-0664
904 7th St Rockford (61104) ***(G-18650)***
**Thoughtly Corp** ... 772 559-2008
750 N Rush St Apt 1906 Chicago (60611) ***(G-6721)***
**Thrall Enterprises Inc (PA)** ... 312 621-8200
180 N Stetson Ave Chicago (60601) ***(G-6722)***
**Thread & Gage Co Inc** ... 815 675-2305
3000 N Us Highway 12 Spring Grove (60081) ***(G-20367)***
**Threads of Time** ... 217 431-9202
207 S Buchanan St Danville (61832) ***(G-7769)***

# ALPHABETIC SECTION — Tin Tree Gifts

**Threads Up Inc** .................................................. 630 595-2297
1060 Entry Dr Bensenville (60106) *(G-2002)*

**Three Angels Printing Svcs Inc** .................................. 630 333-4305
1105 S Westwood Ave Addison (60101) *(G-313)*

**Three Castle Press Inc** .......................................... 630 540-0120
213 Mayfield Dr Streamwood (60107) *(G-20676)*

**Three Guys Pasta LLC** ........................................... 708 932-5555
11225 W Grand Ave Northlake (60164) *(G-16455)*

**Three Hands Technologies** ...................................... 847 680-5358
462 Harrison Ct Vernon Hills (60061) *(G-21212)*

**Three JS Industries Inc** ........................................ 847 640-6080
701 Landmeier Rd Elk Grove Village (60007) *(G-9777)*

**Three Penguin Ice, University Park** Also called Tinley Ice Company *(G-21064)*

**Three R Plastics Inc** ........................................... 815 675-0844
1801 Holian Dr Spring Grove (60081) *(G-20368)*

**Three Star Mfg Co Inc** .......................................... 847 526-2222
375 Hollow Hill Rd Wauconda (60084) *(G-21510)*

**Three Z Printing, Teutopolis** Also called Three-Z Printing Co *(G-20857)*

**Three-Z Printing Co (PA)** ....................................... 217 857-3153
902 W Main St Teutopolis (62467) *(G-20857)*

**Thrice Publishing Nfp** .......................................... 630 776-0478
734 Berwick Pl Roselle (60172) *(G-18982)*

**Thrift Medical Products** ....................................... 630 857-3548
1701 Quincy Ave Naperville (60540) *(G-15765)*

**Thrift n Swift** ................................................. 847 455-1350
9651 Franklin Ave Franklin Park (60131) *(G-10606)*

**Thrift-Remsen Printers, Rockford** Also called Lind-Remsen Printing Co Inc *(G-18470)*

**Thrifty Nckel Amrcn Clssifieds, Champaign** Also called Want ADS of Champaign Inc *(G-3558)*

**Thrilled LLC** ................................................... 312 404-1929
555 W Jackson Blvd # 400 Chicago (60661) *(G-6723)*

**Thrushwood Frms Qlty Meats Inc** ................................ 309 343-5193
2860 W Main St Galesburg (61401) *(G-10778)*

**Thryselius Machining Inc** ..................................... 630 365-9191
44w480 Keslinger Rd Elburn (60119) *(G-8915)*

**Thryselius Stamping Inc** ...................................... 630 232-0795
28 S 8th St Geneva (60134) *(G-10872)*

**Thule Inc** ..................................................... 847 455-2420
7609 Industrial Dr Forest Park (60130) *(G-10254)*

**Thule Chicago, Forest Park** Also called Thule Inc *(G-10254)*

**Thunder Tool Corp** ............................................. 708 544-4742
2800 S 18th Ave Broadview (60155) *(G-2616)*

**Thunderbird LLC (PA)** .......................................... 847 718-9300
1501 Oakton St Elk Grove Village (60007) *(G-9778)*

**Thurne USA, Chicago** Also called Mww Food Processing USA LLC *(G-5838)*

**Thurow Tool Works Inc** ......................................... 630 377-6403
41 W 523 Rr 64 Saint Charles (60175) *(G-19283)*

**Thybar Corporation (PA)** ....................................... 630 543-5300
913 S Kay Ave Addison (60101) *(G-314)*

**Thycurb Fabricating, Addison** Also called Thybar Corporation *(G-314)*

**Thyssenkrupp Auto Sales Techno, Danville** Also called Thyssenkrupp Presta Cold Forgi *(G-7774)*

**Thyssenkrupp Automotve Sales &, Danville** Also called Thyssenkrupp Crankshaft Co LLC *(G-7770)*

**Thyssenkrupp Crankshaft Co LLC (HQ)** .......................... 217 431-0060
1000 Lynch Rd Danville (61834) *(G-7770)*

**Thyssenkrupp Crankshaft Co LLC** ............................... 217 444-5230
1000 Lynch Rd Danville (61834) *(G-7771)*

**Thyssenkrupp Crankshaft Co LLC** ............................... 217 444-5400
1200 International Pl Danville (61834) *(G-7772)*

**Thyssenkrupp Crankshaft Co LLC** ............................... 217 444-5500
75 Walz Crk Danville (61834) *(G-7773)*

**Thyssenkrupp Elevator Corp** ................................... 312 733-8025
940 W Adams St Chicago (60607) *(G-6724)*

**Thyssenkrupp Materials NA Inc** ................................ 630 563-3365
905 Carlow Dr Bolingbrook (60490) *(G-2378)*

**Thyssenkrupp North America Inc (HQ)** .......................... 312 525-2800
111 W Jackson Blvd # 2400 Chicago (60604) *(G-6725)*

**Thyssenkrupp Presta Cold Forgi** ............................... 217 431-4212
69 Walz Crk Danville (61834) *(G-7774)*

**Thyssenkrupp Stainless N Amer, Bannockburn** Also called Mexinox USA Inc *(G-1261)*

**Thyssnkrupp Prsta Danville LLC** ............................... 217 444-5500
75 Walz Crk Danville (61834) *(G-7775)*

**TI International Ltd** ......................................... 847 689-0233
2260 Commonwealth Ave North Chicago (60064) *(G-16188)*

**TI Squared Technologies Inc** .................................. 541 367-2929
1019 W Wise Rd Ste 101 Schaumburg (60193) *(G-19763)*

**Tia Tynette Designs Inc** ...................................... 219 440-2859
2600 Troy Cir Olympia Fields (60461) *(G-16806)*

**Tianhe Stem Cell** ............................................. 630 723-1968
6398 Holly Ct Lisle (60532) *(G-13672)*

**Tibor Machine Products Inc (PA)** .............................. 708 499-0017
7400 W 100th Pl Bridgeview (60455) *(G-2534)*

**Tibor Machine Products Inc** ................................... 309 786-3052
2832 5th St Ste 2 Rock Island (61201) *(G-18207)*

**Tickle Asphalt Co Ltd** ........................................ 309 787-1308
700 4th St W Milan (61264) *(G-14806)*

**Tidd Printing Co** ............................................. 708 749-1200
2709 Ridgeland Ave Berwyn (60402) *(G-2076)*

**Tiem Engineering Corporation** ................................. 630 553-7484
202 Beaver St Yorkville (60560) *(G-22672)*

**Tiesenbach, Marion** Also called Hauhinco LP *(G-14264)*

**Tifb Media Group Inc** ......................................... 844 862-4391
7608 Lockwood Ave Burbank (60459) *(G-2810)*

**Tiffany Stained Glass Ltd** .................................... 312 642-0680
428 Des Plaines Ave Ste 1 Forest Park (60130) *(G-10255)*

**Tiger Accessory Group LLC (HQ)** ............................... 847 821-9630
6700 Wildlife Way Long Grove (60047) *(G-13902)*

**Tiger Tool Inc** ............................................... 888 551-4490
410 Windy Point Dr Glendale Heights (60139) *(G-11084)*

**Tiger Tool Supply, Inc., Glendale Heights** Also called Tiger Tool Inc *(G-11084)*

**Tigerflex Corporation** ........................................ 847 439-1766
801 Estes Ave Elk Grove Village (60007) *(G-9779)*

**Tighe Publishing Services Inc** ................................ 773 281-9100
1700 W Irvng Park Rd # 210 Chicago (60613) *(G-6726)*

**Tii Technical Educatn Systems** ................................ 847 428-3085
56 E End Dr Gilberts (60136) *(G-10939)*

**Tilestar, Tinley Park** Also called Midland Product LLC *(G-20932)*

**Tillock Steel Supply and Salv, Baldwin** Also called Higman LLC *(G-1251)*

**Tilton Pattern Works Inc** ..................................... 217 442-1502
21204 Rileysburg Rd Danville (61834) *(G-7776)*

**Tim Detwiler Enterprises Inc** ................................. 815 758-9950
1140 S 7th St Dekalb (60115) *(G-8127)*

**Tim Wallace Ldscp Sup Co Inc (PA)** ............................ 630 759-6813
1481 W Boughton Rd Bolingbrook (60490) *(G-2379)*

**Timberline Manufacturing, Downers Grove** Also called Dover Energy Automation LLC *(G-8432)*

**Timberline Pallet & Skid Inc** ................................. 309 752-1770
2500 8th Ave East Moline (61244) *(G-8695)*

**Timberside Woodworking** ....................................... 217 578-3201
715 N Cr 125 E Arthur (61911) *(G-922)*

**Time Embroidery** .............................................. 847 364-4371
2201 Lively Blvd Elk Grove Village (60007) *(G-9780)*

**Time Out Chicago Partners Lllp** ............................... 312 924-9555
247 S State St Ste 1700 Chicago (60604) *(G-6727)*

**Time Records Publishing and Bo** ............................... 618 996-3803
2537 Wards Mill Rd Marion (62959) *(G-14291)*

**Timeout Devices Inc** .......................................... 847 729-6543
2718 Covert Rd Glenview (60025) *(G-11209)*

**Timepilot Corporation** ........................................ 630 879-6400
340 Mckee St Batavia (60510) *(G-1507)*

**Times Energy** ................................................. 773 444-9282
11241 S Natoma Ave Worth (60482) *(G-22635)*

**Times Record Company** ......................................... 309 582-5112
219 S College Ave Aledo (61231) *(G-373)*

**Times Republic (HQ)** .......................................... 815 432-5227
1492 E Walnut St Watseka (60970) *(G-21431)*

**Times Republic** ............................................... 217 283-5111
308 E Main St Hoopeston (60942) *(G-12119)*

**Times-Leader, Mc Leansboro** Also called Newspaper Holding Inc *(G-14466)*

**Times-Press Publishing Co** .................................... 815 673-3771
115 Oak St Streator (61364) *(G-20708)*

**Times-Tribune, Troy** Also called Newsprint Ink Inc *(G-21010)*

**Timewell Tile, Timewell** Also called C & L Tiling Inc *(G-20884)*

**Timken Company** ............................................... 618 594-4545
2210 Franklin St Carlyle (62231) *(G-3060)*

**Timken Company** ............................................... 309 692-8150
8415 N Allen Rd Ste 208 Peoria (61615) *(G-17469)*

**Timken Drives LLC (HQ)** ....................................... 815 589-2211
901 19th Ave Fulton (61252) *(G-10706)*

**Timken Drives LLC** ............................................ 312 274-9710
875 N Michigan Ave Chicago (60611) *(G-6728)*

**Timken Gears & Services Inc** .................................. 708 720-9400
8529 192nd St Mokena (60448) *(G-14911)*

**Timken Rail Bearing Service, Carlyle** Also called Timken Company *(G-3060)*

**Timkensteel Chicago Sales Off, Tinley Park** Also called Timkensteel Corporation *(G-20948)*

**Timkensteel Corporation** ...................................... 708 263-6868
18660 Graphic Dr Ste 202 Tinley Park (60477) *(G-20948)*

**Timothy Anderson Corporation** ................................. 815 398-8371
700 20th St Rockford (61104) *(G-18651)*

**Timothy Darrey** ............................................... 847 231-2277
1153 Lee St Bldg 223 Des Plaines (60016) *(G-8286)*

**Timothy Helgoth** .............................................. 217 224-8008
839 Jersey St Quincy (62301) *(G-17894)*

**Timpte Industries Inc** ........................................ 309 820-1095
2312 W Market St Bloomington (61705) *(G-2231)*

**Tin HLA Health Svcs** .......................................... 708 633-0426
7809 Joliet Dr S Tinley Park (60477) *(G-20949)*

**Tin Man Heating & Cooling Inc** ................................ 630 267-3232
419 Rathbone Ave Aurora (60506) *(G-1225)*

**Tin Mans Garage Inc** .......................................... 630 262-0752
39w869 Midan Dr Unit B Elburn (60119) *(G-8916)*

**Tin Maung** .................................................... 217 233-1405
1770 E Lake Shore Dr Decatur (62521) *(G-7953)*

**Tin Tree Gifts** ............................................... 630 935-8086
2720 Stuart Kaplan Dr Aurora (60503) *(G-1086)*

**Tindall Associates Inc** ........ 708 403-7775
10727 Winterset Dr Orland Park (60467) ***(G-16898)***
**Tindall Composites, Godfrey** *Also called Richard Tindall* ***(G-11233)***
**Tinex Technology Corp** ........ 630 904-5368
4759 Clearwater Ln Naperville (60564) ***(G-15830)***
**Tini Martini** ........ 773 269-2900
2169 N Milwaukee Ave Chicago (60647) ***(G-6729)***
**Tinley Ice Company** ........ 708 532-8777
450 Central Ave Ste A University Park (60484) ***(G-21064)***
**Tinney Tool & Machine Co** ........ 618 236-7273
815 N Church St Belleville (62220) ***(G-1679)***
**Tinscape LLC** ........ 630 236-7236
1050 Stockton Ct Aurora (60502) ***(G-1087)***
**Tinsley Steel Inc** ........ 618 656-5231
2 Oasis Dr Edwardsville (62025) ***(G-8817)***
**Tipps Casing Pulling Company** ........ 618 847-7986
Hc 15 Fairfield (62837) ***(G-10156)***
**Tips, Yorkville** *Also called Titan Injection Parts & Svc* ***(G-22673)***
**Tisch Granite & Marble, Belleville** *Also called Tisch Monuments Inc* ***(G-1680)***
**Tisch Monuments Inc (PA)** ........ 618 233-3017
17 N 3rd St Belleville (62220) ***(G-1680)***
**Tisco Parts, Rockford** *Also called Woods Equipment Company* ***(G-18688)***
**Tishma Engineering LLC** ........ 847 755-1200
850 Pratt Blvd Elk Grove Village (60007) ***(G-9781)***
**Tishma Technologies, Schaumburg** *Also called Nortech Packaging LLC* ***(G-19668)***
**Tison & Hall Concrete Products** ........ 618 253-7808
210 N Commercial St Harrisburg (62946) ***(G-11605)***
**Titan Industries Inc** ........ 309 440-1010
100 Prspect Dr Deer Crk Deer Creek Deer Creek (61733) ***(G-7966)***
**Titan Injection Parts & Svc** ........ 630 882-8455
204 Beaver St Ste A Yorkville (60560) ***(G-22673)***
**Titan International Inc** ........ 217 221-4498
2701 Spruce St Quincy (62301) ***(G-17895)***
**Titan International Inc (PA)** ........ 217 228-6011
2701 Spruce St Quincy (62301) ***(G-17896)***
**Titan Metals Inc** ........ 630 752-9700
180 W Lake Dr Glendale Heights (60139) ***(G-11085)***
**Titan Steel Corporation** ........ 815 726-4900
2201 W Haven Ave New Lenox (60451) ***(G-15920)***
**Titan Tire Corporation** ........ 217 228-6011
2701 Spruce St Quincy (62301) ***(G-17897)***
**Titan Tool Company Inc** ........ 847 671-0045
10001 Pacific Ave Franklin Park (60131) ***(G-10607)***
**Titan Tool Works LLC** ........ 630 221-1080
615 Kimberly Dr Carol Stream (60188) ***(G-3255)***
**Titan Tyre Corporation** ........ 217 228-6011
3769 Us Highway 20 E Freeport (61032) ***(G-10692)***
**Titan US LLC** ........ 331 212-5953
1585 Beverly Ct Ste 112 Aurora (60502) ***(G-1088)***
**Titan Wheel Corp Illinois** ........ 217 228-6023
2701 Spruce St Quincy (62301) ***(G-17898)***
**Titanium Insulation Inc** ........ 708 932-5927
14533 Turner Ave Midlothian (60445) ***(G-14770)***
**Titanium Ventures Group LLC** ........ 312 375-3526
329 W Evergreen Ave Chicago (60610) ***(G-6730)***
**Titus Enterprises LLC** ........ 773 441-7222
2s766 Winchester Cir W Warrenville (60555) ***(G-21364)***
**Tj Tool Inc** ........ 630 543-3595
1212 W National Ave Addison (60101) ***(G-315)***
**Tj Wire Forming Inc** ........ 630 628-9209
824 S Kay Ave Addison (60101) ***(G-316)***
**Tja Health LLC**
2501-2505 Reeves Rd Joliet (60436) ***(G-12582)***
**Tjmj Inc** ........ 312 315-7780
1 S Dearborn St Ste 2100 Chicago (60603) ***(G-6731)***
**Tkg Sweeping & Services LLC** ........ 847 505-1400
345 N Lakewood Ave Waukegan (60085) ***(G-21628)***
**Tkk USA Inc (HQ)** ........ 847 439-7821
2550 Golf Rd Ste 800 Rolling Meadows (60008) ***(G-18783)***
**Tks Control Systems Inc** ........ 630 554-3020
88 Templeton Dr Oswego (60543) ***(G-16937)***
**TKT Enterprises Inc (PA)** ........ 630 307-9355
95 Chancellor Dr Roselle (60172) ***(G-18983)***
**TLC Industries, Schaumburg** *Also called Tender Loving Care Inds Inc* ***(G-19759)***
**Tlk Industries Inc** ........ 847 359-3200
130 Prairie Lake Rd Ste A East Dundee (60118) ***(G-8659)***
**Tlk Tool & Stamping Inc** ........ 224 293-6941
130 Prairie Lake Rd Ste C East Dundee (60118) ***(G-8660)***
**Tlm Enterprises Inc** ........ 815 284-5040
213 W 1st St Dixon (61021) ***(G-8356)***
**Tls Windsled Inc** ........ 815 262-5791
507 W 10th St Belvidere (61008) ***(G-1789)***
**Tm Autoworks** ........ 630 766-8250
480 Industrial Dr Bensenville (60106) ***(G-2003)***
**Tmb Industries Inc (PA)** ........ 312 280-2565
980 N Michigan Ave # 11400 Chicago (60611) ***(G-6732)***
**Tmb Publishing Inc** ........ 847 564-1127
6201 W Howard St Ste 201 Niles (60714) ***(G-16043)***
**Tmf Plastic Solutions LLC** ........ 630 552-7575
12127b Galena Rd Plano (60545) ***(G-17677)***
**Tmf Polymer Solutions Inc** ........ 630 552-7575
12127b Galena Rd Plano (60545) ***(G-17678)***
**Tmf Polymer Solutions Inc (PA)** ........ 541 479-7484
12127b Galena Rd Plano (60545) ***(G-17679)***
**TMI, Norridge** *Also called Transformer Manufacturers Inc* ***(G-16110)***
**TMI, Fairbury** *Also called Technical Metals Inc* ***(G-10133)***
**TMJ Architectural LLC** ........ 815 388-7820
430 Everett Ave Crystal Lake (60014) ***(G-7666)***
**Tmk Ipsco** ........ 630 874-0078
2650 Warrenville Rd # 700 Downers Grove (60515) ***(G-8533)***
**Tml Inc** ........ 847 382-1550
223 W Main St Barrington (60010) ***(G-1308)***
**Tms International LLC** ........ 618 451-7840
22nd & Edwardsville Rd Granite City (62040) ***(G-11307)***
**Tms International LLC** ........ 815 939-9460
1 Nucor Way Bourbonnais (60914) ***(G-2408)***
**Tms Manufacturing Co** ........ 847 353-8000
3555 W 123rd St Alsip (60803) ***(G-535)***
**Tms Mfg / Wc Richards Co, Alsip** *Also called Tms Manufacturing Co* ***(G-535)***
**Tmw Enterprises Paving & Maint** ........ 630 350-7717
179 George St Bensenville (60106) ***(G-2004)***
**Tmz Metal Fabricating Inc** ........ 815 230-3071
23807 W Andrew Rd Unit C Plainfield (60585) ***(G-17658)***
**Tne McDonough Democrat Inc** ........ 309 837-3343
833 N Lafayette St Macomb (61455) ***(G-14133)***
**Tni Packaging Inc** ........ 630 293-3030
333 Charles Ct Ste 101 West Chicago (60185) ***(G-21781)***
**Tnp Machinery Co Inc** ........ 708 344-7750
9860 Derby Ln Westchester (60154) ***(G-21858)***
**TNT Plastics Inc** ........ 847 895-6921
1425 Wright Blvd Schaumburg (60193) ***(G-19764)***
**Toastmaster, Elgin** *Also called Middleby Corporation* ***(G-9111)***
**Toby Small Engine Repair** ........ 708 699-6021
22704 Millard Ave Richton Park (60471) ***(G-17980)***
**Toco** ........ 618 257-8626
825 W Main St Belleville (62220) ***(G-1681)***
**Today Gourmet Foods III LLC** ........ 847 401-9192
1087 Country Glen Ln Carol Stream (60188) ***(G-3256)***
**Todays Advantage Inc** ........ 618 463-0612
192 Alton Square Mall Dr A Alton (62002) ***(G-593)***
**Todays Temptations Inc** ........ 773 385-5355
1900 N Austin Ave Ste 72 Chicago (60639) ***(G-6733)***
**Todd Scanlan** ........ 217 585-1717
3112 Normandy Rd Springfield (62703) ***(G-20545)***
**Toffee Time** ........ 309 788-2466
2510 22 1/2 Ave Rock Island (61201) ***(G-18208)***
**Toggle Inc (PA)** ........ 323 882-6339
2004 Wattles Dr Chicago (60614) ***(G-6734)***
**Togo Packing Co Inc** ........ 800 575-3365
2125 Rochester Rd Montgomery (60538) ***(G-15067)***
**Toho Technology Inc** ........ 773 583-7183
4809 N Ravenswood Ave Chicago (60640) ***(G-6735)***
**Tolar Group LLC** ........ 847 668-9485
641 S Humphrey Ave Oak Park (60304) ***(G-16689)***
**Toledo Democrat** ........ 217 849-2000
116 Court House Sq Toledo (62468) ***(G-20967)***
**Toledo Machine & Welding Inc** ........ 217 849-2251
607 E Illinois Rt 121 Toledo (62468) ***(G-20968)***
**Toledo Screw Machine Products** ........ 815 877-8213
5257 Northrock Dr Rockford (61103) ***(G-18652)***
**Tolerance Manufacturing Inc** ........ 847 244-8836
1435 10th St Waukegan (60085) ***(G-21629)***
**Tolerances Grinding Co Inc** ........ 630 543-6066
1020 W National Ave Addison (60101) ***(G-317)***
**Tom Crown Mute Co** ........ 708 352-1039
130 N La Grange Rd # 315 La Grange (60525) ***(G-12747)***
**Tom McCowan Enterprises Inc** ........ 217 369-9352
1004 E Pennsylvania Ave Urbana (61801) ***(G-21103)***
**Tom Tom Tamales & Baking Co, Chicago** *Also called Tom Tom Tamales Mfg Co Inc* ***(G-6736)***
**Tom Tom Tamales Mfg Co Inc** ........ 773 523-5675
4750 S Washtenaw Ave Chicago (60632) ***(G-6736)***
**Tom Zosel Associates Ltd** ........ 847 540-6543
3880 Salem Lake Dr Ste B Long Grove (60047) ***(G-13903)***
**Tomantron Inc** ........ 708 532-2456
17942 66th Ave Tinley Park (60477) ***(G-20950)***
**Tomco Die & Kellering Co** ........ 847 678-8113
10025 Franklin Ave Franklin Park (60131) ***(G-10608)***
**Tomcyndi Inc** ........ 773 847-5400
822 W Exchange Ave Chicago (60609) ***(G-6737)***
**Tomek Iron Originals** ........ 773 788-1750
6059 S Oak Park Ave Chicago (60638) ***(G-6738)***
**Tomen America Inc** ........ 847 439-8500
25 Nw Point Boulev Ste 490 Elk Grove Village (60007) ***(G-9782)***
**Tomenson Machine Works Inc** ........ 630 377-7670
1150 Powis Rd West Chicago (60185) ***(G-21782)***
**Tomermo Inc** ........ 815 229-5077
5127 28th Ave Rockford (61109) ***(G-18653)***
**Tomko Machine Works Inc** ........ 630 244-0902
20w067 Pleasantdale Dr Lemont (60439) ***(G-13266)***

**Tommy Ho Jewelers** 312 368-8593
5 S Wabash Ave Ste 1503 Chicago (60603) ***(G-6739)***
**Tommy Rock, Bloomingdale** *Also called Artistries By Tommy Musto Inc* ***(G-2094)***
**Tompkins Aluminum Foundry Inc** 815 438-5578
23876 Prophet Rd Rock Falls (61071) ***(G-18154)***
**Toms Signs** 630 377-8525
6n592 Il Route 25 Saint Charles (60174) ***(G-19284)***
**Tomson Railings, Mokena** *Also called Tomsons Products Inc* ***(G-14912)***
**Tomsons Products Inc** 708 479-7030
18800 Wolf Rd Mokena (60448) ***(G-14912)***
**Tondinis Wrecker Service** 618 997-9884
2200 S Court St Marion (62959) ***(G-14292)***
**Tone Products Inc** 708 681-3660
2129 N 15th Ave Melrose Park (60160) ***(G-14702)***
**Toner Tech Plus** 815 625-7006
1304 Lincoln St Rock Falls (61071) ***(G-18155)***
**Tonerhead Inc** 815 331-3200
3106 N Us Highway 12 Spring Grove (60081) ***(G-20369)***
**Tonica News** 815 442-8419
242 S Lasalle St Tonica (61370) ***(G-20975)***
**Tonjon Company** 630 208-1173
1450 Meadows Rd Geneva (60134) ***(G-10873)***
**Tony Patterson** 773 487-4000
623 E 89th St Chicago (60619) ***(G-6740)***
**Tony Weishaar** 217 774-2774
Hwy 16 One 16th Mile E Shelbyville (62565) ***(G-19917)***
**Tony's Welding & Repair Svc, Shelbyville** *Also called Tony Weishaar* ***(G-19917)***
**Tonys Bakery** 847 599-1590
1117 Washington St Waukegan (60085) ***(G-21630)***
**Tonys Welding Service Inc** 618 532-9353
624 N Elm St Centralia (62801) ***(G-3436)***
**Tool & Die, Elk Grove Village** *Also called Lauber Tool Co Inc* ***(G-9587)***
**Tool Automation Enterprises** 708 799-6847
1516 175th St Ste A East Hazel Crest (60429) ***(G-8666)***
**Tool Engrg Consulting Mfg LLC** 815 316-2304
2932 Eastrock Dr Rockford (61109) ***(G-18654)***
**Tool Rite Industries Inc** 630 406-6161
570 S River St Batavia (60510) ***(G-1508)***
**Tool World, Arthur** *Also called Doerock Inc* ***(G-895)***
**Tool-Masters Tool & Stamp Inc** 815 465-6830
204 N Stanley St Grant Park (60940) ***(G-11316)***
**Toolex Corporation** 630 458-0001
1204 W Capitol Dr Addison (60101) ***(G-318)***
**Tooling Solutions Inc** 847 472-9940
1515 Commerce Dr Elgin (60123) ***(G-9212)***
**Toolmasters LLC (PA)** 815 968-0961
1204 Milford Ave Rockford (61109) ***(G-18655)***
**Toolmasters LLC** 815 645-2224
206 S Walnut St Stillman Valley (61084) ***(G-20629)***
**Tools Aviation LLC** 630 377-7260
3850 Swenson Ave Saint Charles (60174) ***(G-19285)***
**Toolweld Inc** 847 854-8013
1750 Cumberland Pkwy # 8 Algonquin (60102) ***(G-407)***
**Tootsie Roll Company Inc** 773 838-3400
7401 S Cicero Ave Chicago (60629) ***(G-6741)***
**Tootsie Roll Industries, Chicago** *Also called Tri International Co* ***(G-6769)***
**Tootsie Roll Industries Inc (PA)** 773 838-3400
7401 S Cicero Ave Chicago (60629) ***(G-6742)***
**Tootsie Roll Industries LLC (HQ)** 773 245-4202
7401 S Cicero Ave Chicago (60629) ***(G-6743)***
**Top Ace Inc** 847 581-0550
8440 Callie Ave Unit 612 Morton Grove (60053) ***(G-15241)***
**Top Block & Brick Inc** 815 747-3159
84 N Frentress Lake Rd East Dubuque (61025) ***(G-8626)***
**Top Dollar Slots** 779 210-4884
6590 N Alpine Rd Loves Park (61111) ***(G-14002)***
**Top Gallant Inc** 847 981-5521
648 Dauphine Ct Unit E Elk Grove Village (60007) ***(G-9783)***
**Top Hat Company Inc (PA)** 847 256-6565
2407 Birchwood Ln Wilmette (60091) ***(G-22267)***
**Top Metal Buyers Inc (PA)** 314 421-2721
808 Walnut Ave East Saint Louis (62201) ***(G-8773)***
**Top Metal Recycling, East Saint Louis** *Also called Top Metal Buyers Inc* ***(G-8773)***
**Top Notch Silk Screening** 773 847-6335
3382 S Archer Ave Chicago (60608) ***(G-6744)***
**Top Notch Tool & Supply Inc** 815 633-6295
3175 Tuggle Dr Cherry Valley (61016) ***(G-3648)***
**Top Shelf Quilts Inc** 815 806-1694
10 Elwood St Frankfort (60423) ***(G-10370)***
**Top Tobacco LP (PA)** 847 832-9700
2301 Ravine Way Glenview (60025) ***(G-11210)***
**Topiarius** 773 475-7784
2950 W Carroll Ave Ste 2 Chicago (60612) ***(G-6745)***
**Topilonio, Collinsville** *Also called Alao Temitope* ***(G-7313)***
**Toppert Jetting Service Inc (PA)** 309 755-2240
510 Main St Hillsdale (61257) ***(G-11904)***
**Tops By Dieter, Woodridge** *Also called Dieter Construction Inc* ***(G-22470)***
**Topvox Corporation** 847 842-0900
600 Hart Rd Ste 260 Barrington (60010) ***(G-1309)***
**Topweb LLC** 773 975-0400
5450 N Northwest Hwy Chicago (60630) ***(G-6746)***
**Topy Precision Mfg Inc (HQ)** 847 228-5902
1375 Lunt Ave Elk Grove Village (60007) ***(G-9784)***
**Topz Dairy Products Co** 815 726-5700
505 Bennett Ave Joliet (60433) ***(G-12583)***
**Tora Print Svcs** 773 252-1000
1500 N Greenview Ave Chicago (60642) ***(G-6747)***
**Torblo Inc** 815 941-2684
7075 Lisbon Rd Morris (60450) ***(G-15135)***
**Torgo Inc** 800 360-5910
2033 Milwaukee Ave # 352 Riverwoods (60015) ***(G-18045)***
**Tornado Industries LLC** 817 551-6507
333 Charles Ct Ste 109 West Chicago (60185) ***(G-21783)***
**Tornos Technologies US Corp (PA)** 630 812-2040
840 Parkview Blvd Lombard (60148) ***(G-13869)***
**Torqeedo Inc** 815 444-8806
171 Erick St Ste A1 Crystal Lake (60014) ***(G-7667)***
**Torque-Traction Integration** 815 759-7388
2001 Eastwood Dr Sterling (61081) ***(G-20617)***
**Torrence Machine & Tool Co** 815 469-1850
18830 82nd Ave Mokena (60448) ***(G-14913)***
**Torstenson Glass Co (PA)** 773 525-0435
3233 N Sheffield Ave Chicago (60657) ***(G-6748)***
**Tortilleria Atotonilco Inc** 773 523-0800
1850 W 47th St Chicago (60609) ***(G-6749)***
**Tortilleria Industries, Chicago** *Also called El Popocatapetl Industries Inc* ***(G-4710)***
**Tortilleria La Mexicana, Chicago** *Also called La Mexicana Tortilleria Inc* ***(G-5425)***
**Tortilleria Laf Marias LLC** 224 399-9902
922 Washington St Waukegan (60085) ***(G-21631)***
**Toshiba America Electronic** 847 484-2400
2150 E Lake Cook Rd Buffalo Grove (60089) ***(G-2782)***
**Toshware Inc** 217 896-2437
111 E Lafayette St Monticello (61856) ***(G-15087)***
**Total Control Sports Inc** 708 486-5800
2000 S 25th Ave Ste C Broadview (60155) ***(G-2617)***
**Total Conveyor Services Inc** 630 860-2471
208 Pamela Dr Bensenville (60106) ***(G-2005)***
**Total Design Fashion Jewelry, Highland Park** *Also called Total Design Jewelry Inc* ***(G-11878)***
**Total Design Jewelry Inc** 847 433-5333
3100 Skokie Valley Rd 1n Highland Park (60035) ***(G-11878)***
**Total Engineered Products Inc** 630 543-9006
908 S Westwood Ave Addison (60101) ***(G-319)***
**Total Graphics Services Inc** 847 675-0800
8343 Niles Center Rd Skokie (60077) ***(G-20101)***
**Total Look** 847 382-6646
101 Lions Dr Ste 114 Barrington (60010) ***(G-1310)***
**Total Plastics Inc** 847 593-5000
505 Busse Rd Elk Grove Village (60007) ***(G-9785)***
**Total Printing Systems, Newton** *Also called TPS Enterprises Inc* ***(G-15950)***
**Total Titanium Inc** 618 473-2429
281 Kennedy Dr Red Bud (62278) ***(G-17950)***
**Total Tooling Technology Inc** 847 437-5135
1475 Elmhurst Rd Elk Grove Village (60007) ***(G-9786)***
**Totalworks Inc** 773 489-4313
2240 N Elston Ave Chicago (60614) ***(G-6750)***
**Toth Automotive** 708 474-5137
1621 Thornton Lansing Rd Lansing (60438) ***(G-13190)***
**Touch Quest, Rosemont** *Also called Digital Minds Inc* ***(G-18998)***
**Touchpointcare LLC** 866 713-6590
215 E Park Ave Ste D Libertyville (60048) ***(G-13391)***
**Touchsensor Technologies LLC** 630 221-9000
203 N Gables Blvd Wheaton (60187) ***(G-21987)***
**Touchtunes Music Corporation** 847 253-8708
450 Remington Rd Schaumburg (60173) ***(G-19765)***
**Tough Electric Inc** 630 236-8332
717 Jackson St Aurora (60505) ***(G-1226)***
**Touhy Diagnostic At Home LLC** 847 803-1111
1293 Rand Rd Des Plaines (60016) ***(G-8287)***
**Tour Industries Inc (PA)** 847 854-9400
1188 Starwood Pass Lake In The Hills (60156) ***(G-13008)***
**Tower Automotive Operations I** 773 646-6550
12350 S Avenue O Chicago (60633) ***(G-6751)***
**Tower Metal Products LP (PA)** 847 806-7200
1965 Pratt Blvd Elk Grove Village (60007) ***(G-9787)***
**Tower Oil & Technology Co** 773 927-6161
4300 S Tripp Ave Chicago (60632) ***(G-6752)***
**Tower Plastics Mfg Inc** 847 788-1700
181 Shore Ct Ste 2 Burr Ridge (60527) ***(G-2885)***
**Tower Printing & Design** 630 495-1976
2211 S Highland Ave 5a Lombard (60148) ***(G-13870)***
**Tower Rock Stone Company (PA)** 618 281-4106
250 W Sand Bank Rd Columbia (62236) ***(G-7364)***
**Tower Tool & Engineering Inc** 815 654-1115
11052 Raleigh Ct Machesney Park (61115) ***(G-14112)***
**Tower Works Inc** 630 557-2221
47w543 Perry Rd Maple Park (60151) ***(G-14204)***
**Towerleaf LLC** 847 985-1937
1680 Wright Blvd Schaumburg (60193) ***(G-19766)***
**Towers Holdings, Northfield** *Also called Towers Media Holdings Inc* ***(G-16421)***

**Towers Media Holdings Inc** 312 993-1550
1 Northfield Plz Ste 300 Northfield (60093) *(G-16421)*
**Town Hall Archery, Belleville** *Also called Town Hall Sports Inc (G-1682)*
**Town Hall Sports Inc** 618 235-9881
5901 Cool Sports Rd Belleville (62223) *(G-1682)*
**Town Square Publications LLC** 847 427-4633
155 E Arlington Hts Rd Arlington Heights (60005) *(G-856)*
**Towne Machine Tool Company** 217 442-4910
407 S College St Danville (61832) *(G-7777)*
**Townley Engrg & Mfg Co Inc** 618 273-8271
607 Sutton Rd Eldorado (62930) *(G-8924)*
**Towntees, Wheaton** *Also called Kmf Enterprises Inc (G-21961)*
**Tox- Pressotechnik LLC** 630 447-4600
4250 Weaver Pkwy Warrenville (60555) *(G-21365)*
**Toyal America Inc** 630 505-2160
1717 N Naper Blvd Ste 201 Naperville (60563) *(G-15766)*
**Toyal America Inc (HQ)** 815 740-3000
17401 Broadway St Lockport (60441) *(G-13749)*
**Toyo Ink International Corp** 630 930-5100
710 W Belden Ave Ste B Addison (60101) *(G-320)*
**Toyo Ink International Corp (HQ)** 866 969-8696
1225 N Michael Dr Wood Dale (60191) *(G-22432)*
**Toyo Pump North America** 815 806-1414
1520 Monarch Ave New Lenox (60451) *(G-15921)*
**Toyo USA Manufacturing Inc** 309 827-8836
818 Avalon Way Bloomington (61705) *(G-2232)*
**Toyo-Precision USA Mfg Inc, Bloomington** *Also called Toyo USA Manufacturing Inc (G-2232)*
**Toyoda Machinery USA Corp, Arlington Heights** *Also called Jtekt Toyoda Americas Corp (G-786)*
**Toyota Boshoku Illinois LLC** 618 943-5300
100 Trim Masters Dr Lawrenceville (62439) *(G-13205)*
**TPC Metals LLC (PA)** 330 479-9510
7000 S Adams St Willowbrook (60527) *(G-22234)*
**Tpf Liquidation Co** 847 362-0028
28160 Keith Rd Lake Forest (60045) *(G-12971)*
**Tpr America Inc** 847 446-5336
10 N Martingale Rd Schaumburg (60173) *(G-19767)*
**TPS Enterprises Inc** 618 783-2978
201 S Gregory Dr Newton (62448) *(G-15950)*
**Tra-Doc Communications, Rockford** *Also called T D C Inc (G-18639)*
**Trac Equipment Company Inc** 309 647-5066
12 Enterprise Dr Canton (61520) *(G-2993)*
**Track Master Inc** 815 675-6603
7451 Spring Grove Rd Spring Grove (60081) *(G-20370)*
**Track My Foreclosures LLC** 877 782-8187
107 N State St Ste 1 Monticello (61856) *(G-15088)*
**Traco Industries Inc** 815 675-6603
7451 Spring Grove Rd A Spring Grove (60081) *(G-20371)*
**Tracoinsa USA** 309 287-7046
108 S Center St Gridley (61744) *(G-11411)*
**Tractronics** 630 527-0000
1212 S Naper Blvd Naperville (60540) *(G-15767)*
**Tracy Electric Inc** 618 943-6205
1308 Jefferson St Lawrenceville (62439) *(G-13206)*
**Trade Industries** 618 643-4321
Rr 5 Mc Leansboro (62859) *(G-14469)*
**Trade Label & Decal (PA)** 630 773-0447
1285 Hamilton Pkwy Itasca (60143) *(G-12367)*
**Trade Print, Chicago** *Also called Print Rite Inc (G-6189)*
**Trade-Mark Coffee Corporation (PA)** 847 382-4200
8 Lakeside Ln North Barrington (60010) *(G-16155)*
**Trademark Cabinet Corporation** 847 478-9393
101 Schelter Rd Ste 201b Lincolnshire (60069) *(G-13486)*
**Trademark Products, Elk Grove Village** *Also called S and S Associates Inc (G-9722)*
**Tradevolve Inc** 847 987-9411
4211 Alex Ln Crystal Lake (60014) *(G-7668)*
**Tradin Post Newspaper, Peoria** *Also called Peoria Post Inc (G-17426)*
**Trading Square Company Inc** 630 960-0606
6434 S Cass Ave Westmont (60559) *(G-21925)*
**Tradingscreen Inc** 312 447-0100
566 W Adams St Ste 350 Chicago (60661) *(G-6753)*
**Traeyne Corporation** 309 936-7878
17982 E 2350th St Atkinson (61235) *(G-945)*
**Traffco Products LLC** 773 374-6645
7731 S South Chicago Ave Chicago (60619) *(G-6754)*
**Traffic Control & Protection** 630 293-0026
31w 351 N Ave West Chicago (60185) *(G-21784)*
**Traffic Sign Store, The, Bloomington** *Also called Road Ready Signs (G-2219)*
**Trafficcom (HQ)** 773 997-8351
425 W Randolph St Chicago (60606) *(G-6755)*
**Trafficguard Direct LLC** 815 899-8471
1730 Afton Rd Sycamore (60178) *(G-20820)*
**Trailers Inc** 217 472-6000
1839 Saint Pauls Ch Rd Chapin (62628) *(G-3588)*
**Trailers Machine & Welding, Chapin** *Also called Trailers Inc (G-3588)*
**Tramac, Buffalo Grove** *Also called Maclean Fastener Services LLC (G-2729)*
**Tramco Pump Co** 312 243-5800
1500 W Adams St Chicago (60607) *(G-6756)*
**Tramec Hill Fastener, Rock Falls** *Also called Hill Holdings Inc (G-18135)*
**Trane US Inc** 309 691-4224
8718 N University St Peoria (61615) *(G-17470)*
**Trane US Inc** 708 532-8004
18452 West Creek Dr Tinley Park (60477) *(G-20951)*
**Trans-Astro, South Beloit** *Also called McCleary Inc (G-20160)*
**Transagra International Inc (PA)** 312 856-1010
155 N Michigan Ave # 720 Chicago (60601) *(G-6757)*
**Transcedar Limited** 618 262-4153
916 Empire St Mount Carmel (62863) *(G-15284)*
**Transcend Corp** 847 395-6630
90 Mcmillen Rd Antioch (60002) *(G-658)*
**Transcendia Inc (PA)** 847 678-1800
9201 Belmont Ave Franklin Park (60131) *(G-10609)*
**Transcendia Inc** 847 678-1800
9201 Belmont Ave Ste 100a Franklin Park (60131) *(G-10610)*
**Transco Products Inc** 815 672-2197
1215 E 12th St Streator (61364) *(G-20709)*
**Transco Products Inc (HQ)** 312 427-2818
200 N La Salle St # 1550 Chicago (60601) *(G-6758)*
**Transco Railway Products Inc (HQ)** 312 427-2818
200 N La Salle St # 1550 Chicago (60601) *(G-6759)*
**Transco Railway Products Inc** 419 562-1031
200 N La Salle St # 1550 Chicago (60601) *(G-6760)*
**Transcontinental Cold Storage, Hillsdale** *Also called Tyson Fresh Meats Inc (G-11906)*
**Transfer Logistics Inc** 773 646-0529
11600 S Burley Ave Chicago (60617) *(G-6761)*
**Transformer Manufacturers Inc** 708 457-1200
7051 W Wilson Ave Norridge (60706) *(G-16110)*
**Transilwrap Company Inc** 847 678-1800
9201 Belmont Ave Ste 100a Franklin Park (60131) *(G-10611)*
**Translogic Corporation** 847 392-3700
1951 Rohlwing Rd Ste C Rolling Meadows (60008) *(G-18784)*
**Translucent Publishing Corp** 312 447-5450
222 W Ontario St Ste 410 Chicago (60654) *(G-6762)*
**Transpac USA** 847 605-1616
1515 E Wdfield Rd Ste 340 Schaumburg (60173) *(G-19768)*
**Transparent Container Co Inc (PA)** 708 449-8520
325 S Lombard Rd Addison (60101) *(G-321)*
**Transparent Container Co Inc** 630 543-1818
1110 W National Ave Addison (60101) *(G-322)*
**Transparent Container Co Inc** 708 449-8520
325 S Lombard Rd Addison (60101) *(G-323)*
**Transparent Container Co Inc** 630 860-2666
625 Thomas Dr Bensenville (60106) *(G-2006)*
**Transportation Eqp Advisors** 847 318-7575
6250 N River Rd Ste 5000 Rosemont (60018) *(G-19037)*
**Transportation Illinois Dept** 217 785-0288
701 N Macarthur Blvd Springfield (62702) *(G-20546)*
**Transportation Tech Industires, Rockford** *Also called Gunite Corporation (G-18408)*
**Transworld Plastic Films Inc** 815 561-7117
150 N 15th St Rochelle (61068) *(G-18112)*
**Tranter Phe Inc** 217 227-3470
30241 W Frontage Rd Farmersville (62533) *(G-10184)*
**Traube Canvas Products Inc** 618 281-0696
1727 Bluffview Dr Dupo (62239) *(G-8581)*
**Travel Caddy Inc** 847 621-7000
700 Touhy Ave Elk Grove Village (60007) *(G-9788)*
**Travel Hammock Inc** 847 486-0005
8136 Monticello Ave Skokie (60076) *(G-20102)*
**Traveler Printing, Peoria** *Also called Elise S Allen (G-17354)*
**Travelon, Elk Grove Village** *Also called Travel Caddy Inc (G-9788)*
**Traxco Inc** 847 669-1545
11416 Kiley Dr Huntley (60142) *(G-12180)*
**TRC Environmental Corp** 630 953-9046
7521 Brush Hill Dr Burr Ridge (60527) *(G-2886)*
**Trd Manufacturing Inc** 815 654-7775
10914 N 2nd St Machesney Park (61115) *(G-14113)*
**Treasure Island Foods Inc** 312 440-1144
75 W Elm St Chicago (60610) *(G-6763)*
**Treasure Island Foods Inc** 773 880-8880
2121 N Clybourn Ave # 9 Chicago (60614) *(G-6764)*
**Treasure Island Foods Inc** 312 642-1105
1639 N Wells St Chicago (60614) *(G-6765)*
**Treasure Keeper Inc** 630 761-1500
1355 Paramount Pkwy Batavia (60510) *(G-1509)*
**Treasure Keeper X, Batavia** *Also called Treasure Keeper Inc (G-1509)*
**Treated Water Outsourcing, Naperville** *Also called Nalco Company LLC (G-15705)*
**Treatment Products Ltd** 773 626-8888
4701 W Augusta Blvd Chicago (60651) *(G-6766)*
**Trebor Enterprises Ltd** 815 235-1700
927 W Stephenson St Freeport (61032) *(G-10693)*
**Trebor Sales Corporation (PA)** 630 434-0040
2021 Midwest Rd Ste 307 Oak Brook (60523) *(G-16564)*
**Tredegar Film Products Corp** 847 438-2111
351 Oakwood Rd Lake Zurich (60047) *(G-13138)*

**Tree Towns Reprographics Inc** ... 630 832-0209
1041 S Il Route 83 Elmhurst (60126) *(G-9951)*
**Tree-O Lumber Inc** ... 618 357-2576
5492 Woodhaven Rd Pinckneyville (62274) *(G-17553)*
**Treehouse Foods Inc (PA)** ... 708 483-1300
2021 Spring Rd Ste 600 Oak Brook (60523) *(G-16565)*
**Treehouse Private Brands Inc** ... 630 455-5265
3250 Lacey Rd Ste 600 Downers Grove (60515) *(G-8534)*
**Treehouse Private Brands Inc** ... 815 389-2745
1450 Pate Plaza Dr South Beloit (61080) *(G-20170)*
**Treetop Marketing Inc** ... 877 249-0479
717 Main St Batavia (60510) *(G-1510)*
**Trekon Company Inc** ... 309 925-7942
115 E South St Tremont (61568) *(G-20986)*
**Trellborg Sling Sltions US Inc** ... 630 539-5500
20 N Martingale Rd # 210 Schaumburg (60173) *(G-19769)*
**Trellborg Sling Sltions US Inc** ... 630 289-1500
901 Phoenix Lake Ave Streamwood (60107) *(G-20677)*
**Trelleborg Slng Slns Strmwd, Streamwood** *Also called Trellborg Sling Sltions US Inc (G-20677)*
**Tremont Kitchen Tops Inc** ... 309 925-5736
100 N West St Tremont (61568) *(G-20987)*
**Trend Machinery Inc** ... 630 655-0030
7475 S Madison St Ste 5 Burr Ridge (60527) *(G-2887)*
**Trend Publishing Inc** ... 312 654-2300
625 N Michigan Ave # 1100 Chicago (60611) *(G-6767)*
**Trend Setters Ltd** ... 309 929-7012
22500 State Route 9 Tremont (61568) *(G-20988)*
**Trend Technologies LLC** ... 847 640-2382
737 Fargo Ave Elk Grove Village (60007) *(G-9789)*
**Trendler Inc** ... 773 284-6600
4540 W 51st St Chicago (60632) *(G-6768)*
**Trendy Screenprinting** ... 815 895-0081
155 E Maplewood Dr Sycamore (60178) *(G-20821)*
**Trenton Sun** ... 618 224-9422
15 W Broadway Trenton (62293) *(G-20998)*
**Tres Joli Designs Ltd** ... 847 520-3903
634 Wheeling Rd Wheeling (60090) *(G-22168)*
**Treudt Corporation** ... 630 293-0500
131 Fremont St West Chicago (60185) *(G-21785)*
**Tri City Canvas Products Inc (PA)** ... 618 797-1662
3240 W Chain Of Rocks Rd A Granite City (62040) *(G-11308)*
**Tri City Sheet Metal** ... 630 232-4255
701 May St Geneva (60134) *(G-10874)*
**Tri Cnty Prgnncy Prenting Svcs** ... 847 231-4651
888 E Belvidere Rd # 124 Grayslake (60030) *(G-11364)*
**Tri County Journal, Tuscola** *Also called Tuscola Journal Incorporated (G-21026)*
**Tri County Lift Trucks Inc** ... 847 838-0183
1020 Anita Ave Antioch (60002) *(G-659)*
**Tri County Scribe, Augusta** *Also called Augusta Eagle (G-951)*
**Tri Family Oil Co (PA)** ... 618 654-1137
2103 Saint Michael Ct N Highland (62249) *(G-11813)*
**Tri Guards Inc** ... 847 537-8444
80 N Lively Blvd Elk Grove Village (60007) *(G-9790)*
**Tri Industies, Vernon Hills** *Also called Tri Industries Nfp (G-21213)*
**Tri Industries Nfp** ... 773 754-3100
780 Corporate Woods Pkwy Vernon Hills (60061) *(G-21213)*
**Tri International Co** ... 773 838-3400
7401 S Cicero Ave Chicago (60629) *(G-6769)*
**Tri Kote Inc** ... 618 262-4156
1126 W 3rd St Mount Carmel (62863) *(G-15285)*
**Tri R** ... 224 399-7786
1921 Industrial Dr Libertyville (60048) *(G-13392)*
**Tri Sect Corporation** ... 847 524-1119
717 Morse Ave Schaumburg (60193) *(G-19770)*
**Tri Star Cabinet & Top Co Inc (PA)** ... 815 485-2564
1000 S Cedar Rd New Lenox (60451) *(G-15922)*
**Tri Star Manufacturing, Schaumburg** *Also called Lynda Hervas (G-19627)*
**Tri Star Metals LLC (HQ)** ... 815 232-1600
611 W Lamm Rd Freeport (61032) *(G-10694)*
**Tri Star Plowing** ... 847 584-5070
876 Asbury Ln Schaumburg (60193) *(G-19771)*
**Tri State Acid Co Inc** ... 618 676-1111
110 Industrial Park Clay City (62824) *(G-7268)*
**Tri State Aluminum Products** ... 815 877-6081
6300 Forest Hills Rd Loves Park (61111) *(G-14003)*
**Tri State Cut Stone & Brick Co, Frankfort** *Also called Tri-State Cut Stone Co (G-10371)*
**Tri State Recycling Service** ... 708 865-9939
301 W Lake St Frnt 1 Northlake (60164) *(G-16456)*
**Tri Vantage LLC** ... 630 530-5333
957 N Oaklawn Ave Elmhurst (60126) *(G-9952)*
**Tri-Cam Inc** ... 815 226-9200
2730 Eastrock Dr Rockford (61109) *(G-18656)*
**Tri-City Gold Exchange Inc** ... 708 331-5995
470 E 147th St Harvey (60426) *(G-11678)*
**Tri-City Heat Treat Co Inc** ... 309 786-2689
2020 5th St Rock Island (61201) *(G-18209)*
**Tri-City Ready-Mix** ... 618 439-2071
302 E Bond St Benton (62812) *(G-2042)*
**Tri-City Sports Inc** ... 217 224-2489
4360 Broadway St Quincy (62305) *(G-17899)*
**Tri-Con Materials Inc (PA)** ... 815 872-3206
308 W Railroad Ave Princeton (61356) *(G-17762)*
**Tri-Cor Industries Inc** ... 618 589-9890
1035 Eastgate Dr Ste 2 O Fallon (62269) *(G-16481)*
**Tri-County Chemical Inc (PA)** ... 618 273-2071
2441 Public Rd Eldorado (62930) *(G-8925)*
**Tri-County Chemical Inc** ... 618 268-4318
20 Lebanon Rd Galatia (62935) *(G-10713)*
**Tri-County Concrete Inc** ... 815 786-2179
331 W Church St Sandwich (60548) *(G-19378)*
**Tri-Cunty Wldg Fabrication LLC** ... 217 543-3304
1031 E Columbia St Arthur (61911) *(G-923)*
**Tri-Dim Filter Corporation** ... 847 695-5822
999 Raymond St Elgin (60120) *(G-9213)*
**Tri-Lite Inc** ... 773 384-7765
1642 N Besly Ct Chicago (60642) *(G-6770)*
**Tri-Par Die and Mold Corp** ... 630 232-8800
670 Sundown Rd South Elgin (60177) *(G-20229)*
**Tri-Part Screw Products Inc** ... 815 654-7311
10739 N 2nd St Machesney Park (61115) *(G-14114)*
**Tri-Star Engineering Inc** ... 847 595-3377
2455 Pan Am Blvd Elk Grove Village (60007) *(G-9791)*
**Tri-State Alum & Vinyl Pdts, Loves Park** *Also called Tri State Aluminum Products (G-14003)*
**Tri-State Asphalt LLC** ... 815 942-0080
1362 Bungalow Rd Morris (60450) *(G-15136)*
**Tri-State Asphalt Emulsions, Elgin** *Also called Cgk Enterprises Inc (G-8985)*
**Tri-State Asphalt Emulsions, Morris** *Also called Cgk Enterprises Inc (G-15102)*
**Tri-State Cut Stone Co** ... 815 469-7550
10333 Vans Dr Frankfort (60423) *(G-10371)*
**Tri-State Food Equipment** ... 217 228-1550
1605 Chestnut St Quincy (62301) *(G-17900)*
**Tri-State Producing Developing** ... 618 393-2176
1060 W Main St Olney (62450) *(G-16798)*
**Tri-Tech Molding** ... 847 263-7769
21547 W Morton Dr Lake Villa (60046) *(G-13028)*
**Tri-Tech Sltons Consulting Inc** ... 847 941-0199
259 N Woodland Dr Mount Prospect (60056) *(G-15379)*
**Tri-Tower Printing Inc** ... 847 640-6633
1701 Golf Rd Ste L01 Rolling Meadows (60008) *(G-18785)*
**Tri-Zee Services Inc** ... 630 543-8677
415 W Belden Ave Ste A Addison (60101) *(G-324)*
**Triad Circuits Inc** ... 847 283-8600
3135 N Oak Grove Ave Waukegan (60087) *(G-21632)*
**Triad Controls Inc (PA)** ... 630 443-9343
3715 Swenson Ave Saint Charles (60174) *(G-19286)*
**Triad Cutting Tools Svc & Mfg** ... 847 352-0459
1025 Lunt Ave Ste E Schaumburg (60193) *(G-19772)*
**Triad Oil Inc** ... 815 485-9535
1613 Andrea Dr New Lenox (60451) *(G-15923)*
**Triad Trucking LLC** ... 847 833-9276
836 S Arlington Hts Rd Elk Grove Village (60007) *(G-9792)*
**Trialco Inc (PA)** ... 708 757-4200
900 E Lincoln Hwy Ste 1 Chicago Heights (60411) *(G-7132)*
**Triangle, Skokie** *Also called Expercolor Inc (G-19997)*
**Triangle Concrete Co Inc** ... 309 853-4334
1201 New St Kewanee (61443) *(G-12695)*
**Triangle Dies and Supplies Inc (PA)** ... 630 454-3200
1436 Louis Bork Dr Batavia (60510) *(G-1511)*
**Triangle Engineered Products, Bensenville** *Also called Standard Car Truck Company (G-1998)*
**Triangle Metals Div, Hoffman Estates** *Also called Thomas Engineering Inc (G-12065)*
**Triangle Metals Division, Rockford** *Also called Thomas Engineering Inc (G-18648)*
**Triangle Package Machinery Co (PA)** ... 773 889-0200
6655 W Diversey Ave Chicago (60707) *(G-6771)*
**Triangle Printers Inc** ... 847 675-3700
3737 Chase Ave Skokie (60076) *(G-20103)*
**Triangle Screen Print Inc** ... 847 678-9200
10353 Franklin Ave Franklin Park (60131) *(G-10612)*
**Triangle Technologies Inc** ... 630 736-3318
687 Bonded Pkwy Streamwood (60107) *(G-20678)*
**Tribeam Inc** ... 847 409-9497
1323 S Fernandez Ave Arlington Heights (60005) *(G-857)*
**Tribune Finance Service Center** ... 312 595-0783
435 N Michigan Ave Fl 2 Chicago (60611) *(G-6772)*
**Tribune Freedom Center, Chicago** *Also called Chicago Tribune Company (G-4358)*
**Tribune Media Company** ... 708 498-0584
3333 Warrenville Rd # 750 Lisle (60532) *(G-13673)*
**Tribune Publishing Company LLC (HQ)** ... 312 222-9100
435 N Michigan Ave Fl 2 Chicago (60611) *(G-6773)*
**Tribune Publishing Company LLC** ... 312 832-6711
435 N Michigan Ave Fl 2 Chicago (60611) *(G-6774)*
**Tribune Tower** ... 312 981-7200
435 N Michigan Ave Fl 2 Chicago (60611) *(G-6775)*
**Tricast/Presfore Corporation** ... 815 459-1820
169 Virginia Rd Crystal Lake (60014) *(G-7669)*
**Tricel Corporation** ... 847 336-1321
2100 Swanson Ct Gurnee (60031) *(G-11515)*

ALPHABETIC

# Trick Percussion Products Inc — ALPHABETIC SECTION

**Trick Percussion Products Inc** .......... 847 342-2019
17 E University Dr  Arlington Heights  (60004)  *(G-858)*

**Trico Belting & Supply Company** .......... 773 261-0988
5450 W Roosevelt Rd  Chicago  (60644)  *(G-6776)*

**Trico Technologies Inc** .......... 847 662-9224
209 Ambrogio Dr  Gurnee  (60031)  *(G-11516)*

**Tricon Inds Mfg & Eqp Sls** .......... 815 379-2090
28524 1250 E St  Walnut  (61376)  *(G-21331)*

**Tricor International Inc** .......... 630 629-1213
678 E Western Ave  Lombard  (60148)  *(G-13871)*

**Tricor Systems Inc** .......... 847 742-5542
1650 Todd Farm Dr  Elgin  (60123)  *(G-9214)*

**Tricounty, Antioch** *Also called Tri County Lift Trucks Inc* *(G-659)*

**Tridan International, Danville** *Also called Kaydon Acquisition Xii Inc* *(G-7740)*

**Trident Industries** .......... 847 285-1316
1900 E Golf Rd Ste L100  Schaumburg  (60173)  *(G-19773)*

**Trident Machine Co** .......... 815 968-1585
3491 N Meridian Rd  Rockford  (61101)  *(G-18657)*

**Trident Manufacturing Inc** .......... 847 464-0140
14n2 Prairie St  Pingree Grove  (60140)  *(G-17557)*

**Trident Software Corp** .......... 847 219-8777
1183 S Scoville Ave  Niles  (60714)  *(G-16044)*

**Triezenberg Millwork Co** .......... 708 489-9062
4737 138th St Ste 202  Crestwood  (60445)  *(G-7506)*

**Trifab Inc** .......... 847 838-2083
606 Longview Dr  Antioch  (60002)  *(G-660)*

**Trigon International Corp** .......... 630 978-9990
4000 Sussex Ave  Aurora  (60504)  *(G-1089)*

**Trim Suits By Show-Off Inc** .......... 630 894-0100
48 Congress Cir W  Roselle  (60172)  *(G-18984)*

**Trim-Tex Inc (PA)** .......... 847 679-3000
3700 W Pratt Ave  Lincolnwood  (60712)  *(G-13540)*

**Trimaco LLC** .......... 919 674-3476
1215 Landmeier Rd  Elk Grove Village  (60007)  *(G-9793)*

**Trimark Screen Printing Inc** .......... 630 629-2823
710 E Western Ave Ste C  Lombard  (60148)  *(G-13872)*

**Trinity Brand Industries Inc** .......... 708 482-4980
5342 East Ave  Countryside  (60525)  *(G-7447)*

**Trinity Machined Products Inc** .......... 630 876-6992
2560 White Oak Cir  Aurora  (60502)  *(G-1090)*

**Trinity Structural Towers Inc** .......... 217 935-7900
10000 Tabor Rd  Clinton  (61727)  *(G-7290)*

**Trio Foundry Inc (PA)** .......... 630 892-1676
1985 Aucutt Rd  Montgomery  (60538)  *(G-15068)*

**Trio Foundry Inc** .......... 815 786-6616
924 W Church St  Sandwich  (60548)  *(G-19379)*

**Trio Wire Products Inc** .......... 815 469-2148
141 Ontario St  Frankfort  (60423)  *(G-10372)*

**Triple B Manufacturing Co Inc** .......... 618 566-2888
620 Industrial St  Mascoutah  (62258)  *(G-14360)*

**Triple Edge Manufacturing Inc** .......... 847 468-9156
320 Production Dr  South Elgin  (60177)  *(G-20230)*

**Triple R Graphics, Mokena** *Also called Rrr Graphics & Film Corp* *(G-14901)*

**Triplett Enterprises Inc** .......... 708 333-9421
16613 Kilbourne Ave  Oak Forest  (60452)  *(G-16592)*

**Triplex Marine Ltd** .......... 815 485-0202
1110 E Haven Ave  New Lenox  (60451)  *(G-15924)*

**Triplex Sales Company Inc** .......... 847 839-8442
1143 Tower Rd  Schaumburg  (60173)  *(G-19774)*

**Tripnary LLC** .......... 512 554-1911
233 E Wacker Dr  Chicago  (60601)  *(G-6777)*

**Tripp Lite, Chicago** *Also called Trippe Manufacturing Company* *(G-6778)*

**Trippe Manufacturing Company** .......... 773 869-1111
1111 W 35th St Fl 12  Chicago  (60609)  *(G-6778)*

**Triseal Corporation** .......... 815 648-2473
11920 Price Rd  Hebron  (60034)  *(G-11728)*

**Triseal Worldwide, Hebron** *Also called Triseal Corporation* *(G-11728)*

**Trisure Closures Worldwide, Carol Stream** *Also called American Flange & Mfg Co Inc* *(G-3098)*

**Tritech International LLC** .......... 847 888-0333
1710 Todd Farm Dr  Elgin  (60123)  *(G-9215)*

**Triton Industries Inc (PA)** .......... 773 384-3700
1020 N Kolmar Ave  Chicago  (60651)  *(G-6779)*

**Triton Manufacturing Co Inc (PA)** .......... 708 587-4000
5700 W Triton Way  Monee  (60449)  *(G-15004)*

**Triumph Books Corp** .......... 312 337-0747
814 N Franklin St Fl 3  Chicago  (60610)  *(G-6780)*

**Triumph Packaging Georgia LLC** .......... 312 251-9600
736 N Western Ave Ste 352  Lake Forest  (60045)  *(G-12972)*

**Triumph Packaging Group** .......... 312 251-9600
736 N Western Ave Ste 352  Lake Forest  (60045)  *(G-12973)*

**Triumph Truss & Steel Company** .......... 815 522-6000
1250 Larkin Ave Ste 200  Elgin  (60123)  *(G-9216)*

**Triumph Twist Drill Co Inc** .......... 815 459-6250
301 Industrial Rd  Crystal Lake  (60012)  *(G-7670)*

**Trivial Development Corp** .......... 630 860-2500
1035 Hilltop Dr  Itasca  (60143)  *(G-12368)*

**Triwater Holdings LLC** .......... 847 457-1812
1915 Windridge Dr  Lake Forest  (60045)  *(G-12974)*

**Triwire Inc** .......... 815 633-7707
2201 Range Rd  Loves Park  (61111)  *(G-14004)*

**Trizetto Corporation** .......... 630 369-5300
1240 E Diehl Rd Ste 200  Naperville  (60563)  *(G-15768)*

**Trmg LLP** .......... 847 441-4122
790 W Frontage Rd Ste 416  Northfield  (60093)  *(G-16422)*

**Tro Manufacturing Company Inc** .......... 847 455-3755
2610 Edgington St  Franklin Park  (60131)  *(G-10613)*

**Trojan Oil Inc** .......... 618 754-3474
953 N 1300th St  Newton  (62448)  *(G-15951)*

**Tronc Inc (PA)** .......... 312 222-9100
435 N Michigan Ave  Chicago  (60611)  *(G-6781)*

**Tronox Incorporated** .......... 203 705-3704
2 Washington Ave  Madison  (62060)  *(G-14154)*

**Tropar Trophy Manufacturing Co** .......... 630 787-1900
839 N Central Ave  Wood Dale  (60191)  *(G-22433)*

**Trophies and Awards Plus** .......... 708 754-7127
3344 Chicago Rd Ste 3  Steger  (60475)  *(G-20578)*

**Trophies By George** .......... 630 497-1212
239 Cedarfield Dr  Bartlett  (60103)  *(G-1381)*

**Trophytime Inc** .......... 217 351-7958
223 S Locust St  Champaign  (61820)  *(G-3550)*

**Trotters Manufacturing Inc** .......... 217 364-4540
101 S West St  Buffalo  (62515)  *(G-2649)*

**Trottie Publishing Group Inc** .......... 708 344-5975
9930 Derby Ln Ste 102  Westchester  (60154)  *(G-21859)*

**Trouw Nutrition Usa LLC** .......... 618 651-1521
145 Matter Dr  Highland  (62249)  *(G-11814)*

**Trouw Nutrition Usa LLC (HQ)** .......... 618 654-2070
115 Executive Dr  Highland  (62249)  *(G-11815)*

**Trouw Nutrition Usa LLC** .......... 618 654-2070
1 Ultraway Dr  Highland  (62249)  *(G-11816)*

**Trouw Nutrition Usa LLC** .......... 618 654-2070
145 Matter Dr  Highland  (62249)  *(G-11817)*

**Troxel Industries Inc** .......... 217 431-8674
580 N J St  Tilton  (61833)  *(G-20883)*

**Troy Design & Manufacturing Co** .......... 773 646-0804
12359 S Burley Ave  Chicago  (60633)  *(G-6782)*

**Trp, Elgin** *Also called Thomas Research Products LLC* *(G-9211)*

**Trp Acquisition Corp (PA)** .......... 630 261-2380
1000 N Rohlwing Rd Ste 46  Lombard  (60148)  *(G-13873)*

**Tru Coat Plating and Finishing** .......... 708 544-3940
130 Mannheim Rd  Bellwood  (60104)  *(G-1725)*

**Tru Fragrance & Beauty LLC** .......... 630 563-4110
7725 S Quincy St  Willowbrook  (60527)  *(G-22235)*

**Tru Serv Corp** .......... 773 695-5674
8600 W Bryn Mawr Ave  Chicago  (60631)  *(G-6783)*

**Tru Vue Inc (HQ)** .......... 708 485-5080
9400 W 55th St  Countryside  (60525)  *(G-7448)*

**Tru-Colour Products LLC** .......... 630 447-0559
27575 Ferry Rd Fl 2  Warrenville  (60555)  *(G-21366)*

**Tru-Cut Inc** .......... 847 639-2090
231 Jandus Rd  Cary  (60013)  *(G-3377)*

**Tru-Cut Machine Incorporated** .......... 815 422-5047
480 S Oak St  Saint Anne  (60964)  *(G-19127)*

**Tru-Cut Production Inc** .......... 815 335-2215
211 W Main St  Winnebago  (61088)  *(G-22298)*

**Tru-Cut Tool & Supply Co** .......... 708 396-1122
1480 S Wolf Rd  Wheeling  (60090)  *(G-22169)*

**Tru-Guard Manufacturing Co** .......... 773 568-5264
10733 S Michigan Ave  Chicago  (60628)  *(G-6784)*

**Tru-Machine Co Inc** .......... 815 675-6735
7502 Mayo Ct Unit 3  Spring Grove  (60081)  *(G-20372)*

**Tru-Native Enterprises** .......... 630 409-3258
50 W Commercial Ave  Addison  (60101)  *(G-325)*

**Tru-Native Enterprises** .......... 630 409-3258
50 W Commercial Ave  Addison  (60101)  *(G-326)*

**Tru-Native N'Genuity, Addison** *Also called Tru-Native Enterprises* *(G-325)*

**Tru-Native N'Genuity, Addison** *Also called Tru-Native Enterprises* *(G-326)*

**Tru-Tone Finishing Inc (PA)** .......... 630 543-5520
128 S Lombard Rd  Addison  (60101)  *(G-327)*

**Tru-Vu Monitors Inc** .......... 847 259-2344
925 E Rand Rd Ste 200  Arlington Heights  (60004)  *(G-859)*

**Tru-Way Inc** .......... 708 562-3690
36 W Lake St  Northlake  (60164)  *(G-16457)*

**Truckers Oil Pros Inc** .......... 773 523-8990
2756 W 35th St  Chicago  (60632)  *(G-6785)*

**Trucut, Cary** *Also called Horizon Steel Treating Inc* *(G-3351)*

**Trudeau Approved Products Inc** .......... 312 924-7230
3 Grant Sq 332  Hinsdale  (60521)  *(G-11967)*

**True Dimension, Addison** *Also called Formar Inc* *(G-122)*

**True Lacrosse LLC** .......... 630 359-3857
131 Eisenhower Ln N  Lombard  (60148)  *(G-13874)*

**True Line Mold and Engrg Corp** .......... 815 648-2739
12205 Hansen Rd  Hebron  (60034)  *(G-11729)*

**True Royalty Scents** .......... 309 992-0688
2404 N Elmwood Ave  Peoria  (61604)  *(G-17471)*

**True Sun Dried Tomatoes, Manteno** *Also called Sono Italiano Corporation* *(G-14193)*

**True Value, Lebanon** *Also called Prescription Plus Ltd* *(G-13216)*

**True Value Company**....847 639-5383
201 Jandus Rd Cary (60013) ***(G-3378)***
**True Value Company (PA)**....773 695-5000
8600 W Bryn Mawr Ave 100s Chicago (60631) ***(G-6786)***
**True-Cut Wire EDM Div, Rockford** *Also called Industrial Molds Inc* ***(G-18430)***
**Trueline Inc**....309 378-2571
7095 Shaffer Dr Downs (61736) ***(G-8548)***
**Truepad LLC**....847 274-6898
180 N Wabash Ave Ste 730 Chicago (60601) ***(G-6787)***
**Truequest Communications LLC**....312 356-9900
53 W Jackson Blvd # 1140 Chicago (60604) ***(G-6788)***
**Trufab Group USA LLC**....630 994-3286
550 Albion Ave Ste 90 Schaumburg (60193) ***(G-19775)***
**Trumans Brands LLC**....224 302-5605
1541 S Shields Dr Waukegan (60085) ***(G-21633)***
**Trump Direct, Decatur** *Also called Trump Printing Inc* ***(G-7954)***
**Trump Printing Inc**....217 429-9001
1591 N Water St Decatur (62526) ***(G-7954)***
**Truss Components Inc (PA)**....800 678-7877
607 N Main St Ste 100 Columbia (62236) ***(G-7365)***
**Truss Slater, Virden** *Also called Lumberyard Suppliers Inc* ***(G-21298)***
**Trustwave Holdings Inc (HQ)**....312 750-0950
70 W Madison St Ste 600 Chicago (60602) ***(G-6789)***
**Trusty Warns Inc (PA)**....630 766-9015
229 N Central Ave Wood Dale (60191) ***(G-22434)***
**Truth Labs LLC**....312 291-9035
212 W Superior St Ste 505 Chicago (60654) ***(G-6790)***
**TRW Active Passive Safety Tech, Marshall** *Also called TRW Automotive US LLC* ***(G-14330)***
**TRW Automotive US LLC**....217 826-3011
902 S 2nd St Marshall (62441) ***(G-14330)***
**Try Our Pallets Inc**....708 343-0166
37 S 9th Ave Maywood (60153) ***(G-14436)***
**Tryad Specialties Inc (PA)**....630 549-0079
2015 Dean St Ste 6 Saint Charles (60174) ***(G-19287)***
**Trymark Print Production LLC**....630 668-7800
155 Internationale Blvd Glendale Heights (60139) ***(G-11086)***
**Tryson Metal Stampg & Mfg Inc**....630 628-6570
230 S La Londe Ave Addison (60101) ***(G-328)***
**Tryson Metal Stampg & Mfg Inc (PA)**....630 458-0591
311 S Stewart Ave Addison (60101) ***(G-329)***
**Trz Race Cars, Frankfort** *Also called T R Z Motorsports Inc* ***(G-10367)***
**TSA Processing Chicago Inc**....630 860-5900
520 Thomas Dr Bensenville (60106) ***(G-2007)***
**TSC Ferrite International, Toledo** *Also called TSC Pyroferric International* ***(G-20969)***
**TSC Ferrite International, Wadsworth** *Also called TSC International Inc* ***(G-21328)***
**TSC Ferrite International, Wadsworth** *Also called Ferrite International Company* ***(G-21322)***
**TSC International Inc**....847 249-4900
39105 Magnetics Blvd Wadsworth (60083) ***(G-21328)***
**TSC Pyroferric International (PA)**....217 849-2230
507 E Madison Toledo (62468) ***(G-20969)***
**Tsd Manufacturing Co Inc**....630 238-8750
825 Chase Ave Elk Grove Village (60007) ***(G-9794)***
**Tsf Net Inc**....815 246-7295
402 S Ottawa St Earlville (60518) ***(G-8597)***
**Tsm Inc**....815 544-5012
6859 Belford Indus Dr Belvidere (61008) ***(G-1790)***
**Tst/Impreso Inc**....630 775-9555
450 S Lombard Rd Ste C Addison (60101) ***(G-330)***
**Tsv Adhesive Systems Inc**....815 464-5606
9411 Corsair Rd Frankfort (60423) ***(G-10373)***
**TT Technologies Inc**....630 851-8200
2020 E New York St Aurora (60502) ***(G-1091)***
**Tts Granite Inc (PA)**....708 755-5200
3225 Louis Sherman Dr Steger (60475) ***(G-20579)***
**Tu-Star Manufacturing Co Inc**....815 338-5760
1200 Cobblestone Way Woodstock (60098) ***(G-22619)***
**Tube & Pipe Association Intl**....815 399-8700
2135 Point Blvd Elgin (60123) ***(G-9217)***
**Tube Line Stainless, Carol Stream** *Also called Core Pipe Products Inc* ***(G-3138)***
**Tube Pierce Manufacturing, Franklin Park** *Also called Henry Tool & Die Co* ***(G-10486)***
**Tubular Steel Inc**....630 515-5000
519 N Cass Ave Ste 202 Westmont (60559) ***(G-21926)***
**Tucker Company Division, Schaumburg** *Also called Component Products Inc* ***(G-19477)***
**Tuf-Guard, Frankfort** *Also called Dunhill Corp* ***(G-10315)***
**Tuf-Tite Inc**....847 550-1011
1200 Flex Ct Lake Zurich (60047) ***(G-13139)***
**Tuff Shed Inc**....847 704-1147
1408 E Northwest Hwy Palatine (60074) ***(G-17083)***
**Tuftads, Bensenville** *Also called Bls Enterprises Inc* ***(G-1844)***
**Tuminello Enterprizes Inc (PA)**....815 416-1007
1351 East St Morris (60450) ***(G-15137)***
**Tuminello Enterprizes Inc**....815 416-1007
1351 East St Morris (60450) ***(G-15138)***
**Tunnel Vision Consulting Group**....773 367-7292
8844 S Jeffery Blvd Chicago (60617) ***(G-6791)***
**Turasky Meats, Springfield** *Also called Y T Packing Co* ***(G-20550)***
**Turbine Charging Unit, Bolingbrook** *Also called ABB Inc* ***(G-2276)***
**Turbo Tool & Mold Co**....708 615-1730
3045 S 26th Ave Broadview (60155) ***(G-2618)***
**Turfmapp Inc**....703 473-5678
3550 N Lake Shore Dr Chicago (60657) ***(G-6792)***
**Turk Electric Sign Co**....773 736-9300
3434 N Cicero Ave 3436 Chicago (60641) ***(G-6793)***
**Turn Key Forging, Elk Grove Village** *Also called Klein Tools Inc* ***(G-9577)***
**Turnco Inc**....708 756-6565
2200 S Halsted St Chicago Heights (60411) ***(G-7133)***
**Turnco Products, Chicago Heights** *Also called Turnco Inc* ***(G-7133)***
**Turner Agward**....773 669-8559
5642 W Div St Ste 212 Chicago (60651) ***(G-6794)***
**Turner Jct Prtg & Litho Svc**....630 293-1377
850 Meadowview Xing Ste 2 West Chicago (60185) ***(G-21786)***
**Turner Sand & Gravel Inc**....618 586-2486
15250 N 1720th St Palestine (62451) ***(G-17096)***
**Turnroth Sign Company Inc**....815 625-1155
1207 E Rock Falls Rd Rock Falls (61071) ***(G-18156)***
**Turtle Drain, Wauconda** *Also called Standing Water Solutions Inc* ***(G-21503)***
**Turtle Island Inc**....815 759-9000
1910 Bay Rd Johnsburg (60051) ***(G-12443)***
**Turtle Wax Carwash & Car Appea, Addison** *Also called Turtle Wax Inc* ***(G-331)***
**Turtle Wax Inc (PA)**....630 455-3700
2250 W Pinehurst Blvd # 150 Addison (60101) ***(G-331)***
**Tuschall Engineering Co Inc**....630 655-9100
15w700 79th St Unit 1 Burr Ridge (60527) ***(G-2888)***
**Tuscola Journal Incorporated**....217 253-5086
115 W Sale St Tuscola (61953) ***(G-21026)***
**Tuscola Packaging Group LLC**....734 268-2877
211 E Buckner St Tuscola (61953) ***(G-21027)***
**Tuscola Stone Company**....217 253-4705
1199 E Us Highway 36 Tuscola (61953) ***(G-21028)***
**Tuskin Equipment Corporation**....630 466-5590
483 N Heartland Dr Ste F Sugar Grove (60554) ***(G-20738)***
**Tussey G K Oil Explrtn & Prdc**....618 948-2871
4th & Main St Saint Francisville (62460) ***(G-19314)***
**Tutco Inc**....630 833-5400
650 W Grand Ave Ste 303 Elmhurst (60126) ***(G-9953)***
**Tuthill Corporation (PA)**....630 382-4900
8500 S Madison St Burr Ridge (60527) ***(G-2889)***
**Tuu Duc Le Inc (PA)**....630 897-6363
110 John St North Aurora (60542) ***(G-16148)***
**Tuxco Corporation**....847 244-2220
4300 Grove Ave Gurnee (60031) ***(G-11517)***
**Tuxhorn Drapery, Springfield** *Also called Afar Imports & Interiors Inc* ***(G-20386)***
**Tvh Parts Co**....847 223-1000
95 S Rte 83 Grayslake (60030) ***(G-11365)***
**Tvj Electroforming Division, Chicago** *Also called Dover Industrial Chrome Inc* ***(G-4638)***
**Tvo Acquisition Corporation (PA)**....708 656-4240
2540 S 50th Ave Cicero (60804) ***(G-7239)***
**Tvp Color Graphics Inc**....630 837-3600
230 Roma Jean Pkwy Streamwood (60107) ***(G-20679)***
**Twain Media Mark Publishing**....217 223-7008
617 Broadway St Quincy (62301) ***(G-17901)***
**Tweeten Fibre Co**....312 733-7878
1756 W Hubbard St Chicago (60622) ***(G-6795)***
**Twg Rsarch Div of Willow Group, Chicago** *Also called Willow Group Inc* ***(G-6988)***
**Twh Water Treatment Industries**....847 457-1813
5600 N River Rd Ste 800 Rosemont (60018) ***(G-19038)***
**Twin Cities Ready Mix Inc**....309 862-1500
1324 Fort Jesse Rd Normal (61761) ***(G-16090)***
**Twin City Awards**....309 452-9291
1531 Fort Jesse Rd Ste 5b Normal (61761) ***(G-16091)***
**Twin City Electric Inc**....309 827-0636
1701 Easy St Ste 5 Bloomington (61701) ***(G-2233)***
**Twin City Tent & Awning Co, Urbana** *Also called Champaign Cnty Tent & Awng Co* ***(G-21077)***
**Twin City Wood Recycling Corp**....309 827-9663
1606 W Oakland Ave Bloomington (61701) ***(G-2234)***
**Twin Mills Timber & Tie Co Inc**....618 932-3662
3268 State Highway 37 West Frankfort (62896) ***(G-21821)***
**Twin States Publishing Co, Watseka** *Also called Times Republic* ***(G-21431)***
**Twin Supplies Ltd**....630 590-5138
1010 Jorie Blvd Ste 124 Oak Brook (60523) ***(G-16566)***
**Twin Towers Embroidery, Belvidere** *Also called Twin Towers Marketing* ***(G-1791)***
**Twin Towers Marketing**....815 544-5554
1231 Logan Ave Belvidere (61008) ***(G-1791)***
**Twinplex Manufacturing Co**....630 595-2040
840 Lively Blvd Wood Dale (60191) ***(G-22435)***
**Twinplex Stamping Company, Wood Dale** *Also called Twinplex Manufacturing Co* ***(G-22435)***
**Twist and Seal, Frankfort** *Also called Midwest Innovative Pdts LLC* ***(G-10343)***
**Two Brothers Brewing Company**....630 393-2337
30w315 Calumet Ave W Warrenville (60555) ***(G-21367)***
**Two Consulting**....630 830-2415
329 Windsor Dr Bartlett (60103) ***(G-1382)***
**Two Figs Baking Co**....847 233-0500
3849 Carnation St Franklin Park (60131) ***(G-10614)***
**Two Four Seven Metal Laser**....847 250-5199
1428 Norwood Ave Itasca (60143) ***(G-12369)***

**Two J S Sheet Metal Works Inc** ....773 436-9424
5828 S Oakley Ave Chicago (60636) *(G-6796)*
**Two JS Copies Now Inc** ....847 292-2679
6725 N Northwest Hwy Chicago (60631) *(G-6797)*
**Two Rivers Oil & Gas Co Inc** ....217 773-3356
116 S Capitol Ave Mount Sterling (62353) *(G-15395)*
**Two Tower Frames Inc** ....773 697-6856
1300 W Belmont Ave # 111 Chicago (60657) *(G-6798)*
**Two Tribes LLC** ....847 272-7711
3607 Lawson Rd Glenview (60026) *(G-11211)*
**Twocanoes Software Inc** ....630 305-9601
34 W Chicago Ave Ste A Naperville (60540) *(G-15769)*
**Twr Service Corporation** ....847 923-0692
940 Lunt Ave Schaumburg (60193) *(G-19776)*
**TWT Marketing Inc** ....773 274-4470
2719 W Lunt Ave Chicago (60645) *(G-6799)*
**Txticon LLC** ....312 860-3378
4027 N Kedvale Ave Chicago (60641) *(G-6800)*
**Ty Miles Incorporated** ....708 344-5480
9855 Derby Ln Westchester (60154) *(G-21860)*
**Ty Precision Automatics Inc** ....815 963-9668
2606 Falund St Rockford (61109) *(G-18658)*
**Tyler Enterprises, Morris** *Also called Masterblend International LLC* *(G-15115)*
**Tyler, Thomas A PHD, New Lenox** *Also called Merit Emplyment Asssment Svcs* *(G-15894)*
**Tylers Fab & Welding Inc** ....217 283-6855
1013 W Main St Hoopeston (60942) *(G-12120)*
**Tylka Printing Inc** ....773 767-3775
4915 W 63rd St Chicago (60638) *(G-6801)*
**Tylu Wireless Technology LLC** ....312 260-7934
3424 S State St Chicago (60616) *(G-6802)*
**Tyndale House Publishers Inc (PA)** ....630 668-8300
351 Executive Dr Carol Stream (60188) *(G-3257)*
**Tyndale House Publishers Inc** ....630 668-8300
370 Executive Dr Carol Stream (60188) *(G-3258)*
**Type Concepts Inc** ....708 361-1005
12216 S Harlem Ave Ste B Palos Heights (60463) *(G-17112)*
**Tyson Fresh Meats Inc** ....815 431-9501
621 E Stevenson Rd Ottawa (61350) *(G-16987)*
**Tyson Fresh Meats Inc** ....847 836-5550
2170 Point Blvd Ste 300 Elgin (60123) *(G-9218)*
**Tyson Fresh Meats Inc** ....309 658-2291
28424 38th Ave N Hillsdale (61257) *(G-11905)*
**Tyson Fresh Meats Inc** ....309 658-3377
28424 38th Ave N Hillsdale (61257) *(G-11906)*
**Tyson Fresh Meats Inc** ....309 965-2565
373 Hwy 117 N Goodfield (61742) *(G-11249)*
**Tza Consulting, Long Grove** *Also called Tom Zosel Associates Ltd* *(G-13903)*
**U Camp Products** ....618 228-5080
449 S Spring St Aviston (62216) *(G-1249)*
**U Keep US In Stitches** ....847 427-8127
1420 S Redwood Dr Mount Prospect (60056) *(G-15380)*
**U Mark Inc** ....618 235-7500
102 Iowa Ave Belleville (62220) *(G-1683)*
**U O P Equitec Services Inc** ....847 391-2000
25 E Algonquin Rd Des Plaines (60016) *(G-8288)*
**U Op** ....847 391-2000
25 E Algonquin Rd Des Plaines (60016) *(G-8289)*
**U R On It** ....847 382-0182
22172 N Hillview Dr Lake Barrington (60010) *(G-12826)*
**U S Co-Tronics Corp** ....815 692-3204
403 E Locust St Fairbury (61739) *(G-10134)*
**U S Colors & Coatings Inc** ....630 879-8898
1180 Lyon Rd Batavia (60510) *(G-1512)*
**U S Concepts Inc** ....630 876-3110
31w21 North Ave West Chicago (60185) *(G-21787)*
**U S Filter Products** ....618 451-1205
3202 W 20th St Granite City (62040) *(G-11309)*
**U S Filters** ....815 932-8154
404 E Broadway St Bradley (60915) *(G-2435)*
**U S Free Press LLC** ....217 847-3361
950 E Us Highway 136 Hamilton (62341) *(G-11541)*
**U S Machine & Tool** ....847 740-0077
331 W Main St Hainesville (60073) *(G-11524)*
**U S Naval Institute** ....800 233-8764
2427 Bond St University Park (60484) *(G-21065)*
**U S Railway Services** ....708 468-8343
8201 183rd St Ste C Tinley Park (60487) *(G-20952)*
**U S Silica Company** ....815 562-7336
1951 Steward Rd Rochelle (61068) *(G-18113)*
**U S Silica Company** ....800 635-7263
727 N 3029th Rd Utica (61373) *(G-21108)*
**U S Silica Company** ....815 434-0188
701 Boyce Memorial Dr Ottawa (61350) *(G-16988)*
**U S Soy LLC** ....217 235-1020
2808 Thomason Dr Mattoon (61938) *(G-14411)*
**U S Storage Group LLC** ....618 482-8000
915 Fairway Park Dr Madison (62060) *(G-14155)*
**U S Tool & Manufacturing Co** ....630 953-1000
1335 W Fullerton Ave Addison (60101) *(G-332)*
**U S Truck Body-Midwest, Streator** *Also called Mid-America Truck Corporation* *(G-20694)*
**U S Weight Inc** ....618 392-0408
4594 E Radio Tower Ln Olney (62450) *(G-16799)*
**U Wash Equipment Co** ....618 466-9442
116 Northport Dr Alton (62002) *(G-594)*
**U-Haul, Washington** *Also called Service Auto Supply* *(G-21392)*
**U-Tracking International Inc** ....312 242-6003
500 N Michigan Ave # 300 Chicago (60611) *(G-6803)*
**U.S.T.H., Wheeling** *Also called US Tsubaki Holdings Inc* *(G-22172)*
**U4g Group LLC** ....847 821-6061
1425 Mchenry Rd Ste 209 Buffalo Grove (60089) *(G-2783)*
**Uarco, Watseka** *Also called Standard Register Inc* *(G-21427)*
**Uberloop Inc** ....630 707-0567
1812 High Grove Ln # 101 Naperville (60540) *(G-15770)*
**Uberlube Inc** ....847 372-3127
2611 Hartzell St Evanston (60201) *(G-10103)*
**Ubipass Inc** ....312 626-4624
5931 Stewart Dr Apt 1021 Willowbrook (60527) *(G-22236)*
**Uca Group Inc** ....847 742-7151
201 N Center St South Elgin (60177) *(G-20231)*
**Ucc Holdings Corporation (HQ)** ....847 473-5900
2100 Norman Dr Waukegan (60085) *(G-21634)*
**UCI, Lake Forest** *Also called United Components LLC* *(G-12977)*
**UCI International Inc** ....847 941-0965
1900 W Field Ct Lake Forest (60045) *(G-12975)*
**UCI-Fram Autobrands, Lake Forest** *Also called UCI International Inc* *(G-12975)*
**Ucp, Morris** *Also called Utility Concrete Products LLC* *(G-15140)*
**Udce Limited** ....630 495-9940
974 N Du Page Ave Lombard (60148) *(G-13875)*
**Udv North America Inc** ....815 267-4400
24440 W 143rd St Plainfield (60544) *(G-17659)*
**Uesco Crane, Alsip** *Also called Uesco Industries Inc* *(G-537)*
**Uesco Industries Inc** ....708 385-7700
5908 W 118th St Alsip (60803) *(G-536)*
**Uesco Industries Inc (PA)** ....800 325-8372
5908 W 118th St Alsip (60803) *(G-537)*
**Ugn Inc (HQ)** ....773 437-2400
18410 Crossing Dr Ste C Tinley Park (60487) *(G-20953)*
**Uhlar Inc** ....815 961-0970
1626 Magnolia St Rockford (61104) *(G-18659)*
**Uhlir Manufacturing Corp** ....773 376-5289
2642 W Cullerton St Chicago (60608) *(G-6804)*
**UIC** ....312 413-7697
1747 W Roosevelt Rd 145 Chicago (60608) *(G-6805)*
**Uic Inc** ....815 744-4477
1225 Channahon Rd Ste 2 Rockdale (60436) *(G-18234)*
**Uico LLC** ....630 592-4400
650 W Grand Ave Ste 308 Elmhurst (60126) *(G-9954)*
**Uk Abrasives Inc** ....847 291-3566
3045 Macarthur Blvd Northbrook (60062) *(G-16378)*
**Uk Sailmakers, Chicago** *Also called Nieman & Considine Inc* *(G-5914)*
**Ulla of Finland** ....773 763-0700
6221 N Leona Ave Chicago (60646) *(G-6806)*
**Ulrich Kaeppler** ....847 290-0220
1693 Elmhurst Rd Elk Grove Village (60007) *(G-9795)*
**Ultimate Distributing Inc** ....847 566-2250
300 E Park St Mundelein (60060) *(G-15565)*
**Ultimate Machining & Engrg Inc** ....815 439-8361
14015 S Van Dyke Rd Plainfield (60544) *(G-17660)*
**Ultimate Screen Printing, Mundelein** *Also called Ultimate Distributing Inc* *(G-15565)*
**Ultimate Sign Co** ....773 282-4595
5511 W Pensacola Ave Chicago (60641) *(G-6807)*
**Ultra Packaging Inc** ....630 595-9820
534 N York Rd Bensenville (60106) *(G-2008)*
**Ultra Play Systems Inc (HQ)** ....618 282-8200
1675 Locust St Red Bud (62278) *(G-17951)*
**Ultra Polishing Inc** ....630 635-2926
640 Pratt Ave N Schaumburg (60193) *(G-19777)*
**Ultra Specialty Holdings Inc** ....847 437-8110
1360 Howard St Elk Grove Village (60007) *(G-9796)*
**Ultra Stamping & Assembly Inc** ....815 874-9888
4590 Hydraulic Rd Rockford (61109) *(G-18660)*
**Ultra-Metric Tool Co** ....773 281-4200
2952 N Leavitt St Chicago (60618) *(G-6808)*
**Ultramark Inc** ....847 981-0400
2420 E Oakton St Ste I Arlington Heights (60005) *(G-860)*
**Ultramatic Equipment Co** ....630 543-4565
848 S Westgate St Addison (60101) *(G-333)*
**Ultrasonic Blind Co** ....847 579-8084
342 4th St Libertyville (60048) *(G-13393)*
**Ultrasonic Power Corporation** ....815 235-6020
239 E Stephenson St Freeport (61032) *(G-10695)*
**Ultrasound Div - Buffalo Grove, Buffalo Grove** *Also called Siemens Med Solutions USA Inc* *(G-2769)*
**Ultratech Inc** ....630 539-3578
251 Covington Dr Bloomingdale (60108) *(G-2140)*
**Ultron Inc** ....618 244-3303
6 Fountain Pl Mount Vernon (62864) *(G-15447)*
**Umf Corporation** ....224 251-7822
5721 W Howard St Niles (60714) *(G-16045)*

**Umf Corporation (PA)**....847 920-0370
4709 Golf Rd Ste 300a Skokie (60076) *(G-20104)*
**Umphreys McGee Inc**....773 880-0024
1530 W Oakdale Ave Chicago (60657) *(G-6809)*
**Umt Wind Down Co**....815 467-7900
105 Indl Dr Minooka (60447) *(G-14848)*
**Umw Inc**....847 352-5252
601 Lunt Ave Schaumburg (60193) *(G-19778)*
**Uncommon Radiant**....773 640-1674
2826 W Fitch Ave Chicago (60645) *(G-6810)*
**Uncommon Threads, Buffalo Grove** *Also called V-Tex Inc (G-2787)*
**Uncommon Usa Inc (PA)**....630 268-9672
1146 N Main St Lombard (60148) *(G-13876)*
**Underground Devices Inc**....847 205-9000
420 Academy Dr Northbrook (60062) *(G-16379)*
**Underwood Dental Laboratories**....217 398-0090
301 S 1st St Champaign (61820) *(G-3551)*
**Undetermined, Chicago** *Also called Westrock Rkt Company (G-6969)*
**UNI Electric Enterprise Inc**....630 372-6312
1889 Seneca Dr Bartlett (60133) *(G-1323)*
**UNI-Glide, Chicago** *Also called Singer Safety Company (G-6516)*
**UNI-Glide Corp**....773 235-2100
2300 N Kilbourn Ave Chicago (60639) *(G-6811)*
**UNI-Label and Tag Corporation**....847 956-8900
1121 Pagni Dr Elk Grove Village (60007) *(G-9797)*
**Unicarriers Americas Corp (HQ)**....800 871-5438
240 N Prospect St Marengo (60152) *(G-14244)*
**Unichem, Elgin** *Also called Universal Chem & Coatings Inc (G-9219)*
**Unichem Corporation**....773 376-8872
1201 W 37th St Chicago (60609) *(G-6812)*
**Unichem International Inc**....847 669-6552
11530 Smith Dr Huntley (60142) *(G-12181)*
**Unicomp Typography Inc**....847 821-0221
1137 Lockwood Ct E Buffalo Grove (60089) *(G-2784)*
**Unicor, Greenville** *Also called Federal Prison Industries (G-11393)*
**Unicor, Pekin** *Also called Federal Prison Industries (G-17262)*
**Unicord Companies, The, Calumet Park** *Also called Unicord Corporation (G-2964)*
**Unicord Corporation**....708 385-7999
12010 S Paulina St Calumet Park (60827) *(G-2964)*
**Unicorn Designs**....847 295-5230
659 N Bank Ln Lake Forest (60045) *(G-12976)*
**Unicut Corporation**....773 525-4210
1770 W Berteau Ave # 505 Chicago (60613) *(G-6813)*
**Unidex Packaging LLC**....630 735-7040
1625 Hunter Rd B Hanover Park (60133) *(G-11592)*
**Unifab Mfg Inc**....630 682-8970
450 Saint Paul Blvd Carol Stream (60188) *(G-3259)*
**Unified Distributors, Arlington Heights** *Also called Unified Solutions Corp (G-861)*
**Unified Solutions Corp**....847 478-9100
3456 N Ridge Ave Ste 200 Arlington Heights (60004) *(G-861)*
**Unified Tool Die & Mfg Co Inc**....847 678-3773
9331 Seymour Ave Schiller Park (60176) *(G-19878)*
**Unified Wire and Cable Company**....815 748-4876
338 Wurlitzer Dr Dekalb (60115) *(G-8128)*
**Uniflex of America Ltd**....847 519-1100
1088 National Pkwy Schaumburg (60173) *(G-19779)*
**Unilever Manufacturing US Inc**....847 541-8868
385 Sumac Rd Wheeling (60090) *(G-22170)*
**Unilock Chicago Inc**....630 892-9191
301 E Sullivan Rd Aurora (60505) *(G-1227)*
**Unimin Corporation**....815 667-5102
402 Mill St Utica (61373) *(G-21109)*
**Unimin Corporation**....815 732-2121
1446 W Devils Backbone Rd Oregon (61061) *(G-16833)*
**Unimin Corporation**....815 539-6734
S Peru St Troy Grove (61372) *(G-21013)*
**Unimin Corporation**....618 747-2338
32079 State Highway 127 Tamms (62988) *(G-20826)*
**Unimin Corporation**....618 747-2311
32079 State Highway 127 Tamms (62988) *(G-20827)*
**Unimin Corporation**....815 431-2200
4000 Baker Rd Ottawa (61350) *(G-16989)*
**Unimin Corporation**....815 434-5363
4000 Baker Rd Ottawa (61350) *(G-16990)*
**Unimin Specialty Minerals, Tamms** *Also called Unimin Corporation (G-20826)*
**Unimin Specialty Minerals, Tamms** *Also called Unimin Corporation (G-20827)*
**Unimode Inc**....773 343-6754
11s104 S Jackson St Burr Ridge (60527) *(G-2890)*
**Union Ave Auto Inc**....708 754-3899
3236 Union Ave Steger (60475) *(G-20580)*
**Union Carbide Corporation**....708 396-3000
12840 S Pulaski Rd Alsip (60803) *(G-538)*
**Union Drainage District**....618 445-2843
Rr 1 Mount Erie (62446) *(G-15294)*
**Union Foods Inc**....201 327-2828
233 N Michigan Ave Chicago (60601) *(G-6814)*
**Union Iron Inc (HQ)**....217 429-5148
3550 E Mound Rd Decatur (62521) *(G-7955)*
**Union Pacific Railroad Company**....309 637-9322
3918 Sw Adams St Peoria (61605) *(G-17472)*
**Union Special LLC**....847 669-5101
1 Union Special Plz Huntley (60142) *(G-12182)*
**Union Street Tin Co**....312 379-8200
350 S Northwest Hwy Park Ridge (60068) *(G-17227)*
**Union Tank Car Company (HQ)**....312 431-3111
175 W Jackson Blvd # 2100 Chicago (60604) *(G-6815)*
**Union Tank Car Company**....815 942-7391
8805 Tabler Rd Morris (60450) *(G-15139)*
**Union Tank Car Company**....312 431-3111
175 W Jackson Blvd # 2100 Chicago (60604) *(G-6816)*
**Unipaq Inc**....773 252-3000
2426 W Lyndale St Chicago (60647) *(G-6817)*
**Uniphase Inc**....630 584-4747
425 38th Ave Saint Charles (60174) *(G-19288)*
**Uniqema Americas**....773 376-9000
4650 S Racine Ave Chicago (60609) *(G-6818)*
**Unique Assembly & Decorating**....630 241-4300
2550 Wisconsin Ave Downers Grove (60515) *(G-8535)*
**Unique Blister Company**....630 289-1232
1296 Humbracht Cir Bartlett (60103) *(G-1383)*
**Unique Checkout Systems**....773 522-4400
2312 17th St Franklin Park (60131) *(G-10615)*
**Unique Concrete Concepts Inc**....618 466-0700
26860 State Highway 16 Jerseyville (62052) *(G-12427)*
**Unique Designs**....309 454-1226
408 Lumbertown Rd Normal (61761) *(G-16092)*
**Unique Envelope Corporation**....773 586-0330
5958 S Oak Park Ave Chicago (60638) *(G-6819)*
**Unique Indoor Comfort**....847 362-1910
624 2nd St Libertyville (60048) *(G-13394)*
**Unique Novelty & Manufacturing**....217 538-2014
200 S Main St Fillmore (62032) *(G-10190)*
**Unique Novelty Mfg & Sales, Fillmore** *Also called Unique Novelty & Manufacturing (G-10190)*
**Unique Plastics, Schaumburg** *Also called WJ Die Mold Inc (G-19791)*
**Unique Prtrs Lithographers Inc**....708 656-8900
5500 W 31st St Cicero (60804) *(G-7240)*
**Unique Targets, Lisle** *Also called Hunter Marketing Inc (G-13601)*
**Unique/Active LLC**....708 656-8900
5500 W 31st St Cicero (60804) *(G-7241)*
**Unistrut Construction, Addison** *Also called Unistrut International Corp (G-334)*
**Unistrut International Corp**....630 773-3460
2171 W Executive Dr # 100 Addison (60101) *(G-334)*
**Unistrut International Corp (HQ)**....800 882-5543
16100 Lathrop Ave Harvey (60426) *(G-11679)*
**Unit Step Company, Colona** *Also called Leonards Unit Step of Moline (G-7345)*
**Unit Step Company of Peoria**....309 674-4392
510 Townhall Rd Metamora (61548) *(G-14751)*
**Unitech Industries Inc**....847 357-8800
1461 Elmhurst Rd Elk Grove Village (60007) *(G-9798)*
**United Adhesives Inc**....224 436-0077
820 Port Clinton Ct E Buffalo Grove (60089) *(G-2785)*
**United Amercn Healthcare Corp (PA)**....313 393-4571
303 E Wacker Dr Ste 1040 Chicago (60601) *(G-6820)*
**United American Metals, Chicago** *Also called RE Met Corp (G-6300)*
**United Automation Inc**....847 394-7903
280 Camp Mcdonald Rd A Wheeling (60090) *(G-22171)*
**United Awning, Antioch** *Also called United Canvas Inc (G-661)*
**United Bindery Service**....312 243-0240
1845 W Carroll Ave Chicago (60612) *(G-6821)*
**United Canvas Inc**....847 395-1470
25434 W Il Route 173 Antioch (60002) *(G-661)*
**United Carborator, Schiller Park** *Also called United Remanufacturing Co Inc (G-19881)*
**UNITED CARBURATOR, Schiller Park** *Also called United Remanufacturing Co Inc (G-19880)*
**United Carburator, Schiller Park** *Also called United Carburetor Inc (G-19879)*
**United Carburetor Inc (PA)**....773 777-1223
9550 Soreng Ave Schiller Park (60176) *(G-19879)*
**United Chemi-Con Inc (HQ)**....847 696-2000
1701 Golf Rd Ste 1-1200 Rolling Meadows (60008) *(G-18786)*
**United Cmra Binocular Repr LLC**....630 595-2525
2525 Busse Rd Elk Grove Village (60007) *(G-9799)*
**United Communications Corp**....847 746-1515
2711 Sheridan Rd Ste 202 Zion (60099) *(G-22698)*
**United Communications Corp**....847 746-4700
2711 Shrridon Rd Unit 202 Zion (60099) *(G-22699)*
**United Components LLC (HQ)**....812 867-4516
1900 W Field Ct Lake Forest (60045) *(G-12977)*
**United Container Corporation**....773 342-2200
1350 N Elston Ave Chicago (60642) *(G-6822)*
**United Conveyor Corporation (HQ)**....847 473-5900
2100 Norman Dr Waukegan (60085) *(G-21635)*
**United Conveyor Supply Company**....708 344-8050
2025 N 15th Ave Melrose Park (60160) *(G-14703)*
**United Conveyor Supply Company (HQ)**....847 672-5100
2100 Norman Dr Waukegan (60085) *(G-21636)*
**United Craftsmen Ltd**....815 626-7802
1500 W 4th St Sterling (61081) *(G-20618)*

**United Displaycraft, Des Plaines** *Also called United Wire Craft Inc (G-8291)*
**United Educators Inc (PA)** ....847 234-3700
900 W North Shore Dr # 279 Lake Bluff (60044) **(G-12868)**
**United Electronics Corp Inc** ....847 671-6034
3615 Wolf Rd Franklin Park (60131) **(G-10616)**
**United Engravers Inc** ....847 301-3740
618 Pratt Ave N Schaumburg (60193) **(G-19780)**
**United Fence Co Inc** ....773 924-0773
722 W 49th Pl Chicago (60609) **(G-6823)**
**United Food Ingredients Inc** ....630 655-9494
15w700 S Frontage Rd Burr Ridge (60527) **(G-2891)**
**United Fuel Savers LLC** ....312 725-4993
516 N Ogden Ave Chicago (60642) **(G-6824)**
**United Gasket Corporation** ....708 656-3700
1633 S 55th Ave Cicero (60804) **(G-7242)**
**United Gilsonite Laboratories** ....217 243-7878
550 Capitol Way Jacksonville (62650) **(G-12415)**
**United Granite & Marble** ....815 582-3345
321 Airport Dr Joliet (60431) **(G-12584)**
**United Graphics Llc** ....217 235-7161
2916 Marshall Ave Mattoon (61938) **(G-14412)**
**United Graphics Indiana Inc** ....217 235-7161
2916 Marshall Ave Mattoon (61938) **(G-14413)**
**United Graphics Mailing Group, Bensenville** *Also called United Letter Service Inc (G-2009)*
**United Industries Illinois Ltd** ....847 526-9485
270 Jamie Ln Wauconda (60084) **(G-21511)**
**United Laboratories Inc (PA)** ....630 377-0900
320 37th Ave Saint Charles (60174) **(G-19289)**
**United Letter Service Inc** ....312 408-2404
1231 N Ellis St Bensenville (60106) **(G-2009)**
**United Lithograph Inc** ....847 803-1700
1670 S River Rd Des Plaines (60018) **(G-8290)**
**United Machine Works Inc** ....847 352-5252
601 Lunt Ave Schaumburg (60193) **(G-19781)**
**United Maint Wldg & McHy C** ....708 458-1705
5252 W 73rd St Bedford Park (60638) **(G-1588)**
**United Oil Co** ....309 378-3049
405 S Seminary St Downs (61736) **(G-8549)**
**United Press Inc (del)** ....847 482-0597
211 Northampton Ln Lincolnshire (60069) **(G-13487)**
**United Press International Inc** ....847 864-9450
1561 Darrow Ave Evanston (60201) **(G-10104)**
**United Printers Inc** ....773 376-1955
1540 W 44th St Chicago (60609) **(G-6825)**
**United Rawhide Mfg Co** ....847 692-2791
1315 Linden Ave Park Ridge (60068) **(G-17228)**
**United Ready Mix Inc (PA)** ....309 676-3287
1 Leland St Peoria (61602) **(G-17473)**
**United Remanufacturing Co Inc (HQ)** ....773 777-1223
9550 Soreng Ave Schiller Park (60176) **(G-19880)**
**United Remanufacturing Co Inc** ....847 678-2233
9550 Soreng Ave Schiller Park (60176) **(G-19881)**
**United Seating & Mobility LLC** ....309 699-0509
125 Thunderbird Ln Ste 1 East Peoria (61611) **(G-8737)**
**United Skilled Inc** ....815 874-9696
3412 Precision Dr Rockford (61109) **(G-18661)**
**United Skys LLC** ....847 546-7776
702 Magna Dr Round Lake (60073) **(G-19069)**
**United Sportsmens Company** ....815 599-5690
1931 Route 75 E Freeport (61032) **(G-10696)**
**United Spring & Manufacturing** ....773 384-8464
830 N Pulaski Rd Chicago (60651) **(G-6826)**
**United Standard Industries Inc** ....847 724-0350
2062 Lehigh Ave Glenview (60026) **(G-11212)**
**United States Audio Corp (PA)** ....312 316-2929
411 Crabtree Ln Glenview (60025) **(G-11213)**
**United States Audio Corp** ....312 316-2929
1658 W 35th St Chicago (60609) **(G-6827)**
**United States Filter/Iwt** ....815 877-3041
4669 Shepherd Trl Rockford (61103) **(G-18662)**
**United States Gear Corporation** ....773 821-5450
1020 W 119th St Chicago (60643) **(G-6828)**
**United States Gypsum Company (HQ)** ....312 606-4000
550 W Adams St Ste 1300 Chicago (60661) **(G-6829)**
**United States Steel Corp** ....618 451-3456
1951 State St Granite City (62040) **(G-11310)**
**United Steel & Fasteners Inc** ....630 250-0900
1500 Industrial Dr Itasca (60143) **(G-12370)**
**United Steel Perforating/ARC** ....630 942-7300
325 Windy Point Dr Glendale Heights (60139) **(G-11087)**
**United Systems Incorporated** ....708 479-1450
9704 194th St Mokena (60448) **(G-14914)**
**United Tactical Systems LLC (PA)** ....877 887-3773
28101 N Ballard Dr Ste F Lake Forest (60045) **(G-12978)**
**United Technologies Corp** ....630 516-3460
655 W Grand Ave Ste 320 Elmhurst (60126) **(G-9955)**
**United Technologies Corp** ....815 226-6000
4747 Harrison Ave Rockford (61108) **(G-18663)**
**United Tool and Engineering Co** ....815 389-3021
4095 Prairie Hill Rd South Beloit (61080) **(G-20171)**
**United Toolers of Illinois** ....779 423-0548
7203 Clinton Rd Loves Park (61111) **(G-14005)**
**United Universal Inds Inc** ....815 727-4445
20620 Burl Ct Ste 1 Joliet (60433) **(G-12585)**
**United Validation & Com** ....815 953-6068
1728 E 1700 North Rd Watseka (60970) **(G-21432)**
**United Wire Craft Inc** ....847 375-3800
333 E Touhy Ave Des Plaines (60018) **(G-8291)**
**United Woodworking Inc** ....847 352-3066
729 Lunt Ave Schaumburg (60193) **(G-19782)**
**Unitel Technologies Inc** ....847 297-2265
479 E Bus Ctr Dr Ste 105 Mount Prospect (60056) **(G-15381)**
**Unitex Industries Inc (PA)** ....708 524-0664
7001 North Ave Ste 203 Oak Park (60302) **(G-16690)**
**Unitrol Electronics Inc** ....847 480-0115
702 Landwehr Rd Northbrook (60062) **(G-16380)**
**Unity Baking Company LLC** ....630 360-6099
1130 Kenilworth Pl Aurora (60506) **(G-1228)**
**Unity Hardwoods LLC** ....708 701-2943
5950 W 66th St Unit C Chicago (60638) **(G-6830)**
**Universal Air Filter Company (HQ)** ....618 271-7300
1624 Sauget Indus Pkwy East Saint Louis (62206) **(G-8774)**
**Universal Beauty Products Inc** ....847 805-4100
500 Wall St Glendale Heights (60139) **(G-11088)**
**Universal Broaching Inc** ....847 228-1440
1203 Pagni Dr Elk Grove Village (60007) **(G-9800)**
**Universal Chem & Coatings Inc (PA)** ....847 931-1700
1975 Fox Ln Elgin (60123) **(G-9219)**
**Universal Chem & Coatings Inc** ....847 297-2001
1124 Elmhurst Rd Elk Grove Village (60007) **(G-9801)**
**Universal Coatings Inc** ....708 756-7000
3001 Louis Sherman Dr Steger (60475) **(G-20581)**
**Universal Die Cast Corporation** ....815 633-1702
11500 Summerwood Dr Machesney Park (61115) **(G-14115)**
**Universal Digital Printing** ....708 389-0133
3314 147th St Midlothian (60445) **(G-14771)**
**Universal Display Products, Des Plaines** *Also called Timothy Darrey (G-8286)*
**Universal Drilling and Cutting, Lombard** *Also called Udce Limited (G-13875)*
**Universal Electric Foundry Inc** ....312 421-7233
1523 W Hubbard St Chicago (60642) **(G-6831)**
**Universal Feeder Inc** ....815 633-0752
5299 Irving Blvd Machesney Park (61115) **(G-14116)**
**Universal Hdd, Lake Zurich** *Also called Universal Hrzntal Drctnal Drlg (G-13140)*
**Universal Holdings Inc** ....224 353-6198
2800 W Higgins Rd Ste 210 Hoffman Estates (60169) **(G-12066)**
**Universal Holdings I LLC** ....773 847-1005
70 W Madison St Ste 2300 Chicago (60602) **(G-6832)**
**Universal Hovercraft Amer Inc** ....815 963-1200
1218 Buchanan St Rockford (61101) **(G-18664)**
**Universal Hrzntal Drctnal Drlg** ....847 847-3300
1221 Flex Ct Lake Zurich (60047) **(G-13140)**
**Universal Instrument Company, Lake Barrington** *Also called Norman P Moeller (G-12821)*
**Universal Lighting & Clg Sup, Chicago** *Also called Universal Lighting Corporation (G-6833)*
**Universal Lighting Corporation** ....773 927-2000
3084 S Lock St Chicago (60608) **(G-6833)**
**Universal Metal Hose, South Holland** *Also called Hyspan Precision Products Inc (G-20279)*
**Universal Overall Company** ....312 226-3336
1060 W Van Buren St Chicago (60607) **(G-6834)**
**Universal Pallet Inc** ....815 928-8546
368 S Michigan Ave Bradley (60915) **(G-2436)**
**Universal Printing, Arlington Heights** *Also called Suburban Press Inc (G-847)*
**Universal Saw Mill, Springerton** *Also called Don Poore Saw Mill Inc (G-20382)*
**Universal Scientific Ill Inc, Elk Grove Village** *Also called Universal Scientific Ill Inc (G-9802)*
**Universal Scientific Ill Inc** ....847 228-6464
2101 Arthur Ave Elk Grove Village (60007) **(G-9802)**
**Universal Trnspt Systems LLC** ....312 994-2349
474 N Lake Shore Dr # 5805 Chicago (60611) **(G-6835)**
**Universal-Spc Inc** ....847 742-4400
412 N State St Elgin (60123) **(G-9220)**
**Universal Cat LLC** ....708 753-8070
111 E 34th St S Chicago Hts (60411) **(G-19114)**
**University of Chicago** ....773 702-1722
1427 E 60th St Chicago (60637) **(G-6836)**
**University of Chicago** ....773 702-7000
11030 S Langley Ave Chicago (60628) **(G-6837)**
**University of Chicago** ....773 702-9780
6101 S Blackstone Ave Chicago (60637) **(G-6838)**
**University of Chicago Press, Chicago** *Also called University of Chicago (G-6837)*
**University of Illinois** ....217 333-9350
54 E Gregory Dr Champaign (61820) **(G-3552)**
**University Printing, Chicago** *Also called B P I Printing & Duplicating (G-4021)*
**University Printing Co Inc** ....773 525-2400
4001 N Ravenswood Ave # 304 Chicago (60613) **(G-6839)**
**University Sport Shop, Peoria** *Also called Senn Enterprises Inc (G-17450)*
**Unlimited Svcs Wisconsin Inc** ....815 399-0282
10108 Forest Hills Rd Machesney Park (61115) **(G-14117)**
**Unlimited Wares Inc** ....773 234-4867
6216 Oakton St Morton Grove (60053) **(G-15242)**

**Unytite Inc** ....815 224-2221
1 Unytite Dr Peru (61354) *(G-17529)*
**UOP LLC** ....303 791-0311
50 E Algonquin Rd Des Plaines (60016) *(G-8292)*
**UOP LLC** ....708 442-3681
2820 N Southport Ave Chicago (60657) *(G-6840)*
**UOP LLC** ....847 391-2000
175 W Oakton St Des Plaines (60018) *(G-8293)*
**UOP LLC** ....847 391-2540
201 W Oakton St Ste 2 Des Plaines (60018) *(G-8294)*
**UOP LLC** ....708 442-7400
8400 Joliet Rd Ste 100 Mc Cook (60525) *(G-14460)*
**Up North Printing Inc** ....630 584-8675
1519 E Main St Ste 600 Saint Charles (60174) *(G-19290)*
**Upchurch Ready Mix Concrete** ....618 235-6222
950 West Blvd Belleville (62221) *(G-1684)*
**Upchurch Ready Mix Concrete** ....618 286-4808
200 N 2nd St Dupo (62239) *(G-8582)*
**Upham & Walsh Lumber Co** ....847 519-1010
2155 Stnngton Ave Ste 209 Hoffman Estates (60169) *(G-12067)*
**Upholstered Walls By Anne Mari** ....847 202-0642
419 S Rose St Palatine (60067) *(G-17084)*
**Upholstred Walls By Anne Marie, Palatine** *Also called Upholstered Walls By Anne Mari (G-17084)*
**Upland Concrete** ....224 699-9909
563 Commonwealth Dr # 1000 East Dundee (60118) *(G-8661)*
**Upm North America, Naperville** *Also called Upm-Kymmene Inc (G-15771)*
**Upm Raflatac Inc** ....815 285-6100
101 E Corporate Dr Dixon (61021) *(G-8357)*
**Upm-Kymmene Inc** ....630 922-2500
55 Shuman Blvd Ste 400 Naperville (60563) *(G-15771)*
**Upper Deck Sports Bar** ....815 517-0682
241 E Lincoln Hwy Dekalb (60115) *(G-8129)*
**Upper Limits Midwest Inc** ....217 679-4315
1205 S 2nd St Ste B Springfield (62704) *(G-20547)*
**Upper Urban Green Prprty Maint** ....312 218-5903
3135 S Throop St Chicago (60608) *(G-6841)*
**Uppercase Living - Indepndent** ....309 657-3054
4415 S Newcastle Ct Mapleton (61547) *(G-14214)*
**Upright Network Services** ....630 595-5559
101 Eastern Ave Bensenville (60106) *(G-2010)*
**UPS Authorized Retailer** ....708 354-8772
106 W Calendar Ave La Grange (60525) *(G-12748)*
**UPS Power Management Inc** ....844 877-2288
4940 S Kilbourn Ave Chicago (60632) *(G-6842)*
**UPS Store of Elmhurst, The, Elmhurst** *Also called Bb Services LLC (G-9837)*
**UPS Stores 2872, The, Chicago** *Also called Weary & Baity Inc (G-6947)*
**Upshot Putter Company, Aurora** *Also called Welding Company of America (G-1231)*
**Upstaging Inc (PA)** ....815 899-9888
821 Park Ave Sycamore (60178) *(G-20822)*
**Upward Bound** ....773 265-1370
3501 W Fillmore St Chicago (60624) *(G-6843)*
**Ur Inc** ....630 450-5279
859 Ravinia Ct Batavia (60510) *(G-1513)*
**Urantia Corp** ....773 248-6616
533 W Diversey Pkwy Chicago (60614) *(G-6844)*
**Urantia Foundation (PA)** ....773 525-3319
533 W Diversey Pkwy Chicago (60614) *(G-6845)*
**Urban Apple LLC** ....312 912-1377
7027 N Ridge Blvd Chicago (60645) *(G-6846)*
**Urban Home Furniture & ACC Inc** ....630 761-3200
1375 Kingsland Dr Batavia (60510) *(G-1514)*
**Urban Imaging Group Inc** ....773 961-7500
3246 N Elston Ave Chicago (60618) *(G-6847)*
**Urban Outfitters Inc** ....312 573-2573
8 E Walton St Chicago (60611) *(G-6848)*
**Urban RE Mix LLC** ....312 360-0011
2361 S State St Chicago (60616) *(G-6849)*
**Urban Research Press Inc** ....773 994-7200
840 E 87th St Ste 1 Chicago (60619) *(G-6850)*
**Urban Services of America (PA)** ....847 278-3210
1901 N Roselle Rd Ste 740 Schaumburg (60195) *(G-19783)*
**Urdu Times** ....773 274-3100
7061 N Kedzie Ave # 1102 Chicago (60645) *(G-6851)*
**Uresil LLC** ....847 982-0200
5418 Touhy Ave Skokie (60077) *(G-20105)*
**Urpoint LLC** ....773 919-9002
2089 Edgeview Dr New Lenox (60451) *(G-15925)*
**Urway Design and Manufacturing** ....847 674-7464
8101 Monticello Ave Skokie (60076) *(G-20106)*
**US Acrylic LLC** ....847 837-4800
1320 Harris Rd Libertyville (60048) *(G-13395)*
**US Adhesives** ....312 829-7438
1735 W Carroll Ave Chicago (60612) *(G-6852)*
**US Audio, Glenview** *Also called United States Audio Corp (G-11213)*
**US Catholic Magazine** ....312 236-7782
205 W Monroe St Fl 9 Chicago (60606) *(G-6853)*
**US Chrome Corp Illinois** ....815 544-3487
305 Herbert Rd Kingston (60145) *(G-12708)*
**US Conveyor Tech Mfg Inc** ....309 359-4088
30000 State Route 9 Mackinaw (61755) *(G-14119)*
**US Conveyor Technologies** ....309 359-4088
30000 State Route 9 Mackinaw (61755) *(G-14120)*
**US Fabg & Mine Svcs Inc** ....618 983-7850
11196 Illinois Steel Rd Johnston City (62951) *(G-12448)*
**US Fireplace Products Inc** ....888 290-8181
110 Albrecht Dr Lake Bluff (60044) *(G-12869)*
**US Foods Culinary Eqp Sups LLC (PA)** ....847 720-8000
9399 W Higgins Rd Ste 500 Rosemont (60018) *(G-19039)*
**US Gear, Chicago** *Also called Axletech International LLC (G-4007)*
**US Golf Manufacturing** ....309 797-9820
1612 7th St Moline (61265) *(G-14974)*
**US Hose Corp (PA)** ....815 886-1140
815 Forestwood Dr Romeoville (60446) *(G-18874)*
**US Ignition, Chadwick** *Also called Chadwick Manufacturing Ltd (G-3440)*
**US International Inc** ....312 671-9207
1950 W Armitage Ave # 1 Chicago (60622) *(G-6854)*
**US International Supply, Chicago** *Also called US International Inc (G-6854)*
**US Lbm Ridout Holdings LLC (HQ)** ....877 787-5267
1000 Corporate Grove Dr Buffalo Grove (60089) *(G-2786)*
**US Minerals Inc (PA)** ....219 864-0909
18635 West Creek Dr Ste 2 Tinley Park (60477) *(G-20954)*
**US Minerals Inc** ....618 785-2217
11000 Baldwin Rd Baldwin (62217) *(G-1252)*
**US Minerals Inc** ....217 534-2370
796 Cips Trl Coffeen (62017) *(G-7306)*
**US Paving Inc** ....630 653-4900
849 N Main St Glen Ellyn (60137) *(G-10992)*
**US Plating Co Inc** ....773 522-7300
2136 S Sawyer Ave Chicago (60623) *(G-6855)*
**US Post Co Inc** ....815 675-9313
2701 N Us Highway 12 A Spring Grove (60081) *(G-20373)*
**US Shredder Castings Group Inc** ....309 359-3151
4408 N Rockwood Dr Peoria (61615) *(G-17474)*
**US Silica** ....312 589-7539
200 N La Salle St # 2100 Chicago (60601) *(G-6856)*
**US Smokeless Tob Mfg Co LLC** ....804 274-2000
11601 Copenhagen Ct Franklin Park (60131) *(G-10617)*
**US Soy, Mattoon** *Also called U S Soy LLC (G-14411)*
**US Specialty Packaging Inc** ....847 836-1115
2760 Spectrum Dr Elgin (60124) *(G-9221)*
**US Tsubaki Holdings Inc (HQ)** ....847 459-9500
301 E Marquardt Dr Wheeling (60090) *(G-22172)*
**US Tsubaki Power Transm LLC (HQ)** ....847 459-9500
301 E Marquardt Dr Wheeling (60090) *(G-22173)*
**US Vision Inc** ....847 367-0420
4 Hawthorn Ctr Vernon Hills (60061) *(G-21214)*
**USA Drives Inc** ....630 323-1282
7900 S Madison St Burr Ridge (60527) *(G-2892)*
**USA Elevators, Lake Zurich** *Also called Elevators USA Incorporated (G-13068)*
**USA Embroidery** ....309 692-1391
1605 W Candletree Dr # 102 Peoria (61614) *(G-17475)*
**USA Hoist Company, Chicago** *Also called Mid-American Elevator Co Inc (G-5727)*
**USA Hoist Company, Joliet** *Also called Mid-American Elevator Co Inc (G-12541)*
**USA Hoist Company Inc (HQ)** ....815 740-1890
1000 Sak Dr Unit A Crest Hill (60403) *(G-7470)*
**USA Industrial Export Corp** ....312 391-5552
707 Skokie Blvd Ste 600 Northbrook (60062) *(G-16381)*
**USA Machine Rebuilders** ....815 547-6542
816 E Pleasant St Belvidere (61008) *(G-1792)*
**USA Printworks LLC** ....815 206-0854
1525 W Lake Shore Dr Woodstock (60098) *(G-22620)*
**USA Star Group of Company** ....773 456-6677
4403 N Broadway St Chicago (60640) *(G-6857)*
**USA Technologies Inc** ....309 495-0829
801 Sw Jefferson Ave Peoria (61605) *(G-17476)*
**USA Today, Aurora** *Also called Gannett Stllite Info Ntwrk LLC (G-1013)*
**USA Today Inc** ....815 987-1400
99 E State St Rockford (61104) *(G-18665)*
**Usa/Docufinish, Yorkville** *Also called McKillip Industries Inc (G-22664)*
**Usac Aeronautics Ria-Jmtc** ....949 680-8167
1 Rock Islnd Arl Bldg 210 Rock Island (61299) *(G-18210)*
**Usach Technologies Inc (HQ)** ....847 888-0148
1524 Davis Rd Elgin (60123) *(G-9222)*
**Used Solutions Inc** ....815 759-5000
531 Tenby Way Algonquin (60102) *(G-408)*
**USG Corporation** ....847 970-5200
700 N Us Highway 45 Libertyville (60048) *(G-13396)*
**USG Corporation (PA)** ....312 436-4000
550 W Adams St Chicago (60661) *(G-6858)*
**Usmss Inc** ....708 409-9010
2428 Pinecrest Ln Westchester (60154) *(G-21861)*
**USP Holdings Inc** ....847 604-6100
6250 N Rver Rd Ste 10100 Des Plaines (60018) *(G-8295)*
**USspice Mill Inc** ....773 378-6800
4537 W Fulton St Chicago (60624) *(G-6859)*
**Ust Inc** ....847 957-5104
11601 Copenhagen Ct Franklin Park (60131) *(G-10618)*

ALPHABETIC

**Usway Corporation (PA)**.......773 338-9688
150 W Maple St Apt 1003 Chicago (60610) ***(G-6860)***
**UTC Aerospace Systems, Rockford** *Also called Goodrich Corporation* ***(G-18402)***
**UTC Aerospace Systems, Rockford** *Also called Goodrich Corporation* ***(G-18403)***
**UTC Railcar Repair Svcs LLC**.......312 431-5053
161 N Clark St Chicago (60601) ***(G-6861)***
**Utica Stone Co Inc**.......815 667-4690
773 N 27th Rd Utica (61373) ***(G-21110)***
**Utica Terminal Inc**.......815 667-5131
715 N 27th Rd Utica (61373) ***(G-21111)***
**Uticor Technology, Carol Stream** *Also called Avg Advanced Technologies LP* ***(G-3110)***
**Utility Business Media Inc**.......815 459-1796
360 Memorial Dr Ste 10 Crystal Lake (60014) ***(G-7671)***
**Utility Concrete Products LLC**.......815 416-1000
2495 Bungalow Rd Morris (60450) ***(G-15140)***
**UTILITY SAFETY & OPS LEADERSHI, Crystal Lake** *Also called Utility Business Media Inc* ***(G-7671)***
**Utlx Manufacturing Inc**.......419 698-3820
175 W Jackson Blvd Chicago (60604) ***(G-6862)***
**Uv Process Supply, Chicago** *Also called Con-Trol-Cure Inc* ***(G-4442)***
**Uwd Inc**.......815 316-3080
9135 N 2nd St Ste 100 Roscoe (61073) ***(G-18925)***
**Uxm Studio Inc**.......773 359-1333
707 N Iowa Ave Villa Park (60181) ***(G-21288)***
**Uzhavoor Fuels Inc**.......630 401-6173
707 N Galena Ave Dixon (61021) ***(G-8358)***
**V & A Manufacturing**.......630 595-1072
1054 Fairway Dr Bensenville (60106) ***(G-2011)***
**V & C Converters**.......708 251-5635
3511 Illinois St Lansing (60438) ***(G-13191)***
**V & L Enterprises Inc**.......847 541-1760
422 Mercantile Ct Wheeling (60090) ***(G-22174)***
**V & N Concrete Products Inc**.......815 293-0315
35 Forestwood Dr Romeoville (60446) ***(G-18875)***
**V & N Metal Products Inc**.......773 436-1855
2320 W 78th St Chicago (60620) ***(G-6863)***
**V & S Tool Co**.......847 891-0780
129 Dunlap Pl Schaumburg (60194) ***(G-19784)***
**V & V Supremo Foods Inc (PA)**.......312 733-5652
2141 S Throop St Chicago (60608) ***(G-6864)***
**V A M D Inc**.......773 631-8400
7035 W Higgins Ave Chicago (60656) ***(G-6865)***
**V A Robinson Ltd**.......773 205-4364
2850 N Pulaski Rd Ste 4r Chicago (60641) ***(G-6866)***
**V and F Transformer Corp (PA)**.......630 497-8070
31w222 W Bartlett Rd Bartlett (60103) ***(G-1384)***
**V and L Polishing Co**.......630 543-5999
341 W Interstate Rd Addison (60101) ***(G-335)***
**V Brothers Machine Co**.......708 652-0062
4900 W 16th St Cicero (60804) ***(G-7243)***
**V C P Inc**.......847 658-5090
901 W Algonquin Rd Algonquin (60102) ***(G-409)***
**V C P Printing, Algonquin** *Also called V C P Inc* ***(G-409)***
**V C T, Downers Grove** *Also called Versatile Card Technology Inc* ***(G-8536)***
**V F G, Aurora** *Also called Valley Fastener Group LLC* ***(G-1229)***
**V Formusa Co**.......224 938-9360
2150 Oxford Rd Des Plaines (60018) ***(G-8296)***
**V J Dolan & Company Inc**.......773 237-0100
1830 N Laramie Ave Chicago (60639) ***(G-6867)***
**V J I, Bedford Park** *Also called Vegetable Juices Inc* ***(G-1589)***
**V J Mattson Company**.......708 479-1990
713 Jennifer Ct New Lenox (60451) ***(G-15926)***
**V M I, Elgin** *Also called Vecchio Manufacturing of Ill* ***(G-9224)***
**V P Anodizing Inc**.......773 622-9100
1819 N Lorel Ave Chicago (60639) ***(G-6868)***
**V P Plating, Chicago** *Also called Pariso Inc* ***(G-6082)***
**V W Broaching Service Inc**.......773 533-9000
3250 W Lake St Chicago (60624) ***(G-6869)***
**V&F Transformer, Bartlett** *Also called V and F Transformer Corp* ***(G-1384)***
**V-Cam Inc**.......217 835-4381
201 N 7th St Benld (62009) ***(G-1807)***
**V-Tex Inc**.......847 325-4140
1027 Busch Pkwy Buffalo Grove (60089) ***(G-2787)***
**V2 Flow Controls LLC**.......708 945-9331
8608 Tullamore Dr Tinley Park (60487) ***(G-20955)***
**Vac Serve Inc**.......224 766-6445
4240 Oakton St Skokie (60076) ***(G-20107)***
**Vac-Matic Corporation (PA)**.......630 543-4518
2 S Lincoln Ave Addison (60101) ***(G-336)***
**Vactor Manufacturing Inc**.......815 672-3171
1621 S Illinois St Streator (61364) ***(G-20710)***
**Vacudyne Incorporated (HQ)**.......708 757-5200
375 E Joe Orr Rd Chicago Heights (60411) ***(G-7134)***
**Vacumet Corp**.......708 562-7290
200 W North Ave Northlake (60164) ***(G-16458)***
**Val Custom Cabinets & Flrg Inc**.......708 790-8373
2656 American Ln Elk Grove Village (60007) ***(G-9803)***

**Val-Matic Valve and Mfg Corp (PA)**.......630 941-7600
905 S Riverside Dr Elmhurst (60126) ***(G-9956)***
**Val-Matic Valve and Mfg Corp**.......630 993-4078
303 S Rohlwing Rd Addison (60101) ***(G-337)***
**Valbruna Stainless Inc**.......630 871-5524
370 Village Dr Carol Stream (60188) ***(G-3260)***
**Valee Inc (PA)**.......847 364-6464
859 Oakton St Elk Grove Village (60007) ***(G-9804)***
**Valent Biosciences Corporation (HQ)**.......847 968-4700
870 Technology Way # 100 Libertyville (60048) ***(G-13397)***
**Valent USA, Libertyville** *Also called Valent Biosciences Corporation* ***(G-13397)***
**Valentino Vineyards & Winery, Long Grove** *Also called Valentino Vineyards Inc* ***(G-13904)***
**Valentino Vineyards Inc**.......847 634-2831
5175 Aptakisic Rd Long Grove (60047) ***(G-13904)***
**Valid Secure Solutions LLC**.......260 633-0728
1011 Warrenville Rd # 450 Lisle (60532) ***(G-13674)***
**Valid Usa Inc (HQ)**.......630 852-8200
1011 Warrenville Rd # 450 Lisle (60532) ***(G-13675)***
**Valley Concrete Inc**.......815 725-2422
19515 Ne Frontage Rd Joliet (60404) ***(G-12586)***
**Valley Custom Woodwork Inc**.......815 544-3939
1626 Industrial Ct Belvidere (61008) ***(G-1793)***
**Valley Fastener Group LLC**.......630 548-5679
5s250 Frontenac Rd Naperville (60563) ***(G-15772)***
**Valley Fastener Group LLC (PA)**.......630 299-8910
1490 Mitchell Rd Aurora (60505) ***(G-1229)***
**Valley Fastener Group LLC**.......708 343-2496
3302 Bloomingdale Ave Melrose Park (60160) ***(G-14704)***
**Valley Fasteners Group, Naperville** *Also called Valley Fastener Group LLC* ***(G-15772)***
**Valley Meats LLC**.......309 799-7341
2302 1st St Sr Coal Valley (61240) ***(G-7299)***
**Valley Quarry**.......309 462-3003
772 175th St Saint Augustine (61474) ***(G-19128)***
**Valley Racing Inc**.......708 946-1440
325 W 323rd St Beecher (60401) ***(G-1603)***
**Valley Run Stone Inc**.......630 553-7974
6369 Whitetail Ridge Ct Yorkville (60560) ***(G-22674)***
**Valley View Industries Hc Inc**.......800 323-9369
13834 Kostner Ave Crestwood (60445) ***(G-7507)***
**Valley View Industries Inc (PA)**.......815 358-2236
7551e 2500 N Rd Cornell (61319) ***(G-7382)***
**Valley View Specialties, Crestwood** *Also called Valley View Industries Hc Inc* ***(G-7507)***
**Valmont Ctngs Empire Glvnizing, Franklin Park** *Also called Valmont Industries Inc* ***(G-10619)***
**Valmont Industries Inc**.......773 625-0354
10909 Franklin Ave Franklin Park (60131) ***(G-10619)***
**Valspar**.......815 962-9969
200 Sayre St Rockford (61104) ***(G-18666)***
**Valspar**.......309 743-7133
3560 5th Ave East Moline (61244) ***(G-8696)***
**Valspar Coatings, Wheeling** *Also called Valspar Corporation* ***(G-22175)***
**Valspar Corporation**.......815 962-9986
1215 Nelson Blvd Rockford (61104) ***(G-18667)***
**Valspar Corporation**.......815 987-3701
1215 Nelson Blvd Rockford (61104) ***(G-18668)***
**Valspar Corporation**.......815 933-5561
901 N Greenwood Ave Kankakee (60901) ***(G-12657)***
**Valspar Corporation**.......708 469-7194
6880 River Rd Unit 22 Hodgkins (60525) ***(G-11985)***
**Valspar Corporation**.......847 541-9000
1191 Wheeling Rd Wheeling (60090) ***(G-22175)***
**Valspar Corporation**.......708 720-0600
21901 Central Ave Matteson (60443) ***(G-14380)***
**Valspar Corporation**.......847 541-9000
300 Gilman Ave Wheeling (60090) ***(G-22176)***
**Valspar Corporation**.......815 962-9986
1215 Nelson Blvd Rockford (61104) ***(G-18669)***
**Value Added Services & Tech**.......847 888-8232
164 Division St Ste 315 Elgin (60120) ***(G-9223)***
**Value Engineered Products**.......708 867-6777
1700 Hicks Rd Rolling Meadows (60008) ***(G-18787)***
**Value Link 1 Enterprises**.......630 833-6243
240 N Michigan Ave Villa Park (60181) ***(G-21289)***
**Van Bergen & Greener, Maywood** *Also called Weldon Corporation* ***(G-14437)***
**Van Cleave Woodworking Inc**.......847 424-8200
1919 Milton Ave Northbrook (60062) ***(G-16382)***
**Van Craft Industry of Del Edel (HQ)**.......708 430-6670
8938 Ridgeland Ave Oak Lawn (60453) ***(G-16646)***
**Van Diest Supply Company**.......815 232-6053
1771 Lincoln Dr Freeport (61032) ***(G-10697)***
**Van Drunen Farms, Momence** *Also called R J Van Drunen & Sons Inc* ***(G-14987)***
**Van Drunen Farms, Momence** *Also called R J Van Drunen & Sons Inc* ***(G-14988)***
**Van Heusen, Tuscola** *Also called Pvh Corp* ***(G-21022)***
**Van Heusen, Aurora** *Also called Pvh Corp* ***(G-1071)***
**Van Jakob Vineyard, Pomona** *Also called Von Jakob Vineyard Limited* ***(G-17695)***
**Van L Speakerworks Inc**.......773 769-0773
5704 N Western Ave Chicago (60659) ***(G-6870)***

**Van Lancker Steven**.....309 764-2221
310 15th St Moline (61265) ***(G-14975)***
**Van Leer Containers Inc (HQ)**.....708 371-4777
4300 W 130th St Alsip (60803) ***(G-539)***
**Van Meter Graphx Inc**.....847 465-0600
970 Seton Ct Wheeling (60090) ***(G-22177)***
**Van Meter Mail, Wheeling** *Also called Van Meter Graphx Inc* ***(G-22177)***
**Van Norman Molding Company LLC**.....708 430-4343
9615 S 76th Ave Oak Lawn (60455) ***(G-16647)***
**Van Pelt Corporation**.....313 365-3600
2930 Morton Dr East Moline (61244) ***(G-8697)***
**Van Stockum Kristine**.....847 914-0015
827 Woodward Ave Deerfield (60015) ***(G-8064)***
**Van Voorst Lumber Company Inc**.....815 426-2544
1 Center St Union Hill (60969) ***(G-21039)***
**Van-Packer Co**.....309 895-2311
302 Mill St Buda (61314) ***(G-2648)***
**Vanart Engineering Company**.....847 678-6255
3504 River Rd Franklin Park (60131) ***(G-10620)***
**Vanco Printers Division, Rockford** *Also called Ideal Advertising & Printing* ***(G-18426)***
**Vandalia Electric Mtr Svc Inc**.....618 283-0068
561 Il 185 Vandalia (62471) ***(G-21128)***
**Vandalia Ready-Mix, Vandalia** *Also called Mid-Illinois Concrete Inc* ***(G-21116)***
**Vandalia Sand & Gravel Inc**.....618 283-4029
Rr 2 Vandalia (62471) ***(G-21129)***
**Vandee Mfg Co Div, Batavia** *Also called Vandeventer Mfg Co Inc* ***(G-1515)***
**Vanderbosch Tj & Assoc Inc**.....815 344-3210
1614 S River Rd McHenry (60051) ***(G-14568)***
**Vandeventer Mfg Co Inc**.....630 879-2511
812 Main St Batavia (60510) ***(G-1515)***
**Vanee Foods Company**.....708 449-7300
5418 Mcdermott Dr Berkeley (60163) ***(G-2050)***
**Vanex Color, Mount Vernon** *Also called Vanex Inc* ***(G-15448)***
**Vanex Inc**.....618 244-1413
1700 Shawnee St Mount Vernon (62864) ***(G-15448)***
**Vanfab Inc**.....815 426-2544
1 Center St Union Hill (60969) ***(G-21040)***
**Vangard Distribution Inc**.....708 484-9895
2905 Ridgeland Ave Berwyn (60402) ***(G-2077)***
**Vangard Distribution Inc (PA)**.....708 588-8400
9501 Southview Ave Brookfield (60513) ***(G-2646)***
**Vanguard Chemical Corporation**.....312 751-0717
429 W Ohio St Chicago (60654) ***(G-6871)***
**Vanguard Energy Services LLC**.....630 955-1500
850 E Diehl Rd Ste 142 Naperville (60563) ***(G-15773)***
**Vanguard Solutions Group Inc**.....630 545-1600
800 Roosevelt Rd Ste E410 Glen Ellyn (60137) ***(G-10993)***
**Vanguard Tool & Engineering Co**.....847 981-9595
555 W Carboy Rd Mount Prospect (60056) ***(G-15382)***
**Vanities Inc**.....847 483-0240
212 W University Dr Arlington Heights (60004) ***(G-862)***
**Vanlab, Wauconda** *Also called Synergy Flavors NY Company LLC* ***(G-21507)***
**Vans Inc**.....847 673-0628
4999 Old Orchard Ctr K13 Skokie (60077) ***(G-20108)***
**Vanseal Corporation**.....618 283-4700
815 Payne Dr Vandalia (62471) ***(G-21130)***
**Vantage Oleochemicals Inc**.....773 376-9000
4650 S Racine Ave Chicago (60609) ***(G-6872)***
**Vantage Oleochemicals Inc (HQ)**.....773 376-9000
4650 S Racine Ave Chicago (60609) ***(G-6873)***
**Vantage Oleochemicals Inc**.....773 376-9000
4650 S Racine Ave Chicago (60609) ***(G-6874)***
**Vantage Specialties Inc (PA)**.....847 244-3410
3938 Porett Dr Gurnee (60031) ***(G-11518)***
**Vantage Specialties Inc**.....847 244-3410
4650 S Racine Ave Chicago (60609) ***(G-6875)***
**Vapor Bus International, Buffalo Grove** *Also called Vapor Corporation* ***(G-2788)***
**Vapor Corporation**.....847 777-6400
1010 Johnson Dr Buffalo Grove (60089) ***(G-2788)***
**Vapor Power International, Franklin Park** *Also called VPI Acquisition Company LLC* ***(G-10624)***
**Var Graphics**.....708 456-2028
1743 N 75th Ct Elmwood Park (60707) ***(G-9975)***
**Varda Graphics, Skokie** *Also called Publishers Row* ***(G-20067)***
**Varex Imaging Corporation**.....847 279-5121
425 Barclay Blvd Lincolnshire (60069) ***(G-13488)***
**Vargyas Networks Inc**.....630 929-3610
2200 Ogden Ave Ste 240 Lisle (60532) ***(G-13676)***
**Vari-Op Company**.....847 623-7667
1209 Pine St Apt 6 Waukegan (60085) ***(G-21637)***
**Variable Operations Tech Inc**.....815 479-8528
1145 Paltronics Ct Crystal Lake (60014) ***(G-7672)***
**Varimed Division, Elk Grove Village** *Also called UNI-Label and Tag Corporation* ***(G-9797)***
**Varisport Inc**.....847 480-1366
3386 Commercial Ave Northbrook (60062) ***(G-16383)***
**Varn International Inc**.....630 406-6501
1333 N Kirk Rd Batavia (60510) ***(G-1516)***
**Varsity Logistics Inc**.....650 392-7979
1 Parkway N Ste 400s Deerfield (60015) ***(G-8065)***
**Varsity Publications Inc**.....309 353-4570
309 Railroad Ave Pekin (61554) ***(G-17292)***
**Varsity Striping & Cnstr Co**.....217 352-2203
2601 W Cardinal Rd Champaign (61822) ***(G-3553)***
**Vas Design Inc**.....773 794-1368
3356 N Milwaukee Ave Chicago (60641) ***(G-6876)***
**Vasco Data Security Inc (de)**.....630 932-8844
1901 S Meyers Rd Ste 210 Oakbrook Terrace (60181) ***(G-16721)***
**Vast, Elgin** *Also called Value Added Services & Tech* ***(G-9223)***
**Vast Market, Zion** *Also called K-Log Inc* ***(G-22690)***
**Vator Accessories Inc**.....630 876-8370
1090 Atlantic Dr West Chicago (60185) ***(G-21788)***
**Vaughan & Bushnell Mfg Co (PA)**.....815 648-2446
11414 Maple Ave Hebron (60034) ***(G-11730)***
**Vaughan & Bushnell Mfg Co**.....309 772-2131
201 W Main St Bushnell (61422) ***(G-2909)***
**Vaughn & Sons Machine Shop**.....618 842-9048
Hwy 45 Fairfield (62837) ***(G-10157)***
**Vault Arts Collective**.....217 599-1215
100 N Main St Tuscola (61953) ***(G-21029)***
**Vault Shop**.....630 699-0307
2827 Sun Valley Rd Lisle (60532) ***(G-13677)***
**Vauto Inc (HQ)**.....630 590-2000
1901 S Meyers Rd Ste 700 Oakbrook Terrace (60181) ***(G-16722)***
**Vaxcel International Co Ltd**.....630 260-0067
121 E North Ave Carol Stream (60188) ***(G-3261)***
**Vcna Prairie, Pontiac** *Also called Southfield Corporation* ***(G-17711)***
**Vcna Prairie Inc (PA)**.....708 458-0400
7601 W 79th St Ste 1 Bridgeview (60455) ***(G-2535)***
**Vcna Prairie Inc**.....312 733-0094
865 N Peoria St Chicago (60642) ***(G-6877)***
**Vcna Prairie Illinois Inc**.....708 458-0400
7601 W 79th St Ste 1 Bridgeview (60455) ***(G-2536)***
**Vcna Prairie Indiana Inc**.....708 458-0400
7601 W 79th St Ste 1 Bridgeview (60455) ***(G-2537)***
**Veal Tech Inc**.....630 554-0410
15 Stonehill Rd Oswego (60543) ***(G-16938)***
**Vecchio Manufacturing of Ill (PA)**.....847 742-8429
801d N State St Unit D Elgin (60123) ***(G-9224)***
**Vector Custom Fabricating Inc**.....312 421-5161
2128 W Fulton St Chicago (60612) ***(G-6878)***
**Vector Engineering & Mfg Corp**.....708 474-3900
17506 Chicago Ave Lansing (60438) ***(G-13192)***
**Vector Mold & Tool Inc**.....847 437-0110
412 Norman Ct Des Plaines (60016) ***(G-8297)***
**Vector Packaging, Oak Brook** *Also called Vector USA Inc* ***(G-16567)***
**Vector USA Inc (HQ)**.....630 434-0040
2021 Midwest Rd Ste 307 Oak Brook (60523) ***(G-16567)***
**Vee Pak LLC (PA)**.....708 482-8881
6710 River Rd Hodgkins (60525) ***(G-11986)***
**Vee Pak LLC**.....708 482-8881
5321 Dansher Rd Countryside (60525) ***(G-7449)***
**Veeco Manufacturing Inc**.....312 666-0900
1930 George St Ste A Melrose Park (60160) ***(G-14705)***
**Veeder-Root Company**.....309 797-1762
4926 5th Ave Moline (61265) ***(G-14976)***
**Veejay Plastics Inc**.....847 683-2954
395 S Main St Burlington (60109) ***(G-2814)***
**Veejay Plstic Injction Molding, Burlington** *Also called Kunverji Enterprise Corp* ***(G-2812)***
**Vees Collectibles, Frankfort** *Also called DJB Corporation* ***(G-10313)***
**Vega Molded Products Inc**.....847 428-7761
122 Industrial Dr Gilberts (60136) ***(G-10940)***
**Vega Technology & Systems**.....630 855-5068
7980 Kingsbury Dr Bartlett (60133) ***(G-1324)***
**Vega Wave Systems Inc**.....630 562-9433
1275 W Roosevelt Rd # 104 West Chicago (60185) ***(G-21789)***
**Vegetable Juices Inc**.....708 924-9500
7400 S Narragansett Ave Bedford Park (60638) ***(G-1589)***
**Vegter Steel Fabrication, Morrison** *Also called American Piping Group Inc* ***(G-15141)***
**Vehicle Improvement Pdts Inc**.....847 395-7250
151 S Ram Rd Antioch (60002) ***(G-662)***
**Vej Holdings LLC**.....630 219-1582
1717 N Naper Blvd Ste 108 Naperville (60563) ***(G-15774)***
**Vek Screw Machine Products**.....630 543-5557
777 W Winthrop Ave Addison (60101) ***(G-338)***
**Velasquez & Sons Muffler Shop**.....847 740-6990
507 W Rollins Rd Round Lake Beach (60073) ***(G-19080)***
**Velocity International Inc**.....773 570-6441
100 N Field Dr Ste 160 Lake Forest (60045) ***(G-12979)***
**Velocity Software LLC**.....800 351-6893
1042 E Maple St Lombard (60148) ***(G-13877)***
**Velsicol Chemical LLC**.....847 813-7888
10400 W Higgins Rd # 600 Rosemont (60018) ***(G-19040)***
**Veltex Corporation (PA)**.....312 235-4014
123 W Madison St Ste 1500 Chicago (60602) ***(G-6879)***
**Veneer Specialties Inc**.....630 754-8550
1385 101st St Ste F Lemont (60439) ***(G-13267)***
**Venetian Monument Company**.....312 829-9622
527 N Western Ave Chicago (60612) ***(G-6880)***

ALPHABETIC

Vent Fabrics, Chicago ALPHABETIC SECTION

**Vent Fabrics, Chicago** *Also called Ventfabrics Inc* ***(G-6883)***
**Vent Products Co Inc**...773 521-1900
1901 S Kilbourn Ave Chicago (60623) ***(G-6881)***
**Vent Ure Air**...708 652-7200
1855 S 54th Ave Chicago (60804) ***(G-6882)***
**Ventec USA LLC**...847 621-2261
720 Lee St Elk Grove Village (60007) ***(G-9805)***
**Ventfabrics Inc**...773 775-4477
5520 N Lynch Ave Chicago (60630) ***(G-6883)***
**Ventura Foods LLC**...708 877-5150
201 Armory Dr Thornton (60476) ***(G-20876)***
**Venture Design Incorporated**...630 369-1148
2250 Allegany Dr Naperville (60565) ***(G-15775)***
**Venture Publishing Inc**...217 359-5940
1807 N Federal Dr Urbana (61801) ***(G-21104)***
**Venturedyne Ltd**...708 597-7550
4101 W 126th St Chicago (60803) ***(G-6884)***
**Venturedyne Ltd**...708 597-7090
4101 W 126th St Alsip (60803) ***(G-540)***
**Venus Laboratories Inc (PA)**...630 595-1900
111 S Rohlwing Rd Addison (60101) ***(G-339)***
**Venus Printing Inc**...847 985-7510
549 Morse Ave Schaumburg (60193) ***(G-19785)***
**Venus Processing & Storage**...847 455-0496
2401 Rose St Franklin Park (60131) ***(G-10621)***
**Veolia Es Industrial Svcs Inc**...708 652-0575
6001 W Pershing Rd Cicero (60804) ***(G-7244)***
**Vep, Rolling Meadows** *Also called Value Engineered Products* ***(G-18787)***
**Verdasee Solutions Inc**...847 265-9441
17825 W Pond Ridge Cir Gurnee (60031) ***(G-11519)***
**Verena Solutions LLC**...314 651-1908
650 W Lake St Ste 110 Chicago (60661) ***(G-6885)***
**Veritas Steel LLC (PA)**...630 423-8708
2300 Cabot Dr Ste 425 Lisle (60532) ***(G-13678)***
**Veritiv Operating Company**...800 347-9279
100 E Oakton St Des Plaines (60018) ***(G-8298)***
**Verlo Mat of Skokie-Evanston**...847 966-9988
7927 Golf Rd Morton Grove (60053) ***(G-15243)***
**Verlo Mattress Factory, Morton Grove** *Also called Verlo Mat of Skokie-Evanston* ***(G-15243)***
**Verlo Mattress of Lake Geneva**...815 455-2570
5150 Northwest Hwy Ste 1 Crystal Lake (60014) ***(G-7673)***
**Vermilion Steel Fabrication**...217 442-5300
3295 E Main St Ste A Danville (61834) ***(G-7778)***
**Vernon Micheal**...217 735-4005
1100 Home Ave Lincoln (62656) ***(G-13421)***
**Vernon Township Offices**...847 634-4600
3050 N Main St Buffalo Grove (60089) ***(G-2789)***
**Verona Rubber Works Inc**...815 673-2929
31577 N 1250 East Rd Blackstone (61313) ***(G-2089)***
**Verona Rubber Works Inc (PA)**...815 673-2929
31577 N 1250 East Rd Blackstone (61313) ***(G-2090)***
**Verone Publishing Inc**...773 866-0811
5421 Ne Rver Rd Apt 1605 Chicago (60656) ***(G-6886)***
**Versa Press Inc**...309 822-0260
1465 Spring Bay Rd East Peoria (61611) ***(G-8738)***
**Versatech LLC**...217 342-3500
1609 W Wernsing Ave Ste D Effingham (62401) ***(G-8860)***
**Versatile Card Technology Inc (PA)**...630 852-5600
5200 Thatcher Rd Downers Grove (60515) ***(G-8536)***
**Versatile Machining, Brighton** *Also called Gail E Stephens* ***(G-2540)***
**Versatile Materials Inc**...773 924-3700
600 W 52nd St Chicago (60609) ***(G-6887)***
**Versatility Tl Works Mfg Inc**...708 389-8909
11532 S Mayfield Ave Alsip (60803) ***(G-541)***
**Verson Enterprises Inc**...847 364-2600
870 Cambridge Dr Elk Grove Village (60007) ***(G-9806)***
**Vertec Biosolvents Inc**...630 960-0600
1441 Branding Ave Ste 100 Downers Grove (60515) ***(G-8537)***
**Vertex Inc**...630 328-2600
40 Shuman Blvd Ste 160 Naperville (60563) ***(G-15776)***
**Vertex Chemical Corporation**...618 286-5207
3101 Carondelet Ave Dupo (62239) ***(G-8583)***
**Vertex Consulting Services Inc**...313 492-5154
935 N Plum Grove Rd Ste D Schaumburg (60173) ***(G-19786)***
**Vertex Distribution**...847 437-0400
1680 Elmhurst Rd Elk Grove Village (60007) ***(G-9807)***
**Vertex Fasteners, Des Plaines** *Also called Leggett & Platt Incorporated* ***(G-8223)***
**Vertex International Inc**...312 242-1864
2015 Spring Rd Ste 215 Oak Brook (60523) ***(G-16568)***
**Vertical Blinds Factory, Niles** *Also called 9161 Corporation* ***(G-15953)***
**Vertical Blinds Factory, Chicago** *Also called Offsprings Inc* ***(G-5969)***
**Vertical Software Inc**...309 633-0700
409 Keller St Bartonville (61607) ***(G-1399)***
**Vertical Tower Partner**...217 819-3040
2626 Midwest Ct Champaign (61822) ***(G-3554)***
**Vertical Web Media LLC**...312 362-0076
125 S Wacker Dr Ste 1900 Chicago (60606) ***(G-6888)***
**Vertidrapes Manufacturing Inc**...773 478-9272
3910 N Central Park Ave Chicago (60618) ***(G-6889)***
**Vertisse Inc**...224 532-5145
9244 Trinity Dr Lake In The Hills (60156) ***(G-13009)***
**Vertiv Group Corporation**...630 579-5000
995 Oak Creek Dr Lombard (60148) ***(G-13878)***
**VERU HEALTHCARE, Chicago** *Also called Female Health Company* ***(G-4835)***
**Vestas-American Wind Tech Inc**...815 646-4280
6250 Rte 1475 Tiskilwa (61368) ***(G-20960)***
**Vestergaard Company Inc (PA)**...815 759-9102
1721 Oak Dr McHenry (60050) ***(G-14569)***
**Vestibular Technologies LLC (PA)**...618 993-7561
1207 Early Bird Ln Marion (62959) ***(G-14293)***
**Vestis Group, Palatine** *Also called Consolidated Mill Supply Inc* ***(G-17016)***
**Vestitrak Intl Inc**...312 236-7100
70 W Madison St Ste 1400 Chicago (60602) ***(G-6890)***
**Vesuvius Crucible Company (HQ)**...217 351-5000
1404 Newton Dr Champaign (61822) ***(G-3555)***
**Vesuvius U S A Corporation (HQ)**...217 351-5000
1404 Newton Dr Champaign (61822) ***(G-3556)***
**Vesuvius U S A Corporation**...708 757-7880
333 State St Chicago Heights (60411) ***(G-7135)***
**Vesuvius U S A Corporation**...217 897-1145
Hwy 136 E Fisher (61843) ***(G-10192)***
**Vesuvius U S A Corporation**...217 345-7044
955 N 5th St Charleston (61920) ***(G-3614)***
**Veteran Greens LLC**...773 599-9689
7552 S Union Ave Chicago (60620) ***(G-6891)***
**Veterans Parking Lot Maint**...815 245-7584
240 Mchenry Ave Woodstock (60098) ***(G-22621)***
**Vfn Fiberglass Inc**...630 543-0232
330 W Factory Rd Addison (60101) ***(G-340)***
**Vhd Inc**...815 544-2169
6833 Irene Rd Belvidere (61008) ***(G-1794)***
**Vl Inc**...618 277-8703
1801 N Belt W Ste 4 Belleville (62226) ***(G-1685)***
**Via Times News Organization, Chicago** *Also called Verone Publishing Inc* ***(G-6886)***
**Vibgyor Optical Systems Corp**...847 818-0788
1140 N Phelps Ave Arlington Heights (60004) ***(G-863)***
**Vibgyor Optics Inc**...847 818-0788
1140 N Phelps Ave Arlington Heights (60004) ***(G-864)***
**Vibra Tech, Glen Ellyn** *Also called Vibra-Tech Engineers Inc* ***(G-10994)***
**Vibra-Tech Engineers Inc**...630 858-0681
777 Roosevelt Rd Ste 110 Glen Ellyn (60137) ***(G-10994)***
**Vibracoustic Usa Inc**...618 382-5891
1500 E Main St Carmi (62821) ***(G-3081)***
**Vibracoustic Usa Inc**...618 382-2318
102 Industrial Ave Carmi (62821) ***(G-3082)***
**Vibro/Dynamics Corporation**...708 345-2050
2443 Braga Dr Broadview (60155) ***(G-2619)***
**Vic Cook System, Alton** *Also called Softhaus Ltd* ***(G-590)***
**Vicari Tool & Plastics Inc**...847 671-9430
3350 Schierhorn Ct Franklin Park (60131) ***(G-10622)***
**Viclarity Inc**...201 214-5405
300 N Lasalle St Chicago (60654) ***(G-6892)***
**Vicma Tool Co**...847 541-0177
505 Harvester Ct Ste J Wheeling (60090) ***(G-22178)***
**Vicron Optical Inc**...847 412-5530
1020 Milwaukee Ave # 235 Deerfield (60015) ***(G-8066)***
**Victaulic Company**...630 585-2919
1207 Bilter Rd Ste 103 Aurora (60502) ***(G-1092)***
**Victor Consulting**...847 267-8012
42 Cumberland Dr 2a Lincolnshire (60069) ***(G-13489)***
**Victor Envelope Mfg Corp**...630 616-2750
301 Arthur Ct Bensenville (60106) ***(G-2012)***
**Victor Food Products**...773 478-9529
4194 N Elston Ave Chicago (60618) ***(G-6893)***
**Victor Levy Jewelry Co Inc**...312 782-5297
29 E Madison St Ste 1640 Chicago (60602) ***(G-6894)***
**Victor's Food, Chicago** *Also called Victor Food Products* ***(G-6893)***
**Victoria Amplifier Company**...630 369-3527
1504 Newman Ct Naperville (60564) ***(G-15831)***
**Victory Division of Planter, Chicago** *Also called Planter Inc* ***(G-6135)***
**Victory Medical Equipment, Decatur** *Also called Victory Pharmacy Decatur Inc* ***(G-7956)***
**Victory Pharmacy Decatur Inc**...217 429-8650
163 N Water St Decatur (62523) ***(G-7956)***
**Vida Enterprises Inc**...312 808-0088
3000 S Throop St Chicago (60608) ***(G-6895)***
**Vidas Angels, Chicago** *Also called Vida Enterprises Inc* ***(G-6895)***
**Vidasym Inc**...847 680-6072
1673 Cedar Glen Dr Libertyville (60048) ***(G-13398)***
**Video Gaming Technologies Inc**...847 776-3516
963 N Carmel Dr Palatine (60074) ***(G-17085)***
**Video Refurbishing Svcs Inc**...847 844-7366
850 Commerce Pkwy Carpentersville (60110) ***(G-3304)***
**Video Surveillance, Oak Lawn** *Also called Chicago Cardinal Communication* ***(G-16610)***
**Videojet Systems, Wood Dale** *Also called Videojet Technologies Inc* ***(G-22436)***
**Videojet Technologies Inc**...630 238-3900
1855 Estes Ave Elk Grove Village (60007) ***(G-9808)***
**Videojet Technologies Inc**...618 235-6804
1 Marsh Dr Belleville (62220) ***(G-1686)***

ALPHABETIC SECTION Voodoo Ride LLC

**Videojet Technologies Inc (HQ)**.....630 860-7300
1500 N Mittel Blvd Wood Dale (60191) ***(G-22436)***
**Vidicon LLC**.....815 756-9600
300 Harvestore Dr Dekalb (60115) ***(G-8130)***
**Vienna Beef Ltd (PA)**.....773 278-7800
2501 N Damen Ave Chicago (60647) ***(G-6896)***
**Vies Nails**.....773 281-6485
3511 N Lincoln Ave Fl 1 Chicago (60657) ***(G-6897)***
**Vietnow National Headquarters**.....815 395-8484
1835 Broadway Rockford (61104) ***(G-18670)***
**Vigil Printing Inc**.....773 794-8808
4415 W Lawrence Ave Chicago (60630) ***(G-6898)***
**Vigo Coal Operating Co Inc**.....618 262-7022
7790 Highway 15 Mount Carmel (62863) ***(G-15286)***
**Viking Awards Inc**.....630 833-1733
846 N York St Ste A Elmhurst (60126) ***(G-9957)***
**Viking Metal Cabinet Co LLC**.....800 776-7767
420 N Main St Montgomery (60538) ***(G-15069)***
**Viking Metal Cabinet Company**.....630 863-7234
420 N Main St Montgomery (60538) ***(G-15070)***
**Viking Printing & Copying Inc**.....312 341-0985
53 W Jackson Blvd Lbby Chicago (60604) ***(G-6899)***
**Villa Marie Wine & Banquet Ctr**.....618 345-3100
6633 E Main St Maryville (62062) ***(G-14347)***
**Village Hampshire Trtmnt Plant**.....847 683-2064
350 Mill Ave Hampshire (60140) ***(G-11564)***
**Village Hebron Water Sewage**.....815 648-2353
12007 Prairie Ave Hebron (60034) ***(G-11731)***
**Village Itasca Nature Center, Itasca** *Also called Spring Brook Nature Center* ***(G-12358)***
**Village of Mt Zion**.....217 864-4212
433 N State Route 121 Mount Zion (62549) ***(G-15457)***
**Village Press Inc**.....847 362-1856
124 E Church St Libertyville (60048) ***(G-13399)***
**Village Typographers Inc**.....618 235-6756
1381 Rocky Creek Ct Belleville (62220) ***(G-1687)***
**Village Vintner Winery Brewry**.....847 658-4900
2380 Esplanade Dr Algonquin (60102) ***(G-410)***
**Vilutis and Co Inc**.....815 469-2116
22535 S Center Rd Frankfort (60423) ***(G-10374)***
**Vince & Sons Pasta Co, Bridgeview** *Also called Jo MO Enterprises Inc* ***(G-2503)***
**Vincent Castillo, Harvard** *Also called Cartel Holdings Inc* ***(G-11625)***
**Vincor Ltd (PA)**.....708 534-0008
5652 W Monee Manhattan Rd Monee (60449) ***(G-15005)***
**Vindee Industries Inc**.....815 469-3300
965 Lambrecht Dr Frankfort (60423) ***(G-10375)***
**Vins & Vignobles LLC**.....312 375-7656
40 E Northwest Hwy # 211 Mount Prospect (60056) ***(G-15383)***
**Vins Bbq LLC**.....847 302-3259
506 Lotus Ln Glenview (60025) ***(G-11214)***
**Vintaj Natural Brass Co**.....815 776-9300
5140 W Us Highway 20 A Galena (61036) ***(G-10733)***
**Vinyl Graphics Inc**.....708 579-1234
35 E Plainfield Rd Ste 2 Countryside (60525) ***(G-7450)***
**Vinyl Life North**.....630 906-9686
661 Dewig Ct North Aurora (60542) ***(G-16149)***
**Vinylworks Inc**.....815 477-9680
8550 Ridgefield Rd Ste E Crystal Lake (60012) ***(G-7674)***
**Viobin USA, Monticello** *Also called McShares Inc* ***(G-15079)***
**Viola Ice Cream Shoppe**.....309 596-2131
1003 13th St Viola (61486) ***(G-21295)***
**Virden Recorder, Virden** *Also called Gold Nugget Publications Inc* ***(G-21297)***
**Virtu**.....773 235-3790
2034 N Damen Ave Chicago (60647) ***(G-6900)***
**Vis-O-Graphic Inc**.....630 590-6100
1220 W National Ave Addison (60101) ***(G-341)***
**Vis-O-Graphic Printing, Addison** *Also called Vis-O-Graphic Inc* ***(G-341)***
**Visco Electric LLC**.....630 336-7824
3n75 Woodcreek Ln West Chicago (60185) ***(G-21790)***
**Visco Technologies Usa Inc**.....847 993-3047
511 W Golf Rd Arlington Heights (60005) ***(G-865)***
**Viscofan Usa Inc**.....217 444-8000
915 Michigan St Danville (61834) ***(G-7779)***
**Viscosity Oil Company (HQ)**.....630 850-4000
600 Joliet Rd Ste H Willowbrook (60527) ***(G-22237)***
**Visibility Inc**.....312 616-5900
225 N Michigan Ave Fl 16 Chicago (60601) ***(G-6901)***
**Vision I Systems**.....312 326-9188
2416 S Canal St Chicago (60616) ***(G-6902)***
**Vision Integrated Graphics (PA)**.....312 373-6300
208 S Jefferson St Fl 3 Chicago (60661) ***(G-6903)***
**Vision Integrated Graphics**.....708 570-7900
605 Territorial Dr Ste A Bolingbrook (60440) ***(G-2380)***
**Vision Machine & Fabrication**.....618 965-3199
1102 N Cherry St Steeleville (62288) ***(G-20564)***
**Vision Pickling and Proc Inc**.....815 264-7755
9341 State Route 23 Waterman (60556) ***(G-21410)***
**Vision Sales & Marketing Inc**.....708 496-6016
5620 W 51st Forest Vw St Chicago (60638) ***(G-6904)***
**Vision Sales Incorporated (PA)**.....630 483-1900
1264 Appaloosa Way Bartlett (60103) ***(G-1385)***
**Vision Vocation Guide, Chicago** *Also called Truequest Communications LLC* ***(G-6788)***
**Visionary Sleep LLC**.....224 829-0440
1721 Moon Lake Blvd Hoffman Estates (60169) ***(G-12068)***
**Visionary Solutions Inc**.....847 296-9615
129 Rawls Rd Des Plaines (60018) ***(G-8299)***
**Visiplex Inc**.....847 918-0250
1287 Barclay Blvd Buffalo Grove (60089) ***(G-2790)***
**Visiplex Inc**.....847 229-0250
1287 Barclay Blvd Ste 100 Buffalo Grove (60089) ***(G-2791)***
**Viskase Companies Inc (HQ)**.....630 874-0700
333 E Butterfield Rd # 400 Lombard (60148) ***(G-13879)***
**Viskase Corporation (HQ)**.....630 874-0700
333 E Bttrfeld Rd Ste 400 Lombard (60148) ***(G-13880)***
**Visos Machine Shop & Mfg**.....630 372-3925
686 Bonded Pkwy Streamwood (60107) ***(G-20680)***
**Vista Woodworking**.....815 922-2297
500 Joyce Rd Unit B Joliet (60436) ***(G-12587)***
**Visual Imaging, Fulton** *Also called Visual Marketing Solutions* ***(G-10707)***
**Visual Information Tech Inc**.....217 841-2155
60 Hazelwood Dr Champaign (61820) ***(G-3557)***
**Visual Marketing Inc**.....312 664-9177
154 W Erie St Chicago (60654) ***(G-6905)***
**Visual Marketing Solutions**.....815 589-3848
800 20th Ave Fulton (61252) ***(G-10707)***
**Visual Persuasion Inc**.....815 899-6609
337 E State St Sycamore (60178) ***(G-20823)***
**Vita Food Products Inc (PA)**.....312 738-4500
2222 W Lake St Chicago (60612) ***(G-6906)***
**Vita-V Energy Co Inc**.....630 999-8961
168 N Brandon Dr Glendale Heights (60139) ***(G-11089)***
**Vital Chemicals USA LLC**.....630 778-0330
280 Shuman Blvd Ste 145 Naperville (60563) ***(G-15777)***
**Vital Proteins LLC (PA)**.....224 544-9110
545 Busse Rd Elk Grove Village (60007) ***(G-9809)***
**Vital Proteins LLC**.....224 544-9110
1564 N Damen Ave Ste 208 Chicago (60622) ***(G-6907)***
**Vital Signs USA**.....630 832-9600
791 N Industrial Dr Elmhurst (60126) ***(G-9958)***
**Vitamins Inc**.....773 483-4640
315 Fullerton Ave Carol Stream (60188) ***(G-3262)***
**Vitel Industries Inc**.....847 299-9750
1026 North Ave Ste A Des Plaines (60016) ***(G-8300)***
**Vitelli Concrete Products Inc**.....708 754-5846
2410 S Halsted St Chicago Heights (60411) ***(G-7136)***
**Vitner Chips, Ottawa** *Also called R and B Distributors Inc* ***(G-16981)***
**Viva Solutions Inc**.....312 332-8882
2 E Illinois St Lemont (60439) ***(G-13268)***
**Vivor LLC**.....312 967-6379
222 Merchandise Mart Plz Chicago (60654) ***(G-6908)***
**Vizr Tech LLC**.....312 420-4466
400 N Mcclurg Ct Apt 2906 Chicago (60611) ***(G-6909)***
**Vlahos Electric Service Dr**.....224 764-2335
1707 N Dale Ave Arlington Heights (60004) ***(G-866)***
**Vlasici Hardwood Floors Co**.....815 505-4308
1959 Somerset Dr Romeoville (60446) ***(G-18876)***
**Vm Electronics LLC**.....847 663-9310
5080 N Kimberly Ave # 110 Chicago (60630) ***(G-6910)***
**Vma Group Inc**.....847 877-7039
13 Saint Clair Ln Vernon Hills (60061) ***(G-21215)***
**Vmr Chicago LLC**.....312 649-6673
34 E Oak St Fl 7 Chicago (60611) ***(G-6911)***
**Vo-Tech, Crystal Lake** *Also called Variable Operations Tech Inc* ***(G-7672)***
**Voco Tool & Mfg Inc**.....708 771-3800
1441 Circle Ave Forest Park (60130) ***(G-10256)***
**Voestalpine Nortrak Inc**.....217 876-9160
690 E Kenwood Ave Decatur (62526) ***(G-7957)***
**Voestlpine Precision Strip LLC**.....847 227-5272
901 Morse Ave Elk Grove Village (60007) ***(G-9810)***
**Vogel Manufacturing Co Inc**.....217 536-6946
10862 N 1000th Rd Effingham (62401) ***(G-8861)***
**Vogel/Hill Corporation**.....773 235-6916
3935 W Shakespeare Ave Chicago (60647) ***(G-6912)***
**Voges Inc (PA)**.....618 233-2760
100 N 24th St Belleville (62226) ***(G-1688)***
**Voice**.....630 966-8642
314 N Lake St Ste 2 Aurora (60506) ***(G-1230)***
**Volflex Inc**.....708 478-1117
10838 Walnut Ln Mokena (60448) ***(G-14915)***
**Voltronics Inc**.....773 625-1779
7746 W Addison St Chicago (60634) ***(G-6913)***
**Von Jakob Vineyard Limited**.....618 893-4500
1309 Sadler Rd Pomona (62975) ***(G-17695)***
**Vonberg Valve Inc**.....847 259-3800
3800 Industrial Ave Rolling Meadows (60008) ***(G-18788)***
**Vonco Products LLC**.....847 356-2323
201 Park Ave Lake Villa (60046) ***(G-13029)***
**Vondrak Publishing Co Inc**.....773 476-4800
7676 W 63rd St Summit Argo (60501) ***(G-20768)***
**Voodoo Ride LLC**.....312 944-0465
1341 W Fullerton Ave # 255 Chicago (60614) ***(G-6914)***

ALPHABETIC

**Voortman USA Corp**....815 468-6300
26200 S Whiting Way Ste 1 Monee (60449) *(G-15006)*
**Voris Communication Co Inc (PA)**....630 898-4268
5656 Mcdermott Dr Berkeley (60163) *(G-2051)*
**Voris Communication Co Inc**....630 231-2425
399 Wegner Dr West Chicago (60185) *(G-21791)*
**Vorne Industries Inc**....630 250-9378
1445 Industrial Dr Itasca (60143) *(G-12371)*
**Vorteq Coil Finishers LLC**....847 455-7200
11440 W Addison St Franklin Park (60131) *(G-10623)*
**Vortex Media Group Inc**....630 717-9541
1118 Knoll Dr Naperville (60565) *(G-15778)*
**Vosges Ltd (PA)**....773 388-5560
2950 N Oakley Ave Chicago (60618) *(G-6915)*
**Vosges Haut Chocolate, Chicago** *Also called Vosges Ltd (G-6915)*
**Voss Belting & Specialty Co**....847 673-8900
6965 N Hamlin Ave Ste 1 Lincolnwood (60712) *(G-13541)*
**Voss Electric Inc**....708 596-6000
15241 Commercial Ave Harvey (60426) *(G-11680)*
**Voss Engineering Inc**....847 673-8900
6965 N Hamlin Ave Ste 1 Lincolnwood (60712) *(G-13542)*
**Voss Pattern Works Inc**....618 233-4242
123 Iowa Ave Belleville (62220) *(G-1689)*
**Voyager Enterprise Inc**....815 436-2431
15507 S Route 59 Plainfield (60544) *(G-17661)*
**Voyant Diagnostics Inc**....630 456-6340
1600 S Ind Ave Apt 1101 Chicago (60616) *(G-6916)*
**Vp Plastics and Engrg Inc**....847 689-8900
1270 S Waukegan Rd Waukegan (60085) *(G-21638)*
**VPI Acquisition Company LLC (PA)**....630 694-5500
551 S County Line Rd Franklin Park (60131) *(G-10624)*
**Vpnvantagecom**....877 998-4678
415 W Golf Rd Ste 5 Arlington Heights (60005) *(G-867)*
**Vr Printing Co Inc**....630 980-2315
1979 Bloomingdale Rd Glendale Heights (60139) *(G-11090)*
**Vrg Controls LLC**....773 230-1543
467 Ridge Rd Highland Park (60035) *(G-11879)*
**Vrmc LLC**....612 210-1868
3000 Woodcreek Dr Ste 300 Downers Grove (60515) *(G-8538)*
**Vs Mfg Co**....224 475-1190
715 Rose Rd Lake Zurich (60047) *(G-13141)*
**Vst America Inc**....847 952-3800
85 W Algonquin Rd 215 Arlington Heights (60005) *(G-868)*
**Vtsi, Bartlett** *Also called Vega Technology & Systems (G-1324)*
**Vtw, Alsip** *Also called Versatility Tl Works Mfg Inc (G-541)*
**Vulcan Construction Mtls LLC**....630 955-8500
1000 E Warrenville Rd # 100 Naperville (60563) *(G-15779)*
**Vulcan Equipment, Forrest** *Also called Slagel Manufacturing Inc (G-10267)*
**Vulcan Ladder Usa LLC**....847 526-6321
710 Wood Creek Ct Island Lake (60042) *(G-12220)*
**Vulcan Materials Company**....262 639-2803
1000 E Warrenville Rd # 100 Naperville (60563) *(G-15780)*
**Vulcan Materials Company**....815 899-7204
12502 Lloyd Rd Sycamore (60178) *(G-20824)*
**Vuteq Usa Inc**....309 452-9933
2222 W College Ave Normal (61761) *(G-16093)*
**Vvf Illinois Services LLC**....630 892-4381
2000 Aucutt Rd Montgomery (60538) *(G-15071)*
**Vyaire Medical Inc (PA)**....847 362-8088
26125 N Riverwoods Blvd Mettawa (60045) *(G-14764)*
**W & K Machining Inc**....708 430-9000
4711 W 120th St Alsip (60803) *(G-542)*
**W & W Associates Inc**....847 719-1760
704 Telser Rd Lake Zurich (60047) *(G-13142)*
**W & W Harp Co, Chicago** *Also called W & W Musical Instrument Co (G-6917)*
**W & W Musical Instrument Co**....773 278-4210
3868 W Grand Ave Chicago (60651) *(G-6917)*
**W A M Computers International**....217 324-6926
211 N State St Litchfield (62056) *(G-13699)*
**W A Rice Seed Company**....618 498-5538
1108 W Carpenter St Jerseyville (62052) *(G-12428)*
**W A Whitney Co (HQ)**....815 964-6771
650 Race St Rockford (61101) *(G-18671)*
**W Bozarth Logging**....618 658-4016
540 Hillside Ln Vienna (62995) *(G-21226)*
**W C S, Saint Charles** *Also called RR Donnelley & Sons Company (G-19254)*
**W D Mold Finishing Inc**....847 678-8449
3923 Wesley Ter Schiller Park (60176) *(G-19882)*
**W Diamond Group Corporation (PA)**....646 647-2791
1680 E Touhy Ave Des Plaines (60018) *(G-8301)*
**W G N Flag & Decorating Co**....773 768-8076
798488 S Chicago Ave Chicago (60617) *(G-6918)*
**W H A M, Mason City** *Also called Mason City Banner Times (G-14365)*
**W H Maze Company (PA)**....815 223-1742
1100 Water St Peru (61354) *(G-17530)*
**W H Maze Company**....815 223-8290
100 Church St Peru (61354) *(G-17531)*
**W H Miner Div, Geneva** *Also called Miner Enterprises Inc (G-10849)*
**W I C S, Springfield** *Also called Wyzz Inc (G-20548)*
**W J Dennis & Company**....847 697-4800
1111 Davis Rd Ste B Elgin (60123) *(G-9225)*
**W Kost Manufacturing Co Inc**....847 428-0600
70 W Madison St Ste 2300 Chicago (60602) *(G-6919)*
**W L & J Enterprises Inc**....708 946-0999
31745 S Dixie Hwy Beecher (60401) *(G-1604)*
**W L Engler Distributing Inc**....630 898-5400
4 Gastville St Aurora (60503) *(G-1093)*
**W M Plastics Inc**....815 578-8888
5151 Bolger Ct McHenry (60050) *(G-14570)*
**W N G S Inc**....847 451-1224
11415 Melrose Ave Franklin Park (60131) *(G-10625)*
**W R B Refinery LLC**....618 255-2345
900 S Central Ave Roxana (62084) *(G-19087)*
**W R Grace & Co**....773 838-3200
4099 W 71st St Chicago (60629) *(G-6920)*
**W R Grace & Co**....708 458-0340
4001 W 71st St Chicago (60629) *(G-6921)*
**W R Grace & Co**....414 354-4400
6051 W 65th St Chicago (60638) *(G-6922)*
**W R Grace & Co - Conn**....708 458-0340
6050 W 51st St Chicago (60638) *(G-6923)*
**W R Grace & Co- Conn**....708 458-9700
6051 W 65th St Chicago (60638) *(G-6924)*
**W R Grace Construction Pdts, Chicago** *Also called W R Grace & Co- Conn (G-6924)*
**W R Grace Davison Chemical Div, Chicago** *Also called W R Grace & Co (G-6920)*
**W R Pabich Manufacturing Co**....773 486-4141
2323 N Knox Ave Chicago (60639) *(G-6925)*
**W R S Inc**....630 279-0400
675 W Saint Charles Rd Elmhurst (60126) *(G-9959)*
**W R Typesetting Co**....847 966-1315
8120 River Dr Ste 2 Morton Grove (60053) *(G-15244)*
**W S C Inc**....312 372-1121
70 W Madison St Ste 2300 Chicago (60602) *(G-6926)*
**W S Darley & Co**....630 735-3500
325 Spring Lake Dr Itasca (60143) *(G-12372)*
**W S Hampshire, Hampshire** *Also called Western Slate Company (G-11565)*
**W W Barthel & Co**....847 392-5643
220 W Campus Dr Ste C Arlington Heights (60004) *(G-869)*
**W W Belt Inc**....708 788-1855
6440 Ogden Ave Berwyn (60402) *(G-2078)*
**W Whorton & Co**....773 445-2400
9029 S Western Ave Chicago (60643) *(G-6927)*
**W-D Tool Engineering Company**....773 638-2688
3128 W Grand Ave Chicago (60622) *(G-6928)*
**W-F Professional Assoc Inc**....847 945-8050
400 Lake Cook Rd Ste 207 Deerfield (60015) *(G-8067)*
**W-R Industries Inc**....312 733-5200
2303 W 18th St Chicago (60608) *(G-6929)*
**W.R. Typesetting Co., Morton Grove** *Also called W R Typesetting Co (G-15244)*
**W/M Display Group, Chicago** *Also called Wiremasters Incorporated (G-7005)*
**W/S Packaging Group Inc**....847 658-7363
1310 Zange Dr Algonquin (60102) *(G-411)*
**Wabash Container Corporation**....618 263-3586
1015 W 9th St Mount Carmel (62863) *(G-15287)*
**Wabash Mines, Keensburg** *Also called Alpha Natural Resources Inc (G-12660)*
**Wabash Production & Dev**....618 847-7401
4 Petroleum Blvd Fairfield (62837) *(G-10158)*
**Wabash Publishing Co Inc (PA)**....312 939-5900
906 S Wabash Ave Chicago (60605) *(G-6930)*
**Wabash Valley Service Co**....618 393-2971
1201 S Whittle Ave Olney (62450) *(G-16800)*
**Wabel Tool Company**....217 429-3656
1020 E Eldorado St Decatur (62521) *(G-7958)*
**Wabtec, Chicago** *Also called Cardwell Westinghouse Company (G-4241)*
**Wabtec Global Services, Chicago** *Also called Westinghouse A Brake Tech Corp (G-6965)*
**Wachs Technical Services Inc**....847 537-8800
100 Shepard Ave Wheeling (60090) *(G-22179)*
**Waco, Chicago** *Also called Wilkens-Anderson Company (G-6979)*
**Waco Manufacturing Co Inc**....312 733-0054
2233 W Ferdinand St Chicago (60612) *(G-6931)*
**Wag Industries Inc**....847 329-8932
4117 Grove St Skokie (60076) *(G-20109)*
**Wagenate Entps Holdings LLC**....773 503-1306
14331 S Clark St Riverdale (60827) *(G-18026)*
**Wagner Brass Foundry, Chicago** *Also called Bronze Memorial Inc (G-4175)*
**Wagner Brass Foundry Inc**....773 276-7907
1838 N Elston Ave Chicago (60642) *(G-6932)*
**Wagner International LLC**....224 619-9247
105 W Townline Rd Ste 160 Vernon Hills (60061) *(G-21216)*
**Wagner Printing Co (PA)**....630 941-7961
1 E Spring St Freeport (61032) *(G-10698)*
**Wagner Pump & Supply Co Inc**....847 526-8573
809 Lake Shore Dr Wauconda (60084) *(G-21512)*
**Wagner Systems Inc**....630 503-2400
300 Airport Rd Unit 1 Elgin (60123) *(G-9226)*
**Wagner Zip-Change Inc**....708 681-4100
3100 W Hirsch St Melrose Park (60160) *(G-14706)*

ALPHABETIC SECTION
Wastequip Saint Louis

**Wagners Custom Wood Design** ....847 487-2788
4035 Roberts Rd Island Lake (60042) *(G-12221)*
**Wagners LLC** ....815 889-4101
2812 E 1100 North Rd Milford (60953) *(G-14815)*
**Wah King Noodle Co Inc** ....773 684-8000
5770 S Perry Ave Chicago (60621) *(G-6933)*
**Wah King Noodle Co Inc (PA)** ....323 268-0222
5770 S Perry Ave Chicago (60621) *(G-6934)*
**Wahl Clipper Corporation (PA)** ....815 625-6525
2900 Locust St Sterling (61081) *(G-20619)*
**Wahl Clipper Corporation** ....815 625-6525
2902 Locust St Sterling (61081) *(G-20620)*
**Waipuna Systems, Downers Grove** *Also called Waipuna USA Inc (G-8539)*
**Waipuna USA Inc** ....630 514-0364
5126 Walnut Ave Downers Grove (60515) *(G-8539)*
**Waist Up Imprntd Sprtswear LLC** ....847 963-1400
422 S Vermont St Palatine (60067) *(G-17086)*
**Walach Manufacturing Co Inc** ....773 836-2060
5049 W Diversey Ave Chicago (60639) *(G-6935)*
**Walco Tool & Engineering Corp** ....815 834-0225
18954 Airport Rd Romeoville (60446) *(G-18877)*
**Waldmann Lighting Company** ....847 520-1060
9 Century Dr Wheeling (60090) *(G-22180)*
**Waldos Sports Corner Inc** ....309 688-2425
1306 E Seiberling Ave Peoria (61616) *(G-17477)*
**Walega Precision Company Inc** ....630 682-5000
205 Kehoe Blvd Ste 3 Carol Stream (60188) *(G-3263)*
**Walern Form Grinding, Rockford** *Also called Form Walern Grinding Inc (G-18391)*
**Walk 4 Life Inc** ....815 439-2340
1981c Wiesbrook Rd Oswego (60543) *(G-16939)*
**Walker's Bluff, Carterville** *Also called Cellar LLC (G-3311)*
**Walker's Repair Shop, Pittsfield** *Also called Owen Walker (G-17572)*
**Walker's Supersaver Foods, Charleston** *Also called Charleston County Market (G-3593)*
**Wall-Fill, Aurora** *Also called Wallfill Co (G-1094)*
**Wall-Fill Company -** ....630 668-3400
649 Childs St Ste 3 Wheaton (60187) *(G-21988)*
**Wallace Auto Parts & Svcs Inc** ....618 268-4446
5605 Highway 34 N Raleigh (62977) *(G-17912)*
**Wallace Enterprises Inc** ....309 496-1230
3121 187th Street Ct N East Moline (61244) *(G-8698)*
**Wallace Industries Inc** ....815 389-8999
530 Eastern Ave South Beloit (61080) *(G-20172)*
**Wallace/Haskin Corp** ....630 789-2882
900 Ogden Ave 181 Downers Grove (60515) *(G-8540)*
**Wallfill Co** ....630 499-9591
2246 Kealsy Ln Aurora (60503) *(G-1094)*
**Wally's Printing, Aurora** *Also called Roskuszka & Sons Inc (G-1210)*
**Wallys Precision Machining** ....708 205-2950
1025 N 27th Ave Melrose Park (60160) *(G-14707)*
**Walman Optical Company** ....309 787-0000
1280 11th St W Milan (61264) *(G-14807)*
**Walneck's Cycle Trader, Downers Grove** *Also called Walnecks Inc (G-8541)*
**Walnecks Inc** ....630 985-2097
7923 Janes Ave Downers Grove (60517) *(G-8541)*
**Walnut Creek Hardwood** ....815 389-3317
851 Doner Dr South Beloit (61080) *(G-20173)*
**Walnut Custom Homes Inc (PA)** ....815 379-2151
300 Wyanet Rd Walnut (61376) *(G-21332)*
**Walnut Custom Homes Inc** ....815 379-2151
300 Wyanet Rd Walnut (61376) *(G-21333)*
**Walnut Grove Packaging** ....217 268-5112
578 E County Road 200n Arcola (61910) *(G-687)*
**Walnut St Winery Plus Saunas** ....217 498-9800
309 S Walnut St Rochester (62563) *(G-18123)*
**Walt Ltd** ....312 337-2756
433 W Armitage Ave Chicago (60614) *(G-6936)*
**Walt Machine and Tool Inc** ....815 754-6484
302 W Lincoln Hwy Ste 6 Cortland (60112) *(G-7396)*
**Walter & Kathy Anczerewicz (PA)** ....708 448-3676
12807 S Harlem Ave Palos Heights (60463) *(G-17113)*
**Walter Barr Inc** ....630 325-7265
655 Executive Dr Willowbrook (60527) *(G-22238)*
**Walter H Jelly & Co Inc** ....847 455-4235
2822 Birch St Franklin Park (60131) *(G-10626)*
**Walter Lagestee Inc** ....708 957-2974
2345 183rd St Ste 2 Homewood (60430) *(G-12106)*
**Walter Louis Chem & Assoc Inc** ....217 223-2017
530 S 5th St Quincy (62301) *(G-17902)*
**Walter Louis Fluid Tech, Quincy** *Also called Walter Louis Chem & Assoc Inc (G-17902)*
**Walter Payton Power Eqp LLC (HQ)** ....708 656-7700
930 W 138th St Riverdale (60827) *(G-18027)*
**Walter Tool & Mfg Inc** ....847 697-7230
1535 Commerce Dr Elgin (60123) *(G-9227)*
**Walters Buildings, Fairfield** *Also called Jack Walters & Sons Corp (G-10145)*
**Walters Distributing Company** ....847 468-0941
1625 Dundee Ave Ste D Elgin (60120) *(G-9228)*
**Walters Metal Fabrication Inc** ....618 931-5551
3660 State Route 111 Granite City (62040) *(G-11311)*
**Walts Food Center, Homewood** *Also called Walter Lagestee Inc (G-12106)*

**Waltz Brothers Inc** ....847 520-1122
10 W Waltz Dr Wheeling (60090) *(G-22181)*
**Wam Ventures Inc** ....312 214-6136
70 W Madison St Ste 1403 Chicago (60602) *(G-6937)*
**Wampach Woodwork Inc** ....847 742-1900
1650 Shanahan Dr South Elgin (60177) *(G-20232)*
**Wand Enterprises Inc (PA)** ....847 433-0231
1029 Green Bay Rd Highland Park (60035) *(G-11880)*
**Wand Tool Company, Highland Park** *Also called Wand Enterprises Inc (G-11880)*
**Wand Tool Enterprise** ....847 433-0231
1029 Green Bay Rd Highland Park (60035) *(G-11881)*
**Wandfluh of America Inc** ....847 566-5700
909 E High St Mundelein (60060) *(G-15566)*
**Wangren Machine, Rolling Meadows** *Also called Apex Tool Works Inc (G-18710)*
**Want ADS of Champaign Inc (PA)** ....217 356-4804
505 E University Ave C Champaign (61820) *(G-3558)*
**Wanxiang New Energy LLC** ....815 226-0884
5985 Logistics Pkwy Rockford (61109) *(G-18672)*
**Wanxiang USA Holdings Corp (HQ)** ....847 622-8838
88 Airport Rd Ste 100 Elgin (60123) *(G-9229)*
**Wapro Inc** ....888 927-8677
150 N Michigan Ave Chicago (60601) *(G-6938)*
**Warbler Digital Inc** ....312 924-1056
20 N Wacker Dr Ste 1200 Chicago (60606) *(G-6939)*
**Warbler of Illinois Company** ....301 520-0438
3127 Village Office Pl Champaign (61822) *(G-3559)*
**Ward C N C Machining, Rockford** *Also called Spare Part Solutions Inc (G-18624)*
**Ward Cnc Machining** ....815 637-1490
7480 Forest Hills Rd Loves Park (61111) *(G-14006)*
**Wardzala Industries Inc** ....847 288-9909
9330 Grand Ave Franklin Park (60131) *(G-10627)*
**Warfield Electric Company Inc (PA)** ....815 469-4094
175 Industry Ave Frankfort (60423) *(G-10376)*
**Wargaming (usa) Inc (PA)** ....312 258-0500
651 W Washington Blvd # 600 Chicago (60661) *(G-6940)*
**Wargaming West, Chicago** *Also called Wargaming (usa) Inc (G-6940)*
**Warming Systems** ....800 663-7831
7706 Industrial Dr Unit D Lake Villa (60046) *(G-13030)*
**Warner Harvey Lee Farm Inc** ....217 849-2548
556 County Road 800 E Toledo (62468) *(G-20970)*
**Warner Electric Indus Pdts, South Beloit** *Also called Warner Electric LLC (G-20174)*
**Warner Electric LLC** ....815 566-4683
6593 Revlon Dr Plant 1 1 Plant Belvidere (61008) *(G-1795)*
**Warner Electric LLC (HQ)** ....815 389-4300
449 Gardner St South Beloit (61080) *(G-20174)*
**Warner Farms, Toledo** *Also called Warner Harvey Lee Farm Inc (G-20970)*
**Warner Industries Inc** ....708 458-0627
6551 W 74th St Bedford Park (60638) *(G-1590)*
**Warner Machine Products Inc** ....815 338-2100
2705 S Il Route 47 Woodstock (60098) *(G-22622)*
**Warner Offset Inc** ....847 695-9400
640 Stevenson Rd South Elgin (60177) *(G-20233)*
**Warp Bros, Chicago** *Also called Flex-O-Glass Inc (G-4858)*
**Warren Oil MGT Co IL LLC** ....618 997-5951
201 N 4th St Marion (62959) *(G-14294)*
**Warren Service Company** ....618 384-2117
1714 Oak St Carmi (62821) *(G-3083)*
**Warren Wiersema Signs** ....815 589-3001
1701 9th Ave Fulton (61252) *(G-10708)*
**Warrior Logging & Perforagine** ....618 662-7373
174 Lincoln Rd Flora (62839) *(G-10220)*
**Warrior Well Services Inc** ....618 662-7710
745 Cedardom Dr Flora (62839) *(G-10221)*
**Warthog Inc** ....815 540-7197
2615 Yonge St Rockford (61101) *(G-18673)*
**Warwick Publishing Company** ....630 584-3871
2601 E Main St Saint Charles (60174) *(G-19291)*
**Waseet America** ....708 430-1950
6000 W 79th St Ste 203 Bedford Park (60459) *(G-1591)*
**Washburn Graficolor Inc** ....630 596-0880
1255 E Bailey Rd Naperville (60565) *(G-15781)*
**Washington Courier** ....309 444-3139
100 Ford Ln Washington (61571) *(G-21394)*
**Washington Equipment Company, Eureka** *Also called Columbus McKinnon Corporation (G-9995)*
**Washington Mills Hennepin Inc** ....815 925-7302
13230 Prairie Indl Pkwy Hennepin (61327) *(G-11735)*
**Washington Mills Tonawanda** ....815 925-7302
City Rd 875 E Hennepin (61327) *(G-11736)*
**Washington URS Div** ....309 578-8113
14009 Old Galena Rd Mossville (61552) *(G-15255)*
**Washington Woodworking** ....309 339-0913
1514 Willow Dr Washington (61571) *(G-21395)*
**Wasowski Jacek** ....847 693-1878
9a E Dundee Quarter Dr A Palatine (60074) *(G-17087)*
**Wastequip LLC** ....618 271-6250
2701 Converse Ave East Saint Louis (62207) *(G-8775)*
**Wastequip Saint Louis** ....216 292-0625
2701 Converse Ave East Saint Louis (62207) *(G-8776)*

ALPHABETIC

**Watchfire Enterprises Inc (HQ)**..........217 442-0611
1015 Maple St Danville (61832) ***(G-7780)***
**Watchfire Signs LLC (HQ)**..........217 442-0611
1015 Maple St Danville (61832) ***(G-7781)***
**Watchfire Tech Holdings I Inc (PA)**..........217 442-6971
1015 Maple St Danville (61832) ***(G-7782)***
**Watchfire Tech Holdings II Inc (HQ)**..........217 442-0611
1015 Maple St Danville (61832) ***(G-7783)***
**Water & Gas Technologies**..........708 829-3254
8046 W 128th Pl Palos Park (60464) ***(G-17134)***
**Water & Oil Technologies Inc**..........630 892-2007
52 Eastfield Rd Montgomery (60538) ***(G-15072)***
**Water Dynamics Inc (PA)**..........630 584-8475
1553 Allen Ln Saint Charles (60174) ***(G-19292)***
**Water Inc**..........815 626-8844
2404 Locust St Sterling (61081) ***(G-20621)***
**Water Products Company III Inc**..........630 553-0840
1213 Badger St Yorkville (60560) ***(G-22675)***
**Water Saver Faucet Co (PA)**..........312 666-5500
701 W Erie St Chicago (60654) ***(G-6941)***
**Water Services Company of Ill**..........847 697-6623
390 Sadler Ave Elgin (60120) ***(G-9230)***
**Waterman Winery & Vineyards**..........815 264-3268
11582 Waterman Rd Waterman (60556) ***(G-21411)***
**Watermat Company, Glen Ellyn** *Also called H2o Pod Inc* ***(G-10972)***
**Waters Associates, Wood Dale** *Also called Waters Technologies Corp* ***(G-22437)***
**Waters Industries Inc**..........847 783-5900
213 W Main St West Dundee (60118) ***(G-21803)***
**Waters Technologies Corp**..........630 766-6249
1360 N Wood Dale Rd Ste C Wood Dale (60191) ***(G-22437)***
**Waters Technologies Corp**..........508 482-8365
4559 Paysphere Cir Chicago (60674) ***(G-6942)***
**Waters Wire EDM Service**..........630 640-3534
2719 Curtiss St Downers Grove (60515) ***(G-8542)***
**Waterway Rv LLC Mfg Home**..........312 207-1835
2 N Riverside Plz Ste 800 Chicago (60606) ***(G-6943)***
**Watlow Richmond, Richmond** *Also called Claud S Gordon Company* ***(G-17960)***
**Watson Foods Co Inc**..........847 245-8404
1711 E Grand Ave Lindenhurst (60046) ***(G-13550)***
**Watson Inc**..........217 824-4440
1900 S Spresser St Taylorville (62568) ***(G-20846)***
**Watt Publishing Co (PA)**..........815 966-5400
303 N Main St Ste 500 Rockford (61101) ***(G-18674)***
**Watt Publishing Co**..........815 966-5400
303 N Main St Ste 500 Rockford (61101) ***(G-18675)***
**Wattcore Inc**..........571 482-6777
6208 Oakton St Morton Grove (60053) ***(G-15245)***
**Watters Fishmarket, Hamburg** *Also called Betty Watters* ***(G-11526)***
**Wauconda Tool & Engineering Co**..........847 608-0602
690 Church Rd Elgin (60123) ***(G-9231)***
**Wauconda Tool & Engrg LLC (HQ)**..........847 658-4588
821 W Algonquin Rd Algonquin (60102) ***(G-412)***
**Waukegan Architectural Inc**..........847 746-9077
3505 16th St Zion (60099) ***(G-22700)***
**Waukegan Ready Mix, Waukegan** *Also called Thelen Sand & Gravel Inc* ***(G-21625)***
**Waukegan Steel LLC**..........847 662-2810
1201 Belvidere Rd Waukegan (60085) ***(G-21639)***
**Waupaca Foundry Inc**..........217 347-0600
1500 Heartland Blvd Effingham (62401) ***(G-8862)***
**Wave Mechanics Neon**..........312 829-9283
450 N Leavitt St Chicago (60612) ***(G-6944)***
**Waverly Journal**..........217 435-9221
130 S Pearl St Waverly (62692) ***(G-21645)***
**Waves Fluid Solutions LLC**..........630 765-7533
350 S Schmale Rd Ste 17 Carol Stream (60188) ***(G-3264)***
**Waveteam LLC**..........630 323-0277
10 Hampshire West 260 S Hinsdale (60527) ***(G-11968)***
**Waxman Candles Inc**..........773 929-3000
3044 N Lincoln Ave Chicago (60657) ***(G-6945)***
**Waxstar Inc**..........708 755-3530
3224 Butler St S Chicago Hts (60411) ***(G-19115)***
**Wayland Ready Mix Concrete Svc**..........309 833-2064
1343 W Jackson St Macomb (61455) ***(G-14134)***
**Waymore Power Co Inc**..........618 729-3876
8334 Piasa Rd Piasa (62079) ***(G-17543)***
**Wayne County Press Inc**..........618 842-2662
213 E Main St Fairfield (62837) ***(G-10159)***
**Wayne County Well Surveys Inc**..........618 842-9116
2225 Industrial Dr Fairfield (62837) ***(G-10160)***
**Wayne Engineering (PA)**..........847 674-7166
8242 Christiana Ave Skokie (60076) ***(G-20110)***
**Wayne Printing Company (PA)**..........309 691-2496
7917 N Kckapoo Edwards Rd Edwards (61528) ***(G-8785)***
**Wayne Printing Company**..........309 691-2496
7917 N Kckapoo Edwards Rd Edwards (61528) ***(G-8786)***
**Wayne Wagoner Printing, Edwards** *Also called Wayne Printing Company* ***(G-8786)***
**Waypoint Enterprises**..........847 551-9213
2328 Stonegate Rd Algonquin (60102) ***(G-413)***
**Wb Tray LLC**..........618 918-3821
115 Harting Dr Centralia (62801) ***(G-3437)***
**WCI, Chicago** *Also called Wood Creations Incorporated* ***(G-7022)***
**Wctu Press (PA)**..........847 864-1396
1730 Chicago Ave Evanston (60201) ***(G-10105)***
**We Are Done LLC**..........708 598-7100
8407 S 77th Ave Bridgeview (60455) ***(G-2538)***
**We Clean**..........708 574-2551
5845 Victoria Dr Oak Forest (60452) ***(G-16593)***
**We Innovex Inc**..........847 291-3553
3045 Macarthur Blvd Northbrook (60062) ***(G-16384)***
**We International**..........618 549-1784
54 Oakview Rd Carbondale (62901) ***(G-3026)***
**We Love Soy Inc**..........630 629-9667
905 N Ridge Ave Ste 8 Lombard (60148) ***(G-13881)***
**We-B-Print Inc**..........309 353-8801
1107 N 8th St Pekin (61554) ***(G-17293)***
**Weakley Enterprises Inc**..........815 498-3429
119 W Market St Somonauk (60552) ***(G-20130)***
**Weakley Printing & Sign Shop**..........847 473-4466
1550 Green Bay Rd North Chicago (60064) ***(G-16189)***
**Wealth Partners Publishing Inc**..........312 854-2522
1136 S Delano Ct W B201 Chicago (60605) ***(G-6946)***
**Wear Cote International Inc**..........309 793-1250
101 10th St Rock Island (61201) ***(G-18211)***
**Wear-Flex Slings, Chicago** *Also called MHS Ltd* ***(G-5716)***
**Weary & Baity Inc**..........312 943-6197
333 W North Ave Ste F Chicago (60610) ***(G-6947)***
**Weatherford Signs**..........618 529-2000
219 Weatherford Ln Carbondale (62902) ***(G-3027)***
**Weatherguard Buildings**..........217 894-6213
1654 E 2950th St Clayton (62324) ***(G-7270)***
**Weathertop Woodcraft**
26w282 Macarthur Ave Carol Stream (60188) ***(G-3265)***
**Weaver Equipment LLC**..........618 833-5521
1240 Mount Pleasant Rd Buncombe (62912) ***(G-2802)***
**Weaver Equitment Co, Buncombe** *Also called Weaver Equipment LLC* ***(G-2802)***
**Web Printing Control, Arlington Heights** *Also called Wpc Machinery Corp* ***(G-874)***
**Web Printing Controls Co Inc (PA)**..........618 842-2664
3350 W Salt Creek Ln # 110 Arlington Heights (60005) ***(G-870)***
**Web Printing Controls Co Inc**..........618 842-2664
600 Us Highway 45 Ste A Fairfield (62837) ***(G-10161)***
**WEb Production & Fabg Inc**..........312 733-6800
448 N Artesian Ave Chicago (60612) ***(G-6948)***
**Webb-Mason Inc**..........630 428-5838
280 Shuman Blvd Ste 200 Naperville (60563) ***(G-15782)***
**Webcrafters Inc**..........847 658-6661
1530 Farmhill Dr Algonquin (60102) ***(G-414)***
**Webe Ink**..........618 498-7620
103 Lincoln Ave Jerseyville (62052) ***(G-12429)***
**Weber Flavors, Wheeling** *Also called Edgar A Weber & Company* ***(G-22043)***
**Weber Flavors, Wheeling** *Also called Edgar A Weber & Company* ***(G-22044)***
**Weber Grills, Palatine** *Also called Weber-Stephen Products LLC* ***(G-17088)***
**Weber Grills, Palatine** *Also called Weber-Stephen Products LLC* ***(G-17089)***
**Weber Marking Systems Inc (PA)**..........847 364-8500
711 W Algonquin Rd Arlington Heights (60005) ***(G-871)***
**Weber Meat Inc**..........217 357-2130
515 Miller St Carthage (62321) ***(G-3319)***
**Weber Metal Products Inc**..........815 844-3169
10702 E 1400 North Rd Chenoa (61726) ***(G-3636)***
**Weber Metals Inc**..........847 951-7920
1076 E Park Ave Libertyville (60048) ***(G-13400)***
**Weber Packaging Solutions Inc, Arlington Heights** *Also called Weber Marking Systems Inc* ***(G-871)***
**Weber Press Inc**..........773 561-9815
5746 N Western Ave Chicago (60659) ***(G-6949)***
**Weber-Stephen Products LLC (PA)**..........847 934-5700
1415 S Roselle Rd Palatine (60067) ***(G-17088)***
**Weber-Stephen Products LLC**..........224 836-8536
306 E Helen Rd Palatine (60067) ***(G-17089)***
**Weber-Stephen Products LLC**..........847 669-4900
11811 Oak Creek Pkwy Huntley (60142) ***(G-12183)***
**Webqa Incorporated (PA)**..........630 985-1300
900 S Frontage Rd Ste 110 Woodridge (60517) ***(G-22523)***
**Websolutions Technology Inc**..........630 375-6833
3817 Mccoy Dr Ste 105 Aurora (60504) ***(G-1095)***
**Webster-Hoff Corporation**..........630 858-8030
704 E Fullerton Ave Glendale Heights (60139) ***(G-11091)***
**Webzonepro.com, Deerfield** *Also called Medical ID Fashions Company* ***(G-8035)***
**Wec Welding and Machining LLC (HQ)**..........847 680-8100
1 Energy Dr Lake Bluff (60044) ***(G-12870)***
**Wecaretoo, Chicago** *Also called TWT Marketing Inc* ***(G-6799)***
**Weco Trading Inc (PA)**..........847 615-1020
21 N Skokie Hwy Ste 101 Lake Bluff (60044) ***(G-12871)***
**Wedco Molded Products**..........630 455-6711
7409 S Quincy St Willowbrook (60527) ***(G-22239)***
**Wedding Brand Investors LLC**..........847 887-0071
1225 Karl Ct Wauconda (60084) ***(G-21513)***
**Wedding Pages of Chicago, The, Elk Grove Village** *Also called Chambers Marketing Options* ***(G-9364)***

**Wedgworths Inc (PA)**.....863 682-2153
1101 Skokie Blvd Ste 400 Northbrook (60062) ***(G-16385)***
**Wednesday Journal Inc**.....708 386-5555
141 S Oak Park Ave Ste 1 Oak Park (60302) ***(G-16691)***
**Wedron Flux Div, Serena** *Also called Kona Blackbird Inc* ***(G-19892)***
**Wedron Silica Company**.....815 433-2449
3450 E 2056 Rd Wedron (60557) ***(G-21646)***
**Weeb Enterprises LLC**.....815 861-2625
770 Peninsula Dr Wauconda (60084) ***(G-21514)***
**Weekly James**.....815 786-8203
1305 Vale St Sandwich (60548) ***(G-19380)***
**Weekly Journals**.....815 459-4040
7717 S Il Route 31 Crystal Lake (60014) ***(G-7675)***
**Weekly Newspaper, Goreville** *Also called Goreville Gazette* ***(G-11253)***
**Weekly Visitor**.....815 845-2328
101 E Burrall Ave Scales Mound (61075) ***(G-19416)***
**Weeks Seatcovers, Springfield** *Also called Bill Weeks Inc* ***(G-20397)***
**Weetech Inc**.....847 775-7240
1300 N Skokie Hwy Ste 104 Gurnee (60031) ***(G-11520)***
**Weg Electric Motors**.....630 226-5688
2 Gateway Ct Bolingbrook (60440) ***(G-2381)***
**Wehrle Lumber Co Inc**.....618 283-4859
820 E 1900 Ave Vandalia (62471) ***(G-21131)***
**Wehrli Custom Fabrication**.....630 277-8239
417 Borden Ave Sycamore (60178) ***(G-20825)***
**Wehrli Equipment Co Inc**.....630 717-4150
1805 High Grove Ln # 117 Naperville (60540) ***(G-15783)***
**WEI TO Associates Inc**.....708 747-6660
21750 Main St Unit 27 Matteson (60443) ***(G-14381)***
**WEI-Chuan USA Inc**.....708 352-8886
6845 Santa Fe Dr Hodgkins (60525) ***(G-11987)***
**Weidenmiller Co**.....630 250-2500
1464 Industrial Dr Itasca (60143) ***(G-12373)***
**Weigh Right Automatic Scale Co**.....815 726-4626
612a Mills Rd Joliet (60433) ***(G-12588)***
**Weiland Fast Trac Inc**.....847 438-7996
3386 Rfd Long Grove (60047) ***(G-13905)***
**Weiland Metal Products Company**.....773 631-4210
6437 N Avondale Ave Chicago (60631) ***(G-6950)***
**Weiland Welding Inc**.....815 580-8079
4727 Lindbloom Ln Cherry Valley (61016) ***(G-3649)***
**Weiler Engineering Inc**.....847 697-4900
1395 Gateway Dr Elgin (60124) ***(G-9232)***
**Weiler Rubber Technologies LLC**.....773 826-8900
4223 W Lake St Chicago (60624) ***(G-6951)***
**Weimer Design & Print Ltd Inc**.....630 393-3334
3s25 State Route 59 Warrenville (60555) ***(G-21368)***
**Weiner Optical Inc**.....708 848-4040
1100 Lake St Ste 180 Oak Park (60301) ***(G-16692)***
**Weiskamp Screen Printing**.....217 398-8428
312 S Neil St Champaign (61820) ***(G-3560)***
**Weiss Monument Works Inc**.....618 398-1811
9904 W Main St Belleville (62223) ***(G-1690)***
**Welch Bros Inc (PA)**.....847 741-6134
1050 Saint Charles St Elgin (60120) ***(G-9233)***
**Welch Bros Inc**.....815 547-3000
1000 Town Hall Rd Belvidere (61008) ***(G-1796)***
**Welch Packaging LLC**.....630 916-8090
1000 N Main St Lombard (60148) ***(G-13882)***
**Welch Packaging LLC**.....708 813-1520
5300 Dansher Rd Countryside (60525) ***(G-7451)***
**Welch Steel Products Inc**.....847 741-2623
333 Hammond Ave Elgin (60120) ***(G-9234)***
**Weld-Rite Service Inc**.....708 458-6000
6715 W 73rd St Bedford Park (60638) ***(G-1592)***
**Weldbend Corporation**.....708 594-1700
6600 S Harlem Ave Argo (60501) ***(G-697)***
**Welding Apparatus Company**.....773 252-7670
87 Honing Rd Fox Lake (60020) ***(G-10284)***
**Welding Company of America**.....630 806-2000
335 E Sullivan Rd Aurora (60505) ***(G-1231)***
**Welding Fabrication, Loves Park** *Also called Rrb Fabrication Inc* ***(G-13989)***
**Welding Shop**.....773 785-1305
109 W 103rd St Chicago (60628) ***(G-6952)***
**Welding Specialties**.....708 798-5388
17300 Laflin Ave East Hazel Crest (60429) ***(G-8667)***
**Weldon Corporation**.....708 343-4700
1818 Madison St Maywood (60153) ***(G-14437)***
**Weldstar Company (PA)**.....630 859-3100
1750 Mitchell Rd Aurora (60505) ***(G-1232)***
**Weldstar Company**.....708 534-6419
1100 Hamilton Ave University Park (60484) ***(G-21066)***
**Welkins LLC**.....877 319-3504
3000 Woodcreek Dr Ste 300 Downers Grove (60515) ***(G-8543)***
**Wellington Drive Tech US**.....847 922-5098
1407 Barclay Blvd Buffalo Grove (60089) ***(G-2792)***
**Welliver & Sons Inc**.....815 874-2400
1540 New Milford Schl Rd Rockford (61109) ***(G-18676)***
**Wellmark Int Farnam Co**.....925 948-4000
1501 E Wdfeld Rd Ste 200w Schaumburg (60173) ***(G-19787)***
**Wellness Center Usa Inc (PA)**.....847 925-1885
2500 W Higgins Rd Ste 770 Hoffman Estates (60169) ***(G-12069)***
**Wellness Monitoring, Chicago** *Also called Carematix Inc* ***(G-4242)***
**Wells Janitorial Service Inc**.....872 226-9983
11006 S Michigan Ave # 5 Chicago (60628) ***(G-6953)***
**Wells Lamont Indust Group LLC**.....800 247-3295
6640 W Touhy Ave Niles (60714) ***(G-16046)***
**Wells Pet Stores, Monmouth** *Also called Midwestern Pet Foods Inc* ***(G-15019)***
**Wells Printing Co, Oak Park** *Also called Charles Chauncey Wells Inc* ***(G-16657)***
**Wells Sinkware Corp**.....312 850-3466
916 W 21st St Chicago (60608) ***(G-6954)***
**Wells-Gardner, Countryside** *Also called American Gaming & Elec Inc* ***(G-7414)***
**Wellspring Investments LLC**.....773 736-1213
5470 N Elston Ave Chicago (60630) ***(G-6955)***
**Welsch Ready Mix, Morris** *Also called T H Davidson & Co Inc* ***(G-15134)***
**Welsh Industries Ltd**.....815 756-1111
6 Evergreen Cir Dekalb (60115) ***(G-8131)***
**Wema Vogtland America LLC**.....815 544-0526
4793 Colt Rd Rockford (61109) ***(G-18677)***
**Wemco Inc**.....708 388-1980
11721 S Austin Ave Alsip (60803) ***(G-543)***
**Wenco Manufacturing Co Inc**.....630 377-7474
11n261 Muirhead Rd Elgin (60124) ***(G-9235)***
**Wendell Adams (PA)**.....217 345-9587
1286 W State St Charleston (61920) ***(G-3615)***
**Wenesco Inc**.....773 283-3004
4700 W Montrose Ave Chicago (60641) ***(G-6956)***
**Wenger Woodcraft**.....217 578-3440
676 N County Road 250 E Tuscola (61953) ***(G-21030)***
**Wengers Springbrook Cheese Inc**.....815 865-5855
12805 N Spring Brook Rd Davis (61019) ***(G-7809)***
**Wenlyn Screw Company Inc**.....630 766-0050
810 Maple Ln Bensenville (60106) ***(G-2013)***
**Wenner Media LLC**.....312 660-3040
333 N Michigan Ave # 1105 Chicago (60601) ***(G-6957)***
**Wenona Food & Fuel**.....815 853-4141
3075 Il Route 17 Wenona (61377) ***(G-21649)***
**Wenona Index, Henry** *Also called Henry News Republican* ***(G-11743)***
**Werner Co**.....815 459-6020
420 E Terra Cotta Ave Crystal Lake (60014) ***(G-7676)***
**Werner Co**.....847 455-8001
850 N Arlington Hts Rd Itasca (60143) ***(G-12374)***
**Wernze Farms Inc**.....618 569-4820
20563 N 400th St Annapolis (62413) ***(G-609)***
**Wertheimer Box & Paper Corp**.....312 829-4545
7950 Joliet Rd Ste 100 Mc Cook (60525) ***(G-14461)***
**Wes Tech Printing Graphic**.....630 520-9041
1555 W Hawthorne Ln West Chicago (60185) ***(G-21792)***
**Wes-Tech Inc**.....847 541-5070
720 Dartmouth Ln Buffalo Grove (60089) ***(G-2793)***
**Wes-Tech Automtn Solutions LLC**.....847 541-5070
720 Dartmouth Ln Buffalo Grove (60089) ***(G-2794)***
**Wesco, Chicago** *Also called Sterling Spring LLC* ***(G-6591)***
**Wesco, Chicago** *Also called Sterling Spring LLC* ***(G-6592)***
**Wesco International Inc**.....630 513-4864
737 N Oaklawn Ave Elmhurst (60126) ***(G-9960)***
**Wesco Spring Company**.....773 838-3350
4501 S Knox Ave Chicago (60632) ***(G-6958)***
**Wescom Products**.....217 932-5292
503 Ne 15th St Casey (62420) ***(G-3392)***
**Wesdar Technologies Inc**.....630 761-0965
924 Vineyard Ln Aurora (60502) ***(G-1096)***
**Wesley-Jessen Corporation Del**.....847 294-3000
333 Howard Ave Des Plaines (60018) ***(G-8302)***
**Wesling Products Inc**.....773 533-2850
2912 W Lake St Chicago (60612) ***(G-6959)***
**West Agro Inc**.....847 298-5505
1855 S Mount Prospect Rd Des Plaines (60018) ***(G-8303)***
**West Central Fs Inc**.....309 375-6904
686 N Depot Rd Wataga (61488) ***(G-21399)***
**West Chicago Printing Company, West Chicago** *Also called Treudt Corporation* ***(G-21785)***
**West End Tool & Die Inc**.....815 462-3040
22020 Howell Dr New Lenox (60451) ***(G-15927)***
**West Fuels Inc**.....708 488-8880
7340 Harrison St Forest Park (60130) ***(G-10257)***
**West Laboratories Inc**.....815 935-1630
1305 Harvard Dr Kankakee (60901) ***(G-12658)***
**West Lake Concrete & Rmdlg LLC**.....847 477-8667
2029 N Lavergne Ave Chicago (60639) ***(G-6960)***
**West Liberty Foods LLC**.....603 679-2300
750 S Schmidt Rd Bolingbrook (60440) ***(G-2382)***
**West Machine Products Inc**.....847 740-2404
606 Long Lake Dr Round Lake (60073) ***(G-19070)***
**West Precision Tool Inc**.....630 766-8304
447 Evergreen Ave Bensenville (60106) ***(G-2014)***
**West Publishing Corporation**.....312 894-1690
111 W Jackson Blvd # 1700 Chicago (60604) ***(G-6961)***
**West Salem Knox County Htchy**.....618 456-3601
615 W Church St West Salem (62476) ***(G-21825)***

ALPHABETIC

**West Side Machine Inc** .......................................... 630 243-1069
   11201 S Boyer St Lemont (60439) *(G-13269)*
**West Side Tractor Sales Co** .................................... 815 961-3160
   3110 Prairie Rd Rockford (61102) *(G-18678)*
**West Star Aviation LLC** ......................................... 618 259-3230
   2 Airline Ct East Alton (62024) *(G-8612)*
**West Suburban Journal** .......................................... 708 344-5975
   229 Esprit Ct Bloomingdale (60108) *(G-2141)*
**West Suburban Journal News, Westchester** Also called Trottie Publishing Group Inc *(G-21859)*
**West Suburban Living Magazine, Hillside** Also called C2 Publishing Inc *(G-11912)*
**West Town Plating Inc** ........................................... 708 652-1600
   5243 W 25th Pl Cicero (60804) *(G-7245)*
**West Vly Graphics & Print Inc** ................................. 630 377-7575
   201 S 3rd St Saint Charles (60174) *(G-19293)*
**West Water Inc** .................................................... 312 326-7480
   463 W 24th St Ste 1 Chicago (60616) *(G-6962)*
**West Zwick Corp** .................................................. 217 222-0228
   2132 Glenayre Way Quincy (62305) *(G-17903)*
**Westell Inc (HQ)** .................................................. 630 898-2500
   750 N Commons Dr Aurora (60504) *(G-1097)*
**Westell Technologies Inc (PA)** ................................. 630 898-2500
   750 N Commons Dr Aurora (60504) *(G-1098)*
**Westerling Group** ................................................. 708 547-8488
   5311 Saint Charles Rd Berkeley (60163) *(G-2052)*
**Western Auto Associate Str Co** ............................... 618 357-5555
   9 S Walnut St Pinckneyville (62274) *(G-17554)*
**Western Consolidated Tech Inc** ............................... 815 334-3684
   1425 Lake Ave Woodstock (60098) *(G-22623)*
**Western Digital Tech Inc** ........................................ 949 672-7000
   15535 Collection Ctr Dr Chicago (60693) *(G-6963)*
**Western Illinois Optical Inc** .................................... 309 837-2000
   909 E Grant St Macomb (61455) *(G-14135)*
**Western Illinois Enterprises** ................................... 309 342-5185
   161 N Academy St Galesburg (61401) *(G-10779)*
**Western Lighting Inc** ............................................ 847 451-7200
   2349 17th St Franklin Park (60131) *(G-10628)*
**Western Motor Mfg Co** ......................................... 815 986-2214
   1211 23rd Ave Rockford (61104) *(G-18679)*
**Western Motor Service Div, Rockford** Also called Forest City Auto Electric Co *(G-18386)*
**Western Oil & Gas Dev Co** .................................... 618 544-8646
   9234 E 1050th Ave Robinson (62454) *(G-18075)*
**Western Pece Dyers Fnshers Inc** ............................ 773 523-7000
   122 W 22nd St Oak Brook (60523) *(G-16569)*
**Western Plastics Inc** ............................................ 630 629-3034
   1731 W Armitage Ct Addison (60101) *(G-342)*
**Western Printing Machinery Co (PA)** ....................... 847 678-1740
   9229 Ivanhoe St Schiller Park (60176) *(G-19883)*
**Western Printing Machinery Co** .............................. 847 678-1740
   9228 Ivanhoe St Schiller Park (60176) *(G-19884)*
**Western Railway Devices Corp** .............................. 847 625-8500
   1214 14th St Ste A Waukegan (60085) *(G-21640)*
**Western Railway Equipment, Waukegan** Also called Western Railway Devices Corp *(G-21640)*
**Western Remac Inc (PA)** ....................................... 630 972-7770
   1740 Internationale Pkwy Woodridge (60517) *(G-22524)*
**Western Sand & Gravel Co** .................................... 815 433-1600
   4220 Mbl Dr Ottawa (61350) *(G-16991)*
**Western Slate Company** ....................................... 847 683-4400
   365 Keyes Ave Hampshire (60140) *(G-11565)*
**Western Stoneware, Monmouth** Also called Ws Incorporated of Manmouth *(G-15024)*
**Western Yeast Company Inc** .................................. 309 274-3160
   305 W Ash St Chillicothe (61523) *(G-7172)*
**Western-Cullen-Hayes Inc (PA)** ............................... 773 254-9600
   2700 W 36th Pl Chicago (60632) *(G-6964)*
**Westfalia-Surge Inc** ............................................. 630 759-7346
   1354 Enterprise Dr Romeoville (60446) *(G-18878)*
**Westinghouse, Lake Bluff** Also called Wec Welding and Machining LLC *(G-12870)*
**Westinghouse A Brake Tech Corp** ........................... 708 596-6730
   8401 S Stewart Ave Chicago (60620) *(G-6965)*
**Westmin Corporation** ........................................... 217 224-4570
   2733 Wild Horse Quincy (62305) *(G-17904)*
**Westmont Engineering Company, Broadview** Also called Morey Industries Inc *(G-2598)*
**Westmont Metal Mfg LLC** ..................................... 708 343-0214
   2350 S 27th Ave Broadview (60155) *(G-2620)*
**Westmont Mri Center** .......................................... 630 856-4060
   6311 S Cass Ave Westmont (60559) *(G-21927)*
**Westmore Supply Co** .......................................... 630 627-0278
   250 Westmore Meyers Rd Lombard (60148) *(G-13883)*
**Westosha Airport, Antioch** Also called Thelen Sand & Gravel Inc *(G-656)*
**Westran Thermal Processing LLC** ........................... 815 634-1001
   483 Gardner St South Beloit (61080) *(G-20175)*
**Westrock Cnsmr Packg Group LLC** ........................ 804 444-1000
   1950 N Ruby St Melrose Park (60160) *(G-14708)*
**Westrock Company** ............................................ 630 429-2400
   1601 Mountain St Aurora (60505) *(G-1233)*
**Westrock Converting Company** ............................. 630 783-6700
   365 Crossing Rd Bolingbrook (60440) *(G-2383)*

**Westrock Cp LLC** ................................................ 309 342-0121
   775 S Linwood Rd Galesburg (61401) *(G-10780)*
**Westrock Cp LLC** ................................................ 847 689-4200
   1900 Foss Park Ave North Chicago (60064) *(G-16190)*
**Westrock Cp LLC** ................................................ 708 458-8100
   7601 S 78th Ave Bridgeview (60455) *(G-2539)*
**Westrock Cp LLC** ................................................ 630 924-0104
   965 Muirfield Dr Bartlett (60133) *(G-1325)*
**Westrock Cp LLC** ................................................ 630 384-5200
   450 E North Ave Carol Stream (60188) *(G-3266)*
**Westrock Cp LLC** ................................................ 630 260-3500
   450 E North Ave Carol Stream (60188) *(G-3267)*
**Westrock CP LLC** ................................................ 618 654-2141
   501 Zschokke St Highland (62249) *(G-11818)*
**Westrock CP LLC** ................................................ 630 443-3538
   415 37th Ave Saint Charles (60174) *(G-19294)*
**Westrock CP LLC** ................................................ 773 264-3516
   626 E 111th St Chicago (60628) *(G-6966)*
**Westrock CP LLC** ................................................ 847 625-8284
   3145 Central Ave Waukegan (60085) *(G-21641)*
**Westrock CP LLC** ................................................ 630 655-6951
   8170 S Madison St Burr Ridge (60527) *(G-2893)*
**Westrock CP LLC** ................................................ 630 924-0054
   965 Muirfield Dr Bartlett (60133) *(G-1326)*
**Westrock CP LLC** ................................................ 312 346-6600
   150 N Michigan Ave Chicago (60601) *(G-6967)*
**Westrock CP LLC** ................................................ 708 458-5288
   6131 W 74th St Bedford Park (60638) *(G-1593)*
**Westrock Dspensing Systems Inc** .......................... 847 310-3073
   1325 Remington Rd Ste H Schaumburg (60173) *(G-19788)*
**Westrock Healthcare, Bartlett** Also called Westrock Mwv LLC *(G-1386)*
**Westrock Mwv LLC** ............................................. 773 221-9015
   9540 S Dorchester Ave Chicago (60628) *(G-6968)*
**Westrock Mwv LLC** ............................................. 217 442-2247
   202 Eastgate Dr Danville (61834) *(G-7784)*
**Westrock Mwv LLC** ............................................. 630 289-8537
   1534 Stockton Ct Bartlett (60103) *(G-1386)*
**Westrock Rkt Company** ....................................... 312 346-6600
   222 N La Salle St Chicago (60601) *(G-6969)*
**Westrock Rkt Company** ....................................... 847 649-9231
   1945 Cornell Ave Melrose Park (60160) *(G-14709)*
**Westrock Rkt Company** ....................................... 630 325-9670
   51 Shore Dr Ste 1 Burr Ridge (60527) *(G-2894)*
**Westville Ready Mix Inc** ....................................... 217 267-2082
   1409 English St Westville (61883) *(G-21931)*
**Westway Feed Products LLC** ................................. 309 654-2211
   22220 Route 84 N Cordova (61242) *(G-7380)*
**Westway Trading, Cordova** Also called Westway Feed Products LLC *(G-7380)*
**Westwick Foundry Ltd** ......................................... 815 777-0815
   200 S Main St Galena (61036) *(G-10734)*
**Westwood Lands Inc** ........................................... 618 877-4990
   4 Caine Dr Madison (62060) *(G-14156)*
**Westwood Machine & Tool Co** .............................. 815 626-5090
   1703 Westwood Dr Sterling (61081) *(G-20622)*
**Wet & Forget Usa A New Zealnd** .......................... 847 428-3894
   2521 Tech Dr Ste 209 Elgin (60124) *(G-9236)*
**Wevaultcom LLC** ................................................ 877 938-2858
   190 Liberty Rd Unit 3 Crystal Lake (60014) *(G-7677)*
**Wex Distributors Inc** ........................................... 847 691-5823
   40471 N Bluff Dr Antioch (60002) *(G-663)*
**Wexford Home Corp** ........................................... 847 922-5738
   707 Skokie Blvd Northbrook (60062) *(G-16386)*
**Weyerhaeuser Company** ...................................... 847 439-1111
   1800 Nicholas Blvd Elk Grove Village (60007) *(G-9811)*
**Weyerhaeuser Company** ...................................... 815 987-0395
   1753 23rd Ave Rockford (61104) *(G-18680)*
**Weyerhaeuser Company** ...................................... 630 778-7070
   220 Brookshire Ct Naperville (60540) *(G-15784)*
**Weyerhauser, Naperville** Also called Weyerhaeuser Company *(G-15784)*
**Wf Machining Product, Darien** Also called Willow Farm Product Inc *(G-7804)*
**Wgel Radio, Greenville** Also called Bond Broadcasting Inc *(G-11389)*
**Wgt, Palos Park** Also called Water & Gas Technologies *(G-17134)*
**Whale Manufacturing Inc** ...................................... 847 357-9192
   870 N Ridge Ave Lombard (60148) *(G-13884)*
**Whalen Manufacturing Company** ........................... 309 836-1438
   1270 E Murray St Macomb (61455) *(G-14136)*
**What We Make Inc** ............................................. 331 442-4830
   115 Mill Ave Hampshire (60140) *(G-11566)*
**Wheatland Tube Company, Chicago** Also called John Maneely Company *(G-5316)*
**Wheaton Brace, Carol Stream** Also called Wheaton Resource Corp *(G-3268)*
**Wheaton Cabinetry** ............................................. 815 729-1085
   17238 Weber Rd Lockport (60441) *(G-13750)*
**Wheaton Lines, Peru** Also called Quesse Moving & Storage Inc *(G-17525)*
**Wheaton Plastic Products** .................................... 847 298-5626
   1731 S Mount Prospect Rd Des Plaines (60018) *(G-8304)*
**Wheaton Resource Corp** ...................................... 630 690-5795
   380 S Schmale Rd Ste 121 Carol Stream (60188) *(G-3268)*
**Wheaton Trophy & Engravers** ................................ 630 682-4200
   107 W Front St Ste 3 Wheaton (60187) *(G-21989)*

ALPHABETIC SECTION William Holloway Ltd

**Wheel Worx North LLC** ....309 346-3535
200 Hanna Dr Pekin (61554) **(G-17294)**
**Wheeling Service & Supply** ....815 338-6410
15920 Nelson Rd Woodstock (60098) **(G-22624)**
**Wheels & Deals** ....217 423-6333
170 N Oakdale Blvd Decatur (62522) **(G-7959)**
**Wherry Machine & Welding Inc** ....309 828-5423
11 Carri Dr Bloomington (61705) **(G-2235)**
**Whi Capital Partners (HQ)** ....312 621-0590
191 N Wacker Dr Ste 1500 Chicago (60606) **(G-6970)**
**Whipples Printing Press Inc** ....309 787-3538
2410 119th Avenue Ct W Milan (61264) **(G-14808)**
**Whisco Component Engrg Inc** ....630 790-9785
501 Mitchell Rd Glendale Heights (60139) **(G-11092)**
**Whiskey Acres Distilling Co** ....815 739-8711
11504 Keslinger Rd Dekalb (60115) **(G-8132)**
**Whitacres Country Oaks Shop** ....309 726-1305
704 S Broadway St Hudson (61748) **(G-12127)**
**Whitacres Handcrafted, Hudson** *Also called Whitacres Country Oaks Shop* **(G-12127)**
**White Cap Illinois, Downers Grove** *Also called Silgan White Cap Americas LLC* **(G-8524)**
**White County Coal LLC (HQ)** ....618 382-4651
1525 County Rd 1300 N Carmi (62821) **(G-3084)**
**White Eagle Brands Inc** ....773 631-1764
7257 W Touhy Ave Ste 102 Chicago (60631) **(G-6971)**
**White Eagle Spring &** ....773 384-4455
1637 N Lowell Ave Chicago (60639) **(G-6972)**
**White Graphics Inc** ....630 791-0232
1411 Centre Cir Downers Grove (60515) **(G-8544)**
**White Graphics Printing Svcs** ....630 629-9300
1411 Centre Cir Downers Grove (60515) **(G-8545)**
**White International Inc** ....630 377-9966
2560 Foxfield Rd Ste 200 Saint Charles (60174) **(G-19295)**
**White Jig Grinding** ....847 888-2260
625 Martin Dr South Elgin (60177) **(G-20234)**
**White Land & Mineral Inc** ....618 262-5102
526 N Market St Mount Carmel (62863) **(G-15288)**
**White Oak Resources LLC** ....618 643-5500
18033 County Road 500 E Dahlgren (62828) **(G-7693)**
**White Oak Technology** ....309 228-4201
524 Wedgewood Ter Germantown Hills (61548) **(G-10896)**
**White Owl Winery Incorporated** ....618 928-2898
Rr 1 Flat Rock (62427) **(G-10199)**
**White Picket Media Inc** ....773 769-8400
4611 N Ravenswood Ave # 101 Chicago (60640) **(G-6973)**
**White Pigeon Paper Co Div, Elgin** *Also called Artistic Carton Company* **(G-8958)**
**White Racker Co Inc** ....847 758-1640
420 Lively Blvd Elk Grove Village (60007) **(G-9812)**
**White Sheet Metal** ....217 465-3195
303 N Austin St Paris (61944) **(G-17164)**
**White Star Silo** ....618 523-4735
8320 Wesclin Rd Germantown (62245) **(G-10894)**
**White Stokes Company Inc** ....773 254-5000
4433 W Touhy Ave Ste 207 Lincolnwood (60712) **(G-13543)**
**White Way Sign & Maint Co** ....847 391-0200
2722 N Racine Ave Chicago (60614) **(G-6974)**
**Whiteside Drapery Fabricators** ....847 746-5300
2701 Deborah Ave Ste A Zion (60099) **(G-22701)**
**Whiting Corporation (HQ)** ....708 587-2000
26000 S Whiting Way Ste 1 Monee (60449) **(G-15007)**
**Whitley Products Inc (HQ)** ....574 267-7114
2 N Rverside Plz Ste 1025 Chicago (60606) **(G-6975)**
**Whitney Foods Inc** ....773 842-8511
2541 S Damen Ave Chicago (60608) **(G-6976)**
**Whitney Medical Solutions, Niles** *Also called Whitney Products Inc* **(G-16047)**
**Whitney Products Inc** ....847 966-6161
6153 W Mulford St Ste C Niles (60714) **(G-16047)**
**Whitney Roper LLC** ....815 962-3011
2833 Huffman Blvd Rockford (61103) **(G-18681)**
**Whitney Roper Rockford Inc** ....815 962-3011
2833 Huffman Blvd Rockford (61103) **(G-18682)**
**Whitson Bindery Services** ....847 515-8371
25527 W Brooks Farm Rd Round Lake (60073) **(G-19071)**
**Whittl, Chicago** *Also called Band of Shoppers Inc* **(G-4035)**
**Wholesale Gate Co, Dekalb** *Also called Tim Detwiler Enterprises Inc* **(G-8127)**
**Wholesale Point Inc** ....630 986-1700
260 Shore Ct Burr Ridge (60527) **(G-2895)**
**Wholesome Harvest Baking LLC (HQ)** ....800 550-6810
1011 E Touhy Ave Ste 500 Des Plaines (60018) **(G-8305)**
**Whyte Gate Incorporated** ....847 201-7000
400 S Curran Rd Ste 1 Grayslake (60030) **(G-11366)**
**Wicc Ltd** ....309 444-4125
119 Muller Rd Washington (61571) **(G-21396)**
**Wicks Organ Company** ....618 654-2191
416 Pine St Highland (62249) **(G-11819)**
**Wicks Pipe Organ Company, Highland** *Also called Wicks Organ Company* **(G-11819)**
**Wicoff Inc** ....618 988-8888
3201 S Park Ave Herrin (62948) **(G-11758)**
**Wide Image Incorporated** ....773 279-9183
1187 Tower Rd Schaumburg (60173) **(G-19789)**
**Wiegmann Woodworking** ....618 248-1300
105 Sugar Creek Ln Damiansville (62215) **(G-7700)**
**Wieland Metals Inc (HQ)** ....847 537-3990
567 Northgate Pkwy Wheeling (60090) **(G-22182)**
**Wielgus Product Models Inc** ....312 432-1950
1435 W Fulton St Chicago (60607) **(G-6977)**
**Wieman Fuels LP Gas Company** ....618 632-4015
418 S Belt E Belleville (62220) **(G-1691)**
**Wienmar Inc** ....847 742-9222
1601 N La Fox St South Elgin (60177) **(G-20235)**
**Wiersema Wrren Signs Trck Tstg, Fulton** *Also called Warren Wiersema Signs* **(G-10708)**
**Wikoff Color Corporation** ....847 487-2704
240 Jamie Ln Wauconda (60084) **(G-21515)**
**Wikus Saw Technology Corp** ....630 766-0960
700 W Belden Ave Addison (60101) **(G-343)**
**Wikus Technology** ....630 766-0960
700 W Belden Ave Addison (60101) **(G-344)**
**Wil Lan Company, Lockport** *Also called Bending Specialists LLC* **(G-13706)**
**Wilbert Quincy Vault Co** ....217 224-8557
4128 Wisman Ln Quincy (62305) **(G-17905)**
**Wilbert Shultz Vault Co Inc** ....815 672-2049
115 S Shabbona St Streator (61364) **(G-20711)**
**Wilbert Vault, Sterling** *Also called Sterling Vault Company* **(G-20616)**
**Wilbert Vault Company** ....309 787-5281
636 10th Ave W Milan (61264) **(G-14809)**
**Wilcor Solid Surface Inc** ....630 350-7703
55 Randall St Elk Grove Village (60007) **(G-9813)**
**Wilczak Industrial Parts Inc** ....847 260-5559
9220 Chestnut Ave Franklin Park (60131) **(G-10629)**
**Wildcat Hills** ....618 273-8600
115 Grayson Ln Eldorado (62930) **(G-8926)**
**Wildcat Hlls Cottage Grove Pit, Equality** *Also called Peabody Midwest Mining LLC* **(G-9990)**
**Wilder Farms** ....309 537-3218
271 140th Ave New Boston (61272) **(G-15867)**
**Wildlife Cookie Company** ....630 377-6196
1815 Wallace Ave Ste 305 Saint Charles (60174) **(G-19296)**
**Wildlife Materials Inc** ....618 687-3505
1202 Walnut St Murphysboro (62966) **(G-15586)**
**Wiliams Interactive LLC** ....773 961-1920
2718 W Roscoe St Chicago (60618) **(G-6978)**
**Wilkens-Anderson Company (PA)** ....773 384-4433
4525 W Division St Chicago (60651) **(G-6979)**
**Wilkes & McLean Ltd** ....847 381-3872
17 Lakeside Ln North Barrington (60010) **(G-16156)**
**Wilkos Industries** ....563 249-6691
3199 School Dr Savanna (61074) **(G-19407)**
**Will County Waste** ....708 489-9718
12807 Homan Ave Blue Island (60406) **(G-2272)**
**Will County Well & Pump Co Inc (PA)** ....815 485-2413
1200 S Cedar Rd Ste 1a New Lenox (60451) **(G-15928)**
**Will Don Corp** ....773 276-7081
7171 W 65th St Chicago (60638) **(G-6980)**
**Will Hamms Stained Glass** ....847 255-2230
628 N Highland Ave Arlington Heights (60004) **(G-872)**
**Willard R Schorck** ....217 543-2160
55 E Cr 300 N Arthur (61911) **(G-924)**
**Willdon Corp** ....773 276-7080
7171 W 65th St Chicago (60638) **(G-6981)**
**Wille Bros Co (PA)** ....708 535-4101
11303 Manhattan Monee Rd Monee (60449) **(G-15008)**
**Wille Bros Co** ....708 388-9000
12600 S Hamlin Ct Chicago (60803) **(G-6982)**
**Wille Bros Co** ....815 464-1300
11301 W Mnee Manhattan Rd Monee (60449) **(G-15009)**
**Willenborg Hardwood Inds Inc** ....217 844-2082
15485 E 1900th Ave Effingham (62401) **(G-8863)**
**Willert Company** ....630 860-1620
1144 E Green St Franklin Park (60131) **(G-10630)**
**Willetts Winery & Cellar** ....309 968-7070
105 E Market St Manito (61546) **(G-14177)**
**William Badal** ....815 264-7752
190 W Lincoln Hwy Waterman (60556) **(G-21412)**
**William Charles Cnstr Co LLC (HQ)** ....815 654-4700
5290 Nimtz Rd Loves Park (61111) **(G-14007)**
**William Charles Cnstr Co LLC** ....815 654-4720
4525 Irene Rd Belvidere (61008) **(G-1797)**
**William Dach** ....815 962-3455
4901 W State St Rockford (61102) **(G-18683)**
**William Davis & Co** ....847 395-6860
488 Donin Dr Antioch (60002) **(G-664)**
**William Dudek Manufacturing Co** ....773 622-2727
4901 W Armitage Ave Chicago (60639) **(G-6983)**
**William Frick & Company** ....847 918-3700
2600 Commerce Dr Libertyville (60048) **(G-13401)**
**William Harris Investors, Chicago** *Also called Harris William & Company Inc* **(G-5048)**
**William Harris Lee & Co Inc (PA)** ....312 786-0459
410 S Michigan Ave # 560 Chicago (60605) **(G-6984)**
**William Holloway Ltd** ....847 866-9520
1800 Dempster St Evanston (60202) **(G-10106)**

ALPHABETIC

(PA)=Parent Co (HQ)=Headquarters (DH)=Div Headquarters

## ALPHABETIC SECTION

**William Ingram** .................................................. 217 442-5075
  216 S Gilbert St  Danville (61832)  *(G-7785)*
**William J Kline & Co Inc** ..................................... 815 338-2055
  425 Borden St  Woodstock (60098)  *(G-22625)*
**William N Pasulka** ............................................. 815 339-6300
  15685 State Highway 71  Peru (61354)  *(G-17532)*
**William R Becker** .............................................. 618 378-3337
  760 Route 45 N  Norris City (62869)  *(G-16116)*
**William Street Press, Decatur** *Also called Lee Enterprises Incorporated (G-7905)*
**William W Meyer and Sons (PA)** ........................... 847 918-0111
  1700 Franklin Blvd  Libertyville (60048)  *(G-13402)*
**Williams  White & Company** ................................ 309 797-7650
  600 River Dr  Moline (61265)  *(G-14977)*
**Williams Electronic Games De (HQ)** ...................... 773 961-1000
  3401 N California Ave  Chicago (60618)  *(G-6985)*
**Williams Electronic Games De** ............................. 773 961-1000
  3401 N California Ave  Chicago (60618)  *(G-6986)*
**Williams Halthcare Systems LLC** .......................... 847 741-3650
  158 N Edison Ave  Elgin (60123)  *(G-9237)*
**Williams Welding Service** ................................... 217 235-1758
  14772 Cooks Mills Rd  Humboldt (61931)  *(G-12130)*
**Williams-Hayward Protective Co, Summit Argo** *Also called Willims-Hyward Intl Ctings Inc (G-20769)*
**Williamsburg Press Inc** ...................................... 630 229-0228
  454 Fox Crossing Ave  North Aurora (60542)  *(G-16150)*
**Williamson Energy  LLC** ..................................... 618 983-3020
  18624 Liberty School Rd  Marion (62959)  *(G-14295)*
**Williamson J Hunter & Company** .......................... 847 441-7888
  170 Linden St  Winnetka (60093)  *(G-22315)*
**Willie Washer Mfg Co** ........................................ 847 956-1344
  2101 Greenleaf Ave  Elk Grove Village (60007)  *(G-9814)*
**Willims-Hyward Intl Ctings Inc (PA)** ..................... 708 563-5182
  7425 W 59th St  Summit Argo (60501)  *(G-20769)*
**Willims-Hyward Intl Ctings Inc** ............................ 708 458-0015
  7400 W Archer Ave  Argo (60501)  *(G-698)*
**Willis Publishing** .............................................. 618 497-8272
  1101 E Pine St  Percy (62272)  *(G-17496)*
**Willis Stein & Partners Manage (PA)** ..................... 312 422-2400
  1033 Skokie Blvd Ste 360  Northbrook (60062)  *(G-16387)*
**Willoughbys Auto & Mch Sp** ................................ 815 448-2281
  615 East St  Mazon (60444)  *(G-14441)*
**Willow Creek Energy LLC (PA)** ............................ 312 224-1400
  1 S Wacker Dr Ste 1900  Chicago (60606)  *(G-6987)*
**Willow Farm Product Inc** .................................... 630 395-9246
  8193 S Lemont Rd  Darien (60561)  *(G-7804)*
**Willow Farm Products  Inc** .................................. 630 430-7491
  20w114 97th St  Lemont (60439)  *(G-13270)*
**Willow Group Inc** .............................................. 847 277-9400
  1 E Wacker Dr Ste 2700  Chicago (60601)  *(G-6988)*
**Willow Ridge Glass Inc (PA)** ................................ 630 910-8300
  8102 Lemont Rd Ste 100  Woodridge (60517)  *(G-22525)*
**Willowbrook Sawmill** ......................................... 618 592-3806
  1469 E 1600th Ave  Oblong (62449)  *(G-16737)*
**Wills Milling and Hardwood Inc** ........................... 217 854-9056
  9674 Colt Rd  Carlinville (62626)  *(G-3048)*
**Willy Wonka Candy Factory, Itasca** *Also called Nestle Usa  Inc (G-12330)*
**Wilmar Group LLC** ............................................ 847 421-6595
  818 Larchmont Ln  Lake Forest (60045)  *(G-12980)*
**Wilmette Screw Products** ................................... 773 725-2626
  4432 N Elston Ave  Chicago (60630)  *(G-6989)*
**Wilmington Free Press, Wilmington** *Also called G-W Communications Inc (G-22273)*
**Wilmouth Machine Works  Inc** ............................. 618 372-3189
  1723 Terpening Rd  Brighton (62012)  *(G-2546)*
**Wilpro** ............................................................ 618 382-4667
  205 Industrial Ave  Carmi (62821)  *(G-3085)*
**Wilseys Handmade Sweets LLC** ........................... 314 504-0851
  316 W Park St  Edwardsville (62025)  *(G-8818)*
**Wilson & Wilson Monument Co** ............................ 618 775-6488
  406 W Poplar St  Odin (62870)  *(G-16742)*
**Wilson Kitchens  Inc** ......................................... 618 253-7449
  1653 S Feazel St  Harrisburg (62946)  *(G-11606)*
**Wilson Mfg Screw Mch Pdts** ................................ 815 964-8724
  2500 N Main St Ste 10  Rockford (61103)  *(G-18684)*
**Wilson Printing  Inc** .......................................... 847 949-7800
  309 N Lake St Ste 202  Mundelein (60060)  *(G-15567)*
**Wilson Racket Division, Chicago** *Also called Wilson Sporting Goods Co (G-6991)*
**Wilson Railing & Metal Fabg Co** ........................... 847 662-1747
  640 Wilson Ave  Park City (60085)  *(G-17167)*
**Wilson Sporting Goods Co (HQ)** ........................... 773 714-6400
  8750 W Bryn Mawr Ave Fl 2  Chicago (60631)  *(G-6990)*
**Wilson Sporting Goods Co** .................................. 773 714-6500
  8700 W Bryn Mawr Ave  Chicago (60631)  *(G-6991)*
**Wilson Tool Corporation** .................................... 815 226-0147
  2401 20th St  Rockford (61104)  *(G-18685)*
**Wiltek Inc** ....................................................... 630 922-9200
  3819 Grassmere Rd  Naperville (60564)  *(G-15832)*
**Wilton Brands Inc** ............................................. 815 823-8547
  21350 Sw Frontage Rd  Joliet (60404)  *(G-12589)*
**Wilton Brands LLC (HQ)** ..................................... 630 963-7100
  2240 75th St  Woodridge (60517)  *(G-22526)*
**Wilton Enterprises, Woodridge** *Also called Wilton Industries  Inc (G-22528)*
**Wilton Holdings  Inc (PA)** ................................... 630 963-7100
  2240 75th St  Woodridge (60517)  *(G-22527)*
**Wilton Industries, Joliet** *Also called Wilton Brands Inc (G-12589)*
**Wilton Industries, Woodridge** *Also called Wilton Holdings  Inc (G-22527)*
**Wilton Industries Inc (HQ)** .................................. 630 963-7100
  2240 75th St  Woodridge (60517)  *(G-22528)*
**Wilton Industries Inc** ......................................... 815 834-9390
  1125 Taylor Rd  Romeoville (60446)  *(G-18879)*
**Wimaxspot360.com, Batavia** *Also called Moran  Cristobalian (G-1472)*
**Win Soon Chicago Inc** ........................................ 630 585-7090
  190 Kendall Point Dr  Oswego (60543)  *(G-16940)*
**Win Technologies Incorporated** ........................... 630 236-1020
  800 S Frontenac St Unit 1  Aurora (60504)  *(G-1099)*
**Wincademy Inc** ................................................ 847 445-7886
  34331 N Stonebridge Ln  Grayslake (60030)  *(G-11367)*
**Winchester Ammunition, East Alton** *Also called Olin Corporation (G-8608)*
**Winchester Estates-Div, Rockford** *Also called Littleson Inc (G-18471)*
**Winco Finishing Div, South Elgin** *Also called Custom Aluminum Products  Inc (G-20191)*
**Wind Point Partners  LP (PA)** .............................. 312 255-4800
  676 N Michigan Ave # 3700  Chicago (60611)  *(G-6992)*
**Wind Point Partners Vi  LP (HQ)** .......................... 312 255-4800
  676 N Michigan Ave # 3700  Chicago (60611)  *(G-6993)*
**Windo Well Cover Co** ........................................ 630 554-0366
  2374 Wolf Rd  Oswego (60543)  *(G-16941)*
**Window Coverings, Loves Park** *Also called Znl Corporation (G-14011)*
**Window Fashion Unlimited, Palatine** *Also called Interior Fashions Contract (G-17044)*
**Window Tech Inc** .............................................. 847 272-0739
  1351 Shermer Rd  Northbrook (60062)  *(G-16388)*
**Windsong Press Ltd** .......................................... 847 223-4586
  33403 N Greentree Rd  Grayslake (60030)  *(G-11368)*
**Windward Print Star  Inc** .................................... 309 787-8853
  801 1st St E  Milan (61264)  *(G-14810)*
**Windy Acquisition LLC** ....................................... 630 595-5744
  454 Country Club Dr  Bensenville (60106)  *(G-2015)*
**Windy City Cutting Die  Inc** ................................ 630 521-9410
  104 Foster Ave  Bensenville (60106)  *(G-2016)*
**Windy City Detectors Sales** ................................. 773 774-5445
  6435 N Newark Ave  Chicago (60631)  *(G-6994)*
**Windy City Engineering Inc** ................................. 773 254-8113
  3244 W 30th St  Chicago (60623)  *(G-6995)*
**Windy City Gold Popcorn  Inc** .............................. 708 596-9940
  4855 W 115th St  Alsip (60803)  *(G-544)*
**Windy City Laser Service Inc** ............................... 773 995-0188
  820 W 120th St  Chicago (60643)  *(G-6996)*
**Windy City Media Group** .................................... 773 871-7610
  5315 N Clark St Ste 3  Chicago (60640)  *(G-6997)*
**Windy City Metal Detector Sls, Chicago** *Also called Windy City Detectors Sales (G-6994)*
**Windy City Mutes** ............................................. 630 616-8634
  756 Larson Ln  Bensenville (60106)  *(G-2017)*
**Windy City Parrot  Inc** ....................................... 312 492-9673
  2618 W Walton St  Chicago (60622)  *(G-6998)*
**Windy City Plastics  Inc** ..................................... 773 533-1099
  263 N California Ave  Chicago (60612)  *(G-6999)*
**Windy City Publishers LLC** ................................. 847 925-9434
  1051 S Hiddenbrook Trl  Palatine (60067)  *(G-17090)*
**Windy City Silkscreening  Inc** ............................. 312 842-0030
  2715 S Archer Ave  Chicago (60608)  *(G-7000)*
**Windy City Times, Chicago** *Also called Lambda Publications Inc (G-5448)*
**Windy City Wire and Connectivi (PA)** .................... 630 633-4500
  386 Internationale Dr H  Bolingbrook (60440)  *(G-2384)*
**Windy City Word** .............................................. 773 378-0261
  5090 W Harrison St  Chicago (60644)  *(G-7001)*
**Windy Hill Woodworking Inc** ............................... 309 275-2415
  4 Candle Ridge Rd  Towanda (61776)  *(G-20979)*
**Winery At Shale Lake The, Staunton** *Also called Shale Lake  LLC (G-20558)*
**Winfield Technology Inc** .................................... 630 584-0475
  53 Stirrup Cup Ct  Saint Charles (60174)  *(G-19297)*
**Winfun Usa  LLC** .............................................. 630 942-8464
  551 Roosevelt Rd Ste 137  Glen Ellyn (60137)  *(G-10995)*
**Wings of Roselle LLC** ........................................ 630 529-5700
  840 Lake St Ste 414  Roselle (60172)  *(G-18985)*
**Winhere Brake Parts  Inc** ................................... 630 307-0158
  1331 Schiferl Rd  Bartlett (60103)  *(G-1387)*
**Winkler Products Inc** ........................................ 314 421-1926
  9029 Pin Oak Rd  Edwardsville (62025)  *(G-8819)*
**Winlind Skincare LLC** ........................................ 630 789-9408
  80 Burr Ridge Pkwy  Burr Ridge (60527)  *(G-2896)*
**Winn Star Inc** .................................................. 618 964-1811
  395 S Wolf Creek Rd Fl 1  Carbondale (62902)  *(G-3028)*
**Winnebago Foundry  Inc** .................................... 815 389-3533
  132 Blackhawk Blvd  South Beloit (61080)  *(G-20176)*
**Winner Cutting & Stamping Co** ............................ 630 963-1800
  1245 Warren Ave  Downers Grove (60515)  *(G-8546)*
**Winnetka Mews Condominium Assn** ..................... 847 501-2770
  640 Winnetka Mews  Winnetka (60093)  *(G-22316)*
**Winnetka Sign Co Inc (PA)** ................................. 847 473-9378
  3338 Berwyn Ave Unit 93  North Chicago (60064)  *(G-16191)*

# ALPHABETIC SECTION

**Winning Colors** .................................................. 815 462-4810
345 Jan St Unit C  Manhattan  (60442)  *(G-14171)*
**Winning Stitch** .................................................. 217 348-8279
725 Windsor Rd  Charleston  (61920)  *(G-3616)*
**Winning Streak  Inc** .......................................... 618 277-8191
1580 Decoma Dr  Dupo  (62239)  *(G-8584)*
**Winpak Heat Seal Corp** .................................... 309 477-6600
1821 Riverway Dr  Pekin  (61554)  *(G-17295)*
**Winpak Portion Packaging  Inc** ......................... 708 753-5700
1111 Winpak Way  Sauk Village  (60411)  *(G-19394)*
**Winscribe Usa  Inc (HQ)** .................................. 773 399-1608
8700 W Bryn Mawr Ave 720s  Chicago  (60631)  *(G-7002)*
**Winsight  LLC (HQ)** .......................................... 312 876-0004
300 S Riverside Plz # 1600  Chicago  (60606)  *(G-7003)*
**Winston Pharmaceuticals  Inc (HQ)** ................. 847 362-8200
100 N Fairway Dr Ste 134  Vernon Hills  (60061)  *(G-21217)*
**Winters Welding  Inc** ....................................... 773 860-7735
7122 S Seeley Ave  Chicago  (60636)  *(G-7004)*
**Winzeler Inc** .................................................... 708 867-7971
7355 W Wilson Ave  Harwood Heights  (60706)  *(G-11692)*
**WINZELER GEAR, Harwood Heights** *Also called Winzeler Inc (G-11692)*
**Wirco Inc** ......................................................... 217 398-3200
1700 W Washington St  Champaign  (61821)  *(G-3561)*
**Wire Cloth Filter Mfg, Maywood** *Also called Jsn Inc (G-14426)*
**Wire Mesh  LLC** ............................................... 815 579-8597
42 Marquette Ave  Oglesby  (61348)  *(G-16752)*
**Wireformers  Inc** ............................................. 847 718-1920
500 W Carboy Rd  Mount Prospect  (60056)  *(G-15384)*
**Wireless Chamberlain Products** ....................... 800 282-6225
845 N Larch Ave  Elmhurst  (60126)  *(G-9961)*
**Wireless Express Inc Central** .......................... 309 689-9933
4732 N University St  Peoria  (61614)  *(G-17478)*
**Wireless USA, Quincy** *Also called Wirelessusa Inc (G-17906)*
**Wirelessusa Inc** ............................................... 217 222-4300
2517 W Schneidman Dr E  Quincy  (62305)  *(G-17906)*
**Wiremasters  Incorporated** .............................. 773 254-3700
1040 W 40th St 1050  Chicago  (60609)  *(G-7005)*
**Wiretech  Inc** ................................................... 815 986-9614
521 18th Ave  Rockford  (61104)  *(G-18686)*
**Wirfs Industries Inc** ........................................ 815 344-0635
4021 Main St  McHenry  (60050)  *(G-14571)*
**Wirtz Bev III Metro-Chicago, Cicero** *Also called Wirtz Beverage Illinois LLC (G-7246)*
**Wirtz Beverage Illinois  LLC (PA)** ..................... 847 228-9000
3333 S Laramie Ave  Cicero  (60804)  *(G-7246)*
**Wis - Pak  Inc** .................................................. 217 224-6800
2400 N 30th St  Quincy  (62301)  *(G-17907)*
**Wis-Pak of Quincy, Quincy** *Also called Wis - Pak Inc (G-17907)*
**Wiscon Corp (PA)** ............................................ 708 450-0074
2050 N 15th Ave  Melrose Park  (60160)  *(G-14710)*
**Wiscon Corp** .................................................... 708 450-0074
1931 N 15th Ave  Melrose Park  (60160)  *(G-14711)*
**Wisconsin Cheese, Melrose Park** *Also called Wiscon Corp (G-14710)*
**Wisconsin Cheese, Melrose Park** *Also called Wiscon Corp (G-14711)*
**Wisconsin Flameproof Shop, Montgomery** *Also called Chicago Flameproof WD Spc Corp (G-15037)*
**Wisconsin Wilderness Food Pdts** ..................... 847 735-8661
11 N Skokie Hwy Ste 207  Lake Bluff  (60044)  *(G-12872)*
**Wisdom Adhesives, Elgin** *Also called H E Wisdom & Sons Inc (G-9052)*
**Wisdom Adhesives** .......................................... 847 841-7002
350 River Ridge Dr  Elgin  (60123)  *(G-9238)*
**Wisdom Medical Technology  LLC** ................... 630 803-6383
19 Stonehill Rd  Oswego  (60543)  *(G-16942)*
**Wise Co  Inc** .................................................... 618 594-4091
3750 Industrial Dr  Carlyle  (62231)  *(G-3061)*
**Wise Construction Services** ............................. 630 553-6350
1107 S Bridge St Ste E  Yorkville  (60560)  *(G-22676)*
**Wise Equipment & Rentals Inc** ......................... 847 895-5555
1475 Rodenburg Rd  Schaumburg  (60193)  *(G-19790)*
**Wise Hamlin Plastics, Saint Charles** *Also called Wise Plastics Technologies Inc (G-19298)*
**Wise Plastics Technologies Inc (PA)** ................. 630 584-2307
3810 Stern Ave  Saint Charles  (60174)  *(G-19298)*
**Wise Plastics Technologies Inc** ........................ 847 697-2840
1601 W Hawthorne Ln  West Chicago  (60185)  *(G-21793)*
**Wisepak Foods  LLC** ........................................ 773 772-0072
4225 N Pulaski Rd  Chicago  (60641)  *(G-7006)*
**Wish Bone Rescue** .......................................... 309 212-9210
1007 S Madison St  Bloomington  (61701)  *(G-2236)*
**Wish Collection** ............................................... 205 324-0209
350 N Ogden Ave Ste 100  Chicago  (60607)  *(G-7007)*
**Wishzing** ......................................................... 217 413-8469
320 S East St  Dalton City  (61925)  *(G-7699)*
**Wisniwski Rchard Stl Rule Dies** ....................... 773 282-1144
4422 N Elston Ave  Chicago  (60630)  *(G-7008)*
**Wissmiller & Evans Road Eqp** .......................... 309 725-3598
102 S Jeffrey St  Cooksville  (61730)  *(G-7373)*
**Wissmiller Welding, Cooksville** *Also called Wissmiller & Evans Road Eqp (G-7373)*
**Without A Trace Weaver Inc (PA)** ..................... 773 588-4922
3344 W Bryn Mawr  Chicago  (60659)  *(G-7009)*

**Witron Intgrated Logistics Inc** ......................... 847 398-6130
3721 N Ventura Dr  Arlington Heights  (60004)  *(G-873)*
**Witt Disintegrating Service, Addison** *Also called Ralph Cody Gravrok (G-269)*
**Witte Kendel Die & Mold** .................................. 815 233-9270
657 Youngs Ln  Freeport  (61032)  *(G-10699)*
**Wittenstein  Inc** ............................................... 630 540-5300
1249 Humbracht Cir  Bartlett  (60103)  *(G-1388)*
**Wittenstein Arspc Smlation Inc (PA)** ................ 630 540-5300
1249 Humbracht Cir  Bartlett  (60103)  *(G-1389)*
**Wittwer Brothers Inc** ....................................... 815 522-3589
33462 W County Line Rd  Monroe Center  (61052)  *(G-15025)*
**WJ Die Mold  Inc** ............................................. 847 895-6561
915 Estes Ct  Schaumburg  (60193)  *(G-19791)*
**Wjez Thunder 93 7 Wjbc Wbnq B1** .................... 815 842-6515
315 N Mill St  Pontiac  (61764)  *(G-17712)*
**Wk Drainage, Campbell Hill** *Also called Wk Machine (G-2979)*
**Wk Machine** ..................................................... 618 426-3423
98 Catalpa Ln  Campbell Hill  (62916)  *(G-2979)*
**Wki, Harrisburg** *Also called Wilson Kitchens Inc (G-11606)*
**Wki Holding Company  Inc (PA)** ....................... 847 233-8600
9525 Bryn Mawr Ave # 300  Rosemont  (60018)  *(G-19041)*
**Wm F Meyer Co (PA)** ....................................... 773 772-7272
2211 N Elston Ave Ste 103  Chicago  (60614)  *(G-7010)*
**Wm Huber Cabinet Works** ................................ 773 235-7660
2400 N Campbell Ave  Chicago  (60647)  *(G-7011)*
**Wm W Nugent & Co Inc** .................................... 847 673-8109
3440 Cleveland St  Skokie  (60076)  *(G-20111)*
**Wm Wrigley Jr Company (HQ)** .......................... 312 280-4710
930 W Evergreen Ave  Chicago  (60642)  *(G-7012)*
**Wm Wrigley Jr Company** .................................. 312 644-2121
825 Bluff Rd  Romeoville  (60446)  *(G-18880)*
**Wm Wrigley Jr Company** .................................. 312 205-2300
1300 N North Branch St  Chicago  (60642)  *(G-7013)*
**Wm Wrigley Jr Company** .................................. 312 644-2121
600 W Chicago Ave Ste 500  Chicago  (60654)  *(G-7014)*
**WMS Games Inc (HQ)** ...................................... 773 728-2300
3401 N California Ave  Chicago  (60618)  *(G-7015)*
**WMS Gaming, Chicago** *Also called Williams Electronic Games De (G-6986)*
**WMS Gaming Inc** ............................................. 773 961-1747
3401 N California Ave  Chicago  (60618)  *(G-7016)*
**WMS Gaming Inc (HQ)** ..................................... 773 961-1000
3401 N California Ave  Chicago  (60618)  *(G-7017)*
**WMS Industries Inc (HQ)** ................................. 847 785-3000
3401 N California Ave  Chicago  (60618)  *(G-7018)*
**Wns Publication, Erie** *Also called Review (G-9993)*
**Wns Publications Inc** ....................................... 815 772-7244
100 E Main St  Morrison  (61270)  *(G-15149)*
**Wnta Studio Line** ............................................. 815 874-7861
830 Sandy Hollow Rd  Rockford  (61109)  *(G-18687)*
**Wockhardt Holding Corp** ................................. 847 967-5600
6451 Main St  Morton Grove  (60053)  *(G-15246)*
**Wodack Electric Tool Corp** .............................. 773 287-9866
4627 W Huron St  Chicago  (60644)  *(G-7019)*
**Wold Printing Services Ltd** .............................. 847 546-3110
26639 W Commerce Dr # 402  Volo  (60073)  *(G-21320)*
**Wolf Cabinetry & Ganite** .................................. 847 358-9922
1703 N Rand Rd  Palatine  (60074)  *(G-17091)*
**Wolfam Holdings Corporation** .......................... 312 407-0100
120 W Madison St Ste 510  Chicago  (60602)  *(G-7020)*
**Wolfe Burial Vault Co Inc** ................................. 815 697-2012
310 N Oak St  Chebanse  (60922)  *(G-3632)*
**Wolfram Research  Inc (PA)** ............................. 217 398-0700
100 Trade Centre Dr 6th  Champaign  (61820)  *(G-3562)*
**Wolfsword Press** ............................................. 773 403-1144
7144 N Harlem Ave 325  Chicago  (60631)  *(G-7021)*
**Wolseley Indus Group 3194, Decatur** *Also called Ferguson Enterprises Inc (G-7880)*
**Wolseley Industrial Group, Decatur** *Also called Ferguson Enterprises Inc (G-7881)*
**Wolters Custom Cabinets LLC** ......................... 618 282-3158
8204 State Route 3  Evansville  (62242)  *(G-10108)*
**Wolters Kluwer US Inc (HQ)** ............................. 847 580-5000
2700 Lake Cook Rd  Riverwoods  (60015)  *(G-18046)*
**Woman Christian Temperance Un, Evanston** *Also called Wctu Press (G-10105)*
**Wonder Kids Inc** .............................................. 773 437-8025
1719 Brummel St  Evanston  (60202)  *(G-10107)*
**Wonder Tucky Distillery & Btlg** ........................ 224 678-4396
315 E South St  Woodstock  (60098)  *(G-22626)*
**Wonderlic  Inc** ................................................. 847 680-4900
400 Lakeview Pkwy Ste 200  Vernon Hills  (60061)  *(G-21218)*
**Wonderlin Galleries, Normal** *Also called Frame Mart Inc (G-16071)*
**Wood & Wire, Mundelein** *Also called Ww Displays Inc (G-15568)*
**Wood Creations Incorporated (PA)** ................... 773 772-1375
3918 W Shakespeare Ave  Chicago  (60647)  *(G-7022)*
**Wood Creations Incorporated** .......................... 773 772-1375
4627 W Fullerton Ave  Chicago  (60639)  *(G-7023)*
**Wood Cutters Lane  LLC** ................................. 847 847-2263
129 Heritage Trl  Hainesville  (60030)  *(G-11525)*
**Wood Dale Pipe & Supply Co, Wood Dale** *Also called O Adjust Matic Pump Company (G-22408)*

**Wood Energy Inc**...618 244-1590
3007 Broadway St Mount Vernon (62864) *(G-15449)*
**Wood Labeling Systems Inc**...815 344-8733
4906 Brorson Ln Johnsburg (60051) *(G-12444)*
**Wood River Printing & Pubg Co**...618 254-3134
22 N 1st St Wood River (62095) *(G-22446)*
**Wood Shop**...773 994-6666
441 E 75th St Chicago (60619) *(G-7024)*
**Wood Specialties Incorporated**...217 678-8420
964 E 1100 North Rd Bement (61813) *(G-1803)*
**Wood-N-Ware, Urbana** *Also called Tom McCowan Enterprises Inc (G-21103)*
**Woodards LLC DBA Custom Wroug**...773 283-8113
4464 N Elston Ave Chicago (60630) *(G-7025)*
**Wooded Wonderland**...815 777-1223
610 S Devils Ladder Rd Galena (61036) *(G-10735)*
**Wooden Nickel Pub and Grill**...618 288-2141
171 S Main St Glen Carbon (62034) *(G-10955)*
**Wooden World of Richmond Inc**...815 405-4503
7617 Il Route 31 Richmond (60071) *(G-17974)*
**Woodhaven Woodworks, Springfield** *Also called Todd Scanlan (G-20545)*
**Woodhead Industries LLC (HQ)**...847 353-2500
333 Knightsbridge Pkwy # 200 Lincolnshire (60069) *(G-13490)*
**Woodhill Cabinetry Design Inc**...815 431-0545
3381 N State Route 23 Ottawa (61350) *(G-16992)*
**Woodland Engineering Company**...847 362-0110
122 Baker Rd Lake Bluff (60044) *(G-12873)*
**Woodland Fence Forest Pdts Inc**...630 393-2220
3 S 264 Hc 59 Warrenville (60555) *(G-21369)*
**Woodland Plastics Corp**...630 543-1144
1340 W National Ave Addison (60101) *(G-345)*
**Woodlawn Engineering Co Inc**...630 543-3550
325 W Fay Ave Addison (60101) *(G-346)*
**Woodlogic Custom Millwork Inc**...847 640-4500
505 Bonnie Ln Elk Grove Village (60007) *(G-9815)*
**Woodmac Industries Inc**...708 755-3545
3233 Holeman Ave S Chicago Hts (60411) *(G-19116)*
**Woodmaster Graphics, Lynwood** *Also called Schepel Signs Inc (G-14027)*
**Woodrow Todd**...618 838-9105
1502 N Olive Rd Flora (62839) *(G-10222)*
**Woods Equipment Company**...815 732-2141
1818 Elmwood Rd Ste 2 Rockford (61103) *(G-18688)*
**Woods Equipment Company**...815 732-2141
2606 S Il Route 2 Oregon (61061) *(G-16834)*
**Woods Manufacturing Co Inc**...630 595-6620
735 N Edgewood Ave Ste J Wood Dale (60191) *(G-22438)*
**Woods Mfg and Machining Co**...847 982-9585
8055 Ridgeway Ave Skokie (60076) *(G-20112)*
**Woodshop, The, Chicago** *Also called Wood Shop (G-7024)*
**Woodstock Gardens, Woodstock** *Also called Contempo Industries Inc (G-22553)*
**Woodstock Powersports**...815 308-5705
2055 S Eastwood Dr Woodstock (60098) *(G-22627)*
**Woodstock Special Machining**...815 338-7383
1019 Rail Dr Ste B Woodstock (60098) *(G-22628)*
**Woodward Inc**...847 673-8300
7320 Linder Ave Skokie (60077) *(G-20113)*
**Woodward Inc**...815 877-7441
12533 Wagon Wheel Rd Rockton (61072) *(G-18703)*
**Woodward Inc**...815 877-7441
1 Woodward Loves Park (61111) *(G-14008)*
**Woodward Inc**...815 877-7441
5001 N 2nd St Loves Park (61111) *(G-14009)*
**Woodward Controls Inc (HQ)**...847 673-8300
7320 Linder Ave Skokie (60077) *(G-20114)*
**Woodward International Inc (HQ)**...815 877-7441
5001 N 2nd St Loves Park (61111) *(G-14010)*
**Woodward Mpc, Inc., Niles** *Also called Mpc Products Corporation (G-16010)*
**Woodways Industries LLC**...616 956-3070
850 S Wabash Ave Ste 300 Chicago (60605) *(G-7026)*
**Woodwind Specialists**...217 423-4122
890 W William St Decatur (62522) *(G-7960)*
**Woodwork Apts LLC**...224 595-9691
124 Linden Ave Streamwood (60107) *(G-20681)*
**Woodworkers Shop Inc (PA)**...309 347-5111
13587 E Manito Rd Pekin (61554) *(G-17296)*
**Woodworking Unlimited Inc**...630 469-7023
23w450 Burdette Ave Carol Stream (60188) *(G-3269)*
**Woodx Lumber Inc**...331 979-2171
471 W Wrightwood Ave Elmhurst (60126) *(G-9962)*
**Woody's Ems, Kankakee** *Also called Metzka Inc (G-12638)*
**Woogl Corporation**...847 806-1160
859 Oakton St Elk Grove Village (60007) *(G-9816)*
**Woojin Plaimm Inc**...708 606-5536
1693 W Imperial Ct Mount Prospect (60056) *(G-15385)*
**Woolenwear Co**...847 520-9243
739 Pinecrest Dr Prospect Heights (60070) *(G-17786)*
**Woow Sushi Orland Park LLC**...815 469-5189
19951 S Lagrange Rd Frankfort (60423) *(G-10377)*
**Wordspace Press Limited**...773 292-0292
2259 N Kedzie Blvd Chicago (60647) *(G-7027)*
**Work Area Protection Corp**...630 377-9100
2500 Production Dr Saint Charles (60174) *(G-19299)*
**Work Song Productions, Chicago** *Also called LMS Innovations Inc (G-5528)*
**Workforce On Line, Chicago** *Also called Crain Communications Inc (G-4492)*
**Workhorse Custom Chassis LLC**...765 964-4000
600 Central Ave Ste 220 Highland Park (60035) *(G-11882)*
**Workplace Ink Inc**...312 939-0296
1712 Marguerite St Park Ridge (60068) *(G-17229)*
**Works In Progress Foundation**...847 997-8338
24978 W Lakeview Dr Lake Villa (60046) *(G-13031)*
**Workshop (PA)**...815 777-2211
706 S West St Galena (61036) *(G-10736)*
**Workshop Ltd Inc**...708 458-3222
5900 W 51st St Bedford Park (60638) *(G-1594)*
**Workspace Lyon Products LLC**...630 892-8941
420 N Main St Montgomery (60538) *(G-15073)*
**World Book Direct Marketing, Chicago** *Also called World Book Inc (G-7028)*
**World Book Inc (HQ)**...312 729-5800
180 N La Salle St Ste 900 Chicago (60601) *(G-7028)*
**World Class Technologies Inc**...312 758-3114
70 E Lake St Ste 600 Chicago (60601) *(G-7029)*
**World Class Tool & Machine**...815 962-2081
2422 N Main St Rockford (61103) *(G-18689)*
**World Contract Packagers Inc**...815 624-6501
14392 De La Tour Dr South Beloit (61080) *(G-20177)*
**World Cup Packaging Inc**...815 624-6501
14392 De La Tour Dr South Beloit (61080) *(G-20178)*
**World Dryer Corporation (PA)**...708 449-6950
5700 Mcdermott Dr Berkeley (60163) *(G-2053)*
**World Explorer, Kempton** *Also called Adventures Unlimited (G-12661)*
**World Granite Inc**...815 288-3350
1220 S Galena Ave Dixon (61021) *(G-8359)*
**World Journal Chinese Daily, Chicago** *Also called World Journal LLC (G-7031)*
**World Journal LLC**...312 842-8005
2116 S Archer Ave Chicago (60616) *(G-7030)*
**World Journal LLC**...312 842-8080
2471 S Archer Ave Chicago (60616) *(G-7031)*
**World Kitchen LLC (PA)**...847 233-8600
9525 Bryn Mawr Ave Rosemont (60018) *(G-19042)*
**World Library Publications**...847 678-9300
3708 River Rd Ste 400 Franklin Park (60131) *(G-10631)*
**World of Soul Inc**...773 840-4839
9131 S La Salle St Chicago (60620) *(G-7032)*
**World Richman Mfg Corp**...847 468-8898
2505 Bath Rd Elgin (60124) *(G-9239)*
**World Washer & Stamping Inc**...630 543-6749
763 W Annoreno Dr Addison (60101) *(G-347)*
**World Wide Broach, Arlington Heights** *Also called National Component Sales Inc (G-808)*
**World Wide Fittings Inc (PA)**...847 588-2200
600 Corporate Woods Pkwy Vernon Hills (60061) *(G-21219)*
**World Wide Rotary Die**...630 521-9410
104 Foster Ave Bensenville (60106) *(G-2018)*
**Worldcolor Effingham, Effingham** *Also called Qg LLC (G-8855)*
**Worlds Finest Chocolate Inc (PA)**...773 847-4600
4801 S Lawndale Ave Chicago (60632) *(G-7033)*
**Worldwide Shrimp Company**...847 433-3500
430 Park Ave Ste 2a Highland Park (60035) *(G-11883)*
**Worldwide Tiles Ltd Inc**...708 389-2992
11708 S Mayfield Ave Alsip (60803) *(G-545)*
**Worley Machining Inc**...630 801-9198
601 W New York St Ste 400 Aurora (60506) *(G-1234)*
**Worth Auto Parts, Worth** *Also called Auto Head and Engine Exchange (G-22632)*
**Worth Door Company**...877 379-4947
4203 W Orleans St Mchenry (60050) *(G-14572)*
**Worth Steel and Machine Co**...708 388-6300
4001 W 123rd St Alsip (60803) *(G-546)*
**Worth-Pfaff Innovations Inc (PA)**...847 940-9305
444 Lake Cook Rd Ste 17 Deerfield (60015) *(G-8068)*
**Wortman Printing Company Inc**...217 347-3775
1713 S Banker St Effingham (62401) *(G-8864)*
**Wotkun Group Inc**...708 396-2121
14410 S Western Ave Posen (60469) *(G-17737)*
**Wound Rounds, Schaumburg** *Also called Telemedicine Solutions LLC (G-19758)*
**Woundwear Inc**...847 634-1700
1440 Larchmont Dr Buffalo Grove (60089) *(G-2795)*
**Wow Signs Inc**...847 910-4405
150 Augusta Dr Deerfield (60015) *(G-8069)*
**Wozniak Industries Inc**...630 820-4052
2560 White Oak Cir Aurora (60502) *(G-1100)*
**Wozniak Industries Inc (PA)**...630 954-3400
2 Mid America Plz Ste 700 Oakbrook Terrace (60181) *(G-16723)*
**Wozniak Industries Inc**...708 458-1220
5757 W 65th St Bedford Park (60638) *(G-1595)*
**Wpc Machinery Corp**...630 231-7721
3350 W Salt Creek Ln Arlington Heights (60005) *(G-874)*
**Wpgu-FM, Champaign** *Also called Illini Media Co (G-3499)*
**Wpm, Schiller Park** *Also called Western Printing Machinery Co (G-19883)*
**Wrap & Send Services**...847 329-2559
4909 Old Orchard Ctr Skokie (60077) *(G-20115)*

**Wrap-On Company LLC**....708 496-2150
11756 S Austin Ave Alsip (60803) ***(G-547)***
**Wrapping Inc**....773 871-2898
3600 N Lake Shore Dr Chicago (60613) ***(G-7034)***
**Wrapports LLC (PA)**....312 321-3000
350 N Orleans St 10thf Chicago (60654) ***(G-7035)***
**Wrench**....773 609-1698
1208 W Hubbard St Chicago (60642) ***(G-7036)***
**Wri, Woodridge** *Also called Western Remac Inc* ***(G-22524)***
**Wright Advertising, Cicero** *Also called Wright Quick Signs Inc* ***(G-7247)***
**Wright Metals Inc**....847 267-1212
1405 Valley Rd Bannockburn (60015) ***(G-1267)***
**Wright Quick Signs Inc**....708 652-6020
1347 S Laramie Ave Cicero (60804) ***(G-7247)***
**Wright Technologies Inc**....847 439-4150
1380 Howard St Elk Grove Village (60007) ***(G-9817)***
**Wright Tool & Die Inc**....815 669-2020
4829 Prime Pkwy McHenry (60050) ***(G-14573)***
**Wrightwood Technologies Inc**....312 238-9512
3440 S Dearborn St Ste 39 Chicago (60616) ***(G-7037)***
**Wrigley Manufacturing Co LLC (HQ)**....312 644-2121
410 N Michigan Ave Chicago (60611) ***(G-7038)***
**Wrigley Manufacturing Co LLC**....630 553-4800
2800 State Route 47 Yorkville (60560) ***(G-22677)***
**Wrigley Manufacturing Co LLC**....312 644-2121
1452 N Cherry Ave Chicago (60642) ***(G-7039)***
**Wrigley Midwest, Romeoville** *Also called Wm Wrigley Jr Company* ***(G-18880)***
**Wrigley Sales Company LLC**....312 644-2121
410 N Michigan Ave # 1600 Chicago (60611) ***(G-7040)***
**Wrigley's, Chicago** *Also called Wm Wrigley Jr Company* ***(G-7013)***
**Wrigley's, Chicago** *Also called Wrigley Manufacturing Co LLC* ***(G-7038)***
**Wrigley's, Yorkville** *Also called Wrigley Manufacturing Co LLC* ***(G-22677)***
**Wrigley's, Chicago** *Also called Wrigley Manufacturing Co LLC* ***(G-7039)***
**Write Stuff**....630 365-4425
5n465 Hazelwood Ct Saint Charles (60175) ***(G-19300)***
**Written Word Inc**....630 671-9803
986 Lake St Ste 108 Roselle (60172) ***(G-18986)***
**Ws Incorporated of Manmouth (PA)**....309 734-2161
220 W Franklin Ave Monmouth (61462) ***(G-15024)***
**Wsm Enterprises, Chicago** *Also called Cabworks LLC* ***(G-4209)***
**Wsol, Aurora** *Also called Websolutions Technology Inc* ***(G-1095)***
**Wsw Industrial Maintenance**....773 721-0675
2701 E 105th St Chicago (60617) ***(G-7041)***
**Wuebbels Repair & Sales LLC**....618 648-2227
505 W Market St Mc Leansboro (62859) ***(G-14470)***
**Wunderlich Diamond Tool Corp**....847 437-9904
1330 Howard St Elk Grove Village (60007) ***(G-9818)***
**Wunderlich Doors Inc**....815 727-6430
300 Allen St Joliet (60436) ***(G-12590)***
**Wurst Kitchen Inc (PA)**....630 898-9242
638 2nd Ave Aurora (60505) ***(G-1235)***
**WV Sharp, Chicago** *Also called Wam Ventures Inc* ***(G-6937)***
**Ww Displays Inc**....847 566-6979
401 Wshington Blvd Ste 10 Mundelein (60060) ***(G-15568)***
**WW Engineering Company LLC**....773 376-9494
4321 W 32nd St Chicago (60623) ***(G-7042)***
**WW Henry Company LP**....815 933-8059
150 Mooney Dr Bourbonnais (60914) ***(G-2409)***
**WW Timbers Inc (PA)**....708 423-9112
10150 Virginia Ave Ste K Chicago Ridge (60415) ***(G-7159)***
**Www.agrinews-Pubs.com, La Salle** *Also called Agri-News Publications Inc* ***(G-12760)***
**Www.vltg-Cnvrtr-Transformercom, Roselle** *Also called Saachi Inc* ***(G-18971)***
**Wyckoff Advertising Inc**....630 260-2525
1024 College Ave Wheaton (60187) ***(G-21990)***
**Wyka LLC**....847 298-0740
1515 S Mount Prospect Rd Des Plaines (60018) ***(G-8306)***
**Wyldewood Cellars 2 LLC**....217 469-9463
218 E Lincoln St Saint Joseph (61873) ***(G-19319)***
**Wyman and Company**....708 532-9064
17324 Oak Park Ave Tinley Park (60477) ***(G-20956)***
**Wynright Corporation (HQ)**....847 595-9400
2500 York Rd Elk Grove Village (60007) ***(G-9819)***
**Wyzz Inc**....217 753-5620
2680 E Cook St Springfield (62703) ***(G-20548)***
**X Hale**....847 884-6250
4811 N Olcott Ave # 504 Harwood Heights (60706) ***(G-11693)***
**X-Cel Technologies Inc**....708 802-7400
7800 Graphic Dr Tinley Park (60477) ***(G-20957)***
**X-Cel X-Ray, Crystal Lake** *Also called Arquilla Inc* ***(G-7537)***
**X-L-Engineering Corp (PA)**....847 965-3030
6150 W Mulford St Niles (60714) ***(G-16048)***
**X-L-Engineering Corp**....847 364-4750
330 Crossen Ave Elk Grove Village (60007) ***(G-9820)***
**X-Ray Cassette Repair Co Inc**....815 356-8181
6107 Lou St Crystal Lake (60014) ***(G-7678)***
**X-Tech Innovations Inc**....815 962-4127
424 18th Ave Rockford (61104) ***(G-18690)***
**Xact Wire EDM Corp**....847 516-0903
720 Industrial Dr Ste 126 Cary (60013) ***(G-3379)***
**Xaptum Inc**....847 404-6205
222 Merchandise Mart Pl S Ste 1212 Chicago (60654) ***(G-7043)***
**Xcell International Corp**....630 323-0107
16400 103rd St Lemont (60439) ***(G-13271)***
**Xclusive Auto Sales & Security**....708 897-9990
2410 Oak St Blue Island (60406) ***(G-2273)***
**Xco International Incorporated**....847 428-2400
1082 Rock Road Ln Ste A East Dundee (60118) ***(G-8662)***
**Xd Industries Inc**....630 766-2843
244 James St Bensenville (60106) ***(G-2019)***
**Xd Industries Inc**....847 293-0796
836 E Old Willow Rd Prospect Heights (60070) ***(G-17787)***
**Xena International Inc (PA)**....630 587-2734
39w082 Foxwood Ln Saint Charles (60175) ***(G-19301)***
**Xena International Inc**....815 946-2626
910 S Division Ave Polo (61064) ***(G-17691)***
**Xenia Mfg Inc (PA)**....618 678-2218
1507 Church St Xenia (62899) ***(G-22645)***
**Xenia Mfg Inc**....618 392-7212
1915 Miller Dr Olney (62450) ***(G-16801)***
**Xentris Wireless LLC**....630 693-9700
1250 N Greenbriar Dr A Addison (60101) ***(G-348)***
**Xerox Corporation**....630 983-0172
1435 Foxhill Rd Naperville (60563) ***(G-15785)***
**Xerox Corporation**....217 355-5460
1211 Hagan St Champaign (61820) ***(G-3563)***
**Xerox Corporation**....847 928-5500
5500 Pearl St Ste 100 Rosemont (60018) ***(G-19043)***
**Xerox Corporation**....630 573-0200
2301 W 22nd St Ste 300 Oak Brook (60523) ***(G-16570)***
**Xerox Corporation**....630 573-1000
2301 W 22nd St Ste 300 Hinsdale (60523) ***(G-11969)***
**Xertrex International Inc (PA)**....630 773-4020
1530 Glenlake Ave Itasca (60143) ***(G-12375)***
**Xform Power and Eqp Sups LLC**....773 260-0209
2741 N Pine Grove Ave Chicago (60614) ***(G-7044)***
**Xfpg LLC**....224 513-2010
300 Knightsbridge Pkwy Lincolnshire (60069) ***(G-13491)***
**Xingfa USA Corporation**....360 720-9256
418 W 5th Ave Naperville (60563) ***(G-15786)***
**Xisync LLC**....630 350-9400
655 Wheat Ln Wood Dale (60191) ***(G-22439)***
**Xl Manufacture**....773 271-8900
2717 W Lawrence Ave Chicago (60625) ***(G-7045)***
**Xlogotech Inc**....888 244-5152
5 E College Dr Ste 203 Arlington Heights (60004) ***(G-875)***
**Xmt Solutions LLC**....703 338-9422
1749 N Wells St Apt 2010 Chicago (60614) ***(G-7046)***
**Xomi Instruments Co Ltd**....847 660-4614
1463 Pinehurst Dr Vernon Hills (60061) ***(G-21220)***
**Xpac, Milan** *Also called Export Packaging Co Inc* ***(G-14786)***
**Xpress Printing & Copying Co**....630 980-9600
147 W Irving Park Rd Roselle (60172) ***(G-18987)***
**Xpressigns Inc**....888 303-0640
2470 E Oakton St Arlington Heights (60005) ***(G-876)***
**Xshredders Inc (PA)**....847 205-1875
2855 Shermer Rd Northbrook (60062) ***(G-16389)***
**Xtrem Graphix Solutions Inc**....217 698-6424
1810 W Jefferson St Ste C Springfield (62702) ***(G-20549)***
**Xtreme Dzignz**....309 633-9311
4001 Constitution Dr Bartonville (61607) ***(G-1400)***
**Xtremedata Inc**....847 871-0379
999 N Plaza Dr Ste 570 Schaumburg (60173) ***(G-19792)***
**Xttrium Laboratories Inc (PA)**....773 268-5800
1200 E Business Center Dr # 100 Mount Prospect (60056) ***(G-15386)***
**Xylem, Morton Grove** *Also called ITT Water & Wastewater USA Inc* ***(G-15205)***
**Xylem, Cordova** *Also called Melyx Inc* ***(G-7379)***
**Xylem Inc**....847 966-3700
8200 Austin Ave Morton Grove (60053) ***(G-15247)***
**Y 2 K Electronics Inc**....847 238-9024
2574 United Ln Elk Grove Village (60007) ***(G-9821)***
**Y T Packing Co**....217 522-3345
1129 Taintor Rd Springfield (62702) ***(G-20550)***
**Yale Security Inc**....704 283-2101
9100 Belmont Ave Franklin Park (60131) ***(G-10632)***
**Yamada America Inc**....847 228-9063
955 E Algonquin Rd Arlington Heights (60005) ***(G-877)***
**Yana House**....773 874-7120
7120 S Normal Blvd Chicago (60621) ***(G-7047)***
**Yanfeng US Automotive**....779 552-7300
775 Logistics Dr Belvidere (61008) ***(G-1798)***
**Yanmar (usa) Inc**....847 541-1900
901 Corporate Grove Dr Buffalo Grove (60089) ***(G-2796)***
**Yargus Manufacturing Inc**....217 826-6352
12285 E Main St Marshall (62441) ***(G-14331)***
**Yaskawa America Inc (HQ)**....847 887-7000
2121 Norman Dr Waukegan (60085) ***(G-21642)***

ALPHABETIC

**Yaskawa America Inc**....847 887-7909
1297 E Walnut Ave Des Plaines (60016) ***(G-8307)***
**Yates Complete Concrete, Edwardsville** *Also called David Yates* ***(G-8794)***
**Yates Motloid, Chicago** *Also called Bird-X Inc* ***(G-4112)***
**Yazdan Essie**....847 675-7916
3730 W Morse Ave Lincolnwood (60712) ***(G-13544)***
**Ycl International Inc**....630 873-0768
3118 Whispering Oaks Ln Woodridge (60517) ***(G-22529)***
**Ye Olde Sign Shoppe**....847 228-7446
68 N Lively Blvd Elk Grove Village (60007) ***(G-9822)***
**Yeaman Machine Tech Inc**....847 758-0500
2150 Touhy Ave Elk Grove Village (60007) ***(G-9823)***
**Yeary & Associates Inc**....312 335-1012
1050 N State St Ste Mez3 Chicago (60610) ***(G-7048)***
**Yeary Controls, Chicago** *Also called Yeary & Associates Inc* ***(G-7048)***
**Yeast Printing Inc**....309 833-2845
319 N Lafayette St Macomb (61455) ***(G-14137)***
**Yello, Chicago** *Also called Recsolu Inc* ***(G-6313)***
**Yeomans Pump, Aurora** *Also called Grundfos Water Utility Inc* ***(G-1021)***
**Yer Kiln Me LLC**....309 606-9007
108 N 7th St Wyoming (61491) ***(G-22642)***
**Yes Equipment & Services LLC**....866 799-7743
1151 W Bryn Mawr Ave Itasca (60143) ***(G-12376)***
**Yes Packaging, Chicago** *Also called Yes Print Management Inc* ***(G-7049)***
**Yes Print Management Inc**....312 226-4444
415 N Aberdeen St Ste 2 Chicago (60642) ***(G-7049)***
**Yesco Chicago, Addison** *Also called Omega Sign & Lighting Inc* ***(G-234)***
**Yetee LLC**....630 340-0132
110 Cross St Aurora (60506) ***(G-1236)***
**Yetter Farm Equipment, Colchester** *Also called Yetter Manufacturing Company* ***(G-7309)***
**Yetter M Co Inc Emp B Tr**....309 776-4111
109 S Mcdonough St Colchester (62326) ***(G-7308)***
**Yetter Manufacturing Company**....309 833-1445
1270 E Murray St Macomb (61455) ***(G-14138)***
**Yetter Manufacturing Company (PA)**....309 776-3222
109 S Mcdonough St Colchester (62326) ***(G-7309)***
**Yfy Jupiter Inc**....312 419-8565
445 N Wells St Ste 401 Chicago (60654) ***(G-7050)***
**Yg-1 Tool USA, Vernon Hills** *Also called Sab Tool Supply Co* ***(G-21196)***
**Yhlsoft Inc**....630 355-8033
625 S Wright St Naperville (60540) ***(G-15787)***
**Yield Management Systems LLC**....312 665-1595
2626 N Lakeview Ave # 2501 Chicago (60614) ***(G-7051)***
**Yield360, Morton** *Also called 360 Yield Center LLC* ***(G-15152)***
**Yinlun Usa Inc**....309 291-0843
77 Commerce Dr Morton (61550) ***(G-15185)***
**YKK AP America Inc**....630 582-9602
1000 Stevenson Ct Ste 101 Roselle (60172) ***(G-18988)***
**YMC Corp**....312 842-4900
481 W 26th St Chicago (60616) ***(G-7052)***
**Yockey Oil Incorporated**....618 393-6236
1043 W Main St Olney (62450) ***(G-16802)***
**Yoder John**....217 676-3430
2580 N 1500 East Rd Blue Mound (62513) ***(G-2274)***
**Yoders Portable Buildings LLC (PA)**....618 936-2419
5425 Larkspur Rd Sumner (62466) ***(G-20773)***
**Yolanda Lorente Ltd (PA)**....773 334-4536
4424 N Ravenswood Ave 1 Chicago (60640) ***(G-7053)***
**Yoos Imports, Chicago** *Also called Evoys Corp* ***(G-4791)***
**York Corrugated Container Corp**....630 260-2900
120 W Lake Dr Glendale Heights (60139) ***(G-11093)***
**York International Corporation**....815 946-2351
3820 S Il Route 26 Polo (61064) ***(G-17692)***
**York Spring Co**....847 695-5978
1551 N La Fox St South Elgin (60177) ***(G-20236)***
**Yorke Printe Shoppe Inc**....630 627-4960
930 N Lombard Rd Lombard (60148) ***(G-13885)***
**Yoshino America Corporation**....708 534-1141
2500 Palmer Ave University Park (60484) ***(G-21067)***
**Yotta Pet Products Inc**....217 466-4777
1977 S Central Ave Paris (61944) ***(G-17165)***
**Young Innovations Inc (HQ)**....847 458-5400
2260 Wendt St Algonquin (60102) ***(G-415)***
**Young Innovations Inc (PA)**....847 458-5400
2260 Wendt St Algonquin (60102) ***(G-416)***
**Young Innovations Holdings LLC (PA)**....312 506-5600
111 S Wacker Dr Ste 3350 Chicago (60606) ***(G-7054)***
**Young Os LLC**....847 458-5400
2260 Wendt St Algonquin (60102) ***(G-417)***
**Young Shin Honey Farm, Mount Prospect** *Also called Ys Health Corporation* ***(G-15387)***
**Young Shin USA Limited**....847 598-3611
1320 Tower Rd Ste 111 Schaumburg (60173) ***(G-19793)***
**Youngberg Industries Inc**....815 544-2177
6863 Indy Dr Belvidere (61008) ***(G-1799)***
**Your Custom Cabinetry Corp**....773 290-7247
1609 N 31st Ave Melrose Park (60160) ***(G-14712)***
**Your Images Group Inc**....847 437-6688
1300 Basswood Rd Ste 200 Schaumburg (60173) ***(G-19794)***
**Your Logo Here**....708 258-6666
427 S Governors Hwy Peotone (60468) ***(G-17494)***
**Your Supply Depot Limited**....815 568-4115
207 E Grant Hwy Marengo (60152) ***(G-14245)***
**Your Team Socks**....309 713-1044
8816 N Industrial Rd Peoria (61615) ***(G-17479)***
**Youtopia Inc**....312 593-0859
222 Merchandise Mart Plz # 1212 Chicago (60654) ***(G-7055)***
**Ys Health Corporation**....847 391-9122
411 Kingston Ct Ste A Mount Prospect (60056) ***(G-15387)***
**Yuenger Wood Moulding Inc**....773 735-7100
847 Santa Maria Dr Naperville (60540) ***(G-15788)***
**Yuenger, Wm Mfg Co, Naperville** *Also called Yuenger Wood Moulding Inc* ***(G-15788)***
**Yusraa Inc**....312 608-1916
14828 Cottage Grove Ave Dolton (60419) ***(G-8378)***
**Z & L Machining Inc (PA)**....847 623-9500
3140 Central Ave Waukegan (60085) ***(G-21643)***
**Z A W Collections**....773 568-2031
11145 S Michigan Ave Chicago (60628) ***(G-7056)***
**Z Automation Company**....847 357-0120
163 N Archer Ave Mundelein (60060) ***(G-15569)***
**Z Print Inc**....773 685-4878
5257 N Central Ave Chicago (60630) ***(G-7057)***
**Z-Patch Inc**....618 529-2431
800 W Industrial Park Rd Carbondale (62901) ***(G-3029)***
**Z-Tech Inc**....815 335-7395
1958 S Winnebago Rd Winnebago (61088) ***(G-22299)***
**Zabiha Halal Meat Processors**....630 620-5000
1715 W Cortland Ct Addison (60101) ***(G-349)***
**Zacros America Inc (HQ)**....847 397-6191
1821 Walden Office Sq # 400 Schaumburg (60173) ***(G-19795)***
**Zagone Studio LLC**....773 509-0610
4533 W North Ave Melrose Park (60160) ***(G-14713)***
**Zah Group Inc (PA)**....847 821-5500
450 Bond St Lincolnshire (60069) ***(G-13492)***
**Zaibak Bros (PA)**....312 564-5800
35 E Wacker Dr Fl 9 Chicago (60601) ***(G-7058)***
**Zainab Enterprises Inc**....630 739-0110
684 Phelps Ave Romeoville (60446) ***(G-18881)***
**Zanetis Oil Company**....618 262-4593
319 E 8th St Mount Carmel (62863) ***(G-15289)***
**Zanfel Laboratories Inc (PA)**....309 683-3500
6901 N Knoxville Ave # 200 Peoria (61614) ***(G-17480)***
**Zantech Inc**....309 692-8307
7501 N Harker Dr Peoria (61615) ***(G-17481)***
**Zapp Noodle**....618 979-8863
1407 W Highway 50 Ste 106 O Fallon (62269) ***(G-16482)***
**Zapp Tooling Alloys Inc**....847 599-0351
1528 Saint Paul Ave Gurnee (60031) ***(G-11521)***
**Zaptel Corporation**....847 386-8050
836 S Arlington Hts Rd Elk Grove Village (60007) ***(G-9824)***
**Zarc International Inc**....309 807-2565
529 S Petri Dr Minonk (61760) ***(G-14835)***
**Zb Importing Inc**....708 222-8330
5400 W 35th St Cicero (60804) ***(G-7248)***
**Zebra, Lincolnshire** *Also called Zih Corp* ***(G-13498)***
**Zebra Entp Solutions Corp (HQ)**....847 634-6700
3 Overlook Pt Lincolnshire (60069) ***(G-13493)***
**Zebra Outlet**....312 416-1518
5750 W Bloomingdale Ave Chicago (60639) ***(G-7059)***
**Zebra Software Inc**....847 742-9110
5525 Mallard Ln Hoffman Estates (60192) ***(G-12070)***
**Zebra Technologies Corporation (PA)**....847 634-6700
3 Overlook Pt Lincolnshire (60069) ***(G-13494)***
**Zebra Technologies Corporation**....847 634-6700
6048 Eagle Way Chicago (60678) ***(G-7060)***
**Zebra Technologies Intl LLC (HQ)**....847 634-6700
3 Overlook Pt Lincolnshire (60069) ***(G-13495)***
**Zeco Inc**....847 446-1413
256 Lagoon Dr Northfield (60093) ***(G-16423)***
**Zegers Inc**....708 474-7700
16727 Chicago Ave Lansing (60438) ***(G-13193)***
**Zeigler Chrysler Dodge**....708 956-7700
6539 Ogden Ave Berwyn (60402) ***(G-2079)***
**Zeigler Preowned of Chicago, Berwyn** *Also called Zeigler Chrysler Dodge* ***(G-2079)***
**Zekelman Industries Inc (PA)**....312 275-1600
227 W Monroe St Ste 2600 Chicago (60606) ***(G-7061)***
**Zelda's Sweet Shoppe, Skokie** *Also called Zeldaco Ltd* ***(G-20116)***
**Zeldaco Ltd (PA)**....847 679-0033
4113 Main St Skokie (60076) ***(G-20116)***
**Zell Co**....312 226-9191
329 W 18th St Ste 507 Chicago (60616) ***(G-7062)***
**Zeller + Gmelin Corporation**....630 443-8800
3820 Ohio Ave Ste 1 Saint Charles (60174) ***(G-19302)***
**Zeller Plastik Usa Inc (HQ)**....847 247-7900
1515 Franklin Blvd Libertyville (60048) ***(G-13403)***
**Zeman Mfg Co**....630 960-2300
1996 University Ln Lisle (60532) ***(G-13679)***
**Zen Bakery, MA, Flossmoor** *Also called Pin Hsiao & Associates LLC* ***(G-10227)***

**Zender Enterprises Ltd** .................................................. 773 282-2293
  3692 N Milwaukee Ave  Chicago  (60641)  *(G-7063)*
**Zender Molding Solutions, Chicago** Also called Zender Enterprises Ltd *(G-7063)*
**Zenfab, Chicago** Also called Zenith Fabricating Company *(G-7064)*
**Zenith Electronics Corporation (HQ)** ............................ 847 941-8000
  2000 Millbrook Dr  Lincolnshire  (60069)  *(G-13496)*
**Zenith Fabricating Company** ........................................ 773 622-2601
  1928 N Leamington Ave  Chicago  (60639)  *(G-7064)*
**Zenter Custom Cabinets Inc** ........................................ 847 488-0744
  363 Bluff City Blvd  Elgin  (60120)  *(G-9240)*
**Zero Ground  LLC** ........................................................ 847 360-9500
  2340 Ernie Krueger Cir  Waukegan  (60087)  *(G-21644)*
**Zeta Manufacturing Company** ...................................... 708 301-3766
  13338 W Oak Ct  Homer Glen  (60491)  *(G-12089)*
**ZF Chassis Components  LLC** ..................................... 773 371-4550
  3400 E 126th St  Chicago  (60633)  *(G-7065)*
**ZF Chassis Systems Chicago LLC** .............................. 773 371-4550
  3400 E 126th St  Chicago  (60633)  *(G-7066)*
**ZF Chassis Systems Tuscaloosa, Chicago** Also called ZF Chassis Components LLC *(G-7065)*
**ZF Services  LLC** .......................................................... 734 416-6200
  777 Hickory Hill Dr  Vernon Hills  (60061)  *(G-21221)*
**Zg3 Systems  LLC** ........................................................ 309 745-3398
  25232 Spring Creek Rd  Washington  (61571)  *(G-21397)*
**Zhmin Power, Aurora** Also called Astral Power Systems Inc *(G-1112)*
**Ziemer Usa  Inc** ............................................................ 618 462-9301
  620 E 3rd St  Alton  (62002)  *(G-595)*
**Ziglers Machine and Met Works, Dixon** Also called Ziglers Mch & Met Works Inc *(G-8360)*
**Ziglers Mch & Met Works Inc** ....................................... 815 652-7518
  972 Mile Rd  Dixon  (61021)  *(G-8360)*
**Zih Corp (HQ)** ................................................................ 847 634-6700
  3 Overlook Pt  Lincolnshire  (60069)  *(G-13497)*
**Zih Corp** ......................................................................... 847 634-6700
  3 Overlook Pt  Lincolnshire  (60069)  *(G-13498)*
**Zim Manufacturing Co** .................................................. 773 622-2500
  6100 W Grand Ave  Chicago  (60639)  *(G-7067)*
**Zimco, Chicago** Also called Zimmerman Brush Co *(G-7068)*
**Zimmerman Brush Co** .................................................. 773 761-6331
  6320 N Whipple St  Chicago  (60659)  *(G-7068)*
**Zimmerman Enterprises Inc (PA)** ................................ 847 297-3177
  1216 Rand Rd  Des Plaines  (60016)  *(G-8308)*
**Zing Enterprises  LLC** .................................................. 608 201-9490
  83 Templeton Dr Ste G  Oswego  (60543)  *(G-16943)*
**Zipwhaa Inc** ................................................................... 630 898-4330
  3191 Brockway St  Palatine  (60067)  *(G-17092)*
**Zirlin Interiors Inc** ........................................................ 773 334-5530
  5540 N Broadway St  Chicago  (60640)  *(G-7069)*
**Zirmed Inc** ..................................................................... 312 207-0889
  111 N Canal St Ste 400  Chicago  (60606)  *(G-7070)*
**Zitropack  Ltd** ................................................................ 630 543-1016
  240 S La Londe Ave  Addison  (60101)  *(G-350)*
**Ziv USA Inc (HQ)** .......................................................... 224 735-3961
  5410 Newport Dr Ste 38  Rolling Meadows  (60008)  *(G-18789)*
**Ziyad Brothers Importing, Cicero** Also called Zb Importing  Inc *(G-7248)*
**Zj Industries  Inc (PA)** .................................................. 630 543-6400
  125 W Factory Rd  Addison  (60101)  *(G-351)*
**Znl Corporation** ............................................................ 815 654-0870
  2120 Harlem Rd  Loves Park  (61111)  *(G-14011)*
**Zoe Publications LLC** .................................................. 636 625-6622
  5801 N Cypress Dr # 2905  Peoria  (61615)  *(G-17482)*
**Zoes Mfgco LLC** ........................................................... 312 666-4018
  168 N Sangamon St  Chicago  (60607)  *(G-7071)*
**Zoetis LLC** ..................................................................... 708 757-2592
  400 State St  Chicago Heights  (60411)  *(G-7137)*
**Zoia Monument Company** ............................................ 815 338-0358
  222 Washington St  Woodstock  (60098)  *(G-22629)*
**Zoll-Dental, Niles** Also called Cislak Manufacturing  Inc *(G-15969)*
**Zone Inc** ........................................................................ 630 887-8585
  66 63rd St  Willowbrook  (60527)  *(G-22240)*
**Zookbinders Inc** ........................................................... 847 272-5745
  151 S Pfingsten Rd Ste K  Deerfield  (60015)  *(G-8070)*
**Zorch International  Inc** ............................................... 312 751-8010
  223 W Erie St Ste 5nw  Chicago  (60654)  *(G-7072)*
**Zorin Material Handling Co (PA)** ................................. 773 342-3818
  1937 W Wolfram St  Chicago  (60657)  *(G-7073)*
**Zotos International  Inc** ............................................... 847 390-0984
  10600 W Higgins Rd # 415  Rosemont  (60018)  *(G-19044)*
**Zsi-Foster  Inc** .............................................................. 800 323-7053
  6571 Solutions Ctr  Chicago  (60677)  *(G-7074)*
**Zuchem Inc** ................................................................... 312 997-2150
  2225 W Harrison St Ste F  Chicago  (60612)  *(G-7075)*
**Zuma Corporation** ........................................................ 815 288-7269
  1335 Chicago Ave  Dixon  (61021)  *(G-8361)*
**Zweibel Worldwide Productions** ................................. 312 751-0503
  212 W Superior St Ste 200  Chicago  (60654)  *(G-7076)*

# PRODUCT INDEX

• Product categories are listed in alphabetical order.

## A

ABRASIVE SAND MINING
ABRASIVES
ABRASIVES: Aluminum Oxide Fused
ABRASIVES: Diamond Powder
ABRASIVES: Polishing Rouge
ABRASIVES: Silicon Carbide
ABRASIVES: Tungsten Carbide
ACCELERATION INDICATORS & SYSTEM COMPONENTS: Aerospace
ACCELERATORS: Linear
ACCIDENT INSURANCE CARRIERS
ACCOUNTING SVCS, NEC
ACIDS: Hydrochloric
ACIDS: Inorganic
ACIDS: Sulfuric, Oleum
ACRYLIC RESINS
ACTUATORS: Indl, NEC
ADDITIVE BASED PLASTIC MATERIALS: Plasticizers
ADDRESSING SVCS
ADHESIVES
ADHESIVES & SEALANTS
ADHESIVES: Epoxy
ADVERTISING AGENCIES
ADVERTISING AGENCIES: Consultants
ADVERTISING CURTAINS
ADVERTISING DISPLAY PRDTS
ADVERTISING MATERIAL DISTRIBUTION
ADVERTISING REPRESENTATIVES: Electronic Media
ADVERTISING REPRESENTATIVES: Magazine
ADVERTISING REPRESENTATIVES: Media
ADVERTISING REPRESENTATIVES: Newspaper
ADVERTISING REPRESENTATIVES: Printed Media
ADVERTISING SPECIALTIES, WHOLESALE
ADVERTISING SVCS, NEC
ADVERTISING SVCS: Billboards
ADVERTISING SVCS: Direct Mail
ADVERTISING SVCS: Display
ADVERTISING SVCS: Outdoor
ADVERTISING SVCS: Poster, Outdoor
ADVERTISING SVCS: Transit
AERIAL WORK PLATFORMS
AEROSOLS
AGENTS, BROKERS & BUREAUS: Personal Service
AGRICULTURAL CHEMICALS: Trace Elements
AGRICULTURAL CREDIT INSTITUTIONS
AGRICULTURAL EQPT: BARN, SILO, POULTRY, DAIRY/LIVESTOCK MACH
AGRICULTURAL EQPT: Barn Cleaners
AGRICULTURAL EQPT: Elevators, Farm
AGRICULTURAL EQPT: Fertilizing Machinery
AGRICULTURAL EQPT: Fertilizng, Sprayng, Dustng/Irrigatn Mach
AGRICULTURAL EQPT: Fillers & Unloaders, Silo
AGRICULTURAL EQPT: Grade, Clean & Sort Machines, Fruit/Veg
AGRICULTURAL EQPT: Greens Mowing Eqpt
AGRICULTURAL EQPT: Haying Mach, Mowers, Rakes, Stackers, Etc
AGRICULTURAL EQPT: Loaders, Manure & General Utility
AGRICULTURAL EQPT: Planting Machines
AGRICULTURAL EQPT: Soil Preparation Mach, Exc Turf & Grounds
AGRICULTURAL EQPT: Spreaders, Fertilizer
AGRICULTURAL EQPT: Stackers, Grain
AGRICULTURAL EQPT: Storage Bins, Crop
AGRICULTURAL EQPT: Trailers & Wagons, Farm
AGRICULTURAL EQPT: Turf & Grounds Eqpt
AGRICULTURAL EQPT: Turf Eqpt, Commercial
AGRICULTURAL EQPT: Weeding Machines
AGRICULTURAL LIMESTONE: Ground
AGRICULTURAL LOAN COMPANIES
AGRICULTURAL MACHINERY & EQPT REPAIR
AGRICULTURAL MACHINERY & EQPT: Wholesalers
AIR CLEANING SYSTEMS
AIR CONDITIONERS: Motor Vehicle
AIR CONDITIONING & VENTILATION EQPT & SPLYS: Wholesales

AIR CONDITIONING EQPT
AIR CONDITIONING EQPT, WHOLE HOUSE: Wholesalers
AIR CONDITIONING REPAIR SVCS
AIR CONDITIONING UNITS: Complete, Domestic Or Indl
AIR COOLERS: Metal Plate
AIR CURTAINS
AIR MATTRESSES: Plastic
AIR POLLUTION CONTROL EQPT & SPLYS WHOLESALERS
AIR PURIFICATION EQPT
AIR-CONDITIONING SPLY SVCS
AIRCRAFT & AEROSPACE FLIGHT INSTRUMENTS & GUIDANCE SYSTEMS
AIRCRAFT & HEAVY EQPT REPAIR SVCS
AIRCRAFT ASSEMBLY PLANTS
AIRCRAFT CONTROL SYSTEMS: Electronic Totalizing Counters
AIRCRAFT DEALERS
AIRCRAFT ENGINES & ENGINE PARTS: Airfoils
AIRCRAFT ENGINES & ENGINE PARTS: Mount Parts
AIRCRAFT ENGINES & ENGINE PARTS: Nonelectric Starters
AIRCRAFT ENGINES & ENGINE PARTS: Research & Development, Mfr
AIRCRAFT ENGINES & PARTS
AIRCRAFT EQPT & SPLYS WHOLESALERS
AIRCRAFT FLIGHT INSTRUMENT REPAIR SVCS
AIRCRAFT FUELING SVCS
AIRCRAFT HANGAR OPERATION SVCS
AIRCRAFT MAINTENANCE & REPAIR SVCS
AIRCRAFT PARTS & AUX EQPT: Governors, Propeller Feathering
AIRCRAFT PARTS & AUXILIARY EQPT: Aircraft Training Eqpt
AIRCRAFT PARTS & AUXILIARY EQPT: Assys, Subassemblies/Parts
AIRCRAFT PARTS & AUXILIARY EQPT: Blades, Prop, Metal Or Wood
AIRCRAFT PARTS & AUXILIARY EQPT: Bodies
AIRCRAFT PARTS & AUXILIARY EQPT: Body & Wing Assys & Parts
AIRCRAFT PARTS & AUXILIARY EQPT: Body Assemblies & Parts
AIRCRAFT PARTS & AUXILIARY EQPT: Gears, Power Transmission
AIRCRAFT PARTS & AUXILIARY EQPT: Military Eqpt & Armament
AIRCRAFT PARTS & AUXILIARY EQPT: Refueling Eqpt, In Flight
AIRCRAFT PARTS & AUXILIARY EQPT: Research & Development, Mfr
AIRCRAFT PARTS & AUXILIARY EQPT: Wing Assemblies & Parts
AIRCRAFT PARTS & EQPT, NEC
AIRCRAFT PARTS WHOLESALERS
AIRCRAFT SEATS
AIRCRAFT SERVICING & REPAIRING
AIRCRAFT TURBINES
AIRCRAFT WHEELS
AIRCRAFT: Airplanes, Fixed Or Rotary Wing
AIRLOCKS
ALARMS: Burglar
ALARMS: Fire
ALCOHOL, ETHYL: For Beverage Purposes
ALCOHOL, GRAIN: For Beverage Purposes
ALCOHOL: Ethyl & Ethanol
ALKALIES & CHLORINE
ALL-TERRAIN VEHICLE DEALERS
ALLOYS: Additive, Exc Copper Or Made In Blast Furnaces
ALTERNATORS & GENERATORS: Battery Charging
ALTERNATORS: Automotive
ALUMINUM
ALUMINUM & BERYLLIUM ORES MINING
ALUMINUM PRDTS
ALUMINUM: Coil & Sheet
ALUMINUM: Rolling & Drawing
AMMONIA & AMMONIUM SALTS
AMMONIUM NITRATE OR AMMONIUM SULFATE
AMMUNITION
AMMUNITION: Components

AMMUNITION: Small Arms
AMPLIFIERS
AMPLIFIERS: Parametric
AMPLIFIERS: RF & IF Power
AMUSEMENT & RECREATION SVCS, NEC
AMUSEMENT & RECREATION SVCS: Exhibition & Carnival Op Svcs
AMUSEMENT & RECREATION SVCS: Indoor Or Outdoor Court Clubs
AMUSEMENT & RECREATION SVCS: Scuba & Skin Diving Instruction
AMUSEMENT & RECREATION SVCS: Shooting Range
AMUSEMENT & RECREATION SVCS: Skating Rink Operation
AMUSEMENT & RECREATION SVCS: Tennis Club, Membership
AMUSEMENT & RECREATION SVCS: Tennis Courts, Non-Member
AMUSEMENT MACHINES: Coin Operated
AMUSEMENT PARK DEVICES & RIDES
AMUSEMENT PARK DEVICES & RIDES Carousels Or Merry-Go-Rounds
AMUSEMENT PARK DEVICES & RIDES: Carnival Mach & Eqpt, NEC
AMUSEMENT PARKS
ANALYZERS: Blood & Body Fluid
ANALYZERS: Coulometric, Indl Process
ANALYZERS: Moisture
ANALYZERS: Network
ANALYZERS: Respiratory
ANATOMICAL SPECIMENS & RESEARCH MATERIAL, WHOLESALE
ANESTHETICS: Bulk Form
ANIMAL BASED MEDICINAL CHEMICAL PRDTS
ANIMAL FEED & SUPPLEMENTS: Livestock & Poultry
ANIMAL FEED: Wholesalers
ANIMAL FOOD & SUPPLEMENTS: Bird Food, Prepared
ANIMAL FOOD & SUPPLEMENTS: Dog
ANIMAL FOOD & SUPPLEMENTS: Dog & Cat
ANIMAL FOOD & SUPPLEMENTS: Feather Meal
ANIMAL FOOD & SUPPLEMENTS: Feed Premixes
ANIMAL FOOD & SUPPLEMENTS: Feed Supplements
ANIMAL FOOD & SUPPLEMENTS: Livestock
ANIMAL FOOD & SUPPLEMENTS: Mineral feed supplements
ANIMAL FOOD & SUPPLEMENTS: Pet, Exc Dog & Cat, Canned
ANIMAL FOOD & SUPPLEMENTS: Pet, Exc Dog & Cat, Dry
ANIMAL FOOD & SUPPLEMENTS: Poultry
ANIMAL FOOD & SUPPLEMENTS: Specialty, Mice & Other Pets
ANIMAL OILS: Medicinal Grade, Refined Or Concentrated
ANNEALING: Metal
ANODIZING SVC
ANTENNAS: Radar Or Communications
ANTENNAS: Receiving
ANTENNAS: Satellite, Household Use
ANTIBIOTICS
ANTIFREEZE
ANTIHISTAMINE PREPARATIONS
ANTIQUE & CLASSIC AUTOMOBILE RESTORATION
ANTIQUE AUTOMOBILE DEALERS
ANTIQUE FURNITURE RESTORATION & REPAIR
ANTIQUE REPAIR & RESTORATION SVCS, EXC FURNITURE & AUTOS
ANTIQUE SHOPS
ANTISCALING COMPOUNDS, BOILER
ANTISEPTICS, MEDICINAL
APPAREL ACCESS STORES
APPAREL DESIGNERS: Commercial
APPLIANCE CORDS: Household Electrical Eqpt
APPLIANCE PARTS: Porcelain Enameled
APPLIANCES, HOUSEHOLD: Buttonhole/Eyelet Mach/Attach
APPLIANCES, HOUSEHOLD: Ice Boxes, Metal Or Wood
APPLIANCES, HOUSEHOLD: Kitchen, Major, Exc Refrigs & Stoves
APPLIANCES, HOUSEHOLD: Laundry Machines, Incl Coin-Operated

# PRODUCT INDEX

APPLIANCES, HOUSEHOLD: Refrigs, Mechanical & Absorption
APPLIANCES, HOUSEHOLD: Sewing Machines & Attchmnts, Domestic
APPLIANCES, HOUSEHOLD: Sweepers, Electric
APPLIANCES: Household, Refrigerators & Freezers
APPLIANCES: Major, Cooking
APPLIANCES: Small, Electric
APPLICATIONS SOFTWARE PROGRAMMING
APPRENTICESHIP TRAINING SCHOOLS
AQUARIUMS & ACCESS: Glass
AQUARIUMS & ACCESS: Plastic
ARCHITECTURAL SVCS
ARCHITECTURAL SVCS: Engineering
ARCHITECTURAL SVCS: House Designer
ARMATURE REPAIRING & REWINDING SVC
ARMATURES: Ind
ARSENATES & ARSENITES: Formulated
ART & ORNAMENTAL WARE: Pottery
ART DEALERS & GALLERIES
ART DESIGN SVCS
ART GALLERIES
ART GOODS & SPLYS WHOLESALERS
ART GOODS, WHOLESALE
ART MARBLE: Concrete
ART SCHOOL, EXC COMMERCIAL
ARTIFICIAL FLOWERS & TREES
ARTIST'S MATERIALS & SPLYS
ARTISTS' AGENTS & BROKERS
ARTISTS' EQPT
ARTISTS' MATERIALS, WHOLESALE
ARTISTS' MATERIALS: Boxes, Sketching & Paint
ARTISTS' MATERIALS: Brushes, Air
ARTISTS' MATERIALS: Chalks, Carpenters', Blackboard, Etc
ARTISTS' MATERIALS: Clay, Modeling
ARTISTS' MATERIALS: Eraser Guides & Shields
ARTISTS' MATERIALS: Ink, Drawing, Black & Colored
ARTISTS' MATERIALS: Lettering Instruments
ARTISTS' MATERIALS: Paints, Exc Gold & Bronze
ARTISTS' MATERIALS: Palettes
ARTISTS' MATERIALS: Pencil Holders
ARTISTS' MATERIALS: Pencils & Pencil Parts
ARTISTS' MATERIALS: Wax
ARTWORK: Framed
ASBESTOS PRDTS: Insulation, Molded
ASBESTOS PRDTS: Wick
ASBESTOS PRODUCTS
ASBESTOS REMOVAL EQPT
ASH TRAYS: Stamped Metal
ASPHALT & ASPHALT PRDTS
ASPHALT COATINGS & SEALERS
ASPHALT MIXTURES WHOLESALERS
ASPHALT PLANTS INCLUDING GRAVEL MIX TYPE
ASSEMBLING & PACKAGING SVCS: Cosmetic Kits
ASSEMBLING SVC: Clocks
ASSEMBLING SVC: Plumbing Fixture Fittings, Plastic
ASSOCIATIONS: Bar
ASSOCIATIONS: Business
ASSOCIATIONS: Real Estate Management
ASSOCIATIONS: Trade
ATHLETIC ORGANIZATION
ATOMIZERS
AUCTION SVCS: Livestock
AUDIO & VIDEO EQPT, EXC COMMERCIAL
AUDIO & VIDEO TAPES WHOLESALERS
AUDIO COMPONENTS
AUDIO ELECTRONIC SYSTEMS
AUTO & HOME SUPPLY STORES: Auto & Truck Eqpt & Parts
AUTO & HOME SUPPLY STORES: Automotive Access
AUTO & HOME SUPPLY STORES: Automotive parts
AUTO & HOME SUPPLY STORES: Batteries, Automotive & Truck
AUTO & HOME SUPPLY STORES: Speed Shops, Incl Race Car Splys
AUTO & HOME SUPPLY STORES: Truck Eqpt & Parts
AUTO SPLYS & PARTS, NEW, WHSLE: Exhaust Sys, Mufflers, Etc
AUTOCLAVES: Laboratory
AUTOMATIC REGULATING CNTRLS: Steam Press, Residential/ Comm
AUTOMATIC REGULATING CONTROL: Building Svcs Monitoring, Auto
AUTOMATIC REGULATING CONTROLS: AC & Refrigeration
AUTOMATIC REGULATING CONTROLS: Appliance Regulators

AUTOMATIC REGULATING CONTROLS: Appliance, Exc Air-Cond/Refr
AUTOMATIC REGULATING CONTROLS: Energy Cutoff, Residtl/Comm
AUTOMATIC REGULATING CONTROLS: Gas Burner, Automatic
AUTOMATIC REGULATING CONTROLS: Gradual Switches, Pneumatic
AUTOMATIC REGULATING CONTROLS: Hardware, Environmental Reg
AUTOMATIC REGULATING CONTROLS: Hydronic Circulator, Auto
AUTOMATIC REGULATING CONTROLS: Incinerator, Residential/Comm
AUTOMATIC REGULATING CONTROLS: Pneumatic Relays, Air-Cond
AUTOMATIC REGULATING CONTROLS: Refrigeration, Pressure
AUTOMATIC REGULATING CTRLS: Damper, Pneumatic Or Electric
AUTOMATIC TELLER MACHINES
AUTOMATIC VENDING MACHINES: Mechanisms & Parts
AUTOMOBILE FINANCE LEASING
AUTOMOBILE STORAGE GARAGE
AUTOMOBILES & OTHER MOTOR VEHICLES WHOLESALERS
AUTOMOBILES: Wholesalers
AUTOMOTIVE & TRUCK GENERAL REPAIR SVC
AUTOMOTIVE BATTERIES WHOLESALERS
AUTOMOTIVE BODY SHOP
AUTOMOTIVE BODY, PAINT & INTERIOR REPAIR & MAINTENANCE SVC
AUTOMOTIVE DEALERS, NEC
AUTOMOTIVE EXHAUST REPAIR SVC
AUTOMOTIVE EXTERIOR REPAIR SVCS
AUTOMOTIVE GLASS REPLACEMENT SHOPS
AUTOMOTIVE LETTERING & PAINTING SVCS
AUTOMOTIVE PAINT SHOP
AUTOMOTIVE PARTS, ACCESS & SPLYS
AUTOMOTIVE PARTS: Plastic
AUTOMOTIVE PRDTS: Rubber
AUTOMOTIVE RADIATOR REPAIR SHOPS
AUTOMOTIVE REPAIR SHOPS: Alternators/Generator, Rebuild/Rpr
AUTOMOTIVE REPAIR SHOPS: Diesel Engine Repair
AUTOMOTIVE REPAIR SHOPS: Electrical Svcs
AUTOMOTIVE REPAIR SHOPS: Engine Rebuilding
AUTOMOTIVE REPAIR SHOPS: Engine Repair
AUTOMOTIVE REPAIR SHOPS: Frame Repair Shops
AUTOMOTIVE REPAIR SHOPS: Machine Shop
AUTOMOTIVE REPAIR SHOPS: Springs, Rebuilding & Repair
AUTOMOTIVE REPAIR SHOPS: Torque Converter Repair
AUTOMOTIVE REPAIR SHOPS: Trailer Repair
AUTOMOTIVE REPAIR SHOPS: Truck Engine Repair, Exc Indl
AUTOMOTIVE REPAIR SVC
AUTOMOTIVE SPLYS & PARTS, NEW, WHOL: Testing Eqpt, Electric
AUTOMOTIVE SPLYS & PARTS, NEW, WHOLESALE: Brakes
AUTOMOTIVE SPLYS & PARTS, NEW, WHOLESALE: Clutches
AUTOMOTIVE SPLYS & PARTS, NEW, WHOLESALE: Engines/Eng Parts
AUTOMOTIVE SPLYS & PARTS, NEW, WHOLESALE: Seat Covers
AUTOMOTIVE SPLYS & PARTS, NEW, WHOLESALE: Splys
AUTOMOTIVE SPLYS & PARTS, NEW, WHOLESALE: Stampings
AUTOMOTIVE SPLYS & PARTS, NEW, WHOLESALE: Testing Eqpt, Eng
AUTOMOTIVE SPLYS & PARTS, NEW, WHOLESALE: Tools & Eqpt
AUTOMOTIVE SPLYS & PARTS, NEW, WHOLESALE: Trailer Parts
AUTOMOTIVE SPLYS & PARTS, NEW, WHOLESALE: Wheels
AUTOMOTIVE SPLYS & PARTS, USED, WHOLESALE
AUTOMOTIVE SPLYS & PARTS, WHOLESALE, NEC
AUTOMOTIVE SVCS, EXC REPAIR & CARWASHES: Customizing
AUTOMOTIVE SVCS, EXC REPAIR & CARWASHES: Maintenance
AUTOMOTIVE SVCS, EXC REPAIR: Truck Wash

AUTOMOTIVE SVCS, EXC RPR/CARWASHES: High Perf Auto Rpr/Svc
AUTOMOTIVE TOPS INSTALLATION OR REPAIR: Canvas Or Plastic
AUTOMOTIVE TOWING & WRECKING SVC
AUTOMOTIVE TOWING SVCS
AUTOMOTIVE TRANSMISSION REPAIR SVC
AUTOMOTIVE UPHOLSTERY SHOPS
AUTOMOTIVE WELDING SVCS
AUTOMOTIVE: Bodies
AUTOMOTIVE: Seat Frames, Metal
AUTOMOTIVE: Seating
AVIATION SCHOOL
AWNINGS & CANOPIES
AWNINGS & CANOPIES: Awnings, Fabric, From Purchased Matls
AWNINGS & CANOPIES: Canopies, Fabric, From Purchased Matls
AWNINGS & CANOPIES: Fabric
AWNINGS: Fiberglass
AWNINGS: Metal
AXLES
AXLES: Rolled Or Forged, Made In Steel Mills

# B

BABY FORMULA
BACKHOES
BADGES, WHOLESALE
BADGES: Identification & Insignia
BAGS & CONTAINERS: Textile, Exc Sleeping
BAGS & SACKS: Shipping & Shopping
BAGS: Cellophane
BAGS: Duffle, Canvas, Made From Purchased Materials
BAGS: Flour, Made From Purchased Materials
BAGS: Food Storage & Frozen Food, Plastic
BAGS: Food Storage & Trash, Plastic
BAGS: Garment & Wardrobe, Plastic Film
BAGS: Garment Storage Exc Paper Or Plastic Film
BAGS: Paper
BAGS: Paper, Made From Purchased Materials
BAGS: Plastic
BAGS: Plastic & Pliofilm
BAGS: Plastic, Made From Purchased Materials
BAGS: Pliofilm, Made From Purchased Materials
BAGS: Rubber Or Rubberized Fabric
BAGS: Shipping
BAGS: Textile
BAGS: Trash, Plastic Film, Made From Purchased Materials
BAGS: Vacuum cleaner, Made From Purchased Materials
BAGS: Wardrobe, Closet Access, Made From Purchased Materials
BAIT, FISHING, WHOLESALE
BAKERIES, COMMERCIAL: On Premises Baking Only
BAKERIES: On Premises Baking & Consumption
BAKERY MACHINERY
BAKERY PRDTS: Bagels, Fresh Or Frozen
BAKERY PRDTS: Bakery Prdts, Partially Cooked, Exc frozen
BAKERY PRDTS: Bread, All Types, Fresh Or Frozen
BAKERY PRDTS: Buns, Bread Type, Fresh Or Frozen
BAKERY PRDTS: Cakes, Bakery, Exc Frozen
BAKERY PRDTS: Cakes, Bakery, Frozen
BAKERY PRDTS: Charlotte Russe, Exc Frozen
BAKERY PRDTS: Cookies
BAKERY PRDTS: Cookies & crackers
BAKERY PRDTS: Crackers
BAKERY PRDTS: Croissants, Frozen
BAKERY PRDTS: Doughnuts, Exc Frozen
BAKERY PRDTS: Doughnuts, Frozen
BAKERY PRDTS: Dry
BAKERY PRDTS: Frozen
BAKERY PRDTS: Pies, Bakery, Frozen
BAKERY PRDTS: Pies, Exc Frozen
BAKERY PRDTS: Pretzels
BAKERY PRDTS: Rice Cakes
BAKERY PRDTS: Rolls, Sweet, Frozen
BAKERY PRDTS: Wholesalers
BAKERY: Wholesale Or Wholesale & Retail Combined
BALERS
BALLASTS: Fluorescent
BALLASTS: Lighting
BALLOON SHOPS
BALLOONS: Hot Air
BALLOONS: Rubber Laminated Metal Foil
BALLOONS: Toy & Advertising, Rubber
BANDS: Plastic

# PRODUCT INDEX

BANKS: State Commercial
BANNERS: Fabric
BANQUET HALL FACILITIES
BAR
BARBECUE EQPT
BARBER SHOPS
BARGES BUILDING & REPAIR
BARRELS: Shipping, Metal
BARRICADES: Metal
BARS & BAR SHAPES: Copper & Copper Alloy
BARS & BAR SHAPES: Steel, Hot-Rolled
BARS, COLD FINISHED: Steel, From Purchased Hot-Rolled
BARS, PIPES, PLATES & SHAPES: Lead/Lead Alloy Bars, Pipe
BARS, PLATES & SHEETS: Zinc & Zinc Alloy Bars, Plates, Etc
BARS: Cargo, Stabilizing, Metal
BARS: Concrete Reinforcing, Fabricated Steel
BASEMENT WINDOW AREAWAYS: Concrete
BASES, BEVERAGE
BATH SALTS
BATH SHOPS
BATHROOM ACCESS & FITTINGS: Vitreous China & Earthenware
BATHROOM FIXTURES: Plastic
BATTERIES, EXC AUTOMOTIVE: Wholesalers
BATTERIES: Alkaline, Cell Storage
BATTERIES: Lead Acid, Storage
BATTERIES: Nickel-Cadmium
BATTERIES: Rechargeable
BATTERIES: Storage
BATTERIES: Wet
BATTERY CASES: Plastic Or Plastics Combination
BATTERY CHARGERS
BATTERY CHARGERS: Storage, Motor & Engine Generator Type
BEADS: Unassembled
BEARINGS
BEARINGS & PARTS Ball
BEARINGS: Ball & Roller
BEARINGS: Railroad Car Journal
BEARINGS: Roller & Parts
BEAUTY & BARBER SHOP EQPT
BEAUTY & BARBER SHOP EQPT & SPLYS WHOLESALERS
BEAUTY SALONS
BED SHEETING, COTTON
BEDDING, BEDSPREAD, BLANKET/SHEET: Pillowcase, Purchd Mtrl
BEDDING, BEDSPREADS, BLANKETS & SHEETS: Comforters & Quilts
BEDS: Hospital
BEDS: Inflatable
BEDSPREADS & BED SETS, FROM PURCHASED MATERIALS
BEDSPREADS, COTTON
BEEKEEPERS' SPLYS
BEEKEEPERS' SPLYS: Honeycomb Foundations
BEER & ALE WHOLESALERS
BEER & ALE, WHOLESALE: Beer & Other Fermented Malt Liquors
BEER, WINE & LIQUOR STORES
BEER, WINE & LIQUOR STORES: Beer, Packaged
BEER, WINE & LIQUOR STORES: Wine
BEER, WINE & LIQUOR STORES: Wine & Beer
BELLOWS
BELLOWS ASSEMBLIES: Missiles, Metal
BELTING: Plastic
BELTING: Rubber
BELTS & BELT PRDTS
BELTS: Chain
BELTS: Conveyor, Made From Purchased Wire
BELTS: Seat, Automotive & Aircraft
BENCHES, WORK : Factory
BENCHES: Seating
BENTONITE MINING
BEVERAGE BASES & SYRUPS
BEVERAGE POWDERS
BEVERAGE PRDTS: Brewers' Grain
BEVERAGE PRDTS: Malt Syrup
BEVERAGE PRDTS: Malt, Corn
BEVERAGE STORES
BEVERAGE, NONALCOHOLIC: Iced Tea/Fruit Drink, Bottled/Canned
BEVERAGES, ALCOHOLIC: Ale
BEVERAGES, ALCOHOLIC: Beer

BEVERAGES, ALCOHOLIC: Beer & Ale
BEVERAGES, ALCOHOLIC: Cocktails
BEVERAGES, ALCOHOLIC: Distilled Liquors
BEVERAGES, ALCOHOLIC: Gin
BEVERAGES, ALCOHOLIC: Liquors, Malt
BEVERAGES, ALCOHOLIC: Near Beer
BEVERAGES, ALCOHOLIC: Rum
BEVERAGES, ALCOHOLIC: Scotch Whiskey
BEVERAGES, ALCOHOLIC: Vodka
BEVERAGES, ALCOHOLIC: Wines
BEVERAGES, BEER & ALE, WHOLESALE: Ale
BEVERAGES, NONALCOHOLIC: Bottled & canned soft drinks
BEVERAGES, NONALCOHOLIC: Carbonated
BEVERAGES, NONALCOHOLIC: Carbonated, Canned & Bottled, Etc
BEVERAGES, NONALCOHOLIC: Cider
BEVERAGES, NONALCOHOLIC: Flavoring extracts & syrups, nec
BEVERAGES, NONALCOHOLIC: Fruit Drnks, Under 100% Juice, Can
BEVERAGES, NONALCOHOLIC: Fruit Juices, Concentrtd, Fountain
BEVERAGES, NONALCOHOLIC: Soft Drinks, Canned & Bottled, Etc
BEVERAGES, WINE & DISTILLED ALCOHOLIC, WHOLESALE: Liquor
BEVERAGES, WINE & DISTILLED ALCOHOLIC, WHOLESALE: Neutral Sp
BEVERAGES, WINE & DISTILLED ALCOHOLIC, WHOLESALE: Wine
BIBLE SCHOOL
BICYCLE REPAIR SHOP
BICYCLE SHOPS
BICYCLES, PARTS & ACCESS
BIDETS: Vitreous China
BILLETS: Steel
BILLFOLD INSERTS: Plastic
BILLIARD & POOL TABLES & SPLYS
BILLIARD EQPT & SPLYS WHOLESALERS
BILLING & BOOKKEEPING SVCS
BINDING SVC: Books & Manuals
BINDING SVC: Trade
BIOLOGICAL PRDTS: Blood Derivatives
BIOLOGICAL PRDTS: Coagulation
BIOLOGICAL PRDTS: Exc Diagnostic
BIOLOGICAL PRDTS: Toxin, Viruses/Simlr Substncs, Incl Venom
BIOLOGICAL PRDTS: Vaccines
BIOLOGICAL PRDTS: Veterinary
BIRTH CONTROL DEVICES: Rubber
BLACKBOARDS & CHALKBOARDS
BLACKBOARDS: Slate
BLACKSMITH SHOP
BLADES: Knife
BLADES: Saw, Chain Type
BLADES: Saw, Hand Or Power
BLANKBOOKS & LOOSELEAF BINDERS
BLANKBOOKS: Albums
BLANKBOOKS: Albums, Record
BLANKBOOKS: Checkbooks & Passbooks, Bank
BLANKBOOKS: Diaries
BLANKBOOKS: Ledgers & Ledger Sheets
BLANKBOOKS: Memorandum, Printed
BLANKBOOKS: Passbooks, Bank, Etc
BLANKBOOKS: Scrapbooks
BLANKETS, FROM PURCHASED MATERIALS
BLAST FURNACE & RELATED PRDTS
BLASTING SVC: Sand, Metal Parts
BLINDS & SHADES: Vertical
BLINDS : Window
BLINDS, WOOD
BLOCKS & BRICKS: Concrete
BLOCKS: Brush, Wood, Turned & Shaped
BLOCKS: Chimney Or Fireplace, Concrete
BLOCKS: Landscape Or Retaining Wall, Concrete
BLOCKS: Paving, Asphalt, Not From Refineries
BLOCKS: Paving, Concrete
BLOCKS: Paving, Cut Stone
BLOCKS: Standard, Concrete Or Cinder
BLOCKS: Tackle, Metal
BLOOD RELATED HEALTH SVCS
BLOWER FILTER UNITS: Furnace Blowers
BLOWERS & FANS
BLOWERS & FANS

BLOWERS, TURBO: Indl
BLUEPRINTING SVCS
BOAT BUILDING & REPAIR
BOAT BUILDING & REPAIRING: Fiberglass
BOAT BUILDING & REPAIRING: Kayaks
BOAT BUILDING & REPAIRING: Motorboats, Inboard Or Outboard
BOAT BUILDING & REPAIRING: Pontoons, Exc Aircraft & Inflat
BOAT DEALERS
BOAT DEALERS: Motor
BOAT DEALERS: Outboard
BOAT REPAIR SVCS
BOATS & OTHER MARINE EQPT: Plastic
BOBBINS: Textile Spinning, Made From Purchased Materials
BODIES: Truck & Bus
BODY PARTS: Automobile, Stamped Metal
BOILER & HEATING REPAIR SVCS
BOILER REPAIR SHOP
BOILERS & BOILER SHOP WORK
BOILERS: Low-Pressure Heating, Steam Or Hot Water
BOLTS: Metal
BOOK STORES
BOOK STORES: Children's
BOOKING AGENCIES, THEATRICAL
BOOKS, WHOLESALE
BOOKS: Memorandum, Exc Printed, From Purchased Materials
BOOTS: Women's
BOTTLE CAPS & RESEALERS: Plastic
BOTTLED GAS DEALERS: Propane
BOTTLED WATER DELIVERY
BOTTLES: Plastic
BOTTLES: Vacuum
BOWLING CENTERS
BOWLING EQPT & SPLY STORES
BOWLING EQPT & SPLYS
BOXES & CRATES: Rectangular, Wood
BOXES & SHOOK: Nailed Wood
BOXES: Cash & Stamp, Stamped Metal
BOXES: Corrugated
BOXES: Junction, Electric
BOXES: Mail Or Post Office, Collection/Storage, Sheet Metal
BOXES: Outlet, Electric Wiring Device
BOXES: Packing & Shipping, Metal
BOXES: Paperboard, Folding
BOXES: Paperboard, Set-Up
BOXES: Plastic
BOXES: Solid Fiber
BOXES: Stamped Metal
BOXES: Switch, Electric
BOXES: Wirebound, Wood
BOXES: Wooden
BRAKES & BRAKE PARTS
BRAKES: Metal Forming
BRAKES: Press
BRASS & BRONZE PRDTS: Die-casted
BRASS FOUNDRY, NEC
BRASS ROLLING & DRAWING
BRASSWORK: Ornamental, Structural
BRAZING SVCS
BRAZING: Metal
BRICK, STONE & RELATED PRDTS WHOLESALERS
BRICKS & BLOCKS: Structural
BRICKS : Ceramic Glazed, Clay
BRICKS : Flooring, Clay
BRICKS : Paving, Clay
BRICKS: Clay
BRICKS: Concrete
BRIDAL SHOPS
BRIEFCASES
BROACHING MACHINES
BROADCASTING & COMMS EQPT: Antennas, Transmitting/Comms
BROADCASTING & COMMS EQPT: Rcvr-Transmitter Unt, Transceiver
BROADCASTING & COMMUNICATION EQPT: Transmit-Receiver, Radio
BROADCASTING & COMMUNICATIONS EQPT: Cellular Radio Telephone
BROADCASTING & COMMUNICATIONS EQPT: Studio Eqpt, Radio & TV
BROADCASTING & COMMUNICATIONS EQPT: Transmitting, Radio/TV
BROKERS' SVCS

2017 Harris Illinois Industrial Directory

# PRODUCT INDEX

BROKERS: Commodity Contracts
BROKERS: Food
BROKERS: Log & Lumber
BROKERS: Mortgage, Arranging For Loans
BROKERS: Printing
BRONZE FOUNDRY, NEC
BRONZE ROLLING & DRAWING
BROOMS
BROOMS & BRUSHES
BROOMS & BRUSHES: Household Or Indl
BROOMS & BRUSHES: Paint & Varnish
BROOMS & BRUSHES: Paint Rollers
BROOMS & BRUSHES: Push
BROOMS & BRUSHES: Street Sweeping, Hand Or Machine
BROOMS & BRUSHES: Vacuum Cleaners & Carpet Sweepers
BRUSHES
BRUSHES & BRUSH STOCK CONTACTS: Electric
BUCKLES & PARTS
BUFFING FOR THE TRADE
BUILDING & STRUCTURAL WOOD MBRS: Timbers, Struct, Lam Lumber
BUILDING & STRUCTURAL WOOD MEMBERS
BUILDING CLEANING & MAINTENANCE SVCS
BUILDING COMPONENT CLEANING SVCS
BUILDING COMPONENTS: Structural Steel
BUILDING INSPECTION SVCS
BUILDING MAINTENANCE SVCS, EXC REPAIRS
BUILDING PRDTS & MATERIALS DEALERS
BUILDING PRDTS: Concrete
BUILDING PRDTS: Stone
BUILDINGS & COMPONENTS: Prefabricated Metal
BUILDINGS: Farm & Utility
BUILDINGS: Farm, Prefabricated Or Portable, Wood
BUILDINGS: Mobile, For Commercial Use
BUILDINGS: Portable
BUILDINGS: Prefabricated, Metal
BUILDINGS: Prefabricated, Wood
BUILDINGS: Prefabricated, Wood
BULLETIN BOARDS: Wood
BULLETPROOF VESTS
BUMPERS: Motor Vehicle
BURIAL VAULTS, FIBERGLASS
BURIAL VAULTS: Concrete Or Precast Terrazzo
BURNERS: Gas, Domestic
BURNERS: Gas, Indl
BURNERS: Gas-Oil, Combination
BUS BARS: Electrical
BUSES: Wholesalers
BUSHINGS & BEARINGS
BUSINESS & SECRETARIAL SCHOOLS
BUSINESS ACTIVITIES: Non-Commercial Site
BUSINESS FORMS WHOLESALERS
BUSINESS FORMS: Printed, Continuous
BUSINESS FORMS: Printed, Manifold
BUSINESS FORMS: Unit Sets, Manifold
BUSINESS MACHINE REPAIR, ELECTRIC
BUSINESS SUPPORT SVCS
BUSINESS TRAINING SVCS
BUTADIENE: Indl, Organic, Chemical
BUTTONS

## C

CABINETS & CASES: Show, Display & Storage, Exc Wood
CABINETS: Bathroom Vanities, Wood
CABINETS: Entertainment
CABINETS: Entertainment Units, Household, Wood
CABINETS: Factory
CABINETS: Filing, Wood
CABINETS: Kitchen, Metal
CABINETS: Kitchen, Wood
CABINETS: Office, Metal
CABINETS: Office, Wood
CABINETS: Show, Display, Etc, Wood, Exc Refrigerated
CABINETS: Television, Plastic
CABLE & OTHER PAY TELEVISION DISTRIBUTION
CABLE & PAY TELEVISION SVCS: Subscription
CABLE TELEVISION
CABLE TELEVISION PRDTS
CABLE WIRING SETS: Battery, Internal Combustion Engines
CABLE: Coaxial
CABLE: Fiber
CABLE: Fiber Optic
CABLE: Noninsulated
CABLE: Ropes & Fiber

CABLE: Steel, Insulated Or Armored
CABS: Indl Trucks & Tractors
CAFES
CAGES: Wire
CALCULATING & ACCOUNTING EQPT
CALENDARS, WHOLESALE
CALLIGRAPHER
CAMERAS & RELATED EQPT: Photographic
CAMPGROUNDS
CAMSHAFTS
CAN LIDS & ENDS
CANDLE SHOPS
CANDLES
CANDLES: Wholesalers
CANDY & CONFECTIONS: Cake Ornaments
CANDY & CONFECTIONS: Candy Bars, Including Chocolate Covered
CANDY & CONFECTIONS: Chocolate Candy, Exc Solid Chocolate
CANDY & CONFECTIONS: Cough Drops, Exc Pharmaceutical Preps
CANDY & CONFECTIONS: Fruit & Fruit Peel
CANDY & CONFECTIONS: Fudge
CANDY & CONFECTIONS: Marshmallows
CANDY & CONFECTIONS: Popcorn Balls/Other Trtd Popcorn Prdts
CANDY MAKING GOODS & SPLYS, WHOLESALE
CANDY, NUT & CONFECTIONERY STORE: Popcorn, Incl Caramel Corn
CANDY, NUT & CONFECTIONERY STORES: Candy
CANDY, NUT & CONFECTIONERY STORES: Confectionery
CANDY, NUT & CONFECTIONERY STORES: Produced For Direct Sale
CANDY: Chocolate From Cacao Beans
CANDY: Hard
CANDY: Soft
CANES & TRIMMINGS, EXC PRECIOUS METAL
CANNED SPECIALTIES
CANOPIES: Sheet Metal
CANS: Aluminum
CANS: Metal
CANS: Oil, Metal
CANVAS PRDTS
CANVAS PRDTS, WHOLESALE
CANVAS PRDTS: Air Cushions & Mattresses
CANVAS PRDTS: Convertible Tops, Car/Boat, Fm Purchased Mtrl
CANVAS PRDTS: Shades, Made From Purchased Materials
CAPACITORS & CONDENSERS
CAPACITORS: AC, Motors Or Fluorescent Lamp Ballasts
CAPACITORS: NEC
CAPS & TOPS: Bottle, Stamped Metal
CAPS: Plastic
CAR WASH EQPT
CAR WASHES
CARBIDES
CARBON & GRAPHITE PRDTS, NEC
CARBON BLACK
CARBON PAPER & INKED RIBBONS
CARBON SPECIALTIES Electrical Use
CARBONS: Electric
CARBURETORS
CARDBOARD PRDTS, EXC DIE-CUT
CARDS, PLASTIC, UNPRINTED, WHOLESALE
CARDS: Color
CARDS: Greeting
CARDS: Identification
CARPET & UPHOLSTERY CLEANING SVCS
CARPET LINING: Felt, Exc Woven
CARPETS & RUGS: Tufted
CARPETS, RUGS & FLOOR COVERING
CARPETS: Wilton
CARPORTS: Prefabricated Metal
CARRIAGES: Horse Drawn
CARRIER EQPT: Telephone Or Telegraph
CARRYING CASES, WHOLESALE
CARS & TRUCKS: Indl Mining
CARS: Electric
CARTONS: Egg, Die-Cut, Made From Purchased Materials
CASEMENTS: Aluminum
CASES, WOOD
CASES: Attache'
CASES: Carrying
CASES: Carrying, Clothing & Apparel
CASES: Jewelry

CASES: Nonrefrigerated, Exc Wood
CASES: Packing, Nailed Or Lock Corner, Wood
CASES: Plastic
CASES: Sample Cases
CASES: Shipping, Nailed Or Lock Corner, Wood
CASH REGISTERS WHOLESALERS
CASINGS: Sheet Metal
CASINO HOTELS & MOTELS
CASKETS & ACCESS
CAST STONE: Concrete
CASTERS
CASTINGS GRINDING: For The Trade
CASTINGS: Aerospace, Aluminum
CASTINGS: Aluminum
CASTINGS: Brass, NEC, Exc Die
CASTINGS: Bronze, NEC, Exc Die
CASTINGS: Commercial Investment, Ferrous
CASTINGS: Die, Aluminum
CASTINGS: Die, Copper & Copper Alloy
CASTINGS: Die, Lead & Zinc
CASTINGS: Die, Magnesium & Magnesium-Base Alloy
CASTINGS: Die, Nonferrous
CASTINGS: Die, Titanium
CASTINGS: Die, Zinc
CASTINGS: Ductile
CASTINGS: Gray Iron
CASTINGS: Lead
CASTINGS: Machinery, Aluminum
CASTINGS: Machinery, Copper Or Copper-Base Alloy
CASTINGS: Machinery, Nonferrous, Exc Die or Aluminum Copper
CASTINGS: Precision
CASTINGS: Rubber
CASTINGS: Steel
CASTINGS: Zinc
CAT BOX FILLER
CATALOG & MAIL-ORDER HOUSES
CATALOG SALES
CATALYSTS: Chemical
CATAPULTS
CATCH BASIN COVERS: Concrete
CATERERS
CAULKING COMPOUNDS
CELLULOID PRDTS
CELLULOSE DERIVATIVE MATERIALS
CEMENT & CONCRETE RELATED PRDTS & EQPT: Bituminous
CEMENT ROCK: Crushed & Broken
CEMENT: Clay Refractory
CEMENT: Hydraulic
CEMENT: Linoleum & Tile
CEMENT: Masonry
CEMENT: Portland
CEMETERIES
CEMETERIES: Real Estate Operation
CEMETERY & FUNERAL DIRECTOR'S EQPT & SPLYS WHOLESALERS
CEMETERY MEMORIAL DEALERS
CERAMIC FIBER
CERAMIC FLOOR & WALL TILE WHOLESALERS
CHAIN: Welded, Made From Purchased Wire
CHAINS: Forged
CHAMBERS: Fumigating, Metal Plate
CHAMBERS: Space Simulation, Metal Plate
CHANGE MAKING MACHINES
CHARCOAL: Activated
CHASSIS: Automobile Trailer
CHASSIS: Motor Vehicle
CHEESE WHOLESALERS
CHEMICAL ELEMENTS
CHEMICAL PROCESSING MACHINERY & EQPT
CHEMICAL SPLYS FOR FOUNDRIES
CHEMICALS & ALLIED PRDTS WHOLESALERS, NEC
CHEMICALS & ALLIED PRDTS, WHOL: Food Additives/Preservatives
CHEMICALS & ALLIED PRDTS, WHOL: Gases, Compressed/Liquefied
CHEMICALS & ALLIED PRDTS, WHOLESALE: Aerosols
CHEMICALS & ALLIED PRDTS, WHOLESALE: Alcohols
CHEMICALS & ALLIED PRDTS, WHOLESALE: Chemical Additives
CHEMICALS & ALLIED PRDTS, WHOLESALE: Chemicals, Indl
CHEMICALS & ALLIED PRDTS, WHOLESALE: Chemicals, Indl & Heavy

# PRODUCT INDEX

CHEMICALS & ALLIED PRDTS, WHOLESALE: Chemicals, Rustproofing
CHEMICALS & ALLIED PRDTS, WHOLESALE: Detergent/Soap
CHEMICALS & ALLIED PRDTS, WHOLESALE: Dry Ice
CHEMICALS & ALLIED PRDTS, WHOLESALE: Gelatin
CHEMICALS & ALLIED PRDTS, WHOLESALE: Indl Gases
CHEMICALS & ALLIED PRDTS, WHOLESALE: Oxygen
CHEMICALS & ALLIED PRDTS, WHOLESALE: Plastics Film
CHEMICALS & ALLIED PRDTS, WHOLESALE: Plastics Materials, NEC
CHEMICALS & ALLIED PRDTS, WHOLESALE: Plastics Prdts, NEC
CHEMICALS & ALLIED PRDTS, WHOLESALE: Plastics Sheets & Rods
CHEMICALS & ALLIED PRDTS, WHOLESALE: Polishes, NEC
CHEMICALS & ALLIED PRDTS, WHOLESALE: Polyurethane Prdts
CHEMICALS & ALLIED PRDTS, WHOLESALE: Resins
CHEMICALS & ALLIED PRDTS, WHOLESALE: Resins, Plastics
CHEMICALS & ALLIED PRDTS, WHOLESALE: Resins, Synthetic
CHEMICALS & ALLIED PRDTS, WHOLESALE: Sealants
CHEMICALS & ALLIED PRDTS, WHOLESALE: Silicon Lubricants
CHEMICALS & ALLIED PRDTS, WHOLESALE: Spec Clean/Sanitation
CHEMICALS & ALLIED PRDTS, WHOLESALE: Syn Resin, Rub/Plastic
CHEMICALS & OTHER PRDTS DERIVED FROM COKING
CHEMICALS, AGRICULTURE: Wholesalers
CHEMICALS: Agricultural
CHEMICALS: Alcohols
CHEMICALS: Alkali Metals, Lithium, Cesium, Francium/Rubidium
CHEMICALS: Aluminum Compounds
CHEMICALS: Aluminum Sulfate
CHEMICALS: Anhydrous Ammonia
CHEMICALS: Bleaching Powder, Lime Bleaching Compounds
CHEMICALS: Copper Compounds Or Salts, Inorganic
CHEMICALS: Fluorine, Elemental
CHEMICALS: Fuel Tank Or Engine Cleaning
CHEMICALS: High Purity Grade, Organic
CHEMICALS: High Purity, Refined From Technical Grade
CHEMICALS: Hydrogen Peroxide
CHEMICALS: Inorganic, NEC
CHEMICALS: Lead Compounds/Salts, Inorganic, Not Pigments
CHEMICALS: Medicinal
CHEMICALS: Medicinal, Organic, Uncompounded, Bulk
CHEMICALS: Mercury, Redistilled
CHEMICALS: NEC
CHEMICALS: Nonmetallic Compounds
CHEMICALS: Organic, NEC
CHEMICALS: Phosphates, Defluorinated/Ammoniated, Exc Fertlr
CHEMICALS: Potash Alum
CHEMICALS: Reagent Grade, Refined From Technical Grade
CHEMICALS: Silica Compounds
CHEMICALS: Sulfur Chloride
CHEMICALS: Sulfur, Incl Rcvrd/Refined, Fm Sour Natural Gas
CHEMICALS: Water Treatment
CHESTS: Bank, Metal
CHEWING GUM
CHICKEN SLAUGHTERING & PROCESSING
CHILDBIRTH PREPARATION CLINIC
CHILDREN'S WEAR STORES
CHIMNEY CAPS: Concrete
CHIMNEY CLEANING SVCS
CHINA & GLASS REPAIR SVCS
CHINA FIRING & DECORATING SVCS, TO INDIVIDUAL ORDER
CHINAWARE STORES
CHIROPRACTORS' OFFICES
CHLORINE
CHOCOLATE, EXC CANDY FROM BEANS: Chips, Powder, Block, Syrup
CHOCOLATE, EXC CANDY FROM PURCH CHOC: Chips, Powder, Block
CHRISTMAS NOVELTIES, WHOLESALE
CHRISTMAS TREE LIGHTING SETS: Electric
CHRISTMAS TREE ORNAMENTS: Electric
CHROMATOGRAPHY EQPT
CHUCKS
CHUTES & TROUGHS
CIGARETTE & CIGAR PRDTS & ACCESS
CIGARETTE LIGHTERS
CIRCUIT BOARD REPAIR SVCS
CIRCUIT BOARDS, PRINTED: Television & Radio
CIRCUIT BOARDS: Wiring
CIRCUIT BREAKERS
CIRCUIT BREAKERS: Air
CIRCUITS, INTEGRATED: Hybrid
CIRCUITS: Electronic
CLAMPS & COUPLINGS: Hose
CLAMPS & SHORES: Column
CLAMPS: Ground, Electric-Wiring Devices
CLAMPS: Metal
CLAY MINING
CLAY MINING, COMMON
CLAYS, EXC KAOLIN & BALL
CLEANING & DESCALING SVC: Metal Prdts
CLEANING & DYEING PLANTS, EXC RUGS
CLEANING COMPOUNDS: Rifle Bore
CLEANING EQPT: Blast, Dustless
CLEANING EQPT: Carpet Sweepers, Exc Household Elec Vacuum
CLEANING EQPT: Commercial
CLEANING EQPT: Dirt Sweeping Units, Indl
CLEANING EQPT: Floor Washing & Polishing, Commercial
CLEANING EQPT: High Pressure
CLEANING OR POLISHING PREPARATIONS, NEC
CLEANING PRDTS: Ammonia, Household
CLEANING PRDTS: Automobile Polish
CLEANING PRDTS: Bleaches, Household, Dry Or Liquid
CLEANING PRDTS: Disinfectants, Household Or Indl Plant
CLEANING PRDTS: Drain Pipe Solvents Or Cleaners
CLEANING PRDTS: Drycleaning Preparations
CLEANING PRDTS: Floor Waxes
CLEANING PRDTS: Indl Plant Disinfectants Or Deodorants
CLEANING PRDTS: Laundry Preparations
CLEANING PRDTS: Metal Polish
CLEANING PRDTS: Polishing Preparations & Related Prdts
CLEANING PRDTS: Rug, Upholstery/Dry Clng Detergents/Spotters
CLEANING PRDTS: Sanitation Preparations
CLEANING PRDTS: Sanitation Preps, Disinfectants/Deodorants
CLEANING PRDTS: Specialty
CLEANING PRDTS: Window Cleaning Preparations
CLIPPERS: Hair, Human
CLIPS & FASTENERS, MADE FROM PURCHASED WIRE
CLOSURES: Closures, Stamped Metal
CLOSURES: Plastic
CLOTHESPINS: Plastic
CLOTHING & ACCESS STORES
CLOTHING & ACCESS, WHOLESALE: Leather & Sheep Lined
CLOTHING & ACCESS, WOMEN, CHILD & INFANT, WHSLE: Sportswear
CLOTHING & ACCESS, WOMEN, CHILD/INFANT, WHOLESALE: Child
CLOTHING & ACCESS, WOMEN, CHILDREN & INFANT, WHOL: Handbags
CLOTHING & ACCESS, WOMEN, CHILDREN & INFANT, WHOL: Uniforms
CLOTHING & ACCESS, WOMEN, CHILDREN/INFANT, WHOL: Outerwear
CLOTHING & ACCESS: Costumes, Lodge
CLOTHING & ACCESS: Costumes, Masquerade
CLOTHING & ACCESS: Costumes, Theatrical
CLOTHING & ACCESS: Garters
CLOTHING & ACCESS: Handicapped
CLOTHING & ACCESS: Hospital Gowns
CLOTHING & ACCESS: Men's Miscellaneous Access
CLOTHING & ACCESS: Regalia
CLOTHING & APPAREL STORES: Custom
CLOTHING & FURNISHINGS, MEN'S & BOYS', WHOLESALE: Shirts
CLOTHING & FURNISHINGS, MEN'S & BOYS', WHOLESALE: Umbrellas
CLOTHING & FURNISHINGS, MEN'S & BOYS', WHOLESALE: Uniforms
CLOTHING & FURNISHINGS, MENS & BOYS, WHOL: Sportswear/Work
CLOTHING & FURNISHINGS, MENS & BOYS, WHOLESALE: Apprl Belts
CLOTHING & FURNISHINGS, MENS & BOYS, WHOLESALE: Lined
CLOTHING STORES, NEC
CLOTHING STORES: Formal Wear
CLOTHING STORES: Shirts, Custom Made
CLOTHING STORES: T-Shirts, Printed, Custom
CLOTHING STORES: Unisex
CLOTHING STORES: Work
CLOTHING/ACCESS, WOMEN, CHILDREN/INFANT, WHOL: Apparel Belt
CLOTHING: Academic Vestments
CLOTHING: Access
CLOTHING: Access, Women's & Misses'
CLOTHING: Anklets & Socks
CLOTHING: Aprons, Exc Rubber/Plastic, Women, Misses, Junior
CLOTHING: Aprons, Harness
CLOTHING: Aprons, Waterproof, From Purchased Materials
CLOTHING: Aprons, Work, Exc Rubberized & Plastic, Men's
CLOTHING: Athletic & Sportswear, Men's & Boys'
CLOTHING: Athletic & Sportswear, Women's & Girls'
CLOTHING: Baker, Barber, Lab/Svc Ind Apparel, Washable, Men
CLOTHING: Band Uniforms
CLOTHING: Bathing Suits & Swimwear, Girls, Children & Infant
CLOTHING: Bathing Suits & Swimwear, Knit
CLOTHING: Bathrobes, Mens & Womens, From Purchased Materials
CLOTHING: Belts
CLOTHING: Bibs, Waterproof, From Purchased Materials
CLOTHING: Blouses, Women's & Girls'
CLOTHING: Blouses, Womens & Juniors, From Purchased Mtrls
CLOTHING: Bras & Corsets, Maternity
CLOTHING: Bridal Gowns
CLOTHING: Buntings, Infants'
CLOTHING: Capes, Exc Fur/Rubber, Womens, Misses & Juniors
CLOTHING: Caps, Baseball
CLOTHING: Children & Infants'
CLOTHING: Children's, Girls'
CLOTHING: Clergy Vestments
CLOTHING: Coats & Jackets, Leather & Sheep-Lined
CLOTHING: Coats & Suits, Men's & Boys'
CLOTHING: Coats, Overcoats & Vests
CLOTHING: Cold Weather Knit Outerwear, Including Ski Wear
CLOTHING: Collar & Cuff Sets, Knit
CLOTHING: Costumes
CLOTHING: Disposable
CLOTHING: Down-Filled, Men's & Boys'
CLOTHING: Dresses
CLOTHING: Furs
CLOTHING: Garments, Indl, Men's & Boys
CLOTHING: Gowns & Dresses, Wedding
CLOTHING: Gowns, Plastic
CLOTHING: Hats & Caps, NEC
CLOTHING: Hats & Caps, Police
CLOTHING: Hats & Caps, Uniform
CLOTHING: Hats & Headwear, Knit
CLOTHING: Hats, Silk
CLOTHING: Hosiery, Pantyhose & Knee Length, Sheer
CLOTHING: Hospital, Men's
CLOTHING: Jackets, Field, Military
CLOTHING: Jackets, Tailored Men's & Boys'
CLOTHING: Jeans, Men's & Boys'
CLOTHING: Jerseys, Knit
CLOTHING: Leather & sheep-lined clothing
CLOTHING: Maternity
CLOTHING: Men's & boy's clothing, nec
CLOTHING: Neckwear
CLOTHING: Outerwear, Knit
CLOTHING: Outerwear, Lthr, Wool/Down-Filled, Men, Youth/Boy
CLOTHING: Outerwear, Women's & Misses' NEC
CLOTHING: Robes & Dressing Gowns
CLOTHING: Service Apparel, Women's
CLOTHING: Shirts
CLOTHING: Shirts & T-Shirts, Knit
CLOTHING: Shirts, Dress, Men's & Boys'
CLOTHING: Shirts, Sports & Polo, Men's & Boys'
CLOTHING: Shirts, Uniform, From Purchased Materials
CLOTHING: Socks
CLOTHING: Sportswear, Women's
CLOTHING: Suits, Men's & Boys', From Purchased Materials

# PRODUCT INDEX

CLOTHING: Sweaters & Sweater Coats, Knit
CLOTHING: T-Shirts & Tops, Knit
CLOTHING: T-Shirts & Tops, Women's & Girls'
CLOTHING: Ties, Neck, Men's & Boys', From Purchased Material
CLOTHING: Trousers & Slacks, Men's & Boys'
CLOTHING: Underwear, Women's & Children's
CLOTHING: Uniforms & Vestments
CLOTHING: Uniforms, Ex Athletic, Women's, Misses' & Juniors'
CLOTHING: Uniforms, Men's & Boys'
CLOTHING: Uniforms, Military, Men/Youth, Purchased Materials
CLOTHING: Uniforms, Policemen's, From Purchased Materials
CLOTHING: Uniforms, Team Athletic
CLOTHING: Uniforms, Work
CLOTHING: Warm Weather Knit Outerwear, Including Beachwear
CLOTHING: WarmUp, Jogging & Sweat Suits, Girls' & Children's
CLOTHING: Waterproof Outerwear
CLOTHING: Work Apparel, Exc Uniforms
CLOTHING: Work, Men's
CLUTCHES, EXC VEHICULAR
COAL MINING EXPLORATION & TEST BORING SVC
COAL MINING SERVICES
COAL MINING SVCS: Anthracite, Contract Basis
COAL MINING SVCS: Bituminous, Contract Basis
COAL MINING: Anthracite
COAL MINING: Anthracite, Underground
COAL MINING: Bituminous Coal & Lignite-Surface Mining
COAL MINING: Bituminous Underground
COAL MINING: Bituminous, Auger
COAL MINING: Bituminous, Strip
COAL MINING: Bituminous, Surface, NEC
COAL PREPARATION PLANT: Bituminous or Lignite
COAL, MINERALS & ORES, WHOLESALE: Coal
COAL, MINERALS & ORES, WHOLESALE: Copper Ore
COATED OR PLATED PRDTS
COATING COMPOUNDS: Tar
COATING OR WRAPPING SVC: Steel Pipe
COATING SVC
COATING SVC: Aluminum, Metal Prdts
COATING SVC: Hot Dip, Metals Or Formed Prdts
COATING SVC: Metals & Formed Prdts
COATING SVC: Metals, With Plastic Or Resins
COATING SVC: Rust Preventative
COATING SVC: Silicon
COATINGS: Air Curing
COATINGS: Epoxy
COATINGS: Polyurethane
COCKTAIL LOUNGE
COIL WINDING SVC
COILS & ROD: Extruded, Aluminum
COILS & TRANSFORMERS
COILS, WIRE: Aluminum, Made In Rolling Mills
COILS: Electric Motors Or Generators
COILS: Pipe
COIN COUNTERS
COIN-OPERATED LAUNDRY
COINS & TOKENS: Non-Currency
COKE OVEN PRDTS: Beehive
COKE: Petroleum
COKE: Petroleum & Coal Derivative
COKE: Petroleum, Not From Refineries
COLLECTION AGENCY, EXC REAL ESTATE
COLLECTOR RINGS: Electric Motors Or Generators
COLLEGES, UNIVERSITIES & PROFESSIONAL SCHOOLS
COLOGNES
COLOR LAKES OR TONERS
COLOR PIGMENTS
COLORING & FINISHING SVC: Aluminum Or Formed Prdts
COLORS IN OIL, EXC ARTISTS'
COLORS: Pigments, Inorganic
COLORS: Pigments, Organic
COLUMNS: Concrete
COMFORTERS & QUILTS, FROM MANMADE FIBER OR SILK
COMMERCIAL & INDL SHELVING WHOLESALERS
COMMERCIAL & OFFICE BUILDINGS RENOVATION & REPAIR
COMMERCIAL ART & GRAPHIC DESIGN SVCS
COMMERCIAL ART & ILLUSTRATION SVCS
COMMERCIAL CONTAINERS WHOLESALERS

COMMERCIAL EQPT WHOLESALERS, NEC
COMMERCIAL EQPT, WHOLESALE: Coffee Brewing Eqpt & Splys
COMMERCIAL EQPT, WHOLESALE: Comm Cooking & Food Svc Eqpt
COMMERCIAL EQPT, WHOLESALE: Display Eqpt, Exc Refrigerated
COMMERCIAL EQPT, WHOLESALE: Neon Signs
COMMERCIAL EQPT, WHOLESALE: Restaurant, NEC
COMMERCIAL EQPT, WHOLESALE: Scales, Exc Laboratory
COMMERCIAL EQPT, WHOLESALE: Store Fixtures & Display Eqpt
COMMERCIAL LAUNDRY EQPT
COMMERCIAL PHOTOGRAPHIC STUDIO
COMMERCIAL PRINTING & NEWSPAPER PUBLISHING COMBINED
COMMERCIAL SECTOR REG, LICENSING & INSP, GOVT: Insurance
COMMODITY CONTRACTS BROKERS, DEALERS
COMMON SAND MINING
COMMUNICATIONS EQPT & SYSTEMS, NEC
COMMUNICATIONS EQPT WHOLESALERS
COMMUNICATIONS EQPT: Microwave
COMMUNICATIONS SVCS
COMMUNICATIONS SVCS: Cellular
COMMUNICATIONS SVCS: Data
COMMUNICATIONS SVCS: Electronic Mail
COMMUNICATIONS SVCS: Facsimile Transmission
COMMUNICATIONS SVCS: Internet Connectivity Svcs
COMMUNICATIONS SVCS: Internet Host Svcs
COMMUNICATIONS SVCS: Online Svc Providers
COMMUNICATIONS SVCS: Satellite Earth Stations
COMMUNICATIONS SVCS: Signal Enhancement Network Svcs
COMMUNICATIONS SVCS: Telephone Or Video
COMMUNICATIONS SVCS: Telephone, Local & Long Distance
COMMUNITY DEVELOPMENT GROUPS
COMMUTATORS: Electronic
COMPACT DISCS OR CD'S, WHOLESALE
COMPACT LASER DISCS: Prerecorded
COMPACTORS: Trash & Garbage, Residential
COMPOST
COMPRESSORS, AIR CONDITIONING: Wholesalers
COMPRESSORS: Air & Gas
COMPRESSORS: Air & Gas, Including Vacuum Pumps
COMPRESSORS: Refrigeration & Air Conditioning Eqpt
COMPRESSORS: Repairing
COMPRESSORS: Wholesalers
COMPUTER & COMPUTER SOFTWARE STORES
COMPUTER & COMPUTER SOFTWARE STORES: Peripheral Eqpt
COMPUTER & COMPUTER SOFTWARE STORES: Personal Computers
COMPUTER & COMPUTER SOFTWARE STORES: Printers & Plotters
COMPUTER & COMPUTER SOFTWARE STORES: Software & Access
COMPUTER & COMPUTER SOFTWARE STORES: Software, Bus/Non-Game
COMPUTER & DATA PROCESSING EQPT REPAIR & MAINTENANCE
COMPUTER & OFFICE MACHINE MAINTENANCE & REPAIR
COMPUTER & SFTWR STORE: Modem, Monitor, Terminal/Disk Drive
COMPUTER DATA ESCROW SVCS
COMPUTER DISKETTES WHOLESALERS
COMPUTER FORMS
COMPUTER GRAPHICS SVCS
COMPUTER INTERFACE EQPT: Indl Process
COMPUTER PAPER WHOLESALERS
COMPUTER PERIPHERAL EQPT REPAIR & MAINTENANCE
COMPUTER PERIPHERAL EQPT, NEC
COMPUTER PERIPHERAL EQPT, WHOLESALE
COMPUTER PERIPHERAL EQPT: Graphic Displays, Exc Terminals
COMPUTER PERIPHERAL EQPT: Input Or Output
COMPUTER PROGRAMMING SVCS
COMPUTER PROGRAMMING SVCS: Custom
COMPUTER RELATED MAINTENANCE SVCS
COMPUTER RELATED SVCS, NEC
COMPUTER SERVICE BUREAU
COMPUTER SOFTWARE DEVELOPMENT

COMPUTER SOFTWARE DEVELOPMENT & APPLICATIONS
COMPUTER SOFTWARE SYSTEMS ANALYSIS & DESIGN: Custom
COMPUTER SOFTWARE WRITERS
COMPUTER SOFTWARE WRITERS: Freelance
COMPUTER STORAGE DEVICES, NEC
COMPUTER SYSTEM SELLING SVCS
COMPUTER SYSTEMS ANALYSIS & DESIGN
COMPUTER TERMINALS
COMPUTER TERMINALS: CRT
COMPUTER TIME-SHARING
COMPUTER TRAINING SCHOOLS
COMPUTER-AIDED DESIGN SYSTEMS SVCS
COMPUTER-AIDED ENGINEERING SYSTEMS SVCS
COMPUTER-AIDED MANUFACTURING SYSTEMS SVCS
COMPUTERS, NEC
COMPUTERS, NEC, WHOLESALE
COMPUTERS, PERIPHERALS & SOFTWARE, WHOLESALE: Printers
COMPUTERS, PERIPHERALS & SOFTWARE, WHOLESALE: Software
COMPUTERS, PERIPHERALS/SFTWR, WHOL: Anti-Static Eqpt/Devices
COMPUTERS: Mini
COMPUTERS: Personal
CONCENTRATES, DRINK
CONCENTRATES, FLAVORING, EXC DRINK
CONCRETE BUILDING PRDTS WHOLESALERS
CONCRETE CURING & HARDENING COMPOUNDS
CONCRETE PLANTS
CONCRETE PRDTS
CONCRETE PRDTS, PRECAST, NEC
CONCRETE REINFORCING MATERIAL
CONCRETE: Asphaltic, Not From Refineries
CONCRETE: Dry Mixture
CONCRETE: Ready-Mixed
CONDENSERS: Refrigeration
CONDUITS & FITTINGS: Electric
CONDUITS: Concrete
CONFECTIONERY PRDTS WHOLESALERS
CONFECTIONS & CANDY
CONFINEMENT SURVEILLANCE SYS MAINTENANCE & MONITORING SVCS
CONNECTORS & TERMINALS: Electrical Device Uses
CONNECTORS: Cord, Electric
CONNECTORS: Electrical
CONNECTORS: Electronic
CONNECTORS: Power, Electric
CONSERVATION PROGRAMS ADMINISTRATION SVCS
CONSTRUCTION & MINING MACHINERY WHOLESALERS
CONSTRUCTION & ROAD MAINTENANCE EQPT: Drags, Road
CONSTRUCTION EQPT REPAIR SVCS
CONSTRUCTION EQPT: Attachments
CONSTRUCTION EQPT: Attachments, Snow Plow
CONSTRUCTION EQPT: Attachments, Subsoiler, Tractor Mounted
CONSTRUCTION EQPT: Backhoes, Tractors, Cranes & Similar Eqpt
CONSTRUCTION EQPT: Bucket Or Scarifier Teeth
CONSTRUCTION EQPT: Cabs
CONSTRUCTION EQPT: Crane Carriers
CONSTRUCTION EQPT: Cranes
CONSTRUCTION EQPT: Grinders, Stone, Portable
CONSTRUCTION EQPT: Hammer Mills, Port, Incl Rock/Ore Crush
CONSTRUCTION EQPT: Rock Crushing Machinery, Portable
CONSTRUCTION EQPT: Roofing Eqpt
CONSTRUCTION EQPT: Spreaders, Aggregates
CONSTRUCTION EQPT: Tractors
CONSTRUCTION EQPT: Trucks, Off-Highway
CONSTRUCTION EQPT: Wrecker Hoists, Automobile
CONSTRUCTION MATERIALS, WHOL: Concrete/Cinder Bldg Prdts
CONSTRUCTION MATERIALS, WHOLESALE: Aggregate
CONSTRUCTION MATERIALS, WHOLESALE: Air Ducts, Sheet Metal
CONSTRUCTION MATERIALS, WHOLESALE: Architectural Metalwork
CONSTRUCTION MATERIALS, WHOLESALE: Awnings
CONSTRUCTION MATERIALS, WHOLESALE: Brick, Exc Refractory
CONSTRUCTION MATERIALS, WHOLESALE: Building Stone

# PRODUCT INDEX

CONSTRUCTION MATERIALS, WHOLESALE: Building Stone, Granite
CONSTRUCTION MATERIALS, WHOLESALE: Building Stone, Marble
CONSTRUCTION MATERIALS, WHOLESALE: Building, Exterior
CONSTRUCTION MATERIALS, WHOLESALE: Building, Interior
CONSTRUCTION MATERIALS, WHOLESALE: Cement
CONSTRUCTION MATERIALS, WHOLESALE: Ceramic, Exc Refractory
CONSTRUCTION MATERIALS, WHOLESALE: Clay, Exc Refractory
CONSTRUCTION MATERIALS, WHOLESALE: Concrete Mixtures
CONSTRUCTION MATERIALS, WHOLESALE: Doors, Garage
CONSTRUCTION MATERIALS, WHOLESALE: Doors, Sliding
CONSTRUCTION MATERIALS, WHOLESALE: Drywall Materials
CONSTRUCTION MATERIALS, WHOLESALE: Fiberglass Building Mat
CONSTRUCTION MATERIALS, WHOLESALE: Glass
CONSTRUCTION MATERIALS, WHOLESALE: Grain Storage Bins
CONSTRUCTION MATERIALS, WHOLESALE: Gravel
CONSTRUCTION MATERIALS, WHOLESALE: Joists
CONSTRUCTION MATERIALS, WHOLESALE: Limestone
CONSTRUCTION MATERIALS, WHOLESALE: Masons' Materials
CONSTRUCTION MATERIALS, WHOLESALE: Metal Buildings
CONSTRUCTION MATERIALS, WHOLESALE: Millwork
CONSTRUCTION MATERIALS, WHOLESALE: Molding, All Materials
CONSTRUCTION MATERIALS, WHOLESALE: Pallets, Wood
CONSTRUCTION MATERIALS, WHOLESALE: Paving Materials
CONSTRUCTION MATERIALS, WHOLESALE: Prefabricated Structures
CONSTRUCTION MATERIALS, WHOLESALE: Roof, Asphalt/Sheet Metal
CONSTRUCTION MATERIALS, WHOLESALE: Roofing & Siding Material
CONSTRUCTION MATERIALS, WHOLESALE: Sand
CONSTRUCTION MATERIALS, WHOLESALE: Septic Tanks
CONSTRUCTION MATERIALS, WHOLESALE: Sewer Pipe, Clay
CONSTRUCTION MATERIALS, WHOLESALE: Stone, Crushed Or Broken
CONSTRUCTION MATERIALS, WHOLESALE: Tile & Clay Prdts
CONSTRUCTION MATERIALS, WHOLESALE: Veneer
CONSTRUCTION MATERIALS, WHOLESALE: Wallboard
CONSTRUCTION MATERIALS, WHOLESALE: Windows
CONSTRUCTION MATLS, WHOL: Composite Board Prdts, Woodboard
CONSTRUCTION MATLS, WHOL: Lumber, Rough, Dressed/Finished
CONSTRUCTION MTRLS, WHOL: Exterior Flat Glass, Plate/Window
CONSTRUCTION SAND MINING
CONSTRUCTION SITE PREPARATION SVCS
CONSTRUCTION: Agricultural Building
CONSTRUCTION: Airport Runway
CONSTRUCTION: Athletic & Recreation Facilities
CONSTRUCTION: Bridge
CONSTRUCTION: Commercial & Institutional Building
CONSTRUCTION: Commercial & Office Building, New
CONSTRUCTION: Concrete Patio
CONSTRUCTION: Condominium
CONSTRUCTION: Dam
CONSTRUCTION: Drainage System
CONSTRUCTION: Elevated Highway
CONSTRUCTION: Farm Building
CONSTRUCTION: Food Prdts Manufacturing or Packing Plant
CONSTRUCTION: Heavy Highway & Street
CONSTRUCTION: Indl Building & Warehouse
CONSTRUCTION: Indl Building, Prefabricated
CONSTRUCTION: Indl Buildings, New, NEC
CONSTRUCTION: Irrigation System
CONSTRUCTION: Mausoleum
CONSTRUCTION: Multi-Family Housing
CONSTRUCTION: Oil & Gas Pipeline Construction
CONSTRUCTION: Pharmaceutical Manufacturing Plant
CONSTRUCTION: Power Plant
CONSTRUCTION: Railroad & Subway
CONSTRUCTION: Residential, Nec
CONSTRUCTION: Retaining Wall
CONSTRUCTION: Scaffolding
CONSTRUCTION: Sewer Line
CONSTRUCTION: Single-Family Housing
CONSTRUCTION: Single-family Housing, New
CONSTRUCTION: Street Sign Installation & Mntnce
CONSTRUCTION: Street Surfacing & Paving
CONSTRUCTION: Swimming Pools
CONSTRUCTION: Tennis Court
CONSTRUCTION: Truck & Automobile Assembly Plant
CONSTRUCTION: Tunnel
CONSTRUCTION: Utility Line
CONSTRUCTION: Waste Water & Sewage Treatment Plant
CONSTRUCTION: Water & Sewer Line
CONSTRUCTION: Water Main
CONSULTING SVC: Actuarial
CONSULTING SVC: Business, NEC
CONSULTING SVC: Computer
CONSULTING SVC: Data Processing
CONSULTING SVC: Educational
CONSULTING SVC: Engineering
CONSULTING SVC: Financial Management
CONSULTING SVC: Human Resource
CONSULTING SVC: Management
CONSULTING SVC: Marketing Management
CONSULTING SVC: Motion Picture
CONSULTING SVC: Online Technology
CONSULTING SVC: Sales Management
CONSULTING SVC: Telecommunications
CONSULTING SVCS, BUSINESS: Agricultural
CONSULTING SVCS, BUSINESS: Communications
CONSULTING SVCS, BUSINESS: Energy Conservation
CONSULTING SVCS, BUSINESS: Environmental
CONSULTING SVCS, BUSINESS: Lighting
CONSULTING SVCS, BUSINESS: Publishing
CONSULTING SVCS, BUSINESS: Safety Training Svcs
CONSULTING SVCS, BUSINESS: Sys Engnrg, Exc Computer/Prof
CONSULTING SVCS, BUSINESS: Systems Analysis & Engineering
CONSULTING SVCS, BUSINESS: Testing, Educational Or Personnel
CONSULTING SVCS: Oil
CONTACT LENSES
CONTACTS: Electrical
CONTAINERS, GLASS: Food
CONTAINERS, GLASS: Medicine Bottles
CONTAINERS, GLASS: Packers' Ware
CONTAINERS: Air Cargo, Metal
CONTAINERS: Cargo, Wood
CONTAINERS: Cargo, Wood & Metal Combination
CONTAINERS: Cargo, Wood & Wood With Metal
CONTAINERS: Corrugated
CONTAINERS: Foil, Bakery Goods & Frozen Foods
CONTAINERS: Food & Beverage
CONTAINERS: Food, Folding, Made From Purchased Materials
CONTAINERS: Food, Liquid Tight, Including Milk
CONTAINERS: Food, Wood Wirebound
CONTAINERS: Frozen Food & Ice Cream
CONTAINERS: Glass
CONTAINERS: Metal
CONTAINERS: Plastic
CONTAINERS: Plywood & Veneer, Wood
CONTAINERS: Sanitary, Food
CONTAINERS: Shipping & Mailing, Fiber
CONTAINERS: Shipping, Wood
CONTAINERS: Wood
CONTAINMENT VESSELS: Reactor, Metal Plate
CONTRACTORS: Access Flooring System Installation
CONTRACTORS: Antenna Installation
CONTRACTORS: Asbestos Removal & Encapsulation
CONTRACTORS: Asphalt
CONTRACTORS: Awning Installation
CONTRACTORS: Boiler & Furnace
CONTRACTORS: Boiler Maintenance Contractor
CONTRACTORS: Boring, Building Construction
CONTRACTORS: Building Eqpt & Machinery Installation
CONTRACTORS: Building Front Installation, Metal
CONTRACTORS: Building Sign Installation & Mntnce
CONTRACTORS: Cable Splicing Svcs
CONTRACTORS: Cable TV Installation
CONTRACTORS: Caisson Drilling
CONTRACTORS: Carpentry Work
CONTRACTORS: Carpentry, Cabinet & Finish Work
CONTRACTORS: Carpentry, Cabinet Building & Installation
CONTRACTORS: Carpentry, Finish & Trim Work
CONTRACTORS: Closed Circuit Television Installation
CONTRACTORS: Commercial & Office Building
CONTRACTORS: Communications Svcs
CONTRACTORS: Computer Installation
CONTRACTORS: Concrete
CONTRACTORS: Concrete Breaking, Street & Highway
CONTRACTORS: Concrete Pumping
CONTRACTORS: Concrete Reinforcement Placing
CONTRACTORS: Construction Site Cleanup
CONTRACTORS: Countertop Installation
CONTRACTORS: Decontamination Svcs
CONTRACTORS: Demolition, Building & Other Structures
CONTRACTORS: Directional Oil & Gas Well Drilling Svc
CONTRACTORS: Dock Eqpt Installation, Indl
CONTRACTORS: Drapery Track Installation
CONTRACTORS: Driveway
CONTRACTORS: Electric Power Systems
CONTRACTORS: Electrical
CONTRACTORS: Electronic Controls Installation
CONTRACTORS: Energy Management Control
CONTRACTORS: Environmental Controls Installation
CONTRACTORS: Erection & Dismantling, Poured Concrete Forms
CONTRACTORS: Excavating
CONTRACTORS: Excavating Slush Pits & Cellars Svcs
CONTRACTORS: Exterior Wall System Installation
CONTRACTORS: Fence Construction
CONTRACTORS: Fiberglass Work
CONTRACTORS: Fire Detection & Burglar Alarm Systems
CONTRACTORS: Floor Laying & Other Floor Work
CONTRACTORS: Flooring
CONTRACTORS: Fountain Installation
CONTRACTORS: Garage Doors
CONTRACTORS: Gas Field Svcs, NEC
CONTRACTORS: General Electric
CONTRACTORS: Geothermal Drilling
CONTRACTORS: Glass Tinting, Architectural & Automotive
CONTRACTORS: Glass, Glazing & Tinting
CONTRACTORS: Gutters & Downspouts
CONTRACTORS: Heating & Air Conditioning
CONTRACTORS: Heating Systems Repair & Maintenance Svc
CONTRACTORS: Highway & Street Construction, General
CONTRACTORS: Highway & Street Paving
CONTRACTORS: Highway & Street Resurfacing
CONTRACTORS: Highway Sign & Guardrail Construction & Install
CONTRACTORS: Home & Office Intrs Finish, Furnish/Remodel
CONTRACTORS: Hydraulic Eqpt Installation & Svcs
CONTRACTORS: Kitchen & Bathroom Remodeling
CONTRACTORS: Kitchen Cabinet Installation
CONTRACTORS: Land Reclamation
CONTRACTORS: Lighting Conductor Erection
CONTRACTORS: Machine Rigging & Moving
CONTRACTORS: Machinery Installation
CONTRACTORS: Marble Installation, Interior
CONTRACTORS: Marble Masonry, Exterior
CONTRACTORS: Masonry & Stonework
CONTRACTORS: Mechanical
CONTRACTORS: Metal Ceiling Construction & Repair Work
CONTRACTORS: Millwrights
CONTRACTORS: Oil & Gas Building, Repairing & Dismantling Svc
CONTRACTORS: Oil & Gas Field Geological Exploration Svcs
CONTRACTORS: Oil & Gas Field Geophysical Exploration Svcs
CONTRACTORS: Oil & Gas Field Salt Water Impound/Storing Svc
CONTRACTORS: Oil & Gas Well Casing Cement Svcs
CONTRACTORS: Oil & Gas Well Drilling Svc
CONTRACTORS: Oil & Gas Well Foundation Grading Svcs
CONTRACTORS: Oil & Gas Well On-Site Foundation Building Svcs
CONTRACTORS: Oil & Gas Well Plugging & Abandoning Svcs
CONTRACTORS: Oil & Gas Wells Pumping Svcs
CONTRACTORS: Oil & Gas Wells Svcs
CONTRACTORS: Oil Field Haulage Svcs

# PRODUCT INDEX

CONTRACTORS: Oil Field Lease Tanks: Erectg, Clng/Rprg Svcs
CONTRACTORS: Oil Field Mud Drilling Svcs
CONTRACTORS: Oil Field Pipe Testing Svcs
CONTRACTORS: Oil Sampling Svcs
CONTRACTORS: Oil/Gas Well Construction, Rpr/Dismantling Svcs
CONTRACTORS: On-Site Welding
CONTRACTORS: Ornamental Metal Work
CONTRACTORS: Painting & Wall Covering
CONTRACTORS: Painting, Commercial
CONTRACTORS: Painting, Indl
CONTRACTORS: Patio & Deck Construction & Repair
CONTRACTORS: Pavement Marking
CONTRACTORS: Pipe Laying
CONTRACTORS: Plumbing
CONTRACTORS: Pollution Control Eqpt Installation
CONTRACTORS: Precast Concrete Struct Framing & Panel Placing
CONTRACTORS: Prefabricated Window & Door Installation
CONTRACTORS: Process Piping
CONTRACTORS: Refrigeration
CONTRACTORS: Rock Removal
CONTRACTORS: Roofing
CONTRACTORS: Roofing & Gutter Work
CONTRACTORS: Safety & Security Eqpt
CONTRACTORS: Sandblasting Svc, Building Exteriors
CONTRACTORS: Screening, Window & Door
CONTRACTORS: Septic System
CONTRACTORS: Sheet Metal Work, NEC
CONTRACTORS: Sheet metal Work, Architectural
CONTRACTORS: Siding
CONTRACTORS: Single-family Home General Remodeling
CONTRACTORS: Skylight Installation
CONTRACTORS: Solar Energy Eqpt
CONTRACTORS: Sound Eqpt Installation
CONTRACTORS: Spa & Hot Tub Construction & Installation
CONTRACTORS: Standby Or Emergency Power Specialization
CONTRACTORS: Steam Cleaning, Building Exterior
CONTRACTORS: Stone Masonry
CONTRACTORS: Storage Tank Erection, Metal
CONTRACTORS: Store Fixture Installation
CONTRACTORS: Structural Iron Work, Structural
CONTRACTORS: Structural Steel Erection
CONTRACTORS: Svc Station Eqpt
CONTRACTORS: Svc Station Eqpt Installation, Maint & Repair
CONTRACTORS: Textile Warping
CONTRACTORS: Tile Installation, Ceramic
CONTRACTORS: Underground Utilities
CONTRACTORS: Ventilation & Duct Work
CONTRACTORS: Warm Air Heating & Air Conditioning
CONTRACTORS: Water Intake Well Drilling Svc
CONTRACTORS: Water Well Drilling
CONTRACTORS: Waterproofing
CONTRACTORS: Well Acidizing Svcs
CONTRACTORS: Well Chemical Treating Svcs
CONTRACTORS: Well Cleaning Svcs
CONTRACTORS: Well Logging Svcs
CONTRACTORS: Window Treatment Installation
CONTRACTORS: Windows & Doors
CONTRACTORS: Wood Floor Installation & Refinishing
CONTRACTORS: Wrecking & Demolition
CONTROL CIRCUIT DEVICES
CONTROL EQPT: Electric
CONTROL EQPT: Electric Buses & Locomotives
CONTROL EQPT: Noise
CONTROL PANELS: Electrical
CONTROLS & ACCESS: Indl, Electric
CONTROLS & ACCESS: Motor
CONTROLS: Access, Motor
CONTROLS: Adjustable Speed Drive
CONTROLS: Air Flow, Refrigeration
CONTROLS: Automatic Temperature
CONTROLS: Crane & Hoist, Including Metal Mill
CONTROLS: Electric Motor
CONTROLS: Environmental
CONTROLS: Numerical
CONTROLS: Relay & Ind
CONTROLS: Thermostats
CONTROLS: Thermostats, Built-in
CONTROLS: Water Heater
CONVENTION & TRADE SHOW SVCS
CONVERTERS: Data
CONVERTERS: Frequency
CONVERTERS: Phase Or Rotary, Electrical
CONVERTERS: Power, AC to DC
CONVERTERS: Rotary, Electrical
CONVERTERS: Torque, Exc Auto
CONVEYOR SYSTEMS
CONVEYOR SYSTEMS: Belt, General Indl Use
CONVEYOR SYSTEMS: Bucket Type
CONVEYOR SYSTEMS: Bulk Handling
CONVEYOR SYSTEMS: Pneumatic Tube
CONVEYOR SYSTEMS: Robotic
CONVEYORS & CONVEYING EQPT
CONVEYORS: Overhead
COOKING & FOOD WARMING EQPT: Commercial
COOKING & FOODWARMING EQPT: Coffee Brewing
COOKING & FOODWARMING EQPT: Commercial
COOKING & FOODWARMING EQPT: Popcorn Machines, Commercial
COOKING EQPT, HOUSEHOLD: Ranges, Gas
COOKING WARE, EXC PORCELAIN ENAMELED
COOLERS & ICE CHESTS: Polystyrene Foam
COOLING TOWERS: Metal
COOLING TOWERS: Wood
COPPER ORE MILLING & PREPARATION
COPPER: Bars, Primary
COPPER: Cathodes, Primary
COPPER: Rolling & Drawing
COPY MACHINES WHOLESALERS
CORD & TWINE
CORE WASH OR WAX
CORK & CORK PRDTS
CORK & CORK PRDTS: Insulating Material
CORRECTIONAL INSTITUTIONS
CORRUGATED PRDTS: Boxes, Partition, Display Items, Sheet/Pad
COSMETIC PREPARATIONS
COSMETICS & TOILETRIES
COSMETICS WHOLESALERS
COSMETOLOGIST
COSMETOLOGY & PERSONAL HYGIENE SALONS
COSTUME JEWELRY & NOVELTIES: Bracelets, Exc Precious Metals
COSTUME JEWELRY & NOVELTIES: Earrings, Exc Precious Metals
COSTUME JEWELRY & NOVELTIES: Exc Semi & Precious
COSTUME JEWELRY & NOVELTIES: Keychains, Exc Precious Metal
COSTUME JEWELRY & NOVELTIES: Pins, Exc Precious Metals
COSTUME JEWELRY & NOVELTIES: Rosaries & Sm Religious Items
COSTUME JEWELRY & NOVELTIES: Watchbands, Base Metal
COSTUME JEWELRY/NOVELTS: Cuff-Link/Stud, Exc Prec Metal/Gem
COSTUMES & WIGS STORES
COUNTER & SINK TOPS
COUNTERS & COUNTING DEVICES
COUNTERS OR COUNTER DISPLAY CASES, EXC WOOD
COUNTERS OR COUNTER DISPLAY CASES, WOOD
COUNTING DEVICES: Controls, Revolution & Timing
COUNTING DEVICES: Electromechanical
COUNTING DEVICES: Gauges, Press Temp Corrections Computing
COUNTING DEVICES: Odometers
COUNTING DEVICES: Pedometers
COUNTING DEVICES: Revolution
COUNTING DEVICES: Tachometer, Centrifugal
COUPLINGS, EXC PRESSURE & SOIL PIPE
COUPLINGS: Shaft
COURIER OR MESSENGER SVCS
COURIER SVCS, AIR: Package Delivery, Private
COURIER SVCS: Ground
COURIER SVCS: Package By Vehicle
COVERS: Automobile Seat
COVERS: Automotive, Exc Seat & Tire
COVERS: Metal Plate
COVERS: Slip Made Of Fabric, Plastic, Etc.
CRACKED CASTING REPAIR SVCS
CRANE & AERIAL LIFT SVCS
CRANES: Indl Plant
CRANES: Locomotive
CRANES: Overhead
CRANKSHAFTS & CAMSHAFTS: Machining
CREATIVE SVCS: Advertisers, Exc Writers
CREDIT CLEARINGHOUSE SVC
CREDIT INST, SHORT-TERM BUSINESS: Financing Dealers
CREDIT INSTITUTIONS, SHORT-TERM BUSINESS: Mercantile Finance
CREMATORIES
CROWNS & CLOSURES
CRUDE PETROLEUM & NATURAL GAS PRODUCTION
CRUDE PETROLEUM & NATURAL GAS PRODUCTION
CRUDE PETROLEUM PRODUCTION
CRUDES: Cyclic, Organic
CRYSTALS
CUBICLES: Electric Switchboard Eqpt
CULTURE MEDIA
CULVERTS: Sheet Metal
CUPS & PLATES: Foamed Plastics
CUPS: Plastic Exc Polystyrene Foam
CURBING: Granite Or Stone
CURTAIN & DRAPERY FIXTURES: Poles, Rods & Rollers
CURTAIN WALLS: Building, Steel
CURTAINS: Window, From Purchased Materials
CUSHIONS & PILLOWS
CUSHIONS & PILLOWS: Bed, From Purchased Materials
CUSHIONS & PILLOWS: Hassocks, Textile, Purchased Materials
CUSHIONS: Carpet & Rug, Foamed Plastics
CUSTOM COMPOUNDING OF RUBBER MATERIALS
CUSTOMIZING SVCS
CUT STONE & STONE PRODUCTS
CUTLERY
CUTLERY WHOLESALERS
CUTLERY: Table, Exc Metal Handled
CUTOUTS: Cardboard, Die-Cut, Made From Purchased Materials
CUTOUTS: Distribution
CUTTING EQPT: Milling
CUTTING SVC: Paper, Exc Die-Cut
CUTTING SVC: Paperboard
CYCLIC CRUDES & INTERMEDIATES
CYCLONES: Indl, Metal Plate
CYLINDER & ACTUATORS: Fluid Power
CYLINDERS: Pressure
CYLINDERS: Pump

# D

DAIRY EQPT
DAIRY PRDTS STORE: Ice Cream, Packaged
DAIRY PRDTS STORE: Milk
DAIRY PRDTS STORES
DAIRY PRDTS WHOLESALERS: Fresh
DAIRY PRDTS: Butter
DAIRY PRDTS: Cheese
DAIRY PRDTS: Cream Substitutes
DAIRY PRDTS: Custard, Frozen
DAIRY PRDTS: Dairy Based Desserts, Frozen
DAIRY PRDTS: Dietary Supplements, Dairy & Non-Dairy Based
DAIRY PRDTS: Dips & Spreads, Cheese Based
DAIRY PRDTS: Dips & Spreads, Sour Cream Based
DAIRY PRDTS: Dried Milk
DAIRY PRDTS: Evaporated Milk
DAIRY PRDTS: Frozen Desserts & Novelties
DAIRY PRDTS: Ice Cream & Ice Milk
DAIRY PRDTS: Ice Cream, Bulk
DAIRY PRDTS: Ice Cream, Packaged, Molded, On Sticks, Etc.
DAIRY PRDTS: Imitation Cheese
DAIRY PRDTS: Milk & Cream, Cultured & Flavored
DAIRY PRDTS: Milk Preparations, Dried
DAIRY PRDTS: Milk, Condensed & Evaporated
DAIRY PRDTS: Milk, Fluid
DAIRY PRDTS: Milk, Processed, Pasteurized, Homogenized/Btld
DAIRY PRDTS: Natural Cheese
DAIRY PRDTS: Powdered Buttermilk
DAIRY PRDTS: Powdered Milk
DAIRY PRDTS: Processed Cheese
DAIRY PRDTS: Whey, Powdered
DAIRY PRDTS: Whipped Topping, Exc Frozen Or Dry Mix
DAIRY PRDTS: Yogurt Mix
DAIRY PRDTS: Yogurt, Exc Frozen
DAIRY PRDTS: Yogurt, Frozen
DATA ENTRY SVCS
DATA PROCESSING & PREPARATION SVCS
DATA PROCESSING SVCS
DECORATIVE WOOD & WOODWORK

# PRODUCT INDEX

DEFENSE SYSTEMS & EQPT
DEGREASING MACHINES
DEHYDRATION EQPT
DELIVERY SVCS, BY VEHICLE
DEMONSTRATION SVCS
DENTAL EQPT
DENTAL EQPT & SPLYS
DENTAL EQPT & SPLYS WHOLESALERS
DENTAL EQPT & SPLYS: Dental Hand Instruments, NEC
DENTAL EQPT & SPLYS: Dental Materials
DENTAL EQPT & SPLYS: Denture Materials
DENTAL EQPT & SPLYS: Enamels
DENTAL EQPT & SPLYS: Gold
DENTAL EQPT & SPLYS: Laboratory
DENTAL EQPT & SPLYS: Orthodontic Appliances
DENTAL EQPT & SPLYS: Sterilizers
DENTAL EQPT & SPLYS: Teeth, Artificial, Exc In Dental Labs
DENTAL INSTRUMENT REPAIR SVCS
DENTISTS' OFFICES & CLINICS
DENTURE CLEANERS
DEPARTMENT STORES
DEPARTMENT STORES: Country General
DEPILATORIES, COSMETIC
DERMATOLOGICALS
DERRICKS: Oil & Gas Field
DESIGN SVCS, NEC
DESIGN SVCS: Commercial & Indl
DESIGN SVCS: Computer Integrated Systems
DESIGN SVCS: Hand Tools
DESIGNS SVCS: Scenery, Theatrical
DETECTION APPARATUS: Electronic/Magnetic Field, Light/Heat
DETECTION EQPT: Magnetic Field
DETECTIVE SVCS
DETECTORS: Water Leak
DIAGNOSTIC SUBSTANCES
DIAGNOSTIC SUBSTANCES OR AGENTS: Blood Derivative
DIAGNOSTIC SUBSTANCES OR AGENTS: In Vitro
DIAGNOSTIC SUBSTANCES OR AGENTS: Microbiology & Virology
DIAGNOSTIC SUBSTANCES OR AGENTS: Radioactive
DIAMOND SETTER SVCS
DIAMONDS, GEMS, WHOLESALE
DIAMONDS: Cutting & Polishing
DIAPERS: Cloth
DIAPERS: Disposable
DIATHERMY EQPT
DIE CUTTING SVC: Paper
DIE SETS: Presses, Metal Stamping
DIES & TOOLS: Special
DIES: Cutting, Exc Metal
DIES: Extrusion
DIES: Paper Cutting
DIES: Plastic Forming
DIES: Steel Rule
DIES: Wire Drawing & Straightening
DIMENSION STONE: Buildings
DIODES: Light Emitting
DIRECT SELLING ESTABLISHMENTS, NEC
DIRECT SELLING ESTABLISHMENTS: Food Svcs
DIRECT SELLING ESTABLISHMENTS: Food, Mobile, Exc Coffee-Cart
DIRECT SELLING ESTABLISHMENTS: Milk Delivery
DIRECT SELLING ESTABLISHMENTS: Telemarketing
DISINFECTING SVCS
DISK DRIVES: Computer
DISKETTE DUPLICATING SVCS
DISPENSERS: Soap
DISPENSING EQPT & PARTS, BEVERAGE: Beer
DISPENSING EQPT & PARTS, BEVERAGE: Coolers, Milk/Water, Elec
DISPENSING EQPT & PARTS, BEVERAGE: Fountain/Other Beverage
DISPENSING EQPT & PARTS, BEVERAGE: Fountains, Parts/Access
DISPENSING EQPT & PARTS, BEVERAGE: Siphons, Soda Water
DISPLAY CASES: Refrigerated
DISPLAY FIXTURES: Showcases, Wood, Exc Refrigerated
DISPLAY FIXTURES: Wood
DISPLAY ITEMS: Corrugated, Made From Purchased Materials
DISPLAY ITEMS: Solid Fiber, Made From Purchased Materials
DISPLAY LETTERING SVCS

DISPLAY STANDS: Merchandise, Exc Wood
DISTILLERS DRIED GRAIN & SOLUBLES
DISTRIBUTORS: Motor Vehicle Engine
DIVING EQPT STORES
DOCK EQPT & SPLYS, INDL
DOCKS: Marinas, Prefabricated, Wood
DOOR & WINDOW REPAIR SVCS
DOOR FRAMES: Concrete
DOOR FRAMES: Wood
DOOR MATS: Rubber
DOOR OPERATING SYSTEMS: Electric
DOORS & WINDOWS WHOLESALERS: All Materials
DOORS & WINDOWS: Screen & Storm
DOORS & WINDOWS: Storm, Metal
DOORS: Fire, Metal
DOORS: Folding, Plastic Or Plastic Coated Fabric
DOORS: Garage, Overhead, Metal
DOORS: Garage, Overhead, Wood
DOORS: Glass
DOORS: Rolling, Indl Building Or Warehouse, Metal
DOORS: Safe & Vault, Metal
DOORS: Screen, Metal
DOORS: Wooden
DOWELS & DOWEL RODS
DRAFTING SPLYS WHOLESALERS
DRAFTING SVCS
DRAINAGE PRDTS: Concrete
DRAINING OR PUMPING OF METAL MINES
DRAPERIES & CURTAINS
DRAPERIES & DRAPERY FABRICS, COTTON
DRAPERIES: Plastic & Textile, From Purchased Materials
DRAPERY & UPHOLSTERY STORES: Curtains
DRAPERY & UPHOLSTERY STORES: Draperies
DRIED FRUITS WHOLESALERS
DRILL BITS
DRILLING MACHINERY & EQPT: Oil & Gas
DRILLING MACHINERY & EQPT: Water Well
DRILLING MUD COMPOUNDS, CONDITIONERS & ADDITIVES
DRILLS & DRILLING EQPT: Mining
DRINK MIXES, NONALCOHOLIC: Cocktail
DRINKING FOUNTAINS: Metal, Nonrefrigerated
DRINKING PLACES: Alcoholic Beverages
DRINKING PLACES: Bars & Lounges
DRINKING PLACES: Night Clubs
DRINKING PLACES: Tavern
DRINKING PLACES: Wine Bar
DRINKING WATER COOLERS WHOLESALERS: Mechanical
DRIVE CHAINS: Bicycle Or Motorcycle
DRIVE SHAFTS
DRIVES: High Speed Indl, Exc Hydrostatic
DRIVES: Hydrostatic
DROP CLOTHS: Fabric
DRUG STORES
DRUG TESTING KITS: Blood & Urine
DRUGS & DRUG PROPRIETARIES, WHOL: Biologicals/Allied Prdts
DRUGS & DRUG PROPRIETARIES, WHOLESALE
DRUGS & DRUG PROPRIETARIES, WHOLESALE: Animal Medicines
DRUGS & DRUG PROPRIETARIES, WHOLESALE: Medicinals/Botanicals
DRUGS & DRUG PROPRIETARIES, WHOLESALE: Pharmaceuticals
DRUGS & DRUG PROPRIETARIES, WHOLESALE: Vitamins & Minerals
DRUGS AFFECTING NEOPLASMS & ENDOCRINE SYSTEMS
DRUMS: Brake
DRUMS: Fiber
DRUMS: Magnetic
DRUMS: Shipping, Metal
DRYCLEANING & LAUNDRY SVCS: Commercial & Family
DRYCLEANING EQPT & SPLYS: Commercial
DRYCLEANING PLANTS
DRYERS & REDRYERS: Indl
DUCTING: Metal Plate
DUCTING: Plastic
DUCTS: Sheet Metal
DUMBWAITERS
DUMPSTERS: Garbage
DURABLE GOODS WHOLESALERS, NEC
DUST OR FUME COLLECTING EQPT: Indl
DYES & PIGMENTS: Organic
DYNAMOMETERS

# E

EARTH SCIENCE SVCS
EARTHS: Ground Or Otherwise Treated
EATING PLACES
ECCLESIASTICAL WARE, NEC
EDUCATIONAL PROGRAM ADMINISTRATION, GOVT: Level Of Govt
EDUCATIONAL SVCS
EDUCATIONAL SVCS, NONDEGREE GRANTING: Continuing Education
ELASTIC BRAID & NARROW WOVEN FABRICS
ELASTOMERS
ELECTRIC FENCE CHARGERS
ELECTRIC MOTOR & GENERATOR AUXILIARY PARTS
ELECTRIC MOTOR REPAIR SVCS
ELECTRIC WATER HEATERS WHOLESALERS
ELECTRICAL APPARATUS & EQPT WHOLESALERS
ELECTRICAL APPLIANCES, TELEVISIONS & RADIOS WHOLESALERS
ELECTRICAL CONSTRUCTION MATERIALS WHOLESALERS
ELECTRICAL CURRENT CARRYING WIRING DEVICES
ELECTRICAL DISCHARGE MACHINING, EDM
ELECTRICAL EQPT & SPLYS
ELECTRICAL EQPT FOR ENGINES
ELECTRICAL EQPT REPAIR & MAINTENANCE
ELECTRICAL EQPT REPAIR SVCS
ELECTRICAL EQPT: Automotive, NEC
ELECTRICAL EQPT: Household
ELECTRICAL GOODS, WHOLESALE: Alarms & Signaling Eqpt
ELECTRICAL GOODS, WHOLESALE: Batteries, Storage, Indl
ELECTRICAL GOODS, WHOLESALE: Burglar Alarm Systems
ELECTRICAL GOODS, WHOLESALE: Circuit Breakers
ELECTRICAL GOODS, WHOLESALE: Citizens Band Radios
ELECTRICAL GOODS, WHOLESALE: Connectors
ELECTRICAL GOODS, WHOLESALE: Electrical Appliances, Major
ELECTRICAL GOODS, WHOLESALE: Electrical Entertainment Eqpt
ELECTRICAL GOODS, WHOLESALE: Electronic Parts
ELECTRICAL GOODS, WHOLESALE: Fans, Household
ELECTRICAL GOODS, WHOLESALE: Fire Alarm Systems
ELECTRICAL GOODS, WHOLESALE: Generators
ELECTRICAL GOODS, WHOLESALE: High Fidelity Eqpt
ELECTRICAL GOODS, WHOLESALE: Household Appliances, NEC
ELECTRICAL GOODS, WHOLESALE: Light Bulbs & Related Splys
ELECTRICAL GOODS, WHOLESALE: Lighting Fittings & Access
ELECTRICAL GOODS, WHOLESALE: Lighting Fixtures, Comm & Indl
ELECTRICAL GOODS, WHOLESALE: Magnetic Recording Tape
ELECTRICAL GOODS, WHOLESALE: Motor Ctrls, Starters & Relays
ELECTRICAL GOODS, WHOLESALE: Motors
ELECTRICAL GOODS, WHOLESALE: Paging & Signaling Eqpt
ELECTRICAL GOODS, WHOLESALE: Panelboards
ELECTRICAL GOODS, WHOLESALE: Radio Parts & Access, NEC
ELECTRICAL GOODS, WHOLESALE: Resistors
ELECTRICAL GOODS, WHOLESALE: Safety Switches
ELECTRICAL GOODS, WHOLESALE: Security Control Eqpt & Systems
ELECTRICAL GOODS, WHOLESALE: Semiconductor Devices
ELECTRICAL GOODS, WHOLESALE: Signaling, Eqpt
ELECTRICAL GOODS, WHOLESALE: Sound Eqpt
ELECTRICAL GOODS, WHOLESALE: Switches, Exc Electronic, NEC
ELECTRICAL GOODS, WHOLESALE: Telephone & Telegraphic Eqpt
ELECTRICAL GOODS, WHOLESALE: Telephone Eqpt
ELECTRICAL GOODS, WHOLESALE: Transformer & Transmission Eqpt
ELECTRICAL GOODS, WHOLESALE: Transformers
ELECTRICAL GOODS, WHOLESALE: Video Eqpt
ELECTRICAL GOODS, WHOLESALE: Wire & Cable
ELECTRICAL GOODS, WHOLESALE: Wire & Cable, Building
ELECTRICAL GOODS, WHOLESALE: Wire & Cable, Power
ELECTRICAL HOUSEHOLD APPLIANCE REPAIR

# PRODUCT INDEX

ELECTRICAL INDL APPARATUS, NEC
ELECTRICAL MEASURING INSTRUMENT REPAIR & CALIBRATION SVCS
ELECTRICAL SPLYS
ELECTRICAL SUPPLIES: Porcelain
ELECTRODES: Thermal & Electrolytic
ELECTROLYZING SVC: Steel, Light Gauge
ELECTROMEDICAL EQPT
ELECTROMEDICAL EQPT WHOLESALERS
ELECTROMETALLURGICAL PRDTS
ELECTRON BEAM: Cutting, Forming, Welding
ELECTRON TUBES
ELECTRON TUBES: Cathode Ray
ELECTRON TUBES: Parts
ELECTRON TUBES: Transmitting
ELECTRONIC COMPONENTS
ELECTRONIC DEVICES: Solid State, NEC
ELECTRONIC EQPT REPAIR SVCS
ELECTRONIC LOADS & POWER SPLYS
ELECTRONIC PARTS & EQPT WHOLESALERS
ELECTRONIC TRAINING DEVICES
ELECTROPLATING & PLATING SVC
ELEMENTARY & SECONDARY SCHOOLS, SPECIAL EDUCATION
ELEVATOR: Grain, Storage Only
ELEVATORS & EQPT
ELEVATORS WHOLESALERS
ELEVATORS: Installation & Conversion
EMBALMING FLUID
EMBLEMS: Embroidered
EMBOSSING SVC: Paper
EMBOSSING SVCS: Diplomas, Resolutions, Etc
EMBROIDERING & ART NEEDLEWORK FOR THE TRADE
EMBROIDERING SVC
EMBROIDERING SVC: Schiffli Machine
EMBROIDERY ADVERTISING SVCS
EMERGENCY ALARMS
EMPLOYMENT AGENCY SVCS
ENAMELING SVC: Metal Prdts, Including Porcelain
ENAMELS
ENCLOSURES: Electronic
ENCLOSURES: Screen
ENCODERS: Digital
ENERGY MEASUREMENT EQPT
ENGINE PARTS & ACCESS: Internal Combustion
ENGINE REBUILDING: Diesel
ENGINE REBUILDING: Gas
ENGINEERING SVCS
ENGINEERING SVCS: Building Construction
ENGINEERING SVCS: Chemical
ENGINEERING SVCS: Civil
ENGINEERING SVCS: Electrical Or Electronic
ENGINEERING SVCS: Energy conservation
ENGINEERING SVCS: Heating & Ventilation
ENGINEERING SVCS: Industrial
ENGINEERING SVCS: Machine Tool Design
ENGINEERING SVCS: Marine
ENGINEERING SVCS: Mechanical
ENGINEERING SVCS: Pollution Control
ENGINEERING SVCS: Professional
ENGINEERING SVCS: Structural
ENGINES & ENGINE PARTS: Guided Missile, Research & Develpt
ENGINES: Diesel & Semi-Diesel Or Duel Fuel
ENGINES: Gasoline, NEC
ENGINES: Internal Combustion, NEC
ENGINES: Jet Propulsion
ENGINES: Marine
ENGINES: Steam
ENGRAVING SVC, NEC
ENGRAVING SVC: Jewelry & Personal Goods
ENGRAVING SVCS
ENGRAVINGS: Plastic
ENTERTAINERS & ENTERTAINMENT GROUPS
ENTERTAINMENT PROMOTION SVCS
ENTERTAINMENT SVCS
ENVELOPES
ENVELOPES WHOLESALERS
ENZYMES
EPOXY RESINS
EQUIPMENT: Pedestrian Traffic Control
EQUIPMENT: Rental & Leasing, NEC
ESCALATORS: Passenger & Freight
ETCHING & ENGRAVING SVC
ETCHING SVC: Metal

ETCHING SVC: Photochemical
ETHERS
ETHYLENE
ETHYLENE OXIDE
ETHYLENE-PROPYLENE RUBBERS: EPDM Polymers
EXCAVATING MACHINERY & EQPT WHOLESALERS
EXHAUST SYSTEMS: Eqpt & Parts
EXPANSION JOINTS: Rubber
EXPLOSIVES
EXPLOSIVES, EXC AMMO & FIREWORKS WHOLESALERS
EXTENSION CORDS
EXTERMINATING & FUMIGATING SVCS
EXTRACTS, FLAVORING
EYEGLASSES
EYEGLASSES: Sunglasses
EYELASHES, ARTIFICIAL
EYES & HOOKS Screw
EYES: Artificial
Ethylene Glycols

## F

FABRIC STORES
FABRICATED METAL PRODUCTS, NEC
FABRICS & CLOTH: Quilted
FABRICS & CLOTHING: Rubber Coated
FABRICS: Alpacas, Mohair, Woven
FABRICS: Apparel & Outerwear, Cotton
FABRICS: Awning Stripes, Cotton
FABRICS: Bags & Bagging, Cotton
FABRICS: Bandage Cloth, Cotton
FABRICS: Broadwoven, Cotton
FABRICS: Broadwoven, Synthetic Manmade Fiber & Silk
FABRICS: Broadwoven, Wool
FABRICS: Canvas & Heavy Coarse, Cotton
FABRICS: Coated Or Treated
FABRICS: Cotton, Narrow
FABRICS: Denims
FABRICS: Fiberglass, Broadwoven
FABRICS: Filter Cloth, Cotton
FABRICS: Furniture Denim
FABRICS: Glass & Fiberglass, Broadwoven
FABRICS: Jersey Cloth
FABRICS: Laminated
FABRICS: Luggage, Cotton
FABRICS: Metallized
FABRICS: Nonwoven
FABRICS: Nylon, Broadwoven
FABRICS: Polypropylene, Broadwoven
FABRICS: Print, Cotton
FABRICS: Resin Or Plastic Coated
FABRICS: Satin
FABRICS: Scrub Cloths
FABRICS: Shoe Laces, Exc Leather
FABRICS: Stretch, Cotton
FABRICS: Tapestry, Cotton
FABRICS: Trimmings
FABRICS: Trimmings, Textile
FABRICS: Upholstery, Cotton
FABRICS: Upholstery, Wool
FABRICS: Wall Covering, From Manmade Fiber Or Silk
FABRICS: Weft Or Circular Knit
FABRICS: Woven, Narrow Cotton, Wool, Silk
FACILITIES SUPPORT SVCS
FACSIMILE COMMUNICATION EQPT
FAMILY CLOTHING STORES
FANS, BLOWING: Indl Or Commercial
FANS, EXHAUST: Indl Or Commercial
FANS, VENTILATING: Indl Or Commercial
FANS: Ceiling
FARM & GARDEN MACHINERY WHOLESALERS
FARM MACHINERY REPAIR SVCS
FARM PRDTS, RAW MATERIALS, WHOLESALE: Broomcorn
FARM PRDTS, RAW MATERIALS, WHOLESALE: Farm Animals
FARM SPLY STORES
FARM SPLYS WHOLESALERS
FARM SPLYS, WHOLESALE: Beekeeping Splys, Nondurable
FARM SPLYS, WHOLESALE: Feed
FARM SPLYS, WHOLESALE: Fertilizers & Agricultural Chemicals
FARM SPLYS, WHOLESALE: Harness Eqpt
FARM SPLYS, WHOLESALE: Limestone, Agricultural
FARM SPLYS, WHOLESALE: Saddlery
FASTENERS WHOLESALERS

FASTENERS: Brads, Alum, Brass/Other Nonferrous Metal/Wire
FASTENERS: Metal
FASTENERS: Metal
FASTENERS: Notions, NEC
FASTENERS: Notions, Zippers
FASTENERS: Wire, Made From Purchased Wire
FATTY ACID ESTERS & AMINOS
FAUCETS & SPIGOTS: Metal & Plastic
FEATHERS: Dusters
FEDERAL CROP INSURANCE CORP
FELT PARTS
FELT, WHOLESALE
FELT: Polishing
FENCE POSTS: Iron & Steel
FENCES OR POSTS: Ornamental Iron Or Steel
FENCING DEALERS
FENCING MATERIALS: Plastic
FENCING MATERIALS: Snow Fence, Wood
FENCING MATERIALS: Wood
FENCING: Chain Link
FENDERS: Automobile, Stamped Or Pressed Metal
FERRITES
FERROUS METALS: Reclaimed From Clay
FERTILIZER, AGRICULTURAL: Wholesalers
FERTILIZERS: NEC
FERTILIZERS: Nitrogen Solutions
FERTILIZERS: Nitrogenous
FERTILIZERS: Phosphatic
FIBER & FIBER PRDTS: Acrylic
FIBER & FIBER PRDTS: Fluorocarbon
FIBER & FIBER PRDTS: Organic, Noncellulose
FIBER & FIBER PRDTS: Polyester
FIBER & FIBER PRDTS: Protein
FIBER & FIBER PRDTS: Synthetic Cellulosic
FIBER & FIBER PRDTS: Vinyl
FIBER OPTICS
FIELD WAREHOUSING SVCS
FILE FOLDERS
FILLERS & SEALERS: Putty
FILLERS & SEALERS: Putty, Wood
FILLERS & SEALERS: Wood
FILM & SHEET: Unsuppported Plastic
FILM BASE: Cellulose Acetate Or Nitrocellulose Plastics
FILM: Motion Picture
FILTER CLEANING SVCS
FILTER ELEMENTS: Fluid & Hydraulic Line
FILTERING MEDIA: Pottery
FILTERS
FILTERS & SOFTENERS: Water, Household
FILTERS & STRAINERS: Pipeline
FILTERS: Air
FILTERS: Air Intake, Internal Combustion Engine, Exc Auto
FILTERS: Gasoline, Internal Combustion Engine, Exc Auto
FILTERS: General Line, Indl
FILTERS: Motor Vehicle
FILTERS: Oil, Internal Combustion Engine, Exc Auto
FILTERS: Paper
FILTRATION DEVICES: Electronic
FINANCIAL INVESTMENT ADVICE
FINANCIAL SVCS
FINDINGS & TRIMMINGS: Apparel
FINDINGS & TRIMMINGS: Fabric
FINGERNAILS, ARTIFICIAL
FINISHERS: Concrete & Bituminous, Powered
FINISHING AGENTS
FINISHING AGENTS: Leather
FINISHING SVCS
FIRE ARMS, SMALL: Guns Or Gun Parts, 30 mm & Below
FIRE ARMS, SMALL: Machine Guns & Grenade Launchers
FIRE ARMS, SMALL: Machine Guns/Machine Gun Parts, 30mm/below
FIRE ARMS, SMALL: Revolvers Or Revolver Parts, 30 mm & Below
FIRE ARMS, SMALL: Rifles Or Rifle Parts, 30 mm & below
FIRE CONTROL OR BOMBING EQPT: Electronic
FIRE DETECTION SYSTEMS
FIRE ESCAPES
FIRE EXTINGUISHER CHARGES
FIRE EXTINGUISHER SVC
FIRE EXTINGUISHERS, WHOLESALE
FIRE EXTINGUISHERS: Portable
FIRE OR BURGLARY RESISTIVE PRDTS
FIRE PROTECTION EQPT
FIREARMS & AMMUNITION, EXC SPORTING, WHOLESALE

*2017 Harris Illinois Industrial Directory*

# PRODUCT INDEX

FIREARMS, EXC SPORTING, WHOLESALE
FIREARMS: Large, Greater Than 30mm
FIREARMS: Small, 30mm or Less
FIREFIGHTING APPARATUS
FIREPLACE & CHIMNEY MATERIAL: Concrete
FIREPLACE EQPT & ACCESS
FIREWOOD, WHOLESALE
FIREWORKS
FISH & SEAFOOD PROCESSORS: Canned Or Cured
FISH & SEAFOOD PROCESSORS: Fresh Or Frozen
FISH & SEAFOOD WHOLESALERS
FISH FOOD
FISHING EQPT: Lures
FISHING EQPT: Nets & Seines
FITTINGS & ASSEMBLIES: Hose & Tube, Hydraulic Or Pneumatic
FITTINGS & SPECIALTIES: Steam
FITTINGS: Pipe
FITTINGS: Pipe, Fabricated
FIXTURES & EQPT: Kitchen, Metal, Exc Cast Aluminum
FIXTURES & EQPT: Kitchen, Porcelain Enameled
FIXTURES: Cut Stone
FLAGPOLES
FLAGS: Fabric
FLAT GLASS: Building
FLAT GLASS: Construction
FLAT GLASS: Picture
FLAT GLASS: Sheet
FLAT GLASS: Tempered
FLAT GLASS: Window, Clear & Colored
FLAVORS OR FLAVORING MATERIALS: Synthetic
FLIGHT RECORDERS
FLOOR COVERING STORES
FLOOR COVERING STORES: Carpets
FLOOR COVERING STORES: Floor Tile
FLOOR COVERING: Plastic
FLOOR COVERINGS WHOLESALERS
FLOOR COVERINGS: Asphalted-Felt Base, Linoleum Or Carpet
FLOOR COVERINGS: Rubber
FLOOR COVERINGS: Textile Fiber
FLOORING & GRATINGS: Open, Construction Applications
FLOORING & SIDING: Metal
FLOORING: Hard Surface
FLOORING: Hardwood
FLORIST TELEGRAPH SVCS
FLORIST: Flowers, Fresh
FLORISTS
FLORISTS' SPLYS, WHOLESALE
FLOWER ARRANGEMENTS: Artificial
FLOWERS: Artificial & Preserved
FLUID METERS & COUNTING DEVICES
FLUID POWER PUMPS & MOTORS
FLUID POWER VALVES & HOSE FITTINGS
FLUORSPAR MINING
FLUXES
FM & AM RADIO TUNERS
FOAM RUBBER
FOAM RUBBER, WHOLESALE
FOAMS & RUBBER, WHOLESALE
FOIL & LEAF: Metal
FOIL OR LEAF: Gold
FOIL: Aluminum
FOOD CASINGS: Plastic
FOOD COLORINGS
FOOD PRDTS, BREAKFAST: Cereal, Corn Flakes
FOOD PRDTS, BREAKFAST: Cereal, Infants' Food
FOOD PRDTS, BREAKFAST: Cereal, Rice: Cereal Breakfast Food
FOOD PRDTS, CANNED OR FRESH PACK: Fruit Juices
FOOD PRDTS, CANNED OR FRESH PACK: Vegetable Juices
FOOD PRDTS, CANNED, NEC
FOOD PRDTS, CANNED: Applesauce
FOOD PRDTS, CANNED: Baby Food
FOOD PRDTS, CANNED: Barbecue Sauce
FOOD PRDTS, CANNED: Beans & Bean Sprouts
FOOD PRDTS, CANNED: Beans, Baked Without Meat
FOOD PRDTS, CANNED: Beans, Without Meat
FOOD PRDTS, CANNED: Catsup
FOOD PRDTS, CANNED: Ethnic
FOOD PRDTS, CANNED: Fruit Juices, Fresh
FOOD PRDTS, CANNED: Fruits
FOOD PRDTS, CANNED: Fruits
FOOD PRDTS, CANNED: Fruits & Fruit Prdts

FOOD PRDTS, CANNED: Italian
FOOD PRDTS, CANNED: Jams, Including Imitation
FOOD PRDTS, CANNED: Jams, Jellies & Preserves
FOOD PRDTS, CANNED: Jellies, Edible, Including Imitation
FOOD PRDTS, CANNED: Mexican, NEC
FOOD PRDTS, CANNED: Pizza Sauce
FOOD PRDTS, CANNED: Puddings, Exc Meat
FOOD PRDTS, CANNED: Soups
FOOD PRDTS, CANNED: Spaghetti & Other Pasta Sauce
FOOD PRDTS, CANNED: Tamales
FOOD PRDTS, CANNED: Tomato Sauce.
FOOD PRDTS, CANNED: Tomatoes
FOOD PRDTS, CANNED: Tortillas
FOOD PRDTS, CANNED: Vegetable Purees
FOOD PRDTS, CANNED: Vegetables
FOOD PRDTS, CANNED: Vegetables
FOOD PRDTS, CONFECTIONERY, WHOLESALE: Candy
FOOD PRDTS, CONFECTIONERY, WHOLESALE: Nuts, Salted/Roasted
FOOD PRDTS, CONFECTIONERY, WHOLESALE: Potato Chips
FOOD PRDTS, CONFECTIONERY, WHOLESALE: Snack Foods
FOOD PRDTS, DAIRY, WHOLESALE: Dried Or Canned
FOOD PRDTS, DAIRY, WHOLESALE: Frozen Dairy Desserts
FOOD PRDTS, FISH & SEAFOOD, WHOLESALE: Fresh
FOOD PRDTS, FISH & SEAFOOD: Chowders, Frozen
FOOD PRDTS, FISH & SEAFOOD: Fish, Canned & Cured
FOOD PRDTS, FISH & SEAFOOD: Fresh, Prepared
FOOD PRDTS, FISH & SEAFOOD: Fresh/Frozen Chowder, Soup/Stew
FOOD PRDTS, FISH & SEAFOOD: Seafood, Frozen, Prepared
FOOD PRDTS, FISH & SEAFOOD: Shrimp, Frozen, Prepared
FOOD PRDTS, FROZEN, WHOLESALE: Dinners
FOOD PRDTS, FROZEN: Dinners, Packaged
FOOD PRDTS, FROZEN: Ethnic Foods, NEC
FOOD PRDTS, FROZEN: Fruit Juice, Concentrates
FOOD PRDTS, FROZEN: Fruits & Vegetables
FOOD PRDTS, FROZEN: Fruits, Juices & Vegetables
FOOD PRDTS, FROZEN: Lunches, Packaged
FOOD PRDTS, FROZEN: NEC
FOOD PRDTS, FROZEN: Pizza
FOOD PRDTS, FROZEN: Potato Prdts
FOOD PRDTS, FROZEN: Snack Items
FOOD PRDTS, FROZEN: Spaghetti & Meatballs
FOOD PRDTS, FROZEN: Vegetables, Exc Potato Prdts
FOOD PRDTS, FROZEN: Waffles
FOOD PRDTS, FRUITS & VEG, FRESH, WHOL: Banana Ripening Svc
FOOD PRDTS, MEAT & MEAT PRDTS, WHOLESALE: Brokers
FOOD PRDTS, MEAT & MEAT PRDTS, WHOLESALE: Cured Or Smoked
FOOD PRDTS, MEAT & MEAT PRDTS, WHOLESALE: Fresh
FOOD PRDTS, WHOLESALE: Baking Splys
FOOD PRDTS, WHOLESALE: Beverages, Exc Coffee & Tea
FOOD PRDTS, WHOLESALE: Breading Mixes
FOOD PRDTS, WHOLESALE: Coffee & Tea
FOOD PRDTS, WHOLESALE: Coffee, Green Or Roasted
FOOD PRDTS, WHOLESALE: Condiments
FOOD PRDTS, WHOLESALE: Cookies
FOOD PRDTS, WHOLESALE: Cooking Oils & Shortenings
FOOD PRDTS, WHOLESALE: Flavorings & Fragrances
FOOD PRDTS, WHOLESALE: Flour
FOOD PRDTS, WHOLESALE: Grain Elevators
FOOD PRDTS, WHOLESALE: Grains
FOOD PRDTS, WHOLESALE: Health
FOOD PRDTS, WHOLESALE: Honey
FOOD PRDTS, WHOLESALE: Natural & Organic
FOOD PRDTS, WHOLESALE: Pasta & Rice
FOOD PRDTS, WHOLESALE: Pizza Splys
FOOD PRDTS, WHOLESALE: Rice, Polished
FOOD PRDTS, WHOLESALE: Salt, Edible
FOOD PRDTS, WHOLESALE: Sauces
FOOD PRDTS, WHOLESALE: Shortening, Vegetable
FOOD PRDTS, WHOLESALE: Soups, Exc Frozen
FOOD PRDTS, WHOLESALE: Specialty
FOOD PRDTS, WHOLESALE: Spices & Seasonings
FOOD PRDTS, WHOLESALE: Water, Distilled
FOOD PRDTS, WHOLESALE: Wine Makers' Eqpt & Splys
FOOD PRDTS: Animal & marine fats & oils
FOOD PRDTS: Bran & Middlings, Exc Rice
FOOD PRDTS: Bread Crumbs, Exc Made In Bakeries

FOOD PRDTS: Breakfast Bars
FOOD PRDTS: Cake Fillings, Exc Fruit
FOOD PRDTS: Cereals
FOOD PRDTS: Chewing Gum Base
FOOD PRDTS: Chicken, Processed, Fresh
FOOD PRDTS: Chicken, Processed, Frozen
FOOD PRDTS: Chili Pepper Or Powder
FOOD PRDTS: Cocoa, Instant
FOOD PRDTS: Coffee
FOOD PRDTS: Coffee Extracts
FOOD PRDTS: Coffee Roasting, Exc Wholesale Grocers
FOOD PRDTS: Coffee Substitutes
FOOD PRDTS: Compound Shortenings
FOOD PRDTS: Cooking Oils, Refined Vegetable, Exc Corn
FOOD PRDTS: Corn & other vegetable starches
FOOD PRDTS: Corn Chips & Other Corn-Based Snacks
FOOD PRDTS: Corn Meal
FOOD PRDTS: Cottonseed Oil, Cake & Meal
FOOD PRDTS: Dessert Mixes & Fillings
FOOD PRDTS: Desserts, Ready-To-Mix
FOOD PRDTS: Dough, Pizza, Prepared
FOOD PRDTS: Doughs, Frozen Or Refrig From Purchased Flour
FOOD PRDTS: Dressings, Salad, Raw & Cooked Exc Dry Mixes
FOOD PRDTS: Dried & Dehydrated Fruits, Vegetables & Soup Mix
FOOD PRDTS: Edible Oil Prdts, Exc Corn Oil
FOOD PRDTS: Edible fats & oils
FOOD PRDTS: Eggs, Processed
FOOD PRDTS: Eggs, Processed, Dehydrated
FOOD PRDTS: Emulsifiers
FOOD PRDTS: Fat Substitutes
FOOD PRDTS: Flour
FOOD PRDTS: Flour & Other Grain Mill Products
FOOD PRDTS: Flour Mixes & Doughs
FOOD PRDTS: Flour, Blended From Purchased Flour
FOOD PRDTS: Flours & Flour Mixes, From Purchased Flour
FOOD PRDTS: Fresh Vegetables, Peeled Or Processed
FOOD PRDTS: Fruit Juices
FOOD PRDTS: Fruit Juices, Dehydrated
FOOD PRDTS: Fruit Pops, Frozen
FOOD PRDTS: Fruits & Vegetables, Pickled
FOOD PRDTS: Fruits, Dehydrated Or Dried
FOOD PRDTS: Fruits, Dried Or Dehydrated, Exc Freeze-Dried
FOOD PRDTS: Gluten Feed
FOOD PRDTS: Granola & Energy Bars, Nonchocolate
FOOD PRDTS: Honey
FOOD PRDTS: Horseradish, Exc Sauce
FOOD PRDTS: Ice, Blocks
FOOD PRDTS: Ice, Cubes
FOOD PRDTS: Instant Coffee
FOOD PRDTS: Macaroni Prdts, Dry, Alphabet, Rings Or Shells
FOOD PRDTS: Macaroni, Noodles, Spaghetti, Pasta, Etc
FOOD PRDTS: Malt
FOOD PRDTS: Meat Meal & Tankage, Inedible
FOOD PRDTS: Milled Corn By-Prdts
FOOD PRDTS: Mixes, Bread & Roll From Purchased Flour
FOOD PRDTS: Mixes, Cake, From Purchased Flour
FOOD PRDTS: Mixes, Doughnut From Purchased Flour
FOOD PRDTS: Mixes, Flour
FOOD PRDTS: Mixes, Gravy, Dry
FOOD PRDTS: Mixes, Pancake From Purchased Flour
FOOD PRDTS: Mixes, Pizza From Purchased Flour
FOOD PRDTS: Mixes, Sauces, Dry
FOOD PRDTS: Mixes, Seasonings, Dry
FOOD PRDTS: Mustard, Prepared
FOOD PRDTS: Noodles, Uncooked, Packaged W/Other Ingredients
FOOD PRDTS: Nuts & Seeds
FOOD PRDTS: Oils & Fats, Animal
FOOD PRDTS: Olive Oil
FOOD PRDTS: Onion Fries
FOOD PRDTS: Oriental Noodles
FOOD PRDTS: Pasta, Rice/Potatoes, Uncooked, Pkgd
FOOD PRDTS: Pasta, Uncooked, Packaged With Other Ingredients
FOOD PRDTS: Peanut Butter
FOOD PRDTS: Pickles, Vinegar
FOOD PRDTS: Pizza Doughs From Purchased Flour
FOOD PRDTS: Popcorn, Popped
FOOD PRDTS: Popcorn, Unpopped
FOOD PRDTS: Pork Rinds

# PRODUCT INDEX

FOOD PRDTS: Potato & Corn Chips & Similar Prdts
FOOD PRDTS: Potato Chips & Other Potato-Based Snacks
FOOD PRDTS: Potatoes, Dried
FOOD PRDTS: Potatoes, Dried, Packaged With Other Ingredients
FOOD PRDTS: Poultry Sausage, Lunch Meats/Other Poultry Prdts
FOOD PRDTS: Poultry, Processed, Frozen
FOOD PRDTS: Preparations
FOOD PRDTS: Prepared Meat Sauces Exc Tomato & Dry
FOOD PRDTS: Prepared Sauces, Exc Tomato Based
FOOD PRDTS: Prepared Vegetable Sauces Exc Tomato & Dry
FOOD PRDTS: Raw cane sugar
FOOD PRDTS: Rice, Milled
FOOD PRDTS: Rice, Packaged & Seasoned
FOOD PRDTS: Salad Oils, Refined Vegetable, Exc Corn
FOOD PRDTS: Salads
FOOD PRDTS: Sandwiches
FOOD PRDTS: Seasonings & Spices
FOOD PRDTS: Shortening & Solid Edible Fats
FOOD PRDTS: Soup Mixes
FOOD PRDTS: Soup Mixes, Dried
FOOD PRDTS: Soybean Oil, Deodorized
FOOD PRDTS: Soybean Powder
FOOD PRDTS: Soybean Protein Concentrates & Isolates
FOOD PRDTS: Spices, Including Ground
FOOD PRDTS: Starch, Indl
FOOD PRDTS: Starches
FOOD PRDTS: Sugar
FOOD PRDTS: Sugar Syrup From Sugar Beets
FOOD PRDTS: Sugar, Beet
FOOD PRDTS: Sugar, Cane
FOOD PRDTS: Sugar, Granulated Cane, Purchd Raw Sugar/Syrup
FOOD PRDTS: Sugar, Ground
FOOD PRDTS: Sugar, Liquid Cane Prdts, Exc Refined
FOOD PRDTS: Sugar, Maple, Indl
FOOD PRDTS: Syrup, Pancake, Blended & Mixed
FOOD PRDTS: Syrups
FOOD PRDTS: Tea
FOOD PRDTS: Tortilla Chips
FOOD PRDTS: Tortillas
FOOD PRDTS: Turkey, Processed, NEC
FOOD PRDTS: Variety Meats, Poultry
FOOD PRDTS: Vegetable Oil Mills, NEC
FOOD PRDTS: Vegetable Oil, Refined, Exc Corn
FOOD PRDTS: Vegetable Shortenings, Exc Corn Oil
FOOD PRDTS: Vegetables, Dehydrated Or Dried
FOOD PRDTS: Vegetables, Dried or Dehydrated Exc Freeze-Dried
FOOD PRDTS: Vinegar
FOOD PRDTS: Wheat Flour
FOOD PRDTS: Wheat gluten
FOOD PRDTS: Yeast
FOOD PRODUCTS MACHINERY
FOOD STORES: Delicatessen
FOOD STORES: Grocery, Chain
FOOD STORES: Grocery, Independent
FOOD STORES: Supermarkets
FOOD STORES: Supermarkets, Chain
FOOD WARMING EQPT: Commercial
FOOTWEAR, WHOLESALE: Shoe Access
FOOTWEAR, WHOLESALE: Shoes
FOOTWEAR: Cut Stock
FORGINGS
FORGINGS: Aircraft, Ferrous
FORGINGS: Anchors
FORGINGS: Armor Plate, Iron Or Steel
FORGINGS: Automotive & Internal Combustion Engine
FORGINGS: Bearing & Bearing Race, Nonferrous
FORGINGS: Construction Or Mining Eqpt, Ferrous
FORGINGS: Engine Or Turbine, Nonferrous
FORGINGS: Gear & Chain
FORGINGS: Iron & Steel
FORGINGS: Machinery, Ferrous
FORGINGS: Nonferrous
FORGINGS: Nuclear Power Plant, Ferrous
FORMS: Concrete, Sheet Metal
FOUNDRIES: Aluminum
FOUNDRIES: Brass, Bronze & Copper
FOUNDRIES: Gray & Ductile Iron
FOUNDRIES: Iron
FOUNDRIES: Nonferrous
FOUNDRIES: Steel

FOUNDRY MACHINERY & EQPT
FOUNTAIN SUPPLIES WHOLESALERS
FOUNTAINS: Concrete
FRACTIONATION PRDTS OF CRUDE PETROLEUM, HYDROCARBONS, NEC
FRAMES & FRAMING WHOLESALE
FRANCHISES, SELLING OR LICENSING
FREEZERS: Household
FREIGHT FORWARDING ARRANGEMENTS
FREIGHT FORWARDING ARRANGEMENTS: Domestic
FREIGHT TRANSPORTATION ARRANGEMENTS
FRICTION MATERIAL, MADE FROM POWDERED METAL
FRUIT & VEGETABLE MARKETS
FRUIT STANDS OR MARKETS
FRUITS & VEGETABLES WHOLESALERS: Fresh
FRUITS: Artificial & Preserved
FUEL ADDITIVES
FUEL BRIQUETTES OR BOULETS, MADE WITH PETROLEUM BINDER
FUEL DEALERS: Wood
FUEL OIL DEALERS
FUEL TREATING
FUELS: Diesel
FUELS: Ethanol
FUELS: Gas, Liquefied
FUELS: Jet
FULLER'S EARTH MINING
FUND RAISING ORGANIZATION, NON-FEE BASIS
FUNERAL HOME
FUNERAL HOMES & SVCS
FUNGICIDES OR HERBICIDES
FURNACE CASINGS: Sheet Metal
FURNACES & OVENS: Fuel-Fired
FURNACES & OVENS: Indl
FURNITURE & CABINET STORES: Cabinets, Custom Work
FURNITURE & CABINET STORES: Custom
FURNITURE & FIXTURES Factory
FURNITURE PARTS: Metal
FURNITURE REFINISHING SVCS
FURNITURE REPAIR & MAINTENANCE SVCS
FURNITURE STOCK & PARTS: Carvings, Wood
FURNITURE STOCK & PARTS: Dimension Stock, Hardwood
FURNITURE STOCK & PARTS: Frames, Upholstered Furniture, Wood
FURNITURE STOCK & PARTS: Hardwood
FURNITURE STORES
FURNITURE STORES: Cabinets, Kitchen, Exc Custom Made
FURNITURE STORES: Custom Made, Exc Cabinets
FURNITURE STORES: Office
FURNITURE STORES: Outdoor & Garden
FURNITURE STORES: Unfinished
FURNITURE UPHOLSTERY REPAIR SVCS
FURNITURE WHOLESALERS
FURNITURE, BARBER & BEAUTY SHOP
FURNITURE, GARDEN: Concrete
FURNITURE, HOUSEHOLD: Wholesalers
FURNITURE, MATTRESSES: Wholesalers
FURNITURE, OFFICE: Wholesalers
FURNITURE, OUTDOOR & LAWN: Wholesalers
FURNITURE, PUBLIC BUILDING: Wholesalers
FURNITURE, WHOLESALE: Bar
FURNITURE, WHOLESALE: Beds & Bedding
FURNITURE, WHOLESALE: Chairs
FURNITURE, WHOLESALE: Lockers
FURNITURE, WHOLESALE: Restaurant, NEC
FURNITURE: Bar furniture
FURNITURE: Bed Frames & Headboards, Wood
FURNITURE: Bedroom, Wood
FURNITURE: Beds, Household, Incl Folding & Cabinet, Metal
FURNITURE: Bedsprings, Assembled
FURNITURE: Bookcases & Stereo Cabinets, Metal
FURNITURE: Bookcases, Office, Wood
FURNITURE: Box Springs, Assembled
FURNITURE: Cabinets & Filing Drawers, Office, Exc Wood
FURNITURE: Cabinets & Vanities, Medicine, Metal
FURNITURE: Cafeteria
FURNITURE: Chairs, Household Upholstered
FURNITURE: Chairs, Household Wood
FURNITURE: Chairs, Office Exc Wood
FURNITURE: Chairs, Office Wood
FURNITURE: Chests, Cedar
FURNITURE: China Closets
FURNITURE: Church
FURNITURE: Church, Cut Stone
FURNITURE: Coffee Tables, Wood

FURNITURE: Console Tables, Wood
FURNITURE: Desks & Tables, Office, Exc Wood
FURNITURE: Desks, Household, Wood
FURNITURE: Desks, Metal
FURNITURE: Desks, Wood
FURNITURE: Fiberglass & Plastic
FURNITURE: Foundations & Platforms
FURNITURE: Garden, Exc Wood, Metal, Stone Or Concrete
FURNITURE: Hammocks, Metal Or Fabric & Metal Combined
FURNITURE: Hospital
FURNITURE: Household, Metal
FURNITURE: Household, NEC
FURNITURE: Household, Novelty, Metal
FURNITURE: Household, Upholstered On Metal Frames
FURNITURE: Household, Upholstered, Exc Wood Or Metal
FURNITURE: Household, Wood
FURNITURE: Hydraulic Barber & Beauty Shop Chairs
FURNITURE: Institutional, Exc Wood
FURNITURE: Juvenile, Wood
FURNITURE: Juvenile, Wood
FURNITURE: Kitchen & Dining Room
FURNITURE: Kitchen & Dining Room, Metal
FURNITURE: Laboratory
FURNITURE: Lawn & Garden, Except Wood & Metal
FURNITURE: Lawn, Exc Wood, Metal, Stone Or Concrete
FURNITURE: Lawn, Metal
FURNITURE: Lawn, Wood
FURNITURE: Library
FURNITURE: Living Room, Upholstered On Wood Frames
FURNITURE: Mattresses & Foundations
FURNITURE: Mattresses, Box & Bedsprings
FURNITURE: Mattresses, Innerspring Or Box Spring
FURNITURE: NEC
FURNITURE: Novelty, Wood
FURNITURE: Office, Exc Wood
FURNITURE: Office, Wood
FURNITURE: Outdoor, Wood
FURNITURE: Picnic Tables Or Benches, Park
FURNITURE: Porch & Swings, Wood
FURNITURE: Rattan
FURNITURE: Restaurant
FURNITURE: School
FURNITURE: Sleep
FURNITURE: Stadium
FURNITURE: Stools With Casters, Metal, Exc Home Or Office
FURNITURE: Storage Chests, Household, Wood
FURNITURE: Table Tops, Marble
FURNITURE: Tables & Table Tops, Wood
FURNITURE: Tables, Household, Metal
FURNITURE: Tables, Office, Exc Wood
FURNITURE: Tables, Office, Wood
FURNITURE: Television, Wood
FURNITURE: Unfinished, Wood
FURNITURE: Upholstered
FUSES & FUSE EQPT
FUSES: Electric
Furs

# G

GAMBLING: Lotteries
GAMES & TOYS: Air Rifles
GAMES & TOYS: Banks
GAMES & TOYS: Blocks
GAMES & TOYS: Board Games, Children's & Adults'
GAMES & TOYS: Cars, Play, Children's Vehicles
GAMES & TOYS: Child Restraint Seats, Automotive
GAMES & TOYS: Craft & Hobby Kits & Sets
GAMES & TOYS: Darts & Dart Games
GAMES & TOYS: Doll Carriages & Carts
GAMES & TOYS: Doll Clothing
GAMES & TOYS: Engines, Miniature
GAMES & TOYS: Game Machines, Exc Coin-Operated
GAMES & TOYS: Kits, Science, Incl Microscopes/Chemistry Sets
GAMES & TOYS: Models, Airplane, Toy & Hobby
GAMES & TOYS: Models, Automobile & Truck, Toy & Hobby
GAMES & TOYS: Models, Boat & Ship, Toy & Hobby
GAMES & TOYS: Models, Railroad, Toy & Hobby
GAMES & TOYS: Puzzles
GAMES & TOYS: Rocking Horses
GAMES & TOYS: Sleds, Children's
GAMES & TOYS: Strollers, Baby, Vehicle
GAMES & TOYS: Structural Toy Sets
GAMES & TOYS: Toy Guns
GAMES & TOYS: Trains & Eqpt, Electric & Mechanical

# PRODUCT INDEX

GAMES & TOYS: Wagons, Coaster, Express & Play, Children's
GARAGE DOOR REPAIR SVCS
GARBAGE CONTAINERS: Plastic
GARBAGE DISPOSERS & COMPACTORS: Commercial
GAS & HYDROCARBON LIQUEFACTION FROM COAL
GAS & OIL FIELD EXPLORATION SVCS
GAS & OIL FIELD SVCS, NEC
GAS FIELD MACHINERY & EQPT
GAS PROCESSING SVC
GAS PRODUCTION & DISTRIBUTION: Mixed Natural & Manufactured
GAS STATIONS
GAS: Refinery
GASES & LIQUIFIED PETROLEUM GASES
GASES: Acetylene
GASES: Carbon Dioxide
GASES: Flourinated Hydrocarbon
GASES: Helium
GASES: Hydrogen
GASES: Indl
GASES: Neon
GASES: Nitrogen
GASES: Oxygen
GASKET MATERIALS
GASKETS
GASKETS & SEALING DEVICES
GASOLINE FILLING STATIONS
GASTROINTESTINAL OR GENITOURINARY SYSTEM DRUGS
GATES: Dam, Metal Plate
GATES: Ornamental Metal
GAUGES
GEARS
GEARS & GEAR UNITS: Reduction, Exc Auto
GEARS: Power Transmission, Exc Auto
GELATIN
GEM STONES MINING, NEC: Natural
GEMSTONE & INDL DIAMOND MINING SVCS
GENEALOGICAL INVESTIGATION SVCS
GENERAL & INDUSTRIAL LOAN INSTITUTIONS
GENERAL COUNSELING SVCS
GENERAL MERCHANDISE, NONDURABLE, WHOLESALE
GENERATING APPARATUS & PARTS: Electrical
GENERATION EQPT: Electronic
GENERATOR REPAIR SVCS
GENERATORS SETS: Motor, Automotive
GENERATORS: Automotive & Aircraft
GENERATORS: Electric
GENERATORS: Storage Battery Chargers
GENERATORS: Vehicles, Gas-Electric Or Oil-Electric
GERIATRIC SOCIAL SVCS
GIFT SHOP
GIFT, NOVELTY & SOUVENIR STORES: Party Favors
GIFT, NOVELTY & SOUVENIR STORES: Trading Cards, Sports
GIFTS & NOVELTIES: Wholesalers
GIFTWARE: Brass
GLACE, FOR GLAZING FOOD
GLASS FABRICATORS
GLASS PRDTS, FROM PURCHASED GLASS: Art
GLASS PRDTS, FROM PURCHASED GLASS: Glassware
GLASS PRDTS, FROM PURCHASED GLASS: Glassware, Indl
GLASS PRDTS, FROM PURCHASED GLASS: Insulating
GLASS PRDTS, FROM PURCHASED GLASS: Mirrored
GLASS PRDTS, FROM PURCHASED GLASS: Mirrors, Framed
GLASS PRDTS, FROM PURCHASED GLASS: Novelties, Fruit, Etc
GLASS PRDTS, FROM PURCHASED GLASS: Sheet, Bent
GLASS PRDTS, FROM PURCHASED GLASS: Windshields
GLASS PRDTS, PRESSED OR BLOWN: Blocks & Bricks
GLASS PRDTS, PRESSED OR BLOWN: Bulbs, Electric Lights
GLASS PRDTS, PRESSED OR BLOWN: Glassware, Art Or Decorative
GLASS PRDTS, PRESSED OR BLOWN: Glassware, Novelty
GLASS PRDTS, PRESSED OR BLOWN: Optical
GLASS PRDTS, PRESSED OR BLOWN: Ornaments, Christmas Tree
GLASS PRDTS, PRESSED OR BLOWN: Scientific Glassware
GLASS PRDTS, PRESSED OR BLOWN: Tubing
GLASS PRDTS, PRESSED/BLOWN: Glassware, Art, Decor/Novelty
GLASS PRDTS, PURCHD GLASS: Furniture Top, Cut, Beveld/Polshd
GLASS PRDTS, PURCHSD GLASS: Ornamental, Cut, Engraved/D-cor
GLASS STORE: Leaded Or Stained
GLASS STORES
GLASS: Fiber
GLASS: Flat
GLASS: Indl Prdts
GLASS: Insulating
GLASS: Pressed & Blown, NEC
GLASS: Safety
GLASS: Stained
GLASS: Tempered
GLASSWARE STORES
GLASSWARE WHOLESALERS
GLASSWARE: Cut & Engraved
GLASSWARE: Laboratory
GLASSWARE: Laboratory & Medical
GLOBAL POSITIONING SYSTEMS & EQPT
GLOVES & MITTENS DYEING & FINISHING
GLOVES: Fabric
GLOVES: Leather
GLOVES: Leather, Work
GLOVES: Plastic
GLOVES: Safety
GLOVES: Work
GLOVES: Woven Or Knit, From Purchased Materials
GLUE
GO-CART DEALERS
GOLD ORE MINING
GOLD ORES
GOLF CARTS: Powered
GOLF CLUB & EQPT REPAIR SVCS
GOLF DRIVING RANGES
GOLF EQPT
GOLF GOODS & EQPT
GOURMET FOOD STORES
GOVERNMENT, EXECUTIVE OFFICES: Local
GOVERNMENT, EXECUTIVE OFFICES: Mayors'
GOVERNMENT, GENERAL: Administration
GOVERNORS: Diesel Engine, Pump
GRADING SVCS
GRAIN & FIELD BEANS WHOLESALERS
GRANITE: Crushed & Broken
GRANITE: Cut & Shaped
GRANITE: Dimension
GRANITE: Dimension
GRAPHIC ARTS & RELATED DESIGN SVCS
GRAPHIC LAYOUT SVCS: Printed Circuitry
GRATINGS: Open Steel Flooring
GRATINGS: Tread, Fabricated Metal
GRAVE MARKERS: Concrete
GRAVEL & PEBBLE MINING
GRAVEL MINING
GREASES & INEDIBLE FATS, RENDERED
GREETING CARD PAINTING BY HAND
GREETING CARD SHOPS
GREETING CARDS WHOLESALERS
GRILLES & REGISTERS: Ornamental Metal Work
GRINDING SVC: Precision, Commercial Or Indl
GRINDING SVCS: Ophthalmic Lens, Exc Prescription
GRINDSTONES: Artificial
GRIPS OR HANDLES: Rubber
GROCERIES WHOLESALERS, NEC
GROCERIES, GENERAL LINE WHOLESALERS
GROMMETS: Rubber
GROUTING EQPT: Concrete
GUARD SVCS
GUARDS: Machine, Sheet Metal
GUIDED MISSILES & SPACE VEHICLES: Research & Development
GUIDED MISSILES/SPACE VEHICLE PARTS/AUX EQPT: Research/Devel
GUM & WOOD CHEMICALS
GUN PARTS MADE TO INDIVIDUAL ORDER
GUN STOCKS: Wood
GUNSMITHS
GUTTERS
GUTTERS: Sheet Metal
GYPSUM PRDTS

## H

HAIR & HAIR BASED PRDTS
HAIR ACCESS WHOLESALERS
HAIR ACCESS: Rubber
HAIR CARE PRDTS
HAIR CURLERS: Beauty Shop
HAIR DRESSING, FOR THE TRADE
HAIR REPLACEMENT & WEAVING SVCS
HAIR STYLIST: Men
HAMPERS: Solid Fiber, Made From Purchased Materials
HAND TOOLS, NEC: Wholesalers
HANDBAG STORES
HANDBAGS
HANDBAGS: Women's
HANDLES: Brush Or Tool, Plastic
HANDLES: Wood
HANGERS: Garment, Plastic
HANGERS: Garment, Wire
HARD RUBBER PRDTS, NEC
HARDWARE
HARDWARE & BUILDING PRDTS: Plastic
HARDWARE & EQPT: Stage, Exc Lighting
HARDWARE STORES
HARDWARE STORES: Builders'
HARDWARE STORES: Chainsaws
HARDWARE STORES: Door Locks & Lock Sets
HARDWARE STORES: Pumps & Pumping Eqpt
HARDWARE STORES: Snowblowers
HARDWARE STORES: Tools
HARDWARE STORES: Tools, Hand
HARDWARE STORES: Tools, Power
HARDWARE WHOLESALERS
HARDWARE, WHOLESALE: Bolts
HARDWARE, WHOLESALE: Builders', NEC
HARDWARE, WHOLESALE: Casters & Glides
HARDWARE, WHOLESALE: Chains
HARDWARE, WHOLESALE: Furniture, NEC
HARDWARE, WHOLESALE: Nuts
HARDWARE, WHOLESALE: Power Tools & Access
HARDWARE, WHOLESALE: Screws
HARDWARE, WHOLESALE: Security Devices, Locks
HARDWARE, WHOLESALE: Staples
HARDWARE: Builders'
HARDWARE: Cabinet
HARDWARE: Casket
HARDWARE: Door Opening & Closing Devices, Exc Electrical
HARDWARE: Furniture
HARDWARE: Furniture, Builders' & Other Household
HARDWARE: Luggage
HARDWARE: Piano
HARDWARE: Plastic
HARDWARE: Rubber
HARNESS ASSEMBLIES: Cable & Wire
HARNESS WIRING SETS: Internal Combustion Engines
HARNESSES, HALTERS, SADDLERY & STRAPS
HEADPHONES: Radio
HEALTH & ALLIED SERVICES, NEC
HEALTH & WELFARE COUNCIL
HEALTH AIDS: Exercise Eqpt
HEALTH AIDS: Vaporizers
HEALTH FOOD & SUPPLEMENT STORES
HEALTH SCREENING SVCS
HEARING AIDS
HEARING TESTING SVCS
HEAT EMISSION OPERATING APPARATUS
HEAT EXCHANGERS: After Or Inter Coolers Or Condensers, Etc
HEAT TREATING SALTS
HEAT TREATING: Metal
HEATERS: Induction & Dielectric
HEATERS: Room & Wall, Including Radiators
HEATERS: Space, Exc Electric
HEATERS: Swimming Pool, Electric
HEATING & AIR CONDITIONING EQPT & SPLYS WHOLESALERS
HEATING & AIR CONDITIONING UNITS, COMBINATION
HEATING EQPT & SPLYS
HEATING EQPT: Complete
HEATING EQPT: Induction
HEATING PADS, ELECTRIC
HEATING UNITS & DEVICES: Indl, Electric
HELICOPTERS
HELMETS: Athletic
HELP SUPPLY SERVICES
HIGH ENERGY PARTICLE PHYSICS EQPT
HIGHWAY & STREET MAINTENANCE SVCS
HITCHES: Trailer
HOBBY & CRAFT SPLY STORES

# PRODUCT INDEX

HOBBY SUPPLIES, WHOLESALE
HOBBY, TOY & GAME STORES: Arts & Crafts & Splys
HOBBY, TOY & GAME STORES: Children's Toys & Games, Exc Dolls
HOBBY, TOY & GAME STORES: Dolls & Access
HOBBY, TOY & GAME STORES: Hobbies, NEC
HOISTING SLINGS
HOISTS
HOISTS: Mine
HOLDERS, PAPER TOWEL, GROCERY BAG, ETC: Plastic
HOLDERS: Gas, Metal Plate
HOLDING COMPANIES: Banks
HOLDING COMPANIES: Investment, Exc Banks
HOLDING COMPANIES: Personal, Exc Banks
HOME DELIVERY NEWSPAPER ROUTES
HOME ENTERTAINMENT EQPT: Electronic, NEC
HOME ENTERTAINMENT REPAIR SVCS
HOME FOR THE MENTALLY RETARDED
HOME FURNISHINGS WHOLESALERS
HOME IMPROVEMENT & RENOVATION CONTRACTOR AGENCY
HOMEFURNISHING STORE: Bedding, Sheet, Blanket,Spread/Pillow
HOMEFURNISHING STORES: Beddings & Linens
HOMEFURNISHING STORES: Brooms
HOMEFURNISHING STORES: Lighting Fixtures
HOMEFURNISHING STORES: Mirrors
HOMEFURNISHING STORES: Pictures, Wall
HOMEFURNISHING STORES: Pottery
HOMEFURNISHING STORES: Venetian Blinds
HOMEFURNISHING STORES: Wicker, Rattan, Or Reed
HOMEFURNISHING STORES: Window Furnishings
HOMEFURNISHING STORES: Window Shades, NEC
HOMEFURNISHINGS & SPLYS, WHOLESALE: Decorative
HOMEFURNISHINGS, WHOLESALE: Aluminumware
HOMEFURNISHINGS, WHOLESALE: Blinds, Vertical
HOMEFURNISHINGS, WHOLESALE: Carpets
HOMEFURNISHINGS, WHOLESALE: Curtains
HOMEFURNISHINGS, WHOLESALE: Draperies
HOMEFURNISHINGS, WHOLESALE: Fireplace Eqpt & Access
HOMEFURNISHINGS, WHOLESALE: Floor Cushion & Padding
HOMEFURNISHINGS, WHOLESALE: Kitchenware
HOMEFURNISHINGS, WHOLESALE: Linens, Table
HOMEFURNISHINGS, WHOLESALE: Mirrors/Pictures, Framed/Unframd
HOMEFURNISHINGS, WHOLESALE: Window Covering Parts & Access
HOMEFURNISHINGS, WHOLESALE: Wood Flooring
HOMES, MODULAR: Wooden
HOMES: Log Cabins
HONEYCOMB CORE & BOARD: Made From Purchased Materials
HOODS: Range, Sheet Metal
HOOKS: Gate
HORNS: Marine, Electric
HOSE: Air Line Or Air Brake, Rubber Or Rubberized Fabric
HOSE: Automobile, Plastic
HOSE: Cotton Fabric, Rubber Lined
HOSE: Flexible Metal
HOSE: Heater, Plastic
HOSE: Plastic
HOSE: Rubber
HOSES & BELTING: Rubber & Plastic
HOSPITAL EQPT REPAIR SVCS
HOTEL & MOTEL RESERVATION SVCS
HOTELS & MOTELS
HOUSEHOLD APPLIANCE PARTS: Wholesalers
HOUSEHOLD APPLIANCE STORES: Electric
HOUSEHOLD APPLIANCE STORES: Electric Household Appliance, Sm
HOUSEHOLD APPLIANCE STORES: Electric Household, Major
HOUSEHOLD ARTICLES, EXC FURNITURE: Cut Stone
HOUSEHOLD ARTICLES, EXC KITCHEN: Pottery
HOUSEHOLD FURNISHINGS, NEC
HOUSEWARE STORES
HOUSEWARES, ELECTRIC, EXC COOKING APPLIANCES & UTENSILS
HOUSEWARES, ELECTRIC: Air Purifiers, Portable
HOUSEWARES, ELECTRIC: Appliances, Personal
HOUSEWARES, ELECTRIC: Bedcoverings
HOUSEWARES, ELECTRIC: Cooking Appliances
HOUSEWARES, ELECTRIC: Dryers, Hand & Face
HOUSEWARES, ELECTRIC: Fans, Desk
HOUSEWARES, ELECTRIC: Fans, Exhaust & Ventilating
HOUSEWARES, ELECTRIC: Heaters, Immersion
HOUSEWARES, ELECTRIC: Heaters, Tape
HOUSEWARES, ELECTRIC: Heating Units, Electric Appliances
HOUSEWARES, ELECTRIC: Humidifiers, Household
HOUSEWARES, ELECTRIC: Irons, Household
HOUSEWARES, ELECTRIC: Lighters, Cigarette
HOUSEWARES, ELECTRIC: Massage Machines, Exc Beauty/Barber
HOUSEWARES, ELECTRIC: Ovens, Portable
HOUSEWARES, ELECTRIC: Radiators
HOUSEWARES, ELECTRIC: Shoe Polishers
HOUSEWARES, ELECTRIC: Toasters
HOUSEWARES: Bowls, Wood
HOUSEWARES: Dishes, China
HOUSEWARES: Dishes, Plastic
HOUSEWARES: Household & Commercial, Vitreous China
HOUSEWARES: Kettles & Skillets, Cast Iron
HOUSEWARES: Pots & Pans, Glass
HOUSING COMPONENTS: Prefabricated, Concrete
HOUSINGS: Business Machine, Sheet Metal
HOUSINGS: Motor
HOUSINGS: Pressure
HUB CAPS: Automobile, Stamped Metal
HUMIDIFIERS & DEHUMIDIFIERS
HUMIDIFYING EQPT, EXC PORTABLE
HYDRAULIC EQPT REPAIR SVC
HYDRAULIC FLUIDS: Synthetic Based
HYDROPONIC EQPT
Hard Rubber & Molded Rubber Prdts

## I

ICE
ICE CREAM & ICES WHOLESALERS
ICE WHOLESALERS
ICE: Dry
IDENTIFICATION PLATES
IDENTIFICATION TAGS, EXC PAPER
IGNEOUS ROCK: Crushed & Broken
IGNITION APPARATUS & DISTRIBUTORS
IGNITION SYSTEMS: Internal Combustion Engine
INCINERATORS
INDL & PERSONAL SVC PAPER WHOLESALERS
INDL & PERSONAL SVC PAPER, WHOL: Bags, Paper/Disp Plastic
INDL & PERSONAL SVC PAPER, WHOL: Boxes, Corrugtd/Solid Fiber
INDL & PERSONAL SVC PAPER, WHOL: Boxes, Paperbrd/Plastic
INDL & PERSONAL SVC PAPER, WHOL: Container, Paper/Plastic
INDL & PERSONAL SVC PAPER, WHOL: Cups, Disp, Plastic/Paper
INDL & PERSONAL SVC PAPER, WHOL: Paper, Wrap/Coarse/Prdts
INDL & PERSONAL SVC PAPER, WHOLESALE: Boxes & Containers
INDL & PERSONAL SVC PAPER, WHOLESALE: Paperboard & Prdts
INDL & PERSONAL SVC PAPER, WHOLESALE: Press Sensitive Tape
INDL & PERSONAL SVC PAPER, WHOLESALE: Shipping Splys
INDL CONTRACTORS: Exhibit Construction
INDL DIAMONDS WHOLESALERS
INDL EQPT SVCS
INDL GASES WHOLESALERS
INDL MACHINERY & EQPT WHOLESALERS
INDL MACHINERY REPAIR & MAINTENANCE
INDL PATTERNS: Foundry Cores
INDL PATTERNS: Foundry Patternmaking
INDL PROCESS INSTR: Transmit, Process Variables
INDL PROCESS INSTRUMENTS: Analyzers
INDL PROCESS INSTRUMENTS: Boiler Controls, Power & Marine
INDL PROCESS INSTRUMENTS: Chromatographs
INDL PROCESS INSTRUMENTS: Control
INDL PROCESS INSTRUMENTS: Controllers, Process Variables
INDL PROCESS INSTRUMENTS: Data Loggers
INDL PROCESS INSTRUMENTS: Digital Display, Process Variables
INDL PROCESS INSTRUMENTS: Draft Gauges
INDL PROCESS INSTRUMENTS: Elements, Primary
INDL PROCESS INSTRUMENTS: Indl Flow & Measuring
INDL PROCESS INSTRUMENTS: Level & Bulk Measuring
INDL PROCESS INSTRUMENTS: Temperature
INDL PROCESS INSTRUMENTS: Water Quality Monitoring/Cntrl Sys
INDL SALTS WHOLESALERS
INDL SPLYS WHOLESALERS
INDL SPLYS, WHOL: Fasteners, Incl Nuts, Bolts, Screws, Etc
INDL SPLYS, WHOLESALE: Abrasives
INDL SPLYS, WHOLESALE: Adhesives, Tape & Plasters
INDL SPLYS, WHOLESALE: Bearings
INDL SPLYS, WHOLESALE: Bins & Containers, Storage
INDL SPLYS, WHOLESALE: Cordage
INDL SPLYS, WHOLESALE: Drums, New Or Reconditioned
INDL SPLYS, WHOLESALE: Fasteners & Fastening Eqpt
INDL SPLYS, WHOLESALE: Filters, Indl
INDL SPLYS, WHOLESALE: Gaskets
INDL SPLYS, WHOLESALE: Gaskets & Seals
INDL SPLYS, WHOLESALE: Gears
INDL SPLYS, WHOLESALE: Pipeline Wrappings, Anti-Corrosive
INDL SPLYS, WHOLESALE: Plastic Bottles
INDL SPLYS, WHOLESALE: Power Transmission, Eqpt & Apparatus
INDL SPLYS, WHOLESALE: Rubber Goods, Mechanical
INDL SPLYS, WHOLESALE: Seals
INDL SPLYS, WHOLESALE: Signmaker Eqpt & Splys
INDL SPLYS, WHOLESALE: Springs
INDL SPLYS, WHOLESALE: Staplers & Tackers
INDL SPLYS, WHOLESALE: Textile Printers' Splys
INDL SPLYS, WHOLESALE: Tools
INDL SPLYS, WHOLESALE: Tools, NEC
INDL SPLYS, WHOLESALE: Valves & Fittings
INDL SPLYS, WHOLESALE: Wheels
INDL TOOL GRINDING SVCS
INDUCTORS
INDUSTRIAL & COMMERCIAL EQPT INSPECTION SVCS
INERTIAL GUIDANCE SYSTEMS
INFRARED OBJECT DETECTION EQPT
INGOT, EXTRUSION: Extrusion ingot, aluminum: rolling mills
INGOTS: Steel
INK OR WRITING FLUIDS
INK: Gravure
INK: Letterpress Or Offset
INK: Lithographic
INK: Printing
INK: Screen process
INSECTICIDES
INSECTICIDES & PESTICIDES
INSPECTION & TESTING SVCS
INSTR, MEASURE & CONTROL: Gauge, Oil Pressure & Water Temp
INSTRUMENTS & METERS: Measuring, Electric
INSTRUMENTS, LAB: Spectroscopic/Optical Properties Measuring
INSTRUMENTS, LABORATORY: Analyzers, Thermal
INSTRUMENTS, LABORATORY: Blood Testing
INSTRUMENTS, LABORATORY: Infrared Analytical
INSTRUMENTS, LABORATORY: Photomicrographic
INSTRUMENTS, LABORATORY: Ultraviolet Analytical
INSTRUMENTS, MEASURING & CNTRL: Gauges, Auto, Computer
INSTRUMENTS, MEASURING & CNTRL: Geophysical/Meteorological
INSTRUMENTS, MEASURING & CNTRL: Radiation & Testing, Nuclear
INSTRUMENTS, MEASURING & CNTRL: Testing, Abrasion, Etc
INSTRUMENTS, MEASURING & CNTRLG: Aircraft & Motor Vehicle
INSTRUMENTS, MEASURING & CNTRLG: Thermometers/Temp Sensors
INSTRUMENTS, MEASURING & CNTRLNG: Nuclear Instrument Modules
INSTRUMENTS, MEASURING & CNTRLNG: Wind Direction Indicators
INSTRUMENTS, MEASURING & CONTROLLING: Breathalyzers
INSTRUMENTS, MEASURING & CONTROLLING: Gas Detectors
INSTRUMENTS, MEASURING & CONTROLLING: Gauges, Rain
INSTRUMENTS, MEASURING & CONTROLLING: Surveying & Drafting

# PRODUCT INDEX

INSTRUMENTS, MEASURING & CONTROLLING: Transits, Surveyors'
INSTRUMENTS, MEASURING & CONTROLLING: Ultrasonic Testing
INSTRUMENTS, MEASURING & CONTROLLING: Weather Tracking
INSTRUMENTS, MEASURING/CNTRL: Gauging, Ultrasonic Thickness
INSTRUMENTS, MEASURING/CNTRL: Hydrometers, Exc Indl Process
INSTRUMENTS, MEASURING/CNTRLG: Fare Registers, St Cars/Buses
INSTRUMENTS, MEASURING/CNTRLG: Fire Detect Sys, Non-Electric
INSTRUMENTS, MEASURING/CNTRLNG: Med Diagnostic Sys, Nuclear
INSTRUMENTS, OPTICAL: Alignment & Display
INSTRUMENTS, OPTICAL: Elements & Assemblies, Exc Ophthalmic
INSTRUMENTS, OPTICAL: Lenses, All Types Exc Ophthalmic
INSTRUMENTS, OPTICAL: Magnifying, NEC
INSTRUMENTS, OPTICAL: Mirrors
INSTRUMENTS, OPTICAL: Test & Inspection
INSTRUMENTS, SURGICAL & MED: Cleaning Eqpt, Ultrasonic Med
INSTRUMENTS, SURGICAL & MEDI: Knife Blades/Handles, Surgical
INSTRUMENTS, SURGICAL & MEDICAL: Blood & Bone Work
INSTRUMENTS, SURGICAL & MEDICAL: Blood Pressure
INSTRUMENTS, SURGICAL & MEDICAL: Blood Transfusion
INSTRUMENTS, SURGICAL & MEDICAL: Cannulae
INSTRUMENTS, SURGICAL & MEDICAL: Hemodialysis
INSTRUMENTS, SURGICAL & MEDICAL: Inhalation Therapy
INSTRUMENTS, SURGICAL & MEDICAL: Lasers, Surgical
INSTRUMENTS, SURGICAL & MEDICAL: Muscle Exercise, Ophthalmic
INSTRUMENTS, SURGICAL & MEDICAL: Needles, Suture
INSTRUMENTS, SURGICAL & MEDICAL: Ophthalmic
INSTRUMENTS, SURGICAL & MEDICAL: Retinoscopes
INSTRUMENTS, SURGICAL & MEDICAL: Suction Therapy
INSTRUMENTS, SURGICAL/MED: Microsurgical, Exc Electromedical
INSTRUMENTS: Ammeters & Voltmeters, Automotive
INSTRUMENTS: Analytical
INSTRUMENTS: Combustion Control, Indl
INSTRUMENTS: Digital Panel Meters, Electricity Measuring
INSTRUMENTS: Elec Lab Stds, Resist, Inductance/Capacitance
INSTRUMENTS: Electrocardiographs
INSTRUMENTS: Electrolytic Conductivity, Indl
INSTRUMENTS: Electronic, Analog-Digital Converters
INSTRUMENTS: Endoscopic Eqpt, Electromedical
INSTRUMENTS: Eye Examination
INSTRUMENTS: Flow, Indl Process
INSTRUMENTS: Generators Tachometer
INSTRUMENTS: Humidity, Indl Process
INSTRUMENTS: Indicating, Electric
INSTRUMENTS: Indl Process Control
INSTRUMENTS: Infrared, Indl Process
INSTRUMENTS: Laser, Scientific & Engineering
INSTRUMENTS: Liquid Level, Indl Process
INSTRUMENTS: Measurement, Indl Process
INSTRUMENTS: Measuring & Controlling
INSTRUMENTS: Measuring Electricity
INSTRUMENTS: Measuring, Electrical Power
INSTRUMENTS: Measuring, Electrical Quantities
INSTRUMENTS: Medical & Surgical
INSTRUMENTS: Meters, Integrating Electricity
INSTRUMENTS: Multimeters
INSTRUMENTS: Oscillographs & Oscilloscopes
INSTRUMENTS: Potentiometric
INSTRUMENTS: Radio Frequency Measuring
INSTRUMENTS: Signal Generators & Averagers
INSTRUMENTS: Temperature Measurement, Indl
INSTRUMENTS: Test, Digital, Electronic & Electrical Circuits
INSTRUMENTS: Test, Electrical, Engine
INSTRUMENTS: Test, Electronic & Electric Measurement
INSTRUMENTS: Test, Electronic & Electrical Circuits
INSTRUMENTS: Testing, Semiconductor
INSTRUMENTS: Thermal Conductive, Indl
INSTRUMENTS: Time Code Generators
INSTRUMENTS: Transducers, Volts, Amperes, Watts, VARs & Freq
INSTRUMENTS: Vibration
INSTRUMENTS: Viscometer, Indl Process
INSULATION & CUSHIONING FOAM: Polystyrene
INSULATION MATERIALS WHOLESALERS
INSULATION: Felt
INSULATION: Fiberglass
INSULATORS & INSULATION MATERIALS: Electrical
INSURANCE CARRIERS: Life
INSURANCE PROFESSIONAL STANDARDS SVCS
INSURANCE: Agents, Brokers & Service
INTEGRATED CIRCUITS, SEMICONDUCTOR NETWORKS, ETC
INTERCOMMUNICATION EQPT REPAIR SVCS
INTERCOMMUNICATIONS SYSTEMS: Electric
INTERIOR DECORATING SVCS
INTERIOR DESIGN SVCS, NEC
INTERIOR DESIGNING SVCS
INTERMEDIATES Cyclic, Organic
INTRAVENOUS SOLUTIONS
INVENTORY COMPUTING SVCS
INVESTMENT ADVISORY SVCS
INVESTMENT CLUBS
INVESTMENT FIRM: General Brokerage
INVESTMENT FUNDS, NEC
INVESTMENT FUNDS: Open-Ended
INVESTORS, NEC
INVESTORS: Real Estate, Exc Property Operators
IRON & STEEL PRDTS: Hot-Rolled
IRON ORES
IRON OXIDES
IRON: Sponge
IRONING BOARDS
IRRADIATION EQPT: Nuclear
IRRIGATION EQPT WHOLESALERS

## J

JACKS: Hydraulic
JANITORIAL & CUSTODIAL SVCS
JANITORIAL EQPT & SPLYS WHOLESALERS
JARS: Plastic
JEWELERS' FINDINGS & MATERIALS
JEWELERS' FINDINGS & MATERIALS: Castings
JEWELRY & PRECIOUS STONES WHOLESALERS
JEWELRY APPAREL
JEWELRY FINDINGS & LAPIDARY WORK
JEWELRY REPAIR SVCS
JEWELRY STORES
JEWELRY STORES: Clocks
JEWELRY STORES: Precious Stones & Precious Metals
JEWELRY STORES: Silverware
JEWELRY STORES: Watches
JEWELRY, PREC METAL: Mountings, Pens, Lthr, Etc, Gold/Silver
JEWELRY, PRECIOUS METAL: Cases
JEWELRY, PRECIOUS METAL: Cigar & Cigarette Access
JEWELRY, PRECIOUS METAL: Medals, Precious Or Semi-precious
JEWELRY, PRECIOUS METAL: Mountings & Trimmings
JEWELRY, PRECIOUS METAL: Rings, Finger
JEWELRY, PRECIOUS METAL: Rosaries/Other Sm Religious Article
JEWELRY, PRECIOUS METAL: Settings & Mountings
JEWELRY, WHOLESALE
JEWELRY: Decorative, Fashion & Costume
JEWELRY: Precious Metal
JIGS & FIXTURES
JIGS: Welding Positioners
JOB PRINTING & NEWSPAPER PUBLISHING COMBINED
JOB TRAINING & VOCATIONAL REHABILITATION SVCS
JOINTS & COUPLINGS
JOINTS: Ball Except aircraft & Auto
JOINTS: Expansion
JOINTS: Swivel & Universal, Exc Aircraft & Auto
JOISTS: Long-Span Series, Open Web Steel

## K

KAOLIN MINING
KEYBOARDS: Computer Or Office Machine
KITCHEN CABINET STORES, EXC CUSTOM
KITCHEN CABINETS WHOLESALERS
KITCHEN TOOLS & UTENSILS WHOLESALERS
KITCHEN UTENSILS: Bakers' Eqpt, Wood
KITCHEN UTENSILS: Food Handling & Processing Prdts, Wood
KITCHENWARE STORES
KITCHENWARE: Plastic
KITS: Plastic
KNIVES: Agricultural Or Indl
KNURLING

## L

LABELS: Cotton, Printed
LABELS: Paper, Made From Purchased Materials
LABELS: Woven
LABORATORIES, TESTING: Metallurgical
LABORATORIES, TESTING: Product Testing
LABORATORIES, TESTING: Product Testing, Safety/Performance
LABORATORIES, TESTING: Radiation
LABORATORIES, TESTING: Seed
LABORATORIES, TESTING: Veterinary
LABORATORIES, TESTING: Welded Joint Radiographing
LABORATORIES: Biological
LABORATORIES: Biological Research
LABORATORIES: Biotechnology
LABORATORIES: Commercial Nonphysical Research
LABORATORIES: Dental
LABORATORIES: Dental, Artificial Teeth Production
LABORATORIES: Dental, Crown & Bridge Production
LABORATORIES: Dental, Denture Production
LABORATORIES: Electronic Research
LABORATORIES: Medical
LABORATORIES: Neurological
LABORATORIES: Noncommercial Research
LABORATORIES: Physical Research, Commercial
LABORATORIES: Testing
LABORATORIES: Testing
LABORATORIES: Urinalysis
LABORATORY APPARATUS & FURNITURE
LABORATORY APPARATUS & FURNITURE: Worktables
LABORATORY APPARATUS, EXC HEATING & MEASURING
LABORATORY APPARATUS: Bunsen Burners
LABORATORY APPARATUS: Calibration Tapes, Phy Testing Mach
LABORATORY APPARATUS: Calorimeters
LABORATORY APPARATUS: Evaporation
LABORATORY APPARATUS: Freezers
LABORATORY APPARATUS: Laser Beam Alignment Device
LABORATORY APPARATUS: Metal Periphery Dir Rdg Diameter Tape
LABORATORY APPARATUS: Sample Preparation Apparatus
LABORATORY APPARATUS: Shakers & Stirrers
LABORATORY CHEMICALS: Organic
LABORATORY EQPT, EXC MEDICAL: Wholesalers
LABORATORY EQPT: Clinical Instruments Exc Medical
LABORATORY EQPT: Incubators
LABORATORY EQPT: Measuring
LABORATORY EQPT: Sterilizers
LADDER & WORKSTAND COMBINATION ASSEMBLIES: Metal
LADDERS: Metal
LADDERS: Portable, Metal
LAMINATED PLASTICS: Plate, Sheet, Rod & Tubes
LAMINATING MATERIALS
LAMINATING SVCS
LAMP & LIGHT BULBS & TUBES
LAMP BULBS & TUBES, ELEC: Lead-In Wires, From Purchased Wire
LAMP BULBS & TUBES, ELECTRIC: Electric Light
LAMP BULBS & TUBES, ELECTRIC: For Specialized Applications
LAMP BULBS & TUBES, ELECTRIC: Light, Complete
LAMP BULBS & TUBES, ELECTRIC: Photoflash & Photoflood
LAMP BULBS & TUBES/PARTS, ELECTRIC: Generalized Applications
LAMP FRAMES: Wire
LAMP REPAIR & MOUNTING SVCS
LAMP SHADES: Metal
LAMP STORES
LAMPS: Boudoir, Residential
LAMPS: Incandescent, Filament
LAMPS: Table, Residential
LAMPS: Ultraviolet
LAND SUBDIVISION & DEVELOPMENT
LANTERNS
LAPIDARY WORK: Jewel Cut, Drill, Polish, Recut/Setting
LASER SYSTEMS & EQPT
LASERS: Welding, Drilling & Cutting Eqpt
LATH: Expanded Metal
LATHES
LAUNDRY & GARMENT SVCS, NEC: Diapers

# PRODUCT INDEX

LAUNDRY & GARMENT SVCS, NEC: Garment Making, Alter & Repair
LAUNDRY & GARMENT SVCS: Dressmaking, Matl Owned By Customer
LAUNDRY EQPT: Commercial
LAUNDRY EQPT: Household
LAWN & GARDEN EQPT
LAWN & GARDEN EQPT STORES
LAWN & GARDEN EQPT: Blowers & Vacuums
LAWN & GARDEN EQPT: Edgers
LAWN & GARDEN EQPT: Grass Catchers, Lawn Mower
LAWN & GARDEN EQPT: Lawnmowers, Residential, Hand Or Power
LAWN & GARDEN EQPT: Tractors & Eqpt
LAWN MOWER REPAIR SHOP
LEAD & ZINC
LEAD & ZINC
LEAD & ZINC ORES
LEAD ORE MINING
LEAD PENCILS & ART GOODS
LEASING & RENTAL SVCS: Computer Hardware, Exc Finance
LEASING & RENTAL SVCS: Cranes & Aerial Lift Eqpt
LEASING & RENTAL: Boats & Ships
LEASING & RENTAL: Computers & Eqpt
LEASING & RENTAL: Construction & Mining Eqpt
LEASING & RENTAL: Medical Machinery & Eqpt
LEASING & RENTAL: Mobile Home Sites
LEASING & RENTAL: Office Machines & Eqpt
LEASING & RENTAL: Trucks, Without Drivers
LEASING: Passenger Car
LEASING: Residential Buildings
LEASING: Shipping Container
LEATHER GOODS, EXC FOOTWEAR, GLOVES, LUGGAGE/BELTING, WHOL
LEATHER GOODS: Boxes
LEATHER GOODS: Cases
LEATHER GOODS: Embossed
LEATHER GOODS: Garments
LEATHER GOODS: Harnesses Or Harness Parts
LEATHER GOODS: Money Holders
LEATHER GOODS: NEC
LEATHER GOODS: Personal
LEATHER GOODS: Safety Belts
LEATHER GOODS: Sewing Cases
LEATHER GOODS: Wallets
LEATHER TANNING & FINISHING
LEATHER: Accessory Prdts
LEATHER: Artificial
LEATHER: Bag
LEATHER: Case
LEATHER: Rawhide
LEGAL & TAX SVCS
LEGAL COUNSEL & PROSECUTION: Attorney General's Office
LEGAL OFFICES & SVCS
LEGAL SVCS: Taxation Law
LENS COATING: Ophthalmic
LENSES: Plastic, Exc Optical
LETTERS: Cardboard, Die-Cut, Made From Purchased Materials
LICENSE TAGS: Automobile, Stamped Metal
LIGHTERS, CIGARETTE & CIGAR, WHOLESALE
LIGHTING EQPT: Flashlights
LIGHTING EQPT: Locomotive & Railroad Car Lights
LIGHTING EQPT: Motor Vehicle
LIGHTING EQPT: Motor Vehicle, Flasher Lights
LIGHTING EQPT: Motor Vehicle, NEC
LIGHTING EQPT: Motorcycle Lamps
LIGHTING EQPT: Outdoor
LIGHTING EQPT: Reflectors, Metal, For Lighting Eqpt
LIGHTING EQPT: Spotlights
LIGHTING FIXTURES WHOLESALERS
LIGHTING FIXTURES, NEC
LIGHTING FIXTURES: Airport
LIGHTING FIXTURES: Decorative Area
LIGHTING FIXTURES: Fluorescent, Commercial
LIGHTING FIXTURES: Gas
LIGHTING FIXTURES: Indl & Commercial
LIGHTING FIXTURES: Marine
LIGHTING FIXTURES: Motor Vehicle
LIGHTING FIXTURES: Ornamental, Commercial
LIGHTING FIXTURES: Public
LIGHTING FIXTURES: Residential
LIGHTING FIXTURES: Residential, Electric
LIGHTING FIXTURES: Street
LIME
LIMESTONE & MARBLE: Dimension
LIMESTONE: Crushed & Broken
LIMESTONE: Cut & Shaped
LIMESTONE: Dimension
LIMESTONE: Ground
LINEN SPLY SVC: Apron
LINENS: Napkins, Fabric & Nonwoven, From Purchased Materials
LINER BRICK OR PLATES: Sewer Or Tank Lining, Vitrified Clay
LINER STRIPS: Rubber
LINERS & COVERS: Fabric
LINERS & LINING
LININGS: Apparel, Made From Purchased Materials
LININGS: Safe & Vault, Metal
LIQUEFIED PETROLEUM GAS DEALERS
LIQUEFIED PETROLEUM GAS WHOLESALERS
LIQUID CRYSTAL DISPLAYS
LITHOGRAPHIC PLATES
LIVESTOCK WHOLESALERS, NEC
LOADS: Electronic
LOCK & KEY SVCS
LOCKS
LOCKS & LOCK SETS, WHOLESALE
LOCKS: Safe & Vault, Metal
LOCKSMITHS
LOCOMOTIVES & PARTS
LOG SPLITTERS
LOGGING
LOGGING CAMPS & CONTRACTORS
LOGGING: Stump Harvesting
LOGGING: Timber, Cut At Logging Camp
LOGGING: Wood Chips, Produced In The Field
LOOSELEAF BINDERS
LOOSELEAF BINDERS: Library
LOTIONS OR CREAMS: Face
LOUDSPEAKERS
LUBRICANTS: Corrosion Preventive
LUBRICATING EQPT: Indl
LUBRICATING OIL & GREASE WHOLESALERS
LUBRICATING SYSTEMS: Centralized
LUGGAGE & BRIEFCASES
LUGGAGE & LEATHER GOODS STORES
LUGGAGE WHOLESALERS
LUGGAGE: Traveling Bags
LUGGAGE: Wardrobe Bags
LUMBER & BLDG MATLS DEALER, RET: Garage Doors, Sell/Install
LUMBER & BLDG MTRLS DEALERS, RET: Closets, Interiors/Access
LUMBER & BLDG MTRLS DEALERS, RET: Doors, Storm, Wood/Metal
LUMBER & BLDG MTRLS DEALERS, RET: Planing Mill Prdts/Lumber
LUMBER & BLDG MTRLS DEALERS, RET: Windows, Storm, Wood/Metal
LUMBER & BUILDING MATERIAL DEALERS, RETAIL: Roofing Material
LUMBER & BUILDING MATERIALS DEALER, RET: Door & Window Prdts
LUMBER & BUILDING MATERIALS DEALER, RET: Masonry Matls/Splys
LUMBER & BUILDING MATERIALS DEALERS, RETAIL: Brick
LUMBER & BUILDING MATERIALS DEALERS, RETAIL: Cement
LUMBER & BUILDING MATERIALS DEALERS, RETAIL: Countertops
LUMBER & BUILDING MATERIALS DEALERS, RETAIL: Sand & Gravel
LUMBER & BUILDING MATERIALS DEALERS, RETAIL: Tile, Ceramic
LUMBER & BUILDING MATERIALS RET DEALERS: Millwork & Lumber
LUMBER & BUILDING MATLS DEALERS, RET: Screens, Door/Window
LUMBER & BUILDING MTRLS DEALERS, RET: Insulation Mtrl, Bldg
LUMBER: Flooring, Dressed, Softwood
LUMBER: Hardboard
LUMBER: Hardwood Dimension
LUMBER: Hardwood Dimension & Flooring Mills
LUMBER: Kiln Dried
LUMBER: Panels, Plywood, Softwood
LUMBER: Plywood, Hardwood
LUMBER: Plywood, Hardwood or Hardwood Faced
LUMBER: Plywood, Prefinished, Hardwood
LUMBER: Resawn, Small Dimension
LUMBER: Treated
LUMBER: Veneer, Hardwood

# M

MACHINE PARTS: Stamped Or Pressed Metal
MACHINE SHOPS
MACHINE TOOL ACCESS: Balancing Machines
MACHINE TOOL ACCESS: Boring Attachments
MACHINE TOOL ACCESS: Broaches
MACHINE TOOL ACCESS: Cams
MACHINE TOOL ACCESS: Cutting
MACHINE TOOL ACCESS: Diamond Cutting, For Turning, Etc
MACHINE TOOL ACCESS: Dresser, Abrasive Wheel Or Other
MACHINE TOOL ACCESS: Drill Bushings, Drilling Jig
MACHINE TOOL ACCESS: Drills
MACHINE TOOL ACCESS: Hopper Feed Devices
MACHINE TOOL ACCESS: Knives, Metalworking
MACHINE TOOL ACCESS: Machine Attachments & Access, Drilling
MACHINE TOOL ACCESS: Milling Machine Attachments
MACHINE TOOL ACCESS: Pushers
MACHINE TOOL ACCESS: Tool Holders
MACHINE TOOL ACCESS: Tools & Access
MACHINE TOOL ATTACHMENTS & ACCESS
MACHINE TOOLS & ACCESS
MACHINE TOOLS, METAL CUTTING: Brushing
MACHINE TOOLS, METAL CUTTING: Centering
MACHINE TOOLS, METAL CUTTING: Cutoff
MACHINE TOOLS, METAL CUTTING: Drilling
MACHINE TOOLS, METAL CUTTING: Drilling & Boring
MACHINE TOOLS, METAL CUTTING: Electrochemical Milling
MACHINE TOOLS, METAL CUTTING: Exotic, Including Explosive
MACHINE TOOLS, METAL CUTTING: Grind, Polish, Buff, Lapp
MACHINE TOOLS, METAL CUTTING: Home Workshop
MACHINE TOOLS, METAL CUTTING: Keysetting
MACHINE TOOLS, METAL CUTTING: Lathes
MACHINE TOOLS, METAL CUTTING: Milling, Chemical
MACHINE TOOLS, METAL CUTTING: Numerically Controlled
MACHINE TOOLS, METAL CUTTING: Pipe Cutting & Threading
MACHINE TOOLS, METAL CUTTING: Planers
MACHINE TOOLS, METAL CUTTING: Plasma Process
MACHINE TOOLS, METAL CUTTING: Screw & Thread
MACHINE TOOLS, METAL CUTTING: Tool Replacement & Rpr Parts
MACHINE TOOLS, METAL CUTTING: Vertical Turning & Boring
MACHINE TOOLS, METAL FORMING: Bending
MACHINE TOOLS, METAL FORMING: Container, Metal Incl Cans
MACHINE TOOLS, METAL FORMING: Crimping, Metal
MACHINE TOOLS, METAL FORMING: Die Casting & Extruding
MACHINE TOOLS, METAL FORMING: Electroforming
MACHINE TOOLS, METAL FORMING: Forming, Metal Deposit
MACHINE TOOLS, METAL FORMING: Headers
MACHINE TOOLS, METAL FORMING: High Energy Rate
MACHINE TOOLS, METAL FORMING: Magnetic Forming
MACHINE TOOLS, METAL FORMING: Marking
MACHINE TOOLS, METAL FORMING: Mechanical, Pneumatic Or Hyd
MACHINE TOOLS, METAL FORMING: Presses, Hyd & Pneumatic
MACHINE TOOLS, METAL FORMING: Pressing
MACHINE TOOLS, METAL FORMING: Rebuilt
MACHINE TOOLS, METAL FORMING: Robots, Pressing, Extrudg, Etc
MACHINE TOOLS, METAL FORMING: Spring Winding & Forming
MACHINE TOOLS: Metal Cutting
MACHINE TOOLS: Metal Forming
MACHINERY & EQPT FINANCE LEASING
MACHINERY & EQPT, AGRICULTURAL, WHOL: Farm Eqpt Parts/Splys
MACHINERY & EQPT, AGRICULTURAL, WHOLESALE: Agricultural, NEC
MACHINERY & EQPT, AGRICULTURAL, WHOLESALE: Dairy

# PRODUCT INDEX

MACHINERY & EQPT, AGRICULTURAL, WHOLESALE: Farm Implements
MACHINERY & EQPT, AGRICULTURAL, WHOLESALE: Landscaping Eqpt
MACHINERY & EQPT, AGRICULTURAL, WHOLESALE: Lawn
MACHINERY & EQPT, AGRICULTURAL, WHOLESALE: Lawn & Garden
MACHINERY & EQPT, AGRICULTURAL, WHOLESALE: Livestock Eqpt
MACHINERY & EQPT, AGRICULTURAL, WHOLESALE: Tractors
MACHINERY & EQPT, INDL, WHOL: Controlling Instruments/Access
MACHINERY & EQPT, INDL, WHOL: Environ Pollution Cntrl, Air
MACHINERY & EQPT, INDL, WHOLESALE: Chemical Process
MACHINERY & EQPT, INDL, WHOLESALE: Conveyor Systems
MACHINERY & EQPT, INDL, WHOLESALE: Cranes
MACHINERY & EQPT, INDL, WHOLESALE: Drilling Bits
MACHINERY & EQPT, INDL, WHOLESALE: Drilling, Exc Bits
MACHINERY & EQPT, INDL, WHOLESALE: Engines & Parts, Diesel
MACHINERY & EQPT, INDL, WHOLESALE: Engines, Gasoline
MACHINERY & EQPT, INDL, WHOLESALE: Engs & Parts, Air-Cooled
MACHINERY & EQPT, INDL, WHOLESALE: Engs/Transportation Eqpt
MACHINERY & EQPT, INDL, WHOLESALE: Food Manufacturing
MACHINERY & EQPT, INDL, WHOLESALE: Food Product Manufacturng
MACHINERY & EQPT, INDL, WHOLESALE: Fuel Injection Systems
MACHINERY & EQPT, INDL, WHOLESALE: Hoists
MACHINERY & EQPT, INDL, WHOLESALE: Hydraulic Systems
MACHINERY & EQPT, INDL, WHOLESALE: Indl Machine Parts
MACHINERY & EQPT, INDL, WHOLESALE: Instruments & Cntrl Eqpt
MACHINERY & EQPT, INDL, WHOLESALE: Lift Trucks & Parts
MACHINERY & EQPT, INDL, WHOLESALE: Machine Tools & Access
MACHINERY & EQPT, INDL, WHOLESALE: Machine Tools & Metalwork
MACHINERY & EQPT, INDL, WHOLESALE: Measure/Test, Electric
MACHINERY & EQPT, INDL, WHOLESALE: Metal Refining
MACHINERY & EQPT, INDL, WHOLESALE: Packaging
MACHINERY & EQPT, INDL, WHOLESALE: Paint Spray
MACHINERY & EQPT, INDL, WHOLESALE: Paper Manufacturing
MACHINERY & EQPT, INDL, WHOLESALE: Petroleum Industry
MACHINERY & EQPT, INDL, WHOLESALE: Plastic Prdts Machinery
MACHINERY & EQPT, INDL, WHOLESALE: Pneumatic Tools
MACHINERY & EQPT, INDL, WHOLESALE: Processing & Packaging
MACHINERY & EQPT, INDL, WHOLESALE: Recycling
MACHINERY & EQPT, INDL, WHOLESALE: Robots
MACHINERY & EQPT, INDL, WHOLESALE: Safety Eqpt
MACHINERY & EQPT, INDL, WHOLESALE: Sewing
MACHINERY & EQPT, INDL, WHOLESALE: Tapping Attachments
MACHINERY & EQPT, INDL, WHOLESALE: Tool & Die Makers
MACHINERY & EQPT, INDL, WHOLESALE: Water Pumps
MACHINERY & EQPT, INDL, WHOLESALE: Woodworking
MACHINERY & EQPT, WHOLESALE: Concrete Processing
MACHINERY & EQPT, WHOLESALE: Construction, General
MACHINERY & EQPT, WHOLESALE: Contractors Materials
MACHINERY & EQPT, WHOLESALE: Logging
MACHINERY & EQPT, WHOLESALE: Masonry
MACHINERY & EQPT, WHOLESALE: Oil Field Eqpt
MACHINERY & EQPT: Electroplating
MACHINERY & EQPT: Farm
MACHINERY & EQPT: Gas Producers, Generators/Other Rltd Eqpt
MACHINERY & EQPT: Liquid Automation
MACHINERY & EQPT: Metal Finishing, Plating Etc
MACHINERY & EQPT: Petroleum Refinery
MACHINERY & EQPT: Vibratory Parts Handling Eqpt
MACHINERY BASES
MACHINERY, CALCULATING: Adding
MACHINERY, COMMERCIAL LAUNDRY & Drycleaning: Ironers
MACHINERY, COMMERCIAL LAUNDRY: Extractors
MACHINERY, COMMERCIAL LAUNDRY: Washing, Incl Coin-Operated
MACHINERY, EQPT & SUPPLIES: Parking Facility
MACHINERY, FOOD PRDTS: Beverage
MACHINERY, FOOD PRDTS: Chocolate Processing
MACHINERY, FOOD PRDTS: Confectionery
MACHINERY, FOOD PRDTS: Cutting, Chopping, Grinding, Mixing
MACHINERY, FOOD PRDTS: Dies, Biscuit Cutting
MACHINERY, FOOD PRDTS: Food Processing, Smokers
MACHINERY, FOOD PRDTS: Grinders, Commercial
MACHINERY, FOOD PRDTS: Ovens, Bakery
MACHINERY, FOOD PRDTS: Packing House
MACHINERY, FOOD PRDTS: Processing, Fish & Shellfish
MACHINERY, FOOD PRDTS: Roasting, Coffee, Peanut, Etc.
MACHINERY, FOOD PRDTS: Sausage Stuffers
MACHINERY, LUBRICATION: Automatic
MACHINERY, MAILING: Canceling
MACHINERY, MAILING: Mailing
MACHINERY, MAILING: Postage Meters
MACHINERY, METALWORKING: Assembly, Including Robotic
MACHINERY, METALWORKING: Coil Winding, For Springs
MACHINERY, METALWORKING: Coilers, Metalworking
MACHINERY, METALWORKING: Coiling
MACHINERY, METALWORKING: Cutting & Slitting
MACHINERY, METALWORKING: Rotary Slitters, Metalworking
MACHINERY, OFFICE: Embossing, Store Or Office
MACHINERY, OFFICE: Paper Handling
MACHINERY, OFFICE: Perforators
MACHINERY, OFFICE: Shorthand
MACHINERY, OFFICE: Time Clocks & Time Recording Devices
MACHINERY, PACKAGING: Bread Wrapping
MACHINERY, PACKAGING: Canning, Food
MACHINERY, PACKAGING: Carton Packing
MACHINERY, PACKAGING: Packing & Wrapping
MACHINERY, PACKAGING: Vacuum
MACHINERY, PACKAGING: Wrapping
MACHINERY, PAPER INDUSTRY: Coating & Finishing
MACHINERY, PAPER INDUSTRY: Converting, Die Cutting & Stampng
MACHINERY, PAPER INDUSTRY: Cutting
MACHINERY, PAPER INDUSTRY: Paper Mill, Plating, Etc
MACHINERY, PAPER INDUSTRY: Pulp Mill
MACHINERY, PRINTING TRADE: Type, Lead, Steel, Brass, Etc
MACHINERY, PRINTING TRADES: Bookbinding Machinery
MACHINERY, PRINTING TRADES: Copy Holders
MACHINERY, PRINTING TRADES: Electrotyping
MACHINERY, PRINTING TRADES: Plates
MACHINERY, PRINTING TRADES: Presses, Envelope
MACHINERY, PRINTING TRADES: Presses, Gravure
MACHINERY, PRINTING TRADES: Printing Trade Parts & Attchts
MACHINERY, SERVICING: Coin-Operated, Exc Dry Clean & Laundry
MACHINERY, SEWING: Bag Seaming & Closing
MACHINERY, SEWING: Sewing & Hat & Zipper Making
MACHINERY, TEXTILE: Creels
MACHINERY, TEXTILE: Dyeing
MACHINERY, TEXTILE: Embroidery
MACHINERY, TEXTILE: Fiber & Yarn Preparation
MACHINERY, TEXTILE: Knot Tying
MACHINERY, TEXTILE: Printing
MACHINERY, TEXTILE: Silk Screens
MACHINERY, TEXTILE: Spinning
MACHINERY, TEXTILE: Yarn Texturizing
MACHINERY, WOODWORKING: Cabinet Makers'
MACHINERY, WOODWORKING: Furniture Makers
MACHINERY, WOODWORKING: Sanding, Exc Portable Floor Sanders
MACHINERY, WOODWORKING: Saws, Power, Bench & Table
MACHINERY/EQPT, INDL, WHOL: Cleaning, High Press, Sand/Steam
MACHINERY/EQPT, INDL, WHOL: Machinist Precision Measrng Tool
MACHINERY: Ammunition & Explosives Loading
MACHINERY: Assembly, Exc Metalworking
MACHINERY: Automobile Garage, Frame Straighteners
MACHINERY: Automotive Maintenance
MACHINERY: Automotive Related
MACHINERY: Banking
MACHINERY: Binding
MACHINERY: Blasting, Electrical
MACHINERY: Bottling & Canning
MACHINERY: Brewery & Malting
MACHINERY: Broom Making
MACHINERY: Cement Making
MACHINERY: Concrete Prdts
MACHINERY: Construction
MACHINERY: Cryogenic, Industrial
MACHINERY: Custom
MACHINERY: Deburring
MACHINERY: Die Casting
MACHINERY: Drill Presses
MACHINERY: Electrical Discharge Erosion
MACHINERY: Electronic Component Making
MACHINERY: Electronic Teaching Aids
MACHINERY: Engraving
MACHINERY: Extruding
MACHINERY: Folding
MACHINERY: Gear Cutting & Finishing
MACHINERY: General, Industrial, NEC
MACHINERY: Glassmaking
MACHINERY: Grinding
MACHINERY: Ice Cream
MACHINERY: Ice Making
MACHINERY: Industrial, NEC
MACHINERY: Kilns
MACHINERY: Knitting
MACHINERY: Labeling
MACHINERY: Lapping
MACHINERY: Marking, Metalworking
MACHINERY: Metalworking
MACHINERY: Milling
MACHINERY: Mining
MACHINERY: Optical Lens
MACHINERY: Ozone
MACHINERY: Packaging
MACHINERY: Paint Making
MACHINERY: Paper Industry Miscellaneous
MACHINERY: Pharmacuitical
MACHINERY: Photographic Reproduction
MACHINERY: Plastic Working
MACHINERY: Polishing & Buffing
MACHINERY: Printing Presses
MACHINERY: Recycling
MACHINERY: Riveting
MACHINERY: Road Construction & Maintenance
MACHINERY: Robots, Molding & Forming Plastics
MACHINERY: Rubber Working
MACHINERY: Saw & Sawing
MACHINERY: Semiconductor Manufacturing
MACHINERY: Separation Eqpt, Magnetic
MACHINERY: Service Industry, NEC
MACHINERY: Sheet Metal Working
MACHINERY: Sifting & Screening
MACHINERY: Snow Making
MACHINERY: Specialty
MACHINERY: Stone Working
MACHINERY: Textile
MACHINERY: Tire Shredding
MACHINERY: Tobacco Prdts
MACHINERY: Wire Drawing
MACHINERY: Woodworking
MACHINES: Forming, Sheet Metal
MACHINISTS' TOOLS & MACHINES: Measuring, Metalworking Type
MACHINISTS' TOOLS: Measuring, Precision
MACHINISTS' TOOLS: Precision
MACHINISTS' TOOLS: Scales, Measuring, Precision
MAGAZINES, WHOLESALE
MAGNESIUM
MAGNETIC INK & OPTICAL SCANNING EQPT
MAGNETIC RESONANCE IMAGING DEVICES: Nonmedical
MAGNETIC SHIELDS, METAL
MAGNETIC TAPE, AUDIO: Prerecorded
MAGNETS: Ceramic
MAGNETS: Permanent
MAIL PRESORTING SVCS
MAIL-ORDER BOOK CLUBS

# PRODUCT INDEX

MAIL-ORDER HOUSE, NEC
MAIL-ORDER HOUSES: Arts & Crafts Eqpt & Splys
MAIL-ORDER HOUSES: Automotive Splys & Eqpt
MAIL-ORDER HOUSES: Books, Exc Book Clubs
MAIL-ORDER HOUSES: Cards
MAIL-ORDER HOUSES: Clothing, Exc Women's
MAIL-ORDER HOUSES: Educational Splys & Eqpt
MAIL-ORDER HOUSES: Electronic Kits & Parts
MAIL-ORDER HOUSES: Food
MAIL-ORDER HOUSES: Gift Items
MAIL-ORDER HOUSES: Record & Tape, Music Or Video Club
MAIL-ORDER HOUSES: Religious Merchandise
MAIL-ORDER HOUSES: Women's Apparel
MAILING LIST: Management
MAILING SVCS, NEC
MANAGEMENT CONSULTING SVCS: Administrative
MANAGEMENT CONSULTING SVCS: Automation & Robotics
MANAGEMENT CONSULTING SVCS: Business
MANAGEMENT CONSULTING SVCS: Distribution Channels
MANAGEMENT CONSULTING SVCS: Foreign Trade
MANAGEMENT CONSULTING SVCS: General
MANAGEMENT CONSULTING SVCS: Hospital & Health
MANAGEMENT CONSULTING SVCS: Industrial
MANAGEMENT CONSULTING SVCS: Industrial & Labor
MANAGEMENT CONSULTING SVCS: Industry Specialist
MANAGEMENT CONSULTING SVCS: Maintenance
MANAGEMENT CONSULTING SVCS: Manufacturing
MANAGEMENT CONSULTING SVCS: Merchandising
MANAGEMENT CONSULTING SVCS: Real Estate
MANAGEMENT CONSULTING SVCS: Training & Development
MANAGEMENT CONSULTING SVCS: Transportation
MANAGEMENT SERVICES
MANAGEMENT SVCS: Administrative
MANAGEMENT SVCS: Business
MANAGEMENT SVCS: Construction
MANAGEMENT SVCS: Financial, Business
MANAGEMENT SVCS: Hotel Or Motel
MANAGEMENT SVCS: Industrial
MANAGEMENT SVCS: Restaurant
MANHOLES & COVERS: Metal
MANHOLES COVERS: Concrete
MANICURE PREPARATIONS
MANNEQUINS
MANUFACTURED & MOBILE HOME DEALERS
MANUFACTURING INDUSTRIES, NEC
MARBLE, BUILDING: Cut & Shaped
MARBLE: Dimension
MARINE CARGO HANDLING SVCS
MARINE CARGO HANDLING SVCS: Loading
MARINE HARDWARE
MARINE RELATED EQPT
MARINE SPLY DEALERS
MARINE SPLYS WHOLESALERS
MARKERS
MARKETS: Meat & fish
MARKING DEVICES
MARKING DEVICES: Canceling Stamps, Hand, Rubber Or Metal
MARKING DEVICES: Embossing Seals & Hand Stamps
MARKING DEVICES: Printing Dies, Marking Mach, Rubber/Plastic
MARKING DEVICES: Screens, Textile Printing
MARKING DEVICES: Seal Presses, Notary & Hand
MARKING DEVICES: Stationary Embossers, Personal
MASQUERADE OR THEATRICAL COSTUMES STORES
MASSAGE MACHINES, ELECTRIC: Barber & Beauty Shops
MASTIC ROOFING COMPOSITION
MATCHES & MATCH BOOKS
MATCHES, WHOLESALE
MATERIAL GRINDING & PULVERIZING SVCS NEC
MATERIALS HANDLING EQPT WHOLESALERS
MATERNITY WEAR STORES
MATS & MATTING, MADE FROM PURCHASED WIRE
MATS, MATTING & PADS: Aircraft, Floor, Exc Rubber Or Plastic
MATS, MATTING & PADS: Nonwoven
MATS, ROOFING: Mineral Wool
MATTRESS STORES
MAUSOLEUMS
MEAT & FISH MARKETS: Freezer Provisioners, Meat
MEAT & MEAT PRDTS WHOLESALERS
MEAT CUTTING & PACKING
MEAT MARKETS
MEAT PRDTS: Beef Stew, From Purchased Meat
MEAT PRDTS: Boneless Meat, From Purchased Meat
MEAT PRDTS: Boxed Beef, From Slaughtered Meat
MEAT PRDTS: Canned Exc Baby Food, From Slaughtered Meat
MEAT PRDTS: Corned Beef, From Purchased Meat
MEAT PRDTS: Cured Meats, From Purchased Meat
MEAT PRDTS: Dried Beef, From Purchased Meat
MEAT PRDTS: Dried, From Slaughtered Meat
MEAT PRDTS: Frozen
MEAT PRDTS: Ham, Roasted, From Purchased Meat
MEAT PRDTS: Hams & Picnics, From Slaughtered Meat
MEAT PRDTS: Lamb, From Slaughtered Meat
MEAT PRDTS: Luncheon Meat, From Purchased Meat
MEAT PRDTS: Meat By-Prdts, From Slaughtered Meat
MEAT PRDTS: Pork, From Slaughtered Meat
MEAT PRDTS: Prepared Beef Prdts From Purchased Beef
MEAT PRDTS: Prepared Pork Prdts, From Purchased Meat
MEAT PRDTS: Sausage Casings, Natural
MEAT PRDTS: Sausages & Related Prdts, From Purchased Meat
MEAT PRDTS: Sausages, From Purchased Meat
MEAT PRDTS: Sausages, From Slaughtered Meat
MEAT PRDTS: Smoked
MEAT PRDTS: Snack Sticks, Incl Jerky, From Purchased Meat
MEAT PRDTS: Spreads, Sandwich, From Purchased Meat
MEAT PRDTS: Veal, From Slaughtered Meat
MEAT PROCESSED FROM PURCHASED CARCASSES
MEAT PROCESSING MACHINERY
MEATS, PACKAGED FROZEN: Wholesalers
MECHANISMS: Coin-Operated Machines
MEDIA BUYING AGENCIES
MEDIA: Magnetic & Optical Recording
MEDICAL & HOSPITAL EQPT WHOLESALERS
MEDICAL & HOSPITAL SPLYS: Radiation Shielding Garments
MEDICAL & SURGICAL SPLYS: Abdominal Support, Braces/Trusses
MEDICAL & SURGICAL SPLYS: Bandages & Dressings
MEDICAL & SURGICAL SPLYS: Braces, Orthopedic
MEDICAL & SURGICAL SPLYS: Clothing, Fire Resistant & Protect
MEDICAL & SURGICAL SPLYS: Cosmetic Restorations
MEDICAL & SURGICAL SPLYS: Crutches & Walkers
MEDICAL & SURGICAL SPLYS: Drapes, Surgical, Cotton
MEDICAL & SURGICAL SPLYS: Gauze, Surgical
MEDICAL & SURGICAL SPLYS: Gynecological Splys & Appliances
MEDICAL & SURGICAL SPLYS: Infant Incubators
MEDICAL & SURGICAL SPLYS: Ligatures
MEDICAL & SURGICAL SPLYS: Limbs, Artificial
MEDICAL & SURGICAL SPLYS: Models, Anatomical
MEDICAL & SURGICAL SPLYS: Orthopedic Appliances
MEDICAL & SURGICAL SPLYS: Personal Safety Eqpt
MEDICAL & SURGICAL SPLYS: Prosthetic Appliances
MEDICAL & SURGICAL SPLYS: Respiratory Protect Eqpt, Personal
MEDICAL & SURGICAL SPLYS: Splints, Pneumatic & Wood
MEDICAL & SURGICAL SPLYS: Sponges
MEDICAL & SURGICAL SPLYS: Supports, Abdominal, Ankle, Etc
MEDICAL & SURGICAL SPLYS: Swabs, Sanitary Cotton
MEDICAL & SURGICAL SPLYS: Technical Aids, Handicapped
MEDICAL & SURGICAL SPLYS: Welders' Hoods
MEDICAL EQPT REPAIR SVCS, NON-ELECTRIC
MEDICAL EQPT: Diagnostic
MEDICAL EQPT: Electromedical Apparatus
MEDICAL EQPT: Heart-Lung Machines, Exc Iron Lungs
MEDICAL EQPT: Laser Systems
MEDICAL EQPT: Patient Monitoring
MEDICAL EQPT: PET Or Position Emission Tomography Scanners
MEDICAL EQPT: Ultrasonic Scanning Devices
MEDICAL EQPT: Ultrasonic, Exc Cleaning
MEDICAL EQPT: X-Ray Apparatus & Tubes, Radiographic
MEDICAL EQPT: X-ray Generators
MEDICAL FIELD ASSOCIATION
MEDICAL SVCS ORGANIZATION
MEDICAL TRAINING SERVICES
MEDICAL X-RAY MACHINES & TUBES WHOLESALERS
MEDICAL, DENTAL & HOSPITAL EQPT, WHOL: Dentists' Prof Splys
MEDICAL, DENTAL & HOSPITAL EQPT, WHOL: Hospital Eqpt & Splys
MEDICAL, DENTAL & HOSPITAL EQPT, WHOL: Hosptl Eqpt/Furniture
MEDICAL, DENTAL & HOSPITAL EQPT, WHOL: Surgical Eqpt & Splys
MEDICAL, DENTAL & HOSPITAL EQPT, WHOLESALE: Artificial Limbs
MEDICAL, DENTAL & HOSPITAL EQPT, WHOLESALE: Dental Lab
MEDICAL, DENTAL & HOSPITAL EQPT, WHOLESALE: Hearing Aids
MEDICAL, DENTAL & HOSPITAL EQPT, WHOLESALE: Hosp Furniture
MEDICAL, DENTAL & HOSPITAL EQPT, WHOLESALE: Med Eqpt & Splys
MEDICAL, DENTAL & HOSPITAL EQPT, WHOLESALE: Medical Lab
MEDICAL, DENTAL & HOSPITAL EQPT, WHOLESALE: Orthopedic
MEMBERSHIP ORGANIZATIONS, BUSINESS: Contractors' Association
MEMBERSHIP ORGANIZATIONS, BUSINESS: Merchants' Association
MEMBERSHIP ORGANIZATIONS, NEC: Charitable
MEMBERSHIP ORGANIZATIONS, PROFESSIONAL: Health Association
MEMBERSHIP ORGANIZATIONS, REL: Christian Reformed Church
MEMBERSHIP ORGANIZATIONS, REL: Churches, Temples & Shrines
MEMBERSHIP ORGANIZATIONS, RELIGIOUS: Brethren Church
MEMBERSHIP ORGANIZATIONS, RELIGIOUS: Catholic Church
MEMBERSHIP ORGANIZATIONS, RELIGIOUS: Church Of Christ
MEMBERSHIP ORGANIZATIONS, RELIGIOUS: Nonchurch
MEMBERSHIP ORGANIZATIONS: Reading Rooms/Other Cultural Orgs
MEMBERSHIP ORGS, CIVIC, SOCIAL & FRATERNAL: Condo Assoc
MEMBERSHIP ORGS, CIVIC, SOCIAL/FRAT: Educator's Assoc
MEMBERSHIP SPORTS & RECREATION CLUBS
MEMORIALS, MONUMENTS & MARKERS
MEN'S & BOYS' CLOTHING ACCESS STORES
MEN'S & BOYS' CLOTHING STORES
MEN'S & BOYS' CLOTHING WHOLESALERS, NEC
MEN'S & BOYS' SPORTSWEAR CLOTHING STORES
MEN'S & BOYS' SPORTSWEAR WHOLESALERS
MEN'S CLOTHING STORES: Everyday, Exc Suits & Sportswear
MENTAL HEALTH CLINIC, OUTPATIENT
METAL & STEEL PRDTS: Abrasive
METAL COMPONENTS: Prefabricated
METAL CUTTING SVCS
METAL DETECTORS
METAL FABRICATORS: Architechtural
METAL FABRICATORS: Plate
METAL FABRICATORS: Sheet
METAL FABRICATORS: Structural, Ship
METAL FINISHING SVCS
METAL MINING SVCS
METAL ORES, NEC
METAL RESHAPING & REPLATING SVCS
METAL SERVICE CENTERS & OFFICES
METAL SLITTING & SHEARING
METAL SPINNING FOR THE TRADE
METAL STAMPING, FOR THE TRADE
METAL STAMPINGS: Ornamental
METAL STAMPINGS: Perforated
METAL TREATING COMPOUNDS
METAL TREATING: Cryogenic
METALS SVC CENTERS & WHOL: Structural Shapes, Iron Or Steel
METALS SVC CENTERS & WHOLESALERS: Bars, Metal
METALS SVC CENTERS & WHOLESALERS: Casting, Rough,Iron/Steel
METALS SVC CENTERS & WHOLESALERS: Copper Prdts
METALS SVC CENTERS & WHOLESALERS: Flat Prdts, Iron Or Steel
METALS SVC CENTERS & WHOLESALERS: Foundry Prdts
METALS SVC CENTERS & WHOLESALERS: Iron & Steel Prdt, Ferrous
METALS SVC CENTERS & WHOLESALERS: Misc Nonferrous Prdts

# PRODUCT INDEX

METALS SVC CENTERS & WHOLESALERS: Nonferrous Sheets, Etc
METALS SVC CENTERS & WHOLESALERS: Pig Iron
METALS SVC CENTERS & WHOLESALERS: Pipe & Tubing, Steel
METALS SVC CENTERS & WHOLESALERS: Rods, Wire, Exc Insulated
METALS SVC CENTERS & WHOLESALERS: Sheets, Metal
METALS SVC CENTERS & WHOLESALERS: Steel
METALS SVC CENTERS & WHOLESALERS: Steel Decking
METALS SVC CENTERS & WHOLESALERS: Tubing, Metal
METALS SVC CENTERS/WHOL: Forms, Steel Concrete Construction
METALS SVC CTRS & WHOLESALERS: Aluminum Bars, Rods, Etc
METALS SVC CTRS & WHOLESALERS: Copper Sheets, Plates, NEC
METALS: Precious NEC
METALS: Precious, Secondary
METALS: Primary Nonferrous, NEC
METALWORK: Miscellaneous
METALWORK: Ornamental
METALWORKING MACHINERY WHOLESALERS
METERING DEVICES: Gasoline Dispensing
METERING DEVICES: Integrating & Totalizing, Gas & Liquids
METERING DEVICES: Positive Displacement Meters
METERING DEVICES: Water Quality Monitoring & Control Systems
METERS: Audio
METERS: Demand
MGMT CONSULTING SVCS: Matls, Incl Purch, Handle & Invntry
MICA PRDTS
MICROCIRCUITS, INTEGRATED: Semiconductor
MICROFILM SVCS
MICROMETERS
MICROPHONES
MICROPROCESSORS
MICROSCOPES
MICROWAVE COMPONENTS
MICROWAVE OVENS: Household
MILL PRDTS: Structural & Rail
MILLINERY SUPPLIES: Cap Fronts & Visors
MILLINERY SUPPLIES: Veils & Veiling, Bridal, Funeral, Etc
MILLING: Cereal Flour, Exc Rice
MILLING: Corn Grits & Flakes, For Brewers' Use
MILLING: Grain Cereals, Cracked
MILLING: Grains, Exc Rice
MILLWORK
MINERAL MINING: Nonmetallic
MINERAL WOOL
MINERAL WOOL INSULATION PRDTS
MINERALS: Ground Or Otherwise Treated
MINERALS: Ground or Treated
MINIATURE GOLF COURSES
MINING EQPT: Locomotives & Parts
MINING EXPLORATION & DEVELOPMENT SVCS
MINING MACHINERY & EQPT WHOLESALERS
MINING MACHINES & EQPT: Augers
MINING MACHINES & EQPT: Bits, Rock, Exc Oil/Gas Field Tools
MINING MACHINES & EQPT: Cleaning, Mineral
MINING MACHINES & EQPT: Crushers, Stationary
MINING MACHINES & EQPT: Loading, Underground, Mobile
MINING MACHINES & EQPT: Mineral Beneficiation
MINING MACHINES & EQPT: Sedimentation, Mineral
MINING MACHINES & EQPT: Shuttle Cars, Underground
MINING MACHINES & EQPT: Stamping Mill Machinery
MIRRORS: Motor Vehicle
MISC FIN INVEST ACT: Shares, RE, Entertain & Eqpt, Sales
MISCELLANEOUS FINANCIAL INVEST ACT: Oil/Gas Lease Brokers
MISSILE GUIDANCE SYSTEMS & EQPT
MISSILES: Guided
MITTENS: Leather
MIXING EQPT
MIXTURES & BLOCKS: Asphalt Paving
MOBILE COMMUNICATIONS EQPT
MOBILE HOME FRAMES
MOBILE HOMES
MOBILE HOMES WHOLESALERS
MOBILE HOMES: Personal Or Private Use
MODELS
MODELS: General, Exc Toy
MODULES: Computer Logic
MODULES: Solid State
MOLDED RUBBER PRDTS
MOLDING COMPOUNDS
MOLDING SAND MINING
MOLDINGS & TRIM: Metal, Exc Automobile
MOLDINGS & TRIM: Wood
MOLDINGS OR TRIM: Automobile, Stamped Metal
MOLDINGS, ARCHITECTURAL: Plaster Of Paris
MOLDINGS: Picture Frame
MOLDS: Indl
MOLDS: Plastic Working & Foundry
MONASTERIES
MONUMENTS & GRAVE MARKERS, EXC TERRAZZO
MONUMENTS & GRAVE MARKERS, WHOLESALE
MONUMENTS: Concrete
MONUMENTS: Cut Stone, Exc Finishing Or Lettering Only
MOPEDS & PARTS
MOPS: Floor & Dust
MORTAR
MOTION PICTURE & VIDEO PRODUCTION SVCS
MOTION PICTURE & VIDEO PRODUCTION SVCS: Commercials, TV
MOTION PICTURE & VIDEO PRODUCTION SVCS: Educational
MOTION PICTURE EQPT
MOTION PICTURE PRODUCTION ALLIED SVCS
MOTION PICTURE PRODUCTION SVCS
MOTOR & GENERATOR PARTS: Electric
MOTOR CONTROL CENTERS
MOTOR HOMES
MOTOR INN
MOTOR REBUILDING SVCS, EXC AUTOMOTIVE
MOTOR REPAIR SVCS
MOTOR SCOOTERS & PARTS
MOTOR VEHICLE ASSEMBLY, COMPLETE: Ambulances
MOTOR VEHICLE ASSEMBLY, COMPLETE: Autos, Incl Specialty
MOTOR VEHICLE ASSEMBLY, COMPLETE: Buses, All Types
MOTOR VEHICLE ASSEMBLY, COMPLETE: Fire Department Vehicles
MOTOR VEHICLE ASSEMBLY, COMPLETE: Military Motor Vehicle
MOTOR VEHICLE ASSEMBLY, COMPLETE: Motor Buses
MOTOR VEHICLE ASSEMBLY, COMPLETE: Reconnaissance Cars
MOTOR VEHICLE ASSEMBLY, COMPLETE: Snow Plows
MOTOR VEHICLE ASSEMBLY, COMPLETE: Truck & Tractor Trucks
MOTOR VEHICLE ASSEMBLY, COMPLETE: Truck Tractors, Highway
MOTOR VEHICLE ASSEMBLY, COMPLETE: Wreckers, Tow Truck
MOTOR VEHICLE ASSY, COMPLETE: Street Sprinklers & Sweepers
MOTOR VEHICLE DEALERS: Automobiles, New & Used
MOTOR VEHICLE DEALERS: Cars, Used Only
MOTOR VEHICLE DEALERS: Trucks, Tractors/Trailers, New & Used
MOTOR VEHICLE PARTS & ACCESS: Air Conditioner Parts
MOTOR VEHICLE PARTS & ACCESS: Axel Housings & Shafts
MOTOR VEHICLE PARTS & ACCESS: Bearings
MOTOR VEHICLE PARTS & ACCESS: Body Components & Frames
MOTOR VEHICLE PARTS & ACCESS: Brakes, Air
MOTOR VEHICLE PARTS & ACCESS: Choker Rods
MOTOR VEHICLE PARTS & ACCESS: Clutches
MOTOR VEHICLE PARTS & ACCESS: Connecting Rods
MOTOR VEHICLE PARTS & ACCESS: Cylinder Heads
MOTOR VEHICLE PARTS & ACCESS: Electrical Eqpt
MOTOR VEHICLE PARTS & ACCESS: Engines & Parts
MOTOR VEHICLE PARTS & ACCESS: Engs & Trans,Factory, Rebuilt
MOTOR VEHICLE PARTS & ACCESS: Fuel Systems & Parts
MOTOR VEHICLE PARTS & ACCESS: Gas Tanks
MOTOR VEHICLE PARTS & ACCESS: Gears
MOTOR VEHICLE PARTS & ACCESS: Governors
MOTOR VEHICLE PARTS & ACCESS: Heaters
MOTOR VEHICLE PARTS & ACCESS: Horns
MOTOR VEHICLE PARTS & ACCESS: Instrument Board Assemblies
MOTOR VEHICLE PARTS & ACCESS: Mufflers, Exhaust
MOTOR VEHICLE PARTS & ACCESS: Oil Pumps
MOTOR VEHICLE PARTS & ACCESS: Thermostats
MOTOR VEHICLE PARTS & ACCESS: Trailer Hitches
MOTOR VEHICLE PARTS & ACCESS: Transmission Housings Or Parts
MOTOR VEHICLE PARTS & ACCESS: Transmissions
MOTOR VEHICLE PARTS & ACCESS: Universal Joints
MOTOR VEHICLE PARTS & ACCESS: Wheel rims
MOTOR VEHICLE PARTS & ACCESS: Wiring Harness Sets
MOTOR VEHICLE RADIOS WHOLESALERS
MOTOR VEHICLE SPLYS & PARTS WHOLESALERS: New
MOTOR VEHICLE: Radiators
MOTOR VEHICLE: Shock Absorbers
MOTOR VEHICLE: Steering Mechanisms
MOTOR VEHICLE: Wheels
MOTOR VEHICLES & CAR BODIES
MOTOR VEHICLES, WHOLESALE: Truck bodies
MOTORCYCLE & BICYCLE PARTS: Frames
MOTORCYCLE & BICYCLE PARTS: Gears
MOTORCYCLE ACCESS
MOTORCYCLE DEALERS
MOTORCYCLE PARTS & ACCESS DEALERS
MOTORCYCLE PARTS: Wholesalers
MOTORCYCLE RACING
MOTORCYCLE REPAIR SHOPS
MOTORCYCLES & RELATED PARTS
MOTORS: Electric
MOTORS: Generators
MOTORS: Starting, Automotive & Aircraft
MOTORS: Torque
MOUNTING SVC: Maps & Samples
MOUTHWASHES
MOVING SVC: Local
MOWERS & ACCESSORIES
MULTILITHING SVCS
MUSEUMS
MUSEUMS & ART GALLERIES
MUSIC DISTRIBUTION APPARATUS
MUSIC DISTRIBUTION SYSTEM SVCS
MUSIC RECORDING PRODUCER
MUSIC SCHOOLS
MUSIC VIDEO PRODUCTION SVCS
MUSICAL ENTERTAINERS
MUSICAL INSTRUMENT PARTS & ACCESS, WHOLESALE
MUSICAL INSTRUMENT REPAIR
MUSICAL INSTRUMENTS & ACCESS: Carrying Cases
MUSICAL INSTRUMENTS & ACCESS: NEC
MUSICAL INSTRUMENTS & ACCESS: Pipe Organs
MUSICAL INSTRUMENTS & PARTS: Brass
MUSICAL INSTRUMENTS & PARTS: Percussion
MUSICAL INSTRUMENTS & PARTS: Woodwind
MUSICAL INSTRUMENTS & SPLYS STORES
MUSICAL INSTRUMENTS & SPLYS STORES: Brass Instruments
MUSICAL INSTRUMENTS & SPLYS STORES: String instruments
MUSICAL INSTRUMENTS WHOLESALERS
MUSICAL INSTRUMENTS: Clarinets & Parts
MUSICAL INSTRUMENTS: Electric & Electronic
MUSICAL INSTRUMENTS: Guitars & Parts, Electric & Acoustic
MUSICAL INSTRUMENTS: Harmonicas
MUSICAL INSTRUMENTS: Harps & Parts
MUSICAL INSTRUMENTS: Organ Parts & Materials
MUSICAL INSTRUMENTS: Organs
MUSICAL INSTRUMENTS: Strings, Instrument

# N

NAIL SALONS
NAILS WHOLESALERS
NAILS: Steel, Wire Or Cut
NAME PLATES: Engraved Or Etched
NAMEPLATES
NATIONAL SECURITY FORCES
NATURAL GAS COMPRESSING SVC, On-Site
NATURAL GAS DISTRIBUTION TO CONSUMERS
NATURAL GAS LIQUIDS PRODUCTION
NATURAL GAS LIQUIDS PRODUCTION
NATURAL GAS PRODUCTION
NATURAL GAS TRANSMISSION
NATURAL GAS TRANSMISSION & DISTRIBUTION
NATURAL GASOLINE PRODUCTION
NATURAL PROPANE PRODUCTION
NAVIGATIONAL SYSTEMS & INSTRUMENTS
NEEDLES
NETTING: Plastic
NEW & USED CAR DEALERS
NEWS DEALERS & NEWSSTANDS

# PRODUCT INDEX

NEWS FEATURE SYNDICATES
NEWS SYNDICATES
NEWSPAPERS & PERIODICALS NEWS REPORTING SVCS
NEWSPAPERS, WHOLESALE
NEWSSTAND
NICKEL ALLOY
NONAROMATIC CHEMICAL PRDTS
NONCLASSIFIABLE ESTABLISHMENTS
NONCURRENT CARRYING WIRING DEVICES
NONDURABLE GOODS WHOLESALERS, NEC
NONFERROUS: Rolling & Drawing, NEC
NONMETALLIC MINERALS DEVELOPMENT & TEST BORING SVC
NONMETALLIC MINERALS: Support Activities, Exc Fuels
NOTIONS: Button Backs & Parts
NOTIONS: Pins, Hair, Exc Rubber
NOTIONS: Pins, Straight, Steel Or Brass
NOVELTIES
NOVELTIES & SPECIALTIES: Metal
NOVELTIES: Plastic
NOVELTY SHOPS
NOZZLES & SPRINKLERS Lawn Hose
NOZZLES: Fire Fighting
NOZZLES: Spray, Aerosol, Paint Or Insecticide
NUCLEAR FUELS SCRAP REPROCESSING
NUCLEAR REACTORS: Military Or Indl
NURSERIES & LAWN & GARDEN SPLY STORE, RET: Fountain, Outdoor
NURSERIES & LAWN & GARDEN SPLY STORES, RETAIL: Fertilizer
NURSERIES & LAWN & GARDEN SPLY STORES, RETAIL: Lawn Ornament
NURSERIES & LAWN & GARDEN SPLY STORES, RETAIL: Top Soil
NURSERIES & LAWN/GARDEN SPLY STORE, RET: Lawnmowers/Tractors
NURSERIES & LAWN/GARDEN SPLY STORES, RET: Garden Splys/Tools
NURSERIES/LAWN/GARDEN SPLY STORE, RET: Grdn Tractors/Tillers
NURSERY & GARDEN CENTERS
NURSING CARE FACILITIES: Skilled
NUTRITION SVCS
NUTS: Metal

## O

OCHER MINING
OFFICE EQPT & ACCESSORY CUSTOMIZING SVCS
OFFICE EQPT WHOLESALERS
OFFICE FIXTURES: Wood
OFFICE FURNITURE REPAIR & MAINTENANCE SVCS
OFFICE MACHINES, NEC
OFFICE SPLY & STATIONERY STORES
OFFICE SPLY & STATIONERY STORES: Office Forms & Splys
OFFICE SPLY & STATIONERY STORES: Writing Splys
OFFICE SPLYS, NEC, WHOLESALE
OFFICES & CLINICS OF DENTISTS: Dental Clinic
OFFICES & CLINICS OF DENTISTS: Dental Clinics & Offices
OFFICES & CLINICS OF DOCTORS OF MEDICINE: Dermatologist
OFFICES & CLINICS OF DOCTORS OF MEDICINE: Gynecologist
OFFICES & CLINICS CARRYING DRS OF MEDICINE: Med Clinic, Pri Care
OFFICES & CLINICS OF DRS, MED: Specialized Practitioners
OFFICES & CLINICS OF HEALTH PRACTITIONERS: Nutrition
OFFICES & CLINICS OF HEALTH PRACTITIONERS: Physical Therapy
OFFICES & CLINICS OF HEALTH PRACTITIONERS: Speech Therapist
OIL & GAS FIELD EQPT: Drill Rigs
OIL & GAS FIELD MACHINERY
OIL FIELD MACHINERY & EQPT
OIL FIELD SVCS, NEC
OIL TREATING COMPOUNDS
OILS & ESSENTIAL OILS
OILS & GREASES: Blended & Compounded
OILS & GREASES: Lubricating
OILS, ANIMAL OR VEGETABLE, WHOLESALE
OILS: Cutting
OILS: Essential
OILS: Lubricating
OILS: Lubricating
OILS: Peppermint
OINTMENTS
ON-LINE DATABASE INFORMATION RETRIEVAL SVCS
OPERATOR TRAINING, COMPUTER
OPERATOR: Apartment Buildings
OPERATOR: Nonresidential Buildings
OPHTHALMIC GOODS
OPHTHALMIC GOODS WHOLESALERS
OPHTHALMIC GOODS: Eyewear, Protective
OPHTHALMIC GOODS: Frames & Parts, Eyeglass & Spectacle
OPHTHALMIC GOODS: Frames, Lenses & Parts, Eyeglasses
OPHTHALMIC GOODS: Goggles, Sun, Safety, Indl, Etc
OPHTHALMIC GOODS: Lenses, Ophthalmic
OPHTHALMIC GOODS: Spectacles
OPTICAL GOODS STORES
OPTICAL GOODS STORES: Contact Lenses, Prescription
OPTICAL GOODS STORES: Eyeglasses, Prescription
OPTICAL GOODS STORES: Opticians
OPTICAL INSTRUMENT REPAIR SVCS
OPTICAL INSTRUMENTS & APPARATUS
OPTICAL INSTRUMENTS & LENSES
OPTICAL ISOLATORS
OPTICAL SCANNING SVCS
OPTOMETRISTS' OFFICES
ORAL PREPARATIONS
ORDNANCE
ORGAN TUNING & REPAIR SVCS
ORGANIZATIONS & UNIONS: Labor
ORGANIZATIONS: Educational Research Agency
ORGANIZATIONS: Medical Research
ORGANIZATIONS: Professional
ORGANIZATIONS: Religious
ORGANIZATIONS: Research Institute
ORGANIZATIONS: Safety Research, Noncommercial
ORGANIZATIONS: Scientific Research Agency
ORGANIZATIONS: Veterans' Membership
ORGANIZERS, CLOSET & DRAWER Plastic
ORNAMENTS: Christmas Tree, Exc Electrical & Glass
ORNAMENTS: Lawn
OSCILLATORS
OSCILLATORS
OUTBOARD MOTORS & PARTS
OUTLETS: Electric, Convenience
OUTREACH PROGRAM
OVENS: Cremating
OVENS: Distillation, Charcoal & Coke
OVENS: Infrared
OVENS: Laboratory

## P

PACKAGE DESIGN SVCS
PACKAGED FROZEN FOODS WHOLESALERS, NEC
PACKAGING & LABELING SVCS
PACKAGING MATERIALS, INDL: Wholesalers
PACKAGING MATERIALS, WHOLESALE
PACKAGING MATERIALS: Paper
PACKAGING MATERIALS: Paper, Coated Or Laminated
PACKAGING MATERIALS: Paper, Thermoplastic Coated
PACKAGING MATERIALS: Paperboard Backs For Blister/Skin Pkgs
PACKAGING MATERIALS: Plastic Film, Coated Or Laminated
PACKAGING MATERIALS: Polystyrene Foam
PACKAGING MATERIALS: Resinous Impregnated Paper
PACKAGING: Blister Or Bubble Formed, Plastic
PACKING & CRATING SVC
PACKING & CRATING SVCS: Containerized Goods For Shipping
PACKING MATERIALS: Mechanical
PACKING SVCS: Shipping
PACKING: Metallic
PADS & PADDING: Insulator, Cordage
PADS: Desk, Exc Paper
PADS: Mattress
PAGERS: One-way
PAGING SVCS
PAILS: Plastic
PAILS: Shipping, Metal
PAINT & PAINTING SPLYS STORE
PAINT STORE
PAINTING SVC: Metal Prdts
PAINTS & ADDITIVES
PAINTS & ALLIED PRODUCTS
PAINTS & VARNISHES: Plastics Based
PAINTS, VARNISHES & SPLYS WHOLESALERS
PAINTS, VARNISHES & SPLYS, WHOLESALE: Colors & Pigments
PAINTS, VARNISHES & SPLYS, WHOLESALE: Paints
PAINTS: Oil Or Alkyd Vehicle Or Water Thinned
PAINTS: Waterproof
PALLET REPAIR SVCS
PALLETIZERS & DEPALLETIZERS
PALLETS
PALLETS & SKIDS: Wood
PALLETS: Metal
PALLETS: Plastic
PALLETS: Solid Fiber, Made From Purchased Materials
PALLETS: Wood & Metal Combination
PALLETS: Wooden
PANEL & DISTRIBUTION BOARDS & OTHER RELATED APPARATUS
PANEL & DISTRIBUTION BOARDS: Electric
PANELS, CORRUGATED: Plastic
PANELS, FLAT: Plastic
PANELS: Building, Metal
PANELS: Building, Plastic, NEC
PANELS: Building, Wood
PANELS: Control & Metering, Generator
PANELS: Wood
PAPER & BOARD: Die-cut
PAPER & ENVELOPES: Writing, Made From Purchased Materials
PAPER & PAPER PRDTS: Crepe, Made From Purchased Materials
PAPER CONVERTING
PAPER MANUFACTURERS: Exc Newsprint
PAPER NAPKINS WHOLESALERS
PAPER PRDTS
PAPER PRDTS: Book Covers
PAPER PRDTS: Feminine Hygiene Prdts
PAPER PRDTS: Pressed & Molded Pulp & Fiber Prdts
PAPER PRDTS: Sanitary
PAPER PRDTS: Sanitary Tissue Paper
PAPER PRDTS: Toilet Paper, Made From Purchased Materials
PAPER PRDTS: Towels, Napkins/Tissue Paper, From Purchd Mtrls
PAPER PRDTS: Wrappers, Blank, Made From Purchased Materials
PAPER, WHOLESALE: Fine
PAPER, WHOLESALE: Printing
PAPER, WHOLESALE: Writing
PAPER: Absorbent
PAPER: Adhesive
PAPER: Art
PAPER: Bank Note
PAPER: Book
PAPER: Business Form
PAPER: Cardboard
PAPER: Catalog
PAPER: Chemically Treated, Made From Purchased Materials
PAPER: Coated & Laminated, NEC
PAPER: Coated, Exc Photographic, Carbon Or Abrasive
PAPER: Filter
PAPER: Gift Wrap
PAPER: Gummed, Made From Purchased Materials
PAPER: Insulation Siding
PAPER: Kraft
PAPER: Lithograph
PAPER: Newsprint
PAPER: Packaging
PAPER: Printer
PAPER: Specialty
PAPER: Tissue
PAPER: Wallpaper
PAPER: Waxed, Made From Purchased Materials
PAPER: Wrapping & Packaging
PAPER: Writing
PAPERBOARD
PAPERBOARD CONVERTING
PAPERBOARD PRDTS: Building Insulating & Packaging
PAPERBOARD PRDTS: Container Board
PAPERBOARD PRDTS: Folding Boxboard
PAPERBOARD PRDTS: Packaging Board
PAPERBOARD: Liner Board
PAPETERIES & WRITING PAPER SETS

PAPIER-MACHE PRDTS, EXC STATUARY & ART GOODS
PARKERIZING SVC

# PRODUCT INDEX

PARKING LOTS
PARTICLEBOARD
PARTITIONS & FIXTURES: Except Wood
PARTITIONS: Solid Fiber, Made From Purchased Materials
PARTITIONS: Wood & Fixtures
PARTS: Metal
PASTES: Metal
PATCHING PLASTER: Household
PATENT OWNERS & LESSORS
PATIENT MONITORING EQPT WHOLESALERS
PATTERNS: Indl
PAVERS
PAVING MATERIALS: Prefabricated, Concrete
PAVING MIXTURES
PAYROLL SVCS
PEAT GRINDING SVCS
PENCILS & PENS WHOLESALERS
PENS & PARTS: Ball Point
PENS & PARTS: Stylographic
PENS & PENCILS: Mechanical, NEC
PENSION & RETIREMENT PLAN CONSULTANTS
PERFUME: Concentrated
PERFUME: Perfumes, Natural Or Synthetic
PERFUMES
PERLITE: Processed
PERSONAL & HOUSEHOLD GOODS REPAIR, NEC
PERSONAL CREDIT INSTITUTIONS: Finance Licensed Loan Co's, Sm
PERSONAL DOCUMENT & INFORMATION SVCS
PERSONAL INVESTIGATION SVCS
PERSONAL SHOPPING SVCS
PEST CONTROL IN STRUCTURES SVCS
PEST CONTROL SVCS
PESTICIDES WHOLESALERS
PET FOOD WHOLESALERS
PET SPLYS
PET SPLYS WHOLESALERS
PETROLEUM & PETROLEUM PRDTS, WHOL Svc Station Splys, Petro
PETROLEUM & PETROLEUM PRDTS, WHOLESALE Fuel Oil
PETROLEUM & PETROLEUM PRDTS, WHOLESALE Petroleum Brokers
PETROLEUM & PETROLEUM PRDTS, WHOLESALE Petroleum Terminals
PETROLEUM & PETROLEUM PRDTS, WHOLESALE: Bulk Stations
PETROLEUM BULK STATIONS & TERMINALS
PETROLEUM PRDTS WHOLESALERS
PETROLEUM REFINERY INSPECTION SVCS
PETS & PET SPLYS, WHOLESALE
PHARMACEUTICAL PREPARATIONS: Adrenal
PHARMACEUTICAL PREPARATIONS: Druggists' Preparations
PHARMACEUTICAL PREPARATIONS: Medicines, Capsule Or Ampule
PHARMACEUTICAL PREPARATIONS: Pills
PHARMACEUTICAL PREPARATIONS: Powders
PHARMACEUTICAL PREPARATIONS: Proprietary Drug PRDTS
PHARMACEUTICAL PREPARATIONS: Solutions
PHARMACEUTICAL PREPARATIONS: Tablets
PHARMACEUTICALS
PHARMACEUTICALS: Medicinal & Botanical Prdts
PHARMACIES & DRUG STORES
PHONOGRAPH RECORDS: Prerecorded
PHOSPHATE ROCK MINING
PHOSPHATES
PHOSPHORIC ACID
PHOTOCOPY MACHINES
PHOTOCOPY SPLYS WHOLESALERS
PHOTOCOPYING & DUPLICATING SVCS
PHOTOELECTRIC DEVICES: Magnetic
PHOTOENGRAVING SVC
PHOTOFINISHING LABORATORIES
PHOTOFINISHING LABORATORIES
PHOTOFLASH EQPT
PHOTOGRAPH DEVELOPING & RETOUCHING SVCS
PHOTOGRAPHIC & OPTICAL GOODS EQPT REPAIR SVCS
PHOTOGRAPHIC EQPT & CAMERAS, WHOLESALE
PHOTOGRAPHIC EQPT & SPLYS
PHOTOGRAPHIC EQPT & SPLYS WHOLESALERS
PHOTOGRAPHIC EQPT & SPLYS, WHOLESALE: Motion Picture Camera
PHOTOGRAPHIC EQPT & SPLYS, WHOLESALE: Project, Motion/Slide
PHOTOGRAPHIC EQPT & SPLYS: Blueprint Cloth/Paper, Sensitized
PHOTOGRAPHIC EQPT & SPLYS: Develpg Mach/Eqpt, Still/Motion
PHOTOGRAPHIC EQPT & SPLYS: Film, Sensitized
PHOTOGRAPHIC EQPT & SPLYS: Graphic Arts Plates, Sensitized
PHOTOGRAPHIC EQPT & SPLYS: Printing Eqpt
PHOTOGRAPHIC EQPT & SPLYS: Printing Frames
PHOTOGRAPHIC EQPT & SPLYS: Toners, Prprd, Not Chem Plnts
PHOTOGRAPHIC EQPT & SPLYS: Tripods, Camera & Projector
PHOTOGRAPHIC EQPT REPAIR SVCS
PHOTOGRAPHIC PEOCESSING CHEMICALS
PHOTOGRAPHIC PROCESSING EQPT & CHEMICALS
PHOTOGRAPHY SVCS: Commercial
PHOTOGRAPHY SVCS: Portrait Studios
PHOTOGRAPHY SVCS: Still Or Video
PHOTOTYPESETTING SVC
PHOTOVOLTAIC Solid State
PHYSICAL EXAMINATION & TESTING SVCS
PHYSICAL EXAMINATION SVCS, INSURANCE
PHYSICIANS' OFFICES & CLINICS: Medical doctors
PICNIC JUGS: Plastic
PICTURE FRAMES: Metal
PICTURE FRAMES: Wood
PICTURE FRAMING SVCS, CUSTOM
PICTURE PROJECTION EQPT
PIECE GOODS & NOTIONS WHOLESALERS
PIECE GOODS, NOTIONS & DRY GOODS, WHOL: Textile Converters
PIECE GOODS, NOTIONS & DRY GOODS, WHOL: Textiles, Woven
PIECE GOODS, NOTIONS & DRY GOODS, WHOL: Trimmings, Apparel
PIECE GOODS, NOTIONS & DRY GOODS, WHOLESALE: Fabrics
PIECE GOODS, NOTIONS & DRY GOODS, WHOLESALE: Sewing Access
PIECE GOODS, NOTIONS & OTHER DRY GOODS, WHOL: Flags/Banners
PIECE GOODS, NOTIONS & OTHER DRY GOODS, WHOLESALE: Fabrics
PIECE GOODS, NOTIONS & OTHER DRY GOODS, WHOLESALE: Notions
PIECE GOODS, NOTIONS/DRY GOODS, WHOL: Drapery Mtrl, Woven
PIECE GOODS, NOTIONS/DRY GOODS, WHOL: Fabrics, Synthetic
PIECE GOODS, NOTIONS/DRY GOODS, WHOL: Sewing Splys/Notions
PIGMENTS, INORGANIC: Zinc Oxide, Zinc Sulfide
PILLOWS: Sponge Rubber
PILLOWS: Stereo
PINS
PINS: Dowel
PIPE & FITTING: Fabrication
PIPE & FITTINGS: Cast Iron
PIPE & TUBES: Aluminum
PIPE & TUBES: Copper & Copper Alloy
PIPE & TUBES: Seamless
PIPE CLEANERS
PIPE JOINT COMPOUNDS
PIPE, PRESSURE: Reinforced Concrete
PIPE, SEWER: Concrete
PIPE: Concrete
PIPE: Copper
PIPE: Plastic
PIPE: Seamless Steel
PIPE: Sewer, Cast Iron
PIPE: Sheet Metal
PIPELINE TERMINAL FACILITIES: Independent
PIPELINES: Crude Petroleum
PIPELINES: Natural Gas
PIPELINES: Refined Petroleum
PIPES & FITTINGS: Fiber, Made From Purchased Materials
PIPES & TUBES
PIPES & TUBES: Steel
PIPES & TUBES: Welded
PIPES: Steel & Iron
PISTONS & PISTON RINGS
PLANING MILLS: Millwork
PLANT FOOD, WHOLESALE
PLANT HORMONES
PLANTERS & FLOWER POTS, WHOLESALE
PLANTERS: Plastic
PLANTING MACHINERY & EQPT WHOLESALERS
PLAQUES: Clay, Plaster/Papier-Mache, Factory Production
PLAQUES: Picture, Laminated
PLASMAS
PLASTER & PLASTERBOARD
PLASTER WORK: Ornamental & Architectural
PLASTIC COLORING & FINISHING
PLASTIC PRDTS
PLASTIC PRDTS REPAIR SVCS
PLASTICIZERS, ORGANIC: Cyclic & Acyclic
PLASTICS FILM & SHEET
PLASTICS FILM & SHEET: Polyethylene
PLASTICS FILM & SHEET: Polypropylene
PLASTICS FILM & SHEET: Vinyl
PLASTICS FINISHED PRDTS: Laminated
PLASTICS MATERIAL & RESINS
PLASTICS MATERIALS, BASIC FORMS & SHAPES WHOLESALERS
PLASTICS PROCESSING
PLASTICS SHEET: Packing Materials
PLASTICS: Blow Molded
PLASTICS: Casein
PLASTICS: Cast
PLASTICS: Extruded
PLASTICS: Finished Injection Molded
PLASTICS: Injection Molded
PLASTICS: Molded
PLASTICS: Polystyrene Foam
PLASTICS: Thermoformed
PLATE WORK: For Nuclear Industry
PLATE WORK: Metalworking Trade
PLATED WARE, ALL METALS
PLATEMAKING SVC: Color Separations, For The Printing Trade
PLATES
PLATES: Aluminum
PLATES: Paper, Made From Purchased Materials
PLATES: Sheet & Strip, Exc Coated Prdts
PLATES: Steel
PLATES: Truss, Metal
PLATING & FINISHING SVC: Decorative, Formed Prdts
PLATING & POLISHING SVC
PLATING COMPOUNDS
PLATING SVC: Chromium, Metals Or Formed Prdts
PLATING SVC: Electro
PLATING SVC: Gold
PLATING SVC: NEC
PLAYGROUND EQPT
PLEATING & STITCHING FOR TRADE: Permanent Pleating/Pressing
PLEATING & STITCHING SVC
PLUGS: Electric
PLUMBING & HEATING EQPT & SPLY, WHOLESALE: Hydronic Htg Eqpt
PLUMBING & HEATING EQPT & SPLYS WHOLESALERS
PLUMBING & HEATING EQPT & SPLYS, WHOL: Fireplaces, Prefab
PLUMBING & HEATING EQPT & SPLYS, WHOL: Pipe/Fitting, Plastic
PLUMBING & HEATING EQPT & SPLYS, WHOL: Plumbing Fitting/Sply
PLUMBING & HEATING EQPT & SPLYS, WHOL: Water Purif Eqpt
PLUMBING & HEATING EQPT & SPLYS, WHOLESALE: Boilers, Steam
PLUMBING FIXTURES
PLUMBING FIXTURES: Brass, Incl Drain Cocks, Faucets/Spigots
PLUMBING FIXTURES: Plastic
PLUMBING FIXTURES: Vitreous
PLUMBING FIXTURES: Vitreous China
POINT OF SALE DEVICES
POLE LINE HARDWARE
POLISHING SVC: Metals Or Formed Prdts
POLYCARBONATE RESINS
POLYMETHYL METHACRYLATE RESINS: Plexiglas
POLYPROPYLENE RESINS
POLYSTYRENE RESINS
POLYSULFIDES
POLYTETRAFLUOROETHYLENE RESINS
POLYURETHANE RESINS

# PRODUCT INDEX

POLYVINYL CHLORIDE RESINS
POLYVINYLIDENE CHLORIDE RESINS
POPCORN & SUPPLIES WHOLESALERS
POPULAR MUSIC GROUPS OR ARTISTS
PORCELAIN ENAMELED PRDTS & UTENSILS
POSTERS
POTASH MINING
POTTERY: Laboratory & Indl
POTTING SOILS
POULTRY & SMALL GAME SLAUGHTERING & PROCESSING
POULTRY SLAUGHTERING & PROCESSING
POWDER: Aluminum Atomized
POWDER: Iron
POWDER: Metal
POWER DISTRIBUTION BOARDS: Electric
POWER GENERATORS
POWER MOWERS WHOLESALERS
POWER SPLY CONVERTERS: Static, Electronic Applications
POWER SUPPLIES: All Types, Static
POWER SUPPLIES: Transformer, Electronic Type
POWER SWITCHING EQPT
POWER TOOLS, HAND: Cartridge-Activated
POWER TOOLS, HAND: Drill Attachments, Portable
POWER TOOLS, HAND: Drills & Drilling Tools
POWER TOOLS, HAND: Grinders, Portable, Electric Or Pneumatic
POWER TOOLS, HAND: Hammers, Portable, Elec/Pneumatic, Chip
POWER TOOLS, HAND: Sanders
POWER TRANSMISSION EQPT WHOLESALERS
POWER TRANSMISSION EQPT: Mechanical
POWER TRANSMISSION EQPT: Vehicle
PRECAST TERRAZZO OR CONCRETE PRDTS
PRECIOUS METALS
PRECIOUS STONES & METALS, WHOLESALE
PRECIOUS STONES WHOLESALERS
PRERECORDED TAPE, COMPACT DISC & RECORD STORES
PRERECORDED TAPE, COMPACT DISC & RECORD STORES: Compact Disc
PRERECORDED TAPE, COMPACT DISC & RECORD STORES: Records
PRESS CLIPPING SVC
PRESS SVCS
PRESSED & MOLDED PULP PRDTS, NEC: From Purchased Materials
PRESSED FIBER & MOLDED PULP PRDTS, EXC FOOD PRDTS
PRESSES
PRESTRESSED CONCRETE PRDTS
PRIMARY FINISHED OR SEMIFINISHED SHAPES
PRIMARY METAL PRODUCTS
PRINT CARTRIDGES: Laser & Other Computer Printers
PRINTED CIRCUIT BOARDS
PRINTERS & PLOTTERS
PRINTERS' SVCS: Folding, Collating, Etc
PRINTERS: Computer
PRINTERS: Magnetic Ink, Bar Code
PRINTING & BINDING: Book Music
PRINTING & BINDING: Books
PRINTING & BINDING: Textbooks
PRINTING & EMBOSSING: Plastic Fabric Articles
PRINTING & ENGRAVING: Card, Exc Greeting
PRINTING & ENGRAVING: Financial Notes & Certificates
PRINTING & ENGRAVING: Invitation & Stationery
PRINTING & ENGRAVING: Poster & Decal
PRINTING & STAMPING: Fabric Articles
PRINTING & WRITING PAPER WHOLESALERS
PRINTING INKS WHOLESALERS
PRINTING MACHINERY
PRINTING MACHINERY, EQPT & SPLYS: Wholesalers
PRINTING TRADES MACHINERY & EQPT REPAIR SVCS
PRINTING, COMMERCIAL Newspapers, NEC
PRINTING, COMMERCIAL: Announcements, NEC
PRINTING, COMMERCIAL: Bags, Plastic, NEC
PRINTING, COMMERCIAL: Business Forms, NEC
PRINTING, COMMERCIAL: Calendars, NEC
PRINTING, COMMERCIAL: Certificates, Stock, NEC
PRINTING, COMMERCIAL: Coupons, NEC
PRINTING, COMMERCIAL: Decals, NEC
PRINTING, COMMERCIAL: Directories, Exc Telephone, NEC
PRINTING, COMMERCIAL: Envelopes, NEC
PRINTING, COMMERCIAL: Imprinting
PRINTING, COMMERCIAL: Invitations, NEC
PRINTING, COMMERCIAL: Labels & Seals, NEC
PRINTING, COMMERCIAL: Letterpress & Screen
PRINTING, COMMERCIAL: Literature, Advertising, NEC
PRINTING, COMMERCIAL: Magazines, NEC
PRINTING, COMMERCIAL: Menus, NEC
PRINTING, COMMERCIAL: Promotional
PRINTING, COMMERCIAL: Publications
PRINTING, COMMERCIAL: Ready
PRINTING, COMMERCIAL: Screen
PRINTING, COMMERCIAL: Stationery, NEC
PRINTING, LITHOGRAPHIC: Advertising Posters
PRINTING, LITHOGRAPHIC: Calendars
PRINTING, LITHOGRAPHIC: Calendars & Cards
PRINTING, LITHOGRAPHIC: Color
PRINTING, LITHOGRAPHIC: Decals
PRINTING, LITHOGRAPHIC: Fashion Plates
PRINTING, LITHOGRAPHIC: Forms & Cards, Business
PRINTING, LITHOGRAPHIC: Forms, Business
PRINTING, LITHOGRAPHIC: Letters, Circular Or Form
PRINTING, LITHOGRAPHIC: Maps
PRINTING, LITHOGRAPHIC: Menus
PRINTING, LITHOGRAPHIC: Newspapers
PRINTING, LITHOGRAPHIC: Offset & photolithographic printing
PRINTING, LITHOGRAPHIC: On Metal
PRINTING, LITHOGRAPHIC: Posters
PRINTING, LITHOGRAPHIC: Posters & Decals
PRINTING, LITHOGRAPHIC: Promotional
PRINTING, LITHOGRAPHIC: Publications
PRINTING, LITHOGRAPHIC: Transfers, Decalcomania Or Dry
PRINTING, LITHOGRAPHIC: Wrappers
PRINTING: Books
PRINTING: Books
PRINTING: Checkbooks
PRINTING: Commercial, NEC
PRINTING: Flexographic
PRINTING: Gravure, Business Form & Card
PRINTING: Gravure, Calendar & Card, Exc Business
PRINTING: Gravure, Cards, Exc Greeting
PRINTING: Gravure, Cards, Playing
PRINTING: Gravure, Circulars
PRINTING: Gravure, Envelopes
PRINTING: Gravure, Fashion Plates
PRINTING: Gravure, Job
PRINTING: Gravure, Labels
PRINTING: Gravure, Magazines, No Publishing On-Site
PRINTING: Gravure, Music, Sheet, No Publishing On-Site
PRINTING: Gravure, Post Cards, Picture
PRINTING: Gravure, Rotogravure
PRINTING: Gravure, Visiting Cards
PRINTING: Laser
PRINTING: Letterpress
PRINTING: Lithographic
PRINTING: Manmade Fiber & Silk, Broadwoven Fabric
PRINTING: Offset
PRINTING: Pamphlets
PRINTING: Photo-Offset
PRINTING: Photolithographic
PRINTING: Plisse, Broadwoven Fabrics, Cotton
PRINTING: Roller, Broadwoven Fabrics, Cotton
PRINTING: Roller, Manmade Fiber & Silk, Broadwoven Fabric
PRINTING: Rotogravure
PRINTING: Screen, Broadwoven Fabrics, Cotton
PRINTING: Screen, Fabric
PRINTING: Screen, Manmade Fiber & Silk, Broadwoven Fabric
PRINTING: Thermography
PRODUCT STERILIZATION SVCS
PROFESSIONAL & SEMI-PROFESSIONAL SPORTS CLUBS
PROFESSIONAL EQPT & SPLYS, WHOLESALE: Analytical Instruments
PROFESSIONAL EQPT & SPLYS, WHOLESALE: Bank
PROFESSIONAL EQPT & SPLYS, WHOLESALE: Engineers', NEC
PROFESSIONAL EQPT & SPLYS, WHOLESALE: Optical Goods
PROFESSIONAL EQPT & SPLYS, WHOLESALE: Precision Tools
PROFESSIONAL EQPT & SPLYS, WHOLESALE: Scientific & Engineerg
PROFESSIONAL INSTRUMENT REPAIR SVCS
PROFESSIONAL SCHOOLS
PROFILE SHAPES: Unsupported Plastics
PROGRAMMERS: Indl Process
PROMOTERS OF SHOWS & EXHIBITIONS
PROMOTION SVCS
PROPELLERS: Boat & Ship, Cast
PROPERTY DAMAGE INSURANCE
PROPULSION UNITS: Guided Missiles & Space Vehicles
PROTECTION EQPT: Lightning
PROTECTIVE FOOTWEAR: Rubber Or Plastic
PUBLIC FINANCE, TAXATION & MONETARY POLICY OFFICES
PUBLIC RELATIONS & PUBLICITY SVCS
PUBLIC RELATIONS SVCS
PUBLISHERS: Art Copy
PUBLISHERS: Art Copy & Poster
PUBLISHERS: Atlases
PUBLISHERS: Book
PUBLISHERS: Book Clubs, No Printing
PUBLISHERS: Books, No Printing
PUBLISHERS: Catalogs
PUBLISHERS: Comic Books, No Printing
PUBLISHERS: Directories, NEC
PUBLISHERS: Directories, Telephone
PUBLISHERS: Globe Cover Maps
PUBLISHERS: Magazines, No Printing
PUBLISHERS: Maps
PUBLISHERS: Miscellaneous
PUBLISHERS: Music Book
PUBLISHERS: Music Book & Sheet Music
PUBLISHERS: Music, Book
PUBLISHERS: Music, Sheet
PUBLISHERS: Newsletter
PUBLISHERS: Newspaper
PUBLISHERS: Newspapers, No Printing
PUBLISHERS: Pamphlets, No Printing
PUBLISHERS: Periodical Statistical Reports, No Printing
PUBLISHERS: Periodical, With Printing
PUBLISHERS: Periodicals, Magazines
PUBLISHERS: Periodicals, No Printing
PUBLISHERS: Posters
PUBLISHERS: Shopping News
PUBLISHERS: Technical Manuals
PUBLISHERS: Telephone & Other Directory
PUBLISHERS: Textbooks, No Printing
PUBLISHERS: Trade journals, No Printing
PUBLISHING & BROADCASTING: Internet Only
PUBLISHING & PRINTING: Art Copy
PUBLISHING & PRINTING: Book Clubs
PUBLISHING & PRINTING: Book Music
PUBLISHING & PRINTING: Books
PUBLISHING & PRINTING: Catalogs
PUBLISHING & PRINTING: Comic Books
PUBLISHING & PRINTING: Directories, NEC
PUBLISHING & PRINTING: Guides
PUBLISHING & PRINTING: Magazines: publishing & printing
PUBLISHING & PRINTING: Music, Book
PUBLISHING & PRINTING: Newsletters, Business Svc
PUBLISHING & PRINTING: Newspapers
PUBLISHING & PRINTING: Pamphlets
PUBLISHING & PRINTING: Patterns, Paper
PUBLISHING & PRINTING: Periodical Statistical Reports
PUBLISHING & PRINTING: Shopping News
PUBLISHING & PRINTING: Technical Manuals
PUBLISHING & PRINTING: Textbooks
PUBLISHING & PRINTING: Trade Journals
PUBLISHING & PRINTING: Yearbooks
PULLEYS: Metal
PULLEYS: Power Transmission
PULP MILLS
PULP MILLS: Mech Pulp, Incl Groundwood & Thermomechanical
PULP MILLS: Mechanical & Recycling Processing
PULP MILLS: Wood Based Pulp, NEC
PUMP JACKS & OTHER PUMPING EQPT: Indl
PUMPS
PUMPS & PARTS: Indl
PUMPS & PUMPING EQPT REPAIR SVCS
PUMPS & PUMPING EQPT WHOLESALERS
PUMPS: Domestic, Water Or Sump
PUMPS: Fluid Power
PUMPS: Gasoline, Measuring Or Dispensing
PUMPS: Hydraulic Power Transfer
PUMPS: Measuring & Dispensing
PUMPS: Oil, Measuring Or Dispensing
PUMPS: Vacuum, Exc Laboratory
PUNCHES: Forming & Stamping
PURIFICATION & DUST COLLECTION EQPT
PUSHCARTS

# PRODUCT INDEX

PYROMETER TUBES

## Q

QUARTZ CRYSTALS: Electronic
QUILTING SVC & SPLYS, FOR THE TRADE

## R

RACE CAR OWNERS
RACE TRACK OPERATION
RACEWAYS
RACKS & SHELVING: Household, Wood
RACKS: Bicycle, Automotive
RACKS: Display
RACKS: Magazine, Wood
RACKS: Pallet, Exc Wood
RACKS: Railroad Car, Vehicle Transportation, Steel
RACKS: Trash, Metal Rack
RACQUET RESTRINGING & EQPT REPAIR SVCS
RADAR SYSTEMS & EQPT
RADIATORS: Stationary Engine
RADIO & TELEVISION COMMUNICATIONS EQUIPMENT
RADIO & TELEVISION RECEIVER INSTALLATION SVCS
RADIO & TELEVISION REPAIR
RADIO BROADCASTING & COMMUNICATIONS EQPT
RADIO BROADCASTING STATIONS
RADIO COMMUNICATIONS: Airborne Eqpt
RADIO COMMUNICATIONS: Carrier Eqpt
RADIO RECEIVER NETWORKS
RADIO REPAIR SHOP, NEC
RADIO, TELEVISION & CONSUMER ELECTRONICS STORES: Antennas
RADIO, TELEVISION & CONSUMER ELECTRONICS STORES: Eqpt, NEC
RADIO, TV & CONSUMER ELEC STORES: Automotive Sound Eqpt
RADIO, TV & CONSUMER ELEC STORES: High Fidelity Stereo Eqpt
RADIO, TV/CONSUMER ELEC STORES: Antennas, Satellite Dish
RAIL & STRUCTURAL SHAPES: Aluminum rail & structural shapes
RAILINGS: Prefabricated, Metal
RAILINGS: Wood
RAILROAD CAR RENTING & LEASING SVCS
RAILROAD CAR REPAIR SVCS
RAILROAD CARGO LOADING & UNLOADING SVCS
RAILROAD EQPT
RAILROAD EQPT & SPLYS WHOLESALERS
RAILROAD EQPT, EXC LOCOMOTIVES
RAILROAD EQPT: Brakes, Air & Vacuum
RAILROAD EQPT: Cars & Eqpt, Dining
RAILROAD EQPT: Cars & Eqpt, Dining
RAILROAD EQPT: Cars & Eqpt, Interurban
RAILROAD EQPT: Cars & Eqpt, Train, Freight Or Passenger
RAILROAD EQPT: Cars, Maintenance
RAILROAD EQPT: Cars, Motor
RAILROAD EQPT: Cars, Rebuilt
RAILROAD EQPT: Locomotives & Parts, Electric Or Nonelectric
RAILROAD MAINTENANCE & REPAIR SVCS
RAILROAD RELATED EQPT: Railway Track
RAILROADS: Long Haul
RAILS: Elevator, Guide
RAILS: Steel Or Iron
RAMPS: Prefabricated Metal
RAZORS, RAZOR BLADES
REAL ESTATE AGENCIES & BROKERS
REAL ESTATE AGENCIES: Leasing & Rentals
REAL ESTATE AGENCIES: Residential
REAL ESTATE AGENTS & MANAGERS
REAL ESTATE FIDUCIARIES' OFFICES
REAL ESTATE INVESTMENT TRUSTS
REAL ESTATE OPERATORS, EXC DEVELOPERS: Commercial/Indl Bldg
REAMERS
RECEIVERS: Radio Communications
RECLAIMED RUBBER: Reworked By Manufacturing Process
RECORD BLANKS: Phonographic
RECORDING HEADS: Speech & Musical Eqpt
RECORDING TAPE: Video, Blank
RECORDS & TAPES: Prerecorded
RECORDS OR TAPES: Masters
RECOVERY SVC: Iron Ore, From Open Hearth Slag
RECOVERY SVCS: Metal
RECREATIONAL CAMPS

RECREATIONAL SPORTING EQPT REPAIR SVCS
RECREATIONAL VEHICLE DEALERS
RECREATIONAL VEHICLE PARTS & ACCESS STORES
RECREATIONAL VEHICLE REPAIRS
RECTIFIERS: Electrical Apparatus
RECTIFIERS: Electronic, Exc Semiconductor
RECYCLABLE SCRAP & WASTE MATERIALS WHOLESALERS
RECYCLING: Paper
REFINERS & SMELTERS: Aluminum
REFINERS & SMELTERS: Brass, Secondary
REFINERS & SMELTERS: Copper
REFINERS & SMELTERS: Copper, Secondary
REFINERS & SMELTERS: Gold
REFINERS & SMELTERS: Nonferrous Metal
REFINERS & SMELTERS: Tin, Primary
REFINERS & SMELTERS: Zinc, Primary, Including Zinc Residue
REFINING LUBRICATING OILS & GREASES, NEC
REFINING: Petroleum
REFRACTORIES: Clay
REFRACTORIES: Graphite, Carbon Or Ceramic Bond
REFRACTORIES: Nonclay
REFRACTORY MATERIALS WHOLESALERS
REFRIGERATION & HEATING EQUIPMENT
REFRIGERATION EQPT & SPLYS WHOLESALERS
REFRIGERATION EQPT & SPLYS, WHOLESALE: Beverage Dispensers
REFRIGERATION EQPT & SPLYS, WHOLESALE: Commercial Eqpt
REFRIGERATION EQPT & SPLYS, WHOLESALE: Ice Making Machines
REFRIGERATION EQPT: Complete
REFRIGERATION SVC & REPAIR
REFRIGERATORS & FREEZERS WHOLESALERS
REFUSE SYSTEMS
REGISTERS: Air, Metal
REGULATORS: Generator Voltage
REGULATORS: Line Voltage
REGULATORS: Steam Fittings
REGULATORS: Transmission & Distribution Voltage
REGULATORS: Transmission & Distribution Voltage
REHABILITATION CTR, RESIDENTIAL WITH HEALTH CARE INCIDENTAL
REINSURANCE CARRIERS: Accident & Health
RELAYS & SWITCHES: Indl, Electric
RELAYS: Control Circuit, Ind
RELAYS: Electric Power
RELAYS: Electronic Usage
RELIGIOUS SPLYS WHOLESALERS
REMOVERS & CLEANERS
REMOVERS: Paint
RENDERING PLANT
RENTAL CENTERS: General
RENTAL CENTERS: Party & Banquet Eqpt & Splys
RENTAL CENTERS: Tools
RENTAL SVCS: Aircraft
RENTAL SVCS: Bicycle & Motorcycle
RENTAL SVCS: Business Machine & Electronic Eqpt
RENTAL SVCS: Carpet & Upholstery Cleaning Eqpt
RENTAL SVCS: Costume
RENTAL SVCS: Electronic Eqpt, Exc Computers
RENTAL SVCS: Floor Maintenance Eqpt
RENTAL SVCS: Live Plant
RENTAL SVCS: Recreational Vehicle
RENTAL SVCS: Sound & Lighting Eqpt
RENTAL SVCS: Tent & Tarpaulin
RENTAL SVCS: Tuxedo
RENTAL SVCS: Video Cassette Recorder & Access
RENTAL SVCS: Work Zone Traffic Eqpt, Flags, Cones, Etc
RENTAL: Video Tape & Disc
REPAIR SERVICES, NEC
REPRODUCTION SVCS: Video Tape Or Disk
RESEARCH & DEVELOPMENT SVCS, COMMERCIAL: Engineering Lab
RESEARCH, DEVELOPMENT & TEST SVCS, COMM: Cmptr Hardware Dev
RESEARCH, DEVELOPMENT & TEST SVCS, COMM: Research, Exc Lab
RESEARCH, DEVELOPMENT & TESTING SVCS, COMM: Agricultural
RESEARCH, DEVELOPMENT & TESTING SVCS, COMM: Research Lab
RESEARCH, DEVELOPMENT & TESTING SVCS, COMMERCIAL: Business

RESEARCH, DEVELOPMENT & TESTING SVCS, COMMERCIAL: Education
RESEARCH, DEVELOPMENT & TESTING SVCS, COMMERCIAL: Energy
RESEARCH, DEVELOPMENT & TESTING SVCS, COMMERCIAL: Medical
RESEARCH, DEVELOPMENT & TESTING SVCS, COMMERCIAL: Physical
RESEARCH, DEVELOPMENT SVCS, COMMERCIAL: Indl Lab
RESEARCH, DVLPT & TEST SVCS, COMM: Mkt Analysis or Research
RESEARCH, DVLPT & TESTING SVCS, COMM: Mkt, Bus & Economic
RESEARCH, DVLPT & TESTING SVCS, COMM: Survey, Mktg
RESIDENTIAL CARE FOR CHILDREN
RESIDENTIAL MENTAL HEALTH & SUBSTANCE ABUSE FACILITIES
RESIDENTIAL REMODELERS
RESINS: Custom Compound Purchased
RESISTORS
RESISTORS & RESISTOR UNITS
RESISTORS: Networks
RESPIRATORS
RESPIRATORY SYSTEM DRUGS
RESPIRATORY THERAPY CLINIC
RESTAURANT EQPT REPAIR SVCS
RESTAURANT EQPT: Carts
RESTAURANT EQPT: Food Wagons
RESTAURANT EQPT: Sheet Metal
RESTAURANTS: Delicatessen
RESTAURANTS:Full Svc, American
RESTAURANTS:Full Svc, Barbecue
RESTAURANTS:Full Svc, Ethnic Food
RESTAURANTS:Full Svc, Family
RESTAURANTS:Full Svc, Family, Independent
RESTAURANTS:Full Svc, Italian
RESTAURANTS:Full Svc, Mexican
RESTAURANTS:Full Svc, Steak
RESTAURANTS:Limited Svc, Chicken
RESTAURANTS:Limited Svc, Coffee Shop
RESTAURANTS:Limited Svc, Fast-Food, Chain
RESTAURANTS:Limited Svc, Fast-Food, Independent
RESTAURANTS:Limited Svc, Ice Cream Stands Or Dairy Bars
RESTAURANTS:Limited Svc, Pizza
RESTAURANTS:Limited Svc, Pizzeria, Chain
RESTAURANTS:Limited Svc, Pizzeria, Independent
RESTAURANTS:Ltd Svc, Ice Cream, Soft Drink/Fountain Stands
RESTRAINTS
RETAIL BAKERY: Bagels
RETAIL BAKERY: Bread
RETAIL BAKERY: Cakes
RETAIL BAKERY: Cookies
RETAIL BAKERY: Doughnuts
RETAIL BAKERY: Pastries
RETAIL BAKERY: Pretzels
RETAIL LUMBER YARDS
RETAIL STORES, NEC
RETAIL STORES: Air Purification Eqpt
RETAIL STORES: Alarm Signal Systems
RETAIL STORES: Alcoholic Beverage Making Eqpt & Splys
RETAIL STORES: Architectural Splys
RETAIL STORES: Artificial Limbs
RETAIL STORES: Audio-Visual Eqpt & Splys
RETAIL STORES: Awnings
RETAIL STORES: Banners
RETAIL STORES: Business Machines & Eqpt
RETAIL STORES: Canvas Prdts
RETAIL STORES: Cleaning Eqpt & Splys
RETAIL STORES: Communication Eqpt
RETAIL STORES: Concrete Prdts, Precast
RETAIL STORES: Drafting Eqpt & Splys
RETAIL STORES: Educational Aids & Electronic Training Mat
RETAIL STORES: Electronic Parts & Eqpt
RETAIL STORES: Engine & Motor Eqpt & Splys
RETAIL STORES: Farm Eqpt & Splys
RETAIL STORES: Farm Machinery, NEC
RETAIL STORES: Fire Extinguishers
RETAIL STORES: Flags
RETAIL STORES: Foam & Foam Prdts
RETAIL STORES: Gravestones, Finished
RETAIL STORES: Hearing Aids

# PRODUCT INDEX

RETAIL STORES: Hospital Eqpt & Splys
RETAIL STORES: Ice
RETAIL STORES: Insecticides
RETAIL STORES: Medical Apparatus & Splys
RETAIL STORES: Mobile Telephones & Eqpt
RETAIL STORES: Monuments, Finished To Custom Order
RETAIL STORES: Motors, Electric
RETAIL STORES: Orthopedic & Prosthesis Applications
RETAIL STORES: Perfumes & Colognes
RETAIL STORES: Pet Food
RETAIL STORES: Photocopy Machines
RETAIL STORES: Picture Frames, Ready Made
RETAIL STORES: Religious Goods
RETAIL STORES: Rubber Stamps
RETAIL STORES: Safety Splys & Eqpt
RETAIL STORES: Swimming Pools, Above Ground
RETAIL STORES: Telephone & Communication Eqpt
RETAIL STORES: Tents
RETAIL STORES: Tombstones
RETAIL STORES: Typewriters & Business Machines
RETAIL STORES: Vaults & Safes
RETAIL STORES: Water Purification Eqpt
RETAIL STORES: Welding Splys
RETREADING MATERIALS: Tire
REUPHOLSTERY & FURNITURE REPAIR
REUPHOLSTERY SVCS
REWINDING SVCS
RIBBONS & BOWS
RIBBONS: Machine, Inked Or Carbon
RIDING STABLES
RIVETS: Metal
ROAD CONSTRUCTION EQUIPMENT WHOLESALERS
ROAD MATERIALS: Bituminous, Not From Refineries
ROBOTS: Assembly Line
ROBOTS: Indl Spraying, Painting, Etc
ROCKETS: Space & Military
RODS: Plastic
RODS: Steel & Iron, Made In Steel Mills
ROLL COVERINGS: Rubber
ROLLED OR DRAWN SHAPES, NEC: Copper & Copper Alloy
ROLLERS & FITTINGS: Window Shade
ROLLING MACHINERY: Steel
ROLLING MILL EQPT: Picklers & Pickling Lines
ROLLING MILL MACHINERY
ROLLING MILL ROLLS: Cast Steel
ROLLS & BLANKETS, PRINTERS': Rubber Or Rubberized Fabric
ROLLS & ROLL COVERINGS: Rubber
ROLLS: Rubber, Solid Or Covered
ROOF DECKS
ROOFING MATERIALS: Asphalt
ROOFING MATERIALS: Sheet Metal
ROOM COOLERS: Portable
ROPE
ROTORS: Motor
RUBBER
RUBBER PRDTS
RUBBER PRDTS: Appliance, Mechanical
RUBBER PRDTS: Automotive, Mechanical
RUBBER PRDTS: Mechanical
RUBBER PRDTS: Silicone
RUBBER PRDTS: Sponge
RUBBER STAMP, WHOLESALE
RUBBER STRUCTURES: Air-Supported
RUGS : Tufted
RULERS: Metal
RUST RESISTING

## S

SAFES & VAULTS: Metal
SAFETY EQPT & SPLYS WHOLESALERS
SAFETY INSPECTION SVCS
SAILS
SALES PROMOTION SVCS
SALT
SALT & SULFUR MINING
SAMPLE BOOKS
SAND & GRAVEL
SAND MINING
SAND RIDDLES: Hand Sifting Or Screening Apparatus
SAND: Hygrade
SAND: Silica
SANDBLASTING EQPT
SANDBLASTING SVC: Building Exterior
SANITARY SVC, NEC

SANITARY SVCS: Chemical Detoxification
SANITARY SVCS: Dead Animal Disposal
SANITARY SVCS: Environmental Cleanup
SANITARY SVCS: Hazardous Waste, Collection & Disposal
SANITARY SVCS: Incinerator, Operation Of
SANITARY SVCS: Medical Waste Disposal
SANITARY SVCS: Refuse Collection & Disposal Svcs
SANITARY SVCS: Rubbish Collection & Disposal
SANITARY SVCS: Waste Materials, Recycling
SANITARY WARE: Metal
SANITATION CHEMICALS & CLEANING AGENTS
SASHES: Door Or Window, Metal
SATCHELS
SATELLITE COMMUNICATIONS EQPT
SATELLITES: Communications
SAW BLADES
SAWING & PLANING MILLS
SAWING & PLANING MILLS: Custom
SAWMILL MACHINES
SAWS & SAWING EQPT
SCAFFOLDING WHOLESALERS
SCAFFOLDS: Mobile Or Stationary, Metal
SCALE REPAIR SVCS
SCALES & BALANCES, EXC LABORATORY
SCALES: Baby
SCALES: Bathroom
SCALES: Indl
SCALES: Truck
SCANNING DEVICES: Optical
SCHOOL SPLYS, EXC BOOKS: Wholesalers
SCHOOLS: Vocational, NEC
SCIENTIFIC INSTRUMENTS WHOLESALERS
SCRAP & WASTE MATERIALS, WHOLESALE: Auto Wrecking For Scrap
SCRAP & WASTE MATERIALS, WHOLESALE: Ferrous Metal
SCRAP & WASTE MATERIALS, WHOLESALE: Junk & Scrap
SCRAP & WASTE MATERIALS, WHOLESALE: Metal
SCRAP & WASTE MATERIALS, WHOLESALE: Nonferrous Metals Scrap
SCRAP & WASTE MATERIALS, WHOLESALE: Paper
SCRAP & WASTE MATERIALS, WHOLESALE: Paper & Cloth Materials
SCREENS: Projection
SCREENS: Window, Metal
SCREENS: Woven Wire
SCREW MACHINE PRDTS
SCREW MACHINES
SCREWS: Metal
SEALANTS
SEALING COMPOUNDS: Sealing, synthetic rubber or plastic
SEALS: Hermetic
SEALS: Oil, Leather
SEALS: Oil, Rubber
SEARCH & DETECTION SYSTEMS, EXC RADAR
SEARCH & NAVIGATION SYSTEMS
SEAT BELTS: Automobile & Aircraft
SEATING: Chairs, Table & Arm
SEATING: Railroad
SEATING: Transportation
SECRETARIAL SVCS
SECURITY & COMMODITY EXCHANGES
SECURITY CONTROL EQPT & SYSTEMS
SECURITY DEVICES
SECURITY GUARD SVCS
SECURITY PROTECTIVE DEVICES MAINTENANCE & MONITORING SVCS
SECURITY SYSTEMS SERVICES
SEEDS & BULBS WHOLESALERS
SEEDS: Coated Or Treated, From Purchased Seeds
SELF-PROPELLED AIRCRAFT DEALER
SEMICONDUCTOR CIRCUIT NETWORKS
SEMICONDUCTOR DEVICES: Wafers
SEMICONDUCTORS & RELATED DEVICES
SENSORS: Infrared, Solid State
SENSORS: Radiation
SENSORS: Temperature For Motor Windings
SENSORS: Temperature, Exc Indl Process
SEPARATORS: Metal Plate
SEPTIC TANK CLEANING SVCS
SEPTIC TANKS: Concrete
SEWAGE & WATER TREATMENT EQPT
SEWAGE TREATMENT SYSTEMS & EQPT
SEWER CLEANING & RODDING SVC
SEWER CLEANING EQPT: Power
SEWER INSPECTION SVCS

SEWING CONTRACTORS
SEWING KITS: Novelty
SEWING MACHINE REPAIR SHOP
SEWING MACHINES & PARTS: Household
SEWING MACHINES & PARTS: Indl
SEWING, NEEDLEWORK & PIECE GOODS STORES
SEWING, NEEDLEWORK & PIECE GOODS STORES: Fabric, Remnants
SEWING, NEEDLEWORK & PIECE GOODS STORES: Sewing & Needlework
SEXTANTS
SHADES: Lamp & Light, Residential
SHADES: Window
SHAPES & PILINGS, STRUCTURAL: Steel
SHAPES: Extruded, Aluminum, NEC
SHAPES: Flat, Rolled, Aluminum, NEC
SHEATHING: Asphalt Saturated
SHEET METAL SPECIALTIES, EXC STAMPED
SHEETING: Laminated Plastic
SHEETS & STRIPS: Aluminum
SHEETS: Fabric, From Purchased Materials
SHEETS: Solid Fiber, Made From Purchased Materials
SHELLAC
SHELTERED WORKSHOPS
SHELVES & SHELVING: Wood
SHELVING: Office & Store, Exc Wood
SHIELDS OR ENCLOSURES: Radiator, Sheet Metal
SHIMS: Metal
SHIP BLDG/RPRG: Submersible Marine Robots, Manned/Unmanned
SHIP BUILDING & REPAIRING: Lighters, Marine
SHIP BUILDING & REPAIRING: Offshore Sply Boats
SHIP BUILDING & REPAIRING: Rigging, Marine
SHIPBUILDING & REPAIR
SHOCK ABSORBERS: Indl
SHOE & BOOT ACCESS
SHOE MATERIALS: Counters
SHOE MATERIALS: Plastic
SHOE MATERIALS: Quarters
SHOE MATERIALS: Rands
SHOE MATERIALS: Rubber
SHOE MATERIALS: Uppers
SHOE STORES
SHOE STORES: Athletic
SHOE STORES: Boots, Men's
SHOE STORES: Boots, Women's
SHOE STORES: Custom & Orthopedic
SHOE STORES: Men's
SHOES & BOOTS WHOLESALERS
SHOES: Infants' & Children's
SHOES: Men's
SHOES: Orthopedic, Men's
SHOES: Orthopedic, Women's
SHOES: Plastic Or Rubber
SHOES: Rubber Or Rubber Soled Fabric Uppers
SHOES: Women's
SHOES: Women's, Dress
SHOPPING CENTERS & MALLS
SHOT PEENING SVC
SHOWCASES & DISPLAY FIXTURES: Office & Store
SHOWER STALLS: Metal
SHOWER STALLS: Plastic & Fiberglass
SHREDDERS: Indl & Commercial
SHUTTERS, DOOR & WINDOW: Metal
SHUTTERS, DOOR & WINDOW: Plastic
SHUTTERS: Door, Wood
SHUTTERS: Window, Wood
SIDING & STRUCTURAL MATERIALS: Wood
SIDING: Sheet Metal
SIGN LETTERING & PAINTING SVCS
SIGN PAINTING & LETTERING SHOP
SIGNALING APPARATUS: Electric
SIGNALING DEVICES: Sound, Electrical
SIGNALS: Railroad, Electric
SIGNALS: Traffic Control, Electric
SIGNALS: Transportation
SIGNS & ADVERTISING SPECIALTIES
SIGNS & ADVERTISING SPECIALTIES: Artwork, Advertising
SIGNS & ADVERTISING SPECIALTIES: Letters For Signs, Metal
SIGNS & ADVERTISING SPECIALTIES: Novelties
SIGNS & ADVERTISING SPECIALTIES: Scoreboards, Electric
SIGNS & ADVERTISING SPECIALTIES: Signs

# PRODUCT INDEX

SIGNS & ADVERTSG SPECIALTIES: Displays/Cutouts Window/Lobby
SIGNS, ELECTRICAL: Wholesalers
SIGNS, EXC ELECTRIC, WHOLESALE
SIGNS: Electrical
SIGNS: Neon
SILICA MINING
SILICON WAFERS: Chemically Doped
SILICONES
SILK SCREEN DESIGN SVCS
SILOS: Concrete, Prefabricated
SILOS: Meal
SILVER ORE MINING
SILVER ORES
SILVERSMITHS
SILVERWARE & PLATED WARE
SIMULATORS: Flight
SINKS: Vitreous China
SIRENS: Vehicle, Marine, Indl & Warning
SKIDS: Wood
SKYLIGHTS
SLAB & TILE, ROOFING: Concrete
SLAB & TILE: Precast Concrete, Floor
SLAG: Crushed Or Ground
SLATE: Crushed & Broken
SLAUGHTERING & MEAT PACKING
SLIDES & EXHIBITS: Prepared
SLINGS: Lifting, Made From Purchased Wire
SLINGS: Rope
SLOT MACHINES
SMOKE DETECTORS
SNIPS: Tinners'
SNOW PLOWING SVCS
SNOW REMOVAL EQPT: Residential
SOAPS & DETERGENTS
SOAPS & DETERGENTS: Glycerin, Crude Or Refined, From Fats
SOAPS & DETERGENTS: Textile
SOCIAL CLUBS
SOCIAL SVCS, HANDICAPPED
SOCIAL SVCS: Individual & Family
SOCKETS & RECEPTACLES: Lamp, Electric Wiring Devices
SOCKETS: Electric
SOFT DRINKS WHOLESALERS
SOFTWARE PUBLISHERS: Application
SOFTWARE PUBLISHERS: Business & Professional
SOFTWARE PUBLISHERS: Computer Utilities
SOFTWARE PUBLISHERS: Education
SOFTWARE PUBLISHERS: Home Entertainment
SOFTWARE PUBLISHERS: NEC
SOFTWARE PUBLISHERS: Operating Systems
SOFTWARE PUBLISHERS: Publisher's
SOFTWARE PUBLISHERS: Word Processing
SOFTWARE TRAINING, COMPUTER
SOIL TESTING KITS
SOLAR CELLS
SOLAR HEATING EQPT
SOLDERING EQPT: Electrical, Exc Handheld
SOLDERS
SOLENOIDS
SOLVENTS
SOLVENTS: Organic
SOUND EFFECTS & MUSIC PRODUCTION: Motion Picture
SOUND EQPT: Electric
SOUND RECORDING STUDIOS
SOUND REPRODUCING EQPT
SOYBEAN PRDTS
SPACE VEHICLE EQPT
SPARK PLUGS: Internal Combustion Engines
SPEAKER MONITORS
SPEAKER SYSTEMS
SPEAKERS BUREAU
SPECIAL EVENTS DECORATION SVCS
SPECIALTY FOOD STORES: Coffee
SPECIALTY FOOD STORES: Health & Dietetic Food
SPECIALTY FOOD STORES: Juices, Fruit Or Vegetable
SPECIALTY FOOD STORES: Soft Drinks
SPECIALTY FOOD STORES: Vitamin
SPECULATIVE BUILDERS: Single-Family Housing
SPEED CHANGERS
SPICE & HERB STORES
SPINDLES: Textile
SPOOLS: Indl
SPORTING & ATHLETIC GOODS: Bags, Golf
SPORTING & ATHLETIC GOODS: Bases, Baseball
SPORTING & ATHLETIC GOODS: Basketball Eqpt & Splys, NEC
SPORTING & ATHLETIC GOODS: Bowling Alleys & Access
SPORTING & ATHLETIC GOODS: Camping Eqpt & Splys
SPORTING & ATHLETIC GOODS: Dartboards & Access
SPORTING & ATHLETIC GOODS: Darts & Table Sports Eqpt & Splys
SPORTING & ATHLETIC GOODS: Dumbbells & Other Weight Eqpt
SPORTING & ATHLETIC GOODS: Exercising Cycles
SPORTING & ATHLETIC GOODS: Fish & Bait Baskets Or Creels
SPORTING & ATHLETIC GOODS: Fishing Bait, Artificial
SPORTING & ATHLETIC GOODS: Fishing Eqpt
SPORTING & ATHLETIC GOODS: Fishing Tackle, General
SPORTING & ATHLETIC GOODS: Game Calls
SPORTING & ATHLETIC GOODS: Gymnasium Eqpt
SPORTING & ATHLETIC GOODS: Hockey Eqpt & Splys, NEC
SPORTING & ATHLETIC GOODS: Hooks, Fishing
SPORTING & ATHLETIC GOODS: Hunting Eqpt
SPORTING & ATHLETIC GOODS: Indian Clubs
SPORTING & ATHLETIC GOODS: Lacrosse Eqpt & Splys, NEC
SPORTING & ATHLETIC GOODS: Masks, Hockey, Baseball, Etc
SPORTING & ATHLETIC GOODS: Pools, Swimming, Exc Plastic
SPORTING & ATHLETIC GOODS: Pools, Swimming, Plastic
SPORTING & ATHLETIC GOODS: Protective Sporting Eqpt
SPORTING & ATHLETIC GOODS: Reels, Fishing
SPORTING & ATHLETIC GOODS: Rods & Rod Parts, Fishing
SPORTING & ATHLETIC GOODS: Shafts, Golf Club
SPORTING & ATHLETIC GOODS: Shuffleboards & Shuffleboard Eqpt
SPORTING & ATHLETIC GOODS: Skateboards
SPORTING & ATHLETIC GOODS: Skates & Parts, Roller
SPORTING & ATHLETIC GOODS: Soccer Eqpt & Splys
SPORTING & ATHLETIC GOODS: Softball Eqpt, Splys
SPORTING & ATHLETIC GOODS: Strings, Tennis Racket
SPORTING & ATHLETIC GOODS: Target Shooting Eqpt
SPORTING & ATHLETIC GOODS: Targets, Archery & Rifle Shooting
SPORTING & ATHLETIC GOODS: Team Sports Eqpt
SPORTING & ATHLETIC GOODS: Track & Field Athletic Eqpt
SPORTING & ATHLETIC GOODS: Water Sports Eqpt
SPORTING & REC GOODS, WHOLESALE: Boats, Canoes, Etc/Eqpt
SPORTING & RECREATIONAL GOODS & SPLYS WHOLESALERS
SPORTING & RECREATIONAL GOODS, WHOLESALE: Athletic Goods
SPORTING & RECREATIONAL GOODS, WHOLESALE: Bicycle
SPORTING & RECREATIONAL GOODS, WHOLESALE: Boat Access & Part
SPORTING & RECREATIONAL GOODS, WHOLESALE: Bowling
SPORTING & RECREATIONAL GOODS, WHOLESALE: Diving
SPORTING & RECREATIONAL GOODS, WHOLESALE: Exercise
SPORTING & RECREATIONAL GOODS, WHOLESALE: Fishing
SPORTING & RECREATIONAL GOODS, WHOLESALE: Fishing Tackle
SPORTING & RECREATIONAL GOODS, WHOLESALE: Fitness
SPORTING & RECREATIONAL GOODS, WHOLESALE: Golf
SPORTING & RECREATIONAL GOODS, WHOLESALE: Hunting
SPORTING CAMPS
SPORTING FIREARMS WHOLESALERS
SPORTING GOODS
SPORTING GOODS STORES, NEC
SPORTING GOODS STORES: Archery Splys
SPORTING GOODS STORES: Bait & Tackle
SPORTING GOODS STORES: Firearms
SPORTING GOODS STORES: Fishing Eqpt
SPORTING GOODS STORES: Hunting Eqpt
SPORTING GOODS STORES: Martial Arts Eqpt & Splys
SPORTING GOODS STORES: Playground Eqpt
SPORTING GOODS STORES: Skiing Eqpt
SPORTING GOODS STORES: Team sports Eqpt
SPORTING GOODS STORES: Tennis Goods & Eqpt
SPORTING GOODS: Archery
SPORTING GOODS: Hammocks, Fabric, Made From Purchased Mat
SPORTING/ATHLETIC GOODS: Gloves, Boxing, Handball, Etc
SPORTS APPAREL STORES
SPOUTING: Plastic & Fiberglass Reinforced
SPOUTS: Sheet Metal
SPRAY BULBS: Rubber
SPRAYING & DUSTING EQPT
SPRAYING EQPT: Agricultural
SPRAYS: Artificial & Preserved
SPRINGS: Coiled Flat
SPRINGS: Cold Formed
SPRINGS: Hot Wound, Exc Wire
SPRINGS: Instrument, Precision
SPRINGS: Leaf, Automobile, Locomotive, Etc
SPRINGS: Mechanical, Precision
SPRINGS: Precision
SPRINGS: Steel
SPRINGS: Torsion Bar
SPRINGS: Wire
SPRINKLING SYSTEMS: Fire Control
SPROCKETS: Power Transmission
STACKING MACHINES: Automatic
STAGE LIGHTING SYSTEMS
STAINLESS STEEL
STAINLESS STEEL WARE
STAIRCASES & STAIRS, WOOD
STAMPING SVC: Book, Gold
STAMPINGS: Automotive
STAMPINGS: Metal
STAPLES
STAPLES, MADE FROM PURCHASED WIRE
STARTERS & CONTROLLERS: Motor, Electric
STARTERS: Electric Motor
STARTERS: Motor
STARTING EQPT: Street Cars
STATE CREDIT UNIONS, NOT FEDERALLY CHARTERED
STATIC ELIMINATORS: Ind
STATIONARY & OFFICE SPLYS, WHOLESALE: Manifold Business Form
STATIONARY & OFFICE SPLYS, WHOLESALE: Marking Devices
STATIONARY & OFFICE SPLYS, WHOLESALE: Office Filing Splys
STATIONARY & OFFICE SPLYS, WHOLESALE: Stationery
STATIONARY & OFFICE SPLYS, WHOLESALE: Writing Ink
STATIONER'S SUNDRIES: Rubber
STATIONARY & OFFICE SPLYS WHOLESALERS
STATIONERY PRDTS
STATIONERY: Made From Purchased Materials
STATORS REWINDING SVCS
STATUARY & OTHER DECORATIVE PRDTS: Nonmetallic
STATUARY GOODS, EXC RELIGIOUS: Wholesalers
STATUES: Nonmetal
STEEL & ALLOYS: Tool & Die
STEEL FABRICATORS
STEEL MILLS
STEEL SHEET: Cold-Rolled
STEEL WOOL
STEEL, COLD-ROLLED: Flat Bright, From Purchased Hot-Rolled
STEEL, COLD-ROLLED: Sheet Or Strip, From Own Hot-Rolled
STEEL, COLD-ROLLED: Strip NEC, From Purchased Hot-Rolled
STEEL, COLD-ROLLED: Strip Or Wire
STEEL, HOT-ROLLED: Sheet Or Strip
STEEL: Cold-Rolled
STEEL: Laminated
STEERING SYSTEMS & COMPONENTS
STENCILS
STEREOGRAPHS: Photographic Message Svcs
STERILIZERS, BARBER & BEAUTY SHOP
STITCHING SVCS
STOCK CAR RACING
STOCK SHAPES: Plastic
STONE: Cast Concrete
STONE: Dimension, NEC
STONE: Quarrying & Processing, Own Stone Prdts
STONES: Abrasive
STONEWARE PRDTS: Pottery
STOOLS: Factory
STORE FIXTURES, EXC REFRIGERATED: Wholesalers
STORE FIXTURES: Exc Wood

# PRODUCT INDEX

STORE FIXTURES: Wood
STORES: Auto & Home Supply
STORES: Drapery & Upholstery
STRADDLE CARRIERS: Mobile
STRAINERS: Line, Piping Systems
STRAPPING
STRAPS: Apparel Webbing
STRAPS: Webbing, Woven
STRAW GOODS
STRAWS: Drinking, Made From Purchased Materials
STRINGING BEADS
STRIPS: Copper & Copper Alloy
STRUCTURAL SUPPORT & BUILDING MATERIAL: Concrete
STUDIOS: Artist
STUDIOS: Artists & Artists' Studios
STUDIOS: Sculptor's
STUDS & JOISTS: Sheet Metal
STYLING SVCS: Wigs
STYRENE RESINS, NEC
SUBPRESSES, METALWORKING
SUGAR SUBSTITUTES: Organic
SUNDRIES & RELATED PRDTS: Medical & Laboratory, Rubber
SUNGLASSES, WHOLESALE
SUPERMARKETS & OTHER GROCERY STORES
SURFACE ACTIVE AGENTS
SURFACE ACTIVE AGENTS: Emulsifiers, Exc Food & Pharmaceuticl
SURFACE ACTIVE AGENTS: Oils & Greases
SURFACE ACTIVE AGENTS: Processing Assistants
SURGICAL & MEDICAL INSTRUMENTS WHOLESALERS
SURGICAL APPLIANCES & SPLYS
SURGICAL APPLIANCES & SPLYS
SURGICAL EQPT: See Also Instruments
SURGICAL IMPLANTS
SURVEYING & MAPPING: Land Parcels
SUSPENSION SYSTEMS: Acoustical, Metal
SVC ESTABLISH EQPT, WHOL: Extermination/Fumigatn Eqpt/Splys
SVC ESTABLISHMENT EQPT & SPLYS WHOLESALERS
SVC ESTABLISHMENT EQPT, WHOL: Cleaning & Maint Eqpt & Splys
SVC ESTABLISHMENT EQPT, WHOL: Concrete Burial Vaults & Boxes
SVC ESTABLISHMENT EQPT, WHOL: Liquor Dispensing Eqpt/Sys
SVC ESTABLISHMENT EQPT, WHOLESALE: Beauty Parlor Eqpt & Sply
SVC ESTABLISHMENT EQPT, WHOLESALE: Cemetery Splys & Eqpt
SVC ESTABLISHMENT EQPT, WHOLESALE: Engraving Eqpt & Splys
SVC ESTABLISHMENT EQPT, WHOLESALE: Firefighting Eqpt
SVC ESTABLISHMENT EQPT, WHOLESALE: Laundry Eqpt & Splys
SVC ESTABLISHMENT EQPT, WHOLESALE: Locksmith Eqpt & Splys
SVC ESTABLISHMENT EQPT, WHOLESALE: Restaurant Splys
SVC ESTABLISHMENT EQPT, WHOLESALE: Taxidermist Tools & Eqpt
SWEEPING COMPOUNDS
SWIMMING POOL & HOT TUB CLEANING & MAINTENANCE SVCS
SWIMMING POOL SPLY STORES
SWIMMING POOLS, EQPT & SPLYS: Wholesalers
SWITCHBOARD OPERATIONS: Private Branch Exchanges
SWITCHBOARDS & PARTS: Power
SWITCHES
SWITCHES: Electric Power
SWITCHES: Electric Power, Exc Snap, Push Button, Etc
SWITCHES: Electronic
SWITCHES: Electronic Applications
SWITCHES: Flow Actuated, Electrical
SWITCHES: Solenoid
SWITCHES: Starting, Fluorescent
SWITCHES: Stepping
SWITCHES: Time, Electrical Switchgear Apparatus
SWITCHGEAR & SWITCHBOARD APPARATUS
SWITCHGEAR & SWITCHGEAR ACCESS, NEC
SWITCHING EQPT: Radio & Television Communications
SYNTHETIC RESIN FINISHED PRDTS, NEC
SYRUPS, DRINK
SYRUPS, FLAVORING, EXC DRINK
SYRUPS: Pharmaceutical
SYSTEMS ENGINEERING: Computer Related
SYSTEMS INTEGRATION SVCS
SYSTEMS INTEGRATION SVCS: Local Area Network
SYSTEMS INTEGRATION SVCS: Office Computer Automation
SYSTEMS SOFTWARE DEVELOPMENT SVCS

# T

TABLE OR COUNTERTOPS, PLASTIC LAMINATED
TABLECLOTHS & SETTINGS
TABLETS: Bronze Or Other Metal
TABLEWARE OR KITCHEN ARTICLES: Whiteware, Fine Semivitreous
TAGS & LABELS: Paper
TAGS: Paper, Blank, Made From Purchased Paper
TAILORS: Custom
TALLOW: Animal
TANK REPAIR & CLEANING SVCS
TANK REPAIR SVCS
TANKS & OTHER TRACKED VEHICLE CMPNTS
TANKS: For Tank Trucks, Metal Plate
TANKS: Fuel, Including Oil & Gas, Metal Plate
TANKS: Lined, Metal
TANKS: Plastic & Fiberglass
TANKS: Standard Or Custom Fabricated, Metal Plate
TANKS: Water, Metal Plate
TAPE DRIVES
TAPE MEASURES
TAPE RECERTIFICATION SVCS
TAPE STORAGE UNITS: Computer
TAPE: Instrumentation Type, Blank
TAPE: Rubber
TAPES, ADHESIVE: Masking, Made From Purchased Materials
TAPES, ADHESIVE: Medical
TAPES: Coated Fiberglass, Pipe Sealing Or Insulating
TAPES: Fabric
TAPES: Gummed, Cloth Or Paper Based, From Purchased Matls
TAPES: Magnetic
TAPES: Plastic Coated
TAPES: Pressure Sensitive
TAPES: Pressure Sensitive, Rubber
TAPS
TARPAULINS
TARPAULINS, WHOLESALE
TAX RETURN PREPARATION SVCS
TECHNICAL & TRADE SCHOOLS, NEC
TECHNICAL MANUAL PREPARATION SVCS
TECHNICAL WRITING SVCS
TELECOMMUNICATION EQPT REPAIR SVCS, EXC TELEPHONES
TELECOMMUNICATION SYSTEMS & EQPT
TELECOMMUNICATIONS CARRIERS & SVCS: Wired
TELECOMMUNICATIONS CARRIERS & SVCS: Wireless
TELECONFERENCING SVCS
TELEMARKETING BUREAUS
TELEPHONE ANSWERING SVCS
TELEPHONE BOOTHS, EXC WOOD
TELEPHONE CENTRAL OFFICE EQPT: Dial Or Manual
TELEPHONE EQPT INSTALLATION
TELEPHONE EQPT: Modems
TELEPHONE EQPT: NEC
TELEPHONE STATION EQPT & PARTS: Wire
TELEPHONE SVCS
TELEPHONE SWITCHING EQPT: Toll Switching
TELEPHONE: Autotransformers For Switchboards
TELEPHONE: Fiber Optic Systems
TELEPHONE: Headsets
TELEPHONE: Sets, Exc Cellular Radio
TELESCOPES
TELETYPEWRITERS
TELEVISION BROADCASTING & COMMUNICATIONS EQPT
TELEVISION BROADCASTING STATIONS
TELEVISION FILM PRODUCTION SVCS
TELEVISION SETS
TELEVISION: Cameras
TELEVISION: Closed Circuit Eqpt
TELEVISION: Monitors
TEMPERING: Metal
TEMPORARY HELP SVCS
TENTS: All Materials
TERMINAL BOARDS
TERRAZZO PRECAST PRDTS
TEST BORING SVCS: Nonmetallic Minerals
TEST KITS: Pregnancy
TESTERS: Battery
TESTERS: Environmental
TESTERS: Hardness
TESTERS: Logic Circuit
TESTERS: Physical Property
TESTERS: Water, Exc Indl Process
TESTING SVCS
TEXTILE & APPAREL SVCS
TEXTILE BAGS WHOLESALERS
TEXTILE FABRICATORS
TEXTILE FINISHING: Chem Coat/Treat, Man, Broadwoven, Cotton
TEXTILE FINISHING: Chem Coating/Treating, Broadwoven, Cotton
TEXTILE FINISHING: Chemical Coating Or Treating
TEXTILE FINISHING: Dyeing, Broadwoven, Cotton
TEXTILE FINISHING: Dyeing, Finishing & Printng, Linen Fabric
TEXTILE FINISHING: Embossing, Linen, Broadwoven
TEXTILE FINISHING: Flocking, Cotton, Broadwoven
TEXTILE PRDTS: Hand Woven & Crocheted
TEXTILE: Finishing, Cotton Broadwoven
TEXTILE: Finishing, Raw Stock NEC
TEXTILE: Goods, NEC
TEXTILES: Flock
TEXTILES: Jute & Flax Prdts
TEXTILES: Linen Fabrics
TEXTILES: Linings, Carpet, Exc Felt
TEXTILES: Mill Waste & Remnant
TEXTILES: Padding & Wadding
TEXTILES: Wool Waste, Processes
THEATRICAL LIGHTING SVCS
THEATRICAL PRODUCERS & SVCS
THEATRICAL SCENERY
THEOLOGICAL SEMINARIES
THERMOCOUPLES
THERMOCOUPLES: Indl Process
THERMOMETERS: Liquid-In-Glass & Bimetal
THERMOMETERS: Medical, Digital
THERMOPLASTIC MATERIALS
THERMOPLASTICS
THERMOSTAT REPAIR SVCS
THREAD: All Fibers
THREAD: Crochet
THYROID PREPARATIONS
TIES, FORM: Metal
TILE: Brick & Structural, Clay
TILE: Clay, Drain & Structural
TILE: Concrete, Drain
TILE: Mosaic, Ceramic
TILE: Terrazzo Or Concrete, Precast
TILE: Wall & Floor, Ceramic
TILE: Wall, Ceramic
TIMING DEVICES: Electronic
TIN
TIRE CORD & FABRIC
TIRE CORD & FABRIC: Indl, Reinforcing
TIRE CORD & FABRIC: Steel
TIRE DEALERS
TIRE INFLATORS: Hand Or Compressor Operated
TIRE SUNDRIES OR REPAIR MATERIALS: Rubber
TIRES & INNER TUBES
TIRES & TUBES WHOLESALERS
TIRES & TUBES, WHOLESALE: Automotive
TIRES & TUBES, WHOLESALE: Truck
TIRES, USED, WHOLESALE
TIRES: Agricultural, Pneumatic
TIRES: Auto
TIRES: Cushion Or Solid Rubber
TIRES: Plastic
TITANIUM MILL PRDTS
TOBACCO & TOBACCO PRDTS WHOLESALERS
TOBACCO LEAF PROCESSING
TOBACCO STORES & STANDS
TOBACCO: Chewing
TOBACCO: Chewing & Snuff
TOBACCO: Cigarettes
TOBACCO: Cigars
TOBACCO: Smoking
TOILET PREPARATIONS
TOILET SEATS: Wood
TOILETRIES, COSMETICS & PERFUME STORES
TOILETRIES, WHOLESALE: Hair Preparations

# PRODUCT INDEX

TOILETRIES, WHOLESALE: Perfumes
TOILETRIES, WHOLESALE: Toilet Soap
TOILETRIES, WHOLESALE: Toiletries
TOILETS: Portable Chemical, Plastics
TOLL OPERATIONS
TOLLS: Caulking
TOMBSTONES: Terrazzo Or Concrete, Precast
TOOL & DIE STEEL
TOOL REPAIR SVCS
TOOLS: Carpenters', Including Levels & Chisels, Exc Saws
TOOLS: Hand
TOOLS: Hand, Carpet Layers
TOOLS: Hand, Hammers
TOOLS: Hand, Ironworkers'
TOOLS: Hand, Masons'
TOOLS: Hand, Mechanics
TOOLS: Hand, Plumbers'
TOOLS: Hand, Power
TOOTHPASTES, GELS & TOOTHPOWDERS
TOWELETTES: Premoistened
TOWELS: Knit
TOWERS, SECTIONS: Transmission, Radio & Television
TOWING SVCS: Marine
TOYS
TOYS & HOBBY GOODS & SPLYS, WHOL: Toy Novelties & Amusements
TOYS & HOBBY GOODS & SPLYS, WHOLESALE: Arts/Crafts Eqpt/Sply
TOYS & HOBBY GOODS & SPLYS, WHOLESALE: Educational Toys
TOYS & HOBBY GOODS & SPLYS, WHOLESALE: Model Kits
TOYS & HOBBY GOODS & SPLYS, WHOLESALE: Puzzles
TOYS & HOBBY GOODS & SPLYS, WHOLESALE: Toys & Games
TOYS & HOBBY GOODS & SPLYS, WHOLESALE: Toys, NEC
TOYS & HOBBY GOODS & SPLYS, WHOLESALE: Video Games
TOYS, HOBBY GOODS & SPLYS WHOLESALERS
TOYS: Dolls, Stuffed Animals & Parts
TOYS: Electronic
TOYS: Kites
TOYS: Paint Sets, Children's
TOYS: Rubber
TOYS: Video Game Machines
TRADE SHOW ARRANGEMENT SVCS
TRAILER COACHES: Automobile
TRAILERS & CHASSIS: Camping
TRAILERS & PARTS: Boat
TRAILERS & PARTS: Truck & Semi's
TRAILERS & TRAILER EQPT
TRAILERS: Bodies
TRAILERS: Semitrailers, Truck Tractors
TRANSDUCERS: Electrical Properties
TRANSDUCERS: Pressure
TRANSFORMERS: Control
TRANSFORMERS: Distribution
TRANSFORMERS: Distribution, Electric
TRANSFORMERS: Electric
TRANSFORMERS: Electronic
TRANSFORMERS: Florescent Lighting
TRANSFORMERS: Flyback
TRANSFORMERS: Lighting, Street & Airport
TRANSFORMERS: Meters, Electronic
TRANSFORMERS: Power Related
TRANSFORMERS: Specialty
TRANSFORMERS: Voltage Regulating
TRANSLATION & INTERPRETATION SVCS
TRANSMISSIONS: Motor Vehicle
TRANSPORTATION AGENTS & BROKERS
TRANSPORTATION ARRANGEMENT SVCS, PASS: Sightseeing Tour Co's
TRANSPORTATION BROKERS: Truck
TRANSPORTATION EPQT & SPLYS, WHOLESALE: Marine Crafts/Splys
TRANSPORTATION EPQT/SPLYS, WHOL: Space Propulsion Unit/Part
TRANSPORTATION EQPT & SPLYS WHOLESALERS, NEC
TRANSPORTATION EQUIPMENT, NEC
TRANSPORTATION PROGRAMS REGULATION & ADMINISTRATION SVCS
TRANSPORTATION SVCS, WATER: Water Taxis
TRANSPORTATION SVCS: Airport Limousine, Scheduled Svcs
TRANSPORTATION SVCS: Railroads, Interurban
TRANSPORTATION: Bus Transit Systems
TRANSPORTATION: Deep Sea Domestic Freight
TRANSPORTATION: Transit Systems, NEC
TRAPS: Animal, Iron Or Steel
TRAPS: Stem
TRAVEL AGENCIES
TRAVEL TRAILERS & CAMPERS
TRAVELER ACCOMMODATIONS, NEC
TRAYS: Cable, Metal Plate
TRAYS: Plastic
TRIM: Window, Wood
TROPHIES, NEC
TROPHIES, PLATED, ALL METALS
TROPHIES, WHOLESALE
TROPHIES: Metal, Exc Silver
TROPHY & PLAQUE STORES
TRUCK & BUS BODIES: Automobile Wrecker Truck
TRUCK & BUS BODIES: Beverage Truck
TRUCK & BUS BODIES: Bus Bodies
TRUCK & BUS BODIES: Car Carrier
TRUCK & BUS BODIES: Dump Truck
TRUCK & BUS BODIES: Motor Vehicle, Specialty
TRUCK & BUS BODIES: Truck Cabs, Motor Vehicles
TRUCK & BUS BODIES: Truck, Motor Vehicle
TRUCK & BUS BODIES: Utility Truck
TRUCK & BUS BODIES: Van Bodies
TRUCK & FREIGHT TERMINALS & SUPPORT ACTIVITIES
TRUCK BODIES: Body Parts
TRUCK BODY SHOP
TRUCK FINANCE LEASING
TRUCK GENERAL REPAIR SVC
TRUCK PAINTING & LETTERING SVCS
TRUCK PARTS & ACCESSORIES: Wholesalers
TRUCKING & HAULING SVCS: Coal, Local
TRUCKING & HAULING SVCS: Contract Basis
TRUCKING & HAULING SVCS: Heavy Machinery, Local
TRUCKING & HAULING SVCS: Heavy, NEC
TRUCKING & HAULING SVCS: Liquid, Local
TRUCKING & HAULING SVCS: Machinery, Heavy
TRUCKING & HAULING SVCS: Mobile Homes
TRUCKING & HAULING SVCS: Trailer/Container On Flat Car
TRUCKING, DUMP
TRUCKING: Except Local
TRUCKING: Local, With Storage
TRUCKING: Local, Without Storage
TRUCKS & TRACTORS: Industrial
TRUCKS, INDL: Wholesalers
TRUCKS: Forklift
TRUCKS: Indl
TRUSSES & FRAMING: Prefabricated Metal
TRUSSES: Wood, Floor
TRUSSES: Wood, Roof
TRUST MANAGEMENT SVCS: Personal Investment
TUB CONTAINERS: Plastic
TUBE & TUBING FABRICATORS
TUBES: Extruded Or Drawn, Aluminum
TUBES: Hard Rubber
TUBES: Paper
TUBES: Paper Or Fiber, Chemical Or Electrical Uses
TUBES: Steel & Iron
TUBES: Television
TUBES: Traveling Wave
TUBES: Wrought, Welded Or Lock Joint
TUBING, COLD-DRAWN: Mech Or Hypodermic Sizes, Stainless
TUBING: Copper
TUBING: Electrical Use, Quartz
TUBING: Flexible, Metallic
TUBING: Plastic
TUBING: Seamless
TUCKING FOR THE TRADE
TURBINES & TURBINE GENERATOR SET UNITS: Gas, Complete
TURBINES & TURBINE GENERATOR SETS
TURBINES & TURBINE GENERATOR SETS & PARTS
TURBINES: Hydraulic, Complete
TURBINES: Steam
TURBO-GENERATORS
TURBO-SUPERCHARGERS: Aircraft
TURKEY PROCESSING & SLAUGHTERING
TWINE PRDTS
TYPESETTING SVC
TYPESETTING SVC: Computer
TYPESETTING SVC: Hand Composition
TYPOGRAPHY

## U

ULTRASONIC EQPT: Cleaning, Exc Med & Dental
UMBRELLAS & CANES
UNDERGROUND GOLD MINING
UNDERGROUND IRON ORE MINING
UNIFORM STORES
UNIT TRAIN LOADING FACILITY, BITUMINOUS OR LIGNITE
UNIVERSITY
UNSUPPORTED PLASTICS: Tile
UPHOLSTERY MATERIAL
UPHOLSTERY WORK SVCS
URANIUM ORE MINING, NEC
UREA
USED BOOK STORES
USED CAR DEALERS
USED MERCHANDISE STORES: Art Objects, Antique
USED MERCHANDISE STORES: Clothing & Shoes
USED MERCHANDISE STORES: Office Furniture
UTENSILS: Cast Aluminum, Cooking Or Kitchen
UTENSILS: Cast Aluminum, Hospital
UTENSILS: Household, Cooking & Kitchen, Metal
UTENSILS: Household, Metal, Exc Cast
UTILITY TRAILER DEALERS

## V

VACUUM CLEANER STORES
VACUUM CLEANERS: Household
VACUUM CLEANERS: Indl Type
VACUUM PUMPS & EQPT: Laboratory
VACUUM SYSTEMS: Air Extraction, Indl
VALUE-ADDED RESELLERS: Computer Systems
VALVE REPAIR SVCS, INDL
VALVES
VALVES & PARTS: Gas, Indl
VALVES & PIPE FITTINGS
VALVES & REGULATORS: Pressure, Indl
VALVES Solenoid
VALVES: Aerosol, Metal
VALVES: Aircraft, Control, Hydraulic & Pneumatic
VALVES: Control, Automatic
VALVES: Electrohydraulic Servo, Metal
VALVES: Engine
VALVES: Fluid Power, Control, Hydraulic & pneumatic
VALVES: Indl
VALVES: Plumbing & Heating
VALVES: Regulating & Control, Automatic
VALVES: Regulating, Process Control
VALVES: Water Works
VARIETY STORE MERCHANDISE, WHOLESALE
VARIETY STORES
VARNISHES, NEC
VARNISHES: Lithographic
VARNISHING SVC: Metal Prdts
VAULTS & SAFES WHOLESALERS
VEHICLES: All Terrain
VEHICLES: Children's, Exc Bicycles
VEHICLES: Recreational
VENDING MACHINE OPERATORS: Food
VENDING MACHINES & PARTS
VENETIAN BLINDS & SHADES
VENTILATING EQPT: Metal
VENTILATING EQPT: Sheet Metal
VENTURE CAPITAL COMPANIES
VETERINARY PHARMACEUTICAL PREPARATIONS
VETERINARY PRDTS: Instruments & Apparatus
VIBRATORS: Concrete Construction
VIDEO & AUDIO EQPT, WHOLESALE
VIDEO CAMERA-AUDIO RECORDERS: Household Use
VIDEO EQPT
VIDEO PRODUCTION SVCS
VIDEO TAPE PRODUCTION SVCS
VIDEO TAPE WHOLESALERS, RECORDED
VINYL RESINS, NEC
VISES: Machine
VISUAL COMMUNICATIONS SYSTEMS
VISUAL EFFECTS PRODUCTION SVCS
VITAMINS: Natural Or Synthetic, Uncompounded, Bulk
VITAMINS: Pharmaceutical Preparations
VOCATIONAL REHABILITATION AGENCY
VOCATIONAL TRAINING AGENCY
VOLCANIC ROCK: Dimension

# PRODUCT INDEX

## W

WALLBOARD: Decorated, Made From Purchased Materials
WALLBOARD: Gypsum
WALLPAPER STORE
WALLS: Curtain, Metal
WAREHOUSE CLUBS STORES
WAREHOUSING & STORAGE FACILITIES, NEC
WAREHOUSING & STORAGE, REFRIGERATED: Cold Storage Or Refrig
WAREHOUSING & STORAGE, REFRIGERATED: Frozen Or Refrig Goods
WAREHOUSING & STORAGE: Bulk St & Termnls, Hire, Petro/Chem
WAREHOUSING & STORAGE: General
WAREHOUSING & STORAGE: General
WAREHOUSING & STORAGE: Household Goods
WAREHOUSING & STORAGE: Miniwarehouse
WAREHOUSING & STORAGE: Refrigerated
WARM AIR HEATING & AC EQPT & SPLYS, WHOL: Dust Collecting
WARM AIR HEATING & AC EQPT & SPLYS, WHOLESALE Air Filters
WARM AIR HEATING & AC EQPT & SPLYS, WHOLESALE Heat Exchgrs
WARM AIR HEATING/AC EQPT/SPLYS, WHOL Warm Air Htg Eqpt/Splys
WASHCLOTHS & BATH MITTS, FROM PURCHASED MATERIALS
WASHERS
WASHERS: Lock
WASHERS: Metal
WASHERS: Plastic
WASHERS: Rubber
WASTE CLEANING SVCS
WATCH REPAIR SVCS
WATCHES
WATCHES & PARTS, WHOLESALE
WATER HEATERS
WATER PURIFICATION EQPT: Household
WATER PURIFICATION PRDTS: Chlorination Tablets & Kits
WATER SOFTENER SVCS
WATER SOFTENING WHOLESALERS
WATER SUPPLY
WATER TREATMENT EQPT: Indl
WATER: Distilled
WATER: Mineral, Carbonated, Canned & Bottled, Etc
WATER: Pasteurized & Mineral, Bottled & Canned
WATER: Pasteurized, Canned & Bottled, Etc
WATERPROOFING COMPOUNDS
WAVEGUIDE STRUCTURES: Accelerating
WAVEGUIDES & FITTINGS
WAX REMOVERS
WAX Sealing wax
WAXES: Mineral, Natural
WAXES: Petroleum, Not Produced In Petroleum Refineries
WEATHER STRIPS: Metal
WEAVING MILL, BROADWOVEN FABRICS: Wool Or Similar Fabric
WEIGHING MACHINERY & APPARATUS
WELDING & CUTTING APPARATUS & ACCESS, NEC
WELDING EQPT
WELDING EQPT & SPLYS WHOLESALERS
WELDING EQPT & SPLYS: Electrodes
WELDING EQPT & SPLYS: Gas
WELDING EQPT & SPLYS: Resistance, Electric
WELDING EQPT & SPLYS: Wire, Bare & Coated
WELDING EQPT REPAIR SVCS
WELDING EQPT: Electric
WELDING MACHINES & EQPT: Ultrasonic
WELDING REPAIR SVC
WELDING SPLYS, EXC GASES: Wholesalers
WELDING TIPS: Heat Resistant, Metal
WELDMENTS
WELL CASINGS: Iron & Steel, Made In Steel Mills
WESTERN APPAREL STORES
WET CORN MILLING
WHEEL & CASTER REPAIR SVCS
WHEELCHAIR LIFTS
WHEELCHAIRS
WHEELS
WHEELS & BRAKE SHOES: Railroad, Cast Iron
WHEELS & GRINDSTONES, EXC ARTIFICIAL: Abrasive
WHEELS, GRINDING: Artificial
WHEELS: Abrasive
WHEELS: Disc, Wheelbarrow, Stroller, Etc, Stamped Metal
WHEELS: Polishing
WHEELS: Railroad Car, Cast Steel
WHEELS: Rolled, Locomotive
WHISTLES
WICKER PRDTS
WIG & HAIRPIECE STORES
WIGS & HAIRPIECES
WINCHES
WIND CHIMES
WINDINGS: Coil, Electronic
WINDMILLS: Electric Power Generation
WINDMILLS: Farm Type
WINDOW & DOOR FRAMES
WINDOW BLIND CLEANING SVCS
WINDOW BLIND REPAIR SVCS
WINDOW CLEANING SVCS
WINDOW FRAMES & SASHES: Plastic
WINDOW FRAMES, MOLDING & TRIM: Vinyl
WINDOW FURNISHINGS WHOLESALERS
WINDOW SASHES, WOOD
WINDOW SCREENING: Plastic
WINDOW SQUEEGEES
WINDOWS: Frames, Wood
WINDOWS: Storm, Wood
WINDOWS: Wood
WINDSHIELD WIPER SYSTEMS
WINDSHIELDS: Plastic
WINE & DISTILLED ALCOHOLIC BEVERAGES WHOLESALERS
WINE CELLARS, BONDED: Wine, Blended
WIRE
WIRE & CABLE: Aluminum
WIRE & CABLE: Aluminum
WIRE & CABLE: Nonferrous, Automotive, Exc Ignition Sets
WIRE & CABLE: Nonferrous, Building
WIRE & WIRE PRDTS
WIRE CLOTH & WOVEN WIRE PRDTS, MADE FROM PURCHASED WIRE
WIRE FABRIC: Welded Steel
WIRE FENCING & ACCESS WHOLESALERS
WIRE MATERIALS: Aluminum
WIRE MATERIALS: Copper
WIRE MATERIALS: Steel
WIRE PRDTS: Ferrous Or Iron, Made In Wiredrawing Plants
WIRE PRDTS: Steel & Iron
WIRE ROPE CENTERS
WIRE WINDING OF PURCHASED WIRE
WIRE: Communication
WIRE: Mesh
WIRE: Nonferrous
WIRE: Steel, Insulated Or Armored
WIRE: Wire, Ferrous Or Iron
WOMEN'S & CHILDREN'S CLOTHING WHOLESALERS, NEC
WOMEN'S & GIRLS' SPORTSWEAR WHOLESALERS
WOMEN'S CLOTHING STORES
WOMEN'S CLOTHING STORES: Ready-To-Wear
WOMEN'S FULL & KNEE LENGTH HOSIERY DYEING & FINISHING
WOMEN'S SPECIALTY CLOTHING STORES
WOMEN'S SPORTSWEAR STORES
WOOD EXTRACT PRDTS
WOOD FENCING WHOLESALERS
WOOD PRDTS
WOOD PRDTS: Applicators
WOOD PRDTS: Brackets
WOOD PRDTS: Chair Cane, Rattan Or Reed
WOOD PRDTS: Door Trim
WOOD PRDTS: Handles, Tool
WOOD PRDTS: Laundry
WOOD PRDTS: Marquetry
WOOD PRDTS: Moldings, Unfinished & Prefinished
WOOD PRDTS: Mulch Or Sawdust
WOOD PRDTS: Mulch, Wood & Bark
WOOD PRDTS: Newel Posts
WOOD PRDTS: Outdoor, Structural
WOOD PRDTS: Panel Work
WOOD PRDTS: Planters & Window Boxes
WOOD PRDTS: Poles
WOOD PRDTS: Porch Work
WOOD PRDTS: Signboards
WOOD PRDTS: Stepladders
WOOD PRDTS: Tackle Blocks
WOOD PRDTS: Trophy Bases
WOOD PRDTS: Window Backs, Store Or Lunchroom, Prefabricated
WOOD PRODUCTS: Reconstituted
WOOD SHAVINGS BALES, MULCH TYPE, WHOLESALE
WOOD TREATING: Millwork
WOOD TREATING: Railroad Cross-Ties
WOOD TREATING: Structural Lumber & Timber
WOOD TREATING: Wood Prdts, Creosoted
WOODWORK & TRIM: Exterior & Ornamental
WOODWORK & TRIM: Interior & Ornamental
WOODWORK: Carved & Turned
WOODWORK: Interior & Ornamental, NEC
WOODWORK: Ornamental, Cornices, Mantels, Etc.
WORD PROCESSING SVCS
WOVEN WIRE PRDTS, NEC
WREATHS: Artificial
WRENCHES
WRITING FOR PUBLICATION SVCS

## X

X-RAY EQPT & TUBES
X-RAY EQPT REPAIR SVCS

# PRODUCT SECTION

```
                    ┌─────────────────────────────────────────┐    Indicates approximate employment figure
                    │ BOXES: Folding                          │    A = Over 500 employees, B = 251-500
Product category ───│ Edgar & Son Paperboard ........ G ... 999 999-9999   C = 101-250, D = 51-100, E = 20-50
                    │   Yourtown (G-11480)                    │    F = 10-19, G = 3-9
                    │ Ready Box Co ................... E ... 999 999-9999  ── Business phone
City ───────────────│   Anytown (G-7097)                      │
                    └─────────────────────────────────────────┘    Geographic Section entry number where full
                                                                    company information appears.
```

*See footnotes for symbols and codes identification.*
- Refer to the Industrial Product Index preceding this section to locate product headings.

### ABRASIVE SAND MINING
Fjcj LLC .................................................... F ....... 618 785-2217
  Baldwin *(G-1250)*

### ABRASIVES
Abrasic 90 Inc ........................................ E ....... 800 447-4248
  Niles *(G-15955)*
Abrasive-Form LLC ................................ E ....... 630 220-3437
  Bloomingdale *(G-2091)*
Anchor Abrasives Company ................. E ....... 708 444-4300
  Tinley Park *(G-20893)*
Bates Abrasive Products Inc ............... E ....... 773 586-8700
  Chicago *(G-4054)*
Covidien LP ............................................. C ....... 815 744-3766
  Joliet *(G-12478)*
Dura Wax Company ................................ F ....... 815 385-5000
  McHenry *(G-14499)*
Electro-Glo Distribution Inc ................... G ....... 815 224-4030
  La Salle *(G-12771)*
Harsco Corporation ................................ F ....... 217 237-4335
  Pawnee *(G-17234)*
Ideal Industries Inc ............................... C ....... 815 895-1108
  Sycamore *(G-20801)*
K & K Abrasives & Supplies .................. E ....... 773 582-9500
  Chicago *(G-5341)*
Kona Blackbird Inc ................................. F ....... 815 792-8750
  Serena *(G-19892)*
Marvel Abrasives Products LLC ........... F ....... 800 621-0673
  Chicago *(G-5637)*
Meinhardt Diamond Tool Co ................. G ....... 773 267-3260
  Chicago *(G-5681)*
Rh Preyda Company ............................. F ....... 212 880-1477
  Chicago *(G-6348)*
S & J Industrial Supply Corp ................. F ....... 708 339-1708
  South Holland *(G-20303)*
Saint-Gobain Abrasives Inc .................. C ....... 630 238-3300
  Carol Stream *(G-3231)*
Sand-Rite Manufacturing Co ................ G ....... 312 997-2200
  Melrose Park *(G-14691)*
Sandtech Inc .......................................... F ....... 847 470-9595
  Morton Grove *(G-15234)*
Schram Enterprises Inc ........................ E ....... 708 345-2252
  Melrose Park *(G-14693)*
U S Silica Company .............................. C ....... 815 434-0188
  Ottawa *(G-16988)*
Uk Abrasives Inc .................................. E ....... 847 291-3566
  Northbrook *(G-16378)*
Ultramatic Equipment Co ..................... E ....... 630 543-4565
  Addison *(G-333)*
US Minerals Inc .................................... F ....... 219 864-0909
  Tinley Park *(G-20954)*
US Minerals Inc .................................... F ....... 618 785-2217
  Baldwin *(G-1252)*
US Minerals Inc .................................... F ....... 217 534-2370
  Coffeen *(G-7306)*
Washington Mills Hennepin Inc ........... D ....... 815 925-7302
  Hennepin *(G-11735)*

### ABRASIVES: Aluminum Oxide Fused
Global Material Tech Inc ...................... C ....... 773 247-6000
  Chicago *(G-4958)*

### ABRASIVES: Diamond Powder
Engis Corporation .................................. C ....... 847 808-9400
  Wheeling *(G-22047)*

### ABRASIVES: Polishing Rouge
Agsco Corporation ................................ E ....... 847 520-4455
  Wheeling *(G-21999)*

### ABRASIVES: Silicon Carbide
Washington Mills Tonawanda ............. D ....... 815 925-7302
  Hennepin *(G-11736)*

### ABRASIVES: Tungsten Carbide
Carbco Manufacturing Inc .................... F ....... 630 377-1410
  Saint Charles *(G-19150)*

### ACCELERATION INDICATORS & SYSTEM COMPONENTS: Aerospace
Cadicam Inc .......................................... E ....... 847 394-3610
  Wheeling *(G-22023)*
Kaney Group LLC ................................ G ....... 815 986-4359
  Rockford *(G-18453)*
Northrop Grumman Technical ............. C ....... 847 259-2396
  Rolling Meadows *(G-18754)*
S Flying Inc .......................................... E ....... 618 586-9999
  Palestine *(G-17095)*
Waltz Brothers Inc ............................... E ....... 847 520-1122
  Wheeling *(G-22181)*

### ACCELERATORS: Linear
Accu Cut Inc ......................................... G ....... 815 229-3525
  Rockford *(G-18252)*
Rockford Linear Motion LLC ............... G ....... 815 961-7900
  Rockford *(G-18578)*

### ACCIDENT INSURANCE CARRIERS
Caterpillar Inc ....................................... A ....... 309 675-1000
  Peoria *(G-17326)*
Caterpillar Inc ....................................... B ....... 888 614-4328
  Peoria *(G-17328)*
Caterpillar Inc ....................................... B ....... 309 675-6590
  Peoria *(G-17333)*

### ACCOUNTING SVCS, NEC
Paragon International Inc .................... F ....... 847 240-2981
  Schaumburg *(G-19682)*

### ACIDS: Hydrochloric
Brainerd Chemical Midwest LLC ........ G ....... 918 622-1214
  Danville *(G-7707)*
Remuriate LLC ..................................... G ....... 815 220-5050
  La Salle *(G-12783)*
Xingfa USA Corporation ...................... G ....... 360 720-9256
  Naperville *(G-15786)*

### ACIDS: Inorganic
Solvay USA Inc .................................... E ....... 708 371-2000
  Blue Island *(G-2271)*

### ACIDS: Sulfuric, Oleum
Phosphate Resource Ptrs .................... A ....... 847 739-1200
  Lake Forest *(G-12945)*

### ACRYLIC RESINS
Akrylix Inc ............................................. F ....... 773 869-9005
  Frankfort *(G-10291)*
De Enterprises Inc ............................... F ....... 708 345-8088
  Broadview *(G-2571)*

### ACTUATORS: Indl, NEC
Thomson Linear LLC ........................... C ....... 815 568-8001
  Marengo *(G-14243)*

### ADDITIVE BASED PLASTIC MATERIALS: Plasticizers
Raytech Machining Fabrication ........... E ....... 618 932-2511
  West Frankfort *(G-21816)*

### ADDRESSING SVCS
Assemble and Mail Group Inc ............. G ....... 309 473-2006
  Heyworth *(G-11764)*
J K Printing & Mailing Inc .................... G ....... 847 432-7717
  Highland Park *(G-11846)*

### ADHESIVES
A J Adhesives Inc ................................ G ....... 708 210-1111
  South Holland *(G-20238)*
Aabbitt Adhesives Inc ......................... D ....... 773 227-2700
  Chicago *(G-3701)*
Aabbitt Adhesives Inc ......................... E ....... 773 723-6780
  Chicago *(G-3702)*
Armitage Industries Inc ....................... F ....... 847 288-9090
  Franklin Park *(G-10400)*
Campbell Camie Inc ............................ E ....... 314 968-3222
  Downers Grove *(G-8403)*
Chicago Adhesive Products ................ G ....... 630 978-7766
  Aurora *(G-983)*
CP Moyen Co ....................................... G ....... 847 673-6866
  Skokie *(G-19988)*
Cyberbond LLC .................................... E ....... 630 761-0341
  Batavia *(G-1436)*
Emulsicoat Inc ..................................... F ....... 217 344-7775
  Urbana *(G-21081)*
H E Wisdom & Sons Inc ..................... E ....... 847 841-7002
  Elgin *(G-9052)*
HB Fuller Adhesives LLC .................... E ....... 815 357-6726
  Morris *(G-15110)*
HB Fuller Cnstr Pdts Inc ..................... C ....... 630 978-7766
  Aurora *(G-1023)*
HB Fuller Cnstr Pdts Inc ..................... F ....... 847 776-4375
  Palatine *(G-17035)*
Henkel Corporation ............................. D ....... 847 468-9200
  Elgin *(G-9064)*
ITW Dynatec ........................................ G ....... 847 657-4830
  Glenview *(G-11151)*
Lintec of America Inc .......................... G ....... 847 229-0547
  Schaumburg *(G-19619)*
Mafomsic Incorporated ....................... F ....... 630 279-2005
  Elmhurst *(G-9905)*
Morton International LLC .................... C ....... 312 807-2696
  Chicago *(G-5807)*
Morton Intl Inc Adhsves Spclty .......... G ....... 815 653-2042
  Ringwood *(G-17993)*
Nalco Company LLC ........................... A ....... 630 305-1000
  Naperville *(G-15703)*
National Casein New Jersey Inc ........ G ....... 773 846-7300
  Chicago *(G-5862)*
North Shore Consultants Inc ............. G ....... 847 290-1599
  Elk Grove Village *(G-9655)*
Palm Labs Adhesives LLC .................. G ....... 773 799-8470
  Chicago *(G-6064)*
PPG Architectural Finishes Inc .......... G ....... 847 336-2355
  Gurnee *(G-11487)*
PPG Architectural Finishes Inc .......... E ....... 630 773-8484
  Itasca *(G-12344)*
PPG Architectural Finishes Inc .......... G ....... 630 820-8692
  Aurora *(G-1067)*
Roman Holdings Corporation ............. D ....... 708 891-0770
  Calumet City *(G-2953)*
Rust-Oleum Corporation ..................... D ....... 815 967-4258
  Rockford *(G-18600)*
Sandstrom Products Company ........... E ....... 309 523-2121
  Port Byron *(G-17723)*

**Sanford LP** ............ A ....... 770 418-7000
Downers Grove *(G-8518)*
**Sanford Chemical Co Inc** ............ F ....... 847 437-3530
Elk Grove Village *(G-9727)*
**Simpson Strong-Tie Company Inc** ............ E ....... 630 293-2800
West Chicago *(G-21773)*
**Spartan Adhesives Coatings Co** ............ F ....... 815 459-8500
Crystal Lake *(G-7652)*
**Strytech Adhesives** ............ G ....... 847 509-7566
Northbrook *(G-16373)*
**Surebond Inc** ............ E ....... 630 762-0606
Saint Charles *(G-19275)*
**Surebonder Adhesives Inc** ............ G ....... 847 487-4583
Wauconda *(G-21505)*
**Testor Corporation** ............ D ....... 815 962-6654
Rockford *(G-18644)*
**Tsv Adhesive Systems Inc** ............ E ....... 815 464-5606
Frankfort *(G-10373)*
**Wisdom Adhesives** ............ G ....... 847 841-7002
Elgin *(G-9238)*
**WW Henry Company LP** ............ D ....... 815 933-8059
Bourbonnais *(G-2409)*

## ADHESIVES & SEALANTS

**Adco Global Inc** ............ G ....... 847 282-3485
Lincolnshire *(G-13424)*
**All Weather Courts Inc** ............ G ....... 217 364-4546
Dawson *(G-7816)*
**Bradley Adhsive Applctions Inc** ............ C ....... 630 443-8424
Saint Charles *(G-19145)*
**Chase Corporation** ............ E ....... 847 866-8500
Evanston *(G-10022)*
**Chem Spec Corporation** ............ G ....... 847 891-2133
Elburn *(G-8879)*
**Chicago Latex Products Inc** ............ F ....... 815 459-9680
Crystal Lake *(G-7552)*
**Chromium Industries Inc** ............ E ....... 773 287-3716
Chicago *(G-4373)*
**Daubert Industries Inc** ............ F ....... 630 203-6800
Burr Ridge *(G-2834)*
**Dip Seal Plastics Inc** ............ G ....... 815 398-3533
Rockford *(G-18345)*
**Eco-Pur Solutions LLC** ............ G ....... 630 917-8789
Chicago *(G-4692)*
**Eco-Pur Solutions LLC** ............ G ....... 630 226-2300
Romeoville *(G-18818)*
**Emecole Inc** ............ F ....... 815 372-2493
Romeoville *(G-18819)*
**Essentra International LLC** ............ G ....... 866 800-0775
Westchester *(G-21840)*
**Fitz Chem Corporation** ............ E ....... 630 467-8383
Itasca *(G-12264)*
**Fontana Associates Inc** ............ G ....... 888 707-8273
Arlington Heights *(G-755)*
**G J Nikolas & Co Inc** ............ E ....... 708 544-0320
Bellwood *(G-1706)*
**Glue Inc** ............ G ....... 312 451-4018
Chicago *(G-4962)*
**Green Products LLC** ............ F ....... 815 407-0900
Romeoville *(G-18829)*
**H A Gartenberg & Company** ............ F ....... 847 821-7590
Buffalo Grove *(G-2700)*
**H E Wisdom & Sons Inc** ............ G ....... 847 841-7002
Elgin *(G-9053)*
**Highland Supply Corporation** ............ B ....... 618 654-2161
Highland *(G-11794)*
**Illinois Tool Works Inc** ............ C ....... 708 342-6000
Mokena *(G-14872)*
**Illinois Tool Works Inc** ............ B ....... 847 724-7500
Glenview *(G-11141)*
**Illinois Tool Works Inc** ............ C ....... 630 372-2150
Bartlett *(G-1353)*
**Illinois Tool Works Inc** ............ C ....... 847 783-5500
Elgin *(G-9072)*
**J & J Industries Inc** ............ G ....... 630 595-8878
Bensenville *(G-1925)*
**Jjc Epoxy Inc** ............ G ....... 630 231-5600
West Chicago *(G-21728)*
**Lectro Stik Corp** ............ E ....... 630 894-1355
Glendale Heights *(G-11040)*
**Mapei Corporation** ............ D ....... 630 293-5800
West Chicago *(G-21737)*
**Miller Purcell Co Inc** ............ G ....... 815 485-2142
New Lenox *(G-15897)*
**Morton Salt Inc** ............ C ....... 312 807-2000
Chicago *(G-5809)*
**Nataz Specialty Coatings Inc** ............ F ....... 773 247-7030
Chicago *(G-5856)*
**ND Industries Inc** ............ E ....... 847 498-3600
Northbrook *(G-16318)*
**Nu-Puttie Corporation** ............ E ....... 708 681-1040
Maywood *(G-14433)*
**Olon Industries Inc (us)** ............ E ....... 630 232-4705
Geneva *(G-10858)*
**Opticote Inc** ............ E ....... 847 678-8900
Franklin Park *(G-10544)*
**Owens Corning Sales LLC** ............ E ....... 708 594-6935
Argo *(G-695)*
**Pierce & Stevens Chemical** ............ G ....... 630 653-3800
Carol Stream *(G-3214)*
**Porcelain Enamel Finishers** ............ G ....... 312 808-1560
Chicago *(G-6157)*
**PPG Architectural Finishes Inc** ............ D ....... 773 523-6333
Chicago *(G-6161)*
**PPG Architectural Finishes Inc** ............ B ....... 217 584-1323
Meredosia *(G-14734)*
**PPG Industries Inc** ............ E ....... 773 646-5900
Chicago *(G-6163)*
**Protective Products Intl** ............ G ....... 847 526-1180
Wauconda *(G-21495)*
**Rhopac Fabricated Products LLC** ............ E ....... 847 362-3300
Libertyville *(G-13376)*
**Right/Pointe Company** ............ D ....... 815 754-5700
Dekalb *(G-8115)*
**RM Lucas Co** ............ E ....... 773 523-4300
Chicago *(G-6365)*
**RM Lucas Co** ............ E ....... 773 523-4300
Alsip *(G-522)*
**Roman Decorating Products LLC** ............ E ....... 708 891-0770
Calumet City *(G-2952)*
**Rust-Oleum Corporation** ............ C ....... 847 367-7700
Vernon Hills *(G-21195)*
**Saf-T-Lok International Corp** ............ E ....... 630 495-2001
Lombard *(G-13850)*
**Sandstrom Products Company** ............ F ....... 309 523-2121
Port Byron *(G-17724)*
**Sigma Coatings Inc** ............ G ....... 630 628-5305
Addison *(G-290)*
**Simpson Strong-Tie Company Inc** ............ E ....... 630 613-5100
Addison *(G-293)*
**Ski Seal Coating Inc** ............ G ....... 708 246-5656
Countryside *(G-7442)*
**Specialty Cnstr Brands Inc** ............ F ....... 630 851-0782
Aurora *(G-1081)*
**Spl-Usa LLC** ............ G ....... 312 807-2000
Chicago *(G-6562)*
**Tape Case Ltd** ............ E ....... 847 299-7880
Elk Grove Village *(G-9768)*
**Tempel Steel Company** ............ A ....... 773 250-8000
Chicago *(G-6698)*
**Therm-O-Web Inc** ............ E ....... 847 520-5200
Wheeling *(G-22167)*
**United Gilsonite Laboratories** ............ E ....... 217 243-7878
Jacksonville *(G-12415)*
**Universal Chem & Coatings Inc** ............ E ....... 847 931-1700
Elgin *(G-9219)*
**Universal Chem & Coatings Inc** ............ E ....... 847 297-2001
Elk Grove Village *(G-9801)*
**US Adhesives** ............ G ....... 312 829-7438
Chicago *(G-6852)*
**Versatile Materials Inc** ............ G ....... 773 924-3700
Chicago *(G-6887)*
**Vibracoustic Usa Inc** ............ E ....... 618 382-5891
Carmi *(G-3081)*
**W R Grace & Co- Conn** ............ F ....... 708 458-9700
Chicago *(G-6924)*

## ADHESIVES: Epoxy

**Sika Corporation** ............ G ....... 815 431-1080
Ottawa *(G-16985)*
**United Adhesives Inc** ............ G ....... 224 436-0077
Buffalo Grove *(G-2785)*

## ADVERTISING AGENCIES

**3b Media Inc** ............ F ....... 312 563-9363
Chicago *(G-3667)*
**Ad Images** ............ G ....... 847 956-1887
Elk Grove Village *(G-9269)*
**American Tape Measures** ............ G ....... 312 208-0282
Chicago *(G-3877)*
**Athena Design Group Inc** ............ E ....... 312 733-2828
Chicago *(G-3974)*
**Baka Vitaliy** ............ G ....... 773 370-5522
Chicago *(G-4027)*
**Blue Software LLC** ............ D ....... 773 957-1669
Chicago *(G-4126)*
**Catalog Designers Inc** ............ G ....... 847 228-0025
Elk Grove Village *(G-9359)*
**Corbett Accel Healthcare Grp C** ............ G ....... 312 475-2505
Chicago *(G-4467)*
**Del Great Frame Up Systems Inc** ............ F ....... 847 808-1955
Franklin Park *(G-10456)*
**Early Bird Advertising Inc** ............ G ....... 847 253-1423
Prospect Heights *(G-17777)*
**Edge Communication** ............ G ....... 708 749-7818
Berwyn *(G-2062)*
**Edwards Creative Services LLC** ............ F ....... 309 756-0199
Milan *(G-14784)*
**Fanning Communications Inc** ............ G ....... 708 293-1430
Crestwood *(G-7488)*
**Gammon Group Inc** ............ G ....... 815 722-6400
Shorewood *(G-19927)*
**Geomentum Inc** ............ B ....... 630 729-7500
Downers Grove *(G-8447)*
**Geomentum Inc** ............ G ....... 630 729-7500
Downers Grove *(G-8448)*
**Grove Design & Advertising Inc** ............ G ....... 815 459-4552
Crystal Lake *(G-7585)*
**Holsolutions Inc** ............ G ....... 888 847-5467
Frankfort *(G-10327)*
**Ideal Advertising & Printing** ............ F ....... 815 965-1713
Rockford *(G-18426)*
**Leo Burnett Company Inc** ............ C ....... 312 220-5959
Chicago *(G-5493)*
**Mallof Abruzino Nash Mktg Inc** ............ E ....... 630 929-5200
Carol Stream *(G-3188)*
**McIntyre & Associates** ............ G ....... 847 639-8050
Fox Lake *(G-10278)*
**Media Unlimited Inc** ............ G ....... 630 527-0900
Naperville *(G-15816)*
**Prime Market Targeting Inc** ............ E ....... 815 469-4555
Frankfort *(G-10353)*
**Promark Advertising Specialtie** ............ G ....... 618 483-6025
Altamont *(G-554)*
**Wright Quick Signs Inc** ............ G ....... 708 652-6020
Cicero *(G-7247)*
**Wyckoff Advertising Inc** ............ G ....... 630 260-2525
Wheaton *(G-21990)*

## ADVERTISING AGENCIES: Consultants

**Bpn Chicago** ............ E ....... 312 799-4100
Chicago *(G-4154)*
**Dard Products Inc** ............ C ....... 847 328-5000
Evanston *(G-10025)*
**Integrated Media Inc** ............ F ....... 217 854-6260
Carlinville *(G-3040)*
**Legend Promotions** ............ G ....... 847 438-3528
Lake Zurich *(G-13095)*
**Phoenix Graphics Inc** ............ G ....... 847 699-9520
Des Plaines *(G-8255)*

## ADVERTISING CURTAINS

**Erell Manufacturing Company** ............ F ....... 847 427-3000
Elk Grove Village *(G-9464)*

## ADVERTISING DISPLAY PRDTS

**America Display Inc** ............ F ....... 708 430-7000
Bridgeview *(G-2463)*
**Amt Corp** ............ G ....... 847 459-6177
Deerfield *(G-7977)*
**Assemblers Inc** ............ C ....... 773 378-3000
Chicago *(G-3965)*
**CWI Displays Corp** ............ F ....... 773 277-0040
Chicago *(G-4528)*
**James Coleman Company** ............ F ....... 847 963-8100
Rolling Meadows *(G-18735)*
**Orbus LLC** ............ C ....... 630 226-1155
Woodridge *(G-22506)*
**Orbus LLC** ............ C ....... 847 647-1012
Des Plaines *(G-8247)*
**Roberts Colonial House Inc** ............ F ....... 708 331-6233
South Holland *(G-20301)*
**Two Consulting** ............ G ....... 630 830-2415
Bartlett *(G-1382)*

## ADVERTISING MATERIAL DISTRIBUTION

**Coca-Cola Refreshments USA Inc** ............ F ....... 217 348-1001
Charleston *(G-3595)*

## ADVERTISING REPRESENTATIVES: Electronic Media

**Global Technologies I LLC** ............ D ....... 312 255-8350
Chicago *(G-4960)*
**Publishing Properties LLC** ............ G ....... 312 321-2299
Chicago *(G-6223)*
**Sun- Tmes Mdia Productions LLC** ............ G ....... 312 321-2299
Chicago *(G-6620)*

# PRODUCT SECTION

## AGRICULTURAL EQPT: Barn Cleaners

Sun-Times Media  LLC .................F ...... 312 321-2299
  Chicago  *(G-6622)*
Sun-Times Media Operations LLC ...G ...... 312 321-2299
  Chicago  *(G-6625)*

### ADVERTISING REPRESENTATIVES: Magazine

Gospel Synergy Magazine Inc ............G ...... 708 272-6640
  Calumet Park  *(G-2961)*

### ADVERTISING REPRESENTATIVES: Media

Movie Facts Inc ............................E ...... 847 299-9700
  Des Plaines  *(G-8238)*
National School Services Inc ..........E ...... 847 438-3859
  Long Grove  *(G-13899)*
Schaumburg Review .......................F ...... 847 998-3400
  Chicago  *(G-6450)*
Time Records Publishing and Bo ....G ...... 618 996-3803
  Marion  *(G-14291)*
Vondrak Publishing Co Inc .............E ...... 773 476-4800
  Summit Argo  *(G-20768)*

### ADVERTISING REPRESENTATIVES: Newspaper

Lee Enterprises Incorporated ..........C ...... 618 529-5454
  Carbondale  *(G-3014)*

### ADVERTISING REPRESENTATIVES: Printed Media

Alpha Pages  LLC ..........................G ...... 847 733-1740
  Chicago  *(G-3830)*
Penton Media  Inc ..........................G ...... 212 204-4200
  Chicago  *(G-6100)*

### ADVERTISING SPECIALTIES, WHOLESALE

A Cut Above Engraving Inc ............G ...... 708 671-9800
  Palos Park  *(G-17126)*
Anbek Inc ....................................G ...... 815 434-7340
  Ottawa  *(G-16947)*
ASap Specialties Inc Del ...............G ...... 847 223-7699
  Grayslake  *(G-11321)*
B Gunther & Co ............................F ...... 630 969-5595
  Lisle  *(G-13567)*
Badge-A-Minit Ltd .........................E ...... 815 883-8822
  Oglesby  *(G-16746)*
Brown Wood Products Company ....F ...... 847 673-4780
  Lincolnwood  *(G-13503)*
C & E Specialties  Inc ....................E ...... 815 229-9230
  Rockford  *(G-18294)*
Cacini Inc ....................................G ...... 847 884-1162
  Schaumburg  *(G-19467)*
Classique Signs & Engrv Inc ..........G ...... 217 228-7446
  Quincy  *(G-17813)*
Cloz Companies  Inc .....................E ...... 773 247-8879
  Skokie  *(G-19983)*
Diversified Adtee  Inc ....................E ...... 309 454-2555
  Normal  *(G-16069)*
E I T Inc ......................................G ...... 630 359-3543
  Naperville  *(G-15649)*
Edventure Promotions Inc ..............G ...... 312 440-1800
  Chicago  *(G-4702)*
Express Prtg & Promotions Inc .......G ...... 847 498-9640
  Northbrook  *(G-16253)*
Flow-Eze Company .......................F ...... 815 965-1062
  Rockford  *(G-18383)*
Image Plus Inc .............................G ...... 630 852-4920
  Downers Grove  *(G-8463)*
Insight Advertising Inc ...................G ...... 847 647-0004
  Niles  *(G-15989)*
John Parker Advertising Co ...........G ...... 217 892-4118
  Rantoul  *(G-17931)*
K & L Looseleaf Products  Inc .......D ...... 847 357-9733
  Elk Grove Village  *(G-9568)*
Kingsbury Enterprises Inc .............G ...... 708 535-7590
  Oak Forest  *(G-16586)*
Lee-Wel Printing Corporation ........G ...... 630 682-0935
  Wheaton  *(G-21966)*
M C F Printing Company ...............G ...... 630 279-0301
  Elmhurst  *(G-9904)*
Mbh Promotions Inc .....................G ...... 847 634-2411
  Buffalo Grove  *(G-2733)*
Printers Ink of Paris Inc .................G ...... 217 463-2552
  Paris  *(G-17158)*
Printing Plus of Roselle Inc ...........G ...... 630 893-0410
  Roselle  *(G-18963)*

R & R Creative Graphics Inc ..........G ...... 630 208-4724
  Geneva  *(G-10861)*
S & R Monogramming  Inc .............G ...... 630 369-5468
  Winfield  *(G-22292)*
Sign-A-Rama of Buffalo Grove .......G ...... 847 215-1535
  Buffalo Grove  *(G-2771)*
Skyward Promotions Inc ................G ...... 815 969-0909
  Rockford  *(G-18619)*
Stans Sportsworld Inc ...................G ...... 217 359-8474
  Champaign  *(G-3547)*
Tryad Specialties Inc ....................F ...... 630 549-0079
  Saint Charles  *(G-19287)*
Veltex Corporation ........................E ...... 312 235-4014
  Chicago  *(G-6879)*
Viking Awards Inc .........................G ...... 630 833-1733
  Elmhurst  *(G-9957)*
Voris Communication Co Inc .........D ...... 630 231-2425
  West Chicago  *(G-21791)*

### ADVERTISING SVCS, NEC

Embroid ME ................................G ...... 815 485-4155
  New Lenox  *(G-15880)*
Modern Methods Creative  Inc ......G ...... 309 263-4100
  Peoria  *(G-17410)*

### ADVERTISING SVCS: Billboards

Roman Signs ...............................G ...... 847 381-3425
  Barrington  *(G-1302)*

### ADVERTISING SVCS: Direct Mail

A and K Prtg & Graphic Design .....G ...... 618 244-3525
  Mount Vernon  *(G-15396)*
Advertisers Bindery Inc .................F ...... 312 939-4995
  Chicago  *(G-3776)*
American Litho  Incorporated ........A ...... 630 682-0600
  Carol Stream  *(G-3099)*
Athena Design Group Inc .............E ...... 312 733-2828
  Chicago  *(G-3974)*
Card Prsnlzation Solutions LLC ....E ...... 630 543-2630
  Glendale Heights  *(G-11014)*
Communication Technologies Inc ..E ...... 630 384-0900
  Glendale Heights  *(G-11017)*
Fgs-IL LLC ..................................G ...... 630 375-8500
  Aurora  *(G-1007)*
Flyerinc Corporation .....................G ...... 630 655-3400
  Oak Brook  *(G-16515)*
Group O  Inc ................................E ...... 309 736-8100
  Milan  *(G-14790)*
Integrated Print Graphics Inc ........G ...... 847 695-6777
  South Elgin  *(G-20206)*
Lists & Letters .............................F ...... 847 520-5207
  Wheeling  *(G-22095)*
Mac Graphics Group Inc ..............G ...... 630 620-7200
  Oakbrook Terrace  *(G-16716)*
Marketing Card Technology  LLC ..D ...... 630 985-7900
  Darien  *(G-7799)*
National Data Svcs Chicago Inc ....C ...... 630 597-9100
  Carol Stream  *(G-3204)*
Peterson Publication Services ......G ...... 630 469-6732
  Glen Ellyn  *(G-10987)*
Psa Equity  LLC ............................F ...... 847 478-6000
  Buffalo Grove  *(G-2757)*
R R Donnelley & Sons Company ...B ...... 312 326-8000
  Chicago  *(G-6270)*
Rasmussen Press Inc ...................G
  Bensenville  *(G-1976)*
RR Donnelley & Sons Company ....C ...... 312 236-8000
  Chicago  *(G-6404)*
S R Bastien Co ............................F ...... 847 858-1175
  Evanston  *(G-10093)*
V C P Inc ....................................E ...... 847 658-5090
  Algonquin  *(G-409)*
Vigil Printing Inc ..........................G ...... 773 794-8808
  Chicago  *(G-6898)*

### ADVERTISING SVCS: Display

American Advertising Assoc Inc ....G ...... 773 312-5110
  Chicago  *(G-3847)*
Animated Advg Techniques Inc .....G ...... 312 372-4694
  Chicago  *(G-3908)*
Design Phase Inc .........................E ...... 847 473-0077
  Waukegan  *(G-21550)*
Duo North America .......................G ...... 312 421-7755
  Chicago  *(G-4652)*
J Wallace & Associates  Inc ..........G ...... 630 960-4221
  Downers Grove  *(G-8467)*
Johnson Rolan Co Inc ..................G ...... 309 674-9671
  Peoria  *(G-17394)*

M G M Displays Inc ......................G ...... 708 594-3699
  Chicago  *(G-5580)*
Schellerer Corporation  Inc ...........D ...... 630 980-4567
  Bloomingdale  *(G-2135)*

### ADVERTISING SVCS: Outdoor

Adams Outdoor Advg Ltd Partnr ....E ...... 309 692-2482
  Peoria  *(G-17302)*
Edwards Creative Services  LLC ...F ...... 309 756-0199
  Milan  *(G-14784)*
Key Outdoor Inc ...........................G ...... 815 224-4742
  La Salle  *(G-12780)*
Turnroth Sign Company Inc ..........F ...... 815 625-1155
  Rock Falls  *(G-18156)*
Wright Quick Signs Inc .................G ...... 708 652-6020
  Cicero  *(G-7247)*

### ADVERTISING SVCS: Poster, Outdoor

Nite Lite Signs & Balloons Inc ......G ...... 630 953-2866
  Addison  *(G-229)*

### ADVERTISING SVCS: Transit

Edwards Creative Services  LLC ...F ...... 309 756-0199
  Milan  *(G-14784)*

### AERIAL WORK PLATFORMS

Dlc Inc ........................................F ...... 224 567-8656
  Park Ridge  *(G-17190)*
Skyjack Equipment  Inc .................E ...... 630 797-3299
  Saint Charles  *(G-19263)*
Skyjack Inc ..................................G ...... 630 262-0005
  Saint Charles  *(G-19264)*
USA Hoist Company  Inc ...............E ...... 815 740-1890
  Crest Hill  *(G-7470)*

### AEROSOLS

Chase Products Co ......................D ...... 708 865-1000
  Broadview  *(G-2566)*
Claire-Sprayway Inc .....................D ...... 630 628-3000
  Downers Grove  *(G-8413)*
Custom Blending & Pckaging of ....F ...... 618 286-1140
  Dupo  *(G-8569)*
Full-Fill Industries  LLC .................E ...... 217 286-3532
  Henning  *(G-11737)*
K-G Spray-Pak Inc .......................G ...... 630 543-7600
  Downers Grove  *(G-8469)*
Plz Aeroscience Corporation ........E ...... 630 628-3000
  Downers Grove  *(G-8505)*
Slide Products  Inc .......................F ...... 847 541-7220
  Wheeling  *(G-22153)*
We Are Done LLC ........................E ...... 708 598-7100
  Bridgeview  *(G-2538)*

### AGENTS, BROKERS & BUREAUS: Personal Service

Clifford W Estes Co Inc ................F ...... 815 433-0944
  Ottawa  *(G-16955)*
County Tool & Die ........................G ...... 217 324-6527
  Litchfield  *(G-13683)*
Swenson Technology  Inc .............F ...... 708 587-2300
  Monee  *(G-15003)*

### AGRICULTURAL CHEMICALS: Trace Elements

Sem Minerals LP .........................D ...... 217 224-8766
  Quincy  *(G-17890)*

### AGRICULTURAL CREDIT INSTITUTIONS

Deere & Company ........................A ...... 309 765-8000
  Moline  *(G-14925)*
John Deere AG Holdings Inc ........G ...... 309 765-8000
  Moline  *(G-14946)*

### AGRICULTURAL EQPT: BARN, SILO, POULTRY, DAIRY/LIVESTOCK MACH

King Systems Inc .........................G ...... 309 879-2668
  Dahinda  *(G-7688)*

### AGRICULTURAL EQPT: Barn Cleaners

Davis Welding & Manfctg  Inc .......F ...... 217 784-5480
  Gibson City  *(G-10899)*

---

Employee Codes: A=Over 500 employees, B=251-500
C=101-250, D=51-100, E=20-50, F=10-19, G=3-9

## AGRICULTURAL EQPT: Elevators, Farm

Davidson Grain Incorporated ............. E ...... 815 384-3208
  Creston *(G-7471)*
Paw Paw Co-Operative Grain ............. G ...... 815 627-2071
  Paw Paw *(G-17233)*
Union Iron Inc ............................. E ...... 217 429-5148
  Decatur *(G-7955)*

## AGRICULTURAL EQPT: Fertilizing Machinery

Precision Tank & Equipment Co ........... E ...... 217 452-7228
  Virginia *(G-21307)*
R&R Flight Service ........................ G ...... 815 538-2599
  Earlville *(G-8596)*
Yargus Manufacturing Inc ................. E ...... 217 826-6352
  Marshall *(G-14331)*

## AGRICULTURAL EQPT: Fertilizng, Sprayng, Dustng/Irrigatn Mach

360 Yield Center LLC ..................... E ...... 309 263-4360
  Morton *(G-15152)*

## AGRICULTURAL EQPT: Fillers & Unloaders, Silo

Dspc Company ............................. E ...... 815 997-1116
  Rockford *(G-18353)*

## AGRICULTURAL EQPT: Grade, Clean & Sort Machines, Fruit/Veg

Prater Industries Inc ..................... D ...... 630 679-3200
  Bolingbrook *(G-2359)*

## AGRICULTURAL EQPT: Greens Mowing Eqpt

Midwest Sport Turf Systems LLC ......... F ...... 630 923-8342
  Plainfield *(G-17627)*

## AGRICULTURAL EQPT: Haying Mach, Mowers, Rakes, Stackers, Etc

Mathews Company ......................... D ...... 815 459-2210
  Crystal Lake *(G-7606)*

## AGRICULTURAL EQPT: Loaders, Manure & General Utility

Avant Tecno USA Inc ...................... E ...... 847 380-9822
  Arlington Heights *(G-720)*

## AGRICULTURAL EQPT: Planting Machines

Dutch Prairie Conveyors ................... G ...... 618 349-6177
  Shobonier *(G-19921)*

## AGRICULTURAL EQPT: Soil Preparation Mach, Exc Turf & Grounds

Kongskilde Industries Inc ................. C ...... 309 452-3300
  Hudson *(G-12124)*

## AGRICULTURAL EQPT: Spreaders, Fertilizer

Doyle Equipment Mfg Co .................. D ...... 217 222-1592
  Quincy *(G-17821)*
Spreader Inc .............................. G ...... 217 568-7219
  Gifford *(G-10910)*

## AGRICULTURAL EQPT: Stackers, Grain

Custom Grain Systems LLC ............... G ...... 812 881-8175
  Lawrenceville *(G-13197)*

## AGRICULTURAL EQPT: Storage Bins, Crop

Arrows Up Inc ............................. G ...... 847 305-2550
  Arlington Heights *(G-717)*
Gsi Group LLC ............................ G ...... 217 226-4401
  Assumption *(G-932)*
Gsi Group LLC ............................ C ...... 217 287-6244
  Taylorville *(G-20839)*
Gsi Holdings Corp ......................... G ...... 217 226-4421
  Assumption *(G-933)*

## AGRICULTURAL EQPT: Trailers & Wagons, Farm

Cronkhite Industries Inc ................... F ...... 217 443-3700
  Danville *(G-7711)*

E Z Trail Inc ............................... E ...... 217 543-3471
  Arthur *(G-899)*

## AGRICULTURAL EQPT: Turf & Grounds Eqpt

Ecoturf Midwest Inc ....................... G ...... 630 350-9500
  Bensenville *(G-1888)*
Outdoor Space LLC ....................... E ...... 773 857-5296
  Chicago *(G-6026)*

## AGRICULTURAL EQPT: Turf Eqpt, Commercial

Ideal Turf Inc .............................. G ...... 309 691-3362
  Peoria *(G-17384)*
Mega International Ltd .................... G ...... 309 764-5310
  Moline *(G-14956)*

## AGRICULTURAL EQPT: Weeding Machines

Waipuna USA Inc .......................... G ...... 630 514-0364
  Downers Grove *(G-8539)*

## AGRICULTURAL LIMESTONE: Ground

Central Stone Company ................... F ...... 309 776-3900
  Colchester *(G-7307)*
Meyer Material Co Merger Corp .......... D ...... 815 943-2605
  Harvard *(G-11641)*
Mining International LLC .................. E ...... 815 722-0900
  Joliet *(G-12543)*
Tuscola Stone Company .................. F ...... 217 253-4705
  Tuscola *(G-21028)*

## AGRICULTURAL LOAN COMPANIES

Cnh Industrial America LLC ............... E ...... 706 629-5572
  Burr Ridge *(G-2832)*

## AGRICULTURAL MACHINERY & EQPT REPAIR

Birkeys Farm Store Inc .................... E ...... 217 337-1772
  Urbana *(G-21073)*
Grower Equipment & Supply Co .......... F ...... 847 223-3100
  Hainesville *(G-11523)*
Wittwer Brothers Inc ...................... G ...... 815 522-3589
  Monroe Center *(G-15025)*

## AGRICULTURAL MACHINERY & EQPT: Wholesalers

Bill Chandler Farms ....................... G ...... 618 752-7551
  Noble *(G-16049)*
GKN Walterscheid Inc ..................... C ...... 630 972-9300
  Woodridge *(G-22486)*

## AIR CLEANING SYSTEMS

Bact Process Systems Inc ................ G ...... 847 577-0950
  Arlington Heights *(G-721)*
Heidolph NA LLC .......................... F ...... 224 265-9600
  Elk Grove Village *(G-9520)*
Midwest Air Pro Inc ....................... G ...... 773 622-4566
  Chicago *(G-5741)*
Schubert Environmental Eqp Inc ......... F ...... 630 307-9400
  Glendale Heights *(G-11067)*

## AIR CONDITIONERS: Motor Vehicle

Sigma Coachair Group (us) Inc .......... G ...... 847 541-4446
  Wheeling *(G-22151)*

## AIR CONDITIONING & VENTILATION EQPT & SPLYS: Wholesales

Aen Industries Inc ........................ F ...... 708 758-3000
  Chicago Heights *(G-7077)*
Anytime Heating & AC .................... F ...... 630 851-6696
  Naperville *(G-15796)*
Ruyle Incorporated ........................ E ...... 309 674-6644
  Springfield *(G-20516)*

## AIR CONDITIONING EQPT

Dupage Mechanical ....................... G ...... 630 620-1122
  Wheeling *(G-22038)*
Oceanaire Inc ............................. F ...... 847 583-0311
  Morton Grove *(G-15225)*
Sendra Service Corp ...................... G ...... 815 462-0061
  New Lenox *(G-15910)*
Voges Inc ................................. D ...... 618 233-2760
  Belleville *(G-1688)*

## AIR CONDITIONING EQPT, WHOLE HOUSE: Wholesalers

Dupage Mechanical ....................... G ...... 630 620-1122
  Wheeling *(G-22038)*

## AIR CONDITIONING REPAIR SVCS

Evans Heating and Air Inc ................ G ...... 217 483-8440
  Chatham *(G-3619)*
White Sheet Metal ........................ G ...... 217 465-3195
  Paris *(G-17164)*

## AIR CONDITIONING UNITS: Complete, Domestic Or Indl

Bergstrom Climate Systems LLC ......... B ...... 815 874-7821
  Rockford *(G-18281)*
Honeywell International Inc ............... D ...... 847 797-4000
  Arlington Heights *(G-768)*
Lennox Industries Inc .................... D ...... 630 378-7054
  Romeoville *(G-18839)*

## AIR COOLERS: Metal Plate

Diesel Radiator Co ........................ D ...... 708 865-7299
  Melrose Park *(G-14619)*
Elkay Manufacturing Company ........... B ...... 815 273-7001
  Savanna *(G-19397)*

## AIR CURTAINS

H D A Fans Inc ............................ G ...... 630 627-2087
  Elk Grove Village *(G-9514)*

## AIR MATTRESSES: Plastic

B & M Plastic Inc .......................... F ...... 847 258-4437
  Elk Grove Village *(G-9328)*
Clover Plastics LLC ....................... G ...... 630 473-6488
  West Chicago *(G-21683)*
Pliant LLC ................................. A ...... 812 424-2904
  Rolling Meadows *(G-18763)*

## AIR POLLUTION CONTROL EQPT & SPLYS WHOLESALERS

Bee Clean Specialties LLC ............... G ...... 847 451-0844
  Schaumburg *(G-19458)*

## AIR PURIFICATION EQPT

Aen Industries Inc ........................ F ...... 708 758-3000
  Chicago Heights *(G-7077)*
Altair Corporation (del) ................... E ...... 847 634-9540
  Lincolnshire *(G-13426)*
Architectural Fan Coil Inc ................ G ...... 312 399-1203
  Chicago *(G-3942)*
Bee Clean Specialties LLC ............... G ...... 847 451-0844
  Schaumburg *(G-19458)*
Bofa Americas Inc ........................ G ...... 618 205-5007
  Staunton *(G-20553)*
Calutech Inc .............................. G ...... 708 614-0228
  Orland Park *(G-16845)*
Chatham Corporation ..................... F ...... 847 634-5506
  Lincolnshire *(G-13436)*
Chicago Plastic Systems Inc ............. E ...... 815 455-4599
  Crystal Lake *(G-7553)*
Hydrosil International Ltd ................ G ...... 847 741-1600
  East Dundee *(G-8645)*
Mason Engineering & Designing ......... E ...... 630 595-5000
  Inverness *(G-12209)*
Met-Pro Technologies LLC ............... E ...... 630 775-0707
  Wood Dale *(G-22398)*
Paul D Stark & Associates ............... G ...... 630 964-7111
  Downers Grove *(G-8500)*
Promark Associates Inc .................. G ...... 847 676-1894
  Skokie *(G-20064)*
Sanders Inc .............................. E ...... 815 634-4611
  Morris *(G-15129)*
Scrubair Systems Inc .................... E ...... 847 550-8061
  Lake Zurich *(G-13129)*

## AIR-CONDITIONING SPLY SVCS

Caldwell Plumbing Co .................... F ...... 630 588-8900
  Wheaton *(G-21938)*

# PRODUCT SECTION

## AIRCRAFT PARTS & AUXILIARY EQPT: Military Eqpt & Armament

### AIRCRAFT & AEROSPACE FLIGHT INSTRUMENTS & GUIDANCE SYSTEMS

Armstrong Aerospace Inc .................G  847 250-5132
  Itasca  (G-12231)
Csiteq LLC .................................D  312 265-1509
  Chicago  (G-4512)
Mpc Products Corporation ..............A  847 673-8300
  Niles  (G-16010)
Mpc Products Corporation ..............G  847 673-8300
  Niles  (G-16011)

### AIRCRAFT & HEAVY EQPT REPAIR SVCS

Alpha Services II Inc ......................E  618 997-9999
  Marion  (G-14252)
Midwest Aero Support Inc ...............E  815 398-9202
  Machesney Park  (G-14092)
P J Repair Service Inc ....................F  618 548-5690
  Salem  (G-19341)
Phoenix Welding Co Inc .................F  630 616-1700
  Franklin Park  (G-10549)
Wallace Auto Parts & Svcs Inc ........E  618 268-4446
  Raleigh  (G-17912)

### AIRCRAFT ASSEMBLY PLANTS

Aerostars Inc ................................G  847 736-8171
  Cary  (G-3323)
Aviation Services Group Inc ............G  708 425-4700
  Chicago Ridge  (G-7139)
Calumet Motorsports Inc ................G  708 895-0398
  Lansing  (G-13158)
Donath Aircraft Service ..................G  217 528-6667
  Springfield  (G-20429)
Elan Express Inc ...........................E  815 713-1190
  Rockford  (G-18361)
Gulfstream Aerospace Corp ............A  630 470-9146
  Naperville  (G-15667)
Ibanum Manufacturing LLC .............G  815 262-5373
  Rockford  (G-18425)
Illini Aerofab Inc ............................G  217 425-2971
  Decatur  (G-7891)
Jet Aviation St Louis Inc .................D  618 646-8000
  Cahokia  (G-2923)
Learjet Inc ....................................B  847 553-0172
  Des Plaines  (G-8222)
Mitchell Arcft Expendables LLC .......E  847 516-3773
  Cary  (G-3360)
Northstar Aerospace (usa) Inc ........G  708 728-2000
  Bedford Park  (G-1567)
Quad City Ultralight Aircraft ............F  309 764-3515
  Moline  (G-14966)
SC Aviation Inc .............................G  800 416-4176
  Saint Charles  (G-19259)
Textron Inc ...................................D  815 961-5293
  Rockford  (G-18646)

### AIRCRAFT CONTROL SYSTEMS: Electronic Totalizing Counters

Midwest Aero Support Inc ...............E  815 398-9202
  Machesney Park  (G-14092)

### AIRCRAFT DEALERS

Olivers Helicopters Inc ...................G  847 697-7346
  Gilberts  (G-10930)
Textron Aviation Inc .......................G  630 443-5080
  West Chicago  (G-21779)

### AIRCRAFT ENGINES & ENGINE PARTS: Airfoils

Jetpower LLC ................................F  847 856-8359
  Gurnee  (G-11462)

### AIRCRAFT ENGINES & ENGINE PARTS: Mount Parts

Danville Metal Stamping Co Inc .......F  217 446-0647
  Danville  (G-7712)
Danville Metal Stamping Co Inc .......F  217 446-0647
  Danville  (G-7713)
Danville Metal Stamping Co Inc .......G  217 446-0647
  Danville  (G-7714)

### AIRCRAFT ENGINES & ENGINE PARTS: Nonelectric Starters

Essex Electro Engineers Inc ............E  847 891-4444
  Schaumburg  (G-19521)

### AIRCRAFT ENGINES & ENGINE PARTS: Research & Development, Mfr

Air International C W T US ..............G  217 422-1896
  Decatur  (G-7825)
CTS Electronic Components Inc ......D  630 577-8800
  Lisle  (G-13580)
Innovative Design and RES Inc .......G  217 322-3907
  Rushville  (G-19093)

### AIRCRAFT ENGINES & PARTS

AAR Aircraft Services Inc ................E  630 227-2000
  Wood Dale  (G-22326)
AAR Corp ......................................D  630 227-2000
  Wood Dale  (G-22328)
Aero-Cables Corp ..........................G  815 609-6600
  Oswego  (G-16902)
Area Diesel Service Inc .................E  217 854-2641
  Carlinville  (G-3030)
Arrow Gear Company .....................C  630 969-7640
  Downers Grove  (G-8389)
Chemring Energetic Devices Inc .....C  630 969-0620
  Downers Grove  (G-8408)
Doncasters Inc ..............................C  217 465-6500
  Paris  (G-17146)
General Machinery & Mfg Co ..........F  773 235-3700
  Chicago  (G-4928)
Heligear Acquisition Co ..................C  708 728-2000
  Bedford Park  (G-1553)
Heligear Acquisition Co ..................G  708 728-2055
  Burr Ridge  (G-2850)
Honeywell .....................................E  815 235-5500
  Freeport  (G-10663)
Honeywell International Inc .............A  630 960-5282
  Darien  (G-7796)
Honeywell International Inc .............A  630 922-0138
  Naperville  (G-15810)
Honeywell International Inc .............A  480 353-3020
  Chicago  (G-5106)
Honeywell International Inc .............A  847 701-3038
  Palatine  (G-17037)
Honeywell International Inc .............B  630 377-6580
  Saint Charles  (G-19193)
Honeywell International Inc .............A  973 455-2000
  Chicago  (G-5107)
Honeywell International Inc .............A  309 383-4045
  Metamora  (G-14742)
Honeywell International Inc .............G  217 431-3710
  Danville  (G-7734)
I D Rockford Shop Inc ....................G  815 335-1150
  Winnebago  (G-22297)
Midwest Fuel Injection Svc Corp ......F  847 991-7867
  Palatine  (G-17056)
Precoat Metals ..............................E  618 451-0909
  Granite City  (G-11300)
Superior Joining Tech Inc ................E  815 282-7581
  Machesney Park  (G-14109)
United Technologies Corp ...............B  630 516-3460
  Elmhurst  (G-9955)
United Technologies Corp ...............B  815 226-6000
  Rockford  (G-18663)
Universal Trnspt Systems LLC ........F  312 994-2349
  Chicago  (G-6835)
UOP LLC .......................................D  303 791-0311
  Des Plaines  (G-8292)
Woodward Inc ...............................A  815 877-7441
  Loves Park  (G-14009)

### AIRCRAFT EQPT & SPLYS WHOLESALERS

Koerner Aviation Inc ......................G  815 932-4222
  Kankakee  (G-12636)

### AIRCRAFT FLIGHT INSTRUMENT REPAIR SVCS

Heligear Acquisition Co ..................C  708 728-2000
  Bedford Park  (G-1553)

### AIRCRAFT FUELING SVCS

Jet Aviation St Louis Inc .................D  618 646-8000
  Cahokia  (G-2923)

### AIRCRAFT HANGAR OPERATION SVCS

Thelen Sand & Gravel Inc ...............D  847 838-8800
  Antioch  (G-656)

### AIRCRAFT MAINTENANCE & REPAIR SVCS

AAR Corp ......................................D  630 227-2000
  Wood Dale  (G-22328)
Jme Technologies Inc ....................G  815 477-8800
  Crystal Lake  (G-7595)
Skandia Inc ...................................D  815 393-4600
  Davis Junction  (G-7815)

### AIRCRAFT PARTS & AUX EQPT: Governors, Propeller Feathering

CEF Industries LLC ........................C  630 628-2299
  Addison  (G-71)

### AIRCRAFT PARTS & AUXILIARY EQPT: Aircraft Training Eqpt

Frasca International Inc .................C  217 344-9200
  Urbana  (G-21089)

### AIRCRAFT PARTS & AUXILIARY EQPT: Assys, Subassemblies/Parts

Cyn Industries Inc .........................F  773 895-4324
  Chicago  (G-4531)
Hamilton Sundstrand Corp .............A  815 226-6000
  Rockford  (G-18411)
S I A Inc .......................................G  708 361-3100
  Palos Heights  (G-17109)
TI International Ltd ........................G  847 689-0233
  North Chicago  (G-16188)

### AIRCRAFT PARTS & AUXILIARY EQPT: Blades, Prop, Metal Or Wood

Prograf LLC ..................................G  815 234-4848
  Villa Park  (G-21280)

### AIRCRAFT PARTS & AUXILIARY EQPT: Bodies

Jetpower LLC ................................F  847 856-8359
  Gurnee  (G-11462)

### AIRCRAFT PARTS & AUXILIARY EQPT: Body & Wing Assys & Parts

Aertrade LLC ................................G  630 428-4440
  Aurora  (G-954)
Boeing Company ...........................B  312 544-2000
  Chicago  (G-4136)
Jsn Inc ..........................................E  708 410-1800
  Maywood  (G-14426)
Mpc Products Corporation ..............A  847 673-8300
  Niles  (G-16010)
Mpc Products Corporation ..............G  847 673-8300
  Niles  (G-16011)

### AIRCRAFT PARTS & AUXILIARY EQPT: Body Assemblies & Parts

Advanced Precision Mfg Inc ...........E  847 981-9800
  Elk Grove Village  (G-9276)
Brunswick International Ltd ............G  847 735-4700
  Lake Forest  (G-12889)

### AIRCRAFT PARTS & AUXILIARY EQPT: Gears, Power Transmission

A J R Industries Inc .......................E  847 439-0380
  Elk Grove Village  (G-9250)
Aircraft Gear Corporation ...............D  815 877-7473
  Loves Park  (G-13916)
Auxitrol SA ....................................G  815 874-2471
  Rockford  (G-18272)
Nsa (chi) Liquidating Corp ..............F  708 728-2000
  Elmhurst  (G-9916)

### AIRCRAFT PARTS & AUXILIARY EQPT: Military Eqpt & Armament

Shadowtech Labs Inc ....................G  630 413-4478
  Willowbrook  (G-22231)

Employee Codes: A=Over 500 employees, B=251-500
C=101-250, D=51-100, E=20-50, F=10-19, G=3-9

# AIRCRAFT PARTS & AUXILIARY EQPT: Refueling Eqpt, In Flight

## AIRCRAFT PARTS & AUXILIARY EQPT: Refueling Eqpt, In Flight

Airport Aviation Professionals .........G....... 773 948-6631
  Chicago *(G-3788)*
Kemell Enterprises LLC .........G....... 618 671-1513
  Belleville *(G-1641)*

## AIRCRAFT PARTS & AUXILIARY EQPT: Research & Development, Mfr

Azimuth Cnc Inc .........F....... 815 399-4433
  Rockford *(G-18274)*
Electronica Aviation LLC .........G....... 407 498-1092
  Chicago *(G-4722)*
Titus Enterprises LLC .........G....... 773 441-7222
  Warrenville *(G-21364)*

## AIRCRAFT PARTS & AUXILIARY EQPT: Wing Assemblies & Parts

Xclusive Auto Sales & Security .........G....... 708 897-9990
  Blue Island *(G-2273)*

## AIRCRAFT PARTS & EQPT, NEC

AAR Allen Services Inc .........D....... 630 227-2410
  Wood Dale *(G-22327)*
AAR Supply Chain Inc .........C....... 630 227-2000
  Wood Dale *(G-22329)*
Air Land and Sea Interiors .........G....... 630 834-1717
  Villa Park *(G-21234)*
American Concorde Systems .........F....... 773 342-9951
  Streamwood *(G-20642)*
American Science and Tech Corp .........G....... 312 433-3800
  Chicago *(G-3872)*
Armstrong Aerospace Inc .........D....... 630 285-0200
  Itasca *(G-12232)*
Calport Aviation Company .........G....... 630 588-8091
  Bartlett *(G-1317)*
Chucking Machine Products Inc .........D....... 847 678-1192
  Franklin Park *(G-10431)*
CMC Electronics Aurora LLC .........D....... 630 556-9619
  Sugar Grove *(G-20720)*
Engineering Prototype Inc .........F....... 708 447-3155
  Riverside *(G-18030)*
Fgc Plasma Solutions LLC .........G....... 954 591-1429
  Lemont *(G-13235)*
Fiberforge Corporation .........E....... 970 945-9377
  Chicago *(G-4840)*
Gail E Stephens .........G....... 618 372-0140
  Brighton *(G-2540)*
Gpe Controls Inc .........F....... 708 236-6000
  Hillside *(G-11917)*
Ibanum Manufacturing LLC .........G....... 815 262-5373
  Rockford *(G-18425)*
Ingenium Aerospace LLC .........F....... 815 525-2000
  Rockford *(G-18431)*
Logan Actuator Co .........G....... 815 943-9500
  Harvard *(G-11640)*
Makerite Mfg Co Inc .........E....... 815 389-3902
  Roscoe *(G-18906)*
Mitchell Aircraft Products .........G....... 815 331-8609
  McHenry *(G-14536)*
Multax Corporation .........D....... 309 266-9765
  Morton *(G-15170)*
Quad City Ultralight Aircraft .........F....... 309 764-3515
  Moline *(G-14966)*
Qualiseal Technology LLC .........D....... 708 887-6080
  Harwood Heights *(G-11690)*
Seginus Inc .........G....... 630 800-2795
  Oswego *(G-16933)*
Skandia Inc .........D....... 815 393-4600
  Davis Junction *(G-7815)*
South Subn Logistics Sups Corp .........G....... 312 804-3401
  Harvey *(G-11675)*
Systems & Electronics Inc .........E....... 847 228-0985
  Elk Grove Village *(G-9766)*
Textron Aviation Inc .........G....... 630 443-5080
  West Chicago *(G-21779)*
Thales Visionix Inc .........D....... 630 375-2008
  Aurora *(G-1224)*
Trident Machine Co .........G....... 815 968-1585
  Rockford *(G-18657)*
Usac Aeronautics Ria-Jmtc .........E....... 949 680-8167
  Rock Island *(G-18210)*
Vestergaard Company Inc .........G....... 815 759-9102
  McHenry *(G-14569)*
Video Refurbishing Svcs Inc .........E....... 847 844-7366
  Carpentersville *(G-3304)*

Vonberg Valve Inc .........E....... 847 259-3800
  Rolling Meadows *(G-18788)*
Wittenstein Arspc Smlation Inc .........G....... 630 540-5300
  Bartlett *(G-1389)*
Woodward Inc .........B....... 815 877-7441
  Loves Park *(G-14008)*

## AIRCRAFT PARTS WHOLESALERS

AAR Supply Chain Inc .........C....... 630 227-2000
  Wood Dale *(G-22329)*
Jet Aviation St Louis Inc .........D....... 618 646-8000
  Cahokia *(G-2923)*

## AIRCRAFT SEATS

B/E Aerospace Inc .........C....... 561 791-5000
  Hanover Park *(G-11576)*

## AIRCRAFT SERVICING & REPAIRING

Jet Aviation St Louis Inc .........D....... 618 646-8000
  Cahokia *(G-2923)*

## AIRCRAFT TURBINES

Woodward International Inc .........G....... 815 877-7441
  Loves Park *(G-14010)*

## AIRCRAFT WHEELS

Beringer Aero Usa Inc .........G....... 708 667-7891
  Chicago *(G-4085)*

## AIRCRAFT: Airplanes, Fixed Or Rotary Wing

Boeing Aerospace - Tams Inc .........G....... 312 544-2000
  Chicago *(G-4135)*
Boeing Company .........B....... 312 544-2000
  Chicago *(G-4136)*
Boeing Company .........G....... 847 240-0767
  Schaumburg *(G-19465)*
Boeing LTS Inc .........B....... 312 544-2000
  Chicago *(G-4138)*
Textron Aviation Inc .........G....... 630 443-5080
  West Chicago *(G-21779)*

## AIRLOCKS

Rotary Airlock LLC .........E....... 800 883-8955
  Rock Falls *(G-18150)*

## ALARMS: Burglar

All Tech Systems & Install .........G....... 815 609-0685
  Plainfield *(G-17579)*
Ametek Inc .........E....... 630 621-3121
  West Chicago *(G-21658)*
RF Technologies Inc .........E....... 618 377-2654
  Buffalo Grove *(G-2759)*

## ALARMS: Fire

Global Fire Control Inc .........G....... 309 314-0919
  East Moline *(G-8680)*
Harrington Signal Inc .........E....... 309 762-0731
  Moline *(G-14942)*
Synergistic Tech Solutions Inc .........G....... 224 360-6165
  Mundelein *(G-15562)*

## ALCOHOL, ETHYL: For Beverage Purposes

Mgpi Processing Inc .........C....... 309 353-3990
  Pekin *(G-17275)*

## ALCOHOL, GRAIN: For Beverage Purposes

Illinois Corn Processing LLC .........D....... 309 353-3990
  Pekin *(G-17268)*

## ALCOHOL: Ethyl & Ethanol

Adkins Energy LLC .........E....... 815 369-9173
  Lena *(G-13272)*
Aventine Renewable Energy .........D....... 309 347-9200
  Pekin *(G-17255)*
Big River Resources Galva LLC .........C....... 309 932-2033
  Galva *(G-10784)*
Center Ethanol Company LLC .........E....... 618 875-3008
  Sauget *(G-19384)*
Green Plains Madison LLC .........E....... 618 451-8195
  Madison *(G-14147)*
Illinois River Energy LLC .........D....... 815 561-0650
  Rochelle *(G-18095)*

Lincolnland Agri-Energy LLC .........E....... 618 586-2321
  Palestine *(G-17094)*
Mgpi Processing Inc .........C....... 309 353-3990
  Pekin *(G-17275)*
One Earth Energy LLC .........E....... 217 784-5321
  Gibson City *(G-10905)*
Patriot Renewable Fuels LLC .........D....... 309 935-5700
  Annawan *(G-611)*

## ALKALIES & CHLORINE

Arkema Inc .........C....... 708 385-2188
  Alsip *(G-436)*
Aspen API Inc .........F....... 847 635-0985
  Des Plaines *(G-8152)*
Clorox Products Mfg Co .........C....... 847 229-5500
  Wheeling *(G-22028)*
Coral Chemical Company .........E....... 847 246-6666
  Zion *(G-22680)*
Korex Chicago LLC .........E....... 708 458-4890
  Chicago *(G-5406)*
Occidental Chemical Corp .........F....... 618 482-6346
  Sauget *(G-19388)*
Olin Corporation .........F....... 618 258-5668
  East Alton *(G-8607)*
Petra Industries Inc .........F....... 618 271-0022
  East Saint Louis *(G-8765)*

## ALL-TERRAIN VEHICLE DEALERS

Outdoor Power Inc .........F....... 217 228-9890
  Quincy *(G-17865)*

## ALLOYS: Additive, Exc Copper Or Made In Blast Furnaces

Hickman Williams & Company .........F....... 630 574-2150
  Oak Brook *(G-16521)*
Masters & Alloy LLC .........G....... 312 582-1880
  Alsip *(G-489)*
Miller and Company LLC .........E....... 847 696-2400
  Rosemont *(G-19017)*

## ALTERNATORS & GENERATORS: Battery Charging

A E Iskra Inc .........G....... 815 874-4022
  Rockford *(G-18240)*

## ALTERNATORS: Automotive

A E Iskra Inc .........G....... 815 874-4022
  Rockford *(G-18239)*
Powermaster .........G....... 630 957-4019
  West Chicago *(G-21759)*

## ALUMINUM

Century Aluminum Company .........C....... 312 696-3101
  Chicago *(G-4275)*
Duval Group Ltd .........G....... 847 949-7001
  Mundelein *(G-15495)*
Huml Industries Inc .........G....... 847 426-8061
  Gilberts *(G-10923)*
New Century Performance Inc .........G....... 618 466-6383
  Godfrey *(G-11230)*
Penn Aluminum Intl LLC .........G....... 618 684-2146
  Murphysboro *(G-15579)*
Reynolds Packaging Kama Inc .........C....... 815 468-8300
  Manteno *(G-14192)*

## ALUMINUM & BERYLLIUM ORES MINING

Alro Steel Corporation .........E....... 708 202-3200
  Melrose Park *(G-14591)*

## ALUMINUM PRDTS

Afco Industries Inc .........G....... 618 742-6469
  Olmsted *(G-16757)*
Al3 Inc .........G....... 847 441-7888
  Winnetka *(G-22300)*
American Alum Extrusion Co LLC .........G....... 877 896-2236
  Roscoe *(G-18889)*
Architctural Grilles Sunshades .........F....... 708 479-9458
  Mokena *(G-14854)*
Central Tool Specialities Co .........G....... 630 543-6351
  Addison *(G-72)*
Crown Cork & Seal Usa Inc .........C....... 815 933-9351
  Bradley *(G-2417)*
Custom Aluminum Products Inc .........D....... 847 717-5000
  Genoa *(G-10877)*

| | | |
|---|---|---|
| Custom Aluminum Products Inc | B | 847 717-5000 |
| South Elgin (G-20191) | | |
| Durable Inc | A | 847 541-4400 |
| Wheeling (G-22039) | | |
| Efco Corporation | E | 630 378-4720 |
| Bolingbrook (G-2303) | | |
| Imageworks Manufacturing Inc | E | 708 503-1122 |
| Park Forest (G-17172) | | |
| Maytec Inc | G | 847 429-0321 |
| Dundee (G-8564) | | |
| Metal Impact South LLC | F | 847 718-9300 |
| Elk Grove Village (G-9621) | | |
| Monda Window & Door Corp | E | 773 254-8888 |
| Chicago (G-5792) | | |
| Petersen Aluminum Corporation | D | 847 228-7150 |
| Elk Grove Village (G-9676) | | |
| Rotation Dynamics Corporation | E | 630 769-9700 |
| Chicago (G-6398) | | |
| Sapa Extrusions Inc | E | 847 233-9105 |
| Rosemont (G-19030) | | |
| Sapa Extrusions Inc | C | 877 710-7272 |
| Rosemont (G-19031) | | |
| Sapa Extrusions North Amer LLC | G | 877 922-7272 |
| Rosemont (G-19032) | | |
| Signa Group Inc | G | 847 386-7639 |
| Northfield (G-16417) | | |
| Sno Gem Inc | F | 888 766-4367 |
| McHenry (G-14555) | | |
| Sternberg Lanterns Inc | C | 847 588-3400 |
| Roselle (G-18980) | | |
| T A U Inc | G | 708 841-5757 |
| Dolton (G-8377) | | |
| Transco Products Inc | E | 815 672-2197 |
| Streator (G-20709) | | |
| Werner Co | A | 847 455-8001 |
| Itasca (G-12374) | | |
| William Dach | F | 815 962-3455 |
| Rockford (G-18683) | | |

## ALUMINUM: Coil & Sheet

| | | |
|---|---|---|
| Climco Coils Company | C | 815 772-3717 |
| Morrison (G-15143) | | |
| Sea Converting Inc | F | 630 694-9178 |
| Wood Dale (G-22420) | | |

## ALUMINUM: Rolling & Drawing

| | | |
|---|---|---|
| American Alum Extrusion Co LLC | G | 877 896-2236 |
| Roscoe (G-18889) | | |
| Corus America Inc | E | 847 585-2599 |
| Schaumburg (G-19486) | | |
| Lapham-Hickey Steel Corp | C | 708 496-6111 |
| Chicago (G-5459) | | |
| Msystems Group LLC | G | 630 567-3930 |
| Saint Charles (G-19224) | | |

## AMMONIA & AMMONIUM SALTS

| | | |
|---|---|---|
| Pcs Nitrogen Trinidad Corp | C | 847 849-4200 |
| Northbrook (G-16334) | | |

## AMMONIUM NITRATE OR AMMONIUM SULFATE

| | | |
|---|---|---|
| East Dbque Ntrgn Frtlizers LLC | C | 815 747-3101 |
| East Dubuque (G-8617) | | |

## AMMUNITION

| | | |
|---|---|---|
| General Dynamics Ordnance | C | 618 985-8211 |
| Marion (G-14261) | | |

## AMMUNITION: Components

| | | |
|---|---|---|
| Alanson Manufacturing LLC | F | 773 762-2530 |
| Chicago (G-3795) | | |
| Maxon Shooters Supplies Inc | G | 847 298-4867 |
| Des Plaines (G-8228) | | |

## AMMUNITION: Small Arms

| | | |
|---|---|---|
| A & S Arms Inc | G | 224 267-5670 |
| Antioch (G-612) | | |
| Civilian Force Arms Inc | G | 630 926-6982 |
| Yorkville (G-22652) | | |
| Rampart LLC | G | 847 367-8960 |
| Lake Forest (G-12950) | | |
| RR Defense Systems Inc | G | 312 446-9167 |
| Elk Grove Village (G-9721) | | |

## AMPLIFIERS

| | | |
|---|---|---|
| Key Car Stereo | G | 217 446-4556 |
| Oakwood (G-16726) | | |
| Nantsound Inc | F | 847 939-6101 |
| Park Ridge (G-17210) | | |
| Victoria Amplifier Company | F | 630 369-3527 |
| Naperville (G-15831) | | |

## AMPLIFIERS: Parametric

| | | |
|---|---|---|
| R B Manufacturing Inc | E | 815 522-3100 |
| Kirkland (G-12716) | | |

## AMPLIFIERS: RF & IF Power

| | | |
|---|---|---|
| Amplivox Sound Systems LLC | E | 800 267-5486 |
| Northbrook (G-16204) | | |
| Crescend Technologies LLC | E | 847 908-5400 |
| Schaumburg (G-19490) | | |

## AMUSEMENT & RECREATION SVCS, NEC

| | | |
|---|---|---|
| Embroid ME | G | 815 485-4155 |
| New Lenox (G-15880) | | |

## AMUSEMENT & RECREATION SVCS: Exhibition & Carnival Op Svcs

| | | |
|---|---|---|
| Alpine Amusement Co Inc | G | 708 233-9131 |
| Oak Lawn (G-16600) | | |

## AMUSEMENT & RECREATION SVCS: Indoor Or Outdoor Court Clubs

| | | |
|---|---|---|
| Bernard Cffey Vtrans Fundation | G | 630 687-0033 |
| Naperville (G-15605) | | |

## AMUSEMENT & RECREATION SVCS: Scuba & Skin Diving Instruction

| | | |
|---|---|---|
| Scuba Sports Inc | G | 217 787-3483 |
| Springfield (G-20519) | | |

## AMUSEMENT & RECREATION SVCS: Shooting Range

| | | |
|---|---|---|
| Best Technology Systems Inc | F | 815 254-9554 |
| Plainfield (G-17582) | | |

## AMUSEMENT & RECREATION SVCS: Skating Rink Operation

| | | |
|---|---|---|
| Good Times Roll | G | 217 285-4885 |
| Pittsfield (G-17569) | | |

## AMUSEMENT & RECREATION SVCS: Tennis Club, Membership

| | | |
|---|---|---|
| St Clair Tennis Club LLC | G | 618 632-1400 |
| O Fallon (G-16480) | | |

## AMUSEMENT & RECREATION SVCS: Tennis Courts, Non-Member

| | | |
|---|---|---|
| St Clair Tennis Club LLC | G | 618 632-1400 |
| O Fallon (G-16480) | | |

## AMUSEMENT MACHINES: Coin Operated

| | | |
|---|---|---|
| B and B Amusement Illinois LLC | G | 309 585-2077 |
| Bloomington (G-2145) | | |
| Blast Zone | F | 847 996-0100 |
| Vernon Hills (G-21151) | | |
| Cobraco Manufacturing Inc | E | 847 726-5800 |
| Lake Zurich (G-13055) | | |
| Delaval Manufacturing | G | 847 298-5505 |
| Des Plaines (G-8179) | | |
| Design Plus Industries Inc | G | 309 697-9778 |
| Peoria (G-17349) | | |
| Fun Industries Inc | F | 309 755-5021 |
| East Moline (G-8679) | | |
| Grand Products Inc | C | 800 621-6101 |
| Elk Grove Village (G-9506) | | |
| Namco America Inc | E | 847 264-5610 |
| Elk Grove Village (G-9645) | | |
| Stern Pinball Inc | D | 708 345-7700 |
| Elk Grove Village (G-9757) | | |
| Williams Electronic Games De | B | 773 961-1000 |
| Chicago (G-6985) | | |
| Williams Electronic Games De | F | 773 961-1000 |
| Chicago (G-6986) | | |
| WMS Games Inc | F | 773 728-2300 |
| Chicago (G-7015) | | |
| WMS Industries Inc | D | 847 785-3000 |
| Chicago (G-7018) | | |

## AMUSEMENT PARK DEVICES & RIDES

| | | |
|---|---|---|
| Affri Inc | G | 224 374-0931 |
| Wood Dale (G-22333) | | |
| Chicago Park District | D | 708 857-2653 |
| Chicago Ridge (G-7142) | | |
| County Tool & Die | G | 217 324-6527 |
| Litchfield (G-13683) | | |
| Diamond Industrial Sales Ltd | G | 630 858-3687 |
| Glen Ellyn (G-10966) | | |
| Donaldson Company Inc | C | 309 667-2885 |
| New Windsor (G-15930) | | |
| Dunteman and Co | G | 309 772-2166 |
| Bushnell (G-2902) | | |
| Idex Mpt Inc | D | 630 530-3333 |
| Elmhurst (G-9884) | | |
| K1 Speed-Illinois Inc | G | 847 941-9400 |
| Buffalo Grove (G-2715) | | |
| Lake County Technologies Inc | G | 847 658-1330 |
| Barrington (G-1285) | | |
| Metals USA Rockford | F | 815 874-8536 |
| Rockford (G-18497) | | |
| Playing With Fusion Inc | G | 309 258-7259 |
| Mackinaw (G-14118) | | |
| R/K Industries Inc | F | 847 526-2222 |
| Wauconda (G-21498) | | |
| Senior PLC | G | 630 372-3511 |
| Bartlett (G-1376) | | |
| Spec Check LLC | G | 773 270-0003 |
| Mundelein (G-15559) | | |
| Threads Up Inc | G | 630 595-2297 |
| Bensenville (G-2002) | | |
| Visos Machine Shop & Mfg | G | 630 372-3925 |
| Streamwood (G-20680) | | |

## AMUSEMENT PARK DEVICES & RIDES Carousels Or Merry-Go-Rounds

| | | |
|---|---|---|
| Dan Horenberger | F | 818 394-0028 |
| Marengo (G-14224) | | |

## AMUSEMENT PARK DEVICES & RIDES: Carnival Mach & Eqpt, NEC

| | | |
|---|---|---|
| Alpine Amusement Co Inc | G | 708 233-9131 |
| Oak Lawn (G-16600) | | |

## AMUSEMENT PARKS

| | | |
|---|---|---|
| Fox Valley Park District | D | 630 892-1550 |
| Aurora (G-1157) | | |

## ANALYZERS: Blood & Body Fluid

| | | |
|---|---|---|
| Output Medical Inc | G | 630 430-8024 |
| Chicago (G-6027) | | |

## ANALYZERS: Coulometric, Indl Process

| | | |
|---|---|---|
| Uic Inc | G | 815 744-4477 |
| Rockdale (G-18234) | | |

## ANALYZERS: Moisture

| | | |
|---|---|---|
| Moisture Detection Inc | G | 847 426-0464 |
| Hoffman Estates (G-12024) | | |

## ANALYZERS: Network

| | | |
|---|---|---|
| Abundant Venture Innovation AC | G | 312 291-1910 |
| Chicago (G-3712) | | |
| Amerinet of Michigan Inc | G | 708 466-0110 |
| Naperville (G-15795) | | |
| Brandt Assoc | G | 847 362-0556 |
| Lake Bluff (G-12837) | | |
| Cyber Innovation Labs LLC | G | 847 804-4724 |
| Mount Prospect (G-15325) | | |
| Hipskind Tech Sltons Group Inc | E | 630 920-0960 |
| Oakbrook Terrace (G-16712) | | |
| Telcom Innovations Group LLC | E | 630 350-0700 |
| Itasca (G-12366) | | |

## ANALYZERS: Respiratory

| | | |
|---|---|---|
| Intellidrain Inc | G | 312 725-4332 |
| Evanston (G-10058) | | |
| IV & Respiratory Care Services | E | 618 398-2720 |
| Belleville (G-1639) | | |

# ANATOMICAL SPECIMENS & RESEARCH MATERIAL, WHOLESALE

**3M Dekalb Distribution** ..................E....... 815 756-5087
Dekalb *(G-8071)*

## ANESTHETICS: Bulk Form

**Janssen Pharmaceutica Inc**..................F....... 312 750-0507
Chicago *(G-5279)*

## ANIMAL BASED MEDICINAL CHEMICAL PRDTS

**Animal Center International** ..................G....... 217 214-0536
Quincy *(G-17792)*
**Wellmark Int Farnam Co** ..................B....... 925 948-4000
Schaumburg *(G-19787)*

## ANIMAL FEED & SUPPLEMENTS: Livestock & Poultry

**Agresearch Inc** ..................F....... 815 726-0410
Joliet *(G-12451)*
**Archer-Daniels-Midland Company** ..................E....... 217 342-3986
Effingham *(G-8824)*
**Archer-Daniels-Midland Company** ..................E....... 217 424-5858
Decatur *(G-7837)*
**Archer-Daniels-Midland Company** ..................F....... 217 732-6678
Lincoln *(G-13404)*
**Archer-Daniels-Midland Company** ..................D....... 217 424-5785
Decatur *(G-7839)*
**Archer-Daniels-Midland Company** ..................F....... 815 362-2180
German Valley *(G-10890)*
**Archer-Daniels-Midland Company** ..................G....... 618 432-7194
Patoka *(G-17230)*
**Ardent Mills LLC** ..................E....... 618 826-2371
Chester *(G-3650)*
**B B Milling Co Inc** ..................G....... 217 376-3131
Emden *(G-9983)*
**Blackwing For Pets Inc**..................G....... 203 762-8620
Antioch *(G-624)*
**Cargill Incorporated** ..................F....... 618 662-8070
Flora *(G-10202)*
**Cargill Dry Corn Ingrdents Inc**..................G....... 217 465-5331
Paris *(G-17143)*
**Cloverleaf Feed Co Inc** ..................G....... 217 589-5010
Roodhouse *(G-18882)*
**Darling Ingredients Inc**..................E....... 309 476-8111
Lynn Center *(G-14016)*
**Darling International Inc**..................E....... 708 388-3223
Blue Island *(G-2245)*
**Dawes LLC** ..................F....... 847 577-2020
Arlington Heights *(G-745)*
**Effingham Equity Inc**..................F....... 217 268-5128
Arcola *(G-668)*
**Garver Feeds** ..................E....... 217 422-2201
Decatur *(G-7884)*
**Gsi Group LLC** ..................D....... 217 463-8016
Paris *(G-17149)*
**Helfter Enterprises Inc** ..................F....... 309 522-5505
Osco *(G-16899)*
**Howard Pet Products Inc** ..................G....... 973 398-3038
Saint Charles *(G-19194)*
**Hueber LLC** ..................F....... 815 393-4879
Creston *(G-7472)*
**Jbs United Inc** ..................F....... 217 285-2121
Pittsfield *(G-17570)*
**Lebanon Seaboard Corporation** ..................E....... 217 446-0983
Danville *(G-7746)*
**Liberty Feed Mill** ..................F....... 217 645-3441
Liberty *(G-13296)*
**M & W Feed Service** ..................G....... 815 858-2412
Elizabeth *(G-9243)*
**Mendota Agri-Products Inc** ..................E....... 815 539-5633
Mendota *(G-14724)*
**Mgp Ingredients Illinois Inc** ..................C....... 309 353-3990
Pekin *(G-17274)*
**Pcs Phosphate Company Inc** ..................E....... 815 795-5111
Marseilles *(G-14316)*
**Purina Mills LLC** ..................E....... 618 283-2291
Vandalia *(G-21122)*
**Reconserve Of Illinois Inc** ..................E....... 708 354-4641
Hodgkins *(G-11981)*
**Roanoke Milling Co** ..................G....... 309 923-5731
Roanoke *(G-18054)*
**Trouw Nutrition Usa LLC** ..................E....... 618 651-1521
Highland *(G-11814)*
**Trouw Nutrition Usa LLC** ..................E....... 618 654-2070
Highland *(G-11815)*
**Trouw Nutrition Usa LLC** ..................E....... 618 654-2070
Highland *(G-11816)*
**Trouw Nutrition Usa LLC** ..................E....... 618 654-2070
Highland *(G-11817)*
**Veal Tech Inc** ..................G....... 630 554-0410
Oswego *(G-16938)*
**Western Yeast Company Inc** ..................E....... 309 274-3160
Chillicothe *(G-7172)*
**Zoetis LLC** ..................D....... 708 757-2592
Chicago Heights *(G-7137)*

## ANIMAL FEED: Wholesalers

**Archer-Daniels-Midland Company** ..................G....... 618 432-7194
Patoka *(G-17230)*
**Farmers Mill Inc** ..................E....... 618 445-2114
Albion *(G-362)*
**Jbs United Inc** ..................E....... 309 747-2196
Gridley *(G-11407)*
**Jbs United Inc** ..................F....... 217 285-2121
Pittsfield *(G-17570)*
**Pcs Phosphate Company Inc** ..................E....... 815 795-5111
Marseilles *(G-14316)*
**Shaars International Inc** ..................G....... 815 315-0717
Rockford *(G-18614)*

## ANIMAL FOOD & SUPPLEMENTS: Bird Food, Prepared

**Bill Chandler Farms** ..................G....... 618 752-7551
Noble *(G-16049)*
**Rare Birds Inc** ..................G....... 847 259-7286
Arlington Heights *(G-828)*
**Siemer Enterprises Inc** ..................E....... 217 857-3171
Teutopolis *(G-20855)*
**Wagners LLC** ..................E....... 815 889-4101
Milford *(G-14815)*

## ANIMAL FOOD & SUPPLEMENTS: Dog

**Diddy Dogs Inc** ..................G....... 815 517-0451
Dekalb *(G-8088)*
**Nestle Usa Inc** ..................C....... 847 808-5300
Buffalo Grove *(G-2748)*
**Papmpered Pups** ..................G....... 815 782-8383
Joliet *(G-12549)*
**Pet Factory Inc** ..................C....... 847 281-8054
Mundelein *(G-15544)*
**Pet-Ag Inc** ..................E....... 847 683-2288
Hampshire *(G-11558)*
**Phelps Industries LLC** ..................G....... 815 397-0236
Rockford *(G-18535)*
**Yotta Pet Products Inc** ..................F....... 217 466-4777
Paris *(G-17165)*

## ANIMAL FOOD & SUPPLEMENTS: Dog & Cat

**Evangers Dog and Cat Fd Co Inc** ..................E....... 847 537-0102
Wheeling *(G-22050)*
**Hartz Mountain Corporation** ..................E....... 847 517-2596
Schaumburg *(G-19548)*
**Kraft Heinz Foods Company** ..................C....... 847 291-3900
Northbrook *(G-16290)*
**Lincoln Bark LLC** ..................G....... 800 428-4027
Chicago *(G-5506)*
**Mars Incorporated** ..................G....... 630 878-8877
Wheaton *(G-21968)*
**Midwestern Pet Foods Inc** ..................E....... 309 734-3121
Monmouth *(G-15019)*
**Nobu Nutritional Baking Co Inc** ..................E....... 847 344-7336
Schaumburg *(G-19667)*
**Pedigree Ovens Inc** ..................E....... 815 943-8144
Harvard *(G-11643)*
**Pet Celebrations Inc** ..................G....... 630 832-6549
Elmhurst *(G-9921)*

## ANIMAL FOOD & SUPPLEMENTS: Feather Meal

**Packers By Products Inc** ..................F....... 618 271-0660
National Stock Yards *(G-15851)*

## ANIMAL FOOD & SUPPLEMENTS: Feed Premixes

**Furst-Mcness Company** ..................D....... 800 435-5100
Freeport *(G-10659)*
**Herris Group LLC** ..................G....... 630 908-7393
Willowbrook *(G-22214)*
**Mont Eagle Products Inc** ..................G....... 618 455-3344
Sainte Marie *(G-19325)*

## ANIMAL FOOD & SUPPLEMENTS: Feed Supplements

**Nutriad Inc** ..................E....... 847 214-4860
Hampshire *(G-11556)*
**Pet-Ag Inc** ..................E....... 847 683-2288
Hampshire *(G-11558)*
**Prince Agri Products Inc** ..................E....... 217 222-8854
Quincy *(G-17872)*
**Quality Liquid Feeds Inc** ..................F....... 815 224-1553
La Salle *(G-12782)*
**Transagra International Inc** ..................G....... 312 856-1010
Chicago *(G-6757)*
**Westway Feed Products LLC** ..................E....... 309 654-2211
Cordova *(G-7380)*
**White International Inc** ..................E....... 630 377-9966
Saint Charles *(G-19295)*

## ANIMAL FOOD & SUPPLEMENTS: Livestock

**Agribase International Inc** ..................G....... 847 810-0167
Schaumburg *(G-19426)*
**Altair Corporation (del)** ..................E....... 847 634-9540
Lincolnshire *(G-13426)*
**Archer-Daniels-Midland Company** ..................E....... 217 222-7100
Quincy *(G-17793)*
**B&A Livestock Feed Company LLC** ..................E....... 618 245-6422
Farina *(G-10173)*
**Dekalb Feeds Inc** ..................D....... 815 625-4546
Rock Falls *(G-18131)*
**Griswold Feed Inc** ..................G....... 815 432-2811
Watseka *(G-21417)*
**Jbs United Inc** ..................E....... 309 747-2196
Gridley *(G-11407)*
**Kent Nutrition Group Inc** ..................F....... 815 874-2411
Rockford *(G-18456)*
**Kent Nutrition Group Inc** ..................F....... 217 323-1216
Beardstown *(G-1523)*
**Morgan Robt Inc** ..................E....... 217 466-4777
Paris *(G-17154)*

## ANIMAL FOOD & SUPPLEMENTS: Mineral feed supplements

**Sem Minerals LP** ..................D....... 217 224-8766
Quincy *(G-17890)*

## ANIMAL FOOD & SUPPLEMENTS: Pet, Exc Dog & Cat, Canned

**All-Feed Proc & Packg Inc** ..................F....... 309 629-0001
Alpha *(G-425)*
**All-Feed Proc & Packg Inc** ..................G....... 309 932-3119
Galva *(G-10782)*

## ANIMAL FOOD & SUPPLEMENTS: Pet, Exc Dog & Cat, Dry

**Cherry Valley Feed Supplies** ..................G....... 815 332-7665
Cherry Valley *(G-3640)*

## ANIMAL FOOD & SUPPLEMENTS: Poultry

**Lokman Enterprises Inc** ..................G....... 773 654-0525
Chicago *(G-5534)*
**Tate Lyle Ingrdnts Amricas LLC** ..................G....... 309 473-2721
Heyworth *(G-11766)*

## ANIMAL FOOD & SUPPLEMENTS: Specialty, Mice & Other Pets

**Chatham Corporation** ..................F....... 847 634-5506
Lincolnshire *(G-13436)*

## ANIMAL OILS: Medicinal Grade, Refined Or Concentrated

**RITA Corporation** ..................E....... 815 337-2500
Crystal Lake *(G-7642)*

## ANNEALING: Metal

**Riverdale Pltg Heat Trting LLC** ..................E....... 708 849-2050
Riverdale *(G-18024)*

## ANODIZING SVC

**Accent Metal Finishing Inc** ..................F....... 847 678-7420
Schiller Park *(G-19798)*
**Ace Anodizing Impregnating Inc** ..................D....... 708 547-6680
Hillside *(G-11907)*

All-Brite Anodizing Co Inc.................E....... 708 562-0502
  Northlake  (G-16425)
Aluminum Coil Anodizing Corp..........C....... 630 837-4000
  Streamwood  (G-20641)
Anodizing Specialists Ltd..................G....... 847 437-9495
  Elk Grove Village  (G-9308)
Automatic Anodizing Corp..................E....... 773 478-3304
  Chicago  (G-3991)
Bright Metals Finishing Corp..............G....... 773 486-2312
  Chicago  (G-4169)
Dana Anodizing Inc..............................F....... 773 486-2312
  Chicago  (G-4550)
Finishing Company................................C....... 630 559-0808
  Addison  (G-117)
MBA Manufacturing Inc......................G....... 847 566-2555
  Mundelein  (G-15525)
Meto-Grafics Inc...................................F....... 847 639-0044
  Crystal Lake  (G-7609)
Mikes Anodizing Co..............................E....... 773 722-5778
  Chicago  (G-5758)
P B A Corp.............................................F....... 312 666-7370
  Chicago  (G-6039)
Petersen Finishing Corporation..........G....... 847 228-7150
  Elk Grove Village  (G-9677)
Saporito Finishing Co..........................D....... 708 222-5300
  Cicero  (G-7228)
Saporito Finishing Co..........................G....... 708 222-5300
  Chicago  (G-6443)

## ANTENNAS: Radar Or Communications

Whisco Component Engrg Inc.............F....... 630 790-9785
  Glendale Heights  (G-11092)

## ANTENNAS: Receiving

Dynomax Inc..........................................E....... 224 542-1031
  Lincolnshire  (G-13445)
Futaba Corporation of America...........E....... 847 884-1444
  Schaumburg  (G-19534)
Kp Performance Inc..............................G....... 780 809-1908
  Melrose Park  (G-14667)
Molex  LLC.............................................A....... 630 969-4550
  Lisle  (G-13625)
Molex  LLC.............................................G....... 630 527-4363
  Bolingbrook  (G-2345)
Molex Premise Networks Inc..............A....... 866 733-6659
  Lisle  (G-13628)
Panasonic Corp North America...........G....... 630 801-0359
  Aurora  (G-1062)
Tedds Cstm Installations Inc................G....... 815 485-6800
  New Lenox  (G-15918)

## ANTENNAS: Satellite, Household Use

Joseph C Rakers...................................G....... 618 670-6995
  Pocahontas  (G-17683)
Perfectvision Mfg Inc............................C....... 630 226-9890
  Bolingbrook  (G-2357)
Satellink Inc..........................................G....... 618 983-5555
  Johnston City  (G-12445)

## ANTIBIOTICS

Zoetis LLC..............................................D....... 708 757-2592
  Chicago Heights  (G-7137)

## ANTIFREEZE

Honeywell International Inc.................G....... 630 554-5342
  Oswego  (G-16921)
Illinois Oil Products Inc........................F....... 309 788-1896
  Rock Island  (G-18183)
Planet Earth Antifreeze Inc..................G....... 815 282-2463
  Loves Park  (G-13976)
Prestone Products Corporation............D....... 708 371-3000
  Alsip  (G-513)
Prestone Products Corporation............G....... 203 731-8185
  Lake Forest  (G-12948)
Prestone Products Corporation............C....... 847 482-2045
  Lake Forest  (G-12949)

## ANTIHISTAMINE PREPARATIONS

Abbott Products  Inc.............................B....... 847 937-6100
  Abbott Park  (G-7)

## ANTIQUE & CLASSIC AUTOMOBILE RESTORATION

Restorations Unlimited II Inc...............G....... 847 639-5818
  Cary  (G-3367)

## ANTIQUE AUTOMOBILE DEALERS

Heartland Classics Inc..........................G....... 618 783-4444
  Newton  (G-15941)

## ANTIQUE FURNITURE RESTORATION & REPAIR

Lee Armand & Co Ltd..........................E....... 312 455-1200
  Chicago  (G-5483)

## ANTIQUE REPAIR & RESTORATION SVCS, EXC FURNITURE & AUTOS

Marshall Bauer......................................G....... 847 236-1847
  Bannockburn  (G-1260)
Tiffany Stained Glass Ltd.....................E....... 312 642-0680
  Forest Park  (G-10255)

## ANTIQUE SHOPS

Stained Glass of Peoria........................G....... 309 674-7929
  Peoria  (G-17461)

## ANTISCALING COMPOUNDS, BOILER

Global Water Technology Inc..............E....... 708 349-9991
  Orland Park  (G-16862)

## ANTISEPTICS, MEDICINAL

Ortho Molecular Products Inc.............E....... 815 337-0089
  Woodstock  (G-22596)

## APPAREL ACCESS STORES

Athletic Outfitters Inc..........................G....... 815 942-6696
  Morris  (G-15094)
Nali Inc.................................................E....... 708 442-8710
  Clarendon Hills  (G-7259)

## APPAREL DESIGNERS: Commercial

Diamond Icic Corporation...................E....... 309 269-8652
  Rock Island  (G-18175)

## APPLIANCE CORDS: Household Electrical Eqpt

Best Rep Company Corporation..........G....... 847 451-6644
  Franklin Park  (G-10411)
Coles Craft Corporation.......................G....... 630 858-8171
  Glen Ellyn  (G-10963)
D & D Manufacturing Inc....................G....... 888 300-6869
  Bolingbrook  (G-2296)
Rent-A-Center Inc................................G....... 773 376-8883
  Chicago  (G-6335)

## APPLIANCE PARTS: Porcelain Enameled

Voges Inc..............................................D....... 618 233-2760
  Belleville  (G-1688)

## APPLIANCES, HOUSEHOLD: Buttonhole/Eyelet Mach/Attach

Quantum Precision Inc.........................E....... 630 692-1545
  West Chicago  (G-21762)

## APPLIANCES, HOUSEHOLD: Ice Boxes, Metal Or Wood

Scotsman Industries  Inc.....................D....... 847 215-4501
  Vernon Hills  (G-21199)

## APPLIANCES, HOUSEHOLD: Kitchen, Major, Exc Refrigs & Stoves

Appliance Repair...................................G....... 708 456-1020
  Norridge  (G-16096)
Mic Quality Service Inc........................E....... 847 778-5676
  Chicago  (G-5719)
Rampro Facilities Svcs Corp................G....... 224 639-6378
  Gurnee  (G-11498)
Tablecraft Products Co Inc..................D....... 847 855-9000
  Gurnee  (G-11512)

## APPLIANCES, HOUSEHOLD: Laundry Machines, Incl Coin-Operated

Eastgate Cleaners.................................G....... 630 627-9494
  Lombard  (G-13794)

## APPLIANCES, HOUSEHOLD: Refrigs, Mechanical & Absorption

Sphinx Panel and Door Inc..................G....... 618 351-9266
  Cobden  (G-7305)

## APPLIANCES, HOUSEHOLD: Sewing Machines & Attchmnts, Domestic

Threads of Time....................................G....... 217 431-9202
  Danville  (G-7769)

## APPLIANCES, HOUSEHOLD: Sweepers, Electric

Aerus Electrolux....................................G....... 847 949-4222
  Mundelein  (G-15465)

## APPLIANCES: Household, Refrigerators & Freezers

Craig Industries Inc..............................D....... 217 228-2421
  Quincy  (G-17816)
Dover Corporation................................C....... 630 541-1540
  Downers Grove  (G-8431)
Flurida Group Inc.................................G....... 310 513-0888
  Naperville  (G-15806)
H A Phillips & Co..................................E....... 630 377-0050
  Dekalb  (G-8095)
Tri-State Food Equipment...................G....... 217 228-1550
  Quincy  (G-17900)

## APPLIANCES: Major, Cooking

Axis International Marketing...............C....... 847 297-0744
  Des Plaines  (G-8154)
BR Machine Inc....................................F....... 815 434-0427
  Ottawa  (G-16950)
Global Contract Mfg Inc......................G....... 312 432-6200
  Chicago  (G-4957)
Marshall Middleby Inc.........................C....... 847 289-0204
  Elgin  (G-9100)
Sun Ovens International  Inc..............F....... 630 208-7273
  Elburn  (G-8911)

## APPLIANCES: Small, Electric

Akinsun Heat Co Inc............................F....... 630 289-9506
  Streamwood  (G-20640)
American Fuel Economy Inc................G....... 815 433-3226
  Ottawa  (G-16946)
Extractor Corporation..........................F....... 847 742-3532
  South Elgin  (G-20196)
Keating of Chicago Inc........................E....... 815 569-2324
  Capron  (G-2996)
Newhaven Display Intl Inc..................E....... 847 844-8795
  Elgin  (G-9118)
Tempro International Corp..................G....... 847 677-5370
  Skokie  (G-20100)
Tonjon Company...................................F....... 630 208-1173
  Geneva  (G-10873)

## APPLICATIONS SOFTWARE PROGRAMMING

Hybris (us) Corporation......................E....... 312 265-5010
  Chicago  (G-5128)
Lightfoot Technologies Inc..................G....... 331 302-1297
  Naperville  (G-15690)
Truth Labs  LLC....................................F....... 312 291-9035
  Chicago  (G-6790)

## APPRENTICESHIP TRAINING SCHOOLS

Bandjwet Enterprises Inc....................E....... 847 797-9250
  Rolling Meadows  (G-18715)

## AQUARIUMS & ACCESS: Glass

Midwest Tropical Entps Inc.................E....... 847 679-6666
  Skokie  (G-20040)

## AQUARIUMS & ACCESS: Plastic

Midwest Tropical Entps Inc.................E....... 847 679-6666
  Skokie  (G-20040)

## ARCHITECTURAL SVCS

Fastsigns...............................................G....... 847 675-1600
  Lincolnwood  (G-13509)
Gerald R Page Corporation..................F....... 847 398-5575
  Prospect Heights  (G-17779)

# ARCHITECTURAL SVCS

Lingle Design Group Inc .................. E ...... 815 369-9155
  Lena  (G-13280)

## ARCHITECTURAL SVCS: Engineering

Floline Archtctral Systems LLC .......... F ..... 815 733-5044
  Plainfield  (G-17600)

## ARCHITECTURAL SVCS: House Designer

Home Design Alternatives Inc ............ E ...... 314 731-1427
  Schaumburg  (G-19558)

## ARMATURE REPAIRING & REWINDING SVC

Acme Control Service Inc .................. E ...... 773 774-9191
  Chicago  (G-3732)
Cox Electric Motor Service .................. G ...... 217 344-2458
  Urbana  (G-21080)
Dreisilker Electric Motors Inc ............... C ...... 630 469-7510
  Glen Ellyn  (G-10967)
Flolo Corporation ............................... G ...... 847 249-0880
  Gurnee  (G-11448)
Integrated Power Services LLC ............ E ...... 708 877-5310
  Thornton  (G-20874)
Jasiek Motor Rebuilding Inc ................. G ...... 815 883-3678
  Oglesby  (G-16750)
Lawrence Maddock ............................ F ...... 847 394-1698
  Arlington Heights  (G-792)
New Cie Inc ...................................... F ...... 815 224-1485
  La Salle  (G-12781)
New Cie Inc ...................................... E ...... 815 224-1511
  Peru  (G-17522)
Precision Drive & Control Inc .............. G ...... 815 235-7595
  Freeport  (G-10680)
Quality Armature Inc .......................... G ...... 773 622-3951
  Chicago  (G-6245)
Rathje Enterprises Inc ........................ B ...... 217 423-2593
  Decatur  (G-7932)
Richards Electric Motor Co .................. E ...... 217 222-7154
  Quincy  (G-17887)

## ARMATURES: Ind

Active Tool and Machine Inc ................ F ...... 708 599-0022
  Oak Lawn  (G-16598)

## ARSENATES & ARSENITES: Formulated

Tri-County Chemical Inc ...................... G ...... 618 268-4318
  Galatia  (G-10713)

## ART & ORNAMENTAL WARE: Pottery

In The Attic Inc .................................. G ...... 847 949-5077
  Mundelein  (G-15509)

## ART DEALERS & GALLERIES

Wood Shop ........................................ G ...... 773 994-6666
  Chicago  (G-7024)

## ART DESIGN SVCS

Fortman & Associates Ltd .................... F ...... 847 524-0741
  Elk Grove Village  (G-9488)
Mk Signs Inc ...................................... E ...... 773 545-4444
  Chicago  (G-5777)
Targin Sign Systems Inc ...................... G ...... 630 766-7667
  Wood Dale  (G-22427)

## ART GALLERIES

Okaw Valley Woodworking LLC ............ F ...... 217 543-5180
  Arthur  (G-916)

## ART GOODS & SPLYS WHOLESALERS

Sws Industries Inc .............................. E ...... 904 482-0091
  Woodstock  (G-22616)

## ART GOODS, WHOLESALE

Chase Group LLC ................................ F ...... 847 564-2000
  Northbrook  (G-16219)

## ART MARBLE: Concrete

Blue Pearl Stone Tech LLC .................. G ...... 708 698-5700
  La Grange  (G-12726)
Concrete & Marble Polishing & ............ G ...... 773 968-6897
  Prospect Heights  (G-17774)

## ART SCHOOL, EXC COMMERCIAL

Creative Curricula Inc .......................... G ...... 815 363-9419
  McHenry  (G-14491)

## ARTIFICIAL FLOWERS & TREES

Brees Studio Inc .................................. F ...... 618 687-3331
  Murphysboro  (G-15573)
Lcg Sales Inc ...................................... D ...... 773 378-7455
  Chicago  (G-5476)

## ARTIST'S MATERIALS & SPLYS

Graphic Chemical & Ink Co .................. F ...... 630 832-6004
  Villa Park  (G-21257)

## ARTISTS' AGENTS & BROKERS

Bio Star Films LLC .............................. G ...... 773 254-5959
  Chicago  (G-4108)
Quarasan Group Inc ............................ D ...... 312 981-2540
  Chicago  (G-6254)
Strictly Stainless Inc ............................ G ...... 847 885-2890
  Hoffman Estates  (G-12061)

## ARTISTS' EQPT

Leisure Time Products Inc .................... G ...... 847 287-2863
  Prospect Heights  (G-17782)

## ARTISTS' MATERIALS, WHOLESALE

James Howard Co ................................ G ...... 815 497-2831
  Compton  (G-7366)

## ARTISTS' MATERIALS: Boxes, Sketching & Paint

Bio Packaging Films LLC ...................... F ...... 847 566-4444
  Mundelein  (G-15477)

## ARTISTS' MATERIALS: Brushes, Air

Badger Air Brush Co ............................ D ...... 847 678-3104
  Franklin Park  (G-10409)
Paasche Airbrush Co ............................ D ...... 773 867-9191
  Chicago  (G-6048)
Rust-Oleum Corporation ...................... D ...... 815 967-4258
  Rockford  (G-18600)
Testor Corporation .............................. D ...... 815 962-6654
  Rockford  (G-18644)

## ARTISTS' MATERIALS: Chalks, Carpenters', Blackboard, Etc

Egan Visual/West Inc .......................... G ...... 800 266-2387
  Chicago  (G-4704)
Fernandez Windows Corp ...................... G ...... 773 762-2365
  Chicago  (G-4837)

## ARTISTS' MATERIALS: Clay, Modeling

Polyform Products Company ................ E ...... 847 427-0020
  Elk Grove Village  (G-9685)

## ARTISTS' MATERIALS: Eraser Guides & Shields

Erasermitt Incorporated ...................... G ...... 312 842-2855
  Chicago  (G-4771)

## ARTISTS' MATERIALS: Ink, Drawing, Black & Colored

Hydro Ink Corp .................................. G ...... 847 674-0057
  Skokie  (G-20014)

## ARTISTS' MATERIALS: Lettering Instruments

On Paint It Company .......................... G ...... 219 765-5639
  Dekalb  (G-8112)

## ARTISTS' MATERIALS: Paints, Exc Gold & Bronze

Duro Art Industries Inc ........................ D ...... 773 743-3430
  Chicago  (G-4657)

## ARTISTS' MATERIALS: Palettes

Miller Pallet ...................................... F ...... 217 589-4411
  Roodhouse  (G-18883)

## ARTISTS' MATERIALS: Pencil Holders

E W Enterprises Inc ............................ G ...... 618 345-2244
  Collinsville  (G-7320)

## ARTISTS' MATERIALS: Pencils & Pencil Parts

Stentech Inc ...................................... G ...... 630 833-4747
  Elmhurst  (G-9944)

## ARTISTS' MATERIALS: Wax

Lectro Stik Corp .................................. E ...... 630 894-1355
  Glendale Heights  (G-11040)

## ARTWORK: Framed

I T C W Inc ........................................ B ...... 630 305-8849
  Naperville  (G-15671)
Online Merchant Systems LLC .............. G ...... 847 973-2337
  Ingleside  (G-12197)
Thrilled LLC ...................................... G ...... 312 404-1929
  Chicago  (G-6723)

## ASBESTOS PRDTS: Insulation, Molded

Asbestos Control & Envmtl Svc ............ F ...... 630 690-0189
  Eola  (G-9988)

## ASBESTOS PRDTS: Wick

Wise Construction Services .................. G ...... 630 553-6350
  Yorkville  (G-22676)

## ASBESTOS PRODUCTS

Celtic Environmental ............................ G ...... 708 442-5823
  Chicago Ridge  (G-7140)

## ASBESTOS REMOVAL EQPT

Asbestos Control & Envmtl Svc ............ F ...... 630 690-0189
  Eola  (G-9988)
Bunn-O-Matic Corporation .................. G ...... 217 529-6601
  Springfield  (G-20402)

## ASH TRAYS: Stamped Metal

Creative Metal Products ...................... F ...... 773 638-3200
  Chicago  (G-4500)

## ASPHALT & ASPHALT PRDTS

Allied Asphalt Paving Co Inc ................ F ...... 847 824-2848
  Franklin Park  (G-10390)
Allied Asphalt Paving Co Inc ................ E ...... 630 289-6080
  Elgin  (G-8943)
Arrow Road Construction Co ................ C ...... 847 437-0700
  Mount Prospect  (G-15310)
Asphalt Products Inc ............................ E ...... 618 943-4716
  Lawrenceville  (G-13195)
Certified Asphalt Paving ...................... G ...... 847 441-5000
  Northfield  (G-16396)
Cgk Enterprises Inc ............................ G ...... 847 888-1362
  Elgin  (G-8985)
Corrective Asphalt Mtls LLC ................ G ...... 618 254-3855
  South Roxana  (G-20312)
Crowley-Sheppard Asphalt Inc ............ F ...... 708 499-2900
  Chicago Ridge  (G-7145)
Curran Contracting Company .............. E ...... 815 455-5100
  Crystal Lake  (G-7562)
Done Rite Sealcoating Inc .................... G ...... 630 830-5310
  Streamwood  (G-20651)
Emulsions Inc .................................... G ...... 618 943-2615
  Lawrenceville  (G-13199)
ET Simonds Materials Company ............ E ...... 618 457-8191
  Carbondale  (G-3007)
Frank S Johnson & Company ................ G ...... 847 492-1660
  Evanston  (G-10039)
Geske and Sons Inc ............................ G ...... 815 459-2407
  Crystal Lake  (G-7582)
Geske and Sons Inc ............................ F ...... 815 459-2407
  Crystal Lake  (G-7581)
Gorman Brothers Ready Mix Inc .......... F ...... 618 498-2173
  Jerseyville  (G-12422)
Howell Asphalt Company ...................... G ...... 217 234-8877
  Mattoon  (G-14393)
Illinois Road Contractors Inc ................ E ...... 217 245-6181
  Jacksonville  (G-12393)
Illinois Valley Paving Co ...................... E ...... 217 422-1010
  Elwin  (G-9977)
Louis Marsch Inc ................................ E ...... 217 526-3723
  Morrisonville  (G-15151)

# PRODUCT SECTION

Pothole Pros .................................... G ...... 847 815-5789
  Elgin *(G-9144)*
Reliable Asphalt Corporation ............ F ...... 773 254-1121
  Chicago *(G-6328)*
Reliable Asphalt Corporation ............ G ...... 630 497-8700
  Bartlett *(G-1368)*
Savanna Quarry Inc ......................... G ...... 815 273-4208
  Savanna *(G-19405)*
Seneca Petroleum Co Inc ................. E ...... 630 257-2268
  Lemont *(G-13262)*
Tri-State Asphalt LLC ........................ G ...... 815 942-0080
  Morris *(G-15136)*

## ASPHALT COATINGS & SEALERS

Allied Asphalt Paving Co Inc ............. E ...... 630 289-6080
  Elgin *(G-8943)*
Asphalt Maint Systems Inc ................ F ...... 815 986-6977
  South Beloit *(G-20139)*
Atlas Roofing Corporation ................. E ...... 309 752-7121
  East Moline *(G-8670)*
Black Rock Milling and Pav Co .......... F ...... 847 952-0700
  Arlington Heights *(G-726)*
Bonsal American Inc ......................... D ...... 847 678-6220
  Franklin Park *(G-10415)*
Complete Asphalt Service Co ............ G ...... 217 285-6099
  Pittsfield *(G-17567)*
Crown Coatings Company ................. F ...... 630 365-9925
  Elburn *(G-8881)*
D N M Sealcoating Inc ....................... G ...... 630 365-1816
  Elburn *(G-8882)*
Don Anderson Co ............................. G ...... 618 495-2511
  Hoffman *(G-11988)*
Emulsicoat Inc .................................. F ...... 217 344-7775
  Urbana *(G-21081)*
Harsco Corporation ........................... F ...... 217 237-4335
  Pawnee *(G-17234)*
Jax Asphalt Company Inc .................. F ...... 618 244-0500
  Mount Vernon *(G-15418)*
Lifetime Rooftile Company ................ G ...... 630 355-7922
  Naperville *(G-15689)*
Miller Purcell Co Inc .......................... G ...... 815 485-2142
  New Lenox *(G-15897)*
Nataz Specialty Coatings Inc ............. F ...... 773 247-7030
  Chicago *(G-5856)*
Nu-Puttie Corporation ........................ E ...... 708 681-1040
  Maywood *(G-14433)*
Omnimax International Inc ................ G ...... 309 747-2937
  Gridley *(G-11410)*
Owens Corning Sales LLC ................ B ...... 708 594-6911
  Argo *(G-694)*
Owens Corning Sales LLC ................ E ...... 708 594-6935
  Argo *(G-695)*
Plote Inc ............................................ D ...... 847 695-9467
  Hoffman Estates *(G-12037)*
Pure Asphalt Company ...................... F ...... 773 247-7030
  Chicago *(G-6228)*
R E Burke Roofing Co Inc ................. F ...... 847 675-5010
  Skokie *(G-20068)*
RM Lucas Co .................................... E ...... 773 523-4300
  Alsip *(G-522)*
Sheet Metal Supply Ltd ...................... G ...... 847 478-8500
  Mundelein *(G-15557)*
St Louis Flexicore Inc ....................... F ...... 618 531-8691
  East Saint Louis *(G-8770)*

## ASPHALT MIXTURES WHOLESALERS

Marathon Petroleum Company LP ...... G ...... 618 829-3288
  Saint Elmo *(G-19308)*

## ASPHALT PLANTS INCLUDING GRAVEL MIX TYPE

Byron Blacktop Inc ............................ G ...... 815 234-8115
  Byron *(G-2914)*
Chicago Materials Corporation ........... E ...... 630 257-5600
  Lemont *(G-13232)*
Jamesons Asphalt Service ................. G ...... 630 830-7266
  Streamwood *(G-20659)*
Jordan Services ................................ G ...... 630 416-6701
  Lisle *(G-13611)*
L & N Structures Inc ......................... E ...... 815 426-2164
  Herscher *(G-11759)*
Peter Baker & Son Co ....................... F ...... 815 344-1640
  Mc Henry *(G-14462)*
Streator Asphalt Inc .......................... G ...... 815 426-2164
  Herscher *(G-11762)*
Streator Asphalt Inc .......................... G ...... 815 672-8683
  Streator *(G-20703)*
Utica Terminal Inc ............................. G ...... 815 667-5131
  Utica *(G-21111)*

## ASSEMBLING & PACKAGING SVCS: Cosmetic Kits

Assemble and Mail Group Inc ............ G ...... 309 473-2006
  Heyworth *(G-11764)*

## ASSEMBLING SVC: Clocks

Instrument Services Inc ..................... G ...... 815 623-2993
  Machesney Park *(G-14082)*

## ASSEMBLING SVC: Plumbing Fixture Fittings, Plastic

Sergio Barajas .................................. G ...... 708 238-7614
  La Grange *(G-12744)*

## ASSOCIATIONS: Bar

American Bar Association .................. A ...... 312 988-5000
  Chicago *(G-3851)*

## ASSOCIATIONS: Business

Chester White Swine Rcord Assn ...... G ...... 309 691-0151
  Peoria *(G-17341)*
Tube & Pipe Association Intl .............. D ...... 815 399-8700
  Elgin *(G-9217)*
USA Today Inc .................................. G ...... 815 987-1400
  Rockford *(G-18665)*
W A M Computers International .......... G ...... 217 324-6926
  Litchfield *(G-13699)*

## ASSOCIATIONS: Real Estate Management

Belboz Corp ...................................... G ...... 708 856-6099
  Dolton *(G-8366)*

## ASSOCIATIONS: Trade

American Supply Association .............. F ...... 630 467-0000
  Itasca *(G-12228)*
Associated Equipment Distrs ............. E ...... 630 574-0650
  Schaumburg *(G-19448)*
Comptia Learning LLC ....................... F ...... 630 678-8490
  Downers Grove *(G-8415)*
Fabricators & Mfrs Assn Intl .............. E ...... 815 399-8700
  Elgin *(G-9033)*
National Association Realtors ............ C ...... 800 874-6500
  Chicago *(G-5857)*
National Association Realtors ............ C ...... 800 874-6500
  Chicago *(G-5858)*
National Sporting Goods Assn ........... F ...... 847 296-6742
  Mount Prospect *(G-15353)*

## ATHLETIC ORGANIZATION

Jr Royals Athletics ............................. E ...... 224 659-2906
  Elgin *(G-9085)*

## ATOMIZERS

3dp Unlimited ................................... G ...... 815 389-5667
  Roscoe *(G-18887)*
3M Dekalb Distribution ...................... E ...... 815 756-5087
  Dekalb *(G-8071)*
Acme Finishing Company LLC .......... F ...... 847 640-7890
  Elk Grove Village *(G-9264)*
American Alum Extrusion Co LLC ...... F ...... 877 896-2236
  Roscoe *(G-18889)*
DPM Solutions LLC ........................... G ...... 630 285-1170
  Itasca *(G-12254)*
Fuyao Glass Illinois Inc ..................... G ...... 217 864-2392
  Decatur *(G-7883)*
General Precision Mfg LLC ................ G ...... 847 624-4969
  Elk Grove Village *(G-9497)*
Ihi Turbo America Co ........................ D ...... 217 774-9571
  Shelbyville *(G-19908)*
Illinois Bottle Mfg Co ......................... D ...... 847 595-9000
  Elk Grove Village *(G-9533)*
Integrated Industries Inc ................... G ...... 773 299-1970
  Chicago *(G-5208)*
Integrated Mfg Tech LLC ................... G ...... 618 282-8306
  Red Bud *(G-17943)*
ITW Bldg Components Group ............ G ...... 847 634-1900
  Glenview *(G-11150)*
Jr Industries LLC .............................. F ...... 773 908-5317
  Chicago *(G-5332)*
L & M Hardware Ltd .......................... G ...... 312 805-2752
  Downers Grove *(G-8471)*
Lincoln Green Mazda Inc .................. F ...... 217 391-2400
  Springfield *(G-20470)*
Makray Manufacturing Company ........ E ...... 847 260-5408
  Schiller Park *(G-19844)*
Mp Manufacturing Inc ........................ G ...... 815 334-1112
  Woodstock *(G-22593)*
Nascote Industries Inc ....................... G ...... 618 327-3286
  Nashville *(G-15842)*
Pegasus Mfg Inc ............................... F ...... 309 342-9337
  Galesburg *(G-10770)*
Plastic Container Corporation ............ D ...... 217 352-2722
  Urbana *(G-21098)*
Potash Holding Company Inc ............ G ...... 847 849-4200
  Northbrook *(G-16341)*
Roll-A-Way Conveyors Inc ................ G ...... 847 336-5033
  Gurnee *(G-11500)*
Smith Industrial Rubber & Plas .......... F ...... 815 874-5364
  Rockford *(G-18622)*
Tropar Trophy Manufacturing Co ....... G ...... 630 787-1900
  Wood Dale *(G-22433)*
Yetter Manufacturing Company ......... E ...... 309 833-1445
  Macomb *(G-14138)*

## AUCTION SVCS: Livestock

Banner Publications .......................... G ...... 309 338-3294
  Cuba *(G-7679)*

## AUDIO & VIDEO EQPT, EXC COMMERCIAL

Aco Inc ............................................. E ...... 773 774-5200
  Chicago *(G-3735)*
Amplivox Sound Systems LLC ........... E ...... 800 267-5486
  Northbrook *(G-16204)*
Audio Video Electronics LLC .............. G ...... 847 983-4761
  Skokie *(G-19961)*
AVI-Spl Employee ............................. B ...... 847 437-7712
  Schaumburg *(G-19454)*
Bretford Manufacturing Inc ................ B ...... 847 678-2545
  Franklin Park *(G-10416)*
Cco Holdings LLC ............................. G ...... 618 505-3505
  Troy *(G-21003)*
Cco Holdings LLC ............................. G ...... 618 651-6486
  Highland *(G-11777)*
Chamberlain Manufacturing Corp ....... A ...... 630 279-3600
  Oak Brook *(G-16500)*
Cinemaquest Inc ............................... G ...... 847 603-7649
  Gurnee *(G-11433)*
Crystal Partners Inc .......................... G ...... 847 882-0467
  Schaumburg *(G-19493)*
Decibel Audio Inc .............................. G ...... 773 862-6700
  Chicago *(G-4569)*
Elexa Consumer Products Inc ........... B ...... 773 794-1300
  Deerfield *(G-8006)*
G T C Industries Inc ......................... G ...... 708 369-9815
  Naperville *(G-15661)*
Heil Sound Ltd .................................. F ...... 618 257-3000
  Fairview Heights *(G-10168)*
Home Specialty Connection Inc ......... G ...... 815 363-1934
  Chicago *(G-5103)*
Identatronics Inc ............................... E ...... 847 437-2654
  Crystal Lake *(G-7591)*
J P Goldenne Incorporated ................ F ...... 847 776-5063
  Palatine *(G-17045)*
Knowles Corporation ......................... D ...... 630 250-5100
  Itasca *(G-12295)*
Mechanical Music Corp ..................... F ...... 847 398-5444
  Arlington Heights *(G-801)*
Newhaven Display Intl Inc ................. E ...... 847 844-8795
  Elgin *(G-9118)*
Northrop Grumman Systems Corp ..... A ...... 847 259-9600
  Rolling Meadows *(G-18753)*
Nueva Vida Productions Inc .............. G ...... 708 444-8474
  Tinley Park *(G-20935)*
Peterson Intl Entp Ltd ....................... F ...... 847 541-3700
  Wheeling *(G-22121)*
Philips Lighting N Amer Corp ............ G ...... 708 307-3000
  Roselle *(G-18962)*
Precision Electronics Inc ................... F ...... 847 599-1799
  Gurnee *(G-11490)*
Robotics Technologies Inc ................ G ...... 815 722-7650
  Joliet *(G-12570)*
Sansui America Inc ........................... C ...... 618 392-7000
  Olney *(G-16796)*
Sonistic ............................................. G ...... 217 377-9698
  Champaign *(G-3542)*
Sony Electronics Inc .......................... G ...... 630 773-7500
  Carol Stream *(G-3242)*
Tech Upgraders ................................ G ...... 877 324-8940
  Maywood *(G-14435)*
Techpol Automation Inc ..................... F ...... 847 347-4765
  Des Plaines *(G-8285)*
Touchtunes Music Corporation .......... E ...... 847 253-8708
  Schaumburg *(G-19765)*

# AUDIO & VIDEO EQPT, EXC COMMERCIAL

United States Audio Corp .................G....... 312 316-2929
Chicago (G-6827)
Wireless Chamberlain Products ...........E ....... 800 282-6225
Elmhurst (G-9961)
Zenith Electronics Corporation ............E ....... 847 941-8000
Lincolnshire (G-13496)

## AUDIO & VIDEO TAPES WHOLESALERS

Buzzfire Incorporated .........................F ....... 630 572-9200
Oak Brook (G-16496)
Holsolutions Inc ................................G....... 888 847-5467
Frankfort (G-10327)

## AUDIO COMPONENTS

Bose Corporation ...............................G....... 630 575-8044
Hinsdale (G-11942)
Bose Corporation ...............................G....... 630 585-6654
Aurora (G-971)
Connecteriors LLC .............................G....... 773 549-3333
Chicago (G-4449)
Mitek Corporation ...............................C ....... 815 367-3000
Winslow (G-22318)
Sound Enhancement Products Inc .......E ....... 847 639-4646
Glendale Heights (G-11070)
United States Audio Corp ....................F ....... 312 316-2929
Glenview (G-11213)

## AUDIO ELECTRONIC SYSTEMS

Advanced Audio Devices LLC ..............G....... 847 604-9630
Lake Forest (G-12875)
Audio Supply Inc ................................G....... 847 549-6086
Mundelein (G-15472)
Buzzfire Incorporated .........................F ....... 630 572-9200
Oak Brook (G-16496)
Foster Electric (usa) Inc ......................G....... 847 310-8200
Schaumburg (G-19532)
John Hardy Co ...................................G....... 847 864-8060
Evanston (G-10059)
K C Audio ..........................................G....... 708 636-4928
Alsip (G-477)
Maxxsonics Usa Inc ...........................E ....... 847 540-7700
Libertyville (G-13350)
Organized Noise Inc ..........................G....... 630 820-9855
Aurora (G-1059)
Prescotts Inc .....................................G....... 815 626-2996
Sterling (G-20605)
Rf Communications Inc ......................F ....... 630 420-8882
Naperville (G-15741)
Shockyave Customs ..........................G....... 815 469-9141
Frankfort (G-10363)
Studio Technologies Inc .....................F ....... 847 676-9177
Skokie (G-20093)
Sytek Audio Systems Corp .................F ....... 847 345-6971
Palatine (G-17077)

## AUTO & HOME SUPPLY STORES: Auto & Truck Eqpt & Parts

Blanke Industries Incorporated ............G....... 847 487-2780
Wauconda (G-21448)
Genuine Parts Company .....................F ....... 630 293-1300
Chicago (G-4938)
Goreville Auto Parts & Mch Sp ............G....... 618 995-2375
Goreville (G-11251)
Iggys Auto Parts .................................F ....... 708 452-9790
Norridge (G-16102)
L & T Services Inc .............................G....... 815 397-6260
Rockford (G-18458)
Rursch Specialties Inc .......................G....... 309 795-1502
Reynolds (G-17953)

## AUTO & HOME SUPPLY STORES: Automotive Access

Folk Race Cars ..................................G....... 815 629-2418
Durand (G-8585)
Heartland Classics Inc .......................G....... 618 783-4444
Newton (G-15941)
Joes Automotive Inc ...........................G....... 815 937-9281
Kankakee (G-12630)
Pauls Mc Culloch Sales .....................G....... 217 323-2159
Beardstown (G-1526)
Sustainable Holding Inc .....................G....... 773 324-0407
Chicago (G-6643)

## AUTO & HOME SUPPLY STORES: Automotive parts

A Len Radiator Shoppe Inc ..................G....... 630 852-5445
Downers Grove (G-8384)
CC Distributing Services Inc ................G....... 800 931-2668
Crestwood (G-7480)
Donnelly Automotive Machine ..............F ....... 217 428-7414
Decatur (G-7877)
Kankakee Spring and Alignment ..........G....... 815 932-6718
Kankakee (G-12633)
L A Motors Incorporated .....................G....... 773 736-7305
Chicago (G-5421)
Lakenburges Motor Co .......................G....... 618 523-4231
Germantown (G-10893)
Moran Auto Parts and Mch Sp .............F ....... 309 663-6449
Bloomington (G-2203)
Murrays Disc Auto Stores Inc ..............G....... 847 458-7179
Lake In The Hills (G-12999)
Murrays Disc Auto Stores Inc ..............G....... 708 430-8155
Bridgeview (G-2511)
Murrays Disc Auto Stores Inc ..............G....... 847 882-4384
Schaumburg (G-19659)
Niles Auto Parts .................................G....... 847 215-2549
Lincolnshire (G-13468)
O K Jobbers Inc ................................G....... 217 728-7378
Sullivan (G-20756)
Oreillys Auto Parts Store .....................G....... 847 360-0012
Waukegan (G-21599)
Part Stop Inc .....................................G....... 618 377-5238
Bethalto (G-2082)
Prince Race Car Engineering ..............G....... 815 625-8116
Sterling (G-20606)
R & C Auto Supply Corp ....................G....... 815 625-4414
Sterling (G-20609)
Standard Lifts & Equipment Inc ...........G....... 414 444-1000
Hanover Park (G-11591)
Transcedar Limited ............................E ....... 618 262-4153
Mount Carmel (G-15284)
Wallace Auto Parts & Svcs Inc ............G....... 618 268-4446
Raleigh (G-17912)

## AUTO & HOME SUPPLY STORES: Batteries, Automotive & Truck

Batteries Plus 287 .............................G....... 630 279-3478
Villa Park (G-21237)
Dale Schawitsch ................................G....... 217 224-5161
Quincy (G-17817)
Gingrich Enterprises Inc .....................E ....... 309 923-7312
Roanoke (G-18050)
Interstate All Battery Center ................F ....... 217 214-1069
Quincy (G-17840)
Interstate Battery System Intl ..............G....... 708 424-2288
Oak Lawn (G-16626)
Larrys Better Built Battery ..................G....... 618 758-2011
Coulterville (G-7401)

## AUTO & HOME SUPPLY STORES: Speed Shops, Incl Race Car Splys

Car Shop Inc .....................................G....... 309 797-4188
Moline (G-14920)
Nelson Enterprises Inc .......................G....... 815 633-1100
Roscoe (G-18910)
Rj Race Cars Inc ...............................G....... 309 343-7575
Galesburg (G-10774)

## AUTO & HOME SUPPLY STORES: Truck Eqpt & Parts

Area Diesel Service Inc ......................E ....... 217 854-2641
Carlinville (G-3030)
Hypermax Engineering Inc .................F ....... 847 428-5655
Gilberts (G-10924)
Kleinhoffer Manufacturing Inc .............G....... 815 725-3638
Joliet (G-12527)
Mickey Truck Bodies Inc ....................G....... 309 827-8227
Bloomington (G-2197)
P & A Driveline & Machine Inc ............G....... 630 860-7474
Bensenville (G-1962)

## AUTO SPLYS & PARTS, NEW, WHSLE: Exhaust Sys, Mufflers, Etc

CC Distributing Services Inc ................G....... 800 931-2668
Crestwood (G-7480)

## AUTOCLAVES: Laboratory

Daigger Scientific Inc .........................E ....... 800 621-7193
Vernon Hills (G-21155)

## AUTOMATIC REGULATING CNTRLS: Steam Press, Residential/ Comm

Boyleston 21st Century LLC ...............G....... 708 387-2012
Brookfield (G-2625)

## AUTOMATIC REGULATING CONTROL: Building Svcs Monitoring, Auto

233 Skydeck LLC ...............................G....... 312 875-9448
Chicago (G-3665)
Dundee Design LLC ...........................G....... 847 494-2360
East Dundee (G-8634)
Johnson Controls Inc .........................E ....... 815 397-5147
Rockford (G-18448)
Johnson Controls Inc .........................F ....... 217 793-8858
Springfield (G-20464)
Schneider Elc Buildings LLC ...............B ....... 815 381-5000
Rockford (G-18608)
Schneider Elc Buildings LLC ...............G....... 815 227-4000
Rockford (G-18609)
Schneider Elc Holdings Inc .................A ....... 717 944-5460
Schaumburg (G-19722)

## AUTOMATIC REGULATING CONTROLS: AC & Refrigeration

Hansen Technologies Corp ..................D ....... 706 335-5551
Burr Ridge (G-2849)
Siemens Industry Inc ..........................D ....... 847 520-9084
Buffalo Grove (G-2766)
Siemens Industry Inc ..........................A ....... 847 215-1000
Buffalo Grove (G-2767)
Siemens Industry Inc ..........................D ....... 309 664-2460
Bloomington (G-2223)
Siemens Industry Inc ..........................D ....... 847 215-1000
Buffalo Grove (G-2768)
Siemens Industry Inc ..........................D ....... 301 419-2600
Hoffman Estates (G-12052)
Temperature Equipment Corp ..............G....... 847 429-0818
Elgin (G-9209)
Temprite Company .............................E ....... 630 293-5910
West Chicago (G-21778)

## AUTOMATIC REGULATING CONTROLS: Appliance Regulators

Emerson Electric Co ...........................D ....... 847 585-8300
Elgin (G-9027)

## AUTOMATIC REGULATING CONTROLS: Appliance, Exc Air-Cond/Refr

Reliable Appliance and Ref ..................G....... 847 581-9520
Morton Grove (G-15233)
Sonne Industries LLC .........................G....... 630 235-6734
Naperville (G-15750)

## AUTOMATIC REGULATING CONTROLS: Energy Cutoff, Residtl/Comm

Vanguard Energy Services LLC ............E ....... 630 955-1500
Naperville (G-15773)

## AUTOMATIC REGULATING CONTROLS: Gas Burner, Automatic

Eclipse Inc ........................................D ....... 815 877-3031
Rockford (G-18356)
Indesco Oven Products Inc .................G....... 217 622-6345
Petersburg (G-17536)

## AUTOMATIC REGULATING CONTROLS: Gradual Switches, Pneumatic

Intech Industries Inc ...........................F ....... 847 487-5599
Wauconda (G-21473)

## AUTOMATIC REGULATING CONTROLS: Hardware, Environmental Reg

Ronald Allen ......................................F ....... 314 568-1446
Cahokia (G-2925)

# PRODUCT SECTION

## AUTOMOTIVE PARTS, ACCESS & SPLYS

### AUTOMATIC REGULATING CONTROLS: Hydronic Circulator, Auto

Jql Electronics Inc .................................F ....... 630 873-2020
   Rolling Meadows *(G-18736)*

### AUTOMATIC REGULATING CONTROLS: Incinerator, Residential/Comm

Cdc Enterprises Inc ...............................G ....... 815 790-4205
   Johnsburg *(G-12432)*

### AUTOMATIC REGULATING CONTROLS: Pneumatic Relays, Air-Cond

SMC Corporation of America .................E ....... 630 449-0600
   Aurora *(G-1080)*

### AUTOMATIC REGULATING CONTROLS: Refrigeration, Pressure

H A Phillips & Co ..................................E ....... 630 377-0050
   Dekalb *(G-8095)*

### AUTOMATIC REGULATING CTRLS: Damper, Pneumatic Or Electric

Control Equipment Company Inc ............F ....... 847 891-7500
   Schaumburg *(G-19482)*
ITW Motion ............................................F ....... 708 720-0300
   Frankfort *(G-10335)*

### AUTOMATIC TELLER MACHINES

Alliance Service Co ................................G ....... 708 746-5026
   Frankfort *(G-10292)*
Asai Chicago .........................................F ....... 708 239-0133
   Alsip *(G-437)*
Cummins - Allison Corp .........................B ....... 847 759-6403
   Mount Prospect *(G-15320)*
Diebold Incorporated .............................D ....... 847 598-3300
   Schaumburg *(G-19504)*
Harvard State Bank ................................G ....... 815 943-4400
   Harvard *(G-11635)*
Jpmorgan Chase Bank Nat Assn ...........G ....... 847 392-1600
   Prospect Heights *(G-17781)*
Jpmorgan Chase Bank Nat Assn ...........G ....... 708 868-1274
   Calumet City *(G-2944)*
Jpmorgan Chase Bank Nat Assn ...........G ....... 815 462-2800
   New Lenox *(G-15889)*
Jpmorgan Chase Bank Nat Assn ...........G ....... 847 726-4000
   Lake Zurich *(G-13094)*
Jpmorgan Chase Bank Nat Assn ...........G ....... 217 353-4234
   Champaign *(G-3504)*
Kahuna LLC ...........................................F ....... 888 357-8472
   Bloomington *(G-2188)*
OHare Shell Partners Inc .......................G ....... 847 678-1900
   Schiller Park *(G-19855)*
PNC Financial Svcs Group Inc ...............G ....... 630 420-8400
   Naperville *(G-15728)*

### AUTOMATIC VENDING MACHINES: Mechanisms & Parts

Manufctrng-Resourcing Intl Inc ..............F ....... 217 821-3733
   Shumway *(G-19933)*

### AUTOMOBILE FINANCE LEASING

Navistar International Corp .....................A ....... 331 332-5000
   Lisle *(G-13633)*

### AUTOMOBILE STORAGE GARAGE

Springfield Welding & Auto Bdy .............E ....... 217 523-5365
   Springfield *(G-20534)*

### AUTOMOBILES & OTHER MOTOR VEHICLES WHOLESALERS

Hertz Corporation ..................................G ....... 630 897-0956
   Montgomery *(G-15046)*
North Shore Truck & Equipment ............G ....... 847 887-0200
   Lake Bluff *(G-12860)*

### AUTOMOBILES: Wholesalers

Eaton Corporation ..................................C ....... 815 562-2107
   Rochelle *(G-18087)*

### AUTOMOTIVE & TRUCK GENERAL REPAIR SVC

A Len Radiator Shoppe Inc ....................G ....... 630 852-5445
   Downers Grove *(G-8384)*
Amis Inc .................................................G ....... 708 598-9700
   Bridgeview *(G-2465)*
Bi-Phase Technologies LLC ..................F ....... 952 886-6450
   Wood Dale *(G-22344)*
California Muffler and Brakes .................G ....... 773 776-8990
   Chicago *(G-4215)*
Carnaghi Towing & Repair Inc ...............F ....... 217 446-0333
   Tilton *(G-20878)*
Chicago Drive Line Inc ...........................G ....... 708 385-1900
   Alsip *(G-445)*
CK Acquisition Holdings Inc ...................F ....... 773 646-0115
   Chicago *(G-4391)*
Eden Fuels LLC .....................................G ....... 847 676-9470
   Skokie *(G-19991)*
G&G Machine Shop Inc .........................G ....... 217 892-9696
   Rantoul *(G-17928)*
Gerardo and Quintana Auto Elc .............G ....... 773 424-0634
   Chicago *(G-4947)*
Holstein Garage Inc ...............................G ....... 630 668-0328
   Wheaton *(G-21952)*
Jimmy Diesel Inc ....................................G ....... 708 482-4500
   Wheaton *(G-21959)*
Lakenburges Motor Co ...........................G ....... 618 523-4231
   Germantown *(G-10893)*
Larry Pontnack ......................................G ....... 815 732-7751
   Oregon *(G-16827)*
Larrys Garage & Machine Shop .............G ....... 815 968-8416
   Rockford *(G-18462)*
Legend Racing Enterprises Inc ..............G ....... 847 923-8979
   Schaumburg *(G-19614)*
MCI Service Parts Inc ............................D ....... 419 994-4141
   Des Plaines *(G-8230)*
Mickey Truck Bodies Inc ........................F ....... 309 827-8227
   Bloomington *(G-2197)*
Mikes Inc ................................................G ....... 618 254-4491
   South Roxana *(G-20314)*
Petron Oil Production Inc .......................G ....... 618 783-4486
   Newton *(G-15946)*
Polar Corporation ...................................E ....... 618 548-3660
   Salem *(G-19343)*
Prince Race Car Engineering .................G ....... 815 625-8116
   Sterling *(G-20606)*
R & C Auto Supply Corp .........................G ....... 815 625-4414
   Sterling *(G-20609)*
Redi-Weld & Mfg Co Inc .........................G ....... 815 455-4460
   Lake In The Hills *(G-13004)*
Service Auto Supply ...............................F ....... 309 444-9704
   Washington *(G-21392)*
Springfield Welding & Auto Bdy .............E ....... 217 523-5365
   Springfield *(G-20534)*
Zimmerman Enterprises Inc ...................F ....... 847 297-3177
   Des Plaines *(G-8308)*

### AUTOMOTIVE BATTERIES WHOLESALERS

Dale Schawitsch ....................................G ....... 217 224-5161
   Quincy *(G-17817)*

### AUTOMOTIVE BODY SHOP

Grace Auto Body Frame .........................G ....... 847 963-1234
   Palatine *(G-17030)*
Kurts Carstar Collision Ctr .....................F ....... 618 345-4519
   Maryville *(G-14343)*
Midamerica Industries Inc ......................G ....... 309 787-5119
   Milan *(G-14793)*
Phils Auto Body .....................................G ....... 773 847-7156
   Chicago *(G-6117)*
Springfield Welding & Auto Bdy .............E ....... 217 523-5365
   Springfield *(G-20534)*
Union Ave Auto Inc ................................G ....... 708 754-3899
   Steger *(G-20580)*

### AUTOMOTIVE BODY, PAINT & INTERIOR REPAIR & MAINTENANCE SVC

D D Sales Inc .........................................E ....... 217 857-3196
   Teutopolis *(G-20851)*
Folk Race Cars ......................................G ....... 815 629-2418
   Durand *(G-8585)*
Lou Plucinski .........................................G ....... 815 758-7888
   Dekalb *(G-8103)*
Winning Colors ......................................G ....... 815 462-4810
   Manhattan *(G-14171)*

### AUTOMOTIVE DEALERS, NEC

Prestige Motor Works Inc .......................G ....... 630 780-6439
   Naperville *(G-15823)*

### AUTOMOTIVE EXHAUST REPAIR SVC

Aledo Welding Enterprises Inc ...............G ....... 309 582-2019
   Aledo *(G-367)*
C & D Rebuilders ...................................G ....... 618 273-9862
   Eldorado *(G-8918)*
Velasquez & Sons Muffler Shop ............G ....... 847 740-6990
   Round Lake Beach *(G-19080)*

### AUTOMOTIVE EXTERIOR REPAIR SVCS

Moultri Cnty Hstrcl/Gnlgcl Sct ................F ....... 217 728-4085
   Sullivan *(G-20754)*

### AUTOMOTIVE GLASS REPLACEMENT SHOPS

Glass America Midwest Inc ....................G ....... 877 743-7237
   Elmhurst *(G-9875)*
Harmon Inc .............................................D ....... 312 726-5050
   Chicago *(G-5046)*
Illinois Valley Glass & Mirror ..................F ....... 309 682-6603
   Peoria *(G-17387)*
Martin Glass Company ...........................F ....... 618 277-1946
   Belleville *(G-1652)*
Roscoe Glass Co ...................................G ....... 815 623-6268
   Roscoe *(G-18916)*
T G Automotive ......................................E ....... 630 916-7818
   Lombard *(G-13863)*

### AUTOMOTIVE LETTERING & PAINTING SVCS

Quality Spraying Screen Prtg .................E ....... 630 584-8324
   Saint Charles *(G-19248)*

### AUTOMOTIVE PAINT SHOP

Biddison Autobody .................................G ....... 309 673-6277
   Peoria *(G-17318)*
Jorge A Cruz ..........................................G ....... 773 722-2828
   Chicago *(G-5324)*
Tm Autoworks ........................................G ....... 630 766-8250
   Bensenville *(G-2003)*

### AUTOMOTIVE PARTS, ACCESS & SPLYS

A&G Manufacturing Inc ..........................E ....... 815 562-2107
   Rochelle *(G-18076)*
Accurate Engine & Machine Inc ............G ....... 773 237-4942
   Chicago *(G-3719)*
Air Land and Sea Interiors .....................E ....... 630 834-1717
   Villa Park *(G-21234)*
Aisin Mfg Illinois LLC .............................D ....... 618 998-8333
   Marion *(G-14250)*
Aisin Mfg Illinois LLC .............................A ....... 618 998-8333
   Marion *(G-14251)*
Amerex Corporation ...............................E ....... 309 382-4389
   North Pekin *(G-16192)*
Amsoil Inc ..............................................G ....... 630 595-8385
   Bensenville *(G-1835)*
Anthony Liftgates Inc .............................C ....... 815 842-3383
   Pontiac *(G-17696)*
Antolin Interiors Usa Inc ........................B ....... 618 327-4416
   Nashville *(G-15833)*
Arco Automotive Elec Svc Co ................G ....... 708 422-2976
   Oak Lawn *(G-16603)*
Area Diesel Service Inc .........................E ....... 217 854-2641
   Carlinville *(G-3030)*
Arrow Gear Company .............................C ....... 630 969-7640
   Downers Grove *(G-8389)*
Auto Meter Products Inc ........................C ....... 815 991-2292
   Sycamore *(G-20788)*
Autoparts Holdings Ltd ..........................A ....... 203 830-7800
   Lake Forest *(G-12883)*
Axletech International LLC .....................F ....... 877 547-3907
   Chicago *(G-4007)*
Bill Weeks Inc ........................................G ....... 217 523-8735
   Springfield *(G-20397)*
Boler Company ......................................F ....... 630 773-9111
   Itasca *(G-12236)*
Boler Company ......................................G ....... 630 910-2800
   Woodridge *(G-22457)*
Borgwarner Inc .......................................C ....... 248 754-9200
   Bellwood *(G-1699)*
Borgwarner Inc .......................................E ....... 248 754-9200
   Frankfort *(G-10302)*

---

Employee Codes: A=Over 500 employees, B=251-500
C=101-250, D=51-100, E=20-50, F=10-19, G=3-9

2017 Harris Illinois Industrial Directory

## AUTOMOTIVE PARTS, ACCESS & SPLYS — PRODUCT SECTION

| Company | Col | Phone |
|---|---|---|
| Borgwarner Inc — Dixon *(G-8325)* | G | 815 288-1462 |
| Boyce Industries Inc — Melrose Park *(G-14604)* | F | 708 345-0455 |
| Brake Parts Inc LLC — Litchfield *(G-13682)* | G | 217 324-2161 |
| Brunos Automotive Products — Addison *(G-62)* | G | 630 458-0043 |
| C & M Engineering — Bourbonnais *(G-2391)* | G | 815 932-3388 |
| Cavanaugh Government Group LLC — Bridgeview *(G-2475)* | F | 630 210-8668 |
| Central Hydraulics Inc — El Paso *(G-8866)* | G | 309 527-5238 |
| Champion Laboratories Inc — Albion *(G-358)* | B | 803 684-3205 |
| Chicago Transmission Parts — Chicago *(G-4355)* | G | 773 427-6100 |
| Chucking Machine Products Inc — Franklin Park *(G-10431)* | D | 847 678-1192 |
| City Subn Auto Svc Goodyear — Chicago *(G-4389)* | G | 773 355-5550 |
| Cosmos Manufacturing Inc — S Chicago Hts *(G-19102)* | C | 708 756-1400 |
| Cross Tread Industries Inc — Willow Springs *(G-22194)* | F | 630 850-7100 |
| CTS Automotive LLC — Lisle *(G-13578)* | C | 630 614-7201 |
| Cummins Filtration Inc — Crystal Lake *(G-7561)* | G | 931 526-9551 |
| Dana Auto Systems Group LLC — Lisle *(G-13582)* | D | 630 960-4200 |
| Dana Sealing Manufacturing LLC — Robinson *(G-18061)* | B | 618 544-8651 |
| Danfoss Power Solutions US Co — Freeport *(G-10652)* | C | 815 233-4200 |
| Doga USA Corporation — Huntley *(G-12138)* | F | 847 669-8529 |
| Dow Chemical Company — Kankakee *(G-12611)* | E | 815 933-5514 |
| Dura Products Corporation — Bradley *(G-2420)* | G | 815 939-1399 |
| Eagle Wings Industries Inc — Rantoul *(G-17925)* | B | 217 892-4322 |
| Eaton Corporation — Rochelle *(G-18087)* | C | 815 562-2107 |
| Eberspaecher North America Inc — Belvidere *(G-1750)* | G | 815 544-1421 |
| Engine Rebuilders & Supply — Stone Park *(G-20634)* | G | 708 338-1113 |
| Exress Motor and Lift Parts — Frankfort *(G-10320)* | G | 630 327-2000 |
| Ezee Roll Manufacturing Co — Hoopeston *(G-12110)* | G | 217 339-2279 |
| FCA US LLC — Naperville *(G-15657)* | A | 630 637-3000 |
| FCA US LLC — Lisle *(G-13588)* | A | 630 724-2321 |
| Federal-Mogul Corporation — McHenry *(G-14506)* | C | 815 271-9600 |
| Flex-N-Gate Corporation — Urbana *(G-21087)* | A | 217 255-5025 |
| Flex-N-Gate Corporation — Urbana *(G-21088)* | A | 217 278-2400 |
| Fox Enterprises Inc — Saint Charles *(G-19188)* | G | 630 513-9010 |
| Fram Group Operations LLC — Lake Forest *(G-12899)* | B | 800 890-2075 |
| Frantz Manufacturing Company — Sterling *(G-20593)* | D | 815 564-0991 |
| Gates Corporation — Galesburg *(G-10752)* | G | 309 343-7171 |
| Gem Manufacturing Corporation — Addison *(G-130)* | G | 630 458-0014 |
| General Motors LLC — Bolingbrook *(G-2313)* | C | 815 733-0668 |
| Genuine Parts Company — Chicago *(G-4938)* | F | 630 293-1300 |
| GKN Stromag Inc — Woodridge *(G-22485)* | E | 937 433-3882 |
| Glk Enterprises Inc — Antioch *(G-636)* | G | 847 395-7368 |
| Grupo Antolin Illinois Inc — Belvidere *(G-1759)* | C | 815 544-8020 |
| Gunite Corporation — Rockford *(G-18408)* | B | 815 964-3301 |
| Hardy Radiator Repair — Quincy *(G-17834)* | G | 217 223-8320 |
| Hoosier Stamping & Mfg Corp — Grayville *(G-11371)* | E | 618 375-2057 |
| Iggys Auto Parts — Norridge *(G-16102)* | F | 708 452-9790 |
| Illinois Tool Works Inc — Mokena *(G-14873)* | C | 708 479-7200 |
| Illinois Tool Works Inc — Mazon *(G-14438)* | C | 815 448-7300 |
| Illinois Tool Works Inc — Tinley Park *(G-20922)* | C | 708 479-7200 |
| Interstate Power Systems Inc — Carol Stream *(G-3174)* | F | 630 871-1111 |
| Interstate Power Systems Inc — Rockford *(G-18440)* | D | 952 854-2044 |
| ITW Deltar Seat Component — Elmhurst *(G-9890)* | G | 630 993-9990 |
| ITW Global Investments Inc — Glenview *(G-11152)* | G | 847 724-7500 |
| Jasiek Motor Rebuilding Inc — Oglesby *(G-16750)* | G | 815 883-3678 |
| Johnson Controls Inc — Chicago *(G-5319)* | C | 312 829-5956 |
| Kackert Enterprises Inc — Aurora *(G-1179)* | G | 630 898-9339 |
| Kccdd Inc — Galesburg *(G-10762)* | D | 309 344-2030 |
| Kiene Diesel Accessories Inc — Addison *(G-167)* | E | 630 543-7170 |
| Kleinhoffer Manufacturing Inc — Joliet *(G-12527)* | G | 815 725-3638 |
| Koehler Enterprises Inc — Franklin Park *(G-10513)* | G | 847 451-4966 |
| L & M Screw Machine Products — Montgomery *(G-15052)* | F | 630 801-0455 |
| Lemfco Inc — Galena *(G-10729)* | E | 815 777-0242 |
| Lgb Industries — Cary *(G-3357)* | G | 847 639-1691 |
| Line Craft Tool Company Inc — Lombard *(G-13820)* | C | 630 932-1182 |
| Mag Daddy LLC — Lake Zurich *(G-13098)* | G | 847 719-5600 |
| Magna Extros Intrors Amer Inc — Nashville *(G-15838)* | B | 618 327-2136 |
| Makerite Mfg Co Inc — Roscoe *(G-18906)* | E | 815 389-3902 |
| Mann+hummel Filtration Tech — McHenry *(G-14526)* | F | 800 407-9263 |
| Mann+hummel Filtration Technol — McHenry *(G-14527)* | G | 815 759-7744 |
| Mat Holdings Inc — Long Grove *(G-13897)* | D | 847 821-9630 |
| Maxim Inc — Springfield *(G-20475)* | F | 217 544-7015 |
| MCI Service Parts Inc — Des Plaines *(G-8230)* | D | 419 994-4141 |
| Methode Electronics Inc — Carthage *(G-3316)* | A | 217 357-3941 |
| Midamerica Industries Inc — Milan *(G-14793)* | G | 309 787-5119 |
| Molor Products Company — Oswego *(G-16927)* | F | 630 375-5999 |
| Motec Inc — Downers Grove *(G-8490)* | G | 630 241-9595 |
| Motor Coach Inds Intl Inc — Des Plaines *(G-8235)* | F | 847 285-2000 |
| Motor Row Development Corp — Chicago *(G-5813)* | G | 773 525-3311 |
| Murrays Disc Auto Stores Inc — Lake In The Hills *(G-12999)* | G | 847 458-7179 |
| National Cycle Inc — Maywood *(G-14430)* | C | 708 343-0400 |
| Navistar Inc — Lisle *(G-13629)* | C | 331 332-5000 |
| Navistar International Corp — Lisle *(G-13633)* | A | 331 332-5000 |
| Naylor Automotive Engrg Co Inc — Chicago *(G-5875)* | F | 773 582-6900 |
| Ogden Top & Trim Shop Inc — Berwyn *(G-2070)* | G | 708 484-5422 |
| Omron Automotive Elec Inc — Saint Charles *(G-19229)* | A | 630 443-6800 |
| Pack 2000 Inc — Springfield *(G-20496)* | G | 217 529-4408 |
| Piston Automotive LLC — Belvidere *(G-1779)* | G | 313 541-8789 |
| Plews Inc — Dixon *(G-8339)* | G | 815 288-3344 |
| Premiere Auto Service — Chicago *(G-6179)* | G | 773 275-8785 |
| Prestige Motor Works Inc — Naperville *(G-15823)* | G | 630 780-6439 |
| Quincy Torque Converter Inc — Quincy *(G-17882)* | G | 217 228-0852 |
| Randall Manufacturing LLC — Elmhurst *(G-9925)* | D | 630 782-0001 |
| RE-Do-It Corp — Broadview *(G-2607)* | G | 708 343-7125 |
| Realwheels Corporation — Gurnee *(G-11499)* | E | 847 662-7722 |
| Rj Race Cars Inc — Galesburg *(G-10774)* | F | 309 343-7575 |
| Robert Bosch LLC — Broadview *(G-2610)* | B | 248 876-1000 |
| Rock Valley Antique Auto Parts — Stillman Valley *(G-20627)* | G | 815 645-2272 |
| SKF USA Inc — Elgin *(G-9186)* | D | 847 742-0700 |
| Somic America Inc — Bensenville *(G-1995)* | G | 630 274-4423 |
| Sumitomo Machinery Corp Amer — Glendale Heights *(G-11078)* | E | 630 752-0200 |
| Sure Plus Manufacturing Co — Chicago Heights *(G-7128)* | D | 708 756-3100 |
| Symbol Tool Inc — Skokie *(G-20098)* | G | 847 674-1080 |
| T & T Machine Shop — Gurnee *(G-11511)* | G | 847 244-2020 |
| T G Automotive — Lombard *(G-13863)* | E | 630 916-7818 |
| T J Van Der Bosch & Associates — McHenry *(G-14567)* | G | 815 344-3210 |
| Tenneco Automotive Oper Co Inc — Lincolnshire *(G-13485)* | C | 847 821-0757 |
| Tenneco Inc — Lake Forest *(G-12967)* | D | 847 482-5000 |
| Tesla Motors Inc — Chicago *(G-6704)* | F | 312 733-9780 |
| Thyssenkrupp Crankshaft Co LLC — Danville *(G-7771)* | E | 217 444-5230 |
| Torque-Traction Integration — Sterling *(G-20617)* | G | 815 759-7388 |
| Toyo USA Manufacturing Inc — Bloomington *(G-2232)* | F | 309 827-8836 |
| Toyota Boshoku Illinois LLC — Lawrenceville *(G-13205)* | B | 618 943-5300 |
| UCI International Inc — Lake Forest *(G-12975)* | E | 847 941-0965 |
| Ugn Inc — Tinley Park *(G-20953)* | D | 773 437-2400 |
| United Components LLC — Lake Forest *(G-12977)* | E | 812 867-4516 |
| United Gasket Corporation — Cicero *(G-7242)* | D | 708 656-3700 |
| US Tsubaki Power Transm LLC — Wheeling *(G-22173)* | C | 847 459-9500 |
| Vehicle Improvement Pdts Inc — Antioch *(G-662)* | G | 847 395-7250 |
| Vfn Fiberglass Inc — Addison *(G-340)* | F | 630 543-0232 |
| Vibracoustic Usa Inc — Carmi *(G-3082)* | C | 618 382-2318 |
| Vuteq Usa Inc — Normal *(G-16093)* | C | 309 452-9933 |
| Wanxiang USA Holdings Corp — Elgin *(G-9229)* | F | 847 622-8838 |
| Ycl International Inc — Woodridge *(G-22529)* | E | 630 873-0768 |
| Zeigler Chrysler Dodge — Berwyn *(G-2079)* | G | 708 956-7700 |
| ZF Chassis Components LLC — Chicago *(G-7065)* | B | 773 371-4550 |
| ZF Chassis Systems Chicago LLC — Chicago *(G-7066)* | C | 773 371-4550 |
| ZF Services LLC — Vernon Hills *(G-21221)* | G | 734 416-6200 |

### AUTOMOTIVE PARTS: Plastic

| Company | Col | Phone |
|---|---|---|
| Creative Conveniences By K&E — Lake Zurich *(G-13059)* | G | 847 975-8526 |
| Extruded Solutions Inc — Carol Stream *(G-3149)* | G | 630 871-6450 |
| Flex-N-Gate Chicago LLC — Urbana *(G-21084)* | G | 217 255-5098 |
| Heidts Automotive LLC — Lake Zurich *(G-13083)* | G | 847 487-0150 |
| International Automotive — Belvidere *(G-1765)* | B | 815 544-2102 |
| John Thomas Inc — Dixon *(G-8334)* | E | 815 288-5443 |
| Loop Automotive LLC — Chicago *(G-5539)* | E | 847 912-9090 |

Martinez Management Inc .................. G ...... 847 822-7202
  Algonquin (G-399)
Nascote Industries Inc ........................ D ...... 419 324-3392
  Belvidere (G-1774)
Prestige Motor Works Inc .................... G ...... 630 780-6439
  Naperville (G-15823)
Tmf Polymer Solutions Inc .................. F ...... 630 552-7575
  Plano (G-17678)
Tmf Polymer Solutions Inc .................. G ...... 541 479-7484
  Plano (G-17679)

### AUTOMOTIVE PRDTS: Rubber

A Lakin & Sons Inc ............................... E ...... 773 871-6360
  Montgomery (G-15026)
Lakin General Corporation ................... D ...... 773 871-6360
  Montgomery (G-15054)

### AUTOMOTIVE RADIATOR REPAIR SHOPS

A Len Radiator Shoppe Inc ................... G ...... 630 852-5445
  Downers Grove (G-8384)
Bushnell Welding & Radiator ................ G ...... 309 772-9289
  Bushnell (G-2900)
Hardy Radiator Repair .......................... F ...... 217 223-8320
  Quincy (G-17834)
Jones Garrison Sons Mch Works ........... G ...... 618 847-2161
  Fairfield (G-10147)
Rex Radiator and Welding Co ............... G ...... 312 421-1531
  Chicago (G-6343)
Rex Radiator and Welding Co ............... G ...... 630 595-4664
  Bensenville (G-1977)
Rex Radiator and Welding Co ............... G ...... 847 428-1112
  East Dundee (G-8655)

### AUTOMOTIVE REPAIR SHOPS: Alternators/Generator, Rebuild/Rpr

Lawrence Maddock ............................. F ...... 847 394-1698
  Arlington Heights (G-792)

### AUTOMOTIVE REPAIR SHOPS: Diesel Engine Repair

Cummins Crosspoint LLC ..................... E ...... 309 452-4454
  Normal (G-16068)
Gateway Industrial Power Inc ............... C ...... 888 865-8675
  Collinsville (G-7327)
Gateway Industrial Power Inc ............... G ...... 309 821-1035
  Bloomington (G-2169)
Waymore Power Co Inc ........................ F ...... 618 729-3876
  Piasa (G-17543)

### AUTOMOTIVE REPAIR SHOPS: Electrical Svcs

Dooley Brothers Plumbing & Htg ........... G ...... 309 852-2720
  Kewanee (G-12680)
Mr Auto Electric ................................... G ...... 217 523-3659
  Springfield (G-20485)

### AUTOMOTIVE REPAIR SHOPS: Engine Rebuilding

Engine Rebuilders & Supply .................. G ...... 708 338-1113
  Stone Park (G-20634)

### AUTOMOTIVE REPAIR SHOPS: Engine Repair

L A Motors Incorporated ...................... G ...... 773 736-7305
  Chicago (G-5421)
Murrays Disc Auto Stores Inc ............... G ...... 847 882-4384
  Schaumburg (G-19659)
Oreillys Auto Parts Store ..................... G ...... 847 360-0012
  Waukegan (G-21599)
Union Ave Auto Inc .............................. G ...... 708 754-3899
  Steger (G-20580)

### AUTOMOTIVE REPAIR SHOPS: Frame Repair Shops

Botts Welding and Trck Svc Inc ............ E ...... 815 338-0594
  Woodstock (G-22546)

### AUTOMOTIVE REPAIR SHOPS: Machine Shop

Custom Machining & Design LLC .......... G ...... 847 364-2601
  Elk Grove Village (G-9403)

G&G Machine Shop Inc ........................ G ...... 217 892-9696
  Rantoul (G-17928)
H&S Machine & Tools Inc .................... G ...... 618 451-0164
  Granite City (G-11283)
Jasiek Motor Rebuilding Inc ................. G ...... 815 883-3678
  Oglesby (G-16750)
Mac-Weld Inc ...................................... G ...... 618 529-1828
  Carbondale (G-3015)
Springfield Welding & Auto Bdy ............ E ...... 217 523-5365
  Springfield (G-20534)
Trailers Inc ......................................... G ...... 217 472-6000
  Chapin (G-3588)

### AUTOMOTIVE REPAIR SHOPS: Springs, Rebuilding & Repair

Kankakee Spring and Alignment ........... G ...... 815 932-6718
  Kankakee (G-12633)

### AUTOMOTIVE REPAIR SHOPS: Torque Converter Repair

Dynamic Manufacturing Inc .................. D ...... 708 547-7081
  Hillside (G-11915)

### AUTOMOTIVE REPAIR SHOPS: Trailer Repair

Bierman Welding Inc ............................ F ...... 217 342-2050
  Effingham (G-8827)
Load Redi Inc ...................................... G ...... 217 784-4200
  Gibson City (G-10904)

### AUTOMOTIVE REPAIR SHOPS: Truck Engine Repair, Exc Indl

Cummins Dist Holdco Inc ..................... E ...... 309 787-4300
  Rock Island (G-18170)

### AUTOMOTIVE REPAIR SVC

Accurate Engine & Machine Inc ............ G ...... 773 237-4942
  Chicago (G-3719)
Acme Auto Electric Co ......................... G ...... 708 754-5420
  S Chicago Hts (G-19098)
Amy Schutt ......................................... G ...... 618 994-7405
  Carrier Mills (G-3305)
Arco Automotive Elec Svc Co ............... G ...... 708 422-2976
  Oak Lawn (G-16603)
Deyco Inc ........................................... G ...... 630 553-5666
  Yorkville (G-22656)
Gerardo and Quintana Auto Elc ............. G ...... 773 424-0634
  Chicago (G-4947)
L A Motors Incorporated ...................... G ...... 773 736-7305
  Chicago (G-5421)
Lous Spring and Welding Shop ............. G ...... 815 223-4282
  Peru (G-17517)
Mark S Machine Shop Inc .................... G ...... 815 895-3955
  Sycamore (G-20809)
Naylor Automotive Engrg Co Inc ........... F ...... 773 582-6900
  Chicago (G-5875)
Rex Radiator and Welding Co ............... G ...... 815 725-6655
  Rockdale (G-18230)

### AUTOMOTIVE SPLYS & PARTS, NEW, WHOL: Testing Eqpt, Electric

Autonomoustuff LLC ............................ G ...... 314 270-2123
  Morton (G-15153)

### AUTOMOTIVE SPLYS & PARTS, NEW, WHOLESALE: Brakes

Brake Parts Inc LLC ............................. G ...... 217 324-2161
  Litchfield (G-13682)
Performance Manufacturing .................. G ...... 630 231-8099
  West Chicago (G-21756)

### AUTOMOTIVE SPLYS & PARTS, NEW, WHOLESALE: Clutches

Surge Clutch & Drive Line Co ............... G ...... 708 331-1352
  South Holland (G-20307)

### AUTOMOTIVE SPLYS & PARTS, NEW, WHOLESALE: Engines/Eng Parts

Hendrix Industrial Gastrux Inc .............. G ...... 847 526-1700
  Wauconda (G-21467)
Mac-Weld Inc ...................................... G ...... 618 529-1828
  Carbondale (G-3015)

Premiere Auto Service ......................... G ...... 773 275-8785
  Chicago (G-6179)
Speed Tech Technology Inc .................. G ...... 847 516-2001
  Cary (G-3372)
TKT Enterprises Inc ............................. E ...... 630 307-9355
  Roselle (G-18983)
Tpr America Inc ................................... G ...... 847 446-5336
  Schaumburg (G-19767)

### AUTOMOTIVE SPLYS & PARTS, NEW, WHOLESALE: Seat Covers

Wise Co Inc ........................................ C ...... 618 594-4091
  Carlyle (G-3061)

### AUTOMOTIVE SPLYS & PARTS, NEW, WHOLESALE: Splys

Group O Inc ........................................ B ...... 309 736-8311
  Milan (G-14789)
Joes Automotive Inc ............................ G ...... 815 937-9281
  Kankakee (G-12630)
R & O Specialties Incorporated ............. D ...... 309 736-8660
  Milan (G-14800)

### AUTOMOTIVE SPLYS & PARTS, NEW, WHOLESALE: Stampings

Versatility TI Works Mfg Inc ................. F ...... 708 389-8909
  Alsip (G-541)

### AUTOMOTIVE SPLYS & PARTS, NEW, WHOLESALE: Testing Eqpt, Eng

Affri Inc ............................................. G ...... 224 374-0931
  Wood Dale (G-22333)

### AUTOMOTIVE SPLYS & PARTS, NEW, WHOLESALE: Tools & Eqpt

Fibro Inc ............................................. F ...... 815 229-1300
  Rockford (G-18382)

### AUTOMOTIVE SPLYS & PARTS, NEW, WHOLESALE: Trailer Parts

Neals Trailer Sales .............................. G ...... 217 792-5136
  Lincoln (G-13416)
Tri City Canvas Products Inc ................ F ...... 618 797-1662
  Granite City (G-11308)

### AUTOMOTIVE SPLYS & PARTS, NEW, WHOLESALE: Wheels

Otr Wheel Engineering Inc .................... E ...... 217 223-7705
  Quincy (G-17864)

### AUTOMOTIVE SPLYS & PARTS, USED, WHOLESALE

G T Motoring Inc .................................. G ...... 847 466-7463
  Elk Grove Village (G-9491)
Velasquez & Sons Muffler Shop ............ G ...... 847 740-6990
  Round Lake Beach (G-19080)

### AUTOMOTIVE SPLYS & PARTS, WHOLESALE, NEC

A Len Radiator Shoppe Inc ................... G ...... 630 852-5445
  Downers Grove (G-8384)
Andrews Automotive Company .............. F ...... 773 768-1122
  Chicago (G-3903)
Arco Automotive Elec Svc Co ............... G ...... 708 422-2976
  Oak Lawn (G-16603)
Boley Tool & Machine Works Inc ........... C ...... 309 694-2722
  East Peoria (G-8703)
Brake Parts Inc India LLC .................... F ...... 815 363-9000
  McHenry (G-14484)
Flexitech Inc ....................................... C ...... 309 664-7828
  Bloomington (G-2165)
Genuine Parts Company ....................... F ...... 630 293-1300
  Chicago (G-4938)
H & D Motor Service ............................ G ...... 217 342-3262
  Altamont (G-552)
Honeywell International Inc .................. A ...... 847 391-2000
  Des Plaines (G-8205)
Instrument Services Inc ....................... G ...... 815 623-2993
  Machesney Park (G-14082)
Just Parts Inc ..................................... G ...... 815 756-2184
  Cortland (G-7390)

## AUTOMOTIVE SPLYS & PARTS, WHOLESALE, NEC

L & T Services Inc .................................G....... 815 397-6260
  Rockford *(G-18458)*
L M C Automotive Inc ..............................G....... 618 235-5242
  Belleville *(G-1647)*
Loop Automotive LLC ..............................E....... 847 912-9090
  Chicago *(G-5539)*
Midwest Driveshaft Inc ............................G....... 630 513-9292
  Saint Charles *(G-19221)*
Moran Auto Parts and Mch Sp ................F....... 309 663-6449
  Bloomington *(G-2203)*
Niles Auto Parts .......................................G....... 847 215-2549
  Lincolnshire *(G-13468)*
O K Jobbers Inc ......................................G....... 217 728-7378
  Sullivan *(G-20756)*
Robert Bosch LLC ...................................B....... 248 876-1000
  Broadview *(G-2610)*
Shima American Corporation ..................F....... 630 760-4330
  Itasca *(G-12353)*
Standard Indus & Auto Eqp Inc ..............E....... 630 289-9500
  Hanover Park *(G-11590)*
Suburban Driveline Inc ...........................G....... 630 941-7101
  Villa Park *(G-21286)*
Toth Automotive .......................................F....... 708 474-5137
  Lansing *(G-13190)*
United Components LLC .........................E....... 812 867-4516
  Lake Forest *(G-12977)*
United Remanufacturing Co Inc ..............G....... 773 777-1223
  Schiller Park *(G-19880)*
Vuteq Usa Inc ..........................................C....... 309 452-9933
  Normal *(G-16093)*
Zeigler Chrysler Dodge ...........................G....... 708 956-7700
  Berwyn *(G-2079)*
ZF Chassis Components LLC ................B....... 773 371-4550
  Chicago *(G-7065)*
ZF Chassis Systems Chicago LLC .........C....... 773 371-4550
  Chicago *(G-7066)*

### AUTOMOTIVE SVCS, EXC REPAIR & CARWASHES: Customizing

Midwest Marketing Distrs Inc ...................F....... 309 688-8858
  Peoria *(G-17408)*
Mobilty Works ...........................................G....... 815 254-2000
  Plainfield *(G-17629)*

### AUTOMOTIVE SVCS, EXC REPAIR & CARWASHES: Maintenance

Bazaar Inc ................................................D....... 708 583-1800
  River Grove *(G-18006)*
Fleetpride Inc ...........................................F....... 630 455-6881
  Willowbrook *(G-22212)*
William Ingram .........................................G....... 217 442-5075
  Danville *(G-7785)*

### AUTOMOTIVE SVCS, EXC REPAIR: Truck Wash

Dundee Truck & Trlr Works LLC ..............G....... 224 484-8182
  East Dundee *(G-8635)*

### AUTOMOTIVE SVCS, EXC RPR/CARWASHES: High Perf Auto Rpr/Svc

Continental Auto Systems Inc ..................G....... 847 862-5000
  Deer Park *(G-7969)*
Legend Racing Enterprises Inc ................G....... 847 923-8979
  Schaumburg *(G-19614)*
Prestige Motor Works Inc .........................G....... 630 780-6439
  Naperville *(G-15823)*

### AUTOMOTIVE TOPS INSTALLATION OR REPAIR: Canvas Or Plastic

Bill Weeks Inc ..........................................G....... 217 523-8735
  Springfield *(G-20397)*
Illinois Central Gulf Car Shop ..................D....... 618 533-8281
  Centralia *(G-3418)*

### AUTOMOTIVE TOWING & WRECKING SVC

Tondinis Wrecker Service ........................G....... 618 997-9884
  Marion *(G-14292)*

### AUTOMOTIVE TOWING SVCS

Carnaghi Towing & Repair Inc .................F....... 217 446-0333
  Tilton *(G-20878)*
City Subn Auto Svc Goodyear .................G....... 773 355-5550
  Chicago *(G-4389)*

### AUTOMOTIVE TRANSMISSION REPAIR SVC

Dynamic Manufacturing Inc ......................D....... 708 547-7081
  Hillside *(G-11915)*
Gates Inc ..................................................G....... 217 335-2378
  Barry *(G-1313)*

### AUTOMOTIVE UPHOLSTERY SHOPS

Custom Canvas LLC ................................G....... 847 587-0225
  Ingleside *(G-12188)*
Heartland Classics Inc .............................G....... 618 783-4444
  Newton *(G-15941)*
Ogden Top & Trim Shop Inc ....................G....... 708 484-5422
  Berwyn *(G-2070)*

### AUTOMOTIVE WELDING SVCS

Adermanns Welding & Mch & Co ............G....... 217 342-3234
  Effingham *(G-8822)*
Botts Welding and Trck Svc Inc ...............E....... 815 338-0594
  Woodstock *(G-22546)*
Bushnell Welding & Radiator ...................G....... 309 772-9289
  Bushnell *(G-2900)*
Cimino Machine Corp ..............................F....... 773 767-7000
  Chicago *(G-4378)*
Floyds Welding Service ...........................G....... 618 395-2414
  Olney *(G-16767)*
Holstein Garage Inc .................................G....... 630 668-0328
  Wheaton *(G-21952)*
Jones Brothers Mch & Wldg Inc ...............G....... 618 945-4609
  Bridgeport *(G-2453)*
Larrys Garage & Machine Shop ...............G....... 815 968-8416
  Rockford *(G-18462)*
Mark S Machine Shop Inc ........................G....... 815 895-3955
  Sycamore *(G-20809)*
Pekin Weldors Inc ....................................F....... 309 382-3627
  North Pekin *(G-16193)*
Rex Radiator and Welding Co ..................G....... 630 595-4664
  Bensenville *(G-1977)*
Robert Davis & Son Inc ...........................G....... 815 889-4168
  Milford *(G-14814)*
Robertson Repair .....................................G....... 618 895-2593
  Sims *(G-19941)*
Springfield Welding & Auto Bdy ................E....... 217 523-5365
  Springfield *(G-20534)*
Xd Industries Inc ......................................F....... 630 766-2843
  Bensenville *(G-2019)*

### AUTOMOTIVE: Bodies

Automotive Metal Specialist .....................G....... 309 383-2980
  Germantown Hills *(G-10895)*
Hot Rod Chassis & Cycle Inc ...................G....... 630 458-0808
  Addison *(G-150)*
Jorge A Cruz ............................................G....... 773 722-2828
  Chicago *(G-5324)*
Kurts Carstar Collision Ctr ........................F....... 618 345-4519
  Maryville *(G-14343)*
Midwest Remanufacturing LLC ................G....... 708 496-9100
  Bedford Park *(G-1565)*
Phils Auto Body ........................................G....... 773 847-7156
  Chicago *(G-6117)*
T J Van Der Bosch & Associates .............E....... 815 344-3210
  McHenry *(G-14567)*
Tenneco Intl Holdg Corp ..........................G....... 847 482-5000
  Lake Forest *(G-12968)*
Tm Autoworks ..........................................G....... 630 766-8250
  Bensenville *(G-2003)*
Vanderbosch Tj & Assoc Inc ....................G....... 815 344-3210
  McHenry *(G-14568)*

### AUTOMOTIVE: Seat Frames, Metal

John Thomas Inc .....................................E....... 815 288-2343
  Dixon *(G-8334)*
Tvh Parts Co ............................................E....... 847 223-1000
  Grayslake *(G-11365)*

### AUTOMOTIVE: Seating

Adient US LLC .........................................C....... 815 895-2095
  Sycamore *(G-20785)*
Johnson Controls Inc ...............................E....... 815 288-3859
  Dixon *(G-8335)*
Johnson Controls Inc ...............................E....... 309 427-2800
  East Peoria *(G-8719)*
Johnson Controls Inc ...............................D....... 630 573-0897
  Oak Brook *(G-16527)*
Johnson Controls Inc ...............................E....... 331 212-3800
  Aurora *(G-1038)*
Johnson Controls Inc ...............................E....... 847 364-1500
  Arlington Heights *(G-785)*

Johnson Controls Inc ...............................D....... 630 279-0050
  Elmhurst *(G-9892)*
Johnson Controls Inc ...............................G....... 630 351-9407
  Bloomingdale *(G-2110)*
The United Group Inc ..............................E....... 847 816-7100
  Lake Forest *(G-12970)*
Yanfeng US Automotive ...........................A....... 779 552-7300
  Belvidere *(G-1798)*

### AVIATION SCHOOL

Koerner Aviation Inc ................................G....... 815 932-4222
  Kankakee *(G-12636)*

### AWNINGS & CANOPIES

Awnings Over Chicagoland Inc ................G....... 847 233-0310
  Franklin Park *(G-10406)*
Eclipse Awnings Inc .................................F....... 708 636-3160
  Evergreen Park *(G-10113)*

### AWNINGS & CANOPIES: Awnings, Fabric, From Purchased Matls

Americana Building Pdts Inc ....................D....... 618 548-2800
  Salem *(G-19326)*
Berg Industries Inc ..................................F....... 815 874-1588
  Rockford *(G-18280)*
Blake Co Inc ............................................G....... 815 962-3852
  Rockford *(G-18287)*
Brian Robert Awning Co ..........................G....... 847 679-1140
  Skokie *(G-19970)*
Evanston Awning Company .....................F....... 847 864-4520
  Evanston *(G-10032)*
Hunzinger Williams Inc ............................G....... 847 381-1878
  Lake Barrington *(G-12810)*
Kankakee Tent & Awning Co ...................G....... 815 932-8000
  Kankakee *(G-12634)*
Midwest Awnings Inc ...............................G....... 309 762-3339
  Cameron *(G-2970)*
Nuyen Awning Co ....................................G....... 630 892-3995
  Aurora *(G-1197)*
Stritzel Awnng Svc/Aurra Tent ................E....... 630 420-2000
  Plainfield *(G-17654)*
Traube Canvas Products Inc ...................F....... 618 281-0696
  Dupo *(G-8581)*

### AWNINGS & CANOPIES: Canopies, Fabric, From Purchased Matls

Shelter Systems .......................................G....... 773 281-9270
  Chicago *(G-6495)*

### AWNINGS & CANOPIES: Fabric

Chesterfield Awning Co Inc .....................F....... 708 596-4434
  South Holland *(G-20256)*
Eclipse Awnings Inc .................................F....... 708 636-3160
  Evergreen Park *(G-10113)*
Thatcher Oaks Inc ...................................E....... 630 833-5700
  Elmhurst *(G-9950)*

### AWNINGS: Fiberglass

Acme Awning Co Inc ...............................G....... 847 446-0153
  Lake Zurich *(G-13035)*
Glasstek Inc .............................................G....... 630 978-9897
  Naperville *(G-15807)*

### AWNINGS: Metal

Advance Awnair Corp ..............................F....... 708 422-2730
  Orland Park *(G-16838)*
Americana Building Pdts Inc ....................D....... 618 548-2800
  Salem *(G-19326)*
Awnings Unlimited Inc .............................G....... 708 485-6769
  Brookfield *(G-2622)*
Charles Atwater Assoc Inc ......................G....... 815 678-4813
  Richmond *(G-17959)*
Logan Square Aluminum Sup Inc ............D....... 847 985-1700
  Schaumburg *(G-19622)*
Npi Holding Corp ......................................G....... 217 391-1229
  Springfield *(G-20488)*
Nudo Products Inc ...................................C....... 217 528-5636
  Springfield *(G-20490)*
Professional Metal Company ...................E....... 630 983-9777
  Naperville *(G-15733)*
Rijon Manufacturing Company .................G....... 708 388-2295
  Blue Island *(G-2266)*
Shademaker Products Corp .....................G....... 773 955-0998
  Chicago *(G-6488)*

# PRODUCT SECTION

## BAGS: Pliofilm, Made From Purchased Materials

Tri State Aluminum Products .......... F ...... 815 877-6081
  Loves Park *(G-14003)*

### AXLES

Chicago Drive Line Inc .......... G ...... 708 385-1900
  Alsip *(G-445)*
Mattoon Precision Mfg .......... C ...... 217 235-6000
  Mattoon *(G-14399)*
Strange Engineering Inc .......... D ...... 847 663-1701
  Morton Grove *(G-15239)*
Thyssenkrupp North America Inc .......... E ...... 312 525-2800
  Chicago *(G-6725)*

### AXLES: Rolled Or Forged, Made In Steel Mills

Keystone-Calumet Inc .......... E ...... 708 753-1200
  Chicago Heights *(G-7110)*

### BABY FORMULA

Mead Johnson Nutrition Company .......... E ...... 312 466-5800
  Chicago *(G-5671)*

### BACKHOES

Jcb Inc .......... G ...... 912 704-2995
  Aurora *(G-1037)*
Sebens Backhoe Service Inc .......... G ...... 217 762-7365
  Monticello *(G-15084)*

### BADGES, WHOLESALE

Dbp Communications Inc .......... G ...... 312 263-1569
  Chicago *(G-4566)*
Finer Line Inc .......... F ...... 847 884-1611
  Schaumburg *(G-19527)*
P F Pettibone & Co .......... G ...... 815 344-7811
  Crystal Lake *(G-7624)*

### BADGES: Identification & Insignia

Marking Specialists/Poly .......... F ...... 847 793-8100
  Buffalo Grove *(G-2731)*

### BAGS & CONTAINERS: Textile, Exc Sleeping

ABG Bag Inc .......... F ...... 815 963-9525
  Rockford *(G-18247)*
Inventive Concepts Intl LLC .......... G ...... 847 350-6102
  Glendale Heights *(G-11035)*
Keeper Thermal Bag Co Inc .......... G ...... 630 213-0125
  Bartlett *(G-1359)*
Ryan Products Inc .......... G ...... 847 670-9071
  Arlington Heights *(G-833)*

### BAGS & SACKS: Shipping & Shopping

Westrock Rkt Company .......... A ...... 312 346-6600
  Chicago *(G-6969)*

### BAGS: Cellophane

Keenpac LLC .......... G ...... 845 291-8680
  Morton Grove *(G-15209)*
Peelmaster Packaging Corp .......... E ...... 847 966-6161
  Niles *(G-16015)*

### BAGS: Duffle, Canvas, Made From Purchased Materials

Advance Tools LLC .......... G ...... 855 685-0633
  Glenview *(G-11097)*
Deady Brian Rfg Inc .......... G ...... 708 479-8249
  Orland Park *(G-16853)*
Hunter-Nusport Inc .......... G ...... 815 254-7520
  Plainfield *(G-17607)*

### BAGS: Flour, Made From Purchased Materials

Morris Packaging LLC .......... G ...... 309 663-9100
  Bloomington *(G-2204)*
Pride Packaging LLC .......... G ...... 309 663-9100
  Bloomington *(G-2215)*

### BAGS: Food Storage & Frozen Food, Plastic

Kleer Pak Mfg Co Inc .......... E ...... 630 543-0208
  Addison *(G-169)*
McCook Cold Storage Corp .......... E ...... 708 387-2585
  Mc Cook *(G-14452)*
Morris Packaging LLC .......... G ...... 309 663-9100
  Bloomington *(G-2204)*
Pactiv LLC .......... A ...... 847 482-2000
  Lake Forest *(G-12935)*
R Popernik Co Inc .......... F ...... 773 434-4300
  Chicago *(G-6269)*
Vej Holdings LLC .......... G ...... 630 219-1582
  Naperville *(G-15774)*

### BAGS: Food Storage & Trash, Plastic

Pactiv LLC .......... C ...... 317 390-5306
  Grant Park *(G-11312)*
Pactiv LLC .......... C ...... 708 924-2402
  Bridgeview *(G-2518)*
Pactiv LLC .......... C ...... 815 469-2112
  Frankfort *(G-10346)*
Pactiv LLC .......... C ...... 217 479-1144
  Jacksonville *(G-12404)*
Pactiv LLC .......... C
  Lincolnshire *(G-13469)*
Vida Enterprises Inc .......... G ...... 312 808-0088
  Chicago *(G-6895)*

### BAGS: Garment & Wardrobe, Plastic Film

Fischer Paper Products Inc .......... D ...... 847 395-6060
  Antioch *(G-632)*

### BAGS: Garment Storage Exc Paper Or Plastic Film

Vida Enterprises Inc .......... G ...... 312 808-0088
  Chicago *(G-6895)*

### BAGS: Paper

Duro Hilex Poly LLC .......... D ...... 708 385-8674
  Alsip *(G-459)*
Gateway Packaging Company .......... C ...... 618 451-0010
  Granite City *(G-11279)*
Gateway Packaging Company LLC .......... C ...... 618 415-0010
  Granite City *(G-11280)*
Graphic Packaging Intl Inc .......... C ...... 630 260-6500
  Carol Stream *(G-3163)*
Lexington Leather Goods Co .......... F ...... 773 287-7500
  Chicago *(G-5499)*
Midwesco Filter Resources Inc .......... C ...... 540 773-4780
  Niles *(G-16006)*
Mondi Romeoville Inc .......... D ...... 630 378-9886
  Romeoville *(G-18850)*
Waxstar Inc .......... G ...... 708 755-3530
  S Chicago Hts *(G-19115)*

### BAGS: Paper, Made From Purchased Materials

Bag and Barrier Corporation .......... G ...... 217 849-3271
  Toledo *(G-20961)*
Bagcraftpapercon I LLC .......... C ...... 620 856-2800
  Chicago *(G-4025)*
Bagmakers Inc .......... B ...... 815 923-2247
  Union *(G-21033)*
Fischer Paper Products Inc .......... D ...... 847 395-6060
  Antioch *(G-632)*

### BAGS: Plastic

ABG Bag Inc .......... F ...... 815 963-9525
  Rockford *(G-18247)*
Advanced Custom Shapes .......... F ...... 618 684-2222
  Murphysboro *(G-15570)*
Ampac Flexibles LLC .......... D ...... 630 439-3160
  Hanover Park *(G-11574)*
Bag and Barrier Corporation .......... G ...... 217 849-3271
  Toledo *(G-20961)*
Bagcraftpapercon I LLC .......... C ...... 620 856-2800
  Chicago *(G-4025)*
Coveris Holding Corp .......... G ...... 773 877-3300
  Chicago *(G-4483)*
Drumheller Bag Corporation .......... D ...... 309 676-1006
  Peoria *(G-17350)*
Duro Hilex Poly LLC .......... D ...... 708 385-8674
  Alsip *(G-459)*
E-Z Products Inc .......... F ...... 847 551-9199
  Gilberts *(G-10918)*
Envision Inc .......... G ...... 847 735-0789
  Lake Forest *(G-12897)*
Flex-O-Glass Inc .......... D ...... 773 261-5200
  Chicago *(G-4858)*
Flex-Pak Packaging Products .......... F ...... 630 761-3335
  Batavia *(G-1448)*
Foodhandler Inc .......... D ...... 866 931-3613
  Elk Grove Village *(G-9484)*
Highland Supply Corporation .......... B ...... 618 654-2161
  Highland *(G-11794)*
Kam Group Inc .......... F ...... 630 679-9668
  Bolingbrook *(G-2330)*
Kapak Company LLC .......... G ...... 952 541-0730
  Hanover Park *(G-11584)*
Natural Packaging Inc .......... G ...... 708 246-3420
  La Grange *(G-12740)*
Pactiv Intl Holdings Inc .......... A ...... 847 482-2000
  Lake Forest *(G-12934)*
Pak Source Inc .......... E ...... 309 786-7374
  Rock Island *(G-18191)*
Plastics D-E-F .......... G ...... 312 226-4337
  Chicago *(G-6137)*
Pliant LLC .......... A ...... 812 424-2904
  Rolling Meadows *(G-18763)*
Pregis LLC .......... A ...... 847 597-2200
  Deerfield *(G-8049)*
Printpack Inc .......... F ...... 847 888-7150
  Elgin *(G-9148)*
Renew Packaging LLC .......... G ...... 312 421-6699
  Chicago *(G-6333)*
Silgan Plastics LLC .......... G ...... 618 662-4471
  Flora *(G-10217)*
Waxstar Inc .......... G ...... 708 755-3530
  S Chicago Hts *(G-19115)*

### BAGS: Plastic & Pliofilm

Aargus Industries Inc .......... G ...... 847 325-4444
  Wheeling *(G-21994)*
Aargus Plastics Inc .......... C ...... 847 325-4444
  Wheeling *(G-21995)*
Pactiv LLC .......... B ...... 217 243-3311
  Jacksonville *(G-12405)*
Poly Plastics Films Corp .......... G ...... 815 636-0821
  Machesney Park *(G-14098)*
Pride Packaging LLC .......... G ...... 309 663-9100
  Bloomington *(G-2215)*
Procon Pacific LLC .......... F ...... 630 575-0551
  Oak Brook *(G-16556)*
Quality Bags Inc .......... F ...... 630 543-9800
  Addison *(G-263)*

### BAGS: Plastic, Made From Purchased Materials

Ampac Holdings LLC .......... F ...... 847 639-3530
  Cary *(G-3326)*
Bagmakers Inc .......... B ...... 815 923-2247
  Union *(G-21033)*
Bio Industries Inc .......... D ...... 847 215-8999
  Wheeling *(G-22014)*
Brohman Industries Inc .......... F ...... 630 761-8160
  Chicago *(G-4174)*
Dart Container Michigan LLC .......... G ...... 312 221-1245
  Chicago *(G-4560)*
Diamond Cellophane Pdts Inc .......... E ...... 847 418-3000
  Northbrook *(G-16242)*
Engineered Materials Inc .......... G ...... 847 821-8280
  Buffalo Grove *(G-2691)*
Essentra Packaging US Inc .......... G ...... 704 418-8692
  Westchester *(G-21841)*
Fisher Container Corp .......... D ...... 847 541-0000
  Buffalo Grove *(G-2694)*
Fisher Container Holdings LLC .......... G ...... 847 541-0000
  Buffalo Grove *(G-2695)*
Golden Bag Company Inc .......... F ...... 847 836-7766
  East Dundee *(G-8639)*
Jacobson Acqstion Holdings LLC .......... C ...... 847 623-1414
  Waukegan *(G-21574)*
Laminet Cover Company .......... E ...... 773 622-6700
  Chicago *(G-5451)*
Packaging Personified Inc .......... C ...... 630 653-1655
  Carol Stream *(G-3210)*
Vilutis and Co Inc .......... E ...... 815 469-2116
  Frankfort *(G-10374)*
Vonco Products LLC .......... E ...... 847 356-2323
  Lake Villa *(G-13029)*

### BAGS: Pliofilm, Made From Purchased Materials

Lawrence Packaging Intl .......... G ...... 630 682-2600
  Wheaton *(G-21965)*

---

Employee Codes: A=Over 500 employees, B=251-500
C=101-250, D=51-100, E=20-50, F=10-19, G=3-9

2017 Harris Illinois Industrial Directory

## BAGS: Rubber Or Rubberized Fabric

**Smith Industrial Rubber & Plas** ....F .... 815 874-5364
Rockford *(G-18622)*

## BAGS: Shipping

**Bulk Lift International LLC** ....G .... 847 428-6059
Carpentersville *(G-3277)*
**Langston Bag of Peoria LLC** ....D .... 309 676-1006
Peoria *(G-17399)*

## BAGS: Textile

**Ajr Enterprises Inc** ....C .... 630 377-8886
Saint Charles *(G-19132)*
**Amcraft Manufacturing Inc** ....F .... 847 439-4565
Elk Grove Village *(G-9294)*
**Bearse Manufacturing Co** ....D .... 773 235-8710
Chicago *(G-4068)*
**Beas Bags** ....G .... 847 486-1943
Glenview *(G-11106)*
**Block and Company Inc** ....C .... 847 537-7200
Wheeling *(G-22015)*
**J Design Works Inc** ....G .... 847 812-0891
Bolingbrook *(G-2326)*
**Jarries Shoe Bags** ....G .... 773 379-4044
Chicago *(G-5280)*
**Midwesco Filter Resources Inc** ....C .... 540 773-4780
Niles *(G-16006)*
**Omg Handbags LLC** ....G .... 847 337-9499
Chicago *(G-5989)*
**Sea-Rich Corp** ....G .... 773 261-6633
Chicago *(G-6464)*
**Terre Haute Tent & Awning Inc** ....F .... 812 235-6068
South Holland *(G-20309)*

## BAGS: Trash, Plastic Film, Made From Purchased Materials

**Colonial Bag Corporation** ....D .... 630 690-3999
Carol Stream *(G-3134)*

## BAGS: Vacuum cleaner, Made From Purchased Materials

**Studley Products Inc** ....C .... 309 663-2313
Bloomington *(G-2226)*

## BAGS: Wardrobe, Closet Access, Made From Purchased Materials

**Closet Concept** ....G .... 217 375-4214
Milford *(G-14811)*

## BAIT, FISHING, WHOLESALE

**Outback USA Inc** ....G .... 863 699-2220
Saint Charles *(G-19231)*

## BAKERIES, COMMERCIAL: On Premises Baking Only

**2 Figs Baking Co Inc** ....G .... 847 778-2936
Des Plaines *(G-8135)*
**Ace Bakeries** ....F .... 312 225-4973
Chicago *(G-3726)*
**American Kitchen Delights Inc** ....D .... 708 210-3200
Harvey *(G-11656)*
**Athenian Foods Co** ....F .... 708 343-6700
Melrose Park *(G-14596)*
**B&L Services Inc** ....G .... 630 257-1688
Lemont *(G-13226)*
**Bakery Crescent Corporation** ....G .... 847 956-6470
Arlington Heights *(G-722)*
**Bear-Stewart Corporation** ....E .... 773 276-0400
Chicago *(G-4065)*
**Bimbo Bakeries Usa Inc** ....E .... 773 254-3578
Chicago *(G-4107)*
**Bimbo Bakeries Usa Inc** ....D .... 815 626-6797
Rock Falls *(G-18127)*
**Bodines Baking Company** ....G .... 217 853-7707
Decatur *(G-7846)*
**Butera Finer Foods Inc** ....D .... 708 456-5939
Norridge *(G-16097)*
**Caribbean American Bkg Co Inc** ....G .... 773 761-0700
Chicago *(G-4244)*
**Casa Nostra Bakery Co Inc** ....F .... 847 455-5175
Franklin Park *(G-10424)*
**Charles Cicero Fingerhut** ....F .... 708 652-3643
Chicago *(G-4290)*
**Charleston County Market** ....D .... 217 345-7031
Charleston *(G-3593)*
**Chateau Food Products Inc** ....F .... 708 863-4207
Chicago *(G-4296)*
**Chicago Pastry Inc** ....D .... 630 529-6161
Bloomingdale *(G-2100)*
**Cub Foods Inc** ....C .... 309 689-0140
Peoria *(G-17347)*
**Cupcakeologist LLC** ....G .... 630 656-2272
Bolingbrook *(G-2294)*
**DAmatos Bakery** ....F .... 312 733-5456
Chicago *(G-4547)*
**Dinkels Bakery Inc** ....E .... 773 281-7300
Chicago *(G-4605)*
**Distinctive Foods LLC** ....E .... 847 459-3600
Bensenville *(G-1880)*
**Dominicks Finer Foods Inc** ....D .... 630 584-1750
Saint Charles *(G-19173)*
**Dominos Pastries Inc** ....G .... 773 889-3549
Hickory Hills *(G-11769)*
**Dunajec Bakery & Deli** ....F .... 773 585-9611
Bridgeview *(G-2485)*
**El Moro De Letran Churros & Ba** ....F .... 312 733-3173
Chicago *(G-4708)*
**Enjoy Life Natural Brands LLC** ....E .... 773 632-2163
Chicago *(G-4756)*
**Entrust Services LLC** ....G .... 630 699-9132
Naperville *(G-15654)*
**European Classic Bakery** ....G .... 773 774-8755
Chicago *(G-4783)*
**Father Marcellos & Son** ....C .... 312 654-2565
Chicago *(G-4820)*
**Faustos Bakery** ....G .... 847 255-9049
Arlington Heights *(G-753)*
**Flirty Cupcakes LLC** ....G .... 312 545-1096
Chicago *(G-4862)*
**Fortuna Baking Company** ....G .... 630 681-3000
Carol Stream *(G-3154)*
**G & K Baking LLC** ....G .... 630 415-8687
Oak Brook *(G-16517)*
**Gold Coast Baking Co** ....G .... 630 620-1849
Addison *(G-137)*
**Golosinas El Canto** ....G .... 847 625-5103
Waukegan *(G-21564)*
**Gonnella Baking Co** ....D .... 630 820-3433
Aurora *(G-1020)*
**Gourmet Frog Pastry Shop** ....G .... 847 433-7038
Highland Park *(G-11837)*
**Harners Bakery Restaurant** ....D .... 630 892-5545
North Aurora *(G-16133)*
**Hearthside Food Solutions LLC** ....B .... 815 853-4348
Wenona *(G-21648)*
**Herbs Bakery Inc** ....F .... 847 741-0249
Elgin *(G-9065)*
**Herman Seekamp Inc** ....C .... 630 628-6555
Addison *(G-145)*
**Hermanitas Cupcakes** ....G .... 708 620-9396
Calumet City *(G-2943)*
**Highland Baking Company Inc** ....A .... 847 677-2789
Northbrook *(G-16270)*
**Jewel Osco Inc** ....C .... 773 728-7730
Chicago *(G-5299)*
**Jewel Osco Inc** ....C .... 773 784-1922
Chicago *(G-5300)*
**Jewel Osco Inc** ....C .... 708 352-0120
Countryside *(G-7435)*
**Jewel Osco Inc** ....D .... 630 859-1212
Aurora *(G-1177)*
**Jewel Osco Inc** ....C .... 847 854-2692
Algonquin *(G-395)*
**Jewel Osco Inc** ....C .... 847 677-3331
Skokie *(G-20019)*
**Jewel Osco Inc** ....C .... 630 584-4594
Saint Charles *(G-19202)*
**Jewel Osco Inc** ....C .... 847 428-3547
West Dundee *(G-21798)*
**Jewel Osco Inc** ....C .... 630 355-2172
Naperville *(G-15681)*
**Jewel Osco Inc** ....D .... 630 226-1892
Bolingbrook *(G-2328)*
**Jewel Osco Inc** ....C .... 815 464-5352
Frankfort *(G-10336)*
**Jewel-Osco Inc** ....C .... 847 296-7786
Des Plaines *(G-8216)*
**Kellogg Company** ....C .... 630 941-0300
Elmhurst *(G-9897)*
**Kerry Inc** ....G .... 847 595-1003
Elk Grove Village *(G-9572)*
**Keystone Bakery Holdings LLC** ....G .... 603 792-3113
Deerfield *(G-8024)*
**Korinek & Co Inc** ....G .... 708 652-2870
Cicero *(G-7210)*
**Kroger Co** ....C .... 309 694-6298
East Peoria *(G-8722)*
**Kroger Co** ....C .... 815 332-7267
Rockford *(G-18457)*
**La Chicanita Bakery** ....F .... 630 499-8845
Aurora *(G-1180)*
**La Dolce Bella Cupcakes** ....G .... 847 987-3738
Lockport *(G-13725)*
**Leas Baking Company LLC** ....G .... 708 710-3404
Homer Glen *(G-12082)*
**Leesons Cakes Inc** ....G .... 708 429-1330
Tinley Park *(G-20930)*
**Lucksfood** ....G .... 773 878-7778
Chicago *(G-5557)*
**Mangel and Co** ....F .... 847 634-0730
Long Grove *(G-13894)*
**Marzeya Bakery Inc** ....G .... 773 374-7855
Chicago *(G-5642)*
**Mel-O-Cream Donuts** ....F .... 217 544-4644
Springfield *(G-20476)*
**Melinda I Rhodes** ....G .... 815 569-2789
Capron *(G-2997)*
**Milano Bakery Inc** ....E .... 815 727-2253
Joliet *(G-12542)*
**Miss Joans Cupcakes** ....G .... 630 881-5707
Bolingbrook *(G-2343)*
**Mybread LLC** ....G .... 312 600-9633
Chicago *(G-5843)*
**Nauvoo Mill & Bakery** ....G .... 217 453-6734
Nauvoo *(G-15854)*
**Niemann Foods Foundation** ....C .... 217 222-0190
Quincy *(G-17862)*
**Niemann Foods Foundation** ....C .... 217 793-4091
Springfield *(G-20487)*
**Original Ferrara Inc** ....F .... 312 666-2200
Chicago *(G-6011)*
**Orland Park Bakery Ltd** ....E .... 708 349-8516
Orland Park *(G-16881)*
**Piemonte Bakery Company Inc** ....E .... 815 962-4833
Rockford *(G-18536)*
**Quality Croutons Inc** ....E .... 773 927-8200
Chicago *(G-6246)*
**Rain Creek Baking Corp** ....G .... 559 347-9960
Glendale Heights *(G-11063)*
**Red Hen Bread Inc** ....E .... 773 342-6823
Elmhurst *(G-9927)*
**River City Cupcake LLC** ....G .... 309 613-1312
Pekin *(G-17287)*
**Riverside Bake Shop** ....E .... 815 385-0044
McHenry *(G-14552)*
**Roma Bakeries Inc** ....F .... 815 964-6737
Rockford *(G-18596)*
**Royal Oak Farm Inc** ....F .... 815 648-4141
Harvard *(G-11646)*
**Schnuck Markets Inc** ....C .... 618 466-0825
Godfrey *(G-11237)*
**Schulze and Burch Biscuit Co** ....B .... 773 927-6622
Chicago *(G-6455)*
**Smallcakes Cupcakery of South** ....G .... 773 433-0059
South Barrington *(G-20132)*
**Sunset Food Mart Inc** ....C .... 847 234-0854
Lake Forest *(G-12964)*
**Superior Baking Stone Inc** ....G .... 815 726-4610
Joliet *(G-12580)*
**Sweet Temptations Cupcake** ....G .... 309 212-2637
Bloomington *(G-2228)*
**Tags Bakery Inc** ....E .... 847 328-1200
Evanston *(G-10100)*
**Tam Tav Bakery Inc** ....E .... 773 764-8877
Chicago *(G-6669)*
**Tarte Cupcakery Company** ....G .... 312 898-2103
Lansing *(G-13189)*
**Tonys Bakery** ....G .... 847 599-1590
Waukegan *(G-21630)*
**Tortilleria Atotonilco Inc** ....E .... 773 523-0800
Chicago *(G-6749)*
**Treasure Island Foods Inc** ....D .... 312 642-1105
Chicago *(G-6765)*
**Treasure Island Foods Inc** ....C .... 773 880-8880
Chicago *(G-6764)*
**Treasure Island Foods Inc** ....D .... 312 440-1144
Chicago *(G-6763)*
**Unity Baking Company LLC** ....G .... 630 360-6099
Aurora *(G-1228)*
**Walter Lagestee Inc** ....C .... 708 957-2974
Homewood *(G-12106)*
**Zeldaco Ltd** ....F .... 847 679-0033
Skokie *(G-20116)*

# PRODUCT SECTION

## BAKERIES: On Premises Baking & Consumption

| Company | Code | Phone |
|---|---|---|
| Ace Bakeries — Chicago (G-3726) | F | 312 225-4973 |
| Athenian Foods Co — Melrose Park (G-14596) | F | 708 343-6700 |
| Chipita America Inc — Westchester (G-21832) | E | 708 731-2434 |
| DAmatos Bakery Inc — Chicago (G-4548) | G | 312 733-6219 |
| Harners Bakery Restaurant — North Aurora (G-16133) | D | 630 892-5545 |
| Herbs Bakery Inc — Elgin (G-9065) | F | 847 741-0249 |
| Jewel Osco Inc — Chicago (G-5300) | C | 773 784-1922 |
| Marzeya Bakery Inc — Chicago (G-5642) | G | 773 374-7855 |
| OBrothers Bakery Inc — Waukegan (G-21597) | G | 847 249-0091 |
| Original Ferrara Inc — Chicago (G-6011) | F | 312 666-2200 |
| Orland Park Bakery Ltd — Orland Park (G-16881) | E | 708 349-8516 |
| Riverside Bake Shop — McHenry (G-14552) | E | 815 385-0044 |
| Sunset Food Mart Inc — Lake Forest (G-12964) | C | 847 234-0854 |
| Tags Bakery Inc — Evanston (G-10100) | E | 847 328-1200 |
| Tam Tav Bakery Inc — Chicago (G-6669) | E | 773 764-8877 |
| Tortilleria Atotonilco Inc — Chicago (G-6749) | E | 773 523-0800 |

## BAKERY MACHINERY

| Company | Code | Phone |
|---|---|---|
| Angel Equipment LLC — Glenview (G-11101) | G | 815 455-4320 |
| CMC America Corporation — Joliet (G-12475) | F | 815 726-4337 |
| Custom Systems Inc — Granite City (G-11272) | G | 314 355-4575 |
| Practical Baker Equipment — Harvard (G-11644) | G | 815 943-8730 |
| Precision Service — Collinsville (G-7337) | G | 618 345-2047 |

## BAKERY PRDTS: Bagels, Fresh Or Frozen

| Company | Code | Phone |
|---|---|---|
| Pinnacle Foods Group LLC — Mattoon (G-14406) | B | 217 235-3181 |
| Wholesome Harvest Baking LLC — Des Plaines (G-8305) | E | 800 550-6810 |

## BAKERY PRDTS: Bakery Prdts, Partially Cooked, Exc frozen

| Company | Code | Phone |
|---|---|---|
| Cathys Sweet Creations — Plainfield (G-17585) | G | 815 886-6769 |

## BAKERY PRDTS: Bread, All Types, Fresh Or Frozen

| Company | Code | Phone |
|---|---|---|
| Anns Bakery Inc — Chicago (G-3912) | G | 773 384-5562 |
| C & C Bakery Inc — Chicago (G-4199) | G | 773 276-4233 |
| Gonnella Baking Co — Schaumburg (G-19539) | D | 312 733-2020 |
| Gonnella Baking Co — Schaumburg (G-19540) | D | 312 733-2020 |
| Gonnella Baking Co — Schaumburg (G-19541) | D | 847 884-8829 |
| Gonnella Frozen Products LLC — Schaumburg (G-19542) | C | 847 884-8829 |
| Grecian Delight Foods Inc — Elk Grove Village (G-9511) | E | 847 364-1010 |
| Kim & Sctts Grmet Pretzels Inc — Chicago (G-5383) | D | 800 578-9478 |
| Labriola Baking Company LLC — Alsip (G-483) | C | 708 377-0400 |
| Lewis Brothers Bakeries Inc — Anna (G-607) | G | 618 833-5185 |
| Maplehurst Bakeries LLC — Chicago (G-5610) | E | 773 826-1245 |
| Marconi Bakery Company — Chicago Heights (G-7111) | F | 708 757-6315 |
| Neuman Bakery Specialties Inc — Addison (G-227) | F | 630 916-8909 |
| Rjl Inc — Alsip (G-521) | C | 708 385-4884 |
| Rubschlager Baking Corporation — Chicago (G-6413) | G | 773 826-1245 |
| Zb Importing Inc — Cicero (G-7248) | D | 708 222-8330 |

## BAKERY PRDTS: Buns, Bread Type, Fresh Or Frozen

| Company | Code | Phone |
|---|---|---|
| East Balt Bakery of Florida — Chicago (G-4680) | B | 407 933-2222 |

## BAKERY PRDTS: Cakes, Bakery, Exc Frozen

| Company | Code | Phone |
|---|---|---|
| Arlington Specialties Inc — Elk Grove Village (G-9313) | G | 847 545-9500 |
| Auntie Mmmms — Camp Point (G-2971) | G | 217 509-6012 |
| Baker & Nosh — Chicago (G-4029) | G | 773 989-7393 |
| Bom Bon Corp — Chicago (G-4140) | G | 773 277-8777 |
| Callies Cuties Inc — Plainfield (G-17583) | G | 815 566-6885 |
| Emack & Bolios — Peoria (G-17357) | | 309 682-3530 |
| Homer Vintage Bakery — Homer (G-12075) | G | 217 896-2538 |
| Jr Bakery — Chicago (G-5331) | E | 773 465-6733 |
| La Bella Chrstnas Kitchens Inc — German Valley (G-10891) | G | 815 801-1600 |
| Linx Enterprises LLC — Chicago (G-5516) | G | 224 409-2206 |
| Morningfields — Park Ridge (G-17209) | G | 847 309-8460 |
| Nak Won Korean Bakery — Chicago (G-5850) | G | 773 588-8769 |
| National Biscuit Company — Chicago (G-5860) | G | 773 925-0654 |
| New Chicago Wholesale Bky Inc — Elk Grove Village (G-9650) | E | 847 981-1600 |
| Say Cheese Cake — Centralia (G-3431) | G | 618 532-6001 |
| Sugar Monkey Cupcakes Inc — Naperville (G-15829) | G | 630 527-1869 |
| Sweet Annies Bakery Inc — Flossmoor (G-10231) | F | 708 297-7066 |
| Thats So Sweet — Lexington (G-13294) | G | 903 331-7221 |

## BAKERY PRDTS: Cakes, Bakery, Frozen

| Company | Code | Phone |
|---|---|---|
| Elis Cheesecake Company — Chicago (G-4730) | C | 773 205-3800 |
| K & A Bread LLC — Chicago Heights (G-7107) | D | 708 757-7750 |
| New Chicago Wholesale Bky Inc — Elk Grove Village (G-9650) | E | 847 981-1600 |
| Sweet Creation By Sheila — Glenwood (G-11220) | G | 708 754-7938 |
| Vienna Beef Ltd — Chicago (G-6896) | E | 773 278-7800 |
| Wilseys Handmade Sweets LLC — Edwardsville (G-8818) | G | 314 504-0851 |

## BAKERY PRDTS: Charlotte Russe, Exc Frozen

| Company | Code | Phone |
|---|---|---|
| Dixie Cream Donut Shop — West Frankfort (G-21806) | E | 618 937-4866 |

## BAKERY PRDTS: Cookies

| Company | Code | Phone |
|---|---|---|
| Carols Cookies Inc — Northbrook (G-16217) | G | 847 831-4500 |
| Christian Wolf Inc — Bartelso (G-1314) | G | 618 667-9522 |
| Cookie Kingdom Inc — Oglesby (G-16747) | D | 815 883-3331 |
| Fortella Company Inc — Chicago (G-4876) | G | 312 567-9000 |
| Golden Dragon Fortune Cookies — Chicago (G-4973) | F | 312 842-8199 |
| Harvest Valley Bakery Inc — La Salle (G-12774) | E | 815 224-9030 |
| Herman Seekamp Inc — Addison (G-145) | G | 630 628-6555 |
| Keebler Company — Aurora (G-1039) | E | 630 820-9457 |
| Kellogg Company — Elmhurst (G-9897) | C | 630 941-0300 |
| Matts Cookie Company — Wheeling (G-22103) | G | 847 537-3888 |
| Mondelez Global LLC — Chicago (G-5793) | E | 773 925-4300 |
| Old Colony Baking Company Inc — Spring Valley (G-20377) | G | 847 498-5434 |
| Paleo Prime LLC — Chicago (G-6059) | G | 312 659-6596 |
| Pures Food Specialties LLC — Broadview (G-2605) | E | 708 344-8884 |
| Sugar/Spice Extraordinry Treat — Evanston (G-10098) | F | 847 864-7800 |
| Treehouse Private Brands Inc — South Beloit (G-20170) | C | 815 389-2745 |
| Wex Distributors Inc — Antioch (G-663) | G | 847 691-5823 |
| Wildlife Cookie Company — Saint Charles (G-19296) | G | 630 377-6196 |

## BAKERY PRDTS: Cookies & crackers

| Company | Code | Phone |
|---|---|---|
| Casa Nostra Bakery Co Inc — Franklin Park (G-10424) | F | 847 455-5175 |
| Charleston County Market — Charleston (G-3593) | D | 217 345-7031 |
| Cheryl & Co — Oak Park (G-16658) | C | 708 386-1255 |
| Chicago Pastry Inc — Bloomingdale (G-2100) | D | 630 529-6161 |
| Chipita America Inc — Westchester (G-21832) | E | 708 731-2434 |
| Cookie Dough Creations Co — Naperville (G-15635) | G | 630 369-4833 |
| DAmatos Bakery Inc — Chicago (G-4548) | G | 312 733-6219 |
| Dinkels Bakery Inc — Chicago (G-4605) | E | 773 281-7300 |
| Hop Kee Incorporated — Chicago (G-5109) | E | 312 791-9111 |
| Jewel Osco Inc — Skokie (G-20019) | C | 847 677-3331 |
| Jewel Osco Inc — Naperville (G-15681) | C | 630 355-2172 |
| Jr Bakery — Chicago (G-5331) | E | 773 465-6733 |
| Katys LLC — Oak Park (G-16672) | G | 708 522-9814 |
| Keebler Foods Company — Elmhurst (G-9896) | E | 630 833-2900 |
| Kroger Co — Rockford (G-18457) | C | 815 332-7267 |
| Maiers Bakery — Morton Grove (G-15216) | G | 847 967-8042 |
| Market Square Food Company — Park City (G-17166) | F | 847 599-6070 |
| Mondelez Global LLC — Naperville (G-15699) | B | 630 369-1909 |
| Quality Croutons Inc — Chicago (G-6246) | E | 773 927-8200 |
| Roma Bakeries Inc — Rockford (G-18596) | F | 815 964-6737 |
| Schulze and Burch Biscuit Co — Chicago (G-6455) | B | 773 927-6622 |
| Stress Free Cookies Inc — Chicago (G-6605) | E | 312 856-7686 |
| Tags Bakery Inc — Evanston (G-10100) | E | 847 328-1200 |
| Walter Lagestee Inc — Homewood (G-12106) | C | 708 957-2974 |

## BAKERY PRDTS: Crackers

| Company | Code | Phone |
|---|---|---|
| Lofthouse Bakery Products Inc — Downers Grove (G-8479) | G | 630 455-5229 |
| Mondelez Global LLC — Deerfield (G-8037) | C | 847 943-4000 |
| Th Foods Inc — Loves Park (G-14000) | G | 702 565-2816 |
| Th Foods Inc — Loves Park (G-14001) | C | 800 896-2396 |
| Treehouse Private Brands Inc — Downers Grove (G-8534) | E | 630 455-5265 |

## BAKERY PRDTS: Croissants, Frozen

| Company | Code | Phone |
|---|---|---|
| Forno Palese Baking Company — Bartlett (G-1348) | F | 630 595-5502 |

Employee Codes: A=Over 500 employees, B=251-500, C=101-250, D=51-100, E=20-50, F=10-19, G=3-9

## BAKERY PRDTS: Doughnuts, Exc Frozen

**Amling Donuts Inc** .............................. E ....... 847 426-5327
Carpentersville (G-3274)
**B N K Inc** ............................................ G ....... 630 231-5640
West Chicago (G-21664)
**Bellwood Dunkin Donuts** .................... F ....... 708 401-5601
Bellwood (G-1695)
**Brown & Meyers Inc** ........................... G ....... 618 524-3838
Metropolis (G-14752)
**By Dozen Bakery Inc** .......................... G ....... 815 636-0668
Machesney Park (G-14063)
**Dimples Donuts** .................................. G ....... 630 406-0303
Batavia (G-1438)
**Do-Rite Donuts** ................................... G ....... 312 422-0150
Chicago (G-4619)
**Donut Palace** ...................................... G ....... 618 692-0532
Edwardsville (G-8795)
**Dunkin Donuts** .................................... E ....... 708 460-3088
Orland Park (G-16857)
**Express Donuts Enterprise Inc** ........... F ....... 630 510-9310
Wheaton (G-21947)
**Home Cut Donuts Inc** ......................... G ....... 815 726-2132
Joliet (G-12511)
**Honey Fluff Doughnuts** ...................... G ....... 708 579-1826
Countryside (G-7431)
**Jay Elka** .............................................. F ....... 847 540-7776
Lake Zurich (G-13091)
**Mel-O-Cream Donuts** ......................... G ....... 217 528-2303
Springfield (G-20477)
**Narima Inc** .......................................... G ....... 847 818-9620
Rolling Meadows (G-18748)
**Spunky Dunker Donuts** ...................... G ....... 847 358-7935
Palatine (G-17076)
**Walter & Kathy Anczerewicz** .............. G ....... 708 448-3676
Palos Heights (G-17113)

## BAKERY PRDTS: Doughnuts, Frozen

**Herman Seekamp Inc** ......................... C ....... 630 628-6555
Addison (G-145)
**Keystone Bakery Holdings LLC** ......... G ....... 603 792-3113
Deerfield (G-8024)
**Mel-O-Cream Donuts Intl Inc** ............. D ....... 217 483-1825
Springfield (G-20478)

## BAKERY PRDTS: Dry

**Baked By Betsy Inc** ............................. G ....... 847 292-1434
Wilmette (G-22242)
**Blissful Brownies Inc** .......................... G ....... 541 308-0226
Lake Forest (G-12887)
**Deerfield Bakery** ................................. G ....... 847 520-0068
Buffalo Grove (G-2683)
**Dobake Bakeries Inc** .......................... F ....... 630 620-1849
Addison (G-96)
**Griffin Industries LLC** ......................... G ....... 815 357-8200
Seneca (G-19886)
**Mybread LLC** ...................................... G ....... 312 600-9633
Chicago (G-5843)

## BAKERY PRDTS: Frozen

**Bear-Stewart Corporation** .................. E ....... 773 276-0400
Chicago (G-4065)
**Caramel-A Bakery Ltd** ........................ E ....... 773 227-2635
Chicago (G-4235)
**Cloverhill Pastry-Vend LLC** ................ D ....... 773 745-9800
Chicago (G-4408)
**Conagra Brands Inc** ........................... D ....... 630 455-5200
Downers Grove (G-8817)
**Earthgrains Refrigertd Dough P** ......... A ....... 630 455-5200
Downers Grove (G-8438)
**Goldies Baking Inc** ............................. F ....... 224 757-0820
Volo (G-21313)
**Griffin Industries LLC** ......................... G ....... 815 357-8200
Seneca (G-19886)
**Hillshire Brands Company** .................. B ....... 312 614-6000
Chicago (G-5089)
**Quality Bakeries LLC** ......................... F ....... 630 553-7377
Saint Charles (G-19247)
**Rich Products Corporation** ................. A ....... 815 729-4509
Crest Hill (G-7466)
**Rich Products Corporation** ................. A ....... 309 886-2465
Washington (G-21390)
**Solublend Technologies LLC** ............. G ....... 815 534-7578
Frankfort (G-10364)

## BAKERY PRDTS: Pies, Bakery, Frozen

**Imanis Original Bean Pies & F** ........... G ....... 773 716-7007
Chicago (G-5163)

## BAKERY PRDTS: Pies, Exc Frozen

**Hillshire Brands Company** .................. F ....... 630 991-5100
Downers Grove (G-8458)

## BAKERY PRDTS: Pretzels

**P Double Corporation** ......................... F ....... 630 585-7160
Aurora (G-1061)

## BAKERY PRDTS: Rice Cakes

**Quaker Oats Company** ....................... A ....... 312 821-1000
Chicago (G-6242)

## BAKERY PRDTS: Rolls, Sweet, Frozen

**Aryzta LLC** .......................................... C ....... 708 498-2300
Northlake (G-16428)

## BAKERY PRDTS: Wholesalers

**Athenian Foods Co** ............................. F ....... 708 343-6700
Melrose Park (G-14596)
**Chicago Pastry Inc** ............................. D ....... 630 529-6161
Bloomingdale (G-2100)
**Dinkels Bakery Inc** ............................. E ....... 773 281-7300
Chicago (G-4605)
**Highland Baking Company Inc** ........... A ....... 847 677-2789
Northbrook (G-16270)
**Korinek & Co Inc** ................................ G ....... 708 652-2870
Cicero (G-7210)
**La Bella Chrstnas Kitchens Inc** .......... G ....... 815 801-1600
German Valley (G-10891)
**Leesons Cakes Inc** ............................. G ....... 708 429-1330
Tinley Park (G-20930)
**Mangel and Co** ................................... F ....... 847 634-0730
Long Grove (G-13894)
**Milano Bakery Inc** .............................. E ....... 815 727-2253
Joliet (G-12542)
**New Chicago Wholesale Bky Inc** ....... E ....... 847 981-1600
Elk Grove Village (G-9650)
**Original Ferrara Inc** ............................ F ....... 312 666-2200
Chicago (G-6011)
**Riverside Bake Shop** .......................... E ....... 815 385-0044
McHenry (G-14552)
**Roma Bakeries Inc** ............................. F ....... 815 964-6737
Rockford (G-18596)
**Tam Tav Bakery Inc** ........................... E ....... 773 764-8877
Chicago (G-6669)
**Tom Tom Tamales Mfg Co Inc** ........... F ....... 773 523-5675
Chicago (G-6736)

## BAKERY: Wholesale Or Wholesale & Retail Combined

**American Blue Rbbon Hldngs LLC** ..... D ....... 708 687-7650
Oak Forest (G-16573)
**Bimbo Bakeries Usa Inc** .................... E ....... 309 797-4968
Moline (G-14919)
**Bullards Bakery** .................................. G ....... 618 842-6666
Fairfield (G-10137)
**Cbc Restaurant Corp** ......................... D ....... 773 463-0665
Chicago (G-4260)
**Chicago Bread Company** ................... F ....... 630 620-1849
Addison (G-73)
**Chicago Pastry Inc** ............................. C ....... 630 972-0404
Bolingbrook (G-2286)
**Christys Kitchen** ................................. G ....... 815 735-6791
La Salle (G-12768)
**Cookie Dough Creations Co** ............... E ....... 630 369-4833
Naperville (G-15635)
**DAmatos Bakery Inc** .......................... G ....... 312 733-6219
Chicago (G-4548)
**Doughnut Boy** .................................... G ....... 773 463-6328
Lincolnshire (G-13444)
**East Balt Commissary LLC** ................ G ....... 773 376-4444
Chicago (G-4681)
**Folsoms Bakery Inc** ........................... F ....... 815 622-7870
Rock Falls (G-18132)
**Gadgetworld Enterprises Inc** ............. G ....... 773 703-0796
Chicago (G-4907)
**Gold Standard Baking Inc** ................. C ....... 773 523-2333
Chicago (G-4971)
**Gordon Hann** ..................................... E ....... 630 761-1835
Batavia (G-1451)
**Happy Dog Barkery** ........................... F ....... 630 512-0822
Downers Grove (G-8453)
**Illinois Baking** ..................................... G ....... 773 995-7200
Chicago (G-5154)
**Kerry Ingredients & Flavours** ............. E ....... 847 595-1003
Elk Grove Village (G-9573)
**La Conchita Bakery** ............................ G ....... 847 623-4094
Waukegan (G-21578)
**La Luc Bakery Inc** .............................. G ....... 847 740-0303
Round Lake (G-19061)
**Labaquette Kedzie Inc** ....................... G ....... 773 925-0455
Chicago (G-5429)
**Le Petit Pain Holdings LLC** ................ G ....... 312 981-3770
Chicago (G-5478)
**Leonards Bakery** ................................ G ....... 847 564-4977
Northbrook (G-16294)
**Liborio Baking Co Inc** ........................ G ....... 708 452-7222
River Grove (G-18010)
**Maiers Bakery** .................................... G ....... 847 967-8042
Morton Grove (G-15216)
**Mandys Kitchen & Grill** ...................... G ....... 630 348-2264
Bolingbrook (G-2339)
**Manna Organics LLC** ........................ F ....... 630 795-0500
Lisle (G-13618)
**Mariegold Bake Shoppe** .................... G ....... 773 561-1978
Chicago (G-5617)
**OBrothers Bakery Inc** ........................ G ....... 847 249-0091
Waukegan (G-21597)
**Pin Hsiao & Associates LLC** .............. E ....... 206 818-0155
Flossmoor (G-10227)
**Red Hen Corporation** ......................... G ....... 312 433-0436
Elmhurst (G-9928)
**Roesers Bakery** .................................. E ....... 773 489-6900
Chicago (G-6379)
**Rolfs Patisserie Inc** ............................ C ....... 847 675-6565
Lincolnwood (G-13534)
**Sara Lee Baking Group** ..................... G ....... 217 585-3462
Springfield (G-20518)
**Swirlcup** .............................................. G ....... 847 229-2200
Lincolnshire (G-13483)
**Todays Temptations Inc** ..................... F ....... 773 385-5355
Chicago (G-6733)
**Two Figs Baking Co** ........................... G ....... 847 233-0500
Franklin Park (G-10614)

## BALERS

**Coyote Transportation Inc** ................. G ....... 630 204-5729
Bensenville (G-1869)

## BALLASTS: Fluorescent

**Radionic Industries Inc** ...................... C ....... 773 804-0100
Chicago (G-6282)

## BALLASTS: Lighting

**Lumenergi Inc** .................................... E ....... 866 921-4652
Chicago (G-5564)

## BALLOON SHOPS

**Fanfest Corporation** ........................... G ....... 847 658-2000
Crystal Lake (G-7576)

## BALLOONS: Hot Air

**A R B C Inc** ........................................ F ....... 815 777-6006
Galena (G-10714)
**Strauss Facter Assoc Inc** ................... G ....... 847 759-1100
Park Ridge (G-17224)

## BALLOONS: Rubber Laminated Metal Foil

**CTI Industries Corporation** ................ C ....... 847 382-1000
Lake Barrington (G-12804)

## BALLOONS: Toy & Advertising, Rubber

**A R B C Inc** ........................................ F ....... 815 777-6006
Galena (G-10714)
**Balloon Art By Dj** ................................ G ....... 815 736-6123
Newark (G-15932)
**Boss Balloon Company Inc** ................ G ....... 309 852-2131
Kewanee (G-12672)
**Boss Holdings Inc** .............................. D ....... 309 852-2131
Kewanee (G-12673)
**CTI Industries Corporation** ................ D ....... 800 284-5605
Lake Zurich (G-13060)

## BANDS: Plastic

**Tni Packaging Inc** .............................. G ....... 630 293-3030
West Chicago (G-21781)

## BANKS: State Commercial

**Harris Bmo Bank National Assn** ........ E ....... 815 886-1900
Romeoville (G-18830)

# PRODUCT SECTION

### BANNERS: Fabric
- Action Advertising Inc .......... G .... 312 791-0660
  Chicago *(G-3740)*
- Fabric Images Inc .......... D .... 847 488-9877
  Elgin *(G-9032)*

### BANQUET HALL FACILITIES
- City Living Design Inc .......... G .... 312 335-0711
  Chicago *(G-4383)*
- Hidden Lake Winery Ltd .......... E .... 618 228-9111
  Aviston *(G-1244)*

### BAR
- Murphys Pub .......... G .... 847 526-1431
  Wauconda *(G-21488)*

### BARBECUE EQPT
- Apache Supply .......... G .... 708 409-1040
  Melrose Park *(G-14595)*
- Belson Outdoors LLC .......... E .... 630 897-8489
  North Aurora *(G-16120)*
- Chadwick Manufacturing Ltd .......... G .... 815 684-5152
  Chadwick *(G-3440)*
- Home & Leisure Lifestyles LLC .......... G .... 618 651-0358
  Highland *(G-11797)*
- Homefire Hearth Inc .......... G .... 815 997-1123
  Rockford *(G-18422)*
- Kalamazoo Outdoor Gourmet LLC .......... G .... 312 423-8770
  Chicago *(G-5353)*
- Weber-Stephen Products LLC .......... B .... 847 934-5700
  Palatine *(G-17088)*
- Weber-Stephen Products LLC .......... G .... 224 836-8536
  Palatine *(G-17089)*
- Weber-Stephen Products LLC .......... F .... 847 669-4900
  Huntley *(G-12183)*

### BARBER SHOPS
- Abyss Salon Inc .......... G .... 312 880-0263
  Chicago *(G-3713)*

### BARGES BUILDING & REPAIR
- Midland Manufacturing Corp .......... C .... 847 677-0333
  Skokie *(G-20039)*

### BARRELS: Shipping, Metal
- Mauser Usa LLC .......... G .... 773 261-2332
  Chicago *(G-5657)*

### BARRICADES: Metal
- Builders Chicago Corporation .......... D .... 224 654-2122
  Rosemont *(G-18991)*
- Energy Absorption Systems Inc .......... E .... 312 467-6750
  Chicago *(G-4750)*
- Infrastructure Def Tech LLC .......... G .... 800 379-1822
  Belvidere *(G-1763)*
- Nafisco Inc .......... F .... 815 372-3300
  Romeoville *(G-18851)*
- North American Safety Products .......... G .... 815 469-1144
  Mokena *(G-14888)*
- Quixote Transportation Safety .......... D .... 312 467-6750
  Chicago *(G-6260)*

### BARS & BAR SHAPES: Copper & Copper Alloy
- Ampco Metal Incorporated .......... E .... 847 437-6000
  Arlington Heights *(G-711)*

### BARS & BAR SHAPES: Steel, Hot-Rolled
- Kaltband North America Inc .......... F .... 773 248-6684
  Chicago *(G-5355)*

### BARS, COLD FINISHED: Steel, From Purchased Hot-Rolled
- A & A Steel Fabricating Co .......... F .... 708 389-4499
  Posen *(G-17726)*
- Corey Steel Company .......... C .... 800 323-2750
  Cicero *(G-7185)*
- Krueger and Company .......... E .... 630 833-5650
  Elmhurst *(G-9899)*
- Nelsen Steel and Wire LP .......... D .... 847 671-9700
  Franklin Park *(G-10540)*
- Niagara Lasalle Corporation .......... C .... 708 596-2700
  South Holland *(G-20293)*

- Taubensee Steel & Wire Company .......... C .... 847 459-5100
  Wheeling *(G-22164)*
- Tinsley Steel Inc .......... G .... 618 656-5231
  Edwardsville *(G-8817)*
- Worth Steel and Machine Co .......... E .... 708 388-6300
  Alsip *(G-546)*

### BARS, PIPES, PLATES & SHAPES: Lead/Lead Alloy Bars, Pipe
- Nuclear Power Outfitters LLC .......... F .... 630 963-0320
  Lisle *(G-13634)*

### BARS, PLATES & SHEETS: Zinc & Zinc Alloy Bars, Plates, Etc
- Midland Industries Inc .......... E .... 312 664-7300
  Chicago *(G-5734)*

### BARS: Cargo, Stabilizing, Metal
- Black Mountain Products Inc .......... G .... 224 655-5955
  McHenry *(G-14482)*
- Durabilt Dyvex Inc .......... F .... 708 397-4673
  Broadview *(G-2573)*
- V & N Metal Products Inc .......... G .... 773 436-1855
  Chicago *(G-6863)*

### BARS: Concrete Reinforcing, Fabricated Steel
- Advance Welding & Equipment .......... F .... 630 759-3334
  Countryside *(G-7411)*
- Advanced Assembly .......... G .... 630 379-6158
  Streamwood *(G-20639)*
- American Classic Rebar Corp .......... G .... 708 225-1010
  South Holland *(G-20243)*
- Bohler .......... G .... 630 883-3000
  Elgin *(G-8969)*
- Dayton Superior Corporation .......... G .... 219 476-4106
  Kankakee *(G-12608)*
- Duroweld Company Inc .......... E .... 847 680-3064
  Lake Bluff *(G-12841)*
- Gerdau Ameristeel US Inc .......... F .... 815 544-9651
  Belvidere *(G-1756)*
- Great Lakes Stair & Steel Inc .......... G .... 708 430-2323
  Chicago Ridge *(G-7148)*
- H3 Group LLC .......... F .... 309 222-6027
  Peoria *(G-17377)*
- Headhunter2000 Inc .......... G .... 708 533-3769
  Northlake *(G-16438)*
- J and D Installers Inc .......... G .... 847 288-0783
  Franklin Park *(G-10501)*
- L & M Welding Inc .......... F .... 773 237-8500
  Chicago *(G-5419)*
- Lockport Steel Fabricators LLC .......... D .... 815 726-6281
  Lockport *(G-13728)*
- Mercedes Fabrication .......... F .... 708 709-9240
  Chicago Heights *(G-7112)*
- Metals and Services Inc .......... D .... 630 627-2900
  Addison *(G-202)*
- OMalley Welding and Fabg .......... G .... 630 553-1604
  Yorkville *(G-22667)*
- On Target Grinding and Mfg .......... G .... 708 418-3905
  Lynwood *(G-14022)*
- Steel Fabricating Inc .......... F .... 815 977-5355
  Rockford *(G-18633)*
- Steel Rebar Manufacturing LLC .......... G .... 618 920-2748
  Centreville *(G-3438)*
- Superior Metalcraft Inc .......... F .... 708 418-8940
  Lansing *(G-13188)*
- Thirteen Rf Inc .......... E .... 618 687-1313
  Murphysboro *(G-15585)*
- Vermilion Steel Fabrication .......... G .... 217 442-5300
  Danville *(G-7778)*

### BASEMENT WINDOW AREAWAYS: Concrete
- S & M Basements .......... G .... 618 533-1939
  Centralia *(G-3430)*
- Windo Well Cover Co .......... G .... 630 554-0366
  Oswego *(G-16941)*

### BASES, BEVERAGE
- Beverage Flavors Intl LLC .......... F .... 773 248-3860
  Chicago *(G-4097)*
- Insight Beverages Inc .......... G .... 847 438-1598
  Lake Zurich *(G-13089)*
- Insight Beverages Inc .......... F .... 847 438-1598
  Lake Zurich *(G-13090)*

- Lansing Wings Inc .......... G .... 708 895-3300
  Lansing *(G-13171)*
- Mondelez Global LLC .......... C .... 847 943-4000
  Deerfield *(G-8037)*
- Supreme Juice Co .......... F .... 773 277-5800
  Chicago *(G-6639)*

### BATH SALTS
- Oak Court Creations .......... G .... 815 467-7676
  Minooka *(G-14845)*

### BATH SHOPS
- Stonecrafters Inc .......... E .... 815 363-8730
  Lakemoor *(G-13148)*

### BATHROOM ACCESS & FITTINGS: Vitreous China & Earthenware
- Wonder Kids Inc .......... G .... 773 437-8025
  Evanston *(G-10107)*

### BATHROOM FIXTURES: Plastic
- Carstin Brands Inc .......... D .... 217 543-3331
  Arthur *(G-885)*
- Northwest Marble Products .......... E .... 630 860-2288
  Hoffman Estates *(G-12072)*

### BATTERIES, EXC AUTOMOTIVE: Wholesalers
- Batteries Plus 287 .......... G .... 630 279-3478
  Villa Park *(G-21237)*
- Gingrich Enterprises Inc .......... E .... 309 923-7312
  Roanoke *(G-18050)*
- Interstate All Battery Center .......... F .... 217 214-1069
  Quincy *(G-17840)*
- Interstate Battery System Intl .......... G .... 708 424-2288
  Oak Lawn *(G-16626)*
- Storage Battery Systems LLC .......... G .... 630 221-1700
  Carol Stream *(G-3251)*

### BATTERIES: Alkaline, Cell Storage
- Duracell Company .......... G .... 203 796-4000
  Chicago *(G-4655)*
- Newly Weds Foods Inc .......... D .... 773 628-6900
  Chicago *(G-5900)*
- Spectrum Brands Inc .......... G .... 815 285-6500
  Dixon *(G-8353)*

### BATTERIES: Lead Acid, Storage
- Exide Technologies .......... C .... 630 862-2200
  Aurora *(G-1005)*
- Exide Technologies .......... D .... 678 566-9000
  Lombard *(G-13798)*

### BATTERIES: Nickel-Cadmium
- Hubbell Power Systems Inc .......... F .... 618 797-5000
  Edwardsville *(G-8803)*

### BATTERIES: Rechargeable
- A123 Systems LLC .......... G .... 617 778-5700
  Elgin *(G-8930)*
- Advanced Battery LLC .......... F .... 309 755-7775
  Milan *(G-14772)*
- All Cell Technologies LLC .......... E .... 773 922-1155
  Chicago *(G-3805)*
- Iterna LLC .......... E .... 630 585-7400
  Aurora *(G-1035)*
- National Power Corp .......... E .... 773 685-2662
  Chicago *(G-5867)*
- Palladium Energy Group Inc .......... D .... 630 410-7900
  Woodridge *(G-22507)*
- Technical Power Systems Inc .......... E .... 630 719-1471
  Lisle *(G-13670)*

### BATTERIES: Storage
- Batteries Plus 287 .......... G .... 630 279-3478
  Villa Park *(G-21237)*
- Bell City Battery Mfg Inc .......... G .... 618 233-0437
  Belleville *(G-1611)*
- Crown Battery Manufacturing Co .......... G .... 630 530-8060
  Villa Park *(G-21247)*
- Crown Battery Manufacturing Co .......... G .... 708 946-2535
  Beecher *(G-1597)*
- Ecolocap Solutions Inc .......... G .... 866 479-7041
  Barrington *(G-1279)*

## BATTERIES: Storage

Enersys .................................................. D ...... 630 455-4872
  Lisle *(G-13587)*
Firefly International Enrgy Co ............... G ...... 781 937-0619
  Peoria *(G-17361)*
Ill Battery Spxcialists L ......................... G ...... 773 478-8600
  Chicago *(G-5153)*
Interstate All Battery Center ................. F ...... 217 214-1069
  Quincy *(G-17840)*
Interstate Battery System Intl ................ G ...... 708 424-2288
  Oak Lawn *(G-16626)*
Inventus Power Holdings Inc ................ D ...... 630 410-7900
  Woodridge *(G-22498)*
Johnson Contrls Btry Group Inc ............ B ...... 630 232-4270
  Geneva *(G-10842)*
P L R Sales Inc ..................................... G ...... 217 733-2245
  Fairmount *(G-10164)*
Performance Battery Group Inc ............ G ...... 630 293-5505
  West Chicago *(G-21755)*
Storage Battery Systems LLC ............... G ...... 630 221-1700
  Carol Stream *(G-3251)*

## BATTERIES: Wet

Exide Technologies ................................ C ...... 630 862-2200
  Aurora *(G-1005)*
Exide Technologies ................................ D ...... 678 566-9000
  Lombard *(G-13798)*
Larrys Better Built Battery ..................... G ...... 618 758-2011
  Coulterville *(G-7401)*

## BATTERY CASES: Plastic Or Plastics Combination

GE Polymers LLC ................................... G ...... 312 674-7434
  Hinsdale *(G-11947)*
Jessup Manufacturing Company .......... D ...... 815 385-6650
  Mchenry *(G-14517)*

## BATTERY CHARGERS

Charles Industries Ltd ........................... D ...... 217 932-2068
  Casey *(G-3381)*
Inventus Power Inc ................................ C ...... 630 410-7900
  Woodridge *(G-22496)*
La Marche Mfg Co ................................. C ...... 847 299-1188
  Des Plaines *(G-8220)*
Master Control Systems Inc .................. E ...... 847 295-1010
  Lake Bluff *(G-12856)*
Nexergy Tauber LLC .............................. A ...... 708 316-4407
  Westchester *(G-21851)*
Radionic Hi-Tech Inc .............................. D ...... 773 804-0100
  Chicago *(G-6281)*
Safecharge LLC ..................................... G ...... 248 866-9428
  Chicago *(G-6426)*
Schumacher Electric Corp ..................... D ...... 847 385-1600
  Mount Prospect *(G-15372)*
Schumacher Electric Corp ..................... E ...... 217 283-5551
  Hoopeston *(G-12115)*

## BATTERY CHARGERS: Storage, Motor & Engine Generator Type

Heng Tuo Usa Inc .................................. G ...... 630 705-1898
  Oakbrook Terrace *(G-16710)*
Luon Energy LLC ................................... G ...... 217 419-2678
  Savoy *(G-19411)*
UPS Power Management Inc ................. F ...... 844 877-2288
  Chicago *(G-6842)*

## BEADS: Unassembled

A Beadtiful Thing ................................... G ...... 630 236-5913
  Aurora *(G-953)*

## BEARINGS

Aurora Bearing Company ...................... B ...... 630 897-8941
  Montgomery *(G-15027)*
Babbitting Service Inc ............................ D ...... 847 841-8008
  South Elgin *(G-20184)*
Composite Bearings Mfg ....................... F ...... 630 595-8334
  Wood Dale *(G-22354)*
Nb Corporation of America ................... E ...... 630 295-8880
  Hanover Park *(G-11586)*
Technymon Technology USA Inc .......... G ...... 630 787-0501
  Wood Dale *(G-22428)*

## BEARINGS & PARTS Ball

American NTN Bearing Mfg Corp .......... B ...... 847 741-4545
  Elgin *(G-8950)*
American NTN Bearing Mfg Corp .......... E ...... 847 671-5450
  Schiller Park *(G-19801)*
Frantz Manufacturing Company ........... D ...... 815 625-7063
  Sterling *(G-20592)*
Mechanical Power Inc ........................... E ...... 847 487-0070
  Wauconda *(G-21481)*
NTN USA Corporation ............................ G ...... 847 298-4652
  Mount Prospect *(G-15357)*
Pacific Bearing Corp .............................. E ...... 815 389-5600
  Roscoe *(G-18911)*
Precision Plastic Ball Co ........................ G ...... 847 678-2255
  Franklin Park *(G-10559)*

## BEARINGS: Ball & Roller

Allegion S&S US Holding Co .................. C ...... 815 875-3311
  Princeton *(G-17742)*
Alternative Bearings Corp ..................... E ...... 847 240-9630
  Schaumburg *(G-19435)*
Bearings Manufacturing Company ....... F ...... 773 583-6703
  Chicago *(G-4067)*
HRB America Corporation ..................... G ...... 630 513-1800
  Saint Charles *(G-19195)*
Peer Bearing Company .......................... C ...... 877 600-7337
  Waukegan *(G-21600)*
Roberts Swiss Inc .................................. E ...... 630 467-9100
  Itasca *(G-12348)*
SKF USA Inc .......................................... G ...... 847 742-0700
  Elgin *(G-9185)*
SKF USA Inc .......................................... G ...... 847 742-0700
  Elgin *(G-9186)*
Thomson Linear LLC ............................. C ...... 815 568-8001
  Marengo *(G-14243)*
Timken Company ................................... G ...... 309 692-8150
  Peoria *(G-17469)*

## BEARINGS: Railroad Car Journal

Lv Ventures Inc ...................................... G ...... 312 993-1800
  Chicago *(G-5571)*

## BEARINGS: Roller & Parts

Ccty USA Bearing Co ............................. G ...... 847 540-8196
  Lake Zurich *(G-13051)*
Frantz Manufacturing Company ........... G ...... 815 625-3333
  Sterling *(G-20591)*
NTN Bearing Corporation ...................... G ...... 847 298-7500
  Macomb *(G-14127)*
NTN-Bower Corporation ......................... G ...... 309 837-0440
  Macomb *(G-14128)*
NTN-Bower Corporation ......................... A ...... 309 837-0322
  Macomb *(G-14129)*

## BEAUTY & BARBER SHOP EQPT

A Stucki Company .................................. E ...... 618 498-4442
  Jerseyville *(G-12416)*
Accurate Parts Mfg Co ........................... E ...... 630 616-4125
  Bensenville *(G-1813)*
Alpha Industries Inc .............................. G ...... 847 945-1740
  Deerfield *(G-7974)*
Anfinsen Plastic Moulding Inc .............. E ...... 630 554-4100
  Oswego *(G-16904)*
Belvedere Usa LLC ................................ E ...... 815 544-3131
  Belvidere *(G-1736)*
Buhrke Industries LLC ........................... E ...... 847 981-7550
  Downers Grove *(G-8400)*
Ccar Industries ...................................... G ...... 217 345-3300
  Charleston *(G-3591)*
Clown Global Brands LLC ..................... G ...... 847 564-5950
  Northbrook *(G-16227)*
Conair Corporation ................................ E ...... 203 351-9000
  Rantoul *(G-17924)*
E2 Manufacturing Group LLC ............... G ...... 224 399-9608
  Waukegan *(G-21554)*
Gilster-Mary Lee Corporation ............... G ...... 618 826-3102
  Chester *(G-3656)*
Hearthside Food Solutions LLC ........... C ...... 217 784-4238
  Gibson City *(G-10901)*
Hu-Friedy Mfg Co LLC ........................... F ...... 847 257-4500
  Des Plaines *(G-8206)*
Hue Circle Inc ........................................ G ...... 224 567-8116
  Glenview *(G-11138)*
Idex Mpt Inc ........................................... G ...... 630 530-3333
  Elmhurst *(G-9884)*
In Aaw Hair Emporium LLC ................... G ...... 779 227-1450
  Joliet *(G-12515)*
Ironwood Mfg Inc ................................... G ...... 630 778-8963
  Naperville *(G-15679)*
Jf Industries Inc .................................... G ...... 773 775-8840
  Chicago *(G-5301)*
Leapfrog Product Dev LLC .................... F ...... 312 229-0089
  Chicago *(G-5480)*
Linx ........................................................ G ...... 847 910-5303
  Chicago *(G-5515)*
Medline Industries Inc .......................... F ...... 847 557-2400
  Libertyville *(G-13352)*
Mgn Tool & Mfg Co Inc .......................... G ...... 630 849-3575
  Carol Stream *(G-3195)*
Quad-Illinois Inc .................................... F ...... 847 836-1115
  Elgin *(G-9155)*
Riverside Memorial Co .......................... G ...... 217 323-1280
  Beardstown *(G-1527)*
Riviera Tan Spa (del) ............................. G ...... 618 466-1012
  Godfrey *(G-11235)*
Scimatco Office ..................................... E ...... 630 879-1306
  Batavia *(G-1494)*
Skin Care Systems ................................ G ...... 312 644-9067
  Chicago *(G-6521)*
Technical Power Systems Inc ............... E ...... 630 719-1471
  Lisle *(G-13670)*
Trident Industries .................................. F ...... 847 285-1316
  Schaumburg *(G-19773)*
Troy Design & Manufacturing Co ......... G ...... 773 646-0804
  Chicago *(G-6782)*
Veeco Manufacturing Inc ....................... E ...... 312 666-0900
  Melrose Park *(G-14705)*

## BEAUTY & BARBER SHOP EQPT & SPLYS WHOLESALERS

Bee Sales Comapny ............................... D ...... 847 600-4400
  Niles *(G-15965)*
Hue Circle Inc ........................................ G ...... 224 567-8116
  Glenview *(G-11138)*

## BEAUTY SALONS

Cindys Nail & Hair Care ........................ G ...... 847 234-0780
  Lake Forest *(G-12891)*
D-Orum Corporation .............................. F ...... 773 567-2064
  Chicago *(G-4538)*
Ecoco Inc ............................................... E ...... 773 745-7700
  Chicago *(G-4693)*
Gbn Nails LLC ....................................... G ...... 773 881-8880
  Chicago *(G-4921)*
Glass Artistry ........................................ G ...... 847 998-5800
  Northbrook *(G-16265)*
Kim Tiffani Institute LLC ....................... D ...... 312 260-9000
  Lincolnwood *(G-13519)*
Lab TEC Cosmt By Marzena Inc ........... F ...... 630 396-3970
  Addison *(G-176)*
Skin Care Systems ................................ G ...... 312 644-9067
  Chicago *(G-6521)*

## BED SHEETING, COTTON

Alpha Bedding LLC ............................... F ...... 847 550-5110
  Lake Zurich *(G-13039)*

## BEDDING, BEDSPREAD, BLANKET/SHEET: Pillowcase, Purchd Mtrl

Personalized Pillows Co ........................ G ...... 847 226-7393
  Wadsworth *(G-21325)*

## BEDDING, BEDSPREADS, BLANKETS & SHEETS: Comforters & Quilts

Quiltmaster Inc ...................................... E ...... 847 426-6741
  Carpentersville *(G-3300)*

## BEDS: Hospital

Kci Satellite .......................................... G ...... 800 664-2602
  Pittsfield *(G-17571)*
Kreg Medical Inc ................................... G ...... 312 829-8904
  Melrose Park *(G-14668)*

## BEDS: Inflatable

Aero Products Holdings Inc .................. E ...... 847 485-3200
  Schaumburg *(G-19424)*
Eaton Inflatable LLC ............................. E ...... 312 664-7867
  Chicago *(G-4685)*
Polygroup Services NA Inc ................... G ...... 847 851-9995
  East Dundee *(G-8653)*

## BEDSPREADS & BED SETS, FROM PURCHASED MATERIALS

Tailored Inc ........................................... G ...... 708 387-9854
  Brookfield *(G-2643)*

# PRODUCT SECTION

Unitex Industries Inc .................................. G ...... 708 524-0664
  Oak Park  *(G-16690)*

## BEDSPREADS, COTTON

Dec Art Designs Inc ................................... G ...... 312 329-0553
  Northbrook  *(G-16240)*

## BEEKEEPERS' SPLYS

Sweet Beginnings LLC ............................... G ...... 773 638-7058
  Chicago  *(G-6647)*

## BEEKEEPERS' SPLYS: Honeycomb Foundations

Dadant & Sons Inc ..................................... D ...... 217 847-3324
  Hamilton  *(G-11533)*

## BEER & ALE WHOLESALERS

Church Street Brewing Co LLC ................ G ...... 630 438-5725
  Itasca  *(G-12244)*

## BEER & ALE, WHOLESALE: Beer & Other Fermented Malt Liquors

Dresbach Distributing Co .......................... G ...... 815 223-0116
  Peru  *(G-17507)*
Finchs Beer Company  LLC ...................... G ...... 773 919-8012
  Chicago  *(G-4844)*
RJ Distributing Co ...................................... E ...... 309 685-2794
  East Peoria  *(G-8731)*

## BEER, WINE & LIQUOR STORES

Cub Foods Inc ............................................. C ...... 309 689-0140
  Peoria  *(G-17347)*

## BEER, WINE & LIQUOR STORES: Beer, Packaged

Walter Lagestee Inc ................................... C ...... 708 957-2974
  Homewood  *(G-12106)*

## BEER, WINE & LIQUOR STORES: Wine

Bella Terra Winery  LLC ............................. F ...... 618 658-8882
  Creal Springs  *(G-7453)*
Kickapoo Creek Winery ............................ G ...... 309 495-9463
  Edwards  *(G-8782)*
Mangel and Co ............................................ E ...... 847 459-3100
  Buffalo Grove  *(G-2730)*
Waterman Winery & Vineyards ................ G ...... 815 264-3268
  Waterman  *(G-21411)*

## BEER, WINE & LIQUOR STORES: Wine & Beer

Two Brothers Brewing Company ............ G ...... 630 393-2337
  Warrenville  *(G-21367)*

## BELLOWS

Brock Industrial Services  LLC ................. E ...... 815 730-3350
  Joliet  *(G-12467)*
Commercial Dynamics Inc ........................ G ...... 847 439-5300
  Arlington Heights  *(G-737)*
Flex-Weld Inc .............................................. D ...... 815 334-3662
  Woodstock  *(G-22567)*
James Walker Mfg Co ............................... E ...... 708 754-4020
  Glenwood  *(G-11217)*
Microlution Inc ............................................ E ...... 773 282-6495
  Chicago  *(G-5724)*

## BELLOWS ASSEMBLIES: Missiles, Metal

Duraflex Inc ................................................. E ...... 847 462-1007
  Cary  *(G-3336)*

## BELTING: Plastic

Chemi-Flex LLC .......................................... E ...... 630 627-9650
  Lombard  *(G-13776)*
Molds & Tooling ......................................... E ...... 630 627-9650
  Lombard  *(G-13828)*

## BELTING: Rubber

Bando Usa Inc ............................................ E ...... 630 773-6600
  Itasca  *(G-12234)*
Voss Belting & Specialty Co .................... E ...... 847 673-8900
  Lincolnwood  *(G-13541)*

## BELTS & BELT PRDTS

Ammeraal Beltech Inc ............................... G ...... 847 673-1736
  Skokie  *(G-19954)*

## BELTS: Chain

John King Usa  Inc .................................... G ...... 309 698-9250
  East Peoria  *(G-8718)*

## BELTS: Conveyor, Made From Purchased Wire

Ammeraal Beltech Inc ............................... D ...... 847 673-6720
  Skokie  *(G-19955)*
Trico Belting & Supply Company ........... F ...... 773 261-0988
  Chicago  *(G-6776)*

## BELTS: Seat, Automotive & Aircraft

Deyco Inc ..................................................... G ...... 630 553-5666
  Yorkville  *(G-22656)*
Hooker Custom Harness Inc .................... G ...... 815 233-5478
  Freeport  *(G-10666)*

## BENCHES, WORK : Factory

L & D Group Inc .......................................... B ...... 630 892-8941
  Montgomery  *(G-15051)*
Macon Metal Products Co ........................ G ...... 217 824-7205
  Taylorville  *(G-20842)*

## BENCHES: Seating

Center-111 W Burnham Wash LLC ......... E ...... 312 368-6320
  Chicago  *(G-4269)*
J C Decaux New York Inc ......................... E ...... 312 456-2999
  Chicago  *(G-5258)*
T2 Site Amenities Incorporated .............. G ...... 847 579-9003
  Highland Park  *(G-11876)*

## BENTONITE MINING

Amcol International Corp ......................... E ...... 847 851-1500
  Hoffman Estates  *(G-11991)*
American Colloid Company ..................... E ...... 618 452-8143
  Granite City  *(G-11263)*
American Colloid Company ..................... F ...... 304 882-2123
  Elgin  *(G-8947)*
American Colloid Company ..................... E ...... 847 851-1700
  Hoffman Estates  *(G-11992)*

## BEVERAGE BASES & SYRUPS

Passion Fruit Drink Inc ............................. G ...... 708 769-4749
  South Holland  *(G-20296)*

## BEVERAGE POWDERS

Inside Beverages ....................................... C ...... 847 438-1338
  Lake Zurich  *(G-13088)*
Kraft Foods Asia PCF Svcs LLC ............. C ...... 847 943-4000
  Deerfield  *(G-8026)*
Kraft Heinz Company ................................ C ...... 847 646-2000
  Glenview  *(G-11160)*
Kruger North America Inc ....................... F ...... 708 851-3670
  Oak Park  *(G-16673)*
Mondelez International Inc ...................... A ...... 847 943-4000
  Deerfield  *(G-8038)*
Treehouse Foods Inc ................................ B ...... 708 483-1300
  Oak Brook  *(G-16565)*
Ur Inc ............................................................ G ...... 630 450-5279
  Batavia  *(G-1513)*

## BEVERAGE PRDTS: Brewers' Grain

Rolling Meadows Brewery  LLC .............. G ...... 217 725-2492
  Springfield  *(G-20514)*

## BEVERAGE PRDTS: Malt Syrup

Alao  Temitope ............................................ F ...... 331 454-3333
  Collinsville  *(G-7313)*

## BEVERAGE PRDTS: Malt, Corn

Warner  Harvey Lee Farm Inc ................. G ...... 217 849-2548
  Toledo  *(G-20970)*

## BEVERAGE STORES

Balon International Corp .......................... E ...... 773 379-7779
  Chicago  *(G-4034)*
Coca-Cola Refreshments USA Inc ......... F ...... 217 348-1001
  Charleston  *(G-3595)*

# BEVERAGES, ALCOHOLIC: Beer & Ale

Insight Beverages Inc ............................... F ...... 847 438-1598
  Lake Zurich  *(G-13090)*
Jel Sert Co ................................................... B ...... 630 231-7590
  West Chicago  *(G-21727)*

## BEVERAGE, NONALCOHOLIC: Iced Tea/Fruit Drink, Bottled/Canned

Home Juice Corp ........................................ G ...... 708 681-2678
  Melrose Park  *(G-14654)*

## BEVERAGES, ALCOHOLIC: Ale

Aero Alehouse ............................................ G ...... 815 977-5602
  Loves Park  *(G-13914)*
Ale Syndicate Brewers  LLC .................... G ...... 773 340-2337
  Chicago  *(G-3799)*
Church Street Brewing Co LLC .............. G ...... 630 438-5725
  Itasca  *(G-12244)*
Colleagues of Beer  Inc ............................ G ...... 847 727-3318
  Grayslake  *(G-11327)*
Wirtz Beverage Illinois  LLC ..................... C ...... 847 228-9000
  Cicero  *(G-7246)*

## BEVERAGES, ALCOHOLIC: Beer

Aldi Inc ......................................................... F ...... 815 877-0861
  Machesney Park  *(G-14055)*
Anheuser-Busch LLC ................................ C ...... 708 206-2881
  Country Club Hills  *(G-7404)*
Anheuser-Busch LLC ................................ C ...... 630 512-9002
  Lisle  *(G-13561)*
Argus Brewery ............................................ G ...... 773 941-4050
  Chicago  *(G-3944)*
Blue Island Beer Co .................................. G ...... 708 954-8085
  Blue Island  *(G-2239)*
Bob C Beverages  LLC .............................. G ...... 847 520-7582
  Wheeling  *(G-22016)*
Caulfields Restaurant Ltd ........................ E ...... 708 798-1599
  Flossmoor  *(G-10223)*
Chicago Beverage Systems LLC ............ E ...... 773 826-4100
  Chicago  *(G-4305)*
Cicerone Certification Program .............. G ...... 773 549-4800
  Chicago  *(G-4377)*
Crushed Grapes Ltd .................................. G ...... 618 659-3530
  Millstadt  *(G-14822)*
Crystal Lake Beer Company ................... F ...... 779 220-9288
  Crystal Lake  *(G-7559)*
Emmetts Tavern & Brewing Co ............... G ...... 630 434-8500
  Downers Grove  *(G-8441)*
Emmetts Tavern & Brewing Co ............... G ...... 630 480-7181
  Wheaton  *(G-21945)*
Emmetts Tavern & Brewing Co ............... F ...... 847 359-1533
  Palatine  *(G-17025)*
Emmetts Tavern & Brewing Co ............... E ...... 847 428-4500
  West Dundee  *(G-21796)*
Finchs Beer Company  LLC ...................... G ...... 773 919-8012
  Chicago  *(G-4844)*
Forbidden Root  A Benefit LLC ............... G ...... 312 464-7910
  Chicago  *(G-4871)*
Glazers Stoller Distrg LLC ....................... G ...... 847 350-3200
  Franklin Park  *(G-10479)*
Golden Eagle Distributing LLC ............... F ...... 618 993-8900
  Marion  *(G-14263)*
Haymarket Brewing Company  LLC ....... G ...... 312 638-0700
  Chicago  *(G-5056)*
Lincoln Park Brewery Inc ......................... D ...... 312 915-0071
  Chicago  *(G-5507)*
Millercoors LLC .......................................... A ...... 312 496-2700
  Chicago  *(G-5760)*
Resco 8 LLC ................................................ D ...... 773 772-4422
  Chicago  *(G-6336)*
Rock Bottom Minneapolis Inc ................. D ...... 312 755-9339
  Chicago  *(G-6373)*
St Nicholas Brewing Co ........................... G ...... 618 318-3556
  Du Quoin  *(G-8558)*
Tenth and Blake Beer Company ............. F ...... 312 496-2759
  Chicago  *(G-6702)*

## BEVERAGES, ALCOHOLIC: Beer & Ale

Apple Rush Company ............................... G ...... 847 730-5324
  Glenview  *(G-11104)*
Breakroom Brewery ................................... G ...... 773 564-9534
  Chicago  *(G-4160)*
Carlyle Brewing Co ................................... G ...... 815 963-2739
  Rockford  *(G-18297)*
City Beverage LLC .................................... D ...... 708 333-4360
  Markham  *(G-14302)*
Drewrys Brewing Company ..................... G ...... 815 385-9115
  McHenry  *(G-14498)*

Employee Codes: A=Over 500 employees, B=251-500
C=101-250, D=51-100, E=20-50, F=10-19, G=3-9

# BEVERAGES, ALCOHOLIC: Beer & Ale

Fulton Street Brewery LLC .............E....... 312 915-0071
  Chicago (G-4896)
Goose Holdings Inc ........................E....... 312 226-1119
  Chicago (G-4979)
Half Acre Beer Company .................F....... 773 248-4038
  Chicago (G-5035)
Lagunitas Brewing Company ............C....... 773 522-1308
  Chicago (G-5438)
Libertyville Brewing Company ..........D....... 847 362-6688
  Libertyville (G-13343)
Millercoors LLC ..............................E....... 312 496-2700
  Chicago (G-5761)
Only Child Brewing Company LLC .....G....... 847 877-9822
  Gurnee (G-11481)
Pyramid ........................................G....... 708 468-8140
  Tinley Park (G-20940)

## BEVERAGES, ALCOHOLIC: Cocktails

Cliffords Pub Inc ............................G....... 847 259-3000
  Palatine (G-17011)
Kats Meow ....................................G....... 815 747-2113
  East Dubuque (G-8618)
North Shore Distillery LLC ...............G....... 847 574-2499
  Libertyville (G-13363)

## BEVERAGES, ALCOHOLIC: Distilled Liquors

Agave Loco LLC ............................F....... 847 383-6052
  Vernon Hills (G-21142)
Beam Global Spirits & Wine LLC ......C....... 847 948-8888
  Deerfield (G-7990)
Beam Suntory Inc ..........................C....... 847 948-8888
  Deerfield (G-7991)
Callison Distributing LLC ................D....... 618 277-4300
  Belleville (G-1616)
Dtrs Enterprises Inc .......................G....... 630 296-6890
  Bolingbrook (G-2302)
Glunz Fmly Winery Cellars Inc .........E....... 847 548-9463
  Grayslake (G-11342)
Jim Beam Brands Co ......................B....... 847 948-8903
  Deerfield (G-8019)
Koval Inc ......................................F....... 773 944-0089
  Chicago (G-5408)
Rumshine Distilling LLC ..................G....... 217 446-6960
  Tilton (G-20882)
Sazerac North America Inc .............E....... 502 423-5225
  Chicago (G-6448)
Whiskey Acres Distilling Co ............F....... 815 739-8711
  Dekalb (G-8132)

## BEVERAGES, ALCOHOLIC: Gin

Diageo North America Inc ..............E....... 815 267-4400
  Plainfield (G-17591)
Mgp Ingredients Illinois Inc .............C....... 309 353-3990
  Pekin (G-17274)

## BEVERAGES, ALCOHOLIC: Liquors, Malt

Dept 28 Inc ...................................G....... 847 285-1343
  Schaumburg (G-19502)
Dj Liquors Inc ................................G....... 815 645-1145
  Davis Junction (G-7810)
La Casa Del Tequila Corp ...............G....... 708 652-3640
  Cicero (G-7212)

## BEVERAGES, ALCOHOLIC: Near Beer

Metropolitan Brewing LLC ...............G....... 773 474-6893
  Chicago (G-5707)

## BEVERAGES, ALCOHOLIC: Rum

Apostrophe Brands ........................F....... 312 832-0300
  Chicago (G-3924)

## BEVERAGES, ALCOHOLIC: Scotch Whiskey

JK Williams Distilling LLC ...............G....... 309 839-0591
  East Peoria (G-8717)

## BEVERAGES, ALCOHOLIC: Vodka

773 LLC ........................................G....... 312 707-8780
  Chicago (G-3675)
Podhalanska LLC ...........................G....... 630 247-9256
  Lemont (G-13256)

## BEVERAGES, ALCOHOLIC: Wines

Acquaviva Winery LLC ...................G....... 630 365-0333
  Maple Park (G-14197)
August Hill Winery .........................G....... 815 224-8199
  Peru (G-17501)
Augusthill Winery Co .....................G....... 815 667-5211
  Utica (G-21106)
Barrington Cardinal Whse LLC ........G....... 847 387-3676
  Barrington (G-1270)
Baxter Vineyards ...........................G....... 217 453-2528
  Nauvoo (G-15852)
Bella Terra Winery LLC ..................F....... 618 658-8882
  Creal Springs (G-7453)
Benessere Vineyard Inc .................G....... 708 560-9840
  Oak Brook (G-16492)
Bluffs Vineyard & Winery L L C .......G....... 618 763-4447
  Murphysboro (G-15572)
Broken Earth Winery ......................F....... 847 383-5052
  Long Grove (G-13888)
Cellar LLC .....................................G....... 618 956-9900
  Carterville (G-3311)
Coopers Hawk Production LLC ........G....... 708 839-2920
  Countryside (G-7419)
Coopers Hwk Intermedte Holdng .....C....... 708 839-2920
  Countryside (G-7420)
Coopers Hwk Intermedte Holdng .....F....... 708 215-5674
  Countryside (G-7421)
Crushed Grapes Ltd ......................G....... 618 659-3530
  Millstadt (G-14822)
D C Estate Winery .........................G....... 815 218-0573
  South Beloit (G-20143)
De Vine Distributors LLC ................G....... 773 248-7005
  Chicago (G-4567)
Fox Creek Vineyards .....................G....... 618 395-3325
  Olney (G-16768)
Fox Valley Home Brew & Winery .....G....... 630 892-0742
  Aurora (G-1154)
Fox Valley Winery Inc ....................G....... 630 554-0404
  Oswego (G-16919)
Galena Cellars Winery ...................G....... 815 777-3330
  Galena (G-10720)
Galena Cellars Winery ...................E....... 815 777-3429
  Galena (G-10721)
Glunz Fmly Winery Cellars Inc .........E....... 847 548-9463
  Grayslake (G-11342)
Hogg Hollow Winery LLC ................G....... 618 695-9463
  Golconda (G-11239)
Illinois River Winery Inc .................G....... 815 691-8031
  Willowbrook (G-22216)
Kickapoo Creek Winery ..................G....... 309 495-9463
  Edwards (G-8782)
Lau Nae Winery Inc .......................G....... 618 282-9463
  Red Bud (G-17944)
Lavender Crest Winery ...................E....... 309 949-2565
  Colona (G-7344)
Lincoln Heritage Winery LLC ...........G....... 618 833-3783
  Cobden (G-7302)
Lynfred Winery Inc ........................G....... 630 529-9463
  Roselle (G-18953)
Main Street Market Roscoe Inc .......G....... 815 623-6328
  Roscoe (G-18905)
Mary McHelle Winery Vinyrd LLC ....F....... 217 942-6250
  Carrollton (G-3308)
Pheasant Hollow Winery Inc ...........G....... 618 629-2302
  Whittington (G-22188)
Pomona Winery .............................G....... 618 893-2623
  Pomona (G-17694)
Pour It Again Sam Inc ....................G....... 708 474-1744
  Lynwood (G-14023)
Prp Wine International Inc .............F....... 630 995-4500
  Naperville (G-15734)
Rapid Displays Inc ........................D....... 773 927-1500
  Chicago (G-6292)
Rustle Hill Winery LLC ...................G....... 618 893-2700
  Cobden (G-7303)
Shawnee Grapevines LLC ...............G....... 618 893-9463
  Cobden (G-7304)
Shawnee Winery ...........................G....... 618 658-8400
  Vienna (G-21225)
Southern Ill Wine Trail Nfp .............G....... 618 695-9463
  Golconda (G-11242)
Terlato Wine Group Ltd .................E....... 847 604-8900
  Lake Bluff (G-12867)
Terraneo Merchants Inc .................G....... 312 753-9134
  Lincolnwood (G-13539)
Valentino Vineyards Inc .................G....... 847 634-2831
  Long Grove (G-13904)
Vins & Vignobles LLC ....................G....... 312 375-7656
  Mount Prospect (G-15383)
Von Jakob Vineyard Limited ...........G....... 618 893-4500
  Pomona (G-17695)
Waterman Winery & Vineyards .......G....... 815 264-3268
  Waterman (G-21411)
Wyldewood Cellars 2 LLC ...............G....... 217 469-9463
  Saint Joseph (G-19319)

## BEVERAGES, BEER & ALE, WHOLESALE: Ale

Ale Syndicate Brewers LLC .............G....... 773 340-2337
  Chicago (G-3799)

## BEVERAGES, NONALCOHOLIC: Bottled & canned soft drinks

A Barr Ftn Beverage Sls & Svc ........G....... 708 442-2000
  Lyons (G-14028)
American Bottling Company ............E....... 217 356-0577
  Champaign (G-3448)
American Bottling Company ............E....... 815 877-7777
  Loves Park (G-13919)
Brewers Bottlers & Bev Corp ..........G....... 773 262-9711
  Chicago (G-4163)
Chicago Bottling Industries .............G....... 847 885-8093
  Hoffman Estates (G-11999)
Coca ............................................G....... 630 588-8786
  Carol Stream (G-3132)
Coca Cola Fleet Service .................G....... 847 600-2279
  Niles (G-15970)
Coca-Cola Bottling Co Cnsld ...........E....... 217 223-5183
  Quincy (G-17814)
Coca-Cola Btlg Wisconsin Del .........B....... 847 647-0200
  Niles (G-15971)
Coca-Cola Company .......................D....... 847 647-0200
  Niles (G-15972)
Coca-Cola Refreshments USA Inc ...D....... 815 636-7300
  Machesney Park (G-14067)
Coca-Cola Refreshments USA Inc ...D....... 847 647-0200
  Niles (G-15973)
Coca-Cola Refreshments USA Inc ...E....... 309 787-1700
  Rock Island (G-18167)
Coca-Cola Refreshments USA Inc ...E....... 815 933-2653
  Kankakee (G-12605)
Coca-Cola Refreshments USA Inc ...E....... 217 544-4892
  Springfield (G-20420)
Coca-Cola Refreshments USA Inc ...E....... 217 367-1761
  Urbana (G-21078)
Cocacola Bottling Co .....................G....... 815 220-3100
  Peru (G-17505)
Dr Pepper Snapple Group Inc .........D....... 708 947-5000
  Northlake (G-16434)
Dr Pepper/7 Up Bottling Group .......G....... 217 585-1496
  Springfield (G-20430)
Dynamic Nutritionals Inc ................G....... 815 545-9171
  New Lenox (G-15878)
E & J Gallo Winery ........................E....... 630 505-4000
  Lisle (G-13584)
Emmert John ................................F....... 773 292-6580
  Chicago (G-4744)
Essen Nutrition Corporation ...........E....... 630 739-6700
  Romeoville (G-18820)
Fast Forward Energy Inc ................G....... 312 860-0978
  Chicago (G-4815)
Florida Fruit Juices Inc ..................E....... 773 586-6200
  Chicago (G-4863)
Flowers Distributing Inc .................E....... 618 255-1021
  East Alton (G-8601)
Gatorade Company ........................A....... 312 821-1000
  Chicago (G-4918)
Great Lakes Coca-Cola Dist LLC .....C....... 847 227-6500
  Rosemont (G-19004)
Kalena LLC ...................................G....... 773 598-0033
  Chicago (G-5354)
Key Colony Inc ..............................G....... 630 783-8572
  Lemont (G-13237)
Kraft Heinz Foods Company ...........B....... 618 512-9100
  Granite City (G-11290)
Lee Gilster-Mary Corporation .........D....... 815 472-6456
  Momence (G-14983)
P-Americas LLC ............................D....... 312 821-2266
  Chicago (G-6044)
Pepsico Inc ...................................G....... 312 821-1000
  Chicago (G-6105)
Powercoco LLC .............................G....... 614 323-5890
  Chicago (G-6159)
Pursuit Beverage Company LLC ......G....... 888 606-3353
  Lake Zurich (G-13119)
Quaker Oats Company ...................A....... 312 821-1000
  Chicago (G-6242)
Quaker Oats Company ...................C....... 708 458-7090
  Bridgeview (G-2521)
Wis - Pak Inc ................................D....... 217 224-6800
  Quincy (G-17907)

Wonder Tucky Distillery & Btlg............G...... 224 678-4396
Woodstock (G-22626)

## BEVERAGES, NONALCOHOLIC: Carbonated

AD Huesing Corporation ............D....... 309 788-5652
Rock Island (G-18157)
Crisp Container Corporation ................D....... 618 998-0400
Marion (G-14257)
Decatur Bottling Co ...........................D....... 217 429-5415
Decatur (G-7870)
P-Americas LLC ..................................B....... 773 893-2300
Chicago (G-6042)
P-Americas LLC ..................................C....... 773 451-4499
Chicago (G-6043)
P-Americas LLC ..................................C....... 773 624-8013
Chicago (G-6045)
Pepsi Mid America .............................G....... 217 826-8118
Marshall (G-14327)
Pepsi Midamerica Co .........................A....... 618 997-1377
Marion (G-14277)
Pepsi-Cola Chmpign Urbana Btlr ........D....... 217 352-4126
Champaign (G-3523)
Pepsi-Cola General Bottlers VA...........B....... 847 253-1000
Rolling Meadows (G-18762)
Refreshment Services Inc ..................E....... 217 223-8600
Quincy (G-17886)
Refreshment Services Inc ..................E....... 217 522-8841
Springfield (G-20511)
Refreshment Services Inc ..................E....... 217 429-5415
Decatur (G-7933)
Rockys Beverages LLC ......................F....... 312 561-3182
Glenview (G-11194)
Rorke & Riley Specialty B ..................G....... 773 929-2522
Chicago (G-6393)
Springfield Pepsi Cola Btlg Co ............E....... 217 522-8841
Springfield (G-20530)

## BEVERAGES, NONALCOHOLIC: Carbonated, Canned & Bottled, Etc

Balon International Corp ....................E....... 773 379-7779
Chicago (G-4034)
Clover Club Bottling Co Inc ................F....... 773 261-7100
Chicago (G-4406)
Coca-Cola Refreshments USA Inc ......C....... 618 542-2101
Du Quoin (G-8552)
Coca-Cola Refreshments USA Inc ......F....... 217 348-1001
Charleston (G-3595)
Hydrive Sales .....................................G....... 708 478-8194
Mokena (G-14870)
Vision Sales & Marketing Inc .............G....... 708 496-6016
Chicago (G-6904)
Win Soon Chicago Inc ........................C....... 630 585-7090
Oswego (G-16940)

## BEVERAGES, NONALCOHOLIC: Cider

Eckert Orchards Inc ............................C....... 618 233-0513
Belleville (G-1630)
Mangel and Co ....................................E....... 847 459-3100
Buffalo Grove (G-2730)

## BEVERAGES, NONALCOHOLIC: Flavoring extracts & syrups, nec

A Barr Ftn Beverage Sls & Svc ...........G....... 708 442-2000
Lyons (G-14028)
Abelei Inc ...........................................F....... 630 859-1410
North Aurora (G-16117)
Caravan Ingredients Inc ......................D....... 708 849-8590
Dolton (G-8368)
Conagra Fods Fd Ingrdients Inc..........G....... 630 682-5600
Carol Stream (G-3135)
Custom Culinary Inc ...........................D....... 630 299-0500
Oswego (G-16912)
Dawn Food Products Inc ....................C....... 815 933-0600
Bradley (G-2419)
Equi-Chem International Inc ...............F....... 630 784-0432
Carol Stream (G-3146)
FBC Industries Inc .............................G....... 847 839-0880
Rochelle (G-18089)
Fona ...................................................G....... 630 462-1414
Carol Stream (G-3153)
Givaudan Flavors Corporation ............E....... 630 773-8484
Itasca (G-12270)
Green Mountain Flavors Inc................F....... 630 554-9530
Oswego (G-16920)
Gycor International Ltd ......................F....... 630 754-8070
Woodridge (G-22492)

Interntnal Ingredient Mall LLC ............G....... 630 462-1414
Geneva (G-10839)
Lee Gilster-Mary Corporation .............D....... 618 965-3426
Steeleville (G-20561)
Lucta U S A Inc ..................................G....... 847 996-3400
Libertyville (G-13345)
Mh/1993/Foods Inc ............................F....... 708 331-7453
South Holland (G-20290)
Necta Sweet Inc .................................E....... 847 215-9955
Buffalo Grove (G-2742)
Neiman Bros Co Inc ...........................G....... 773 463-3000
Chicago (G-5882)
Nestle Usa Inc ....................................D....... 847 808-5404
Buffalo Grove (G-2747)
NFC Company Inc ..............................G....... 773 472-6468
Chicago (G-5908)
Pepsico Inc ........................................G....... 312 821-1000
Chicago (G-6105)
Roquette America Inc ........................D....... 847 360-0886
Gurnee (G-11501)
Royal Foods & Flavors Inc .................F....... 847 595-9166
Elk Grove Village (G-9720)
Sensient Flavors LLC .........................B....... 317 243-3521
Hoffman Estates (G-12050)
Sensient Flavors LLC .........................F....... 815 857-3691
Amboy (G-599)
Sensient Technologies Corp ..............E....... 708 481-0910
Matteson (G-14378)
Synergy Flavors Inc ...........................D....... 847 487-1011
Wauconda (G-21506)
T Hasegawa USA Inc ..........................E....... 847 559-6060
Northbrook (G-16375)
Tampico Beverages Inc ......................F....... 773 296-0190
Chicago (G-6670)
Vitamins Inc .......................................G....... 773 483-4640
Carol Stream (G-3262)
Watson Inc .........................................E....... 217 824-4440
Taylorville (G-20846)
Wm Wrigley Jr Company ....................B....... 312 280-4710
Chicago (G-7012)

## BEVERAGES, NONALCOHOLIC: Fruit Drnks, Under 100% Juice, Can

Drivnn LLC .........................................G....... 815 222-4447
Loves Park (G-13937)
Vita-V Energy Co Inc ..........................G....... 630 999-8961
Glendale Heights (G-11089)

## BEVERAGES, NONALCOHOLIC: Fruit Juices, Concentrtd, Fountain

Institutional Foods Packing Co ..........E....... 847 904-5250
Glenview (G-11148)
Key Colony Inc ...................................G....... 630 783-8572
Lemont (G-13237)

## BEVERAGES, NONALCOHOLIC: Soft Drinks, Canned & Bottled, Etc

American Bottling Company ...............B....... 708 947-5000
Northlake (G-16426)
American Bottling Company ...............E....... 309 693-2777
Edwards (G-8781)
Berner Food & Beverage LLC ............B....... 815 563-4222
Dakota (G-7694)
Coca-Cola Refreshments USA Inc ......C....... 630 513-5247
Saint Charles (G-19158)
Coca-Cola Refreshments USA Inc ......C....... 708 597-6700
Alsip (G-450)
Coca-Cola Refreshments USA Inc ......C....... 708 597-4700
Chicago (G-4415)
Egg Cream America Inc .....................G....... 847 559-2700
Northbrook (G-16248)
Excel Bottling Co ...............................G....... 618 526-7159
Breese (G-2443)
Ginger Bliss Juice LLC .......................G....... 773 456-0181
Hinsdale (G-11949)
P-Americas LLC ..................................G....... 309 266-2400
Morton (G-15173)
Pepsi Cola Gen Bttlers of Lima ..........G....... 847 253-1000
Rolling Meadows (G-18761)
Pepsi Midamerica ..............................G....... 618 242-6285
Mount Vernon (G-15439)
Pepsi-Cola Gen Bottlers Inc ...............B....... 847 598-3000
Schaumburg (G-19688)

## BEVERAGES, WINE & DISTILLED ALCOHOLIC, WHOLESALE: Liquor

Alto Vinyards Inc ................................F....... 618 893-4898
Alto Pass (G-556)
Callison Distributing LLC ....................D....... 618 277-4300
Belleville (G-1616)
Jamiel Inc ...........................................E....... 217 423-1000
Decatur (G-7898)

## BEVERAGES, WINE & DISTILLED ALCOHOLIC, WHOLESALE: Neutral Sp

Coca-Cola Refreshments USA Inc ......E....... 217 544-4892
Springfield (G-20420)
Vins & Vignobles LLC .........................G....... 312 375-7656
Mount Prospect (G-15383)

## BEVERAGES, WINE & DISTILLED ALCOHOLIC, WHOLESALE: Wine

Bella Terra Winery LLC .....................F....... 618 658-8882
Creal Springs (G-7453)
Coopers Hwk Intermedte Holdng .......C....... 708 839-2920
Countryside (G-7420)
Coopers Hwk Intermedte Holdng .......F....... 708 215-5674
Countryside (G-7421)
De Vine Distributors LLC ...................G....... 773 248-7005
Chicago (G-4567)
E & J Gallo Winery ..............................E....... 630 505-4000
Lisle (G-13584)
Galena Cellars Winery ........................G....... 815 777-3330
Galena (G-10720)
Lincoln Heritage Winery LLC ..............G....... 618 833-3783
Cobden (G-7302)
RJ Distributing Co ..............................E....... 309 685-2794
East Peoria (G-8731)
Terlato Wine Group Ltd .....................E....... 847 604-8900
Lake Bluff (G-12867)

## BIBLE SCHOOL

Moody Bible Inst of Chicago...............A....... 312 329-4000
Chicago (G-5799)

## BICYCLE REPAIR SHOP

In The Attic Inc ..................................G....... 847 949-5077
Mundelein (G-15509)

## BICYCLE SHOPS

Wrench ..............................................G....... 773 609-1698
Chicago (G-7036)

## BICYCLES, PARTS & ACCESS

Brg Sports Inc ....................................F....... 217 893-9300
Rantoul (G-17921)
Brg Sports Inc ....................................C....... 831 461-7500
Rosemont (G-18990)
N Fly Cycle Inc ...................................G....... 815 562-4620
Ashton (G-929)
Pacific Cycle Inc .................................C....... 618 393-2508
Olney (G-16789)

## BIDETS: Vitreous China

BBC Innovation Corporation ..............G....... 847 458-2334
Crystal Lake (G-7540)

## BILLETS: Steel

Keystone Consolidated Inds Inc .........E....... 309 697-7020
Peoria (G-17396)

## BILLFOLD INSERTS: Plastic

Classic Fasteners LLC .......................G....... 630 605-0195
Saint Charles (G-19157)

## BILLIARD & POOL TABLES & SPLYS

Tweeten Fibre Co ...............................E....... 312 733-7878
Chicago (G-6795)

## BILLIARD EQPT & SPLYS WHOLESALERS

Brunswick Corporation ......................B....... 847 735-4700
Lake Forest (G-12888)

## BILLING & BOOKKEEPING SVCS

**American Hosp Assn Svcs Del** ....E .... 312 422-2000
Chicago *(G-3858)*

## BINDING SVC: Books & Manuals

**11th Street Express Prtg Inc** ....F .... 815 968-0208
Rockford *(G-18235)*
**A A Swift Print Inc** ....G .... 847 301-1122
Schaumburg *(G-19418)*
**A To Z Engraving Co Inc** ....G .... 847 526-7396
Wauconda *(G-21435)*
**A To Z Offset Prtg & Pubg Inc** ....G .... 847 966-3016
Skokie *(G-19943)*
**A+ Printing Co** ....G .... 815 968-8181
Rockford *(G-18242)*
**ABS Graphics Inc** ....C .... 630 495-2400
Itasca *(G-12223)*
**Accord Carton Co** ....C .... 708 272-3050
Alsip *(G-428)*
**Acres of Sky Communications** ....G .... 815 493-2560
Lanark *(G-13149)*
**Adams Printing Co** ....G .... 618 529-2396
Carbondale *(G-3000)*
**Adcraft Printers Inc** ....F .... 815 932-6432
Kankakee *(G-12601)*
**All Printing & Graphics Inc** ....F .... 708 450-1512
Broadview *(G-2555)*
**All-Ways Quick Print** ....G .... 708 403-8422
Orland Park *(G-16841)*
**Allegra Network LLC** ....G .... 630 801-9335
Aurora *(G-1104)*
**Allegra Print & Imaging Inc** ....G .... 847 697-1434
Elgin *(G-8942)*
**Alphadigital Inc** ....G .... 708 482-4488
La Grange Park *(G-12752)*
**AlphaGraphics Printshops** ....G .... 630 964-9600
Lisle *(G-13555)*
**American Quick Print Inc** ....G .... 847 253-2700
Wauconda *(G-21441)*
**Apple Graphics Inc** ....G .... 630 389-2222
Batavia *(G-1416)*
**Apple Press Inc** ....G .... 815 224-1451
Peru *(G-17500)*
**Apple Printing Center** ....G .... 630 932-9494
Addison *(G-41)*
**Arch Printing Inc** ....G .... 630 966-0235
Aurora *(G-1110)*
**Art Bookbinders of America** ....E .... 312 226-4100
Chicago *(G-3949)*
**Avid of Illinois Inc** ....F .... 847 698-2775
Saint Charles *(G-19140)*
**B & B Printing Company** ....G .... 217 285-6072
Pittsfield *(G-17561)*
**B F Shaw Printing Company** ....E .... 815 875-4461
Princeton *(G-17744)*
**B J Plastic Molding Co** ....E .... 630 766-3200
Franklin Park *(G-10408)*
**Bailleu & Bailleu Printing Inc** ....G .... 309 852-2517
Kewanee *(G-12670)*
**Barnaby Inc** ....F .... 815 895-6555
Sycamore *(G-20789)*
**Bell Litho Inc** ....D .... 847 952-3300
Elk Grove Village *(G-9338)*
**Benzinger Printing** ....G .... 815 784-6560
Genoa *(G-10875)*
**Bikast Graphics Inc** ....G .... 847 487-8822
Wauconda *(G-21446)*
**Biller Press & Manufacturing** ....G .... 847 395-4111
Antioch *(G-623)*
**Brads Printing Inc** ....G .... 847 662-0447
Waukegan *(G-21531)*
**Branstiter Printing Co** ....G .... 217 245-6533
Jacksonville *(G-12381)*
**Cadore-Miller Printing Inc** ....F .... 708 430-7091
Hickory Hills *(G-11768)*
**Camera Ready Copies Inc** ....E .... 847 215-8611
Prospect Heights *(G-17773)*
**Cameron Printing Inc** ....G .... 630 231-3301
West Chicago *(G-21677)*
**Cannon Ball Marketing Inc** ....G .... 630 971-2127
Lisle *(G-13573)*
**Capitol Impressions Inc** ....E .... 309 633-1400
Peoria *(G-17322)*
**Cardinal Colorprint Prtg Corp** ....E .... 630 467-1000
Itasca *(G-12241)*
**Carter Printing Co Inc** ....G .... 217 227-4464
Farmersville *(G-10183)*
**Case Paluch & Associates Inc** ....G .... 773 465-0098
Chicago *(G-4248)*
**Century Printing** ....G .... 618 632-2486
O Fallon *(G-16465)*
**Cenveo Inc** ....G .... 217 243-4258
Jacksonville *(G-12383)*
**Challenge Printers** ....G .... 773 252-0212
Chicago *(G-4285)*
**Christopher R Cline Prtg Ltd** ....F .... 847 981-0500
Elk Grove Village *(G-9372)*
**Cifuentes Luis & Nicole Inc** ....G .... 847 490-3660
Schaumburg *(G-19472)*
**Cjs Printing** ....G .... 309 968-6585
Manito *(G-14172)*
**Cloverdale Corporation** ....G .... 847 296-9225
Des Plaines *(G-8171)*
**Cmb Printing Inc** ....F .... 630 323-1110
Burr Ridge *(G-2830)*
**Commercial Copy Printing Ctr** ....F .... 847 981-8590
Elk Grove Village *(G-9384)*
**Copy Mat Printing** ....G .... 309 452-1392
Bloomington *(G-2155)*
**Copy Service Inc** ....G .... 815 758-1151
Dekalb *(G-8079)*
**Copy-Mor Inc** ....E .... 312 666-4000
Elmhurst *(G-9856)*
**Cpr Printing Inc** ....F .... 630 377-8420
Geneva *(G-10821)*
**Craftsmen Printing** ....G .... 217 283-9574
Hoopeston *(G-12108)*
**Creative Lithocraft Inc** ....G .... 847 352-7002
Schaumburg *(G-19489)*
**Crossmark Printing Inc** ....F .... 708 532-8263
Tinley Park *(G-20906)*
**D E Asbury Inc** ....F .... 217 222-0617
Hamilton *(G-11532)*
**D G Brandt Inc** ....G .... 815 942-4064
Morris *(G-15105)*
**D L V Printing Service Inc** ....F .... 773 626-1661
Chicago *(G-4537)*
**Dale K Brown** ....G .... 815 338-0222
Woodstock *(G-22558)*
**Darnall Printing** ....G .... 309 827-7212
Bloomington *(G-2161)*
**Darwill Inc** ....C .... 708 449-7770
Hillside *(G-11914)*
**David H Vander Ploeg** ....G .... 708 331-7700
South Holland *(G-20260)*
**DE Asbury Inc** ....E .... 217 222-0617
Quincy *(G-17820)*
**Deadline Prtg Clor Copying LLC** ....G .... 847 437-9000
Elk Grove Village *(G-9419)*
**Deluxe Johnson** ....F .... 847 635-7200
Des Plaines *(G-8182)*
**Demis Printing Inc** ....G .... 773 282-9128
Park Ridge *(G-17189)*
**Denor Graphics Inc** ....F .... 847 364-1130
Elk Grove Village *(G-9423)*
**Design Graphics Inc** ....G .... 815 462-3323
New Lenox *(G-15875)*
**Diamond Graphics of Berwyn** ....G .... 708 749-2500
Berwyn *(G-2060)*
**DMarv Design Specialty Prtrs** ....G .... 708 389-4420
Blue Island *(G-2246)*
**Donnells Printing & Off Pdts** ....G .... 815 842-6541
Pontiac *(G-17698)*
**E & H Graphic Service** ....G .... 708 748-5656
Matteson *(G-14371)*
**Eastrich Printing & Sales** ....G .... 815 232-4216
Freeport *(G-10654)*
**Einstein Crest** ....G .... 847 965-7791
Niles *(G-15977)*
**Elgin Instant Print** ....G .... 847 931-9006
Elgin *(G-9024)*
**Elliott Publishing Inc** ....G .... 217 645-3033
Liberty *(G-13295)*
**Elmhurst Enterprise Group Inc** ....G .... 847 228-5945
Arlington Heights *(G-749)*
**F Weber Printing Co Inc** ....G .... 815 468-6152
Manteno *(G-14183)*
**Fast Printing of Joliet Inc** ....G .... 815 723-0080
Joliet *(G-12492)*
**Fastway Printing Inc** ....G .... 847 882-0950
Schaumburg *(G-19524)*
**Fedex Office & Print Svcs Inc** ....E .... 217 355-3400
Champaign *(G-3485)*
**Fedex Office & Print Svcs Inc** ....F .... 847 475-8650
Evanston *(G-10036)*
**Fedex Office & Print Svcs Inc** ....F .... 815 229-0033
Rockford *(G-18380)*
**Fedex Office & Print Svcs Inc** ....F .... 847 329-9464
Lincolnwood *(G-13510)*
**Fedex Office & Print Svcs Inc** ....E .... 847 729-3030
Glenview *(G-11124)*
**Fedex Office & Print Svcs Inc** ....E .... 309 685-4093
Peoria *(G-17359)*
**Fedex Office & Print Svcs Inc** ....G .... 847 459-8008
Buffalo Grove *(G-2693)*
**Fedex Office & Print Svcs Inc** ....E .... 708 452-0149
Elmwood Park *(G-9970)*
**Fedex Office & Print Svcs Inc** ....G .... 847 823-9360
Park Ridge *(G-17193)*
**Fedex Office & Print Svcs Inc** ....F .... 630 894-1800
Bloomingdale *(G-2108)*
**Fedex Office & Print Svcs Inc** ....E .... 847 670-4100
Arlington Heights *(G-754)*
**Fedex Office & Print Svcs Inc** ....F .... 312 670-4460
Chicago *(G-4831)*
**Fernwood Printers Ltd** ....G .... 630 964-9449
Oak Forest *(G-16581)*
**Fidelity Bindery Company** ....E .... 708 343-6833
Broadview *(G-2578)*
**First Impression of Chicago** ....G .... 773 224-3434
Chicago *(G-4849)*
**Fisheye Services Incorporated** ....G .... 773 942-6314
Chicago *(G-4852)*
**Flash Printing Inc** ....G .... 847 288-9101
Franklin Park *(G-10470)*
**Fleetwood Press Inc** ....G .... 708 485-6811
Brookfield *(G-2632)*
**Floden Enterprises** ....G .... 847 566-7898
Mundelein *(G-15502)*
**FM Graphic Impressions Inc** ....E .... 630 897-8788
Aurora *(G-1153)*
**Forms Design Plus Coleman Prtg** ....G .... 309 685-6000
Peoria *(G-17365)*
**French Studio Ltd** ....G .... 618 942-5328
Herrin *(G-11748)*
**G F Printing** ....G .... 618 797-0576
Granite City *(G-11278)*
**Gamma Alpha Visual** ....G .... 847 956-0633
Elk Grove Village *(G-9496)*
**Gossett Printing Inc** ....G .... 618 548-2583
Salem *(G-19335)*
**Graphics Group LLC** ....D .... 708 867-5500
Chicago *(G-4992)*
**Grasso Graphics Inc** ....G .... 708 489-2060
Alsip *(G-465)*
**Griffith Solutions Inc** ....G .... 847 384-1810
Park Ridge *(G-17201)*
**Grovak Instant Printing Co** ....G .... 847 675-2414
Mount Prospect *(G-15334)*
**Harris Bookbinding LLC** ....E .... 773 287-9414
Downers Grove *(G-8454)*
**Hawthorne Press** ....G .... 708 652-9000
Cicero *(G-7201)*
**Hawthorne Press Inc** ....G .... 847 587-0582
Spring Grove *(G-20336)*
**Heart Printing Inc** ....G .... 847 259-2100
Arlington Heights *(G-764)*
**Heritage Press Inc** ....G .... 847 362-9699
Libertyville *(G-13330)*
**Highland Printers** ....G .... 618 654-5880
Highland *(G-11791)*
**House of Graphics** ....G .... 630 682-0810
Carol Stream *(G-3168)*
**Hq Printers Inc** ....G .... 312 782-2020
Chicago *(G-5125)*
**Hub Printing Company Inc** ....F .... 815 562-7057
Rochelle *(G-18094)*
**Ideal Advertising & Printing** ....F .... 815 965-1713
Rockford *(G-18426)*
**Illinois Office Sup Elect Prtg** ....E .... 815 434-0186
Ottawa *(G-16962)*
**Illinois Tool Works Inc** ....E .... 708 720-0300
Frankfort *(G-10333)*
**Image Print Inc** ....G .... 815 672-1068
Streator *(G-20691)*
**Impression Printing** ....F .... 708 614-8660
Oak Forest *(G-16583)*
**In A Bind Assembly Fulfillment** ....E .... 815 568-6952
Marengo *(G-14231)*
**In-Print Graphics Inc** ....E .... 708 396-1010
Oak Forest *(G-16584)*
**Ink Well Printing** ....G .... 815 224-1366
Peru *(G-17514)*
**Ink Well Printing & Design Ltd** ....G .... 847 923-8060
Schaumburg *(G-19566)*
**Insty Prints Palatine Inc** ....F .... 847 963-0000
Palatine *(G-17042)*
**Insty-Prints of Champaign Inc** ....G .... 217 356-6166
Champaign *(G-3501)*

# PRODUCT SECTION
## BINDING SVC: Books & Manuals

| Company | Code | Phone |
|---|---|---|
| Instyprints of Waukegan Inc — Waukegan (G-21571) | G | 847 336-5599 |
| Integra Graphics and Forms Inc — Crestwood (G-7490) | F | 708 385-0950 |
| International Graphics & Assoc — Saint Charles (G-19196) | F | 630 584-2248 |
| J & J Mr Quick Print Inc — Chicago (G-5251) | G | 773 767-7776 |
| J D Graphic Co Inc — Elk Grove Village (G-9557) | E | 847 364-4000 |
| J F Wagner Printing Co — Northbrook (G-16280) | G | 847 564-0017 |
| Jay Printing — Palatine (G-17046) | G | 847 934-6103 |
| Joes Printing — Chicago (G-5309) | G | 773 545-6063 |
| Johns-Byrne Company — Niles (G-15992) | D | 847 583-3100 |
| Johnson Press America Inc — Pontiac (G-17704) | E | 815 844-5161 |
| Josco Inc — Chicago (G-5326) | G | 708 867-7189 |
| Jph Enterprises Inc — Des Plaines (G-8217) | G | 847 390-0900 |
| Juskie Printing Corp — Downers Grove (G-8468) | G | 630 663-8833 |
| K & M Printing Company Inc — Schaumburg (G-19595) | D | 847 884-1100 |
| K O G Mfg & Bindery Corp — Waukegan (G-21576) | F | 847 263-5050 |
| K R O Enterprises Ltd — Moline (G-14949) | G | 309 797-2213 |
| Kelly Printing Co Inc — Danville (G-7741) | E | 217 443-1792 |
| Kendall Printing Co — Yorkville (G-22663) | G | 630 553-9200 |
| Kens Quick Print Inc — Highland Park (G-11849) | F | 847 831-4410 |
| Kevin Kewney — Quincy (G-17844) | G | 217 228-7444 |
| Key Printing — Kankakee (G-12635) | G | 815 933-1800 |
| Klein Printing Inc — Chicago (G-5387) | G | 773 235-2121 |
| Klh Printing Corp — Wheeling (G-22086) | G | 847 459-0115 |
| Koehler Bindery Inc — Chicago (G-5401) | G | 773 539-7979 |
| Kwik Print Inc — Itasca (G-12299) | G | 630 773-3225 |
| LAC Enterprises Inc — Crystal Lake (G-7601) | G | 815 455-5044 |
| Lake Shore Printing — Skokie (G-20024) | G | 847 679-4110 |
| Lans Printing Inc — Lynwood (G-14021) | G | 708 895-6226 |
| Lasons Label Co — Chicago (G-5464) | G | 773 775-2606 |
| Lee-Wel Printing Corporation — Wheaton (G-21966) | G | 630 682-0935 |
| Leonard Emerson — Divernon (G-8316) | G | 217 628-3441 |
| Lind-Remsen Printing Co Inc — Rockford (G-18470) | F | 815 969-0610 |
| Link-Letters Ltd — Wheeling (G-22094) | F | 847 459-1199 |
| Lists & Letters — Wheeling (G-22095) | F | 847 520-5207 |
| Lynns Printing Co — Alton (G-583) | G | 618 465-7701 |
| M & G Graphics Inc — Chicago (G-5576) | E | 773 247-1596 |
| M O W Printing Inc — Collinsville (G-7331) | F | 618 345-5525 |
| Macoupin County Enquirer Inc — Carlinville (G-3042) | E | 217 854-2534 |
| Mall Graphic Inc — Huntley (G-12161) | F | 847 668-7600 |
| Marcus Press — Bloomingdale (G-2115) | G | 630 351-1857 |
| Mark Twain Press Inc — Mundelein (G-15523) | G | 847 255-2700 |
| Marquardt Printing Company — Willowbrook (G-22220) | E | 630 887-8500 |
| Mason City Banner Times — Mason City (G-14365) | F | 217 482-3276 |
| Master Engraving — Virden (G-21299) | G | 217 965-5885 |
| Mattoon Printing Center — Mattoon (G-14400) | G | 217 234-3100 |
| McGrath Press Inc — Crystal Lake (G-7607) | E | 815 356-5246 |
| Mencarini Enterprises Inc — Rockford (G-18491) | G | 815 398-9565 |
| Merritt & Edwards Corporation — Bloomington (G-2196) | F | 309 828-4741 |
| Metro Printing & Pubg Inc — Millstadt (G-14829) | G | 618 476-9587 |
| Michael Zimmerman — Northbrook (G-16311) | G | 847 272-5560 |
| Mid Central Printing & Mailing — Wilmette (G-22262) | F | 847 251-4040 |
| Mid City Printing Service — Chicago (G-5725) | G | 773 777-5400 |
| Minuteman Press — Countryside (G-7437) | G | 630 541-9122 |
| Minuteman Press — Lombard (G-13827) | G | 630 279-0438 |
| Minuteman Press Inc — Arlington Heights (G-803) | G | 847 577-2411 |
| Minuteman Press Morton Grove — Morton Grove (G-15221) | G | 847 470-0212 |
| Minuteman Press of Rockford — Loves Park (G-13967) | G | 815 633-2992 |
| Modern Printing of Quincy — Quincy (G-17861) | F | 217 223-1063 |
| Msf Graphics Inc — Des Plaines (G-8239) | G | 847 446-6900 |
| Multi Art Press — Chicago (G-5831) | G | 773 775-0515 |
| Multicopy Corp — Northfield (G-16410) | G | 847 446-7015 |
| N Bujarski Inc — Schaumburg (G-19660) | G | 847 884-1600 |
| N P D Inc — Oak Lawn (G-16636) | G | 708 424-6788 |
| New Life Printing & Publishing — Algonquin (G-402) | G | 847 658-4111 |
| Newell & Haney Inc — Belleville (G-1660) | F | 618 277-3660 |
| Northwest Premier Printing — Chicago (G-5940) | G | 773 736-1882 |
| Northwest Printing Inc — Harvard (G-11642) | G | 815 943-7977 |
| Nu-Art Printing — Centralia (G-3425) | G | 618 533-9971 |
| Off The Press — Plainfield (G-17634) | G | 815 436-9612 |
| Office Assistants Inc — Oak Lawn (G-16637) | G | 708 346-0505 |
| Ogden Offset Printers Inc — Chicago (G-5973) | G | 773 284-7797 |
| Olde Print Shoppe Inc — Olney (G-16786) | G | 618 395-3833 |
| On Time Printing and Finishing — Hillside (G-11929) | G | 708 544-4500 |
| Osbon Lithographers — Park Ridge (G-17214) | G | 847 825-7727 |
| P & S Cochran Printers Inc — Peoria (G-17421) | E | 309 691-6668 |
| P H C Enterprises Inc — Vernon Hills (G-21186) | G | 847 816-7373 |
| P P Graphics Inc — Westchester (G-21852) | G | 708 343-2530 |
| Parrot Press — Chicago (G-6087) | G | 773 376-6333 |
| Patrick Impressions LLC — Lemont (G-13250) | G | 630 257-9336 |
| Patton Printing and Graphics — Effingham (G-8852) | G | 217 347-0220 |
| Perma Graphics Printers — New Lenox (G-15901) | G | 815 485-6955 |
| Perryco Inc — Plainfield (G-17638) | F | 815 436-2431 |
| Pinney Printing Company — Sterling (G-20603) | G | 815 626-2727 |
| Pinney Printing Company — Sterling (G-20604) | G | 815 626-2727 |
| PIP Printing Inc — Frankfort (G-10349) | G | 815 464-0075 |
| Prairieland Printing — Washington (G-21387) | G | 309 647-5425 |
| Precision Die Cutting & Finish — Chicago (G-6169) | G | 773 252-5625 |
| Preferred Printing Service — Chicago (G-6175) | G | 312 421-2343 |
| Print & Design Services LLC — Bannockburn (G-1264) | G | 847 317-9001 |
| Print King Inc — Oak Lawn (G-16641) | F | 708 499-3777 |
| Print Turnaround Inc — Arlington Heights (G-822) | F | 847 228-1762 |
| Printed Word Inc — Evanston (G-10091) | G | 847 328-1511 |
| Printing By Joseph — Mokena (G-14898) | G | 708 479-2669 |
| Printing Craftsmen of Joliet — Joliet (G-12555) | G | 815 254-3982 |
| Printing Etc Inc — Rochelle (G-18102) | G | 815 562-6151 |
| Printing Plus — Lockport (G-13739) | G | 708 301-3900 |
| Printing Plus of Roselle Inc — Roselle (G-18963) | G | 630 893-0410 |
| Printing Press of Joliet Inc — Joliet (G-12556) | G | 815 725-0018 |
| Printing Source Inc — Morton Grove (G-15228) | G | 773 588-2930 |
| Printing Works Inc — Elk Grove Village (G-9698) | G | 847 860-1920 |
| Printmeisters Inc — Lansing (G-13180) | G | 708 474-8400 |
| Printsource Plus Inc — Blue Island (G-2265) | G | 708 389-6252 |
| Prism Commercial Printing Ctrs — Chicago (G-6199) | G | 630 834-4443 |
| Pro-Type Printing Inc — Paxton (G-17244) | G | 217 379-4715 |
| Progress Printing Corporation — Chicago (G-6210) | E | 773 927-0123 |
| Quad City Press — Moline (G-14965) | F | 309 764-8142 |
| Quad/Graphics Inc — Mount Morris (G-15297) | A | 815 734-4121 |
| Quality Quickprint Inc — Joliet (G-12560) | F | 815 439-3430 |
| Quality Quickprint Inc — Lockport (G-13740) | F | 815 838-1784 |
| Quickprinters — Macomb (G-14130) | G | 309 833-5250 |
| Quinn Print Inc — Park Ridge (G-17218) | G | 847 823-9100 |
| R & R Bindery Service Inc — Girard (G-10949) | C | 217 627-2143 |
| R R Donnelley & Sons Company — Dwight (G-8591) | A | 815 584-2770 |
| Rapid Print — Peoria (G-17440) | G | 309 673-0826 |
| Ready Press — Palatine (G-17066) | G | 847 358-8655 |
| Redline Press — Lisle (G-13650) | G | 630 690-9828 |
| Remke Printing Inc — Wheeling (G-22137) | G | 847 520-7300 |
| Reprographics — Crystal Lake (G-7638) | G | 815 477-1018 |
| Review Printing Co Inc — Rock Island (G-18199) | G | 309 788-7094 |
| Rickard Circular Folding Co — Chicago (G-6353) | D | 312 243-6300 |
| Rider Dickerson Inc — Bellwood (G-1718) | D | 312 427-2926 |
| Rightway Printing Inc — Glendale Heights (G-11064) | F | 630 790-0444 |
| River Bend Printing — Litchfield (G-13696) | G | 217 324-6056 |
| Ro-Web Inc — Peoria (G-17444) | G | 309 688-2155 |
| Robal Company Inc — Warrenville (G-21361) | F | 630 393-0777 |
| Rodin Enterprises Inc — Wheeling (G-22142) | G | 847 412-1370 |
| Rohrer Litho Inc — Elmhurst (G-9931) | G | 630 833-6610 |
| Rose Business Forms & Printing — Centralia (G-3429) | G | 618 533-3032 |
| Rrr Graphics & Film Corp — Mokena (G-14901) | G | 708 478-4573 |
| Rudin Printing Company Inc — Springfield (G-20515) | F | 217 528-5111 |
| Rusty & Angela Buzzard — Effingham (G-8857) | G | 217 342-9841 |
| S B Liquidating Company — Elk Grove Village (G-9723) | D | 847 758-9500 |
| Salem Times-Commoner Pubg Co — Salem (G-19349) | E | 618 548-3330 |
| Samecwei Inc — Aurora (G-1214) | G | 630 897-7888 |
| Scheiwes Print Shop — Crescent City (G-7456) | G | 815 683-2398 |

Employee Codes: A=Over 500 employees, B=251-500
C=101-250, D=51-100, E=20-50, F=10-19, G=3-9

## BINDING SVC: Books & Manuals

Schommer Inc .................................. G ...... 815 344-1404
  McHenry *(G-14554)*
Service Printing Corporation ............. G ...... 847 669-9620
  Huntley *(G-12176)*
Shawver Press Inc ......................... G ...... 815 772-4700
  Morrison *(G-15148)*
Shoreline Graphics Inc ................... G ...... 847 587-4804
  Ingleside *(G-12198)*
Shree Mahavir Inc .......................... G ...... 312 408-1080
  Chicago *(G-6501)*
Shree Printing Corp ........................ G ...... 773 267-9500
  Chicago *(G-6502)*
Sigley Printing & Off Sup Co ........... G ...... 618 997-5304
  Marion *(G-14287)*
Sir Speedy Printing ......................... G ...... 312 337-0774
  Chicago *(G-6518)*
Sommers & Fahrenbach Inc ............. F ...... 773 478-3033
  Chicago *(G-6543)*
Speedys Quick Print ....................... G ...... 217 431-0510
  Danville *(G-7766)*
Springfield Printing Inc .................... G ...... 217 787-3500
  Springfield *(G-20531)*
Stark Printing Company ................... G ...... 847 234-8430
  Round Lake *(G-19068)*
Stearns Printing of Charleston .......... G ...... 217 345-7518
  Charleston *(G-3613)*
Steve Bortman ................................ G ...... 708 442-1669
  Lyons *(G-14046)*
Swifty Print .................................... G ...... 630 584-9063
  Saint Charles *(G-19276)*
T F N W Inc .................................... G ...... 630 584-7383
  Saint Charles *(G-19277)*
Techprint Inc .................................. F ...... 847 616-0109
  Elk Grove Village *(G-9774)*
Thomas Printing & Sty Co ............... G ...... 618 435-2801
  Benton *(G-2041)*
Tidd Printing Co ............................. G ...... 708 749-1200
  Berwyn *(G-2076)*
Tower Printing & Design .................. G ...... 630 495-1976
  Lombard *(G-13870)*
Tree Towns Reprographics Inc ......... E ...... 630 832-0209
  Elmhurst *(G-9951)*
Tri-Tower Printing Inc ...................... G ...... 847 640-6633
  Rolling Meadows *(G-18785)*
Trump Printing Inc .......................... F ...... 217 429-9001
  Decatur *(G-7954)*
United Lithograph Inc ...................... G ...... 847 803-1700
  Des Plaines *(G-8290)*
Viking Printing & Copying Inc .......... G ...... 312 341-0985
  Chicago *(G-6899)*
Voris Communication Co Inc ........... C ...... 630 898-4268
  Berkeley *(G-2051)*
We-B-Print Inc ............................... G ...... 309 353-8801
  Pekin *(G-17293)*
Weakley Printing & Sign Shop .......... G ...... 847 473-4466
  North Chicago *(G-16189)*
Weimer Design & Print Ltd Inc ......... G ...... 630 393-3334
  Warrenville *(G-21368)*
West Vly Graphics & Print Inc .......... G ...... 630 377-7575
  Saint Charles *(G-19293)*
William Holloway Ltd ....................... G ...... 847 866-9520
  Evanston *(G-10106)*
Wood River Printing & Pubg Co ....... F ...... 618 254-3134
  Wood River *(G-22446)*
Woogl Corporation .......................... E ...... 847 806-1160
  Elk Grove Village *(G-9816)*
Wortman Printing Company Inc ........ G ...... 217 347-3775
  Effingham *(G-8864)*

## BINDING SVC: Trade

Accurate Die Cutting Inc ................. G ...... 847 437-7215
  Elk Grove Village *(G-9261)*
Hopkins Printing & Envelope Co ....... F ...... 630 543-8227
  Addison *(G-148)*
Instant Collating Service Inc ............ F ...... 312 243-4703
  Chicago *(G-5205)*

## BIOLOGICAL PRDTS: Blood Derivatives

Csl Behring LLC .............................. B ...... 815 932-6773
  Bradley *(G-2418)*
Northern Ill Blood Bnk Inc ................ D ...... 815 965-8751
  Rockford *(G-18520)*

## BIOLOGICAL PRDTS: Coagulation

Aspen API Inc ................................ F ...... 847 635-0985
  Des Plaines *(G-8152)*

## BIOLOGICAL PRDTS: Exc Diagnostic

Abbvie Inc ..................................... B ...... 847 932-7900
  North Chicago *(G-16166)*
Abbvie US LLC ............................... C ...... 800 255-5162
  North Chicago *(G-16171)*
Avexis Inc ..................................... F ...... 847 572-8280
  Bannockburn *(G-1254)*
Bioaffinity Inc ................................. G ...... 815 988-5077
  Rockford *(G-18285)*
Bioforce Nanosciences Inc .............. G ...... 515 233-8333
  Chicago *(G-4110)*
Biologos Inc .................................. G ...... 630 801-4740
  Montgomery *(G-15031)*
Bn National Trail ............................. G ...... 618 783-8709
  Newton *(G-15938)*
C & S Chemicals Inc ...................... G ...... 815 722-6671
  Joliet *(G-12470)*
Midwest Bio Manufacturing Div ........ F ...... 815 542-6417
  Tampico *(G-20828)*
Protide Pharmaceuticals Inc ............ G ...... 847 726-3100
  Lake Zurich *(G-13117)*
Ptm Biolabs Inc .............................. G ...... 312 802-6843
  Chicago *(G-6221)*
Quorum Labs LLC .......................... G ...... 618 525-5600
  Eldorado *(G-8921)*
Spherotech Inc ............................... F ...... 847 680-8922
  Lake Forest *(G-12961)*
W-R Industries Inc .......................... G ...... 312 733-5200
  Chicago *(G-6929)*

## BIOLOGICAL PRDTS: Toxin, Viruses/Simlr Substncs, Incl Venom

Roy Winnett ................................... G ...... 309 367-4867
  Metamora *(G-14748)*

## BIOLOGICAL PRDTS: Vaccines

Charles River Laboratories Inc ......... D ...... 309 923-7122
  Roanoke *(G-18049)*

## BIOLOGICAL PRDTS: Veterinary

Cislak Manufacturing Inc ................. E ...... 847 647-1819
  Niles *(G-15969)*
Splash Dog Therapy Inc .................. G ...... 847 296-4007
  Des Plaines *(G-8279)*

## BIRTH CONTROL DEVICES: Rubber

Female Health Company .................. E ...... 312 595-9123
  Chicago *(G-4835)*

## BLACKBOARDS & CHALKBOARDS

Claridge Products and Eqp Inc ......... G ...... 847 991-8822
  Elgin *(G-8992)*

## BLACKBOARDS: Slate

Vecchio Manufacturing of Ill ............. F ...... 847 742-8429
  Elgin *(G-9224)*

## BLACKSMITH SHOP

B J Fehr Machine Co ...................... G ...... 309 923-8691
  Roanoke *(G-18048)*
Fehring Ornamental Iron Works ........ F ...... 217 483-6727
  Chatham *(G-3620)*

## BLADES: Knife

Summerville Consulting Svcs LLC .... G ...... 618 547-7142
  Alma *(G-424)*

## BLADES: Saw, Chain Type

Unicut Corporation .......................... G ...... 773 525-4210
  Chicago *(G-6813)*

## BLADES: Saw, Hand Or Power

Amv International Inc ...................... F ...... 815 282-9990
  Loves Park *(G-13920)*
Contour Saws Inc ........................... C ...... 800 259-6834
  Des Plaines *(G-8174)*
Midwest Saw Inc ............................ G ...... 630 293-4252
  West Chicago *(G-21743)*
Roentgen USA LLC ........................ G ...... 847 787-0135
  Schiller Park *(G-19868)*
Saws Unlimited Inc ......................... G ...... 847 640-7450
  Elk Grove Village *(G-9730)*
Tru-Cut Tool & Supply Co ................ F ...... 708 396-1122
  Wheeling *(G-22169)*
Wikus Saw Technology Corp ........... E ...... 630 766-0960
  Addison *(G-343)*

## BLANKBOOKS & LOOSELEAF BINDERS

Assemble and Mail Group Inc .......... G ...... 309 473-2006
  Heyworth *(G-11764)*
Bindery Maintenance Services ......... G ...... 618 945-7480
  Bridgeport *(G-2449)*
Post Press Production Inc .............. F ...... 630 860-9833
  Elk Grove Village *(G-9688)*
Tower Plastics Mfg Inc .................... G ...... 847 788-1700
  Burr Ridge *(G-2885)*

## BLANKBOOKS: Albums

Zookbinders Inc ............................. D ...... 847 272-5745
  Deerfield *(G-8070)*

## BLANKBOOKS: Albums, Record

George S Music Room ..................... G ...... 773 767-4676
  Chicago *(G-4945)*
Polyvinyl Record Co ........................ G ...... 217 403-1752
  Champaign *(G-3527)*

## BLANKBOOKS: Checkbooks & Passbooks, Bank

Jpmorgan Chase Bank Nat Assn ...... E ...... 630 653-1270
  Carol Stream *(G-3177)*
Systems Service & Supply ............... G ...... 815 725-1836
  Joliet *(G-12581)*

## BLANKBOOKS: Diaries

Johnson Diaries .............................. G ...... 708 478-2882
  Mokena *(G-14877)*

## BLANKBOOKS: Ledgers & Ledger Sheets

Howard Medical Company ................ G ...... 773 278-1440
  Chicago *(G-5122)*

## BLANKBOOKS: Memorandum, Printed

Funeral Register Books Inc .............. F ...... 217 627-3235
  Girard *(G-10946)*
Webcrafters Inc ............................. D ...... 847 658-6661
  Algonquin *(G-414)*

## BLANKBOOKS: Passbooks, Bank, Etc

Harris Bmo Bank National Assn ........ E ...... 815 886-1900
  Romeoville *(G-18830)*

## BLANKBOOKS: Scrapbooks

Chartwell Studio Inc ........................ G ...... 847 868-8674
  Evanston *(G-10021)*
Got 2b Scrappin ............................. G ...... 217 347-3600
  Effingham *(G-8837)*
Heart & Soul Memories Inc .............. G ...... 847 478-1931
  Buffalo Grove *(G-2702)*

## BLANKETS, FROM PURCHASED MATERIALS

Cotton Goods Manufacturing Co ...... F ...... 773 265-0088
  Chicago *(G-4481)*

## BLAST FURNACE & RELATED PRDTS

O & K American Corp ..................... D ...... 773 767-2500
  Chicago *(G-5957)*

## BLASTING SVC: Sand, Metal Parts

Paradigm Coatings LLC .................. G ...... 847 961-6466
  Huntley *(G-12165)*
Specialty Pntg Soda Blastg Inc ........ G ...... 815 577-0006
  Plainfield *(G-17651)*

## BLINDS & SHADES: Vertical

9161 Corporation ............................ G ...... 847 470-8828
  Niles *(G-15953)*
Going Vertical Inc ........................... G ...... 847 669-3377
  Huntley *(G-12142)*
Hansens Mfrs Win Coverings ........... F ...... 815 935-0010
  Bradley *(G-2424)*
Jack Beall Vertical Service In ........... G ...... 847 426-7958
  Carpentersville *(G-3289)*

## PRODUCT SECTION — BLUEPRINTING SVCS

Marvin Feig & Associates Inc .............F ..... 773 384-5228
  Niles (G-16001)
Regent Window Fashions LLC ............G ..... 773 871-6400
  Chicago (G-6324)
Sage Vertical Grdn Systems LLC .........F ..... 312 234-9655
  Chicago (G-6428)
Ultrasonic Blind Co ...........................G ..... 847 579-8084
  Libertyville (G-13393)
Vertical Tower Partner .......................G ..... 217 819-3040
  Champaign (G-3554)

### BLINDS : Window

21st Century Us-Sino Services ...........G ..... 312 808-9328
  Chicago (G-3664)
A B C Blind Inc .................................G ..... 708 877-7100
  Thornton (G-20866)
Blind Connection Inc .........................G ..... 630 728-6275
  Lake In The Hills (G-12989)
Carol Andrzejewski ............................G ..... 630 369-9711
  Naperville (G-15618)
Chicago Blind Company ....................G ..... 815 553-5525
  Joliet (G-12472)
Excitingwindows By Susan Day ..........G ..... 217 652-2821
  Springfield (G-20436)
EZ Blinds and Drapery Inc ................F ..... 708 246-6600
  La Grange (G-12731)
Levolor Window Furnishings Inc .........G ..... 800 346-3278
  Oak Brook (G-16534)
Robert E Bolton ................................G ..... 815 725-7120
  Joliet (G-12569)
Vertidrapes Manufacturing Inc ...........E ..... 773 478-9272
  Chicago (G-6889)
Window Tech Inc ..............................G ..... 847 272-0739
  Northbrook (G-16388)
Znl Corporation .................................G ..... 815 654-0870
  Loves Park (G-14011)

### BLINDS, WOOD

Aspen Shutters Inc ...........................G ..... 847 979-0166
  Schaumburg (G-19447)
Hilling Services Inc ...........................G ..... 618 667-2005
  Troy (G-21008)

### BLOCKS & BRICKS: Concrete

Artistries By Tommy Musto Inc ..........G ..... 630 674-8667
  Bloomingdale (G-2094)
Beelman Ready-Mix Inc ....................G ..... 618 247-3866
  Sandoval (G-19355)
Bricks Inc .........................................F ..... 773 523-5718
  Chicago (G-4164)
Bricks Inc .........................................G ..... 630 897-6926
  Aurora (G-1121)
Contractors Ready-Mix Inc ................G ..... 217 482-5530
  Mason City (G-14362)
Elston Materials LLC .........................G ..... 773 235-3100
  Chicago (G-4736)
Hamilton Concrete Products Co .........G ..... 217 847-3118
  Hamilton (G-11537)
Lion Ornamental Concrete Pdts .........G ..... 630 892-7304
  Montgomery (G-15056)
M & M Exposed Aggregate Co ..........G ..... 847 551-1818
  Carpentersville (G-3291)
Meno Stone Co Inc ..........................E ..... 630 257-9220
  Lemont (G-13241)
Midwest Cement Products Inc ..........G ..... 815 284-2342
  Woosung (G-22630)
Monmouth Ready Mix Corp ..............G ..... 309 734-3211
  Monmouth (G-15021)
Northfield Block Company .................E ..... 847 949-3600
  Mundelein (G-15539)
Quikrete Companies Inc ...................F ..... 309 346-1184
  Pekin (G-17285)
Southfield Corporation .......................F ..... 217 875-5455
  Decatur (G-7941)
Southfield Corporation .......................E ..... 708 458-0400
  Oak Lawn (G-16644)
Swansea Building Products Inc .........F ..... 618 874-6282
  East Saint Louis (G-8772)
Terrell Materials Corporation ..............E ..... 312 376-0105
  Rosemont (G-19036)

### BLOCKS: Brush, Wood, Turned & Shaped

Silvacor Inc ......................................G ..... 630 897-9211
  Aurora (G-1218)

### BLOCKS: Chimney Or Fireplace, Concrete

Fireplace & Chimney Authority ..........E ..... 630 279-8500
  Elmhurst (G-9872)

### BLOCKS: Landscape Or Retaining Wall, Concrete

Mef Construction Inc ........................G ..... 847 741-8601
  Elgin (G-9105)
R & D Concrete Products Inc ...........E ..... 309 787-0264
  Rock Island (G-18195)
Valley View Industries Hc Inc ............E ..... 800 323-9369
  Crestwood (G-7507)

### BLOCKS: Paving, Asphalt, Not From Refineries

All Pro Paving Inc ............................F ..... 815 806-2222
  Steger (G-20566)

### BLOCKS: Paving, Concrete

Paveloc Industries Inc ......................F ..... 815 568-4700
  Marengo (G-14238)
US Paving Inc ..................................E ..... 630 653-4900
  Glen Ellyn (G-10992)

### BLOCKS: Paving, Cut Stone

Unilock Chicago Inc .........................D ..... 630 892-9191
  Aurora (G-1227)

### BLOCKS: Standard, Concrete Or Cinder

Atlas Concrete Products Co ..............F ..... 217 528-7368
  Springfield (G-20390)
Building Products Corp .....................E ..... 618 233-4427
  Belleville (G-1615)
County Materials Corp ......................E ..... 217 352-4181
  Champaign (G-3470)
County Materials Corp ......................E ..... 217 544-4607
  Springfield (G-20422)
Harvey Cement Products Inc ............F ..... 708 333-1900
  Harvey (G-11668)
Lafarge Building Materials Inc ...........D ..... 678 746-2000
  Chicago (G-5434)
Lafarge North America Inc ................C ..... 703 480-3600
  Chicago (G-5435)
Macomb Concrete Products Inc ........G ..... 309 772-3826
  Bushnell (G-2904)
Northfield Block Company .................C ..... 847 816-9000
  Mundelein (G-15538)
Northfield Block Company .................E ..... 815 941-4100
  Morris (G-15123)
Northfield Block Company .................F ..... 708 458-8130
  Berwyn (G-2069)
Sesser Concrete Products Co ...........F ..... 618 625-2811
  Sesser (G-19895)
Tison & Hall Concrete Products .........F ..... 618 253-7808
  Harrisburg (G-11605)
Top Block & Brick Inc .......................F ..... 815 747-3159
  East Dubuque (G-8626)

### BLOCKS: Tackle, Metal

Durabilt Dyvex Inc ............................F ..... 708 397-4673
  Broadview (G-2573)

### BLOOD RELATED HEALTH SVCS

Lemaitre Vascular Inc .......................F ..... 847 462-2191
  Fox River Grove (G-10288)
Samel Botros ....................................G ..... 847 466-5905
  Bloomingdale (G-2134)

### BLOWER FILTER UNITS: Furnace Blowers

Clean and Science USA Co Ltd ........G ..... 847 461-9292
  Schaumburg (G-19473)
Filter Friend Z Inc .............................G ..... 847 824-4049
  Des Plaines (G-8195)
Kap Holdings LLC ............................F ..... 708 948-0226
  Oak Park (G-16671)

### BLOWERS & FANS

Basement Dewatering Systems ........F ..... 309 647-0331
  Canton (G-2981)
Bost Corporation ..............................F ..... 708 450-9234
  Melrose Park (G-14603)
C P Environmental Inc .....................F ..... 630 759-8866
  Romeoville (G-18805)
Camfil USA Inc ................................D ..... 815 459-6600
  Crystal Lake (G-7549)
Catalytic Products Intl Inc .................E ..... 847 438-0334
  Lake Zurich (G-13050)
Communication Coil Inc ....................D ..... 847 671-1333
  Schiller Park (G-19815)
Durable Manufacturing Company ......F ..... 630 766-0398
  Bensenville (G-1885)
Dust Patrol Inc .................................G ..... 309 676-1161
  Peoria (G-17351)
E I P Inc ..........................................G ..... 847 885-3615
  Hoffman Estates (G-12007)
Filtertek Inc ......................................B ..... 815 648-2410
  Hebron (G-11719)
Filtration Group Corporation ..............D ..... 815 726-4600
  Joliet (G-12494)
Filtration Group LLC .........................G ..... 815 726-4600
  Joliet (G-12495)
Freedom Air Filtration Inc .................G ..... 815 744-8999
  Joliet (G-12497)
Frequency Devices Inc .....................F ..... 815 434-7800
  Ottawa (G-16960)
Fuel Tech Inc ...................................C ..... 630 845-4500
  Warrenville (G-21348)
G T C Industries Inc .........................G ..... 708 369-9815
  Naperville (G-15661)
Goose Island Mfg & Supply Corp ......G ..... 708 343-4225
  Lansing (G-13164)
Henry Technologies Inc ....................G ..... 217 483-2406
  Chatham (G-3621)
Industrial Fiberglass Inc ....................F ..... 708 681-2707
  Melrose Park (G-14657)
Industrial Filter Pump Mfg Co ...........D ..... 708 656-7800
  Bedford Park (G-1556)
Jacobs Boiler & Mech Inds Inc .........E ..... 773 385-9900
  Chicago (G-5269)
Keating of Chicago Inc ....................E ..... 815 569-2324
  Capron (G-2996)
Marvel Electric Corporation ...............D ..... 773 327-2644
  Chicago (G-5638)
Master Manufacturing Co ..................F ..... 630 833-7060
  Villa Park (G-21269)
Mity Inc ............................................G ..... 630 365-5030
  Elburn (G-8898)
Monoxivent Systems Inc ...................G ..... 309 764-9605
  Rock Island (G-18190)
Perma-Pipe Intl Holdings Inc ............C ..... 847 966-1000
  Niles (G-16019)
Quality Cleaning Fluids Inc ...............G ..... 847 451-1190
  Franklin Park (G-10566)
Revcor Inc ........................................B ..... 847 428-4411
  Carpentersville (G-3301)
Revcor Inc ........................................G ..... 847 428-4411
  Carpentersville (G-3302)
Robko Flock Coating Company .........G ..... 847 272-6202
  Northbrook (G-16357)
Terre Haute Tent & Awning Inc .........F ..... 812 235-6068
  South Holland (G-20309)
Tri-Dim Filter Corporation .................E ..... 847 695-5822
  Elgin (G-9213)
Vent Products Co Inc .......................E ..... 773 521-1900
  Chicago (G-6881)

### BLOWERS & FANS

Df Fan Services Inc .........................F ..... 630 876-1495
  West Chicago (G-21692)
Jan-Air Inc .......................................E ..... 815 678-4516
  Richmond (G-17964)
Scott Industrial Blower Co ................F ..... 847 426-8800
  Gilberts (G-10936)
William W Meyer and Sons ..............D ..... 847 918-0111
  Libertyville (G-13402)

### BLOWERS, TURBO: Indl

Kturbo USA Inc ................................G ..... 630 406-1473
  Batavia (G-1462)

### BLUEPRINTING SVCS

Cushing and Company ......................E ..... 312 266-8228
  Chicago (G-4518)
Decatur Blue Print Company .............G ..... 217 423-7589
  Decatur (G-7869)
Lake County Press Inc .....................F ..... 847 336-4333
  Waukegan (G-21580)
Merritt & Edwards Corporation ..........F ..... 309 828-4741
  Bloomington (G-2196)
Robal Company Inc ..........................F ..... 630 393-0777
  Warrenville (G-21361)
Tree Towns Reprographics Inc .........E ..... 630 832-0209
  Elmhurst (G-9951)

# BOAT BUILDING & REPAIR

## BOAT BUILDING & REPAIR

| | | |
|---|---|---|
| Air Land and Sea Interiors | G | 630 834-1717 |
| Villa Park (G-21234) | | |
| ARS Marine Inc East Location | G | 815 942-2600 |
| Morris (G-15093) | | |
| Chicago Sea Ray Inc | E | 815 385-2720 |
| Volo (G-21310) | | |
| Final Finish Boat Works | G | 847 603-1345 |
| Antioch (G-631) | | |
| Nautic Global Group LLC | G | 574 457-5731 |
| Chicago (G-5872) | | |
| Oquawka Boats and Fabrications | G | 309 867-2213 |
| Oquawka (G-16812) | | |
| Purity Select Inc | G | 847 275-3821 |
| Northbrook (G-16349) | | |
| Scf Services LLC | E | 314 436-7559 |
| Sauget (G-19389) | | |
| Seavivor Boats | G | 847 297-5953 |
| Des Plaines (G-8270) | | |
| Tls Windsled Inc | G | 815 262-5791 |
| Belvidere (G-1789) | | |
| Union Ave Auto Inc | G | 708 754-3899 |
| Steger (G-20580) | | |

## BOAT BUILDING & REPAIRING: Fiberglass

| | | |
|---|---|---|
| Advocations Inc | G | 815 568-7505 |
| Woodstock (G-22537) | | |
| Brunswick Corporation | B | 847 735-4700 |
| Lake Forest (G-12888) | | |
| Brunswick International Ltd | G | 847 735-4700 |
| Lake Forest (G-12889) | | |
| Crowleys Yacht Yard Lakeside | F | 773 221-9990 |
| Chicago (G-4509) | | |
| Custom Fiberglass of Illinois | G | 309 344-7727 |
| Galesburg (G-10744) | | |
| Elite Power Boats Inc | G | 618 654-6292 |
| Highland (G-11785) | | |
| Karma Yacht Sales LLC | G | 773 254-0200 |
| Chicago (G-5362) | | |
| Landcraft Auto & Marine Inc | F | 708 385-0717 |
| Crestwood (G-7492) | | |
| Leisure Properties LLC | A | 618 937-6426 |
| West Frankfort (G-21811) | | |
| Metro East Fiberglass Repair | G | 618 235-9217 |
| Belleville (G-1658) | | |
| Rinalli Boat Co Inc | G | 618 467-8850 |
| Godfrey (G-11234) | | |

## BOAT BUILDING & REPAIRING: Kayaks

| | | |
|---|---|---|
| P W C Sports | G | 708 516-6183 |
| Tinley Park (G-20936) | | |

## BOAT BUILDING & REPAIRING: Motorboats, Inboard Or Outboard

| | | |
|---|---|---|
| Sereen LLC | G | 386 527-4876 |
| Rockford (G-18612) | | |
| Waypoint Enterprises | G | 847 551-9213 |
| Algonquin (G-413) | | |

## BOAT BUILDING & REPAIRING: Pontoons, Exc Aircraft & Inflat

| | | |
|---|---|---|
| Outback USA Inc | G | 863 699-2220 |
| Saint Charles (G-19231) | | |

## BOAT DEALERS

| | | |
|---|---|---|
| Metro East Fiberglass Repair | G | 618 235-9217 |
| Belleville (G-1658) | | |
| Nieman & Considine Inc | F | 312 326-1053 |
| Chicago (G-5914) | | |
| Seavivor Boats | G | 847 297-5953 |
| Des Plaines (G-8270) | | |

## BOAT DEALERS: Motor

| | | |
|---|---|---|
| Chicago Sea Ray Inc | E | 815 385-2720 |
| Volo (G-21310) | | |
| Karma Yacht Sales LLC | G | 773 254-0200 |
| Chicago (G-5362) | | |

## BOAT DEALERS: Outboard

| | | |
|---|---|---|
| Sereen LLC | G | 386 527-4876 |
| Rockford (G-18612) | | |

## BOAT REPAIR SVCS

| | | |
|---|---|---|
| Accu-Wright Fiberglass Inc | G | 618 337-3318 |
| East Saint Louis (G-8739) | | |
| Bee Boat Co Inc | G | 217 379-2605 |
| Paxton (G-17236) | | |
| Karma Yacht Sales LLC | G | 773 254-0200 |
| Chicago (G-5362) | | |
| Oquawka Boats and Fabrications | G | 309 867-2213 |
| Oquawka (G-16812) | | |

## BOATS & OTHER MARINE EQPT: Plastic

| | | |
|---|---|---|
| Bee Boat Co Inc | G | 217 379-2605 |
| Paxton (G-17236) | | |

## BOBBINS: Textile Spinning, Made From Purchased Materials

| | | |
|---|---|---|
| T J Assemblies Inc | E | 847 671-0060 |
| Franklin Park (G-10603) | | |

## BODIES: Truck & Bus

| | | |
|---|---|---|
| Automotive Metal Specialist | G | 309 383-2980 |
| Germantown Hills (G-10895) | | |
| Biddison Autobody | G | 309 673-6277 |
| Peoria (G-17318) | | |
| Caterpillar Inc | A | 217 475-4000 |
| Decatur (G-7853) | | |
| Fricker Machine Shop & Salvage | F | 618 285-3271 |
| Elizabethtown (G-9245) | | |
| Independent Antique RAD Mfg | G | 847 458-7400 |
| Algonquin (G-393) | | |
| Knapheide Manufacturing Co | F | 217 222-7134 |
| Quincy (G-17846) | | |
| Kurts Carstar Collision Ctr | F | 618 345-4519 |
| Maryville (G-14343) | | |
| MCI Service Parts Inc | D | 419 994-4141 |
| Des Plaines (G-8230) | | |
| McLaughlin Body Co | D | 309 762-7755 |
| Moline (G-14955) | | |
| Mid City Truck Bdy & Equipmemt | F | 630 628-9080 |
| Addison (G-209) | | |
| Navistar Inc | B | 662 494-3421 |
| Lisle (G-13631) | | |
| Navistar Inc | G | 815 230-0060 |
| Plainfield (G-17631) | | |
| Navistar International Corp | A | 331 332-5000 |
| Lisle (G-13633) | | |
| Phils Auto Body | G | 773 847-7156 |
| Chicago (G-6117) | | |
| Polar Corporation | E | 618 548-3660 |
| Salem (G-19343) | | |
| Pools Welding Inc | G | 309 787-2083 |
| Milan (G-14798) | | |
| R & L Truck Service Inc | F | 847 489-7135 |
| Wadsworth (G-21326) | | |
| Summit Tank & Equipment Co | F | 708 594-3040 |
| Mc Cook (G-14459) | | |
| Thule Inc | C | 847 455-2420 |
| Forest Park (G-10254) | | |
| Triseal Corporation | E | 815 648-2473 |
| Hebron (G-11728) | | |
| Wag Industries Inc | F | 847 329-8932 |
| Skokie (G-20109) | | |

## BODY PARTS: Automobile, Stamped Metal

| | | |
|---|---|---|
| Amis Inc | G | 708 598-9700 |
| Bridgeview (G-2465) | | |
| Autogenesis LLC | G | 630 851-9424 |
| Aurora (G-963) | | |
| Bosch Auto Svc Solutions Inc | G | 815 407-3900 |
| Romeoville (G-18803) | | |
| G T Motoring Inc | G | 847 466-7463 |
| Elk Grove Village (G-9491) | | |
| Grace Auto Body Frame | G | 847 963-1234 |
| Palatine (G-17030) | | |
| Illinois Tool Works Inc | G | 708 720-3541 |
| Frankfort (G-10334) | | |
| ITW Dynatec | G | 847 657-4830 |
| Glenview (G-11151) | | |
| Mmma | F | 309 888-8765 |
| Normal (G-16078) | | |
| Rhino Pros | G | 815 235-7767 |
| Freeport (G-10684) | | |
| SPX Corporation | F | 815 407-3915 |
| Romeoville (G-18869) | | |
| Taurus Die Casting LLC | F | 815 316-6160 |
| Rockford (G-18642) | | |
| Waupaca Foundry Inc | C | 217 347-0600 |
| Effingham (G-8862) | | |

## BOILER & HEATING REPAIR SVCS

| | | |
|---|---|---|
| Petro Chem Echer Erhardt LLC | G | 773 847-7535 |
| Chicago (G-6114) | | |

## BOILER REPAIR SHOP

| | | |
|---|---|---|
| Atlas Boiler & Welding Company | G | 815 963-3360 |
| Elgin (G-8960) | | |
| Cruise Boiler and Repr Co Inc | F | 630 279-7111 |
| Elmhurst (G-9860) | | |
| Jacobs Boiler & Mech Inds Inc | E | 773 385-9900 |
| Chicago (G-5269) | | |
| Jarvis Welding Co | G | 309 647-0033 |
| Canton (G-2988) | | |
| JM Industries LLC | E | 708 849-4700 |
| Riverdale (G-18020) | | |
| Murphy Brothers Enterprises | F | 773 874-9020 |
| Chicago (G-5836) | | |
| Rayes Boiler & Welding Ltd | E | 847 675-6655 |
| Skokie (G-20072) | | |
| South Side Bler Wldg Works Inc | G | 708 478-1714 |
| Orland Park (G-16893) | | |
| Spannuth Boiler Co | G | 708 386-1882 |
| Oak Park (G-16687) | | |

## BOILERS & BOILER SHOP WORK

| | | |
|---|---|---|
| Hudson Boiler & Tank Company | F | 312 666-4780 |
| Lockport (G-13722) | | |

## BOILERS: Low-Pressure Heating, Steam Or Hot Water

| | | |
|---|---|---|
| Cruise Boiler and Repr Co Inc | F | 630 279-7111 |
| Elmhurst (G-9860) | | |
| Mfi Industries Inc | F | 708 841-0727 |
| Riverdale (G-18021) | | |

## BOLTS: Metal

| | | |
|---|---|---|
| Ampex Screw Mfg Inc | E | 847 228-1202 |
| Arlington Heights (G-712) | | |
| BBC Fasteners Inc | E | 708 597-9100 |
| Alsip (G-439) | | |
| Chicago Fastener Inc | E | 708 479-9770 |
| Mokena (G-14857) | | |
| Deco Manufacturing Company | E | 217 872-6450 |
| Decatur (G-7875) | | |
| Formed Fastener Mfg Inc | E | 708 496-1219 |
| Bridgeview (G-2492) | | |
| J H Botts LLC | E | 815 726-5885 |
| Joliet (G-12519) | | |
| MNP Precision Parts LLC | C | 815 391-5256 |
| Rockford (G-18509) | | |
| Pearson Fastener Corporation | F | 815 397-4460 |
| Rockford (G-18532) | | |
| Rockford Bolt & Steel Co | E | 815 968-0514 |
| Rockford (G-18567) | | |
| Screws Industries Inc | D | 630 539-9200 |
| Glendale Heights (G-11068) | | |
| Wenco Manufacturing Co Inc | E | 630 377-7474 |
| Elgin (G-9235) | | |

## BOOK STORES

| | | |
|---|---|---|
| Barnes & Noble College | E | 309 677-2320 |
| Peoria (G-17314) | | |
| Fellowship Black Light | G | 773 826-7790 |
| Chicago (G-4834) | | |
| Filmfax Magazine Inc | G | 847 866-7155 |
| Evanston (G-10037) | | |
| Graphic Score Book Co Inc | G | 847 823-7382 |
| Park Ridge (G-17199) | | |
| Polonia Book Store Inc | G | 773 481-6968 |
| Chicago (G-6151) | | |

## BOOK STORES: Children's

| | | |
|---|---|---|
| Phoenix Intl Publications Inc | B | 312 739-4400 |
| Chicago (G-6119) | | |
| Senario LLC | F | 847 882-0677 |
| Schaumburg (G-19725) | | |

## BOOKING AGENCIES, THEATRICAL

| | | |
|---|---|---|
| Haute Noir Media Group Inc | G | 312 869-4526 |
| Chicago (G-5055) | | |

# PRODUCT SECTION

## BOOKS, WHOLESALE

| Company | Code | Phone |
|---|---|---|
| Art Media Resources Inc | G | 312 663-5351 |
| Chicago *(G-3951)* | | |
| Charles H Kerr Publishing Co | G | 773 262-1329 |
| Chicago *(G-4291)* | | |
| Chicago Review Press Inc | E | 312 337-0747 |
| Chicago *(G-4344)* | | |
| Follett School Solutions Inc | C | 815 759-1700 |
| McHenry *(G-14507)* | | |
| P F Pettibone & Co | G | 815 344-7811 |
| Crystal Lake *(G-7624)* | | |
| Psytec Inc | G | 815 758-1415 |
| Dekalb *(G-8114)* | | |

## BOOKS: Memorandum, Exc Printed, From Purchased Materials

| Company | Code | Phone |
|---|---|---|
| House of Doolittle Ltd | E | 847 593-3417 |
| Arlington Heights *(G-769)* | | |

## BOOTS: Women's

| Company | Code | Phone |
|---|---|---|
| Horse Creek Outfitters | G | 217 544-2740 |
| Springfield *(G-20452)* | | |

## BOTTLE CAPS & RESEALERS: Plastic

| Company | Code | Phone |
|---|---|---|
| Berry Global Inc | C | 815 334-5225 |
| Woodstock *(G-22544)* | | |
| Berry Global Inc | G | |
| Lake Bluff *(G-12836)* | | |
| Berry Global Inc | B | 708 396-1470 |
| Alsip *(G-441)* | | |
| Jigsaw Solutions Inc | G | 630 926-1948 |
| Romeoville *(G-18832)* | | |

## BOTTLED GAS DEALERS: Propane

| Company | Code | Phone |
|---|---|---|
| Ferrellgas LP | G | 815 877-7333 |
| Machesney Park *(G-14073)* | | |
| Outback USA Inc | G | 863 699-2220 |
| Saint Charles *(G-19231)* | | |

## BOTTLED WATER DELIVERY

| Company | Code | Phone |
|---|---|---|
| Ds Services of America Inc | F | 800 322-6272 |
| Rockford *(G-18352)* | | |
| Mautino Distributing Co Inc | E | 815 664-4311 |
| Spring Valley *(G-20376)* | | |
| Samuel Rowell | G | 618 942-6970 |
| Herrin *(G-11754)* | | |

## BOTTLES: Plastic

| Company | Code | Phone |
|---|---|---|
| Alpha Packaging Minnesota Inc | G | 507 454-3830 |
| Chicago *(G-3829)* | | |
| Amcor Rigid Plastics Usa LLC | E | 630 406-3500 |
| Batavia *(G-1411)* | | |
| Amcor Rigid Plastics Usa LLC | D | 630 773-3235 |
| Itasca *(G-12227)* | | |
| American National Can Co | G | 630 406-3500 |
| Batavia *(G-1414)* | | |
| CCL Dispensing Systems LLC | D | 847 816-9400 |
| Libertyville *(G-13312)* | | |
| Consolidated Container Co LLC | C | 630 231-7150 |
| West Chicago *(G-21686)* | | |
| Container Specialties Inc | E | 708 615-1400 |
| Franklin Park *(G-10441)* | | |
| Dana Plastic Container Corp | G | 847 670-0650 |
| Arlington Heights *(G-744)* | | |
| Dana Plastic Container Corp | E | 630 529-7878 |
| Roselle *(G-18939)* | | |
| Fitpac Co Ltd | G | 630 428-9077 |
| Bensenville *(G-1899)* | | |
| Graham Packaging Co Europe LLC | C | 630 562-5912 |
| West Chicago *(G-21711)* | | |
| Graham Packaging Co Europe LLC | B | 630 231-0850 |
| West Chicago *(G-21712)* | | |
| Graham Packaging Company LP | E | 630 739-9150 |
| Woodridge *(G-22490)* | | |
| Harbison Corporation | D | 815 224-2633 |
| Peru *(G-17511)* | | |
| Illinois Bottle Mfg Co | D | 847 595-9000 |
| Elk Grove Village *(G-9533)* | | |
| Inhance Technologies LLC | G | 630 231-7515 |
| West Chicago *(G-21719)* | | |
| Innocor Foam Technologies LLC | F | 630 293-0780 |
| West Chicago *(G-21723)* | | |
| Isovac Products LLC | G | 630 679-1740 |
| Romeoville *(G-18831)* | | |
| Lexi Group Inc | G | 866 675-1683 |
| Chicago *(G-5498)* | | |
| Liquid Container Inc | E | 630 562-5812 |
| West Chicago *(G-21733)* | | |
| Logoplaste Chicago LLC | G | 815 230-6961 |
| Plainfield *(G-17619)* | | |
| Logoplaste Fort Worth LLC | G | 815 230-6961 |
| Plainfield *(G-17620)* | | |
| Logoplaste Racine LLC | G | 815 230-6961 |
| Plainfield *(G-17621)* | | |
| Logoplaste Usa Inc | D | 815 230-6961 |
| Plainfield *(G-17622)* | | |
| Petainer Manufacturing USA Inc | F | 630 326-9921 |
| Batavia *(G-1481)* | | |
| Phoenix Unlimited Ltd | G | 847 515-1263 |
| Huntley *(G-12167)* | | |
| Plastic Container Corporation | D | 217 352-2722 |
| Urbana *(G-21098)* | | |
| Plastipak Packaging Inc | B | 217 398-1832 |
| Champaign *(G-3526)* | | |
| Plastipak Packaging Inc | C | 708 385-0721 |
| Alsip *(G-510)* | | |
| Pvc Container Corporation | C | 217 463-6600 |
| Paris *(G-17159)* | | |
| Ring Container Tech LLC | E | 217 875-5084 |
| Decatur *(G-7934)* | | |
| Ring Container Tech LLC | E | 815 229-9110 |
| Rockford *(G-18555)* | | |
| Ringwood Containers LP | G | 815 939-7270 |
| Kankakee *(G-12644)* | | |
| Silgan Plastics LLC | D | 618 662-4471 |
| Flora *(G-10217)* | | |
| Southeastern Container Inc | G | 217 342-9600 |
| Effingham *(G-8858)* | | |
| Wheaton Plastic Products | G | 847 298-5626 |
| Des Plaines *(G-8304)* | | |
| Whitney Products Inc | F | 847 966-6161 |
| Niles *(G-16047)* | | |

## BOTTLES: Vacuum

| Company | Code | Phone |
|---|---|---|
| Tkk USA Inc | G | 847 439-7821 |
| Rolling Meadows *(G-18783)* | | |

## BOWLING CENTERS

| Company | Code | Phone |
|---|---|---|
| Brunswick Corporation | B | 847 735-4700 |
| Lake Forest *(G-12888)* | | |

## BOWLING EQPT & SPLY STORES

| Company | Code | Phone |
|---|---|---|
| K 9 Tag Company Inc | G | 847 304-8247 |
| Waukegan *(G-21575)* | | |

## BOWLING EQPT & SPLYS

| Company | Code | Phone |
|---|---|---|
| Bobs Business Inc | G | 630 238-5790 |
| Bensenville *(G-1845)* | | |
| Bowl-Tronics Enterprises Inc | G | 847 741-4500 |
| Elgin *(G-8970)* | | |

## BOXES & CRATES: Rectangular, Wood

| Company | Code | Phone |
|---|---|---|
| Caisson Inc | E | 815 547-5925 |
| Belvidere *(G-1741)* | | |
| Caisson Industries Inc | F | 815 568-6554 |
| Marengo *(G-14221)* | | |
| Chicago Crate Inc | G | 708 380-4716 |
| Downers Grove *(G-8409)* | | |
| D/C Export & Domestic Pkg Inc | E | 847 593-4200 |
| Elk Grove Village *(G-9415)* | | |
| Hart - Clayton Inc | F | 217 525-1610 |
| Springfield *(G-20448)* | | |
| Induspac Rtp Inc | G | 919 484-9484 |
| Bridgeview *(G-2500)* | | |
| Nefab Packaging N Centl LLC | C | |
| Elk Grove Village *(G-9649)* | | |
| Pallett Wilson | G | 217 543-3555 |
| Sullivan *(G-20757)* | | |
| R & H Products Inc | G | 815 744-4110 |
| Rockdale *(G-18229)* | | |
| Specialty Crate Factory | G | 708 756-2100 |
| Steger *(G-20576)* | | |

## BOXES & SHOOK: Nailed Wood

| Company | Code | Phone |
|---|---|---|
| Arrowtech Pallet & Crating | D | 815 547-9300 |
| Belvidere *(G-1734)* | | |
| Central Wood Products Inc | E | 217 728-4412 |
| Sullivan *(G-20742)* | | |
| Chicago Export Packing Co | F | 773 247-8911 |
| Chicago *(G-4318)* | | |
| Community Support Systems | D | 217 705-4300 |
| Teutopolis *(G-20850)* | | |
| Dexton Enterprises | G | 309 788-1881 |
| Rock Island *(G-18174)* | | |
| Du-Call Miller Plastics Inc | F | 630 964-6020 |
| Batavia *(G-1443)* | | |
| Fca LLC | E | 309 949-3999 |
| Coal Valley *(G-7296)* | | |
| Fca LLC | E | 309 385-2588 |
| Princeville *(G-17765)* | | |
| Jordan Paper Box Company | F | 773 287-5362 |
| Chicago *(G-5323)* | | |
| Kccdd Inc | D | 309 344-2030 |
| Galesburg *(G-10762)* | | |
| Nefab Packaging N Centl LLC | C | |
| Elk Grove Village *(G-9649)* | | |
| Pak Source Inc | E | 309 786-7374 |
| Rock Island *(G-18191)* | | |
| R & H Products Inc | G | 815 744-4110 |
| Rockdale *(G-18229)* | | |
| Trade Industries | E | 618 643-4321 |
| Mc Leansboro *(G-14469)* | | |
| Upham & Walsh Lumber Co | G | 847 519-1010 |
| Hoffman Estates *(G-12067)* | | |

## BOXES: Cash & Stamp, Stamped Metal

| Company | Code | Phone |
|---|---|---|
| Block and Company Inc | C | 847 537-7200 |
| Wheeling *(G-22015)* | | |

## BOXES: Corrugated

| Company | Code | Phone |
|---|---|---|
| Akers Packaging Service Inc | D | 773 731-2900 |
| Chicago *(G-3790)* | | |
| Alois Box Co Inc | E | 708 681-4090 |
| Melrose Park *(G-14590)* | | |
| American Boxboard LLC | E | 708 924-9810 |
| Batavia *(G-1413)* | | |
| Batavia Container Inc | C | 630 879-2100 |
| Batavia *(G-1419)* | | |
| Box Manufacturing Inc | G | 309 637-6228 |
| Peoria *(G-17319)* | | |
| Cameo Container Corporation | C | 773 254-1030 |
| Chicago *(G-4222)* | | |
| Cano Container Corporation | G | 630 585-7500 |
| Aurora *(G-980)* | | |
| Capitol Carton Company | E | 312 563-9690 |
| Chicago *(G-4229)* | | |
| Capitol Carton Company | E | 312 491-2220 |
| Chicago *(G-4230)* | | |
| Cascades Plastics Inc | C | 450 469-3389 |
| Aurora *(G-981)* | | |
| Compak Inc | E | 815 399-2699 |
| Rockford *(G-18320)* | | |
| Corr-Pak Corporation | E | 708 442-7806 |
| Mc Cook *(G-14447)* | | |
| Cross Container Corporation | E | 847 844-3200 |
| Carpentersville *(G-3281)* | | |
| DDN Industries Inc | G | 847 885-8595 |
| Hoffman Estates *(G-12004)* | | |
| Forest Packaging Corporation | E | 847 981-7000 |
| Elk Grove Village *(G-9485)* | | |
| Greif Inc | D | 217 468-2396 |
| Oreana *(G-16817)* | | |
| H Field & Sons Inc | F | 847 434-0970 |
| Arlington Heights *(G-761)* | | |
| Heritage Packaging LLC | E | 217 735-4406 |
| Lincoln *(G-13410)* | | |
| Ideal Box Co | C | 708 594-3100 |
| Chicago *(G-5140)* | | |
| Illinois Valley Container Inc | E | 815 223-7200 |
| Peru *(G-17513)* | | |
| International Paper Company | C | 217 735-1221 |
| Lincoln *(G-13411)* | | |
| Kindlon Enterprises Inc | G | 708 367-4000 |
| Aurora *(G-1043)* | | |
| Liberty Diversified Intl Inc | E | 217 935-8361 |
| Clinton *(G-7285)* | | |
| Liberty Diversified Intl Inc | C | 309 787-6161 |
| Rock Island *(G-18186)* | | |
| Midwest Fibre Products Inc | G | 309 596-2955 |
| Viola *(G-21292)* | | |
| Midwest Packaging & Cont Inc | D | 815 633-6800 |
| Machesney Park *(G-14093)* | | |
| Nation Inc | E | 847 844-7300 |
| Carpentersville *(G-3292)* | | |
| Orora North America | E | 630 613-2600 |
| Lombard *(G-13839)* | | |
| Orora Packaging Solutions | D | 815 895-2343 |
| Sycamore *(G-20812)* | | |
| Packaging Corporation America | G | 618 662-6700 |
| Flora *(G-10213)* | | |
| Pierce Box & Paper Corporation | E | 815 547-0117 |
| Belvidere *(G-1778)* | | |

## BOXES: Corrugated

**Reliable Container Inc** .................... E ....... 630 543-6131
  Addison *(G-274)*
**Rex Carton Company Inc** .................. E ....... 773 581-4115
  Chicago *(G-6342)*
**Royal Box Group LLC** ....................... B ....... 708 656-2020
  Cicero *(G-7225)*
**Royal Box Group LLC** ....................... E ....... 630 543-4464
  Addison *(G-281)*
**Royal Box Group LLC** ....................... F ....... 708 222-4650
  Cicero *(G-7226)*
**Rudd Container Corporation** ............. D ....... 773 847-7600
  Chicago *(G-6414)*
**Sauk Valley Container Corp** .............. F ....... 815 626-9657
  Sterling *(G-20611)*
**Siebs Die Cutting Specialty Co** ......... G ....... 217 735-1432
  Lincoln *(G-13420)*
**Sisco Corporation** ............................ E ....... 618 327-3066
  Nashville *(G-15847)*
**Stand Fast Packaging Pdts Inc** .......... D ....... 630 600-0900
  Carol Stream *(G-3247)*
**Strive Converting Corporation** ........... C ....... 773 227-6000
  Chicago *(G-6607)*
**Sycamore Containers Inc** ................. D ....... 815 895-2343
  Sycamore *(G-20818)*
**Tuscola Packaging Group LLC** ......... G ....... 734 268-2877
  Tuscola *(G-21027)*
**United Container Corporation** ........... E ....... 773 342-2200
  Chicago *(G-6822)*
**Wertheimer Box & Paper Corp** .......... D ....... 312 829-4545
  Mc Cook *(G-14461)*
**Westrock Cp LLC** ............................. C ....... 847 689-4200
  North Chicago *(G-16190)*
**Westrock Cp LLC** ............................. D ....... 630 384-5200
  Carol Stream *(G-3266)*

## BOXES: Junction, Electric

**Appleton Grp LLC** ............................. C ....... 847 268-6000
  Rosemont *(G-18989)*
**Hubbell Wiegmann Inc** ..................... B ....... 618 539-3542
  Freeburg *(G-10637)*

## BOXES: Mail Or Post Office, Collection/Storage, Sheet Metal

**US Post Co Inc** ................................. G ....... 815 675-9313
  Spring Grove *(G-20373)*

## BOXES: Outlet, Electric Wiring Device

**Lew Electric Fittings Co** .................... F ....... 630 665-2075
  Carol Stream *(G-3183)*
**Midwest-Design Inc** ......................... G ....... 708 615-1572
  Broadview *(G-2596)*

## BOXES: Packing & Shipping, Metal

**Mfz Ventures Inc** .............................. G ....... 773 247-4611
  Chicago *(G-5715)*
**Product Service Craft Inc** ................. F ....... 630 964-5160
  Downers Grove *(G-8511)*
**Zenith Fabricating Company** ............ E ....... 773 622-2601
  Chicago *(G-7064)*

## BOXES: Paperboard, Folding

**Accord Carton Co** ............................ C ....... 708 272-3050
  Alsip *(G-428)*
**Artistic Carton Company** .................. E ....... 847 741-0247
  Elgin *(G-8958)*
**Box Form Inc** ................................... E ....... 773 927-8808
  Chicago *(G-4151)*
**Capitol Carton Company** .................. E ....... 312 563-9690
  Chicago *(G-4229)*
**Caraustar Industries Inc** ................... E ....... 773 308-7622
  Chicago *(G-4236)*
**Cartoncraft Inc** ................................. D ....... 630 377-1230
  Saint Charles *(G-19151)*
**Colbert Packaging Corporation** ......... C ....... 847 367-5990
  Lake Forest *(G-12892)*
**Combined Technologies Inc** ............ G ....... 847 968-4855
  Libertyville *(G-13317)*
**Fox Valley Printing Co Inc** ................ F ....... 419 232-3348
  Montgomery *(G-15043)*
**General Converting Inc** .................... D ....... 630 378-9800
  Bolingbrook *(G-2312)*
**Graphic Packaging Holding Co** ........ B ....... 630 260-6500
  Carol Stream *(G-3161)*
**Graphic Packaging Intl Inc** ................ D ....... 618 533-2721
  Centralia *(G-3416)*
**H Field & Sons Inc** ........................... F ....... 847 434-0970
  Arlington Heights *(G-761)*

**Impac Group Inc** ............................... A ....... 708 344-9100
  Melrose Park *(G-14655)*
**Jordan Paper Box Company** ............. F ....... 773 287-5362
  Chicago *(G-5323)*
**Knight Paper Box Company** .............. D ....... 773 585-2035
  Chicago *(G-5390)*
**Master Paper Box Company Inc** ....... F ....... 773 927-0252
  Chicago *(G-5643)*
**MB Box Inc** ...................................... G ....... 815 589-3043
  Fulton *(G-10703)*
**Midwest Fibre Products Inc** .............. E ....... 309 596-2955
  Viola *(G-21292)*
**Nosco Inc** ........................................ B ....... 847 336-4200
  Waukegan *(G-21595)*
**Plasticrest Products Inc** ................... F ....... 773 826-2163
  Chicago *(G-6136)*
**Racine Paper Box Manufacturing** ..... E ....... 773 227-3900
  Chicago *(G-6278)*
**Rex Carton Company Inc** .................. E ....... 773 581-4115
  Chicago *(G-6342)*
**Specialty Box Corp** .......................... F ....... 630 897-7278
  North Aurora *(G-16145)*
**The Calumet Carton Company** ......... D ....... 708 331-7910
  South Holland *(G-20310)*
**United Press Inc (del)** ...................... F ....... 847 482-0597
  Lincolnshire *(G-13487)*
**Westrock Cp LLC** ............................. F ....... 309 342-0121
  Galesburg *(G-10780)*
**Winkler Products Inc** ........................ G ....... 314 421-1926
  Edwardsville *(G-8819)*

## BOXES: Paperboard, Set-Up

**Armbrust Paper Tubes Inc** ................ E ....... 773 586-3232
  Chicago *(G-3945)*
**Bierdeman Box LLC** ........................ E ....... 847 256-0302
  Wilmette *(G-22244)*
**Colbert Packaging Corporation** ......... C ....... 847 367-5990
  Lake Forest *(G-12892)*
**Elegant Acquisition LLC** ................... D ....... 708 652-3400
  Cicero *(G-7194)*
**International Paper Company** ........... E ....... 708 728-1000
  Bedford Park *(G-1557)*
**Jordan Paper Box Company** ............. F ....... 773 287-5362
  Chicago *(G-5323)*
**Master Paper Box Company Inc** ....... F ....... 773 927-0252
  Chicago *(G-5643)*
**Racine Paper Box Manufacturing** ..... E ....... 773 227-3900
  Chicago *(G-6278)*
**Reddi-Pac Inc** .................................. F ....... 847 657-5222
  Glenview *(G-11191)*
**Wabash Container Corporation** ........ E ....... 618 263-3586
  Mount Carmel *(G-15287)*

## BOXES: Plastic

**Accurate Carriers Inc** ....................... F ....... 630 790-3430
  Glendale Heights *(G-11007)*
**Akrylix Inc** ....................................... F ....... 773 869-9005
  Frankfort *(G-10291)*
**Aptargroup International LLC** ........... G ....... 815 477-0424
  Crystal Lake *(G-7536)*
**CTS Automotive LLC** ....................... E ....... 815 385-9480
  McHenry *(G-14493)*
**Home Pdts Intl - N Amer Inc** ............. B ....... 773 890-1010
  Chicago *(G-5102)*
**Plano Molding Company LLC** .......... G ....... 630 552-3111
  Plano *(G-17673)*
**Plasticrest Products Inc** ................... F ....... 773 826-2163
  Chicago *(G-6136)*
**Really Useful Boxes Inc** ................... F ....... 847 238-0444
  Elk Grove Village *(G-9710)*

## BOXES: Solid Fiber

**John J Monaco Products Co Inc** ....... E ....... 708 344-3333
  Melrose Park *(G-14664)*
**Stitch TEC Co Inc** ............................ G ....... 618 327-8054
  Nashville *(G-15848)*
**The Calumet Carton Company** ......... D ....... 708 331-7910
  South Holland *(G-20310)*

## BOXES: Stamped Metal

**Plasticrest Products Inc** ................... F ....... 773 826-2163
  Chicago *(G-6136)*

## BOXES: Switch, Electric

**Honeywell International Inc** .............. G ....... 815 235-5500
  Freeport *(G-10664)*

## BOXES: Wirebound, Wood

**A & M Wood Products Inc** ................ G ....... 630 323-2555
  Burr Ridge *(G-2818)*
**Ockerlund Wood Products Co** .......... E ....... 630 620-1269
  Addison *(G-233)*

## BOXES: Wooden

**D/C Export & Domestic Pkg Inc** ........ E ....... 847 593-4200
  Elk Grove Village *(G-9415)*
**Elm Street Industries Inc** .................. F ....... 309 854-7000
  Kewanee *(G-12681)*
**Extreme Tools Inc** ........................... G ....... 630 202-8324
  Naperville *(G-15656)*
**Ockerlund Industries Inc** .................. E ....... 630 620-1269
  Addison *(G-232)*
**Pierce Packaging Co** ....................... F ....... 815 636-5650
  Loves Park *(G-13974)*
**Pierce Packaging Co** ....................... F ....... 815 636-5656
  Peoria *(G-17428)*
**Pierce Packaging Co** ....................... F ....... 815 636-5656
  Loves Park *(G-13975)*
**Specialty Box Corp** .......................... F ....... 630 897-7278
  North Aurora *(G-16145)*

## BRAKES & BRAKE PARTS

**Bpi Holdings International Inc** ........... C ....... 815 363-9000
  McHenry *(G-14483)*
**Brake Parts Inc India LLC** ................ F ....... 815 363-9000
  McHenry *(G-14484)*
**Brake Parts Inc LLC** ........................ C ....... 815 363-9000
  McHenry *(G-14485)*
**Bremskerl North America Inc** ........... G ....... 847 289-3460
  Bartlett *(G-1337)*
**Gunite Corporation** .......................... B ....... 815 490-6260
  Rockford *(G-18407)*
**Methods Distrs & Mfrs Inc** ................ G ....... 847 973-1449
  Fox Lake *(G-10279)*
**Mid-Illinois Caliper Co Inc** ................ F .......
  Springfield *(G-20482)*
**Morse Automotive Corporation** ......... A ....... 773 843-9000
  Buffalo Grove *(G-2739)*
**Performance Manufacturing** ............. G ....... 630 231-8099
  West Chicago *(G-21756)*
**Rebuilders Enterprises Inc** ............... G ....... 708 430-0030
  Bridgeview *(G-2523)*

## BRAKES: Metal Forming

**Kazmier Tooling Inc** ......................... G ....... 773 586-0300
  Chicago *(G-5366)*
**Kipp Manufacturing Company Inc** .... F ....... 630 768-9051
  Wauconda *(G-21477)*

## BRAKES: Press

**Ceg Subsidiary LLC** ......................... D ....... 618 262-8666
  Mount Carmel *(G-15262)*
**Press Brakes** .................................. G ....... 630 916-1494
  Lombard *(G-13845)*
**R-K Press Brake Dies Inc** ................. F ....... 708 371-1756
  Chicago *(G-6275)*
**Riteway Brake Dies Inc** .................... F ....... 708 430-0795
  Bridgeview *(G-2524)*

## BRASS & BRONZE PRDTS: Die-casted

**Anderson Casting Company Inc** ....... G ....... 312 733-1185
  Chicago *(G-3901)*
**G & W Electric Company** ................. E ....... 708 389-8307
  Blue Island *(G-2251)*
**Mahoney Foundries Inc** .................... E ....... 309 784-2311
  Vermont *(G-21138)*

## BRASS FOUNDRY, NEC

**Altman Pattern and Foundry Co** ........ F ....... 773 586-9100
  Chicago *(G-3839)*
**Calumet Brass Foundry Inc** .............. F ....... 708 849-3040
  Dolton *(G-8367)*
**Cast Technologies Inc** ..................... C ....... 309 676-1715
  Peoria *(G-17323)*
**Illini Foundry Co Inc** ......................... G ....... 309 697-3142
  Peoria *(G-17385)*
**Kvk Foundry Inc** .............................. F ....... 815 695-5212
  Millington *(G-14819)*
**Tricast/Presfore Corporation** ............ G ....... 815 459-1820
  Crystal Lake *(G-7669)*
**Trio Foundry Inc** .............................. E ....... 630 892-1676
  Montgomery *(G-15068)*

# PRODUCT SECTION — BROOMS

### BRASS ROLLING & DRAWING
Gbc Metals LLC .................................. F ...... 618 258-2350
East Alton *(G-8602)*
Gbc Metals LLC .................................. G ...... 618 258-2350
East Alton *(G-8603)*
Global Brass and Copper Inc .............. G ...... 502 873-3000
East Alton *(G-8604)*

### BRASSWORK: Ornamental, Structural
Krum Kreations .................................. G ...... 815 772-8296
Morrison *(G-15145)*

### BRAZING SVCS
Ehrhardt Tool & Machine LLC ............ C ...... 314 436-6900
Granite City *(G-11274)*

### BRAZING: Metal
DK Surface Hardening Inc .................. G ...... 708 233-9095
Bridgeview *(G-2484)*
International Proc Co Amer ................ E ...... 847 437-8400
Elk Grove Village *(G-9553)*
Met Co Industries Inc ......................... E ...... 630 584-5100
Saint Charles *(G-19218)*
Rogers Metal Services Inc .................. E ...... 847 679-4642
Skokie *(G-20078)*
Rogers Metal Services Inc .................. E ...... 847 679-4642
Skokie *(G-20079)*
Standard Heat Treating Co Inc ........... D ...... 708 447-7504
Chicago *(G-6569)*

### BRICK, STONE & RELATED PRDTS WHOLESALERS
Clay Vollmar Products Co ................... G ...... 847 540-5850
Lake Zurich *(G-13054)*
Eagle Stone and Brick Inc ................... G ...... 618 282-6722
Red Bud *(G-17940)*
Jackson County Sand & Grav Co ........ G ...... 618 763-4711
Gorham *(G-11254)*
Kona Blackbird Inc .............................. F ...... 815 792-8750
Serena *(G-19892)*
Ozinga Bros Inc .................................. E ...... 708 326-4200
Mokena *(G-14889)*
Paveloc Industries Inc ......................... F ...... 815 568-4700
Marengo *(G-14238)*
Tri-State Cut Stone Co ....................... E ...... 815 469-7550
Frankfort *(G-10371)*
Western Sand & Gravel Co ................. F ...... 815 433-1600
Ottawa *(G-16991)*

### BRICKS & BLOCKS: Structural
Southfield Corporation ....................... F ...... 217 398-4300
Champaign *(G-3543)*

### BRICKS: Ceramic Glazed, Clay
Selee Corporation ............................... E ...... 847 428-4455
Gilberts *(G-10937)*

### BRICKS: Flooring, Clay
Kona Blackbird Inc .............................. F ...... 815 792-8750
Serena *(G-19892)*

### BRICKS: Paving, Clay
Arrowhead Brick Pavers Inc ................ E ...... 630 393-1584
Warrenville *(G-21342)*
Complete Lawn and Snow Service ..... F ...... 847 776-7287
Palatine *(G-17014)*

### BRICKS: Clay
Red-E-Mix LLC ................................... D ...... 618 654-2166
Highland *(G-11808)*
Richards Brick Company .................... D ...... 618 656-0230
Edwardsville *(G-8812)*

### BRICKS: Concrete
Glen-Gery Corporation ...................... D ...... 815 795-6911
Marseilles *(G-14309)*
New Panel Brick Company of Ill ......... G ...... 847 696-1686
Glenview *(G-11173)*
North Shore Paving Inc ...................... G ...... 847 201-1710
Round Lake Heights *(G-19082)*

### BRIDAL SHOPS
Best Kept Secrets ............................... G ...... 773 431-0353
Blue Island *(G-2238)*
Chambers Marketing Options ............ G ...... 847 584-2626
Elk Grove Village *(G-9364)*
Doris Bridal Boutique ......................... G ...... 847 433-2575
Highwood *(G-11884)*
Duckys Formal Wear Inc .................... G ...... 309 342-5914
Galesburg *(G-10748)*
Jane Stodden Bridals .......................... G ...... 815 223-2091
La Salle *(G-12779)*
Winning Stitch ................................... G ...... 217 348-8279
Charleston *(G-3616)*

### BRIEFCASES
J-Industries Inc .................................. F ...... 815 654-0055
Loves Park *(G-13949)*
Jacobson Acqstion Holdings LLC ....... C ...... 847 623-1414
Waukegan *(G-21574)*

### BROACHING MACHINES
Illinois Broaching Co .......................... G ...... 847 678-3080
Schiller Park *(G-19840)*
Inland Broaching and TI Co LLC ......... G ...... 847 233-0033
Elgin *(G-9077)*
Rockford Broach Inc .......................... F ...... 815 484-0409
Rockford *(G-18568)*
Universal Broaching Inc ..................... F ...... 847 228-1440
Elk Grove Village *(G-9800)*

### BROADCASTING & COMMS EQPT: Antennas, Transmitting/Comms
AF Antronics Inc ................................ G ...... 217 328-0800
Urbana *(G-21068)*
Amphenol Antenna Solutions Inc ...... C ...... 815 399-0001
Rockford *(G-18265)*
Amphenol T&M Antennas Inc ........... F ...... 847 478-5600
Lincolnshire *(G-13428)*
Antenex Inc ....................................... G ...... 847 839-6910
Schaumburg *(G-19444)*
Charles Electronics LLC ..................... G ...... 815 244-7981
Mount Carroll *(G-15290)*
Moran Cristobalian ............................ .......... 630 506-4777
Batavia *(G-1472)*
Nucurrent Inc .................................... .......... 312 575-0388
Chicago *(G-5954)*
Research In Motion Rf Inc ................. .......... 815 444-1095
Crystal Lake *(G-7639)*

### BROADCASTING & COMMS EQPT: Rcvr-Transmitter Unt, Transceiver
Portable Cmmnctns Spclsts ............... G ...... 630 458-1800
Addison *(G-247)*

### BROADCASTING & COMMUNICATION EQPT: Transmit-Receiver, Radio
Las Systems Inc ................................. E ...... 847 462-8100
Woodstock *(G-22582)*
LL Electronics ..................................... G ...... 217 586-6477
Mahomet *(G-14160)*

### BROADCASTING & COMMUNICATIONS EQPT: Cellular Radio Telephone
Acp Tower Holdings LLC .................... G ...... 800 835-8527
Chicago *(G-3737)*
Clearchoice Mobility Inc .................... G ...... 847 986-6313
Round Lake Beach *(G-19074)*
Community Advantage Network ....... G ...... 847 376-8943
Des Plaines *(G-8173)*
Lemko Corporation ........................... E ...... 630 948-3025
Itasca *(G-12302)*
Scrn LLC ............................................ G ...... 847 513-4082
Chicago *(G-6462)*
Tanklink Corporation ......................... E ...... 312 379-8397
Chicago *(G-6673)*
Telular Corporation ........................... D ...... 800 835-8527
Chicago *(G-6692)*
Xentris Wireless LLC .......................... D ...... 630 693-9700
Addison *(G-348)*

### BROADCASTING & COMMUNICATIONS EQPT: Studio Eqpt, Radio & TV
Anywave Communication Tech Inc .... F ...... 847 415-2258
Lincolnshire *(G-13429)*
Jai-S Record Label ............................. G ...... 708 351-4279
Park Forest *(G-17173)*

### BROADCASTING & COMMUNICATIONS EQPT: Transmitting, Radio/TV
BEI Electronics LLC ............................ F ...... 217 224-9600
Quincy *(G-17802)*

### BROKERS' SVCS
Arby Graphic Service Inc ................... F ...... 847 763-0900
Niles *(G-15961)*
Integra Graphics and Forms Inc ........ F ...... 708 385-0950
Crestwood *(G-7490)*
Tailored Printing Inc .......................... G ...... 217 522-6287
Rochester *(G-18122)*

### BROKERS: Commodity Contracts
Huyear Trucking Inc ........................... G ...... 217 854-3551
Carlinville *(G-3039)*

### BROKERS: Food
Chicago Local Foods LLC .................. E ...... 312 432-6575
Chicago *(G-4329)*
Custom Culinary Inc .......................... D ...... 630 299-0500
Oswego *(G-16912)*
Far East Food Inc ............................... G ...... 312 733-1688
Chicago *(G-4813)*
Hensaal Management Group Inc ...... .......... 312 624-8133
Chicago *(G-5074)*
Hong Kong Market Chicago Inc ........ G ...... 312 791-9111
Chicago *(G-5108)*
Hop Kee Incorporated ....................... E ...... 312 791-9111
Chicago *(G-5109)*
Jaali Bean Inc .................................... .......... 312 730-5095
Chicago *(G-5265)*
Kronos Foods Corp ............................ B ...... 773 847-2250
Glendale Heights *(G-11039)*
Mat Capital LLC ................................. G ...... 847 821-9630
Long Grove *(G-13895)*
Rawnature5 LLC ................................ F ...... 312 800-3239
Chicago *(G-6296)*
Zaibak Bros ....................................... F ...... 312 564-5800
Chicago *(G-7058)*

### BROKERS: Log & Lumber
Challinor Wood Products Inc ............ G ...... 847 256-8828
Wilmette *(G-22250)*
Sterling Lumber Company ................. C ...... 708 388-2223
Phoenix *(G-17542)*

### BROKERS: Mortgage, Arranging For Loans
Cummins-American Corp .................. G ...... 847 299-9550
Mount Prospect *(G-15323)*

### BROKERS: Printing
Coyle Print Group Inc ........................ G ...... 847 784-1080
Skokie *(G-19987)*
Galleon Industries Inc ....................... G ...... 708 478-5444
Joliet *(G-12499)*
Lighthouse Printing Inc ..................... G ...... 708 479-7776
New Lenox *(G-15891)*
Village Press Inc ................................ G ...... 847 362-1856
Libertyville *(G-13399)*
Weimer Design & Print Ltd Inc ......... G ...... 630 393-3334
Warrenville *(G-21368)*

### BRONZE FOUNDRY, NEC
Alu-Bra Foundry Inc .......................... D ...... 630 766-3112
Bensenville *(G-1829)*
Intermet Metals Services Inc ............. E ...... 847 605-1300
Schaumburg *(G-19571)*

### BRONZE ROLLING & DRAWING
Universal Electric Foundry Inc ........... E ...... 312 421-7233
Chicago *(G-6831)*

### BROOMS
Humboldt Broom Company .............. G ...... 217 268-3718
Arcola *(G-671)*

---
Employee Codes: A=Over 500 employees, B=251-500
C=101-250, D=51-100, E=20-50, F=10-19, G=3-9

2017 Harris Illinois Industrial Directory

# BROOMS

## PRODUCT SECTION

Luco Mop Company .................................G....... 217 235-1992
  Mattoon *(G-14398)*
Quinn Broom Works Inc .........................E....... 217 923-3181
  Greenup *(G-11385)*

### BROOMS & BRUSHES

Concorde Laboratories Inc .....................G....... 630 717-5300
  Lisle *(G-13576)*
Don Leventhal Group LLC .......................E....... 618 783-4424
  Newton *(G-15939)*
F B Williams Co .....................................G....... 773 233-4255
  Chicago *(G-4802)*
Federal Prison Industries .......................C....... 309 346-8588
  Pekin *(G-17262)*
Freudenberg Household Pdts LP ............G....... 630 270-1400
  Aurora *(G-1010)*
Klm Commercial Sweeping Inc ..............G....... 618 978-9276
  Belleville *(G-1643)*
Libman Company ...................................C....... 217 268-4200
  Arcola *(G-675)*
Nexstep Commercial Pdts LLC ..............G....... 217 379-2377
  Paxton *(G-17238)*
Re-Maid Incorporated ...........................G....... 815 315-0500
  Freeport *(G-10683)*

### BROOMS & BRUSHES: Household Or Indl

E Gornell & Sons Inc .............................E....... 773 489-2330
  Chicago *(G-4665)*
Zimmerman Brush Co .............................D....... 773 761-6331
  Chicago *(G-7068)*

### BROOMS & BRUSHES: Paint & Varnish

True Value Company ..............................G....... 847 639-5383
  Cary *(G-3378)*
True Value Company ..............................B....... 773 695-5000
  Chicago *(G-6786)*

### BROOMS & BRUSHES: Paint Rollers

Newell Operating Company ...................C....... 815 235-4171
  Freeport *(G-10675)*

### BROOMS & BRUSHES: Push

Jones Software Corp .............................G....... 312 952-0011
  Chicago *(G-5322)*
Sherwin-Williams Company ...................G....... 847 251-6115
  Kenilworth *(G-12663)*

### BROOMS & BRUSHES: Street Sweeping, Hand Or Machine

Gosia Cartage Ltd .................................G....... 312 613-8735
  Hodgkins *(G-11975)*

### BROOMS & BRUSHES: Vacuum Cleaners & Carpet Sweepers

Rainbow Dusters International ..............G....... 770 627-3575
  Carol Stream *(G-3227)*

### BRUSHES

Jim Jolly Sales Inc .................................G....... 847 669-7570
  Huntley *(G-12153)*
Team Technologies Inc .........................D....... 630 937-0380
  Batavia *(G-1504)*

### BRUSHES & BRUSH STOCK CONTACTS: Electric

J Ream Manufacturing ...........................G....... 630 983-6945
  Naperville *(G-15680)*

### BUCKLES & PARTS

H L M Sales Inc .....................................G....... 815 455-6922
  Barrington *(G-1283)*
Linda Levinson Designs Inc ...................G....... 312 951-6943
  Chicago *(G-5509)*

### BUFFING FOR THE TRADE

Bucthel Metal Finishing Corp .................F....... 847 427-8704
  Elk Grove Village *(G-9347)*
Courtesy Metal Polishing ......................G....... 630 832-1862
  Villa Park *(G-21246)*
Master Polishing & Buffing ....................G....... 773 731-3883
  Chicago *(G-5644)*

Metal Images Inc ...................................G....... 847 488-9877
  Elgin *(G-9108)*
Rockford Metal Polishing Co .................G....... 815 282-4448
  Loves Park *(G-13984)*

### BUILDING & STRUCTURAL WOOD MBRS: Timbers, Struct, Lam Lumber

Cooper Lake Millworks Inc ....................G....... 217 847-2681
  Hamilton *(G-11530)*
Lamboo Technologies LLC ...................G....... 866 966-2999
  Litchfield *(G-13693)*
WW Timbers Inc ....................................G....... 708 423-9112
  Chicago Ridge *(G-7159)*

### BUILDING & STRUCTURAL WOOD MEMBERS

Central Illinois Truss .............................F....... 309 447-6644
  Deer Creek *(G-7961)*
Central Wood LLC .................................G....... 217 543-2662
  Arcola *(G-666)*
Connor Sports Flooring LLC .................D....... 847 290-9020
  Elk Grove Village *(G-9389)*
Ruff Quality Components .....................E....... 309 662-0425
  Bloomington *(G-2221)*
Strat-O-Span Buildings Inc ...................G....... 618 526-4566
  Breese *(G-2448)*

### BUILDING CLEANING & MAINTENANCE SVCS

New Metal Crafts Inc ............................E....... 312 787-6991
  Lincolnwood *(G-13526)*

### BUILDING COMPONENT CLEANING SVCS

Averus Usa Inc .....................................D....... 800 913-7034
  Elgin *(G-8961)*

### BUILDING COMPONENTS: Structural Steel

Accurate Fabricators Svcs Inc ..............G....... 618 530-7883
  Granite City *(G-11259)*
Ambassador Steel Corporation ...........F....... 815 929-3770
  Bourbonnais *(G-2387)*
Canam Steel Corporation ....................C....... 815 224-9588
  Peru *(G-17502)*
Carpenter Contractors Amer Inc .........B....... 815 544-1699
  Belvidere *(G-1744)*
Central Ill Fbrcation Whse Inc ..............F....... 217 367-2323
  Urbana *(G-21076)*
Delta Erectors Inc ................................F....... 708 267-9721
  Villa Park *(G-21248)*
Dietrich Industries Inc .........................E....... 815 207-0110
  Joliet *(G-12485)*
Hercules Iron Works Inc ......................F....... 312 226-2405
  Chicago *(G-5078)*
Integrated Mfg Tech LLC .....................E....... 618 282-8306
  Red Bud *(G-17943)*
L & M Steel Services Inc .....................F....... 309 755-3713
  East Moline *(G-8684)*
Max Fire Training Inc ...........................F....... 618 210-2079
  Godfrey *(G-11228)*
Ornamental Metalworks Inc ................G....... 217 424-2326
  Decatur *(G-7923)*
Pro-Fab Metals Inc ..............................G....... 618 283-2986
  Vandalia *(G-21121)*
Sheas Iron Works Inc ..........................E....... 847 356-2922
  Lake Villa *(G-13026)*
Steel Span Inc .....................................G....... 815 943-9071
  Harvard *(G-11648)*
Walnut Custom Homes Inc .................E....... 815 379-2151
  Walnut *(G-21333)*
WEb Production & Fabg Inc ................F....... 312 733-6800
  Chicago *(G-6948)*

### BUILDING INSPECTION SVCS

Tuschall Engineering Co Inc ................E....... 630 655-9100
  Burr Ridge *(G-2888)*

### BUILDING MAINTENANCE SVCS, EXC REPAIRS

Equity Concepts Co Inc ......................G....... 815 226-1300
  Rockford *(G-18368)*

### BUILDING PRDTS & MATERIALS DEALERS

Advanced Window Corp .......................E....... 773 379-3500
  Chicago *(G-3773)*

Agusta Mill Works .................................G....... 309 787-4616
  Milan *(G-14773)*
Beelman Ready-Mix Inc .......................F....... 618 526-0260
  Breese *(G-2439)*
Brewer Company ..................................F....... 708 339-9000
  Harvey *(G-11662)*
Charles K Eichen ..................................G....... 217 854-9751
  Carlinville *(G-3034)*
County Materials Corp .........................E....... 217 352-4181
  Champaign *(G-3470)*
County Materials Corp .........................E....... 217 544-4607
  Springfield *(G-20422)*
Creative Cabinetry Inc .........................G....... 708 460-2900
  Orland Park *(G-16851)*
Custom Woodwork & Interiors ............E....... 217 546-0006
  Springfield *(G-20427)*
E-Z Tree Recycling Inc ........................G....... 773 493-8600
  Chicago *(G-4670)*
Effingham Equity Inc ...........................F....... 217 268-5128
  Arcola *(G-668)*
Ellers Custom Cabinets Inc .................F....... 309 633-0101
  Groveland *(G-11415)*
Elston Materials LLC ............................G....... 773 235-3100
  Chicago *(G-4736)*
Franklin Park Building Mtls ..................G....... 847 455-3985
  Franklin Park *(G-10472)*
Gorman Brothers Ready Mix Inc .........G....... 618 498-2173
  Jerseyville *(G-12422)*
Granite Gallery Inc ..............................G....... 773 279-9200
  Chicago *(G-4986)*
H J Mohr & Sons Company .................F....... 708 366-0338
  Oak Park *(G-16667)*
J E Tomes & Associates Inc ...............F....... 708 653-5100
  Blue Island *(G-2258)*
Jesse B Holt Inc ..................................D....... 618 783-3075
  Newton *(G-15942)*
Liese Lumber Co Inc ...........................E....... 618 234-0105
  Belleville *(G-1649)*
Logan Square Aluminum Sup Inc ........D....... 773 235-2500
  Chicago *(G-5530)*
Menoni & Mocogni Inc ........................F....... 847 432-0850
  Highland Park *(G-11854)*
Meyer Material Co Merger Corp .........E....... 815 385-4920
  Elburn *(G-8894)*
Narvick Bros Lumber Co Inc ...............G....... 815 942-1173
  Morris *(G-15121)*
Peoples Coal and Lumber Co .............G....... 815 432-2456
  Watseka *(G-21425)*
Perma-Treat of Illinois Inc ...................E....... 618 997-5646
  Marion *(G-14278)*
Petersen Sand & Gravel Inc ................F....... 815 344-1060
  Lakemoor *(G-13145)*
Ronnie P Faber ....................................G....... 815 626-4561
  Sterling *(G-20610)*
Southfield Corporation ........................E....... 708 458-0400
  Oak Lawn *(G-16644)*
Stahl Lumber Company .......................F....... 309 695-4331
  Wyoming *(G-22640)*
Van Voorst Lumber Company Inc .......E....... 815 426-2544
  Union Hill *(G-21039)*
W H Maze Company .............................E....... 815 223-1742
  Peru *(G-17530)*
Welch Bros Inc ....................................C....... 847 741-6134
  Elgin *(G-9233)*
Welch Bros Inc ....................................G....... 815 547-3000
  Belvidere *(G-1796)*
Western Illinois Enterprises .................G....... 309 342-5185
  Galesburg *(G-10779)*
Wm F Meyer Co ...................................E....... 773 772-7272
  Chicago *(G-7010)*
Wooded Wonderland ..........................G....... 815 777-1223
  Galena *(G-10735)*

### BUILDING PRDTS: Concrete

Architectural Distributors ...................G....... 847 223-5800
  Grayslake *(G-11320)*
Blue Linx Corporation .........................F....... 708 235-4200
  University Park *(G-21045)*
Great Lakes Lifting ..............................G....... 815 931-4825
  Country Club Hills *(G-7407)*
Kodiak Concrete Forms Inc ................G....... 630 773-9339
  Itasca *(G-12298)*
Lane Construction Corporation ..........F....... 815 846-4466
  Shorewood *(G-19929)*
Quick Building Systems Inc ................G....... 708 598-6733
  Palos Hills *(G-17122)*
Spacil Construction Co ......................G....... 708 448-3809
  Palos Heights *(G-17110)*
Sws .......................................................G....... 815 267-7378
  Plainfield *(G-17656)*

# PRODUCT SECTION

## BURNERS: Gas, Indl

Vcna Prairie Inc .................................. A ....... 312 733-0094
   Chicago *(G-6877)*

### BUILDING PRDTS: Stone

Primo Granito LLC ............................... F ....... 773 282-6391
   Chicago *(G-6187)*
Rogan Group Inc .................................. G ....... 708 371-4191
   Merrionette Park *(G-14738)*
Stylenquaza LLC .................................. G ....... 847 981-0191
   Elk Grove Village *(G-9759)*

### BUILDINGS & COMPONENTS: Prefabricated Metal

Alvarez & Marsal Inc ........................... E ....... 312 601-4220
   Chicago *(G-3840)*
American Deck & Sunroom C ................ G ....... 217 586-4840
   Mahomet *(G-14157)*
American Fixture .................................. G ....... 217 429-1300
   Decatur *(G-7832)*
Americana Building Pdts Inc ................ D ....... 618 548-2800
   Salem *(G-19326)*
Atkore International Group Inc ............. A ....... 708 339-1610
   Harvey *(G-11658)*
Atkore Intl Holdings Inc ........................ G ....... 708 225-2051
   Harvey *(G-11659)*
Bluescope Buildings N Amer Inc .......... E ....... 217 348-7676
   Charleston *(G-3590)*
Cardinal Enterprises ............................. G ....... 618 994-4454
   Stonefort *(G-20637)*
Comforts Home Services Inc ............... G ....... 847 856-8002
   Montgomery *(G-15040)*
Craig Industries Inc ............................. D ....... 217 228-2421
   Quincy *(G-17816)*
D & D Construction Co LLC ................. G ....... 217 852-6631
   Dallas City *(G-7695)*
Eagle Companies Inc ........................... G ....... 309 686-9054
   Chillicothe *(G-7164)*
Elfi LLC ................................................ E ....... 815 439-1833
   Chicago *(G-4727)*
Esi Steel & Fabrication ......................... F ....... 618 548-3017
   Salem *(G-19331)*
Heico Companies LLC ......................... F ....... 312 419-8220
   Chicago *(G-5068)*
Kravet Inc ............................................. G ....... 847 870-1414
   Arlington Heights *(G-790)*
McElroy Metal Mill Inc .......................... G ....... 217 935-9421
   Clinton *(G-7287)*
Minority Auto Hdlg Specialists ............. F ....... 708 757-8758
   Chicago Heights *(G-7113)*
Morton Buildings Inc ............................ G ....... 217 357-3713
   Carthage *(G-3317)*
Optimal Construction Svcs Inc ............. G ....... 630 365-5050
   Elburn *(G-8902)*
Penstock Construction Services ........... G ....... 630 816-2456
   Plainfield *(G-17636)*
Rv6 Performance ................................. G ....... 630 346-7998
   Wheaton *(G-21978)*
Steel Span Inc ...................................... F ....... 815 943-9071
   Harvard *(G-11648)*
White Star Silo ...................................... G ....... 618 523-4735
   Germantown *(G-10894)*

### BUILDINGS: Farm & Utility

Arrow Shed LLC ................................... C ....... 618 526-4546
   Breese *(G-2438)*
CST Industries Inc ............................... C ....... 815 756-1551
   Dekalb *(G-8080)*
Morton Buildings Inc ............................ F ....... 630 904-1122
   Streator *(G-20695)*

### BUILDINGS: Farm, Prefabricated Or Portable, Wood

Strat-O-Span Buildings Inc .................. G ....... 618 526-4566
   Breese *(G-2448)*
Yoders Portable Buildings LLC ............. G ....... 618 936-2419
   Sumner *(G-20773)*

### BUILDINGS: Mobile, For Commercial Use

Carlin Mfg A Div Grs Holdg LLC ........... E ....... 559 276-0123
   Naperville *(G-15617)*
Innovative Mobile Marketing ................ F ....... 815 929-1029
   Bourbonnais *(G-2400)*

### BUILDINGS: Portable

American Buildings Company .............. C ....... 309 527-5420
   El Paso *(G-8865)*

Arrow Shed LLC ................................... E ....... 618 526-4546
   Breese *(G-2437)*
Fehring Ornamental Iron Works ........... F ....... 217 483-6727
   Chatham *(G-3620)*
Jack Walters & Sons Corp .................... E ....... 618 842-2642
   Fairfield *(G-10145)*
Mobile Mini Inc ..................................... E ....... 708 297-2004
   Calumet Park *(G-2963)*
Morton Buildings Inc ............................ F ....... 309 936-7282
   Atkinson *(G-944)*
Signa Development Group Inc ............. G ....... 773 418-4506
   Norridge *(G-16108)*
Strat-O-Span Buildings Inc .................. G ....... 618 526-4566
   Breese *(G-2448)*

### BUILDINGS: Prefabricated, Metal

Associated Group Holdings LLC ........... G ....... 312 662-5488
   Chicago *(G-3968)*
Medieval Builders LLC ......................... G ....... 331 245-7791
   Schaumburg *(G-19639)*
Nci Group Inc ....................................... D ....... 309 527-3095
   El Paso *(G-8871)*
Renegade Steel ................................... G ....... 716 903-2506
   Chicago *(G-6332)*
Safety Storage Inc ............................... D ....... 217 345-4422
   Charleston *(G-3610)*

### BUILDINGS: Prefabricated, Wood

Coach House Inc .................................. E ....... 217 543-3761
   Arthur *(G-888)*
Cook Sales Inc ..................................... G ....... 618 893-2114
   Cobden *(G-7301)*
Everlast Portable Buildings .................. G ....... 217 543-4080
   Sullivan *(G-20745)*
Faze Change Produx ........................... E ....... 217 728-2184
   Sullivan *(G-20745)*
K & K Storage Barns LLC .................... F ....... 618 927-0533
   Ewing *(G-10120)*
Schrocks Wood Shop ........................... G ....... 217 773-3842
   Mount Sterling *(G-15394)*
Steel Span Inc ...................................... F ....... 815 943-9071
   Harvard *(G-11648)*
Tuff Shed Inc ....................................... G ....... 847 704-1147
   Palatine *(G-17083)*
W Kost Manufacturing Co Inc ............... C ....... 847 428-0600
   Chicago *(G-6919)*
Walnut Custom Homes Inc .................. G ....... 815 379-2151
   Walnut *(G-21332)*

### BUILDINGS: Prefabricated, Wood

Alply Insulated Panels LLC .................. E ....... 217 324-6700
   Litchfield *(G-13680)*
Frederking Construction Co .................. G ....... 618 483-5031
   Altamont *(G-551)*
Grs Holding LLC ................................... G ....... 630 355-1660
   Naperville *(G-15666)*
Lester Building Systems LLC ............... E ....... 217 348-7676
   Charleston *(G-3603)*
Omni-Tech Systems Inc ....................... G ....... 309 962-2281
   Le Roy *(G-13208)*

### BULLETIN BOARDS: Wood

Vecchio Manufacturing of Ill ................. F ....... 847 742-8429
   Elgin *(G-9224)*

### BULLETPROOF VESTS

Itus Corporation LLC ............................ G ....... 888 537-5661
   Arlington Heights *(G-780)*

### BUMPERS: Motor Vehicle

Cnh Industrial America LLC ................. E ....... 309 965-2233
   Goodfield *(G-11244)*
Flex-N-Gate Corporation ...................... D ....... 217 442-4018
   Danville *(G-7720)*
Flex-N-Gate Corporation ...................... B ....... 217 384-6600
   Urbana *(G-21085)*
Flex-N-Gate Corporation ...................... B ....... 217 384-6600
   Urbana *(G-21086)*
Hendrickson International Corp ............ C ....... 815 727-4031
   Joliet *(G-12510)*
High Impact Fabricating LLC ............... G ....... 708 235-8912
   University Park *(G-21052)*
Magna Exteriors America Inc ............... A ....... 618 327-4381
   Nashville *(G-15837)*
Mendota Welding & Mfg ....................... G ....... 815 539-6944
   Mendota *(G-14727)*

## BURNERS: Gas, Indl

Nascote Industries Inc ......................... A ....... 618 327-3286
   Nashville *(G-15840)*
Nascote Industries Inc ......................... C ....... 618 478-2092
   Nashville *(G-15841)*

### BURIAL VAULTS, FIBERGLASS

Doric Products Inc ............................... D ....... 217 826-6302
   Marshall *(G-14321)*
Greenwood Inc ..................................... F ....... 800 798-4900
   Danville *(G-7728)*

### BURIAL VAULTS: Concrete Or Precast Terrazzo

American Wilbert Vault Corp ................ F ....... 773 238-2746
   Chicago *(G-3883)*
American Wilbert Vault Corp ................ F ....... 708 366-3210
   Bridgeview *(G-2464)*
Beauty Vault LLC .................................. F ....... 773 621-5189
   Chicago *(G-4070)*
C L Vault & Safe Srv ............................. G ....... 708 237-0039
   Oak Lawn *(G-16607)*
Central Concrete Products ................... F ....... 217 673-6111
   Woodson *(G-22530)*
Eagle Burial Vault ................................. G ....... 815 722-8660
   Frankfort *(G-10318)*
Energy Vault LLC ................................. G ....... 847 722-1128
   Chicago *(G-4751)*
Farmington Wilbert Vault Corp ............. F ....... 309 245-2133
   Farmington *(G-10186)*
Forsyth Brothers Concrete Pdts ............ G ....... 217 548-2770
   Fithian *(G-10193)*
Hallen Burial Vault Inc ......................... G ....... 815 544-6138
   Belvidere *(G-1761)*
J P Vincent & Sons Inc ........................ G ....... 815 777-2365
   Galena *(G-10727)*
Kelley Vault Co Inc ............................... F ....... 217 355-5551
   Champaign *(G-3506)*
Knauer Industries Ltd .......................... E ....... 815 725-0246
   Joliet *(G-12528)*
Meatball Vault Original ......................... G ....... 312 285-2090
   Chicago *(G-5673)*
Merz Vault Company Inc ...................... G ....... 618 548-2859
   Salem *(G-19338)*
Northern Illinois Wilbert Vlt .................. G ....... 815 544-3355
   Belvidere *(G-1775)*
Oakwood Memorial Park Inc ................ G ....... 815 433-0313
   Ottawa *(G-16973)*
Peoria Wilbert Vault Co Inc .................. F ....... 309 383-2882
   Metamora *(G-14747)*
Perfection Vault Co Inc ........................ F ....... 217 673-6111
   Woodson *(G-22531)*
Quad Cities Concrete Pdts LLC ............ G ....... 309 787-4919
   Milan *(G-14799)*
Rex Vault Co ........................................ G ....... 618 783-2416
   Newton *(G-15948)*
Schmalz Precast Concrete Mfg ............ G ....... 815 747-3939
   East Dubuque *(G-8622)*
Slavish Inc ............................................ G ....... 309 754-8233
   Matherville *(G-14367)*
Southern Ill Wilbert Vlt Co .................... F ....... 618 942-5845
   Herrin *(G-11756)*
Sterling Vault Company ....................... F ....... 815 625-0077
   Sterling *(G-20616)*
Tanya Shipley ....................................... G ....... 708 476-0433
   Mokena *(G-14910)*
Vault Arts Collective ............................. G ....... 217 599-1215
   Tuscola *(G-21029)*
Vault Shop ............................................ G ....... 630 699-0307
   Lisle *(G-13677)*
Wilbert Quincy Vault Co ....................... G ....... 217 224-8557
   Quincy *(G-17905)*
Wilbert Shultz Vault Co Inc .................. F ....... 815 672-2049
   Streator *(G-20711)*
Wilbert Vault Company ........................ F ....... 309 787-5281
   Milan *(G-14809)*
Wolfe Burial Vault Co Inc ..................... G ....... 815 697-2012
   Chebanse *(G-3632)*

### BURNERS: Gas, Domestic

Midco International Inc ........................ E ....... 773 604-8700
   Chicago *(G-5733)*

### BURNERS: Gas, Indl

Eclipse Combustion Inc ....................... C ....... 815 877-3031
   Rockford *(G-18357)*

## BURNERS: Gas-Oil, Combination

**Eclipse Inc** ... D ... 815 877-3031
Rockford *(G-18356)*

## BUS BARS: Electrical

**Schneider Electric Usa Inc** ... E ... 847 441-2526
Schaumburg *(G-19723)*
**Triton Manufacturing Co Inc** ... D ... 708 587-4000
Monee *(G-15004)*

## BUSES: Wholesalers

**Motor Coach Industries** ... G ... 847 285-2000
Des Plaines *(G-8236)*

## BUSHINGS & BEARINGS

**Aetna Bearing Company** ... E ... 630 694-0024
Franklin Park *(G-10386)*

## BUSINESS & SECRETARIAL SCHOOLS

**Illinois Inst Cntng Legl Ed** ... E ... 217 787-2080
Springfield *(G-20454)*

## BUSINESS ACTIVITIES: Non-Commercial Site

**4 Elements Company** ... G ... 773 236-2284
Mundelein *(G-15461)*
**4g Antenna Shop Inc** ... G ... 815 496-0444
Aurora *(G-952)*
**A & S Arms Inc** ... G ... 224 267-5670
Antioch *(G-612)*
**Abki Tech Service Inc** ... F ... 847 818-8403
Des Plaines *(G-8143)*
**Ace Machine & Tool** ... G ... 815 793-5077
Dekalb *(G-8072)*
**Advanced Cstm Enrgy Sltons Inc** ... D ... 312 428-9540
Chicago *(G-3768)*
**Advanced Robotics Research** ... G ... 630 544-0040
Naperville *(G-15591)*
**Alao Temitope** ... F ... 331 454-3333
Collinsville *(G-7313)*
**Angelo Bruni** ... G ... 773 754-5422
Aurora *(G-957)*
**ARC Mobile LLC** ... F ... 201 838-3410
Western Springs *(G-21863)*
**Beloved Characters Ltd** ... G ... 773 599-0073
Chicago *(G-4079)*
**BJs Welding Services Etc Co** ... G ... 773 964-5836
Chicago *(G-4118)*
**Bold Diagnostics LLC** ... G ... 806 543-5743
Chicago *(G-4139)*
**Bows Arts Inc** ... F ... 847 501-3161
Glenview *(G-11109)*
**Brunet Snow Service Company** ... G ... 847 846-0037
Wood Dale *(G-22347)*
**Buyersvine Inc** ... G ... 630 235-6804
Hinsdale *(G-11943)*
**C & B Services** ... G ... 847 462-8484
Cary *(G-3329)*
**Caples-El Transport Inc** ... G ... 708 300-2727
Calumet City *(G-2936)*
**Captivision Inc** ... G ... 630 235-8763
Bolingbrook *(G-2283)*
**Cash House Music Group LLC** ... G ... 847 471-7401
Indian Creek *(G-12185)*
**Charwat Food Group Ltd** ... G ... 630 847-3473
Hinsdale *(G-11944)*
**CHI Home Improvement Mag Inc** ... G ... 630 801-7788
Aurora *(G-1128)*
**CJ Drilling Inc** ... E ... 847 854-3888
Dundee *(G-8560)*
**Cream Team Logistics LLC** ... F ... 708 541-9128
Phoenix *(G-17540)*
**Cyber Innovation Labs LLC** ... G ... 847 804-4724
Mount Prospect *(G-15325)*
**Dan De Tash Knits** ... G ... 708 970-6238
Maywood *(G-14424)*
**Daves Welding Service Inc** ... G ... 630 655-3224
Darien *(G-7792)*
**Deady Brian Rfg Inc** ... G ... 708 479-8249
Orland Park *(G-16853)*
**Delta Erectors Inc** ... F ... 708 267-9721
Villa Park *(G-21248)*
**Donr Co** ... G ... 773 895-3359
Chicago *(G-4630)*
**Drig Corporation** ... G ... 312 265-1509
Chicago *(G-4644)*
**Drywear Apparel LLC** ... G ... 847 687-8540
Kildeer *(G-12699)*
**Dtrs Enterprises Inc** ... G ... 630 296-6890
Bolingbrook *(G-2302)*
**Edqu Media LLC** ... G ... 773 803-9793
Chicago *(G-4698)*
**Edward J Warren Jr** ... G ... 630 882-8817
Yorkville *(G-22657)*
**Effective Energy Assoc LLC** ... G ... 815 248-9280
Davis *(G-7805)*
**Eli Morris Group LLC** ... G ... 773 314-7173
Chicago *(G-4729)*
**Erasermitt Incorporated** ... G ... 312 842-2855
Chicago *(G-4771)*
**Esquify Inc** ... G ... 917 553-3741
Chicago *(G-4777)*
**Fleming Music Technology Ctr** ... G ... 708 316-8662
Wheaton *(G-21948)*
**Flexxsonic Corporation** ... G ... 847 452-7226
Mount Prospect *(G-15330)*
**Fortitud Inc** ... G ... 312 919-4938
Algonquin *(G-390)*
**Franch & Sons Trnsp Inc** ... G ... 630 392-3307
Addison *(G-123)*
**Gayton Enterprises LLC** ... G ... 847 462-4030
Algonquin *(G-391)*
**Gld Industries Inc** ... G ... 217 390-9594
Champaign *(G-3489)*
**Grier Abrasive Co Inc** ... C ... 708 333-6445
South Holland *(G-20271)*
**Griffard & Associates LLC** ... G ... 217 316-1732
Quincy *(G-17832)*
**Gulf Petroleum LLC** ... G ... 312 803-0373
Chicago *(G-5012)*
**Hallmark Cabinet Company** ... D ... 708 757-7807
Chicago Heights *(G-7102)*
**Hampster Industries Inc** ... G ... 866 280-2287
Mundelein *(G-15507)*
**Healthy-Txt LLC** ... G ... 630 945-1787
Chicago *(G-5063)*
**HI Metals LLC** ... G ... 312 590-3360
Winnetka *(G-22307)*
**Hollywood Tools LLC** ... G ... 773 793-3119
West Chicago *(G-21715)*
**Howard Pet Products Inc** ... E ... 973 398-3038
Saint Charles *(G-19194)*
**Identcorp Industries** ... E ... 708 896-6407
Dolton *(G-8372)*
**Idevconcepts Inc** ... G ... 312 351-1615
Chicago *(G-5142)*
**Illuminight Lighting LLC** ... F ... 312 685-4448
Highland Park *(G-11843)*
**Integrated Lighting Tech Inc** ... G ... 630 750-3786
Bolingbrook *(G-2322)*
**Invisio Communications Inc** ... G ... 412 327-6578
Chicago *(G-5234)*
**Jds Labs Inc** ... G ... 618 366-0475
Collinsville *(G-7329)*
**Jewerly and Beyond** ... G ... 312 833-6785
Schaumburg *(G-19588)*
**Jofas Print Corporation** ... G ... 815 534-5725
Frankfort *(G-10337)*
**John Dagys Media LLC** ... G ... 708 373-0180
Palos Park *(G-17129)*
**Katys LLC** ... G ... 708 522-9814
Oak Park *(G-16672)*
**Kenneth W Templeman** ... G ... 847 912-2740
Volo *(G-21315)*
**L & B Global Power LLC** ... G ... 847 323-0770
Chicago *(G-5417)*
**Legistek LLC** ... G ... 312 399-4891
Chicago *(G-5491)*
**Lexpress Inc** ... G ... 773 517-7095
Prospect Heights *(G-17783)*
**Linkhouse LLC** ... G ... 312 671-2225
Schaumburg *(G-19618)*
**Live Love Hair** ... G ... 530 554-2471
Lansing *(G-13174)*
**Lokman Enterprises Inc** ... G ... 773 654-0525
Chicago *(G-5534)*
**Love Journey Inc** ... G ... 773 447-5591
Chicago *(G-5548)*
**Luon Energy LLC** ... G ... 217 419-2678
Savoy *(G-19411)*
**Made As Intended Inc** ... F ... 630 789-3494
Oak Brook *(G-16538)*
**Marcmetals** ... G ... 847 905-0018
Evanston *(G-10069)*
**Mef Construction Inc** ... G ... 847 741-8601
Elgin *(G-9105)*
**Midwest Mobile Canning LLC** ... G ... 815 861-4515
Crystal Lake *(G-7612)*
**Moran Cristobalian** ... G ... 630 506-4777
Batavia *(G-1472)*
**Natures Appeal Mfg Corp** ... G ... 630 880-6222
Addison *(G-226)*
**Nls Analytics LLC** ... G ... 312 593-0293
Glencoe *(G-11003)*
**Opsdirt LLC** ... G ... 773 412-1179
Chicago *(G-5996)*
**Organnica Inc** ... G ... 312 925-7272
Berwyn *(G-2071)*
**Osmer Woodworking Inc** ... G ... 815 973-5809
Dixon *(G-8338)*
**Paralleldirect LLC** ... G ... 847 748-2025
Lincolnshire *(G-13471)*
**Penstock Construction Services** ... G ... 630 816-2456
Plainfield *(G-17636)*
**Pix2doc LLC** ... G ... 312 925-4010
Lisle *(G-13642)*
**Powercoco LLC** ... G ... 614 323-5890
Chicago *(G-6159)*
**Questily LLC** ... G ... 312 636-6657
Chicago *(G-6256)*
**Rays Electrical Service LLC** ... F ... 847 214-2944
Elgin *(G-9161)*
**Rays Power Wshg Svc Peggy Ray** ... G ... 618 939-6306
Waterloo *(G-21405)*
**Rebel Brands LLC** ... G ... 312 804-0009
Wilmette *(G-22264)*
**Revolution Brands LLC** ... G ... 847 902-3320
Huntley *(G-12173)*
**Rinalli Boat Co Inc** ... G ... 618 467-8850
Godfrey *(G-11234)*
**Rlw Inc** ... G ... 309 352-2499
Green Valley *(G-11380)*
**Ronald Allen** ... F ... 314 568-1446
Cahokia *(G-2925)*
**Roq Innovation LLC** ... G ... 917 770-2403
Chicago *(G-6392)*
**Route 40 Media LLC** ... G ... 309 370-5809
Peoria *(G-17449)*
**Royale Innovation Group Ltd** ... G ... 312 339-1406
Itasca *(G-12351)*
**S Vs Industries Inc** ... G ... 630 408-1083
Hoffman Estates *(G-12047)*
**Saachi Inc** ... G ... 630 775-1700
Roselle *(G-18971)*
**Seat Trans Inc** ... G ... 224 522-1007
Lake In The Hills *(G-13006)*
**See What You Send Inc** ... G ... 781 780-1483
Chicago *(G-6473)*
**Signa Development Group Inc** ... G ... 773 418-4506
Norridge *(G-16108)*
**Southland Voice** ... E ... 708 214-8582
Crete *(G-7519)*
**Ssn LLC** ... G ... 815 978-8729
Byron *(G-2922)*
**Sustainable Holding Inc** ... G ... 773 324-0407
Chicago *(G-6643)*
**T9 Group LLC** ... G ... 847 912-8862
Hawthorn Woods *(G-11705)*
**Take Your Mark Sports LLC** ... G ... 708 655-0525
Western Springs *(G-21874)*
**Tape Case Ltd** ... E ... 847 299-7880
Elk Grove Village *(G-9768)*
**Team Sider Inc** ... G ... 847 767-0107
Highland Park *(G-11877)*
**Terrapin Xpress Inc** ... G ... 866 823-7323
Palos Heights *(G-17111)*
**Third Day Oil & Gas LLC** ... G ... 618 553-5538
Oblong *(G-16736)*
**Tradevolve Inc** ... G ... 847 987-9411
Crystal Lake *(G-7668)*
**Tripnary LLC** ... G ... 512 554-1911
Chicago *(G-6777)*
**Truepad LLC** ... F ... 847 274-6898
Chicago *(G-6787)*
**Turfmapp Inc** ... G ... 703 473-5678
Chicago *(G-6792)*
**Turner Agward** ... G ... 773 669-8559
Chicago *(G-6794)*
**Universal Trnspt Systems LLC** ... F ... 312 994-2349
Chicago *(G-6835)*
**Urpoint LLC** ... G ... 773 919-9002
New Lenox *(G-15925)*
**Veteran Greens LLC** ... G ... 773 599-9689
Chicago *(G-6891)*
**Vida Enterprises Inc** ... G ... 312 808-0088
Chicago *(G-6895)*

**Vulcan Ladder Usa LLC** G 847 526-6321
Island Lake *(G-12220)*
**Weiss Monument Works Inc** G 618 398-1811
Belleville *(G-1690)*
**Wells Janitorial Service Inc** G 872 226-9983
Chicago *(G-6953)*
**Winlind Skincare LLC** G 630 789-9408
Burr Ridge *(G-2896)*
**Wood Cutters Lane LLC** G 847 847-2263
Hainesville *(G-11525)*
**World of Soul Inc** G 773 840-4839
Chicago *(G-7032)*

## BUSINESS FORMS WHOLESALERS

**Aais Services Corporation** G 630 457-3263
Lisle *(G-13552)*
**Accurate Business Controls Inc** G 815 633-5500
Machesney Park *(G-14051)*
**All Purpose Prtg & Bus Forms** G 708 389-9192
Alsip *(G-431)*
**Allan Brooks & Associates Inc** F 847 537-7500
Lake Villa *(G-13010)*
**American Assn Insur Svcs** E 630 681-8347
Lisle *(G-13557)*
**Bfc Forms Service Inc** C 630 879-9240
Batavia *(G-1422)*
**C M J Associates Inc** G 708 636-2995
Oak Lawn *(G-16608)*
**Certified Business Forms Inc** G 773 286-8194
Chicago *(G-4283)*
**Designation Inc** F 847 367-9100
Mundelein *(G-15494)*
**Eagle Printing Company** G 309 762-0771
Moline *(G-14936)*
**Express Prtg & Promotions Inc** G 847 498-9640
Northbrook *(G-16253)*
**Forms Design Plus Coleman Prtg** G 309 685-6000
Peoria *(G-17365)*
**Forms Etc By Marty Walsh** G 708 499-6767
Oak Lawn *(G-16620)*
**Grand Forms & Systems Inc** F 847 259-4600
Arlington Heights *(G-760)*
**Informative Systems Inc** F 217 523-8422
Springfield *(G-20457)*
**Marc Business Forms Inc** F 847 568-9200
Lincolnwood *(G-13524)*
**Medical Records Co** G 847 662-6373
Waukegan *(G-21588)*
**Mid-Central Business Forms** G 309 692-9090
Peoria *(G-17406)*
**Minuteman Press** G 630 584-7383
Saint Charles *(G-19223)*
**Noor International Inc** G 847 985-2300
Bartlett *(G-1320)*
**R & R Creative Graphics Inc** G 630 208-4724
Geneva *(G-10861)*
**Reign Print Solutions Inc** G 847 590-7091
Arlington Heights *(G-830)*
**Rose Business Forms & Printing** G 618 533-3032
Centralia *(G-3429)*
**Roseri Business Forms Inc** G 847 381-8012
Inverness *(G-12211)*
**RR Donnelley & Sons Company** E 312 332-4345
Chicago *(G-6402)*

## BUSINESS FORMS: Printed, Continuous

**Acco Brands Corporation** A 847 541-9500
Lake Zurich *(G-13033)*
**Standard Register Inc** F 815 432-4203
Watseka *(G-21427)*

## BUSINESS FORMS: Printed, Manifold

**Acco Brands USA LLC** B 800 222-6462
Lake Zurich *(G-13034)*
**Acco Brands USA LLC** D 847 272-3700
Lincolnshire *(G-13423)*
**Advance Instant Printing Co** G 312 346-0986
Chicago *(G-3760)*
**American Graphics Network Inc** F 847 729-7220
Glenview *(G-11100)*
**Azusa Inc** G 618 244-6591
Mount Vernon *(G-15399)*
**B & B Printing Company** G 217 285-6072
Pittsfield *(G-17561)*
**Block and Company Inc** C 847 537-7200
Wheeling *(G-22015)*
**Certified Business Forms Inc** G 773 286-8194
Chicago *(G-4283)*
**Computer Business Forms Co** G 773 775-0155
Chicago *(G-4440)*
**Eklunds Typesetting & Prtg LLC** G 630 924-0057
Roselle *(G-18940)*
**Ennis Inc** E 815 875-2000
Princeton *(G-17748)*
**Fast Print Shop** G 618 997-1976
Marion *(G-14259)*
**Forms Etc By Marty Walsh** G 708 499-6767
Oak Lawn *(G-16620)*
**Forms Specialist Inc** G 847 298-2868
Lincolnshire *(G-13449)*
**Frank R Walker Company** G 630 613-9312
Lombard *(G-13802)*
**Gem Acquisition Company Inc** F 773 735-3300
Chicago *(G-4923)*
**Genoa Business Forms Inc** E 815 895-2800
Sycamore *(G-20798)*
**Grand Forms & Systems Inc** F 847 259-4600
Arlington Heights *(G-760)*
**Integrated Print Graphics Inc** D 847 695-6777
South Elgin *(G-20206)*
**J Gooch & Associates Inc** G 217 522-7575
Springfield *(G-20461)*
**K R O Enterprises Ltd** G 309 797-2213
Moline *(G-14949)*
**Kellogg Printing Co** F 309 734-8388
Monmouth *(G-15016)*
**Keneal Industries Inc** F 815 886-1300
Romeoville *(G-18834)*
**Little Doloras** G 708 331-1330
South Holland *(G-20286)*
**M L S Printing Co Inc** G 847 948-8902
Deerfield *(G-8033)*
**M Wells Printing Co** G 312 455-0400
Chicago *(G-5588)*
**Marc Business Forms Inc** F 847 568-9200
Lincolnwood *(G-13524)*
**Midwest Graphic Industries** F 630 509-2972
Bensenville *(G-1952)*
**Moore North America Fin Inc** G 847 607-6000
Chicago *(G-5802)*
**N Bujarski Inc** G 847 884-1600
Schaumburg *(G-19660)*
**Novak Business Forms Inc** E 630 932-9850
Lombard *(G-13834)*
**Perftech Inc** E 630 554-0010
North Aurora *(G-16141)*
**Physicians Record Co Inc** D 800 323-9268
Berwyn *(G-2074)*
**Proform** G 309 676-2535
Peoria *(G-17437)*
**RR Donnelley & Sons Company** C 630 377-2586
Saint Charles *(G-19254)*
**RR Donnelley & Sons Company** D 312 326-8000
Chicago *(G-6403)*
**RR Donnelley & Sons Company** C 217 935-2113
Clinton *(G-7288)*
**Safeguard Scientifics Inc** G 312 234-9828
Chicago *(G-6427)*
**Shanin Company** D 847 676-1200
Lincolnwood *(G-13537)*
**Springfield Printing Inc** G 217 787-3500
Springfield *(G-20531)*
**Standard Register Inc** G 309 693-3700
Peoria *(G-17462)*
**Standard Register Inc** F 630 784-6833
Chicago *(G-6571)*
**Standard Register Inc** G 217 793-1900
Springfield *(G-20535)*
**Standard Register Inc** G 708 560-7600
Oak Forest *(G-16589)*
**Standard Register Inc** G 630 368-0336
Oak Brook *(G-16561)*
**Standard Register Inc** E 815 439-1050
Plainfield *(G-17652)*
**Standard Register Inc** C 630 784-6810
Carol Stream *(G-3248)*

## BUSINESS FORMS: Unit Sets, Manifold

**R & L Business Forms Inc** F 618 939-6535
Waterloo *(G-21404)*

## BUSINESS MACHINE REPAIR, ELECTRIC

**CDs Office Systems Inc** F 630 305-9034
Springfield *(G-20411)*
**CDs Office Systems Inc** D 800 367-1508
Springfield *(G-20410)*
**Konica Minolta** G 630 893-8238
Roselle *(G-18950)*
**Konica Minolta Business Soluti** E 309 671-1360
Peoria *(G-17398)*
**Xerox Corporation** E 630 573-1000
Hinsdale *(G-11969)*

## BUSINESS SUPPORT SVCS

**Aberdon Enterprises** F 847 228-1300
Elk Grove Village *(G-9255)*
**U R On It** G 847 382-0182
Lake Barrington *(G-12826)*

## BUSINESS TRAINING SVCS

**Myeccho LLC** G 224 639-3068
Des Plaines *(G-8240)*

## BUTADIENE: Indl, Organic, Chemical

**Equistar Chemicals LP** E 217 253-3311
Tuscola *(G-21019)*

## BUTTONS

**Acme Button & Buttonhole Co** G 773 907-8400
Chicago *(G-3731)*
**Just Another Button** F 618 667-8531
Troy *(G-21009)*

## CABINETS & CASES: Show, Display & Storage, Exc Wood

**Advert Display Products Inc** G 815 513-5432
Morris *(G-15090)*
**Central Sheet Metal Pdts Inc** E 773 583-2424
Skokie *(G-19976)*
**Diversified Metal Products Inc** E 847 753-9595
Northbrook *(G-16244)*
**HMC Holdings LLC** E 847 541-5070
Buffalo Grove *(G-2705)*
**Imperial Marble Corp** C 815 498-2303
Somonauk *(G-20126)*
**Industrial Enclosure Corp** E 630 898-7499
Aurora *(G-1171)*
**Kewaunee Scientific Corp** G 847 675-7744
Highland Park *(G-11850)*
**Liam Brex** G 630 848-0222
Naperville *(G-15688)*
**Organized Home** G 217 698-6460
Springfield *(G-20494)*
**Plas-Co Inc** F 618 476-1761
Millstadt *(G-14832)*
**T and D Metal Products LLC** G 815 432-4938
Watseka *(G-21430)*
**Tts Granite Inc** E 708 755-5200
Steger *(G-20579)*
**Wilson Kitchens Inc** D 618 253-7449
Harrisburg *(G-11606)*

## CABINETS: Bathroom Vanities, Wood

**Crestwood Custom Cabinets** G 708 385-3167
Crestwood *(G-7485)*
**Crown Coverings Inc** E 630 546-2959
Roselle *(G-18937)*
**Der Holtzmacher Ltd** G 815 895-4887
Sycamore *(G-20792)*
**Kunz Carpentry** G 618 224-7892
Trenton *(G-20994)*
**Lacava LLC** E 773 637-9600
Chicago *(G-5432)*
**Pace Industries Inc** D 312 226-5500
Chicago *(G-6051)*
**Stonetree Fabrication Inc** E 618 332-1700
East Saint Louis *(G-8771)*
**Teds Custom Cabinets Inc** G 773 581-4455
Chicago *(G-6687)*
**Vanities Inc** G 847 483-0240
Arlington Heights *(G-862)*

## CABINETS: Entertainment

**Anderson & Marter Cabinets** G 630 406-9840
Batavia *(G-1415)*
**C M Sell Woodwork** G 847 526-3627
Wauconda *(G-21451)*
**Cabinets By Custom Craft Inc** G 815 637-4001
Roscoe *(G-18891)*
**Cooper Lake Millworks Inc** G 217 847-2681
Hamilton *(G-11530)*
**Creative Wood Concepts Inc** G 773 384-9960
Chicago *(G-4502)*

# CABINETS: Entertainment

Crestwood Custom Cabinets ................G....... 708 385-3167
  Crestwood *(G-7485)*
Eddie Gapastione ..............................G....... 708 430-3881
  Bridgeview *(G-2487)*
Elm Street Industries Inc ....................F....... 309 854-7000
  Kewanee *(G-12681)*
Grays Cabinet Co ................................G....... 618 948-2211
  Saint Francisville *(G-19313)*
HI Tech .................................................G....... 708 957-4210
  Homewood *(G-12100)*
Midwest Woodcrafters Inc ..................G....... 630 665-0901
  Carol Stream *(G-3199)*
Monticello Design & Mfg ...................G....... 217 762-8551
  Monticello *(G-15081)*
Roncin Custom Design .......................G....... 847 669-0260
  Huntley *(G-12175)*
Spirit Concepts Inc ..............................G....... 708 388-4500
  Crestwood *(G-7503)*
Woodhill Cabinetry Design Inc ...........G....... 815 431-0545
  Ottawa *(G-16992)*

## CABINETS: Entertainment Units, Household, Wood

Der Holtzmacher Ltd .........................G....... 815 895-4887
  Sycamore *(G-20792)*
Manufacturing / Woodworking ..........G....... 847 730-4823
  Des Plaines *(G-8226)*
Timberside Woodworking ...................G....... 217 578-3201
  Arthur *(G-922)*

## CABINETS: Factory

Aline International LLC .......................G....... 708 478-2471
  Mokena *(G-14850)*
Anderson & Marter Cabinets ..............G....... 630 406-9840
  Batavia *(G-1415)*
Concord Cabinets Inc .........................F....... 217 894-6507
  Clayton *(G-7269)*
Custom Wood & Laminate Ltd ............G....... 815 727-4168
  Joliet *(G-12481)*
Fortune Brands Home & SEC Inc ......C....... 847 484-4400
  Deerfield *(G-8007)*
Glenview Custom Cabinets Inc ...........G....... 847 345-5754
  Glenview *(G-11130)*
Hylan Design Ltd ................................G....... 312 243-7341
  Chicago *(G-5129)*
Michael Goss Custom Cabinets ..........G....... 217 864-4600
  Argenta *(G-690)*
Perfection Custom Closets & Co ........F....... 847 647-6461
  Niles *(G-16017)*
Phoenix Woodworking Corp ...............E....... 815 338-9338
  Woodstock *(G-22599)*
S L Fixtures Inc .................................G....... 217 423-9907
  Decatur *(G-7937)*
Suzy Cabinet Company Inc ................G....... 708 705-1259
  Bellwood *(G-1724)*

## CABINETS: Filing, Wood

C-V Cstom Cntrtops Cbinets Inc ........F....... 708 388-5066
  Blue Island *(G-2241)*
Cabinet Gallery LLC ...........................G....... 618 882-4801
  Highland *(G-11776)*
Cmp Millwork Co ................................G....... 630 832-6462
  Elmhurst *(G-9851)*
Ideal Cabinet Solutions Inc ................G....... 618 514-7087
  Alhambra *(G-418)*
Manufacturing / Woodworking ..........G....... 847 730-4823
  Des Plaines *(G-8226)*

## CABINETS: Kitchen, Metal

Dpcac LLC ...........................................F....... 630 741-7900
  Itasca *(G-12253)*

## CABINETS: Kitchen, Wood

57th Street Bookcase & Cabinet .........G....... 312 867-1669
  Chicago *(G-3674)*
Aba Custom Woodworking ..................G....... 815 356-9663
  Crystal Lake *(G-7525)*
Ability Cabinet Co Inc ........................G....... 847 678-6678
  Franklin Park *(G-10383)*
Action Cabinet Sales Inc ...................G....... 847 717-0011
  Elgin *(G-8935)*
Adams Street Iron Inc .......................F....... 312 733-3229
  Evergreen Park *(G-10109)*
Aji Custom Cabinets ...........................G....... 847 312-7847
  McHenry *(G-14478)*
Allie Woodworking ..............................G....... 847 244-1919
  Waukegan *(G-21522)*
Allwood Cabinet .................................G....... 773 778-1242
  Chicago *(G-3825)*
Amberleaf Cabinetry Inc ....................F....... 773 247-8282
  Chicago *(G-3844)*
American Custom Woodworking .........F....... 847 526-5900
  Wauconda *(G-11440)*
American Fixture ................................G....... 217 429-1300
  Decatur *(G-7832)*
Ameriscan Designs Inc ......................D....... 773 542-1291
  Chicago *(G-3886)*
Anderson & Marter Cabinets ..............G....... 630 406-9840
  Batavia *(G-1415)*
Anliker Custom Wood .........................F....... 815 657-7510
  Forrest *(G-10260)*
Aspen Cabinet Dist Corp ....................G....... 847 381-4241
  Barrington *(G-1268)*
Austin-Westran LLC ...........................C....... 815 234-2811
  Montgomery *(G-15029)*
Autumn Woods Ltd .............................G....... 630 868-3535
  Wheaton *(G-21937)*
Autumn Woods Ltd .............................E....... 630 668-2080
  Carol Stream *(G-3109)*
B & B Formica Appliers Inc ...............G....... 773 804-1015
  Chicago *(G-4014)*
Becker Jules D Wood Products ..........G....... 847 526-8002
  Wauconda *(G-21445)*
Bell Cabinet & Millwork Co ................G....... 708 425-1200
  Evergreen Park *(G-10110)*
Benchmark Cabinets & Mllwk Inc .......E....... 309 697-5855
  Peoria *(G-17316)*
Birom Cabinetry LLC ..........................G....... 312 286-7132
  Addison *(G-56)*
Bolhuis Woodworking Co ....................G....... 708 333-5100
  Manhattan *(G-14168)*
Brakur Custom Cabinetry Inc .............C....... 630 355-2244
  Shorewood *(G-19923)*
Brian Bequette Cabinetry ..................G....... 618 670-5427
  Staunton *(G-20554)*
Bridgeview Custom Kit Cabinets ........F....... 708 598-1221
  Bridgeview *(G-2472)*
Brighton Cabinetry Inc .......................G....... 217 235-1978
  Mattoon *(G-14385)*
Brighton Cabinetry Inc .......................G....... 217 895-3000
  Neoga *(G-15857)*
Brown Woodworking ...........................G....... 815 477-8333
  Crystal Lake *(G-7544)*
Byttow Enterprises Inc ......................G....... 708 754-4995
  Steger *(G-20570)*
C M Sell Woodwork .............................G....... 847 526-3627
  Wauconda *(G-21451)*
C S C Inc ............................................G....... 217 925-5908
  Dieterich *(G-8312)*
C-V Cstom Cntrtops Cbinets Inc ........F....... 708 388-5066
  Blue Island *(G-2241)*
Cabinet Broker Ltd ............................G....... 847 352-1898
  Elk Grove Village *(G-9354)*
Cabinet Designs .................................G....... 708 614-8603
  Oak Forest *(G-16575)*
Cabinets & Granite Direct LLC ..........F....... 630 588-8886
  Carol Stream *(G-3121)*
Cabinets By Custom Craft Inc ...........G....... 815 637-4001
  Roscoe *(G-18891)*
Cabinets Doors and More LLC ...........G....... 847 395-6334
  Antioch *(G-627)*
Carpenters Millwork Co ....................F....... 708 339-7707
  South Holland *(G-20255)*
Carpenters Millwork Co ....................G....... 708 339-7707
  Villa Park *(G-21241)*
Cassini Cabinetry ..............................G....... 847 244-9755
  Waukegan *(G-21535)*
Charles N Benner Inc .......................E....... 312 829-4300
  Chicago *(G-4293)*
Choice Cabinet Chicago ....................G....... 630 599-1099
  Glendale Heights *(G-11016)*
Closet Works LLC ..............................G....... 630 832-4422
  Elmhurst *(G-9850)*
Con-Temp Cabinets Inc .....................F....... 630 892-7300
  North Aurora *(G-16123)*
Contract Industries Inc .....................E....... 708 458-8150
  Bedford Park *(G-1545)*
Cooper Lake Millworks Inc ................G....... 217 847-2681
  Hamilton *(G-11530)*
Counter Craft Inc ...............................G....... 847 336-8205
  Waukegan *(G-21545)*
County Line Inc .................................E....... 217 268-5056
  Arthur *(G-892)*
Creative Cabinetry Inc ......................G....... 708 460-2900
  Orland Park *(G-16851)*
Creative Cabinets Countertops ..........F....... 217 446-6406
  Danville *(G-7710)*
Creative Designs Kitc ........................E....... 773 327-8400
  Chicago *(G-4497)*
Crown Custom Cabinetry Inc .............G....... 815 942-0432
  Morris *(G-15104)*
Custom Cabinet Refacers Inc ............G....... 847 695-8800
  Elgin *(G-9006)*
Custom Wood Designs Inc .................G....... 708 799-3439
  Crestwood *(G-7486)*
Custom Woodwork & Interiors ...........E....... 217 546-0006
  Springfield *(G-20427)*
Cws Cabinets .....................................G....... 847 258-4468
  Elk Grove Village *(G-9407)*
D & D Counter Tops Co Inc ................G.......
  Machesney Park *(G-14070)*
Daniel M Powers & Assoc Ltd ............D....... 630 685-8400
  Bolingbrook *(G-2299)*
David Hayes .......................................G....... 815 238-7690
  Steward *(G-20623)*
Decams Cabinets Inc .........................G....... 847 360-4970
  Lincolnshire *(G-13442)*
Design Woodworks ..............................G....... 847 566-6603
  Mundelein *(G-15493)*
Dicks Custom Cabinet Shop ..............G....... 815 358-2663
  Cornell *(G-7381)*
Dilaberto Co Inc .................................G....... 630 892-8448
  Aurora *(G-1141)*
Donald Kranz .....................................G....... 847 428-1616
  Carpentersville *(G-3283)*
Dpcac LLC ...........................................F....... 630 741-7900
  Itasca *(G-12253)*
Dvoraks Creations Inc .......................G....... 815 838-2214
  Lockport *(G-13713)*
Eagle Cabinet Inc ..............................G....... 847 289-9992
  Elgin *(G-9018)*
Eddie Gapastione ..............................G....... 708 430-3881
  Bridgeview *(G-2487)*
Edgars Custom Cabinets ...................G....... 847 928-0922
  Franklin Park *(G-10463)*
Edward Hull Cabinet Shop .................G....... 217 864-3011
  Mount Zion *(G-15450)*
Ellers Custom Cabinets Inc ..............F....... 309 633-0101
  Groveland *(G-11415)*
En Pointe Cabinetry ...........................G....... 847 787-0777
  Elk Grove Village *(G-9457)*
Encon Environmental Concepts .........F....... 630 543-1583
  Addison *(G-111)*
Euro-Tech Cabinetry Rmdlg Corp ......G....... 815 254-3876
  Plainfield *(G-17596)*
Forest City Counter Tops Inc .............G....... 815 633-8602
  Loves Park *(G-13942)*
Four Acre Wood Products ..................F....... 217 543-2971
  Arthur *(G-900)*
Fra-Milco Cabinets Co Inc .................G.......
  Frankfort *(G-10323)*
Fraser Millwork Inc ...........................G....... 708 447-3262
  Lyons *(G-14038)*
Garver Inc ..........................................G....... 217 932-2441
  Casey *(G-3383)*
Glenview Custom Cabinets Inc ...........G....... 847 345-5754
  Glenview *(G-11130)*
Gold Seal Cabinets Countertops ........E....... 630 906-0366
  Aurora *(G-1163)*
Grays Cabinet Co ................................G....... 618 948-2211
  Saint Francisville *(G-19313)*
Hansen Custom Cabinet Inc ...............G....... 847 356-1100
  Lake Villa *(G-13015)*
Hci Cabinetry and Design Inc ............G....... 630 584-0266
  Saint Charles *(G-19190)*
Helmuth Custom Kitchens LLC ..........E....... 217 543-3588
  Arthur *(G-904)*
Hester Cabinets & Millwork ...............G....... 815 634-4555
  Coal City *(G-7293)*
Hickory Street Cabinets ....................G....... 618 667-9676
  Troy *(G-21007)*
Hidalgo Fine Cabinetry ......................G....... 630 753-9323
  Naperville *(G-15809)*
Hylan Design Ltd ................................G....... 312 243-7341
  Chicago *(G-5129)*
I Kustom Cabinets Inc .......................G....... 773 343-6858
  Highwood *(G-11885)*
Ideal Cabinet Solutions Inc ................G....... 618 514-7087
  Alhambra *(G-418)*
J K Custom Countertops ....................G....... 630 495-2324
  Lombard *(G-13813)*
J M Lustig Custom Cabinets Co .........F....... 217 342-6661
  Effingham *(G-8840)*
Janik Custom Millwork Inc ................G....... 708 482-4844
  Hodgkins *(G-11977)*
Johnson Custom Cabinets ..................G....... 815 675-9690
  Spring Grove *(G-20339)*

**Joliet Cabinet Company Inc**.....E ....... 815 727-4096
Lockport *(G-13724)*
**Jones Design Group Ltd**.....G ....... 630 462-9340
Winfield *(G-22286)*
**Kabinet Kraft**.....F ....... 618 395-1047
Olney *(G-16775)*
**Kanneberg Custom Kitchens Inc**.....G ....... 815 654-1110
Machesney Park *(G-14084)*
**Kaufmans Custom Cabinets**.....F ....... 217 268-4330
Arcola *(G-673)*
**Kempner Company Inc**.....F ....... 312 733-1606
Chicago *(G-5376)*
**Kessmanns Cabinet Shop & Cnstr**.....G ....... 618 654-2538
Highland *(G-11800)*
**Kitchen Krafters Inc**.....G ....... 815 675-6061
Spring Grove *(G-20341)*
**Koala Cabinets**.....G ....... 630 818-1289
West Chicago *(G-21730)*
**Kowal Custom Cabinet & Furn**.....G ....... 708 597-3367
Blue Island *(G-2260)*
**Kraft Custom Design Inc**.....G ....... 815 485-5506
New Lenox *(G-15890)*
**Krafty Kabinets**.....G ....... 815 369-5250
Lena *(G-13276)*
**Lyko Woodworking & Cnstr**.....G ....... 773 583-4561
Chicago *(G-5573)*
**M & R Custom Millwork**.....G ....... 815 547-8549
Belvidere *(G-1768)*
**Manufacturing / Woodworking**.....G ....... 847 730-4823
Des Plaines *(G-8226)*
**Markham Cabinet Works Inc**.....G ....... 708 687-3074
Midlothian *(G-14767)*
**Markus Cabinet Manufacturing**.....E ....... 618 228-7376
Aviston *(G-1246)*
**Masco Corporation**.....D ....... 847 303-3088
Schaumburg *(G-19633)*
**Master Cabinets**.....G ....... 847 639-1323
Cary *(G-3359)*
**Masterbrand Cabinets Inc**.....B ....... 217 543-3311
Arthur *(G-909)*
**Masterbrand Cabinets Inc**.....G ....... 217 543-3466
Arthur *(G-910)*
**Masterbrand Cabinets Inc**.....G ....... 503 241-4964
Arthur *(G-911)*
**Masters Shop**.....G ....... 217 643-7826
Thomasboro *(G-20860)*
**Mc Laminated Cabinets**.....G ....... 773 301-0393
Franklin Park *(G-10525)*
**Metro Cabinet Refinishers**.....G ....... 217 498-7174
Rochester *(G-18120)*
**Mica Furniture Mfg Inc**.....G ....... 708 430-1150
Addison *(G-205)*
**Middletons Mouldings Inc**.....D ....... 517 278-6610
Schaumburg *(G-19646)*
**Midwest Woodcrafters Inc**.....G ....... 630 665-0901
Carol Stream *(G-3199)*
**Millcraft**.....G ....... 618 426-9819
Campbell Hill *(G-2977)*
**Miller Whiteside Wood Working**.....G ....... 309 827-6470
Mc Lean *(G-14463)*
**Mirek Cabinets**.....G ....... 630 350-8336
Franklin Park *(G-10535)*
**Monarch Mfg Corp Amer**.....E ....... 217 728-2552
Sullivan *(G-20753)*
**Monticello Design & Mfg**.....G ....... 217 762-8551
Monticello *(G-15081)*
**Mueller Custom Cabinetry Inc**.....G ....... 815 448-5448
Mazon *(G-14439)*
**Multiplex Display Fixture Co**.....E ....... 800 325-3350
Dupo *(G-8574)*
**Murray Cabinetry & Tops Inc**.....G ....... 815 672-6992
Streator *(G-20696)*
**Northstar Custom Cabinetry**.....G ....... 708 597-2099
Posen *(G-17733)*
**Northwest Marble Products**.....E ....... 630 860-2288
Hoffman Estates *(G-12072)*
**OGorman Son Carpentry Contrs**.....E ....... 815 485-8997
New Lenox *(G-15898)*
**Okaw Valley Woodworking LLC**.....F ....... 217 543-5180
Arthur *(G-916)*
**Orchard Hill Cabinetry Inc**.....E ....... 312 829-4300
Chicago *(G-6005)*
**Pac Team US Productions LLC**.....G ....... 773 360-8960
Chicago *(G-6049)*
**Parenti & Raffaelli Ltd**.....C ....... 847 253-5550
Mount Prospect *(G-15361)*
**Perkins Construction**.....G ....... 815 233-9655
Freeport *(G-10678)*
**Pintas Cultured Marble**.....E ....... 708 385-3360
Alsip *(G-509)*
**Planks Cabinet Shop Inc**.....G ....... 217 543-2687
Arthur *(G-918)*
**Plas-Co Inc**.....F ....... 618 476-1761
Millstadt *(G-14832)*
**Prairie Woodworks Inc**.....G ....... 309 378-2418
Downs *(G-8547)*
**Pro Cabinets Inc**.....G ....... 618 993-0008
Marion *(G-14284)*
**R & R Custom Cabinet Making**.....G ....... 847 358-6188
Palatine *(G-17065)*
**Rapp Cabinets & Woodworks Inc**.....F ....... 618 736-2955
Dahlgren *(G-7692)*
**Raymond Earl Fine Woodworking**.....G ....... 309 565-7661
Hanna City *(G-11570)*
**Regency Custom Woodworking**.....F ....... 815 689-2117
Cullom *(G-7683)*
**Richard King and Sons**.....G ....... 815 654-0226
Loves Park *(G-13982)*
**Richard Schrock**.....G ....... 217 543-3111
Arthur *(G-920)*
**Riverside Custom Woodworking**.....G ....... 815 589-3608
Fulton *(G-10705)*
**Riverton Cabinet Company**.....E ....... 815 462-5300
New Lenox *(G-15908)*
**Rogan Granitindustrie Inc**.....G ....... 708 758-0050
Lynwood *(G-14025)*
**Romar Cabinet & Top Co Inc**.....D ....... 815 467-4452
Channahon *(G-3584)*
**Roncin Custom Design**.....G ....... 847 669-0260
Huntley *(G-12175)*
**Ronnie P Faber**.....G ....... 815 626-4561
Sterling *(G-20610)*
**Royal Fabricators Inc**.....F ....... 847 775-7466
Wadsworth *(G-21327)*
**Santelli Custom Cabinetry**.....G ....... 708 771-3884
River Forest *(G-18000)*
**Schrock Custom Woodworking**.....G ....... 217 849-3375
Toledo *(G-20965)*
**Seigles Cabinet Center LLC**.....G ....... 224 535-7034
Elgin *(G-9174)*
**Seneca Custom Cabinetry**.....G ....... 815 357-1322
Seneca *(G-19890)*
**Shews Custom Woodworking**.....G ....... 217 737-5543
Lincoln *(G-13419)*
**Sleeping Bear Inc**.....G ....... 630 541-7220
Lisle *(G-13656)*
**Snaidero USA**.....G ....... 312 644-6662
Chicago *(G-6538)*
**Space Organization Ltd**.....F ....... 312 654-1400
Chicago *(G-6548)*
**Specialized Woodwork Inc**.....G ....... 630 627-0450
Lombard *(G-13854)*
**Stancy Woodworking Co Inc**.....F ....... 847 526-0252
Island Lake *(G-12219)*
**T and T Cabinet Co**.....G ....... 815 245-6322
McHenry *(G-14566)*
**T2 Cabinets Inc**.....F ....... 312 593-1507
Chicago *(G-6664)*
**Trademark Cabinet Corporation**.....G ....... 847 478-9393
Lincolnshire *(G-13486)*
**Tri Star Cabinet & Top Co Inc**.....D ....... 815 485-2564
New Lenox *(G-15922)*
**Val Custom Cabinets & Flrg Inc**.....G ....... 708 790-8373
Elk Grove Village *(G-9803)*
**Van Cleave Woodworking Inc**.....G ....... 847 424-8200
Northbrook *(G-16382)*
**Viking Metal Cabinet Co LLC**.....D ....... 800 776-7767
Montgomery *(G-15069)*
**Viking Metal Cabinet Company**.....D ....... 630 863-7234
Montgomery *(G-15070)*
**Wheaton Cabinetry**.....G ....... 815 729-1085
Lockport *(G-13750)*
**Wilcor Solid Surface Inc**.....F ....... 630 350-7703
Elk Grove Village *(G-9813)*
**Wolf Cabinetry & Ganite**.....G ....... 847 358-9922
Palatine *(G-17091)*
**Wolters Custom Cabinets LLC**.....G ....... 618 282-3158
Evansville *(G-10108)*
**Wood Shop**.....G ....... 773 994-6666
Chicago *(G-7024)*
**Wood Specialties Incorporated**.....F ....... 217 678-8420
Bement *(G-1803)*
**Woodhill Cabinetry Design Inc**.....G ....... 815 431-0545
Ottawa *(G-16992)*
**Woodways Industries LLC**.....E ....... 616 956-3070
Chicago *(G-7026)*
**Zenter Custom Cabinets Inc**.....F ....... 847 488-0744
Elgin *(G-9240)*

## *CABINETS: Office, Metal*

**Accurate Custom Cabinets Inc**.....E ....... 630 458-0460
Addison *(G-17)*
**Oak Creek Distribution LLC**.....E ....... 800 244-5263
Waukegan *(G-21596)*

## *CABINETS: Office, Wood*

**Accurate Custom Cabinets Inc**.....E ....... 630 458-0460
Addison *(G-17)*
**Castle Craft Products Inc**.....F ....... 630 279-7494
Villa Park *(G-21242)*
**Complete Custom Woodworks**.....G ....... 309 644-1911
Coal Valley *(G-7294)*
**Grays Cabinet Co**.....G ....... 618 948-2211
Saint Francisville *(G-19313)*
**Kessmanns Cabinet Shop & Cnstr**.....G ....... 618 654-2538
Highland *(G-11800)*

## *CABINETS: Show, Display, Etc, Wood, Exc Refrigerated*

**57th Street Bookcase & Cabinet**.....F ....... 773 363-3038
Chicago *(G-3673)*
**Churchill Cabinet Company**.....E ....... 708 780-0070
Cicero *(G-7182)*
**Con-Temp Cabinets Inc**.....F ....... 630 892-7300
North Aurora *(G-16123)*
**Imperial Kitchens & Bath Inc**.....F ....... 708 485-0020
Brookfield *(G-2635)*
**Kewaunee Scientific Corp**.....G ....... 847 675-7744
Highland Park *(G-11850)*
**Marcy Enterprises Inc**.....G ....... 708 352-7220
La Grange Park *(G-12758)*
**Midwest Display & Mfg Inc**.....G ....... 815 962-2199
Rockford *(G-18505)*
**Omni Craft Inc**.....G ....... 815 838-1285
Lockport *(G-13736)*
**Randal Wood Displays Inc**.....D ....... 630 761-0400
Batavia *(G-1490)*
**Specialized Woodwork Inc**.....G ....... 630 627-0450
Lombard *(G-13854)*
**Wilson Kitchens Inc**.....D ....... 618 253-7449
Harrisburg *(G-11606)*
**Windy Hill Woodworking Inc**.....G ....... 309 275-2415
Towanda *(G-20979)*

## *CABINETS: Television, Plastic*

**Avista Group Corporation**.....F ....... 877 772-8826
Elk Grove Village *(G-9324)*
**Zenith Electronics Corporation**.....E ....... 847 941-8000
Lincolnshire *(G-13496)*

## *CABLE & OTHER PAY TELEVISION DISTRIBUTION*

**Cco Holdings LLC**.....G ....... 618 505-3505
Troy *(G-21003)*
**Cco Holdings LLC**.....G ....... 618 651-6486
Highland *(G-11777)*
**Icon Acquisition Holdings LP**.....G ....... 312 751-8000
Chicago *(G-5136)*
**Skywide Publicity Solutions**.....G ....... 331 425-0341
Aurora *(G-1219)*

## *CABLE & PAY TELEVISION SVCS: Subscription*

**Jklein Enterprises Inc**.....G ....... 618 664-4554
Greenville *(G-11395)*

## *CABLE TELEVISION*

**Fred Kennerly**.....G ....... 815 398-6861
Rockford *(G-18392)*

## *CABLE TELEVISION PRDTS*

**Ed Co**.....E ....... 708 614-0695
Tinley Park *(G-20909)*
**Fred Kennerly**.....G ....... 815 398-6861
Rockford *(G-18392)*

## *CABLE WIRING SETS: Battery, Internal Combustion Engines*

**Appliance Information and Repr**.....G ....... 217 698-8858
Rochester *(G-18115)*
**Julian Elec Svc & Engrg Inc**.....E ....... 630 920-8950
Westmont *(G-21895)*

## CABLE WIRING SETS: Battery, Internal Combustion Engines

Sk Express Inc .................................................C....... 815 748-4388
　Dekalb *(G-8118)*
UNI Electric Enterprise Inc .............................G....... 630 372-6312
　Bartlett *(G-1323)*

## CABLE: Coaxial

Andrew New Zealand Inc .................................E....... 708 873-3507
　Orland Park *(G-16843)*
Commscope Technologies LLC ........................B....... 779 435-6000
　Joliet *(G-12476)*
Industrial Wire Cable II Corp .............................F....... 847 726-8910
　Lake Zurich *(G-13087)*

## CABLE: Fiber

Calvert Systems ...............................................G....... 309 523-3262
　Port Byron *(G-17719)*
Clark Wire & Cable Co Inc ................................E....... 847 949-9944
　Mundelein *(G-15488)*

## CABLE: Fiber Optic

Arris Group Inc ..................................................E....... 630 281-3000
　Lisle *(G-13564)*
Belford Electronics Inc ......................................E....... 630 705-3020
　Addison *(G-52)*
SITech Inc ..........................................................E....... 630 761-3640
　Batavia *(G-1496)*

## CABLE: Noninsulated

Advantage Components Inc .............................E....... 815 725-8644
　Joliet *(G-12450)*
Amsysco Inc .....................................................E....... 630 296-8383
　Romeoville *(G-18798)*
Industrial Wire & Cable Corp ............................E....... 847 726-8910
　Lake Zurich *(G-13086)*
Unistrut International Corp ................................C....... 800 882-5543
　Harvey *(G-11679)*

## CABLE: Ropes & Fiber

Lehigh Consumer Products LLC .......................C....... 630 851-7330
　Aurora *(G-1045)*

## CABLE: Steel, Insulated Or Armored

Southwire Company LLC ..................................D....... 618 662-8341
　Flora *(G-10219)*

## CABS: Indl Trucks & Tractors

Dfk America Inc .................................................G....... 630 324-6793
　Downers Grove *(G-8427)*

## CAFES

Sotish Ltd ..........................................................G....... 708 476-2017
　La Grange *(G-12746)*

## CAGES: Wire

Ameriguard Corporation ...................................G....... 630 986-1900
　Burr Ridge *(G-2822)*
Circle K Industries Inc .......................................F....... 847 949-0363
　Mundelein *(G-15487)*

## CALCULATING & ACCOUNTING EQPT

Business Valuation Group Inc ..........................G....... 312 595-1900
　Chicago *(G-4190)*

## CALENDARS, WHOLESALE

Midwest Promotional Group Co .......................E....... 708 563-0600
　Burr Ridge *(G-2868)*

## CALLIGRAPHER

Little Shop of Papers Ltd ..................................G....... 847 382-7733
　Barrington *(G-1287)*

## CAMERAS & RELATED EQPT: Photographic

Moog Inc ............................................................C....... 847 498-0700
　Northbrook *(G-16314)*
Quickset International Inc .................................D....... 847 498-0700
　Northbrook *(G-16350)*
Robotics Technologies Inc ...............................E....... 815 722-7650
　Joliet *(G-12570)*

## CAMPGROUNDS

Arthur Leo Kuhl .................................................G....... 618 752-5473
　Ingraham *(G-12199)*

Wooded Wonderland .......................................G....... 815 777-1223
　Galena *(G-10735)*

## CAMSHAFTS

Thyssnkrupp Prsta Danville LLC ......................B....... 217 444-5500
　Danville *(G-7775)*

## CAN LIDS & ENDS

Centric Co Inc ....................................................G....... 708 728-9061
　Downers Grove *(G-8407)*
Silgan Containers Mfg Corp .............................C....... 217 283-5501
　Hoopeston *(G-12116)*

## CANDLE SHOPS

Edwin Waldmire & Virginia ...............................G....... 217 498-9375
　Rochester *(G-18117)*
Marley Candles ................................................E....... 815 485-6604
　Mokena *(G-14883)*
Waxman Candles Inc .......................................G....... 773 929-3000
　Chicago *(G-6945)*

## CANDLES

Buh Hines Group LLC ......................................G....... 847 336-1460
　Gurnee *(G-11432)*
C Becky & Company Inc ..................................G....... 847 818-1021
　Mount Prospect *(G-15314)*
Candle Enterprises Inc .....................................G....... 618 526-8070
　Breese *(G-2441)*
Candle-Licious ..................................................E....... 847 488-9982
　Morrison *(G-15142)*
Chicago Candle Company ...............................G....... 773 637-5279
　Chicago *(G-4309)*
Heartland Candle Co ........................................G....... 815 698-2200
　Ashkum *(G-925)*
Imagine That Candle Co ..................................G....... 708 481-6370
　Matteson *(G-14373)*
Kemis Kollections .............................................G....... 773 431-2037
　Chicago *(G-5375)*
Marley Candles ................................................E....... 815 485-6604
　Mokena *(G-14883)*
Mondelez Global LLC .......................................C....... 847 943-4000
　Deerfield *(G-8037)*
Partylite Inc .......................................................E....... 630 845-6025
　Batavia *(G-1480)*
Sassy Primitives Ltd .........................................G....... 815 385-9302
　McCullom Lake *(G-14472)*
Tatine .................................................................G....... 312 733-0173
　Chicago *(G-6678)*
Waxman Candles Inc .......................................G....... 773 929-3000
　Chicago *(G-6945)*

## CANDLES: Wholesalers

Chicago Candle Company ...............................G....... 773 637-5279
　Chicago *(G-4309)*

## CANDY & CONFECTIONS: Cake Ornaments

White Stokes Company Inc ..............................E....... 773 254-5000
　Lincolnwood *(G-13543)*

## CANDY & CONFECTIONS: Candy Bars, Including Chocolate Covered

Eat Investments LLC ........................................E....... 618 624-5350
　O Fallon *(G-16467)*
Forbidden Sweets Inc ......................................F....... 847 838-9692
　Antioch *(G-633)*
Healthful Habits LLC ........................................F....... 224 489-4256
　West Chicago *(G-21714)*
Jessis Hideout ..................................................G....... 618 343-4346
　Caseyville *(G-3398)*
Orbit Room ........................................................F....... 773 588-8540
　Chicago *(G-6004)*

## CANDY & CONFECTIONS: Chocolate Candy, Exc Solid Chocolate

Chocolate Potpourri Ltd ...................................F....... 847 729-8878
　Glenview *(G-11112)*
Morkes Inc .........................................................F....... 847 359-3511
　Palatine *(G-17057)*
Tri International Co ............................................A....... 773 838-3400
　Chicago *(G-6769)*
Zeldaco Ltd .......................................................F....... 847 679-0033
　Skokie *(G-20116)*

## CANDY & CONFECTIONS: Cough Drops, Exc Pharmaceutical Preps

Universal Holdings I LLC ..................................D....... 773 847-1005
　Chicago *(G-6832)*

## CANDY & CONFECTIONS: Fruit & Fruit Peel

All American Nut & Candy Corp .......................F....... 630 595-6473
　Bensenville *(G-1823)*

## CANDY & CONFECTIONS: Fudge

Arndts Stores Inc ..............................................G....... 618 783-2511
　Newton *(G-15937)*
Deli Star Ventures Inc ......................................F....... 618 233-0400
　Belleville *(G-1624)*

## CANDY & CONFECTIONS: Marshmallows

Doumak Inc .......................................................G....... 800 323-0318
　Bensenville *(G-1881)*
Doumak Inc .......................................................D....... 847 981-2180
　Elk Grove Village *(G-9433)*
We Love Soy Inc ...............................................G....... 630 629-9667
　Lombard *(G-13881)*

## CANDY & CONFECTIONS: Popcorn Balls/Other Trtd Popcorn Prdts

Double Good LLC .............................................F....... 630 568-5544
　Burr Ridge *(G-2837)*
Gary Poppins LLC ............................................G....... 847 455-2200
　Franklin Park *(G-10476)*
Larry Ragan ......................................................G....... 618 698-1041
　Belleville *(G-1648)*
McCleary Inc .....................................................C....... 815 389-3053
　South Beloit *(G-20160)*
Mix Match LLC ..................................................F....... 708 201-0009
　Dolton *(G-8373)*
Windy City Gold Popcorn Inc ...........................G....... 708 596-9940
　Alsip *(G-544)*

## CANDY MAKING GOODS & SPLYS, WHOLESALE

Cupcake Holdings LLC ....................................C....... 800 794-5866
　Woodridge *(G-22466)*
Wilton Brands LLC ............................................B....... 630 963-7100
　Woodridge *(G-22526)*
Wilton Holdings Inc ..........................................G....... 630 963-7100
　Woodridge *(G-22527)*
Wilton Industries Inc .........................................B....... 630 963-7100
　Woodridge *(G-22528)*
Wilton Industries Inc .........................................F....... 815 834-9390
　Romeoville *(G-18879)*

## CANDY, NUT & CONFECTIONERY STORE: Popcorn, Incl Caramel Corn

Great American Popcorn Company ................G....... 815 777-4116
　Galena *(G-10725)*

## CANDY, NUT & CONFECTIONERY STORES: Candy

American Convenience Inc ..............................F....... 815 344-6040
　McHenry *(G-14480)*
Baileys Fudge & Fine Gifts Inc ........................G....... 217 231-3834
　Quincy *(G-17799)*
Cora Lee Candies Inc ......................................F....... 847 724-2754
　Glenview *(G-11115)*
Ford Gum & Machine Company Inc ...............F....... 847 955-0003
　Buffalo Grove *(G-2698)*
Galenas Kandy Kitchen ....................................G....... 815 777-0241
　Galena *(G-10723)*
Gayety Candy Co Inc .......................................E....... 708 418-0062
　Lansing *(G-13163)*
Mitchlls Cndies Ice Creams Inc .......................F....... 708 799-3835
　Homewood *(G-12104)*
Morkes Inc .........................................................F....... 847 359-3511
　Palatine *(G-17057)*
Peases Inc ........................................................F....... 217 523-3721
　Springfield *(G-20501)*

## CANDY, NUT & CONFECTIONERY STORES: Confectionery

Long Grove Confectionery Co .........................E....... 847 459-3100
　Buffalo Grove *(G-2728)*

# PRODUCT SECTION

## CANDY, NUT & CONFECTIONERY STORES: Produced For Direct Sale

Altona Co .................................. G ..... 815 232-7819
  Freeport *(G-10645)*

## CANDY: Chocolate From Cacao Beans

Godiva Chocolatier Inc .................. E ..... 630 820-5842
  Aurora *(G-1019)*
Morkes Inc .................................. F ..... 847 359-3511
  Palatine *(G-17057)*
Vosges Ltd .................................. D ..... 773 388-5560
  Chicago *(G-6915)*

## CANDY: Hard

Primrose Candy Co ........................ C ..... 800 268-9522
  Chicago *(G-6188)*

## CANDY: Soft

Baldi Candy Co ............................ E ..... 773 463-7600
  Chicago *(G-4031)*

## CANES & TRIMMINGS, EXC PRECIOUS METAL

Cane Plus .................................. G ..... 217 522-4035
  Springfield *(G-20403)*

## CANNED SPECIALTIES

Archer-Daniels-Midland Company ......... E ..... 309 772-2141
  Bushnell *(G-2897)*
Dial Corporation ........................... C ..... 630 892-4381
  Montgomery *(G-15041)*
Kraft Heinz Foods Company ............... C ..... 847 291-3900
  Northbrook *(G-16290)*
Lee Gilster-Mary Corporation ............ D ..... 618 965-3426
  Steeleville *(G-20561)*
Lynfred Winery Inc ........................ E ..... 630 529-9463
  Roselle *(G-18953)*
McShares Inc .............................. E ..... 217 762-2561
  Monticello *(G-15079)*
Mead Johnson & Company LLC ........... F ..... 847 832-2420
  Chicago *(G-5670)*
Nara Dips Inc ............................. G ..... 773 837-0601
  Dekalb *(G-8108)*
Nestle Usa Inc ............................ D ..... 847 808-5404
  Buffalo Grove *(G-2747)*
Nestle Usa Inc ............................ C ..... 847 808-5300
  Buffalo Grove *(G-2748)*
Nogi Brands LLC .......................... G ..... 312 371-7974
  Chicago *(G-5922)*
Sofrito Foods LLC ......................... G ..... 630 302-8615
  South Elgin *(G-20226)*
Vanee Foods Company ..................... D ..... 708 449-7300
  Berkeley *(G-2050)*
Windy Acquisition LLC .................... E ..... 630 595-5744
  Bensenville *(G-2015)*

## CANOPIES: Sheet Metal

Diversified Cnstr Svcs LLC ............... G ..... 708 344-4900
  Melrose Park *(G-14620)*

## CANS: Aluminum

Fitpac Co Ltd ............................. G ..... 630 428-9077
  Bensenville *(G-1899)*
Rexam Beverage Can Company ........... C ..... 773 247-4646
  Chicago *(G-6345)*

## CANS: Metal

All Container Inc ......................... G ..... 847 677-2100
  Lincolnwood *(G-13502)*
Ardagh Metal Beverage USA Inc ......... D ..... 773 399-3000
  Chicago *(G-3943)*
Ball Corporation .......................... C
  Elgin *(G-8963)*
Brockway Standard Inc ................... G ..... 773 893-2100
  Chicago *(G-4173)*
Bway Corporation ......................... C ..... 847 956-0750
  Elk Grove Village *(G-9351)*
Bway Corporation ......................... C ..... 773 254-8700
  Chicago *(G-4194)*
Bway Parent Company Inc ................ F ..... 773 890-3300
  Chicago *(G-4195)*
Central Can Company Inc ................ C ..... 773 254-8700
  Chicago *(G-4270)*

Certified Tank & Mfg LLC ................ E ..... 217 525-1433
  Springfield *(G-20415)*
Chicago Mtal Sup Fbrcation Inc ......... F ..... 773 227-6200
  Chicago *(G-4336)*
Cooler Concepts Inc ...................... G ..... 815 462-3866
  New Lenox *(G-15872)*
Creative Metal Products .................. F ..... 773 638-3200
  Chicago *(G-4500)*
Crown Cork & Seal Usa Inc .............. C ..... 708 239-5555
  Alsip *(G-452)*
Crown Cork & Seal Usa Inc .............. G ..... 815 933-9351
  Bradley *(G-2417)*
Crown Cork & Seal Usa Inc .............. C ..... 708 239-5000
  Alsip *(G-453)*
Crown Cork & Seal Usa Inc .............. D ..... 217 672-3533
  Warrensburg *(G-21338)*
Crown Cork & Seal Usa Inc .............. C ..... 217 872-6100
  Decatur *(G-7861)*
Crown Cork & Seal Usa Inc .............. G ..... 630 851-7774
  Aurora *(G-989)*
D & B Fabricators & Distrs .............. F ..... 630 325-3811
  Lemont *(G-13234)*
Ds Containers Inc ........................ C ..... 630 406-9600
  Batavia *(G-1442)*
Great Lakes Art Foundry Inc ............. G ..... 847 213-0800
  Skokie *(G-20006)*
Ideal Fabricators Inc ..................... F ..... 217 999-7017
  Mount Olive *(G-15304)*
JL Clark LLC .............................. C ..... 815 961-5609
  Rockford *(G-18447)*
Jlo Metal Products Co A Corp ........... D ..... 773 889-6242
  Chicago *(G-5307)*
Justrite Manufacturing Co LLC ........... C ..... 217 234-7486
  Mattoon *(G-14396)*
Metraflex Company ........................ D ..... 312 738-3800
  Chicago *(G-5706)*
Rexam Beverage Can Company ........... C ..... 847 238-3200
  Elk Grove Village *(G-9715)*
Silgan Containers LLC .................... D ..... 815 562-1250
  Rochelle *(G-18109)*
Silgan Containers Mfg Corp .............. E ..... 847 336-0552
  Waukegan *(G-21616)*
Silgan Equipment Company ............... E ..... 847 336-0552
  Waukegan *(G-21617)*
Silgan White Cap Corporation ........... C ..... 217 398-1600
  Champaign *(G-3539)*
Staffco Inc ................................ G ..... 309 688-3223
  Peoria *(G-17460)*
Willow Farm Product Inc ................. G ..... 630 395-9246
  Darien *(G-7804)*

## CANS: Oil, Metal

Best Metal Corporation ................... E ..... 815 337-0420
  Woodstock *(G-22545)*

## CANVAS PRDTS

A B Kelly Inc ............................. G ..... 847 639-1022
  Cary *(G-3320)*
Acme Awning Co .......................... G ..... 847 446-0153
  Highland Park *(G-11822)*
Air Land and Sea Interiors ............... G ..... 630 834-1717
  Villa Park *(G-21234)*
Awnings By Zip Dee Inc .................. E ..... 847 640-0460
  Elk Grove Village *(G-9326)*
Bloomington Tent & Awning Inc .......... G ..... 309 828-3411
  Bloomington *(G-2150)*
Brumleve Industries Inc .................. F ..... 217 857-3777
  Teutopolis *(G-20847)*
Canvas Creations Inc ..................... G ..... 309 343-5082
  Galesburg *(G-10741)*
Champaign Cnty Tent & Awng Co ....... E ..... 217 328-5749
  Urbana *(G-21077)*
Ed Hill S Custom Canvas ................. G ..... 815 476-5042
  Wilmington *(G-22271)*
Environetics Inc .......................... G ..... 815 838-8331
  Lockport *(G-13715)*
Event Equipment Sales LLC ............... F ..... 708 352-0662
  Hodgkins *(G-11974)*
Flex-O-Glass Inc ......................... D ..... 773 261-5200
  Chicago *(G-4858)*
Haakes Awning ............................ G ..... 618 529-4808
  Carbondale *(G-3009)*
Jelinek & Sons Inc ....................... G ..... 630 355-3474
  Plainfield *(G-17610)*
Johnson Seat & Canvas Shop ............ G ..... 815 756-2037
  Cortland *(G-7389)*
Kroto Inc .................................. E ..... 800 980-1089
  Morton Grove *(G-15210)*
M Putterman & Co LLC ................... G ..... 773 734-1000
  Chicago *(G-5586)*

M Putterman & Co LLC ................... D ..... 773 927-4120
  Chicago *(G-5585)*
Material Control Inc ...................... F ..... 630 892-4274
  Batavia *(G-1467)*
Mpc Containment Systems LLC .......... D ..... 773 927-4121
  Chicago *(G-5822)*
Mpc Containment Systems LLC .......... E ..... 773 734-1000
  Chicago *(G-5823)*
Mpc Group LLC ........................... G ..... 773 927-4120
  Chicago *(G-5824)*
Ogden Top & Trim Shop Inc ............. G ..... 708 484-5422
  Berwyn *(G-2070)*
Ottos Canvas Shop ....................... G ..... 217 543-3307
  Arthur *(G-917)*
Rehabilitation and Vocational ............ E ..... 618 833-5344
  Anna *(G-608)*
Tri City Canvas Products Inc ............ F ..... 618 797-1662
  Granite City *(G-11308)*
Tri Vantage LLC .......................... F ..... 630 530-5333
  Elmhurst *(G-9952)*

## CANVAS PRDTS, WHOLESALE

Brumleve Industries Inc .................. F ..... 217 857-3777
  Teutopolis *(G-20847)*

## CANVAS PRDTS: Air Cushions & Mattresses

Sleep6 LLC ................................ G ..... 844 375-3376
  Chicago *(G-6528)*

## CANVAS PRDTS: Convertible Tops, Car/Boat, Fm Purchased Mtrl

Custom Canvas LLC ....................... G ..... 847 587-0225
  Ingleside *(G-12188)*
Magna Extrors Intrors Amer Inc ......... G ..... 847 548-9170
  Grayslake *(G-11353)*
United Canvas Inc ........................ E ..... 847 395-1470
  Antioch *(G-661)*

## CANVAS PRDTS: Shades, Made From Purchased Materials

Shading Solutions Group Inc ............. G ..... 630 444-2102
  Geneva *(G-10866)*

## CAPACITORS & CONDENSERS

Motor Capacitors Inc ..................... F ..... 773 774-6666
  Wood Dale *(G-22401)*
Ronken Industries Inc .................... E ..... 815 664-5306
  Spring Valley *(G-20380)*

## CAPACITORS: AC, Motors Or Fluorescent Lamp Ballasts

American Electronic Pdts Inc ............ F ..... 630 889-9977
  Oak Brook *(G-16488)*
Elpac Electronics Inc ..................... C ..... 708 316-4407
  Westchester *(G-21839)*
Innovation Plus Power Systems .......... F ..... 630 457-1105
  Saint Charles *(G-19198)*

## CAPACITORS: NEC

Aisin Light Metals LLC ................... G ..... 618 997-7900
  Marion *(G-14249)*
Bycap Inc ................................. E ..... 773 561-4976
  Chicago *(G-4196)*
Elpac Electronics Inc ..................... C ..... 708 316-4407
  Westchester *(G-21839)*
Jbsmwg Corp .............................. F ..... 847 675-1865
  Lincolnwood *(G-13516)*
Knowles Corporation ...................... D ..... 630 250-5100
  Itasca *(G-12295)*
Motor Capacitors Inc ..................... F ..... 773 774-6666
  Wood Dale *(G-22401)*
Murata Electronics N Amer Inc .......... G ..... 847 330-9200
  Schaumburg *(G-19657)*
Pei/Genesis Inc ........................... G ..... 215 673-0400
  Rolling Meadows *(G-18760)*
Standard Condenser Corporation ........ F ..... 847 965-2722
  Morton Grove *(G-15237)*
United Chemi-Con Inc .................... E ..... 847 696-2000
  Rolling Meadows *(G-18786)*

## CAPS & TOPS: Bottle, Stamped Metal

Walter H Jelly & Co Inc .................. G ..... 847 455-4235
  Franklin Park *(G-10626)*

Employee Codes: A=Over 500 employees, B=251-500
C=101-250, D=51-100, E=20-50, F=10-19, G=3-9

# CAPS: Plastic — PRODUCT SECTION

### CAPS: Plastic
- Blackhawk Molding Co Inc .......... D ...... 630 628-6218
  Addison *(G-58)*
- Fliptabs Inc .......... G ...... 815 701-2584
  Wonder Lake *(G-22323)*
- Oakridge Products LLC .......... G ...... 815 363-4700
  McHenry *(G-14538)*
- Selig S LLC .......... G ...... 815 785-2100
  Forrest *(G-10264)*
- Selig Sealing Holdings Inc .......... G ...... 815 785-2100
  Forrest *(G-10265)*

### CAR WASH EQPT
- Avw Equipment Company Inc .......... E ...... 708 343-7738
  Maywood *(G-14417)*
- Big R Car Wash Inc .......... G ...... 217 367-4958
  Urbana *(G-21072)*
- Brite-O-Matic Mfg Inc .......... D ...... 847 956-1100
  Arlington Heights *(G-730)*
- Diskin Systems Inc .......... G ...... 815 276-7288
  Algonquin *(G-387)*
- Enterprises One Stop .......... G ...... 773 924-5506
  Chicago *(G-4761)*
- Galesburg Manufacturing Co .......... E ...... 309 342-3173
  Galesburg *(G-10750)*
- Princeton Fast Stop .......... F ...... 815 872-0706
  Princeton *(G-17758)*
- River North Hand .......... G ...... 312 335-9669
  Chicago *(G-6362)*
- Sparkle Express .......... G ...... 630 375-9801
  Oswego *(G-16935)*
- U Wash Equipment Co .......... G ...... 618 466-9442
  Alton *(G-594)*

### CAR WASHES
- Rays Power Wshg Svc Peggy Ray .......... G ...... 618 939-6306
  Waterloo *(G-21405)*
- Truckers Oil Pros Inc .......... F ...... 773 523-8990
  Chicago *(G-6785)*

### CARBIDES
- Rend Lake Carbide Inc .......... G ...... 618 438-0160
  Benton *(G-2039)*
- Rockform Tooling & Machinery .......... E ...... 770 345-4624
  Rockford *(G-18591)*
- Schwanog LLC .......... G ...... 847 289-1055
  Elgin *(G-9172)*

### CARBON & GRAPHITE PRDTS, NEC
- Aero Industries Inc .......... F ...... 815 943-7818
  Harvard *(G-11618)*
- AMS Seals Inc .......... G ...... 815 609-4977
  Plainfield *(G-17580)*
- Cabot Corporation .......... D ...... 217 253-5752
  Tuscola *(G-21018)*
- Carbon Solutions Group LLC .......... F ...... 312 638-9077
  Chicago *(G-4239)*
- Frantz Manufacturing Company .......... D ...... 815 625-7063
  Sterling *(G-20592)*
- Graphtek LLC .......... F ...... 847 279-1925
  Northbrook *(G-16266)*
- Hickman Williams & Company .......... F ...... 708 656-8818
  Cicero *(G-7202)*
- Industrial Graphite Sales LLC .......... G ...... 815 943-5502
  Harvard *(G-11638)*
- Kirkman Composites .......... G ...... 309 734-5606
  Monmouth *(G-15018)*
- Process Engineering Corp .......... F ...... 815 459-1734
  Crystal Lake *(G-7634)*
- Seal Operation S L .......... G ...... 847 537-8100
  Wheeling *(G-22145)*
- Superior Graphite Co .......... E ...... 708 458-0006
  Chicago *(G-6633)*

### CARBON BLACK
- Cabot Corporation .......... D ...... 217 253-5752
  Tuscola *(G-21018)*

### CARBON PAPER & INKED RIBBONS
- Dauphin Enterprise Inc .......... G ...... 630 893-6300
  Bloomingdale *(G-2101)*
- Illinois Tool Works Inc .......... E ...... 708 720-0300
  Frankfort *(G-10333)*
- Nashua Corporation .......... D ...... 847 692-9130
  Park Ridge *(G-17211)*

### CARBON SPECIALTIES Electrical Use
- Becker Brothers Graphite Corp .......... G ...... 708 410-0700
  Maywood *(G-14418)*
- Rnfl Acquisition LLC .......... E ...... 651 442-6011
  Chicago *(G-6366)*

### CARBONS: Electric
- Industrial Graphite Products .......... G ...... 630 350-0155
  Franklin Park *(G-10498)*

### CARBURETORS
- Borgwarner Inc .......... C ...... 815 288-1462
  Dixon *(G-8324)*
- United Carburetor Inc .......... E ...... 773 777-1223
  Schiller Park *(G-19879)*
- United Remanufacturing Co Inc .......... G ...... 773 777-1223
  Schiller Park *(G-19880)*
- United Remanufacturing Co Inc .......... E ...... 847 678-2233
  Schiller Park *(G-19881)*

### CARDBOARD PRDTS, EXC DIE-CUT
- Integrated Label Corporation .......... F ...... 815 874-2500
  Rockford *(G-18437)*

### CARDS, PLASTIC, UNPRINTED, WHOLESALE
- Universal Holdings Inc .......... F ...... 224 353-6198
  Hoffman Estates *(G-12066)*

### CARDS: Color
- Color Communications Inc .......... C ...... 773 638-1400
  Chicago *(G-4426)*
- Modern Trade Communications .......... F ...... 847 674-2200
  Skokie *(G-20041)*

### CARDS: Greeting
- Advantage Printing Inc .......... G ...... 630 627-7468
  Lombard *(G-13760)*
- Alex Smart Inc .......... G ...... 773 244-9275
  Chicago *(G-3803)*
- Cardthartic LLC .......... F ...... 217 239-5895
  Champaign *(G-3461)*
- Cook Communications Ministries .......... C ...... 847 741-0800
  Elgin *(G-9004)*
- Crest Greetings Inc .......... F ...... 708 210-0800
  Chicago *(G-4503)*
- Florists Transworld Dlvry Inc .......... A ...... 630 719-7800
  Downers Grove *(G-8444)*
- Fsg Crest LLC .......... F ...... 708 210-0800
  Lake In The Hills *(G-12993)*
- Ggc Corp .......... D ...... 847 671-6500
  Schiller Park *(G-19834)*
- Gram Colossal Inc .......... G ...... 847 223-5757
  Grayslake *(G-11343)*
- Harry Otto Printing Company .......... F ...... 630 365-6111
  Elburn *(G-8889)*
- K Chae Corp .......... F ...... 847 763-0077
  Lincolnwood *(G-13518)*
- Karen Young .......... F ...... 312 202-0142
  Chicago *(G-5360)*
- Marketing Card Technology LLC .......... D ...... 630 985-7900
  Darien *(G-7799)*
- National Gift Card Corp .......... E ...... 815 477-4288
  Crystal Lake *(G-7617)*
- P S Greetings Inc .......... F ...... 708 831-5340
  Chicago *(G-6040)*
- P S Greetings Inc .......... F ...... 847 673-7255
  Skokie *(G-20052)*
- Recycled Paper Greetings Inc .......... E ...... 773 348-6410
  Chicago *(G-6314)*
- Salamander Studios Chicago Inc .......... F ...... 773 379-2211
  Chicago *(G-6431)*
- United Press Inc (del) .......... F ...... 847 482-0597
  Lincolnshire *(G-13487)*

### CARDS: Identification
- Computhink Inc .......... F ...... 630 705-9050
  Lombard *(G-13783)*
- Hemmerle Jr Irvin .......... G ...... 630 334-4392
  Naperville *(G-15670)*
- Id3 Inc .......... E ...... 847 734-9781
  Arlington Heights *(G-771)*
- Identatronics Inc .......... E ...... 847 437-2654
  Crystal Lake *(G-7591)*
- Identification Products Mfg Co .......... G ...... 847 367-6452
  Lake Forest *(G-12914)*
- Multi Packaging Solutions Inc .......... G ...... 773 283-9500
  Chicago *(G-5832)*
- National Emergency Med ID Inc .......... G ...... 847 366-1267
  Spring Grove *(G-20351)*
- Oberthur Tech Amer Corp .......... D ...... 630 551-0792
  Naperville *(G-15718)*
- Perfect Plastic Printing Corp .......... C ...... 630 584-1600
  Saint Charles *(G-19234)*
- Psa Equity LLC .......... F ...... 847 478-6000
  Buffalo Grove *(G-2757)*
- Teraco-Il Inc .......... E ...... 630 539-4400
  Roselle *(G-18981)*
- Versatile Card Technology Inc .......... C ...... 630 852-5600
  Downers Grove *(G-8536)*

### CARPET & UPHOLSTERY CLEANING SVCS
- Duraclean International Inc .......... F ...... 847 704-7100
  Arlington Heights *(G-748)*
- Randys Exper-Clean .......... G ...... 217 423-1975
  Decatur *(G-7931)*

### CARPET LINING: Felt, Exc Woven
- Midwest Carpet Recycling Inc .......... E ...... 855 406-8600
  Lake Villa *(G-13021)*

### CARPETS & RUGS: Tufted
- Interfaceflor LLC .......... E ...... 312 775-6307
  Chicago *(G-5212)*
- Interfaceflor LLC .......... E ...... 312 836-3389
  Chicago *(G-5213)*

### CARPETS, RUGS & FLOOR COVERING
- Aspen Carpet Designs .......... G ...... 815 483-8501
  Mokena *(G-14855)*
- Baker Avenue Investments Inc .......... G ...... 309 427-2500
  Washington *(G-21378)*
- Blachford Investments Inc .......... C ...... 630 231-8300
  West Chicago *(G-21671)*
- Ds Production LLC .......... G ...... 708 873-3142
  Orland Park *(G-16856)*
- Eagle Carpet Services Ltd .......... G ...... 956 971-8560
  Addison *(G-105)*
- East West Martial Arts Sups .......... G ...... 773 878-7711
  Chicago *(G-4682)*
- Edward Fields Incorporated .......... G ...... 312 644-0400
  Chicago *(G-4703)*
- Interfaceflor LLC .......... F ...... 312 822-9640
  Chicago *(G-5214)*
- L & L Flooring Inc .......... E ...... 773 935-9314
  Chicago *(G-5418)*
- Mailbox International Inc .......... E ...... 847 541-8466
  Wheeling *(G-22097)*
- Mastercraft Rug Design .......... G ...... 630 655-3393
  Hinsdale *(G-11952)*
- Milliken & Company .......... F ...... 800 241-4826
  Chicago *(G-5763)*
- Minasian Rug Corporation .......... F ...... 847 864-1010
  Evanston *(G-10073)*
- Shaw Industries Group Inc .......... G ...... 312 467-1331
  Chicago *(G-6491)*
- Shiir Rugs LLC .......... E ...... 312 828-0400
  Chicago *(G-6497)*

### CARPETS: Wilton
- Mohawk Industries Inc .......... D ...... 630 972-8000
  Bolingbrook *(G-2344)*

### CARPORTS: Prefabricated Metal
- American Steel Carports Inc .......... F ...... 800 487-4010
  Kewanee *(G-12669)*

### CARRIAGES: Horse Drawn
- Prompt Usa Inc .......... G ...... 309 660-0222
  Minooka *(G-14846)*

### CARRIER EQPT: Telephone Or Telegraph
- Quen-Tel Communication Svc Inc .......... G ...... 815 463-1800
  New Lenox *(G-15903)*

### CARRYING CASES, WHOLESALE
- Bearse Manufacturing Co .......... D ...... 773 235-8710
  Chicago *(G-4068)*

# PRODUCT SECTION

## CASTINGS: Die, Aluminum

Gabriel Enterprises .................................... G ...... 773 342-8705
  Chicago *(G-4906)*

### CARS & TRUCKS: Indl Mining

Daco Products LLC .................................... G ...... 630 373-2245
  North Aurora *(G-16125)*

### CARS: Electric

Park License Service Inc ............................. G ...... 815 633-5511
  Loves Park *(G-13972)*

### CARTONS: Egg, Die-Cut, Made From Purchased Materials

Classic Packaging Corporation .................... G ...... 224 723-5157
  Northbrook *(G-16226)*

### CASEMENTS: Aluminum

Pittco Architectural Mtls Inc ....................... G ...... 800 992-7488
  Elk Grove Village *(G-9682)*

### CASES, WOOD

Kunde Woodwork Inc ................................. G ...... 847 669-2030
  Huntley *(G-12156)*
Wesling Products Inc ................................. G ...... 773 533-2850
  Chicago *(G-6959)*

### CASES: Attache'

Jelco Inc ................................................... F ...... 847 459-5207
  Wheeling *(G-22082)*
McKlein Company LLC ............................... F ...... 773 235-0600
  Chicago *(G-5668)*
Platt Luggage Inc ...................................... D ...... 773 838-2000
  Chicago *(G-6139)*

### CASES: Carrying

Custom Case Co Inc .................................. E ...... 773 585-1164
  Chicago *(G-4521)*
Mfz Ventures Inc ....................................... G ...... 773 247-4611
  Chicago *(G-5715)*
Sukie Group Inc ........................................ F ...... 773 521-1800
  Chicago *(G-6613)*

### CASES: Carrying, Clothing & Apparel

Jans ......................................................... G ...... 815 722-9360
  Joliet *(G-12521)*

### CASES: Jewelry

Tia Tynette Designs Inc .............................. G ...... 219 440-2859
  Olympia Fields *(G-16806)*

### CASES: Nonrefrigerated, Exc Wood

Proto Productions Inc ................................. E ...... 630 628-6626
  Addison *(G-260)*
Roberts Sheet Metal Works Inc ................... E ...... 773 626-3811
  Chicago *(G-6370)*

### CASES: Packing, Nailed Or Lock Corner, Wood

Botkin Lumber Company Inc ....................... E ...... 217 287-2127
  Taylorville *(G-20834)*
Chrometec LLC ......................................... G ...... 630 792-8777
  Lombard *(G-13778)*

### CASES: Plastic

A W Enterprises Inc .................................. E ...... 708 458-8989
  Bedford Park *(G-1531)*
Black Rhino Concealment ........................... G ...... 847 783-6499
  Gilberts *(G-10913)*
Platt Luggage Inc ...................................... D ...... 773 838-2000
  Chicago *(G-6139)*
Time Records Publishing and Bo ................ G ...... 618 996-3803
  Marion *(G-14291)*

### CASES: Sample Cases

Seamcraft International LLC ....................... E ...... 773 417-4002
  Chicago *(G-6466)*
Service & Manufacturing Corp ..................... E ...... 773 287-5500
  Chicago *(G-6481)*

### CASES: Shipping, Nailed Or Lock Corner, Wood

BP Shipping .............................................. F ...... 630 393-1032
  Naperville *(G-15610)*
Export Packaging Co Inc ............................ A ...... 309 756-4288
  Milan *(G-14786)*
Western Illinois Enterprises ........................ G ...... 309 342-5185
  Galesburg *(G-10779)*

### CASH REGISTERS WHOLESALERS

Micros Systems Inc ................................... F ...... 443 285-6000
  Itasca *(G-12316)*

### CASINGS: Sheet Metal

Prairie State Industries Inc ......................... F ...... 847 428-3641
  Carpentersville *(G-3297)*
Service Metal Enterprises ........................... G ...... 630 628-1444
  Addison *(G-288)*
Vanfab Inc ................................................ E ...... 815 426-2544
  Union Hill *(G-21040)*

### CASINO HOTELS & MOTELS

Diamond Icic Corporation ........................... E ...... 309 269-8652
  Rock Island *(G-18175)*

### CASKETS & ACCESS

Dixline Corporation .................................... D ...... 309 932-2011
  Galva *(G-10788)*
Illinois Casket Company .............................. G ...... 773 483-4500
  Chicago *(G-5155)*
Loyal Casket Co ........................................ F ...... 773 722-4065
  Chicago *(G-5549)*
Tolar Group LLC ....................................... E ...... 847 668-9485
  Oak Park *(G-16689)*

### CAST STONE: Concrete

Casey Stone Co ........................................ G ...... 217 857-3425
  Teutopolis *(G-20849)*
Fischer Stone & Materials LLC ................... G ...... 815 233-3232
  Freeport *(G-10656)*

### CASTERS

Beauticontrol ............................................. G ...... 217 223-0382
  Quincy *(G-17801)*
Caster Warehouse Inc ................................ F ...... 847 836-5712
  Carpentersville *(G-3279)*
Pan Pac International Inc ............................ G ...... 847 222-9077
  Arlington Heights *(G-816)*
Payson Casters Inc .................................... C ...... 847 336-6200
  Gurnee *(G-11482)*

### CASTINGS GRINDING: For The Trade

Absolute Grinding and Mfg ......................... F ...... 815 964-1999
  Rockford *(G-18250)*
Action Carbide Grinding Co ........................ G ...... 847 891-9026
  Schaumburg *(G-19422)*
Asteroid Grinding & Mfg Inc ....................... G ...... 847 298-8109
  Des Plaines *(G-8153)*
B & R Grinding Co .................................... G ...... 630 595-7789
  Franklin Park *(G-10407)*
Class A Grinding ....................................... G ...... 815 874-2118
  Rockford *(G-18311)*
Conform Industries Inc .............................. F ...... 630 285-0272
  Schaumburg *(G-19479)*
Empire Hard Chrome Inc ............................ C ...... 773 762-3156
  Chicago *(G-4745)*
Express Grinding Inc ................................. G ...... 847 434-5827
  Elk Grove Village *(G-9472)*
Form Walern Grinding Inc .......................... G ...... 815 874-7000
  Rockford *(G-18391)*
Glenview Grind ......................................... G ...... 847 729-0111
  Glenview *(G-11131)*
Highland Metal Inc .................................... E ...... 708 544-6641
  Hillside *(G-11919)*
Innovative Gringing Inc .............................. G ...... 630 766-4567
  Bensenville *(G-1919)*
Jet Grinding & Manufacturing ..................... F ...... 847 956-8646
  Arlington Heights *(G-783)*
Lrm Grinding Co Inc .................................. D ...... 708 458-7878
  Bridgeview *(G-2504)*
Metro East Manufacturing ........................... F ...... 618 233-0182
  Swansea *(G-20778)*
OHare Precision Metals LLC ....................... E ...... 847 640-6050
  Arlington Heights *(G-811)*

Pioneer Grinding & Mfg Co ......................... G ...... 847 678-6565
  Franklin Park *(G-10551)*
Precision Ground ....................................... F ...... 815 578-2613
  Lakemoor *(G-13146)*
Roll Rite Inc ............................................. G ...... 815 645-8600
  Davis Junction *(G-7814)*
S & B Jig Grinding .................................... G ...... 815 654-7907
  Loves Park *(G-13990)*
Sterling Tool & Manufacturing ..................... G ...... 847 304-1800
  Barrington *(G-1305)*
T & K Precision Grinding ............................ G ...... 708 450-0565
  Melrose Park *(G-14699)*

### CASTINGS: Aerospace, Aluminum

Komet America Holding Inc ........................ G ...... 847 923-8400
  Schaumburg *(G-19602)*
Martin Tool Works Inc ................................ F ...... 847 923-8400
  Schaumburg *(G-19631)*

### CASTINGS: Aluminum

Alcast Company ........................................ D ...... 309 691-5513
  Peoria *(G-17306)*
Alcast Company ........................................ D ...... 309 691-5513
  Peoria *(G-17307)*
Atherton Foundry Products Inc ................... G ...... 708 849-4615
  Riverdale *(G-18015)*
Chester Brass and Aluminum ..................... F ...... 618 826-2391
  Chester *(G-3652)*
Country Cast Products ............................... F ...... 815 777-1070
  Galena *(G-10718)*
Kellermann Manufacturing Inc ..................... G ...... 847 526-7266
  Wauconda *(G-21476)*
Louis Meskan Brass Foundry Inc ................. C ...... 773 237-7662
  Chicago *(G-5547)*
Master Foundry Inc ................................... F ...... 217 223-7396
  Quincy *(G-17856)*
Olson Aluminum Castings Ltd .................... E ...... 815 229-3292
  Rockford *(G-18526)*
Precision Entps Fndry Mch Inc ................... E ...... 815 498-2317
  Somonauk *(G-20129)*
Rockford Foundries Inc .............................. F ...... 815 965-7243
  Rockford *(G-18574)*
Tazewell Machine Works Inc ....................... C ...... 309 347-3181
  Pekin *(G-17291)*
Universal Electric Foundry Inc .................... E ...... 312 421-7233
  Chicago *(G-6831)*
Wagner Brass Foundry Inc ......................... G ...... 773 276-7907
  Chicago *(G-6932)*

### CASTINGS: Brass, NEC, Exc Die

Atherton Foundry Products Inc ................... C ...... 708 849-4615
  Riverdale *(G-18015)*
C B & A Inc .............................................. F ...... 815 561-0255
  Rochelle *(G-18080)*
Louis Meskan Brass Foundry Inc ................. C ...... 773 237-7662
  Chicago *(G-5547)*
Rockford Foundries Inc .............................. F ...... 815 965-7243
  Rockford *(G-18574)*
Tilton Pattern Works Inc ............................. F ...... 217 442-1502
  Danville *(G-7776)*

### CASTINGS: Bronze, NEC, Exc Die

Art Casting of IL Inc .................................. G ...... 815 732-7777
  Oregon *(G-16818)*
Chester Brass and Aluminum ..................... F ...... 618 826-2391
  Chester *(G-3652)*

### CASTINGS: Commercial Investment, Ferrous

Fisher & Ludlow Inc ................................... G ...... 217 324-6106
  Litchfield *(G-13684)*

### CASTINGS: Die, Aluminum

Able Die Casting Corporation ..................... D ...... 847 678-1991
  Schiller Park *(G-19797)*
Acme Alliance LLC .................................... C ...... 847 272-9520
  Northbrook *(G-16196)*
Acme Die Casting LLC ............................... G ...... 847 272-9520
  Northbrook *(G-16197)*
ADC Diecasting LLC .................................. C ...... 847 541-3030
  Elk Grove Village *(G-9271)*
ADC Diecasting LLC .................................. G ...... 847 541-3030
  Elk Grove Village *(G-9272)*
Aluminum Castings Corporation .................. E ...... 309 343-8910
  Galesburg *(G-10737)*
American Electronic Pdts Inc ...................... F ...... 630 889-9977
  Oak Brook *(G-16488)*

Employee Codes: A=Over 500 employees, B=251-500
C=101-250, D=51-100, E=20-50, F=10-19, G=3-9

## CASTINGS: Die, Aluminum

**Ames Metal Products Company** ..........F ....... 773 523-3230
  Wheeling *(G-22005)*
**Anderson Casting Company Inc** ..........G ....... 312 733-1185
  Chicago *(G-3901)*
**Arrow Aluminum Castings Inc** ..........G ....... 815 338-4480
  Woodstock *(G-22542)*
**Belden Energy Solutions Inc** ..........G ....... 800 235-3361
  Elmhurst *(G-9838)*
**Burgess-Norton Mfg Co Inc** ..........E ....... 630 232-4100
  Geneva *(G-10814)*
**C B & A Inc** ..........F ....... 815 561-0255
  Rochelle *(G-18080)*
**Carroll Tool & Manufacturing** ..........G ....... 630 766-3363
  Bensenville *(G-1852)*
**Cast Aluminum Solutions LLC** ..........D ....... 630 482-5325
  Batavia *(G-1426)*
**Chicago White Metal Cast Inc** ..........C ....... 630 595-4424
  Bensenville *(G-1858)*
**Continental Automation Inc** ..........E ....... 630 584-5100
  Saint Charles *(G-19162)*
**Crown Premiums Inc** ..........F ....... 815 469-8789
  Frankfort *(G-10311)*
**Curto-Ligonier Foundries Co** ..........E ....... 708 345-2250
  Melrose Park *(G-14613)*
**Dart Castings Inc** ..........E ....... 708 388-4914
  Alsip *(G-455)*
**Dixline Corporation** ..........F ....... 309 932-2011
  Galva *(G-10787)*
**Dixline Corporation** ..........D ....... 309 932-2011
  Galva *(G-10788)*
**Duro Cast Inc** ..........G ....... 815 498-2317
  Somonauk *(G-20125)*
**Dynacast Inc** ..........C ....... 847 608-2200
  Elgin *(G-9015)*
**Federal Equipment & Svcs Inc** ..........F ....... 847 731-9002
  Zion *(G-22685)*
**G & M Die Casting Company Inc** ..........D ....... 630 595-2340
  Wood Dale *(G-22374)*
**G & W Electric Company** ..........E ....... 708 389-8307
  Blue Island *(G-2251)*
**Lovejoy Industries Inc** ..........G ....... 859 873-6828
  Northbrook *(G-16299)*
**Mahoney Foundries Inc** ..........E ....... 309 784-2311
  Vermont *(G-21138)*
**Master-Cast Inc** ..........E ....... 630 879-3866
  Carol Stream *(G-3191)*
**Mattoon Precision Mfg** ..........C ....... 217 235-6000
  Mattoon *(G-14399)*
**Monnex International Inc** ..........E ....... 847 850-5263
  Buffalo Grove *(G-2738)*
**OFallon Pressure Cast Co** ..........G ....... 618 632-8694
  O Fallon *(G-16472)*
**Precision Entps Fndry Mch Inc** ..........G ....... 815 797-1000
  Somonauk *(G-20128)*
**Precision Entps Fndry Mch Inc** ..........E ....... 815 498-2317
  Somonauk *(G-20129)*
**Prismier LLC** ..........E ....... 630 592-4515
  Woodridge *(G-22511)*
**RCM Industries Inc** ..........C ....... 847 455-1950
  Franklin Park *(G-10571)*
**RCM Industries Inc** ..........C ....... 847 455-1950
  Wheeling *(G-22133)*
**Rockbridge Casting Inc** ..........G ....... 618 753-3188
  Rockbridge *(G-18212)*
**Soldy Manufacturing Inc** ..........D ....... 847 671-3396
  Schiller Park *(G-19875)*
**Spartan Light Metal Pdts Inc** ..........E ....... 618 443-4346
  Sparta *(G-20321)*
**Spartan Light Metal Pdts Inc** ..........A ....... 618 443-4346
  Sparta *(G-20322)*
**Tek-Cast Inc** ..........D ....... 630 422-1458
  Elgin *(G-9205)*
**Tompkins Aluminum Foundry Inc** ..........G ....... 815 438-5578
  Rock Falls *(G-18154)*

## CASTINGS: Die, Copper & Copper Alloy

**Amcast Inc** ..........F ....... 630 766-7450
  Bensenville *(G-1831)*
**Polar Container Corp Inc** ..........G ....... 847 299-5030
  Rosemont *(G-19024)*

## CASTINGS: Die, Lead & Zinc

**Gary W Berger** ..........G ....... 708 588-0200
  Countryside *(G-7427)*

## CASTINGS: Die, Magnesium & Magnesium-Base Alloy

**Chicago White Metal Cast Inc** ..........C ....... 630 595-4424
  Bensenville *(G-1858)*

**Curto-Ligonier Foundries Co** ..........E ....... 708 345-2250
  Melrose Park *(G-14613)*
**Spartan Light Metal Pdts Inc** ..........E ....... 618 443-4346
  Sparta *(G-20321)*
**Spartan Light Metal Pdts Inc** ..........A ....... 618 443-4346
  Sparta *(G-20322)*

## CASTINGS: Die, Nonferrous

**American Cast Products Inc** ..........F ....... 708 895-5152
  Lansing *(G-13156)*
**Continental Automation Inc** ..........E ....... 630 584-5100
  Saint Charles *(G-19162)*
**Edge Mold Corporation** ..........G ....... 630 616-8108
  Bensenville *(G-1889)*
**GM Casting House Inc** ..........F ....... 312 782-7160
  Chicago *(G-4963)*
**Rockbridge Casting Inc** ..........G ....... 618 753-3188
  Rockbridge *(G-18212)*

## CASTINGS: Die, Titanium

**TI Squared Technologies Inc** ..........F ....... 541 367-2929
  Schaumburg *(G-19763)*

## CASTINGS: Die, Zinc

**Accucast Inc** ..........G ....... 815 394-1875
  Rockford *(G-18253)*
**Acme Die Casting LLC** ..........G ....... 847 272-9520
  Northbrook *(G-16197)*
**Allied Die Casting Corporation** ..........E ....... 815 385-9330
  McHenry *(G-14479)*
**Cast Products Inc** ..........C ....... 708 457-1500
  Norridge *(G-16098)*
**Chicago Die Casting Mfg Co** ..........G ....... 847 671-5010
  Franklin Park *(G-10428)*
**Condor Tool & Manufacturing** ..........F ....... 630 628-8200
  Addison *(G-81)*
**Craft Die Casting Corporation** ..........G ....... 773 237-9710
  Chicago *(G-4488)*
**Dart Castings Inc** ..........E ....... 708 388-4914
  Alsip *(G-455)*
**Dynacast Inc** ..........C ....... 847 608-2200
  Elgin *(G-9015)*
**Hub Manufacturing Company Inc** ..........E ....... 773 252-1373
  Chicago *(G-5127)*
**Lovejoy Industries Inc** ..........G ....... 859 873-6828
  Northbrook *(G-16299)*
**Micro Industries Inc** ..........E ....... 815 625-8000
  Rock Falls *(G-18143)*
**Quality Die Casting Co** ..........F ....... 847 214-8840
  Elgin *(G-9156)*
**Quality Metal Finishing Co** ..........C ....... 815 234-2711
  Byron *(G-2918)*
**Serv-All Die & Tool Company** ..........E ....... 815 459-2900
  Crystal Lake *(G-7647)*
**Soldy Manufacturing Inc** ..........D ....... 847 671-3396
  Schiller Park *(G-19875)*
**Taurus Die Casting LLC** ..........F ....... 815 316-6160
  Rockford *(G-18642)*
**Universal Die Cast Corporation** ..........G ....... 815 633-1702
  Machesney Park *(G-14115)*
**Vogel/Hill Corporation** ..........E ....... 773 235-6916
  Chicago *(G-6912)*

## CASTINGS: Ductile

**Galesburg Castings Inc** ..........D ....... 309 343-6178
  Galesburg *(G-10749)*
**Gunite EMI Corporation** ..........B ....... 815 964-7124
  Rockford *(G-18409)*
**Russell Enterprises Inc** ..........E ....... 847 692-6050
  Park Ridge *(G-17221)*
**Standard Car Truck Company** ..........E ....... 847 692-6050
  Rosemont *(G-19033)*
**Waupaca Foundry Inc** ..........C ....... 217 347-0600
  Effingham *(G-8862)*

## CASTINGS: Gray Iron

**American Electronic Pdts Inc** ..........F ....... 630 889-9977
  Oak Brook *(G-16488)*
**Charter Dura-Bar Inc** ..........E ....... 815 338-3900
  Woodstock *(G-22551)*
**Charter Dura-Bar Inc** ..........D ....... 847 854-1044
  Algonquin *(G-383)*
**Decatur Foundry Inc** ..........D ....... 217 429-5261
  Decatur *(G-7871)*
**E Rowe Foundry & Machine Co** ..........D ....... 217 382-4135
  Martinsville *(G-14334)*
**Illini Foundry Co Inc** ..........G ....... 309 697-3142
  Peoria *(G-17385)*
**Kettler Casting Co Inc** ..........E ....... 618 234-5303
  Belleville *(G-1642)*
**Meta TEC of Illinois Inc** ..........D ....... 309 246-2960
  Lacon *(G-12790)*
**State Line Foundries Inc** ..........D ....... 815 389-3921
  Roscoe *(G-18922)*
**Winnebago Foundry Inc** ..........G ....... 815 389-3533
  South Beloit *(G-20176)*

## CASTINGS: Lead

**Knock On Metal Inc** ..........G ....... 312 372-4569
  Chicago *(G-5392)*

## CASTINGS: Machinery, Aluminum

**Custom Fabrications Inc** ..........G ....... 847 531-5912
  Elgin *(G-9007)*
**Sonoco Prtective Solutions Inc** ..........E ....... 815 787-5244
  Dekalb *(G-8119)*

## CASTINGS: Machinery, Copper Or Copper-Base Alloy

**Amsted Rail Company Inc** ..........A ....... 618 452-2111
  Granite City *(G-11264)*
**General Products Intl Ltd** ..........G ....... 847 458-6357
  Lake In The Hills *(G-12994)*

## CASTINGS: Machinery, Nonferrous, Exc Die or Aluminum Copper

**Clark Tashaunda** ..........G ....... 708 247-8274
  Calumet Park *(G-2958)*

## CASTINGS: Precision

**Caterpillar Inc** ..........C ....... 706 779-4620
  Mapleton *(G-14206)*
**Impro Industries Usa Inc** ..........G ....... 630 759-0280
  Bolingbrook *(G-2320)*
**Tempco Electric Heater Corp** ..........B ....... 630 350-2252
  Wood Dale *(G-22429)*

## CASTINGS: Rubber

**Access Casters** ..........G ....... 773 881-4186
  Chicago *(G-3714)*

## CASTINGS: Steel

**Alloys Tech Inc** ..........G ....... 708 248-5041
  S Chicago Hts *(G-19099)*
**Cast Rite Steel Casting Corp** ..........F ....... 312 738-2900
  Chicago *(G-4251)*
**Devco Casting** ..........G ....... 312 456-0076
  Chicago *(G-4587)*
**Kaltband North America Inc** ..........F ....... 773 248-6684
  Chicago *(G-5355)*
**Universal Electric Foundry Inc** ..........E ....... 312 421-7233
  Chicago *(G-6831)*

## CASTINGS: Zinc

**Able Die Casting Corporation** ..........D ....... 847 678-1991
  Schiller Park *(G-19797)*

## CAT BOX FILLER

**Jaffee Investment Partnr LP** ..........C ....... 312 321-1515
  Chicago *(G-5270)*
**Oil-Dri Corporation America** ..........B ....... 312 321-1516
  Chicago *(G-5976)*

## CATALOG & MAIL-ORDER HOUSES

**Anatomical Worldwide LLC** ..........G ....... 312 224-4772
  Evanston *(G-10010)*
**Aquadine Inc** ..........G ....... 800 497-3463
  Harvard *(G-11621)*
**McCormicks Enterprises Inc** ..........E ....... 847 398-8680
  Arlington Heights *(G-800)*
**Narda Inc** ..........F ....... 312 648-2300
  Chicago *(G-5853)*
**Need To Know Inc** ..........G ....... 309 691-3877
  Peoria *(G-17415)*
**Northwoods Wreaths Company** ..........E ....... 847 615-9491
  Lake Forest *(G-12931)*
**Your Supply Depot Limited** ..........G ....... 815 568-4115
  Marengo *(G-14245)*

# PRODUCT SECTION

CHARCOAL: Activated

## CATALOG SALES

Orvis Company Inc ..................................F ...... 312 440-0662
  Chicago  *(G-6019)*

## CATALYSTS: Chemical

Arcturus Performance Pdts LLC ..........G ...... 630 204-0211
  Saint Charles  *(G-19137)*
Catalytic Products Intl Inc .....................E ...... 847 438-0334
  Lake Zurich  *(G-13050)*
Equa Star Chemical Corp ......................G ...... 815 942-7011
  Morris  *(G-15107)*
Gmm Holdings LLC ................................F ...... 312 255-9830
  Chicago  *(G-4966)*
Merichem Chem Rfinery Svcs LLC ......F ...... 847 285-3850
  Schaumburg  *(G-19643)*
U Op .......................................................G ...... 847 391-2000
  Des Plaines  *(G-8289)*
Universial Cat LLC .................................E ...... 708 753-8070
  S Chicago Hts  *(G-19114)*
UOP LLC ................................................C ...... 708 442-3681
  Chicago  *(G-6840)*
UOP LLC ................................................C ...... 847 391-2540
  Des Plaines  *(G-8294)*
W R Grace & Co ....................................C ...... 708 458-0340
  Chicago  *(G-6921)*
W R Grace & Co ....................................C ...... 773 838-3200
  Chicago  *(G-6920)*
Xena International Inc ............................E ...... 815 946-2626
  Polo  *(G-17691)*

## CATAPULTS

Catapult Marketing .................................D ...... 312 216-4460
  Chicago  *(G-4257)*

## CATCH BASIN COVERS: Concrete

Rockford Cement Products Co .............F ...... 815 965-0537
  Rockford  *(G-18571)*

## CATERERS

Biagios Gourmet Foods Inc ...................E ...... 708 867-4641
  Chicago  *(G-4103)*
Creative Cakes LLC ..............................E ...... 708 614-9755
  Tinley Park  *(G-20904)*
Danziger Kosher Catering Inc ...............E ...... 847 982-1818
  Lincolnwood  *(G-13506)*
Eickmans Processing Co Inc ................E ...... 815 247-8451
  Seward  *(G-19896)*
Fema L & L Food Services Inc .............G ...... 217 835-2018
  Benld  *(G-1805)*
Gourmet Gorilla Inc ...............................F ...... 877 219-3663
  Chicago  *(G-4981)*
La Bella Chrstnas Kitchens Inc ............G ...... 815 801-1600
  German Valley  *(G-10891)*
Rt Wholesale .........................................D ...... 847 678-3663
  Schiller Park  *(G-19869)*
William Badal .........................................G ...... 815 264-7752
  Waterman  *(G-21412)*

## CAULKING COMPOUNDS

Roanoke Companies Group Inc ...........G ...... 630 499-5870
  Aurora  *(G-1074)*
Roanoke Companies Group Inc ...........D ...... 630 375-0324
  Aurora  *(G-1075)*
Sarco Putty Company ............................G ...... 773 735-5577
  Chicago  *(G-6444)*

## CELLULOID PRDTS

Viskase Companies Inc .........................D ...... 630 874-0700
  Lombard  *(G-13879)*
Viskase Corporation ..............................D ...... 630 874-0700
  Lombard  *(G-13880)*

## CELLULOSE DERIVATIVE MATERIALS

Scholle Ipn Corporation .........................F ...... 708 562-7290
  Northlake  *(G-16450)*
Vacumet Corp .........................................F ...... 708 562-7290
  Northlake  *(G-16458)*

## CEMENT & CONCRETE RELATED PRDTS & EQPT: Bituminous

Wehrli Equipment Co Inc ......................F ...... 630 717-4150
  Naperville  *(G-15783)*
Wille Bros Co ........................................D ...... 708 535-4101
  Monee  *(G-15008)*

## CEMENT ROCK: Crushed & Broken

Charleston Stone Company ..................E ...... 217 345-6292
  Ashmore  *(G-928)*
Elmhurst-Chicago Stone Company .......E ...... 630 983-6410
  Bolingbrook  *(G-2305)*
St Marys Cement ...................................G ...... 773 995-5100
  Chicago  *(G-6567)*
Valley Quarry .........................................G ...... 309 462-3003
  Saint Augustine  *(G-19128)*

## CEMENT: Clay Refractory

Cimentos N Votorantim Amer Inc .........E ...... 708 458-0400
  Bridgeview  *(G-2477)*

## CEMENT: Hydraulic

Bonsal American Inc ............................D ...... 847 678-6220
  Franklin Park  *(G-10415)*
Buzzi Unicem USA Inc ..........................G ...... 815 768-3660
  Joliet  *(G-12468)*
Coal City Redi-Mix Co Inc ....................F ...... 815 634-4455
  Coal City  *(G-7292)*
Essroc Cement Corp .............................G ...... 708 388-0797
  Riverdale  *(G-18019)*
GBS Liquidating Corp ...........................G ...... 309 342-4155
  Galesburg  *(G-10753)*
Holcim (us) Inc ......................................E ...... 773 731-1320
  Chicago  *(G-5098)*
Lafarge North America Inc ...................G ...... 630 892-1616
  North Aurora  *(G-16137)*
Lafarge North America Inc ...................C ...... 703 480-3600
  Chicago  *(G-5435)*
Lafarge North America Inc ...................G ...... 847 742-6060
  South Elgin  *(G-20213)*
Lafarge North America Inc ...................E ...... 815 741-2090
  Rockdale  *(G-18224)*
Lafarge North America Inc ...................G ...... 618 289-3404
  Cave In Rock  *(G-3403)*
Lafarge North America Inc ...................E ...... 773 372-1000
  Golconda  *(G-11240)*
Lafarge North America Inc ...................C ...... 618 543-7541
  Grand Chain  *(G-11256)*
Lafarge North America Inc ...................F ...... 847 599-0391
  Waukegan  *(G-21579)*
Lafarge North America Inc ...................E ...... 773 372-1000
  Chicago  *(G-5436)*
Lafarge North America Inc ...................E ...... 773 646-5228
  Chicago  *(G-5437)*
Southfield Corporation ...........................C ...... 815 284-3357
  Dixon  *(G-8352)*
Sport Redi-Mix LLC ..............................E ...... 217 355-4222
  Champaign  *(G-3545)*
Sport Redi-Mix LLC ..............................E ...... 217 892-4222
  Rantoul  *(G-17937)*
Sport Redi-Mix LLC ..............................G ...... 217 582-2555
  Ogden  *(G-16745)*
St Marys Cement Inc (us) .....................E ...... 313 842-4600
  Dixon  *(G-8354)*

## CEMENT: Linoleum & Tile

JB Enterprises II Inc .............................E ...... 630 372-8300
  Streamwood  *(G-20660)*

## CEMENT: Masonry

Illinois Cement Company LLC ..............C ...... 815 224-2112
  La Salle  *(G-12776)*
Kona Blackbird Inc ...............................F ...... 815 792-8750
  Serena  *(G-19892)*
Lafarge Building Materials Inc ..............D ...... 678 746-2000
  Chicago  *(G-5434)*
Skyway Cement Company LLC ............F ...... 800 643-1808
  Chicago  *(G-6525)*

## CEMENT: Portland

Cemex Cement Inc ...............................G ...... 773 995-5100
  Chicago  *(G-4268)*
Holcim (us) Inc ......................................G ...... 773 721-8352
  Chicago  *(G-5097)*
Lone Star Industries Inc .......................G ...... 815 883-3173
  Oglesby  *(G-16751)*
Red-E-Mix Transportation LLC .............E ...... 618 654-2166
  Highland  *(G-11809)*

## CEMETERIES

Rex Vault Co .........................................F ...... 618 783-2416
  Newton  *(G-15948)*

## CEMETERIES: Real Estate Operation

Oakwood Memorial Park Inc .................G ...... 815 433-0313
  Ottawa  *(G-16973)*

## CEMETERY & FUNERAL DIRECTOR'S EQPT & SPLYS WHOLESALERS

Angels Heavenly Funeral Home ...........G ...... 773 239-8700
  Chicago  *(G-3907)*
Frigid Fluid Company ............................E ...... 708 836-1215
  Melrose Park  *(G-14645)*
Tolar Group LLC ...................................E ...... 847 668-9485
  Oak Park  *(G-16689)*

## CEMETERY MEMORIAL DEALERS

All Saints Monument Co Inc .................G ...... 847 824-1248
  Des Plaines  *(G-8145)*
American Monument Co ........................G ...... 618 993-8968
  Marion  *(G-14253)*
Arnold Monument Co Inc ......................G ...... 217 546-2102
  Springfield  *(G-20388)*
Czarnik Memorials Inc ..........................G ...... 708 458-4443
  Justice  *(G-12596)*
Meier Granite Company ........................G ...... 847 678-7300
  Franklin Park  *(G-10527)*
Pontiac Granite Company Inc ...............F ...... 815 842-1384
  Pontiac  *(G-17707)*
Stonecrafters Inc ...................................E ...... 815 363-8730
  Lakemoor  *(G-13148)*

## CERAMIC FIBER

Better Earth LLC ...................................G ...... 844 243-6333
  Chicago  *(G-4095)*
Nanophase Technologies Corp .............F ...... 630 771-6747
  Burr Ridge  *(G-2870)*
Nanophase Technologies Corp .............E ...... 630 771-6708
  Romeoville  *(G-18852)*
Pillar Enterprises Inc .............................G ...... 630 966-2566
  North Aurora  *(G-16142)*
Thermal Ceramics Inc ...........................E ...... 217 627-2101
  Girard  *(G-10950)*
Thermionics Corp ..................................F ...... 800 800-5728
  Springfield  *(G-20544)*

## CERAMIC FLOOR & WALL TILE WHOLESALERS

American Bullnose Co Midw .................G ...... 630 238-1300
  Wood Dale  *(G-22340)*
MK Tile Ink .............................................G ...... 773 964-8905
  Chicago  *(G-5778)*

## CHAIN: Welded, Made From Purchased Wire

Durabilt Dyvex Inc .................................F ...... 708 397-4673
  Broadview  *(G-2573)*

## CHAINS: Forged

Timken Drives LLC ...............................C ...... 815 589-2211
  Fulton  *(G-10706)*
Timken Drives LLC ...............................G ...... 312 274-9710
  Chicago  *(G-6728)*

## CHAMBERS: Fumigating, Metal Plate

Pureline Treatment Systems LLC .........E ...... 847 963-8465
  Bensenville  *(G-1970)*

## CHAMBERS: Space Simulation, Metal Plate

3d Flight Simulation Co .........................G ...... 708 560-0701
  Oak Forest  *(G-16571)*

## CHANGE MAKING MACHINES

Singer Data Products Inc .....................G ...... 630 860-6500
  Bensenville  *(G-1991)*

## CHARCOAL: Activated

Calgon Carbon Corporation ..................G ...... 815 741-5452
  Rockdale  *(G-18215)*
McClendon Holdings LLC .....................G ...... 773 251-2314
  Chicago  *(G-5664)*
Plaze Inc ................................................C ...... 630 628-4240
  Downers Grove  *(G-8503)*

---

Employee Codes: A=Over 500 employees, B=251-500
C=101-250, D=51-100, E=20-50, F=10-19, G=3-9

# CHASSIS: Automobile Trailer

## CHASSIS: Automobile Trailer

T & E Enterprises Herscher Inc .......... F ....... 815 426-2761
 Herscher *(G-11763)*

## CHASSIS: Motor Vehicle

Federal Signal Corporation .......... E ....... 708 534-4756
 University Park *(G-21048)*
Federal Signal Corporation .......... E ....... 708 534-3400
 University Park *(G-21050)*
Folk Race Cars .......... G ....... 815 629-2418
 Durand *(G-8585)*
Prince Race Car Engineering .......... G ....... 815 625-8116
 Sterling *(G-20606)*
Taylor Off Road Racing .......... G ....... 815 544-4500
 Belvidere *(G-1788)*
Workhorse Custom Chassis LLC .......... G ....... 765 964-4000
 Highland Park *(G-11882)*

## CHEESE WHOLESALERS

A New Dairy Company .......... E ....... 312 421-1234
 Chicago *(G-3690)*
Cheese Merchants America LLC .......... B ....... 630 221-0580
 Bartlett *(G-1338)*
Kraft Food Ingredients Corp .......... D ....... 901 381-6500
 Glenview *(G-11159)*
Nuestro Queso LLC .......... E ....... 224 366-4320
 Rosemont *(G-19019)*
Randolph Packing Co .......... D ....... 630 830-3100
 Streamwood *(G-20670)*
Wiscon Corp .......... E ....... 708 450-0074
 Melrose Park *(G-14710)*

## CHEMICAL ELEMENTS

Elemental Art Jewelry .......... G ....... 773 844-4812
 Chicago *(G-4725)*
Elements Group .......... G ....... 312 664-2252
 Chicago *(G-4726)*
Essential Elmnts Therapeutic M .......... G ....... 815 623-6810
 Roscoe *(G-18896)*
Pure Element .......... G ....... 309 269-7823
 Moline *(G-14963)*

## CHEMICAL PROCESSING MACHINERY & EQPT

D R Sperry & Co .......... D ....... 630 892-4361
 Aurora *(G-1137)*
G K Enterprises Inc .......... G ....... 708 587-2150
 Monee *(G-14996)*
K R Komarek Inc .......... E ....... 847 956-0060
 Wood Dale *(G-22384)*
Nalco Company LLC .......... A ....... 630 305-1000
 Naperville *(G-15703)*
Nalco Company LLC .......... G ....... 630 305-2451
 Naperville *(G-15705)*
Nalco Holdings LLC .......... A ....... 630 305-1000
 Naperville *(G-15707)*
Norchem Inc .......... F ....... 708 478-4777
 Mokena *(G-14887)*
Prater Industries Inc .......... D ....... 630 679-3200
 Bolingbrook *(G-2359)*
Schold Machine Corporation .......... E ....... 708 458-3788
 Chicago *(G-6454)*
Spf Supplies Inc .......... G ....... 847 454-9081
 Elk Grove Village *(G-9746)*
WEI TO Associates Inc .......... G ....... 708 747-6660
 Matteson *(G-14381)*

## CHEMICAL SPLYS FOR FOUNDRIES

Chem Trade Global .......... G ....... 847 675-2682
 Skokie *(G-19978)*
Harcros Chemicals Inc .......... G ....... 815 740-9971
 Thornton *(G-20872)*
Mid America Intl Inc .......... G ....... 847 635-8303
 Glenview *(G-11169)*
Swenson Technology Inc .......... F ....... 708 587-2300
 Monee *(G-15003)*
T D J Group Inc .......... G ....... 847 639-1113
 Cary *(G-3374)*

## CHEMICALS & ALLIED PRDTS WHOLESALERS, NEC

1717 Chemall Corporation .......... G ....... 224 864-4180
 Mundelein *(G-15460)*
A J Funk & Co .......... G ....... 847 741-6760
 Elgin *(G-8929)*
Air Products and Chemicals Inc .......... D ....... 618 451-0577
 Granite City *(G-11261)*
Airgas USA LLC .......... E ....... 630 231-9260
 West Chicago *(G-21653)*
Americo Chemical Products Inc .......... E ....... 630 588-0830
 Carol Stream *(G-3103)*
AmeriGas .......... D ....... 708 544-1131
 Hillside *(G-11909)*
Cater Chemical Co .......... G ....... 630 980-2300
 Roselle *(G-18930)*
Cedar Concepts Corporation .......... E ....... 773 890-5790
 Chicago *(G-4265)*
Chemix Corp .......... F ....... 708 754-2150
 Glenwood *(G-11215)*
Colorex Chemical Co Inc .......... G ....... 630 238-3124
 Bensenville *(G-1862)*
Delta Products Group Inc .......... F ....... 630 357-5544
 Aurora *(G-1139)*
Dumore Supplies Inc .......... G ....... 312 949-6260
 Chicago *(G-4649)*
Esma Inc .......... G ....... 708 331-0456
 South Holland *(G-20267)*
Gano Welding Supplies Inc .......... F ....... 217 345-3777
 Charleston *(G-3597)*
GE Healthcare Holdings Inc .......... A ....... 847 398-8400
 Arlington Heights *(G-759)*
GL Downs Inc .......... G ....... 618 993-9777
 Marion *(G-14262)*
Henkel Corporation .......... G ....... 847 468-9200
 Elgin *(G-9064)*
Hurst Chemical Company .......... G ....... 815 964-0451
 Rockford *(G-18424)*
Ivanhoe Industries Inc .......... E ....... 847 872-3311
 Zion *(G-22688)*
J & W Counter Tops Inc .......... E ....... 217 544-0876
 Springfield *(G-20460)*
J B Watts Company Inc .......... G ....... 773 643-1855
 Chicago *(G-5256)*
Koch Industries Inc .......... G ....... 312 867-1295
 Chicago *(G-5394)*
Lanxess Corporation .......... E ....... 630 789-8440
 Willowbrook *(G-22219)*
Lasalle Chemical & Supply Co .......... F ....... 847 470-1234
 Morton Grove *(G-15211)*
Lee Quigley Company .......... G ....... 708 563-1600
 Chicago *(G-5484)*
Linde LLC .......... E ....... 630 690-3010
 Carol Stream *(G-3185)*
Liquid Resin International .......... F ....... 618 392-3590
 Olney *(G-16777)*
Litho Research Incorporated .......... G ....... 630 860-7070
 Itasca *(G-12307)*
Major Prime Plastics Inc .......... G ....... 630 953-4111
 Addison *(G-189)*
McClendon Holdings LLC .......... G ....... 773 251-2314
 Chicago *(G-5664)*
North Shore Consultants Inc .......... E ....... 847 290-1599
 Elk Grove Village *(G-9655)*
R & D Clark Ltd .......... F ....... 847 749-2061
 Arlington Heights *(G-825)*
RITA Corporation .......... E ....... 815 337-2500
 Crystal Lake *(G-7642)*
Robert B Scott Ocularists Ltd .......... G ....... 312 782-3558
 Chicago *(G-6367)*
Rock Valley Oil & Chemical Co .......... E ....... 815 654-2400
 Loves Park *(G-13983)*
T9 Group LLC .......... G ....... 847 912-8862
 Hawthorn Woods *(G-11705)*
Tomen America Inc .......... D ....... 847 439-8500
 Elk Grove Village *(G-9782)*
Vanguard Chemical Corporation .......... F ....... 312 751-0717
 Chicago *(G-6871)*
Varn International Inc .......... E ....... 630 406-6501
 Batavia *(G-1516)*
Xena International Inc .......... E ....... 815 946-2626
 Polo *(G-17691)*

## CHEMICALS & ALLIED PRDTS, WHOL: Food Additives/Preservatives

Essen Nutrition Corporation .......... E ....... 630 739-6700
 Romeoville *(G-18820)*
Pmp Fermentation Products Inc .......... F ....... 309 637-0400
 Peoria *(G-17430)*

## CHEMICALS & ALLIED PRDTS, WHOL: Gases, Compressed/Liquefied

Lincoln Electric Company .......... F ....... 630 783-3600
 Bolingbrook *(G-2335)*
Praxair Distribution Inc .......... E ....... 314 664-7900
 Cahokia *(G-2924)*

## CHEMICALS & ALLIED PRDTS, WHOLESALE: Aerosols

Diversified CPC Intl Inc .......... E ....... 815 423-5991
 Channahon *(G-3571)*
Plaze Inc .......... C ....... 630 628-4240
 Downers Grove *(G-8503)*

## CHEMICALS & ALLIED PRDTS, WHOLESALE: Alcohols

Wirtz Beverage Illinois LLC .......... C ....... 847 228-9000
 Cicero *(G-7246)*

## CHEMICALS & ALLIED PRDTS, WHOLESALE: Chemical Additives

Navran Advncd Nanoprdcts Dev .......... G ....... 847 331-0809
 Hoffman Estates *(G-12029)*

## CHEMICALS & ALLIED PRDTS, WHOLESALE: Chemicals, Indl

Amtex Chemicals LLC .......... G ....... 630 268-0085
 Lombard *(G-13764)*
Emco Chemical Distributors Inc .......... C ....... 262 427-0400
 North Chicago *(G-16178)*
Fujifilm Hunt Chem USA Inc .......... E ....... 847 259-8800
 Rolling Meadows *(G-18730)*
Global Water Technology Inc .......... E ....... 708 349-9991
 Orland Park *(G-16862)*
Hallstar Company .......... C ....... 312 554-7400
 Chicago *(G-5036)*
Hallstar Services Corp .......... G ....... 312 554-7400
 Chicago *(G-5037)*
Holland Applied Technologies .......... E ....... 630 325-5130
 Burr Ridge *(G-2851)*
Innovative Molecular Diagnosti .......... G ....... 630 845-8246
 Geneva *(G-10838)*
Interra Global Corporation .......... F ....... 847 292-8600
 Park Ridge *(G-17204)*
Producers Chemical Company .......... E ....... 630 466-4584
 Sugar Grove *(G-20731)*
Stutz Company .......... F ....... 773 287-1068
 Chicago *(G-6610)*
Vantage Oleochemicals Inc .......... C ....... 773 376-9000
 Chicago *(G-6873)*
Vantage Specialties Inc .......... F ....... 847 244-3410
 Chicago *(G-6875)*

## CHEMICALS & ALLIED PRDTS, WHOLESALE: Chemicals, Indl & Heavy

Benetech Inc .......... E ....... 630 844-1300
 Aurora *(G-1119)*
Benetech (taiwan) LLC .......... G ....... 630 844-1300
 Aurora *(G-1120)*
Fitz Chem Corporation .......... E ....... 630 467-8383
 Itasca *(G-12264)*
Illini Fs Inc .......... G ....... 217 442-4737
 Potomac *(G-17738)*
Magnum International Inc .......... G ....... 708 889-9999
 Lansing *(G-13175)*
Mineral Masters Corporation .......... F ....... 630 293-7727
 West Chicago *(G-21744)*
Roquette America Inc .......... D ....... 847 360-0886
 Gurnee *(G-11501)*
T D J Group Inc .......... G ....... 847 639-1113
 Cary *(G-3374)*

## CHEMICALS & ALLIED PRDTS, WHOLESALE: Chemicals, Rustproofing

Daubert Industries Inc .......... F ....... 630 203-6800
 Burr Ridge *(G-2834)*
Ecp Incorporated .......... D ....... 630 754-4200
 Woodridge *(G-22474)*

## CHEMICALS & ALLIED PRDTS, WHOLESALE: Detergent/Soap

Dial Corporation .......... C ....... 630 892-4381
 Montgomery *(G-15041)*
Vision Sales & Marketing Inc .......... G ....... 708 496-6016
 Chicago *(G-6904)*

# PRODUCT SECTION

## CHEMICALS: Bleaching Powder, Lime Bleaching Compounds

### CHEMICALS & ALLIED PRDTS, WHOLESALE: Dry Ice

Continental Carbonic Pdts Inc ............... E ...... 309 346-7515
  Pekin *(G-17257)*

### CHEMICALS & ALLIED PRDTS, WHOLESALE: Gelatin

Al Gelato Chicago LLC ......................... G ...... 847 455-5355
  Franklin Park *(G-10388)*

### CHEMICALS & ALLIED PRDTS, WHOLESALE: Indl Gases

Airgas USA LLC ................................... G ...... 618 439-7207
  Benton *(G-2020)*

### CHEMICALS & ALLIED PRDTS, WHOLESALE: Oxygen

Little Egypt Gas A & Wldg Sups ............ G ...... 618 937-2271
  West Frankfort *(G-21813)*

### CHEMICALS & ALLIED PRDTS, WHOLESALE: Plastics Film

Piper Plastics Inc ................................ D ...... 847 367-0110
  Libertyville *(G-13369)*
Protective Products Intl ...................... G ...... 847 526-1180
  Wauconda *(G-21495)*

### CHEMICALS & ALLIED PRDTS, WHOLESALE: Plastics Materials, NEC

Alpha Omega Plastics Company .......... D ...... 847 956-8777
  Elk Grove Village *(G-9289)*
Cope Plastics Inc ................................ G ...... 309 787-4465
  Rock Island *(G-18168)*
Magnum International Inc ................... G ...... 708 889-9999
  Lansing *(G-13175)*
Peterson Brothers Plastics ................... F ...... 773 286-5666
  Chicago *(G-6111)*
Shannon Industrial Corporation ............ F ...... 815 337-2349
  Woodstock *(G-22609)*
Sherman Plastics Corp ........................ E ...... 630 369-6170
  Naperville *(G-15746)*
Streamwood Plastics Ltd .................... G ...... 847 895-9190
  Schaumburg *(G-19741)*

### CHEMICALS & ALLIED PRDTS, WHOLESALE: Plastics Prdts, NEC

Ability Plastics Inc ............................. E ...... 708 458-4480
  Justice *(G-12594)*
AIM Distribution Inc ............................ F ...... 815 986-2770
  Rockford *(G-18258)*
Bucktown Polymers ............................ G ...... 312 436-1460
  Chicago *(G-4181)*
Cdj Technologies Inc .......................... G ...... 321 277-7807
  Wilmette *(G-22249)*
Fisher Container Corp ........................ D ...... 847 541-0000
  Buffalo Grove *(G-2694)*
Fisher Container Holdings LLC ............ G ...... 847 541-0000
  Buffalo Grove *(G-2695)*
Flow-Eze Company ............................. F ...... 815 965-1062
  Rockford *(G-18383)*
Foodhandler Inc .................................. D ...... 866 931-3613
  Elk Grove Village *(G-9484)*
Mate Technologies Inc ........................ F ...... 847 289-1010
  Elgin *(G-9103)*
Sarj Kalidas LLC ................................ D ...... 708 865-9134
  Chicago *(G-6446)*
Seagon Inc ......................................... G ...... 630 541-5460
  Lisle *(G-13655)*
Transcendia Inc .................................. C ...... 847 678-1800
  Franklin Park *(G-10609)*

### CHEMICALS & ALLIED PRDTS, WHOLESALE: Plastics Sheets & Rods

Cope Plastics Inc ................................ D ...... 618 466-0221
  Alton *(G-568)*
D and K Plastics .................................. G ...... 712 723-5372
  Yorkville *(G-22653)*
Edmik Inc ............................................ E ...... 847 263-0460
  Gurnee *(G-11445)*
Engineered Plastic Pdts Corp ............... E ...... 847 952-8400
  Elk Grove Village *(G-9460)*

Plastic Film Corp America Inc ............. F ...... 630 887-0800
  Romeoville *(G-18857)*
Thyssenkrupp Materials NA Inc ........... G ...... 630 563-3365
  Bolingbrook *(G-2378)*

### CHEMICALS & ALLIED PRDTS, WHOLESALE: Polishes, NEC

Jacob Hay Co ..................................... G ...... 847 215-8880
  Wheeling *(G-22080)*

### CHEMICALS & ALLIED PRDTS, WHOLESALE: Polyurethane Prdts

Guardian Energy Tech Inc .................... F ...... 800 516-0949
  Riverwoods *(G-18038)*

### CHEMICALS & ALLIED PRDTS, WHOLESALE: Resins

Bamberger Polymers Inc ..................... F ...... 630 773-8626
  Itasca *(G-12233)*
Resin Exchange Inc ............................ E ...... 630 628-7266
  Addison *(G-276)*
Resins Inc .......................................... G ...... 847 884-0025
  Hoffman Estates *(G-12043)*

### CHEMICALS & ALLIED PRDTS, WHOLESALE: Resins, Plastics

North American Fund III LP ................. G ...... 312 332-4950
  Chicago *(G-5932)*
Polyone Corporation ........................... D ...... 630 972-0505
  Romeoville *(G-18859)*

### CHEMICALS & ALLIED PRDTS, WHOLESALE: Resins, Synthetic

Major-Prime Plastics Inc ..................... E ...... 630 834-9400
  Villa Park *(G-21267)*

### CHEMICALS & ALLIED PRDTS, WHOLESALE: Sealants

Rae Products and Chem Corp .............. G ...... 708 396-1984
  Alsip *(G-517)*

### CHEMICALS & ALLIED PRDTS, WHOLESALE: Silicon Lubricants

Erbeck One Chem & Lab Sup Inc ......... G ...... 312 203-0078
  Manhattan *(G-14169)*

### CHEMICALS & ALLIED PRDTS, WHOLESALE: Spec Clean/Sanitation

Apco Enterprises Inc .......................... G ...... 708 430-7333
  Bridgeview *(G-2466)*
Quality Cleaning Fluids Inc .................. G ...... 847 451-1190
  Franklin Park *(G-10566)*
United Laboratories Inc ....................... D ...... 630 377-0900
  Saint Charles *(G-19289)*

### CHEMICALS & ALLIED PRDTS, WHOLESALE: Syn Resin, Rub/Plastic

Ricon Colors Inc ................................. F ...... 630 562-9000
  West Chicago *(G-21764)*
Rite Systems East Inc ......................... E ...... 630 293-9174
  West Chicago *(G-21765)*

### CHEMICALS & OTHER PRDTS DERIVED FROM COKING

Apex Material Technologies LLC .......... G ...... 815 727-3010
  Joliet *(G-12456)*
Kusmierek Industries Inc ..................... G ...... 708 258-3100
  Peotone *(G-17490)*

### CHEMICALS, AGRICULTURE: Wholesalers

Van Diest Supply Company ................. G ...... 815 232-6053
  Freeport *(G-10697)*

### CHEMICALS: Agricultural

Agriscience Inc .................................. G ...... 212 365-4214
  Peoria *(G-17304)*
Alpha AG Inc ...................................... G ...... 217 546-2724
  Pleasant Plains *(G-17681)*

Chase Products Co ............................. D ...... 708 865-1000
  Broadview *(G-2566)*
Claire-Sprayway Inc ........................... D ...... 630 628-3000
  Downers Grove *(G-8413)*
Clarke Aquatic Services Inc ................ D ...... 630 894-2000
  Saint Charles *(G-19154)*
Crop Production Services Inc .............. G ...... 217 466-5430
  Kansas *(G-12659)*
Dow Agrosciences LLC ....................... D ...... 630 428-8494
  Naperville *(G-15648)*
Dow Agrosciences LLC ....................... G ...... 815 844-3128
  Pontiac *(G-17699)*
Du Pont Delaware Inc ......................... G ...... 630 285-2700
  Itasca *(G-12255)*
E N P Inc ........................................... G ...... 800 255-4906
  Mendota *(G-14720)*
Gard Rogard Inc ................................. D ...... 847 836-7700
  Carpentersville *(G-3284)*
Harbach Nixon & Willson Inc ............... G ...... 217 935-8378
  Clinton *(G-7283)*
Isky North America Inc ....................... G ...... 937 641-1368
  Chicago *(G-5243)*
J Stewart & Co .................................... G ...... 847 419-9595
  Buffalo Grove *(G-2712)*
Maplehurst Farms Inc ........................ F ...... 815 562-8723
  Rochelle *(G-18097)*
Monsanto Company ............................ D ...... 309 829-6640
  Bloomington *(G-2202)*
Monsanto Company ............................ G ...... 815 264-8153
  Waterman *(G-21408)*
Nufarm Americas Inc .......................... D ...... 708 377-1330
  Alsip *(G-501)*
Precision Laboratories LLC ................. E ...... 800 323-6280
  Waukegan *(G-21606)*
Pro-Tek Products Inc .......................... G ...... 630 293-5100
  Wheaton *(G-21973)*
Smithereen Company .......................... D ...... 800 340-1888
  Niles *(G-16034)*
Smithereen Company Del .................... D ...... 847 675-0010
  Niles *(G-16035)*
Valent Biosciences Corporation ........... D ...... 847 968-4700
  Libertyville *(G-13397)*
Van Diest Supply Company ................. G ...... 815 232-6053
  Freeport *(G-10697)*
West Agro Inc .................................... E ...... 847 298-5505
  Des Plaines *(G-8303)*
Westmin Corporation ......................... G ...... 217 224-4570
  Quincy *(G-17904)*

### CHEMICALS: Alcohols

Archer-Daniels-Midland Company ....... C ...... 309 673-7828
  Peoria *(G-17309)*
RJ Distributing Co .............................. E ...... 309 685-2794
  East Peoria *(G-8731)*

### CHEMICALS: Alkali Metals, Lithium, Cesium, Francium/Rubidium

Amnetic LLC ...................................... G ...... 877 877-3678
  Des Plaines *(G-8149)*
Bellman-Melcor Holdings Inc .............. F ...... 708 532-5000
  Tinley Park *(G-20896)*

### CHEMICALS: Aluminum Compounds

Interra Global Corporation .................. F ...... 847 292-8600
  Park Ridge *(G-17204)*

### CHEMICALS: Aluminum Sulfate

C & S Chemicals Inc ........................... G ...... 815 722-6671
  Joliet *(G-12470)*
Chemtrade Chemicals US LLC ............. E ...... 618 274-4363
  East Saint Louis *(G-8746)*

### CHEMICALS: Anhydrous Ammonia

CF Industries Inc ................................ B ...... 847 405-2400
  Deerfield *(G-7994)*
CF Industries Inc ................................ D ...... 309 654-2218
  Albany *(G-352)*

### CHEMICALS: Bleaching Powder, Lime Bleaching Compounds

Vertex Chemical Corporation .............. F ...... 618 286-5207
  Dupo *(G-8583)*

# CHEMICALS: Copper Compounds Or Salts, Inorganic

### CHEMICALS: Copper Compounds Or Salts, Inorganic

American Chemet Corporation ............F ....... 847 948-0800
   Deerfield *(G-7975)*

### CHEMICALS: Fluorine, Elemental

Solvay Chemicals Inc ........................E ....... 618 274-0755
   East Saint Louis *(G-8769)*

### CHEMICALS: Fuel Tank Or Engine Cleaning

Kop-Coat Inc .....................................F ....... 847 272-2278
   Buffalo Grove *(G-2719)*
Techdrive Inc ....................................G ....... 312 567-3910
   Chicago *(G-6684)*

### CHEMICALS: High Purity Grade, Organic

Covachem LLC .................................F ....... 815 714-8421
   Loves Park *(G-13927)*

### CHEMICALS: High Purity, Refined From Technical Grade

Chemtech Services Inc ....................F ....... 815 838-4800
   Lockport *(G-13709)*
Delta Products Group Inc .................F ....... 630 357-5544
   Aurora *(G-1139)*
Incon Industries Inc ..........................G ....... 630 728-4014
   Saint Charles *(G-19196)*
Pharmasyn Inc .................................G ....... 847 752-8405
   Libertyville *(G-13367)*

### CHEMICALS: Hydrogen Peroxide

Hydrox Chemical Company Inc .......D ....... 847 468-9400
   Elgin *(G-9069)*
McShares Inc ....................................E ....... 217 762-2561
   Monticello *(G-15079)*

### CHEMICALS: Inorganic, NEC

AA-Gem Corporation ........................G ....... 773 539-9303
   Chicago *(G-3699)*
Acl Inc ...............................................F ....... 773 285-0295
   Chicago *(G-3730)*
Advanced Diamond Tech Inc ...........E ....... 815 293-0900
   Romeoville *(G-18791)*
Akzo Nobel Inc .................................C ....... 312 544-7000
   Chicago *(G-3793)*
Americo Chemical Products Inc .......E ....... 630 588-0830
   Carol Stream *(G-3103)*
Aquion Partners Ltd Partnr ..............G ....... 847 437-9400
   Elk Grove Village *(G-9311)*
Arch Chemicals Inc ..........................F ....... 630 955-0401
   Naperville *(G-15600)*
Big River Zinc Corporation ...............E ....... 618 274-5000
   Sauget *(G-19382)*
Boyer Corporation ............................G ....... 708 352-2553
   La Grange *(G-12727)*
BP Amoco Chemical Company ........B ....... 630 420-5111
   Naperville *(G-15608)*
Bullen Midwest Inc ...........................E ....... 773 785-2300
   Chicago *(G-4183)*
Cabot Corporation ............................C ....... 217 253-3370
   Tuscola *(G-21017)*
Cabot Microelectronics Corp ............C ....... 630 375-6631
   Aurora *(G-979)*
Campbell Camie Inc .........................E ....... 314 968-3222
   Downers Grove *(G-8403)*
Carus Corporation ............................D ....... 815 223-1500
   Peru *(G-17503)*
Carus Corporation ............................C ....... 815 223-1500
   La Salle *(G-12766)*
Carus Corporation ............................D ....... 815 223-1565
   La Salle *(G-12767)*
Carus Group Inc ...............................D ....... 815 223-1500
   Peru *(G-17504)*
Cater Chemical Co ...........................G ....... 630 980-2300
   Roselle *(G-18930)*
Clorox Products Mfg Co ...................C ....... 708 728-4200
   Chicago *(G-4404)*
Dauber Company Inc .......................E ....... 815 442-3569
   Tonica *(G-20973)*
Dow Chemical Company ..................E ....... 847 439-2240
   Elk Grove Village *(G-9434)*
Dow Chemical Company ..................C ....... 815 653-2411
   Ringwood *(G-17989)*
Dow Chemical Company ..................D ....... 815 933-8900
   Kankakee *(G-12610)*

DSM Desotech Inc ...........................C ....... 847 697-0400
   Elgin *(G-9013)*
Emco Chemical Distributors Inc ......C ....... 262 427-0400
   North Chicago *(G-16178)*
Entrust Services LLC .......................G ....... 630 699-9132
   Naperville *(G-15654)*
Esma Inc ...........................................G ....... 708 331-0456
   South Holland *(G-20267)*
Eureka Chemical Labs Inc ...............G ....... 773 847-9672
   Chicago *(G-4782)*
Finoric LLC .......................................G ....... 773 829-5811
   Naperville *(G-15658)*
Frank Miller & Sons Inc ....................G ....... 708 201-7200
   Mokena *(G-14863)*
Fusion Chemical Corporation ...........G ....... 847 656-5285
   Park Ridge *(G-17197)*
Gcp Applied Technologies ...............C ....... 410 531-4000
   Bannockburn *(G-1259)*
Gycor International Ltd ....................F ....... 630 754-8070
   Woodridge *(G-22492)*
H A Gartenberg & Company ...........F ....... 847 821-7590
   Buffalo Grove *(G-2700)*
Helena Chemical Company .............F ....... 217 382-4241
   Martinsville *(G-14336)*
Helena Chemical Company .............G ....... 217 234-2726
   Mattoon *(G-14391)*
Honeywell International Inc .............B ....... 618 524-2111
   Metropolis *(G-14754)*
Hussain Shaheen ............................G ....... 630 405-8009
   Bolingbrook *(G-2317)*
Incon Processing LLC .....................E ....... 630 305-8556
   Batavia *(G-1456)*
Innophos Inc ....................................F ....... 773 468-2300
   Chicago *(G-5199)*
J B Watts Company Inc ...................F ....... 773 643-1855
   Chicago *(G-5256)*
J Stilling Enterprises Inc ..................F ....... 630 584-5050
   Saint Charles *(G-19201)*
JM Huber Corporation .....................E ....... 217 224-1100
   Quincy *(G-17841)*
Kafko International Ltd ....................F ....... 847 763-0333
   Skokie *(G-20021)*
Klean-Ko Inc ....................................D ....... 630 620-1860
   Lombard *(G-13816)*
Konzen Chemicals Inc ....................F ....... 708 878-7636
   Matteson *(G-14375)*
Lonza Inc ..........................................D ....... 309 697-7200
   Mapleton *(G-14212)*
Maclee Chemical Company Inc .......F ....... 847 480-0953
   Northbrook *(G-16305)*
Magrabar LLC ..................................F ....... 847 965-7550
   Morton Grove *(G-15215)*
Mason Chemical Company .............F ....... 847 290-1621
   Arlington Heights *(G-799)*
Masters Co Inc .................................E ....... 630 238-9292
   Wood Dale *(G-22396)*
Metal Finishing Research Corp .......F ....... 773 373-0800
   Chicago *(G-5699)*
Milliken & Company .........................D ....... 312 666-2015
   Chicago *(G-5764)*
Murdock Company Inc ....................G ....... 847 566-0050
   Mundelein *(G-15535)*
Nanochem Solutions Inc .................G ....... 708 563-9200
   Naperville *(G-15708)*
Nanochem Solutions Inc .................G ....... 815 224-8480
   Peru *(G-17521)*
National Interchem LLC ..................G ....... 708 597-7777
   Blue Island *(G-2264)*
Nikkin Flux Corp ...............................F ....... 618 656-2125
   Edwardsville *(G-8810)*
NNt Enterprises Incorporated ..........E ....... 630 875-9600
   Itasca *(G-12332)*
Old World Global LLC .....................G ....... 800 323-5440
   Northbrook *(G-16324)*
Old World Inds Holdings LLC ..........G ....... 800 323-5440
   Northbrook *(G-16325)*
Orica USA Inc ...................................E ....... 815 357-8711
   Morris *(G-15125)*
PQ Corporation .................................F ....... 815 667-4241
   Utica *(G-21107)*
PQ Corporation .................................F ....... 847 662-8566
   Gurnee *(G-11488)*
Radco Industries Inc .......................F ....... 630 232-7966
   Elburn *(G-8908)*
Radco Industries Inc .......................E ....... 630 232-7966
   Batavia *(G-1489)*
Regis Technologies Inc ...................D ....... 847 967-6000
   Morton Grove *(G-15232)*
Rhone-Poulenc Basic Chem Co .....G ....... 708 757-6111
   Chicago Heights *(G-7121)*

Sanford Chemical Co Inc ................F ....... 847 437-3530
   Elk Grove Village *(G-9727)*
Scholle Ipn Corporation ...................F ....... 708 562-7290
   Northlake *(G-16450)*
Solvay USA Inc .................................E ....... 708 441-6041
   Chicago Heights *(G-7126)*
Spartan Flame Retardants Inc ........F ....... 815 459-8500
   Crystal Lake *(G-7653)*
Stellar Manufacturing Company ......D ....... 618 823-3761
   Cahokia *(G-2926)*
Toyal America Inc ............................G ....... 630 505-2160
   Naperville *(G-15766)*
Trico Technologies Inc ....................G ....... 847 662-9224
   Gurnee *(G-11516)*
Universal Chem & Coatings Inc ......E ....... 847 297-2001
   Elk Grove Village *(G-9801)*
UOP LLC ...........................................D ....... 708 442-7400
   Mc Cook *(G-14460)*
Vacumet Corp ...................................F ....... 708 562-7290
   Northlake *(G-16458)*
Velsicol Chemical LLC ....................D ....... 847 813-7888
   Rosemont *(G-19040)*
Vernon Micheal ................................F ....... 217 735-4005
   Lincoln *(G-13421)*
Vital Chemicals USA LLC ................G ....... 630 778-0330
   Naperville *(G-15777)*
W R Grace & Co- Conn ...................F ....... 708 458-9700
   Chicago *(G-6924)*
Washington Mills Tonawanda ..........D ....... 815 925-7302
   Hennepin *(G-11736)*

### CHEMICALS: Lead Compounds/Salts, Inorganic, Not Pigments

Powerlab Inc ....................................F ....... 815 273-7718
   Savanna *(G-19404)*

### CHEMICALS: Medicinal

Chemsci Technologies Inc ..............G ....... 815 608-9135
   Belvidere *(G-1746)*
Frontida Biopharm Inc ....................G ....... 215 620-3527
   Aurora *(G-1012)*
Obiter Research LLC ......................F ....... 217 359-1626
   Champaign *(G-3521)*
Synchem Inc ....................................F ....... 847 298-2436
   Elk Grove Village *(G-9764)*

### CHEMICALS: Medicinal, Organic, Uncompounded, Bulk

Organnica Inc ...................................G ....... 312 925-7272
   Berwyn *(G-2071)*
Pelron Corporation ...........................E ....... 708 442-9100
   Mc Cook *(G-14455)*
UOP LLC ...........................................D ....... 708 442-7400
   Mc Cook *(G-14460)*

### CHEMICALS: Mercury, Redistilled

Dfg Mercury Corp .............................G ....... 847 869-7800
   Evanston *(G-10028)*

### CHEMICALS: NEC

Abbott Laboratories ..........................F ....... 847 937-6100
   Abbott Park *(G-2)*
ABM Marking Ltd .............................F ....... 618 277-3773
   Belleville *(G-1606)*
Accusol Incorporated .......................G ....... 773 283-4686
   Oak Lawn *(G-16597)*
Afton Chemical Corporation ............B ....... 618 583-1000
   East Saint Louis *(G-8740)*
All American Chemical Co Inc .........E ....... 847 297-2840
   Melrose Park *(G-14586)*
Alloy Chrome Inc .............................G ....... 847 678-2880
   Schiller Park *(G-19800)*
American Chemical & Eqp Inc ........G ....... 815 675-9199
   Northlake *(G-16427)*
American Colloid Company .............F ....... 815 547-5369
   Belvidere *(G-1731)*
American Colloid Company .............G ....... 618 452-8143
   Granite City *(G-11263)*
American Colloid Company .............F ....... 304 882-2123
   Elgin *(G-8947)*
American Colloid Company .............E ....... 847 851-1700
   Hoffman Estates *(G-11992)*
Americlean Inc .................................F ....... 314 741-8901
   Wood River *(G-22440)*
Apex Engineering Products Corp ....F ....... 630 820-8888
   Aurora *(G-958)*

Arch Chemicals Inc................F ....... 630 955-0401
Naperville (G-15600)
BASF Corporation................B ....... 815 932-9863
Kankakee (G-12603)
Bird-X Inc................E ....... 312 226-2473
Chicago (G-4112)
Black Swan Manufacturing Co................F ....... 773 227-3700
Chicago (G-4121)
Bmi Products Northern Ill Inc................E ....... 847 395-7110
Antioch (G-625)
Bonsal American Inc................D ....... 847 678-6220
Franklin Park (G-10415)
Brite Site Supply Inc................G ....... 773 772-7300
Chicago (G-4171)
Buzz Sales Company Inc................G ....... 815 459-1170
Crystal Lake (G-7546)
C & S Chemicals Inc................G ....... 815 722-6671
Joliet (G-12470)
Cabot Corporation................D ....... 217 253-5752
Tuscola (G-21018)
Campbell Camie Inc................E ....... 314 968-3222
Downers Grove (G-8403)
Cater Chemical Co................G ....... 630 980-2300
Roselle (G-18930)
CCI Manufacturing IL Corp................E ....... 630 685-7534
Lemont (G-13230)
CD Magic Inc................G ....... 708 582-3496
Roselle (G-18931)
Chemical Processing & Acc................G ....... 847 793-2387
Lincolnshire (G-13437)
Chemix Corp................F ....... 708 754-2150
Glenwood (G-11215)
Circle Systems Inc................F ....... 815 286-3271
Hinckley (G-11934)
Claire-Sprayway Inc................D ....... 630 628-3000
Downers Grove (G-8413)
CLC Lubricants Company................E ....... 630 232-7900
Geneva (G-10818)
Compass Minerals Intl Inc................F ....... 773 978-7258
Chicago (G-4438)
Dayton Superior Corporation................C ....... 815 936-3300
Kankakee (G-12609)
De Enterprises Inc................F ....... 708 345-8088
Broadview (G-2571)
Emerald Polymer Additives LLC................D ....... 309 364-2311
Henry (G-11742)
Enterprise Oil Co................E ....... 312 487-2025
Chicago (G-4759)
Enviro Tech International Inc................G ....... 708 343-6641
Melrose Park (G-14634)
Environmental Specialties Inc................G ....... 630 860-7070
Itasca (G-12259)
Frank Miller & Sons Inc................E ....... 708 201-7200
Mokena (G-14863)
Getex Corporation................G ....... 630 993-1300
Hinsdale (G-11948)
Gillette Company................D ....... 847 689-3111
North Chicago (G-16180)
H A Gartenberg & Company................F ....... 847 821-7590
Buffalo Grove (G-2700)
H-O-H Water Technology Inc................E ....... 847 358-7400
Palatine (G-17032)
Hawkins Inc................G ....... 708 258-3797
Peotone (G-17489)
HIG Chemicals Holdings................C ....... 773 376-9000
Chicago (G-5085)
I W M Corporation................G ....... 847 695-0700
Elgin (G-9070)
Illinois Tool Works Inc................E ....... 847 350-0193
Elk Grove Village (G-9536)
Industrial Specialty Chem Inc................E ....... 708 339-1313
South Holland (G-20280)
Industrial Waste Elimination................F ....... 312 498-0880
Peoria (G-17390)
Industrial Water Trtmnt Soltns................G ....... 708 339-1313
Harvey (G-11672)
Ineos Americas LLC................G ....... 630 857-7463
Naperville (G-15673)
Ineos Americas LLC................G ....... 630 857-7000
Lisle (G-13603)
Interra Global Corporation................F ....... 847 292-8600
Park Ridge (G-17204)
Jackson Marking Products Co................F ....... 618 242-7901
Mount Vernon (G-15417)
JM Huber Corporation................E ....... 217 224-1100
Quincy (G-17841)
Klein Tools Inc................D ....... 847 228-6999
Elk Grove Village (G-9577)
Klein Tools Inc................E ....... 847 821-5500
Lincolnshire (G-13461)
Lamar Owings................G ....... 630 232-0564
Geneva (G-10845)
Lawter Inc................E ....... 312 662-5700
Chicago (G-5473)
Litho Research Incorporated................G ....... 630 860-7070
Itasca (G-12307)
Magnetic Inspection Lab Inc................D ....... 847 437-4488
Elk Grove Village (G-9606)
Mapei Corporation................D ....... 630 293-5800
West Chicago (G-21737)
Master Fog LLC................G ....... 773 918-9080
Plainfield (G-17624)
Mc Chemical Company................G ....... 618 965-3668
Steeleville (G-20563)
Mc Chemical Company................E ....... 815 964-7687
Rockford (G-18487)
Metal Finishing Research Corp................F ....... 773 373-0800
Chicago (G-5699)
Micro Surface Corporation................F ....... 815 942-4221
Morris (G-15116)
Miller Purcell Co Inc................G ....... 815 485-2142
New Lenox (G-15897)
Mineral Masters Corporation................F ....... 630 293-7727
West Chicago (G-21744)
Morton Salt Inc................C ....... 312 807-2000
Chicago (G-5809)
Nalco Holding Company................D ....... 630 305-1000
Naperville (G-15706)
Nataz Specialty Coatings Inc................F ....... 773 247-7030
Chicago (G-5856)
Ochem Inc................G ....... 847 403-7044
Des Plaines (G-8246)
Ochem Inc................F ....... 847 403-7044
Chicago (G-5967)
Penray Companies Inc................D ....... 800 323-6329
Wheeling (G-22120)
Polyenviro Labs Inc................G ....... 708 489-0195
Mokena (G-14896)
PQ Corporation................E ....... 815 667-4241
Utica (G-21107)
Pressure Vessel Service Inc................F ....... 773 913-7700
Chicago (G-6182)
Pro TEC Metal Finishing Corp................G ....... 773 384-7853
Chicago (G-6203)
Producers Chemical Company................E ....... 630 466-4584
Sugar Grove (G-20731)
Progressive Solutions Corp................G ....... 847 639-7272
Algonquin (G-405)
PVS Chemical Solutions Inc................E ....... 773 933-8800
Chicago (G-6231)
Quikrete Chicago................D ....... 630 557-8252
Elburn (G-8906)
RPS Products Inc................E ....... 847 683-3400
Hampshire (G-11562)
Rust-Oleum Corporation................C ....... 847 367-7700
Vernon Hills (G-21195)
Rycoline Products LLC................C ....... 773 775-6755
Chicago (G-6417)
Sanford Chemical Co Inc................F ....... 847 437-3530
Elk Grove Village (G-9727)
Seymour of Sycamore Inc................C ....... 815 895-9101
Sycamore (G-20815)
Sika Corporation................G ....... 815 431-1080
Ottawa (G-16985)
Solazyme................G ....... 309 258-5695
Peoria (G-17457)
Solutia Inc................A ....... 618 482-6536
Sauget (G-19390)
Solvay Chemicals Inc................E ....... 618 274-0755
East Saint Louis (G-8769)
Solvay USA Inc................E ....... 708 235-7200
University Park (G-21062)
Specialty Cnstr Brands Inc................F ....... 630 851-0782
Aurora (G-1081)
Steroids Ltd................G ....... 312 996-2364
Chicago (G-6593)
The Euclid Chemical Company................F ....... 815 522-2308
Kirkland (G-12720)
Tower Oil & Technology Co................E ....... 773 927-6161
Chicago (G-6752)
Uniqema Americas................E ....... 773 376-9000
Chicago (G-6818)
United Gilsonite Laboratories................E ....... 217 243-7878
Jacksonville (G-12415)
Vantage Oleochemicals Inc................E ....... 773 376-9000
Chicago (G-6872)
Vantage Oleochemicals Inc................G ....... 773 376-9000
Chicago (G-6874)
Varn International Inc................E ....... 630 406-6501
Batavia (G-1516)
W R Grace & Co- Conn................F ....... 708 458-9700
Chicago (G-6924)
Wenesco Inc................F ....... 773 283-3004
Chicago (G-6956)
Winn Star Inc................G ....... 618 964-1811
Carbondale (G-3028)

## CHEMICALS: Nonmetallic Compounds

Circle Systems Inc................F ....... 815 286-3271
Hinckley (G-11934)

## CHEMICALS: Organic, NEC

Afton Chemical Corporation................B ....... 618 583-1000
East Saint Louis (G-8740)
Akzo Nobel Functional Chem LLC................D ....... 312 544-7000
Chicago (G-3792)
Akzo Nobel Inc................C ....... 312 544-7000
Chicago (G-3793)
Amtex Chemicals LLC................G ....... 630 268-0085
Lombard (G-13764)
Arvens Technology Inc................G ....... 650 776-5443
Peoria (G-17311)
Aspen API Inc................F ....... 847 635-0985
Des Plaines (G-8152)
AST Industries Inc................F ....... 847 455-2300
Franklin Park (G-10405)
Avatar Corporation................D ....... 708 534-5511
University Park (G-21042)
BASF Corporation................B ....... 815 932-9863
Kankakee (G-12603)
Big River Prairie Gold LLC................G ....... 319 753-1100
Galva (G-10783)
BP Amoco Chemical Company................B ....... 630 420-5111
Naperville (G-15608)
Bullen Midwest Inc................E ....... 773 785-2300
Chicago (G-4183)
Campbell Camie Inc................E ....... 314 968-3222
Downers Grove (G-8403)
Cedar Concepts Corporation................E ....... 773 890-5790
Chicago (G-4265)
Clean Motion Inc................F ....... 607 323-1778
Chicago (G-4397)
Custom Chemical Inc................G ....... 217 529-0878
Springfield (G-20426)
Dubois Chemicals Group Inc................G ....... 708 458-2000
Chicago (G-4646)
Dynachem Inc................D ....... 217 662-2136
Westville (G-21929)
Elevance Rnewable Sciences Inc................C ....... 630 296-8880
Woodridge (G-22476)
Emerald Biofuels LLC................G ....... 847 420-0898
Chicago (G-4739)
Emerald One LLC................G ....... 601 529-6793
Chicago (G-4741)
Entrust Services LLC................G ....... 630 699-9132
Naperville (G-15654)
Envirox LLC................E ....... 217 442-8596
Danville (G-7716)
Ethyl Corp................G ....... 618 583-1292
East Saint Louis (G-8751)
Evonik Corporation................C ....... 309 697-6220
Mapleton (G-14209)
Evonik Corporation................G ....... 630 230-0176
Burr Ridge (G-2841)
Global Water Technology Inc................E ....... 708 349-9991
Orland Park (G-16862)
Green Plains Partners LP................F ....... 618 451-4420
Madison (G-14148)
H A Gartenberg & Company................F ....... 847 821-7590
Buffalo Grove (G-2700)
Ha-International LLC................E ....... 630 575-5700
Westmont (G-21888)
Ha-International LLC................E ....... 815 732-3898
Oregon (G-16826)
Ha-Usa Inc................G ....... 630 575-5700
Westmont (G-21889)
Hallstar Company................D ....... 708 594-5947
Bedford Park (G-1552)
Honeywell International Inc................B ....... 618 524-2111
Metropolis (G-14754)
Hurst Chemical Company................G ....... 815 964-0451
Rockford (G-18424)
Hydrox Chemical Company Inc................D ....... 847 468-9400
Elgin (G-9069)
Indorama Ventures Oxide & Glyl................E ....... 800 365-0794
Riverwoods (G-18039)
Ineos Styrolution America LLC................G ....... 815 423-5541
Channahon (G-3576)
Ineos Styrolution America LLC................C ....... 630 820-9500
Aurora (G-1028)

Employee Codes: A=Over 500 employees, B=251-500
C=101-250, D=51-100, E=20-50, F=10-19, G=3-9
2017 Harris Illinois
Industrial Directory
1509
PRODUCT

## CHEMICALS: Organic, NEC

Ivanhoe Industries Inc .... E .... 847 872-3311
  Zion (G-22688)
Koppers Industries Inc .... E .... 708 656-5900
  Cicero (G-7209)
Lanzatech Inc .... D .... 630 439-3050
  Skokie (G-20025)
Liquid Resin International .... E .... 618 392-3590
  Olney (G-16777)
Lonza Inc .... D .... 309 697-7200
  Mapleton (G-14212)
Lyondell Chemical Company .... B .... 815 942-7011
  Morris (G-15114)
Merisant Company .... F .... 312 840-6000
  Chicago (G-5691)
Midwest Biodiesel Products LLC .... F .... 618 254-2920
  South Roxana (G-20313)
Miwon NA .... G .... 630 568-5850
  Willowbrook (G-22224)
National Interchem LLC .... G .... 708 597-7777
  Blue Island (G-2264)
Natures Appeal Mfg Corp .... G .... 630 880-6222
  Addison (G-226)
Nufarm Americas Inc .... D .... 708 377-1330
  Alsip (G-501)
Nutrasweet Company .... G .... 312 873-5000
  Chicago (G-5956)
Pacific Ethanol Canton LLC .... G .... 309 347-9200
  Pekin (G-17278)
Paradigm Bioaviation LLC .... F .... 309 663-2303
  Bloomington (G-2210)
Penray Companies Inc .... D .... 800 323-6329
  Wheeling (G-22120)
Pmp Fermentation Products Inc .... E .... 309 637-0400
  Peoria (G-17430)
Polyenviro Labs Inc .... G .... 708 489-0195
  Mokena (G-14896)
PPG Architectural Finishes Inc .... D .... 773 523-6333
  Chicago (G-6161)
PVS Chemical Solutions Inc .... E .... 773 933-8800
  Chicago (G-6231)
Rahn USA Corp .... E .... 630 851-4220
  Aurora (G-1072)
Reg Seneca LLC .... E .... 888 734-8686
  Seneca (G-19889)
Regis Technologies Inc .... D .... 847 967-6000
  Morton Grove (G-15232)
Reliance Specialty Pdts Inc .... F .... 847 640-8923
  Elk Grove Village (G-9713)
RHO Chemical Company Inc .... F .... 815 727-4791
  Joliet (G-12568)
Roquette America Inc .... D .... 847 360-0886
  Gurnee (G-11501)
SB Boron Corporation .... G .... 708 547-9002
  Bellwood (G-1719)
Solvay Chemicals Inc .... E .... 618 274-0755
  East Saint Louis (G-8769)
Solvay USA Inc .... E .... 708 371-2000
  Blue Island (G-2271)
Standard Rubber Products Co .... E .... 847 593-5630
  Elk Grove Village (G-9751)
Stepan Company .... B .... 815 727-4944
  Elwood (G-9982)
Strebor Specialties LLC .... E .... 618 286-1140
  Dupo (G-8580)
Swi Energy LLC .... G .... 618 465-7277
  Alton (G-592)
Tate Lyle Ingrdnts Amricas LLC .... G .... 309 473-2721
  Heyworth (G-11766)
Water & Oil Technologies Inc .... G .... 630 892-2007
  Montgomery (G-15072)
Xena International Inc .... E .... 815 946-2626
  Polo (G-17691)

## CHEMICALS: Phosphates, Defluorinated/Ammoniated, Exc Fertlr

Innophos Inc .... C .... 708 757-6111
  Chicago Heights (G-7103)
Pcs Phosphate Company Inc .... D .... 847 849-4200
  Northbrook (G-16336)
Potash Corp Ssktchewan Fla Inc .... C .... 847 849-4200
  Northbrook (G-16340)

## CHEMICALS: Potash Alum

Potash Corp Ssktchewan Fla Inc .... C .... 847 849-4200
  Northbrook (G-16339)

## CHEMICALS: Reagent Grade, Refined From Technical Grade

Campbell Science Corp .... F .... 815 962-7415
  Rockford (G-18295)

## CHEMICALS: Silica Compounds

US Silica .... F .... 312 589-7539
  Chicago (G-6856)

## CHEMICALS: Sulfur Chloride

PVS Chemical Solutions Inc .... E .... 773 933-8800
  Chicago (G-6231)

## CHEMICALS: Sulfur, Incl Rcvrd/Refined, Fm Sour Natural Gas

Reagent Chemical & RES Inc .... G .... 618 271-8140
  East Saint Louis (G-8766)

## CHEMICALS: Water Treatment

Arch Chemicals Inc .... G .... 630 365-1720
  Elburn (G-8876)
Bromine Systems Inc .... G .... 630 624-3303
  Addison (G-61)
Custom Chemical Inc .... G .... 217 529-0878
  Springfield (G-20426)
Dober Chemical Corp .... C .... 630 410-7300
  Woodridge (G-22471)
Garratt-Callahan Company .... G .... 630 543-4411
  Addison (G-128)
GE Betz Inc .... E .... 630 543-8480
  Addison (G-129)
Girard Chemical Company .... G .... 630 293-5886
  Bensenville (G-1909)
Rockford Chemical Co .... G .... 815 544-3476
  Belvidere (G-1783)
Siemens Industry Inc .... F .... 618 451-1205
  Granite City (G-11303)
Swanson Water Treatment Inc .... G .... 847 680-1113
  Libertyville (G-13386)

## CHESTS: Bank, Metal

Panek Precision Products Co .... C .... 847 291-9755
  Northbrook (G-16330)

## CHEWING GUM

Ford Gum & Machine Company Inc .... F .... 847 955-0003
  Buffalo Grove (G-2698)
Mid Pack .... .... 773 626-3500
  Chicago (G-5726)
Mondelez Global LLC .... C .... 847 943-4000
  Deerfield (G-8037)
Wm Wrigley Jr Company .... B .... 312 280-4710
  Chicago (G-7012)
Wm Wrigley Jr Company .... .... 312 205-2300
  Chicago (G-7013)
Wm Wrigley Jr Company .... A .... 312 644-2121
  Chicago (G-7014)
Wrigley Manufacturing Co LLC .... A .... 312 644-2121
  Chicago (G-7038)
Wrigley Manufacturing Co LLC .... B .... 630 553-4800
  Yorkville (G-22677)
Wrigley Manufacturing Co LLC .... .... 312 644-2121
  Chicago (G-7039)
Wrigley Sales Company LLC .... F .... 312 644-2121
  Chicago (G-7040)

## CHICKEN SLAUGHTERING & PROCESSING

Charles Autin Limited .... D .... 312 432-0888
  Chicago (G-4289)

## CHILDBIRTH PREPARATION CLINIC

Cambridge Sensors USA LLC .... G .... 877 374-4062
  Plainfield (G-17584)

## CHILDREN'S WEAR STORES

Initial Choice .... F .... 847 234-5884
  Lake Forest (G-12917)
Slick Sugar Inc .... G .... 815 782-7101
  Plainfield (G-17649)

## CHIMNEY CAPS: Concrete

Chimney King LLC .... .... 847 244-8860
  Waukegan (G-21537)

Taurus Safety Products Inc .... G .... 630 620-7940
  Lombard (G-13865)

## CHIMNEY CLEANING SVCS

Lindemann Chimney Service Inc .... F .... 847 918-7994
  Lake Bluff (G-12854)

## CHINA & GLASS REPAIR SVCS

Glass Fx .... G .... 217 359-0048
  Champaign (G-3488)

## CHINA FIRING & DECORATING SVCS, TO INDIVIDUAL ORDER

Besco Awards & Embroidery .... G .... 847 395-4862
  Antioch (G-622)

## CHINAWARE STORES

Georg Jensen Inc .... G .... 312 642-9160
  Chicago (G-4941)

## CHIROPRACTORS' OFFICES

Serola Biomechanics Inc .... F .... 815 636-2780
  Loves Park (G-13991)

## CHLORINE

Arkema Inc .... C .... 708 396-3001
  Alsip (G-435)
Champion Packaging & Dist Inc .... C .... 630 755-4220
  Woodridge (G-22460)

## CHOCOLATE, EXC CANDY FROM BEANS: Chips, Powder, Block, Syrup

American Convenience Inc .... F .... 815 344-6040
  McHenry (G-14480)
Andersons Candy Shop Inc .... F .... 815 678-6000
  Richmond (G-17957)
Baldi Candy Co .... D .... 773 267-5770
  Chicago (G-4032)
Belgian Chocolatier Piron Inc .... G .... 847 864-5504
  Evanston (G-10014)
Chocolat By Daniel .... G .... 815 969-7990
  Rockford (G-18307)
Chocolate Potpourri Ltd .... F .... 847 729-8878
  Glenview (G-11112)
Cora Lee Candies Inc .... F .... 847 724-2754
  Glenview (G-11115)
Dekalb Confectionary Inc .... F .... 815 758-5990
  Dekalb (G-8086)
Galenas Kandy Kitchen .... G .... 815 777-0241
  Galena (G-10723)
Gayety Candy Co Inc .... E .... 708 418-0062
  Lansing (G-13163)
Hershey Company .... .... 800 468-1714
  Deerfield (G-8011)
Hershey Company .... A .... 618 544-3111
  Robinson (G-18064)
John B Sanfilippo & Son Inc .... C .... 847 289-1800
  Elgin (G-9083)
Joyce Greiner .... G .... 618 654-9340
  Highland (G-11799)
Kruger North America Inc .... F .... 708 851-3670
  Oak Park (G-16673)
Mars Chocolate North Amer LLC .... C .... 630 850-9898
  Burr Ridge (G-2864)
Mars Chocolate North Amer LLC .... A .... 662 335-8000
  Chicago (G-5630)
Peases Inc .... F .... 217 529-2912
  Springfield (G-20502)
Sweet Endeavors Inc .... G .... 224 653-2700
  Schaumburg (G-19748)
Worlds Finest Chocolate Inc .... B .... 773 847-4600
  Chicago (G-7033)

## CHOCOLATE, EXC CANDY FROM PURCH CHOC: Chips, Powder, Block

Barry Callebaut USA LLC .... G .... 312 496-7300
  Chicago (G-4047)
Barry Callebaut USA LLC .... B .... 312 496-7300
  Chicago (G-4048)
Blommer Chocolate Company .... D .... 800 621-1606
  Chicago (G-4123)
Cargill Cocoa & Chocolate Inc .... G .... 815 578-2000
  Island Lake (G-12213)

Godiva Chocolatier Inc ............................. F ....... 847 329-8620
  Skokie  (G-20004)
Godiva Chocolatier Inc ............................. F ....... 312 280-1133
  Chicago  (G-4968)
Godiva Chocolatier Inc ............................. E ....... 847 918-0124
  Vernon Hills  (G-21167)
Mondelez Global LLC .............................. C ....... 847 943-4000
  Deerfield  (G-8037)

## CHRISTMAS NOVELTIES, WHOLESALE

Mattarusky Inc ............................................. G ....... 630 469-4125
  Glen Ellyn  (G-10980)
Temple Display Ltd ..................................... G ....... 630 851-3331
  Oswego  (G-16936)

## CHRISTMAS TREE LIGHTING SETS: Electric

American Holiday Lights Inc .................... G ....... 630 769-9999
  Woodridge  (G-22451)
Natures Best Christmas Trees ................ G ....... 815 765-2960
  Poplar Grove  (G-17715)
Santas Best ................................................. F ....... 847 459-3301
  Riverwoods  (G-18043)

## CHRISTMAS TREE ORNAMENTS: Electric

Polygroup Services NA Inc ....................... G ....... 847 851-9995
  East Dundee  (G-8653)

## CHROMATOGRAPHY EQPT

Alltech Associates Inc ................................ D ....... 773 261-2252
  Chicago  (G-3824)
Dionex Corporation .................................... G ....... 847 295-7500
  Bannockburn  (G-1257)
Waters Technologies Corp ........................ F ....... 630 766-6249
  Wood Dale  (G-22437)
Waters Technologies Corp ........................ F ....... 508 482-8365
  Chicago  (G-6942)

## CHUCKS

Electro-Matic Products Co ........................ F ....... 773 235-4010
  Chicago  (G-4720)
Kitagawa Usa Inc ........................................ E ....... 847 310-8198
  Schaumburg  (G-19599)
Kitagawa-Northtech Inc .............................. E ....... 847 310-8787
  Schaumburg  (G-19600)
LFA Industries Inc ...................................... G ....... 630 762-7391
  Saint Charles  (G-19210)
Miyanohitec Machinery Inc ........................ G ....... 847 382-2794
  Barrington  (G-1292)
Reichel Hardware Company Inc .............. G ....... 630 762-7394
  Saint Charles  (G-19252)

## CHUTES & TROUGHS

American Chute Systems Inc ................... G ....... 815 723-7632
  Joliet  (G-12452)

## CIGARETTE & CIGAR PRDTS & ACCESS

A and T Cigarettes Imports ....................... G ....... 847 836-9134
  East Dundee  (G-8627)
Indigo Cigar Factory ................................... G ....... 217 348-1514
  Charleston  (G-3600)

## CIGARETTE LIGHTERS

Sarj Kalidas LLC ......................................... D ....... 708 865-9134
  Chicago  (G-6446)

## CIRCUIT BOARD REPAIR SVCS

Novatronix Inc .............................................. E ....... 630 860-4300
  Wood Dale  (G-22407)

## CIRCUIT BOARDS, PRINTED: Television & Radio

American Controls & Automation ............ G ....... 630 293-8841
  West Chicago  (G-21655)
Bandjwet Enterprises Inc .......................... E ....... 847 797-9250
  Rolling Meadows  (G-18715)
Bestproto Inc ................................................ F ....... 224 387-3280
  Rolling Meadows  (G-18717)
Delta Design Inc .......................................... F ....... 708 424-9400
  Evergreen Park  (G-10112)
Light of Mine LLC ........................................ G ....... 312 840-8570
  Chicago  (G-5503)
Microsun Electronics Corp ........................ F ....... 630 410-7900
  Woodridge  (G-22502)

Ncab Group Usa Inc ................................... F ....... 630 562-5550
  Itasca  (G-12326)
Parth Consultants Inc ................................. F ....... 847 758-1400
  Rolling Meadows  (G-18758)
Quality Surface Mount Inc ......................... E ....... 630 350-8556
  Wood Dale  (G-22415)
RB Manufacturing & Electronics ............. E ....... 815 522-3100
  Kirkland  (G-12717)
Star Electronics Corp ................................. E ....... 847 439-0605
  Elk Grove Village  (G-9755)

## CIRCUIT BOARDS: Wiring

American Prgrssive Crcuits Inc ................ E ....... 630 495-6900
  Addison  (G-37)

## CIRCUIT BREAKERS

Boltswitch Inc ............................................... E ....... 815 459-6900
  Crystal Lake  (G-7542)
Clark Tashaunda ......................................... G ....... 708 247-8274
  Calumet Park  (G-2958)
Eunice Larry ................................................. G ....... 708 339-5678
  South Holland  (G-20268)

## CIRCUIT BREAKERS: Air

Schneider Electric Usa Inc ........................ G ....... 312 697-4770
  Chicago  (G-6452)

## CIRCUITS, INTEGRATED: Hybrid

Hytel Group Inc ............................................ G ....... 847 683-9800
  Hampshire  (G-11551)

## CIRCUITS: Electronic

Absolute Process Instruments .................. E ....... 847 918-3510
  Libertyville  (G-13299)
Accelerated Assemblies Inc ..................... E ....... 630 616-6680
  Elk Grove Village  (G-9259)
Access Assembly LLC ............................... G ....... 847 894-1047
  Mundelein  (G-15463)
Aimtron Corporation ................................... D ....... 630 372-7500
  Palatine  (G-16999)
Air802 Corporation ...................................... G ....... 630 428-3108
  Aurora  (G-956)
American Precision Elec Inc ..................... D ....... 630 510-8080
  Carol Stream  (G-3101)
Andrew Technologies Inc .......................... G ....... 847 520-5770
  Wheeling  (G-22006)
ARC-Tronics Inc .......................................... C ....... 847 437-0211
  Elk Grove Village  (G-9312)
Aria Corporation .......................................... G ....... 847 918-9329
  Libertyville  (G-13304)
Avg Group of Companies ......................... F ....... 630 668-8886
  Carol Stream  (G-3111)
B D C Inc ...................................................... E ....... 847 741-2233
  Elgin  (G-8962)
Bestar Technologies Inc ............................ E ....... 520 439-9204
  Saint Charles  (G-19142)
Blockmaster Electronics Inc ...................... E ....... 847 956-1680
  Elk Grove Village  (G-9345)
C Hofbauer Inc ............................................ G ....... 630 920-1222
  Burr Ridge  (G-2826)
C L Greenslade Sales Inc ......................... G ....... 847 593-3450
  Arlington Heights  (G-733)
C R V Electronics Corp .............................. D ....... 815 675-6500
  Spring Grove  (G-20329)
Cal-Tronics Systems Inc ........................... G ....... 630 350-0044
  Wood Dale  (G-22350)
Capital Advanced Technologies .............. G ....... 630 690-1696
  Carol Stream  (G-3124)
Circom Inc .................................................... E ....... 630 595-4460
  Bensenville  (G-1859)
Cita Technologies LLC .............................. G ....... 847 419-9118
  Buffalo Grove  (G-2673)
Cmetrix Inc ................................................... G ....... 630 595-9800
  Wood Dale  (G-22353)
Continental Assembly Inc ......................... F ....... 773 472-8004
  Chicago  (G-4457)
Daesam Corporation .................................. G ....... 917 653-2000
  Grayslake  (G-11331)
Dalco Marketing Services ......................... G ....... 630 961-3366
  Naperville  (G-15641)
De Amertek Corporation Inc .................... E ....... 630 572-0800
  Lombard  (G-13788)
Delta Circuits Inc ......................................... G ....... 630 876-0691
  West Chicago  (G-21690)
Dynomax Inc ................................................ D ....... 847 680-8833
  Wheeling  (G-22040)
Elan Industries Inc ...................................... F ....... 630 679-2000
  Bolingbrook  (G-2304)

Entropy International Inc USA ................... F ....... 630 834-3872
  Elmhurst  (G-9867)
Excelitas Technologies Corp .................... E ....... 847 537-4277
  Wheeling  (G-22052)
Four Star Tool Inc ....................................... D ....... 224 735-2419
  Rolling Meadows  (G-18729)
G T C Industries Inc ................................... G ....... 708 369-9815
  Naperville  (G-15661)
Hi-Tech Elctronic Pdts Mfg Inc ................. E ....... 815 220-1543
  Oglesby  (G-16749)
His Company Inc ......................................... G ....... 847 885-2922
  Schaumburg  (G-19556)
Integrated Circuits Research .................... G ....... 630 830-9024
  Hanover Park  (G-11583)
Journey Circuits Inc ................................... G ....... 630 283-0604
  Schaumburg  (G-19591)
L I K Inc ........................................................ F ....... 630 213-1282
  Streamwood  (G-20665)
Lace Technologies Inc ............................... F ....... 630 762-3865
  Addison  (G-177)
Lane Technical Sales Inc .......................... E ....... 773 775-1613
  Chicago  (G-5457)
Littelfuse Inc ................................................. A ....... 773 628-1000
  Chicago  (G-5521)
Loda Electronics Co ................................... G ....... 217 386-2554
  Loda  (G-13752)
Matrix Circuits LLC .................................... G ....... 319 367-5000
  Lake Villa  (G-13020)
Midwest Aero Support Inc ......................... G ....... 815 398-9202
  Machesney Park  (G-14092)
Monnex International Inc ........................... E ....... 847 850-5263
  Buffalo Grove  (G-2738)
Murata Electronics N Amer Inc ................ G ....... 847 330-9200
  Schaumburg  (G-19657)
Navatek Resources Inc ............................. G ....... 847 301-0174
  Schaumburg  (G-19662)
Navitas Electronics Corp ........................... E ....... 702 293-4670
  Woodridge  (G-22504)
Northrop Grumman Systems Corp .......... A ....... 847 259-9600
  Rolling Meadows  (G-18753)
Novel Electronic Designs Inc ................... G ....... 309 224-9945
  Chillicothe  (G-7169)
Nusource Inc ................................................ F ....... 847 201-8934
  Round Lake  (G-19064)
On Time Circuits Inc .................................. G ....... 630 955-1110
  Lisle  (G-13636)
Polyera Corporation .................................... E ....... 847 677-7517
  Skokie  (G-20056)
Precision Circuits Inc ................................. F ....... 630 515-9100
  Downers Grove  (G-8510)
Qcircuits Inc ................................................. F ....... 847 797-6678
  Rolling Meadows  (G-18771)
Safemobile Inc ............................................ F ....... 847 818-1649
  Rolling Meadows  (G-18776)
Seagon Inc ................................................... G ....... 630 541-5460
  Lisle  (G-13655)
Sigmatron International Inc ....................... G ....... 847 586-5200
  Elgin  (G-9178)
Sigmatron International Inc ....................... G ....... 847 956-8000
  Elk Grove Village  (G-9737)
Simple Circuits Inc ...................................... G ....... 708 671-9600
  Palos Park  (G-17132)
Skyline International Inc ............................ E ....... 847 357-9077
  Downers Grove  (G-8525)
Sumida America Components Inc .......... F ....... 847 545-6700
  Schaumburg  (G-19742)
Tanvas Inc .................................................... G ....... 773 295-6220
  Chicago  (G-6674)
Tech Star Design and Mfg ........................ F ....... 847 290-8676
  Elk Grove Village  (G-9771)
Teejet Technologies LLC .......................... D ....... 630 665-5002
  Springfield  (G-20542)
The Syntek Group Inc ................................ G ....... 773 279-0131
  Chicago  (G-6710)
Tvh Parts Co ................................................ G ....... 847 223-1000
  Grayslake  (G-11365)
Uico LLC ....................................................... E ....... 630 592-4400
  Elmhurst  (G-9954)

## CLAMPS & COUPLINGS: Hose

American Couplings Co ............................. G ....... 630 323-4442
  Westmont  (G-21875)
Capital Rubber Corporation ...................... F ....... 630 595-6644
  Bensenville  (G-1851)
Freeman Products Inc ............................... G ....... 847 439-1000
  Elk Grove Village  (G-9490)

## CLAMPS & SHORES: Column

Prospan Manufacturing Co ....................... G ....... 630 860-1930
  Bensenville  (G-1967)

# CLAMPS: Ground, Electric-Wiring Devices

### CLAMPS: Ground, Electric-Wiring Devices
Maclean Senior Industries LLC ............E....... 630 350-1600
  Wood Dale *(G-22393)*

### CLAMPS: Metal
Adjustable Clamp Company ..................C....... 312 666-0640
  Chicago *(G-3751)*
Berens Inc ...........................................G....... 815 932-0913
  Kankakee *(G-12604)*
Stanley Hartco Co ................................E....... 847 967-1122
  Skokie *(G-20090)*
Strut & Supply Inc ...............................G....... 847 756-4337
  Lake Barrington *(G-12824)*
Value Engineered Products ..................E....... 708 867-6777
  Rolling Meadows *(G-18787)*
Zsi-Foster Inc .....................................G....... 800 323-7053
  Chicago *(G-7074)*

### CLAY MINING
American Colloid Minerals Co ...............E....... 800 527-9948
  Arlington Heights *(G-709)*

### CLAY MINING, COMMON
Carpentersville Quarry Inc ...................F....... 847 836-1550
  Carpentersville *(G-3278)*
Oil-Dri Corporation America ................B....... 312 321-1516
  Chicago *(G-5976)*

### CLAYS, EXC KAOLIN & BALL
Oil-Dri Corporation America ................D....... 618 745-6881
  Mounds *(G-15259)*

### CLEANING & DESCALING SVC: Metal Prdts
AAM-Ro Corporation .............................F....... 708 343-5543
  Broadview *(G-2552)*
Ace Metal Refinishers Inc ....................F....... 800 323-7147
  Oak Brook *(G-16484)*
Diamond Blast Corporation ..................F....... 708 681-2640
  Melrose Park *(G-14617)*
Great Lakes Finishing Eqp Inc .............G....... 708 345-5300
  South Elgin *(G-20202)*
Redi-Strip Company ............................G....... 630 529-2442
  Roselle *(G-18966)*

### CLEANING & DYEING PLANTS, EXC RUGS
Eastgate Cleaners ...............................G....... 630 627-9494
  Lombard *(G-13794)*

### CLEANING COMPOUNDS: Rifle Bore
300 Below Inc ....................................G....... 217 423-3070
  Decatur *(G-7819)*

### CLEANING EQPT: Blast, Dustless
Disa Holding Corp ...............................G....... 630 820-3000
  Oswego *(G-16913)*

### CLEANING EQPT: Carpet Sweepers, Exc Household Elec Vacuum
Best Way Carpet & Uphl Clg .................G....... 618 544-8585
  Robinson *(G-18057)*

### CLEANING EQPT: Commercial
Clements National Company .................E....... 708 594-5890
  Broadview *(G-2570)*
Detrex Corporation .............................G....... 708 345-3806
  Melrose Park *(G-14616)*
Markham Division 9 Inc ......................E....... 708 503-0657
  Park Forest *(G-17174)*
Meyer Machine & Equipment Inc ..........F....... 847 395-2970
  Antioch *(G-645)*
Minuteman International Inc ................C....... 630 627-6900
  Pingree Grove *(G-17556)*
Minuteman International Inc ................D....... 847 683-5210
  Hampshire *(G-11555)*
Original Systems .................................G....... 847 945-7660
  Riverwoods *(G-18041)*
Producers Envmtl Pdts LLC ..................G....... 630 482-5995
  Batavia *(G-1487)*
Umf Corporation ..................................G....... 224 251-7822
  Niles *(G-16045)*
Umf Corporation ..................................F....... 847 920-0370
  Skokie *(G-20104)*

Wet & Forget Usa  A New Zealnd ..........G....... 847 428-3894
  Elgin *(G-9236)*

### CLEANING EQPT: Dirt Sweeping Units, Indl
Tkg Sweeping & Services  LLC ............G....... 847 505-1400
  Waukegan *(G-21628)*

### CLEANING EQPT: Floor Washing & Polishing, Commercial
Rays Power Wshg Svc Peggy Ray .........G....... 618 939-6306
  Waterloo *(G-21405)*
Selrok Inc ...........................................G....... 630 876-8322
  West Chicago *(G-21770)*
Star Industries  Inc .............................E....... 708 240-4862
  Highland Park *(G-11873)*

### CLEANING EQPT: High Pressure
Fna Ip Holdings Inc .............................D....... 847 348-1500
  Elk Grove Village *(G-9482)*
Getz Fire Equipment Co .......................E....... 309 637-1440
  Peoria *(G-17372)*
James A Freund  LLC ..........................G....... 630 664-7692
  Oswego *(G-16923)*
Jetin Systems Inc ................................F....... 815 726-4686
  Joliet *(G-12522)*
M & M Pump Co ..................................G....... 217 935-2517
  Clinton *(G-7286)*
Ross and White Company ....................F....... 847 516-3900
  Cary *(G-3369)*

### CLEANING OR POLISHING PREPARATIONS, NEC
Apco Enterprises Inc ...........................G....... 708 430-7333
  Bridgeview *(G-2466)*
Apex Engineering Products Corp ..........F....... 630 820-8888
  Aurora *(G-958)*
Chemical Specialties Mfg Corp .............G....... 309 697-5400
  Mapleton *(G-14207)*
Claire-Sprayway Inc ............................E....... 630 628-3000
  Downers Grove *(G-8412)*
Colorex Chemical Co  Inc ....................G....... 630 238-3124
  Bensenville *(G-1862)*
Coral Chemical Company ....................E....... 847 246-6666
  Zion *(G-22680)*
Duraclean International Inc ..................F....... 847 704-7100
  Arlington Heights *(G-748)*
Floor-Chem Inc ...................................G....... 630 789-2152
  Romeoville *(G-18825)*
Houghton International Inc ..................F....... 610 666-4000
  Chicago *(G-5121)*
Kik International Inc ............................F....... 905 660-0444
  Carol Stream *(G-3178)*
Minuteman International Inc ................C....... 630 627-6900
  Pingree Grove *(G-17556)*
Penray Companies Inc ........................D....... 800 323-6329
  Wheeling *(G-22120)*
PLC Corp ............................................G....... 847 247-1900
  Lake Bluff *(G-12863)*
R R Street & Co Inc ............................E....... 773 247-1190
  Chicago *(G-6271)*
Rycoline Products  LLC .......................C....... 773 775-6755
  Chicago *(G-6417)*
Science Solutions LLC .........................G....... 773 261-1197
  Chicago *(G-6458)*
Stellar Blending & Packaging ...............F....... 314 520-7318
  Dupo *(G-8577)*

### CLEANING PRDTS: Ammonia, Household
Champion Packaging & Dist Inc ............G....... 630 755-4220
  Woodridge *(G-22460)*
Formulations Inc .................................G....... 847 674-9141
  Skokie *(G-20001)*

### CLEANING PRDTS: Automobile Polish
Bumper Scuffs ....................................G....... 847 489-7926
  Lake Villa *(G-13011)*
Reed-Union Corporation ......................F....... 312 644-3200
  Chicago *(G-6318)*
Treatment Products  Ltd .....................E....... 773 626-8888
  Chicago *(G-6766)*
Voodoo Ride LLC .................................G....... 312 944-0465
  Chicago *(G-6914)*

### CLEANING PRDTS: Bleaches, Household, Dry Or Liquid
Clorox Hidden Valley Mfg ....................F....... 847 229-5500
  Wheeling *(G-22027)*
Clorox Products Mfg Co ......................C....... 708 728-4200
  Chicago *(G-4404)*

### CLEANING PRDTS: Disinfectants, Household Or Indl Plant
Advanage Diversified Pdts Inc .............F....... 708 331-8390
  Harvey *(G-11650)*

### CLEANING PRDTS: Drain Pipe Solvents Or Cleaners
Detrex Corporation .............................G....... 708 345-3806
  Melrose Park *(G-14616)*
Imagination Products Corp ..................G....... 309 274-6223
  Chillicothe *(G-7167)*

### CLEANING PRDTS: Drycleaning Preparations
Qualitex Company ...............................F....... 773 506-8112
  Chicago *(G-6244)*
R R Street & Co  Inc ...........................F....... 773 254-1277
  Chicago *(G-6272)*

### CLEANING PRDTS: Floor Waxes
Bullen Midwest Inc ..............................E....... 773 785-2300
  Chicago *(G-4183)*
Dura Wax Company .............................F....... 815 385-5000
  McHenry *(G-14499)*

### CLEANING PRDTS: Indl Plant Disinfectants Or Deodorants
Interflo Industries Inc .........................G....... 847 228-0606
  Elk Grove Village *(G-9551)*
Teitelbaum Brothers Inc ......................G....... 847 729-3490
  Glenview *(G-11208)*

### CLEANING PRDTS: Laundry Preparations
Clorox Company ..................................E....... 510 271-7000
  Willowbrook *(G-22204)*

### CLEANING PRDTS: Metal Polish
Electro-Glo Distribution Inc .................G....... 815 224-4030
  La Salle *(G-12771)*
Matchless Metal Polish Company .........E....... 773 924-1515
  Chicago *(G-5649)*

### CLEANING PRDTS: Polishing Preparations & Related Prdts
Cabot Microelectronics Corp ................D....... 630 375-6631
  Aurora *(G-977)*
Zoes Mfgco LLC ..................................F....... 312 666-4018
  Chicago *(G-7071)*

### CLEANING PRDTS: Rug, Upholstery/Dry Clng Detergents/Spotters
Elco Laboratories Inc ..........................D....... 708 534-3000
  University Park *(G-21047)*
R R Street & Co  Inc ...........................E....... 630 416-4244
  Naperville *(G-15736)*

### CLEANING PRDTS: Sanitation Preparations
City of Chicago ...................................E....... 312 744-0940
  Chicago *(G-4384)*
First Ayd Corporation ..........................D....... 847 622-0001
  Elgin *(G-9036)*
Gea Farm Technologies Inc .................C....... 630 548-8200
  Naperville *(G-15662)*
Johnnys Little LLC ...............................G....... 217 243-2570
  Jacksonville *(G-12399)*
Purdy Products Company .....................F....... 847 526-5505
  Wauconda *(G-21497)*

### CLEANING PRDTS: Sanitation Preps, Disinfectants/Deodorants
City of Chicago ...................................E....... 312 746-6583
  Chicago *(G-4387)*

## PRODUCT SECTION — CLOTHING & FURNISHINGS, MENS & BOYS, WHOLESALE: Lined

Ecolab Inc .................................................. E ...... 815 389-8132
  Roscoe *(G-18895)*
Ecolab Inc .................................................. E ...... 815 389-4063
  South Beloit *(G-20144)*

### CLEANING PRDTS: Specialty

300 Below Inc ........................................... G ...... 217 423-3070
  Decatur *(G-7819)*
Atm America Corp ..................................... E ...... 800 298-0030
  Chicago *(G-3986)*
Blue Light Inc .......................................... E ...... 630 400-4539
  Lisle *(G-13570)*
Boyer Corporation .................................... G ...... 708 352-2553
  La Grange *(G-12727)*
Brite Site Supply Inc ............................... G ...... 773 772-7300
  Chicago *(G-4171)*
Clifton Chemical Company ..................... G ...... 815 697-2343
  Chebanse *(G-3630)*
Creative Metal Products .......................... F ...... 773 638-3200
  Chicago *(G-4500)*
Doris Company ........................................ G ...... 224 302-5605
  Waukegan *(G-21553)*
Ecp Incorporated ..................................... D ...... 630 754-4200
  Woodridge *(G-22474)*
First Mate Yacht Detailing ...................... G ...... 847 249-7654
  Waukegan *(G-21560)*
Fola Community Action Services ........... F ...... 773 487-4310
  Chicago *(G-4868)*
Future Environmental Inc ....................... C ...... 708 479-6900
  Mokena *(G-14865)*
Pete Frcano Sons Cstm HM Bldrs ......... F ...... 847 258-4626
  Elk Grove Village *(G-9675)*
R E Z Packaging Inc ................................ G ...... 773 247-0800
  Chicago *(G-6266)*
Scs Company ........................................... E ...... 708 203-4955
  Crestwood *(G-7501)*
Tiger Accessory Group LLC ................... G ...... 847 821-9630
  Long Grove *(G-13902)*
United Laboratories Inc .......................... D ...... 630 377-0900
  Saint Charles *(G-19289)*
Venus Laboratories Inc .......................... E ...... 630 595-1900
  Addison *(G-339)*

### CLEANING PRDTS: Window Cleaning Preparations

A J Funk & Co .......................................... G ...... 847 741-6760
  Elgin *(G-8929)*
Anytime Window Cleaning Inc ............... G ...... 773 235-5677
  Chicago *(G-3919)*
Newby Oil Company Inc ......................... G ...... 815 756-7688
  Sycamore *(G-20810)*

### CLIPPERS: Hair, Human

Wahl Clipper Corporation ....................... A ...... 815 625-6525
  Sterling *(G-20619)*
Wahl Clipper Corporation ....................... F ...... 815 625-6525
  Sterling *(G-20620)*

### CLIPS & FASTENERS, MADE FROM PURCHASED WIRE

Acco Brands USA LLC ............................ B ...... 800 222-6462
  Lake Zurich *(G-13034)*
Acco Brands USA LLC ............................ D ...... 847 272-3700
  Lincolnshire *(G-13423)*
Keats Manufacturing Co ......................... D ...... 847 520-1133
  Wheeling *(G-22083)*
Manufasteners House Iq Inc .................. G ...... 847 705-6538
  Palatine *(G-17053)*
Precitec Corporation ............................... D ...... 847 949-2800
  Mundelein *(G-15547)*

### CLOSURES: Closures, Stamped Metal

Amcor Flexibles LLC ............................... C ...... 224 313-7000
  Buffalo Grove *(G-2656)*
Sorini Manufacturing Corp ..................... E ...... 773 247-5858
  Chicago *(G-6544)*

### CLOSURES: Plastic

Aptargroup Inc ........................................ E ...... 779 220-4430
  Crystal Lake *(G-7534)*
Aptargroup Inc ........................................ B ...... 815 477-0424
  Crystal Lake *(G-7535)*
Mold-Rite Plastics LLC ........................... C ...... 518 561-1812
  Chicago *(G-5790)*
Portola Packaging LLC ........................... E ...... 630 515-8383
  Downers Grove *(G-8506)*

Sun Dome Inc .......................................... F ...... 773 890-5350
  Chicago *(G-6618)*
Zeller Plastik Usa Inc ............................. C ...... 847 247-7900
  Libertyville *(G-13403)*

### CLOTHESPINS: Plastic

Goodco Products LLC ............................ G ...... 630 258-6384
  Countryside *(G-7428)*

### CLOTHING & ACCESS STORES

U R On It .................................................. G ...... 847 382-0182
  Lake Barrington *(G-12826)*

### CLOTHING & ACCESS, WHOLESALE: Leather & Sheep Lined

Loren Girovich ......................................... G ...... 773 334-1444
  Chicago *(G-5541)*

### CLOTHING & ACCESS, WOMEN, CHILD & INFANT, WHSLE: Sportswear

Select Screen Prints & EMB ................... F ...... 309 829-6511
  Bloomington *(G-2222)*

### CLOTHING & ACCESS, WOMEN, CHILD/INFANT, WHOLESALE: Child

Elite Kids ................................................. G ...... 815 451-9600
  Crystal Lake *(G-7572)*

### CLOTHING & ACCESS, WOMEN, CHILDREN & INFANT, WHOL: Handbags

Advance Tools LLC ................................. G ...... 855 685-0633
  Glenview *(G-11097)*

### CLOTHING & ACCESS, WOMEN, CHILDREN & INFANT, WHOL: Uniforms

Chicago Knitting Mills ............................. G ...... 773 463-1464
  Chicago *(G-4326)*

### CLOTHING & ACCESS, WOMEN, CHILDREN/INFANT, WHOL: Outerwear

All In Stitches ......................................... G ...... 309 944-4084
  Geneseo *(G-10796)*
Summit Graphics Inc .............................. F ...... 309 799-5100
  Moline *(G-14973)*

### CLOTHING & ACCESS: Costumes, Lodge

Akshar Limited ........................................ G ...... 815 942-1433
  Morris *(G-15091)*

### CLOTHING & ACCESS: Costumes, Masquerade

Fanfest Corporation ................................ G ...... 847 658-2000
  Crystal Lake *(G-7576)*
Zagone Studio Inc ................................... E ...... 773 509-0610
  Melrose Park *(G-14713)*

### CLOTHING & ACCESS: Costumes, Theatrical

Custom & Hard To Find Wigs ................. F ...... 773 777-0222
  Chicago *(G-4519)*
Facemakers Inc ....................................... F ...... 815 273-3944
  Savanna *(G-19398)*
Facemakers Inc ....................................... E ...... 815 273-3944
  Savanna *(G-19399)*

### CLOTHING & ACCESS: Garters

Wedding Brand Investors LLC .............. E ...... 847 887-0071
  Wauconda *(G-21513)*

### CLOTHING & ACCESS: Handicapped

Roq Innovation LLC ................................ G ...... 917 770-2403
  Chicago *(G-6392)*

### CLOTHING & ACCESS: Hospital Gowns

Baxter Healthcare Corporation ............... E ...... 847 578-4671
  Waukegan *(G-21529)*

### CLOTHING & ACCESS: Men's Miscellaneous Access

Allen Larson ............................................ G ...... 773 454-2210
  Chicago *(G-3811)*
Bazaar Inc ............................................... D ...... 708 583-1800
  River Grove *(G-18006)*
Chicago Harley Davidson Inc ................. G ...... 312 274-9666
  Chicago *(G-4322)*
Chicago Protective Apparel Inc ............. D ...... 847 674-7900
  Skokie *(G-19980)*
Daniel Bruce LLC .................................... F ...... 917 583-1538
  Palatine *(G-17019)*
Demoulin Brothers & Company .............. E ...... 618 533-3810
  Centralia *(G-3411)*
Gennco International Inc ........................ F ...... 847 541-3333
  Wheeling *(G-22062)*
K&G Mens Company Inc ......................... G ...... 708 349-2579
  Orland Park *(G-16871)*
New York & Company Inc ....................... F ...... 630 232-7693
  Geneva *(G-10853)*
New York & Company Inc ....................... F ...... 630 783-2910
  Bolingbrook *(G-2352)*
Nu-Life Inc of Illinois .............................. G ...... 618 943-4500
  Lawrenceville *(G-13203)*
Sieden Sticker USA Ltd .......................... G ...... 312 280-7711
  Chicago *(G-6505)*

### CLOTHING & ACCESS: Regalia

Pollack Service ....................................... D ...... 773 528-8096
  Chicago *(G-6149)*

### CLOTHING & APPAREL STORES: Custom

AM Harper Products Inc ........................ F ...... 312 767-8283
  Chicago *(G-3841)*
American Enlightenment LLC ................ G ...... 773 687-8996
  Chicago *(G-3856)*
American Outfitters Ltd ......................... E ...... 847 623-3959
  Waukegan *(G-21524)*
Fast Lane Threads Custom EMB ........... G ...... 815 544-9898
  Belvidere *(G-1751)*

### CLOTHING & FURNISHINGS, MEN'S & BOYS', WHOLESALE: Shirts

Go Van Goghs Tee Shirt ......................... G ...... 309 342-1112
  Galesburg *(G-10755)*
Screen Machine Incorporated ................ G ...... 847 439-2233
  Elk Grove Village *(G-9732)*

### CLOTHING & FURNISHINGS, MEN'S & BOYS', WHOLESALE: Umbrellas

Shedrain Corporation ............................. G ...... 708 848-5212
  Oak Park *(G-16685)*

### CLOTHING & FURNISHINGS, MEN'S & BOYS', WHOLESALE: Uniforms

Chicago Knitting Mills ............................ G ...... 773 463-1464
  Chicago *(G-4326)*
Compu-Tap Inc ........................................ G ...... 708 594-5773
  Summit Argo *(G-20761)*
High Performance Entp Inc .................... E ...... 773 283-1778
  Chicago *(G-5087)*
Vertex International Inc ......................... G ...... 312 242-1864
  Oak Brook *(G-16568)*

### CLOTHING & FURNISHINGS, MENS & BOYS, WHOL: Sportswear/Work

Athllete LLC ............................................ F ...... 773 829-3752
  Bolingbrook *(G-2279)*
Select Screen Prints & EMB ................... F ...... 309 829-6511
  Bloomington *(G-2222)*

### CLOTHING & FURNISHINGS, MENS & BOYS, WHOLESALE: Apprl Belts

Continent Corp ........................................ G ...... 773 733-1584
  Bolingbrook *(G-2287)*
Randa Accessories Lea Gds LLC .......... D ...... 847 292-8300
  Rosemont *(G-19026)*

### CLOTHING & FURNISHINGS, MENS & BOYS, WHOLESALE: Lined

Loren Girovich ........................................ G ...... 773 334-1444
  Chicago *(G-5541)*

Employee Codes: A=Over 500 employees, B=251-500
C=101-250, D=51-100, E=20-50, F=10-19, G=3-9

# CLOTHING STORES, NEC

## CLOTHING STORES, NEC

Mjt Design and Prtg Entps Inc .............. G ...... 708 240-4323
 Hillside *(G-11926)*

## CLOTHING STORES: Formal Wear

Duckys Formal Wear Inc ...................... G ...... 309 342-5914
 Galesburg *(G-10748)*
Winning Stitch ...................................... G ...... 217 348-8279
 Charleston *(G-3616)*

## CLOTHING STORES: Shirts, Custom Made

Go Van Goghs Tee Shirt ....................... G ...... 309 342-1112
 Galesburg *(G-10755)*

## CLOTHING STORES: T-Shirts, Printed, Custom

Academy Screenprinting Awards ........ G ...... 309 686-0026
 Peoria *(G-17300)*
Camilles of Canton Inc ........................ G ...... 309 647-7403
 Canton *(G-2983)*
Dbp Communications Inc .................... G ...... 312 263-1569
 Chicago *(G-4566)*
Dean Patterson ................................... G ...... 708 430-0477
 Bridgeview *(G-2482)*
Fellowship Black Light ........................ G ...... 773 826-7790
 Chicago *(G-4834)*
High-5 Printwear Inc ........................... G ...... 847 818-0081
 Arlington Heights *(G-765)*
Hole In The Wall Screen Arts ............... G ...... 217 243-9100
 Jacksonville *(G-12391)*
M & P Talking Tees Inc ........................ F ...... 262 495-4000
 Round Lake Beach *(G-19077)*
Mjt Design and Prtg Entps Inc ............ G ...... 708 240-4323
 Hillside *(G-11926)*
Select Screen Prints & EMB ................. F ...... 309 829-6511
 Bloomington *(G-2222)*
Teds Shirt Shack Inc ............................ G ...... 217 224-9705
 Quincy *(G-17892)*

## CLOTHING STORES: Unisex

Elan Furs ............................................... F ...... 317 255-6100
 Morton Grove *(G-15195)*
No Surrender Inc .................................. G ...... 773 929-7920
 Chicago *(G-5920)*
Z A W Collections ................................ G ...... 773 568-2031
 Chicago *(G-7056)*

## CLOTHING STORES: Work

Illinois Glove Company ........................ G ...... 800 342-5458
 Northbrook *(G-16272)*
Magid Glove Safety Mfg Co LLC ......... B ...... 773 384-2070
 Romeoville *(G-18841)*
Mennon Rubber & Safety Pdts ............ G ...... 847 678-8250
 Schiller Park *(G-19849)*

## CLOTHING/ACCESS, WOMEN, CHILDREN/INFANT, WHOL: Apparel Belt

Continent Corp .................................... G ...... 773 733-1584
 Bolingbrook *(G-2287)*

## CLOTHING: Academic Vestments

Herff Jones LLC .................................. C ...... 217 268-4543
 Arcola *(G-670)*
Herff Jones LLC .................................. C ...... 317 612-3705
 Hillside *(G-11918)*

## CLOTHING: Access

Andrea and ME and ME Too ................ G ...... 708 955-3850
 Richton Park *(G-17976)*
Browns Global Exchange ..................... D ...... 708 345-0955
 Maywood *(G-14421)*
Phoebe & Frances ............................... F ...... 847 446-5480
 Winnetka *(G-22314)*
Songear Holding Company LLC ........... G ...... 630 699-1119
 Elmhurst *(G-9939)*
Wish Collection ................................... G ...... 205 324-0209
 Chicago *(G-7007)*

## CLOTHING: Access, Women's & Misses'

Daniel Bruce LLC ................................. F ...... 917 583-1538
 Palatine *(G-17019)*
Doughman Don & Assoc ..................... G ...... 312 321-1011
 Chicago *(G-4636)*

Its A Girl Thing ..................................... F ...... 630 232-2778
 Geneva *(G-10840)*
Jenny Capp Co ..................................... F ...... 773 217-0057
 Chicago *(G-5291)*
Pola Company ..................................... G ...... 847 470-1182
 Niles *(G-16020)*

## CLOTHING: Anklets & Socks

Felice Hosiery Company Inc ................ E ...... 312 922-3710
 Chicago *(G-4833)*

## CLOTHING: Aprons, Exc Rubber/Plastic, Women, Misses, Junior

Quincy Specialties Company ............... G ...... 217 222-4057
 Quincy *(G-17881)*

## CLOTHING: Aprons, Harness

Rock Tops Inc ...................................... G ...... 708 672-1450
 Crete *(G-7518)*

## CLOTHING: Aprons, Waterproof, From Purchased Materials

Petra Manufacturing Co ....................... D ...... 773 622-1475
 Chicago *(G-6113)*

## CLOTHING: Aprons, Work, Exc Rubberized & Plastic, Men's

Quincy Specialties Company ............... G ...... 217 222-4057
 Quincy *(G-17881)*

## CLOTHING: Athletic & Sportswear, Men's & Boys'

Athllete LLC ......................................... F ...... 773 829-3752
 Bolingbrook *(G-2279)*
Bell Sports .......................................... G ...... 309 693-2746
 Rantoul *(G-17919)*
BMW Sportswear Inc .......................... G ...... 773 265-0110
 Chicago *(G-4133)*
Choi Brands Inc ................................... G ...... 773 489-2800
 Chicago *(G-4368)*
Cloz Companies Inc ............................ E ...... 773 247-8879
 Skokie *(G-19983)*
Columbia Sportswear Company .......... C ...... 312 649-3758
 Chicago *(G-4432)*
Express LLC ........................................ E ...... 708 453-0566
 Norridge *(G-16101)*
Jtoor LLC ............................................. G ...... 312 291-8249
 Chicago *(G-5334)*
M Handelsman & Co ........................... F ...... 312 427-0784
 Chicago *(G-5581)*
Pro Image ........................................... G ...... 708 422-7471
 Chicago Ridge *(G-7155)*
Tfo Group LLC .................................... G ...... 608 469-7519
 Chicago *(G-6709)*

## CLOTHING: Athletic & Sportswear, Women's & Girls'

Athllete LLC ......................................... F ...... 773 829-3752
 Bolingbrook *(G-2279)*
Custom By Lamar Inc .......................... F ...... 312 738-2160
 Chicago *(G-4520)*
Laqueus Inc ......................................... F ...... 773 508-1993
 Chicago *(G-5460)*
Srh Holdings Inc ................................. G ...... 847 583-2295
 Niles *(G-16037)*

## CLOTHING: Baker, Barber, Lab/Svc Ind Apparel, Washable, Men

V-Tex Inc ............................................. E ...... 847 325-4140
 Buffalo Grove *(G-2787)*
Woolenwear Co ................................... F ...... 847 520-9243
 Prospect Heights *(G-17786)*

## CLOTHING: Band Uniforms

Demoulin Brothers & Company ........... C ...... 618 664-2000
 Greenville *(G-11391)*

## CLOTHING: Bathing Suits & Swimwear, Girls, Children & Infant

Goldfish Swim School Lincoln ............. E ...... 773 588-7946
 Chicago *(G-4975)*

## CLOTHING: Bathing Suits & Swimwear, Knit

The Lifeguard Store Inc ....................... G ...... 630 548-5500
 Naperville *(G-15764)*

## CLOTHING: Bathrobes, Mens & Womens, From Purchased Materials

Telegraph Hill Inc ................................ G ...... 415 252-9097
 Vernon Hills *(G-21207)*

## CLOTHING: Belts

Loren Girovich .................................... G ...... 773 334-1444
 Chicago *(G-5541)*

## CLOTHING: Bibs, Waterproof, From Purchased Materials

Ryan Products Inc ............................... G ...... 847 670-9071
 Arlington Heights *(G-833)*

## CLOTHING: Blouses, Women's & Girls'

Apparel Works Intl LLC ....................... G ...... 224 235-4240
 Lake Bluff *(G-12832)*
Dyna Comp Inc .................................... G ...... 815 455-5570
 Crystal Lake *(G-7568)*
Joriki LLC ............................................ G ...... 312 848-1136
 Chicago *(G-5325)*
Yolanda Lorente Ltd ............................ E ...... 773 334-4536
 Chicago *(G-7053)*

## CLOTHING: Blouses, Womens & Juniors, From Purchased Mtrls

Besleys Accessories Inc ...................... G ...... 773 561-3300
 Chicago *(G-4089)*

## CLOTHING: Bras & Corsets, Maternity

Golda Inc ............................................. G ...... 217 895-3602
 Neoga *(G-15858)*

## CLOTHING: Bridal Gowns

Best Kept Secrets ................................ G ...... 773 431-0353
 Blue Island *(G-2238)*
Doris Bridal Boutique .......................... G ...... 847 433-2575
 Highwood *(G-11884)*

## CLOTHING: Buntings, Infants'

Moonbeam Babies ............................... G ...... 847 245-7371
 Lindenhurst *(G-13548)*

## CLOTHING: Capes, Exc Fur/Rubber, Womens, Misses & Juniors

Mademoiselle Inc ................................ F ...... 773 394-4555
 Chicago *(G-5596)*

## CLOTHING: Caps, Baseball

Bee Sales Comapny ............................ D ...... 847 600-4400
 Niles *(G-15965)*
Bxb Intl Inc ......................................... G ...... 312 240-1966
 Brookfield *(G-2626)*

## CLOTHING: Children & Infants'

Carters Inc .......................................... G ...... 708 345-6680
 Melrose Park *(G-14605)*
Dino Design Incorporated ................... G ...... 773 763-4223
 Chicago *(G-4606)*

## CLOTHING: Children's, Girls'

Bee Sales Comapny ............................ D ...... 847 600-4400
 Niles *(G-15965)*
Cloz Companies Inc ............................ E ...... 773 247-8879
 Skokie *(G-19983)*
Elite Kids ............................................. G ...... 815 451-9600
 Crystal Lake *(G-7572)*
Lauren Lein Ltd ................................... E ...... 312 527-1714
 Chicago *(G-5468)*
Laurenceleste Inc ................................ G ...... 708 383-3432
 Oak Park *(G-16674)*
Little Journeys Limited ........................ G ...... 847 677-0350
 Skokie *(G-20030)*
Slick Sugar Inc .................................... G ...... 815 782-7101
 Plainfield *(G-17649)*

# PRODUCT SECTION

## CLOTHING: Shirts, Dress, Men's & Boys'

### CLOTHING: Clergy Vestments
American Church Supply .................. G ...... 847 464-4140
Saint Charles *(G-19134)*

### CLOTHING: Coats & Jackets, Leather & Sheep-Lined
Excelled Sheepskin & Lea Coat ........... C ...... 309 852-3341
Kewanee *(G-12682)*
Excelled Sheepskin & Lea Coat ........... E ...... 309 852-3341
Kewanee *(G-12683)*

### CLOTHING: Coats & Suits, Men's & Boys'
Demoulin Brothers & Company ........... C ...... 618 664-2000
Greenville *(G-11391)*
Excelled Sheepskin & Lea Coat ........... C ...... 309 852-3341
Kewanee *(G-12682)*

### CLOTHING: Coats, Overcoats & Vests
Pro-Pak Industries Inc ...................... F ...... 630 876-1050
West Chicago *(G-21761)*

### CLOTHING: Cold Weather Knit Outerwear, Including Ski Wear
Five Brother Inc ............................... G ...... 309 663-6323
Bloomington *(G-2164)*

### CLOTHING: Collar & Cuff Sets, Knit
Bird Dog Bay Inc ............................. G ...... 312 631-3108
Chicago *(G-4111)*

### CLOTHING: Costumes
Andy Dallas & Co ............................. F ...... 217 351-5974
Champaign *(G-3450)*
Learning Curve International ............. E ...... 630 573-7200
Oak Brook *(G-16533)*
Orr Marketing Corp .......................... F ...... 847 401-5171
Elgin *(G-9130)*
Sunnywood Incorporated .................. G ...... 815 675-9777
Spring Grove *(G-20366)*

### CLOTHING: Disposable
Jero Medical Eqp & Sups Inc .............. E ...... 773 305-4193
Chicago *(G-5295)*
Taitt Burial Garments ....................... F ...... 773 483-7424
Chicago *(G-6667)*

### CLOTHING: Down-Filled, Men's & Boys'
Custom By Lamar Inc ....................... F ...... 312 738-2160
Chicago *(G-4520)*

### CLOTHING: Dresses
Caroline Rose Inc ............................. G ...... 708 386-1011
Oak Park *(G-16656)*
Chicago Bridal Store Inc .................... G ...... 773 445-4450
Chicago *(G-4308)*
Donna Karan Company LLC ............... C ...... 630 236-8900
Aurora *(G-996)*
Salmons and Brown .......................... G ...... 312 929-6756
Chicago *(G-6434)*
Yolanda Lorente Ltd ......................... E ...... 773 334-4536
Chicago *(G-7053)*

### CLOTHING: Furs
Excelled Sheepskin & Lea Coat ........... E ...... 309 852-3341
Kewanee *(G-12683)*

### CLOTHING: Garments, Indl, Men's & Boys
Apparel Works Intl LLC ..................... G ...... 224 235-4240
Lake Bluff *(G-12832)*
Rubin Brothers Inc ........................... E ...... 312 942-1111
Chicago *(G-6411)*

### CLOTHING: Gowns & Dresses, Wedding
Alyce Designs Inc ............................. E ...... 847 966-6933
Morton Grove *(G-15187)*
Casa Di Castronovo Inc ..................... G ...... 815 962-4731
Rockford *(G-18299)*
Chicagostyle Weddings ..................... G ...... 847 584-2626
Elk Grove Village *(G-9371)*
Halanick Enterprises Inc .................... E ...... 708 403-3334
Orland Park *(G-16864)*

Igar Bridal Inc .................................. G ...... 224 318-2337
Arlington Heights *(G-772)*
Jane Stodden Bridals ........................ G ...... 815 223-2091
La Salle *(G-12779)*
Matthew Christopher Inc .................. G ...... 212 938-6820
Batavia *(G-1468)*
Mom Dad & ME ................................ G ...... 773 735-9606
Chicago *(G-5791)*
Prestige Wedding Decoration ............. G ...... 847 845-0901
Arlington Heights *(G-820)*
SASI Corporation ............................. E ...... 314 922-7432
Collinsville *(G-7340)*
Urban Outfitters Inc ......................... G ...... 312 573-2573
Chicago *(G-6848)*

### CLOTHING: Gowns, Plastic
Drug Testing Suppliers Inc ................. G ...... 618 208-3810
Godfrey *(G-11224)*
Polyconversions Inc .......................... E ...... 217 893-3330
Rantoul *(G-17935)*

### CLOTHING: Hats & Caps, NEC
American Needle Inc ......................... E ...... 847 215-0011
Buffalo Grove *(G-2657)*
Choice Cap Inc ................................. G ...... 847 588-3443
Niles *(G-15968)*
Hats For You ................................... G ...... 773 481-1611
Chicago *(G-5054)*
Lids Corporation .............................. G ...... 708 873-9606
Orland Park *(G-16873)*

### CLOTHING: Hats & Caps, Police
Midway Cap Company ...................... E ...... 773 384-0911
Chicago *(G-5736)*

### CLOTHING: Hats & Caps, Uniform
Midway Cap Company ...................... E ...... 773 384-0911
Chicago *(G-5737)*

### CLOTHING: Hats & Headwear, Knit
A&B Apparel .................................... G ...... 815 962-5070
Rockford *(G-18241)*

### CLOTHING: Hats, Silk
Jenny Capp Co ................................. F ...... 773 217-0057
Chicago *(G-5291)*

### CLOTHING: Hosiery, Pantyhose & Knee Length, Sheer
Bee Sales Comapny ........................... D ...... 847 600-4400
Niles *(G-15965)*

### CLOTHING: Hospital, Men's
Cintas Corporation ........................... D ...... 708 563-2626
Chicago *(G-4379)*
Gelscrubs ........................................ G ...... 312 243-4612
Chicago *(G-4922)*
Iguanamed LLC ................................ G ...... 312 546-4182
Chicago *(G-5148)*

### CLOTHING: Jackets, Field, Military
Vertex International Inc .................... G ...... 312 242-1864
Oak Brook *(G-16568)*

### CLOTHING: Jackets, Tailored Men's & Boys'
Signature Design & Tailoring .............. F ...... 773 375-4915
Chicago *(G-6510)*

### CLOTHING: Jeans, Men's & Boys'
Guess Inc ........................................ E ...... 312 440-9592
Chicago *(G-5009)*
Lucky Brand Dungarees LLC .............. E ...... 847 550-1647
Deer Park *(G-7972)*

### CLOTHING: Jerseys, Knit
Russell Brands LLC ........................... D ...... 309 454-6737
Normal *(G-16087)*

### CLOTHING: Leather & sheep-lined clothing
Keleen Leathers Inc .......................... F ...... 630 590-5300
Westmont *(G-21898)*

### CLOTHING: Maternity
Golda Inc ........................................ C ...... 217 895-3602
Neoga *(G-15858)*
Second Child ................................... G ...... 773 883-0880
Chicago *(G-6468)*

### CLOTHING: Men's & boy's clothing, nec
Kims Menswear Ltd .......................... G ...... 773 373-2237
Chicago *(G-5385)*
Sansabelt ........................................ G ...... 312 357-5119
Chicago *(G-6440)*

### CLOTHING: Neckwear
Lee Allison Company Inc ................... G ...... 773 276-7172
Chicago *(G-5482)*

### CLOTHING: Outerwear, Knit
Heartfelt Gifts Inc ............................ G ...... 309 852-2296
Kewanee *(G-12690)*

### CLOTHING: Outerwear, Lthr, Wool/Down-Filled, Men, Youth/Boy
Independence Inc ............................. G ...... 312 675-2105
Chicago *(G-5172)*
Vmr Chicago LLC .............................. F ...... 312 649-6673
Chicago *(G-6911)*

### CLOTHING: Outerwear, Women's & Misses' NEC
Anart Inc ........................................ E ...... 708 447-0225
Riverside *(G-18028)*
Chicago Knitting Mills ....................... G ...... 773 463-1464
Chicago *(G-4326)*
Cintas Corporation ........................... D ...... 708 563-2626
Chicago *(G-4379)*
Cloz Companies Inc .......................... E ...... 773 247-8879
Skokie *(G-19983)*
Demoulin Brothers & Company ........... C ...... 618 664-2000
Greenville *(G-11391)*
Fashahnn Corporation ....................... G ...... 773 994-3132
Chicago *(G-4814)*
Gennco International Inc ................... F ...... 847 541-3333
Wheeling *(G-22062)*
Lauren Lein Ltd ................................ E ...... 312 527-1714
Chicago *(G-5468)*
Little Journeys Limited ..................... G ...... 847 677-0350
Skokie *(G-20030)*
Marena Marena Two Inc .................... G ...... 773 327-0619
Chicago *(G-5614)*
Paul Sisti ........................................ G ...... 773 472-5615
Chicago *(G-6091)*
Yolanda Lorente Ltd ......................... E ...... 773 334-4536
Chicago *(G-7053)*

### CLOTHING: Robes & Dressing Gowns
Halanick Enterprises Inc .................... E ...... 708 403-3334
Orland Park *(G-16864)*
Herff Jones LLC ................................ C ...... 317 612-3705
Hillside *(G-11918)*
Maries Custom Made Choir Robes ...... G ...... 773 826-1214
Chicago *(G-5618)*

### CLOTHING: Service Apparel, Women's
Woolenwear Co ................................ F ...... 847 520-9243
Prospect Heights *(G-17786)*

### CLOTHING: Shirts
Dyna Comp Inc ................................ G ...... 815 455-5570
Crystal Lake *(G-7568)*
Riddle McIntyre Inc .......................... G ...... 312 782-3317
Chicago *(G-6355)*
Salmons and Brown .......................... G ...... 312 929-6756
Chicago *(G-6434)*

### CLOTHING: Shirts & T-Shirts, Knit
Inkn Tees ........................................ G ...... 847 244-2266
Waukegan *(G-21570)*
Top Ace Inc ..................................... G ...... 847 581-0550
Morton Grove *(G-15241)*

### CLOTHING: Shirts, Dress, Men's & Boys'
Pvh Corp ........................................ F ...... 217 253-3398
Tuscola *(G-21022)*

Employee Codes: A=Over 500 employees, B=251-500
C=101-250, D=51-100, E=20-50, F=10-19, G=3-9

## CLOTHING: Shirts, Dress, Men's & Boys'

Pvh Corp ..................................... G ...... 630 898-7718
Aurora (G-1071)

### CLOTHING: Shirts, Sports & Polo, Men's & Boys'

Drywear Apparel LLC ............... G ...... 847 687-8540
Kildeer (G-12699)

### CLOTHING: Shirts, Uniform, From Purchased Materials

Silk Screen Express Inc ............ F ...... 708 845-5600
Tinley Park (G-20945)

### CLOTHING: Socks

Bee Sales Comapny ................... D ...... 847 600-4400
Niles (G-15965)
Emeelys Socks and More ......... G ...... 847 529-3026
Chicago (G-4738)
Four White Socks LLC .............. G ...... 312 257-6456
Chicago (G-4879)
Living Royal ............................... F ...... 312 906-7600
Wheeling (G-22096)
Midwest Socks LLC ................... G ...... 773 283-3952
Chicago (G-5749)
Quincy Socks House .................. G ...... 217 506-6106
Quincy (G-17880)
Soy City Sock Co Inc ................. F ...... 217 762-2157
Monticello (G-15085)
Your Team Socks ....................... G ...... 309 713-1044
Peoria (G-17479)

### CLOTHING: Sportswear, Women's

Caroline Rose Inc ....................... G ...... 708 386-1011
Oak Park (G-16656)
Lululemon USA Inc .................... G ...... 773 227-1869
Chicago (G-5560)
Nguyen Chau .............................. G ...... 773 506-1066
Chicago (G-5909)

### CLOTHING: Suits, Men's & Boys', From Purchased Materials

Mancillas International Ltd ......... F ...... 847 441-7748
Winnetka (G-22311)
Oxxford Clothes Xx Inc .............. C ...... 312 829-3600
Chicago (G-6034)

### CLOTHING: Sweaters & Sweater Coats, Knit

Chicago Knitting Mills ................. G ...... 773 463-1464
Chicago (G-4326)
Denise Allen Robinson Inc ......... F ...... 773 275-8080
Chicago (G-4582)
Sue Peterson .............................. G ...... 847 730-3035
Glenview (G-11207)

### CLOTHING: T-Shirts & Tops, Knit

Bxb Intl Inc .................................. G ...... 312 240-1966
Brookfield (G-2626)
Csi Chicago Inc .......................... G ...... 773 665-2226
Chicago (G-4511)
Derbyteescom ............................ G ...... 309 264-1033
Henry (G-11739)
M & G Simplicitees ..................... G ...... 224 372-7426
Lake Villa (G-13018)
Main Street Records .................. G ...... 618 244-2737
Mount Vernon (G-15424)
Mr T Shirt and Dollar Plus ......... G ...... 708 596-9150
Harvey (G-11674)
NRR Corp ................................... F ...... 630 915-8388
Oak Brook (G-16550)
Rfq LLC ...................................... G ...... 815 893-6656
Crystal Lake (G-7640)
Yetee LLC ................................... G ...... 630 340-0132
Aurora (G-1236)

### CLOTHING: T-Shirts & Tops, Women's & Girls'

Forever Fly LLC .......................... G ...... 312 981-9161
Chicago (G-4873)

### CLOTHING: Ties, Neck, Men's & Boys', From Purchased Material

Besleys Accessories Inc ............ G ...... 773 561-3300
Chicago (G-4089)

Corporate Textiles Inc ................ G ...... 847 433-4111
Lincolnwood (G-13505)

### CLOTHING: Trousers & Slacks, Men's & Boys'

Kanan Fashions Inc .................... E ...... 630 240-1234
Oak Brook (G-16530)
Oxxford Clothes Xx Inc .............. C ...... 312 829-3600
Chicago (G-6034)

### CLOTHING: Underwear, Women's & Children's

Maidenform LLC ......................... C ...... 630 898-8419
Aurora (G-1052)

### CLOTHING: Uniforms & Vestments

C H Millery LLC .......................... F ...... 773 476-7525
Chicago (G-4204)
Midwest Pub Safety Outfitters ... F ...... 866 985-0013
Poplar Grove (G-17714)
Nali Inc ....................................... E ...... 708 442-8710
Clarendon Hills (G-7259)

### CLOTHING: Uniforms, Ex Athletic, Women's, Misses' & Juniors'

Advance Uniform Company ....... F ...... 312 922-1797
Chicago (G-3765)
Atlas Uniform Company ............. G ...... 312 492-8527
Chicago (G-3985)
Choi Brands Inc ......................... C ...... 773 489-2800
Chicago (G-4368)
Cintas Corporation ..................... D ...... 708 563-2626
Chicago (G-4379)
Cintas Corporation No 2 ............ G ...... 708 424-4747
Oak Lawn (G-16612)
Iguanamed LLC .......................... G ...... 312 546-4182
Chicago (G-5148)

### CLOTHING: Uniforms, Men's & Boys'

Compu-Tap Inc ........................... G ...... 708 594-5773
Summit Argo (G-20761)

### CLOTHING: Uniforms, Military, Men/Youth, Purchased Materials

Vertex International Inc ............. G ...... 312 242-1864
Oak Brook (G-16568)

### CLOTHING: Uniforms, Policemen's, From Purchased Materials

J G Uniforms Inc ........................ G ...... 773 545-4644
Chicago (G-5259)

### CLOTHING: Uniforms, Team Athletic

Athletic Sewing Mfg Co .............. E ...... 773 589-0361
Chicago (G-3975)
Curt Smith Sporting Goods Inc .. E ...... 618 233-5177
Belleville (G-1621)
Exclusive Pro Sports Ltd ........... E ...... 815 877-8585
Rockford (G-18377)

### CLOTHING: Uniforms, Work

Advance Uniform Company ....... F ...... 312 922-1797
Chicago (G-3765)
Atlas Uniform Company ............. G ...... 312 492-8527
Chicago (G-3985)
Chicago Uniforms Company ...... E ...... 312 913-1006
Chicago (G-4361)
Choi Brands Inc ......................... C ...... 773 489-2800
Chicago (G-4368)
Cintas Corporation ..................... F ...... 708 424-4747
Oak Lawn (G-16611)
Federal Uniform LLC ................. G ...... 847 658-5470
Chicago (G-4823)
High Performance Entp Inc ....... E ...... 773 283-1778
Chicago (G-5087)

### CLOTHING: Warm Weather Knit Outerwear, Including Beachwear

Creative Clothing Created 4 U .. G ...... 847 543-0051
Grayslake (G-11330)

### CLOTHING: WarmUp, Jogging & Sweat Suits, Girls' & Children's

Trim Suits By Show-Off Inc ....... G ...... 630 894-0100
Roselle (G-18984)

### CLOTHING: Waterproof Outerwear

Boss Holdings Inc ...................... D ...... 309 852-2131
Kewanee (G-12673)
Boss Manufacturing Holdings .... F ...... 309 852-2781
Kewanee (G-12675)

### CLOTHING: Work Apparel, Exc Uniforms

G & P Products Inc .................... E ...... 708 442-9667
Lyons (G-14039)
K A & F Group LLC ................... G ...... 847 780-4600
Highland Park (G-11848)

### CLOTHING: Work, Men's

Ai Ind .......................................... E ...... 773 265-6640
Chicago (G-3784)
Compu-Tap Inc ........................... G ...... 708 594-5773
Summit Argo (G-20761)
Demoulin Brothers & Company .. C ...... 618 664-2000
Greenville (G-11391)
Harris Clothing & Uniforms Inc .. F ...... 309 671-4543
Peoria (G-17380)
Magid Glove Safety Mfg Co LLC . B ...... 773 384-2070
Romeoville (G-18841)
Mennon Rubber & Safety Pdts .. G ...... 847 678-8250
Schiller Park (G-19849)
Mighty Mites Awards and Sons . G ...... 847 297-0035
Des Plaines (G-8233)
Standard Safety Equipment Co . E ...... 815 363-8565
McHenry (G-14556)
Universal Overall Company ....... E ...... 312 226-3336
Chicago (G-6834)
W Diamond Group Corporation . A ...... 646 647-2791
Des Plaines (G-8301)

### CLUTCHES, EXC VEHICULAR

Dyneer Corporation .................... B ...... 217 228-6011
Quincy (G-17823)
Marland Clutch ........................... G ...... 800 216-3515
South Beloit (G-20157)
Ringspann Corporation .............. F ...... 847 678-3581
Franklin Park (G-10575)

### COAL MINING EXPLORATION & TEST BORING SVC

Freeman United Coal Mining Co . E ...... 217 698-3300
Springfield (G-20443)
Keyrock Energy LLC .................. E ...... 618 982-9710
Thompsonville (G-20862)

### COAL MINING SERVICES

Coal Field Development Co ....... G ...... 630 653-3700
Carol Stream (G-3131)
Cobra Coal Inc ........................... E ...... 630 560-1050
West Chicago (G-21684)
Exxon Mobil Corporation ........... B ...... 217 854-3291
Carlinville (G-3038)
Fjcj LLC ...................................... F ...... 618 785-2217
Baldwin (G-1250)
Fred Hutson Mineral Products ... G ...... 618 994-4383
Harrisburg (G-11599)
Freeman Energy Corporation .... F ...... 217 698-3949
Springfield (G-20442)
Freeman United Coal Mining Co . C ...... 217 627-2161
Girard (G-10945)
Hamilton County Coal LLC ....... B ...... 618 648-2603
Dahlgren (G-7690)
Icg Illinois .................................... G ...... 217 947-2332
Elkhart (G-9825)
Icg Illinois LLC ........................... F ...... 217 566-3000
Williamsville (G-22191)
Knight Hawk Coal LLC .............. G ...... 618 426-3662
Percy (G-17495)
Knight Hawk Coal LLC .............. C ...... 618 497-2768
Cutler (G-7687)
Mach Mining LLC ....................... G ...... 618 983-3020
Marion (G-14271)
Macoupin Energy LLC ............... F ...... 217 854-3291
Carlinville (G-3043)
Macoupin Energy LLC ............... C ...... 217 854-3291
Carlinville (G-3044)

# PRODUCT SECTION

## COATING SVC: Metals, With Plastic Or Resins

Peabody Arclar Mining LLC .................G....... 618 273-4314
  Equality (G-9989)
Suncoke Energy Inc.............................B....... 630 824-1000
  Lisle (G-13666)
Surface Mining Reclamation Off...........E....... 618 463-6460
  Alton (G-591)
White Oak Resources LLC....................A....... 618 643-5500
  Dahlgren (G-7693)
Wildcat Hills........................................G....... 618 273-8600
  Eldorado (G-8926)

### COAL MINING SVCS: Anthracite, Contract Basis

Seneca Rebuild LLC ............................F....... 618 435-9445
  Macedonia (G-14047)

### COAL MINING SVCS: Bituminous, Contract Basis

Williamson Energy LLC........................E....... 618 983-3020
  Marion (G-14295)

### COAL MINING: Anthracite

Jii Holdings LLC..................................G....... 847 945-5591
  Deerfield (G-8018)

### COAL MINING: Anthracite, Underground

Fabick Mining LLC..............................F....... 618 982-9000
  Norris City (G-16114)

### COAL MINING: Bituminous Coal & Lignite-Surface Mining

Alpha Natural Resources Inc ...............C....... 618 298-2394
  Keensburg (G-12660)
Hillsboro Energy LLC...........................G....... 217 532-3983
  Hillsboro (G-11894)
Hnrc Dissolution Co ............................C....... 618 758-4501
  Coulterville (G-7400)
Keller Group Inc .................................B....... 847 446-7550
  Northfield (G-16405)
Material Service Resources ................D....... 630 325-7736
  Chicago (G-5651)
Peabody Midwest Mining LLC .............C....... 618 276-5006
  Equality (G-9990)
Standard Laboratories Inc ...................E....... 618 539-5836
  Freeburg (G-10642)
Sun Coke International Inc..................D....... 630 824-1000
  Lisle (G-13665)

### COAL MINING: Bituminous Underground

Alpha Natural Resources Inc ...............C....... 618 298-2394
  Keensburg (G-12660)
American Coal Company .....................G....... 618 268-6311
  Galatia (G-10711)
Blue Blaze Coal Cpitl Resource............E....... 309 647-2000
  Canton (G-2982)
Exxon Mobil Corporation .....................B....... 217 854-3291
  Carlinville (G-3038)
Illinois Fuel Company LLC...................D....... 618 275-4486
  Herod (G-11747)
Jewell Resources Corporation .............G....... 276 935-8810
  Lisle (G-13610)
Keller Group Inc .................................B....... 847 446-7550
  Northfield (G-16405)
Knight Hawk Coal LLC ........................G....... 618 426-3662
  Percy (G-17495)
Peabody Coal Company ......................C....... 618 758-2395
  Coulterville (G-7402)
Sun Coke International Inc..................D....... 630 824-1000
  Lisle (G-13665)

### COAL MINING: Bituminous, Auger

Power Planter Inc...............................G....... 217 379-2614
  Loda (G-13754)

### COAL MINING: Bituminous, Strip

Blue Blaze Coal Cpitl Resource............E....... 309 647-2000
  Canton (G-2982)
Illinois Fuel Company LLC...................D....... 618 275-4486
  Herod (G-11747)
Jader Fuel Co Inc ...............................G....... 618 269-3101
  Shawneetown (G-19904)

### COAL MINING: Bituminous, Surface, NEC

White County Coal LLC .......................C....... 618 382-4651
  Carmi (G-3084)

### COAL PREPARATION PLANT: Bituminous or Lignite

Hickman Williams & Company .............F....... 708 656-8818
  Cicero (G-7202)

### COAL, MINERALS & ORES, WHOLESALE: Coal

Fricker Machine Shop & Salvage .........G....... 618 285-3271
  Elizabethtown (G-9245)

### COAL, MINERALS & ORES, WHOLESALE: Copper Ore

American Coal Company .....................G....... 618 268-6311
  Galatia (G-10711)

### COATED OR PLATED PRDTS

Archer Industries & Supplies ...............G....... 773 777-2698
  Chicago (G-3937)
Cobraa Inc ..........................................G....... 618 228-7380
  Aviston (G-1243)

### COATING COMPOUNDS: Tar

American Grinders Inc ........................E....... 815 943-4902
  Harvard (G-11620)
Brewer Company ................................F....... 708 339-9000
  Harvey (G-11662)
Sales Stretcher Enterprises ................F....... 815 223-9681
  Peru (G-17527)

### COATING OR WRAPPING SVC: Steel Pipe

Kobelco Advnced Cting Amer Inc ........A....... 847 520-6000
  Buffalo Grove (G-2717)

### COATING SVC

Aggressive Motorsports Inc .................G....... 847 846-7488
  Batavia (G-1406)
Ambrotos Inc ......................................G....... 815 355-8217
  Crystal Lake (G-7532)
Dt Metronic Inc ...................................G....... 847 593-0945
  Mount Prospect (G-15326)
Legend Dynamix Inc ...........................G....... 847 789-7007
  Antioch (G-641)
Midwest Nameplate Corp ....................G....... 708 614-0606
  Orland Park (G-16875)
Petersburg Power Washing Inc ...........G....... 217 415-9013
  Springfield (G-20504)

### COATING SVC: Aluminum, Metal Prdts

Chicago Anodizing Company ...............D....... 773 533-3737
  Chicago (G-4303)
Finishing Company..............................C....... 630 559-0808
  Addison (G-117)
Marie Gere Corporation .......................C....... 847 540-1154
  Lake Zurich (G-13099)
Micron Metal Finishing LLC ................E....... 708 599-0055
  Bridgeview (G-2508)
Voges Inc ...........................................D....... 618 233-2760
  Belleville (G-1688)

### COATING SVC: Hot Dip, Metals Or Formed Prdts

AAA Galvanizing - Joliet Inc ................E....... 815 284-5001
  Dixon (G-8321)
AAA Galvanizing - Joliet Inc ................D....... 815 723-5000
  Joliet (G-12449)
Rogers Brothers Co ............................. ....... 815 965-5132
  Rockford (G-18594)

### COATING SVC: Metals & Formed Prdts

Accent Metal Finishing Inc ..................F....... 847 678-7420
  Schiller Park (G-19798)
Advance Enameling Co .......................E....... 773 737-7356
  Chicago (G-3758)
Advanced Graphics Tech Inc ...............C....... 817 481-8561
  Darien (G-7787)
Applied Thermal Coatings ...................F....... 815 372-4305
  Romeoville (G-18799)

### COATING SVC: Metals, With Plastic Or Resins

Armoloy of Illinois Inc .........................E....... 815 758-6657
  Dekalb (G-8075)
Chem Processing Inc ..........................D....... 815 874-8118
  Rockford (G-18305)
Chem Processing Inc ..........................F....... 815 965-1037
  Rockford (G-18306)
Core Finishing Inc ..............................D....... 630 521-9635
  Bensenville (G-1866)
Crosslink Coatings Corporation ...........G....... 815 467-7970
  Channahon (G-3568)
Curtis Metal Finishing Company ..........D....... 815 633-6693
  Machesney Park (G-14069)
Diamond Spray Painting Inc ................G....... 630 513-5600
  Saint Charles (G-19171)
Dover Industrial Chrome Inc ...............G....... 773 478-2022
  Chicago (G-4638)
Downey Investments Inc .....................B....... 708 345-8000
  Broadview (G-2572)
E & R Powder Coatings Inc .................E....... 773 523-9510
  Chicago (G-4664)
Enameled Steel and Sign Co ...............E....... 773 481-2270
  Chicago (G-4748)
Finishing Company..............................D....... 630 521-9635
  Bensenville (G-1898)
Joseph Kristan....................................G....... 847 731-3131
  Zion (G-22689)
Krueger and Company .........................E....... 630 833-5650
  Elmhurst (G-9899)
Kvf-Quad Corporation .........................F....... 563 529-1916
  East Moline (G-8683)
Lo-Ko Performance Coatings ...............G....... 708 424-7863
  Oak Lawn (G-16632)
Macon Metal Products Co ...................E....... 217 824-7205
  Taylorville (G-20842)
Metokote Corporation..........................E....... 815 223-1190
  Peru (G-17519)
Midwest Coatings Inc .........................G....... 815 717-8914
  New Lenox (G-15896)
MSC Pre Finish Metals Egv Inc ............C....... 847 439-2210
  Elk Grove Village (G-9640)
Oerlikon Blzers Cating USA Inc ...........F....... 847 619-5541
  Schaumburg (G-19673)
Oerlikon Blzers Cating USA Inc ........... ....... 847 695-5200
  Elgin (G-9127)
Omega Plating Inc ..............................F....... 708 389-5410
  Crestwood (G-7496)
Plastisol Products Inc .........................E....... 630 543-1770
  Addison (G-243)
Polaris Laser Laminations LLC ............G....... 630 444-0760
  West Chicago (G-21758)
Precoat Metals....................................D....... 618 451-0909
  Granite City (G-11300)
Progressive Coating Corp ....................F....... 773 261-8900
  Chicago (G-6212)
Rainbow Art Inc ..................................F....... 312 421-5600
  Chicago (G-6288)
Ro Pal Grinding Inc.............................F....... 815 964-5894
  Rockford (G-18561)
Sealtronix Inc ..................................... ....... 800 878-9864
  Franklin Park (G-10585)
Slipmate Co ........................................E....... 847 289-9200
  Elgin (G-9188)
Sub Source Inc ...................................E....... 815 968-7800
  Rockford (G-18637)
Superior Coating Corporation ..............E....... 815 544-3340
  Belvidere (G-1786)
Thomson Steel Polishing Corp.............G....... 773 586-2345
  Chicago (G-6720)
Transco Products Inc ..........................D....... 312 427-2818
  Chicago (G-6758)
Wear Cote International Inc ................E....... 309 793-1250
  Rock Island (G-18211)
Zegers Inc ..........................................F....... 708 474-7700
  Lansing (G-13193)

### COATING SVC: Metals, With Plastic Or Resins

ABC Coating Company Inc ..................E....... 708 258-9633
  Manteno (G-14180)
Amerigraphics Corp ............................G....... 630 543-9790
  Addison (G-39)
Britt Industries Inc .............................E....... 847 640-1177
  Arlington Heights (G-731)
Casting Impregnators Inc ...................F....... 847 455-1000
  Franklin Park (G-10425)
Clad-Rex Steel LLC .............................E....... 847 455-7373
  Franklin Park (G-10434)
Economic Plastic Coating Inc ..............F....... 708 343-2216
  Melrose Park (G-14627)

# COATING SVC: Metals, With Plastic Or Resins

Epscca .............................................. E ...... 815 568-3020
  Marengo *(G-14227)*
Jet Rack Corp .................................... E ...... 773 586-2150
  Chicago *(G-5298)*
Metal Impregnating Corp ................... G ...... 630 543-3443
  Addison *(G-200)*

## COATING SVC: Rust Preventative

Aqua Coat Inc .................................. G ...... 815 209-0808
  Elgin *(G-8955)*
Wheeling Service & Supply ................ F ...... 815 338-6410
  Woodstock *(G-22624)*

## COATING SVC: Silicon

D N D Coating .................................. G ...... 309 379-3021
  Stanford *(G-20551)*

## COATINGS: Air Curing

Hlh Associates .................................. F ...... 773 646-5900
  Chicago *(G-5092)*
Magnum International Inc ................. G ...... 708 889-9999
  Lansing *(G-13175)*
Mid-Amrica Prtctive Ctings Inc .......... G ...... 630 628-4501
  Addison *(G-210)*
Universal Chem & Coatings Inc ......... E ...... 847 931-1700
  Elgin *(G-9219)*

## COATINGS: Epoxy

BASF Construction Chem LLC ........... G ...... 847 249-4080
  Gurnee *(G-11431)*
Mla Franklin Park Inc ........................ F ...... 847 451-0279
  Franklin Park *(G-10536)*
Neverstrip LLC ................................ G ...... 708 588-9707
  Hinsdale *(G-11955)*

## COATINGS: Polyurethane

Agi Corp ........................................... F ...... 815 708-0502
  Loves Park *(G-13915)*
Polyurethane Products Corp .............. E ...... 630 543-6700
  Addison *(G-246)*

## COCKTAIL LOUNGE

Libertyville Brewing Company ........... D ...... 847 362-6688
  Libertyville *(G-13343)*
Rumshine Distilling LLC .................... G ...... 217 446-6960
  Tilton *(G-20882)*

## COIL WINDING SVC

Mid-America Taping Reeling Inc ........ D ...... 630 629-6646
  Glendale Heights *(G-11048)*
Pillarhouse USA Inc .......................... F ...... 847 593-9080
  Elk Grove Village *(G-9680)*

## COILS & ROD: Extruded, Aluminum

Kloeckner Metals Corporation ........... F ...... 773 646-6363
  Chicago *(G-5388)*
Peerless America Incorporated .......... C ...... 217 342-0400
  Effingham *(G-8853)*

## COILS & TRANSFORMERS

Actown-Electrocoil Inc ...................... G
  Spring Grove *(G-20324)*
Arnold Engineering Co ..................... D ...... 815 568-2000
  Marengo *(G-14218)*
AT&T Corp ....................................... F ...... 312 602-4108
  Chicago *(G-3972)*
Becker Specialty Corporation ............ F ...... 847 766-3555
  Elk Grove Village *(G-9336)*
Blocksmoy Inc .................................. F ...... 847 260-9070
  Franklin Park *(G-10413)*
Charles Industries Ltd ...................... D ...... 217 826-2318
  Marshall *(G-14319)*
Coilcraft Incorporated ...................... G ...... 815 879-4408
  Princeton *(G-17745)*
Coilform Company ........................... G ...... 630 232-8000
  Geneva *(G-10820)*
Communication Coil Inc .................... D ...... 847 671-1333
  Schiller Park *(G-19815)*
Eis .................................................. G ...... 630 530-7500
  Elmhurst *(G-9863)*
Ets-Lindgren Inc ............................... C ...... 630 307-7200
  Wood Dale *(G-22363)*
Forest Electric Company ................... E ...... 708 681-0180
  Melrose Park *(G-14639)*
Magnetic Devices Inc ....................... G ...... 815 459-0077
  Crystal Lake *(G-7605)*
Muntz Industries Inc ........................ E ...... 847 949-8280
  Mundelein *(G-15534)*
North Point Investments Inc ............. G ...... 312 977-4386
  Chicago *(G-5935)*
Permacor Inc ................................... E ...... 708 422-3353
  Oak Lawn *(G-16639)*
Power House Tool Inc ...................... E ...... 815 727-6301
  Joliet *(G-12552)*
Qcircuits Inc .................................... E ...... 618 662-8365
  Flora *(G-10214)*
Qse Inc ............................................ E ...... 815 432-5281
  Watseka *(G-21426)*
Santucci Enterprises ........................ G ...... 773 286-5629
  Chicago *(G-6442)*
Sigmatron International Inc .............. E ...... 847 586-5200
  Elgin *(G-9178)*
Sigmatron International Inc .............. E ...... 847 956-8000
  Elk Grove Village *(G-9737)*
STC Inc ........................................... E ...... 618 643-2555
  Mc Leansboro *(G-14468)*
Stryde Technologies Inc .................... E ...... 510 786-8890
  Evanston *(G-10096)*
Taycorp Inc ..................................... E ...... 630 530-7500
  Elmhurst *(G-9948)*
Taycorp Inc ..................................... E ...... 708 629-0921
  Alsip *(G-533)*
Transformer Manufacturers Inc ......... E ...... 708 457-1200
  Norridge *(G-16110)*
U S Co-Tronics Corp ......................... E ...... 815 692-3204
  Fairbury *(G-10134)*
V and F Transformer Corp ................ D ...... 630 497-8070
  Bartlett *(G-1384)*
Wattcore Inc .................................... E ...... 571 482-6777
  Morton Grove *(G-15245)*

## COILS, WIRE: Aluminum, Made In Rolling Mills

Ashland Aluminum Company Inc ....... F ...... 773 278-6440
  Chicago *(G-3961)*

## COILS: Electric Motors Or Generators

Calumet Armature and Elc LLC ......... E ...... 708 841-6880
  Riverdale *(G-18017)*
U S Co-Tronics Corp ......................... E ...... 815 692-3204
  Fairbury *(G-10134)*

## COILS: Pipe

Integrated Mfg Tech LLC .................. E ...... 618 282-8306
  Red Bud *(G-17943)*

## COIN COUNTERS

Pfingsten Partners LLC ..................... F ...... 312 222-8707
  Chicago *(G-6115)*

## COIN-OPERATED LAUNDRY

Lloyd M Hughes Enterprises Inc ........ G ...... 773 363-6331
  Chicago *(G-5527)*

## COINS & TOKENS: Non-Currency

Jing MEI Industrial USA Inc .............. E ...... 847 671-0800
  Rosemont *(G-19007)*

## COKE OVEN PRDTS: Beehive

Prairie Profile .................................. G ...... 618 846-2116
  Vandalia *(G-21120)*

## COKE: Petroleum

Oxbow Carbon LLC .......................... E ...... 630 257-7751
  Lemont *(G-13247)*
Oxbow Midwest Calcining LLC .......... D ...... 630 257-7751
  Lemont *(G-13248)*

## COKE: Petroleum & Coal Derivative

Raven Energy LLC ........................... G ...... 217 532-3983
  Hillsboro *(G-11899)*

## COKE: Petroleum, Not From Refineries

Koch Industries Inc .......................... E ...... 773 375-3700
  Chicago *(G-5395)*

## COLLECTION AGENCY, EXC REAL ESTATE

Manufctrers Claring Hse of Ill ............ G ...... 773 545-6300
  Chicago *(G-5609)*
Quadramed Corporation .................... E ...... 312 396-0700
  Chicago *(G-6240)*

## COLLECTOR RINGS: Electric Motors Or Generators

Fulling Motor USA Inc ...................... G ...... 847 894-6238
  Park Ridge *(G-17196)*

## COLLEGES, UNIVERSITIES & PROFESSIONAL SCHOOLS

Tanaka Dental Enterprises Inc ........... F ...... 847 679-1610
  Skokie *(G-20099)*

## COLOGNES

Givaudan Fragrances Corp ................ G ...... 847 735-0221
  Lake Forest *(G-12900)*

## COLOR LAKES OR TONERS

Discount Computer Supply Inc .......... G ...... 847 883-8743
  Buffalo Grove *(G-2688)*

## COLOR PIGMENTS

Accel Corporation ............................ E ...... 630 579-6961
  Batavia *(G-1402)*
Kasha Industries Inc ........................ E ...... 618 375-2511
  Grayville *(G-11372)*
Kasha Industries Inc ........................ F ...... 618 375-2511
  Grayville *(G-11373)*

## COLORING & FINISHING SVC: Aluminum Or Formed Prdts

Alton Industries Inc .......................... F ...... 708 865-2000
  Broadview *(G-2556)*

## COLORS IN OIL, EXC ARTISTS'

Finishing Company ........................... C ...... 630 559-0808
  Addison *(G-117)*

## COLORS: Pigments, Inorganic

Allegheny Color Corporation ............. E ...... 815 741-1391
  Rockdale *(G-18213)*
Chromium Industries Inc ................... E ...... 773 287-3716
  Chicago *(G-4373)*
Color Corporation of America ........... D ...... 815 987-3700
  Rockford *(G-18314)*
Colors For Plastics Inc ..................... G ...... 847 437-0033
  Elk Grove Village *(G-9381)*
Colors For Plastics Inc ..................... D ...... 847 437-0033
  Elk Grove Village *(G-9382)*
Fortune International Tech LLC ......... G ...... 847 429-9791
  Hoffman Estates *(G-12011)*
P M S Consolidated .......................... G ...... 847 364-0011
  Elk Grove Village *(G-9668)*
Plastics Color Corp Illinois ................ D ...... 708 868-3800
  Calumet City *(G-2950)*
Polyone Corporation ......................... D ...... 847 364-0011
  Elk Grove Village *(G-9686)*
Prince Minerals LLC ......................... G ...... 646 747-4222
  Quincy *(G-17873)*
Prince Minerals LLC ......................... G ...... 646 747-4200
  Quincy *(G-17874)*
Rust-Oleum Corporation ................... C ...... 847 367-7700
  Vernon Hills *(G-21195)*
Scientific Colors Inc ......................... F ...... 815 741-1391
  Rockdale *(G-18232)*
Solomon Colors Inc .......................... D ...... 217 522-3112
  Springfield *(G-20527)*
Toyal America Inc ............................ G ...... 630 505-2160
  Naperville *(G-15766)*
Toyal America Inc ............................ D ...... 815 740-3000
  Lockport *(G-13749)*
Valspar Corporation .......................... F ...... 815 962-9986
  Rockford *(G-18667)*
Versatile Materials Inc ...................... G ...... 773 924-3700
  Chicago *(G-6887)*

## COLORS: Pigments, Organic

Allegheny Color Corporation ............. E ...... 815 741-1391
  Rockdale *(G-18213)*

# PRODUCT SECTION

## COMMERCIAL PRINTING & NEWSPAPER PUBLISHING COMBINED

Apex Colors .......................................... G ...... 219 764-3301
  Chicago  (G-3921)
General Press Colors Ltd ....................... E ...... 630 543-7878
  Chicago  (G-4931)
HI Tech Colorants ................................. G ...... 630 762-0368
  Saint Charles  (G-19192)
Huntsman P&A Americas LLC ................ G ...... 618 646-2119
  East Saint Louis  (G-8755)
Nb Coatings Inc ................................... C ...... 800 323-3224
  Lansing  (G-13179)
Rite Systems East Inc ........................... E ...... 630 293-9174
  West Chicago  (G-21765)
Scientific Colors Inc ............................. F ...... 815 741-1391
  Rockdale  (G-18232)

### COLUMNS: Concrete

George Pagels Company ....................... G ...... 708 478-7036
  Mokena  (G-14867)

### COMFORTERS & QUILTS, FROM MANMADE FIBER OR SILK

Funquilts Inc ....................................... G ...... 708 445-9871
  Oak Park  (G-16665)

### COMMERCIAL & INDL SHELVING WHOLESALERS

Djr Inc ................................................ F ...... 773 581-5204
  Chicago  (G-4615)
Rwi Holdings Inc .................................. F ...... 630 897-6951
  Aurora  (G-1211)

### COMMERCIAL & OFFICE BUILDINGS RENOVATION & REPAIR

Pete Frcano Sons Cstm HM Bldrs ........... F ...... 847 258-4626
  Elk Grove Village  (G-9675)
Signa Development Group Inc ................ G ...... 773 418-4506
  Norridge  (G-16108)

### COMMERCIAL ART & GRAPHIC DESIGN SVCS

Active Graphics Inc .............................. E ...... 708 656-8900
  Cicero  (G-7176)
Allegra Network LLC ............................. G ...... 815 877-3400
  Belvidere  (G-1730)
Athena Design Group Inc ...................... E ...... 312 733-2828
  Chicago  (G-3974)
Award Designs Inc ............................... G ...... 815 227-1264
  Rockford  (G-18273)
Burgopak Limited ................................. E ...... 312 255-0827
  Chicago  (G-4185)
Case Paluch & Associates Inc ................ G ...... 773 465-0098
  Chicago  (G-4248)
Charleston Graphics Inc ........................ G
  Charleston  (G-3594)
Colors Chicago Inc ............................... G ...... 312 265-1642
  Chicago  (G-4429)
Colorwave Graphics LLC ....................... G ...... 815 397-4293
  Loves Park  (G-13925)
Custom Direct Inc ................................ F ...... 630 529-1936
  Roselle  (G-18938)
Delta Press Inc .................................... E ...... 847 671-3200
  Palatine  (G-17022)
Digital Prtg & Total Graphics ................. G ...... 630 627-7400
  Lombard  (G-13792)
Donnas House of Type Inc ..................... G ...... 217 522-5050
  Athens  (G-938)
Dzro-Bans International Inc ................... G ...... 779 324-2740
  Homewood  (G-12096)
Expercolor Inc ..................................... E ...... 773 465-3400
  Skokie  (G-19997)
F Weber Printing Co Inc ........................ G ...... 815 468-6152
  Manteno  (G-14183)
G T Services of Illionois Inc ................... G ...... 309 925-5111
  Tremont  (G-20982)
Graphics Plus Inc ................................. F ...... 630 968-9073
  Lisle  (G-13597)
Haute Noir Media Group Inc .................. G ...... 312 869-4526
  Chicago  (G-5055)
Henderson Co Inc ................................. F ...... 773 628-7216
  Chicago  (G-5070)
Hopper Graphics Inc ............................. G ...... 708 489-0459
  Palos Heights  (G-17107)
Key One Graphics Services Inc ............... G
  West Dundee  (G-21799)
L P M Inc ............................................ G ...... 847 866-9777
  Evanston  (G-10062)

Legend Promotions ............................... G ...... 847 438-3528
  Lake Zurich  (G-13095)
Linx Enterprises LLC ............................. G ...... 224 409-2206
  Chicago  (G-5516)
M M Marketing .................................... G ...... 815 459-7968
  Crystal Lake  (G-7603)
Mac Graphics Group Inc ........................ G ...... 630 620-7200
  Oakbrook Terrace  (G-16716)
McGrath Press Inc ............................... E ...... 815 356-5246
  Crystal Lake  (G-7607)
Media Unlimited Inc ............................. G ...... 630 527-0900
  Naperville  (G-15816)
Motr Grafx LLC .................................... G ...... 847 600-5656
  Niles  (G-16009)
Mu Dai LLC ......................................... F ...... 312 982-0040
  Chicago  (G-5828)
P N K Ventures Inc ............................... G ...... 630 527-0500
  Naperville  (G-15720)
Printed Word Inc .................................. G ...... 847 328-1511
  Evanston  (G-10091)
Rite-TEC Communications ..................... G ...... 815 459-7712
  Crystal Lake  (G-7643)
S G S Inc ............................................ G ...... 708 544-6061
  Downers Grove  (G-8517)
S M C Graphics ................................... G ...... 708 754-8973
  Chicago Heights  (G-7125)
Shree Printing Corp .............................. G ...... 773 267-9500
  Chicago  (G-6502)
Stark Printing Company ........................ G ...... 847 234-8430
  Round Lake  (G-19068)
Viking Awards Inc ................................ G ...... 630 833-1733
  Elmhurst  (G-9957)
Xtrem Graphix Solutions Inc .................. G ...... 217 698-6424
  Springfield  (G-20549)

### COMMERCIAL ART & ILLUSTRATION SVCS

Morton Suggestion Company LLC ........... G ...... 847 255-4770
  Mount Prospect  (G-15351)

### COMMERCIAL CONTAINERS WHOLESALERS

Greif Inc ............................................. E ...... 630 961-9786
  Naperville  (G-15664)

### COMMERCIAL EQPT WHOLESALERS, NEC

Charleston Industries Inc ...................... G ...... 847 228-7150
  Elk Grove Village  (G-9365)
REB Steel Equipment Corp ..................... E ...... 773 252-0400
  Chicago  (G-6309)
T J S Equipment Inc ............................. G ...... 618 656-8046
  Edwardsville  (G-8816)
Tee Lee Popcorn Inc ............................ G ...... 815 864-2363
  Shannon  (G-19903)

### COMMERCIAL EQPT, WHOLESALE: Coffee Brewing Eqpt & Splys

Classic Vending Inc .............................. E ...... 773 252-7000
  Chicago  (G-4395)

### COMMERCIAL EQPT, WHOLESALE: Comm Cooking & Food Svc Eqpt

Institutional Equipment Inc .................... E ...... 630 771-0990
  Bolingbrook  (G-2321)
Lee Industries Inc ................................ C ...... 847 462-1865
  Elk Grove Village  (G-9590)
Style Rite Restaurant Eqp Co ................. G ...... 630 628-0940
  Addison  (G-299)
Tri-State Food Equipment ...................... G ...... 217 228-1550
  Quincy  (G-17900)
Wag Industries Inc .............................. G ...... 847 329-8932
  Skokie  (G-20109)

### COMMERCIAL EQPT, WHOLESALE: Display Eqpt, Exc Refrigerated

Creative Merchandising Systems ............. G ...... 847 955-9990
  Lincolnshire  (G-13441)
Exclusively Expo .................................. E ...... 630 378-4600
  Romeoville  (G-18821)
Iretired LLC ........................................ E ...... 630 285-9500
  Itasca  (G-12287)
Marietta Corporation ............................ C ...... 773 816-5137
  Chicago  (G-5619)
Richardson Electronics Ltd .................... C ...... 630 208-2278
  Lafox  (G-12795)

### COMMERCIAL EQPT, WHOLESALE: Neon Signs

Neon Design Inc .................................. G ...... 773 880-5020
  Chicago  (G-5886)
Precision Neon Glasswork ..................... G ...... 847 428-1200
  Crystal Lake  (G-7627)
Signet Sign Company ........................... G ...... 630 830-8242
  Bartlett  (G-1377)
Staar Bales Lestarge Inc ....................... G ...... 618 259-6366
  East Alton  (G-8611)

### COMMERCIAL EQPT, WHOLESALE: Restaurant, NEC

American Soda Ftn Exch Inc .................. F ...... 312 733-5000
  Chicago  (G-3875)
Co-Rect Products Inc ........................... E ...... 763 542-9200
  Lincolnshire  (G-13438)
NFC Company Inc ................................ G ...... 773 472-6468
  Chicago  (G-5908)

### COMMERCIAL EQPT, WHOLESALE: Scales, Exc Laboratory

Advanced Weighing Systems Inc ............ G ...... 630 916-6179
  Addison  (G-25)
Florida Metrology LLC .......................... F ...... 630 833-3800
  Villa Park  (G-21252)
Scale-Tronix Inc .................................. F ...... 630 653-3377
  Carol Stream  (G-3235)

### COMMERCIAL EQPT, WHOLESALE: Store Fixtures & Display Eqpt

Advert Display Products Inc ................... G ...... 815 513-5432
  Morris  (G-15090)
B Andrews Inc ..................................... G ...... 847 381-7444
  Barrington  (G-1269)
B Gunther & Co ................................... F ...... 630 969-5595
  Lisle  (G-13567)
Duo Usa Incorporated .......................... G ...... 312 421-7755
  Chicago  (G-4653)
G D S Professional Bus Display .............. E ...... 309 829-3298
  Bloomington  (G-2168)
Prairie Display Chicago Inc .................... G ...... 630 834-8773
  Elmhurst  (G-9922)
Southern Imperial Inc ........................... B ...... 815 877-7041
  Rockford  (G-18623)

### COMMERCIAL LAUNDRY EQPT

Chicago Dryer Company ........................ C ...... 773 235-4430
  Chicago  (G-4317)
Ellis Corporation .................................. D ...... 630 250-9222
  Itasca  (G-12258)

### COMMERCIAL PHOTOGRAPHIC STUDIO

Epic Eye ............................................. G ...... 309 210-6212
  Grand Ridge  (G-11257)
Pro Image ........................................... G ...... 708 422-7471
  Chicago Ridge  (G-7155)
Schellhorn Photo Techniques ................. F ...... 773 267-5141
  Chicago  (G-6451)
Wyckoff Advertising Inc ........................ G ...... 630 260-2525
  Wheaton  (G-21990)

### COMMERCIAL PRINTING & NEWSPAPER PUBLISHING COMBINED

Ada Holding Company Inc ..................... F ...... 312 440-2897
  Chicago  (G-3742)
B F Shaw Printing Company .................. E ...... 815 875-4461
  Princeton  (G-17744)
Bar Code Dr Inc ................................... G ...... 815 547-1001
  Cherry Valley  (G-3639)
Belair Hd Studios LLC ........................... E ...... 312 254-5188
  Chicago  (G-4075)
Belvidere Daily Republican Co ................ E ...... 815 547-0084
  Belvidere  (G-1737)
Carbondale Night Life .......................... F ...... 618 549-2799
  Carbondale  (G-3002)
Carroll County Review .......................... G ...... 815 259-2131
  Thomson  (G-20864)
Central Ill Communications LLC ............. F ...... 217 753-2226
  Springfield  (G-20413)
Community Newsppr Holdings Inc ........... F ...... 217 774-2161
  Shelbyville  (G-19906)
Daily Robinson News Inc ....................... E ...... 618 544-2101
  Robinson  (G-18060)

Employee Codes: A=Over 500 employees, B=251-500
C=101-250, D=51-100, E=20-50, F=10-19, G=3-9

## COMMERCIAL PRINTING & NEWSPAPER PUBLISHING COMBINED

De Boer & Associates .......................... G ....... 630 972-1600
  Bolingbrook *(G-2300)*
Democrat Company Corp .................... G ....... 217 357-2149
  Carthage *(G-3313)*
Fisher Printing Inc ............................... C ....... 708 598-9266
  Bridgeview *(G-2490)*
Gatehouse Media Illinois Ho ................ B ....... 217 788-1300
  Springfield *(G-20446)*
Joong-Ang Daily News ........................ E ....... 847 228-7200
  Elk Grove Village *(G-9564)*
Losangeles Features Syndicate .......... G ....... 847 446-4082
  Winnetka *(G-22310)*
Midwest Suburban Publishing .............. A ....... 708 633-6880
  Tinley Park *(G-20933)*
Okawville Times .................................. G ....... 618 243-5563
  Okawville *(G-16754)*
Ottawa Publishing Co Inc .................... C ....... 815 433-2000
  Ottawa *(G-16975)*
Ottawa Publishing Co Inc .................... F ....... 815 434-3330
  Ottawa *(G-16976)*
Peoria Journal Star Inc ........................ C ....... 585 598-0030
  Peoria *(G-17423)*
Prints Chicago Inc ............................... G ....... 312 243-6481
  Chicago *(G-6197)*
Progress Reporter Inc ......................... G ....... 815 472-2000
  Momence *(G-14986)*
Ramsey News Journal ........................ G ....... 618 423-2411
  Ramsey *(G-17915)*
Tegna Inc ............................................ C ....... 847 490-6657
  Hoffman Estates *(G-12064)*
Times Record Company ...................... E ....... 309 582-5112
  Aledo *(G-373)*
Trenton Sun ........................................ G ....... 618 224-9422
  Trenton *(G-20998)*
Wayne County Press Inc .................... E ....... 618 842-2662
  Fairfield *(G-10159)*

## COMMERCIAL SECTOR REG, LICENSING & INSP, GOVT: Insurance

State of Illinois ..................................... C ....... 312 836-9500
  Chicago *(G-6578)*

## COMMODITY CONTRACTS BROKERS, DEALERS

J and K Printing .................................. G ....... 708 229-9558
  Oak Lawn *(G-16627)*

## COMMON SAND MINING

Lafarge Aggregates III Inc .................. G ....... 847 742-6060
  South Elgin *(G-20212)*
Material Service Corporation ............... E ....... 815 942-1830
  Romeoville *(G-18843)*
Reliable Sand and Gravel Co .............. G ....... 815 385-5020
  McHenry *(G-14551)*
Southfield Corporation ........................ G ....... 217 379-3606
  Paxton *(G-17245)*

## COMMUNICATIONS EQPT & SYSTEMS, NEC

Extentel Wrless Communications ........ G ....... 847 809-3131
  Inverness *(G-12203)*
Lares Technologies LLC ..................... G ....... 630 408-4368
  Oswego *(G-16925)*
Neovision Usa Inc ............................... F ....... 847 533-0541
  Deer Park *(G-7973)*
Quality Service & Installation .............. G ....... 847 352-4000
  Schaumburg *(G-19709)*
Securecom Inc ................................... G ....... 219 314-4537
  Lansing *(G-13183)*
Vpnvantagecom .................................. G ....... 877 998-4678
  Arlington Heights *(G-867)*
Xomi Instruments Co Ltd .................... G ....... 847 660-4614
  Vernon Hills *(G-21220)*

## COMMUNICATIONS EQPT WHOLESALERS

Data Comm For Business Inc .............. F ....... 217 897-1741
  Dewey *(G-8310)*
David Jeskey ..................................... G ....... 630 659-6337
  Saint Charles *(G-19168)*

## COMMUNICATIONS EQPT: Microwave

Andrew International Svcs Corp .......... A ....... 779 435-6000
  Joliet *(G-12455)*
Andrew New Zealand Inc .................... E ....... 708 873-3507
  Orland Park *(G-16843)*
Callpod Inc ......................................... F ....... 312 829-2680
  Chicago *(G-4217)*

Commscope Technologies LLC ........... A ....... 708 236-6600
  Westchester *(G-21835)*
Commscope Technologies LLC ........... A ....... 779 435-6000
  Joliet *(G-12476)*

## COMMUNICATIONS SVCS

Infinite Cnvrgnce Slutions Inc .............. G ....... 224 764-3400
  Arlington Heights *(G-777)*
Telcom Innovations Group LLC ........... E ....... 630 350-0700
  Itasca *(G-12366)*
Valid Secure Solutions LLC ................ F ....... 260 633-0728
  Lisle *(G-13674)*

## COMMUNICATIONS SVCS: Cellular

AT&T Teleholdings Inc ........................ G ....... 800 257-0902
  Chicago *(G-3973)*
Driver Services ................................... G ....... 505 267-8686
  Bensenville *(G-1883)*
Gogo LLC ........................................... B ....... 630 647-1400
  Chicago *(G-4970)*
Gogo LLC ........................................... D ....... 630 647-1400
  Bensenville *(G-1911)*
Motorola Mobility LLC ......................... B ....... 800 668-6765
  Chicago *(G-5817)*
T-Mobile Usa Inc ................................ F ....... 847 289-9988
  South Elgin *(G-20228)*
Tylu Wireless Technology LLC ........... G ....... 312 260-7934
  Chicago *(G-6802)*

## COMMUNICATIONS SVCS: Data

Gogo LLC ........................................... B ....... 630 647-1400
  Chicago *(G-4970)*
Truequest Communications LLC ......... G ....... 312 356-9900
  Chicago *(G-6788)*

## COMMUNICATIONS SVCS: Electronic Mail

H & R Block Inc .................................. F ....... 847 566-5557
  Mundelein *(G-15506)*
H&R Block Inc .................................... F ....... 773 582-3444
  Chicago *(G-5025)*

## COMMUNICATIONS SVCS: Facsimile Transmission

Fedex Office & Print Svcs Inc .............. G ....... 630 759-5784
  Bolingbrook *(G-2308)*

## COMMUNICATIONS SVCS: Internet Connectivity Svcs

Businessmine LLC .............................. G ....... 630 541-8480
  Lombard *(G-13774)*
Eqes Inc ............................................. G ....... 630 858-6161
  Glen Ellyn *(G-10969)*
Vision I Systems ................................ G ....... 312 326-9188
  Chicago *(G-6902)*

## COMMUNICATIONS SVCS: Internet Host Svcs

Capital Merchant Solutions Inc ............ F ....... 309 452-5990
  Bloomington *(G-2152)*
TWT Marketing Inc .............................. G ....... 773 274-4470
  Chicago *(G-6799)*

## COMMUNICATIONS SVCS: Online Svc Providers

Royer Systems Inc ............................. G ....... 217 965-3699
  Virden *(G-21301)*
Tsf Net Inc ......................................... F ....... 815 246-7295
  Earlville *(G-8597)*
Websolutions Technology Inc ............. E ....... 630 375-6833
  Aurora *(G-1095)*
Yamada America Inc .......................... E ....... 847 228-9063
  Arlington Heights *(G-877)*

## COMMUNICATIONS SVCS: Satellite Earth Stations

Fleet Management Solutions Inc ......... E ....... 805 787-0508
  Glenview *(G-11126)*

## COMMUNICATIONS SVCS: Signal Enhancement Network Svcs

Csiteq LLC ......................................... D ....... 312 265-1509
  Chicago *(G-4512)*

GBA Systems Integrators LLC ............ G ....... 913 492-0400
  Moline *(G-14941)*
Hauhinco LP ....................................... E ....... 618 993-5399
  Marion *(G-14264)*
Quixote Corporation ............................ E ....... 312 705-8400
  Chicago *(G-6259)*
Temco Japan Co Ltd .......................... E ....... 847 359-3277
  South Barrington *(G-20134)*

## COMMUNICATIONS SVCS: Telephone Or Video

Buzzfire Incorporated ......................... F ....... 630 572-9200
  Oak Brook *(G-16496)*
Chicago Cardinal Communication ....... F ....... 708 424-1446
  Oak Lawn *(G-16610)*

## COMMUNICATIONS SVCS: Telephone, Local & Long Distance

Zaptel Corporation .............................. G ....... 847 386-8050
  Elk Grove Village *(G-9824)*

## COMMUNITY DEVELOPMENT GROUPS

Mental Health Ctrs Centl Ill ................. D ....... 217 735-1413
  Lincoln *(G-13415)*

## COMMUTATORS: Electronic

E Solutions Business .......................... E ....... 855 324-3339
  Chicago *(G-4668)*

## COMPACT DISCS OR CD'S, WHOLESALE

Aztec Corporation ............................... G
  Downers Grove *(G-8391)*

## COMPACT LASER DISCS: Prerecorded

Aztec Corporation ............................... G
  Downers Grove *(G-8391)*
Cedille Chicago Nfp ............................ G ....... 773 989-2515
  Chicago *(G-4266)*
Corporate Disk Company .................... D ....... 800 634-3475
  McHenry *(G-14489)*
Datasis Corporation ............................ F ....... 847 427-0909
  Elk Grove Village *(G-9417)*
Idea Media Services LLC ................... F ....... 312 226-2900
  Chicago *(G-5138)*
Robert Koester ................................... G ....... 773 539-5001
  Chicago *(G-6368)*
Tony Patterson ................................... G ....... 773 487-4000
  Chicago *(G-6740)*

## COMPACTORS: Trash & Garbage, Residential

Belson Outdoors LLC ......................... E ....... 630 897-8489
  North Aurora *(G-16120)*

## COMPOST

Better Earth Premium Compost ........... G ....... 309 697-0963
  Peoria *(G-17317)*
Green Earth Technologies Inc ............ G ....... 847 991-0436
  Palatine *(G-17031)*
Green Organics Inc ............................ F ....... 630 871-0108
  Carol Stream *(G-3164)*
Kimmy Compost Inc ........................... G ....... 847 372-9201
  Evanston *(G-10061)*
Midwest Intgrted Companies LLC ....... C ....... 847 426-6354
  Gilberts *(G-10926)*
Pearl Valley Organix Inc .................... F ....... 815 443-2170
  Pearl City *(G-17249)*
Veteran Greens LLC ........................... G ....... 773 599-9689
  Chicago *(G-6891)*

## COMPRESSORS, AIR CONDITIONING: Wholesalers

A-L-L Equipment Company ................. G ....... 815 877-7000
  Loves Park *(G-13911)*
Bridgeport Air Comprsr & Tl Co .......... G ....... 618 945-7163
  Bridgeport *(G-2450)*

## COMPRESSORS: Air & Gas

Agro-Chem Inc .................................... F ....... 309 475-8311
  Saybrook *(G-19413)*
Atlas Copco Compressors LLC ........... F ....... 847 640-6067
  Elk Grove Village *(G-9319)*

## PRODUCT SECTION

**COMPUTER PERIPHERAL EQPT, NEC**

Atlas Copco Compressors LLC............F....... 281 590-7500
 Chicago *(G-3979)*
Atlas Copco Comptec Inc...............E....... 847 726-9866
 Hawthorn Woods *(G-11701)*
Buell Manufacturing Company...........G....... 708 447-6320
 Lyons *(G-14033)*
Corken Inc...........................D....... 405 946-5576
 Lake Bluff *(G-12839)*
Cvp Systems Inc......................D....... 630 852-1190
 Downers Grove *(G-8422)*
Ecothermics Corporation..............G....... 217 621-2402
 Peoria *(G-17483)*
Fluid-Aire Dynamics Inc..............E....... 847 678-8388
 Schaumburg *(G-19531)*
Gardner Denver Inc...................D....... 217 222-5400
 Quincy *(G-17828)*
Gardner Denver Inc...................D....... 815 875-3321
 Princeton *(G-17750)*
Harris Equipment Corporation.........E....... 708 343-0866
 Melrose Park *(G-14651)*
Howe Corporation.....................E....... 773 235-0200
 Chicago *(G-5123)*
Idex Corporation.....................B....... 847 498-7070
 Lake Forest *(G-12915)*
Mat Industries LLC...................G....... 847 821-9630
 Long Grove *(G-13898)*
Mayekawa USA Inc.....................F....... 773 516-5070
 Elk Grove Village *(G-9615)*
Nordson Corporation..................E....... 815 784-5025
 Genoa *(G-10881)*
Ohio Medical LLC.....................D....... 847 855-0500
 Gurnee *(G-11479)*
On-Line Compressor Inc...............G....... 847 497-9750
 Johnsburg *(G-12440)*
Ortman-Mccain Co.....................G....... 312 666-2244
 Chicago *(G-6018)*
Rebuilders Enterprises Inc...........G....... 708 430-0030
 Bridgeview *(G-2523)*
Rietschle Inc........................E....... 410 712-4100
 Quincy *(G-17888)*
Ryan Manufacturing Inc...............G....... 815 695-5310
 Newark *(G-15934)*
Scrollex Corporation.................G....... 630 887-8817
 Willowbrook *(G-22230)*
Standard Car Truck Company...........D....... 630 860-5511
 Bensenville *(G-1998)*
Standard Lifts & Equipment Inc.......G....... 414 444-1000
 Hanover Park *(G-11591)*
William W Meyer and Sons.............D....... 847 918-0111
 Libertyville *(G-13402)*

### COMPRESSORS: Air & Gas, Including Vacuum Pumps

Allegion S&S US Holding Co...........C....... 815 875-3311
 Princeton *(G-17742)*
Bridgeport Air Comprsr & TI Co.......G....... 618 945-7163
 Bridgeport *(G-2450)*
Brock Equipment Company..............E....... 815 459-4210
 Woodstock *(G-22547)*
Compressed Air Advisors Inc..........G....... 877 247-2381
 Westchester *(G-21836)*
Gardner Denver Inc...................F....... 209 823-0356
 Princeton *(G-17749)*
Ingersoll-Rand Company...............E....... 704 655-4000
 Chicago *(G-5191)*
Mat Holdings Inc.....................D....... 847 821-9630
 Long Grove *(G-13897)*
Meyer Tool & Manufacturing Inc.......E....... 708 425-9080
 Oak Lawn *(G-16634)*
Quincy Compressor LLC................C....... 217 222-7700
 Quincy *(G-17875)*
Resolute Industrial LLC..............E....... 800 537-9675
 Wheeling *(G-22139)*
Thomas Gardner Denver Inc............E....... 217 222-5400
 Quincy *(G-17893)*

### COMPRESSORS: Refrigeration & Air Conditioning Eqpt

Buell Manufacturing Company..........G....... 708 447-6320
 Lyons *(G-14033)*
Parks Industries LLC.................F....... 618 997-9608
 Marion *(G-14276)*

### COMPRESSORS: Repairing

Compressed Air Advisors Inc..........G....... 877 247-2381
 Westchester *(G-21836)*
Fluid-Aire Dynamics Inc..............E....... 847 678-8388
 Schaumburg *(G-19531)*

### COMPRESSORS: Wholesalers

Compressed Air Advisors Inc..........G....... 877 247-2381
 Westchester *(G-21836)*

### COMPUTER & COMPUTER SOFTWARE STORES

Associate Computer Systems...........G....... 618 997-3653
 Marion *(G-14254)*
Barcoding Inc........................F....... 847 726-7777
 Mundelein *(G-15474)*
Derbytech Inc........................E....... 309 755-2662
 East Moline *(G-8676)*
Ep Technology Corporation USA........D....... 217 351-7888
 Champaign *(G-3482)*
Friedrich Klatt and Associates.............. 773 753-1806
 Chicago *(G-4891)*

### COMPUTER & COMPUTER SOFTWARE STORES: Peripheral Eqpt

Koi Computers Inc....................G....... 630 627-8811
 Lombard *(G-13817)*
Laser Pro............................G....... 847 742-1055
 Elgin *(G-9093)*
Proship Inc..........................G....... 312 332-7447
 Chicago *(G-6217)*

### COMPUTER & COMPUTER SOFTWARE STORES: Personal Computers

Rf Ideas Inc.........................D....... 847 870-1723
 Rolling Meadows *(G-18774)*

### COMPUTER & COMPUTER SOFTWARE STORES: Printers & Plotters

Cityblue Technologies LLC............F....... 309 676-6633
 Peoria *(G-17343)*
Digi Trax Corporation................E....... 847 613-2100
 Lincolnshire *(G-13443)*

### COMPUTER & COMPUTER SOFTWARE STORES: Software & Access

Bantix Technologies LLC..............G....... 630 446-0886
 Glen Ellyn *(G-10960)*
Bishop Engineering Company...........F....... 630 305-9538
 Lisle *(G-13569)*
CDI Computers (us) Corp..............G....... 888 226-5727
 Chicago *(G-4263)*
Information Builders Inc.............G....... 630 971-6700
 Schaumburg *(G-19565)*
Sunrise Hitek Group LLC..............E....... 773 792-8880
 Chicago *(G-6629)*
Tegratecs Development Corp...........G....... 847 397-0088
 Schaumburg *(G-19757)*

### COMPUTER & COMPUTER SOFTWARE STORES: Software, Bus/Non-Game

McCormicks Enterprises Inc...........E....... 847 398-8680
 Arlington Heights *(G-800)*
Mfrontiers LLC.......................G....... 224 513-5312
 Libertyville *(G-13356)*
Precision Computer Methods...........G....... 630 208-8000
 Elburn *(G-8904)*
Savo Group Ltd.......................C....... 312 276-7700
 Chicago *(G-6447)*
Scientific Cmpt Assoc Corp...........G....... 708 771-4567
 River Forest *(G-18001)*

### COMPUTER & DATA PROCESSING EQPT REPAIR & MAINTENANCE

AR Inet Corp.........................G....... 603 380-3903
 Aurora *(G-959)*

### COMPUTER & OFFICE MACHINE MAINTENANCE & REPAIR

Bc Asi Capital II Inc................A....... 708 534-5575
 University Park *(G-21043)*
Blue Gem Computers Inc...............G....... 708 562-5524
 Morris *(G-15098)*
CDs Office Systems Inc...............D....... 800 367-1508
 Springfield *(G-20410)*
Computer Svcs & Consulting Inc.......E....... 855 827-8328
 Chicago *(G-4441)*
Derbytech Inc........................E....... 309 755-2662
 East Moline *(G-8676)*
Ibs Conversions Inc..................D....... 630 571-9100
 Oak Brook *(G-16524)*
National Micro Systems Inc...........G....... 312 566-0414
 Chicago *(G-5865)*
Pinehurst Bus Solutions Corp.........G....... 630 842-6155
 Winfield *(G-22290)*
React Computer Services Inc..........D....... 630 323-6200
 Willowbrook *(G-22229)*
Rico Computers Enterprises Inc.......F....... 708 594-7426
 Chicago *(G-6354)*
Tech Upgraders.................................. 877 324-8940
 Maywood *(G-14435)*
Xerox Corporation....................E....... 630 573-1000
 Hinsdale *(G-11969)*

### COMPUTER & SFTWR STORE: Modem, Monitor, Terminal/Disk Drive

Integrity Technologies LLC...........G....... 850 240-6089
 Elgin *(G-9078)*

### COMPUTER DATA ESCROW SVCS

Secureslice Inc......................E....... 800 984-0494
 Chicago *(G-6470)*

### COMPUTER DISKETTES WHOLESALERS

Xlogotech Inc........................... 888 244-5152
 Arlington Heights *(G-875)*

### COMPUTER FORMS

Multi Packaging Solutions Inc........G....... 773 283-9500
 Chicago *(G-5832)*
Nbs Systems Inc......................E....... 217 999-3472
 Mount Olive *(G-15306)*

### COMPUTER GRAPHICS SVCS

Fanning Communications Inc...........G....... 708 293-1430
 Crestwood *(G-7488)*
Holsolutions Inc.....................G....... 888 847-5467
 Frankfort *(G-10327)*
Integrated Media Inc.................F....... 217 854-6260
 Carlinville *(G-3040)*
SGS International LLC................C....... 309 690-5231
 Peoria *(G-17453)*
Tb Cardworks Llc.....................E....... 847 229-9990
 Palatine *(G-17079)*
Tgrv LLC.............................G....... 815 634-2102
 Bourbonnais *(G-2407)*

### COMPUTER INTERFACE EQPT: Indl Process

Alpha Pages LLC......................G....... 847 733-1740
 Chicago *(G-3830)*
Creative Controls Systems Inc........G....... 815 629-2358
 Rockton *(G-18695)*
Emac Inc.............................E....... 618 529-4525
 Carbondale *(G-3006)*
Lake Electronics Inc.................F....... 847 201-1270
 Volo *(G-21317)*
Sendele Wireless Solutions...........G....... 815 227-4212
 Rockford *(G-18610)*
Sensor Synergy.......................G....... 847 353-8200
 Vernon Hills *(G-21202)*
Surya Electronics Inc................C....... 630 858-8000
 Glendale Heights *(G-11080)*

### COMPUTER PAPER WHOLESALERS

Computer Business Forms Co...........G....... 773 775-0155
 Chicago *(G-4440)*

### COMPUTER PERIPHERAL EQPT REPAIR & MAINTENANCE

L P S Express Inc....................E....... 217 636-7683
 Springfield *(G-20465)*
Midwest Laser Incorporated...........G....... 708 974-0084
 Palos Hills *(G-17119)*

### COMPUTER PERIPHERAL EQPT, NEC

Adazon Inc...........................G....... 847 235-2700
 Lake Forest *(G-12874)*
Allied Telesis Inc...................D....... 312 726-1990
 Chicago *(G-3818)*
Ambir Technology Inc.................G....... 630 530-5400
 Wood Dale *(G-22339)*

---

Employee Codes: A=Over 500 employees, B=251-500
C=101-250, D=51-100, E=20-50, F=10-19, G=3-9

## COMPUTER PERIPHERAL EQPT, NEC

|  | |  |
|---|---|---|
| American Digital Corporation | E | 847 637-4300 |
| Elk Grove Village *(G-9296)* | | |
| Andrew New Zealand Inc | E | 708 873-3507 |
| Orland Park *(G-16843)* | | |
| Antares Computer Systems Inc | G | 773 783-8855 |
| Chicago *(G-3915)* | | |
| Arba Retail Systems Corp | G | 630 620-8566 |
| Naperville *(G-15797)* | | |
| Automated Systems & Control Co | E | 847 735-8310 |
| Lake Bluff *(G-12834)* | | |
| Bigtime Fantasy Sports Inc | G | 630 605-7544 |
| Lombard *(G-13769)* | | |
| Black Box Corporation | F | 312 656-8807 |
| Tinley Park *(G-20899)* | | |
| Bycap Inc | E | 773 561-4976 |
| Chicago *(G-4196)* | | |
| CDI Computers (us) Corp | G | 888 226-5727 |
| Chicago *(G-4263)* | | |
| CDs Office Systems Inc | D | 800 367-1508 |
| Springfield *(G-20410)* | | |
| Cisco Systems Inc | G | 217 363-4500 |
| Champaign *(G-3466)* | | |
| Cobius Halthcare Solutions LLC | G | 847 656-8700 |
| Northbrook *(G-16229)* | | |
| Colorjar LLC | F | 312 489-8510 |
| Chicago *(G-4428)* | | |
| Commscope Technologies LLC | B | 779 435-6000 |
| Joliet *(G-12476)* | | |
| Computerprox | F | 847 516-8560 |
| Elgin *(G-8997)* | | |
| Contemporary Ctrl Systems Inc | E | 630 963-1993 |
| Downers Grove *(G-8419)* | | |
| Current Works Inc | G | 847 497-9650 |
| Johnsburg *(G-12433)* | | |
| Domino Amjet Inc | E | 847 662-3148 |
| Gurnee *(G-11439)* | | |
| Domino Lasers Inc | E | 847 855-1364 |
| Gurnee *(G-11442)* | | |
| Dover Corporation | C | 630 541-1540 |
| Downers Grove *(G-8431)* | | |
| Elfring Fonts Inc | G | 630 377-3520 |
| Saint Charles *(G-19179)* | | |
| Epix Inc | G | 847 465-1818 |
| Buffalo Grove *(G-2692)* | | |
| Gb Marketing Inc | F | 847 367-0101 |
| Vernon Hills *(G-21164)* | | |
| Hausermann Die & Machine Co | F | 630 543-6688 |
| Addison *(G-144)* | | |
| Hoffman J&M Farm Holdings Inc | D | 847 671-6280 |
| Schiller Park *(G-19838)* | | |
| Illinois Tool Works Inc | D | 618 997-1716 |
| Marion *(G-14269)* | | |
| Illinois Tool Works Inc | C | 847 876-9400 |
| Des Plaines *(G-8208)* | | |
| Imageworks Manufacturing Inc | E | 708 503-1122 |
| Park Forest *(G-17172)* | | |
| Lexmark International Inc | E | 847 318-5700 |
| Rosemont *(G-19009)* | | |
| Mextell Inc | E | 630 595-4146 |
| Elmhurst *(G-9911)* | | |
| Micros Systems Inc | F | 443 285-6000 |
| Itasca *(G-12316)* | | |
| Omex Technologies Inc | G | 847 850-5858 |
| Wheeling *(G-22112)* | | |
| Omni Vision Inc | E | 630 893-1720 |
| Glendale Heights *(G-11053)* | | |
| Peradata Technology Corp | E | 631 588-2216 |
| Chicago *(G-6106)* | | |
| Poynting Products Inc | G | 708 386-2139 |
| Oak Park *(G-16680)* | | |
| Source Software Inc | G | 815 922-7717 |
| Lockport *(G-13747)* | | |
| Sparton Aydin LLC | G | 800 772-7866 |
| Schaumburg *(G-19733)* | | |
| Tech Global Inc | F | 847 532-4882 |
| Elgin *(G-9203)* | | |
| Teledyne Lecroy Inc | E | 847 888-0450 |
| Elgin *(G-9206)* | | |
| Timeout Devices Inc | F | 847 729-6543 |
| Glenview *(G-11209)* | | |
| Tomantron Inc | F | 708 532-2456 |
| Tinley Park *(G-20950)* | | |
| Tri-Cor Industries Inc | D | 618 589-9890 |
| O Fallon *(G-16481)* | | |
| Trippe Manufacturing Company | B | 773 869-1111 |
| Chicago *(G-6778)* | | |
| United Universal Inds Inc | E | 815 727-4445 |
| Joliet *(G-12585)* | | |
| Verdasee Solutions Inc | G | 847 265-9441 |
| Gurnee *(G-11519)* | | |
| Wam Ventures Inc | G | 312 214-6136 |
| Chicago *(G-6937)* | | |
| Xerox Corporation | E | 630 573-1000 |
| Hinsdale *(G-11969)* | | |

## COMPUTER PERIPHERAL EQPT, WHOLESALE

|  | |  |
|---|---|---|
| C M F Enterprises Inc | F | 847 526-9499 |
| Wauconda *(G-21450)* | | |
| M & S Technologies Inc | F | 847 763-0500 |
| Niles *(G-15997)* | | |

## COMPUTER PERIPHERAL EQPT: Graphic Displays, Exc Terminals

|  | |  |
|---|---|---|
| Bishop Image Group Inc | G | 312 735-8153 |
| Chicago *(G-4113)* | | |
| Corporate Graphics Inc | G | 630 762-9000 |
| Saint Charles *(G-19164)* | | |
| Display Graphics Systems LLC | G | 800 706-9670 |
| Chicago *(G-4611)* | | |

## COMPUTER PERIPHERAL EQPT: Input Or Output

|  | |  |
|---|---|---|
| Oceancomm Incorporated | G | 800 757-3266 |
| Champaign *(G-3522)* | | |
| Scadaware Inc | F | 309 665-0135 |
| Normal *(G-16088)* | | |
| Somat Corporation | E | 800 578-4260 |
| Champaign *(G-3541)* | | |

## COMPUTER PROGRAMMING SVCS

|  | |  |
|---|---|---|
| Abki Tech Service Inc | F | 847 818-8403 |
| Des Plaines *(G-8143)* | | |
| Anylogic N Amer Ltd Lblty Co | G | 312 635-3344 |
| Chicago *(G-3918)* | | |
| Arxium Inc | C | 847 808-2600 |
| Buffalo Grove *(G-2660)* | | |
| Barcoding Inc | F | 847 726-7777 |
| Mundelein *(G-15474)* | | |
| Ca Inc | D | 631 342-6000 |
| Lisle *(G-13572)* | | |
| Canon Solutions America Inc | D | 630 351-1227 |
| Itasca *(G-12240)* | | |
| Clutch Systems Inc | G | 815 282-7960 |
| Machesney Park *(G-14066)* | | |
| Creative Controls Systems Inc | G | 815 629-2358 |
| Rockton *(G-18695)* | | |
| Cyborg Systems Inc | C | 312 279-7000 |
| Chicago *(G-4529)* | | |
| Information Builders Inc | E | 630 971-6700 |
| Schaumburg *(G-19565)* | | |
| Isewan USA Inc | G | 630 561-2807 |
| Schaumburg *(G-19584)* | | |
| Lab Software Inc | G | 815 521-9116 |
| Minooka *(G-14841)* | | |
| Lattice Incorporated | E | 630 949-3250 |
| Wheaton *(G-21964)* | | |
| Micrograms Inc | G | 815 877-4455 |
| Loves Park *(G-13966)* | | |
| Monotype Imaging Inc | F | 847 718-0400 |
| Elk Grove Village *(G-9635)* | | |
| Monotype Imaging Inc | G | 847 718-0400 |
| Mount Prospect *(G-15350)* | | |
| Mu Dai LLC | F | 312 982-0040 |
| Chicago *(G-5828)* | | |
| National Data Svcs Chicago Inc | C | 630 597-9100 |
| Carol Stream *(G-3204)* | | |
| Oracle Systems Corporation | E | 312 245-1580 |
| Chicago *(G-6002)* | | |
| Pagepath Technologies Inc | G | 630 689-4111 |
| Plano *(G-17671)* | | |
| Pendragon Software Corporation | G | 847 816-9660 |
| Chicago *(G-6099)* | | |
| Poynting Products Inc | G | 708 386-2139 |
| Oak Park *(G-16680)* | | |
| Process and Control Systems | F | 708 293-0557 |
| Alsip *(G-514)* | | |
| Quadramed Corporation | E | 312 396-0700 |
| Chicago *(G-6240)* | | |
| React Computer Services Inc | G | 630 323-6200 |
| Willowbrook *(G-22229)* | | |
| Reliefwatch Inc | G | 646 678-2336 |
| Chicago *(G-6331)* | | |
| Showcase Corporation | C | 312 651-3000 |
| Chicago *(G-6500)* | | |
| Signature Business Systems Inc | F | 847 459-8500 |
| Deerfield *(G-8053)* | | |
| Systems Live Ltd | G | 815 455-3383 |
| Crystal Lake *(G-7657)* | | |
| Thomas A Doan | G | 847 864-8772 |
| Evanston *(G-10102)* | | |
| Thomson Quantitative Analytics | E | 847 610-0574 |
| Chicago *(G-6717)* | | |
| Uxm Studio Inc | G | 773 359-1333 |
| Villa Park *(G-21288)* | | |
| Vargyas Networks Inc | G | 630 929-3610 |
| Lisle *(G-13676)* | | |
| Verdasee Solutions Inc | G | 847 265-9441 |
| Gurnee *(G-11519)* | | |
| Vertex Consulting Services Inc | F | 313 492-5154 |
| Schaumburg *(G-19786)* | | |
| Websolutions Technology Inc | E | 630 375-6833 |
| Aurora *(G-1095)* | | |

## COMPUTER PROGRAMMING SVCS: Custom

|  | |  |
|---|---|---|
| AR Inet Corp | G | 603 380-3903 |
| Aurora *(G-959)* | | |
| Manufacturing Tech Group Inc | G | 815 966-2300 |
| Rockford *(G-18482)* | | |
| Secure Data Inc | F | 618 726-5225 |
| O Fallon *(G-16478)* | | |

## COMPUTER RELATED MAINTENANCE SVCS

|  | |  |
|---|---|---|
| 7000 Inc | F | 312 800-3612 |
| Bolingbrook *(G-2275)* | | |
| Applus Technologies Inc | E | 312 661-1604 |
| Chicago *(G-3927)* | | |
| Palm International Inc | G | 630 357-1437 |
| Naperville *(G-15721)* | | |
| Pinehurst Bus Solutions Corp | G | 630 842-6155 |
| Winfield *(G-22290)* | | |

## COMPUTER RELATED SVCS, NEC

|  | |  |
|---|---|---|
| Joliet Herald Newspaper | E | 815 280-4100 |
| Joliet *(G-12523)* | | |

## COMPUTER SERVICE BUREAU

|  | |  |
|---|---|---|
| Abki Tech Service Inc | F | 847 818-8403 |
| Des Plaines *(G-8143)* | | |
| Be Group Inc | G | 312 436-0301 |
| Chicago *(G-4061)* | | |
| Donnas House of Type Inc | G | 217 522-5050 |
| Athens *(G-938)* | | |
| Precision Reproductions Inc | F | 847 724-0182 |
| Glenview *(G-11184)* | | |
| W R Typesetting Co | G | 847 966-1315 |
| Morton Grove *(G-15244)* | | |

## COMPUTER SOFTWARE DEVELOPMENT

|  | |  |
|---|---|---|
| Access International Inc | E | 312 920-9366 |
| Chicago *(G-3715)* | | |
| Applied Systems Inc | A | 708 534-5575 |
| University Park *(G-21041)* | | |
| Bc Asi Capital II Inc | A | 708 534-5575 |
| University Park *(G-21043)* | | |
| Bigtime Fantasy Sports Inc | G | 630 605-7544 |
| Lombard *(G-13769)* | | |
| Bytebin LLC | G | 312 286-0740 |
| Chicago *(G-4197)* | | |
| Catapult Communications Corp | G | 847 884-0048 |
| Schaumburg *(G-19469)* | | |
| CCH Incorporated | A | 847 267-7000 |
| Riverwoods *(G-18037)* | | |
| Chicago Data Solutions Inc | G | 847 370-4609 |
| Willowbrook *(G-22203)* | | |
| Computer Pwr Solutions III Ltd | E | 618 281-8898 |
| Columbia *(G-7355)* | | |
| Document Publishing Group | E | 847 783-0670 |
| Elgin *(G-9011)* | | |
| Flexera Holdings LP | G | 847 466-4000 |
| Itasca *(G-12265)* | | |
| Flexera Software LLC | B | 800 374-4353 |
| Itasca *(G-12266)* | | |
| High Tech Research Inc | F | 847 215-9797 |
| Deerfield *(G-8012)* | | |
| Idevconcepts Inc | G | 312 351-1615 |
| Chicago *(G-5142)* | | |
| Impact Technologies Inc | G | 708 246-5041 |
| Western Springs *(G-21867)* | | |
| Infosys Limited | E | 630 482-5000 |
| Lisle *(G-13606)* | | |
| Intelligrated Systems Inc | B | 630 985-4350 |
| Woodridge *(G-22495)* | | |
| Isoprime Corporation | G | 630 737-0963 |
| Lisle *(G-13609)* | | |

# PRODUCT SECTION

## COMPUTERS, NEC

J S Paluch Co Inc .................................. C ...... 847 678-9300
  Franklin Park *(G-10502)*
Lansa Inc ........................................... C ...... 630 874-7042
  Downers Grove *(G-8472)*
Lemko Corporation ............................... E ...... 630 948-3025
  Itasca *(G-12302)*
Logicgate Inc ...................................... F ...... 312 279-2775
  Chicago *(G-5533)*
Oas Software Corp ............................... F ...... 630 513-2990
  Saint Charles *(G-19226)*
Paulmar Industries Inc .......................... F ...... 847 395-2520
  Antioch *(G-648)*
Prairie Wi-FI Systems ........................... G ...... 515 988-3260
  Chicago *(G-6167)*
Proship Inc ......................................... G ...... 312 332-7447
  Chicago *(G-6217)*
Screen North Amer Holdings Inc ............. F ...... 847 870-7400
  Rolling Meadows *(G-18777)*
Stenograph LLC ................................... D ...... 630 532-5100
  Elmhurst *(G-9942)*
Structurepoint LLC ............................... F ...... 847 966-4357
  Skokie *(G-20092)*
Tangent Systems Inc ............................ F ...... 847 882-3833
  Hoffman Estates *(G-12062)*

### COMPUTER SOFTWARE DEVELOPMENT & APPLICATIONS

Active Simulations Inc .......................... G ...... 630 747-8393
  Oak Park *(G-16648)*
Aeverie Inc ......................................... G ...... 844 238-3743
  Buffalo Grove *(G-2651)*
Agile Health Technologies Inc ................. E ...... 630 247-5565
  Naperville *(G-15789)*
Applus Technologies Inc ........................ E ...... 312 661-1604
  Chicago *(G-3927)*
Cognizant Tech Solutions Corp ................ E ...... 630 955-0617
  Lisle *(G-13575)*
Cona LLC ........................................... G ...... 773 750-7485
  Chicago *(G-4443)*
Digital H2o Inc .................................... F ...... 847 456-8424
  Chicago *(G-4601)*
Eighty Nine Robotics LLC ...................... G ...... 512 573-9091
  Chicago *(G-4705)*
Endure Holdings Inc ............................. G ...... 224 558-1828
  Plainfield *(G-17594)*
Follett School Solutions Inc ................... C ...... 815 759-1700
  McHenry *(G-14507)*
G2 Crowd Inc ...................................... F ...... 847 748-7559
  Chicago *(G-4904)*
Gatesair Inc ........................................ C ...... 217 222-8200
  Quincy *(G-17830)*
J2sys LLC ........................................... F ...... 630 542-1342
  Clarendon Hills *(G-7257)*
Jones Software Corp ............................ G ...... 312 952-0011
  Chicago *(G-5322)*
Memorable Inc .................................... G ...... 847 272-8207
  Northbrook *(G-16310)*
Next Generation Inc ............................. G ...... 312 953-7514
  Plainfield *(G-17632)*
Pintsch Tiefenbach Us Inc ..................... G ...... 618 993-8513
  Marion *(G-14280)*
Pluribus Games LLC ............................. G ...... 630 770-2043
  Aurora *(G-1204)*
Premier International Entps ................... E ...... 312 857-2200
  Chicago *(G-6177)*
Productive Edge LLC ............................ D ...... 312 561-9000
  Chicago *(G-6207)*
Proquis Inc ......................................... F ...... 847 278-3230
  Elgin *(G-9151)*
Psylotech Inc ...................................... G ...... 847 328-7100
  Evanston *(G-10092)*
Rico Computers Enterprises Inc .............. F ...... 708 594-7426
  Chicago *(G-6354)*
Scadaware Inc ..................................... F ...... 309 665-0135
  Normal *(G-16088)*
Shoppertrak Rct Corporation .................. F ...... 312 529-5300
  Chicago *(G-6498)*
Synergy Technology Group Inc ............... F ...... 773 305-3500
  Chicago *(G-6657)*

### COMPUTER SOFTWARE SYSTEMS ANALYSIS & DESIGN: Custom

Digi Trax Corporation ........................... E ...... 847 613-2100
  Lincolnshire *(G-13443)*
Elemech Inc ........................................ E ...... 630 417-2845
  Aurora *(G-1001)*
Elfring Fonts Inc .................................. G ...... 630 377-3520
  Saint Charles *(G-19179)*
Emac Inc ............................................ E ...... 618 529-4525
  Carbondale *(G-3006)*
Entappia LLC ...................................... G ...... 630 546-4531
  Aurora *(G-1003)*
Infopro Inc ......................................... G ...... 630 978-9231
  Aurora *(G-1029)*
Logical Design Solutions Inc .................. G ...... 630 786-5999
  Aurora *(G-1047)*
Marucco Stddard Frenbach Walsh ............ E ...... 217 698-3535
  Springfield *(G-20474)*
Optimus Advantage LLC ........................ G ...... 847 905-1000
  Chicago *(G-5997)*
Orinoco Systems LLC ............................ G ...... 630 510-0775
  Wheaton *(G-21971)*
Peak Computer Systems Inc ................... F ...... 618 398-5612
  Belleville *(G-1665)*
Phillip Grigalanz .................................. G ...... 219 628-6706
  Jerseyville *(G-12425)*
Pinnakle Technologies Inc ...................... F ...... 630 352-0070
  Aurora *(G-1066)*
Richardson Electronics Ltd ..................... C ...... 630 208-2278
  Lafox *(G-12795)*
Softhaus Ltd ....................................... G ...... 618 463-1140
  Alton *(G-590)*
Tempus Health Inc ............................... E ...... 312 784-4400
  Chicago *(G-6699)*
Tryad Specialties Inc ............................ G ...... 630 549-0079
  Saint Charles *(G-19287)*
Viva Solutions Inc ................................ G ...... 312 332-8882
  Lemont *(G-13268)*

### COMPUTER SOFTWARE WRITERS

Localfix Solutions LLC ........................... G ...... 312 569-0619
  Winfield *(G-22287)*
Picis Clinical Solutions Inc ..................... F ...... 847 993-2200
  Rosemont *(G-19023)*
Recsolu Inc ......................................... E ...... 312 517-3200
  Chicago *(G-6313)*
Western Printing Machinery Co ............... G ...... 847 678-1740
  Schiller Park *(G-19883)*
Western Printing Machinery Co ............... G ...... 847 678-1740
  Schiller Park *(G-19884)*

### COMPUTER SOFTWARE WRITERS: Freelance

Edqu Media LLC ................................... G ...... 773 803-9793
  Chicago *(G-4698)*
Imaging Systems Inc ............................ F ...... 630 875-1100
  Itasca *(G-12283)*

### COMPUTER STORAGE DEVICES, NEC

10th Magnitude LLC ............................. E ...... 224 628-9047
  Chicago *(G-3661)*
Ally Global Corporation ......................... G ...... 773 822-3373
  Chicago *(G-3826)*
Dickson/Unigage Inc ............................. E ...... 630 543-3747
  Addison *(G-92)*
E Mc .................................................. G ...... 217 228-1280
  Quincy *(G-17824)*
E N M Company ................................... G ...... 773 775-8400
  Chicago *(G-4667)*
EMC .................................................. G ...... 480 225-5498
  Channahon *(G-3573)*
File System Labs LLC ........................... F ...... 617 431-4313
  Northbrook *(G-16259)*
Illinoi Eye Surgns/Quantm Visn .............. G ...... 618 315-6560
  Mount Vernon *(G-15414)*
International Bus Mchs Corp .................. C ...... 312 423-6640
  Chicago *(G-5219)*
Interntional Cmpt Concepts Inc .............. E ...... 847 808-7789
  Northbrook *(G-16279)*
Invision Software Inc ........................... F ...... 312 474-7767
  Lisle *(G-13608)*
Loop Limited ....................................... G ...... 312 612-1010
  Evanston *(G-10066)*
Pinehurst Bus Solutions Corp ................. G ...... 630 842-6155
  Winfield *(G-22290)*
Quantum Corporation ........................... D ...... 312 372-2857
  Chicago *(G-6250)*
Quantum Healing ................................. G ...... 217 414-2412
  Mechanicsburg *(G-14575)*
Quantum Legal LLC .............................. G ...... 847 433-4500
  Highland Park *(G-11863)*
Quantum Marketing LLC ....................... G ...... 630 257-7012
  Lemont *(G-13259)*
Quantum Mechanical LLC ...................... G ...... 773 480-8200
  Huntley *(G-12170)*
Quantum Meruit LLC ............................ G ...... 630 283-3555
  Glendale Heights *(G-11061)*
Quantum Nova Technologies .................. G ...... 773 386-6816
  Chicago *(G-6251)*
Quantum Partners LLC .......................... G ...... 312 725-4668
  Chicago *(G-6252)*
Quantum Vision Centers ....................... G ...... 618 656-7774
  Swansea *(G-20780)*
Quantum9 Inc ..................................... G ...... 888 716-0404
  Chicago *(G-6253)*
Western Digital Tech Inc ....................... G ...... 949 672-7000
  Chicago *(G-6963)*
Wevaultcom LLC .................................. E ...... 877 938-2858
  Crystal Lake *(G-7677)*

### COMPUTER SYSTEM SELLING SVCS

Karimi Saifuddin .................................. G ...... 630 379-9344
  Plainfield *(G-17614)*

### COMPUTER SYSTEMS ANALYSIS & DESIGN

Cronus Technologies Inc ....................... D ...... 847 839-0088
  Schaumburg *(G-19491)*
Polysystems Inc ................................... D ...... 312 332-2114
  Chicago *(G-6155)*
Precision Computer Methods .................. G ...... 630 208-8000
  Elburn *(G-8904)*

### COMPUTER TERMINALS

Lightfoot Technologies Inc ..................... G ...... 331 302-1297
  Naperville *(G-15690)*
Luna It Services .................................. G ...... 213 537-2764
  Chicago *(G-5567)*
Pacap LLC .......................................... G ...... 773 754-7089
  Chicago *(G-6050)*
Teledyne Lecroy Inc ............................. E ...... 847 888-0450
  Elgin *(G-9206)*

### COMPUTER TERMINALS: CRT

Kristel Limited Partnership .................... D ...... 630 443-1290
  Saint Charles *(G-19205)*

### COMPUTER TIME-SHARING

Amoco Technology Company (del) ........... C ...... 312 861-6000
  Chicago *(G-3892)*
Polysystems Inc ................................... D ...... 312 332-2114
  Chicago *(G-6155)*

### COMPUTER TRAINING SCHOOLS

Dmi Information Process Center .............. E ...... 773 378-2644
  Chicago *(G-4616)*

### COMPUTER-AIDED DESIGN SYSTEMS SVCS

C Tri Co ............................................. E ...... 309 467-4715
  Eureka *(G-9994)*
Octane Motorsports LLC ........................ G ...... 224 419-5460
  Waukegan *(G-21598)*

### COMPUTER-AIDED ENGINEERING SYSTEMS SVCS

System Software Associates Del .............. E ...... 312 258-6000
  Chicago *(G-6660)*

### COMPUTER-AIDED MANUFACTURING SYSTEMS SVCS

Precision Technologies Inc ..................... G ...... 847 439-5447
  Glendale Heights *(G-11058)*
Tunnel Vision Consulting Group .............. G ...... 773 367-7292
  Chicago *(G-6791)*

### COMPUTERS, NEC

Accelerated Assemblies Inc .................... E ...... 630 616-6680
  Elk Grove Village *(G-9259)*
Ace Pcb Design Inc .............................. G ...... 847 674-8745
  Skokie *(G-19946)*
Alegria Company .................................. C ...... 608 726-2336
  Chicago *(G-3800)*
Apollo Computer Solutions Inc ................ G ...... 312 671-3575
  Downers Grove *(G-8388)*
Bio-Logic Systems Corp ........................ D ...... 847 949-0456
  Mundelein *(G-15478)*
Easy Pay & Data Inc ............................ G ...... 217 398-9729
  Champaign *(G-3476)*
Enghouse Interactive Inc ....................... G ...... 630 472-9669
  Oak Brook *(G-16509)*
Fourier Systems Inc ............................. G ...... 708 478-5333
  Homer Glen *(G-12079)*

Employee Codes: A=Over 500 employees, B=251-500
C=101-250, D=51-100, E=20-50, F=10-19, G=3-9

# COMPUTERS, NEC

General Dynamics Adv Inf Sys .............. C ...... 703 876-3000
  Chicago (G-4926)
George Electronics Inc ......................... G ...... 708 331-1983
  Orland Park (G-16860)
Gld Industries Inc ................................. G ...... 217 390-9594
  Champaign (G-3489)
HP Inc ................................................. D ...... 847 342-2000
  Elk Grove Village (G-9526)
ICC Intrntonal Celsius Concept ............ G ...... 773 993-4405
  Cicero (G-7203)
Integrity Technologies LLC .................. G ...... 850 240-6089
  Elgin (G-9078)
Interntional Cmpt Concepts Inc ........... E ...... 847 808-7789
  Northbrook (G-16279)
Inverom Corporation ............................ G ...... 630 568-5609
  Burr Ridge (G-2858)
Jets Computing Inc ............................. G ...... 618 585-6676
  Bunker Hill (G-2805)
Koi Computers Inc .............................. G ...... 630 627-8811
  Lombard (G-13817)
Konica Minolta ..................................... G ...... 630 893-8238
  Roselle (G-18950)
Konica Minolta Business Soluti ............ E ...... 309 671-1360
  Peoria (G-17398)
Motorola Solutions Inc ......................... G ...... 847 341-3485
  Oak Brook (G-16546)
National Micro Systems Inc ................. G ...... 312 566-0414
  Chicago (G-5865)
Northrop Grumman Systems Corp ...... A ...... 847 259-9600
  Rolling Meadows (G-18753)
Okamura Corp ..................................... G ...... 312 645-0115
  Chicago (G-5977)
Perkins Enterprise Inc ......................... G ...... 708 560-3837
  South Holland (G-20298)
Pinehurst Bus Solutions Corp .............. G ...... 630 842-6155
  Winfield (G-22290)
Retailout Inc ........................................ E ...... 312 786-4312
  Chicago (G-6339)
Rico Computers Enterprises Inc .......... F ...... 708 594-7426
  Chicago (G-6354)
RMC Imaging Inc ................................ G ...... 815 885-4521
  Rockford (G-18560)
Royer Systems Inc .............................. G ...... 217 965-3699
  Virden (G-21301)
Tech Global Inc ................................... G ...... 224 623-2000
  Elgin (G-9204)
Texmac Inc .......................................... G ...... 630 244-4702
  Mundelein (G-15564)
Tri-Cor Industries Inc .......................... D ...... 618 589-9890
  O Fallon (G-16481)
Tunnel Vision Consulting Group .......... G ...... 773 367-7292
  Chicago (G-6791)
W S C Inc ........................................... G ...... 312 372-1121
  Chicago (G-6926)

## COMPUTERS, NEC, WHOLESALE

Decision Systems Company ................ G ...... 815 885-3000
  Roscoe (G-18892)
Derbytech Inc ...................................... E ...... 309 755-2662
  East Moline (G-8676)
HP Inc ................................................. D ...... 847 342-2000
  Elk Grove Village (G-9526)
Illinois Tool Works Inc ......................... E ...... 708 720-0300
  Frankfort (G-10333)
Jeanblanc International Inc ................. G ...... 815 598-3400
  Elizabeth (G-9242)
Panatech Computer Management ....... G ...... 847 678-8848
  Schiller Park (G-19857)
Rmcis Corporation ............................... E ...... 630 955-1310
  Lisle (G-13652)

## COMPUTERS, PERIPHERALS & SOFTWARE, WHOLESALE: Printers

3dp Unlimited ...................................... G ...... 815 389-5667
  Roscoe (G-18887)

## COMPUTERS, PERIPHERALS & SOFTWARE, WHOLESALE: Software

Elfring Fonts Inc .................................. G ...... 630 377-3520
  Saint Charles (G-19179)
G2 Crowd Inc ...................................... F ...... 847 748-7559
  Chicago (G-4904)
Imaging Systems Inc .......................... F ...... 630 875-1100
  Itasca (G-12283)
Kcura LLC ........................................... B ...... 312 263-1177
  Chicago (G-5368)
MCS Management Corp ...................... G ...... 847 680-3707
  Hawthorn Woods (G-11703)

Michaels Ross and Cole Inc ................ F ...... 630 916-0662
  Oak Brook (G-16543)
Pinnakle Technologies Inc .................. F ...... 630 352-0070
  Aurora (G-1066)
Rand McNally & Company .................. B ...... 847 329-8100
  Skokie (G-20069)
Thomson Quantitative Analytics .......... G ...... 847 610-0574
  Chicago (G-6717)

## COMPUTERS, PERIPHERALS/SFTWR, WHOL: Anti-Static Eqpt/Devices

L-Data Corporation ............................. E ...... 312 552-7855
  Chicago (G-5423)

## COMPUTERS: Mini

International Bus Mchs Corp ............... A ...... 847 706-3461
  Schaumburg (G-19572)

## COMPUTERS: Personal

Antares Computer Systems Inc .......... G ...... 773 783-8855
  Chicago (G-3915)
Apple Express ..................................... G ...... 708 483-8168
  Maywood (G-14416)
Baked Apple Pancake House .............. G ...... 630 515-9000
  Downers Grove (G-8393)
HP Inc ................................................. G ...... 847 207-9118
  Palatine (G-17038)
Monroe Associates Inc ........................ G ...... 217 665-3898
  Bethany (G-2085)
Motorola Solutions Inc ......................... G ...... 847 576-8600
  Schaumburg (G-19652)
Urban Apple LLC ................................ G ...... 312 912-1377
  Chicago (G-6846)

## CONCENTRATES, DRINK

Tampico Beverages Inc ....................... G ...... 773 296-0190
  Chicago (G-6671)

## CONCENTRATES, FLAVORING, EXC DRINK

Jel Sert Co .......................................... B ...... 630 231-7590
  West Chicago (G-21727)

## CONCRETE BUILDING PRDTS WHOLESALERS

Carroll Distrg & Cnstr Sup Inc ............ G ...... 630 892-4855
  Aurora (G-1125)
CCS Contractor Eqp & Sup Inc ........... E ...... 630 393-9020
  Naperville (G-15622)
Macomb Concrete Products Inc .......... G ...... 309 772-3826
  Bushnell (G-2904)
Mazel & Co Inc ................................... F ...... 773 533-1600
  Chicago (G-5662)
Stockdale Block Systems LLC ............ G ...... 815 416-1030
  Morris (G-15132)

## CONCRETE CURING & HARDENING COMPOUNDS

Advantech Limited ............................... G ...... 815 397-9133
  Aurora (G-1102)
BASF Construction Chem LLC ............ G ...... 847 249-4080
  Gurnee (G-11431)
Colloid Envmtl Tech Co LLC ............... C ...... 847 851-1500
  Hoffman Estates (G-12002)
Dayton Superior Corporation .............. E ...... 815 732-3136
  Oregon (G-16821)
PPG Architectural Finishes Inc ........... F ...... 847 699-8400
  Des Plaines (G-8259)
Right/Pointe Company ........................ D ...... 815 754-5700
  Dekalb (G-8115)
W R Grace & Co .................................. F ...... 414 354-4400
  Chicago (G-6922)
W R Grace & Co - Conn ...................... C ...... 708 458-0340
  Chicago (G-6923)

## CONCRETE PLANTS

Gayton Enterprises LLC ...................... G ...... 847 462-4030
  Algonquin (G-391)

## CONCRETE PRDTS

A&J Paving Inc .................................... G ...... 773 889-9133
  Chicago (G-3694)
Abel Vault & Monument Co Inc ........... G ...... 309 647-0105
  Canton (G-2980)

American Cast Stone .......................... F ...... 630 291-0250
  Lemont (G-13223)
American Wilbert Vault Corp ............... G ...... 847 824-4415
  Des Plaines (G-8148)
American Wilbert Vault Corp ............... G ...... 847 741-3089
  Elgin (G-8951)
Atlas Concrete Products Co ................ F ...... 217 528-7368
  Springfield (G-20390)
Bricks Inc ............................................ G ...... 630 897-6926
  Aurora (G-1121)
Classical Statuary & Decor ................. G ...... 815 462-3408
  New Lenox (G-15871)
Clay Vollmar Products Co ................... F ...... 773 774-1234
  Chicago (G-4396)
Clay Vollmar Products Co ................... G ...... 847 540-5850
  Lake Zurich (G-13054)
Concrete Products .............................. G ...... 815 339-6395
  Granville (G-11317)
Concrete Specialities Co Inc ............... G ...... 847 608-1200
  Elgin (G-8998)
Contractors Ready-Mix Inc ................. F ...... 217 735-2565
  Lincoln (G-13407)
Cortelyou Excavating .......................... G ...... 309 772-2922
  Bushnell (G-2901)
County Materials Corp ........................ E ...... 217 352-4181
  Champaign (G-3470)
Details Etc .......................................... F ...... 708 932-5543
  Mokena (G-14860)
Elmhurst-Chicago Stone Company ..... F ...... 630 557-2446
  Kaneville (G-12599)
Elmhurst-Chicago Stone Company ..... E ...... 630 983-6410
  Bolingbrook (G-2305)
F H Leinweber Co Inc ......................... G ...... 773 568-7722
  Chicago (G-4803)
Ferber George & Sons ........................ G ...... 217 733-2184
  Fairmount (G-10163)
Forrest Redi-Mix Inc ........................... G ...... 815 657-8241
  Forrest (G-10262)
GBS Liquidating Corp ......................... G ...... 309 342-4155
  Galesburg (G-10753)
Great Lakes Envmtl Mar Del ............... G ...... 312 332-3377
  Chicago (G-4996)
Hahn Industries ................................... G ...... 815 689-2133
  Cullom (G-7682)
Hamel Tire and Concrete Pdts ............ G ...... 618 633-2405
  Hamel (G-11529)
Hamilton Concrete Products Co .......... G ...... 217 847-3118
  Hamilton (G-11537)
Hanson Aggregates East LLC ............. E ...... 815 398-2300
  Rockford (G-18412)
Illinois Cast Stone .............................. G ...... 815 943-6050
  Harvard (G-11637)
J E Tomes & Associates Inc ............... F ...... 708 653-5100
  Blue Island (G-2258)
Lafarge North America Inc .................. C ...... 703 480-3600
  Chicago (G-5435)
Legacy Vulcan LLC ............................. G ...... 773 890-2360
  Chicago (G-5487)
Legacy Vulcan LLC ............................. G ...... 217 963-2196
  Decatur (G-7908)
Lion Ornamental Concrete Pdts .......... G ...... 630 892-7304
  Montgomery (G-15056)
Macomb Concrete Products Inc .......... G ...... 309 772-3826
  Bushnell (G-2904)
Material Haulers Inc ............................ G ...... 815 857-4336
  Schaumburg (G-19636)
Material Service Corporation ............... E ...... 815 838-2400
  Romeoville (G-18842)
McCann Concrete Products Inc .......... G ...... 618 377-3888
  Dorsey (G-8381)
Meyer Material Co Merger Corp ......... D ...... 815 943-2605
  Harvard (G-11641)
Mid-Illinois Concrete Inc ..................... G ...... 618 664-1340
  Greenville (G-11399)
Mid-Illinois Concrete Inc ..................... G ...... 217 345-6404
  Charleston (G-3604)
Mid-Illinois Concrete Inc ..................... E ...... 217 235-5858
  Mattoon (G-14404)
Midwest Cement Products Inc ............ G ...... 815 284-2342
  Woosung (G-22630)
Northfield Block Company .................. G ...... 708 458-8130
  Berwyn (G-2069)
Orlandi Statuary Company .................. D ...... 773 489-0303
  Chicago (G-6015)
Ozinga Concrete Products Inc ............ E ...... 847 426-0920
  Elgin (G-9132)
Ozinga Concrete Products Inc ............ G ...... 708 479-9050
  Hampshire (G-11557)
Ozinga Ready Mix Concrete Inc ......... E ...... 708 326-4200
  Mokena (G-14892)

**Prosser Construction Co** .......F....... 217 774-5032
Shelbyville *(G-19913)*

**Quikrete Chicago** .......D....... 630 557-8252
Elburn *(G-8906)*

**Quikrete Companies Inc** .......F....... 309 346-1184
Pekin *(G-17285)*

**Rochelle Vault Co** .......G....... 815 562-6484
Rochelle *(G-18108)*

**Safe Sheds Inc** .......G....... 888 556-1531
Alma *(G-423)*

**Southern Illinois Vault Co Inc** .......G....... 270 554-4436
Herrin *(G-11757)*

**Southfield Corporation** .......F....... 217 875-5455
Decatur *(G-7941)*

**Stockdale Block Systems LLC** .......G....... 815 416-1030
Morris *(G-15132)*

**Stonecraft Cast Stone LLC** .......G....... 708 653-1477
Steger *(G-20577)*

**V & N Concrete Products Inc** .......F....... 815 293-0315
Romeoville *(G-18875)*

**Vcna Prairie Indiana Inc** .......E....... 708 458-0400
Bridgeview *(G-2537)*

**Vitelli Concrete Products Inc** .......G....... 708 754-5846
Chicago Heights *(G-7136)*

**Welch Bros Inc** .......G....... 815 547-3000
Belvidere *(G-1796)*

## CONCRETE PRDTS, PRECAST, NEC

**Architectural Cast Ston** .......E....... 630 377-4800
West Chicago *(G-21661)*

**Atmi Dynacore LLC** .......G....... 815 838-9492
Lockport *(G-13704)*

**Atmi Precast Inc** .......E....... 630 897-0577
Aurora *(G-1113)*

**Avan Precast Concrete Pdts Inc** .......F....... 708 757-6200
Lynwood *(G-14017)*

**Concrete Specialties Co** .......E....... 847 608-1200
Elgin *(G-8999)*

**Concrete Unit Step Co Inc** .......G....... 618 344-7256
Collinsville *(G-7317)*

**Construction Equipment** .......G....... 618 345-0799
Belleville *(G-1619)*

**Doty & Sons Concrete Products** .......F....... 815 895-2884
Sycamore *(G-20793)*

**Gary & Larry Brown Trucking** .......G....... 618 268-6377
Raleigh *(G-17909)*

**Impact Polymer LLC** .......G....... 847 441-2394
Northfield *(G-16402)*

**Leonards Unit Step Co** .......G....... 815 744-1263
Rockdale *(G-18225)*

**Leonards Unit Step of Moline** .......G....... 309 792-9641
Colona *(G-7345)*

**Lombard Archtctral Prcast Pdts** .......E....... 708 389-1060
Chicago *(G-5535)*

**Lombard Investment Company** .......D....... 708 389-1060
Alsip *(G-484)*

**Mid-Illinois Concrete Inc** .......G....... 217 382-6650
Martinsville *(G-14338)*

**Mid-Illinois Concrete Inc** .......F....... 618 283-1600
Vandalia *(G-21116)*

**Mid-States Concrete Inds LLC** .......D....... 815 389-2277
South Beloit *(G-20162)*

**Midwest Perma-Column Inc** .......G....... 309 589-7949
Edwards *(G-8783)*

**Southern Illinois Redimix Inc** .......F....... 618 993-3600
Marion *(G-14290)*

**Super Mix of Wisconsin Inc** .......G....... 262 859-9000
McHenry *(G-14564)*

**Unit Step Company of Peoria** .......G....... 309 674-4392
Metamora *(G-14751)*

**Utility Concrete Products LLC** .......E....... 815 416-1000
Morris *(G-15140)*

**Van-Packer Co** .......E....... 309 895-2311
Buda *(G-2648)*

**Welch Bros Inc** .......C....... 847 741-6134
Elgin *(G-9233)*

## CONCRETE REINFORCING MATERIAL

**Gateway Construction Company** .......E....... 708 868-2926
Chicago *(G-4917)*

**Hohmann & Barnard Illinois LLC** .......E....... 773 586-6700
Chicago Ridge *(G-7150)*

**Mazel & Co Inc** .......F....... 773 533-1600
Chicago *(G-5662)*

**Midwest Color** .......F....... 847 647-1364
Niles *(G-16007)*

## CONCRETE: Asphaltic, Not From Refineries

**Tmw Enterprises Paving & Maint** .......E....... 630 350-7717
Bensenville *(G-2004)*

## CONCRETE: Dry Mixture

**Bonsal American Inc** .......D....... 847 678-6220
Franklin Park *(G-10415)*

## CONCRETE: Ready-Mixed

**A & L Construction Inc** .......E....... 708 343-1660
Melrose Park *(G-14577)*

**Advanced On-Site Concrete Inc** .......E....... 773 622-7836
Chicago *(G-3771)*

**Atlas Ready Mix Inc** .......G....... 618 271-0774
East Saint Louis *(G-8741)*

**Aztec Material Service Corp** .......G....... 773 521-0909
Chicago *(G-4010)*

**Ballard Bros Inc** .......F....... 217 374-2137
White Hall *(G-22183)*

**Barnett Redi-Mix Inc** .......G....... 618 276-4298
Junction *(G-12593)*

**Bee Line Service Inc** .......G....... 815 233-1812
Freeport *(G-10648)*

**Beelman Ready-Mix Inc** .......G....... 618 357-6120
Pinckneyville *(G-17544)*

**Beelman Ready-Mix Inc** .......E....... 618 646-5300
East Saint Louis *(G-8744)*

**Beelman Ready-Mix Inc** .......G....... 618 244-9600
Mount Vernon *(G-15400)*

**Beelman Ready-Mix Inc** .......G....... 618 247-3866
Sandoval *(G-19355)*

**Beelman Ready-Mix Inc** .......G....... 618 478-2044
Nashville *(G-15834)*

**Beelman Ready-Mix Inc** .......G....... 618 526-0260
Breese *(G-2439)*

**Biochemical Lab** .......G....... 708 447-3923
Riverside *(G-18029)*

**Bleigh Construction Company** .......G....... 217 222-5005
Quincy *(G-17805)*

**Blomberg Bros Inc** .......F....... 618 245-6321
Farina *(G-10174)*

**Bmi Products Northern Ill Inc** .......E....... 847 395-7110
Antioch *(G-625)*

**Bob Barnett Redi-Mix Inc** .......F....... 618 252-3581
Harrisburg *(G-11596)*

**Breckenridge Material Company** .......E....... 618 398-4141
Caseyville *(G-3394)*

**Builders Ready-Mix Co** .......E....... 847 866-6300
Evanston *(G-10018)*

**Canton Redi-Mix Inc** .......F....... 309 668-2261
Canton *(G-2984)*

**Canton Redi-Mix Inc** .......E....... 309 647-0019
Canton *(G-2985)*

**Capitol Ready-Mix Inc** .......E....... 217 528-1100
Springfield *(G-20407)*

**CCI Redi Mix** .......E....... 217 342-2299
Effingham *(G-8829)*

**Charleston Concrete Supply Co** .......F....... 217 345-6404
Charleston *(G-3592)*

**Chris Dj Mix LLC** .......G....... 312 725-3838
Chicago *(G-4369)*

**Cigar Mix & Detail Shop** .......G....... 708 396-1826
Calumet Park *(G-2957)*

**Clinard Ready Mix Inc** .......E....... 217 773-3965
Mount Sterling *(G-15391)*

**Clinton County Materials Corp** .......F....... 618 533-4252
Centralia *(G-3409)*

**Coal City Redi-Mix Co Inc** .......F....... 815 634-4455
Coal City *(G-7292)*

**Community Rady Mix of Pttsfeld** .......G....... 217 285-5548
Pittsfield *(G-17566)*

**Community Readymix Inc** .......E....... 217 245-6668
Jacksonville *(G-12385)*

**Concrete 1 Inc** .......G....... 630 357-1329
Naperville *(G-15634)*

**Concrete Supply LLC** .......G....... 618 646-5300
East Saint Louis *(G-8747)*

**Concrete Supply Tolono Inc** .......G....... 217 485-3100
Urbana *(G-21079)*

**Condominiums Northbrook Cort 1** .......G....... 847 498-1640
Lincolnshire *(G-13439)*

**Continental Materials Corp** .......F....... 312 541-7200
Chicago *(G-4459)*

**Contractors Ready-Mix Inc** .......G....... 217 482-5530
Mason City *(G-14362)*

**Contractors Ready-Mix Inc** .......F....... 217 735-2565
Lincoln *(G-13407)*

**Country Stone Inc** .......E....... 309 787-1744
Milan *(G-14781)*

**County Materials Corp** .......E....... 217 544-4607
Springfield *(G-20422)*

**County Materials Corp** .......E....... 217 352-4181
Champaign *(G-3470)*

**Crazy Horse Concrete Inc** .......E....... 217 523-4420
Springfield *(G-20423)*

**Curry Ready Mix of Petersburg** .......G....... 217 632-2516
Petersburg *(G-17535)*

**Curry Ready-Mix of Decatur** .......F....... 217 428-7177
Decatur *(G-7862)*

**Cyrulik Inc** .......G....... 217 935-6969
Clinton *(G-7280)*

**David Yates** .......G....... 618 656-7879
Edwardsville *(G-8794)*

**Diamond Ready Mix Inc** .......F....... 630 355-5414
Naperville *(G-15645)*

**Dollar Mix** .......G....... 773 582-7110
Chicago *(G-4622)*

**Edwards County Concrete LLC** .......G....... 618 445-2711
Albion *(G-361)*

**Elmhurst-Chicago Stone Company** .......E....... 630 832-4000
Elmhurst *(G-9865)*

**Elmhurst-Chicago Stone Company** .......E....... 630 983-6410
Bolingbrook *(G-2305)*

**Fairfield Ready Mix Inc** .......G....... 618 842-9462
Fairfield *(G-10141)*

**Fehrenbacher Ready-Mix Inc** .......G....... 618 395-2306
Olney *(G-16766)*

**Ferber George & Sons** .......G....... 217 733-2184
Fairmount *(G-10163)*

**Fishstone Studio Inc** .......G....... 815 276-0299
Crystal Lake *(G-7579)*

**Flora Ready Mix Inc** .......G....... 618 662-4818
Flora *(G-10207)*

**Fnh Ready Mix Inc** .......F....... 815 235-1400
Freeport *(G-10657)*

**Forrest Redi-Mix Inc** .......G....... 815 657-8241
Forrest *(G-10262)*

**Fox Redi-Mix Inc** .......G....... 217 774-2110
Shelbyville *(G-19907)*

**Franklin Park Building Mtls** .......G....... 847 455-3985
Franklin Park *(G-10472)*

**Fuller Brothers Ready Mix** .......G....... 217 532-2422
Hillsboro *(G-11891)*

**Gary & Larry Brown Trucking** .......G....... 618 268-6377
Raleigh *(G-17909)*

**GBS Liquidating Corp** .......G....... 309 342-4155
Galesburg *(G-10753)*

**Goreville Concrete Inc** .......E....... 618 995-2670
Goreville *(G-11252)*

**Gorman Brothers Ready Mix Inc** .......F....... 618 498-2173
Jerseyville *(G-12422)*

**Great River Ready Mix Inc** .......F....... 217 847-3515
Hamilton *(G-11535)*

**Grohne Concrete Products Co** .......G....... 217 877-4197
Decatur *(G-7886)*

**Gunther Construction Co** .......G....... 309 343-1032
Galesburg *(G-10756)*

**H J Mohr & Sons Company** .......F....... 708 366-0338
Oak Park *(G-16667)*

**Hahn Ready-Mix Company** .......G....... 309 582-2436
Aledo *(G-369)*

**Hamilton County Concrete Co** .......G....... 618 643-4333
Mc Leansboro *(G-14465)*

**Herman Bade & Sons** .......G....... 217 832-9444
Villa Grove *(G-21228)*

**Illini Concrete Inc** .......F....... 618 235-4141
Belleville *(G-1636)*

**Illini Concrete Inc** .......G....... 618 398-4141
Caseyville *(G-3397)*

**Illini Ready Mix Inc** .......G....... 618 833-7321
Anna *(G-605)*

**Illini Ready Mix Inc** .......G....... 618 734-0287
Carbondale *(G-3011)*

**Illini Ready Mix Inc** .......G....... 618 529-1626
Carbondale *(G-3012)*

**Info Corner Materials Inc** .......F....... 217 566-3561
Springfield *(G-20456)*

**J W Ossola Company Inc** .......G....... 815 339-6112
Granville *(G-11318)*

**J&J Ready Mix Inc** .......G....... 309 676-0579
East Peoria *(G-8716)*

**Jerry Berry Contracting Co** .......G....... 618 594-3339
Carlyle *(G-3055)*

**Joe Hatzer & Son Inc** .......G....... 815 673-5571
Streator *(G-20692)*

**Joe Hatzer & Son Inc** .......G....... 815 672-2161
Streator *(G-20693)*

**JW Ossola Co Inc** .......G....... 815 339-6113
Granville *(G-11319)*



Employee Codes: A=Over 500 employees, B=251-500
C=101-250, D=51-100, E=20-50, F=10-19, G=3-9

2017 Harris Illinois
Industrial Directory

1525

## CONCRETE: Ready-Mixed

Kendall County Concrete Inc ............... E ....... 630 851-9197
Aurora (G-1041)
Lafarge Building Materials Inc ........... D ....... 678 746-2000
Chicago (G-5434)
Lafarge North America Inc ................. C ....... 703 480-3600
Chicago (G-5435)
Lahood Construction Inc ..................... E ....... 309 699-5080
East Peoria (G-8723)
Langheim Ready Mix Inc ..................... G ....... 217 625-2351
Girard (G-10947)
Material Service Corporation .............. E ....... 815 838-2400
Romeoville (G-18842)
Max Miller ............................................ F ....... 708 758-7760
S Chicago Hts (G-19107)
Maxheimer Construction Inc ................ G ....... 309 444-4200
Washington (G-21386)
McLean County Asphalt Co ................. D ....... 309 827-6115
Bloomington (G-2194)
Menoni & Mocogni Inc ......................... F ....... 847 432-0850
Highland Park (G-11854)
Mertel Gravel Company Inc ................ F ....... 815 223-0468
Peru (G-17518)
Metropolis Ready Mix Inc ................... E ....... 618 524-8221
Metropolis (G-14758)
Meyer Material Co Merger Corp .......... E ....... 847 824-4111
Elburn (G-8892)
Meyer Material Co Merger Corp .......... E ....... 815 568-6119
Elburn (G-8893)
Meyer Material Co Merger Corp .......... E ....... 815 385-4920
Elburn (G-8894)
Meyer Material Co Merger Corp .......... E ....... 847 689-9200
Lake Bluff (G-12857)
Meyer Material Co Merger Corp .......... G ....... 815 568-7205
Elburn (G-8895)
Meyer Material Co Merger Corp .......... D ....... 815 943-2605
Harvard (G-11641)
Meyer Material Handling ..................... G ....... 414 768-1631
Elburn (G-8896)
Mid-Illinois Concrete Inc ...................... E ....... 217 235-5858
Mattoon (G-14404)
Mid-Illinois Concrete Inc ...................... G ....... 217 382-6650
Martinsville (G-14338)
Mid-Illinois Concrete Inc ...................... G ....... 618 664-1340
Greenville (G-11399)
Mid-Illinois Concrete Inc ...................... F ....... 618 283-1600
Vandalia (G-21116)
Mindful Mix ........................................... G ....... 847 284-4404
Lake Zurich (G-13105)
Mix Foods LLC ..................................... G ....... 224 338-0377
Ingleside (G-12194)
Mix Kitchen .......................................... G ....... 312 649-0330
Chicago (G-5776)
Mix N Mingle ........................................ G ....... 815 308-5170
Woodstock (G-22592)
Moeller Ready Mix Inc ......................... F ....... 217 243-7471
Jacksonville (G-12402)
Moline Consumers Co ......................... F ....... 309 757-8289
Moline (G-14958)
Monmouth Ready Mix Corp ................. G ....... 309 734-3211
Monmouth (G-15021)
Moultrie County Redi-Mix Co .............. G ....... 217 728-2334
Sullivan (G-20755)
Mt Crmel Stblzation Group Inc ............ E ....... 618 262-5118
Mount Carmel (G-15277)
Myers Concrete & Construction ......... G ....... 815 732-2591
Oregon (G-16828)
Narvick Bros Lumber Co Inc .............. E ....... 815 521-1173
Minooka (G-14844)
Narvick Bros Lumber Co Inc .............. G ....... 815 942-1173
Morris (G-15121)
Newton Ready Mix Inc ......................... F ....... 618 783-8611
Newton (G-15944)
ODaniel Trucking Co ........................... D ....... 618 382-5371
Carmi (G-3076)
Odum Concrete Products Inc ............. G ....... 618 942-4572
Herrin (G-11751)
Odum Concrete Products Inc ............. E ....... 618 993-6211
Marion (G-14275)
Oltman & Sons Inc .............................. G ....... 309 364-2849
Henry (G-11745)
Ozinga Bros Inc ................................... E ....... 708 326-4200
Mokena (G-14889)
Ozinga Bros Inc ................................... D ....... 708 326-4200
Chicago Heights (G-7116)
Ozinga Chicago Ready Mix Con ......... E ....... 708 479-9050
Alsip (G-504)
Ozinga Chicago Ready Mix Con ......... E ....... 312 432-5700
Chicago (G-6035)
Ozinga Chicago Ready Mix Con ......... E ....... 773 862-2817
Chicago (G-6036)
Ozinga Chicago Ready Mix Con ......... E ....... 847 447-0353
Chicago (G-6037)
Ozinga Chicago Ready Mix Con ......... D ....... 312 432-5700
Chicago (G-6038)
Ozinga Indiana Rdymx Con Inc .......... G ....... 708 479-9050
Mokena (G-14890)
Ozinga Materials Inc ........................... F ....... 309 364-3401
Mokena (G-14891)
Ozinga Ready Mix Concrete Inc ......... E ....... 708 326-4200
Mokena (G-14892)
Ozinga S Subn Rdymx Con Inc .......... E ....... 708 479-3080
Mokena (G-14893)
Ozinga S Subn Rdymx Con Inc .......... D ....... 708 326-4201
Mokena (G-14894)
Paxton Ready Mix Inc ......................... G ....... 217 379-2303
Paxton (G-17242)
Pbi Redi Mix & Trucking ..................... E ....... 217 562-3717
Pana (G-17138)
Peoples Coal and Lumber Co ............. F ....... 815 432-2456
Watseka (G-21425)
Pike County Concrete Inc ................... G ....... 217 285-5548
Pittsfield (G-17573)
Poggenpohl LLC ................................. G ....... 217 229-3411
Raymond (G-17939)
Poggenpohl LLC ................................. G ....... 217 824-2020
Taylorville (G-20844)
Point Ready Mix LLC ......................... G ....... 815 578-9100
McHenry (G-14547)
Prairie Central Ready Mix .................. G ....... 217 877-5210
Decatur (G-7928)
Prairie Group Management LLC ........ D ....... 708 458-0400
Bridgeview (G-2519)
Prairie Materials Group ...................... G ....... 815 207-6750
Shorewood (G-19930)
Prarie Material Sales Inc ................... G ....... 847 733-8809
Evanston (G-10090)
Princeton Ready-Mix Inc .................... F ....... 815 875-3359
Princeton (G-17759)
Quad County Ready Mix Swansea .... G ....... 618 257-9530
Swansea (G-20779)
Quad-County Ready Mix Corp ........... F ....... 618 243-6430
Okawville (G-16755)
Quad-County Ready Mix Corp ........... F ....... 618 588-4656
New Baden (G-15863)
Quad-County Ready Mix Corp ........... G ....... 618 526-7130
Breese (G-2446)
Quad-County Ready Mix Corp ........... E ....... 618 244-6973
Mount Vernon (G-15442)
Quad-County Ready Mix Corp ........... F ....... 618 327-3748
Nashville (G-15846)
Quad-County Ready Mix Corp ........... G ....... 618 594-2732
Carlyle (G-3057)
Quad-County Ready Mix Corp ........... F ....... 618 548-2477
Salem (G-19346)
Quad-County Ready Mix Corp ........... F ....... 618 295-3000
Marissa (G-15134)
Quality Ready Mix Concrete Co ......... G ....... 815 589-2013
Fulton (G-10704)
Quality Ready Mix Concrete Co ......... F ....... 815 772-7181
Morrison (G-15147)
Quality Ready Mix Concrete Co ......... G ....... 815 625-0750
Sterling (G-20608)
Quality Ready Mix Concrete Co ......... G ....... 815 288-6416
Dixon (G-8340)
R & L Ready Mix Inc ........................... F ....... 618 544-7514
Robinson (G-18070)
Ranger Redi-Mix & Mtls Inc ............... G ....... 815 337-2662
Woodstock (G-22605)
Rapco Ltd ............................................. G ....... 618 249-6614
Richview (G-17981)
Regional Ready Mix LLC ................... F ....... 815 562-1901
Rochelle (G-18104)
Riber Construction Inc ....................... G ....... 815 584-3337
Dwight (G-8592)
River Redi Mix Inc .............................. G ....... 815 795-2025
Marseilles (G-14317)
Riverstone Group Inc ......................... G ....... 309 757-8297
Moline (G-14967)
Riverstone Group Inc ......................... F ....... 309 788-9543
Rock Island (G-18202)
Roanoke Concrete Products Co ........ F ....... 309 698-7882
East Peoria (G-8732)
Rock River Ready Mix Inc ................. G ....... 815 625-1139
Dixon (G-8345)
Rock River Ready-Mix ........................ E ....... 815 288-2269
Dixon (G-8346)
Rogers Ready Mix & Mtls Inc ............ D ....... 815 234-8212
Byron (G-2920)
Rogers Ready Mix & Mtls Inc ............ G ....... 815 234-8044
Oregon (G-16831)
Rogers Ready Mix & Mtls Inc ............ E ....... 815 874-6626
Rockford (G-18595)
Rogers Ready Mix & Mtls Inc ............ F ....... 815 389-2223
Roscoe (G-18915)
Rogers Redi-Mix Inc ........................... F ....... 618 282-3844
Ruma (G-19088)
Roscoe Ready-Mix Inc ....................... G ....... 815 389-0888
Roscoe (G-18917)
Silver Bros Inc ..................................... G ....... 217 283-7751
Hoopeston (G-12117)
Southern Illinois Redimix Inc ............. F ....... 618 993-3600
Marion (G-14290)
Southfield Corporation ....................... D ....... 708 345-0030
Melrose Park (G-14694)
Southfield Corporation ....................... D ....... 708 563-4056
Addison (G-296)
Southfield Corporation ....................... D ....... 309 676-6121
Morton (G-15181)
Southfield Corporation ....................... E ....... 708 362-2520
Bridgeview (G-2529)
Southfield Corporation ....................... C ....... 815 284-3357
Dixon (G-8352)
Southfield Corporation ....................... F ....... 217 877-5210
Decatur (G-7942)
Southfield Corporation ....................... D ....... 708 458-0400
Bridgeview (G-2530)
Southfield Corporation ....................... E ....... 309 829-1087
Bloomington (G-2225)
Southfield Corporation ....................... E ....... 309 676-0576
Peoria (G-17459)
Southfield Corporation ....................... E ....... 708 458-0400
Oak Lawn (G-16644)
Speedy Redi Mix LLC ......................... E ....... 773 487-2000
Chicago (G-6557)
Spicy Mix Asian and American .......... G ....... 773 295-5765
Chicago (G-6559)
Stahl Lumber Company ...................... F ....... 309 695-4331
Wyoming (G-22640)
Stahl Lumber Company ...................... F ....... 309 385-2552
Wyoming (G-22641)
Staley Concrete Co ............................. E ....... 217 356-9533
Champaign (G-3546)
Sterling-Rock Falls Ready Mix ........... F ....... 815 288-3135
Dixon (G-8355)
Super Mix Inc ....................................... E ....... 815 544-9100
McHenry (G-14561)
Super Mix Inc ....................................... D ....... 815 578-9100
McHenry (G-14562)
Super Mix Concrete LLC .................... G ....... 262 742-2892
McHenry (G-14563)
Super Mix of Wisconsin Inc ............... F ....... 815 578-9100
McHenry (G-14565)
T H Davidson & Co Inc ....................... E ....... 815 464-2000
Oak Forest (G-16591)
T H Davidson & Co Inc ....................... G ....... 815 941-0280
Morris (G-15134)
Thelen Sand & Gravel Inc .................. F ....... 847 662-0760
Waukegan (G-21625)
Thelen Sand & Gravel Inc .................. D ....... 847 838-8800
Antioch (G-656)
Tri-City Ready-Mix .............................. G ....... 618 439-2071
Benton (G-2042)
Tri-County Concrete Inc ..................... G ....... 815 786-2179
Sandwich (G-19378)
Triangle Concrete Co Inc ................... G ....... 309 853-4334
Kewanee (G-12695)
Twin Cities Ready Mix Inc .................. F ....... 309 862-1500
Normal (G-16090)
United Ready Mix Inc .......................... E ....... 309 676-3287
Peoria (G-17473)
Upchurch Ready Mix Concrete .......... G ....... 618 235-6222
Belleville (G-1684)
Upchurch Ready Mix Concrete .......... G ....... 618 286-4808
Dupo (G-8582)
Upland Concrete .................................. G ....... 224 699-9909
East Dundee (G-8661)
Urban RE Mix LLC ............................... G ....... 312 360-0011
Chicago (G-6849)
Valley Concrete Inc ............................. D ....... 815 725-2422
Joliet (G-12586)
Vcna Prairie Inc ................................... D ....... 708 458-0400
Bridgeview (G-2535)
Vcna Prairie Illinois Inc ...................... G ....... 708 458-0400
Bridgeview (G-2536)
Wayland Ready Mix Concrete Svc .... F ....... 309 833-2064
Macomb (G-14134)
Westmore Supply Co .......................... F ....... 630 627-0278
Lombard (G-13883)
Westville Ready Mix Inc ..................... G ....... 217 267-2082
Westville (G-21931)

**Wille Bros Co**.........E....... 815 464-1300
Monee *(G-15009)*
**Wille Bros Co**.........D....... 708 388-9000
Chicago *(G-6982)*
**Winnetka Mews Condominium Assn**....G....... 847 501-2770
Winnetka *(G-22316)*

## CONDENSERS: Refrigeration

**Peerless America Incorporated**.........C....... 217 342-0400
Effingham *(G-8853)*

## CONDUITS & FITTINGS: Electric

**Anamet Electrical Inc**.........C....... 217 234-8844
Mattoon *(G-14382)*
**Anamet Inc**.........G....... 217 234-8844
Glen Ellyn *(G-10958)*
**Atlas Tube (chicago) LLC**.........B....... 773 646-4500
Chicago *(G-3984)*
**Beacon Fas & Components Inc**.........E....... 847 541-0404
Wheeling *(G-22013)*
**Cable Management Products Inc**.........G....... 630 723-0470
Aurora *(G-976)*
**Electri-Flex Company (del)**.........D....... 630 307-1095
Roselle *(G-18941)*
**Electric Conduit Cnstr Co**.........C....... 630 293-4474
Elburn *(G-8886)*
**Electric Conduit Construction**.........F....... 630 859-9310
Elburn *(G-8887)*
**John Maneely Company**.........C....... 773 254-0617
Chicago *(G-5316)*
**Panduit Corp**.........C....... 708 460-1800
Orland Park *(G-16882)*
**Panduit Corp**.........E....... 815 836-1800
Lockport *(G-13737)*
**Panduit Corp**.........A....... 708 532-1800
Tinley Park *(G-20937)*

## CONDUITS: Concrete

**Electric Conduit Cnstr Co**.........C....... 630 293-4474
Elburn *(G-8886)*

## CONFECTIONERY PRDTS WHOLESALERS

**Chipita America Inc**.........E....... 708 731-2434
Westchester *(G-21832)*
**Combined Technologies Inc**.........G....... 847 968-4855
Libertyville *(G-13317)*
**Frito-Lay North America Inc**.........C....... 708 331-7200
Oak Forest *(G-16582)*
**Select Snacks Company Inc**.........D....... 773 933-2167
Chicago *(G-6475)*

## CONFECTIONS & CANDY

**American Convenience Inc**.........F....... 815 344-6040
McHenry *(G-14480)*
**Amy Wertheim**.........G....... 309 830-4361
Atlanta *(G-946)*
**Andersons Candy Shop Inc**.........F....... 815 678-6000
Richmond *(G-17957)*
**Andrews Caramel LLC**.........F....... 773 286-2224
Chicago *(G-3904)*
**Andrews Caramel Apples Inc**.........F....... 773 286-2224
Libertyville *(G-13303)*
**Baileys Fudge & Fine Gifts Inc**.........G....... 217 231-3834
Quincy *(G-17799)*
**Belgian Chocolatier Piron Inc**.........G....... 847 864-5504
Evanston *(G-10014)*
**Bobbie Haycraft**.........G....... 217 856-2194
Humboldt *(G-12128)*
**Cambridge Brands Mfg Inc**.........G....... 773 838-3400
Chicago *(G-4221)*
**Candy Tech LLC**.........F....... 847 229-1011
Park Ridge *(G-17186)*
**Candyality**.........G....... 773 472-7800
Chicago *(G-4226)*
**Capol LLC**.........G....... 224 545-5095
Deerfield *(G-7993)*
**Cellas Confections Inc**.........D....... 773 838-3400
Chicago *(G-4267)*
**Colleens Confection**.........G....... 630 653-2231
Carol Stream *(G-3133)*
**Creative Confections Inc**.........G....... 847 724-0990
Glenview *(G-11117)*
**Das Foods LLC**.........G....... 224 715-9289
Chicago *(G-4561)*
**Doumak Inc**.........D....... 630 594-5400
Bensenville *(G-1882)*
**Element Bars Inc**.........F....... 888 411-3536
Chicago *(G-4723)*
**Fannie May Cnfctons Brands Inc**.........F....... 773 693-9100
Melrose Park *(G-14635)*
**Ferrara Candy Company**.........B....... 708 366-0500
Oakbrook Terrace *(G-16707)*
**Ferrara Candy Company**.........B....... 630 366-0500
Forest Park *(G-10244)*
**Ferrara Candy Company**.........G....... 630 378-4197
Bolingbrook *(G-2309)*
**Ferrara Candy Company**.........F....... 708 432-4407
Bellwood *(G-1705)*
**Ferrara Candy Company**.........B....... 708 488-1892
Forest Park *(G-10245)*
**Galenas Kandy Kitchen**.........G....... 815 777-0241
Galena *(G-10723)*
**Goelitz Confectionery Company**.........C....... 847 689-2225
North Chicago *(G-16181)*
**Hershey Company**.........A....... 618 544-3111
Robinson *(G-18064)*
**Hollingworth Candies Inc**.........E....... 815 838-2275
Lockport *(G-13721)*
**Imaginings 3 Inc**.........E....... 847 647-1370
Niles *(G-15987)*
**Jelly Belly Candy Company**.........C....... 847 689-2225
North Chicago *(G-16183)*
**John B Sanfilippo & Son Inc**.........C....... 847 289-1800
Elgin *(G-9083)*
**Killeen Confectionery LLC**.........G....... 312 804-0009
Wilmette *(G-22258)*
**La Sweet Inc**.........F....... 252 340-0390
Lincolnwood *(G-13520)*
**Long Grove Confectionery Co**.........E....... 847 459-3100
Buffalo Grove *(G-2728)*
**Mars Chocolate North Amer LLC**.........A....... 662 335-8000
Chicago *(G-5630)*
**Mars Chocolate North Amer LLC**.........C....... 630 850-9898
Burr Ridge *(G-2864)*
**Mederer Group**.........G....... 630 860-4587
Bensenville *(G-1948)*
**Mexicandy Distributor Inc**.........G....... 773 847-0024
Chicago *(G-5708)*
**Mondelez Global LLC**.........C....... 815 877-8081
Loves Park *(G-13968)*
**Monogram Creative Group Inc**.........G....... 312 802-1433
Glenview *(G-11170)*
**MSI Green Inc**.........G....... 312 421-6550
Chicago *(G-5826)*
**Nestle Usa Inc**.........D....... 847 957-7850
Franklin Park *(G-10541)*
**Nestle Usa Inc**.........C....... 847 808-5300
Buffalo Grove *(G-2748)*
**Office Snax Inc**.........G....... 630 789-1783
Oak Brook *(G-16552)*
**Peases Inc**.........F....... 217 523-3721
Springfield *(G-20501)*
**Peases Inc**.........F....... 217 529-2912
Springfield *(G-20502)*
**Peerless Confection Company**.........D....... 773 281-6100
Lincolnwood *(G-13529)*
**Princess Foods Inc**.........F....... 847 933-1820
Skokie *(G-20060)*
**Rebel Brands LLC**.........G....... 312 804-0009
Wilmette *(G-22264)*
**Ruckers Mkin Batch Candies Inc**.........E....... 618 945-7778
Bridgeport *(G-2455)*
**Silvestri Sweets Inc**.........F....... 630 232-2500
Geneva *(G-10867)*
**Sweet Company**.........F....... 815 462-4586
Mokena *(G-14909)*
**Taylors Candy Inc**.........E....... 708 371-0332
Alsip *(G-534)*
**Terri Lynn Inc**.........C....... 847 741-1900
Elgin *(G-9210)*
**Toffee Time**.........G....... 309 788-2466
Rock Island *(G-18208)*
**Tootsie Roll Company Inc**.........A....... 773 838-3400
Chicago *(G-6741)*
**Tootsie Roll Industries Inc**.........A....... 773 838-3400
Chicago *(G-6742)*
**Tootsie Roll Industries LLC**.........G....... 773 245-4202
Chicago *(G-6743)*
**Wm Wrigley Jr Company**.........B....... 312 280-4710
Chicago *(G-7012)*
**Wm Wrigley Jr Company**.........A....... 312 644-2121
Chicago *(G-7014)*
**Wrigley Manufacturing Co LLC**.........B....... 630 553-4800
Yorkville *(G-22677)*
**Zb Importing Inc**.........D....... 708 222-8330
Cicero *(G-7248)*

## CONFINEMENT SURVEILLANCE SYS MAINTENANCE & MONITORING SVCS

**Moog Inc**.........E....... 770 987-7550
Northbrook *(G-16313)*

## CONNECTORS & TERMINALS: Electrical Device Uses

**Amerline Enterprises Co Inc**.........E....... 847 671-6554
Schiller Park *(G-19802)*
**Central Rubber Company**.........E....... 815 544-2191
Belvidere *(G-1745)*
**Cinch Connectors Inc**.........D....... 630 705-6001
Lombard *(G-13780)*
**Connomac Corporation**.........E....... 708 482-3434
La Grange *(G-12729)*
**David Jeskey**.........G....... 630 659-6337
Saint Charles *(G-19168)*
**French Corporation**.........E....... 708 354-9000
La Grange *(G-12732)*
**Gateway Cable Inc**.........G....... 630 766-7969
Lisle *(G-13592)*
**Imperial Fabricators Co**.........E....... 773 463-5522
Franklin Park *(G-10495)*
**Itron Corporation Del**.........F....... 708 222-5320
Cicero *(G-7207)*
**J P Goldenne Incorporated**.........F....... 847 776-5063
Palatine *(G-17045)*
**Molex LLC**.........A....... 630 969-4550
Lisle *(G-13625)*
**Molex LLC**.........G....... 630 527-4363
Bolingbrook *(G-2345)*
**Molex LLC**.........F....... 630 512-8787
Downers Grove *(G-8489)*
**Molex International Inc**.........F....... 630 969-4550
Lisle *(G-13627)*
**Molex Premise Networks Inc**.........A....... 866 733-6659
Lisle *(G-13628)*
**Panduit Corp**.........E....... 815 836-1800
Lockport *(G-13737)*
**Remke Industries Inc**.........D....... 847 541-3780
Wheeling *(G-22135)*
**Remke Industries Inc**.........D....... 847 325-7835
Wheeling *(G-22136)*
**Special Mine Services Inc**.........D....... 618 932-2151
West Frankfort *(G-21820)*
**Woodhead Industries LLC**.........B....... 847 353-2500
Lincolnshire *(G-13490)*

## CONNECTORS: Cord, Electric

**Shattuc Cord Specialties Inc**.........F....... 847 360-9500
Waukegan *(G-21615)*

## CONNECTORS: Electrical

**Amphenol Eec Inc**.........E....... 773 463-8343
Chicago *(G-3894)*
**Cinch Connectors Inc**.........B....... 630 705-6001
Lombard *(G-13781)*
**Clements National Company**.........G....... 708 594-5890
Broadview *(G-2569)*
**Eastco Inc**.........G....... 708 499-1701
Oak Lawn *(G-16617)*
**Mac Lean-Fogg Company**.........C....... 847 288-2534
Franklin Park *(G-10519)*
**Pancon Illinois LLC**.........G....... 630 972-6400
Bolingbrook *(G-2356)*
**Possehl Connector Svcs SC Inc**.........E....... 803 366-8316
Elk Grove Village *(G-9687)*
**Sicame Corp**.........D....... 630 238-6680
Aurora *(G-1217)*

## CONNECTORS: Electronic

**Advantage Components Inc**.........E....... 815 725-8644
Joliet *(G-12450)*
**Amphenol Corporation**.........D....... 800 944-6446
Lisle *(G-13559)*
**Amphenol Corporation**.........G....... 847 478-5600
Lincolnshire *(G-13427)*
**Amphenol Fiber Optic Products**.........E....... 630 960-1010
Lisle *(G-13560)*
**B M I Inc**.........C....... 847 839-6000
Schaumburg *(G-19456)*
**Belden Energy Solutions Inc**.........G....... 800 235-3361
Elmhurst *(G-9838)*
**Bragi NA LLC**.........D....... 708 717-5000
Frankfort *(G-10305)*
**C D T Manufacturing Inc**.........G....... 847 679-2361
Skokie *(G-19972)*

## CONNECTORS: Electronic

|  | |  |
|---|---|---|
| Central Rubber Company........E | | 815 544-2191 |
| Belvidere (G-1745) | | |
| Cinch Cnnctivity Solutions Inc........C | | 847 739-0300 |
| Lombard (G-13779) | | |
| Cinch Connectors Inc........D | | 630 705-6001 |
| Lombard (G-13780) | | |
| Continental Automation Inc........E | | 630 584-5100 |
| Saint Charles (G-19162) | | |
| Conxall Corporation........C | | 630 834-7504 |
| Villa Park (G-21245) | | |
| CTS Corporation........C | | 630 577-8800 |
| Lisle (G-13579) | | |
| Custom Assembly LLC........C | | 630 595-4855 |
| Wood Dale (G-22356) | | |
| Data Accessories Inc........G | | 847 669-3640 |
| Huntley (G-12136) | | |
| David Jeskey........G | | 630 659-6337 |
| Saint Charles (G-19168) | | |
| Eastco Inc........G | | 708 499-1701 |
| Oak Lawn (G-16617) | | |
| Element14 Inc........E | | 773 784-5100 |
| Chicago (G-4724) | | |
| Evoys Corp........G | | 773 736-4200 |
| Chicago (G-4791) | | |
| Gage Applied Technologies LLC........E | | 815 838-0005 |
| Lockport (G-13716) | | |
| Glenair Inc........E | | 847 679-8833 |
| Lincolnwood (G-13515) | | |
| Hale Devices Inc........E | | 305 394-4119 |
| Chicago (G-5034) | | |
| Harting Inc of North America........E | | 847 741-2700 |
| Elgin (G-9058) | | |
| Harting Inc of North America........E | | 847 741-1500 |
| Elgin (G-9059) | | |
| Hirose Electric (usa) Inc........D | | 630 282-6700 |
| Downers Grove (G-8459) | | |
| Iconn Systems LLC........E | | 630 827-6000 |
| Lombard (G-13811) | | |
| Ip Media Holdings........E | | 847 714-1177 |
| Wheeling (G-22078) | | |
| Kylon Midwest........G | | 773 699-3640 |
| Chicago (G-5416) | | |
| Mac Lean-Fogg Company........D | | 847 566-0010 |
| Mundelein (G-15521) | | |
| Methode Development Co........D | | 708 867-6777 |
| Chicago (G-5703) | | |
| Methode Electronics Inc........B | | 708 867-6777 |
| Chicago (G-5704) | | |
| Methode Electronics Inc........C | | 847 577-9545 |
| Rolling Meadows (G-18744) | | |
| Methode Electronics Inc........A | | 217 357-3941 |
| Carthage (G-3316) | | |
| Microway Systems Inc........E | | 847 679-8833 |
| Lincolnwood (G-13525) | | |
| Molex LLC........F | | 847 353-2500 |
| Lincolnshire (G-13466) | | |
| Molex LLC........G | | 630 527-4357 |
| Lisle (G-13626) | | |
| Molex LLC........E | | 630 969-4747 |
| Bolingbrook (G-2346) | | |
| Molex LLC........F | | 630 512-8787 |
| Downers Grove (G-8489) | | |
| Molex Incorporated........F | | 630 969-4550 |
| Naperville (G-15698) | | |
| Molex International Inc........F | | 630 969-4550 |
| Lisle (G-13627) | | |
| Nec Display Solutions Amer Inc........G | | 630 467-5000 |
| Itasca (G-12327) | | |
| Newko Tool & Engineering Co........E | | 847 359-1670 |
| Palatine (G-17058) | | |
| Nobility Corporation........E | | 847 677-3204 |
| Skokie (G-20045) | | |
| P K Neuses Incorporated........G | | 847 253-6555 |
| Rolling Meadows (G-18756) | | |
| Switchcraft Inc........B | | 773 792-2700 |
| Chicago (G-6653) | | |
| Switchcraft Holdco Inc........G | | 773 792-2700 |
| Chicago (G-6654) | | |
| Te Connectivity Corporation........D | | 847 680-7400 |
| Mundelein (G-15563) | | |
| United Universal Inds Inc........E | | 815 727-4445 |
| Joliet (G-12585) | | |
| Woodhead Industries LLC........B | | 847 353-2500 |
| Lincolnshire (G-13490) | | |

### CONNECTORS: Power, Electric

| | | |
|---|---|---|
| David Jeskey........G | | 630 659-6337 |
| Saint Charles (G-19168) | | |

### CONSERVATION PROGRAMS ADMINISTRATION SVCS

| | | |
|---|---|---|
| Ill Dept Natural Resources........G | | 217 498-9208 |
| Rochester (G-18118) | | |
| Ill Dept Natural Resources........F | | 217 782-4970 |
| Springfield (G-20453) | | |
| Natural Resources Ill Dept........E | | 618 439-4320 |
| Benton (G-2036) | | |

### CONSTRUCTION & MINING MACHINERY WHOLESALERS

| | | |
|---|---|---|
| Altorfer Power Systems........G | | 309 697-1234 |
| Bartonville (G-1391) | | |
| Anna-Jonesboro Motor Co Inc........G | | 618 833-4486 |
| Anna (G-601) | | |
| C S O Corp........E | | 630 365-6600 |
| Virgil (G-21302) | | |
| Compania Brasileira De T........G | | 319 550-6440 |
| Mount Olive (G-15301) | | |
| Global Track Property USA Inc........G | | 630 213-6863 |
| Bartlett (G-1350) | | |
| Hg-Farley Laserlab USA Inc........E | | 815 874-1400 |
| Rockford (G-18418) | | |
| Mikes Inc........D | | 618 254-4491 |
| South Roxana (G-20314) | | |
| Rogan Group Inc........G | | 708 371-4191 |
| Merrionette Park (G-14738) | | |
| Sauber Manufacturing Company........D | | 630 365-6600 |
| Virgil (G-21303) | | |
| Spl Software Alliance LLC........G | | 309 266-0304 |
| Morton (G-15182) | | |
| USA Hoist Company Inc........E | | 815 740-1890 |
| Crest Hill (G-7470) | | |
| West Side Tractor Sales Co........E | | 815 961-3160 |
| Rockford (G-18678) | | |

### CONSTRUCTION & ROAD MAINTENANCE EQPT: Drags, Road

| | | |
|---|---|---|
| Central Township Road & Bridge........G | | 618 704-5517 |
| Greenville (G-11390) | | |
| Mfs Holdings LLC........E | | 815 385-7700 |
| McHenry (G-14532) | | |
| Steuben Township........F | | 309 208-7073 |
| Sparland (G-20315) | | |

### CONSTRUCTION EQPT REPAIR SVCS

| | | |
|---|---|---|
| Braden Rock Bit........G | | 618 435-4519 |
| Benton (G-2024) | | |
| R W Bradley Supply Company........G | | 217 528-8438 |
| Springfield (G-20510) | | |

### CONSTRUCTION EQPT: Attachments

| | | |
|---|---|---|
| Baird Inc........G | | 217 526-3407 |
| Morrisonville (G-15150) | | |
| C S O Corp........E | | 630 365-6600 |
| Virgil (G-21302) | | |
| Global Track Property USA Inc........G | | 630 213-6863 |
| Bartlett (G-1350) | | |
| Paul Wever Construction Eqp Co........F | | 309 965-2005 |
| Goodfield (G-11248) | | |
| Rockford Rigging Inc........G | | 309 263-0566 |
| Morton (G-15180) | | |
| Sauber Manufacturing Company........D | | 630 365-6600 |
| Virgil (G-21303) | | |
| Woods Equipment Company........D | | 815 732-2141 |
| Oregon (G-16834) | | |

### CONSTRUCTION EQPT: Attachments, Snow Plow

| | | |
|---|---|---|
| Flink Company........E | | 815 673-4321 |
| Streator (G-20688) | | |
| Henderson Products Inc........F | | 847 836-4996 |
| Gilberts (G-10921) | | |
| Tim Wallace Ldscp Sup Co Inc........F | | 630 759-6813 |
| Bolingbrook (G-2379) | | |

### CONSTRUCTION EQPT: Attachments, Subsoiler, Tractor Mounted

| | | |
|---|---|---|
| Ovis Loader Attachments Inc........G | | 618 203-2757 |
| Carbondale (G-3017) | | |

### CONSTRUCTION EQPT: Backhoes, Tractors, Cranes & Similar Eqpt

| | | |
|---|---|---|
| Clarke Equipment Company........G | | 701 241-8700 |
| Woodridge (G-22461) | | |
| Manitou Americas Inc........G | | 262 334-9461 |
| Belvidere (G-1769) | | |
| Mjmc Inc........E | | 708 596-5200 |
| Hazel Crest (G-11713) | | |
| National Tractor Parts Inc........E | | 630 552-4235 |
| Plano (G-17668) | | |

### CONSTRUCTION EQPT: Bucket Or Scarifier Teeth

| | | |
|---|---|---|
| USA Star Group of Company........G | | 773 456-6677 |
| Chicago (G-6857) | | |

### CONSTRUCTION EQPT: Cabs

| | | |
|---|---|---|
| Bergstrom Electrified Systems........G | | 815 874-7821 |
| Rockford (G-18282) | | |
| Bergstrom Inc........B | | 815 874-7821 |
| Rockford (G-18283) | | |
| Bergstrom Parts LLC........G | | 815 874-7821 |
| Rockford (G-18284) | | |
| Interntional Eqp Solutions LLC........D | | 630 570-6880 |
| Oak Brook (G-16526) | | |

### CONSTRUCTION EQPT: Crane Carriers

| | | |
|---|---|---|
| Avanti Motor Carriers Inc........G | | 630 313-9160 |
| Naperville (G-15798) | | |
| Lanigan Holdings LLC........F | | 708 596-5200 |
| Hazel Crest (G-11710) | | |
| Walter Payton Power Eqp LLC........E | | 708 656-7700 |
| Riverdale (G-18027) | | |

### CONSTRUCTION EQPT: Cranes

| | | |
|---|---|---|
| Engineered Fluid Pwr Con Cons........G | | 815 332-3344 |
| Cherry Valley (G-3641) | | |
| Snook Equipment Crane Inc........G | | 815 223-0003 |
| Joliet (G-12577) | | |
| Uesco Industries Inc........G | | 708 385-7700 |
| Alsip (G-536) | | |

### CONSTRUCTION EQPT: Grinders, Stone, Portable

| | | |
|---|---|---|
| Czarnik Precision Grinding Mch........G | | 708 229-9639 |
| Oak Lawn (G-16614) | | |

### CONSTRUCTION EQPT: Hammer Mills, Port, Incl Rock/Ore Crush

| | | |
|---|---|---|
| Genesis III Inc........E | | 815 537-7900 |
| Prophetstown (G-17769) | | |

### CONSTRUCTION EQPT: Rock Crushing Machinery, Portable

| | | |
|---|---|---|
| Flsmidth Pekin LLC........D | | 309 347-3031 |
| Pekin (G-17263) | | |

### CONSTRUCTION EQPT: Roofing Eqpt

| | | |
|---|---|---|
| Illinois Tool Works Inc........F | | 847 918-6473 |
| Libertyville (G-13337) | | |
| Machine Solution Providers Inc........D | | 630 717-7040 |
| Downers Grove (G-8481) | | |
| Omg Inc........E | | 630 228-8377 |
| Addison (G-235) | | |
| Rdi Group Inc........C | | 630 773-4900 |
| Itasca (G-12347) | | |
| Reload Sales Inc........E | | 618 588-2866 |
| New Baden (G-15864) | | |

### CONSTRUCTION EQPT: Spreaders, Aggregates

| | | |
|---|---|---|
| Swenson Spreader LLC........C | | 815 393-4455 |
| Lindenwood (G-13551) | | |

### CONSTRUCTION EQPT: Tractors

| | | |
|---|---|---|
| Caterpillar Inc........B | | 309 675-1000 |
| East Peoria (G-8704) | | |
| Caterpillar Inc........B | | 217 424-1809 |
| Decatur (G-7854) | | |
| Caterpillar Inc........A | | 217 475-4000 |
| Decatur (G-7853) | | |

# PRODUCT SECTION

## CONSTRUCTION MATERIALS, WHOLESALE: Paving Materials

Washington URS Div .................... G ....... 309 578-8113
Mossville *(G-15255)*

### CONSTRUCTION EQPT: Trucks, Off-Highway

Kress Corporation .................... D ....... 309 446-3395
Brimfield *(G-2547)*
Sibor Express Ltd .................... G ....... 773 499-8707
La Grange *(G-12745)*

### CONSTRUCTION EQPT: Wrecker Hoists, Automobile

High Point Recovery Company .................... G ....... 217 821-7777
Toledo *(G-20964)*
S&S Recovery .................... G ....... 217 538-2206
Fillmore *(G-10189)*

### CONSTRUCTION MATERIALS, WHOL: Concrete/Cinder Bldg Prdts

Hamilton Concrete Products Co .................... G ....... 217 847-3118
Hamilton *(G-11537)*
Upland Concrete .................... G ....... 224 699-9909
East Dundee *(G-8661)*

### CONSTRUCTION MATERIALS, WHOLESALE: Aggregate

Rogers Ready Mix & Mtls Inc .................... D ....... 815 234-8212
Byron *(G-2920)*

### CONSTRUCTION MATERIALS, WHOLESALE: Air Ducts, Sheet Metal

Bisco Enterprise Inc .................... F ....... 630 628-1831
Schaumburg *(G-19463)*

### CONSTRUCTION MATERIALS, WHOLESALE: Architectural Metalwork

Carl Stahl Decorcble Innovtns .................... F ....... 312 454-2996
Burr Ridge *(G-2828)*

### CONSTRUCTION MATERIALS, WHOLESALE: Awnings

Acme Awning Co Inc .................... G ....... 847 446-0153
Lake Zurich *(G-13035)*
Anderson Awning & Shutter .................... G ....... 815 654-1155
Machesney Park *(G-14056)*
Tri State Aluminum Products .................... F ....... 815 877-6081
Loves Park *(G-14003)*

### CONSTRUCTION MATERIALS, WHOLESALE: Brick, Exc Refractory

Atlas Concrete Products Co .................... F ....... 217 528-7368
Springfield *(G-20390)*
Bricks Inc .................... G ....... 630 897-6926
Aurora *(G-1121)*
Richards Brick Company .................... D ....... 618 656-0230
Edwardsville *(G-8812)*
Sesser Concrete Products Co .................... F ....... 618 625-2811
Sesser *(G-19895)*
Stone Center Inc .................... G ....... 630 971-2060
Lisle *(G-13664)*

### CONSTRUCTION MATERIALS, WHOLESALE: Building Stone

Lansing Cut Stone Co .................... F ....... 708 474-7515
Lansing *(G-13170)*
Stone Design Inc .................... F ....... 630 790-5715
Glendale Heights *(G-11075)*
Stone Design Inc .................... E ....... 630 790-5715
Glendale Heights *(G-11076)*

### CONSTRUCTION MATERIALS, WHOLESALE: Building Stone, Granite

Midwest Stone Sales Inc .................... F ....... 815 254-6600
Plainfield *(G-17628)*

### CONSTRUCTION MATERIALS, WHOLESALE: Building Stone, Marble

American Marble & Granite Inc .................... G ....... 815 741-1710
Crest Hill *(G-7457)*

House Granite & Marble Corp .................... G ....... 847 928-1111
Schiller Park *(G-19839)*
Marble Emporium Inc .................... E ....... 847 205-4000
Northbrook *(G-16306)*

### CONSTRUCTION MATERIALS, WHOLESALE: Building, Exterior

Arrowtech Pallet & Crating .................... D ....... 815 547-9300
Belvidere *(G-1734)*
Chicago Flameproof WD Spc Corp .................... E ....... 630 859-0009
Montgomery *(G-15037)*
Continental Materials Corp .................... F ....... 312 541-7200
Chicago *(G-4459)*
H J Mohr & Sons Company .................... F ....... 708 366-0338
Oak Park *(G-16667)*
Illinois Tool Works Inc .................... G ....... 708 720-7070
Frankfort *(G-10332)*
Logan Square Aluminum Sup Inc .................... D ....... 847 985-1700
Schaumburg *(G-19622)*
Woodx Lumber Inc .................... G ....... 331 979-2171
Elmhurst *(G-9962)*

### CONSTRUCTION MATERIALS, WHOLESALE: Building, Interior

Architectural Distributors .................... G ....... 847 223-5800
Grayslake *(G-11320)*
Customwood Stairs Inc .................... E ....... 630 739-5252
Romeoville *(G-18815)*

### CONSTRUCTION MATERIALS, WHOLESALE: Cement

Illinois Cement Company LLC .................... C ....... 815 224-2112
La Salle *(G-12776)*

### CONSTRUCTION MATERIALS, WHOLESALE: Ceramic, Exc Refractory

Nidec-Shimpo America Corp .................... E ....... 630 924-7138
Itasca *(G-12331)*

### CONSTRUCTION MATERIALS, WHOLESALE: Clay, Exc Refractory

Amcol International Corp .................... E ....... 847 851-1500
Hoffman Estates *(G-11991)*

### CONSTRUCTION MATERIALS, WHOLESALE: Concrete Mixtures

Advanced On-Site Concrete Inc .................... E ....... 773 622-7836
Chicago *(G-3771)*
Material Service Corporation .................... E ....... 815 838-2400
Romeoville *(G-18842)*
Rock River Ready Mix Inc .................... G ....... 815 288-2260
Dixon *(G-8344)*

### CONSTRUCTION MATERIALS, WHOLESALE: Doors, Garage

Bricks Inc .................... G ....... 630 897-6926
Aurora *(G-1121)*

### CONSTRUCTION MATERIALS, WHOLESALE: Doors, Sliding

Cmp Millwork Co .................... G ....... 630 832-6462
Elmhurst *(G-9851)*
Metal Products Sales Corp .................... G ....... 708 301-6844
Lockport *(G-13732)*

### CONSTRUCTION MATERIALS, WHOLESALE: Drywall Materials

Illinois Fibre Specialty Co .................... E ....... 773 376-1122
Chicago *(G-5157)*
Pro Patch Systems Inc .................... G ....... 847 356-8100
Lake Villa *(G-13024)*

### CONSTRUCTION MATERIALS, WHOLESALE: Fiberglass Building Mat

Npi Holding Corp .................... G ....... 217 391-1229
Springfield *(G-20488)*
Nudo Products Inc .................... C ....... 217 528-5636
Springfield *(G-20490)*

### CONSTRUCTION MATERIALS, WHOLESALE: Glass

Euroview Enterprises LLC .................... E ....... 630 227-3300
Elmhurst *(G-9869)*
House of Color .................... F ....... 708 352-3222
Countryside *(G-7432)*
Moore Memorials .................... F ....... 708 636-6532
Chicago Ridge *(G-7152)*
Shoreline Glass Co Inc .................... E ....... 312 829-9500
Hillside *(G-11933)*

### CONSTRUCTION MATERIALS, WHOLESALE: Grain Storage Bins

Arrows Up Inc .................... G ....... 847 305-2550
Arlington Heights *(G-717)*

### CONSTRUCTION MATERIALS, WHOLESALE: Gravel

Rock River Ready-Mix .................... E ....... 815 288-2269
Dixon *(G-8346)*

### CONSTRUCTION MATERIALS, WHOLESALE: Joists

Heckmann Building Products Inc .................... E ....... 708 865-2403
Melrose Park *(G-14652)*
Selco Industries .................... G ....... 708 499-1060
Chicago Ridge *(G-7158)*

### CONSTRUCTION MATERIALS, WHOLESALE: Limestone

Riverstone Group Inc .................... F ....... 309 933-1123
Cleveland *(G-7271)*

### CONSTRUCTION MATERIALS, WHOLESALE: Masons' Materials

Harvey Cement Products Inc .................... F ....... 708 333-1900
Harvey *(G-11668)*
Northfield Block Company .................... G ....... 708 458-8130
Berwyn *(G-2069)*

### CONSTRUCTION MATERIALS, WHOLESALE: Metal Buildings

Surtreat Construction Svcs LLC .................... G ....... 630 986-0780
Schaumburg *(G-19746)*

### CONSTRUCTION MATERIALS, WHOLESALE: Millwork

Kohout Woodwork Inc .................... G ....... 630 628-6257
Addison *(G-172)*
Mid-West Millwork Wholesale .................... G ....... 618 407-5940
Mascoutah *(G-14356)*
River City Millwork Inc .................... D ....... 800 892-9297
Rockford *(G-18556)*
Triezenberg Millwork Co .................... G ....... 708 489-9062
Crestwood *(G-7506)*

### CONSTRUCTION MATERIALS, WHOLESALE: Molding, All Materials

AGCO Recycling LLC .................... F ....... 217 224-9048
Quincy *(G-17790)*
Southern Mold Finishing Inc .................... F ....... 618 983-5049
Johnston City *(G-12446)*

### CONSTRUCTION MATERIALS, WHOLESALE: Pallets, Wood

F and L Pallets Inc .................... G ....... 773 364-0798
Chicago *(G-4801)*
Northern Pallet and Supply Co .................... F ....... 847 716-1400
Northfield *(G-16412)*

### CONSTRUCTION MATERIALS, WHOLESALE: Paving Materials

Curran Contracting Company .................... G ....... 815 758-8113
Dekalb *(G-8081)*
Lane Construction Corporation .................... F ....... 815 846-4466
Shorewood *(G-19929)*

# CONSTRUCTION MATERIALS, WHOLESALE: Prefabricated Structures

## PRODUCT SECTION

### CONSTRUCTION MATERIALS, WHOLESALE: Prefabricated Structures

- Morton Buildings Inc .................................G....... 217 357-3713
  Carthage *(G-3317)*
- Morton Buildings Inc .................................F....... 309 936-7282
  Atkinson *(G-944)*

### CONSTRUCTION MATERIALS, WHOLESALE: Roof, Asphalt/Sheet Metal

- Chicago Metallic Company LLC ...................C....... 708 563-4600
  Chicago *(G-4334)*
- Crown Coatings Company ..........................F....... 630 365-9925
  Elburn *(G-8881)*

### CONSTRUCTION MATERIALS, WHOLESALE: Roofing & Siding Material

- Cofair Products Inc ..................................G....... 847 626-1500
  Skokie *(G-19985)*
- TMJ Architectural LLC ..............................G....... 815 388-7820
  Crystal Lake *(G-7666)*

### CONSTRUCTION MATERIALS, WHOLESALE: Sand

- Central Stone Company ............................D....... 309 757-8250
  Moline *(G-14921)*
- GBS Liquidating Corp ...............................G....... 309 342-4155
  Galesburg *(G-10753)*
- Mertel Gravel Company Inc .......................F....... 815 223-0468
  Peru *(G-17518)*

### CONSTRUCTION MATERIALS, WHOLESALE: Septic Tanks

- Septic Solutions Inc .................................G....... 217 925-5992
  Dieterich *(G-8314)*

### CONSTRUCTION MATERIALS, WHOLESALE: Sewer Pipe, Clay

- Clay Vollmar Products Co ..........................F....... 773 774-1234
  Chicago *(G-4396)*
- Kieft Bros Inc ...........................................E....... 630 832-8090
  Elmhurst *(G-9898)*

### CONSTRUCTION MATERIALS, WHOLESALE: Stone, Crushed Or Broken

- Central Stone Company ............................F....... 309 776-3900
  Colchester *(G-7307)*
- Gallasi Cut Stone & Marble LLC .................E....... 708 479-9494
  Mokena *(G-14866)*
- Galloy and Van Etten Inc ..........................E....... 773 928-4800
  Chicago *(G-4911)*
- Jacobs Trucking .......................................G....... 618 687-3578
  Murphysboro *(G-15577)*
- Riverstone Group Inc ...............................E....... 309 787-3141
  Milan *(G-14804)*
- Rogers Ready Mix & Mtls Inc ....................F....... 815 389-2223
  Roscoe *(G-18915)*
- Southern Illinois Stone Co ........................E....... 618 995-2392
  Buncombe *(G-2801)*
- Southfield Corporation .............................E....... 815 842-2333
  Pontiac *(G-17711)*
- Southfield Corporation .............................E....... 708 458-0400
  Oak Lawn *(G-16644)*
- T H Davidson & Co Inc .............................E....... 815 464-2000
  Oak Forest *(G-16591)*
- Tuscola Stone Company ...........................F....... 217 253-4705
  Tuscola *(G-21028)*
- William Charles Cnstr Co LLC ...................G....... 815 654-4720
  Belvidere *(G-1797)*

### CONSTRUCTION MATERIALS, WHOLESALE: Tile & Clay Prdts

- Great Lakes Clay & Supply Inc ..................G....... 224 535-8127
  Elgin *(G-9051)*
- Worldwide Tiles Ltd Inc ............................G....... 708 389-2992
  Alsip *(G-545)*

### CONSTRUCTION MATERIALS, WHOLESALE: Veneer

- R S Bacon Veneer Company ......................C....... 630 323-1414
  Lisle *(G-13648)*

### CONSTRUCTION MATERIALS, WHOLESALE: Wallboard

- J & W Counter Tops Inc ............................E....... 217 544-0876
  Springfield *(G-20460)*

### CONSTRUCTION MATERIALS, WHOLESALE: Windows

- Cmp Millwork Co .....................................G....... 630 832-6462
  Elmhurst *(G-9851)*
- Metal Products Sales Corp ........................G....... 708 301-6844
  Lockport *(G-13732)*

### CONSTRUCTION MATLS, WHOL: Composite Board Prdts, Woodboard

- Fca LLC ..................................................E....... 309 792-3444
  Moline *(G-14939)*

### CONSTRUCTION MATLS, WHOL: Lumber, Rough, Dressed/Finished

- Cedar Creek LLC .....................................E....... 618 797-1220
  Granite City *(G-11269)*
- Connor Sports Flooring LLC .....................D....... 847 290-9020
  Elk Grove Village *(G-9389)*
- Enterprise Pallet Inc ................................F....... 815 928-8546
  Bourbonnais *(G-2395)*
- Farrow Lumber Co ...................................F....... 618 734-0255
  Cairo *(G-2929)*
- Great Northern Lumber Inc ......................G....... 708 388-1818
  Blue Island *(G-2254)*
- Perma-Treat of Illinois Inc ........................F....... 618 997-5646
  Marion *(G-14278)*
- Southeast Wood Treating Inc ...................F....... 815 562-5007
  Rochelle *(G-18110)*
- Sterling Lumber Company .......................C....... 708 388-2223
  Phoenix *(G-17542)*
- Tomen America Inc .................................D....... 847 439-8500
  Elk Grove Village *(G-9782)*
- Upham & Walsh Lumber Co .....................G....... 847 519-1010
  Hoffman Estates *(G-12067)*
- Wooded Wonderland ...............................G....... 815 777-1223
  Galena *(G-10735)*
- Woodworkers Shop Inc ............................E....... 309 347-5111
  Pekin *(G-17296)*

### CONSTRUCTION MTRLS, WHOL: Exterior Flat Glass, Plate/Window

- Harmon Inc .............................................D....... 312 726-5050
  Chicago *(G-5046)*
- T J M & Associates Inc ............................G....... 847 382-1993
  Lake Barrington *(G-12825)*
- Torstenson Glass Co ...............................E....... 773 525-0435
  Chicago *(G-6748)*

### CONSTRUCTION SAND MINING

- Clear Lake Sand & Gravel Co ...................F....... 217 725-6999
  Springfield *(G-20419)*
- Jackson County Sand & Grav Co ..............G....... 618 763-4711
  Gorham *(G-11254)*
- Material Service Corporation ...................C....... 708 731-2600
  Westchester *(G-21850)*
- Material Service Resources .....................D....... 630 325-7736
  Chicago *(G-5651)*
- Parkview Sand & Gravel Inc ....................G....... 262 534-4347
  Lake In The Hills *(G-13003)*
- Plote Construction Inc ............................D....... 847 695-9300
  Hoffman Estates *(G-12036)*
- Quality Sand Company Inc ......................G....... 618 346-1070
  Collinsville *(G-7339)*
- Rock River Ready Mix Inc .......................G....... 815 288-2260
  Dixon *(G-8344)*
- Turner Sand & Gravel Inc .......................G....... 618 586-2486
  Palestine *(G-17096)*

### CONSTRUCTION SITE PREPARATION SVCS

- Powell Tree Care Inc ..............................G....... 847 364-1181
  Elk Grove Village *(G-9689)*

### CONSTRUCTION: Agricultural Building

- Better Built Buildings .............................G....... 217 267-7824
  Westville *(G-21928)*
- Morton Buildings Inc ..............................F....... 630 904-1122
  Streator *(G-20695)*
- Morton Buildings Inc ..............................F....... 309 936-7282
  Atkinson *(G-944)*
- West Central Fs Inc ................................G....... 309 375-6904
  Wataga *(G-21399)*

### CONSTRUCTION: Airport Runway

- Lane Construction Corporation ................F....... 815 846-4466
  Shorewood *(G-19929)*

### CONSTRUCTION: Athletic & Recreation Facilities

- Armitage Welding ...................................G....... 773 772-1442
  Chicago *(G-3946)*
- Mef Construction Inc ..............................E....... 847 741-8601
  Elgin *(G-9105)*

### CONSTRUCTION: Bridge

- Hillyer Inc ..............................................D....... 309 837-6434
  Macomb *(G-14125)*
- Riber Construction Inc ...........................F....... 815 584-3337
  Dwight *(G-8592)*

### CONSTRUCTION: Commercial & Institutional Building

- Chicagoland Metal Fabricators .................G....... 847 260-5320
  Franklin Park *(G-10430)*
- Contract Industries Inc ...........................E....... 708 458-8150
  Bedford Park *(G-1545)*
- Creative Designs Kitc .............................E....... 773 327-8400
  Chicago *(G-4497)*
- D Kersey Construction Co .......................G....... 847 919-4980
  Northbrook *(G-16237)*
- ERA Development Group Inc ...................E....... 708 252-6979
  Northbrook *(G-16251)*
- Erect-A-Tube Inc ....................................E....... 815 943-4091
  Harvard *(G-11632)*
- Frederking Construction Co ....................G....... 618 483-5031
  Altamont *(G-551)*
- Spannuth Boiler Co ................................G....... 708 386-1882
  Oak Park *(G-16687)*

### CONSTRUCTION: Commercial & Office Building, New

- Gerald R Page Corporation .....................F....... 847 398-5575
  Prospect Heights *(G-17779)*
- Global Brass and Copper Inc ...................G....... 502 873-3000
  East Alton *(G-8604)*
- Global General Contractors LLC ..............G....... 708 663-0476
  Tinley Park *(G-20918)*
- Morris Construction Inc .........................E....... 618 544-8504
  Robinson *(G-18067)*

### CONSTRUCTION: Concrete Patio

- West Lake Concrete & Rmdlg LLC ...........G....... 847 477-8667
  Chicago *(G-6960)*

### CONSTRUCTION: Condominium

- Global General Contractors LLC ..............G....... 708 663-0476
  Tinley Park *(G-20918)*

### CONSTRUCTION: Dam

- Lane Construction Corporation ...............F....... 815 846-4466
  Shorewood *(G-19929)*

### CONSTRUCTION: Drainage System

- William Charles Cnstr Co LLC .................D....... 815 654-4700
  Loves Park *(G-14007)*

### CONSTRUCTION: Elevated Highway

- Lane Construction Corporation ...............F....... 815 846-4466
  Shorewood *(G-19929)*

### CONSTRUCTION: Farm Building

- Greene Welding & Hardware Inc .............E....... 217 375-4244
  East Lynn *(G-8668)*

### CONSTRUCTION: Food Prdts Manufacturing or Packing Plant

- American Kitchen Delights Inc ................D....... 708 210-3200
  Harvey *(G-11656)*

# PRODUCT SECTION

## CONSTRUCTION: Heavy Highway & Street

- Advanced Asphalt Co .......... E ...... 815 872-9911
  Princeton *(G-17741)*
- Arrow Road Construction Co .......... G ...... 847 658-1140
  Algonquin *(G-378)*
- Cullinan & Sons Inc .......... E ...... 309 925-2711
  Tremont *(G-20981)*
- Curran Contracting Company .......... G ...... 815 758-8113
  Dekalb *(G-8081)*
- Curran Contracting Company .......... E ...... 815 455-5100
  Crystal Lake *(G-7562)*
- Geske and Sons Inc .......... F ...... 815 459-2407
  Crystal Lake *(G-7581)*
- Illinois Valley Paving Co .......... E ...... 217 422-1010
  Elwin *(G-9977)*
- Mt Crmel Stblzation Group Inc .......... E ...... 618 262-5118
  Mount Carmel *(G-15277)*
- Peter Baker & Son Co .......... F ...... 815 344-1640
  Mc Henry *(G-14462)*
- Schulze & Schulze Inc .......... G ...... 618 687-1106
  Murphysboro *(G-15582)*
- Seneca Petroleum Co Inc .......... E ...... 708 396-1100
  Crestwood *(G-7502)*
- Southern Illinois Stone Co .......... F ...... 573 334-5261
  Buncombe *(G-2800)*

## CONSTRUCTION: Indl Building & Warehouse

- Amex Nooter LLC .......... F ...... 708 429-8300
  Tinley Park *(G-20892)*
- I P G Warehouse Ltd .......... E ...... 773 722-5527
  Chicago *(G-5132)*
- Tyndale House Publishers Inc .......... D ...... 630 668-8300
  Carol Stream *(G-3258)*

## CONSTRUCTION: Indl Building, Prefabricated

- Morton Buildings Inc .......... F ...... 309 936-7282
  Atkinson *(G-944)*
- Signa Development Group Inc .......... G ...... 773 418-4506
  Norridge *(G-16108)*

## CONSTRUCTION: Indl Buildings, New, NEC

- Gerald R Page Corporation .......... F ...... 847 398-5575
  Prospect Heights *(G-17779)*
- Grs Holding LLC .......... G ...... 630 355-1660
  Naperville *(G-15666)*
- Kelley Construction Inc .......... B ...... 217 422-1800
  Decatur *(G-7902)*
- Silver Bros Inc .......... G ...... 217 283-7751
  Hoopeston *(G-12117)*

## CONSTRUCTION: Irrigation System

- C & L Tiling Inc .......... D ...... 217 773-3357
  Timewell *(G-20884)*

## CONSTRUCTION: Mausoleum

- St Charles Memorial Works Inc .......... G ...... 630 584-0183
  Saint Charles *(G-19268)*

## CONSTRUCTION: Multi-Family Housing

- Frederking Construction Co .......... G ...... 618 483-5031
  Altamont *(G-551)*

## CONSTRUCTION: Oil & Gas Pipeline Construction

- Csiteq LLC .......... D ...... 312 265-1509
  Chicago *(G-4512)*
- Electric Conduit Cnstr Co .......... C ...... 630 293-4474
  Elburn *(G-8886)*
- L & H Company Inc .......... F ...... 630 571-7200
  Oak Brook *(G-16532)*

## CONSTRUCTION: Pharmaceutical Manufacturing Plant

- Idex Mpt Inc .......... D ...... 630 530-3333
  Elmhurst *(G-9884)*

## CONSTRUCTION: Power Plant

- Onyx Environmental Svcs LLC .......... E ...... 630 218-1500
  Lombard *(G-13838)*

## CONSTRUCTION: Railroad & Subway

- AR Concepts USA Inc .......... G ...... 847 392-4608
  Palatine *(G-17002)*

## CONSTRUCTION: Residential, Nec

- H Borre & Sons Inc .......... G ...... 847 524-8890
  Lake Zurich *(G-13081)*
- Protective Coatings & Waterpro .......... G ...... 708 403-7650
  Orland Park *(G-16886)*
- Slaymaker Fine Art Ltd .......... G ...... 773 348-1450
  Chicago *(G-6526)*

## CONSTRUCTION: Retaining Wall

- Unilock Chicago Inc .......... D ...... 630 892-9191
  Aurora *(G-1227)*

## CONSTRUCTION: Scaffolding

- Gilco Real Estate Company .......... E ...... 847 298-1717
  Des Plaines *(G-8202)*

## CONSTRUCTION: Sewer Line

- William Charles Cnstr Co LLC .......... D ...... 815 654-4700
  Loves Park *(G-14007)*

## CONSTRUCTION: Single-Family Housing

- Bernard Cffey Vtrans Fundation .......... G ...... 630 687-0033
  Naperville *(G-15605)*
- Chicagoland Metal Fabricators .......... G ...... 847 260-5320
  Franklin Park *(G-10430)*
- Duhack Lehn & Associates Inc .......... G ...... 815 777-3460
  Galena *(G-10719)*
- Electric Conduit Cnstr Co .......... C ...... 630 293-4474
  Elburn *(G-8886)*
- Frederking Construction Co .......... G ...... 618 483-5031
  Altamont *(G-551)*
- Global General Contractors LLC .......... G ...... 708 663-0476
  Tinley Park *(G-20918)*
- Heafner Contracting Inc .......... F ...... 618 466-3678
  Godfrey *(G-11225)*
- Luxury Bath Liners Inc .......... G ...... 630 295-9084
  Glendale Heights *(G-11042)*
- Old Blue Illinois Inc .......... F ...... 309 289-7921
  Knoxville *(G-12722)*
- Otten Construction Co Inc .......... G ...... 618 768-4310
  Addieville *(G-13)*
- Poggenpohl LLC .......... G ...... 217 229-3411
  Raymond *(G-17939)*
- Poggenpohl LLC .......... G ...... 217 824-2020
  Taylorville *(G-20844)*
- Scheffler Custom Woodworking .......... G ...... 815 284-6564
  Dixon *(G-8348)*
- Stahl Lumber Company .......... F ...... 309 695-4331
  Wyoming *(G-22640)*
- Surtreat Construction Svcs LLC .......... G ...... 630 986-0780
  Schaumburg *(G-19746)*

## CONSTRUCTION: Single-family Housing, New

- Jack Ruch Quality Homes Inc .......... G ...... 309 663-6595
  Bloomington *(G-2185)*
- Pete Frcano Sons Cstm HM Bldrs .......... F ...... 847 258-4626
  Elk Grove Village *(G-9675)*
- Peters Construction .......... G ...... 773 489-5555
  Chicago *(G-6110)*
- R-Squared Construction Inc .......... G ...... 815 232-7433
  Freeport *(G-10682)*
- Savino Enterprises .......... G ...... 708 385-5277
  Blue Island *(G-2268)*

## CONSTRUCTION: Street Sign Installation & Mntnce

- Traffic Control & Protection .......... E ...... 630 293-0026
  West Chicago *(G-21784)*

## CONSTRUCTION: Street Surfacing & Paving

- A&J Paving Inc .......... G ...... 773 889-9133
  Chicago *(G-3694)*
- Hillyer Inc .......... D ...... 309 837-6434
  Macomb *(G-14125)*

## CONSTRUCTION: Swimming Pools

- Knapheide Manufacturing Co .......... E ...... 217 223-1848
  Quincy *(G-17847)*
- Platinum Aquatech Ltd .......... F ...... 847 537-3800
  Wheeling *(G-22124)*
- Rockford Sewer Co Inc .......... G ...... 815 877-9060
  Loves Park *(G-13987)*
- Royal Fiberglass Pools Inc .......... D ...... 618 266-7089
  Dix *(G-8318)*

## CONSTRUCTION: Tennis Court

- All Weather Courts Inc .......... G ...... 217 364-4546
  Dawson *(G-7816)*
- Schulze & Schulze Inc .......... G ...... 618 687-1106
  Murphysboro *(G-15582)*

## CONSTRUCTION: Truck & Automobile Assembly Plant

- Auto Truck Group LLC .......... C ...... 630 860-5600
  Bartlett *(G-1333)*

## CONSTRUCTION: Tunnel

- Industrial Controls Inc .......... G ...... 630 752-8100
  Batavia *(G-1457)*

## CONSTRUCTION: Utility Line

- Cullinan & Sons Inc .......... E ...... 309 925-2711
  Tremont *(G-20981)*
- Foltz Welding Ltd .......... C ...... 618 432-7777
  Patoka *(G-17231)*
- Mid-America Underground LLC .......... E ...... 630 443-9999
  Aurora *(G-1188)*

## CONSTRUCTION: Waste Water & Sewage Treatment Plant

- Allendale Gravel Co Inc .......... G ...... 618 263-3521
  Allendale *(G-420)*
- Gig Karasek LLC .......... F ...... 630 549-0394
  Saint Charles *(G-19189)*

## CONSTRUCTION: Water & Sewer Line

- Kvd Enterprises LLC .......... G ...... 618 726-5114
  O Fallon *(G-16469)*
- Mef Construction Inc .......... G ...... 847 741-8601
  Elgin *(G-9105)*

## CONSTRUCTION: Water Main

- Hillyer Inc .......... D ...... 309 837-6434
  Macomb *(G-14125)*
- Lake County Grading Co LLC .......... E ...... 847 362-2590
  Libertyville *(G-13341)*

## CONSULTING SVC: Actuarial

- Taloc Usa Inc .......... G ...... 847 665-8222
  Libertyville *(G-13388)*

## CONSULTING SVC: Business, NEC

- 10th Magnitude LLC .......... E ...... 224 628-9047
  Chicago *(G-3661)*
- Ada Holding Company Inc .......... F ...... 312 440-2897
  Chicago *(G-3742)*
- Advantage Press Inc .......... G ...... 630 960-5305
  Lisle *(G-13553)*
- Captains Emporium Inc .......... G ...... 773 972-7609
  Chicago *(G-4234)*
- Continental Usa Inc .......... G ...... 847 823-0958
  Park Ridge *(G-17188)*
- Eco-Pur Solutions LLC .......... G ...... 630 226-2300
  Romeoville *(G-18818)*
- G T C Industries Inc .......... G ...... 708 369-9815
  Naperville *(G-15661)*
- Honeywell Safety Pdts USA Inc .......... C ...... 309 786-7741
  Rock Island *(G-18182)*
- I W M Corporation .......... G ...... 847 695-0700
  Elgin *(G-9070)*
- Ieg LLC .......... E ...... 312 944-1727
  Chicago *(G-5144)*
- Joe Hunt .......... G ...... 618 392-2000
  Olney *(G-16774)*
- Kishknows Inc .......... G ...... 708 252-3648
  Richton Park *(G-17979)*
- L T P LLC .......... C ...... 815 723-9400
  Joliet *(G-12530)*

## CONSULTING SVC: Business, NEC

Logicgate Inc .....................................F........ 312 279-2775
  Chicago (G-5533)
McIlvaine Co .....................................E........ 847 784-0012
  Northfield (G-16408)
Monolithic Industries Inc ....................G........ 630 985-6009
  Woodridge (G-22503)
Motivequest LLC ...............................F........ 847 905-6100
  Evanston (G-10075)
Nas Media Group Inc .........................G........ 312 371-7499
  Olympia Fields (G-16803)
Nas Media Group Inc .........................F........ 773 824-0242
  Chicago (G-5855)
North Shore Consultants Inc ...............G........ 847 290-1599
  Elk Grove Village (G-9655)
Nu-Recycling Technology Inc ..............F........ 630 904-5237
  Naperville (G-15820)
Paragon International Inc ...................F........ 847 240-2981
  Schaumburg (G-19682)
Perry Johnson Inc .............................F........ 847 635-0010
  Rosemont (G-19021)
Pool Center Inc .................................G........ 217 698-7665
  Springfield (G-20505)
Promark Associates Inc .....................G........ 847 676-1894
  Skokie (G-20064)
Pure Flo Bottling Inc .........................G........ 815 963-4797
  Rockford (G-18544)
Quarasan Group Inc ..........................D........ 312 981-2540
  Chicago (G-6254)
Regunathan & Assoc Inc ....................G........ 630 653-0387
  Wheaton (G-21975)
St Louis Scrap Trading LLC ...............G........ 618 307-9002
  Edwardsville (G-8815)
Strategic Applications Inc ..................G........ 847 680-9385
  Lake Villa (G-13027)
Tighe Publishing Services Inc .............F........ 773 281-9100
  Chicago (G-6726)
Two Consulting ..................................G........ 630 830-2415
  Bartlett (G-1382)
W-F Professional Assoc Inc ................G........ 847 945-8050
  Deerfield (G-8067)
Weeb Enterprises LLC .......................G........ 815 861-2625
  Wauconda (G-21514)

## CONSULTING SVC: Computer

Affinnova Inc ....................................G........ 781 464-4700
  Chicago (G-3780)
Aldea Technologies Inc .....................E........ 800 804-0635
  Schaumburg (G-19428)
Amaitis and Associates Inc ................F........ 847 428-1269
  Wood Dale (G-22338)
Ats Commercial Group LLC ................F........ 815 686-2705
  Piper City (G-17558)
Bantix Technologies LLC ...................G........ 630 446-0886
  Glen Ellyn (G-10960)
Buyersvine Inc ..................................G........ 630 235-6804
  Hinsdale (G-11943)
Computer Industry Almanac Inc ..........G........ 847 758-1926
  Arlington Heights (G-738)
Computer Pwr Solutions III Ltd ...........E........ 618 281-8898
  Columbia (G-7355)
Comvigo Inc .....................................G........ 240 255-4093
  Willowbrook (G-22205)
Entappia LLC ....................................G........ 630 546-4531
  Aurora (G-1003)
Friedrich Klatt and Associates ............G........ 773 753-1806
  Chicago (G-4891)
Gld Industries Inc .............................G........ 217 390-9594
  Champaign (G-3489)
Hands of Many LLC ...........................G........ 917 841-9969
  Flossmoor (G-10225)
Imcp Inc ...........................................G........ 630 477-8600
  Itasca (G-12284)
Infopro Inc .......................................G........ 630 978-9231
  Aurora (G-1029)
Infosys Limited .................................E........ 630 482-5000
  Lisle (G-13606)
Logicgate Inc ....................................F........ 312 279-2775
  Chicago (G-5533)
M K Advantage Inc ............................F........ 773 902-5272
  Chicago (G-5583)
Manufacturers News Inc ....................D........ 847 864-7000
  Evanston (G-10068)
Marie Gere Corporation .....................C........ 847 540-1154
  Lake Zurich (G-13099)
Monroe Associates Inc ......................G........ 217 665-3898
  Bethany (G-2085)
National Def Intelligence Inc ..............G........ 630 757-4007
  Naperville (G-15818)
Onx USA LLC ....................................E........ 630 343-8940
  Lisle (G-13637)
Pagepath Technologies Inc ................F........ 630 689-4111
  Plano (G-17671)
Panatech Computer Management ......G........ 847 678-8848
  Schiller Park (G-19857)
Premier International Entps ...............E........ 312 857-2200
  Chicago (G-6177)
Print Management Partners Inc ..........E........ 847 699-2999
  Des Plaines (G-8265)
Quadrant 4 System Corporation .........B........ 855 995-7367
  Schaumburg (G-19706)
Reign Print Solutions Inc ...................G........ 847 590-7091
  Arlington Heights (G-830)
Sedona Inc .......................................C........ 309 736-4104
  Moline (G-14969)
Spend Radar LLC ..............................E........ 312 265-0764
  Chicago (G-6558)
Synergy Technology Group Inc ..........F........ 773 305-3500
  Chicago (G-6657)
Tegratecs Development Corp .............G........ 847 397-0088
  Schaumburg (G-19757)
Tindall Associates Inc .......................F........ 708 403-7775
  Orland Park (G-16898)
Vertical Software Inc .........................F........ 309 633-0700
  Bartonville (G-1399)

## CONSULTING SVC: Data Processing

Ifs North America Inc .......................E........ 888 437-4968
  Itasca (G-12279)

## CONSULTING SVC: Educational

BGF Performance Systems LLC ..........G........ 773 539-7099
  Chicago (G-4101)
LMS Innovations Inc .........................G........ 312 613-2345
  Chicago (G-5528)
Pieces of Learning Inc ......................G........ 618 964-9426
  Marion (G-14279)

## CONSULTING SVC: Engineering

Accelrted Mch Design Engrg LLC .......F........ 815 316-6381
  Rockford (G-18251)
Applied Mechanical Tech LLC ............E........ 815 472-2700
  Momence (G-14978)
Armstrong Aerospace Inc ..................D........ 630 285-0200
  Itasca (G-12232)
Component Tool & Mfg Co .................F........ 708 672-5505
  Crete (G-7510)
Control Panels Inc ............................G........ 815 654-6000
  Rockford (G-18323)
Dike-O-Seal Incorporated ..................F........ 773 254-3224
  Chicago (G-4603)
Enders Process Equipment Corp ........G........ 630 469-3787
  Glendale Heights (G-11022)
Industrial Phrm Resources Inc ...........F........ 630 823-4700
  Bartlett (G-1357)
Marie Gere Corporation .....................C........ 847 540-1154
  Lake Zurich (G-13099)
Meyer Systems ..................................G........ 815 436-7077
  Joliet (G-12540)
Mid-City Die & Mold Corp ..................G........ 773 278-4844
  Chicago (G-5729)
Millennium Mold Design Inc ..............G........ 815 344-9790
  McHenry (G-14535)
Silicon Control Inc ............................G........ 847 215-7947
  Deerfield (G-8054)
Triangle Technologies Inc ..................G........ 630 736-3318
  Streamwood (G-20678)

## CONSULTING SVC: Financial Management

Alvarez & Marsal Inc .........................E........ 312 601-4220
  Chicago (G-3840)
Lehigh Consumer Products LLC .........C........ 630 851-7330
  Aurora (G-1045)

## CONSULTING SVC: Human Resource

Merit Emplyment Asssstment Svcs ....G........ 815 320-3680
  New Lenox (G-15894)

## CONSULTING SVC: Management

7000 Inc ...........................................F........ 312 800-3612
  Bolingbrook (G-2275)
C D Nelson Consulting Inc .................G........ 847 487-4870
  Wauconda (G-21449)
Chad Mazeika ...................................G........ 815 298-8118
  Rockford (G-18303)
Csiteq LLC ........................................D........ 312 265-1509
  Chicago (G-4512)
Datair Employee Benefit Systems ......E........ 630 325-2600
  Westmont (G-21881)
Falex Corporation .............................E........ 630 556-3679
  Sugar Grove (G-20723)
Huntley & Associates Inc ..................G........ 224 381-8500
  Lake Zurich (G-13085)
I T C W Inc .......................................E........ 630 305-8849
  Naperville (G-15671)
Identiti Resources Ltd ......................E........ 847 301-0510
  Schaumburg (G-19562)
Infogix Inc .......................................C........ 630 505-1800
  Naperville (G-15674)
Knowledgeshift Inc ...........................G........ 630 221-8759
  Wheaton (G-21962)
Lenrok Industries Inc ........................G........ 630 628-1946
  Addison (G-179)
Lexi Group Inc ..................................G........ 866 675-1683
  Chicago (G-5498)
McClendon Holdings LLC ...................G........ 773 251-2314
  Chicago (G-5664)
McIlvaine Co .....................................E........ 847 784-0012
  Northfield (G-16408)
NFC Company Inc .............................G........ 773 472-6468
  Chicago (G-5908)
Parth Consultants Inc .......................E........ 847 758-1400
  Rolling Meadows (G-18758)
Roger Fritz & Associates Inc .............G........ 630 355-2614
  Naperville (G-15744)
Screen North Amer Holdings Inc .......F........ 847 870-7400
  Rolling Meadows (G-18777)
State of Illinois ................................C........ 312 836-9500
  Chicago (G-6578)
Tom Zosel Associates Ltd .................D........ 847 540-6543
  Long Grove (G-13903)
Vega Technology & Systems .............G........ 630 855-5068
  Bartlett (G-1324)
Ycl International Inc .........................E........ 630 873-0768
  Woodridge (G-22529)

## CONSULTING SVC: Marketing Management

Allegra Marketing Print Mail ..............G........ 630 790-0444
  Schaumburg (G-19430)
Alliance Creative Group Inc ...............E........ 847 885-1800
  Schaumburg (G-19431)
Bendinger Bruce Crtve Comm In ......G........ 773 871-1179
  Chicago (G-4082)
Chase Security Systems Inc .............G........ 773 594-1919
  Chicago (G-4295)
Custom Direct Inc .............................F........ 630 529-1936
  Roselle (G-18938)
Custom Machining & Design LLC ......G........ 847 364-2601
  Elk Grove Village (G-9403)
Darwill Inc .......................................C........ 708 449-7770
  Hillside (G-11914)
Evo Exhibits LLC ...............................G........ 630 520-0710
  West Chicago (G-21697)
Flyerinc Corporation .........................G........ 630 655-3400
  Oak Brook (G-16515)
Forrest Consulting ............................G........ 630 730-9619
  Glen Ellyn (G-10971)
Fuse LLC ..........................................C........ 708 449-8989
  Berkeley (G-2045)
Gammon Group Inc ...........................G........ 815 722-6400
  Shorewood (G-19927)
Lure Group LLC ................................G........ 630 222-6515
  Bolingbrook (G-2338)
M Wells Printing Co ..........................G........ 312 455-0400
  Chicago (G-5588)
Marketing Analytics Inc ....................D........ 847 733-8459
  Evanston (G-10070)
Orr Marketing Corp ..........................F........ 847 401-5171
  Elgin (G-9130)
Palm International Inc ......................G........ 630 357-1437
  Naperville (G-15721)
Print and Mktg Solutions Group ........E........ 847 498-9640
  Northbrook (G-16344)
Print Management Partners Inc .........E........ 847 699-2999
  Des Plaines (G-8265)
Progrssive Imprssions Intl Inc ...........C........ 309 664-0444
  Bloomington (G-2216)
Segerdahl Graphics Inc .....................B........ 847 541-1080
  Wheeling (G-22148)
Srv Professional Publications ............G........ 847 330-1260
  Schaumburg (G-19739)
Stagnito Partners LLC ......................D........ 224 632-8200
  Deerfield (G-8056)
Tgrv LLC ..........................................G........ 815 634-2102
  Bourbonnais (G-2407)

# PRODUCT SECTION

## CONTAINERS: Corrugated

### CONSULTING SVC: Motion Picture
2nd Cine Inc..................................G...... 773 455-5808
 Elgin *(G-8928)*

### CONSULTING SVC: Online Technology
Baka Vitaliy..................................G...... 773 370-5522
 Chicago *(G-4027)*
Compsoft Tech Sltons Group Inc....F 847 517-9608
 Schaumburg *(G-19478)*
Sunemco Technologies Inc...........G...... 630 369-8947
 Naperville *(G-15758)*
Viva Solutions Inc.........................G...... 312 332-8882
 Lemont *(G-13268)*
Wrapports LLC.............................E...... 312 321-3000
 Chicago *(G-7035)*

### CONSULTING SVC: Sales Management
Am-Don Partnership......................G...... 217 355-7750
 Champaign *(G-3447)*
E I T Inc.........................................G...... 630 359-3543
 Naperville *(G-15649)*
Partners Resource Inc..................G...... 630 620-9161
 Glen Ellyn *(G-10985)*
Scholastic Inc................................E...... 630 443-8197
 Saint Charles *(G-19261)*

### CONSULTING SVC: Telecommunications
Driver Services..............................G...... 505 267-8686
 Bensenville *(G-1883)*
Shield Electronics LLC..................G...... 815 467-4134
 Minooka *(G-14847)*

### CONSULTING SVCS, BUSINESS: Agricultural
Busatis Inc....................................G...... 630 844-9803
 Montgomery *(G-15034)*

### CONSULTING SVCS, BUSINESS: Communications
Ayla Group Inc...............................G...... 630 954-9432
 Bartlett *(G-1334)*
Darwill Inc.....................................C...... 708 449-7770
 Hillside *(G-11914)*

### CONSULTING SVCS, BUSINESS: Energy Conservation
Clean Energy Renewables LLC.....E...... 309 797-4844
 Moline *(G-14922)*
E2s LLC.........................................G...... 708 629-0714
 Alsip *(G-460)*

### CONSULTING SVCS, BUSINESS: Environmental
Blackburn Sampling Inc................G...... 309 342-8429
 Galesburg *(G-10738)*
Pan America Environmental Inc...G...... 847 487-9166
 McHenry *(G-14541)*
Water & Oil Technologies Inc.......G...... 630 892-2007
 Montgomery *(G-15072)*

### CONSULTING SVCS, BUSINESS: Lighting
Lighting Design By Michael Ant....G...... 708 289-4783
 Mokena *(G-14880)*

### CONSULTING SVCS, BUSINESS: Publishing
Cade Communications Inc............G...... 773 477-7184
 Chicago *(G-4210)*
College Bound Publications..........G...... 773 262-5810
 Chicago *(G-4424)*
Forrest Consulting........................G...... 630 730-9619
 Glen Ellyn *(G-10971)*
John C Grafft................................F...... 847 842-9200
 Lake Barrington *(G-12811)*

### CONSULTING SVCS, BUSINESS: Safety Training Svcs
International Tactical Trainin.........G...... 872 221-4886
 Chicago *(G-5223)*

### CONSULTING SVCS, BUSINESS: Sys Engnrg, Exc Computer/Prof
AR Inet Corp.................................G...... 603 380-3903
 Aurora *(G-959)*
Braindok LLC.................................G...... 847 877-1586
 Buffalo Grove *(G-2668)*
Capital Tours & Travel Inc............G...... 847 274-1138
 Skokie *(G-19973)*
Logical Design Solutions Inc........G...... 630 786-5999
 Aurora *(G-1047)*
Prairie Wi-FI Systems...................G...... 515 988-3260
 Chicago *(G-6167)*
Turner Agward..............................G...... 773 669-8559
 Chicago *(G-6794)*

### CONSULTING SVCS, BUSINESS: Systems Analysis & Engineering
Global Tech & Resources Inc.......G...... 630 364-4260
 Rolling Meadows *(G-18732)*
Haran Ventures LLC.....................G...... 217 239-1628
 Champaign *(G-3493)*
Igt Testing Systems Inc................G...... 847 952-2448
 Arlington Heights *(G-773)*

### CONSULTING SVCS, BUSINESS: Testing, Educational Or Personnel
Scholastic Testing Service.............F...... 630 766-7150
 Bensenville *(G-1988)*

### CONSULTING SVCS: Oil
Advanced Lubrication Inc.............G...... 815 932-3288
 Kankakee *(G-12602)*
Howard Energy Corporation..........G...... 618 263-3000
 Mount Carmel *(G-15268)*
Team Energy LLC..........................G...... 618 943-1010
 Bridgeport *(G-2456)*

### CONTACT LENSES
Alcon Laboratories Inc..................E...... 312 751-6200
 Chicago *(G-3797)*
Ciba Vision Inc..............................A...... 847 294-3000
 Des Plaines *(G-8169)*
Wesley-Jessen Corporation Del....A...... 847 294-3000
 Des Plaines *(G-8302)*

### CONTACTS: Electrical
Deringer-Ney Inc...........................E...... 847 566-4100
 Vernon Hills *(G-21157)*

### CONTAINERS, GLASS: Food
Fri Jado Inc...................................G...... 630 633-7944
 Woodridge *(G-22480)*

### CONTAINERS, GLASS: Medicine Bottles
Alexander Technique.....................G...... 847 337-7926
 Evanston *(G-10006)*
Teamdance Illinois........................G...... 815 463-9044
 Geneva *(G-10871)*

### CONTAINERS, GLASS: Packers' Ware
Owens-Brockway Glass Cont Inc..C...... 815 672-3141
 Streator *(G-20699)*

### CONTAINERS: Air Cargo, Metal
AAR Corp.......................................D...... 630 227-2000
 Wood Dale *(G-22328)*
John Bean Technologies Corp......E...... 312 861-5900
 Chicago *(G-5310)*
Majesty Cases Inc.........................E...... 847 546-2558
 Ingleside *(G-12193)*

### CONTAINERS: Cargo, Wood
Blue Comet Transport Inc.............G...... 773 617-9512
 Chicago *(G-4125)*
Cargois Inc....................................F...... 847 357-1901
 Elk Grove Village *(G-9356)*

### CONTAINERS: Cargo, Wood & Metal Combination
Cimc Leasing Usa Inc....................G...... 630 785-6875
 Oakbrook Terrace *(G-16702)*

Raildecks Intermodal.....................G...... 630 442-7676
 Downers Grove *(G-8512)*

### CONTAINERS: Cargo, Wood & Wood With Metal
Arrows Up Inc................................G...... 847 305-2550
 Arlington Heights *(G-717)*

### CONTAINERS: Corrugated
A Trustworthy Sup Source Inc......G...... 773 480-0255
 Chicago *(G-3693)*
Akers Packaging Solutions Inc.....E...... 217 468-2396
 Oreana *(G-16816)*
All-Pak Manufacturing Corp..........D...... 630 851-5859
 Aurora *(G-1103)*
APAC Unlimited Inc......................G...... 847 441-4282
 Northfield *(G-16390)*
Armbrust Paper Tubes Inc............E...... 773 586-3232
 Chicago *(G-3945)*
Blackhawk Corrugated LLC..........E...... 844 270-2296
 Carol Stream *(G-3115)*
Blackhawk Courtyards LLC..........G...... 416 298-8101
 Carol Stream *(G-3116)*
Box USA.........................................G...... 708 562-6000
 Northlake *(G-16429)*
Combined Technologies Inc.........G...... 847 968-4855
 Libertyville *(G-13317)*
Dexton Enterprises.......................G...... 309 788-1881
 Rock Island *(G-18174)*
Elm Street Industries Inc.............F...... 309 854-7000
 Kewanee *(G-12681)*
Fca LLC..........................................E...... 309 949-3999
 Coal Valley *(G-7296)*
Georgia-Pacific LLC......................C...... 217 999-2511
 Mount Olive *(G-15302)*
Georgia-Pacific Bldg Pdts LLC......G...... 630 449-7200
 Aurora *(G-1015)*
Grafcor Packaging Inc..................F...... 815 639-2380
 Loves Park *(G-13945)*
Graphic Packaging Holding Co.....B...... 630 260-6500
 Carol Stream *(G-3161)*
Greif Inc........................................E...... 708 371-4777
 Alsip *(G-466)*
Inglese Box Co Ltd.......................E...... 847 669-1700
 Huntley *(G-12149)*
International Paper Company........C...... 630 896-2061
 Montgomery *(G-15050)*
International Paper Company........C...... 815 398-2100
 Rockford *(G-18439)*
International Paper Company........D...... 708 562-6000
 Northlake *(G-16440)*
International Paper Company........C...... 630 585-3400
 Aurora *(G-1033)*
J H H of Illinois Inc......................F...... 630 293-0739
 West Chicago *(G-21726)*
Jordan Paper Box Company..........F...... 773 287-5362
 Chicago *(G-5323)*
Kodiak LLC....................................E...... 248 545-7520
 Chicago *(G-5398)*
Ockerlund Industries Inc..............E...... 630 620-1269
 Addison *(G-232)*
Packaging Corporation America...F...... 847 388-6000
 Mundelein *(G-15540)*
Packaging Corporation America...G...... 618 934-3100
 Trenton *(G-20995)*
Packaging Corporation America...G...... 773 378-8700
 Chicago *(G-6054)*
Packaging Corporation America...D...... 708 594-5260
 Bedford Park *(G-1570)*
Packaging Corporation America...C...... 847 482-3000
 Lake Forest *(G-12933)*
Pak Source Inc..............................E...... 309 786-7374
 Rock Island *(G-18191)*
PCA International Inc...................C...... 847 482-3000
 Lake Forest *(G-12941)*
SCI Box LLC..................................E...... 618 244-7244
 Mount Vernon *(G-15444)*
Sonoco Products Company...........D...... 630 231-1489
 West Chicago *(G-21775)*
Specialty Box Corp........................F...... 630 897-7278
 North Aurora *(G-16145)*
Stand Fast Group LLC...................D...... 630 600-0900
 Carol Stream *(G-3246)*
Vangard Distribution Inc..............G...... 708 484-9895
 Berwyn *(G-2077)*
Vangard Distribution Inc..............G...... 708 588-8400
 Brookfield *(G-2646)*
Westrock Cp LLC..........................C...... 309 342-0121
 Galesburg *(G-10780)*

Employee Codes: A=Over 500 employees, B=251-500
C=101-250, D=51-100, E=20-50, F=10-19, G=3-9

2017 Harris Illinois
Industrial Directory

1533

# CONTAINERS: Corrugated

Westrock CP LLC .................................. C ...... 618 654-2141
　Highland *(G-11818)*
Westrock CP LLC .................................. D ...... 630 924-0054
　Bartlett *(G-1326)*
Westrock Rkt Company ........................ C ...... 847 649-9231
　Melrose Park *(G-14709)*
York Corrugated Container Corp ......... D ...... 630 260-2900
　Glendale Heights *(G-11093)*

## CONTAINERS: Foil, Bakery Goods & Frozen Foods

C M Holding Co Inc ............................... G ...... 847 438-2171
　Lake Zurich *(G-13048)*
Durable Inc ........................................... A ...... 847 541-4400
　Wheeling *(G-22039)*
Handi-Foil Corp .................................... A ...... 847 520-1000
　Wheeling *(G-22065)*
Handi-Foil Corp .................................... E ...... 847 520-5742
　Wheeling *(G-22066)*
Hfa Inc .................................................. A ...... 847 520-1000
　Wheeling *(G-22069)*
R and R Brokerage Co ......................... C ...... 847 438-4600
　Lake Zurich *(G-13121)*

## CONTAINERS: Food & Beverage

Amcor Rigid Plastics Usa LLC ............. F ...... 630 406-3500
　Batavia *(G-1412)*
Ignite Usa LLC ..................................... E ...... 312 432-6223
　Chicago *(G-5147)*
Jamiel Inc ............................................. G ...... 217 423-1000
　Decatur *(G-7898)*
Kraft Heinz Company ........................... C ...... 847 646-2000
　Glenview *(G-11160)*
Midway Food LLC ................................ G ...... 773 294-0730
　Chicago *(G-5738)*
Rexam Beverage Can Company .......... C ...... 773 399-3000
　Chicago *(G-6344)*
Shenglong Intl Group Corp .................. G ...... 312 388-2345
　Glenview *(G-11195)*
Silgan White Cap Americas LLC ......... F ...... 630 515-8383
　Downers Grove *(G-8524)*

## CONTAINERS: Food, Folding, Made From Purchased Materials

Pactiv LLC ............................................ C ...... 630 262-6335
　Saint Charles *(G-19233)*
Thermal Bags By Ingrid Inc ................. F ...... 847 836-4400
　Gilberts *(G-10938)*

## CONTAINERS: Food, Liquid Tight, Including Milk

International Paper Company .............. C ...... 217 735-1221
　Lincoln *(G-13411)*
Tetra Pak US Holdings Inc .................. C ...... 940 565-8800
　Vernon Hills *(G-21210)*

## CONTAINERS: Food, Wood Wirebound

Elm Street Industries Inc .................... F ...... 309 854-7000
　Kewanee *(G-12681)*

## CONTAINERS: Frozen Food & Ice Cream

Earthgrains Refrigertd Dough P .......... A ...... 630 455-5200
　Downers Grove *(G-8438)*

## CONTAINERS: Glass

Amcor Phrm Packg USA LLC .............. C ...... 847 298-5626
　Des Plaines *(G-8146)*
Anchor Glass Container Corp ............. E ...... 815 672-7761
　Streator *(G-20683)*
Ardagh Glass Inc ................................. D ...... 708 849-4010
　Dolton *(G-8363)*
Ball Foster Glass Container ................ G ...... 708 849-1500
　Dolton *(G-8365)*
Ball Foster Glass Container Co .......... G ...... 217 735-1511
　Lincoln *(G-13406)*
Fitpac Co Ltd ....................................... G ...... 630 428-9077
　Bensenville *(G-1899)*
Gerresheimer Glass Inc ...................... E ...... 708 757-6853
　Chicago Heights *(G-7098)*
Glass Haus .......................................... G ...... 815 459-5849
　McHenry *(G-14510)*
Kavalierglass North Amer Inc ............. E ...... 847 364-7303
　Elk Grove Village *(G-9571)*
Libation Container Inc ........................ F ...... 312 287-4524
　Chicago *(G-5501)*

## CONTAINERS: Metal

American Rack Company ..................... ...... 773 763-7309
　Chicago *(G-3870)*
Central Can Company Inc ................... C ...... 773 254-8700
　Chicago *(G-4270)*
D & B Fabricators & Distrs .................. F ...... 630 325-3811
　Lemont *(G-13234)*
Grafcor Packaging Inc ........................ F ...... 815 639-2380
　Loves Park *(G-13945)*
Greif Inc .............................................. E ...... 815 935-7575
　Bradley *(G-2423)*
Higgins Bros Inc .................................. F ...... 773 523-0124
　Chicago *(G-5086)*
Liberty Diversified Intl Inc .................. E ...... 217 935-8361
　Clinton *(G-7285)*
Production Manufacturing .................. G ...... 217 256-4211
　Warsaw *(G-21371)*
Staffco Inc ........................................... G ...... 309 688-3223
　Peoria *(G-17460)*
Van Leer Containers Inc ..................... C ...... 708 371-4777
　Alsip *(G-539)*
Westrock Cp LLC ................................ C ...... 847 689-4200
　North Chicago *(G-16190)*
Woods Equipment Company ............... D ...... 815 732-2141
　Oregon *(G-16834)*

## CONTAINERS: Plastic

Amcor Phrm Packg USA LLC .............. C ...... 847 298-5626
　Des Plaines *(G-8146)*
Armbrust Paper Tubes Inc ................. E ...... 773 586-3232
　Chicago *(G-3945)*
Bli Legacy Inc ..................................... E ...... 847 428-6059
　Carpentersville *(G-3276)*
Bway Corporation ............................... C ...... 847 956-0750
　Elk Grove Village *(G-9351)*
Bway Corporation ............................... C ...... 773 254-8700
　Chicago *(G-4194)*
Bway Parent Company Inc ................. F ...... 773 890-3300
　Chicago *(G-4195)*
Calumet Container Corp .................... F ...... 773 646-3653
　Chicago *(G-4218)*
Carroll Tool & Manufacturing ............. G ...... 630 766-3363
　Bensenville *(G-1852)*
Consolidated Container Co LLC ........ C ...... 815 943-7828
　Harvard *(G-11628)*
Core-Mark International Inc .............. E ...... 847 593-1800
　Elk Grove Village *(G-9396)*
CTI Industries Corporation ................ C ...... 847 382-1000
　Lake Barrington *(G-12804)*
CTI Industries Corporation ................ D ...... 800 284-5605
　Lake Zurich *(G-13060)*
Flow-Eze Company ............................. F ...... 815 965-1062
　Rockford *(G-18383)*
Gilster-Mary Lee Corporation ............ A ...... 618 826-2361
　Chester *(G-3657)*
Graham Packaging Co Europe LLC ... A ...... 630 293-8616
　West Chicago *(G-21710)*
Graham Packaging Company LP ....... E ...... 630 739-9150
　Woodridge *(G-22490)*
Great Midwest Packaging LLC .......... F ...... 847 395-4500
　Waukegan *(G-21565)*
Greif Inc ............................................. E ...... 815 838-7210
　Lockport *(G-13719)*
Gy Packaging LLC ............................. F ...... 847 272-8803
　Northbrook *(G-16267)*
Hardwood Line Manufacturing Co ..... E ...... 773 463-2600
　Chicago *(G-5045)*
Illinois Bottle Mfg Co ........................ D ...... 847 595-9000
　Elk Grove Village *(G-9533)*
Illinois Tool Works Inc ...................... D ...... 630 773-9301
　Itasca *(G-12282)*
International Mold & Prod LLC ......... G ...... 313 617-5251
　Grayslake *(G-11347)*
Isovac Products LLC ........................ G ...... 630 679-1740
　Romeoville *(G-18831)*
Jarden Corporation ........................... D ...... 201 836-7070
　Aurora *(G-1036)*
JL Clark LLC ..................................... ...... 815 961-5677
　Rockford *(G-18446)*
JL Clark LLC ..................................... C ...... 815 961-5609
　Rockford *(G-18447)*
Jodi Maurer ...................................... G ...... 847 961-5347
　Lake In The Hills *(G-12996)*
Jordan Specialty Plastics Inc .......... G ...... 847 945-5591
　Deerfield *(G-8021)*
Jtec Industries Inc ............................ E ...... 309 698-9301
　East Peoria *(G-8720)*
Lee Gilster-Mary Corporation ........... ...... 618 826-2361
　Chester *(G-3658)*
Lee Gilster-Mary Corporation ........... E ...... 618 443-5676
　Sparta *(G-20318)*
Lee Gilster-Mary Corporation ........... D ...... 815 472-6456
　Momence *(G-14983)*
Mary Lee Packaging Corporation ...... E ...... 618 826-2361
　Chester *(G-3659)*
Matrix Packaging Inc ........................ G ...... 630 458-1942
　Addison *(G-193)*
MCS Midwest LLC ............................ G ...... 630 393-7402
　Aurora *(G-1185)*
Moore-Addison Co ........................... E ...... 630 543-6744
　Addison *(G-220)*
Neomek Incorporated ...................... F ...... 630 879-5400
　Batavia *(G-1475)*
North America Packaging Corp ....... E ...... 630 203-4100
　Oak Brook *(G-16547)*
Olcott Plastics Inc ............................ D ...... 630 584-0555
　Saint Charles *(G-19228)*
Pactiv LLC ........................................ C ...... 217 479-1144
　Jacksonville *(G-12404)*
Paragon Manufacturing Inc ............. D ...... 708 345-1717
　Melrose Park *(G-14681)*
Plano Molding Company LLC .......... G ...... 630 552-9557
　Sandwich *(G-19373)*
Plano Molding Company LLC .......... C ...... 815 786-3331
　Sandwich *(G-19374)*
Plastic Container Corporation ......... D ...... 217 352-2722
　Urbana *(G-21098)*
Polar Tech Industries Inc ................ G ...... 815 784-9000
　Genoa *(G-10882)*
Precision Container Inc .................. G ...... 618 548-2830
　Salem *(G-19344)*
Pylon Plastics Inc ............................ G ...... 630 968-6374
　Lisle *(G-13646)*
RPS Products Inc ............................ E ...... 847 683-3400
　Hampshire *(G-11562)*
Safeway Products Inc ...................... F ...... 815 226-8322
　Rockford *(G-18606)*
Silgan Plastics LLC .......................... ...... 815 334-1200
　Woodstock *(G-22612)*
Snyder Industries Inc ...................... G ...... 630 773-9510
　Bensenville *(G-1993)*
Transparent Container Co Inc ......... E ...... 708 449-8520
　Addison *(G-321)*
Transparent Container Co Inc ......... D ...... 630 543-1818
　Addison *(G-322)*
Transparent Container Co Inc ......... E ...... 630 860-2666
　Bensenville *(G-2006)*
Westrock Dspensing Systems Inc ... G ...... 847 310-3073
　Schaumburg *(G-19788)*
Yoshino America Corporation .......... E ...... 708 534-1141
　University Park *(G-21067)*

## CONTAINERS: Plywood & Veneer, Wood

Chicago Floral Planters Inc ............. G ...... 708 423-2754
　Chicago Ridge *(G-7141)*
Midwest Mktg/Pdctn Mfg Co ............ G ...... 217 256-3414
　Warsaw *(G-21370)*
Production Manufacturing ............... G ...... 217 256-4211
　Warsaw *(G-21371)*

## CONTAINERS: Sanitary, Food

Pactiv LLC ........................................ C ...... 219 924-4120
　Lake Forest *(G-12936)*
Pactiv LLC ........................................ C ...... 630 262-6335
　Saint Charles *(G-19233)*

## CONTAINERS: Shipping & Mailing, Fiber

Advantage Structures LLC .............. G ...... 773 734-9305
　Chicago *(G-3775)*
G T Express Ltd .............................. G ...... 708 338-0303
　Northlake *(G-16437)*

## CONTAINERS: Shipping, Wood

Polamer Inc ..................................... G ...... 773 774-3600
　Chicago *(G-6148)*

## CONTAINERS: Wood

Central Wood Products Inc ............. E ...... 217 728-4412
　Sullivan *(G-20742)*
Cole Pallet Services Corp ............... E ...... 815 758-3226
　Dekalb *(G-8077)*
U S Storage Group LLC .................. F ...... 618 482-8000
　Madison *(G-14155)*
Van Voorst Lumber Company Inc .... G ...... 815 426-2544
　Union Hill *(G-21039)*
Wesling Products Inc ..................... G ...... 773 533-2850
　Chicago *(G-6959)*

# PRODUCT SECTION

## CONTRACTORS: Closed Circuit Television Installation

### CONTAINMENT VESSELS: Reactor, Metal Plate

Powerone Corp .................................. G ...... 630 443-6500
  Saint Charles *(G-19239)*

### CONTRACTORS: Access Flooring System Installation

Imbert Construction Inds Inc .................. G ...... 847 588-3170
  Niles *(G-15988)*
Polymer Nation LLC ............................ G ...... 847 972-2157
  Waukegan *(G-21603)*
Rampro Facilities Svcs Corp ................... G ...... 224 639-6378
  Gurnee *(G-11498)*

### CONTRACTORS: Antenna Installation

Vincor Ltd .................................... F ...... 708 534-0008
  Monee *(G-15005)*

### CONTRACTORS: Asbestos Removal & Encapsulation

Onyx Environmental Svcs LLC ................... E ...... 630 218-1500
  Lombard *(G-13838)*

### CONTRACTORS: Asphalt

Crowley-Sheppard Asphalt Inc .................. F ...... 708 499-2900
  Chicago Ridge *(G-7145)*
F Lee Charles & Sons Inc ...................... G ...... 815 547-7141
  Kirkland *(G-12712)*
Freesen Inc ................................... E ...... 309 827-4554
  Bloomington *(G-2167)*

### CONTRACTORS: Awning Installation

Nuyen Awning Co ............................... G ...... 630 892-3995
  Aurora *(G-1197)*

### CONTRACTORS: Boiler & Furnace

Ed Hartwig Trucking & Excvtg .................. G ...... 309 364-3672
  Henry *(G-11740)*
Hidden Hollow Stables Inc ..................... G ...... 309 243-7979
  Dunlap *(G-8567)*
Moultri Cnty Hstrcl/Gnlgcl Sct ................ F ...... 217 728-4085
  Sullivan *(G-20754)*
Resolute Industrial LLC ....................... E ...... 800 537-9675
  Wheeling *(G-22139)*
White Sheet Metal ............................. G ...... 217 465-3195
  Paris *(G-17164)*

### CONTRACTORS: Boiler Maintenance Contractor

Depue Mechanical Inc .......................... E ...... 815 447-2267
  Depue *(G-8134)*
Hudson Boiler & Tank Company .................. F ...... 312 666-4780
  Lockport *(G-13722)*

### CONTRACTORS: Boring, Building Construction

Mid-America Underground LLC ................... E ...... 630 443-9999
  Aurora *(G-1188)*

### CONTRACTORS: Building Eqpt & Machinery Installation

Assa Abloy Entrance Systems US ................ F ...... 847 228-5600
  Elk Grove Village *(G-9316)*
Avenue Metal Manufacturing Co ................. F ...... 312 243-3483
  Chicago *(G-3999)*
Chevron Commercial Inc ........................ G ...... 618 654-5555
  Highland *(G-11779)*
Fixture Company ............................... G ...... 847 214-3100
  Chicago *(G-4854)*
Great Lakes Mech Svcs Inc ..................... F ...... 708 672-5900
  Lincolnshire *(G-13451)*
Kelly Systems Inc ............................. E ...... 312 733-3224
  Chicago *(G-5374)*
Patrick Holdings Inc .......................... F ...... 815 874-5300
  Rockford *(G-18531)*
Randal Wood Displays Inc ...................... D ...... 630 761-0400
  Batavia *(G-1490)*
Siemens Industry Inc .......................... G ...... 309 664-2460
  Bloomington *(G-2223)*
Sudholt Sheet Metal Inc ....................... G ...... 618 228-7351
  Aviston *(G-1248)*

### CONTRACTORS: Building Front Installation, Metal

Delta Erectors Inc ............................ F ...... 708 267-9721
  Villa Park *(G-21248)*

### CONTRACTORS: Building Sign Installation & Mntnce

Action Advertising Inc ........................ G ...... 312 791-0660
  Chicago *(G-3740)*
Ad Deluxe Sign Company Inc .................... G ...... 815 556-8469
  Plainfield *(G-17576)*
All-Brite Sign Co Inc ......................... F ...... 309 829-1551
  Normal *(G-16063)*
All-Right Sign Inc ............................ F ...... 708 754-6366
  Steger *(G-20567)*
All-Steel Structures Inc ...................... E ...... 708 210-1313
  South Holland *(G-20241)*
American Sign & Lighting Co ................... F ...... 847 258-8151
  Chicago *(G-3874)*
Bella Sign Co ................................. G ...... 630 539-0343
  Roselle *(G-18928)*
Bendsen Signs & Graphics Inc .................. F ...... 217 877-2345
  Decatur *(G-7845)*
Best Neon Sign Co Inc ......................... F ...... 773 586-2700
  Chicago *(G-4093)*
Demond Signs Inc .............................. G ...... 618 624-7260
  O Fallon *(G-16466)*
Friendly Signs Inc ............................ G ...... 815 933-7070
  Kankakee *(G-12618)*
Hardin Signs Inc .............................. F ...... 309 688-4111
  Peoria *(G-17379)*
Holland Design Group Inc ...................... G ...... 847 526-8848
  Wauconda *(G-21470)*
Hughes & Son Inc .............................. G ...... 815 459-1887
  Crystal Lake *(G-7589)*
Image Signs Inc ............................... F ...... 815 282-4141
  Loves Park *(G-13947)*
Midwest Sun-Ray Lighting & Sig ................ F ...... 618 656-2884
  Granite City *(G-11296)*
Mk Signs Inc .................................. G ...... 773 545-4444
  Chicago *(G-5777)*
Monitor Sign Co ............................... G ...... 217 234-2412
  Mattoon *(G-14405)*
North Shore Sign Company ...................... G ...... 847 816-7020
  Libertyville *(G-13364)*
Ozko Sign & Lighting Company .................. G ...... 224 653-8531
  Schaumburg *(G-19676)*
Quatum Structure and Design ................... F ...... 815 741-0733
  Rockdale *(G-18228)*
Roth Neon Sign Company Inc .................... G ...... 618 942-6378
  Herrin *(G-11753)*
Signage Plus Ltd .............................. G ...... 815 485-0300
  Lockport *(G-13744)*
Signet Sign Company ........................... G ...... 630 830-8242
  Bartlett *(G-1377)*
Staar Bales Lestarge Inc ...................... G ...... 618 259-6366
  East Alton *(G-8611)*
Strictly Neon Inc ............................. G ...... 708 597-1616
  Crestwood *(G-7504)*
T Ham Sign Inc ................................ F ...... 618 242-2010
  Opdyke *(G-16811)*

### CONTRACTORS: Cable Splicing Svcs

Express Signs & Lighting Maint ................ F ...... 815 725-9080
  Shorewood *(G-19926)*

### CONTRACTORS: Cable TV Installation

Jklein Enterprises Inc ........................ G ...... 618 664-4554
  Greenville *(G-11395)*

### CONTRACTORS: Caisson Drilling

CJ Drilling Inc ............................... E ...... 847 854-3888
  Dundee *(G-8560)*

### CONTRACTORS: Carpentry Work

Allie Woodworking ............................. G ...... 847 244-1919
  Waukegan *(G-21522)*
Ashland Door Solutions LLC .................... G ...... 773 348-5106
  Elk Grove Village *(G-9315)*
Carpenter Contractors Amer Inc ................ B ...... 815 544-1699
  Belvidere *(G-1744)*
Contract Industries Inc ....................... E ...... 708 458-8150
  Bedford Park *(G-1545)*
Furniture Services Inc ........................ G ...... 847 520-9490
  Wheeling *(G-22060)*
H Borre & Sons Inc ............................ G ...... 847 524-8890
  Lake Zurich *(G-13081)*
Ken Young Construction Co ..................... G ...... 847 358-3026
  Hoffman Estates *(G-12021)*
Lyko Woodworking & Cnstr ...................... G ...... 773 583-4561
  Chicago *(G-5573)*
Perkins Construction .......................... G ...... 815 233-9655
  Freeport *(G-10678)*
Peters Construction ........................... G ...... 773 489-5555
  Chicago *(G-6110)*
Savino Enterprises ............................ G ...... 708 385-5277
  Blue Island *(G-2268)*
Ww Displays Inc ............................... G ...... 847 566-6979
  Mundelein *(G-15568)*

### CONTRACTORS: Carpentry, Cabinet & Finish Work

Aba Custom Woodworking ........................ G ...... 815 356-9663
  Crystal Lake *(G-7525)*
Anderson & Marter Cabinets .................... G ...... 630 406-9840
  Batavia *(G-1415)*
Axis Design Architectual Mllwk ................ F ...... 630 466-4549
  Sugar Grove *(G-20717)*
C S C Inc ..................................... E ...... 217 925-5908
  Dieterich *(G-8312)*
Concord Cabinets Inc .......................... F ...... 217 894-6507
  Clayton *(G-7269)*
Cooper Lake Millworks Inc ..................... G ...... 217 847-2681
  Hamilton *(G-11530)*
Design Woodworks ............................. G ...... 847 566-6603
  Mundelein *(G-15493)*
Eiesland Builders Inc ......................... G ...... 847 998-1731
  Glenview *(G-11123)*
Greenberg Casework Company Inc ................ E ...... 815 624-0288
  South Beloit *(G-20150)*
L Surges Custom Woodwork ...................... G ...... 815 774-9663
  Joliet *(G-12529)*
Orren Pickell Builders Inc .................... F ...... 847 572-5200
  Northfield *(G-16415)*
Rays Countertop Shop Inc ...................... F ...... 217 483-2514
  Glenarm *(G-10997)*
Space Organization Ltd ........................ F ...... 312 654-1400
  Chicago *(G-6548)*
Stairsland .................................... G ...... 708 853-9593
  Lyons *(G-14045)*
Unique Designs ................................ G ...... 309 454-1226
  Normal *(G-16092)*
Wagners Custom Wood Design .................... G ...... 847 487-2788
  Island Lake *(G-12221)*
Wenger Woodcraft .............................. G ...... 217 578-3440
  Tuscola *(G-21030)*
Western Illinois Enterprises .................. G ...... 309 342-5185
  Galesburg *(G-10779)*

### CONTRACTORS: Carpentry, Cabinet Building & Installation

Action Cabinet Sales Inc ...................... G ...... 847 717-0011
  Elgin *(G-8935)*
Baker Elements Inc ............................ F ...... 630 660-8100
  Oak Park *(G-16654)*
Barrington Millwork LLC ....................... G ...... 847 304-0791
  Lake Barrington *(G-12800)*
Creative Cabinetry Inc ........................ G ...... 708 460-2900
  Orland Park *(G-16851)*
Custom Craft Cabinetry ........................ G ...... 630 897-2334
  Aurora *(G-1135)*
Eddie Gapastione .............................. G ...... 708 430-3881
  Bridgeview *(G-2487)*
Imperial Kitchens & Bath Inc .................. F ...... 708 485-0020
  Brookfield *(G-2635)*
OGorman Son Carpentry Contrs .................. G ...... 815 485-8997
  New Lenox *(G-15898)*
Riverton Cabinet Company ...................... E ...... 815 462-5300
  New Lenox *(G-15908)*
Sleeping Bear Inc ............................. G ...... 630 541-7220
  Lisle *(G-13656)*

### CONTRACTORS: Carpentry, Finish & Trim Work

Masters Shop .................................. G ...... 217 643-7826
  Thomasboro *(G-20860)*

### CONTRACTORS: Closed Circuit Television Installation

Quality Intgrted Solutions Inc ................ G ...... 815 464-4772
  Tinley Park *(G-20942)*

---

Employee Codes: A=Over 500 employees, B=251-500
C=101-250, D=51-100, E=20-50, F=10-19, G=3-9

# CONTRACTORS: Commercial & Office Building

### CONTRACTORS: Commercial & Office Building

|  | |  |
|---|---|---|
| Lombard Investment Company ..... D | | 708 389-1060 |
| Alsip *(G-484)* | | |
| Narvick Bros Lumber Co Inc ..... G | | 815 942-1173 |
| Morris *(G-15121)* | | |
| Poggenpohl LLC ..... G | | 217 229-3411 |
| Raymond *(G-17939)* | | |
| Poggenpohl LLC ..... G | | 217 824-2020 |
| Taylorville *(G-20844)* | | |

### CONTRACTORS: Communications Svcs

| Ayla Group Inc ..... G | 630 954-9432 |
|---|---|
| Bartlett *(G-1334)* | |
| Gatesair Inc ..... C | 217 222-8200 |
| Quincy *(G-17830)* | |
| Heil Sound Ltd ..... F | 618 257-3000 |
| Fairview Heights *(G-10168)* | |
| Jax Asphalt Company Inc ..... F | 618 244-0500 |
| Mount Vernon *(G-15418)* | |
| Medical Cmmnctions Systems Inc ..... G | 708 895-4500 |
| Lansing *(G-13176)* | |
| Tellabs Inc ..... E | 630 798-8800 |
| Naperville *(G-15762)* | |

### CONTRACTORS: Computer Installation

| Data Accessories Inc ..... G | 847 669-3640 |
|---|---|
| Huntley *(G-12136)* | |

### CONTRACTORS: Concrete

| Andel Services Inc ..... G | 630 566-0210 |
|---|---|
| Aurora *(G-1109)* | |
| Charles E Mahoney Company ..... E | 618 235-3355 |
| Swansea *(G-20776)* | |
| Christopher Concrete Products ..... G | 618 724-2951 |
| Buckner *(G-2647)* | |
| Cope & Sons Asphalt ..... G | 618 462-2207 |
| Alton *(G-567)* | |
| Engineered Fluid Pwr Con Cons ..... G | 815 332-3344 |
| Cherry Valley *(G-3641)* | |
| Hamilton Concrete Products Co ..... G | 217 847-3118 |
| Hamilton *(G-11537)* | |
| Herman Bade & Sons ..... G | 217 832-9444 |
| Villa Grove *(G-21228)* | |
| Jerry Berry Contracting Co ..... G | 618 594-3339 |
| Carlyle *(G-3055)* | |
| Langheim Ready Mix Inc ..... G | 217 625-2351 |
| Girard *(G-10947)* | |
| Myers Concrete & Construction ..... G | 815 732-2591 |
| Oregon *(G-16828)* | |
| Prosser Construction Co ..... F | 217 774-5032 |
| Shelbyville *(G-19913)* | |
| Rock Road Companies Inc ..... F | 815 874-2441 |
| Rockford *(G-18564)* | |

### CONTRACTORS: Concrete Breaking, Street & Highway

| Orange Crush LLC ..... G | 847 537-7900 |
|---|---|
| Wheeling *(G-22115)* | |
| Orange Crush LLC ..... E | 708 544-9440 |
| Hillside *(G-11930)* | |
| Orange Crush LLC ..... G | 847 428-6176 |
| East Dundee *(G-8650)* | |
| Orange Crush LLC ..... G | 630 739-5560 |
| Romeoville *(G-18856)* | |

### CONTRACTORS: Concrete Pumping

| Gary & Larry Brown Trucking ..... G | 618 268-6377 |
|---|---|
| Raleigh *(G-17909)* | |
| Roscoe Ready-Mix Inc ..... G | 815 389-0888 |
| Roscoe *(G-18917)* | |

### CONTRACTORS: Concrete Reinforcement Placing

| Steel Fabrication and Welding ..... G | 773 343-0731 |
|---|---|
| Cicero *(G-7230)* | |

### CONTRACTORS: Construction Site Cleanup

| Stages Construction Inc ..... G | 773 619-2977 |
|---|---|
| Chicago *(G-6568)* | |

### CONTRACTORS: Countertop Installation

| Carrera Stone Systems of Chica ..... E | 847 566-2277 |
|---|---|
| Mundelein *(G-15483)* | |
| Clover Custom Counters Inc ..... G | 708 598-8912 |
| Bridgeview *(G-2478)* | |
| Design Plus Industries Inc ..... G | 309 697-9778 |
| Peoria *(G-17349)* | |
| Dieter Construction Inc ..... G | 630 960-9662 |
| Woodridge *(G-22470)* | |
| Gerali Custom Design Inc ..... D | 847 760-0500 |
| Elgin *(G-9044)* | |
| Granite Xperts Inc ..... E | 847 364-1900 |
| Franklin Park *(G-10481)* | |
| Kitchen Krafters Inc ..... G | 815 675-6061 |
| Spring Grove *(G-20341)* | |
| R & R Custom Cabinet Making ..... G | 847 358-6188 |
| Palatine *(G-17065)* | |
| Surface Solutions Illinois Inc ..... G | 708 571-3449 |
| Mokena *(G-14907)* | |
| Wienmar Inc ..... C | 847 742-9222 |
| South Elgin *(G-20235)* | |
| Wilcor Solid Surface Inc ..... F | 630 350-7703 |
| Elk Grove Village *(G-9813)* | |

### CONTRACTORS: Decontamination Svcs

| Best Technology Systems Inc ..... F | 815 254-9554 |
|---|---|
| Plainfield *(G-17582)* | |

### CONTRACTORS: Demolition, Building & Other Structures

| Certified Asphalt Paving ..... G | 847 441-5000 |
|---|---|
| Northfield *(G-16396)* | |

### CONTRACTORS: Directional Oil & Gas Well Drilling Svc

| Booth Resources Inc ..... G | 618 662-4955 |
|---|---|
| Flora *(G-10201)* | |
| C&R Directional Boring ..... G | 630 458-0055 |
| Addison *(G-66)* | |
| Coursons Coring & Drilling ..... G | 618 349-8765 |
| Saint Peter *(G-19321)* | |
| Coy Oil Inc ..... G | 618 966-2126 |
| Crossville *(G-7522)* | |
| Jackson Oil Corporation ..... G | 618 263-6521 |
| Mount Carmel *(G-15270)* | |
| Mid-America Underground LLC ..... E | 630 443-9999 |
| Aurora *(G-1188)* | |
| Pep Drilling Co ..... G | 618 242-2205 |
| Mount Vernon *(G-15438)* | |
| Quad Cities Directional Boring ..... G | 309 792-3070 |
| Colona *(G-7346)* | |
| Rays Electrical Service LLC ..... F | 847 214-2944 |
| Elgin *(G-9161)* | |
| Southern Triangle Oil Company ..... F | 618 262-4131 |
| Mount Carmel *(G-15282)* | |
| Universal Hrzntal Drctnal Drlg ..... G | 847 847-3300 |
| Lake Zurich *(G-13140)* | |

### CONTRACTORS: Dock Eqpt Installation, Indl

| Builders Chicago Corporation ..... D | 224 654-2122 |
|---|---|
| Rosemont *(G-18991)* | |
| Fix It Fast Ltd ..... G | 708 401-8320 |
| Midlothian *(G-14766)* | |

### CONTRACTORS: Drapery Track Installation

| Dons Drapery Service ..... G | 815 385-4759 |
|---|---|
| McHenry *(G-14497)* | |

### CONTRACTORS: Driveway

| Fuller Asphalt & Landscape ..... G | 618 797-1169 |
|---|---|
| Granite City *(G-11277)* | |
| Jacobs Trucking ..... G | 618 687-3578 |
| Murphysboro *(G-15577)* | |

### CONTRACTORS: Electric Power Systems

| Current Plus Electric LLC ..... G | 618 394-4827 |
|---|---|
| Belleville *(G-1620)* | |
| Enterprise Service Corporation ..... G | 773 589-2727 |
| Des Plaines *(G-8188)* | |

### CONTRACTORS: Electrical

| Aemm A Electric ..... G | 708 403-6700 |
|---|---|
| Orland Park *(G-16839)* | |
| Al Cook Electric Motors ..... G | 309 653-2337 |
| Adair *(G-11)* | |
| Archer General Contg & Fabg ..... G | 708 757-7902 |
| Steger *(G-20568)* | |
| Cable Electric Company Inc ..... G | 708 458-8900 |
| Oak Lawn *(G-16609)* | |
| Carey Electric Co Inc ..... G | 847 949-9294 |
| Grayslake *(G-11325)* | |
| Connor Electric Services Inc ..... E | 630 823-8230 |
| Schaumburg *(G-19480)* | |
| Cullinan & Sons Inc ..... E | 309 925-2711 |
| Tremont *(G-20981)* | |
| Eberhart Sign & Lighting Co ..... G | 618 656-7256 |
| Edwardsville *(G-8797)* | |
| Erbes Electric ..... G | 815 849-5508 |
| Sublette *(G-20715)* | |
| Hardt Electric ..... G | 312 822-0869 |
| Chicago *(G-5044)* | |
| Heico Companies LLC ..... F | 312 419-8220 |
| Chicago *(G-5068)* | |
| Kavanaugh Electric Inc ..... G | 708 503-1310 |
| Frankfort *(G-10339)* | |
| Kohns Electric ..... G | 309 463-2331 |
| Varna *(G-21134)* | |
| L & H Company Inc ..... F | 630 571-7200 |
| Oak Brook *(G-16532)* | |
| Lightscape Inc ..... E | 847 247-8800 |
| Libertyville *(G-13344)* | |
| Marshall Electric Inc ..... F | 618 382-3932 |
| Carmi *(G-3074)* | |
| Midwest Sun-Ray Lighting & Sig ..... F | 618 656-2884 |
| Granite City *(G-11296)* | |
| Rathje Enterprises Inc ..... B | 217 423-2593 |
| Decatur *(G-7932)* | |
| Rays Electrical Service LLC ..... F | 847 214-2944 |
| Elgin *(G-9161)* | |
| Richards Electric Motor Co ..... E | 217 222-7154 |
| Quincy *(G-17887)* | |
| Saturn Electrical Services Inc ..... G | 630 980-0300 |
| Roselle *(G-18973)* | |
| Twin City Electric Inc ..... E | 309 827-0636 |
| Bloomington *(G-2233)* | |
| Twin Supplies Ltd ..... G | 630 590-5138 |
| Oak Brook *(G-16566)* | |

### CONTRACTORS: Electronic Controls Installation

| Contract Assembly Partners ..... F | 217 960-3352 |
|---|---|
| Hillsboro *(G-11888)* | |
| Humidity 2 Optimization LLC ..... F | 847 991-7488 |
| East Dundee *(G-8644)* | |
| Northwest Instrumentation Inc ..... E | 847 825-0699 |
| Park Ridge *(G-17213)* | |

### CONTRACTORS: Energy Management Control

| Contemprary Enrgy Slutions LLC ..... F | 630 768-3743 |
|---|---|
| Naperville *(G-15801)* | |
| E2s LLC ..... G | 708 629-0714 |
| Alsip *(G-460)* | |
| Global Technologies I LLC ..... D | 312 255-8350 |
| Chicago *(G-4960)* | |
| Lightitech LLC ..... G | 847 910-4177 |
| Chicago *(G-5504)* | |
| Rtenergy LLC ..... F | 773 975-2598 |
| Chicago *(G-6410)* | |

### CONTRACTORS: Environmental Controls Installation

| Johnson Controls Inc ..... F | 217 793-8858 |
|---|---|
| Springfield *(G-20464)* | |

### CONTRACTORS: Erection & Dismantling, Poured Concrete Forms

| West Lake Concrete & Rmdlg LLC ..... G | 847 477-8667 |
|---|---|
| Chicago *(G-6960)* | |

### CONTRACTORS: Excavating

| A E Frasz Inc ..... F | 630 232-6223 |
|---|---|
| Elburn *(G-8872)* | |
| Amigoni Construction ..... G | 309 923-3701 |
| Roanoke *(G-18047)* | |
| Certified Asphalt Paving ..... G | 847 441-5000 |
| Northfield *(G-16396)* | |
| Conmat Inc ..... E | 815 235-2200 |
| Freeport *(G-10651)* | |
| Cortelyou Excavating ..... G | 309 772-2922 |
| Bushnell *(G-2901)* | |
| Ed Hartwig Trucking & Excvtg ..... G | 309 364-3672 |
| Henry *(G-11740)* | |

# PRODUCT SECTION

## CONTRACTORS: Highway & Street Resurfacing

Gorman Brothers Ready Mix Inc ............F....... 618 498-2173
  Jerseyville  *(G-12422)*
Hamilton Concrete Products Co .............G....... 217 847-3118
  Hamilton  *(G-11537)*
Hulse Excavating ....................................G....... 815 796-4106
  Flanagan  *(G-10194)*
J W Ossola Company Inc ........................G....... 815 339-6112
  Granville  *(G-11318)*
Jay A Morris ..............................................G....... 815 432-6440
  Watseka  *(G-21420)*
Jerry Berry Contracting Co .....................G....... 618 594-3339
  Carlyle  *(G-3055)*
Joe Hatzer & Son Inc ..............................G....... 815 673-5571
  Streator  *(G-20692)*
Lake County Grading Co LLC .................E....... 847 362-2590
  Libertyville  *(G-13341)*
Loberg Excavating Inc ............................E....... 815 443-2874
  Pearl City  *(G-17248)*
Mertel Gravel Company Inc ....................F....... 815 223-0468
  Peru  *(G-17518)*
Mid-America Underground LLC ..............E....... 630 443-9999
  Aurora  *(G-1188)*
Myers Concrete & Construction ..............G....... 815 732-2591
  Oregon  *(G-16828)*

## CONTRACTORS: Excavating Slush Pits & Cellars Svcs

T-Rex Excavating Inc ..............................G....... 815 547-9955
  Belvidere  *(G-1787)*
Toppert Jetting Service Inc .....................G....... 309 755-2240
  Hillsdale  *(G-11904)*

## CONTRACTORS: Exterior Wall System Installation

Polymer Nation LLC ................................G....... 847 972-2157
  Waukegan  *(G-21603)*

## CONTRACTORS: Fence Construction

Alfredos Iron Works Inc ..........................E....... 815 748-1177
  Cortland  *(G-7384)*
Bergeron Group Inc ................................E....... 815 741-1635
  Joliet  *(G-12464)*
Industrial Fence Inc ................................E....... 773 521-9900
  Chicago  *(G-5176)*
Invisible Fencing of Quad City ................G....... 309 797-1688
  Moline  *(G-14945)*
Sandoval Fences Corp ............................G....... 773 287-0279
  Chicago  *(G-6438)*
United Fence Co Inc ................................G....... 773 924-0773
  Chicago  *(G-6823)*
William Dach ............................................F....... 815 962-3455
  Rockford  *(G-18683)*
Winters Welding Inc .................................G....... 773 860-7735
  Chicago  *(G-7004)*
Woodland Fence Forest Pdts Inc ............G....... 630 393-2220
  Warrenville  *(G-21369)*

## CONTRACTORS: Fiberglass Work

Accu-Wright Fiberglass Inc .....................G....... 618 337-3318
  East Saint Louis  *(G-8739)*

## CONTRACTORS: Fire Detection & Burglar Alarm Systems

Accurate Security & Lock Corp ...............G....... 815 455-0133
  Lake In The Hills  *(G-12982)*

## CONTRACTORS: Floor Laying & Other Floor Work

Cullinan & Sons Inc ................................E....... 309 925-2711
  Tremont  *(G-20981)*
F H Leinweber Co Inc .............................G....... 708 424-7000
  Oak Lawn  *(G-16619)*
F H Leinweber Co Inc .............................E....... 773 568-7722
  Chicago  *(G-4803)*
Grads Inc .................................................G....... 847 426-3904
  East Dundee  *(G-8641)*

## CONTRACTORS: Flooring

Substrate Technology Inc .......................F....... 815 941-4800
  Morris  *(G-15133)*

## CONTRACTORS: Fountain Installation

Fountain Technologies Ltd ......................E....... 847 537-3677
  Wheeling  *(G-22057)*

## CONTRACTORS: Garage Doors

Allied Garage Door Inc ............................E....... 630 279-0795
  Addison  *(G-29)*
Builders Chicago Corporation .................D....... 224 654-2122
  Rosemont  *(G-18991)*

## CONTRACTORS: Gas Field Svcs, NEC

Harold L Ray Truck & Trctr Svc ..............F....... 618 673-2701
  Cisne  *(G-7252)*

## CONTRACTORS: General Electric

Control Panels Inc ..................................F....... 815 654-6000
  Rockford  *(G-18323)*
Jf Industries Inc .......................................G....... 773 775-8840
  Chicago  *(G-5301)*
K R J Inc ...................................................G....... 309 925-5123
  Tremont  *(G-20983)*
Keller United Elc & Mch Co .....................G....... 217 382-4521
  Martinsville  *(G-14337)*
Phoenix Business Solutions LLC ............E....... 708 388-1330
  Alsip  *(G-508)*
Rathje Enterprises Inc ............................F....... 217 443-0022
  Danville  *(G-7763)*
Sharlen Electric Co ..................................E....... 773 721-0700
  Chicago  *(G-6489)*
Sievert Electric Svc & Sls Co ...................D....... 708 771-1600
  Forest Park  *(G-10253)*
Superior One Electric Inc ........................G....... 630 655-3300
  Westchester  *(G-21856)*
Tracy Electric Inc ....................................E....... 618 943-6205
  Lawrenceville  *(G-13206)*

## CONTRACTORS: Geothermal Drilling

Unique Indoor Comfort ............................F....... 847 362-1910
  Libertyville  *(G-13394)*

## CONTRACTORS: Glass Tinting, Architectural & Automotive

Lou Plucinski ...........................................G....... 815 758-7888
  Dekalb  *(G-8103)*

## CONTRACTORS: Glass, Glazing & Tinting

Botti Studio of Architectural ....................E....... 847 869-5933
  Evanston  *(G-10017)*
Christopher Glass & Aluminum ...............D....... 312 256-8500
  Chicago  *(G-4372)*
Circle Studio Stained Glass ....................G....... 847 432-7249
  Highland Park  *(G-11827)*
Euroview Enterprises LLC ......................E....... 630 227-3300
  Elmhurst  *(G-9869)*
Harmon Inc ..............................................D....... 312 726-5050
  Chicago  *(G-5046)*
Horan Glass Block Inc ............................G....... 773 586-4808
  Chicago  *(G-5111)*
Illinois Valley Glass & Mirror ...................F....... 309 682-6603
  Peoria  *(G-17387)*
Shoreline Glass Co Inc ...........................E....... 312 829-9500
  Hillside  *(G-11933)*
Southern Glass Co .................................G....... 618 532-4281
  Centralia  *(G-3434)*
T J M & Associates Inc ...........................G....... 847 382-1993
  Lake Barrington  *(G-12825)*
Tuminello Enterprizes Inc .......................G....... 815 416-1007
  Morris  *(G-15137)*
Tuminello Enterprizes Inc .......................G....... 815 416-1007
  Morris  *(G-15138)*
Will Hamms Stained Glass .....................F....... 847 255-2230
  Arlington Heights  *(G-872)*
Willow Ridge Glass Inc ...........................F....... 630 910-8300
  Woodridge  *(G-22525)*

## CONTRACTORS: Gutters & Downspouts

GROsse&sons Htg &SHeet Met Inc .......G....... 708 447-8397
  Lyons  *(G-14040)*

## CONTRACTORS: Heating & Air Conditioning

B A P Enterprises Inc .............................G....... 708 849-0900
  Dolton  *(G-8364)*
Custom Fabricating Htg & Coolg ............G....... 815 726-0477
  Joliet  *(G-12480)*
D and S Molding & Dctg Inc ...................G....... 815 399-2734
  Rockford  *(G-18332)*
Elk Grove Custom Sheet Metal ..............F....... 847 352-2845
  Elk Grove Village  *(G-9451)*
Kool Technologies Inc .............................G....... 630 483-2256
  Streamwood  *(G-20662)*
Lemanski Heating & AC ..........................G....... 815 232-4519
  Freeport  *(G-10673)*
Macari Service Center Inc ......................G....... 217 774-4214
  Shelbyville  *(G-19910)*
Mach Mechanical Group LLC .................G....... 630 674-6224
  Naperville  *(G-15815)*
Merz Air Conditioning and Htg ................E....... 217 342-2323
  Effingham  *(G-8845)*
National Metal Works Inc ........................G....... 815 282-5533
  Loves Park  *(G-13969)*
Support Central Inc .................................G....... 702 202-3500
  Skokie  *(G-20096)*
Synergy Mechanical Inc ..........................G....... 708 410-1004
  Westchester  *(G-21857)*
Unique Indoor Comfort ............................F....... 847 362-1910
  Libertyville  *(G-13394)*

## CONTRACTORS: Heating Systems Repair & Maintenance Svc

Service King Plbg Htg Colg Elc ..............G....... 847 458-8900
  Lake In The Hills  *(G-13007)*
Smid Heating & Air ..................................G....... 815 467-0362
  Channahon  *(G-3586)*

## CONTRACTORS: Highway & Street Construction, General

Air Duct Manufacturing Inc .....................G....... 630 620-9866
  Addison  *(G-28)*
Allendale Gravel Co Inc ..........................G....... 618 263-3521
  Allendale  *(G-420)*
Ambraw Asphalt Materials Inc ................E....... 618 943-4716
  Lawrenceville  *(G-13194)*
Charles Sheridan and Sons ....................G....... 847 903-7209
  Evanston  *(G-10020)*
Don Anderson Co ....................................G....... 618 495-2511
  Hoffman  *(G-11988)*
Gunther Construction Co ........................G....... 309 343-1032
  Galesburg  *(G-10756)*
L & H Company Inc .................................F....... 630 571-7200
  Oak Brook  *(G-16532)*
Lumberyard Suppliers Inc ......................F....... 618 931-0315
  Granite City  *(G-11291)*
ODaniel Trucking Co ...............................D....... 618 382-5371
  Carmi  *(G-3076)*

## CONTRACTORS: Highway & Street Paving

Allied Asphalt Paving Co Inc ...................E....... 630 289-6080
  Elgin  *(G-8943)*
Andel Services Inc ..................................G....... 630 566-0210
  Aurora  *(G-1109)*
Arrow Road Construction Co ..................C....... 847 437-0700
  Mount Prospect  *(G-15310)*
Charles E Mahoney Company ................E....... 618 235-3355
  Swansea  *(G-20776)*
Corrective Asphalt Mtls LLC ...................G....... 618 254-3855
  South Roxana  *(G-20312)*
Curran Group Inc ....................................E....... 815 455-5100
  Crystal Lake  *(G-7563)*
Geneva Construction Company ..............G....... 630 892-6536
  North Aurora  *(G-16132)*
McLean County Asphalt Co ....................D....... 309 827-6115
  Bloomington  *(G-2194)*
Peter Baker & Son Co .............................D....... 847 362-3663
  Lake Bluff  *(G-12861)*
Plote Construction Inc ............................G....... 847 695-0422
  Hoffman Estates  *(G-12035)*
Plote Construction Inc ............................D....... 847 695-9300
  Hoffman Estates  *(G-12036)*
Prosser Construction Co ........................F....... 217 774-5032
  Shelbyville  *(G-19913)*
Rock Road Companies Inc .....................G....... 815 874-2441
  Rockford  *(G-18564)*
William Charles Cnstr Co LLC ................D....... 815 654-4700
  Loves Park  *(G-14007)*

## CONTRACTORS: Highway & Street Resurfacing

All Weather Courts Inc ............................G....... 217 364-4546
  Dawson  *(G-7816)*
G & S Asphalt Inc ....................................F....... 217 826-2421
  Marshall  *(G-14322)*

## CONTRACTORS: Highway Sign & Guardrail Construction & Install

Industrial Fence Inc .................................. E ....... 773 521-9900
Chicago *(G-5176)*

## CONTRACTORS: Home & Office Intrs Finish, Furnish/Remodel

Baker Avenue Investments Inc ............. G ....... 309 427-2500
Washington *(G-21378)*
Lincoln Office LLC ................................... D ....... 309 427-2500
Washington *(G-21385)*
Osmer Woodworking Inc ....................... G ....... 815 973-5809
Dixon *(G-8338)*
Systems Unlimited Inc ............................ C ....... 630 285-0010
Itasca *(G-12363)*
Woodworking Unlimited Inc ................... F ....... 630 469-7023
Carol Stream *(G-3269)*

## CONTRACTORS: Hydraulic Eqpt Installation & Svcs

Professional Meters Inc .......................... C ....... 815 942-7000
Morris *(G-15127)*
Rehobot Inc ............................................. G ....... 815 385-7777
McHenry *(G-14550)*
Wandfluh of America Inc ........................ F ....... 847 566-5700
Mundelein *(G-15566)*

## CONTRACTORS: Kitchen & Bathroom Remodeling

Creative Designs Kitc .............................. E ....... 773 327-8400
Chicago *(G-4497)*
Perkins Construction ............................... G ....... 815 233-9655
Freeport *(G-10678)*
Rays Countertop Shop Inc ..................... F ....... 217 483-2514
Glenarm *(G-10997)*
Wenger Woodcraft .................................. G ....... 217 578-3440
Tuscola *(G-21030)*

## CONTRACTORS: Kitchen Cabinet Installation

Hci Cabinetry and Design Inc ................. G ....... 630 584-0266
Saint Charles *(G-19190)*

## CONTRACTORS: Land Reclamation

SF Contracting LLC ................................ E ....... 618 926-1477
Raleigh *(G-17911)*

## CONTRACTORS: Lighting Conductor Erection

Harger Inc ................................................ E ....... 847 548-8700
Grayslake *(G-11345)*

## CONTRACTORS: Machine Rigging & Moving

American Industrial Werks Inc ................ F ....... 847 477-2648
Schaumburg *(G-19437)*
Chicago Flyhouse Incorporated ............. F ....... 773 533-1590
Chicago *(G-4320)*
New Cie Inc ............................................. E ....... 815 224-1511
Peru *(G-17522)*

## CONTRACTORS: Machinery Installation

Aak Mechanical Inc ................................. D ....... 217 935-8501
Clinton *(G-7276)*
Dontech Industries Inc ............................ F ....... 847 428-8222
Gilberts *(G-10917)*
Morey Industries Inc ............................... C ....... 708 343-3220
Broadview *(G-2598)*
R C Industrial Inc .................................... G ....... 309 756-3724
Milan *(G-14801)*
Sardee Industries Inc .............................. G ....... 630 824-4200
Lisle *(G-13654)*

## CONTRACTORS: Marble Installation, Interior

Acme Marble Co Inc ............................... G ....... 630 964-7162
Darien *(G-7786)*
Marble Emporium Inc ............................. E ....... 847 205-4000
Northbrook *(G-16306)*
Stonecrafters Inc .................................... E ....... 815 363-8730
Lakemoor *(G-13148)*

## CONTRACTORS: Marble Masonry, Exterior

Galloy and Van Etten Inc ........................ E ....... 773 928-4800
Chicago *(G-4911)*
Standard Marble & Granite .................... F ....... 773 533-0450
Chicago *(G-6570)*

## CONTRACTORS: Masonry & Stonework

Surface Solutions Illinois Inc .................. G ....... 708 571-3449
Mokena *(G-14907)*
V J Mattson Company ............................ D ....... 708 479-1990
New Lenox *(G-15926)*

## CONTRACTORS: Mechanical

American Industrial Werks Inc ................ F ....... 847 477-2648
Schaumburg *(G-19437)*
Elgin Sheet Metal Co .............................. E ....... 847 742-3486
South Elgin *(G-20194)*
Lake Process Systems Inc ..................... E ....... 847 381-7663
Lake Barrington *(G-12817)*
Miller Roger Weston ............................... G ....... 217 352-0476
Champaign *(G-3514)*
R B Hayward Company .......................... E ....... 847 671-0400
Schiller Park *(G-19864)*
Schneider Elc Buildings LLC .................. B ....... 815 381-5000
Rockford *(G-18608)*
Schneider Elc Buildings LLC .................. G ....... 815 227-4000
Rockford *(G-18609)*
Schneider Elc Holdings Inc .................... A ....... 717 944-5460
Schaumburg *(G-19722)*

## CONTRACTORS: Metal Ceiling Construction & Repair Work

Polymer Nation LLC ................................ G ....... 847 972-2157
Waukegan *(G-21603)*

## CONTRACTORS: Millwrights

Bing Engineering Inc ............................... C ....... 708 228-8005
Frankfort *(G-10300)*
Neiweem Industries Inc .......................... G ....... 847 487-1239
Oakwood Hills *(G-16727)*

## CONTRACTORS: Oil & Gas Building, Repairing & Dismantling Svc

Gholson Pump & Repairs Co ................. G ....... 618 382-4730
Carmi *(G-3069)*
Samtek International Inc ......................... ....... 314 954-4005
Swansea *(G-20782)*

## CONTRACTORS: Oil & Gas Field Geological Exploration Svcs

Howard Energy Corporation ................... G ....... 618 263-3000
Mount Carmel *(G-15268)*

## CONTRACTORS: Oil & Gas Field Geophysical Exploration Svcs

Strata Exploration Inc ............................. G ....... 618 842-2610
Fairfield *(G-10155)*

## CONTRACTORS: Oil & Gas Field Salt Water Impound/Storing Svc

Water & Gas Technologies ..................... G ....... 708 829-3254
Palos Park *(G-17134)*

## CONTRACTORS: Oil & Gas Well Casing Cement Svcs

Glover Oil Field Service Inc .................... F ....... 618 395-3624
Olney *(G-16770)*
M & S Oil Well Cementing Co ................ G ....... 618 262-7962
Mount Carmel *(G-15273)*
Schwartz Oilfield Services ...................... E ....... 618 532-0232
Walnut Hill *(G-21334)*

## CONTRACTORS: Oil & Gas Well Drilling Svc

Baker Hghes Olfld Oprtions Inc .............. F ....... 618 393-2919
Olney *(G-16761)*
Black Bison Water Services LLC ........... G ....... 630 272-5935
Chicago *(G-4119)*
Crystal Precision Drilling ........................ G ....... 815 633-5460
Loves Park *(G-13930)*
Dee Drilling Co ........................................ E ....... 618 262-4136
Mount Carmel *(G-15264)*
Ebers Drilling Co ..................................... G ....... 618 826-5398
Chester *(G-3655)*
Evergreen Energy LLC ........................... G ....... 618 384-9295
Carmi *(G-3067)*
F L Beard Service Corp .......................... E ....... 618 262-5193
Mount Carmel *(G-15265)*
Five P Drilling Inc ................................... E ....... 618 943-9771
Bridgeport *(G-2452)*
G&E Transportation Inc .......................... E ....... 404 350-6497
Chicago *(G-4903)*
Geo N Mitchell Drlg Co Inc ..................... G ....... 618 382-2343
Carmi *(G-3068)*
Glover Oil Field Service Inc .................... F ....... 618 395-3624
Olney *(G-16770)*
J H Robison & Associates Ltd ................ G ....... 847 559-9662
Northbrook *(G-16281)*
Jerry D Graham Oil ................................. ....... 618 548-5540
Salem *(G-19337)*
Kapp Company LLC ............................... G ....... 618 676-1000
Olney *(G-16776)*
Kinoco Inc ............................................... G ....... 618 378-3802
Norris City *(G-16115)*
L C Neelydrilling Inc ................................ G ....... 618 544-2726
Robinson *(G-18065)*
Les Wilson Inc ........................................ C ....... 618 382-4667
Carmi *(G-3073)*
Marion Oelze .......................................... G ....... 618 327-9224
Nashville *(G-15839)*
Murvin & Meier Oil Co ............................ G ....... 847 277-8380
Barrington *(G-1293)*
Quality Drilling Service LLP ................... G ....... 937 663-4715
Alton *(G-587)*
Reef Development Inc ............................ F ....... 618 842-7711
Fairfield *(G-10152)*
Rodgers Bill Oil Min Bits Svc .................. G ....... 618 299-7771
West Salem *(G-21824)*
Royal Drilling & Producing ...................... G ....... 618 966-2221
Crossville *(G-7523)*
Runyon Oil Production Inc ...................... G ....... 618 395-8510
Olney *(G-16794)*
Spartan Petroleum Company ................. G ....... 618 262-4197
Mount Carmel *(G-15283)*
Ta Oil Field Service Inc .......................... G ....... 618 249-9001
Richview *(G-17982)*
Tussey G K Oil Explrtn & Prdc ............... G ....... 618 948-2871
Saint Francisville *(G-19314)*

## CONTRACTORS: Oil & Gas Well Foundation Grading Svcs

Runyon Oil Tools Inc ............................... G ....... 618 395-5045
Olney *(G-16795)*

## CONTRACTORS: Oil & Gas Well On-Site Foundation Building Svcs

Deep Rock Energy Corporation .............. E ....... 618 548-2779
Kinmundy *(G-12709)*

## CONTRACTORS: Oil & Gas Well Plugging & Abandoning Svcs

I D Tool Specialty Company ................... G ....... 815 432-2007
Watseka *(G-21419)*
Precision Plugging and Sls Inc ............... F ....... 618 395-8510
Olney *(G-16792)*

## CONTRACTORS: Oil & Gas Wells Pumping Svcs

Wabash Production & Dev ..................... G ....... 618 847-7401
Fairfield *(G-10158)*
Wilpro ...................................................... G ....... 618 382-4667
Carmi *(G-3085)*

## CONTRACTORS: Oil & Gas Wells Svcs

Abner Trucking Co Inc ............................ G ....... 618 676-1301
Clay City *(G-7261)*
Franklin Well Services Inc ...................... D ....... 812 494-2800
Lawrenceville *(G-13200)*
M & L Well Service Inc ........................... G ....... 618 395-4538
Olney *(G-16779)*
Mason Well Servicing Inc ....................... G ....... 618 375-4411
Grayville *(G-11375)*
Mitchco Farms LLC ................................ F ....... 618 382-5032
Carmi *(G-3075)*
Sids Well Service .................................... G ....... 618 375-5411
Grayville *(G-11377)*
Stewart Producers Inc ............................ G ....... 618 244-3754
Mount Vernon *(G-15446)*

# PRODUCT SECTION

Wayne County Well Surveys Inc............F........ 618 842-9116
  Fairfield  *(G-10160)*

## CONTRACTORS: Oil Field Haulage Svcs

Haggard Well Services Inc..........................G....... 618 262-5060
  Mount Carmel  *(G-15266)*

## CONTRACTORS: Oil Field Lease Tanks: Erectg, Clng/Rprg Svcs

De Vries International Inc.........................E...... 773 248-6695
  Chicago  *(G-4568)*
J B Oil Field Cnstr & Sup..........................G....... 618 936-2350
  Sumner  *(G-20771)*

## CONTRACTORS: Oil Field Mud Drilling Svcs

Marlow Hill Drilling Inc...........................F....... 618 867-2978
  Murphysboro  *(G-15578)*

## CONTRACTORS: Oil Field Pipe Testing Svcs

Buckeye Terminals LLC.............................G....... 217 342-2336
  Effingham  *(G-8828)*
Foltz Welding  Ltd..................................C....... 618 432-7777
  Patoka  *(G-17231)*
McNdt Pipeline Ltd..................................G....... 815 467-5200
  Channahon  *(G-3579)*
Panhandle Eastrn Pipe Line LP................E...... 217 753-1108
  Springfield  *(G-20498)*

## CONTRACTORS: Oil Sampling Svcs

Map Oil Co Inc........................................G....... 618 375-7616
  Grayville  *(G-11374)*

## CONTRACTORS: Oil/Gas Well Construction, Rpr/Dismantling Svcs

1 Heavy Equipment Loading Inc................F....... 773 581-7374
  Bedford Park  *(G-1528)*
Abundance House Treasure Nfp..............G....... 312 788-4316
  Chicago  *(G-3711)*
Craftwood Inc........................................F....... 630 758-1740
  Elmhurst  *(G-9858)*
Crystatech Inc........................................F....... 847 768-0500
  Des Plaines  *(G-8178)*
D Kersey Construction Co........................G....... 847 919-4980
  Northbrook  *(G-16237)*
Dontrell Percy.........................................F....... 773 418-4900
  Chicago  *(G-4631)*
Finite Resources Ltd...............................G....... 618 252-3733
  Harrisburg  *(G-11598)*
Gesells Pump Sales & Service.................G....... 618 439-7354
  Whittington  *(G-22186)*
Global General Contractors LLC..............G....... 708 663-0476
  Tinley Park  *(G-20918)*
Heafner Contracting Inc..........................F....... 618 466-3678
  Godfrey  *(G-11225)*
Jsq Inc..................................................G....... 847 731-8800
  Wadsworth  *(G-21323)*
Local 46 Training Program Tr..................G....... 217 528-4041
  Springfield  *(G-20471)*
Matrix North Amercn Cnstr Inc................G....... 312 754-6605
  Chicago  *(G-5654)*
Mdm Construction Supply  LLC...............G....... 815 847-7340
  Rockford  *(G-18488)*
Patriot Home Improvement Inc................F....... 630 800-1901
  Aurora  *(G-1203)*
Pool Center Inc......................................G....... 217 698-7665
  Springfield  *(G-20505)*
Protus Construction................................G....... 773 405-9999
  Chicago  *(G-6218)*
Purified Lubricants Inc............................E...... 708 478-3500
  Mokena  *(G-14899)*
Stages Construction Inc..........................G....... 773 619-2977
  Chicago  *(G-6568)*
Tri-Zee Services Inc...............................G....... 630 543-8677
  Addison  *(G-324)*

## CONTRACTORS: On-Site Welding

1883 Properties Inc................................D...... 847 537-8800
  Lincolnshire  *(G-13422)*
A&S Machining & Welding Inc................E...... 708 442-4544
  Mc Cook  *(G-14443)*
Alloyweld Inspection Co Inc....................E...... 630 595-2145
  Bensenville  *(G-1827)*
B J Fehr Machine Co..............................G....... 309 923-8691
  Roanoke  *(G-18048)*

Bulaw Welding & Engineering Co ...........D...... 630 228-8300
  Itasca  *(G-12239)*
Cokel Welding Shop..............................G....... 217 357-3312
  Carthage  *(G-3312)*
Curran Group Inc...................................E...... 815 455-5100
  Crystal Lake  *(G-7563)*
D W Terry Welding Company.................F....... 618 433-9722
  Alton  *(G-570)*
Daves Welding Service Inc....................F....... 630 655-3224
  Darien  *(G-7792)*
F Vogelmann and Company....................F....... 815 469-2285
  Frankfort  *(G-10321)*
Fabricators Unlimited Inc.......................E...... 847 223-7986
  Grayslake  *(G-11337)*
Global Field Services Intl Inc..................E...... 847 931-8930
  Elgin  *(G-9048)*
Koenig Machine & Welding Inc...............G....... 217 228-6538
  Quincy  *(G-17849)*
Pools Welding Inc..................................G....... 309 787-2083
  Milan  *(G-14798)*
Pro Machining Inc..................................G....... 815 633-4140
  Loves Park  *(G-13978)*
Pro-Tran Inc..........................................G....... 217 348-9353
  Charleston  *(G-3608)*
Reyco Precision Welding Inc..................F....... 847 593-2947
  Lake Zurich  *(G-13122)*
Shannon & Sons Welding.......................G....... 630 898-7778
  Aurora  *(G-1215)*
Southwick Machine & Design Co............G....... 309 949-2868
  Colona  *(G-7348)*
Tri-Cunty Wldg Fabrication LLC..............G....... 217 543-3304
  Arthur  *(G-923)*
Wec Welding and Machining  LLC..........G....... 847 680-8100
  Lake Bluff  *(G-12870)*
Wissmiller & Evans Road Eqp.................G....... 309 725-3598
  Cooksville  *(G-7373)*
Wittwer Brothers Inc..............................G....... 815 522-3589
  Monroe Center  *(G-15025)*

## CONTRACTORS: Ornamental Metal Work

European Ornamental Iron Works............G....... 630 705-9300
  Addison  *(G-113)*
Fehring Ornamental Iron Works..............F....... 217 483-6727
  Chatham  *(G-3620)*
K D Iron Works......................................G....... 847 991-3039
  Palatine  *(G-17047)*
Legna Iron Works  Inc............................E...... 630 894-8056
  Roselle  *(G-18952)*
Ornamental Iron Shop............................G....... 618 281-6072
  Columbia  *(G-7361)*
Quality Iron Works Inc............................F....... 630 766-0885
  Bensenville  *(G-1971)*
R & I Ornamental Iron Inc......................G....... 847 836-6934
  Gilberts  *(G-10933)*

## CONTRACTORS: Painting & Wall Covering

Artistries By Tommy Musto Inc...............G....... 630 674-8667
  Bloomingdale  *(G-2094)*
Brothers Decorating...............................G....... 815 648-2214
  Hebron  *(G-11715)*
Jones Design Group Ltd.........................G....... 630 462-9340
  Winfield  *(G-22286)*

## CONTRACTORS: Painting, Commercial

Central Illinois Sign Company.................G....... 217 523-4740
  Springfield  *(G-20414)*
Signage Plus Ltd....................................G....... 815 485-0300
  Lockport  *(G-13744)*
Thornton Welding Service Inc.................E...... 217 877-0610
  Decatur  *(G-7952)*

## CONTRACTORS: Painting, Indl

J & C Premier Concepts Inc...................G....... 309 523-2344
  Port Byron  *(G-17720)*
Metal Prep Services Inc.........................G....... 815 874-7631
  Rockford  *(G-18496)*

## CONTRACTORS: Patio & Deck Construction & Repair

Bergeron Group Inc................................E...... 815 741-1635
  Joliet  *(G-12464)*

## CONTRACTORS: Pavement Marking

Varsity Striping & Cnstr Co.....................E...... 217 352-2203
  Champaign  *(G-3553)*

## CONTRACTORS: Safety & Security Eqpt

## CONTRACTORS: Pipe Laying

Lake Process Systems Inc......................E...... 847 381-7663
  Lake Barrington  *(G-12817)*

## CONTRACTORS: Plumbing

Ave Inc..................................................G....... 815 727-0153
  Joliet  *(G-12457)*
F J Murphy & Son Inc............................D...... 217 787-3477
  Springfield  *(G-20437)*
Hamilton Concrete Products Co..............G....... 217 847-3118
  Hamilton  *(G-11537)*
Jupiter Industries Inc.............................G....... 847 925-5120
  Schaumburg  *(G-19592)*
Key West Metal Industries Inc................C....... 708 371-1470
  Crestwood  *(G-7491)*
Kitchen & Bath Gallery...........................G....... 217 214-0310
  Quincy  *(G-17845)*
Marvin Schumaker Plbg Inc....................G....... 815 626-8130
  Sterling  *(G-20597)*
Peter Perella & Co..................................F....... 815 727-4526
  Joliet  *(G-12550)*
Tane Corporation...................................G....... 847 705-7125
  Palatine  *(G-17078)*

## CONTRACTORS: Pollution Control Eqpt Installation

Elk Grove Custom Sheet Metal................F....... 847 352-2845
  Elk Grove Village  *(G-9451)*

## CONTRACTORS: Precast Concrete Struct Framing & Panel Placing

Gcs Steel Installers Inc..........................G....... 630 487-6736
  Montgomery  *(G-15044)*
Lombard Archtctral Prcast Pdts..............E...... 708 389-1060
  Chicago  *(G-5535)*
Lombard Investment Company...............D...... 708 389-1060
  Alsip  *(G-484)*

## CONTRACTORS: Prefabricated Window & Door Installation

Wallfill Co..............................................F....... 630 499-9591
  Aurora  *(G-1094)*

## CONTRACTORS: Process Piping

Melissa A Miller....................................G....... 708 529-7786
  New Lenox  *(G-15893)*
Stainless Specialties Inc........................G....... 618 654-7723
  Pocahontas  *(G-17686)*

## CONTRACTORS: Refrigeration

Hudson Technologies Inc.......................E...... 217 373-1414
  Champaign  *(G-3496)*
Tracy Electric Inc...................................E...... 618 943-6205
  Lawrenceville  *(G-13206)*

## CONTRACTORS: Rock Removal

Civil Constructors Inc.............................G....... 815 858-2691
  Elizabeth  *(G-9241)*

## CONTRACTORS: Roofing

Joiner Sheet Metal & Roofing.................G....... 618 664-9488
  Greenville  *(G-11396)*
L R Gregory and Son Inc........................E...... 847 247-0216
  Lake Bluff  *(G-12852)*
R E Burke Roofing Co Inc......................F....... 847 675-5010
  Skokie  *(G-20068)*
RM Lucas Co.........................................E...... 773 523-4300
  Chicago  *(G-6365)*
RM Lucas Co.........................................E...... 773 523-4300
  Alsip  *(G-522)*

## CONTRACTORS: Roofing & Gutter Work

Cofair Products Inc................................G....... 847 626-1500
  Skokie  *(G-19985)*

## CONTRACTORS: Safety & Security Eqpt

Lane Industries Inc................................E...... 847 498-6650
  Northbrook  *(G-16292)*
National Safety Council..........................B...... 630 285-1121
  Itasca  *(G-12324)*
Siemens Industry Inc.............................A...... 847 215-1000
  Buffalo Grove  *(G-2767)*

---

Employee Codes: A=Over 500 employees, B=251-500
C=101-250, D=51-100, E=20-50, F=10-19, G=3-9

2017 Harris Illinois Industrial Directory

1539

## CONTRACTORS: Sandblasting Svc, Building Exteriors

| | | |
|---|---|---|
| Metal Prep Services Inc | G | 815 874-7631 |
| Rockford (G-18496) | | |
| Stripmasters Illinois Inc | G | 618 452-1060 |
| Granite City (G-11306) | | |
| Thornton Welding Service Inc | E | 217 877-0610 |
| Decatur (G-7952) | | |

## CONTRACTORS: Screening, Window & Door

| | | |
|---|---|---|
| Metaltek Fabricating Inc | F | 708 534-9102 |
| University Park (G-21056) | | |

## CONTRACTORS: Septic System

| | | |
|---|---|---|
| Alternative Wastewater Systems | G | 630 761-8720 |
| Batavia (G-1409) | | |
| Central Concrete Products | E | 217 523-7964 |
| Springfield (G-20412) | | |
| Cortelyou Excavating | G | 309 772-2922 |
| Bushnell (G-2901) | | |
| Gary & Larry Brown Trucking | G | 618 268-6377 |
| Raleigh (G-17909) | | |
| Rochelle Vault Co | G | 815 562-6484 |
| Rochelle (G-18108) | | |
| Rockford Sewer Co Inc | G | 815 877-9060 |
| Loves Park (G-13987) | | |

## CONTRACTORS: Sheet Metal Work, NEC

| | | |
|---|---|---|
| A J Wagner & Son | F | 773 935-1414 |
| Wauconda (G-21434) | | |
| Arrow Sheet Metal Company | E | 815 455-2019 |
| Crystal Lake (G-7538) | | |
| Bing Engineering Inc | C | 708 228-8005 |
| Frankfort (G-10300) | | |
| Cleats Mfg Inc | F | 773 521-0300 |
| Chicago (G-4399) | | |
| Crawford Heating & Cooling Co | D | 309 788-4573 |
| Rock Island (G-18169) | | |
| D/C Industries LLC | G | 630 876-1100 |
| West Chicago (G-21689) | | |
| Elk Grove Custom Sheet Metal | F | 847 352-2845 |
| Elk Grove Village (G-9451) | | |
| Gengler-Lowney Laser Works | F | 630 801-4840 |
| Aurora (G-1161) | | |
| Hohlfider A H Shtmtl Htg Coolg | G | 815 965-9134 |
| Rockford (G-18420) | | |
| John J Rickhoff Shtmtl Co Inc | F | 708 331-2970 |
| Phoenix (G-17541) | | |
| Kirby Sheet Metal Works Inc | E | 773 247-6477 |
| Chicago (G-5386) | | |
| Kwm Gutterman Inc | E | 815 725-9205 |
| Rockdale (G-18223) | | |
| S & S Heating & Sheet Metal | G | 815 933-1993 |
| Bradley (G-2431) | | |

## CONTRACTORS: Sheet metal Work, Architectural

| | | |
|---|---|---|
| Hemingway Chimney Inc | F | 708 333-0355 |
| South Holland (G-20275) | | |
| Nesterowicz & Associates Inc | G | 815 522-4469 |
| Kirkland (G-12715) | | |
| Steel Rebar Manufacturing LLC | G | 618 920-2748 |
| Centreville (G-3438) | | |
| Taloc Usa Inc | G | 847 665-8222 |
| Libertyville (G-13388) | | |

## CONTRACTORS: Siding

| | | |
|---|---|---|
| Boekeloo Heating & Sheet Metal | G | 708 877-6560 |
| Thornton (G-20868) | | |
| Four Seasons Gutter Prote | G | 309 694-4565 |
| East Peoria (G-8710) | | |
| Seamless Gutter Corp | E | 630 495-9800 |
| Lombard (G-13852) | | |
| Wallfill Co | F | 630 499-9591 |
| Aurora (G-1094) | | |

## CONTRACTORS: Single-family Home General Remodeling

| | | |
|---|---|---|
| Basement Dewatering Systems | F | 309 647-0331 |
| Canton (G-2981) | | |
| Bushnell Locker Service | G | 309 772-2783 |
| Bushnell (G-2899) | | |
| Jelinek & Sons Inc | G | 630 355-3474 |
| Plainfield (G-17610) | | |

| | | |
|---|---|---|
| Legna Iron Works Inc | E | 630 894-8056 |
| Roselle (G-18952) | | |
| Netranix Enterprise | F | |
| Bolingbrook (G-2350) | | |
| Penstock Construction Services | G | 630 816-2456 |
| Plainfield (G-17636) | | |
| Raymond Earl Fine Woodworking | G | 309 565-7661 |
| Hanna City (G-11570) | | |

## CONTRACTORS: Skylight Installation

| | | |
|---|---|---|
| Ccsi International Inc | E | 815 544-8385 |
| Garden Prairie (G-10793) | | |
| Midwest Skylite Company Inc | E | 847 214-9505 |
| South Elgin (G-20219) | | |
| United Skys LLC | F | 847 546-7776 |
| Round Lake (G-19069) | | |

## CONTRACTORS: Solar Energy Eqpt

| | | |
|---|---|---|
| Astral Power Systems Inc | G | 630 518-1741 |
| Aurora (G-1112) | | |
| Titus Enterprises LLC | G | 773 441-7222 |
| Warrenville (G-21364) | | |

## CONTRACTORS: Sound Eqpt Installation

| | | |
|---|---|---|
| Pentegra Systems LLC | E | 630 941-6000 |
| Addison (G-238) | | |

## CONTRACTORS: Spa & Hot Tub Construction & Installation

| | | |
|---|---|---|
| Pure Skin LLC | G | 217 679-6267 |
| Springfield (G-20509) | | |

## CONTRACTORS: Standby Or Emergency Power Specialization

| | | |
|---|---|---|
| Smart Surveillance Inc | G | 630 968-5075 |
| Lisle (G-13657) | | |

## CONTRACTORS: Steam Cleaning, Building Exterior

| | | |
|---|---|---|
| All Seasons Heating & AC | G | 217 429-2022 |
| Decatur (G-7831) | | |
| Therma-Kleen Inc | G | 630 718-0212 |
| Plainfield (G-17657) | | |

## CONTRACTORS: Stone Masonry

| | | |
|---|---|---|
| Collinsville Ice & Fuel Co | F | 618 344-3272 |
| Collinsville (G-7315) | | |
| Meno Stone Co Inc | E | 630 257-9220 |
| Lemont (G-13241) | | |

## CONTRACTORS: Storage Tank Erection, Metal

| | | |
|---|---|---|
| JM Industries LLC | E | 708 849-4700 |
| Riverdale (G-18020) | | |
| Matrix Service Inc | F | 618 466-4862 |
| Alton (G-585) | | |

## CONTRACTORS: Store Fixture Installation

| | | |
|---|---|---|
| Suburban Fix & Installation | G | 847 823-4047 |
| Park Ridge (G-17225) | | |

## CONTRACTORS: Structural Iron Work, Structural

| | | |
|---|---|---|
| Lamonica Ornamental Iron Works | G | 773 638-6633 |
| Chicago (G-5452) | | |
| Steel Services Enterprises | E | 708 259-1181 |
| Lansing (G-13187) | | |

## CONTRACTORS: Structural Steel Erection

| | | |
|---|---|---|
| Advance Iron Works Inc | F | 708 798-3540 |
| East Hazel Crest (G-8663) | | |
| Advance Steel Services Inc | | 773 619-2977 |
| Chicago (G-3764) | | |
| Aetna Engineering Works Inc | E | 773 785-0489 |
| Chicago (G-3778) | | |
| Alfredos Iron Works Inc | | 815 748-1177 |
| Cortland (G-7384) | | |
| Atkore International Group Inc | A | 708 339-1610 |
| Harvey (G-11658) | | |
| Atkore Intl Holdings Inc | | 708 225-2051 |
| Harvey (G-11659) | | |

| | | |
|---|---|---|
| Builders Chicago Corporation | D | 224 654-2122 |
| Rosemont (G-18991) | | |
| Chicago Ornamental Iron Inc | E | 773 321-9635 |
| Chicago (G-4338) | | |
| Corsetti Structural Steel Inc | E | 815 726-0186 |
| Joliet (G-12477) | | |
| Fbs Group Inc | F | 773 229-8675 |
| Chicago (G-4821) | | |
| Guardian Construction Pdts Inc | E | 630 820-8899 |
| Naperville (G-15808) | | |
| Hudson Boiler & Tank Company | F | 312 666-4780 |
| Lockport (G-13722) | | |
| Kd Steel Inc | G | 630 201-1619 |
| Westmont (G-21897) | | |
| Lichtnwald - Johnston Ir Works | E | 847 966-1100 |
| Morton Grove (G-15212) | | |
| Marqutte Stl Sup Fbrcation Inc | F | 815 433-0178 |
| Ottawa (G-16968) | | |
| Mechanical Indus Stl Svcs Inc | E | 815 521-1725 |
| Channahon (G-3580) | | |
| Morey Industries Inc | C | 708 343-3220 |
| Broadview (G-2598) | | |
| North Chicago Iron Works Inc | E | 847 689-2000 |
| North Chicago (G-16185) | | |
| Old Style Iron Works Inc | | 773 265-5787 |
| Chicago (G-5980) | | |
| Regal Steel Erectors LLC | E | 847 888-3500 |
| Elgin (G-9162) | | |
| Sandoval Fences Corp | G | 773 287-0279 |
| Chicago (G-6438) | | |
| Tru-Guard Manufacturing Co | G | 773 568-5264 |
| Chicago (G-6784) | | |
| Tuschall Engineering Co Inc | E | 630 655-9100 |
| Burr Ridge (G-2888) | | |
| Unistrut International Corp | C | 800 882-5543 |
| Harvey (G-11679) | | |
| WEb Production & Fabg Inc | F | 312 733-6800 |
| Chicago (G-6948) | | |

## CONTRACTORS: Svc Station Eqpt

| | | |
|---|---|---|
| Emco Wheaton Usa Inc | E | 281 856-1300 |
| Quincy (G-17825) | | |

## CONTRACTORS: Svc Station Eqpt Installation, Maint & Repair

| | | |
|---|---|---|
| R L Hoener Co | E | 217 223-2190 |
| Quincy (G-17883) | | |

## CONTRACTORS: Textile Warping

| | | |
|---|---|---|
| Next Gen Manufacturing Inc | G | 847 289-8444 |
| Elgin (G-9120) | | |

## CONTRACTORS: Tile Installation, Ceramic

| | | |
|---|---|---|
| Contempo Marble & Granite Inc | G | 312 455-0022 |
| Chicago (G-4456) | | |
| MK Tile Ink | G | 773 964-8905 |
| Chicago (G-5778) | | |

## CONTRACTORS: Underground Utilities

| | | |
|---|---|---|
| Jklein Enterprises Inc | G | 618 664-4554 |
| Greenville (G-11395) | | |
| McLean Subsurface Utility | G | 336 988-2520 |
| Decatur (G-7911) | | |

## CONTRACTORS: Ventilation & Duct Work

| | | |
|---|---|---|
| All Seasons Heating & AC | G | 217 429-2022 |
| Decatur (G-7831) | | |
| American Metal Installers & FA | G | 630 993-0812 |
| Villa Park (G-21236) | | |

## CONTRACTORS: Warm Air Heating & Air Conditioning

| | | |
|---|---|---|
| Alton Sheet Metal Corp | F | 618 462-0609 |
| Alton (G-559) | | |
| Anytime Heating & AC | F | 630 851-6696 |
| Naperville (G-15796) | | |
| Bergesch Heating & Cooling | G | 618 259-4620 |
| Alton (G-564) | | |
| Boekeloo Heating & Sheet Metal | G | 708 877-6560 |
| Thornton (G-20868) | | |
| Brex-Arlington Incorporated | F | 847 255-6284 |
| Arlington Heights (G-729) | | |
| Eikenberry Sheet Metal Works | G | 815 625-0955 |
| Sterling (G-20590) | | |

# PRODUCT SECTION

## CONTROLS & ACCESS: Indl, Electric

Elk Heating & Sheet Metal Inc............F....... 618 251-4747
  Wood River *(G-22442)*
Gengler-Lowney Laser Works ............F....... 630 801-4840
  Aurora *(G-1161)*
GROsse&sons Htg &SHeet Met Inc.......G....... 708 447-8397
  Lyons *(G-14040)*
Habegger Corporation............................F....... 309 793-7172
  Rock Island *(G-18178)*
Hohlflder A H Shtmtl Htg Coolg..........G....... 815 965-9134
  Rockford *(G-18420)*
Ibbotson Heating Co .............................E....... 847 253-0866
  Arlington Heights *(G-770)*
J D Refrigeration ..................................G....... 618 345-0041
  Collinsville *(G-7328)*
Keil-Forness Comfort Systems ...........G....... 618 233-3039
  Belleville *(G-1640)*
L M Sheet Metal Inc..............................E....... 815 654-1837
  Loves Park *(G-13957)*
L R Gregory and Son Inc .....................E....... 847 247-0216
  Lake Bluff *(G-12852)*
Lizotte Sheet Metal Inc ........................G....... 618 656-3066
  Edwardsville *(G-8806)*
Montefusco Heating & Shtmtl Co........G....... 309 691-7400
  Peoria *(G-17412)*
Reedy Industries Inc............................F....... 847 729-9450
  Glenview *(G-11192)*
Ring Sheet Metal Heating & AC ...........G....... 309 289-4213
  Knoxville *(G-12723)*
Ruyle Incorporated ...............................E....... 309 674-6644
  Springfield *(G-20516)*
S & S Heating & Sheet Metal ................G....... 815 933-1993
  Bradley *(G-2431)*
Sudholt Sheet Metal Inc ......................G....... 618 228-7351
  Aviston *(G-1248)*
Tri City Sheet Metal .............................G....... 630 232-4255
  Geneva *(G-10874)*

### CONTRACTORS: Water Intake Well Drilling Svc

Grosch Irrigation Company .................F....... 217 482-5479
  Mason City *(G-14364)*
Mashburn Well Drilling ........................G....... 217 794-3728
  Maroa *(G-14306)*
Raimonde Drilling Corp.......................F....... 630 458-0590
  Addison *(G-268)*

### CONTRACTORS: Water Well Drilling

Coursons Coring & Drilling .................G....... 618 349-8765
  Saint Peter *(G-19321)*
Dowell Lynnea ......................................G....... 309 543-3854
  Havana *(G-11694)*
Kohnens Concrete Products Inc .........E....... 618 277-2120
  Germantown *(G-10892)*
Mashburn Well Drilling ........................G....... 217 794-3728
  Maroa *(G-14306)*
Will County Well & Pump Co Inc .........G....... 815 485-2413
  New Lenox *(G-15928)*

### CONTRACTORS: Waterproofing

Protective Coatings & Waterpro ..........G....... 708 403-7650
  Orland Park *(G-16886)*
Ted Muller ............................................G....... 312 435-0978
  Chicago *(G-6686)*

### CONTRACTORS: Well Acidizing Svcs

B & B Tank Truck Construction ...........F....... 618 378-3337
  Norris City *(G-16111)*
Fairfield Acid and Frac Co ...................F....... 618 842-9186
  Fairfield *(G-10140)*
Koontz Services ...................................G....... 618 375-7613
  Carmi *(G-3072)*
M & I Acid Company Inc ......................G....... 618 676-1638
  Clay City *(G-7266)*
Tri State Acid Co Inc ............................G....... 618 676-1111
  Clay City *(G-7268)*

### CONTRACTORS: Well Chemical Treating Svcs

Sims Company Inc ..............................G....... 618 665-3901
  Louisville *(G-13910)*

### CONTRACTORS: Well Cleaning Svcs

Gesell Oil Well Service LLC .................G....... 618 547-7114
  Kinmundy *(G-12710)*

### CONTRACTORS: Well Logging Svcs

Ordner Well Service Inc.......................G....... 618 676-1950
  Clay City *(G-7267)*

### CONTRACTORS: Window Treatment Installation

Energy Solutions Inc ............................G....... 618 465-5404
  Alton *(G-575)*
Regent Window Fashions LLC ............G....... 773 871-6400
  Chicago *(G-6324)*

### CONTRACTORS: Windows & Doors

A Ashland Lock Company ....................F....... 773 348-5106
  Chicago *(G-3684)*
Cofair Products Inc .............................G....... 847 626-1500
  Skokie *(G-19985)*
Doralco Inc ...........................................G....... 708 388-9324
  Alsip *(G-458)*

### CONTRACTORS: Wood Floor Installation & Refinishing

Signature Innovations LLC ..................G....... 847 758-9600
  Elk Grove Village *(G-9739)*

### CONTRACTORS: Wrecking & Demolition

American Industrial Werks Inc ............F....... 847 477-2648
  Schaumburg *(G-19437)*
Lake County Grading Co LLC ..............E....... 847 362-2590
  Libertyville *(G-13341)*
St Louis Scrap Trading LLC ................G....... 618 307-9002
  Edwardsville *(G-8815)*

### CONTROL CIRCUIT DEVICES

Master Control Systems Inc ................E....... 847 295-1010
  Lake Bluff *(G-12856)*

### CONTROL EQPT: Electric

BTR Controls Inc ..................................G....... 847 608-9500
  Elgin *(G-8972)*
Con-Trol-Cure Inc.................................F....... 773 248-0099
  Chicago *(G-4442)*
Control Systems Inc ............................G....... 847 438-6228
  Long Grove *(G-13889)*
Copar Corporation................................E....... 708 496-1859
  Burbank *(G-2807)*
Don Johns Inc ......................................E....... 630 326-9650
  Batavia *(G-1439)*
Dresser Inc ...........................................D....... 847 437-5940
  Elk Grove Village *(G-9435)*
Elcon Inc ...............................................E....... 815 467-9500
  Minooka *(G-14840)*
Enercon Engineering Inc .....................C....... 800 218-8831
  East Peoria *(G-8708)*
Hurletron Incorporated........................E....... 847 680-7022
  Libertyville *(G-13335)*
Interstate Industrial Tech ....................E....... 618 286-4900
  Dupo *(G-8572)*
Jemison Elc Box Swtchboard Inc .......G....... 815 459-4060
  Crystal Lake *(G-7594)*
Joliet Technologies LLC .......................G....... 815 725-9696
  Crest Hill *(G-7461)*
M-1 Tool Works Inc .............................G....... 815 344-1275
  McHenry *(G-14525)*
Machine Control Systems Inc .............G....... 708 389-2160
  Palos Heights *(G-17108)*
Meyer Systems .....................................G....... 815 436-7077
  Joliet *(G-12540)*
Parker-Hannifin Corporation...............C....... 309 266-2200
  Morton *(G-15175)*
Parking Systems Inc ............................G....... 847 891-3819
  Schaumburg *(G-19684)*
Process and Control Systems .............F....... 708 293-0557
  Alsip *(G-514)*
R & D Electronics Inc...........................G....... 847 583-9080
  Niles *(G-16024)*
Rockdale Controls Co Inc ....................F....... 815 436-6181
  Plainfield *(G-17646)*
Sparton Aydin LLC...............................G....... 800 772-7866
  Schaumburg *(G-19733)*
Spectrum Cos International ................G....... 630 879-8008
  Batavia *(G-1497)*
Trend Machinery Inc ...........................G....... 630 655-0030
  Burr Ridge *(G-2887)*
Unitrol Electronics Inc .........................E....... 847 480-0115
  Northbrook *(G-16380)*

Win Technologies Incorporated ..........E....... 630 236-1020
  Aurora *(G-1099)*
Xylem Inc ..............................................D....... 847 966-3700
  Morton Grove *(G-15247)*

### CONTROL EQPT: Electric Buses & Locomotives

International Supply Co.......................D....... 309 249-6211
  Edelstein *(G-8780)*

### CONTROL EQPT: Noise

Blachford Investments Inc ..................C....... 630 231-8300
  West Chicago *(G-21671)*
Rensel-Chicago Inc .............................F....... 773 235-2100
  Chicago *(G-6334)*
Sound Seal Inc .....................................E....... 630 844-1999
  North Aurora *(G-16144)*
Steel-Guard Safety Corp .....................G....... 708 589-4588
  South Holland *(G-20306)*
Wilkes & McLean Ltd ...........................G....... 847 381-3872
  North Barrington *(G-16156)*

### CONTROL PANELS: Electrical

Accu-Fab Incorporated........................E....... 847 541-4230
  Wheeling *(G-21998)*
Cable Electric Company Inc................G....... 708 458-8900
  Oak Lawn *(G-16609)*
Control Panels Inc ...............................F....... 815 654-6000
  Rockford *(G-18323)*
Control Works Inc ................................G....... 630 444-1942
  Saint Charles *(G-19163)*
Cymatics Inc.........................................G....... 630 420-7117
  Naperville *(G-15640)*
Don Johns Inc ......................................E....... 630 326-9650
  Batavia *(G-1439)*
Engineered Fluid Inc............................C....... 618 533-1351
  Centralia *(G-3413)*
Excel Ltd Inc .........................................G....... 847 543-9138
  Grayslake *(G-11336)*
Fox Controls Inc...................................E....... 847 464-5096
  Elgin *(G-9040)*
Inland Tech Holdings LLC ....................E....... 618 476-7678
  Millstadt *(G-14827)*
Its Solar LLC ........................................G....... 618 476-7678
  Millstadt *(G-14828)*
Machine Control Systems Inc .............G....... 708 597-1200
  Alsip *(G-486)*
Machine Control Systems Inc .............G....... 708 389-2160
  Palos Heights *(G-17108)*
Morton Automatic Electric Co .............G....... 309 263-7577
  Morton *(G-15166)*
Northwest Instrumentation Inc ...........E....... 847 825-0699
  Park Ridge *(G-17213)*
Panel Authority Inc ..............................F....... 815 838-0488
  Lockport *(G-13738)*
Panelshopnet Inc .................................G....... 630 692-0214
  Naperville *(G-15821)*
Platt Industrial Control Inc .................G....... 630 833-4388
  Addison *(G-244)*
Prater Industries Inc ...........................D....... 630 679-3200
  Bolingbrook *(G-2359)*
Protection Controls Inc .......................E....... 773 763-3110
  Skokie *(G-20066)*
Quantum Design Inc ...........................D....... 815 885-1300
  Loves Park *(G-13980)*
R G Controls Inc...................................G....... 847 438-3981
  Barrington *(G-1300)*
RLC Industries Inc ...............................G....... 708 837-7300
  La Grange *(G-12743)*
Robotics Technologies Inc ..................E....... 815 722-7650
  Joliet *(G-12570)*
RWS Design and Controls Inc ............E....... 815 654-6000
  Roscoe *(G-18919)*
Schubert Controls Corporation ...........G....... 847 526-8200
  Wauconda *(G-21501)*
Smart Surveillance Inc ........................G....... 630 968-5075
  Lisle *(G-13657)*
Venture Design Incorporated..............F....... 630 369-1148
  Naperville *(G-15775)*

### CONTROLS & ACCESS: Indl, Electric

7 Mile Solutions Inc ............................E....... 847 588-2280
  Niles *(G-15952)*
American Control Elec LLC .................G....... 815 624-6950
  South Beloit *(G-20137)*
Box of Rain Ltd ....................................G....... 847 640-6996
  Arlington Heights *(G-727)*

---

Employee Codes: A=Over 500 employees, B=251-500
C=101-250, D=51-100, E=20-50, F=10-19, G=3-9

2017 Harris Illinois Industrial Directory

1541

Capable Controls Inc ............ D ....... 630 860-6514
Bensenville *(G-1850)*
Control Designs Inc ............ G ....... 847 918-9347
Gurnee *(G-11434)*
Control Research Inc ............ G ....... 847 352-4920
Schaumburg *(G-19483)*
Electro-Matic Products Co ............ F ....... 773 235-4010
Chicago *(G-4720)*
Fivecubits Inc ............ F ....... 925 273-1862
Oak Brook *(G-16514)*
Harrington Signal Inc ............ E ....... 309 762-0731
Moline *(G-14942)*
I P C Automation Inc ............ G ....... 815 759-3934
McHenry *(G-14514)*
Jtekt Toyoda Americas Corp ............ C ....... 847 253-0340
Arlington Heights *(G-786)*
Lumenite Control Technology ............ F ....... 847 455-1450
Franklin Park *(G-10518)*
Meister Industries Inc ............ G ....... 815 623-8919
Roscoe *(G-18907)*
Mission Control Systems Inc ............ F ....... 847 956-7650
Elk Grove Village *(G-9630)*
National Control Holdings ............ B ....... 630 231-5900
West Chicago *(G-21748)*
Questek Manufacturing Corp ............ D ....... 847 428-0300
Elgin *(G-9159)*
Rockwell Automation Inc ............ C ....... 217 373-0800
Champaign *(G-3534)*
Smart Surveillance Inc ............ G ....... 630 968-5075
Lisle *(G-13657)*
Value Added Services & Tech ............ G ....... 847 888-8232
Elgin *(G-9223)*
Woodward Inc ............ G ....... 815 877-7441
Rockton *(G-18703)*

## *CONTROLS & ACCESS: Motor*

Capsonic Automotive Inc ............ F ....... 847 888-7300
Elgin *(G-8978)*
Capsonic Automotive Inc ............ F ....... 847 888-7300
Elgin *(G-8979)*
Capsonic Automotive Inc ............ B ....... 915 872-3585
Chicago *(G-4232)*
Danfoss Inc ............ G ....... 815 639-8600
Loves Park *(G-13935)*
Danfoss LLC ............ C ....... 888 326-3677
Loves Park *(G-13936)*
Eaton Corporation ............ C ....... 815 398-6585
Rockford *(G-18354)*
Eaton Hydraulics LLC ............ G ....... 618 667-2553
Troy *(G-21006)*
Garen Eaton Farms LLC ............ G ....... 217 228-0324
Quincy *(G-17829)*

## *CONTROLS: Access, Motor*

Industrial Controls Inc ............ G ....... 630 752-8100
Batavia *(G-1457)*

## *CONTROLS: Adjustable Speed Drive*

Geitek Automation Inc ............ D ....... 815 385-3500
McHenry *(G-14509)*
Invektek Llc ............ G ....... 312 343-0600
Chicago *(G-5230)*
Mektronix Technology Inc ............ G ....... 847 680-3300
Libertyville *(G-13353)*

## *CONTROLS: Air Flow, Refrigeration*

Holland Safety Equipment Inc ............ G ....... 847 680-9930
Libertyville *(G-13332)*

## *CONTROLS: Automatic Temperature*

Automatic Building Contrls LLC ............ E ....... 847 296-4000
Rolling Meadows *(G-18712)*
Interactive Bldg Solutions LLC ............ F ....... 815 724-0525
Joliet *(G-12518)*
Precision Control Systems ............ D ....... 630 521-0234
Lisle *(G-13643)*
Professional Freezing Svcs LLC ............ G ....... 773 847-7500
Chicago *(G-6208)*

## *CONTROLS: Crane & Hoist, Including Metal Mill*

Terex Utilities Inc ............ G ....... 847 515-7030
Addison *(G-310)*

## *CONTROLS: Electric Motor*

Bodine Electric Company ............ C ....... 773 478-3515
Northfield *(G-16393)*
Continental Auto Systems Inc ............ G ....... 847 862-5000
Deer Park *(G-7969)*
Industrial Service Solutions ............ F ....... 917 609-6979
Chicago *(G-5180)*

## *CONTROLS: Environmental*

Automax Corporation ............ G ....... 630 972-1919
Woodridge *(G-22454)*
Avg Advanced Technologies LP ............ A ....... 630 668-3900
Carol Stream *(G-3110)*
Beneficial Reuse MGT LLC ............ F ....... 312 784-0300
Chicago *(G-4083)*
Biosynergy Inc ............ G ....... 847 956-0471
Elk Grove Village *(G-9342)*
Candy Mfg Co Inc ............ F ....... 847 588-2639
Niles *(G-15966)*
Catalytic Products Intl Inc ............ E ....... 847 438-0334
Lake Zurich *(G-13050)*
Caterpillar Inc ............ B ....... 815 729-5511
Joliet *(G-12471)*
Caviton Inc ............ G ....... 217 621-5746
Urbana *(G-21075)*
Chicago Tank Removal Inc ............ G ....... 312 214-6144
Chicago *(G-4353)*
Creative Controls Systems Inc ............ G ....... 815 629-2358
Rockton *(G-18695)*
Dickson/Unigage Inc ............ E ....... 630 543-3747
Addison *(G-92)*
Eg Group Inc ............ G ....... 309 692-0968
Peoria *(G-17352)*
Elcon Inc ............ E ....... 815 467-9500
Minooka *(G-14840)*
Global Green Products LLC ............ G ....... 708 341-3670
Orland Park *(G-16861)*
Green Ladder Technologies LLC ............ E ....... 630 457-1872
Batavia *(G-1452)*
Gus Berthold Electric Company ............ E ....... 312 243-5767
Chicago *(G-5013)*
Gypsoil Pelletized Pdts LLC ............ F ....... 312 784-0300
Chicago *(G-5015)*
Homecontrolplus Incorporated ............ G ....... 847 823-8414
Park Ridge *(G-17202)*
Honeywell International Inc ............ G ....... 815 235-5500
Freeport *(G-10664)*
Marine Canada Acquisition ............ G ....... 630 513-5809
Saint Charles *(G-19215)*
Mitsubishi Elc Automtn Inc ............ C ....... 847 478-2100
Vernon Hills *(G-21183)*
R & D Electronics Inc ............ G ....... 847 583-9080
Niles *(G-16024)*
Robertshaw Controls Company ............ C ....... 630 260-3400
Itasca *(G-12349)*
Scientific Instruments Inc ............ G ....... 847 679-1242
Skokie *(G-20082)*
Solidyne Corporation ............ F ....... 847 394-3333
Rolling Meadows *(G-18779)*
Solidyne Corporation ............ G ....... 847 394-3333
Hoffman Estates *(G-12056)*
Spring Brook Nature Center ............ G ....... 630 773-5572
Itasca *(G-12358)*
Tempro International Corp ............ G ....... 847 677-5370
Skokie *(G-20100)*
Vent Ure Air ............ G ....... 708 652-7200
Chicago *(G-6882)*
Web Printing Controls Co Inc ............ C ....... 618 842-2664
Fairfield *(G-10161)*

## *CONTROLS: Numerical*

Comet Tool Inc ............ E ....... 847 956-0126
Elk Grove Village *(G-9383)*
Hausermann Controls Co ............ F ....... 630 543-6688
Addison *(G-143)*

## *CONTROLS: Relay & Ind*

ABRA Enterprises Inc ............ G ....... 847 866-6903
Evanston *(G-10001)*
Advanced Engneered Systems Inc ............ E ....... 815 624-7797
South Beloit *(G-20135)*
Advanced Technologies Inc ............ G ....... 847 329-9875
Park Ridge *(G-17178)*
Automated Systems & Control Co ............ G ....... 847 735-8310
Lake Bluff *(G-12834)*
Avg Advanced Technologies LP ............ A ....... 630 668-3900
Carol Stream *(G-3110)*
Burke Tool & Manufacturing Inc ............ G ....... 618 542-6441
Du Quoin *(G-8551)*
Caterpillar Inc ............ B ....... 815 729-5511
Joliet *(G-12471)*
Chamberlain Manufacturing Corp ............ A ....... 630 279-3600
Oak Brook *(G-16500)*
Control Masters Inc ............ G ....... 630 968-2390
Downers Grove *(G-8420)*
Control Solutions LLC ............ D ....... 630 806-7062
Aurora *(G-984)*
Controllink Incorporated ............ E ....... 847 622-1100
Elgin *(G-9002)*
Core Components Inc ............ F ....... 630 690-0520
Carol Stream *(G-3137)*
Creative Controls Systems Inc ............ G ....... 815 629-2358
Rockton *(G-18695)*
D C Grove Electric Inc ............ G ....... 847 587-0864
Fox Lake *(G-10275)*
Dgm Electronics Inc ............ G ....... 815 389-2040
Roscoe *(G-18894)*
Domino Engineering Corp ............ F ....... 217 824-9441
Taylorville *(G-20838)*
Eaton Corporation ............ C ....... 815 562-2107
Rochelle *(G-18087)*
Elemech Inc ............ E ....... 630 417-2845
Aurora *(G-1001)*
Elenco Electronics Inc ............ E ....... 847 541-3800
Wheeling *(G-22046)*
Enercon Engineering Inc ............ D ....... 309 694-1418
East Peoria *(G-8709)*
Envirnmntal Ctrl Solutions Inc ............ G ....... 217 793-8966
Springfield *(G-20435)*
Flolo Corporation ............ G ....... 847 249-0880
Gurnee *(G-11448)*
Gpe Controls Inc ............ F ....... 708 236-6000
Hillside *(G-11917)*
Guardian Consolidated Tech Inc ............ G ....... 815 334-3600
Woodstock *(G-22571)*
Guardian Electric Mfg Co ............ D ....... 815 334-3600
Woodstock *(G-22572)*
Harris Precision Tools Inc ............ G ....... 708 422-5808
Chicago Ridge *(G-7149)*
Harvey Bros Inc ............ F ....... 309 342-3137
Galesburg *(G-10757)*
Hauhinco LP ............ E ....... 618 993-5399
Marion *(G-14264)*
Hausermann Die & Machine Co ............ F ....... 630 543-6688
Addison *(G-144)*
Hella Corporate Center USA Inc ............ B ....... 734 414-0900
Flora *(G-10208)*
Hella Corporate Center USA Inc ............ B ....... 618 662-4402
Flora *(G-10209)*
Hella Electronics Corporation ............ A ....... 618 662-5186
Flora *(G-10210)*
Honeywell International Inc ............ G ....... 815 235-5500
Freeport *(G-10664)*
Ideal Industries Inc ............ C ....... 815 895-1108
Sycamore *(G-20801)*
Industrial Motion Control LLC ............ C ....... 847 459-5200
Wheeling *(G-22076)*
Instrmntation Ctrl Systems Inc ............ F ....... 630 543-6200
Roselle *(G-18947)*
K & W Auto Electric ............ F ....... 217 857-1717
Teutopolis *(G-20853)*
Kackert Enterprises Inc ............ G ....... 630 898-9339
Aurora *(G-1179)*
Keonix Corporation ............ G ....... 847 259-9430
Arlington Heights *(G-788)*
Loda Electronics Co ............ G ....... 217 386-2554
Loda *(G-13752)*
Machine Control Systems Inc ............ G ....... 708 597-1200
Alsip *(G-486)*
Magnetrol International Inc ............ C ....... 630 723-6600
Aurora *(G-1051)*
Martin Automatic Inc ............ C ....... 815 654-4800
Rockford *(G-18483)*
Maurey Instrument Corp ............ F ....... 708 388-9898
Alsip *(G-490)*
Methode Electronics Inc ............ A ....... 217 357-3941
Carthage *(G-3316)*
Meto-Grafics Inc ............ F ....... 847 639-0044
Crystal Lake *(G-7609)*
Meyer Electronic Mfg Svcs Inc ............ G ....... 309 808-4100
Normal *(G-16076)*
Mitsubishi Elc Automtn Inc ............ C ....... 847 478-2100
Vernon Hills *(G-21183)*
Morton Automatic Electric Co ............ G ....... 309 263-7577
Morton *(G-15166)*
Mpc Products Corporation ............ G ....... 847 673-8300
Niles *(G-16011)*

# PRODUCT SECTION  —  CONVEYORS & CONVEYING EQPT

Mpc Products Corporation .................... A ....... 847 673-8300
  Niles  (G-16010)
New Cie Inc ........................................ F ....... 815 224-1485
  La Salle  (G-12781)
Niles Auto Parts ................................. G ....... 847 215-2549
  Lincolnshire  (G-13468)
O C Keckley Company ........................ E ....... 847 674-8422
  Skokie  (G-20048)
Olympic Controls Corp ....................... E ....... 847 742-3566
  Elgin  (G-9128)
Omron Automotive Elec Inc ................ A ....... 630 443-6800
  Saint Charles  (G-19229)
Panatrol Corporation .......................... E ....... 630 655-4700
  Burr Ridge  (G-2874)
Pilz Automtn Safety Ltd Partnr ............ G ....... 734 354-0272
  Chicago  (G-6123)
Power-Io Inc ...................................... E ....... 630 717-7335
  Naperville  (G-15730)
Pro-Quip Incorporated ....................... F ....... 708 352-5732
  La Grange Park  (G-12759)
Process Technologies Group ............... G ....... 630 393-4777
  Warrenville  (G-21360)
Protection Controls Inc ...................... E ....... 773 763-3110
  Skokie  (G-20066)
Rockwell Automation Inc ................... D ....... 414 382-3662
  Burr Ridge  (G-2878)
S & C Electric Company ..................... A ....... 773 338-1000
  Chicago  (G-6419)
Schneider Elc Buildings LLC ............... B ....... 815 381-5000
  Rockford  (G-18608)
Schneider Elc Holdings Inc ................. A ....... 717 944-5460
  Schaumburg  (G-19722)
Scientific Instruments Inc ................... G ....... 847 679-1242
  Skokie  (G-20082)
SE Relays LLC .................................... G ....... 847 827-9880
  Schaumburg  (G-19724)
Siemens Industry Inc .......................... A ....... 847 215-1000
  Buffalo Grove  (G-2767)
Simplex Inc ........................................ C ....... 217 483-1600
  Springfield  (G-20526)
Smart Systems Inc ............................. E ....... 630 343-3333
  Bolingbrook  (G-2372)
Sterling Systems & Controls ............... F ....... 815 625-0852
  Sterling  (G-20615)
Sumitomo Machinery Corp Amer ........ E ....... 630 752-0200
  Glendale Heights  (G-11078)
Tc Electric Controls LLC ..................... G ....... 847 598-3508
  Schaumburg  (G-19755)
Tomantron Inc ................................... F ....... 708 532-2456
  Tinley Park  (G-20950)
Web Printing Controls Co Inc .............. C ....... 618 842-2664
  Fairfield  (G-10161)
Yaskawa America Inc ......................... C ....... 847 887-7000
  Waukegan  (G-21642)
Z-Tech Inc ......................................... G ....... 815 335-7395
  Winnebago  (G-22299)

## CONTROLS: Thermostats

Braeburn Systems LLC ....................... F ....... 866 268-8892
  Montgomery  (G-15033)
Chicago Sensor Inc ............................ G ....... 773 252-9660
  Chicago  (G-4347)
E+e Elektronik Corporation ................ G ....... 508 530-3068
  Schaumburg  (G-19510)

## CONTROLS: Thermostats, Built-in

Goodrich Sensor Systems ................... G ....... 847 546-5749
  Round Lake  (G-19058)

## CONTROLS: Water Heater

A&B Reliable ..................................... G ....... 708 228-6148
  Lemont  (G-13222)
All Precision Mfg LLC ........................ F ....... 217 563-7070
  Nokomis  (G-16055)
Lopez Plumbing Systems Inc .............. G ....... 773 424-8225
  Chicago  (G-5540)
Unitrol Electronics Inc ........................ E ....... 847 480-0115
  Northbrook  (G-16380)

## CONVENTION & TRADE SHOW SVCS

Be Group Inc ..................................... G ....... 312 436-0301
  Chicago  (G-4061)
Stagnito Partners LLC ....................... D ....... 224 632-8200
  Deerfield  (G-8056)

## CONVERTERS: Data

Cisco Systems Inc .............................. B ....... 847 678-6600
  Des Plaines  (G-8170)

Ibs Conversions Inc ............................ D ....... 630 571-9100
  Oak Brook  (G-16524)
Mediarecall Holdings LLC .................. G ....... 847 513-6710
  Northbrook  (G-16309)
Precision Computer Methods .............. G ....... 630 208-8000
  Elburn  (G-8904)
Richardson Electronics Ltd ................. G ....... 630 208-2278
  Lafox  (G-12795)

## CONVERTERS: Frequency

Weldon Corporation ........................... E ....... 708 343-4700
  Maywood  (G-14437)

## CONVERTERS: Phase Or Rotary, Electrical

Ronk Electrical Industries Inc .............. E ....... 217 563-8333
  Nokomis  (G-16061)
Rsf Electronics Inc ............................. F ....... 847 490-0351
  Schaumburg  (G-19714)
Tracy Electric Inc ............................... E ....... 618 943-6205
  Lawrenceville  (G-13206)

## CONVERTERS: Power, AC to DC

Richardson Rfpd Inc .......................... G ....... 630 262-6800
  Geneva  (G-10862)
Synergistic Tech Solutions Inc ............. C ....... 224 360-6165
  Mundelein  (G-15562)

## CONVERTERS: Rotary, Electrical

Switched Source LLC ......................... G ....... 708 207-1479
  Chicago  (G-6655)

## CONVERTERS: Torque, Exc Auto

Midwest Converters Inc ..................... F ....... 815 229-9808
  Rockford  (G-18504)

## CONVEYOR SYSTEMS

Deyco Inc .......................................... G ....... 630 553-5666
  Yorkville  (G-22656)
Ewab Engineering Inc ........................ E ....... 847 247-0015
  Libertyville  (G-13321)
Industrial Kinetics Inc ......................... E ....... 630 655-0300
  Downers Grove  (G-8466)
Krygier Design Inc ............................. F ....... 620 766-1001
  Wood Dale  (G-22387)
Witron Intgrated Logistics Inc ............. C ....... 847 398-6130
  Arlington Heights  (G-873)

## CONVEYOR SYSTEMS: Belt, General Indl Use

Duravant LLC .................................... F ....... 630 635-3910
  Downers Grove  (G-8437)
Erect - O -Veyor Corporation .............. E ....... 630 766-1200
  Franklin Park  (G-10465)
Forbo Siegling LLC ............................ F ....... 630 595-4031
  Wood Dale  (G-22370)
J W Todd Co ..................................... G ....... 630 406-5715
  Aurora  (G-1173)
Lake Fabrication Inc .......................... E ....... 217 832-2761
  Villa Grove  (G-21229)
Rotec Industries Inc ........................... D ....... 630 279-3300
  Hampshire  (G-11561)

## CONVEYOR SYSTEMS: Bucket Type

Joy Technologies Inc .......................... E ....... 618 242-3650
  Mount Vernon  (G-15419)

## CONVEYOR SYSTEMS: Bulk Handling

Align Production Systems LLC ............ E ....... 217 423-6001
  Decatur  (G-7830)
Dover Artificial Lift Intl LLC ................. F ....... 630 743-2563
  Downers Grove  (G-8430)
GMI Packaging Co ............................. E ....... 734 972-7389
  Chicago  (G-4965)
Quantum Services Inc ........................ G ....... 815 230-5893
  Joliet  (G-12561)
Total Conveyor Services Inc ............... E ....... 630 860-2471
  Bensenville  (G-2005)
William W Meyer and Sons ................ D ....... 847 918-0111
  Libertyville  (G-13402)

## CONVEYOR SYSTEMS: Pneumatic Tube

Bankmark Inc .................................... F ....... 847 683-9834
  Hampshire  (G-11542)

Barrington Automation Ltd ................. E ....... 847 458-0900
  Lake In The Hills  (G-12987)
Kelly Systems Inc .............................. E ....... 312 733-3224
  Chicago  (G-5374)
Kongskilde Industries Inc ................... C ....... 309 452-3300
  Hudson  (G-12124)
Neuero Corporation ........................... F ....... 630 231-9020
  West Chicago  (G-21750)
Translogic Corporation ....................... F ....... 847 392-3700
  Rolling Meadows  (G-18784)

## CONVEYOR SYSTEMS: Robotic

Diversified Fleet MGT Inc ................... E ....... 815 578-1051
  McHenry  (G-14496)
Matrix Design LLC ............................. D ....... 847 841-8260
  South Elgin  (G-20217)
Measured Plastics Inc ........................ G ....... 815 939-4408
  Bourbonnais  (G-2402)
Panasonic Corp North America ........... C ....... 847 637-9700
  Buffalo Grove  (G-2750)
Smart Motion Robotics Inc ................. E ....... 815 895-8550
  Sycamore  (G-20817)

## CONVEYORS & CONVEYING EQPT

Acro Magnetics Inc ............................ G ....... 815 943-5018
  Harvard  (G-11617)
Astec Mobile Screens Inc ................... C ....... 815 626-6374
  Sterling  (G-20582)
Automatic Feeder Company Inc .......... F ....... 847 534-2300
  Schaumburg  (G-19450)
Automotion Inc .................................. C ....... 708 229-3700
  Oak Lawn  (G-16605)
Avasarala Inc ..................................... G ....... 847 969-0630
  Palatine  (G-17004)
Barry-Whmller Cont Systems Inc ........ C ....... 630 759-6800
  Romeoville  (G-18802)
Birnberg Machinery Inc ...................... G ....... 847 673-5242
  Skokie  (G-19964)
Bost Corporation ............................... E ....... 708 344-7023
  Maywood  (G-14420)
Canconex Inc ..................................... F ....... 847 458-9955
  Algonquin  (G-382)
Central Manufacturing Company ........ G ....... 309 387-6591
  East Peoria  (G-8705)
Chicago Can Conveyor Corp ............... E ....... 708 430-0988
  Bridgeview  (G-2476)
Chicago Chain and Transm Co ............ E ....... 630 482-9000
  Countryside  (G-7417)
Cmd Conveyor Inc ............................. E ....... 708 237-0996
  Chicago Ridge  (G-7144)
Confab Systems Inc ........................... F ....... 708 388-4103
  Posen  (G-17728)
Container Hdlg Systems Corp ............. E ....... 708 482-9900
  Countryside  (G-7418)
Container Service Group Inc ............... F ....... 815 744-8693
  Rockdale  (G-18218)
Conveyor Installations Inc .................. F ....... 630 859-8900
  Batavia  (G-1433)
Conveyors Plus Inc ............................ C ....... 708 361-1512
  Orland Park  (G-16849)
Cosveyor Inc ..................................... F ....... 630 859-8900
  Batavia  (G-1434)
Custom Machinery Inc ....................... G ....... 847 678-3033
  Schiller Park  (G-19818)
Dematic Corp ..................................... F ....... 630 852-9200
  Lisle  (G-13583)
Diversatech Metalfab LLC .................. E ....... 309 747-4159
  Gridley  (G-11404)
Dspc Company .................................. E ....... 815 997-1116
  Rockford  (G-18353)
Duravant ........................................... G ....... 630 635-3910
  Downers Grove  (G-8436)
Eaglestone Inc ................................... F ....... 630 587-1115
  Saint Charles  (G-19177)
Eirich Machines Inc ............................ D ....... 847 336-2444
  Gurnee  (G-11446)
Engineered Plumbing Spc LLC ............ E ....... 630 682-1555
  Joliet  (G-12491)
Engineering Products Company .......... G ....... 815 436-9055
  Plainfield  (G-17595)
Forte Automation Systems Inc ........... E ....... 815 316-6247
  Machesney Park  (G-14076)
Frantz Manufacturing Company .......... G ....... 815 564-0991
  Sterling  (G-20593)
Gammerler US Corp ........................... E ....... 941 465-4400
  Mount Prospect  (G-15332)
GE Fairchild Mining Equipment .......... D ....... 618 559-3216
  Du Quoin  (G-8555)

Employee Codes: A=Over 500 employees, B=251-500
C=101-250, D=51-100, E=20-50, F=10-19, G=3-9

## CONVEYORS & CONVEYING EQPT

Gsi Group LLC .................................................. C ...... 217 463-1612
  Paris *(G-17148)*
Icon Co ............................................................. G ...... 630 545-2345
  Glen Ellyn *(G-10973)*
Industrial Motion Control LLC ........................ C ...... 847 459-5200
  Wheeling *(G-22076)*
Intelligrated Systems Inc ................................ B ...... 630 985-4350
  Woodridge *(G-22495)*
Kamflex Conveyor Corporation ...................... G ...... 630 682-1555
  Joliet *(G-12526)*
Kanetic Inc ....................................................... E ...... 847 382-9922
  Lake Barrington *(G-12816)*
Kimco USA Inc ................................................. F ...... 800 788-1133
  Marshall *(G-14325)*
L M C Inc .......................................................... G ...... 815 758-3514
  Dekalb *(G-8101)*
Loma International Inc .................................... D ...... 630 588-0900
  Carol Stream *(G-3186)*
Loop Belt Industries Inc ................................. G ...... 630 469-1300
  Glen Ellyn *(G-10978)*
Machinex Technologies Inc ............................ D ...... 773 867-8801
  Chicago *(G-5593)*
Mallard Handling Solutions LLC .................... E ...... 815 625-9491
  Sterling *(G-20596)*
Marvco Tool & Manufacturing ......................... G ...... 847 437-4900
  Elk Grove Village *(G-9612)*
Mid States Corporation ................................... E ...... 708 754-1760
  S Chicago Hts *(G-19109)*
Mid-American Elevator Co Inc ....................... C ...... 773 486-6900
  Chicago *(G-5727)*
Mid-American Elevator Co Inc ....................... E ...... 815 740-1204
  Joliet *(G-12541)*
Morrison Timing Screw Company ................. D ...... 708 331-6600
  Glenwood *(G-11219)*
Payson Casters Inc ......................................... C ...... 847 336-5033
  Gurnee *(G-11483)*
Pre Pack Machinery Inc .................................. G ...... 217 352-1010
  Champaign *(G-3528)*
Precision Conveyor and Erct Co ................... F ...... 779 324-5269
  Frankfort *(G-10350)*
Roll-A-Way Conveyors Inc ............................. G ...... 847 336-5033
  Gurnee *(G-11500)*
RPS Engineering Inc ....................................... F ...... 847 931-1950
  Elgin *(G-9168)*
SA Nat Industrial Cnstr Co Inc ....................... E ...... 618 246-9402
  Mount Vernon *(G-15443)*
Sardee Industries Inc ...................................... G ...... 630 824-4200
  Lisle *(G-13654)*
SBS Steel Belt Systems USA Inc ................... F ...... 847 841-3300
  Gilberts *(G-10935)*
Special Tool Engineering Co .......................... F ...... 773 767-6690
  Chicago *(G-6554)*
Stanford Bettendorf Inc .................................. D ...... 618 548-3555
  Salem *(G-19353)*
Superior Industries Inc ................................... A ...... 309 346-1742
  Pekin *(G-17290)*
Tracoinsa USA ................................................. G ...... 309 287-7046
  Gridley *(G-11411)*
Tricon Inds Mfg & Eqp Sls .............................. E ...... 815 379-2090
  Walnut *(G-21331)*
United Conveyor Corporation ........................ C ...... 847 473-5900
  Waukegan *(G-21635)*
United Systems Incorporated ......................... F ...... 708 479-1450
  Mokena *(G-14914)*
US Conveyor Tech Mfg Inc ............................. E ...... 309 359-4088
  Mackinaw *(G-14119)*
US Conveyor Technologies ........................... F ...... 309 359-4088
  Mackinaw *(G-14120)*
V & C Converters ............................................ G ...... 708 251-5635
  Lansing *(G-13191)*
Wes-Tech Automtn Solutions LLC ................ D ...... 847 541-5070
  Buffalo Grove *(G-2794)*
Wynright Corporation ..................................... D ...... 847 595-9400
  Elk Grove Village *(G-9819)*

### CONVEYORS: Overhead

Rwi Manufacturing Inc .................................... C ...... 800 277-1699
  Aurora *(G-1212)*

### COOKING & FOOD WARMING EQPT: Commercial

A J Antunes & Co ............................................ C ...... 630 784-1000
  Carol Stream *(G-3087)*
A La Cart Inc ................................................... E ...... 847 256-4102
  Highland Park *(G-11820)*
Keating of Chicago Inc ................................... E ...... 815 569-2324
  Capron *(G-2996)*
Middleby Corporation ..................................... E ...... 847 741-3300
  Elgin *(G-9110)*
Omni Containment Systems LLC ................... G ...... 847 468-1772
  Elgin *(G-9129)*
Optimal Automatics Co ................................... G ...... 847 439-9110
  Elk Grove Village *(G-9667)*
Prince Castle LLC ........................................... C ...... 630 462-8800
  Carol Stream *(G-3218)*
Quantum Technical Services Inc ................... E ...... 815 464-1540
  Frankfort *(G-10355)*

### COOKING & FOODWARMING EQPT: Coffee Brewing

Bunn-O-Matic Corporation ............................. G ...... 217 528-8739
  Springfield *(G-20401)*

### COOKING & FOODWARMING EQPT: Commercial

Ali Group North America Corp ....................... E ...... 847 215-6565
  Vernon Hills *(G-21144)*
Food Equipment Technologies Co ................ C ...... 847 719-3000
  Lake Zurich *(G-13075)*
Lee Industries Inc .......................................... C ...... 847 462-1865
  Elk Grove Village *(G-9590)*
Midco International Inc .................................. E ...... 773 604-8700
  Chicago *(G-5733)*
Middleby Corporation ..................................... E ...... 847 741-3300
  Elgin *(G-9111)*
Triplex Sales Company Inc ............................ G ...... 847 839-8442
  Schaumburg *(G-19774)*

### COOKING & FOODWARMING EQPT: Popcorn Machines, Commercial

C Cretors & Co ................................................ D ...... 847 616-6900
  Wood Dale *(G-22348)*

### COOKING EQPT, HOUSEHOLD: Ranges, Gas

Empire Comfort Systems Inc ......................... C ...... 618 233-7420
  Belleville *(G-1631)*
Peerless-Premier Appliance Co .................... D ...... 618 233-0475
  Belleville *(G-1666)*

### COOKING WARE, EXC PORCELAIN ENAMELED

C M Holding Co Inc ........................................ G ...... 847 438-2171
  Lake Zurich *(G-13048)*

### COOLERS & ICE CHESTS: Polystyrene Foam

Tkk USA Inc .................................................... G ...... 847 439-7821
  Rolling Meadows *(G-18783)*

### COOLING TOWERS: Metal

Amsted Industries Incorporated .................... B ...... 312 645-1700
  Chicago *(G-3896)*
Amsted Industries Incorporated .................... F ...... 312 645-1700
  Chicago *(G-3897)*
Evapco Inc ...................................................... E ...... 410 756-2600
  Chicago *(G-4788)*
SPX Cooling Technologies Inc ...................... D ...... 815 873-3767
  Rockford *(G-18630)*
SPX Corporation ............................................. C ...... 847 593-8855
  Elk Grove Village *(G-9749)*
SPX Corporation ............................................. B ...... 815 874-5556
  Rockford *(G-18631)*

### COOLING TOWERS: Wood

Mc Mechanical Contractors Inc ..................... G ...... 708 460-0075
  Orland Park *(G-16874)*

### COPPER ORE MILLING & PREPARATION

Ventec USA LLC ............................................. G ...... 847 621-2261
  Elk Grove Village *(G-9805)*

### COPPER: Bars, Primary

Ampco Metal Incorporated ............................. E ...... 847 437-6000
  Arlington Heights *(G-711)*

### COPPER: Cathodes, Primary

Inter-Trade Global LLC .................................. G ...... 618 954-6119
  Belleville *(G-1637)*

### COPPER: Rolling & Drawing

Ansonia Copper & Brass Inc ......................... C ...... 866 607-7066
  Chicago *(G-3914)*
Chicago Hardware and Fix Co ....................... D ...... 847 455-6609
  Franklin Park *(G-10429)*
Demco Products Inc ....................................... F ...... 708 636-6240
  Oak Lawn *(G-16616)*
Empire Bronze Corp ....................................... F ...... 630 916-9722
  Lombard *(G-13796)*
Fairbanks Wire Corporation .......................... G ...... 847 683-2600
  Hampshire *(G-11550)*
Global Brass Cop Holdings Inc ..................... E ...... 847 240-4700
  Schaumburg *(G-19537)*
Kroh-Wagner Inc ............................................. E ...... 773 252-2031
  Chicago *(G-5412)*
Olin Corporation ............................................. G ...... 618 258-2245
  Brighton *(G-2543)*

### COPY MACHINES WHOLESALERS

Konica Minolta ................................................ G ...... 630 893-8238
  Roselle *(G-18950)*
Konica Minolta Business Soluti ..................... E ...... 309 671-1360
  Peoria *(G-17398)*

### CORD & TWINE

Aamstrand Ropes & Twines Inc .................... F ...... 815 468-2100
  Manteno *(G-14179)*
Erin Rope Corporation ................................... F ...... 708 377-1084
  Blue Island *(G-2250)*
Obies Tackle Co Inc ....................................... G ...... 618 234-5638
  Belleville *(G-1662)*

### CORE WASH OR WAX

Butterfield Color Inc ....................................... E ...... 630 906-1980
  Aurora *(G-1122)*

### CORK & CORK PRDTS

Edgewater Products Company Inc ................ F ...... 708 345-9200
  Melrose Park *(G-14629)*

### CORK & CORK PRDTS: Insulating Material

Cma Inc ............................................................ E ...... 847 848-0674
  Joliet *(G-12474)*
Cma Inc ............................................................ E ...... 630 551-3100
  Oswego *(G-16909)*

### CORRECTIONAL INSTITUTIONS

Federal Prison Industries .............................. F ...... 618 664-6361
  Greenville *(G-11393)*
Federal Prison Industries .............................. C ...... 309 346-8588
  Pekin *(G-17262)*

### CORRUGATED PRDTS: Boxes, Partition, Display Items, Sheet/Pad

Aira Enterprise Inc ......................................... E ...... 708 458-4360
  Bedford Park *(G-1534)*
D/C Export & Domestic Pkg Inc .................... E ...... 847 593-4200
  Elk Grove Village *(G-9415)*
Georg-Pcific Corrugated IV LLC ................... C ...... 630 896-3610
  Aurora *(G-1014)*
International Paper Company ........................ C ...... 708 728-8200
  Chicago *(G-5222)*
J Wallace & Associates Inc ........................... G ...... 630 960-4221
  Downers Grove *(G-8467)*
Murnane Specialties Inc ................................ E ...... 708 449-1200
  Northlake *(G-16444)*
Packaging Corporation America ................... D ...... 708 821-1600
  Chicago *(G-6053)*
Packaging Design Corporation ..................... E ...... 630 323-1354
  Burr Ridge *(G-2873)*
Pry-Bar Company ............................................ F ...... 815 436-3383
  Joliet *(G-12558)*
Welch Packaging LLC .................................... D ...... 708 813-1520
  Countryside *(G-7451)*
Westrock Rkt Company .................................. A ...... 312 346-6600
  Chicago *(G-6969)*
Weyerhaeuser Company ................................. C ...... 847 439-1111
  Elk Grove Village *(G-9811)*

### COSMETIC PREPARATIONS

Bad Girlz Enterprises Inc .............................. C ...... 618 215-1428
  East Saint Louis *(G-8743)*
Clintex Laboratories Inc ................................ E ...... 773 493-9777
  Chicago *(G-4403)*

Colorlab Cosmetics Inc .......... E ...... 815 965-0026
  Rockford (G-18315)
Combe Laboratories Inc .......... C ...... 217 893-4490
  Rantoul (G-17923)
Concept Laboratories Inc .......... D ...... 773 395-7300
  Chicago (G-4446)
Delta Laboratories Inc .......... G ...... 630 351-1798
  Elk Grove Village (G-9421)
Geka Manufacturing Corporation .......... E ...... 224 238-5080
  Elgin (G-9043)
Johnson Publishing Company LLC .......... C ...... 312 322-9200
  Chicago (G-5320)
Juvenesse By Elaine Gayle Inc .......... G ...... 312 944-1211
  Chicago (G-5340)
Maynard Inc .......... G ...... 773 235-5225
  Chicago (G-5661)
Mseed Group LLC .......... G ...... 847 226-1147
  South Holland (G-20292)
New Avon LLC .......... A ...... 847 966-0200
  Morton Grove (G-15224)
Rna Corporation .......... D ...... 708 597-7777
  Blue Island (G-2267)
Skyline Beauty Supply Inc .......... F ...... 773 275-6003
  Franklin Park (G-10589)
Techpack Inc .......... E ...... 847 439-8220
  Elk Grove Village (G-9773)
Vee Pak LLC .......... D ...... 708 482-8881
  Hodgkins (G-11986)
Vee Pak LLC .......... C ...... 708 482-8881
  Countryside (G-7449)
Zanfel Laboratories Inc .......... G ...... 309 683-3500
  Peoria (G-17480)

## COSMETICS & TOILETRIES

4 Elements Company .......... G ...... 773 236-2284
  Mundelein (G-15461)
A & H Manufacturing Inc .......... F ...... 630 543-5900
  Addison (G-14)
Abbott Laboratories .......... A ...... 847 937-6100
  North Chicago (G-16164)
Amedico Laboratories LLC .......... G ...... 347 857-7546
  Oakbrook Terrace (G-16696)
Anjel Scents LLC .......... G ...... 313 729-0719
  Chicago (G-3909)
Art of Shaving - Fl LLC .......... G ...... 847 568-0881
  Skokie (G-19959)
Art of Shaving - Fl LLC .......... G ...... 312 527-1604
  Chicago (G-3952)
Art of Shaving - Fl LLC .......... G ...... 630 684-0277
  Oak Brook (G-16489)
Avlon Industries Inc .......... D ...... 708 344-0709
  Melrose Park (G-14598)
Belle-Aire Fragrances Inc .......... E ...... 847 816-3500
  Mundelein (G-15476)
Collagen Usa Inc .......... G ...... 708 716-0251
  Chicago (G-4423)
Common Scents Mom .......... G ...... 309 389-3216
  Mapleton (G-14208)
Conopco Inc .......... C ...... 773 916-4400
  Chicago (G-4452)
Dallas Scrub .......... G ...... 312 651-6012
  Chicago (G-4546)
Deputante Inc .......... G ...... 773 545-9531
  Chicago (G-4584)
Dhaliwal Labs Illinois LLC .......... D ...... 312 690-7734
  Bedford Park (G-1548)
Dial Corporation .......... C ...... 630 892-4381
  Montgomery (G-15041)
Emlin Cosmetics Inc .......... E ...... 630 860-5773
  Bensenville (G-1892)
Formulations Inc .......... G ...... 847 674-9141
  Skokie (G-20001)
Garcoa Inc .......... D ...... 708 905-5118
  Brookfield (G-2633)
H N C Products Inc .......... E ...... 217 935-9100
  Clinton (G-7281)
Healing Scents .......... G ...... 815 874-0924
  Rockford (G-18415)
Kellyjo Makes Scents .......... G ...... 618 281-4241
  Columbia (G-7359)
Kik Custom Products Inc .......... B ...... 217 442-1400
  Danville (G-7743)
Lasner Bros Inc .......... G ...... 773 935-7383
  Chicago (G-5463)
Luxis International Inc .......... G ...... 800 240-1473
  Dekalb (G-8104)
One Love .......... G ...... 708 832-1740
  Calumet City (G-2947)
Pal Midwest Ltd .......... G ...... 815 965-2981
  Rockford (G-18528)
Pivotal Production LLC .......... G ...... 773 726-7706
  Chicago (G-6134)
Princeton Chemicals Inc .......... G ...... 847 975-6210
  Highland Park (G-11862)
Punch Skin Care Inc .......... E ...... 702 333-2510
  Chicago (G-6227)
Pure Essential Supply Inc .......... G
  Saint Charles (G-19245)
Rose Laboratories Inc .......... E ...... 815 740-1121
  Joliet (G-12571)
San Telmo Ltd .......... G ...... 847 842-9115
  Barrington (G-1304)
Schmit Laboratories Inc .......... E ...... 773 476-0072
  Glendale Heights (G-11066)
Sigan America LLC .......... G ...... 815 431-9830
  Ottawa (G-16983)
Special Scents Inc .......... E ...... 708 596-9370
  Harvey (G-11676)
Spike Nanotech Inc .......... G ...... 847 504-6273
  Matteson (G-14379)
Suretint Technologies LLC .......... F ...... 847 509-3625
  Mount Prospect (G-15377)
True Royalty Scents .......... G ...... 309 992-0688
  Peoria (G-17471)
Trumans Brands LLC .......... F ...... 224 302-5605
  Waukegan (G-21633)
Unilever Manufacturing US Inc .......... G ...... 847 541-8868
  Wheeling (G-22170)
W-R Industries Inc .......... G ...... 312 733-5200
  Chicago (G-6929)

## COSMETICS WHOLESALERS

Avlon Industries Inc .......... D ...... 708 344-0709
  Melrose Park (G-14598)
Juvenesse By Elaine Gayle Inc .......... G ...... 312 944-1211
  Chicago (G-5340)

## COSMETOLOGIST

Payne Chauna .......... G ...... 618 580-2584
  Belleville (G-1664)

## COSMETOLOGY & PERSONAL HYGIENE SALONS

Patty Style Shop .......... G ...... 618 654-2015
  Highland (G-11805)

## COSTUME JEWELRY & NOVELTIES: Bracelets, Exc Precious Metals

Medical ID Fashions Company .......... G ...... 847 404-6789
  Deerfield (G-8035)

## COSTUME JEWELRY & NOVELTIES: Earrings, Exc Precious Metals

Alessco Inc .......... F ...... 773 327-7919
  Chicago (G-3801)

## COSTUME JEWELRY & NOVELTIES: Exc Semi & Precious

Total Design Jewelry Inc .......... G ...... 847 433-5333
  Highland Park (G-11878)

## COSTUME JEWELRY & NOVELTIES: Keychains, Exc Precious Metal

S & S Keytax Inc .......... F ...... 708 656-9221
  Chicago (G-6421)

## COSTUME JEWELRY & NOVELTIES: Pins, Exc Precious Metals

R S Owens & Co Inc .......... B ...... 773 282-6000
  Chicago (G-6273)
Ribbon Supply Comp .......... F ...... 773 237-7979
  Chicago (G-6350)

## COSTUME JEWELRY & NOVELTIES: Rosaries & Sm Religious Items

Anthos and Co LLC .......... G ...... 773 744-6813
  Inverness (G-12202)

## COSTUME JEWELRY & NOVELTIES: Watchbands, Base Metal

JP Leatherworks Inc .......... G ...... 847 317-9804
  Deerfield (G-8022)

## COSTUME JEWELRY/NOVELTS: Cuff-Link/Stud, Exc Prec Metal/Gem

Bird Dog Bay Inc .......... G ...... 312 631-3108
  Chicago (G-4111)

## COSTUMES & WIGS STORES

Custom & Hard To Find Wigs .......... F ...... 773 777-0222
  Chicago (G-4519)

## COUNTER & SINK TOPS

Alexander Lumber Co .......... G ...... 217 429-2729
  Decatur (G-7827)
All Stone Inc .......... G ...... 815 529-1754
  Romeoville (G-18793)
Beachys Counter Tops Inc .......... F ...... 217 543-2143
  Arthur (G-882)
Booths and Upholstery By Ray .......... G ...... 773 523-3355
  Chicago (G-4144)
Brothers Leal LLC .......... G ...... 708 385-4400
  Alsip (G-443)
Counter Craft Inc .......... G ...... 847 336-8205
  Waukegan (G-21545)
Countertop Creations .......... G ...... 618 736-2700
  Dahlgren (G-7689)
Crown Coverings Inc .......... E ...... 630 546-2959
  Roselle (G-18937)
Custom Countertop Creations .......... F ...... 847 695-8800
  South Elgin (G-20192)
D & D Counter Tops Co Inc .......... G
  Machesney Park (G-14070)
Dieter Construction Inc .......... G ...... 630 960-9662
  Woodridge (G-22470)
DK Knutsen .......... G ...... 815 626-4388
  Sterling (G-20589)
Granite Xperts Inc .......... E ...... 847 364-1900
  Franklin Park (G-10481)
Graniteworks .......... G ...... 815 288-3350
  Dixon (G-8333)
K & D Counter Tops Inc .......... E ...... 618 224-9630
  Trenton (G-20992)
Kitchen Krafters Inc .......... G ...... 815 675-6061
  Spring Grove (G-20341)
Kraft Custom Design Inc .......... G ...... 815 485-5506
  New Lenox (G-15890)
Midwest Fabrication-Countertop .......... G ...... 217 528-0571
  Springfield (G-20483)
New Age Surfaces LLC .......... G ...... 630 226-0011
  Romeoville (G-18853)
Royal Fabricators Inc .......... F ...... 847 775-7466
  Wadsworth (G-21327)
Stone Fabricators Company .......... G ...... 847 788-8296
  Arlington Heights (G-845)
Surface Solutions Illinois Inc .......... G ...... 708 571-3449
  Mokena (G-14907)
Tremont Kitchen Tops Inc .......... G ...... 309 925-5736
  Tremont (G-20987)

## COUNTERS & COUNTING DEVICES

ARC-Tronics Inc .......... C ...... 847 437-0211
  Elk Grove Village (G-9312)
Flodyne Inc .......... G ...... 630 563-3600
  Hanover Park (G-11581)
Otak International Inc .......... G ...... 630 373-9229
  Melrose Park (G-14679)
Shoppertrak Rct Corporation .......... F ...... 312 529-5300
  Chicago (G-6498)
Spartanics Ltd .......... E ...... 847 394-5700
  Rolling Meadows (G-18781)
Tml Inc .......... G ...... 847 382-1550
  Barrington (G-1308)
Woodward Inc .......... F ...... 847 673-8300
  Skokie (G-20113)

## COUNTERS OR COUNTER DISPLAY CASES, EXC WOOD

Cabinet Designs .......... G ...... 708 614-8603
  Oak Forest (G-16575)
Gerali Custom Design Inc .......... D ...... 847 760-0500
  Elgin (G-9044)
Jbc Holding Co .......... G ...... 217 347-7701
  Effingham (G-8841)

# COUNTERS OR COUNTER DISPLAY CASES, EXC WOOD

Mikron Designs Inc .................. G ...... 847 726-3990
Lake Zurich (G-13103)

## COUNTERS OR COUNTER DISPLAY CASES, WOOD

Collinsville Custom Kitchens .......... F ...... 618 288-2000
Maryville (G-14340)
Hallmark Cabinet Company ............ D ...... 708 757-7807
Chicago Heights (G-7102)
J & W Counter Tops Inc .............. E ...... 217 544-0876
Springfield (G-20460)
Maxwell Counters Inc ................ E ...... 309 928-2848
Farmer City (G-10179)
Murray Cabinetry & Tops Inc ......... G ...... 815 672-6992
Streator (G-20696)
Wilcor Solid Surface Inc ............. F ...... 630 350-7703
Elk Grove Village (G-9813)

## COUNTING DEVICES: Controls, Revolution & Timing

Danaher Corporation ................. F ...... 800 866-6659
Gurnee (G-11437)
Dynapar Corporation ................. C ...... 847 662-2666
Gurnee (G-11443)

## COUNTING DEVICES: Electromechanical

Line Group Inc ...................... E ...... 847 593-6810
Arlington Heights (G-793)
Nep Electronics Inc ................. C ...... 630 595-8500
Wood Dale (G-22405)

## COUNTING DEVICES: Gauges, Press Temp Corrections Computing

G H Meiser & Co .................... E ...... 708 388-7867
Posen (G-17730)

## COUNTING DEVICES: Odometers

O E M Marketing Inc ................. F ...... 847 985-9490
Schaumburg (G-19671)

## COUNTING DEVICES: Pedometers

Walk 4 Life Inc ..................... F ...... 815 439-2340
Oswego (G-16939)

## COUNTING DEVICES: Revolution

E N M Company ..................... D ...... 773 775-8400
Chicago (G-4667)

## COUNTING DEVICES: Tachometer, Centrifugal

Auto Meter Products Inc ............. C ...... 815 991-2292
Sycamore (G-20788)

## COUPLINGS, EXC PRESSURE & SOIL PIPE

RF Mau Co .......................... F ...... 847 329-9731
Lincolnwood (G-13533)
Victaulic Company ................... B ...... 630 585-2919
Aurora (G-1092)

## COUPLINGS: Shaft

Lovejoy Inc ......................... C ...... 630 852-0500
Downers Grove (G-8480)
Mathis Energy LLC .................. G ...... 309 925-3177
Tremont (G-20984)
Rexnord Industries LLC ............. D ...... 630 969-1770
Downers Grove (G-8515)

## COURIER OR MESSENGER SVCS

Ocs America Inc .................... E ...... 630 595-0111
Wood Dale (G-22409)

## COURIER SVCS, AIR: Package Delivery, Private

Continental Usa Inc ................. G ...... 847 823-0958
Park Ridge (G-17188)

## COURIER SVCS: Ground

Bb Services LLC ................... G ...... 630 941-8122
Elmhurst (G-9837)

Open Kitchens Inc .................. E ...... 312 666-5334
Chicago (G-5995)

## COURIER SVCS: Package By Vehicle

Leg Up LLC ......................... G ...... 312 282-2725
Chicago (G-5486)
UPS Authorized Retailer ............. G ...... 708 354-8772
La Grange (G-12748)

## COVERS: Automobile Seat

Bill Weeks Inc ...................... G ...... 217 523-8735
Springfield (G-20397)

## COVERS: Automotive, Exc Seat & Tire

Leader Accessories LLC ............. G ...... 877 662-9808
Rockton (G-18698)

## COVERS: Metal Plate

Imbert Construction Inds Inc ........ G ...... 847 588-3170
Niles (G-15988)

## COVERS: Slip Made Of Fabric, Plastic, Etc.

Ameriguard Corporation ............. G ...... 630 986-1900
Burr Ridge (G-2822)

## CRACKED CASTING REPAIR SVCS

Franklin Maintenance ................ G ...... 815 284-6806
Dixon (G-8332)
Metalock Corporation ................ F ...... 815 666-1560
Crest Hill (G-7463)
Ramsey Welding Inc ................ E ...... 618 483-6248
Altamont (G-555)

## CRANE & AERIAL LIFT SVCS

Coast Crane Company ............... C ...... 847 215-6500
Buffalo Grove (G-2674)
Sheas Iron Works Inc ............... G ...... 847 356-2922
Lake Villa (G-13026)

## CRANES: Indl Plant

Handling Systems Inc ............... E ...... 708 352-1213
La Grange (G-12735)

## CRANES: Locomotive

W N G S Inc ........................ E ...... 847 451-1224
Franklin Park (G-10625)

## CRANES: Overhead

Gh Cranes Corporation .............. G ...... 815 277-5328
Frankfort (G-10325)
Lanco International Inc .............. B ...... 708 596-5200
Hazel Crest (G-11709)
Uesco Industries Inc ................ E ...... 800 325-8372
Alsip (G-537)

## CRANKSHAFTS & CAMSHAFTS: Machining

Abacus Manufacturing Group Inc .... G ...... 815 654-7050
Rockford (G-18245)
Allen Popovich ...................... G ...... 815 712-7404
Custer Park (G-7686)
Chrome Crankshaft Company LLC .. F ...... 815 725-9030
Joliet (G-12473)
Precision Dynamics Inc ............. G ...... 815 877-1592
Machesney Park (G-14099)
Regent Automotive Engineering ...... G ...... 773 889-5744
Chicago (G-6323)
Riser Machine Corp ................. F ...... 708 532-2313
New Lenox (G-15907)
Southern Illinois Crankshafts ........ F ...... 618 282-4100
Ruma (G-19089)

## CREATIVE SVCS: Advertisers, Exc Writers

Phoenix Graphix .................... G ...... 618 531-3664
Pinckneyville (G-17551)

## CREDIT CLEARINGHOUSE SVC

Manufctrers Claring Hse of Ill ....... G ...... 773 545-6300
Chicago (G-5609)

## CREDIT INST, SHORT-TERM BUSINESS: Financing Dealers

Navistar Inc ........................ C ...... 331 332-5000
Lisle (G-13629)

## CREDIT INSTITUTIONS, SHORT-TERM BUSINESS: Mercantile Finance

Caterpillar Inc ...................... B ...... 309 675-6590
Peoria (G-17333)

## CREMATORIES

Sterling Vault Company ............. F ...... 815 625-0077
Sterling (G-20616)
Wilbert Shultz Vault Co Inc ......... F ...... 815 672-2049
Streator (G-20711)

## CROWNS & CLOSURES

Alcon Tool & Mfg Co Inc ............ F ...... 773 545-8742
Chicago (G-3798)
American Flange & Mfg Co Inc ..... E ...... 630 665-7900
Carol Stream (G-3098)
Galena Manufacturing Co Inc ....... G ...... 815 777-2078
Galena (G-10722)
Kile Machine & Tool Inc ............. E ...... 217 446-8616
Danville (G-7744)
Kipp Manufacturing Company Inc .... F ...... 630 768-9051
Wauconda (G-21477)
Product Service Craft Inc ........... F ...... 630 964-5160
Downers Grove (G-8511)

## CRUDE PETROLEUM & NATURAL GAS PRODUCTION

Brookstone Resources Inc .......... G ...... 618 382-2893
Carmi (G-3062)
Collins Brothers Oil Corp ........... G ...... 618 244-1093
Mount Vernon (G-15404)
Deep Rock Energy Corporation ..... F ...... 618 548-2779
Salem (G-19329)
Glover Oil Field Service Inc ........ F ...... 618 395-3624
Olney (G-16770)
Gulf Coast Exploration Inc .......... G ...... 847 226-4654
Highland Park (G-11838)
L & J Producers Inc ................ G ...... 217 932-5639
Casey (G-3387)
Murphy USA Inc .................... E ...... 815 337-2440
Woodstock (G-22595)
Murphy USA Inc .................... D ...... 815 936-6144
Kankakee (G-12639)
Oelze Equipment Company LLC .... E ...... 618 327-9111
Nashville (G-15845)
Petco Petroleum Corporation ....... D ...... 618 242-8718
Mount Vernon (G-15440)
Petron Oil Production Inc .......... G ...... 618 783-4486
Newton (G-15946)
R & D Oil Producers ............... G ...... 217 773-9299
Mount Sterling (G-15393)
R H Johnson Oil Co Inc ............ G ...... 630 668-3649
Wheaton (G-21974)
Rex Energy Corporation ............ E ...... 618 943-8700
Bridgeport (G-2454)
Ron Absher ......................... G ...... 618 382-4646
Carmi (G-3079)
Shawnee Exploration Partners ...... G ...... 618 382-3223
Carmi (G-3080)
St Pierre Oil Company Inc .......... G ...... 618 783-4441
Newton (G-15949)
Steven A Zanetis ................... G ...... 618 393-2176
Olney (G-16797)

## CRUDE PETROLEUM & NATURAL GAS PRODUCTION

BP Products North America Inc .... G ...... 630 420-4300
Naperville (G-15609)
Chicap Pipe Line Company ......... F ...... 708 479-1219
Mokena (G-14858)
Concord Well Service Inc .......... G ...... 618 395-4405
Olney (G-16765)
D & Z Exploration Inc .............. G ...... 618 829-3274
Saint Elmo (G-19305)
Ensource Inc ....................... G ...... 312 912-1048
Chicago (G-4758)
Gulf Petroleum LLC ................ G ...... 312 803-0373
Chicago (G-5012)
Jbl - Alton ......................... G ...... 618 466-0411
Alton (G-580)

Kerogen Resources Inc....G....618 382-3114
Carmi (G-3071)
Midco Petroleum Inc....G....630 655-2198
Westmont (G-21906)
Midwest Oil LLC....G....309 456-3663
Good Hope (G-11243)
Midwest Radiant Oil and Gas....G....618 476-1303
Millstadt (G-14830)
MRC Global (us) Inc....F....314 231-3400
Granite City (G-11297)
Murvin & Meir Oil Co....G....618 395-4405
Olney (G-16783)
Natural Gas Pipeline Amer LLC....E....618 495-2211
Centralia (G-3423)
Natural Gas Pipeline Amer LLC....E....618 829-3224
Saint Elmo (G-19309)
River City Oil LLC....G....309 693-2249
Peoria (G-17442)
Rodgers Bill Oil Min Bits Svc....G....618 299-7771
West Salem (G-21824)
Roosevelt Mobile....G....630 293-7630
West Chicago (G-21766)
Star Energy Corp Inc....G....618 584-3631
Flat Rock (G-10197)
UOP LLC....D....708 442-7400
Mc Cook (G-14460)
Warren Oil MGT Co IL LLC....G....618 997-5951
Marion (G-14294)
Zanetis Oil Company....G....618 262-4593
Mount Carmel (G-15289)

## CRUDE PETROLEUM PRODUCTION

Ashley Oil Co....G....217 932-2112
Casey (G-3380)
B Quad Oil Inc....G....618 656-4419
Edwardsville (G-8790)
Basin Transports....G....618 829-3323
Saint Elmo (G-19303)
Basnetts Investments....G....618 842-4040
Fairfield (G-10136)
Belden Enterprises LP....F....618 829-3274
Saint Elmo (G-19304)
Bell Brothers....G....618 544-2157
Robinson (G-18055)
Bertram Oil Co....G....618 546-1122
Robinson (G-18056)
Bi-Petro Inc....E....217 535-0181
Springfield (G-20396)
Booth Oil Co Inc....G....618 662-7696
Flora (G-10200)
Booth Resources Inc....G....618 662-4955
Flora (G-10201)
Brehm Oil Inc....F....618 242-4620
Mount Vernon (G-15402)
Bruce McCullough....G....217 773-3130
Mount Sterling (G-15390)
Budmark Oil Company Inc....G....618 937-2495
West Frankfort (G-21805)
Carter Anna Brooks LLC....G....618 382-3939
Carmi (G-3065)
Citation Oil & Gas Corp....E....618 966-2101
Crossville (G-7521)
Continental Resources Ill Inc....E....618 242-1717
Mount Vernon (G-15405)
D Little Drilling....G....618 943-3721
Saint Francisville (G-19312)
Dedica Energy Corporation....G....217 235-9191
Mattoon (G-14388)
Duncan Oil Company Inc....G....618 548-2923
Salem (G-19330)
ES Investments Inc....G....618 345-6151
Collinsville (G-7323)
Evans Talaiha....G....618 327-8200
Nashville (G-15835)
Finks Oil Co Inc....G....618 548-5757
Salem (G-19333)
Friend Oil Co....G....618 842-9161
Fairfield (G-10142)
Herman L Loeb LLC....E....618 943-2227
Lawrenceville (G-13202)
Hocking Oil Company Inc....G....618 263-3258
Mount Carmel (G-15267)
Horizontal Systems Inc....G....217 932-6218
Casey (G-3385)
Howard Energy Corporation....G....618 263-3000
Mount Carmel (G-15268)
J R G Oil Co Inc....G....618 842-9131
Fairfield (G-10144)
J W Rudy Co Inc....F....618 676-1616
Clay City (G-7265)
Jarvis Bros & Marcell Inc....G....217 422-3120
Decatur (G-7899)
Jarvis Drilling Co....G....217 422-3120
Decatur (G-7900)
Jim Haley Oil Production Co....F....618 382-7338
Carmi (G-3070)
Lampley Oil Inc....G....618 439-6288
Benton (G-2034)
Lawrence Oil Company Inc....G....618 262-4138
Mount Carmel (G-15272)
Mitchco Farms LLC....F....618 382-5032
Carmi (G-3075)
Murvin Oil Company....E....618 393-2124
Olney (G-16784)
New Triangle Oil Company....G....618 262-4131
Mount Carmel (G-15278)
Orion Petro Corporation....G....618 244-2370
Mount Vernon (G-15436)
Pawnee Oil Corporation....F....217 522-5440
Springfield (G-20500)
Phosphate Resource Ptrs....A....847 739-1200
Lake Forest (G-12945)
Pool & Pool Oil Productions....G....618 544-7590
Robinson (G-18069)
R & W Oil Company....G....618 686-3084
Louisville (G-13909)
Republic Oil Co Inc....G....618 842-7591
Fairfield (G-10153)
Revelle Resources Inc....G....217 875-7336
Forsyth (G-10271)
Robinson Production Inc....G....618 842-6111
Fairfield (G-10154)
Ronnie Joe Graham....G....618 548-5544
Salem (G-19348)
Ross Oil Co Inc....G....618 592-3808
Oblong (G-16733)
Shulman Brothers Inc....G....618 283-3253
Vandalia (G-21124)
Smoco Inc....G....618 662-6458
Flora (G-10218)
Southern Triangle Oil Company....F....618 262-4131
Mount Carmel (G-15282)
Spartan Petroleum Company....G....618 262-4197
Mount Carmel (G-15283)
Stewart Producers Inc....G....618 244-3754
Mount Vernon (G-15446)
Team Energy LLC....G....618 943-1010
Bridgeport (G-2456)
Tipps Casing Pulling Company....G....618 847-7986
Fairfield (G-10156)
Tri Family Oil Co....G....618 654-1137
Highland (G-11813)
Tri-State Producing Developing....G....618 393-2176
Olney (G-16798)
Trojan Oil Inc....G....618 754-3474
Newton (G-15951)
Tussey G K Oil Explrtn & Prdc....G....618 948-2871
Saint Francisville (G-19314)
Two Rivers Oil & Gas Co Inc....G....217 773-3356
Mount Sterling (G-15395)
Western Oil & Gas Dev Co....F....618 544-8646
Robinson (G-18075)
White Land & Mineral Inc....G....618 262-5102
Mount Carmel (G-15288)
William R Becker....F....618 378-3337
Norris City (G-16116)
Wood Energy Inc....G....618 244-1590
Mount Vernon (G-15449)
Yockey Oil Incorporated....G....618 393-6236
Olney (G-16802)

## CRUDES: Cyclic, Organic

BP Amoco Chemical Company....B....630 420-5111
Naperville (G-15608)

## CRYSTALS

Netcom Inc....C....847 537-6300
Wheeling (G-22106)
Rubicon Technology Inc....C....847 295-7000
Bensenville (G-1983)

## CUBICLES: Electric Switchboard Eqpt

J & A Sheet Metal Shop Inc....E....773 276-3739
Chicago (G-5250)

## CULTURE MEDIA

3abn....G....618 627-4651
Thompsonville (G-20861)
Laboratory Media Corporation....F....630 897-8000
Montgomery (G-15053)

## CULVERTS: Sheet Metal

Energy Culvert Co Inc....G....618 942-7381
Energy (G-9986)
Monmouth Metal Culvert Co....G....309 734-7723
Monmouth (G-15020)

## CUPS & PLATES: Foamed Plastics

All-Vac Industries Inc....F....847 675-2290
Skokie (G-19948)
Dart Container Corp Illinois....D....630 896-4631
North Aurora (G-16126)
Dart Container Corp Illinois....C....630 896-4631
North Aurora (G-16127)
Master Containers Inc....F....863 425-5571
Lake Forest (G-12924)

## CUPS: Plastic Exc Polystyrene Foam

Lily-Canada Holding Corp....G....847 831-4800
Highland Park (G-11852)
Northwestern Cup & Logo Inc....G....773 874-8000
Chicago (G-5942)
Prairie Packaging Inc....G....708 563-8670
Bridgeview (G-2520)
SCC Holding Company LLC....A....847 444-5000
Lake Forest (G-12958)
Solo Cup Company....C....847 831-4800
Lincolnshire (G-13480)
Solo Cup Company LLC....C....847 444-5000
Lincolnshire (G-13481)
Solo Cup Investment Corp....E....847 831-4800
Highland Park (G-11872)
Solo Cup Operating Corporation....C....847 444-5000
Chicago (G-6541)

## CURBING: Granite Or Stone

Heartland Granite Inc....E....630 499-8000
Aurora (G-1025)
Insignia Stone....G....815 463-9802
New Lenox (G-15886)
Optimum Granite & Marble Inc....G....800 920-6033
South Elgin (G-20222)

## CURTAIN & DRAPERY FIXTURES: Poles, Rods & Rollers

Baker Drapery Corporation....G....309 691-3295
Peoria (G-17313)
Blind Williamson & Drapery....G....309 694-7339
East Peoria (G-8702)
Dezign Sewing Inc....G....773 549-4336
Chicago (G-4590)
Dons Drapery Service....G....815 385-4759
McHenry (G-14497)
Draperyland Inc....F....630 521-1000
Wood Dale (G-22360)
House of Atlas LLC....G....847 491-1800
Evanston (G-10054)
Image Custom Drapery....G....630 837-0107
Bartlett (G-1354)
Offsprings Inc....G....773 525-1800
Chicago (G-5969)
Olshaws Interior Services....G....312 421-3131
Chicago (G-5985)
Ottos Drapery Service Inc....G....773 777-7755
Chicago (G-6024)
Roberts Draperies Center Inc....G....847 255-4040
Mount Prospect (G-15370)
Shade Aire Company....G....815 623-7597
Roscoe (G-18921)
Unitex Industries Inc....G....708 524-0664
Oak Park (G-16690)
Zirlin Interiors Inc....E....773 334-5530
Chicago (G-7069)

## CURTAIN WALLS: Building, Steel

Delta Erectors Inc....F....708 267-9721
Villa Park (G-21248)

PRODUCT

## CURTAINS: Window, From Purchased Materials

**Cdc Group Inc**.....E..... 847 480-8830
Chicago *(G-4262)*

## CUSHIONS & PILLOWS

**Bean Products Inc**.....E..... 312 666-3600
Chicago *(G-4064)*
**Eastern Accents Inc**.....C..... 773 604-7300
Chicago *(G-4683)*
**Ileesh Products LLC**.....G..... 847 383-6695
Vernon Hills *(G-21172)*
**Pacific Coast Feather Company**.....G..... 847 827-1210
Des Plaines *(G-8248)*
**Pyar & Company LLC**.....G..... 312 451-5073
Chicago *(G-6232)*

## CUSHIONS & PILLOWS: Bed, From Purchased Materials

**Encompass Group LLC**.....E..... 847 680-3388
Mundelein *(G-15499)*
**Pillow Factory Inc**.....F..... 847 680-3388
Buffalo Grove *(G-2752)*

## CUSHIONS & PILLOWS: Hassocks, Textile, Purchased Materials

**Peterson Dermond Design LLC**.....G..... 414 383-5029
Evanston *(G-10085)*

## CUSHIONS: Carpet & Rug, Foamed Plastics

**Engineered Plastic Components**.....C..... 217 892-2026
Rantoul *(G-17927)*

## CUSTOM COMPOUNDING OF RUBBER MATERIALS

**Verona Rubber Works Inc**.....F..... 815 673-2929
Blackstone *(G-2090)*

## CUSTOMIZING SVCS

**A J R International Inc**.....D..... 800 232-3965
Glendale Heights *(G-11006)*

## CUT STONE & STONE PRODUCTS

**Acme Marble Co Inc**.....G..... 630 964-7162
Darien *(G-7786)*
**American Marble & Granite Inc**.....G..... 815 741-1710
Crest Hill *(G-7457)*
**Arnold Monument Co Inc**.....G..... 217 546-2102
Springfield *(G-20388)*
**Beutel Corporation**.....G..... 309 786-8134
Rock Island *(G-18164)*
**Cline Concrete Products**.....F..... 217 283-5012
Hoopeston *(G-12107)*
**Clugston Tibbitts Funeral Home**.....G..... 309 833-2188
Macomb *(G-14122)*
**Contemporary Marble Inc**.....G..... 618 281-6200
Columbia *(G-7357)*
**Contractors Ready-Mix Inc**.....G..... 217 482-5530
Mason City *(G-14362)*
**Country Stone Inc**.....E..... 309 787-1744
Milan *(G-14781)*
**Creative Cabinetry Inc**.....G..... 708 460-2900
Orland Park *(G-16851)*
**Creative Inds Terrazzo Pdts**.....G..... 773 235-9088
Chicago *(G-4499)*
**Custom Stone Wrks Acqstion Inc**.....G..... 630 669-1119
Cortland *(G-7386)*
**Czarnik Memorials Inc**.....G..... 708 458-4443
Justice *(G-12596)*
**Daprato Rigali Inc**.....E..... 773 763-5511
Chicago *(G-4557)*
**Dtk Construction Inc**.....G..... 312 296-2762
Wheeling *(G-22037)*
**Effingham Monument Co Inc**.....G..... 217 857-6085
Effingham *(G-8835)*
**F Lee Charles & Sons Inc**.....G..... 815 547-7141
Kirkland *(G-12712)*
**G & L Counter Tops Corporation**.....F..... 815 786-2244
Sandwich *(G-19364)*
**Gallasi Cut Stone & Marble LLC**.....E..... 708 479-9494
Mokena *(G-14866)*
**Galloy and Van Etten Inc**.....E..... 773 928-4800
Chicago *(G-4911)*
**Gast Monuments Inc**.....G..... 773 262-2400
Chicago *(G-4916)*
**GBS Liquidating Corp**.....G..... 309 342-4155
Galesburg *(G-10753)*
**Granite Works LLC**.....G..... 847 837-1688
Mundelein *(G-15503)*
**J W Reynolds Monument Co Inc**.....G..... 618 833-6014
Anna *(G-606)*
**Jacksonville Monument Co**.....G..... 217 245-2514
Jacksonville *(G-12397)*
**Lansing Cut Stone Co**.....F..... 708 474-7515
Lansing *(G-13170)*
**Lonnies Stonecrafters Inc**.....F..... 815 316-6565
Rockford *(G-18473)*
**Luxury MBL & Gran Design Inc**.....G..... 773 656-2125
Chicago *(G-5570)*
**Machine & Design**.....G..... 630 858-6416
Glen Ellyn *(G-10979)*
**Material Service Corporation**.....E..... 217 732-2117
Athens *(G-939)*
**Meier Granite Company**.....G..... 847 678-7300
Franklin Park *(G-10527)*
**Mendota Monument Co**.....G..... 815 539-7276
Mendota *(G-14725)*
**Meno Stone Co Inc**.....E..... 630 257-9220
Lemont *(G-13241)*
**Milano Direct**.....G..... 847 566-1387
Mundelein *(G-15532)*
**Moore Memorials**.....F..... 708 636-6532
Chicago Ridge *(G-7152)*
**Newton Ready Mix Inc**.....F..... 618 783-8611
Newton *(G-15944)*
**Nu-Dell Manufacturing Co Inc**.....F..... 847 803-4500
Chicago *(G-5953)*
**Pana Monument Co**.....G..... 217 562-5121
Pana *(G-17136)*
**Peter Troost Monument Co**.....G..... 773 585-0242
Chicago *(G-6109)*
**Pontiac Granite Company Inc**.....F..... 815 842-1384
Pontiac *(G-17707)*
**Regal Cut Stone LLC**.....F..... 773 826-8796
Chicago *(G-6320)*
**Spence Monuments Co**.....G..... 217 348-5992
Charleston *(G-3612)*
**St Charles Memorial Works Inc**.....G..... 630 584-0183
Saint Charles *(G-19268)*
**Stone Center Inc**.....G..... 630 971-2060
Lisle *(G-13664)*
**Stone Design Inc**.....F..... 630 790-5715
Glendale Heights *(G-11075)*
**Stone Design Inc**.....E..... 630 790-5715
Glendale Heights *(G-11076)*
**Stonecasters LLC**.....D..... 847 526-5200
Wauconda *(G-21504)*
**Superior Home Products Inc**.....G..... 217 726-9300
Springfield *(G-20540)*
**Tisch Monuments Inc**.....G..... 618 233-3017
Belleville *(G-1680)*
**Tri-State Cut Stone Co**.....E..... 815 469-7550
Frankfort *(G-10371)*
**Venetian Monument Company**.....F..... 312 829-9622
Chicago *(G-6880)*
**Weiss Monument Works Inc**.....G..... 618 398-1811
Belleville *(G-1690)*
**Wendell Adams**.....E..... 217 345-9587
Charleston *(G-3615)*
**Wilson & Wilson Monument Co**.....F..... 618 775-6488
Odin *(G-16742)*
**World Granite Inc**.....G..... 815 288-3350
Dixon *(G-8359)*
**Worldwide Tiles Ltd Inc**.....G..... 708 389-2992
Alsip *(G-545)*
**Zoia Monument Company**.....G..... 815 338-0358
Woodstock *(G-22629)*

## CUTLERY

**Alps Group Inc**.....G..... 815 469-3800
Chicago *(G-3833)*
**Anjay Traders Inc**.....G..... 847 888-8562
Elgin *(G-8954)*
**Custom Cutting Tools Inc**.....G..... 815 986-0320
Loves Park *(G-13931)*
**Estwing Manufacturing Co Inc**.....B..... 815 397-9521
Rockford *(G-18370)*
**Harris Precision Tools Inc**.....G..... 708 422-5808
Chicago Ridge *(G-7149)*
**Kernel Kutter Inc**.....G..... 815 877-1515
Machesney Park *(G-14085)*
**SCC Holding Company LLC**.....A..... 847 444-5000
Lake Forest *(G-12958)*
**Solo Cup Company**.....C..... 847 831-4800
Lincolnshire *(G-13480)*
**Solo Cup Company LLC**.....C..... 847 444-5000
Lincolnshire *(G-13481)*
**Solo Cup Investment Corp**.....E..... 847 831-4800
Highland Park *(G-11872)*
**Solo Cup Operating Corporation**.....C..... 847 444-5000
Chicago *(G-6541)*
**Superior Knife Inc**.....E..... 847 982-2280
Skokie *(G-20095)*
**W A Whitney Co**.....C..... 815 964-6771
Rockford *(G-18671)*
**Wallace/Haskin Corp**.....G..... 630 789-2882
Downers Grove *(G-8540)*
**Whitney Roper LLC**.....D..... 815 962-3011
Rockford *(G-18681)*
**Whitney Roper Rockford Inc**.....D..... 815 962-3011
Rockford *(G-18682)*
**World Kitchen LLC**.....C..... 847 233-8600
Rosemont *(G-19042)*

## CUTLERY WHOLESALERS

**Primedge Inc**.....C..... 224 265-6600
Elk Grove Village *(G-9697)*

## CUTLERY: Table, Exc Metal Handled

**Goodco Products LLC**.....G..... 630 258-6384
Countryside *(G-7428)*

## CUTOUTS: Cardboard, Die-Cut, Made From Purchased Materials

**Siebs Die Cutting Specialty Co**.....G..... 217 735-1432
Lincoln *(G-13420)*

## CUTOUTS: Distribution

**Kms Industries LLC**.....G..... 331 225-2671
Addison *(G-171)*

## CUTTING EQPT: Milling

**Rend Lake Carbide Inc**.....G..... 618 438-0160
Benton *(G-2039)*

## CUTTING SVC: Paper, Exc Die-Cut

**Olympic Bindery Inc**.....D..... 847 577-8132
Arlington Heights *(G-813)*

## CUTTING SVC: Paperboard

**Diecrafters Inc**.....E..... 708 656-3336
Cicero *(G-7190)*
**Global Abrasive Products Inc**.....E..... 630 543-9466
Addison *(G-136)*

## CYCLIC CRUDES & INTERMEDIATES

**Colors For Plastics Inc**.....G..... 847 437-0033
Elk Grove Village *(G-9381)*
**Colors For Plastics Inc**.....D..... 847 437-0033
Elk Grove Village *(G-9382)*
**Miller Purcell Co Inc**.....G..... 815 485-2142
New Lenox *(G-15897)*
**Navran Advncd Nanoprdcts Dev**.....G..... 847 331-0809
Hoffman Estates *(G-12029)*
**Polyone Corporation**.....D..... 630 972-0505
Romeoville *(G-18859)*
**Scientific Colors Inc**.....C..... 815 744-5650
Rockdale *(G-18233)*
**Stepan Company**.....B..... 815 727-4944
Elwood *(G-9982)*
**U S Colors & Coatings Inc**.....G..... 630 879-8898
Batavia *(G-1512)*

## CYCLONES: Indl, Metal Plate

**Paul D Stark & Associates**.....G..... 630 964-7111
Downers Grove *(G-8500)*

## CYLINDER & ACTUATORS: Fluid Power

**Bimba Manufacturing Company**.....E..... 708 534-7997
Manteno *(G-14181)*
**Bimba Manufacturing Company**.....E..... 708 534-8544
Frankfort *(G-10299)*
**Blac Inc**.....D..... 630 279-6400
Elmhurst *(G-9840)*
**Brake Parts Inc LLC**.....G..... 217 324-2161
Litchfield *(G-13682)*

# PRODUCT SECTION

## DAIRY PRDTS: Frozen Desserts & Novelties

Dresser Inc .................................................. D .... 847 437-5940
  Elk Grove Village *(G-9435)*
Ergo Help Inc ............................................... G .... 847 593-0722
  Arlington Heights *(G-750)*
Gpe Controls Inc .......................................... F .... 708 236-6000
  Hillside *(G-11917)*
Hadady Machining Company Inc ............... F .... 708 474-8620
  Lansing *(G-13165)*
Ken Elliott Co Inc ......................................... G .... 618 466-8200
  Godfrey *(G-11226)*
Kitagawa Usa Inc ........................................ E .... 847 310-8198
  Schaumburg *(G-19599)*
Master Hydraulics & Machining .................. F .... 847 895-5578
  Schaumburg *(G-19635)*
Mead Fluid Dynamics Inc ........................... E .... 773 685-6800
  Chicago *(G-5669)*
Mpc Products Corporation .......................... G .... 847 673-8300
  Niles *(G-16011)*
RE-Do-It Corp .............................................. G .... 708 343-7125
  Broadview *(G-2607)*
Sarco Hydraulics Inc ................................... E .... 217 324-6577
  Litchfield *(G-13697)*
T J Brooks Co .............................................. G .... 847 680-0350
  Libertyville *(G-13387)*
T Mac Cylinders Inc .................................... G .... 815 877-7090
  Roscoe *(G-18923)*
Tuxco Corporation ....................................... F .... 847 244-2220
  Gurnee *(G-11517)*
Walach Manufacturing Co Inc ..................... F .... 773 836-2060
  Chicago *(G-6935)*

### CYLINDERS: Pressure

Hoerbiger-Origa Corporation ...................... D .... 800 283-1377
  Glendale Heights *(G-11030)*
Maccarb Inc ................................................ D .... 877 427-2499
  Elgin *(G-9098)*
Midwest Hydra-Line Inc .............................. G .... 309 674-6570
  Peoria *(G-17407)*
Midwest Hydra-Line Inc .............................. F .... 309 342-6171
  Galesburg *(G-10768)*
Reino Tool & Manufacturing Co .................. F .... 773 588-5800
  Chicago *(G-6326)*
Rockford Air Devices Inc ............................ F .... 815 654-3330
  Machesney Park *(G-14104)*

### CYLINDERS: Pump

Davis Welding & Manfctg Inc ...................... F .... 217 784-5480
  Gibson City *(G-10899)*
Olive Mount Mart ........................................ G .... 773 476-4964
  Chicago *(G-5982)*
Pokorney Manufacturing Co ....................... G .... 630 458-0406
  Addison *(G-245)*
Rrp Enterprises Inc ..................................... G .... 847 455-5674
  Franklin Park *(G-10577)*
S C C Pumps Inc ........................................ G .... 847 593-8495
  Arlington Heights *(G-834)*
Trd Manufacturing Inc ................................. E .... 815 654-7775
  Machesney Park *(G-14113)*

### DAIRY EQPT

Gea Farm Technologies Inc ....................... C .... 630 548-8200
  Naperville *(G-15662)*

### DAIRY PRDTS STORE: Ice Cream, Packaged

Al Gelato Chicago LLC ............................... G .... 847 455-5355
  Franklin Park *(G-10388)*

### DAIRY PRDTS STORE: Milk

Oberweis Dairy Inc ..................................... F .... 847 368-9060
  Arlington Heights *(G-810)*
Oberweis Dairy Inc ..................................... E .... 630 906-6455
  Oswego *(G-16928)*
Oberweis Dairy Inc ..................................... E .... 708 660-1350
  Oak Park *(G-16678)*
Oberweis Dairy Inc ..................................... F .... 630 782-0141
  Elmhurst *(G-9917)*
Oberweis Dairy Inc ..................................... F .... 847 290-9222
  Rolling Meadows *(G-18755)*
Oberweis Dairy Inc ..................................... E .... 630 474-0284
  Glen Ellyn *(G-10983)*

### DAIRY PRDTS STORES

GF Parent LLC ............................................ G .... 312 255-4800
  Chicago *(G-4949)*
Wiscon Corp ................................................ E .... 708 450-0074
  Melrose Park *(G-14711)*

### DAIRY PRDTS WHOLESALERS: Fresh

Cacique USA .............................................. G .... 630 766-0059
  Wood Dale *(G-22349)*
Milk Products Holdings N Amer .................. E .... 847 928-1600
  Rosemont *(G-19016)*
Prairie Pure Cheese .................................... G .... 815 568-5000
  Marengo *(G-14240)*
Savencia Cheese USA LLC ........................ G .... 815 369-4577
  Lena *(G-13283)*

### DAIRY PRDTS: Butter

Danish Maid Butter Company ..................... F .... 773 731-8787
  Chicago *(G-4556)*
Hoogwegt US Inc ........................................ D .... 847 918-8787
  Lake Forest *(G-12905)*
Madison Farms Butter Company ................. F .... 217 854-2547
  Carlinville *(G-3045)*
Old Heritage Creamery LLC ....................... G .... 217 268-4355
  Arcola *(G-680)*
Prairie Farms Dairy Inc ............................... G .... 618 451-5600
  Granite City *(G-11299)*

### DAIRY PRDTS: Cheese

Avanti Foods Company ............................... E .... 815 379-2155
  Walnut *(G-21329)*
Berner Food & Beverage LLC .................... B .... 815 865-5136
  Rock City *(G-18124)*
Bn Delfi USA Inc ......................................... G .... 847 280-0447
  Elgin *(G-8968)*
Brewster Cheese Company ........................ F .... 815 947-3361
  Stockton *(G-20630)*
Cacique USA .............................................. G .... 630 766-0059
  Wood Dale *(G-22349)*
Charwat Food Group Ltd ............................ G .... 630 847-3473
  Hinsdale *(G-11944)*
Cheese Merchants America LLC ............... G .... 630 221-0580
  Bartlett *(G-1338)*
El Encanto Products Inc ............................. F .... 773 940-1807
  Chicago *(G-4707)*
Hoogwegt US Inc ........................................ D .... 847 918-8787
  Lake Forest *(G-12905)*
Kraft Fods Ltin Amer Holdg LLC ................ F .... 847 646-2000
  Northfield *(G-16406)*
Kraft Heinz Foods Company ...................... F .... 847 646-2000
  Northfield *(G-16407)*
Kraft Heinz Foods Company ...................... F .... 217 378-1900
  Champaign *(G-3507)*
Ludwig Dairy Products Inc ......................... G .... 847 860-8646
  Elk Grove Village *(G-9599)*
Mancuso Cheese Company ....................... F .... 815 722-2475
  Joliet *(G-12536)*
Mondelez Global LLC ................................. C .... 847 943-4000
  Deerfield *(G-8037)*
Nuestro Queso LLC .................................... G .... 815 443-2100
  Kent *(G-12666)*
Nuestro Queso LLC .................................... E .... 224 366-4320
  Rosemont *(G-19019)*
Prairie Farms Dairy Inc ............................... G .... 618 451-5600
  Granite City *(G-11299)*
Prairie Pure Cheese .................................... G .... 815 568-5000
  Marengo *(G-14240)*
Savencia Cheese USA LLC ........................ G .... 815 369-4577
  Lena *(G-13283)*
V Formusa Co ............................................. F .... 224 938-9360
  Des Plaines *(G-8296)*
Wengers Springbrook Cheese Inc .............. F .... 815 865-5855
  Davis *(G-7809)*
Wiscon Corp ................................................ E .... 708 450-0074
  Melrose Park *(G-14711)*
Wiscon Corp ................................................ E .... 708 450-0074
  Melrose Park *(G-14710)*

### DAIRY PRDTS: Cream Substitutes

Bay Valley Foods LLC ................................ D .... 815 239-2631
  Pecatonica *(G-17251)*
Treehouse Foods Inc .................................. B .... 708 483-1300
  Oak Brook *(G-16565)*

### DAIRY PRDTS: Custard, Frozen

Gregs Frozen Custard Company ................ G .... 847 837-4175
  Mundelein *(G-15504)*

### DAIRY PRDTS: Dairy Based Desserts, Frozen

Baldwin Richardson Foods Co .................... G .... 815 464-9994
  Oakbrook Terrace *(G-16698)*

### DAIRY PRDTS: Dietary Supplements, Dairy & Non-Dairy Based

Health King Enterprise Inc ......................... G .... 312 567-9978
  Chicago *(G-5059)*
Liqua Fit Inc ................................................ G .... 630 965-8067
  Grayslake *(G-11351)*
Saasoom LLC ............................................. G .... 630 561-7300
  Saint Charles *(G-19258)*
Salud Natural Entrepreneur Inc .................. E .... 224 789-7400
  Waukegan *(G-21611)*
Salud Natural Entrepreneur Inc .................. E .... 224 789-7400
  Waukegan *(G-21612)*
Vital Proteins LLC ....................................... E .... 224 544-9110
  Chicago *(G-6907)*
Vital Proteins LLC ....................................... E .... 224 544-9110
  Elk Grove Village *(G-9809)*

### DAIRY PRDTS: Dips & Spreads, Cheese Based

Berner Food & Beverage LLC .................... B .... 815 563-4222
  Dakota *(G-7694)*
Handcut Foods LLC .................................... D .... 312 239-0381
  Chicago *(G-5040)*
Saputo Cheese USA Inc ............................. D .... 847 267-1100
  Lincolnshire *(G-13476)*

### DAIRY PRDTS: Dips & Spreads, Sour Cream Based

Berner Food & Beverage LLC .................... B .... 815 563-4222
  Dakota *(G-7694)*

### DAIRY PRDTS: Dried Milk

Fonterra (usa) Inc ....................................... D .... 847 928-1600
  Rosemont *(G-19002)*

### DAIRY PRDTS: Evaporated Milk

Nestle Usa Inc ............................................ C .... 309 263-2651
  Morton *(G-15172)*
Nestle Usa Inc ............................................ C .... 217 243-9175
  Jacksonville *(G-12403)*
Nestle Usa Inc ............................................ C .... 630 773-2090
  Itasca *(G-12330)*
Nestle Usa Inc ............................................ E .... 630 505-5387
  Naperville *(G-15711)*
Nestle Usa Inc ............................................ C .... 309 829-1031
  Bloomington *(G-2206)*
Nestle Usa Inc ............................................ C .... 847 808-5300
  Buffalo Grove *(G-2748)*

### DAIRY PRDTS: Frozen Desserts & Novelties

Al Gelato Chicago LLC ............................... G .... 847 455-5355
  Franklin Park *(G-10388)*
Annies Frozen Custard ............................... E .... 618 656-0289
  Edwardsville *(G-8787)*
Baked .......................................................... G .... 773 384-7655
  Chicago *(G-4028)*
Deja Investments Inc .................................. G .... 630 408-9222
  Bolingbrook *(G-2301)*
Five Star Desserts and Foods .................... G .... 773 375-5100
  Chicago *(G-4853)*
Flamingos Icecream .................................... G .... 708 749-4287
  Berwyn *(G-2066)*
Gayety Candy Co Inc ................................. G .... 708 418-0062
  Lansing *(G-13163)*
Gelato Enterprises LLC .............................. F .... 847 432-2233
  Highland Park *(G-11835)*
Gelato Enterprises LLC .............................. F .... 630 210-8457
  Naperville *(G-15663)*
Hershey Creamery Company ..................... F .... 708 339-4656
  South Holland *(G-20276)*
Huddlestun Creamery Inc ........................... F .... 815 609-1893
  Joliet *(G-12512)*
Icream Group LLC ...................................... G .... 773 342-2834
  Chicago *(G-5137)*
Instantwhip-Chicago Inc ............................. F .... 773 235-5588
  Chicago *(G-5206)*
Joint Asia Dev Group LLC .......................... E .... 847 223-1804
  Grayslake *(G-11349)*
Kent Precision Foods Group Inc ................ E .... 630 226-0071
  Bolingbrook *(G-2331)*
Lezza Spumoni and Desserts Inc ............... E .... 708 547-5969
  Bellwood *(G-1712)*
Lorenzos Delectable LLC ........................... G .... 773 791-3327
  Chicago *(G-5542)*
Los Mangos ................................................ G .... 773 542-1522
  Chicago *(G-5544)*

## DAIRY PRDTS: Frozen Desserts & Novelties

ME and Gia Inc .................................... G ...... 708 583-1111
　Elmwood Park *(G-9972)*
Mitchlls Cndies Ice Creams Inc ........... F ...... 708 799-3835
　Homewood *(G-12104)*
Paleteria El Sabor ................................ G ...... 312 243-2308
　Chicago *(G-6061)*
Prairie Farms Dairy Inc ..................... G ...... 618 451-5600
　Granite City *(G-11299)*
Prairie Farms Dairy Inc ..................... E ...... 618 632-3632
　O Fallon *(G-16476)*
Prairie Farms Dairy Inc ..................... D ...... 217 423-3459
　Decatur *(G-7929)*
Red Mango Rockford .......................... G ...... 815 282-1020
　Rockford *(G-18551)*
Suzys Swirl LLC ................................ G ...... 847 855-9987
　Gurnee *(G-11510)*
Sweet Pops By Cindy ......................... G ...... 630 294-0640
　Wheaton *(G-21982)*
Union Foods Inc ................................ G ...... 201 327-2828
　Chicago *(G-6814)*
Viola Ice Cream Shoppe ..................... G ...... 309 596-2131
　Viola *(G-21295)*
We Love Soy Inc ................................ G ...... 630 629-9667
　Lombard *(G-13881)*

### DAIRY PRDTS: Ice Cream & Ice Milk

Cold Stone Creamery 488 ................... G
　South Elgin *(G-20190)*
Muller-Pinehurst Dairy Inc ................ C ...... 815 968-0441
　Rockford *(G-18512)*
Panchos Ice Cream ............................. G ...... 773 254-3141
　Chicago *(G-6067)*
Roesers Bakery ................................... E ...... 773 489-6900
　Chicago *(G-6379)*

### DAIRY PRDTS: Ice Cream, Bulk

Gyood .................................................. G ...... 773 360-8810
　Chicago *(G-5014)*
Homers Ice Cream Inc ....................... E ...... 847 251-0477
　Wilmette *(G-22254)*
La Nueva Michoacana ........................ G ...... 815 722-3720
　Joliet *(G-12531)*
Neveria Michoacana LLC ................... G ...... 630 783-3518
　Bolingbrook *(G-2351)*
Paleteria Azteca Inc .......................... G ...... 773 277-1423
　Chicago *(G-6060)*
Paleteria El Sabor De Michoacn ......... G ...... 773 376-3880
　Chicago *(G-6062)*
Smooches Ice Cream ......................... G ...... 708 370-0282
　Chicago *(G-6537)*

### DAIRY PRDTS: Ice Cream, Packaged, Molded, On Sticks, Etc.

Conopco Inc ...................................... G ...... 847 520-8002
　Buffalo Grove *(G-2677)*
Sisler Dairy Products Company ......... G ...... 815 376-2913
　Ohio *(G-16753)*

### DAIRY PRDTS: Imitation Cheese

We Love Soy Inc ................................ G ...... 630 629-9667
　Lombard *(G-13881)*

### DAIRY PRDTS: Milk & Cream, Cultured & Flavored

Muller-Pinehurst Dairy Inc ................ C ...... 815 968-0441
　Rockford *(G-18512)*
Socius Ingredients LLC ..................... F ...... 847 440-0156
　Evanston *(G-10094)*

### DAIRY PRDTS: Milk Preparations, Dried

Erie Group International Inc .............. D ...... 309 659-2233
　Rochelle *(G-18088)*

### DAIRY PRDTS: Milk, Condensed & Evaporated

Abbott Laboratories ........................... A ...... 847 938-8717
　North Chicago *(G-16163)*
Corefx Ingredients LLC ..................... G ...... 773 271-2663
　Chicago *(G-4468)*
Corefx Ingredients LLC ..................... F ...... 773 271-2663
　Orangeville *(G-16814)*
Emsur USA LLC ................................ E ...... 847 274-9450
　Elk Grove Village *(G-9456)*
Lifeway Foods Inc ............................. B ...... 847 967-1010
　Morton Grove *(G-15213)*

Milk Products Holdings N Amer ......... E ...... 847 928-1600
　Rosemont *(G-19016)*
MSI Green Inc .................................... G ...... 312 421-6550
　Chicago *(G-5826)*
Rich Products Corporation ................ D ...... 847 581-1749
　Niles *(G-16027)*
Rich Products Corporation ................ C ...... 847 459-5400
　Wheeling *(G-22140)*

### DAIRY PRDTS: Milk, Fluid

Bay Valley Foods LLC ....................... ......... 815 239-2631
　Pecatonica *(G-17251)*
Berner Food & Beverage LLC .......... E ...... 815 865-5136
　Rock City *(G-18124)*
Chester Dairy Company Inc ............. F ...... 618 826-2394
　Chester *(G-3653)*
Chester Dairy Company Inc ............. G ...... 618 826-2395
　Chester *(G-3654)*
Dean Foods Company ....................... D
　Rockford *(G-18338)*
Dean Foods Company ....................... D ...... 217 428-6726
　Decatur *(G-7867)*
Deja Investments Inc ........................ G ...... 630 408-9222
　Bolingbrook *(G-2301)*
Douglas Graybill ................................ G ...... 815 218-1749
　Freeport *(G-10653)*
Erie Group International Inc .............. D ...... 309 659-2233
　Rochelle *(G-18088)*
Kilgus Farmstead Inc ........................ G ...... 815 692-6080
　Fairbury *(G-10129)*
Kraft Heinz Foods Company ............. D ...... 217 378-1900
　Champaign *(G-3507)*
Lifeway Foods Inc ............................. B ...... 847 967-1010
　Morton Grove *(G-15213)*
Midwest Ice Cream Company LLC ... G ...... 630 879-0800
　Batavia *(G-1470)*
Midwest Ice Cream Company LLC ... F ...... 815 544-2105
　Belvidere *(G-1772)*
Pet OFallon LLC ................................ D ...... 618 628-3300
　O Fallon *(G-16473)*
Prairie Farms Dairy Inc ..................... F ...... 217 245-4413
　Jacksonville *(G-12408)*
Prairie Farms Dairy Inc ..................... G ...... 618 451-5600
　Granite City *(G-11299)*
Rich Products Corporation ................ D ...... 847 581-1749
　Niles *(G-16027)*

### DAIRY PRDTS: Milk, Processed, Pasteurized, Homogenized/Btld

Dean Foods Company ....................... C ...... 847 669-5123
　Huntley *(G-12137)*
Dean Foods Company ....................... C ...... 815 943-7375
　Harvard *(G-11630)*
East Side Jersey Dairy Inc ............... E ...... 217 854-2547
　Carlinville *(G-3036)*
Oberweis Dairy Inc ........................... F ...... 847 368-9060
　Arlington Heights *(G-810)*
Oberweis Dairy Inc ........................... E ...... 630 906-6455
　Oswego *(G-16928)*
Oberweis Dairy Inc ........................... E ...... 708 660-1350
　Oak Park *(G-16678)*
Oberweis Dairy Inc ........................... F ...... 630 782-0141
　Elmhurst *(G-9917)*
Oberweis Dairy Inc ........................... F ...... 847 290-9222
　Rolling Meadows *(G-18755)*
Oberweis Dairy Inc ........................... E ...... 630 474-0284
　Glen Ellyn *(G-10983)*
Prairie Farms Dairy Inc ..................... E ...... 217 223-5530
　Quincy *(G-17869)*
Prairie Farms Dairy Inc ..................... D ...... 618 393-2128
　Olney *(G-16791)*
Prairie Farms Dairy Inc ..................... E ...... 217 854-2547
　Carlinville *(G-3047)*
Prairie Farms Dairy Inc ..................... E ...... 618 632-3632
　O Fallon *(G-16476)*
Prairie Farms Dairy Inc ..................... E ...... 618 457-4167
　Carbondale *(G-3018)*
Prairie Farms Dairy Inc ..................... C ...... 309 686-2400
　Peoria *(G-17434)*
Prairie Farms Dairy Inc ..................... D ...... 217 423-3459
　Decatur *(G-7929)*

### DAIRY PRDTS: Natural Cheese

Bel Brands Usa Inc ........................... E ...... 312 462-1500
　Chicago *(G-4072)*
Carl Buddig and Company ................. E ...... 708 798-0900
　Homewood *(G-12093)*
Churny Company Inc ........................ B ...... 847 646-5500
　Chicago *(G-4375)*

Conagra Dairy Foods Company ........ B ...... 630 848-0975
　Chicago *(G-4445)*
GF Parent LLC .................................. ......... 312 255-4800
　Chicago *(G-4949)*
Kolb-Lena Inc ................................... D ...... 815 369-4577
　Lena *(G-13275)*
Kraft Heinz Company ........................ C ...... 847 646-2000
　Glenview *(G-11160)*
Marcoot Jersey Creamery LLC .......... F ...... 618 664-1110
　Greenville *(G-11398)*
Saputo Cheese USA Inc .................... C ...... 847 267-1100
　Lincolnshire *(G-13475)*
Topz Dairy Products Co .................... F ...... 815 726-5700
　Joliet *(G-12583)*
Two Tribes LLC ................................. G ...... 847 272-7711
　Glenview *(G-11211)*
V & V Supremo Foods Inc ................. C ...... 312 733-5652
　Chicago *(G-6864)*

### DAIRY PRDTS: Powdered Buttermilk

Hoogwegt US Inc .............................. D ...... 847 918-8787
　Lake Forest *(G-12905)*

### DAIRY PRDTS: Powdered Milk

Kelly Flour Company ......................... G ...... 312 933-3104
　Chicago *(G-5373)*

### DAIRY PRDTS: Processed Cheese

G&G Kraft Build ................................ G ...... 773 744-6522
　Wood Dale *(G-22375)*
Karens Krafts .................................... ......... 217 466-8100
　Paris *(G-17151)*
Kraft Foods Asia PCF Svcs LLC ....... G ...... 847 943-4000
　Deerfield *(G-8026)*
Kraft Heinz Foods Company ............. C ...... 847 646-3690
　Glenview *(G-11161)*
Kraft Services ................................... G ...... 309 662-6178
　Bloomington *(G-2191)*
La Hispamex Food Products Inc ....... G ...... 708 780-1808
　Cicero *(G-7213)*
Mondelez International Inc ............... A ...... 847 943-4000
　Deerfield *(G-8038)*
Sheri Lyn Kraft ................................. G ...... 847 724-4718
　Glenview *(G-11196)*

### DAIRY PRDTS: Whey, Powdered

Armada Nutrition LLC ....................... G ...... 931 451-7808
　Carol Stream *(G-3105)*

### DAIRY PRDTS: Whipped Topping, Exc Frozen Or Dry Mix

Instantwhip-Chicago Inc ................... F ...... 773 235-5588
　Chicago *(G-5206)*

### DAIRY PRDTS: Yogurt Mix

Muller Quaker Dairy LLC ................... C ...... 312 821-1000
　Chicago *(G-5830)*

### DAIRY PRDTS: Yogurt, Exc Frozen

Lulus Real Froyo ............................... G ...... 630 299-3854
　Aurora *(G-1049)*
Starfruit LLC ..................................... ......... 312 527-3674
　Chicago *(G-6576)*

### DAIRY PRDTS: Yogurt, Frozen

Amani Froyo LLC .............................. G ...... 941 744-1111
　Oakbrook Terrace *(G-16695)*

## DATA ENTRY SVCS

Information Resources Inc ................ B ...... 312 474-3154
　Bartlett *(G-1318)*

## DATA PROCESSING & PREPARATION SVCS

Imaging Systems Inc ........................ F ...... 630 875-1100
　Itasca *(G-12283)*
Innerworkings Inc ............................. D ...... 312 642-3700
　Chicago *(G-5198)*
Microdynamics Corporation ............... C ...... 630 276-0527
　Naperville *(G-15697)*
Reprographics ................................... G ...... 815 477-1018
　Crystal Lake *(G-7638)*
Sebis Direct Inc ................................ E ...... 312 243-9300
　Bedford Park *(G-1584)*

Tempus Health Inc ....E .... 312 784-4400
Chicago *(G-6699)*
Vertex Consulting Services Inc ....F .... 313 492-5154
Schaumburg *(G-19786)*

## DATA PROCESSING SVCS

Accuity Inc ....B .... 847 676-9600
Evanston *(G-10003)*
Negs & Litho Inc ....G .... 847 647-7770
Chicago *(G-5881)*
Overt Press Inc ....E .... 773 284-0909
Chicago *(G-6029)*
Pactiv LLC ....C ....
Lincolnshire *(G-13469)*
Tri-Cor Industries Inc ....D .... 618 589-9890
O Fallon *(G-16481)*

## DECORATIVE WOOD & WOODWORK

Aba Custom Woodworking ....G .... 815 356-9663
Crystal Lake *(G-7525)*
Adel Woodworks ....G .... 815 886-9006
Romeoville *(G-18790)*
All American Wood Register Co ....F .... 815 356-1000
Crystal Lake *(G-7528)*
Archi-Cepts ....G .... 618 594-8810
Carlyle *(G-3052)*
Brown Woodworking ....G .... 815 477-8333
Crystal Lake *(G-7544)*
Caldwell Woodworks ....G .... 217 566-2434
Williamsville *(G-22190)*
Curtis Woodworking Inc ....G .... 815 544-3543
Belvidere *(G-1748)*
Delleman Associates & Corp ....G .... 708 345-9520
Maywood *(G-14425)*
Dusty Lane Wood Products ....G .... 618 426-9045
Campbell Hill *(G-2975)*
Forest Awards & Engraving ....G .... 630 595-2242
Wood Dale *(G-22371)*
Herschberger Wood Working ....G .... 217 543-4075
Arthur *(G-905)*
Hexacomb Corporation ....G .... 847 955-7984
Buffalo Grove *(G-2704)*
Jack Ruch Quality Homes Inc ....G .... 309 663-6595
Bloomington *(G-2185)*
Jacobs Reproduction ....G .... 618 374-2198
Elsah *(G-9976)*
Joseph Woodworking Corporation ....F .... 847 233-9766
Schiller Park *(G-19841)*
Kaufman Woodworking ....G .... 217 543-3607
Arthur *(G-906)*
Kaufmans Custom Cabinets ....F .... 217 268-4330
Arcola *(G-673)*
Kohout Woodwork Inc ....G .... 630 628-6257
Addison *(G-172)*
Little Creek Woodworking ....G .... 217 543-2815
Arthur *(G-908)*
Macks Wood Working ....G .... 630 953-2559
Lombard *(G-13823)*
Orren Pickell Builders Inc ....F .... 847 572-5200
Northfield *(G-16415)*
Powers Woodworking ....G .... 630 663-9644
Woodridge *(G-22509)*
Premium Wood Products Inc ....E .... 815 787-3669
Dekalb *(G-8113)*
R Maderite Inc ....G .... 773 235-1515
Chicago *(G-6268)*
R S Bacon Veneer Company ....C .... 630 323-1414
Lisle *(G-13648)*
Roselle Custom Woodwork LLC ....G .... 630 980-5655
Roselle *(G-18969)*
Silver Line ....G .... 708 832-9100
Calumet City *(G-2954)*
Stancy Woodworking Co Inc ....F .... 847 526-0252
Island Lake *(G-12219)*
Star Cabinetry ....G .... 773 725-4651
Chicago *(G-6575)*
Tender Loving Care Inds Inc ....D .... 847 891-0230
Schaumburg *(G-19759)*
Tepromark International Inc ....G .... 847 329-7881
Chicago *(G-6703)*
Todd Scanlan ....G .... 217 585-1717
Springfield *(G-20545)*
Vas Design Inc ....G .... 773 794-1368
Chicago *(G-6876)*
Woodlogic Custom Millwork Inc ....E .... 847 640-4500
Elk Grove Village *(G-9815)*
Woodwind Specialists ....G .... 217 423-4122
Decatur *(G-7960)*

## DEFENSE SYSTEMS & EQPT

Bizstarterscom LLC ....G .... 847 305-4626
Arlington Heights *(G-725)*
Ctg Advanced Materials LLC ....E .... 630 226-9080
Bolingbrook *(G-2292)*
Lg Innotek USA Inc ....G .... 847 941-8713
Lincolnshire *(G-13462)*
Navistar Defense LLC ....E .... 331 332-3500
Lisle *(G-13632)*
Raytheon Company ....B .... 630 295-6394
Rolling Meadows *(G-18773)*

## DEGREASING MACHINES

Graymills Corporation ....D .... 773 477-4100
Broadview *(G-2582)*
Therma-Kleen Inc ....G .... 630 718-0212
Plainfield *(G-17657)*

## DEHYDRATION EQPT

Davenport Dryer L L C ....G .... 309 786-1500
Moline *(G-14923)*
Kitchy Koo Gourmet Co ....G .... 708 499-5236
Oak Lawn *(G-16629)*

## DELIVERY SVCS, BY VEHICLE

Lexpress Inc ....G .... 773 517-7095
Prospect Heights *(G-17783)*
Tolar Group LLC ....E .... 847 668-9485
Oak Park *(G-16689)*

## DEMONSTRATION SVCS

Modern Printing Colors Inc ....F .... 708 681-5678
Broadview *(G-2597)*

## DENTAL EQPT

Allstar Dental Inc ....G .... 847 325-5134
Vernon Hills *(G-21145)*
Goldman Products Inc ....E .... 847 526-1166
Wauconda *(G-21465)*
Lemoy International Inc ....G .... 847 427-0840
Elk Grove Village *(G-9594)*
Nordent Manufacturing Inc ....E .... 847 437-4780
Elk Grove Village *(G-9653)*

## DENTAL EQPT & SPLYS

Acquamed Technologies Inc ....G .... 630 728-4014
Oswego *(G-16901)*
Apex Dental Materials Inc ....G .... 847 719-1133
Lake Zurich *(G-13042)*
Artistic Dental Studio Inc ....E .... 630 679-8686
Bolingbrook *(G-2278)*
Bennett Technologies Inc ....F .... 708 389-9501
Tinley Park *(G-20897)*
Ched Markay Inc ....G .... 847 566-3307
Mundelein *(G-15486)*
Coralite Dental Products Inc ....G .... 847 679-3400
Skokie *(G-19986)*
Denbur Inc ....G .... 630 986-9667
Westmont *(G-21882)*
Dental Arts Laboratories Inc ....G .... 309 342-3117
Galesburg *(G-10745)*
Dental Crafts Lab Inc ....G .... 815 872-3221
Princeton *(G-17746)*
Dental Laboratory Inc ....E .... 630 262-3700
Geneva *(G-10823)*
Dental Technologies Inc ....D .... 847 677-5500
Lincolnwood *(G-13507)*
Dental USA Inc ....F .... 815 363-8003
McHenry *(G-14495)*
Dentalez Alabama Inc ....C .... 773 624-4330
Chicago *(G-4583)*
Dentsply Sirona Inc ....C .... 847 640-4800
Des Plaines *(G-8183)*
Dove Dental Studio ....G .... 847 679-2434
Niles *(G-15975)*
Duquoin Dental Associates ....G .... 618 542-8832
Du Quoin *(G-8553)*
Fred Pigg Dental Lab ....G .... 618 439-6829
Benton *(G-2028)*
Fricke Dental Manufacturing Co ....G .... 630 540-1900
Streamwood *(G-20657)*
Fricke International Inc ....F .... 630 833-2627
Villa Park *(G-21253)*
Gc America Inc ....C .... 708 597-0900
Alsip *(G-463)*
Gc Manufacturing America LLC ....D .... 708 597-0900
Alsip *(G-464)*
Harry J Bosworth Company ....E .... 847 679-3400
Evanston *(G-10050)*
Healthdentl LLC ....G .... 800 845-5172
Plainfield *(G-17605)*
Holland Specialty Co ....E .... 309 697-9262
Peoria *(G-17383)*
J L Lawrence & Co ....G .... 217 235-3622
Mattoon *(G-14394)*
Lang Dental Mfg Co Inc ....F .... 847 215-6622
Wheeling *(G-22089)*
Lmpl Management Corporation ....G .... 708 636-2443
Oak Lawn *(G-16631)*
Mandis Dental Laboratory ....G .... 618 345-3777
Collinsville *(G-7334)*
Northwest Dental Prosthetics ....G .... 773 505-9191
Chicago *(G-5938)*
Odl Inc ....D .... 815 434-0655
Ottawa *(G-16974)*
Oratech Inc ....E .... 217 793-2735
Springfield *(G-20493)*
Sunstar Americas Inc ....B .... 773 777-4000
Schaumburg *(G-19744)*
Tanaka Dental Enterprises Inc ....F .... 847 679-1610
Skokie *(G-20099)*
Underwood Dental Laboratories ....F .... 217 398-0090
Champaign *(G-3551)*
Young Innovations Inc ....D .... 847 458-5400
Algonquin *(G-415)*
Young Innovations Inc ....D .... 847 458-5400
Algonquin *(G-416)*
Young Innovations Holdings LLC ....G .... 312 506-5600
Chicago *(G-7054)*
Young Os LLC ....E .... 847 458-5400
Algonquin *(G-417)*

## DENTAL EQPT & SPLYS WHOLESALERS

Lemoy International Inc ....G .... 847 427-0840
Elk Grove Village *(G-9594)*
Omar Medical Supplies Inc ....E .... 708 922-4377
Chicago *(G-5988)*

## DENTAL EQPT & SPLYS: Dental Hand Instruments, NEC

Cislak Manufacturing Inc ....E .... 847 647-1819
Niles *(G-15969)*
Hu-Friedy Mfg Co LLC ....B .... 773 975-3975
Chicago *(G-5126)*
M & N Dental ....G .... 815 678-0036
Richmond *(G-17966)*

## DENTAL EQPT & SPLYS: Dental Materials

American Dental Products Inc ....E .... 630 238-0275
Bensenville *(G-1832)*
Bisco Inc ....D .... 847 534-6000
Schaumburg *(G-19464)*
Reliance Dental Mfg Co ....G .... 708 597-6694
Alsip *(G-518)*

## DENTAL EQPT & SPLYS: Denture Materials

Astron Dental Corporation ....F .... 847 726-8787
Lake Zurich *(G-13044)*
Prime Dental Manufacturing ....E .... 773 283-2914
Chicago *(G-6185)*

## DENTAL EQPT & SPLYS: Enamels

Anthony Collins ....G .... 847 566-5350
Mundelein *(G-15470)*
Brite Dental PC ....E .... 773 735-8353
Chicago *(G-4170)*
James Street Dental P C ....G .... 630 232-9535
Geneva *(G-10841)*
Landman Dental ....G .... 312 266-6480
Chicago *(G-5456)*
Naper Dental ....G .... 630 369-6818
Naperville *(G-15709)*
North Halsted Dental Spa ....G .... 773 296-0325
Chicago *(G-5934)*
Perfect Smiles ....G .... 708 687-6100
Oak Forest *(G-16587)*
Smile Lee Faces ....G .... 773 376-9999
Chicago *(G-6534)*
Smile of Brookfield ....G .... 708 485-7754
Brookfield *(G-2642)*

# DENTAL EQPT & SPLYS: Gold

### DENTAL EQPT & SPLYS: Gold
Harris and Discount Supplies............................G....... 847 726-3800
  Lake Zurich *(G-13082)*

### DENTAL EQPT & SPLYS: Laboratory
Strictly Dentures..............................................G....... 815 969-0531
  Rockford *(G-18635)*

### DENTAL EQPT & SPLYS: Orthodontic Appliances
Prairie Orthodontics PC ................................F....... 847 249-8800
  Gurnee *(G-11489)*
Spiraltech Superior Dental Imp ....................F....... 312 440-7777
  Chicago *(G-6561)*

### DENTAL EQPT & SPLYS: Sterilizers
Integrated Medical Tech Inc .........................G....... 309 662-3614
  Bloomington *(G-2183)*

### DENTAL EQPT & SPLYS: Teeth, Artificial, Exc In Dental Labs
Martin Dental Laboratory Inc ........................F....... 708 597-8880
  Lockport *(G-13731)*
Myerson LLC ...................................................G....... 312 432-8200
  Chicago *(G-5844)*

### DENTAL INSTRUMENT REPAIR SVCS
Nordent Manufacturing Inc ............................E....... 847 437-4780
  Elk Grove Village *(G-9653)*

### DENTISTS' OFFICES & CLINICS
Bisco Inc ...........................................................D....... 847 534-6000
  Schaumburg *(G-19464)*
Dove Dental Studio .........................................G....... 847 679-2434
  Niles *(G-15975)*
Fricke Dental Manufacturing Co ..................G....... 630 540-1900
  Streamwood *(G-20657)*
Harry J Bosworth Company ..........................E....... 847 679-3400
  Evanston *(G-10050)*

### DENTURE CLEANERS
Holland Specialty Co .....................................E....... 309 697-9262
  Peoria *(G-17383)*

### DEPARTMENT STORES
Angelo Bruni ....................................................G....... 773 754-5422
  Aurora *(G-957)*

### DEPARTMENT STORES: Country General
Reasons Inc .....................................................G....... 309 537-3424
  Buffalo Prairie *(G-2797)*

### DEPILATORIES, COSMETIC
Bioelements Inc ..............................................F....... 773 525-3509
  Chicago *(G-4109)*

### DERMATOLOGICALS
Therapeutic Skin Care ...................................G....... 630 244-1833
  Lombard *(G-13868)*

### DERRICKS: Oil & Gas Field
Country Side Woodworking ..........................F....... 217 543-4190
  Arthur *(G-890)*

### DESIGN SVCS, NEC
4ever Printing Inc ...........................................G....... 847 222-1525
  Arlington Heights *(G-699)*
Amazing Cabinets & Design Corp ...............G....... 773 405-0174
  Elk Grove Village *(G-9292)*
Cabinet Broker Ltd .........................................G....... 847 352-1898
  Elk Grove Village *(G-9354)*
Concepts Magnet ............................................G....... 847 253-3351
  Mount Prospect *(G-15318)*
D5 Design Met Fabrication LLC ...................G....... 773 770-4705
  Chicago *(G-4539)*
Fordoc Incorporated .......................................G....... 708 452-8400
  River Grove *(G-18009)*
Group 329 LLC ................................................G....... 312 828-0200
  Chicago *(G-5005)*
Heat Seal Tooling Corporation .....................G....... 815 626-6009
  Rock Falls *(G-18134)*

Kohler Co ..........................................................E....... 847 635-8071
  Glenview *(G-11156)*
Legacy 3d LLC ................................................F....... 815 727-5454
  Crest Hill *(G-7462)*
M & G Simplicitees ........................................G....... 224 372-7426
  Lake Villa *(G-13018)*
Manufcture Dsign Innvation Inc ..................... 773 526-7773
  West Chicago *(G-21736)*
Met-L-Flo Inc ...................................................F....... 630 409-9860
  Sugar Grove *(G-20729)*
Randal Wood Displays Inc ............................D....... 630 761-0400
  Batavia *(G-1490)*
Rutherford & Associates ................................ 630 365-5263
  Saint Charles *(G-19257)*
Sadannah Group LLC ...................................G....... 630 357-2300
  Naperville *(G-15745)*
Signtastic Inc ...................................................G....... 708 598-4749
  Palos Hills *(G-17125)*
Spectrum Cos International .........................G....... 630 879-8008
  Batavia *(G-1497)*
Sunrise Hitek Service Inc .............................E....... 773 792-8880
  Chicago *(G-6630)*
Swath International Limited .......................... 815 654-4800
  Rockford *(G-18638)*
Taico Design Products Inc ............................ 773 871-9086
  Chicago *(G-6665)*
Tecnova Electronics Inc ................................D....... 847 336-6160
  Waukegan *(G-21623)*
Telcom Innovations Group LLC ...................E....... 630 350-0700
  Itasca *(G-12366)*
Tgrv LLC ...........................................................G....... 815 634-2102
  Bourbonnais *(G-2407)*
Tlk Industries Inc ............................................D....... 847 359-3200
  East Dundee *(G-8659)*
Wesdar Technologies Inc .............................. 630 761-0965
  Aurora *(G-1096)*

### DESIGN SVCS: Commercial & Indl
Active Automation Inc ....................................F....... 847 427-8100
  Elk Grove Village *(G-9268)*
Corporation Supply Co Inc ............................E....... 312 726-3375
  Chicago *(G-4476)*
Device Technologies Inc ............................... 630 553-7178
  Yorkville *(G-22655)*
E Gornell & Sons Inc .....................................E....... 773 489-2330
  Chicago *(G-4665)*
Gil Instruments Co .......................................... 815 459-8764
  Crystal Lake *(G-7583)*
M & R Printing Inc ..........................................G....... 847 398-2500
  Rolling Meadows *(G-18742)*
Pmb Industries Inc ..........................................G....... 708 442-4515
  La Grange *(G-12742)*
Scientific Instruments Inc .............................. 847 679-1242
  Skokie *(G-20082)*
Universal Feeder Inc .....................................G....... 815 633-0752
  Machesney Park *(G-14116)*
William Frick & Company .............................E....... 847 918-3700
  Libertyville *(G-13401)*

### DESIGN SVCS: Computer Integrated Systems
Agile Health Technologies Inc .....................E....... 630 247-5565
  Naperville *(G-15789)*
Applus Technologies Inc .............................E....... 312 661-1604
  Chicago *(G-3927)*
Cleo Communications Inc ............................G....... 815 654-8110
  Rockford *(G-18312)*
Controllink Incorporated ................................E....... 847 622-1100
  Elgin *(G-9002)*
Dimension Data North Amer Inc .................F....... 847 278-6413
  Schaumburg *(G-19505)*
GE Intelligent Platforms Inc ........................G....... 630 829-4000
  Lisle *(G-13593)*
Infinite Cnvrgnce Slutions Inc ..................... 224 764-3400
  Arlington Heights *(G-777)*
Isewa LLC ........................................................F....... 847 877-1586
  Buffalo Grove *(G-2711)*
Koi Computers Inc .........................................G....... 630 627-8811
  Lombard *(G-13817)*
M13 Inc ..............................................................E....... 847 310-1913
  Schaumburg *(G-19629)*
Matrix Circuits Inc .......................................... 319 367-5000
  Lake Villa *(G-13020)*
Merge Healthcare Incorporated ...................C....... 312 565-6868
  Chicago *(G-5690)*
Mu Dai LLC ......................................................F....... 312 982-0040
  Chicago *(G-5828)*
National School Services Inc ......................E....... 847 438-3859
  Long Grove *(G-13899)*

Palm International Inc ...................................G....... 630 357-1437
  Naperville *(G-15721)*
Pervasive Health Inc ......................................G....... 312 257-2967
  Chicago *(G-6107)*
Phillip Grigalanz ..............................................G....... 219 628-6706
  Jerseyville *(G-12425)*
Pinehurst Bus Solutions Corp .....................G....... 630 842-6155
  Winfield *(G-22290)*
Quadramed Corporation ................................E....... 312 396-0700
  Chicago *(G-6240)*
Richardson Electronics Ltd .........................C....... 630 208-2200
  Lafox *(G-12796)*
Smartsignal Corporation ...............................D....... 630 829-4000
  Lisle *(G-13658)*
Vertex Consulting Services Inc ...................F....... 313 492-5154
  Schaumburg *(G-19786)*

### DESIGN SVCS: Hand Tools
T N T Industries Inc .......................................F....... 630 879-1522
  Batavia *(G-1503)*

### DESIGNS SVCS: Scenery, Theatrical
Guess Whackit & Hope Inc ...........................G....... 773 342-4273
  Chicago *(G-5010)*
Ivan Carlson Associates Inc ........................E....... 312 829-4616
  Chicago *(G-5248)*

### DETECTION APPARATUS: Electronic/Magnetic Field, Light/Heat
Checkpoint Systems Inc ...............................D....... 630 771-4240
  Romeoville *(G-18809)*
Ecolotech Asl Inc ............................................G....... 630 859-0485
  Aurora *(G-1142)*
Graceland Custom Products Inc .................F....... 630 616-4143
  Bensenville *(G-1912)*
Intex Systems Corp ........................................G....... 630 636-6594
  Oswego *(G-16922)*
Smart Pixel Inc ................................................G....... 630 771-0206
  Bolingbrook *(G-2371)*

### DETECTION EQPT: Magnetic Field
Metrasens Inc .................................................E....... 603 541-6509
  Lisle *(G-13622)*

### DETECTIVE SVCS
National Def Intelligence Inc .......................G....... 630 757-4007
  Naperville *(G-15818)*

### DETECTORS: Water Leak
CAM Co Inc ......................................................F....... 630 556-3110
  Big Rock *(G-2086)*

### DIAGNOSTIC SUBSTANCES
3primedx Inc ....................................................G....... 312 621-0643
  Chicago *(G-3668)*
Abbott Laboratories .......................................F....... 847 937-6100
  Abbott Park *(G-2)*
Abbott Laboratories .......................................G....... 224 361-7129
  Elk Grove Village *(G-9254)*
Abbott Laboratories .......................................A....... 224 667-6100
  Abbott Park *(G-1)*
Abbott Laboratories .......................................A....... 847 938-8717
  North Chicago *(G-16163)*
Abbott Laboratories ........................................ 847 937-6100
  North Chicago *(G-16164)*
Abbott Molecular Inc ......................................G....... 224 361-7800
  Des Plaines *(G-8141)*
Abbott Molecular Inc ......................................D....... 224 361-7800
  Des Plaines *(G-8142)*
Amoco Technology Company (del) ............C....... 312 861-6000
  Chicago *(G-3892)*
Bion Enterprises Ltd ......................................E....... 847 544-5044
  Des Plaines *(G-8159)*
Cairo Diagnostic Center ................................F....... 618 734-1500
  Cairo *(G-2927)*
Chemprobe Inc ................................................G....... 847 231-4534
  Grayslake *(G-11326)*
Cooper Equipment Company Inc ................G....... 708 367-1291
  Crete *(G-7511)*
GE Healthcare Holdings Inc ........................A....... 847 398-8400
  Arlington Heights *(G-759)*
Innovative Molecular Diagnosti ...................G....... 630 845-8246
  Geneva *(G-10838)*
Nuclin Diagnostics Inc ...................................G....... 847 498-5210
  Northbrook *(G-16320)*

# PRODUCT SECTION — DIES & TOOLS: Special

Ohmx Corporation .................................. F ...... 847 491-8500
  Evanston *(G-10081)*
Open Advanced Mri Crystl .................... G ...... 815 444-1330
  Crystal Lake *(G-7623)*
Pyramid Sciences Inc ........................... G ...... 630 974-6110
  Burr Ridge *(G-2876)*
Regis Technologies Inc ......................... D ...... 847 967-6000
  Morton Grove *(G-15232)*

## DIAGNOSTIC SUBSTANCES OR AGENTS: Blood Derivative

Baxalta Export Corporation .................... G ...... 224 948-2000
  Deerfield *(G-7981)*
Baxalta US Inc ...................................... F ...... 312 648-2244
  Chicago *(G-4056)*
Baxalta US Inc ...................................... D ...... 847 948-2000
  Round Lake *(G-19052)*
Baxalta World Trade LLC ...................... G ...... 224 948-2000
  Deerfield *(G-7982)*
Baxalta Worldwide LLC ......................... G ...... 224 948-2000
  Deerfield *(G-7983)*
Baxter Healthcare Corporation .............. C ...... 847 948-3206
  Spring Grove *(G-20328)*
Baxter Healthcare Corporation .............. E ...... 847 578-4671
  Waukegan *(G-21529)*
Baxter International Inc ......................... A ...... 224 948-2000
  Deerfield *(G-7988)*
Ortho-Clinical Diagnostics Inc ................ C ...... 618 281-3882
  Columbia *(G-7362)*

## DIAGNOSTIC SUBSTANCES OR AGENTS: In Vitro

Chem-Impex International Inc ............... E ...... 630 350-5015
  Wood Dale *(G-22351)*
Glucosentient Inc ................................. G ...... 217 487-4087
  Champaign *(G-3490)*
Prenosis Inc ......................................... G ...... 949 246-3113
  Champaign *(G-3530)*
Voyant Diagnostics Inc ......................... G ...... 630 456-6340
  Chicago *(G-6916)*

## DIAGNOSTIC SUBSTANCES OR AGENTS: Microbiology & Virology

Kim Laboratories Inc ............................ G ...... 217 337-6666
  Rantoul *(G-17932)*
Muhammad Sotavia ............................. G ...... 708 966-2262
  Orland Park *(G-16877)*

## DIAGNOSTIC SUBSTANCES OR AGENTS: Radioactive

Petnet Solutions Inc ............................ G ...... 847 297-3721
  Des Plaines *(G-8252)*

## DIAMOND SETTER SVCS

Blando G Mfg Jewelers ........................ G ...... 708 387-0014
  Brookfield *(G-2624)*

## DIAMONDS, GEMS, WHOLESALE

Hy Spreckman & Sons Inc .................... F ...... 312 236-2173
  Skokie *(G-20013)*
Norkin Jewelry Co Inc ........................... E ...... 312 782-7311
  Chicago *(G-5928)*
North American Jewelers Inc ................. D ...... 312 425-9000
  Chicago *(G-5933)*
Steinmetz R (us) Ltd ............................ G ...... 312 332-0990
  Chicago *(G-6586)*

## DIAMONDS: Cutting & Polishing

144 International Inc ............................ F ...... 847 426-8881
  West Dundee *(G-21794)*
Diamond Die & Bevel Cutng LLC .......... E ...... 224 387-3200
  Wheeling *(G-22034)*
Precise Lapping Grinding Corp ............. F ...... 708 615-0240
  Melrose Park *(G-14683)*
S G Nelson & Co ................................ G ...... 630 668-7900
  Wheaton *(G-21979)*
Steinmetz R (us) Ltd ........................... G ...... 312 332-0990
  Chicago *(G-6586)*

## DIAPERS: Cloth

Jac US Inc .......................................... E ...... 312 421-2268
  Chicago *(G-5267)*

## DIAPERS: Disposable

Bottoms Up Inc ................................... G ...... 847 336-0040
  Waukegan *(G-21530)*

## DIATHERMY EQPT

Sullivan Home Health Products ............. G ...... 217 532-6366
  Hillsboro *(G-11900)*

## DIE CUTTING SVC: Paper

Capital Prtg & Die Cutng Inc ................. G ...... 630 896-5520
  Aurora *(G-1124)*
Graphic Arts Finishing Company ........... D ...... 708 345-8484
  Melrose Park *(G-14648)*
Intra-Cut Die Cutting Inc ....................... F ...... 773 775-6228
  Chicago *(G-5228)*
PMC Converting Corp .......................... G ...... 773 481-2269
  Chicago *(G-6142)*

## DIE SETS: Presses, Metal Stamping

Amity Die and Stamping Co .................. E ...... 847 680-6600
  Lake Forest *(G-12879)*
Ammentorp Tool Company Inc .............. G ...... 847 671-9290
  Franklin Park *(G-10395)*
Atomic Engineering Co ......................... F ...... 847 228-1387
  Elk Grove Village *(G-9320)*
Barco Stamping Co .............................. E ...... 630 293-5155
  West Chicago *(G-21666)*
Capitol City Tool & Design .................... E ...... 217 544-9250
  Springfield *(G-20406)*
CGR Technologies Inc .......................... E ...... 847 934-7622
  Palatine *(G-17010)*
Chirch Global Mfg LLC .......................... F ...... 815 385-5600
  Cary *(G-3330)*
Dms Inc ............................................... E ...... 847 726-2828
  Lake Zurich *(G-13063)*
Ehrhardt Tool & Machine LLC ............... C ...... 314 436-6900
  Granite City *(G-11274)*
ERA Tool and Manufacturing Co ........... E ...... 847 298-6333
  Zion *(G-22684)*
Erva Tool & Die Company ..................... E ...... 773 533-7806
  Chicago *(G-4775)*
Harig Manufacturing Corp ..................... E ...... 847 647-9500
  Skokie *(G-20011)*
J F Schroeder Company Inc ................. E ...... 847 357-8600
  Arlington Heights *(G-781)*
Jenco Metal Products Inc ..................... F ...... 847 956-0550
  Mount Prospect *(G-15340)*
PDQ Tool & Stamping Co ..................... E ...... 708 841-3000
  Dolton *(G-8374)*
Pecora Tool & Die Co Inc ..................... E ...... 847 524-1275
  Schaumburg *(G-19686)*
Riverside Tool & Die Co ....................... F ...... 309 689-0104
  Peoria *(G-17443)*
Rj Stuckel Co Inc ................................. E ...... 800 789-7220
  Elk Grove Village *(G-9716)*
Sierra Manufacturing Corp ................... E ...... 630 458-8830
  Addison *(G-289)*
Tauber Brothers Tool & Die Co ............. E ...... 708 867-9100
  Chicago *(G-6679)*
Wireformers Inc ................................... E ...... 847 718-1920
  Mount Prospect *(G-15384)*

## DIES & TOOLS: Special

3d Industries Inc ................................. E ...... 630 616-8702
  Bensenville *(G-1808)*
A M Tool & Die ..................................... E ...... 847 398-7530
  Rolling Meadows *(G-18706)*
Ability Tool Co ...................................... G ...... 815 633-5909
  Machesney Park *(G-14050)*
AC Precision Tool Inc ........................... G ...... 630 797-5161
  Saint Charles *(G-19131)*
Action Rotary Die Inc ........................... E ...... 630 628-6830
  Addison *(G-21)*
Action Tool & Mfg Inc .......................... E ...... 815 874-5775
  Rockford *(G-18256)*
Altman Manufacturing Co Inc ............... F ...... 630 963-0031
  Lisle *(G-13556)*
American Die Supplies Acquisit ............ G ...... 630 766-6226
  Wood Dale *(G-22341)*
Arrow Engineering Inc .......................... E ...... 815 397-0862
  Rockford *(G-18270)*
Astro Tool Co Inc ................................. E ...... 630 876-3402
  West Chicago *(G-21663)*
Austin Tool & Die Co ............................ D ...... 847 509-5800
  Northbrook *(G-16209)*
Azimuth Cnc Inc .................................. F ...... 815 399-4433
  Rockford *(G-18274)*
B L I Tool & Die Inc ............................. G ...... 217 434-9106
  Fowler *(G-10272)*
B Radtke and Sons Inc ........................ G ...... 847 546-3999
  Round Lake Park *(G-19083)*
Bahr Tool & Die Co .............................. G ...... 847 392-4447
  Wheeling *(G-22012)*
Bel-Air Manufacturing Inc .................... F ...... 773 276-7550
  Chicago *(G-4074)*
Bennett Metal Products Inc .................. D ...... 618 244-1911
  Mount Vernon *(G-15401)*
Best Brake Die Inc ............................... G ...... 708 388-1896
  Crestwood *(G-7477)*
Bi-Link Metal Specialties Inc ................ C ...... 630 858-5900
  Bloomingdale *(G-2096)*
Big 3 Precision Products Inc ................ C ...... 618 533-3251
  Centralia *(G-3405)*
Briergate Tool & Engrg Co ................... F ...... 630 766-7050
  Bensenville *(G-1846)*
Bronson & Bratton Inc ......................... C ...... 630 986-1815
  Burr Ridge *(G-2825)*
BT & E Co ........................................... G ...... 815 544-6431
  Belvidere *(G-1740)*
Cdv Corp ............................................. F ...... 815 397-3903
  Rockford *(G-18300)*
County Tool & Die ................................ G ...... 217 324-6527
  Litchfield *(G-13683)*
Custom Tool & Gage Co Inc ................. G ...... 847 671-5306
  Franklin Park *(G-10450)*
Cut Rite Die Co ................................... G ...... 847 394-0492
  Arlington Heights *(G-742)*
D & D Tooling Inc ................................. C ...... 630 759-0015
  Bolingbrook *(G-2298)*
Daley Automation LLC ......................... G ...... 630 384-9900
  Naperville *(G-15642)*
Davis Machine Company Inc ................ G ...... 815 723-9121
  Joliet *(G-12484)*
Dice Mold & Engineering Inc ................ G ...... 630 773-3595
  Itasca *(G-12250)*
Die Craft Metal Products ...................... G ...... 847 593-1433
  Elk Grove Village *(G-9427)*
Die Darrell .......................................... G ...... 309 282-9112
  Eureka *(G-9997)*
Domeny Tool & Stamping Company ..... F ...... 847 526-5700
  Wauconda *(G-21454)*
Double M Machine Inc ......................... G ...... 815 692-4676
  Fairbury *(G-10123)*
Dovee Manufacturing Inc ..................... G ...... 847 437-8122
  Elgin *(G-9012)*
East Side Tool & Die Co Inc ................. F ...... 618 397-1633
  Caseyville *(G-3395)*
Embeddedkits ..................................... E ...... 847 401-7488
  Streamwood *(G-20654)*
Extrusion Tooling Technology .............. G ...... 847 526-1606
  Wauconda *(G-21461)*
Fabrik Industries Inc ............................ B ...... 815 385-9480
  McHenry *(G-14505)*
Federal Signal Corporation .................. B ...... 630 954-2000
  Oak Brook *(G-16510)*
Fidelity Tool & Mold Ltd ....................... F ...... 630 879-2300
  Batavia *(G-1447)*
Forster Products Inc ............................ E ...... 815 493-6360
  Lanark *(G-13154)*
Forster Tool & Mfg Co Inc ................... G ...... 630 616-8177
  Bensenville *(G-1902)*
G & M Die Casting Company Inc .......... D ...... 630 595-2340
  Wood Dale *(G-22374)*
Gail E Stephens ................................... G ...... 618 372-0140
  Brighton *(G-2540)*
Geo T Schmidt Inc ............................... D ...... 847 647-7117
  Niles *(G-15982)*
George Hansen & Co Inc ..................... F ...... 630 628-8700
  Addison *(G-134)*
Gerhard Designing & Mfg Inc ............... E ...... 708 599-4664
  Bridgeview *(G-2494)*
Graffs Tooling Center Inc ..................... G ...... 618 357-5005
  Pinckneyville *(G-17549)*
Header Die and Tool Inc ....................... G ...... 815 397-0123
  Rockford *(G-18414)*
Henry Tool & Die Co ............................. G ...... 847 671-1361
  Franklin Park *(G-10486)*
Hill Engineering Inc ............................. E ...... 630 315-5070
  Carol Stream *(G-3166)*
Horizon Die Company Inc ..................... E ...... 847 426-8558
  East Dundee *(G-8643)*
Icon Metalcraft Inc ............................... C ...... 630 766-5600
  Wood Dale *(G-22381)*
Idea Tool & Manufacturing Co .............. D ...... 312 476-1080
  Chicago *(G-5139)*
Iemco Corporation ............................... G ...... 773 728-4400
  Chicago *(G-5145)*

---

Employee Codes: A=Over 500 employees, B=251-500
C=101-250, D=51-100, E=20-50, F=10-19, G=3-9

## DIES & TOOLS: Special

Imperial Punch & Manufacturing ............F ....... 815 226-8200
 Rockford  *(G-18428)*
Industrial Park Machine & Tool..............F ....... 708 754-7080
 S Chicago Hts  *(G-19105)*
International Cutting Die Inc..................E ....... 708 343-3333
 Melrose Park  *(G-14660)*
J & J Carbide & Tool  Inc ..........................E ....... 708 489-0300
 Alsip  *(G-475)*
J & S Tool Inc ............................................G .....
 Chicago  *(G-5254)*
Jamco Tool & Cams Inc ............................G ....... 847 678-0280
 Franklin Park  *(G-10505)*
Jensen and Son Inc ..................................G ....... 815 895-3855
 Sycamore  *(G-20803)*
JM Tool & Die  LLC ....................................G ....... 630 595-1274
 Bensenville  *(G-1929)*
Kenmode Tool and Engrg Inc ...................C ....... 847 658-5041
 Algonquin  *(G-396)*
Kensen Tool & Die Inc ..............................F ....... 847 455-0150
 Franklin Park  *(G-10512)*
L E D Tool & Die Inc ..................................E ....... 708 597-2505
 Chicago  *(G-5422)*
L T L Co ......................................................F ....... 815 874-0913
 Rockford  *(G-18459)*
Lew-El Tool & Manufacturing Co ............F ....... 773 804-1133
 Chicago  *(G-5497)*
Line Group  Inc ..........................................E ....... 847 593-6810
 Arlington Heights  *(G-793)*
Loren Tool & Manufacturing Co ..............G ....... 630 595-0100
 Franklin Park  *(G-10517)*
Lorette Dies Inc ........................................G ....... 630 279-9682
 Elmhurst  *(G-9902)*
Machine Works  Inc ..................................F ....... 708 597-1665
 Alsip  *(G-487)*
Manor Tool and Mfg Co ............................E ....... 847 678-2020
 Schiller Park  *(G-19845)*
Marathon Cutting Die  Inc ........................E ....... 847 398-5165
 Wheeling  *(G-22101)*
McCurdy Tool & Machining Co ................D ....... 815 765-2117
 Caledonia  *(G-2933)*
Micron Engineering Co .............................G ....... 815 455-2888
 Crystal Lake  *(G-7611)*
Mid-States Forging Die-Tool ....................G ....... 815 226-2313
 Rockford  *(G-18502)*
Midwest Machine Tool  Inc .......................G ....... 815 427-8665
 Saint Anne  *(G-19124)*
Mik Tool & Die Co  Inc ...............................F ....... 847 487-4311
 Wauconda  *(G-21484)*
National Header Die Corp ........................F ....... 815 636-7201
 Rockford  *(G-18516)*
Natural Products  Inc ................................F ....... 847 509-5835
 Northbrook  *(G-16317)*
North American Die Castng Assn ............G ....... 773 202-1000
 Chicago  *(G-5931)*
Odom Tool and Technology  Inc ..............G ....... 815 895-8545
 Sycamore  *(G-20811)*
Panzer Tool Corp ......................................G ....... 630 519-5214
 Lombard  *(G-13841)*
Performance Stamping Co  Inc ................E ....... 847 426-2233
 Carpentersville  *(G-3295)*
Precise Rotary Die Inc ..............................E ....... 847 678-0001
 Schiller Park  *(G-19861)*
Precision Process Corp ............................E ....... 847 640-9820
 Elk Grove Village  *(G-9695)*
Precision Tool & Die Company ................F ....... 217 864-3371
 Mount Zion  *(G-15455)*
Procraft Engraving Inc .............................G ....... 847 673-1500
 Skokie  *(G-20062)*
Production Fabg & Stamping Inc ............F ....... 708 755-5468
 S Chicago Hts  *(G-19111)*
Qualitek Manufacturing  Inc ....................E ....... 847 336-7570
 Gurnee  *(G-11496)*
Quantum Engineering  Inc .......................E ....... 847 640-1340
 Elk Grove Village  *(G-9703)*
Radius Machine & Tool Inc ......................F ....... 847 662-7690
 Gurnee  *(G-11497)*
Ray Tool & Engineering  Inc .....................E ....... 630 587-0000
 Saint Charles  *(G-19251)*
Risk Never Die Inc ....................................G ....... 708 240-4194
 Chicago  *(G-6360)*
Rockford Tool and Mfg Co .......................F ....... 815 398-5876
 Rockford  *(G-18588)*
Rockford Toolcraft  Inc .............................C ....... 815 398-5507
 Rockford  *(G-18589)*
S & S Tool Company .................................E ....... 847 891-0780
 Schaumburg  *(G-19715)*
Schwarz Bros Manufacturing Co .............E ....... 309 342-5814
 Galesburg  *(G-10776)*
Select Tool & Die  Inc ................................G ....... 630 372-0300
 Bartlett  *(G-1372)*

Serv-All Die & Tool Company ...................E ....... 815 459-2900
 Crystal Lake  *(G-7647)*
Sharp Metal Products ..............................G ....... 847 439-5393
 Elk Grove Village  *(G-9735)*
Shelby Tool & Die Inc ...............................G ....... 217 774-2189
 Shelbyville  *(G-19915)*
Sopher Design & Manufacturing .............G ....... 309 699-6419
 East Peoria  *(G-8735)*
Spannagel Tool & Die ...............................G ....... 630 969-7575
 Downers Grove  *(G-8526)*
Standard Machine & Tool Corp ...............F ....... 309 762-6431
 Moline  *(G-14972)*
Sterling Die Inc .........................................G ....... 216 267-1300
 Glendale Heights  *(G-11074)*
Suruga USA Corp .......................................E ....... 630 628-0989
 Schaumburg  *(G-19747)*
T R Jones Machine Co Inc ........................G ....... 815 356-5000
 Machesney Park  *(G-14111)*
Technical Tool Enterprise ........................G ....... 630 893-3390
 Addison  *(G-307)*
Ternkirst Tl & Die & Mch Works ..............F ....... 847 437-8360
 Elk Grove Village  *(G-9776)*
Titan Tool Company Inc ...........................G ....... 847 671-0045
 Franklin Park  *(G-10607)*
Tool-Masters Tool & Stamp Inc ...............G ....... 815 465-6830
 Grant Park  *(G-11316)*
Tower Tool & Engineering Inc .................F ....... 815 654-1115
 Machesney Park  *(G-14112)*
Ultra Polishing Inc ....................................E ....... 630 635-2926
 Schaumburg  *(G-19777)*
Vhd  Inc ......................................................E ....... 815 544-2169
 Belvidere  *(G-1794)*
W A Whitney Co .........................................C ....... 815 964-6771
 Rockford  *(G-18671)*
Walt  Ltd ....................................................G ....... 312 337-2756
 Chicago  *(G-6936)*
West End Tool & Die  Inc ..........................G ....... 815 462-3040
 New Lenox  *(G-15927)*
Windy City Cutting Die  Inc ......................G ....... 630 521-9410
 Bensenville  *(G-2016)*
World Wide Rotary Die .............................G ....... 630 521-9410
 Bensenville  *(G-2018)*

### DIES: Cutting, Exc Metal

Atlas Die  LLC ............................................D ....... 630 351-5140
 Glendale Heights  *(G-11009)*

### DIES: Extrusion

Best Metal Extrusions  Inc .......................E ....... 847 981-0797
 Elk Grove Village  *(G-9341)*
Metal Impact LLC .....................................D ....... 847 718-0192
 Elk Grove Village  *(G-9620)*

### DIES: Paper Cutting

Best Cutting Die Co .................................C ....... 847 675-5522
 Skokie  *(G-19963)*

### DIES: Plastic Forming

Able Die & Mold Inc ..................................G ....... 773 282-3652
 Chicago  *(G-3709)*
Witte Kendel Die & Mold..........................G ....... 815 233-9270
 Freeport  *(G-10699)*

### DIES: Steel Rule

Alcon Tool & Mfg Co Inc ...........................F ....... 773 545-8742
 Chicago  *(G-3798)*
C & S Steel Rule Die Co Inc ......................G ....... 773 254-4027
 Chicago  *(G-4202)*
Converting Technology  Inc .....................D ....... 847 290-0590
 Elk Grove Village  *(G-9392)*
Creative Steel Rule Dies Inc.....................F ....... 630 307-8880
 Glendale Heights  *(G-11019)*
Dax Steel Rule Dies Inc ............................G ....... 708 448-4436
 Orland Park  *(G-16852)*
Die Cut Group Inc .....................................G ....... 630 629-9211
 Lombard  *(G-13790)*
Die Pros Inc ...............................................G ....... 630 543-2025
 Addison  *(G-93)*
Die World Steel Rule Dies ........................G ....... 815 399-8675
 Rockford  *(G-18344)*
Durabuilt Die Corp ...................................F ....... 847 437-2086
 Elk Grove Village  *(G-9437)*
F & S Engraving  Inc ..................................E ....... 847 870-8400
 Mount Prospect  *(G-15328)*
Johnson Steel Rule Die Co ......................F ....... 773 921-4334
 Chicago  *(G-5321)*
Mid-City Die & Mold Corp ........................G ....... 773 278-4844
 Chicago  *(G-5729)*

Triangle Dies and Supplies Inc ................D ....... 630 454-3200
 Batavia  *(G-1511)*

### DIES: Wire Drawing & Straightening

Southern Steel and Wire Inc ...................G ....... 618 654-2161
 Highland  *(G-11812)*

### DIMENSION STONE: Buildings

Granitex  Corp ..........................................G ....... 630 888-1838
 Elmhurst  *(G-9879)*

### DIODES: Light Emitting

American Led Ltg Solutions LLC ..............G ....... 847 931-1900
 Elgin  *(G-8949)*
Bare Development  Inc ............................F ....... 708 352-2273
 Countryside  *(G-7415)*
CPA Systems  Incorporated .....................G ....... 630 858-3057
 Glen Ellyn  *(G-10965)*
Integrated Lighting Tech Inc ...................G ....... 630 750-3786
 Bolingbrook  *(G-2322)*
Led Industries  Inc ....................................E ....... 888 700-7815
 Spring Grove  *(G-20345)*
LED Rite  LLC .............................................G ....... 847 683-8000
 Hampshire  *(G-11553)*
Solid State Luminaires  LLC ....................G ....... 877 775-4733
 Saint Charles  *(G-19266)*
Tech Oasis International  Inc ...................F ....... 847 302-1590
 Gurnee  *(G-11513)*

### DIRECT SELLING ESTABLISHMENTS, NEC

Nak Won Korean Bakery ..........................G ....... 773 588-8769
 Chicago  *(G-5850)*
Simonton Holdings  Inc ............................F ....... 304 428-8261
 Deerfield  *(G-8055)*

### DIRECT SELLING ESTABLISHMENTS: Food Svcs

Kronos Foods Corp ...................................B ....... 773 847-2250
 Glendale Heights  *(G-11039)*

### DIRECT SELLING ESTABLISHMENTS: Food, Mobile, Exc Coffee-Cart

Cindys Pocket Kitchen .............................G ....... 815 388-8385
 Harvard  *(G-11627)*

### DIRECT SELLING ESTABLISHMENTS: Milk Delivery

Oberweis Dairy  Inc ...................................F ....... 847 368-9060
 Arlington Heights  *(G-810)*
Oberweis Dairy  Inc ...................................E ....... 630 906-6455
 Oswego  *(G-16928)*
Oberweis Dairy  Inc ...................................E ....... 708 660-1350
 Oak Park  *(G-16678)*
Oberweis Dairy  Inc ...................................F ....... 630 782-0141
 Elmhurst  *(G-9917)*
Oberweis Dairy  Inc ...................................F ....... 847 290-9222
 Rolling Meadows  *(G-18755)*
Oberweis Dairy  Inc ...................................E ....... 630 474-0284
 Glen Ellyn  *(G-10983)*

### DIRECT SELLING ESTABLISHMENTS: Telemarketing

Darwill  Inc ................................................C ....... 708 449-7770
 Hillside  *(G-11914)*
Evo Exhibits  LLC ......................................G ....... 630 520-0710
 West Chicago  *(G-21697)*

### DISINFECTING SVCS

Sterigenics US  LLC ..................................E .....
 Willowbrook  *(G-22233)*

### DISK DRIVES: Computer

Ckd USA Corporation ................................E ....... 847 368-0539
 Rolling Meadows  *(G-18722)*
Xlogotech Inc .............................................G ....... 888 244-5152
 Arlington Heights  *(G-875)*

### DISKETTE DUPLICATING SVCS

Voris Communication Co Inc ...................D ....... 630 231-2425
 West Chicago  *(G-21791)*

# PRODUCT SECTION

## DISPENSERS: Soap
Midland Product LLC .................F..... 708 444-8200
  Tinley Park *(G-20932)*

## DISPENSING EQPT & PARTS, BEVERAGE: Beer
Banner Equipment Co ..................E..... 815 941-9600
  Morris *(G-15097)*

## DISPENSING EQPT & PARTS, BEVERAGE: Coolers, Milk/Water, Elec
Elkay Manufacturing Company .......C..... 815 493-8850
  Lanark *(G-13153)*
Haskris Co ...................................D..... 847 956-6420
  Elk Grove Village *(G-9517)*

## DISPENSING EQPT & PARTS, BEVERAGE: Fountain/Other Beverage
Cornelius Inc ................................B..... 630 539-6850
  Glendale Heights *(G-11018)*
Natural Choice Corporation .........F..... 815 874-4444
  Rockford *(G-18518)*
Perfection Equipment Inc ............E..... 847 244-7200
  Gurnee *(G-11485)*

## DISPENSING EQPT & PARTS, BEVERAGE: Fountains, Parts/Access
American Soda Ftn Exch Inc ........F..... 312 733-5000
  Chicago *(G-3875)*

## DISPENSING EQPT & PARTS, BEVERAGE: Siphons, Soda Water
Standing Water Solutions Inc .....G..... 847 469-8876
  Wauconda *(G-21503)*

## DISPLAY CASES: Refrigerated
John F Mate Co .............................G..... 847 381-8131
  Lake Barrington *(G-12812)*

## DISPLAY FIXTURES: Showcases, Wood, Exc Refrigerated
Redbox Workshop Ltd ..................E..... 773 478-7077
  Chicago *(G-6316)*

## DISPLAY FIXTURES: Wood
Alex Displays & Co ......................F..... 312 829-2948
  Chicago *(G-3802)*
Display Worldwide LLC ................G..... 815 439-2695
  Plainfield *(G-17592)*
Duo Usa Incorporated .................G..... 312 421-7755
  Chicago *(G-4653)*
Laminated Components Inc ........E..... 815 648-4811
  Hebron *(G-11723)*
Marv-O-Lus Manufacturing Co .....F..... 773 826-1717
  Chicago *(G-5636)*
Multiplex Display Fixture Co .......E..... 800 325-3350
  Dupo *(G-8574)*
Pac Team US Productions LLC ..G..... 773 360-8960
  Chicago *(G-6049)*
Proto Productions Inc .................E..... 630 628-6626
  Addison *(G-260)*
Ww Displays Inc ..........................F..... 847 566-6979
  Mundelein *(G-15568)*

## DISPLAY ITEMS: Corrugated, Made From Purchased Materials
Kodiak LLC ...................................E..... 773 284-9975
  Chicago *(G-5399)*
Menasha Packaging Company LLC ..C..... 773 227-6000
  Chicago *(G-5685)*
Menasha Packaging Company LLC ..B..... 312 880-4620
  Chicago *(G-5686)*
Menasha Packaging Company LLC ..B..... 309 787-1747
  Rock Island *(G-18188)*
Precision Die Cutting & Finish .....G..... 773 252-5625
  Chicago *(G-6169)*
Sonoco Display & Packaging LLC ..F..... 630 789-1111
  Westmont *(G-21922)*

## DISPLAY ITEMS: Solid Fiber, Made From Purchased Materials
Ameriguard Corporation ..............G..... 630 986-1900
  Burr Ridge *(G-2822)*
Premier Packaging Systems Inc .G..... 847 996-6860
  Mundelein *(G-15548)*

## DISPLAY LETTERING SVCS
Effingham Signs & Graphics .......G..... 217 347-8711
  Effingham *(G-8836)*

## DISPLAY STANDS: Merchandise, Exc Wood
Maasscorp Inc ..............................G..... 763 383-1400
  Rockford *(G-18478)*

## DISTILLERS DRIED GRAIN & SOLUBLES
Mega International Ltd ................G..... 309 764-5310
  Moline *(G-14956)*
Mid-Oak Distillery Inc ..................G..... 708 925-9318
  Crestwood *(G-7495)*
Udv North America Inc ................G..... 815 267-4400
  Plainfield *(G-17659)*

## DISTRIBUTORS: Motor Vehicle Engine
Borgwarner Transm Systems Inc ..F..... 708 731-4540
  Melrose Park *(G-14602)*
General Air Compressor Inc ........G..... 630 860-1717
  Bensenville *(G-1907)*
Motion Industries Inc ...................G..... 847 760-6630
  Elgin *(G-9113)*
Northrop Grmmn Spce & Mssn Sys ..F..... 630 773-6900
  Itasca *(G-12333)*

## DIVING EQPT STORES
Scuba Sports Inc .........................G..... 217 787-3483
  Springfield *(G-20519)*

## DOCK EQPT & SPLYS, INDL
H and D Distribution Inc .............G..... 847 247-2011
  Libertyville *(G-13328)*

## DOCKS: Marinas, Prefabricated, Wood
Bitter End Yacht Club Intl ............F..... 312 506-6205
  Chicago *(G-4115)*

## DOOR & WINDOW REPAIR SVCS
Boom Company Inc ......................G..... 847 459-6199
  Wheeling *(G-22018)*

## DOOR FRAMES: Concrete
Jgr Commercial Solutions Inc ....G..... 847 669-7010
  Huntley *(G-12152)*

## DOOR FRAMES: Wood
Alliance Door and Hardware LLC ..G..... 630 451-7070
  Bridgeview *(G-2461)*
Nelson Door Co .............................. 217 543-3489
  Arthur *(G-913)*

## DOOR MATS: Rubber
Superior Mfg Group - Europe ......F..... 708 458-4600
  Chicago *(G-6635)*

## DOOR OPERATING SYSTEMS: Electric
Assa Abloy Entrance Systems US ..F..... 847 228-5600
  Elk Grove Village *(G-9316)*
Chamberlain Group Inc ...............G..... 630 833-0618
  Oak Brook *(G-16498)*
Chamberlain Group Inc ...............B..... 630 279-3600
  Oak Brook *(G-16499)*
Chamberlain Manufacturing Corp ..A..... 630 279-3600
  Oak Brook *(G-16500)*
Gate Systems Corporation ..........G..... 847 731-6700
  Gurnee *(G-11452)*
Kamstra Door Service Inc ...........G..... 708 895-9990
  Lansing *(G-13167)*
Marantec America Corporation ..G..... 847 596-6400
  Gurnee *(G-11469)*
Mi-Jack Systems & Tech LLC .....F..... 708 596-3780
  Hazel Crest *(G-11712)*
Perimeter Access Sys Svcs Inc ..F..... 630 556-4283
  Elburn *(G-8903)*
Pro Access Systems Inc ..............F..... 630 426-0022
  Elburn *(G-8905)*
Tricor International Inc ................E..... 630 629-1213
  Lombard *(G-13871)*
Yale Security Inc ..........................D..... 704 283-2101
  Franklin Park *(G-10632)*

## DOORS & WINDOWS WHOLESALERS: All Materials
A-Ok Inc ........................................E..... 815 943-7431
  Harvard *(G-11616)*
Absolute Windows Inc ..................E..... 708 599-9191
  Oak Lawn *(G-16594)*
ERA Development Group Inc ......E..... 708 252-6979
  Northbrook *(G-16251)*
Kramer Window Co ......................G..... 708 343-4780
  Maywood *(G-14427)*
Specialty Crate Factory ...............G..... 708 756-2100
  Steger *(G-20576)*

## DOORS & WINDOWS: Screen & Storm
Aluminite of Paris .........................G..... 217 463-2233
  Paris *(G-17140)*
Pegas Window Inc .......................G..... 773 394-6466
  Chicago *(G-6097)*
Tri State Aluminum Products ......F..... 815 877-6081
  Loves Park *(G-14003)*

## DOORS & WINDOWS: Storm, Metal
Kramer Window Co ......................G..... 708 343-4780
  Maywood *(G-14427)*
Lang Exterior Inc ..........................G..... 773 737-4500
  Chicago *(G-5458)*
Tempco Products Co ...................D..... 618 544-3175
  Robinson *(G-18074)*

## DOORS: Fire, Metal
Fix It Fast Ltd ...............................F..... 708 401-8320
  Midlothian *(G-14766)*

## DOORS: Folding, Plastic Or Plastic Coated Fabric
Mueller Door Company .................E..... 815 385-8550
  Wauconda *(G-21487)*

## DOORS: Garage, Overhead, Metal
Builders Chicago Corporation .....D..... 224 654-2122
  Rosemont *(G-18991)*
C B M Plastics Inc .......................F..... 217 543-3870
  Arthur *(G-883)*
C H I Overhead Doors Inc ............B..... 217 543-2135
  Arthur *(G-884)*
Hormann LLC ................................C..... 877 654-6762
  Montgomery *(G-15047)*
Hormann LLC ................................G..... 630 859-3000
  Montgomery *(G-15048)*
Neisewander Enterprises Inc .......A..... 815 288-1431
  Dixon *(G-8337)*
Overhead Door Corporation ........G..... 630 775-9118
  Itasca *(G-12338)*
Overhead Door Solutions Inc ......G..... 847 359-3667
  Palatine *(G-17062)*
Raynor Mfg Co ..............................A..... 815 288-1431
  Dixon *(G-8341)*
Raynor Mfg Co ..............................D..... 815 288-1431
  Dixon *(G-8342)*

## DOORS: Garage, Overhead, Wood
Allied Garage Door Inc ................E..... 630 279-0795
  Addison *(G-29)*
Central Illinois Door .....................G..... 309 828-0087
  Bloomington *(G-2154)*
Clopay Building Pdts Co Inc ........G..... 708 346-0901
  Chicago Ridge *(G-7143)*
Neisewander Enterprises Inc .......A..... 815 288-1431
  Dixon *(G-8337)*

## DOORS: Glass
Clear View Industries Inc ............G..... 815 267-3593
  Plainfield *(G-17588)*
Doralco Inc ....................................E..... 708 388-9324
  Alsip *(G-458)*
Glass Concepts LLC ....................F..... 773 650-0520
  Chicago *(G-4954)*

# DOORS: Rolling, Indl Building Or Warehouse, Metal

**Allied Garage Door Inc** .................... E ..... 630 279-0795
  Addison *(G-29)*
**Dynaco Usa Inc** ............................... E ..... 847 562-4910
  Mundelein *(G-15497)*
**Power-Sonic Corporation** ................ G ..... 309 752-7750
  East Moline *(G-8690)*
**Steel-Guard Safety Corp** .................. G ..... 708 589-4588
  South Holland *(G-20306)*

## DOORS: Safe & Vault, Metal

**Promus Equity Partners LLC** ............ F ..... 312 784-3990
  Chicago *(G-6216)*

## DOORS: Screen, Metal

**Midwest Screens LLC** ...................... G ..... 847 557-5015
  Antioch *(G-646)*
**Quanex Screens LLC** ........................ G ..... 217 463-2233
  Paris *(G-17160)*

## DOORS: Wooden

**Accurate Cstm Sash Mllwk Corp** ........ G ..... 708 423-0423
  Oak Lawn *(G-16595)*
**Custom Crafted Door Inc** ................... F ..... 309 527-5075
  El Paso *(G-8867)*
**Decore-Ative Specialties** ................... B ..... 630 947-6294
  Cary *(G-3334)*
**Harold Prefinished Wood Inc** ............ F ..... 618 548-1414
  Salem *(G-19336)*
**Landquist & Son Inc** ......................... E ..... 847 674-6600
  Mokena *(G-14878)*
**Masonite Corporation** ....................... D ..... 630 584-6330
  West Chicago *(G-21740)*
**Overhead Door Corporation** ............. G ..... 630 775-9118
  Itasca *(G-12338)*
**S R Door Inc** ..................................... E ..... 815 227-1148
  Rockford *(G-18603)*
**Torblo Inc** ......................................... G ..... 815 941-2684
  Morris *(G-15135)*
**US Lbm Ridout Holdings LLC** .......... G ..... 877 787-5267
  Buffalo Grove *(G-2786)*

## DOWELS & DOWEL RODS

**Chicago Dowel Company Inc** ........... D ..... 773 622-2000
  Chicago *(G-4315)*
**Excel Group Holdings Inc** ................ E ..... 630 773-1815
  Itasca *(G-12261)*

## DRAFTING SPLYS WHOLESALERS

**Numeridex Incorporated** ................... F ..... 847 541-8840
  Wheeling *(G-22111)*

## DRAFTING SVCS

**Associated Design Inc** ...................... F ..... 708 974-9100
  Palos Hills *(G-17114)*

## DRAINAGE PRDTS: Concrete

**C & L Tiling Inc** ................................. D ..... 217 773-3357
  Timewell *(G-20885)*
**Southern Illinois Stone Co** ................ F ..... 573 334-5261
  Buncombe *(G-2800)*

## DRAINING OR PUMPING OF METAL MINES

**Ave Inc** ............................................. G ..... 815 727-0153
  Joliet *(G-12457)*

## DRAPERIES & CURTAINS

**A B Kelly Inc** ..................................... G ..... 847 639-1022
  Cary *(G-3320)*
**ADM International Inc** ....................... F ..... 773 774-2400
  North Chicago *(G-16173)*
**Baker Drapery Corporation** .............. G ..... 309 691-3295
  Peoria *(G-17313)*
**Berg Industries Inc** ........................... F ..... 815 874-1588
  Rockford *(G-18280)*
**Dezign Sewing Inc** ........................... G ..... 773 549-4336
  Chicago *(G-4590)*
**Dons Drapery Service** ...................... G ..... 815 385-4759
  McHenry *(G-14497)*
**Drapery House Inc** ........................... G ..... 847 318-1161
  Park Ridge *(G-17191)*
**Drapery Room Inc** ............................ F ..... 708 301-3374
  Homer Glen *(G-12077)*
**Draperyland Inc** ................................ F ..... 630 521-1000
  Wood Dale *(G-22360)*
**Drexel House of Drapes Inc** ............. G ..... 618 624-5415
  Belleville *(G-1627)*
**Indecor Inc** ....................................... F ..... 773 561-7670
  Morton Grove *(G-15202)*
**Interior Fashions Contract** ................ G ..... 847 358-6050
  Palatine *(G-17044)*
**North-West Drapery Service** ............ G ..... 773 282-7117
  Chicago *(G-5937)*
**Roberts Draperies Center Inc** ........... G ..... 847 255-4040
  Mount Prospect *(G-15370)*
**Rogers Custom Trims Inc** ................ G ..... 773 745-6577
  Chicago *(G-6380)*
**Shade Aire Company** ....................... G ..... 815 623-7597
  Roscoe *(G-18921)*
**Slagel Drapery Service** ..................... G ..... 815 692-3834
  Fairbury *(G-10132)*
**Tazewell Floor Covering Inc** ............. F ..... 309 266-6371
  Morton *(G-15184)*
**Tenggren-Mehl Co Inc** ...................... G ..... 773 763-3290
  Chicago *(G-6700)*
**Tres Joli Designs Ltd** ....................... G ..... 847 520-3903
  Wheeling *(G-22168)*
**Zirlin Interiors Inc** ............................. E ..... 773 334-5530
  Chicago *(G-7069)*

## DRAPERIES & DRAPERY FABRICS, COTTON

**A B C Blind Inc** ................................. G ..... 708 877-7100
  Thornton *(G-20866)*
**Annas Draperies & Associates** ......... G ..... 773 282-1365
  Chicago *(G-3911)*
**Drapery Room Inc** ............................ F ..... 708 301-3374
  Homer Glen *(G-12077)*
**F & L Drapery Inc** ............................. G ..... 815 932-8997
  Saint Anne *(G-19122)*
**Kempco Window Treatments Inc** ...... E ..... 708 754-4484
  Chicago Heights *(G-7108)*

## DRAPERIES: Plastic & Textile, From Purchased Materials

**A D Specialty Sewing** ....................... G ..... 847 639-0390
  Fox River Grove *(G-10285)*
**Aracon Drpery Vntian Blind Ltd** ........ G ..... 773 252-1281
  Chicago *(G-3930)*
**E J Self Furniture** ............................. G ..... 847 394-0899
  Mount Prospect *(G-15327)*
**Loraes Drapery Workroom Inc** ......... G ..... 847 358-7999
  Palatine *(G-17051)*
**Marvin Feig & Associates Inc** ........... F ..... 773 384-5228
  Niles *(G-16001)*
**Olshaws Interior Services** ................. G ..... 312 421-3131
  Chicago *(G-5985)*
**Parenteau Studios** ............................ E ..... 312 337-8015
  Chicago *(G-6081)*
**Shade Brookline Co** ......................... F ..... 773 274-5513
  Chicago *(G-6487)*
**Tailored Inc** ...................................... G ..... 708 387-9854
  Brookfield *(G-2643)*
**Unitex Industries Inc** ........................ G ..... 708 524-0664
  Oak Park *(G-16690)*
**Whiteside Drapery Fabricators** ......... F ..... 847 746-5300
  Zion *(G-22701)*

## DRAPERY & UPHOLSTERY STORES: Curtains

**Annas Draperies & Associates** ......... G ..... 773 282-1365
  Chicago *(G-3911)*
**Ensembles Inc** .................................. G ..... 630 527-0004
  Naperville *(G-15805)*

## DRAPERY & UPHOLSTERY STORES: Draperies

**Afar Imports & Interiors Inc** .............. G ..... 217 744-3262
  Springfield *(G-20386)*
**Drapery House Inc** ........................... G ..... 847 318-1161
  Park Ridge *(G-17191)*
**Draperyland Inc** ................................ F ..... 630 521-1000
  Wood Dale *(G-22360)*
**Drexel House of Drapes Inc** ............. G ..... 618 624-5415
  Belleville *(G-1627)*
**Hansens Mfrs Win Coverings** ........... F ..... 815 935-0010
  Bradley *(G-2424)*
**Roberts Draperies Center Inc** ........... G ..... 847 255-4040
  Mount Prospect *(G-15370)*
**Tres Joli Designs Ltd** ....................... G ..... 847 520-3903
  Wheeling *(G-22168)*

## DRIED FRUITS WHOLESALERS

**TEC Foods Inc** .................................. E ..... 800 315-8002
  Chicago *(G-6683)*

## DRILL BITS

**Galaxy Industries Inc** ........................ D ..... 847 639-8580
  Cary *(G-3345)*
**Irwin Industrial Tool Company** .......... C ..... 815 235-4171
  Freeport *(G-10669)*
**Mincon Inc** ........................................ E ..... 618 435-3404
  Benton *(G-2035)*
**Quality Tech Tool Inc** ........................ E ..... 847 690-9643
  Bensenville *(G-1973)*
**Tru-Cut Inc** ....................................... D ..... 847 639-2090
  Cary *(G-3377)*

## DRILLING MACHINERY & EQPT: Oil & Gas

**Dover Corporation** ............................ C ..... 630 541-1540
  Downers Grove *(G-8431)*
**FMC Subsea Service Inc** .................. E ..... 312 861-6174
  Chicago *(G-4864)*
**Oil Filter Recyclers Inc** ..................... E ..... 309 329-2131
  Astoria *(G-935)*

## DRILLING MACHINERY & EQPT: Water Well

**Azcon Inc** ......................................... F ..... 815 548-7000
  Sterling *(G-20583)*
**Innerweld Cover Co** .......................... F ..... 847 497-3009
  Mundelein *(G-15511)*

## DRILLING MUD COMPOUNDS, CONDITIONERS & ADDITIVES

**Aldridge Electric Inc** ......................... B ..... 847 680-5200
  Libertyville *(G-13300)*

## DRILLS & DRILLING EQPT: Mining

**Midwest Machine Tool Inc** ................ G ..... 815 427-8665
  Saint Anne *(G-19124)*

## DRINK MIXES, NONALCOHOLIC: Cocktail

**Jo Snow Inc** ...................................... G ..... 773 732-3045
  Chicago *(G-5308)*

## DRINKING FOUNTAINS: Metal, Nonrefrigerated

**Elkay Manufacturing Company** ......... B ..... 815 273-7001
  Savanna *(G-19397)*

## DRINKING PLACES: Alcoholic Beverages

**Andrias Food Group Inc** .................... E ..... 618 632-4866
  O Fallon *(G-16461)*
**Father Marcellos & Son** .................... C ..... 312 654-2565
  Chicago *(G-4820)*
**Goose Holdings Inc** .......................... E ..... 312 226-1119
  Chicago *(G-4979)*
**Hometown Hangout LLC** ................... E ..... 309 639-2108
  Williamsfield *(G-22189)*
**Rock Bottom Minneapolis Inc** ........... D ..... 312 755-9339
  Chicago *(G-6373)*

## DRINKING PLACES: Bars & Lounges

**Haymarket Brewing Company LLC** .... G ..... 312 638-0700
  Chicago *(G-5056)*

## DRINKING PLACES: Night Clubs

**Tini Martini** ........................................ G ..... 773 269-2900
  Chicago *(G-6729)*

## DRINKING PLACES: Tavern

**Broken Oar Inc** .................................. G ..... 847 639-9468
  Port Barrington *(G-17718)*

## DRINKING PLACES: Wine Bar

**Galena Cellars Winery** ...................... G ..... 815 777-3330
  Galena *(G-10720)*
**Tavern On Prospect Ltd** ................... G ..... 309 693-8677
  Peoria *(G-17466)*

# PRODUCT SECTION

## EATING PLACES

### DRINKING WATER COOLERS WHOLESALERS: Mechanical

Natural Choice Corporation ............. F ..... 815 874-4444
  Rockford *(G-18518)*
Superior Water Services Inc ............ G ..... 309 691-9287
  Peoria *(G-17464)*

### DRIVE CHAINS: Bicycle Or Motorcycle

Wrench ......................................... G ..... 773 609-1698
  Chicago *(G-7036)*

### DRIVE SHAFTS

Aluminum Drive Line Products ........... G ..... 708 946-9777
  Beecher *(G-1596)*
Dana Driveshaft Mfg LLC ................. E ..... 815 626-6700
  Sterling *(G-20588)*
Drive Shaft Unlimited Inc ................. G ..... 708 447-2211
  Lyons *(G-14036)*
Johnson Power Ltd ......................... E ..... 708 345-4300
  Broadview *(G-2588)*
Midwest Driveshaft Inc .................... G ..... 630 513-9292
  Saint Charles *(G-19221)*
Quarter Master Industries Inc ........... E ..... 847 540-8999
  Lake Zurich *(G-13120)*
Suburban Driveline Inc .................... G ..... 630 941-7101
  Villa Park *(G-21286)*
Surge Clutch & Drive Line Co ........... G ..... 708 331-1352
  South Holland *(G-20307)*

### DRIVES: High Speed Indl, Exc Hydrostatic

Arrow Gear Company ...................... C ..... 630 969-7640
  Downers Grove *(G-8389)*

### DRIVES: Hydrostatic

Hydro-Gear Inc .............................. C ..... 217 728-2581
  Sullivan *(G-20748)*
Kocsis Technologies Inc .................. G ..... 708 597-4177
  Alsip *(G-482)*

### DROP CLOTHS: Fabric

Chicago Dropcloth Tarpaulin Co ........ E ..... 773 588-3123
  Chicago *(G-4316)*

### DRUG STORES

Jewel Osco Inc .............................. C ..... 847 882-6477
  Hoffman Estates *(G-12020)*
Pharmedium Healthcare Corp ........... E ..... 847 457-2300
  Lake Forest *(G-12944)*
Prescription Plus Ltd ....................... F ..... 618 537-6202
  Lebanon *(G-13216)*

### DRUG TESTING KITS: Blood & Urine

First Step Womens Center ............... G ..... 217 523-0100
  Springfield *(G-20441)*

### DRUGS & DRUG PROPRIETARIES, WHOL: Biologicals/Allied Prdts

Chem-Impex International Inc ........... E ..... 630 350-5015
  Wood Dale *(G-22351)*

### DRUGS & DRUG PROPRIETARIES, WHOLESALE

Daito Pharmaceuticals Amer Inc ........ G ..... 847 205-0800
  Northbrook *(G-16238)*
Dashire Inc ................................... F ..... 847 236-0776
  Deerfield *(G-8003)*

### DRUGS & DRUG PROPRIETARIES, WHOLESALE: Animal Medicines

First Priority Inc ............................. D ..... 847 531-1215
  Elgin *(G-9037)*
Pet King Brands Inc ....................... G ..... 630 241-3905
  Westmont *(G-21911)*

### DRUGS & DRUG PROPRIETARIES, WHOLESALE: Medicinals/Botanicals

GE Healthcare Holdings Inc ............. A ..... 847 398-8500
  Arlington Heights *(G-759)*

### DRUGS & DRUG PROPRIETARIES, WHOLESALE: Pharmaceuticals

Avocet Polymer Tech Inc ................. G ..... 773 523-2872
  Chicago *(G-4001)*
Espee Biopharma & Finechem LLC ... G ..... 888 851-6667
  Schaumburg *(G-19520)*
Fresenius Kabi Usa Inc ................... B ..... 708 450-7500
  Melrose Park *(G-14640)*
Jewel Osco Inc .............................. C ..... 847 882-6477
  Hoffman Estates *(G-12020)*
Lundbeck LLC ............................... C ..... 847 282-1000
  Deerfield *(G-8031)*
Medimmune LLC ............................ G ..... 847 356-3274
  Lindenhurst *(G-13547)*
Ravens Wood Pharmacy .................. G ..... 708 667-0525
  Chicago *(G-6295)*
Sagent Pharmaceuticals Inc ............. D ..... 847 908-1600
  Schaumburg *(G-19717)*
Symbria Rx Services LLC ................ E ..... 630 981-8000
  Woodridge *(G-22520)*

### DRUGS & DRUG PROPRIETARIES, WHOLESALE: Vitamins & Minerals

Glanbia Performance Ntrtn Inc .......... C ..... 630 236-0097
  Downers Grove *(G-8451)*
Healthy Life Nutraceutics Inc ............ ..... 201 253-9053
  Deerfield *(G-8010)*
Natures Best Inc ............................ E ..... 631 232-3355
  Downers Grove *(G-8493)*
Natures Sources LLC ...................... G ..... 847 663-9168
  Niles *(G-16013)*

### DRUGS AFFECTING NEOPLASMS & ENDOCRINE SYSTEMS

Becton Dickinson and Company ........ G ..... 630 428-3499
  Naperville *(G-15604)*

### DRUMS: Brake

Gunite EMI Corporation ................... B ..... 815 964-7124
  Rockford *(G-18409)*
Winhere Brake Parts Inc .................. G ..... 630 307-0158
  Bartlett *(G-1387)*

### DRUMS: Fiber

Fibre Drum Company ...................... E ..... 815 933-3222
  Kankakee *(G-12616)*
Greif Inc ...................................... E ..... 630 961-1842
  Naperville *(G-15665)*

### DRUMS: Magnetic

Estad Stamping & Mfg Co ................ E ..... 217 442-4600
  Danville *(G-7717)*

### DRUMS: Shipping, Metal

Chicago Steel Container Corp ........... E ..... 773 277-2244
  Chicago *(G-4350)*
Meyer Steel Drum Inc ..................... E ..... 773 522-3030
  Chicago *(G-5712)*
Meyer Steel Drum Inc ..................... ..... 773 376-8376
  Chicago *(G-5713)*
Mobile Mini Inc ............................... E ..... 708 297-2004
  Calumet Park *(G-2963)*
Zorin Material Handling Co ............... G ..... 773 342-3818
  Chicago *(G-7073)*

### DRYCLEANING & LAUNDRY SVCS: Commercial & Family

Workshop ..................................... E ..... 815 777-2211
  Galena *(G-10736)*

### DRYCLEANING EQPT & SPLYS: Commercial

Eminent Technologies LLC ............... G ..... 630 416-2311
  Naperville *(G-15653)*
Solvair LLC ................................... F ..... 630 416-4244
  Naperville *(G-15749)*

### DRYCLEANING PLANTS

Regency Hand Laundry .................... G ..... 773 871-3950
  Chicago *(G-6322)*
Rkc Cleaner I Corp ......................... F ..... 630 904-0477
  Naperville *(G-15824)*

### DRYERS & REDRYERS: Indl

Henderson Engineering Co Inc .......... G ..... 815 786-9471
  Sandwich *(G-19368)*
Paul D Stark & Associates ............... G ..... 630 964-7111
  Downers Grove *(G-8500)*

### DUCTING: Metal Plate

Mach Mechanical Group LLC ............ G ..... 630 674-6224
  Naperville *(G-15815)*

### DUCTING: Plastic

Lakeland Plastics Inc ..................... E ..... 847 680-1550
  Mundelein *(G-15517)*

### DUCTS: Sheet Metal

Advanced Metalcraft Inc .................. F ..... 847 451-0771
  Franklin Park *(G-10384)*
Cleats Mfg Inc ............................... F ..... 773 521-0300
  Chicago *(G-4399)*
Cleats Mfg Inc ............................... F ..... 773 542-0453
  Chicago *(G-4400)*
Crawford Heating & Cooling Co ......... D ..... 309 788-4573
  Rock Island *(G-18169)*
Daniel & Sons Mech Contrs Inc ........ F ..... 618 997-2822
  Marion *(G-14258)*
Elgin Sheet Metal Co ...................... E ..... 847 742-3486
  South Elgin *(G-20194)*
Lindemann Chimney Service Inc ....... F ..... 847 918-7994
  Lake Bluff *(G-12854)*
Macari Service Center Inc ............... ..... 217 774-4214
  Shelbyville *(G-19910)*
Safe-Air of Illinois Inc ..................... E ..... 708 652-9100
  Cicero *(G-7227)*
Synergy Mechanical Inc ................... G ..... 708 410-1004
  Westchester *(G-21857)*

### DUMBWAITERS

Otis Elevator Company .................... F ..... 618 529-3411
  Carbondale *(G-3016)*

### DUMPSTERS: Garbage

Captain Hook Inc ........................... G ..... 309 565-7676
  Hanna City *(G-11567)*
D & P Construction Co Inc ............... E ..... 773 714-9330
  Chicago *(G-4535)*
Wastequip LLC .............................. E ..... 618 271-6250
  East Saint Louis *(G-8775)*

### DURABLE GOODS WHOLESALERS, NEC

AEP Inc ........................................ G ..... 618 466-7668
  Alton *(G-558)*

### DUST OR FUME COLLECTING EQPT: Indl

Blowers LLC .................................. E ..... 708 594-1800
  Elmhurst *(G-9841)*
Bost Corporation ............................ E ..... 708 344-7023
  Maywood *(G-14420)*
Custom Systems Inc ....................... G ..... 314 355-4575
  Granite City *(G-11272)*

### DYES & PIGMENTS: Organic

Clariant Plas Coatings USA Inc ......... D ..... 630 562-9700
  West Chicago *(G-21682)*
Polyone Corporation ........................ D ..... 847 364-0011
  Elk Grove Village *(G-9686)*

### DYNAMOMETERS

Star Test Dynamometer Inc .............. G ..... 309 452-0371
  Normal *(G-16089)*

### EARTH SCIENCE SVCS

Toppert Jetting Service Inc ............... G ..... 309 755-2240
  Hillsdale *(G-11904)*

### EARTHS: Ground Or Otherwise Treated

Oil-Dri Corporation America .............. D ..... 312 321-1515
  Chicago *(G-5975)*

### EATING PLACES

Aero Alehouse ............................... G ..... 815 977-5602
  Loves Park *(G-13914)*

---

Employee Codes: A=Over 500 employees, B=251-500
C=101-250, D=51-100, E=20-50, F=10-19, G=3-9

2017 Harris Illinois Industrial Directory

# EATING PLACES

Amity Packing Company Inc..............D........312 942-0270
  Chicago (G-3889)
Bellaflora Foods Ltd..........................E........773 252-6113
  Chicago (G-4077)
Campeche Restaurant Inc...................G........815 776-9950
  Galena (G-10716)
Caulfields Restaurant Ltd...................E........708 798-1599
  Flossmoor (G-10223)
Consumers Packing Co Inc.................D........708 344-0047
  Melrose Park (G-14611)
Coopers Hwk Intermedte Holdng..........C........708 839-2920
  Countryside (G-7420)
Coopers Hwk Intermedte Holdng..........F........708 215-5674
  Countryside (G-7421)
Cornerstone Communications..............E........773 989-2087
  Chicago (G-4471)
Doreens Pizza Inc...............................F........708 862-7499
  Calumet City (G-2937)
Elis Cheesecake Company..................C........773 205-3800
  Chicago (G-4730)
Express Donuts Enterprise Inc.............F........630 510-9310
  Wheaton (G-21947)
Fooda Inc...........................................E........312 752-4352
  Chicago (G-4869)
Gonnella Baking Co............................D........312 733-2020
  Schaumburg (G-19539)
Hidden Hollow Stables Inc..................G........309 243-7979
  Dunlap (G-8567)
Homers Ice Cream Inc........................E........847 251-0477
  Wilmette (G-22254)
Hometown Hangout LLC.....................G........309 639-2108
  Williamsfield (G-22189)
Italia Foods Inc..................................E........847 397-4479
  Schaumburg (G-19585)
Jewel Osco Inc..................................C........815 464-5352
  Frankfort (G-10336)
Kernel Kutter Inc................................G........815 877-1515
  Machesney Park (G-14085)
Lau Nae Winery Inc............................G........618 282-9463
  Red Bud (G-17944)
Lincoln Park Brewery Inc....................D........312 915-0071
  Chicago (G-5507)
Lynfred Winery Inc.............................E........630 529-9463
  Roselle (G-18953)
Mandys Kitchen & Grill......................G........630 348-2264
  Bolingbrook (G-2339)
Mariegold Bake Shoppe.....................G........773 561-1978
  Chicago (G-5617)
Marion Oelze.....................................G........618 327-9224
  Nashville (G-15839)
Meats By Linz Inc..............................E........708 862-0830
  Calumet City (G-2946)
Napco Inc..........................................E........630 406-1100
  Batavia (G-1474)
Niemann Foods Foundation.................C........217 222-0190
  Quincy (G-17862)
Niemann Foods Foundation.................C........217 793-4091
  Springfield (G-20487)
Open Kitchens Inc.............................E........312 666-5334
  Chicago (G-5995)
Pastificio Inc.....................................G........847 432-5459
  Highwood (G-11887)
Plochman Inc....................................E........815 468-3434
  Manteno (G-14190)
Raymond Brothers Inc........................F........847 928-9300
  Schiller Park (G-19866)
Ron & Pats Pizza Shack....................G........847 395-5005
  Antioch (G-653)
Royal Oak Farm Inc...........................F........815 648-4141
  Harvard (G-11646)
Schau Southeast Sushi Inc.................E........630 783-1000
  Woodridge (G-22516)
Schnuck Markets Inc.........................C........618 466-0825
  Godfrey (G-11237)
Stiglmeier Sausage Co Inc..................F........847 537-9988
  Wheeling (G-22157)
Union Foods Inc................................G........201 327-2828
  Chicago (G-6814)

## ECCLESIASTICAL WARE, NEC

Empire Bronze Corp...........................F........630 916-9722
  Lombard (G-13796)

## EDUCATIONAL PROGRAM ADMINISTRATION, GOVT: Level Of Govt

Max Fire Training Inc........................F........618 210-2079
  Godfrey (G-11228)

## EDUCATIONAL SVCS

African American Ctr For Hnb..............D........618 549-3965
  Park Forest (G-17168)
Care Education Group Inc...................G........708 361-4110
  Palos Park (G-17127)
Great Books Foundation......................E........312 332-5870
  Chicago (G-4994)
Iep Quality Inc...................................G........217 840-0570
  Champaign (G-3497)
LMS Innovations Inc..........................G........312 613-2345
  Chicago (G-5528)
Mold Shields Inc................................G........708 983-5931
  Villa Park (G-21271)
Peopleadmin Inc.................................E........877 637-5800
  Chicago (G-6102)
Thinkcercacom Inc.............................F........224 412-3722
  Chicago (G-6714)

## EDUCATIONAL SVCS, NONDEGREE GRANTING: Continuing Education

Cengage Learning Inc.........................G........630 554-0821
  Downers Grove (G-8406)
M T M Assn For Standards & RES.......G........847 299-1111
  Des Plaines (G-8224)
National Association Realtors...............C........800 874-6500
  Chicago (G-5857)
National Association Realtors...............C........800 874-6500
  Chicago (G-5858)

## ELASTIC BRAID & NARROW WOVEN FABRICS

Lea & Sachs Inc................................F........847 296-8000
  Des Plaines (G-8221)

## ELASTOMERS

Miner Elastomer Products Corp...........E........630 232-3000
  Geneva (G-10848)

## ELECTRIC FENCE CHARGERS

Invisible Fencing of Quad City............G........309 797-1688
  Moline (G-14945)

## ELECTRIC MOTOR & GENERATOR AUXILIARY PARTS

Kaman Automation Inc.......................F........847 273-9050
  Schaumburg (G-19596)
Torqeedo Inc......................................G........815 444-8806
  Crystal Lake (G-7667)

## ELECTRIC MOTOR REPAIR SVCS

Accurate Elc Mtr & Pump Co..............G........708 448-2792
  Worth (G-22631)
Addison Electric Inc............................E........800 517-4871
  Addison (G-22)
Al Cook Electric Motors......................G........309 653-2337
  Adair (G-11)
All Electric Mtr Repr Svc Inc...............F........773 925-2404
  Chicago (G-3806)
Avana Electric Motors Inc...................F........847 588-0400
  Elk Grove Village (G-9323)
Bak Electric.......................................G........708 458-3578
  Bridgeview (G-2469)
Bellwood Electric Motors Inc...............G........708 544-7223
  Bellwood (G-1696)
Belmont Electro Co Inc......................G........773 472-4641
  Brookfield (G-2623)
BP Elc Mtrs Pump & Svc Inc..............G........773 539-4343
  Skokie (G-19967)
Calumet Armature and Elc LLC...........E........708 841-6880
  Riverdale (G-18017)
Cameron Electric Motor Corp..............F........312 939-5770
  Chicago (G-4223)
Decatur Industrial Elc Inc....................E........217 428-6621
  Decatur (G-7872)
Dependable Electric............................G........618 592-3314
  Oblong (G-16732)
Ebling Electric Company.....................E........312 455-1885
  Chicago (G-4688)
Electric Motor Corp............................G........773 725-1050
  Chicago (G-4719)
Elmot Inc...........................................G........773 791-7039
  Chicago (G-4734)
Erbes Electric....................................G........815 849-5508
  Sublette (G-20715)

# PRODUCT SECTION

First Electric Motor Shop Inc..............G........217 698-0672
  Springfield (G-20440)
Flolo Corporation................................E........630 595-1010
  West Chicago (G-21703)
Foremost Electric & Transm Inc..........E........309 699-2200
  Peoria (G-17364)
Gem Electric Motor Repair..................G........815 756-5317
  Dekalb (G-8094)
Goding Electric Company....................F........630 858-7700
  Glendale Heights (G-11029)
H & H Motor Service Inc....................G........708 652-6100
  Cicero (G-7199)
Heise Industries Inc...........................G........847 223-2410
  Grayslake (G-11346)
Hills Electric Motor Service.................G........815 625-0305
  Rock Falls (G-18136)
Hopcroft Electric Inc..........................G........618 288-7302
  Glen Carbon (G-10952)
Iesco Inc............................................E........708 594-1250
  Chicago (G-5146)
Industrial Service Solutions.................F........917 609-6979
  Chicago (G-5180)
Inman Electric Motors Inc..................E........815 223-2288
  La Salle (G-12778)
J & J Electric Motor Repair Sp............G........217 529-0015
  Springfield (G-20459)
Joes Automotive Inc...........................G........815 937-9281
  Kankakee (G-12630)
Kankakee Industrial Tech....................F........815 933-6683
  Bradley (G-2425)
Keller United Elc & Mch Co...............G........217 382-4521
  Martinsville (G-14337)
Lakenburges Motor Co.......................G........618 523-4231
  Germantown (G-10893)
Lange Electric Inc..............................G........217 347-7626
  Effingham (G-8843)
Lee Foss Electric Motor Svc...............G........708 681-5335
  Melrose Park (G-14670)
M H Electric Motor & Ctrl Corp..........G........630 393-3736
  Warrenville (G-21350)
Melton Electric Co.............................G........309 697-1422
  Peoria (G-17405)
Metzka Inc........................................G........815 932-6363
  Kankakee (G-12638)
Midwest Elc Mtr Inc Danville.............G........217 442-5656
  Danville (G-7756)
Midwest Motor Specialists Inc............G........815 942-0083
  Morris (G-15118)
Park Electric Motor Service................G........217 442-1977
  Danville (G-7759)
Rockford Electric Equipment Co.........G........815 398-4096
  Rockford (G-18573)
Sandner Electric Co Inc.....................G........618 932-2179
  West Frankfort (G-21818)
Schaeffer Electric Co.........................G........618 592-3231
  Oblong (G-16734)
Service Pro Electric Mtr Repr..............G........630 766-1215
  Bensenville (G-1990)
Steiner Electric Company...................E........312 421-7220
  Chicago (G-6584)
Vandalia Electric Mtr Svc Inc..............G........618 283-0068
  Vandalia (G-21128)
Voss Electric Inc................................G........708 596-6000
  Harvey (G-11680)
Yaskawa America Inc........................C........847 887-7000
  Waukegan (G-21642)

## ELECTRIC WATER HEATERS WHOLESALERS

Metropolitan Industries Inc.................C........815 886-9200
  Romeoville (G-18845)

## ELECTRICAL APPARATUS & EQPT WHOLESALERS

Al Cook Electric Motors......................G........309 653-2337
  Adair (G-11)
Arrow Edm Inc...................................F........217 893-4277
  Rantoul (G-17918)
Automated Design Corp......................G........630 783-1150
  Romeoville (G-18801)
C R V Electronics Corp......................D........815 675-6500
  Spring Grove (G-20329)
Calumet Armature and Elc LLC...........E........708 841-6880
  Riverdale (G-18017)
Chicago Chain and Transm Co...........E........630 482-9000
  Countryside (G-7417)
Chicago Technical Sales Inc...............G........630 889-7121
  Oakbrook Terrace (G-16701)

# PRODUCT SECTION — ELECTRICAL EQPT & SPLYS

| Company | Code | Phone |
|---|---|---|
| City Screen Inc | G | 773 588-5642 |
| Chicago (G-4388) | | |
| Core Components Inc | F | 630 690-0520 |
| Carol Stream (G-3137) | | |
| Dalco Marketing Services | G | 630 961-3366 |
| Naperville (G-15641) | | |
| Dreisilker Electric Motors Inc | C | 630 469-7510 |
| Glen Ellyn (G-10967) | | |
| Dumore Supplies Inc | F | 312 949-6260 |
| Chicago (G-4649) | | |
| Eazypower Corporation | E | 773 278-5000 |
| Chicago (G-4686) | | |
| Enersys | D | 630 455-4872 |
| Lisle (G-13587) | | |
| Hallmark Industries Inc | F | 847 301-8050 |
| Schaumburg (G-19546) | | |
| Industrial Controls Inc | G | 630 752-8100 |
| Batavia (G-1457) | | |
| Inter-Market Inc | G | 847 729-5330 |
| Glenview (G-11149) | | |
| Motor Coach Industries | G | 847 285-2000 |
| Des Plaines (G-8236) | | |
| New Cie Inc | E | 815 224-1511 |
| Peru (G-17522) | | |
| New Cie Inc | F | 815 224-1485 |
| La Salle (G-12781) | | |
| North Point Investments Inc | G | 312 977-4386 |
| Chicago (G-5935) | | |
| Numeridex Incorporated | F | 847 541-8840 |
| Wheeling (G-22111) | | |
| Panduit Corp | A | 708 532-1800 |
| Tinley Park (G-20937) | | |
| Panduit Corp | E | 815 836-1800 |
| Lockport (G-13737) | | |
| Philips Lighting N Amer Corp | C | 800 825-5844 |
| Rosemont (G-19022) | | |
| Precision Drive & Control Inc | G | 815 235-7595 |
| Freeport (G-10680) | | |
| Psytronics Inc | G | 847 719-1371 |
| Lake Zurich (G-13118) | | |
| Robertson Transformer Co | E | 708 388-2315 |
| Crestwood (G-7500) | | |
| Rockford Electric Equipment Co | G | 815 398-4096 |
| Rockford (G-18573) | | |
| Special Mine Services Inc | D | 618 932-2151 |
| West Frankfort (G-21820) | | |
| Square 1 Precision Ltg Inc | G | 708 343-1500 |
| Melrose Park (G-14695) | | |
| Steiner Electric Company | E | 312 421-7220 |
| Chicago (G-6584) | | |
| Summit Design Solutions Inc | G | 847 836-8183 |
| East Dundee (G-8657) | | |
| Tent Maker Industrial Sup Inc | G | 847 469-6070 |
| Wauconda (G-21509) | | |
| V and F Transformer Corp | D | 630 497-8070 |
| Bartlett (G-1384) | | |
| Wesco International Inc | G | 630 513-4864 |
| Elmhurst (G-9960) | | |

## ELECTRICAL APPLIANCES, TELEVISIONS & RADIOS WHOLESALERS

| Company | Code | Phone |
|---|---|---|
| AVI-Spl Employee | B | 847 437-7712 |
| Schaumburg (G-19454) | | |
| Cco Holdings LLC | G | 618 505-3505 |
| Troy (G-21003) | | |
| Cco Holdings LLC | G | 618 651-6486 |
| Highland (G-11777) | | |
| Portable Cmmnctons Spclsts | G | 630 458-1800 |
| Addison (G-247) | | |
| Sansui America Inc | C | 618 392-7000 |
| Olney (G-16796) | | |

## ELECTRICAL CONSTRUCTION MATERIALS WHOLESALERS

| Company | Code | Phone |
|---|---|---|
| Matrix North Amercn Cnstr Inc | G | 312 754-6605 |
| Chicago (G-5654) | | |

## ELECTRICAL CURRENT CARRYING WIRING DEVICES

| Company | Code | Phone |
|---|---|---|
| Aco Inc | E | 773 774-5200 |
| Chicago (G-3735) | | |
| Alan Manufacturing Corp | G | 815 568-6836 |
| Marengo (G-14217) | | |
| Alcon Tool & Mfg Co Inc | F | 773 545-8742 |
| Chicago (G-3798) | | |
| American Bare Conductor Inc | E | 815 224-3422 |
| La Salle (G-12762) | | |
| Americor Electronics Ltd | F | 847 956-6200 |
| Elk Grove Village (G-9300) | | |
| Belden Energy Solutions Inc | G | 800 235-3361 |
| Elmhurst (G-9838) | | |
| Connector Concepts Inc | F | 847 541-4020 |
| Mundelein (G-15491) | | |
| Cooper B-Line Inc | C | 618 667-6779 |
| Troy (G-21004) | | |
| CTS Automotive LLC | C | 630 614-7201 |
| Lisle (G-13578) | | |
| Data Cable Technologies Inc | F | 630 226-5600 |
| Romeoville (G-18816) | | |
| Dcx-Chol Enterprises Inc | E | 309 353-4455 |
| Pekin (G-17258) | | |
| Dqm Inc | F | 630 692-0633 |
| Oswego (G-16914) | | |
| Eagle Connector Corporation | F | 847 593-8737 |
| Elk Grove Village (G-9446) | | |
| Excel Specialty Corp | E | 773 262-7575 |
| Lake Forest (G-12898) | | |
| Flex-Weld Inc | D | 815 334-3662 |
| Woodstock (G-22567) | | |
| General Electric Company | C | 309 664-1513 |
| Bloomington (G-2170) | | |
| GKN Stromag Inc | E | 937 433-3882 |
| Woodridge (G-22485) | | |
| Grayhill Inc | C | 847 428-6990 |
| Carpentersville (G-3285) | | |
| Gus Berthold Electric Company | E | 312 243-5767 |
| Chicago (G-5013) | | |
| Hauhinco LP | F | 618 993-5399 |
| Marion (G-14264) | | |
| Heil Sound Ltd | F | 618 257-3000 |
| Fairview Heights (G-10168) | | |
| Hubbell Incorporated | F | 972 756-1184 |
| Aurora (G-19024) | | |
| Ideal Industries Inc | C | 815 895-1108 |
| Sycamore (G-20801) | | |
| Ideal Industries Inc | E | 815 895-5181 |
| Sycamore (G-20802) | | |
| Ideal Industries Inc | C | 815 895-5181 |
| Sycamore (G-20800) | | |
| Ideal Industries Inc | D | 815 758-2656 |
| Dekalb (G-8098) | | |
| Illinois Tool Works Inc | C | 847 876-9400 |
| Des Plaines (G-8208) | | |
| Inglot Electronics Corp | D | 773 286-5881 |
| Chicago (G-5192) | | |
| Ki Industries Inc | F | 708 449-1990 |
| Berkeley (G-2046) | | |
| Leviton Manufacturing Co Inc | D | 630 539-0249 |
| Bloomingdale (G-2113) | | |
| Leviton Manufacturing Co Inc | C | 630 443-0500 |
| Saint Charles (G-19209) | | |
| Lutamar Electrical Assemblies | E | 847 679-5400 |
| Skokie (G-20032) | | |
| M E Barber Co Inc | G | 217 428-4591 |
| Decatur (G-7909) | | |
| Magnetrol International Inc | C | 630 723-6600 |
| Aurora (G-1051) | | |
| Methode Development Co | D | 708 867-6777 |
| Chicago (G-5703) | | |
| Methode Electronics Inc | G | 847 577-9545 |
| Rolling Meadows (G-18744) | | |
| Methode Electronics Inc | A | 217 357-3941 |
| Carthage (G-3316) | | |
| Methode Electronics Inc | B | 708 867-6777 |
| Chicago (G-5704) | | |
| Micro West Ltd | G | 630 766-7160 |
| Bensenville (G-1949) | | |
| Midwest Fiber Solutions | G | 217 971-7400 |
| Springfield (G-20484) | | |
| Mpc Products Corporation | G | 847 673-8300 |
| Niles (G-16012) | | |
| Porch Electric LLC | G | 815 368-3230 |
| Lostant (G-13908) | | |
| Process Screw Products Inc | E | 815 864-2220 |
| Shannon (G-19901) | | |
| Rockford Rigging Inc | F | 309 263-0566 |
| Roscoe (G-18914) | | |
| Rrp Enterprises Inc | G | 847 455-5674 |
| Franklin Park (G-10577) | | |
| S & C Electric Company | A | 773 338-1000 |
| Chicago (G-6419) | | |
| S-P Products Inc | G | 847 593-8595 |
| Elk Grove Village (G-9725) | | |
| Safco LLC | G | 847 677-3204 |
| Skokie (G-20081) | | |
| Simple Assemblies Inc | G | 708 212-7494 |
| New Lenox (G-15911) | | |
| Simplex Inc | C | 217 483-1600 |
| Springfield (G-20526) | | |
| Skach Manufacturing Co Inc | E | 847 395-3560 |
| Antioch (G-655) | | |
| Switchcraft Inc | B | 773 792-2700 |
| Chicago (G-6653) | | |
| Switchcraft Holdco Inc | G | 773 792-2700 |
| Chicago (G-6654) | | |
| Twin City Electric Inc | E | 309 827-0636 |
| Bloomington (G-2233) | | |
| U S Tool & Manufacturing Co | E | 630 953-1000 |
| Addison (G-332) | | |
| United Universal Inds Inc | E | 815 727-4445 |
| Joliet (G-12585) | | |
| Unlimited Svcs Wisconsin Inc | E | 815 399-0282 |
| Machesney Park (G-14117) | | |
| Western-Cullen-Hayes Inc | D | 773 254-9600 |
| Chicago (G-6964) | | |
| Woodward Controls Inc | C | 847 673-8300 |
| Skokie (G-20114) | | |

## ELECTRICAL DISCHARGE MACHINING, EDM

| Company | Code | Phone |
|---|---|---|
| Abet Industries Corporation | G | 708 482-8282 |
| La Grange Park (G-12751) | | |
| Alicona Manufacturing Inc | G | 630 736-2718 |
| Bartlett (G-1330) | | |
| EDM Scorpio Inc | G | 847 931-5164 |
| Elgin (G-9020) | | |
| Electroform Company | E | 815 633-1113 |
| Machesney Park (G-14072) | | |
| Inventive Mfg Inc | F | 847 647-9500 |
| Skokie (G-20018) | | |
| Master Cut E D M Inc | G | 847 534-0343 |
| Schaumburg (G-19634) | | |
| Xact Wire EDM Corp | F | 847 516-0903 |
| Cary (G-3379) | | |

## ELECTRICAL EQPT & SPLYS

| Company | Code | Phone |
|---|---|---|
| 2d2c Inc | G | 847 543-0980 |
| Gurnee (G-11416) | | |
| Access Japan LLC | G | 773 583-7183 |
| Chicago (G-3716) | | |
| Aemm A Electric | G | 708 403-6700 |
| Orland Park (G-16839) | | |
| Agrowtek Inc | G | 847 380-3009 |
| Gurnee (G-11420) | | |
| Aim Inc | G | 630 941-0027 |
| Elmhurst (G-9831) | | |
| Ambient Lightning and Electric | G | 708 529-3434 |
| Oak Lawn (G-16601) | | |
| Asco Power Technologies LP | G | 630 505-4050 |
| Warrenville (G-21343) | | |
| Associate General Labs Inc | G | 847 678-2717 |
| Franklin Park (G-10404) | | |
| Axon Electric LLC | G | 630 834-4090 |
| Lake In The Hills (G-12986) | | |
| Azz Incorporated | D | 815 723-5000 |
| Joliet (G-12459) | | |
| Bechara Sim | F | 847 913-9950 |
| Buffalo Grove (G-2662) | | |
| Bin Long & Electric | G | 309 758-5407 |
| Adair (G-12) | | |
| Brighter Electric Inc | G | 630 325-4915 |
| Willowbrook (G-22202) | | |
| Burr Ridge Lighting Inc | G | 630 323-4850 |
| Westmont (G-21878) | | |
| Carey Electric Co Inc | G | 847 949-9294 |
| Grayslake (G-11325) | | |
| Cdc Enterprises Inc | G | 815 790-4205 |
| Johnsburg (G-12432) | | |
| Cecomp Electronics Inc | E | 847 918-3510 |
| Libertyville (G-13313) | | |
| Coating & Systems Integration | F | 312 335-1848 |
| Chicago (G-4414) | | |
| Commscope Technologies LLC | A | 708 236-6600 |
| Westchester (G-21835) | | |
| Connor Electric Services Inc | E | 630 823-8230 |
| Schaumburg (G-19480) | | |
| Corporate Electric Inc | G | 847 963-2800 |
| Schaumburg (G-19485) | | |
| Current Plus Electric LLC | G | 618 394-4827 |
| Belleville (G-1620) | | |
| Custom Tool Inc | F | 217 465-8538 |
| Paris (G-17145) | | |
| Domino Amjet Inc | E | 847 662-3148 |
| Gurnee (G-11439) | | |
| E N M Company | D | 773 775-8400 |
| Chicago (G-4667) | | |
| East West Martial Arts Sups | G | 773 878-7711 |
| Chicago (G-4682) | | |

Employee Codes: A=Over 500 employees, B=251-500, C=101-250, D=51-100, E=20-50, F=10-19, G=3-9

Edison Electric G 815 464-1006
Frankfort (G-10319)
Elec Easel G 815 444-9700
Crystal Lake (G-7571)
Electri-Flex Company (del) D 630 307-1095
Roselle (G-18941)
Electric Grand G 630 363-8893
Montgomery (G-15042)
Electro-Technic Products Inc F 773 561-2349
Chicago (G-4721)
Elenco Electronics Inc E 847 541-3800
Wheeling (G-22046)
Enginuity Communications Corp E 630 444-0778
Saint Charles (G-19182)
Excarb Inc G 217 493-8477
Champaign (G-3484)
Eztech Manufacturing Inc F 630 293-0010
West Chicago (G-21700)
Fortitud Inc G 312 919-4938
Algonquin (G-390)
Foulk Electric Inc G 309 435-7006
Canton (G-2986)
Fryman Electric G 309 387-6540
Pekin (G-17264)
Genesis Electric & Tech Inc G 847 258-5218
Elk Grove Village (G-9498)
Gerardo and Quintana Auto Elc G 773 424-0634
Chicago (G-4947)
Giba Electric G 773 685-4420
Chicago (G-4951)
Gilbert Electric G 618 458-7235
Fults (G-10710)
Global Manufacturing G 630 908-7633
Willowbrook (G-22213)
Hardt Electric G 312 822-0869
Chicago (G-5044)
Heuft Usa Inc F 630 395-9521
Downers Grove (G-8457)
Hopcroft Electric Inc G 618 288-7302
Glen Carbon (G-10952)
Hubbell Power Systems Inc F 618 797-5000
Edwardsville (G-8803)
IMS Engineered Products LLC C 847 391-8100
Des Plaines (G-8211)
Industrial Enclosure Corp E 630 898-7499
Aurora (G-1171)
Intown Electric G 847 305-4816
Arlington Heights (G-779)
Inventus Power (illinois) LLC C 630 410-7900
Woodridge (G-22497)
James J Sandoval G 734 717-7555
Lombard (G-13814)
Jardis Industries Inc F 630 773-5600
Itasca (G-12290)
Jarvis Electric G 618 806-2767
O Fallon (G-16468)
Jescorp Inc D 847 378-1200
Elk Grove Village (G-9562)
Jess Electric G 217 243-7946
Jacksonville (G-12398)
Kavanaugh Electric Inc G 708 503-1310
Frankfort (G-10339)
Kaybee Engineering Company Inc E 630 968-7100
Westmont (G-21896)
Klass Electric Company Inc F 847 437-5555
Elk Grove Village (G-9576)
Kohns Electric G 309 463-2331
Varna (G-21134)
Lecip Inc G 312 626-2525
Bensenville (G-1939)
Lee Electric G 618 244-6810
Mount Vernon (G-15422)
Littelfuse Inc G 217 531-3100
Champaign (G-3511)
Lutamar Electrical Assemblies E 847 679-5400
Skokie (G-20032)
Mac Lean-Fogg Company C 847 288-2534
Franklin Park (G-10519)
Magnetrol International Inc C 630 723-6600
Aurora (G-1051)
Marmon Engineered Components E 312 372-9500
Chicago (G-5623)
Midwest Tool Inc G 773 588-1313
Chicago (G-5751)
Migatron Corporation E 815 338-5800
Woodstock (G-22590)
Mikus Elc & Generators Inc G 224 757-5534
Volo (G-21319)
Mkc Electric G 630 844-9700
Montgomery (G-15061)
Motor Sport Marketing Group E 618 654-6750
Highland (G-11803)
Newhaven Display Intl Inc E 847 844-8795
Elgin (G-9118)
Nova Systems Ltd G 630 879-2296
Aurora (G-1195)
Occly LLC G 773 969-5080
Chicago (G-5966)
Omron Electronics LLC C 847 843-7900
Hoffman Estates (G-12033)
Panduit Corp A 708 532-1800
Tinley Park (G-20937)
Panduit Corp E 815 836-1800
Lockport (G-13737)
Penco Electric G 847 423-2159
Niles (G-16016)
Plug-In Electric Charge Inc G 224 856-5229
Hoffman Estates (G-12038)
Prime Devices Corporation F 847 729-2550
Willow Springs (G-22198)
Probotix G 309 691-2643
Peoria (G-17436)
Protection Controls Inc E 773 763-3110
Skokie (G-20066)
Raynor Mfg Co A 815 288-1431
Dixon (G-8341)
Rein Electric G 224 433-6936
Libertyville (G-13375)
Request Electric G 217 629-7789
Riverton (G-18034)
Roman Electric G 773 777-9246
Chicago (G-6388)
Roundtble Hlthcare Partners LP E 847 482-9275
Lake Forest (G-12954)
S & S Electric Service G 708 366-5800
Forest Park (G-10252)
Scis Air Security Corporation G 847 671-9502
Schiller Park (G-19872)
Service King Plbg Htg Colg Elc G 847 458-8900
Lake In The Hills (G-13007)
Spurt Inc G 847 571-6497
Northbrook (G-16370)
SRC Electric LLC G 224 404-6103
Elk Grove Village (G-9750)
Superior One Electric Inc G 630 655-3300
Westchester (G-21856)
Sustanable Infrastructures Inc G 815 341-1447
Frankfort (G-10366)
Swiatek Electric G 331 225-3052
Elmhurst (G-9946)
Tenneco Automotive Oper Co Inc C 847 482-5000
Lake Forest (G-12965)
Thomas & Betts Corp G 630 444-2151
Saint Charles (G-19282)
Tii Technical Educatn Systems G 847 428-3085
Gilberts (G-10939)
Toho Technology Inc G 773 583-7183
Chicago (G-6735)
Unified Tool Die & Mfg Co Inc F 847 678-3773
Schiller Park (G-19878)
United Universal Inds Inc E 815 727-4445
Joliet (G-12585)
Visco Electric LLC G 630 336-7824
West Chicago (G-21790)
Vlahos Electric Service Dr G 224 764-2335
Arlington Heights (G-866)
Weg Electric Motors G 630 226-5688
Bolingbrook (G-2381)
Wesco International Inc G 630 513-4864
Elmhurst (G-9960)
Wildlife Materials Inc E 618 687-3505
Murphysboro (G-15586)

## ELECTRICAL EQPT FOR ENGINES

Aerodyne Incorporated G 773 588-2905
Chicago (G-3777)
Amerline Enterprises Co Inc E 847 671-6554
Schiller Park (G-19802)
Ark Technologies Inc C 630 377-8855
Saint Charles (G-19138)
Continental Automotive Inc E 847 862-6300
Deer Park (G-7970)
D C Grove Electric Inc G 847 587-0864
Fox Lake (G-10275)
Egan Wagner Corporation G 630 985-8007
Woodridge (G-22475)
Excel Specialty Corp E 773 262-7575
Lake Forest (G-12898)
Fram Group Operations LLC B 800 890-2075
Lake Forest (G-12899)
Harvey Bros Inc F 309 342-3137
Galesburg (G-10757)
Innovation Specialists Inc G 815 372-9001
New Lenox (G-15885)
J & B Truck Services Ltd G 708 430-8760
Bridgeview (G-2501)
K & W Auto Electric F 217 857-1717
Teutopolis (G-20853)
Kold-Ban International Ltd E 847 658-8561
Lake In The Hills (G-12997)
Major Wire Incorporated F 708 457-0121
Norridge (G-16105)
Mat Engine Technologies LLC G 847 821-9630
Long Grove (G-13896)
MTA USA Corp G 847 847-5503
Schaumburg (G-19656)
Niles Auto Parts G 847 215-2549
Lincolnshire (G-13468)
P & G Keene Elec Rbldrs LLC E 708 430-5770
Bridgeview (G-2516)
Thyssenkrupp Presta Cold Forgi E 217 431-4212
Danville (G-7774)

## ELECTRICAL EQPT REPAIR & MAINTENANCE

A J R International Inc D 800 232-3965
Glendale Heights (G-11006)
Ad Deluxe Sign Company Inc G 815 556-8469
Plainfield (G-17576)
B J Fehr Machine Co G 309 923-8691
Roanoke (G-18048)
C/B Machine Tool Corp G 847 288-1807
Franklin Park (G-10422)
Caterpillar Globl Min Amer LLC D 618 982-9000
Carrier Mills (G-3306)
Century Signs Inc F 217 224-7419
Quincy (G-17812)
Cooper Equipment Company Inc G 708 367-1291
Crete (G-7511)
Cortelyou Machine & Welding G 618 592-3961
Oblong (G-16730)
Cox Electric Motor Service G 217 344-2458
Urbana (G-21080)
FH Ayer Manufacturing Co E 708 755-0550
Chicago Heights (G-7097)
Hurst Enterprises Inc G 708 344-9291
Glendale Heights (G-11032)
Industrial Welder Rebuilders G 708 371-5688
Alsip (G-473)
Integrated Power Services LLC E 708 877-5310
Thornton (G-20874)
Jacobs Boiler & Mech Inds Inc E 773 385-9900
Chicago (G-5269)
L M Machine Shop Inc G 815 625-3256
Rock Falls (G-18141)
Midwest Design & Automtn Inc G 618 392-2892
Olney (G-16781)
Midwest Machine Service Inc F 708 229-1122
Alsip (G-494)
Napier Machine & Welding Inc G 217 525-8740
Springfield (G-20486)
National Machine Repair Inc F 708 672-7711
Crete (G-7517)
Niese Walter Machine Mfg Co G 773 774-7337
Chicago (G-5915)
S-P-D Incorporated G 847 882-9820
Palatine (G-17070)
Smart Inc G 847 464-4160
Hampshire (G-11563)
Thornton Welding Service Inc E 217 877-0610
Decatur (G-7952)
White Way Sign & Maint Co C 847 391-0200
Chicago (G-6974)

## ELECTRICAL EQPT REPAIR SVCS

ABRA Enterprises Inc G 847 866-6903
Evanston (G-10001)
Huygen Corporation G 815 455-2200
Crystal Lake (G-7590)
Johnson Controls Inc F 217 793-8858
Springfield (G-20464)

## ELECTRICAL EQPT: Automotive, NEC

Bill West Enterprises Inc G 217 886-2591
Jacksonville (G-12378)
Carnation Enterprises G 847 804-5928
Niles (G-15967)
County Packaging Inc D 708 597-1100
Crestwood (G-7484)

# PRODUCT SECTION

## ELECTRICAL GOODS, WHOLESALE: Panelboards

Elc Industries Corp ............................. E ...... 630 851-1616
  Aurora *(G-1144)*
Joes Automotive Inc ........................... G ...... 815 937-9281
  Kankakee *(G-12630)*
Kromray Hydraulic McHy Inc ............. G ...... 630 257-8655
  Lemont *(G-13238)*
Midtronics Inc ..................................... D ...... 630 323-2800
  Willowbrook *(G-22222)*
Plasmatreat USA Inc .......................... F ...... 847 783-0622
  Elgin *(G-9138)*
Southern Ill Auto Elec Inc .................. F ...... 618 587-3308
  Tilden *(G-20877)*

### ELECTRICAL EQPT: Household

Eazypower Corporation ...................... E ...... 773 278-5000
  Chicago *(G-4686)*
Eazypower Corporation ...................... G ...... 773 278-5000
  Chicago *(G-4687)*
Intermountain Electronics Inc ........... G ...... 618 339-6743
  Centralia *(G-3419)*
Temple Display Ltd ............................. G ...... 630 851-3331
  Oswego *(G-16936)*

### ELECTRICAL GOODS, WHOLESALE: Alarms & Signaling Eqpt

Siemens Industry Inc ......................... A ...... 847 215-1000
  Buffalo Grove *(G-2767)*

### ELECTRICAL GOODS, WHOLESALE: Batteries, Storage, Indl

Johnson Contrls Btry Group Inc ........ B ...... 630 232-4270
  Geneva *(G-10842)*

### ELECTRICAL GOODS, WHOLESALE: Burglar Alarm Systems

Audio Installers Inc ............................ F ...... 815 969-7500
  Loves Park *(G-13923)*

### ELECTRICAL GOODS, WHOLESALE: Circuit Breakers

Chicago Circuits Corporation ............. F ...... 847 238-1623
  Elk Grove Village *(G-9367)*
Oakland Industries Ltd ....................... E ...... 847 827-7600
  Mount Prospect *(G-15358)*

### ELECTRICAL GOODS, WHOLESALE: Citizens Band Radios

Wirelessusa Inc .................................. G ...... 217 222-4300
  Quincy *(G-17906)*

### ELECTRICAL GOODS, WHOLESALE: Connectors

Harting Inc of North America ............. E ...... 847 741-1500
  Elgin *(G-9059)*
Omnitronix Corporation ..................... F ...... 630 837-1400
  Streamwood *(G-20668)*

### ELECTRICAL GOODS, WHOLESALE: Electrical Appliances, Major

Appliance Repair ................................ G ...... 708 456-1020
  Norridge *(G-16096)*

### ELECTRICAL GOODS, WHOLESALE: Electrical Entertainment Eqpt

Gb Marketing Inc ................................ F ...... 847 367-0101
  Vernon Hills *(G-21164)*
Prager Associates .............................. G ...... 309 691-1565
  Peoria *(G-17433)*

### ELECTRICAL GOODS, WHOLESALE: Electronic Parts

Bisco Intl Inc ....................................... G ...... 708 544-6308
  Hillside *(G-11911)*
Hanjitech Inc ....................................... G ...... 847 707-5611
  Chicago *(G-5041)*
Huygen Corporation ........................... G ...... 815 455-2200
  Crystal Lake *(G-7590)*
Marshall Wolf Automation Inc ........... E ...... 847 658-8130
  Algonquin *(G-398)*
Morrell Incorporated .......................... F ...... 630 858-4600
  Glendale Heights *(G-11050)*
Nep Electronics Inc ............................ C ...... 630 595-8500
  Wood Dale *(G-22405)*
Nu-Way Electronics Inc ..................... G ...... 847 437-7120
  Elk Grove Village *(G-9657)*
Omron Automotive Elec Inc .............. A ...... 630 443-6800
  Saint Charles *(G-19229)*
Omron Electronics LLC ...................... C ...... 847 843-7900
  Hoffman Estates *(G-12033)*

### ELECTRICAL GOODS, WHOLESALE: Fans, Household

Df Fan Services Inc ............................ F ...... 630 876-1495
  West Chicago *(G-21692)*

### ELECTRICAL GOODS, WHOLESALE: Fire Alarm Systems

Flame Guard Usa LLC ........................ G ...... 815 219-4074
  Lake Barrington *(G-12806)*

### ELECTRICAL GOODS, WHOLESALE: Generators

Ees Inc ................................................ G ...... 708 343-1800
  Stone Park *(G-20633)*
Industrial Welder Rebuilders .............. G ...... 708 371-5688
  Alsip *(G-473)*
Kackert Enterprises Inc ...................... G ...... 630 898-9339
  Aurora *(G-1179)*
Lionheart Critical Pow ........................ E ...... 847 291-1413
  Huntley *(G-12159)*
Peoria Midwest Equipment Inc ......... G ...... 309 454-6800
  Normal *(G-16083)*
Unique Indoor Comfort ...................... G ...... 847 362-1910
  Libertyville *(G-13394)*
Xform Power and Eqp Sups LLC ....... G ...... 773 260-0209
  Chicago *(G-7044)*

### ELECTRICAL GOODS, WHOLESALE: High Fidelity Eqpt

Acoustic Avenue Inc .......................... F ...... 217 544-9810
  Springfield *(G-20385)*

### ELECTRICAL GOODS, WHOLESALE: Household Appliances, NEC

Mfp Holding Co ................................... G ...... 312 666-3366
  Chicago *(G-5714)*
Xfpg LLC ............................................. B ...... 224 513-2010
  Lincolnshire *(G-13491)*

### ELECTRICAL GOODS, WHOLESALE: Light Bulbs & Related Splys

Advanced Micro Lites Inc ................... G ...... 630 365-5450
  Elburn *(G-8874)*
Aero-Tech Light Bulb Co .................... F ...... 847 534-6580
  Schaumburg *(G-19425)*
Stone Lighting LLC ............................ G ...... 312 240-0400
  Flossmoor *(G-10230)*

### ELECTRICAL GOODS, WHOLESALE: Lighting Fittings & Access

Rgb Lights Inc .................................... F ...... 312 421-6080
  Chicago *(G-6346)*
Usway Corporation ............................. G ...... 773 338-9688
  Chicago *(G-6860)*

### ELECTRICAL GOODS, WHOLESALE: Lighting Fixtures, Comm & Indl

First Light Inc ..................................... G ...... 630 520-0017
  West Chicago *(G-21701)*
Holiday Bright Lights Inc ................... G ...... 312 226-8281
  Chicago *(G-5099)*
New Metal Crafts Inc ......................... E ...... 312 787-6991
  Lincolnwood *(G-13526)*
Shinetoo Lighting America LLC ......... G ...... 877 957-7317
  Des Plaines *(G-8274)*

### ELECTRICAL GOODS, WHOLESALE: Magnetic Recording Tape

Paragon Group Inc ............................. G ...... 847 526-1800
  Wauconda *(G-21491)*

### ELECTRICAL GOODS, WHOLESALE: Motor Ctrls, Starters & Relays

Envirnmntal Ctrl Solutions Inc .......... G ...... 217 793-8966
  Springfield *(G-20435)*
Midwest Elc Mtr Inc Danville ............. G ...... 217 442-5656
  Danville *(G-7756)*
Nusource Inc ...................................... F ...... 847 201-8934
  Round Lake *(G-19064)*

### ELECTRICAL GOODS, WHOLESALE: Motors

Accurate Elc Mtr & Pump Co ............. G ...... 708 448-2792
  Worth *(G-22631)*
Addison Electric Inc ........................... E ...... 800 517-4871
  Addison *(G-22)*
Avana Electric Motors Inc ................. F ...... 847 588-0400
  Elk Grove Village *(G-9323)*
Bellwood Electric Motors Inc ............ G ...... 708 544-7223
  Bellwood *(G-1696)*
Bodine Electric Company .................. C ...... 773 478-3515
  Northfield *(G-16393)*
BP Elc Mtrs Pump & Svc Inc ............. G ...... 773 539-4343
  Skokie *(G-19967)*
Cox Electric Motor Service ................ G ...... 217 344-2458
  Urbana *(G-21080)*
Flolo Corporation ............................... G ...... 847 249-0880
  Gurnee *(G-11448)*
Flolo Corporation ............................... E ...... 630 595-1010
  West Chicago *(G-21703)*
Foremost Electric & Transm Inc ....... E ...... 309 699-2200
  Peoria *(G-17364)*
Gem Electric Motor Repair ................ G ...... 815 756-5317
  Dekalb *(G-8094)*
Goding Electric Company .................. F ...... 630 858-7700
  Glendale Heights *(G-11029)*
Heise Industries Inc ........................... G ...... 847 223-2410
  Grayslake *(G-11346)*
Hills Electric Motor Service ............... G ...... 815 625-0305
  Rock Falls *(G-18136)*
Hopcroft Electric Inc .......................... G ...... 618 288-7302
  Glen Carbon *(G-10952)*
Industrial Service Solutions .............. F ...... 917 609-6979
  Chicago *(G-5180)*
Inman Electric Motors Inc ................. E ...... 815 223-2288
  La Salle *(G-12778)*
J Ream Manufacturing ....................... G ...... 630 983-6945
  Naperville *(G-15680)*
Kaman Automation Inc ...................... F ...... 847 273-9050
  Schaumburg *(G-19596)*
Kankakee Industrial Tech .................. F ...... 815 933-6683
  Bradley *(G-2425)*
Lange Electric Inc .............................. G ...... 217 347-7626
  Effingham *(G-8843)*
M R Glenn Electric Inc ....................... E ...... 708 479-9200
  Lockport *(G-13729)*
Melton Electric Co .............................. G ...... 309 697-1422
  Peoria *(G-17405)*
Metzka Inc .......................................... G ...... 815 932-6363
  Kankakee *(G-12638)*
Park Electric Motor Service ............... G ...... 217 442-1977
  Danville *(G-7759)*
Richards Electric Motor Co ............... G ...... 217 222-7154
  Quincy *(G-17887)*
Sandner Electric Co Inc ..................... G ...... 618 932-2179
  West Frankfort *(G-21818)*
Spg Usa Inc ........................................ G ...... 847 439-4949
  Elk Grove Village *(G-9747)*
Union Special LLC ............................. C ...... 847 669-5101
  Huntley *(G-12182)*
Vandalia Electric Mtr Svc Inc ............ G ...... 618 283-0068
  Vandalia *(G-21128)*
Yaskawa America Inc ........................ C ...... 847 887-7909
  Des Plaines *(G-8307)*
Yaskawa America Inc ........................ C ...... 847 887-7000
  Waukegan *(G-21642)*

### ELECTRICAL GOODS, WHOLESALE: Paging & Signaling Eqpt

Visiplex Inc ......................................... F ...... 847 229-0250
  Buffalo Grove *(G-2791)*

### ELECTRICAL GOODS, WHOLESALE: Panelboards

Industrial Electric Svc Inc ................. G ...... 708 997-2090
  Bartlett *(G-1356)*

Employee Codes: A=Over 500 employees, B=251-500, C=101-250, D=51-100, E=20-50, F=10-19, G=3-9

# ELECTRICAL GOODS, WHOLESALE: Radio Parts & Access, NEC

### ELECTRICAL GOODS, WHOLESALE: Radio Parts & Access, NEC
Amis Inc .................................... G ....... 708 598-9700
  Bridgeview *(G-2465)*

### ELECTRICAL GOODS, WHOLESALE: Resistors
Ohmite Holding LLC ................. E ....... 847 258-0300
  Warrenville *(G-21352)*

### ELECTRICAL GOODS, WHOLESALE: Safety Switches
Bircher America Inc ................. G ....... 847 952-3730
  Schaumburg *(G-19462)*

### ELECTRICAL GOODS, WHOLESALE: Security Control Eqpt & Systems
Ionit Technologies Inc .............. E ....... 847 205-9651
  Northfield *(G-16403)*
No Surrender Inc ...................... G ....... 773 929-7920
  Chicago *(G-5920)*

### ELECTRICAL GOODS, WHOLESALE: Semiconductor Devices
Component Sales Incorporated ... F ....... 630 543-9666
  Addison *(G-79)*

### ELECTRICAL GOODS, WHOLESALE: Signaling, Eqpt
Autonomoustuff LLC ................ G ....... 314 270-2123
  Morton *(G-15153)*
Nafisco Inc ................................ F ....... 815 372-3300
  Romeoville *(G-18851)*

### ELECTRICAL GOODS, WHOLESALE: Sound Eqpt
Amplivox Sound Systems LLC .... E ....... 800 267-5486
  Northbrook *(G-16204)*
Foster Electric (usa) Inc .......... F ....... 847 310-8200
  Schaumburg *(G-19532)*
OEM Solutions Inc ................... G ....... 708 574-8893
  Oak Brook *(G-16551)*

### ELECTRICAL GOODS, WHOLESALE: Switches, Exc Electronic, NEC
Data Accessories Inc ............... G ....... 847 669-3640
  Huntley *(G-12136)*

### ELECTRICAL GOODS, WHOLESALE: Telephone & Telegraphic Eqpt
Wescom Products ..................... G ....... 217 932-5292
  Casey *(G-3392)*

### ELECTRICAL GOODS, WHOLESALE: Telephone Eqpt
AT&T Teleholdings Inc .............. G ....... 800 257-0902
  Chicago *(G-3973)*
Charles Industries Ltd ............. D ....... 217 932-5294
  Casey *(G-3382)*
Custom Canvas LLC ................. G ....... 847 587-0225
  Ingleside *(G-12188)*

### ELECTRICAL GOODS, WHOLESALE: Transformer & Transmission Eqpt
Aldonex Inc .............................. F ....... 708 547-5663
  Bellwood *(G-1693)*
Custom Millers Supply Inc ........ G ....... 309 734-6312
  Monmouth *(G-15011)*
McC Technology Inc ................. F ....... 630 377-7200
  Saint Charles *(G-19216)*

### ELECTRICAL GOODS, WHOLESALE: Transformers
Philips Lighting N Amer Corp ... E ....... 708 307-3000
  Roselle *(G-18962)*

### ELECTRICAL GOODS, WHOLESALE: Video Eqpt
Pfingsten Partners LLC ............ F ....... 312 222-8707
  Chicago *(G-6115)*

### ELECTRICAL GOODS, WHOLESALE: Wire & Cable
Cable Company ......................... E ....... 847 437-5267
  Elk Grove Village *(G-9355)*
Clark Wire & Cable Co Inc ....... E ....... 847 949-9944
  Mundelein *(G-15488)*
Hamalot Inc .............................. E ....... 847 944-1500
  Schaumburg *(G-19547)*
Manu Industries Inc ................. F ....... 847 891-6412
  Schaumburg *(G-19630)*
Monona Holdings LLC .............. G ....... 630 946-0630
  Naperville *(G-15700)*
Partex Marking Systems Inc .... G ....... 630 516-0400
  Lombard *(G-13842)*
Quality Cable & Components Inc ... E ....... 309 695-3435
  Wyoming *(G-22639)*

### ELECTRICAL GOODS, WHOLESALE: Wire & Cable, Building
Advantage Direct Inc ............... F ....... 847 427-1185
  Elk Grove Village *(G-9279)*

### ELECTRICAL GOODS, WHOLESALE: Wire & Cable, Power
Pro-Pak Industries Inc ............. F ....... 630 876-1050
  West Chicago *(G-21761)*

### ELECTRICAL HOUSEHOLD APPLIANCE REPAIR
Appliance Repair ...................... G ....... 708 456-1020
  Norridge *(G-16096)*

### ELECTRICAL INDL APPARATUS, NEC
Powerone Corp ......................... G ....... 630 443-6500
  Saint Charles *(G-19239)*

### ELECTRICAL MEASURING INSTRUMENT REPAIR & CALIBRATION SVCS
Allied Instrument Service Inc ... F ....... 708 788-1912
  Berwyn *(G-2056)*

### ELECTRICAL SPLYS
Decatur Industrial Elc Inc ........ E ....... 217 428-6621
  Decatur *(G-7872)*
Johnson Controls Inc ............... E ....... 309 427-2800
  East Peoria *(G-8719)*
Johnson Controls Inc ............... G ....... 312 829-5956
  Chicago *(G-5319)*
Rathje Enterprises Inc ............. B ....... 217 423-2593
  Decatur *(G-7932)*
Telegartner Inc ......................... E ....... 630 616-7600
  Franklin Park *(G-10605)*
Uesco Industries Inc ................ G ....... 800 325-8372
  Alsip *(G-537)*

### ELECTRICAL SUPPLIES: Porcelain
Dpcac LLC ................................ F ....... 630 741-7900
  Itasca *(G-12253)*
Ferro Corporation .................... C ....... 847 623-0370
  Waukegan *(G-21559)*
Johnson Sign Co ....................... G ....... 847 678-2092
  Franklin Park *(G-10509)*
Porcelain Enamel Finishers ..... G ....... 312 808-1560
  Chicago *(G-6157)*
Senna Design LLC .................... G ....... 847 821-7877
  Vernon Hills *(G-21201)*
Voges Inc .................................. D ....... 618 233-2760
  Belleville *(G-1688)*

### ELECTRODES: Thermal & Electrolytic
Hausermann Die & Machine Co ... F ....... 630 543-6688
  Addison *(G-144)*
Starex Inc ................................. G ....... 847 918-5555
  Libertyville *(G-13384)*

### ELECTROLYZING SVC: Steel, Light Gauge
Koderhandt Inc ......................... G ....... 618 233-4808
  Belleville *(G-1645)*

### ELECTROMEDICAL EQPT
Acoustic Medsystems Inc ......... G ....... 217 355-8888
  Savoy *(G-19408)*
Arxium Inc ................................ C ....... 847 808-2600
  Buffalo Grove *(G-2660)*
Axios Medtech Inc .................... G ....... 312 224-7856
  Round Lake Beach *(G-19072)*
Barrington Clinical Partners ..... G ....... 847 508-9737
  Barrington *(G-1271)*
Bio-Logic Systems Corp ........... D ....... 847 949-0456
  Mundelein *(G-15478)*
Domino Lasers Inc ................... E ....... 847 855-1364
  Gurnee *(G-11442)*
Elmed Incorporated .................. E ....... 630 543-2792
  Glendale Heights *(G-11021)*
Henderson Engineering Co Inc ... G ....... 815 786-9471
  Sandwich *(G-19368)*
Interexpo Ltd ............................ F ....... 847 489-7056
  Kildeer *(G-12700)*
Jones Medical Instrument Co ... E ....... 630 571-1980
  Oak Brook *(G-16528)*
Lifeline Scientific Inc .............. E ....... 847 294-0300
  Itasca *(G-12304)*
Lifewatch Technologies Inc ..... D ....... 800 633-3361
  Rosemont *(G-19014)*
Medtex Health Services Inc ..... G ....... 630 789-0330
  Clarendon Hills *(G-7258)*
Memorial Breast Diagnstc Svcs ... G ....... 217 788-4042
  Springfield *(G-20479)*
Metritrack Inc ........................... G ....... 708 498-3578
  Hillside *(G-11925)*
Natus Medical Incorporated ..... F ....... 847 949-5200
  Mundelein *(G-15536)*
Northgate Technologies Inc ..... E ....... 847 608-8900
  Elgin *(G-9126)*
Olympus America Inc ............... F ....... 630 953-2080
  Lombard *(G-13836)*
Omex Technologies Inc ............ G ....... 847 850-5858
  Wheeling *(G-22112)*
Omron Healthcare Inc .............. G ....... 847 680-6200
  Lake Forest *(G-12932)*
Positron Corporation ................ E ....... 317 576-0183
  Westmont *(G-21912)*
Retmap Inc ................................ G ....... 312 224-8938
  Grayslake *(G-11361)*
Siemens Med Solutions USA Inc ... F ....... 847 793-4429
  Buffalo Grove *(G-2769)*
Siemens Med Solutions USA Inc ... D ....... 847 304-7700
  Hoffman Estates *(G-12053)*
Snap Diagnostics LLC ............... F ....... 847 777-0000
  Wheeling *(G-22154)*
System Science Corporation .... G ....... 708 214-2264
  Chicago *(G-6659)*
Thermatome Corporation ......... G ....... 312 772-2201
  Chicago *(G-6712)*
Thermopol Inc .......................... G ....... 815 422-0400
  Saint Anne *(G-19126)*
Vestibular Technologies LLC ... G ....... 618 993-7561
  Marion *(G-14293)*

### ELECTROMEDICAL EQPT WHOLESALERS
Interexpo Ltd ............................ F ....... 847 489-7056
  Kildeer *(G-12700)*
Lifewatch Technologies Inc ..... D ....... 800 633-3361
  Rosemont *(G-19014)*
Medical Specialties Distrs LLC ... E ....... 630 307-6200
  Hanover Park *(G-11585)*

### ELECTROMETALLURGICAL PRDTS
Prince Minerals LLC ................. G ....... 646 747-4222
  Quincy *(G-17873)*
Prince Minerals LLC ................. G ....... 646 747-4200
  Quincy *(G-17874)*
SWB Inc .................................... G ....... 847 438-1800
  Lake Zurich *(G-13136)*
Tempel Steel Company ............. A ....... 773 250-8000
  Chicago *(G-6697)*
Tempel Steel Company ............. F ....... 847 244-5330
  Old Mill Creek *(G-16756)*
Tempel Steel Company ............. A ....... 773 250-8000
  Chicago *(G-6696)*
Tempel Steel Company ............. A ....... 773 250-8000
  Chicago *(G-6698)*

## PRODUCT SECTION

### ELECTRON BEAM: Cutting, Forming, Welding

Sciaky Inc ..................................... E ...... 708 594-3841
  Chicago  *(G-6456)*
Trigon International Corp ................. E ...... 630 978-9990
  Aurora  *(G-1089)*

### ELECTRON TUBES

Dcx-Chol Enterprises Inc ................. E ...... 309 353-4455
  Pekin  *(G-17258)*
Northrop Grumman Systems Corp ..... A ...... 847 259-9600
  Rolling Meadows  *(G-18753)*
Rcl Electronics .............................. G ...... 630 834-0156
  Addison  *(G-271)*

### ELECTRON TUBES: Cathode Ray

Light of Mine LLC ........................... G ...... 312 840-8570
  Chicago  *(G-5503)*
Thomas Electronics Inc .................. E ...... 315 923-2051
  Addison  *(G-312)*

### ELECTRON TUBES: Parts

Richardson Electronics Ltd .............. C ...... 630 208-2200
  Lafox  *(G-12796)*

### ELECTRON TUBES: Transmitting

F & L Electronics LLC ..................... F ...... 217 586-2132
  Mahomet  *(G-14158)*

### ELECTRONIC COMPONENTS

Americut Wire Edm Inc .................... F ...... 847 675-1754
  Skokie  *(G-19952)*
C & B Services .............................. G ...... 847 462-8484
  Cary  *(G-3329)*
Compu Doc Inc .............................. G ...... 630 554-5800
  Oswego  *(G-16910)*
Elgo Electronic Inc ......................... G ...... 630 626-1639
  Bartlett  *(G-1344)*
Ot Systems Limited ........................ G ...... 630 554-9178
  Plano  *(G-17669)*
Seaco Data Systems Inc ................. D ...... 630 876-2169
  Carol Stream  *(G-3237)*
Value Link 1 Enterprises ................. G ...... 630 833-6243
  Villa Park  *(G-21289)*

### ELECTRONIC DEVICES: Solid State, NEC

Dynawave Corporation .................... F ...... 630 232-4945
  Geneva  *(G-10826)*
Power Electronics Intl Inc ................ E ...... 847 836-2071
  East Dundee  *(G-8654)*
Thermoelectric Coolg Amer Corp ..... G ...... 773 342-4900
  Chicago  *(G-6713)*

### ELECTRONIC EQPT REPAIR SVCS

Bowl-Tronics Enterprises Inc ........... G ...... 847 741-4500
  Elgin  *(G-8970)*
Elcon Inc ...................................... E ...... 815 467-9500
  Minooka  *(G-14840)*
Municipal Electronics Inc ................. G ...... 217 877-8601
  Decatur  *(G-7920)*
Murata Electronics N Amer Inc ........ G ...... 847 330-9200
  Schaumburg  *(G-19657)*
Rockford Electric Equipment Co ...... G ...... 815 398-4096
  Rockford  *(G-18573)*
Yale Security Inc ........................... D ...... 704 283-2101
  Franklin Park  *(G-10632)*

### ELECTRONIC LOADS & POWER SPLYS

Advanced Strobe Products Inc ........ D ...... 708 867-3100
  Chicago  *(G-3772)*
Lifesafety Power Inc ...................... F ...... 224 324-4240
  Mundelein  *(G-15520)*
Light To Form LLC ......................... E ...... 847 498-5832
  Northbrook  *(G-16296)*
Limitless Innovations Inc ................ E ...... 855 843-4828
  McHenry  *(G-14522)*
Power Equipment Company ............. E ...... 815 754-4090
  Cortland  *(G-7394)*
Sumida America Inc ....................... E ...... 847 545-6700
  Schaumburg  *(G-19743)*
T&L International Mfg/Dist Inc ........ G ...... 309 830-7238
  Farmer City  *(G-10182)*
TRW Automotive US LLC ................ B ...... 217 826-3011
  Marshall  *(G-14330)*

VI Inc ........................................... G ...... 618 277-8703
  Belleville  *(G-1685)*

### ELECTRONIC PARTS & EQPT WHOLESALERS

Ally Global Corporation ................... G ...... 773 822-3373
  Chicago  *(G-3826)*
ASap Specialties Inc Del ................. G ...... 847 223-7699
  Grayslake  *(G-11321)*
Autotech Tech Ltd Partnr ................ G ...... 630 668-8886
  Carol Stream  *(G-3108)*
Bechara Sim .................................. F ...... 847 913-9950
  Buffalo Grove  *(G-2662)*
Belford Electronics Inc .................... E ...... 630 705-3020
  Addison  *(G-52)*
Cisco Systems Inc ......................... B ...... 847 678-6600
  Des Plaines  *(G-8170)*
Communication Coil Inc .................. D ...... 847 671-1333
  Schiller Park  *(G-19815)*
Consolidated Elec Wire & Cable ...... D ...... 847 455-8830
  Franklin Park  *(G-10440)*
Dytec Midwest Inc .......................... E ...... 847 255-3200
  Rolling Meadows  *(G-18726)*
George Electronics Inc .................... G ...... 708 331-1983
  Orland Park  *(G-16860)*
Gepco International Inc ................... E ...... 847 795-9555
  Des Plaines  *(G-8201)*
Heuft Usa Inc ................................. F ...... 630 395-9521
  Downers Grove  *(G-8457)*
Hirose Electric (usa) Inc .................. D ...... 630 282-6700
  Downers Grove  *(G-8459)*
Inglot Electronics Corp .................... D ...... 773 286-5881
  Chicago  *(G-5192)*
Jme Technologies Inc ..................... G ...... 815 477-8800
  Crystal Lake  *(G-7595)*
Limitless Innovations Inc ................. E ...... 855 843-4828
  McHenry  *(G-14522)*
Loma International Inc .................... D ...... 630 588-0900
  Carol Stream  *(G-3186)*
Midwest Cad Design Inc .................. G ...... 847 397-0220
  Schaumburg  *(G-19647)*
Nielsen & Bainbridge LLC ................ D ...... 708 546-2135
  Bridgeview  *(G-2514)*
Northern Technologies Inc ............... G ...... 440 246-6999
  Warrenville  *(G-21351)*
Pactra Corp ................................... G ...... 847 281-0308
  Vernon Hills  *(G-21187)*
Richardson Electronics Ltd .............. C ...... 630 208-2200
  Lafox  *(G-12796)*
Rittal Corp ..................................... A ...... 847 240-4600
  Schaumburg  *(G-19712)*
Sumida America Inc ....................... E ...... 847 545-6700
  Schaumburg  *(G-19743)*
Tellurian Technologies Inc ............... C ...... 847 934-4141
  Arlington Heights  *(G-854)*
Touchsensor Technologies LLC ....... B ...... 630 221-9000
  Wheaton  *(G-21987)*
Unified Solutions Corp .................... E ...... 847 478-9100
  Arlington Heights  *(G-861)*
Vincor Ltd ..................................... F ...... 708 534-0008
  Monee  *(G-15005)*

### ELECTRONIC TRAINING DEVICES

Kidde Fire Triner Holdings LLC ........ G ...... 312 219-7900
  Chicago  *(G-5381)*
Midwest Assembly & Packg Inc ....... G
  Wauconda  *(G-21483)*
Northern Illi Electrcl Jnt App ............ F ...... 815 969-8484
  Rockford  *(G-18521)*
Pipeline Trading Systems LLC .......... G ...... 312 212-4288
  Chicago  *(G-6128)*
Three Hands Technologies ............... G ...... 847 680-5358
  Vernon Hills  *(G-21212)*
Tricor Systems Inc ......................... E ...... 847 742-5542
  Elgin  *(G-9214)*

### ELECTROPLATING & PLATING SVC

Ameriplate Inc ............................... E ...... 815 744-8585
  Joliet  *(G-12453)*
Chris Plating Inc ............................ E ...... 847 729-9271
  Northbrook  *(G-16223)*
Electrolizing Inc ............................. G ...... 815 758-6657
  Dekalb  *(G-8089)*
Perfection Plating Inc ..................... C ...... 847 593-6506
  Elk Grove Village  *(G-9673)*
Selective Plating Inc ....................... E ...... 630 543-1380
  Addison  *(G-286)*
Unitech Industries Inc ..................... F ...... 847 357-8800
  Elk Grove Village  *(G-9798)*

### ELEMENTARY & SECONDARY SCHOOLS, SPECIAL EDUCATION

Route 40 Media LLC ....................... G ...... 309 370-5809
  Peoria  *(G-17449)*

### ELEVATOR: Grain, Storage Only

Archer-Daniels-Midland Company .... E ...... 217 224-1800
  Quincy  *(G-17794)*
Gateway Fs Inc .............................. G ...... 618 824-6631
  Venedy  *(G-21136)*

### ELEVATORS & EQPT

Adams Elevator Equipment Co ........ E ...... 847 581-2900
  Chicago  *(G-3743)*
Cabworks LLC ............................... G ...... 773 588-1731
  Chicago  *(G-4209)*
D A Matot Inc ................................ D ...... 708 547-1888
  Bellwood  *(G-1702)*
Elevator Cable & Supply Co ............ G ...... 708 338-9700
  Broadview  *(G-2574)*
Elevators USA Incorporated ............ G ...... 847 847-1856
  Lake Zurich  *(G-13068)*
Formula Systems North America ..... G ...... 847 350-0655
  Elk Grove Village  *(G-9486)*
Harris Companies Inc ..................... F ...... 217 578-2231
  Atwood  *(G-947)*
Integrated Display Systems ............. F ...... 708 298-9661
  Cicero  *(G-7206)*
Kafka Manufacturing Co .................. G ...... 708 771-0970
  Forest Park  *(G-10250)*
Kone Elevator ................................ C ...... 309 764-6771
  Moline  *(G-14950)*
Lifts of Illinois Inc .......................... G ...... 309 923-7450
  Roanoke  *(G-18052)*
Long Elevator and Mch Co Inc ........ D ...... 217 629-9648
  Springfield  *(G-20472)*
Mitsubishi Electric Us Inc ................ E ...... 708 354-2900
  Countryside  *(G-7439)*
Otis Elevator Company ................... D ...... 312 454-1616
  Chicago  *(G-6023)*
Quality Elevator Products Inc .......... E ...... 847 581-0085
  Niles  *(G-16023)*
United Technologies Corp ................ B ...... 815 226-6000
  Rockford  *(G-18663)*
Vator Accessories Inc ..................... G ...... 630 876-8370
  West Chicago  *(G-21788)*

### ELEVATORS WHOLESALERS

Home Mobility Solutions Inc ............ G ...... 630 800-7800
  Downers Grove  *(G-8461)*
Lifts of Illinois Inc .......................... G ...... 309 923-7450
  Roanoke  *(G-18052)*
Otis Elevator Company ................... F ...... 618 529-3411
  Carbondale  *(G-3016)*
Parts Specialists Inc ...................... G ...... 708 371-2444
  Posen  *(G-17734)*

### ELEVATORS: Installation & Conversion

Colley Elevator Company ................. E ...... 630 766-7230
  Bensenville  *(G-1861)*
Jeffrey Elevator Co Inc .................... F ...... 847 524-2400
  Schaumburg  *(G-19587)*
Kone Inc ....................................... A ...... 630 577-1650
  Lisle  *(G-13614)*
Lifts of Illinois Inc .......................... G ...... 309 923-7450
  Roanoke  *(G-18052)*
Mid-American Elevator Co Inc ......... C ...... 773 486-6900
  Chicago  *(G-5727)*
Mid-American Elevator Co Inc ......... E ...... 815 740-1204
  Joliet  *(G-12541)*

### EMBALMING FLUID

Frigid Fluid Company ...................... E ...... 708 836-1215
  Melrose Park  *(G-14645)*

### EMBLEMS: Embroidered

Ameri-Tex ..................................... G ...... 847 247-0777
  Mundelein  *(G-15469)*
American EMB & Screen Prtg LLC ... G ...... 630 766-2825
  Glendale Heights  *(G-11008)*
Chicago Knitting Mills .................... G ...... 773 463-1464
  Chicago  *(G-4326)*
Cq Industries Inc ........................... G ...... 630 530-0177
  Elmhurst  *(G-9857)*
Fast Lane Threads Custom EMB ...... G ...... 815 544-9898
  Belvidere  *(G-1751)*

## EMBLEMS: Embroidered

Midwest Swiss Embroideries Co .......... E ....... 773 631-7120
 Chicago  (G-5750)
Personalized Threads ........................... G ....... 815 431-1815
 Ottawa  (G-16978)
Stitch Magic Usa Inc ............................ E ....... 847 836-5000
 West Dundee  (G-21802)
Stitchables Embroidery ........................ G ....... 217 322-3000
 Rushville  (G-19096)
Trading Square Company Inc ............. G ....... 630 960-0606
 Westmont  (G-21925)
Tryad Specialties Inc ........................... F ....... 630 549-0079
 Saint Charles  (G-19287)
Welsh Industries Ltd ............................ E ....... 815 756-1111
 Dekalb  (G-8131)
Winning Stitch ...................................... G ....... 217 348-8279
 Charleston  (G-3616)

## EMBOSSING SVC: Paper

Capital Prtg & Die Cutng Inc ................ G ....... 630 896-5520
 Aurora  (G-1124)
Capitol Impressions Inc ....................... E ....... 309 633-1400
 Peoria  (G-17322)
Classic Impressions Inc ...................... G
 Oswego  (G-16908)
Creative Lithocraft Inc ......................... F ....... 847 352-7002
 Schaumburg  (G-19488)
Creative Lithocraft Inc ......................... G ....... 847 352-7002
 Schaumburg  (G-19489)
H A Friend & Company Inc ................. E ....... 847 746-1248
 Zion  (G-22687)
Illinois Valley Printing  Inc ................... G ....... 309 674-4942
 Peoria  (G-17388)
Lasersketch Ltd ................................... F ....... 630 243-6360
 Romeoville  (G-18837)
Midwest Gold Stampers  Inc ............... F ....... 773 775-5253
 Chicago  (G-5744)
Redeen Engraving Inc ........................ G ....... 847 593-6500
 Elk Grove Village  (G-9712)

## EMBOSSING SVCS: Diplomas, Resolutions, Etc

A Cut Above Engraving Inc ................. G ....... 708 671-9800
 Palos Park  (G-17126)

## EMBROIDERING & ART NEEDLEWORK FOR THE TRADE

A Plus Apparel .................................... G ....... 815 675-2117
 Spring Grove  (G-20323)
Action Screen Print  Inc ...................... F ....... 630 393-1990
 Warrenville  (G-21340)
All In Stitches ...................................... G ....... 309 944-4084
 Geneseo  (G-10796)
ASap Specialties Inc Del .................... G ....... 847 223-7699
 Grayslake  (G-11321)
Athletic Outfitters  Inc ......................... G ....... 815 942-6696
 Morris  (G-15094)
B & B Custom TS & Gifts .................... G ....... 618 463-0443
 Alton  (G-562)
Barnes & Noble College ..................... E ....... 309 677-2320
 Peoria  (G-17314)
Bean Stich Inc .................................... G ....... 630 422-1269
 Bensenville  (G-1841)
Camilles of Canton Inc ....................... G ....... 309 647-7403
 Canton  (G-2983)
Chicago Printing and EMB Inc ............ G ....... 630 628-1777
 Addison  (G-75)
Classic Embroidery  Inc ...................... F ....... 708 485-7034
 Chicago  (G-4392)
Cloz Companies  Inc ........................... E ....... 773 247-8879
 Skokie  (G-19983)
Cubby Hole of Carlinville Inc .............. F ....... 217 854-8511
 Carlinville  (G-3035)
Custom AP & Promotions Inc ............. G ....... 815 398-9823
 Rockford  (G-18326)
D & D Embroidery ............................... G ....... 309 266-7092
 Morton  (G-15156)
D & J International Inc ........................ F ....... 847 966-9260
 Niles  (G-15974)
Digistitch Embroidery & Design .......... G ....... 773 229-8630
 Chicago  (G-4598)
Dilars Embroidery & Monograms ........ G ....... 815 338-6066
 Woodstock  (G-22560)
Doras Spinning Wheel Inc .................. G ....... 618 466-1900
 Alton  (G-571)
Dpe Incorporated ................................ G ....... 773 306-0105
 Chicago  (G-4640)
Elegant Embroidery  Inc ..................... G ....... 847 540-8003
 Lake Zurich  (G-13067)
Embroidery Choices ........................... G ....... 708 597-9093
 Blue Island  (G-2249)
Embroidery Services Inc .................... G ....... 847 588-2660
 Niles  (G-15978)
Essential Creations ............................ G ....... 773 238-1700
 Chicago  (G-4779)
Fielders Choice .................................. G ....... 618 937-2294
 West Frankfort  (G-21807)
First Impression .................................. G ....... 815 883-3357
 Oglesby  (G-16748)
Galaxy Embroidery  Inc ...................... G ....... 312 243-8991
 Chicago  (G-4908)
Gavina Graphics ................................. F ....... 217 345-9228
 Charleston  (G-3598)
Hermans  Inc ...................................... E ....... 309 206-4892
 Rock Island  (G-18181)
Hyperstitch ......................................... F ....... 815 568-0590
 Marengo  (G-14230)
Illinois Embroidery Service ................. G ....... 618 526-8006
 Breese  (G-2445)
Janes Lettering Service Inc ................ G ....... 309 243-7669
 Dunlap  (G-8568)
Langa Resource Group Inc ................ G ....... 618 462-1899
 Alton  (G-581)
M&M Embroidery Corp ....................... G ....... 847 209-1086
 Palatine  (G-17052)
Minor League Inc ............................... G ....... 618 548-8040
 Salem  (G-19339)
Mt Greenwood Embroidery ................. G ....... 773 779-5798
 Chicago  (G-5827)
Nelson Enterprises Inc ....................... G ....... 815 633-1100
 Roscoe  (G-18910)
Orland Sports Ltd ............................... G ....... 773 685-3711
 Chicago  (G-6014)
Reel Mate Mfg Co ............................... G ....... 708 423-8005
 Oak Lawn  (G-16643)
Select Screen Prints & EMB .............. F ....... 309 829-6511
 Bloomington  (G-2222)
Senn Enterprises Inc .......................... G ....... 309 673-4384
 Peoria  (G-17451)
Senn Enterprises Inc .......................... F ....... 309 637-1147
 Peoria  (G-17450)
Sports Designs & Graphics ................ E ....... 217 342-2777
 Effingham  (G-8859)
Stans Sportsworld Inc ......................... G ....... 217 359-8474
 Champaign  (G-3547)
Star Silkscreen Design Inc ................. G ....... 217 877-0804
 Decatur  (G-7943)
Stitchin Image .................................... G ....... 815 578-9890
 Richmond  (G-17973)
T Graphics .......................................... G ....... 618 592-4145
 Oblong  (G-16735)
Town Hall Sports Inc ........................... F ....... 618 235-9881
 Belleville  (G-1682)
Waist Up Imprntd Sprtswear LLC ....... G ....... 847 963-1400
 Palatine  (G-17086)
Wellspring Investments LLC ............... G ....... 773 736-1213
 Chicago  (G-6955)
Winning Streak  Inc ............................ E ....... 618 277-8191
 Dupo  (G-8584)

## EMBROIDERING SVC

A B S Embroidery Inc ......................... G ....... 708 597-7785
 Alsip  (G-427)
All Stars -N- Stitches Inc .................... G ....... 618 435-5555
 Benton  (G-2021)
Allstar Embroidery .............................. G ....... 847 913-1133
 Buffalo Grove  (G-2555)
Bee Designs Embroidery & Scree ...... G ....... 815 393-4593
 Malta  (G-14165)
Bullseye Imprinting & EMB ................. G ....... 630 834-8175
 Elmhurst  (G-9844)
C & C Embroidery Inc ......................... G ....... 815 777-6167
 Galena  (G-10715)
Cottage Collage .................................. G ....... 847 541-7205
 Buffalo Grove  (G-2681)
Design Loft Imaging Inc ..................... G ....... 847 439-2486
 Elk Grove Village  (G-9425)
Downtown Sports ............................... G ....... 815 284-2255
 Dixon  (G-8330)
Embroidery Experts Inc ..................... G ....... 847 403-0200
 Vernon Hills  (G-21160)
Embroidery Express Inc ..................... G ....... 630 365-9393
 Elburn  (G-8888)
Ensign Emblem Ltd ............................ D ....... 217 877-8224
 Decatur  (G-7879)
Expressions By Christine Inc .............. F ....... 217 223-2750
 Quincy  (G-17827)
Femina Sport Inc ................................ G ....... 630 271-1876
 Downers Grove  (G-8442)
Harlan Vance Company ..................... F ....... 309 888-4804
 Normal  (G-16072)
I D Togs .............................................. G ....... 618 235-1538
 Belleville  (G-1635)
Image Plus Inc .................................... G ....... 630 852-4920
 Downers Grove  (G-8463)
J C Embroidery & Screen Print ........... G ....... 630 595-4670
 Bensenville  (G-1926)
Midwest Stitch .................................... G ....... 815 394-1516
 Rockford  (G-18507)
Promotional TS ................................... G ....... 312 243-8991
 Chicago  (G-6215)
Sango Embroidery .............................. G ....... 773 582-4354
 Chicago  (G-6439)
Sewing Salon ..................................... G ....... 217 345-3886
 Charleston  (G-3611)
Shirt Tales .......................................... G ....... 618 662-4572
 Flora  (G-10216)
Signature of Chicago Inc .................... G ....... 630 271-1876
 Downers Grove  (G-8523)
Time Embroidery ................................ G ....... 847 364-4371
 Elk Grove Village  (G-9780)
Twin Towers Marketing ....................... G ....... 815 544-5554
 Belvidere  (G-1791)
U Keep US In Stitches ........................ G ....... 847 427-8127
 Mount Prospect  (G-15380)
U R On It ............................................. G ....... 847 382-0182
 Lake Barrington  (G-12826)
USA Embroidery ................................. G ....... 309 692-1391
 Peoria  (G-17475)
Visual Persuasion Inc ......................... F ....... 815 899-6609
 Sycamore  (G-20823)
Woolenwear Inc .................................. F ....... 847 520-9243
 Prospect Heights  (G-17786)

## EMBROIDERING SVC: Schiffli Machine

Midwest Swiss Embroideries Co .......... E ....... 773 631-7120
 Chicago  (G-5750)

## EMBROIDERY ADVERTISING SVCS

Ad Images ........................................... G ....... 847 956-1887
 Elk Grove Village  (G-9269)
Ameri-Tex ........................................... G ....... 847 247-0777
 Mundelein  (G-15469)
C & C Sport Stop ................................ G ....... 618 632-7812
 O Fallon  (G-16464)
C M F Enterprises Inc ......................... F ....... 847 526-9499
 Wauconda  (G-21450)
Energy Tees ........................................ G ....... 708 771-0000
 Forest Park  (G-10240)
Spirit Warrior Inc ................................. G ....... 708 614-0020
 Orland Park  (G-16895)
Visual Persuasion Inc ......................... F ....... 815 899-6609
 Sycamore  (G-20823)
Wagner International  LLC .................. G ....... 224 619-9247
 Vernon Hills  (G-21216)

## EMERGENCY ALARMS

Jeron Electronic Systems  Inc ............. D ....... 773 275-1900
 Niles  (G-15991)
Magnum Machining LLC ..................... G ....... 815 678-6800
 Richmond  (G-17967)
Marine Technologies Inc ..................... E ....... 847 546-9001
 Volo  (G-21318)
Pacific Electronics Corp ...................... F ....... 815 206-5450
 Woodstock  (G-22598)
Regional Emrgncy Dispatch Ctr .......... F ....... 847 498-5748
 Northbrook  (G-16354)
Siemens Industry  Inc ......................... A ....... 847 215-1000
 Buffalo Grove  (G-2767)
Simplexgrinnell LP .............................. B ....... 630 268-1863
 Addison  (G-292)
Simplexgrinnell LP .............................. D ....... 309 694-8000
 East Peoria  (G-8734)
Tri-Lite  Inc ......................................... E ....... 773 384-7765
 Chicago  (G-6770)
Wireless Chamberlain Products .......... E ....... 800 282-6225
 Elmhurst  (G-9961)

## EMPLOYMENT AGENCY SVCS

American Data Centre Inc .................. G ....... 847 358-7111
 Palatine  (G-17000)
Wesco International Inc ...................... G ....... 630 513-4864
 Elmhurst  (G-9960)

# PRODUCT SECTION

## ENAMELING SVC: Metal Prdts, Including Porcelain

Acme Finishing Company Inc............D....... 847 640-7890
  Elk Grove Village *(G-9265)*
DLP Coatings Inc................................E....... 847 350-0113
  Elk Grove Village *(G-9430)*

## ENAMELS

American Powder Coatings Inc...........E....... 630 762-0100
  Saint Charles *(G-19135)*
Rust-Oleum Corporation.....................D....... 815 967-4258
  Rockford *(G-18600)*
Testor Corporation.............................D....... 815 962-6654
  Rockford *(G-18644)*
U S Colors & Coatings Inc..................G....... 630 879-8898
  Batavia *(G-1512)*

## ENCLOSURES: Electronic

Equipto Electronics Corp....................E....... 630 897-4691
  Aurora *(G-1147)*
G & M Manufacturing Corp..................E....... 815 455-1900
  Crystal Lake *(G-7580)*
Larsen Manufacturing LLC..................C....... 847 970-9600
  Mundelein *(G-15519)*
Laystrom Manufacturing Co.................D....... 773 342-4800
  Chicago *(G-5474)*
MNP Precision Parts LLC....................C....... 815 391-5256
  Rockford *(G-18509)*
New Dimension Models........................G....... 815 935-1001
  Aroma Park *(G-879)*
Perfection Spring Stmping Corp...........D....... 847 437-3900
  Mount Prospect *(G-15362)*
Rittal Corp........................................A....... 847 240-4600
  Schaumburg *(G-19712)*
Tellenar Inc......................................F....... 815 356-8044
  Crystal Lake *(G-7663)*

## ENCLOSURES: Screen

Chicago Enclosures...........................G....... 708 344-6600
  Melrose Park *(G-14609)*
Singer Safety Company........................F....... 773 235-2100
  Chicago *(G-6516)*

## ENCODERS: Digital

Bar Codes Inc...................................F....... 800 351-9962
  Chicago *(G-4039)*
Evanston Graphic Imaging Inc............G....... 847 869-7446
  Evanston *(G-10033)*

## ENERGY MEASUREMENT EQPT

E2s LLC...........................................G....... 708 629-0714
  Alsip *(G-460)*

## ENGINE PARTS & ACCESS: Internal Combustion

Boley Tool & Machine Works Inc..........C....... 309 694-2722
  East Peoria *(G-8703)*
Nelson Enterprises Inc.......................G....... 815 633-1100
  Roscoe *(G-18910)*
Sierra International LLC......................C....... 217 324-9400
  Litchfield *(G-13698)*
Tpr America Inc................................G....... 847 446-5336
  Schaumburg *(G-19767)*
Wuebbels Repair & Sales LLC.............G....... 618 648-2227
  Mc Leansboro *(G-14470)*

## ENGINE REBUILDING: Diesel

Dura Products Corporation.................G....... 815 939-1399
  Bradley *(G-2420)*
Honeywell International Inc.................A....... 847 391-2000
  Des Plaines *(G-8205)*
Jimmy Diesel Inc...............................G....... 708 482-4500
  Wheaton *(G-21959)*
L S Diesel Repair Inc.........................G....... 217 283-5537
  Hoopeston *(G-12112)*
Precision Engine Rebuilders................G....... 815 254-2333
  Plainfield *(G-17642)*

## ENGINE REBUILDING: Gas

B & S Auto Rebuilders Inc..................G....... 773 283-3763
  Chicago *(G-4017)*
C & M Engineering.............................G....... 815 932-3388
  Bourbonnais *(G-2391)*

## ENGINEERING SVCS

ARINC Incorporated...........................E....... 800 633-6882
  O Fallon *(G-16463)*
Art Cnc Machining LLC.......................G....... 708 907-3090
  Bridgeview *(G-2468)*
Automated Systems & Control Co........G....... 847 735-8310
  Lake Bluff *(G-12834)*
Bc Asi Capital II Inc..........................A....... 708 534-5575
  University Park *(G-21043)*
Bing Engineering Inc.........................C....... 708 228-8005
  Frankfort *(G-10300)*
Cast21 Inc........................................G....... 847 772-8547
  Champaign *(G-3462)*
Charter Dura-Bar Inc.........................C....... 815 338-7800
  Woodstock *(G-22552)*
Circom Inc........................................E....... 630 595-4460
  Bensenville *(G-1859)*
Control Masters Inc...........................G....... 630 968-2390
  Downers Grove *(G-8420)*
Deyco Inc.........................................G....... 630 553-5666
  Yorkville *(G-22656)*
Diversified Cnstr Svcs LLC..................G....... 708 344-4900
  Melrose Park *(G-14620)*
Elgin National Industries Inc................F....... 630 434-7200
  Downers Grove *(G-8440)*
Emac Inc..........................................E....... 618 529-4525
  Carbondale *(G-3006)*
Engineering Finshg Systems LLC........E....... 815 893-6090
  Elmhurst *(G-9866)*
Gama Electronics Inc.........................F....... 815 356-9600
  Woodstock *(G-22569)*
General Electro Corporation................F....... 630 595-8989
  Bensenville *(G-1908)*
Ghetzler Aero-Power Corp..................G....... 224 513-5636
  Vernon Hills *(G-21165)*
Global Water Technology Inc..............E....... 708 349-9991
  Orland Park *(G-16862)*
Hpd LLC...........................................C....... 815 436-3013
  Plainfield *(G-17606)*
Icon Mech Cnstr & Engrg LLC............G....... 618 452-0035
  Granite City *(G-11287)*
IMS Companies LLC..........................D....... 847 391-8100
  Des Plaines *(G-8210)*
Integral Automation Inc.....................F....... 630 654-4300
  Burr Ridge *(G-2856)*
International Mold & Prod LLC.............G....... 313 617-5251
  Grayslake *(G-11347)*
Ionit Technologies Inc.......................E....... 847 205-9651
  Northfield *(G-16403)*
Lake County Tool Works North............G....... 847 662-4542
  Wadsworth *(G-21324)*
Linde North America Inc....................E....... 630 257-3612
  Lockport *(G-13726)*
Loda Electronics Co..........................G....... 217 386-2554
  Loda *(G-13752)*
M H Detrick Company.........................E....... 708 479-5085
  Mokena *(G-14882)*
Matrix IV Inc....................................E....... 815 338-4500
  Woodstock *(G-22588)*
McLean Subsurface Utility..................G....... 336 988-2520
  Decatur *(G-7911)*
Mid-States Concrete Inds LLC............D....... 815 389-2277
  South Beloit *(G-20162)*
Midwest Cad Design Inc....................G....... 847 397-0220
  Schaumburg *(G-19647)*
Midwest Control Corp........................F....... 708 599-1331
  Bridgeview *(G-2509)*
Modern Process Equipment Inc..........E....... 773 254-3929
  Chicago *(G-5784)*
Neomek Incorporated........................G....... 630 879-5400
  Batavia *(G-1475)*
Newko Tool & Engineering Co.............E....... 847 359-1670
  Palatine *(G-17058)*
Octane Motorsports LLC....................G....... 224 419-5460
  Waukegan *(G-21598)*
Onyx Environmental Svcs LLC.............G....... 630 218-1500
  Lombard *(G-13838)*
Performance Pattern & Mch Inc..........E....... 309 676-0907
  Peoria *(G-17427)*
Plastic Services Group......................G....... 847 368-1444
  Arlington Heights *(G-818)*
Precision Metal Technologies..............F....... 847 228-6630
  Rolling Meadows *(G-18768)*
Royale Innovation Group Ltd..............G....... 312 339-1406
  Itasca *(G-12351)*
S & C Electric Company.....................A....... 773 338-1000
  Chicago *(G-6419)*
S Flying Inc......................................F....... 618 586-9999
  Palestine *(G-17095)*
Senior PLC........................................G....... 630 372-3511
  Bartlett *(G-1376)*
Sigenics Inc.....................................F....... 312 448-8000
  Chicago *(G-6506)*
SPEP Acquisition Corp.......................E....... 310 608-0693
  Bolingbrook *(G-2375)*
U Op................................................G....... 847 391-2000
  Des Plaines *(G-8289)*
Walters Metal Fabrication Inc.............D....... 618 931-5551
  Granite City *(G-11311)*
Wynright Corporation.........................D....... 847 595-9400
  Elk Grove Village *(G-9819)*

## ENGINEERING SVCS: Building Construction

Elliott Aviation Arcft Sls Inc................G....... 309 799-3183
  Milan *(G-14785)*
Global General Contractors LLC..........G....... 708 663-0476
  Tinley Park *(G-20918)*
Matrix North Amercn Cnstr Inc............G....... 312 754-6605
  Chicago *(G-5654)*
Osmer Woodworking Inc.....................G....... 815 973-5809
  Dixon *(G-8338)*
Ozinga Ready Mix Concrete Inc..........E....... 708 326-4200
  Mokena *(G-14892)*
Stages Construction Inc.....................G....... 773 619-2977
  Chicago *(G-6568)*

## ENGINEERING SVCS: Chemical

Agriscience Inc.................................G....... 212 365-4214
  Peoria *(G-17304)*
Gig Karasek LLC................................F....... 630 549-0394
  Saint Charles *(G-19189)*

## ENGINEERING SVCS: Civil

I A E Inc..........................................G....... 219 882-2400
  Oak Park *(G-16670)*
Structurepoint LLC............................F....... 847 966-4357
  Skokie *(G-20092)*

## ENGINEERING SVCS: Electrical Or Electronic

Anderson Engrg New Prague Inc.........G....... 630 736-0900
  Streamwood *(G-20643)*
Aria Corporation................................G....... 847 918-9329
  Libertyville *(G-13304)*
Bishop Engineering Company..............F....... 630 305-9538
  Lisle *(G-13569)*
Calvert Systems................................G....... 309 523-3262
  Port Byron *(G-17719)*
Control Works Inc.............................G....... 630 444-1942
  Saint Charles *(G-19163)*
Elemech Inc......................................E....... 630 417-2845
  Aurora *(G-1001)*
Imagineering Inc...............................E....... 847 806-0003
  Elk Grove Village *(G-9541)*
Industrial Controls Inc.......................G....... 630 752-8100
  Batavia *(G-1457)*
Lectro Graphics Inc...........................G....... 847 537-3592
  Wheeling *(G-22091)*
Nova Systems Ltd.............................G....... 630 879-2296
  Aurora *(G-1195)*
Online Electronics Inc........................E....... 847 871-1700
  Elk Grove Village *(G-9666)*
RWS Design and Controls Inc.............E....... 815 654-6000
  Roscoe *(G-18919)*
S & M Group Inc...............................F....... 630 766-1000
  Wood Dale *(G-22418)*
Spurt Inc.........................................G....... 847 571-6497
  Northbrook *(G-16370)*

## ENGINEERING SVCS: Energy conservation

Clean Energy Renewables LLC............E....... 309 797-4844
  Moline *(G-14922)*
Elfi LLC...........................................E....... 815 439-1833
  Chicago *(G-4727)*

## ENGINEERING SVCS: Heating & Ventilation

Honeywell International Inc.................D....... 847 797-4000
  Arlington Heights *(G-768)*

## ENGINEERING SVCS: Industrial

Americhem Systems Inc.....................F....... 630 495-9300
  Aurora *(G-1106)*
Gerb Vibration Control Systems..........G....... 630 724-1660
  Lisle *(G-13595)*

# ENGINEERING SVCS: Machine Tool Design

## ENGINEERING SVCS: Machine Tool Design

- All Cnc Solutions Inc ............................G...... 847 972-1139
  Skokie *(G-19947)*
- Bartell Corporation ...............................G...... 847 854-3232
  Algonquin *(G-380)*
- Design Systems Inc ...............................E...... 309 263-7706
  Morton *(G-15157)*
- Ehrhardt Tool & Machine LLC ...............C...... 314 436-6900
  Granite City *(G-11274)*
- Ingenious Concepts Inc ..........................G...... 630 539-8059
  Medinah *(G-14576)*
- Matt Pak Inc ..........................................D...... 847 451-4018
  Franklin Park *(G-10523)*
- Ramco Group LLC .................................F...... 847 639-9899
  Crystal Lake *(G-7636)*
- Sloan Industries Inc ................................E...... 630 350-1614
  Wood Dale *(G-22423)*

## ENGINEERING SVCS: Marine

- Great Lakes Envmtl Mar Del .................G...... 312 332-3377
  Chicago *(G-4996)*

## ENGINEERING SVCS: Mechanical

- Design Technology Inc ...........................E...... 630 920-1300
  Westmont *(G-21883)*
- Dynamic Automation Inc .........................G...... 312 782-8555
  Lincolnwood *(G-13508)*
- Eighty Nine Robotics LLC .......................G...... 512 573-9091
  Chicago *(G-4705)*
- Langham Engineering ............................G...... 815 223-5250
  Peru *(G-17516)*
- Livingston Products Inc ..........................F...... 847 808-0900
  Waukegan *(G-21581)*
- MEA Inc .................................................E...... 847 766-9040
  Elk Grove Village *(G-9616)*
- Medco Inc ..............................................F...... 847 296-3021
  Des Plaines *(G-8231)*
- Specialized Liftruck Svcs LLC ................F...... 708 552-2705
  Bedford Park *(G-1585)*
- Technique Engineering Inc .....................F...... 847 816-1870
  Waukegan *(G-21622)*
- Titan US LLC .........................................G...... 331 212-5953
  Aurora *(G-1088)*
- Z-Tech Inc .............................................G...... 815 335-7395
  Winnebago *(G-22299)*

## ENGINEERING SVCS: Pollution Control

- C P Environmental Inc ...........................F...... 630 759-8866
  Romeoville *(G-18805)*

## ENGINEERING SVCS: Professional

- Concept and Design Services ................G...... 847 259-1675
  Mount Prospect *(G-15317)*
- Earthsafe Systems Inc ...........................F...... 312 226-7600
  Chicago *(G-4679)*
- Intratek Inc ............................................G...... 847 640-0007
  Elk Grove Village *(G-9554)*
- Vibra-Tech Engineers Inc ......................G...... 630 858-0681
  Glen Ellyn *(G-10994)*

## ENGINEERING SVCS: Structural

- Structural Design Corp ..........................G...... 847 816-3816
  Libertyville *(G-13385)*
- Versatech LLC .......................................C...... 217 342-3500
  Effingham *(G-8860)*

## ENGINES & ENGINE PARTS: Guided Missile, Research & Develpt

- Starfire Industries LLC ..........................E...... 217 721-4165
  Champaign *(G-3548)*

## ENGINES: Diesel & Semi-Diesel Or Duel Fuel

- Caterpillar Inc ........................................A...... 309 675-1000
  Peoria *(G-17326)*
- Caterpillar Inc ........................................G...... 815 729-5511
  Rockdale *(G-18216)*
- Caterpillar Inc ........................................B...... 888 614-4328
  Peoria *(G-17328)*
- Caterpillar Inc ........................................B...... 309 675-6590
  Peoria *(G-17333)*
- Global Cmpnent Tech Amrcas Inc .........E...... 815 568-4507
  Marengo *(G-14229)*
- Heavy Quip Incorporated .......................F...... 312 368-7997
  Chicago *(G-5067)*
- Navistar Inc ............................................C...... 331 332-5000
  Lisle *(G-13629)*
- Navistar International Corp ....................A...... 331 332-5000
  Lisle *(G-13633)*
- Quincy Compressor LLC ........................C...... 217 222-7700
  Quincy *(G-17875)*

## ENGINES: Gasoline, NEC

- Speed Tech Technology Inc ...................G...... 847 516-2001
  Cary *(G-3372)*
- Unicarriers Americas Corp .....................B...... 800 871-5438
  Marengo *(G-14244)*

## ENGINES: Internal Combustion, NEC

- American Speed Enterprises .................G...... 309 764-3601
  Moline *(G-14917)*
- Caterpillar Gb LLC .................................G...... 309 675-1000
  Peoria *(G-17325)*
- Conley Precision Engines Inc ................F...... 630 858-3160
  Glen Ellyn *(G-10964)*
- Cummins - Allison Corp .........................B...... 847 759-6403
  Mount Prospect *(G-15320)*
- Cummins - Allison Corp .........................D...... 847 299-9550
  Mount Prospect *(G-15321)*
- Cummins - Allison Corp .........................C...... 847 299-9550
  Mount Prospect *(G-15322)*
- Cummins - Allison Corp .........................F...... 630 833-2285
  Elmhurst *(G-9862)*
- Cummins Crosspoint LLC ......................E...... 309 452-4454
  Normal *(G-16068)*
- Cummins Dist Holdco Inc ......................E...... 309 787-4300
  Rock Island *(G-18170)*
- Cummins Inc ..........................................E...... 309 787-4300
  Rock Island *(G-18171)*
- Cummins Npower LLC ...........................E...... 708 579-9222
  Hodgkins *(G-11973)*
- Cummins-American Corp .......................G...... 847 299-9550
  Mount Prospect *(G-15323)*
- Engine Efficiency Systems LLC .............F...... 630 590-5241
  Burr Ridge *(G-2838)*
- Iet-Meco .................................................C...... 217 465-6575
  Paris *(G-17150)*
- Jasiek Motor Rebuilding Inc ...................G...... 815 883-3678
  Oglesby *(G-16750)*
- Navistar Inc ............................................C......
  Melrose Park *(G-14675)*
- Navistar Inc ............................................B...... 317 352-4500
  Melrose Park *(G-14676)*
- Npt Automotive Machine Shop ..............G...... 618 233-1344
  Belleville *(G-1661)*
- Perkins Engines Inc ...............................E...... 309 578-7364
  Mossville *(G-15254)*
- Progress Rail Locomotive Inc ................A...... 800 255-5355
  Mc Cook *(G-14456)*
- Progress Rail Locomotive Inc ................F...... 708 387-5510
  Mc Cook *(G-14457)*
- R & C Auto Supply Corp ........................G...... 815 625-4414
  Sterling *(G-20609)*
- Waymore Power Co Inc .........................F...... 618 729-3876
  Piasa *(G-17543)*

## ENGINES: Jet Propulsion

- Chicago Jet Group LLC ..........................E...... 630 466-3600
  Sugar Grove *(G-20719)*

## ENGINES: Marine

- B & M Automotive ..................................G...... 309 637-4977
  Peoria *(G-17312)*
- Marine Engine and Drive S ....................G...... 630 606-6124
  West Chicago *(G-21739)*

## ENGINES: Steam

- Union Iron Inc ........................................E...... 217 429-5148
  Decatur *(G-7955)*

## ENGRAVING SVC, NEC

- Fresh Concept Enterprises Inc ..............G...... 815 254-7295
  Plainfield *(G-17601)*

## ENGRAVING SVC: Jewelry & Personal Goods

- Ace Engraving & Specialties Co ............G...... 815 759-2093
  McHenry *(G-14476)*
- Addison Engraving Inc ...........................G...... 630 833-9123
  Villa Park *(G-21232)*
- Art Clay World Usa Inc ..........................G...... 708 857-8800
  Oak Lawn *(G-16604)*
- B&B Awards and Recognition Inc .........G...... 309 828-9698
  Bloomington *(G-2146)*
- Comet Die & Engraving Company .........D...... 630 833-5600
  Elmhurst *(G-9854)*
- Finer Line Inc ........................................F...... 847 884-1611
  Schaumburg *(G-19527)*
- Hoeing Die & Mold Engraving ...............G...... 630 543-0006
  Addison *(G-147)*
- Johnos Inc .............................................G...... 630 897-6929
  Aurora *(G-1178)*
- M J Burton Engraving Co ......................G...... 217 223-7273
  Quincy *(G-17854)*
- Trophies and Awards Plus .....................G...... 708 754-7127
  Steger *(G-20578)*
- Viking Awards Inc ..................................G...... 630 833-1733
  Elmhurst *(G-9957)*
- Wheaton Trophy & Engravers ................G...... 630 682-4200
  Wheaton *(G-21989)*

## ENGRAVING SVCS

- Amkine Inc .............................................F...... 847 526-7088
  Wauconda *(G-21442)*
- Benzinger Printing .................................G...... 815 784-6560
  Genoa *(G-10875)*
- Bertco Enterprises Inc ...........................G...... 618 234-9283
  Belleville *(G-1614)*
- C F C Interantional ................................G...... 708 753-0679
  Chicago Heights *(G-7085)*
- Cook Merritt .........................................G...... 630 980-3070
  Roselle *(G-18934)*
- Finer Line Inc ........................................F...... 847 884-1611
  Schaumburg *(G-19527)*
- George Lauterer Corporation ................E...... 312 913-1881
  Chicago *(G-4943)*
- Light Waves LLC ..................................F...... 847 251-1622
  Wilmette *(G-22259)*
- M J Burton Engraving Co ......................G...... 217 223-7273
  Quincy *(G-17854)*
- Monograms & More ..............................G...... 630 789-8424
  Burr Ridge *(G-2869)*
- Nathan Winston Service Inc ..................G...... 815 758-4545
  Dekalb *(G-8109)*
- National Rubber Stamp Co Inc ..............G...... 773 281-6522
  Chicago *(G-5868)*
- Procraft Engraving Inc ...........................G...... 847 673-1500
  Skokie *(G-20062)*
- Standex International Corp ...................E...... 630 588-0400
  Carol Stream *(G-3249)*
- Trophies By George ..............................G...... 630 497-1212
  Bartlett *(G-1381)*
- Walnut Creek Hardwood .......................G...... 815 389-3317
  South Beloit *(G-20173)*

## ENGRAVINGS: Plastic

- A To Z Engraving Co Inc .......................G...... 847 526-7396
  Wauconda *(G-21435)*
- Lens Lenticlear Lenticular .....................F...... 630 467-0900
  Itasca *(G-12303)*

## ENTERTAINERS & ENTERTAINMENT GROUPS

- Ikan Creations LLC ...............................G...... 312 204-7333
  Chicago *(G-5150)*
- Linx Enterprises LLC ............................G...... 224 409-2206
  Chicago *(G-5516)*
- Windsong Press Ltd .............................G...... 847 223-4586
  Grayslake *(G-11368)*

## ENTERTAINMENT PROMOTION SVCS

- Deshamusic Inc .....................................G...... 818 257-2716
  Chicago *(G-4585)*

## ENTERTAINMENT SVCS

- Megamedia Enterprises Inc ...................F...... 773 889-0880
  Chicago *(G-5680)*

## ENVELOPES

- American Graphics Network Inc ............F...... 847 729-7220
  Glenview *(G-11100)*
- Cenveo Inc ............................................D...... 773 267-1717
  Chicago *(G-4279)*
- Cenveo Corporation ..............................C...... 312 286-6400
  Chicago *(G-4281)*
- Diamond Envelope Corporation ............D...... 630 499-2800
  Aurora *(G-995)*
- Federal Envelope Company ..................D...... 630 595-2000
  Bensenville *(G-1896)*

# PRODUCT SECTION — EYEGLASSES

Forest Envelope Company .......................... E ....... 630 515-1200
 Bolingbrook (G-2311)
Gaw-Ohara Envelope Co ............................ E ....... 773 638-1200
 Chicago (G-4920)
Gluetech Inc ............................................... F ....... 847 455-2707
 Wood Dale (G-22377)
Gordon Caplan Inc ..................................... G ....... 773 489-3300
 Chicago (G-4980)
Graphic Industries Inc ................................ E ....... 847 357-9870
 South Elgin (G-20201)
Mackay Mitchell Envelope Co ..................... G ....... 847 418-3866
 Northbrook (G-16304)
Managed Marketing Inc ............................. G ....... 847 279-8260
 Wheeling (G-22098)
Overt Press Inc .......................................... E ....... 773 284-0909
 Chicago (G-6029)
Roodhouse Envelope Co ............................ D ....... 217 589-4321
 Roodhouse (G-18884)
Royal Envelope Corporation ....................... D ....... 773 376-1212
 Chicago (G-6401)
Service Envelope Corporation .................... E ....... 847 559-0004
 Northbrook (G-16362)
The Calumet Carton Company ................... D ....... 708 331-7910
 South Holland (G-20310)
Trekon Company Inc ................................. G ....... 309 925-7942
 Tremont (G-20986)
Unique Envelope Corporation .................... E ....... 773 586-0330
 Chicago (G-6819)

## ENVELOPES WHOLESALERS

Envelopes Only Inc ................................... E ....... 630 213-2500
 Streamwood (G-20655)
Gordon Caplan Inc ..................................... G ....... 773 489-3300
 Chicago (G-4980)

## ENZYMES

Chem Free Solutions .................................. G ....... 630 541-7931
 Darien (G-7791)
Enzymes Incorporated ................................ G ....... 847 487-5401
 Wauconda (G-21460)
Interface Protein Tech Inc .......................... D ....... 630 963-8809
 Lisle (G-13607)
Natures Sources LLC ................................ G ....... 847 663-9168
 Niles (G-16013)

## EPOXY RESINS

Corro-Shield International Inc .................... F ....... 847 298-7770
 Elk Grove Village (G-9397)
Kns Companies Inc .................................... F ....... 630 665-9010
 Carol Stream (G-3181)

## EQUIPMENT: Pedestrian Traffic Control

Km Enterprises Inc .................................... F ....... 618 204-0888
 Mount Vernon (G-15420)

## EQUIPMENT: Rental & Leasing, NEC

Amber Soft Inc .......................................... F ....... 630 377-6945
 Lake Barrington (G-12799)
Bloomington Tent & Awning Inc ................ G ....... 309 828-3411
 Bloomington (G-2150)
Breeze Printing Co .................................... F ....... 217 824-2233
 Taylorville (G-20835)
CCS Contractor Eqp & Sup Inc .................. E ....... 630 393-9020
 Naperville (G-15622)
Champaign Cnty Tent & Awng Co ............. E ....... 217 328-5749
 Urbana (G-21077)
Chicago Rivet & Machine Co ..................... C ....... 630 357-8500
 Naperville (G-15627)
Coast Crane Company ............................... C ....... 847 215-6500
 Buffalo Grove (G-2674)
Ds Services of America Inc ....................... C ....... 773 586-8600
 Chicago (G-4645)
Essannay Show It Inc ................................ G ....... 312 733-5511
 Chicago (G-4778)
Florida Metrology LLC ............................. F ....... 630 833-3800
 Villa Park (G-21252)
Gilco Real Estate Company ....................... E ....... 847 298-1717
 Des Plaines (G-8202)
Grate Signs Inc .......................................... E ....... 815 729-9700
 Joliet (G-12503)
Grs Holding LLC ....................................... G ....... 630 355-1660
 Naperville (G-15666)
Hinckley & Schmitt Inc ............................. A ....... 773 586-8600
 Chicago (G-5091)
Mobile Air Inc ............................................ F ....... 847 755-0586
 Glendale Heights (G-11049)
Narvick Bros Lumber Co Inc ..................... G ....... 815 942-1173
 Morris (G-15121)

Praxair Distribution Inc .............................. E ....... 314 664-7900
 Cahokia (G-2924)

## ESCALATORS: Passenger & Freight

Kone Inc .................................................... A ....... 630 577-1650
 Lisle (G-13614)

## ETCHING & ENGRAVING SVC

Acme Metallizing Co Inc ............................ F ....... 773 767-7000
 Chicago (G-3733)
Amex Nooter LLC ..................................... G ....... 708 429-8300
 Tinley Park (G-20892)
Bertco Enterprises Inc ................................ G ....... 618 234-9283
 Belleville (G-1614)
Bishops Engrv & Trophy Svc Inc ................ G ....... 773 777-5014
 Chicago (G-4114)
Crown Trophy ............................................ G ....... 309 699-1766
 East Peoria (G-8707)
Iemco Corporation ..................................... G ....... 773 728-4400
 Chicago (G-5145)
Meto-Grafics Inc ........................................ F ....... 847 639-0044
 Crystal Lake (G-7609)
Monogram of Evanston Inc ........................ G ....... 847 864-8100
 Evanston (G-10074)
Oerlikon ..................................................... E ....... 847 619-5541
 Schaumburg (G-19672)
Safeway Services Rockford Inc ................. E ....... 815 986-1504
 Rockford (G-18607)

## ETCHING SVC: Metal

Etch-Tech Inc ............................................. G ....... 630 833-4234
 Elmhurst (G-9868)
Lifetime Creations ..................................... G ....... 708 895-2770
 Lansing (G-13172)
Ostrom & Co Inc ........................................ F ....... 503 281-6469
 Winfield (G-22288)
Rebechini Studio Inc .................................. F ....... 847 364-8600
 Elk Grove Village (G-9711)

## ETCHING SVC: Photochemical

Faspro Technologies Inc ............................ F ....... 847 364-9999
 Elk Grove Village (G-9476)

## ETHERS

LLC Ethersonic Techno .............................. G ....... 708 441-4730
 Matteson (G-14376)

## ETHYLENE

C U Plastic LLC ........................................ G ....... 888 957-9993
 Rochelle (G-18081)
Marquis Energy LLC ................................. E ....... 815 925-7300
 Hennepin (G-11734)

## ETHYLENE OXIDE

Union Carbide Corporation ........................ D ....... 708 396-3000
 Alsip (G-538)

## ETHYLENE-PROPYLENE RUBBERS: EPDM Polymers

Advanced Polymer Alloys LLC ................... G ....... 847 836-8119
 Carpentersville (G-3272)
J6 Polymers LLC ....................................... G ....... 815 517-1179
 Dekalb (G-8099)
Mexichem Specialty Resins Inc ................. F ....... 309 364-2154
 Henry (G-11744)

## EXCAVATING MACHINERY & EQPT WHOLESALERS

Birkeys Farm Store Inc .............................. E ....... 217 337-1772
 Urbana (G-21073)

## EXHAUST SYSTEMS: Eqpt & Parts

CC Distributing Services Inc ...................... G ....... 800 931-2668
 Crestwood (G-7480)
Delphi Automotive Systems LLC ................ E ....... 847 391-2000
 Des Plaines (G-8180)
Hendrix Industrial Gastrux Inc ................... E ....... 847 526-1700
 Wauconda (G-21467)
Parker Fabrication Inc ................................ E ....... 309 266-8413
 Morton (G-15174)

## EXPANSION JOINTS: Rubber

Flexicraft Industries Inc ............................. F ....... 312 738-3588
 Chicago (G-4861)

## EXPLOSIVES

Buckley Powder Co .................................. F ....... 217 285-5531
 Pittsfield (G-17562)
Dyno Nobel Inc ......................................... F ....... 217 285-5621
 Barry (G-1312)
Dyno Nobel Inc ......................................... E ....... 217 285-5531
 Detroit (G-8309)
Evenson Explosives LLC .......................... E ....... 815 942-5800
 Morris (G-15108)
General Dynamics Ordnance ..................... C ....... 618 985-8211
 Marion (G-14261)
Hanley Industries Inc ................................ E ....... 618 465-8892
 Alton (G-577)
Orica USA Inc ........................................... E ....... 815 357-8711
 Morris (G-15125)

## EXPLOSIVES, EXC AMMO & FIREWORKS WHOLESALERS

Orica USA Inc ........................................... E ....... 815 357-8711
 Morris (G-15125)

## EXTENSION CORDS

Appleton Grp LLC ..................................... C ....... 847 268-6000
 Rosemont (G-18989)
Power Port Products Inc ........................... E ....... 630 628-9102
 Addison (G-249)

## EXTERMINATING & FUMIGATING SVCS

Smithereen Company Del .......................... D ....... 847 675-0010
 Niles (G-16035)

## EXTRACTS, FLAVORING

Dennco Inc ................................................ G ....... 708 862-0070
 Burnham (G-2816)
Edgar A Weber & Company ....................... E ....... 847 215-1980
 Wheeling (G-22043)
Edgar A Weber & Company ....................... E ....... 847 215-1980
 Wheeling (G-22044)
Edlong Corporation .................................... D ....... 847 439-9230
 Elk Grove Village (G-9449)
Flavorchem Corporation ............................ D ....... 630 932-8100
 Downers Grove (G-8443)
Fona International Inc ................................ G ....... 630 578-8600
 Saint Charles (G-19185)
Fona International Inc ................................ E ....... 630 578-8600
 Geneva (G-10827)
Fona Uk Ltd ............................................... C ....... 331 442-5779
 Geneva (G-10828)
H B Taylor Co ............................................ E ....... 773 254-4805
 Chicago (G-5020)
La Boost Inc .............................................. G ....... 630 444-1755
 Saint Charles (G-19206)
Northwestern Flavors LLC ........................ E ....... 630 231-6111
 West Chicago (G-21752)
Ocean Cliff Corporation ............................. G ....... 847 729-9074
 Glenview (G-11176)
Silesia Flavors Inc ..................................... E ....... 847 645-0270
 Hoffman Estates (G-12054)
Stepan Company ....................................... B ....... 847 446-7500
 Northfield (G-16419)
Sterling Extract Company Inc .................... G ....... 847 451-9728
 Franklin Park (G-10595)
Synergy Flavors NY Company LLC ........... E ....... 585 232-6648
 Wauconda (G-21507)
Wm Wrigley Jr Company ........................... A ....... 312 644-2121
 Chicago (G-7014)

## EYEGLASSES

Bahk Eye Center Inc ................................. G ....... 773 561-1199
 Chicago (G-4026)
Essilor Laboratories Amer Inc ................... E ....... 309 787-2727
 Rock Island (G-18176)
Eye Candy Optics Corporation ................... G ....... 773 697-7370
 Chicago (G-4800)
Family Eye Care ........................................ G ....... 708 614-2311
 Tinley Park (G-20912)
Midwest Uncuts Inc ................................... F ....... 312 664-3131
 Chicago (G-5752)
Tammy Smith ............................................. G ....... 618 372-8410
 Brighton (G-2545)
Vicron Optical Inc ...................................... F ....... 847 412-5530
 Deerfield (G-8066)

---

Employee Codes: A=Over 500 employees, B=251-500
C=101-250, D=51-100, E=20-50, F=10-19, G=3-9

## EYEGLASSES: Sunglasses

**Jim Maui Inc** .................................................. G ...... 888 666-5905
Peoria  *(G-17392)*

### EYELASHES, ARTIFICIAL

**Manhattan Eyelash EXT Sew On** .......... G ...... 847 818-8774
Arlington Heights  *(G-798)*

### EYES & HOOKS Screw

**Southern Imperial Inc** ............................... G ...... 815 877-7041
Loves Park  *(G-13993)*

### EYES: Artificial

**Dean B Scott** ............................................... G ...... 630 960-4455
Downers Grove  *(G-8425)*
**Eye Surgeons of Libertyville** .................. G ...... 847 362-3811
Libertyville  *(G-13322)*
**Eyewearplanet Com Inc** ........................... G ...... 847 513-6203
Northbrook  *(G-16254)*
**Henderson Eye Center** ............................. F ...... 217 698-9477
Springfield  *(G-20451)*
**Illinois Retina Institute SC** ...................... F ...... 309 589-1880
Peoria  *(G-17386)*
**Robert B Scott Ocularists Ltd** ................. G ...... 312 782-3558
Chicago  *(G-6367)*

### Ethylene Glycols

**Compania Brasileira De T** ........................ G ...... 319 550-6440
Mount Olive  *(G-15301)*

### FABRIC STORES

**A D Specialty Sewing** ............................... G ...... 847 639-0390
Fox River Grove  *(G-10285)*
**Duracrest Fabrics** ..................................... G ...... 847 350-0030
Elk Grove Village  *(G-9438)*

### FABRICATED METAL PRODUCTS, NEC

**Adk Products Inc** ...................................... G ...... 847 710-0021
Elk Grove Village  *(G-9274)*
**Dva Metal Fabrication Inc** ....................... G ...... 224 577-8217
Mundelein  *(G-15496)*
**Kenneth W Templeman** ............................ G ...... 847 912-2740
Volo  *(G-21315)*
**Lindsay Metal Madness Inc** .................... G ...... 815 568-4560
Marengo  *(G-14235)*
**Macholl Metal Fabrication** ...................... G ...... 815 597-1908
Garden Prairie  *(G-10795)*
**Mc Metals & Fabricating Inc** ................... G ...... 847 961-5242
Huntley  *(G-12163)*
**Robin L Barnhouse** .................................. G ...... 309 737-5431
Joy  *(G-12592)*
**Viking Metal Cabinet Co LLC** .................. D ...... 800 776-7767
Montgomery  *(G-15069)*

### FABRICS & CLOTH: Quilted

**Advanced Flexible Mtls LLC** .................... F ...... 770 222-6000
Chicago  *(G-3769)*
**Donghia Showrooms Inc** ......................... G ...... 312 822-0766
Chicago  *(G-4627)*
**Rock Tops Inc** ........................................... G ...... 708 672-1450
Crete  *(G-7518)*

### FABRICS & CLOTHING: Rubber Coated

**Custom Product Innovations** .................. G ...... 618 628-0111
Lebanon  *(G-13214)*
**Ljm Equipment Co** ................................... G ...... 847 291-0162
Northbrook  *(G-16297)*

### FABRICS: Alpacas, Mohair, Woven

**Salt Creek Alpacas Inc** ............................ G ...... 309 530-7904
Farmer City  *(G-10181)*

### FABRICS: Apparel & Outerwear, Cotton

**Chicor Inc** .................................................. G ...... 630 953-6154
Oak Brook  *(G-16501)*
**Dpe Incorporated** ..................................... G ...... 773 306-0105
Chicago  *(G-4640)*
**Hartmarx Corporation** .............................. F ...... 312 357-5325
Chicago  *(G-5051)*
**Netranix Enterprise** .................................. F
Bolingbrook  *(G-2350)*
**Rubin Manufacturing Inc** ........................ B ...... 312 942-1111
Chicago  *(G-6412)*

**Vitel Industries Inc** ................................... G ...... 847 299-9750
Des Plaines  *(G-8300)*

### FABRICS: Awning Stripes, Cotton

**Haakes Awning** ......................................... G ...... 618 529-4808
Carbondale  *(G-3009)*
**Rt Properties & Cnstr Corp** ..................... G ...... 708 913-7607
Riverdale  *(G-18025)*

### FABRICS: Bags & Bagging, Cotton

**Jacobson Acqstion Holdings LLC** ......... C ...... 847 623-1414
Waukegan  *(G-21574)*
**Sea-Rich Corp** ........................................... G ...... 773 261-6633
Chicago  *(G-6464)*
**Sultry Satchels** .......................................... G ...... 773 873-5718
Chicago  *(G-6615)*

### FABRICS: Bandage Cloth, Cotton

**Tru-Colour Products LLC** ....................... G ...... 630 447-0559
Warrenville  *(G-21366)*

### FABRICS: Broadwoven, Cotton

**I M M Inc** .................................................... F ...... 773 767-3700
Chicago  *(G-5131)*
**Veltex Corporation** ................................... E ...... 312 235-4014
Chicago  *(G-6879)*

### FABRICS: Broadwoven, Synthetic Manmade Fiber & Silk

**BP Amoco Chemical Company** ............... B ...... 630 420-5111
Naperville  *(G-15608)*
**Haakes Awning** ......................................... G ...... 618 529-4808
Carbondale  *(G-3009)*
**Loomcraft Textile & Supply Co** .............. E ...... 847 680-0000
Vernon Hills  *(G-21182)*
**MHS Ltd** ..................................................... F ...... 773 736-3333
Chicago  *(G-5716)*
**Ogden Top & Trim Shop Inc** ................... G ...... 708 484-5422
Berwyn  *(G-2070)*
**Robert Stern Industries Inc** .................... G ...... 630 983-9765
Naperville  *(G-15742)*

### FABRICS: Broadwoven, Wool

**Aurora Spclty Txtles Group Inc** ............. D ...... 800 864-0303
Yorkville  *(G-22650)*
**Modern Specialties Company** ................ G ...... 312 648-5800
Chicago  *(G-5785)*

### FABRICS: Canvas & Heavy Coarse, Cotton

**Jo-Ann Stores LLC** ................................... F ...... 847 394-9742
Arlington Heights  *(G-784)*

### FABRICS: Coated Or Treated

**Ace Anodizing Impregnating Inc** ........... D ...... 708 547-6680
Hillside  *(G-11907)*
**Advanced Flxble Composites Inc** .......... D ...... 847 658-3938
Lake In The Hills  *(G-12983)*
**Allerton Charter Coach** ........................... G ...... 217 344-2600
Champaign  *(G-3445)*
**Brasel Products Inc** ................................. G ...... 630 879-3759
Batavia  *(G-1424)*
**Jessup Manufacturing Company** .......... E ...... 847 362-0961
Lake Bluff  *(G-12851)*
**Metal Impregnating Corp** ........................ G ...... 630 543-3443
Addison  *(G-200)*
**Stickon Adhesive Inds Inc** ...................... E ...... 847 593-5959
Arlington Heights  *(G-844)*

### FABRICS: Cotton, Narrow

**F Hyman & Co** ........................................... G ...... 312 664-3810
Chicago  *(G-4804)*

### FABRICS: Denims

**Henry-Lee & Company LLC** ................... F ...... 312 648-1575
Chicago  *(G-5073)*

### FABRICS: Fiberglass, Broadwoven

**Accu-Wright Fiberglass Inc** .................... G ...... 618 337-3318
East Saint Louis  *(G-8739)*
**Fiberglass Solutions Corp** ...................... G ...... 630 458-0756
Addison  *(G-116)*
**Jalaa Fiberglass Inc** ................................. G ...... 217 923-3433
Greenup  *(G-11384)*

**Kabert Industries Inc** ............................... G ...... 630 833-2115
Villa Park  *(G-21262)*
**Mahans Fiberglass** ................................... G ...... 309 562-7349
Easton  *(G-8777)*
**Seco** ........................................................... G ...... 618 748-9227
Mound City  *(G-15257)*

### FABRICS: Filter Cloth, Cotton

**Hygienic Fabrics & Filters Inc** ................ G ...... 815 493-2502
Lanark  *(G-13155)*
**Terre Haute Tent & Awning Inc** .............. F ...... 812 235-6068
South Holland  *(G-20309)*

### FABRICS: Furniture Denim

**Anees Upholstery** ..................................... G ...... 312 243-2919
Chicago  *(G-3906)*
**City Living Design Inc** ............................. G ...... 312 335-0711
Chicago  *(G-4383)*

### FABRICS: Glass & Fiberglass, Broadwoven

**Fiberteq LLC** .............................................. D ...... 217 431-2111
Danville  *(G-7719)*

### FABRICS: Jersey Cloth

**Jr Royals Athletics** ................................... E ...... 224 659-2906
Elgin  *(G-9085)*

### FABRICS: Laminated

**Seal Tech Services** ................................... G ...... 847 776-0043
Palatine  *(G-17072)*

### FABRICS: Luggage, Cotton

**Home For All Heros Nfp** .......................... G ...... 309 808-2789
Bloomington  *(G-2180)*

### FABRICS: Metallized

**J M Fabricating Inc** .................................. G ...... 815 359-2024
Harmon  *(G-11595)*
**Vacumet Corp** ............................................ F ...... 708 562-7290
Northlake  *(G-16458)*

### FABRICS: Nonwoven

**Cowtan and Tout Inc** ................................ F ...... 312 644-0717
Chicago  *(G-4485)*
**Fibertex Nonwovens LLC** ........................ D ...... 815 349-3200
Ingleside  *(G-12189)*
**Midwest Nonwovens LLC** ........................ E ...... 618 337-9662
Sauget  *(G-19387)*

### FABRICS: Nylon, Broadwoven

**Srm Industries Inc** ................................... G ...... 847 735-0077
Lake Forest  *(G-12963)*

### FABRICS: Polypropylene, Broadwoven

**Kobawala Poly-Pack Inc** .......................... E ...... 312 664-3810
Naperville  *(G-15684)*
**Neptune USA Inc** ...................................... G ...... 847 987-3804
Schaumburg  *(G-19663)*
**Sea-Rich Corp** ........................................... G ...... 773 261-6633
Chicago  *(G-6464)*

### FABRICS: Print, Cotton

**DLS Custom Embroidery Inc** .................. E ...... 847 593-5957
Elk Grove Village  *(G-9431)*

### FABRICS: Resin Or Plastic Coated

**Engineered Polymr Solutions Inc** .......... E ...... 815 987-3700
Rockford  *(G-18366)*
**Engineered Polymr Solutions Inc** .......... E ...... 815 568-4205
Marengo  *(G-14226)*
**H E Wisdom & Sons Inc** .......................... E ...... 847 841-7002
Elgin  *(G-9052)*

### FABRICS: Satin

**Girls In White Satin** .................................. G ...... 217 245-5400
Jacksonville  *(G-12389)*

### FABRICS: Scrub Cloths

**Olivia R Aguilar-Camacho** ....................... G ...... 773 600-6864
Chicago  *(G-5984)*

## FABRICS: Shoe Laces, Exc Leather

Shoelace Inc ....G.... 847 854-2500
Crystal Lake (G-7650)

## FABRICS: Stretch, Cotton

Moss Holding Company ....C.... 847 238-4200
Elk Grove Village (G-9636)

## FABRICS: Tapestry, Cotton

Toco ....G.... 618 257-8626
Belleville (G-1681)

## FABRICS: Trimmings

A & R Screening LLC ....F.... 708 598-2480
Bridgeview (G-2457)

Alternative TS ....G.... 618 257-0230
Belleville (G-1608)

American Name Plate & Metal De ....E.... 773 376-1400
Chicago (G-3867)

Art Newvo Incorporated ....G.... 847 838-0304
Antioch (G-619)

Ashland Screening Corporation ....E.... 708 758-8800
Chicago Heights (G-7080)

Authority Screenprint & EMB ....G.... 630 236-0289
Plainfield (G-17581)

B and A Screen Printing ....G.... 217 762-2632
Monticello (G-15074)

Bailleu & Bailleu Printing Inc ....G.... 309 852-2517
Kewanee (G-12670)

Bikast Graphics Inc ....G.... 847 487-8822
Wauconda (G-21446)

Bow Brothers Co Inc ....G.... 217 359-0555
Champaign (G-3457)

Brownfield Sports Inc ....G.... 217 367-8321
Urbana (G-21074)

Carl Gorr Printing Co ....G.... 815 338-3191
Woodstock (G-22549)

Color Tone Printing ....G.... 708 385-1442
Blue Island (G-2242)

Creative Clothing Created 4 U ....G.... 847 543-0051
Grayslake (G-11330)

Custom Monogramming ....G.... 815 625-9044
Rock Falls (G-18130)

Custom Telephone Printing Inc ....F.... 815 338-0000
Woodstock (G-22557)

Custom Trophies ....G.... 217 422-3353
Decatur (G-7863)

Darnall Printing ....G.... 309 827-7212
Bloomington (G-2161)

Desk & Door Nameplate Company ....F.... 815 806-8670
Frankfort (G-10312)

DMarv Design Specialty Prtrs ....G.... 708 389-4420
Blue Island (G-2246)

Earl Ad Inc ....G.... 312 666-7106
Chicago (G-4673)

ESP T-Shirt Co Inc ....G.... 630 393-1033
Warrenville (G-21346)

Fantastic Lettering Inc ....G.... 773 685-7650
Chicago (G-4812)

G and D Enterprises Inc ....E.... 847 981-8661
Arlington Heights (G-757)

Gabriel Enterprises ....G.... 773 342-8705
Chicago (G-4906)

George Lauterer Corporation ....E.... 312 913-1881
Chicago (G-4943)

Go Van Goghs Tee Shirt ....G.... 309 342-1112
Galesburg (G-10755)

Good Impressions Inc ....G.... 847 831-4317
Highland Park (G-11836)

Graphic Screen Printing Inc ....G.... 708 429-3330
Orland Park (G-16863)

Hangables Inc ....F.... 847 673-9770
Skokie (G-20010)

Hazen Display Corporation ....E.... 815 248-2925
Davis (G-7806)

Hi-Five Sportswear Inc ....G.... 815 637-6044
Machesney Park (G-14079)

Hole In The Wall Screen Arts ....G.... 217 243-9100
Jacksonville (G-12391)

Image Plus Inc ....G.... 630 852-4920
Downers Grove (G-8463)

J & D Instant Signs ....G.... 847 965-2800
Morton Grove (G-15206)

Johnson Rolan Co Inc ....G.... 309 674-9671
Peoria (G-17394)

K and A Graphics Inc ....G.... 847 244-2345
Gurnee (G-11463)

Lee-Wel Printing Corporation ....G.... 630 682-0935
Wheaton (G-21966)

Linda Levinson Designs Inc ....G.... 312 951-6943
Chicago (G-5509)

Lloyd Midwest Graphics ....G.... 815 282-8828
Machesney Park (G-14089)

Lochman Ref Silk Screen Co ....F.... 847 475-6266
Evanston (G-10065)

Locker Room Screen Printing ....G.... 630 759-2533
Bolingbrook (G-2337)

M Wells Printing Co ....G.... 312 455-0400
Chicago (G-5588)

Mer-Pla Inc ....F.... 847 530-9798
Chicago (G-5687)

Mexacali Silkscreen Inc ....G.... 630 628-9313
Addison (G-203)

Midwest Stitch ....G.... 815 394-1516
Rockford (G-18507)

Mighty Mites Awards and Sons ....G.... 847 297-0035
Des Plaines (G-8233)

Minerva Sportswear Inc ....F.... 309 661-2387
Bloomington (G-2201)

Nancys Lettering Shop ....G.... 217 345-6007
Charleston (G-3605)

Need To Know Inc ....G.... 309 691-3877
Peoria (G-17415)

Nu-Art Printing ....G.... 618 533-9971
Centralia (G-3425)

Offworld Designs ....G.... 815 786-7080
Sandwich (G-19372)

Olympic Trophy and Awards Co ....F.... 773 631-9500
Chicago (G-5987)

Paddock Industries Inc ....F.... 618 277-1580
Smithton (G-20123)

Papyrus Press Inc ....F.... 773 342-0700
Chicago (G-6074)

Plastics Printing Group Inc ....F.... 312 421-7980
Chicago (G-6138)

Precision Screen Specialties ....G.... 630 762-9548
Saint Charles (G-19241)

Printing Works Inc ....G.... 847 860-1920
Elk Grove Village (G-9698)

Priority Print ....G.... 708 485-7080
Brookfield (G-2641)

Qst Industries Inc ....E.... 312 930-9400
Chicago (G-6237)

Qst Industries Inc ....D.... 312 930-9400
Chicago (G-6238)

Quality Spraying Screen Prtg ....E.... 630 584-8324
Saint Charles (G-19248)

R J S Silk Screening Co ....G.... 708 974-3009
Palos Hills (G-17123)

Rainbow Art Inc ....F.... 312 421-5600
Chicago (G-6288)

Rico Industries Inc ....D.... 312 427-0313
Niles (G-16028)

Ronald J Nixon ....G.... 708 748-8130
Park Forest (G-17175)

RR Donnelley & Sons Company ....D.... 630 762-7600
Saint Charles (G-19256)

Scheiwes Print Shop ....G.... 815 683-2398
Crescent City (G-7456)

Screen Graphics ....G.... 309 699-8513
Pekin (G-17288)

Screen Machine Incorporated ....G.... 847 439-2233
Elk Grove Village (G-9732)

Select Screen Prints & EMB ....F.... 309 829-6511
Bloomington (G-2222)

Shree Mahavir Inc ....G.... 312 408-1080
Chicago (G-6501)

Signature Label of Illinois ....G.... 618 283-5145
Vandalia (G-21125)

Signcraft Screenprint Inc ....C.... 815 777-3030
Galena (G-10731)

Sport Connection ....G.... 630 980-1787
Roselle (G-18979)

Stevens Sign Co Inc ....G.... 708 562-4888
Northlake (G-16453)

T J Marche Ltd ....G.... 618 445-2314
Albion (G-366)

Teds Shirt Shack Inc ....G.... 217 224-9705
Quincy (G-17892)

Think Ink Inc ....G.... 815 459-4565
Crystal Lake (G-7665)

Top Notch Silk Screening ....G.... 773 847-6335
Chicago (G-6744)

Triangle Screen Print Inc ....F.... 847 678-9200
Franklin Park (G-10612)

Trimark Screen Printing Inc ....G.... 630 629-2823
Lombard (G-13872)

Type Concepts Inc ....G.... 708 361-1005
Palos Heights (G-17112)

Ultimate Distributing Inc ....G.... 847 566-2250
Mundelein (G-15565)

Wagner Zip-Change Inc ....E.... 708 681-4100
Melrose Park (G-14706)

Waldos Sports Corner Inc ....G.... 309 688-2425
Peoria (G-17477)

Weiskamp Screen Printing ....G.... 217 398-8428
Champaign (G-3560)

Winning Stitch ....G.... 217 348-8279
Charleston (G-3616)

## FABRICS: Trimmings, Textile

Rogers Custom Trims Inc ....G.... 773 745-6577
Chicago (G-6380)

## FABRICS: Upholstery, Cotton

Nolte & Tyson Inc ....F.... 847 551-3313
Gilberts (G-10929)

## FABRICS: Upholstery, Wool

EW Bredemeier and Co ....F.... 773 237-1600
Chicago (G-4793)

## FABRICS: Wall Covering, From Manmade Fiber Or Silk

Maya Romanoff Corporation ....E.... 773 465-6909
Skokie (G-20034)

## FABRICS: Weft Or Circular Knit

Chicago Knitting Mills ....G.... 773 463-1464
Chicago (G-4326)

## FABRICS: Woven, Narrow Cotton, Wool, Silk

Chase Corporation ....E.... 847 866-8500
Evanston (G-10022)

Harbor Village LLC ....G.... 773 338-2222
Chicago (G-5043)

Shoelace Inc ....G.... 847 854-2500
Kildeer (G-12704)

Technical Sealants Inc ....F.... 815 777-9797
Galena (G-10732)

UNI-Label and Tag Corporation ....E.... 847 956-8900
Elk Grove Village (G-9797)

Voss Belting & Specialty Co ....E.... 847 673-8900
Lincolnwood (G-13541)

## FACILITIES SUPPORT SVCS

Pitney Bowes Inc ....E.... 800 784-4224
Itasca (G-12341)

## FACSIMILE COMMUNICATION EQPT

Pitney Bowes Inc ....E.... 800 784-4224
Itasca (G-12341)

## FAMILY CLOTHING STORES

Five Brother Inc ....G.... 309 663-6323
Bloomington (G-2164)

Teds Shirt Shack Inc ....G.... 217 224-9705
Quincy (G-17892)

Tgrv LLC ....G.... 815 634-2102
Bourbonnais (G-2407)

Thrilled LLC ....G.... 312 404-1929
Chicago (G-6723)

## FANS, BLOWING: Indl Or Commercial

Eclipse Inc ....D.... 815 877-3031
Rockford (G-18356)

Illinois Blower Inc ....D.... 847 639-5500
Cary (G-3352)

Mellish & Murray Co ....F.... 312 733-3513
Chicago (G-5683)

## FANS, EXHAUST: Indl Or Commercial

Car - Mon Products Inc ....E.... 847 695-9000
Elgin (G-8981)

Homewerks Worldwide LLC ....E.... 877 319-3757
Lake Bluff (G-12849)

Muffler ....G.... 217 344-1676
Urbana (G-21095)

# FANS, VENTILATING: Indl Or Commercial

### FANS, VENTILATING: Indl Or Commercial

Conservation Technology Ltd .............D...... 847 559-5500
  Northbrook (G-16232)
New York Blower Company ................D...... 217 347-3233
  Effingham (G-8849)

### FANS: Ceiling

Matthews-Gerbar Ltd ...........................G........ 847 680-9043
  Libertyville (G-13348)
Matthewsgerbar Ltd .............................G........ 847 680-9043
  Libertyville (G-13349)

### FARM & GARDEN MACHINERY WHOLESALERS

Gsi Group LLC .....................................D...... 618 283-9792
  Vandalia (G-21115)
Mega International Ltd .........................G...... 309 764-5310
  Moline (G-14956)
Michaels Equipment Co .......................G...... 618 524-8560
  Metropolis (G-14759)
Wabash Valley Service Co ...................F...... 618 393-2971
  Olney (G-16800)

### FARM MACHINERY REPAIR SVCS

Greene Welding & Hardware Inc .........E...... 217 375-4244
  East Lynn (G-8668)
Lake Fabrication Inc ............................E...... 217 832-2761
  Villa Grove (G-21229)
Midwest Machine Tool Inc ...................G...... 815 427-8665
  Saint Anne (G-19124)
Needham Shop Inc ..............................G...... 630 557-9019
  Kaneville (G-12600)
Trotters Manufacturing Co ...................G...... 217 364-4540
  Buffalo (G-2649)

### FARM PRDTS, RAW MATERIALS, WHOLESALE: Broomcorn

Thomas Monahan Company .................F...... 217 268-5771
  Arcola (G-686)

### FARM PRDTS, RAW MATERIALS, WHOLESALE: Farm Animals

Millstadt Rendering Company ..............E...... 618 538-5312
  Belleville (G-1659)

### FARM SPLY STORES

Piatt County Service Co .......................G........ 217 678-5511
  Bement (G-1801)

### FARM SPLYS WHOLESALERS

Archer-Daniels-Midland Company .......G...... 618 483-6171
  Altamont (G-549)
Birkeys Farm Store Inc ........................E...... 217 337-1772
  Urbana (G-21073)
Brandt Consolidated Inc ......................E...... 217 547-5800
  Springfield (G-20399)
Brandt Consolidated Inc ......................G...... 309 365-7201
  Lexington (G-13291)
Cloverleaf Feed Co Inc ........................G...... 217 589-5010
  Roodhouse (G-18882)
Effingham Equity Inc ...........................F...... 217 268-5128
  Arcola (G-668)
Hayden Mills Inc ..................................E...... 618 962-3136
  Omaha (G-16807)
Helena Chemical Company .................G...... 217 234-2726
  Mattoon (G-14391)
Hueber LLC .........................................F...... 815 393-4879
  Creston (G-7472)
M & W Feed Service ............................G...... 815 858-2412
  Elizabeth (G-9243)
Mont Eagle Products Inc .....................G...... 618 455-3344
  Sainte Marie (G-19325)
South Central Fs Inc ...........................E...... 618 283-1557
  Vandalia (G-21126)

### FARM SPLYS, WHOLESALE: Beekeeping Splys, Nondurable

Prairie Profile .......................................G....... 618 846-2116
  Vandalia (G-21120)

### FARM SPLYS, WHOLESALE: Feed

American Milling Company ..................F...... 309 347-6888
  Pekin (G-17253)
B B Milling Co Inc ................................G...... 217 376-3131
  Emden (G-9983)
Furst-Mcness Company ......................D...... 800 435-5100
  Freeport (G-10659)
Liberty Feed Mill ..................................F...... 217 645-3441
  Liberty (G-13296)
Siemer Enterprises Inc .......................E...... 217 857-3171
  Teutopolis (G-20855)
Wabash Valley Service Co ...................F...... 618 393-2971
  Olney (G-16800)

### FARM SPLYS, WHOLESALE: Fertilizers & Agricultural Chemicals

Brandt Consolidated Inc .....................F...... 217 438-6158
  Auburn (G-948)
Prairieland Fs Inc ................................G...... 309 329-2162
  Astoria (G-936)

### FARM SPLYS, WHOLESALE: Harness Eqpt

Mast Harness Shop ............................E...... 217 543-3463
  Campbell Hill (G-2976)

### FARM SPLYS, WHOLESALE: Limestone, Agricultural

Blomberg Bros Inc ..............................F...... 618 245-6321
  Farina (G-10174)

### FARM SPLYS, WHOLESALE: Saddlery

Choice Usa LLC ..................................G....... 847 428-2252
  Gilberts (G-10915)

### FASTENERS WHOLESALERS

R-B Industries Inc ...............................E...... 847 647-4020
  Niles (G-16026)

### FASTENERS: Brads, Alum, Brass/Other Nonferrous Metal/Wire

Jjj Brass and Aluminum Foundry .........G...... 608 363-9225
  South Beloit (G-20153)

### FASTENERS: Metal

Ecf Holdings LLC ................................E...... 224 723-5524
  Northbrook (G-16246)
Gemco ................................................E...... 217 446-7900
  Danville (G-7726)
Hilti Inc ...............................................G...... 847 364-9818
  Elmhurst (G-9882)
Topy Precision Mfg Inc .......................D...... 847 228-5902
  Elk Grove Village (G-9784)

### FASTENERS: Metal

Cleats Mfg Inc ....................................F...... 773 521-0300
  Chicago (G-4399)
Driv-Lok Inc ........................................G...... 815 895-8161
  Sycamore (G-20794)
Hunter-Stevens Company Inc .............F...... 847 671-5014
  Franklin Park (G-10493)
Illinois Tool Works Inc .........................E...... 708 681-3891
  Broadview (G-2585)
Metal Mfg LLC ....................................C...... 815 432-4595
  Watseka (G-21423)
Termax Corporation ............................C...... 847 519-1500
  Lake Zurich (G-13137)
United Steel & Fasteners Inc .............G...... 630 250-0900
  Itasca (G-12370)

### FASTENERS: Notions, NEC

Afi Industries Inc ................................E...... 630 462-0400
  Carol Stream (G-3092)
American Fas & Components .............G...... 815 397-2698
  Rockford (G-18262)
Ample Supply Company ......................E...... 815 895-3500
  Sycamore (G-20786)
Anixter Inc ..........................................E...... 512 989-4254
  Glenview (G-11102)
Blue Ribbon Fastener Company .........F...... 847 673-1248
  Skokie (G-19966)
Brighton-Best Intl Inc ..........................G...... 562 808-8000
  Aurora (G-974)
Component Hardware Inc ...................G...... 847 458-8181
  Gilberts (G-10916)
Contmid Inc ........................................G...... 708 747-1200
  Park Forest (G-17170)
Ecf Holdings LLC ................................G...... 224 723-5524
  Northbrook (G-16246)
Engineered Components Co ...............E...... 847 985-8000
  Elgin (G-9028)
Excell Fastener Solutions Inc .............G...... 630 424-3360
  Lombard (G-13797)
Forest City Technologies Inc ..............E...... 815 965-5880
  Rockford (G-18389)
Greenslade Fastener Svcs LLC ..........G...... 815 398-4073
  Rockford (G-18406)
Hawk Fastener Services .....................F...... 708 489-2000
  Alsip (G-472)
Ideal Supply Inc .................................G...... 847 961-5900
  Huntley (G-12146)
Illinois Tool Works Inc .........................C...... 708 342-6000
  Mokena (G-14872)
Illinois Tool Works Inc .........................B...... 847 724-7500
  Glenview (G-11141)
Illinois Tool Works Inc .........................G...... 630 372-2150
  Bartlett (G-1353)
Illinois Tool Works Inc .........................C...... 847 783-5500
  Elgin (G-9072)
Inland Fastener Inc ............................F...... 630 293-3800
  West Chicago (G-21720)
L & M Screw Machine Products .........F...... 630 801-0455
  Montgomery (G-15052)
Lawrence Screw Products Inc ............D...... 708 867-5150
  Harwood Heights (G-11686)
Lhs Inc ...............................................G...... 630 832-3875
  Elmhurst (G-9901)
Marmon Industrial LLC ......................G...... 312 372-9500
  Chicago (G-5626)
Multitech Cold Forming LLC ..............E...... 630 949-8200
  Carol Stream (G-3201)
Nbs Corporation .................................G...... 847 860-8856
  Elk Grove Village (G-9648)
Pecson Distributors LLC ....................G...... 815 342-7977
  Beecher (G-1601)
Safety Socket LLC .............................E...... 224 484-6222
  Gilberts (G-10934)
Sanco Industries Inc .........................F...... 847 243-8675
  Kildeer (G-12703)
Signode Packaging Systems Corp ....D...... 800 323-2464
  Glenview (G-11203)
Supreme Screw Inc ...........................G...... 630 226-9000
  Romeoville (G-18872)
Vertex Distribution .............................G...... 847 437-0400
  Elk Grove Village (G-9807)

### FASTENERS: Notions, Zippers

Minigrip Inc .......................................D...... 845 680-2710
  Ottawa (G-16969)

### FASTENERS: Wire, Made From Purchased Wire

Klimp Industries Inc ..........................G...... 630 682-0752
  Carol Stream (G-3179)
Klimp Industries Inc ..........................G...... 630 790-0600
  Carol Stream (G-3180)

### FATTY ACID ESTERS & AMINOS

Vantage Oleochemicals Inc ..............C...... 773 376-9000
  Chicago (G-6873)
Vantage Specialties Inc ...................D...... 847 244-3410
  Gurnee (G-11518)

### FAUCETS & SPIGOTS: Metal & Plastic

PSI Systems North America Inc ........G...... 630 830-9435
  Bartlett (G-1366)
Water Saver Faucet Co ....................C...... 312 666-5500
  Chicago (G-6941)

### FEATHERS: Dusters

Modern Specialties Company ...........G...... 312 648-5800
  Chicago (G-5785)

### FEDERAL CROP INSURANCE CORP

Associated Agri-Business Inc ...........G...... 618 498-2977
  Jerseyville (G-12417)
Associated Agri-Business Inc ...........G...... 618 498-2977
  Eldred (G-8927)

# PRODUCT SECTION

### FELT PARTS
Biz Pins Inc .................................................. G ....... 847 695-6212
　Elgin *(G-8967)*
Filter Technology Inc ................................. E ....... 773 523-7200
　Bedford Park *(G-1550)*
Fourell Corp ................................................ G ....... 217 742-3186
　Winchester *(G-22279)*
Metric Felt Co ............................................. G ....... 708 479-7979
　Mokena *(G-14885)*

### FELT, WHOLESALE
Supreme Felt & Abrasives Inc ................. E ....... 708 344-0134
　Cicero *(G-7234)*

### FELT: Polishing
Gilday Services ........................................... G ....... 847 395-0853
　Antioch *(G-635)*

### FENCE POSTS: Iron & Steel
CHS Acquisition Corp ................................ C ....... 708 756-5648
　Chicago Heights *(G-7090)*
Frazer Manufacturing Corp ..................... G ....... 815 625-5411
　Rock Falls *(G-18133)*

### FENCES OR POSTS: Ornamental Iron Or Steel
Electrostatic Concepts Inc ........................ F ....... 630 585-5080
　Naperville *(G-15804)*
Industrial Fence Inc .................................. E ....... 773 521-9900
　Chicago *(G-5176)*
Iron Castle Inc ............................................ F ....... 773 890-0575
　Chicago *(G-5238)*
Mike Meier & Sons Fence Mfg ................ E ....... 847 587-1111
　Spring Grove *(G-20347)*
Mueller Orna Ir Works Inc ........................ F ....... 847 758-9941
　Elk Grove Village *(G-9643)*
Neiweem Industries Inc ............................ G ....... 847 487-1239
　Oakwood Hills *(G-16727)*
Osorio Iron Works ..................................... F ....... 773 772-4060
　Chicago *(G-6022)*
Sandoval Fences Corp ............................... G ....... 773 287-0279
　Chicago *(G-6438)*
Winters Welding Inc .................................. G ....... 773 860-7735
　Chicago *(G-7004)*

### FENCING DEALERS
Mike Meier & Sons Fence Mfg ................ E ....... 847 587-1111
　Spring Grove *(G-20347)*
Ornamental Iron Shop ............................... G ....... 618 281-6072
　Columbia *(G-7361)*
William Dach ............................................... F ....... 815 962-3455
　Rockford *(G-18683)*
Woodland Fence Forest Pdts Inc ............ G ....... 630 393-2220
　Warrenville *(G-21369)*

### FENCING MATERIALS: Plastic
Katco Enterprises LLC .............................. G ....... 217 429-5855
　Decatur *(G-7901)*
Plastival Inc ................................................. B ....... 847 931-4771
　Elgin *(G-9142)*
Steel Guard Inc .......................................... F ....... 773 342-6265
　Chicago *(G-6580)*

### FENCING MATERIALS: Snow Fence, Wood
Iron Castle Inc ............................................ F ....... 773 890-0575
　Chicago *(G-5238)*

### FENCING MATERIALS: Wood
Bergeron Group Inc ................................... E ....... 815 741-1635
　Joliet *(G-12464)*
Mike Meier & Sons Fence Mfg ................ E ....... 847 587-1111
　Spring Grove *(G-20347)*

### FENCING: Chain Link
Master-Halco Inc ........................................ E ....... 618 395-4365
　Olney *(G-16780)*
Master-Halco Inc ........................................ G ....... 630 293-5560
　West Chicago *(G-21741)*
Stephens Pipe & Steel LLC ...................... E ....... 800 451-2612
　North Aurora *(G-16146)*

### FENDERS: Automobile, Stamped Or Pressed Metal
Gs Custom Works Inc ................................ G ....... 815 233-4724
　Freeport *(G-10661)*

### FERRITES
Permacor Inc ............................................... E ....... 708 422-3353
　Oak Lawn *(G-16639)*
TSC Pyroferric International .................... C ....... 217 849-2230
　Toledo *(G-20969)*

### FERROUS METALS: Reclaimed From Clay
Progress Rail Services Corp ..................... G ....... 309 343-6176
　Galesburg *(G-10771)*

### FERTILIZER, AGRICULTURAL: Wholesalers
Brandt Consolidated Inc .......................... G ....... 217 626-1123
　Farmer City *(G-10178)*
F S Gateway Inc ......................................... G ....... 618 458-6588
　Fults *(G-10709)*
Harbach Gillan & Nixon Inc ..................... G ....... 217 794-5117
　Maroa *(G-14305)*
Harbach Gillan & Nixon Inc ..................... F ....... 217 935-8378
　Clinton *(G-7282)*
Huyear Trucking Inc ................................. G ....... 217 854-3551
　Carlinville *(G-3039)*
Illini Fs Inc .................................................. G ....... 217 442-4737
　Potomac *(G-17738)*
Miller Fertilizer Inc ................................... G ....... 217 382-4241
　Casey *(G-3390)*
Millers Fertilizer & Feed ........................... G ....... 217 783-6321
　Cowden *(G-7452)*
Potash Holding Company Inc .................. G ....... 847 849-4200
　Northbrook *(G-16341)*
Randolph Agricultural Services ............... G ....... 309 473-3256
　Heyworth *(G-11765)*
South Central Fs Inc ................................. F ....... 217 849-2242
　Toledo *(G-20966)*

### FERTILIZERS: NEC
Allerton Supply Company ......................... F ....... 217 896-2522
　Homer *(G-12074)*
Anp Inc ......................................................... G ....... 309 757-0372
　Moline *(G-14918)*
Archer-Daniels-Midland Company ........... G ....... 618 483-6171
　Altamont *(G-549)*
Bio Green Inc .............................................. G ....... 847 740-9637
　Volo *(G-21308)*
Brandt Consolidated Inc .......................... E ....... 217 547-5800
　Springfield *(G-20399)*
Brandt Consolidated Inc .......................... G ....... 217 626-1123
　Farmer City *(G-10178)*
Brandt Consolidated Inc .......................... G ....... 309 365-7201
　Lexington *(G-13291)*
Brandt Consolidated Inc .......................... F ....... 217 438-6158
　Auburn *(G-948)*
CF Industries Nitrogen Llc ....................... C ....... 847 405-2400
　Deerfield *(G-7997)*
Crop Production Services Inc ................. G ....... 217 427-2181
　Catlin *(G-3401)*
E N P Inc ..................................................... G ....... 815 539-7471
　Mendota *(G-14721)*
E N P Inc ..................................................... G ....... 800 255-4906
　Mendota *(G-14720)*
Evergreen Fs Inc ........................................ G ....... 815 934-5422
　Cullom *(G-7681)*
F S Gateway Inc ......................................... G ....... 618 458-6588
　Fults *(G-10709)*
Garden Prairie Organics LLC .................. G ....... 815 597-1318
　Garden Prairie *(G-10794)*
Harbach Gillan & Nixon Inc ..................... F ....... 217 935-8378
　Clinton *(G-7282)*
Hayden Mills Inc ......................................... E ....... 618 962-3136
　Omaha *(G-16807)*
Hyponex Corporation ................................. E ....... 815 772-2167
　Morrison *(G-15144)*
Kreider Services Incorporated ................ D ....... 815 288-6691
　Dixon *(G-8336)*
Lebanon Seaboard Corporation ............... E ....... 217 446-0983
　Danville *(G-7746)*
Masterblend International LLC ............... G ....... 815 423-5551
　Morris *(G-15115)*
Miller Fertilizer Inc ................................... G ....... 217 382-4241
　Casey *(G-3390)*
Millers Fertilizer & Feed ........................... F ....... 217 783-6321
　Cowden *(G-7452)*
Myers Inc ..................................................... G ....... 309 725-3710
　Varna *(G-21135)*
Piatt County Service Co ........................... G ....... 217 678-5511
　Bement *(G-1801)*
Piatt County Service Co ........................... G ....... 217 489-2411
　Mansfield *(G-14178)*
Prairieland Fs Inc ....................................... G ....... 309 329-2162
　Astoria *(G-936)*
Randolph Agricultural Services ............... G ....... 309 473-3256
　Heyworth *(G-11765)*
South Central Fs Inc ................................. F ....... 217 849-2242
　Toledo *(G-20966)*
South Central Fs Inc ................................. E ....... 618 283-1557
　Vandalia *(G-21126)*
Van Diest Supply Company ...................... G ....... 815 232-6053
　Freeport *(G-10697)*
Wabash Valley Service Co ........................ F ....... 618 393-2971
　Olney *(G-16800)*
Wedgworths Inc .......................................... E ....... 863 682-2153
　Northbrook *(G-16385)*
West Central Fs Inc ................................... G ....... 309 375-6904
　Wataga *(G-21399)*

### FERTILIZERS: Nitrogen Solutions
Rentech Development Corp ...................... C ....... 815 747-3101
　East Dubuque *(G-8620)*
Terra Nitrogen Company LP ................... G ....... 847 405-2400
　Deerfield *(G-8062)*

### FERTILIZERS: Nitrogenous
Bio Green Inc .............................................. G ....... 847 740-9637
　Volo *(G-21308)*
CF Industries Enterprises Inc ................. G ....... 847 405-2400
　Deerfield *(G-7995)*
CF Industries Holdings Inc ...................... B ....... 847 405-2400
　Deerfield *(G-7996)*
CF Industries Nitrogen LLC .................... F ....... 847 405-2400
　Deerfield *(G-7998)*
CF Industries Nitrogen Llc ...................... G ....... 847 405-2400
　Deerfield *(G-7997)*
CF Industries Sales LLC .......................... B ....... 847 405-2400
　Deerfield *(G-7999)*
Crop Production Services Inc ................. G ....... 815 853-4078
　Wenona *(G-21647)*
E N P Inc ..................................................... G ....... 800 255-4906
　Mendota *(G-14720)*
E N P Inc ..................................................... G ....... 815 539-7471
　Mendota *(G-14721)*
Fertilizer Inc ................................................ G ....... 708 458-8615
　Chicago *(G-4838)*
Fertilizer Inc ................................................ G ....... 708 458-8615
　Bedford Park *(G-1549)*
Gateway Fs Inc ........................................... G ....... 618 824-6631
　Venedy *(G-21136)*
Harbach Gillan & Nixon Inc ..................... F ....... 217 935-8378
　Clinton *(G-7282)*
Harbach Gillan & Nixon Inc ..................... G ....... 217 794-5117
　Maroa *(G-14305)*
Michel Fertilizer & Equipment ................ G ....... 618 242-6000
　Mount Vernon *(G-15425)*
Pcs Nitrogen Inc ......................................... D ....... 847 849-4200
　Northbrook *(G-16332)*
Pcs Nitrogen Fertilizer LP ....................... F ....... 847 849-4200
　Northbrook *(G-16333)*
Pcs Ntrgen Frtlzer Oprtons Inc .............. D ....... 847 849-4200
　Northbrook *(G-16335)*
Potash Corp Ssktchewan Fla Inc ............ C ....... 847 849-4200
　Northbrook *(G-16339)*
Potash Corp Ssktchewan Fla Inc ............ G ....... 847 849-4200
　Northbrook *(G-16340)*
Solution Designs Inc ................................. G ....... 847 680-7788
　Vernon Hills *(G-21203)*
Sun Ag Inc ................................................... G ....... 309 726-1331
　Hudson *(G-12126)*
Sunrise AG Service Company ................. G ....... 309 538-4287
　Kilbourne *(G-12698)*
Veolia Es Industrial Svcs Inc .................. F ....... 708 652-0575
　Cicero *(G-7244)*

### FERTILIZERS: Phosphatic
CF Industries Holdings Inc ...................... B ....... 847 405-2400
　Deerfield *(G-7996)*
CF Industries Nitrogen LLC .................... F ....... 847 405-2400
　Deerfield *(G-7998)*
Gateway Fs Inc ........................................... G ....... 618 824-6631
　Venedy *(G-21136)*
Occidental Chemical Corp ........................ F ....... 773 284-0079
　Chicago *(G-5965)*

# FERTILIZERS: Phosphatic

Pcs Nitrogen Inc ..................................... D ...... 847 849-4200
  Northbrook *(G-16332)*
Pcs Phosphate Company Inc ............... D ...... 847 849-4200
  Northbrook *(G-16336)*
Phosphate Resource Ptrs ..................... A ...... 847 739-1200
  Lake Forest *(G-12945)*
Potash Corp Ssktchewan Fla Inc .......... C ...... 847 849-4200
  Northbrook *(G-16339)*
Potash Corp Ssktchewan Fla Inc .......... C ...... 847 849-4200
  Northbrook *(G-16340)*
Sun Ag Inc ............................................. G ...... 309 726-1331
  Hudson *(G-12126)*

## FIBER & FIBER PRDTS: Acrylic

Acrylic Design Works Inc ..................... F ...... 773 843-1300
  Chicago *(G-3738)*

## FIBER & FIBER PRDTS: Fluorocarbon

Honeywell International Inc .................. E
  Danville *(G-7733)*

## FIBER & FIBER PRDTS: Organic, Noncellulose

Gig Karasek LLC ................................... F ...... 630 549-0394
  Saint Charles *(G-19189)*

## FIBER & FIBER PRDTS: Polyester

Fairfield Processing Corp ...................... E ...... 618 452-8404
  Granite City *(G-11276)*

## FIBER & FIBER PRDTS: Protein

RITA Corporation .................................. E ...... 815 337-2500
  Crystal Lake *(G-7642)*

## FIBER & FIBER PRDTS: Synthetic Cellulosic

Higgins Bros Inc ................................... F ...... 773 523-0124
  Chicago *(G-5086)*
Iten Industries Inc ................................. G ...... 630 543-2820
  Addison *(G-155)*
Lanxess Corporation ............................ E ...... 630 789-8440
  Willowbrook *(G-22219)*

## FIBER & FIBER PRDTS: Vinyl

Magnetic Occasions & More Inc .......... G ...... 815 462-4141
  New Lenox *(G-15892)*
Vinylworks Inc ...................................... G ...... 815 477-9680
  Crystal Lake *(G-7674)*

## FIBER OPTICS

Advanced Fiber Products LLC ............. G ...... 847 768-9001
  Des Plaines *(G-8144)*
Elite Fiber Optics LLC .......................... E ...... 630 225-9454
  Oak Brook *(G-16506)*
Neolight Labs LLC ............................... G ...... 312 242-1773
  Ingleside *(G-12195)*

## FIELD WAREHOUSING SVCS

Adams Elevator Equipment Co ............ E ...... 847 581-2900
  Chicago *(G-3743)*

## FILE FOLDERS

Acco Brands USA LLC ......................... B ...... 800 222-6462
  Lake Zurich *(G-13034)*
Warwick Publishing Company .............. D ...... 630 584-3871
  Saint Charles *(G-19291)*

## FILLERS & SEALERS: Putty

Black Swan Manufacturing Co .............. F ...... 773 227-3700
  Chicago *(G-4121)*
Nu-Puttie Corporation .......................... E ...... 708 681-1040
  Maywood *(G-14433)*
Sarco Putty Company .......................... G ...... 773 735-5577
  Chicago *(G-6444)*

## FILLERS & SEALERS: Putty, Wood

Atlas Putty Products Co ....................... D ...... 708 429-5858
  Tinley Park *(G-20895)*

## FILLERS & SEALERS: Wood

Sherwin-Williams Company .................. G ...... 847 573-0240
  Libertyville *(G-13380)*
Sherwin-Williams Company .................. G ...... 815 337-0942
  Woodstock *(G-22611)*
Sherwin-Williams Company .................. G ...... 847 478-0677
  Long Grove *(G-13901)*
Sherwin-Williams Company .................. G ...... 708 409-4728
  Westchester *(G-21854)*
Sherwin-Williams Company .................. G ...... 815 254-3559
  Romeoville *(G-18868)*

## FILM & SHEET: Unsuppported Plastic

Abbott Plastics & Supply Co ................. E ...... 815 874-8500
  Rockford *(G-18246)*
Avery Dennison Corporation ................ D ...... 877 214-0909
  Niles *(G-15962)*
Bema Inc .............................................. G ...... 630 279-7800
  Elmhurst *(G-9839)*
Catalina Coating & Plas Inc .................. F ...... 847 806-1340
  Elk Grove Village *(G-9358)*
CFC International Inc ........................... G ...... 708 891-3456
  Chicago Heights *(G-7086)*
CFC International Corporation .............. C ...... 708 323-4131
  Chicago Heights *(G-7087)*
Co-Ordinated Packaging Inc ................. F ...... 847 559-8877
  Northbrook *(G-16228)*
Cope Plastics Inc ................................. F ...... 630 226-1664
  Bolingbrook *(G-2288)*
Custom Films Inc ................................. F ...... 217 826-2326
  Marshall *(G-14320)*
Custom Plastics of Peoria .................... ...... 309 697-2888
  Bartonville *(G-1394)*
Design Packaging Company Inc ........... E ...... 847 835-3327
  Glencoe *(G-10998)*
E-Z Products Inc .................................. ...... 847 551-9199
  Gilberts *(G-10918)*
Environetics Inc ................................... F ...... 815 838-8331
  Lockport *(G-13715)*
Exclusively Expo .................................. E ...... 630 378-4600
  Romeoville *(G-18821)*
Fisher Container Corp ......................... D ...... 847 541-0000
  Buffalo Grove *(G-2694)*
Fisher Container Holdings LLC ............ ...... 847 541-0000
  Buffalo Grove *(G-2695)*
Fox Enterprises Inc .............................. ...... 630 513-9010
  Saint Charles *(G-19188)*
H H Interantional Inc ............................ ...... 847 697-7805
  Elgin *(G-9054)*
Highland Supply Corporation ................ B ...... 618 654-2161
  Highland *(G-11794)*
Jordan Specialty Plastics Inc ................ E ...... 847 945-5591
  Deerfield *(G-8021)*
Kns Companies Inc .............................. F ...... 630 665-9010
  Carol Stream *(G-3181)*
Major Prime Plastics Inc ....................... ...... 630 953-4111
  Addison *(G-189)*
Midwest Lminating Coatings Inc ........... E ...... 708 653-9500
  Alsip *(G-493)*
Midwest Marketing Distrs Inc ............... ...... 309 663-6972
  Bloomington *(G-2199)*
Midwest Marketing Distrs Inc ............... F ...... 309 688-8858
  Peoria *(G-17408)*
Minigrip Inc .......................................... D ...... 845 680-2710
  Ottawa *(G-16969)*
Multi-Plastics Inc .................................. E ...... 630 226-0580
  Bolingbrook *(G-2348)*
Polyair Inter Pack Inc ........................... ...... 773 995-1818
  Chicago *(G-6153)*
Reynolds Food Packaging LLC ............ C ...... 847 482-3500
  Lake Forest *(G-12953)*
Sandee Manufacturing Co .................... ...... 847 671-1335
  Franklin Park *(G-10581)*
Senoplast USA ..................................... G ...... 630 898-0731
  Aurora *(G-1077)*
Summit Plastics Inc .............................. ...... 815 578-8700
  McHenry *(G-14558)*
Transilwrap Company Inc .................... ...... 847 678-1800
  Franklin Park *(G-10611)*
Transworld Plastic Films Inc ................. F ...... 815 561-7117
  Rochelle *(G-18112)*

## FILM BASE: Cellulose Acetate Or Nitrocellulose Plastics

Sofiflex LLC ......................................... F ...... 847 261-4849
  Schiller Park *(G-19874)*
W R Grace & Co ................................... C ...... 773 838-3200
  Chicago *(G-6920)*

## FILM: Motion Picture

Chicago Film Archive Nfp ..................... G ...... 773 478-3799
  Chicago *(G-4319)*

Motus Digital Llc .................................. E ...... 972 943-0008
  Des Plaines *(G-8237)*

## FILTER CLEANING SVCS

All Seasons Heating & AC ................... G ...... 217 429-2022
  Decatur *(G-7831)*

## FILTER ELEMENTS: Fluid & Hydraulic Line

Doms Incorporated .............................. E ...... 847 838-6723
  Antioch *(G-630)*

## FILTERING MEDIA: Pottery

Spouts of Water Inc ............................. G ...... 303 570-5104
  Des Plaines *(G-8280)*

## FILTERS

Arrow Pneumatics Inc .......................... D ...... 708 343-6177
  Broadview *(G-2559)*
Camfil USA Inc ..................................... D ...... 815 459-6600
  Crystal Lake *(G-7549)*
Champion Laboratories Inc .................. A ...... 618 445-6011
  Albion *(G-357)*
Filter Monkey LLC ............................... G ...... 630 773-4402
  Itasca *(G-12263)*
Filter Renew Tecnologies ..................... G ...... 815 344-2200
  McCullom Lake *(G-14471)*
Filters To You ....................................... G ...... 815 939-0700
  Bradley *(G-2421)*
Flow Pro Products Inc ......................... F ...... 815 836-1900
  Bolingbrook *(G-2310)*
Gutter Masters ..................................... G ...... 309 686-1234
  Peoria *(G-17376)*
H2o Filter Inc ....................................... G ...... 630 963-3303
  Lisle *(G-13598)*
Helix International Inc ........................... ...... 847 709-0666
  Elk Grove Village *(G-9521)*
Illinois Tool Works Inc ........................... F ...... 708 720-0300
  Frankfort *(G-10329)*
Industrial Filter Pump Mfg Co ............... G ...... 708 656-7800
  Cicero *(G-7205)*
Inlet & Pipe Protection Inc ................... G ...... 630 355-3288
  Naperville *(G-15811)*
Intech Industries Inc ............................. F ...... 847 487-5599
  Wauconda *(G-21473)*
Leaffilter North LLC .............................. E ...... 630 595-9605
  Wood Dale *(G-22390)*
Mavea LLC ........................................... G ...... 905 712-2045
  Elgin *(G-9104)*
Norman Filter Company LLC ................ D ...... 708 233-5521
  Bridgeview *(G-2515)*
Nsk-America Corporation ..................... F ...... 847 843-7664
  Hoffman Estates *(G-12031)*
Quality Cleaning Fluids Inc ................... G ...... 847 451-1190
  Franklin Park *(G-10566)*
Smb Toolroom Inc ................................ G ...... 309 353-7396
  Pekin *(G-17289)*
Smith Power Transmission Co .............. G ...... 773 526-5512
  Chicago *(G-6535)*
U S Filter Products ............................... G ...... 618 451-1205
  Granite City *(G-11309)*
U S Filters ............................................ G ...... 815 932-8154
  Bradley *(G-2435)*
United States Filter/Iwt ......................... G ...... 815 877-3041
  Rockford *(G-18662)*

## FILTERS & SOFTENERS: Water, Household

Amber Soft Inc ..................................... F ...... 630 377-6945
  Lake Barrington *(G-12799)*
Amsoil Inc ............................................ G ...... 630 595-8385
  Bensenville *(G-1835)*
Aquion Inc ............................................ D ...... 847 725-3000
  Roselle *(G-18926)*
Durable Manufacturing Company ......... F ...... 630 766-0398
  Bensenville *(G-1885)*
J II Inc ................................................. D ...... 847 432-8979
  Highland Park *(G-11845)*
Liquitech Inc ........................................ G ...... 630 693-0500
  Lombard *(G-13821)*
Pure N Natural Systems Inc ................. F ...... 630 372-9681
  Morton Grove *(G-15230)*
RPS Products Inc ................................ E ...... 847 683-3400
  Hampshire *(G-11562)*

## FILTERS & STRAINERS: Pipeline

Csiteq LLC ........................................... D ...... 312 265-1509
  Chicago *(G-4512)*

## PRODUCT SECTION

Mity Inc ..................................................G........ 630 365-5030
  Elburn *(G-8898)*
Perma-Pipe Intl Holdings Inc ..................C........ 847 966-1000
  Niles *(G-16019)*
Water Products Company III Inc ...............E........ 630 553-0840
  Yorkville *(G-22675)*

### FILTERS: Air

Aeropulse LLC .....................................G........ 215 245-7600
  Romeoville *(G-18792)*
American Air Filter Co Inc ......................D........ 502 637-0011
  Chicago *(G-3848)*
Creasey Construction III Inc ...................F........ 217 546-1277
  Springfield *(G-20424)*
Diablo Furnaces LLC ............................F........ 815 636-7502
  Machesney Park *(G-14071)*
Filtration Group LLC .............................D........ 630 968-1563
  Oak Brook *(G-16512)*
Flanders Corporation .............................C........ 815 472-4230
  Momence *(G-14980)*
Greenlees Filter LLC .............................D........ 708 366-3256
  Vernon Hills *(G-21169)*
Henderson Engineering Co Inc ................G........ 815 786-9471
  Sandwich *(G-19368)*
Lilly Air Systems Co Inc .........................F........ 630 773-2225
  Itasca *(G-12305)*
Murdock Company Inc ..........................G........ 847 566-0050
  Mundelein *(G-15535)*
Permatron Corporation ...........................E........ 847 434-1421
  Elk Grove Village *(G-9674)*
Smith Filter Corporation .........................E........ 309 764-8324
  Moline *(G-14971)*
Solberg International Ltd .......................G........ 630 616-4400
  Itasca *(G-12355)*
Solberg Mfg Inc ...................................D........ 630 616-4400
  Itasca *(G-12356)*
Solberg Mfg Inc ...................................E........ 630 773-1363
  Itasca *(G-12357)*
Storms Industries Inc ............................E........ 312 243-7480
  Chicago *(G-6601)*
Universal Air Filter Company ...................E........ 618 271-7300
  East Saint Louis *(G-8774)*

### FILTERS: Air Intake, Internal Combustion Engine, Exc Auto

Bedford Rakim ....................................G........ 773 749-3086
  Lansing *(G-13157)*
Byrne & Schaefer Inc ...........................G........ 815 727-5000
  Lockport *(G-13708)*
Clean and Science USA Co Ltd ...............G........ 847 461-9292
  Schaumburg *(G-19473)*
Daves Auto Repair ...............................G........ 630 682-4411
  Carol Stream *(G-3140)*
Donaldson Company Inc .......................E........ 815 288-3374
  Dixon *(G-8329)*
Precision Grinding and Mch Inc ...............G........
  Joliet *(G-12553)*
Tane Corporation .................................G........ 847 705-7125
  Palatine *(G-17078)*

### FILTERS: Gasoline, Internal Combustion Engine, Exc Auto

Central Illinois Mfg Co ...........................D........ 217 762-8184
  Bement *(G-1800)*

### FILTERS: General Line, Indl

American Precision Machining .................F........ 847 455-1720
  Franklin Park *(G-10392)*
Averus Usa Inc ....................................D........ 800 913-7034
  Elgin *(G-8961)*
Century Filter Products Inc .....................G........ 773 477-1790
  Chicago *(G-4276)*
Evoqua Water Technologies LLC .............G........ 618 451-1205
  Granite City *(G-11275)*
Industrial Filter Pump Mfg Co ..................D........ 708 656-7800
  Bedford Park *(G-1556)*
International Filter Mfg Corp ...................F........ 217 324-2303
  Litchfield *(G-13688)*
Robko Flock Coating Company ...............G........ 847 272-6202
  Northbrook *(G-16357)*
Textile Industries Inc ............................G........ 312 829-3112
  Chicago *(G-6706)*
Tri-Dim Filter Corporation ......................E........ 847 695-5822
  Elgin *(G-9213)*
Waves Fluid Solutions LLC ....................G........ 630 765-7533
  Carol Stream *(G-3264)*

### FILTERS: Motor Vehicle

Champion Laboratories Inc ....................A........ 618 445-6011
  Albion *(G-356)*
Champion Laboratories Inc ....................A........ 618 445-6011
  Albion *(G-359)*
Champion Laboratories Inc ....................C........ 618 445-6011
  Albion *(G-360)*
Jsn Inc ...............................................E........ 708 410-1800
  Maywood *(G-14426)*

### FILTERS: Oil, Internal Combustion Engine, Exc Auto

Advanced Filtration Systems Inc ..............C........ 217 351-3073
  Champaign *(G-3444)*

### FILTERS: Paper

USA Technologies Inc ...........................C........ 309 495-0829
  Peoria *(G-17476)*

### FILTRATION DEVICES: Electronic

Barnes International Inc ........................C........ 815 964-8661
  Rockford *(G-18276)*
Cemec Inc ..........................................G........ 630 495-9696
  Downers Grove *(G-8405)*
Daly Engineered Filtration Inc .................G........ 708 355-1550
  Naperville *(G-15643)*
Erbeck One Chem & Lab Sup Inc ...........C........ 312 203-0078
  Manhattan *(G-14169)*
Federal-Mogul Corporation .....................C........ 815 271-9600
  McHenry *(G-14506)*
Netcom Inc .........................................C........ 847 537-6300
  Wheeling *(G-22106)*
Perma-Pipe Intl Holdings Inc ..................C........ 847 966-1000
  Niles *(G-16019)*
Te Connectivity Corporation ...................D........ 847 680-7400
  Mundelein *(G-15563)*

### FINANCIAL INVESTMENT ADVICE

American Medical Association .................A........ 312 464-5000
  Chicago *(G-3863)*
Envestnet Inc ......................................C........ 312 827-2800
  Chicago *(G-4763)*

### FINANCIAL SVCS

Business Valuation Group Inc .................G........ 312 595-1900
  Chicago *(G-4190)*
Envestnet Inc ......................................C........ 312 827-2800
  Chicago *(G-4763)*
Envestnet Rtrment Slutions LLC ..............C........ 312 827-7957
  Chicago *(G-4764)*
Lbe Ltd ..............................................G........ 847 907-4959
  Kildeer *(G-12701)*
Q Lotus Holdings Inc ............................G........ 312 379-1800
  Chicago *(G-6234)*

### FINDINGS & TRIMMINGS: Apparel

Arbetman & Associates .........................G........ 708 386-8586
  Oak Park *(G-16653)*

### FINDINGS & TRIMMINGS: Fabric

Russell Doot Inc ..................................G........ 312 527-1437
  Chicago *(G-6415)*

### FINGERNAILS, ARTIFICIAL

Crystal Nails McHenry ...........................G........ 815 363-5498
  McHenry *(G-14492)*
Gbn Nails LLC .....................................G........ 773 881-8880
  Chicago *(G-4921)*

### FINISHERS: Concrete & Bituminous, Powered

West Lake Concrete & Rmdlg LLC ..........G........ 847 477-8667
  Chicago *(G-6960)*

### FINISHING AGENTS

Ilf Technologies LLC .............................G........ 630 789-9770
  Willowbrook *(G-22215)*

### FINISHING AGENTS: Leather

ISachs Sons Inc ...................................F........ 312 733-2815
  Chicago *(G-5240)*

### FIRE EXTINGUISHER SVC

Sadelco USA Corp ...............................G........ 847 781-8844
  Hoffman Estates *(G-12048)*
Sanford Chemical Co Inc ......................F........ 847 437-3530
  Elk Grove Village *(G-9727)*

### FINISHING SVCS

Gmk Finishing .....................................G........ 630 837-0568
  Bartlett *(G-1351)*
Quantum Color Graphics LLC .................C........ 847 967-3600
  Morton Grove *(G-15231)*

### FIRE ARMS, SMALL: Guns Or Gun Parts, 30 mm & Below

A & S Arms Inc ...................................G........ 224 267-5670
  Antioch *(G-612)*
Art Jewel Enterprises Ltd ......................F........ 630 260-0400
  Carol Stream *(G-3106)*
Civilian Force Arms Inc .........................G........ 630 926-6982
  Yorkville *(G-22652)*
Devil Dog Arms Inc ..............................G........ 847 790-4004
  Lake Zurich *(G-13062)*
Fim Engineering LLC ............................G........ 773 880-8841
  Milford *(G-14812)*
Nelson-Whittaker Ltd ............................G........ 815 459-6000
  Crystal Lake *(G-7618)*
Northern Ordinance Corporation ..............G........ 815 675-6400
  Spring Grove *(G-20352)*
Oglesby & Oglesby Gunmakers ...............G........ 217 487-7100
  Springfield *(G-20492)*
Phalanx Training Inc .............................G........ 847 859-9156
  Evanston *(G-10086)*
Rock River Arms Inc ............................D........ 309 792-5780
  Colona *(G-7347)*

### FIRE ARMS, SMALL: Machine Guns & Grenade Launchers

Ar1510 LLC ........................................F........ 309 944-6939
  Geneseo *(G-10798)*
Double Nickel LLC ...............................G........ 618 476-3200
  Millstadt *(G-14823)*

### FIRE ARMS, SMALL: Machine Guns/Machine Gun Parts, 30mm/below

Pro Tech Engineering ............................G........ 309 475-2502
  Saybrook *(G-19414)*

### FIRE ARMS, SMALL: Revolvers Or Revolver Parts, 30 mm & Below

Dynamic Door Service Inc ......................G........ 847 885-4751
  Elgin *(G-9016)*

### FIRE ARMS, SMALL: Rifles Or Rifle Parts, 30 mm & below

Gregory Martin ....................................G........ 815 265-4527
  Gilman *(G-10943)*
McGowen Rifle Barrels ..........................G........ 815 937-9816
  Saint Anne *(G-19123)*

### FIRE CONTROL OR BOMBING EQPT: Electronic

Dalmatian Fire Equipment Ltd .................G........ 708 201-1730
  Dolton *(G-8369)*

### FIRE DETECTION SYSTEMS

Brk Brands Inc ....................................C........ 630 851-7330
  Aurora *(G-975)*
Fire Sentry Corporation .........................E........ 714 694-0823
  Lincolnshire *(G-13448)*

### FIRE ESCAPES

Rockford Ornamental Iron Inc .................F........ 815 633-1162
  Rockford *(G-18581)*

### FIRE EXTINGUISHER CHARGES

Rampro Facilities Svcs Corp ...................G........ 224 639-6378
  Gurnee *(G-11498)*

### FIRE EXTINGUISHER SVC

Rampro Facilities Svcs Corp ...................G........ 224 639-6378
  Gurnee *(G-11498)*

# FIRE EXTINGUISHERS, WHOLESALE

### FIRE EXTINGUISHERS, WHOLESALE
Flame Guard Usa LLC ............................ G ..... 815 219-4074
  Lake Barrington *(G-12806)*
Quality Intgrted Solutions Inc ............... G ..... 815 464-4772
  Tinley Park *(G-20942)*

### FIRE EXTINGUISHERS: Portable
Amerex Corporation ............................... E ..... 309 382-4389
  North Pekin *(G-16192)*
Arrow Sales & Service Inc ...................... G ..... 815 223-0251
  La Salle *(G-12765)*
Bella Casa ............................................... G ..... 630 455-5900
  Hinsdale *(G-11941)*
First Alert Inc ......................................... G ..... 630 499-3295
  Aurora *(G-1009)*
Flame Guard Usa LLC ............................ G ..... 815 219-4074
  Lake Barrington *(G-12806)*
Oval Fire Products Corporation ............. G ..... 630 635-5000
  Glendale Heights *(G-11055)*

### FIRE OR BURGLARY RESISTIVE PRDTS
A - Square Manufacturing Inc ................ F ..... 800 628-6720
  Chicago *(G-3681)*
A - Square Manufacturing Inc ................ E ..... 800 628-6720
  Chicago *(G-3682)*
Austin-Westran LLC ............................... C ..... 815 234-2811
  Montgomery *(G-15029)*
Fotofab LLC ........................................... E ..... 773 463-6211
  Chicago *(G-4877)*
G & M Metal Fabricators Inc ................. D ..... 847 678-6501
  Franklin Park *(G-10473)*
Group Industries Inc .............................. E ..... 708 877-6200
  Thornton *(G-20871)*
Key West Metal Industries Inc ............... C ..... 708 371-1470
  Crestwood *(G-7491)*
Millenia Products Group Inc .................. C ..... 630 458-0401
  Itasca *(G-12318)*
Noise Barriers LLC ................................ E ..... 847 843-0500
  Libertyville *(G-13362)*
Suburban Metalcraft Inc ........................ G ..... 847 678-7550
  Franklin Park *(G-10598)*
Titan Metals Inc ..................................... E ..... 630 752-9700
  Glendale Heights *(G-11085)*
Viking Metal Cabinet Company ............. D ..... 630 863-7234
  Montgomery *(G-15070)*

### FIRE PROTECTION EQPT
Aquarius Fluid Products Inc .................. G ..... 847 289-9090
  Elgin *(G-8957)*
Citizenprime LLC ................................... G ..... 708 995-1241
  Mokena *(G-14859)*
Evac Systems Fire & Rescue ................ F ..... 309 764-7812
  Moline *(G-14937)*
PAcrimson Fire Risk Svcs Inc ............... G ..... 630 424-3400
  Lombard *(G-13840)*
Paratech Incorporated ........................... D ..... 815 469-3911
  Frankfort *(G-10348)*
Roodhouse Fire Protection Dst ............. E ..... 217 589-5134
  Roodhouse *(G-18885)*

### FIREARMS & AMMUNITION, EXC SPORTING, WHOLESALE
D S Arms Incorporated ......................... F ..... 847 277-7258
  Lake Barrington *(G-12805)*
Shaars International Inc ........................ G ..... 815 315-0717
  Rockford *(G-18614)*

### FIREARMS, EXC SPORTING, WHOLESALE
Civilian Force Arms Inc ......................... G ..... 630 926-6982
  Yorkville *(G-22652)*

### FIREARMS: Large, Greater Than 30mm
Devil Dog Arms Inc ............................... G ..... 847 790-4004
  Lake Zurich *(G-13062)*

### FIREARMS: Small, 30mm or Less
D S Arms Incorporated ......................... F ..... 847 277-7258
  Lake Barrington *(G-12805)*
Olin Corporation .................................... C ..... 618 258-2000
  East Alton *(G-8608)*
RR Defense Systems Inc ...................... G ..... 312 446-9167
  Elk Grove Village *(G-9721)*
Springfield Inc ....................................... C ..... 309 944-5631
  Geneseo *(G-10805)*

### FIREFIGHTING APPARATUS
Amkus Inc .............................................. E ..... 630 515-1800
  Downers Grove *(G-8387)*
Oregon Fire Protection Dst ................... E ..... 815 732-7214
  Oregon *(G-16830)*

### FIREPLACE & CHIMNEY MATERIAL: Concrete
Tagitsold Inc ......................................... G ..... 630 724-1800
  Downers Grove *(G-8529)*
US Fireplace Products Inc .................... G ..... 888 290-8181
  Lake Bluff *(G-12869)*

### FIREPLACE EQPT & ACCESS
Innerweld Cover Co .............................. F ..... 847 497-3009
  Mundelein *(G-15511)*

### FIREWOOD, WHOLESALE
Dg Wood Processing ............................. F ..... 217 543-2128
  Arthur *(G-894)*
E-Z Tree Recycling Inc .......................... G ..... 773 493-8600
  Chicago *(G-4670)*

### FIREWORKS
Jamaica Pyrotechnics ............................ G ..... 217 649-2902
  Philo *(G-17539)*
Lumina Inc ............................................. G ..... 312 829-8970
  Chicago *(G-5565)*
Nostalgia Pyrotechnics Inc .................... G ..... 309 522-5136
  Osco *(G-16900)*

### FISH & SEAFOOD PROCESSORS: Canned Or Cured
Kraft Heinz Foods Company ................. C ..... 847 291-3900
  Northbrook *(G-16290)*
Sokol and Company .............................. D ..... 708 482-8250
  Countryside *(G-7443)*

### FISH & SEAFOOD PROCESSORS: Fresh Or Frozen
Betty Watters ......................................... G ..... 618 232-1150
  Hamburg *(G-11526)*
Midway Food LLC ................................. G ..... 773 294-0730
  Chicago *(G-5738)*
Rich Products Corporation .................... D ..... 847 581-1749
  Niles *(G-16027)*
Wisepak Foods LLC .............................. E ..... 773 772-0072
  Chicago *(G-7006)*

### FISH & SEAFOOD WHOLESALERS
Honey Foods Inc ................................... G ..... 847 928-9300
  Franklin Park *(G-10488)*

### FISH FOOD
Aqua-Tech Co ....................................... G ..... 847 383-7075
  Elgin *(G-8956)*
Fish King Inc ......................................... G ..... 773 736-4974
  Chicago *(G-4850)*
Lockport Fish Pantry ............................. G ..... 815 588-3543
  Lockport *(G-13727)*
Oceanic Food Express Inc .................... G ..... 847 480-7217
  Northbrook *(G-16322)*

### FISHING EQPT: Lures
Biospawn Lure Co ................................. G ..... 773 458-0752
  Evanston *(G-10016)*
Cast Industries Inc ................................ E ..... 217 522-8292
  Springfield *(G-20409)*
Jerry H Simpson .................................... G ..... 618 654-3235
  Highland *(G-11798)*
Luck E Strike Corporation ..................... F ..... 630 313-2408
  Geneva *(G-10847)*
Obies Tackle Co Inc .............................. G ..... 618 234-5638
  Belleville *(G-1662)*
Reeves Lure Co ..................................... G ..... 217 864-3493
  Lovington *(G-14012)*

### FISHING EQPT: Nets & Seines
Douglas Net Company ........................... F ..... 815 427-6350
  Saint Anne *(G-19119)*
Nichols Net & Twine Inc ........................ G ..... 618 797-0211
  Granite City *(G-11298)*

## PRODUCT SECTION

### FITTINGS & ASSEMBLIES: Hose & Tube, Hydraulic Or Pneumatic
A Len Radiator Shoppe Inc .................... G ..... 630 852-5445
  Downers Grove *(G-8384)*
Adair Enterprises Inc ............................ F ..... 847 640-7789
  Elk Grove Village *(G-9270)*
All Type Hydraulics Corp ...................... G ..... 618 585-4844
  Bunker Hill *(G-2803)*
Hurst Manufacturing Co ........................ F ..... 309 756-9960
  Milan *(G-14791)*
J C Hose & Tube Inc ............................. G ..... 630 543-4747
  Addison *(G-157)*
Jason of Illinois Inc ............................... E ..... 630 752-0600
  Carol Stream *(G-3176)*
Nagano International Corp .................... G ..... 847 537-0011
  Buffalo Grove *(G-2741)*
Nanco Sales Co Inc ............................... G ..... 630 892-9820
  Aurora *(G-1193)*
Quad City Hose ..................................... E ..... 563 386-8936
  Taylor Ridge *(G-20830)*
Royal Brass Inc ..................................... G ..... 618 439-6341
  Benton *(G-2040)*
T & T Distribution Inc ........................... G ..... 815 223-0715
  Peru *(G-17528)*
Whitley Products Inc ............................. F ..... 574 267-7114
  Chicago *(G-6975)*

### FITTINGS & SPECIALTIES: Steam
Steamgard LLC ..................................... E ..... 847 913-8400
  Vernon Hills *(G-21204)*

### FITTINGS: Pipe
Advanced Plbg & Pipe Fitting ............... G ..... 618 554-2677
  Newton *(G-15936)*
Dixon Brass ........................................... E ..... 630 323-3716
  Westmont *(G-21885)*
Dvcc Inc ................................................ E ..... 630 323-3105
  Westmont *(G-21886)*
Flocon Inc ............................................. G ..... 815 943-5893
  Harvard *(G-11633)*
Mechanical Engineering Pdts ................ G ..... 312 421-3375
  Chicago *(G-5674)*
MRC Global (us) Inc ............................. F ..... 815 729-7742
  Joliet *(G-12544)*
Process Piping Inc ................................ G ..... 708 717-0513
  Tinley Park *(G-20939)*

### FITTINGS: Pipe, Fabricated
Chicago Pipe Bending & Coil Co .......... F ..... 773 379-1918
  Chicago *(G-4339)*
Duraflex Inc .......................................... E ..... 847 462-1007
  Cary *(G-3336)*
Illco Inc ................................................. G ..... 815 725-9100
  Joliet *(G-12513)*
Lafox Manufacturing Corp ..................... G ..... 630 232-0266
  Lafox *(G-12794)*

### FIXTURES & EQPT: Kitchen, Metal, Exc Cast Aluminum
Style Rite Restaurant Eqp Co ............... G ..... 630 628-0940
  Addison *(G-299)*

### FIXTURES & EQPT: Kitchen, Porcelain Enameled
Elkay Vrgnia Dcrative Surfaces ............ F ..... 630 574-8484
  Oak Brook *(G-16508)*
Exclusive Stone ..................................... G ..... 847 593-6963
  Elk Grove Village *(G-9470)*
Fountain Products Inc ........................... G ..... 630 991-7237
  Elgin *(G-9039)*
Pt Holdings Inc ..................................... G ..... 217 691-1793
  Springfield *(G-20508)*

### FIXTURES: Cut Stone
Imperial Marble Corp ............................. C ..... 815 498-2303
  Somonauk *(G-20126)*

### FLAGPOLES
Uncommon Usa Inc ............................... F ..... 630 268-9672
  Lombard *(G-13876)*

### FLAGS: Fabric
E I T Inc ................................................ G ..... 630 359-3543
  Naperville *(G-15649)*

# PRODUCT SECTION — FLUID POWER PUMPS & MOTORS

**George Lauterer Corporation** .......... E ...... 312 913-1881
Chicago *(G-4943)*

**J C Schultz Enterprises Inc** .......... D ...... 800 323-9127
Batavia *(G-1459)*

**McCormicks Enterprises Inc** .......... E ...... 847 398-8680
Arlington Heights *(G-800)*

**Seasonal Designs Inc** .......... E ...... 847 688-0280
Waukegan *(G-21613)*

**W G N Flag & Decorating Co** .......... F ...... 773 768-8076
Chicago *(G-6918)*

## FLAT GLASS: Building

**Chicago Tempered Glass Inc** .......... F ...... 773 583-2300
Chicago *(G-4354)*

**Glass America Midwest Inc** .......... G ...... 203 932-0248
Elmhurst *(G-9876)*

## FLAT GLASS: Construction

**S R Door Inc** .......... E ...... 815 227-1148
Rockford *(G-18603)*

## FLAT GLASS: Picture

**Tru Vue Inc** .......... C ...... 708 485-5080
Countryside *(G-7448)*

## FLAT GLASS: Sheet

**Engineered Glass Products LLC** .......... D ...... 312 326-4710
Chicago *(G-4752)*

## FLAT GLASS: Tempered

**Euroview Enterprises LLC** .......... E ...... 630 227-3300
Elmhurst *(G-9869)*

**Willow Ridge Glass Inc** .......... F ...... 630 910-8300
Woodridge *(G-22525)*

## FLAT GLASS: Window, Clear & Colored

**Allpro Fleet Maint Systems** .......... G ...... 708 430-1400
Burbank *(G-2806)*

**Crystal Win & Door Systems Ltd** .......... E ...... 773 376-6688
Chicago *(G-4510)*

**Energy-Glazed Systems Inc** .......... F ...... 847 223-4500
Grayslake *(G-11334)*

**Harmon Inc** .......... D ...... 312 726-5050
Chicago *(G-5046)*

## FLAVORS OR FLAVORING MATERIALS: Synthetic

**Bada Beans** .......... G ...... 630 655-0693
Hinsdale *(G-11940)*

**Givaudan Flavors Corporation** .......... E ...... 630 773-8484
Itasca *(G-12270)*

**Givaudan Flavors Corporation** .......... C ...... 847 608-6200
Elgin *(G-9047)*

**Prinova Solutions LLC** .......... E ...... 630 868-0359
Carol Stream *(G-3221)*

**Sensient Flavors** .......... C ...... 847 645-7002
Hoffman Estates *(G-12049)*

## FLIGHT RECORDERS

**Korean Air** .......... G ...... 773 686-2730
Chicago *(G-5405)*

## FLOOR COVERING STORES

**Afar Imports & Interiors Inc** .......... G ...... 217 744-3262
Springfield *(G-20386)*

**Alumafloor & More Inc** .......... G ...... 630 628-0226
Addison *(G-31)*

**L & L Flooring Inc** .......... E ...... 773 935-9314
Chicago *(G-5418)*

**Ridgefield Industries Co LLC** .......... E ...... 800 569-0316
Crystal Lake *(G-7641)*

**Rogers Custom Trims Inc** .......... G ...... 773 745-6577
Chicago *(G-6380)*

**Sealmaster Inc** .......... F ...... 847 480-7325
Northbrook *(G-16360)*

## FLOOR COVERING STORES: Carpets

**Tazewell Floor Covering Inc** .......... F ...... 309 266-6371
Morton *(G-15184)*

## FLOOR COVERING STORES: Floor Tile

**MK Tile Ink** .......... G ...... 773 964-8905
Chicago *(G-5778)*

## FLOOR COVERING: Plastic

**Sap Acquisition Co LLC** .......... E ...... 847 229-1600
Buffalo Grove *(G-2761)*

**Superior American Plastics Co** .......... E ...... 847 229-1600
Buffalo Grove *(G-2778)*

## FLOOR COVERINGS WHOLESALERS

**Corsaw Hardwood Lumber Inc** .......... F ...... 309 293-2055
Smithfield *(G-20119)*

**Hakwood** .......... 630 219-3388
Naperville *(G-15669)*

## FLOOR COVERINGS: Asphalted-Felt Base, Linoleum Or Carpet

**Carpets By Kuniej** .......... G ...... 815 232-9060
Freeport *(G-10650)*

**Owens Corning Sales LLC** .......... E ...... 708 594-6935
Argo *(G-695)*

## FLOOR COVERINGS: Rubber

**Alessco Inc** .......... F ...... 773 327-7919
Chicago *(G-3801)*

## FLOOR COVERINGS: Textile Fiber

**Protect Assoc** .......... G ...... 847 446-8664
Northbrook *(G-16348)*

## FLOORING & GRATINGS: Open, Construction Applications

**Essential Flooring Inc** .......... G ...... 630 788-3121
Oswego *(G-16916)*

**Fisher & Ludlow Inc** .......... D ...... 815 932-1200
Bourbonnais *(G-2396)*

**Oldcastle Precast Inc** .......... F ...... 309 661-4608
Normal *(G-16082)*

## FLOORING & SIDING: Metal

**Alumafloor & More Inc** .......... G ...... 630 628-0226
Addison *(G-31)*

## FLOORING: Hard Surface

**Kitchen & Bath Gallery** .......... 217 214-0310
Quincy *(G-17845)*

**Surface Shields Inc** .......... E ...... 708 226-9810
Orland Park *(G-16896)*

## FLOORING: Hardwood

**Access Flooring Co Inc** .......... G ...... 847 781-0100
Hoffman Estates *(G-11989)*

**Connor Sports Flooring LLC** .......... D ...... 847 290-9020
Elk Grove Village *(G-9389)*

**Flooring Warehouse Direct Inc** .......... G ...... 815 730-6767
Homer Glen *(G-12078)*

**Grads Inc** .......... G ...... 847 426-3904
East Dundee *(G-8641)*

**Hakwood** .......... 630 219-3388
Naperville *(G-15669)*

**Historic Timber & Plank Inc** .......... E ...... 618 372-4546
Brighton *(G-2542)*

**Ridgefield Industries Co LLC** .......... E ...... 800 569-0316
Crystal Lake *(G-7641)*

**T J P Investments Inc** .......... G ...... 309 673-8383
Peoria *(G-17465)*

**Unity Hardwoods LLC** .......... F ...... 708 701-2943
Chicago *(G-6830)*

**Vlasici Hardwood Floors Co** .......... G ...... 815 505-4308
Romeoville *(G-18876)*

## FLORIST TELEGRAPH SVCS

**Florists Transworld Dlvry Inc** .......... A ...... 630 719-7800
Downers Grove *(G-8444)*

## FLORIST: Flowers, Fresh

**Albert F Amling LLC** .......... C ...... 630 333-1720
Elmhurst *(G-9832)*

**Mangel and Co** .......... E ...... 847 459-3100
Buffalo Grove *(G-2730)*

## FLORISTS

**Cub Foods Inc** .......... C ...... 309 689-0140
Peoria *(G-17347)*

**Hts Hancock Transcriptions Svc** .......... E ...... 217 379-9241
Paxton *(G-17237)*

**Kroger Co** .......... C ...... 309 694-6298
East Peoria *(G-8722)*

**Kroger Co** .......... C ...... 815 332-7267
Rockford *(G-18457)*

**Niemann Foods Foundation** .......... C ...... 217 222-0190
Quincy *(G-17862)*

**Niemann Foods Foundation** .......... C ...... 217 793-4091
Springfield *(G-20487)*

**Schnuck Markets Inc** .......... C ...... 618 466-0825
Godfrey *(G-11237)*

**Sunset Food Mart Inc** .......... C ...... 847 234-0854
Lake Forest *(G-12964)*

**Treasure Island Foods Inc** .......... D ...... 312 440-1144
Chicago *(G-6763)*

**Treasure Island Foods Inc** .......... C ...... 773 880-8880
Chicago *(G-6764)*

**Walter Lagestee Inc** .......... C ...... 708 957-2974
Homewood *(G-12106)*

## FLORISTS' SPLYS, WHOLESALE

**Florists Transworld Dlvry Inc** .......... A ...... 630 719-7800
Downers Grove *(G-8444)*

## FLOWER ARRANGEMENTS: Artificial

**Design Merchants** .......... G ...... 630 208-1850
Geneva *(G-10825)*

**Floralstar Enterprises** .......... G ...... 847 726-0124
Hawthorn Woods *(G-11702)*

**K M I International Corp** .......... G ...... 630 627-6300
Addison *(G-164)*

## FLOWERS: Artificial & Preserved

**Albert F Amling LLC** .......... C ...... 630 333-1720
Elmhurst *(G-9832)*

**Southern Blooms LLC** .......... G ...... 618 565-1111
Murphysboro *(G-15584)*

## FLUID METERS & COUNTING DEVICES

**Avg Advanced Technologies LP** .......... A ...... 630 668-3900
Carol Stream *(G-3110)*

**Erdco Engineering Corporation** .......... E ...... 847 328-0550
Evanston *(G-10031)*

**International Traffic Corp** .......... G ...... 815 675-1430
Spring Grove *(G-20338)*

**Kinetic Fit Works Inc** .......... G ...... 630 340-5168
Galena *(G-10728)*

**Langham Engineering** .......... G ...... 815 223-5250
Peru *(G-17516)*

**Metraflex Company** .......... D ...... 312 738-3800
Chicago *(G-5706)*

**Rauckman Utility Products LLC** .......... G ...... 618 234-0001
Belleville *(G-1668)*

## FLUID POWER PUMPS & MOTORS

**American Electronic Pdts Inc** .......... F ...... 630 889-9977
Oak Brook *(G-16488)*

**Applied Hydraulic Services** .......... G ...... 773 638-8500
Chicago *(G-3925)*

**Applied Hydraulics Corporation** .......... G ...... 773 638-8500
Chicago *(G-3926)*

**Caterpillar Inc** .......... B ...... 815 729-5511
Joliet *(G-12471)*

**Central Hydraulics Inc** .......... G ...... 309 527-5238
El Paso *(G-8866)*

**Danfoss Power Solutions US Co** .......... C ...... 815 233-4200
Freeport *(G-10652)*

**Deltrol Corp** .......... C ...... 708 547-0500
Bellwood *(G-1703)*

**Grand Specialties Co** .......... F ...... 630 629-8000
Oak Brook *(G-16520)*

**Highland Mch & Screw Pdts Co** .......... D ...... 618 654-2103
Highland *(G-11788)*

**Idex Corporation** .......... B ...... 847 498-7070
Lake Forest *(G-12915)*

**Leading Edge Group Inc** .......... C ...... 815 316-3500
Rockford *(G-18464)*

**Mechanical Engineering Pdts** .......... G ...... 312 421-3375
Chicago *(G-5674)*

**New Dimensions Precision Mac** .......... D ...... 815 923-8300
Union *(G-21037)*

**Rdh Inc of Rockford** .......... F ...... 815 874-9421
Rockford *(G-18550)*

**Rhino Tool Company** .......... F ...... 309 853-5555
Kewanee *(G-12694)*

**Tomenson Machine Works Inc** .......... D ...... 630 377-7670
West Chicago *(G-21782)*

---

Employee Codes: A=Over 500 employees, B=251-500
C=101-250, D=51-100, E=20-50, F=10-19, G=3-9

# FLUID POWER PUMPS & MOTORS

Tramco Pump Co ............................................. E ....... 312 243-5800
  Chicago *(G-6756)*
Tuxco Corporation ......................................... F ....... 847 244-2220
  Gurnee *(G-11517)*
Wes-Tech Inc ................................................. G ...... 847 541-5070
  Buffalo Grove *(G-2793)*

## FLUID POWER VALVES & HOSE FITTINGS

Bristol Hose & Fitting Inc ............................... E ....... 708 492-3456
  Northlake *(G-16430)*
Bristol Transport Inc ..................................... E ....... 708 343-6411
  Northlake *(G-16431)*
Deltrol Corp .................................................. C ....... 708 547-0500
  Bellwood *(G-1703)*
Deublin Company ......................................... C ....... 847 689-8600
  Waukegan *(G-21551)*
Flexitech Inc ................................................. C ....... 309 664-7828
  Bloomington *(G-2165)*
Flow Valves International LLC ..................... G ...... 847 866-1188
  Evanston *(G-10038)*
James Walker Mfg Co .................................. E ....... 708 754-4020
  Glenwood *(G-11217)*
Kepner Products Company .......................... D ...... 630 279-1550
  Villa Park *(G-21264)*
Lsl Precision Machining Inc ......................... E ....... 815 633-4701
  Loves Park *(G-13962)*
Mac Lean-Fogg Company ............................ D ...... 847 566-0010
  Mundelein *(G-15521)*
Milliken Valve LLC ........................................ G ...... 610 861-8803
  Aurora *(G-1190)*
Mj Works Hose & Fitting LLC ....................... G ...... 708 995-5723
  Mokena *(G-14886)*
Parker-Hannifin Corporation ........................ C ....... 847 258-6200
  Elk Grove Village *(G-9670)*
Plews Inc ...................................................... C ....... 815 288-3344
  Dixon *(G-8339)*
Reber Welding Service ................................ G ...... 217 774-3441
  Shelbyville *(G-19914)*
Rehobot Inc .................................................. G ...... 815 385-7777
  McHenry *(G-14550)*
Seals & Components Inc ............................. G ...... 708 895-5222
  Lansing *(G-13182)*
Standard Truck Parts Inc ............................. G ...... 815 726-4486
  Joliet *(G-12578)*
Trellborg Sling Sltions US Inc ...................... D ...... 630 289-1500
  Streamwood *(G-20677)*
Woods Manufacturing Co Inc ...................... G ...... 630 595-6620
  Wood Dale *(G-22438)*

## FLUORSPAR MINING

Hastie Mining & Trucking ............................. E ....... 618 289-4536
  Cave In Rock *(G-3402)*

## FLUXES

C & S Fabrication Services Inc ................... G ...... 815 363-8510
  Johnsburg *(G-12431)*
Holland LP .................................................... C ....... 708 672-2300
  Crete *(G-7515)*
Kona Blackbird Inc ....................................... F ....... 815 792-8750
  Serena *(G-19892)*
La-Co Industries Inc .................................... G ...... 847 427-3220
  Elk Grove Village *(G-9582)*
Qualitek International Inc ............................. E ....... 630 628-8083
  Addison *(G-262)*

## FM & AM RADIO TUNERS

Wirelessusa Inc ............................................ G ...... 217 222-4300
  Quincy *(G-17906)*

## FOAM RUBBER

Dennis Carnes ............................................. G ...... 618 244-1770
  Mount Vernon *(G-15410)*
Reilly Foam Corp .......................................... E ....... 630 392-2680
  Naperville *(G-15740)*
Secon Rubber and Plastics Inc ................... E ....... 618 282-7700
  Red Bud *(G-17948)*

## FOAM RUBBER, WHOLESALE

Reilly Foam Corp .......................................... E ....... 630 392-2680
  Naperville *(G-15740)*

## FOAMS & RUBBER, WHOLESALE

Fairchild Industries Inc ................................. E ....... 847 550-9580
  Lake Zurich *(G-13071)*

## FOIL & LEAF: Metal

Bagcraftpapercon I LLC .............................. C ....... 620 856-2800
  Chicago *(G-4025)*
D W Machine Products Inc .......................... G ...... 618 654-2161
  Highland *(G-11782)*
Highland Supply Corporation ...................... B ....... 618 654-2161
  Highland *(G-11794)*
Pactiv LLC .................................................... E ....... 847 482-2000
  Lake Forest *(G-12937)*
Pactiv LLC .................................................... C ....... 217 479-1144
  Jacksonville *(G-12404)*
Tinscape LLC ............................................... G ...... 630 236-7236
  Aurora *(G-1087)*
Winpak Heat Seal Corp ............................... D ...... 309 477-6600
  Pekin *(G-17295)*

## FOIL OR LEAF: Gold

Kurz Transfer Products LP ......................... G ...... 847 228-0001
  Elk Grove Village *(G-9580)*

## FOIL: Aluminum

Midwest Lminating Coatings Inc ................. E ....... 708 653-9500
  Alsip *(G-493)*
Pactiv LLC .................................................... E ....... 847 482-2000
  Lake Forest *(G-12937)*
Reynolds Consumer Products LLC ............. E ....... 217 479-1126
  Jacksonville *(G-12411)*
Reynolds Consumer Products LLC ............. G ...... 217 479-1466
  Jacksonville *(G-12412)*
Reynolds Consumer Products LLC ............. B ....... 847 482-3500
  Lake Forest *(G-12952)*
Reynolds Food Packaging ........................... F ....... 815 465-2115
  Grant Park *(G-11314)*

## FOOD CASINGS: Plastic

Damron Corporation ..................................... E ....... 773 265-2724
  Chicago *(G-4549)*
Lake Pacific Partners LLC ........................... B ....... 312 578-1110
  Chicago *(G-5440)*
Pactiv LLC .................................................... A ....... 847 482-2000
  Lake Forest *(G-12935)*
Pactiv LLC .................................................... C ....... 815 469-2112
  Frankfort *(G-10346)*
Teepak Usa LLC .......................................... C ....... 217 446-6460
  Danville *(G-7767)*
Vector USA Inc ............................................. F ....... 630 434-0040
  Oak Brook *(G-16567)*
Viscofan Usa Inc .......................................... C ....... 217 444-8000
  Danville *(G-7779)*

## FOOD COLORINGS

Kosto Food Products Company .................. F ....... 847 487-2600
  Wauconda *(G-21478)*
Sethness Products Company ..................... F ....... 847 329-2080
  Skokie *(G-20083)*

## FOOD PRDTS, BREAKFAST: Cereal, Corn Flakes

Mary Lee Packaging Corporation ............... E ....... 618 826-2361
  Chester *(G-3659)*

## FOOD PRDTS, BREAKFAST: Cereal, Infants' Food

Care Child Companies ................................ G ...... 630 295-6770
  Bloomingdale *(G-2099)*

## FOOD PRDTS, BREAKFAST: Cereal, Rice: Cereal Breakfast Food

General Mills Inc .......................................... F ....... 630 577-3800
  Lisle *(G-13594)*

## FOOD PRDTS, CANNED OR FRESH PACK: Fruit Juices

H J M P Corp ................................................ C ....... 708 345-5370
  Melrose Park *(G-14650)*
Kraft Heinz Foods Company ....................... B ....... 618 512-9100
  Granite City *(G-11290)*
Odwalla Inc .................................................. E ....... 773 687-8667
  Chicago *(G-5968)*

## FOOD PRDTS, CANNED OR FRESH PACK: Vegetable Juices

Vegetable Juices Inc ................................... D ...... 708 924-9500
  Bedford Park *(G-1589)*

## FOOD PRDTS, CANNED, NEC

AA Superb Food Corporation ..................... E ....... 773 927-3233
  Chicago *(G-3698)*
Beatrice Companies Inc .............................. E ....... 602 225-2000
  Chicago *(G-4069)*

## FOOD PRDTS, CANNED: Applesauce

Planks Apple Butter ..................................... G ...... 217 268-4933
  Arcola *(G-681)*

## FOOD PRDTS, CANNED: Baby Food

Kraft Heinz Company ................................... B ....... 412 456-5700
  Chicago *(G-5410)*

## FOOD PRDTS, CANNED: Barbecue Sauce

Andrias Food Group Inc .............................. G ...... 618 632-3118
  O Fallon *(G-16462)*
Andrias Food Group Inc .............................. E ....... 618 632-4866
  O Fallon *(G-16461)*
Captain Curts Food Products ...................... E ....... 773 783-8400
  Chicago *(G-4233)*
Dingo Inc ...................................................... G ...... 217 868-5615
  Effingham *(G-8832)*
Legacy Foods Mfg LLC ............................... F ....... 847 595-9106
  Elk Grove Village *(G-9592)*
Raymond Brothers Inc ................................. F ....... 847 928-9300
  Schiller Park *(G-19866)*
Vins Bbq LLC .............................................. G ...... 847 302-3259
  Glenview *(G-11214)*

## FOOD PRDTS, CANNED: Beans & Bean Sprouts

Hong Kong Market Chicago Inc .................. G ...... 312 791-9111
  Chicago *(G-5108)*
Hop Kee Incorporated ................................. E ....... 312 791-9111
  Chicago *(G-5109)*

## FOOD PRDTS, CANNED: Beans, Baked Without Meat

Earthgrains .................................................. G ...... 630 859-8782
  North Aurora *(G-16128)*

## FOOD PRDTS, CANNED: Beans, Without Meat

Teasdale Foods Inc ..................................... D ...... 217 283-7771
  Hoopeston *(G-12118)*

## FOOD PRDTS, CANNED: Catsup

Kraft Heinz Foods Company ....................... E ....... 630 505-0170
  Lisle *(G-13615)*

## FOOD PRDTS, CANNED: Ethnic

Avoco International LLC .............................. G ...... 847 795-0200
  Elk Grove Village *(G-9325)*
Jaali Bean Inc .............................................. G ...... 312 730-5095
  Chicago *(G-5265)*

## FOOD PRDTS, CANNED: Fruit Juices, Fresh

Florida Fruit Juices Inc ................................ E ....... 773 586-6200
  Chicago *(G-4863)*

## FOOD PRDTS, CANNED: Fruits

Nestle Usa Inc ............................................. C ....... 847 808-5300
  Buffalo Grove *(G-2748)*

## FOOD PRDTS, CANNED: Fruits

Bay Valley Foods LLC ................................. D ...... 773 927-7700
  Chicago *(G-4058)*
Beatrice Companies Inc .............................. E ....... 602 225-2000
  Chicago *(G-4069)*
Cider Gould & Apple .................................... G ...... 630 365-2233
  Elburn *(G-8880)*
Juice Tyme Inc ............................................. F ....... 773 579-1291
  Chicago *(G-5335)*
Key Colony Inc ............................................. G ...... 630 783-8572
  Lemont *(G-13237)*

## PRODUCT SECTION

## FOOD PRDTS, FROZEN: Dinners, Packaged

Kraft Heinz Foods Company ............... C ..... 847 291-3900
  Northbrook *(G-16290)*
Kraft Heinz Foods Company ............... B ..... 815 338-7000
  Woodstock *(G-22580)*
Lawrence Foods Inc .............................. C ..... 847 437-2400
  Elk Grove Village *(G-9588)*
Lynfred Winery Inc ................................. E ..... 630 529-9463
  Roselle *(G-18953)*
Mancuso Cheese Company ................... F ..... 815 722-2475
  Joliet *(G-12536)*
Mullen Foods LLC ................................... G ..... 773 716-9001
  Chicago *(G-5829)*
V Formusa Co ........................................... F ..... 224 938-9360
  Des Plaines *(G-8296)*
Wisconsin Wilderness Food Pdts ........ G ..... 847 735-8661
  Lake Bluff *(G-12872)*

### FOOD PRDTS, CANNED: Fruits & Fruit Prdts

MSI Green Inc .......................................... G ..... 312 421-6550
  Chicago *(G-5826)*

### FOOD PRDTS, CANNED: Italian

Alm Distributors LLC ............................ G ..... 708 865-8000
  Melrose Park *(G-14589)*
Ciprianis Pasta & Sauce Inc ................. E ..... 630 851-3086
  Aurora *(G-1131)*
Michaelangelo Foods LLC ..................... G ..... 773 425-3498
  Chicago *(G-5720)*
Pastorelli Food Products Inc ................ G ..... 312 455-1006
  Chicago *(G-6089)*
Stevie S Italian Foods Inc ..................... G ..... 217 793-9693
  Springfield *(G-20538)*

### FOOD PRDTS, CANNED: Jams, Including Imitation

Bear-Stewart Corporation ..................... E ..... 773 276-0400
  Chicago *(G-4065)*
Millers Country Crafts Inc ..................... G ..... 618 426-3108
  Ava *(G-1240)*

### FOOD PRDTS, CANNED: Jams, Jellies & Preserves

Kuntry Kettle ............................................ G ..... 618 426-1600
  Ava *(G-1238)*
Margies Brands Inc ................................. E ..... 773 643-1417
  Chicago *(G-5615)*
Treehouse Foods Inc ............................. B ..... 708 483-1300
  Oak Brook *(G-16565)*

### FOOD PRDTS, CANNED: Jellies, Edible, Including Imitation

Stewart Ingrdients Systems Inc ........... F ..... 312 254-3539
  Chicago *(G-6596)*

### FOOD PRDTS, CANNED: Mexican, NEC

Ebro Foods Inc ........................................ D ..... 773 696-0150
  Chicago *(G-4690)*
Mexico Enterprise Corporation ............ G ..... 920 568-8900
  Chicago *(G-5710)*
Ole Mexican Foods Inc .......................... E ..... 708 458-3296
  Bedford Park *(G-1568)*
Quay Corporation Inc ............................. F ..... 847 676-4233
  Lincolnwood *(G-13531)*

### FOOD PRDTS, CANNED: Pizza Sauce

Nation Pizza Products LP ..................... A ..... 847 397-3320
  Schaumburg *(G-19661)*
Pastorelli Food Products Inc ................ G ..... 312 455-1006
  Chicago *(G-6089)*
Russo Wholesale Meat Inc .................... G ..... 708 385-0500
  Alsip *(G-525)*

### FOOD PRDTS, CANNED: Puddings, Exc Meat

Treehouse Foods Inc ............................. B ..... 708 483-1300
  Oak Brook *(G-16565)*

### FOOD PRDTS, CANNED: Soups

Essen Nutrition Corporation ................. E ..... 630 739-6700
  Romeoville *(G-18820)*

### FOOD PRDTS, CANNED: Spaghetti & Other Pasta Sauce

Berner Food & Beverage LLC ............... B ..... 815 563-4222
  Dakota *(G-7694)*
Pappone Inc ............................................. G ..... 630 234-4738
  Chicago *(G-6073)*
R&B Foods Inc ......................................... E ..... 847 590-0059
  Mount Prospect *(G-15367)*
Rana Meal Solutions LLC ...................... F ..... 630 581-4100
  Bartlett *(G-1367)*
Rana Meal Solutions LLC ...................... C ..... 630 581-4100
  Oak Brook *(G-16558)*
Sokol and Company ............................... D ..... 708 482-8250
  Countryside *(G-7443)*

### FOOD PRDTS, CANNED: Tamales

Castro Foods Wholesale Inc ................. E ..... 773 869-0641
  Chicago *(G-4253)*
Mexifeast Foods Inc ............................... G ..... 773 356-6386
  Chicago *(G-5711)*
Supreme Tamale Co ............................... G ..... 773 622-3777
  Elk Grove Village *(G-9763)*
Tom Tom Tamales Mfg Co Inc .............. F ..... 773 523-5675
  Chicago *(G-6736)*

### FOOD PRDTS, CANNED: Tomato Sauce.

Kraft Heinz Company ............................. B ..... 412 456-5700
  Chicago *(G-5410)*
Simply Salsa LLC ..................................... G ..... 815 514-3993
  Homer Glen *(G-12087)*

### FOOD PRDTS, CANNED: Tomatoes

78 Brand Co ............................................. G ..... 312 344-1602
  Chicago *(G-3676)*
Iya Foods LLC .......................................... G ..... 630 854-7107
  North Aurora *(G-16135)*
Mullins Food Products Inc .................... B ..... 708 344-3224
  Broadview *(G-2599)*

### FOOD PRDTS, CANNED: Tortillas

Lpz Inc ....................................................... G ..... 773 579-6120
  Chicago *(G-5551)*

### FOOD PRDTS, CANNED: Vegetable Purees

Hooray Puree Inc .................................... G ..... 312 515-0266
  Park Ridge *(G-17203)*

### FOOD PRDTS, CANNED: Vegetables

General Mills Inc ..................................... E ..... 815 544-7399
  Belvidere *(G-1754)*
Seneca Foods Corporation ................... E ..... 309 385-4301
  Princeville *(G-17766)*

### FOOD PRDTS, CANNED: Vegetables

Del Monte Foods Inc .............................. G ..... 309 968-7033
  Manito *(G-14173)*
Del Monte Foods Inc .............................. F ..... 815 562-1359
  Rochelle *(G-18084)*
Del Monte Foods Inc .............................. F ..... 630 836-8131
  Rochelle *(G-18085)*

### FOOD PRDTS, CONFECTIONERY, WHOLESALE: Candy

Amy Wertheim .......................................... G ..... 309 830-4361
  Atlanta *(G-946)*
Cora Lee Candies Inc ............................. F ..... 847 724-2754
  Glenview *(G-11115)*
Vision Sales & Marketing Inc ................ G ..... 708 496-6016
  Chicago *(G-6904)*

### FOOD PRDTS, CONFECTIONERY, WHOLESALE: Nuts, Salted/Roasted

Anton-Argires Inc ................................... G ..... 708 388-6250
  Alsip *(G-434)*
Specialty Nut & Bky Sup Co Inc ........... G ..... 630 268-8500
  Addison *(G-297)*

### FOOD PRDTS, CONFECTIONERY, WHOLESALE: Potato Chips

Frito-Lay North America Inc ................. F ..... 815 468-3940
  Manteno *(G-14184)*

### FOOD PRDTS, CONFECTIONERY, WHOLESALE: Snack Foods

African American Ctr For Hnb .............. D ..... 618 549-3965
  Park Forest *(G-17168)*
Dessertwerks Inc .................................... G ..... 847 487-8239
  Libertyville *(G-13319)*
Hensaal Management Group Inc ......... G ..... 312 624-8133
  Chicago *(G-5074)*
Laredo Foods Inc .................................... E ..... 773 762-1500
  Chicago *(G-5461)*
Mix Match LLC ......................................... F ..... 708 201-0009
  Dolton *(G-8373)*

### FOOD PRDTS, DAIRY, WHOLESALE: Dried Or Canned

Kraft Food Ingredients Corp ................. D ..... 901 381-6500
  Glenview *(G-11159)*
Quay Corporation Inc ............................. F ..... 847 676-4233
  Lincolnwood *(G-13531)*

### FOOD PRDTS, DAIRY, WHOLESALE: Frozen Dairy Desserts

Al Gelato Chicago LLC ........................... G ..... 847 455-5355
  Franklin Park *(G-10388)*
Lorenzos Delectable LLC ...................... G ..... 773 791-3327
  Chicago *(G-5542)*

### FOOD PRDTS, FISH & SEAFOOD, WHOLESALE: Fresh

Betty Watters .......................................... G ..... 618 232-1150
  Hamburg *(G-11526)*

### FOOD PRDTS, FISH & SEAFOOD: Chowders, Frozen

King Midas Seafood Entps Inc ............. G ..... 847 566-2192
  Mundelein *(G-15516)*

### FOOD PRDTS, FISH & SEAFOOD: Fish, Canned & Cured

Vita Food Products Inc ......................... D ..... 312 738-4500
  Chicago *(G-6906)*

### FOOD PRDTS, FISH & SEAFOOD: Fresh, Prepared

Dar Enterprises Inc ................................ G ..... 815 961-8748
  Rockford *(G-18334)*

### FOOD PRDTS, FISH & SEAFOOD: Fresh/Frozen Chowder, Soup/Stew

Vanee Foods Company .......................... D ..... 708 449-7300
  Berkeley *(G-2050)*

### FOOD PRDTS, FISH & SEAFOOD: Seafood, Frozen, Prepared

Open Waters Seafood Company ........... G ..... 847 329-8585
  Skokie *(G-20051)*

### FOOD PRDTS, FISH & SEAFOOD: Shrimp, Frozen, Prepared

Worldwide Shrimp Company ................ E ..... 847 433-3500
  Highland Park *(G-11883)*

### FOOD PRDTS, FROZEN, WHOLESALE: Dinners

Jo MO Enterprises Inc .......................... F ..... 708 599-8098
  Bridgeview *(G-2503)*

### FOOD PRDTS, FROZEN: Dinners, Packaged

Nestle Prepared Foods Company ........ B ..... 630 671-3721
  Glendale Heights *(G-11051)*
On-Cor Frozen Foods LLC .................... E ..... 630 692-2283
  Aurora *(G-1199)*
On-Cor Frozen Foods LLC .................... D ..... 630 692-2283
  Aurora *(G-1200)*
WEI-Chuan USA Inc ................................ F ..... 708 352-8886
  Hodgkins *(G-11987)*

# FOOD PRDTS, FROZEN: Ethnic Foods, NEC

## FOOD PRDTS, FROZEN: Ethnic Foods, NEC

Beatrice Companies Inc .................................. E ...... 602 225-2000
  Chicago *(G-4069)*
Italia Foods Inc ............................................. E ...... 847 397-4479
  Schaumburg *(G-19585)*
Kasias Deli Inc .............................................. F ...... 312 666-2900
  Chicago *(G-5363)*
Moon Guy Hong Food Inc ............................ F ...... 773 927-3233
  Chicago *(G-5801)*

## FOOD PRDTS, FROZEN: Fruit Juice, Concentrates

Greenwood Associates Inc ........................... F ...... 847 579-5500
  Niles *(G-15985)*

## FOOD PRDTS, FROZEN: Fruits & Vegetables

R J Van Drunen & Sons Inc ......................... D ...... 815 472-3211
  Momence *(G-14989)*
R J Van Drunen & Sons Inc ......................... D ...... 815 472-3100
  Momence *(G-14987)*
R J Van Drunen & Sons Inc ......................... E ...... 830 422-2167
  Momence *(G-14988)*

## FOOD PRDTS, FROZEN: Fruits, Juices & Vegetables

H J M P Corp ................................................ C ...... 708 345-5370
  Melrose Park *(G-14650)*
Harvest Food Group Inc ............................... F ...... 773 847-3313
  Chicago *(G-5052)*
Juice Tyme Inc ............................................. F ...... 773 579-1291
  Chicago *(G-5335)*
Key Colony Inc ............................................. G ...... 630 783-8572
  Lemont *(G-13237)*
Kraft Heinz Foods Company ........................ B ...... 618 512-9100
  Granite City *(G-11290)*
Kraft Heinz Foods Company ........................ C ...... 847 291-3900
  Northbrook *(G-16290)*
Lawlor Marketing ......................................... G ...... 847 357-1080
  Arlington Heights *(G-791)*
Maaldar Pukhtoon Group LLC ..................... G ...... 630 696-1723
  Glendale Heights *(G-11044)*
Premier Beverage Solutions LLC ................ G ...... 309 369-7117
  East Peoria *(G-8728)*
Shady Creek Vineyard Inc ........................... G ...... 847 275-7979
  Palatine *(G-17073)*

## FOOD PRDTS, FROZEN: Lunches, Packaged

Luvo Usa LLC ............................................. D ...... 847 485-8595
  Schaumburg *(G-19625)*
Luvo Usa LLC ............................................. F ...... 847 485-8595
  Schaumburg *(G-19626)*

## FOOD PRDTS, FROZEN: NEC

A New Dairy Company ................................ E ...... 312 421-1234
  Chicago *(G-3690)*
Ajinomoto Windsor Inc ................................. C ...... 815 452-2361
  Toluca *(G-20972)*
Aryzta LLC ................................................... C ...... 815 306-7171
  Romeoville *(G-18800)*
BF Manufacturing LLC ................................. D ...... 312 446-1163
  Chicago *(G-4100)*
Biagios Gourmet Foods Inc ......................... E ...... 708 867-4641
  Chicago *(G-4103)*
Chateau Food Products Inc ......................... F ...... 708 863-4207
  Chicago *(G-4296)*
Conagra Brands Inc .................................... C ...... 312 549-5000
  Chicago *(G-4444)*
Conagra Brands Inc .................................... C ...... 630 857-1000
  Naperville *(G-15633)*
Danziger Kosher Catering Inc ..................... E ...... 847 982-1818
  Lincolnwood *(G-13506)*
Dfg Confectionary LLC ................................ B ...... 847 412-1961
  Northbrook *(G-16241)*
Dianas Bananas Inc .................................... F ...... 773 638-6800
  Chicago *(G-4594)*
Distinctive Foods LLC .................................. F ...... 847 459-3600
  Wheeling *(G-22036)*
Distinctive Foods LLC .................................. E ...... 847 459-3600
  Bensenville *(G-1880)*
Fema L & L Food Services Inc .................... G ...... 217 835-2018
  Benld *(G-1805)*
General Mills Inc .......................................... E ...... 815 544-7399
  Belvidere *(G-1754)*
General Mills Green Giant ........................... G ...... 815 547-5311
  Belvidere *(G-1755)*

Givaudan Flavors Corporation ..................... C ...... 630 682-5600
  Carol Stream *(G-3158)*
Globus Food Products LLC ......................... G ...... 847 378-8221
  Elk Grove Village *(G-9505)*
Gonnella Baking Co ..................................... D ...... 312 733-2020
  Schaumburg *(G-19539)*
Greg El- Inc ................................................. F ...... 773 478-9050
  Chicago *(G-5001)*
Heartland Harvest Inc .................................. G ...... 815 932-2100
  Kankakee *(G-12621)*
Herman Seekamp Inc .................................. C ...... 630 628-6555
  Addison *(G-145)*
Kraft Heinz Company ................................... B ...... 412 456-5700
  Chicago *(G-5410)*
Kraft Heinz Foods Company ........................ C ...... 847 291-3900
  Northbrook *(G-16290)*
Leggero Foods ............................................. G ...... 815 871-9640
  Rockford *(G-18466)*
Lezza Spumoni and Desserts Inc ................ E ...... 708 547-5969
  Bellwood *(G-1712)*
Mjs-Cn LLC ................................................. F ...... 630 580-7200
  Carol Stream *(G-3200)*
O Chilli Frozen Foods Inc ............................ E ...... 847 562-1991
  Northbrook *(G-16321)*
Open Kitchens Inc ....................................... E ...... 312 666-5334
  Chicago *(G-5995)*
Paani Foods Inc ........................................... F ...... 312 420-4624
  Chicago *(G-6047)*
Pinnacle Foods Group LLC ......................... B ...... 618 829-3275
  Saint Elmo *(G-19310)*
Pinnacle Foods Group LLC ......................... C ...... 731 343-4995
  Centralia *(G-3426)*
Supreme Tamale Co .................................... G ...... 773 622-3777
  Elk Grove Village *(G-9763)*

## FOOD PRDTS, FROZEN: Pizza

Afs Classico LLC ........................................ E ...... 309 786-8833
  Rock Island *(G-18158)*
Avanti Foods Company ................................ G ...... 815 379-2155
  Walnut *(G-21329)*
Champion Foods LLC .................................. G ...... 815 648-2725
  Hebron *(G-11716)*
Doreens Pizza Inc ....................................... F ...... 708 862-7499
  Calumet City *(G-2937)*
Home Run Inn Frozen Foods Corp .............. D ...... 630 783-9696
  Woodridge *(G-22494)*
Kraft Pizza Company Inc ............................. E ...... 847 646-2000
  Glenview *(G-11163)*
Little Lady Foods Inc ................................... F ...... 847 806-1440
  Elk Grove Village *(G-9597)*
Lorenzo Frozen Foods Ltd .......................... G ...... 708 343-7670
  Westchester *(G-21848)*
McCain Usa Inc ........................................... C ...... 800 938-7799
  Lisle *(G-13621)*
Nation Pizza Products LP ............................ A ...... 847 397-3320
  Schaumburg *(G-19661)*
Preziosio Ltd ................................................ F ...... 630 393-0920
  Warrenville *(G-21359)*
RCM Smith Inc ............................................. F ...... 309 786-8833
  Rock Island *(G-18197)*
Reggios Pizza Inc ........................................ D ...... 773 488-1411
  Chicago *(G-6325)*
Rollys Convenient Foods Inc ....................... G ...... 630 766-4070
  Bensenville *(G-1979)*
Teresa Foods Inc ......................................... F ...... 708 258-6200
  Peotone *(G-17493)*

## FOOD PRDTS, FROZEN: Potato Prdts

McCain Foods Usa Inc ................................ B ...... 630 955-0400
  Lisle *(G-13620)*
McCain Usa Inc ........................................... C ...... 800 938-7799
  Lisle *(G-13621)*

## FOOD PRDTS, FROZEN: Snack Items

Hearthside Food Solutions LLC ................... E ...... 630 967-3600
  Downers Grove *(G-8456)*
Mondelez Intl Holdings LLC ........................ G ...... 800 572-3847
  Deerfield *(G-8039)*

## FOOD PRDTS, FROZEN: Spaghetti & Meatballs

Jo MO Enterprises Inc ................................. F ...... 708 599-8098
  Bridgeview *(G-2503)*

## FOOD PRDTS, FROZEN: Vegetables, Exc Potato Prdts

General Mills Inc .......................................... E ...... 815 544-7399
  Belvidere *(G-1754)*
Midway Food LLC ........................................ G ...... 773 294-0730
  Chicago *(G-5738)*

## FOOD PRDTS, FROZEN: Waffles

Creapan USA Corp ...................................... G ...... 312 836-3704
  Chicago *(G-4496)*

## FOOD PRDTS, FRUITS & VEG, FRESH, WHOL: Banana Ripening Svc

Hong Kong Market Chicago Inc ................... G ...... 312 791-9111
  Chicago *(G-5108)*
Hop Kee Incorporated ................................. E ...... 312 791-9111
  Chicago *(G-5109)*

## FOOD PRDTS, MEAT & MEAT PRDTS, WHOLESALE: Brokers

F & Y Enterprises Inc .................................. E ...... 847 526-0620
  Wauconda *(G-21462)*

## FOOD PRDTS, MEAT & MEAT PRDTS, WHOLESALE: Cured Or Smoked

H & B Hams ................................................. G ...... 618 372-8690
  Brighton *(G-2541)*
Meats By Linz Inc ........................................ E ...... 708 862-0830
  Calumet City *(G-2946)*

## FOOD PRDTS, MEAT & MEAT PRDTS, WHOLESALE: Fresh

Allens Farm Quality Meats ........................... G ...... 217 896-2532
  Homer *(G-12073)*
Amity Packing Company Inc ........................ D ...... 312 942-0270
  Chicago *(G-3889)*
B B M Packing Co Inc ................................. G ...... 312 243-1061
  Chicago *(G-4019)*
Bruss Company ........................................... C ...... 773 282-2900
  Chicago *(G-4179)*
C & F Packing Co Inc .................................. E ...... 847 245-2000
  Lake Villa *(G-13012)*
Columbus Meats Inc .................................... G ...... 312 829-2480
  Chicago *(G-4433)*
Danielson Food Products Inc ....................... E ...... 773 285-2111
  Chicago *(G-4555)*
Eickmans Processing Co Inc ....................... G ...... 815 247-8451
  Seward *(G-19896)*
Fabbri Sausage Manufacturing .................... E ...... 312 829-6363
  Chicago *(G-4808)*
H C Schau & Son Inc .................................. C ...... 630 783-1000
  Woodridge *(G-22493)*
Hansen Packing Co ..................................... G ...... 618 498-3714
  Jerseyville *(G-12423)*
Jones Packing Co ........................................ G ...... 815 943-4488
  Harvard *(G-11639)*
Kelly Corned Beef Co Chicago ..................... E ...... 773 588-2882
  Chicago *(G-5372)*
Korte Meat Processing Inc .......................... G ...... 618 654-3813
  Highland *(G-11801)*
Moweaqua Packing Plant ............................ G ...... 217 768-4714
  Moweaqua *(G-15458)*
Nationwide Foods Inc .................................. B ...... 773 787-4900
  Chicago *(G-5869)*
Nea Agora Packing Co ................................ G ...... 312 421-5130
  Chicago *(G-5878)*
Olympia Meat Packers Inc ........................... G ...... 312 666-2222
  Chicago *(G-5986)*
Park Packing Company Inc ......................... E ...... 773 254-0100
  Chicago *(G-6083)*
Portillos Food Service Inc ............................ E ...... 630 620-0460
  Addison *(G-248)*
Prince Meat Co ............................................ F ...... 815 729-2333
  Darien *(G-7801)*
Rapid Foods Inc ........................................... G ...... 708 366-0321
  Shorewood *(G-19931)*
Roma Packing Co ........................................ G ...... 773 927-7371
  Chicago *(G-6386)*
Ryan Meat Company ................................... G ...... 773 783-3840
  Chicago *(G-6416)*
Seifferts Locker & Meat Proc ....................... F ...... 618 594-3921
  Carlyle *(G-3058)*
Y T Packing Co ............................................ F ...... 217 522-3345
  Springfield *(G-20550)*

## PRODUCT SECTION

## FOOD PRDTS: Cereals

### FOOD PRDTS, WHOLESALE: Baking Splys

Bear-Stewart Corporation ............................ E ...... 773 276-0400
  Chicago *(G-4065)*
J R Short Milling Company ....................... G ...... 815 937-2635
  Kankakee *(G-12627)*

### FOOD PRDTS, WHOLESALE: Beverages, Exc Coffee & Tea

A Barr Ftn Beverage Sls & Svc .................. G ...... 708 442-2000
  Lyons *(G-14028)*
Atlantic Beverage Company Inc ................ G ...... 847 412-6200
  Northbrook *(G-16207)*
Gatorade Company ...................................... A ...... 312 821-1000
  Chicago *(G-4918)*
H J M P Corp ................................................ C ...... 708 345-5370
  Melrose Park *(G-14650)*

### FOOD PRDTS, WHOLESALE: Breading Mixes

Red Hen Bread Inc ....................................... E ...... 773 342-6823
  Elmhurst *(G-9927)*

### FOOD PRDTS, WHOLESALE: Coffee & Tea

Farmer Bros Co ............................................ G ...... 217 787-7565
  Springfield *(G-20438)*

### FOOD PRDTS, WHOLESALE: Coffee, Green Or Roasted

Napco Inc ...................................................... E ...... 630 406-1100
  Batavia *(G-1474)*

### FOOD PRDTS, WHOLESALE: Condiments

Clorox Hidden Valley Mfg ........................... F ...... 847 229-5500
  Wheeling *(G-22027)*
Dell Cove Spice Co ..................................... G ...... 312 339-8389
  Chicago *(G-4577)*

### FOOD PRDTS, WHOLESALE: Cookies

Blissful Brownies Inc ................................... G ...... 541 308-0226
  Lake Forest *(G-12887)*
Carols Cookies Inc ...................................... G ...... 847 831-4500
  Northbrook *(G-16217)*

### FOOD PRDTS, WHOLESALE: Cooking Oils & Shortenings

Mexifeast Foods Inc .................................... G ...... 773 356-6386
  Chicago *(G-5711)*

### FOOD PRDTS, WHOLESALE: Flavorings & Fragrances

Givaudan Fragrances Corp ........................ G ...... 847 735-0221
  Lake Forest *(G-12900)*
Lucta U S A Inc ............................................ G ...... 847 996-3400
  Libertyville *(G-13345)*

### FOOD PRDTS, WHOLESALE: Flour

Ardent Mills LLC .......................................... E ...... 618 826-2371
  Chester *(G-3650)*
Neiman Bros Co Inc .................................... E ...... 773 463-3000
  Chicago *(G-5882)*

### FOOD PRDTS, WHOLESALE: Grain Elevators

ADM Grain Company ................................... E ...... 217 424-5200
  Decatur *(G-7820)*
Archer-Daniels-Midland Company ............ G ...... 618 483-6171
  Altamont *(G-549)*
Archer-Daniels-Midland Company ............ E ...... 217 224-1800
  Quincy *(G-17794)*
Archer-Daniels-Midland Company ............ A ...... 312 634-8100
  Chicago *(G-3941)*
Archer-Daniels-Midland Company ............ E ...... 217 424-5413
  Decatur *(G-7835)*
Cargill Dry Corn Ingrdents Inc ................... E ...... 217 465-5331
  Paris *(G-17143)*
F S Gateway Inc .......................................... G ...... 618 458-6588
  Fults *(G-10709)*
Hueber Inc .................................................... F ...... 815 393-4879
  Creston *(G-7472)*
South Central Fs Inc ................................... F ...... 217 849-2242
  Toledo *(G-20966)*

### FOOD PRDTS, WHOLESALE: Grains

Archer-Daniels-Midland Company ............ F ...... 815 362-2180
  German Valley *(G-10890)*
Archer-Daniels-Midland Company ............ E ...... 309 772-2141
  Bushnell *(G-2897)*
Jbs United Inc .............................................. F ...... 217 285-2121
  Pittsfield *(G-17570)*
Liberty Feed Mill .......................................... F ...... 217 645-3441
  Liberty *(G-13296)*
Tomen America Inc ..................................... D ...... 847 439-8500
  Elk Grove Village *(G-9782)*
White International Inc ................................ E ...... 630 377-9966
  Saint Charles *(G-19295)*

### FOOD PRDTS, WHOLESALE: Health

Glanbia Performance Ntrtn Inc .................. C ...... 630 236-0097
  Downers Grove *(G-8451)*

### FOOD PRDTS, WHOLESALE: Honey

Millers Country Crafts Inc ........................... G ...... 618 426-3108
  Ava *(G-1240)*

### FOOD PRDTS, WHOLESALE: Natural & Organic

Iya Foods LLC .............................................. G ...... 630 854-7107
  North Aurora *(G-16135)*
Nestle Usa Inc ............................................. D ...... 847 808-5404
  Buffalo Grove *(G-2747)*

### FOOD PRDTS, WHOLESALE: Pasta & Rice

Golden Grain Company ............................... G ...... 708 458-7020
  Bridgeview *(G-2495)*
Wah King Noodle Co Inc ............................ F ...... 323 268-0222
  Chicago *(G-6934)*

### FOOD PRDTS, WHOLESALE: Pizza Splys

Avanti Foods Company ............................... E ...... 815 379-2155
  Walnut *(G-21329)*
Grant Park Packing Company Inc ............. E ...... 312 421-4096
  Franklin Park *(G-10482)*
Mancuso Cheese Company ........................ F ...... 815 722-2475
  Joliet *(G-12536)*
Randolph Packing Co ................................. D ...... 630 830-3100
  Streamwood *(G-20670)*
Russo Wholesale Meat Inc ........................ G ...... 708 385-0500
  Alsip *(G-525)*

### FOOD PRDTS, WHOLESALE: Rice, Polished

International Golden Foods Inc ................. F ...... 630 860-5552
  Bensenville *(G-1921)*
Sunrise Distributors Inc .............................. G ...... 630 400-8786
  Elk Grove Village *(G-9761)*

### FOOD PRDTS, WHOLESALE: Salt, Edible

K+s Salt LLC ................................................ G ...... 844 789-3991
  Chicago *(G-5347)*

### FOOD PRDTS, WHOLESALE: Sauces

Andrias Food Group Inc ............................. E ...... 618 632-4866
  O Fallon *(G-16461)*
Sokol and Company ................................... D ...... 708 482-8250
  Countryside *(G-7443)*

### FOOD PRDTS, WHOLESALE: Shortening, Vegetable

Abitec Corporation ...................................... E ...... 217 465-8577
  Paris *(G-17139)*

### FOOD PRDTS, WHOLESALE: Soups, Exc Frozen

Turtle Island Inc .......................................... F ...... 815 759-9000
  Johnsburg *(G-12443)*

### FOOD PRDTS, WHOLESALE: Specialty

American Kitchen Delights Inc .................. D ...... 708 210-3200
  Harvey *(G-11656)*
Olive and Vinnies ........................................ G ...... 630 534-6457
  Glen Ellyn *(G-10984)*
Plumrose Usa Inc ....................................... D ...... 732 257-6600
  Downers Grove *(G-8504)*
V & V Supremo Foods Inc ......................... C ...... 312 733-5652
  Chicago *(G-6864)*

Zb Importing Inc .......................................... D ...... 708 222-8330
  Cicero *(G-7248)*

### FOOD PRDTS, WHOLESALE: Spices & Seasonings

La Criolla Inc ................................................ E ...... 312 243-8882
  Chicago *(G-5424)*
Laredo Foods Inc ........................................ E ...... 773 762-1500
  Chicago *(G-5461)*
USspice Mill Inc ........................................... F ...... 773 378-6800
  Chicago *(G-6859)*
Vej Holdings LLC ........................................ G ...... 630 219-1582
  Naperville *(G-15774)*
Vita Food Products Inc .............................. C ...... 312 738-4500
  Chicago *(G-6906)*

### FOOD PRDTS, WHOLESALE: Water, Distilled

Ds Services of America Inc ....................... C ...... 773 586-8600
  Chicago *(G-4645)*
Hinckley & Schmitt Inc ............................... A ...... 773 586-8600
  Chicago *(G-5091)*

### FOOD PRDTS, WHOLESALE: Wine Makers' Eqpt & Splys

Crushed Grapes Ltd ................................... G ...... 618 659-3530
  Millstadt *(G-14822)*
Fox Valley Home Brew & Winery .............. G ...... 630 892-0742
  Aurora *(G-1154)*

### FOOD PRDTS: Animal & marine fats & oils

Abitec Corporation ...................................... E ...... 217 465-8577
  Paris *(G-17139)*
Ace Grease Service Inc ............................. G ...... 618 781-1207
  Millstadt *(G-14820)*
Bunge Oils Inc ............................................. D ...... 815 939-3631
  Bradley *(G-2415)*
Darling Ingredients Inc ............................... E ...... 309 476-8111
  Lynn Center *(G-14016)*
McShares Inc ............................................... E ...... 217 762-2561
  Monticello *(G-15079)*
Micro Surface Corporation ......................... F ...... 815 942-4221
  Morris *(G-15116)*
Millstadt Rendering Company .................... E ...... 618 538-5312
  Belleville *(G-1659)*
Potter Rendering Co ................................... G ...... 580 924-2414
  Buffalo Grove *(G-2755)*
Sdr Corp ....................................................... G ...... 773 638-1800
  Chicago *(G-6463)*
Specialized Separators Inc ........................ F ...... 815 316-0626
  Rockford *(G-18625)*
Sustainable Sourcing LLC ......................... F ...... 815 714-8055
  Mokena *(G-14908)*

### FOOD PRDTS: Bran & Middlings, Exc Rice

Salud Natural Entrepreneur Inc ................ E ...... 224 789-7400
  Waukegan *(G-21612)*

### FOOD PRDTS: Bread Crumbs, Exc Made In Bakeries

Best Croutons LLC ..................................... F ...... 773 927-8200
  Chicago *(G-4091)*
Jbc Holding Co ............................................ G ...... 217 347-7701
  Effingham *(G-8841)*
Newly Weds Foods Inc ............................... A ...... 773 489-7000
  Chicago *(G-5899)*

### FOOD PRDTS: Breakfast Bars

CGC Corporation ......................................... D ...... 773 838-3400
  Chicago *(G-4284)*

### FOOD PRDTS: Cake Fillings, Exc Fruit

Sokol and Company ................................... D ...... 708 482-8250
  Countryside *(G-7443)*

### FOOD PRDTS: Cereals

BF Foods Inc ................................................ E ...... 773 252-6113
  Chicago *(G-4099)*
General Mills Inc .......................................... D ...... 630 844-1125
  Montgomery *(G-15045)*
General Mills Inc .......................................... B ...... 630 231-1140
  Calumet City *(G-2939)*
Gilster-Mary Lee Corporation .................... A ...... 618 826-2361
  Chester *(G-3657)*

---

Employee Codes: A=Over 500 employees, B=251-500
C=101-250, D=51-100, E=20-50, F=10-19, G=3-9

## FOOD PRDTS: Cereals

|  | |  |
|---|---|---|
| Hearthside Food Solutions LLC | E | 630 967-3600 |
| Downers Grove (G-8456) | | |
| Kellogg Company | B | 773 254-0900 |
| Chicago (G-5370) | | |
| Kellogg Company | F | 217 258-3251 |
| Mattoon (G-14397) | | |
| Kellogg Company | E | 630 820-9457 |
| Oak Brook (G-16531) | | |
| Kellogg Company | A | 773 995-7200 |
| Chicago (G-5371) | | |
| Kraft Foods Asia PCF Svcs LLC | G | 847 943-4000 |
| Deerfield (G-8026) | | |
| Kraft Heinz Company | C | 847 646-2000 |
| Glenview (G-11160) | | |
| Lee Gilster-Mary Corporation | G | 618 826-2361 |
| Chester (G-3658) | | |
| Lee Gilster-Mary Corporation | E | 618 443-5676 |
| Sparta (G-20318) | | |
| Mondelez Global LLC | B | 630 369-1909 |
| Naperville (G-15699) | | |
| Mondelez International Inc | | 847 943-4000 |
| Deerfield (G-8038) | | |
| Quaker Manufacturing LLC | F | 312 222-7111 |
| Chicago (G-6241) | | |
| Quaker Oats Company | A | 312 821-1000 |
| Chicago (G-6242) | | |
| Quaker Oats Company | A | 217 443-4995 |
| Danville (G-7761) | | |
| Quaker Oats Europe Inc | G | 312 821-1000 |
| Chicago (G-6243) | | |
| Treehouse Private Brands Inc | F | 630 455-5265 |
| Downers Grove (G-8534) | | |

## FOOD PRDTS: Chewing Gum Base

|  | |  |
|---|---|---|
| Wm Wrigley Jr Company | C | 312 644-2121 |
| Romeoville (G-18880) | | |

## FOOD PRDTS: Chicken, Processed, Fresh

|  | |  |
|---|---|---|
| Aspen Foods Inc | C | 312 829-7282 |
| Chicago (G-3964) | | |
| Jcg Industries Inc | C | 312 829-7282 |
| Chicago (G-5286) | | |
| New Specialty Products Inc | E | 773 847-0230 |
| Chicago (G-5894) | | |

## FOOD PRDTS: Chicken, Processed, Frozen

|  | |  |
|---|---|---|
| Lean Protein Team LLC | G | 440 525-1532 |
| Chicago (G-5479) | | |
| Love ME Tenders LLC | G | 847 564-2533 |
| Northbrook (G-16298) | | |

## FOOD PRDTS: Chili Pepper Or Powder

|  | |  |
|---|---|---|
| Mexico Distributor Inc | G | |
| Chicago (G-5709) | | |

## FOOD PRDTS: Cocoa, Instant

|  | |  |
|---|---|---|
| Inside Beverages | C | 847 438-1338 |
| Lake Zurich (G-13088) | | |

## FOOD PRDTS: Coffee

|  | |  |
|---|---|---|
| Central Mountain Coffee LLC | G | 309 981-0094 |
| Galesburg (G-10743) | | |
| Crushed Grapes Ltd | G | 618 659-3530 |
| Millstadt (G-14822) | | |
| Fratelli Coffee Company | G | 847 671-7300 |
| Schiller Park (G-19832) | | |
| Healthwise Gourmet Coffees | G | 847 382-3230 |
| Deer Park (G-7971) | | |
| Hillshire Brands Company | C | 847 956-7575 |
| Elk Grove Village (G-9524) | | |
| Hmshost Corporation | E | 847 678-2098 |
| Schiller Park (G-19837) | | |
| Javamania Coffee Roastery Inc | G | 815 885-3654 |
| Loves Park (G-13951) | | |
| Napco Inc | E | 630 406-1100 |
| Batavia (G-1474) | | |
| Sparrow Coffee Roastery | G | 321 648-6415 |
| Westchester (G-21855) | | |
| Trade-Mark Coffee Corporation | F | 847 382-4200 |
| North Barrington (G-16155) | | |
| Two Brothers Brewing Company | G | 630 393-2337 |
| Warrenville (G-21367) | | |

## FOOD PRDTS: Coffee Extracts

|  | |  |
|---|---|---|
| Coffee Brewmasters Usa LLC | F | 773 294-9665 |
| Buffalo Grove (G-2675) | | |

|  | |  |
|---|---|---|
| Insight Beverages Inc | F | 847 438-1598 |
| Lake Zurich (G-13090) | | |
| Limitless Coffee LLC | E | 630 779-3778 |
| Chicago (G-5505) | | |

## FOOD PRDTS: Coffee Roasting, Exc Wholesale Grocers

|  | |  |
|---|---|---|
| Farmer Bros Co | G | 217 787-7565 |
| Springfield (G-20438) | | |
| Kraft Foods Asia PCF Svcs LLC | G | 847 943-4000 |
| Deerfield (G-8026) | | |
| Kraft Heinz Company | | 847 646-2000 |
| Glenview (G-11160) | | |
| Mondelez International Inc | A | 847 943-4000 |
| Deerfield (G-8038) | | |
| Nuri Corp | F | 847 940-7134 |
| Deerfield (G-8044) | | |
| Stewarts Prvate Blend Fods Inc | E | 773 489-2500 |
| Carol Stream (G-3250) | | |

## FOOD PRDTS: Coffee Substitutes

|  | |  |
|---|---|---|
| Kws Cereals Usa LLC | G | 815 200-2666 |
| Champaign (G-3508) | | |

## FOOD PRDTS: Compound Shortenings

|  | |  |
|---|---|---|
| South Chicago Packing LLC | D | 708 589-2400 |
| South Holland (G-20305) | | |
| South Chicago Packing LLC | D | 708 589-2400 |
| Chicago (G-6546) | | |

## FOOD PRDTS: Cooking Oils, Refined Vegetable, Exc Corn

|  | |  |
|---|---|---|
| A-F Acquisition LLC | F | 773 978-5130 |
| Chicago (G-3695) | | |
| Beatrice Companies Inc | E | 602 225-2000 |
| Chicago (G-4069) | | |
| Fgfi LLC | E | 708 598-0909 |
| Countryside (G-7424) | | |
| Pastorelli Food Products Inc | E | 312 455-1006 |
| Chicago (G-6089) | | |

## FOOD PRDTS: Corn & other vegetable starches

|  | |  |
|---|---|---|
| Tate & Lyle Americas LLC | E | 847 396-7500 |
| Hoffman Estates (G-12063) | | |
| Tate & Lyle Americas LLC | C | 217 421-2964 |
| Decatur (G-7949) | | |

## FOOD PRDTS: Corn Chips & Other Corn-Based Snacks

|  | |  |
|---|---|---|
| El Popocatapetl Industries Inc | D | 773 843-0888 |
| Chicago (G-4709) | | |
| Larry Ragan | G | 618 698-1041 |
| Belleville (G-1648) | | |
| Snak-King Corp | C | 815 232-6700 |
| Freeport (G-10689) | | |

## FOOD PRDTS: Corn Meal

|  | |  |
|---|---|---|
| Cargill Dry Corn Ingrdents Inc | G | 217 465-5331 |
| Paris (G-17143) | | |

## FOOD PRDTS: Cottonseed Oil, Cake & Meal

|  | |  |
|---|---|---|
| Lee Gilster-Mary Corporation | C | 618 533-4808 |
| Centralia (G-3421) | | |

## FOOD PRDTS: Dessert Mixes & Fillings

|  | |  |
|---|---|---|
| Creative Contract Packg LLC | D | 630 851-6226 |
| Aurora (G-987) | | |
| Dennco Inc | G | 708 862-0070 |
| Burnham (G-2816) | | |
| Holton Food Products Company | F | 708 352-5599 |
| La Grange (G-12736) | | |
| Home Style | | 847 455-5000 |
| Franklin Park (G-10487) | | |

## FOOD PRDTS: Desserts, Ready-To-Mix

|  | |  |
|---|---|---|
| Essen Nutrition Corporation | E | 630 739-6700 |
| Romeoville (G-18820) | | |
| Jel Sert Co | B | 630 231-7590 |
| West Chicago (G-21727) | | |
| Solo Foods | G | 800 328-7656 |
| Countryside (G-7444) | | |

## FOOD PRDTS: Dough, Pizza, Prepared

|  | |  |
|---|---|---|
| LLC Urban Farmer | F | 815 468-7200 |
| Manteno (G-14187) | | |

## FOOD PRDTS: Doughs, Frozen Or Refrig From Purchased Flour

|  | |  |
|---|---|---|
| Loders Croklaan BV | C | 815 730-5200 |
| Channahon (G-3577) | | |

## FOOD PRDTS: Dressings, Salad, Raw & Cooked Exc Dry Mixes

|  | |  |
|---|---|---|
| Earthgrains Refrigertd Dough P | A | 630 455-5200 |
| Downers Grove (G-8438) | | |
| Kraft Foods Asia PCF Svcs LLC | G | 847 943-4000 |
| Deerfield (G-8026) | | |
| Kraft Heinz Company | C | 847 646-2000 |
| Glenview (G-11160) | | |
| Kraft Heinz Foods Company | C | 847 646-2000 |
| Glenview (G-11162) | | |
| Mizkan America Inc | E | 847 590-0059 |
| Mount Prospect (G-15347) | | |
| Mondelez International Inc | A | 847 943-4000 |
| Deerfield (G-8038) | | |
| Mullins Food Products Inc | B | 708 344-3224 |
| Broadview (G-2599) | | |
| Treehouse Private Brands Inc | F | 630 455-5265 |
| Downers Grove (G-8534) | | |

## FOOD PRDTS: Dried & Dehydrated Fruits, Vegetables & Soup Mix

|  | |  |
|---|---|---|
| Bernard Food Industries Inc | D | 847 869-5222 |
| Evanston (G-10015) | | |
| Goodhome Foods Inc | G | 847 816-6832 |
| Lake Forest (G-12903) | | |
| Karlin Foods Corp | F | 847 441-8330 |
| Northfield (G-16404) | | |
| Kent Precision Foods Group Inc | E | 630 226-0071 |
| Bolingbrook (G-2331) | | |
| Kent Precision Foods Group Inc | E | 630 226-0498 |
| Bolingbrook (G-2332) | | |
| R J Van Drunen & Sons Inc | D | 815 472-3211 |
| Momence (G-14989) | | |
| Swiss Products LP | E | 773 394-6480 |
| Chicago (G-6651) | | |

## FOOD PRDTS: Edible Oil Prdts, Exc Corn Oil

|  | |  |
|---|---|---|
| Grante Foods International LLC | F | 773 751-9551 |
| Elk Grove Village (G-9507) | | |
| Loders Croklaan BV | C | 815 730-5200 |
| Channahon (G-3577) | | |
| Loders Croklaan Usa LLC | C | 815 730-5200 |
| Channahon (G-3578) | | |

## FOOD PRDTS: Edible fats & oils

|  | |  |
|---|---|---|
| Ach Food Companies Inc | C | 708 458-8690 |
| Summit Argo (G-20759) | | |
| All Fresh Food Products | G | 847 864-5030 |
| Evanston (G-10007) | | |
| Allfresh Food Products Inc | G | 847 869-3100 |
| Evanston (G-10008) | | |
| Archer-Daniels-Midland Company | E | 217 224-1800 |
| Quincy (G-17794) | | |
| Avatar Corporation | D | 708 534-5511 |
| University Park (G-21042) | | |
| Bunge Oils Inc | D | 815 939-3631 |
| Bradley (G-2415) | | |
| Cargill Incorporated | F | 773 375-7255 |
| Chicago (G-4243) | | |
| Cfc Inc | D | 847 257-8920 |
| Des Plaines (G-8163) | | |
| Darling Ingredients Inc | E | 217 482-3261 |
| Mason City (G-14363) | | |
| Dawn Food Products Inc | C | 815 933-0600 |
| Bradley (G-2419) | | |
| Midwest Processing Company | D | 217 424-5200 |
| Decatur (G-7916) | | |
| Stratas Foods LLC | E | 217 424-5660 |
| Decatur (G-7945) | | |
| V Formusa Co | F | 224 938-9360 |
| Des Plaines (G-8296) | | |

## FOOD PRDTS: Eggs, Processed

|  | |  |
|---|---|---|
| Pelbo Americas Inc | G | 630 395-7788 |
| Naperville (G-15723) | | |

# PRODUCT SECTION

## FOOD PRDTS: Eggs, Processed, Dehydrated

Kelly Flour Company .................................. G ...... 312 933-3104
  Chicago **(G-5373)**

## FOOD PRDTS: Emulsifiers

FBC Industries Inc .................................... G ...... 847 241-6143
  Schaumburg **(G-19525)**
FBC Industries Inc .................................... G ...... 847 839-0880
  Rochelle **(G-18089)**
Kosto Food Products Company ................... F ...... 847 487-2600
  Wauconda **(G-21478)**

## FOOD PRDTS: Fat Substitutes

Fibergel Technologies Inc ........................... G ...... 847 549-6002
  Mundelein **(G-15500)**

## FOOD PRDTS: Flour

Ardent Mills LLC ........................................ C ...... 618 463-4411
  Alton **(G-561)**
J R Short Milling Company ......................... G ...... 815 937-2635
  Kankakee **(G-12627)**
McShares Inc ............................................. E ...... 217 762-2561
  Monticello **(G-15079)**
McShares Inc ............................................. E ...... 217 762-2561
  Monticello **(G-15080)**
TEC Foods Inc ........................................... E ...... 800 315-8002
  Chicago **(G-6683)**

## FOOD PRDTS: Flour & Other Grain Mill Products

ADM Grain Company ................................. E ...... 217 424-5200
  Decatur **(G-7820)**
Agritech Worldwide Inc .............................. F ...... 847 549-6002
  Mundelein **(G-15466)**
American Milling Company ........................ F ...... 309 347-6888
  Pekin **(G-17253)**
Archer-Daniels-Midland Company .............. E ...... 217 424-5200
  Decatur **(G-7838)**
Archer-Daniels-Midland Company .............. C ...... 309 673-7828
  Peoria **(G-17309)**
Ardent Mills LLC ........................................ E ...... 618 826-2371
  Chester **(G-3650)**
Bio Fuels By American Farmers ................. F ...... 561 859-6251
  Benton **(G-2023)**
Bunge Milling Inc ....................................... C ...... 217 442-1801
  Danville **(G-7708)**
Dix McGuire Commodities LLC ................... G ...... 847 496-5320
  Palatine **(G-17023)**
Farmers Mill Inc ........................................ G ...... 618 445-2114
  Albion **(G-362)**
Hayden Mills Inc ........................................ E ...... 618 962-3136
  Omaha **(G-16807)**
Hodgson Mill Inc ........................................ C ...... 217 347-0105
  Effingham **(G-8839)**
J R Short Milling Company ......................... C ...... 815 937-2633
  Kankakee **(G-12628)**
Nauvoo Mill & Bakery ................................ G ...... 217 453-6734
  Nauvoo **(G-15854)**
New Alliance Production LLC ..................... E ...... 309 928-3123
  Farmer City **(G-10180)**
Nu-World Amaranth Inc ............................. G ...... 630 369-6819
  Naperville **(G-15717)**
Pillsbury Company LLC ............................. G ...... 847 541-8888
  Buffalo Grove **(G-2753)**
Problend-Eurogerm LLC ............................ G ...... 847 221-5004
  Rolling Meadows **(G-18770)**
Quaker Oats Company ............................... A ...... 217 443-4995
  Danville **(G-7761)**
Roanoke Milling Co .................................... G ...... 309 923-5731
  Roanoke **(G-18054)**
Ron & Pats Pizza Shack ............................. G ...... 847 395-5005
  Antioch **(G-653)**
Sunrise Distributors Inc ............................. G ...... 630 400-8786
  Elk Grove Village **(G-9761)**
U S Soy LLC .............................................. F ...... 217 235-1020
  Mattoon **(G-14411)**

## FOOD PRDTS: Flour Mixes & Doughs

Barilla America Inc .................................... D ...... 515 956-4400
  Northbrook **(G-16211)**
Bear-Stewart Corporation .......................... E ...... 773 276-0400
  Chicago **(G-4065)**
Brolite Products Incorporated .................... E ...... 630 830-0340
  Streamwood **(G-20646)**
Dominos Pizza LLC .................................... E ...... 630 783-0738
  Woodridge **(G-22472)**
Glen Lake Inc ............................................. F ...... 630 668-3492
  Carol Stream **(G-3159)**
Lee Gilster-Mary Corporation .................... D ...... 618 965-3426
  Steeleville **(G-20561)**
Parke & Son Inc ........................................ G ...... 217 875-0572
  Decatur **(G-7925)**
Simple Mills LLC ....................................... G ...... 312 600-6196
  Chicago **(G-6514)**
Watson Foods Co Inc ................................. D ...... 847 245-8404
  Lindenhurst **(G-13550)**
Watson Inc ................................................ G ...... 217 824-4440
  Taylorville **(G-20846)**

## FOOD PRDTS: Flour, Blended From Purchased Flour

Fleetchem LLC .......................................... G ...... 708 957-5311
  Flossmoor **(G-10224)**
Gilster-Mary Lee Corporation ..................... A ...... 618 826-2361
  Chester **(G-3657)**
Lee Gilster-Mary Corporation .................... G ...... 618 826-2361
  Chester **(G-3658)**
Lee Gilster-Mary Corporation .................... E ...... 618 443-5676
  Sparta **(G-20318)**
Lee Gilster-Mary Corporation .................... G ...... 815 472-6456
  Momence **(G-14983)**

## FOOD PRDTS: Flours & Flour Mixes, From Purchased Flour

Continental Mills Inc .................................. C ...... 217 540-4000
  Effingham **(G-8830)**
Quaker Oats Company ............................... A ...... 312 821-1000
  Chicago **(G-6242)**
Quaker Oats Europe Inc ............................. G ...... 312 821-1000
  Chicago **(G-6243)**

## FOOD PRDTS: Fresh Vegetables, Peeled Or Processed

Taylor Farms Illinois Inc ............................ B ...... 312 226-3328
  Chicago **(G-6680)**

## FOOD PRDTS: Fruit Juices

Dulce Vida Juice Bar LLC .......................... G ...... 224 236-5045
  Hanover Park **(G-11579)**
J J Mata Inc .............................................. G ...... 773 750-0643
  Chicago **(G-5260)**
Mautino Distributing Co Inc ....................... E ...... 815 664-4311
  Spring Valley **(G-20376)**
Natural Distribution Company .................... G ...... 630 350-1700
  Wood Dale **(G-22403)**

## FOOD PRDTS: Fruit Juices, Dehydrated

Americas Food Technologies Inc ................ E ...... 708 532-1222
  Tinley Park **(G-20891)**

## FOOD PRDTS: Fruit Pops, Frozen

Jel Sert Co ................................................. B ...... 630 231-7590
  West Chicago **(G-21727)**

## FOOD PRDTS: Fruits & Vegetables, Pickled

E Formella & Sons Inc ............................... E ...... 708 598-0909
  Countryside **(G-7422)**

## FOOD PRDTS: Fruits, Dehydrated Or Dried

Handcut Foods LLC ................................... D ...... 312 239-0381
  Chicago **(G-5040)**
Hot Mexican Peppers Inc ........................... G ...... 773 843-9774
  Chicago **(G-5118)**
Terri Lynn Inc ............................................ C ...... 847 741-1900
  Elgin **(G-9210)**

## FOOD PRDTS: Fruits, Dried Or Dehydrated, Exc Freeze-Dried

H A Gartenberg & Company ....................... F ...... 847 821-7590
  Buffalo Grove **(G-2700)**

## FOOD PRDTS: Gluten Feed

Mgp Ingredients Illinois Inc ....................... C ...... 309 353-3990
  Pekin **(G-17274)**
Mgpi Processing Inc .................................. C ...... 309 353-3990
  Pekin **(G-17275)**

## FOOD PRDTS: Granola & Energy Bars, Nonchocolate

Alabaster Box Creations LLC ..................... G ...... 708 473-6880
  Oak Forest **(G-16572)**
Nature S American Co ............................... G ...... 630 246-4776
  Lombard **(G-13832)**
Quaker Oats Company ............................... A ...... 312 821-1000
  Chicago **(G-6242)**

## FOOD PRDTS: Honey

Sweet Beginnings LLC ............................... G ...... 773 638-7058
  Chicago **(G-6647)**
Ys Health Corporation ................................ F ...... 847 391-9122
  Mount Prospect **(G-15387)**

## FOOD PRDTS: Horseradish, Exc Sauce

Fournie Farms Inc ..................................... E ...... 618 344-8527
  Collinsville **(G-7325)**

## FOOD PRDTS: Ice, Blocks

Collinsville Ice & Fuel Co ........................... F ...... 618 344-3272
  Collinsville **(G-7315)**
Just Ice Inc ............................................... G ...... 773 301-7323
  Chicago **(G-5337)**

## FOOD PRDTS: Ice, Cubes

Sisler Dairy Products Company .................. G ...... 815 376-2913
  Ohio **(G-16753)**

## FOOD PRDTS: Instant Coffee

Berner Food & Beverage LLC ..................... B ...... 815 563-4222
  Dakota **(G-7694)**
Sweet Company ........................................ F ...... 815 462-4586
  Mokena **(G-14909)**

## FOOD PRDTS: Macaroni Prdts, Dry, Alphabet, Rings Or Shells

Gilster-Mary Lee Corporation ..................... A ...... 618 826-2361
  Chester **(G-3657)**
Golden Grain Company .............................. G ...... 708 458-7020
  Bridgeview **(G-2495)**
Lee Gilster-Mary Corporation .................... G ...... 618 826-2361
  Chester **(G-3658)**
Lee Gilster-Mary Corporation .................... E ...... 618 443-5676
  Sparta **(G-20318)**
Lee Gilster-Mary Corporation .................... D ...... 815 472-6456
  Momence **(G-14983)**
Mareta Ravioli Inc ..................................... F ...... 815 856-2621
  Leonore **(G-13286)**

## FOOD PRDTS: Macaroni, Noodles, Spaghetti, Pasta, Etc

Bellaflora Foods Ltd .................................. E ...... 773 252-6113
  Chicago **(G-4077)**
General Mills Inc ....................................... B ...... 630 231-1140
  Calumet City **(G-2939)**
Jo MO Enterprises Inc ............................... F ...... 708 599-8098
  Bridgeview **(G-2503)**
Kraft Heinz Company ................................ B ...... 412 456-5700
  Chicago **(G-5410)**
Kraft Heinz Foods Company ...................... D ...... 217 378-1900
  Champaign **(G-3507)**
Lee Gilster-Mary Corporation .................... B ...... 618 965-3449
  Steeleville **(G-20562)**
Lee Gilster-Mary Corporation .................... D ...... 618 965-3426
  Steeleville **(G-20561)**
Mary Lee Packaging Corporation ................ E ...... 618 826-2361
  Chester **(G-3659)**
Oriental Noodle ......................................... G ...... 773 279-1595
  Chicago **(G-6009)**
Pastafresh Co ............................................ G ...... 773 745-5888
  Chicago **(G-6088)**
Pastificio Inc ............................................. G ...... 847 432-5459
  Highwood **(G-11887)**
Stevie S Italian Foods Inc .......................... G ...... 217 793-9693
  Springfield **(G-20538)**

## FOOD PRDTS: Malt

Archer-Daniels-Midland Company .............. D ...... 217 424-5200
  Decatur **(G-7836)**
Archer-Daniels-Midland Company .............. A ...... 312 634-8100
  Chicago **(G-3941)**
Archer-Daniels-Midland Company .............. E ...... 217 424-5413
  Decatur **(G-7835)**

---

Employee Codes: A=Over 500 employees, B=251-500
C=101-250, D=51-100, E=20-50, F=10-19, G=3-9

# FOOD PRDTS: Malt

Mid Country Malt Supply .................. G ...... 708 339-7005
  South Holland  (G-20291)
Muntons Malted Ingredients Inc .......... G ...... 630 812-1600
  Lombard  (G-13830)

## FOOD PRDTS: Meat Meal & Tankage, Inedible

Darling Ingredients Inc .................. E ...... 217 482-3261
  Mason City  (G-14363)

## FOOD PRDTS: Milled Corn By-Prdts

Gro Alliance LLC ........................ E ...... 217 792-3355
  Mount Pulaski  (G-15388)

## FOOD PRDTS: Mixes, Bread & Roll From Purchased Flour

Kerry Inc ................................ D ...... 708 450-3260
  Melrose Park  (G-14666)

## FOOD PRDTS: Mixes, Cake, From Purchased Flour

Arlington Specialties Inc ................ G ...... 847 545-9500
  Elk Grove Village  (G-9313)
Inside Beverages ........................ C ...... 847 438-1338
  Lake Zurich  (G-13088)

## FOOD PRDTS: Mixes, Doughnut From Purchased Flour

Joshi Brothers Inc ...................... E ...... 847 895-0200
  Schaumburg  (G-19590)

## FOOD PRDTS: Mixes, Flour

Bay Foods Inc .......................... E ...... 312 346-5757
  Chicago  (G-4057)
General Mills Inc ....................... E ...... 309 342-9165
  Galesburg  (G-10754)
General Mills Inc ....................... F ...... 630 577-3800
  Lisle  (G-13594)

## FOOD PRDTS: Mixes, Gravy, Dry

Custom Culinary Inc .................... D ...... 630 928-4898
  Lombard  (G-13787)
Swiss Products LP ...................... E ...... 773 394-6480
  Chicago  (G-6651)

## FOOD PRDTS: Mixes, Pancake From Purchased Flour

Arro Corporation ........................ E ...... 708 352-7412
  Hodgkins  (G-11971)
Arro Corporation ........................ C ...... 708 352-8200
  Hodgkins  (G-11970)
Arro Corporation ........................ G ...... 773 978-1251
  Chicago  (G-3947)
Gust-John Foods & Pdts Corp ............ G ...... 630 879-8700
  Batavia  (G-1453)
Hodgson Mill Inc ........................ C ...... 217 347-0105
  Effingham  (G-8839)

## FOOD PRDTS: Mixes, Pizza From Purchased Flour

Diversfied III Green Works LLC ........... D ...... 773 544-7777
  Chicago  (G-4613)
Russo Wholesale Meat Inc .............. G ...... 708 385-0500
  Alsip  (G-525)

## FOOD PRDTS: Mixes, Sauces, Dry

Culinary Co-Pack Inc ................... G ...... 847 451-1551
  Franklin Park  (G-10447)
Johnny Vans Smokehouse ............... G ...... 773 750-1589
  Chicago  (G-5318)
Swagger Foods Corporation ............. E ...... 847 913-1200
  Vernon Hills  (G-21205)

## FOOD PRDTS: Mixes, Seasonings, Dry

Char Crust Co Inc ..................... G ...... 773 528-0600
  Chicago  (G-4288)
Griffith Foods Group Inc ................ F ...... 708 371-0900
  Alsip  (G-467)
Griffith Foods Inc ...................... B ...... 708 371-0900
  Alsip  (G-468)
Griffith Foods Worldwide Inc ............ G ...... 708 371-0900
  Alsip  (G-469)

Papys Foods Inc ........................ E ...... 815 385-3313
  McHenry  (G-14542)
Royal Foods & Flavors Inc .............. F ...... 847 595-9166
  Elk Grove Village  (G-9720)
Sono Italiano Corporation ............... G ...... 817 472-8903
  Manteno  (G-14193)
Vanee Foods Company .................. D ...... 708 449-7300
  Berkeley  (G-2050)

## FOOD PRDTS: Mustard, Prepared

Boetje Foods Inc ....................... G ...... 309 788-4352
  Rock Island  (G-18165)
Flaherty Incorporated ................... F ...... 773 472-8456
  Skokie  (G-20000)
Plochman Inc .......................... E ...... 815 468-3434
  Manteno  (G-14190)

## FOOD PRDTS: Noodles, Uncooked, Packaged W/Other Ingredients

Good World Noodle Inc ................. G ...... 312 326-0441
  Chicago  (G-4977)
New Taste Good Noodle Inc ............. G ...... 312 842-8980
  Chicago  (G-5897)

## FOOD PRDTS: Nuts & Seeds

Anton-Argires Inc ...................... G ...... 708 388-6250
  Alsip  (G-434)
Peases Inc ............................ F ...... 217 529-2912
  Springfield  (G-20502)
Regal Health Foods Intl Inc ............. E ...... 773 252-1044
  Chicago  (G-6321)
Specialty Nut & Bky Sup Co Inc ......... G ...... 630 268-8500
  Addison  (G-297)
Terri Lynn Inc ......................... C ...... 847 741-1900
  Elgin  (G-9210)

## FOOD PRDTS: Oils & Fats, Animal

Mendota Agri-Products Inc ............. E ...... 815 539-5633
  Mendota  (G-14724)

## FOOD PRDTS: Olive Oil

Old Town Oil Evanston ................. G ...... 312 787-9595
  Evanston  (G-10082)
Olive and Vinnies ...................... G ...... 630 534-6457
  Glen Ellyn  (G-10984)
Olive Leclaire Oil Co ................... G ...... 888 255-1867
  Yorkville  (G-22666)
Olive Oil Market Place .................. G ...... 618 304-3769
  Godfrey  (G-11231)
Olive Oil Marketplace Inc ............... G ...... 618 304-3769
  Alton  (G-586)
Olive Oils & More LLC ................. G ...... 618 656-4645
  Edwardsville  (G-8811)
Olive Spartathlon Oil & Gre ............. G ...... 312 782-9855
  Chicago  (G-5983)
Stevie S Italian Foods Inc .............. G ...... 217 793-9693
  Springfield  (G-20538)

## FOOD PRDTS: Onion Fries

Michaels Dawg House LLC .............. G ...... 847 485-7600
  Palatine  (G-17055)

## FOOD PRDTS: Oriental Noodles

Oakland Noodle Company ............... G ...... 217 346-2322
  Oakland  (G-16724)
Real Taste Noodles Mfg Inc ............. G ...... 312 738-1893
  Chicago  (G-6303)
Three Guys Pasta LLC .................. E ...... 708 932-5555
  Northlake  (G-16455)
YMC Corp ............................. F ...... 312 842-4900
  Chicago  (G-7052)

## FOOD PRDTS: Pasta, Rice/Potatoes, Uncooked, Pkgd

Baja Sales Inc ......................... G ...... 708 672-9245
  Crete  (G-7508)
Foulds Inc ............................. E ...... 414 964-1428
  Libertyville  (G-13325)
Jo MO Enterprises Inc .................. F ...... 708 599-8098
  Bridgeview  (G-2503)
Pastafresh Co ......................... G ...... 773 745-5888
  Chicago  (G-6088)

## FOOD PRDTS: Pasta, Uncooked, Packaged With Other Ingredients

Archer-Daniels-Midland Company ........ D ...... 224 544-5980
  Lake Bluff  (G-12833)
E3 Artisan Inc ......................... F ...... 815 575-9315
  Woodstock  (G-22564)
Nestle Usa Inc ......................... C ...... 847 808-5300
  Buffalo Grove  (G-2748)
Perfect Pasta Inc ...................... G ...... 630 543-8300
  Addison  (G-239)
Wah King Noodle Co Inc ............... F ...... 323 268-0222
  Chicago  (G-6934)

## FOOD PRDTS: Peanut Butter

Beatrice Companies Inc ................. E ...... 602 225-2000
  Chicago  (G-4069)
John B Sanfilippo & Son Inc ............ C ...... 847 289-1800
  Elgin  (G-9083)
Peanut Butter Partners LLC ............. G ...... 847 489-5322
  Glen Ellyn  (G-10986)

## FOOD PRDTS: Pickles, Vinegar

Kraft Heinz Foods Company ............ B ...... 815 338-7000
  Woodstock  (G-22580)
North Star Pickle LLC .................. F ...... 847 970-5555
  Lake Zurich  (G-13109)
Pickles Sorrel Inc ...................... F ...... 773 379-4748
  Chicago  (G-6121)

## FOOD PRDTS: Pizza Doughs From Purchased Flour

Nation Pizza Products LP ............... A ...... 847 397-3320
  Schaumburg  (G-19661)

## FOOD PRDTS: Popcorn, Popped

Gary Poppins LLC ...................... G ...... 847 455-2200
  Franklin Park  (G-10476)
Great American Popcorn Company ....... G ...... 815 777-4116
  Galena  (G-10725)
Marianne Strawn ....................... G ...... 309 447-6612
  Deer Creek  (G-7965)
Tpf Liquidation Co ..................... D ...... 847 362-0028
  Lake Forest  (G-12971)

## FOOD PRDTS: Popcorn, Unpopped

Cornfields LLC ........................ C ...... 847 263-7000
  Waukegan  (G-21544)
Gilster-Mary Lee Corporation ............ A ...... 618 826-2361
  Chester  (G-3657)
Great American Popcorn Company ....... G ...... 815 777-4116
  Galena  (G-10725)
Lee Gilster-Mary Corporation ............ G ...... 618 826-2361
  Chester  (G-3658)
Lee Gilster-Mary Corporation ............ E ...... 618 443-5676
  Sparta  (G-20318)
Lee Gilster-Mary Corporation ............ D ...... 815 472-6456
  Momence  (G-14983)
Tee Lee Popcorn Inc ................... E ...... 815 864-2363
  Shannon  (G-19903)
Tpf Liquidation Co ..................... D ...... 847 362-0028
  Lake Forest  (G-12971)

## FOOD PRDTS: Pork Rinds

Evans Food Group Ltd ................. E ...... 773 254-7400
  Chicago  (G-4786)
Evans Foods Inc ...................... D ...... 773 254-7400
  Chicago  (G-4787)

## FOOD PRDTS: Potato & Corn Chips & Similar Prdts

Altona Co ............................. G ...... 815 232-7819
  Freeport  (G-10645)
Chipita America Inc ................... E ...... 708 731-2434
  Westchester  (G-21832)
Chips Aleeces Pita .................... G ...... 309 699-8859
  East Peoria  (G-8706)
Frito-Lay North America Inc ............ C ...... 217 532-5040
  Hillsboro  (G-11890)
Frito-Lay North America Inc ............ E ...... 618 997-2865
  Marion  (G-14260)
John B Sanfilippo & Son Inc ........... C ...... 847 289-1800
  Elgin  (G-9083)
Pepsico Inc ........................... G ...... 312 821-1000
  Chicago  (G-6105)

## PRODUCT SECTION

## FOOD PRDTS: Preparations

| Company | Code | Phone |
|---|---|---|
| Quality Snack Foods Inc | D | 708 377-7120 |
| Alsip (G-515) | | |
| R and B Distributors Inc | G | 815 433-6843 |
| Ottawa (G-16981) | | |
| Safe Fair Food Company LLC | F | 904 930-4277 |
| Chicago (G-6424) | | |
| Select Snacks Company Inc | D | 773 933-2167 |
| Chicago (G-6475) | | |
| Tee Lee Popcorn Inc | E | 815 864-2363 |
| Shannon (G-19903) | | |
| Wisconsin Wilderness Food Pdts | G | 847 735-8661 |
| Lake Bluff (G-12872) | | |

### FOOD PRDTS: Potato Chips & Other Potato-Based Snacks

| Company | Code | Phone |
|---|---|---|
| Frito-Lay North America Inc | E | 217 776-2320 |
| Sidney (G-19936) | | |
| Kitchen Cooked Inc | E | 309 245-2191 |
| Farmington (G-10187) | | |
| Kitchen Cooked Inc | E | 309 772-2798 |
| Bushnell (G-2903) | | |
| Mrs Fishers Inc | F | 815 964-9114 |
| Rockford (G-18511) | | |
| Ole Saltys of Rockford Inc | G | 815 637-2447 |
| Rockford (G-18525) | | |
| Ole Saltys of Rockford Inc | G | 815 637-2447 |
| Loves Park (G-13970) | | |
| Revolution Companies Inc | E | 800 826-4083 |
| Chicago (G-6341) | | |

### FOOD PRDTS: Potatoes, Dried

| Company | Code | Phone |
|---|---|---|
| Bran-Zan Holdings LLC | F | 847 342-0000 |
| Arlington Heights (G-728) | | |
| Noon Hour Food Products Inc | E | 312 382-1177 |
| Chicago (G-5924) | | |

### FOOD PRDTS: Potatoes, Dried, Packaged With Other Ingredients

| Company | Code | Phone |
|---|---|---|
| Marges Aunt Potato Salad | G | 708 612-2300 |
| Brookfield (G-2637) | | |

### FOOD PRDTS: Poultry Sausage, Lunch Meats/Other Poultry Prdts

| Company | Code | Phone |
|---|---|---|
| Nduja Artisans Co | G | 312 550-6991 |
| Chicago (G-5877) | | |

### FOOD PRDTS: Poultry, Processed, Frozen

| Company | Code | Phone |
|---|---|---|
| Midway Food LLC | G | 773 294-0730 |
| Chicago (G-5738) | | |

### FOOD PRDTS: Preparations

| Company | Code | Phone |
|---|---|---|
| Abelei Inc | F | 630 859-1410 |
| North Aurora (G-16117) | | |
| Agritech Worldwide Inc | F | 847 549-6002 |
| Mundelein (G-15466) | | |
| Altona Co | G | 815 232-7819 |
| Freeport (G-10645) | | |
| American Tristar Inc | E | 920 872-2181 |
| Saint Charles (G-19136) | | |
| American Tristar Inc | G | 630 262-5500 |
| Geneva (G-10809) | | |
| Archer-Daniels-Midland Company | E | 309 772-2141 |
| Bushnell (G-2897) | | |
| Arts Tamales | G | 309 367-2850 |
| Metamora (G-14739) | | |
| Athenian Foods Co | F | 708 343-6700 |
| Melrose Park (G-14596) | | |
| Avani Spices LLC | G | 847 532-1075 |
| Algonquin (G-379) | | |
| Barkaat Foods LLC | F | 773 376-8723 |
| Chicago (G-4042) | | |
| Bay Valley Foods LLC | E | 708 409-5300 |
| Oak Brook (G-16491) | | |
| Bear-Stewart Corporation | E | 773 276-0400 |
| Chicago (G-4065) | | |
| Bellisario Holdings LLC | G | 847 867-2960 |
| Park Ridge (G-17183) | | |
| Bernard Food Industries Inc | D | 847 869-5222 |
| Evanston (G-10015) | | |
| Canadian Harvest LP | F | 309 343-7808 |
| Galesburg (G-10740) | | |
| Canyon Foods Inc | G | 773 890-9888 |
| Chicago (G-4228) | | |
| Caravan Ingredients Inc | D | 708 849-8590 |
| Dolton (G-8368) | | |
| Chateau Food Products Inc | F | 708 863-4207 |
| Chicago (G-4296) | | |
| Christian Wolf Inc | G | 618 667-9522 |
| Bartelso (G-1314) | | |
| Cindys Pocket Kitchen | G | 815 388-8385 |
| Harvard (G-11627) | | |
| Clown Global Brands LLC | G | 847 564-5950 |
| Northbrook (G-16227) | | |
| Coki Foods LLC | G | 708 261-5758 |
| Elmhurst (G-9852) | | |
| Conagra Brands Inc | C | 312 549-5000 |
| Chicago (G-4444) | | |
| Conagra Brands Inc | C | 630 857-1000 |
| Naperville (G-15633) | | |
| Contract Packaging Plus Inc | G | 708 356-1100 |
| Bensenville (G-1865) | | |
| Culinary Co-Pack Incorporated | G | 847 451-1551 |
| Franklin Park (G-10448) | | |
| Custom Culinary Inc | D | 630 299-0500 |
| Oswego (G-16912) | | |
| Deja Investments Inc | G | 630 408-9222 |
| Bolingbrook (G-2301) | | |
| Delobian Foods | G | 773 564-0913 |
| Chicago (G-4578) | | |
| Dkb Industries LLC | F | 630 450-4151 |
| Naperville (G-15802) | | |
| E I Du Pont De Nemours & Co | D | 815 259-3311 |
| Thomson (G-20865) | | |
| El-Ranchero Food Products | E | 773 847-9167 |
| Chicago (G-4716) | | |
| Equi-Chem International Inc | F | 630 784-0432 |
| Carol Stream (G-3146) | | |
| Euphoria Catering and Events | G | 630 301-4369 |
| Aurora (G-1148) | | |
| Event Catering Group | G | 708 534-3100 |
| Chicago Heights (G-7096) | | |
| Far East Food Inc | G | 312 733-1688 |
| Chicago (G-4813) | | |
| Favorite Foods | G | 847 401-7126 |
| Northbrook (G-16256) | | |
| Fema L & L Food Services Inc | G | 217 835-2018 |
| Benld (G-1805) | | |
| Flaherty Incorporated | G | 773 472-8456 |
| Skokie (G-20000) | | |
| Food Service | D | 815 933-0725 |
| Kankakee (G-12617) | | |
| Fresh Express Incorporated | E | 630 736-3900 |
| Streamwood (G-20656) | | |
| Frito-Lay North America Inc | F | 815 468-3940 |
| Manteno (G-14184) | | |
| Frito-Lay North America Inc | C | 708 331-7200 |
| Oak Forest (G-16582) | | |
| Futuro Foods Inc | G | 773 418-2720 |
| Chicago (G-4898) | | |
| General Mills Inc | B | 630 231-1140 |
| Calumet City (G-2939) | | |
| Georgies Greek Tasty Food Inc | G | 773 987-1298 |
| Chicago (G-4946) | | |
| Gilster-Mary Lee Corporation | G | 618 272-3261 |
| Ridgway (G-17985) | | |
| Givaudan Flavors Corporation | C | 630 682-5600 |
| Carol Stream (G-3158) | | |
| Golden State Foods Corp | C | 618 537-6121 |
| Lebanon (G-13215) | | |
| Gonnella Baking Co | D | 312 733-2020 |
| Schaumburg (G-19539) | | |
| Grecian Delight Foods Inc | C | 847 364-1010 |
| Elk Grove Village (G-9511) | | |
| Gycor International Ltd | F | 630 754-8070 |
| Woodridge (G-22492) | | |
| H C Schau & Son Inc | C | 630 783-1000 |
| Woodridge (G-22493) | | |
| Herman Seekamp Inc | C | 630 628-6555 |
| Addison (G-145) | | |
| Hop Kee Incorporated | E | 312 791-9111 |
| Chicago (G-5109) | | |
| Ingredients Inc | G | 847 419-9595 |
| Buffalo Grove (G-2708) | | |
| Instantwhip-Chicago Inc | F | 773 235-5588 |
| Chicago (G-5206) | | |
| Italia Foods Inc | E | 847 397-4479 |
| Schaumburg (G-19585) | | |
| Ixtapa Foods | G | 773 788-9701 |
| Chicago (G-5249) | | |
| Jimmybars | G | 888 676-7971 |
| Chicago (G-5305) | | |
| John B Sanfilippo & Son Inc | C | 847 690-8432 |
| Elgin (G-9084) | | |
| Kanbo International (us) Inc | G | 630 873-6320 |
| Oakbrook Terrace (G-16713) | | |
| Kerry Holding Co | D | 309 747-3534 |
| Gridley (G-11408) | | |
| Kerry Inc | D | 309 747-3534 |
| Gridley (G-11409) | | |
| Kerry Inc | D | 708 450-3260 |
| Melrose Park (G-14666) | | |
| Kraft Food Ingredients Corp | D | 901 381-6500 |
| Glenview (G-11159) | | |
| Kraft Heinz Foods Company | B | 618 451-4820 |
| Granite City (G-11289) | | |
| Kraft Heinz Foods Company | C | 217 378-1900 |
| Champaign (G-3507) | | |
| Kruger North America Inc | F | 708 851-3670 |
| Oak Park (G-16673) | | |
| La Criolla Inc | E | 312 243-8882 |
| Chicago (G-5424) | | |
| Laredo Foods Inc | G | 773 762-1500 |
| Chicago (G-5461) | | |
| Lawrence Foods Inc | C | 847 437-2400 |
| Elk Grove Village (G-9588) | | |
| Lcv Company | G | 309 738-6452 |
| East Moline (G-8685) | | |
| Lee Gilster-Mary Corporation | D | 618 965-3426 |
| Steeleville (G-20561) | | |
| Liborio Baking Co Inc | G | 708 452-7222 |
| River Grove (G-18010) | | |
| Little Lady Foods Inc | G | 847 806-1440 |
| Elk Grove Village (G-9597) | | |
| Ludis Foods Adams Inc | G | 312 939-2877 |
| Chicago (G-5558) | | |
| Mangel and Co | F | 847 634-0730 |
| Long Grove (G-13894) | | |
| Mead Johnson & Company LLC | F | 847 832-2420 |
| Chicago (G-5670) | | |
| Mondelez Global LLC | E | 773 925-4300 |
| Chicago (G-5793) | | |
| Monterey Mushrooms Inc | G | 815 875-4436 |
| Princeton (G-17755) | | |
| Moon Guy Hong Food Inc | F | 773 927-3233 |
| Chicago (G-5801) | | |
| My Own Meals Inc | G | 773 378-6505 |
| Chicago (G-5841) | | |
| My Own Meals Inc | G | 847 948-1118 |
| Deerfield (G-8042) | | |
| Necta Sweet Inc | E | 847 215-9955 |
| Buffalo Grove (G-2742) | | |
| Neiman Bros Co Inc | F | 773 463-3000 |
| Chicago (G-5882) | | |
| Nestle Usa Inc | D | 847 808-5404 |
| Buffalo Grove (G-2747) | | |
| Nu-World Amaranth Inc | G | 630 369-6819 |
| Naperville (G-15717) | | |
| Nutrivo LLC | E | 630 270-1700 |
| Aurora (G-1196) | | |
| O Chilli Frozen Foods Inc | E | 847 562-1991 |
| Northbrook (G-16321) | | |
| On-Cor Frozen Foods LLC | E | 630 692-2283 |
| Aurora (G-1199) | | |
| Open Kitchens Inc | C | 312 666-5334 |
| Chicago (G-5994) | | |
| Open Kitchens Inc | E | 312 666-5334 |
| Chicago (G-5995) | | |
| OSI Group LLC | F | 630 851-6600 |
| Aurora (G-1201) | | |
| Pennant Foods | G | 708 752-8730 |
| Alsip (G-506) | | |
| PO Food Specialists Ltd | G | 847 517-8315 |
| Hoffman Estates (G-12040) | | |
| Pop Box LLC | F | 630 509-2281 |
| Chicago (G-6156) | | |
| Princess Foods Inc | F | 847 933-1820 |
| Skokie (G-20060) | | |
| Prinova Solutions LLC | E | 630 868-0359 |
| Carol Stream (G-3221) | | |
| Quaker Oats Company | A | 217 443-4995 |
| Danville (G-7761) | | |
| R J Van Drunen & Sons Inc | D | 815 472-3211 |
| Momence (G-14989) | | |
| Rawnature5 LLC | F | 312 800-3239 |
| Chicago (G-6296) | | |
| Revolution Brands LLC | G | 847 902-3320 |
| Huntley (G-12173) | | |
| Roma Bakeries Inc | F | 815 964-6737 |
| Rockford (G-18596) | | |
| Rt Wholesale | D | 847 678-3663 |
| Schiller Park (G-19869) | | |
| S&J Food Management Corp | G | 630 323-9296 |
| Hinsdale (G-11961) | | |
| Schau Southeast Sushi Inc | E | 630 783-1000 |
| Woodridge (G-22516) | | |

Employee Codes: A=Over 500 employees, B=251-500
C=101-250, D=51-100, E=20-50, F=10-19, G=3-9

## FOOD PRDTS: Preparations

Schulze and Burch Biscuit Co..............B........773 927-6622
 Chicago (G-6455)
Sdr Corp........................................G........773 638-1800
 Chicago (G-6463)
Seneca Foods Corporation...................E........309 545-2233
 Manito (G-14176)
Sims Family Holdings LLC.................D........847 488-1230
 Elgin (G-9183)
Snak-King Corp...............................C........815 232-6700
 Freeport (G-10689)
Sotiros Foods Inc............................G........708 371-0002
 Alsip (G-529)
Stepan Specialty Products LLC............G........847 446-7500
 Northfield (G-16420)
Sweetener Supply Corporation..............G........708 484-3455
 Berwyn (G-2075)
Tara International LP.......................G........708 354-7050
 Hodgkins (G-11984)
Teresa Foods Inc.............................F........708 258-6200
 Peotone (G-17493)
Thomas Proestler.............................G........630 971-0185
 Lisle (G-13671)
Today Gourmet Foods III LLC...............G........847 401-9192
 Carol Stream (G-3256)
United Food Ingredients Inc................G........630 655-9494
 Burr Ridge (G-2891)
Wah King Noodle Co Inc....................G........773 684-8000
 Chicago (G-6933)
Whitney Foods Inc...........................F........773 842-8511
 Chicago (G-6976)
Wisconsin Wilderness Food Pdts...........G........847 735-8661
 Lake Bluff (G-12872)
Xena International Inc......................G........630 587-2734
 Saint Charles (G-19301)
Zaibak Bros...................................F........312 564-5800
 Chicago (G-7058)

## FOOD PRDTS: Prepared Meat Sauces Exc Tomato & Dry

Andrias Food Group Inc....................G........618 632-3118
 O Fallon (G-16462)
Andrias Food Group Inc....................E........618 632-4866
 O Fallon (G-16461)

## FOOD PRDTS: Prepared Sauces, Exc Tomato Based

Fgfi LLC.......................................E........708 598-0909
 Countryside (G-7424)
Foods & Things Inc..........................G........618 526-4478
 Breese (G-2444)

## FOOD PRDTS: Prepared Vegetable Sauces Exc Tomato & Dry

Simply Salsa LLC.............................G........815 514-3993
 Homer Glen (G-12087)

## FOOD PRDTS: Raw cane sugar

Westway Feed Products LLC................F........309 654-2211
 Cordova (G-7380)

## FOOD PRDTS: Rice, Milled

International Golden Foods Inc............F........630 860-5552
 Bensenville (G-1921)

## FOOD PRDTS: Rice, Packaged & Seasoned

Golden Hill Ingredients LLC................G........773 406-3409
 Chicago (G-4974)
Quaker Oats Company......................A........312 821-1000
 Chicago (G-6242)

## FOOD PRDTS: Salad Oils, Refined Vegetable, Exc Corn

Ventura Foods LLC..........................E........708 877-5150
 Thornton (G-20876)

## FOOD PRDTS: Salads

Dean Food Products Company.............E........847 678-1680
 Franklin Park (G-10455)

## FOOD PRDTS: Sandwiches

Calma Optima Foods.........................G........847 962-8329
 Franklin Park (G-10423)

Chicago Oriental Cnstr Inc..................G........312 733-9633
 Chicago (G-4337)

## FOOD PRDTS: Seasonings & Spices

Aakash Spices & Produce Inc..............F........773 916-4100
 Chicago (G-3703)
Dell Cove Spice Co...........................G........312 339-8389
 Chicago (G-4577)
El Tradicional.................................G........773 925-0335
 Chicago (G-4712)
Famar Flavor LLC.............................E........708 926-2951
 Crestwood (G-7487)
Granadino Food Services Corp.............F........708 717-2930
 Lombard (G-13805)
Hensaal Management Group Inc..........G........312 624-8133
 Chicago (G-5074)
John Morrell & Co............................C........630 993-8763
 Bolingbrook (G-2329)
Nanas Kitchen Inc............................G........815 363-8500
 Johnsburg (G-12439)
R J Van Drunen & Sons Inc................D........815 472-3100
 Momence (G-14987)
R J Van Drunen & Sons Inc................E........830 422-2167
 Momence (G-14988)
Sentry Seasonings Inc......................E........630 530-5370
 Elmhurst (G-9938)

## FOOD PRDTS: Shortening & Solid Edible Fats

Mahoney Environmental Inc................E........815 730-2087
 Joliet (G-12535)

## FOOD PRDTS: Soup Mixes

Custom Culinary Inc.........................D........630 928-4898
 Lombard (G-13787)
K M J Enterprises Inc.......................E........847 688-1200
 Gurnee (G-11465)
TEC Foods Inc................................E........800 315-8002
 Chicago (G-6683)

## FOOD PRDTS: Soup Mixes, Dried

Turtle Island Inc..............................F........815 759-9000
 Johnsburg (G-12443)
Vanee Foods Company......................D........708 449-7300
 Berkeley (G-2050)

## FOOD PRDTS: Soybean Oil, Deodorized

Clarkson Soy Products LLC................G........217 763-9511
 Cerro Gordo (G-3439)

## FOOD PRDTS: Soybean Powder

Devansoy Inc..................................G........712 792-9665
 Rock City (G-18125)

## FOOD PRDTS: Soybean Protein Concentrates & Isolates

Bunge North America Foundation..........C........217 784-8261
 Gibson City (G-10898)

## FOOD PRDTS: Spices, Including Ground

Arlington Specialties Inc...................G........847 545-9500
 Elk Grove Village (G-9313)
Josephs Food Products Co Inc............C........708 338-4090
 Broadview (G-2589)
USspice Mill Inc..............................F........773 378-6800
 Chicago (G-6859)

## FOOD PRDTS: Starch, Indl

PPG Architectural Finishes Inc............D........773 523-6333
 Chicago (G-6161)

## FOOD PRDTS: Starches

Ktm Industries Inc...........................G........217 224-5861
 Quincy (G-17850)

## FOOD PRDTS: Sugar

Bn Delfi USA Inc..............................G........847 280-0447
 Elgin (G-8968)
Combined Technologies Inc................G........847 968-4855
 Libertyville (G-13317)
Domino Foods Inc............................F........773 646-2203
 Chicago (G-4625)

Zuchem Inc....................................G........312 997-2150
 Chicago (G-7075)

## FOOD PRDTS: Sugar Syrup From Sugar Beets

Jo Snow Inc...................................G........773 732-3045
 Chicago (G-5308)

## FOOD PRDTS: Sugar, Beet

Inter-Trade Global LLC......................G........618 954-6119
 Belleville (G-1637)
Lee Gilster-Mary Corporation..............B........618 965-3449
 Steeleville (G-20562)
Merisant Us Inc...............................C........815 929-2700
 Manteno (G-14188)
Sweet Specialty Solutions LLC............E........630 739-9151
 Lemont (G-13265)

## FOOD PRDTS: Sugar, Cane

Domino Foods Inc............................E........773 254-8282
 Chicago (G-4624)
Lee Gilster-Mary Corporation..............B........618 965-3449
 Steeleville (G-20562)
Necta Sweet Inc..............................E........847 215-9955
 Buffalo Grove (G-2742)
Pullman Sugar LLC..........................E........773 260-9180
 Chicago (G-6225)

## FOOD PRDTS: Sugar, Granulated Cane, Purchd Raw Sugar/Syrup

Inter-Trade Global LLC......................G........618 954-6119
 Belleville (G-1637)

## FOOD PRDTS: Sugar, Ground

Sugar Factory Rosemont LLC..............F........847 349-9161
 Rosemont (G-19034)

## FOOD PRDTS: Sugar, Liquid Cane Prdts, Exc Refined

Nablus Sweets Inc............................E........708 205-6534
 Chicago (G-5847)

## FOOD PRDTS: Sugar, Maple, Indl

Hogback Haven Maple Farm................G........815 291-9440
 Orangeville (G-16815)

## FOOD PRDTS: Syrup, Pancake, Blended & Mixed

Gust-John Foods & Pdts Corp.............G........630 879-8700
 Batavia (G-1453)

## FOOD PRDTS: Syrups

Margies Brands Inc..........................E........773 643-1417
 Chicago (G-5615)
Mary Lee Packaging Corporation.........E........618 826-2361
 Chester (G-3659)

## FOOD PRDTS: Tea

Damron Corporation.........................E........773 265-2724
 Chicago (G-4549)
Insight Beverages Inc.......................F........847 438-1598
 Lake Zurich (G-13090)
Sparrow Coffee Roastery...................G........321 648-6415
 Westchester (G-21855)
Stewarts Prvate Blend Fods Inc...........E........773 489-2500
 Carol Stream (G-3250)

## FOOD PRDTS: Tortilla Chips

Azteca Foods Inc.............................C........708 563-6600
 Chicago (G-4012)
Donkey Brands LLC..........................F........630 251-2007
 Carol Stream (G-3144)
El-Ranchero Food Products................F........773 843-0430
 Chicago (G-4715)
El-Ranchero Food Products................E........773 847-9167
 Chicago (G-4716)
Masa Uno Inc..................................G........708 749-4866
 Berwyn (G-2068)
McCleary Inc...................................C........815 389-3053
 South Beloit (G-20160)

# PRODUCT SECTION

## FOOD PRDTS: Tortillas

- Azteca Foods Inc .......................... C ..... 708 563-6600
  Chicago *(G-4012)*
- Castro Foods Wholesale Inc ........ E ..... 773 869-0641
  Chicago *(G-4253)*
- El Popocatapetl Industries Inc .... E ..... 312 421-6143
  Chicago *(G-4710)*
- El-Milagro Inc ............................... B ..... 773 579-6120
  Chicago *(G-4713)*
- El-Milagro Inc ............................... C ..... 773 650-1614
  Chicago *(G-4714)*
- La Mexicana Tortilleria Inc .......... E ..... 773 247-5443
  Chicago *(G-5425)*
- Los Gamas Inc .............................. G ..... 872 829-3514
  Chicago *(G-5543)*
- Munoz Flour Tortilleria Inc .......... F ..... 773 523-1837
  Chicago *(G-5833)*
- Sabinas Food Products Inc .......... E ..... 312 738-2412
  Chicago *(G-6423)*
- Sunny Day Distributing Inc .......... G ..... 630 779-8466
  Cortland *(G-7395)*
- Tortilleria Laf Marias LLC ............ G ..... 224 399-9902
  Waukegan *(G-21631)*

## FOOD PRDTS: Turkey, Processed, NEC

- Gift Check Program 2013 Inc ...... G ..... 630 986-5081
  Downers Grove *(G-8450)*

## FOOD PRDTS: Variety Meats, Poultry

- Handcut Foods LLC ...................... D ..... 312 239-0381
  Chicago *(G-5040)*

## FOOD PRDTS: Vegetable Oil Mills, NEC

- Abitec Corporation ....................... E ..... 217 465-8577
  Paris *(G-17139)*
- Bio Fuels By American Farmers .. F ..... 561 859-6251
  Benton *(G-2023)*
- Bunge Oils Inc .............................. E ..... 815 523-8129
  Bradley *(G-2414)*
- Dawn Food Products Inc ............. C ..... 815 933-0600
  Bradley *(G-2419)*
- Syngenta Seeds Inc .................... F ..... 217 253-5646
  Tuscola *(G-21024)*

## FOOD PRDTS: Vegetable Oil, Refined, Exc Corn

- Archer-Daniels-Midland Company ..... D ..... 217 224-1875
  Quincy *(G-17796)*

## FOOD PRDTS: Vegetable Shortenings, Exc Corn Oil

- Olive Oil Store Inc ....................... G ..... 630 262-0210
  Geneva *(G-10856)*

## FOOD PRDTS: Vegetables, Dehydrated Or Dried

- Griffith Laboratories USA Inc ..... E ..... 773 523-7509
  Chicago *(G-5004)*
- R J Van Drunen & Sons Inc ........ D ..... 815 472-3100
  Momence *(G-14987)*
- R J Van Drunen & Sons Inc ........ E ..... 830 422-2167
  Momence *(G-14988)*

## FOOD PRDTS: Vegetables, Dried or Dehydrated Exc Freeze-Dried

- Sono Italiano Corporation ........... G ..... 817 472-8903
  Manteno *(G-14193)*

## FOOD PRDTS: Vinegar

- Consumer Vinegar and Spice ..... G ..... 708 354-1144
  La Grange *(G-12730)*
- Fleischmanns Vinegar Co Inc ..... F ..... 773 523-2817
  Chicago *(G-4856)*
- Mizkan America Inc ..................... E ..... 847 590-0059
  Mount Prospect *(G-15347)*
- Mizkan America Holdings Inc ..... G ..... 847 590-0059
  Mount Prospect *(G-15348)*
- National Vinegar Co ..................... F ..... 618 395-1011
  Olney *(G-16785)*
- Pastorelli Food Products Inc ...... G ..... 312 455-1006
  Chicago *(G-6089)*

## FOOD PRDTS: Wheat Flour

- Archer-Daniels-Midland Company ..... G ..... 217 424-5236
  Decatur *(G-7834)*
- Archer-Daniels-Midland Company ..... A ..... 312 634-8100
  Chicago *(G-3941)*
- Archer-Daniels-Midland Company ..... E ..... 217 424-5413
  Decatur *(G-7835)*
- Mennel Milling Co ........................ F ..... 217 999-2161
  Mount Olive *(G-15305)*
- Roquette America Inc ................. G ..... 630 232-2157
  Geneva *(G-10864)*

## FOOD PRDTS: Wheat gluten

- Enjoy Life Natural Brands LLC .. E ..... 773 632-2163
  Chicago *(G-4756)*

## FOOD PRDTS: Yeast

- American Yeast Corp Tennessee .. G ..... 630 932-1290
  Addison *(G-38)*
- Sensient Technologies Corp ....... E ..... 708 481-0910
  Matteson *(G-14378)*

## FOOD PRODUCTS MACHINERY

- American Extrusion Intl Corp ..... E ..... 815 624-6616
  South Beloit *(G-20138)*
- American Metal Installers & FA .. G ..... 630 993-0812
  Villa Park *(G-21236)*
- APV Consolidated Inc .................. F ..... 847 678-4300
  Schiller Park *(G-19804)*
- Beacon Inc ..................................... F ..... 708 544-9900
  Alsip *(G-440)*
- Cartpac Inc .................................... E ..... 630 283-8979
  Carol Stream *(G-3125)*
- Cobatco Inc ................................... F ..... 309 676-2663
  Peoria *(G-17344)*
- Colborne Acquisition Co LLC ...... E ..... 847 371-0101
  Lake Forest *(G-12893)*
- Comtec Industries Ltd ................. G ..... 630 759-9000
  Woodridge *(G-22465)*
- Cornelius Inc ................................. B ..... 630 539-6850
  Glendale Heights *(G-11018)*
- Corrigan Corporation America ... F ..... 800 462-6478
  Gurnee *(G-11435)*
- Crm North America LLC ............. G ..... 708 603-3475
  Franklin Park *(G-10446)*
- Cvp Systems Inc .......................... D ..... 630 852-1190
  Downers Grove *(G-8422)*
- D W Ram Manufacturing Co ....... E ..... 708 633-7900
  Tinley Park *(G-20908)*
- Dontech Industries Inc ............... F ..... 847 428-8222
  Gilberts *(G-10917)*
- Dover Prtg Identification Inc ...... D ..... 630 541-1540
  Downers Grove *(G-8434)*
- Eirich Machines Inc ..................... F ..... 847 336-2444
  Gurnee *(G-11446)*
- F & S Engraving Inc .................... E ..... 847 870-8400
  Mount Prospect *(G-15328)*
- Felste Co Inc ................................. G ..... 217 283-4884
  Hoopeston *(G-12111)*
- Formax Inc ..................................... E ..... 708 479-3000
  Mokena *(G-14862)*
- G K Enterprises Inc ..................... G ..... 708 587-2150
  Monee *(G-14996)*
- Galena Garlic Co .......................... G ..... 331 248-0342
  Geneva *(G-10829)*
- Great Lakes Service Chicago ..... G ..... 630 627-4022
  Lombard *(G-13806)*
- Gsi Group LLC .............................. D ..... 618 283-9792
  Vandalia *(G-21115)*
- Heat and Control Inc ................... D ..... 309 342-5518
  Galesburg *(G-10758)*
- Hot Food Boxes Inc ..................... E ..... 773 533-5912
  Chicago *(G-5117)*
- Institutional Equipment Inc ........ E ..... 630 771-0990
  Bolingbrook *(G-2321)*
- John Bean Technologies Corp ... E ..... 312 861-5900
  Chicago *(G-5310)*
- Keating of Chicago Inc ............... F ..... 815 569-2324
  Capron *(G-2996)*
- Lee Industries Inc ........................ C ..... 847 462-1865
  Elk Grove Village *(G-9590)*
- Mc Brady Engineering Inc .......... F ..... 815 744-8900
  Rockdale *(G-18226)*
- Mc Cleary Equipment Inc ............ G ..... 815 389-3053
  South Beloit *(G-20159)*
- Middleby Corporation .................. E ..... 847 741-3300
  Elgin *(G-9110)*
- Middleby Corporation .................. E ..... 847 741-3300
  Elgin *(G-9111)*
- Middleby Worldwide Inc .............. G ..... 847 741-3300
  Elgin *(G-9112)*
- Modern Food Concepts Inc ........ G ..... 815 534-5747
  Frankfort *(G-10344)*
- Mww Food Processing USA LLC .. G ..... 800 582-1574
  Chicago *(G-5838)*
- Optimal Automatics Co ................ G ..... 847 439-9110
  Elk Grove Village *(G-9667)*
- Packers Supplies & Eqp LLC ..... G ..... 630 543-5810
  Addison *(G-236)*
- Prater Industries Inc ................... D ..... 630 679-3200
  Bolingbrook *(G-2359)*
- Pre Pack Machinery Inc .............. G ..... 217 352-1010
  Champaign *(G-3528)*
- Q-Matic Technologies Inc ........... G ..... 847 263-7324
  Carol Stream *(G-3224)*
- Rockdale Controls Co Inc ........... F ..... 815 436-6181
  Plainfield *(G-17646)*
- S G Acquisition Inc ...................... F ..... 815 624-6501
  South Beloit *(G-20168)*
- Sojuz Ent ....................................... G ..... 847 215-9400
  Bensenville *(G-1994)*
- Solo Cup Operating Corporation .. D ..... 847 444-5000
  Lincolnshire *(G-13482)*
- Speco Inc ....................................... E ..... 847 678-4240
  Schiller Park *(G-19876)*
- Stanford Bettendorf Inc .............. D ..... 618 548-3555
  Salem *(G-19353)*
- Terrace Holding Company .......... A ..... 708 652-5600
  Cicero *(G-7238)*
- Towne Machine Tool Company .. F ..... 217 442-4910
  Danville *(G-7777)*
- Vilutis and Co Inc ......................... E ..... 815 469-2116
  Frankfort *(G-10374)*
- Vision Machine & Fabrication .... G ..... 618 965-3199
  Steeleville *(G-20564)*
- Wag Industries Inc ...................... F ..... 847 329-8932
  Skokie *(G-20109)*
- Wemco Inc ..................................... F ..... 708 388-1980
  Alsip *(G-543)*
- World Cup Packaging Inc ........... G ..... 815 624-6501
  South Beloit *(G-20178)*

## FOOD STORES: Delicatessen

- Andys Deli and Mikolajczyk ....... E ..... 773 722-1000
  Chicago *(G-3905)*
- Vienna Beef Ltd ............................ E ..... 773 278-7800
  Chicago *(G-6896)*

## FOOD STORES: Grocery, Chain

- Niemann Foods Foundation ........ C ..... 217 222-0190
  Quincy *(G-17862)*
- Treasure Island Foods Inc .......... D ..... 312 642-1105
  Chicago *(G-6765)*

## FOOD STORES: Grocery, Independent

- AM Ko Oriental Foods .................. G ..... 217 398-2922
  Champaign *(G-3446)*
- Charleston County Market ......... D ..... 217 345-7031
  Charleston *(G-3593)*
- George Nottoli & Sons Inc .......... G ..... 773 589-1010
  Chicago *(G-4944)*
- Koenemann Sausage Co ............. G ..... 815 385-6260
  Volo *(G-21316)*
- Olive Oil Marketplace Inc ............ G ..... 618 304-3769
  Alton *(G-586)*
- Treasure Island Foods Inc .......... D ..... 312 440-1144
  Chicago *(G-6763)*

## FOOD STORES: Supermarkets

- Cub Foods Inc ............................... C ..... 309 689-0140
  Peoria *(G-17347)*
- Niemann Foods Foundation ........ C ..... 217 793-4091
  Springfield *(G-20487)*

## FOOD STORES: Supermarkets, Chain

- Dominicks Finer Foods Inc ........ D ..... 630 584-1750
  Saint Charles *(G-19173)*
- Jewel Osco Inc ............................. C ..... 630 948-6000
  Itasca *(G-12291)*
- Jewel Osco Inc ............................. C ..... 630 355-2172
  Naperville *(G-15681)*
- Jewel Osco Inc ............................. D ..... 630 226-1892
  Bolingbrook *(G-2328)*
- Jewel Osco Inc ............................. C ..... 773 728-7730
  Chicago *(G-5299)*

## FOOD STORES: Supermarkets, Chain

Jewel Osco Inc .................................... C ...... 773 784-1922
  Chicago (G-5300)
Jewel Osco Inc .................................... C ...... 847 677-3331
  Skokie (G-20019)
Jewel Osco Inc .................................... C ...... 708 352-0120
  Countryside (G-7435)
Jewel Osco Inc .................................... C ...... 630 584-4594
  Saint Charles (G-19202)
Jewel Osco Inc .................................... D ...... 630 859-1212
  Aurora (G-1177)
Jewel Osco Inc .................................... C ...... 815 464-5352
  Frankfort (G-10336)
Jewel Osco Inc .................................... C ...... 847 428-3547
  West Dundee (G-21798)
Jewel Osco Inc .................................... C ...... 847 854-2692
  Algonquin (G-395)
Jewel-Osco Inc .................................... C ...... 847 296-7786
  Des Plaines (G-8216)
Kroger Co .......................................... C ...... 309 694-6298
  East Peoria (G-8722)
Schnuck Markets Inc ........................... C ...... 618 466-0825
  Godfrey (G-11237)

### FOOD WARMING EQPT: Commercial

Carter Hoffmann LLC ......................... C ...... 847 362-5500
  Mundelein (G-15484)

### FOOTWEAR, WHOLESALE: Shoe Access

Marietta Corporation ............................ C ...... 773 816-5137
  Chicago (G-5619)

### FOOTWEAR, WHOLESALE: Shoes

A&B Apparel ....................................... G ...... 815 962-5070
  Rockford (G-18241)
Angelo Bruni ....................................... G ...... 773 754-5422
  Aurora (G-957)
Leos Dancewear Inc ........................... D ...... 773 889-7700
  River Forest (G-17998)
Mennon Rubber & Safety Pdts ............ G ...... 847 678-8250
  Schiller Park (G-19849)

### FOOTWEAR: Cut Stock

Zoes Mfgco LLC ................................. F ...... 312 666-4018
  Chicago (G-7071)

### FORGINGS

Adrian Orgas Gheorghe ...................... G ...... 773 355-1200
  Palatine (G-16997)
Allied Gear Co .................................... G ...... 773 287-8742
  Chicago (G-3815)
Anderson Shumaker Company ............ E ...... 773 287-0874
  Chicago (G-3902)
Andrew McDonald ............................... G ...... 618 867-2323
  De Soto (G-7818)
Arrow Gear Company .......................... C ...... 630 969-7640
  Downers Grove (G-8389)
C & F Forge Company ........................ G ...... 847 455-6609
  Franklin Park (G-10420)
Carmona Gear Cutting ........................ G ...... 815 963-8236
  Rockford (G-18298)
Chicago Hardware and Fix Co ............ D ...... 847 455-6609
  Franklin Park (G-10429)
Cleveland Hdwr & Forging Co ............ D ...... 630 896-9850
  Aurora (G-1132)
Cornell Forge Company ...................... D ...... 708 458-1582
  Chicago (G-4470)
Dekalb Forge Company ...................... D ...... 815 756-3538
  Dekalb (G-8087)
E M Glabus Co Inc ............................. F ...... 630 766-3027
  Bensenville (G-1887)
Forge Resources Group LLC .............. G ...... 815 758-6400
  Dekalb (G-8093)
Forgings & Stampings Inc .................. E ...... 815 962-5597
  Rockford (G-18390)
Gear & Repair ..................................... G ...... 708 387-0144
  Brookfield (G-2634)
Gears Gears Gears Inc ....................... G ...... 708 366-6555
  Harwood Heights (G-11685)
General Forging Die Co Inc ................ E ...... 815 874-4224
  Rockford (G-18397)
Great Lakes Forge Company .............. G ...... 773 277-2800
  Chicago (G-4997)
Group Industries Inc ........................... E ...... 708 877-6200
  Thornton (G-20871)
Hadley Gear Manufacturing Co ........... F ...... 773 722-1030
  Chicago (G-5028)
HM Manufacturing Inc ........................ F ...... 847 487-8700
  Wauconda (G-21469)
Hurst Enterprises Inc ......................... G ...... 708 344-9291
  Glendale Heights (G-11032)
I Forge Company LLC ....................... ...... 815 535-0600
  Rock Falls (G-18137)
Jernberg Industries LLC .................... C ...... 773 268-3004
  Chicago (G-5294)
Jernberg Industries LLC .................... C ...... 630 972-7000
  Bolingbrook (G-2327)
Kautzmann Machine Works Inc .......... G ...... 847 455-9105
  Franklin Park (G-10511)
Kd Steel Inc ....................................... G ...... 630 201-1619
  Westmont (G-21897)
Kdk Upset Forging Co ....................... E ...... 708 388-8770
  Blue Island (G-2259)
Keller Group Inc ................................. B ...... 847 446-7550
  Northfield (G-16405)
Lawndale Forging & Tool Works ......... G ...... 773 277-2800
  Chicago (G-5471)
Lehigh Consumer Products LLC ........ C ...... 630 851-7330
  Aurora (G-1045)
Machine Tool Acc & Mfg Co ............... G ...... 773 489-0903
  Chicago (G-5592)
Master Guard Security Co .................. G ...... 618 398-7749
  East Saint Louis (G-8760)
Metform LLC ...................................... C ...... 815 273-2201
  Savanna (G-19400)
Metform LLC ...................................... G ...... 847 566-0010
  Mundelein (G-15531)
Metform LLC ...................................... E ...... 815 273-0230
  Savanna (G-19401)
Modern Gear & Machine Inc .............. F ...... 630 350-9173
  Bensenville (G-1953)
Moline Forge Inc ................................ D ...... 309 762-5506
  Moline (G-14960)
Moore-Addison Co ............................. E ...... 630 543-6744
  Addison (G-220)
Norforge and Machining Inc ............... D ...... 309 772-3124
  Bushnell (G-2907)
Park-Hio Frged McHned Pdts LLC ..... D ...... 708 652-6691
  Chicago (G-6084)
Phoenix Trading Chicago Inc ............. G ...... 847 304-5181
  Lake Barrington (G-12822)
Productigear Inc ................................. E ...... 773 847-4505
  Chicago (G-6205)
Products In Motion Inc ....................... G ...... 815 213-7251
  Rock Falls (G-18146)
Rail Exchange Inc ............................. E ...... 708 757-3317
  Chicago Heights (G-7119)
Rj Link International Inc ..................... G ...... 815 874-8110
  Rockford (G-18559)
Rockford Drop Forge Company ......... D ...... 815 963-9611
  Rockford (G-18572)
Rockford Jobbing Service Inc ............ G ...... 815 398-8661
  Rockford (G-18576)
RT Blackhawk Mch Pdts Inc .............. G ...... 815 389-3632
  South Beloit (G-20167)
Sbic America Inc ............................... G ...... 847 303-5430
  Schaumburg (G-19719)
Schmid Tool & Engineering Corp ....... E ...... 630 333-1733
  Villa Park (G-21283)
Scot Forge Company ......................... D ...... 847 678-6000
  Franklin Park (G-10584)
Stanley Hartco Co ............................. E ...... 847 967-1122
  Skokie (G-20090)
Star Forge Inc ................................... D ...... 815 235-7750
  Freeport (G-10691)
Stock Gears Inc ................................. F ...... 224 653-9489
  Elk Grove Village (G-9758)
Sumitomo Machinery Corp Amer ....... E ...... 630 752-0200
  Glendale Heights (G-11078)
Thyssenkrupp Crankshaft Co LLC ..... C ...... 217 444-5400
  Danville (G-7772)
Thyssenkrupp Crankshaft Co LLC ..... C ...... 217 444-5500
  Danville (G-7773)
Tomek Iron Originals ......................... G ...... 773 788-1750
  Chicago (G-6738)
Tomko Machine Works Inc ................ G ...... 630 244-0902
  Lemont (G-13266)
US Tsubaki Power Transm LLC ........ C ...... 847 459-9500
  Wheeling (G-22173)
Welch Steel Products Inc ................. F ...... 847 741-2623
  Elgin (G-9234)
Wozniak Industries Inc ..................... C ...... 708 458-1220
  Bedford Park (G-1595)
Wozniak Industries Inc ..................... G ...... 630 954-3400
  Oakbrook Terrace (G-16723)

### FORGINGS: Aircraft, Ferrous

Scot Forge Company ......................... B ...... 815 675-1000
  Spring Grove (G-20364)

### FORGINGS: Anchors

Simpson Strong-Tie Company Inc ...... E ...... 630 613-5100
  Addison (G-293)

### FORGINGS: Armor Plate, Iron Or Steel

Malca-Amit North America Inc ........... G ...... 312 346-1507
  Chicago (G-5606)
Prime Stainless Products LLC ........... G ...... 847 678-0800
  Schiller Park (G-19863)

### FORGINGS: Automotive & Internal Combustion Engine

Kishwaukee Forge Company .............. E ...... 815 758-4451
  Cortland (G-7391)
Thyssenkrupp Crankshaft Co LLC ..... C ...... 217 431-0060
  Danville (G-7770)

### FORGINGS: Bearing & Bearing Race, Nonferrous

Standard Precision Grinding Co ........ F ...... 708 474-1211
  Lansing (G-13185)
Voss Engineering Inc ........................ E ...... 847 673-8900
  Lincolnwood (G-13542)

### FORGINGS: Construction Or Mining Eqpt, Ferrous

Caterpillar Inc ................................... G ...... 815 729-5511
  Rockdale (G-18216)
Caterpillar Inc ................................... G ...... 309 675-4408
  Peoria (G-17329)
Chicago Clamp Company .................. G ...... 708 343-8311
  Broadview (G-2567)
Dayton Superior Corporation ............. C ...... 815 936-3300
  Kankakee (G-12609)
Velocity International Inc ................... G ...... 773 570-6441
  Lake Forest (G-12979)

### FORGINGS: Engine Or Turbine, Nonferrous

Burgess-Norton Mfg Co Inc ............... E ...... 630 232-4100
  Geneva (G-10814)
Genacc LLC ..................................... G ...... 309 253-9034
  Peoria (G-17370)

### FORGINGS: Gear & Chain

Eagle Gear & Manufacturing Co ........ F ...... 630 628-6100
  Addison (G-106)
Emco Gears Inc ................................ E ...... 847 220-4327
  Elk Grove Village (G-9454)
Engelhardt Enterprises Inc ................ G ...... 847 277-7070
  Inverness (G-12208)
Gear Products & Mfg Inc .................. G ...... 708 344-0875
  Bridgeview (G-2493)
Innovative Rack & Gear Company ..... F ...... 630 766-2652
  Wood Dale (G-22382)
Loch Precision Technologies ............ G ...... 847 438-1400
  Lake Zurich (G-13096)

### FORGINGS: Iron & Steel

Advantage Tool and Mold Inc ........... G ...... 847 301-9020
  Elk Grove Village (G-9280)
C & F Forge Company ...................... G ...... 847 455-6609
  Franklin Park (G-10420)

### FORGINGS: Machinery, Ferrous

Mitsutoyo-Kiko USA Inc .................... G ...... 847 981-5200
  Rolling Meadows (G-18745)

### FORGINGS: Nonferrous

Acme Screw Co ................................ F ...... 815 332-7548
  Cherry Valley (G-3637)
Anchor-Harvey Components LLC ...... D ...... 815 233-3833
  Freeport (G-10646)
Anderson Shumaker Company .......... E ...... 773 287-0874
  Chicago (G-3902)
Boler Ventures LLC .......................... G ...... 630 773-9111
  Itasca (G-12237)
Jernberg Industries LLC ................... C ...... 773 268-3004
  Chicago (G-5294)
Midwest Brass Forging Co ................ E ...... 847 678-7023
  Franklin Park (G-10532)

## PRODUCT SECTION

### FORGINGS: Nuclear Power Plant, Ferrous

Exelon Corporation................................A ...... 815 357-6761
  Marseilles *(G-14308)*

### FORMS: Concrete, Sheet Metal

3 D Concrete Design Inc......................G ...... 847 297-7968
  Des Plaines *(G-8136)*
Carroll Distrg & Cnstr Sup Inc.............G ...... 815 464-0100
  Frankfort *(G-10308)*
Carroll Distrg & Cnstr Sup Inc.............G ...... 630 892-4855
  Aurora *(G-1125)*
Carroll Distrg & Cnstr Sup Inc.............G ...... 630 243-0272
  Lemont *(G-13229)*
Carroll Distrg & Cnstr Sup Inc.............G ...... 815 941-1548
  Morris *(G-15100)*
Carroll Distrg & Cnstr Sup Inc.............G ...... 309 449-6044
  Hopedale *(G-12121)*
Carroll Distrg & Cnstr Sup Inc.............G ...... 217 223-8126
  Quincy *(G-17810)*
Carroll Distrg & Cnstr Sup Inc.............F ...... 630 369-6520
  Naperville *(G-15619)*
CCS Contractor Eqp & Sup Inc............E ...... 630 393-9020
  Naperville *(G-15622)*
Dayton Superior Corporation...............A ...... 847 391-4700
  Elk Grove Village *(G-9418)*
Dee Concrete Accessories....................F ...... 708 452-0250
  Norridge *(G-16099)*
Forming America Ltd............................E ...... 888 993-1304
  West Chicago *(G-21706)*
Gerdau Ameristeel US Inc....................E ...... 815 547-0400
  Belvidere *(G-1757)*
Luebbers Welding & Mfg Inc................F ...... 618 594-2489
  Carlyle *(G-3056)*
Starmont Manufacturing Co..................G ...... 815 939-1041
  Kankakee *(G-12653)*

### FOUNDRIES: Aluminum

Able Die Casting Corporation..............D ...... 847 678-1991
  Schiller Park *(G-19797)*
Acme Die Casting LLC..........................G ...... 847 272-9520
  Northbrook *(G-16197)*
Altman & Koehler Foundry....................G ...... 773 373-7737
  Chicago *(G-3838)*
Altman Pattern and Foundry Co............F ...... 773 586-9100
  Chicago *(G-3839)*
Alu-Bra Foundry Inc..............................D ...... 630 766-3112
  Bensenville *(G-1829)*
Amcast Inc............................................F ...... 630 766-7450
  Bensenville *(G-1831)*
AMS LLC...............................................G ...... 773 904-7740
  Chicago *(G-3895)*
Anderson Casting Company Inc............G ...... 312 733-1185
  Chicago *(G-3901)*
Arrow Aluminum Castings Inc..............G ...... 815 338-4480
  Woodstock *(G-22542)*
Becks Light Gauge Aluminum Co.........F ...... 847 290-9990
  Elk Grove Village *(G-9337)*
Cast Technologies Inc..........................C ...... 309 676-1715
  Peoria *(G-17323)*
Chicago Alum Castings Co Inc.............G ...... 773 762-3009
  Chicago *(G-4301)*
Curto-Ligonier Foundries Co.................E ...... 708 345-2250
  Melrose Park *(G-14613)*
D R Sperry & Co...................................D ...... 630 892-4361
  Aurora *(G-1137)*
Du Page Precision Products Co............D ...... 630 849-2940
  Aurora *(G-998)*
Dynacast Inc.........................................C ...... 847 608-2200
  Elgin *(G-9015)*
Illini Foundry Co Inc.............................G ...... 309 697-3142
  Peoria *(G-17385)*
Jsp Mold...............................................G ...... 815 225-7110
  Milledgeville *(G-14817)*
Kvk Foundry Inc....................................F ...... 815 695-5212
  Millington *(G-14819)*
Marble Machine Inc..............................G ...... 217 442-0746
  Danville *(G-7752)*
Nelson - Harkins Inds Inc.....................E ...... 773 478-6243
  Chicago *(G-5884)*
Quincy Foundry & Pattern Co...............G ...... 217 222-0718
  Quincy *(G-17877)*
R&R Racing of Palm Beach Inc............G ...... 618 937-6767
  West Frankfort *(G-21815)*
RCM Industries Inc...............................C ...... 847 455-1950
  Wheeling *(G-22133)*
Reynolds Manufacturing Company........E ...... 309 787-8600
  Milan *(G-14803)*
Robert Kellerman & Co..........................G ...... 847 526-7266
  Wauconda *(G-21500)*

Spartan Light Metal Pdts Inc................E ...... 618 443-4346
  Sparta *(G-20321)*
Tompkins Aluminum Foundry Inc.........G ...... 815 438-5578
  Rock Falls *(G-18154)*
Tricast/Presfore Corporation................G ...... 815 459-1820
  Crystal Lake *(G-7669)*
Trio Foundry Inc...................................E ...... 815 786-6616
  Sandwich *(G-19379)*
Trio Foundry Inc...................................E ...... 630 892-1676
  Montgomery *(G-15068)*

### FOUNDRIES: Brass, Bronze & Copper

AJ Oster LLC........................................C ...... 630 260-0950
  Carol Stream *(G-3094)*
Amcast Inc............................................F ...... 630 766-7450
  Bensenville *(G-1831)*
American Bare Conductor Inc..............E ...... 815 224-3422
  La Salle *(G-1420)*
Ampco Metal Incorporated...................E ...... 847 437-6000
  Arlington Heights *(G-711)*
Anderson Casting Company Inc............G ...... 312 733-1185
  Chicago *(G-3901)*
Aurora Metals Division LLC..................C ...... 630 844-4900
  Montgomery *(G-15028)*
Bearing Sales Corporation....................E ...... 773 282-8686
  Chicago *(G-4066)*
Covey Machine Inc...............................F ...... 773 650-1530
  Chicago *(G-4484)*
F Kreutzer & Co....................................G ...... 773 826-5767
  Chicago *(G-4805)*
Fiberlink LLC........................................E ...... 312 951-8500
  Chicago *(G-4841)*
Imperial Punch & Manufacturing..........F ...... 815 226-8200
  Rockford *(G-18428)*
Mahoney Foundries Inc........................E ...... 309 784-2311
  Vermont *(G-21138)*
Reynolds Manufacturing Company........E ...... 309 787-8600
  Milan *(G-14803)*
Universal Electric Foundry Inc.............E ...... 312 421-7233
  Chicago *(G-6831)*
Wagner Brass Foundry Inc..................E ...... 773 276-7907
  Chicago *(G-6932)*

### FOUNDRIES: Gray & Ductile Iron

Amsted Industries Incorporated...........B ...... 312 645-1700
  Chicago *(G-3896)*
Burgess-Norton Mfg Co Inc.................E ...... 630 232-4100
  Geneva *(G-10814)*
Castwell Products LLC.........................C ...... 847 966-9552
  Skokie *(G-19974)*
Caterpillar Inc......................................A ...... 309 633-8788
  Mapleton *(G-14205)*
Charter Dura-Bar Inc............................C ...... 815 338-7800
  Woodstock *(G-22552)*
Demco Products Inc.............................F ...... 708 636-6240
  Oak Lawn *(G-16616)*
E H Baare Corporation..........................C ...... 618 546-1575
  Robinson *(G-18062)*
F J Murphy & Son Inc..........................D ...... 217 787-3477
  Springfield *(G-20437)*
Group Industries Inc............................E ...... 708 877-6200
  Thornton *(G-20871)*
Johnston & Jennings Inc......................G ...... 708 757-5375
  Chicago Heights *(G-7106)*
Lemfco Inc............................................E ...... 815 777-0242
  Galena *(G-10729)*
M H Detrick Company...........................E ...... 708 479-5085
  Mokena *(G-14882)*
Ptc Tubular Products LLC.....................C ...... 815 692-4900
  Fairbury *(G-10131)*
Reynolds Manufacturing Company........E ...... 309 787-8600
  Milan *(G-14803)*
Rj Link International Inc.......................E ...... 815 874-8110
  Rockford *(G-18559)*
Timkensteel Corporation.......................G ...... 708 263-6868
  Tinley Park *(G-20948)*
Tmb Industries Inc................................F ...... 312 280-2565
  Chicago *(G-6732)*
Westwick Foundry Ltd..........................E ...... 815 777-0815
  Galena *(G-10734)*

### FOUNDRIES: Iron

Advanced Pattern Works LLC..............G ...... 618 346-9039
  Collinsville *(G-7312)*
Du Page Precision Products Co............D ...... 630 849-2940
  Aurora *(G-998)*
M H Detrick Company...........................E ...... 708 479-5085
  Mokena *(G-14882)*

Wirco Inc..............................................D ...... 217 398-3200
  Champaign *(G-3561)*

### FOUNDRIES: Nonferrous

Acme Die Casting LLC..........................G ...... 847 272-9520
  Northbrook *(G-16197)*
Altman & Koehler Foundry....................G ...... 773 373-7737
  Chicago *(G-3838)*
Amcast Inc............................................F ...... 630 766-7450
  Bensenville *(G-1831)*
Ames Metal Products Company............F ...... 773 523-3230
  Wheeling *(G-22005)*
Anderson Casting Company Inc............G ...... 312 733-1185
  Chicago *(G-3901)*
Avan Tool & Die Co Inc.........................F ...... 773 287-1670
  Chicago *(G-3996)*
Batavia Foundry and Machine Co.........G ...... 630 879-1319
  Batavia *(G-1420)*
Charter Dura-Bar Inc............................C ...... 815 338-7800
  Woodstock *(G-22552)*
Clinkenbeard & Associates Inc............E ...... 815 226-0291
  Rockford *(G-18313)*
Curto-Ligonier Foundries Co.................E ...... 708 345-2250
  Melrose Park *(G-14613)*
Du Page Precision Products Co............D ...... 630 849-2940
  Aurora *(G-998)*
Dynacast Inc.........................................C ...... 847 608-2200
  Elgin *(G-9015)*
G & W Electric Company......................E ...... 708 389-8307
  Blue Island *(G-2251)*
Illini Foundry Co Inc.............................G ...... 309 697-3142
  Peoria *(G-17385)*
Ipsen Inc...............................................E ...... 815 239-2385
  Pecatonica *(G-17252)*
Kabert Industries Inc............................G ...... 630 833-2115
  Villa Park *(G-21262)*
Kettler Casting Co Inc..........................E ...... 618 234-5303
  Belleville *(G-1642)*
Lemfco Inc............................................E ...... 815 777-0242
  Galena *(G-10729)*
Libco Industries Inc..............................F ...... 815 623-7677
  Roscoe *(G-18902)*
Mahoney Foundries Inc........................E ...... 309 784-2311
  Vermont *(G-21138)*
Marble Machine Inc..............................G ...... 217 442-0746
  Danville *(G-7752)*
Master Foundry Inc..............................F ...... 217 223-7396
  Quincy *(G-17856)*
Quincy Foundry & Pattern Co...............G ...... 217 222-0718
  Quincy *(G-17877)*
Reynolds Manufacturing Company........E ...... 309 787-8600
  Milan *(G-14803)*
Robert Kellerman & Co..........................G ...... 847 526-7266
  Wauconda *(G-21500)*
Rockbridge Casting Inc........................G ...... 618 753-3188
  Rockbridge *(G-18212)*
Rockford Foundries Inc........................F ...... 815 965-7243
  Rockford *(G-18574)*
Sarcol...................................................G ...... 773 533-3000
  Chicago *(G-6445)*
Spartan Light Metal Pdts Inc................E ...... 618 443-4346
  Sparta *(G-20321)*
Tompkins Aluminum Foundry Inc.........G ...... 815 438-5578
  Rock Falls *(G-18154)*
Tricast/Presfore Corporation................G ...... 815 459-1820
  Crystal Lake *(G-7669)*
Trio Foundry Inc...................................E ...... 815 786-6616
  Sandwich *(G-19379)*
Trio Foundry Inc...................................E ...... 630 892-1676
  Montgomery *(G-15068)*
Universal Electric Foundry Inc.............E ...... 312 421-7233
  Chicago *(G-6831)*
Wagner Brass Foundry Inc..................E ...... 773 276-7907
  Chicago *(G-6932)*
Wishzing..............................................E ...... 217 413-8469
  Dalton City *(G-7699)*

### FOUNDRIES: Steel

Allquip Co Inc.......................................G ...... 309 944-6153
  Geneseo *(G-10797)*
Combined Metals Holding Inc..............C ...... 708 547-8800
  Bellwood *(G-1701)*
Componenta USA LLC..........................G ...... 309 691-7000
  Peoria *(G-17345)*
Dee Erectors Inc...................................G ...... 630 327-1185
  Downers Grove *(G-8426)*
Du Page Precision Products Co............D ...... 630 849-2940
  Aurora *(G-998)*
E H Baare Corporation..........................C ...... 618 546-1575
  Robinson *(G-18062)*

## FOUNDRIES: Steel

FMC Corporation .................................. D ..... 815 824-2153
  Lee *(G-13217)*
Illinois Ni Cast LLC ............................. G ..... 217 398-3200
  Champaign *(G-3500)*
Lmt Usa Inc ...................................... G ..... 630 969-5412
  Waukegan *(G-21583)*
Monett Metals Inc ................................ G ..... 773 478-8888
  Chicago *(G-5794)*
Neenah Foundry Co ................................ G ..... 800 558-5075
  Frankfort *(G-10345)*
Nisshin Holding Inc .............................. G ..... 847 290-5100
  Rolling Meadows *(G-18750)*
Scot Forge Company ............................... D ..... 847 678-6000
  Franklin Park *(G-10584)*
Set Enterprises of Mi Inc ........................ F ..... 708 758-1111
  Sauk Village *(G-19393)*
T & H Lemont Inc ................................. D ..... 708 482-1800
  Countryside *(G-7446)*
Voestlpine Precision Strip LLC ................... D ..... 847 227-5272
  Elk Grove Village *(G-9810)*

## FOUNDRY MACHINERY & EQPT

Asta Service Inc ................................. G ..... 630 271-0960
  Lisle *(G-13565)*
Chatham Corporation .............................. F ..... 847 634-5506
  Lincolnshire *(G-13436)*
Disa Holding Corp ................................ G ..... 630 820-3000
  Oswego *(G-16913)*
Hunter Foundry Machinery Corp .................... D ..... 847 397-5110
  Schaumburg *(G-19560)*
International Molding Mch Co ..................... G ..... 708 354-1380
  La Grange Park *(G-12757)*
Pekay Machine & Engrg Co Inc ..................... F ..... 312 829-5530
  Chicago *(G-6098)*
Simpson Technologies Corp ........................ E ..... 630 978-2700
  Aurora *(G-1079)*

## FOUNTAIN SUPPLIES WHOLESALERS

Fountain Technologies Ltd ........................ E ..... 847 537-3677
  Wheeling *(G-22057)*

## FOUNTAINS: Concrete

Aqua Control Inc ................................. E ..... 815 664-4900
  Spring Valley *(G-20374)*
Fountain Technologies Ltd ........................ E ..... 847 537-3677
  Wheeling *(G-22057)*

## FRACTIONATION PRDTS OF CRUDE PETROLEUM, HYDROCARBONS, NEC

Arland Clean Fuels LLC ........................... G ..... 847 868-8580
  Evanston *(G-10011)*

## FRAMES & FRAMING WHOLESALE

Frame House Inc .................................. G ..... 708 383-1616
  Oak Park *(G-16663)*
Mercurys Green LLC ............................... E ..... 708 865-9134
  Franklin Park *(G-10528)*
Michels Frame Shop ............................... G ..... 847 647-7366
  Niles *(G-16004)*
Picture Frame Fulfillment LLC .................... D ..... 847 260-5071
  Franklin Park *(G-10550)*
Sarj USA Inc ..................................... E ..... 708 865-9134
  Franklin Park *(G-10582)*
Seshin USA Inc ................................... G ..... 847 550-5556
  Lake Zurich *(G-13130)*

## FRANCHISES, SELLING OR LICENSING

Duraclean International Inc ...................... F ..... 847 704-7100
  Arlington Heights *(G-748)*
H & R Block Inc .................................. F ..... 847 566-5557
  Mundelein *(G-15506)*
H&R Block Inc .................................... F ..... 773 582-3444
  Chicago *(G-5025)*

## FREEZERS: Household

Lambright Distributors ........................... G ..... 217 543-2083
  Arthur *(G-907)*

## FREIGHT FORWARDING ARRANGEMENTS

Minority Auto Hdlg Specialists ................... F ..... 708 757-8758
  Chicago Heights *(G-7113)*

## FREIGHT FORWARDING ARRANGEMENTS: Domestic

Driver Services .................................. G ..... 505 267-8686
  Bensenville *(G-1883)*

## FREIGHT TRANSPORTATION ARRANGEMENTS

Adrian Orgas Gheorghe ............................ G ..... 773 355-1200
  Palatine *(G-16997)*
Aerostar Global Logistics Inc .................... F ..... 630 396-7890
  Lombard *(G-13761)*
Corr-Pak Corporation ............................. E ..... 708 442-7806
  Mc Cook *(G-14447)*
Kdm Enterprises LLC .............................. ..... 877 591-9768
  Carpentersville *(G-3290)*
Kuchar Combine Performance ....................... ..... 217 854-9838
  Carlinville *(G-3041)*
Luna Mattress Transport Inc ...................... F ..... 773 847-1812
  Chicago *(G-5568)*

## FRICTION MATERIAL, MADE FROM POWDERED METAL

Gpi Manufacturing Inc ............................ E ..... 847 615-8900
  Lake Bluff *(G-12847)*
Pma Friction Products Inc ........................ D ..... 630 406-9119
  Batavia *(G-1484)*
PSM Industries Inc ............................... E ..... 815 337-8800
  Woodstock *(G-22602)*
Webster-Hoff Corporation ......................... D ..... 630 858-8030
  Glendale Heights *(G-11091)*

## FRUIT & VEGETABLE MARKETS

Eckert Orchards Inc .............................. C ..... 618 233-0513
  Belleville *(G-1630)*
Veteran Greens LLC ............................... G ..... 773 599-9689
  Chicago *(G-6891)*

## FRUIT STANDS OR MARKETS

Bobs Market & Greenhouse ......................... ..... 217 442-8155
  Danville *(G-7706)*

## FRUITS & VEGETABLES WHOLESALERS: Fresh

Veteran Greens LLC ............................... G ..... 773 599-9689
  Chicago *(G-6891)*

## FRUITS: Artificial & Preserved

Midwest Foods Mfg Inc ............................ E ..... 847 455-4636
  Franklin Park *(G-10533)*

## FUEL ADDITIVES

Caibros Americas LLC ............................. ..... 312 593-3128
  Highland Park *(G-11826)*
Cartel Holdings Inc .............................. ..... 815 334-0250
  Harvard *(G-11625)*
Commax Inc ....................................... ..... 847 995-0994
  Schaumburg *(G-19476)*
ET Products LLC .................................. G ..... 800 325-5746
  Burr Ridge *(G-2839)*
Hydrophi Tech Group Inc .......................... ..... 630 981-0098
  Oak Brook *(G-16523)*

## FUEL BRIQUETTES OR BOULETS, MADE WITH PETROLEUM BINDER

Chemalloy Company LLC ............................ E .....
  Rosemont *(G-18993)*

## FUEL DEALERS: Wood

E-Z Tree Recycling Inc ........................... G ..... 773 493-8600
  Chicago *(G-4670)*
Powell Tree Care Inc ............................. G ..... 847 364-1181
  Elk Grove Village *(G-9689)*

## FUEL OIL DEALERS

Times Energy ..................................... G ..... 773 444-9282
  Worth *(G-22635)*
Westmore Supply Co ............................... F ..... 630 627-0278
  Lombard *(G-13883)*

## FUEL TREATING

Debourg Corp ..................................... G ..... 815 338-7852
  Bull Valley *(G-2798)*
Opw Fueling Components Inc ....................... G ..... 708 485-4200
  Hodgkins *(G-11980)*

## FUELS: Diesel

Blackhawk Biofuels LLC ........................... E ..... 217 431-6600
  Freeport *(G-10649)*
Drig Corporation ................................. ..... 312 265-1509
  Chicago *(G-4644)*
Patriot Fuels Biodiesel LLC ...................... F ..... 309 935-5700
  Annawan *(G-610)*
Synsel Energy Inc ................................ G ..... 630 516-1284
  Elmhurst *(G-9947)*

## FUELS: Ethanol

Afs Inc .......................................... F ..... 847 437-2345
  Arlington Heights *(G-703)*
AMP Americas LLC ................................. F ..... 312 300-6700
  Chicago *(G-3893)*
Ashland Fuel & Quick Lube ........................ G ..... 773 434-8870
  Chicago *(G-3962)*
Austins Saloon & Eatery .......................... G ..... 847 549-1972
  Libertyville *(G-13305)*
Bala & Anula Fuels Inc ........................... G ..... 630 766-1807
  Bensenville *(G-1840)*
Big Rver Rsrces W Brlngton LLC ................... G ..... 309 734-8423
  Monmouth *(G-15010)*
Biovantage Fuels LLC ............................. F ..... 815 544-6028
  Belvidere *(G-1738)*
Bps Fuels Inc .................................... G ..... 217 452-7608
  Virginia *(G-21304)*
Breakfast Fuel LLC ............................... G ..... 847 251-3835
  Wilmette *(G-22247)*
Cheers Food and Fuel 240 ......................... G ..... 618 995-9153
  Goreville *(G-11250)*
Cheers Food Fuel ................................. G ..... 618 827-4836
  Dongola *(G-8379)*
Chrisman Fuel .................................... G ..... 217 463-3400
  Paris *(G-17144)*
Cooper Oil Co .................................... G ..... 708 349-2893
  Orland Park *(G-16850)*
Ecolocap Solutions Inc ........................... G ..... 866 479-7041
  Barrington *(G-1279)*
Eden Fuels LLC ................................... G ..... 847 676-9470
  Skokie *(G-19991)*
Executive Performance Fuel LLC ................... G ..... 847 364-1933
  Elk Grove Village *(G-9471)*
Freedom Fuel & Food Inc .......................... G ..... 773 233-5350
  Chicago *(G-4888)*
Friends Fuel ..................................... G ..... 773 434-9387
  Chicago *(G-4892)*
Fryer To Fuel Inc ................................ G ..... 309 654-2875
  Cordova *(G-7375)*
Fuel Fitness ..................................... ..... 708 367-0707
  Crete *(G-7513)*
Fuel Research & Instrument Co .................... G ..... 630 953-2459
  Lombard *(G-13804)*
Gateway Fuels Inc ................................ G ..... 618 248-5000
  Albers *(G-354)*
H&Z Fuel & Food Inc .............................. G ..... 815 399-9108
  Rockford *(G-18410)*
Harvey Fuels ..................................... G ..... 708 339-0777
  Harvey *(G-11669)*
Havanah Fuel ..................................... G ..... 309 543-2211
  Havana *(G-11696)*
Hinman Specialty Fuels ........................... G ..... 847 868-6026
  Evanston *(G-10051)*
Horizon Fuel Cell Americas ....................... G ..... 312 316-8050
  Chicago *(G-5112)*
Hucks Food Fuel .................................. F ..... 618 286-5111
  Dupo *(G-8571)*
Illini Fs Inc .................................... G ..... 217 442-4737
  Potomac *(G-17738)*
Jagjita Corp ..................................... G ..... 217 374-6016
  White Hall *(G-22185)*
K&H Fuel ......................................... G ..... 815 405-4364
  Frankfort *(G-10338)*
L & W Fuels ...................................... G ..... 815 848-8360
  Fairbury *(G-10130)*
Lakeview Energy LLC .............................. E ..... 312 386-5897
  Chicago *(G-5446)*
Midtown Fuels .................................... G ..... 217 347-7191
  Effingham *(G-8846)*
Midwest Bio Fuel Inc ............................. G ..... 309 965-2612
  Goodfield *(G-11247)*
Nikli Fuels Inc .................................. G ..... 309 363-2425
  Pekin *(G-17276)*

# PRODUCT SECTION — FURNITURE STORES

Omega Partners .................................. G ...... 618 254-0603
 Hartford *(G-11613)*
Patriot Fuels LLC ................................ G ...... 847 551-5946
 East Dundee *(G-8651)*
Pro Fuel Nine Inc ............................... G ...... 309 867-3375
 Oquawka *(G-16813)*
R & P Fuels ....................................... G ...... 630 855-2358
 Hoffman Estates *(G-12042)*
Rocket Fuel Inc .................................. F ...... 207 520-9075
 Chicago *(G-6374)*
Rsb Fuels Inc .................................... G ...... 217 999-4409
 Mount Olive *(G-15307)*
Saint Mary Fuel Company .................. G ...... 773 918-1681
 Chicago *(G-6429)*
Speedway .......................................... G ...... 815 463-0840
 New Lenox *(G-15912)*
Stateline Renewable Fuels LLC .......... G ...... 608 931-4634
 Buffalo Grove *(G-2776)*
Swissport Fueling Incorpo .................. G ...... 773 203-5419
 Chicago *(G-6652)*
United Fuel Savers LLC ...................... G ...... 312 725-4993
 Chicago *(G-6824)*
Uzhavoor Fuels Inc ............................ G ...... 630 401-6173
 Dixon *(G-8358)*
Wenona Food & Fuel .......................... G ...... 815 853-4141
 Wenona *(G-21649)*
West Fuels Inc ................................... G ...... 708 488-8880
 Forest Park *(G-10257)*
Wieman Fuels LP Gas Company ......... G ...... 618 632-5150
 Belleville *(G-1691)*

## FUELS: Gas, Liquefied

Gateway Propane LLC ........................ G ...... 618 286-3005
 East Carondelet *(G-8614)*

## FUELS: Jet

Esi Fuel & Energy Group LLC ............. G ...... 716 465-4289
 Collinsville *(G-7324)*

## FULLER'S EARTH MINING

Profile Products LLC ........................... E ...... 847 215-1144
 Buffalo Grove *(G-2756)*

## FUND RAISING ORGANIZATION, NON-FEE BASIS

R L Allen Industries ............................ G ...... 618 667-2544
 Troy *(G-21011)*

## FUNERAL HOME

Clugston Tibbitts Funeral Home .......... G ...... 309 833-2188
 Macomb *(G-14122)*
Greenwood Inc ................................... F ...... 800 798-4900
 Danville *(G-7728)*
Keepes Funeral Home Inc ................... F ...... 618 262-5200
 Mount Carmel *(G-15271)*

## FUNERAL HOMES & SVCS

Merz Vault Company Inc .................... E ...... 618 548-2859
 Salem *(G-19338)*
Northern Illinois Wilbert Vlt ................. G ...... 815 544-3355
 Belvidere *(G-1775)*
St Charles Memorial Works Inc ........... G ...... 630 584-0183
 Saint Charles *(G-19268)*

## FUNGICIDES OR HERBICIDES

Dow Chemical Company ..................... E ...... 815 933-5514
 Kankakee *(G-12611)*
E I Du Pont De Nemours & Co ............ E ...... 309 527-5115
 El Paso *(G-8868)*
Frank Miller & Sons Inc ...................... E ...... 708 201-7200
 Mokena *(G-14863)*
Pfizer Inc ........................................... D ...... 847 639-3020
 Cary *(G-3363)*
Sanford Chemical Co Inc .................... F ...... 847 437-3530
 Elk Grove Village *(G-9727)*

## FURNACE CASINGS: Sheet Metal

Goose Island Mfg & Supply Corp ......... G ...... 708 343-4225
 Lansing *(G-13164)*
Temp Excel Properties LLC ................ G ...... 847 844-3845
 Elgin *(G-9207)*
W L Engler Distributing Inc ................. G ...... 630 898-5400
 Aurora *(G-1093)*

## FURNACES & OVENS: Fuel-Fired

Burdett Burner Mfg Inc ....................... G ...... 630 617-5060
 Villa Park *(G-21239)*

## FURNACES & OVENS: Indl

Amiberica Inc .................................... E ...... 773 247-3600
 Chicago *(G-3888)*
Anderson Msnry Refr Spcialists .......... G ...... 847 540-8885
 Lake Zurich *(G-13041)*
Armil/Cfs Inc ...................................... G ...... 708 339-6810
 South Holland *(G-20247)*
Austin-Westran LLC ............................ C ...... 815 234-2811
 Byron *(G-2912)*
Campbell International Inc .................. E ...... 408 661-0794
 Wauconda *(G-21452)*
Chicago Brick Oven LLC ..................... G ...... 630 359-4793
 Elmhurst *(G-9847)*
Coating & Systems Integration ............ F ...... 312 335-1848
 Chicago *(G-4414)*
Dane Industries LLC ........................... G ...... 815 234-2811
 Byron *(G-2915)*
Fish Oven and Equipment Corp ........... E ...... 847 526-8686
 Wauconda *(G-21463)*
G & M Fabricating Inc ........................ G ...... 815 282-1744
 Roscoe *(G-18898)*
Grieve Corporation ............................. D ...... 847 546-8225
 Round Lake *(G-19059)*
Henry Technologies Inc ...................... G ...... 217 483-2406
 Chatham *(G-3621)*
Infratrol LLC ...................................... G ...... 779 475-3098
 Byron *(G-2916)*
Ipsen Inc ........................................... C ...... 815 332-4941
 Cherry Valley *(G-3645)*
Ipsen Inc ........................................... G ...... 815 239-2385
 Pecatonica *(G-17252)*
J N Machinery Corp ........................... G ...... 224 699-9161
 East Dundee *(G-8648)*
M H Detrick Company ......................... G ...... 708 479-5085
 Mokena *(G-14882)*
McEnglevan Indus Frnc Mfg Inc .......... G ...... 217 446-0941
 Danville *(G-7753)*
Moffitt Co .......................................... G ...... 847 678-5450
 Schiller Park *(G-19853)*
Northpoint Heating & Air Cond ............ G ...... 847 731-1067
 Zion *(G-22692)*
Pioneer Express ................................. G ...... 217 236-3022
 Perry *(G-17497)*
Precision Quincy Ovens LLC ............... E ...... 302 602-8738
 South Beloit *(G-20164)*
Quincy Lab Inc ................................... G ...... 773 622-2428
 Chicago *(G-6258)*
Thermal Solutions Inc ......................... G ...... 217 352-7019
 Savoy *(G-19412)*
Tks Control Systems Inc .................... F ...... 630 554-3020
 Oswego *(G-16937)*
Westran Thermal Processing LLC ....... E ...... 815 634-1001
 South Beloit *(G-20175)*

## FURNITURE & CABINET STORES: Cabinets, Custom Work

57th Street Bookcase & Cabinet .......... F ...... 773 363-3038
 Chicago *(G-3673)*
Ameriscan Designs Inc ....................... D ...... 773 542-1291
 Chicago *(G-3886)*
Benchmark Cabinets & Mllwk Inc ........ E ...... 309 697-5855
 Peoria *(G-17316)*
Bolhuis Woodworking Co .................... G ...... 708 333-5100
 Manhattan *(G-14168)*
Creative Cabinetry Inc ........................ G ...... 708 460-2900
 Orland Park *(G-16851)*
Dicks Custom Cabinet Shop ................ G ...... 815 358-2663
 Cornell *(G-7381)*
Encon Environmental Concepts ........... F ...... 630 543-1583
 Addison *(G-111)*
Fra-Milco Cabinets Co Inc .................. G
 Frankfort *(G-10323)*
Glenview Custom Cabinets Inc ........... G ...... 847 345-5754
 Glenview *(G-11130)*
Hansen Custom Cabinet Inc ............... G ...... 847 356-1100
 Lake Villa *(G-13015)*
Hickory Street Cabinets ..................... G ...... 618 667-9676
 Troy *(G-21007)*
Miller Whiteside Wood Working .......... G ...... 309 827-6470
 Mc Lean *(G-14463)*
Rose Custom Cabinets Inc .................. G ...... 847 816-4800
 Mundelein *(G-15553)*
Scheffler Custom Woodworking ........... G ...... 815 284-6564
 Dixon *(G-8348)*

Unique Designs ................................. G ...... 309 454-1226
 Normal *(G-16092)*
Wagners Custom Wood Design ........... G ...... 847 487-2788
 Island Lake *(G-12221)*

## FURNITURE & CABINET STORES: Custom

Bernhard Woodwork Ltd ..................... E ...... 847 291-1040
 Northbrook *(G-16214)*
Manufacturing / Woodworking ............. G ...... 847 730-4823
 Des Plaines *(G-8226)*
Stonetree Fabrication Inc ................... G ...... 618 332-1700
 East Saint Louis *(G-8771)*

## FURNITURE & FIXTURES Factory

Akerue Industries LLC ........................ E ...... 847 395-3300
 Antioch *(G-615)*
Display Plan Lpdg .............................. E ...... 773 525-3787
 Chicago *(G-4612)*
Edsal Manufacturing Co Inc ................ A ...... 773 475-3020
 Chicago *(G-4699)*
Edsal Manufacturing Co Inc ................ D ...... 773 475-3013
 Chicago *(G-4700)*
Finishing Touch ................................. G ...... 309 789-6444
 Cuba *(G-7680)*
Kewaunee Scientific Corp ................... G ...... 847 675-7744
 Highland Park *(G-11850)*
Marshall Furniture Inc ........................ E ...... 847 395-9350
 Antioch *(G-643)*
Pollard Bros Mfg Co ........................... F ...... 773 763-6868
 Chicago *(G-6150)*
Railcraft Nexim Design ....................... G ...... 309 937-2360
 Cambridge *(G-2969)*

## FURNITURE PARTS: Metal

Chadwick Manufacturing Ltd ............... G ...... 815 684-5152
 Chadwick *(G-3440)*
Trendler Inc ....................................... E ...... 773 284-6600
 Chicago *(G-6768)*

## FURNITURE REFINISHING SVCS

Doll Furniture Co Inc .......................... G ...... 309 452-2606
 Normal *(G-16070)*
Mastercraft Furn Rfinishing Inc ........... F ...... 773 722-5730
 Chicago *(G-5647)*

## FURNITURE REPAIR & MAINTENANCE SVCS

Gmk Finishing ................................... G ...... 630 837-0568
 Bartlett *(G-1351)*

## FURNITURE STOCK & PARTS: Carvings, Wood

Greatlakes Architectural Millw ............. E ...... 312 829-7110
 Chicago *(G-5000)*
Signature Innovations LLC .................. G ...... 847 758-9600
 Elk Grove Village *(G-9739)*

## FURNITURE STOCK & PARTS: Dimension Stock, Hardwood

Hardwood Lumber Products Co ........... G ...... 309 538-4411
 Kilbourne *(G-12697)*
New Line Hardwoods Inc .................... D ...... 309 657-7621
 Beardstown *(G-1524)*

## FURNITURE STOCK & PARTS: Frames, Upholstered Furniture, Wood

Redbox Workshop Ltd ........................ E ...... 773 478-7077
 Chicago *(G-6316)*

## FURNITURE STOCK & PARTS: Hardwood

Heartland Hardwoods Inc ................... E ...... 217 844-3312
 Effingham *(G-8838)*
Riverside Custom Woodworking .......... G ...... 815 589-3608
 Fulton *(G-10705)*

## FURNITURE STORES

Aero Products Holdings Inc ................. E ...... 847 485-3200
 Schaumburg *(G-19424)*
Albert Vivo Upholstery Co Inc ............. G ...... 312 226-7779
 Burr Ridge *(G-2821)*
Athletic & Sports Seating ................... G ...... 630 837-5566
 Streamwood *(G-20644)*
B & B Formica Appliers Inc ................. F ...... 773 804-1015
 Chicago *(G-4014)*

---

Employee Codes: A=Over 500 employees, B=251-500
C=101-250, D=51-100, E=20-50, F=10-19, G=3-9

2017 Harris Illinois Industrial Directory

# FURNITURE STORES

Bright Designs Inc .................................. G ...... 847 428-6012
  Dundee (G-8559)
Caroline Cole Inc .................................... F ...... 618 233-0600
  Belleville (G-1617)
Coles Appliance & Furn Co .................... G ...... 773 525-1797
  Chicago (G-4422)
Compx Security Products Inc ................ D ...... 847 234-1864
  Grayslake (G-11329)
Doll Furniture Co Inc ............................. G ...... 309 452-2606
  Normal (G-16070)
Euromarket Designs Inc ........................ A ...... 847 272-2888
  Northbrook (G-16252)
Furniture Services Inc ........................... G ...... 847 520-9490
  Wheeling (G-22060)
Hanley Design Inc .................................. G ...... 309 682-9665
  Peoria (G-17378)
Hylan Design Ltd .................................... G ...... 312 243-7341
  Chicago (G-5129)
Interior Tectonics LLC ........................... G ...... 312 515-7779
  Chicago (G-5215)
Jans ......................................................... G ...... 815 722-9360
  Joliet (G-12521)
Kaufmans Custom Cabinets .................. F ...... 217 268-4330
  Arcola (G-673)
Kunz Carpentry ...................................... G ...... 618 224-7892
  Trenton (G-20994)
Montauk Chicago Inc ............................. G ...... 312 951-5688
  Chicago (G-5797)
Petro Enterprises Inc ............................. G ...... 708 425-1551
  Chicago Ridge (G-7153)
Piersons Mattress Inc ............................ G ...... 309 637-8455
  Peoria (G-17429)
Railcraft Nexim Design .......................... G ...... 309 937-2360
  Cambridge (G-2969)
Riverton Cabinet Company .................... E ...... 815 462-5300
  New Lenox (G-15908)
Whitacres Country Oaks Shop ............... F ...... 309 726-1305
  Hudson (G-12127)

## FURNITURE STORES: Cabinets, Kitchen, Exc Custom Made

Kitchen & Bath Gallery .......................... G ...... 217 214-0310
  Quincy (G-17845)

## FURNITURE STORES: Custom Made, Exc Cabinets

Counter Craft Inc ................................... G ...... 847 336-8205
  Waukegan (G-21545)
Scibor Upholstering & Gallery ............... G ...... 708 671-9700
  Chicago (G-6457)

## FURNITURE STORES: Office

Gazette Democrat ................................. E ...... 618 833-2150
  Anna (G-603)
James Ray Monroe Corporation ............ F ...... 618 532-4575
  Centralia (G-3420)
OfficeMax North America Inc ................ E ...... 815 748-3007
  Dekalb (G-8111)
Vertisse Inc ........................................... G ...... 224 532-5145
  Lake In The Hills (G-13009)

## FURNITURE STORES: Outdoor & Garden

Cabinets Doors and More LLC ............... G ...... 847 395-6334
  Antioch (G-627)

## FURNITURE STORES: Unfinished

Finishing Touch ..................................... G ...... 309 789-6444
  Cuba (G-7680)

## FURNITURE UPHOLSTERY REPAIR SVCS

Marks Custom Seating ........................... G ...... 630 980-8270
  Roselle (G-18956)

## FURNITURE WHOLESALERS

ADM International Inc ........................... F ...... 773 774-2400
  North Chicago (G-16173)
American Trade & Coml Svc LLC ........... F ...... 202 910-8808
  Chicago (G-3879)
Norix Group Inc ..................................... E ...... 630 231-1331
  West Chicago (G-21751)
Petro Enterprises Inc ............................ G ...... 708 425-1551
  Chicago Ridge (G-7153)
Urban Home Furniture & ACC Inc ......... E ...... 630 761-3200
  Batavia (G-1514)

Veeco Manufacturing Inc ...................... E ...... 312 666-0900
  Melrose Park (G-14705)

## FURNITURE, BARBER & BEAUTY SHOP

Buff & Go Inc ......................................... G ...... 773 719-4436
  Chicago (G-4182)

## FURNITURE, GARDEN: Concrete

M & M Exposed Aggregate Co ............... G ...... 847 551-1818
  Carpentersville (G-3291)

## FURNITURE, HOUSEHOLD: Wholesalers

Athletic & Sports Seating ...................... G ...... 630 837-5566
  Streamwood (G-20644)
Ligo Products Inc .................................. E ...... 708 478-1800
  Mokena (G-14881)
Melvin Wolf and Associates Inc ............. G ...... 847 433-9098
  Highland Park (G-11853)

## FURNITURE, MATTRESSES: Wholesalers

Wicoff Inc .............................................. E ...... 618 988-8888
  Herrin (G-11758)

## FURNITURE, OFFICE: Wholesalers

Franz Stationery Company Inc ............. F ...... 847 593-0060
  Lake Barrington (G-12807)
H A Friend & Company Inc ................... E ...... 847 746-1248
  Zion (G-22687)
Nova Solutions Inc ................................ E ...... 217 342-7070
  Effingham (G-8851)
Roevolution 226 LLC ............................. G ...... 773 658-4022
  Riverwoods (G-18042)
Vertisse Inc ........................................... G ...... 224 532-5145
  Lake In The Hills (G-13009)

## FURNITURE, OUTDOOR & LAWN: Wholesalers

Prescription Plus Ltd ............................ F ...... 618 537-6202
  Lebanon (G-13216)

## FURNITURE, PUBLIC BUILDING: Wholesalers

Mfp Holding Co ..................................... G ...... 312 666-3366
  Chicago (G-5714)

## FURNITURE, WHOLESALE: Bar

Bar Stool Depotcom ............................. G ...... 815 727-7294
  Joliet (G-12460)

## FURNITURE, WHOLESALE: Beds & Bedding

Nolte & Tyson Inc .................................. F ...... 847 551-3313
  Gilberts (G-10929)

## FURNITURE, WHOLESALE: Chairs

Choice Furnishings Inc ......................... F ...... 847 329-0004
  Skokie (G-19982)
Ortho Seating LLC ............................... F ...... 773 276-3539
  Chicago (G-6017)

## FURNITURE, WHOLESALE: Lockers

REB Steel Equipment Corp .................... E ...... 773 252-0400
  Chicago (G-6309)
Safecharge LLC ..................................... G ...... 248 866-9428
  Chicago (G-6426)

## FURNITURE, WHOLESALE: Restaurant, NEC

Event Equipment Sales LLC .................. F ...... 708 352-0662
  Hodgkins (G-11974)

## FURNITURE: Bar furniture

Booths and Upholstery By Ray ............. G ...... 773 523-3355
  Chicago (G-4144)
Regal Manufacturing Co ....................... E ...... 630 628-6867
  Addison (G-273)
Wag Industries Inc ................................ F ...... 847 329-8932
  Skokie (G-20109)

## FURNITURE: Bed Frames & Headboards, Wood

Custom Window Accents ...................... F ...... 815 943-7651
  Harvard (G-11629)
Rooms Redux Chicago Inc .................... F ...... 312 835-1192
  Chicago (G-6390)

## FURNITURE: Bedroom, Wood

D D G Inc ............................................... G ...... 847 412-0277
  Northbrook (G-16236)
Douglas County Wood Products ........... G ...... 217 543-2888
  Arthur (G-896)

## FURNITURE: Beds, Household, Incl Folding & Cabinet, Metal

Durable Design Products Inc ................ G ...... 708 707-1147
  River Forest (G-17997)
Melvin Wolf and Associates Inc ............. G ...... 847 433-9098
  Highland Park (G-11853)

## FURNITURE: Bedsprings, Assembled

Leggett & Platt Incorporated ................ E ...... 630 801-0609
  North Aurora (G-16138)

## FURNITURE: Bookcases & Stereo Cabinets, Metal

Metal Box International Inc .................. C ...... 847 455-8500
  Franklin Park (G-10529)

## FURNITURE: Bookcases, Office, Wood

Djr Inc .................................................... F ...... 773 581-5204
  Chicago (G-4615)

## FURNITURE: Box Springs, Assembled

Leggett & Platt Incorporated ................ D
  Chicago (G-5488)
Leggett & Platt Incorporated ................ G ...... 708 458-1800
  Chicago (G-5489)
National Bedding Company LLC ........... C ...... 847 645-0200
  Hoffman Estates (G-12028)
National Bedding Company LLC ........... E ...... 847 645-0200
  Hoffman Estates (G-12027)
US Specialty Packaging Inc .................. F ...... 847 836-1115
  Elgin (G-9221)

## FURNITURE: Cabinets & Filing Drawers, Office, Exc Wood

IMS Engineered Products LLC .............. C ...... 847 391-8100
  Des Plaines (G-8211)

## FURNITURE: Cabinets & Vanities, Medicine, Metal

Pace Industries Inc ............................... D ...... 312 226-5500
  Chicago (G-6051)

## FURNITURE: Cafeteria

Norix Group Inc ..................................... E ...... 630 231-1331
  West Chicago (G-21751)

## FURNITURE: Chairs, Household Upholstered

E J Self Furniture .................................. G ...... 847 394-0899
  Mount Prospect (G-15327)
La-Z-Boy Incorporated .......................... C ...... 773 384-4440
  Chicago (G-5428)

## FURNITURE: Chairs, Household Wood

Athletic & Sports Seating ...................... G ...... 630 837-5566
  Streamwood (G-20644)
Choice Furnishings Inc ......................... F ...... 847 329-0004
  Skokie (G-19982)

## FURNITURE: Chairs, Office Exc Wood

Mlp Seating Corp ................................... E ...... 847 956-1700
  Elk Grove Village (G-9633)
Ortho Seating LLC ............................... F ...... 773 276-3539
  Chicago (G-6017)

# PRODUCT SECTION

## FURNITURE: Chairs, Office Wood

Nightingale Corp .................................. D ....... 800 363-8954
  Chicago *(G-5916)*

## FURNITURE: Chests, Cedar

Gro Products Inc ................................. G ....... 815 308-5423
  Woodstock *(G-22570)*

## FURNITURE: China Closets

A Closet Wholesaler ............................ F ....... 312 654-1400
  Chicago *(G-3685)*

## FURNITURE: Church

Atwood-Hamlin Mfg Co Inc ................... F ....... 815 678-7291
  Richmond *(G-17958)*
Heritage Rstoration Design Inc ............ G ....... 309 637-5404
  Peoria *(G-17382)*
Pep Industries Inc ............................... F ....... 630 833-0404
  Villa Park *(G-21276)*
Roberts and Downey Chapel Eqp .......... G ....... 217 795-2391
  Argenta *(G-692)*

## FURNITURE: Church, Cut Stone

Pep Industries Inc ............................... F ....... 630 833-0404
  Villa Park *(G-21276)*

## FURNITURE: Coffee Tables, Wood

Signature Innovations LLC .................. G ....... 847 758-9600
  Elk Grove Village *(G-9739)*

## FURNITURE: Console Tables, Wood

Chillin Products Inc ............................ G ....... 815 725-7253
  Rockdale *(G-18217)*

## FURNITURE: Desks & Tables, Office, Exc Wood

Kimball Office Inc ............................... F ....... 800 349-9827
  Chicago *(G-5384)*

## FURNITURE: Desks, Household, Wood

Whitacres Country Oaks Shop ............. F ....... 309 726-1305
  Hudson *(G-12127)*

## FURNITURE: Desks, Metal

Groupe Lacasse LLC ........................... E ....... 312 670-9100
  Chicago *(G-5006)*
Ise Inc .............................................. E ....... 703 319-0390
  Chicago *(G-5241)*
L & D Group Inc ................................. B ....... 630 892-8941
  Montgomery *(G-15051)*

## FURNITURE: Desks, Wood

Groupe Lacasse LLC ........................... E ....... 312 670-9100
  Chicago *(G-5006)*
Systems Unlimited Inc ........................ C ....... 630 285-0010
  Itasca *(G-12363)*

## FURNITURE: Fiberglass & Plastic

Patio Plus .......................................... G ....... 815 433-2399
  Ottawa *(G-16977)*

## FURNITURE: Foundations & Platforms

Pace Foundation ................................ E ....... 309 691-3553
  Peoria *(G-17422)*

## FURNITURE: Garden, Exc Wood, Metal, Stone Or Concrete

Gensler Gardens Inc ........................... G ....... 815 874-9634
  Davis Junction *(G-7813)*

## FURNITURE: Hammocks, Metal Or Fabric & Metal Combined

Smart Solar Inc .................................. F ....... 813 343-5770
  Libertyville *(G-13382)*

## FURNITURE: Hospital

Kinsman Enterprises Inc ..................... G ....... 618 932-3838
  West Frankfort *(G-21810)*

Mpd Medical Systems Inc ................... G ....... 815 477-0707
  Crystal Lake *(G-7616)*

## FURNITURE: Household, Metal

Austin-Westran LLC ............................ C ....... 815 234-2811
  Montgomery *(G-15029)*
Chicago American Mfg LLC .................. C ....... 773 376-0100
  Chicago *(G-4302)*
Chicagos Finest Ironworks ................... G ....... 708 895-4484
  Lansing *(G-13159)*
European Ornamental Iron Works ......... G ....... 630 705-9300
  Addison *(G-113)*
Glober Manufacturing Company ............ F ....... 847 829-4883
  Cary *(G-3349)*
Richardson Ironworks LLC .................. G ....... 217 359-3333
  Champaign *(G-3533)*
Viking Metal Cabinet Co LLC ................ D ....... 800 776-7767
  Montgomery *(G-15069)*
Viking Metal Cabinet Company ............. D ....... 630 863-7234
  Montgomery *(G-15070)*

## FURNITURE: Household, NEC

Jagoli ............................................... G ....... 312 563-0583
  Chicago *(G-5271)*
Mitchel Home .................................... G ....... 773 205-9902
  Chicago *(G-5773)*
Rustic Woodcrafts .............................. G ....... 618 584-3912
  Flat Rock *(G-10196)*

## FURNITURE: Household, Novelty, Metal

Evan Lewis Inc .................................. G ....... 773 539-0402
  Chicago *(G-4784)*

## FURNITURE: Household, Upholstered On Metal Frames

Parenteau Studios .............................. E ....... 312 337-8015
  Chicago *(G-6081)*
Tesko Welding & Mfg Co ..................... D ....... 708 452-0045
  Norridge *(G-16109)*

## FURNITURE: Household, Upholstered, Exc Wood Or Metal

Albert Vivo Upholstery Co Inc .............. G ....... 312 226-7779
  Burr Ridge *(G-2821)*
American Trade & Coml Svc LLC .......... F ....... 202 910-8808
  Chicago *(G-3879)*
Bi State Furniture Inc ......................... G ....... 309 662-6562
  Bloomington *(G-2148)*
Petro Enterprises Inc ......................... G ....... 708 425-1551
  Chicago Ridge *(G-7153)*

## FURNITURE: Household, Wood

AB&d Custom Furniture Inc ................. E ....... 708 922-9061
  Homewood *(G-12090)*
Aba Custom Woodworking .................... G ....... 815 356-9663
  Crystal Lake *(G-7525)*
Addison Interiors Company ................... F ....... 630 628-1345
  Addison *(G-23)*
Allie Woodworking .............................. G ....... 847 244-1919
  Waukegan *(G-21522)*
Amish Country Heirlooms LLC .............. G ....... 217 253-9200
  Tuscola *(G-21015)*
Amtab Manufacturing Corp .................. G ....... 630 301-7600
  Aurora *(G-1107)*
Bell Cabinet & Millwork Co .................. G ....... 708 425-1200
  Evergreen Park *(G-10110)*
Bender Mat Fctry Fton Slepshop ........... G ....... 217 328-1700
  Urbana *(G-21071)*
Bill Weeks Inc ................................... G ....... 217 523-8735
  Springfield *(G-20397)*
Bright Designs Inc ............................. G ....... 847 428-6012
  Dundee *(G-8559)*
Butcher Block Furn By Oneill ............... G ....... 312 666-9144
  Chicago *(G-4193)*
Carson Properties Inc ......................... E ....... 630 832-3322
  Elmhurst *(G-9845)*
Chicago Booth Mfg Inc ........................ F ....... 773 378-8400
  Chicago *(G-4307)*
Chicago Honeymooners LLC ................. G ....... 312 399-5699
  Chicago *(G-4323)*
Chicagos Finest Ironworks ................... G ....... 708 895-4484
  Lansing *(G-13159)*
City Living Design Inc ......................... G ....... 312 335-0711
  Chicago *(G-4383)*
Closet Works Inc ............................... E ....... 630 832-3322
  Elmhurst *(G-9849)*

Country Workshop .............................. G ....... 217 543-4094
  Arthur *(G-891)*
Creative Wood Concepts Inc ................ G ....... 773 384-9960
  Chicago *(G-4502)*
Custom Designs By Georgio ................. F ....... 847 233-0410
  Franklin Park *(G-10449)*
Custom Wood Designs Inc ................... G ....... 708 799-3439
  Crestwood *(G-7486)*
Debcor Inc ........................................ G ....... 708 333-2191
  South Holland *(G-20261)*
Dicks Custom Cabinet Shop ................. G ....... 815 358-2663
  Cornell *(G-7381)*
Diebolds Cabinet Shop ........................ G ....... 773 772-3076
  Chicago *(G-4597)*
Eddie Gapastione ............................... G ....... 708 430-3881
  Bridgeview *(G-2487)*
Fredman Bros Furniture Co Inc ............. E ....... 309 674-2011
  Peoria *(G-17366)*
Gavin Woodworking Inc ...................... G ....... 815 786-2242
  Sandwich *(G-19365)*
Glober Manufacturing Company ............ F ....... 847 829-4883
  Cary *(G-3349)*
Grant Wood Works .............................. G ....... 847 328-4349
  Evanston *(G-10046)*
Great Spirit Hardwoods LLC ................. G ....... 224 801-1969
  East Dundee *(G-8642)*
Green Gables Country Store ................ D ....... 309 897-7160
  Bradford *(G-2411)*
Guess Whackit & Hope Inc .................. G ....... 773 342-4273
  Chicago *(G-5010)*
Hanley Design Inc .............................. G ....... 309 682-9665
  Peoria *(G-17378)*
Human Svc Ctr Southern Metro E ......... E ....... 618 282-6233
  Red Bud *(G-17942)*
Hylan Design Ltd ............................... G ....... 312 243-7341
  Chicago *(G-5129)*
Imperial Kitchens & Bath Inc ............... F ....... 708 485-0020
  Brookfield *(G-2635)*
Innovative Mktg Solutions Inc .............. F ....... 630 227-4300
  Schaumburg *(G-19568)*
International Wood Design Inc ............. G ....... 773 227-9270
  Chicago *(G-5224)*
J & J Woodwork Furniture Inc .............. G ....... 708 563-9581
  Chicago *(G-5253)*
J & M Representatives Inc .................. D ....... 217 268-4504
  Arcola *(G-672)*
J M Lustig Custom Cabinets Co ............ F ....... 217 342-6661
  Effingham *(G-8840)*
JAm International Co Ltd .................... G ....... 847 827-6391
  Deerfield *(G-8016)*
Jbc Holding Co .................................. G ....... 217 347-7701
  Effingham *(G-8841)*
Joliet Cabinet Company Inc ................. E ....... 815 727-4096
  Lockport *(G-13724)*
Kaufmans Custom Cabinets .................. F ....... 217 268-4330
  Arcola *(G-673)*
Kinser Woodworks .............................. G ....... 618 549-4540
  Makanda *(G-14163)*
Kowal Custom Cabinet & Furn .............. G ....... 708 597-3367
  Blue Island *(G-2260)*
Kunz Carpentry .................................. G ....... 618 224-7892
  Trenton *(G-20994)*
Laverns Wood Items ........................... G ....... 217 268-4544
  Arcola *(G-674)*
Legacy Woodwork Inc ......................... G ....... 847 451-7602
  Franklin Park *(G-10515)*
Leggett & Platt Incorporated ................ E ....... 630 801-0609
  North Aurora *(G-16138)*
M Inc ............................................... G ....... 312 853-0512
  Chicago *(G-5582)*
Master Cabinets ................................. G ....... 847 639-1323
  Cary *(G-3359)*
Mastercraft Furn Rfnishing Inc ............. F ....... 773 722-5730
  Chicago *(G-5647)*
Meier Granite Company ....................... G ....... 847 678-7300
  Franklin Park *(G-10527)*
Mica Furniture Mfg Inc ....................... G ....... 708 430-1150
  Addison *(G-205)*
Michael Scott Inc ............................... F ....... 847 965-8700
  Deerfield *(G-8036)*
Miller Whiteside Wood Working ............ G ....... 309 827-6470
  Mc Lean *(G-14463)*
Mobilia Inc ....................................... E ....... 708 865-0700
  Bellwood *(G-1715)*
Morningside Woodcraft ........................ G ....... 217 268-4313
  Arcola *(G-679)*
Muhs Funiture Manufacturing ............... G ....... 618 723-2590
  Noble *(G-16052)*
O & I Woodworking ............................. G ....... 217 543-3155
  Arthur *(G-914)*

Employee Codes: A=Over 500 employees, B=251-500
C=101-250, D=51-100, E=20-50, F=10-19, G=3-9

# FURNITURE: Household, Wood

Okaw Valley Woodworking LLC ............F ..... 217 543-5180
  Arthur *(G-916)*
Old Blue Illinois Inc ................................F ..... 309 289-7921
  Knoxville *(G-12722)*
ONeill Products Inc .............................G ..... 312 243-3413
  Chicago *(G-5991)*
Patio Plus ...........................................G ..... 815 433-2399
  Ottawa *(G-16977)*
Philip Reinisch Company .....................F ..... 312 644-6776
  Naperville *(G-15726)*
Planks Cabinet Shop Inc .....................G ..... 217 543-2687
  Arthur *(G-918)*
Prairie Woodworks Inc .........................G ..... 309 378-2418
  Downs *(G-8547)*
R Maderite Inc ...................................G ..... 847 785-0875
  North Chicago *(G-16186)*
Riverside Custom Woodworking ...........G ..... 815 589-3608
  Fulton *(G-10705)*
Roncin Custom Design ........................G ..... 847 669-0260
  Huntley *(G-12175)*
Rose Custom Cabinets Inc ...................E ..... 847 816-4800
  Mundelein *(G-15553)*
Royal Fabricators Inc ..........................F ..... 847 775-7466
  Wadsworth *(G-21327)*
Shews Custom Woodworking ...............G ..... 217 737-5543
  Lincoln *(G-13419)*
Specialized Woodwork Inc ...................G ..... 630 627-0450
  Lombard *(G-13854)*
Spirit Concepts Inc .............................G ..... 708 388-4500
  Crestwood *(G-7503)*
Stancy Woodworking Co Inc ................F ..... 847 526-0252
  Island Lake *(G-12219)*
Suburban Laminating Inc ....................G ..... 708 389-6106
  Melrose Park *(G-14697)*
Tables Inc ..........................................G ..... 630 365-0741
  Elburn *(G-8912)*
United Woodworking Inc .....................E ..... 847 352-3066
  Schaumburg *(G-19782)*
Van Cleave Woodworking Inc ...............G ..... 847 424-8200
  Northbrook *(G-16382)*
Verlo Mattress of Lake Geneva .............G ..... 815 455-2570
  Crystal Lake *(G-7673)*
Waco Manufacturing Co Inc .................F ..... 312 733-0054
  Chicago *(G-6931)*
What We Make Inc .............................G ..... 331 442-4830
  Hampshire *(G-11566)*
Wicks Organ Company ........................E ..... 618 654-2191
  Highland *(G-11819)*
Wooden World of Richmond Inc ...........G ..... 815 405-4503
  Richmond *(G-17974)*

## FURNITURE: Hydraulic Barber & Beauty Shop Chairs

Ecologic Industries LLC .......................E ..... 847 234-5855
  Gurnee *(G-11444)*
Fiberforge Corporation ........................E ..... 970 945-9377
  Chicago *(G-4840)*
Hagen Manufacturing Inc ....................G ..... 224 735-2099
  Wheeling *(G-22064)*
Zarc International Inc .........................F ..... 309 807-2565
  Minonk *(G-14835)*

## FURNITURE: Institutional, Exc Wood

Abundant Living Christian Ctr ..............G ..... 708 896-6181
  Dolton *(G-8362)*
Booths and Upholstery By Ray .............G ..... 773 523-3355
  Chicago *(G-4144)*
Chicago American Mfg LLC .................C ..... 773 376-0100
  Chicago *(G-4302)*
Chicago Booth Mfg Inc ........................F ..... 773 378-8400
  Chicago *(G-4307)*
Correctional Technologies Inc ..............F ..... 630 455-0811
  Willowbrook *(G-22207)*
Egan Visual/West Inc .........................G ..... 800 266-2387
  Chicago *(G-4704)*
Fortune Brands Home & SEC Inc .........C ..... 847 484-4400
  Deerfield *(G-8007)*
Hanley Design Inc ..............................G ..... 309 682-9665
  Peoria *(G-17378)*
Jcdecaux Chicago LLC ........................E ..... 312 456-2999
  Chicago *(G-5285)*
Kinsman Enterprises Inc .....................G ..... 618 932-3838
  West Frankfort *(G-21810)*
Mfp Holding Co ..................................G ..... 312 666-3366
  Chicago *(G-5714)*
Nu-Dell Manufacturing Co Inc .............F ..... 847 803-4500
  Chicago *(G-5953)*
Partners Resource Inc ........................G ..... 630 620-9161
  Glen Ellyn *(G-10985)*

Patio Plus ...........................................G ..... 815 433-2399
  Ottawa *(G-16977)*
Redbox Workshop Ltd ..........................E ..... 773 478-7077
  Chicago *(G-6316)*
Sedia Systems Inc ..............................G ..... 312 212-8010
  Chicago *(G-6471)*
Serious Energy Inc ..............................E ..... 312 515-4606
  Chicago *(G-6478)*
Stevens Cabinets Inc ..........................B ..... 217 857-7100
  Teutopolis *(G-20856)*
Vecchio Manufacturing of Ill ................F ..... 847 742-8429
  Elgin *(G-9224)*
Waco Manufacturing Co Inc .................F ..... 312 733-0054
  Chicago *(G-6931)*
Wise Co Inc ........................................C ..... 618 594-4091
  Carlyle *(G-3061)*

## FURNITURE: Juvenile, Wood

Stevens Cabinets Inc ..........................B ..... 217 857-7100
  Teutopolis *(G-20856)*
Tender Loving Care Inds Inc ................D ..... 847 891-0230
  Schaumburg *(G-19759)*

## FURNITURE: Juvenile, Wood

Meadowbrook LLC ..............................G ..... 312 475-9903
  Chicago *(G-5672)*

## FURNITURE: Kitchen & Dining Room

South Side HM Kit Emporium Inc ..........G ..... 217 322-3708
  Rushville *(G-19095)*

## FURNITURE: Kitchen & Dining Room, Metal

US Foods Culinary Eqp Sups LLC .........G ..... 847 720-8000
  Rosemont *(G-19039)*

## FURNITURE: Laboratory

Kewaunee Scientific Corp .....................G ..... 847 675-7744
  Highland Park *(G-11850)*
Prime Industries Inc ............................E ..... 630 833-6821
  Lisle *(G-13645)*

## FURNITURE: Lawn & Garden, Except Wood & Metal

Bw Dallas LLC ....................................G ..... 847 441-1892
  Northfield *(G-16394)*
Westerling Group ................................G ..... 708 547-8488
  Berkeley *(G-2052)*

## FURNITURE: Lawn, Exc Wood, Metal, Stone Or Concrete

Suncast Corporation .............................A ..... 630 879-2050
  Batavia *(G-1501)*

## FURNITURE: Lawn, Metal

Dixline Corporation ..............................F ..... 309 932-2011
  Galva *(G-10787)*
Henry Crown and Company ..................C ..... 312 236-6300
  Chicago *(G-5072)*

## FURNITURE: Lawn, Wood

Cabinets Doors and More LLC ..............G ..... 847 395-6334
  Antioch *(G-627)*
Chicago Wicker & Trading Co ...............E ..... 708 563-2890
  Alsip *(G-447)*

## FURNITURE: Library

Harrier Interior Products .......................G ..... 847 934-1310
  Palatine *(G-17033)*
Library Furniture Intl ............................G ..... 847 564-9497
  Northbrook *(G-16295)*

## FURNITURE: Living Room, Upholstered On Wood Frames

Trp Acquisition Corp ............................G ..... 630 261-2380
  Lombard *(G-13873)*

## FURNITURE: Mattresses & Foundations

HMK Mattress Holdings LLC .................G ..... 773 472-7390
  Chicago *(G-5094)*
HMK Mattress Holdings LLC .................G ..... 847 798-8023
  Schaumburg *(G-19557)*

HMK Mattress Holdings LLC .................G ..... 708 429-0704
  Orland Park *(G-16865)*
Hospitality Products LLC ......................G ..... 630 359-5075
  Addison *(G-149)*
Illini Mattress Company Inc ..................G ..... 217 359-0156
  Champaign *(G-3498)*
Innocor Inc .........................................B ..... 630 231-0622
  West Chicago *(G-21721)*
Made Rite Bedding Company ...............F ..... 847 349-5886
  Franklin Park *(G-10520)*
Quality Sleep Shop Inc .........................G ..... 708 246-2224
  La Grange Highlands *(G-12750)*
Serta Inc ............................................G ..... 847 645-0200
  Hoffman Estates *(G-12051)*
Wicoff Inc ...........................................G ..... 618 988-8888
  Herrin *(G-11758)*

## FURNITURE: Mattresses, Box & Bedsprings

Corsicana Bedding LLC .......................C ..... 630 264-0032
  Aurora *(G-1134)*
L A Bedding Corp ................................G ..... 773 715-9641
  Chicago *(G-5420)*
Leggett & Platt Incorporated ................D ..... 815 233-0022
  Freeport *(G-10672)*
Luna Mattress Transport Inc .................F ..... 773 847-1812
  Chicago *(G-5568)*
Magic Sleep Mattress Co Inc ................E ..... 815 795-6942
  Marseilles *(G-14314)*
Parenteau Studios ...............................E ..... 312 337-8015
  Chicago *(G-6081)*
Robin Hood Mat & Quilting Corp ..........G ..... 312 953-2960
  Chicago *(G-6371)*
Shevick Sales Corp .............................G ..... 312 487-2865
  Niles *(G-16033)*
Ther A Pedic Midwest Inc ....................G ..... 309 788-0401
  Rock Island *(G-18206)*
Verlo Mat of Skokie-Evanston ...............G ..... 847 966-9988
  Morton Grove *(G-15243)*
Verlo Mattress of Lake Geneva .............G ..... 815 455-2570
  Crystal Lake *(G-7673)*
Visionary Sleep LLC ............................C ..... 224 829-0440
  Hoffman Estates *(G-12068)*

## FURNITURE: Mattresses, Innerspring Or Box Spring

Bedding Group Inc ..............................E ..... 309 788-0401
  Rock Island *(G-18162)*
Bemco Mattress Inc ............................E ..... 217 529-0777
  Springfield *(G-20395)*
Bender Mat Fctry Fton Slepshop ...........B ..... 217 328-1700
  Urbana *(G-21071)*
Estee Bedding Company ......................E ..... 800 521-7378
  Chicago *(G-4780)*
Piersons Mattress Inc ..........................G ..... 309 637-8455
  Peoria *(G-17429)*
Royal Bedding Company Inc ................D ..... 847 645-0200
  Hoffman Estates *(G-12045)*

## FURNITURE: NEC

Classic Remix .....................................G ..... 312 915-0521
  Chicago *(G-4394)*
K K O Inc ...........................................G ..... 815 569-2324
  Capron *(G-2995)*
Lacava ...............................................G ..... 773 637-9600
  Chicago *(G-5431)*
Montauk Chicago Inc ...........................G ..... 312 951-5688
  Chicago *(G-5797)*

## FURNITURE: Novelty, Wood

Lee Weitzman Furniture Inc ..................G ..... 312 243-3009
  Chicago *(G-5485)*

## FURNITURE: Office, Exc Wood

Almacen Inc ........................................G ..... 847 934-7955
  Inverness *(G-12201)*
Austin-Westran LLC .............................C ..... 815 234-2811
  Montgomery *(G-15029)*
Baker Avenue Investments Inc .............G ..... 309 427-2500
  Washington *(G-21378)*
Bretford Manufacturing Inc ..................B ..... 847 678-2545
  Franklin Park *(G-10416)*
C-V Cstom Cntrtops Cbinets Inc ..........F ..... 708 388-5066
  Blue Island *(G-2241)*
Capitol Carton Company ......................E ..... 312 563-9690
  Chicago *(G-4229)*
Central Radiator Cabinet Co ................G ..... 773 539-1700
  Lena *(G-13274)*

# PRODUCT SECTION

## FURNITURE: Upholstered

Debcor Inc .................................................. G ....... 708 333-2191
  South Holland *(G-20261)*
Dirtt Envmtl Solutions Inc ....................... C ....... 312 245-2870
  Chicago *(G-4609)*
Edsal Manufacturing Co Inc ..................... A ....... 773 475-3020
  Chicago *(G-4699)*
Edsal Manufacturing Co Inc ..................... D ....... 773 475-3013
  Chicago *(G-4700)*
Fanmar Inc ............................................... E ....... 708 563-0505
  Elk Grove Village *(G-9475)*
Fellowes Trading Company ...................... G ....... 630 893-1600
  Itasca *(G-12262)*
Hanley Design Inc .................................... G ....... 309 682-9665
  Peoria *(G-17378)*
K-Log Inc .................................................. E ....... 847 872-6611
  Zion *(G-22690)*
Lincoln Office LLC .................................... D ....... 309 427-2500
  Washington *(G-21385)*
Marvel Group Inc ..................................... C ....... 773 523-4804
  Chicago *(G-5639)*
Marvel Group Inc ..................................... C ....... 773 523-4804
  Chicago *(G-5640)*
Marvel Group Inc ..................................... F ....... 773 523-4804
  Chicago *(G-5641)*
Mayline Investments Inc ......................... G ....... 847 948-9340
  Northbrook *(G-16307)*
Metal Box International Inc .................... C ....... 847 455-8500
  Franklin Park *(G-10529)*
Niedermaier Inc ....................................... E ....... 312 492-9400
  Chicago *(G-5913)*
Paoli Inc ................................................... G ....... 312 644-5509
  Chicago *(G-6070)*
Pointe International Company ................ F ....... 847 550-7001
  Lake Zurich *(G-13115)*
Rome Metal Mfg Inc ................................ G ....... 773 287-1755
  Chicago *(G-6389)*
Steel Solutions USA ................................ G ....... 815 432-4938
  Watseka *(G-21428)*
Steelcase Inc ........................................... F ....... 312 321-3720
  Chicago *(G-6581)*
T J Van Der Bosch & Associates ............. E ....... 815 344-3210
  McHenry *(G-14567)*
Techline Studio ........................................ G ....... 212 674-1813
  Palatine *(G-17080)*
Vertisse Inc .............................................. G ....... 224 532-5145
  Lake In The Hills *(G-13009)*
Viking Metal Cabinet Co LLC ................... D ....... 800 776-7767
  Montgomery *(G-15069)*
Viking Metal Cabinet Company ............... D ....... 630 863-7234
  Montgomery *(G-15070)*
Waco Manufacturing Co Inc .................... F ....... 312 733-0054
  Chicago *(G-6931)*

## FURNITURE: Office, Wood

AB&d Custom Furniture Inc .................... E ....... 708 922-9061
  Homewood *(G-12090)*
Aba Custom Woodworking ...................... G ....... 815 356-9663
  Crystal Lake *(G-7525)*
Almacen Inc ............................................. G ....... 847 934-7955
  Inverness *(G-12201)*
B & B Formica Appliers Inc ..................... F ....... 773 804-1015
  Chicago *(G-4014)*
Bretford Manufacturing Inc ..................... B ....... 847 678-2545
  Franklin Park *(G-10416)*
Crestwood Custom Cabinets ................... G ....... 708 385-3167
  Crestwood *(G-7485)*
Daniel M Powers & Assoc Ltd ................. D ....... 630 685-8400
  Bolingbrook *(G-2299)*
Debcor Inc ............................................... G ....... 708 333-2191
  South Holland *(G-20261)*
Diebolds Cabinet Shop ............................ G ....... 773 772-3076
  Chicago *(G-4597)*
Dirtt Envmtl Solutions Inc ....................... C ....... 312 245-2870
  Chicago *(G-4609)*
Donald Kranz ........................................... G ....... 847 428-1616
  Carpentersville *(G-3283)*
Eddie Gapastione .................................... G ....... 708 430-3881
  Bridgeview *(G-2487)*
Egan Visual/West Inc .............................. G ....... 800 266-2387
  Chicago *(G-4704)*
Gianni Incorporated ................................ D ....... 708 863-6696
  Cicero *(G-7198)*
Global Industries Inc ............................... F ....... 630 681-2818
  Glendale Heights *(G-11028)*
Herner-Geissler Wdwkg Corp .................. D ....... 312 226-3400
  Chicago *(G-5081)*
J K Custom Countertops ......................... G ....... 630 495-1224
  Lombard *(G-13813)*
J M Lustig Custom Cabinets Co .............. F ....... 217 342-6661
  Effingham *(G-8840)*
K-Log Inc .................................................. E ....... 847 872-6611
  Zion *(G-22690)*
Lacava LLC ............................................... E ....... 773 637-9600
  Chicago *(G-5432)*
Magnuson Group Inc ............................... F ....... 630 783-8100
  Woodridge *(G-22501)*
Marcy Enterprises Inc ............................. G ....... 708 352-7220
  La Grange Park *(G-12758)*
Marvel Group Inc ..................................... C ....... 773 523-4804
  Chicago *(G-5639)*
Mastercraft Furn Rfnishing Inc ............... G ....... 773 722-5730
  Chicago *(G-5647)*
Mayline Investments Inc ......................... G ....... 847 948-9340
  Northbrook *(G-16307)*
Mlp Seating Corp ..................................... G ....... 847 956-1700
  Elk Grove Village *(G-9633)*
Mobilia Inc ............................................... E ....... 708 865-0700
  Bellwood *(G-1715)*
Newtec Window & Door Inc .................... E ....... 773 869-9888
  Chicago *(G-5905)*
Nova Solutions Inc .................................. E ....... 217 342-7070
  Effingham *(G-8851)*
Pio Woodworking Inc ............................... G ....... 630 628-6900
  Addison *(G-241)*
Regency Custom Woodworking ............... F ....... 815 689-2117
  Cullom *(G-7683)*
Rieke Office Interiors Inc ........................ D ....... 847 622-9711
  Elgin *(G-9165)*
Roevolution 226 LLC ............................... G ....... 773 658-4022
  Riverwoods *(G-18042)*
S & J Woodproducts ................................ G ....... 815 973-1970
  Rockford *(G-18601)*
Stay Straight Manufacturing ................... G ....... 312 226-2137
  Chicago *(G-6579)*
Steelcase Inc ........................................... F ....... 312 321-3720
  Chicago *(G-6581)*
Vertisse Inc .............................................. G ....... 224 532-5145
  Lake In The Hills *(G-13009)*
Wm Huber Cabinet Works ....................... E ....... 773 235-7660
  Chicago *(G-7011)*
Woodhill Cabinetry Design Inc ................ G ....... 815 431-0545
  Ottawa *(G-16992)*

## FURNITURE: Outdoor, Wood

Acrylic Ventures Inc ................................ F ....... 847 901-4440
  Glenview *(G-11094)*
Five Star Industries Inc .......................... E ....... 618 542-4880
  Du Quoin *(G-8554)*
Urban Home Furniture & ACC Inc ........... E ....... 630 761-3200
  Batavia *(G-1514)*

## FURNITURE: Picnic Tables Or Benches, Park

Belson Outdoors LLC ............................... E ....... 630 897-8489
  North Aurora *(G-16120)*
Ill Dept Natural Resources ...................... G ....... 217 498-9208
  Rochester *(G-18118)*
Picnic Tables Inc ..................................... G ....... 630 482-6200
  Batavia *(G-1482)*

## FURNITURE: Porch & Swings, Wood

Pfingsten Partners Fund IV LP ................ B ....... 312 222-8707
  Chicago *(G-6116)*

## FURNITURE: Rattan

House of Rattan Inc ................................ G ....... 630 627-8160
  Lombard *(G-13810)*

## FURNITURE: Restaurant

American Metalcraft Inc .......................... D ....... 800 333-9133
  Franklin Park *(G-10391)*
Buhlwork Design Guild ............................ G ....... 630 325-5340
  Oak Brook *(G-16495)*
Chicago Booth Mfg Inc ............................ F ....... 773 378-8400
  Chicago *(G-4307)*
Contract Industries Inc ........................... G ....... 708 458-8150
  Bedford Park *(G-1545)*
DLM Manufacturing Inc ........................... G ....... 815 964-3800
  Rockford *(G-18348)*
E-J Industries Inc .................................... D ....... 312 226-5023
  Chicago *(G-4669)*
Lena Mercantile ....................................... G ....... 815 369-9955
  Lena *(G-13278)*
Marmon Ret & End User Tech Inc ........... G ....... 312 372-9500
  Chicago *(G-5628)*

## FURNITURE: School

James Howard Co .................................... G ....... 815 497-2831
  Compton *(G-7366)*
K-Log Inc .................................................. E ....... 847 872-6611
  Zion *(G-22690)*
Pointe International Company ................ F ....... 847 550-7001
  Lake Zurich *(G-13115)*
Sage Clover ............................................. G ....... 630 220-9600
  Winfield *(G-22293)*
Sandlock Sandbox LLC ............................ G ....... 630 963-9422
  Westmont *(G-21919)*

## FURNITURE: Sleep

Fredman Bros Furniture Co Inc .............. E ....... 309 674-2011
  Peoria *(G-17366)*

## FURNITURE: Stadium

Irwin Seating Company ........................... C ....... 618 483-6157
  Altamont *(G-553)*

## FURNITURE: Stools With Casters, Metal, Exc Home Or Office

Waco Manufacturing Co Inc .................... F ....... 312 733-0054
  Chicago *(G-6931)*

## FURNITURE: Storage Chests, Household, Wood

Chicagoland Closets LLC ......................... E ....... 630 906-0000
  Aurora *(G-1130)*
Quesse Moving & Storage Inc ................. G ....... 815 223-0253
  Peru *(G-17525)*

## FURNITURE: Table Tops, Marble

Central Illinois Granite Inc ..................... G ....... 309 263-6880
  Morton *(G-15155)*
Factory Plaza Inc .................................... E ....... 630 616-9999
  Bensenville *(G-1895)*
Patterson Products .................................. E ....... 618 723-2688
  Noble *(G-16053)*

## FURNITURE: Tables & Table Tops, Wood

E J Self Furniture ................................... G ....... 847 394-0899
  Mount Prospect *(G-15327)*

## FURNITURE: Tables, Household, Metal

Austin-Westran LLC ................................ C ....... 815 234-2811
  Byron *(G-2912)*

## FURNITURE: Tables, Office, Exc Wood

Amtab Manufacturing Corp ..................... D ....... 630 301-7600
  Aurora *(G-1107)*
Tables Inc ................................................ G ....... 630 365-0741
  Elburn *(G-8912)*

## FURNITURE: Tables, Office, Wood

Amtab Manufacturing Corp ..................... D ....... 630 301-7600
  Aurora *(G-1107)*

## FURNITURE: Television, Wood

Zenith Electronics Corporation ............... E ....... 847 941-8000
  Lincolnshire *(G-13496)*

## FURNITURE: Unfinished, Wood

Churchill Cabinet Company ..................... E ....... 708 780-0070
  Cicero *(G-7182)*
Trendler Inc ............................................. E ....... 773 284-6600
  Chicago *(G-6768)*

## FURNITURE: Upholstered

Addison Interiors Company ..................... F ....... 630 628-1345
  Addison *(G-23)*
Booths and Upholstery By Ray ............... G ....... 773 523-3355
  Chicago *(G-4144)*
Brusic-Rose Inc ....................................... E ....... 708 458-9900
  Bedford Park *(G-1542)*
Coles Appliance & Furn Co ..................... G ....... 773 525-1797
  Chicago *(G-4422)*
Custom Cabinet Man Inc ......................... G ....... 847 249-0007
  Gurnee *(G-11436)*
Custom Craft Cabinetry ........................... G ....... 630 897-2334
  Aurora *(G-1135)*

## FURNITURE: Upholstered

E M C Industry .................................. G ...... 217 543-2894
  Arthur  *(G-898)*
Groupe Lacasse LLC ............................ E ...... 312 670-9100
  Chicago  *(G-5006)*
Knapp Industrial Wood ........................ F ...... 815 657-8854
  Forrest  *(G-10263)*
M & R Custom Millwork ....................... G ...... 815 547-8549
  Belvidere  *(G-1768)*
New Image Upholstery ......................... F ...... 630 542-5560
  South Elgin  *(G-20221)*
Nolte & Tyson Inc .................................. F ...... 847 551-3313
  Gilberts  *(G-10929)*
Parenteau Studios ................................ E ...... 312 337-8015
  Chicago  *(G-6081)*
Patrick Cabinetry Inc ........................... G ...... 630 307-9333
  Bloomingdale  *(G-2126)*
Scibor Upholstering & Gallery ............. G ...... 708 671-9700
  Chicago  *(G-6457)*
Sherwood Industries Inc ..................... F ...... 847 626-0300
  Niles  *(G-16032)*
Shoppe De Lee Inc ............................... G ...... 847 350-0580
  Elk Grove Village  *(G-9736)*
Tables Inc .............................................. G ...... 630 365-0741
  Elburn  *(G-8912)*
Vinyl Life North ..................................... G ...... 630 906-9686
  North Aurora  *(G-16149)*

## FUSES & FUSE EQPT

Littelfuse Inc ......................................... A ...... 773 628-1000
  Chicago  *(G-5521)*

## FUSES: Electric

Fuseco ................................................... G ...... 847 749-4158
  Rolling Meadows  *(G-18731)*
S & C Electric Company ....................... A ...... 773 338-1000
  Chicago  *(G-6419)*

## Furs

Elan Furs ............................................... F ...... 317 255-6100
  Morton Grove  *(G-15195)*

## GAMBLING: Lotteries

WMS Industries Inc ............................... D ...... 847 785-3000
  Chicago  *(G-7018)*

## GAMES & TOYS: Air Rifles

Airgun Designs USA Inc ....................... G ...... 847 520-7507
  Cary  *(G-3324)*

## GAMES & TOYS: Banks

Citizens Bank National Assn ................ G ...... 708 755-0741
  Chicago Heights  *(G-7092)*
Harris Skokie ......................................... G ...... 847 675-6300
  Skokie  *(G-20012)*
Ing Bank Fsb ........................................ G ...... 312 981-1236
  Chicago  *(G-5190)*
Liberty Classics Inc ............................... G ...... 847 367-1288
  Libertyville  *(G-13342)*

## GAMES & TOYS: Blocks

Click-Block Corporation ....................... E ...... 847 749-1651
  Rolling Meadows  *(G-18723)*

## GAMES & TOYS: Board Games, Children's & Adults'

Rapid Displays Inc ................................ C ...... 773 927-5000
  Chicago  *(G-6291)*

## GAMES & TOYS: Cars, Play, Children's Vehicles

Quicker Engineering .............................. G ...... 815 675-6516
  Spring Grove  *(G-20360)*

## GAMES & TOYS: Child Restraint Seats, Automotive

Safe Traffic System Inc ........................ G ...... 847 233-0365
  Lincolnwood  *(G-13536)*
Star Sleigh ............................................. F ...... 630 858-2576
  Glen Ellyn  *(G-10991)*

## GAMES & TOYS: Craft & Hobby Kits & Sets

Craft World Inc ...................................... G ...... 800 654-6114
  Loves Park  *(G-13928)*
Edwin Waldmire & Virginia .................. G ...... 217 498-9375
  Rochester  *(G-18117)*
Made By Hands Inc .............................. G ...... 773 761-4200
  Chicago  *(G-5595)*
Virtu ....................................................... G ...... 773 235-3790
  Chicago  *(G-6900)*

## GAMES & TOYS: Darts & Dart Games

Merlin Technologies Inc ....................... G ...... 630 232-9223
  Rockford  *(G-18493)*

## GAMES & TOYS: Doll Carriages & Carts

Standard Container Co of Edgar .......... E ...... 847 438-1510
  Lake Zurich  *(G-13134)*

## GAMES & TOYS: Doll Clothing

Jiminees Inc .......................................... G ...... 630 295-8002
  Roselle  *(G-18949)*

## GAMES & TOYS: Engines, Miniature

Conley Precision Engines Inc ............... F ...... 630 858-3160
  Glen Ellyn  *(G-10964)*

## GAMES & TOYS: Game Machines, Exc Coin-Operated

AGS Partners LLC ................................. D ...... 630 446-7777
  Itasca  *(G-12224)*
Arkadian Gaming LLC .......................... G ...... 708 377-5656
  Orland Park  *(G-16844)*
Novomatic Americas Sales LLC ........... G ...... 224 802-2974
  Mount Prospect  *(G-15356)*
Video Gaming Technologies Inc .......... G ...... 847 776-3516
  Palatine  *(G-17085)*

## GAMES & TOYS: Kits, Science, Incl Microscopes/Chemistry Sets

American Science & Surplus Inc .......... F ...... 773 763-0313
  Chicago  *(G-3871)*
Science Supply Solutions ..................... G ...... 847 981-5500
  Bensenville  *(G-1989)*

## GAMES & TOYS: Models, Airplane, Toy & Hobby

Great Planes Model Mfg Inc ................ E ...... 217 367-2707
  Urbana  *(G-21090)*

## GAMES & TOYS: Models, Automobile & Truck, Toy & Hobby

Branch Lines Ltd ................................... G ...... 847 256-4294
  Wilmette  *(G-22245)*
Diecasm LLC ......................................... G ...... 877 343-2276
  Buffalo Grove  *(G-2687)*

## GAMES & TOYS: Models, Boat & Ship, Toy & Hobby

Octura Models Inc ................................ G ...... 847 674-7351
  Skokie  *(G-20049)*

## GAMES & TOYS: Models, Railroad, Toy & Hobby

Accurail Inc ............................................ F ...... 630 365-6400
  Elburn  *(G-8873)*
Huff & Puff Industries Ltd .................... G ...... 847 381-8255
  North Barrington  *(G-16152)*
Scale Railroad Equipment .................... G ...... 630 682-9170
  Carol Stream  *(G-3234)*

## GAMES & TOYS: Puzzles

Picture Perfect Puzzles LLC ................. G ...... 847 838-0848
  Lake Villa  *(G-13022)*
Puzzles Bus Off Solutions Inc .............. G ...... 773 891-7688
  Chicago  *(G-6230)*

## GAMES & TOYS: Rocking Horses

Rocking Horse ....................................... G ...... 773 486-0011
  Chicago  *(G-6375)*

## GAMES & TOYS: Sleds, Children's

Pacific Cycle Inc .................................... C ...... 618 393-2508
  Olney  *(G-16789)*

## GAMES & TOYS: Strollers, Baby, Vehicle

Nelson-Whittaker Ltd ........................... E ...... 815 459-6000
  Crystal Lake  *(G-7618)*

## GAMES & TOYS: Structural Toy Sets

Mackin Group LLC ................................ G ...... 847 245-4201
  Lake Villa  *(G-13019)*

## GAMES & TOYS: Toy Guns

Budd AA Inc .......................................... G ...... 630 879-1740
  North Aurora  *(G-16121)*

## GAMES & TOYS: Trains & Eqpt, Electric & Mechanical

Lake County C V Joints Inc .................. G ...... 847 537-7588
  Wheeling  *(G-22088)*
Narita Manufacturing Inc ..................... F ...... 248 345-1777
  Belvidere  *(G-1773)*
Oakridge Corporation ........................... G ...... 630 435-5900
  Lemont  *(G-13245)*

## GAMES & TOYS: Wagons, Coaster, Express & Play, Children's

Radio Flyer Inc ...................................... E ...... 773 637-7100
  Chicago  *(G-6279)*

## GARAGE DOOR REPAIR SVCS

Builders Chicago Corporation .............. D ...... 224 654-2122
  Rosemont  *(G-18991)*

## GARBAGE CONTAINERS: Plastic

AAA Trash .............................................. G ...... 618 775-1365
  Odin  *(G-16738)*
Cwi ........................................................ G ...... 618 443-2030
  Sparta  *(G-20316)*
Kevs Kans Inc ....................................... G ...... 309 303-3999
  Roanoke  *(G-18051)*
Will County Waste ................................ G ...... 708 489-9718
  Blue Island  *(G-2272)*

## GARBAGE DISPOSERS & COMPACTORS: Commercial

Area Disposal Service Inc .................... F ...... 217 935-1300
  Clinton  *(G-7278)*
Azcon Inc .............................................. F ...... 815 548-7000
  Sterling  *(G-20583)*
Covington Service Installation ............. G ...... 309 376-4921
  Carlock  *(G-3049)*

## GAS & HYDROCARBON LIQUEFACTION FROM COAL

Murphy USA .......................................... G ...... 815 578-9053
  Johnsburg  *(G-12438)*

## GAS & OIL FIELD EXPLORATION SVCS

Angel Rose Energy LLC ........................ G ...... 618 392-3700
  Olney  *(G-16760)*
Baker Hghes Olfld Oprtions Inc ........... F ...... 618 393-2919
  Olney  *(G-16761)*
Bell Brothers ......................................... G ...... 618 544-2157
  Robinson  *(G-18055)*
Benchmark Properties Ltd ................... G ...... 618 395-7023
  Olney  *(G-16762)*
Crawford County Oil LLC ..................... E ...... 618 544-3493
  Robinson  *(G-18058)*
Digital H2o Inc ...................................... F ...... 847 456-8424
  Chicago  *(G-4601)*
East End Express Lube Inc ................... G ...... 618 257-1049
  Belleville  *(G-1629)*
Energy Group Inc .................................. E ...... 847 836-2000
  Dundee  *(G-8561)*
J H Robison & Associates Ltd .............. G ...... 847 559-9662
  Northbrook  *(G-16281)*
Laron Oil Corporation ........................... G ...... 847 836-2000
  Dundee  *(G-8563)*
Lla Exploration Inc ................................ G ...... 217 623-4096
  Taylorville  *(G-20841)*

# PRODUCT SECTION — GASOLINE FILLING STATIONS

Martin Exploration Mgt Co .................... G ....... 708 385-6500
  Alsip *(G-488)*
Mid States Salvage ................................. G ....... 618 842-6741
  Fairfield *(G-10150)*
Midco Exploration Inc ............................ G ....... 630 655-2198
  Westmont *(G-21905)*
Mohican Petroleum Inc .......................... G ....... 312 782-6385
  Chicago *(G-5788)*
Moran Properties Inc ............................. G ....... 312 440-1962
  Chicago *(G-5804)*
Murphy USA Inc ..................................... E ....... 630 801-4950
  Montgomery *(G-15063)*
Northern Illinois Gas Company ............. E ....... 630 983-8676
  Kankakee *(G-12640)*
Northern Illinois Gas Company ............. F ....... 217 357-3105
  Carthage *(G-3318)*
Northern Illinois Gas Company ............. C ....... 630 983-8676
  Crystal Lake *(G-7620)*
Northern Illinois Gas Company ............. D ....... 815 433-3850
  Ottawa *(G-16972)*
Northern Illinois Gas Company ............. C ....... 815 693-3907
  Joliet *(G-12546)*
Northern Illinois Gas Company ............. F ....... 815 223-8097
  Mendota *(G-14729)*
Ofgd Inc ................................................. G ....... 708 283-7101
  Olympia Fields *(G-16804)*
Tenexco Inc ........................................... G ....... 708 771-7870
  River Forest *(G-18003)*
Third Day Oil & Gas LLC ...................... G ....... 618 553-5538
  Oblong *(G-16736)*
Times Energy ........................................ G ....... 773 444-9282
  Worth *(G-22635)*
Woodrow Todd ...................................... G ....... 618 838-9105
  Flora *(G-10222)*

## GAS & OIL FIELD SVCS, NEC

Clinton Oil Corp ..................................... G ....... 815 356-1124
  Crystal Lake *(G-7555)*
Evergreen Marathon .............................. G ....... 708 636-5700
  Evergreen Park *(G-10114)*
Pyrophase Inc ....................................... G ....... 773 324-8645
  Chicago *(G-6233)*
R Energy LLC ....................................... G ....... 618 382-7313
  Carmi *(G-3077)*
Ta Oil Field Service Inc ........................ G ....... 618 249-9001
  Richview *(G-17982)*
United Oil Co ........................................ G ....... 309 378-3049
  Downs *(G-8549)*

## GAS FIELD MACHINERY & EQPT

Mueller Co LLC ..................................... E ....... 217 423-4471
  Decatur *(G-7918)*

## GAS PROCESSING SVC

East St Louis Trml & Stor Co ................ E ....... 618 271-2185
  East Saint Louis *(G-8749)*

## GAS PRODUCTION & DISTRIBUTION: Mixed Natural & Manufactured

Vantage Specialties Inc ......................... D ....... 847 244-3410
  Gurnee *(G-11518)*

## GAS STATIONS

BP Products North America Inc ............. G ....... 630 420-4300
  Naperville *(G-15609)*
Joe Anthony & Associates ..................... G ....... 708 935-0804
  Richton Park *(G-17978)*
K & J Synthetic Lubricants .................... G ....... 630 628-1011
  Addison *(G-162)*
Murphy USA ......................................... G ....... 815 578-9053
  Johnsburg *(G-12438)*
Murphy USA Inc ................................... E ....... 815 337-2440
  Woodstock *(G-22595)*
Murphy USA Inc ................................... D ....... 815 936-6144
  Kankakee *(G-12639)*

## GAS: Refinery

Murphy Oil Usa Inc ............................... G ....... 217 442-7882
  Danville *(G-7757)*
Shell Oil Company ................................ C ....... 618 254-7371
  Wood River *(G-22445)*

## GASES & LIQUIFIED PETROLEUM GASES

Lub-Tek Petroleum Products ................. G ....... 815 741-0414
  Joliet *(G-12534)*

Suma America Inc ................................ G ....... 847 427-7880
  Wood Dale *(G-22425)*

## GASES: Acetylene

Gano Welding Supplies Inc ................... F ....... 217 345-3777
  Charleston *(G-3597)*

## GASES: Carbon Dioxide

Continental Carbonic Pdts Inc ............... E ....... 217 428-2068
  Decatur *(G-7859)*
Linde North America Inc ....................... E ....... 309 353-9717
  Pekin *(G-17273)*
Maccarb Inc .......................................... G ....... 877 427-2499
  Elgin *(G-9098)*

## GASES: Flourinated Hydrocarbon

Hudson Technologies Inc ...................... E ....... 217 373-1414
  Champaign *(G-3496)*
Solvay USA Inc ..................................... E ....... 708 235-7200
  University Park *(G-21062)*

## GASES: Helium

Boc Global Helium Inc .......................... C ....... 630 897-1900
  Montgomery *(G-15032)*
Hands To Work Railroading .................. G ....... 708 489-9776
  Alsip *(G-470)*

## GASES: Hydrogen

Industrial Gas Products Inc ................... G ....... 618 337-1030
  East Saint Louis *(G-8757)*

## GASES: Indl

Aeropres Corporation ............................ G ....... 815 478-3266
  Manhattan *(G-14167)*
Air Products and Chemicals Inc ............ E ....... 618 452-5335
  Granite City *(G-11260)*
Air Products and Chemicals Inc ............ E ....... 815 223-2924
  La Salle *(G-12761)*
Air Products and Chemicals Inc ............ D ....... 618 451-0577
  Granite City *(G-11261)*
Air Products and Chemicals Inc ............ E ....... 815 423-5032
  Channahon *(G-3564)*
Airgas Inc .............................................. E ....... 773 785-3000
  Chicago *(G-3787)*
Airgas Inc .............................................. E ....... 773 785-3000
  Chicago *(G-3786)*
Airgas USA LLC .................................... E ....... 708 482-8400
  Countryside *(G-7413)*
Airgas USA LLC .................................... E ....... 630 231-9260
  West Chicago *(G-21653)*
Airgas USA LLC .................................... E ....... 708 354-0813
  Countryside *(G-7412)*
Airgas USA LLC .................................... E ....... 618 439-7207
  Benton *(G-2020)*
AmeriGas ............................................... D ....... 708 544-1131
  Hillside *(G-11909)*
Brewer Company .................................. F ....... 708 339-9000
  Harvey *(G-11662)*
C P Contractor ...................................... G ....... 630 235-2381
  Hanover Park *(G-11577)*
Continental Carbonic Pdts Inc ............... E ....... 309 346-7515
  Pekin *(G-17257)*
Diversified CPC Intl Inc ......................... E ....... 815 423-5991
  Channahon *(G-3571)*
Ilmo Products Company ....................... E ....... 217 245-2183
  Jacksonville *(G-12394)*
Linde LLC ............................................. E ....... 630 515-2576
  Naperville *(G-15692)*
Linde LLC ............................................. E ....... 630 690-3010
  Carol Stream *(G-3185)*
Linde North America Inc ....................... E ....... 630 257-3612
  Lockport *(G-13726)*
Matheson Tri-Gas Inc ........................... F ....... 309 697-1933
  Mapleton *(G-14213)*
Matheson Tri-Gas Inc ........................... E ....... 815 727-2202
  Joliet *(G-12539)*
Praxair Inc ............................................. E ....... 847 428-3405
  Gilberts *(G-10932)*
Praxair Distribution Inc ......................... E ....... 314 664-7900
  Cahokia *(G-2924)*
Weldstar Company ................................ E ....... 630 859-3100
  Aurora *(G-1232)*

## GASES: Neon

Neon Moon Ltd ..................................... G ....... 847 849-3200
  Algonquin *(G-401)*

Neon Nights Dj Svc ............................... G ....... 309 820-9000
  Bloomington *(G-2205)*
Quality Neon Service ............................ G ....... 847 299-2969
  Des Plaines *(G-8266)*
Shinn Enterprises ................................. G ....... 217 698-3344
  Springfield *(G-20523)*

## GASES: Nitrogen

Amer Nitrogen Co ................................. G ....... 847 681-1068
  Highland Park *(G-11823)*
Linde LLC ............................................. E ....... 618 251-5217
  Hartford *(G-11611)*
Nitrogen Labs Inc ................................. G ....... 312 504-8134
  Champaign *(G-3520)*

## GASES: Oxygen

Linde Gas North America LLC .............. F ....... 630 857-6460
  Broadview *(G-2592)*

## GASKET MATERIALS

Pres-On Corporation ............................. E ....... 630 628-2255
  Bolingbrook *(G-2360)*
Supreme Felt & Abrasives Inc ............... E ....... 708 344-0134
  Cicero *(G-7234)*

## GASKETS

American Gasket Tech Inc .................... D ....... 630 543-1510
  Addison *(G-36)*
Cal-Ill Gasket Co ................................... F ....... 773 287-9605
  Chicago *(G-4213)*
Chicago-Wilcox Mfg Co ........................ E ....... 708 339-5000
  South Holland *(G-20257)*
Excelsior Inc ......................................... G ....... 815 987-2900
  Rockford *(G-18376)*
Excelsior Inc ......................................... E ....... 815 987-2900
  Rockford *(G-18375)*
Gasket & Seal Fabricators Inc ............... E ....... 314 241-3673
  East Saint Louis *(G-8752)*
Ilpea Industries Inc ............................... D ....... 309 343-3332
  Galesburg *(G-10760)*
Lamons Gasket Company ..................... G ....... 815 744-3902
  Joliet *(G-12532)*
M Cor Inc .............................................. E ....... 630 860-1150
  Bensenville *(G-1943)*
Midwest Sealing Products Inc ............... E ....... 847 459-2202
  Buffalo Grove *(G-2737)*
Rhopac Fabricated Products LLC ......... E ....... 847 362-3300
  Libertyville *(G-13376)*
Standard Rubber Products Co .............. E ....... 847 593-5630
  Elk Grove Village *(G-9751)*
Winner Cutting & Stamping Co ............. F ....... 630 963-1800
  Downers Grove *(G-8546)*

## GASKETS & SEALING DEVICES

All American Washer Werks Inc ............ E ....... 847 566-9091
  Mundelein *(G-15468)*
Federal-Mogul Corporation ................... E ....... 248 354-7700
  Berwyn *(G-2065)*
Grumen Manufacturing Inc ................... G ....... 847 473-2233
  Gurnee *(G-11455)*
Hennig Gasket & Seals Inc ................... G ....... 312 243-8270
  Chicago *(G-5071)*
John Crane Inc ..................................... A ....... 312 605-7800
  Chicago *(G-5313)*
John Crane Inc ..................................... E ....... 847 967-2400
  Morton Grove *(G-15207)*
L A D Specialties .................................. G ....... 708 430-1588
  Oak Lawn *(G-16630)*
Punch Products Manufacturing ............. E ....... 773 533-2800
  Chicago *(G-6226)*
Qcc LLC ................................................ C ....... 708 867-5400
  Harwood Heights *(G-11689)*
Rutgers Enterprises Inc ........................ E ....... 847 674-7666
  Lincolnwood *(G-13535)*
Sealtec ................................................. F ....... 630 692-0633
  Oswego *(G-16932)*
SKF USA Inc ......................................... D ....... 847 742-0700
  Elgin *(G-9186)*
Southland Industries Inc ....................... E ....... 757 543-5701
  Bannockburn *(G-1265)*

## GASOLINE FILLING STATIONS

Carnaghi Towing & Repair Inc .............. F ....... 217 446-0333
  Tilton *(G-20878)*
Citgo Petroleum Corporation ................ F ....... 847 734-7611
  Lemont *(G-13233)*

---

Employee Codes: A=Over 500 employees, B=251-500
C=101-250, D=51-100, E=20-50, F=10-19, G=3-9

2017 Harris Illinois Industrial Directory

1595

# GASOLINE FILLING STATIONS

Equilon Enterprises LLC .............................F ....... 312 733-1849
  Chicago *(G-4768)*
Lakenburges Motor Co .............................G ....... 618 523-4231
  Germantown *(G-10893)*

## GASTROINTESTINAL OR GENITOURINARY SYSTEM DRUGS

Joseph B Pigato MD Ltd .............................G ....... 815 937-2122
  Kankakee *(G-12631)*

## GATES: Dam, Metal Plate

BJs Welding Services Etc Co .....................G ....... 773 964-5836
  Chicago *(G-4118)*

## GATES: Ornamental Metal

Tim Detwiler Enterprises Inc .....................G ....... 815 758-9950
  Dekalb *(G-8127)*

## GAUGES

Accu-Grind Manufacturing Inc ..................F ....... 847 526-2700
  Wauconda *(G-21437)*
Active Grinding & Mfg Co .........................F ....... 708 344-0510
  Broadview *(G-2554)*
Air Gage Company .....................................C ....... 847 695-0911
  Elgin *(G-8941)*
Barcor Inc ..................................................F ....... 847 940-0750
  Bannockburn *(G-1255)*
Crown Tool Company Inc .........................G ....... 630 766-3050
  Bensenville *(G-1872)*
Custom Tool & Gage Co Inc ....................G ....... 847 671-5306
  Franklin Park *(G-10450)*
Dundick Corporation .................................E ....... 708 656-6363
  Cicero *(G-7192)*
Gage Assembly Co ....................................D ....... 847 679-5180
  Lincolnwood *(G-13512)*
K Systems Corporation ..............................G ....... 708 449-0400
  Hillside *(G-11921)*
Thread & Gage Co Inc ..............................G ....... 815 675-2305
  Spring Grove *(G-20367)*

## GEARS

Blaz-Man Gear Inc ....................................G ....... 708 599-9700
  Bridgeview *(G-2471)*
Clark Gear Works Inc ................................G ....... 630 561-2320
  Carol Stream *(G-3130)*
Excel Gear Inc ..........................................G ....... 815 623-3414
  Roscoe *(G-18897)*
J & L Gear Incorporated ...........................F ....... 630 832-1880
  Villa Park *(G-21259)*
Ken Elliott Co Inc .......................................G ....... 618 466-8200
  Godfrey *(G-11226)*
Process Screw Products Inc .....................G ....... 815 864-2220
  Shannon *(G-19901)*
Raycar Gear & Machine Company ...........E ....... 815 874-3948
  Rockford *(G-18549)*
Schafer Gear Works Roscoe LLC ............C ....... 815 874-4327
  Roscoe *(G-18920)*

## GEARS & GEAR UNITS: Reduction, Exc Auto

Gam Enterprises Inc .................................E ....... 847 649-2500
  Mount Prospect *(G-15331)*
Geitek Automation Inc ...............................D ....... 815 385-3500
  McHenry *(G-14509)*
Hydraulicnet LLC .......................................F ....... 630 543-7630
  Addison *(G-151)*
Overton Chicago Gear Corp ......................D ....... 773 638-0508
  Chicago *(G-6030)*

## GEARS: Power Transmission, Exc Auto

Allied Gear Co ...........................................G ....... 773 287-8742
  Chicago *(G-3815)*
Circle Gear & Machine Co Inc ..................E ....... 708 652-1000
  Cicero *(G-7184)*
Engelhardt Gear Co ...................................E ....... 847 766-7070
  Elk Grove Village *(G-9458)*
Hadley Gear Manufacturing Co .................F ....... 773 722-1030
  Chicago *(G-5028)*
Ll Gear Inc .................................................G ....... 630 226-1688
  Romeoville *(G-18840)*
Martin Sprocket & Gear Inc ......................F ....... 847 298-8844
  Des Plaines *(G-8227)*
Prophet Gear Co .......................................E ....... 815 537-2002
  Prophetstown *(G-17771)*
Reliance Gear Corporation ........................D ....... 630 543-6640
  Addison *(G-275)*

## GELATIN

Gelita USA Chicago ...................................F ....... 708 891-8400
  Calumet City *(G-2938)*
In3gredients Inc .........................................G ....... 312 577-4275
  Chicago *(G-5171)*

## GEM STONES MINING, NEC: Natural

Professional Gem Sciences Inc .................G ....... 312 920-1541
  Chicago *(G-6209)*

## GEMSTONE & INDL DIAMOND MINING SVCS

Diamond Icic Corporation ..........................E ....... 309 269-8652
  Rock Island *(G-18175)*

## GENEALOGICAL INVESTIGATION SVCS

Moultri Cnty Hstrcl/Gnlgcl Sct ....................F ....... 217 728-4085
  Sullivan *(G-20754)*

## GENERAL & INDUSTRIAL LOAN INSTITUTIONS

Knowles Elec Holdings Inc ........................A ....... 630 250-5100
  Itasca *(G-12296)*

## GENERAL COUNSELING SVCS

Kccdd Inc ..................................................D ....... 309 344-2030
  Galesburg *(G-10762)*

## GENERAL MERCHANDISE, NONDURABLE, WHOLESALE

Bee Sales Comapny ..................................D ....... 847 600-4400
  Niles *(G-15965)*
C B E Inc ...................................................G ....... 630 571-2610
  Oak Brook *(G-16497)*
Corporation Supply Co Inc ........................E ....... 312 726-3375
  Chicago *(G-4476)*
D S Arms Incorporated .............................F ....... 847 277-7258
  Lake Barrington *(G-12805)*
Hanjitech Inc .............................................G ....... 847 707-5611
  Chicago *(G-5041)*

## GENERATING APPARATUS & PARTS: Electrical

Alternative Technologies ...........................G ....... 888 858-4678
  Melrose Park *(G-14592)*
Ees Inc ......................................................G ....... 708 343-1800
  Stone Park *(G-20633)*
Mecc Alte Inc ............................................F ....... 815 344-0530
  McHenry *(G-14530)*

## GENERATION EQPT: Electronic

A J R International Inc ..............................D ....... 800 232-3965
  Glendale Heights *(G-11006)*
Ametek Inc ................................................C ....... 847 596-7000
  Waukegan *(G-21526)*
B&Bimc LLC ..............................................G ....... 815 433-5100
  Ottawa *(G-16948)*
Charles Industries Ltd ..............................D ....... 847 806-6300
  Rolling Meadows *(G-18719)*
Dalec Electronics Inc ................................G ....... 847 671-7676
  South Holland *(G-20259)*
Delta-Unibus Corp .....................................C ....... 708 409-1200
  Northlake *(G-16433)*
Ees Inc ......................................................G ....... 708 343-1800
  Stone Park *(G-20633)*
Hauhinco LP .............................................E ....... 618 993-5399
  Marion *(G-14264)*
Heico Ohmite LLC ....................................F ....... 847 258-0300
  Rolling Meadows *(G-18733)*
Jf Industries Inc ........................................G ....... 773 775-8840
  Chicago *(G-5301)*
Panatrol Corporation .................................G ....... 630 655-4700
  Burr Ridge *(G-2874)*
Powell Electrical Systems Inc ...................C ....... 708 409-1200
  Northlake *(G-16447)*
Powell Electrical Systems Inc ...................C ....... 708 409-1200
  Northlake *(G-16448)*
Powervar Inc .............................................C ....... 847 596-7000
  Waukegan *(G-21604)*
Powervar Holdings LLC ...........................C ....... 800 369-7179
  Waukegan *(G-21605)*
Slaughter Company Inc ............................F ....... 847 932-3662
  Lake Forest *(G-12960)*
We International .......................................G ....... 618 549-1784
  Carbondale *(G-3026)*

## GENERATOR REPAIR SVCS

Lionheart Critical Pow ...............................E ....... 847 291-1413
  Huntley *(G-12159)*

## GENERATORS SETS: Motor, Automotive

H R Larke Corp .........................................G ....... 847 204-2776
  Crystal Lake *(G-7586)*

## GENERATORS: Automotive & Aircraft

C & D Rebuilders .......................................G ....... 618 273-9862
  Eldorado *(G-8918)*
Dale Schawitsch ........................................G ....... 217 224-5161
  Quincy *(G-17817)*

## GENERATORS: Electric

Powersource Generator Rentals ...............G ....... 847 587-3991
  Fox Lake *(G-10281)*

## GENERATORS: Storage Battery Chargers

Performance Battery Group Inc ................G ....... 630 293-5505
  West Chicago *(G-21755)*

## GENERATORS: Vehicles, Gas-Electric Or Oil-Electric

Eco Green Analytics LLC ..........................G ....... 847 691-1148
  Deerfield *(G-8005)*
Innova Global LLC ....................................G ....... 630 568-5609
  Burr Ridge *(G-2853)*

## GERIATRIC SOCIAL SVCS

Oakland Noodle Company ........................G ....... 217 346-2322
  Oakland *(G-16724)*

## GIFT SHOP

Academy Screenprinting Awards ..............G ....... 309 686-0026
  Peoria *(G-17300)*
Baileys Fudge & Fine Gifts Inc .................G ....... 217 231-3834
  Quincy *(G-17799)*
Crabtree & Evelyn Ltd ...............................G ....... 630 898-3478
  Aurora *(G-985)*
Euromarket Designs Inc ............................A ....... 847 272-2888
  Northbrook *(G-16252)*
Galena Cellars Winery ..............................G ....... 815 777-3330
  Galena *(G-10720)*
Heartfelt Gifts Inc ......................................G ....... 309 852-2296
  Kewanee *(G-12690)*
In The Attic Inc .........................................G ....... 847 949-5077
  Mundelein *(G-15509)*
Initial Choice .............................................F ....... 847 234-5884
  Lake Forest *(G-12917)*
Kickapoo Creek Winery ............................G ....... 309 495-9463
  Edwards *(G-8782)*
Little Shop of Papers Ltd ..........................G ....... 847 382-7733
  Barrington *(G-1287)*
M J Burton Engraving Co .........................G ....... 217 223-7273
  Quincy *(G-17854)*
Mangel and Co ..........................................E ....... 847 459-3100
  Buffalo Grove *(G-2730)*
Marley Candles .........................................E ....... 815 485-6604
  Mokena *(G-14883)*
Missouri Wood Craft Inc ...........................G ....... 217 453-2204
  Nauvoo *(G-15853)*
Monograms & More ..................................G ....... 630 789-8424
  Burr Ridge *(G-2869)*
Royal Oak Farm Inc ..................................F ....... 815 648-4141
  Harvard *(G-11646)*
Thia & Co ..................................................G ....... 630 510-9770
  Wheaton *(G-21986)*
Twin City Awards ......................................G ....... 309 452-9291
  Normal *(G-16091)*
Virtu ...........................................................G ....... 773 235-3790
  Chicago *(G-6900)*
Workshop ..................................................E ....... 815 777-2211
  Galena *(G-10736)*

## GIFT, NOVELTY & SOUVENIR STORES: Party Favors

Paper Moon Recycling Inc ........................G ....... 847 548-8875
  Grayslake *(G-11358)*

## GIFT, NOVELTY & SOUVENIR STORES: Trading Cards, Sports

Fielders Choice .............................. G ...... 618 937-2294
  West Frankfort  (G-21807)

## GIFTS & NOVELTIES: Wholesalers

A Jule Enterprise Inc ........................ G ...... 312 243-6950
  Chicago  (G-3689)
Afar Imports & Interiors Inc ................ G ...... 217 744-3262
  Springfield  (G-20386)
Alpha Acrylic Design ........................ G ...... 847 818-8178
  Arlington Heights  (G-708)
Award Concepts Inc ......................... E ...... 630 513-7801
  Saint Charles  (G-19141)
Bella Casa .................................... G ...... 630 455-5900
  Hinsdale  (G-11941)
Bestpysanky Inc ............................. G ...... 877 797-2659
  Morton Grove  (G-15189)
C Becky & Company Inc ..................... G ...... 847 818-1021
  Mount Prospect  (G-15314)
Crabtree & Evelyn Ltd ....................... G ...... 630 898-3478
  Aurora  (G-985)
Fragrance Island ............................. G ...... 773 488-2700
  Chicago  (G-4881)
George Lauterer Corporation ................ E ...... 312 913-1881
  Chicago  (G-4943)
Morton Suggestion Company LLC .......... G ...... 847 255-4770
  Mount Prospect  (G-15351)
Recycled Paper Greetings Inc ............... E ...... 773 348-6410
  Chicago  (G-6314)
Reel Life Dvd LLC ........................... G ...... 708 579-1360
  Western Springs  (G-21872)

## GIFTWARE: Brass

Berkshire Investments LLC .................. D ...... 708 656-7900
  Cicero  (G-7180)

## GLACE, FOR GLAZING FOOD

Capol LLC ..................................... G ...... 224 545-5095
  Deerfield  (G-7993)

## GLASS FABRICATORS

Bertco Enterprises Inc ....................... G ...... 618 234-9283
  Belleville  (G-1614)
Biomerieux Inc ............................... E ...... 630 628-6055
  Lombard  (G-13771)
Boom Company Inc .......................... G ...... 847 459-6199
  Wheeling  (G-22018)
Central Illinois Glass & ....................... G ...... 309 367-4242
  Metamora  (G-14741)
Circle Studio Stained Glass .................. G ...... 847 432-7249
  Highland Park  (G-11827)
Circle Studio Stained Glass .................. G ...... 773 588-4848
  Chicago  (G-4380)
Cristaux Inc ................................... G ...... 773 775-6020
  Elk Grove Village  (G-9400)
Diamond J Glass ............................. G ...... 847 973-2741
  Fox Lake  (G-10276)
Dorma Usa Inc ................................ D ...... 717 336-3881
  Steeleville  (G-20560)
Dorma Usa Inc ................................ D ...... 847 295-2700
  Lake Bluff  (G-12840)
Drehobl Art Glass Company ................. G ...... 773 286-2566
  Chicago  (G-4643)
Energy-Glazed Systems Inc ................. F ...... 847 223-4500
  Grayslake  (G-11334)
Engineered Glass Products LLC ............ C ...... 312 326-4710
  Chicago  (G-4754)
Engineered Glass Products LLC ............ D ...... 312 326-4710
  Chicago  (G-4752)
Engineered Glass Products LLC ............ E ...... 773 843-1964
  Chicago  (G-4753)
Geneva Glassworks Inc ...................... G ...... 630 232-1200
  Geneva  (G-10830)
Gerresheimer Glass Inc ...................... C ...... 708 757-6853
  Chicago Heights  (G-7098)
Glass Dimensions Inc ........................ F ...... 708 410-2305
  Melrose Park  (G-14647)
Glazed Structures Inc ........................ F ...... 847 223-4560
  Grayslake  (G-11341)
Harmon Inc .................................... D ...... 312 726-5050
  Chicago  (G-5046)
Hunter Manufacturing Group Inc ............ G ...... 859 254-7573
  Lake Forest  (G-12911)
Legend Dynamix Inc .......................... G ...... 847 789-7007
  Antioch  (G-641)
Martin Glass Company ....................... F ...... 618 277-1946
  Belleville  (G-1652)
Metal Products Sales Corp ................... G ...... 708 301-6844
  Lockport  (G-13732)
Meyer Glass Design Inc ...................... F ...... 847 675-7219
  Evanston  (G-10071)
Montclare Scientific Glass .................... .......... 847 255-6870
  Arlington Heights  (G-805)
Montrose Glass & Mirror Corp ............... G ...... 773 478-6433
  Chicago  (G-5798)
Mth Enterprises LLC .......................... D ...... 708 498-1100
  Hillside  (G-11928)
Norman P Moeller ............................. G ...... 847 991-3933
  Lake Barrington  (G-12821)
OBrien Scntfic GL Blowing LLC .............. G ...... 217 762-3636
  Monticello  (G-15082)
OHara Autoglass Inc .......................... G ...... 217 323-2300
  Beardstown  (G-1525)
Oi Glass Containers Oi G9 ................... G ...... 815 672-1548
  Streator  (G-20698)
Panel Window Co Inc ......................... G ...... 708 485-0310
  Brookfield  (G-2640)
Pilkington North America Inc ................ C ...... 815 433-0932
  Ottawa  (G-16979)
Precision Screen Specialties ................ G ...... 630 762-9548
  Saint Charles  (G-19241)
River City Millwork Inc ........................ D ...... 800 892-9297
  Rockford  (G-18556)
Roscoe Glass Co .............................. G ...... 815 623-6268
  Roscoe  (G-18916)
S P Industries Inc ............................. E ...... 847 228-2851
  Elk Grove Village  (G-9724)
Safelite Glass Corp ........................... G ...... 877 800-2727
  Decatur  (G-7938)
Shoreline Glass Co Inc ....................... G ...... 312 829-9500
  Hillside  (G-11933)
Southern Glass Co ............................ G ...... 618 532-4281
  Centralia  (G-3434)
Stained Glass of Peoria ....................... G ...... 309 674-7929
  Peoria  (G-17461)
Strategic Materials Inc ........................ G ...... 773 523-2200
  Chicago  (G-6602)
Temp-Tech Industries Inc .................... E ...... 773 586-2800
  Chicago  (G-6694)
Tonjon Company .............................. F ...... 630 208-1173
  Geneva  (G-10873)
Torstenson Glass Co .......................... E ...... 773 525-0435
  Chicago  (G-6748)
Total Look ...................................... .......... 847 382-6646
  Barrington  (G-1310)
Tuminello Enterprizes Inc .................... G ...... 815 416-1007
  Morris  (G-15137)
Tuminello Enterprizes Inc .................... G ...... 815 416-1007
  Morris  (G-15138)
Weathertop Woodcraft ....................... G ......
  Carol Stream  (G-3265)

## GLASS PRDTS, FROM PURCHASED GLASS: Art

Lotton Art Glass Co ........................... G ...... 708 672-1400
  Crete  (G-7516)
Sheri Law Art Glass Ltd ....................... G ...... 708 301-2800
  Homer Glen  (G-12086)

## GLASS PRDTS, FROM PURCHASED GLASS: Glassware

Lead n Glass Tm ............................... F ...... 847 255-2074
  Wheeling  (G-22090)
Monogram of Evanston Inc .................. F ...... 847 864-8100
  Evanston  (G-10074)

## GLASS PRDTS, FROM PURCHASED GLASS: Glassware, Indl

Enameled Steel and Sign Co ................. E ...... 773 481-2270
  Chicago  (G-4748)

## GLASS PRDTS, FROM PURCHASED GLASS: Insulating

Duo Plex Glass Ltd ............................ G ...... 708 532-4422
  Orland Park  (G-16858)
Hillside Industries Inc ........................ C ...... 708 498-1100
  Hillside  (G-11920)
Illinois Valley Glass & Mirror ................. F ...... 309 682-6603
  Peoria  (G-17387)

## GLASS PRDTS, FROM PURCHASED GLASS: Mirrored

Alfred Robinson ............................... G ...... 773 487-5777
  Chicago  (G-3804)
Henry Baron Enterprises Inc ................. G ...... 847 681-2755
  Highland Park  (G-11840)
Lester L Brossard Co .......................... F ...... 815 338-7825
  Woodstock  (G-22585)
Quality Glass and Mirror Inc ................. G ...... 847 290-1707
  Mount Prospect  (G-15366)
See All Industries Inc ......................... F ...... 773 927-3232
  Chicago  (G-6472)

## GLASS PRDTS, FROM PURCHASED GLASS: Mirrors, Framed

Sarj USA Inc ................................... E ...... 708 865-9134
  Franklin Park  (G-10582)

## GLASS PRDTS, FROM PURCHASED GLASS: Novelties, Fruit, Etc

Bards Products Inc ............................ F ...... 800 323-5499
  Mundelein  (G-15475)
Glass Haus ..................................... G ...... 815 459-5849
  McHenry  (G-14510)
Howw Manufacturing Company Inc ........ E ...... 847 382-4380
  Lake Barrington  (G-12809)
Skyline Design Inc ............................ D ...... 773 278-4660
  Chicago  (G-6524)

## GLASS PRDTS, FROM PURCHASED GLASS: Sheet, Bent

Brenda Miller .................................. G ...... 618 678-2639
  Xenia  (G-22643)

## GLASS PRDTS, FROM PURCHASED GLASS: Windshields

Glass America Midwest Inc .................. G ...... 877 743-7237
  Elmhurst  (G-9875)
Pro Glass Corporation ........................ G ...... 630 553-3141
  Bristol  (G-2549)
Safelite Glass Corp ............................ G ...... 815 436-6333
  Crest Hill  (G-7467)
Safelite Glass Corp ............................ G ...... 877 800-2727
  Champaign  (G-3535)

## GLASS PRDTS, PRESSED OR BLOWN: Blocks & Bricks

Lang Exterior Inc .............................. D ...... 773 737-4500
  Chicago  (G-5458)

## GLASS PRDTS, PRESSED OR BLOWN: Bulbs, Electric Lights

Tadd LLC ....................................... F ...... 847 380-3540
  Cary  (G-3375)

## GLASS PRDTS, PRESSED OR BLOWN: Glassware, Art Or Decorative

Amkine Inc ..................................... F ...... 847 526-7088
  Wauconda  (G-21442)
Finer Line Inc .................................. F ...... 847 884-1611
  Schaumburg  (G-19527)
Libation Container Inc ........................ F ...... 312 287-4524
  Chicago  (G-5501)

## GLASS PRDTS, PRESSED OR BLOWN: Glassware, Novelty

Hunter Mfg LLP ................................ D ...... 859 254-7573
  Lake Forest  (G-12912)

## GLASS PRDTS, PRESSED OR BLOWN: Optical

Spectragen Incorporated ..................... G ...... 847 982-0481
  Naperville  (G-15752)
Tacom Hq Inc .................................. G ...... 630 251-8919
  Sheridan  (G-19919)

# GLASS PRDTS, PRESSED OR BLOWN: Ornaments, Christmas Tree

## GLASS PRDTS, PRESSED OR BLOWN: Ornaments, Christmas Tree

Mattarusky Inc .................................. G ...... 630 469-4125
  Glen Ellyn *(G-10980)*

## GLASS PRDTS, PRESSED OR BLOWN: Scientific Glassware

OBrien Scntfic GL Blowing LLC ............ G ...... 217 762-3636
  Monticello *(G-15082)*

## GLASS PRDTS, PRESSED OR BLOWN: Tubing

Cleavenger Associates Inc .................. G ...... 630 221-0007
  Winfield *(G-22284)*

## GLASS PRDTS, PRESSED/BLOWN: Glassware, Art, Decor/Novelty

Altamira Art Glass ............................... G ...... 708 848-3799
  Oak Park *(G-16652)*
Arttig Art ............................................. G ...... 847 804-8001
  Wheeling *(G-22008)*
Sotish Ltd ........................................... G ...... 708 476-2017
  La Grange *(G-12746)*

## GLASS PRDTS, PURCHD GLASS: Furniture Top, Cut, Beveld/Polshd

J K Custom Countertops ..................... G ...... 630 495-2324
  Lombard *(G-13813)*

## GLASS PRDTS, PURCHSD GLASS: Ornamental, Cut, Engraved/D- cor

Besco Awards & Embroidery ............... G ...... 847 395-4862
  Antioch *(G-622)*
Ostrom & Co Inc ................................ F ...... 503 281-6469
  Winfield *(G-22288)*
Slee Corporation ................................ E ...... 773 777-2444
  Chicago *(G-6527)*

## GLASS STORE: Leaded Or Stained

Stained Glass of Peoria ...................... G ...... 309 674-7929
  Peoria *(G-17461)*
T J M & Associates Inc ....................... G ...... 847 382-1993
  Lake Barrington *(G-12825)*
U R On It ............................................ G ...... 847 382-0182
  Lake Barrington *(G-12826)*

## GLASS STORES

Duo Plex Glass Ltd ............................. G ...... 708 532-4422
  Orland Park *(G-16858)*
Fuyao Glass Illinois Inc ....................... C ...... 217 864-2392
  Decatur *(G-7883)*
Martin Glass Company ....................... F ...... 618 277-1946
  Belleville *(G-1652)*
Montrose Glass & Mirror Corp ............. G ...... 773 478-6433
  Chicago *(G-5798)*
Oldcastle Buildingenvelope Inc ............ G ...... 773 523-8400
  Chicago *(G-5981)*
Shoreline Glass Co Inc ....................... E ...... 312 829-9500
  Hillside *(G-11933)*

## GLASS: Fiber

Industrial Fiberglass Inc ..................... F ...... 708 681-2707
  Melrose Park *(G-14657)*

## GLASS: Flat

Cat I Manufacturing Inc ...................... C ...... 847 931-1200
  South Elgin *(G-20188)*
Duo Plex Glass Ltd ............................. G ...... 708 532-4422
  Orland Park *(G-16858)*
Engineered Glass Products LLC ......... E ...... 773 843-1964
  Chicago *(G-4753)*
Fuyao Glass Illinois Inc ....................... C ...... 217 864-2392
  Decatur *(G-7883)*
Glazed Structures Inc ........................ F ...... 847 223-4560
  Grayslake *(G-11341)*
Great Lakes GL & Mirror Corp ............ G ...... 847 647-1036
  Niles *(G-15984)*
Higgins Glass Studio LLC ................... G ...... 708 447-2787
  Riverside *(G-18031)*
Horan Glass Block Inc ........................ G ...... 773 586-4808
  Chicago *(G-5111)*

Jacksonville Art Glass Inc .................. G ...... 217 245-0500
  Jacksonville *(G-12395)*
Montrose Glass & Mirror Corp ............. G ...... 773 478-6433
  Chicago *(G-5798)*
Pilkington North America Inc ............... C ...... 630 545-0063
  Glendale Heights *(G-11057)*
Pilkington North America Inc ............... C ...... 815 433-0932
  Ottawa *(G-16979)*
Pittsburgh Glass Works LLC ............... C ...... 630 879-5100
  Batavia *(G-1483)*
Pontiac Recyclers Inc ......................... C ...... 815 844-6419
  Pontiac *(G-17708)*
Thermal Ceramics Inc ........................ E ...... 217 627-2101
  Girard *(G-10950)*

## GLASS: Indl Prdts

Montclare Scientific Glass ................... G ...... 847 255-6870
  Arlington Heights *(G-805)*
Nippon Electric Glass Amer Inc ........... G ...... 630 285-8323
  Schaumburg *(G-19665)*

## GLASS: Insulating

Lang Exterior Inc ................................ D ...... 773 737-4500
  Chicago *(G-5458)*

## GLASS: Pressed & Blown, NEC

Alpha Precision Inc ............................. F ...... 630 553-7331
  Yorkville *(G-22648)*
Barcor Inc .......................................... F ...... 847 940-0750
  Bannockburn *(G-1255)*
James R Wilbat Glass Studio .............. G ...... 847 940-0015
  Deerfield *(G-8017)*
Libbey Inc .......................................... C ...... 630 818-3400
  West Chicago *(G-21731)*
Lotton Art Glass Co ............................ G ...... 708 672-1400
  Crete *(G-7516)*
Mac Lean-Fogg Company ................... C ...... 847 288-2534
  Franklin Park *(G-10519)*
Norman P Moeller ............................... G ...... 847 991-3933
  Lake Barrington *(G-12821)*
Prairie Fire Glass Inc .......................... G ...... 217 762-3332
  Monticello *(G-15083)*
Punch Products Manufacturing ........... E ...... 773 533-2800
  Chicago *(G-6226)*
Quality Coating Co ............................. F ...... 815 875-3228
  Princeton *(G-17761)*
Thermal Ceramics Inc ........................ E ...... 217 627-2101
  Girard *(G-10950)*
Waters Industries Inc .......................... E ...... 847 783-5900
  West Dundee *(G-21803)*
Wki Holding Company Inc .................. D ...... 847 233-8600
  Rosemont *(G-19041)*
World Kitchen LLC ............................. C ...... 847 233-8600
  Rosemont *(G-19042)*

## GLASS: Safety

Sharp Bullet Resistant Pdts ................. G ...... 815 726-2626
  Joliet *(G-12574)*

## GLASS: Stained

Botti Studio of Architectural ................. E ...... 847 869-5933
  Evanston *(G-10017)*
G & R Stained Glass .......................... G ...... 847 455-7026
  Franklin Park *(G-10474)*
Glass Fx ............................................. G ...... 217 359-0048
  Champaign *(G-3488)*
Tiffany Stained Glass Ltd .................... G ...... 312 642-0680
  Forest Park *(G-10255)*
Will Hamms Stained Glass .................. F ...... 847 255-2230
  Arlington Heights *(G-872)*

## GLASS: Tempered

Oldcastle Buildingenvelope Inc ............ G ...... 773 523-8400
  Chicago *(G-5981)*
Oldcastle Buildingenvelope Inc ............ G ...... 630 250-7270
  Elk Grove Village *(G-9663)*

## GLASSWARE STORES

Altamira Art Glass ............................... G ...... 708 848-3799
  Oak Park *(G-16652)*
Crystal Cave ...................................... F ...... 847 251-1160
  Glenview *(G-11118)*
Higgins Glass Studio LLC ................... G ...... 708 447-2787
  Riverside *(G-18031)*

## GLASSWARE WHOLESALERS

McCracken Label Co .......................... E ...... 773 581-8860
  Chicago *(G-5666)*

## GLASSWARE: Cut & Engraved

Art Crystal II Enterprises Inc ................ E ...... 630 739-0222
  Lyons *(G-14030)*
Crystal Cave ...................................... F ...... 847 251-1160
  Glenview *(G-11118)*

## GLASSWARE: Laboratory

Supertek Scientific LLC ...................... G ...... 630 345-3450
  Villa Park *(G-21287)*

## GLASSWARE: Laboratory & Medical

Pure 111 ............................................. G ...... 618 558-7888
  Caseyville *(G-3400)*

## GLOBAL POSITIONING SYSTEMS & EQPT

OEM Solutions Inc .............................. G ...... 708 574-8893
  Oak Brook *(G-16551)*
Safemobile Inc ................................... F ...... 847 818-1649
  Rolling Meadows *(G-18776)*
STC Inc .............................................. E ...... 618 643-2555
  Mc Leansboro *(G-14468)*

## GLOVES & MITTENS DYEING & FINISHING

Omar Medical Supplies Inc ................. E ...... 708 922-4377
  Chicago *(G-5988)*

## GLOVES: Fabric

Boss Manufacturing Holdings .............. F ...... 309 852-2781
  Kewanee *(G-12675)*
Klein Tools Inc ................................... D ...... 847 228-6999
  Elk Grove Village *(G-9577)*
Klein Tools Inc ................................... E ...... 847 821-5500
  Lincolnshire *(G-13461)*
Kunz Glove Co Inc ............................. E ...... 312 733-8780
  Chicago *(G-5414)*
PW Masonry Inc ................................. G ...... 847 573-0510
  Libertyville *(G-13372)*

## GLOVES: Leather

Boss Manufacturing Holdings .............. F ...... 309 852-2781
  Kewanee *(G-12675)*

## GLOVES: Leather, Work

Boss Holdings Inc .............................. D ...... 309 852-2131
  Kewanee *(G-12673)*
Boss Manufacturing Company ............ D ...... 309 852-2131
  Kewanee *(G-12674)*
Kunz Glove Co Inc ............................. E ...... 312 733-8780
  Chicago *(G-5414)*
Magid Glove Safety Mfg Co LLC ......... B ...... 773 384-2070
  Romeoville *(G-18841)*
Magid Glove Safety Mfg Co LLC ......... B ...... 773 384-2070
  Chicago *(G-5601)*
Nationwide Glove Co Inc .................... D ...... 618 252-7192
  Harrisburg *(G-11602)*

## GLOVES: Plastic

Oak Technical LLC ............................. G ...... 931 455-7011
  Matteson *(G-14377)*

## GLOVES: Safety

Boss Manufacturing Holdings .............. F ...... 309 852-2781
  Kewanee *(G-12675)*

## GLOVES: Work

Boss Holdings Inc .............................. D ...... 309 852-2131
  Kewanee *(G-12673)*
Magid Glove Safety Mfg Co LLC ......... B ...... 773 384-2070
  Romeoville *(G-18841)*
Magid Glove Safety Mfg Co LLC ......... B ...... 773 384-2070
  Chicago *(G-5601)*
Nationwide Glove Co Inc .................... D ...... 618 252-7192
  Harrisburg *(G-11602)*
Wells Lamont Indust Group LLC ......... A ...... 800 247-3295
  Niles *(G-16046)*

## PRODUCT SECTION — GRAPHIC ARTS & RELATED DESIGN SVCS

### GLOVES: Woven Or Knit, From Purchased Materials

Illinois Glove Company .................... G ...... 800 342-5458
Northbrook *(G-16272)*

### GLUE

HB Fuller Company ........................... G ...... 847 358-9555
Aurora *(G-1024)*
National Casein Company ................. E ...... 773 846-7300
Chicago *(G-5861)*
National Casein of California ............ D ...... 773 846-7300
Chicago *(G-5863)*

### GO-CART DEALERS

Hopkins Saws & Karts Inc ................ G ...... 618 756-2778
Belle Rive *(G-1605)*

### GOLD ORE MINING

Coeur Mining Inc ............................... D ...... 312 489-5800
Chicago *(G-4419)*

### GOLD ORES

Billy Cash For Gold Inc .................... G ...... 773 905-2447
Melrose Park *(G-14600)*

### GOLF CARTS: Powered

Brewer Utility Systems Inc ............... G ...... 217 224-5975
Quincy *(G-17808)*

### GOLF CLUB & EQPT REPAIR SVCS

Custom Golf By Tanis ....................... G ...... 708 481-4433
Matteson *(G-14369)*

### GOLF DRIVING RANGES

Pro Circle Golf Centers Inc .............. G ...... 815 675-2747
Spring Grove *(G-20359)*

### GOLF EQPT

Custom Golf By Tanis ....................... G ...... 708 481-4433
Matteson *(G-14369)*
Dreamworld Golf ............................... G ...... 847 803-4757
Des Plaines *(G-8186)*
EJL Custom Golf Clubs Inc .............. G ...... 630 654-8887
Willowbrook *(G-22210)*
Infiniti Golf ......................................... G ...... 630 520-0626
West Chicago *(G-21718)*
Par Golf Supply Inc .......................... E ...... 847 891-1222
Schaumburg *(G-19681)*
Pro Circle Golf Centers Inc .............. G ...... 815 675-2747
Spring Grove *(G-20359)*
US Golf Manufacturing ..................... G ...... 309 797-9820
Moline *(G-14974)*

### GOLF GOODS & EQPT

Brewer Utility Systems Inc ............... G ...... 217 224-5975
Quincy *(G-17808)*
Custom Golf By Tanis ....................... G ...... 708 481-4433
Matteson *(G-14369)*
EJL Custom Golf Clubs Inc .............. G ...... 630 654-8887
Willowbrook *(G-22210)*
Pro Circle Golf Centers Inc .............. G ...... 815 675-2747
Spring Grove *(G-20359)*

### GOURMET FOOD STORES

Larry Ragan ...................................... G ...... 618 698-1041
Belleville *(G-1648)*
Pappone Inc ..................................... G ...... 630 234-4738
Chicago *(G-6073)*
Pastificio Inc .................................... G ...... 847 432-5459
Highwood *(G-11887)*

### GOVERNMENT, EXECUTIVE OFFICES: Local

City of Chicago ................................. E ...... 312 744-0940
Chicago *(G-4384)*

### GOVERNMENT, EXECUTIVE OFFICES: Mayors'

City of Pekin ..................................... F ...... 309 477-2325
Pekin *(G-17256)*

### GOVERNMENT, GENERAL: Administration

City of Chicago ................................. G ...... 773 581-8000
Chicago *(G-4386)*

### GOVERNORS: Diesel Engine, Pump

Concentric Itasca Inc ....................... D ...... 630 268-1528
Itasca *(G-12246)*

### GRADING SVCS

Thelen Sand & Gravel Inc ................ D ...... 847 838-8800
Antioch *(G-656)*

### GRAIN & FIELD BEANS WHOLESALERS

Cargill Incorporated ......................... G ...... 815 942-0932
Morris *(G-15099)*
Effingham Equity Inc ........................ F ...... 217 268-5128
Arcola *(G-668)*
Maplehurst Farms Inc ..................... F ...... 815 562-8723
Rochelle *(G-18097)*

### GRANITE: Crushed & Broken

Martin Marietta Materials Inc ........... F ...... 618 285-6267
Golconda *(G-11241)*
Pacific Granites Inc .......................... G ...... 312 835-7777
Chicago *(G-6052)*

### GRANITE: Cut & Shaped

AA Rigoni Brothers Inc .................... E ...... 815 838-9770
Lockport *(G-13701)*
Accorn Gran Natural Stone Inc ....... G ...... 312 663-5000
Chicago *(G-3718)*
Carrera Stone Systems of Chica .... G ...... 847 566-2277
Mundelein *(G-15483)*
Condor Granites Intl Inc .................. G ...... 847 635-7214
Elgin *(G-9000)*
Cosmos Granite & Marble Corp ..... G ...... 630 595-8025
Wood Dale *(G-22355)*
D & H Granite and Marble Sup ....... E ...... 773 869-9988
Chicago *(G-4533)*
Earth Stone Products III Inc ............ G ...... 847 671-3000
Schiller Park *(G-19822)*
Euro Marble & Granite Inc .............. F ...... 847 233-0700
Schiller Park *(G-19827)*
Geokat Granite ................................ G ...... 773 265-1423
Chicago *(G-4940)*
Global Stone Inc .............................. G ...... 847 718-1418
Elk Grove Village *(G-9502)*
Granite Designs of Ilinois ................ G ...... 773 772-5300
Chicago *(G-4985)*
Granite Mountain Inc ....................... G ...... 708 774-1442
New Lenox *(G-15884)*
House Granite & Marble Corp ........ G ...... 847 928-1111
Schiller Park *(G-19839)*
Kitchen Transformation Inc ............. F ...... 847 758-1905
Elk Grove Village *(G-9574)*
Midwest Stone Sales Inc ................ G ...... 815 254-6600
Plainfield *(G-17628)*
Monumental Art Works .................... G ...... 708 389-3038
Blue Island *(G-2263)*
United Granite & Marble ................. G ...... 815 582-3345
Joliet *(G-12584)*
Wasowski Jacek .............................. G ...... 847 693-1878
Palatine *(G-17087)*

### GRANITE: Dimension

Eastern Kitchen & Bath ................... G ...... 312 492-7248
Chicago *(G-4684)*

### GRANITE: Dimension

Blue Pearl Stone Tech LLC ............. G ...... 708 698-5700
La Grange *(G-12726)*
C & V Granite Inc ............................. G ...... 847 966-0275
Morton Grove *(G-15191)*
Picture Stone Inc ............................. G ...... 773 875-5021
Mount Prospect *(G-15365)*

### GRAPHIC ARTS & RELATED DESIGN SVCS

A To Z Type & Graphic Inc .............. G ...... 312 587-1887
Chicago *(G-3692)*
All-Brite Sign Co Inc ........................ F ...... 309 829-1551
Normal *(G-16063)*
Allied Graphics Inc .......................... G ...... 847 419-8830
Buffalo Grove *(G-2654)*
Alta Vista Graphic Corporation ....... F ...... 773 267-2530
Chicago *(G-3835)*
Anderson Safford Mkg Graphics .... F ...... 847 827-8968
Des Plaines *(G-8150)*
Apollo Printing Inc ........................... G ...... 815 741-3065
Homewood *(G-12091)*
ASap Specialties Inc Del ................ G ...... 847 223-7699
Grayslake *(G-11321)*
Bach & Associates .......................... G ...... 618 277-1652
Belleville *(G-1610)*
Baseline Graphics Inc ..................... G ...... 630 964-9566
Downers Grove *(G-8395)*
Baum Holdings Inc .......................... G ...... 847 488-0650
South Elgin *(G-20185)*
Bindery & Distribution Service ....... G ...... 847 550-7000
South Barrington *(G-20131)*
Carlberg Design Inc ........................ G ...... 217 341-3291
Petersburg *(G-17534)*
Chicago Mltlingua Graphics Inc ..... F ...... 847 386-7187
Northfield *(G-16397)*
Comet Conection Inc ...................... G ...... 312 243-5400
Alsip *(G-451)*
Corporate Graphics Inc ................... G ...... 630 762-9000
Saint Charles *(G-19164)*
Crosstech Communications Inc ..... E ...... 312 382-0111
Chicago *(G-4506)*
Dicianni Graphics Incorporated ..... F ...... 630 833-5100
Addison *(G-91)*
Edwards Creative Services LLC .... F ...... 309 756-0199
Milan *(G-14784)*
First Impression of Chicago ........... G ...... 773 224-3434
Chicago *(G-4849)*
G & G Studios /Broadway Prtg ...... F ...... 815 933-8181
Bradley *(G-2422)*
Gammon Group Inc ......................... G ...... 815 722-6400
Shorewood *(G-19927)*
Gfx International Inc ........................ G ...... 847 543-7179
Grayslake *(G-11340)*
Gh Printing Co Inc ........................... E ...... 630 960-4115
Downers Grove *(G-8449)*
Group 329 LLC ................................ G ...... 312 828-0200
Chicago *(G-5005)*
Haapanen Brothers Inc ................... D ...... 847 662-2233
Gurnee *(G-11457)*
Ideal/Mikron Inc ............................... G ...... 847 873-0254
Mount Prospect *(G-15336)*
Inde Enterprises Inc ........................ E ...... 815 338-8844
Woodstock *(G-22574)*
Innovtive Design Graphics Corp .... G ...... 847 475-7772
Evanston *(G-10057)*
Jamali Kopy Kat Printing Inc .......... G ...... 708 544-6164
Bellwood *(G-1711)*
Jans Graphics Inc ............................ F ...... 312 644-4700
Chicago *(G-5278)*
Josephs Printing Service ................ G ...... 847 724-4429
Glenview *(G-11154)*
Just Your Type Inc ........................... G ...... 847 864-8890
Evanston *(G-10060)*
Laser Expressions Ltd .................... G ...... 847 419-9600
Buffalo Grove *(G-2721)*
Lloyd Midwest Graphics ................. G ...... 815 282-8828
Machesney Park *(G-14089)*
Luttrell Engraving Inc ...................... E ...... 708 489-3800
Alsip *(G-485)*
Pelegan Inc ...................................... G ...... 708 442-9797
Riverside *(G-18033)*
Phoenix Marketing Services .......... F ...... 630 616-8000
Mundelein *(G-15546)*
Prime Market Targeting Inc ............ E ...... 815 469-4555
Frankfort *(G-10353)*
R R Donnelley & Sons Company ... B ...... 312 326-8000
Chicago *(G-6270)*
Royal Publishing Inc ....................... G ...... 309 343-4007
Galesburg *(G-10775)*
RR Donnelley & Sons Company .... C ...... 312 236-8000
Chicago *(G-6404)*
Sadannah Group LLC ..................... G ...... 630 357-2300
Naperville *(G-15745)*
Sandra E Greene ............................ G ...... 815 469-0092
Frankfort *(G-10361)*
Sharp Graphics Inc ......................... G ...... 847 966-7000
Skokie *(G-20085)*
Shoreline Graphics Inc ................... G ...... 847 587-4804
Ingleside *(G-12198)*
Sign & Banner Express ................... G ...... 630 783-9700
Bolingbrook *(G-2368)*
Speedpro Imaging ........................... G ...... 847 856-8220
Gurnee *(G-11506)*
Unicomp Typography Inc ................ G ...... 847 821-0221
Buffalo Grove *(G-2784)*
Van Meter Graphx Inc ..................... G ...... 847 465-0600
Wheeling *(G-22177)*

---

Employee Codes: A=Over 500 employees, B=251-500
C=101-250, D=51-100, E=20-50, F=10-19, G=3-9

# GRAPHIC ARTS & RELATED DESIGN SVCS
# PRODUCT SECTION

Vis-O-Graphic Inc .................................. E ...... 630 590-6100
 Addison  *(G-341)*
Washburn Graficolor Inc ...................... G ...... 630 596-0880
 Naperville  *(G-15781)*
Wyckoff Advertising Inc ....................... G ...... 630 260-2525
 Wheaton  *(G-21990)*

## GRAPHIC LAYOUT SVCS: Printed Circuitry

Laux Grafix Inc ......................................... 618 337-4558
 East Saint Louis  *(G-8759)*

## GRATINGS: Open Steel Flooring

Metalex Corporation ............................. C ...... 847 362-5400
 Libertyville  *(G-13355)*
WEb Production & Fabg Inc ................ F ...... 312 733-6800
 Chicago  *(G-6948)*

## GRATINGS: Tread, Fabricated Metal

Barnett-Bates Corporation ................... F ...... 815 726-5223
 Joliet  *(G-12461)*
Cooper B-Line Inc .................................. C ...... 618 357-5353
 Pinckneyville  *(G-17546)*
Gs Metals Corp ....................................... C ...... 618 357-5353
 Pinckneyville  *(G-17550)*
Midwest Cage Company ...................... G ...... 815 806-0005
 Frankfort  *(G-10342)*
Paco Corporation .................................. F ...... 708 430-2424
 Bridgeview  *(G-2517)*

## GRAVE MARKERS: Concrete

Spence Monuments Co ....................... G ...... 217 348-5992
 Charleston  *(G-3612)*

## GRAVEL & PEBBLE MINING

Valley Run Stone Inc ............................. E ...... 630 553-7974
 Yorkville  *(G-22674)*

## GRAVEL MINING

A E Frasz Inc .......................................... F ...... 630 232-6223
 Elburn  *(G-8872)*
Allendale Gravel Co Inc ....................... G ...... 618 263-3521
 Allendale  *(G-420)*
Amigoni Construction ........................... G ...... 309 923-3701
 Roanoke  *(G-18047)*
C & H Gravel C Inc ................................ G ...... 217 857-3425
 Teutopolis  *(G-20848)*
Edk Construction Inc ............................ G ...... 630 853-3484
 Darien  *(G-7793)*
Elmhurst-Chicago Stone Company ... E ...... 630 832-4000
 Elmhurst  *(G-9865)*
Fox Ridge Stone Co .............................. G ...... 630 554-9101
 Oswego  *(G-16918)*
Hastie Mining & Trucking ..................... E ...... 618 289-4536
 Cave In Rock  *(G-3402)*
Lake County Grading Co LLC ............. G ...... 847 362-2590
 Libertyville  *(G-13341)*
Legacy Vulcan LLC ............................... F ...... 815 895-6501
 Sycamore  *(G-20807)*
Petersen Sand & Gravel Inc ................ F ...... 815 344-1060
 Lakemoor  *(G-13145)*
Plote Construction Inc .......................... E ...... 847 695-0422
 Hoffman Estates  *(G-12035)*
Prosser Construction Co ...................... F ...... 217 774-5032
 Shelbyville  *(G-19913)*
Southfield Corporation .......................... E ...... 309 676-0576
 Peoria  *(G-17459)*

## GREASES & INEDIBLE FATS, RENDERED

Darling Ingredients Inc ......................... E ...... 773 376-5550
 Chicago  *(G-4559)*
Kostelac Grease Service Inc ............... E ...... 314 436-7166
 Belleville  *(G-1646)*

## GREETING CARD PAINTING BY HAND

Card Dynamix LLC ................................ C ...... 630 685-4060
 Romeoville  *(G-18806)*

## GREETING CARD SHOPS

Jane Stodden Bridals ........................... G ...... 815 223-2091
 La Salle  *(G-12779)*

## GREETING CARDS WHOLESALERS

C Becky & Company Inc ...................... G ...... 847 818-1021
 Mount Prospect  *(G-15314)*

Crest Greetings Inc ............................... F ...... 708 210-0800
 Chicago  *(G-4503)*
Fsg Crest LLC ........................................ F ...... 708 210-0800
 Lake In The Hills  *(G-12993)*

## GRILLES & REGISTERS: Ornamental Metal Work

Birdsell Machine & Orna Inc ............... G ...... 217 243-5849
 Jacksonville  *(G-12379)*

## GRINDING SVC: Precision, Commercial Or Indl

A J Carbide Grinding ............................ G ...... 847 675-5112
 Skokie  *(G-19942)*
A-B Die Mold Inc ................................... F ...... 847 658-1199
 Bartlett  *(G-1327)*
Abrasive West LLC ............................... G ...... 630 736-0818
 Bartlett  *(G-1328)*
Accu-Grind Manufacturing Inc ............ F ...... 847 526-2700
 Wauconda  *(G-21437)*
B S Grinding Inc .................................... G ...... 847 787-0770
 Elk Grove Village  *(G-9332)*
BT & E Co ............................................... G ...... 815 544-6431
 Belvidere  *(G-1740)*
Century Mold & Tool Co ....................... E ...... 847 364-5858
 Elk Grove Village  *(G-9362)*
Contour Tool Works Inc ........................ E ...... 847 947-4700
 Palatine  *(G-17018)*
Ever Ready Pin & Manufacturing ....... D ...... 815 874-4949
 Rockford  *(G-18371)*
Grind Lap Services Inc ........................ G ...... 630 458-1111
 Addison  *(G-139)*
Kasha Industries Inc ............................. E ...... 618 375-2511
 Grayville  *(G-11372)*
Nb Finishing Inc .................................... F ...... 847 364-7500
 Melrose Park  *(G-14677)*
Pioneer Service Inc .............................. E ...... 630 628-0249
 Addison  *(G-242)*
Prospect Grinding Incorporated ......... G ...... 847 229-9240
 Wheeling  *(G-22129)*
Ro Pal Grinding Inc .............................. F ...... 815 964-5894
 Rockford  *(G-18561)*
S & S Tool Company ............................. G ...... 847 891-0780
 Schaumburg  *(G-19715)*
Sterling Tool & Manufacturing ............. G ...... 847 304-1800
 Barrington  *(G-1305)*

## GRINDING SVCS: Ophthalmic Lens, Exc Prescription

Edgebrook Eyecare ............................... F ...... 815 397-5959
 Rockford  *(G-18358)*

## GRINDSTONES: Artificial

C M C Industries Inc ............................. F ...... 630 377-0530
 Saint Charles  *(G-19147)*
Radiac Abrasives Inc ........................... C ...... 618 548-4200
 Salem  *(G-19347)*

## GRIPS OR HANDLES: Rubber

Go Steady LLC ...................................... G ...... 630 293-3243
 West Chicago  *(G-21709)*

## GROCERIES WHOLESALERS, NEC

Ach Food Companies Inc .................... C ...... 708 458-8690
 Summit Argo  *(G-20759)*
American Bottling Company ................ B ...... 708 947-5000
 Northlake  *(G-16426)*
Chipita America Inc .............................. E ...... 708 731-2434
 Westchester  *(G-21832)*
Coca-Cola Refreshments USA Inc .... C ...... 630 513-5247
 Saint Charles  *(G-19158)*
Coca-Cola Refreshments USA Inc .... C ...... 708 597-6700
 Alsip  *(G-450)*
Coca-Cola Refreshments USA Inc .... D ...... 708 597-4700
 Chicago  *(G-4415)*
E & J Gallo Winery ................................ G ...... 630 505-4000
 Lisle  *(G-13584)*
Goodhome Foods Inc ........................... G ...... 847 816-6832
 Lake Forest  *(G-12903)*
Grante Foods International LLC .......... F ...... 773 751-9551
 Elk Grove Village  *(G-9507)*
Hillshire Brands Company ................... C ...... 847 956-7575
 Elk Grove Village  *(G-9524)*
Ixtapa Foods .......................................... G ...... 773 788-9701
 Chicago  *(G-5249)*

Jewel Osco Inc ...................................... C ...... 630 584-4594
 Saint Charles  *(G-19202)*
Lee Gilster-Mary Corporation .............. F ...... 618 533-4808
 Centralia  *(G-3421)*
Natural Distribution Company ............. G ...... 630 350-1700
 Wood Dale  *(G-22403)*
Noon Hour Food Products Inc ............ E ...... 312 382-1177
 Chicago  *(G-5924)*
Sotiros Foods Inc .................................. G ...... 708 371-0002
 Alsip  *(G-529)*
Vienna Beef Ltd ..................................... F ...... 773 278-7800
 Chicago  *(G-6896)*

## GROCERIES, GENERAL LINE WHOLESALERS

Abitec Corporation ................................ E ...... 217 465-8577
 Paris  *(G-17139)*
Arro Corporation .................................... C ...... 708 352-8200
 Hodgkins  *(G-11970)*
Arro Corporation .................................... G ...... 773 978-1251
 Chicago  *(G-3947)*
Arro Corporation .................................... E ...... 708 352-7412
 Hodgkins  *(G-11971)*
Dfg Confectionary LLC ......................... B ...... 847 412-1961
 Northbrook  *(G-16241)*
Dzro-Bans International Inc ................. G ...... 779 324-2740
 Homewood  *(G-12096)*
Goodhome Foods Inc ........................... G ...... 847 816-6832
 Lake Forest  *(G-12903)*
Hodgson Mill Inc ................................... C ...... 217 347-0105
 Effingham  *(G-8839)*
Ixtapa Foods .......................................... G ...... 773 788-9701
 Chicago  *(G-5249)*
Iya Foods LLC ....................................... G ...... 630 854-7107
 North Aurora  *(G-16135)*
Koenemann Sausage Co ..................... G ...... 815 385-6260
 Volo  *(G-21316)*
Michael Lewis Company ...................... C ...... 708 688-2200
 Mc Cook  *(G-14453)*
Pennant Foods ....................................... G ...... 708 752-8730
 Alsip  *(G-506)*
Simu Ltd ................................................. F ...... 630 350-1900
 Wood Dale  *(G-22422)*
Sotiros Foods Inc .................................. G ...... 708 371-0002
 Alsip  *(G-529)*
Thomas Proestler .................................. G ...... 630 971-0185
 Lisle  *(G-13671)*
V Formusa Co ........................................ F ...... 224 938-9360
 Des Plaines  *(G-8296)*

## GROMMETS: Rubber

Rahco Rubber Inc ................................. D ...... 847 298-4200
 Des Plaines  *(G-8267)*

## GROUTING EQPT: Concrete

Black-Jack Grout Pumps Inc ............... G ...... 815 494-2904
 Rockford  *(G-18286)*

## GUARD SVCS

Embassy Security Group Inc .............. E ...... 800 627-1325
 Orland Park  *(G-16859)*

## GUARDS: Machine, Sheet Metal

Hennig Inc .............................................. G ...... 815 636-9900
 Machesney Park  *(G-14078)*

## GUIDED MISSILES & SPACE VEHICLES: Research & Development

Branmark Strategy Group LLC ........... G ...... 847 849-9080
 Glenview  *(G-11110)*

## GUIDED MISSILES/SPACE VEHICLE PARTS/AUX EQPT: Research/Devel

Azimuth Cnc Inc .................................... F ...... 815 399-4433
 Rockford  *(G-18274)*
Wilson Tool Corporation ....................... E ...... 815 226-0147
 Rockford  *(G-18685)*

## GUM & WOOD CHEMICALS

Ryano Resins Inc .................................. G ...... 630 621-5677
 Aurora  *(G-1076)*

# PRODUCT SECTION

# HARDWARE

### GUN PARTS MADE TO INDIVIDUAL ORDER
**Oglesby & Oglesby Gunmakers** .......... G ...... 217 487-7100
Springfield *(G-20492)*

### GUN STOCKS: Wood
**Plano Synergy Holding Inc** .................. E ...... 630 552-3111
Plano *(G-17674)*

### GUNSMITHS
**Maxon Shooters Supplies Inc** ................ G ...... 847 298-4867
Des Plaines *(G-8228)*
**McGowen Rifle Barrels** .......................... G ...... 815 937-9816
Saint Anne *(G-19123)*

### GUTTERS
**Four Seasons Gutter Prote** .................... G ...... 309 694-4565
East Peoria *(G-8710)*

### GUTTERS: Sheet Metal
**American Home Aluminium Co** ............ G ...... 773 925-9442
Calumet Park *(G-2956)*
**Illinois Valley Gutters Inc** ...................... G ...... 309 698-8140
East Peoria *(G-8713)*
**Rollex Corporation** .................................. C ...... 847 437-3000
Elk Grove Village *(G-9717)*
**Wallfill Co** ................................................. F ...... 630 499-9591
Aurora *(G-1094)*

### GYPSUM PRDTS
**Continental Studios Inc** ......................... E ...... 773 542-0309
Chicago *(G-4460)*
**Creative Perky Cuisine LLC** .................. G ...... 312 870-0282
Tinley Park *(G-20905)*
**New Ngc Inc** ............................................. D ...... 847 623-8100
Waukegan *(G-21592)*
**Owens Corning Sales LLC** .................... D ...... 815 226-4627
Rockford *(G-18527)*
**Patrick Industries Inc** ............................. D ...... 630 595-0595
Franklin Park *(G-10548)*
**United States Gypsum Company** ......... B ...... 312 606-4000
Chicago *(G-6829)*
**USG Corporation** ..................................... F ...... 847 970-5200
Libertyville *(G-13396)*
**USG Corporation** ..................................... B ...... 312 436-4000
Chicago *(G-6858)*

### HAIR & HAIR BASED PRDTS
**Afam Concept Inc** ................................... C ...... 773 838-1336
Chicago *(G-3779)*
**Beachwaver** .............................................. E ...... 224 513-5817
Libertyville *(G-13308)*
**Hairline Creations Inc** ............................. F ...... 773 282-5454
Chicago *(G-5032)*
**Interntonal Hair Solutions LLC** ............. G ...... 404 474-3547
Schaumburg *(G-19574)*
**QS Luxurious Hair & Shoes Inc** ........... G ...... 773 556-6092
Bellwood *(G-1716)*
**Schmit Laboratories Inc** ........................ E ...... 773 476-0072
Glendale Heights *(G-11066)*

### HAIR ACCESS WHOLESALERS
**Maxi-Vac Inc** ............................................ G ...... 224 699-9760
Addison *(G-194)*

### HAIR ACCESS: Rubber
**Bows Arts Inc** .......................................... F ...... 847 501-3161
Glenview *(G-11109)*

### HAIR CARE PRDTS
**American Blending & Filling Co** ............ D ...... 847 689-1000
Waukegan *(G-21523)*
**Biocare Labs Inc** .................................... G ...... 708 496-8657
Bedford Park *(G-1541)*
**BMC 1092 Inc** .......................................... E ...... 708 544-2200
Broadview *(G-2563)*
**Ecoco Inc** ................................................. E ...... 773 745-7700
Chicago *(G-4693)*
**Hollywood International Co** ................... E ...... 708 926-9437
Blue Island *(G-2256)*
**Luster Products Inc** ................................ B ...... 773 579-1800
Chicago *(G-5569)*
**Market Ready Inc** ................................... G ...... 847 689-1000
Waukegan *(G-21586)*

**Namaste Laboratories LLC** .................... D ...... 708 824-1393
Chicago *(G-5851)*
**Natural Beginnings** ................................ G ...... 773 457-0509
Plainfield *(G-17630)*
**Safe Effective Alternatives** .................... F ...... 618 236-2727
Belleville *(G-1675)*
**Selected Chemical Products Co** ........... E ...... 847 623-2224
Waukegan *(G-21614)*
**Summit Laboratories Inc** ....................... E ...... 708 333-2995
Harvey *(G-11677)*
**Zotos International Inc** .......................... C ...... 847 390-0984
Rosemont *(G-19044)*

### HAIR CURLERS: Beauty Shop
**Alliance For Illinois Mfg** ......................... G ...... 773 594-9292
Chicago *(G-3813)*
**Cindys Nail & Hair Care** ........................ G ...... 847 234-0780
Lake Forest *(G-12891)*
**Live Love Hair** ......................................... G ...... 530 554-2471
Lansing *(G-13174)*

### HAIR DRESSING, FOR THE TRADE
**Kim Tiffani Institute LLC** ....................... D ...... 312 260-9000
Lincolnwood *(G-13519)*

### HAIR REPLACEMENT & WEAVING SVCS
**Interntonal Hair Solutions LLC** ............. G ...... 404 474-3547
Schaumburg *(G-19574)*
**Payne Chauna** ............................................... 618 580-2584
Belleville *(G-1664)*

### HAIR STYLIST: Men
**Casper Ernest E Hairgoods** ................... G ...... 773 545-2800
Chicago *(G-4249)*

### HAMPERS: Solid Fiber, Made From Purchased Materials
**Westrock Rkt Company** ......................... E ...... 630 325-9670
Burr Ridge *(G-2894)*

### HAND TOOLS, NEC: Wholesalers
**Advance Equipment Mfg Co** .................. F ...... 773 287-8220
Chicago *(G-3759)*
**Doerock Inc** ..................................................... 217 543-2101
Arthur *(G-895)*
**Rockford Commercial Whse Inc** ........... G ...... 815 623-8400
Machesney Park *(G-14105)*

### HANDBAG STORES
**Bag and Barrier Corporation** ................. G ...... 217 849-3271
Toledo *(G-20961)*
**Bxb Intl Inc** .............................................. G ...... 312 240-1966
Brookfield *(G-2626)*

### HANDBAGS
**Ipurse Inc** ................................................ F ...... 312 344-3449
Chicago *(G-5236)*

### HANDBAGS: Women's
**Coach Inc** ................................................ F ...... 630 232-0667
Geneva *(G-10819)*
**Coach Inc** ................................................ E ...... 708 349-1053
Orland Park *(G-16848)*

### HANDLES: Brush Or Tool, Plastic
**Altamont Co** ............................................ D ...... 800 626-5774
Thomasboro *(G-20859)*
**Phoenix Electric Mfg Co** ........................ E ...... 773 477-8855
Chicago *(G-6118)*

### HANDLES: Wood
**Nikwood Products Inc** ........................... G ...... 309 658-2341
Hillsdale *(G-11902)*
**Vaughan & Bushnell Mfg Co** ................. F ...... 815 648-2446
Hebron *(G-11730)*

### HANGERS: Garment, Plastic
**Applied Arts & Sciences Inc** ................. G ...... 407 288-8228
Mokena *(G-14853)*

### HANGERS: Garment, Wire
**Hangables Inc** ......................................... F ...... 847 673-9770
Skokie *(G-20010)*

### HARD RUBBER PRDTS, NEC
**Voss Belting & Specialty Co** .................. E ...... 847 673-8900
Lincolnwood *(G-13541)*

### HARDWARE
**9161 Corporation** .................................... G ...... 847 470-8828
Niles *(G-15953)*
**Aco Inc** .................................................... E ...... 773 774-5200
Chicago *(G-3735)*
**Advanced Machine & Engrg Co** ............. C ...... 815 962-6076
Rockford *(G-18257)*
**Afc Cable Systems Inc** .......................... B ...... 508 998-1131
Harvey *(G-11651)*
**Agena Manufacturing Co** ....................... E ...... 630 668-5086
Carol Stream *(G-3093)*
**Alan Manufacturing Corp** ...................... G ...... 815 568-6836
Marengo *(G-14217)*
**Aldon Co** .................................................. F ...... 847 623-8800
Waukegan *(G-21521)*
**Allquip Co Inc** ......................................... G ...... 309 944-6153
Geneseo *(G-10797)*
**American Partsmith Inc** ......................... G ...... 630 520-0432
West Chicago *(G-21656)*
**Antolin Interiors Usa Inc** ....................... B ...... 618 327-4416
Nashville *(G-15833)*
**Ashland Door Solutions LLC** ................. G ...... 773 348-5106
Elk Grove Village *(G-9315)*
**Baker Drapery Corporation** ................... G ...... 309 691-3295
Peoria *(G-17313)*
**Baron Manufacturing Co LLC** ................ E ...... 630 628-9110
Itasca *(G-12235)*
**Braun Manufacturing Co Inc** ................. E ...... 847 635-2050
Mount Prospect *(G-15313)*
**Caterpillar Inc** ......................................... A ...... 309 578-2473
Mossville *(G-15250)*
**Chas O Larson Co** .................................. E ...... 815 625-0503
Rock Falls *(G-18129)*
**Chicago Car Seal Company** ................... G ...... 773 278-9400
Chicago *(G-4310)*
**Chicago Hardware and Fix Co** ............... D ...... 847 455-6609
Franklin Park *(G-10429)*
**Cooper B-Line Inc** .................................. A ...... 618 654-2184
Highland *(G-11780)*
**Creative Steel Fabricators** ..................... E ...... 847 803-2090
Des Plaines *(G-8177)*
**Crosby Group LLC** ................................. C ...... 708 333-3005
Harvey *(G-11663)*
**Crown Metal Manufacturing Co** ............ E ...... 630 279-9800
Elmhurst *(G-9859)*
**Del Storm Products Inc** ......................... F ...... 217 446-3377
Danville *(G-7715)*
**Du Bro Products Inc** .............................. E ...... 847 526-2136
Wauconda *(G-21456)*
**Dumore Supplies Inc** ............................. F ...... 312 949-6260
Chicago *(G-4649)*
**Dura Operating LLC** ............................... C ...... 815 947-3333
Stockton *(G-20631)*
**Duratrack Inc** .......................................... E ...... 847 806-0202
Elk Grove Village *(G-9439)*
**E R Wagner Manufacturing Co** .............. C ...... 708 485-3400
Brookfield *(G-2630)*
**Engert Co Inc** .......................................... E ...... 847 673-1633
Skokie *(G-19993)*
**Estwing Manufacturing Co Inc** .............. B ...... 815 397-9521
Rockford *(G-18370)*
**F B Williams Co** ..................................... F ...... 773 233-4255
Chicago *(G-4802)*
**Fenix Manufacturing LLC** ...................... G ...... 815 208-0755
Fulton *(G-10700)*
**First Choice Building Pdts Inc** .............. F ...... 630 350-2770
Wood Dale *(G-22368)*
**Geib Industries Inc** ................................ E ...... 847 455-4550
Bensenville *(G-1906)*
**Hendrickson International Corp** ............ C ...... 815 727-4031
Joliet *(G-12510)*
**Hyspan Precision Products Inc** ............. E ...... 773 277-0700
South Holland *(G-20279)*
**I Hardware Direct Inc** ............................ G ...... 708 325-0000
Westmont *(G-21892)*
**Illinois Steel Service Inc** ....................... D ...... 312 926-7440
Chicago *(G-5158)*
**Industrial Rubber & Sup Entp** ............... G ...... 217 429-3747
Decatur *(G-7895)*
**Inland Fastener Inc** ................................ F ...... 630 293-3800
West Chicago *(G-21720)*

Employee Codes: A=Over 500 employees, B=251-500
C=101-250, D=51-100, E=20-50, F=10-19, G=3-9

2017 Harris Illinois Industrial Directory

# HARDWARE  PRODUCT SECTION

Jerome Remien Corporation ............F ...... 847 806-0888
  Elk Grove Village *(G-9561)*
Kemper Industries .........................G ...... 217 826-5712
  Marshall *(G-14324)*
MHS Ltd .......................................F ...... 773 736-3333
  Chicago *(G-5716)*
Neisewander Enterprises Inc .........A ...... 815 288-1431
  Dixon *(G-8337)*
Norforge and Machining Inc .........D ...... 309 772-3124
  Bushnell *(G-2907)*
OBerry Enterprises Inc ...................G ...... 815 728-9480
  Ringwood *(G-17994)*
Peerless Industries Inc ...................B ...... 630 375-5100
  Aurora *(G-1063)*
Plews Inc .......................................C ...... 815 288-3344
  Dixon *(G-8339)*
Practechal Marketing .....................G ...... 847 486-8600
  Glenview *(G-11183)*
Prater Industries Inc .....................D ...... 630 679-3200
  Bolingbrook *(G-2359)*
Precision Brand Products Inc ........E ...... 630 969-7200
  Downers Grove *(G-8509)*
Quality Hnge A Div Spreme Hnge ...E ...... 708 534-7801
  University Park *(G-21061)*
Reichel Hardware Company Inc .....G ...... 630 762-7394
  Saint Charles *(G-19252)*
Rockford Process Control Inc ........C ...... 815 966-2000
  Rockford *(G-18583)*
Royal Brass Inc .............................G ...... 618 439-6341
  Benton *(G-2040)*
Rutland Inc ....................................E ...... 217 245-7810
  Jacksonville *(G-12413)*
S & D Products Inc .......................E ...... 630 372-2325
  Bartlett *(G-1370)*
Seamless Gutter Corp ....................E ...... 630 495-9800
  Lombard *(G-13852)*
Shapco Inc .....................................G ...... 847 229-1439
  Wheeling *(G-22149)*
SPEP Acquisition Corp ...................E ...... 310 608-0693
  Bolingbrook *(G-2375)*
Standard Truck Parts Inc ...............G ...... 815 726-4486
  Joliet *(G-12578)*
Stock Gears Inc .............................F ...... 224 653-9489
  Elk Grove Village *(G-9758)*
Tables Inc .......................................G ...... 630 365-0741
  Elburn *(G-8912)*
Tekni-Plex Inc ................................E ...... 217 935-8311
  Clinton *(G-7289)*
Thermos LLC ..................................E ...... 847 439-7821
  Schaumburg *(G-19760)*
U S Tool & Manufacturing Co .......E ...... 630 953-1000
  Addison *(G-332)*
Unistrut International Corp ...........C ...... 800 882-5543
  Harvey *(G-11679)*
V & N Metal Products Inc .............G ...... 773 436-1855
  Chicago *(G-6863)*
Van Craft Industry of Del Edel .....G ...... 708 430-6670
  Oak Lawn *(G-16646)*
Venturedyne Ltd ............................E ...... 708 597-7550
  Chicago *(G-6884)*
W J Dennis & Company .................F ...... 847 697-4800
  Elgin *(G-9225)*
Weiland Metal Products Company ...G ...... 773 631-4210
  Chicago *(G-6950)*
William Dudek Manufacturing Co ...E ...... 773 622-2727
  Chicago *(G-6983)*
Wind Point Partners Vi LP ............G ...... 312 255-4800
  Chicago *(G-6993)*
Wozniak Industries Inc ..................C ...... 708 458-1220
  Bedford Park *(G-1595)*
Zirlin Interiors Inc ........................E ...... 773 334-5530
  Chicago *(G-7069)*

## HARDWARE & BUILDING PRDTS: Plastic

Advanced Drainage Systems Inc ...F ...... 815 539-2160
  Mendota *(G-14714)*
Dayton Superior Corporation .......C ...... 815 936-3300
  Kankakee *(G-12609)*
Dike-O-Seal Incorporated ..............F ...... 773 254-3224
  Chicago *(G-4603)*
Dukane Ias LLC .............................D ...... 630 797-4900
  Saint Charles *(G-19176)*
Entrigue Designs ...........................G ...... 708 647-6159
  Homewood *(G-12097)*
Fiberglass Innovations LLC ..........F ...... 815 962-9338
  Rockford *(G-18381)*
Illinois Tool Works Inc ..................C ...... 708 479-7200
  Mokena *(G-14873)*
Illinois Tool Works Inc ..................G ...... 708 479-7200
  Tinley Park *(G-20922)*

Jay Cee Plastic Fabricators ...........F ...... 773 276-1920
  Chicago *(G-5284)*
Kalle USA Inc ................................G ...... 847 775-0781
  Gurnee *(G-11466)*
Kastalon Inc ...................................D ...... 708 389-2210
  Alsip *(G-478)*
L & P Guarding LLC .....................C ...... 708 325-0400
  Bedford Park *(G-1560)*
Nu-Dell Manufacturing Co Inc ......F ...... 847 803-4500
  Chicago *(G-5953)*
Pexco LLC .....................................C ...... 847 296-5511
  Des Plaines *(G-8253)*
Quixote Corporation ......................E ...... 312 705-8400
  Chicago *(G-6259)*
Sno Gem Inc .................................F ...... 888 766-4367
  McHenry *(G-14555)*
Specialized Woodwork Inc ............F ...... 630 627-0450
  Lombard *(G-13854)*
Tri Guards Inc ................................F ...... 847 537-8444
  Elk Grove Village *(G-9790)*
Tuf-Tite Inc ....................................F ...... 847 550-1011
  Lake Zurich *(G-13139)*
W J Dennis & Company .................F ...... 847 697-4800
  Elgin *(G-9225)*
White Eagle Brands Inc ................G ...... 773 631-1764
  Chicago *(G-6971)*

## HARDWARE & EQPT: Stage, Exc Lighting

UIC ................................................F ...... 312 413-7697
  Chicago *(G-6805)*

## HARDWARE STORES

Anixter Inc .....................................E ...... 512 989-4254
  Glenview *(G-11102)*
Ashland Door Solutions LLC ........G ...... 773 348-5106
  Elk Grove Village *(G-9315)*
Chicago Clamp Company ..............G ...... 708 343-8311
  Broadview *(G-2567)*
Continental Midland ......................G ...... 708 441-1000
  Calumet Park *(G-2960)*
Dumore Supplies Inc ....................F ...... 312 949-6260
  Chicago *(G-4649)*
Four Seasons Ace Hardware .........G ...... 618 439-2101
  Benton *(G-2027)*
Giovannini Metals Corp .................G ...... 815 842-0500
  Pontiac *(G-11702)*
Koson Tool Inc ..............................G ...... 815 277-2107
  Frankfort *(G-10340)*
Peoples Coal and Lumber Co ........F ...... 815 432-2456
  Watseka *(G-21425)*
Prescription Plus Ltd ....................F ...... 618 537-6202
  Lebanon *(G-13216)*
Reasons Inc ...................................G ...... 309 537-3424
  Buffalo Prairie *(G-2797)*
Upper Limits Midwest Inc ............G ...... 217 679-4315
  Springfield *(G-20547)*
Value Link 1 Enterprises ..............G ...... 630 833-6243
  Villa Park *(G-21289)*

## HARDWARE STORES: Builders'

A Ashland Lock Company ..............F ...... 773 348-5106
  Chicago *(G-3684)*
Greene Welding & Hardware Inc ...E ...... 217 375-4244
  East Lynn *(G-8668)*

## HARDWARE STORES: Chainsaws

Outdoor Power Inc ........................F ...... 217 228-9890
  Quincy *(G-17865)*
Owen Walker .................................G ...... 217 285-4012
  Pittsfield *(G-17572)*

## HARDWARE STORES: Door Locks & Lock Sets

Kaser Power Equipment Inc .........G ...... 309 289-2176
  Knoxville *(G-12721)*
Lovatt & Radcliffe Ltd .................G ...... 815 568-9797
  Skokie *(G-20031)*

## HARDWARE STORES: Pumps & Pumping Eqpt

S C C Pumps Inc ...........................G ...... 847 593-8495
  Arlington Heights *(G-834)*
Wagner Pump & Supply Co Inc ....G ...... 847 526-8573
  Wauconda *(G-21512)*

## HARDWARE STORES: Snowblowers

Wissmiller & Evans Road Eqp .......G ...... 309 725-3598
  Cooksville *(G-7373)*

## HARDWARE STORES: Tools

Correct Tool Inc .............................F ...... 630 595-6055
  Bensenville *(G-1867)*
Form Relief Tool Co Inc ................F ...... 815 393-4263
  Davis Junction *(G-7812)*
Line Craft Tool Company Inc ........C ...... 630 932-1182
  Lombard *(G-13820)*
Quality Tech Tool Inc ....................E ...... 847 690-9643
  Bensenville *(G-1973)*
Sab Tool Supply Co .......................G ...... 847 634-3700
  Vernon Hills *(G-21196)*
Sport Redi-Mix LLC .......................E ...... 217 355-4222
  Champaign *(G-3545)*

## HARDWARE STORES: Tools, Hand

Doerock Inc ...................................G ...... 217 543-2101
  Arthur *(G-895)*

## HARDWARE STORES: Tools, Power

Performance Lawn & Power ..........G ...... 217 857-3717
  Teutopolis *(G-20854)*

## HARDWARE WHOLESALERS

Advance Tools LLC ........................G ...... 855 685-0633
  Glenview *(G-11097)*
Champion Chisel Works Inc .........F ...... 815 535-0647
  Rock Falls *(G-18128)*
Continental Midland ......................G ...... 708 441-1000
  Calumet Park *(G-2960)*
CR Laurence Co Inc ......................G ...... 773 242-2871
  Cicero *(G-7186)*
Engert Co Inc .................................E ...... 847 673-1633
  Skokie *(G-19993)*
J & W Counter Tops Inc ................E ...... 217 544-0876
  Springfield *(G-20460)*
Konekt Inc .....................................G ...... 773 733-0471
  Chicago *(G-5403)*
Mechanics Planing Mill Inc ...........E ...... 618 288-3000
  Glen Carbon *(G-10954)*
OBerry Enterprises Inc ..................G ...... 815 728-9480
  Ringwood *(G-17994)*
SPEP Acquisition Corp ..................E ...... 310 608-0693
  Bolingbrook *(G-2375)*
True Value Company .....................G ...... 847 639-5383
  Cary *(G-3378)*
True Value Company .....................B ...... 773 695-5000
  Chicago *(G-6786)*
UNI-Glide Corp ..............................G ...... 773 235-2100
  Chicago *(G-6811)*

## HARDWARE, WHOLESALE: Bolts

Beacon Fas & Components Inc .....E ...... 847 541-0404
  Wheeling *(G-22013)*
Sanco Industries Inc .....................F ...... 847 243-8675
  Kildeer *(G-12703)*
Slsb LLC .........................................D ...... 618 219-4115
  Madison *(G-14153)*

## HARDWARE, WHOLESALE: Builders', NEC

Beno J Gundlach Company ...........E ...... 618 233-1781
  Belleville *(G-1613)*
Fna Ip Holdings Inc ......................D ...... 847 348-1500
  Elk Grove Village *(G-9482)*
Hersheys Metal Meister LLC .........E ...... 217 234-4700
  Claremont *(G-7256)*
La Force Inc ..................................G ...... 630 325-1950
  Willowbrook *(G-22218)*
Simpson Strong-Tie Company Inc ...E ...... 630 613-5100
  Addison *(G-293)*

## HARDWARE, WHOLESALE: Casters & Glides

Clark Caster Co .............................G ...... 708 366-1913
  Forest Park *(G-10238)*

## HARDWARE, WHOLESALE: Chains

Galva Iron and Metal Co Inc ........G ...... 309 932-3450
  Galva *(G-10789)*
Timken Drives LLC ........................C ...... 815 589-2211
  Fulton *(G-10706)*

## PRODUCT SECTION

### HARDWARE, WHOLESALE: Furniture, NEC

Innovative Components Inc .................E ....... 847 885-9050
  Schaumburg  (G-19567)

### HARDWARE, WHOLESALE: Nuts

Ability Fasteners Inc ........................F ....... 847 593-4230
  Elk Grove Village  (G-9256)

### HARDWARE, WHOLESALE: Power Tools & Access

Dun-Rite Tool & Machine Co ...............E ...... 815 758-5464
  Cortland  (G-7388)
Eazypower Corporation ......................G ....... 773 278-5000
  Chicago  (G-4687)

### HARDWARE, WHOLESALE: Screws

Air Stamping Inc ..............................F ....... 217 342-1283
  Effingham  (G-8823)
Archer Screw Products Inc .................D ....... 847 451-1150
  Franklin Park  (G-10399)
Cold Headers Inc ..............................F ....... 773 775-7900
  Chicago  (G-4421)
Gateway Screw & Rivet Inc ................E ....... 630 539-2232
  Glendale Heights  (G-11026)
Illinois Tool Works Inc ........................B ....... 630 595-3500
  Roselle  (G-18946)
Komar Screw Corp ............................E ....... 847 965-9090
  Niles  (G-15995)
Lombard Swiss Screw Company .........E ....... 630 576-5096
  Addison  (G-183)

### HARDWARE, WHOLESALE: Security Devices, Locks

Patt Supply Corporation ......................F ....... 708 442-3901
  Lyons  (G-14043)

### HARDWARE, WHOLESALE: Staples

ITW Bldg Components Group ...............G ....... 847 634-1900
  Glenview  (G-11150)

### HARDWARE: Builders'

Amos Industries Inc ..........................F ....... 630 393-0606
  Warrenville  (G-21341)
Architctral Bldrs Hdwr Mfg Inc .............E ....... 630 875-9900
  Itasca  (G-12230)
Dorma Usa Inc .................................D ....... 717 336-3881
  Steeleville  (G-20560)
Grand Specialties Co .........................F ....... 630 629-8000
  Oak Brook  (G-16520)
Heckmann Building Products Inc .........E ....... 708 865-2403
  Melrose Park  (G-14652)
In Midwest Service Enterprises ...........G ....... 217 224-1932
  Quincy  (G-17839)

### HARDWARE: Cabinet

Amazing Cabinets & Design Corp ........G ....... 773 405-0174
  Elk Grove Village  (G-9292)
Avoca Ridge Ltd ................................G ....... 815 692-4772
  Fairbury  (G-10122)
Nova Wildcat Amerock LLC ................F ....... 815 266-6416
  Freeport  (G-10677)
Royal Kitchen & Bathroom Cabin ........G ....... 847 588-0011
  Niles  (G-16029)
S L Fixtures Inc .................................G ....... 217 423-9907
  Decatur  (G-7937)
Sweet Manufacturing Corp .................E ....... 847 546-5575
  Chicago  (G-6648)

### HARDWARE: Casket

Dixline Corporation ...........................D ....... 309 932-2011
  Galva  (G-10788)
Dixline Corporation ...........................F ....... 309 932-2011
  Galva  (G-10787)
Estad Stamping & Mfg Co ..................E ....... 217 442-4600
  Danville  (G-7717)
General Machinery & Mfg Co ..............F ....... 773 235-3700
  Chicago  (G-4928)
Kraig Corporation ..............................E ....... 847 928-0630
  Franklin Park  (G-10514)

### HARDWARE: Door Opening & Closing Devices, Exc Electrical

Leatherneck Hardware Inc .................E ....... 217 431-3096
  Danville  (G-7745)
Midwest Group Dist & Svcs Inc ...........G ....... 708 597-0059
  Alsip  (G-492)

### HARDWARE: Furniture

Compx Security Products Inc ..............D ....... 847 234-1864
  Grayslake  (G-11329)
Focus Marketing Group Inc .................G ....... 815 363-2525
  Johnsburg  (G-12434)
Haddock Tool & Manufacturing ............G ....... 815 786-2739
  Sandwich  (G-19367)
Illinois Fibre Specialty Co ....................E ....... 773 376-1122
  Chicago  (G-5157)
Innovative Components Inc .................E ....... 847 885-9050
  Schaumburg  (G-19567)
Tolerance Manufacturing Inc ...............F ....... 847 244-8836
  Waukegan  (G-21629)

### HARDWARE: Furniture, Builders' & Other Household

Allegion S&S US Holding Co ..............C ....... 815 875-3311
  Princeton  (G-17742)

### HARDWARE: Luggage

Remin Laboratories Inc ......................D ....... 815 723-1940
  Joliet  (G-12566)

### HARDWARE: Piano

Adams Machine Shop .......................G ....... 630 851-6060
  Naperville  (G-15590)

### HARDWARE: Plastic

Jeffrey Jae Inc ...................................E ....... 847 394-1313
  Arlington Heights  (G-782)
Rand Manufacturing Network Inc ........G ....... 847 299-8884
  Wheeling  (G-22132)

### HARDWARE: Rubber

Edgewater Products Company Inc .......F ....... 708 345-9200
  Melrose Park  (G-14629)
Finzer Holding LLC ...........................F ....... 847 390-6200
  Des Plaines  (G-8198)

### HARNESS ASSEMBLIES: Cable & Wire

Advanced Technologies Inc ................G ....... 847 329-9875
  Park Ridge  (G-17178)
Bryton Technology Inc .......................C ....... 309 995-3379
  Toulon  (G-20976)
C & C Electronics Inc ........................F ....... 847 550-0177
  Mundelein  (G-15481)
Camtek Inc .......................................D ....... 309 661-0348
  Bloomington  (G-2151)
Capsonic Automotive Inc ....................F ....... 847 888-7300
  Elgin  (G-8979)
Casco Manufacturing Inc ....................E ....... 630 771-9555
  Bolingbrook  (G-2285)
Central Industries of Indiana ................A ....... 618 943-2311
  Lawrenceville  (G-13196)
Cinch Cnnctivity Solutions Inc .............C ....... 847 739-0300
  Lombard  (G-13779)
Delta Design Inc ................................F ....... 708 424-9400
  Evergreen Park  (G-10112)
Delta Design Inc ................................F ....... 708 424-9400
  Evergreen Park  (G-10111)
Excel Specialty Corp ..........................E ....... 773 262-7575
  Lake Forest  (G-12898)
Flp Industries LLC .............................F ....... 847 215-8650
  Wheeling  (G-22054)
Gateway Cable Co .............................G ....... 630 766-7969
  Bensenville  (G-1905)
Gil Instruments Co .............................G ....... 815 459-8764
  Crystal Lake  (G-7583)
Grand Products Inc ............................C ....... 800 621-6101
  Elk Grove Village  (G-9506)
Hart Electric LLC ...............................E ....... 815 368-3341
  Lostant  (G-13906)
IMS Companies LLC .........................D ....... 847 391-8100
  Des Plaines  (G-8210)
Julian Elec Svc & Engrg Inc ................E ....... 630 920-8950
  Westmont  (G-21895)
Manu-TEC of Illinois LLC ....................F ....... 630 543-3022
  Addison  (G-190)

Millennium Electronics Inc ...................D ....... 815 479-9755
  Crystal Lake  (G-7613)
Mk Test Systems Americas Inc ...........G ....... 773 569-3778
  Lake Barrington  (G-12820)
Nep Electronics Inc ............................C ....... 630 595-8500
  Wood Dale  (G-22405)
Nu-Way Electronics Inc ......................E ....... 847 437-7120
  Elk Grove Village  (G-9657)
Omnitronix Corporation ......................F ....... 630 837-1400
  Streamwood  (G-20668)
Partec Inc .........................................C ....... 847 678-9520
  Franklin Park  (G-10547)
Quality Cable & Components Inc ........E ....... 309 695-3435
  Wyoming  (G-22639)
Sentral Assemblies LLC .....................D ....... 847 478-9720
  Lincolnshire  (G-13477)
Sentral Group LLC .............................G ....... 847 478-9720
  Lincolnshire  (G-13478)
Sub-Sem Inc .....................................E ....... 815 459-4139
  Crystal Lake  (G-7655)
Triton Manufacturing Co Inc ................D ....... 708 587-4000
  Monee  (G-15004)
Unlimited Svcs Wisconsin Inc .............E ....... 815 399-0282
  Machesney Park  (G-14117)
Zero Ground LLC ..............................F ....... 847 360-9500
  Waukegan  (G-21644)

### HARNESS WIRING SETS: Internal Combustion Engines

Aeromotive Services Inc .....................F ....... 224 535-9220
  Elgin  (G-8939)
Barcar Manufacturing Inc ...................G ....... 630 365-5200
  Elburn  (G-8877)
Elc Industries Corp ............................C ....... 630 851-1616
  Aurora  (G-1143)
Midwest Aero Support Inc ...................E ....... 815 398-9202
  Machesney Park  (G-14092)
Monona Holdings LLC .......................G ....... 630 946-0630
  Naperville  (G-15700)
Sentral Group LLC .............................G ....... 847 478-9720
  Lincolnshire  (G-13478)
Xenia Mfg Inc ....................................C ....... 618 678-2218
  Xenia  (G-22645)
Xenia Mfg Inc ....................................E ....... 618 392-7212
  Olney  (G-16801)

### HARNESSES, HALTERS, SADDLERY & STRAPS

Spirit Industries Inc ............................G ....... 217 285-4500
  Griggsville  (G-11414)

### HEADPHONES: Radio

Bem Wireless LLC .............................F ....... 815 337-0541
  Algonquin  (G-381)
Bozki Inc ..........................................G ....... 312 767-2122
  Chicago  (G-4152)
Jds Labs Inc .....................................G ....... 618 366-0475
  Collinsville  (G-7329)

### HEALTH & ALLIED SERVICES, NEC

Perez Health Incorporated ..................G ....... 708 788-0101
  Berwyn  (G-2072)

### HEALTH & WELFARE COUNCIL

National Safety Council ......................B ....... 630 285-1121
  Itasca  (G-12324)

### HEALTH AIDS: Exercise Eqpt

J & C Premier Concepts Inc ................G ....... 309 523-2344
  Port Byron  (G-17720)
Life Fitness Inc ..................................B ....... 847 288-3300
  Rosemont  (G-19010)
Life Fitness Inc ..................................G ....... 847 288-3300
  Franklin Park  (G-10516)
Life Fitness Inc ..................................C ....... 800 494-6344
  Rosemont  (G-19011)
Reflex Fitness Products Inc ................F ....... 309 756-1050
  Milan  (G-14802)
Septic Solutions Inc ...........................G ....... 217 925-5992
  Dieterich  (G-8314)
Varisport Inc .....................................E ....... 847 480-1366
  Northbrook  (G-16383)
Xmt Solutions LLC .............................G ....... 703 338-9422
  Chicago  (G-7046)

Employee Codes: A=Over 500 employees, B=251-500
C=101-250, D=51-100, E=20-50, F=10-19, G=3-9

# HEALTH AIDS: Vaporizers

### HEALTH AIDS: Vaporizers
Power Industries Inc .................................. G ....... 630 443-0671
  Saint Charles  (G-19238)
Quick Nic Juice LLC .................................. F ....... 815 315-8523
  Sandwich  (G-19376)
Upper Limits Midwest Inc .......................... G ....... 217 679-4315
  Springfield  (G-20547)

### HEALTH FOOD & SUPPLEMENT STORES
Helmuth Custom Kitchens LLC ................... E ....... 217 543-3588
  Arthur  (G-904)

### HEALTH SCREENING SVCS
Medical Screening Labs Inc ....................... E ....... 847 647-7911
  Niles  (G-16002)

### HEARING AIDS
Accuquest Hearing Center Inc .................. G ....... 847 588-1895
  Niles  (G-15956)
Accutone Hearing Aid Inc ......................... G ....... 773 545-3279
  Evanston  (G-10004)
Audibel Hearing Center ............................ G ....... 217 670-1183
  Springfield  (G-20391)
Beltone Corporation .................................. D ....... 847 832-3300
  Glenview  (G-11107)
Etymotic Research Inc .............................. E ....... 847 228-0006
  Elk Grove Village  (G-9465)
Gohear LLC .............................................. G ....... 847 574-7829
  Lake Forest  (G-12902)
Hearing Aid Warehouse Inc ...................... G ....... 217 431-4700
  Danville  (G-7730)
Hearing Associates PC ............................. F ....... 847 662-9300
  Gurnee  (G-11459)
Hearwell .................................................... G ....... 217 824-5210
  Taylorville  (G-20840)
Knowles Electronics LLC .......................... A ....... 630 250-5100
  Itasca  (G-12297)
Lloyd American Corporation ..................... F ....... 815 964-4191
  Rockford  (G-18472)
Mimosa Acoustics Inc ............................... G ....... 217 359-9740
  Champaign  (G-3515)
Phonak LLC .............................................. A ....... 630 821-5000
  Warrenville  (G-21354)
SC Industries Inc ...................................... G ....... 312 366-3899
  Chicago  (G-6449)

### HEARING TESTING SVCS
Gohear LLC .............................................. G ....... 847 574-7829
  Lake Forest  (G-12902)
Mimosa Acoustics Inc ............................... G ....... 217 359-9740
  Champaign  (G-3515)

### HEAT EMISSION OPERATING APPARATUS
Delta-Therm Corporation ........................... F ....... 847 526-2407
  Crystal Lake  (G-7566)

### HEAT EXCHANGERS: After Or Inter Coolers Or Condensers, Etc
Alfa Laval Inc ........................................... C ....... 630 354-6090
  Wood Dale  (G-22334)
Energy Solutions Inc ................................ G ....... 618 465-5404
  Alton  (G-575)
Roney Machine Works Inc ....................... E ....... 618 462-4113
  Alton  (G-588)
Yinlun Usa Inc .......................................... G ....... 309 291-0843
  Morton  (G-15185)

### HEAT TREATING SALTS
Houghton International Inc ....................... F ....... 610 666-4000
  Chicago  (G-5121)
Philos Technologies Inc ........................... G ....... 630 945-2933
  Buffalo Grove  (G-2751)

### HEAT TREATING: Metal
300 Below Inc .......................................... G ....... 217 423-3070
  Decatur  (G-7819)
Advanced Heat Treating Inc .................... E ....... 815 877-8593
  Loves Park  (G-13913)
Advanced Thermal Processing ................. G ....... 630 595-9000
  Bensenville  (G-1820)
Arrow Gear Company ............................... C ....... 630 969-7640
  Downers Grove  (G-8389)
Beechner Heat Treating Co Inc ................ G ....... 815 397-4314
  Rockford  (G-18279)
Bodycote Thermal Proc Inc ...................... D ....... 708 236-5360
  Melrose Park  (G-14601)
Bonell Manufacturing Company ................ E ....... 708 849-1770
  Riverdale  (G-18016)
Bulaw Welding & Engineering Co ............. D ....... 630 228-8300
  Itasca  (G-12239)
Bwt LLC .................................................... E ....... 708 410-8000
  Northlake  (G-16432)
Bwt LLC .................................................... E ....... 630 210-4577
  Rockford  (G-18293)
C/B Machine Tool Corp ............................ G ....... 847 288-1807
  Franklin Park  (G-10422)
Certified Heat Treating Co ........................ F ....... 309 693-7711
  Peoria  (G-17340)
Chem-Plate Industries Inc ........................ E ....... 708 345-3588
  Maywood  (G-14422)
Chem-Plate Industries Inc ........................ D ....... 847 640-1600
  Elk Grove Village  (G-9366)
Cooley Wire Products Mfg Co .................. E ....... 847 678-8585
  Schiller Park  (G-19816)
Curtis Metal Finishing Company ............... F ....... 815 282-1433
  Machesney Park  (G-14068)
Diamond Heat Treat Inc ........................... G ....... 815 873-1348
  Rockford  (G-18343)
Eklund Metal Treating Inc ........................ G ....... 815 877-7436
  Loves Park  (G-13939)
F P M LLC ................................................ C ....... 847 228-2525
  Elk Grove Village  (G-9473)
F P M LLC ................................................ C ....... 815 332-4961
  Cherry Valley  (G-3643)
Fpm Heat Treating .................................... F ....... 815 332-4961
  Cherry Valley  (G-3644)
Fpm Heat Treatment ................................ E ....... 847 274-7269
  Itasca  (G-12267)
General Surface Hardening ...................... E ....... 312 226-5472
  Chicago  (G-4933)
Golfers Family Corporation ...................... E ....... 815 968-0094
  Rockford  (G-18401)
Horizon Steel Treating Inc ....................... D ....... 847 639-4030
  Cary  (G-3351)
Howell Welding Corporation ..................... G ....... 630 616-1100
  Franklin Park  (G-10489)
Hudapack Mtal Treating III Inc ................. G ....... 630 793-1916
  Glendale Heights  (G-11031)
Induction Heat Treating Corp ................... E ....... 815 477-7788
  Crystal Lake  (G-7592)
K V F Company ........................................ E ....... 847 437-5100
  Elk Grove Village  (G-9569)
K V F Company ........................................ F ....... 847 437-5019
  Elk Grove Village  (G-9570)
Lapham-Hickey Steel Corp ...................... C ....... 708 496-6111
  Chicago  (G-5459)
Metals Technology Corporation ................ G ....... 630 221-2500
  Carol Stream  (G-3193)
Metform LLC ............................................ E ....... 815 273-0230
  Savanna  (G-19401)
Mp Steel Chicago LLC ............................. G ....... 773 242-0853
  Chicago  (G-5820)
Nitrex Inc ................................................. E ....... 630 851-5880
  Aurora  (G-1058)
Precision Chrome Inc .............................. E ....... 847 587-1515
  Fox Lake  (G-10282)
Precision Metal Technologies .................. F ....... 847 228-6630
  Rolling Meadows  (G-18768)
Progressive Steel Treating Inc ................. E ....... 815 877-2571
  Loves Park  (G-13979)
R-M Industries Inc ................................... F ....... 630 543-3071
  Addison  (G-267)
Rockford Heat Treaters Inc ..................... G ....... 815 874-0089
  Rockford  (G-18575)
Salman Metal ........................................... G ....... 630 359-5110
  Elmhurst  (G-9933)
Scientific Metal Treating Co .................... E ....... 630 582-0071
  Roselle  (G-18975)
Standard Heat Treating LLC .................... E ....... 773 242-0853
  Cicero  (G-7229)
Superheat Fgh Services Inc .................... G ....... 708 478-0205
  New Lenox  (G-15915)
Supertech Holdings Inc ........................... G ....... 708 478-0205
  New Lenox  (G-15916)
Tc Industries Inc ..................................... C ....... 815 459-2401
  Crystal Lake  (G-7660)
Tempel Steel Company ........................... A ....... 773 250-8000
  Chicago  (G-6696)
Terra Cotta Holdings Co ......................... G ....... 815 459-2400
  Crystal Lake  (G-7664)
Thermo Techniques LLC ......................... E ....... 217 446-1407
  Danville  (G-7768)
Tri-City Heat Treat Co Inc ....................... D ....... 309 786-2689
  Rock Island  (G-18209)
Wec Welding and Machining LLC ............ G ....... 847 680-8100
  Lake Bluff  (G-12870)

### HEATERS: Induction & Dielectric
IDI Fabrication Inc ................................... E ....... 630 783-2246
  Lemont  (G-13236)

### HEATERS: Room & Wall, Including Radiators
All Wood or Metal Radiator Cov .............. G ....... 773 973-7328
  Chicago  (G-3809)

### HEATERS: Space, Exc Electric
Empire Comfort Systems Inc ................... C ....... 618 233-7420
  Belleville  (G-1631)

### HEATERS: Swimming Pool, Electric
Superheat Fgh Services Inc .................... G ....... 618 251-9450
  New Lenox  (G-15914)

### HEATING & AIR CONDITIONING EQPT & SPLYS WHOLESALERS
Ecolab Inc ............................................... E ....... 815 729-7334
  Joliet  (G-12488)
Ecolab Inc ............................................... E ....... 847 350-2229
  Elk Grove Village  (G-9448)
Frigel North America Inc ........................ F ....... 847 540-0160
  East Dundee  (G-8636)
Illco Inc ................................................... G ....... 815 725-9100
  Joliet  (G-12513)
Lennox Industries Inc ............................. D ....... 630 378-7054
  Romeoville  (G-18839)
Mucci Kirkpatrick Sheet Metal ................ G ....... 815 433-3350
  Ottawa  (G-16970)
Quality Filter Services ............................ G ....... 618 654-3716
  Highland  (G-11807)

### HEATING & AIR CONDITIONING UNITS, COMBINATION
Bernard Cffey Vtrans Fundation .............. G ....... 630 687-0033
  Naperville  (G-15605)
Eclipse Usa Inc ...................................... G ....... 773 816-0886
  Elmwood Park  (G-9967)
EZ Comfort Heating & AC ...................... G ....... 630 289-2020
  Elgin  (G-9031)
Synergy Mech Solutions Inc ................... G ....... 847 437-4500
  Elk Grove Village  (G-9765)

### HEATING EQPT & SPLYS
Aldrico Inc .............................................. E ....... 309 695-2311
  Wyoming  (G-22636)
All American Wood Register Co .............. F ....... 815 356-1000
  Crystal Lake  (G-7528)
American Fuel Economy Inc ................... G ....... 815 433-3226
  Ottawa  (G-16946)
BP Solar International Inc ....................... A ....... 301 698-4200
  Naperville  (G-15611)
Custom Linear Grille Inc ......................... G ....... 847 520-5511
  Wheeling  (G-22033)
Easy Heat Inc ......................................... E ....... 847 268-6000
  Rosemont  (G-19000)
Filtran Holdings LLC ............................... G ....... 847 635-6670
  Des Plaines  (G-8196)
Filtran LLC .............................................. C ....... 847 635-6670
  Des Plaines  (G-8197)
Goose Island Mfg & Supply Corp ............ G ....... 708 343-4225
  Lansing  (G-13164)
Grieve Corporation ................................. D ....... 847 546-8225
  Round Lake  (G-19059)
Guntner US ............................................. G ....... 847 781-0900
  Schaumburg  (G-19545)
Hardy Radiator Repair ............................ F ....... 217 223-8320
  Quincy  (G-17834)
Industries Publication Inc ....................... E ....... 630 357-5269
  Lisle  (G-13602)
Ipsen Inc ................................................. E ....... 815 239-2385
  Pecatonica  (G-17252)
R & D Electronics Inc ............................. G ....... 847 583-9080
  Niles  (G-16024)
Spirotherm Inc ........................................ G ....... 630 307-2662
  Glendale Heights  (G-11071)
Sws Industries Inc ................................. E ....... 904 482-0091
  Woodstock  (G-22616)
Tri-State Food Equipment ....................... G ....... 217 228-1550
  Quincy  (G-17900)

## PRODUCT SECTION — HOME FURNISHINGS WHOLESALERS

### HEATING EQPT: Complete

- Airdronic Test & Balance Inc ........... G ..... 815 561-0339
  Rochelle *(G-18077)*
- American Fuel Economy Inc ............. G ..... 815 433-3226
  Ottawa *(G-16946)*
- Big M Manufacturing LLC ................. G ..... 217 824-9372
  Taylorville *(G-20833)*
- Flinn & Dreffein Engrg Co .................. E ..... 847 272-6374
  Northbrook *(G-16260)*
- Frigel North America Inc .................... F ..... 847 540-0160
  East Dundee *(G-8636)*
- Habegger Corporation ........................ F ..... 309 793-7172
  Rock Island *(G-18178)*
- Haggerty Corporation .......................... G ..... 309 793-4328
  Rock Island *(G-18179)*
- Kelco Industries Inc ............................. G ..... 815 334-3600
  Woodstock *(G-22577)*
- Temperature Equipment Corp ............ G ..... 815 229-2935
  Rockford *(G-18643)*

### HEATING EQPT: Induction

- Mellish & Murray Co ............................ F ..... 312 379-0335
  Chicago *(G-5684)*
- Precision Chrome Inc .......................... E ..... 847 587-1515
  Fox Lake *(G-10282)*

### HEATING PADS, ELECTRIC

- Cabot Microelectronics Corp ............. D ..... 630 375-6631
  Aurora *(G-978)*

### HEATING UNITS & DEVICES: Indl, Electric

- Acra Electric Corporation .................. D ..... 847 678-8870
  Schiller Park *(G-19799)*
- Akinsun Heat Co Inc ........................... F ..... 630 289-9506
  Streamwood *(G-20640)*
- Calco Controls Inc .............................. F ..... 847 639-3858
  Crystal Lake *(G-7548)*
- Delta-Therm Corporation .................... F ..... 847 526-2407
  Crystal Lake *(G-7566)*
- Fast Heat Inc ....................................... C ..... 630 359-6300
  Elmhurst *(G-9871)*
- Goodman Distribution Inc .................. G ..... 773 376-8214
  Chicago *(G-4978)*
- Hts Chicago Inc .................................. G ..... 630 352-3690
  Wheaton *(G-21954)*
- Oakley Industrial McHy Inc ................ E ..... 847 966-0052
  Elk Grove Village *(G-9660)*
- Tempco Electric Heater Corp ............. B ..... 630 350-2252
  Wood Dale *(G-22429)*
- Tempro International Corp ................. G ..... 847 677-5370
  Skokie *(G-20100)*
- Tutco Inc ............................................. C ..... 630 833-5400
  Elmhurst *(G-9953)*
- Zeman Mfg Co .................................... E ..... 630 960-2300
  Lisle *(G-13679)*

### HELICOPTERS

- Helivalues ........................................... G ..... 847 487-8258
  Wauconda *(G-21466)*
- Kaman Industrial Tech Corp .............. E ..... 317 248-8355
  Wood Dale *(G-22385)*
- Olivers Helicopters Inc ....................... G ..... 847 697-7346
  Gilberts *(G-10930)*
- United Technologies Corp .................. B ..... 815 226-6000
  Rockford *(G-18663)*

### HELMETS: Athletic

- Bell Racing Usa LLC .......................... G ..... 217 239-5355
  Champaign *(G-3456)*
- Bell Sports Inc .................................... D ..... 217 893-9300
  Rantoul *(G-17920)*
- Brg Sports Inc .................................... F ..... 217 893-9300
  Rantoul *(G-17921)*
- Brg Sports Inc .................................... C ..... 831 461-7500
  Rosemont *(G-18990)*
- Park View Manufacturing Corp ......... D ..... 618 548-9054
  Salem *(G-19342)*
- Riddell Inc .......................................... C ..... 847 292-1472
  Rosemont *(G-19027)*

### HELP SUPPLY SERVICES

- National Emergency Med ID Inc ....... G ..... 847 366-1267
  Spring Grove *(G-20351)*
- Wind Point Partners LP ..................... F ..... 312 255-4800
  Chicago *(G-6992)*

### HIGH ENERGY PARTICLE PHYSICS EQPT

- Rtenergy LLC ..................................... F ..... 773 975-2598
  Chicago *(G-6410)*
- United Technologies Corp ................. B ..... 815 226-6000
  Rockford *(G-18663)*

### HIGHWAY & STREET MAINTENANCE SVCS

- Illinois Road Contractors Inc ............. E ..... 217 245-6181
  Jacksonville *(G-12393)*
- Louis Marsch Inc ................................ E ..... 217 526-3723
  Morrisonville *(G-15151)*

### HITCHES: Trailer

- Great Lakes Forge Company ............ G ..... 773 277-2800
  Chicago *(G-4997)*
- Kerins Industries Inc .......................... G ..... 630 515-9111
  Darien *(G-7798)*

### HOBBY & CRAFT SPLY STORES

- Made By Hands Inc ........................... G ..... 773 761-4200
  Chicago *(G-5595)*

### HOBBY SUPPLIES, WHOLESALE

- Central RC Hobbies ........................... G ..... 309 686-8004
  Peoria *(G-17339)*

### HOBBY, TOY & GAME STORES: Arts & Crafts & Splys

- Smart Creations Inc ........................... G ..... 847 433-3451
  Highland Park *(G-11869)*

### HOBBY, TOY & GAME STORES: Children's Toys & Games, Exc Dolls

- Midwest Rail Junction ........................ G ..... 815 963-0200
  Rockford *(G-18506)*

### HOBBY, TOY & GAME STORES: Dolls & Access

- Jiminees Inc ........................................ G ..... 630 295-8002
  Roselle *(G-18949)*

### HOBBY, TOY & GAME STORES: Hobbies, NEC

- Central RC Hobbies ........................... G ..... 309 686-8004
  Peoria *(G-17339)*
- Fanfest Corporation ............................ G ..... 847 658-2000
  Crystal Lake *(G-7576)*
- Hands To Work Railroading ............... G ..... 708 489-9776
  Alsip *(G-470)*

### HOISTING SLINGS

- Liftex Corporation ............................... E ..... 847 782-0572
  Gurnee *(G-11467)*

### HOISTS

- Columbus McKinnon Corporation ..... C ..... 800 548-2930
  Eureka *(G-9995)*
- Columbus McKinnon Corporation ..... E ..... 630 783-1195
  Woodridge *(G-22463)*
- Peerless Chain Company .................. G ..... 708 339-0545
  South Holland *(G-20297)*
- Ramseys Machine Co ........................ G ..... 217 824-2320
  Taylorville *(G-20845)*
- Sievert Electric Svc & Sls Co ............. D ..... 708 771-1600
  Forest Park *(G-10253)*

### HOISTS: Mine

- Logan Actuator Co .............................. G ..... 815 943-9500
  Harvard *(G-11640)*

### HOLDERS, PAPER TOWEL, GROCERY BAG, ETC: Plastic

- C Line Products Inc ............................ D ..... 847 827-6661
  Mount Prospect *(G-15315)*
- Com-Pac International Inc ................. C ..... 618 529-2421
  Carbondale *(G-3004)*
- Urpoint LLC ........................................ G ..... 773 919-9002
  New Lenox *(G-15925)*
- Vision Sales & Marketing Inc ............. G ..... 708 496-6016
  Chicago *(G-6904)*

### HOLDERS: Gas, Metal Plate

- Midwest Can Company ...................... E ..... 708 615-1400
  Melrose Park *(G-14673)*

### HOLDING COMPANIES: Banks

- T H K Holdings of America LLC ......... G ..... 847 310-1111
  Schaumburg *(G-19750)*

### HOLDING COMPANIES: Investment, Exc Banks

- Atkore Intl Holdings Inc ...................... G ..... 708 225-2051
  Harvey *(G-11659)*
- Coveris Holding Corp ......................... G ..... 773 877-3300
  Chicago *(G-4483)*
- Fisher Container Holdings LLC ......... G ..... 847 541-0000
  Buffalo Grove *(G-2695)*
- Hovi Industries Incorporated ............. E ..... 815 512-7500
  Bolingbrook *(G-2316)*
- Industrial Service Solutions ............... F ..... 917 609-6979
  Chicago *(G-5180)*
- Madison Inds Holdings LLC .............. G ..... 312 277-0156
  Chicago *(G-5598)*
- Mat Capital LLC .................................. G ..... 847 821-9630
  Long Grove *(G-13895)*
- Npi Holding Corp ................................ G ..... 217 391-1229
  Springfield *(G-20488)*
- Omc Investors LLC ............................ C ..... 847 855-6220
  Gurnee *(G-11480)*
- Roevolution 226 LLC ......................... G ..... 773 658-4022
  Riverwoods *(G-18042)*
- Sentral Group LLC ............................. G ..... 847 478-9720
  Lincolnshire *(G-13478)*
- Tag-Barton LLC .................................. G ..... 217 428-0711
  Decatur *(G-7948)*
- Thyssenkrupp North America Inc ..... E ..... 312 525-2800
  Chicago *(G-6725)*
- US Lbm Ridout Holdings LLC ........... G ..... 877 787-5267
  Buffalo Grove *(G-2786)*

### HOLDING COMPANIES: Personal, Exc Banks

- Baker Avenue Investments Inc ......... G ..... 309 427-2500
  Washington *(G-21378)*
- Industrial Water Trtmnt Soltns ........... G ..... 708 339-1313
  Harvey *(G-11672)*
- Pharmdium Hlthcare Hldings Inc ...... G ..... 800 523-7749
  Lake Forest *(G-12943)*
- Pt Holdings Inc ................................... G ..... 217 691-1793
  Springfield *(G-20508)*

### HOME DELIVERY NEWSPAPER ROUTES

- Phoenix Press Inc .............................. G ..... 630 833-2281
  Villa Park *(G-21277)*

### HOME ENTERTAINMENT EQPT: Electronic, NEC

- Digital Living Inc ................................. G ..... 708 434-1197
  Oak Park *(G-16659)*
- Relay Systems America Inc .............. F ..... 815 730-0100
  Joliet *(G-12565)*
- Senario LLC ....................................... F ..... 847 882-0677
  Schaumburg *(G-19725)*
- William N Pasulka ............................... G ..... 815 339-6300
  Peru *(G-17532)*

### HOME ENTERTAINMENT REPAIR SVCS

- Acoustic Avenue Inc .......................... F ..... 217 544-9810
  Springfield *(G-20385)*
- Sota Service Ctr By Bodinets ............ G ..... 608 538-3500
  Dekalb *(G-8120)*
- Van L Speakerworks Inc .................... G ..... 773 769-0773
  Chicago *(G-6870)*

### HOME FOR THE MENTALLY RETARDED

- Community Support Systems ............ D ..... 217 705-4300
  Teutopolis *(G-20850)*

### HOME FURNISHINGS WHOLESALERS

- Amk Enterprises Chicago Inc ............ G ..... 312 523-7212
  Chicago *(G-3890)*
- Del Great Frame Up Systems Inc ..... F ..... 847 808-1955
  Franklin Park *(G-10456)*
- Granite Xperts Inc .............................. E ..... 847 364-1900
  Franklin Park *(G-10481)*

---

Employee Codes: A=Over 500 employees, B=251-500
C=101-250, D=51-100, E=20-50, F=10-19, G=3-9

# HOME FURNISHINGS WHOLESALERS

**PRODUCT SECTION**

Larson-Juhl US LLC .................................. D .... 630 307-9700
 Roselle *(G-18951)*
Lexi Group Inc ......................................... G .... 866 675-1683
 Chicago *(G-5498)*

## HOME IMPROVEMENT & RENOVATION CONTRACTOR AGENCY

Crosscom Inc ........................................... F .... 630 871-5500
 Wheaton *(G-21942)*
Ornamental Iron Shop .............................. G .... 618 281-6072
 Columbia *(G-7361)*

## HOMEFURNISHING STORE: Bedding, Sheet, Blanket,Spread/Pillow

Standard Container Co of Edgar .............. E .... 847 438-1510
 Lake Zurich *(G-13134)*

## HOMEFURNISHING STORES: Beddings & Linens

Eastern Accents Inc ................................. C .... 773 604-7300
 Chicago *(G-4683)*

## HOMEFURNISHING STORES: Brooms

Luco Mop Company .................................. G .... 217 235-1992
 Mattoon *(G-14398)*

## HOMEFURNISHING STORES: Lighting Fixtures

Acculight LLC ........................................... G .... 630 847-1000
 Elk Grove Village *(G-9260)*

## HOMEFURNISHING STORES: Mirrors

Montrose Glass & Mirror Corp ................. G .... 773 478-6433
 Chicago *(G-5798)*

## HOMEFURNISHING STORES: Pictures, Wall

Picture Frame Fulfillment LLC .................. D .... 847 260-5071
 Franklin Park *(G-10550)*
Supreme Frame & Moulding Co ............... F .... 312 930-9056
 Chicago *(G-6638)*

## HOMEFURNISHING STORES: Pottery

Great Lakes Clay & Supply Inc ................ G .... 224 535-8127
 Elgin *(G-9051)*

## HOMEFURNISHING STORES: Venetian Blinds

Olshaws Interior Services ......................... G .... 312 421-3131
 Chicago *(G-5985)*

## HOMEFURNISHING STORES: Wicker, Rattan, Or Reed

House of Rattan Inc .................................. G .... 630 627-8160
 Lombard *(G-13810)*
Wise Construction Services ..................... G .... 630 553-6350
 Yorkville *(G-22676)*

## HOMEFURNISHING STORES: Window Furnishings

9161 Corporation ...................................... G .... 847 470-8828
 Niles *(G-15953)*
Loomcraft Textile & Supply Co ................. E .... 847 680-0000
 Vernon Hills *(G-21182)*
Offsprings Inc ........................................... G .... 773 525-1800
 Chicago *(G-5969)*
Regent Window Fashions LLC ................. G .... 773 871-6400
 Chicago *(G-6324)*
Roberts Draperies Center Inc .................. G .... 847 255-4040
 Mount Prospect *(G-15370)*

## HOMEFURNISHING STORES: Window Shades, NEC

Drapery House Inc .................................... G .... 847 318-1161
 Park Ridge *(G-17191)*
Midwest Marketing Distrs Inc ................... G .... 309 663-6972
 Bloomington *(G-2199)*
Midwest Marketing Distrs Inc ................... F .... 309 688-8858
 Peoria *(G-17408)*

## HOMEFURNISHINGS & SPLYS, WHOLESALE: Decorative

Limitless Innovations Inc .......................... E .... 855 843-4828
 McHenry *(G-14522)*
Little Journeys Limited ............................. G .... 847 677-0350
 Skokie *(G-20030)*
Pingotopia Inc .......................................... F .... 847 503-9333
 Northbrook *(G-16338)*
World Dryer Corporation .......................... E .... 708 449-6950
 Berkeley *(G-2053)*

## HOMEFURNISHINGS, WHOLESALE: Aluminumware

Axis International Marketing .................... C .... 847 297-0744
 Des Plaines *(G-8154)*

## HOMEFURNISHINGS, WHOLESALE: Blinds, Vertical

Unitex Industries Inc ................................ G .... 708 524-0664
 Oak Park *(G-16690)*

## HOMEFURNISHINGS, WHOLESALE: Carpets

Milliken & Company .................................. F .... 800 241-4826
 Chicago *(G-5763)*

## HOMEFURNISHINGS, WHOLESALE: Curtains

Cdc Group Inc .......................................... E .... 847 480-8830
 Chicago *(G-4262)*

## HOMEFURNISHINGS, WHOLESALE: Draperies

ADM International Inc .............................. F .... 773 774-2400
 North Chicago *(G-16173)*
Baker Drapery Corporation ...................... G .... 309 691-3295
 Peoria *(G-17313)*
Dons Drapery Service .............................. G .... 815 385-4759
 McHenry *(G-14497)*
Kempco Window Treatments Inc ............. E .... 708 754-4484
 Chicago Heights *(G-7108)*

## HOMEFURNISHINGS, WHOLESALE: Fireplace Eqpt & Access

Citizenprime LLC ..................................... G .... 708 995-1241
 Mokena *(G-14859)*

## HOMEFURNISHINGS, WHOLESALE: Floor Cushion & Padding

Jab Distributors LLC ................................ E .... 847 998-6901
 Wheeling *(G-22079)*

## HOMEFURNISHINGS, WHOLESALE: Kitchenware

Cupcake Holdings LLC ............................ C .... 800 794-5866
 Woodridge *(G-22466)*
Rays Countertop Shop Inc ....................... F .... 217 483-2514
 Glenarm *(G-10997)*
Wilton Brands LLC ................................... B .... 630 963-7100
 Woodridge *(G-22526)*
Wilton Holdings Inc .................................. G .... 630 963-7100
 Woodridge *(G-22527)*
Wilton Industries Inc ................................ B .... 630 963-7100
 Woodridge *(G-22528)*
Wilton Industries Inc ................................ F .... 815 834-9390
 Romeoville *(G-18879)*
Xcell International Corp ........................... D .... 630 323-0107
 Lemont *(G-13271)*
Xfpg LLC .................................................. B .... 224 513-2010
 Lincolnshire *(G-13491)*

## HOMEFURNISHINGS, WHOLESALE: Linens, Table

Pyar & Company LLC .............................. G .... 312 451-5073
 Chicago *(G-6232)*

## HOMEFURNISHINGS, WHOLESALE: Mirrors/Pictures, Framed/Unframd

Reel Life Dvd LLC ................................... G .... 708 579-1360
 Western Springs *(G-21872)*

## HOMEFURNISHINGS, WHOLESALE: Window Covering Parts & Access

Ensembles Inc ......................................... G .... 630 527-0004
 Naperville *(G-15805)*
Vertidrapes Manufacturing Inc ................ E .... 773 478-9272
 Chicago *(G-6889)*

## HOMEFURNISHINGS, WHOLESALE: Wood Flooring

Moultrie County Hardwoods LLC ............. G
 Arthur *(G-912)*
Ridgefield Industries Co LLC ................... E .... 800 569-0316
 Crystal Lake *(G-7641)*
Signature Innovations LLC ...................... G .... 847 758-9600
 Elk Grove Village *(G-9739)*

## HOMES, MODULAR: Wooden

Contempri Industries Inc ......................... E .... 618 357-5361
 Pinckneyville *(G-17545)*
Csi Manufacturing Inc .............................. E .... 309 937-2653
 Cambridge *(G-2967)*
Homeway Homes Inc ............................... D .... 309 965-2312
 Deer Creek *(G-7964)*
Norridge Jewelry ...................................... G .... 312 984-1036
 Chicago *(G-5929)*

## HOMES: Log Cabins

Otten Construction Co Inc ....................... G .... 618 768-4310
 Addieville *(G-13)*
Snagamon Valley Log Builders ................ G .... 217 632-7609
 Petersburg *(G-17538)*

## HONEYCOMB CORE & BOARD: Made From Purchased Materials

Pactiv LLC ................................................ D .... 618 934-4311
 Trenton *(G-20996)*
Tricel Corporation .................................... F .... 847 336-1321
 Gurnee *(G-11515)*

## HOODS: Range, Sheet Metal

All Seasons Heating & AC ....................... G .... 217 429-2022
 Decatur *(G-7831)*

## HOOKS: Gate

Alltec Gates Inc ........................................ G .... 708 301-9361
 Tinley Park *(G-20889)*

## HORNS: Marine, Electric

Buell Manufacturing Company ................. G .... 708 447-6320
 Lyons *(G-14033)*

## HOSE: Air Line Or Air Brake, Rubber Or Rubberized Fabric

Power Port Products Inc .......................... E .... 630 628-9102
 Addison *(G-249)*

## HOSE: Automobile, Plastic

Bristol Hose & Fitting Inc ......................... E .... 708 492-3456
 Northlake *(G-16430)*

## HOSE: Cotton Fabric, Rubber Lined

Robbi Joy Eklow ....................................... G .... 847 223-0460
 Third Lake *(G-20858)*

## HOSE: Flexible Metal

Able Metal Hose Inc ................................ F .... 630 543-9620
 Addison *(G-15)*
Afc Cable Systems Inc ............................ B .... 508 998-1131
 Harvey *(G-11651)*
Anamet Inc ............................................... G .... 217 234-8844
 Glen Ellyn *(G-10958)*
Electri-Flex Company (del) ...................... D .... 630 307-1095
 Roselle *(G-18941)*
Flextron Inc .............................................. F .... 630 543-5995
 Addison *(G-119)*
Senior Holdings Inc ................................. C .... 630 837-1811
 Bartlett *(G-1373)*
Senior Operations LLC ............................ B .... 630 837-1811
 Bartlett *(G-1375)*

## PRODUCT SECTION

### HOSE: Heater, Plastic
Kanaflex Corporation Illinois .......... G ...... 847 634-6100
  Vernon Hills (G-21177)

### HOSE: Plastic
Tigerflex Corporation .......... A ...... 847 439-1766
  Elk Grove Village (G-9779)

### HOSE: Rubber
Gates Corporation .......... C ...... 309 343-7171
  Galesburg (G-10752)
Gusco Silicone Rbr & Svcs LLC .......... G ...... 773 770-5008
  Aurora (G-1165)
Suncast Corporation .......... A ...... 630 879-2050
  Batavia (G-1501)
W J Dennis & Company .......... F ...... 847 697-4800
  Elgin (G-9225)

### HOSES & BELTING: Rubber & Plastic
Ammeraal Beltech Inc .......... D ...... 847 673-6720
  Skokie (G-19953)
Behabelt USA .......... G ...... 630 521-9835
  Bensenville (G-1842)
Bristol Transport Inc .......... E ...... 708 343-6411
  Northlake (G-16431)
Caterpillar Inc .......... A ...... 309 578-2473
  Mossville (G-15250)
Geib Industries Inc .......... E ...... 847 455-4550
  Bensenville (G-1906)
Industrial Rubber & Sup Entp .......... G ...... 217 429-3747
  Decatur (G-7895)
Jason of Illinois Inc .......... E ...... 630 752-0600
  Carol Stream (G-3176)
Kemper Industries .......... G ...... 217 826-5712
  Marshall (G-14324)
Kuriyama of America Inc .......... D ...... 847 755-0360
  Schaumburg (G-19608)
Lanmar Inc .......... G ...... 800 233-5520
  Northbrook (G-16293)
Pix North America Inc .......... E ...... 217 516-8348
  Danville (G-7760)
Quad City Hose .......... E ...... 563 386-8936
  Taylor Ridge (G-20830)
Royal Brass Inc .......... G ...... 618 439-6341
  Benton (G-2040)
Team Products Inc .......... F ...... 815 244-6100
  Mount Carroll (G-15293)
Western Consolidated Tech Inc .......... G ...... 815 334-3684
  Woodstock (G-22623)

### HOSPITAL EQPT REPAIR SVCS
Amity Hospital Services Inc .......... G ...... 708 206-3970
  Country Club Hills (G-7403)

### HOTEL & MOTEL RESERVATION SVCS
Bitter End Yacht Club Intl .......... F ...... 312 506-6205
  Chicago (G-4115)

### HOTELS & MOTELS
Raynor Mfg Co .......... A ...... 815 288-1431
  Dixon (G-8341)

### HOUSEHOLD APPLIANCE PARTS: Wholesalers
Ameriguard Corporation .......... G ...... 630 986-1900
  Burr Ridge (G-2822)
Diehl Controls North Amer Inc .......... E ...... 630 955-9055
  Naperville (G-15646)

### HOUSEHOLD APPLIANCE STORES: Electric
Doctors Choice Inc .......... G ...... 312 666-1111
  Chicago (G-4621)
Gier Radio & Television Inc .......... G ...... 815 722-8514
  Joliet (G-12502)
Macari Service Center Inc .......... G ...... 217 774-4214
  Shelbyville (G-19910)
Reasons Inc .......... G ...... 309 537-3424
  Buffalo Prairie (G-2797)

### HOUSEHOLD APPLIANCE STORES: Electric Household Appliance, Sm
Coles Appliance & Furn Co .......... G ...... 773 525-1797
  Chicago (G-4422)

### HOUSEHOLD APPLIANCE STORES: Electric Household, Major
Fna Ip Holdings Inc .......... D ...... 847 348-1500
  Elk Grove Village (G-9482)

### HOUSEHOLD ARTICLES, EXC FURNITURE: Cut Stone
Wienmar Inc .......... C ...... 847 742-9222
  South Elgin (G-20235)

### HOUSEHOLD ARTICLES, EXC KITCHEN: Pottery
Haeger Industries Inc .......... D ...... 847 426-3441
  West Dundee (G-21797)

### HOUSEHOLD FURNISHINGS, NEC
A D Specialty Sewing .......... G ...... 847 639-0390
  Fox River Grove (G-10285)
Besleys Accessories Inc .......... G ...... 773 561-3300
  Chicago (G-4089)
Caroline Cole Inc .......... F ...... 618 233-0600
  Belleville (G-1617)
Envision Unlimited .......... C ...... 773 651-1100
  Chicago (G-4766)
Green Energy Solutions Inc .......... F ...... 708 672-1900
  Crete (G-7514)
I M M Inc .......... F ...... 773 767-3700
  Chicago (G-5131)
Interior Fashions Contract .......... G ...... 847 358-6050
  Palatine (G-17044)
Qst Industries Inc .......... E ...... 312 930-9400
  Chicago (G-6237)
Rome Metal Mfg Inc .......... G ...... 773 287-1755
  Chicago (G-6389)
Slagel Drapery Service .......... G ...... 815 692-3834
  Fairbury (G-10132)

### HOUSEWARE STORES
Al Bar Laboratories Inc .......... F ...... 847 251-1218
  Wilmette (G-22241)
Century Molded Plastics Inc .......... E ...... 847 729-3455
  Glenview (G-11111)

### HOUSEWARES, ELECTRIC, EXC COOKING APPLIANCES & UTENSILS
Baier Home Center .......... G ...... 815 457-2300
  Cissna Park (G-7253)
Bath Solutions Inc .......... F ...... 817 429-2318
  Chicago (G-4055)
Sensible Designs Online Inc .......... G ...... 708 267-8924
  Orland Park (G-16890)
Xfpg LLC .......... B ...... 224 513-2010
  Lincolnshire (G-13491)

### HOUSEWARES, ELECTRIC: Air Purifiers, Portable
Blueair Inc .......... F ...... 888 258-3247
  Chicago (G-4127)
Boneco North America Corp .......... G ...... 630 983-3294
  Naperville (G-15607)
Radovent Illinois LLC .......... G ...... 847 637-0297
  Arlington Heights (G-827)

### HOUSEWARES, ELECTRIC: Appliances, Personal
Western Auto Associate Str Co .......... G ...... 618 357-5555
  Pinckneyville (G-17554)

### HOUSEWARES, ELECTRIC: Bedcoverings
Alpha Bedding LLC .......... F ...... 847 550-5110
  Lake Zurich (G-13039)

### HOUSEWARES, ELECTRIC: Cooking Appliances
Mh Equipment Company .......... D ...... 217 443-7210
  Danville (G-7755)

### HOUSEWARES, ELECTRIC: Dryers, Hand & Face
American Dryer Inc .......... E ...... 734 421-2400
  Berkeley (G-2043)
Dyson B2b Inc .......... E ...... 312 469-5950
  Chicago (G-4661)
World Dryer Corporation .......... E ...... 708 449-6950
  Berkeley (G-2053)

### HOUSEWARES, ELECTRIC: Fans, Desk
O2cool LLC .......... E ...... 312 951-6700
  Chicago (G-5960)

### HOUSEWARES, ELECTRIC: Fans, Exhaust & Ventilating
Clements National Company .......... G ...... 708 594-5890
  Broadview (G-2569)

### HOUSEWARES, ELECTRIC: Heaters, Immersion
Expo Engineered Inc .......... G ...... 708 780-7155
  Cicero (G-7196)

### HOUSEWARES, ELECTRIC: Heaters, Tape
Thermosoft International Corp .......... E ...... 847 279-3800
  Vernon Hills (G-21211)

### HOUSEWARES, ELECTRIC: Heating Units, Electric Appliances
General Electric Company .......... F ...... 708 780-2600
  Cicero (G-7197)

### HOUSEWARES, ELECTRIC: Humidifiers, Household
Bestair Pro .......... G ...... 847 683-3400
  Hampshire (G-11543)

### HOUSEWARES, ELECTRIC: Irons, Household
Conair Corporation .......... E ...... 203 351-9000
  Rantoul (G-17924)

### HOUSEWARES, ELECTRIC: Lighters, Cigarette
Hotvapes Ltd .......... F ...... 775 468-8273
  Chicago (G-5120)

### HOUSEWARES, ELECTRIC: Massage Machines, Exc Beauty/Barber
Tifb Media Group Inc .......... G ...... 844 862-4391
  Burbank (G-2810)

### HOUSEWARES, ELECTRIC: Ovens, Portable
Sun Ovens International Inc .......... F ...... 630 208-7273
  Elburn (G-8911)

### HOUSEWARES, ELECTRIC: Radiators
Menk Usa LLC .......... E ...... 815 626-9730
  Sterling (G-20598)

### HOUSEWARES, ELECTRIC: Shoe Polishers
Beck Shoe Products Company .......... G ...... 618 656-5819
  Edwardsville (G-8792)

### HOUSEWARES, ELECTRIC: Toasters
Hamilton Beach Brands Inc .......... E ...... 847 252-7036
  Hoffman Estates (G-12015)

### HOUSEWARES: Bowls, Wood
Elegant Concepts Ltd .......... G ...... 708 456-9590
  Elmwood Park (G-9968)

### HOUSEWARES: Dishes, China
Pickard Incorporated .......... D ...... 847 395-3800
  Antioch (G-650)

Employee Codes: A=Over 500 employees, B=251-500
C=101-250, D=51-100, E=20-50, F=10-19, G=3-9

## HOUSEWARES: Dishes, Plastic

|  |  |  |
|---|---|---|
| Alpha Acrylic Design | Arlington Heights (G-708) | G 847 818-8178 |
| D&W Fine Pack Holdings LLC | Elk Grove Village (G-9413) | G 847 378-1200 |
| D&W Fine Pack LLC | Lake Zurich (G-13061) | G 800 323-0422 |
| D&W Fine Pack LLC | Elk Grove Village (G-9414) | A 847 378-1200 |
| EMC Innovations Inc | Joliet (G-12490) | G 815 741-2546 |
| Frederics Frame Studio Inc | Chicago (G-4886) | F 312 243-2950 |
| Global Contract Mfg Inc | Chicago (G-4957) | G 312 432-6200 |
| Innoware Plastic Inc | Lake Forest (G-12918) | C 678 690-5100 |
| Jr Plastics LLC | Chicago (G-5333) | C 773 523-5454 |
| Mat Capital LLC | Long Grove (G-13895) | G 847 821-9630 |
| Mgs Mfg Group Inc | Libertyville (G-13358) | E 847 968-4335 |
| Microthincom Inc | Bensenville (G-1950) | F 630 543-0501 |
| Mid Oaks Investments LLC | Buffalo Grove (G-2736) | G 847 215-3475 |
| Molor Products Company | Oswego (G-16927) | F 630 375-5999 |
| Solo Cup Operating Corporation | Lincolnshire (G-13482) | D 847 444-5000 |
| Tenex Corporation | Buffalo Grove (G-2780) | E 847 504-0400 |
| Thermform Engineered Qulty LLC | Huntley (G-12179) | D 847 669-5291 |
| US Acrylic LLC | Libertyville (G-13395) | D 847 837-4800 |

## HOUSEWARES: Household & Commercial, Vitreous China

|  |  |  |
|---|---|---|
| Spring (usa) Corporation | Naperville (G-15754) | F 630 527-8600 |

## HOUSEWARES: Kettles & Skillets, Cast Iron

|  |  |  |
|---|---|---|
| Sunrise Distributors Inc | Elk Grove Village (G-9761) | G 630 400-8786 |

## HOUSEWARES: Pots & Pans, Glass

|  |  |  |
|---|---|---|
| Harris Potteries LP | Northbrook (G-16268) | G 847 564-5544 |

## HOUSING COMPONENTS: Prefabricated, Concrete

|  |  |  |
|---|---|---|
| Bernard Cffey Vtrans Fundation | Naperville (G-15605) | G 630 687-0033 |
| Englewood Co Op | Chicago (G-4755) | G 773 873-1201 |

## HOUSINGS: Business Machine, Sheet Metal

|  |  |  |
|---|---|---|
| IMS Engineered Products LLC | Des Plaines (G-8211) | C 847 391-8100 |
| K B Metal Company | Washburn (G-21376) | G 309 248-7355 |
| Prismier LLC | Woodridge (G-22511) | E 630 592-4515 |

## HOUSINGS: Motor

|  |  |  |
|---|---|---|
| Power Enclosures Inc | Chillicothe (G-7170) | F 309 274-9000 |

## HOUSINGS: Pressure

|  |  |  |
|---|---|---|
| Murdock Company Inc | Mundelein (G-15535) | G 847 566-0050 |

## HUB CAPS: Automobile, Stamped Metal

|  |  |  |
|---|---|---|
| Marmon Industries LLC | Chicago (G-5627) | G 312 372-9500 |

## HUMIDIFIERS & DEHUMIDIFIERS

|  |  |  |
|---|---|---|
| Pure N Natural Systems Inc | Morton Grove (G-15230) | F 630 372-9681 |

## HUMIDIFYING EQPT, EXC PORTABLE

|  |  |  |
|---|---|---|
| Galmar Enterprises Inc | New Lenox (G-15883) | G 815 463-9826 |

## HYDRAULIC EQPT REPAIR SVC

|  |  |  |
|---|---|---|
| Central Hydraulics Inc | El Paso (G-8866) | G 309 527-5238 |
| Cylinder Services Inc | Sugar Grove (G-20721) | G 630 466-9820 |
| Master Hydraulics & Machining | Schaumburg (G-19635) | F 847 895-5578 |
| Midwestern Mch Hydraulics Inc | Mount Vernon (G-15426) | F 618 246-9440 |
| RE-Do-It Corp | Broadview (G-2607) | G 708 343-7125 |
| Sarco Hydraulics Inc | Litchfield (G-13697) | E 217 324-6577 |

## HYDRAULIC FLUIDS: Synthetic Based

|  |  |  |
|---|---|---|
| Houghton International Inc | Chicago (G-5121) | F 610 666-4000 |

## HYDROPONIC EQPT

|  |  |  |
|---|---|---|
| Modern Sprout LLC | Chicago (G-5786) | G 312 342-2114 |

## Hard Rubber & Molded Rubber Prdts

|  |  |  |
|---|---|---|
| Dyneer Corporation | Quincy (G-17823) | B 217 228-6011 |
| Jvi Inc | Lincolnwood (G-13517) | E 847 675-1560 |
| Weiland Fast Trac Inc | Long Grove (G-13905) | G 847 438-7996 |

## ICE

|  |  |  |
|---|---|---|
| Carnaghi Towing & Repair Inc | Tilton (G-20878) | F 217 446-0333 |
| Four Seasons Ace Hardware | Benton (G-2027) | G 618 439-2101 |
| Home City Ice | Chicago (G-5101) | F 773 622-9400 |
| Home City Ice Company | Decatur (G-7889) | F 217 877-7733 |
| International Ice Bagging Syst | Glencoe (G-11000) | G 312 633-4000 |
| Muller-Pinehurst Dairy Inc | Rockford (G-18512) | C 815 968-0441 |
| Pro Rep Sale IL | Barrington (G-1299) | F 847 382-1592 |
| Sislers Ice Inc | Dekalb (G-8117) | E 815 756-6903 |
| Tinley Ice Company | University Park (G-21064) | E 708 532-8777 |

## ICE CREAM & ICES WHOLESALERS

|  |  |  |
|---|---|---|
| Jel Sert Co | West Chicago (G-21727) | B 630 231-7590 |
| Joint Asia Dev Group LLC | Grayslake (G-11349) | E 847 223-1804 |
| Mitchlls Cndies Ice Creams Inc | Homewood (G-12104) | F 708 799-3835 |

## ICE WHOLESALERS

|  |  |  |
|---|---|---|
| Powerone Corp | Saint Charles (G-19239) | G 630 443-6500 |

## ICE: Dry

|  |  |  |
|---|---|---|
| Continental Carbonic Pdts Inc | Decatur (G-7858) | G 217 428-2080 |
| Dixie Carbonic Inc | Decatur (G-7876) | D 217 428-2068 |

## IDENTIFICATION PLATES

|  |  |  |
|---|---|---|
| R L Allen Industries | Troy (G-21011) | G 618 667-2544 |
| Zing Enterprises LLC | Oswego (G-16943) | G 608 201-9490 |

## IDENTIFICATION TAGS, EXC PAPER

|  |  |  |
|---|---|---|
| Bocks Cattle-Identi Co Inc | Mattoon (G-14384) | G 217 234-6634 |
| C H Hanson Company | Naperville (G-15613) | D 630 848-2000 |
| Edmark Visual Identification | Chicago (G-4696) | G 800 923-8333 |

## IGNEOUS ROCK: Crushed & Broken

|  |  |  |
|---|---|---|
| Gateway Crushing & Screening | East Saint Louis (G-8753) | E 618 337-1954 |
| Monmouth Stone Co | Monmouth (G-15022) | F 309 734-7951 |

## IGNITION APPARATUS & DISTRIBUTORS

|  |  |  |
|---|---|---|
| Charlotte Louise Tate | Chicago (G-4294) | G 773 849-3236 |
| Nidec Motor Corporation | Des Plaines (G-8241) | D 847 439-3760 |

## IGNITION SYSTEMS: Internal Combustion Engine

|  |  |  |
|---|---|---|
| Motorola Solutions Inc | Schaumburg (G-19652) | C 847 576-8600 |

## INCINERATORS

|  |  |  |
|---|---|---|
| Elastec Inc | Carmi (G-3066) | C 618 382-2525 |
| Enders Process Equipment Corp | Glendale Heights (G-11022) | G 630 469-3787 |
| Midco International Inc | Chicago (G-5733) | E 773 604-8700 |

## INDL & PERSONAL SVC PAPER WHOLESALERS

|  |  |  |
|---|---|---|
| Hollymatic Corporation | Countryside (G-7430) | D 708 579-3700 |
| Inglese Box Co Ltd | Huntley (G-12149) | E 847 669-1700 |
| Iten Industries Inc | Addison (G-155) | G 630 543-2820 |
| Michael Lewis Company | Mc Cook (G-14453) | C 708 688-2200 |
| Nanco Sales Co Inc | Aurora (G-1193) | G 630 892-9820 |
| Nielsen & Bainbridge LLC | Bridgeview (G-2514) | D 708 546-2135 |
| Qualified Innovation Inc | Sugar Grove (G-20732) | F 630 556-4136 |
| Simu Ltd | Wood Dale (G-22422) | G 630 350-1060 |
| Terrapin Xpress Inc | Palos Heights (G-17111) | G 866 823-7323 |

## INDL & PERSONAL SVC PAPER, WHOL: Bags, Paper/Disp Plastic

|  |  |  |
|---|---|---|
| Poly Plastics Films Corp | Machesney Park (G-14098) | G 815 636-0821 |
| Renew Packaging LLC | Chicago (G-6333) | G 312 421-6699 |
| Sea-Rich Corp | Chicago (G-6464) | G 773 261-6633 |

## INDL & PERSONAL SVC PAPER, WHOL: Boxes, Corrugtd/Solid Fiber

|  |  |  |
|---|---|---|
| Georgia-Pacific LLC | Mount Olive (G-15302) | C 217 999-2511 |
| Pry-Bar Company | Joliet (G-12558) | F 815 436-3383 |
| Rudd Container Corporation | Chicago (G-6414) | D 773 847-7600 |
| Westrock Cp LLC | Galesburg (G-10780) | C 309 342-0121 |

## INDL & PERSONAL SVC PAPER, WHOL: Boxes, Paperbrd/Plastic

|  |  |  |
|---|---|---|
| Co-Ordinated Packaging Inc | Northbrook (G-16228) | F 847 559-8877 |

## INDL & PERSONAL SVC PAPER, WHOL: Container, Paper/Plastic

|  |  |  |
|---|---|---|
| Pactiv LLC | Lake Forest (G-12935) | A 847 482-2000 |

## PRODUCT SECTION — INDL MACHINERY & EQPT WHOLESALERS

### INDL & PERSONAL SVC PAPER, WHOL: Cups, Disp, Plastic/Paper
- Amic Global Inc ........................... G ....... 847 600-3590
  Buffalo Grove *(G-2659)*

### INDL & PERSONAL SVC PAPER, WHOL: Paper, Wrap/Coarse/Prdts
- Orora North America ...................... D ....... 630 613-2600
  Lombard *(G-13839)*
- Orora Packaging Solutions .............. D ....... 815 895-2343
  Sycamore *(G-20812)*

### INDL & PERSONAL SVC PAPER, WHOLESALE: Boxes & Containers
- H Field & Sons Inc ........................ F ....... 847 434-0970
  Arlington Heights *(G-761)*

### INDL & PERSONAL SVC PAPER, WHOLESALE: Paperboard & Prdts
- Roll Source Paper .......................... G ....... 630 875-0308
  Itasca *(G-12350)*

### INDL & PERSONAL SVC PAPER, WHOLESALE: Press Sensitive Tape
- Hugh Courtright & Co Ltd ............... F ....... 708 534-8400
  Monee *(G-14997)*
- Strata-Tac Inc ............................... F ....... 630 879-9388
  Saint Charles *(G-19272)*

### INDL & PERSONAL SVC PAPER, WHOLESALE: Shipping Splys
- Compak Inc .................................. E ....... 815 399-2699
  Rockford *(G-18320)*
- Heritage Packaging LLC ................. E ....... 217 735-4406
  Lincoln *(G-13410)*
- Primedia Source LLC ..................... G ....... 630 553-8451
  Yorkville *(G-22670)*
- Quad-Illinois Inc ............................ F ....... 847 836-1115
  Elgin *(G-9155)*
- Weary & Baity Inc ......................... G ....... 312 943-6197
  Chicago *(G-6947)*

### INDL CONTRACTORS: Exhibit Construction
- General Exhibits and Displays ......... D ....... 847 934-1943
  Inverness *(G-12204)*
- Howard Displays Inc ...................... F
  Highland Park *(G-11841)*
- Proto Productions Inc .................... E ....... 630 628-6626
  Addison *(G-260)*

### INDL DIAMONDS WHOLESALERS
- Diamond Industrial Sales Ltd .......... G ....... 630 858-3687
  Glen Ellyn *(G-10966)*

### INDL EQPT SVCS
- AAA Press Specialists Inc .............. F ....... 847 818-1100
  Arlington Heights *(G-701)*
- BSB International Corp ................... G ....... 847 791-9272
  Bensenville *(G-1848)*
- C P Environmental Inc .................... F ....... 630 759-8866
  Romeoville *(G-18805)*
- Cryogenic Systems Equipment ........ E ....... 708 385-4216
  Blue Island *(G-2244)*
- D & N Deburring Co Inc .................. G ....... 847 451-7702
  Franklin Park *(G-10452)*
- Dover Prtg Identification Inc ........... D ....... 630 541-1540
  Downers Grove *(G-8434)*
- Dumore Supplies Inc ...................... F ....... 312 949-6260
  Chicago *(G-4649)*
- Electron Beam Technologies Inc ..... C ....... 815 935-2211
  Kankakee *(G-12612)*
- Elmot Inc ...................................... G ....... 773 791-7039
  Chicago *(G-4734)*
- Erowa Technology Inc .................... F ....... 847 290-0295
  Arlington Heights *(G-751)*
- Gti Spindle Technology Inc ............. F ....... 309 820-7887
  Bloomington *(G-2175)*
- Industrial Mint Wldg Machining ...... D ....... 773 376-6526
  Chicago *(G-5178)*
- Kelly Systems Inc .......................... E ....... 312 733-3224
  Chicago *(G-5374)*

- Meta TEC Development Inc ............ G ....... 309 246-2960
  Lacon *(G-12789)*
- Meyer Machine & Equipment Inc ..... F ....... 847 395-2970
  Antioch *(G-645)*
- North Shore Truck & Equipment ...... G ....... 847 887-0200
  Lake Bluff *(G-12860)*
- Patrick Holdings Inc ....................... F ....... 815 874-5300
  Rockford *(G-18531)*
- Plating International Inc ................. F ....... 847 451-2101
  Franklin Park *(G-10554)*
- Quality Machine Tool Services ........ G ....... 847 776-0073
  Schaumburg *(G-19708)*
- Richards Electric Motor Co ............. E ....... 217 222-7154
  Quincy *(G-17887)*
- Sloan Industries Inc ....................... E ....... 630 350-1614
  Wood Dale *(G-22423)*
- Stickon Adhesive Inds Inc .............. F ....... 847 593-5959
  Arlington Heights *(G-844)*
- Stolp Gore Company ...................... G ....... 630 904-5180
  Plainfield *(G-17653)*
- Wehrli Equipment Co Inc ................ F ....... 630 717-4150
  Naperville *(G-15783)*
- Windy City Laser Service Inc .......... G ....... 773 995-0188
  Chicago *(G-6996)*

### INDL GASES WHOLESALERS
- Airgas Inc ..................................... F ....... 773 785-3000
  Chicago *(G-3786)*
- Airgas USA LLC ............................. E ....... 708 354-0813
  Countryside *(G-7412)*
- American Welding & Gas Inc .......... E ....... 630 527-2550
  Stone Park *(G-20632)*
- Boc Global Helium Inc .................... C ....... 630 897-1900
  Montgomery *(G-15032)*
- Maccarb Inc .................................. G ....... 877 427-2499
  Elgin *(G-9098)*

### INDL MACHINERY & EQPT WHOLESALERS
- AAM-Ro Corporation ....................... F ....... 708 343-5543
  Broadview *(G-2552)*
- Active Automation Inc .................... F ....... 847 427-8100
  Elk Grove Village *(G-9268)*
- Air Mite Devices Inc ...................... E ....... 224 338-0071
  Round Lake *(G-19051)*
- Airgas Inc ..................................... F ....... 773 785-3000
  Chicago *(G-3786)*
- Al Cook Electric Motors .................. G ....... 309 653-2337
  Adair *(G-11)*
- Alfa Controls Inc ........................... G ....... 847 978-9245
  Wheeling *(G-22001)*
- Altak Inc ....................................... D ....... 630 622-0300
  Bloomingdale *(G-2092)*
- American Specialty Toy .................. G ....... 312 222-0984
  Chicago *(G-3876)*
- Amj Industries Inc ......................... F ....... 815 654-9000
  Rockford *(G-18264)*
- Automatic Production Equipment .... G ....... 847 439-1448
  Elk Grove Village *(G-9321)*
- Baley Enterprises Inc ..................... E ....... 708 681-0900
  Melrose Park *(G-14599)*
- Belden Machine Corporation ........... F ....... 708 344-4600
  Broadview *(G-2561)*
- C U Services LLC .......................... G ....... 847 439-2303
  Elk Grove Village *(G-9352)*
- CDL Technology Inc ....................... E ....... 630 543-5240
  Addison *(G-70)*
- Century Filter Products Inc ............ G ....... 773 477-1790
  Chicago *(G-4276)*
- Chicago Chain and Transm Co ........ E ....... 630 482-9000
  Countryside *(G-7417)*
- Chicago Heights Star Tool and ....... F ....... 708 758-2525
  Chicago Heights *(G-7089)*
- Chicago Metal Fabricators Inc ........ D ....... 773 523-5755
  Chicago *(G-4332)*
- Clybourn Metal Finishing Co ........... G ....... 773 525-8162
  Chicago *(G-4409)*
- Coe Equipment Inc ........................ G ....... 217 498-7200
  Rochester *(G-18116)*
- Control Weigh ................................ G ....... 847 540-8260
  Buffalo Grove *(G-2679)*
- Corrugated Converting Eqp ............. F ....... 618 532-2138
  Centralia *(G-3410)*
- Craftsman Tool & Mold Co .............. G ....... 630 851-8700
  Aurora *(G-986)*
- Custom Blades & Tools Inc ............. G ....... 630 860-7650
  Bensenville *(G-1875)*
- Disa Holding Corp .......................... G ....... 630 820-3000
  Oswego *(G-16913)*
- Doyle Equipment Mfg Co ................ D ....... 217 222-1592
  Quincy *(G-17821)*

- DTS America Inc ............................ G ....... 847 783-0401
  East Dundee *(G-8633)*
- Dura Products Corporation ............. G ....... 815 939-1399
  Bradley *(G-2420)*
- Dynamesh Inc ................................ E ....... 630 293-5454
  Batavia *(G-1444)*
- Earthsafe Systems Inc ................... F ....... 312 226-7600
  Chicago *(G-4679)*
- EJ Cady & Company ...................... G ....... 847 537-2239
  Wheeling *(G-22045)*
- Enerstar Inc .................................. G ....... 847 350-3400
  Bensenville *(G-1893)*
- Engineered Abrasives Inc .............. E ....... 662 582-4143
  Alsip *(G-462)*
- Fna Ip Holdings Inc ....................... D ....... 847 348-1500
  Elk Grove Village *(G-9482)*
- Frantz Manufacturing Company ...... D ....... 815 625-7063
  Sterling *(G-20592)*
- Fusibond Piping Systems Inc ......... F ....... 630 969-4488
  Downers Grove *(G-8446)*
- Hartland Cutting Tools Inc ............. F ....... 847 639-9400
  Cary *(G-3350)*
- Hausermann Die & Machine Co ...... F ....... 630 543-6688
  Addison *(G-144)*
- HEF Corporation ............................ E ....... 708 343-0866
  Melrose Park *(G-14653)*
- Hfo Chicago LLC ............................ F ....... 847 258-2850
  Elk Grove Village *(G-9523)*
- Hoerbiger-Origa Corporation ........... D ....... 800 283-1377
  Glendale Heights *(G-11030)*
- Holland Applied Technologies ......... E ....... 630 325-5130
  Burr Ridge *(G-2851)*
- Hugh Courtright & Co Ltd ............... F ....... 708 534-8400
  Monee *(G-14997)*
- Hydra Fold Auger Inc ..................... G ....... 217 379-2614
  Loda *(G-13751)*
- Hyster-Yale Group Inc ................... E ....... 217 443-7416
  Danville *(G-7736)*
- I W M Corporation .......................... G ....... 847 695-0700
  Elgin *(G-9070)*
- Illinois Lift Equipment Inc .............. G ....... 888 745-0577
  West Chicago *(G-21717)*
- Illinois Oil Products Inc .................. F ....... 309 788-1896
  Rock Island *(G-18183)*
- Industrial Filter Pump Mfg Co ........ D ....... 708 656-7800
  Bedford Park *(G-1556)*
- Inlet & Pipe Protection Inc ............. G ....... 630 355-3288
  Naperville *(G-15811)*
- Intelligrated Systems Inc ............... B ....... 630 985-4350
  Woodridge *(G-22495)*
- Interlake Mecalux Inc .................... B ....... 708 344-9999
  Melrose Park *(G-14659)*
- Interstate Power Systems Inc ........ F ....... 630 871-1111
  Carol Stream *(G-3174)*
- Interstate Power Systems Inc ........ D ....... 952 854-2044
  Rockford *(G-18440)*
- Inverom Corporation ...................... G ....... 630 568-5609
  Burr Ridge *(G-2858)*
- ITT Water & Wastewater USA Inc ... F ....... 708 342-0484
  Tinley Park *(G-20924)*
- J A K Enterprises Inc .................... G ....... 217 422-3881
  Decatur *(G-7897)*
- Jamco Products Inc ....................... D ....... 815 624-0400
  South Beloit *(G-20152)*
- Jardis Industries Inc ..................... E ....... 630 860-5959
  Itasca *(G-12289)*
- Jn Pump Holdings Inc .................... F ....... 708 754-2940
  Chicago Heights *(G-7105)*
- Knapheide Manufacturing Co .......... E ....... 217 223-1848
  Quincy *(G-17847)*
- Kwalyti Tling McHy Rblding Inc ...... F ....... 630 761-8040
  Batavia *(G-1463)*
- L & J Engineering Inc .................... E ....... 708 236-6000
  Hillside *(G-11922)*
- Lab Ten LLC .................................. E ....... 815 877-1410
  Machesney Park *(G-14087)*
- Lamco Slings & Rigging Inc ........... E ....... 309 764-7400
  Moline *(G-14952)*
- Lc Holdings of Delaware Inc .......... G ....... 847 940-3550
  Deerfield *(G-8028)*
- Lewis Paper Place Inc ................... E ....... 847 808-1343
  Wheeling *(G-22093)*
- Liberty Machinery Company ........... F ....... 847 276-2761
  Lincolnshire *(G-13463)*
- Litho Research Incorporated .......... G ....... 630 860-7070
  Itasca *(G-12307)*
- Loma International Inc .................. D ....... 630 588-0900
  Carol Stream *(G-3186)*
- Maac Machinery Co Inc ................. E ....... 630 665-1700
  Carol Stream *(G-3187)*

---

Employee Codes: A=Over 500 employees, B=251-500, C=101-250, D=51-100, E=20-50, F=10-19, G=3-9

## INDL MACHINERY & EQPT WHOLESALERS

Maxi-Vac Inc .................................................. G ........ 224 699-9760
  Addison *(G-194)*
Mega International Ltd .................................. G ........ 309 764-5310
  Moline *(G-14956)*
Midstate Manufacturing Company ............... C ........ 309 342-9555
  Galesburg *(G-10767)*
Mitsubishi Heavy Inds Amer Inc ................... F ........ 630 693-4700
  Addison *(G-217)*
Mity Inc .......................................................... G ........ 630 365-5030
  Elburn *(G-8898)*
Mueller Mfg Corp .......................................... E ........ 847 640-1666
  Elk Grove Village *(G-9642)*
Newssor Manufacturing Inc ......................... G ........ 618 259-1174
  East Alton *(G-8606)*
Nidec-Shimpo America Corp ....................... E ........ 630 924-7138
  Itasca *(G-12331)*
Nissei America Inc ...................................... G ........ 847 228-5000
  Elk Grove Village *(G-9652)*
NNt Enterprises Incorporated ...................... E ........ 630 875-9600
  Itasca *(G-12332)*
O Adjust Matic Pump Company .................. G ........ 630 766-1490
  Wood Dale *(G-22408)*
Original Systems ......................................... G ........ 847 945-7660
  Riverwoods *(G-18041)*
Polar Corporation ......................................... E ........ 618 548-3660
  Salem *(G-19343)*
Prime Devices Corporation ......................... G ........ 847 729-2550
  Willow Springs *(G-22198)*
Pro-Quip Incorporated ................................. F ........ 708 352-5732
  La Grange Park *(G-12759)*
Process Mechanical Inc ............................... G ........ 630 416-7021
  Naperville *(G-15732)*
Proto-Cutter Inc ............................................ G ........ 815 232-2300
  Freeport *(G-10681)*
R G Hanson Company Inc ........................... F ........ 309 661-9200
  Bloomington *(G-2217)*
Randall Publishing Inc ................................. F ........ 847 437-6604
  Elk Grove Village *(G-9709)*
Red Bud Industries Inc ................................ C ........ 618 282-3801
  Red Bud *(G-17947)*
Robert Brysiewicz Incorporated .................. G ........ 630 289-0903
  Bartlett *(G-1369)*
Smart Motion Robotics Inc ......................... G ........ 815 895-8550
  Sycamore *(G-20817)*
Stein Inc ....................................................... D ........ 618 452-0836
  Granite City *(G-11305)*
Stutz Company ............................................ F ........ 773 287-1068
  Chicago *(G-6610)*
Terco Inc ...................................................... E ........ 630 894-8828
  Bloomingdale *(G-2139)*
Thomas Engineering Inc .............................. D ........ 847 358-5800
  Hoffman Estates *(G-12065)*
Trac Equipment Company Inc ..................... G ........ 309 647-5066
  Canton *(G-2993)*
Triumph Twist Drill Co Inc ........................... B ........ 815 459-6250
  Crystal Lake *(G-7670)*
Tru-Cut Tool & Supply Co ............................ F ........ 708 396-1122
  Wheeling *(G-22169)*
Uesco Industries Inc ................................... E ........ 708 385-7700
  Alsip *(G-536)*
Ultra Packaging Inc ..................................... G ........ 630 595-9820
  Bensenville *(G-2008)*
Ultramatic Equipment Co ............................ G ........ 630 543-4565
  Addison *(G-333)*
Wehrli Equipment Co Inc ............................. F ........ 630 717-4150
  Naperville *(G-15783)*
Weldstar Company ...................................... G ........ 708 534-6419
  University Park *(G-21066)*
Wynright Corporation ................................... D ........ 847 595-9400
  Elk Grove Village *(G-9819)*

### INDL MACHINERY REPAIR & MAINTENANCE

Acsys Lasertechnik US Inc ......................... G ........ 224 699-9572
  Elgin *(G-8934)*
Action Turbine Repair Svc Inc ..................... F ........ 708 924-9601
  Summit Argo *(G-20760)*
Allen Popovich ............................................. G ........ 815 712-7404
  Custer Park *(G-7686)*
Allied Instrument Service Inc ...................... F ........ 708 788-1912
  Berwyn *(G-2056)*
Automatic Machinery Resources ................ G ........ 630 543-4944
  Addison *(G-48)*
Best Rep Company Corporation .................. G ........ 847 451-6644
  Franklin Park *(G-10411)*
Bonell Manufacturing Company .................. E ........ 708 849-1770
  Riverdale *(G-18016)*
Bos Machine Tool Services Inc ................... F ........ 309 658-2223
  Hillsdale *(G-11901)*
Bourn & Koch Inc ......................................... D ........ 815 965-4013
  Rockford *(G-18290)*

Cartpac Inc ................................................... E ........ 630 283-8979
  Carol Stream *(G-3125)*
Cloos Robotic Welding Inc .......................... F ........ 847 923-9988
  Schaumburg *(G-19474)*
Commercial Machine Services .................... F ........ 847 806-1901
  Elk Grove Village *(G-9386)*
Control Works Inc ........................................ G ........ 630 444-1942
  Saint Charles *(G-19163)*
Dainichi Machinery Inc ................................ G ........ 630 681-1572
  Carol Stream *(G-3139)*
David Schutte .............................................. G ........ 217 223-5464
  Quincy *(G-17818)*
E & H Graphic Service ................................. G ........ 708 748-5656
  Matteson *(G-14371)*
Gilday Services ............................................ G ........ 847 395-0853
  Antioch *(G-635)*
HB Coatings LLC .......................................... G ........ 618 215-8161
  Madison *(G-14149)*
Industrial Instrument Svc Corp .................... G ........ 773 581-3355
  Chicago *(G-5177)*
Lipscomb Engineering Inc ........................... G ........ 630 231-3833
  West Chicago *(G-21732)*
McCloskey Eyman Mlone Mfg Svcs ............ G ........ 309 647-4000
  Canton *(G-2991)*
Melissa A Miller .......................................... G ........ 708 529-7786
  New Lenox *(G-15893)*
Mj Snyder Ironworks Inc ............................. G ........ 217 826-6440
  Marshall *(G-14326)*
Modern Fluid Technology Inc ...................... G ........ 815 356-0001
  Crystal Lake *(G-7614)*
Paperchine Inc ............................................. G ........ 815 389-8200
  Rockton *(G-18700)*
Pillarhouse USA Inc ..................................... F ........ 847 593-9080
  Elk Grove Village *(G-9680)*
Robey Packaging Eqp & Svc ....................... G ........ 708 758-8250
  Chicago Heights *(G-7123)*
S G Acquisition Inc ...................................... F ........ 815 624-6501
  South Beloit *(G-20168)*
Service Cutting & Welding .......................... G ........ 773 622-8366
  Chicago *(G-6482)*
Total Tooling Technology Inc ....................... F ........ 847 437-5135
  Elk Grove Village *(G-9786)*
Tox- Pressotechnik LLC ............................... G ........ 630 447-4600
  Warrenville *(G-21365)*
Uesco Industries Inc ................................... E ........ 800 325-8372
  Alsip *(G-537)*
Usach Technologies Inc .............................. E ........ 847 888-0148
  Elgin *(G-9222)*
Wemco Inc ................................................... F ........ 708 388-1980
  Alsip *(G-543)*
World Cup Packaging Inc ............................ G ........ 815 624-6501
  South Beloit *(G-20178)*
WW Engineering Company LLC .................. F ........ 773 376-9494
  Chicago *(G-7042)*

### INDL PATTERNS: Foundry Cores

Cores For You Inc ........................................ E ........ 217 847-3233
  Hamilton *(G-11531)*
Johnson Pattern & Mch Works ................... E ........ 815 433-2775
  Ottawa *(G-16964)*
Midstate Core Co ......................................... E ........ 217 429-2673
  Decatur *(G-7914)*

### INDL PATTERNS: Foundry Patternmaking

Apex Pattern Works ..................................... G ........ 309 346-2905
  Pekin *(G-17254)*
Arnette Pattern Co Inc ................................. G ........ 618 451-7700
  Granite City *(G-11268)*
D & M Pattern Co ......................................... G ........ 217 877-0064
  Decatur *(G-7864)*
Olson Aluminum Castings Ltd .................... E ........ 815 229-3292
  Rockford *(G-18526)*
Park Products Inc ........................................ G ........ 630 543-2474
  Addison *(G-237)*
Prs Inc .......................................................... G ........ 630 620-7259
  Lombard *(G-13846)*

### INDL PROCESS INSTR: Transmit, Process Variables

Autrol Corporation of America .................... G ........ 847 779-5000
  Schaumburg *(G-19451)*
Landairsea Systems Inc .............................. F ........ 847 462-8100
  Woodstock *(G-22581)*

### INDL PROCESS INSTRUMENTS: Analyzers

Electronic System Design Inc ..................... G ........ 847 358-8212
  Bensenville *(G-1890)*

### INDL PROCESS INSTRUMENTS: Boiler Controls, Power & Marine

Fuel Tech Inc ................................................ C ........ 630 845-4500
  Warrenville *(G-21348)*

### INDL PROCESS INSTRUMENTS: Chromatographs

Orochem Technologies Inc .......................... E ........ 630 210-8300
  Naperville *(G-15719)*

### INDL PROCESS INSTRUMENTS: Control

ARI Industries Inc ........................................ D ........ 630 953-9100
  Addison *(G-44)*
Charnor Inc .................................................. D ........ 309 787-2427
  Milan *(G-14778)*
Janco Process Controls Inc ......................... E ........ 847 526-0800
  Wauconda *(G-21475)*
Modern Fluid Technology Inc ...................... G ........ 815 356-0001
  Crystal Lake *(G-7614)*
Schneider Elc Buildings LLC ....................... B ........ 815 381-5000
  Rockford *(G-18608)*
Schneider Elc Holdings Inc ......................... A ........ 717 944-5460
  Schaumburg *(G-19722)*
Sterling Products Inc ................................... D ........ 847 273-7700
  Schaumburg *(G-19740)*
Tecnova Electronics Inc .............................. D ........ 847 336-6160
  Waukegan *(G-21623)*

### INDL PROCESS INSTRUMENTS: Controllers, Process Variables

Mid-American Elevator Co Inc ..................... C ........ 773 486-6900
  Chicago *(G-5727)*
Mid-American Elevator Co Inc ..................... E ........ 815 740-1204
  Joliet *(G-12541)*
Northern Technologies Inc .......................... E ........ 440 246-6999
  Warrenville *(G-21351)*

### INDL PROCESS INSTRUMENTS: Data Loggers

Embedor Technologies Inc .......................... G ........ 202 681-0359
  Champaign *(G-3480)*

### INDL PROCESS INSTRUMENTS: Digital Display, Process Variables

Airways Video Inc ........................................ G ........ 773 539-8400
  Chicago *(G-3789)*
Liveone Inc .................................................. G ........ 312 282-2320
  Chicago *(G-5525)*
Starhouse Inc ............................................... G ........ 630 679-0979
  Lockport *(G-13748)*
Tomantron Inc .............................................. F ........ 708 532-2456
  Tinley Park *(G-20950)*

### INDL PROCESS INSTRUMENTS: Draft Gauges

Indev Gauging Systems Inc ........................ E ........ 815 282-4463
  Rockford *(G-18429)*
Indev Gauging Systems Inc ........................ G ........ 815 282-4463
  Loves Park *(G-13948)*

### INDL PROCESS INSTRUMENTS: Elements, Primary

Principal Instruments Inc ............................ G ........ 815 469-8159
  Frankfort *(G-10354)*
V2 Flow Controls LLC .................................. G ........ 708 945-9331
  Tinley Park *(G-20955)*

### INDL PROCESS INSTRUMENTS: Indl Flow & Measuring

Nordson Asymtek Inc ................................... C ........ 760 431-1919
  Chicago *(G-5926)*

### INDL PROCESS INSTRUMENTS: Level & Bulk Measuring

Magnetrol International Inc ......................... C ........ 630 723-6600
  Aurora *(G-1051)*

# PRODUCT SECTION

## INDL SPLYS, WHOLESALE: Rubber Goods, Mechanical

### INDL PROCESS INSTRUMENTS: Temperature

Dickson/Unigage Inc............................E....... 630 543-3747
  Addison *(G-92)*
Eclipse Inc..............................................D....... 815 877-3031
  Rockford *(G-18356)*

### INDL PROCESS INSTRUMENTS: Water Quality Monitoring/Cntrl Sys

Automated Logic Corporation...............F....... 630 852-1700
  Lisle *(G-13566)*
Azcon Inc................................................F....... 815 548-7000
  Sterling *(G-20583)*
Enerstar Inc...........................................G...... 847 350-3400
  Bensenville *(G-1893)*
Ffg Restoration Inc................................F....... 708 240-4873
  Broadview *(G-2577)*
G-M Services.........................................G...... 618 532-2324
  Centralia *(G-3415)*
Pan America Environmental Inc...........G...... 847 487-9166
  McHenry *(G-14541)*
Village Hampshire Trtmnt Plant............G...... 847 683-2064
  Hampshire *(G-11564)*
Village Hebron Water Sewage..............G...... 815 648-2353
  Hebron *(G-11731)*

### INDL SALTS WHOLESALERS

Compass Minerals Intl Inc.....................F....... 773 978-7258
  Chicago *(G-4438)*
K+s Salt LLC..........................................G...... 844 789-3991
  Chicago *(G-5347)*

### INDL SPLYS WHOLESALERS

ABM Marking Ltd...................................F....... 618 277-3773
  Belleville *(G-1606)*
Afc Cable Systems Inc..........................B....... 508 998-1131
  Harvey *(G-11651)*
American Industrial Direct LLC.............E....... 800 382-1200
  Elgin *(G-8948)*
Blastline USA Inc...................................G...... 630 871-0147
  Carol Stream *(G-3118)*
Chase Fasteners Inc.............................E....... 708 345-0335
  Melrose Park *(G-14608)*
Coding Solutions Inc.............................F....... 630 377-5825
  Saint Charles *(G-19159)*
Darbe Products Company Inc..............G...... 630 985-0769
  Woodridge *(G-22468)*
David Linderholm..................................G...... 847 336-3755
  Waukegan *(G-21548)*
Dixon Brass............................................E....... 630 323-3716
  Westmont *(G-21885)*
Dvcc Inc.................................................E....... 630 323-3105
  Westmont *(G-21886)*
Fca LLC..................................................E....... 309 949-3999
  Coal Valley *(G-7296)*
Fca LLC..................................................E....... 309 385-2588
  Princeville *(G-17765)*
Fca LLC..................................................E....... 309 792-3444
  Moline *(G-14939)*
Flexicraft Industries Inc.........................F....... 312 738-3588
  Chicago *(G-4861)*
Gear & Repair........................................G...... 708 387-0144
  Brookfield *(G-2634)*
Graphic Pallet & Transport....................E....... 630 904-4951
  Plainfield *(G-17604)*
Group O Inc...........................................B....... 309 736-8311
  Milan *(G-14789)*
Illinois Tool Works Inc...........................C...... 847 299-2222
  Des Plaines *(G-8209)*
Ingersoll-Rand Company......................E....... 630 530-3800
  Elmhurst *(G-9886)*
Jacob Hay Co........................................G...... 847 215-8880
  Wheeling *(G-22080)*
Jason of Illinois Inc...............................E....... 630 752-0600
  Carol Stream *(G-3176)*
Kocour Inc..............................................E....... 773 847-1111
  Chicago *(G-5397)*
Laminart Inc...........................................E....... 800 323-7624
  Schaumburg *(G-19612)*
Lbs Marketing Ltd..................................G...... 815 965-5234
  Rockford *(G-18463)*
Litho Research Incorporated................G...... 630 860-7070
  Itasca *(G-12307)*
M Cor Inc...............................................F....... 630 860-1150
  Bensenville *(G-1943)*
Midwest Cnstr Svcs Inc Peoria.............F....... 309 697-1000
  Bartonville *(G-1397)*

Nuair Filter Company LLC....................F....... 309 888-4331
  Normal *(G-16081)*
Omar Medical Supplies Inc..................E....... 708 922-4377
  Chicago *(G-5988)*
Primedia Source LLC...........................G...... 630 553-8451
  Yorkville *(G-22670)*
R & D Clark Ltd.....................................G...... 847 749-2061
  Arlington Heights *(G-825)*
R & O Specialties Incorporated............D...... 309 736-8660
  Milan *(G-14800)*
Reel Life Dvd LLC.................................G...... 708 579-1360
  Western Springs *(G-21872)*
Resource Plastics Inc...........................D...... 708 389-3558
  Alsip *(G-519)*
RR Donnelley Printing Co LP...............G...... 312 326-8000
  Chicago *(G-6405)*
S & J Industrial Supply Corp................E....... 708 339-1708
  South Holland *(G-20303)*
Samuel Strapping Systems Inc...........D...... 630 783-8900
  Woodridge *(G-22515)*
Semler Industries Inc............................E....... 847 671-5650
  Franklin Park *(G-10586)*
Shima American Corporation................G...... 630 760-4330
  Itasca *(G-12353)*
Steel-Guard Safety Corp......................E....... 708 589-4588
  South Holland *(G-20306)*
Superior Mfg Group - Europe..............E....... 708 458-4600
  Chicago *(G-6635)*
United Remanufacturing Co Inc...........G...... 773 777-1223
  Schiller Park *(G-19880)*
Wallace/Haskin Corp............................E....... 630 789-2882
  Downers Grove *(G-8540)*

### INDL SPLYS, WHOL: Fasteners, Incl Nuts, Bolts, Screws, Etc

Classic Fasteners LLC..........................G...... 630 605-0195
  Saint Charles *(G-19157)*
Component Hardware Inc.....................G...... 847 458-8181
  Gilberts *(G-10916)*
Engineered Components Co................E....... 847 985-8000
  Elgin *(G-9028)*
Great Lakes Washer Company.............F....... 630 887-7447
  Burr Ridge *(G-2846)*
Intech Industries Inc.............................F....... 847 487-5599
  Wauconda *(G-21473)*
Set Screw & Mfg Co.............................E....... 847 717-3700
  Elgin *(G-9176)*

### INDL SPLYS, WHOLESALE: Abrasives

Abrasic 90 Inc........................................E....... 800 447-4248
  Niles *(G-15955)*
Agsco Corporation................................E....... 847 520-4455
  Wheeling *(G-21999)*
Bronson & Bratton Inc..........................C...... 630 986-1815
  Burr Ridge *(G-2825)*
K & K Abrasives & Supplies.................E....... 773 582-9500
  Chicago *(G-5341)*

### INDL SPLYS, WHOLESALE: Adhesives, Tape & Plasters

Adhes Tape Technology Inc..................G...... 847 496-7949
  Arlington Heights *(G-702)*
C H Hanson Company..........................D...... 630 848-2000
  Naperville *(G-15613)*
Fontana Associates Inc........................G...... 888 707-8273
  Arlington Heights *(G-755)*
Lanmar Inc.............................................E....... 800 233-5520
  Northbrook *(G-16293)*
Strata-Tac Inc........................................F....... 630 879-9388
  Saint Charles *(G-19272)*
Tape Case Ltd.......................................E....... 847 299-7880
  Elk Grove Village *(G-9768)*

### INDL SPLYS, WHOLESALE: Bearings

Alternative Bearings Corp.....................G...... 847 240-9630
  Schaumburg *(G-19435)*
Bearing Sales Corporation...................E....... 773 282-8686
  Chicago *(G-4066)*
Ccty USA Bearing Co...........................E....... 847 540-8196
  Lake Zurich *(G-13051)*
Composite Bearings Mfg......................F....... 630 595-8334
  Wood Dale *(G-22354)*
Inpro/Seal LLC.......................................C...... 309 787-8940
  Rock Island *(G-18184)*
NTN USA Corporation..........................C...... 847 298-4652
  Mount Prospect *(G-15357)*

Voss Engineering Inc............................E....... 847 673-8900
  Lincolnwood *(G-13542)*

### INDL SPLYS, WHOLESALE: Bins & Containers, Storage

Arrows Up Inc........................................G...... 847 305-2550
  Arlington Heights *(G-717)*
Stack-On Products Co..........................C...... 847 526-1611
  Wauconda *(G-21502)*

### INDL SPLYS, WHOLESALE: Cordage

Tri Vantage LLC....................................F....... 630 530-5333
  Elmhurst *(G-9952)*

### INDL SPLYS, WHOLESALE: Drums, New Or Reconditioned

Higgins Bros Inc....................................F....... 773 523-0124
  Chicago *(G-5086)*
Meyer Steel Drum Inc...........................E....... 773 522-3030
  Chicago *(G-5712)*
Meyer Steel Drum Inc...........................C...... 773 376-8376
  Chicago *(G-5713)*
Polycorp Illinois Inc..............................D...... 773 847-7575
  Chicago *(G-6154)*

### INDL SPLYS, WHOLESALE: Fasteners & Fastening Eqpt

J B Watts Company Inc........................G...... 773 643-1855
  Chicago *(G-5256)*

### INDL SPLYS, WHOLESALE: Filters, Indl

Bisco Enterprise Inc.............................F....... 630 628-1831
  Schaumburg *(G-19463)*
Filter Kleen Inc......................................G...... 708 447-4666
  Lyons *(G-14037)*
Murdock Company Inc.........................G...... 847 566-0050
  Mundelein *(G-15535)*

### INDL SPLYS, WHOLESALE: Gaskets

Capital Rubber Corporation..................F....... 630 595-6644
  Bensenville *(G-1851)*
Plastic Specialties & Tech Inc..............E....... 847 781-2414
  Schaumburg *(G-19693)*

### INDL SPLYS, WHOLESALE: Gaskets & Seals

Hennig Gasket & Seals Inc...................G...... 312 243-8270
  Chicago *(G-5071)*
Non-Metals Inc......................................G...... 630 378-9866
  Bolingbrook *(G-2354)*

### INDL SPLYS, WHOLESALE: Gears

Omni Gear and Machine Corp..............F....... 815 723-4327
  Joliet *(G-12548)*
Smith Power Transmission Co..............G...... 773 526-5512
  Chicago *(G-6535)*

### INDL SPLYS, WHOLESALE: Pipeline Wrappings, Anti-Corrosive

Buckeye Terminals LLC........................G...... 217 342-2336
  Effingham *(G-8828)*

### INDL SPLYS, WHOLESALE: Plastic Bottles

Decorative Industries Inc.....................E....... 773 229-0015
  Chicago *(G-4570)*

### INDL SPLYS, WHOLESALE: Power Transmission, Eqpt & Apparatus

Chicago Chain and Transm Co.............E....... 630 482-9000
  Countryside *(G-7417)*
Nidec-Shimpo America Corp................E....... 630 924-7138
  Itasca *(G-12331)*
US Tsubaki Holdings Inc......................C...... 847 459-9500
  Wheeling *(G-22172)*
US Tsubaki Power Transm LLC............C...... 847 459-9500
  Wheeling *(G-22173)*

### INDL SPLYS, WHOLESALE: Rubber Goods, Mechanical

Accurate Products Incorporated...........E....... 773 878-2200
  Chicago *(G-3722)*

## INDL SPLYS, WHOLESALE: Rubber Goods, Mechanical

Allstates Rubber & Tool Corp .................F ....... 708 342-1030
Tinley Park (G-20888)
Industrial Rubber & Sup Entp ................G ....... 217 429-3747
Decatur (G-7895)
ONeill Products Inc ...................................G ....... 312 243-3413
Chicago (G-5991)

### INDL SPLYS, WHOLESALE: Seals

AMS Seals Inc ............................................G ....... 815 609-4977
Plainfield (G-17580)
Lochman Ref Silk Screen Co ...................F ....... 847 475-6266
Evanston (G-10065)
Rt Enterprises Inc ....................................F ....... 847 675-1444
Skokie (G-20080)
Waves Fluid Solutions LLC ......................G ....... 630 765-7533
Carol Stream (G-3264)

### INDL SPLYS, WHOLESALE: Signmaker Eqpt & Splys

Component Products Inc ..........................E ....... 847 301-1000
Schaumburg (G-19477)
Mich Enterprises Inc .................................F ....... 630 616-9000
Wood Dale (G-22399)

### INDL SPLYS, WHOLESALE: Springs

Ascent Mfg Co ...........................................E ....... 847 806-6600
Elk Grove Village (G-9314)
Mid-West Spring & Stamping Inc ............G ....... 630 739-3800
Romeoville (G-18848)
R & G Spring Co Inc .................................G ....... 847 228-5640
Elk Grove Village (G-9706)

### INDL SPLYS, WHOLESALE: Staplers & Tackers

Ample Supply Company ............................E ....... 815 895-3500
Sycamore (G-20786)

### INDL SPLYS, WHOLESALE: Textile Printers' Splys

Chicago Silk Screen Sup Co Inc ..............E ....... 312 666-1213
Chicago (G-4349)
Sg2 ............................................................G ....... 847 779-5500
Skokie (G-20084)

### INDL SPLYS, WHOLESALE: Tools

Carroll Tool & Manufacturing ....................G ....... 630 766-3363
Bensenville (G-1852)
General Cutng Tl Svc & Mfg Inc ...............F ....... 847 677-8770
Lincolnwood (G-13513)
Gki Incorporated .......................................E ....... 815 459-2330
Rockford (G-18398)
Imprex International Inc ...........................F ....... 847 364-4930
Arlington Heights (G-775)
Tapco USA Inc ..........................................G ....... 815 877-4039
Loves Park (G-13998)
Top Notch Tool & Supply Inc ...................G ....... 815 633-6295
Cherry Valley (G-3648)
Universal Broaching Inc ...........................F ....... 847 228-1440
Elk Grove Village (G-9800)

### INDL SPLYS, WHOLESALE: Tools, NEC

Belcar Products Inc ..................................G ....... 630 462-1950
Carol Stream (G-3113)
Bridgeport Air Comprsr & Tl Co ...............G ....... 618 945-7163
Bridgeport (G-2450)
Sieber Tool Engineering LP ......................F ....... 630 462-9370
Carol Stream (G-3240)

### INDL SPLYS, WHOLESALE: Valves & Fittings

Barnett-Bates Corporation ........................F ....... 815 726-5223
Joliet (G-12461)
Cleavenger Associates Inc ......................G ....... 630 221-0007
Winfield (G-22284)
Industrial Pipe and Supply Co ..................E ....... 708 652-7511
Chicago (G-5179)
Lewis Process Systems Inc .....................F ....... 630 510-8200
Carol Stream (G-3184)
Mj Works Hose & Fitting LLC ...................G ....... 708 995-5723
Mokena (G-14886)
O C Keckley Company .............................E ....... 847 674-8422
Skokie (G-20048)

### INDL SPLYS, WHOLESALE: Wheels

Diagrind Inc ...............................................F ....... 708 460-4333
Orland Park (G-16854)
Hayes Abrasives Inc ................................F ....... 217 532-6850
Hillsboro (G-11892)

### INDL TOOL GRINDING SVCS

A&W Tool Inc ............................................G ....... 815 653-1700
Ringwood (G-17986)
Diamond Edge Manufacturing ..................G ....... 630 458-1630
Addison (G-89)
Kmp Tool Grinding Inc ..............................G ....... 847 205-9640
Northbrook (G-16288)
Sterling Tool & Manufacturing ..................G ....... 847 304-1800
Barrington (G-1305)

### INDUCTORS

Induction Innovations Inc ........................G ....... 847 836-6933
Elgin (G-9076)
Marvel Electric Corporation ......................E ....... 847 671-0632
Schiller Park (G-19846)

### INDUSTRIAL & COMMERCIAL EQPT INSPECTION SVCS

Nordex Usa Inc .........................................D ....... 208 383-6500
Chicago (G-5925)
X-Tech Innovations Inc ............................G ....... 815 962-4127
Rockford (G-18690)

### INERTIAL GUIDANCE SYSTEMS

Engility Corporation ..................................G ....... 847 583-1216
Skokie (G-19994)
Engility Corporation ..................................G ....... 708 596-8245
Harvey (G-11665)

### INFRARED OBJECT DETECTION EQPT

Epir Technologies Inc ...............................E ....... 630 771-0203
Bolingbrook (G-2307)

### INGOT, EXTRUSION: Extrusion ingot, aluminum: rolling mills

Plastic Power Extrusions Corp .................E ....... 847 233-9901
Schiller Park (G-19859)
Werner Co .................................................E ....... 815 459-6020
Crystal Lake (G-7676)

### INGOTS: Steel

A Finkl & Sons Co ....................................B ....... 773 975-2510
Chicago (G-3687)

### INK OR WRITING FLUIDS

An Environmental Inks .............................F ....... 800 728-8200
West Chicago (G-21659)
Central Chemical and Service .................F ....... 630 653-9200
Carol Stream (G-3126)
Chemsong Inc ...........................................F .......
Glen Ellyn (G-10962)
Crosslink Coatings Corporation ...............G ....... 815 467-7970
Channahon (G-3568)
Domino Amjet Inc .....................................E ....... 847 662-3148
Gurnee (G-11439)
Domino Amjet Inc .....................................D ....... 847 244-2501
Gurnee (G-11440)
Graphic Sciences Inc ...............................G ....... 630 226-0994
Bolingbrook (G-2314)
I S C America Inc .....................................G ....... 630 616-1331
Wood Dale (G-22380)
Ink Smart Inc ............................................G ....... 708 349-9555
Orland Park (G-16868)
Interactive Inks Coatings Corp .................F ....... 847 289-8710
South Elgin (G-20208)
INX International Ink Co ...........................E ....... 630 681-7200
West Chicago (G-21724)
INX International Ink Co ...........................G ....... 630 382-1800
Schaumburg (G-19581)
INX International Ink Co ...........................E ....... 630 681-7100
West Chicago (G-21725)
Modern Printing Colors Inc ......................F ....... 708 681-5678
Broadview (G-2597)
Phoenix Inks and Coatings LLC ..............F ....... 630 972-2500
Lemont (G-13255)
Sun Chemical Corporation .......................G ....... 630 513-5348
Saint Charles (G-19274)

Zeller + Gmelin Corporation .....................G ....... 630 443-8800
Saint Charles (G-19302)

### INK: Gravure

Buzz Sales Company Inc .........................G ....... 815 459-1170
Crystal Lake (G-7546)
Graphic Chemical & Ink Co .....................F ....... 630 832-6004
Villa Park (G-21257)

### INK: Letterpress Or Offset

Central Ink Corporation ............................D ....... 630 231-6500
West Chicago (G-21679)

### INK: Lithographic

Cudner & OConnor Co .............................F ....... 773 826-0200
Chicago (G-4514)
Scientific Colors Inc .................................C ....... 815 744-5650
Rockdale (G-18233)

### INK: Printing

ABM Marking Ltd .....................................F ....... 618 277-3773
Belleville (G-1606)
Actega North America Inc .......................G ....... 847 690-9310
Elk Grove Village (G-9267)
Alden & Ott Printing Inks Co ...................D ....... 847 956-6830
Arlington Heights (G-706)
Alden & Ott Printing Inks Co ...................F ....... 847 364-6817
Mount Prospect (G-15309)
CIS Systems Inc ......................................G ....... 847 827-0747
Glenview (G-11114)
Domino Holdings Inc ...............................D ....... 847 244-2501
Gurnee (G-11441)
Environmental Inks & Coding ..................F ....... 630 231-7313
West Chicago (G-21696)
Environmental Specialties Inc .................G ....... 630 860-7070
Itasca (G-12259)
Flint Group US LLC .................................E ....... 630 526-9903
Batavia (G-1450)
Flint Group US LLC .................................F ....... 618 349-8384
Saint Peter (G-19322)
Gibbon America Inc .................................F ....... 847 931-1255
Elgin (G-9045)
Gibbon America II Corp ...........................F ....... 847 931-1255
Elgin (G-9046)
Hostmann Steinberg Inc ..........................F ....... 502 968-5961
Kankakee (G-12622)
Hostmann Steinberg Inc ..........................F ....... 815 401-5493
Bourbonnais (G-2399)
Hubergroup Usa Inc ................................D ....... 815 929-9293
Kankakee (G-12623)
Hurst Chemical Company .......................G ....... 815 964-0451
Rockford (G-18424)
Hydro Ink Corp .........................................F ....... 847 674-0057
Skokie (G-20014)
I C T W Ink ................................................G ....... 630 893-4658
Roselle (G-18945)
I Q Infinity LLC .........................................G ....... 773 651-2556
Chicago (G-5133)
I S C America Inc .....................................G ....... 630 616-1331
Wood Dale (G-22380)
Ink Systems Inc .......................................F ....... 847 427-2200
Elk Grove Village (G-9547)
INX Digital International Co .....................F ....... 630 382-1800
Schaumburg (G-19576)
INX Group Ltd ..........................................G ....... 708 799-1993
Homewood (G-12103)
INX Group Ltd ..........................................G ....... 630 382-1800
Schaumburg (G-19577)
INX International Ink Co ...........................D ....... 630 382-1800
Schaumburg (G-19578)
INX International Ink Co ...........................E ....... 630 681-7200
West Chicago (G-21724)
INX International Ink Co ...........................E ....... 708 496-3600
Chicago (G-5235)
INX International Ink Co ...........................E ....... 800 233-4657
Schaumburg (G-19579)
INX International Ink Co ...........................E ....... 630 382-1800
Schaumburg (G-19580)
INX International Ink Co ...........................F ....... 630 382-1800
Schaumburg (G-19581)
INX International Ink Co ...........................E ....... 630 681-7100
West Chicago (G-21725)
L P S Express Inc ....................................G ....... 217 636-7683
Springfield (G-20465)
Laser Technology Group Inc ...................F ....... 847 524-4088
Elk Grove Village (G-9586)
Midwest Ink Co ........................................E ....... 708 345-7177
Broadview (G-2595)

# PRODUCT SECTION

## INSTRUMENTS, MEASURING/CNTRL: Hydrometers, Exc Indl Process

Paper Graphics Inc .................................. G ...... 847 276-2727
  Lincolnshire *(G-13470)*
Precision Ink Corporation ........................ F ...... 847 952-1500
  Elk Grove Village *(G-9694)*
R A Kerley Ink Engineers Inc .................. E ...... 708 344-1295
  Broadview *(G-2606)*
Springbox Inc ............................................ G ...... 708 921-9944
  Flossmoor *(G-10229)*
Sun Chemical Corporation ...................... C ...... 708 562-0550
  Northlake *(G-16454)*
Sun Chemical Corporation ...................... D ...... 815 939-0136
  Kankakee *(G-12655)*
Thrall Enterprises Inc .............................. F ...... 312 621-8200
  Chicago *(G-6722)*
Toyo Ink International Corp ..................... F ...... 630 930-5100
  Addison *(G-320)*
Toyo Ink International Corp ..................... F ...... 866 969-8696
  Wood Dale *(G-22432)*
U S Colors & Coatings Inc ...................... G ...... 630 879-8898
  Batavia *(G-1512)*
Wikoff Color Corporation ........................ G ...... 847 487-2704
  Wauconda *(G-21515)*

### INK: Screen process

Kolorcure Corporation ............................. E ...... 630 879-9050
  Batavia *(G-1460)*

### INSECTICIDES

FMC Corporation ..................................... E ...... 309 695-2571
  Wyoming *(G-22638)*
Nufarm Americas Inc ............................... D ...... 708 756-2010
  Chicago Heights *(G-7115)*

### INSECTICIDES & PESTICIDES

Cardinal Professional Products ............... G ...... 714 761-3292
  Decatur *(G-7850)*
Clarke Group Inc ..................................... C ...... 630 894-2000
  Saint Charles *(G-19155)*
Clarke Mosquito Ctrl Pdts Inc ................. C ...... 630 894-2000
  Saint Charles *(G-19156)*
Wellmark Int Farnam Co ......................... B ...... 925 948-4000
  Schaumburg *(G-19787)*

### INSPECTION & TESTING SVCS

Research and Testing Worx Inc .............. G ...... 815 734-7346
  Mount Morris *(G-15299)*
Sub Source Inc ........................................ E ...... 815 968-7800
  Rockford *(G-18637)*

### INSTR, MEASURE & CONTROL: Gauge, Oil Pressure & Water Temp

Alphagage ................................................ G ...... 815 391-6400
  Rockford *(G-18260)*
Water Services Company of Ill ............... G ...... 847 697-6623
  Elgin *(G-9230)*

### INSTRUMENTS & METERS: Measuring, Electric

Design Technology Inc ............................ E ...... 630 920-1300
  Westmont *(G-21883)*
Innovative Sports Training Inc ................ G ...... 773 244-6470
  Chicago *(G-5201)*
P K Neuses Incorporated ........................ G ...... 847 253-6555
  Rolling Meadows *(G-18756)*
S Himmelstein and Company .................. E ...... 847 843-3300
  Hoffman Estates *(G-12046)*

### INSTRUMENTS, LAB: Spectroscopic/Optical Properties Measuring

Omex Technologies Inc ........................... G ...... 847 850-5858
  Wheeling *(G-22112)*
Slipchip Corporation ................................ F ...... 312 550-5600
  Chicago *(G-6531)*

### INSTRUMENTS, LABORATORY: Analyzers, Thermal

Sterigenics US LLC ................................. E ...... 630 285-9121
  Itasca *(G-12360)*

### INSTRUMENTS, LABORATORY: Blood Testing

Abbott Laboratories ................................. A ...... 224 667-6100
  Abbott Park *(G-1)*

Cambridge Sensors USA LLC ................ G ...... 877 374-4062
  Plainfield *(G-17584)*

### INSTRUMENTS, LABORATORY: Infrared Analytical

Enhanced Plasmonics LLC ..................... G ...... 904 238-9270
  Evanston *(G-10030)*

### INSTRUMENTS, LABORATORY: Photomicrographic

St Imaging Inc ......................................... F ...... 847 501-3344
  Northbrook *(G-16371)*

### INSTRUMENTS, LABORATORY: Ultraviolet Analytical

Prime Systems Inc .................................. E ...... 630 681-2100
  Carol Stream *(G-3217)*

### INSTRUMENTS, MEASURING & CNTRL: Gauges, Auto, Computer

Tunnel Vision Consulting Group .............. G ...... 773 367-7292
  Chicago *(G-6791)*

### INSTRUMENTS, MEASURING & CNTRL: Geophysical/Meteorological

Geotest Instrument Corp ......................... G ...... 847 869-7645
  Burr Ridge *(G-2845)*

### INSTRUMENTS, MEASURING & CNTRL: Radiation & Testing, Nuclear

7 Mile Solutions Inc ................................. E ...... 847 588-2280
  Niles *(G-15952)*
Gamma Products Inc .............................. F ...... 708 974-4100
  Palos Hills *(G-17117)*

### INSTRUMENTS, MEASURING & CNTRL: Testing, Abrasion, Etc

EJ Cady & Company ............................... G ...... 847 537-2239
  Wheeling *(G-22045)*
Kiene Diesel Accessories Inc ................. E ...... 630 543-7170
  Addison *(G-167)*
Kocour Co ................................................ E ...... 773 847-1111
  Chicago *(G-5397)*
Libco Industries Inc ................................. F ...... 815 623-7677
  Roscoe *(G-18902)*
Schultes Precision Mfg Inc ...................... D ...... 847 465-0300
  Buffalo Grove *(G-2763)*
Technics Inc ............................................. G ...... 630 215-3742
  Bolingbrook *(G-2377)*

### INSTRUMENTS, MEASURING & CNTRLG: Aircraft & Motor Vehicle

Emissions Systems Incorporated ............ G ...... 847 669-8044
  Lake In The Hills *(G-12991)*
TRC Environmental Corp ........................ G ...... 630 953-9046
  Burr Ridge *(G-2886)*

### INSTRUMENTS, MEASURING & CNTRLG: Thermometers/Temp Sensors

7000 Inc .................................................... F ...... 312 800-3612
  Bolingbrook *(G-2275)*
Biosynergy Inc ......................................... G ...... 847 956-0471
  Elk Grove Village *(G-9342)*
Durex International Corp ......................... C ...... 847 639-5600
  Cary *(G-3338)*
Ewikon Molding Tech Inc ........................ G ...... 815 874-7270
  Rockford *(G-18373)*
I C Innovations Inc .................................. G ...... 847 279-7888
  Highland Park *(G-11842)*
Melt Design Inc ........................................ F ...... 630 443-4000
  Saint Charles *(G-19217)*
Q Sales Llc .............................................. G ...... 708 271-9842
  Hazel Crest *(G-11714)*
Taylor Precision Products Inc ................. F ...... 630 954-1250
  Oak Brook *(G-16563)*

### INSTRUMENTS, MEASURING & CNTRLNG: Nuclear Instrument Modules

Coinstar Procurement LLC ..................... G ...... 630 424-4788
  Oakbrook Terrace *(G-16703)*

M I E America Inc .................................... F ...... 847 981-6100
  Elk Grove Village *(G-9603)*

### INSTRUMENTS, MEASURING & CNTRLNG: Wind Direction Indicators

Clean Energy Renewables LLC .............. E ...... 309 797-4844
  Moline *(G-14922)*

### INSTRUMENTS, MEASURING & CONTROLLING: Breathalyzers

Linde Gas North America LLC ................ F ...... 708 345-0894
  Broadview *(G-2593)*

### INSTRUMENTS, MEASURING & CONTROLLING: Gas Detectors

B&W Technologies Inc ............................ G ...... 888 749-8878
  Lincolnshire *(G-13430)*
DOD Technologies Inc ............................ G ...... 815 788-5200
  Cary *(G-3335)*
First Alert Inc ........................................... G ...... 630 499-3295
  Aurora *(G-1009)*
Honeywell Analytics Inc .......................... C ...... 847 955-8200
  Lincolnshire *(G-13454)*

### INSTRUMENTS, MEASURING & CONTROLLING: Gauges, Rain

Innoquest Inc ........................................... G ...... 815 337-8555
  Woodstock *(G-22575)*

### INSTRUMENTS, MEASURING & CONTROLLING: Surveying & Drafting

Crain Enterprises Inc .............................. D ...... 618 748-9227
  Mound City *(G-15256)*
Germann Instruments Inc ....................... G ...... 847 329-9999
  Evanston *(G-10042)*
Humboldt Mfg Co .................................... E ...... 708 456-6300
  Elgin *(G-9068)*
S & W Manufacturing Co Inc .................. E ...... 630 595-5044
  Bensenville *(G-1984)*

### INSTRUMENTS, MEASURING & CONTROLLING: Transits, Surveyors'

Polmax LLC ............................................. C ...... 708 843-8300
  Alsip *(G-511)*

### INSTRUMENTS, MEASURING & CONTROLLING: Ultrasonic Testing

Midwest Ultrasonics Inc .......................... G ...... 630 434-9458
  Darien *(G-7800)*
Migatron Corporation ............................... E ...... 815 338-5800
  Woodstock *(G-22590)*
Santec Systems Inc ................................ F ...... 847 215-8884
  Arlington Heights *(G-835)*
Sonoscan Inc ........................................... D ...... 847 437-6400
  Elk Grove Village *(G-9744)*
Ultrasonic Power Corporation ................. E ...... 815 235-6020
  Freeport *(G-10695)*

### INSTRUMENTS, MEASURING & CONTROLLING: Weather Tracking

Outdoor Environments LLC ..................... G ...... 847 325-5000
  Buffalo Grove *(G-2749)*

### INSTRUMENTS, MEASURING/CNTRL: Gauging, Ultrasonic Thickness

Assurance Technologies Inc ................... F ...... 630 550-5000
  Bartlett *(G-1331)*
Gpe Controls Inc ..................................... F ...... 708 236-6000
  Hillside *(G-11917)*
Trinity Brand Industries Inc .................... F ...... 708 482-4980
  Countryside *(G-7447)*

### INSTRUMENTS, MEASURING/CNTRL: Hydrometers, Exc Indl Process

Norman P Moeller .................................... G ...... 847 991-3933
  Lake Barrington *(G-12821)*

Employee Codes: A=Over 500 employees, B=251-500
C=101-250, D=51-100, E=20-50, F=10-19, G=3-9

## INSTRUMENTS, MEASURING/CNTRLG: Fare Registers, St Cars/Buses

Cubic Trnsp Systems Inc .................... G ...... 312 257-3242
Chicago (G-4513)

## INSTRUMENTS, MEASURING/CNTRLG: Fire Detect Sys, Non-Electric

H S I Fire and Safety Group .............. G ...... 847 427-8340
Elk Grove Village (G-9515)

## INSTRUMENTS, MEASURING/CNTRLNG: Med Diagnostic Sys, Nuclear

Joseph Ringelstein ............................ G ...... 708 955-7467
Norridge (G-16103)
Safersonic Us Inc ............................. G ...... 847 274-1534
Highland Park (G-11867)
Siemens Med Solutions USA Inc ....... D ...... 847 304-7700
Hoffman Estates (G-12053)
Touhy Diagnostic At Home LLC ........ F ...... 847 803-1111
Des Plaines (G-8287)

## INSTRUMENTS, OPTICAL: Alignment & Display

Oakley Inc ........................................ G ...... 312 787-2545
Chicago (G-5962)

## INSTRUMENTS, OPTICAL: Elements & Assemblies, Exc Ophthalmic

Kreischer Optics Ltd .......................... F ...... 815 344-4220
McHenry (G-14518)

## INSTRUMENTS, OPTICAL: Lenses, All Types Exc Ophthalmic

Beastgrip Co ..................................... G ...... 312 283-5283
Des Plaines (G-8157)
Karl Lambrecht Corp .......................... E ...... 773 472-5442
Chicago (G-5361)
Lens Lenticlear Lenticular .................. F ...... 630 467-0900
Itasca (G-12303)
Lenscrafters Crafters ......................... F ...... 618 632-2312
Fairview Heights (G-10170)

## INSTRUMENTS, OPTICAL: Magnifying, NEC

Identity Optical Lab .......................... G ...... 309 807-3160
Normal (G-16073)

## INSTRUMENTS, OPTICAL: Mirrors

H L Clausing Inc ............................... G ...... 847 676-0330
Skokie (G-20008)
Tonjon Company ............................... F ...... 630 208-1173
Geneva (G-10873)

## INSTRUMENTS, OPTICAL: Test & Inspection

Gaertner Scientific Corp .................... E ...... 847 673-5006
Skokie (G-20003)
Jme Technologies Inc ....................... G ...... 815 477-8800
Crystal Lake (G-7595)

## INSTRUMENTS, SURGICAL & MED: Cleaning Eqpt, Ultrasonic Med

Esma Inc .......................................... G ...... 708 331-0456
South Holland (G-20267)

## INSTRUMENTS, SURGICAL & MEDI: Knife Blades/Handles, Surgical

Beaver-Visitec Intl Inc ....................... G ...... 847 739-3219
Lake Forest (G-12886)

## INSTRUMENTS, SURGICAL & MEDICAL: Blood & Bone Work

Accuro Medical Products LLC ............ G ...... 800 669-4757
Chicago (G-3724)
Life Spine Inc ................................... E ...... 847 884-6117
Huntley (G-12158)
Monogen Inc ..................................... E ...... 847 573-6700
Chicago (G-5796)
Murray Inc ........................................ D ...... 847 620-7990
North Barrington (G-16153)

Patterson Medical Products Inc ......... C ...... 630 393-6671
Warrenville (G-21353)
Smart Medical Technology Inc .......... F ...... 630 964-1689
Darien (G-7802)
Sysmex America Inc ......................... C ...... 847 996-4500
Lincolnshire (G-13484)
Thermopol Inc ................................... G ...... 815 422-0400
Saint Anne (G-19126)
Tianhe Stem Cell .............................. F ...... 630 723-1968
Lisle (G-13672)

## INSTRUMENTS, SURGICAL & MEDICAL: Blood Pressure

Bold Diagnostics LLC ........................ G ...... 806 543-5743
Chicago (G-4139)
Endotronix Inc .................................. G ...... 630 504-2861
Woodridge (G-22478)
Medical Screening Labs Inc .............. E ...... 847 647-7911
Niles (G-16002)

## INSTRUMENTS, SURGICAL & MEDICAL: Blood Transfusion

Baxter World Trade Corporation ........ F ...... 224 948-2000
Deerfield (G-7989)

## INSTRUMENTS, SURGICAL & MEDICAL: Cannulae

Sunset Halthcare Solutions Inc ......... E ...... 877 578-6738
Chicago (G-6631)

## INSTRUMENTS, SURGICAL & MEDICAL: Hemodialysis

Aksys Ltd ......................................... D ...... 847 229-2020
Lincolnshire (G-13425)
Akzo Nobel Inc ................................. C ...... 312 544-7000
Chicago (G-3793)

## INSTRUMENTS, SURGICAL & MEDICAL: Inhalation Therapy

Ltc Holdings Inc ............................... C ...... 847 249-5900
Waukegan (G-21585)

## INSTRUMENTS, SURGICAL & MEDICAL: Lasers, Surgical

Novian Health Inc ............................. G ...... 312 266-7200
Chicago (G-5948)

## INSTRUMENTS, SURGICAL & MEDICAL: Muscle Exercise, Ophthalmic

Stretch CHI ...................................... G ...... 773 420-9355
Chicago (G-6606)

## INSTRUMENTS, SURGICAL & MEDICAL: Needles, Suture

Manan Tool & Manufacturing ............ A ...... 847 637-3333
Wheeling (G-22100)

## INSTRUMENTS, SURGICAL & MEDICAL: Ophthalmic

Beaver-Visitec Intl Holdings .............. B ...... 847 739-3219
Lake Forest (G-12885)
Stereo Optical Company Inc ............. F ...... 773 867-0380
Chicago (G-6589)

## INSTRUMENTS, SURGICAL & MEDICAL: Retinoscopes

Advanced Retinal Institute Inc .......... G ...... 617 821-5597
Oak Park (G-16649)

## INSTRUMENTS, SURGICAL & MEDICAL: Suction Therapy

Precision Products Mfg Intl ............... E ...... 847 299-8500
Des Plaines (G-8262)

## INSTRUMENTS, SURGICAL/MED: Microsurgical, Exc Electromedical

Novo Surgical Inc ............................. F ...... 877 860-6686
Oak Brook (G-16549)

## INSTRUMENTS: Ammeters & Voltmeters, Automotive

Bittle .............................................. G ...... 618 539-6099
Freeburg (G-10633)

## INSTRUMENTS: Analytical

Abbott Laboratories .......................... A ...... 847 938-8717
North Chicago (G-16163)
Abbott Molecular Inc ......................... G ...... 224 361-7800
Des Plaines (G-8141)
Abbott Molecular Inc ......................... D ...... 224 361-7800
Des Plaines (G-8142)
Ag-Defense Systems Inc ................... G ...... 309 495-7258
Peoria (G-17303)
Akzo Nobel Inc ................................. C ...... 312 544-7000
Chicago (G-3793)
Beckman Coulter Inc ........................ G ...... 800 526-3821
Wood Dale (G-22343)
Bio-RAD Laboratories Inc ................. B ...... 847 699-2217
Des Plaines (G-8158)
Cbana Labs Inc ................................ G ...... 217 819-5201
Champaign (G-3463)
Design Scientific Inc ......................... G ...... 616 582-5225
Wilmette (G-22251)
EJ Cady & Company .......................... G ...... 847 537-2239
Wheeling (G-22045)
EMD Millipore Corporation ................ C ...... 815 937-8270
Kankakee (G-12613)
EMD Millipore Corporation ................ B ...... 815 932-9017
Kankakee (G-12614)
Fisher Scientific Company LLC ......... C ...... 412 490-8300
Hanover Park (G-11580)
Gaertner Scientific Corp .................... E ...... 847 673-5006
Skokie (G-20003)
Hach Company .................................. C ...... 800 227-4224
Chicago (G-5026)
Huygen Corporation .......................... G ...... 815 455-2200
Crystal Lake (G-7590)
Igt Testing Systems Inc .................... G ...... 847 952-2448
Arlington Heights (G-773)
Illinois Instruments Inc .................... E ...... 815 344-6212
Johnsburg (G-12436)
Illinois Tool Works Inc ...................... C ...... 847 295-6500
Lake Bluff (G-12850)
Jrd Labs LLC .................................... G ...... 847 818-1076
Elk Grove Village (G-9565)
L A M Inc De .................................... G ...... 630 860-9700
Wood Dale (G-22388)
Lachata Design Ltd .......................... G ...... 708 946-2757
Beecher (G-1599)
McCrone Associates Inc ................... G ...... 630 887-7100
Westmont (G-21904)
Parr Instrument Company ................. D ...... 309 762-7716
Moline (G-14961)
Progroup Instrument Inc .................. G ...... 618 466-2815
Godfrey (G-11232)
Regis Technologies Inc .................... D ...... 847 967-6000
Morton Grove (G-15232)
Scientific Instruments Inc ................. G ...... 847 679-1242
Skokie (G-20082)
Sensor 21 Inc ................................... G ...... 847 561-6233
Mundelein (G-15556)
Sherwood Industries Inc ................... F ...... 847 626-0300
Niles (G-16032)
Spectroclick Inc ................................ G ...... 217 356-4829
Champaign (G-3544)
Supertek Scientific LLC .................... G ...... 630 345-3450
Villa Park (G-21287)
UOP LLC .......................................... G ...... 847 391-2000
Des Plaines (G-8293)
Verson Enterprises Inc ..................... F ...... 847 364-2600
Elk Grove Village (G-9806)

## INSTRUMENTS: Combustion Control, Indl

Benetech Inc .................................... E ...... 630 844-1300
Aurora (G-1119)
Benetech (taiwan) LLC ..................... G ...... 630 844-1300
Aurora (G-1120)

## INSTRUMENTS: Digital Panel Meters, Electricity Measuring

Professional Meters Inc .................... C ...... 815 942-7000
Morris (G-15127)

# PRODUCT SECTION

# INSTRUMENTS: Measuring & Controlling

### INSTRUMENTS: Elec Lab Stds, Resist, Inductance/Capacitance

LAB Equipment Inc .................................. E ...... 630 595-4288
  Itasca *(G-12301)*

### INSTRUMENTS: Electrocardiographs

Lifewatch Corp ....................................... G ...... 847 720-2100
  Rosemont *(G-19012)*
Lifewatch Services Inc ........................... B ...... 847 720-2100
  Rosemont *(G-19013)*
Universal Holdings Inc ........................... F ...... 224 353-6198
  Hoffman Estates *(G-12066)*

### INSTRUMENTS: Electrolytic Conductivity, Indl

Dots UT Inc ............................................ G ...... 217 390-3286
  Champaign *(G-3475)*

### INSTRUMENTS: Electronic, Analog-Digital Converters

Deif Inc .................................................. G ...... 970 530-2261
  Wood Dale *(G-22359)*
Frequency Devices Inc ........................... F ...... 815 434-7800
  Ottawa *(G-16960)*
Oso Technologies Inc ............................. G ...... 844 777-2575
  Urbana *(G-21096)*
Phoenix Converting LLC ........................ F ...... 630 285-1500
  Itasca *(G-12339)*
Suffolk Business Group Inc .................... G ...... 847 404-2486
  Bartlett *(G-1379)*

### INSTRUMENTS: Endoscopic Eqpt, Electromedical

Cortek Endoscopy Inc ............................. G ...... 847 526-2266
  Wauconda *(G-21453)*
Mobile Endoscopix LLC .......................... G ...... 847 380-8992
  Northbrook *(G-16312)*

### INSTRUMENTS: Eye Examination

Precision Vision Inc ............................... G ...... 815 223-2022
  Woodstock *(G-22601)*

### INSTRUMENTS: Flow, Indl Process

Fms USA Inc .......................................... G ...... 847 519-4400
  Hoffman Estates *(G-12010)*

### INSTRUMENTS: Generators Tachometer

Sfc of Illinois Inc ................................... E ...... 815 745-2100
  Warren *(G-21336)*

### INSTRUMENTS: Humidity, Indl Process

Harry J Trainor ...................................... G ...... 630 493-1163
  Downers Grove *(G-8455)*
Humidity 2 Optimization LLC ................. F ...... 847 991-7488
  East Dundee *(G-8644)*

### INSTRUMENTS: Indicating, Electric

Schweitzer Engrg Labs Inc ..................... D ...... 847 362-8304
  Lake Zurich *(G-13128)*

### INSTRUMENTS: Indl Process Control

Active Grinding & Mfg Co ...................... F ...... 708 344-0510
  Broadview *(G-2554)*
Advanced Technologies Inc .................... G ...... 847 329-9875
  Park Ridge *(G-17178)*
Air Gage Company ................................. G ...... 847 695-0911
  Elgin *(G-8941)*
Altera Corporation ................................. G ...... 847 240-0313
  Schaumburg *(G-19434)*
Auto Meter Products Inc ........................ C ...... 815 991-2292
  Sycamore *(G-20788)*
Axode Corp ............................................ G ...... 312 578-9897
  Chicago *(G-4008)*
Barcor Inc .............................................. F ...... 847 940-0750
  Bannockburn *(G-1255)*
Caterpillar Inc ........................................ B ...... 815 729-5511
  Joliet *(G-12471)*
Chino Works America Inc ...................... G ...... 630 328-0014
  Arlington Heights *(G-735)*
Cognex Corporation ............................... G ...... 630 505-9990
  Naperville *(G-15631)*

Competition Electronics Inc ................... G ...... 815 874-8001
  Rockford *(G-18321)*
Dalec Controls Inc ................................. G ...... 847 671-7676
  South Holland *(G-20258)*
Danaher Corporation ............................. G ...... 815 568-8001
  Marengo *(G-14225)*
Danfoss LLC .......................................... C ...... 888 326-3677
  Loves Park *(G-13936)*
Decatur Aeration and Temp ................... F ...... 217 733-2800
  Fairmount *(G-10162)*
Dinamica Generale Us Inc ..................... G ...... 815 751-9916
  Elgin *(G-9010)*
Doncasters Inc ...................................... G ...... 217 465-6500
  Paris *(G-17146)*
Electro-Matic Products Co ..................... F ...... 773 235-4010
  Chicago *(G-4720)*
Erdco Engineering Corporation .............. E ...... 847 328-0550
  Evanston *(G-10031)*
Frequency Devices Inc ........................... F ...... 815 434-7800
  Ottawa *(G-16960)*
FSI Technologies Inc .............................. E ...... 630 932-9380
  Lombard *(G-13803)*
Goodrich Corporation ............................ D ...... 815 226-6000
  Rockford *(G-18402)*
Goodrich Corporation ............................ D ...... 815 226-6000
  Rockford *(G-18403)*
Hadady Machining Company Inc ........... F ...... 708 474-8620
  Lansing *(G-13165)*
Hauhinco LP .......................................... F ...... 618 993-5399
  Marion *(G-14264)*
Hexagon Metrology Inc .......................... G ...... 312 624-8786
  Chicago *(G-5083)*
Honeywell International Inc ................... C ...... 618 940-0401
  Metropolis *(G-14755)*
Imada Inc .............................................. E ...... 847 562-0834
  Northbrook *(G-16273)*
Jjs Global Ventures Inc .......................... G ...... 847 999-4313
  Schaumburg *(G-19589)*
Lumenite Control Technology ................ F ...... 847 455-1450
  Franklin Park *(G-10518)*
Mar-TEC Research Inc ............................ E ...... 630 879-1200
  Batavia *(G-1465)*
Martin Automatic Inc ............................ C ...... 815 654-4800
  Rockford *(G-18483)*
Master Control Systems Inc ................... E ...... 847 295-1010
  Lake Bluff *(G-12856)*
Mech-Tronics Corporation ..................... D ...... 708 344-9823
  Melrose Park *(G-14671)*
Mid-American Elevator Eqp Co .............. E ...... 773 486-6900
  Chicago *(G-5728)*
National Micro Systems Inc ................... G ...... 312 566-0414
  Chicago *(G-5865)*
Oakland Industries Ltd .......................... E ...... 847 827-7600
  Mount Prospect *(G-15358)*
Omron Healthcare Inc ........................... D ...... 847 680-6200
  Lake Forest *(G-12932)*
Proceq USA Inc ..................................... G ...... 847 623-9570
  Gurnee *(G-11491)*
Process Technologies Group .................. G ...... 630 393-4777
  Warrenville *(G-21360)*
Prostat Corporation ............................... G ...... 630 238-8883
  Bensenville *(G-1968)*
Protection Controls Inc .......................... E ...... 773 763-3110
  Skokie *(G-20066)*
Robertshaw Controls Company .............. G ...... 815 591-2417
  Hanover *(G-11573)*
Robertshaw Controls Company .............. G ...... 630 260-3400
  Itasca *(G-12349)*
Rosemount Inc ...................................... G ...... 217 877-5278
  Decatur *(G-7935)*
Schrader-Bridgeport Intl Inc .................. G ...... 815 288-3344
  Dixon *(G-8349)*
Semler Industries Inc ............................ E ...... 847 671-5650
  Franklin Park *(G-10586)*
Silicon Control Inc ................................. E ...... 847 215-7947
  Deerfield *(G-8054)*
Superior Graphite Co ............................. E ...... 708 458-0006
  Chicago *(G-6633)*
Taylor Precision Products Inc ................. F ...... 630 954-1250
  Oak Brook *(G-16563)*
Thermo Fisher Scientific Inc .................. G
  Bannockburn *(G-1266)*
Thread & Gage Co Inc ........................... G ...... 815 675-2305
  Spring Grove *(G-20367)*
Tii Technical Educatn Systems ............... E ...... 847 428-3085
  Gilberts *(G-10939)*
Tricor Systems Inc ................................. G ...... 847 742-5542
  Elgin *(G-9214)*
UOP LLC ................................................ G ...... 847 391-2000
  Des Plaines *(G-8293)*

Veeder-Root Company ........................... G ...... 309 797-1762
  Moline *(G-14976)*
Yaskawa America Inc ............................ C ...... 847 887-7000
  Waukegan *(G-21642)*

### INSTRUMENTS: Infrared, Indl Process

Fjw Optical Systems Inc ........................ F ...... 847 358-2500
  Palatine *(G-17029)*

### INSTRUMENTS: Laser, Scientific & Engineering

Amoco Technology Company (del) ......... C ...... 312 861-6000
  Chicago *(G-3892)*
Laser Products Industries Inc ................. G ...... 877 679-1300
  Romeoville *(G-18836)*

### INSTRUMENTS: Liquid Level, Indl Process

Monitor Technologies LLC ..................... E ...... 630 365-9403
  Elburn *(G-8899)*

### INSTRUMENTS: Measurement, Indl Process

Clean Energy Renewables LLC ............... E ...... 309 797-4844
  Moline *(G-14922)*
Dadant & Sons Inc ................................ F ...... 217 852-3324
  Dallas City *(G-7696)*
Fusion Systems Incorporated ................. E ...... 630 323-4115
  Burr Ridge *(G-2843)*
Metrology Resource Group Inc .............. G ...... 815 703-3141
  Rockford *(G-18498)*
Midwest Energy Management Inc .......... G ...... 630 759-6007
  Lombard *(G-13826)*
Process Mechanical Inc ......................... G ...... 630 416-7021
  Naperville *(G-15732)*
T T T Inc ................................................ G ...... 630 860-7499
  Wood Dale *(G-22426)*
Technical Sales Midwest Inc .................. G ...... 847 855-2457
  Gurnee *(G-11514)*
Vorne Industries Inc .............................. G ...... 630 250-9378
  Itasca *(G-12371)*
Xisync LLC ............................................. C ...... 630 350-9400
  Wood Dale *(G-22439)*

### INSTRUMENTS: Measuring & Controlling

Aixacct Systems Inc ............................... G ...... 952 303-4077
  Wheaton *(G-21935)*
Amerex Corporation ............................... E ...... 309 382-4389
  North Pekin *(G-16192)*
Asm Sensors Inc .................................... F ...... 630 832-3202
  Elmhurst *(G-9834)*
Auto Meter Products Inc ........................ C ...... 815 991-2292
  Sycamore *(G-20788)*
Autonics USA Inc ................................... G ...... 847 680-8160
  Mundelein *(G-15473)*
Barcor Inc .............................................. F ...... 847 831-2650
  Highland Park *(G-11824)*
Barcor Inc .............................................. F ...... 847 940-0750
  Bannockburn *(G-1255)*
Cabot McRlectronics Polsg Corp ............ E ...... 630 543-6682
  Addison *(G-67)*
CAM Co Inc ........................................... F ...... 630 556-3110
  Big Rock *(G-2086)*
Cd LLC ................................................... F ...... 312 275-5747
  Chicago *(G-4261)*
Celinco Inc ............................................. G ...... 815 964-2256
  Rockford *(G-18301)*
Centurion Non Destructive Tstg ............. F ...... 630 736-5500
  Streamwood *(G-20648)*
Chicago Dial Indicator Company ............ E ...... 847 827-7186
  Des Plaines *(G-8164)*
Circle Systems Inc ................................. F ...... 815 286-3271
  Hinckley *(G-11934)*
Converting Systems Inc ......................... G ...... 847 519-0232
  Schaumburg *(G-19484)*
CTS Corporation .................................... C ...... 630 577-8800
  Lisle *(G-13579)*
Deatak Inc ............................................. F ...... 815 322-2013
  McHenry *(G-14494)*
Deere & Company .................................. A ...... 309 765-2960
  Moline *(G-14933)*
Dual Mfg Co Inc ..................................... F ...... 773 267-4457
  Franklin Park *(G-10460)*
Dynamicsignals LLC ............................... E ...... 815 838-0005
  Lockport *(G-13714)*
Elcon Inc ................................................ E ...... 815 467-9500
  Minooka *(G-14840)*
Erdco Engineering Corporation .............. E ...... 847 328-0550
  Evanston *(G-10031)*

---

Employee Codes: A=Over 500 employees, B=251-500
C=101-250, D=51-100, E=20-50, F=10-19, G=3-9

# INSTRUMENTS: Measuring & Controlling

Fluid Manufacturing Services .......... G ..... 800 458-5262
  Lake Bluff *(G-12844)*
Honeywell International Inc .......... G ..... 815 235-5500
  Freeport *(G-10664)*
Illinois Tool Works Inc .......... E ..... 847 657-5300
  Glenview *(G-11143)*
Illinois Tool Works Inc .......... C ..... 847 295-6500
  Lake Bluff *(G-12850)*
Industrial Measurement Systems .......... G ..... 630 236-5901
  Aurora *(G-1027)*
Jones Medical Instrument Co .......... E ..... 630 571-1980
  Oak Brook *(G-16528)*
Jordan Industrial Controls Inc .......... E ..... 217 864-4444
  Mount Zion *(G-15453)*
Keson Industries Inc .......... E ..... 630 820-4200
  Aurora *(G-1042)*
L & J Engineering Inc .......... E ..... 708 236-6000
  Hillside *(G-11922)*
L & J Holding Company Ltd .......... D ..... 708 236-6000
  Hillside *(G-11923)*
L A M Inc De .......... G ..... 630 860-9700
  Wood Dale *(G-22388)*
Landauer Inc .......... C ..... 708 755-7000
  Glenwood *(G-11218)*
Livorsi Marine Inc .......... E ..... 847 548-5900
  Grayslake *(G-11352)*
Luster Leaf Products Inc .......... G ..... 815 337-5560
  Woodstock *(G-22586)*
Martin Engineering Company .......... C ..... 309 852-2384
  Neponset *(G-15859)*
Material Testing Tech Inc .......... F ..... 847 215-1211
  Wheeling *(G-22102)*
Mech-Tronics Corporation .......... G ..... 708 344-0202
  Melrose Park *(G-14672)*
Mitsubishi Elc Automtn Inc .......... C ..... 847 478-2100
  Vernon Hills *(G-21183)*
Nova Systems Ltd .......... G ..... 630 879-2296
  Aurora *(G-1195)*
Omron Healthcare Inc .......... D ..... 847 680-6200
  Lake Forest *(G-12932)*
One Plus Corp .......... E ..... 847 498-0955
  Northbrook *(G-16326)*
Parking Systems Inc .......... G ..... 847 891-3819
  Schaumburg *(G-19684)*
Power House Tool Inc .......... E ..... 815 727-6301
  Joliet *(G-12552)*
Praxsym Inc .......... F ..... 217 897-1744
  Fisher *(G-10191)*
Product Feeding Solutions Inc .......... G ..... 630 709-9546
  Chicago Ridge *(G-7156)*
Prostat Corporation .......... G ..... 630 238-8883
  Bensenville *(G-1968)*
Psylotech Inc .......... G ..... 847 328-7100
  Evanston *(G-10092)*
R & D Clark Ltd .......... G ..... 847 749-2061
  Arlington Heights *(G-825)*
Ryeson Corporation .......... D ..... 847 455-8677
  Carol Stream *(G-3230)*
Scientific Instruments Inc .......... G ..... 847 679-1242
  Skokie *(G-20082)*
Sigenics Inc .......... F ..... 312 448-8000
  Chicago *(G-6506)*
Sikora Automation Incorporated .......... G ..... 630 833-0298
  Addison *(G-291)*
Simpson Electric Company .......... E ..... 847 697-2260
  Elgin *(G-9182)*
Ssh Environmental Inds Inc .......... G ..... 312 573-6413
  Chicago *(G-6566)*
Stevens Instrument Company .......... G ..... 847 336-9375
  Waukegan *(G-21620)*
Teledyne Lecroy Inc .......... E ..... 847 888-0450
  Elgin *(G-9206)*
Tempro International Corp .......... G ..... 847 677-5370
  Skokie *(G-20100)*
Tricor Systems Inc .......... E ..... 847 742-5542
  Elgin *(G-9214)*
Venturedyne Ltd .......... E ..... 708 597-7090
  Alsip *(G-540)*
Vibra-Tech Engineers Inc .......... G ..... 630 858-0681
  Glen Ellyn *(G-10994)*
Wellness Center Usa Inc .......... G ..... 847 925-1885
  Hoffman Estates *(G-12069)*
Wilkens-Anderson Company .......... E ..... 773 384-4433
  Chicago *(G-6979)*
Worth-Pfaff Innovations Inc .......... G ..... 847 940-9305
  Deerfield *(G-8068)*

## INSTRUMENTS: Measuring Electricity

Accushim Inc .......... G ..... 708 442-6448
  Lyons *(G-14029)*
Acl Inc .......... F ..... 773 285-0295
  Chicago *(G-3730)*
Agilent Technologies Inc .......... G ..... 800 227-9770
  Chicago *(G-3782)*
Agilent Technologies Inc .......... A ..... 847 690-0431
  Arlington Heights *(G-704)*
Aiknow Inc .......... F ..... 312 391-9452
  Naperville *(G-15790)*
Air Gage Company .......... C ..... 847 695-0911
  Elgin *(G-8941)*
Atlas Material Tstg Tech LLC .......... C ..... 773 327-4520
  Mount Prospect *(G-15311)*
B+b Smartworx Inc .......... G ..... 815 433-5100
  Ottawa *(G-16949)*
Bolingbrook Communications Inc .......... A ..... 630 759-9500
  Lisle *(G-13571)*
C E R Machining & Tooling Ltd .......... G ..... 708 442-9614
  Lyons *(G-14034)*
Cobalt Tool & Manufacturing .......... G ..... 630 530-8898
  Villa Park *(G-21243)*
CSM Products Inc .......... G ..... 815 444-1671
  Crystal Lake *(G-7560)*
Davies Molding LLC .......... C ..... 630 510-8188
  Carol Stream *(G-3141)*
Electronic System Design Inc .......... E ..... 847 358-8212
  Bensenville *(G-1890)*
Erdco Engineering Corporation .......... E ..... 847 328-0550
  Evanston *(G-10031)*
Falex Corporation .......... E ..... 630 556-3679
  Sugar Grove *(G-20723)*
Heidenhain Corporation .......... D ..... 847 490-1191
  Schaumburg *(G-19551)*
I P C Automation Inc .......... G ..... 815 759-3934
  McHenry *(G-14514)*
Illinois Tool Works Inc .......... E ..... 847 657-5300
  Glenview *(G-11143)*
Illinois Tool Works Inc .......... C ..... 847 295-6500
  Lake Bluff *(G-12850)*
Langham Engineering .......... G ..... 815 223-5250
  Peru *(G-17516)*
National Technical Systems Inc .......... F ..... 815 315-9250
  Rockford *(G-18517)*
Nidec-Shimpo America Corp .......... E ..... 630 924-7138
  Itasca *(G-12331)*
Prostat Corporation .......... G ..... 630 238-8883
  Bensenville *(G-1968)*
Silicon Control Inc .......... G ..... 847 215-7947
  Deerfield *(G-8054)*
Simpson Electric Company .......... E ..... 847 697-2260
  Elgin *(G-9182)*
Tellurian Technologies Inc .......... G ..... 847 934-4141
  Arlington Heights *(G-854)*
Transformer Manufacturers Inc .......... E ..... 708 457-1200
  Norridge *(G-16110)*
Weetech Inc .......... G ..... 847 775-7240
  Gurnee *(G-11520)*

## INSTRUMENTS: Measuring, Electrical Power

Ideal Industries Inc .......... C ..... 815 895-5181
  Sycamore *(G-20800)*
Ideal Industries Inc .......... C ..... 815 895-1108
  Sycamore *(G-20801)*

## INSTRUMENTS: Measuring, Electrical Quantities

F T I Inc .......... E ..... 312 943-4015
  Chicago *(G-4807)*

## INSTRUMENTS: Medical & Surgical

1 Federal Supply Source Inc .......... G ..... 708 964-2222
  Steger *(G-20565)*
Abbott Laboratories .......... A ..... 847 938-8717
  North Chicago *(G-16163)*
Abbott Point of Care Inc .......... 847 937-6100
  Abbott Park *(G-6)*
Abrasive West LLC .......... G ..... 630 736-0818
  Bartlett *(G-1328)*
Access Medical Supply Inc .......... G ..... 847 891-6210
  Schaumburg *(G-19420)*
Accessing Your Abilities Inc .......... G ..... 309 761-4016
  Kewanee *(G-12667)*
Addition Technology Inc .......... F ..... 847 297-8419
  Lombard *(G-13759)*
Adhereon Corporation .......... G ..... 312 997-5002
  Chicago *(G-3750)*
Alicona Manufacturing Inc .......... G ..... 630 736-2718
  Bartlett *(G-1330)*
Allcare Inc .......... G ..... 630 830-7486
  Saint Charles *(G-19133)*
Amar Plastics Inc .......... F ..... 630 627-4105
  Addison *(G-32)*
American Medical Industries .......... G ..... 847 918-9800
  Lake Bluff *(G-12829)*
Amerisrcbergen Solutions Group .......... E ..... 847 808-2600
  Buffalo Grove *(G-2658)*
Argentum Medical LLC .......... E ..... 888 551-0188
  Geneva *(G-10810)*
Attune Medical .......... E ..... 312 994-0174
  Chicago *(G-3988)*
Avalign Technologies Inc .......... E ..... 855 282-5446
  Bannockburn *(G-1253)*
Bandgrip Inc .......... G ..... 844 968-6322
  Chicago *(G-4036)*
Baxalta Export Corporation .......... G ..... 224 948-2000
  Deerfield *(G-7981)*
Baxalta World Trade LLC .......... G ..... 224 948-2000
  Deerfield *(G-7982)*
Baxalta Worldwide LLC .......... G ..... 224 948-2000
  Deerfield *(G-7983)*
Baxter Diagnostics Inc .......... F ..... 201 337-1212
  Buffalo Grove *(G-2661)*
Baxter Global Holdings II Inc .......... G ..... 847 948-2000
  Deerfield *(G-7984)*
Baxter Healthcare Corporation .......... A ..... 224 270-6300
  Round Lake *(G-19053)*
Baxter Healthcare Corporation .......... G ..... 847 367-2544
  Vernon Hills *(G-21148)*
Baxter Healthcare Corporation .......... E ..... 847 578-4671
  Waukegan *(G-21529)*
Baxter Healthcare Corporation .......... B ..... 847 948-2000
  Deerfield *(G-7986)*
Baxter Healthcare Corporation .......... G ..... 847 948-2000
  Deerfield *(G-7987)*
Baxter International Inc .......... A ..... 224 948-2000
  Deerfield *(G-7988)*
Baxter V Mueller .......... G ..... 847 774-6800
  Niles *(G-15964)*
Becton Dickinson and Company .......... G ..... 630 743-2006
  Downers Grove *(G-8396)*
Beecken Petty Okeefe & Co LLC .......... A ..... 312 435-0300
  Chicago *(G-4071)*
Bio-Logic Systems Corp .......... D ..... 847 949-0456
  Mundelein *(G-15478)*
Biosynergy Inc .......... G ..... 847 956-0471
  Elk Grove Village *(G-9342)*
Bosley Medical Institute .......... G ..... 312 642-5252
  Chicago *(G-4148)*
Brainlab Inc .......... C ..... 800 784-7700
  Westchester *(G-21831)*
Briteseed LLC .......... G ..... 206 384-0311
  Chicago *(G-4172)*
C & S Chemicals Inc .......... G ..... 815 722-6671
  Joliet *(G-12470)*
Cardinal Health Inc .......... B ..... 847 578-4443
  Waukegan *(G-21532)*
Cardinal Health 200 LLC .......... C ..... 847 473-3200
  Waukegan *(G-21533)*
Cardinal Health 200 LLC .......... E ..... 847 689-8410
  Waukegan *(G-21534)*
Carefusion Corporation .......... D ..... 858 617-2000
  Vernon Hills *(G-21153)*
Carstens Incorporated .......... D ..... 708 669-1500
  Chicago *(G-4245)*
Cast21 Inc .......... G ..... 847 772-8547
  Champaign *(G-3462)*
Cell-Safe Life Sciences LLC .......... G ..... 847 674-7075
  Skokie *(G-19975)*
Chucking Machine Products Inc .......... D ..... 847 678-1192
  Franklin Park *(G-10431)*
Coeur Inc .......... F ..... 815 648-1093
  Hebron *(G-11717)*
Corpak Medsystems Inc .......... C ..... 847 537-4601
  Buffalo Grove *(G-2680)*
Creative Bedding Technologies .......... G ..... 815 444-9088
  Crystal Lake *(G-7558)*
Csl Behring LLC .......... B ..... 815 932-6773
  Bradley *(G-2418)*
D-M-S Holdings Inc .......... C ..... 847 680-6811
  Waukegan *(G-21547)*
Doctors Choice Inc .......... G ..... 312 666-1111
  Chicago *(G-4621)*
Eagle Medical Concepts Inc .......... G ..... 618 475-3671
  Fairview Heights *(G-10167)*
Elas Tek Molding Inc .......... E ..... 815 675-9012
  Spring Grove *(G-20335)*
Elmed Incorporated .......... E ..... 630 543-2792
  Glendale Heights *(G-11021)*
Endepth Vision Systems LLC .......... G ..... 630 329-7909
  Lisle *(G-13586)*

# PRODUCT SECTION

## INSTRUMENTS: Test, Electronic & Electrical Circuits

Feelsure Health Corporation.................G....... 847 446-7881
  Winnetka  (G-22306)
Fetzer Surgical LLC.................................G....... 630 635-2520
  Schaumburg  (G-19526)
Flexxsonic Corporation.........................G....... 847 452-7226
  Mount Prospect  (G-15330)
Gema Inc.................................................G....... 773 508-6690
  Chicago  (G-4924)
Global Endoscopy Inc...........................G....... 847 910-5836
  Elk Grove Village  (G-9501)
Good Lite Co.........................................G....... 847 841-1145
  Elgin  (G-9050)
Griffith Company...................................G....... 847 524-4173
  Schaumburg  (G-19544)
Hearing Screening Assoc LLC..............G....... 855 550-9427
  Arlington Heights  (G-763)
Hill-Rom Holdings Inc...........................B....... 312 819-7200
  Chicago  (G-5088)
Hollister Incorporated...........................B....... 847 680-1000
  Libertyville  (G-13333)
Hospital Therapy Products Inc..............F....... 630 766-7101
  Wood Dale  (G-22379)
Inland Midwest Corporation..................E....... 773 775-2111
  Elmhurst  (G-9887)
Integrated Medical Tech Inc.................G....... 309 662-3614
  Bloomington  (G-2183)
Intratherm LLC.....................................G....... 630 333-5419
  Naperville  (G-15677)
J Stone Inc............................................E....... 847 325-5660
  Mundelein  (G-15513)
Janin Group Inc....................................G....... 630 554-8906
  Oswego  (G-16924)
Jones Medical Instrument Co...............E....... 630 571-1980
  Oak Brook  (G-16528)
Kdk Upset Forging Co..........................E....... 708 388-8770
  Blue Island  (G-2259)
Kimberly-Clark Corporation..................C....... 815 886-7872
  Romeoville  (G-18835)
Labthermics Technologies....................G....... 217 351-7722
  Champaign  (G-3509)
Lakeview Equipment Co.......................G....... 847 548-7705
  Round Lake  (G-19062)
Lavezzi Precision Inc............................C....... 630 582-1230
  Bloomingdale  (G-2112)
Leica Microsystems Inc........................G....... 847 405-0123
  Buffalo Grove  (G-2725)
Lemoy International Inc........................G....... 847 427-0840
  Elk Grove Village  (G-9594)
Lsi Industries Inc...................................D....... 773 878-1100
  Chicago  (G-5555)
Ludwig Medical Inc...............................G....... 217 342-6570
  Effingham  (G-8844)
Mallinckrodt LLC...................................E....... 618 664-2111
  Greenville  (G-11397)
Manan Medical Products Inc................D....... 847 637-3333
  Wheeling  (G-22099)
Medical Adherence Tech Inc................G....... 847 525-6300
  Winnetka  (G-22312)
Medigroup Inc.......................................G....... 630 554-5533
  Oswego  (G-16926)
Medline Industries Inc..........................A....... 847 949-5500
  Northfield  (G-16409)
Medline Industries Inc..........................B....... 847 949-2056
  Mundelein  (G-15528)
Medline Industries Inc..........................B....... 847 949-5500
  Waukegan  (G-21589)
Medtec Applications Inc.......................G....... 224 353-6752
  Glendale Heights  (G-11047)
Medtex Health Services Inc.................G....... 630 789-0330
  Clarendon Hills  (G-7258)
Medtronic Inc........................................G....... 815 444-2500
  Crystal Lake  (G-7608)
Medtronic Inc........................................E....... 630 627-6677
  Lombard  (G-13824)
Nemera Buffalo Grove LLC..................B....... 847 541-7900
  Buffalo Grove  (G-2743)
Nemera Buffalo Grove LLC..................G....... 847 325-3629
  Buffalo Grove  (G-2744)
Nemera Buffalo Grove LLC..................G....... 847 325-3628
  Buffalo Grove  (G-2745)
Nemera US Holding Inc........................F....... 847 325-3620
  Buffalo Grove  (G-2746)
Newmedical Technology Inc.................E....... 847 412-1000
  Northbrook  (G-16319)
Nexhand Inc..........................................G....... 619 820-2988
  Chicago  (G-5906)
Nordent Manufacturing Inc...................E....... 847 437-4780
  Elk Grove Village  (G-9653)
Northgate Technologies Inc..................E....... 847 608-8900
  Elgin  (G-9126)

Nuclin Diagnostics Inc..........................G....... 847 498-5210
  Northbrook  (G-16320)
Ohio Medical LLC..................................D....... 847 855-0500
  Gurnee  (G-11479)
Omc Investors LLC...............................G....... 847 855-6220
  Gurnee  (G-11480)
Omnicare Group Inc.............................G....... 708 949-8802
  Homer Glen  (G-12084)
Omron Healthcare Inc..........................D....... 847 680-6200
  Lake Forest  (G-12932)
Opticent Inc...........................................G....... 410 829-7384
  Evanston  (G-10083)
Organ Recovery Systems Inc..............F....... 847 824-2600
  Itasca  (G-12337)
Phenome Technologies Inc..................G....... 847 962-1273
  Lincolnshire  (G-13474)
Philips Medical Systems Clevel............G....... 630 585-2000
  Aurora  (G-1065)
Photonicare Inc.....................................G....... 405 880-7209
  Champaign  (G-3525)
Prodico Technologies LLC....................G....... 312 498-5152
  Chicago  (G-6204)
Resonance Medical LLC......................G....... 229 292-2094
  Chicago  (G-6337)
Rexam Devices LLC.............................G....... 847 325-3629
  Buffalo Grove  (G-2758)
Reznik Instrument Co...........................G....... 847 673-3444
  Skokie  (G-20075)
Richard Wolf Med Instrs Corp..............G....... 847 913-1113
  Vernon Hills  (G-21193)
River Bank Laboratories Inc.................F....... 630 232-2207
  Geneva  (G-10863)
Salter Labs............................................G....... 661 854-3166
  Lake Forest  (G-12956)
Salter Labs............................................E....... 847 739-3224
  Lake Forest  (G-12957)
Savex Manufacturing Company............G....... 630 668-7219
  Carol Stream  (G-3233)
Siemens Hlthcare Dgnostics Inc..........E....... 847 267-5300
  Deerfield  (G-8052)
Simpex Medical Inc..............................G....... 847 757-9928
  Mount Prospect  (G-15374)
Sonoma Orthopedic Products Inc........F....... 847 807-4378
  Buffalo Grove  (G-2774)
Spinecraft LLC......................................F....... 630 920-7300
  Westmont  (G-21923)
Star Cushion Products Inc...................F....... 618 539-7070
  Freeburg  (G-10643)
Steris Corporation................................F....... 847 455-2881
  Franklin Park  (G-10594)
Superior Surgical Instrumen TS...........G....... 630 628-8437
  Addison  (G-301)
Supertek Scientific LLC........................G....... 630 345-3450
  Villa Park  (G-21287)
Teleflex Incorporated............................D....... 847 259-7400
  Arlington Heights  (G-853)
Thermatome Corporation.....................G....... 312 772-2201
  Chicago  (G-6712)
Thrift Medical Products........................G....... 630 857-3548
  Naperville  (G-15765)
Total Titanium Inc.................................E....... 618 473-2429
  Red Bud  (G-17950)
United Amercn Healthcare Corp..........F....... 313 393-4571
  Chicago  (G-6820)
Vyaire Medical Inc................................F....... 847 362-8088
  Mettawa  (G-14764)
Welkins LLC..........................................G....... 877 319-3504
  Downers Grove  (G-8543)
Whitney Products Inc...........................F....... 847 966-6161
  Niles  (G-16047)
Wholesale Point Inc.............................F....... 630 986-1700
  Burr Ridge  (G-2895)
Wisdom Medical Technology LLC........G....... 630 803-6383
  Oswego  (G-16942)

## INSTRUMENTS: Meters, Integrating Electricity

L & B Global Power LLC......................G....... 847 323-0770
  Chicago  (G-5417)
Wb Tray LLC.........................................E....... 618 918-3821
  Centralia  (G-3437)

## INSTRUMENTS: Multimeters

Nu Vision Media Inc............................G....... 773 495-5254
  Chicago  (G-5952)

## INSTRUMENTS: Oscillographs & Oscilloscopes

Elenco Electronics Inc..........................E....... 847 541-3800
  Wheeling  (G-22046)

## INSTRUMENTS: Potentiometric

Maurey Instrument Corp......................F....... 708 388-9898
  Alsip  (G-490)

## INSTRUMENTS: Radio Frequency Measuring

Haynes-Bent Inc...................................F....... 630 845-3316
  Wilmington  (G-22274)

## INSTRUMENTS: Signal Generators & Averagers

Adams Elevator Equipment Co............E....... 847 581-2900
  Chicago  (G-3743)

## INSTRUMENTS: Temperature Measurement, Indl

Ascon Corp............................................G....... 630 482-2950
  Batavia  (G-1417)
Atlas Material Tstg Tech LLC...............C....... 773 327-4520
  Mount Prospect  (G-15311)
Claud S Gordon Company....................B....... 815 678-2211
  Richmond  (G-17960)
Durex International Corp......................C....... 847 639-5600
  Cary  (G-3338)
Heng Tuo Usa Inc.................................G....... 630 705-1898
  Oakbrook Terrace  (G-16710)

## INSTRUMENTS: Test, Digital, Electronic & Electrical Circuits

Creative Science Activities...................G....... 847 870-1746
  Prospect Heights  (G-17775)
Nanofast Inc..........................................E....... 312 943-4223
  Chicago  (G-5852)

## INSTRUMENTS: Test, Electrical, Engine

Protec Equipment Resources Inc.........G....... 847 434-5808
  Schaumburg  (G-19702)
Sigmatron International Inc.................G....... 847 586-5200
  Elgin  (G-9178)
Sigmatron International Inc.................G....... 847 956-8000
  Elk Grove Village  (G-9737)
Stevens Instrument Company..............G....... 847 336-9375
  Waukegan  (G-21620)

## INSTRUMENTS: Test, Electronic & Electric Measurement

Associated Research Inc......................E....... 847 367-4077
  Lake Forest  (G-12881)
B T Technology Inc...............................G....... 217 322-3768
  Rushville  (G-19090)
Dytec Midwest Inc................................G....... 847 255-3200
  Rolling Meadows  (G-18726)
Fox Meter Inc........................................G....... 630 968-3635
  Lisle  (G-13590)
Gld Industries Inc.................................G....... 217 390-9594
  Champaign  (G-3489)
Nls Analytics LLC..................................G....... 312 593-0293
  Glencoe  (G-11003)
Premium Test Equipment Corp............G....... 630 400-2681
  Warrenville  (G-21358)
TEC Rep Corporation...........................F....... 630 627-9110
  Lombard  (G-13866)

## INSTRUMENTS: Test, Electronic & Electrical Circuits

Centurion Non Destructive Tstg...........F....... 630 736-5500
  Streamwood  (G-20648)
Cymatics Inc..........................................G....... 630 420-7117
  Naperville  (G-15640)
Eagle Test Systems Inc........................E....... 847 367-8282
  Buffalo Grove  (G-2689)
Huygen Corporation..............................G....... 815 455-2200
  Crystal Lake  (G-7590)
International Electro Magnetic..............G....... 847 358-4622
  Wheeling  (G-22077)
Methode Electronics Inc.......................B....... 708 867-6777
  Chicago  (G-5704)

## INSTRUMENTS: Test, Electronic & Electrical Circuits

**Monolithic Industries Inc**................G....... 630 985-6009
Woodridge *(G-22503)*
**Teledyne Lecroy Inc**...........................E....... 847 888-0450
Elgin *(G-9206)*

### INSTRUMENTS: Testing, Semiconductor

**Sk Hynix America Inc**..........................G....... 847 925-0196
Schaumburg *(G-19729)*

### INSTRUMENTS: Thermal Conductive, Indl

**Controlled Thermal Processing**...........G....... 847 651-5511
Streamwood *(G-20650)*
**Luse Thermal Technologies LLC**........G....... 630 862-2600
Aurora *(G-1050)*

### INSTRUMENTS: Time Code Generators

**Dgm Electronics Inc**...........................G....... 815 389-2040
Roscoe *(G-18894)*

### INSTRUMENTS: Transducers, Volts, Amperes, Watts, VARs & Freq

**Identcorp Industries**...........................E....... 708 896-6407
Dolton *(G-8372)*

### INSTRUMENTS: Vibration

**Anamet Inc**........................................G....... 217 234-8844
Glen Ellyn *(G-10958)*
**SKF USA Inc**......................................D....... 847 742-0700
Elgin *(G-9186)*

### INSTRUMENTS: Viscometer, Indl Process

**Mettler-Toledo LLC**............................E....... 630 790-3355
Aurora *(G-1054)*

### INSULATION & CUSHIONING FOAM: Polystyrene

**Ade Inc**..............................................E....... 773 646-3400
Chicago *(G-3746)*
**Armacell LLC**.....................................D....... 708 596-9501
South Holland *(G-20246)*
**Eagle Panel System Inc**......................G....... 618 326-7132
Mulberry Grove *(G-15459)*
**Hunter Panels LLC**............................D....... 847 671-2516
Franklin Park *(G-10492)*
**Insulco Inc**.........................................F....... 309 353-6145
Pekin *(G-17270)*
**K & S Service & Rental Corp**.............F....... 630 279-4292
Elmhurst *(G-9893)*
**Minnesota Diversified Pdts Inc**..........E....... 815 539-3106
Mendota *(G-14728)*
**Pregis LLC**.........................................A....... 847 597-2200
Deerfield *(G-8049)*
**Punch Products Manufacturing**..........E....... 773 533-2800
Chicago *(G-6226)*
**Remco Technology Inc**.......................F....... 847 329-8090
Skokie *(G-20074)*

### INSULATION MATERIALS WHOLESALERS

**Hersheys Metal Meister LLC**..............E....... 217 234-4700
Claremont *(G-7256)*
**Insulators Supply Inc**.........................G....... 847 394-2836
Prospect Heights *(G-17780)*
**Meyer Enterprises LLC**......................G....... 309 698-0062
East Peoria *(G-8725)*

### INSULATION: Felt

**Thermohelp Inc**.................................G....... 847 821-7130
Buffalo Grove *(G-2781)*

### INSULATION: Fiberglass

**Atlas Roofing Corporation**..................E....... 309 752-7121
East Moline *(G-8670)*
**Fbm Galaxy Inc**.................................E....... 847 362-0925
Lake Bluff *(G-12843)*
**Mary E Fisher**....................................G....... 618 964-1528
Marion *(G-14273)*
**Owens-Corning Fiberglass Tech**........G....... 708 563-9091
Argo *(G-696)*

### INSULATORS & INSULATION MATERIALS: Electrical

**Guardian Energy Tech Inc**..................F....... 800 516-0949
Riverwoods *(G-18038)*
**Illinois Tool Works Inc**........................D....... 847 537-8800
Lincolnshire *(G-13457)*
**Jpmorgan Chase & Co**......................F....... 773 978-3408
Chicago *(G-5329)*
**Jpmorgan Chase Bank Nat Assn**......G....... 773 994-2490
Chicago *(G-5330)*
**Jpmorgan Chase Bank Nat Assn**......G....... 847 685-0490
Park Ridge *(G-17205)*
**Resinite Corporation**..........................C....... 847 537-4250
Wheeling *(G-22138)*

### INSURANCE CARRIERS: Life

**Gibson Insurance Inc**.........................G....... 217 864-4877
Mount Zion *(G-15451)*

### INSURANCE PROFESSIONAL STANDARDS SVCS

**Aais Services Corporation**..................G....... 630 457-3263
Lisle *(G-13552)*
**American Assn Insur Svcs**.................G....... 630 681-8347
Lisle *(G-13557)*

### INSURANCE: Agents, Brokers & Service

**Frank S Johnson & Company**............G....... 847 492-1660
Evanston *(G-10039)*
**Gibson Insurance Inc**.........................G....... 217 864-4877
Mount Zion *(G-15451)*
**Vej Holdings LLC**...............................G....... 630 219-1582
Naperville *(G-15774)*

### INTEGRATED CIRCUITS, SEMICONDUCTOR NETWORKS, ETC

**Analog Devices Inc**............................G....... 847 519-3669
Schaumburg *(G-19441)*
**GBA Systems Integrators LLC**..........G....... 913 492-0400
Moline *(G-14941)*
**Konekt Inc**..........................................G....... 773 733-0471
Chicago *(G-5403)*
**Microchip Technology Inc**..................E....... 630 285-0071
Itasca *(G-12315)*
**Precision Technologies Inc**.................G....... 847 439-5447
Glendale Heights *(G-11058)*
**Smart Controls LLC**...........................G....... 618 394-0300
Fairview Heights *(G-10171)*
**Visco Technologies Usa Inc**...............E....... 847 993-3047
Arlington Heights *(G-865)*
**Xtremedata Inc**..................................E....... 847 871-0379
Schaumburg *(G-19792)*

### INTERCOMMUNICATION EQPT REPAIR SVCS

**Portable Cmmnctons Spclsts**............G....... 630 458-1800
Addison *(G-247)*

### INTERCOMMUNICATIONS SYSTEMS: Electric

**AVI-Spl Employee**..............................B....... 847 437-7712
Schaumburg *(G-19454)*
**Data Comm For Business Inc**............F....... 217 897-1741
Dewey *(G-8310)*
**McC Technology Inc**..........................F....... 630 377-7200
Saint Charles *(G-19216)*
**Motorola Mobility LLC**........................E....... 847 523-5000
Chicago *(G-5816)*
**Pro Intercom LLC**..............................F....... 224 406-7108
Algonquin *(G-404)*
**Procomm Inc Hoopeston Illinois**........E....... 815 268-4303
Onarga *(G-16809)*
**Stenograph LLC**.................................D....... 630 532-5100
Elmhurst *(G-9942)*
**Talk-A-Phone Co**...............................D....... 773 539-1100
Niles *(G-16039)*

### INTERIOR DECORATING SVCS

**Cleavenger Associates Inc**.................G....... 630 221-0007
Winfield *(G-22284)*
**Lloyd M Hughes Enterprises Inc**........G....... 773 363-6331
Chicago *(G-5527)*

## PRODUCT SECTION

**Modagrafics Inc**..................................D....... 800 860-3169
Rolling Meadows *(G-18746)*

### INTERIOR DESIGN SVCS, NEC

**Afar Imports & Interiors Inc**...............G....... 217 744-3262
Springfield *(G-20386)*
**Amk Enterprises Chicago Inc**............G....... 312 523-7212
Chicago *(G-3890)*
**Baker Avenue Investments Inc**..........G....... 309 427-2500
Washington *(G-21378)*
**Botti Studio of Architectural**...............E....... 847 869-5933
Evanston *(G-10017)*
**Buhlwork Design Guild**......................G....... 630 325-5340
Oak Brook *(G-16495)*
**Elliott Aviation Arcft Sls Inc**................G....... 309 799-3183
Milan *(G-14785)*
**Lincoln Office LLC**..............................D....... 309 427-2500
Washington *(G-21385)*

### INTERIOR DESIGNING SVCS

**Draperyland Inc**..................................F....... 630 521-1000
Wood Dale *(G-22360)*
**Eastern Accents Inc**..........................C....... 773 604-7300
Chicago *(G-4683)*
**Essex Electro Engineers Inc**..............E....... 847 891-4444
Schaumburg *(G-19521)*
**Loyola Paper Company**.....................E....... 847 956-7770
Elk Grove Village *(G-9598)*
**M L Rongo Inc**....................................E....... 630 540-1120
Bartlett *(G-1360)*
**Michels Frame Shop**.........................G....... 847 647-7366
Niles *(G-16004)*
**Mosaic Construction**..........................G....... 847 504-0177
Northbrook *(G-16315)*
**Panache Editions Ltd**.........................G....... 847 921-8574
Glencoe *(G-11005)*
**Shade Aire Company**........................G....... 815 623-7597
Roscoe *(G-18921)*

### INTERMEDIATES Cyclic, Organic

**Stepan Company**...............................B....... 847 446-7500
Northfield *(G-16419)*

### INTRAVENOUS SOLUTIONS

**Anritsu Infivis Inc**...............................E....... 847 419-9729
Elk Grove Village *(G-9309)*
**Baxter World Trade Corporation**.......F....... 224 948-2000
Deerfield *(G-7989)*
**Fresenius Usa Inc**..............................E....... 773 262-7147
Chicago *(G-4890)*

### INVENTORY COMPUTING SVCS

**Paragon International Inc**...................F....... 847 240-2981
Schaumburg *(G-19682)*

### INVESTMENT ADVISORY SVCS

**American Association of Indivi**...........E....... 312 280-0170
Chicago *(G-3850)*

### INVESTMENT CLUBS

**Harris William & Company Inc**...........E....... 312 621-0590
Chicago *(G-5048)*
**Whi Capital Partners**.........................F....... 312 621-0590
Chicago *(G-6970)*

### INVESTMENT FIRM: General Brokerage

**Lake Pacific Partners LLC**................B....... 312 578-1110
Chicago *(G-5440)*
**Pfingsten Partners LLC**.....................F....... 312 222-8707
Chicago *(G-6115)*
**Wanxiang USA Holdings Corp**..........F....... 847 622-8838
Elgin *(G-9229)*

### INVESTMENT FUNDS, NEC

**Mid Oaks Investments LLC**...............G....... 847 215-3475
Buffalo Grove *(G-2736)*

### INVESTMENT FUNDS: Open-Ended

**Roundtble Hlthcare Partners LP**........E....... 847 482-9275
Lake Forest *(G-12954)*

### INVESTORS, NEC

**Lv Ventures Inc**..................................E....... 312 993-1758
Chicago *(G-5572)*

## PRODUCT SECTION — JEWELRY, PREC METAL: Mountings, Pens, Lthr, Etc, Gold/Silver

**Shore Capital Partners LLC** .................. F ... 312 348-7580
Chicago *(G-6499)*
**Tmb Industries Inc** ................................ F ... 312 280-2565
Chicago *(G-6732)*
**Willis Stein & Partners Manage** ........... E ... 312 422-2400
Northbrook *(G-16387)*
**Wind Point Partners Vi LP** ................... G ... 312 255-4800
Chicago *(G-6993)*

### INVESTORS: Real Estate, Exc Property Operators

**Le Claire Investment Inc** ...................... G ... 309 757-8250
Moline *(G-14953)*

### IRON & STEEL PRDTS: Hot-Rolled

**Economy Iron Inc** ................................. F ... 708 343-1777
Melrose Park *(G-14628)*
**TSA Processing Chicago Inc** ................ G ... 630 860-5900
Bensenville *(G-2007)*

### IRON ORES

**Q Lotus Holdings Inc** ........................... G ... 312 379-1800
Chicago *(G-6234)*
**Regal Converting Co Inc** ...................... F ... 630 257-3581
Lockport *(G-13742)*

### IRON OXIDES

**Huntsman P&A Americas LLC** .............. E ... 618 646-2119
East Saint Louis *(G-8755)*

### IRON: Sponge

**Connelly-Gpm Inc** ................................ E ... 773 247-7231
Chicago *(G-4451)*

### IRONING BOARDS

**Home Pdts Intl - N Amer Inc** ................ B ... 773 890-1010
Chicago *(G-5102)*

### IRRADIATION EQPT: Nuclear

**Starfire Industries LLC** ......................... E ... 217 721-4165
Champaign *(G-3548)*

### IRRIGATION EQPT WHOLESALERS

**Dowell Lynnea** ..................................... G ... 309 543-3854
Havana *(G-11694)*

### JACKS: Hydraulic

**Central Hydraulics Inc** ......................... G ... 309 527-5238
El Paso *(G-8866)*
**Jahns Structure Jacking System** .......... G ... 630 365-2455
Elburn *(G-8890)*
**Rehobot Inc** .......................................... G ... 815 385-7777
McHenry *(G-14550)*
**Walach Manufacturing Co Inc** .............. F ... 773 836-2060
Chicago *(G-6935)*

### JANITORIAL & CUSTODIAL SVCS

**Klean-Ko Inc** ........................................ D ... 630 620-1860
Lombard *(G-13816)*
**Rampro Facilities Svcs Corp** ................ G ... 224 639-6378
Gurnee *(G-11498)*
**Wells Janitorial Service Inc** .................. G ... 872 226-9983
Chicago *(G-6953)*
**Workshop** ............................................ E ... 815 777-2211
Galena *(G-10736)*

### JANITORIAL EQPT & SPLYS WHOLESALERS

**Brite Site Supply Inc** ............................ G ... 773 772-7300
Chicago *(G-4171)*
**Dura Wax Company** ............................. F ... 815 385-5000
McHenry *(G-14499)*
**GL Downs Inc** ...................................... G ... 618 993-9777
Marion *(G-14262)*
**Nanco Sales Co Inc** .............................. G ... 630 892-9820
Aurora *(G-1193)*

### JARS: Plastic

**Xcell International Corp** ....................... D ... 630 323-0107
Lemont *(G-13271)*

### JEWELERS' FINDINGS & MATERIALS

**North American Jewelers Inc** ............... D ... 312 425-9000
Chicago *(G-5933)*

### JEWELERS' FINDINGS & MATERIALS: Castings

**Branchfield Casting** ............................. E ... 309 932-2278
Galva *(G-10786)*
**M B Jewelers Inc** ................................. ... 312 853-3490
Chicago *(G-5579)*

### JEWELRY & PRECIOUS STONES WHOLESALERS

**Diamond Icic Corporation** ................... E ... 309 269-8652
Rock Island *(G-18175)*
**Edgar H Fey Jewelers Inc** ..................... E ... 708 352-4115
Naperville *(G-15651)*
**Pearl Perfect Inc** .................................. E ... 847 679-6251
Morton Grove *(G-15227)*
**S G Nelson & Co** .................................. G ... 630 668-7900
Wheaton *(G-21979)*
**Tia Tynette Designs Inc** ....................... ... 219 440-2859
Olympia Fields *(G-16806)*

### JEWELRY APPAREL

**A G Mitchells Jewelers Ltd** .................. F ... 847 394-0820
Arlington Heights *(G-700)*
**Georg Jensen Inc** ................................ G ... 312 642-9160
Chicago *(G-4941)*
**Patricia Locke Ltd** ................................ F ... 847 949-2303
Mundelein *(G-15543)*
**Vintaj Natural Brass Co** ....................... G ... 815 776-9300
Galena *(G-10733)*

### JEWELRY FINDINGS & LAPIDARY WORK

**Alex and Ani LLC** ................................. G ... 630 574-2329
Oak Brook *(G-16486)*
**C D Nelson Consulting Inc** ................... G ... 847 487-4870
Wauconda *(G-21449)*
**Dimend Scaasi Ltd** .............................. G ... 312 857-1700
Chicago *(G-4604)*
**Israel Levy Diamnd Cutters Inc** ........... E ... 312 368-8540
Chicago *(G-5244)*
**Micro Lapping & Grinding Co** .............. G ... 847 455-5446
Franklin Park *(G-10531)*

### JEWELRY REPAIR SVCS

**Diamondaire Corp** ............................... G ... 630 355-7464
Saint Charles *(G-19172)*
**Emerald City Jewelry Inc** ..................... G ... 217 222-8896
Quincy *(G-17826)*
**Hustedt Manufacturing Jewelers** ........ G ... 217 784-8462
Gibson City *(G-10903)*
**Kaye Lee & Company Inc** .................... G ... 312 236-9686
Chicago *(G-5365)*
**Masud Jewelers Inc** ............................. ... 312 236-0547
Chicago *(G-5648)*
**Michael P Jones** .................................. G ... 217 787-7457
Springfield *(G-20481)*
**Norkin Jewelry Co Inc** ......................... E ... 312 782-7311
Chicago *(G-5928)*
**Rodger Murphy** ................................... G ... 309 582-2202
Aledo *(G-372)*
**Roger Burke Jewelers Inc** .................... F ... 309 692-0210
Peoria *(G-17445)*
**Simon Zelikman** .................................. G ... 847 338-8031
Oakwood Hills *(G-16728)*
**Unicorn Designs** .................................. G ... 847 295-5230
Lake Forest *(G-12976)*
**Victor Levy Jewelry Co Inc** .................. G ... 312 782-5297
Chicago *(G-6894)*

### JEWELRY STORES

**A G Mitchells Jewelers Ltd** .................. F ... 847 394-0820
Arlington Heights *(G-700)*
**Azteca Jewelry** .................................... G ... 773 929-0796
Chicago *(G-4013)*
**Bing Yeung Jewelers Inc** ..................... G ... 708 749-4800
Berwyn *(G-2057)*
**David Nelson Exquisite Jewelry** .......... G ... 815 741-4702
Joliet *(G-12483)*
**Emerald City Jewelry Inc** ..................... G ... 217 222-8896
Quincy *(G-17826)*
**G Blando Jewelers Inc** ......................... G ... 630 627-7963
Countryside *(G-7425)*
**Hakimian Gem Co** ............................... G ... 312 236-6969
Chicago *(G-5033)*
**Jordan Gold Inc** ................................... G ... 708 430-7008
Oak Lawn *(G-16628)*
**Marion Oelze** ...................................... G ... 618 327-9224
Nashville *(G-15839)*
**Nali Inc** ................................................ E ... 708 442-8710
Clarendon Hills *(G-7259)*
**Rodger Murphy** ................................... G ... 309 582-2202
Aledo *(G-372)*
**Ross Designs Ltd** ................................. G ... 847 831-7669
Highland Park *(G-11866)*
**T J Marche Ltd** .................................... G ... 618 445-2314
Albion *(G-366)*
**Tommy Ho Jewelers** ........................... G ... 312 368-8593
Chicago *(G-6739)*

### JEWELRY STORES: Clocks

**Instrument Services Inc** ...................... G ... 815 623-2993
Machesney Park *(G-14082)*

### JEWELRY STORES: Precious Stones & Precious Metals

**A M Lee Inc** ......................................... G ... 847 291-1777
Northbrook *(G-16195)*
**Alan Rocca Ltd** .................................... E ... 630 323-5800
Oak Brook *(G-16485)*
**Blando G Mfg Jewelers** ....................... G ... 708 387-0014
Brookfield *(G-2624)*
**Burdeens Jewelry Ltd** ......................... G ... 847 459-8980
Buffalo Grove *(G-2671)*
**Charles Horberg Jewelers Inc** ............. G ... 312 263-4924
Chicago *(G-4292)*
**D&M Perlman Fine Jwly Gift LLC** ........ G ... 847 426-8881
West Dundee *(G-21795)*
**Daniels Jewelry & Mfg Co** ................... G ... 847 998-5222
Glenview *(G-11120)*
**Edgar H Fey Jewelers Inc** ..................... E ... 708 352-4115
Naperville *(G-15651)*
**Eve J Alfille Ltd** .................................... G ... 847 869-7920
Evanston *(G-10035)*
**Faye Jewellery Chez** ........................... G ... 815 477-1818
Crystal Lake *(G-7577)*
**Frank S Bender Inc** .............................. G ... 847 441-7370
Northfield *(G-16399)*
**H Watson Jewelry Co** .......................... G ... 312 236-1104
Chicago *(G-5024)*
**Kaye Lee & Company Inc** .................... G ... 312 236-9686
Chicago *(G-5365)*
**Leo A Bachrach Jewelers Inc** .............. G ... 312 263-3111
Chicago *(G-5492)*
**Lester Lampert Inc** ............................. E ... 312 944-6888
Chicago *(G-5495)*
**Michals Accessory Mart Inc** ................ G ... 312 263-0066
Chicago *(G-5721)*
**Perle & Sons Jewelers Inc** ................... G ... 630 357-3357
Naperville *(G-15724)*
**Razny Jewelers Ltd** ............................. E ... 630 932-4900
Addison *(G-270)*
**Richards Fine Jewelry & Design** ......... G ... 847 697-4053
South Elgin *(G-20224)*
**Roger Burke Jewelers Inc** .................... F ... 309 692-0210
Peoria *(G-17445)*
**Solari R Mfg Jewelers** ......................... G ... 847 823-4354
Park Ridge *(G-17222)*
**Tri-City Gold Exchange Inc** .................. F ... 708 331-5995
Harvey *(G-11678)*
**Unicorn Designs** .................................. G ... 847 295-5230
Lake Forest *(G-12976)*

### JEWELRY STORES: Silverware

**Al Bar Laboratories Inc** ....................... F ... 847 251-1218
Wilmette *(G-22241)*
**Georg Jensen Inc** ................................ G ... 312 642-9160
Chicago *(G-4941)*
**Westerling Group** ............................... G ... 708 547-8488
Berkeley *(G-2052)*

### JEWELRY STORES: Watches

**Bxb Intl Inc** .......................................... G ... 312 240-1966
Brookfield *(G-2626)*

### JEWELRY, PREC METAL: Mountings, Pens, Lthr, Etc, Gold/Silver

**Award Emblem Mfg Co Inc** .................. F ... 630 739-0800
Bolingbrook *(G-2281)*

---

Employee Codes: A=Over 500 employees, B=251-500
C=101-250, D=51-100, E=20-50, F=10-19, G=3-9

## JEWELRY, PRECIOUS METAL: Cases

**Mfz Ventures Inc**......G...... 773 247-4611
Chicago *(G-5715)*

## JEWELRY, PRECIOUS METAL: Cigar & Cigarette Access

**ISA Chicago**......G...... 630 317-7169
Carol Stream *(G-3175)*

## JEWELRY, PRECIOUS METAL: Medals, Precious Or Semiprecious

**Mint Masters Inc**......E...... 847 451-1133
Franklin Park *(G-10534)*
**Park-Ohio Industries Inc**......D...... 708 652-6691
Chicago *(G-6085)*
**R S Owens & Co Inc**......B...... 773 282-6000
Chicago *(G-6273)*

## JEWELRY, PRECIOUS METAL: Mountings & Trimmings

**Blando G Mfg Jewelers**......G...... 708 387-0014
Brookfield *(G-2624)*

## JEWELRY, PRECIOUS METAL: Rings, Finger

**Bliss Ring Company Inc**......F...... 847 446-3440
Winnetka *(G-22304)*
**David Nelson Exquisite Jewelry**......G...... 815 741-4702
Joliet *(G-12483)*
**Fashion Craft Corporation**......E...... 847 998-0092
Highland Park *(G-11832)*
**Herff Jones LLC**......F...... 815 756-4743
Dekalb *(G-8096)*
**Herff Jones LLC**......D...... 773 463-1144
Chicago *(G-5079)*
**Herff Jones LLC**......F...... 217 351-9500
Champaign *(G-3494)*
**Herff Jones LLC**......G...... 708 425-0130
Oak Lawn *(G-16625)*
**Jostens Inc**......E...... 217 483-8989
Chatham *(G-3623)*
**Razny Jewelers Ltd**......E...... 630 932-4900
Addison *(G-270)*
**Trebor Enterprises Ltd**......G...... 815 235-1700
Freeport *(G-10693)*

## JEWELRY, PRECIOUS METAL: Rosaries/Other Sm Religious Article

**Kesher Stam**......G...... 773 973-7826
Chicago *(G-5378)*

## JEWELRY, PRECIOUS METAL: Settings & Mountings

**Eve J Alfille Ltd**......E...... 847 869-7920
Evanston *(G-10035)*
**Fine Gold Mfg Jewelers**......G...... 630 323-9600
Hinsdale *(G-11946)*
**Hy Spreckman & Sons Inc**......F...... 312 236-2173
Skokie *(G-20013)*
**Kaye Lee & Company Inc**......G...... 312 236-9686
Chicago *(G-5365)*
**Michael P Jones**......G...... 217 787-7457
Springfield *(G-20481)*
**Roger Burke Jewelers Inc**......F...... 309 692-0210
Peoria *(G-17445)*
**S G Nelson & Co**......G...... 630 668-7900
Wheaton *(G-21979)*

## JEWELRY, WHOLESALE

**Alomar Inc**......G...... 312 855-0714
Chicago *(G-3827)*
**Azteca Jewelry**......G...... 773 929-0796
Chicago *(G-4013)*
**Charles Horberg Jewelers Inc**......G...... 312 263-4924
Chicago *(G-4292)*
**Diamondaire Corp**......G...... 630 355-7464
Saint Charles *(G-19172)*
**Faye Jewellery Chez**......G...... 815 477-1818
Crystal Lake *(G-7577)*
**Jason Lau Jewelry**......G...... 312 750-1028
Chicago *(G-5282)*
**Rahmanims Imports Inc**......G...... 312 236-2200
Chicago *(G-6284)*
**Total Design Jewelry Inc**......G...... 847 433-5333
Highland Park *(G-11878)*

## JEWELRY: Decorative, Fashion & Costume

**Acme Button & Buttonhole Co**......G...... 773 907-8400
Chicago *(G-3731)*
**Bee-Jay Industries Inc**......F...... 708 867-4431
Bloomingdale *(G-2095)*
**Blandings Ltd**......G...... 773 478-3542
Chicago *(G-4122)*
**D & D Sukach Inc**......G...... 815 895-3377
Sycamore *(G-20790)*
**Dan De Tash Knits**......G...... 708 970-6238
Maywood *(G-14424)*
**Daniels Jewelry & Mfg Co**......G...... 847 998-5222
Glenview *(G-11120)*
**Diamondaire Corp**......G...... 630 355-7464
Saint Charles *(G-19172)*
**Faiths Designs**......G...... 773 768-5804
Chicago *(G-4810)*
**Hustedt Manufacturing Jewelers**......G...... 217 784-8462
Gibson City *(G-10903)*
**Jewerly and Beyond**......G...... 312 833-6785
Schaumburg *(G-19588)*
**Jordan Gold Inc**......G...... 708 430-7008
Oak Lawn *(G-16628)*
**K Fleye Designs**......G...... 773 531-0716
Chicago *(G-5342)*
**Pearl Perfect Inc**......E...... 847 679-6251
Morton Grove *(G-15227)*
**Replacement Services LLC**......F...... 618 398-9880
Belleville *(G-1669)*
**Smart Creations Inc**......G...... 847 433-3451
Highland Park *(G-11869)*
**Solari R Mfg Jewelers**......G...... 847 823-4354
Park Ridge *(G-17222)*
**Sunnywood Incorporated**......G...... 815 675-9777
Spring Grove *(G-20366)*
**Swarovski North America Ltd**......G...... 847 680-5150
Vernon Hills *(G-21206)*
**Swarovski US Holding Limited**......G...... 847 679-8670
Skokie *(G-20097)*
**Ulla of Finland**......G...... 773 763-0700
Chicago *(G-6806)*

## JEWELRY: Precious Metal

**A M Lee Inc**......G...... 847 291-1777
Northbrook *(G-16195)*
**Accents By Fred**......G...... 708 366-9850
Forest Park *(G-10234)*
**Afshar Inc**......G...... 773 645-8922
Chicago *(G-3781)*
**Alan Rocca Ltd**......E...... 630 323-5800
Oak Brook *(G-16485)*
**Alomar Inc**......G...... 312 855-0714
Chicago *(G-3827)*
**Award Concepts Inc**......E...... 630 513-7801
Saint Charles *(G-19141)*
**Azteca Jewelry**......G...... 773 929-0796
Chicago *(G-4013)*
**Bee-Jay Industries Inc**......F...... 708 867-4431
Bloomingdale *(G-2095)*
**Bing Yeung Jewelers Inc**......G...... 708 749-4800
Berwyn *(G-2057)*
**Blandings Ltd**......G...... 773 478-3542
Chicago *(G-4122)*
**Burdeens Jewelry Ltd**......G...... 847 459-8980
Buffalo Grove *(G-2671)*
**Cabanas Manufacturing Jewelers**......G...... 312 726-0333
Chicago *(G-4208)*
**Casting House Inc**......F...... 312 782-7160
Chicago *(G-4252)*
**Charles Horberg Jewelers Inc**......G...... 312 263-4924
Chicago *(G-4292)*
**D&M Perlman Fine Jwly Gift LLC**......G...... 847 426-8881
West Dundee *(G-21795)*
**Dalzell & Company**......G...... 815 477-8816
Crystal Lake *(G-7565)*
**Edgar H Fey Jewelers Inc**......E...... 708 352-4115
Naperville *(G-15651)*
**Emerald City Jewelry Inc**......G...... 217 222-8896
Quincy *(G-17826)*
**Faye Jewellery Chez**......G...... 815 477-1818
Crystal Lake *(G-7577)*
**Frank S Bender Inc**......G...... 847 441-7370
Northfield *(G-16399)*
**G Blando Jewelers Inc**......G...... 630 627-7963
Countryside *(G-7425)*
**General Design Jewelers Inc**......G...... 312 201-9047
Chicago *(G-4925)*
**George Erckman Jewelers**......G...... 312 263-7380
Chicago *(G-4942)*
**H Watson Jewelry Co**......G...... 312 236-1104
Chicago *(G-5024)*
**Hakimian Gem Co**......G...... 312 236-6969
Chicago *(G-5033)*
**Herff Jones LLC**......C...... 317 612-3705
Hillside *(G-11918)*
**Hustedt Manufacturing Jewelers**......G...... 217 784-8462
Gibson City *(G-10903)*
**Jamex Jewelry Inc**......G...... 312 726-7867
Chicago *(G-5275)*
**Jason Lau Jewelry**......G...... 312 750-1028
Chicago *(G-5282)*
**John Buechner Inc**......G...... 312 263-2226
Chicago *(G-5312)*
**Joseph C Wolf**......G...... 312 332-3135
Chicago *(G-5327)*
**Jostens Inc**......E...... 630 963-3500
Lisle *(G-13612)*
**La Ron Jewelers**......G...... 312 263-3898
Chicago *(G-5427)*
**Lana Unlimited Co**......G...... 312 226-7050
Lake Forest *(G-12923)*
**Leo A Bachrach Jewelers Inc**......G...... 312 263-3111
Chicago *(G-5492)*
**Lester Lampert Inc**......E...... 312 944-6888
Chicago *(G-5495)*
**M B Jewelers Inc**......G...... 312 853-3490
Chicago *(G-5579)*
**Made As Intended Inc**......F...... 630 789-3494
Oak Brook *(G-16538)*
**Masud Jewelers Inc**......G...... 312 236-0547
Chicago *(G-5648)*
**Medaowview Ventures II Inc**......E...... 847 965-1700
Morton Grove *(G-15218)*
**Michals Accessory Mart Inc**......G...... 312 263-0066
Chicago *(G-5721)*
**Mtm Jostens Inc**......G...... 815 875-1111
Princeton *(G-17756)*
**Mtm Recognition Corporation**......C...... 815 875-1111
Princeton *(G-17757)*
**Norkin Jewelry Co Inc**......E...... 312 782-7311
Chicago *(G-5928)*
**Perle & Sons Jewelers Inc**......G...... 630 357-3357
Naperville *(G-15724)*
**Rahmanims Imports Inc**......G...... 312 236-2200
Chicago *(G-6284)*
**Richards Fine Jewelry & Design**......G...... 847 697-4053
South Elgin *(G-20224)*
**Rodger Murphy**......G...... 309 582-2202
Aledo *(G-372)*
**Rosengard Sue Jwly Design Ltd**......G...... 312 733-1133
Chicago *(G-6396)*
**Ross Designs Ltd**......G...... 847 831-7669
Highland Park *(G-11866)*
**Simon Zelikman**......G...... 847 338-8031
Oakwood Hills *(G-16728)*
**Therese Crowe Design Ltd**......G...... 312 269-0039
Chicago *(G-6711)*
**Tommy Ho Jewelers**......G...... 312 368-8593
Chicago *(G-6739)*
**Tri-City Gold Exchange Inc**......F...... 708 331-5995
Harvey *(G-11678)*
**Unicorn Designs**......G...... 847 295-5230
Lake Forest *(G-12976)*
**Victor Levy Jewelry Co Inc**......G...... 312 782-5297
Chicago *(G-6894)*

## JIGS & FIXTURES

**Grove Plastic Inc**......F...... 847 678-8244
Franklin Park *(G-10484)*
**K & H Tool Co**......G...... 630 766-4588
Bensenville *(G-1931)*
**Precision Engineering & Dev Co**......E...... 630 834-5956
Villa Park *(G-21278)*
**R & R Machining Inc**......G...... 217 835-4579
Benld *(G-1806)*
**Republic Drill**......G...... 708 865-7666
Melrose Park *(G-14686)*
**Roscoe Tool & Manufacturing**......E...... 815 633-8808
Roscoe *(G-18918)*
**White Jig Grinding**......G...... 847 888-2260
South Elgin *(G-20234)*

## JIGS: Welding Positioners

**Alm Materials Handling LLC**......E...... 815 673-5546
Streator *(G-20682)*
**Alm Positioners Inc**......G...... 309 787-6200
Rock Island *(G-18159)*

## JOB PRINTING & NEWSPAPER PUBLISHING COMBINED

Arthur Graphic Clarion .................................. G ....... 217 543-2151
  Arthur *(G-881)*
Augusta Eagle ................................................ G ....... 217 392-2715
  Augusta *(G-951)*
Breeze Printing Co ........................................ F ....... 217 824-2233
  Taylorville *(G-20835)*
Bunker Hill Publication ................................ G ....... 618 585-4411
  Bunker Hill *(G-2804)*
Centralia Press Ltd ...................................... D ....... 618 532-5604
  Centralia *(G-3408)*
Farina News ................................................. G ....... 618 245-6216
  Farina *(G-10176)*
Golden Prairie News .................................... G ....... 217 226-3721
  Assumption *(G-931)*
Greenup Press Inc ....................................... G ....... 217 923-3704
  Greenup *(G-11383)*
Kaneland Publications Inc .......................... F ....... 630 365-6446
  Saint Charles *(G-19203)*
KK Stevens Publishing Co .......................... E ....... 309 329-2151
  Astoria *(G-934)*
Liberty Group Publishing ............................ F ....... 309 944-1779
  Geneseo *(G-10802)*
Mason City Banner Times ........................... F ....... 217 482-3276
  Mason City *(G-14365)*
Perryco Inc ................................................... G ....... 217 322-3321
  Rushville *(G-19094)*
Rankin Publishing Inc ................................. F ....... 217 268-4959
  Arcola *(G-683)*
Toledo Democrat .......................................... G ....... 217 849-2000
  Toledo *(G-20967)*

## JOB TRAINING & VOCATIONAL REHABILITATION SVCS

Envision Unlimited ....................................... C ....... 773 651-1100
  Chicago *(G-4766)*
Fulton County Rehabilitation ...................... E ....... 309 647-6510
  Canton *(G-2987)*
Mental Health Ctrs Centl Ill ....................... D ....... 217 735-1413
  Lincoln *(G-13415)*
Park Lawn Association Inc ......................... F ....... 708 425-7377
  Oak Lawn *(G-16638)*
Rehabilitation and Vocational .................... E ....... 618 833-5344
  Anna *(G-608)*
Simformotion LLC ........................................ F ....... 309 263-7595
  Peoria *(G-17456)*

## JOINTS & COUPLINGS

La Salle Co Esda .......................................... G ....... 815 433-5622
  Ottawa *(G-16966)*

## JOINTS: Ball Except aircraft & Auto

Hyspan Precision Products Inc ................. E ....... 773 277-0700
  South Holland *(G-20279)*

## JOINTS: Expansion

Anamet Inc .................................................... G ....... 217 234-8844
  Glen Ellyn *(G-10958)*
Commercial Fabricators Inc ....................... G ....... 708 594-1199
  Bridgeview *(G-2479)*
Lichtnwald - Johnston Ir Works ................. E ....... 847 966-1100
  Morton Grove *(G-15212)*
Metraflex Company ..................................... D ....... 312 738-3800
  Chicago *(G-5706)*

## JOINTS: Swivel & Universal, Exc Aircraft & Auto

Flex-Weld Inc ............................................... D ....... 815 334-3662
  Woodstock *(G-22567)*
NTN USA Corporation .................................. C ....... 847 298-4652
  Mount Prospect *(G-15357)*

## JOISTS: Long-Span Series, Open Web Steel

C M I Novacast Inc ...................................... F ....... 847 699-9020
  Des Plaines *(G-8161)*
Gooder-Henrichsen Company Inc ............. D ....... 708 757-5030
  Chicago Heights *(G-7100)*

## KAOLIN MINING

Huber Carbonates LLC ............................... G ....... 217 224-8737
  Quincy *(G-17837)*

## KEYBOARDS: Computer Or Office Machine

Art Cnc Machining LLC ............................... G ....... 708 907-3090
  Bridgeview *(G-2468)*
Grayhill Inc .................................................. B ....... 708 354-1040
  La Grange *(G-12734)*
Tunnel Vision Consulting Group ................ G ....... 773 367-7292
  Chicago *(G-6791)*

## KITCHEN CABINET STORES, EXC CUSTOM

Cabinets & Granite Direct LLC .................. F ....... 630 588-8886
  Carol Stream *(G-3121)*
Edward Hull Cabinet Shop ......................... G ....... 217 864-3011
  Mount Zion *(G-15450)*
Harts Top and Cabinet Shop ...................... G ....... 708 957-4666
  Country Club Hills *(G-7408)*
Hickory Street Cabinets ............................. G ....... 618 667-9676
  Troy *(G-21007)*
Kabinet Kraft ............................................... F ....... 618 395-1047
  Olney *(G-16775)*
Markham Cabinet Works Inc ..................... G ....... 708 687-3074
  Midlothian *(G-14767)*
Regency Custom Woodworking ................. F ....... 815 689-2117
  Cullom *(G-7683)*
Teds Custom Cabinets Inc ........................ G ....... 773 581-4455
  Chicago *(G-6687)*
Wenger Woodcraft ....................................... G ....... 217 578-3440
  Tuscola *(G-21030)*
Wilson Kitchens Inc .................................... D ....... 618 253-7449
  Harrisburg *(G-11606)*

## KITCHEN CABINETS WHOLESALERS

Cabinets & Granite Direct LLC .................. F ....... 630 588-8886
  Carol Stream *(G-3121)*
Creative Cabinets Countertops ................. F ....... 217 446-6406
  Danville *(G-7710)*
Gold Seal Cabinets Countertops ............... E ....... 630 906-0366
  Aurora *(G-1163)*
Hci Cabinetry and Design Inc ................... G ....... 630 584-0266
  Saint Charles *(G-19190)*
Lead n Glass Tm ......................................... F ....... 847 255-2074
  Wheeling *(G-22090)*
Orren Pickell Builders Inc ......................... F ....... 847 572-5200
  Northfield *(G-16415)*
Stonecrafters Inc ....................................... G ....... 815 363-8730
  Lakemoor *(G-13148)*

## KITCHEN TOOLS & UTENSILS WHOLESALERS

R/K Industries Inc ...................................... F ....... 847 526-2222
  Wauconda *(G-21498)*
Superior Knife Inc ...................................... E ....... 847 982-2280
  Skokie *(G-20095)*

## KITCHEN UTENSILS: Bakers' Eqpt, Wood

House On The Hill Inc ................................ G ....... 630 279-4455
  Wheaton *(G-21953)*
John Joda Post 54 ...................................... G ....... 815 692-3222
  Fairbury *(G-10128)*

## KITCHEN UTENSILS: Food Handling & Processing Prdts, Wood

Axis Design Architectual Mllwk ................. F ....... 630 466-4549
  Sugar Grove *(G-20717)*
New SBL Inc ................................................. E ....... 773 376-8280
  Chicago *(G-5893)*
Swagath Group Inc ..................................... G ....... 847 640-6446
  Arlington Heights *(G-849)*

## KITCHENWARE STORES

Euromarket Designs Inc ............................. A ....... 847 272-2888
  Northbrook *(G-16252)*
Tri-State Food Equipment ......................... G ....... 217 228-1550
  Quincy *(G-17900)*
US Foods Culinary Eqp Sups LLC ............. F ....... 847 720-8000
  Rosemont *(G-19039)*
World Kitchen LLC ...................................... C ....... 847 233-8600
  Rosemont *(G-19042)*

## KITCHENWARE: Plastic

Limitless Innovations Inc ........................... E ....... 855 843-4828
  McHenry *(G-14522)*
Pactiv LLC .................................................... C ....... 708 496-2900
  Bedford Park *(G-1571)*
Prairie Packaging Inc ................................. E ....... 708 496-1172
  Bedford Park *(G-1575)*
Prairie Packaging Inc ................................. F ....... 708 496-2900
  Chicago *(G-6166)*
Schweppe Inc ............................................... G ....... 630 627-3550
  Addison *(G-284)*

## KITS: Plastic

Rust-Oleum Corporation ............................. D ....... 815 967-4258
  Rockford *(G-18600)*
Testor Corporation ...................................... D ....... 815 962-6654
  Rockford *(G-18644)*
Universal Hovercraft Amer Inc .................. F ....... 815 963-1200
  Rockford *(G-18664)*

## KNIVES: Agricultural Or Indl

Gartech Manufacturing Co ......................... E ....... 217 324-6527
  Litchfield *(G-13686)*
Precision Industrial Knife .......................... F ....... 630 350-7898
  Wood Dale *(G-22412)*

## KNURLING

Roll Rite Inc ................................................. G ....... 815 645-8600
  Davis Junction *(G-7814)*

## LABELS: Cotton, Printed

Sato Lbling Solutions Amer Inc ................. D ....... 630 771-4200
  Romeoville *(G-18866)*

## LABELS: Paper, Made From Purchased Materials

Brohman Industries Inc ............................. F ....... 630 761-8160
  Chicago *(G-4174)*
Diversfied Lbling Slutions Inc .................. D ....... 630 625-1225
  Itasca *(G-12252)*
Gateway Packaging Company .................. C ....... 618 451-0010
  Granite City *(G-11279)*
Identi-Graphics Inc ..................................... G ....... 630 801-4845
  Montgomery *(G-15049)*
Trade Label & Decal ................................... G ....... 630 773-0447
  Itasca *(G-12367)*

## LABELS: Woven

W & W Associates Inc ................................ G ....... 847 719-1760
  Lake Zurich *(G-13142)*

## LABORATORIES, TESTING: Metallurgical

Magnetic Inspection Lab Inc ..................... D ....... 847 437-4488
  Elk Grove Village *(G-9606)*
Quality Circle Machine Inc ........................ G ....... 708 474-1160
  Lynwood *(G-14024)*

## LABORATORIES, TESTING: Product Testing

Skandia Inc .................................................. D ....... 815 393-4600
  Davis Junction *(G-7815)*
Superior Joining Tech Inc ......................... E ....... 815 282-7581
  Machesney Park *(G-14109)*

## LABORATORIES, TESTING: Product Testing, Safety/Performance

Atlas Material Tstg Tech LLC .................... E ....... 773 327-4520
  Chicago *(G-3983)*
Atlas Material Tstg Tech LLC .................... C ....... 773 327-4520
  Mount Prospect *(G-15311)*

## LABORATORIES, TESTING: Radiation

Landauer Inc ................................................ C ....... 708 755-7000
  Glenwood *(G-11218)*

## LABORATORIES, TESTING: Seed

Pioneer Hi-Bred Intl Inc ............................. F ....... 309 962-2931
  Le Roy *(G-13209)*

## LABORATORIES, TESTING: Veterinary

Shaars International Inc ............................ G ....... 815 315-0717
  Rockford *(G-18614)*

## LABORATORIES, TESTING: Welded Joint Radiographing

Jay RS Steel & Welding Inc ....................... G ....... 847 949-9353
  Mundelein *(G-15514)*

## LABORATORIES: Biological

### LABORATORIES: Biological
Interface Protein Tech Inc .................. D ...... 630 963-8809
  Lisle *(G-13607)*

### LABORATORIES: Biological Research
Isovac Products LLC ........................... G ...... 630 679-1740
  Romeoville *(G-18831)*

### LABORATORIES: Biotechnology
Sigenics Inc ....................................... F ...... 312 448-8000
  Chicago *(G-6506)*

### LABORATORIES: Commercial Nonphysical Research
Group O Inc ....................................... E ...... 309 736-8100
  Milan *(G-14790)*
Night Vision Corporation .................... G ...... 847 677-7611
  Lincolnwood *(G-13527)*

### LABORATORIES: Dental
American Dental Products Inc ............. E ...... 630 238-0275
  Bensenville *(G-1832)*
Artistic Dental Studio Inc ................... E ...... 630 679-8686
  Bolingbrook *(G-2278)*
Dental Arts Laboratories Inc .............. G ...... 309 342-3117
  Galesburg *(G-10745)*
Dental Laboratory Inc ........................ E ...... 630 262-3700
  Geneva *(G-10823)*
J L Lawrence & Co ............................ G ...... 217 235-3622
  Mattoon *(G-14394)*
Lmpl Management Corporation ........... G ...... 708 636-2443
  Oak Lawn *(G-16631)*
Martin Dental Laboratory Inc .............. F ...... 708 597-8880
  Lockport *(G-13731)*
Oratech Inc ....................................... E ...... 217 793-2735
  Springfield *(G-20493)*
Tanaka Dental Enterprises Inc ............ F ...... 847 679-1610
  Skokie *(G-20099)*
Underwood Dental Laboratories .......... F ...... 217 398-0090
  Champaign *(G-3551)*

### LABORATORIES: Dental, Artificial Teeth Production
Odl Inc .............................................. D ...... 815 434-0655
  Ottawa *(G-16974)*

### LABORATORIES: Dental, Crown & Bridge Production
Bennett Technologies Inc ................... F ...... 708 389-9501
  Tinley Park *(G-20897)*
Dental Crafts Lab Inc ......................... G ...... 815 872-3221
  Princeton *(G-17746)*
Mandis Dental Laboratory ................... G ...... 618 345-3777
  Collinsville *(G-7334)*

### LABORATORIES: Dental, Denture Production
Fred Pigg Dental Lab .......................... G ...... 618 439-6829
  Benton *(G-2028)*

### LABORATORIES: Electronic Research
Emac Inc ........................................... E ...... 618 529-4525
  Carbondale *(G-3006)*
Imagineering Inc ................................ E ...... 847 806-0003
  Elk Grove Village *(G-9541)*
Spectrum Cos International ................ G ...... 630 879-8008
  Batavia *(G-1497)*
Tech Star Design and Mfg .................. F ...... 847 290-8676
  Elk Grove Village *(G-9771)*

### LABORATORIES: Medical
African American Ctr For Hnb ............. D ...... 618 549-3965
  Park Forest *(G-17168)*
Biomerieux Inc .................................. E ...... 630 628-6055
  Lombard *(G-13771)*

### LABORATORIES: Neurological
Naurex Inc ........................................ G ...... 847 871-0377
  Evanston *(G-10078)*

### LABORATORIES: Noncommercial Research
Elliot Institute For Social SC .............. G ...... 217 525-8202
  Springfield *(G-20434)*

### LABORATORIES: Physical Research, Commercial
Abbott Laboratories ........................... C ...... 847 937-6100
  North Chicago *(G-16161)*
Abbott Products Inc .......................... B ...... 847 937-6100
  Abbott Park *(G-7)*
Associate General Labs Inc ................ G ...... 847 678-2717
  Franklin Park *(G-10404)*
Blue Pearl Stone Tech LLC ................ G ...... 708 698-5700
  La Grange *(G-12726)*
Cabot Microelectronics Corp .............. C ...... 630 375-6631
  Aurora *(G-979)*
Chicago Dscovery Solutions LLC ........ G ...... 815 609-2071
  Plainfield *(G-17586)*
Circom Inc ........................................ E ...... 630 595-4460
  Bensenville *(G-1859)*
Dawes LLC ........................................ F ...... 847 577-2020
  Arlington Heights *(G-745)*
DSM Desotech Inc ............................. G ...... 847 697-0400
  Elgin *(G-9013)*
Elona Biotechnologies Inc .................. F ...... 317 865-4770
  Chicago *(G-4735)*
Epir Technologies Inc ........................ G ...... 630 771-0203
  Bolingbrook *(G-2307)*
Firefly International Enrgy Co ............ G ...... 781 937-0619
  Peoria *(G-17361)*
Genesis Electric & Tech Inc ............... G ...... 847 258-5218
  Elk Grove Village *(G-9498)*
Honeywell International Inc ............... D ...... 847 797-4000
  Arlington Heights *(G-768)*
Illinois Foundation Seeds Inc ............. F ...... 217 485-6420
  Tolono *(G-20971)*
Incon Processing LLC ........................ E ...... 630 305-8556
  Batavia *(G-1456)*
INX International Ink Co .................... E ...... 630 681-7100
  West Chicago *(G-21725)*
Norfolk Medical Products Inc ............. F ...... 847 674-7075
  Skokie *(G-20046)*
Pharmasyn Inc ................................... G ...... 847 752-8405
  Libertyville *(G-13367)*
Provisur Technologies ........................ G ...... 312 284-4698
  Chicago *(G-6219)*
R & D Clark Ltd ................................. G ...... 847 749-2061
  Arlington Heights *(G-825)*
Silicon Control Inc ............................ G ...... 847 215-7947
  Deerfield *(G-8054)*
Starfire Industries LLC ....................... E ...... 217 721-4165
  Champaign *(G-3548)*
Swenson Technology Inc ................... F ...... 708 587-2300
  Monee *(G-15003)*
Systems & Electronics Inc ................. E ...... 847 228-0985
  Elk Grove Village *(G-9766)*
Tagore Technology Inc ...................... G ...... 847 790-3799
  Arlington Heights *(G-851)*
Websolutions Technology Inc ............. E ...... 630 375-6833
  Aurora *(G-1095)*
Willims-Hyward Intl Ctings Inc ........... F ...... 708 458-0015
  Argo *(G-698)*

### LABORATORIES: Testing
Alloyweld Inspection Co Inc ............... E ...... 630 595-2145
  Bensenville *(G-1827)*
Lifewatch Services Inc ....................... B ...... 847 720-2100
  Rosemont *(G-19013)*

### LABORATORIES: Testing
Agrochem Inc .................................... F ...... 847 564-1304
  Northbrook *(G-16201)*
Alloyweld Inspection Co Inc ............... E ...... 630 595-2145
  Bensenville *(G-1827)*
Associate General Labs Inc ................ G ...... 847 678-2717
  Franklin Park *(G-10404)*
Biomerieux Inc .................................. G ...... 630 628-6055
  Lombard *(G-13771)*
Cemec Inc ........................................ G ...... 630 495-9696
  Downers Grove *(G-8405)*
Centurion Non Destructive Tstg ......... F ...... 630 736-5500
  Streamwood *(G-20648)*
Design Scientific Inc ......................... G ...... 616 582-5225
  Wilmette *(G-22251)*
FH Ayer Manufacturing Co ................. F ...... 708 755-0550
  Chicago Heights *(G-7097)*
Incon Processing LLC ........................ G ...... 630 305-8556
  Batavia *(G-1456)*
McNdt Pipeline Ltd ............................ G ...... 815 467-5200
  Channahon *(G-3579)*
Perten Instruments Inc ..................... E ...... 217 585-9440
  Springfield *(G-20503)*
Pharmaceutical Labs and Cons I ......... G ...... 630 359-3831
  Addison *(G-240)*
Professional Gem Sciences Inc ........... G ...... 312 920-1541
  Chicago *(G-6209)*
Sigenics Inc ...................................... F ...... 312 448-8000
  Chicago *(G-6506)*
Sonoscan Inc .................................... D ...... 847 437-6400
  Elk Grove Village *(G-9744)*
Standard Laboratories Inc .................. E ...... 618 539-5836
  Freeburg *(G-10642)*
Unified Solutions Corp ....................... E ...... 847 478-9100
  Arlington Heights *(G-861)*
Verson Enterprises Inc ...................... F ...... 847 364-2600
  Elk Grove Village *(G-9806)*

### LABORATORIES: Urinalysis
Colormetric Laboratories Inc .............. G ...... 847 803-3737
  Des Plaines *(G-8172)*

### LABORATORY APPARATUS & FURNITURE
Atlas Material Tstg Tech LLC .............. C ...... 773 327-4520
  Mount Prospect *(G-15311)*
B T Technology Inc ........................... G ...... 217 322-3768
  Rushville *(G-19090)*
Biosynergy Inc .................................. G ...... 847 956-0471
  Elk Grove Village *(G-9342)*
Blair Company ................................... G ...... 847 439-3980
  Elk Grove Village *(G-9343)*
Colormetric Laboratories Inc .............. G ...... 847 803-3737
  Des Plaines *(G-8172)*
David Martin ..................................... G ...... 217 564-2440
  Ivesdale *(G-12377)*
Gardner Denver Inc ........................... E ...... 847 676-8800
  Niles *(G-15981)*
K H Steuernagel Technical Ltg ............ G ...... 773 327-4520
  Chicago *(G-5343)*
L A M Inc De ..................................... G ...... 630 860-9700
  Wood Dale *(G-22388)*
Laboratory Builders Inc ..................... G ...... 630 598-0216
  Burr Ridge *(G-2862)*
Leica Microsystems Inc ..................... C ...... 847 405-0123
  Buffalo Grove *(G-2726)*
Ludwig Medical Inc ............................ G ...... 217 342-6570
  Effingham *(G-8844)*
Modernfold Doors of Chicago ............. G ...... 630 654-4560
  Westmont *(G-21908)*
Norman P Moeller ............................. G ...... 847 991-3933
  Lake Barrington *(G-12821)*
OBrien Scntfic GL Blowing LLC .......... G ...... 217 762-3636
  Monticello *(G-15082)*
Preston Industries Inc ...................... C ...... 847 647-2900
  Niles *(G-16022)*
Scientific Instruments Inc ................. G ...... 847 679-1242
  Skokie *(G-20082)*
Sirius Automation Inc ....................... F ...... 847 607-9378
  Buffalo Grove *(G-2773)*
Wrightwood Technologies Inc ............ G ...... 312 238-9512
  Chicago *(G-7037)*

### LABORATORY APPARATUS & FURNITURE: Worktables
Suburban Surgical Co ........................ G ...... 847 537-9320
  Wheeling *(G-22159)*

### LABORATORY APPARATUS, EXC HEATING & MEASURING
Celinco Inc ....................................... G ...... 815 964-2256
  Rockford *(G-18301)*
Innovative Projects Lab Inc ............... G ...... 847 605-2125
  Schaumburg *(G-19569)*

### LABORATORY APPARATUS: Bunsen Burners
Humboldt Mfg Co ............................... E ...... 708 456-6300
  Elgin *(G-9068)*

### LABORATORY APPARATUS: Calibration Tapes, Phy Testing Mach
Florida Metrology LLC ........................ F ...... 630 833-3800
  Villa Park *(G-21252)*
Hcs Hahn Calibration Service ............. G ...... 847 567-2500
  Lincolnshire *(G-13453)*
Novel Products Inc ............................ G ...... 815 624-4888
  Rockton *(G-18699)*

## LABORATORY APPARATUS: Calorimeters

Parr Instrument Company ............... D .... 309 762-7716
  Moline *(G-14961)*

## LABORATORY APPARATUS: Evaporation

Swenson Technology Inc ............... F ...... 708 587-2300
  Monee *(G-15003)*

## LABORATORY APPARATUS: Freezers

Preferred Freezer Services of ........ F ...... 773 254-9500
  Chicago *(G-6174)*

## LABORATORY APPARATUS: Laser Beam Alignment Device

Amoco Technology Company (del) .... C .... 312 861-6000
  Chicago *(G-3892)*
Scanlab America Inc .......................... G ...... 630 797-2044
  Saint Charles *(G-19260)*

## LABORATORY APPARATUS: Metal Periphery Dir Rdg Diameter Tape

R L Kolbi Company .......................... F ...... 847 506-1440
  Arlington Heights *(G-826)*

## LABORATORY APPARATUS: Sample Preparation Apparatus

Illinois Tool Works Inc ...................... C ...... 847 295-6500
  Lake Bluff *(G-12850)*

## LABORATORY APPARATUS: Shakers & Stirrers

Heidolph NA LLC ............................... F ...... 224 265-9600
  Elk Grove Village *(G-9520)*

## LABORATORY CHEMICALS: Organic

Akzo Nobel Surfc Chemistry LLC ..... F ...... 312 544-7000
  Chicago *(G-3794)*
Elona Biotechnologies Inc ................ F ...... 317 865-4770
  Chicago *(G-4735)*
Franmar Chemical .............................. G ...... 309 829-5952
  Bloomington *(G-2166)*
Numat Technologies Inc ................... G ...... 301 233-5329
  Skokie *(G-20047)*
Tempil Inc ........................................... G ...... 908 757-8300
  Elk Grove Village *(G-9775)*

## LABORATORY EQPT, EXC MEDICAL: Wholesalers

Blair Company ................................... G ...... 847 439-3980
  Elk Grove Village *(G-9343)*
Fisher Scientific Company LLC ......... C ...... 412 490-8300
  Hanover Park *(G-11580)*
Flinn Scientific Inc ............................. C ...... 800 452-1261
  Batavia *(G-1449)*
Hugh Courtright & Co Ltd ................. F ...... 708 534-8400
  Monee *(G-14997)*
Laboratory Media Corporation ......... F ...... 630 897-8000
  Montgomery *(G-15053)*

## LABORATORY EQPT: Clinical Instruments Exc Medical

Dual Mfg Co Inc ................................. F ...... 773 267-4457
  Franklin Park *(G-10460)*
Intermerican Clinical Svcs Inc .......... G ...... 773 252-1147
  Chicago *(G-5217)*
Perez Health Incorporated ................ G ...... 708 788-0101
  Berwyn *(G-2072)*

## LABORATORY EQPT: Incubators

1 Federal Supply Source Inc ............. G ...... 708 964-2222
  Steger *(G-20565)*

## LABORATORY EQPT: Measuring

Perten Instruments Inc ..................... E ...... 217 585-9440
  Springfield *(G-20503)*
Supertek Scientific LLC ..................... G ...... 630 345-3450
  Villa Park *(G-21287)*

## LABORATORY EQPT: Sterilizers

Amity Hospital Services Inc ............. G ...... 708 206-3970
  Country Club Hills *(G-7403)*
Reviss Services Inc ........................... G ...... 847 680-4522
  Vernon Hills *(G-21192)*
Sterigenics US LLC ............................ E ...... 847 855-0727
  Gurnee *(G-11508)*
Sterigenics US LLC ............................ E
  Willowbrook *(G-22233)*

## LADDER & WORKSTAND COMBINATION ASSEMBLIES: Metal

Ojedas Welding Co ............................ G ...... 708 595-3799
  Maywood *(G-14434)*

## LADDERS: Metal

Innerweld Cover Co ........................... F ...... 847 497-3009
  Mundelein *(G-15511)*
Louisville Ladder Inc ......................... G ...... 309 692-1895
  Peoria *(G-17402)*
Vulcan Ladder Usa LLC ..................... G ...... 847 526-6321
  Island Lake *(G-12220)*

## LADDERS: Portable, Metal

Werner Co ........................................... E ...... 815 459-6020
  Crystal Lake *(G-7676)*

## LAMINATED PLASTICS: Plate, Sheet, Rod & Tubes

Accurate Partitions Corp .................. G ...... 708 442-6801
  Mc Cook *(G-14444)*
Ameriscan Designs Inc ..................... D ...... 773 542-1291
  Chicago *(G-3886)*
C Line Products Inc ........................... D ...... 847 827-6661
  Mount Prospect *(G-15315)*
Card Dynamix LLC ............................. C ...... 630 685-4060
  Romeoville *(G-18806)*
Carl Gorr Printing Co ........................ G ...... 815 338-3191
  Woodstock *(G-22549)*
Catalina Coating & Plas Inc .............. F ...... 847 806-1340
  Elk Grove Village *(G-9358)*
CFC International Inc ........................ G ...... 708 891-3456
  Chicago Heights *(G-7086)*
Coilform Company ............................ G ...... 630 232-8000
  Geneva *(G-10820)*
Cortube Products Co ........................ G ...... 708 429-6700
  Tinley Park *(G-20903)*
Custom Films Inc .............................. F ...... 217 826-2326
  Marshall *(G-14320)*
Dana Plastic Container Corp ............ E ...... 630 529-7878
  Roselle *(G-18939)*
Designed Plastics Inc ....................... E ...... 630 694-7300
  Bensenville *(G-1879)*
E-Jay Plastics Co .............................. F ...... 630 543-4000
  Addison *(G-104)*
Glazed Structures Inc ....................... F ...... 847 223-4560
  Grayslake *(G-11341)*
James Injection Molding Co ............. E ...... 847 564-3820
  Northbrook *(G-16283)*
John Maneely Company .................... C ...... 773 254-0617
  Chicago *(G-5316)*
Lakone Company ............................... D ...... 630 892-4251
  Montgomery *(G-15055)*
Olon Industries Inc (us) .................... E ...... 630 232-4705
  Geneva *(G-10858)*
Photo Techniques Corp .................... E ...... 630 690-9360
  Carol Stream *(G-3213)*
Pro Glass Corporation ...................... G ...... 630 553-3141
  Bristol *(G-2549)*
R & R Custom Cabinet Making ......... G ...... 847 358-6188
  Palatine *(G-17065)*
Richard Tindall ................................... 618 433-8107
  Godfrey *(G-11233)*
T J Kellogg Inc .................................. G ...... 815 969-0524
  Rockford *(G-18640)*
Tempel Steel Company ..................... A ...... 773 250-8000
  Chicago *(G-6698)*
Upm Raflatac Inc .............................. C ...... 815 285-6100
  Dixon *(G-8357)*

## LAMINATING MATERIALS

D & K Group Inc ................................ E ...... 847 956-0160
  Elk Grove Village *(G-9409)*
D & K International Inc ..................... E ...... 847 439-3423
  Elk Grove Village *(G-9410)*

## LAMINATING SVCS

Bellen Container Corporation .......... E ...... 847 741-5600
  Elgin *(G-8964)*
GM Laminating & Mounting Corp .... G ...... 630 941-7979
  Elmhurst *(G-9878)*
Identatronics Inc ................................ E ...... 847 437-2654
  Crystal Lake *(G-7591)*
Sign Identity Inc ................................ G ...... 630 942-1400
  Glen Ellyn *(G-10989)*

## LAMP & LIGHT BULBS & TUBES

Aco Inc ............................................... E ...... 773 774-5200
  Chicago *(G-3735)*
Advanced Micro Lites Inc ................. G ...... 630 365-5450
  Elburn *(G-8874)*
Advanced Strobe Products Inc ........ D ...... 708 867-3100
  Chicago *(G-3772)*
American Light Bulb Mfg Inc ........... D ...... 843 464-0755
  Schaumburg *(G-19439)*
Cec Industries Ltd ............................ E ...... 847 821-1199
  Lincolnshire *(G-13434)*
Dontech Industries Inc ..................... F ...... 847 428-8222
  Gilberts *(G-10917)*
Eden Park Illumination Inc ............... G ...... 217 403-1866
  Champaign *(G-3478)*
Keating of Chicago Inc .................... E ...... 815 569-2324
  Capron *(G-2996)*
Lampholders Assemblies Inc ........... G ...... 773 205-0005
  Chicago *(G-5453)*
Light Matrix Inc ................................. G ...... 847 590-0856
  Palatine *(G-17050)*
Mattson Lamp Plant .......................... G ...... 217 258-9390
  Mattoon *(G-14401)*
Modern Lighting Tech LLC ............... G ...... 312 624-9267
  Chicago *(G-5782)*
National Direct Lighting ................... E ...... 708 371-4950
  Alsip *(G-497)*
North American Lighting Inc ........... A ...... 618 548-6249
  Salem *(G-19340)*
Royal Haeger Lamp Co ..................... E ...... 309 837-9966
  Macomb *(G-14132)*
Universal Lighting Corporation ....... G ...... 773 927-2000
  Chicago *(G-6833)*

## LAMP BULBS & TUBES, ELEC: Lead-In Wires, From Purchased Wire

Anixter Inc ......................................... C ...... 800 323-8167
  Glenview *(G-11103)*
Bz Bearing & Power Inc .................... G ...... 877 850-3993
  Hickory Hills *(G-11767)*

## LAMP BULBS & TUBES, ELECTRIC: Electric Light

Acculight LLC .................................... G ...... 630 847-1000
  Elk Grove Village *(G-9260)*
Amglo Kemlite Laboratories Inc ...... D ...... 630 238-3031
  Bensenville *(G-1834)*

## LAMP BULBS & TUBES, ELECTRIC: For Specialized Applications

Santas Best ....................................... F ...... 847 459-3301
  Riverwoods *(G-18043)*

## LAMP BULBS & TUBES, ELECTRIC: Light, Complete

Orion Media Logistics Inc ................. G ...... 847 866-6215
  Evanston *(G-10084)*

## LAMP BULBS & TUBES, ELECTRIC: Photoflash & Photoflood

General Electric Company ............... C ...... 217 235-4081
  Mattoon *(G-14389)*

## LAMP BULBS & TUBES/PARTS, ELECTRIC: Generalized Applications

Malcolite Corporation ....................... D ...... 847 562-1350
  Deerfield *(G-8034)*
S A W Co ........................................... G ...... 630 678-5400
  Lombard *(G-13849)*

Employee Codes: A=Over 500 employees, B=251-500
C=101-250, D=51-100, E=20-50, F=10-19, G=3-9

# LAMP FRAMES: Wire

### LAMP FRAMES: Wire
Paramount Wire Specialties..............F....... 773 252-5636
  Chicago *(G-6080)*

### LAMP REPAIR & MOUNTING SVCS
Bellows Shoppe................................G....... 847 446-5533
  Winnetka *(G-22303)*

### LAMP SHADES: Metal
Lampshade Inc..................................F....... 773 522-2300
  Chicago *(G-5454)*

### LAMP STORES
Bellows Shoppe................................G....... 847 446-5533
  Winnetka *(G-22303)*
Rainbow Lighting...............................E....... 847 480-1136
  Northbrook *(G-16352)*
Smart Solar Inc.................................F....... 813 343-5770
  Libertyville *(G-13382)*

### LAMPS: Boudoir, Residential
Stone Lighting LLC...........................F....... 312 240-0400
  Flossmoor *(G-10230)*

### LAMPS: Incandescent, Filament
Aero-Tech Light Bulb Co..................F....... 847 534-6580
  Schaumburg *(G-19425)*
Comet Neon......................................G....... 630 668-6366
  Lombard *(G-13782)*
Radionic Hi-Tech Inc........................D....... 773 804-0100
  Chicago *(G-6281)*

### LAMPS: Table, Residential
Royal Haeger Lamp Co.....................E....... 309 837-9966
  Macomb *(G-14132)*

### LAMPS: Ultraviolet
AAA Press Specialists Inc................F....... 847 818-1100
  Arlington Heights *(G-701)*
Ddk Scientific Corporation................G....... 618 235-2849
  Belleville *(G-1623)*

### LAND SUBDIVISION & DEVELOPMENT
Creative Designs Kitc......................E....... 773 327-8400
  Chicago *(G-4497)*
Elmer L Larson L C..........................F....... 815 895-4837
  Sycamore *(G-20797)*
Jack Ruch Quality Homes Inc..........G....... 309 663-6595
  Bloomington *(G-2185)*
Plote Construction Inc.....................D....... 847 695-9300
  Hoffman Estates *(G-12036)*

### LANTERNS
Designed For Just For You..............G....... 309 221-2667
  Macomb *(G-14124)*

### LAPIDARY WORK: Jewel Cut, Drill, Polish, Recut/Setting
Edmund D Schmelzie & Sons..........G....... 312 782-7230
  Chicago *(G-4697)*

### LASER SYSTEMS & EQPT
Amt (additive Mfg Tech Inc..............G....... 847 258-4475
  Elk Grove Village *(G-9304)*
Domino Lasers Inc..........................E....... 847 855-1364
  Gurnee *(G-11442)*
Laser Energy Systems....................G....... 815 282-8200
  Loves Park *(G-13959)*
Novanta Inc.....................................G....... 781 266-5700
  Newton *(G-15945)*
Windy City Laser Service Inc..........G....... 773 995-0188
  Chicago *(G-6996)*

### LASERS: Welding, Drilling & Cutting Eqpt
Alliance Laser Sales Inc..................E....... 847 487-1945
  Wauconda *(G-21438)*
Allmetal Inc.....................................D....... 630 250-8090
  Itasca *(G-12225)*
Bystronic Inc...................................C....... 847 214-0300
  Elgin *(G-8974)*
Charlotte Dmg Inc............................G....... 630 227-3900
  Itasca *(G-12243)*

HK America Inc................................G....... 630 916-0200
  Lombard *(G-13809)*
O R Lasertechnology Inc.................F....... 847 593-5711
  Elk Grove Village *(G-9659)*
Presentation Studios Intl LLC...........F....... 312 733-8160
  Chicago *(G-6180)*
United Amercn Healthcare Corp.....F....... 313 393-4571
  Chicago *(G-6820)*

### LATH: Expanded Metal
Expanded Metal Products Corp........F....... 773 735-4500
  Chicago *(G-4795)*
Metalex Corporation.........................C....... 847 362-8300
  Libertyville *(G-13354)*

### LATHES
T&J Turning Inc................................G....... 309 738-8762
  Colona *(G-7349)*
Trigon International Corp..................E....... 630 978-9990
  Aurora *(G-1089)*

### LAUNDRY & GARMENT SVCS, NEC: Diapers
Bottoms Up Inc.................................G....... 847 336-0040
  Waukegan *(G-21530)*

### LAUNDRY & GARMENT SVCS, NEC: Garment Making, Alter & Repair
Igar Bridal Inc..................................G....... 224 318-2337
  Arlington Heights *(G-772)*
Sewing Salon...................................G....... 217 345-3886
  Charleston *(G-3611)*

### LAUNDRY & GARMENT SVCS: Dressmaking, Matl Owned By Customer
Paul Sisti........................................G....... 773 472-5615
  Chicago *(G-6091)*

### LAUNDRY EQPT: Commercial
Jetin Systems Inc............................F....... 815 726-4686
  Joliet *(G-12522)*
L T P LLC........................................C....... 815 723-9400
  Joliet *(G-12530)*
New Spin Cycle................................G....... 773 952-7490
  Chicago *(G-5895)*
Qualitex Company............................F....... 773 506-8112
  Chicago *(G-6244)*
Ross and White Company................F....... 847 516-3900
  Cary *(G-3369)*

### LAUNDRY EQPT: Household
C Streeter Enterprise.......................G....... 773 858-4388
  Chicago *(G-4205)*
Coin Macke Laundry........................G....... 847 459-1109
  Wheeling *(G-22029)*
Iron-A-Way LLC...............................E....... 309 266-7232
  Morton *(G-15161)*

### LAWN & GARDEN EQPT
A Yard Materials Co.........................G....... 815 385-4560
  Mchenry *(G-14474)*
Bartonville Equipment Rental...........G....... 309 633-0227
  Bartonville *(G-1392)*
Beall Manufacturing Inc...................E....... 618 259-8154
  East Alton *(G-8599)*
Coleman Lawn Equipment Inc.........G....... 618 529-0181
  Carbondale *(G-3003)*
Contempo Industries Inc..................D....... 815 337-6267
  Woodstock *(G-22553)*
Echo Incorporated............................A....... 847 540-8400
  Lake Zurich *(G-13064)*
Echo Incorporated............................E....... 847 540-3500
  Lake Zurich *(G-13065)*
Fiskars Brands Inc..........................B....... 309 690-2200
  Peoria *(G-17363)*
Grower Equipment & Supply Co.....F....... 847 223-3100
  Hainesville *(G-11523)*
Hipro Manufacturing Inc..................E....... 815 432-5271
  Watseka *(G-21418)*
Hyponex Corporation.......................F....... 815 772-2167
  Morrison *(G-15144)*
Jeffs Small Engine Inc....................G....... 630 904-6840
  Plainfield *(G-17609)*
Lutz Corp.........................................G....... 800 203-7740
  Normal *(G-16075)*

Oldcastle Lawn & Garden Inc........F....... 618 274-1222
  East Saint Louis *(G-8763)*
Precision Products Inc..................C....... 217 735-1590
  Lincoln *(G-13418)*
Ryan Manufacturing Inc................G....... 815 695-5310
  Newark *(G-15934)*
Sawier..............................................E....... 630 297-8588
  Downers Grove *(G-8519)*
Valley View Industries Hc Inc.........E....... 800 323-9369
  Crestwood *(G-7507)*
Vaughan & Bushnell Mfg Co..........F....... 815 648-2446
  Hebron *(G-11730)*
Zuma Corporation............................G....... 815 288-7269
  Dixon *(G-8361)*

### LAWN & GARDEN EQPT STORES
Gentry Small Engine Repair............G....... 217 849-3378
  Toledo *(G-20963)*
Wise Equipment & Rentals Inc.......F....... 847 895-5555
  Schaumburg *(G-19790)*

### LAWN & GARDEN EQPT: Blowers & Vacuums
David Taylor....................................E....... 217 222-6480
  Quincy *(G-17819)*
Tuthill Corporation...........................E....... 630 382-4900
  Burr Ridge *(G-2889)*

### LAWN & GARDEN EQPT: Edgers
Alpha Omega Profile Extrusion........F....... 847 956-8777
  Elk Grove Village *(G-9290)*

### LAWN & GARDEN EQPT: Grass Catchers, Lawn Mower
M Martinez Inc.................................G....... 847 740-6364
  Round Lake Heights *(G-19081)*

### LAWN & GARDEN EQPT: Lawnmowers, Residential, Hand Or Power
Kunz Engineering Inc......................G....... 815 539-6954
  Mendota *(G-14723)*

### LAWN & GARDEN EQPT: Tractors & Eqpt
Deere & Company............................A....... 309 765-8000
  Moline *(G-14925)*
John Deere AG Holdings Inc..........G....... 309 765-8000
  Moline *(G-14946)*

### LAWN MOWER REPAIR SHOP
Lakenburges Motor Co....................G....... 618 523-4231
  Germantown *(G-10893)*
Outdoor Power Inc...........................F....... 217 228-9890
  Quincy *(G-17865)*
Peoria Midwest Equipment Inc.......G....... 309 454-6800
  Normal *(G-16083)*
Wise Equipment & Rentals Inc.......F....... 847 895-5555
  Schaumburg *(G-19790)*

### LEAD & ZINC
Mayco Manufacturing LLC...............E....... 618 451-4400
  Granite City *(G-11292)*

### LEAD & ZINC
Big River Zinc Corporation..............G....... 618 274-5000
  Sauget *(G-19382)*
Mayco-Granite City Inc...................E....... 618 451-4400
  Granite City *(G-11293)*

### LEAD & ZINC ORES
Big River Zinc Corporation..............G....... 618 274-5000
  Sauget *(G-19382)*
Midland Coal Company....................G....... 309 362-2795
  Trivoli *(G-21000)*

### LEAD ORE MINING
Ebers Drilling Co..............................G....... 618 826-5398
  Chester *(G-3655)*

### LEAD PENCILS & ART GOODS
Alexander Manufacturing Co...........D....... 309 728-2224
  Towanda *(G-20978)*

# PRODUCT SECTION

Chicago Ink & Research Co Inc..............G....... 847 395-1078
  Antioch *(G-628)*
Cushing and Company........................E....... 312 266-8228
  Chicago *(G-4518)*
Hobbico Inc.................................E....... 217 367-2707
  Urbana *(G-21091)*
James Howard Co............................G....... 815 497-2831
  Compton *(G-7366)*
Moldworks Inc..............................G....... 815 520-8819
  Roscoe *(G-18908)*
Sanford LP..................................A....... 770 418-7000
  Downers Grove *(G-8518)*

## LEASING & RENTAL SVCS: Computer Hardware, Exc Finance

Datasis Corporation........................F....... 847 427-0909
  Elk Grove Village *(G-9417)*

## LEASING & RENTAL SVCS: Cranes & Aerial Lift Eqpt

Bendsen Signs & Graphics Inc..............F....... 217 877-2345
  Decatur *(G-7845)*
Coast Crane Company.......................C....... 847 215-6500
  Buffalo Grove *(G-2674)*
Floyd Steel Erectors Inc..................F....... 630 238-8383
  Wood Dale *(G-22369)*
Joe Hatzer & Son Inc......................G....... 815 673-5571
  Streator *(G-20692)*

## LEASING & RENTAL: Boats & Ships

Outback USA Inc............................G....... 863 699-2220
  Saint Charles *(G-19231)*

## LEASING & RENTAL: Computers & Eqpt

Essannay Show It Inc......................G....... 312 733-5511
  Chicago *(G-4778)*
Information Builders Inc..................E....... 630 971-6700
  Schaumburg *(G-19565)*
Pinehurst Bus Solutions Corp..............G....... 630 842-6155
  Winfield *(G-22290)*

## LEASING & RENTAL: Construction & Mining Eqpt

Altorfer Power Systems....................G....... 309 697-1234
  Bartonville *(G-1391)*
L & N Structures Inc......................E....... 815 426-2164
  Herscher *(G-11759)*
Lanco International Inc...................B....... 708 596-5200
  Hazel Crest *(G-11709)*
Lee Jensen Sales Co Inc...................E....... 815 459-0929
  Crystal Lake *(G-7602)*
Midwest Cnstr Svcs Inc Peoria.............F....... 309 697-1000
  Bartonville *(G-1397)*
Patrick Holdings Inc......................F....... 815 874-5300
  Rockford *(G-18531)*
Rotec Industries Inc......................D....... 630 279-3300
  Hampshire *(G-11561)*
USA Hoist Company Inc.....................E....... 815 740-1890
  Crest Hill *(G-7470)*

## LEASING & RENTAL: Medical Machinery & Eqpt

Hill-Rom Holdings Inc.....................B....... 312 819-7200
  Chicago *(G-5088)*

## LEASING & RENTAL: Mobile Home Sites

Littleson Inc..............................G....... 815 968-8349
  Rockford *(G-18471)*
Southmoor Estates Inc.....................G....... 815 756-1299
  Dekalb *(G-8121)*

## LEASING & RENTAL: Office Machines & Eqpt

Nexus Supply Consortium Inc...............G....... 630 649-2868
  Bolingbrook *(G-2353)*

## LEASING & RENTAL: Trucks, Without Drivers

City Subn Auto Svc Goodyear...............G....... 773 355-5550
  Chicago *(G-4389)*
Doll Furniture Co Inc.....................G....... 309 452-2606
  Normal *(G-16070)*
Grace Auto Body Frame.....................G....... 847 963-1234
  Palatine *(G-17030)*

Grs Holding LLC............................G....... 630 355-1660
  Naperville *(G-15666)*
Pauls Mc Culloch Sales....................G....... 217 323-2159
  Beardstown *(G-1526)*
Printing Works Inc........................G....... 847 860-1920
  Elk Grove Village *(G-9698)*
Service Auto Supply........................F....... 309 444-9704
  Washington *(G-21392)*

## LEASING: Passenger Car

Lgb Industries.............................G....... 847 639-1691
  Cary *(G-3357)*

## LEASING: Residential Buildings

Anns Printing & Copying Co................G....... 618 656-6878
  Edwardsville *(G-8788)*

## LEASING: Shipping Container

Mobile Mini Inc............................E....... 708 297-2004
  Calumet Park *(G-2963)*

## LEATHER GOODS, EXC FOOTWEAR, GLOVES, LUGGAGE/BELTING, WHOL

American Trade & Coml Svc LLC.............F....... 202 910-8808
  Chicago *(G-3879)*
Keleen Leathers Inc.......................F....... 630 590-5300
  Westmont *(G-21898)*
Rico Industries Inc.......................D....... 312 427-0313
  Niles *(G-16028)*

## LEATHER GOODS: Boxes

American Trade & Coml Svc LLC.............F....... 202 910-8808
  Chicago *(G-3879)*

## LEATHER GOODS: Cases

A W Enterprises Inc.......................E....... 708 458-8989
  Bedford Park *(G-1531)*
Hertzberg Ernst & Sons....................E....... 773 525-3518
  Chicago *(G-5082)*

## LEATHER GOODS: Embossed

Hertzberg Ernst & Sons....................E....... 773 525-3518
  Chicago *(G-5082)*

## LEATHER GOODS: Garments

Boston Leather Inc........................E....... 815 622-1635
  Sterling *(G-20585)*

## LEATHER GOODS: Harnesses Or Harness Parts

Choice Usa LLC.............................G....... 847 428-2252
  Gilberts *(G-10915)*
Mast Harness Shop.........................E....... 217 543-3463
  Campbell Hill *(G-2976)*

## LEATHER GOODS: Money Holders

Toshware Inc...............................E....... 217 896-2437
  Monticello *(G-15087)*

## LEATHER GOODS: NEC

Cocajo Blades & Leather...................G....... 217 370-6634
  Franklin *(G-10378)*
Elite Manufacturer LLC....................G....... 779 777-3857
  Streamwood *(G-20653)*

## LEATHER GOODS: Personal

Medacta Usa Inc............................D....... 312 878-2381
  Chicago *(G-5675)*
Plasticrest Products Inc..................F....... 773 826-2163
  Chicago *(G-6136)*
Randa Accessories Lea Gds LLC.............D....... 847 292-8300
  Rosemont *(G-19026)*
World Richman Mfg Corp....................F....... 847 468-8898
  Elgin *(G-9239)*

## LEATHER GOODS: Safety Belts

W W Belt Inc...............................G....... 708 788-1855
  Berwyn *(G-2078)*

## LEATHER GOODS: Sewing Cases

Elegant Acquisition LLC...................D....... 708 652-3400
  Cicero *(G-7194)*

## LEATHER GOODS: Wallets

J-Industries Inc...........................F....... 815 654-0055
  Loves Park *(G-13949)*
Loren Girovich.............................G....... 773 334-1444
  Chicago *(G-5541)*
Rico Industries Inc.......................D....... 312 427-0313
  Niles *(G-16028)*

## LEATHER TANNING & FINISHING

Angelo Bruni...............................G....... 773 754-5422
  Aurora *(G-957)*
Darling Ingredients Inc...................E....... 618 271-8190
  National Stock Yards *(G-15850)*
Excelled Sheepskin & Lea Coat.............C....... 309 852-3341
  Kewanee *(G-12682)*
Tyson Fresh Meats Inc.....................F....... 847 836-5550
  Elgin *(G-9218)*
Zoes Mfgco LLC.............................F....... 312 666-4018
  Chicago *(G-7071)*

## LEATHER: Accessory Prdts

Brighton Collectibles LLC.................E....... 847 674-6719
  Skokie *(G-19971)*

## LEATHER: Artificial

Phoenix Leather Goods LLC.................G....... 815 267-3926
  Plainfield *(G-17639)*

## LEATHER: Bag

Unidex Packaging LLC......................F....... 630 735-7040
  Hanover Park *(G-11592)*

## LEATHER: Case

Sukie Group Inc............................F....... 773 521-1800
  Chicago *(G-6613)*

## LEATHER: Rawhide

United Rawhide Mfg Co.....................G....... 847 692-2791
  Park Ridge *(G-17228)*

## LEGAL & TAX SVCS

CCH Incorporated...........................A....... 847 267-7000
  Riverwoods *(G-18037)*

## LEGAL COUNSEL & PROSECUTION: Attorney General's Office

State Attorney Appellate..................G....... 217 782-3397
  Springfield *(G-20536)*

## LEGAL OFFICES & SVCS

Alexeter Technologies LLC.................F....... 847 419-1507
  Wheeling *(G-22000)*
American Bar Foundation...................D....... 312 988-6500
  Chicago *(G-3852)*
C M S Publishing Inc......................G....... 708 839-9201
  Willow Springs *(G-22193)*
Education Partners Project Ltd............G....... 773 675-6643
  Chicago *(G-4701)*
Inside Council.............................F....... 312 654-3500
  Chicago *(G-5204)*
State of Illinois..........................C....... 312 836-9500
  Chicago *(G-6578)*

## LEGAL SVCS: Taxation Law

Vernon Township Offices...................E....... 847 634-4600
  Buffalo Grove *(G-2789)*

## LENS COATING: Ophthalmic

Opticote Inc...............................E....... 847 678-8900
  Franklin Park *(G-10544)*

## LENSES: Plastic, Exc Optical

Pactiv LLC.................................C....... 847 451-1480
  Franklin Park *(G-10545)*

## LETTERS: Cardboard, Die-Cut, Made From Purchased Materials

Acco Brands USA LLC .................................D....... 847 272-3700
  Lincolnshire *(G-13423)*
Mich Enterprises Inc....................................F....... 630 616-9000
  Wood Dale *(G-22399)*

## LICENSE TAGS: Automobile, Stamped Metal

10 4 Irp Inc .....................................................G....... 708 485-1040
  Brookfield *(G-2621)*
Aable License Consultants ......................G....... 708 836-1235
  Westchester *(G-21827)*
City of Danville ............................................G....... 217 442-1564
  Tilton *(G-20879)*
Headly Manufacturing Co ..........................D....... 708 338-0800
  Broadview *(G-2584)*
S & S Keytax Inc..........................................F....... 708 656-9221
  Chicago *(G-6421)*
Secretary of State Illinois .........................G....... 217 466-5220
  Paris *(G-17161)*
Secretary of State Illinois .........................G....... 217 782-4850
  Springfield *(G-20520)*
Secretary of State Illinois .........................G....... 708 388-9199
  Midlothian *(G-14768)*
Secretary of State Illinois .........................G....... 217 243-4327
  Jacksonville *(G-12414)*
Secretary of State Illinois .........................F....... 773 660-4963
  Chicago *(G-6469)*
Steibel License Service ............................G....... 618 233-7555
  Swansea *(G-20783)*

## LIGHTERS, CIGARETTE & CIGAR, WHOLESALE

Sarj Kalidas LLC .........................................D....... 708 865-9134
  Chicago *(G-6446)*

## LIGHTING EQPT: Flashlights

First Alert Inc ..............................................G....... 630 499-3295
  Aurora *(G-1009)*
First-Light Usa LLC ....................................F....... 217 687-4048
  Seymour *(G-19897)*
Press A Light Corporation ........................F....... 630 231-6566
  West Chicago *(G-21760)*
Promier Products Inc .................................F....... 815 223-3393
  Peru *(G-17524)*

## LIGHTING EQPT: Locomotive & Railroad Car Lights

Progress Rail Locomotive Inc ..................A....... 800 255-5355
  Mc Cook *(G-14456)*

## LIGHTING EQPT: Motor Vehicle

Federal Signal Corporation ......................D....... 630 954-2000
  Oak Brook *(G-16510)*
L & T Services Inc ......................................G....... 815 397-6260
  Rockford *(G-18458)*
Tiger Accessory Group LLC .....................G....... 847 821-9630
  Long Grove *(G-13902)*

## LIGHTING EQPT: Motor Vehicle, Flasher Lights

Tool Automation Enterprises ....................G....... 708 799-6847
  East Hazel Crest *(G-8666)*

## LIGHTING EQPT: Motor Vehicle, NEC

North American Lighting Inc....................A....... 217 465-6600
  Paris *(G-17155)*
North American Lighting Inc....................A....... 618 548-6249
  Salem *(G-19340)*
North American Lighting Inc....................B....... 618 662-4483
  Flora *(G-10212)*
Tri-Lite Inc ....................................................E....... 773 384-7765
  Chicago *(G-6770)*

## LIGHTING EQPT: Motorcycle Lamps

River View Motor Sports Inc ....................G....... 309 467-4569
  Congerville *(G-7371)*

## LIGHTING EQPT: Outdoor

Afterdark Outdoor Lighting ......................G....... 708 243-1228
  Lockport *(G-13702)*
Lightscape Inc.............................................E....... 847 247-8800
  Libertyville *(G-13344)*
Schreder Lighting LLC ...............................E....... 847 621-5130
  Addison *(G-282)*

## LIGHTING EQPT: Reflectors, Metal, For Lighting Eqpt

Plastic Technologies Inc ...........................E....... 847 841-8610
  Elgin *(G-9140)*

## LIGHTING EQPT: Spotlights

Comcast Corporation .................................E....... 217 498-3274
  Quincy *(G-17815)*
Spotlight Youth Theater ............................G....... 847 516-2298
  Cary *(G-3373)*

## LIGHTING FIXTURES WHOLESALERS

American Holiday Lights Inc....................G....... 630 769-9999
  Woodridge *(G-22451)*
Arris Group Inc............................................E....... 630 281-3000
  Lisle *(G-13564)*
Dado Lighting LLC .....................................G....... 877 323-6584
  Western Springs *(G-21866)*
Eagle High Mast Ltg Co Inc .....................G....... 847 473-3800
  Waukegan *(G-21555)*
Good Earth Lighting Inc ...........................E....... 847 808-1133
  Mount Prospect *(G-15333)*
Lakeshore Lighting LLC ............................G....... 847 989-5843
  Mundelein *(G-15518)*
Lbl Lighting LLC ..........................................F....... 708 755-2100
  Skokie *(G-20028)*
Lumenart Ltd ...............................................G....... 773 254-0744
  Chicago *(G-5562)*
Microlite Corporation .................................G....... 630 876-0500
  West Chicago *(G-21742)*
Vaxcel International Co Ltd .....................E....... 630 260-0067
  Carol Stream *(G-3261)*

## LIGHTING FIXTURES, NEC

APL Engineered Materials Inc .................G....... 217 367-1340
  Urbana *(G-21070)*
Apolinski John ............................................G....... 847 696-3156
  Park Ridge *(G-17181)*
Big Beam Emergency Systems Inc........E....... 815 459-6100
  Crystal Lake *(G-7541)*
Bilt-Rite Metal Products Inc ....................E....... 815 495-2211
  Leland *(G-13218)*
Carmen Matthew LLC ...............................D....... 630 784-7500
  Elgin *(G-8984)*
Clements National Company ...................G....... 708 594-5890
  Broadview *(G-2569)*
Cyclops Industrial Inc................................G....... 815 962-1984
  Rockford *(G-18329)*
D2 Lighting LLC ..........................................G....... 708 243-9059
  La Grange Highlands *(G-12749)*
David Michael Productions ......................F....... 630 972-9640
  Woodridge *(G-22469)*
Duroweld Company Inc ............................G....... 847 680-3064
  Lake Bluff *(G-12841)*
Eagle High Mast Ltg Co Inc .....................G....... 847 473-3800
  Waukegan *(G-21555)*
Efficient Energy Lighting Inc ..................G....... 630 272-9388
  Sycamore *(G-20796)*
Elcast Manufacturing Inc .........................E....... 630 628-1992
  Addison *(G-107)*
Est Lighting Inc ...........................................E....... 847 612-1705
  Richmond *(G-17962)*
F G Lighting Inc...........................................G....... 847 295-0445
  Lake Bluff *(G-12842)*
Flex Lighting II LLC ....................................E....... 312 929-3488
  Chicago *(G-4857)*
Good Earth Lighting Inc ...........................E....... 847 808-1133
  Mount Prospect *(G-15333)*
Ilight Technologies Inc .............................F....... 312 876-8630
  Chicago *(G-5152)*
Illuminight Lighting LLC ...........................F....... 312 685-4448
  Highland Park *(G-11843)*
Intex Lighting LLC .....................................G....... 847 380-2027
  Schaumburg *(G-19575)*
Lakeshore Lighting LLC ............................G....... 847 989-5843
  Mundelein *(G-15518)*
Lampholders Assemblies Inc ..................G....... 773 205-0005
  Chicago *(G-5453)*
Lighting Innovations Inc ..........................E....... 630 889-8100
  Saint Charles *(G-19211)*
Lightitech LLC .............................................G....... 847 910-4177
  Chicago *(G-5504)*
Litetronics Technologies Inc ...................G....... 708 333-6707
  Chicago *(G-5518)*
Microlite Corporation .................................G....... 630 876-0500
  West Chicago *(G-21742)*
Midwest Sign & Lighting Inc ....................G....... 708 365-5555
  Country Club Hills *(G-7410)*
Musco Sports Lighting LLC .....................G....... 630 876-0500
  Batavia *(G-1473)*
North American Signal Co .......................E....... 847 537-8888
  Wheeling *(G-22108)*
Northern Lighting & Power Inc ................G....... 708 383-9926
  Oak Park *(G-16677)*
Poem Lighting Company ..........................G....... 847 395-1768
  Antioch *(G-651)*
Productworks LLC ......................................G....... 224 406-8810
  Northbrook *(G-16347)*
Radionic Hi-Tech Inc..................................D....... 773 804-0100
  Chicago *(G-6281)*
SC Lighting .................................................G....... 630 849-3384
  Schaumburg *(G-19720)*
Sensio America LLC ..................................F....... 877 501-5337
  Carol Stream *(G-3238)*
Shinetoo Lighting America LLC ..............G....... 877 957-7317
  Des Plaines *(G-8274)*
Spurt Inc ......................................................G....... 847 571-6497
  Northbrook *(G-16370)*
Square 1 Precision Ltg Inc ......................G....... 708 343-1500
  Melrose Park *(G-14695)*
Sternberg Lanterns Inc.............................C....... 847 588-3400
  Roselle *(G-18980)*
Track Master Inc ........................................G....... 815 675-6603
  Spring Grove *(G-20370)*
Transco Products Inc ................................G....... 815 672-2197
  Streator *(G-20709)*
Twin Supplies Ltd .......................................F....... 630 590-5138
  Oak Brook *(G-16566)*
Western Lighting Inc .................................F....... 847 451-7200
  Franklin Park *(G-10628)*

## LIGHTING FIXTURES: Airport

Tactical Lighting Systems Inc.................F....... 800 705-0518
  Addison *(G-306)*

## LIGHTING FIXTURES: Decorative Area

Boston Warehouse Trading Corp ...........G....... 630 992-5604
  Aurora *(G-972)*
Group O Inc .................................................D....... 309 736-8660
  Milan *(G-14788)*

## LIGHTING FIXTURES: Fluorescent, Commercial

Everlights Inc ..............................................F....... 773 734-9873
  Skokie *(G-19996)*
Louvers International Inc .........................E....... 630 782-9977
  Elmhurst *(G-9903)*
Morris Kurtzon Incorporated ...................E....... 773 277-2121
  Chicago *(G-5806)*
Wallace/Haskin Corp .................................G....... 630 789-2882
  Downers Grove *(G-8540)*
Western Lighting Inc .................................F....... 847 451-7200
  Franklin Park *(G-10628)*

## LIGHTING FIXTURES: Gas

Modern Home Products Corp ..................E....... 847 395-6556
  Antioch *(G-647)*

## LIGHTING FIXTURES: Indl & Commercial

555 International Inc .................................E....... 773 869-0555
  Chicago *(G-3671)*
555 International Inc .................................E....... 773 847-1400
  Chicago *(G-3670)*
Advanced Specialty Lighting ...................C....... 708 867-3140
  Harwood Heights *(G-11681)*
Afx Inc ..........................................................E....... 847 249-5970
  Waukegan *(G-21519)*
Amerilights Inc ............................................G....... 847 219-1476
  Bloomingdale *(G-2093)*
Appleton Grp LLC .......................................C....... 847 268-6000
  Rosemont *(G-18989)*
Astral Power Systems Inc ........................G....... 630 518-1741
  Aurora *(G-1112)*
Avtec Inc ......................................................F....... 618 337-7800
  East Saint Louis *(G-8742)*
Blackjack Lighting ......................................G....... 847 941-0588
  Buffalo Grove *(G-2666)*
Challenger Lighting Co Inc ......................E....... 847 717-4700
  Batavia *(G-1429)*

# PRODUCT SECTION

## LIMESTONE: Crushed & Broken

Conservation Tech III LLC .................. G ....... 847 559-5500
  Northbrook *(G-16231)*
Conservation Technology Ltd .............. D ....... 847 559-5500
  Northbrook *(G-16232)*
Contemprary Enrgy Slutions LLC ........ F ....... 630 768-3743
  Naperville *(G-15801)*
Cooper Lighting LLC .......................... D ....... 847 956-8400
  Elk Grove Village *(G-9394)*
Dado Lighting LLC .............................. G ....... 877 323-6584
  Western Springs *(G-21866)*
Dva Mayday Corporation .................... G ....... 847 848-7555
  Village of Lakewood *(G-21290)*
Eclipse Lighting Inc ............................. E ....... 847 260-0333
  Schiller Park *(G-19823)*
Esco Lighting Inc ................................ E ....... 773 427-7000
  Chicago *(G-4776)*
Eti Solid State Lighting Inc ................. E ....... 855 384-7754
  Vernon Hills *(G-21162)*
First Light Inc ..................................... G ....... 630 520-0017
  West Chicago *(G-21701)*
Fli Products LLC ................................. G ....... 630 520-0017
  West Chicago *(G-21702)*
Focal Point Lighting Inc ...................... C ....... 773 247-9494
  Chicago *(G-4866)*
Focal Point LLC ................................... C ....... 773 247-9494
  Chicago *(G-4867)*
Glamox Aqua Signal Corporation ....... F ....... 847 639-6412
  Cary *(G-3348)*
H A Framburg & Company .................. E ....... 708 547-5757
  Bellwood *(G-1708)*
Holiday Bright Lights Inc .................... G ....... 312 226-8281
  Chicago *(G-5099)*
Jarvis Corp ......................................... E ....... 800 363-1075
  Elk Grove Village *(G-9560)*
Lamp Co of America Inc ..................... G ....... 630 584-4001
  Saint Charles *(G-19207)*
Larentia Led LLC ................................. F ....... 312 291-9111
  Chicago *(G-5462)*
Leading Energy Designs Ltd ............... G ....... 815 382-8852
  Woodstock *(G-22583)*
Led Business Solutions LLC ............... F ....... 844 464-5337
  Downers Grove *(G-8474)*
Led Lighting Inc .................................. F ....... 847 412-4880
  Buffalo Grove *(G-2723)*
Lighting Design By Michael Ant .......... G ....... 708 289-4783
  Mokena *(G-14880)*
Neptun Light Inc ................................. G ....... 847 735-8330
  Lake Forest *(G-12929)*
New Star Custom Lighting Co ............ E ....... 773 254-7827
  Chicago *(G-5896)*
North Star Lighting LLC ...................... D ....... 708 681-4330
  Elmhurst *(G-9915)*
Paul D Metal Products Inc .................. D ....... 773 847-1400
  Chicago *(G-6090)*
Philips Lighting N Amer Corp .............. C ....... 800 825-5844
  Rosemont *(G-19022)*
Productworks LLC ............................... G ....... 224 406-8810
  Northbrook *(G-16347)*
Pure Lighting LLC ............................... G ....... 773 770-1130
  Chicago *(G-6229)*
Rainbow Lighting ................................ E ....... 847 480-1136
  Northbrook *(G-16352)*
Rgb Lights Inc .................................... F ....... 312 421-6080
  Chicago *(G-6346)*
S-P Products Inc ................................. F ....... 847 593-8595
  Elk Grove Village *(G-9725)*
Security Lighting Systems Inc ............ E ....... 800 544-4848
  Rolling Meadows *(G-18778)*
Square 1 Precision Ltg Inc ................. G ....... 708 343-1500
  Melrose Park *(G-14695)*
Sustanble Sltions Amer Led LLC ........ F ....... 866 323-3494
  Chicago *(G-6644)*
Tri-Lite Inc ........................................... E ....... 773 384-7765
  Chicago *(G-6770)*
Twin Supplies Ltd ................................ F ....... 630 590-5138
  Oak Brook *(G-16566)*
Waldmann Lighting Company ............. E ....... 847 520-1060
  Wheeling *(G-22180)*

### LIGHTING FIXTURES: Marine

Glamox Aqua Signal Corporation ........ F ....... 847 639-6412
  Cary *(G-3348)*

### LIGHTING FIXTURES: Motor Vehicle

Elc Industries Corp ............................. C ....... 630 851-1616
  Aurora *(G-1143)*
Elc Industries Corp ............................. E ....... 630 851-1616
  Aurora *(G-1144)*
Els Electronic Lighting Spc ................. G ....... 708 453-3666
  Elmwood Park *(G-9969)*

Lecip Inc ............................................. G ....... 312 626-2525
  Bensenville *(G-1939)*
Mellish & Murray Co ........................... F ....... 312 733-3513
  Chicago *(G-5683)*
Progress Rail Locomotive Inc ............. F ....... 708 387-5510
  Mc Cook *(G-14457)*

### LIGHTING FIXTURES: Ornamental, Commercial

New Metal Crafts Inc .......................... E ....... 312 787-6991
  Lincolnwood *(G-13526)*
Sternberg Lanterns Inc ....................... C ....... 847 588-3400
  Roselle *(G-18980)*

### LIGHTING FIXTURES: Public

Advanced Cstm Enrgy Sltons Inc ........ D ....... 312 428-9540
  Chicago *(G-3768)*

### LIGHTING FIXTURES: Residential

Advanced Micro Lites Inc .................... G ....... 630 365-5450
  Elburn *(G-8874)*
Afx Inc ................................................. C ....... 847 249-5970
  Waukegan *(G-21519)*
Astral Power Systems Inc ................... G ....... 630 518-1741
  Aurora *(G-1112)*
Cooper Lighting LLC .......................... G ....... 312 595-2770
  Elk Grove Village *(G-9393)*
Cooper Lighting LLC .......................... D ....... 847 956-8400
  Elk Grove Village *(G-9394)*
Eclipse Lighting Inc ............................. E ....... 847 260-0333
  Schiller Park *(G-19823)*
Elcast Manufacturing Inc ..................... E ....... 630 628-1992
  Addison *(G-107)*
Fanmar Inc .......................................... E ....... 708 563-0505
  Elk Grove Village *(G-9475)*
Fli Products LLC ................................. G ....... 630 520-0017
  West Chicago *(G-21702)*
Gerber Manufacturing (gm) LLC ......... F ....... 708 478-0100
  Mokena *(G-14868)*
Greencast Services Inc ....................... G ....... 630 723-8000
  Hinsdale *(G-11950)*
H A Framburg & Company .................. E ....... 708 547-5757
  Bellwood *(G-1708)*
H E Associates Inc .............................. G ....... 630 553-6382
  Yorkville *(G-22661)*
Intermatic Incorporated ...................... A ....... 815 675-2321
  Spring Grove *(G-20337)*
Io Lighting LLC .................................... F ....... 847 735-7000
  Vernon Hills *(G-21176)*
K&I Light Kandi Led Inc ...................... G ....... 773 745-1533
  Chicago *(G-5345)*
Lamp Co of America Inc ..................... G ....... 630 584-4001
  Saint Charles *(G-19207)*
Larentia Led LLC ................................. F ....... 312 291-9111
  Chicago *(G-5462)*
Lifespan Brands LLC .......................... F ....... 630 315-3300
  Elk Grove Village *(G-9595)*
Lightolier Genlyte Inc ......................... D ....... 847 364-8250
  Elk Grove Village *(G-9596)*
Lumenart Ltd ....................................... G ....... 773 254-0744
  Chicago *(G-5563)*
Lumenart Ltd ....................................... G ....... 773 254-0744
  Chicago *(G-5562)*
Metomic Corporation ........................... E ....... 773 247-4716
  Chicago *(G-5705)*
Midwest Sun-Ray Lighting & Sig ......... F ....... 618 656-2884
  Granite City *(G-11296)*
New Metal Crafts Inc .......................... E ....... 312 787-6991
  Lincolnwood *(G-13526)*
Pace Industries Inc ............................. D ....... 312 226-5500
  Chicago *(G-6051)*
Paramount Wire Specialties ............... F ....... 773 252-5636
  Chicago *(G-6080)*
Productworks LLC ............................... G ....... 224 406-8810
  Northbrook *(G-16347)*
Rgb Lights Inc .................................... F ....... 312 421-6080
  Chicago *(G-6346)*
Sternberg Lanterns Inc ....................... C ....... 847 588-3400
  Roselle *(G-18980)*
Uncommon Radiant ............................. G ....... 773 640-1674
  Chicago *(G-6810)*
Vaxcel International Co Ltd ................ E ....... 630 260-0067
  Carol Stream *(G-3261)*
Western Lighting Inc .......................... F ....... 847 451-7200
  Franklin Park *(G-10628)*

### LIGHTING FIXTURES: Residential, Electric

Artemide Inc ....................................... G ....... 312 475-0100
  Chicago *(G-3954)*
Jr Lighting Design Inc ......................... G ....... 708 460-6319
  Tinley Park *(G-20926)*
Lbl Lighting LLC .................................. F ....... 708 755-2100
  Skokie *(G-20028)*
Tri-Lite Inc ........................................... E ....... 773 384-7765
  Chicago *(G-6770)*

### LIGHTING FIXTURES: Street

City of Pekin ....................................... F ....... 309 477-2325
  Pekin *(G-17256)*

### LIME

Heisler Stone Co Inc ........................... G ....... 815 244-2685
  Mount Carroll *(G-15291)*
Jacobs Trucking .................................. G ....... 618 687-3578
  Murphysboro *(G-15577)*
Lafarge Building Materials Inc ............ D ....... 678 746-2000
  Chicago *(G-5434)*
Mineral Products Inc ........................... G ....... 618 433-3150
  Galatia *(G-10712)*

### LIMESTONE & MARBLE: Dimension

JKS Ventures Inc ................................. G ....... 708 345-9344
  Melrose Park *(G-14662)*

### LIMESTONE: Crushed & Broken

Anna Quarries Inc ............................... E ....... 618 833-5121
  Anna *(G-600)*
Argyle Cut Stone Co ........................... E ....... 847 456-6210
  Des Plaines *(G-8151)*
Callender Construction Co Inc ............ F ....... 217 285-2161
  Pittsfield *(G-17563)*
Central Stone Company ...................... G ....... 217 327-4300
  Chambersburg *(G-3443)*
Civil Constructors Inc ......................... G ....... 815 858-2691
  Elizabeth *(G-9241)*
Collinson Stone Co ............................. F ....... 309 787-7983
  Milan *(G-14780)*
Columbia Quarry Company ................. E ....... 618 281-7631
  Columbia *(G-7354)*
Columbia Quarry Company ................. E ....... 618 939-8833
  Waterloo *(G-21400)*
Conmat Inc .......................................... E ....... 815 235-2200
  Freeport *(G-10651)*
Elmer L Larson L C ............................. F ....... 815 895-4837
  Sycamore *(G-20797)*
H&H Crushing Inc ................................ G ....... 309 275-0643
  West Peoria *(G-21822)*
Hastie Mining & Trucking ................... E ....... 618 289-4536
  Cave In Rock *(G-3402)*
Heisler Stone Co Inc ........................... G ....... 815 244-2685
  Mount Carroll *(G-15291)*
Huyear Trucking Inc ............................ G ....... 217 854-3551
  Carlinville *(G-3039)*
Kimmaterials Inc ................................. G ....... 618 466-0352
  Godfrey *(G-11227)*
Le Claire Investment Inc .................... G ....... 309 757-8250
  Moline *(G-14953)*
Legacy Vulcan LLC ............................. E ....... 815 468-8141
  Manteno *(G-14186)*
Macklin Inc .......................................... F ....... 815 562-4803
  Rochelle *(G-18096)*
Martha Lacey ...................................... G ....... 217 723-4380
  Pearl *(G-17247)*
Material Service Corporation .............. C ....... 708 731-2600
  Westchester *(G-21850)*
Material Service Corporation .............. E ....... 217 732-2117
  Athens *(G-939)*
Material Service Corporation .............. D ....... 708 877-6540
  Thornton *(G-20875)*
Mid-America Carbonates LLC ............. G ....... 217 222-3500
  Quincy *(G-17858)*
Mill Creek Mining Inc .......................... G ....... 309 787-1414
  Milan *(G-14794)*
Nokomis Quarry Company .................. F ....... 217 563-2011
  Nokomis *(G-16059)*
Omni Materials Inc .............................. E ....... 618 262-5118
  Mount Carmel *(G-15279)*
R L ONeal & Sons ................................ F ....... 309 458-3350
  Plymouth *(G-17682)*
Riverstone Group Inc .......................... F ....... 309 523-3159
  Hillsdale *(G-11903)*
Riverstone Group Inc .......................... F ....... 309 933-1123
  Cleveland *(G-7271)*

# LIMESTONE: Crushed & Broken

Riverstone Group Inc .................... E ...... 309 787-3141
  Milan  (G-14804)
Savanna Quarry Inc ..................... G ...... 815 273-4208
  Savanna  (G-19405)
Shawnee Stone LLC ..................... F ...... 618 548-1585
  Salem  (G-19350)
Southern Illinois Stone Co ............. F ...... 573 334-5261
  Buncombe  (G-2800)
Southfield Corporation .................. E ...... 815 842-2333
  Pontiac  (G-17711)
Southfield Corporation .................. F ...... 815 468-8700
  Manteno  (G-14194)
Stolle Casper Quar & Contg Co ....... E ...... 618 337-5212
  Dupo  (G-8579)
Tower Rock Stone Company ............ F ...... 618 281-4106
  Columbia  (G-7364)
Tri-State Cut Stone Co .................. G ...... 815 469-7550
  Frankfort  (G-10371)
Utica Stone Co Inc ....................... G ...... 815 667-4690
  Utica  (G-21110)
Valley View Industries Inc .............. E ...... 815 358-2236
  Cornell  (G-7382)
Vulcan Construction Mtls LLC .......... E ...... 630 955-8500
  Naperville  (G-15779)
Vulcan Materials Company .............. F ...... 262 639-2803
  Naperville  (G-15780)
Vulcan Materials Company .............. E ...... 815 899-7204
  Sycamore  (G-20824)
William Charles Cnstr Co LLC ......... G ...... 815 654-4720
  Belvidere  (G-1797)

## LIMESTONE: Cut & Shaped

Argyle Cut Stone Co ..................... E ...... 847 456-6210
  Des Plaines  (G-8151)
Liberty Limestone Inc ................... G ...... 815 385-5011
  McHenry  (G-14521)

## LIMESTONE: Dimension

Anna Quarries Inc ....................... E ...... 618 833-5121
  Anna  (G-600)
Joliet Sand and Gravel Company ...... D ...... 815 741-2090
  Rockdale  (G-18222)
Lafarge Aggregates III Inc ............. G ...... 847 742-6060
  South Elgin  (G-20212)
Material Service Corporation .......... D ...... 708 485-8211
  Mc Cook  (G-14451)
Nokomis Quarry Company ............... F ...... 217 563-2011
  Nokomis  (G-16059)
Pana Limestone Company ............... G ...... 217 562-4231
  Pana  (G-17135)

## LIMESTONE: Ground

Calhoun Quarry Incorporated .......... F ...... 618 396-2229
  Batchtown  (G-1517)
Calhoun Quarry Incorporated .......... G ...... 618 576-9223
  Hardin  (G-11593)
Central Limestone Company Inc ....... F ...... 815 736-6341
  Morris  (G-15101)
Central Stone Company .................. D ...... 309 757-8250
  Moline  (G-14921)
Central Stone Company .................. F ...... 217 723-4410
  Pittsfield  (G-17565)
Central Stone Company .................. F ...... 217 224-7330
  Quincy  (G-17811)
Gray Quarries Inc ........................ F ...... 217 847-2712
  Hamilton  (G-11534)
Iola Quarry Inc ........................... F ...... 217 682-3865
  Mode  (G-14849)
Material Service Corporation .......... E ...... 217 563-2531
  Nokomis  (G-16058)
Mining International LLC ............... F ...... 630 232-4246
  Geneva  (G-10850)
Quality Lime Company ................... F ...... 217 826-2343
  Marshall  (G-14328)
Renner Quarries Ltd ..................... G ...... 815 288-6699
  Dixon  (G-8343)
Southern Illinois Stone Co ............. E ...... 618 995-2392
  Buncombe  (G-2801)

## LINEN SPLY SVC: Apron

NRR Corp .................................. F ...... 630 915-8388
  Oak Brook  (G-16550)

## LINENS: Napkins, Fabric & Nonwoven, From Purchased Materials

Ameritex Industries Inc ................. F ...... 217 324-4044
  Litchfield  (G-13681)

## LINER BRICK OR PLATES: Sewer Or Tank Lining, Vitrified Clay

Colloid Envmtl Tech Co LLC ............ C ...... 847 851-1500
  Hoffman Estates  (G-12002)

## LINER STRIPS: Rubber

Bls Enterprises Inc ...................... F ...... 630 766-1300
  Bensenville  (G-1844)

## LINERS & COVERS: Fabric

Creative Covers Inc ..................... G ...... 708 233-6880
  Bridgeview  (G-2480)
Polyair Inter Pack Inc .................. G ...... 773 995-1818
  Chicago  (G-6153)
Seamcraft International LLC ........... E ...... 773 417-4002
  Chicago  (G-6466)

## LINERS & LINING

Bulk Lift International LLC ............ G ...... 847 428-6059
  Carpentersville  (G-3277)
Chicago Tank Lining Sales ............. G ...... 847 328-0500
  Evanston  (G-10023)
Resist-A-Line Industries Inc .......... G ...... 815 650-3177
  Joliet  (G-12567)
Tacknologies .............................. G ...... 630 729-9900
  Woodridge  (G-22521)

## LININGS: Apparel, Made From Purchased Materials

Mid State Graphics ...................... G ...... 309 772-3843
  Bushnell  (G-2906)

## LININGS: Safe & Vault, Metal

Variable Operations Tech Inc .......... E ...... 815 479-8528
  Crystal Lake  (G-7672)

## LIQUEFIED PETROLEUM GAS DEALERS

AmeriGas ................................... D ...... 708 544-1131
  Hillside  (G-11909)
Mills Machine Inc ........................ G ...... 815 273-4707
  Savanna  (G-19403)
Zorin Material Handling Co ............ G ...... 773 342-3818
  Chicago  (G-7073)

## LIQUEFIED PETROLEUM GAS WHOLESALERS

AmeriGas ................................... D ...... 708 544-1131
  Hillside  (G-11909)
Drig Corporation ......................... G ...... 312 265-1509
  Chicago  (G-4644)

## LIQUID CRYSTAL DISPLAYS

Global Display Solutions Inc .......... E ...... 815 282-2328
  Rockford  (G-18399)
Innolux Technology USA Inc ........... E ...... 847 490-5315
  Hoffman Estates  (G-12018)
Richardson Electronics Ltd ............ C ...... 630 208-2278
  Lafox  (G-12795)

## LITHOGRAPHIC PLATES

Autotype Americas Incorporated ...... G ...... 847 818-8262
  Rolling Meadows  (G-18713)
Color Smiths Inc ......................... E ...... 708 562-0061
  Elmhurst  (G-9853)
Dupli Group Inc .......................... G ...... 773 549-5285
  Chicago  (G-4654)
Graphics Plus Inc ........................ F ...... 630 968-9073
  Lisle  (G-13597)

## LIVESTOCK WHOLESALERS, NEC

Golden Valley Hardscapes LLC ........ G ...... 309 654-2261
  Cordova  (G-7376)
Tyson Fresh Meats Inc .................. F ...... 309 965-2565
  Goodfield  (G-11249)

## LOADS: Electronic

Consolidated Elec Wire & Cable ...... D ...... 847 455-8830
  Franklin Park  (G-10440)

## LOCK & KEY SVCS

Agena Manufacturing Co ................ E ...... 630 668-5086
  Carol Stream  (G-3093)

## LOCKS

A Ashland Lock Company ................ F ...... 773 348-5106
  Chicago  (G-3684)
Eastern Company ......................... C ...... 847 537-1800
  Wheeling  (G-22041)
Expert Locksmith Inc .................... G ...... 917 751-9267
  Chicago  (G-4796)
Fort Lock Corporation .................. E ...... 708 456-1100
  Grayslake  (G-11338)
Lovatt & Radcliffe Ltd .................. G ...... 815 568-9797
  Skokie  (G-20031)

## LOCKS & LOCK SETS, WHOLESALE

Eastern Company ......................... C ...... 847 537-1800
  Wheeling  (G-22041)

## LOCKS: Safe & Vault, Metal

Jerome Remien Corporation ............ F ...... 847 806-0888
  Elk Grove Village  (G-9561)

## LOCKSMITHS

A Ashland Lock Company ................ F ...... 773 348-5106
  Chicago  (G-3684)
Lovatt & Radcliffe Ltd .................. G ...... 815 568-9797
  Skokie  (G-20031)

## LOCOMOTIVES & PARTS

G&E Transportation Inc ................. E ...... 404 350-6497
  Chicago  (G-4903)
Hadady Corporation ...................... E ...... 219 322-7417
  South Holland  (G-20274)
National Railway Equipment Co ....... C ...... 618 242-6590
  Mount Vernon  (G-15432)
National Railway Equipment Co ....... C ...... 309 755-6800
  Silvis  (G-19939)
National Railway Equipment Co ....... C ...... 618 241-9270
  Mount Vernon  (G-15433)
Relco Locomotives Inc ................... D ...... 630 968-0670
  Lisle  (G-13651)
Tenneco Intl Holdg Corp ................ G ...... 847 482-5000
  Lake Forest  (G-12968)

## LOG SPLITTERS

Brave Products Inc ...................... G ...... 815 672-0551
  Streator  (G-20684)
Ramsplitter Log Splitters Inc ......... G ...... 815 398-4726
  Rockford  (G-18547)
Speeco Incorporated .................... C ...... 303 279-5544
  Oregon  (G-16832)

## LOGGING

Beeman & Sons Inc ...................... F ...... 217 232-4268
  Martinsville  (G-14332)
Big Creek Forestry & Logging L ...... G ...... 217 822-8282
  Marshall  (G-14318)
Billy & Rachel Poignant ................ G ...... 309 713-5500
  Lacon  (G-12785)
Bourrette Logging ....................... G ...... 815 591-3761
  Hanover  (G-11571)
Brian Kinney ............................. G ...... 309 206-4219
  Rock Island  (G-18166)
Christiansen Sawmill and Log ........ G ...... 815 315-7520
  Caledonia  (G-2931)
Dust Logging LLC ........................ G ...... 217 844-2305
  Effingham  (G-8834)
Ericson S Log & Lumber Co ........... G ...... 309 667-2147
  New Windsor  (G-15931)
Frank E Galloway ....................... G ...... 618 948-2578
  Sumner  (G-20770)
G & C Enterprises Inc .................. G ...... 618 747-2272
  Jonesboro  (G-12591)
Heartland Hardwoods Inc .............. E ...... 217 844-3312
  Effingham  (G-8838)
Illiana Real Log Homes Inc ........... G ...... 815 471-4004
  Milford  (G-14813)
K D Custom Sawing Logging ........... G ...... 309 231-4805
  Green Valley  (G-11379)
Kelly & Son Forestry & Log LLC ..... G ...... 815 275-6687
  Crystal Lake  (G-7598)
Larry Musgrave Logging ................ G ...... 618 842-6386
  Fairfield  (G-10148)

## PRODUCT SECTION — LUMBER & BUILDING MATERIALS DEALER, RET: Masonry Matls/Splys

**Lonnie Hickam** .......... G ....... 618 893-4223
Pomona *(G-17693)*
**Mid-State Timber & Veneer Co** .......... G ....... 618 423-2619
Ramsey *(G-17914)*
**Poignant Logging** .......... G ....... 309 246-5647
Lacon *(G-12791)*
**Rlw Inc** .......... G ....... 309 352-2499
Green Valley *(G-11380)*
**Warrior Logging & Perforagine** .......... G ....... 618 662-7373
Flora *(G-10220)*
**Warrior Well Services Inc** .......... G ....... 618 662-7710
Flora *(G-10221)*

### LOGGING CAMPS & CONTRACTORS

**Jack Shepard Logging** .......... G ....... 618 845-3496
Ullin *(G-21031)*
**Russell Ferrell** .......... G ....... 217 847-3954
Hamilton *(G-11540)*
**W Bozarth Logging** .......... G ....... 618 658-4016
Vienna *(G-21226)*

### LOGGING: Stump Harvesting

**Cnv Enterprises Inc** .......... G ....... 815 405-6762
Plainfield *(G-17589)*

### LOGGING: Timber, Cut At Logging Camp

**Loneoak Timber & Veneere Co** .......... G ....... 618 426-3065
Ava *(G-1239)*
**Tallwood** .......... G ....... 815 786-8186
Plano *(G-17676)*

### LOGGING: Wood Chips, Produced In The Field

**Powell Tree Care Inc** .......... G ....... 847 364-1181
Elk Grove Village *(G-9689)*

### LOOSELEAF BINDERS

**Acco Brands Corporation** .......... A ....... 847 541-9500
Lake Zurich *(G-13033)*
**Advance Bindery Co** .......... F ....... 847 662-2418
Waukegan *(G-21518)*
**Americas Community Bankers** .......... E ....... 312 644-3100
Chicago *(G-3884)*
**Beta Pak Inc** .......... F ....... 708 466-7844
Sugar Grove *(G-20718)*
**Counter Cft Svc Systems & Pdts** .......... G ....... 630 629-7336
Lombard *(G-13785)*
**General Loose Leaf Bindery Inc** .......... E ....... 847 244-9700
Waukegan *(G-21562)*
**Jacobson Acqstion Holdings LLC** .......... C ....... 847 623-1414
Waukegan *(G-21574)*
**K & L Looseleaf Products Inc** .......... D ....... 847 357-9733
Elk Grove Village *(G-9568)*
**Michael Lewis Company** .......... C ....... 708 688-2200
Mc Cook *(G-14453)*
**Protek Inc** .......... G ....... 888 536-5466
Saint Charles *(G-19243)*
**Simu Ltd** .......... F ....... 630 350-1060
Wood Dale *(G-22422)*

### LOOSELEAF BINDERS: Library

**J-Industries Inc** .......... F ....... 815 654-0055
Loves Park *(G-13949)*

### LOTIONS OR CREAMS: Face

**Bethany Pharmacol Co Inc** .......... G ....... 217 665-3395
Bethany *(G-2084)*
**Dzro-Bans International Inc** .......... G ....... 779 324-2740
Homewood *(G-12096)*
**Jindilli Beverages LLC** .......... G ....... 630 581-5697
Burr Ridge *(G-2860)*
**Luxurious Lathers Ltd** .......... G ....... 844 877-7627
Hinsdale *(G-11951)*
**Paket Corporation** .......... E ....... 773 221-7300
Chicago *(G-6057)*
**RITA Corporation** .......... E ....... 815 337-2500
Crystal Lake *(G-7642)*
**Solab Inc** .......... F ....... 708 544-2200
Bellwood *(G-1722)*

### LOUDSPEAKERS

**Advance Tools LLC** .......... G ....... 855 685-0633
Glenview *(G-11097)*
**Quam-Nichols Company** .......... C ....... 773 488-5800
Chicago *(G-6249)*

### LUBRICANTS: Corrosion Preventive

**Castrol Industrial N Amer Inc** .......... C ....... 877 641-1600
Naperville *(G-15620)*
**Dynacron** .......... G ....... 773 378-0736
Chicago *(G-4659)*
**Ingersoll-Rand Company** .......... E ....... 704 655-4000
Chicago *(G-5191)*
**Ivanhoe Industries Inc** .......... G ....... 847 566-7170
Mundelein *(G-15512)*
**Lubrication Enterprises LLC** .......... G ....... 800 537-7683
Plainfield *(G-17623)*
**M R O Solutions LLC** .......... G ....... 847 588-2480
Niles *(G-15998)*
**Nalco Company LLC** .......... A ....... 630 305-1000
Naperville *(G-15703)*
**Nalco Holdings LLC** .......... A ....... 630 305-1000
Naperville *(G-15707)*
**Safety Compound Corporation** .......... E ....... 630 953-1515
Lombard *(G-13851)*

### LUBRICATING EQPT: Indl

**Gaunt Industries Inc** .......... G ....... 847 671-0776
Franklin Park *(G-10477)*
**Illini Hi-Reach Inc** .......... F ....... 847 428-3311
East Dundee *(G-8646)*
**LDI Industries Inc** .......... D ....... 847 669-7510
Huntley *(G-12157)*
**Lsp Industries Inc** .......... F ....... 815 226-8090
Rockford *(G-18474)*
**Pulsarlube USA Inc** .......... G ....... 847 593-5300
Elk Grove Village *(G-9700)*
**Standard Indus & Auto Eqp Inc** .......... E ....... 630 289-9500
Hanover Park *(G-11590)*

### LUBRICATING OIL & GREASE WHOLESALERS

**Famous Lubricants Inc** .......... G ....... 773 268-2555
Chicago *(G-4811)*
**Fuchs Corporation** .......... G ....... 800 323-7755
Harvey *(G-11667)*
**K & J Synthetic Lubricants** .......... G ....... 630 628-1011
Addison *(G-162)*
**Lubeq Corporation** .......... F ....... 847 931-1020
Elgin *(G-9096)*
**Motor Oil Inc** .......... G ....... 847 956-7550
Elk Grove Village *(G-9639)*
**Petrochem Inc** .......... G ....... 630 513-6350
Saint Charles *(G-19235)*

### LUBRICATING SYSTEMS: Centralized

**Wm W Nugent & Co Inc** .......... E ....... 847 673-8109
Skokie *(G-20111)*

### LUGGAGE & BRIEFCASES

**A W Enterprises Inc** .......... E ....... 708 458-8989
Bedford Park *(G-1531)*
**Art Jewel Enterprises Ltd** .......... F ....... 630 260-0400
Carol Stream *(G-3106)*
**Du-Call Miller Plastics Inc** .......... F ....... 630 964-6020
Batavia *(G-1443)*
**Ips & Luggage Co Inc** .......... G ....... 630 894-2414
Roselle *(G-18948)*
**LC Industries Inc** .......... E ....... 312 455-0500
Elk Grove Village *(G-9589)*
**Midwest Fibre Products Inc** .......... E ....... 309 596-2955
Viola *(G-21292)*
**Plano Molding Company LLC** .......... C ....... 815 786-3331
Sandwich *(G-19374)*

### LUGGAGE & LEATHER GOODS STORES

**Keleen Leathers Inc** .......... E ....... 630 590-5300
Westmont *(G-21898)*
**Phoenix Leather Goods LLC** .......... F ....... 815 267-3926
Plainfield *(G-17639)*
**Randa Accessories Lea Gds LLC** .......... D ....... 847 292-8300
Rosemont *(G-19026)*

### LUGGAGE WHOLESALERS

**Sukie Group Inc** .......... F ....... 773 521-1800
Chicago *(G-6613)*

### LUGGAGE: Traveling Bags

**Kingport Industries LLC** .......... G ....... 847 480-5745
Northbrook *(G-16287)*
**Travel Caddy Inc** .......... E ....... 847 621-7000
Elk Grove Village *(G-9788)*

### LUGGAGE: Wardrobe Bags

**Hartmann** .......... G ....... 618 684-6814
Murphysboro *(G-15576)*

### LUMBER & BLDG MATLS DEALER, RET: Garage Doors, Sell/Install

**Allied Garage Door Inc** .......... E ....... 630 279-0795
Addison *(G-29)*
**Hormann LLC** .......... G ....... 630 859-3000
Montgomery *(G-15048)*

### LUMBER & BLDG MTRLS DEALERS, RET: Closets, Interiors/Access

**RTC Industries Inc** .......... B ....... 847 640-2400
Rolling Meadows *(G-18775)*

### LUMBER & BLDG MTRLS DEALERS, RET: Doors, Storm, Wood/Metal

**Accurate Cstm Sash Mllwk Corp** .......... G ....... 708 423-0423
Oak Lawn *(G-16595)*
**Barneys Aluminum Specialties** .......... G ....... 815 723-5341
Joliet *(G-12462)*
**Cornerstone Building Products** .......... G ....... 217 543-2829
Arthur *(G-889)*
**Defender Steel Door & Window** .......... E ....... 708 780-7320
Cicero *(G-7188)*
**Metal Products Sales Corp** .......... G ....... 708 301-6844
Lockport *(G-13732)*

### LUMBER & BLDG MTRLS DEALERS, RET: Planing Mill Prdts/Lumber

**Lumberyard Suppliers Inc** .......... E ....... 217 965-4911
Virden *(G-21298)*

### LUMBER & BLDG MTRLS DEALERS, RET: Windows, Storm, Wood/Metal

**Drexel House of Drapes Inc** .......... G ....... 618 624-5415
Belleville *(G-1627)*
**Tuminello Enterprizes Inc** .......... G ....... 815 416-1007
Morris *(G-15137)*
**Tuminello Enterprizes Inc** .......... G ....... 815 416-1007
Morris *(G-15138)*

### LUMBER & BUILDING MATERIAL DEALERS, RETAIL: Roofing Material

**Acme Awning Co** .......... G ....... 847 446-0153
Highland Park *(G-11822)*

### LUMBER & BUILDING MATERIALS DEALER, RET: Door & Window Prdts

**Kamstra Door Service Inc** .......... G ....... 708 895-9990
Lansing *(G-13167)*

### LUMBER & BUILDING MATERIALS DEALER, RET: Masonry Matls/Splys

**Architectural Cast Ston** .......... E ....... 630 377-4800
West Chicago *(G-21661)*
**Beelman Ready-Mix Inc** .......... G ....... 618 478-2044
Nashville *(G-15834)*
**Beelman Ready-Mix Inc** .......... G ....... 618 357-6120
Pinckneyville *(G-17544)*
**Exclusive Stone** .......... G ....... 847 593-6963
Elk Grove Village *(G-9470)*
**Gary & Larry Brown Trucking** .......... G ....... 618 268-6377
Raleigh *(G-17909)*
**Lion Ornamental Concrete Pdts** .......... G ....... 630 892-7304
Montgomery *(G-15056)*
**Monmouth Ready Mix Corp** .......... G ....... 309 734-3211
Monmouth *(G-15021)*
**Odum Concrete Products Inc** .......... G ....... 618 942-4572
Herrin *(G-11751)*
**Southern Illinois Redimix Inc** .......... F ....... 618 993-3600
Marion *(G-14290)*
**Tamms Industries Inc** .......... D ....... 815 522-3394
Kirkland *(G-12719)*

# LUMBER & BUILDING MATERIALS DEALERS, RETAIL: Brick

## PRODUCT SECTION

### LUMBER & BUILDING MATERIALS DEALERS, RETAIL: Brick

- Bricks Inc .................................................. G ...... 630 897-6926
  Aurora  *(G-1121)*
- Glen-Gery Corporation ............................. D ...... 815 795-6911
  Marseilles  *(G-14309)*
- Southfield Corporation ............................. F ...... 217 875-5455
  Decatur  *(G-7941)*
- Tison & Hall Concrete Products .............. F ...... 618 253-7808
  Harrisburg  *(G-11605)*

### LUMBER & BUILDING MATERIALS DEALERS, RETAIL: Cement

- Prarie Material Sales Inc ......................... G ...... 847 733-8809
  Evanston  *(G-10090)*
- Upland Concrete ..................................... G ...... 224 699-9909
  East Dundee  *(G-8661)*
- Wille Bros Co .......................................... D ...... 708 388-9000
  Chicago  *(G-6982)*

### LUMBER & BUILDING MATERIALS DEALERS, RETAIL: Countertops

- Granite Mountain Inc .............................. G ...... 708 774-1442
  New Lenox  *(G-15884)*
- Rays Countertop Shop Inc ...................... F ...... 217 483-2514
  Glenarm  *(G-10997)*

### LUMBER & BUILDING MATERIALS DEALERS, RETAIL: Sand & Gravel

- Quad-County Ready Mix Corp ................ G ...... 618 295-3000
  Marissa  *(G-14297)*
- Rockford Sand & Gravel Co .................... E ...... 815 654-4700
  Loves Park  *(G-13986)*

### LUMBER & BUILDING MATERIALS DEALERS, RETAIL: Tile, Ceramic

- MK Tile Ink ............................................. G ...... 773 964-8905
  Chicago  *(G-5778)*

### LUMBER & BUILDING MATERIALS RET DEALERS: Millwork & Lumber

- Bailey Hardwoods Inc ............................. G ...... 217 529-6800
  Springfield  *(G-20394)*
- Bull Valley Hardwood .............................. G ...... 815 701-9400
  Woodstock  *(G-22548)*
- Custom Crafted Door Inc ........................ F ...... 309 527-5075
  El Paso  *(G-8867)*
- Great Spirit Hardwoods LLC ................... G ...... 224 801-1969
  East Dundee  *(G-8642)*
- John Tobin Millwork Co .......................... G ...... 630 832-3780
  Villa Park  *(G-21260)*
- R Maderite Inc ........................................ G ...... 773 235-1515
  Chicago  *(G-6268)*
- Triezenberg Millwork Co ......................... G ...... 708 489-9062
  Crestwood  *(G-7506)*
- Wille Bros Co .......................................... D ...... 708 535-4101
  Monee  *(G-15008)*

### LUMBER & BUILDING MATLS DEALERS, RET: Screens, Door/Window

- Boom Company Inc ................................ G ...... 847 459-6199
  Wheeling  *(G-22018)*

### LUMBER & BUILDING MTRLS DEALERS, RET: Insulation Mtrl, Bldg

- Insulators Supply Inc .............................. G ...... 847 394-2836
  Prospect Heights  *(G-17780)*

### LUMBER: Flooring, Dressed, Softwood

- K&S International Inc ............................. G ...... 847 229-0202
  Buffalo Grove  *(G-2714)*
- Mechanics Planing Mill Inc ..................... E ...... 618 288-3000
  Glen Carbon  *(G-10954)*
- Oltenia Inc .............................................. G ...... 773 987-2888
  Norridge  *(G-16107)*

### LUMBER: Hardboard

- Craftmaster Manufacturing Inc .............. A ...... 800 405-2233
  Chicago  *(G-4490)*
- Iten Industries Inc .................................. G ...... 630 543-2820
  Addison  *(G-155)*

### LUMBER: Hardwood Dimension

- Woodworkers Shop Inc ........................... E ...... 309 347-5111
  Pekin  *(G-17296)*
- Woodx Lumber Inc .................................. G ...... 331 979-2171
  Elmhurst  *(G-9962)*

### LUMBER: Hardwood Dimension & Flooring Mills

- Art Jewel Enterprises Ltd ....................... F ...... 630 260-0400
  Carol Stream  *(G-3106)*
- Bond Brothers Hardwoods ..................... G ...... 618 272-4811
  Ridgway  *(G-17983)*
- Boyd Sawmill ......................................... G ...... 618 735-2056
  Dix  *(G-8317)*
- Builders Warehouse Inc ......................... G ...... 309 672-1760
  Peoria  *(G-17320)*
- Central Illinois Hardwood ....................... G ...... 309 352-2363
  Green Valley  *(G-11378)*
- Christiansen Sawmill and Log ................ G ...... 815 315-7520
  Caledonia  *(G-2931)*
- Eichen Lumber Co Inc ............................ G ...... 217 854-9751
  Carlinville  *(G-3037)*
- Enterprise Pallet Inc .............................. F ...... 815 928-8546
  Bourbonnais  *(G-2395)*
- Ericson S Log & Lumber Co ................... G ...... 309 667-2147
  New Windsor  *(G-15931)*
- G L Beaumont Lumber Company ........... F ...... 618 423-2323
  Ramsey  *(G-17913)*
- Great Northern Lumber Inc .................... D ...... 708 388-1818
  Blue Island  *(G-2254)*
- Lohrberg Lumber .................................... F ...... 618 473-2061
  Waterloo  *(G-21402)*
- Moultrie County Hardwoods LLC ............ G
  Arthur  *(G-912)*
- Outdoors Synergy Products Tech ........... D ...... 630 552-3111
  Plano  *(G-17670)*
- Simonton Hardwood Lumber LLC ........... F ...... 618 594-2132
  Carlyle  *(G-3059)*
- Tree-O Lumber Inc ................................. G ...... 618 357-2576
  Pinckneyville  *(G-17553)*
- Wooded Wonderland ............................... G ...... 815 777-1223
  Galena  *(G-10735)*
- Woodmac Industries Inc ......................... F ...... 708 755-3545
  S Chicago Hts  *(G-19116)*

### LUMBER: Kiln Dried

- Cairo Dry Kilns Inc ................................. E ...... 618 734-1039
  Cairo  *(G-2928)*

### LUMBER: Panels, Plywood, Softwood

- Westrock CP LLC .................................... D ...... 312 346-6600
  Chicago  *(G-6967)*

### LUMBER: Plywood, Hardwood

- Aircraft Plywood Mfg Inc ........................ G ...... 618 654-6740
  Highland  *(G-11775)*
- Challinor Wood Products Inc ................. G ...... 847 256-8828
  Wilmette  *(G-22250)*
- Chalon Wood Products Inc .................... G ...... 630 243-9793
  Lemont  *(G-13231)*
- Great Northern Lumber Inc .................... D ...... 708 388-1818
  Blue Island  *(G-2254)*
- L Land Hardwoods .................................. ....... 708 496-9000
  Bedford Park  *(G-1561)*
- Lumberyard Suppliers Inc ...................... E ...... 217 965-4911
  Virden  *(G-21298)*
- Veneer Specialties Inc ............................ F ...... 630 754-8550
  Lemont  *(G-13267)*

### LUMBER: Plywood, Hardwood or Hardwood Faced

- Westrock CP LLC .................................... D ...... 312 346-6600
  Chicago  *(G-6967)*

### LUMBER: Plywood, Prefinished, Hardwood

- R S Bacon Veneer Company ................... G ...... 331 777-4762
  Lisle  *(G-13649)*

### LUMBER: Resawn, Small Dimension

- Liese Lumber Co Inc .............................. E ...... 618 234-0105
  Belleville  *(G-1649)*

### LUMBER: Treated

- Chicago Flameproof WD Spc Corp ......... E ...... 630 859-0009
  Montgomery  *(G-15037)*
- Great Lakes Art Foundry Inc .................. G ...... 847 213-0800
  Skokie  *(G-20006)*
- Great Northern Lumber Inc .................... D ...... 708 388-1818
  Blue Island  *(G-2254)*
- Nu Again ................................................ F ...... 630 564-5590
  Bartlett  *(G-1364)*
- Perma-Treat of Illinois Inc ..................... F ...... 618 997-5646
  Marion  *(G-14278)*
- T P I Inc ................................................. G ...... 847 888-0232
  Elgin  *(G-9201)*

### LUMBER: Veneer, Hardwood

- R S Bacon Veneer Company ................... C ...... 630 323-1414
  Lisle  *(G-13648)*

### MACHINE PARTS: Stamped Or Pressed Metal

- A & M Tool Co Inc .................................. E ...... 847 215-8140
  Wheeling  *(G-21993)*
- Able Barmilling & Mfg Co Inc ................. F ...... 708 343-5666
  Melrose Park  *(G-14580)*
- Accurate CNc Machining Inc .................. G ...... 815 623-6516
  Roscoe  *(G-18888)*
- Alcon Tool & Mfg Co Inc ........................ F ...... 773 545-8742
  Chicago  *(G-3798)*
- Amtec Precision Products Inc ................ D ...... 847 695-8030
  Elgin  *(G-8953)*
- Barrington Automation Ltd .................... E ...... 847 458-0900
  Lake In The Hills  *(G-12987)*
- Blue Chip Mfg LLC ................................. G ...... 630 553-6321
  Oswego  *(G-16905)*
- C N C HI-Tech Inc .................................. E ...... 847 201-8151
  Volo  *(G-21309)*
- Cicero Plastic Products Inc .................... E ...... 815 886-9522
  Romeoville  *(G-18811)*
- Crystal Precision Drilling ........................ G ...... 815 633-5460
  Loves Park  *(G-13930)*
- CSI Cutting Specialist Inc ...................... D ...... 731 352-5351
  East Alton  *(G-8600)*
- Custom Machinery Inc ............................ G ...... 847 678-3033
  Schiller Park  *(G-19818)*
- Dart Technology Inc ............................... G ...... 847 534-0357
  Schaumburg  *(G-19499)*
- Domeny Tool & Stamping Company ...... F ...... 847 526-5700
  Wauconda  *(G-21454)*
- Force Manufacturing Inc ........................ G ...... 847 265-6500
  Lake Villa  *(G-13013)*
- G & Z Industries Inc .............................. E ...... 847 215-2300
  Wheeling  *(G-22061)*
- G T L Technologies Inc .......................... G ...... 630 469-9818
  Glendale Heights  *(G-11025)*
- Gingrich Enterprises Inc ........................ E ...... 309 923-7312
  Roanoke  *(G-18050)*
- Graphic Parts Intl Inc ............................. F ...... 773 725-4900
  Chicago  *(G-4990)*
- Headly Manufacturing Co ....................... D ...... 708 338-0800
  Broadview  *(G-2583)*
- Horizon Die Company Inc ...................... E ...... 847 426-8558
  East Dundee  *(G-8643)*
- I C Universal Inc .................................... G ...... 630 766-1169
  Bensenville  *(G-1918)*
- Icon Power Roller Inc ............................ E ...... 630 545-2345
  Marseilles  *(G-14310)*
- Kr Machine ............................................. ....... 815 248-2250
  Durand  *(G-8586)*
- Lorbern Mfg Inc ..................................... E ...... 847 301-8600
  Schaumburg  *(G-19623)*
- Mark Development Corporation ............. C ...... 815 339-2226
  Mark  *(G-14298)*
- Mercury Products Corp ........................... C ...... 847 524-4400
  Schaumburg  *(G-19641)*
- Mercury Products Corp ........................... ....... 847 524-4400
  Schaumburg  *(G-19642)*
- Meridian Parts Inc .................................. E ...... 630 718-1995
  Naperville  *(G-15696)*
- North Amercn Acquisition Corp .............. C ...... 847 695-8030
  Elgin  *(G-9125)*
- Northfield Holdings LLC ......................... E ...... 847 755-0700
  Schaumburg  *(G-19669)*
- Patko Tool & Manufacturing ................... G ...... 630 616-8802
  Bensenville  *(G-1963)*
- Pro Machining Inc .................................. F ...... 815 633-4140
  Loves Park  *(G-13978)*
- R Hansel & Son Inc ................................ G ...... 815 784-5500
  Genoa  *(G-10883)*
- R Z Tool Inc ........................................... F ...... 847 647-2350
  Niles  *(G-16025)*

Rail Exchange Inc ... E ... 708 757-3317
Chicago Heights *(G-7119)*
Rockwell Metal Products Inc ... G ... 773 762-7030
Chicago *(G-6377)*
Rursch Specialties Inc ... G ... 309 795-1502
Reynolds *(G-17953)*
S & L Tool Co Inc ... G ... 847 455-5550
Franklin Park *(G-10579)*
Spare Part Solutions Inc ... F ... 815 637-1490
Rockford *(G-18624)*
Technical Metals Inc ... D ... 815 692-4643
Fairbury *(G-10133)*
Tru-Machine Co Inc ... G ... 815 675-6735
Spring Grove *(G-20372)*
United Standard Industries Inc ... D ... 847 724-0350
Glenview *(G-11212)*

## *MACHINE SHOPS*

Absolute Turn Inc ... E ... 847 459-4629
Wheeling *(G-21997)*
Ace Coating Enterprises Inc ... F ... 708 547-6680
Hillside *(G-11908)*
Ace Machining of Rockford Inc ... G ... 815 398-3200
Rockford *(G-18255)*
Addison Precision Products ... F ... 815 857-4466
Amboy *(G-596)*
Advantage Machining Inc ... E ... 630 897-1220
Aurora *(G-1101)*
All Cnc Solutions Inc ... G ... 847 972-1139
Skokie *(G-19947)*
Allied Machine Tool & Dye ... G ... 708 388-7676
Crestwood *(G-7475)*
Allied Welding Inc ... E ... 309 274-6227
Chillicothe *(G-7161)*
American Drilling Inc ... E ... 847 850-5090
Wheeling *(G-22003)*
AP Machine Inc ... F ... 708 450-1010
Melrose Park *(G-14594)*
Aurora Custom Machining Inc ... D ... 630 859-2638
Aurora *(G-1115)*
Auto Head and Engine Exchange ... G ... 708 448-8762
Worth *(G-22632)*
Avers Machine & Mfg Inc ... E ... 847 447-3430
Schiller Park *(G-19807)*
B & B Tool Co ... E ... 815 229-5792
Rockford *(G-18275)*
B & G Machine Inc ... G ... 618 262-2269
Mount Carmel *(G-15261)*
B A P Enterprises Inc ... G ... 708 849-0900
Dolton *(G-8364)*
Barton Manufacturing LLC ... E ... 217 428-0711
Decatur *(G-7843)*
Bc Machine ... G ... 815 962-7884
Rockford *(G-18278)*
BSB International Corp ... G ... 847 791-9272
Bensenville *(G-1848)*
C D Tools Machining Inc ... G ... 773 859-2028
Addison *(G-65)*
C E R Machining & Tooling Ltd ... G ... 708 442-9614
Lyons *(G-14034)*
Caffero Tool & Mfg ... D ... 224 293-2600
Streamwood *(G-20647)*
Carmona Gear Cutting ... G ... 815 963-8236
Rockford *(G-18298)*
Cmg Precision Machining Co Inc ... G ... 630 759-8080
Romeoville *(G-18813)*
Cope Plastics Inc ... D ... 618 466-0221
Alton *(G-568)*
Custom Superfinishing Grinding ... G ... 847 699-9710
Rosemont *(G-18997)*
Cutting Edge Machining Inc ... G ... 847 427-1392
Elk Grove Village *(G-9406)*
D E Specialty Tool & Mfg Inc ... E ... 847 678-0004
Franklin Park *(G-10453)*
Daco Incorporated ... F ... 630 897-8797
North Aurora *(G-16124)*
Davis Machine Company Inc ... G ... 815 723-9121
Joliet *(G-12484)*
DNp Enterprises Inc ... G ... 630 628-7210
Addison *(G-95)*
Dura Feed Inc ... G ... 815 395-1115
Loves Park *(G-13938)*
Dynamic Machining Inc ... G ... 815 675-3330
Spring Grove *(G-20334)*
E & F Tool Company Inc ... F ... 815 729-1305
Joliet *(G-12486)*
Eastwood Enterprises Inc ... D ... 847 940-4008
Deerfield *(G-8004)*
Ed Weitekamp Inc ... G ... 217 229-4239
Raymond *(G-17938)*
Eww Enterprise Inc ... G ... 815 463-9607
New Lenox *(G-15881)*
Excel Machining Inc ... G ... 773 585-6666
Chicago *(G-4794)*
G Messmore Company ... G ... 708 343-8114
Broadview *(G-2581)*
General Machine & Tl Works Inc ... F ... 312 337-2177
Chicago *(G-4927)*
Geo T Schmidt Inc ... D ... 847 647-7117
Niles *(G-15982)*
Goellner Inc ... C ... 815 962-6076
Rockford *(G-18400)*
Goreville Auto Parts & Mch Sp ... G ... 618 995-2375
Goreville *(G-11251)*
Grebner Machine & Tool Inc ... G ... 309 248-7768
Washburn *(G-21375)*
Gti Spindle Technology Inc ... F ... 309 820-7887
Bloomington *(G-2175)*
H & H Machining ... G ... 309 365-7010
Lexington *(G-13292)*
Hfo Chicago LLC ... F ... 847 258-2850
Elk Grove Village *(G-9523)*
Indiana Precision Inc ... F ... 765 361-0247
Danville *(G-7739)*
J & S Machine Works Inc ... G ... 708 344-2101
Melrose Park *(G-14661)*
Janssen Machine Inc ... F ... 815 877-9901
Loves Park *(G-13950)*
Jda Aqua Cutting Inc ... G ... 815 485-8028
New Lenox *(G-15888)*
Jdb Machining Inc ... G ... 708 749-9596
Forest View *(G-10258)*
Jdb Manufacturing Company ... G ... 708 749-9596
Forest View *(G-10259)*
Jim Sterner Machines ... G ... 815 962-8983
Rockford *(G-18445)*
K D Industries Illinois Inc ... G ... 309 854-7100
Kewanee *(G-12691)*
Keeper Corp ... G ... 630 773-9393
Itasca *(G-12292)*
Kemp Manufacturing Company ... E ... 309 682-7292
Peoria *(G-17395)*
Kohlert Manufacturing Corp ... G ... 630 584-0013
Saint Charles *(G-19204)*
Komax Corporation ... D ... 847 537-6640
Buffalo Grove *(G-2718)*
L A T Enterprise Inc ... G ... 630 543-5533
Addison *(G-174)*
L T Properties Inc ... G ... 217 423-8772
Decatur *(G-7904)*
Lays Mining Service Inc ... E ... 618 244-6570
Mount Vernon *(G-15421)*
Lenrok Industries Inc ... G ... 630 628-1946
Addison *(G-179)*
Littell LLC ... E ... 630 916-6662
Schaumburg *(G-19620)*
Machine Works of Decatur Inc ... G ... 217 428-3896
Decatur *(G-7910)*
Machining Systems Corporation ... G ... 708 385-7903
Crestwood *(G-7493)*
Magnet-Schultz Amer Holdg LLC ... G ... 630 789-0600
Westmont *(G-21901)*
Magnet-Schultz America Inc ... D ... 630 789-0600
Westmont *(G-21902)*
Marion Tool & Die Inc ... D ... 309 266-6551
Morton *(G-15162)*
Messer Machine ... G ... 815 398-6248
Rockford *(G-18494)*
Metal Works Machine Inc ... G ... 217 868-5111
Shumway *(G-19934)*
Metric Machine Shop Inc ... G ... 847 439-9891
Elk Grove Village *(G-9623)*
Midway Grinding Inc ... E ... 847 439-7424
Elk Grove Village *(G-9627)*
Milco Precision Machining Inc ... F ... 630 628-5730
Addison *(G-216)*
Mk Systems Incorporated ... F ... 847 709-6180
Elk Grove Village *(G-9632)*
New Lenox Machine Co Inc ... F ... 815 584-4866
Dwight *(G-8589)*
Numalliance - North Amer Inc ... G ... 847 439-4500
Elk Grove Village *(G-9658)*
Octane Motorsports LLC ... G ... 224 419-5460
Waukegan *(G-21598)*
Olney Machine & Design Inc ... G ... 618 392-6634
Olney *(G-16788)*
Olon Industries Inc (us) ... E ... 630 232-4705
Geneva *(G-10858)*
P & H Manufacturing Co ... D ... 217 774-2123
Shelbyville *(G-19911)*
PDQ Machine Inc ... G ... 815 282-7575
Machesney Park *(G-14096)*
Plastak Inc ... G ... 630 466-4100
Sugar Grove *(G-20730)*
Prairie Manufacturing Inc ... G ... 815 498-1593
Somonauk *(G-20127)*
Precision Laser Marking Inc ... G ... 630 628-8575
Addison *(G-251)*
Precision Metal Crafters Inc ... F ... 847 816-3244
Libertyville *(G-13371)*
Price Machine Inc ... G ... 217 892-8958
Dewey *(G-8311)*
Pride Machine & Tool Co Inc ... F ... 708 343-7190
Melrose Park *(G-14684)*
Pro Arc Inc ... E ... 815 877-1804
Loves Park *(G-13977)*
Pro-Qua Inc ... G ... 630 543-5644
Addison *(G-258)*
Production Tool Companies LLC ... E ... 773 288-4400
Chicago *(G-6206)*
R Machining Inc ... G ... 217 532-2174
Butler *(G-2910)*
Rah Enterprises Inc ... G ... 217 223-1970
Quincy *(G-17885)*
Rix Enterprise Inc ... G ... 618 996-8237
Creal Springs *(G-7454)*
Romtech Machining Inc ... G ... 630 543-7039
Addison *(G-280)*
Rutherford & Associates ... G ... 630 365-5263
Saint Charles *(G-19257)*
S & S Machining Services Inc ... G ... 708 758-8300
Lynwood *(G-14026)*
S D Custom Machining ... G ... 618 544-7007
Robinson *(G-18072)*
Sas Industrial Machinery Inc ... G ... 847 455-5526
Franklin Park *(G-10583)*
Shredderhotlinecom Company ... C ... 815 674-5802
Streator *(G-20701)*
Solutions Manufacturing Inc ... E ... 847 310-4506
Hoffman Estates *(G-12057)*
Southern IL Crankshaft Inc ... F ... 618 282-4100
Red Bud *(G-17949)*
Southwick Machine & Design Co ... G ... 309 949-2868
Colona *(G-7348)*
Summit Mold Inc ... G ... 815 865-5809
Davis *(G-7807)*
Swebco Mfg Inc ... E ... 815 636-7160
Machesney Park *(G-14110)*
Tag-Barton LLC ... G ... 217 428-0711
Decatur *(G-7948)*
Ter-Son Corporation ... D ... 309 274-6227
Chillicothe *(G-7171)*
Thompson Industries Inc ... E ... 815 899-6670
Sycamore *(G-20819)*
Thunderbird LLC ... G ... 847 718-9300
Elk Grove Village *(G-9778)*
Total Titanium Inc ... E ... 618 473-2429
Red Bud *(G-17950)*
Traxco Inc ... G ... 847 669-1545
Huntley *(G-12180)*
Trinity Machined Products Inc ... E ... 630 876-6992
Aurora *(G-1090)*
Trufab Group USA LLC ... E ... 630 994-3286
Schaumburg *(G-19775)*
Vek Screw Machine Products ... G ... 630 543-5557
Addison *(G-338)*
W-D Tool Engineering Company ... F ... 773 638-2688
Chicago *(G-6928)*
Wachs Technical Services Inc ... E ... 847 537-8800
Wheeling *(G-22179)*
Walco Tool & Engineering Corp ... D ... 815 834-0225
Romeoville *(G-18877)*
Wilczak Industrial Parts Inc ... G ... 847 260-5559
Franklin Park *(G-10629)*
Zeco Inc ... G ... 847 446-1413
Northfield *(G-16423)*

## *MACHINE TOOL ACCESS: Balancing Machines*

Balanstar Corporation ... F ... 773 261-5034
Chicago *(G-4030)*
Stuhr Manufacturing Co ... F ... 815 398-2460
Rockford *(G-18636)*

## *MACHINE TOOL ACCESS: Boring Attachments*

Grove Industrial ... G ... 815 385-4800
Johnsburg *(G-12435)*

Employee Codes: A=Over 500 employees, B=251-500
C=101-250, D=51-100, E=20-50, F=10-19, G=3-9
2017 Harris Illinois
Industrial Directory
1631
PRODUCT

# MACHINE TOOL ACCESS: Boring Attachments

Machine Tool Acc & Mfg Co .................. G ..... 773 489-0903
   Chicago *(G-5592)*

## MACHINE TOOL ACCESS: Broaches

J M Resources Inc ................................. F ..... 630 690-7337
   Elgin *(G-9080)*
Universal Broaching Inc ......................... F ..... 847 228-1440
   Elk Grove Village *(G-9800)*

## MACHINE TOOL ACCESS: Cams

Cams Inc ............................................... G ..... 773 929-3656
   Chicago *(G-4225)*
Elgin CAM Co ....................................... G ..... 847 741-1757
   Elgin *(G-9021)*
Sacco-Camex Inc .................................. G ..... 630 595-8090
   Franklin Park *(G-10580)*

## MACHINE TOOL ACCESS: Cutting

Abbco Inc .............................................. E ..... 630 595-7115
   Elk Grove Village *(G-9253)*
Alfa Mfg Industries Inc .......................... E ..... 847 470-9595
   Morton Grove *(G-15186)*
Circle Cutting Tools Inc ......................... G ..... 815 398-4153
   Rockford *(G-18310)*
Damen Carbide Tool Company Inc ......... E ..... 630 766-7875
   Wood Dale *(G-22357)*
Federal Signal Corporation .................... D ..... 630 954-2000
   Oak Brook *(G-16510)*
Illinois Carbide Tool Co Inc .................... F ..... 847 244-1110
   Waukegan *(G-21569)*
Intrepid Tool Industries LLC .................. E ..... 773 467-4200
   Chicago *(G-5229)*
Kitamura Machinery USA Inc ................. F ..... 847 520-7755
   Wheeling *(G-22084)*
Klein Tools Inc ....................................... G ..... 815 282-0530
   Machesney Park *(G-14086)*
Maverick Tool Company Inc ................... E ..... 630 766-2313
   Bensenville *(G-1947)*
Midwest Tool & Manufacturing ............... G ..... 815 282-6754
   Machesney Park *(G-14094)*
Mitsubishi Materials USA Corp ............... F ..... 847 519-1601
   Schaumburg *(G-19649)*
New World Products Inc ........................ G ..... 630 690-5625
   Carol Stream *(G-3205)*
OSG Usa Inc .......................................... C ..... 630 274-2100
   Bensenville *(G-1961)*
Progrssive Cmponents Intl Corp ............. D ..... 847 487-1000
   Wauconda *(G-21494)*
Regal Cutting Tools Inc ......................... C ..... 815 389-3461
   Roscoe *(G-18912)*
Rockform Tooling & Machinery .............. G ..... 815 398-7650
   Rockford *(G-18592)*
Sandtech Inc ......................................... F ..... 847 470-9595
   Morton Grove *(G-15234)*
Sieber Tool Engineering LP ................... F ..... 630 462-9370
   Carol Stream *(G-3240)*
Spie Tool Co .......................................... E ..... 847 891-6556
   Schaumburg *(G-19738)*
Techny Precision Mfg Inc ...................... F ..... 630 543-7065
   Addison *(G-308)*
Tool Engrg Consulting Mfg LLC ............. G ..... 815 316-2304
   Rockford *(G-18654)*
Toolmasters LLC ................................... E ..... 815 968-0961
   Rockford *(G-18655)*
Triad Cutting Tools Svc & Mfg ............... G ..... 847 352-0459
   Schaumburg *(G-19772)*
Triumph Twist Drill Co Inc ..................... B ..... 815 459-6250
   Crystal Lake *(G-7670)*
Udce Limited ......................................... G ..... 630 495-9940
   Lombard *(G-13875)*
Wenco Manufacturing Co Inc ................. E ..... 630 377-7474
   Elgin *(G-9235)*

## MACHINE TOOL ACCESS: Diamond Cutting, For Turning, Etc

Accu-Cut Diamond Tool Company .......... F ..... 708 457-8800
   Norridge *(G-16095)*
Meinhardt Diamond Tool Co .................. G ..... 773 267-3260
   Chicago *(G-5681)*
Saint-Gobain Abrasives Inc ................... C ..... 630 868-8060
   Carol Stream *(G-3232)*
Shape-Master Tool Co ........................... E ..... 815 522-6186
   Kirkland *(G-12718)*
Wunderlich Diamond Tool Corp ............. F ..... 847 437-9904
   Elk Grove Village *(G-9818)*

## MACHINE TOOL ACCESS: Dresser, Abrasive Wheel Or Other

Industrial Diamond Products ................. E ..... 847 272-7840
   Northbrook *(G-16276)*

## MACHINE TOOL ACCESS: Drill Bushings, Drilling Jig

Acme Industrial Company ...................... C ..... 847 428-3911
   Carpentersville *(G-3271)*
National Bushing & Mfg ......................... G ..... 847 847-1553
   Lake Zurich *(G-13108)*

## MACHINE TOOL ACCESS: Drills

Brunner & Lay Inc ................................. C ..... 847 678-3232
   Elmhurst *(G-9843)*
Cjt Koolcarb Inc .................................... C ..... 630 690-5933
   Carol Stream *(G-3129)*
Infinity Tool Mfg LLC ............................. G ..... 618 439-4042
   Benton *(G-2031)*
Precision Dormer LLC ........................... C ..... 800 877-3745
   Elgin *(G-9146)*

## MACHINE TOOL ACCESS: Hopper Feed Devices

Custom Feeder Co of Rockford .............. E ..... 815 654-2444
   Loves Park *(G-13932)*
Jerhen Industries Inc ............................ D ..... 815 397-0400
   Rockford *(G-18443)*
Universal Feeder Inc ............................. G ..... 815 633-0752
   Machesney Park *(G-14116)*

## MACHINE TOOL ACCESS: Knives, Metalworking

General Cutng Tl Svc & Mfg Inc ............ F ..... 847 677-8770
   Lincolnwood *(G-13513)*

## MACHINE TOOL ACCESS: Machine Attachments & Access, Drilling

Chicago Quadrill Co ............................... G ..... 847 824-4196
   Des Plaines *(G-8167)*

## MACHINE TOOL ACCESS: Milling Machine Attachments

Bourn & Bourn Inc ................................ C ..... 815 965-4013
   Rockford *(G-18289)*

## MACHINE TOOL ACCESS: Pushers

Pixel Pushers Incorporated ................... ..... 847 550-6560
   Lake Zurich *(G-13114)*

## MACHINE TOOL ACCESS: Tool Holders

Eri America Inc ...................................... ..... 847 550-9710
   Lake Zurich *(G-13070)*
Haimer Usa LLC .................................... G ..... 630 833-1500
   Villa Park *(G-21258)*

## MACHINE TOOL ACCESS: Tools & Access

2I Technologies LLC .............................. G ..... 312 526-3900
   Chicago *(G-3666)*
Alcon Tool & Mfg Co Inc ........................ F ..... 773 545-8742
   Chicago *(G-3798)*
Ammentorp Tool Company Inc .............. G ..... 847 671-9290
   Franklin Park *(G-10395)*
Burnex Corporation ............................... E ..... 815 728-1317
   Ringwood *(G-17988)*
Coordinate Machine Company ............... E ..... 630 894-9880
   Roselle *(G-18935)*
G & S Manufacturing Inc ....................... ..... 847 674-7666
   Bannockburn *(G-1258)*
Harig Manufacturing Corp ..................... E ..... 847 647-9500
   Skokie *(G-20011)*
Heim Group ........................................... ..... 708 496-7403
   Chicago *(G-5069)*
Hilti Inc .................................................. ..... 847 364-9818
   Elmhurst *(G-9882)*
Pace Machinery Group Inc ................... F ..... 630 377-1750
   Wasco *(G-21373)*
Park Products Inc ................................. ..... 630 543-2474
   Addison *(G-237)*
Tag Sales Co Inc .................................. ..... 630 990-3434
   Hinsdale *(G-11966)*
Thermoplastec Inc ................................ F ..... 815 873-9288
   Rockford *(G-18647)*

## MACHINE TOOL ATTACHMENTS & ACCESS

3d Manufacturing Corporation ............... G ..... 815 806-9200
   Frankfort *(G-10290)*
A J Manufacturing Co Inc ...................... G ..... 630 832-2828
   Elmhurst *(G-9828)*
Belden Tools Inc ................................... E ..... 708 344-4600
   Broadview *(G-2562)*
Bertsche Engineering Corp .................... F ..... 847 537-8757
   Buffalo Grove *(G-2664)*
Edmik Inc .............................................. E ..... 847 263-0460
   Gurnee *(G-11445)*
H R Slater Co Inc .................................. F ..... 312 666-1855
   Chicago *(G-5023)*
J & J Carbide & Tool Inc ....................... E ..... 708 489-0300
   Alsip *(G-475)*
Kut-Rite Tool Company ......................... F ..... 630 837-8130
   Streamwood *(G-20664)*
Matheu Tool Works Inc ......................... ..... 773 327-9274
   Chicago *(G-5652)*
Mid-West Feeder Inc ............................. E ..... 815 544-2994
   Belvidere *(G-1771)*
Retondo Enterprises Inc ....................... ..... 630 837-8130
   Streamwood *(G-20671)*
S Vs Industries Inc ................................ ..... 630 408-1083
   Hoffman Estates *(G-12047)*
Tornos Technologies US Corp ................ G ..... 630 812-2040
   Lombard *(G-13869)*

## MACHINE TOOLS & ACCESS

A R Tech & Tool Inc .............................. G ..... 708 599-5745
   Bridgeview *(G-2458)*
A&W Tool Inc ........................................ ..... 815 653-1700
   Ringwood *(G-17986)*
ADS LLC ................................................ D ..... 256 430-3366
   Burr Ridge *(G-2820)*
Advanced Machine Co Inc ..................... ..... 773 545-9790
   Chicago *(G-3770)*
Advent Tool & Mfg Inc .......................... F ..... 847 395-9707
   Antioch *(G-613)*
Alliance Tool & Manufacturing ............... F ..... 708 345-5444
   Maywood *(G-14415)*
Allkut Tool Incorporated ........................ ..... 815 476-9656
   Wilmington *(G-22269)*
American Machine Tools Inc .................. G ..... 773 775-6285
   Chicago *(G-3861)*
Arrow Engineering Inc .......................... E ..... 815 397-0862
   Rockford *(G-18270)*
Asko Inc ................................................ E ..... 773 785-4515
   South Holland *(G-20248)*
Assurance Technologies Inc .................. F ..... 630 550-5000
   Bartlett *(G-1331)*
Atm America Corp ................................. E ..... 800 298-0030
   Chicago *(G-3986)*
Auto Meter Products Inc ....................... C ..... 815 991-2292
   Sycamore *(G-20788)*
Autocut Machine Co .............................. G ..... 815 436-1900
   Elwood *(G-9978)*
Belcar Products Inc .............................. ..... 630 462-1950
   Carol Stream *(G-3113)*
Besly Cutting Tools Inc ......................... F ..... 815 389-2231
   South Beloit *(G-20141)*
Big Kser Precision Tooling Inc ............... E ..... 847 228-7660
   Hoffman Estates *(G-11996)*
Blackhawk Industrial Dist Inc ................. F ..... 773 736-9600
   Carol Stream *(G-3117)*
C & C Tooling Inc .................................. F ..... 630 543-5523
   Addison *(G-63)*
Carbco Manufacturing Inc ..................... F ..... 630 377-1410
   Saint Charles *(G-19150)*
Center Tool Company Inc ...................... G ..... 847 683-7559
   Hampshire *(G-11544)*
Champion Chisel Works Inc .................. F ..... 815 535-0647
   Rock Falls *(G-18128)*
Chicago Hardware and Fix Co ............... D ..... 847 455-6609
   Franklin Park *(G-10429)*
Craftstech Inc ....................................... E ..... 847 758-3100
   Elk Grove Village *(G-9398)*
Custom Cutting Tools Inc ...................... G ..... 815 986-0320
   Loves Park *(G-13931)*
Custom Cuttingedge Tool Inc ................ G ..... 847 622-0457
   Batavia *(G-1435)*
Custom Machining & Design LLC ........... G ..... 847 364-2601
   Elk Grove Village *(G-9403)*
Custom Tool Inc .................................... F ..... 217 465-8538
   Paris *(G-17145)*
D & R Ekstrom Carlson Co .................... G ..... 815 394-1744
   Rockford *(G-18331)*

# PRODUCT SECTION

## MACHINE TOOLS, METAL CUTTING: Home Workshop

David Linderholm ...................................G....... 847 336-3755
  Waukegan *(G-21548)*
Del-Co-West Inc .....................................F....... 309 799-7543
  Milan *(G-14783)*
Design Systems Inc ................................E....... 309 263-7706
  Morton *(G-15157)*
Die Specialty Co .....................................G....... 312 303-5738
  La Grange Park *(G-12755)*
Dmg Mori Usa Inc ..................................D....... 847 593-5400
  Hoffman Estates *(G-12006)*
Dover Energy Automation LLC ..............E....... 630 541-1540
  Downers Grove *(G-8432)*
Dynacut Industries Inc ...........................E....... 630 462-1900
  Carol Stream *(G-3145)*
EJ Cady & Company ..............................G....... 847 537-2239
  Wheeling *(G-22045)*
Emtech Machining & Grinding ..............G....... 815 338-1580
  Woodstock *(G-22565)*
Engineering Products Company ............G....... 815 436-9055
  Plainfield *(G-17595)*
Engis Corporation ..................................C....... 847 808-9400
  Wheeling *(G-22047)*
Estwing Manufacturing Co Inc ...............B....... 815 397-9521
  Rockford *(G-18370)*
Fox Machine & Tool Inc .........................G....... 847 357-1845
  Elk Grove Village *(G-9489)*
Fulton Corporation ..................................D....... 815 589-3211
  Fulton *(G-10701)*
Galaxy Sourcing Inc ...............................G....... 630 532-5003
  Villa Park *(G-21254)*
Gator Products Inc .................................G....... 847 836-0581
  Gilberts *(G-10919)*
Gki Incorporated .....................................E....... 815 459-2330
  Rockford *(G-18398)*
Greenlee Diamond Tool Co ....................E....... 866 451-3316
  Elk Grove Village *(G-9512)*
Guide Line Industries Inc .......................F....... 815 777-3722
  Scales Mound *(G-19415)*
Hallmark Industries Inc ..........................F....... 847 301-8050
  Schaumburg *(G-19546)*
Harris Precision Tools Inc ......................G....... 708 422-5808
  Chicago Ridge *(G-7149)*
Hartland Cutting Tools Inc .....................F....... 847 639-9400
  Cary *(G-3350)*
Heidenhain Holding Inc .........................G....... 716 661-1700
  Schaumburg *(G-19552)*
Henry Technologies Inc .........................G....... 217 483-2406
  Chatham *(G-3621)*
Hg-Farley Laserlab USA Inc ..................G....... 815 874-1400
  Rockford *(G-18418)*
Holden Industries Inc ............................F....... 847 940-1500
  Deerfield *(G-8013)*
Ideal Industries Inc ................................C....... 815 895-1108
  Sycamore *(G-20801)*
Illinois Broaching Co ..............................G....... 847 678-3080
  Schiller Park *(G-19840)*
Imprex International Inc .........................G....... 847 364-4930
  Arlington Heights *(G-775)*
Industrial Instrument Svc Corp ..............G....... 773 581-3355
  Chicago *(G-5177)*
Ingersoll Cutting Tool Company ............B....... 815 387-6600
  Rockford *(G-18432)*
Ingersoll Machine Tools Inc ..................C....... 815 987-6000
  Rockford *(G-18433)*
Inland Tool Company .............................E....... 217 792-3206
  Mount Pulaski *(G-15389)*
Intech Industries Inc ..............................F....... 847 487-5599
  Wauconda *(G-21473)*
Ivan Schwenker .....................................G....... 630 543-7798
  Addison *(G-156)*
J H Benedict Co Inc ...............................D....... 309 694-3111
  East Peoria *(G-8715)*
Jamco Tool & Cams Inc ........................F....... 847 678-0280
  Franklin Park *(G-10505)*
Johnson Pattern & Mch Works ..............G....... 815 433-2775
  Ottawa *(G-16964)*
K-C Tool Co ............................................G....... 630 983-5960
  Naperville *(G-15683)*
Kaydon Acquisition Xii Inc ....................E....... 217 443-3592
  Danville *(G-7740)*
Kennametal Inc ......................................F....... 309 578-1888
  Mossville *(G-15253)*
Kennametal Inc ......................................E....... 630 963-2910
  Lisle *(G-13613)*
Kennametal Inc ......................................C....... 815 226-0650
  Rockford *(G-18454)*
Keonix Corporation ................................G....... 847 259-9430
  Arlington Heights *(G-788)*
Kile Machine & Tool Inc ........................G....... 217 446-8616
  Danville *(G-7744)*

Kmp Tool Grinding Inc ...........................G....... 847 205-9640
  Northbrook *(G-16288)*
L & M Screw Machine Products .............F....... 630 801-0455
  Montgomery *(G-15052)*
Lmt Onsrud LP .......................................G....... 847 362-1560
  Waukegan *(G-21582)*
Lmt Usa Inc ............................................G....... 630 969-5412
  Waukegan *(G-21583)*
Logan Actuator Co .................................G....... 815 943-9500
  Harvard *(G-11640)*
Logan Graphic Products Inc ..................D....... 847 526-5515
  Wauconda *(G-21479)*
Machine Technology Inc ........................G....... 815 444-4837
  Crystal Lake *(G-7604)*
Magna-Lock Usa Inc .............................F....... 815 962-8700
  Rockford *(G-18480)*
Merit Tool Engineering Co Inc ...............G....... 773 283-1114
  Chicago *(G-5694)*
Method Molds Inc ..................................G....... 815 877-0191
  Loves Park *(G-13965)*
Midland Manufacturing Corp .................G....... 847 677-0333
  Skokie *(G-20039)*
Moldtronics Inc ......................................E....... 630 968-7000
  Downers Grove *(G-8488)*
NNt Enterprises Incorporated ................G....... 630 875-9600
  Itasca *(G-12332)*
P K Neuses Incorporated ......................G....... 847 253-6555
  Rolling Meadows *(G-18756)*
PDQ Machine Inc ..................................G....... 815 282-7575
  Machesney Park *(G-14096)*
Pontiac Engraving .................................G....... 630 834-4424
  Bensenville *(G-1965)*
Porcelain Enamel Finishers ...................G....... 312 808-1560
  Chicago *(G-6157)*
Port Byron Machine Inc .........................G....... 309 523-9111
  Port Byron *(G-17722)*
Precision Brand Products Inc ................G....... 630 969-7200
  Downers Grove *(G-8509)*
Precision Masters ..................................E....... 815 397-3894
  Rockford *(G-18539)*
Precision Tool & Die Company ..............F....... 217 864-3371
  Mount Zion *(G-15455)*
Prince Industries Inc .............................C....... 630 588-0088
  Carol Stream *(G-3220)*
Prototype & Production Co ....................E....... 847 419-1553
  Wheeling *(G-22130)*
Rdh Inc of Rockford ...............................F....... 815 874-9421
  Rockford *(G-18550)*
Rockford Jobbing Service Inc ...............G....... 815 398-8661
  Rockford *(G-18576)*
Roll McHning Tech Slutions Inc ............E....... 815 372-9100
  Romeoville *(G-18864)*
Roll Rite Inc ...........................................G....... 815 645-8600
  Davis Junction *(G-7814)*
S & J Industrial Supply Corp .................F....... 708 339-1708
  South Holland *(G-20303)*
S & W Manufacturing Co Inc .................E....... 630 595-5044
  Bensenville *(G-1984)*
Schaefer Technologies LLC ..................G....... 630 406-9377
  Batavia *(G-1493)*
Sensible Products Inc ............................G....... 773 774-7400
  Chicago *(G-6477)*
Shelby Tool & Die Inc ............................G....... 217 774-2189
  Shelbyville *(G-19915)*
Sollami Company ...................................E....... 618 988-1521
  Herrin *(G-11755)*
Stock Gears Inc .....................................F....... 224 653-9489
  Elk Grove Village *(G-9758)*
Tag Tool Services Incorporated .............E....... 309 694-2400
  East Peoria *(G-8736)*
Technical Tool Enterprise ......................G....... 630 893-3390
  Addison *(G-307)*
Techniks LLC .........................................E....... 815 689-2748
  Cullom *(G-7685)*
Thermal-Tech Systems Inc ...................G....... 630 639-5115
  West Chicago *(G-21780)*
Thomas Packaging LLC ........................F....... 847 392-1652
  Rolling Meadows *(G-18782)*
Top Notch Tool & Supply Inc .................G....... 815 633-6295
  Cherry Valley *(G-3648)*
Tox- Pressotechnik LLC ........................G....... 630 447-4600
  Warrenville *(G-21365)*
Tri-Star Engineering Inc ........................E....... 847 595-3377
  Elk Grove Village *(G-9791)*
Vanguard Tool & Engineering Co ..........F....... 847 981-9595
  Mount Prospect *(G-15382)*
W A Whitney Co ....................................C....... 815 964-6771
  Rockford *(G-18671)*
Wema Vogtland America LLC ................F....... 815 544-0526
  Rockford *(G-18677)*

West Precision Tool Inc ........................F....... 630 766-8304
  Bensenville *(G-2014)*
Willow Farm Products Inc ....................G....... 630 430-7491
  Lemont *(G-13270)*
Wozniak Industries Inc ........................G....... 708 458-1220
  Bedford Park *(G-1595)*
Yana House ..........................................G....... 773 874-7120
  Chicago *(G-7047)*
Z-Patch Inc ...........................................E....... 618 529-2431
  Carbondale *(G-3029)*

## MACHINE TOOLS, METAL CUTTING: Brushing

Above & Beyond Black Oxiding ...........G....... 708 345-7100
  Melrose Park *(G-14581)*

## MACHINE TOOLS, METAL CUTTING: Centering

Stuhr Manufacturing Co ......................F....... 815 398-2460
  Rockford *(G-18636)*

## MACHINE TOOLS, METAL CUTTING: Cutoff

Harris Precision Tools Inc ...................G....... 708 422-5808
  Chicago Ridge *(G-7149)*
Huml Industries Inc .............................G....... 847 426-8061
  Gilberts *(G-10923)*
Kiene Diesel Accessories Inc .............E....... 630 543-7170
  Addison *(G-167)*
R T M Precision Machining Inc ...........G....... 630 595-0946
  Carol Stream *(G-3226)*

## MACHINE TOOLS, METAL CUTTING: Drilling

Tri-Cam Inc ..........................................F....... 815 226-9200
  Rockford *(G-18656)*

## MACHINE TOOLS, METAL CUTTING: Drilling & Boring

Advanced Machine & Engrg Co ...........C....... 815 962-6076
  Rockford *(G-18257)*
Midwest Turned Products LLC ............G....... 847 551-4482
  Gilberts *(G-10927)*
N W Horizontal Boring .........................G....... 618 566-9117
  Mascoutah *(G-14358)*
Rdh Inc of Rockford .............................F....... 815 874-9421
  Rockford *(G-18550)*
TT Technologies Inc ............................D....... 630 851-8200
  Aurora *(G-1091)*

## MACHINE TOOLS, METAL CUTTING: Electrochemical Milling

ABRA Enterprises Inc .........................G....... 847 866-6903
  Evanston *(G-10001)*

## MACHINE TOOLS, METAL CUTTING: Exotic, Including Explosive

Alliance Tool & Manufacturing .............F....... 708 345-5444
  Maywood *(G-14415)*
Composite Cutter Tech Inc ..................G....... 847 740-6875
  Volo *(G-21311)*
Hi-Tech Manufacturing LLC .................C....... 847 678-1616
  Schiller Park *(G-19836)*
Tauber Brothers Tool & Die Co ............E....... 708 867-9100
  Chicago *(G-6679)*

## MACHINE TOOLS, METAL CUTTING: Grind, Polish, Buff, Lapp

Hausermann Abrading Process Co ......F....... 630 543-6688
  Addison *(G-142)*
Lc Holdings of Delaware Inc ...............G....... 847 940-3550
  Deerfield *(G-8028)*
Precision Chrome Inc ..........................E....... 847 587-1515
  Fox Lake *(G-10282)*
Raymond Alstom .................................G....... 630 369-3700
  Naperville *(G-15739)*

## MACHINE TOOLS, METAL CUTTING: Home Workshop

Air Mite Devices Inc ............................E....... 224 338-0071
  Round Lake *(G-19051)*
B & B Machine Inc ...............................G....... 309 786-3279
  Rock Island *(G-18160)*

---

Employee Codes: A=Over 500 employees, B=251-500
C=101-250, D=51-100, E=20-50, F=10-19, G=3-9

2017 Harris Illinois Industrial Directory

## MACHINE TOOLS, METAL CUTTING: Keysetting

Hoffman J&M Farm Holdings Inc .......... D ....... 847 671-6280
Schiller Park *(G-19838)*

## MACHINE TOOLS, METAL CUTTING: Lathes

Dainichi Machinery Inc ............................ G ....... 630 681-1572
Carol Stream *(G-3139)*
Hyundai Wia Machine Amer Corp .......... E ....... 201 636-5600
Itasca *(G-12277)*

## MACHINE TOOLS, METAL CUTTING: Milling, Chemical

Engineered Mills Inc .............................. G ....... 847 548-0044
Grayslake *(G-11335)*

## MACHINE TOOLS, METAL CUTTING: Numerically Controlled

Accelrted Mch Design Engrg LLC .......... F ....... 815 316-6381
Rockford *(G-18251)*
Dearborn Tool & Mfg Inc ......................... E ....... 630 655-1260
Burr Ridge *(G-2836)*
Miyano Machinery USA Inc ..................... E ....... 630 766-4141
Elk Grove Village *(G-9631)*
Peddinghaus Corporation ........................ C ....... 815 937-3800
Bradley *(G-2428)*
R B Evans Co ......................................... G ....... 630 365-3554
Elburn *(G-8907)*
S & S Tool Company .............................. G ....... 847 891-0780
Schaumburg *(G-19715)*
Walter Tool & Mfg Inc ............................. F ....... 847 697-7230
Elgin *(G-9227)*

## MACHINE TOOLS, METAL CUTTING: Pipe Cutting & Threading

Rothenberger Usa Inc ............................ E ....... 815 397-7617
Loves Park *(G-13988)*

## MACHINE TOOLS, METAL CUTTING: Planers

Bourn & Bourn Inc ................................. C ....... 815 965-4013
Rockford *(G-18289)*

## MACHINE TOOLS, METAL CUTTING: Plasma Process

Electron Beam Technologies Inc ............. C ....... 815 935-2211
Kankakee *(G-12612)*

## MACHINE TOOLS, METAL CUTTING: Screw & Thread

Cutting Tool Innovations Inc ................... G ....... 630 766-4839
Bensenville *(G-1877)*
Folkerts Manufacturing Inc ..................... G ....... 815 968-7426
Rockford *(G-18385)*

## MACHINE TOOLS, METAL CUTTING: Tool Replacement & Rpr Parts

AC Precision Tool Inc ............................ G ....... 630 797-5161
Saint Charles *(G-19131)*
AG Precision Inc ................................... G ....... 847 724-7786
Glenview *(G-11098)*
Chicago Cnc Machining Co ..................... G ....... 708 352-1255
Hodgkins *(G-11972)*
Condor Machine Tool ............................. G ....... 773 767-5985
Chicago *(G-4447)*
Ctc Machine Service Inc ........................ G ....... 630 876-5120
West Chicago *(G-21688)*
Endofix Ltd ............................................ G ....... 708 715-3472
Brookfield *(G-2631)*
Jakes McHning Rbilding Svc Inc ............. E ....... 630 892-3291
Aurora *(G-1175)*
Laser Technologies Inc .......................... C ....... 630 761-1200
Naperville *(G-15686)*
M & M Tooling Inc .................................. G ....... 630 595-8834
Wood Dale *(G-22392)*
Machine Medics LLC .............................. G ....... 309 633-5454
Peoria *(G-17404)*
Prototype & Production Co ..................... G ....... 847 419-1553
Wheeling *(G-22130)*
Technox Machine & Mfg Inc .................... E ....... 773 745-6800
Chicago *(G-6685)*
Umt Wind Down Co ................................ E ....... 815 467-7900
Minooka *(G-14848)*

Versatility TI Works Mfg Inc .................... F ....... 708 389-8909
Alsip *(G-541)*
Walega Precision Company Inc .............. G ....... 630 682-5000
Carol Stream *(G-3263)*

## MACHINE TOOLS, METAL CUTTING: Vertical Turning & Boring

Honor Med Maskiner Corp ...................... G ....... 847 741-9400
Elgin *(G-9066)*

## MACHINE TOOLS, METAL FORMING: Bending

Giant Globes Inc .................................... G ....... 773 772-2917
Chicago *(G-4950)*

## MACHINE TOOLS, METAL FORMING: Container, Metal Incl Cans

Ives-Way Products Inc ............................ G ....... 847 740-0658
Round Lake Beach *(G-19076)*

## MACHINE TOOLS, METAL FORMING: Crimping, Metal

MB Corp & Associates ............................ F ....... 847 214-8843
South Elgin *(G-20218)*
Uniflex of America Ltd ........................... G ....... 847 519-1100
Schaumburg *(G-19779)*

## MACHINE TOOLS, METAL FORMING: Die Casting & Extruding

Park Engineering Inc .............................. E ....... 847 455-1424
Franklin Park *(G-10546)*
Service Machine Jobs ............................ G ....... 815 986-3033
Rockford *(G-18613)*
Simpson Technologies ............................ E ....... 630 978-2700
Aurora *(G-1078)*

## MACHINE TOOLS, METAL FORMING: Electroforming

10x Microstructures LLC ........................ G ....... 847 215-7448
Wheeling *(G-21991)*
Woodstock Special Machining ................. G ....... 815 338-7383
Woodstock *(G-22628)*

## MACHINE TOOLS, METAL FORMING: Forming, Metal Deposit

Dreis and Krump Mfg Co ........................ E ....... 708 258-1200
Peotone *(G-17488)*
Terry Tool & Machining Corp .................. G ....... 847 289-1054
East Dundee *(G-8658)*
Whitney Roper LLC ................................ D ....... 815 962-3011
Rockford *(G-18681)*

## MACHINE TOOLS, METAL FORMING: Headers

First Header Die Inc .............................. G ....... 815 282-5161
Machesney Park *(G-14075)*
Precision Header Tooling Inc .................. F ....... 815 874-9116
Rockford *(G-18538)*

## MACHINE TOOLS, METAL FORMING: High Energy Rate

Innovate Technologies Inc ...................... G ....... 630 587-4220
Saint Charles *(G-19197)*

## MACHINE TOOLS, METAL FORMING: Magnetic Forming

A & A Magnetics Inc .............................. F ....... 815 338-6054
Woodstock *(G-22532)*

## MACHINE TOOLS, METAL FORMING: Marking

Geo T Schmidt Inc ................................. D ....... 847 647-7117
Niles *(G-15982)*
Kwik Mark Inc ....................................... G ....... 815 363-8268
McHenry *(G-14519)*
Marsh Shipping Supply Co LLC .............. F ....... 618 343-1006
Collinsville *(G-7335)*
Rae Products and Chem Corp ................ G ....... 708 396-1984
Alsip *(G-517)*

## MACHINE TOOLS, METAL FORMING: Mechanical, Pneumatic Or Hyd

Ajax Tool Works Inc .............................. D ....... 847 455-5420
Franklin Park *(G-10387)*
Williams White & Company .................... C ....... 309 797-7650
Moline *(G-14977)*

## MACHINE TOOLS, METAL FORMING: Presses, Hyd & Pneumatic

Hastings Manufacturing Inc .................... E ....... 800 338-8688
Millstadt *(G-14825)*
Sterling Products Inc ............................. D ....... 847 273-7700
Schaumburg *(G-19740)*

## MACHINE TOOLS, METAL FORMING: Pressing

L M C Inc ............................................... G ....... 815 758-3514
Dekalb *(G-8101)*
Venturedyne Ltd .................................... E ....... 708 597-7550
Chicago *(G-6884)*

## MACHINE TOOLS, METAL FORMING: Rebuilt

Kwalyti Tling McHy Rblding Inc ............... F ....... 630 761-8040
Batavia *(G-1463)*
New Lenox Machine Co Inc ..................... F ....... 815 584-4866
Dwight *(G-8589)*
Nor Service Inc ..................................... E ....... 815 232-8379
Freeport *(G-10676)*
Tox- Pressotechnik LLC ......................... G ....... 630 447-4600
Warrenville *(G-21365)*

## MACHINE TOOLS, METAL FORMING: Robots, Pressing, Extrudg, Etc

Cloos Robotic Welding Inc ..................... F ....... 847 923-9988
Schaumburg *(G-19474)*

## MACHINE TOOLS, METAL FORMING: Spring Winding & Forming

Accurate Spring Tech Inc ....................... F ....... 815 344-3333
McHenry *(G-14475)*
Integral Automation Inc ......................... F ....... 630 654-4300
Burr Ridge *(G-2856)*

## MACHINE TOOLS: Metal Cutting

1883 Properties Inc ............................... D ....... 847 537-8800
Lincolnshire *(G-13422)*
A&W Tool Inc ........................................ G ....... 815 653-1700
Ringwood *(G-17986)*
Abbco Inc .............................................. E ....... 630 595-7115
Elk Grove Village *(G-9253)*
Acsys Lasertechnik US Inc ..................... G ....... 224 699-9572
Elgin *(G-8934)*
ADK Arms Inc ....................................... G ....... 847 981-9800
Elk Grove Village *(G-9273)*
ADS LLC ............................................... D ....... 256 430-3366
Burr Ridge *(G-2820)*
American Machine Tools Inc ................... G ....... 773 775-6285
Chicago *(G-3861)*
Automatic Production Equipment ............ G ....... 847 439-1448
Elk Grove Village *(G-9321)*
Belcar Products Inc ............................... G ....... 630 462-1950
Carol Stream *(G-3113)*
Belden Machine Corporation ................... F ....... 708 344-4600
Broadview *(G-2561)*
Bertsche Engineering Corp ..................... F ....... 847 537-8757
Buffalo Grove *(G-2664)*
Beverly Shear Mfg Corporation ............... G ....... 773 233-2063
Chicago *(G-4098)*
Bilz Tool Company ................................. F ....... 630 495-3996
Lombard *(G-13770)*
Bley LLC ............................................... D ....... 847 290-0117
Elk Grove Village *(G-9344)*
Bos Machine Tool Services Inc ............... F ....... 309 658-2223
Hillsdale *(G-11901)*
Bourn & Koch Inc .................................. D ....... 815 965-4013
Rockford *(G-18290)*
Branson Ultrasonics Corp ....................... G ....... 847 229-0800
Buffalo Grove *(G-2669)*
Bystronic Inc ......................................... C ....... 847 214-0300
Elgin *(G-8974)*
C D T Manufacturing Inc ........................ G ....... 847 679-2361
Skokie *(G-19972)*
Cdv Corp ............................................... F ....... 815 397-3903
Rockford *(G-18300)*

**CH Machining Company** G 630 595-1050
Bensenville *(G-1856)*
**Chad Mazeika** G 815 298-8118
Rockford *(G-18303)*
**Charlotte Dmg Inc** G 630 227-3900
Itasca *(G-12243)*
**Chicago Grinding & Machine Co** E 708 343-4399
Melrose Park *(G-14610)*
**Circle Cutting Tools Inc** G 815 398-4153
Rockford *(G-18310)*
**Crown Tool Company Inc** G 630 766-3050
Bensenville *(G-1872)*
**Custom Cutting Tools Inc** G 815 986-0320
Loves Park *(G-13931)*
**Custom Tool Inc** F 217 465-8538
Paris *(G-17145)*
**Del-Co-West Inc** F 309 799-7543
Milan *(G-14783)*
**Diamond Edge Manufactoring** G 630 458-1630
Addison *(G-89)*
**Dmg Charlotte LLC** F 704 583-1193
Hoffman Estates *(G-12005)*
**Dmg Mori Usa Inc** D 847 593-5400
Hoffman Estates *(G-12006)*
**Emhart Teknologies LLC** F 877 364-2781
Chicago *(G-4743)*
**Engineered Abrasives Inc** E 662 582-4143
Alsip *(G-462)*
**Engis Corporation** C 847 808-9400
Wheeling *(G-22047)*
**Fordoc Incorporated** G 708 452-8400
River Grove *(G-18009)*
**Form Relief Tool Co Inc** F 815 393-4263
Davis Junction *(G-7812)*
**Gail E Stephens** G 618 372-0140
Brighton *(G-2540)*
**Greenlee Textron Inc** D 815 397-7070
Rockford *(G-18405)*
**Gymtek Incorporated** F 815 547-0771
Belvidere *(G-1760)*
**Hartland Cutting Tools Inc** F 847 639-9400
Cary *(G-3350)*
**Hfd Manufacturing Inc** G 847 263-5050
Waukegan *(G-21568)*
**Hobsource** G 847 229-9120
Mount Prospect *(G-15335)*
**Holden Industries Inc** F 847 940-1500
Deerfield *(G-8013)*
**Hottinger Bldwin Msrements Inc** E 217 328-5359
Champaign *(G-3495)*
**Ibanum Manufacturing LLC** G 815 262-5373
Rockford *(G-18425)*
**Illinois Electro Deburring Co** F 847 678-5010
Franklin Park *(G-10494)*
**Ingersoll Machine Tools Inc** C 815 987-6000
Rockford *(G-18433)*
**Ingersoll Prod Systems LLC** D 815 637-8500
Rockford *(G-18434)*
**Intrepid Tool Industries LLC** E 773 467-4200
Chicago *(G-5229)*
**Isewan USA Inc** G 630 561-2807
Schaumburg *(G-19584)*
**J & L Gear Incorporated** F 630 832-1880
Villa Park *(G-21259)*
**Jtekt Toyoda Americas Corp** C 847 253-0340
Arlington Heights *(G-786)*
**Komet America Holding Inc** G 847 923-8400
Schaumburg *(G-19602)*
**Komet of America Inc** C 847 923-8400
Schaumburg *(G-19603)*
**Logan Graphic Products Inc** D 847 526-5515
Wauconda *(G-21479)*
**Machine Technology Inc** F 815 795-6818
Marseilles *(G-14313)*
**Magnetrol International Inc** C 630 723-6600
Aurora *(G-1051)*
**Manan Tool & Manufacturing** A 847 637-3333
Wheeling *(G-22100)*
**Master Machine Group** G 847 472-9940
Elgin *(G-9101)*
**Metal Cutting Tools Corp** C 815 226-0650
Rockford *(G-18495)*
**Micro Machines Intl LLC** G 815 985-3652
Rockford *(G-18499)*
**Modern Specialties Company** G 312 648-5800
Chicago *(G-5785)*
**Nicholas Machine & Tool Inc** G 847 298-2035
Rosemont *(G-19018)*
**NNt Enterprises Incorporated** E 630 875-9600
Itasca *(G-12332)*
**Onsrud Machine Corp** E 847 520-5300
Northbrook *(G-16327)*
**OSG Power Tools Inc** C 630 561-4008
Bensenville *(G-1960)*
**OSG Usa Inc** E 630 790-1400
Glendale Heights *(G-11054)*
**Pioneer Service Inc** E 630 628-0249
Addison *(G-242)*
**Port Byron Machine Inc** G 309 523-9111
Port Byron *(G-17722)*
**Ppt Industrial Machines Inc** E 800 851-3586
Mount Carmel *(G-15281)*
**Prater Industries Inc** D 630 679-3200
Bolingbrook *(G-2359)*
**Precision McHned Cmponents Inc** E 630 759-5555
Romeoville *(G-18860)*
**Precision Tool & Die Company** F 217 864-3371
Mount Zion *(G-15455)*
**Process Screw Products Inc** E 815 864-2220
Shannon *(G-19901)*
**Rabbit Tool USA Inc** G 309 793-4375
Rock Island *(G-18196)*
**Radiac Abrasives Inc** E 630 898-0315
Oswego *(G-16931)*
**Ramco Group LLC** F 847 639-9899
Crystal Lake *(G-7636)*
**Reliance Tool & Mfg Co** E 847 695-1235
Elgin *(G-9164)*
**Reliance Tool & Mfg Co** E 847 455-4350
Franklin Park *(G-10573)*
**Resco Products Co** G 847 455-3776
Franklin Park *(G-10574)*
**Robbins Hdd LLC** F 847 955-0050
Lake Zurich *(G-13123)*
**Roberts Swiss Inc** E 630 467-9100
Itasca *(G-12348)*
**Roll Rite Inc** G 815 645-8600
Davis Junction *(G-7814)*
**Sacco-Camex Inc** G 630 595-8090
Franklin Park *(G-10580)*
**Schram Enterprises Inc** E 708 345-2252
Melrose Park *(G-14693)*
**Serien Manufacturing Inc** G 815 337-1447
Woodstock *(G-22608)*
**Service Machine Jobs** G 815 986-3033
Rockford *(G-18613)*
**Specialty Enterprises Inc** G 630 595-7808
Franklin Park *(G-10592)*
**Swisstronics Corp** G 708 403-8877
Orland Park *(G-16897)*
**Synax Inc** F 224 352-2927
Buffalo Grove *(G-2779)*
**Thread & Gage Co Inc** G 815 675-2305
Spring Grove *(G-20367)*
**Tiger Tool Inc** G 888 551-4490
Glendale Heights *(G-11084)*
**Tooling Solutions Inc** G 847 472-9940
Elgin *(G-9212)*
**Total Tooling Technology Inc** F 847 437-5135
Elk Grove Village *(G-9786)*
**Tvo Acquisition Corporation** E 708 656-4240
Cicero *(G-7239)*
**Ty Miles Incorporated** E 708 344-5480
Westchester *(G-21860)*
**USA Machine Rebuilders** G 815 547-6542
Belvidere *(G-1792)*
**Variable Operations Tech Inc** E 815 479-8528
Crystal Lake *(G-7672)*
**Vaughn & Sons Machine Shop** G 618 842-9048
Fairfield *(G-10157)*
**Voortman USA Corp** F 815 468-6300
Monee *(G-15006)*
**We Innovex Inc** G 847 291-3553
Northbrook *(G-16384)*
**Wec Welding and Machining LLC** G 847 680-8100
Lake Bluff *(G-12870)*
**West Precision Tool Inc** F 630 766-8304
Bensenville *(G-2014)*

## *MACHINE TOOLS: Metal Forming*

**A J Carbide Grinding** G 847 675-5112
Skokie *(G-19942)*
**Advanced Prototype Molding** G 847 202-4200
Palatine *(G-16998)*
**Alan Manufacturing Corp** G 815 568-6836
Marengo *(G-14217)*
**Altman Manufacturing Co Inc** F 630 963-0031
Lisle *(G-13556)*
**American Machine Tools Inc** G 773 775-6285
Chicago *(G-3861)*
**Ardagh Conversion Systems Inc** G 847 438-4100
Lake Zurich *(G-13043)*
**Bohl Machine & Tool Company** E 309 799-5122
Milan *(G-14777)*
**Centric Mfg Solutions Inc** G 815 315-9258
Chicago *(G-4273)*
**Clements National Company** G 708 594-5890
Broadview *(G-2569)*
**Continental Automation Inc** E 630 584-5100
Saint Charles *(G-19162)*
**Cutting Edge Industries Inc** G 847 678-1777
Franklin Park *(G-10451)*
**D R Sperry & Co** D 630 892-4361
Aurora *(G-1137)*
**Deringer-Ney Inc** E 847 566-4100
Vernon Hills *(G-21157)*
**Dover Europe Inc** G 630 541-1540
Downers Grove *(G-8433)*
**Duo-Fast Corporation** E 847 944-2288
Glenview *(G-11122)*
**Elgalabwater LLC** G 630 343-5251
Woodridge *(G-22477)*
**Epcor Industrial Inc** G 847 545-9212
Elk Grove Village *(G-9461)*
**Formtek Inc** F 630 285-1500
Lisle *(G-13589)*
**Hersheys Metal Meister LLC** E 217 234-4700
Claremont *(G-7256)*
**Illinois Tool Works Inc** C 630 595-3500
Itasca *(G-12281)*
**Infinity Metal Spinning Inc** G 773 731-4467
Chicago *(G-5183)*
**Ingenious Concepts Inc** G 630 539-8059
Medinah *(G-14576)*
**John J Rickhoff Shtmtl Co Inc** F 708 331-2970
Phoenix *(G-17541)*
**Komori America Corporation** D 847 806-9000
Rolling Meadows *(G-18739)*
**Kwm Gutterman Inc** E 815 725-9205
Rockdale *(G-18223)*
**Littell International Inc** E 630 622-4950
Schaumburg *(G-19621)*
**Lotus Creative Innovations LLC** G 815 440-8999
Compton *(G-7367)*
**Madison Capital Partners Corp** G 312 277-0323
Chicago *(G-5597)*
**Mead Products LLC** G 847 541-9500
Lake Zurich *(G-13100)*
**Metro Tool Company** G 847 673-6790
Skokie *(G-20037)*
**Mgb Engineering Company** E 847 956-7444
Elk Grove Village *(G-9624)*
**Mikes Machinery Rebuilders** G 630 543-6400
Addison *(G-215)*
**Mzm Manufacturing Inc** G 815 624-8666
Roscoe *(G-18909)*
**Ocm Inc** G 847 462-4258
Wauconda *(G-21490)*
**Petrak Industries Incorporated** E 815 483-2290
Joliet *(G-12551)*
**Ppt Industrial Machines Inc** E 800 851-3586
Mount Carmel *(G-15281)*
**Precision Service Mtr Inc** F 630 628-9900
Addison *(G-253)*
**Punch Products Manufacturing** E 773 533-2800
Chicago *(G-6226)*
**Rapid Air** G 815 397-2578
Rockford *(G-18548)*
**Rock Valley Die Sinking Inc** F 815 874-5511
Rockford *(G-18565)*
**Sieber Tool Engineering LP** F 630 462-9370
Carol Stream *(G-3240)*
**Sloan Industries Inc** E 630 350-1614
Wood Dale *(G-22423)*
**Summit Tooling Inc** F 815 385-7500
McHenry *(G-14559)*
**Sure-Way Die Designs Inc** F 630 323-0370
Westmont *(G-21924)*
**Versatech LLC** C 217 342-3500
Effingham *(G-8860)*
**W A Whitney Co** C 815 964-6771
Rockford *(G-18671)*
**Wardzala Industries Inc** F 847 288-9909
Franklin Park *(G-10627)*

## *MACHINERY & EQPT FINANCE LEASING*

**AT&T Teleholdings Inc** G 800 257-0902
Chicago *(G-3973)*
**Marmon Industrial LLC** G 312 372-9500
Chicago *(G-5626)*

# MACHINERY & EQPT, AGRICULTURAL, WHOL: Farm Eqpt Parts/Splys  PRODUCT SECTION

## MACHINERY & EQPT, AGRICULTURAL, WHOL: Farm Eqpt Parts/Splys

Shoup Manufacturing Co Inc ............... E ....... 815 933-4439
Kankakee (G-12648)

## MACHINERY & EQPT, AGRICULTURAL, WHOLESALE: Agricultural, NEC

Seedburo Equipment Company Inc ...... F ....... 312 738-3700
Des Plaines (G-8271)

## MACHINERY & EQPT, AGRICULTURAL, WHOLESALE: Dairy

Gea Farm Technologies Inc ............... C ....... 630 548-8200
Naperville (G-15662)

## MACHINERY & EQPT, AGRICULTURAL, WHOLESALE: Farm Implements

Birkeys Farm Store Inc ...................... E ....... 217 337-1772
Urbana (G-21073)

## MACHINERY & EQPT, AGRICULTURAL, WHOLESALE: Landscaping Eqpt

Corsaw Hardwood Lumber Inc ........... F ....... 309 293-2055
Smithfield (G-20119)
Oly Ola Edging Inc ........................... F ....... 630 833-3033
Villa Park (G-21274)

## MACHINERY & EQPT, AGRICULTURAL, WHOLESALE: Lawn

Siemer Enterprises Inc ...................... E ....... 217 857-3171
Teutopolis (G-20855)

## MACHINERY & EQPT, AGRICULTURAL, WHOLESALE: Lawn & Garden

Cobraco Manufacturing Inc ............... E ....... 847 726-5800
Lake Zurich (G-13055)
Grower Equipment & Supply Co ......... F ....... 847 223-3100
Hainesville (G-11523)
Power Equipment Company ............... E ....... 815 754-4090
Cortland (G-7394)

## MACHINERY & EQPT, AGRICULTURAL, WHOLESALE: Livestock Eqpt

Gsi Group LLC ................................. C ....... 217 463-1612
Paris (G-17148)

## MACHINERY & EQPT, AGRICULTURAL, WHOLESALE: Tractors

National Tractor Parts Inc .................. E ....... 630 552-4235
Plano (G-17668)
Woods Equipment Company ............. D ....... 815 732-2141
Oregon (G-16834)

## MACHINERY & EQPT, INDL, WHOL: Controlling Instruments/Access

Automax Corporation ........................ G ....... 630 972-1919
Woodridge (G-22454)
Novaspect Inc .................................. C ....... 847 956-8020
Schaumburg (G-19670)

## MACHINERY & EQPT, INDL, WHOL: Environ Pollution Cntrl, Air

C P Environmental Inc ...................... F ....... 630 759-8866
Romeoville (G-18805)
Enders Process Equipment Corp ........ G ....... 630 469-3787
Glendale Heights (G-11022)

## MACHINERY & EQPT, INDL, WHOLESALE: Chemical Process

Benetech Inc ................................... E ....... 630 844-1300
Aurora (G-1119)
Benetech (taiwan) LLC ..................... G ....... 630 844-1300
Aurora (G-1120)

## MACHINERY & EQPT, INDL, WHOLESALE: Conveyor Systems

Centec Automation Inc ..................... G ....... 847 791-9430
Palatine (G-17009)
Engineering Products Company ......... G ....... 815 436-9055
Plainfield (G-17595)
Franklin Automation Inc .................... F ....... 630 466-1900
Sugar Grove (G-20725)
Machinex Technologies Inc ............... D ....... 773 867-8801
Chicago (G-5593)
Payson Casters Inc .......................... G ....... 847 336-5033
Gurnee (G-11483)
Sardee Industries Inc ....................... G ....... 630 824-4200
Lisle (G-13654)
Siemens Industry Inc ....................... G ....... 309 664-2460
Bloomington (G-2223)
Visionary Solutions Inc ..................... G ....... 847 296-9615
Des Plaines (G-8299)

## MACHINERY & EQPT, INDL, WHOLESALE: Cranes

Coast Crane Company ..................... G ....... 847 215-6500
Buffalo Grove (G-2674)
Lanco International Inc ..................... B ....... 708 596-5200
Hazel Crest (G-11709)

## MACHINERY & EQPT, INDL, WHOLESALE: Drilling Bits

Bit Brokers International Ltd .............. G ....... 618 435-5811
West Frankfort (G-21804)
Rodgers Bill Oil Min Bits Svc ............. G ....... 618 299-7771
West Salem (G-21824)
T & T Carbide ................................. G ....... 618 439-7253
Logan (G-13755)
T & T Distribution Inc ....................... E ....... 815 223-0715
Peru (G-17528)

## MACHINERY & EQPT, INDL, WHOLESALE: Drilling, Exc Bits

Galaxy Industries Inc ........................ D ....... 847 639-8580
Cary (G-3345)
TT Technologies Inc ......................... D ....... 630 851-8200
Aurora (G-1091)

## MACHINERY & EQPT, INDL, WHOLESALE: Engines & Parts, Diesel

American Diesel Tube Corp ............... F ....... 630 628-1830
Addison (G-35)
Area Diesel Service Inc .................... E ....... 217 854-2641
Carlinville (G-3030)
Concentric Itasca Inc ....................... D ....... 630 268-1528
Itasca (G-12246)
Cummins Crosspoint LLC ................. E ....... 309 452-4454
Normal (G-16068)
Cummins Npower LLC ...................... E ....... 708 579-9222
Hodgkins (G-11973)
Du Page Precision Products Co ......... D ....... 630 849-2940
Aurora (G-998)
Industrial Welder Rebuilders ............. G ....... 708 371-5688
Alsip (G-473)
Midwest Fuel Injction Svc Corp .......... F ....... 847 991-7867
Palatine (G-17056)
Tuscola Packaging Group LLC .......... G ....... 734 268-2877
Tuscola (G-21027)
Yanmar (usa) Inc ............................. G ....... 847 541-1900
Buffalo Grove (G-2796)

## MACHINERY & EQPT, INDL, WHOLESALE: Engines, Gasoline

Kaser Power Equipment Inc .............. G ....... 309 289-2176
Knoxville (G-12721)
Owen Walker .................................. G ....... 217 285-4012
Pittsfield (G-17572)

## MACHINERY & EQPT, INDL, WHOLESALE: Engs & Parts, Air-Cooled

Cummins Dist Holdco Inc .................. E ....... 309 787-4300
Rock Island (G-18170)

## MACHINERY & EQPT, INDL, WHOLESALE: Engs/Transportation Eqpt

Kackert Enterprises Inc .................... G ....... 630 898-9339
Aurora (G-1179)

## MACHINERY & EQPT, INDL, WHOLESALE: Food Manufacturing

Bc International ............................... G ....... 847 674-7384
Skokie (G-19962)
Bz Bearing & Power Inc .................... G ....... 877 850-3993
Hickory Hills (G-11767)
Packers Supplies & Eqp LLC ............. G ....... 630 543-5810
Addison (G-236)

## MACHINERY & EQPT, INDL, WHOLESALE: Food Product Manufacturng

Melissa A Miller ............................... G ....... 708 529-7786
New Lenox (G-15893)

## MACHINERY & EQPT, INDL, WHOLESALE: Fuel Injection Systems

Caterpillar Inc ................................. B ....... 815 842-6000
Pontiac (G-17697)

## MACHINERY & EQPT, INDL, WHOLESALE: Hoists

Handling Systems Inc ...................... E ....... 708 352-1213
La Grange (G-12735)

## MACHINERY & EQPT, INDL, WHOLESALE: Hydraulic Systems

Certified Power Inc .......................... E ....... 847 573-3800
Mundelein (G-15485)
Erie Vehicle Company ...................... F ....... 773 536-6300
Chicago (G-4772)
Flodyne Inc .................................... G ....... 630 563-3600
Hanover Park (G-11581)
Force America Inc ........................... F ....... 815 730-3600
Joliet (G-12496)
Geib Industries Inc .......................... G ....... 847 455-4550
Bensenville (G-1906)
Headco Industries Inc ...................... F ....... 847 640-6490
Elk Grove Village (G-9519)
Headco Industries Inc ...................... G ....... 815 729-4016
Joliet (G-12509)
Jrm International Inc ........................ G ....... 815 282-9330
Loves Park (G-13955)
Master Mechanic Mfg Inc .................. G ....... 847 573-3812
Mundelein (G-15524)
Morrell Incorporated ........................ F ....... 630 858-4600
Glendale Heights (G-11050)
Tetra Pak Inc .................................. D ....... 847 955-6000
Vernon Hills (G-21208)

## MACHINERY & EQPT, INDL, WHOLESALE: Indl Machine Parts

Industrial Phrm Resources Inc ........... F ....... 630 823-4700
Bartlett (G-1357)
Meadoweld Machine Inc ................... G ....... 815 623-3939
South Beloit (G-20161)
Rjg Enterprises Ltd .......................... G ....... 847 752-2065
Grayslake (G-11362)

## MACHINERY & EQPT, INDL, WHOLESALE: Instruments & Cntrl Eqpt

Fox Controls Inc .............................. E ....... 847 464-5096
Elgin (G-9040)
Process Technologies Group ............. G ....... 630 393-4777
Warrenville (G-21360)
S-P-D Incorporated .......................... G ....... 847 882-9820
Palatine (G-17070)
Worth-Pfaff Innovations Inc .............. G ....... 847 940-9305
Deerfield (G-8068)

## MACHINERY & EQPT, INDL, WHOLESALE: Lift Trucks & Parts

Alm Materials Handling LLC .............. E ....... 815 673-5546
Streator (G-20682)
Bolzoni Auramo Inc ......................... E ....... 708 957-8809
Homewood (G-12092)

# PRODUCT SECTION — MACHINERY & EQPT: Electroplating

Komatsu Forklift USA LLC .................... E ...... 847 437-5800
 Rolling Meadows (G-18738)
Manitowoc Lifts and Mfg LLC ................ G ...... 815 748-9500
 Dekalb (G-8105)
R&R Equipment Plus1 Inc ...................... F ...... 708 529-3931
 Chicago Ridge (G-7157)
Systems Equipment Services ................ G ...... 708 535-1273
 Oak Forest (G-16590)
Tvh Parts Co ........................................... E ...... 847 223-1000
 Grayslake (G-11365)
Unicarriers Americas Corp ..................... B ...... 800 871-5438
 Marengo (G-14244)

## MACHINERY & EQPT, INDL, WHOLESALE: Machine Tools & Access

Abbott Machine Co ................................. F ...... 618 465-1898
 Alton (G-557)
Erowa Technology Inc ............................ F ...... 847 290-0295
 Arlington Heights (G-751)
Fibro Inc ................................................. F ...... 815 229-1300
 Rockford (G-18382)
Line Craft Tool Company Inc ................. C ...... 630 932-1182
 Lombard (G-13820)
Madden Ventures Inc ............................. G ...... 847 487-0644
 Mundelein (G-15522)
Mitsubishi Materials USA Corp .............. G ...... 847 519-1601
 Schaumburg (G-19649)
Rockform Tooling & Machinery .............. G ...... 815 398-7650
 Rockford (G-18592)
Spencer and Krahn Mch Tl Sls ............... G ...... 815 282-3300
 Rockford (G-18627)
Techniks LLC ......................................... E ...... 815 689-2748
 Cullom (G-7685)

## MACHINERY & EQPT, INDL, WHOLESALE: Machine Tools & Metalwork

Accushim Inc .......................................... G ...... 708 442-6448
 Lyons (G-14029)
Belcar Products Inc ................................ G ...... 630 462-1950
 Carol Stream (G-3113)
Crd Enterprises Inc ................................ G ...... 847 438-4299
 Lake Zurich (G-13058)
J Schneerberger Corp ............................ G ...... 847 888-3498
 Elgin (G-9081)
Jtekt Toyoda Americas Corp .................. C ...... 847 253-0340
 Arlington Heights (G-786)
Kinast Inc ................................................ G ...... 217 852-3525
 Dallas City (G-7698)
Lmt Usa Inc ............................................ G ...... 630 969-5412
 Waukegan (G-21583)
OSG Usa Inc .......................................... E ...... 630 790-1400
 Glendale Heights (G-11054)
Pillarhouse USA Inc ............................... F ...... 847 593-9080
 Elk Grove Village (G-9680)
Powernail Company ............................... E ...... 800 323-1653
 Lake Zurich (G-13116)

## MACHINERY & EQPT, INDL, WHOLESALE: Measure/Test, Electric

Dickson/Unigage Inc .............................. E ...... 630 543-3747
 Addison (G-92)
Geotest Instrument Corp ........................ G ...... 847 869-7645
 Burr Ridge (G-2845)
Heidenhain Corporation ......................... D ...... 847 490-1191
 Schaumburg (G-19551)
Heidenhain Holding Inc .......................... G ...... 716 661-1700
 Schaumburg (G-19552)
O E M Marketing Inc .............................. F ...... 847 985-9490
 Schaumburg (G-19671)

## MACHINERY & EQPT, INDL, WHOLESALE: Metal Refining

American Chemical & Eqp Inc ................ G ...... 815 675-9199
 Northlake (G-16427)
Amic Global Inc ...................................... G ...... 847 600-3590
 Buffalo Grove (G-2659)
Chemical Processing & Acc ................... G ...... 847 793-2387
 Lincolnshire (G-13437)

## MACHINERY & EQPT, INDL, WHOLESALE: Packaging

Birnberg Machinery Inc .......................... G ...... 847 673-5242
 Skokie (G-19964)
Fromm Airpad Inc ................................... F ...... 630 393-9790
 Warrenville (G-21347)
Quad-Illinois Inc ..................................... F ...... 847 836-1115
 Elgin (G-9155)
Weary & Baity Inc .................................. G ...... 312 943-6197
 Chicago (G-6947)

## MACHINERY & EQPT, INDL, WHOLESALE: Paint Spray

Bjs Enterprises Inc ................................. G ...... 815 432-5176
 Watseka (G-21416)
Blastline USA Inc ................................... G ...... 630 871-0147
 Carol Stream (G-3118)

## MACHINERY & EQPT, INDL, WHOLESALE: Paper Manufacturing

Paperchine Inc ....................................... C ...... 815 389-8200
 Rockton (G-18700)

## MACHINERY & EQPT, INDL, WHOLESALE: Petroleum Industry

American Welding & Gas Inc ................. E ...... 630 527-2550
 Stone Park (G-20632)
R L Hoener Co ....................................... E ...... 217 223-2190
 Quincy (G-17883)

## MACHINERY & EQPT, INDL, WHOLESALE: Plastic Prdts Machinery

Universal Holdings Inc ........................... F ...... 224 353-6198
 Hoffman Estates (G-12066)

## MACHINERY & EQPT, INDL, WHOLESALE: Pneumatic Tools

Don Johns Inc ........................................ E ...... 630 326-9650
 Batavia (G-1439)
SMC Corporation of America ................. E ...... 630 449-0600
 Aurora (G-1080)

## MACHINERY & EQPT, INDL, WHOLESALE: Processing & Packaging

Ingersoll-Rand Company ........................ E ...... 630 530-3800
 Elmhurst (G-9886)
Stickon Adhesive Inds Inc ...................... E ...... 847 593-5959
 Arlington Heights (G-844)
Tramco Pump Co .................................. E ...... 312 243-5800
 Chicago (G-6756)

## MACHINERY & EQPT, INDL, WHOLESALE: Recycling

Nu-Recycling Technology Inc ................. F ...... 630 904-5237
 Naperville (G-15820)
T2 Site Amenities Incorporated .............. G ...... 847 579-9003
 Highland Park (G-11876)

## MACHINERY & EQPT, INDL, WHOLESALE: Robots

Innovative Automation ............................ G ...... 708 418-8720
 Lansing (G-13166)

## MACHINERY & EQPT, INDL, WHOLESALE: Safety Eqpt

American Labelmark Company .............. C ...... 773 478-0900
 Chicago (G-3859)
Fisher Scientific Company LLC .............. C ...... 412 490-8300
 Hanover Park (G-11580)
Guardian Equipment Inc ........................ E ...... 312 447-8100
 Chicago (G-5007)
John Thomas Inc ................................... E ...... 815 288-2343
 Dixon (G-8334)
National Safety Council ......................... B ...... 630 285-1121
 Itasca (G-12324)
North American Safety Products ............ G ...... 815 469-1144
 Mokena (G-14888)

## MACHINERY & EQPT, INDL, WHOLESALE: Sewing

Union Special LLC ................................. C ...... 847 669-5101
 Huntley (G-12182)

## MACHINERY & EQPT, INDL, WHOLESALE: Tapping Attachments

Tek Pak Inc ............................................ D ...... 630 406-0560
 Batavia (G-1506)

## MACHINERY & EQPT, INDL, WHOLESALE: Tool & Die Makers

Patkus Machine Co ................................ G ...... 815 398-7818
 Rockford (G-18530)
Progrssive Cmponents Intl Corp ............ D ...... 847 487-1000
 Wauconda (G-21494)
Tritech International LLC ........................ G ...... 847 888-0333
 Elgin (G-9215)

## MACHINERY & EQPT, INDL, WHOLESALE: Water Pumps

Semler Industries Inc ............................. E ...... 847 671-5650
 Franklin Park (G-10586)

## MACHINERY & EQPT, INDL, WHOLESALE: Woodworking

U S Concepts Inc ................................... F ...... 630 876-3110
 West Chicago (G-21787)

## MACHINERY & EQPT, WHOLESALE: Concrete Processing

CCS Contractor Eqp & Sup Inc ............. E ...... 630 393-9020
 Naperville (G-15622)

## MACHINERY & EQPT, WHOLESALE: Construction, General

Elston Materials LLC .............................. G ...... 773 235-3100
 Chicago (G-4736)
Grover Welding Company ...................... G ...... 847 966-3119
 Skokie (G-20007)
Jcb Inc .................................................... G ...... 912 704-2995
 Aurora (G-1037)
Lanigan Holdings LLC ............................ F ...... 708 596-5200
 Hazel Crest (G-11710)
Lee Jensen Sales Co Inc ....................... E ...... 815 459-0929
 Crystal Lake (G-7602)
Otak International Inc ............................. G ...... 630 373-9229
 Melrose Park (G-14679)
R W Bradley Supply Company .............. G ...... 217 528-8438
 Springfield (G-20510)
Rahn Equipment Company ................... G ...... 217 431-1232
 Danville (G-7762)

## MACHINERY & EQPT, WHOLESALE: Contractors Materials

Carroll Distrg & Cnstr Sup Inc ................ G ...... 630 243-0272
 Lemont (G-13229)
Carroll Distrg & Cnstr Sup Inc ................ G ...... 815 941-1548
 Morris (G-15100)
Carroll Distrg & Cnstr Sup Inc ................ G ...... 309 449-6044
 Hopedale (G-12121)
Carroll Distrg & Cnstr Sup Inc ................ G ...... 217 223-8126
 Quincy (G-17810)
Carroll Distrg & Cnstr Sup Inc ................ F ...... 630 369-6520
 Naperville (G-15619)
Outdoor Power Inc ................................. F ...... 217 228-9890
 Quincy (G-17865)

## MACHINERY & EQPT, WHOLESALE: Logging

Ramsplitter Log Splitters Inc .................. G ...... 815 398-4726
 Rockford (G-18547)

## MACHINERY & EQPT, WHOLESALE: Masonry

Galaxy Industries Inc ............................. D ...... 847 639-8580
 Cary (G-3345)

## MACHINERY & EQPT, WHOLESALE: Oil Field Eqpt

Vaughn & Sons Machine Shop .............. G ...... 618 842-9048
 Fairfield (G-10157)

## MACHINERY & EQPT: Electroplating

Hardwood Line Manufacturing Co .......... E ...... 773 463-2600
 Chicago (G-5045)

Employee Codes: A=Over 500 employees, B=251-500
C=101-250, D=51-100, E=20-50, F=10-19, G=3-9

## MACHINERY & EQPT: Electroplating

Ransburg Corporation .................. B ...... 847 724-7500
  Glenview *(G-11190)*
Rapid Electroplating Process .......... G ...... 708 344-2504
  Melrose Park *(G-14685)*
Sterling Systems Sales Corp .......... G ...... 630 584-3580
  Saint Charles *(G-19271)*

### MACHINERY & EQPT: Farm

A & P Grain Systems Inc ............. F ...... 815 827-3079
  Maple Park *(G-14196)*
AGCO Corporation .................... E ...... 630 406-3248
  Batavia *(G-1404)*
Alamo Group (il) Inc ................. E ...... 217 784-4261
  Gibson City *(G-10897)*
Alvarez & Marsal Inc ................ E ...... 312 601-4220
  Chicago *(G-3840)*
Aqua Control Inc ..................... E ...... 815 664-4900
  Spring Valley *(G-20374)*
B J Fehr Machine Co ................. G ...... 309 923-8691
  Roanoke *(G-18048)*
B T Brown Manufacturing ............ G ...... 815 947-3633
  Kent *(G-12665)*
Beall Manufacturing Inc ............. E ...... 618 259-8154
  East Alton *(G-8599)*
Birkeys Farm Store Inc .............. E ...... 217 337-1772
  Urbana *(G-21073)*
Brian Burcar .......................... G ...... 815 856-2271
  Leonore *(G-13285)*
Bushnell Illinois Tank Co ............ D ...... 309 772-3106
  Bushnell *(G-2898)*
Calmer Corn Heads Inc .............. E ...... 309 629-9000
  Lynn Center *(G-14015)*
Caterpillar Brazil LLC ................ G ...... 309 675-1000
  Peoria *(G-17324)*
Charles Crane ........................ G ...... 815 258-5375
  Clifton *(G-7273)*
Christopher Concrete Products ...... G ...... 618 724-2951
  Buckner *(G-2647)*
Circle K Industries Inc ............... F ...... 847 949-0363
  Mundelein *(G-15487)*
Cline Concrete Products ............. F ...... 217 283-5012
  Hoopeston *(G-12107)*
Cnh Capital America LLC ............ E ...... 630 887-2233
  Burr Ridge *(G-2831)*
Cnh Industrial America LLC ......... G ...... 847 263-5793
  Waukegan *(G-21539)*
Cnh Industrial America LLC ......... E ...... 309 965-2233
  Goodfield *(G-11244)*
Cnh Industrial America LLC ......... C ...... 309 965-2217
  Goodfield *(G-11245)*
Cnh Industrial America LLC ......... C ...... 630 887-2233
  Burr Ridge *(G-2833)*
Cnh Industrial America LLC ......... E ...... 706 629-5572
  Burr Ridge *(G-2832)*
CST Industries Inc ................... C ...... 815 756-1551
  Dekalb *(G-8080)*
D & B Fabricators & Distrs .......... F ...... 630 325-3811
  Lemont *(G-13234)*
Davenport Tractor Inc ................ G ...... 309 781-8305
  Milan *(G-14782)*
David Taylor .......................... E ...... 217 222-6480
  Quincy *(G-17819)*
Dawn Equipment Company Inc ...... F ...... 815 899-8000
  Sycamore *(G-20791)*
Deere & Company .................... A ...... 309 765-8000
  Moline *(G-14925)*
Deere & Company .................... A ...... 309 748-0580
  Moline *(G-14926)*
Deere & Company .................... E ...... 309 765-3177
  Moline *(G-14927)*
Deere & Company .................... A ...... 309 765-8000
  Moline *(G-14928)*
Deere & Company .................... A ...... 800 765-9588
  East Moline *(G-8674)*
Deere & Company .................... G ...... 309 765-8000
  East Moline *(G-8675)*
Deere & Company .................... E ...... 309 748-8260
  Moline *(G-14931)*
Deere & Company .................... F ...... 309 765-8000
  Moline *(G-14932)*
Deere & Company .................... A ...... 309 765-8277
  Moline *(G-14934)*
Dsi Inc ................................ G ...... 309 965-5110
  Goodfield *(G-11246)*
Factory Direct Worldwide LLC ....... F ...... 847 272-6464
  Wheeling *(G-22053)*
Farmweld Inc ......................... E ...... 217 857-6423
  Teutopolis *(G-20852)*
Fehr Cab Interiors .................... G ...... 815 692-3355
  Fairbury *(G-10124)*

Genwoods Holdco LLC ............... A ...... 815 732-2141
  Oregon *(G-16825)*
Globetec Midwest Partners LLC .... G ...... 847 608-9300
  South Elgin *(G-20200)*
H W Hostetler & Sons ................ G ...... 815 438-7816
  Deer Grove *(G-7967)*
Hcc Inc ............................... C ...... 815 539-9371
  Mendota *(G-14722)*
Henry A Engelhart .................... E ...... 217 563-2176
  Nokomis *(G-16057)*
Hipro Manufacturing Inc ............. E ...... 815 432-5271
  Watseka *(G-21418)*
Hypermax Engineering Inc .......... F ...... 847 428-5655
  Gilberts *(G-10924)*
J & J Equipment Inc ................. G ...... 309 449-5442
  Hopedale *(G-12122)*
John Deere AG Holdings Inc ........ G ...... 309 765-8000
  Moline *(G-14946)*
John Deere Cnstr & For Co ......... F ...... 309 765-8000
  Moline *(G-14947)*
Kinast Inc ............................ G ...... 217 852-3525
  Dallas City *(G-7698)*
Korhumel Inc ......................... G ...... 847 330-0335
  Schaumburg *(G-19604)*
Ksem Inc ............................. G ...... 618 656-5388
  Edwardsville *(G-8805)*
Ksi Conveyor Inc .................... D ...... 815 457-2403
  Cissna Park *(G-7255)*
Licon Inc ............................. E ...... 618 485-2222
  Ashley *(G-927)*
Lmt Inc ............................... F ...... 309 932-3311
  Galva *(G-10792)*
Manitou Americas Inc ................ G ...... 262 334-9461
  Belvidere *(G-1769)*
McLaughlin Body Co ................. D ...... 309 762-7755
  Moline *(G-14955)*
Meteer Inc ........................... G ...... 217 636-7280
  Athens *(G-940)*
Midwest Bio-Systems Inc ........... G ...... 815 438-7200
  Tampico *(G-20829)*
Ndy Manufacturing Inc .............. G ...... 815 426-2330
  Bonfield *(G-2385)*
Neuero Corporation .................. F ...... 630 231-9020
  West Chicago *(G-21750)*
Newton Implement Partnership ..... E ...... 618 783-8716
  Newton *(G-15943)*
Ogden Metalworks Inc .............. G ...... 217 582-2552
  Ogden *(G-16743)*
P & H Manufacturing Co ............. D ...... 217 774-2123
  Shelbyville *(G-19911)*
Polar Container Corp Inc ............ G ...... 847 299-5030
  Rosemont *(G-19024)*
Quality Metal Works Inc ............. G ...... 309 379-5311
  Stanford *(G-20552)*
R K Products Inc ..................... G ...... 309 792-1927
  East Moline *(G-8693)*
Seedburo Equipment Company Inc .. F ...... 312 738-3700
  Des Plaines *(G-8271)*
Shoup Manufacturing Co Inc ....... E ...... 815 933-4439
  Kankakee *(G-12648)*
Sopher Design & Manufacturing ..... G ...... 309 699-6419
  East Peoria *(G-8735)*
Speeco Incorporated ................. C ...... 303 279-5544
  Oregon *(G-16832)*
Star Forge Inc ....................... G ...... 815 235-7750
  Freeport *(G-10691)*
Straightline AG Inc ................... G ...... 217 963-1270
  Harristown *(G-11608)*
Trusty Warns Inc .................... E ...... 630 766-9015
  Wood Dale *(G-22434)*
Weaver Equipment LLC .............. G ...... 618 833-5521
  Buncombe *(G-2802)*
Whalen Manufacturing Company .... G ...... 309 836-1438
  Macomb *(G-14136)*
Woods Equipment Company ........ D ...... 815 732-2141
  Rockford *(G-18688)*
Yetter Manufacturing Company ..... D ...... 309 776-3222
  Colchester *(G-7309)*

### MACHINERY & EQPT: Gas Producers, Generators/Other Rltd Eqpt

Cleavenger Associates Inc .......... G ...... 630 221-0007
  Winfield *(G-22284)*
Specialized Separators Inc .......... F ...... 815 316-0626
  Rockford *(G-18625)*

### MACHINERY & EQPT: Liquid Automation

Bowl Doctors Inc ..................... G ...... 815 282-6009
  Machesney Park *(G-14060)*

Component Products Inc ............. E ...... 847 301-1000
  Schaumburg *(G-19477)*
DTS America Inc ..................... G ...... 847 783-0401
  East Dundee *(G-8633)*
Komax Systems Rockford Inc ...... D ...... 815 885-8800
  Loves Park *(G-13956)*
Online Inc ............................ F ...... 815 363-8008
  McHenry *(G-14540)*
Progressive Recovery Inc ........... D ...... 618 286-5000
  Dupo *(G-8575)*

### MACHINERY & EQPT: Metal Finishing, Plating Etc

American Rack Company ............ E ...... 773 763-7309
  Chicago *(G-3870)*
Amiberica Inc ........................ E ...... 773 247-3600
  Chicago *(G-3888)*
Brown Metal Products Ltd ........... G ...... 309 936-7384
  Atkinson *(G-943)*
Crw Finishing Inc .................... E ...... 630 495-4994
  Addison *(G-84)*
Desco Inc ............................ G ...... 847 439-2130
  Elk Grove Village *(G-9424)*
Electro-Glo Distribution Inc ......... G ...... 815 224-4030
  La Salle *(G-12771)*
Fanuc America Corporation ......... E ...... 847 898-5000
  Hoffman Estates *(G-12009)*
K&J Finishing Inc .................... F ...... 815 965-9655
  Rockford *(G-18451)*
Meminger Metal Finishing Inc ...... F ...... 309 582-3363
  Aledo *(G-371)*
Morrell Incorporated ................. F ...... 630 858-4600
  Glendale Heights *(G-11050)*
ROC Industries Inc .................. G ...... 618 277-6044
  Belleville *(G-1670)*
Stutz Company ...................... F ...... 773 287-1068
  Chicago *(G-6610)*

### MACHINERY & EQPT: Petroleum Refinery

Leonard Associates Inc .............. E ...... 815 226-9609
  Rockford *(G-18467)*
Unitel Technologies Inc .............. F ...... 847 297-2265
  Mount Prospect *(G-15381)*

### MACHINERY & EQPT: Vibratory Parts Handling Eqpt

Masterfeed Corporation .............. G ...... 630 879-1133
  Batavia *(G-1466)*

### MACHINERY BASES

Fox Metal Services Inc .............. F ...... 847 439-9696
  Carol Stream *(G-3155)*
G & M Fabricating Inc ............... G ...... 815 282-1744
  Roscoe *(G-18898)*
Hadady Corporation .................. E ...... 219 322-7417
  South Holland *(G-20274)*
JMS Metals Inc ...................... G ...... 618 443-1000
  Sparta *(G-20317)*
Millenia Specialty Metals LLC ...... G ...... 630 458-0401
  Itasca *(G-12319)*
Millenia Trucking LLC ............... E ...... 630 458-0401
  Itasca *(G-12320)*
Roll Roll Met Fabricators Inc ........ E ...... 773 434-1315
  Chicago *(G-6384)*
Serra Laser Precision LLC .......... D ...... 847 367-0282
  Libertyville *(G-13379)*
Skol Mfg Co .......................... E ...... 773 878-5959
  Chicago *(G-6522)*
Tc Industries Inc ..................... C ...... 815 459-2401
  Crystal Lake *(G-7660)*
Terra Cotta Holdings Co ............. E ...... 815 459-2400
  Crystal Lake *(G-7664)*
Tu-Star Manufacturing Co Inc ...... G ...... 815 338-5760
  Woodstock *(G-22619)*
Vibro/Dynamics Corporation ........ E ...... 708 345-2050
  Broadview *(G-2619)*

### MACHINERY, CALCULATING: Adding

B & M Machine Inc .................. G ...... 630 350-8950
  Bensenville *(G-1838)*

### MACHINERY, COMMERCIAL LAUNDRY & Drycleaning: Ironers

Cmv Sharper Finish Inc ............. E ...... 773 276-4800
  Chicago *(G-4411)*

# PRODUCT SECTION

## MACHINERY, PACKAGING: Canning, Food

Rkc Cleaner I Corp .............................. F ...... 630 904-0477
Naperville  (G-15824)

### MACHINERY, COMMERCIAL LAUNDRY: Extractors

Extractor Corporation .......................... F ...... 847 742-3532
South Elgin  (G-20196)

### MACHINERY, COMMERCIAL LAUNDRY: Washing, Incl Coin-Operated

B-Clean Laundromat Inc ....................... G ...... 678 983-5492
Chicago  (G-4022)

### MACHINERY, EQPT & SUPPLIES: Parking Facility

Federal Signal Corporation ................... D ...... 630 954-2000
Oak Brook  (G-16510)
Parking Systems Inc ............................. G ...... 847 891-3819
Schaumburg  (G-19684)
Spacesaver Parking Company ................ G ...... 773 486-6900
Chicago  (G-6549)

### MACHINERY, FOOD PRDTS: Beverage

Alberti Enterprises Inc .......................... G ...... 847 810-7610
Lake Forest  (G-12877)
Choice Treat Equipment Mfg ................. G ...... 708 442-2004
Lyons  (G-14035)
IMI McR Inc ........................................ E ...... 309 734-6282
Monmouth  (G-15014)

### MACHINERY, FOOD PRDTS: Chocolate Processing

Blommer Machinery Company ............... G ...... 312 226-7700
Chicago  (G-4124)

### MACHINERY, FOOD PRDTS: Confectionery

Savage Bros Company ......................... D ...... 847 981-3000
Elk Grove Village  (G-9728)

### MACHINERY, FOOD PRDTS: Cutting, Chopping, Grinding, Mixing

Aaron Process Equipment Co Inc ........... E ...... 630 350-2200
Bensenville  (G-1810)
Houpt Revolving Cutters Inc .................. G ...... 618 395-1913
Olney  (G-16771)

### MACHINERY, FOOD PRDTS: Dies, Biscuit Cutting

Weidenmiller Co .................................. F ...... 630 250-2500
Itasca  (G-12373)

### MACHINERY, FOOD PRDTS: Food Processing, Smokers

Home Fires Inc .................................... G ...... 815 967-4100
Rockford  (G-18421)
R S Cryo Equipment Inc ....................... G ...... 815 468-6115
Manteno  (G-14191)
Titan Injection Parts & Svc .................... G ...... 630 882-8455
Yorkville  (G-22673)

### MACHINERY, FOOD PRDTS: Grinders, Commercial

Bauermeister Inc .................................. G ...... 901 363-0921
Vernon Hills  (G-21146)
Modern Process Equipment Inc ............. E ...... 773 254-3929
Chicago  (G-5784)
Wallace/Haskin Corp ............................ G ...... 630 789-2882
Downers Grove  (G-8540)

### MACHINERY, FOOD PRDTS: Ovens, Bakery

Mario Escobar .................................... G ...... 773 202-8497
Chicago  (G-5621)
Marshall Middleby Inc .......................... C ...... 847 289-0204
Elgin  (G-9100)
Rational Cooking Systems Inc .............. D ...... 224 366-3500
Rolling Meadows  (G-18772)

### MACHINERY, FOOD PRDTS: Packing House

Nimco Corporation .............................. D ...... 815 459-4200
Crystal Lake  (G-7619)

### MACHINERY, FOOD PRDTS: Processing, Fish & Shellfish

Gregor Jonsson Associates Inc ............. E ...... 847 247-4200
Lake Forest  (G-12904)

### MACHINERY, FOOD PRDTS: Roasting, Coffee, Peanut, Etc.

Bravilor Bonamat LLC .......................... F ...... 630 423-9400
Aurora  (G-973)
Rancilio North America Inc .................. E ...... 630 427-1703
Woodridge  (G-22513)

### MACHINERY, FOOD PRDTS: Sausage Stuffers

Gilberts Craft Sausages LLC ................ G ...... 630 923-8969
Wheaton  (G-21950)

### MACHINERY, LUBRICATION: Automatic

Concep Machine Co Inc ...................... F ...... 847 498-9740
Northbrook  (G-16230)

### MACHINERY, MAILING: Canceling

Taloc Usa Inc .................................... G ...... 847 665-8222
Libertyville  (G-13388)

### MACHINERY, MAILING: Mailing

Direct Mail Equipment Services ............ G ...... 815 485-7010
New Lenox  (G-15876)
Multimail Solutions ............................. G ...... 847 516-9977
Cary  (G-3361)
Pitney Bowes Inc ................................ E ...... 773 755-5808
Chicago  (G-6131)
Pitney Bowes Inc ................................ E ...... 800 784-4224
Itasca  (G-12341)

### MACHINERY, MAILING: Postage Meters

Pitney Bowes Inc ................................ E ...... 312 209-2216
Schaumburg  (G-19691)
Pitney Bowes Inc ................................ F ...... 312 419-7114
Chicago  (G-6132)
Pitney Bowes Inc ................................ D ...... 630 435-7476
Lisle  (G-13640)
Pitney Bowes Inc ................................ D ...... 630 435-7500
Lisle  (G-13641)
Singer Data Products Inc .................... G ...... 630 860-6500
Bensenville  (G-1991)

### MACHINERY, METALWORKING: Assembly, Including Robotic

Accelrted Mch Design Engrg LLC ......... F ...... 815 316-6381
Rockford  (G-18251)
Active Automation Inc ........................ F ...... 847 427-8100
Elk Grove Village  (G-9268)
Advanced Robotics Research .............. G ...... 630 544-0040
Naperville  (G-15591)
Advantage Machining Inc ................... G ...... 630 897-1220
Aurora  (G-1101)
Amber Engineering and Mfg Co ........... G ...... 847 595-6966
Elk Grove Village  (G-9293)
Ats Sortimat USA LLC ....................... D ...... 847 925-1234
Rolling Meadows  (G-18711)
Bartell Corporation ........................... G ...... 847 854-3232
Algonquin  (G-380)
Central Machines Inc ........................ E ...... 847 634-6900
Lincolnshire  (G-13435)
Continental Automation Inc ............... G ...... 630 584-5100
Saint Charles  (G-19162)
Custom Assembly Solutions Inc ......... F ...... 847 224-5800
Schaumburg  (G-19495)
Feeder Corporation of America .......... F ...... 708 343-4900
Melrose Park  (G-14638)
Hilscher North America Inc ............... F ...... 630 505-5301
Lisle  (G-13600)
Jerhen Industries Inc ....................... D ...... 815 397-0400
Rockford  (G-18443)
P-K Tool & Mfg Co .......................... D ...... 773 235-4700
Chicago  (G-6046)
Performance Design Inc ................... G ...... 847 719-1535
Lake Zurich  (G-13113)
Qc Service Associates Inc ................ E ...... 309 755-6785
East Moline  (G-8691)
R+d Custom Automation Inc ............. F ...... 847 395-3330
Lake Villa  (G-13025)
Schaffer Tool & Design Inc ............... G ...... 630 876-3800
West Chicago  (G-21769)
Sigmatron International Inc .............. G ...... 847 586-5200
Elgin  (G-9178)
Sigmatron International Inc .............. G ...... 847 956-8000
Elk Grove Village  (G-9737)
Sortimat Technology LP ................... D ...... 847 925-1234
Rolling Meadows  (G-18780)
Tellenar Inc ................................... F ...... 815 356-8044
Crystal Lake  (G-7663)
Tool Rite Industries Inc .................... G ...... 630 406-6161
Batavia  (G-1508)
United Automation Inc ..................... G ...... 847 394-7903
Wheeling  (G-22171)
Wes-Tech Automtn Solutions LLC ..... D ...... 847 541-5070
Buffalo Grove  (G-2794)

### MACHINERY, METALWORKING: Coil Winding, For Springs

Jardis Industries Inc ........................ F ...... 630 773-5600
Itasca  (G-12290)

### MACHINERY, METALWORKING: Coilers, Metalworking

Stalex Inc ..................................... G ...... 630 627-9401
Lombard  (G-13858)

### MACHINERY, METALWORKING: Coiling

Remington Industries Inc ................. F ...... 815 385-1987
Johnsburg  (G-12441)

### MACHINERY, METALWORKING: Cutting & Slitting

Navillus Woodworks LLC ................. G ...... 312 375-2680
Chicago  (G-5874)

### MACHINERY, METALWORKING: Rotary Slitters, Metalworking

Braner Usa Inc ............................... E ...... 847 671-6210
Schiller Park  (G-19809)

### MACHINERY, OFFICE: Embossing, Store Or Office

Your Supply Depot Limited ............... G ...... 815 568-4115
Marengo  (G-14245)

### MACHINERY, OFFICE: Paper Handling

Copar Corporation ......................... E ...... 708 496-1859
Burbank  (G-2807)

### MACHINERY, OFFICE: Perforators

American Perforator Company .......... G ...... 815 469-4300
Frankfort  (G-10294)
Cummins - Allison Corp .................. D ...... 847 299-9550
Mount Prospect  (G-15321)
Cummins - Allison Corp .................. C ...... 847 299-9550
Mount Prospect  (G-15322)
Cummins - Allison Corp .................. F ...... 630 833-2285
Elmhurst  (G-9862)

### MACHINERY, OFFICE: Shorthand

Stenograph LLC ........................... D ...... 630 532-5100
Elmhurst  (G-9942)

### MACHINERY, OFFICE: Time Clocks & Time Recording Devices

SBA Wireless Inc .......................... E ...... 847 215-8720
Buffalo Grove  (G-2762)

### MACHINERY, PACKAGING: Bread Wrapping

Pandaderia El Acambaro ................ G ...... 312 666-6316
Chicago  (G-6069)

### MACHINERY, PACKAGING: Canning, Food

Econopin ..................................... G ...... 708 599-5002
Bridgeview  (G-2486)
Frings America Inc ....................... G ...... 630 851-5826
Aurora  (G-1011)

## MACHINERY, PACKAGING: Carton Packing

Cartpac Inc .................................. E ..... 630 283-8979
  Carol Stream *(G-3125)*

## MACHINERY, PACKAGING: Packing & Wrapping

I T W Inc ..................................... C ..... 847 657-6171
  Glenview *(G-11140)*
Jescorp Inc .................................. D ..... 847 378-1200
  Elk Grove Village *(G-9562)*
John R Nalbach Engineering Co ..... E ..... 708 579-9100
  Countryside *(G-7436)*
Knight Packaging Group Inc ......... G ..... 773 585-2035
  Chicago *(G-5389)*
Point Five Packaging LLC ............. G ..... 847 678-5016
  Schiller Park *(G-19860)*
Signode Industrial Group LLC ....... E ..... 847 483-1490
  Glenview *(G-11199)*
Sjd Direct Midwest LLC ................ G ..... 618 931-2151
  Edwardsville *(G-8814)*
Tegrant Holding Corp .................... A ..... 815 756-8451
  Dekalb *(G-8126)*

## MACHINERY, PACKAGING: Vacuum

All-Vac Industries Inc ................... F ..... 847 675-2290
  Skokie *(G-19948)*
Henkelman Inc ............................. G ..... 331 979-2013
  Elmhurst *(G-9881)*
Robert L Murphy .......................... G ..... 708 424-0277
  Evergreen Park *(G-10118)*

## MACHINERY, PACKAGING: Wrapping

Arpac LLC .................................... C ..... 847 678-9034
  Schiller Park *(G-19805)*

## MACHINERY, PAPER INDUSTRY: Coating & Finishing

Platit Inc ...................................... G ..... 847 680-5270
  Libertyville *(G-13370)*

## MACHINERY, PAPER INDUSTRY: Converting, Die Cutting & Stampng

Midwest Gold Stampers Inc ......... F ..... 773 775-5253
  Chicago *(G-5744)*
United Gasket Corporation ........... D ..... 708 656-3700
  Cicero *(G-7242)*

## MACHINERY, PAPER INDUSTRY: Cutting

Rosenthal Manufacturing Co Inc ... E ..... 847 714-0404
  Northbrook *(G-16358)*

## MACHINERY, PAPER INDUSTRY: Paper Mill, Plating, Etc

Gy Packaging LLC ....................... F ..... 847 272-8803
  Northbrook *(G-16267)*

## MACHINERY, PAPER INDUSTRY: Pulp Mill

Gt Flow Technology Inc ................ G ..... 815 636-9982
  Roscoe *(G-18899)*

## MACHINERY, PRINTING TRADE: Type, Lead, Steel, Brass, Etc

Global Brass and Copper Inc ........ G ..... 618 258-5330
  East Alton *(G-8605)*
Group 3 Envelope F & S Type ....... G ..... 630 766-1230
  Bensenville *(G-1914)*

## MACHINERY, PRINTING TRADES: Bookbinding Machinery

Klai-Co Idntification Pdts Inc ......... E ..... 847 573-0375
  Lake Forest *(G-12921)*
Smart Inc ..................................... G ..... 847 464-4160
  Hampshire *(G-11563)*
Southern Illinois McHy Co Inc ....... D ..... 217 868-5431
  Shumway *(G-19935)*
Stolp Gore Company .................... G ..... 630 904-5180
  Plainfield *(G-17653)*

## MACHINERY, PRINTING TRADES: Copy Holders

Zebra Outlet ................................. F ..... 312 416-1518
  Chicago *(G-7059)*

## MACHINERY, PRINTING TRADES: Electrotyping

Vm Electronics LLC ..................... G ..... 847 663-9310
  Chicago *(G-6910)*

## MACHINERY, PRINTING TRADES: Plates

Aaxis Engravers Inc ..................... G ..... 224 629-4045
  Bensenville *(G-1811)*
Anderson & Vreeland-Illinois ........ F ..... 847 255-2110
  Arlington Heights *(G-713)*
Banner Moulded Products ........... E ..... 708 452-0033
  River Grove *(G-18005)*
Bisco Intl Inc ............................... G ..... 708 544-6308
  Hillside *(G-11911)*
Color Smiths Inc .......................... E ..... 708 562-0061
  Elmhurst *(G-9853)*
K and A Graphics Inc ................... G ..... 847 244-2345
  Gurnee *(G-11463)*
Luttrell Engraving Inc ................... E ..... 708 489-3800
  Alsip *(G-485)*
Oec Graphics-Chicago LLC .......... E ..... 630 455-6700
  Willowbrook *(G-22227)*
Plate and Pre-Press Management ... G ..... 847 352-0462
  Schaumburg *(G-19694)*
Tanic Rubber Plate Co ................. G ..... 630 896-2122
  Aurora *(G-1223)*

## MACHINERY, PRINTING TRADES: Presses, Envelope

Paw Office Machines Inc ............. ..... 815 363-9780
  McHenry *(G-14543)*

## MACHINERY, PRINTING TRADES: Presses, Gravure

Martin Automatic Inc .................... C ..... 815 654-4800
  Rockford *(G-18483)*

## MACHINERY, PRINTING TRADES: Printing Trade Parts & Attchts

C & C Printing Controls Inc .......... G ..... 630 810-0484
  Downers Grove *(G-8401)*
Sun Graphic Inc .......................... E ..... 773 775-6755
  Chicago *(G-6619)*

## MACHINERY, SERVICING: Coin-Operated, Exc Dry Clean & Laundry

Butterfield Cleaners ..................... G ..... 847 816-7060
  Mundelein *(G-15480)*
Regency Hand Laundry ............... G ..... 773 871-3950
  Chicago *(G-6322)*

## MACHINERY, SEWING: Bag Seaming & Closing

Carlson Sti Inc ............................. G ..... 630 232-2460
  Elgin *(G-8982)*
Duravant LLC ............................... F ..... 630 635-3910
  Downers Grove *(G-8437)*

## MACHINERY, SEWING: Sewing & Hat & Zipper Making

SMS Technical Services LLC ....... G ..... 708 479-1333
  Mokena *(G-14903)*
Star Cutter Co .............................. G ..... 231 264-5661
  Hoffman Estates *(G-12058)*

## MACHINERY, TEXTILE: Creels

Manufacturers Alliance Corp ........ F ..... 847 696-1600
  Villa Park *(G-21268)*

## MACHINERY, TEXTILE: Dyeing

Innovo Corp ................................. F ..... 847 616-0063
  Elk Grove Village *(G-9548)*

## MACHINERY, TEXTILE: Embroidery

Initial Impressions Inc .................. G ..... 630 208-9399
  Geneva *(G-10836)*
Peerless ...................................... G ..... 773 294-2667
  Chicago *(G-6096)*

## MACHINERY, TEXTILE: Fiber & Yarn Preparation

Cy Laser LLC ............................... G ..... 630 208-1931
  Geneva *(G-10822)*

## MACHINERY, TEXTILE: Knot Tying

Forest Lee LLC ............................ G ..... 312 379-0032
  Chicago *(G-4872)*

## MACHINERY, TEXTILE: Printing

M & R Printing Equipment Inc ...... B ..... 800 736-6431
  Roselle *(G-18954)*
M&R Holdings Inc ........................ C ..... 630 858-6101
  Roselle *(G-18955)*

## MACHINERY, TEXTILE: Silk Screens

David H Pool ................................ G ..... 847 695-5007
  Elgin *(G-9009)*
Modern Graphic Systems Inc ....... G ..... 773 476-6898
  Chicago *(G-5781)*
On Time Decorations Inc ............. F ..... 708 357-6072
  Cicero *(G-7224)*
Signature Label of Illinois ............. G ..... 618 283-5145
  Vandalia *(G-21125)*
Summit Graphics Inc ................... ..... 309 799-5100
  Moline *(G-14973)*

## MACHINERY, TEXTILE: Spinning

Natural Fiber Welding Inc ............. G ..... 309 685-3591
  Peoria *(G-17414)*

## MACHINERY, TEXTILE: Yarn Texturizing

Cargill Incorporated ..................... F ..... 217 872-7653
  Decatur *(G-7851)*

## MACHINERY, WOODWORKING: Cabinet Makers'

Bona Fide Corp ............................ G ..... 847 970-8693
  Wheeling *(G-22017)*
Bw Exhibits .................................. G ..... 847 697-9224
  Gilberts *(G-10914)*
Quality Cove ................................ G ..... 618 684-5900
  Murphysboro *(G-15581)*
Yazdan Essie ............................... G ..... 847 675-7916
  Lincolnwood *(G-13544)*
Your Custom Cabinetry Corp ........ G ..... 773 290-7247
  Melrose Park *(G-14712)*

## MACHINERY, WOODWORKING: Furniture Makers

Coalesse ..................................... F ..... 312 622-6269
  Chicago *(G-4413)*
D M O Inc .................................... G ..... 815 756-3638
  Cortland *(G-7387)*
Little Creek Woodworking ............ G ..... 217 543-2815
  Arthur *(G-908)*

## MACHINERY, WOODWORKING: Sanding, Exc Portable Floor Sanders

Crl Industries Inc ......................... G ..... 847 940-3550
  Deerfield *(G-8002)*
Lc Holdings of Delaware Inc ........ G ..... 847 940-3550
  Deerfield *(G-8028)*
Sand-Rite Manufacturing Co ........ G ..... 312 997-2200
  Melrose Park *(G-14691)*

## MACHINERY, WOODWORKING: Saws, Power, Bench & Table

Marvco Tool & Manufacturing ....... G ..... 847 437-4900
  Elk Grove Village *(G-9612)*
White Oak Technology .................. G ..... 309 228-4201
  Germantown Hills *(G-10896)*

# PRODUCT SECTION

## MACHINERY/EQPT, INDL, WHOL: Cleaning, High Press, Sand/Steam

M & M Pump Co ..................................... G ....... 217 935-2517
  Clinton *(G-7286)*
Therma-Kleen Inc ................................. G ....... 630 718-0212
  Plainfield *(G-17657)*

## MACHINERY/EQPT, INDL, WHOL: Machinist Precision Measrng Tool

Sparx EDM Inc ....................................... G ....... 847 722-7577
  Streamwood *(G-20674)*

## MACHINERY: Ammunition & Explosives Loading

Black Market Parts Inc ........................ G ....... 630 562-9400
  West Chicago *(G-21672)*

## MACHINERY: Assembly, Exc Metalworking

Advanced Engneered Systems Inc .... E ....... 815 624-7797
  South Beloit *(G-20135)*
Assemtech Inc ....................................... E ....... 630 876-4990
  West Chicago *(G-21662)*
Ats Sortimat USA LLC .......................... D ....... 847 925-1234
  Rolling Meadows *(G-18711)*
Automatic Feeder Company Inc ........ F ....... 847 534-2300
  Schaumburg *(G-19450)*
Automation Systems Inc ..................... E ....... 847 671-9515
  Melrose Park *(G-14597)*
Barrington Automation Ltd ................. E ....... 847 458-0900
  Lake In The Hills *(G-12987)*
Boley Tool & Machine Works Inc ....... C ....... 309 694-2722
  East Peoria *(G-8703)*
Centec Automation Inc ........................ G ....... 847 791-9430
  Palatine *(G-17009)*
Concept and Design Services ............ G ....... 847 259-1675
  Mount Prospect *(G-15317)*
Diamond Machine Werks Inc ............. E ....... 847 437-0665
  Arlington Heights *(G-746)*
Eberle Manufacturing Company ........ F ....... 847 215-0100
  Wheeling *(G-22042)*
G & W Technical Corporation ............. G ....... 847 487-0990
  Island Lake *(G-12215)*
Intertech Development Company ...... D ....... 847 679-3377
  Skokie *(G-20017)*
Numerical Control Incorporated ........ G ....... 708 389-8140
  Alsip *(G-502)*
Pro Techmation Inc .............................. G ....... 815 459-5909
  Crystal Lake *(G-7632)*
Trueline Inc ............................................. E ....... 309 378-2571
  Downs *(G-8548)*
Western Slate Company ...................... D ....... 847 683-4400
  Hampshire *(G-11565)*

## MACHINERY: Automobile Garage, Frame Straighteners

American Industrial Direct LLC .......... E ....... 800 382-1200
  Elgin *(G-8948)*
McLaughlin Body Co ............................ D ....... 309 762-7755
  Moline *(G-14955)*
Rapid Line Industries Inc ................... F ....... 815 727-4362
  Joliet *(G-12563)*

## MACHINERY: Automotive Maintenance

Atlas Maintenance Service Inc .......... G ....... 773 486-3386
  Chicago *(G-3981)*
Pro Tools & Equipment Inc ................ G ....... 847 838-6666
  Antioch *(G-652)*
Speed Bleeder Products Co ............... G ....... 815 736-6296
  Newark *(G-15935)*

## MACHINERY: Automotive Related

Ace Machine & Tool .............................. G ....... 815 793-5077
  Dekalb *(G-8072)*
Dover Artificial Lift Intl LLC ................ F ....... 630 743-2563
  Downers Grove *(G-8430)*
Gaither Tool Co ...................................... G ....... 217 245-0545
  Jacksonville *(G-12388)*
Globe Lift LLC ........................................ G ....... 630 844-4247
  Aurora *(G-1162)*
Guzzler Manufacturing Inc ................. G ....... 815 672-3171
  Streator *(G-20690)*
Hackett Precision Company Inc ........ E ....... 615 227-3136
  Chicago *(G-5027)*
Haussermann Usa LLC ........................ G ....... 847 272-9850
  Northbrook *(G-16269)*
I T R Inc ................................................... E ....... 217 245-4478
  Jacksonville *(G-12392)*
Kps Capital Partners LP ....................... G ....... 630 972-7000
  Bolingbrook *(G-2333)*
Multitech Industries Inc ...................... E ....... 630 784-9200
  Carol Stream *(G-3202)*
Multitech McHned Cmponents LLC .. E ....... 630 949-8200
  Carol Stream *(G-3203)*
Nal Worldwide Holdings Inc ............... B ....... 630 261-3100
  Addison *(G-225)*
Pollmann North America Inc ............. E ....... 815 834-1122
  Romeoville *(G-18858)*
SMC Corporation of America .............. E ....... 630 449-0600
  Aurora *(G-1080)*
T & S Business Group LLC .................. E ....... 815 432-7084
  Watseka *(G-21429)*
Waupaca Foundry Inc .......................... C ....... 217 347-0600
  Effingham *(G-8862)*

## MACHINERY: Banking

Jpmorgan Chase Bank Nat Assn ....... G ....... 847 663-1235
  Niles *(G-15994)*
Talaris Inc ............................................... C ....... 630 577-1000
  Lisle *(G-13669)*

## MACHINERY: Binding

Acco Brands USA LLC .......................... E ....... 708 280-4702
  Addison *(G-16)*
Deluxe Stitcher Company Inc ............ D ....... 847 455-4400
  Franklin Park *(G-10457)*
Identification Products Mfg Co .......... G ....... 847 367-6452
  Lake Forest *(G-12914)*
Klai-Co Idntification Pdts Inc ............. E ....... 847 573-0375
  Lake Forest *(G-12921)*
Laminting Bnding Solutions Inc ....... G ....... 847 573-0375
  Lake Forest *(G-12922)*
Lane Industries Inc .............................. E ....... 847 498-6650
  Northbrook *(G-16292)*
Plastic Binding Laminating Inc ......... G ....... 847 573-0375
  Lake Forest *(G-12946)*
Sws Industries Inc ............................... E ....... 904 482-0091
  Woodstock *(G-22616)*

## MACHINERY: Blasting, Electrical

Brigitflex Inc .......................................... F ....... 847 741-1452
  Elgin *(G-8971)*
Engineered Abrasives Inc .................. E ....... 662 582-4143
  Alsip *(G-462)*

## MACHINERY: Bottling & Canning

Midwest Mobile Canning LLC ............ G ....... 815 861-4515
  Crystal Lake *(G-7612)*

## MACHINERY: Brewery & Malting

5 Rabbit Cerveceria Inc ...................... F ....... 312 265-8316
  Chicago *(G-3669)*

## MACHINERY: Broom Making

Carlson Tool & Machine Company .... F ....... 630 232-2460
  Elgin *(G-8983)*

## MACHINERY: Cement Making

Eirich Machines Inc ............................. D ....... 847 336-2444
  Gurnee *(G-11446)*

## MACHINERY: Concrete Prdts

Calser Corp ............................................. G ....... 618 277-0329
  Swansea *(G-20775)*
Gisco Inc ................................................. G ....... 630 910-3000
  Darien *(G-7795)*
Saint-Gobain Abrasives Inc ................ C ....... 630 868-8060
  Carol Stream *(G-3232)*
Substrate Technology Inc ................... G ....... 815 941-4800
  Morris *(G-15133)*

## MACHINERY: Construction

Aaron Engnered Process Eqp Inc ..... G ....... 630 350-2200
  Bensenville *(G-1809)*
APL Logistics Americas Ltd ............... E ....... 630 783-0200
  Woodridge *(G-22453)*
Associated Professionals ................... G ....... 847 931-0095
  Elgin *(G-8959)*
Brunner & Lay Inc ................................. C ....... 847 678-3232
  Elmhurst *(G-9843)*
Caterpillar Global Mining LLC ........... E ....... 618 378-3441
  Norris City *(G-16112)*
Caterpillar Inc ........................................ A ....... 309 675-1000
  Peoria *(G-17326)*
Caterpillar Inc ........................................ B ....... 815 729-5511
  Joliet *(G-12471)*
Caterpillar Inc ........................................ A ....... 630 859-5000
  Montgomery *(G-15036)*
Caterpillar Inc ........................................ B ....... 815 584-4887
  Dwight *(G-8588)*
Caterpillar Inc ........................................ E ....... 309 675-5681
  Peoria *(G-17327)*
Caterpillar Inc ........................................ B ....... 309 578-2086
  Washington *(G-21380)*
Caterpillar Inc ........................................ B ....... 309 266-4294
  Mossville *(G-15248)*
Caterpillar Inc ........................................ B ....... 903 712-4505
  Mossville *(G-15249)*
Caterpillar Inc ........................................ B ....... 888 614-4328
  Peoria *(G-17328)*
Caterpillar Inc ........................................ A ....... 309 578-2473
  Mossville *(G-15250)*
Caterpillar Inc ........................................ E ....... 309 675-1000
  Peoria *(G-17330)*
Caterpillar Inc ........................................ B ....... 309 578-8250
  Peoria *(G-17331)*
Caterpillar Inc ........................................ B ....... 309 675-1000
  Peoria *(G-17332)*
Caterpillar Inc ........................................ B ....... 309 494-0138
  East Peoria *(G-8699)*
Caterpillar Inc ........................................ B ....... 309 675-6590
  Peoria *(G-17333)*
Caterpillar Luxembourg LLC .............. G ....... 309 675-1000
  Peoria *(G-17334)*
Caterpillar Power Systems ................. G ....... 309 675-1000
  Peoria *(G-17335)*
Chartrand Equipment Co Inc ............. G ....... 618 853-2314
  Ellis Grove *(G-9826)*
Cnh Industrial America LLC ............... E ....... 706 629-5572
  Burr Ridge *(G-2832)*
Coast Crane Company ........................ C ....... 847 215-6500
  Buffalo Grove *(G-2674)*
CPM Co Inc ............................................. E ....... 815 385-7700
  McHenry *(G-14490)*
CTS Advanced Materials LLC ............ E ....... 630 226-9080
  Bolingbrook *(G-2293)*
D & B Fabricators & Distrs ................. F ....... 630 325-3811
  Lemont *(G-13234)*
Deere & Company ................................. A ....... 309 765-8000
  Moline *(G-14925)*
Division 5 Metals Inc ........................... G ....... 815 901-5001
  Kirkland *(G-12711)*
Doosan Infracore America Corp ....... G ....... 847 437-1010
  Elk Grove Village *(G-9432)*
Dover Europe Inc .................................. C ....... 630 541-1540
  Downers Grove *(G-8433)*
Eirich Machines Inc ............................. D ....... 847 336-2444
  Gurnee *(G-11446)*
G&D Intgrted Mfg Logistics Inc ......... B ....... 309 284-6700
  Morton *(G-15160)*
Gemtar Inc .............................................. G ....... 618 548-1353
  Salem *(G-19334)*
Heico Companies LLC ......................... F ....... 312 419-8220
  Chicago *(G-5068)*
Inertia Machine Corporation .............. E ....... 815 233-1619
  Freeport *(G-10667)*
Interstate Mechanical Inc ................... G ....... 312 961-9291
  Chicago *(G-5227)*
Ism Machinery Incorporated ............. G ....... 847 231-8002
  Libertyville *(G-13339)*
John Deere AG Holdings Inc .............. G ....... 309 765-8000
  Moline *(G-14946)*
Jrb Attachments LLC ........................... C ....... 319 378-3696
  Oak Brook *(G-16529)*
K R Komarek Inc .................................... E ....... 847 956-0060
  Wood Dale *(G-22384)*
Koflo Corporation ................................. F ....... 847 516-3700
  Cary *(G-3356)*
Komatsu America Corp ....................... B ....... 847 437-5800
  Rolling Meadows *(G-18737)*
L T Properties Inc ................................. G ....... 217 423-8772
  Decatur *(G-7904)*
Lanco International Inc ....................... B ....... 708 596-5200
  Hazel Crest *(G-11709)*
Lee Industries Inc ................................ C ....... 847 462-1865
  Elk Grove Village *(G-9590)*
Maimin Technology Group Inc .......... E ....... 847 263-8200
  Gurnee *(G-11468)*

Employee Codes: A=Over 500 employees, B=251-500
C=101-250, D=51-100, E=20-50, F=10-19, G=3-9

# MACHINERY: Construction

Mi-Jack Products Inc .................... B ...... 708 596-5200
  Hazel Crest (G-11711)
Midwest Cnstr Svcs Inc Peoria ...... F ...... 309 697-1000
  Bartonville (G-1397)
Midwest Mixing Inc ....................... G ...... 708 422-8100
  Chicago Ridge (G-7151)
Mj Snyder Ironworks Inc ............... G ...... 217 826-6440
  Marshall (G-14326)
North Point Investments Inc ......... G ...... 312 977-4386
  Chicago (G-5935)
Paladin Brands International H ..... .. ...... 319 378-3696
  Oak Brook (G-16554)
Prella Technologies Inc ................. .. ...... 630 400-0626
  Huntley (G-12168)
Rhino Tool Company ...................... F ...... 309 853-5555
  Kewanee (G-12694)
Ringwood Company ....................... D ...... 708 458-6000
  Bedford Park (G-1579)
Roadsafe Traffic Systems Inc ........ G ...... 217 629-7139
  Riverton (G-18036)
Spreader Inc .................................. .. ...... 217 568-7219
  Gifford (G-10910)
Stevenson Sales & Service LLC .... G ...... 630 972-0330
  Bolingbrook (G-2376)
Terramac LLC ................................ G ...... 630 365-4800
  Elburn (G-8914)
Troxel Industries Inc ..................... E ...... 217 431-8674
  Tilton (G-20883)
US Shredder Castings Group Inc .. G ...... 309 359-3151
  Peoria (G-17474)
W R Grace & Co- Conn .................. F ...... 708 458-9700
  Chicago (G-6924)
West Side Tractor Sales Co ........... E ...... 815 961-3160
  Rockford (G-18678)

## MACHINERY: Cryogenic, Industrial

Cryogenic Systems Equipment ...... E ...... 708 385-4216
  Blue Island (G-2244)

## MACHINERY: Custom

Acme Industries Inc ...................... C ...... 847 296-3346
  Elk Grove Village (G-9266)
Air Caster LLC ............................... E ...... 217 877-1237
  Decatur (G-7824)
All Cut Inc ...................................... G ...... 630 910-6505
  Darien (G-7788)
Argo Manufacturing Co .................. F ...... 630 377-1750
  Wasco (G-21372)
Ats Sortimat USA LLC .................... D ...... 847 925-1234
  Rolling Meadows (G-18711)
Aura Systems Inc .......................... E ...... 217 423-4100
  Decatur (G-7842)
Automated Design Corp ................ G ...... 630 783-1150
  Romeoville (G-18801)
Automated Mfg Solutions Inc ........ G ...... 815 477-2428
  Crystal Lake (G-7539)
Axis Manufacturing Inc ................. F ...... 847 350-0200
  Elk Grove Village (G-9327)
Bams Manufacturing Co Inc .......... G ...... 800 206-0613
  Elk Grove Village (G-9334)
Banner Service Corporation .......... C ...... 630 653-7500
  Carol Stream (G-3112)
Bbs Automation Chicago Inc ........ C ...... 630 351-3000
  Bartlett (G-1335)
Big 3 Precision Products Inc ......... F ...... 618 533-3251
  Centralia (G-3405)
C N C Central Inc .......................... G ...... 630 595-1453
  Bensenville (G-1849)
Concepts and Controls Inc ............ F ...... 847 478-9296
  Buffalo Grove (G-2676)
Crown Machine Inc ....................... E ...... 815 877-7700
  Rockford (G-18325)
Custom Machinery Inc ................... G ...... 847 678-3033
  Schiller Park (G-19818)
Daley Automation LLC ................... G ...... 630 384-9900
  Naperville (G-15642)
Datum Machine Works Inc ............ F ...... 815 877-8502
  Rockford (G-18336)
Datum Tool and Mfg Inc ................ .. ...... 847 742-4092
  South Elgin (G-20193)
David L Knoche ............................. .. ...... 618 466-7120
  Godfrey (G-11223)
Elastec Inc .................................... C ...... 618 382-2525
  Carmi (G-3066)
Elburn Metal Stamping Inc ........... E ...... 630 365-2500
  Elburn (G-8885)
Excel Machine & Tool ................... G ...... 815 467-1177
  Channahon (G-3574)
F N Smith Corporation .................. E ...... 815 732-2171
  Oregon (G-16824)

Folk Race Cars .............................. G ...... 815 629-2418
  Durand (G-8585)
Fox Machine & Tool Inc ................ G ...... 847 357-1845
  Elk Grove Village (G-9489)
Franklin Automation Inc ............... F ...... 630 466-1900
  Sugar Grove (G-20725)
Gail E Stephens ............................ G ...... 618 372-0140
  Brighton (G-2540)
General Machine and Tool Inc ..... G ...... 815 727-4342
  Lockport (G-13717)
Harvard Factory Automation Inc .. F ...... 815 943-1195
  Harvard (G-11634)
Haumiller Engineering Company .. C ...... 847 695-9111
  Elgin (G-9060)
Hess Machine Inc ......................... G ...... 618 887-4444
  Marine (G-14246)
IMI Manufacturing Inc ................... .. ...... 630 771-0003
  Bolingbrook (G-2319)
Jbw Machining Inc ........................ F ...... 847 451-0276
  Franklin Park (G-10508)
Johnson Pattern & Mch Works ..... E ...... 815 433-2775
  Ottawa (G-16964)
Kopis Machine Co Inc ................... E ...... 630 543-4138
  Addison (G-173)
Livingston Products Inc ................ F ...... 847 808-0900
  Waukegan (G-21581)
Meta TEC of Illinois Inc ................. D ...... 309 246-2960
  Lacon (G-12790)
Midaco Corporation ...................... E ...... 847 593-8420
  Elk Grove Village (G-9626)
Orat Inc ......................................... G ...... 630 567-6728
  Saint Charles (G-19230)
Pacific Bearing Corp ..................... C ...... 815 389-5600
  Roscoe (G-18911)
Paragon Automation Inc ............... F ...... 847 593-0434
  Elk Grove Village (G-9669)
Park Engineering Inc .................... .. ...... 847 455-1424
  Franklin Park (G-10546)
Parsons Company Inc .................. C ...... 309 467-9100
  Roanoke (G-18053)
Patlin Enterprises Inc ................... .. ...... 815 675-6606
  Spring Grove (G-20355)
Peters Machine Works Inc ........... F ...... 708 496-3005
  Oak Lawn (G-16640)
Pgi Mfg LLC .................................. D ...... 800 821-3475
  Rockford (G-18534)
Phillip Rodgers ............................. .. ...... 815 877-5461
  Loves Park (G-13973)
Pmb Industries Inc ....................... .. ...... 708 442-4515
  La Grange (G-12742)
Prosco Inc .................................... G ...... 847 336-1323
  Gurnee (G-11493)
Qc Components & Sales Inc ......... F ...... 630 268-0644
  Lombard (G-13847)
R G Hanson Company Inc ............ F ...... 309 661-9200
  Bloomington (G-2217)
Reba Machine Corp ...................... .. ...... 630 595-1272
  Wood Dale (G-22416)
Rj Link International Inc ............... F ...... 815 874-8110
  Rockford (G-18559)
Rockford Linear Actuation ............ .. ...... 815 986-4400
  Rockford (G-18577)
Romed Industries Corporation ..... G ...... 847 362-3900
  Lake Zurich (G-13124)
Sandbagger LLC ........................... D ...... 630 876-2400
  Elmhurst (G-9934)
SEC Design Technologies Inc ...... F ...... 847 680-0439
  Libertyville (G-13378)
Service Machine Jobs .................. G ...... 815 986-3033
  Rockford (G-18613)
Sst Forming Roll Inc .................... .. ...... 847 215-6812
  Buffalo Grove (G-2775)
Taylor Design Inc .......................... .. ...... 815 389-3991
  Roscoe (G-18924)
Tower Tool & Engineering Inc ...... F ...... 815 654-1115
  Machesney Park (G-14112)
Triple Edge Manufacturing Inc ..... G ...... 847 468-9156
  South Elgin (G-20230)
Tsd Manufacturing Co Inc ............ F ...... 630 238-8750
  Elk Grove Village (G-9794)
USA Industrial Export Corp ........... G ...... 312 391-5552
  Northbrook (G-16381)
Whale Manufacturing Inc ............. G ...... 847 357-9192
  Lombard (G-13884)
X-Cel Technologies Inc ................. F ...... 708 802-7400
  Tinley Park (G-20957)
X-Tech Innovations Inc ................. G ...... 815 962-4127
  Rockford (G-18690)
Z-Tech Inc ..................................... G ...... 815 335-7395
  Winnebago (G-22299)

## MACHINERY: Deburring

Crw Finishing Inc .......................... E ...... 630 495-4994
  Addison (G-84)
Precise Lapping Grinding Corp ..... F ...... 708 615-0240
  Melrose Park (G-14683)
Redin Parts Inc ............................. G ...... 815 398-1010
  Rockford (G-18553)
Robert Bosch LLC ......................... B ...... 248 876-1000
  Broadview (G-2610)
Ultramatic Equipment Co ............. E ...... 630 543-4565
  Addison (G-333)

## MACHINERY: Die Casting

Crd Enterprises Inc ....................... G ...... 847 438-4299
  Lake Zurich (G-13058)
Die Cast Machinery LLC ............... F ...... 847 360-9170
  Waukegan (G-21552)
DJB Corporation ............................ .. ...... 815 469-7533
  Frankfort (G-10313)
Kaufman-Worthen Machinery Inc . G ...... 847 360-9170
  Waukegan (G-21577)
Precision Entps Fndry Mch Inc ..... G ...... 815 797-1000
  Somonauk (G-20128)

## MACHINERY: Drill Presses

Midwest Machine Tool Inc ............ G ...... 815 427-8665
  Saint Anne (G-19124)

## MACHINERY: Electrical Discharge Erosion

Edmpartscom Inc .......................... .. ...... 630 427-1603
  Darien (G-7794)
J Francis & Assoc .......................... G ...... 309 697-5931
  Bartonville (G-1395)

## MACHINERY: Electronic Component Making

CIC North America Inc .................. G ...... 847 873-0860
  Rolling Meadows (G-18721)
Etel Inc ......................................... .. ...... 847 519-3380
  Schaumburg (G-19523)
Felix Partners LLC ........................ .. ...... 847 648-8449
  Rolling Meadows (G-18728)
Hanjitech Inc ................................ G ...... 847 707-5611
  Chicago (G-5041)
Renu Electronics Private Ltd ........ G ...... 630 879-8412
  Batavia (G-1491)
Rex Morioka ................................. G ...... 847 651-9400
  Schiller Park (G-19867)
Srmd Solutions LLC ...................... .. ...... 217 925-5773
  Dieterich (G-8315)

## MACHINERY: Electronic Teaching Aids

Spartanics Ltd .............................. E ...... 847 394-5700
  Rolling Meadows (G-18781)

## MACHINERY: Engraving

Able Engravers Inc ....................... G ...... 847 676-3737
  Skokie (G-19945)

## MACHINERY: Extruding

Lens Lenticlear Lenticular ............ F ...... 630 467-0900
  Itasca (G-12303)

## MACHINERY: Folding

C F Anderson & Co ........................ F ...... 312 341-0850
  Chicago (G-4203)

## MACHINERY: Gear Cutting & Finishing

Kautzmann Machine Works Inc .... G ...... 847 455-9105
  Franklin Park (G-10511)
Modern Gear & Machine Inc ......... F ...... 630 350-9173
  Bensenville (G-1953)
Sterling Gear Inc .......................... F ...... 815 438-4327
  Deer Grove (G-7968)

## MACHINERY: General, Industrial, NEC

Aberdon Enterprises ..................... F ...... 847 228-1300
  Elk Grove Village (G-9255)
Apf US Inc ..................................... G ...... 217 304-0027
  Danville (G-7702)
Dtc Products Inc ........................... .. ...... 630 513-3323
  Saint Charles (G-19174)
Intellgent Prcsses Automtn Inc .... G ...... 630 656-1215
  Addison (G-154)

# PRODUCT SECTION

## MACHINERY: Optical Lens

Rotospray Mfg Inc..................................G....... 708 478-3307
  Mokena *(G-14900)*

### MACHINERY: Glassmaking

Bystronic Inc.........................................C....... 847 214-0300
  Elgin *(G-8974)*
CR Laurence Co Inc............................G....... 773 242-2871
  Cicero *(G-7186)*

### MACHINERY: Grinding

Blackhawk Industrial Dist Inc................F....... 773 736-9600
  Carol Stream *(G-3117)*
Fives Landis Corp................................D....... 815 389-2251
  South Beloit *(G-20146)*
Grindal Company..................................E....... 630 250-8950
  Itasca *(G-12273)*
J Schneerberger Corp..........................G....... 847 888-3498
  Elgin *(G-9081)*
Kmp Tool Grinding Inc..........................G....... 847 205-9640
  Northbrook *(G-16288)*
Spencer and Krahn Mch Tl Sls............G....... 815 282-3300
  Rockford *(G-18627)*
Usach Technologies Inc......................E....... 847 888-0148
  Elgin *(G-9222)*

### MACHINERY: Ice Cream

Carrier Commercial Rfrgn Inc..............A....... 815 624-8333
  Rockton *(G-18693)*
HC Duke & Son LLC............................C....... 309 755-4553
  East Moline *(G-8681)*

### MACHINERY: Ice Making

Scotsman Group Inc.............................D....... 847 215-4500
  Vernon Hills *(G-21197)*
Scotsman Ice Systems........................E....... 847 215-4500
  Vernon Hills *(G-21198)*

### MACHINERY: Industrial, NEC

H&S Machine & Tools Inc....................G....... 618 451-0164
  Granite City *(G-11283)*
Indar Ventures LLC..............................F....... 708 343-4900
  Melrose Park *(G-14656)*
Kern Precision.......................................G....... 331 979-0954
  Addison *(G-166)*
ND Manifold..........................................G....... 815 923-4305
  Union *(G-21036)*
Pull X Machines Inc 933......................G....... 847 952-9977
  Elgin *(G-9153)*
RMH Enterprises..................................G....... 630 525-5552
  Wheaton *(G-21976)*
Southern IL Precision..........................G....... 618 643-3340
  Mc Leansboro *(G-14467)*
Tbw Machining Inc...............................F....... 847 524-1501
  Schaumburg *(G-19754)*
Tru-Vu Monitors Inc.............................G....... 847 259-2344
  Arlington Heights *(G-859)*

### MACHINERY: Kilns

Bailey Business Group........................G....... 618 548-3566
  Salem *(G-19327)*
Chicago Kiln Service...........................G....... 847 436-0919
  Rolling Meadows *(G-18720)*
Yer Kiln Me LLC...................................G....... 309 606-9007
  Wyoming *(G-22642)*

### MACHINERY: Knitting

Initially Ewe..........................................G....... 708 246-7777
  Western Springs *(G-21868)*

### MACHINERY: Labeling

F C D Inc...............................................E....... 847 498-3711
  Northbrook *(G-16255)*
Mii Inc....................................................F....... 630 879-3000
  Batavia *(G-1471)*

### MACHINERY: Lapping

John Crane Inc.....................................E....... 815 459-0420
  Crystal Lake *(G-7596)*
Micro Lapping & Grinding Co..............E....... 847 455-5446
  Franklin Park *(G-10531)*

### MACHINERY: Marking, Metalworking

Lester Manufacturing Inc....................E....... 815 986-1172
  Rockford *(G-18468)*

### MACHINERY: Metalworking

Arcam Cad To Metal Inc......................G....... 630 357-5700
  Naperville *(G-15599)*
Automation Systems Inc.....................E....... 847 671-9515
  Melrose Park *(G-14597)*
Bams Manufacturing Co Inc................G....... 800 206-0613
  Elk Grove Village *(G-9334)*
Beverly Shear Mfg Corporation..........G....... 773 233-2063
  Chicago *(G-4098)*
Black Bros Co......................................D....... 815 539-7451
  Mendota *(G-14717)*
Burns Machine Company....................E....... 815 434-3131
  Ottawa *(G-16952)*
C E R Machining & Tooling Ltd...........G....... 708 442-9614
  Lyons *(G-14034)*
Canny Innovative Solutions Inc..........G....... 847 323-1271
  Grayslake *(G-11323)*
Court & Slope Inc.................................G....... 847 697-3600
  Elgin *(G-9005)*
Crl Industries Inc.................................G....... 847 940-3550
  Deerfield *(G-8002)*
Custom Machinery Inc.........................G....... 847 678-3033
  Schiller Park *(G-19818)*
Darda Enterprises Inc.........................F....... 847 270-0410
  Palatine *(G-17020)*
Deluxe Stitcher Company Inc.............D....... 847 455-4400
  Franklin Park *(G-10457)*
Dmtg North America LLC....................G....... 815 637-8500
  Rockford *(G-18349)*
Dooling Machine Products Inc............G....... 618 254-0724
  Hartford *(G-11610)*
Engineered Abrasives Inc...................E....... 662 582-4143
  Alsip *(G-462)*
Gerhard Designing & Mfg Inc.............E....... 708 599-4664
  Bridgeview *(G-2494)*
GMC Technologies Inc........................G....... 847 426-8618
  East Dundee *(G-8638)*
Greenlee Textron Inc...........................D....... 815 397-7070
  Rockford *(G-18405)*
Hansel Walter J & Assoc Inc..............G....... 815 678-6065
  Richmond *(G-17963)*
Illinois Tool Works Inc.........................G....... 618 997-1716
  Marion *(G-14269)*
Junker Inc..............................................G....... 630 231-3770
  West Chicago *(G-21729)*
K R Komarek Inc...................................E....... 847 956-0060
  Wood Dale *(G-22384)*
Kormex Metal Craft Inc.......................G....... 630 953-8856
  Lombard *(G-13818)*
Lane Tool & Mfg Co Inc......................E....... 847 622-1506
  South Elgin *(G-20216)*
Lc Holdings of Delaware Inc...............G....... 847 940-3550
  Deerfield *(G-8028)*
Leggett & Platt Incorporated...............D....... 847 768-6139
  Des Plaines *(G-8223)*
Lipscomb Engineering Inc..................G....... 630 231-1833
  West Chicago *(G-21732)*
Littell LLC.............................................G....... 630 916-6662
  Schaumburg *(G-19620)*
Littell International Inc........................G....... 630 622-4950
  Schaumburg *(G-19621)*
Magnum Steel Works Inc....................D....... 618 244-5190
  Mount Vernon *(G-15423)*
Marvco Tool & Manufacturing.............E....... 847 437-4900
  Elk Grove Village *(G-9612)*
Master Machine Craft Inc....................E....... 815 874-3078
  Rockford *(G-18484)*
Master Manufacturing Co....................F....... 630 833-7060
  Villa Park *(G-21269)*
Meadoweld Machine Inc......................G....... 815 623-3939
  South Beloit *(G-20161)*
Medford Aero Arms LLC.....................G....... 773 961-7686
  Chicago *(G-5676)*
Merit Tool Engineering Co Inc............G....... 773 283-1114
  Chicago *(G-5694)*
Mfw Services Inc.................................G....... 708 522-5879
  South Holland *(G-20289)*
North America O M C G Inc.................G....... 630 860-1016
  Bensenville *(G-1956)*
Omiotek Coil Spring Co......................G....... 630 495-4056
  Lombard *(G-13837)*
Onsrud Machine Corp.........................E....... 847 520-5300
  Northbrook *(G-16327)*
Park Tool & Machine Co Inc..............G....... 630 530-5110
  Villa Park *(G-21275)*
Precision Tool & Die Company...........F....... 217 864-3371
  Mount Zion *(G-15455)*
Prototype & Production Co.................E....... 847 419-1553
  Wheeling *(G-22130)*
Red Bud Industries Inc.......................C....... 618 282-3801
  Red Bud *(G-17947)*
Robert Brysiewicz Incorporated.........G....... 630 289-0903
  Bartlett *(G-1369)*
Schmid Tool & Engineering Corp......E....... 630 333-1733
  Villa Park *(G-21283)*
Spinco Tool & Fabe.............................G....... 815 578-8600
  Wonder Lake *(G-22325)*
T & K Tool & Manufacturing Co..........G....... 815 338-0954
  Woodstock *(G-22617)*
Titan Tool Company Inc......................G....... 847 671-0045
  Franklin Park *(G-10607)*
Ty Miles Incorporated.........................E....... 708 344-5480
  Westchester *(G-21860)*
U S Concepts Inc.................................F....... 630 876-3110
  West Chicago *(G-21787)*
Ultramatic Equipment Co....................E....... 630 543-4565
  Addison *(G-333)*
Used Solutions Inc..............................F....... 815 759-5000
  Algonquin *(G-408)*
Variable Operations Tech Inc.............E....... 815 479-8528
  Crystal Lake *(G-7672)*
Vindee Industries Inc.........................E....... 815 469-3300
  Frankfort *(G-10375)*
W A Whitney Co...................................C....... 815 964-6771
  Rockford *(G-18671)*
Z-Tech Inc............................................G....... 815 335-7395
  Winnebago *(G-22299)*
Zj Industries Inc..................................F....... 630 543-6400
  Addison *(G-351)*

### MACHINERY: Milling

Extrude Hone LLC...............................E....... 847 669-5355
  Huntley *(G-12139)*
I-N-I Machining Inc..............................G....... 309 496-1002
  East Moline *(G-8682)*
Mid-West Millwork Wholesale............G....... 618 407-5940
  Mascoutah *(G-14356)*
United Tool and Engineering Co........D....... 815 389-3021
  South Beloit *(G-20171)*

### MACHINERY: Mining

Caterpillar Globl Min Amer LLC.........D....... 618 982-9000
  Carrier Mills *(G-3306)*
Dry Systems Technologies LLC........E....... 630 427-2051
  Woodridge *(G-22473)*
Dry Systems Technologies LLC........F....... 618 658-3000
  Vienna *(G-21222)*
Elgin Equipment Group LLC..............G....... 630 434-7200
  Downers Grove *(G-8439)*
Elgin National Industries Inc.............F....... 630 434-7200
  Downers Grove *(G-8440)*
Freedom Material Resources Inc......F....... 618 937-6415
  West Frankfort *(G-21808)*
G&D Integrated Services Inc............E....... 309 284-6700
  Morton *(G-15159)*
GE Fairchild Mining Equipment.........D....... 618 559-3216
  Du Quoin *(G-8555)*
Gundlach Equipment Corporation.....D....... 618 233-7208
  Belleville *(G-1633)*
Kennametal Inc....................................C....... 815 226-0650
  Rockford *(G-18454)*
Komatsu America Corp.......................C....... 309 672-7000
  Peoria *(G-17397)*
Komatsu America Corp.......................B....... 847 437-5800
  Rolling Meadows *(G-18737)*
Lashcon Inc..........................................F....... 217 742-3186
  Winchester *(G-22281)*
Logan Actuator Co..............................E....... 815 943-9500
  Harvard *(G-11640)*
Martin Engineering Company.............C....... 309 852-2384
  Neponset *(G-15859)*
Roe Machine Inc..................................E....... 618 983-5524
  West Frankfort *(G-21817)*
Sollami Company.................................E....... 618 988-1521
  Herrin *(G-11755)*
Terrasource Global Corporation........D....... 618 641-6985
  Belleville *(G-1678)*
Townley Engrg & Mfg Co Inc..............F....... 618 273-8271
  Eldorado *(G-8924)*
Wallace Auto Parts & Svcs Inc..........E....... 618 268-4446
  Raleigh *(G-17912)*

### MACHINERY: Optical Lens

Vst America Inc...................................G....... 847 952-3800
  Arlington Heights *(G-868)*

## MACHINERY: Ozone

**Ozonology Inc** ...G ... 847 998-8808
Northbrook *(G-16329)*

## MACHINERY: Packaging

**Algus Packaging Inc** ...D ... 815 756-1881
Dekalb *(G-8073)*
**American Packaging McHy Inc** ...E ... 815 337-8580
Woodstock *(G-22539)*
**Ats Sortimat USA LLC** ...D ... 847 925-1234
Rolling Meadows *(G-18711)*
**Automtic Lquid Pckg Sltons LLC** ...E ... 847 372-3336
Arlington Heights *(G-719)*
**Barrington Packaging Systems** ...G ... 847 382-8063
Barrington *(G-1272)*
**Birnberg Machinery Inc** ...G ... 847 673-5242
Skokie *(G-19964)*
**Bms Manufacturing Company Inc** ...E ... 309 787-3158
Milan *(G-14776)*
**Bprex Healthcare Packaging Inc** ...D ... 800 537-0178
Buffalo Grove *(G-2667)*
**British Cnvrtng Sltns Nrth AME** ...E ... 281 764-6651
Elmhurst *(G-9842)*
**Burghof Engineering & Mfg Co** ...E ... 847 634-0737
Lincolnshire *(G-13433)*
**C N C Central Inc** ...G ... 630 595-1453
Bensenville *(G-1849)*
**Competitive Edge Opportunities** ...G ... 815 322-2164
Lakemoor *(G-13143)*
**Cvp Systems Inc** ...D ... 630 852-1190
Downers Grove *(G-8422)*
**Dover Europe Inc** ...G ... 630 541-1540
Downers Grove *(G-8433)*
**Dover Prtg Identification Inc** ...D ... 630 541-1540
Downers Grove *(G-8434)*
**Duravant** ...G ... 630 635-3910
Downers Grove *(G-8436)*
**Duravant LLC** ...F ... 630 635-3910
Downers Grove *(G-8437)*
**Eoe Inc** ...F ... 847 550-1665
Lake Zurich *(G-13069)*
**Fromm Airpad Inc** ...F ... 630 393-9790
Warrenville *(G-21347)*
**Fuji Impulse American Corp** ...G ... 847 236-9190
Deerfield *(G-8008)*
**Gama Electronics Inc** ...F ... 815 356-9600
Woodstock *(G-22569)*
**Gateway Packaging Company LLC** ...C ... 618 415-0010
Granite City *(G-11280)*
**Graphbury Machines LLC** ...G ... 754 779-4285
Chicago *(G-4988)*
**Illinois Tool Works Inc** ...E ... 708 720-0300
Frankfort *(G-10333)*
**Illinois Tool Works Inc** ...E ... 847 215-8925
Buffalo Grove *(G-2706)*
**Illinois Tool Works Inc** ...E ... 217 345-2166
Charleston *(G-3599)*
**Illinois Tool Works Inc** ...D ... 618 997-1716
Marion *(G-14269)*
**Integrated Packg & Fastener** ...D ... 847 439-5730
Elk Grove Village *(G-9550)*
**Korpack Inc** ...F ... 630 213-3600
Bloomingdale *(G-2111)*
**Libco Industries Inc** ...F ... 815 623-7677
Roscoe *(G-18902)*
**Mamata Enterprises Inc** ...G ... 941 205-0227
Montgomery *(G-15059)*
**Marquette Enterprises LLC** ...G ... 877 689-0001
Waukegan *(G-21587)*
**Marsh Shipping Supply Co LLC** ...F ... 618 343-1006
Collinsville *(G-7335)*
**Martin Automatic Inc** ...C ... 815 654-4800
Rockford *(G-18483)*
**Mid America Ems Industries** ...G ... 630 916-8203
Schaumburg *(G-19645)*
**Millwood Inc** ...F ... 708 343-7341
Melrose Park *(G-14674)*
**Mssc LLC** ...G ... 618 343-1006
Collinsville *(G-7336)*
**Nortech Packaging LLC** ...G ... 847 884-1805
Schaumburg *(G-19668)*
**Park Lawn Association Inc** ...F ... 708 425-7377
Oak Lawn *(G-16638)*
**Pioneer Container McHy Inc** ...G ... 618 533-7833
Centralia *(G-3427)*
**PMI Cartoning Inc** ...D ... 847 437-1427
Elk Grove Village *(G-9684)*
**Pre Pack Machinery Inc** ...G ... 217 352-1010
Champaign *(G-3528)*
**Prototype Equipment Corp** ...D ... 847 596-9000
Waukegan *(G-21609)*
**Purchasing Services Ltd Inc** ...E ... 618 566-8100
Mascoutah *(G-14359)*
**R P Grollman Co Inc** ...G ... 847 607-0294
Highland Park *(G-11864)*
**Robert Bosch LLC** ...B ... 248 876-1000
Broadview *(G-2610)*
**Rollstock Inc** ...G ... 708 579-3700
Countryside *(G-7441)*
**Rosenthal Manufacturing Co Inc** ...E ... 847 714-0404
Northbrook *(G-16358)*
**S G Acquisition Inc** ...F ... 815 624-6501
South Beloit *(G-20168)*
**Sardee Industries Inc** ...G ... 630 824-4200
Lisle *(G-13654)*
**Serac Inc** ...E ... 630 510-9343
Carol Stream *(G-3239)*
**Signode Corporation** ...A ... 800 527-1499
Glenview *(G-11197)*
**Signode Industrial Group LLC** ...G ... 630 268-9999
Glenview *(G-11201)*
**Sj Converting LLC** ...G ... 630 262-6640
West Chicago *(G-21774)*
**Suburban Machine Corporation** ...E ... 847 808-9095
Wheeling *(G-22158)*
**T & T Machinery Inc** ...G ... 708 366-8747
River Forest *(G-18002)*
**Taisei Lamick USA Inc** ...F ... 847 258-3283
Elk Grove Village *(G-9767)*
**Tegrant Alloyd Brands Inc** ...B ... 815 756-8451
Dekalb *(G-8124)*
**Terco Inc** ...E ... 630 894-8828
Bloomingdale *(G-2139)*
**Tetra Pak Inc** ...D ... 847 955-6000
Vernon Hills *(G-21208)*
**Trebor Sales Corporation** ...F ... 630 434-0040
Oak Brook *(G-16564)*
**Triangle Package Machinery Co** ...C ... 773 889-0200
Chicago *(G-6771)*
**Triangle Technologies Inc** ...G ... 630 736-3318
Streamwood *(G-20678)*
**Ultra Packaging Inc** ...G ... 630 595-9820
Bensenville *(G-2008)*
**Unique Blister Company** ...F ... 630 289-1232
Bartlett *(G-1383)*
**Weigh Right Automatic Scale Co** ...G ... 815 726-4626
Joliet *(G-12588)*
**Winpak Portion Packaging Inc** ...F ... 708 753-5700
Sauk Village *(G-19394)*
**World Cup Packaging Inc** ...G ... 815 624-6501
South Beloit *(G-20178)*
**Yeaman Machine Tech Inc** ...E ... 847 758-0500
Elk Grove Village *(G-9823)*
**Z Automation Company** ...E ... 847 357-0120
Mundelein *(G-15569)*
**Zitropack Ltd** ...F ... 630 543-1016
Addison *(G-350)*

## MACHINERY: Paint Making

**Engineering Finshg Systems LLC** ...E ... 815 893-6090
Elmhurst *(G-9866)*
**Fluid Management Inc** ...B ... 847 537-0880
Wheeling *(G-22055)*
**Wagner Systems Inc** ...E ... 630 503-2400
Elgin *(G-9226)*

## MACHINERY: Paper Industry Miscellaneous

**Birnberg Machinery Inc** ...G ... 847 673-5242
Skokie *(G-19964)*
**Black Bros Co** ...D ... 815 539-7451
Mendota *(G-14717)*
**Culmac Inc** ...E ... 309 944-5197
Geneseo *(G-10800)*
**Emt International Inc** ...G ... 630 655-4145
Westmont *(G-21887)*
**Finishers Exchange** ...G ... 847 462-0533
Fox River Grove *(G-10286)*
**Hfd Manufacturing Inc** ...G ... 847 263-5050
Waukegan *(G-21568)*
**Keene Technology Inc** ...D ... 815 624-8989
South Beloit *(G-20155)*
**Mayatech Corporation** ...E ... 847 297-0930
Des Plaines *(G-8229)*
**Paperchine Inc** ...C ... 815 389-8200
Rockton *(G-18700)*
**Quality Converting Inc** ...G ... 847 669-9094
Huntley *(G-12169)*
**Quipp Inc** ...F ... 305 623-8700
Glenview *(G-11186)*
**Ringwood Company** ...D ... 708 458-6000
Bedford Park *(G-1579)*
**Ultra Packaging Inc** ...G ... 630 595-9820
Bensenville *(G-2008)*

## MACHINERY: Pharmaciutical

**Accelrted Mch Design Engrg LLC** ...F ... 815 316-6381
Rockford *(G-18251)*
**Asahi Kasei Bioprocess Inc** ...E ... 847 834-0800
Glenview *(G-11105)*
**Dabrico Inc** ...E ... 815 939-0580
Bourbonnais *(G-2393)*
**Hygeia Industries Inc** ...F ... 847 380-2030
Glenview *(G-11139)*
**Industrial Phrm Resources Inc** ...F ... 630 823-4700
Bartlett *(G-1357)*
**Kirby Lester LLC** ...D ... 847 984-3377
Lake Forest *(G-12920)*
**Thomas Engineering Inc** ...D ... 847 358-5800
Hoffman Estates *(G-12065)*
**Thomas Engineering Inc** ...E ... 815 398-0280
Rockford *(G-18648)*
**United Validation & Com** ...G ... 815 953-6068
Watseka *(G-21432)*
**Weiler Engineering Inc** ...D ... 847 697-4900
Elgin *(G-9232)*

## MACHINERY: Photographic Reproduction

**George Wilson** ...G ... 847 342-1111
Prospect Heights *(G-17778)*

## MACHINERY: Plastic Working

**Black Bros Co** ...D ... 815 539-7451
Mendota *(G-14717)*
**CDL Technology Inc** ...E ... 630 543-5240
Addison *(G-70)*
**Credit Card Systems Inc** ...F ... 847 459-8320
Wheeling *(G-22031)*
**E P M Sales Co Inc** ...E ... 630 761-2051
Batavia *(G-1445)*
**Ewikon Molding Tech Inc** ...G ... 815 874-7270
Rockford *(G-18373)*
**Hastings Manufacturing Inc** ...E ... 800 338-8688
Millstadt *(G-14825)*
**Hmt Manufacturing Inc** ...E ... 847 473-2310
North Chicago *(G-16182)*
**Maac Machinery Co Inc** ...E ... 630 665-1700
Carol Stream *(G-3187)*
**Mamata Enterprises Inc** ...G ... 941 205-0227
Montgomery *(G-15059)*
**Mgb Engineering Company** ...E ... 847 956-7444
Elk Grove Village *(G-9624)*
**Midwest Innovations Inc** ...G ... 815 578-1401
McHenry *(G-14533)*
**Plastics Color Corporation** ...G ... 708 868-3800
Calumet City *(G-2951)*
**Prinsco Inc** ...E ... 815 635-3131
Chatsworth *(G-3627)*
**Processing Tech Intl LLC** ...D ... 630 585-5800
Aurora *(G-1070)*
**RAO Design International Inc** ...G ... 847 671-6182
Schiller Park *(G-19865)*
**Rdn Manufacturing Company Inc** ...E ... 630 893-4500
Bloomingdale *(G-2130)*
**Sterling Products Inc** ...D ... 847 273-7700
Schaumburg *(G-19740)*
**Tek Pak Inc** ...D ... 630 406-0560
Batavia *(G-1506)*
**Tuskin Equipment Corporation** ...G ... 630 466-5590
Sugar Grove *(G-20738)*

## MACHINERY: Polishing & Buffing

**Glaser USA Inc** ...G ... 847 362-7878
Lake Forest *(G-12901)*

## MACHINERY: Printing Presses

**Global Web Systems Inc** ...F ... 630 782-9690
Elk Grove Village *(G-9504)*
**Goss International LLC** ...E ... 630 796-7560
Woodridge *(G-22488)*
**Heidelberg USA Inc** ...D ... 847 550-0915
Barrington *(G-1284)*
**Mmpcu Limited** ...G ... 217 355-0500
Champaign *(G-3516)*
**Printers Repair Parts Inc** ...E ... 847 288-9000
Franklin Park *(G-10562)*
**Schlesinger Machinery Inc** ...G ... 630 766-4074
Bensenville *(G-1987)*

# PRODUCT SECTION

## MACHINERY: Recycling

All Metal Recycling Company ..................G....... 847 530-4825
  Villa Park  (G-21235)
Americlean Inc .......................................F....... 314 741-8901
  Wood River  (G-22440)
Arcoa Group Inc ....................................E....... 847 693-7519
  Waukegan  (G-21527)
Cortes Enterprise Inc ...........................G....... 779 777-1061
  Cortland  (G-7385)
ER&r Inc ................................................G....... 847 791-5671
  Northbrook  (G-16250)
Fortune Metal Midwest LLC ..................E....... 630 778-7776
  Sandwich  (G-19363)
Harris Metals & Recycling......................G....... 217 235-1808
  Mattoon  (G-14390)
Kuusakoski Philadelphia LLC ................D....... 215 533-8323
  Plainfield  (G-17616)
Maren Engineering Corporation ............E....... 708 333-6250
  South Holland  (G-20287)
Midwest Electronics Recycling ..............G....... 847 249-7011
  Waukegan  (G-21591)
Nu-Recycling Technology Inc ................F....... 630 904-5237
  Naperville  (G-15820)

## MACHINERY: Riveting

Chicago Rivet & Machine Co .................C....... 630 357-8500
  Naperville  (G-15627)
Ebe Industrial LLC ................................F....... 815 379-2400
  Walnut  (G-21330)

## MACHINERY: Road Construction & Maintenance

Bonnell Industries Inc ...........................D....... 815 284-3819
  Dixon  (G-8323)
ED Etnyre & Co .....................................B....... 815 732-2116
  Oregon  (G-16822)
Etnyre International Ltd .......................B....... 815 732-2116
  Oregon  (G-16823)
Millstadt Township ...............................G....... 618 476-3592
  Millstadt  (G-14831)
Pilot Township Road District ................G....... 815 426-6221
  Herscher  (G-11761)
S & S Maintenance................................G....... 815 725-9263
  Wilmington  (G-22277)

## MACHINERY: Robots, Molding & Forming Plastics

Isis3d LLC..............................................G....... 516 426-5410
  Chicago  (G-5242)

## MACHINERY: Rubber Working

LAB Equipment Inc ...............................E....... 630 595-4288
  Itasca  (G-12301)

## MACHINERY: Saw & Sawing

E H Wachs .............................................G....... 815 943-4785
  Lincolnshire  (G-13446)
Meadoweld Machine Inc .......................G....... 815 623-3939
  South Beloit  (G-20161)

## MACHINERY: Semiconductor Manufacturing

R & G Machine Shop Inc ......................F....... 217 342-6622
  Effingham  (G-8856)

## MACHINERY: Separation Eqpt, Magnetic

Acro Magnetics Inc ...............................G....... 815 943-5018
  Harvard  (G-11617)

## MACHINERY: Service Industry, NEC

Prinzings of Rockford............................G....... 815 874-9654
  Rockford  (G-18541)
We Clean ...............................................G....... 708 574-2551
  Oak Forest  (G-16593)

## MACHINERY: Sheet Metal Working

Straightline Erectors Inc ......................G....... 708 430-5426
  Oak Lawn  (G-16645)
Whitney Roper Rockford Inc.................D....... 815 962-3011
  Rockford  (G-18682)

## MACHINERY: Sifting & Screening

Classic Fasteners LLC ..........................G....... 630 605-0195
  Saint Charles  (G-19157)

## MACHINERY: Snow Making

Brunet Snow Service Company.............G....... 847 846-0037
  Wood Dale  (G-22347)

## MACHINERY: Specialty

Quality Fastener Products Inc ..............G....... 224 330-3162
  Elgin  (G-9157)
Six Oaks Company ................................G....... 312 343-4037
  Chicago  (G-6519)

## MACHINERY: Stone Working

Kinast Inc ..............................................G....... 217 852-3525
  Dallas City  (G-7698)

## MACHINERY: Textile

Birnberg Machinery Inc.........................G....... 847 673-5242
  Skokie  (G-19964)
Forte Automation Systems Inc ............E....... 815 316-6247
  Machesney Park  (G-14076)
Handy Button Machine Co ....................E....... 847 459-0900
  Wheeling  (G-22067)

## MACHINERY: Tire Shredding

Gone For Good.......................................G....... 217 753-0414
  Springfield  (G-20447)

## MACHINERY: Tobacco Prdts

Vacudyne Incorporated .........................E....... 708 757-5200
  Chicago Heights  (G-7134)

## MACHINERY: Wire Drawing

Blachford Enterprises Inc .....................E....... 630 231-8300
  West Chicago  (G-21670)
C B Ferrari Incorporated .......................G....... 847 756-4100
  Lake Barrington  (G-12801)
Drawing Technology Inc .......................G....... 815 877-5133
  Rockford  (G-18351)
International Technologies Inc .............G....... 847 301-9005
  Schaumburg  (G-19573)
J & C Premier Concepts Inc .................G....... 309 523-2344
  Port Byron  (G-17720)
Rockford Systems LLC ..........................D....... 815 874-7891
  Rockford  (G-18587)

## MACHINERY: Woodworking

Black Bros Co ........................................D....... 815 539-7451
  Mendota  (G-14717)
Doll Furniture Co Inc ............................G....... 309 452-2606
  Normal  (G-16070)
Elliott Aviation Arcft Sls Inc .................G....... 309 799-3183
  Milan  (G-14785)
Onsrud Machine Corp ...........................E....... 847 520-5300
  Northbrook  (G-16327)
Prairie State Machine LLC ....................G....... 217 543-3768
  Arthur  (G-919)
SA Industries Inc..................................G....... 847 730-4823
  Des Plaines  (G-8269)
Total Tooling Technology Inc................F....... 847 437-5135
  Elk Grove Village  (G-9786)

## MACHINES: Forming, Sheet Metal

Comet Roll & Machine Company...........E....... 630 268-1407
  Saint Charles  (G-19161)
Mac-Ster Inc..........................................F....... 847 830-7013
  Addison  (G-185)

## MACHINISTS' TOOLS & MACHINES: Measuring, Metalworking Type

Alpha Swiss Industries Inc ...................G....... 815 455-3031
  Crystal Lake  (G-7530)
Precision Gage Company ......................F....... 630 655-2121
  Burr Ridge  (G-2875)
Ryeson Corporation ..............................D....... 847 455-8677
  Carol Stream  (G-3230)

## MACHINISTS' TOOLS: Measuring, Precision

Glen Products .......................................G....... 847 998-1361
  Glenview  (G-11129)
Keson Industries Inc.............................E....... 630 820-4200
  Aurora  (G-1042)
L S Starrett Co ......................................G....... 847 816-9999
  Vernon Hills  (G-21178)

## MAGNETIC SHIELDS, METAL

Nex Gen Manufacturing Inc ..................G....... 847 487-7077
  Wauconda  (G-21489)
Roscoe Tool & Manufacturing ...............E....... 815 633-8808
  Roscoe  (G-18918)

## MACHINISTS' TOOLS: Precision

Ability Tool Co ......................................E....... 815 633-5909
  Machesney Park  (G-14050)
Automatic Precision Inc .......................E....... 708 867-1116
  Chicago  (G-3992)
Comet Tool Inc .....................................E....... 847 956-0126
  Elk Grove Village  (G-9383)
Forster Products Inc ............................E....... 815 493-6360
  Lanark  (G-13154)
Fotofabrication Corp ............................E....... 773 463-6211
  Chicago  (G-4878)
P-K Tool & Mfg Co................................D....... 773 235-4700
  Chicago  (G-6046)
Pfeifer Industries LLC ...........................E....... 630 596-9000
  Naperville  (G-15725)
Powertronics Surgitech USA Inc ..........G....... 630 305-4261
  Naperville  (G-15731)
Precision Prismatic Inc ........................G....... 708 424-0905
  Chicago Ridge  (G-7154)
Reino Tool & Manufacturing Co ............F....... 773 588-5800
  Chicago  (G-6326)
Team Cnc Inc ........................................G....... 630 377-2723
  Saint Charles  (G-19280)
Thomas-Zientz Group Inc .....................G....... 847 395-2363
  Antioch  (G-657)

## MACHINISTS' TOOLS: Scales, Measuring, Precision

Central Illinois Scale Co .......................G....... 309 697-0033
  Peoria  (G-17338)
Metrom LLC (not Llc) ............................G....... 847 847-7233
  Lake Zurich  (G-13102)
Scale-Tronix Inc ....................................F....... 630 653-3377
  Carol Stream  (G-3235)
Shinwa Measuring Tools Corp ..............G....... 847 598-3701
  Schaumburg  (G-19726)

## MAGAZINES, WHOLESALE

Desert Southwest Fitness Inc ..............G....... 520 292-0011
  Champaign  (G-3474)
Sherman Media Company Inc ...............G....... 312 335-1962
  Lake Forest  (G-12959)

## MAGNESIUM

Chicago Magnesium ..............................G....... 708 926-9531
  Dixmoor  (G-8319)
Elektron N Magnesium Amer Inc ..........D....... 618 452-5190
  Madison  (G-14144)

## MAGNETIC INK & OPTICAL SCANNING EQPT

Pos Plus LLC .........................................F....... 618 993-7587
  Marion  (G-14282)
Tangent Systems Inc ............................F....... 847 882-3833
  Hoffman Estates  (G-12062)

## MAGNETIC RESONANCE IMAGING DEVICES: Nonmedical

Forest City Diagnostic Imaging .............E....... 815 398-1300
  Rockford  (G-18387)
Imed Glenview ......................................G....... 847 298-2200
  Glenview  (G-11146)
Morton Grove Med Imaging LLC ...........E....... 847 213-2700
  Morton Grove  (G-15222)
O2m Technologies LLC .........................G....... 773 910-8533
  Chicago  (G-5961)
Peoria Open M R I ................................G....... 309 692-7674
  Peoria  (G-17425)
Prairie Glen Imaging Ctr LLC ................G....... 847 296-5366
  Des Plaines  (G-8260)
Smart Scan Mri LLC ..............................G....... 847 623-4000
  Gurnee  (G-11505)
Westmont Mri Center ...........................G....... 630 856-4060
  Westmont  (G-21927)

## MAGNETIC SHIELDS, METAL

American Partsmith Inc ........................G....... 630 520-0432
  West Chicago  (G-21656)
JL Clark LLC ..........................................C....... 815 961-5609
  Rockford  (G-18447)

---

Employee Codes: A=Over 500 employees, B=251-500
C=101-250, D=51-100, E=20-50, F=10-19, G=3-9

# MAGNETIC SHIELDS, METAL

### PRODUCT SECTION

Laird Technologies Inc ..................C...... 847 839-6900
 Schaumburg *(G-19610)*
Manufacturers Inv Group LLC ............E...... 630 285-0800
 Itasca *(G-12310)*
TSC International Inc ....................F...... 847 249-4900
 Wadsworth *(G-21328)*

## *MAGNETIC TAPE, AUDIO: Prerecorded*

Acta Publications ..........................G...... 773 989-3036
 Chicago *(G-3739)*
Advanced Audio Technology Inc........G...... 630 665-3344
 Carol Stream *(G-3090)*

## *MAGNETS: Ceramic*

Arnold Magnetic Tech Corp ..............E...... 815 568-2000
 Marengo *(G-14219)*
Hitachi Metals America LLC ............F...... 847 364-7200
 Arlington Heights *(G-766)*

## *MAGNETS: Permanent*

Morris Magnetics Inc ......................E...... 847 487-0829
 Wauconda *(G-21486)*

## *MAIL PRESORTING SVCS*

Rightsource Digital Svcs Inc .............F...... 888 774-2201
 Chicago *(G-6357)*

## *MAIL-ORDER BOOK CLUBS*

Caxton Club ..................................G...... 312 266-8825
 Chicago *(G-4259)*

## *MAIL-ORDER HOUSE, NEC*

D S Arms Incorporated ....................F...... 847 277-7258
 Lake Barrington *(G-12805)*
Dinkels Bakery Inc .........................E...... 773 281-7300
 Chicago *(G-4605)*
Euromarket Designs Inc ...................A...... 847 272-2888
 Northbrook *(G-16252)*
Franz Stationery Company Inc ..........F...... 847 593-0060
 Lake Barrington *(G-12807)*
Road Runner Sports Inc ...................F...... 847 719-8941
 Palatine *(G-17068)*
Simonton Holdings Inc ....................F...... 304 428-8261
 Deerfield *(G-8055)*
Spirit Warrior Inc ............................... 708 614-0020
 Orland Park *(G-16895)*
Waxman Candles Inc ......................G...... 773 929-3000
 Chicago *(G-6945)*

## *MAIL-ORDER HOUSES: Arts & Crafts Eqpt & Splys*

Dick Blick Company ........................C...... 309 343-6181
 Galesburg *(G-10747)*

## *MAIL-ORDER HOUSES: Automotive Splys & Eqpt*

American Speed Enterprises .............G...... 309 764-3601
 Moline *(G-14917)*

## *MAIL-ORDER HOUSES: Books, Exc Book Clubs*

Adventures Unlimited .....................G...... 815 253-6390
 Kempton *(G-12661)*
World Book Inc ..............................E...... 312 729-5800
 Chicago *(G-7028)*

## *MAIL-ORDER HOUSES: Cards*

Crest Greetings Inc ........................F...... 708 210-0800
 Chicago *(G-4503)*

## *MAIL-ORDER HOUSES: Clothing, Exc Women's*

Freddie Bear Sports ........................F...... 708 532-4133
 Tinley Park *(G-20916)*

## *MAIL-ORDER HOUSES: Educational Splys & Eqpt*

C W Publications Inc .....................G...... 800 554-5537
 Sterling *(G-20586)*

## *MAIL-ORDER HOUSES: Electronic Kits & Parts*

A and T Labs Incorporated ...............G...... 630 668-8562
 Wheaton *(G-21932)*

## *MAIL-ORDER HOUSES: Food*

Advertising Premiums Inc.................G...... 888 364-9710
 Mount Prospect *(G-15308)*
Prince Meat Co ..............................F...... 815 729-2333
 Darien *(G-7801)*

## *MAIL-ORDER HOUSES: Gift Items*

A Jule Enterprise Inc .......................G...... 312 243-6950
 Chicago *(G-3689)*

## *MAIL-ORDER HOUSES: Record & Tape, Music Or Video Club*

Aztec Corporation ..........................G .....
 Downers Grove *(G-8391)*
Marshall Pubg & Promotions ............G...... 224 238-3530
 Barrington *(G-1289)*
Polyvinyl Record Co ........................G...... 217 403-1752
 Champaign *(G-3527)*
Sandes Quynetta ..........................G...... 815 275-4876
 Freeport *(G-10687)*

## *MAIL-ORDER HOUSES: Religious Merchandise*

Bible Truth Publishers Inc.................G...... 630 543-1441
 Addison *(G-55)*

## *MAIL-ORDER HOUSES: Women's Apparel*

Trim Suits By Show-Off Inc ..............G...... 630 894-0100
 Roselle *(G-18984)*

## *MAILING LIST: Management*

American Association of Indivi .........E...... 312 280-0170
 Chicago *(G-3850)*

## *MAILING SVCS, NEC*

Allegra Print & Imaging Inc ..............F...... 847 697-1434
 Elgin *(G-8942)*
Alliance Graphics ...........................G...... 312 280-8000
 Chicago *(G-3814)*
Better News Papers Inc ...................G...... 618 566-8282
 Mascoutah *(G-14348)*
Caldwell Letter Service Inc ..............E...... 773 847-0708
 Chicago *(G-4214)*
Chicago Tribune Company ...............A...... 312 222-3232
 Chicago *(G-4357)*
Cision US Inc .................................C...... 312 922-2400
 Chicago *(G-4381)*
Com-Graphics Inc ..........................D...... 312 226-0900
 Chicago *(G-4434)*
Consumerbase LLC ........................C...... 312 600-8000
 Chicago *(G-4455)*
D G Printing Inc ............................E...... 847 397-7779
 Schaumburg *(G-19498)*
Des Plaines Journal Inc...................D...... 847 299-5511
 Des Plaines *(G-8184)*
First String Enterprises Inc ..............E...... 708 614-1200
 Tinley Park *(G-20913)*
Havana Printing & Mailing ...............F...... 309 543-2000
 Havana *(G-11695)*
Herald Publications ........................F...... 618 566-8282
 Mascoutah *(G-14353)*
Kevron Printing & Design Inc ...........F...... 708 229-7725
 Hickory Hills *(G-11772)*
Little Doloras ..................................G...... 708 331-1330
 South Holland *(G-20286)*
Metropolitan Graphic Arts Inc ..........E...... 847 566-9502
 Gurnee *(G-11471)*
Mid Central Printing & Mailing .........F...... 847 251-4040
 Wilmette *(G-22262)*
Negs & Litho Inc ............................F...... 847 647-7770
 Chicago *(G-5881)*
Practical Communications Inc .........E...... 773 754-3250
 Schaumburg *(G-19699)*
Precision Dialogue Direct Inc ...........D...... 773 237-2264
 Chicago *(G-6168)*
Printing Plus ..................................F...... 708 301-3900
 Lockport *(G-13739)*
Professnl Mling Prtg Svcs Inc ..........F...... 630 510-1000
 Carol Stream *(G-3222)*

Reliable Mail Services Inc ................F...... 847 677-6245
 Skokie *(G-20073)*
Tgrv LLC .......................................G...... 815 634-2102
 Bourbonnais *(G-2407)*
United Letter Service Inc .................F...... 312 408-2404
 Bensenville *(G-2009)*
Van Meter Graphx Inc .....................G...... 847 465-0600
 Wheeling *(G-22177)*
Voris Communication Co Inc ...........D...... 630 231-2425
 West Chicago *(G-21791)*
Your Images Group Inc ...................G...... 847 437-6688
 Schaumburg *(G-19794)*
Zell Co ..........................................G...... 312 226-9191
 Chicago *(G-7062)*

## *MANAGEMENT CONSULTING SVCS: Administrative*

Association Management Center .....D...... 847 375-4700
 Chicago *(G-3971)*

## *MANAGEMENT CONSULTING SVCS: Automation & Robotics*

Active Automation Inc .....................F...... 847 427-8100
 Elk Grove Village *(G-9268)*
Concepts and Controls Inc ..............F...... 847 478-9296
 Buffalo Grove *(G-2676)*
Eighty Nine Robotics LLC ................G...... 512 573-9091
 Chicago *(G-4705)*
Hydrotec Systems Company Inc ......G...... 815 624-6644
 Tiskilwa *(G-20959)*
Indesco Oven Products Inc..............G...... 217 622-6345
 Petersburg *(G-17536)*
R+d Custom Automation Inc ...........E...... 847 395-3330
 Lake Villa *(G-13025)*
Senformatics LLC ..........................G...... 217 419-2571
 Champaign *(G-3536)*

## *MANAGEMENT CONSULTING SVCS: Business*

Allen Entertainment Management .....E...... 630 752-0903
 Carol Stream *(G-3096)*
Alligator Rec & Artist MGT Inc .........F...... 773 973-7736
 Chicago *(G-3819)*
Education Partners Project Ltd .........G...... 773 675-6643
 Chicago *(G-4701)*
Media Associates Intl Inc ................F...... 630 260-9063
 Carol Stream *(G-3192)*
National Sporting Goods Assn ..........F...... 847 296-6742
 Mount Prospect *(G-15353)*
Scholl Communications Inc .............G...... 847 945-1891
 Deerfield *(G-8051)*
Simplement Inc ..............................G...... 702 560-5332
 Northfield *(G-16418)*

## *MANAGEMENT CONSULTING SVCS: Distribution Channels*

Raytrans Distribution Svcs Inc..........F...... 708 503-9940
 Chicago *(G-6297)*

## *MANAGEMENT CONSULTING SVCS: Foreign Trade*

ADS LLC ........................................D...... 256 430-3366
 Burr Ridge *(G-2820)*
Mandus Group Ltd .........................F...... 309 786-1507
 Rock Island *(G-18187)*

## *MANAGEMENT CONSULTING SVCS: General*

Proquis Inc ....................................F...... 847 278-3230
 Elgin *(G-9151)*

## *MANAGEMENT CONSULTING SVCS: Hospital & Health*

Care Education Group Inc................G...... 708 361-4110
 Palos Park *(G-17127)*
Dorenfest Group Ltd ......................D...... 312 464-3000
 Chicago *(G-4632)*
Globepharm Inc ............................G...... 847 914-0922
 Deerfield *(G-8009)*
Jero Medical Eqp & Sups Inc ...........E...... 773 305-4193
 Chicago *(G-5295)*
Medcore International LLC ..............G...... 630 645-9900
 Oak Brook *(G-16540)*
Quadramed Corporation .................E...... 312 396-0700
 Chicago *(G-6240)*

# PRODUCT SECTION

# MANUFACTURING INDUSTRIES, NEC

### MANAGEMENT CONSULTING SVCS: Industrial

Chemsong Inc .................................. F .....
 Glen Ellyn *(G-10962)*
Mar-TEC Research Inc ................... E ...... 630 879-1200
 Batavia *(G-1465)*

### MANAGEMENT CONSULTING SVCS: Industrial & Labor

Private Studios ............................... G ...... 217 367-3530
 Urbana *(G-21099)*
Tropar Trophy Manufacturing Co .. E ...... 630 787-1900
 Wood Dale *(G-22433)*

### MANAGEMENT CONSULTING SVCS: Industry Specialist

Broadcast Electronics Inc .............. C ...... 217 224-9600
 Quincy *(G-17809)*
Met-L-Flo Inc .................................. F ...... 630 409-9860
 Sugar Grove *(G-20729)*
Modern Fluid Technology Inc ....... G ...... 815 356-0001
 Crystal Lake *(G-7614)*

### MANAGEMENT CONSULTING SVCS: Maintenance

New Lenox Machine Co Inc ........... F ...... 815 584-4866
 Dwight *(G-8589)*
Specialized Liftruck Svcs LLC ........ F ...... 708 552-2705
 Bedford Park *(G-1585)*

### MANAGEMENT CONSULTING SVCS: Manufacturing

DFT Inc ........................................... G ...... 630 628-8352
 Addison *(G-87)*
Gary W Berger ................................ G ...... 708 588-0200
 Countryside *(G-7427)*
Precision Products Mfg Intl ........... E ...... 847 299-8500
 Des Plaines *(G-8262)*

### MANAGEMENT CONSULTING SVCS: Merchandising

Action Advertising Inc .................. G ...... 312 791-0660
 Chicago *(G-3740)*

### MANAGEMENT CONSULTING SVCS: Real Estate

Omron Automotive Elec Inc .......... A ...... 630 443-6800
 Saint Charles *(G-19229)*

### MANAGEMENT CONSULTING SVCS: Training & Development

Be Group Inc .................................. G ...... 312 436-0301
 Chicago *(G-4061)*
Cengage Learning Inc .................... G ...... 630 554-0821
 Downers Grove *(G-8406)*
L C Mold Inc ................................... E ...... 847 593-5004
 Rolling Meadows *(G-18740)*

### MANAGEMENT CONSULTING SVCS: Transportation

G&E Transportation Inc ................. E ...... 404 350-6497
 Chicago *(G-4903)*

### MANAGEMENT SERVICES

Barry Callebaut USA LLC ............... G ...... 312 496-7300
 Chicago *(G-4047)*
Del Monte Foods Inc ..................... F ...... 630 836-8131
 Rochelle *(G-18085)*
Deshamusic Inc ............................. G ...... 818 257-2716
 Chicago *(G-4585)*
Essentra Packaging US Inc ............ G ...... 704 418-8692
 Westchester *(G-21841)*
Grupo Antolin Illinois Inc ............... C ...... 815 544-8020
 Belvidere *(G-1759)*
Kkt Chillers Inc .............................. F ...... 847 734-1600
 Elk Grove Village *(G-9575)*
Madison Capital Partners Corp ..... G ...... 312 277-0323
 Chicago *(G-5597)*
Medcore International LLC ............ G ...... 630 645-9900
 Oak Brook *(G-16540)*

Natural Gas Pipeline Amer LLC ..... F ...... 815 426-2151
 Herscher *(G-11760)*
Prairie Area Library System .......... E ...... 309 799-3155
 Coal Valley *(G-7298)*
Quantum Color Graphics LLC ....... C ...... 847 967-3600
 Morton Grove *(G-15231)*
Ripa LLC ........................................ G ...... 708 938-1600
 Broadview *(G-2609)*
Southfield Corporation .................. D ...... 708 345-0030
 Melrose Park *(G-14694)*
Subaru of America Inc ................... E ...... 630 250-4740
 Itasca *(G-12361)*

### MANAGEMENT SVCS: Administrative

Barry Callebaut USA LLC ............... B ...... 312 496-7300
 Chicago *(G-4048)*
Charles Industries Ltd ................... D ...... 217 826-2318
 Marshall *(G-14319)*
Fanning Communications Inc ....... G ...... 708 293-1430
 Crestwood *(G-7488)*
Impact Technologies Inc ................ G ...... 708 246-5041
 Western Springs *(G-21867)*
Moody Bible Inst of Chicago ......... E ...... 312 329-2102
 Chicago *(G-5800)*

### MANAGEMENT SVCS: Business

Bailey Business Group ................... G ...... 618 548-3566
 Salem *(G-19327)*
Diversified Fleet MGT Inc .............. F ...... 815 578-1051
 McHenry *(G-14496)*
Secure Data Inc ............................. F ...... 618 726-5225
 O Fallon *(G-16478)*
Valley Meats LLC ........................... E ...... 309 799-7341
 Coal Valley *(G-7299)*

### MANAGEMENT SVCS: Construction

Stages Construction Inc ................ G ...... 773 619-2977
 Chicago *(G-6568)*

### MANAGEMENT SVCS: Financial, Business

American Data Centre Inc ............. G ...... 847 358-7111
 Palatine *(G-17000)*

### MANAGEMENT SVCS: Hotel Or Motel

Parker International Pdts Inc ........ D ...... 815 524-5831
 Vernon Hills *(G-21188)*

### MANAGEMENT SVCS: Industrial

Swenson Technology Inc ............... F ...... 708 587-2300
 Monee *(G-15003)*

### MANAGEMENT SVCS: Restaurant

Coopers Hwk Intermedte Holdng .. C ...... 708 839-2920
 Countryside *(G-7420)*
Coopers Hwk Intermedte Holdng .. F ...... 708 215-5674
 Countryside *(G-7421)*

### MANHOLES & COVERS: Metal

Ej Usa Inc ....................................... F ...... 815 740-1640
 New Lenox *(G-15879)*

### MANHOLES COVERS: Concrete

Di Cicco Concrete Products .......... F ...... 708 754-5691
 Chicago Heights *(G-7095)*
Skelcher Concrete Products .......... G ...... 618 457-2930
 Carbondale *(G-3023)*
Unique Concrete Concepts Inc ..... F ...... 618 466-0700
 Jerseyville *(G-12427)*

### MANICURE PREPARATIONS

Abyss Salon Inc ............................. G ...... 312 880-0263
 Chicago *(G-3713)*
Affirmed LLC ................................. G ...... 847 550-0170
 Lake Zurich *(G-13037)*
Be Products Inc ............................. G ...... 312 201-9669
 Chicago *(G-4062)*
Signature Nail Systems LLC .......... G ...... 888 445-2786
 Quincy *(G-17891)*
Vies Nails ....................................... G ...... 773 281-6485
 Chicago *(G-6897)*

### MANNEQUINS

Orlandi Statuary Company ........... D ...... 773 489-0303
 Chicago *(G-6015)*

Research Mannikins Inc ................ F ...... 618 426-3456
 Ava *(G-1242)*

### MANUFACTURED & MOBILE HOME DEALERS

Southmoor Estates Inc .................. G ...... 815 756-1299
 Dekalb *(G-8121)*

### MANUFACTURING INDUSTRIES, NEC

3 Goldenstar Inc ............................ F ...... 847 963-0451
 Palatine *(G-16994)*
312 Aquaponics LLC ..................... G ...... 312 469-0239
 Des Plaines *(G-8137)*
425 Manufacturing ........................ G ...... 815 873-7066
 Rockford *(G-18236)*
A Wiley & Associates ..................... G ...... 815 343-7401
 Ottawa *(G-16945)*
ABC Beverage Mfg Inc ................... G ...... 708 449-2600
 Northlake *(G-16424)*
Aci Plastics Manufacturing ........... G ...... 630 629-0400
 Addison *(G-19)*
Advance Manufacturing ................ G ...... 618 245-6515
 Farina *(G-10172)*
Al Mite Manufacturing Co Inc ....... G ...... 815 654-0720
 Machesney Park *(G-14054)*
Amk Enterprises Chicago Inc ........ G ...... 312 523-7212
 Chicago *(G-3890)*
Android Industries LLC .................. G ...... 815 544-4165
 Belvidere *(G-1733)*
AR Industries ................................. G ...... 630 543-0282
 Addison *(G-43)*
Atlas Manufacturing ...................... G ...... 773 327-3005
 Chicago *(G-3982)*
Auth-Florence Mfg ......................... G .....
 Glendale Heights *(G-11010)*
B and K Mueller Industries ............ G ...... 847 290-1108
 Elk Grove Village *(G-9330)*
Baker Manufacturing LLC .............. G ...... 847 362-3663
 Lake Bluff *(G-12835)*
Baumbach Manufacturing ............. G ...... 630 941-0505
 Elmhurst *(G-9836)*
Bogart Industries LLC .................... G ...... 224 242-4578
 Elburn *(G-8878)*
Bork Industries .............................. G ...... 630 365-5517
 Maple Park *(G-14198)*
Borse Industries Inc ...................... G ...... 630 325-1210
 Willowbrook *(G-22201)*
Bw Industries ................................. G ...... 630 784-1020
 Winfield *(G-22283)*
C & J Industries ............................. G ...... 708 757-4495
 Sauk Village *(G-19391)*
Cargo Support Industries Inc ........ G .....
 Inverness *(G-12207)*
Cell Parts Manufacturing Co ......... G ...... 847 669-9690
 Huntley *(G-12135)*
Chicago Art Center Co ................... G ...... 773 817-2725
 Chicago *(G-4304)*
Circle T Mfg ................................... G ...... 217 728-4834
 Sullivan *(G-20744)*
Cjj Industries Inc ........................... G ...... 708 921-9290
 La Grange Park *(G-12753)*
Crutcher Mfg .................................. G ...... 309 725-3545
 Cooksville *(G-7372)*
Crutcher Mfg .................................. G ...... 309 724-8206
 Ellsworth *(G-9827)*
Cultivated Energy Group Inc ........ G ...... 312 203-8833
 Hebron *(G-11718)*
Curlee Mfg ..................................... G ...... 847 268-6517
 Rosemont *(G-18995)*
Danko Industries ........................... G ...... 630 882-6070
 Yorkville *(G-22654)*
Diamond Quality Manufacturing ... G ...... 815 521-4184
 Channahon *(G-3570)*
Duchossois Industries Inc Non ..... G ...... 630 279-3600
 Oak Brook *(G-16504)*
Dyno Manufacturing Inc ................ G ...... 618 451-6609
 Madison *(G-14143)*
Elite Industries .............................. G ...... 224 433-6988
 Gurnee *(G-11447)*
F & A Industries Company LLC ..... G ...... 630 504-9839
 Oak Lawn *(G-16618)*
Fab Con Industries Inc .................. G ...... 618 969-9040
 Eldorado *(G-8920)*
Flurry Industries Inc ...................... G ...... 630 882-8361
 Yorkville *(G-22658)*
Freitas P Sabah .............................. G ...... 708 386-8934
 Oak Park *(G-16664)*
Genetics Development Corp ......... G ...... 847 283-9780
 Lake Bluff *(G-12845)*

Employee Codes: A=Over 500 employees, B=251-500
C=101-250, D=51-100, E=20-50, F=10-19, G=3-9

2017 Harris Illinois
Industrial Directory

**Goble Manufacturing Inc**..........G..... 217 932-5615
Casey *(G-3384)*
**Godbey Industries**..........G..... 773 769-4391
Chicago *(G-4967)*
**Green Giant**..........G..... 815 544-0438
Belvidere *(G-1758)*
**H V Manufacturing Vanguar**..........G..... 847 229-5502
Wheeling *(G-22063)*
**Hi-Tech Builidng Systems**..........G..... 847 526-5310
Wauconda *(G-21468)*
**Holm Industries**..........G..... 309 343-3332
Galesburg *(G-10759)*
**Infamous Industries Inc**..........G..... 708 789-2326
Hickory Hills *(G-11771)*
**Inspira Industries Inc**..........G..... 630 907-2123
North Aurora *(G-16134)*
**J B Burling Group Ltd**..........G..... 773 327-5362
Chicago *(G-5255)*
**J Garvin Industries**..........G..... 708 819-1148
Evergreen Park *(G-10116)*
**Kkj Industries LLC**..........G..... 630 202-9160
Villa Park *(G-21265)*
**Km4 Manufacturing**..........G..... 708 924-5150
Bedford Park *(G-1559)*
**Knapheide Mfg Co**..........E..... 217 223-1848
Quincy *(G-17848)*
**Kriese Mfg**..........G..... 815 748-2683
Cortland *(G-7392)*
**Kunverji Enterprise Corp**..........F..... 847 683-2954
Burlington *(G-2812)*
**Ledretrofitting Inc**..........G..... 815 347-5047
Glen Ellyn *(G-10975)*
**M Squared Industries LLC**..........G..... 708 606-2603
Chicago *(G-5587)*
**Mac Medical Inc**..........G..... 618 719-6757
Belleville *(G-1650)*
**Marca Industries Inc**..........E..... 773 884-4500
Burbank *(G-2808)*
**Mbs Manufacturing**..........G..... 630 227-0300
Franklin Park *(G-10524)*
**Metrom Rail LLC**..........F..... 847 874-7233
Crystal Lake *(G-7610)*
**Midstate Industries**..........G..... 217 268-3900
Sullivan *(G-20752)*
**Midwest Nameplate Corp**..........G..... 708 614-0606
Orland Park *(G-16875)*
**Mold Repair and Manufacturing**..........G..... 815 477-1332
Crystal Lake *(G-7615)*
**Monty Burcenski**..........G..... 815 838-0934
Lockport *(G-13733)*
**Morris Industries Inc**..........G..... 630 739-1502
Lemont *(G-13243)*
**Mpc Containment Intl LLC**..........D..... 773 927-4120
Chicago *(G-5821)*
**Murff Enterprises LLC**..........G..... 203 685-5556
Chicago *(G-5834)*
**Northwstern Globl Hlth Fndtion**..........G..... 214 207-9485
Chicago *(G-5943)*
**Omega Door Frame Products**..........E..... 630 773-9900
Itasca *(G-12335)*
**Performance Manufacturing**..........G..... 630 231-8099
West Chicago *(G-21756)*
**Phoenix Industries Inc**..........G..... 708 478-5474
Mokena *(G-14895)*
**Pioneer Industries Intl Inc**..........G..... 630 543-7676
Itasca *(G-12340)*
**Platinum Touch Industries LLC**..........G..... 773 775-9988
Des Plaines *(G-8256)*
**Pollack Manufacturing Co LLC**..........G..... 815 520-8415
Crystal Lake *(G-7626)*
**Pratt Industries**..........D..... 630 254-0271
Sauk Village *(G-19392)*
**Prospan Manufacturing**..........G..... 847 815-0191
Rosemont *(G-19025)*
**Pru Dent Mfg Inc**..........G..... 847 301-1170
Schaumburg *(G-19703)*
**Rexnord Industries LLC**..........C..... 630 719-2345
Downers Grove *(G-8516)*
**Ringmaster Mfg**..........G..... 815 675-4230
Spring Grove *(G-20362)*
**River North Industries Inc**..........G..... 773 600-4960
Spring Grove *(G-20363)*
**Riverview Mfg House SA**..........G..... 815 625-1459
Rock Falls *(G-18148)*
**Roses Moulding By Design Inc**..........E..... 847 549-9200
Mundelein *(G-15554)*
**Ryan Industries**..........G..... 708 479-7600
Mokena *(G-14902)*
**S & S Mfg Solutions LLC**..........G..... 815 838-1960
Lockport *(G-13743)*
**Scientific Manufacturing Inc**..........G..... 847 414-5658
Sleepy Hollow *(G-20118)*
**Sean Matthew Innovations Inc**..........G..... 815 455-4525
Crystal Lake *(G-7646)*
**Sentry Spring & Mfg Co**..........G..... 847 584-9391
Elk Grove Village *(G-9734)*
**Seven Mfg Inc**..........G..... 815 356-8102
Crystal Lake *(G-7648)*
**Shermar Industries LLC**..........G..... 847 378-8073
Des Plaines *(G-8273)*
**SKW Industries LLC**..........F..... 773 261-8900
Chicago *(G-6523)*
**Smh2 Manufacturing LLC**..........G..... 773 793-6643
Chicago *(G-6533)*
**Snowball Industries**..........G..... 773 316-0051
Chicago *(G-6540)*
**Star Lite Mfg**..........G..... 630 595-8338
Wood Dale *(G-22424)*
**Stock Manufacturing Co LLC**..........G..... 773 265-6640
Chicago *(G-6597)*
**Sustainable Holding Inc**..........G..... 773 324-0407
Chicago *(G-6643)*
**Swan Manufacturing Co**..........E..... 309 441-6985
Geneseo *(G-10806)*
**Synergetic Industries**..........G..... 309 321-8145
Morton *(G-15183)*
**T P R Resources Inc**..........G..... 630 443-9060
Saint Charles *(G-19278)*
**Tishma Engineering LLC**..........G..... 847 755-1200
Elk Grove Village *(G-9781)*
**US International Inc**..........G..... 312 671-9207
Chicago *(G-6854)*
**Utlx Manufacturing Inc**..........G..... 419 698-3820
Chicago *(G-6862)*
**Visionary Solutions Inc**..........G..... 847 296-9615
Des Plaines *(G-8299)*
**Vrmc LLC**..........G..... 612 210-1868
Downers Grove *(G-8538)*
**Vs Mfg Co**..........G..... 224 475-1190
Lake Zurich *(G-13141)*
**Waterway Rv LLC Mfg Home**..........G..... 312 207-1835
Chicago *(G-6943)*
**Western Sand & Gravel Co**..........F..... 815 433-1600
Ottawa *(G-16991)*
**Wikus Technology**..........G..... 630 766-0960
Addison *(G-344)*
**Wilton Brands Inc**..........F..... 815 823-8547
Joliet *(G-12589)*
**Wotkun Group Inc**..........G..... 708 396-2121
Posen *(G-17737)*
**Write Stuff**..........G..... 630 365-4425
Saint Charles *(G-19300)*
**Xd Industries Inc**..........G..... 847 293-0796
Prospect Heights *(G-17787)*
**Xl Manufacture**..........G..... 773 271-8900
Chicago *(G-7045)*
**Yetter M Co Inc Emp B Tr**..........G..... 309 776-4111
Colchester *(G-7308)*
**Zeta Manufacturing Company**..........G..... 708 301-3766
Homer Glen *(G-12089)*

## MARBLE, BUILDING: Cut & Shaped

**Absolute Stoneworks Inc**..........G..... 708 652-7600
Cicero *(G-7175)*
**Botti Studio of Architectural**..........E..... 847 869-5933
Evanston *(G-10017)*
**Contempo Marble & Granite Inc**..........G..... 312 455-0022
Chicago *(G-4456)*
**Creative Marble Inc**..........G..... 217 359-7271
Champaign *(G-3471)*
**Marble Emporium Inc**..........E..... 847 205-4000
Northbrook *(G-16306)*
**Natural Stone Inc**..........G..... 847 735-1129
Lake Bluff *(G-12858)*
**Pintas Cultured Marble**..........E..... 708 385-3360
Alsip *(G-509)*
**Standard Marble & Granite**..........F..... 773 533-0450
Chicago *(G-6570)*
**Stonecrafters Inc**..........E..... 815 363-8730
Lakemoor *(G-13148)*

## MARBLE: Dimension

**PC Marble Inc**..........E..... 708 385-3360
Alsip *(G-505)*

## MARINE CARGO HANDLING SVCS

**Blue Comet Transport Inc**..........G..... 773 617-9512
Chicago *(G-4125)*

## MARINE CARGO HANDLING SVCS: Loading

**Metropolis Ready Mix Inc**..........E..... 618 524-8221
Metropolis *(G-14758)*

## MARINE HARDWARE

**Custom Stainless Steel Inc**..........F..... 618 435-2605
Benton *(G-2026)*
**Meyer Engineering Co**..........G..... 847 746-1500
Winthrop Harbor *(G-22319)*
**Top Gallant Inc**..........F..... 847 981-5521
Elk Grove Village *(G-9783)*

## MARINE RELATED EQPT

**Marine Canada Acquisition**..........G..... 630 513-5809
Saint Charles *(G-19215)*
**Prime Group Inc**..........G..... 312 922-3883
Chicago *(G-6186)*

## MARINE SPLY DEALERS

**Cyn Industries Inc**..........F..... 773 895-4324
Chicago *(G-4531)*

## MARINE SPLYS WHOLESALERS

**Cyn Industries Inc**..........F..... 773 895-4324
Chicago *(G-4531)*

## MARKERS

**Premier Packaging Corp**..........G..... 815 469-7951
Frankfort *(G-10352)*
**U Mark Inc**..........E..... 618 235-7500
Belleville *(G-1683)*

## MARKETS: Meat & fish

**Hartrich Meats Inc**..........G..... 618 455-3172
Sainte Marie *(G-19324)*
**Jewel Osco Inc**..........C..... 847 428-3547
West Dundee *(G-21798)*
**Jewel Osco Inc**..........D..... 630 226-1892
Bolingbrook *(G-2328)*
**Jewel Osco Inc**..........C..... 815 464-5352
Frankfort *(G-10336)*
**Jewel-Osco Inc**..........C..... 847 296-7786
Des Plaines *(G-8216)*
**Park Packing Company Inc**..........E..... 773 254-0100
Chicago *(G-6083)*
**Raber Packing Company**..........E..... 309 673-0721
Peoria *(G-17439)*
**T & J Meatpacking Inc**..........D..... 708 757-6930
Chicago Heights *(G-7129)*
**Treasure Island Foods Inc**..........D..... 312 440-1144
Chicago *(G-6763)*
**V A M D Inc**..........G..... 773 631-8400
Chicago *(G-6865)*

## MARKING DEVICES

**A & E Rubber Stamp Corp**..........G..... 312 575-1416
Chicago *(G-3679)*
**A 1 Marking Products**..........G..... 309 762-6096
Moline *(G-14916)*
**A To Z Engraving Co Inc**..........G..... 847 526-7396
Wauconda *(G-21435)*
**All-Brite Sign Co Inc**..........F..... 309 829-1551
Normal *(G-16063)*
**Anderson Safford Mkg Graphics**..........F..... 847 827-8968
Des Plaines *(G-8150)*
**Bendsen Signs & Graphics Inc**..........F..... 217 877-2345
Decatur *(G-7845)*
**Bertco Enterprises Inc**..........G..... 618 234-9283
Belleville *(G-1614)*
**C H Hanson Company**..........D..... 630 848-2000
Naperville *(G-15613)*
**C H Hanson Company**..........F..... 630 848-2000
Naperville *(G-15614)*
**Chicago Ink & Research Co Inc**..........G..... 847 395-1078
Antioch *(G-628)*
**Dans Rubber Stamp & Signs**..........G..... 815 964-5603
Rockford *(G-18333)*
**Gadge Signs Inc**..........G..... 815 462-4490
New Lenox *(G-15882)*
**Iemco Corporation**..........G..... 773 728-4400
Chicago *(G-5145)*
**Illinois Tool Works Inc**..........D..... 618 997-1716
Marion *(G-14269)*
**Jackson Marking Products Co**..........F..... 618 242-7901
Mount Vernon *(G-15417)*

## PRODUCT SECTION
## MEAT CUTTING & PACKING

Joes Printing .................................................. G ....... 773 545-6063
 Chicago *(G-5309)*
K and A Graphics Inc ...................................... G ....... 847 244-2345
 Gurnee *(G-11463)*
Kellogg Printing Co ......................................... F ....... 309 734-8388
 Monmouth *(G-15016)*
Keneal Industries Inc ...................................... F ....... 815 886-1300
 Romeoville *(G-18834)*
Keson Industries Inc ...................................... E ....... 630 820-4200
 Aurora *(G-1042)*
Kiwi Coders Corp ........................................... E ....... 847 541-4511
 Wheeling *(G-22085)*
Letters Unlimited Inc ...................................... G ....... 847 891-7811
 Schaumburg *(G-19615)*
Mich Enterprises Inc ...................................... F ....... 630 616-9000
 Wood Dale *(G-22399)*
Millennium Marking Company ....................... E ....... 847 806-1750
 Elk Grove Village *(G-9629)*
Nameplate Robinson & Precision ................... G ....... 847 678-2255
 Franklin Park *(G-10538)*
Nathan Winston Service Inc ........................... G ....... 815 758-4545
 Dekalb *(G-8109)*
National Rubber Stamp Co Inc ...................... G ....... 773 281-6522
 Chicago *(G-5868)*
Navitor Inc ...................................................... B ....... 800 323-0253
 Harwood Heights *(G-11687)*
Nelson - Harkins Inds Inc .............................. E ....... 773 478-6243
 Chicago *(G-5884)*
Pro-Pak Industries Inc ................................... F ....... 630 876-1050
 West Chicago *(G-21761)*
Professional Sales Associates ...................... G ....... 847 487-1900
 Wauconda *(G-21493)*
Pylon Plastics Inc .......................................... G ....... 630 968-6374
 Lisle *(G-13646)*
Rebechini Studio Inc ..................................... F ....... 847 364-8600
 Elk Grove Village *(G-9711)*
Richards Sthman Rbr Stamps LLC ............... G ....... 217 522-6801
 Springfield *(G-20512)*
Shawver Press Inc ......................................... G ....... 815 772-4700
 Morrison *(G-15148)*
Wagner Zip-Change Inc ................................ E ....... 708 681-4100
 Melrose Park *(G-14706)*
Weakley Printing & Sign Shop ...................... G ....... 847 473-4466
 North Chicago *(G-16189)*

### MARKING DEVICES: Canceling Stamps, Hand, Rubber Or Metal

Take Your Mark Sports LLC ......................... G ....... 708 655-0525
 Western Springs *(G-21874)*

### MARKING DEVICES: Embossing Seals & Hand Stamps

S and S Associates Inc ................................ G ....... 847 584-0033
 Elk Grove Village *(G-9722)*

### MARKING DEVICES: Printing Dies, Marking Mach, Rubber/Plastic

B&H Machine Inc .......................................... F ....... 618 281-3737
 Columbia *(G-7351)*

### MARKING DEVICES: Screens, Textile Printing

Blue Monkey Graphics Inc ............................ G ....... 708 488-9501
 Forest Park *(G-10235)*
Hookset Enterprises LLC ............................. G ....... 224 374-1936
 Northbrook *(G-16271)*
Village Press Inc .......................................... G ....... 847 362-1856
 Libertyville *(G-13399)*

### MARKING DEVICES: Seal Presses, Notary & Hand

Education Partners Project Ltd .................... G ....... 773 675-6643
 Chicago *(G-4701)*

### MARKING DEVICES: Stationary Embossers, Personal

Promoframes LLC ........................................ G ....... 866 566-7224
 Schaumburg *(G-19701)*

### MASQUERADE OR THEATRICAL COSTUMES STORES

Andy Dallas & Co ......................................... F ....... 217 351-5974
 Champaign *(G-3450)*

Fanfest Corporation ...................................... G ....... 847 658-2000
 Crystal Lake *(G-7576)*

### MASSAGE MACHINES, ELECTRIC: Barber & Beauty Shops

Elia Day Spa ................................................. F ....... 708 535-1450
 Oak Forest *(G-16579)*

### MASTIC ROOFING COMPOSITION

Ted Muller ..................................................... G ....... 312 435-0978
 Chicago *(G-6686)*

### MATCHES & MATCH BOOKS

Atlas Match LLC ........................................... D ....... 815 469-2314
 Western Springs *(G-21864)*
Bradley Industries Inc .................................. E ....... 815 469-2314
 Frankfort *(G-10304)*

### MATCHES, WHOLESALE

Goodco Products LLC .................................. G ....... 630 258-6384
 Countryside *(G-7428)*

### MATERIAL GRINDING & PULVERIZING SVCS NEC

Kemp Manufacturing Company ..................... E ....... 309 682-7292
 Peoria *(G-17395)*
Polycorp Illinois Inc ...................................... D ....... 773 847-7575
 Chicago *(G-6154)*
Rockford Quality Grinding Inc ..................... F ....... 815 227-9001
 Rockford *(G-18584)*
Sturtevant Inc .............................................. G ....... 630 613-8968
 Lombard *(G-13861)*

### MATERIALS HANDLING EQPT WHOLESALERS

Allquip Co Inc .............................................. G ....... 309 944-6153
 Geneseo *(G-10797)*
Allstates Rubber & Tool Corp ...................... F ....... 708 342-1030
 Tinley Park *(G-20888)*
Crane Equipment & Services Inc ................. E ....... 309 467-6262
 Eureka *(G-9996)*
Ergo Help Inc ............................................... G ....... 847 593-0722
 Arlington Heights *(G-750)*
Jcb Inc .......................................................... G ....... 912 704-2995
 Aurora *(G-1037)*
Mailbox International Inc ............................. G ....... 847 541-8466
 Wheeling *(G-22097)*
Material Control Inc ..................................... F ....... 630 892-4274
 Batavia *(G-1467)*
REB Steel Equipment Corp ........................... E ....... 773 252-0400
 Chicago *(G-6309)*
Schaumburg Specialties Co ........................ G ....... 847 451-0070
 Schaumburg *(G-19721)*
W N G S Inc .................................................. G ....... 847 451-1224
 Franklin Park *(G-10625)*

### MATERNITY WEAR STORES

Golda Inc ...................................................... C ....... 217 895-3602
 Neoga *(G-15858)*

### MATS & MATTING, MADE FROM PURCHASED WIRE

Logan Graphic Products Inc ........................ D ....... 847 526-5515
 Wauconda *(G-21479)*
Tru Vue Inc .................................................. C ....... 708 485-5080
 Countryside *(G-7448)*

### MATS, MATTING & PADS: Aircraft, Floor, Exc Rubber Or Plastic

Skandia Inc .................................................. D ....... 815 393-4600
 Davis Junction *(G-7815)*

### MATS, MATTING & PADS: Nonwoven

Lessy Messy LLC ......................................... F ....... 708 790-7589
 Naperville *(G-15814)*

### MATS, ROOFING: Mineral Wool

Owens Corning Sales LLC ........................... B ....... 708 594-6911
 Argo *(G-694)*

### MATTRESS STORES

L & W Bedding Inc ....................................... G ....... 309 762-6019
 Moline *(G-14951)*
National Bedding Company LLC .................. E ....... 847 645-0200
 Hoffman Estates *(G-12027)*
Verlo Mat of Skokie-Evanston ...................... G ....... 847 966-9988
 Morton Grove *(G-15243)*
Verlo Mattress of Lake Geneva .................... G ....... 815 455-2570
 Crystal Lake *(G-7673)*
Wicoff Inc ...................................................... G ....... 618 988-8888
 Herrin *(G-11758)*

### MAUSOLEUMS

J W Reynolds Monument Co Inc ................. G ....... 618 833-6014
 Anna *(G-606)*

### MEAT & FISH MARKETS: Freezer Provisioners, Meat

Professional Freezing Svcs LLC .................. G ....... 773 847-7500
 Chicago *(G-6208)*

### MEAT & MEAT PRDTS WHOLESALERS

Advertising Premiums Inc ............................ G ....... 888 364-9710
 Mount Prospect *(G-15308)*
American Food Distrs Corp .......................... F ....... 708 331-1982
 Harvey *(G-11655)*
Atlantic Beverage Company Inc .................. G ....... 847 412-6200
 Northbrook *(G-16207)*
Ba Le Meat Processing & Whl Co ............... F ....... 773 506-2499
 Chicago *(G-4023)*
Branding Iron Holdings Inc ......................... G ....... 618 337-8400
 Sauget *(G-19383)*
Calihan Pork Processors Inc ....................... D ....... 309 674-9175
 Peoria *(G-17321)*
Charles Autin Limited .................................. D ....... 312 432-0888
 Chicago *(G-4289)*
Charwat Food Group Ltd ............................. G ....... 630 847-3473
 Hinsdale *(G-11944)*
Consumers Packing Co Inc ......................... D ....... 708 344-0047
 Melrose Park *(G-14611)*
Dreymiller & Kray Inc .................................. G ....... 847 683-2271
 Hampshire *(G-11547)*
Grant Park Packing Company Inc ............... E ....... 312 421-4096
 Franklin Park *(G-10482)*
Jbs Usa LLC ................................................. E ....... 217 323-3774
 Beardstown *(G-1522)*
John J Moesle Wholesale Meats ................. F ....... 773 847-4900
 Chicago *(G-5315)*
Lena AJS Maid Meats ................................... F ....... 815 369-4522
 Lena *(G-13277)*
Old Fashioned Meat Co Inc ......................... G ....... 312 421-4555
 Chicago *(G-5978)*
OSI Industries LLC ...................................... C ....... 630 231-9090
 West Chicago *(G-21754)*
OSI Industries LLC ...................................... B ....... 773 847-2000
 Chicago *(G-6021)*
Peoria Packing Ltd ...................................... F ....... 312 226-2600
 Chicago *(G-6104)*
Plumrose Usa Inc ........................................ E ....... 732 257-6600
 Downers Grove *(G-8504)*
Quay Corporation Inc .................................. F ....... 847 676-4233
 Lincolnwood *(G-13531)*
Russo Wholesale Meat Inc .......................... G ....... 708 385-0500
 Alsip *(G-525)*
Schau Southeast Sushi Inc ......................... E ....... 630 783-1000
 Woodridge *(G-22516)*
Smithfield Farmland Corp ............................ A ....... 309 734-5353
 Monmouth *(G-15023)*
T & J Meatpacking Inc ................................. D ....... 708 757-6930
 Chicago Heights *(G-7129)*
Tomcyndi Inc ................................................ E ....... 773 847-5400
 Chicago *(G-6737)*
Tru-Native Enterprises ................................. G ....... 630 409-3258
 Addison *(G-325)*
Tru-Native Enterprises ................................. G ....... 630 409-3258
 Addison *(G-326)*
V A M D Inc .................................................. G ....... 773 631-8400
 Chicago *(G-6865)*
Vej Holdings LLC .......................................... G ....... 630 219-1582
 Naperville *(G-15774)*
Vienna Beef Ltd ........................................... E ....... 773 278-7800
 Chicago *(G-6896)*

### MEAT CUTTING & PACKING

Allens Farm Quality Meats .......................... G ....... 217 896-2532
 Homer *(G-12073)*

Employee Codes: A=Over 500 employees, B=251-500
C=101-250, D=51-100, E=20-50, F=10-19, G=3-9

2017 Harris Illinois Industrial Directory

# MEAT CUTTING & PACKING

## PRODUCT SECTION

Amelio Bros Meats .................................G..... 708 300-2920
  Richton Park *(G-17975)*
American Food Distrs Corp ....................F..... 708 331-1982
  Harvey *(G-11655)*
Amity Packing Company Inc .................D..... 312 942-0270
  Chicago *(G-3889)*
Antioch Packing House ..........................G..... 847 838-6800
  Antioch *(G-618)*
Belmont Sausage Company ....................E..... 847 357-1515
  Elk Grove Village *(G-9340)*
Bruss Company ......................................C..... 773 282-2900
  Chicago *(G-4179)*
Bushnell Locker Service ........................G..... 309 772-2783
  Bushnell *(G-2899)*
Butterball LLC ........................................B..... 800 575-3365
  Montgomery *(G-15035)*
Calihan Pork Processors Inc .................D..... 309 674-9175
  Peoria *(G-17321)*
Cargill Meat Solutions Corp ...................C..... 630 739-1746
  Woodridge *(G-22458)*
Cass Meats .............................................G..... 217 452-3072
  Virginia *(G-21305)*
Chenoa Locker Inc .................................G..... 815 945-7323
  Chenoa *(G-3633)*
Cherry Meat Packers Inc ........................E..... 773 927-1200
  Chicago *(G-4297)*
Chicago Meat Authority Inc ....................B..... 773 254-3811
  Chicago *(G-4331)*
City Foods Inc ........................................C..... 773 523-1566
  Chicago *(G-4382)*
Consumers Packing Co Inc ...................D..... 708 344-0047
  Melrose Park *(G-14611)*
Country Village Meats .............................G..... 815 849-5532
  Sublette *(G-20714)*
Dawn Food Products Inc ........................G..... 815 933-0600
  Bradley *(G-2419)*
Deer Processing .....................................F..... 309 799-5994
  Coal Valley *(G-7295)*
Dutch Valley Meats Inc ...........................G..... 217 543-3354
  Arthur *(G-897)*
Earlville Cold Stor Lckr LLC ....................G..... 815 246-9469
  Earlville *(G-8593)*
Ed Kabrick Beef Inc ................................G..... 217 656-3263
  Plainville *(G-17662)*
Edgar County Locker Service .................G..... 217 466-5000
  Paris *(G-17147)*
Eureka Locker Inc ..................................F..... 309 467-2731
  Eureka *(G-9998)*
Fabbri Sausage Manufacturing ...............E..... 312 829-6363
  Chicago *(G-4808)*
Farina Locker Service .............................G..... 618 245-6491
  Farina *(G-10175)*
Farmers Packing Inc ...............................F..... 618 445-3822
  Albion *(G-363)*
Farmington Locker/Ice Plant Co .............G..... 309 245-4621
  Farmington *(G-10185)*
Fema L & L Food Services Inc ...............G..... 217 835-2018
  Benld *(G-1805)*
Galloway Como Processing ....................G..... 815 626-0305
  Sterling *(G-20594)*
Golden Locker Inc ..................................G..... 217 696-4456
  Camp Point *(G-2973)*
Great Lakes Packing Co Intl ...................G..... 773 927-6660
  Chicago *(G-4998)*
Gridley Meats Inc ....................................G..... 309 747-2120
  Gridley *(G-11405)*
Hansen Packing Co ................................G..... 618 498-3714
  Jerseyville *(G-12423)*
Hartrich Meats Inc ..................................G..... 618 455-3172
  Sainte Marie *(G-19324)*
Honey Foods Inc ....................................G..... 847 928-9300
  Franklin Park *(G-10488)*
J Brodie Meat Products Inc ....................F..... 309 342-1500
  Galesburg *(G-10761)*
Jancorp LLC ...........................................G..... 217 892-4830
  Rantoul *(G-17929)*
Jbs Usa LLC ...........................................E..... 217 323-3774
  Beardstown *(G-1522)*
Johnsons Processing Plant ....................G..... 815 684-5183
  Chadwick *(G-3442)*
Jones Packing Co ...................................G..... 815 943-4488
  Harvard *(G-11639)*
Kelly Corned Beef Co Chicago ...............E..... 773 588-2882
  Chicago *(G-5372)*
Korte Meat Processing Inc .....................G..... 618 654-3813
  Highland *(G-11801)*
Lake Pacific Partners LLC ......................B..... 312 578-1110
  Chicago *(G-5440)*
Lena AJS Maid Meats .............................F..... 815 369-4522
  Lena *(G-13277)*

Magros Processing .................................G..... 217 438-2880
  Springfield *(G-20473)*
Mangold Networks ..................................... 224 402-0068
  West Dundee *(G-21800)*
Meats By Linz Inc ...................................E..... 708 862-0830
  Calumet City *(G-2946)*
Momence Packing Co .............................B..... 815 472-6485
  Momence *(G-14984)*
Morris Meat Packing Co Inc ...................G..... 708 865-8566
  Maywood *(G-14429)*
Moweaqua Packing Plant .......................G..... 217 768-4714
  Moweaqua *(G-15458)*
National Beef Packing Co LLC ...............G..... 312 332-6166
  Chicago *(G-5859)*
Nea Agora Packing Co ...........................G..... 312 421-5130
  Chicago *(G-5878)*
Olympia Meat Packers Inc .....................G..... 312 666-2222
  Chicago *(G-5986)*
Oriental Kitchen Corporation ..................G..... 312 738-2850
  Chicago *(G-6007)*
Paris Frozen Foods Inc ..........................G..... 217 532-3822
  Hillsboro *(G-11897)*
Park Packing Company Inc ....................E..... 773 254-0100
  Chicago *(G-6083)*
Peer Foods Inc .......................................G..... 773 927-1440
  Chicago *(G-6095)*
Peoria Packing Ltd .................................F..... 312 226-2600
  Chicago *(G-6104)*
Peoria Packing Ltd .................................F..... 815 465-9824
  Grant Park *(G-11313)*
Pluesters Quality Meat Co .....................G..... 618 396-2224
  Hardin *(G-11594)*
Pork King Packing Inc ............................C..... 815 568-8024
  Marengo *(G-14239)*
Prince Meat Co ......................................F..... 815 729-2333
  Darien *(G-7801)*
Raber Packing Company ........................G..... 309 673-0721
  Peoria *(G-17439)*
Reasons Inc ............................................G..... 309 537-3424
  Buffalo Prairie *(G-2797)*
Rochelle Foods LLC ...............................A..... 815 562-4141
  Rochelle *(G-18105)*
Ryan Meat Company ..............................G..... 773 783-3840
  Chicago *(G-6416)*
Smithfield Farmland Corp .......................G..... 815 747-8809
  East Dubuque *(G-8623)*
Smithfield Farmland Corp .......................A..... 309 734-5353
  Monmouth *(G-15023)*
Smithfield Foods Inc ...............................F..... 312 577-5650
  Chicago *(G-6536)*
Specialty Foods Holdings Inc .................G..... 630 599-5900
  Lombard *(G-13855)*
Spectrum Preferred Meats Inc ...............D..... 815 946-3816
  Mount Morris *(G-15300)*
Steinbach Provision Company ................G..... 773 538-1511
  Chicago *(G-6583)*
Stiglmeier Sausage Co Inc .....................F..... 847 537-9988
  Wheeling *(G-22157)*
Togo Packing Co Inc ..............................B..... 800 575-3365
  Montgomery *(G-15067)*
Tomcyndi Inc ..........................................E..... 773 847-5400
  Chicago *(G-6737)*
Tyson Fresh Meats Inc ...........................F..... 847 836-5550
  Elgin *(G-9218)*
Tyson Fresh Meats Inc ...........................C..... 309 658-3377
  Hillsdale *(G-11906)*
Tyson Fresh Meats Inc ...........................F..... 309 965-2565
  Goodfield *(G-11249)*
Victor Food Products ..............................G..... 773 478-9529
  Chicago *(G-6893)*
Weber Meat Inc .......................................G..... 217 357-2130
  Carthage *(G-3319)*
Y T Packing Co .......................................F..... 217 522-3345
  Springfield *(G-20550)*
Zabiha Halal Meat Processors ................G..... 630 620-5000
  Addison *(G-349)*

## MEAT MARKETS

Allens Farm Quality Meats .....................G..... 217 896-2532
  Homer *(G-12073)*
Antioch Packing House ..........................G..... 847 838-6800
  Antioch *(G-618)*
Cass Meats .............................................G..... 217 452-3072
  Virginia *(G-21305)*
Columbus Meats Inc ...............................G..... 312 829-2480
  Chicago *(G-4433)*
Country Village Meats .............................G..... 815 849-5532
  Sublette *(G-20714)*
Cub Foods Inc ........................................C..... 309 689-0140
  Peoria *(G-17347)*

Dreymiller & Kray Inc ..............................G..... 847 683-2271
  Hampshire *(G-11547)*
Eickmans Processing Co Inc .................E..... 815 247-8451
  Seward *(G-19896)*
Elburn Market Inc ...................................E..... 630 365-6461
  Elburn *(G-8884)*
Farmington Locker/Ice Plant Co .............G..... 309 245-4621
  Farmington *(G-10185)*
Gridley Meats Inc ....................................G..... 309 747-2120
  Gridley *(G-11405)*
Jones Packing Co ...................................G..... 815 943-4488
  Harvard *(G-11639)*
Korte Meat Processing Inc .....................G..... 618 654-3813
  Highland *(G-11801)*
M E F Corp .............................................F..... 815 965-8604
  Rockford *(G-18477)*
Moweaqua Packing Plant .......................G..... 217 768-4714
  Moweaqua *(G-15458)*
Nea Agora Packing Co ...........................G..... 312 421-5130
  Chicago *(G-5878)*
Olympia Meat Packers Inc .....................G..... 312 666-2222
  Chicago *(G-5986)*
Peoria Packing Ltd .................................G..... 312 226-2600
  Chicago *(G-6104)*
Pluesters Quality Meat Co .....................G..... 618 396-2224
  Hardin *(G-11594)*
Polancics Meats & Tenderloins ..............G..... 815 433-0324
  Ottawa *(G-16980)*
Seifferts Locker & Meat Proc ..................F..... 618 594-3921
  Carlyle *(G-3058)*
Weber Meat Inc .......................................G..... 217 357-2130
  Carthage *(G-3319)*
Wurst Kitchen Inc ...................................G..... 630 898-9242
  Aurora *(G-1235)*
Y T Packing Co .......................................F..... 217 522-3345
  Springfield *(G-20550)*

### MEAT PRDTS: Beef Stew, From Purchased Meat

Lorenzo Frozen Foods Ltd .....................G..... 708 343-7670
  Westchester *(G-21848)*

### MEAT PRDTS: Boneless Meat, From Purchased Meat

Chicago Local Foods LLC ......................E..... 312 432-6575
  Chicago *(G-4329)*
Greenridge Farm Inc ..............................E..... 847 434-1803
  Elk Grove Village *(G-9513)*
Ogden Foods LLC ..................................E..... 773 277-8207
  Chicago *(G-5970)*
Ogden Foods LLC ..................................G..... 773 801-0125
  Chicago *(G-5971)*

### MEAT PRDTS: Boxed Beef, From Slaughtered Meat

Aurora Packing Company Inc .................C..... 630 897-0551
  North Aurora *(G-16119)*
Tyson Fresh Meats Inc ...........................B..... 815 431-9501
  Ottawa *(G-16987)*
Tyson Fresh Meats Inc ...........................C..... 309 658-2291
  Hillsdale *(G-11905)*
Valley Meats LLC ....................................E..... 309 799-7341
  Coal Valley *(G-7299)*

### MEAT PRDTS: Canned Exc Baby Food, From Slaughtered Meat

Bar-B-Que Industries Inc ........................F..... 773 227-5400
  Chicago *(G-4040)*
Sommers Fare LLC ................................E..... 877 377-9797
  Mundelein *(G-15558)*

### MEAT PRDTS: Corned Beef, From Purchased Meat

Bar-B-Que Industries Inc ........................F..... 773 227-5400
  Chicago *(G-4040)*
Lodolce Meat Co Inc ..............................G..... 708 863-4655
  Cicero *(G-7216)*
Nationwide Foods Inc .............................B..... 773 787-4900
  Chicago *(G-5869)*

### MEAT PRDTS: Cured Meats, From Purchased Meat

Dabecca Natural Foods Inc ....................C..... 773 291-1428
  Chicago *(G-4540)*

# PRODUCT SECTION

## MEAT PROCESSED FROM PURCHASED CARCASSES

### MEAT PRDTS: Dried Beef, From Purchased Meat

F & Y Enterprises Inc.................................E...... 847 526-0620
  Wauconda *(G-21462)*

### MEAT PRDTS: Dried, From Slaughtered Meat

H A Gartenberg & Company.....................F...... 847 821-7590
  Buffalo Grove *(G-2700)*

### MEAT PRDTS: Frozen

Capitol Wholesale Meats Inc....................B...... 708 485-4800
  Mc Cook *(G-14446)*
Holten Meat Inc.......................................D...... 618 337-8400
  Sauget *(G-19386)*
Original Greek Specialties.......................E...... 773 735-2250
  Chicago *(G-6012)*

### MEAT PRDTS: Ham, Roasted, From Purchased Meat

Honey Bear Ham......................................E...... 312 942-1160
  Chicago *(G-5105)*

### MEAT PRDTS: Hams & Picnics, From Slaughtered Meat

John Hofmeister & Son Inc......................D...... 773 847-0700
  Chicago *(G-5314)*
Plumrose Usa Inc....................................E...... 732 257-6600
  Downers Grove *(G-8504)*
Smithfield Global Products Inc................G...... 630 281-5000
  Lisle *(G-13659)*

### MEAT PRDTS: Lamb, From Slaughtered Meat

Grecian Delight Foods Inc......................C...... 847 364-1010
  Elk Grove Village *(G-9511)*
Halsted Packing House Co.....................G...... 312 421-5147
  Chicago *(G-5038)*

### MEAT PRDTS: Luncheon Meat, From Purchased Meat

Crawford Sausage Co Inc.......................E...... 773 277-3095
  Chicago *(G-4495)*

### MEAT PRDTS: Meat By-Prdts, From Slaughtered Meat

Best Chicago Meat Company LLC..........F...... 773 523-8161
  Chicago *(G-4090)*
Stewart Brothers Packing Co.................G...... 217 422-7741
  Decatur *(G-7944)*
T & J Meatpacking Inc............................D...... 708 757-6930
  Chicago Heights *(G-7129)*

### MEAT PRDTS: Pork, From Slaughtered Meat

Grant Park Packing Company Inc..........E...... 312 421-4096
  Franklin Park *(G-10482)*
Rose Packing Company Inc...................A...... 708 458-9300
  Chicago *(G-6395)*

### MEAT PRDTS: Prepared Beef Prdts From Purchased Beef

Charles Autin Limited.............................D...... 312 432-0888
  Chicago *(G-4289)*
Farmington Foods Inc............................C...... 708 771-3600
  Forest Park *(G-10243)*
Kronos Foods Corp................................B...... 773 847-2250
  Glendale Heights *(G-11039)*
New Specialty Products Inc...................E...... 773 847-0230
  Chicago *(G-5894)*
Specialty Foods Holdings Inc................G...... 630 599-5900
  Lombard *(G-13855)*
Stampede Meat Inc................................A...... 773 376-4300
  Bridgeview *(G-2531)*
Vienna Beef Ltd.....................................E...... 773 278-7800
  Chicago *(G-6896)*

### MEAT PRDTS: Prepared Pork Prdts, From Purchased Meat

Bridgford Foods Corporation..................B...... 312 733-0300
  Chicago *(G-4168)*
Charwat Food Group Ltd.......................G...... 630 847-3473
  Hinsdale *(G-11944)*

John J Moesle Wholesale Meats.............F...... 773 847-4900
  Chicago *(G-5315)*
Polancics Meats & Tenderloins..............G...... 815 433-0324
  Ottawa *(G-16980)*

### MEAT PRDTS: Sausage Casings, Natural

Interntional Casings Group Inc..............D...... 773 376-9200
  Chicago *(G-5225)*
Viscofan Usa Inc....................................D...... 217 444-8000
  Danville *(G-7779)*

### MEAT PRDTS: Sausages & Related Prdts, From Purchased Meat

Bende Inc................................................G...... 847 913-0304
  Vernon Hills *(G-21150)*
Direct Marketing 1 Corporation..............E...... 773 234-9122
  Chicago *(G-4608)*
Ifa International Inc................................F...... 847 566-0008
  Mundelein *(G-15508)*
Russo Wholesale Meat Inc....................G...... 708 385-0500
  Alsip *(G-525)*

### MEAT PRDTS: Sausages, From Purchased Meat

Andys Deli and Mikolajczyk....................E...... 773 722-1000
  Chicago *(G-3905)*
Atk Foods Inc.........................................E...... 312 829-2250
  Chicago *(G-3976)*
C & F Packing Co Inc.............................C...... 847 245-2000
  Lake Villa *(G-13012)*
Cherry Meat Packers Inc.......................E...... 773 927-1200
  Chicago *(G-4297)*
Elburn Market Inc...................................G...... 630 365-6461
  Elburn *(G-8884)*
Fabbri Sausage Manufacturing..............E...... 312 829-6363
  Chicago *(G-4808)*
Fema L & L Food Services Inc..............G...... 217 835-2018
  Benld *(G-1805)*
Gurman Food Co....................................F...... 847 837-1100
  Mundelein *(G-15505)*
Makowskis Real Sausage Co................G...... 312 842-5330
  Chicago *(G-5605)*
New Packing Company...........................F...... 312 666-1314
  Chicago *(G-5892)*
Oriental Kitchen Corporation..................G...... 312 738-2850
  Chicago *(G-6007)*
Oriental Kitchen Corporation..................G...... 312 738-2850
  Chicago *(G-6008)*
Oscars Foods Inc...................................G...... 773 622-6822
  Chicago *(G-6020)*
Parker House Sausage Company..........E...... 773 538-1112
  Chicago *(G-6086)*
Roma Packing Co..................................G...... 773 927-7371
  Chicago *(G-6386)*
Smolich Bros..........................................G...... 815 727-2144
  Joliet *(G-12576)*
Stiglmeier Sausage Co Inc.....................F...... 847 537-9988
  Wheeling *(G-22157)*

### MEAT PRDTS: Sausages, From Slaughtered Meat

Heinkels Packing Company Inc.............E...... 217 428-4401
  Decatur *(G-7888)*

### MEAT PRDTS: Smoked

A New Dairy Company............................E...... 312 421-1234
  Chicago *(G-3690)*
Carl Buddig and Company.....................E...... 708 798-0900
  Homewood *(G-12093)*
Food Purveyors Logistics.......................F...... 630 229-6168
  Naperville *(G-15659)*
Sparrer Sausage Company Inc..............C...... 773 762-3334
  Chicago *(G-6551)*

### MEAT PRDTS: Snack Sticks, Incl Jerky, From Purchased Meat

Bert Packing Co Inc................................G...... 312 733-0346
  Chicago *(G-4087)*
Paxton Packing LLC...............................F...... 623 707-5604
  Paxton *(G-17241)*

### MEAT PRDTS: Spreads, Sandwich, From Purchased Meat

Michaels Dawg House LLC...................G...... 847 485-7600
  Palatine *(G-17055)*

### MEAT PRDTS: Veal, From Slaughtered Meat

Brown Packing Company Inc................E...... 708 849-7990
  South Holland *(G-20253)*

### MEAT PROCESSED FROM PURCHASED CARCASSES

A P Deli IV Inc.......................................F...... 708 335-4462
  Hazel Crest *(G-11706)*
Alef Sausage Inc....................................F...... 847 968-2533
  Mundelein *(G-15467)*
Allens Farm Quality Meats.....................G...... 217 896-2532
  Homer *(G-12073)*
Another Chance Community Dev...........E...... 773 998-1641
  Chicago *(G-3913)*
Arts Tamales..........................................G...... 309 367-2850
  Metamora *(G-14739)*
Atlantic Beverage Company Inc............G...... 847 412-6200
  Northbrook *(G-16207)*
B B M Packing Co Inc............................G...... 312 243-1061
  Chicago *(G-4019)*
Ba Le Meat Processing & Whl Co.........F...... 773 506-2499
  Chicago *(G-4023)*
Beatrice Companies Inc........................G...... 602 225-2000
  Chicago *(G-4069)*
Belmont Sausage Company..................G...... 847 357-1515
  Elk Grove Village *(G-9340)*
Bob Evans Farms Inc............................D...... 309 932-2194
  Galva *(G-10785)*
Branding Iron Holdings Inc...................G...... 618 337-8400
  Sauget *(G-19383)*
Brown Packing Company Inc................E...... 708 849-7990
  South Holland *(G-20253)*
Bruss Company.....................................C...... 773 282-2900
  Chicago *(G-4179)*
Carroll County Locker............................G...... 815 493-2370
  Lanark *(G-13151)*
Cass Meats............................................G...... 217 452-3072
  Virginia *(G-21305)*
Columbus Meats Inc..............................G...... 312 829-2480
  Chicago *(G-4433)*
Conagra Brands Inc...............................G...... 312 549-5000
  Chicago *(G-4444)*
Conagra Brands Inc...............................C...... 630 857-1000
  Naperville *(G-15633)*
Consumers Packing Co Inc...................D...... 708 344-0047
  Melrose Park *(G-14611)*
Country Village Meats............................G...... 815 849-5532
  Sublette *(G-20714)*
Creta Farms Usa LLC............................G...... 630 282-5964
  Bolingbrook *(G-2291)*
Danielson Food Products Inc................E...... 773 285-2111
  Chicago *(G-4555)*
Dawn Food Products Inc.......................C...... 815 933-0600
  Bradley *(G-2419)*
Dons Meat Market..................................G...... 309 968-6026
  Manito *(G-14174)*
Dreymiller & Kray Inc.............................G...... 847 683-2271
  Hampshire *(G-11547)*
Earlville Cold Stor Lckr LLC...................G...... 815 246-9469
  Earlville *(G-8593)*
Ed Kabrick Beef Inc...............................G...... 217 656-3263
  Plainville *(G-17662)*
Edgar County Locker Service................G...... 217 466-5000
  Paris *(G-17147)*
Eickmans Processing Co Inc................G...... 815 247-8451
  Seward *(G-19896)*
Emmel Inc..............................................G...... 847 254-5178
  Lake In The Hills *(G-12992)*
Equitrade Group.....................................G...... 312 499-9500
  Chicago *(G-4770)*
Eureka Locker Inc..................................F...... 309 467-2731
  Eureka *(G-9998)*
Farina Locker Service............................G...... 618 245-6491
  Farina *(G-10175)*
Farmington Locker/Ice Plant Co............G...... 309 245-4621
  Farmington *(G-10185)*
Freda Custom Foods Inc.......................C...... 847 412-5900
  Northbrook *(G-16261)*
Freedom Sausage Inc............................F...... 815 792-8276
  Earlville *(G-8594)*
George Nottoli & Sons Inc.....................G...... 773 589-1010
  Chicago *(G-4944)*

---

Employee Codes: A=Over 500 employees, B=251-500
C=101-250, D=51-100, E=20-50, F=10-19, G=3-9

## MEAT PROCESSED FROM PURCHASED CARCASSES

Givaudan Flavors Corporation .......... C ...... 630 682-5600
  Carol Stream (G-3158)
Glenmark Industries Ltd .......... C ...... 773 927-4800
  Chicago (G-4955)
Golden Locker Inc .......... G ...... 217 696-4456
  Camp Point (G-2973)
Grante Foods International LLC .......... F ...... 773 751-9551
  Elk Grove Village (G-9507)
Grecian Delight Foods Inc .......... C ...... 847 364-1010
  Elk Grove Village (G-9511)
Gridley Meats Inc .......... G ...... 309 747-2120
  Gridley (G-11405)
H & B Hams .......... G ...... 618 372-8690
  Brighton (G-2541)
Halsted Packing House Co .......... G ...... 312 421-5147
  Chicago (G-5038)
Hansen Packing Co .......... G ...... 618 498-3714
  Jerseyville (G-12423)
Hartrich Meats Inc .......... G ...... 618 455-3172
  Sainte Marie (G-19324)
Hillshire Brands Company .......... B ...... 312 614-6000
  Chicago (G-5089)
Hillshire Brands Company .......... B ...... 800 727-2533
  Rochelle (G-18093)
Hillshire Brands Company .......... E ...... 312 614-6000
  Chicago (G-5090)
Hillshire Brands Company .......... G ...... 847 310-9400
  Schaumburg (G-19555)
Houser Meats .......... G ...... 217 322-4994
  Rushville (G-19092)
J Brodie Meat Products Inc .......... F ...... 309 342-1500
  Galesburg (G-10761)
Johnsons Processing Plant .......... G ...... 815 684-5183
  Chadwick (G-3442)
Jones Packing Co .......... G ...... 815 943-4488
  Harvard (G-11639)
Koenemann Sausage Co .......... G ...... 815 385-6260
  Volo (G-21316)
Korte Meat Processing Inc .......... G ...... 618 654-3813
  Highland (G-11801)
Kraft Foods Asia PCF Svcs LLC .......... G ...... 847 943-4000
  Deerfield (G-8026)
Lake Pacific Partners LLC .......... B ...... 312 578-1110
  Chicago (G-5440)
Land OFrost Inc .......... C ...... 708 474-7100
  Lansing (G-13169)
Lena AJS Maid Meats .......... F ...... 815 369-4522
  Lena (G-13277)
M E F Corp .......... F ...... 815 965-8604
  Rockford (G-18477)
Meats By Linz Inc .......... E ...... 708 862-0830
  Calumet City (G-2946)
Momence Packing Co .......... B ...... 815 472-6485
  Momence (G-14984)
Mondelez International Inc .......... A ...... 847 943-4000
  Deerfield (G-8038)
Morris Meat Packing Co Inc .......... G ...... 708 865-8566
  Maywood (G-14429)
Moweaqua Packing Plant .......... G ...... 217 768-4714
  Moweaqua (G-15458)
Nea Agora Packing Co .......... G ...... 312 421-5130
  Chicago (G-5878)
O Chilli Frozen Foods Inc .......... E ...... 847 562-1991
  Northbrook (G-16321)
Old Fashioned Meat Co Inc .......... G ...... 312 421-4555
  Chicago (G-5978)
On-Cor Frozen Foods LLC .......... D ...... 630 692-2283
  Aurora (G-1200)
On-Cor Frozen Foods LLC .......... E ...... 630 692-2283
  Aurora (G-1199)
OSI Industries LLC .......... C ...... 630 231-9090
  West Chicago (G-21754)
OSI Industries LLC .......... B ...... 773 847-2000
  Chicago (G-6021)
OSI International Foods Ltd .......... D ...... 630 851-6600
  Aurora (G-1060)
Papa Charlies Inc .......... E ...... 773 522-7900
  Chicago (G-6071)
Park Packing Company Inc .......... E ...... 773 254-0100
  Chicago (G-6083)
Plumrose Usa Inc .......... E ...... 732 257-6600
  Downers Grove (G-8504)
Portillos Food Service Inc .......... E ...... 630 620-0460
  Addison (G-248)
Powers John .......... G ...... 309 742-8929
  Elmwood (G-9965)
Preferred Foods Products Inc .......... F ...... 773 847-0230
  Chicago (G-6173)
Prince Meat Co .......... F ...... 815 729-2333
  Darien (G-7801)

R&R Meat Co .......... G ...... 270 898-6296
  Metropolis (G-14761)
Randolph Packing Co .......... D ...... 630 830-3100
  Streamwood (G-20670)
Rapid Foods Inc .......... G ...... 708 366-0321
  Shorewood (G-19931)
Rochelle Foods LLC .......... A ...... 815 562-4141
  Rochelle (G-18105)
Rose Packing Company Inc .......... A ...... 708 458-9300
  Chicago (G-6395)
Ryan Meat Company .......... G ...... 773 783-3840
  Chicago (G-6416)
Seifferts Locker & Meat Proc .......... F ...... 618 594-3921
  Carlyle (G-3058)
Smithfield Farmland Corp .......... A ...... 309 734-5353
  Monmouth (G-15023)
Steinbach Provision Company .......... G ...... 773 538-1511
  Chicago (G-6583)
T & J Meatpacking Inc .......... D ...... 708 757-6930
  Chicago Heights (G-7129)
Tomcyndi Inc .......... E ...... 773 847-5400
  Chicago (G-6737)
Tyson Fresh Meats Inc .......... F ...... 847 836-5550
  Elgin (G-9218)
V A M D Inc .......... G ...... 773 631-8400
  Chicago (G-6865)
William Badal .......... G ...... 815 264-7752
  Waterman (G-21412)
Wurst Kitchen Inc .......... G ...... 630 898-9242
  Aurora (G-1235)
Y T Packing Co .......... F ...... 217 522-3345
  Springfield (G-20550)

## MEAT PROCESSING MACHINERY

Cozzini LLC .......... C ...... 773 478-9700
  Chicago (G-4486)
E-Quip Manufacturing Co .......... E ...... 815 464-0053
  Frankfort (G-10317)
Hollymatic Corporation .......... D ...... 708 579-3700
  Countryside (G-7430)
Miles Bros .......... G ...... 618 937-4115
  West Frankfort (G-21814)
Primedge Inc .......... C ...... 224 265-6600
  Elk Grove Village (G-9697)
Rantoul Foods LLC .......... B ...... 217 892-4178
  Rantoul (G-17936)
Stephen Paoli Mfg Corp .......... F ...... 815 965-0621
  Rockford (G-18634)
TEC Systems Inc .......... F ...... 815 722-2800
  New Lenox (G-15917)
Tyson Fresh Meats Inc .......... F ...... 847 836-5550
  Elgin (G-9218)

## MEATS, PACKAGED FROZEN: Wholesalers

B B M Packing Co Inc .......... G ...... 312 243-1061
  Chicago (G-4019)
Bruss Company .......... C ...... 773 282-2900
  Chicago (G-4179)
Fabbri Sausage Manufacturing .......... E ...... 312 829-6363
  Chicago (G-4808)
Nationwide Foods Inc .......... B ...... 773 787-4900
  Chicago (G-5869)
Randolph Packing Co .......... D ...... 630 830-3100
  Streamwood (G-20670)

## MECHANISMS: Coin-Operated Machines

Advanced Technologies Inc .......... G ...... 847 329-9875
  Park Ridge (G-17178)

## MEDIA BUYING AGENCIES

7000 Inc .......... F ...... 312 800-3612
  Bolingbrook (G-2275)

## MEDIA: Magnetic & Optical Recording

Acro Magnetics Inc .......... G ...... 815 943-5018
  Harvard (G-11617)
Arba Retail Systems Corp .......... G ...... 630 620-8566
  Naperville (G-15797)
Bpn Chicago .......... E ...... 312 799-4100
  Chicago (G-4154)
Magna-Flux International .......... G ...... 815 623-7634
  Roscoe (G-18904)
Magnetic Occasions & More Inc .......... G ...... 815 462-4141
  New Lenox (G-15892)

## MEDICAL & HOSPITAL EQPT WHOLESALERS

1 Federal Supply Source Inc .......... G ...... 708 964-2222
  Steger (G-20565)
Airgas USA LLC .......... E ...... 708 354-0813
  Countryside (G-7412)
Cardinal Health Inc .......... B ...... 847 578-4443
  Waukegan (G-21532)
Covidien LP .......... C ...... 815 744-3766
  Joliet (G-12478)
D-M-S Holdings Inc .......... C ...... 847 680-6811
  Waukegan (G-21547)
Mac Medical Inc .......... G ...... 618 719-6757
  Belleville (G-1650)
McClendon Holdings LLC .......... G ...... 773 251-2314
  Chicago (G-5664)
Medela LLC .......... C ...... 800 435-8316
  McHenry (G-14531)
Medtex Health Services Inc .......... G ...... 630 789-0330
  Clarendon Hills (G-7258)
Sage Products LLC .......... B ...... 815 455-4700
  Cary (G-3370)
Titus Enterprises LLC .......... G ...... 773 441-7222
  Warrenville (G-21364)
Vicron Optical Inc .......... F ...... 847 412-5530
  Deerfield (G-8066)
Wholesale Point Inc .......... F ...... 630 986-1700
  Burr Ridge (G-2895)

## MEDICAL & HOSPITAL SPLYS: Radiation Shielding Garments

Accurate Radiation Shielding .......... G ...... 847 639-5533
  Cary (G-3321)

## MEDICAL & SURGICAL SPLYS: Abdominal Support, Braces/Trusses

Milvia .......... G ...... 312 527-3403
  Chicago (G-5766)

## MEDICAL & SURGICAL SPLYS: Bandages & Dressings

Hollister Wound Care LLC .......... G ...... 847 996-6000
  Libertyville (G-13334)
Newmedical Technology Inc .......... E ...... 847 412-1000
  Northbrook (G-16319)

## MEDICAL & SURGICAL SPLYS: Braces, Orthopedic

Comprhnsive Prsthtics Orthtics .......... F ...... 708 387-9700
  Brookfield (G-2628)
Keller Orthotics Inc .......... F ...... 773 929-4700
  Chicago (G-5369)
Midwest Orthotic Services LLC .......... E ...... 773 930-3770
  Chicago (G-5748)
O & P Kinetic .......... G ...... 815 401-7260
  Bourbonnais (G-2404)
Pal Health Technologies Inc .......... D ...... 309 347-8785
  Pekin (G-17280)
Therapeutic Envisions Inc .......... G ...... 720 323-7032
  Libertyville (G-13390)

## MEDICAL & SURGICAL SPLYS: Clothing, Fire Resistant & Protect

Salisbury Elec Safety LLC .......... B ...... 877 406-4501
  Bolingbrook (G-2365)

## MEDICAL & SURGICAL SPLYS: Cosmetic Restorations

Cosmedent Inc .......... E ...... 312 644-9388
  Chicago (G-4478)
Landau Real Estate Svcs LLC .......... G ...... 312 379-9146
  Chicago (G-5455)
Lemaitre Vascular Inc .......... F ...... 847 462-2191
  Fox River Grove (G-10288)

## MEDICAL & SURGICAL SPLYS: Crutches & Walkers

Go Steady LLC .......... G ...... 630 293-3243
  West Chicago (G-21709)

# PRODUCT SECTION

# MEDICAL EQPT: Electromedical Apparatus

### MEDICAL & SURGICAL SPLYS: Drapes, Surgical, Cotton

Brandt Interiors ................................................. G ....... 847 251-3543
  Wilmette  *(G-22246)*

### MEDICAL & SURGICAL SPLYS: Gauze, Surgical

Brasel Products Inc ........................................... G ....... 630 879-3759
  Batavia  *(G-1424)*
Modern Aids Inc ................................................ E ....... 847 437-8600
  Elk Grove Village  *(G-9634)*

### MEDICAL & SURGICAL SPLYS: Gynecological Splys & Appliances

Medgyn Products Inc ........................................ D ....... 630 627-4105
  Addison  *(G-197)*

### MEDICAL & SURGICAL SPLYS: Infant Incubators

Mhub .................................................................. G ....... 773 580-1485
  Chicago  *(G-5717)*

### MEDICAL & SURGICAL SPLYS: Ligatures

Star Cushion Products Inc ................................ F ....... 618 539-7070
  Freeburg  *(G-10643)*

### MEDICAL & SURGICAL SPLYS: Limbs, Artificial

Hanger Prosthetics & ........................................ G ....... 217 429-6656
  Decatur  *(G-7887)*
Hanger Prosthetics & ........................................ D ....... 708 371-9999
  Oak Lawn  *(G-16624)*
Hanger Prosthetics & ........................................ G ....... 847 623-6080
  Gurnee  *(G-11458)*
Hanger Prosthetics & ........................................ G ....... 630 820-5656
  Aurora  *(G-1022)*
Hanger Prsthetcs & Ortho Inc ........................... G ....... 708 957-0240
  Hazel Crest  *(G-11708)*
Illiana Orthopedics Inc ....................................... G ....... 708 532-0061
  Tinley Park  *(G-20921)*
Koebers Prosthetic Orthpd Lab ........................ G ....... 309 676-2276
  Chicago  *(G-5400)*
Psyonic Inc ........................................................ G ....... 773 888-3252
  Champaign  *(G-3531)*
Quad City Prosthetics Inc ................................. F ....... 309 676-2276
  Rock Island  *(G-18194)*
Replacement Arts Inc ....................................... G ....... 708 922-0580
  Posen  *(G-17735)*
Ronald S Lefors Bs Cpo ................................... G ....... 618 259-1969
  East Alton  *(G-8610)*
Scheck Siress Prosthetics Inc .......................... C ....... 630 424-0392
  Oak Park  *(G-16684)*
Tuu Duc Le Inc .................................................. G ....... 630 897-6363
  North Aurora  *(G-16148)*

### MEDICAL & SURGICAL SPLYS: Models, Anatomical

Anatomical Worldwide LLC .............................. G ....... 312 224-4772
  Evanston  *(G-10010)*

### MEDICAL & SURGICAL SPLYS: Orthopedic Appliances

Bergmann Orthotic Laboratory ......................... G ....... 847 729-7923
  Glenview  *(G-11108)*
Cera Ltd ............................................................ G ....... 773 334-1042
  Chicago  *(G-4282)*
Dreher Orthopedic Industries ........................... G ....... 708 848-4646
  Oak Park  *(G-16661)*
Hanger Inc ........................................................ E ....... 708 679-1006
  Matteson  *(G-14372)*
Hanger Prosthetics & ........................................ G ....... 847 478-8154
  Lincolnshire  *(G-13452)*
Howmedica Osteonics Corp .............................. G ....... 309 663-6414
  Bloomington  *(G-2181)*
Joliet Orthotics ................................................... G ....... 708 798-1767
  Flossmoor  *(G-10226)*
JP Orthotics ...................................................... G ....... 217 885-3047
  Quincy  *(G-17843)*
Kinetic Orthotic Inc ........................................... G ....... 708 246-9266
  Western Springs  *(G-21869)*
Neo Orthotics Inc ............................................. G ....... 309 699-0354
  East Peoria  *(G-8726)*

Northern Prosthetics ......................................... G ....... 815 226-0444
  Rockford  *(G-18522)*
Optech Ortho & Prosth Svcs ............................. G ....... 815 932-8564
  Kankakee  *(G-12642)*
Orthotic & Prosthetic Assoc .............................. G ....... 217 789-1450
  Springfield  *(G-20495)*
Permobil Inc ...................................................... F ....... 847 568-0001
  Skokie  *(G-20054)*
Prosthetic Orthotic Specialist ........................... G ....... 309 454-8733
  Normal  *(G-16085)*
Rinella Orthotics Inc ......................................... G ....... 815 717-8970
  New Lenox  *(G-15906)*
Serola Biomechanics Inc .................................. F ....... 815 636-2780
  Loves Park  *(G-13991)*
World Class Technologies Inc .......................... G ....... 312 758-3114
  Chicago  *(G-7029)*

### MEDICAL & SURGICAL SPLYS: Personal Safety Eqpt

Fall Protection Systems Inc ............................. E ....... 618 452-7000
  Madison  *(G-14145)*
Plastic Specialists America ............................. G ....... 847 406-7547
  Gurnee  *(G-11486)*
Prointegration Tech LLC ................................... G ....... 618 409-3233
  Highland  *(G-11806)*
Sellstrom Manufacturing Co ............................. D ....... 800 323-7402
  Elgin  *(G-9175)*
Standard Safety Equipment Co ........................ E ....... 815 363-8565
  McHenry  *(G-14556)*
Steel-Guard Safety Corp .................................. G ....... 708 589-4588
  South Holland  *(G-20306)*
Steiner Industries Inc ....................................... D ....... 773 588-3444
  Chicago  *(G-6585)*
Triad Controls Inc ............................................ G ....... 630 443-9343
  Saint Charles  *(G-19286)*
Weeb Enterprises LLC ..................................... G ....... 815 861-2625
  Wauconda  *(G-21514)*

### MEDICAL & SURGICAL SPLYS: Prosthetic Appliances

Bioconcepts Inc ................................................ G ....... 630 986-0007
  Burr Ridge  *(G-2824)*
D J Peters Orthopedics Ltd .............................. G ....... 309 664-6930
  Bloomington  *(G-2159)*
Delta Molding LLC ............................................ G ....... 847 414-7773
  Buffalo Grove  *(G-2685)*
Hanger Inc ........................................................ E ....... 847 695-6955
  McHenry  *(G-14511)*
Hanger Prosthetics & ........................................ G ....... 618 997-1451
  Herrin  *(G-11749)*
Hanger Prosthetics & Orthotics ........................ E ....... 618 288-8920
  Maryville  *(G-14341)*
Hanger Prsthetcs & Ortho Inc ........................... G ....... 815 937-0241
  Kankakee  *(G-12620)*
Hanger Prsthetcs & Ortho Inc ........................... G ....... 815 744-9944
  Joliet  *(G-12508)*
Optech Ortho & Prosth Svcs ............................. G ....... 708 364-9700
  Orland Park  *(G-16880)*
Payne Chauna .................................................. G ....... 618 580-2584
  Belleville  *(G-1664)*
Pro-Orthotics Inc ............................................... G ....... 708 326-1554
  Orland Park  *(G-16885)*
Prosthetics Orthotics Han ................................. G ....... 847 695-6955
  McHenry  *(G-14549)*
Srt Prosthetics Orthotics LLC ........................... G ....... 847 855-0030
  Gurnee  *(G-11507)*

### MEDICAL & SURGICAL SPLYS: Respiratory Protect Eqpt, Personal

Rondex Products Incorporated ........................ F ....... 815 226-0452
  Rockford  *(G-18597)*

### MEDICAL & SURGICAL SPLYS: Splints, Pneumatic & Wood

Gregory Lamar & Assoc Inc ............................. G ....... 312 595-1545
  Chicago  *(G-5002)*

### MEDICAL & SURGICAL SPLYS: Sponges

Integrated Medical Tech Inc ............................. G ....... 309 662-3614
  Bloomington  *(G-2183)*

### MEDICAL & SURGICAL SPLYS: Supports, Abdominal, Ankle, Etc

New Step Orthotic Lab Inc ............................... F ....... 618 208-4444
  Maryville  *(G-14345)*

### MEDICAL & SURGICAL SPLYS: Swabs, Sanitary Cotton

Clinere Products Inc ......................................... G ....... 847 837-4020
  Mundelein  *(G-15489)*

### MEDICAL & SURGICAL SPLYS: Technical Aids, Handicapped

R W G Manufacturing Inc ................................. G ....... 708 755-8035
  S Chicago Hts  *(G-19112)*

### MEDICAL & SURGICAL SPLYS: Welders' Hoods

Sourcennex International Co ............................ G ....... 847 251-5500
  Wilmette  *(G-22266)*
Tri R ................................................................... G ....... 224 399-7786
  Libertyville  *(G-13392)*

### MEDICAL EQPT REPAIR SVCS, NON-ELECTRIC

Griffith Company ............................................... G ....... 847 524-4173
  Schaumburg  *(G-19544)*

### MEDICAL EQPT: Diagnostic

7000 Inc ........................................................... F ....... 312 800-3612
  Bolingbrook  *(G-2275)*
Abbott Laboratories .......................................... B ....... 847 935-5509
  North Chicago  *(G-16162)*
Abbott Laboratories .......................................... A ....... 847 937-6100
  Abbott Park  *(G-3)*
Abbott Laboratories .......................................... A ....... 224 667-6100
  Abbott Park  *(G-1)*
Abbott Laboratories Inc .................................... A ....... 224 668-2076
  Abbott Park  *(G-4)*
Addison Central Pathology ............................... G ....... 847 685-9326
  Chicago  *(G-3744)*
African American Ctr For Hnb .......................... D ....... 618 549-3965
  Park Forest  *(G-17168)*
American Biooptics LLC ................................... G ....... 847 467-0628
  Evanston  *(G-10009)*
American Imaging MGT Inc .............................. E ....... 708 236-8500
  Westchester  *(G-21829)*
American Imaging MGT Inc .............................. G ....... 847 564-8500
  Deerfield  *(G-7976)*
Atch Inc ............................................................. G ....... 847 295-5055
  Lake Forest  *(G-12882)*
Diagnostic Photonics Inc .................................. G ....... 312 320-5478
  Chicago  *(G-4592)*
Elite Imaging .................................................... F ....... 618 632-2900
  East Saint Louis  *(G-8750)*
Feelsure Health Corparation ............................ G ....... 847 823-0137
  Park Ridge  *(G-17194)*
Hospira Inc ....................................................... A ....... 224 212-2000
  Lake Forest  *(G-12908)*
Hospira Inc ....................................................... C ....... 224 212-6244
  Lake Forest  *(G-12909)*
Hospira Worldwide LLC ................................... G ....... 224 212-2000
  Lake Forest  *(G-12910)*
ISS Medical Inc ................................................ G ....... 217 359-8681
  Champaign  *(G-3503)*
Leica Microsystems Inc .................................... C ....... 847 405-0123
  Buffalo Grove  *(G-2726)*
MD Technologies Inc ........................................ F ....... 815 598-3143
  Elizabeth  *(G-9244)*
Merge Healthcare Incorporated ........................ C ....... 312 565-6868
  Chicago  *(G-5690)*
Nrtx LLC ............................................................ G ....... 224 717-0465
  Chicago  *(G-5951)*
Provena Randalwood Open Mri ........................ E ....... 630 587-9917
  Geneva  *(G-10860)*
Rockford Wellness & Diagnostic ....................... G ....... 815 708-0125
  Rockford  *(G-18590)*
Siemens Med Solutions USA Inc ..................... D ....... 847 304-7700
  Schaumburg  *(G-19727)*

### MEDICAL EQPT: Electromedical Apparatus

CTS Automotive LLC ........................................ C ....... 630 614-7201
  Lisle  *(G-13578)*
General Electric Company ................................ B ....... 847 304-7400
  Hoffman Estates  *(G-12013)*
Healthlight LLC ................................................. F ....... 224 231-0342
  Schaumburg  *(G-19550)*
Isovac Products LLC ........................................ G ....... 630 679-1740
  Romeoville  *(G-18831)*
Medical Specialties Distrs LLC ......................... E ....... 630 307-6200
  Hanover Park  *(G-11585)*

## MEDICAL EQPT: Heart-Lung Machines, Exc Iron Lungs

Cardiac Imaging Inc .................................... F ...... 630 834-7100
  Oakbrook Terrace *(G-16700)*
Fredrick Hoy ............................................... G ...... 309 691-4410
  Peoria *(G-17367)*

## MEDICAL EQPT: Laser Systems

Aespheptics Medical Ltd ............................. G ...... 630 416-1400
  Lombard *(G-13762)*
Dermatique Laser & Skin ............................ F ...... 630 262-2515
  Geneva *(G-10824)*
Samel Botros .............................................. G ...... 847 466-5905
  Bloomingdale *(G-2134)*

## MEDICAL EQPT: PET Or Position Emission Tomography Scanners

ADM Imaging Inc ........................................ G ...... 630 834-7100
  Wheaton *(G-21934)*

## MEDICAL EQPT: Patient Monitoring

7000 Inc ..................................................... F ...... 312 800-3612
  Bolingbrook *(G-2275)*
Dupage Chropractic Centre Ltd .................. G ...... 630 858-9780
  Glen Ellyn *(G-10968)*
Touchpointcare LLC .................................. G ...... 866 713-6590
  Libertyville *(G-13391)*

## MEDICAL EQPT: Ultrasonic Scanning Devices

Apana Inc .................................................. G ...... 309 303-4007
  Peoria *(G-17308)*
Carematix Inc ............................................. E ...... 312 627-9300
  Chicago *(G-4242)*
Nanocytomics LLC ..................................... G ...... 847 467-2868
  Evanston *(G-10077)*
Smart Scan Mri LLC .................................. G ...... 847 623-4000
  Gurnee *(G-11505)*
Verena Solutions LLC ................................ G ...... 314 651-1908
  Chicago *(G-6885)*

## MEDICAL EQPT: Ultrasonic, Exc Cleaning

Axiosonic LLC ........................................... F ...... 217 342-3412
  Effingham *(G-8826)*
Ctg Advanced Materials LLC ..................... E ...... 630 226-9080
  Bolingbrook *(G-2292)*
Victory Pharmacy Decatur Inc ................... E ...... 217 429-8650
  Decatur *(G-7956)*

## MEDICAL EQPT: X-Ray Apparatus & Tubes, Radiographic

Wallace Enterprises Inc ............................. G ...... 309 496-1230
  East Moline *(G-8698)*

## MEDICAL EQPT: X-ray Generators

Sedecal Usa Inc ........................................ E ...... 847 394-6960
  Arlington Heights *(G-837)*

## MEDICAL FIELD ASSOCIATION

American Assn Endodontists ..................... E ...... 312 266-7255
  Chicago *(G-3849)*
American Assn Nurosurgeons Inc .............. E ...... 847 378-0500
  Rolling Meadows *(G-18709)*
American Cllege Chest Physcans ............... D ...... 224 521-9800
  Glenview *(G-11099)*
American Medical Association ................... A ...... 312 464-5000
  Chicago *(G-3863)*
American Soc Plastic Surgeons ................. D ...... 847 228-9900
  Arlington Heights *(G-710)*
International College Surgeons .................. G ...... 312 642-6502
  Chicago *(G-5220)*

## MEDICAL SVCS ORGANIZATION

Smart Scan Mri LLC .................................. G ...... 847 623-4000
  Gurnee *(G-11505)*

## MEDICAL TRAINING SERVICES

Tanaka Dental Enterprises Inc ................... F ...... 847 679-1610
  Skokie *(G-20099)*

## MEDICAL X-RAY MACHINES & TUBES WHOLESALERS

Arquilla Inc ................................................. F ...... 815 455-2470
  Crystal Lake *(G-7537)*

## MEDICAL, DENTAL & HOSPITAL EQPT, WHOL: Dentists' Prof Splys

Dental Laboratory Inc ................................. E ...... 630 262-3700
  Geneva *(G-10823)*

## MEDICAL, DENTAL & HOSPITAL EQPT, WHOL: Hospital Eqpt & Splys

Accurate Radiation Shielding ..................... G ...... 847 639-5533
  Cary *(G-3321)*
C R Kesner Company ................................ G ...... 630 232-8118
  Geneva *(G-10816)*
Omron Healthcare Inc ................................ D ...... 847 680-6200
  Lake Forest *(G-12932)*
Richard Ochwat Specialty Entp .................. G ...... 630 682-0800
  Carol Stream *(G-3228)*

## MEDICAL, DENTAL & HOSPITAL EQPT, WHOL: Hosptl Eqpt/Furniture

Faxitron X-Ray LLC .................................... E ...... 847 465-9729
  Lincolnshire *(G-13447)*
Mark Industries ........................................... G ...... 847 487-8670
  Wauconda *(G-21480)*
Medifix Inc .................................................. G ...... 847 965-1898
  Morton Grove *(G-15219)*
Shenglong Intl Group Corp ........................ G ...... 312 388-2345
  Glenview *(G-11195)*
Umf Corporation ........................................ F ...... 847 920-0370
  Skokie *(G-20104)*

## MEDICAL, DENTAL & HOSPITAL EQPT, WHOL: Surgical Eqpt & Splys

Akorn Inc .................................................... F ...... 847 625-1100
  Gurnee *(G-11425)*
Akorn Inc .................................................... C ...... 847 279-6100
  Lake Forest *(G-12876)*
Tetra Medical Supply Corp ........................ F ...... 847 647-0590
  Niles *(G-16040)*

## MEDICAL, DENTAL & HOSPITAL EQPT, WHOLESALE: Artificial Limbs

Gema Inc .................................................... G ...... 773 508-6690
  Chicago *(G-4924)*
O & P Kinetic ............................................. G ...... 815 401-7260
  Bourbonnais *(G-2404)*

## MEDICAL, DENTAL & HOSPITAL EQPT, WHOLESALE: Dental Lab

Bird-X Inc ................................................... E ...... 312 226-2473
  Chicago *(G-4112)*

## MEDICAL, DENTAL & HOSPITAL EQPT, WHOLESALE: Hearing Aids

Gohear LLC ............................................... G ...... 847 574-7829
  Lake Forest *(G-12902)*

## MEDICAL, DENTAL & HOSPITAL EQPT, WHOLESALE: Hosp Furniture

Blair Company ........................................... G ...... 847 439-3980
  Elk Grove Village *(G-9343)*

## MEDICAL, DENTAL & HOSPITAL EQPT, WHOLESALE: Med Eqpt & Splys

Brainlab Inc ................................................ C ...... 800 784-7700
  Westchester *(G-21831)*
Cino Incorporated ...................................... G ...... 630 377-7242
  Saint Charles *(G-19153)*
Doctors Choice Inc .................................... G ...... 312 666-1111
  Chicago *(G-4621)*
Fenwal Inc ................................................. B ...... 847 550-2300
  Lake Zurich *(G-13072)*
Fenwal Holdings Inc .................................. B ...... 847 550-2300
  Lake Zurich *(G-13073)*
General Bandages Inc ............................... F ...... 847 966-8383
  Park Ridge *(G-17198)*
Good Lite Co .............................................. G ...... 847 841-1145
  Elgin *(G-9050)*
Howard Medical Company ........................ G ...... 773 278-1440
  Chicago *(G-5122)*
Indilab Inc .................................................. E ...... 847 928-1050
  Franklin Park *(G-10496)*
Jero Medical Eqp & Sups Inc .................... E ...... 773 305-4193
  Chicago *(G-5295)*
Medgyn Products Inc ................................. D ...... 630 627-4105
  Addison *(G-197)*
Mobility Connection Inc ............................. G ...... 815 965-8090
  Rockford *(G-18510)*
Nestle Usa Inc ........................................... D ...... 847 808-5404
  Buffalo Grove *(G-2747)*
Northgate Technologies Inc ....................... E ...... 847 608-8900
  Elgin *(G-9126)*
Richard Wolf Med Instrs Corp ................... C ...... 847 913-1113
  Vernon Hills *(G-21193)*
Simpex Medical Inc ................................... G ...... 847 757-9928
  Mount Prospect *(G-15374)*
Sullivan Home Health Products ................ G ...... 217 532-6366
  Hillsboro *(G-11900)*
Victory Pharmacy Decatur Inc ................... E ...... 217 429-8650
  Decatur *(G-7956)*

## MEDICAL, DENTAL & HOSPITAL EQPT, WHOLESALE: Medical Lab

Asahi Kasei Bioprocess Inc ....................... E ...... 847 834-0800
  Glenview *(G-11105)*
Baxter Healthcare Corporation .................. E ...... 847 578-4671
  Waukegan *(G-21529)*
Spraying Systems Co ................................ F ...... 630 665-5001
  Aurora *(G-1082)*

## MEDICAL, DENTAL & HOSPITAL EQPT, WHOLESALE: Orthopedic

Medacta Usa Inc ........................................ D ...... 312 878-2381
  Chicago *(G-5675)*
Serola Biomechanics Inc ........................... F ...... 815 636-2780
  Loves Park *(G-13991)*

## MEMBERSHIP ORGANIZATIONS, BUSINESS: Contractors' Association

Be Group Inc .............................................. G ...... 312 436-0301
  Chicago *(G-4061)*
Shading Solutions Group Inc ..................... G ...... 630 444-2102
  Geneva *(G-10866)*

## MEMBERSHIP ORGANIZATIONS, BUSINESS: Merchants' Association

Narda Inc ................................................... F ...... 312 648-2300
  Chicago *(G-5853)*

## MEMBERSHIP ORGANIZATIONS, NEC: Charitable

Spudnik Press Cooperative ....................... F ...... 312 563-0302
  Chicago *(G-6564)*

## MEMBERSHIP ORGANIZATIONS, PROFESSIONAL: Health Association

Christian Cnty Mntal Hlth Assn ................. D ...... 217 824-9675
  Taylorville *(G-20836)*

## MEMBERSHIP ORGANIZATIONS, REL: Christian Reformed Church

Marantha Wrld Rvval Ministries ................. G ...... 773 384-7717
  Chicago *(G-5611)*

## MEMBERSHIP ORGANIZATIONS, REL: Churches, Temples & Shrines

Community Gospel Center ........................ G ...... 773 486-7661
  Chicago *(G-4436)*

## MEMBERSHIP ORGANIZATIONS, RELIGIOUS: Brethren Church

Church of Brethren Inc .............................. D ...... 847 742-5100
  Elgin *(G-8990)*

# PRODUCT SECTION

## METAL FABRICATORS: Architechtural

### MEMBERSHIP ORGANIZATIONS, RELIGIOUS: Catholic Church

Saints Volo & Olha Uk Cath Par............G...... 312 829-5209
  Chicago *(G-6430)*

### MEMBERSHIP ORGANIZATIONS, RELIGIOUS: Church Of Christ

St Johns United Church Christ............G...... 847 491-6686
  Evanston *(G-10095)*

### MEMBERSHIP ORGANIZATIONS, RELIGIOUS: Nonchurch

Baptist General Conference............D...... 800 323-4215
  Arlington Heights *(G-723)*
Theosophical Society In Amer............G...... 630 665-0130
  Wheaton *(G-21984)*

### MEMBERSHIP ORGANIZATIONS: Reading Rooms/Other Cultural Orgs

Theosophical Society In Amer............F...... 630 665-0123
  Wheaton *(G-21985)*

### MEMBERSHIP ORGS, CIVIC, SOCIAL & FRATERNAL: Condo Assoc

Condominiums Northbrook Cort 1............G...... 847 498-1640
  Lincolnshire *(G-13439)*
J R G Oil Co Inc............G...... 618 842-9131
  Fairfield *(G-10144)*
Winnetka Mews Condominium Assn............G...... 847 501-2770
  Winnetka *(G-22316)*

### MEMBERSHIP ORGS, CIVIC, SOCIAL/FRAT: Educator's Assoc

Theosophical Society In Amer............G...... 630 665-0130
  Wheaton *(G-21984)*
Theosophical Society In Amer............F...... 630 665-0123
  Wheaton *(G-21985)*

### MEMBERSHIP SPORTS & RECREATION CLUBS

Good Sam Enterprises LLC............E...... 847 229-6720
  Lincolnshire *(G-13450)*

### MEMORIALS, MONUMENTS & MARKERS

All Saints Monument Co Inc............G...... 847 824-1248
  Des Plaines *(G-8145)*
American Monument Co............G...... 618 993-8968
  Marion *(G-14253)*
Jack R Phillips............G...... 618 242-8411
  Mount Vernon *(G-15416)*
Keepes Funeral Home Inc............F...... 618 262-5200
  Mount Carmel *(G-15271)*
Monumental Manufacturing Co............D...... 708 544-0916
  Hillside *(G-11927)*
Nashville Memorial Co............G...... 618 327-8492
  Nashville *(G-15843)*

### MEN'S & BOYS' CLOTHING ACCESS STORES

Duckys Formal Wear Inc............G...... 309 342-5914
  Galesburg *(G-10748)*
Gcg Corp............G...... 847 298-2285
  Glenview *(G-11128)*
Hugo Boss Usa Inc............F...... 847 517-1461
  Schaumburg *(G-19559)*

### MEN'S & BOYS' CLOTHING STORES

A&B Apparel............G...... 815 962-5070
  Rockford *(G-18241)*
BMW Sportswear Inc............G...... 773 265-0110
  Chicago *(G-4133)*
Fashahnn Corporation............G...... 773 994-3132
  Chicago *(G-4814)*
Signature Design & Tailoring............F...... 773 375-4915
  Chicago *(G-6510)*
W Diamond Group Corporation............A...... 646 647-2791
  Des Plaines *(G-8301)*

### MEN'S & BOYS' CLOTHING WHOLESALERS, NEC

ASap Specialties Inc Del............G...... 847 223-7699
  Grayslake *(G-11321)*
Bird Dog Bay Inc............G...... 312 631-3108
  Chicago *(G-4111)*
Dzro-Bans International Inc............ 779 324-2740
  Homewood *(G-12096)*
Gabriel Enterprises............G...... 773 342-8705
  Chicago *(G-4906)*
Mennon Rubber & Safety Pdts............G...... 847 678-8250
  Schiller Park *(G-19849)*

### MEN'S & BOYS' SPORTSWEAR CLOTHING STORES

B JS Printables............G...... 618 656-8625
  Edwardsville *(G-8789)*
Fielders Choice............G...... 618 937-2294
  West Frankfort *(G-21807)*
Johnos Inc............G...... 630 897-6929
  Aurora *(G-1178)*
Minerva Sportswear Inc............F...... 309 661-2387
  Bloomington *(G-2201)*
Te Shurt Shop Inc............F...... 217 344-1226
  Champaign *(G-3549)*

### MEN'S & BOYS' SPORTSWEAR WHOLESALERS

American Outfitters Ltd............E...... 847 623-3959
  Waukegan *(G-21524)*
Art-Flo Shirt & Lettering Co............E...... 708 656-5422
  Chicago *(G-3953)*
B and A Screen Printing............G...... 217 762-2632
  Monticello *(G-15074)*
B JS Printables............G...... 618 656-8625
  Edwardsville *(G-8789)*
Chicago Shirt & Lettering Co............G...... 773 745-0222
  Chicago *(G-4348)*
Hermans Inc............E...... 309 206-4892
  Rock Island *(G-18181)*
Ronald J Nixon............G...... 708 748-8130
  Park Forest *(G-17175)*

### MEN'S CLOTHING STORES: Everyday, Exc Suits & Sportswear

Custom By Lamar Inc............F...... 312 738-2160
  Chicago *(G-4520)*

### MENTAL HEALTH CLINIC, OUTPATIENT

Mental Health Ctrs Centl Ill............D...... 217 735-1413
  Lincoln *(G-13415)*

### METAL & STEEL PRDTS: Abrasive

Arcelor Mittal USA LLC............F...... 312 899-3500
  Chicago *(G-3932)*
Avec Inc............G...... 217 670-0439
  Naperville *(G-15799)*
Higman LLC............G...... 618 785-2545
  Baldwin *(G-1251)*
Severstal US Holdings II Inc............E...... 708 756-0400
  Hinsdale *(G-11964)*

### METAL COMPONENTS: Prefabricated

Ward Cnc Machining............G...... 815 637-1490
  Loves Park *(G-14006)*

### METAL CUTTING SVCS

Accurate Metals Illinois LLC............F...... 815 966-6320
  Rockford *(G-18254)*
Fox Metal Services Inc............F...... 847 439-9696
  Carol Stream *(G-3155)*
Laser Plus Technologies LLC............G...... 847 787-9017
  Elk Grove Village *(G-9585)*
Polaris Laser Laminations LLC............G...... 630 444-0760
  West Chicago *(G-21758)*
Production Fabg & Stamping Inc............F...... 708 755-5468
  S Chicago Hts *(G-19111)*
Progress Rail Services Corp............E...... 309 963-4425
  Danvers *(G-7701)*

### METAL DETECTORS

Minelab Americas Inc............F...... 630 401-8150
  Lisle *(G-13624)*

Windy City Detectors Sales............G...... 773 774-5445
  Chicago *(G-6994)*

### METAL FABRICATORS: Architechtural

555 International Inc............E...... 773 847-1400
  Chicago *(G-3670)*
Aj Welding Services............G...... 708 843-2701
  Oak Park *(G-16651)*
Alert Tubing Fabricators Inc............G...... 847 253-7237
  Schaumburg *(G-19429)*
Alfredos Iron Works Inc............E...... 815 748-1177
  Cortland *(G-7384)*
American Stair Corporation Inc............D...... 815 886-9600
  Romeoville *(G-18796)*
Amron Stair Works Inc............F...... 847 426-4800
  Gilberts *(G-10912)*
Anchor Welding & Fabrication............G...... 815 937-1640
  Aroma Park *(G-878)*
Ancient Graffiti Inc............E...... 847 726-5800
  Lake Zurich *(G-13040)*
Architectural Metals LLC............F...... 815 654-2370
  Loves Park *(G-13922)*
AS Fabricating Inc............G...... 618 242-7438
  Mount Vernon *(G-15398)*
Atkore International Group Inc............A...... 708 339-1610
  Harvey *(G-11658)*
Atkore Intl Holdings Inc............G...... 708 225-2051
  Harvey *(G-11659)*
Bailey Hardwoods Inc............G...... 217 529-6800
  Springfield *(G-20394)*
Barker Metal Craft Inc............G...... 773 588-9300
  Chicago *(G-4043)*
Botti Studio of Architectural............E...... 847 869-5933
  Evanston *(G-10017)*
Builders Ironworks Inc............G...... 708 672-1047
  Crete *(G-7509)*
Capitol Wood Works LLC............D...... 217 522-5553
  Springfield *(G-20408)*
Chase Security Systems Inc............G...... 773 594-1919
  Chicago *(G-4295)*
Chicago Metal Rolled Pdts Co............D...... 773 523-5757
  Chicago *(G-4333)*
Chicago Metallic Company LLC............C...... 708 563-4600
  Chicago *(G-4334)*
Chicago Ornamental Iron Inc............E...... 773 321-9635
  Chicago *(G-4338)*
Christopher Glass & Aluminum............D...... 312 256-8500
  Chicago *(G-4372)*
City Screen Inc............G...... 773 588-5642
  Chicago *(G-4388)*
Concrete Unit Step Co Inc............G...... 618 344-7256
  Collinsville *(G-7317)*
Custom Linear Grille Inc............G...... 847 520-5511
  Wheeling *(G-22033)*
Daves Welding Service Inc............G...... 630 655-3224
  Darien *(G-7792)*
David Architectural Metals Inc............E...... 773 376-3200
  Chicago *(G-4563)*
DSI Spaceframes Inc............E...... 630 607-0045
  Addison *(G-99)*
Dynamic Iron Inc............G...... 708 672-7617
  Park Forest *(G-17171)*
Economy Iron Inc............F...... 708 343-1777
  Melrose Park *(G-14628)*
Ed Stan Fabricating Co............G...... 708 863-7668
  Chicago *(G-4694)*
Empire Bronze Corp............F...... 630 916-9722
  Lombard *(G-13796)*
European Ornamental Iron Works............G...... 630 705-9300
  Addison *(G-113)*
Fariss John............G...... 815 433-3803
  Moline *(G-14938)*
Fbs Group Inc............F...... 773 229-8675
  Chicago *(G-4821)*
Fehring Ornamental Iron Works............F...... 217 483-6727
  Chatham *(G-3620)*
Fisher & Ludlow Inc............D...... 217 324-6106
  Litchfield *(G-13685)*
G & M Fabricating Inc............G...... 815 282-1744
  Roscoe *(G-18898)*
Gemini Steel Inc............G...... 815 472-4462
  Momence *(G-14981)*
Gilco Real Estate Company............E...... 847 298-1717
  Des Plaines *(G-8202)*
Goose Island Mfg & Supply Corp............G...... 708 343-4225
  Lansing *(G-13164)*
Handi Products Inc............E...... 847 816-7525
  Libertyville *(G-13329)*
Hercules Iron Works Inc............F...... 312 226-2405
  Chicago *(G-5078)*

ITW Blding Cmponents Group Inc ... E ... 217 324-0303
Litchfield (G-13689)

J B Metal Works Inc ... G ... 847 824-4253
Des Plaines (G-8215)

J C Schultz Enterprises Inc ... D ... 800 323-9127
Batavia (G-1459)

J H Botts LLC ... E ... 815 726-5885
Joliet (G-12519)

Jack Rush Quality Homes Inc ... G ... 309 663-6595
Bloomington (G-2185)

John F Mate Co ... G ... 847 381-8131
Lake Barrington (G-12812)

Kelley Ornamental Iron LLC ... E ... 309 697-9870
East Peoria (G-8721)

Kelley Ornamental Iron LLC ... F ... 309 820-7540
Bloomington (G-2189)

Kencor Stairs & Woodworking ... G ... 630 279-8980
Villa Park (G-21263)

Ki Industries Inc ... E ... 708 449-1990
Berkeley (G-2046)

Lamonica Ornamental Iron Works ... G ... 773 638-6633
Chicago (G-5452)

Lawndale Forging & Tool Works ... G ... 773 277-2800
Chicago (G-5471)

Leggs Manufacturing ... G ... 618 842-9847
Fairfield (G-10149)

Legna Iron Works Inc ... E ... 630 894-8056
Roselle (G-18952)

Leonards Unit Step of Moline ... G ... 309 792-9641
Colona (G-7345)

Lickenbrock & Sons Inc ... G ... 618 632-4977
O Fallon (G-16470)

Lizotte Sheet Metal Inc ... G ... 618 656-3066
Edwardsville (G-8806)

Mechanical Indus Stl Svcs Inc ... E ... 815 521-1725
Channahon (G-3580)

Metal Edge Inc ... F ... 708 756-4696
S Chicago Hts (G-19108)

Milk Design Company ... G ... 312 563-6455
Posen (G-17732)

Mj Snyder Ironworks Inc ... G ... 217 826-6440
Marshall (G-14326)

Montefusco Heating & Shtmtl Co ... G ... 309 691-7400
Peoria (G-17412)

Nci Group Inc ... D ... 309 527-3095
El Paso (G-8871)

Nelson - Harkins Inds Inc ... E ... 773 478-6243
Chicago (G-5884)

Nicks Metal Fabg & Sons ... F ... 708 485-1170
Brookfield (G-2639)

North Chicago Iron Works Inc ... E ... 847 689-2000
North Chicago (G-16185)

Old Style Iron Works Inc ... G ... 773 265-5787
Chicago (G-5980)

Orsolinis Welding & Fabg ... F ... 773 722-9855
Chicago (G-6016)

P & M Ornamental Ir Works Inc ... F ... 708 267-2868
Melrose Park (G-14680)

P I W Corporation ... F ... 708 301-5100
Homer Glen (G-12085)

Paul D Metal Products Inc ... D ... 773 847-1400
Chicago (G-6090)

Quality Iron Works Inc ... F ... 630 766-0885
Bensenville (G-1971)

R & B Metal Products Inc ... E ... 815 338-1890
Woodstock (G-22603)

R & I Ornamental Iron Inc ... E ... 847 836-6934
Gilberts (G-10933)

Selvaggio Orna & Strl Stl Inc ... E ... 217 528-4077
Springfield (G-20521)

Sheas Iron Works Inc ... E ... 847 356-2922
Lake Villa (G-13026)

Sno Gem Inc ... F ... 888 766-4367
McHenry (G-14555)

South Subn Wldg & Fabg Co Inc ... G ... 708 385-7160
Posen (G-17736)

Steel Construction Svcs Inc ... G ... 815 678-7509
Richmond (G-17972)

Steel Guard Inc ... F ... 773 342-6265
Chicago (G-6580)

Steelwerks of Chicago LLC ... G ... 312 792-9593
Chicago (G-6582)

Stevenson Fabrication Svcs Inc ... G ... 815 468-7941
Manteno (G-14195)

Tinsley Steel Inc ... G ... 618 656-5231
Edwardsville (G-8817)

Tuschall Engineering Co Inc ... E ... 630 655-9100
Burr Ridge (G-2888)

United Conveyor Supply Company ... E ... 708 344-8050
Melrose Park (G-14703)

United Fence Co Inc ... G ... 773 924-0773
Chicago (G-6823)

V & N Metal Products Inc ... G ... 773 436-1855
Chicago (G-6863)

Vector Custom Fabricating Inc ... F ... 312 421-5161
Chicago (G-6878)

W G N Flag & Decorating Co ... F ... 773 768-8076
Chicago (G-6918)

Weber Metals Inc ... G ... 847 951-7920
Libertyville (G-13400)

Werner Co ... A ... 847 455-8001
Itasca (G-12374)

## METAL FABRICATORS: Plate

A & A Steel Fabricating Co ... F ... 708 389-4499
Posen (G-17726)

Abbey Metal Services Inc ... F ... 773 568-0330
Chicago (G-3704)

Ae2009 Technologies Inc ... E ... 708 331-0025
South Holland (G-20240)

Allquip Co Inc ... G ... 309 944-6153
Geneseo (G-10797)

American Rack Company ... E ... 773 763-7309
Chicago (G-3870)

Anchor Welding & Fabrication ... G ... 815 937-1640
Aroma Park (G-878)

Anderson Awning & Shutter ... G ... 815 654-1155
Machesney Park (G-14056)

AS Fabricating Inc ... G ... 618 242-7438
Mount Vernon (G-15398)

Associated Rack Corporation ... F ... 616 554-6004
Chicago (G-3970)

Atlas Boiler & Welding Company ... G ... 815 963-3360
Elgin (G-8960)

Atlas Tool & Die Works Inc ... D ... 708 442-1661
Lyons (G-14031)

Barker Metal Craft Inc ... G ... 773 588-9300
Chicago (G-4043)

Beaver Creek Enterprises Inc ... F ... 815 723-9455
Joliet (G-12463)

Blommer Machinery Company ... G ... 312 226-7700
Chicago (G-4124)

BR Machine Inc ... F ... 815 434-0427
Ottawa (G-16950)

Burns Machine Company ... E ... 815 434-1660
Ottawa (G-16953)

C J Holdings Inc ... G ... 309 274-3141
Chillicothe (G-7163)

Central Manufacturing Company ... G ... 309 387-6591
East Peoria (G-8705)

Chadwick Manufacturing Ltd ... G ... 815 684-5152
Chadwick (G-3440)

Colfax Welding & Fabricating ... G ... 847 359-4433
Palatine (G-17013)

Contech Engnered Solutions LLC ... E ... 217 529-5461
Springfield (G-20421)

Corrugated Converting Eqp ... F ... 618 532-2138
Centralia (G-3410)

CST Industries Inc ... C ... 815 756-1551
Dekalb (G-8080)

Cyclops Welding Co ... G ... 815 223-0685
La Salle (G-12769)

D & D Manufacturing ... G ... 815 339-9100
Hennepin (G-11733)

Debcor Inc ... G ... 708 333-2191
South Holland (G-20261)

Dee Concrete Accessories ... F ... 708 452-0250
Norridge (G-16099)

Deere & Company ... E ... 309 765-8000
Moline (G-14930)

Dill Brothers Inc ... F ... 847 746-8323
Zion (G-22682)

Dip Seal Plastics Inc ... G ... 815 398-3533
Rockford (G-18345)

E H Baare Corporation ... C ... 618 546-1575
Robinson (G-18062)

EC Harms Met Fabricators Inc ... F ... 309 385-2132
Princeville (G-17764)

Ed Stan Fabricating Co ... G ... 708 863-7668
Chicago (G-4694)

Edmik Inc ... E ... 847 263-0460
Gurnee (G-11445)

Eirich Machines Inc ... D ... 847 336-2444
Gurnee (G-11446)

Ekstrom Carlson Fabricating Co ... G ... 815 226-1511
Rockford (G-18360)

Elite Fabrication Inc ... G ... 773 274-4474
Chicago (G-4731)

Evapco Inc ... C ... 217 923-3431
Greenup (G-11382)

Fabtek Aero Ltd ... F ... 630 552-3622
Plano (G-17664)

G & M Fabricating Inc ... G ... 815 282-1744
Roscoe (G-18898)

G E Mathis Company ... D ... 773 586-3800
Chicago (G-4900)

G K Enterprises Inc ... G ... 708 587-2150
Monee (G-14996)

Gateway Fabricators Inc ... G ... 618 271-5700
East Saint Louis (G-8754)

Gpe Controls Inc ... F ... 708 236-6000
Hillside (G-11917)

Great Lakes Art Foundry Inc ... G ... 847 213-0800
Skokie (G-20006)

H A Phillips & Co ... E ... 630 377-0050
Dekalb (G-8095)

HEF Corporation ... E ... 708 343-0866
Melrose Park (G-14653)

Howe Corporation ... E ... 773 235-0200
Chicago (G-5123)

Illinois Rack Enterprises Inc ... E ... 815 385-5750
Lakemoor (G-13144)

Illinois Tool Works Inc ... C ... 708 325-2300
Bridgeview (G-2498)

Industrial Maintenance & McHy ... G ... 815 726-0030
Mokena (G-14874)

J & G Fabricating Inc ... G ... 708 385-9147
Blue Island (G-2257)

J B Metal Works Inc ... G ... 847 824-4253
Des Plaines (G-8215)

J H Botts LLC ... E ... 815 726-5885
Joliet (G-12519)

Jet Rack Corp ... E ... 773 586-2150
Chicago (G-5298)

Jiffy Metal Products Inc ... G ... 773 626-8090
Chicago (G-5303)

JT Cullen Co Inc ... D ... 815 589-2412
Fulton (G-10702)

Kennamtal Tricon Mtls Svcs Inc ... E ... 708 235-0563
University Park (G-21053)

Kodiak Concrete Forms Inc ... G ... 630 773-9339
Itasca (G-12298)

Lawndale Forging & Tool Works ... G ... 773 277-2800
Chicago (G-5471)

Lee Industries Inc ... C ... 847 462-1865
Elk Grove Village (G-9590)

Lewis Process Systems Inc ... F ... 630 510-8200
Carol Stream (G-3184)

Lizotte Sheet Metal Inc ... G ... 618 656-3066
Edwardsville (G-8806)

Madison Inds Holdings LLC ... G ... 312 277-0156
Chicago (G-5598)

Mailbox International Inc ... G ... 847 541-8466
Wheeling (G-22097)

Mendota Welding & Mfg ... G ... 815 539-6944
Mendota (G-14727)

Midwest Imperial Steel ... F ... 815 469-1072
Oak Lawn (G-16635)

Midwest Pipe Supports Inc ... G ... 630 665-6400
Bartlett (G-1319)

Mj Snyder Ironworks Inc ... G ... 217 826-6440
Marshall (G-14326)

Montefusco Heating & Shtmtl Co ... G ... 309 691-7400
Peoria (G-17412)

Newman Welding & Machine Shop ... G ... 618 435-5591
Benton (G-2037)

Osbornes Mch Weld Fabrication ... G ... 217 795-4716
Argenta (G-691)

Paasche Airbrush Co ... D ... 773 867-9191
Chicago (G-6048)

Peerless America Incorporated ... C ... 217 342-0400
Effingham (G-8853)

Petro Chem Echer Erhardt LLC ... G ... 773 847-7535
Chicago (G-6114)

Pools Welding Inc ... G ... 309 787-2083
Milan (G-14798)

Precision Tank & Equipment Co ... F ... 217 636-7023
Athens (G-942)

Pro-Fab Inc ... E ... 309 263-8454
Morton (G-15178)

Pryco Inc ... E ... 217 364-4467
Mechanicsburg (G-14574)

R & B Metal Products Inc ... E ... 815 338-1890
Woodstock (G-22603)

R-M Industries Inc ... F ... 630 543-3071
Addison (G-267)

Rayes Boiler & Welding Ltd ... G ... 847 675-6655
Skokie (G-20072)

Realwheels Corporation ... E ... 847 662-7722
Gurnee (G-11499)

Redi-Weld & Mfg Co Inc ....G.... 815 455-4460
Lake In The Hills (G-13004)
Rome Metal Mfg Inc ....G.... 773 287-1755
Chicago (G-6389)
Ross and White Company ....F.... 847 516-3900
Cary (G-3369)
Shew Brothers Inc ....G.... 618 997-4414
Marion (G-14286)
Simplex Inc ....C.... 217 483-1600
Springfield (G-20526)
South Subn Wldg & Fabg Co Inc ....G.... 708 385-7160
Posen (G-17736)
Specialized Separators Inc ....F.... 815 316-0626
Rockford (G-18625)
Squibb Tank Company ....F.... 618 548-0141
Salem (G-19352)
Staffco Inc ....G.... 309 688-3223
Peoria (G-17460)
Superior Fabrication & Machine ....G.... 217 762-5512
Monticello (G-15086)
Temprite Company ....E.... 630 293-5910
West Chicago (G-21778)
Tinsley Steel Inc ....G.... 618 656-5231
Edwardsville (G-8817)
Traco Industries Inc ....G.... 815 675-6603
Spring Grove (G-20371)
Tranter Phe Inc ....F.... 217 227-3470
Farmersville (G-10184)
Ucc Holdings Corporation ....F.... 847 473-5900
Waukegan (G-21634)
Unistrut International Corp ....D.... 630 773-3460
Addison (G-334)
United Conveyor Supply Company ....D.... 847 672-5100
Waukegan (G-21636)
United Conveyor Supply Company ....E.... 708 344-8050
Melrose Park (G-14703)
V & N Metal Products Inc ....G.... 773 436-1855
Chicago (G-6863)
VPI Acquisition Company LLC ....E.... 630 694-5500
Franklin Park (G-10624)
Whiting Corporation ....C.... 708 587-2000
Monee (G-15007)
Wilkos Industries ....G.... 563 249-6691
Savanna (G-19407)
Youngberg Industries Inc ....D.... 815 544-2177
Belvidere (G-1799)

## METAL FABRICATORS: Sheet

555 International Inc ....E.... 773 847-1400
Chicago (G-3670)
A & A Steel Fabricating Co ....F.... 708 389-4499
Posen (G-17726)
A G Welding ....G.... 773 261-0575
Chicago (G-3688)
A Hartlett & Sons Inc ....G.... 815 338-0109
Woodstock (G-22533)
A J Wagner & Son ....F.... 773 935-1414
Wauconda (G-21434)
A&S Machining & Welding Inc ....E.... 708 442-4544
Mc Cook (G-14443)
Abbott Scott Manufacturing Co ....E.... 773 342-7200
Chicago (G-3706)
Ability Fasteners Inc ....F.... 847 593-4230
Elk Grove Village (G-9256)
Ablaze Welding & Fabricating ....G.... 815 965-0046
Rockford (G-18248)
Ace Metal Spinning Inc ....F.... 708 389-5635
Alsip (G-430)
Adler Norco Inc ....F.... 847 473-3600
Mundelein (G-15464)
Aetna Engineering Works Inc ....E.... 773 785-0489
Chicago (G-3778)
Afc Cable Systems Inc ....B.... 508 998-1131
Harvey (G-11651)
Agena Manufacturing Co ....E.... 630 668-5086
Carol Stream (G-3093)
Albert J Wagner & Son LLC ....F.... 815 459-1287
Crystal Lake (G-7527)
Alert Tubing Fabricators Inc ....G.... 847 253-7237
Schaumburg (G-19429)
All Style Awning Corporation ....G.... 708 343-2323
Melrose Park (G-14587)
All-Vac Industries Inc ....F.... 847 675-2290
Skokie (G-19948)
Allmetal Inc ....E.... 630 350-2524
Wood Dale (G-22335)
Alloy Welding Corp ....E.... 708 345-6756
Melrose Park (G-14588)
Allquip Co Inc ....G.... 309 944-6153
Geneseo (G-10797)
Allstate Metal Fabricators Inc ....G.... 630 860-1500
Wood Dale (G-22336)
American Chute Systems Inc ....G.... 815 723-7632
Joliet (G-12452)
American Fuel Economy Inc ....G.... 815 433-3226
Ottawa (G-16946)
American Metal Installers & FA ....G.... 630 993-0812
Villa Park (G-21236)
American Shtmtl Fbricators Inc ....F.... 708 877-7200
Thornton (G-20867)
Anchor Welding & Fabrication ....G.... 815 937-1640
Aroma Park (G-878)
Anderson Awning & Shutter ....G.... 815 654-1155
Machesney Park (G-14056)
Angle Metal Manufacturing Co ....G.... 847 437-8666
Elk Grove Village (G-9306)
Anytime Heating & AC ....F.... 630 851-6696
Naperville (G-15796)
Aquarius Metal Products Inc ....F.... 847 659-9266
Huntley (G-12132)
Archer Industries & Supplies ....G.... 773 777-2698
Chicago (G-3937)
Arntzen Corporation ....E.... 815 334-0788
Woodstock (G-22541)
Arrow Sheet Metal Company ....E.... 815 455-2019
Crystal Lake (G-7538)
Art Wire Works Inc ....F.... 708 458-3993
Bedford Park (G-1538)
AS Fabricating Inc ....G.... 618 242-7438
Mount Vernon (G-15398)
Associated Rack Corporation ....F.... 616 554-6004
Chicago (G-3970)
Astoria Wire Products Inc ....D.... 708 496-9950
Bedford Park (G-1539)
Austin-Westran LLC ....C.... 815 234-2811
Byron (G-2912)
Austin-Westran LLC ....C.... 815 234-2811
Montgomery (G-15029)
B & D Independence Inc ....E.... 618 262-7117
Mount Carmel (G-15260)
B & G Sheet Metal ....G.... 773 265-6121
Chicago (G-4015)
B & J Wire Inc ....E.... 877 787-9473
Chicago (G-4016)
B M I Inc ....C.... 847 839-6000
Schaumburg (G-19456)
Barker Metal Craft Inc ....G.... 773 588-9300
Chicago (G-4043)
Bartec Orb Inc ....E.... 773 927-8600
Chicago (G-4051)
Beverly Shear Mfg Corporation ....G.... 773 233-2063
Chicago (G-4098)
Bill West Enterprises Inc ....G.... 217 886-2591
Jacksonville (G-12378)
Bilt-Rite Metal Products Inc ....E.... 815 495-2211
Leland (G-13218)
Bing Engineering Inc ....C.... 708 228-8005
Frankfort (G-10300)
Boekeloo Heating & Sheet Metal ....G.... 708 877-6560
Thornton (G-20868)
Brex-Arlington Incorporated ....F.... 847 255-6284
Arlington Heights (G-729)
Brian Burcar ....G.... 815 856-2271
Leonore (G-13285)
Busatis Inc ....G.... 630 844-9803
Montgomery (G-15034)
Buww Coverings Incorporated ....E.... 815 394-1985
Rockford (G-18292)
C J Holdings Inc ....G.... 309 274-3141
Chillicothe (G-7163)
C Keller Manufacturing Inc ....E.... 630 833-5593
Villa Park (G-21240)
Central Machining Service ....G.... 217 422-7472
Decatur (G-7855)
Central Sheet Metal Pdts Inc ....E.... 773 583-2424
Skokie (G-19976)
Cgi Automated Mfg Inc ....E.... 815 221-5300
Romeoville (G-18808)
Charles Industries Ltd ....D.... 217 893-8335
Rantoul (G-17922)
Chesterfield Awning Co Inc ....F.... 708 596-4434
South Holland (G-20256)
Chicago Metal Rolled Pdts Co ....D.... 773 523-5757
Chicago (G-4333)
Chicagoland Metal Fabricators ....G.... 847 260-5320
Franklin Park (G-10430)
Chris Industries Inc ....E.... 847 729-9292
Northbrook (G-16222)
Christensen Precision Products ....G.... 630 543-6525
Addison (G-76)
City Screen Inc ....G.... 773 588-5642
Chicago (G-4388)
Classic Sheet Metal Inc ....D.... 630 694-0300
Franklin Park (G-10435)
Cobra Metal Works Inc ....C.... 847 214-8400
Elgin (G-8993)
Colfax Welding & Fabricating ....G.... 847 359-4433
Palatine (G-17013)
Columbus Industries Inc ....F.... 309 245-1010
Fairview (G-10165)
Control Equipment Company Inc ....F.... 847 891-7500
Schaumburg (G-19482)
Cooper B-Line Inc ....A.... 618 654-2184
Highland (G-11780)
Corrpak Inc ....G.... 618 758-2755
Coulterville (G-7399)
Craftsman Custom Metals LLC ....D.... 847 655-0040
Schiller Park (G-19817)
Creative Steel Fabricators ....G.... 847 803-2090
Des Plaines (G-8177)
Crown Concepts Corporation ....E.... 815 941-1081
Morris (G-15103)
Custom Fabricating Htg & Coolg ....G.... 815 726-0477
Joliet (G-12480)
Custom Fit Shtmetal Roofg Corp ....F.... 773 227-9019
Chicago (G-4522)
Custom Linear Grille Inc ....G.... 847 520-5511
Wheeling (G-22033)
Cyclops Welding Co ....G.... 815 223-0685
La Salle (G-12769)
D L Sheet Metal ....G.... 708 599-5538
Palos Hills (G-17116)
D W Terry Welding Company ....G.... 618 433-9722
Alton (G-570)
Dadant & Sons Inc ....F.... 217 852-3324
Dallas City (G-7696)
Daniel Mfg Inc ....F.... 309 963-4227
Carlock (G-3050)
Daves Welding Service Inc ....G.... 630 655-3224
Darien (G-7792)
Delaney Sheet Metal Co ....G.... 847 991-9579
Palatine (G-17021)
Demco Inc ....F.... 708 345-4822
Melrose Park (G-14615)
Depue Mechanical Inc ....E.... 815 447-2267
Depue (G-8134)
Diemasters Manufacturing Inc ....C.... 847 640-9900
Elk Grove Village (G-9429)
Duroweld Company Inc ....E.... 847 680-3064
Lake Bluff (G-12841)
Dynacoil Inc ....E.... 847 731-3300
Zion (G-22683)
E-M Metal Fabricator ....G.... 847 593-9970
Elk Grove Village (G-9444)
Ed Stan Fabricating Co ....G.... 708 863-7668
Chicago (G-4694)
Eikenberry Sheet Metal Works ....G.... 815 625-0955
Sterling (G-20590)
Ekstrom Carlson Fabricating Co ....G.... 815 226-1511
Rockford (G-18360)
Elite Machining Co ....G.... 708 308-0947
Bridgeview (G-2488)
Elite Manufacturing Tech Inc ....C.... 630 351-5757
Bloomingdale (G-2106)
Elk Grove Custom Sheet Metal ....F.... 847 352-2845
Elk Grove Village (G-9451)
Elk Heating & Sheet Metal Inc ....F.... 618 251-4747
Wood River (G-22442)
Emerald Machine Inc ....G.... 773 924-3659
Chicago (G-4740)
Enterprise AC & Htg Co ....G.... 708 430-2212
Chicago Ridge (G-7147)
Esi Steel & Fabrication ....F.... 618 548-3017
Salem (G-19331)
Estes Laser & Mfg Inc ....F.... 847 301-8231
Schaumburg (G-19522)
Ets-Lindgren Inc ....C.... 630 307-7200
Wood Dale (G-22363)
Extreme Manufacturing Inc ....G.... 630 350-8566
Wood Dale (G-22364)
Ezee Roll Manufacturing Co ....G.... 217 339-2279
Hoopeston (G-12110)
Eztech Manufacturing Inc ....F.... 630 293-0010
West Chicago (G-21700)
F Kreutzer & Co ....G.... 773 826-5767
Chicago (G-4805)
F Vogelmann and Company ....F.... 815 469-2285
Frankfort (G-10321)
Fab Werks Inc ....E.... 815 724-0317
Crest Hill (G-7458)



Employee Codes: A=Over 500 employees, B=251-500
C=101-250, D=51-100, E=20-50, F=10-19, G=3-9
2017 Harris Illinois
Industrial Directory
1657

**Fab-Rite Sheet Metal** .......... F ....... 847 228-0300
Des Plaines ***(G-8193)***
**Fabricating Machinery Sales** .......... E ....... 630 350-2266
Wood Dale ***(G-22366)***
**Famaco Corp** .......... E ....... 217 442-4412
Tilton ***(G-20881)***
**Fanmar Inc** .......... E ....... 708 563-0505
Elk Grove Village ***(G-9475)***
**Farmweld Inc** .......... E ....... 217 857-6423
Teutopolis ***(G-20852)***
**Fbs Group Inc** .......... F ....... 773 229-8675
Chicago ***(G-4821)***
**Feralloy Corporation** .......... E ....... 503 286-8869
Chicago ***(G-4836)***
**Formtec Inc** .......... E ....... 630 752-9700
Glendale Heights ***(G-11024)***
**Fox Metal Services Inc** .......... F ....... 847 439-9696
Carol Stream ***(G-3155)***
**Fulton Metal Works Inc** .......... G ....... 217 476-8223
Ashland ***(G-926)***
**G & M Fabricating Inc** .......... G ....... 815 282-1744
Roscoe ***(G-18898)***
**G Branch Corp** .......... D ....... 630 458-1909
Addison ***(G-125)***
**General Machinery & Mfg Co** .......... F ....... 773 235-3700
Chicago ***(G-4928)***
**Gengler-Lowney Laser Works** .......... F ....... 630 801-4840
Aurora ***(G-1161)***
**Giovanini Metals Corp** .......... G ....... 815 842-0500
Pontiac ***(G-17702)***
**Glazed Structures Inc** .......... F ....... 847 223-4560
Grayslake ***(G-11341)***
**GLC Industries Inc** .......... E ....... 630 628-5870
Addison ***(G-135)***
**Gma Inc** .......... G ....... 630 595-1255
Bensenville ***(G-1910)***
**Grimm Metal Fabricators Inc** .......... E ....... 630 792-1710
Lombard ***(G-13807)***
**GROsse&sons Htg &SHeet Met Inc** .......... G ....... 708 447-8397
Lyons ***(G-14040)***
**Group Industries Inc** .......... E ....... 708 877-6200
Thornton ***(G-20871)***
**Helander Metal Spinning Co** .......... E ....... 630 268-9292
Lombard ***(G-13808)***
**Hendrick Metal Products LLC** .......... D ....... 847 742-7002
Elgin ***(G-9062)***
**Hennessy Sheet Metal** .......... G ....... 708 754-6342
S Chicago Hts ***(G-19104)***
**Heritage Sheet Metal Inc** .......... G ....... 847 724-8449
Glenview ***(G-11137)***
**Hi-Grade Welding and Mfg LLC** .......... E ....... 847 640-8172
Schaumburg ***(G-19553)***
**Highland Mch & Screw Pdts Co** .......... D ....... 618 654-2103
Highland ***(G-11788)***
**Hogg Welding Inc** .......... G ....... 708 339-0033
Harvey ***(G-11670)***
**Hohlfider A H Shtmtl Htg Coolg** .......... G ....... 815 965-9134
Rockford ***(G-18420)***
**Hontech International Corp** .......... F ....... 847 364-9800
Elk Grove Village ***(G-9525)***
**Hot Food Boxes Inc** .......... E ....... 773 533-5912
Chicago ***(G-5117)***
**Howler Fabrication & Wldg Inc** .......... E ....... 630 293-9300
West Chicago ***(G-21716)***
**Hpl Stampings Inc** .......... E ....... 847 540-1400
Lake Zurich ***(G-13084)***
**I F & G Metal Craft Co** .......... G ....... 847 488-0630
South Elgin ***(G-20204)***
**Ibbotson Heating Co** .......... E ....... 847 253-0866
Arlington Heights ***(G-770)***
**Illinois Valley Glass & Mirror** .......... F ....... 309 682-6603
Peoria ***(G-17387)***
**ILmachine Company Inc** .......... F ....... 847 243-9900
Wheeling ***(G-22074)***
**Ironform Holdings Co** .......... F ....... 312 374-4810
Chicago ***(G-5239)***
**J & G Fabricating Inc** .......... G ....... 708 385-9147
Blue Island ***(G-2257)***
**J & I Son Tool Company Inc** .......... G ....... 847 455-4200
Franklin Park ***(G-10500)***
**J & M Fab Metals Inc** .......... G ....... 815 758-0354
Marengo ***(G-14232)***
**J B Metal Works Inc** .......... G ....... 847 824-4253
Des Plaines ***(G-8215)***
**J F Schroeder Company Inc** .......... E ....... 847 357-8600
Arlington Heights ***(G-781)***
**J K Manufacturing Co** .......... D ....... 708 563-2500
Bedford Park ***(G-1558)***
**J-TEC Metal Products Inc** .......... F ....... 630 875-1300
Itasca ***(G-12288)***
**John J Rickhoff Shtmtl Co Inc** .......... F ....... 708 331-2970
Phoenix ***(G-17541)***
**Joiner Sheet Metal & Roofing** .......... G ....... 618 664-9488
Greenville ***(G-11396)***
**JT Cullen Co Inc** .......... D ....... 815 589-2412
Fulton ***(G-10702)***
**K & K Tool & Die Inc** .......... F ....... 309 829-4479
Bloomington ***(G-2187)***
**K Three Welding Service Inc** .......... G ....... 708 563-2911
Chicago ***(G-5344)***
**Kaiser Manufacturing Co** .......... C ....... 773 235-4705
Chicago ***(G-5352)***
**Kcp Metal Fabrications Inc** .......... E ....... 773 775-0318
Chicago ***(G-5367)***
**Keil-Forness Comfort Systems** .......... G ....... 618 233-3039
Belleville ***(G-1640)***
**Kelley Construction Inc** .......... B ....... 217 422-1800
Decatur ***(G-7902)***
**Kemper Industries** .......... G ....... 217 826-5712
Marshall ***(G-14324)***
**Kim Gough** .......... G ....... 309 734-3511
Monmouth ***(G-15017)***
**Kirby Sheet Metal Works Inc** .......... E ....... 773 247-6477
Chicago ***(G-5386)***
**Kormex Metal Craft Inc** .......... E ....... 630 953-8856
Lombard ***(G-13818)***
**Kroh-Wagner Inc** .......... E ....... 773 252-2031
Chicago ***(G-5412)***
**L M Sheet Metal Inc** .......... E ....... 815 654-1837
Loves Park ***(G-13957)***
**L R Gregory and Son Inc** .......... E ....... 847 247-0216
Lake Bluff ***(G-12852)***
**L/J Fabricators Inc** .......... E ....... 815 397-9099
Rockford ***(G-18460)***
**Lakefront Roofing Supply** .......... E ....... 773 509-0400
Chicago ***(G-5443)***
**Lamco Slings & Rigging Inc** .......... E ....... 309 764-7400
Moline ***(G-14952)***
**Laser Center Corporation** .......... E ....... 630 422-1975
Bensenville ***(G-1938)***
**Laystrom Manufacturing Co** .......... D ....... 773 342-4800
Chicago ***(G-5474)***
**Lemanski Heating & AC** .......... G ....... 815 232-4519
Freeport ***(G-10673)***
**Lewis Process Systems Inc** .......... F ....... 630 510-8200
Carol Stream ***(G-3184)***
**Licon Inc** .......... G ....... 618 485-2222
Ashley ***(G-927)***
**Lizotte Sheet Metal Inc** .......... G ....... 618 656-3066
Edwardsville ***(G-8806)***
**Lmt Usa Inc** .......... G ....... 630 969-5412
Waukegan ***(G-21583)***
**Macon Metal Products Co** .......... E ....... 217 824-7205
Taylorville ***(G-20842)***
**Mailbox International Inc** .......... G ....... 847 541-8466
Wheeling ***(G-22097)***
**Marsha Lega Studio Inc** .......... G
Joliet ***(G-12537)***
**MB Machine Inc** .......... F ....... 815 864-3555
Shannon ***(G-19900)***
**Mech-Tronics Corporation** .......... D ....... 708 344-9823
Melrose Park ***(G-14671)***
**Mellish & Murray Co** .......... F ....... 312 379-0335
Chicago ***(G-5684)***
**Mendota Welding & Mfg** .......... G ....... 815 539-6944
Mendota ***(G-14727)***
**Merz Air Conditioning and Htg** .......... E ....... 217 342-2323
Effingham ***(G-8845)***
**Metal Box International Inc** .......... C ....... 847 455-8500
Franklin Park ***(G-10529)***
**Metal Spinners Inc** .......... E ....... 815 625-0390
Rock Falls ***(G-18142)***
**Metal Strip Buiding Products** .......... G ....... 847 742-8500
Itasca ***(G-12314)***
**Metalex Corporation** .......... C ....... 847 362-5400
Libertyville ***(G-13355)***
**Metals and Services Inc** .......... D ....... 630 627-2900
Addison ***(G-202)***
**Midwest Awnings Inc** .......... G ....... 309 762-3339
Cameron ***(G-2970)***
**Midwest Skylite Service Inc** .......... G ....... 847 214-9505
Schaumburg ***(G-19648)***
**Mj Celco International LLC** .......... E ....... 847 671-1900
Schiller Park ***(G-19852)***
**Mj Snyder Ironworks Inc** .......... G ....... 217 826-6440
Marshall ***(G-14326)***
**Montana Metal Products LLC** .......... C ....... 847 803-6600
Des Plaines ***(G-8234)***
**Montefusco Heating & Shtmtl Co** .......... G ....... 309 691-7400
Peoria ***(G-17412)***
**Morton Metalcraft Co PA** .......... E ....... 309 266-7176
Morton ***(G-15169)***
**Mucci Kirkpatrick Sheet Metal** .......... G ....... 815 433-3350
Ottawa ***(G-16970)***
**Multimetal Products Corp** .......... E ....... 847 662-9110
Gurnee ***(G-11475)***
**National Metal Works Inc** .......... G ....... 815 282-5533
Loves Park ***(G-13969)***
**Nature House Inc** .......... D ....... 217 833-2393
Griggsville ***(G-11413)***
**Nelson Manufacturing Co Inc** .......... F ....... 815 229-0161
Rockford ***(G-18519)***
**Neomek Incorporated** .......... F ....... 630 879-5400
Batavia ***(G-1475)***
**Nesterowicz & Associates Inc** .......... G ....... 815 522-4469
Kirkland ***(G-12715)***
**North Shore Truck & Equipment** .......... G ....... 847 887-0200
Lake Bluff ***(G-12860)***
**Nova Metals Inc** .......... F ....... 630 690-4300
Carol Stream ***(G-3206)***
**Nu-Way Industries Inc** .......... C ....... 847 298-7710
Des Plaines ***(G-8244)***
**Odin Industries Inc** .......... F ....... 630 365-2475
Elburn ***(G-8901)***
**Olympia Manufacturing Inc** .......... G ....... 309 387-2633
East Peoria ***(G-8727)***
**Omega Products Inc** .......... G ....... 618 939-3445
Waterloo ***(G-21403)***
**Omnimax International Inc** .......... E ....... 770 449-7066
Bedford Park ***(G-1569)***
**Osbornes Mch Weld Fabrication** .......... G ....... 217 795-4716
Argenta ***(G-691)***
**Paasche Airbrush Co** .......... D ....... 773 867-9191
Chicago ***(G-6048)***
**Parker Fabrication Inc** .......... E ....... 309 266-8413
Morton ***(G-15174)***
**Pep Industries Inc** .......... F ....... 630 833-0404
Villa Park ***(G-21276)***
**Peter Lehman Inc** .......... G ....... 847 395-7997
Antioch ***(G-649)***
**Peter Perella & Co** .......... F ....... 815 727-4526
Joliet ***(G-12550)***
**Pittsfield Mch Tl & Wldg Co** .......... G ....... 217 656-4000
Payson ***(G-17246)***
**Pools Welding Inc** .......... G ....... 309 787-2083
Milan ***(G-14798)***
**Powdered Metal Tech LLC** .......... G ....... 630 852-0500
Downers Grove ***(G-8507)***
**Precision Metal Products Inc** .......... F ....... 630 458-0100
Addison ***(G-252)***
**Premier Manufacturing Corp** .......... F ....... 847 640-6644
Addison ***(G-254)***
**Pro-Tech Metal Specialties Inc** .......... E ....... 630 279-7094
Elmhurst ***(G-9923)***
**Pro-Tran Inc** .......... G ....... 217 348-9353
Charleston ***(G-3608)***
**Production Fabg & Stamping Inc** .......... F ....... 708 755-5468
S Chicago Hts ***(G-19111)***
**Production Manufacturing** .......... G ....... 217 256-4211
Warsaw ***(G-21371)***
**Progressive Sheet Metal Inc** .......... G ....... 773 376-1155
Chicago ***(G-6213)***
**Pyramid Manufacturing Corp** .......... D ....... 630 443-0141
Saint Charles ***(G-19246)***
**Quad-Metal Inc** .......... F ....... 630 953-0907
Addison ***(G-261)***
**Quality Fabricators Inc** .......... D ....... 630 543-0540
Addison ***(G-264)***
**Quality Metal Works Inc** .......... G ....... 309 379-5311
Stanford ***(G-20552)***
**Quanex Homeshield LLC** .......... E ....... 815 635-3171
Chatsworth ***(G-3628)***
**Quicksilver Mechanical Inc** .......... G ....... 847 577-1564
Arlington Heights ***(G-824)***
**R & B Metal Products Inc** .......... E ....... 815 338-1890
Woodstock ***(G-22603)***
**R B White Inc** .......... E ....... 309 452-5816
Normal ***(G-16086)***
**R E Burke Roofing Co Inc** .......... F ....... 847 675-5010
Skokie ***(G-20068)***
**R&R Rf Inc** .......... E ....... 847 669-3720
Rock Falls ***(G-18147)***
**Redi-Weld & Mfg Co Inc** .......... G ....... 815 455-4460
Lake In The Hills ***(G-13004)***
**Reliable Autotech Usa LLC** .......... G ....... 815 945-7838
Chenoa ***(G-3635)***
**Remin Laboratories Inc** .......... D ....... 815 723-1940
Joliet ***(G-12566)***
**Rettick Enterprises Inc** .......... G ....... 309 275-4967
Bloomington ***(G-2218)***

# PRODUCT SECTION — METAL SERVICE CENTERS & OFFICES

| Company | Code | Phone |
|---|---|---|
| Rogers Precision Machining — Freeport (G-10685) | F | 815 233-0065 |
| S & S Heating & Sheet Metal — Bradley (G-2431) | G | 815 933-1993 |
| S & S Welding & Fabrication — Elgin (G-9170) | G | 847 742-7344 |
| San Mateo Inc — Bensenville (G-1985) | E | 630 860-6991 |
| Schubert Environmental Eqp Inc — Glendale Heights (G-11067) | F | 630 307-9400 |
| Seamless Gutter Corp — Lombard (G-13852) | E | 630 495-9800 |
| Service Sheet Metal Works Inc — Chicago (G-6483) | F | 773 229-0031 |
| Shamrock Manufacturing Co Inc — South Holland (G-20304) | G | 708 331-7776 |
| Shannon & Sons Welding — Aurora (G-1215) | G | 630 898-7778 |
| Sheas Iron Works Inc — Lake Villa (G-13026) | E | 847 356-2922 |
| Sheet Metal Connectors Inc — Rockford (G-18615) | F | 815 874-4600 |
| Sheet Metal Supply Ltd — Mundelein (G-15557) | G | 847 478-8500 |
| Sheet Metal Werks Inc — Arlington Heights (G-840) | D | 847 827-4700 |
| Sheets & Cylinder Welding Inc — Chicago (G-6494) | G | 800 442-2200 |
| Shew Brothers Inc — Marion (G-14286) | G | 618 997-4414 |
| Silver Machine Shop Inc — Champaign (G-3540) | E | 217 359-5717 |
| Smid Heating & Air — Channahon (G-3586) | G | 815 467-0362 |
| South Subn Wldg & Fabg Co Inc — Posen (G-17736) | G | 708 385-7160 |
| Southwick Machine & Design Co — Colona (G-7348) | G | 309 949-2868 |
| Spartan Sheet Metal Inc — Chicago (G-6553) | G | 773 895-7266 |
| Spiral-Helix Inc — Bensenville (G-1996) | F | 224 659-7870 |
| Star Forge Inc — Freeport (G-10691) | D | 815 235-7750 |
| Steel Services Enterprises — Lansing (G-13187) | E | 708 259-1181 |
| Steel Span Inc — Harvard (G-11648) | F | 815 943-9071 |
| Stuecklen Manufacturing Co — Franklin Park (G-10596) | G | 847 678-5130 |
| Sturdee Metal Products Inc — New Lenox (G-15913) | G | 773 523-3074 |
| Suburban Welding & Steel LLC — Franklin Park (G-10599) | F | 847 678-1264 |
| Sudholt Sheet Metal Inc — Aviston (G-1248) | G | 618 228-7351 |
| Sugar River Machine Shop — South Beloit (G-20169) | E | 815 624-0214 |
| Superior Fabrication & Machine — Monticello (G-15086) | G | 217 762-5512 |
| T & L Sheet Metal Inc — Addison (G-304) | F | 630 628-7960 |
| T/J Fabricators Inc — Addison (G-305) | D | 630 543-2293 |
| Tandem Industries Inc — Saint Charles (G-19279) | G | 630 761-6615 |
| Tassos Metal Inc — Lombard (G-13864) | G | 630 953-1333 |
| Tcr Systems LLC — Decatur (G-7951) | D | 217 877-5622 |
| Tewell Bros Machine Inc — Tuscola (G-21025) | F | 217 253-6303 |
| Thybar Corporation — Addison (G-314) | E | 630 543-5300 |
| Thyssenkrupp Materials NA Inc — Bolingbrook (G-2378) | G | 630 563-3365 |
| Tin Mans Garage Inc — Elburn (G-8916) | G | 630 262-0752 |
| Tinsley Steel Inc — Edwardsville (G-8817) | G | 618 656-5231 |
| Tlk Industries Inc — East Dundee (G-8659) | D | 847 359-3200 |
| Traco Industries Inc — Spring Grove (G-20371) | G | 815 675-6603 |
| Transco Products Inc — Streator (G-20709) | E | 815 672-2197 |
| Tri City Sheet Metal — Geneva (G-10874) | G | 630 232-4255 |
| Troxel Industries Inc — Tilton (G-20883) | E | 217 431-8674 |
| Tru-Way Inc — Northlake (G-16457) | E | 708 562-3690 |
| Tu-Star Manufacturing Co Inc — Woodstock (G-22619) | G | 815 338-5760 |
| Two J S Sheet Metal Works Inc — Chicago (G-6796) | G | 773 436-9424 |
| Ultratech Inc — Bloomingdale (G-2140) | E | 630 539-3578 |
| Unifab Mfg Inc — Carol Stream (G-3259) | E | 630 682-8970 |
| Unique Checkout Systems — Franklin Park (G-10615) | F | 773 522-4400 |
| Unistrut International Corp — Addison (G-334) | D | 630 773-3460 |
| United Canvas Inc — Antioch (G-661) | G | 847 395-1470 |
| United Conveyor Supply Company — Melrose Park (G-14703) | E | 708 344-8050 |
| V & N Metal Products Inc — Chicago (G-6863) | G | 773 436-1855 |
| Venus Processing & Storage — Franklin Park (G-10621) | G | 847 455-0496 |
| Viking Metal Cabinet Co LLC — Montgomery (G-15069) | D | 800 776-7767 |
| Viking Metal Cabinet Company — Montgomery (G-15070) | D | 630 863-7234 |
| W A Whitney Co — Rockford (G-18671) | C | 815 964-6771 |
| Wagner Zip-Change Inc — Melrose Park (G-14706) | E | 708 681-4100 |
| Waukegan Architectural Inc — Zion (G-22700) | G | 847 746-9077 |
| Welding Specialties — East Hazel Crest (G-8667) | G | 708 798-5388 |
| White Sheet Metal — Paris (G-17164) | G | 217 465-3195 |
| William Dudek Manufacturing Co — Chicago (G-6983) | E | 773 622-2727 |
| Wilson Railing & Metal Fabg Co — Park City (G-17167) | G | 847 662-1747 |
| Wiltek Inc — Naperville (G-15832) | G | 630 922-9200 |
| Wirfs Industries Inc — McHenry (G-14571) | F | 815 344-0635 |
| Woodlawn Engineering Co Inc — Addison (G-346) | E | 630 543-3550 |
| Woods Mfg and Machining Co — Skokie (G-20112) | F | 847 982-9585 |
| Wozniak Industries Inc — Oakbrook Terrace (G-16723) | G | 630 954-3400 |
| Wright Metals Inc — Bannockburn (G-1267) | G | 847 267-1212 |

## METAL FABRICATORS: Structural, Ship

| Company | Code | Phone |
|---|---|---|
| Veritas Steel LLC — Lisle (G-13678) | C | 630 423-8708 |

## METAL FINISHING SVCS

| Company | Code | Phone |
|---|---|---|
| A & B Metal Polishing Inc — Chicago (G-3678) | F | 773 847-1077 |
| Ace Metal Refinishers Inc — Lombard (G-13758) | G | 630 778-9200 |
| Alliance Specialties Corp — Wauconda (G-21439) | F | 847 487-1945 |
| Ata Finishing Corp — Skokie (G-19960) | G | 847 677-8560 |
| Bar Processing Corporation — Chicago Heights (G-7081) | E | 708 757-4570 |
| Budding Polishing & Met Finshg — South Holland (G-20254) | G | 708 396-1166 |
| Castle Metal Finishing Corp — Schiller Park (G-19811) | G | 847 678-6041 |
| Delta Secondary Inc — Bensenville (G-1878) | E | 630 766-1180 |
| Dixline Corporation — Galva (G-10787) | F | 309 932-2011 |
| DS Polishing & Metal Finshg — East Moline (G-8677) | G | 309 755-0544 |
| Electrohone Technologies Inc — McHenry (G-14501) | G | 815 363-5536 |
| Enameled Steel and Sign Co — Chicago (G-4748) | G | 773 481-2270 |
| Envirocoat Inc — Skokie (G-19995) | G | 847 673-3649 |
| G L Tool and Manufacturing Co — Addison (G-126) | F | 630 628-1992 |
| Gatto Industrial Platers Inc — Chicago (G-4919) | G | 773 287-0100 |
| Gyro Processing Inc — Chicago (G-5016) | G | 800 491-0733 |
| Illinois Electro Deburring Co — Franklin Park (G-10494) | F | 847 678-5010 |
| K V F Company — Elk Grove Village (G-9569) | E | 847 437-5100 |
| K V F Company — Elk Grove Village (G-9570) | F | 847 437-5019 |
| Lee Quigley Company — Chicago (G-5484) | G | 708 563-1600 |
| Main Steel Polishing Co Inc — Elk Grove Village (G-9608) | E | 847 916-1220 |
| Markham Industry Inc — Woodstock (G-22587) | G | 815 338-0116 |
| Neiland Custom Products — Malta (G-14166) | G | 815 825-2233 |
| Oerlikon Blzers Cating USA Inc — Schaumburg (G-19673) | F | 847 619-5541 |
| Performance Auto Salon Inc — Manteno (G-14189) | E | 815 468-6882 |
| Precise Finishing Co Inc — Franklin Park (G-10558) | E | 847 451-2077 |
| R C Industries Inc — Chicago (G-6265) | F | 773 378-1118 |
| Reliable Plating Corporation — Chicago (G-6330) | D | 312 421-4747 |
| Spider Company Inc — Rockford (G-18629) | D | 815 961-8200 |
| Transcend Corp — Antioch (G-658) | G | 847 395-6630 |
| Twr Service Corporation — Schaumburg (G-19776) | F | 847 923-0692 |
| Universal Coatings Inc — Steger (G-20581) | G | 708 756-7000 |

## METAL MINING SVCS

| Company | Code | Phone |
|---|---|---|
| Able Electropolishing Co Inc — Chicago (G-3710) | E | 773 277-1600 |
| Caterpillar Inc — Mossville (G-15251) | A | 309 675-6223 |
| Coeur Capital Inc — Chicago (G-4418) | G | 312 489-5800 |
| Ingersoll-Rand Company — Elmhurst (G-9886) | E | 630 530-3800 |
| Regal Johnson Co — Bolingbrook (G-2364) | G | 630 885-0688 |
| SF Contracting LLC — Raleigh (G-17911) | G | 618 926-1477 |
| T Cat Enterprise Inc — Franklin Park (G-10602) | G | 630 330-6800 |

## METAL ORES, NEC

| Company | Code | Phone |
|---|---|---|
| Staging By Tish — Downers Grove (G-8527) | G | 630 852-9595 |

## METAL RESHAPING & REPLATING SVCS

| Company | Code | Phone |
|---|---|---|
| Bellows Shoppe — Winnetka (G-22303) | G | 847 446-5533 |
| Great Lakes Mech Svcs Inc — Lincolnshire (G-13451) | F | 708 672-5900 |
| Jet Rack Corp — Chicago (G-5298) | E | 773 586-2150 |
| Ralph Cody Gravrok — Addison (G-269) | G | 630 628-9570 |

## METAL SERVICE CENTERS & OFFICES

| Company | Code | Phone |
|---|---|---|
| Alter Trading Corporation — Quincy (G-17791) | | 217 223-0156 |
| Andscot Co Inc — Franklin Park (G-10396) | G | 847 455-5800 |
| Arcon Ring and Specialty Corp — Carol Stream (G-3104) | F | 630 682-5252 |
| Central Ill Fbrcation Whse Inc — Urbana (G-21076) | F | 217 367-2323 |
| Century Spring Corporation — Chicago (G-4277) | G | 800 237-5225 |
| Cerro Flow Products LLC — Sauget (G-19385) | C | 618 337-6000 |
| Chicago Tube and Iron Company — Romeoville (G-18810) | E | 815 834-2500 |
| Commercial Metals Company — Kankakee (G-12606) | G | 815 928-9600 |
| D L Austin Steel Supply Corp — Collinsville (G-7319) | G | 618 345-7200 |
| Energy Culvert Co Inc — Energy (G-9986) | G | 618 942-7381 |
| Fairbanks Wire Corporation — Hampshire (G-11550) | G | 847 683-2600 |
| Harris Steel Company — Cicero (G-7200) | D | 708 656-5500 |

---

Employee Codes: A=Over 500 employees, B=251-500, C=101-250, D=51-100, E=20-50, F=10-19, G=3-9

**Heidtman Steel Products Inc** ....D ....... 618 451-0052
Granite City *(G-11284)*
**Heidtman Steel Products Inc** ....D ....... 618 451-0052
Granite City *(G-11285)*
**Henry Baron Enterprises Inc** ....G ....... 847 681-2755
Highland Park *(G-11840)*
**Hickman Williams & Company** ....F ....... 630 574-2150
Oak Brook *(G-16521)*
**Illinois Tool Works Inc** ....E ....... 847 215-8925
Buffalo Grove *(G-2706)*
**Intermet Metals Services Inc** ....E ....... 847 605-1300
Schaumburg *(G-19571)*
**J C Schultz Enterprises Inc** ....D ....... 800 323-9127
Batavia *(G-1459)*
**K-Met Industries Inc** ....F ....... 708 534-3300
Monee *(G-14998)*
**Lindsay Metal Madness Inc** ....G ....... 815 568-4560
Marengo *(G-14235)*
**M C Steel Inc** ....E ....... 847 350-9618
Antioch *(G-642)*
**Marmon Holdings Inc** ....D ....... 312 372-9500
Chicago *(G-5625)*
**Mid-State Industries Oper Inc** ....E ....... 217 268-3900
Arcola *(G-676)*
**Morgan Bronze Products Inc** ....D ....... 847 526-6000
Lake Zurich *(G-13106)*
**Olympic Steel Inc** ....E ....... 847 584-4000
Schaumburg *(G-19675)*
**Petersen Aluminum Corporation** ....D ....... 847 228-7150
Elk Grove Village *(G-9676)*
**Precision Steel Warehouse Inc** ....C ....... 800 323-0740
Franklin Park *(G-10560)*
**R W Bradley Supply Company** ....G ....... 217 528-8438
Springfield *(G-20510)*
**Raco Steel Company** ....E ....... 708 339-2958
Markham *(G-14304)*
**Scot Industries Inc** ....D ....... 630 466-7591
Sugar Grove *(G-20734)*
**Steel Whse Quad Cities LLC** ....E ....... 309 756-1089
Rock Island *(G-18205)*
**Tempel Steel Company** ....A ....... 773 250-8000
Chicago *(G-6696)*
**Thyssenkrupp Materials NA Inc** ....G ....... 630 563-3365
Bolingbrook *(G-2378)*
**Union Tank Car Company** ....C ....... 312 431-3111
Chicago *(G-6815)*

## METAL SLITTING & SHEARING

**D B M Services Corp** ....G ....... 630 964-5678
Lisle *(G-13581)*

## METAL SPINNING FOR THE TRADE

**Ace Metal Spinning Inc** ....F ....... 708 389-5635
Alsip *(G-430)*
**AM Metal Spinning Co Inc** ....G ....... 630 616-8634
Bensenville *(G-1830)*
**Bingaman-Precision Metal Spini** ....E ....... 847 392-5620
Rolling Meadows *(G-18718)*
**Century Metal Spinning Co Inc** ....E ....... 630 595-3900
Bensenville *(G-1855)*
**Columbia Metal Spinning Co** ....D ....... 773 685-2800
Chicago *(G-4431)*
**Craft Metal Spinning Co** ....F ....... 773 685-4700
Chicago *(G-4489)*
**Mayfair Metal Spinning Co Inc** ....G ....... 847 358-7450
Palatine *(G-17054)*
**Metal Spinners Inc** ....E ....... 815 625-0390
Rock Falls *(G-18142)*
**Precision Metal Spinning Corp** ....E ....... 847 392-5672
Rolling Meadows *(G-18767)*
**Spectracrafts Ltd** ....G ....... 847 824-4117
Lombard *(G-13856)*
**Sterling Metal Craft Inc** ....F ....... 708 652-4590
Cicero *(G-7231)*
**Stuecklen Manufacturing Co** ....G ....... 847 678-5130
Franklin Park *(G-10596)*

## METAL STAMPING, FOR THE TRADE

**Acme Spinning Company Inc** ....F ....... 773 927-2711
Chicago *(G-3734)*
**Allied Production Drilling** ....F ....... 815 969-0940
Rockford *(G-18259)*
**American Industrial Company** ....F ....... 847 855-9200
Gurnee *(G-11427)*
**Amity Die and Stamping Co** ....E ....... 847 680-6600
Lake Forest *(G-12879)*
**Animated Manufacturing Company** ....F ....... 708 333-6688
South Holland *(G-20245)*
**Archer Manufacturing Corp** ....E ....... 773 585-7181
Chicago *(G-3938)*
**Aro Metal Stamping Company Inc** ....E ....... 630 351-7676
Roselle *(G-18927)*
**Atlantic Engineering** ....G ....... 847 782-1762
Zion *(G-22679)*
**Bel-Air Manufacturing Inc** ....F ....... 773 276-7550
Chicago *(G-4074)*
**Bi-Link Metal Specialties Inc** ....C ....... 630 858-5900
Bloomingdale *(G-2096)*
**Braun Manufacturing Co Inc** ....E ....... 847 635-2050
Mount Prospect *(G-15313)*
**Burnex Corporation** ....E ....... 815 728-1317
Ringwood *(G-17988)*
**C & C Can Co Inc** ....G ....... 312 421-2372
Chicago *(G-4200)*
**C & J Metal Products Inc** ....F ....... 847 455-0766
Franklin Park *(G-10421)*
**C Keller Manufacturing Inc** ....E ....... 630 833-5593
Villa Park *(G-21240)*
**Carlson Capitol Mfg Co** ....F ....... 815 398-3110
Rockford *(G-18296)*
**Chicago Cutting Die Co** ....D ....... 847 509-5800
Northbrook *(G-16221)*
**Custom Metal Products Corp** ....E ....... 815 397-3306
Rockford *(G-18328)*
**Dial Tool Industries Inc** ....D ....... 630 543-3600
Addison *(G-88)*
**Ed Stan Fabricating Co** ....G ....... 708 863-7668
Chicago *(G-4694)*
**Elburn Metal Stamping Inc** ....E ....... 630 365-2500
Elburn *(G-8885)*
**ERA Tool and Manufacturing Co** ....E ....... 847 298-6333
Zion *(G-22684)*
**Erva Tool & Die Company** ....G ....... 773 533-7806
Chicago *(G-4775)*
**Estad Stamping & Mfg Co** ....E ....... 217 442-4600
Danville *(G-7717)*
**Exton Corp** ....C ....... 847 391-8100
Des Plaines *(G-8192)*
**F B Williams Co** ....G ....... 773 233-4255
Chicago *(G-4802)*
**Fabricators Unlimited Inc** ....G ....... 847 223-7986
Grayslake *(G-11337)*
**Form-All Spring Stamping Inc** ....E ....... 630 595-8833
Bensenville *(G-1900)*
**Formco Metal Products Inc** ....E ....... 630 766-4441
Wood Dale *(G-22372)*
**Fox Valley Stamping Company** ....F ....... 847 741-2277
South Elgin *(G-20198)*
**G & M Metal Fabricators Inc** ....D ....... 847 678-6501
Franklin Park *(G-10473)*
**Gilbert Spring Corporation** ....E ....... 773 486-6030
Chicago *(G-4952)*
**Harig Manufacturing Corp** ....E ....... 847 647-9500
Skokie *(G-20011)*
**Hpl Stampings Inc** ....E ....... 847 540-1400
Lake Zurich *(G-13084)*
**Hub Manufacturing Company Inc** ....E ....... 773 252-1373
Chicago *(G-5127)*
**Hudson Tool & Die Co** ....F ....... 847 678-8710
Franklin Park *(G-10491)*
**Industrial Park Machine & Tool** ....F ....... 708 754-7080
S Chicago Hts *(G-19105)*
**International Spring Company** ....D ....... 847 470-8170
Morton Grove *(G-15203)*
**J F Schroeder Company Inc** ....E ....... 847 357-8600
Arlington Heights *(G-781)*
**Jenco Metal Products Inc** ....F ....... 847 956-0550
Mount Prospect *(G-15340)*
**Jiffy Metal Products Inc** ....G ....... 773 626-8090
Chicago *(G-5303)*
**Jlo Metal Products Co A Corp** ....D ....... 773 889-6242
Chicago *(G-5307)*
**Johnson Tool Company** ....G ....... 708 453-8600
Huntley *(G-12154)*
**K-Metal Products Incorporated** ....G ....... 773 476-2700
Chicago *(G-5349)*
**Kaman Tool Corporation** ....G ....... 708 652-9023
Cicero *(G-7208)*
**Kensen Tool & Die Inc** ....F ....... 847 455-0150
Franklin Park *(G-10512)*
**Kier Mfg Co** ....G ....... 630 953-9500
Addison *(G-168)*
**Kosmos Tool Inc** ....F ....... 815 675-2200
Spring Grove *(G-20343)*
**Kuester Tool & Die Inc** ....E ....... 217 223-1955
Quincy *(G-17851)*
**Lewis Spring and Mfg Company** ....E ....... 847 588-7030
Niles *(G-15996)*
**Lindy Manufacturing Company** ....E ....... 630 963-4126
Downers Grove *(G-8476)*
**Line Group Inc** ....E ....... 847 593-6810
Arlington Heights *(G-793)*
**Lsa United Inc** ....C ....... 773 476-7439
Lombard *(G-13822)*
**M Ward Manufacturing Co Inc** ....E ....... 847 864-4786
Evanston *(G-10067)*
**Macon Metal Products Co** ....E ....... 217 824-7205
Taylorville *(G-20842)*
**Major Die & Engineering Co** ....F ....... 630 773-3444
Itasca *(G-12309)*
**Manor Tool and Mfg Co** ....E ....... 847 678-2020
Schiller Park *(G-19845)*
**Masonite Corporation** ....D ....... 630 584-6330
West Chicago *(G-21740)*
**Micromatic Spring Stamping Inc** ....E ....... 630 607-0141
Addison *(G-208)*
**Mueller Mfg Corp** ....E ....... 847 640-1666
Elk Grove Village *(G-9642)*
**Nelson Manufacturing Co Inc** ....F ....... 815 229-0161
Rockford *(G-18519)*
**New Process Steel LP** ....D ....... 708 389-3482
Alsip *(G-499)*
**Nu-Way Industries Inc** ....C ....... 847 298-7710
Des Plaines *(G-8244)*
**Odm Tool & Mfg Co Inc** ....D ....... 708 485-6130
Hodgkins *(G-11978)*
**OHare Spring Company Inc** ....E ....... 847 298-1360
Elk Grove Village *(G-9662)*
**Omiotek Coil Spring Co** ....D ....... 630 495-4056
Lombard *(G-13837)*
**P T L Manufacturing Inc** ....E ....... 618 277-6789
Belleville *(G-1663)*
**P-K Tool & Mfg Co** ....D ....... 773 235-4700
Chicago *(G-6046)*
**Paragon Spring Company** ....E ....... 773 489-6300
Chicago *(G-6076)*
**Parkway Metal Products Inc** ....D ....... 847 789-4000
Des Plaines *(G-8251)*
**Performance Stamping Co Inc** ....E ....... 847 426-2233
Carpentersville *(G-3295)*
**Precise Stamping Inc** ....E ....... 630 897-6477
North Aurora *(G-16143)*
**Precision Stamping Pdts Inc** ....E ....... 847 678-0800
Schiller Park *(G-19862)*
**Premier Metal Works Inc** ....G ....... 312 226-7414
Chicago *(G-6178)*
**Principal Manufacturing Corp** ....B ....... 708 865-7500
Broadview *(G-2603)*
**Production Fabg & Stamping Inc** ....F ....... 708 755-5468
S Chicago Hts *(G-19111)*
**Ramcel Engineering Co** ....D ....... 847 272-6980
Northbrook *(G-16353)*
**Reliable Machine Company** ....E ....... 815 968-8803
Rockford *(G-18554)*
**Reliable Metal Stamping Co Inc** ....F ....... 773 625-1177
Franklin Park *(G-10572)*
**Reliance Tool & Mfg Co** ....E ....... 847 695-1235
Elgin *(G-9164)*
**Ri-Del Mfg Inc** ....D ....... 312 829-8720
Chicago *(G-6349)*
**Rijon Manufacturing Company** ....G ....... 708 388-2295
Blue Island *(G-2266)*
**Rj Stuckel Co Inc** ....E ....... 800 789-7220
Elk Grove Village *(G-9716)*
**Rtm Trend Industries Inc** ....E ....... 847 455-4350
Franklin Park *(G-10578)*
**Service Stampings of IL Inc** ....E ....... 630 894-7880
Roselle *(G-18977)*
**Skill-Di Inc** ....F ....... 708 544-6080
Bellwood *(G-1721)*
**Smith & Richardson Mfg Co** ....E ....... 630 232-2581
Geneva *(G-10868)*
**Smithco Fabricators Inc** ....F ....... 847 678-1619
Schiller Park *(G-19873)*
**St Charles Stamping Inc** ....F ....... 630 584-2029
Saint Charles *(G-19269)*
**Stanley Spring & Stamping Corp** ....D ....... 773 777-2600
Chicago *(G-6572)*
**Stanron Corporation** ....D ....... 773 777-2600
Chicago *(G-6573)*
**Stumpfoll Tool & Mfg** ....G ....... 312 733-2632
Chicago *(G-6609)*
**Sundstrom Pressed Steel Co** ....E ....... 773 721-2237
Chicago *(G-6626)*
**Superior Metal Products Inc** ....F ....... 630 466-1150
Sugar Grove *(G-20737)*
**Sure-Way Die Designs Inc** ....F ....... 630 323-0370
Westmont *(G-21924)*

# PRODUCT SECTION — METALS SVC CTRS & WHOLESALERS: Aluminum Bars, Rods, Etc

T N T Industries Inc .................................. F ....... 630 879-1522
  Batavia *(G-1503)*
Tauber Brothers Tool & Die Co .............. E ....... 708 867-9100
  Chicago *(G-6679)*
Tempel Holdings Inc ................................ G ....... 773 250-8000
  Chicago *(G-6695)*
Tempel Steel Company ............................ A ....... 773 250-8000
  Chicago *(G-6696)*
Three Star Mfg Co Inc ............................. G ....... 847 526-2222
  Wauconda *(G-21510)*
Thryselius Stamping Inc .......................... G ....... 630 232-0795
  Geneva *(G-10872)*
Triton Industries Inc ................................. C ....... 773 384-3700
  Chicago *(G-6779)*
Tro Manufacturing Company Inc ............ E ....... 847 455-3755
  Franklin Park *(G-10613)*
Tryson Metal Stampg & Mfg Inc ............ G ....... 630 628-6570
  Addison *(G-328)*
Tryson Metal Stampg & Mfg Inc ............. E ....... 630 458-0591
  Addison *(G-329)*
Twinplex Manufacturing Co ..................... F ....... 630 595-2040
  Wood Dale *(G-22435)*
Ultra Stamping & Assembly Inc .............. E ....... 815 874-9888
  Rockford *(G-18660)*
Unified Tool Die & Mfg Co Inc ................ F ....... 847 678-3773
  Schiller Park *(G-19878)*
Vanart Engineering Company ................. E ....... 847 678-6255
  Franklin Park *(G-10620)*
Vindee Industries Inc ............................... E ....... 815 469-3300
  Frankfort *(G-10375)*
Voco Tool & Mfg Inc ................................ G ....... 708 771-3800
  Forest Park *(G-10256)*
Wauconda Tool & Engineering Co .......... E ....... 847 608-0602
  Elgin *(G-9231)*
Wauconda Tool & Engrg LLC .................. D ....... 847 658-4588
  Algonquin *(G-412)*
Willie Washer Mfg Co ............................... C ....... 847 956-1344
  Elk Grove Village *(G-9814)*
Wireformers Inc ........................................ E ....... 847 718-1920
  Mount Prospect *(G-15384)*

## *METAL STAMPINGS: Ornamental*

Mj Celco International LLC ..................... E ....... 847 671-1900
  Schiller Park *(G-19852)*
T A U Inc ................................................... G ....... 708 841-5757
  Dolton *(G-8377)*

## *METAL STAMPINGS: Perforated*

Accurate Perforating Co Inc ................... D ....... 773 254-3232
  Chicago *(G-3721)*
American Metal Perforating Inc .............. F ....... 773 523-8884
  Chicago *(G-3866)*
Metalex Corporation ................................ C ....... 847 362-8300
  Libertyville *(G-13354)*
United Steel Perforating/ARC ................. E ....... 630 942-7300
  Glendale Heights *(G-11087)*

## *METAL TREATING COMPOUNDS*

Advanced Finishing ................................. G ....... 815 964-3367
  Belvidere *(G-1728)*
Fuchs Corporation ................................... G ....... 800 323-7755
  Harvey *(G-11667)*
Technic Inc ............................................... G ....... 773 262-2662
  Arlington Heights *(G-852)*

## *METAL TREATING: Cryogenic*

Controlled Thermal Processing ............... G ....... 847 651-5511
  Streamwood *(G-20650)*
Dippit Inc .................................................. G ....... 630 762-6500
  West Chicago *(G-21693)*

## *METALS SVC CENTERS & WHOL: Structural Shapes, Iron Or Steel*

American Steel Fabricators Inc ............... F ....... 847 807-4200
  Melrose Park *(G-14593)*
Azcon Inc .................................................. F ....... 815 548-7000
  Sterling *(G-20583)*
Michelmann Steel Cnstr Co ..................... E ....... 217 222-0555
  Quincy *(G-17857)*
Mutual Svcs Highland Pk Inc ................... F ....... 847 432-3815
  Highland Park *(G-11858)*
Van Pelt Corporation ............................... E ....... 313 365-3600
  East Moline *(G-8697)*

## *METALS SVC CENTERS & WHOLESALERS: Bars, Metal*

Charter Dura-Bar Inc ............................... E ....... 815 338-3900
  Woodstock *(G-22551)*
Lapham-Hickey Steel Corp ..................... C ....... 708 496-6111
  Chicago *(G-5459)*

## *METALS SVC CENTERS & WHOLESALERS: Casting, Rough, Iron/Steel*

R C Castings Inc ...................................... G ....... 708 331-1882
  South Holland *(G-20300)*

## *METALS SVC CENTERS & WHOLESALERS: Copper Prdts*

Chris Industries Inc ................................. E ....... 847 729-9292
  Northbrook *(G-16222)*

## *METALS SVC CENTERS & WHOLESALERS: Flat Prdts, Iron Or Steel*

Feralloy Corporation ................................ E ....... 503 286-8869
  Chicago *(G-4836)*
JT Cullen Co Inc ...................................... G ....... 815 589-2412
  Fulton *(G-10702)*
Millenia Specialty Metals LLC ................. G ....... 630 458-0401
  Itasca *(G-12319)*
Millenia Trucking LLC .............................. G ....... 630 458-0401
  Itasca *(G-12320)*

## *METALS SVC CENTERS & WHOLESALERS: Foundry Prdts*

Asta Service Inc ....................................... G ....... 630 271-0960
  Lisle *(G-13565)*
Vesuvius Crucible Company .................... G ....... 217 351-5000
  Champaign *(G-3555)*

## *METALS SVC CENTERS & WHOLESALERS: Iron & Steel Prdt, Ferrous*

Adams Street Iron Inc ............................. F ....... 312 733-3229
  Evergreen Park *(G-10109)*
Illinois Steel Service Inc .......................... D ....... 312 926-7440
  Chicago *(G-5158)*
Lickenbrock & Sons Inc .......................... G ....... 618 632-4977
  O Fallon *(G-16470)*
Millenia Metals LLC ................................. D ....... 630 458-0401
  Itasca *(G-12317)*
O Brien Bill ............................................... G ....... 630 980-5571
  Geneva *(G-10854)*
Prime Stainless Products LLC ................ G ....... 847 678-0800
  Schiller Park *(G-19863)*

## *METALS SVC CENTERS & WHOLESALERS: Misc Nonferrous Prdts*

Becks Light Gauge Aluminum Co ........... F ....... 847 290-9990
  Elk Grove Village *(G-9337)*

## *METALS SVC CENTERS & WHOLESALERS: Nonferrous Sheets, Etc*

Harris Metals & Recycling ....................... G ....... 217 235-1808
  Mattoon *(G-14390)*

## *METALS SVC CENTERS & WHOLESALERS: Pig Iron*

Miller and Company LLC ......................... E ....... 847 696-2400
  Rosemont *(G-19017)*

## *METALS SVC CENTERS & WHOLESALERS: Pipe & Tubing, Steel*

Chicago Pipe Bending & Coil Co ............ F ....... 773 379-1918
  Chicago *(G-4339)*
Illinois Meter Inc ...................................... G ....... 618 438-6039
  Benton *(G-2030)*
Stephens Pipe & Steel LLC .................... E ....... 800 451-2612
  North Aurora *(G-16146)*

## *METALS SVC CENTERS & WHOLESALERS: Rods, Wire, Exc Insulated*

Avasarala Inc ............................................ G ....... 847 969-0630
  Palatine *(G-17004)*

## *METALS SVC CENTERS & WHOLESALERS: Sheets, Metal*

Custom Plastics of Peoria ....................... G ....... 309 697-2888
  Bartonville *(G-1394)*
New Process Steel LP ............................. D ....... 708 389-3482
  Alsip *(G-499)*

## *METALS SVC CENTERS & WHOLESALERS: Steel*

A2 Sales LLC ........................................... D ....... 708 924-1200
  Bedford Park *(G-1532)*
Allegheny Ludlum LLC ............................ E ....... 708 974-8801
  Bridgeview *(G-2460)*
Ameralloy Steel Corporation ................... G ....... 847 967-0600
  Morton Grove *(G-15188)*
American Grinding & Machine Co .......... D ....... 773 889-4343
  Chicago *(G-3857)*
Arntzen Corporation ................................ E ....... 815 334-0788
  Woodstock *(G-22541)*
Awerkamp Machine Co ............................ F ....... 217 222-3490
  Quincy *(G-17798)*
Banner Service Corporation .................... C ....... 630 653-7500
  Carol Stream *(G-3112)*
Central Illinois Steel Company ............... E ....... 217 854-3251
  Carlinville *(G-3032)*
Galva Iron and Metal Co Inc ................... G ....... 309 932-3450
  Galva *(G-10789)*
Hofmeister Wldg & Fabrication .............. F ....... 217 833-2451
  Griggsville *(G-11412)*
Kennamtal Tricon Mtls Svcs Inc ............. E ....... 708 235-0563
  University Park *(G-21053)*
Lexington Steel Corporation ................... D ....... 708 594-9200
  Oak Brook *(G-16536)*
Madison Inds Holdings LLC .................... G ....... 312 277-0156
  Chicago *(G-5598)*
Mervis Industries Inc .............................. G ....... 217 753-1492
  Springfield *(G-20480)*
Metals and Services Inc .......................... D ....... 630 627-2900
  Addison *(G-202)*
Millers Eureka Inc .................................... F ....... 312 666-9383
  Chicago *(G-5762)*
Multiplex Industries Inc ........................... G ....... 630 906-9780
  Montgomery *(G-15062)*
SE Steel Inc ............................................. G ....... 847 350-9618
  Antioch *(G-654)*
Soudan Metals Company Inc .................. C ....... 773 548-7600
  Chicago *(G-6545)*
Steel Rebar Manufacturing LLC .............. G ....... 618 920-2748
  Centreville *(G-3438)*

## *METALS SVC CENTERS & WHOLESALERS: Steel Decking*

Advance Steel Services Inc .................... G ....... 773 619-2977
  Chicago *(G-3764)*

## *METALS SVC CENTERS & WHOLESALERS: Tubing, Metal*

Chicago Tube and Iron Company ........... E ....... 309 787-4947
  Milan *(G-14779)*
D & W Mfg Co Inc .................................... E ....... 773 533-1542
  Chicago *(G-4536)*
Modern Tube LLC .................................... G ....... 877 848-3300
  Bloomingdale *(G-2118)*
Tubular Steel Inc ..................................... G ....... 630 515-5000
  Westmont *(G-21926)*

## *METALS SVC CENTERS/WHOL: Forms, Steel Concrete Construction*

Deslauriers Inc ......................................... E ....... 708 544-4455
  La Grange Park *(G-12754)*
Forming America Ltd .............................. E ....... 888 993-1304
  West Chicago *(G-21706)*

## *METALS SVC CTRS & WHOLESALERS: Aluminum Bars, Rods, Etc*

Aluminum Coil Anodizing Corp ............... C ....... 630 837-4000
  Streamwood *(G-20641)*
Corey Steel Company .............................. C ....... 800 323-2750
  Cicero *(G-7185)*
Mandel Metals Inc ................................... D ....... 847 455-6606
  Franklin Park *(G-10521)*
Penn Aluminum Intl LLC ......................... C ....... 618 684-2146
  Murphysboro *(G-15579)*

---

Employee Codes: A=Over 500 employees, B=251-500
C=101-250, D=51-100, E=20-50, F=10-19, G=3-9

2017 Harris Illinois Industrial Directory

## METALS SVC CTRS & WHOLESALERS: Copper Sheets, Plates, NEC

Alconix Usa Inc ... G ... 847 717-7407
Elk Grove Village *(G-9284)*

## METALS: Precious NEC

Academy Corp ... G ... 847 359-3000
Palatine *(G-16995)*
Chicago Precious Mtls Exch LLC ... G ... 312 854-7084
Chicago *(G-4341)*
Elite Precious Metals Inc ... G ... 312 929-3055
Chicago *(G-4732)*
Tanaka Kikinzoku Intl Amer Inc ... G ... 224 653-8309
Schaumburg *(G-19752)*
Tanaka Kknzoku Intrnational Kk ... G ... 224 653-8309
Schaumburg *(G-19753)*
TPC Metals LLC ... G ... 330 479-9510
Willowbrook *(G-22234)*

## METALS: Precious, Secondary

Enviro-Chem Inc ... G ... 847 549-7797
Vernon Hills *(G-21161)*
Reclamation LLC ... G ... 510 441-2305
Chicago *(G-6311)*
Sims Rcycl Sltons Holdings Inc ... C ... 847 455-8800
Franklin Park *(G-10587)*
Sims Recycling Solutions Inc ... G ... 847 455-8800
Franklin Park *(G-10588)*

## METALS: Primary Nonferrous, NEC

AG Medical Systems Inc ... F ... 847 458-3100
Lake In The Hills *(G-12984)*
Ames Metal Products Company ... F ... 773 523-3230
Wheeling *(G-22005)*
AMS Store and Shred LLC ... F ... 847 458-3100
Lake In The Hills *(G-12985)*
Big River Zinc Corporation ... G ... 618 274-5000
Sauget *(G-19382)*
Cambridge-Lee Industries LLC ... F ... 708 388-0121
Alsip *(G-444)*
Horizon Metals Inc ... F ... 773 478-8888
Chicago *(G-5113)*
Jason Incorporated ... C ... 847 362-8300
Libertyville *(G-13340)*
Powerlab Inc ... F ... 815 273-7718
Savanna *(G-19404)*
Refiners House ... G ... 708 922-0772
Olympia Fields *(G-16805)*
Rockford Rigging Inc ... F ... 309 263-0566
Roscoe *(G-18914)*

## METALWORK: Miscellaneous

A & S Steel Specialties Inc ... E ... 815 838-8188
Lockport *(G-13700)*
All-Steel Structures Inc ... E ... 708 210-1313
South Holland *(G-20241)*
American Steel Fabricators Inc ... F ... 847 807-4200
Melrose Park *(G-14593)*
Bergst Special Tools Inc ... G ... 630 543-1020
Addison *(G-53)*
Central Steel Fabricators ... E ... 708 652-2037
Broadview *(G-2565)*
Chicago Metal Rolled Pdts Co ... D ... 773 523-5757
Chicago *(G-4333)*
Chicago Ornamental Iron Inc ... E ... 773 321-9635
Chicago *(G-4338)*
Crown Premiums Inc ... F ... 815 469-8789
Frankfort *(G-10311)*
Dixline Corporation ... D ... 309 932-2011
Galva *(G-10788)*
Dixline Corporation ... F ... 309 932-2011
Galva *(G-10787)*
Elfi LLC ... E ... 815 439-1833
Chicago *(G-4727)*
Fabco Enterprises Inc ... G ... 708 333-4644
Harvey *(G-11666)*
FHB Lighting Inc ... G ... 888 364-8802
Palatine *(G-17028)*
Gerdau Ameristeel US Inc ... E ... 815 547-0400
Belvidere *(G-1757)*
Gmh Metal Fabrication Inc ... G ... 309 253-6429
East Peoria *(G-8711)*
HI Metals LLC ... G ... 312 590-3360
Winnetka *(G-22307)*
Illinois Steel Service Inc ... D ... 312 926-7440
Chicago *(G-5158)*
Jason Incorporated ... C ... 847 362-8300
Libertyville *(G-13340)*
JC Metalcrafters Inc ... G ... 815 942-9891
Morris *(G-15111)*
Kroh-Wagner Inc ... E ... 773 252-2031
Chicago *(G-5412)*
Ladder Industries Inc ... E ... 800 360-6789
Deerfield *(G-8027)*
Luren Precision Chicago Co Ltd ... G ... 847 882-1388
Schaumburg *(G-19624)*
Marsha Lega Studio Inc ... G
Joliet *(G-12537)*
MB Steel Company Inc ... F ... 618 877-7000
Madison *(G-14152)*
MBI Tools LLC ... G ... 815 844-0937
Pontiac *(G-17706)*
Metal Strip Buiding Products ... G ... 847 742-8500
Itasca *(G-12314)*
MMC Precision Holdings Corp ... G ... 309 266-7176
Morton *(G-15164)*
Morton Industrial Group Inc ... D ... 309 266-7176
Morton *(G-15167)*
Morton Metalcraft Co PA ... E ... 309 266-7176
Morton *(G-15169)*
Nucor Steel Kankakee Inc ... B ... 815 937-3131
Bourbonnais *(G-2403)*
Olin Engineered Systems Inc ... G ... 618 258-2874
East Alton *(G-8609)*
R W Bradley Supply Company ... G ... 217 528-8438
Springfield *(G-20510)*
Schmolz Bckenbach USA Holdings ... G ... 630 682-3900
Carol Stream *(G-3236)*
Sitexpedite LLC ... E ... 847 245-2185
Lindenhurst *(G-13549)*
Steelwerks of Chicago LLC ... G ... 312 792-9593
Chicago *(G-6582)*
Trinity Machined Products Inc ... E ... 630 876-6992
Aurora *(G-1090)*
Van Pelt Corporation ... E ... 313 365-3600
East Moline *(G-8697)*
Ziglers Mch & Met Works Inc ... G ... 815 652-7518
Dixon *(G-8360)*

## METALWORK: Ornamental

Aetna Engineering Works Inc ... E ... 773 785-0489
Chicago *(G-3778)*
Chicagos Finest Iron Works ... F ... 773 646-4484
Chicago *(G-4365)*
Chicagos Finest Ironworks ... G ... 708 895-4484
Lansing *(G-13159)*
Crosstree Inc ... G ... 773 227-1234
Chicago *(G-4507)*
D5 Design Met Fabrication LLC ... G ... 773 770-4705
Chicago *(G-4539)*
Ibarra Group LLC ... G ... 773 650-0503
Chicago *(G-5135)*
Imperial Stone Collection ... G ... 847 640-8817
Elk Grove Village *(G-9543)*
King Metal Co ... G ... 708 388-3845
Alsip *(G-479)*
Leonards Unit Step Co ... G ... 815 744-1263
Rockdale *(G-18225)*
P & P Artec Inc ... F ... 630 860-2990
Wood Dale *(G-22410)*
Pep Industries Inc ... F ... 630 833-0404
Villa Park *(G-21276)*
Technetics Group LLC ... G ... 708 887-6080
Harwood Heights *(G-11691)*
Tru-Guard Manufacturing Co ... G ... 773 568-5264
Chicago *(G-6784)*
Waukegan Architectural Inc ... G ... 847 746-9077
Zion *(G-22700)*
Waukegan Steel LLC ... E ... 847 662-2810
Waukegan *(G-21639)*

## METALWORKING MACHINERY WHOLESALERS

Barnes International Inc ... C ... 815 964-8661
Rockford *(G-18276)*
Handi Products Inc ... E ... 847 816-7525
Libertyville *(G-13329)*
Industrial Instrument Svc Corp ... G ... 773 581-3355
Chicago *(G-5177)*
McLean Manufacturing Company ... G ... 847 277-9912
Lake Barrington *(G-12819)*
Miyano Machinery USA Inc ... E ... 630 766-4141
Elk Grove Village *(G-9631)*
Muntz Industries Inc ... E ... 847 949-8280
Mundelein *(G-15534)*
Usach Technologies Inc ... E ... 847 888-0148
Elgin *(G-9222)*

## METERING DEVICES: Gasoline Dispensing

Opw Fuel MGT Systems Inc ... G ... 708 352-9617
Hodgkins *(G-11979)*
Professional Meters Inc ... C ... 815 942-7000
Morris *(G-15127)*

## METERING DEVICES: Integrating & Totalizing, Gas & Liquids

Advance Engineering Corp ... E ... 847 760-9421
Elgin *(G-8937)*

## METERING DEVICES: Positive Displacement Meters

Liquid Controls LLC ... C ... 847 295-1050
Lake Bluff *(G-12855)*

## METERING DEVICES: Water Quality Monitoring & Control Systems

Bc Enterprises ... G ... 618 655-0784
Edwardsville *(G-8791)*

## METERS: Audio

Singer Data Products Inc ... G ... 630 860-6500
Bensenville *(G-1991)*
Singer Medical Products Inc ... G ... 630 860-6500
Bensenville *(G-1992)*

## METERS: Demand

Etcon Corp ... F ... 630 325-6100
Burr Ridge *(G-2840)*

## MGMT CONSULTING SVCS: Matls, Incl Purch, Handle & Invntry

Mennies Machine Company ... C ... 815 339-2226
Mark *(G-14299)*

## MICA PRDTS

GL Downs Inc ... G ... 618 993-9777
Marion *(G-14262)*

## MICROCIRCUITS, INTEGRATED: Semiconductor

Zenith Electronics Corporation ... E ... 847 941-8000
Lincolnshire *(G-13496)*

## MICROFILM SVCS

Com-Graphics Inc ... D ... 312 226-0900
Chicago *(G-4434)*
Forman Co Inc ... G ... 309 734-3413
Monmouth *(G-15012)*
Microdynamics Corporation ... C ... 630 276-0527
Naperville *(G-15697)*

## MICROMETERS

Bradley Machining Inc ... F ... 630 543-2875
Addison *(G-59)*
Spectris Holdings Inc ... F ... 847 680-3709
Libertyville *(G-13383)*

## MICROPHONES

Shure Incorporated ... F ... 847 520-4404
Wheeling *(G-22150)*

## MICROPROCESSORS

Digital Optics Tech Inc ... G ... 847 358-2592
Rolling Meadows *(G-18725)*
Intel Corp ... G ... 847 602-1170
Long Grove *(G-13891)*
Intel East ... G ... 312 725-2014
Mount Prospect *(G-15338)*
Sparton Aubrey LLC ... E ... 386 740-5381
Schaumburg *(G-19732)*
Sparton Corporation ... B ... 847 762-5800
Schaumburg *(G-19734)*
Sparton Design Services LLC ... G ... 847 762-5800
Schaumburg *(G-19735)*

# PRODUCT SECTION

# MILLWORK

| Company | Code | Phone |
|---|---|---|
| Sparton Emt LLC | G | 800 772-7866 |
| Schaumburg (G-19736) | | |
| Sparton led LLC | D | 847 762-5800 |
| Schaumburg (G-19737) | | |
| Systems Intel | G | 847 842-0120 |
| Barrington (G-1307) | | |
| Worth Door Company | G | 877 379-4947 |
| Mchenry (G-14572) | | |

## MICROSCOPES

| Company | Code | Phone |
|---|---|---|
| Alicona Corporation | G | 630 372-9900 |
| Bartlett (G-1329) | | |
| McCrone Associates Inc | G | 630 887-7100 |
| Westmont (G-21904) | | |

## MICROWAVE COMPONENTS

| Company | Code | Phone |
|---|---|---|
| Formcraft Tool Company | F | 773 476-8727 |
| Chicago (G-4874) | | |

## MICROWAVE OVENS: Household

| Company | Code | Phone |
|---|---|---|
| Microwave RES & Applications | G | 630 480-7456 |
| Carol Stream (G-3197) | | |

## MILL PRDTS: Structural & Rail

| Company | Code | Phone |
|---|---|---|
| Guardian Construction Pdts Inc | E | 630 820-8899 |
| Naperville (G-15808) | | |
| Progress Rail Services Corp | E | 309 963-4425 |
| Danvers (G-7701) | | |
| Rmi Inc | F | 708 756-5640 |
| Chicago Heights (G-7122) | | |

## MILLINERY SUPPLIES: Cap Fronts & Visors

| Company | Code | Phone |
|---|---|---|
| Gcg Corp | G | 847 298-2285 |
| Glenview (G-11128) | | |

## MILLINERY SUPPLIES: Veils & Veiling, Bridal, Funeral, Etc

| Company | Code | Phone |
|---|---|---|
| Angels Heavenly Funeral Home | G | 773 239-8700 |
| Chicago (G-3907) | | |
| Hamsher Lakeside Funerals | G | 847 587-2100 |
| Fox Lake (G-10277) | | |

## MILLING: Cereal Flour, Exc Rice

| Company | Code | Phone |
|---|---|---|
| ADM Milling Co | E | 312 666-2465 |
| Chicago (G-3753) | | |

## MILLING: Corn Grits & Flakes, For Brewers' Use

| Company | Code | Phone |
|---|---|---|
| Temperance Beer Company LLC | G | 847 864-1000 |
| Evanston (G-10101) | | |

## MILLING: Grain Cereals, Cracked

| Company | Code | Phone |
|---|---|---|
| Natures American Co | G | 630 246-4274 |
| Chicago (G-5870) | | |

## MILLING: Grains, Exc Rice

| Company | Code | Phone |
|---|---|---|
| Kws Cereals Usa LLC | G | 815 200-2666 |
| Champaign (G-3508) | | |

## MILLWORK

| Company | Code | Phone |
|---|---|---|
| A and J Development Plus LLC | G | 630 470-9539 |
| Plainfield (G-17575) | | |
| Ability Cabinet Co Inc | G | 847 678-6678 |
| Franklin Park (G-10383) | | |
| Adams Street Iron Inc | F | 312 733-3229 |
| Evergreen Park (G-10109) | | |
| All American Wood Register Co | F | 815 356-1000 |
| Crystal Lake (G-7528) | | |
| Allie Woodworking | G | 847 244-1919 |
| Waukegan (G-21522) | | |
| American Custom Woodworking | F | 847 526-5900 |
| Wauconda (G-21440) | | |
| American Woodworks | G | 630 279-1629 |
| Sleepy Hollow (G-20117) | | |
| Ameriscan Designs Inc | D | 773 542-1291 |
| Chicago (G-3886) | | |
| Anderson Awning & Shutter | G | 815 654-1155 |
| Machesney Park (G-14056) | | |
| Architectural Woodworking | G | 847 259-3331 |
| Prospect Heights (G-17772) | | |
| Baker Elements Inc | F | 630 660-8100 |
| Oak Park (G-16654) | | |
| Barrington Millwork LLC | G | 847 304-0791 |
| Lake Barrington (G-12800) | | |
| Barsanti Woodwork Corporation | E | 773 284-6888 |
| Chicago (G-4050) | | |
| Beloit Pattern Works | F | 815 389-2578 |
| South Beloit (G-20140) | | |
| Blueberry Woodworking Inc | G | 773 230-7179 |
| Franklin Park (G-10414) | | |
| Bond Brothers Hardwoods | G | 618 272-4811 |
| Ridgway (G-17983) | | |
| Brown Woodworking | G | 815 477-8333 |
| Crystal Lake (G-7544) | | |
| Byttow Enterprises Inc | G | 708 754-4995 |
| Steger (G-20570) | | |
| CA Custom Woodworking | G | 630 201-6154 |
| Oswego (G-16906) | | |
| Cabinets Doors and More LLC | G | 847 395-6334 |
| Antioch (G-627) | | |
| Cain Millwork Inc | D | 815 561-9700 |
| Rochelle (G-18082) | | |
| Caldwell Woodworks | G | 217 566-2434 |
| Williamsville (G-22190) | | |
| Carpenters Millwork Co | F | 708 339-7707 |
| South Holland (G-20255) | | |
| Carpenters Millwork Co | G | 708 339-7707 |
| Villa Park (G-21241) | | |
| Chicago School Woodworking LLC | G | 773 275-1170 |
| Chicago (G-4346) | | |
| Christos Woodworking | G | 708 975-5045 |
| Alsip (G-448) | | |
| City Screen Inc | G | 773 588-5642 |
| Chicago (G-4388) | | |
| Cmp Millwork Co | G | 630 832-6462 |
| Elmhurst (G-9851) | | |
| Contract Industries Inc | E | 708 458-8150 |
| Bedford Park (G-1545) | | |
| Cooper Lake Millworks Inc | G | 217 847-2681 |
| Hamilton (G-11530) | | |
| Corsaw Hardwood Lumber Inc | F | 309 293-2055 |
| Smithfield (G-20119) | | |
| Crea and Crea | G | 630 292-5625 |
| Bartlett (G-1339) | | |
| Creswell Woodworking CA | G | 847 381-9222 |
| Woodstock (G-22556) | | |
| Curtis Woodworking Inc | G | 815 544-3543 |
| Belvidere (G-1748) | | |
| Custom Wood Creations | G | 618 346-2208 |
| Collinsville (G-7318) | | |
| Custom Woodworking Inc | G | 630 584-7106 |
| Saint Charles (G-19166) | | |
| Customwood Stairs Inc | G | 630 739-5252 |
| Romeoville (G-18815) | | |
| Dandurand Custom Woodworking | G | 708 489-6440 |
| Posen (G-17729) | | |
| Daniel M Powers & Assoc Ltd | D | 630 685-8400 |
| Bolingbrook (G-2299) | | |
| Decorators Supply Corporation | E | 773 847-6300 |
| Chicago (G-4571) | | |
| Deem Woodworks | G | 217 832-9614 |
| Villa Grove (G-21227) | | |
| Del Great Frame Up Systems Inc | F | 847 808-1955 |
| Franklin Park (G-10456) | | |
| Demeter Millwork LLC | G | 312 224-4440 |
| Chicago (G-4581) | | |
| Duhack Lehn & Associates Inc | G | 815 777-3460 |
| Galena (G-10719) | | |
| Dunigan Custom Woodworking | G | 708 351-5213 |
| Homewood (G-12095) | | |
| Eiesland Builders Inc | E | 847 998-1731 |
| Glenview (G-11123) | | |
| Elite Custom Woodworking | G | 630 888-4322 |
| Batavia (G-1446) | | |
| European Wood Works Inc | G | 773 662-6607 |
| Carol Stream (G-3148) | | |
| FM Woodworking | G | 847 533-1545 |
| Lake Zurich (G-13074) | | |
| Fraser Millwork Inc | G | 708 447-3262 |
| Lyons (G-14038) | | |
| Furniture Services Inc | G | 847 520-9490 |
| Wheeling (G-22060) | | |
| G & M Woodworking Inc | G | 708 425-4013 |
| Oak Lawn (G-16622) | | |
| Gavin Woodworking Inc | G | 815 786-2242 |
| Sandwich (G-19365) | | |
| Geo J Rothan Co | E | 309 674-5189 |
| Peoria (G-17371) | | |
| George Drowne Cabinet Sand | G | 847 234-1487 |
| Lake Bluff (G-12846) | | |
| Georgia-Pacific LLC | D | 847 885-3920 |
| Hoffman Estates (G-12014) | | |
| Glendale Woodworking | G | 630 545-1520 |
| Glendale Heights (G-11027) | | |
| Gmk Finishing | G | 630 837-0568 |
| Bartlett (G-1351) | | |
| Grays Cabinet Co | G | 618 948-2211 |
| Saint Francisville (G-19313) | | |
| H & H Custom Woodworking Inc | E | 815 932-6820 |
| Bourbonnais (G-2398) | | |
| H & M Woodworks | G | 608 289-3141 |
| Hamilton (G-11536) | | |
| Heartland Hardwoods Inc | E | 217 844-3312 |
| Effingham (G-8838) | | |
| HK Woodwork | G | 773 964-2468 |
| Wheeling (G-22071) | | |
| Hogan Woodwork Inc | G | 708 354-4525 |
| Countryside (G-7429) | | |
| Hylan Design Ltd | G | 312 243-7341 |
| Chicago (G-5129) | | |
| Imperial Store Fixtures Inc | G | 773 348-1137 |
| Chicago (G-5168) | | |
| Imperial Woodworking Entps Inc | E | 847 358-6920 |
| Palatine (G-17040) | | |
| Janik Custom Millwork Inc | G | 708 482-4844 |
| Hodgkins (G-11977) | | |
| Jay A Morris | G | 815 432-6440 |
| Watseka (G-21420) | | |
| Jeld-Wen Inc | D | 217 893-4444 |
| Rantoul (G-17930) | | |
| Jelinek & Sons Inc | G | 630 355-3474 |
| Plainfield (G-17610) | | |
| Jj Wood Working | G | 708 426-6854 |
| Bridgeview (G-2502) | | |
| Jlm Woodworking | G | 309 275-8259 |
| Normal (G-16074) | | |
| Jmi Crafted Coml Mllwk Inc | F | 708 331-6331 |
| Harvey (G-11673) | | |
| John Tobin Millwork Co | G | 630 832-3780 |
| Villa Park (G-21260) | | |
| Kabinet Kraft | F | 618 395-1047 |
| Olney (G-16775) | | |
| Kep Woodworking | F | 847 480-9545 |
| Northbrook (G-16286) | | |
| Kozin Woodwork US | G | 815 568-8918 |
| Marengo (G-14234) | | |
| L Surges Custom Woodwork | G | 815 774-9663 |
| Joliet (G-12529) | | |
| Lyko Woodworking & Cnstr | G | 773 583-4561 |
| Chicago (G-5573) | | |
| M & R Custom Millwork | G | 815 547-8549 |
| Belvidere (G-1768) | | |
| Majestic Archtctural Wdwrk Inc | G | 708 240-8484 |
| Bellwood (G-1713) | | |
| Master Cabinets | G | 847 639-1323 |
| Cary (G-3359) | | |
| May Wood Industries Inc | F | 708 489-1515 |
| Chicago (G-5660) | | |
| Mc Dist & Mfg Co | F | 630 628-5180 |
| Addison (G-195) | | |
| Menard Inc | D | 815 474-6767 |
| Plano (G-17666) | | |
| Menard Inc | D | 708 346-9144 |
| Evergreen Park (G-10117) | | |
| Menard Inc | D | 715 876-5911 |
| Plano (G-17667) | | |
| Menard Inc | E | 708 780-0260 |
| Cicero (G-7220) | | |
| Merkel Woodworking Inc | G | 630 458-0700 |
| Addison (G-199) | | |
| Metal Products Sales Corp | G | 708 301-6844 |
| Lockport (G-13732) | | |
| Metrie | E | 815 717-2660 |
| New Lenox (G-15895) | | |
| Midwest Woodcrafters Inc | G | 630 665-0901 |
| Carol Stream (G-3199) | | |
| Miller Whiteside Wood Working | G | 309 827-6470 |
| Mc Lean (G-14463) | | |
| Minimill Technologies Inc | G | 315 857-7107 |
| Chicago (G-5768) | | |
| Missouri Wood Craft Inc | G | 217 453-2204 |
| Nauvoo (G-15853) | | |
| Mjf Woodworking | G | 815 679-6700 |
| McHenry (G-14537) | | |
| Monticello Design & Mfg | G | 217 762-8551 |
| Monticello (G-15081) | | |
| Moonlight Woodworking | G | 815 728-9121 |
| Ringwood (G-17992) | | |
| Mulvain Woodworks | G | 815 248-2305 |
| Durand (G-8587) | | |
| Navillus Woodworks LLC | G | 312 375-2680 |
| Chicago (G-5874) | | |

# MILLWORK

Olivet Woodworking .................G....... 773 505-5225
  Lake Zurich  *(G-13111)*
Osmer Woodworking Inc ............G....... 815 973-5809
  Dixon  *(G-8338)*
Performance Lawn & Power ........G....... 217 857-3717
  Teutopolis  *(G-20854)*
Peters Construction ..................G....... 773 489-5555
  Chicago  *(G-6110)*
Phoenix Art Woodworks...............G....... 847 279-1576
  Wheeling  *(G-22122)*
Pinnacle Wood Products Inc .......G....... 815 385-0792
  McHenry  *(G-14544)*
Pio Woodworking Inc..................G....... 630 628-6900
  Addison  *(G-241)*
Prairie Woodworks Inc ...............G....... 309 378-2418
  Downs  *(G-8547)*
Pro Woodworking ......................G....... 708 508-5948
  Bedford Park  *(G-1576)*
R W G Manufacturing Inc ...........G....... 708 755-8035
  S Chicago Hts  *(G-19112)*
Ramar Industries Inc .................G....... 847 451-0445
  Franklin Park  *(G-10569)*
Raynor Mfg Co ...........................A....... 815 288-1431
  Dixon  *(G-8341)*
Remmert Studios Inc .................G....... 815 933-4867
  Orland Park  *(G-16887)*
Rhyme or Reason Woodworking ...G....... 217 678-8301
  Bement  *(G-1802)*
Richard King and Sons ...............G....... 815 654-0226
  Loves Park  *(G-13982)*
River City Millwork Inc................D....... 800 892-9297
  Rockford  *(G-18556)*
Rs Woodworking .......................G....... 815 476-1818
  Wilmington  *(G-22275)*
Scheffler Custom Woodworking ....G....... 815 284-6564
  Dixon  *(G-8348)*
Schrocks Woodworking ..............G....... 217 578-3259
  Arthur  *(G-921)*
Scott Lind Owner ......................G....... 847 323-9140
  Lake In The Hills  *(G-13005)*
Skokie Millwork Inc ....................G....... 847 673-7868
  Skokie  *(G-20087)*
Stancy Woodworking Co Inc .......F....... 847 526-0252
  Island Lake  *(G-12219)*
Stine Woodworking LLC .............G....... 618 885-2229
  Dow  *(G-8383)*
Stovers Fine Woodworking Inc ....G....... 630 557-0072
  Maple Park  *(G-14203)*
Sugarcreek Woodworking ...........G....... 618 584-3817
  Flat Rock  *(G-10198)*
Suzy Cabinet Company Inc .........G....... 708 705-1259
  Bellwood  *(G-1724)*
Temp-Tech Industries Inc ............E....... 773 586-2800
  Chicago  *(G-6694)*
Tree-O Lumber Inc .....................E....... 618 357-2576
  Pinckneyville  *(G-17553)*
Tri State Aluminum Products .......F....... 815 877-6081
  Loves Park  *(G-14003)*
Triezenberg Millwork Co .............G....... 708 489-9062
  Crestwood  *(G-7506)*
Tru-Guard Manufacturing Co ......G....... 773 568-5264
  Chicago  *(G-6784)*
Unimode Inc .............................G....... 773 343-6754
  Burr Ridge  *(G-2890)*
Vista Woodworking ....................G....... 815 922-2297
  Joliet  *(G-12587)*
Washington Woodworking ..........G....... 309 339-0913
  Washington  *(G-21395)*
West Zwick Corp .......................G....... 217 222-0228
  Quincy  *(G-17903)*
Wiegmann Woodworking ............G....... 618 248-1300
  Damiansville  *(G-7700)*
Willard R Schorck .......................F....... 217 543-2160
  Arthur  *(G-924)*
Wills Milling and Hardwood Inc ....E....... 217 854-9056
  Carlinville  *(G-3048)*
Wood Creations Incorporated .....G....... 773 772-1375
  Chicago  *(G-7022)*
Wood Creations Incorporated .....G....... 773 772-1375
  Chicago  *(G-7023)*
Wood Cutters Lane LLC .............G....... 847 847-2263
  Hainesville  *(G-11525)*
Wooden World of Richmond Inc ..G....... 815 405-4503
  Richmond  *(G-17974)*
Woodwork Apts LLC ..................G....... 224 595-9691
  Streamwood  *(G-20681)*

## MINERAL MINING: Nonmetallic

Mulch It Inc ..............................G....... 847 566-9372
  Mundelein  *(G-15533)*

## MINERAL WOOL

J & J Industries Inc ...................G....... 630 595-8878
  Bensenville  *(G-1925)*
Johns Manville Corporation ........C....... 815 744-1545
  Rockdale  *(G-18221)*
Safe-T-Quip Corporation .............F....... 773 235-2100
  Chicago  *(G-6425)*
Silbrico Corporation ...................D....... 708 354-3350
  Hodgkins  *(G-11983)*
Tex Trend Inc ............................E....... 847 215-6796
  Wheeling  *(G-22166)*

## MINERAL WOOL INSULATION PRDTS

Advance Thermal Corp ..............E....... 630 595-5150
  Wood Dale  *(G-22331)*
Advance Thermal Corp ..............D....... 630 595-5150
  Wood Dale  *(G-22332)*
USG Corporation ......................F....... 847 970-5200
  Libertyville  *(G-13396)*
USG Corporation ......................B....... 312 436-4000
  Chicago  *(G-6858)*

## MINERALS: Ground Or Otherwise Treated

Prince Minerals Inc ...................F....... 618 285-6558
  Rosiclare  *(G-19049)*

## MINERALS: Ground or Treated

C-E Minerals Inc .......................E....... 618 285-6558
  Rosiclare  *(G-19047)*
Dauber Company Inc ................E....... 815 442-3569
  Tonica  *(G-20973)*
Harsco Corporation ...................F....... 217 237-4335
  Pawnee  *(G-17234)*
Holcim (us) Inc .........................E....... 773 731-1320
  Chicago  *(G-5098)*
John Crane Inc .........................E....... 815 459-0420
  Crystal Lake  *(G-7596)*
Material Service Corporation ......D....... 708 877-6540
  Thornton  *(G-20875)*
McGill Asphalt Construction Co ..F....... 708 924-1755
  Chicago  *(G-5667)*
Mineral Products Inc .................F....... 618 433-3150
  Galatia  *(G-10712)*
Minerals Technologies Inc ..........G....... 847 851-1500
  Hoffman Estates  *(G-12022)*
Oil-Dri Corporation America .......D....... 618 745-6881
  Mounds  *(G-15259)*
Polyform Products Company .....E....... 847 427-0020
  Elk Grove Village  *(G-9685)*
Sem Minerals LP .......................D....... 217 224-8766
  Quincy  *(G-17890)*
Unimin Corporation ...................E....... 815 667-5102
  Utica  *(G-21109)*
Washington Mills Tonawanda ......D....... 815 925-7302
  Hennepin  *(G-11736)*

## MINIATURE GOLF COURSES

Okawville Times ........................E....... 618 243-5563
  Okawville  *(G-16754)*

## MINING EQPT: Locomotives & Parts

Heavy Equipment Products ........G....... 630 377-3005
  Saint Charles  *(G-19191)*

## MINING EXPLORATION & DEVELOPMENT SVCS

Caterpillar Inc ...........................B....... 309 494-0858
  Aurora  *(G-1126)*
Metal Sprmarkets Chicago Niles ..G....... 847 647-2423
  Niles  *(G-16003)*
Ultron Inc .................................F....... 618 244-3303
  Mount Vernon  *(G-15447)*

## MINING MACHINERY & EQPT WHOLESALERS

Komatsu America Corp ..............B....... 847 437-5800
  Rolling Meadows  *(G-18737)*

## MINING MACHINES & EQPT: Augers

Hydra Fold Auger Inc .................G....... 217 379-2614
  Loda  *(G-13751)*

## MINING MACHINES & EQPT: Bits, Rock, Exc Oil/Gas Field Tools

Braden Rock Bit ........................G....... 618 435-4519
  Benton  *(G-2024)*

## MINING MACHINES & EQPT: Cleaning, Mineral

O-Cedar Commercial .................G....... 217 379-2377
  Paxton  *(G-17240)*

## MINING MACHINES & EQPT: Crushers, Stationary

Drumbeaters of America Inc ......F....... 630 365-5527
  Elburn  *(G-8883)*

## MINING MACHINES & EQPT: Loading, Underground, Mobile

Fibro Inc ..................................F....... 815 229-1300
  Rockford  *(G-18382)*

## MINING MACHINES & EQPT: Mineral Beneficiation

Carroll International Corp ...........F....... 630 983-5979
  Lake Forest  *(G-12890)*
Centrifugal Services Inc .............D....... 618 268-4850
  Raleigh  *(G-17908)*

## MINING MACHINES & EQPT: Sedimentation, Mineral

Fox International Corp ...............F....... 773 465-3634
  Chicago  *(G-4880)*

## MINING MACHINES & EQPT: Shuttle Cars, Underground

Alpha Services II Inc .................E....... 618 997-9999
  Marion  *(G-14252)*

## MINING MACHINES & EQPT: Stamping Mill Machinery

American Equipment & Mch Inc ..D....... 618 533-3857
  Centralia  *(G-3404)*

## MIRRORS: Motor Vehicle

Sure Plus Manufacturing Co .......D....... 708 756-3100
  Chicago Heights  *(G-7128)*

## MISC FIN INVEST ACT: Shares, RE, Entertain & Eqpt, Sales

Equity Concepts Co Inc .............G....... 815 226-1300
  Rockford  *(G-18368)*

## MISCELLANEOUS FINANCIAL INVEST ACT: Oil/Gas Lease Brokers

Vigo Coal Operating Co Inc .......C....... 618 262-7022
  Mount Carmel  *(G-15286)*

## MISSILE GUIDANCE SYSTEMS & EQPT

Chemring Energetic Devices Inc ..C....... 630 969-0620
  Downers Grove  *(G-8408)*

## MISSILES: Guided

Boeing Company .......................B....... 312 544-2000
  Chicago  *(G-4136)*
Boeing Company .......................G....... 847 240-0767
  Schaumburg  *(G-19465)*

## MITTENS: Leather

Nexx Business Solutions Inc ......G....... 708 252-1958
  Oakbrook Terrace  *(G-16717)*

## MIXING EQPT

Fluid Mnagement Operations LLC ..G....... 847 537-0880
  Wheeling  *(G-22056)*

## MIXTURES & BLOCKS: Asphalt Paving

**Advanced Asphalt Co**............E....... 815 872-9911
Princeton *(G-17741)*
**Ambraw Asphalt Materials Inc**............E....... 618 943-4716
Lawrenceville *(G-13194)*
**Anytime Blacktopping**............G....... 618 931-6958
Granite City *(G-11266)*
**Arrow Asphalt Paving**............G....... 618 277-3009
Swansea *(G-20774)*
**Arrow Road Construction Co**............G....... 847 658-1140
Algonquin *(G-378)*
**Asphalt Maintenance**............G....... 815 234-7325
Byron *(G-2911)*
**Bonsal American Inc**............D....... 847 678-6220
Franklin Park *(G-10415)*
**Cgk Enterprises Inc**............E....... 815 942-0080
Morris *(G-15102)*
**Charles E Mahoney Company**............E....... 618 235-3355
Swansea *(G-20776)*
**Chaulsetts Painting**............G....... 618 931-6958
Granite City *(G-11270)*
**Christ Bros Products LLC**............G....... 618 537-6174
Lebanon *(G-13212)*
**Clean Sweep Environmental Inc**............G....... 630 879-8750
Batavia *(G-1431)*
**Consolidated Paving Inc**............G....... 309 693-3505
Peoria *(G-17346)*
**Cope & Sons Asphalt**............G....... 618 462-2207
Alton *(G-567)*
**County Asphalt Inc**............G....... 618 224-9033
Trenton *(G-20990)*
**Cullinan & Sons Inc**............E....... 309 925-2711
Tremont *(G-20981)*
**Curran Contracting Company**............G....... 815 758-8113
Dekalb *(G-8081)*
**Don Anderson Co**............G....... 618 495-2511
Hoffman *(G-11988)*
**Dougherty E J Oil & Stone Sup**............G....... 618 271-4414
East Saint Louis *(G-8748)*
**Emulsicoat Inc**............F....... 217 344-7775
Urbana *(G-21081)*
**Fahrner Asphalt Sealers LLC**............G....... 815 986-1180
Rockford *(G-18379)*
**Ferro Asphalt Company**............G....... 815 744-6633
Rockdale *(G-18219)*
**Freesen Inc**............E....... 309 827-4554
Bloomington *(G-2167)*
**Fuller Asphalt & Landscape**............G....... 618 797-1169
Granite City *(G-11277)*
**G & S Asphalt Inc**............F....... 217 826-2421
Marshall *(G-14322)*
**General Contractor Inc**............G....... 618 533-5213
Sandoval *(G-19357)*
**Geneva Construction Company**............G....... 630 892-6536
North Aurora *(G-16132)*
**Hassebrock Asphalt Sealing**............G....... 618 566-7214
Mascoutah *(G-14352)*
**Hillyer Inc**............D....... 309 837-6434
Macomb *(G-14125)*
**Jax Asphalt Company Inc**............F....... 618 244-0500
Mount Vernon *(G-15418)*
**Lafarge North America Inc**............C....... 703 480-3600
Chicago *(G-5435)*
**Marathon Petroleum Company LP**............G....... 618 829-3288
Saint Elmo *(G-19308)*
**Maul Asphalt Sealcoating Inc**............E....... 630 420-8765
Naperville *(G-15695)*
**Orange Crush LLC**............E....... 708 544-9440
Hillside *(G-11930)*
**Orange Crush LLC**............G....... 847 428-6176
East Dundee *(G-8650)*
**Orange Crush LLC**............G....... 630 739-5560
Romeoville *(G-18856)*
**Orange Crush LLC**............G....... 847 537-7900
Wheeling *(G-22115)*
**Owens Corning Sales LLC**............E....... 708 594-6935
Argo *(G-695)*
**Peter Baker & Son Co**............D....... 847 362-3663
Lake Bluff *(G-12861)*
**Plote Construction Inc**............D....... 847 695-9300
Hoffman Estates *(G-12036)*
**Plote Inc**............D....... 847 695-9467
Hoffman Estates *(G-12037)*
**Prosser Construction Co**............F....... 217 774-5032
Shelbyville *(G-19913)*
**Quikrete Companies Inc**............F....... 309 346-1184
Pekin *(G-17285)*
**Rock Road Companies Inc**............F....... 815 874-2441
Rockford *(G-18564)*
**Route 66 Asphalt Company**............G....... 630 739-6633
Lemont *(G-13260)*
**Sandeno Inc**............G....... 815 730-9415
Rockdale *(G-18231)*
**Schulze & Schulze Inc**............G....... 618 687-1106
Murphysboro *(G-15582)*
**Sealmaster Inc**............F....... 847 480-7325
Northbrook *(G-16360)*
**Sealmaster/Alsip**............G....... 708 489-0900
Alsip *(G-527)*
**Sherwin Industries Inc**............E....... 815 234-8007
Byron *(G-2921)*
**St Clair Tennis Club LLC**............G....... 618 632-1400
O Fallon *(G-16480)*
**Streator Asphalt Inc**............G....... 815 672-8683
Streator *(G-20703)*
**Taft Street Company Inc**............G....... 217 544-3471
Springfield *(G-20541)*
**Terry Terri Mulgrew**............G....... 815 747-6248
East Dubuque *(G-8625)*
**Thorworks Industries Inc**............G....... 815 969-0664
Rockford *(G-18650)*
**Veterans Parking Lot Maint**............G....... 815 245-7584
Woodstock *(G-22621)*
**William Charles Cnstr Co LLC**............D....... 815 654-4700
Loves Park *(G-14007)*

## MOBILE COMMUNICATIONS EQPT

**Iic Acquisitions II LLC**............G....... 217 224-9600
Quincy *(G-17838)*
**Kvh Industries Inc**............E....... 708 444-2800
Tinley Park *(G-20927)*
**Motorola Mobility LLC**............B....... 800 668-6765
Chicago *(G-5817)*
**Motorola Solutions Inc**............C....... 847 538-6959
Northbrook *(G-16316)*
**T-Mobile Usa Inc**............F....... 847 289-9988
South Elgin *(G-20228)*
**Team Cast Inc**............G....... 312 263-0033
Chicago *(G-6682)*
**Tribeam Inc**............G....... 847 409-9497
Arlington Heights *(G-857)*

## MOBILE HOME FRAMES

**Shur Co of Illinois**............G....... 217 877-8277
Decatur *(G-7940)*

## MOBILE HOMES

**Gerald Graff**............E....... 312 343-2612
Lincolnwood *(G-13514)*
**Mobil Trailer Transport Inc**............E....... 630 993-1200
Villa Park *(G-21270)*
**Southmoor Estates Inc**............G....... 815 756-1299
Dekalb *(G-8121)*
**Superior Mobile Home Service**............G....... 708 672-7799
Crete *(G-7520)*

## MOBILE HOMES WHOLESALERS

**Herman Bade & Sons**............G....... 217 832-9444
Villa Grove *(G-21228)*

## MOBILE HOMES: Personal Or Private Use

**Skiman Sales Inc**............G....... 847 888-8200
Elgin *(G-9187)*

## MODELS

**Acme Design Inc**............G....... 847 841-7400
Elgin *(G-8932)*
**Models Plus Inc**............E....... 847 231-4300
Grayslake *(G-11354)*
**Rock Island Cannon Company**............G....... 309 786-1507
Rock Island *(G-18203)*
**Wielgus Product Models Inc**............E....... 312 432-1950
Chicago *(G-6977)*

## MODELS: General, Exc Toy

**Associated Design Inc**............F....... 708 974-9100
Palos Hills *(G-17114)*
**Capital Pttern Model Works Inc**............G....... 630 469-8200
Glendale Heights *(G-11013)*
**Denoyer - Geppert Science Co**............E....... 800 621-1014
Skokie *(G-19990)*
**E J Kupjack & Associates Inc**............G....... 847 823-6661
Chicago *(G-4666)*
**Evergreen Scale Models Inc**............F....... 224 567-8099
Des Plaines *(G-8191)*
**Paradigm Development Group Inc**............F....... 847 545-9600
Winfield *(G-22289)*
**Sun Pattern & Model Inc**............E....... 630 293-3366
West Chicago *(G-21777)*

## MODULES: Computer Logic

**Components Express Inc**............E....... 630 257-0605
Woodridge *(G-22464)*
**Linear Dimensions Inc**............F....... 312 321-1810
Chicago *(G-5511)*

## MODULES: Solid State

**Coinstar Procurement LLC**............G....... 630 424-4788
Oakbrook Terrace *(G-16703)*
**Inland Tech Holdings LLC**............E....... 618 476-7678
Millstadt *(G-14827)*
**Touchsensor Technologies LLC**............B....... 630 221-9000
Wheaton *(G-21987)*

## MOLDED RUBBER PRDTS

**Accurate Products Incorporated**............E....... 773 878-2200
Chicago *(G-3722)*
**Aero Rubber Company Inc**............E....... 800 662-1009
Tinley Park *(G-20886)*
**Aztec Products**............G....... 217 726-8631
Springfield *(G-20393)*
**Central Rbr Extrusions III Inc**............G....... 618 654-1171
Highland *(G-11778)*
**Custom Seal & Rubber Products**............G....... 888 356-2966
Mount Morris *(G-15295)*
**Diamond Tool & Mold Inc**............G....... 630 543-7011
Addison *(G-90)*
**Flexan LLC**............C....... 773 685-6446
Chicago *(G-4860)*
**Gusco Silicone Rbr & Svcs LLC**............G....... 773 770-5008
Aurora *(G-1165)*
**Kelco Industries Inc**............G....... 815 334-3600
Woodstock *(G-22577)*
**Loop Attachment Co**............G....... 847 922-0642
Chicago *(G-5538)*
**Midwest Sealing Products Inc**............E....... 847 459-2202
Buffalo Grove *(G-2737)*
**Omni Products Inc**............G....... 815 344-3100
McHenry *(G-14539)*
**Polyonics Rubber Co**............G....... 815 765-2033
Poplar Grove *(G-17716)*
**Roho Inc**............C....... 618 277-9173
Belleville *(G-1672)*
**Roho Inc**............C....... 618 234-4899
Belleville *(G-1673)*
**Rutgers Enterprises Inc**............G....... 847 674-7666
Lincolnwood *(G-13535)*
**Southland Industries Inc**............E....... 757 543-5701
Bannockburn *(G-1265)*
**Verona Rubber Works Inc**............F....... 815 673-2929
Blackstone *(G-2089)*

## MOLDING COMPOUNDS

**A Schulman Inc**............E....... 847 426-3350
Carpentersville *(G-3270)*
**Acomtech Mold Inc**............G....... 847 741-3537
Elgin *(G-8933)*
**Advanced Prototype Molding**............G....... 847 202-4200
Palatine *(G-16998)*
**Akshar Plastic Inc**............E....... 815 635-3536
Bloomington *(G-2142)*
**Camryn Industries LLC**............C....... 815 544-1900
Belvidere *(G-1743)*
**Catlyst Reaction LLC**............G....... 708 941-4616
Markham *(G-14301)*
**Chicago Latex Products Inc**............F....... 815 459-9680
Crystal Lake *(G-7552)*
**Clarich Mold Corp**............F....... 708 865-8120
Westchester *(G-21833)*
**Clear Lam Packaging Inc**............D....... 847 378-1200
Elk Grove Village *(G-9377)*
**LL Display Group Ltd**............E....... 847 982-0231
Lincolnwood *(G-13522)*
**Mossan Inc**............G....... 857 247-4122
Schaumburg *(G-19650)*
**Snyder Industries Inc**............D....... 630 773-9510
Bensenville *(G-1993)*
**Underground Devices Inc**............F....... 847 205-9000
Northbrook *(G-16379)*

## MOLDING SAND MINING

**Snyder Industries Inc**............D....... 630 773-9510
Bensenville *(G-1993)*

## MOLDINGS & TRIM: Metal, Exc Automobile

**Group Industries Inc** ....E .... 708 877-6200
Thornton *(G-20871)*
**Kroh-Wagner Inc** ....E .... 773 252-2031
Chicago *(G-5412)*

## MOLDINGS & TRIM: Wood

**A & M Wood Products Inc** ....G .... 630 323-2555
Burr Ridge *(G-2818)*

## MOLDINGS OR TRIM: Automobile, Stamped Metal

**Kipp Manufacturing Company Inc** ....F .... 630 768-9051
Wauconda *(G-21477)*

## MOLDINGS, ARCHITECTURAL: Plaster Of Paris

**Quality Molding Products LLC** ....G .... 224 308-4167
Grayslake *(G-11360)*

## MOLDINGS: Picture Frame

**A Jule Enterprise Inc** ....G .... 312 243-6950
Chicago *(G-3689)*
**Artistic Framing Inc** ....C .... 847 808-0200
Wheeling *(G-22007)*
**Bravura Moulding Company** ....G .... 262 633-1882
Lake Bluff *(G-12838)*
**Frame Mart Inc** ....G .... 309 452-0658
Normal *(G-16071)*
**Jorh Frame & Moulding Co Inc** ....G .... 708 747-3440
Matteson *(G-14374)*
**Larson-Juhl US LLC** ....D .... 630 307-9700
Roselle *(G-18951)*
**Nielsen & Bainbridge LLC** ....D .... 708 546-2135
Bridgeview *(G-2514)*
**Northwest Frame Company Inc** ....G .... 847 359-0987
Palatine *(G-17059)*
**Nu-Dell Manufacturing Co Inc** ....F .... 847 803-4500
Chicago *(G-5953)*
**Supreme Frame & Moulding Co** ....F .... 312 930-9056
Chicago *(G-6638)*
**Woodmac Industries Inc** ....F .... 708 755-3545
S Chicago Hts *(G-19116)*
**Wyman and Company** ....G .... 708 532-9064
Tinley Park *(G-20956)*

## MOLDS: Indl

**A & C Mold Company Inc** ....E .... 630 587-0177
Saint Charles *(G-19130)*
**Admo** ....D .... 847 741-5777
Elgin *(G-8936)*
**Advanced Digital & Mold Inc** ....G .... 630 595-8242
Bensenville *(G-1818)*
**Allstar Tool & Molds Inc** ....F .... 630 766-0162
Bensenville *(G-1828)*
**Amt (additive Mfg Tech Inc** ....G .... 847 258-4475
Elk Grove Village *(G-9304)*
**ARC Industries Inc** ....E .... 847 303-5005
Schaumburg *(G-19446)*
**Assurance Clg Restoration LLC** ....F .... 630 444-3600
Saint Charles *(G-19139)*
**Atlas Die LLC** ....D .... 630 351-5140
Glendale Heights *(G-11009)*
**B A Die Mold Inc** ....F .... 630 978-4747
Aurora *(G-965)*
**Ballek Die Mold Inc** ....F .... 847 885-2300
Hoffman Estates *(G-11993)*
**Bg Die Mold Inc** ....G .... 847 961-5861
Huntley *(G-12133)*
**Cameo Mold Corp** ....F .... 630 876-1340
West Chicago *(G-21676)*
**Canny Tool & Mold Corporation** ....G .... 847 548-1573
Grayslake *(G-11324)*
**Carroll Industrial Molds Inc** ....F .... 815 225-7250
Milledgeville *(G-14816)*
**Challenge Tool Co** ....G .... 847 640-8085
Elk Grove Village *(G-9363)*
**Comet Die & Engraving Company** ....D .... 630 833-5600
Elmhurst *(G-9854)*
**Complete Mold Polishing Inc** ....G .... 630 406-7668
Batavia *(G-1432)*
**Con Mold** ....G .... 708 442-6002
Hillside *(G-11913)*
**Country Cast Products** ....F .... 815 777-1070
Galena *(G-10718)*
**Craftsman Tool & Mold Co** ....E .... 630 851-8700
Aurora *(G-986)*
**Crystal Die and Mold Inc** ....E .... 847 658-6535
Rolling Meadows *(G-18724)*
**Custom Mold Services** ....E .... 847 364-6589
Mount Prospect *(G-15324)*
**Dangios** ....G .... 773 533-3000
Chicago *(G-4552)*
**Die Mold Jig Grinding & Mfg** ....G .... 847 228-1444
Elk Grove Village *(G-9428)*
**Dragon Die Mold Inc** ....G .... 630 836-0699
Warrenville *(G-21345)*
**Edge Mold Corporation** ....G .... 630 616-8108
Bensenville *(G-1889)*
**Elba Tool Co Inc** ....F .... 847 895-4100
Bloomingdale *(G-2105)*
**Emerson Industries LLC** ....F .... 630 279-0920
Villa Park *(G-21250)*
**Ewikon Molding Tech Inc** ....G .... 815 874-7270
Rockford *(G-18373)*
**Furnel Inc** ....E .... 630 543-0885
Addison *(G-124)*
**Glenwood Tool & Mold Inc** ....F .... 630 289-3400
Bartlett *(G-1349)*
**Haaker Mold Co Inc** ....G .... 847 253-8103
Arlington Heights *(G-762)*
**Hausermann Die & Machine Co** ....F .... 630 543-6688
Addison *(G-144)*
**Helm Tool Company Incorporated** ....E .... 847 952-9528
Elk Grove Village *(G-9522)*
**Heritage Mold Incorporated** ....F .... 815 397-1117
Rockford *(G-18417)*
**Illinois Mold Builders Inc** ....F .... 847 526-0400
Wauconda *(G-21471)*
**Inc Midwest Die Mold** ....G .... 224 353-6417
Schaumburg *(G-19564)*
**Industrial Molded Products** ....G .... 847 358-2160
Mundelein *(G-15510)*
**Iplastics LLC** ....D .... 309 444-8884
Washington *(G-21383)*
**Jbw Machining Inc** ....F .... 847 451-0276
Franklin Park *(G-10508)*
**JC Tool and Mold Inc** ....G .... 630 483-2203
Streamwood *(G-20661)*
**Jsp Mold** ....G .... 815 225-7110
Milledgeville *(G-14817)*
**Kelco Industries Inc** ....G .... 815 334-3600
Woodstock *(G-22577)*
**Kyowa Industrial Co Ltd USA** ....F .... 847 459-3500
Wheeling *(G-22087)*
**Libco Industries Inc** ....F .... 815 623-7677
Roscoe *(G-18902)*
**Magic Mold Removal** ....G .... 630 486-0912
Aurora *(G-1183)*
**Manufcture Dsign Innvation Inc** ....G .... 773 526-7773
West Chicago *(G-21736)*
**Matrix Tooling Inc** ....D .... 630 595-6144
Wood Dale *(G-22397)*
**Metro Tool Company** ....G .... 847 673-6790
Skokie *(G-20037)*
**Micro Mold Corporation** ....G .... 630 628-0777
Addison *(G-207)*
**Midwest Tool Technology** ....G .... 630 207-6076
Elburn *(G-8897)*
**Millennium Mold & Tool** ....G .... 847 438-5600
Lake Zurich *(G-13104)*
**Mold Express Inc** ....G .... 773 766-0874
Chicago *(G-5789)*
**Mp Mold Inc** ....G .... 630 613-8086
Addison *(G-223)*
**Nemeth Tool Inc** ....G .... 630 595-0409
Wood Dale *(G-22404)*
**Pelco Tool & Mold Inc** ....E .... 630 871-1010
Glendale Heights *(G-11056)*
**Phoenix Tool Corp** ....F .... 847 956-1886
Elk Grove Village *(G-9679)*
**Plastic Products Company Inc** ....C .... 309 762-6532
Moline *(G-14962)*
**Plaza Tool & Mold Co** ....G .... 847 537-2320
Wheeling *(G-22125)*
**Pro Built Tool & Mold Inc** ....G .... 815 436-9088
Plainfield *(G-17645)*
**Pro-Mold Incorporated** ....D .... 630 893-3594
Roselle *(G-18964)*
**Soldy Manufacturing Inc** ....D .... 847 671-3396
Schiller Park *(G-19875)*
**Star Die Molding Inc** ....D .... 847 766-7952
Elk Grove Village *(G-9754)*
**Surfacetec Corp** ....F .... 630 521-0001
Franklin Park *(G-10600)*
**Vicma Tool Co** ....G .... 847 541-0177
Wheeling *(G-22178)*
**Voss Pattern Works Inc** ....G .... 618 233-4242
Belleville *(G-1689)*
**Wapro Inc** ....G .... 888 927-8677
Chicago *(G-6938)*
**William J Kline & Co Inc** ....F .... 815 338-2055
Woodstock *(G-22625)*
**Wirco Inc** ....D .... 217 398-3200
Champaign *(G-3561)*
**Zender Enterprises Ltd** ....G .... 773 282-2293
Chicago *(G-7063)*

## MOLDS: Plastic Working & Foundry

**3-D Mold & Tool Inc** ....G .... 847 870-7150
Wheeling *(G-21992)*
**A-1 Tool Corporation** ....D .... 708 345-5000
Melrose Park *(G-14579)*
**APT Tool Inc** ....G .... 815 337-0051
Woodstock *(G-22540)*
**Chicago Mold Engrg Co Inc** ....D .... 630 584-1311
Saint Charles *(G-19152)*
**Do-Rite Die & Engineering Co** ....F .... 708 754-4355
S Chicago Hts *(G-19103)*
**Glo-Mold Inc** ....F .... 847 671-1762
Schiller Park *(G-19835)*
**Hatcher Associates Inc** ....F .... 773 252-2171
Chicago *(G-5053)*
**Industrial Modern Pattern** ....G .... 847 296-4930
Rosemont *(G-19006)*
**Industrial Molds Inc** ....D .... 815 397-2971
Rockford *(G-18430)*
**J R Mold Inc** ....G .... 630 289-2192
Streamwood *(G-20658)*
**Janler Corporation** ....E .... 773 774-0166
Chicago *(G-5277)*
**Lens Lenticlear Lenticular** ....F .... 630 467-0900
Itasca *(G-12303)*
**Method Molds Inc** ....G .... 815 877-0191
Loves Park *(G-13965)*
**Monarch Manufacturing** ....G .... 630 519-4580
Lombard *(G-13829)*
**Northern Illinois Mold Corp** ....F .... 847 669-2100
Dundee *(G-8565)*
**P M Mold Company** ....E .... 847 923-5400
Schaumburg *(G-19678)*
**P M Mold Company** ....E .... 847 923-5400
Schaumburg *(G-19679)*
**RAO Design International Inc** ....G .... 847 671-6182
Schiller Park *(G-19865)*
**Sterling Tool & Manufacturing** ....G .... 847 304-1800
Barrington *(G-1305)*
**Wright Tool & Die Inc** ....F .... 815 669-2020
McHenry *(G-14573)*

## MONASTERIES

**Marytown** ....E .... 847 367-7800
Libertyville *(G-13347)*

## MONUMENTS & GRAVE MARKERS, EXC TERRAZZO

**Kowalski Memorials Inc** ....G .... 630 462-7226
Carol Stream *(G-3182)*
**Monumental Art Works** ....G .... 708 389-3038
Blue Island *(G-2263)*

## MONUMENTS & GRAVE MARKERS, WHOLESALE

**Tolar Group LLC** ....E .... 847 668-9485
Oak Park *(G-16689)*

## MONUMENTS: Concrete

**Bobs Market & Greenhouse** ....G .... 217 442-8155
Danville *(G-7706)*
**Elite Monument Co** ....G .... 217 532-6080
Hillsboro *(G-11889)*

## MONUMENTS: Cut Stone, Exc Finishing Or Lettering Only

**Bevel Granite Co Inc** ....D .... 708 388-9060
Merrionette Park *(G-14736)*
**King & Sons Monuments** ....G .... 815 786-6321
Sandwich *(G-19371)*
**Old Capitol Monument Works Inc** ....G .... 217 324-5673
Vandalia *(G-21118)*

# PRODUCT SECTION

## MOTOR VEHICLE ASSEMBLY, COMPLETE: Truck Tractors, Highway

Reynolds Rock of Ages .................. F ...... 618 658-2911
  Vienna  (G-21224)
Rogan Granitindustrie Inc ............... G ...... 708 758-0050
  Merrionette Park  (G-14737)
Rogan Granitindustrie Inc ............... G ...... 708 758-0050
  Lynwood  (G-14025)

### MOPEDS & PARTS

Monahan Partners Inc ................... F ...... 217 268-5758
  Arcola  (G-678)

### MOPS: Floor & Dust

Don Leventhal Group LLC ............... E ...... 618 783-4424
  Newton  (G-15939)
FHP-Berner USA LP ...................... E ...... 630 270-1400
  Aurora  (G-1008)
Freudenberg Household Pdts LP ....... C ...... 630 270-1400
  Aurora  (G-1010)
Libman Company .......................... C ...... 217 268-4200
  Arcola  (G-675)

### MORTAR

Maxi-Mix Inc ................................. G ...... 773 489-6747
  Chicago  (G-5658)

### MOTION PICTURE & VIDEO PRODUCTION SVCS

Edqu Media LLC ............................ G ...... 773 803-9793
  Chicago  (G-4698)
Linx Enterprises LLC ...................... G ...... 224 409-2206
  Chicago  (G-5516)
Towers Media Holdings Inc ............. D ...... 312 993-1550
  Northfield  (G-16421)

### MOTION PICTURE & VIDEO PRODUCTION SVCS: Commercials, TV

Gfx International Inc ....................... C ...... 847 543-7179
  Grayslake  (G-11340)

### MOTION PICTURE & VIDEO PRODUCTION SVCS: Educational

Learning Seed LLC ........................ G ...... 847 540-8855
  Chicago  (G-5481)

### MOTION PICTURE EQPT

2nd Cine Inc ................................. G ...... 773 455-5808
  Elgin  (G-8928)
Essannay Show It Inc .................... G ...... 312 733-5511
  Chicago  (G-4778)
Imac Motion Control Corp ............... G ...... 847 741-4622
  Elgin  (G-9073)

### MOTION PICTURE PRODUCTION ALLIED SVCS

Personify ...................................... F ...... 217 840-2638
  Urbana  (G-21097)

### MOTION PICTURE PRODUCTION SVCS

Icon Acquisition Holdings LP ........... G ...... 312 751-8000
  Chicago  (G-5136)

### MOTOR & GENERATOR PARTS: Electric

Alfa Controls Inc ........................... G ...... 847 978-9245
  Wheeling  (G-22001)
Alin Machining Company Inc .......... C ...... 708 681-1043
  Melrose Park  (G-14585)
Brook Crompton Usa Inc ................ G ...... 708 893-0690
  South Holland  (G-20252)
Djh Industries Inc .......................... E ...... 309 246-8456
  Lacon  (G-12786)
Encap Technologies Inc ................. F ...... 510 337-2700
  Palatine  (G-17026)
Encap Technologies Inc ................. B ...... 510 337-2700
  Palatine  (G-17027)
Kap Holdings LLC ......................... F ...... 708 948-0226
  Oak Park  (G-16671)
R&R Equipment Plus1 Inc .............. F ...... 708 529-3931
  Chicago Ridge  (G-7157)
Stable Beginning Corporation ......... E ...... 815 745-2100
  Warren  (G-21337)
Waves Fluid Solutions LLC ............. G ...... 630 765-7533
  Carol Stream  (G-3264)

### MOTOR CONTROL CENTERS

Siemens Industry Inc ..................... C
  West Chicago  (G-21771)

### MOTOR HOMES

Mobilty Works ............................... G ...... 815 254-2000
  Plainfield  (G-17629)

### MOTOR INN

River View Motor Sports Inc ........... G ...... 309 467-4569
  Congerville  (G-7371)

### MOTOR REBUILDING SVCS, EXC AUTOMOTIVE

Amj Industries Inc ......................... F ...... 815 654-9000
  Rockford  (G-18264)
Automatic Machinery Resources ..... G ...... 630 543-4944
  Addison  (G-48)
C and C Machine Tool Service ....... G ...... 630 810-0484
  Downers Grove  (G-8402)
Endeavor Technologies Inc ............ E ...... 630 562-0300
  Saint Charles  (G-19181)
Fdf Armature Inc ........................... G ...... 630 458-0452
  Addison  (G-115)
Fontela Electric Incorporated ......... F ...... 630 932-1600
  Addison  (G-121)
L A Motors Incorporated ................ G ...... 773 736-7305
  Chicago  (G-5421)
M R Glenn Electric Inc .................. E ...... 708 479-9200
  Lockport  (G-13729)
Murrays Disc Auto Stores Inc ......... G ...... 847 458-7179
  Lake In The Hills  (G-12999)
Murrays Disc Auto Stores Inc ......... G ...... 847 882-4384
  Schaumburg  (G-19659)
Murrays Disc Auto Stores Inc ......... G ...... 708 430-8155
  Bridgeview  (G-2511)
Oreillys Auto Parts Store ................ G ...... 847 360-0012
  Waukegan  (G-21599)

### MOTOR REPAIR SVCS

Anna-Jonesboro Motor Co Inc ........ G ...... 618 833-4486
  Anna  (G-601)
Decatur Industrial Elc Inc ............... E ...... 618 244-1066
  Mount Vernon  (G-15409)
Fleetpride Inc ............................... F ...... 630 455-6881
  Willowbrook  (G-22212)
Fluid Pump Service Inc .................. G ...... 847 228-0750
  Elk Grove Village  (G-9480)
Harvey Bros Inc ............................ F ...... 309 342-3137
  Galesburg  (G-10757)
Metroeast Motorsports Inc ............. G ...... 618 628-2466
  O Fallon  (G-16471)
Pauls Mc Culloch Sales ................. G ...... 217 323-2159
  Beardstown  (G-1526)

### MOTOR SCOOTERS & PARTS

Genuine Scooters LLC ................... G ...... 773 271-8514
  Chicago  (G-4939)
Pruett Enterprises Inc .................... G ...... 618 235-6184
  Belleville  (G-1667)
T G Enterprises Inc ....................... F ...... 309 662-0508
  Bloomington  (G-2229)

### MOTOR VEHICLE ASSEMBLY, COMPLETE: Ambulances

Light of Mine LLC .......................... G ...... 312 840-8570
  Chicago  (G-5503)

### MOTOR VEHICLE ASSEMBLY, COMPLETE: Autos, Incl Specialty

Android Indstres- Blvidere LLC ....... C ...... 815 547-3742
  Belvidere  (G-1732)
Blackjack Customs ........................ G ...... 847 361-5225
  North Chicago  (G-16175)
Brunos Automotive Products .......... G ...... 630 458-0043
  Addison  (G-62)
Chassis Service Unlimited ............. G ...... 847 336-2305
  Waukegan  (G-21536)
Dakkota Integrated Systems LLC ... D ...... 517 694-6500
  Chicago  (G-4545)
High Speed Welding Inc ................ G ...... 630 971-8929
  Westmont  (G-21891)
Innova Uev LLC ............................ F ...... 630 568-5609
  Burr Ridge  (G-2855)
John Beyer Race Cars ................... G ...... 773 779-5313
  Chicago  (G-5311)
Kens Street Rod Repair ................. G ...... 815 874-1811
  Rockford  (G-18455)
Legend Racing Enterprises Inc ...... G ...... 847 923-8979
  Schaumburg  (G-19614)
Midwest Coach Builders Inc .......... G ...... 630 690-1420
  Carol Stream  (G-3198)
Midwest Hot Rods Inc .................... F ...... 815 254-7637
  Plainfield  (G-17626)
Restorations Unlimited II Inc .......... G ...... 847 639-5818
  Cary  (G-3367)
Rj Race Cars Inc ........................... F ...... 309 343-7575
  Galesburg  (G-10774)
T R Z Motorsports Inc .................... G ...... 815 806-0838
  Frankfort  (G-10367)

### MOTOR VEHICLE ASSEMBLY, COMPLETE: Buses, All Types

Motor Coach Inds Intl Inc ............... C ...... 847 285-2000
  Des Plaines  (G-8235)
Motor Coach Industries .................. C ...... 847 285-2000
  Des Plaines  (G-8236)

### MOTOR VEHICLE ASSEMBLY, COMPLETE: Fire Department Vehicles

Alexis Fire Equipment Company ..... D ...... 309 482-6121
  Alexis  (G-375)
Crete Twp ..................................... G ...... 708 672-3111
  Crete  (G-7512)
Odin Fire Protection District ........... E ...... 618 775-8292
  Odin  (G-16741)
Sentinel Emrgncy Solutions LLC .... E ...... 618 539-3863
  Freeburg  (G-10640)

### MOTOR VEHICLE ASSEMBLY, COMPLETE: Military Motor Vehicle

Performance Military Group Inc ...... G ...... 847 325-4450
  Lincolnshire  (G-13473)

### MOTOR VEHICLE ASSEMBLY, COMPLETE: Motor Buses

Liberty Coach Inc .......................... D ...... 847 578-4600
  North Chicago  (G-16184)

### MOTOR VEHICLE ASSEMBLY, COMPLETE: Reconnaissance Cars

Heartland Classics Inc ................... G ...... 618 783-4444
  Newton  (G-15941)

### MOTOR VEHICLE ASSEMBLY, COMPLETE: Snow Plows

Enterprise Service Corporation ...... G ...... 773 589-2727
  Des Plaines  (G-8188)
Koenig Body & Equipment Inc ....... E ...... 309 673-7435
  West Peoria  (G-21823)

### MOTOR VEHICLE ASSEMBLY, COMPLETE: Truck & Tractor Trucks

Direct Dimension Inc ..................... G ...... 815 479-1936
  Algonquin  (G-386)
Hertz Corporation .......................... G ...... 630 897-0956
  Montgomery  (G-15046)
Jenner Precision Inc ...................... F ...... 815 692-6655
  Fairbury  (G-10127)
Navistar Inc ................................... D ...... 630 963-0769
  Downers Grove  (G-8494)
Navistar Inc ................................... D ...... 331 332-5000
  Lisle  (G-13630)
Navistar International Corp ............. A ...... 331 332-5000
  Lisle  (G-13633)
Rahn Equipment Company ............ G ...... 217 431-1232
  Danville  (G-7762)

### MOTOR VEHICLE ASSEMBLY, COMPLETE: Truck Tractors, Highway

Dierzen-Kewanee Heavy Inds ........ D ...... 309 853-2316
  Kewanee  (G-12679)

## MOTOR VEHICLE ASSEMBLY, COMPLETE: Wreckers, Tow Truck

Mares Service Inc .................. G ...... 708 656-1660
Cicero (G-7218)

## MOTOR VEHICLE ASSY, COMPLETE: Street Sprinklers & Sweepers

Elgin Sweeper Company .................. B ...... 847 741-5370
Elgin (G-9026)

## MOTOR VEHICLE DEALERS: Automobiles, New & Used

Birkeys Farm Store Inc .................. E ...... 217 337-1772
Urbana (G-21073)
City Subn Auto Svc Goodyear .................. G ...... 773 355-5550
Chicago (G-4389)
Lincoln Green Mazda Inc .................. F ...... 217 391-2400
Springfield (G-20470)
Motor Sport Marketing Group .................. E ...... 618 654-6750
Highland (G-11803)
Pilla Exec Inc .................. G ...... 312 882-8263
Chicago (G-6122)
Subaru of America Inc .................. E ...... 630 250-4740
Itasca (G-12361)
Union Ave Auto Inc .................. G ...... 708 754-3899
Steger (G-20580)

## MOTOR VEHICLE DEALERS: Cars, Used Only

Metzger Welding Service .................. G ...... 217 234-2851
Mattoon (G-14403)
Weg Electric Motors .................. G ...... 630 226-5688
Bolingbrook (G-2381)

## MOTOR VEHICLE DEALERS: Trucks, Tractors/Trailers, New & Used

Great Dane Limited Partnership .................. D ...... 773 254-5533
Kewanee (G-12689)

## MOTOR VEHICLE PARTS & ACCESS: Air Conditioner Parts

Bison Gear & Engineering Corp .................. C ...... 630 377-0153
Saint Charles (G-19143)
T/CCI Manufacturing LLC .................. C ...... 217 423-0066
Decatur (G-7947)

## MOTOR VEHICLE PARTS & ACCESS: Axel Housings & Shafts

Power Plus Products Inc .................. F ...... 773 788-9794
Bedford Park (G-1574)

## MOTOR VEHICLE PARTS & ACCESS: Bearings

Ggb North America LLC .................. E ...... 847 775-1859
Waukegan (G-21563)
Nta Precision Axle Corporation .................. B ...... 630 690-6300
Carol Stream (G-3207)

## MOTOR VEHICLE PARTS & ACCESS: Body Components & Frames

Johnson Controls Inc .................. D ...... 630 279-0050
Elmhurst (G-9892)
Qwik-Tip Inc .................. G ...... 847 640-7387
Elk Grove Village (G-9705)
Waltz Brothers Inc .................. E ...... 847 520-1122
Wheeling (G-22181)

## MOTOR VEHICLE PARTS & ACCESS: Brakes, Air

Air-X Remanufacturing Corp .................. G ...... 708 598-0044
Bridgeview (G-2459)
Airbrake Products Inc .................. F ...... 708 594-1110
Orland Park (G-16840)

## MOTOR VEHICLE PARTS & ACCESS: Choker Rods

Kama Enterprises Inc .................. G ...... 773 551-9642
Chicago (G-5356)

## MOTOR VEHICLE PARTS & ACCESS: Clutches

Advanced Machine Products Inc .................. G ...... 618 254-4112
Hartford (G-11609)
Clutch Systems Inc .................. G ...... 815 282-7960
Machesney Park (G-14066)
Matrix International Ltd .................. G ...... 815 389-3771
South Beloit (G-20158)
Warner Electric LLC .................. C ...... 815 389-4300
South Beloit (G-20174)

## MOTOR VEHICLE PARTS & ACCESS: Connecting Rods

Precision Cnncting Rod Svc Inc .................. F ...... 708 345-3700
Broadview (G-2602)

## MOTOR VEHICLE PARTS & ACCESS: Cylinder Heads

Accurate Auto Manufacturing Co .................. G ...... 618 244-0727
Mount Vernon (G-15397)
Little Egypt Gas A & Wldg Sups .................. G ...... 618 937-2271
West Frankfort (G-21813)

## MOTOR VEHICLE PARTS & ACCESS: Electrical Eqpt

Autonomoustuff LLC .................. G ...... 314 270-2123
Morton (G-15153)
CK Acquisition Holdings Inc .................. F ...... 773 646-0115
Chicago (G-4391)
Just Parts Inc .................. G ...... 815 756-2184
Cortland (G-7390)
Mr Auto Electric .................. G ...... 217 523-3659
Springfield (G-20485)

## MOTOR VEHICLE PARTS & ACCESS: Engines & Parts

Acme Auto Electric Co .................. G ...... 708 754-5420
S Chicago Hts (G-19098)
Alloy Tech .................. G ...... 217 253-3939
Tuscola (G-21014)
American Speed Enterprises .................. G ...... 309 764-3601
Moline (G-14917)
Andersen Machine & Welding Inc .................. G ...... 815 232-4664
Freeport (G-10647)
Arsco .................. F ...... 708 755-1733
Chicago Heights (G-7079)
Elgin Industries Inc .................. C ...... 847 742-1720
Elgin (G-9023)
Engine Solutions Inc .................. G ...... 815 979-2312
Rockford (G-18365)
Fire Chariot LLC .................. G ...... 815 561-3688
Rochelle (G-18090)
Ft Motors Inc .................. F ...... 773 737-5581
Chicago (G-4893)
Jordan Industries Inc .................. F ...... 847 945-5591
Deerfield (G-8020)
K & W Auto Electric .................. F ...... 217 857-1717
Teutopolis (G-20853)
Larry Pontnack .................. G ...... 815 732-7751
Oregon (G-16827)
Mercury Products Corp .................. G ...... 847 524-4400
Schaumburg (G-19641)
Mercury Products Corp .................. G ...... 847 524-4400
Schaumburg (G-19642)
Pactiv LLC .................. C
Lincolnshire (G-13469)
Php Racengines Inc .................. G ...... 847 526-9393
Wauconda (G-21492)
Premiere Motorsports LLC .................. G ...... 708 634-0007
Plainfield (G-17644)
Tenneco Global Holdings Inc .................. F ...... 847 482-5000
Lake Forest (G-12966)
U S Tool & Manufacturing Co .................. E ...... 630 953-1000
Addison (G-332)
Vogel Manufacturing Co Inc .................. G ...... 217 536-6946
Effingham (G-8861)

## MOTOR VEHICLE PARTS & ACCESS: Engs & Trans,Factory, Rebuilt

R & R Engines and Parts Inc .................. G ...... 630 628-1545
Addison (G-266)
TKT Enterprises Inc .................. E ...... 630 307-9355
Roselle (G-18983)

Windy City Engineering Inc .................. F ...... 773 254-8113
Chicago (G-6995)

## MOTOR VEHICLE PARTS & ACCESS: Fuel Systems & Parts

American Diesel Tube Corp .................. F ...... 630 628-1830
Addison (G-35)
Bi-Phase Technologies LLC .................. F ...... 952 886-6450
Wood Dale (G-22344)
Borgwarner Inc .................. C ...... 815 288-1462
Dixon (G-8324)
Pryco Inc .................. E ...... 217 364-4467
Mechanicsburg (G-14574)

## MOTOR VEHICLE PARTS & ACCESS: Gas Tanks

Gs Custom Works Inc .................. G ...... 815 233-4724
Freeport (G-10661)

## MOTOR VEHICLE PARTS & ACCESS: Gears

American Gear Inc .................. F ...... 815 537-5111
Prophetstown (G-17767)
Cloyes Gear and Products Inc .................. E ...... 630 420-0900
Naperville (G-15630)
Global Gear & Machining LLC .................. C ...... 630 969-9400
Downers Grove (G-8452)
IMS Companies LLC .................. D ...... 847 391-8100
Des Plaines (G-8210)
S A Gear Company Inc .................. E ...... 708 496-0395
Bedford Park (G-1582)
United States Gear Corporation .................. G ...... 773 821-5450
Chicago (G-6828)

## MOTOR VEHICLE PARTS & ACCESS: Governors

Precision Governors LLC .................. E ...... 815 229-5300
Rockford (G-18537)

## MOTOR VEHICLE PARTS & ACCESS: Heaters

Bergstrom Inc .................. D ...... 847 394-4013
Joliet (G-12465)
Illinois Tool Works Inc .................. D ...... 630 993-9990
Elmhurst (G-9885)

## MOTOR VEHICLE PARTS & ACCESS: Horns

Buell Manufacturing Company .................. G ...... 708 447-6320
Lyons (G-14033)

## MOTOR VEHICLE PARTS & ACCESS: Instrument Board Assemblies

Aisin Electronics Illinois LLC .................. C ...... 618 997-9800
Marion (G-14248)
Julian Elec Svc & Engrg Inc .................. E ...... 630 920-8950
Westmont (G-21895)

## MOTOR VEHICLE PARTS & ACCESS: Mufflers, Exhaust

California Muffler and Brakes .................. G ...... 773 776-8990
Chicago (G-4215)
Velasquez & Sons Muffler Shop .................. G ...... 847 740-6990
Round Lake Beach (G-19080)

## MOTOR VEHICLE PARTS & ACCESS: Oil Pumps

Harbison-Fischer Inc .................. G ...... 618 375-3841
Grayville (G-11369)

## MOTOR VEHICLE PARTS & ACCESS: Thermostats

Freeman Products Inc .................. G ...... 847 439-1000
Elk Grove Village (G-9490)
Transcedar Limited .................. E ...... 618 262-4153
Mount Carmel (G-15284)

## MOTOR VEHICLE PARTS & ACCESS: Trailer Hitches

Great Lakes Forge Company .................. G ...... 773 277-2800
Chicago (G-4997)

# PRODUCT SECTION

# MOTORCYCLE REPAIR SHOPS

Precision Truck Products Inc .................E  618 548-9011
  Salem *(G-19345)*

## MOTOR VEHICLE PARTS & ACCESS: Transmission Housings Or Parts

Amtec Precision Products Inc ...............D  847 695-8030
  Elgin *(G-8953)*
Borgwarner Transm Systems Inc ..........B  815 469-7819
  Chicago *(G-4145)*
Kay Manufacturing Company ................C  708 862-6800
  Calumet City *(G-2945)*
North Amercn Acquisition Corp .............C  847 695-8030
  Elgin *(G-9125)*

## MOTOR VEHICLE PARTS & ACCESS: Transmissions

Bedford Rakim .......................................G  773 759-3947
  South Holland *(G-20249)*
Borgwarner Transm Systems ................A  708 547-2600
  Bellwood *(G-1700)*
Borgwarner Transm Systems Inc ..........B  815 469-2721
  Frankfort *(G-10303)*
Dynamic Manufacturing Inc ...................D  708 343-8753
  Melrose Park *(G-14623)*
Dynamic Manufacturing Inc ...................D  708 681-0682
  Melrose Park *(G-14624)*
Dynamic Manufacturing Inc ...................D  708 547-7081
  Hillside *(G-11915)*
Dynamic Manufacturing Inc ...................E  708 343-8753
  Melrose Park *(G-14625)*
Finish Line Transmission Inc .................G  630 350-7776
  Wood Dale *(G-22367)*
Jimmy Diesel Inc ..................................G  708 482-4500
  Wheaton *(G-21959)*
Michelangelo & Donata Burdi ................F  773 427-1437
  Chicago *(G-5722)*
Walters Distributing Company ...............G  847 468-0941
  Elgin *(G-9228)*

## MOTOR VEHICLE PARTS & ACCESS: Universal Joints

Aircraft Gear Corporation .....................D  815 877-7473
  Loves Park *(G-13916)*
Federal-Mogul Corporation ...................E  248 354-7700
  Berwyn *(G-2065)*
GKN America Corp ...............................F  630 972-9300
  Woodridge *(G-22483)*
Thyssenkrupp Crankshaft Co LLC .........C  217 431-0060
  Danville *(G-7770)*
Thyssenkrupp Crankshaft Co LLC .........C  217 444-5500
  Danville *(G-7773)*

## MOTOR VEHICLE PARTS & ACCESS: Wheel rims

Advance Wheel Corporation .................D  773 471-5734
  Chicago *(G-3766)*

## MOTOR VEHICLE PARTS & ACCESS: Wiring Harness Sets

Infinitybox LLC .....................................G  847 232-1991
  Elk Grove Village *(G-9545)*

## MOTOR VEHICLE RADIOS WHOLESALERS

Audio Installers Inc ..............................F  815 969-7500
  Loves Park *(G-13923)*
Robert Bosch LLC ................................B  248 876-1000
  Broadview *(G-2610)*

## MOTOR VEHICLE SPLYS & PARTS WHOLESALERS: New

A Lakin & Sons Inc ..............................E  773 871-6360
  Montgomery *(G-15026)*
American Industrial Direct LLC ..............E  800 382-1200
  Elgin *(G-8948)*
Chicago Drive Line Inc .........................G  708 385-1900
  Alsip *(G-445)*
Elgin Industries Inc ..............................C  847 742-1720
  Elgin *(G-9023)*
General Motors LLC ..............................C  815 733-0668
  Bolingbrook *(G-2313)*
GKN North America Services Inc ..........F  630 972-9300
  Woodridge *(G-22484)*
Hella Corporate Center USA Inc ...........B  734 414-0900
  Flora *(G-10208)*
Illini/Altco Inc .......................................D  847 549-0321
  Vernon Hills *(G-21173)*
Koehler Enterprises Inc ........................G  847 451-4966
  Franklin Park *(G-10513)*
Mann+hummel Filtration Tech ...............F  800 407-9263
  McHenry *(G-14526)*
MCI Service Parts Inc ..........................D  419 994-4141
  Des Plaines *(G-8230)*
Riken Corporation of America ...............C  847 673-1400
  Skokie *(G-20076)*
Tvh Parts Co ........................................E  847 223-1000
  Grayslake *(G-11365)*
United Gasket Corporation ...................D  708 656-3700
  Cicero *(G-7242)*

## MOTOR VEHICLE: Radiators

Caterpillar Inc ......................................B  815 842-6000
  Pontiac *(G-17697)*
Independent Antique RAD Mfg ..............G  847 458-7400
  Algonquin *(G-393)*
National Porges Radiator Corp .............F  773 224-3000
  Chicago *(G-5866)*

## MOTOR VEHICLE: Shock Absorbers

Taw Enterprises LLC ...........................G  618 466-0134
  Godfrey *(G-11238)*
Tenneco Automotive Oper Co Inc ..........C  847 482-5000
  Lake Forest *(G-12965)*
Tenneco Intl Holdg Corp .......................C  847 482-5000
  Lake Forest *(G-12968)*

## MOTOR VEHICLE: Steering Mechanisms

Precision Remanufacturing Inc ..............F  773 489-7225
  Chicago *(G-6171)*
United Remanufacturing Co Inc .............E  847 678-2233
  Schiller Park *(G-19881)*

## MOTOR VEHICLE: Wheels

Accuride Corporation ............................C  630 454-4299
  Batavia *(G-1403)*
Accuride Corporation ............................C  630 568-3914
  Hinsdale *(G-11938)*
American Vulko Tread Corp ..................F  847 956-1300
  Elk Grove Village *(G-9299)*
American Wheel Corp ...........................E  708 458-9141
  Chicago *(G-3882)*
Clement Industries Inc Del ....................E  708 458-9141
  Bedford Park *(G-1544)*
Marmon Industries LLC ........................G  312 372-9500
  Chicago *(G-5627)*
Otr Wheel Engineering Inc ....................F  217 223-7705
  Quincy *(G-17864)*
Titan International Inc ..........................B  217 228-6011
  Quincy *(G-17896)*

## MOTOR VEHICLES & CAR BODIES

4x4 Headquarters LLC .........................G  217 540-5337
  Effingham *(G-8820)*
Alcon Components ...............................G  847 788-0901
  Arlington Heights *(G-705)*
Amerex Corporation .............................E  309 382-4389
  North Pekin *(G-16192)*
Bergstrom Inc ......................................G  847 394-4013
  Joliet *(G-12465)*
Bill West Enterprises Inc ......................G  217 886-2591
  Jacksonville *(G-12378)*
Chicago Motorcars ...............................E  630 221-1800
  West Chicago *(G-21680)*
ED Etnyre & Co ...................................B  815 732-2116
  Oregon *(G-16822)*
FCA US LLC ........................................G  630 724-2321
  Lisle *(G-13588)*
Federal Signal Corporation ...................G  630 954-2000
  Oak Brook *(G-16510)*
Federal Signal Credit Corp ...................G  630 954-2000
  Oak Brook *(G-16511)*
Fs Depot Inc ........................................G  847 468-2350
  University Park *(G-21051)*
Heat Armor LLC ...................................F  773 938-1030
  Chicago *(G-5066)*
Hopperstad Customs ............................G  815 547-7534
  Belvidere *(G-1762)*
Illinois Sterling Ltd ...............................G  847 526-5151
  Wauconda *(G-21472)*
Maxim Inc ............................................G  217 544-7015
  Springfield *(G-20475)*
Mickey Truck Bodies Inc ......................F  309 827-8227
  Bloomington *(G-2197)*
Mobility Works .....................................G  815 254-2000
  Plainfield *(G-17629)*
Navistar Inc .........................................C  331 332-5000
  Lisle *(G-13629)*
Navistar Inc .........................................C  331 332-5000
  Joliet *(G-12545)*
Nippon Sharyo Mfg LLC .......................G  815 562-8600
  Rochelle *(G-18101)*
Peters Body Shop & Towing Inc ...........G  217 223-5250
  Quincy *(G-17867)*
Powertrain Technology Inc ...................G  847 458-2323
  Algonquin *(G-403)*
R/A Hoerr Inc .......................................G  309 691-8789
  Edwards *(G-8784)*
SAE Customs Inc .................................G  855 723-2878
  Round Lake *(G-19066)*
Subaru of America Inc .........................E  630 250-4740
  Itasca *(G-12361)*
Tesla Motors Inc ..................................F  312 733-9780
  Chicago *(G-6704)*
Vuteq Usa Inc ......................................C  309 452-9933
  Normal *(G-16093)*

## MOTOR VEHICLES, WHOLESALE: Truck bodies

Bonnell Industries Inc ..........................D  815 284-3819
  Dixon *(G-8323)*
Koenig Body & Equipment Inc ..............E  309 673-7435
  West Peoria *(G-21823)*
Mark S Machine Shop Inc .....................G  815 895-3955
  Sycamore *(G-20809)*
Mid City Truck Bdy & Equipmemt ..........F  630 628-9080
  Addison *(G-209)*

## MOTORCYCLE & BICYCLE PARTS: Frames

Colnago America Inc ............................G  312 239-6666
  Chicago *(G-4425)*

## MOTORCYCLE & BICYCLE PARTS: Gears

David Taylor .........................................E  217 222-6480
  Quincy *(G-17819)*
Sram LLC ............................................D  312 664-8800
  Chicago *(G-6565)*

## MOTORCYCLE ACCESS

Gs Custom Works Inc ...........................G  815 233-4724
  Freeport *(G-10661)*
National Cycle Inc ................................C  708 343-0400
  Maywood *(G-14430)*

## MOTORCYCLE DEALERS

Decatur Industrial Elc Inc .....................E  618 244-1066
  Mount Vernon *(G-15409)*
Lo-Ko Performance Coatings ................G  708 424-7863
  Oak Lawn *(G-16632)*
Metroeast Motorsports Inc ....................G  618 628-2466
  O Fallon *(G-16471)*
T G Enterprises Inc ..............................F  309 662-0508
  Bloomington *(G-2229)*
Valley Racing Inc .................................G  708 946-1440
  Beecher *(G-1603)*
Weiland Fast Trac Inc ..........................G  847 438-7996
  Long Grove *(G-13905)*

## MOTORCYCLE PARTS & ACCESS DEALERS

Service Pro Electric Mtr Repr ...............G  630 766-1215
  Bensenville *(G-1990)*
W L & J Enterprises Inc .......................G  708 946-0999
  Beecher *(G-1604)*

## MOTORCYCLE PARTS: Wholesalers

Franks Maintenance & Engrg ...............G  847 475-1003
  Evanston *(G-10040)*

## MOTORCYCLE RACING

Valley Racing Inc .................................G  708 946-1440
  Beecher *(G-1603)*

## MOTORCYCLE REPAIR SHOPS

Metroeast Motorsports Inc ....................G  618 628-2466
  O Fallon *(G-16471)*
Midwest Design & Automtn Inc .............G  618 392-2892
  Olney *(G-16781)*
Valley Racing Inc .................................G  708 946-1440
  Beecher *(G-1603)*

# MOTORCYCLES & RELATED PARTS　　　　　　　　　　　　　　　　　　　　　　　　　PRODUCT SECTION

## MOTORCYCLES & RELATED PARTS

Black Magic Customs Inc ............................ G ...... 815 786-1977
  Sandwich *(G-19360)*
Chopper Mm LLC ...................................... G ...... 309 875-3544
  Maquon *(G-14215)*
Jh Choppers LLC ...................................... G ...... 618 420-2500
  Maryville *(G-14342)*
Taurus Cycle ............................................. G ...... 309 454-1565
  Bloomington *(G-2230)*
World of Soul Inc ...................................... G ...... 773 840-4839
  Chicago *(G-7032)*

## MOTORS: Electric

Bodine Electric Company ............................ C ...... 773 478-3515
  Northfield *(G-16393)*
Broad Ocean Motors LLC ............................ E ...... 630 908-4720
  Westmont *(G-21877)*
Charles R Frontczak .................................. G ...... 224 392-4151
  Rockford *(G-18304)*
Ddu Magnetics Inc .................................... G ...... 708 325-6587
  Lynwood *(G-14019)*
Digitaldrive Tech ....................................... G ...... 630 510-1580
  Wheaton *(G-21944)*
Dlt Electric LLC ......................................... F ...... 630 552-4115
  Plano *(G-17663)*
Eastview Manufacturing Inc ........................ G ...... 847 741-2514
  Elgin *(G-9019)*
Electric Motor Corp ................................... E ...... 773 725-1050
  Chicago *(G-4719)*
Electric Vehicle Technologies ...................... E ...... 847 673-8330
  Skokie *(G-19992)*
Forest City Auto Electric Co ....................... F ...... 815 963-4350
  Rockford *(G-18386)*
Geitek Automation Inc ................................ D ...... 815 385-3500
  McHenry *(G-14509)*
Hallmark Industries Inc .............................. F ...... 847 301-8050
  Schaumburg *(G-19546)*
Haran Technologies LLC ............................ G ...... 217 239-1628
  Champaign *(G-3492)*
Haran Ventures LLC .................................. G ...... 217 239-1628
  Champaign *(G-3493)*
Howland Technology Inc ............................ F ...... 847 965-9808
  Morton Grove *(G-15200)*
Jordan Industries Inc ................................. F ...... 847 945-5591
  Deerfield *(G-8020)*
L & H Company Inc ................................... F ...... 630 571-7200
  Oak Brook *(G-16532)*
Moons Industries America Inc .................... A ...... 630 833-5940
  Itasca *(G-12322)*
Nidec Motor Corporation ............................ D ...... 847 439-3760
  Elk Grove Village *(G-9651)*
Schneider Elc Buildings LLC ...................... B ...... 815 381-5000
  Rockford *(G-18608)*
Schneider Elc Holdings Inc ........................ A ...... 717 944-5460
  Schaumburg *(G-19722)*
Sfc of Illinois Inc ....................................... E ...... 815 745-2100
  Warren *(G-21336)*
Spg Usa Inc ............................................. E ...... 847 439-4949
  Elk Grove Village *(G-9747)*
Warfield Electric Company Inc ................... E ...... 815 469-4094
  Frankfort *(G-10376)*
Wodack Electric Tool Corp ........................ F ...... 773 287-9866
  Chicago *(G-7019)*
Yaskawa America Inc ................................ C ...... 847 887-7000
  Waukegan *(G-21642)*
Yaskawa America Inc ................................ C ...... 847 887-7909
  Des Plaines *(G-8307)*

## MOTORS: Generators

Advanced Ozone Tech Inc ......................... F ...... 630 964-1300
  Downers Grove *(G-8385)*
Al Cook Electric Motors ............................. G ...... 309 653-2337
  Adair *(G-11)*
Altorfer Power Systems ............................. G ...... 309 697-1234
  Bartonville *(G-1391)*
American Total Engine Co ......................... G ...... 847 623-2737
  Ingleside *(G-12186)*
Applied Mechanical Tech LLC .................... E ...... 815 472-2700
  Momence *(G-14978)*
Atlas Copco Compressors LLC ................. F ...... 281 590-7500
  Chicago *(G-3979)*
Baldor Electric Company .......................... C ...... 630 296-1400
  Bolingbrook *(G-2282)*
Belmont Electro Co Inc ............................. G ...... 773 472-4641
  Brookfield *(G-2623)*
Bison Gear & Engineering Corp ................ C ...... 630 377-0153
  Saint Charles *(G-19143)*
Bolingbrook Communications Inc .............. A ...... 630 759-9500
  Lisle *(G-13571)*

Cemec Inc ............................................... G ...... 630 495-9696
  Downers Grove *(G-8405)*
Charles Industries Ltd ............................... D ...... 217 826-2318
  Marshall *(G-14319)*
Coilform Company .................................... G ...... 630 232-8000
  Geneva *(G-10820)*
Communication Coil Inc ............................ D ...... 847 671-1333
  Schiller Park *(G-19815)*
Con-Trol-Cure Inc .................................... F ...... 773 248-0099
  Chicago *(G-4442)*
D C Grove Electric Inc ............................... G ...... 847 587-0864
  Fox Lake *(G-10275)*
Elm Products Corp ................................... E ...... 847 336-0020
  Waukegan *(G-21557)*
Engine Rebuilders & Supply ...................... G ...... 708 338-1113
  Stone Park *(G-20634)*
Federal Prison Industries .......................... C ...... 309 346-8588
  Pekin *(G-17262)*
Flolo Corporation ..................................... G ...... 847 249-0880
  Gurnee *(G-11448)*
General Manufacturing LLC ...................... D ...... 708 345-8600
  Melrose Park *(G-14646)*
GKN Stromag Inc ..................................... G ...... 937 433-3882
  Woodridge *(G-22485)*
Hardin Industries LLC .............................. G ...... 309 246-8456
  Lacon *(G-12787)*
Harvey Bros Inc ....................................... F ...... 309 342-3137
  Galesburg *(G-10757)*
Hopcroft Electric Inc ................................. G ...... 618 288-7302
  Glen Carbon *(G-10952)*
Illinois Tool Works Inc ............................... C ...... 847 876-9400
  Des Plaines *(G-8208)*
Industrial Welder Rebuilders ..................... G ...... 708 371-5688
  Alsip *(G-473)*
Inglot Electronics Corp ............................. D ...... 773 286-5881
  Chicago *(G-5192)*
Inman Electric Motors Inc ......................... E ...... 815 223-2288
  La Salle *(G-12778)*
Integrated Power Services LLC ................. E ...... 708 877-5310
  Thornton *(G-20874)*
ITT Water & Wastewater USA Inc ............... G ...... 847 966-3700
  Morton Grove *(G-15205)*
Jardis Industries Inc ................................. F ...... 630 773-5600
  Itasca *(G-12290)*
Jasiek Motor Rebuilding Inc ...................... G ...... 815 883-3678
  Oglesby *(G-16750)*
Jomar Electric Coil Mfg Inc ....................... G ...... 630 279-1494
  Villa Park *(G-21261)*
Kackert Enterprises Inc ............................ G ...... 630 898-9339
  Aurora *(G-1179)*
Kaybee Engineering Company Inc ............. G ...... 630 968-7100
  Westmont *(G-21896)*
Lenhardt Tool and Die Company ............... D ...... 618 462-1075
  Alton *(G-582)*
M R Glenn Electric Inc .............................. E ...... 708 479-9200
  Lockport *(G-13729)*
Magnetic Coil Manufacturing Co ................ E ...... 630 787-1948
  Wood Dale *(G-22395)*
Magnetic Devices Inc ............................... G ...... 815 459-0077
  Crystal Lake *(G-7605)*
Maurey Instrument Corp ........................... F ...... 708 388-9898
  Alsip *(G-490)*
Morrell Incorporated ................................. F ...... 630 858-4600
  Glendale Heights *(G-11050)*
Motormakers De Kalb Credit Un ................ G ...... 815 756-6331
  Chicago *(G-5814)*
Mpc Products Corporation ........................ A ...... 847 673-8300
  Niles *(G-16010)*
Mpc Products Corporation ........................ A ...... 847 673-8300
  Niles *(G-16011)*
Nelco Coil Supply Company ..................... E ...... 847 259-7517
  Mount Prospect *(G-15354)*
Netgain Motors Inc ................................... G ...... 630 243-9100
  Lockport *(G-13735)*
North Point Investments Inc ..................... G ...... 312 977-4386
  Chicago *(G-5935)*
Northrop Grumman Systems Corp ............. A ...... 847 259-9600
  Rolling Meadows *(G-18753)*
Pre Fnish Mtals Mrrisville Inc .................... D ...... 847 439-2211
  Elk Grove Village *(G-9691)*
Progress Rail Locomotive Inc ................... A ...... 800 255-5355
  Mc Cook *(G-14456)*
Progress Rail Locomotive Inc ................... F ...... 708 387-5510
  Mc Cook *(G-14457)*
Provisur Technologies .............................. G ...... 312 284-4698
  Chicago *(G-6219)*
Qcircuits Inc ............................................ G ...... 618 662-8365
  Flora *(G-10214)*
Rathje Enterprises Inc .............................. F ...... 217 443-0022
  Danville *(G-7763)*

Robertson Transformer Co ........................ E ...... 708 388-2315
  Crestwood *(G-7500)*
Ronk Electrical Industries Inc .................... E ...... 217 563-8333
  Nokomis *(G-16062)*
Rotary Dryer Parts Inc .............................. G ...... 217 877-2787
  Decatur *(G-7936)*
Saco USA (il)inc ...................................... G ...... 815 877-8832
  Rockford *(G-18605)*
Santucci Enterprises ................................ G ...... 773 286-5629
  Chicago *(G-6442)*
Synergy Power Group LLC ....................... E ...... 618 247-3200
  Sandoval *(G-19359)*
Teledyne Lecroy Inc ................................. G ...... 847 888-0450
  Elgin *(G-9206)*
Transformer Manufacturers Inc ................. E ...... 708 457-1200
  Norridge *(G-16110)*
Ultrasonic Power Corporation ................... E ...... 815 235-6020
  Freeport *(G-10695)*
UOP LLC .................................................. E ...... 847 391-2000
  Des Plaines *(G-8293)*
Voss Electric Inc ...................................... E ...... 708 596-6000
  Harvey *(G-11680)*
Wellington Drive Tech US ......................... G ...... 847 922-5098
  Buffalo Grove *(G-2792)*
Western Motor Mfg Co .............................. G ...... 815 986-2214
  Rockford *(G-18679)*
Xform Power and Eqp Sups LLC ............... G ...... 773 260-0209
  Chicago *(G-7044)*

## MOTORS: Starting, Automotive & Aircraft

A and D Industrial Ignition ........................ G ...... 773 992-4040
  Franklin Park *(G-10380)*
Quick Start Pdts & Solutions ..................... F ...... 815 562-5414
  Rochelle *(G-18103)*
Robert Bosch LLC .................................... B ...... 248 876-1000
  Broadview *(G-2610)*

## MOTORS: Torque

American Electronic Pdts Inc .................... F ...... 630 889-9977
  Oak Brook *(G-16488)*
Brown Line Metal Works LLC ................... G ...... 312 884-7644
  Chicago *(G-4178)*

## MOUNTING SVC: Maps & Samples

GM Laminating & Mounting Corp .............. G ...... 630 941-7979
  Elmhurst *(G-9878)*

## MOUTHWASHES

Prevention Health Sciences Inc ................. G ...... 618 252-6922
  Raleigh *(G-17910)*

## MOVING SVC: Local

Bing Engineering Inc ................................ C ...... 708 228-8005
  Frankfort *(G-10300)*

## MOWERS & ACCESSORIES

Hevco Industries ...................................... G ...... 708 344-1342
  Aurora *(G-1169)*
Yanmar (usa) Inc ..................................... G ...... 847 541-1900
  Buffalo Grove *(G-2796)*

## MULTILITHING SVCS

Tri-Tower Printing Inc ............................... G ...... 847 640-6633
  Rolling Meadows *(G-18785)*

## MUSEUMS

International College Surgeons ................. G ...... 312 642-6502
  Chicago *(G-5220)*

## MUSEUMS & ART GALLERIES

Antioch Fine Arts Foundation .................... G ...... 847 838-2274
  Antioch *(G-617)*
Fox Valley Park District ............................. D ...... 630 892-1550
  Aurora *(G-1157)*
Sand Sculpture Co ................................... G ...... 815 334-9101
  Woodstock *(G-22607)*

## MUSIC DISTRIBUTION APPARATUS

Linx Enterprises LLC ................................ G ...... 224 409-2206
  Chicago *(G-5516)*

## MUSIC DISTRIBUTION SYSTEM SVCS

Deshamusic Inc ....................................... G ...... 818 257-2716
  Chicago *(G-4585)*

## MUSIC RECORDING PRODUCER

Bailey Business Group..................G...... 618 548-3566
  Salem *(G-19327)*
Drag City..................................G...... 312 455-1015
  Chicago *(G-4642)*
Linx Enterprises LLC....................G...... 224 409-2206
  Chicago *(G-5516)*

## MUSIC SCHOOLS

Flynn Guitars Inc.........................G...... 800 585-9555
  Wilmette *(G-22252)*

## MUSIC VIDEO PRODUCTION SVCS

Ikan Creations LLC.....................G...... 312 204-7333
  Chicago *(G-5150)*

## MUSICAL ENTERTAINERS

Fleming Music Technology Ctr......G...... 708 316-8662
  Wheaton *(G-21948)*
Kaelco Entrmt Holdings Inc..........G...... 217 600-7815
  Champaign *(G-3505)*
Time Records Publishing and Bo...G...... 618 996-3803
  Marion *(G-14291)*

## MUSICAL INSTRUMENT PARTS & ACCESS, WHOLESALE

Pjla Music..................................G...... 847 382-3212
  Barrington *(G-1297)*

## MUSICAL INSTRUMENT REPAIR

Schilke Music Products Inc..........E...... 708 343-8858
  Melrose Park *(G-14692)*
W & W Musical Instrument Co......E...... 773 278-4210
  Chicago *(G-6917)*

## MUSICAL INSTRUMENTS & ACCESS: Carrying Cases

Mechanical Music Corp................F...... 847 398-5444
  Arlington Heights *(G-801)*

## MUSICAL INSTRUMENTS & ACCESS: NEC

American Plating & Mfg Co...........F...... 773 890-4907
  Chicago *(G-3869)*
Analog Outfitters Inc..................G...... 217 202-6134
  Rantoul *(G-17917)*
Intelligent Instrument Sy..............G...... 630 323-3911
  Burr Ridge *(G-2857)*
Lothson Guitars.........................G...... 815 756-2031
  Dekalb *(G-8102)*
Mechanical Music Corp................F...... 847 398-5444
  Arlington Heights *(G-801)*
Music Connection Inc..................G...... 708 364-7590
  Orland Park *(G-16878)*
Peterson Elctr-Msical Pdts Inc......E...... 708 388-3311
  Alsip *(G-507)*
Schaff International LLC..............E...... 847 438-4560
  Lake Zurich *(G-13125)*
Schilke Music Products Inc..........E...... 708 343-8858
  Melrose Park *(G-14692)*
Suntimez Entertainment..............G...... 630 747-0712
  Cicero *(G-7232)*
Tom Crown Mute Co....................G...... 708 352-1039
  La Grange *(G-12747)*
Umphreys McGee Inc...................G...... 773 880-0024
  Chicago *(G-6809)*
Windy City Mutes.......................G...... 630 616-8634
  Bensenville *(G-2017)*

## MUSICAL INSTRUMENTS & ACCESS: Pipe Organs

Buzard Pipe Organ Builders LLC...F...... 217 352-1955
  Champaign *(G-3459)*
Wicks Organ Company.................E...... 618 654-2191
  Highland *(G-11819)*

## MUSICAL INSTRUMENTS & PARTS: Brass

Pjla Music..................................G...... 847 382-3212
  Barrington *(G-1297)*

## MUSICAL INSTRUMENTS & PARTS: Percussion

Fugate Inc..................................G...... 309 472-6830
  Washington *(G-21382)*
Trick Percussion Products Inc......G...... 847 342-2019
  Arlington Heights *(G-858)*

## MUSICAL INSTRUMENTS & PARTS: Woodwind

North Okaw Woodworking.............G...... 217 856-2178
  Humboldt *(G-12129)*

## MUSICAL INSTRUMENTS & SPLYS STORES

3b Media Inc..............................F...... 312 563-9363
  Chicago *(G-3667)*
Flynn Guitars Inc.........................G...... 800 585-9555
  Wilmette *(G-22252)*
W & W Musical Instrument Co......E...... 773 278-4210
  Chicago *(G-6917)*

## MUSICAL INSTRUMENTS & SPLYS STORES: Brass Instruments

McCormicks Enterprises Inc.........E...... 847 398-8680
  Arlington Heights *(G-800)*

## MUSICAL INSTRUMENTS & SPLYS STORES: String instruments

Lothson Guitars.........................G...... 815 756-2031
  Dekalb *(G-8102)*
Lyon & Healy Holding Corp..........E...... 312 786-1881
  Chicago *(G-5575)*

## MUSICAL INSTRUMENTS WHOLESALERS

Antigua Casa Sherry-Brener........G...... 773 737-1711
  Chicago *(G-3916)*
Engelhardt-Link Inc....................G...... 847 593-5850
  Elk Grove Village *(G-9459)*
Mechanical Music Corp................F...... 847 398-5444
  Arlington Heights *(G-801)*
PM Woodwind Repair Inc.............G...... 847 869-7049
  Evanston *(G-10088)*

## MUSICAL INSTRUMENTS: Clarinets & Parts

Interntnal Mscal Suppliers Inc......G...... 847 774-2938
  Glen Ellyn *(G-10974)*

## MUSICAL INSTRUMENTS: Electric & Electronic

Schneider Pipe Organs Inc...........G...... 217 871-4807
  Kenney *(G-12664)*

## MUSICAL INSTRUMENTS: Guitars & Parts, Electric & Acoustic

Flynn Guitars Inc.........................G...... 800 585-9555
  Wilmette *(G-22252)*
Music Solutions.........................F...... 630 759-3033
  Bolingbrook *(G-2349)*

## MUSICAL INSTRUMENTS: Harmonicas

Harrison Harmonicas LLC.............G...... 312 379-9427
  Chicago *(G-5049)*

## MUSICAL INSTRUMENTS: Harps & Parts

Lyon & Healy Harps Inc...............E...... 312 786-1881
  Chicago *(G-5574)*
Lyon & Healy Holding Corp..........E...... 312 786-1881
  Chicago *(G-5575)*
W & W Musical Instrument Co......E...... 773 278-4210
  Chicago *(G-6917)*

## MUSICAL INSTRUMENTS: Organ Parts & Materials

Daves Electronic Service.............F...... 217 283-5010
  Hoopeston *(G-12109)*

## MUSICAL INSTRUMENTS: Organs

Berghaus Pipe Organ Builders......E...... 708 544-4052
  Bellwood *(G-1698)*
C P O Inc..................................G...... 630 898-7733
  Aurora *(G-1123)*
Hammond Suzuki Usa Inc............E...... 630 543-0277
  Addison *(G-141)*
Midi Music Center Inc.................E...... 708 352-3388
  Wood Dale *(G-22400)*

## MUSICAL INSTRUMENTS: Strings, Instrument

Engelhardt-Link Inc....................G...... 847 593-5850
  Elk Grove Village *(G-9459)*
William Harris Lee & Co Inc.........E...... 312 786-0459
  Chicago *(G-6984)*

## NAIL SALONS

Total Look..................................G...... 847 382-6646
  Barrington *(G-1310)*

## NAILS WHOLESALERS

Sales Stretcher Enterprises.........F...... 815 223-9681
  Peru *(G-17527)*

## NAILS: Steel, Wire Or Cut

Estad Stamping & Mfg Co............E...... 217 442-4600
  Danville *(G-7717)*
Illinois Tool Works Inc.................G...... 847 821-2170
  Vernon Hills *(G-21174)*
L & J Industrial Staples Inc..........G...... 815 864-3337
  Shannon *(G-19899)*
W H Maze Company....................E...... 815 223-1742
  Peru *(G-17530)*
W H Maze Company....................D...... 815 223-8290
  Peru *(G-17531)*

## NAME PLATES: Engraved Or Etched

Durable Engravers Inc................E...... 630 766-6420
  Franklin Park *(G-10461)*
Forest Awards & Engraving..........G...... 630 595-2242
  Wood Dale *(G-22371)*
Mobile Air Inc............................F...... 847 755-0586
  Glendale Heights *(G-11049)*
Nameplate Robinson & Precision..G...... 847 678-2255
  Franklin Park *(G-10538)*
National Rubber Stamp Co Inc.....G...... 773 281-6522
  Chicago *(G-5868)*
Photo Techniques Corp...............E...... 630 690-9360
  Carol Stream *(G-3213)*
Porcelain Enamel Finishers..........G...... 312 808-1560
  Chicago *(G-6157)*

## NAMEPLATES

American Name Plate & Metal De..E...... 773 376-1400
  Chicago *(G-3867)*
Cypress Multigraphics LLC...........E...... 708 633-1166
  Tinley Park *(G-20907)*
Gabel & Schubert Bronze............F...... 773 878-6800
  Chicago *(G-4905)*
Signcraft Screenprint Inc............C...... 815 777-3030
  Galena *(G-10731)*

## NATIONAL SECURITY FORCES

Dla Document Services................F...... 618 256-4686
  Scott Air Force Base *(G-19885)*

## NATURAL GAS COMPRESSING SVC, On-Site

ANR Pipeline Company.................G...... 309 667-2158
  New Windsor *(G-15929)*

## NATURAL GAS DISTRIBUTION TO CONSUMERS

La Quinta Gas Pipeline Company..G...... 217 430-6781
  Quincy *(G-17852)*
Northern Illinois Gas Company.....E...... 630 983-8676
  Kankakee *(G-12640)*
Northern Illinois Gas Company.....F...... 217 357-3105
  Carthage *(G-3318)*
Northern Illinois Gas Company.....C...... 630 983-8676
  Crystal Lake *(G-7620)*
Northern Illinois Gas Company.....D...... 815 433-3850
  Ottawa *(G-16972)*
Northern Illinois Gas Company.....C...... 815 693-3907
  Joliet *(G-12546)*
Northern Illinois Gas Company.....F...... 815 223-8097
  Mendota *(G-14729)*

## NATURAL GAS LIQUIDS PRODUCTION
Aux Sable Liquid Products LP .............. E ....... 815 941-5800
  Morris (G-15095)
Aux Sable Midstream LLC ..................... E ....... 815 941-5800
  Morris (G-15096)

## NATURAL GAS LIQUIDS PRODUCTION
Enterprise Products Company ............. G ....... 708 534-6266
  Monee (G-14993)
Ferrellgas LP ............................................ G ....... 815 877-7333
  Machesney Park (G-14073)
FMC Technologies Inc ........................... G ....... 312 803-4321
  Chicago (G-4865)

## NATURAL GAS PRODUCTION
La Quinta Gas Pipeline Company ........ G ....... 217 430-6781
  Quincy (G-17852)
Midco Production Co Inc ........................ G ....... 630 655-2198
  Westmont (G-21907)
Natural Gas Pipeline Amer LLC ........... F ....... 815 426-2151
  Herscher (G-11760)

## NATURAL GAS TRANSMISSION
Natural Gas Pipeline Amer LLC ........... E ....... 618 495-2211
  Centralia (G-3423)
Natural Gas Pipeline Amer LLC ........... E ....... 618 829-3224
  Saint Elmo (G-19309)

## NATURAL GAS TRANSMISSION & DISTRIBUTION
Northern Illinois Gas Company ............ E ....... 630 983-8676
  Kankakee (G-12640)
Northern Illinois Gas Company ............ F ....... 217 357-3105
  Carthage (G-3318)
Northern Illinois Gas Company ........... C ....... 630 983-8676
  Crystal Lake (G-7620)
Northern Illinois Gas Company ........... D ....... 815 433-3850
  Ottawa (G-16972)
Northern Illinois Gas Company ........... C ....... 815 693-3907
  Joliet (G-12546)

## NATURAL GASOLINE PRODUCTION
15679 Wadsworth Inc ............................. G ....... 847 662-4561
  Wadsworth (G-21321)
Alliance Pipeline Inc .............................. G ....... 815 941-5874
  Morris (G-15092)

## NATURAL PROPANE PRODUCTION
Ferrellgas LP ............................................ G ....... 815 599-8967
  Machesney Park (G-14074)

## NAVIGATIONAL SYSTEMS & INSTRUMENTS
Auxitrol SA ............................................... G ....... 815 874-2471
  Rockford (G-18272)
Brunswick International Ltd ................. G ....... 847 735-4700
  Lake Forest (G-12889)
Kvh Industries Inc ................................. E ....... 708 444-2800
  Tinley Park (G-20927)
Navigo Technologies LLC ..................... G ....... 312 560-9257
  Geneva (G-10852)
Navman Wireless North Amer Ltd ...... E ....... 866 527-9896
  Glenview (G-11172)
Zebra Entp Solutions Corp .................. E ....... 847 634-6700
  Lincolnshire (G-13493)

## NEEDLES
Newell Operating Company ................. C ....... 815 235-4171
  Freeport (G-10675)

## NETTING: Plastic
Shannon Industries Inc ........................ G ....... 815 338-8960
  Woodstock (G-22610)

## NEW & USED CAR DEALERS
Diecasm LLC ........................................... G ....... 877 343-2276
  Buffalo Grove (G-2687)

## NEWS DEALERS & NEWSSTANDS
Bureau Valley Chief ............................... G ....... 815 646-4731
  Tiskilwa (G-20958)
Chrisman Leader .................................... G ....... 217 269-2811
  Chrisman (G-7173)

## NEWS FEATURE SYNDICATES
Chicago Tribune Company ................... A ....... 312 222-3232
  Chicago (G-4357)

## NEWS SYNDICATES
Sun Times News Agency ....................... G ....... 815 672-1260
  Streator (G-20706)

## NEWSPAPERS & PERIODICALS NEWS REPORTING SVCS
Central Ill Communications LLC .......... F ....... 217 753-2226
  Springfield (G-20413)

## NEWSPAPERS, WHOLESALE
Ocs America Inc ..................................... E ....... 630 595-0111
  Wood Dale (G-22409)
Paddock Publications Inc .................... D ....... 630 955-3500
  Lisle (G-13638)

## NEWSSTAND
Daily Egyptian Siu Newspaper ............. D ....... 618 536-3311
  Carbondale (G-3005)
Herald Whig Quincy ............................... G ....... 217 222-7600
  Quincy (G-17835)
Ocs America Inc ..................................... E ....... 630 595-0111
  Wood Dale (G-22409)

## NICKEL ALLOY
Alloy Rod Products Inc ......................... G ....... 815 562-8200
  Aurora (G-1105)
Daniel J Nickel & Assocs PC ............... G ....... 312 345-1850
  Chicago (G-4553)
Double Nickel Holdings LLC ................ G ....... 618 476-3200
  Millstadt (G-14824)
Nickel Putter .......................................... G ....... 312 337-7888
  Chicago (G-5911)
Nickels Electric ...................................... G ....... 309 676-1350
  Peoria (G-17418)
Nickels Quarters LLC ............................ G ....... 630 514-5779
  Downers Grove (G-8495)
Wooden Nickel Pub and Grill ............... G ....... 618 288-2141
  Glen Carbon (G-10955)

## NONAROMATIC CHEMICAL PRDTS
Indilab Inc .............................................. E ....... 847 928-1050
  Franklin Park (G-10496)

## NONCLASSIFIABLE ESTABLISHMENTS
Apser Laboratory Inc ........................... D ....... 630 543-3333
  Addison (G-42)

## NONCURRENT CARRYING WIRING DEVICES
Aco Inc ..................................................... E ....... 773 774-5200
  Chicago (G-3735)
Chase Corporation ................................. F ....... 630 752-3622
  Wheaton (G-21940)
Chase Corporation ................................. F ....... 708 385-4679
  Palos Heights (G-17101)
Chicago Switchboard Co Inc ............... E ....... 630 833-2266
  Elmhurst (G-9848)
Eaton Corporation ................................. A ....... 217 732-3131
  Lincoln (G-13409)
Excel Specialty Corp ............................. E ....... 773 262-7575
  Lake Forest (G-12898)
Methode Development Co .................... D ....... 708 867-6777
  Chicago (G-5703)
Minerallac Company ............................. G ....... 630 543-7080
  Hampshire (G-11554)
Questek Manufacturing Corp .............. D ....... 847 428-0300
  Elgin (G-9159)
Taurus Safety Products Inc ................ G ....... 630 620-7940
  Lombard (G-13865)
Vertiv Group Corporation .................... E ....... 630 579-5000
  Lombard (G-13878)

## NONDURABLE GOODS WHOLESALERS, NEC
Modern Methods Creative Inc ............. G ....... 309 263-4100
  Peoria (G-17410)

## NONFERROUS: Rolling & Drawing, NEC
American/Jebco Corporation ............... C ....... 847 455-3150
  Franklin Park (G-10394)

Cooper B-Line Inc .................................. A ....... 618 654-2184
  Highland (G-11780)
Dupage Products Group ....................... D ....... 630 969-7200
  Downers Grove (G-8435)
Guardian Rollform LLC ......................... D ....... 847 382-8074
  Lake Barrington (G-12808)
Hadley Gear Manufacturing Co ........... F ....... 773 722-1030
  Chicago (G-5028)
Red Devil Manufacturing Co ................ G ....... 847 215-1377
  Wheeling (G-22134)
Suburban Industries Inc ...................... F ....... 630 766-3773
  Franklin Park (G-10597)
Tinsley Steel Inc .................................... G ....... 618 656-5231
  Edwardsville (G-8817)
Townley Engrg & Mfg Co Inc ................ F ....... 618 273-8271
  Eldorado (G-8924)
Wagner Zip-Change Inc ........................ E ....... 708 681-4100
  Melrose Park (G-14706)

## NONMETALLIC MINERALS DEVELOPMENT & TEST BORING SVC
Montana Minerals Dev Co ..................... G ....... 800 426-5564
  Arlington Heights (G-804)

## NONMETALLIC MINERALS: Support Activities, Exc Fuels
Harsco Corporation ............................... G ....... 309 347-1962
  Pekin (G-17266)
Hastie Mining & Trucking ..................... G ....... 618 285-3600
  Rosiclare (G-19048)
Illinois Valley Minerals LLC ................. G ....... 815 442-8402
  Tonica (G-20974)
Raimonde Drilling Corp ........................ F ....... 630 458-0590
  Addison (G-268)
Vigo Coal Operating Co Inc ................. C ....... 618 262-7022
  Mount Carmel (G-15286)

## NOTIONS: Button Backs & Parts
Handy Button Machine Co .................... E ....... 847 459-0900
  Wheeling (G-22067)
Matchless Parisian Novelty Inc ........... G ....... 773 924-1515
  Chicago (G-5650)

## NOTIONS: Pins, Hair, Exc Rubber
STA-Rite Ginnie Lou Inc ....................... F ....... 217 774-3921
  Shelbyville (G-19916)

## NOTIONS: Pins, Straight, Steel Or Brass
Aerofast Inc ............................................ E ....... 630 668-6575
  Carol Stream (G-3091)

## NOVELTIES
Creative Werks LLC ............................... E ....... 630 860-2222
  Bartlett (G-1340)
Creative Werks LLC ............................... E ....... 630 860-2222
  Bensenville (G-1871)
Hangables Inc ......................................... F ....... 847 673-9770
  Skokie (G-20010)
M & A Grocery ........................................ G ....... 708 749-9786
  Stickney (G-20624)
Marshall Manufacturing LLC ............... G ....... 312 914-7288
  Chicago (G-5631)
Ramona Sedivy ...................................... G ....... 630 983-1902
  Naperville (G-15738)
Slagel Manufacturing Inc ..................... E ....... 815 688-3318
  Forrest (G-10267)

## NOVELTIES & SPECIALTIES: Metal
Lynda Hervas .......................................... G ....... 847 985-1690
  Schaumburg (G-19627)
Metal Strip Buiding Products .............. G ....... 847 742-8500
  Itasca (G-12314)
Midland Metal Products Co .................. D ....... 773 927-5700
  Chicago (G-5735)
Midland Stamping and Fabg Corp ....... D ....... 847 678-7573
  Schiller Park (G-19851)
Progressive Bronze Works Inc ............ E ....... 773 463-5500
  Chicago (G-6211)
Renner & Co ............................................ F ....... 847 639-4900
  Cary (G-3366)
Wiremasters Incorporated ................... E ....... 773 254-3700
  Chicago (G-7005)

## PRODUCT SECTION

### OFFICE SPLY & STATIONERY STORES: Office Forms & Splys

### NOVELTIES: Plastic
- Adams Apple Distributing LP .......... E ...... 847 832-9900
  Glenview *(G-11095)*
- Spirit Foodservice Inc .......... C ...... 214 634-1393
  Lake Forest *(G-12962)*

### NOVELTY SHOPS
- Andy Dallas & Co .......... F ...... 217 351-5974
  Champaign *(G-3450)*
- Budget Signs .......... F ...... 618 259-4460
  Wood River *(G-22441)*
- Compu-Tap Inc .......... G ...... 708 594-5773
  Summit Argo *(G-20761)*

### NOZZLES & SPRINKLERS Lawn Hose
- Fiskars Brands Inc .......... F ...... 800 635-7668
  Peoria *(G-17362)*
- Leyden Lawn Sprinklers .......... E ...... 630 665-5520
  Glen Ellyn *(G-10976)*
- Suncast Corporation .......... A ...... 630 879-2050
  Batavia *(G-1501)*

### NOZZLES: Fire Fighting
- Max Fire Training Inc .......... F ...... 618 210-2079
  Godfrey *(G-11228)*

### NOZZLES: Spray, Aerosol, Paint Or Insecticide
- Lechler Inc .......... D ...... 630 377-6611
  Saint Charles *(G-19208)*
- Spraying Systems Co .......... A ...... 630 665-5000
  Glendale Heights *(G-11072)*
- Spraying Systems Co .......... F ...... 630 665-5001
  Aurora *(G-1082)*
- Spraying Systems Midwest Inc .......... G ...... 630 665-5000
  Glendale Heights *(G-11073)*
- Strebor Specialties LLC .......... E ...... 618 286-1140
  Dupo *(G-8580)*

### NUCLEAR FUELS SCRAP REPROCESSING
- Lattice Energy LLC .......... G ...... 312 861-0115
  Chicago *(G-5466)*

### NUCLEAR REACTORS: Military Or Indl
- Spectrum Technologies Intl Ltd .......... G ...... 630 961-5244
  Woodridge *(G-22518)*

### NURSERIES & LAWN & GARDEN SPLY STORE, RET: Fountain, Outdoor
- Smart Solar Inc .......... F ...... 813 343-5770
  Libertyville *(G-13382)*

### NURSERIES & LAWN & GARDEN SPLY STORES, RETAIL: Fertilizer
- Allerton Supply Company .......... F ...... 217 896-2522
  Homer *(G-12074)*
- Piatt County Service Co .......... G ...... 217 489-2411
  Mansfield *(G-14178)*
- Piatt County Service Co .......... G ...... 217 678-5511
  Bement *(G-1801)*
- Sun Ag Inc .......... G ...... 309 726-1331
  Hudson *(G-12126)*

### NURSERIES & LAWN & GARDEN SPLY STORES, RETAIL: Lawn Ornament
- In The Attic Inc .......... G ...... 847 949-5077
  Mundelein *(G-15509)*

### NURSERIES & LAWN & GARDEN SPLY STORES, RETAIL: Top Soil
- Jacobs Trucking .......... G ...... 618 687-3578
  Murphysboro *(G-15577)*
- Markman Peat Corp .......... E ...... 815 772-4014
  Morrison *(G-15146)*

### NURSERIES & LAWN/GARDEN SPLY STORE, RET: Lawnmowers/Tractors
- Gibson Insurance Inc .......... G ...... 217 864-4877
  Mount Zion *(G-15451)*
- Lakenburges Motor Co .......... G ...... 618 523-4231
  Germantown *(G-10893)*
- Outdoor Power Inc .......... F ...... 217 228-9890
  Quincy *(G-17865)*
- Owen Walker .......... G ...... 217 285-4012
  Pittsfield *(G-17572)*
- Peoria Midwest Equipment Inc .......... G ...... 309 454-6800
  Normal *(G-16083)*
- West Side Tractor Sales Co .......... E ...... 815 961-3160
  Rockford *(G-18678)*

### NURSERIES & LAWN/GARDEN SPLY STORES, RET: Garden Splys/Tools
- Albert F Amling LLC .......... C ...... 630 333-1720
  Elmhurst *(G-9832)*
- Gds Enterprises .......... G ...... 217 543-3681
  Arthur *(G-901)*
- Kaser Power Equipment Inc .......... G ...... 309 289-2176
  Knoxville *(G-12721)*

### NURSERIES/LAWN/GARDEN SPLY STORE, RET: Grdn Tractors/Tillers
- Service Auto Supply .......... F ...... 309 444-9704
  Washington *(G-21392)*

### NURSERY & GARDEN CENTERS
- Tim Wallace Ldscp Sup Co Inc .......... F ...... 630 759-6813
  Bolingbrook *(G-2379)*
- West Central Fs Inc .......... G ...... 309 375-6904
  Wataga *(G-21399)*

### NURSING CARE FACILITIES: Skilled
- McKnights Long Term Care News .......... G ...... 847 559-2884
  Northbrook *(G-16308)*
- Willims-Hyward Intl Ctings Inc .......... F ...... 708 458-0015
  Argo *(G-698)*

### NUTRITION SVCS
- Wellness Center Usa Inc .......... G ...... 847 925-1885
  Hoffman Estates *(G-12069)*

### NUTS: Metal
- Aztech Engineering Inc .......... E ...... 630 236-3200
  Aurora *(G-964)*
- Century Fasteners & Mch Co Inc .......... F ...... 773 463-3900
  Skokie *(G-19977)*
- Folkerts Manufacturing Inc .......... G ...... 815 968-7426
  Rockford *(G-18385)*
- Hill Holdings Inc .......... E ...... 815 625-6600
  Rock Falls *(G-18135)*
- Locknut Technology Inc .......... G ...... 630 628-5330
  Addison *(G-182)*
- Mac Lean-Fogg Company .......... D ...... 847 566-0010
  Mundelein *(G-15521)*
- Security Locknut LLC .......... F ...... 847 970-4050
  Vernon Hills *(G-21200)*

### OCHER MINING
- Flint Hills Resources LP .......... D ...... 815 224-1525
  Peru *(G-17509)*

### OFFICE EQPT & ACCESSORY CUSTOMIZING SVCS
- Addison Business Systems Inc .......... G ...... 708 371-5454
  Palos Heights *(G-17098)*
- Laser Innovations Inc .......... F ...... 217 522-8580
  Springfield *(G-20467)*

### OFFICE EQPT WHOLESALERS
- Carnation Enterprises .......... G ...... 847 804-5928
  Niles *(G-15967)*
- CDs Office Systems Inc .......... D ...... 800 367-1508
  Springfield *(G-20410)*
- CDs Office Systems Inc .......... G ...... 217 351-5046
  Champaign *(G-3464)*
- CDs Office Systems Inc .......... F ...... 630 305-9034
  Springfield *(G-20411)*
- H A Friend & Company Inc .......... E ...... 847 746-1248
  Zion *(G-22687)*
- Klai-Co Idntification Pdts Inc .......... F ...... 847 573-0375
  Lake Forest *(G-12921)*
- Komori America Corporation .......... D ...... 847 806-9000
  Rolling Meadows *(G-18739)*
- Sws Industries Inc .......... E ...... 904 482-0091
  Woodstock *(G-22616)*
- Xerox Corporation .......... E ...... 630 573-1000
  Hinsdale *(G-11969)*

### OFFICE FIXTURES: Wood
- Contract Industries Inc .......... E ...... 708 458-8150
  Bedford Park *(G-1545)*
- Hanley Design Inc .......... G ...... 309 682-9665
  Peoria *(G-17378)*
- Hire-Nelson Company Inc .......... E ...... 630 543-9400
  Addison *(G-146)*

### OFFICE FURNITURE REPAIR & MAINTENANCE SVCS
- Gavin Woodworking Inc .......... G ...... 815 786-2242
  Sandwich *(G-19365)*

### OFFICE MACHINES, NEC
- Lason Inc .......... G ...... 217 893-1515
  Rantoul *(G-17933)*
- Neopost R Meadows .......... G ...... 630 467-0604
  Itasca *(G-12329)*

### OFFICE SPLY & STATIONERY STORES
- A 1 Marking Products .......... G ...... 309 762-6096
  Moline *(G-14916)*
- Ashleys Inc .......... G ...... 630 794-0804
  Hinsdale *(G-11939)*
- CDs Office Systems Inc .......... F ...... 630 305-9034
  Springfield *(G-20411)*
- W/S Packaging Group Inc .......... G ...... 847 658-7363
  Algonquin *(G-411)*
- Write Stuff .......... G ...... 630 365-4425
  Saint Charles *(G-19300)*

### OFFICE SPLY & STATIONERY STORES: Office Forms & Splys
- Balsley Printing Inc .......... G ...... 815 637-8787
  Rockton *(G-18691)*
- Capitol Impressions Inc .......... E ...... 309 633-1400
  Peoria *(G-17322)*
- Clover Technologies Group LLC .......... B ...... 815 431-8100
  Ottawa *(G-16957)*
- Copy Service Inc .......... G ...... 815 758-1151
  Dekalb *(G-8079)*
- Corporation Supply Co Inc .......... E ...... 312 726-3375
  Chicago *(G-4476)*
- Dans Printing & Off Sups Inc .......... F ...... 708 687-3055
  Oak Forest *(G-16577)*
- Donnells Printing & Off Pdts .......... G ...... 815 842-6541
  Pontiac *(G-17698)*
- East Moline Herald Print Inc .......... G ...... 309 755-5224
  East Moline *(G-8678)*
- Fast Print Shop .......... G ...... 618 997-1976
  Marion *(G-14259)*
- Franz Stationery Company Inc .......... F ...... 847 593-0060
  Lake Barrington *(G-12807)*
- Gallery Office Pdts & Prtrs .......... G ...... 708 798-2220
  Homewood *(G-12099)*
- Gazette Democrat .......... E ...... 618 833-2150
  Anna *(G-603)*
- Go Calendars .......... G ...... 847 816-1563
  Vernon Hills *(G-21166)*
- Gold Nugget Publications Inc .......... E ...... 217 965-3355
  Virden *(G-21297)*
- Hardin County Independent .......... F ...... 618 287-2361
  Elizabethtown *(G-9246)*
- Hub Printing Company Inc .......... G ...... 815 562-7057
  Rochelle *(G-18094)*
- James Ray Monroe Corporation .......... F ...... 618 532-4575
  Centralia *(G-3420)*
- Jds Printing Inc .......... G ...... 630 208-1195
  Glendale Heights *(G-11037)*
- Merritt & Edwards Corporation .......... F ...... 309 828-4741
  Bloomington *(G-2196)*
- Mid-Central Business Forms .......... G ...... 309 692-9090
  Peoria *(G-17406)*
- OfficeMax North America Inc .......... E ...... 815 748-3007
  Dekalb *(G-8111)*
- Reign Print Solutions Inc .......... G ...... 847 590-7091
  Arlington Heights *(G-830)*
- Ro-Web Inc .......... G ...... 309 688-2155
  Peoria *(G-17444)*
- Selnar Inc .......... G ...... 309 699-3977
  East Peoria *(G-8733)*

---

Employee Codes: A=Over 500 employees, B=251-500
C=101-250, D=51-100, E=20-50, F=10-19, G=3-9

2017 Harris Illinois Industrial Directory

## OFFICE SPLY & STATIONERY STORES: Office Forms & Splys

Sigley Printing & Off Sup Co .................... G ....... 618 997-5304
  Marion *(G-14287)*
Supreme Screw Inc .................................. G ....... 630 226-9000
  Romeoville *(G-18872)*
Weimer Design & Print Ltd Inc ................. G ....... 630 393-3334
  Warrenville *(G-21368)*
Xertrex International Inc ........................... E ....... 630 773-4020
  Itasca *(G-12375)*

### OFFICE SPLY & STATIONERY STORES: Writing Splys

A & E Rubber Stamp Corp ........................ G ....... 312 575-1416
  Chicago *(G-3679)*

### OFFICE SPLYS, NEC, WHOLESALE

Bar Codes Inc .......................................... F ....... 800 351-9962
  Chicago *(G-4039)*
Franz Stationery Company Inc ................. F ....... 847 593-0060
  Lake Barrington *(G-12807)*
Graphic Source Group Inc ....................... G ....... 847 854-2670
  Lake In The Hills *(G-12995)*
H A Friend & Company Inc ....................... E ....... 847 746-1248
  Zion *(G-22687)*
J M Printers Inc ....................................... F ....... 815 727-1579
  Crest Hill *(G-7459)*
Klai-Co Idntification Pdts Inc ..................... E ....... 847 573-0375
  Lake Forest *(G-12921)*
Lewis Paper Place Inc ............................. G ....... 847 808-1343
  Wheeling *(G-22093)*
Rehabilitation and Vocational .................. E ....... 618 833-5344
  Anna *(G-608)*
S G C M Corp .......................................... G ....... 630 953-2428
  Oakbrook Terrace *(G-16720)*

### OFFICES & CLINICS OF DENTISTS: Dental Clinic

Indilab Inc ............................................... E ....... 847 928-1050
  Franklin Park *(G-10496)*

### OFFICES & CLINICS OF DENTISTS: Dental Clinics & Offices

Lmpl Management Corporation ............... G ....... 708 636-2443
  Oak Lawn *(G-16631)*

### OFFICES & CLINICS OF DOCTORS OF MEDICINE: Dermatologist

Michael A Greenberg MD Ltd ................... F ....... 847 364-4717
  Elk Grove Village *(G-9625)*

### OFFICES & CLINICS OF DOCTORS OF MEDICINE: Gynecologist

Samel Botros .......................................... G ....... 847 466-5905
  Bloomingdale *(G-2134)*

### OFFICES & CLINICS OF DRS OF MEDICINE: Med Clinic, Pri Care

First Step Womens Center ...................... G ....... 217 523-0100
  Springfield *(G-20441)*

### OFFICES & CLINICS OF DRS, MED: Specialized Practitioners

Dean Prsthtic Orthtic Svcs Ltd .................. G ....... 847 475-7080
  Evanston *(G-10026)*

### OFFICES & CLINICS OF HEALTH PRACTITIONERS: Nutrition

Natures Best Inc ..................................... E ....... 631 232-3355
  Downers Grove *(G-8493)*

### OFFICES & CLINICS OF HEALTH PRACTITIONERS: Physical Therapy

Deborah Morris Gulbrandson Pt ............... F ....... 847 639-4140
  Cary *(G-3333)*

### OFFICES & CLINICS OF HEALTH PRACTITIONERS: Speech Therapist

Janelle Publications Inc .......................... G ....... 815 756-2300
  Dekalb *(G-8100)*

## OIL & GAS FIELD EQPT: Drill Rigs

H & H Drilling Co ..................................... G ....... 618 529-3697
  Carbondale *(G-3008)*

## OIL & GAS FIELD MACHINERY

Arid Technologies Inc .............................. E ....... 630 681-8500
  Wheaton *(G-21936)*
Bartec Orb Inc ......................................... E ....... 773 927-8600
  Chicago *(G-4051)*
Cortelyou Machine & Welding .................. G ....... 618 592-3961
  Oblong *(G-16730)*
Emerson Electric Co ................................ G ....... 312 803-4321
  Chicago *(G-4742)*
Green Investment Group Inc .................... G ....... 618 465-7277
  Alton *(G-576)*
Maass Midwest Mfg Inc ........................... G ....... 847 669-5135
  Huntley *(G-12160)*
Proppant Frac Sand LLC ......................... G ....... 815 942-2467
  Morris *(G-15128)*
Royal Brass Inc ....................................... G ....... 618 439-6341
  Benton *(G-2040)*
Triad Oil Inc ............................................ G ....... 815 485-9535
  New Lenox *(G-15923)*
Trusty Warns Inc .................................... E ....... 630 766-9015
  Wood Dale *(G-22434)*
U O P Equitec Services Inc ...................... A ....... 847 391-2000
  Des Plaines *(G-8288)*

## OIL FIELD MACHINERY & EQPT

Big Als Machines Inc .............................. G ....... 618 963-2619
  Enfield *(G-9987)*
Dnow LP ................................................. G ....... 618 842-9176
  Fairfield *(G-10139)*
Dover Artificial Lift Intl LLC ....................... F ....... 630 743-2563
  Downers Grove *(G-8430)*
Gemtar Inc .............................................. G ....... 618 548-1353
  Salem *(G-19334)*
Squibb Tank Company ............................ G ....... 618 548-0141
  Salem *(G-19352)*

## OIL FIELD SVCS, NEC

B & B Equipment .................................... F ....... 217 562-2511
  Assumption *(G-930)*
Baker Hghes Oilfld Oprtions Inc ............... F ....... 618 393-2919
  Olney *(G-16761)*
Bangert Casing Pulling Corp ................... G ....... 618 676-1411
  Clay City *(G-7262)*
Campbell Energy LLC ............................. G ....... 618 382-3939
  Carmi *(G-3063)*
Citation Oil & Gas Corp ............................ G ....... 618 548-2331
  Odin *(G-16739)*
Concord Oil & Gas Corporation ............... E ....... 618 393-2124
  Olney *(G-16764)*
Cross Oil & Well Service Inc .................... F ....... 618 592-4609
  Oblong *(G-16731)*
Duncan Oil Company Inc ......................... G ....... 618 548-2923
  Salem *(G-19330)*
F L Beard Service Corp ........................... E ....... 618 262-5193
  Mount Carmel *(G-15265)*
Feller Oilfield Service Inc ......................... F ....... 618 267-5650
  Saint Elmo *(G-19307)*
M & L Well Service Inc ............................ G ....... 618 393-7144
  Olney *(G-16778)*
Mid-States Services LLC ........................ F ....... 618 842-4726
  Fairfield *(G-10151)*
Oelze Equipment Company LLC ............. G ....... 618 327-9111
  Nashville *(G-15845)*
P J Repair Service Inc ............................ F ....... 618 548-5690
  Salem *(G-19341)*
Petco Petroleum Corporation .................. G ....... 630 654-1740
  Hinsdale *(G-11956)*
Pinnacle Exploration Corp ....................... G ....... 618 395-8100
  Olney *(G-16790)*
Roark Oil Field Services Inc .................... G ....... 618 382-4703
  Carmi *(G-3078)*
Seip Service & Supply Inc ....................... G ....... 618 532-1923
  Centralia *(G-3432)*
Tdw Services Inc .................................... F ....... 815 407-0675
  Romeoville *(G-18873)*
Tri Kote Inc ............................................. G ....... 618 262-4156
  Mount Carmel *(G-15285)*
Warren Service Company ....................... G ....... 618 384-2117
  Carmi *(G-3083)*

## OIL TREATING COMPOUNDS

Afton Chemical Corporation .................... E ....... 708 728-1546
  Bedford Park *(G-1533)*
Express Care .......................................... G ....... 815 521-2185
  Channahon *(G-3575)*
Lubrizol Corporation ............................... F ....... 630 355-3605
  Naperville *(G-15694)*

## OILS & ESSENTIAL OILS

Fragrance Island ..................................... G ....... 773 488-2700
  Chicago *(G-4881)*
Jeanblanc International Inc ...................... G ....... 815 598-3400
  Elizabeth *(G-9242)*

## OILS & GREASES: Blended & Compounded

Calumet Lubr Co Ltd Partnr ..................... F ....... 708 832-2463
  Burnham *(G-2815)*
CLC Lubricants Company ....................... E ....... 630 232-7900
  Geneva *(G-10818)*
Clean Harbors Wichita LLC ..................... G ....... 815 675-1272
  Spring Grove *(G-20330)*
Harris Lubricants .................................... G ....... 708 849-1935
  Dolton *(G-8370)*
Illinois Oil Products Inc ............................ F ....... 309 788-1896
  Rock Island *(G-18183)*
Konzen Chemicals Inc ............................ G ....... 708 878-7636
  Matteson *(G-14375)*
Motor Oil Inc ........................................... F ....... 847 956-7550
  Elk Grove Village *(G-9639)*
Mullen Circle Brand Inc .......................... G ....... 847 676-1880
  Skokie *(G-20042)*
Perkins Products Inc .............................. E ....... 708 458-2000
  Bedford Park *(G-1572)*
Premium Oil Company ............................ F ....... 815 963-3800
  Rockford *(G-18540)*
Strebor Specialties LLC .......................... E ....... 618 286-1140
  Dupo *(G-8580)*
Syn-Tech Ltd .......................................... E ....... 630 628-3044
  Addison *(G-303)*
Truckers Oil Pros Inc .............................. F ....... 773 523-8990
  Chicago *(G-6785)*
Viscosity Oil Company ............................ E ....... 630 850-4000
  Willowbrook *(G-22237)*

## OILS & GREASES: Lubricating

Ameriflon Ltd .......................................... G ....... 847 541-6000
  Wheeling *(G-22004)*
Amsoil Inc .............................................. G ....... 630 595-8385
  Bensenville *(G-1835)*
Avatar Corporation .................................. D ....... 708 534-5511
  University Park *(G-21042)*
Bioblend Lubricants Intl .......................... G ....... 630 227-1800
  Joliet *(G-12466)*
Boyer Corporation ................................... G ....... 708 352-2553
  La Grange *(G-12727)*
Campbell Camie Inc ............................... E ....... 314 968-3222
  Downers Grove *(G-8403)*
Cargill Incorporated ................................ F ....... 773 375-7255
  Chicago *(G-4243)*
Castrol Industrial N Amer Inc .................. C ....... 877 641-1600
  Naperville *(G-15620)*
Chemix Corp .......................................... F ....... 708 754-2150
  Glenwood *(G-11215)*
Chemtool Incorporated ........................... C ....... 815 957-4140
  Rockton *(G-18694)*
Chemtool Incorporated ........................... D ....... 815 459-1250
  Crystal Lake *(G-7551)*
Claire-Sprayway Inc ............................... D ....... 630 628-3000
  Downers Grove *(G-8413)*
Comet Supply Inc ................................... G ....... 309 444-2712
  Washington *(G-21381)*
Darling Ingredients Inc ............................ G ....... 217 482-3261
  Mason City *(G-14363)*
Ecli Products LLC ................................... E ....... 630 449-5000
  Aurora *(G-1000)*
Enterprise Oil Co .................................... E ....... 312 487-2025
  Chicago *(G-4759)*
Famous Lubricants Inc ........................... G ....... 773 268-2555
  Chicago *(G-4811)*
Filter Kleen Inc ....................................... G ....... 708 447-4666
  Lyons *(G-14037)*
Fuchs Corporation .................................. G ....... 800 323-7755
  Harvey *(G-11667)*
Growmark Energy LLC ........................... G ....... 309 557-6000
  Bloomington *(G-2174)*
Havoline Xpress Lube LLC ..................... G ....... 847 221-5724
  Palatine *(G-17034)*
Havoline Xpress Lube LLC ..................... F ....... 224 757-5628
  Round Lake *(G-19060)*
Ideas Inc ................................................ G ....... 630 620-2010
  Lombard *(G-13812)*

# PRODUCT SECTION

## OPTICAL GOODS STORES: Eyeglasses, Prescription

Ideas Inc .................................................G...... 708 596-1055
  Harvey  *(G-11671)*
Jcl Specialty Products Inc ....................G...... 815 806-2202
  Mokena  *(G-14876)*
Jx Nippon Oil & Energy Lubrica ...........F...... 847 413-2188
  Schaumburg  *(G-19594)*
K & J Synthetic Lubricants ....................G...... 630 628-1011
  Addison  *(G-162)*
Kostelac Grease Service Inc ..................E...... 314 436-7166
  Belleville  *(G-1646)*
Lub-Tek Petroleum Products ..................G...... 815 741-0414
  Joliet  *(G-12534)*
Lubrication Technology Inc ....................G...... 740 574-5150
  Aurora  *(G-1048)*
Midwest Recycling Co ...........................E...... 815 744-4922
  Rockdale  *(G-18227)*
Nalco Holding Company .......................D...... 630 305-1000
  Naperville  *(G-15706)*
Nanolube Inc .........................................G...... 630 706-1250
  Lombard  *(G-13831)*
Olympic Petroleum Corporation ............D...... 847 995-0996
  Schaumburg  *(G-19674)*
Olympic Petroleum Corporation ............D...... 708 876-7900
  Cicero  *(G-7223)*
Pdv Midwest Refining LLC ...................A...... 630 257-7761
  Lemont  *(G-13254)*
Polartech Additives Inc .........................E...... 708 458-8450
  Bedford Park  *(G-1573)*
Polyenviro Labs Inc ..............................G...... 708 489-0195
  Mokena  *(G-14896)*
Rilco Fluid Care .....................................E...... 309 788-1854
  Rock Island  *(G-18200)*
Rock Valley Oil & Chemical Co ..............E...... 815 654-2400
  Loves Park  *(G-13983)*
Rs Used Oil Services Inc ......................G...... 618 781-1717
  Roxana  *(G-19085)*
Sandstrom Products Company ..............F...... 309 523-2121
  Port Byron  *(G-17724)*
Shima American Corporation .................F...... 630 760-4330
  Itasca  *(G-12353)*
Spartacus Group Inc .............................F...... 815 637-1574
  Machesney Park  *(G-14108)*
Specialized Separators Inc ....................F...... 815 316-0626
  Rockford  *(G-18625)*
Superior Graphite Co .............................E...... 708 458-0006
  Chicago  *(G-6633)*
Tower Oil & Technology Co ....................E...... 773 927-6161
  Chicago  *(G-6752)*
Uberlube Inc ..........................................G...... 847 372-3127
  Evanston  *(G-10103)*

### OILS, ANIMAL OR VEGETABLE, WHOLESALE

Archer-Daniels-Midland Company .........D...... 217 224-1875
  Quincy  *(G-17796)*
Vantage Specialties Inc ........................F...... 847 244-3410
  Chicago  *(G-6875)*

### OILS: Cutting

Illini Coolant Management Corp ............F...... 847 966-1079
  Morton Grove  *(G-15201)*
Mistic Metal Mover Inc ..........................G...... 815 875-1371
  Princeton  *(G-17754)*

### OILS: Essential

Arbor Products ......................................G...... 847 653-6210
  Park Ridge  *(G-17182)*
Sensory Essence Inc ............................G...... 847 526-3645
  Island Lake  *(G-12218)*
Super-Dri Corp ......................................G...... 708 599-8700
  Bridgeview  *(G-2532)*

### OILS: Lubricating

Apple Lube Center ................................G...... 217 787-7035
  Springfield  *(G-20387)*
E Z Lube ...............................................G...... 815 439-3980
  Joliet  *(G-12487)*
Lamson Oil Company ............................G...... 815 226-8090
  Rockford  *(G-18461)*
Power Lube LLC ...................................G...... 847 806-7022
  Elk Grove Village  *(G-9690)*

### OILS: Lubricating

Atm America Corp .................................E...... 800 298-0030
  Chicago  *(G-3986)*
CAM Tek Lubricants Inc ........................G...... 708 477-3000
  Orland Park  *(G-16846)*

Gtx Inc ..................................................G...... 847 699-7421
  Des Plaines  *(G-8203)*
High Performance Lubr LLC .................G...... 815 468-3535
  Manteno  *(G-14185)*
Huels Oil Company ...............................F...... 877 338-6277
  Carlyle  *(G-3054)*
Nalco Company LLC .............................A...... 630 305-1000
  Naperville  *(G-15703)*
Nalco Holdings LLC ..............................A...... 630 305-1000
  Naperville  *(G-15707)*
Speedco Inc .........................................G...... 618 931-1575
  Granite City  *(G-11304)*
William Ingram .....................................G...... 217 442-5075
  Danville  *(G-7785)*

### OILS: Peppermint

Wm Wrigley Jr Company ......................B...... 312 280-4710
  Chicago  *(G-7012)*
Wm Wrigley Jr Company ......................A...... 312 644-2121
  Chicago  *(G-7014)*

### OINTMENTS

Blistex Inc ............................................C...... 630 571-2870
  Oak Brook  *(G-16493)*
Blistex Inc ............................................G...... 630 571-2870
  Oak Brook  *(G-16494)*

### ON-LINE DATABASE INFORMATION RETRIEVAL SVCS

AR Inet Corp ........................................G...... 603 380-3903
  Aurora  *(G-959)*
Calutech Inc .........................................G...... 708 614-0228
  Orland Park  *(G-16845)*
Penton Media Inc .................................G...... 212 204-4200
  Chicago  *(G-6100)*

### OPERATOR TRAINING, COMPUTER

Friedrich Klatt and Associates ..............G...... 773 753-1806
  Chicago  *(G-4891)*
Mbm Business Assistance Inc .............G...... 217 398-6600
  Champaign  *(G-3512)*
Tunnel Vision Consulting Group ...........G...... 773 367-7292
  Chicago  *(G-6791)*

### OPERATOR: Apartment Buildings

Christopher Concrete Products .............G...... 618 724-2951
  Buckner  *(G-2647)*
Patty Style Shop ..................................G...... 618 654-2015
  Highland  *(G-11805)*

### OPERATOR: Nonresidential Buildings

D D G Inc .............................................G...... 847 412-0277
  Northbrook  *(G-16236)*
Littleson Inc .........................................G...... 815 968-8349
  Rockford  *(G-18471)*
Upper Urban Green Prprty Maint ..........G...... 312 218-5903
  Chicago  *(G-6841)*

### OPHTHALMIC GOODS

Asico LLC ............................................F...... 630 986-8032
  Westmont  *(G-21876)*
C & S Chemicals Inc ............................G...... 815 722-6671
  Joliet  *(G-12470)*
Clear Sight Inc .....................................G...... 630 323-3590
  Westmont  *(G-21880)*
G T Laboratories Inc .............................G...... 847 998-4776
  Lisle  *(G-13591)*
Hoya Corporation .................................C...... 618 281-3344
  Columbia  *(G-7358)*
Hoya Lens of Chicago Inc ....................E...... 847 678-4700
  Franklin Park  *(G-10490)*
Illmo R/X Service .................................G...... 217 877-1192
  Decatur  *(G-7893)*
Innova Systems Inc .............................G...... 630 920-8880
  Burr Ridge  *(G-2854)*
Lights Prosthetic Eyes Inc ....................G...... 309 676-3663
  Peoria  *(G-17401)*
M & S Technologies Inc .......................F...... 847 763-0500
  Niles  *(G-15997)*
Night Vision Corporation ......................G...... 847 677-7611
  Lincolnwood  *(G-13527)*
Quality Optical Inc ................................G...... 773 561-0870
  Chicago  *(G-6247)*
US Vision Inc .......................................G...... 847 367-0420
  Vernon Hills  *(G-21214)*

Walman Optical Company ....................E...... 309 787-0000
  Milan  *(G-14807)*
Waters Industries Inc ...........................E...... 847 783-5900
  West Dundee  *(G-21803)*
Weiner Optical Inc ................................G...... 708 848-4040
  Oak Park  *(G-16692)*
Ziemer Usa Inc ....................................F...... 618 462-9301
  Alton  *(G-595)*

### OPHTHALMIC GOODS WHOLESALERS

Asico LLC ............................................F...... 630 986-8032
  Westmont  *(G-21876)*
Hoya Lens of Chicago Inc ....................E...... 847 678-4700
  Franklin Park  *(G-10490)*
Illmo R/X Service .................................F...... 217 877-1192
  Decatur  *(G-7893)*
Two Tower Frames Inc .........................G...... 773 697-6856
  Chicago  *(G-6798)*
Western Ilinois Optical Inc ....................G...... 309 837-2000
  Macomb  *(G-14135)*

### OPHTHALMIC GOODS: Eyewear, Protective

Independent Eyewear Mfg LLC ............D...... 847 537-0008
  Vernon Hills  *(G-21175)*

### OPHTHALMIC GOODS: Frames & Parts, Eyeglass & Spectacle

Western Ilinois Optical Inc ....................G...... 309 837-2000
  Macomb  *(G-14135)*

### OPHTHALMIC GOODS: Frames, Lenses & Parts, Eyeglasses

Reding Optics Inc .................................G...... 708 301-2020
  Lockport  *(G-13741)*

### OPHTHALMIC GOODS: Goggles, Sun, Safety, Indl, Etc

One Way Safety LLC ............................G...... 708 579-0229
  La Grange  *(G-12741)*

### OPHTHALMIC GOODS: Lenses, Ophthalmic

My Eye Doctor ......................................G...... 847 325-4440
  Buffalo Grove  *(G-2740)*
My Eye Doctor ......................................G...... 312 782-4208
  Chicago  *(G-5839)*
Scuba Optics Inc ..................................G...... 815 625-7272
  Rock Falls  *(G-18151)*
Seoco Inc .............................................G...... 815 874-9565
  Rockford  *(G-18611)*

### OPHTHALMIC GOODS: Spectacles

Black Spectacles Blog ..........................G...... 312 884-9091
  Park Ridge  *(G-17184)*
Spectacle Zoom LLC ............................G...... 504 352-7237
  Des Plaines  *(G-8278)*

### OPTICAL GOODS STORES

Bahk Eye Center Inc ............................G...... 773 561-1199
  Chicago  *(G-4026)*
Eyelation LLC .......................................F...... 888 308-4703
  Tinley Park  *(G-20911)*
J A K Enterprises Inc ............................G...... 217 422-3881
  Decatur  *(G-7897)*
Weiner Optical Inc ................................G...... 708 848-4040
  Oak Park  *(G-16692)*

### OPTICAL GOODS STORES: Contact Lenses, Prescription

My Eye Doctor ......................................G...... 312 782-4208
  Chicago  *(G-5839)*

### OPTICAL GOODS STORES: Eyeglasses, Prescription

Edgebrook Eyecare ...............................F...... 815 397-5959
  Rockford  *(G-18358)*
Hoya Lens of Chicago Inc ....................E...... 847 678-4700
  Franklin Park  *(G-10490)*
Quality Optical Inc ................................G...... 773 561-0870
  Chicago  *(G-6247)*

---

Employee Codes: A=Over 500 employees, B=251-500
C=101-250, D=51-100, E=20-50, F=10-19, G=3-9

# OPTICAL GOODS STORES: Opticians — PRODUCT SECTION

### OPTICAL GOODS STORES: Opticians
- My Eye Doctor .................................................. G ...... 847 325-4440
  Buffalo Grove *(G-2740)*

### OPTICAL INSTRUMENT REPAIR SVCS
- Cortek Endoscopy Inc ..................................... G ...... 847 526-2266
  Wauconda *(G-21453)*

### OPTICAL INSTRUMENTS & APPARATUS
- Community Gospel Center .............................. G ...... 773 486-7661
  Chicago *(G-4436)*
- Intra Action Corp ............................................. E ...... 708 547-6644
  Bellwood *(G-1710)*

### OPTICAL INSTRUMENTS & LENSES
- Cabot McRlectronics Polsg Corp ..................... E ...... 630 543-6682
  Addison *(G-67)*
- Elmed Incorporated ......................................... E ...... 630 543-2792
  Glendale Heights *(G-11021)*
- Illinois Tool Works Inc ..................................... C ...... 847 295-6500
  Lake Bluff *(G-12850)*
- J A K Enterprises Inc ...................................... G ...... 217 422-3881
  Decatur *(G-7897)*
- Laurel Industries Inc ....................................... E ...... 847 432-8204
  Highland Park *(G-11851)*
- Leica McRosystems Holdings Inc ................... F ...... 800 248-0123
  Buffalo Grove *(G-2724)*
- Leica Microsystems Inc .................................. G ...... 847 405-0123
  Buffalo Grove *(G-2725)*
- Leica Microsystems Inc .................................. C ...... 847 405-0123
  Buffalo Grove *(G-2726)*
- Omex Technologies Inc ................................... G ...... 847 850-5858
  Wheeling *(G-22112)*
- Opti-Vue Inc .................................................... G ...... 630 274-6121
  Bensenville *(G-1959)*
- Precision Vision Inc ........................................ G ...... 815 223-2022
  Woodstock *(G-22601)*
- Quality Msrement Solutions Inc ...................... G ...... 630 406-1618
  Naperville *(G-15735)*
- Quality Optical Inc ........................................... G ...... 773 561-0870
  Chicago *(G-6247)*
- Scuva Optics Inc ............................................. G ...... 815 625-6195
  Rock Falls *(G-18152)*
- Solarscope LLC ............................................... G ...... 847 579-0024
  Highland Park *(G-11871)*
- Strausberger Assoc Sls & Mktg ..................... G ...... 630 553-3447
  Yorkville *(G-22671)*
- Two Tower Frames Inc ................................... G ...... 773 697-6856
  Chicago *(G-6798)*
- Vega Technology & Systems .......................... G ...... 630 855-5068
  Bartlett *(G-1324)*
- Vibgyor Optical Systems Corp ........................ E ...... 847 818-0788
  Arlington Heights *(G-863)*
- Vibgyor Optics Inc ........................................... E ...... 847 818-0788
  Arlington Heights *(G-864)*
- Wayne Engineering ......................................... G ...... 847 674-7166
  Skokie *(G-20110)*

### OPTICAL ISOLATORS
- Jql Electronics Inc ........................................... F ...... 630 873-2020
  Rolling Meadows *(G-18736)*

### OPTICAL SCANNING SVCS
- Rightsource Digital Svcs Inc ........................... F ...... 888 774-2201
  Chicago *(G-6357)*

### OPTOMETRISTS' OFFICES
- Eye Surgeons of Libertyville ........................... G ...... 847 362-3811
  Libertyville *(G-13322)*

### ORAL PREPARATIONS
- Lakeview Oral and Maxillofacia ...................... G ...... 773 327-9500
  Chicago *(G-5447)*
- Tja Health LLC ................................................ G .....
  Joliet *(G-12582)*

### ORDNANCE
- Contract Assembly Partners ........................... F ...... 217 960-3352
  Hillsboro *(G-11888)*
- General Dynamics Ordnance .......................... C ...... 618 985-8211
  Marion *(G-14261)*
- United Tactical Systems LLC ......................... E ...... 877 887-3773
  Lake Forest *(G-12978)*

### ORGAN TUNING & REPAIR SVCS
- Berghaus Pipe Organ Builders ....................... E ...... 708 544-4052
  Bellwood *(G-1698)*
- Buzard Pipe Organ Builders LLC .................... F ...... 217 352-1955
  Champaign *(G-3459)*
- C P O Inc ......................................................... G ...... 630 898-7733
  Aurora *(G-1123)*
- Daves Electronic Service ................................ F ...... 217 283-5010
  Hoopeston *(G-12109)*
- Schneider Pipe Organs Inc ............................. G ...... 217 871-4807
  Kenney *(G-12664)*

### ORGANIZATIONS & UNIONS: Labor
- Local 46 Training Program Tr .......................... G ...... 217 528-4041
  Springfield *(G-20471)*

### ORGANIZATIONS: Educational Research Agency
- About Learning Inc .......................................... F ...... 847 487-1800
  Wauconda *(G-21436)*

### ORGANIZATIONS: Medical Research
- Clarus Therapeutics Inc .................................. G ...... 847 562-4300
  Northbrook *(G-16225)*

### ORGANIZATIONS: Professional
- American Association of Indivi ........................ E ...... 312 280-0170
  Chicago *(G-3850)*
- American Soc HM Inspectors Inc ................... F ...... 847 759-2820
  Des Plaines *(G-8147)*
- Associated Equipment Distrs .......................... E ...... 630 574-0650
  Schaumburg *(G-19448)*

### ORGANIZATIONS: Religious
- Central Ill Communications LLC ...................... F ...... 217 753-2226
  Springfield *(G-20413)*
- Chicago Jewish News ..................................... F ...... 847 966-0606
  Skokie *(G-19979)*
- Christian National Womans ............................. G ...... 847 864-1396
  Evanston *(G-10024)*
- Christian Specialized Services ........................ G ...... 217 546-7338
  Springfield *(G-20418)*
- Christian Wolf Inc ............................................ G ...... 618 667-9522
  Bartelso *(G-1314)*
- Cook Communications Ministries ................... C ...... 847 741-0800
  Elgin *(G-9004)*
- Crusade Enterprises Inc .................................. G ...... 618 662-4461
  Flora *(G-10205)*
- Evang Lthn Ch Dr Mrtn Luth KG ..................... F ...... 773 380-2540
  Chicago *(G-4785)*
- Interntnal Awkening Ministries ........................ G ...... 630 653-8616
  Wheaton *(G-21958)*
- Moody Bible Inst of Chicago ............................ A ...... 312 329-4000
  Chicago *(G-5799)*
- Paddock Industries Inc .................................... F ...... 618 277-1580
  Smithton *(G-20123)*
- Templegate Publishers .................................... G ...... 217 522-3353
  Springfield *(G-20543)*
- Urantia Corp .................................................... F ...... 773 248-6616
  Chicago *(G-6844)*
- Urantia Foundation .......................................... F ...... 773 525-3319
  Chicago *(G-6845)*

### ORGANIZATIONS: Research Institute
- African American Ctr For Hnb ......................... D ...... 618 549-3965
  Park Forest *(G-17168)*
- American Bar Foundation ................................ D ...... 312 988-6500
  Chicago *(G-3852)*

### ORGANIZATIONS: Safety Research, Noncommercial
- Microwave RES & Applications ....................... G ...... 630 480-7456
  Carol Stream *(G-3197)*

### ORGANIZATIONS: Scientific Research Agency
- 1717 Chemall Corporation ............................... G ...... 224 864-4180
  Mundelein *(G-15460)*
- Advanced Robotics Research ......................... G ...... 630 544-0040
  Naperville *(G-15591)*
- Mp Technologies LLC ..................................... G ...... 847 491-4253
  Evanston *(G-10076)*

### ORGANIZATIONS: Veterans' Membership
- John Joda Post 54 ........................................... G ...... 815 692-3222
  Fairbury *(G-10128)*
- Vietnow National Headquarters ...................... G ...... 815 395-8484
  Rockford *(G-18670)*

### ORGANIZERS, CLOSET & DRAWER Plastic
- Bannon Enterprises Inc ................................... G ...... 847 529-9265
  Geneva *(G-10811)*
- Mountain Horizions Inc ................................... E ...... 630 501-0190
  Addison *(G-222)*
- Quality Custom Closets ................................... G ...... 773 307-1105
  Glenview *(G-11185)*

### ORNAMENTS: Christmas Tree, Exc Electrical & Glass
- Polygroup Services NA Inc ............................. G ...... 847 851-9995
  East Dundee *(G-8653)*

### ORNAMENTS: Lawn
- Rome Industries Inc ........................................ G ...... 309 691-7120
  Peoria *(G-17448)*

### OSCILLATORS
- Connor-Winfield Corp ...................................... C ...... 630 851-4722
  Aurora *(G-1133)*
- John Hauter Dremel ........................................ G ...... 800 437-3635
  Mount Prospect *(G-15341)*

### OSCILLATORS
- FSI Technologies Inc ...................................... E ...... 630 932-9380
  Lombard *(G-13803)*
- Radio Controlled Models Inc ........................... G ...... 847 740-8726
  Round Lake Beach *(G-19079)*

### OUTBOARD MOTORS & PARTS
- Brunswick Corporation .................................... B ...... 847 735-4700
  Lake Forest *(G-12888)*
- Brunswick International Ltd ............................. G ...... 847 735-4700
  Lake Forest *(G-12889)*

### OUTLETS: Electric, Convenience
- 2d2c Inc .......................................................... G ...... 847 543-0980
  Gurnee *(G-11416)*
- Dollar Express ................................................. G ...... 815 399-9719
  Rockford *(G-18350)*
- Garvin Industries Inc ....................................... E ...... 847 455-0188
  Franklin Park *(G-10475)*

### OUTREACH PROGRAM
- Cornerstone Community Outreach ................. F ...... 773 506-4904
  Chicago *(G-4472)*

### OVENS: Cremating
- Aquagreen Dispositions LLC .......................... G ...... 708 606-0211
  Monee *(G-14992)*

### OVENS: Distillation, Charcoal & Coke
- Uic Inc ............................................................. G ...... 815 744-4477
  Rockdale *(G-18234)*

### OVENS: Infrared
- Oxytech Systems Inc ...................................... F ...... 847 888-8611
  Carpentersville *(G-3293)*

### OVENS: Laboratory
- Aalborg Company ............................................ G ...... 708 246-8858
  Western Springs *(G-21862)*
- Grieve Corporation .......................................... D ...... 847 546-8225
  Round Lake *(G-19059)*
- Quincy Lab Inc ................................................ E ...... 773 622-2428
  Chicago *(G-6258)*

### PACKAGE DESIGN SVCS
- Bar Code Graphics Inc .................................... F ...... 312 664-0700
  Chicago *(G-4038)*
- Cornerstone Communications ......................... E ...... 773 989-2087
  Chicago *(G-4471)*
- Forest Packaging Corporation ........................ E ...... 847 981-7000
  Elk Grove Village *(G-9485)*

Mii Inc.....F 630 879-3000
Batavia (G-1471)
Pregis Holding I Corporation.....F 847 597-2200
Deerfield (G-8046)

## PACKAGED FROZEN FOODS WHOLESALERS, NEC

Doreens Pizza Inc.....F 708 862-7499
Calumet City (G-2937)
Ed Kabrick Beef Inc.....G 217 656-3263
Plainville (G-17662)
Great Lakes Coca-Cola Dist LLC.....C 847 227-6500
Rosemont (G-19004)
Koch Meat Co Inc.....B 847 384-5940
Chicago (G-5396)
Lena AJS Maid Meats.....F 815 369-4522
Lena (G-13277)
Lorenzo Frozen Foods Ltd.....G 708 343-7670
Westchester (G-21848)
Michael Lewis Company.....C 708 688-2200
Mc Cook (G-14453)
Paani Foods Inc.....F 312 420-4624
Chicago (G-6047)
Simu Ltd.....F 630 350-1060
Wood Dale (G-22422)
WEI-Chuan USA Inc.....F 708 352-8886
Hodgkins (G-11987)

## PACKAGING & LABELING SVCS

Alltemated Inc.....E 847 394-5800
Arlington Heights (G-707)
Assemblers Inc.....C 773 378-3000
Chicago (G-3965)
Bankier Companies Inc.....C 847 647-6565
Niles (G-15963)
Bli Legacy Inc.....E 847 428-6059
Carpentersville (G-3276)
Clifton Chemical Company.....G 815 697-2343
Chebanse (G-3630)
Contract Packaging Plus Inc.....G 708 356-1100
Bensenville (G-1865)
Corr-Pak Corporation.....E 708 442-7806
Mc Cook (G-14447)
County Packaging Inc.....D 708 597-1100
Crestwood (G-7484)
Eagle Express Mail LLC.....G 618 377-6245
Bethalto (G-2081)
Emco Chemical Distributors Inc.....C 262 427-0400
North Chicago (G-16178)
Fedex Corporation.....F 847 918-7730
Vernon Hills (G-21163)
Fedex Office & Print Svcs Inc.....F 312 341-9644
Chicago (G-4827)
Fedex Office & Print Svcs Inc.....F 312 755-0325
Chicago (G-4828)
Fedex Office & Print Svcs Inc.....F 312 595-0768
Chicago (G-4829)
Fedex Office & Print Svcs Inc.....F 312 663-1149
Chicago (G-4830)
Gc Packaging LLC.....D 630 758-4100
Elmhurst (G-9874)
General Assembly & Mfg Corp.....E 847 516-6462
Cary (G-3346)
Lee Gilster-Mary Corporation.....B 618 965-3449
Steeleville (G-20562)
Major-Prime Plastics Inc.....E 630 834-9400
Villa Park (G-21267)
Marietta Corporation.....C 773 816-5137
Chicago (G-5619)
Midwest Packaging & Cont Inc.....D 815 633-6800
Machesney Park (G-14093)
Multi-Pack Solutions LLC.....D 847 635-6772
Mount Prospect (G-15352)
Paket Corporation.....E 773 221-7300
Chicago (G-6057)
Papys Foods Inc.....E 815 385-3313
McHenry (G-14542)
Park Lawn Association Inc.....F 708 425-7377
Oak Lawn (G-16638)
Patt Supply Corporation.....F 708 442-3901
Lyons (G-14043)
Phoenix Unlimited Ltd.....G 847 515-1263
Huntley (G-12167)
Quality Croutons Inc.....E 773 927-8200
Chicago (G-6246)
R & R Creative Graphics Inc.....G 630 208-4724
Geneva (G-10861)
Randolph Packing Co.....D 630 830-3100
Streamwood (G-20670)
Rose Laboratories Inc.....E 815 740-1121
Joliet (G-12571)
RPS Products Inc.....E 847 683-3400
Hampshire (G-11562)
Schmit Laboratories Inc.....E 773 476-0072
Glendale Heights (G-11066)
Service Packaging Design Inc.....G 847 966-6592
Morton Grove (G-15236)
Stellar Blending & Packaging.....F 314 520-7318
Dupo (G-8577)
Sunstar Pharmaceutical Inc.....D 773 777-4000
Elgin (G-9198)
Tara International LP.....D 708 354-7050
Hodgkins (G-11984)
Taylors Candy Inc.....E 708 371-0332
Alsip (G-534)
Treatment Products Ltd.....E 773 626-8888
Chicago (G-6766)
Unified Solutions Corp.....E 847 478-9100
Arlington Heights (G-861)
Vegetable Juices Inc.....D 708 924-9500
Bedford Park (G-1589)
Wisconsin Wilderness Food Pdts.....G 847 735-8661
Lake Bluff (G-12872)

## PACKAGING MATERIALS, INDL: Wholesalers

Sherwood Industries Inc.....F 847 626-0300
Niles (G-16032)
Titan US LLC.....G 331 212-5953
Aurora (G-1088)

## PACKAGING MATERIALS, WHOLESALE

Acme Finishing Company LLC.....F 847 640-7890
Elk Grove Village (G-9264)
All-Pak Manufacturing Corp.....D 630 851-5859
Aurora (G-1103)
Alliance Creative Group Inc.....E 847 885-1800
Schaumburg (G-19431)
Americo Chemical Products Inc.....E 630 588-0830
Carol Stream (G-3103)
Emsur USA LLC.....E 847 274-9450
Elk Grove Village (G-9456)
Fromm Airpad Inc.....F 630 393-9790
Warrenville (G-21347)
Illinois Tool Works Inc.....E 217 345-2166
Charleston (G-3599)
Market Connect Inc.....G 847 726-6788
Kildeer (G-12702)
Midpoint Packaging LLC.....G 630 613-9922
Downers Grove (G-8487)
Morton Group Ltd.....G 847 831-2766
Highland Park (G-11857)
Pak Source Inc.....E 309 786-7374
Rock Island (G-18191)
Pregis Holding I Corporation.....F 847 597-2200
Deerfield (G-8046)
Pregis Innovative Packg LLC.....E 847 597-2200
Deerfield (G-8047)
S and K Packaging Incorporated.....G 563 582-8895
East Dubuque (G-8621)
S Vs Industries Inc.....G 630 408-1083
Hoffman Estates (G-12047)
Schwarz Paper Company LLC.....C 847 966-2550
Morton Grove (G-15235)
Signode Intl Holdings LLC.....F 800 648-8864
Glenview (G-11202)
Stickon Adhesive Inds Inc.....E 847 593-5959
Arlington Heights (G-844)
Tni Packaging Inc.....G 630 293-3030
West Chicago (G-21781)

## PACKAGING MATERIALS: Paper

Allegra Print & Imaging Inc.....G 847 697-1434
Elgin (G-8942)
American Graphics Network Inc.....F 847 729-7220
Glenview (G-11100)
American Name Plate & Metal De.....E 773 376-1400
Chicago (G-3867)
Applied Products Inc.....E 815 633-3825
Machesney Park (G-14057)
Arcadia Press Inc.....F 847 451-6390
Franklin Park (G-10398)
Avery Dnnson Ret Info Svcs LLC.....G 626 304-2000
Chicago (G-4000)
B & B Printing Company.....G 217 285-6072
Pittsfield (G-17561)
Bagcraftpapercon I LLC.....C 620 856-2800
Chicago (G-4025)
Bemis Packaging Inc.....E 708 544-1600
Bellwood (G-1697)
Bucktown Polymers.....G 312 436-1460
Chicago (G-4181)
Burgopak Limited.....E 312 255-0827
Chicago (G-4185)
Catty Corporation.....D 815 943-2143
Harvard (G-11626)
Clear Lam Packaging Inc.....B 847 439-8570
Elk Grove Village (G-9376)
Daubert Cromwell LLC.....E 708 293-7750
Alsip (G-456)
Deco Adhesive Pdts 1985 Ltd.....E 847 472-2100
Elk Grove Village (G-9420)
Dresbach Distributing Co.....G 815 223-0116
Peru (G-17507)
Ennis Inc.....E 815 875-2000
Princeton (G-17748)
Flex-O-Glass Inc.....E 815 288-1424
Dixon (G-8331)
Formel Industries Inc.....E 847 928-5100
Franklin Park (G-10471)
Framarx Corporation.....E 708 755-3530
Steger (G-20572)
General Packaging Products Inc.....D 312 226-5611
Chicago (G-4929)
Great Midwest Packaging LLC.....F 847 395-4500
Waukegan (G-21565)
Griffith Solutions Inc.....G 847 384-1810
Park Ridge (G-17201)
H S Crocker Company Inc.....D 847 669-3600
Huntley (G-12143)
Hanlon Group Ltd.....G 773 525-3666
Chicago (G-5042)
Illinois Tag Co.....E 773 626-0542
Carol Stream (G-3169)
Ken Don LLC.....G 708 596-4910
Markham (G-14303)
Label Graphics Co Inc.....F 815 648-2478
Hebron (G-11722)
Labels Unlimited Incorporated.....E 773 523-7500
Chicago (G-5430)
Lasons Label Co.....G 773 775-2606
Chicago (G-5464)
Miller Products Inc.....E 708 534-5111
University Park (G-21058)
Miracle Press Company.....F 773 722-6176
Chicago (G-5770)
Multi Packaging Solutions Inc.....G 773 283-9500
Chicago (G-5832)
Nashua Corporation.....D 847 692-9130
Park Ridge (G-17211)
No Surrender Inc.....G 773 929-7920
Chicago (G-5920)
Noor International Inc.....G 847 985-2300
Bartlett (G-1320)
Odra Inc.....G 847 249-2910
Gurnee (G-11478)
Packaging Dynamics Corporation.....B 773 254-8000
Chicago (G-6055)
Packaging Prtg Specialists Inc.....F 630 513-8060
Saint Charles (G-19232)
Perryco Inc.....F 815 436-2431
Plainfield (G-17638)
Photo Techniques Corp.....E 630 690-9360
Carol Stream (G-3213)
Pioneer Labels Inc.....C 618 546-5418
Robinson (G-18068)
Preferred Printing Service.....G 312 421-2343
Chicago (G-6175)
Pregis Holding I Corporation.....F 847 597-2200
Deerfield (G-8046)
Pregis Innovative Packg LLC.....E 847 597-2200
Deerfield (G-8047)
Pregis LLC.....A 847 597-2200
Deerfield (G-8049)
Prime Label & Packaging LLC.....D 630 227-1300
Wood Dale (G-22414)
Prime Label Group LLC.....G 773 630-8793
Batavia (G-1486)
Printpack Inc.....C 847 888-7150
Elgin (G-9148)
RR Donnelley & Sons Company.....D 630 762-7600
Saint Charles (G-19256)
RTC Industries Inc.....D 847 640-2400
Chicago (G-6409)
Seshin USA Inc.....G 847 550-5556
Lake Zurich (G-13130)
Signature Label of Illinois.....G 618 283-5145
Vandalia (G-21125)

PRODUCT

Employee Codes: A=Over 500 employees, B=251-500
C=101-250, D=51-100, E=20-50, F=10-19, G=3-9
2017 Harris Illinois
Industrial Directory
1677

## PACKAGING MATERIALS: Paper

Stepac USA Corporation ..................G....... 630 296-2000
  Romeoville  *(G-18870)*
Stephen Fossler Company ..............D....... 847 635-7200
  Des Plaines  *(G-8281)*
Surface Guard Inc ...........................D....... 630 236-8250
  Aurora  *(G-1084)*
Transparent Container Co Inc .........D....... 708 449-8520
  Addison  *(G-323)*
Transparent Container Co Inc .........E....... 630 860-2666
  Bensenville  *(G-2006)*
Triumph Packaging Georgia LLC .....G....... 312 251-9600
  Lake Forest  *(G-12972)*
Triumph Packaging Group ................E....... 312 251-9600
  Lake Forest  *(G-12973)*
UNI-Label and Tag Corporation .......E....... 847 956-8900
  Elk Grove Village  *(G-9797)*
Westrock Cnsmr Packg Group LLC ...A....... 804 444-1000
  Melrose Park  *(G-14708)*

## PACKAGING MATERIALS: Paper, Coated Or Laminated

Hexacomb Corporation ....................G....... 847 955-7984
  Buffalo Grove  *(G-2704)*
Lbp Manufacturing LLC ....................D....... 800 545-6200
  Cicero  *(G-7215)*
Midwest Lminating Coatings Inc ......E....... 708 653-9500
  Alsip  *(G-493)*
Nation Inc .........................................E....... 847 844-7300
  Carpentersville  *(G-3292)*
Packaging Dynamics Oper Co ..........G....... 773 843-8000
  Chicago  *(G-6056)*
Pregis LLC ........................................D....... 618 934-4311
  Trenton  *(G-20997)*
Selig Sealing Products Inc ...............G....... 815 785-2100
  Forrest  *(G-10266)*
Tetra Pak Inc ....................................D....... 815 873-1222
  Rockford  *(G-18645)*
Tetra Pak Inc ....................................D....... 847 955-6000
  Vernon Hills  *(G-21208)*
Tetra Pak Materials LP .....................D....... 847 955-6000
  Vernon Hills  *(G-21209)*
Xshredders Inc .................................D....... 847 205-1875
  Northbrook  *(G-16389)*

## PACKAGING MATERIALS: Paper, Thermoplastic Coated

MEI LLC ............................................G....... 630 285-1505
  Itasca  *(G-12313)*
Signode Industrial Group LLC ..........E....... 847 724-6100
  Glenview  *(G-11200)*

## PACKAGING MATERIALS: Paperboard Backs For Blister/Skin Pkgs

Pure Skin LLC ..................................G....... 217 679-6267
  Springfield  *(G-20509)*
Tegrant Corporation ..........................D....... 630 879-0121
  Batavia  *(G-1505)*

## PACKAGING MATERIALS: Plastic Film, Coated Or Laminated

Acorn Diversified Inc ........................F....... 708 478-1051
  Orland Park  *(G-16837)*
Amcor Flexibles LLC ........................C....... 224 313-7000
  Buffalo Grove  *(G-2656)*
Ampac Flexicon LLC ........................E....... 630 439-3160
  Hanover Park  *(G-11575)*
Ampac Flexicon LLC ........................D....... 847 639-3530
  Cary  *(G-3325)*
Dart Container Michigan LLC ...........G....... 312 221-1245
  Chicago  *(G-4560)*
Elite Extrusion Technology Inc .........G....... 630 485-2020
  Saint Charles  *(G-19180)*
Fisher Container Corp ......................D....... 847 541-0000
  Buffalo Grove  *(G-2694)*
Fisher Container Holdings LLC ........G....... 847 541-0000
  Buffalo Grove  *(G-2695)*
Forestree Inc ....................................G....... 708 598-8789
  Oak Brook  *(G-16516)*
Iam Acquisition LLC .........................E....... 847 259-7800
  Wheeling  *(G-22073)*
Navis Industries Inc .........................G....... 224 293-2000
  Elgin  *(G-9117)*
Petra Manufacturing Co ....................G....... 773 622-1475
  Chicago  *(G-6113)*
Polyair Inter Pack Inc .......................D....... 773 995-1818
  Chicago  *(G-6153)*

Pro-Pak Industries Inc .....................F....... 630 876-1050
  West Chicago  *(G-21761)*
Quality Bags Inc ...............................F....... 630 543-9800
  Addison  *(G-263)*
Rapak LLC ........................................C....... 630 296-2000
  Romeoville  *(G-18862)*
SJS Packaging Inc ...........................G....... 630 855-4755
  Streamwood  *(G-20673)*
Tegrant Corporation ..........................B....... 815 756-8451
  Dekalb  *(G-8125)*
World Contract Packagers Inc .........G....... 815 624-6501
  South Beloit  *(G-20177)*
Zacros America Inc .........................G....... 847 397-6191
  Schaumburg  *(G-19795)*

## PACKAGING MATERIALS: Polystyrene Foam

Co-Ordinated Packaging Inc ............F....... 847 559-8877
  Northbrook  *(G-16228)*
Cpg Finance Inc ...............................A....... 773 877-3300
  Chicago  *(G-4487)*
Cushioneer Inc .................................D....... 815 748-5505
  Dekalb  *(G-8083)*
Elongated Plastics Inc .....................G....... 224 456-0559
  Northbrook  *(G-16249)*
Epe Industries Usa Inc ....................F....... 800 315-0336
  Elk Grove Village  *(G-9462)*
Evergreen Resource Inc ..................G....... 630 428-9077
  Naperville  *(G-15655)*
Focus Poly ........................................G....... 847 981-6890
  Elk Grove Village  *(G-9483)*
Form Plastics Company ...................D....... 630 443-1400
  Saint Charles  *(G-19187)*
Grafcor Packaging Inc .....................F....... 815 963-1300
  Rockford  *(G-18404)*
Greg Waters .....................................G....... 618 798-9758
  Granite City  *(G-11282)*
Illinois Tool Works Inc .....................E....... 217 345-2166
  Charleston  *(G-3599)*
Mailbox Plus .....................................G....... 847 577-1737
  Mount Prospect  *(G-15345)*
Midpoint Packaging LLC ..................G....... 630 613-9922
  Downers Grove  *(G-8487)*
Northern Products Company ............D....... 708 597-8501
  Alsip  *(G-500)*
Polar Tech Industries Inc ................G....... 815 784-9000
  Genoa  *(G-10882)*
Polyair Inter Pack Inc .......................D....... 773 995-1818
  Chicago  *(G-6153)*
Positive Packaging Inc ....................G....... 847 392-4405
  Rolling Meadows  *(G-18765)*
Pregis LLC ........................................G....... 331 425-6264
  Aurora  *(G-1068)*
Pregis LLC ........................................D....... 847 597-9330
  Deerfield  *(G-8048)*
Rock-Tenn Company .......................E....... 815 756-8913
  Dekalb  *(G-8116)*
Sales Midwest Prtg & Packg Inc .....G....... 309 764-5544
  Moline  *(G-14968)*
Sealed Air Corporation .....................D....... 708 352-8700
  Hodgkins  *(G-11982)*
Silgan Equipment Company .............E....... 847 336-0552
  Waukegan  *(G-21617)*
Sonoco Display & Packaging LLC ....D....... 630 972-1990
  Bolingbrook  *(G-2373)*
Sonoco Protective Solutions ............E....... 847 398-0110
  Arlington Heights  *(G-841)*
Superb Packaging Inc .....................G....... 847 579-1870
  Highland Park  *(G-11874)*
Volflex Inc .........................................E....... 708 478-1117
  Mokena  *(G-14915)*
Westrock Converting Company ........G....... 630 783-6700
  Bolingbrook  *(G-2383)*
Wrap & Send Services .....................F....... 847 329-2559
  Skokie  *(G-20115)*
Wrapping Inc .....................................G....... 773 871-2898
  Chicago  *(G-7034)*

## PACKAGING MATERIALS: Resinous Impregnated Paper

Signode Industrial Group LLC ..........E....... 847 724-7500
  Glenview  *(G-11198)*
Signode Industrial Group LLC ..........E....... 815 939-6192
  Kankakee  *(G-12649)*
Signode Intl Holdings LLC ...............F....... 800 648-8864
  Glenview  *(G-11202)*

## PACKAGING: Blister Or Bubble Formed, Plastic

Algus Packaging Inc ........................D....... 815 756-1881
  Dekalb  *(G-8073)*
Dordan Manufacturing Company ......E....... 815 334-0087
  Woodstock  *(G-22562)*
Rohrer Corporation ...........................E....... 847 961-5920
  Huntley  *(G-12174)*
Tegrant Alloyd Brands Inc ...............B....... 815 756-8451
  Dekalb  *(G-8124)*
Tegrant Holding Corp .......................A....... 815 756-8451
  Dekalb  *(G-8126)*
Thermo-Pak Co .................................E....... 630 860-1303
  Wood Dale  *(G-22431)*
Vp Plastics and Engrg Inc ................E....... 847 689-8900
  Waukegan  *(G-21638)*
Wind Point Partners LP ....................F....... 312 255-4800
  Chicago  *(G-6992)*

## PACKING & CRATING SVC

Atlas Putty Products Co ...................D....... 708 429-5858
  Tinley Park  *(G-20895)*
D/C Export & Domestic Pkg Inc .......E....... 847 593-4200
  Elk Grove Village  *(G-9415)*
Export Packaging Co Inc .................A....... 309 756-4288
  Milan  *(G-14786)*
Smart Motion Robotics Inc ..............E....... 815 895-8550
  Sycamore  *(G-20817)*

## PACKING & CRATING SVCS: Containerized Goods For Shipping

Weyerhaeuser Company ...................G....... 815 987-0395
  Rockford  *(G-18680)*

## PACKING MATERIALS: Mechanical

CFC International Corporation ..........C....... 708 323-4131
  Chicago Heights  *(G-7087)*
Innovative Automation ......................G....... 708 418-8720
  Lansing  *(G-13166)*
Unipaq Inc ........................................G....... 773 252-3000
  Chicago  *(G-6817)*
Vangard Distribution Inc ..................E....... 708 484-9895
  Berwyn  *(G-2077)*
Vangard Distribution Inc ..................G....... 708 588-8400
  Brookfield  *(G-2646)*

## PACKING SVCS: Shipping

C & C Electronics Inc .......................F....... 847 550-0177
  Mundelein  *(G-15481)*
Chicago Export Packing Co ..............G....... 773 247-8911
  Chicago  *(G-4318)*
Eagle Express Mail LLC ...................G....... 618 377-6245
  Bethalto  *(G-2081)*
Fca LLC ............................................E....... 309 792-3444
  Moline  *(G-14939)*
Kafko International Ltd ....................E....... 847 763-0333
  Skokie  *(G-20021)*
Pierce Packaging Co ........................F....... 815 636-5650
  Loves Park  *(G-13974)*
Pierce Packaging Co ........................G....... 815 636-5656
  Peoria  *(G-17428)*
Pierce Packaging Co ........................F....... 815 636-5656
  Loves Park  *(G-13975)*
Tiem Engineering Corporation ..........F....... 630 553-7484
  Yorkville  *(G-22672)*

## PACKING: Metallic

Union Street Tin Co ..........................G....... 312 379-8200
  Park Ridge  *(G-17227)*

## PADS & PADDING: Insulator, Cordage

Mac Lean-Fogg Company ..................C....... 847 288-2534
  Franklin Park  *(G-10519)*

## PADS: Desk, Exc Paper

G & M Industries Inc ........................G....... 618 344-6655
  Collinsville  *(G-7326)*

## PADS: Mattress

Innocor Foam Tech W Chcago LLC ...E....... 732 945-6222
  West Chicago  *(G-21722)*
Jab Distributors LLC ........................E....... 847 998-6901
  Wheeling  *(G-22079)*

**L & W Bedding Inc** ....G.... 309 762-6019
Moline *(G-14951)*

## *PAGERS: One-way*

**Visiplex Inc** ....F.... 847 229-0250
Buffalo Grove *(G-2791)*

## *PAGING SVCS*

**Chicago Cardinal Communication** ....F.... 708 424-1446
Oak Lawn *(G-16610)*

## *PAILS: Plastic*

**North America Packaging Corp** ....C.... 630 845-8726
Peotone *(G-17491)*

## *PAILS: Shipping, Metal*

**Arrows Up Inc** ....G.... 847 305-2550
Arlington Heights *(G-717)*
**Cleveland Steel Container Corp** ....E.... 708 258-0700
Peotone *(G-17486)*

## *PAINT & PAINTING SPLYS STORE*

**Sherwin-Williams Company** ....G.... 847 251-6115
Kenilworth *(G-12663)*
**Sherwin-Williams Company** ....G.... 847 573-0240
Libertyville *(G-13380)*
**Sherwin-Williams Company** ....C.... 618 662-4415
Flora *(G-10215)*
**Sherwin-Williams Company** ....G.... 815 337-0942
Woodstock *(G-22611)*
**Sherwin-Williams Company** ....G.... 847 478-0677
Long Grove *(G-13901)*
**Sherwin-Williams Company** ....G.... 708 409-4728
Westchester *(G-21854)*
**Sherwin-Williams Company** ....G.... 815 254-3559
Romeoville *(G-18868)*
**Wm F Meyer Co** ....E.... 773 772-7272
Chicago *(G-7010)*

## *PAINT STORE*

**C2 Premium Paint** ....G.... 847 251-6906
Wilmette *(G-22248)*

## *PAINTING SVC: Metal Prdts*

**A R C Electro Refinishers Inc** ....G.... 708 681-5535
Bellwood *(G-1692)*
**Coating Methods Incorporated** ....F.... 847 428-8800
Carpentersville *(G-3280)*
**Coatings Applications Inc** ....E.... 847 238-9408
Elk Grove Village *(G-9380)*
**Electrostatic Concepts Inc** ....F.... 630 585-5080
Naperville *(G-15804)*
**Group O Inc** ....B.... 309 736-8311
Milan *(G-14789)*
**Industrial Finishing Inc** ....F.... 847 451-4230
Franklin Park *(G-10497)*
**Material Sciences Corporation** ....E.... 847 439-2210
Elk Grove Village *(G-9613)*
**Qc Finishers Inc** ....E.... 847 678-2660
Franklin Park *(G-10565)*
**R & O Specialties Incorporated** ....D.... 309 736-8660
Milan *(G-14800)*
**Reliable Autotech Usa LLC** ....G.... 815 945-7838
Chenoa *(G-3635)*
**Smithco Fabricators Inc** ....F.... 847 678-1619
Schiller Park *(G-19873)*
**Specialty Pntg Soda Blastg Inc** ....G.... 815 577-0006
Plainfield *(G-17651)*
**Tru-Tone Finishing Inc** ....E.... 630 543-5520
Addison *(G-327)*
**Willis Stein & Partners Manage** ....E.... 312 422-2400
Northbrook *(G-16387)*

## *PAINTS & ADDITIVES*

**Akzo Nobel Inc** ....C.... 312 544-7000
Chicago *(G-3793)*
**Behr Process Corporation** ....D.... 630 289-6247
Bartlett *(G-1336)*
**Behr Process Corporation** ....D.... 708 753-0136
Chicago Heights *(G-7082)*
**Behr Process Corporation** ....D.... 708 753-1820
Lynwood *(G-14018)*
**Behr Process Corporation** ....C.... 708 757-6350
Chicago Heights *(G-7083)*
**Carbit Corporation** ....E.... 312 280-2300
Chicago *(G-4237)*
**Engineered Polymr Solutions Inc** ....E.... 815 987-3700
Rockford *(G-18366)*
**Finishes Unlimited Inc** ....F.... 630 466-4881
Sugar Grove *(G-20724)*
**Tru Serv Corp** ....F.... 773 695-5674
Chicago *(G-6783)*
**True Value Company** ....G.... 847 639-5383
Cary *(G-3378)*
**True Value Company** ....B.... 773 695-5000
Chicago *(G-6786)*

## *PAINTS & ALLIED PRODUCTS*

**Acm Inc** ....G.... 847 473-1991
North Chicago *(G-16172)*
**Alpha Coating Technologies LLC** ....E.... 630 268-8787
Addison *(G-30)*
**American Rack Company** ....E.... 773 763-7309
Chicago *(G-3870)*
**Armitage Industries Inc** ....F.... 847 288-9090
Franklin Park *(G-10400)*
**Ata Finishing Corp** ....G.... 847 677-8560
Skokie *(G-19960)*
**Automatic Anodizing Corp** ....E.... 773 478-3304
Chicago *(G-3991)*
**Autonomic Materials Inc** ....F.... 217 863-2023
Champaign *(G-3455)*
**Basement Dewatering Systems** ....F.... 309 647-0331
Canton *(G-2981)*
**Central Chemical and Service** ....F.... 630 653-9200
Carol Stream *(G-3126)*
**Chase Corporation** ....E.... 847 866-8500
Evanston *(G-10022)*
**Chase Products Co** ....D.... 708 865-1000
Broadview *(G-2566)*
**Chemix Corp** ....F.... 708 754-2150
Glenwood *(G-11215)*
**Chicago Latex Products Inc** ....F.... 815 459-9680
Crystal Lake *(G-7552)*
**Chromium Industries Inc** ....E.... 773 287-3716
Chicago *(G-4373)*
**Clariant Plas Coatings USA Inc** ....D.... 630 562-9700
West Chicago *(G-21682)*
**Coatings International Inc** ....E.... 847 455-1400
Franklin Park *(G-10439)*
**Color Corporation of America** ....D.... 815 987-3700
Rockford *(G-18314)*
**Contract Transportation Sys Co** ....C.... 217 342-5757
Effingham *(G-8831)*
**D and R Tech** ....G.... 224 353-6693
Schaumburg *(G-19497)*
**Dick Blick Company** ....C.... 309 343-6181
Galesburg *(G-10747)*
**Dip Seal Plastics Inc** ....G.... 815 398-3533
Rockford *(G-18345)*
**DSM Desotech Inc** ....C.... 847 697-0400
Elgin *(G-9013)*
**F H Leinweber Co Inc** ....E.... 773 568-7722
Chicago *(G-4803)*
**Federated Paint Mfg Co** ....F.... 708 345-4848
Chicago *(G-4824)*
**Gibraltar Chemical Works Inc** ....F.... 708 333-0600
South Holland *(G-20270)*
**Hallstar Company** ....D.... 708 594-5947
Bedford Park *(G-1552)*
**I Pulloma Paints** ....F.... 847 426-4140
Carpentersville *(G-3287)*
**If Walls Could Talk** ....G.... 847 219-5527
South Elgin *(G-20205)*
**Inhance Technologies LLC** ....E.... 630 231-7515
West Chicago *(G-21719)*
**International Paint LLC** ....F.... 847 623-4200
Waukegan *(G-21572)*
**Jet Rack Corp** ....E.... 773 586-2150
Chicago *(G-5298)*
**Jfb Hart Coatings Inc** ....F.... 630 783-1917
Plainfield *(G-17612)*
**Knott So Shabby** ....G.... 618 281-6002
Columbia *(G-7360)*
**Kns Companies Inc** ....F.... 630 665-9010
Carol Stream *(G-3181)*
**Lawter Inc** ....E.... 312 662-5700
Chicago *(G-5473)*
**Mate Technologies Inc** ....F.... 847 289-1010
Elgin *(G-9103)*
**Metro Paint Supplies** ....G.... 708 385-7701
Crestwood *(G-7494)*
**Midwest Powder Coatings Inc** ....E.... 630 587-2918
Saint Charles *(G-19222)*
**Miller Purcell Co Inc** ....G.... 815 485-2142
New Lenox *(G-15897)*
**Morton Nippon Coatings** ....G.... 708 868-7403
Lansing *(G-13178)*
**Morton Salt Inc** ....C.... 312 807-2000
Chicago *(G-5809)*
**Nataz Specialty Coatings Inc** ....F.... 773 247-7030
Chicago *(G-5856)*
**National Coatings Inc** ....E.... 309 342-4184
Galesburg *(G-10769)*
**One Shot LLC** ....E.... 773 646-5900
Chicago *(G-5990)*
**Owens Corning Sales LLC** ....E.... 708 594-6935
Argo *(G-695)*
**Penray Companies Inc** ....D.... 800 323-6329
Wheeling *(G-22120)*
**Pioneer Powder Coatings LLC** ....E.... 847 671-1100
Franklin Park *(G-10552)*
**Plastic Services and Products** ....D.... 708 868-3800
Calumet City *(G-2948)*
**Plastics Color Corp Illinois** ....D.... 708 868-3800
Calumet City *(G-2950)*
**Polymer Nation LLC** ....G.... 847 972-2157
Waukegan *(G-21603)*
**Polyone Corporation** ....D.... 847 364-0011
Elk Grove Village *(G-9686)*
**Polyone Corporation** ....D.... 630 972-0505
Romeoville *(G-18859)*
**Porcelain Enamel Finishers** ....G.... 312 808-1560
Chicago *(G-6157)*
**Powder Coat Plus** ....G.... 217 228-0081
Quincy *(G-17868)*
**PPG Architectural Finishes Inc** ....G.... 309 673-3761
Peoria *(G-17432)*
**PPG Industries Inc** ....E.... 773 646-5900
Chicago *(G-6162)*
**PPG Industries Inc** ....E.... 630 879-5100
Batavia *(G-1485)*
**PPG Industries Inc** ....G.... 708 597-7044
Alsip *(G-512)*
**PPG Industries Inc** ....E.... 847 742-3340
Elgin *(G-9145)*
**PPG Industries Inc** ....G.... 618 206-2250
O Fallon *(G-16475)*
**PPG Industries Inc** ....E.... 312 666-2277
Chicago *(G-6164)*
**PPG Industries Inc** ....E.... 847 991-0620
Rolling Meadows *(G-18766)*
**PPG Industries Inc** ....E.... 217 757-9080
Springfield *(G-20506)*
**PPG Industries Inc** ....G.... 708 345-1515
Stone Park *(G-20636)*
**PPG Industries Inc** ....G.... 630 960-3600
Westmont *(G-21913)*
**Premium Products Inc** ....F.... 630 553-6160
Yorkville *(G-22669)*
**Prescription Plus Ltd** ....F.... 618 537-6202
Lebanon *(G-13216)*
**Quality Coating Co** ....F.... 815 875-3228
Princeton *(G-17761)*
**R C Industries Inc** ....F.... 773 378-1118
Chicago *(G-6265)*
**Richards Company II Inc** ....F.... 708 385-6633
Alsip *(G-520)*
**Rock-Tred 2 LLC** ....E.... 888 762-5873
Waukegan *(G-21610)*
**Sandstrom Products Company** ....E.... 309 523-2121
Port Byron *(G-17723)*
**Sandstrom Products Company** ....F.... 309 523-2121
Port Byron *(G-17724)*
**Sherwin-Williams Company** ....C.... 618 662-4415
Flora *(G-10215)*
**Tamms Industries Inc** ....D.... 815 522-3394
Kirkland *(G-12719)*
**Technical Coatings Co** ....E.... 708 343-6000
Melrose Park *(G-14701)*
**Tennant Company** ....E.... 773 376-7132
Chicago *(G-6701)*
**Tms Manufacturing Co** ....G.... 847 353-8000
Alsip *(G-535)*
**Universal Chem & Coatings Inc** ....E.... 847 297-2001
Elk Grove Village *(G-9801)*
**Valspar** ....G.... 309 743-7133
East Moline *(G-8696)*
**Valspar Corporation** ....C.... 815 933-5561
Kankakee *(G-12657)*
**Valspar Corporation** ....D.... 708 469-7194
Hodgkins *(G-11985)*
**Valspar Corporation** ....D.... 847 541-9000
Wheeling *(G-22175)*
**Valspar Corporation** ....C.... 708 720-0600
Matteson *(G-14380)*

PRODUCT

Employee Codes: A=Over 500 employees, B=251-500
C=101-250, D=51-100, E=20-50, F=10-19, G=3-9

2017 Harris Illinois
Industrial Directory

1679

# PAINTS & ALLIED PRODUCTS

Valspar Corporation .................... D ....... 847 541-9000
  Wheeling (G-22176)
Voges Inc .................................... D ....... 618 233-2760
  Belleville (G-1688)
Willims-Hyward Intl Ctings Inc ... E ....... 708 563-5182
  Summit Argo (G-20769)
Willims-Hyward Intl Ctings Inc ... F ....... 708 458-0015
  Argo (G-698)

## PAINTS & VARNISHES: Plastics Based

Nb Coatings Inc ......................... C ....... 800 323-3224
  Lansing (G-13179)

## PAINTS, VARNISHES & SPLYS WHOLESALERS

Benjamin Moore & Co ................ C ....... 708 343-6000
  Carol Stream (G-3114)
Federal Equipment & Svcs Inc ... F ....... 847 731-9002
  Zion (G-22685)
Global Material Tech Inc ............. C ....... 773 247-6000
  Chicago (G-4958)
PPG Architectural Finishes Inc ... G ....... 309 673-3761
  Peoria (G-17432)
Sherwin-Williams Company ........ G ....... 847 573-0240
  Libertyville (G-13380)
Sherwin-Williams Company ................ 815 337-0942
  Woodstock (G-22611)
Sherwin-Williams Company ........ G ....... 847 478-0677
  Long Grove (G-13901)
Sherwin-Williams Company ........ G ....... 708 409-4728
  Westchester (G-21854)
Sherwin-Williams Company ........ G ....... 815 254-3559
  Romeoville (G-18868)

## PAINTS, VARNISHES & SPLYS, WHOLESALE: Colors & Pigments

Fortune International Tech LLC ... G ....... 847 429-9791
  Hoffman Estates (G-12011)

## PAINTS, VARNISHES & SPLYS, WHOLESALE: Paints

Akzo Nobel Coatings Inc ............ E ....... 630 792-1619
  Lombard (G-13763)
Metro Paint Supplies .................. E ....... 708 385-7701
  Crestwood (G-7494)
Richards Company II Inc ............ F ....... 708 385-6633
  Alsip (G-520)
United Gilsonite Laboratories ..... E ....... 217 243-7878
  Jacksonville (G-12415)
Wm F Meyer Co ......................... E ....... 773 772-7272
  Chicago (G-7010)

## PAINTS: Oil Or Alkyd Vehicle Or Water Thinned

Akzo Nobel Coatings Inc ............ E ....... 630 792-1619
  Lombard (G-13763)
Akzo Nobel Coatings Inc ............ F ....... 847 623-4200
  Waukegan (G-21520)
Seymour of Sycamore Inc .......... C ....... 815 895-9101
  Sycamore (G-20815)
Vanex Inc .................................... E ....... 618 244-1413
  Mount Vernon (G-15448)

## PAINTS: Waterproof

PPG Industries Inc ..................... E ....... 773 646-5900
  Chicago (G-6163)
Rust-Oleum Corporation ............. C ....... 847 367-7700
  Vernon Hills (G-21195)

## PALLET REPAIR SVCS

Cardinal Pallet Co ...................... E ....... 773 725-5387
  Chicago (G-4240)
Commercial Pallet Inc ................. E ....... 312 226-6699
  Chicago (G-4435)
Lake Street Pallets .................... G ....... 773 889-2266
  Chicago (G-5441)
Mills Pallet ................................. F ....... 773 533-6458
  Chicago (G-5765)
Murrihy Pallet Co ....................... E ....... 615 370-7000
  Chicago (G-5837)
Round Lake Pallets Inc .............. G ....... 847 637-6162
  Round Lake (G-19065)

## PALLETIZERS & DEPALLETIZERS

Pallet Repair Systems Inc .......... F ....... 217 291-0009
  Jacksonville (G-12406)

## PALLETS

3v Pallet ..................................... G ....... 708 620-7790
  South Holland (G-20237)
3v Pallet ..................................... G ....... 708 333-1113
  Harvey (G-11649)
815 Pallets Inc ........................... E ....... 815 678-0012
  Richmond (G-17954)
All Pallet Service ....................... G ....... 618 451-7545
  Granite City (G-11262)
American Pallet Co Inc .............. D ....... 847 662-5525
  Waukegan (G-21525)
Amerigreen Pallets ..................... G ....... 309 698-3463
  East Peoria (G-8700)
ASAP Pallets Inc ........................ F ....... 630 350-7689
  Franklin Park (G-10402)
ASAP Pallets Inc ........................ G ....... 630 917-0180
  Bellwood (G-1694)
Ash Pallet Management Inc ....... D ....... 847 473-5700
  Antioch (G-620)
Ash Pallet Management Inc ....... G ....... 847 473-5700
  Franklin Park (G-10403)
Bach Timber & Pallet Inc ........... G ....... 815 885-3774
  Caledonia (G-2930)
Badger Pallet Inc ........................ G ....... 815 943-1147
  Harvard (G-11623)
Best Pallet Company LLC .......... F ....... 815 637-1500
  Loves Park (G-13924)
Best Pallet Company LLC .......... G ....... 312 242-4009
  Chicago (G-4094)
Cantarero Pallets Inc ................. G ....... 773 413-7017
  Chicago (G-4227)
Central States Pallets ................ G ....... 217 494-2710
  Chatham (G-3617)
Champion Wood Pallets Inc ....... G ....... 630 801-8036
  Aurora (G-1127)
Chicago Heights Pallets Co ....... F ....... 708 757-7641
  Chicago Heights (G-7088)
Chicago Pallet Service II Inc ...... G ....... 847 439-8330
  Elk Grove Village (G-9369)
Corr-Pak Corporation ................. E ....... 708 442-7806
  Mc Cook (G-14447)
Craft Pallet Inc ........................... G ....... 618 437-5382
  INA (G-12184)
D & E Pallet Inc ......................... G ....... 708 891-4307
  Chicago (G-4532)
Darios Pallets Corp .................... G ....... 312 421-3413
  Chicago (G-4558)
Diaz Pallets ................................ G ....... 630 340-3736
  Aurora (G-1140)
Dixon Pallet Service ................... G ....... 773 238-9569
  Chicago (G-4614)
Eam Pallets ................................ G ....... 708 333-0596
  Harvey (G-11664)
Earthwise Recycled Pallet ......... G ....... 618 286-6015
  Dupo (G-8570)
Edgar Pallets ............................. G ....... 773 454-8919
  Chicago (G-4695)
F and L Pallets Inc .................... G ....... 773 364-0798
  Chicago (G-4801)
G & S Pallets ............................. G ....... 630 574-2741
  Oak Brook (G-16518)
General Pallet ............................ G ....... 773 660-8550
  Chicago (G-4930)
Glitter Your Pallet ...................... G ....... 708 516-8494
  Homer Glen (G-12080)
Great Lakes Lumber and Pallet .. G ....... 773 243-6839
  Park Ridge (G-17200)
Guero Pallets ............................. G ....... 312 593-4276
  Chicago (G-5008)
HMM Pallets Inc ......................... G ....... 773 927-3448
  Chicago (G-5095)
Hope Pallet Inc .......................... G ....... 815 412-4606
  Rockdale (G-18220)
Illinois Pallets Inc ....................... G ....... 773 640-9228
  Willow Springs (G-22197)
Industrial Pallets LLC ................. G ....... 708 351-8783
  Glendale Heights (G-11034)
Industrial Service Pallet Inc ........ G ....... 708 655-4963
  Melrose Park (G-14658)
J&A Pallets Service Inc ............. F ....... 708 333-6601
  Chicago Heights (G-7104)
Joliet Pallets .............................. G ....... 815 370-7000
  Joliet (G-12524)
Joseph B Krisher ....................... G ....... 618 677-2016
  Mascoutah (G-14354)
Lakeland Pallets Inc .................. G ....... 616 949-9515
  Geneva (G-10844)
Los Primos Pallets Inc ............... G ....... 773 418-3584
  Chicago (G-5545)
M and M Pallet Inc .................... G ....... 708 272-4447
  Blue Island (G-2261)
Morris Pallet Skids Inc ............... G ....... 618 786-2241
  Dow (G-8382)
Muro Pallets Corp ...................... G ....... 773 640-8606
  Chicago (G-5835)
Nefab Packaging N Centl LLC ... C
  Elk Grove Village (G-9649)
Newport Pallet ........................... G ....... 217 662-6577
  Georgetown (G-10889)
Northern Illinois Pallet Inc ......... G ....... 815 236-9242
  Fox Lake (G-10280)
Pallet Base LLC ......................... G ....... 312 316-6137
  Chicago (G-6063)
Pallet Recyclers Inc ................... G ....... 815 432-4022
  Watseka (G-21424)
Pallet Solution ............................ G ....... 773 837-8677
  Streamwood (G-20669)
Pallet Wrapz .............................. F ....... 847 729-5850
  Glenview (G-11178)
Pallet Wrapz Inc ........................ G ....... 847 729-5850
  Glenview (G-11179)
Pallets International Holding ...... G ....... 773 391-7223
  South Holland (G-20294)
Pallets Shop .............................. G ....... 618 920-6875
  Springfield (G-20497)
Premium Pallets ......................... G ....... 217 974-0155
  Springfield (G-20507)
Rock Valley Pallet Company ..... G ....... 815 654-4850
  Machesney Park (G-14102)
S & S Pallet Corp ...................... E ....... 618 219-3218
  Granite City (G-11301)
Schroeders Pallet Service .......... G ....... 708 371-9046
  Blue Island (G-2269)
Singleton Pallets Co ................... G ....... 708 687-7006
  Oak Forest (G-16588)
Sotos Pallets Inc ........................ G ....... 815 338-7750
  Woodstock (G-22613)
Timberline Pallet & Skid Inc ...... F ....... 309 752-1770
  East Moline (G-8695)

## PALLETS & SKIDS: Wood

A & F Pallet Service Inc ............ F ....... 773 767-9500
  Chicago (G-3680)
AA Pallet Inc .............................. E ....... 773 536-3699
  Chicago (G-3697)
Advance Pallet Incorporated ..... E ....... 847 697-5700
  South Elgin (G-20179)
AGCO Recycling LLC ................ E ....... 217 224-9048
  Quincy (G-17790)
Aldon Co ..................................... F ....... 847 623-8800
  Waukegan (G-21521)
Bob Ulrichs Pallets .................... E ....... 217 224-2568
  Quincy (G-17806)
Chicago Pallet Service Inc ........ E ....... 847 439-8754
  Elk Grove Village (G-9368)
Commercial Pallet Inc ................ E ....... 312 226-6699
  Chicago (G-4435)
Community Support Systems .... D ....... 217 705-4300
  Teutopolis (G-20850)
Crossroad Crating & Pallet ........ G ....... 815 657-8409
  Forrest (G-10261)
Edison Pallet & Wood Products  G ....... 630 653-3416
  Winfield (G-22285)
Eds Pallet Service ..................... F ....... 618 248-5386
  Albers (G-353)
Fca LLC ..................................... E ....... 309 385-2588
  Princeville (G-17765)
Fulton County Rehabilitation ..... E ....... 309 647-6510
  Canton (G-2987)
Go Jo Pallets & Supplies Inc .... F ....... 815 254-1631
  Plainfield (G-17603)
Graphic Pallet & Transport ........ E ....... 630 904-4951
  Plainfield (G-17604)
Hammer Enterprises Inc ............ F ....... 217 662-8225
  Georgetown (G-10888)
Harvey Pallets Inc ..................... C ....... 708 293-1831
  Blue Island (G-2255)
Hill Top Pallet ............................. G ....... 618 426-9810
  Ava (G-1237)
Human Svc Ctr Southern Metro E .. E ....... 618 282-6233
  Red Bud (G-17942)
J & J Quality Pallets Inc ............ E ....... 618 262-6426
  Mount Carmel (G-15269)
Jo Go Pallet & Supplies ............ F ....... 815 254-1631
  Plainfield (G-17613)

## PRODUCT SECTION

### PAPER & BOARD: Die-cut

Lake Street Pallets ............................... G ...... 773 889-2266
  Chicago (G-5441)
Lottus Inc ............................................ G ...... 847 691-9464
  Glenview (G-11166)
McKean Pallet Co ................................ G ...... 309 246-7543
  Lacon (G-12788)
Mental Health Ctrs Centl Ill ................. D ...... 217 735-1413
  Lincoln (G-13415)
Mobile Pallet Service Inc .................... F ...... 630 231-6597
  West Chicago (G-21745)
Northwest Pallet Supply Co ................ C ...... 815 544-6001
  Belvidere (G-1777)
Pak Source Inc ................................... E ...... 309 786-7374
  Rock Island (G-18191)
Pallet Solution Inc .............................. E ...... 618 445-2316
  Albion (G-364)
Palletmaxx Inc .................................... G ...... 708 385-9595
  Crestwood (G-7497)
Pallets Plus Inc ................................... G ...... 847 318-1853
  Park Ridge (G-17215)
Progressive Recycling Systems ......... G ...... 217 291-0009
  Jacksonville (G-12410)
R & H Products Inc ............................ G ...... 815 744-4110
  Rockdale (G-18229)
R & R Services Illinois Inc .................. G ...... 217 424-2602
  Decatur (G-7930)
Rbj Inc ................................................ F ...... 309 344-5066
  Galesburg (G-10772)
Simonton Hardwood Lumber LLC ...... F ...... 618 594-2132
  Carlyle (G-3059)
Trade Industries ................................. E ...... 618 643-4321
  Mc Leansboro (G-14469)
Try Our Pallets Inc ............................. G ...... 708 343-0166
  Maywood (G-14436)
Twin City Wood Recycling Corp ......... G ...... 309 827-9663
  Bloomington (G-2234)
Universal Pallet Inc ............................ G ...... 815 928-8546
  Bradley (G-2436)
Upham & Walsh Lumber Co ............... G ...... 847 519-1010
  Hoffman Estates (G-12067)

### PALLETS: Metal

Chicago Pallet Service Inc ................. E ...... 847 439-8330
  Maywood (G-14423)
Marcells Pallet Inc ............................. G ...... 773 265-1200
  Chicago (G-5612)
Midaco Corporation ........................... E ...... 847 593-8420
  Elk Grove Village (G-9626)

### PALLETS: Plastic

Chem-Tainer Industries Inc ............... G ...... 630 932-7778
  Lombard (G-13775)
Greif Inc ............................................ E ...... 815 935-7575
  Bradley (G-2423)
Illinois Tool Works Inc ....................... E ...... 630 773-9300
  Itasca (G-12280)
One Way Solutions LLC .................... G ...... 847 446-0872
  Northfield (G-16414)
Plastic Products Inc .......................... E ...... 847 874-3440
  Schaumburg (G-19692)
Plastipak Packaging Inc ................... B ...... 217 398-1832
  Champaign (G-3526)
Plastipak Packaging Inc ................... C ...... 708 385-0721
  Alsip (G-510)
Transparent Container Co Inc .......... D ...... 708 449-8520
  Addison (G-323)

### PALLETS: Solid Fiber, Made From Purchased Materials

Wehrle Lumber Co Inc ...................... F ...... 618 283-4859
  Vandalia (G-21131)

### PALLETS: Wood & Metal Combination

Dexton Enterprises ........................... G ...... 309 788-1881
  Rock Island (G-18174)

### PALLETS: Wooden

ADP Pallet Inc ................................... F ...... 773 638-3800
  Chicago (G-3755)
Arrowtech Pallet & Crating ................ D ...... 815 547-9300
  Belvidere (G-1734)
Botkin Lumber Company Inc ............. E ...... 217 287-2127
  Taylorville (G-20834)
Cardinal Pallet Co ............................. G ...... 773 725-5387
  Chicago (G-4240)
Central Wood Products Inc ............... E ...... 217 728-4412
  Sullivan (G-20742)

Cleary Pallet Sales Inc ....................... E ...... 815 784-3048
  Genoa (G-10876)
Cole Pallet Services Corp .................. E ...... 815 758-3226
  Dekalb (G-8077)
Corsaw Hardwood Lumber Inc .......... F ...... 309 293-2055
  Smithfield (G-20119)
D and D Pallets .................................. F ...... 630 800-1102
  Aurora (G-1136)
Decatur Wood Products LLC ............. E ...... 217 424-2602
  Decatur (G-7874)
Dg Wood Processing ......................... F ...... 217 543-2128
  Arthur (G-894)
Enterprise Pallet Inc .......................... F ...... 815 928-8546
  Bourbonnais (G-2395)
Equstock LLC .................................... F ...... 866 962-4686
  Loves Park (G-13940)
Export Packaging Co Inc ................... A ...... 309 756-4288
  Milan (G-14786)
Fca LLC ............................................. F ...... 309 792-3444
  Moline (G-14939)
Georgetown Wood and Pallet Co ....... E ...... 217 662-2563
  Georgetown (G-10887)
Hardwood Lumber Products Co ........ F ...... 309 538-4411
  Kilbourne (G-12697)
Ifco .................................................... G ...... 630 226-0650
  Bolingbrook (G-2318)
Jjm Products LLC .............................. G ...... 630 319-9325
  Westmont (G-21894)
Kccdd Inc .......................................... G ...... 309 344-2030
  Galesburg (G-10762)
Kirk Wood Products Inc .................... G ...... 309 829-6661
  Bloomington (G-2190)
M & M Paltech Inc ............................. D ...... 630 350-7890
  Belvidere (G-1767)
Malvaes Solutions Incorporated ........ G ...... 773 823-1034
  Chicago (G-5608)
Midwest Wood Inc ............................. F ...... 815 273-3333
  Savanna (G-19402)
Mills Pallet ......................................... G ...... 773 533-6458
  Chicago (G-5765)
Momence Pallet Corporation ............. E ...... 815 472-6451
  Momence (G-14985)
Murrihy Pallet Co ............................... G ...... 615 370-7000
  Chicago (G-5837)
Northern Pallet and Supply Co .......... F ...... 847 716-1400
  Northfield (G-16412)
Pallett Wilson .................................... G ...... 217 543-3555
  Sullivan (G-20757)
Piece Works Specialists Inc .............. F ...... 309 266-7016
  Morton (G-15177)
Quality Pallets Inc ............................. E ...... 217 459-2655
  Windsor (G-22282)
R K J Pallets Inc ................................ F ...... 708 493-0701
  Bellwood (G-1717)
Rose Pallet LLC ................................. G ...... 708 333-3000
  Bridgeview (G-2525)
Round Lake Pallets Inc ..................... G ...... 847 637-6162
  Round Lake (G-19065)
Sterling Lumber Company ................ C ...... 708 388-2223
  Phoenix (G-17542)
Steve Forrest .................................... F ...... 815 765-9040
  Poplar Grove (G-17717)
Walnut Grove Packaging ................... G ...... 217 268-5112
  Arcola (G-687)
Workshop Ltd Inc .............................. G ...... 708 458-3222
  Bedford Park (G-1594)

### PANEL & DISTRIBUTION BOARDS & OTHER RELATED APPARATUS

Agnes & Chris Gulik ......................... G ...... 847 931-9641
  Elgin (G-8940)
Marshall Electric Inc ......................... F ...... 618 382-3932
  Carmi (G-3074)
Midwest Control Corp ....................... F ...... 708 599-1331
  Bridgeview (G-2509)
Schneider Electric Usa Inc ............... C ...... 630 428-3849
  Schiller Park (G-19871)

### PANEL & DISTRIBUTION BOARDS: Electric

AKD Controls Inc .............................. G ...... 815 633-4586
  Machesney Park (G-14053)
G & F Manufacturing Co Inc ............. E ...... 708 424-4170
  Oak Lawn (G-16621)
General Electric Company ............... G ...... 309 664-1513
  Bloomington (G-2170)
Industrial Electric Svc Inc ................. G ...... 708 997-2090
  Bartlett (G-1356)
Kinney Electrical Mfg Co .................. D ...... 847 742-9600
  Elgin (G-9090)

Marshall Wolf Automation Inc ........... E ...... 847 658-8130
  Algonquin (G-398)

### PANELS, CORRUGATED: Plastic

Andrews Automotive Company ......... F ...... 773 768-1122
  Chicago (G-3903)
Floline Archtctral Systems LLC ......... F ...... 815 733-5044
  Plainfield (G-17600)

### PANELS, FLAT: Plastic

Sek Corporation ................................ E ...... 630 762-0606
  Saint Charles (G-19262)

### PANELS: Building, Metal

Petersen Aluminum Corporation ....... D ...... 847 228-7150
  Elk Grove Village (G-9676)

### PANELS: Building, Plastic, NEC

Crane Composites Inc ...................... B ...... 815 467-8600
  Channahon (G-3566)
Crane Composites Inc ...................... D ...... 630 378-9580
  Bolingbrook (G-2289)
Crane Composites Inc ...................... C ...... 815 467-1437
  Channahon (G-3567)

### PANELS: Building, Wood

McDonnell Components Inc ............. D ...... 815 547-9555
  Belvidere (G-1770)
R & N Components Co ..................... G ...... 217 543-3495
  Tuscola (G-21023)

### PANELS: Control & Metering, Generator

A C Gentrol Inc ................................. E ...... 309 274-5486
  Chillicothe (G-7160)
Simplex Inc ....................................... C ...... 217 483-1600
  Springfield (G-20526)

### PANELS: Wood

Klaman Hardwood ............................ G ...... 217 972-7888
  Decatur (G-7903)
R-Squared Construction Inc ............. G ...... 815 232-7433
  Freeport (G-10682)
Walnut Creek Hardwood ................... G ...... 815 389-3317
  South Beloit (G-20173)

### PAPER & BOARD: Die-cut

11th Street Express Prtg Inc ............. F ...... 815 968-0208
  Rockford (G-18235)
Ade Inc .............................................. E ...... 773 646-3400
  Chicago (G-3746)
Alloyd Brands ................................... G ...... 843 383-7000
  Batavia (G-1408)
Andrews Converting LLC .................. E ...... 708 352-2555
  La Grange (G-12725)
Animated Advg Techniques Inc ........ G ...... 312 372-4694
  Chicago (G-3908)
Artistic Carton Company .................. G ...... 847 741-0247
  Elgin (G-8958)
B Allan Graphics Inc ......................... F ...... 708 396-1704
  Alsip (G-438)
Business Forms Finishing Svc ......... G ...... 773 229-0230
  Chicago (G-4187)
Butler Bros Steel Rule Die Co ........... G ...... 815 630-4629
  Shorewood (G-19924)
Carson Printing Inc .......................... G ...... 847 836-0900
  East Dundee (G-8629)
Creative Label Inc ............................. D ...... 847 981-3800
  Elk Grove Village (G-9399)
Creative Lithocraft Inc ...................... G ...... 847 352-7002
  Schaumburg (G-19489)
Deco Adhesive Pdts 1985 Ltd .......... E ...... 847 472-2100
  Elk Grove Village (G-9420)
Delta Press Inc ................................. E ...... 847 671-3200
  Palatine (G-17022)
Graphic Converting Inc .................... B ...... 630 758-4100
  Elmhurst (G-9880)
Impression Printing .......................... F ...... 708 614-8660
  Oak Forest (G-16583)
Lee-Wel Printing Corporation ........... G ...... 630 682-0935
  Wheaton (G-21966)
M S A Printing Inc ............................. G ...... 847 593-5699
  Elk Grove Village (G-9604)
M Wells Printing Co .......................... G ...... 312 455-0400
  Chicago (G-5588)
McGrath Press Inc ............................ E ...... 815 356-5246
  Crystal Lake (G-7607)

Employee Codes: A=Over 500 employees, B=251-500
C=101-250, D=51-100, E=20-50, F=10-19, G=3-9

## PAPER & BOARD: Die-cut

Midwest Cortland Inc .................... E ....... 847 671-0376
  Addison *(G-211)*
Midwest Index Inc ........................ D ....... 847 995-8425
  Addison *(G-212)*
Plastics Printing Group Inc ........ F ....... 312 421-7980
  Chicago *(G-6138)*
Potomac Corporation ................... C ....... 847 259-0546
  Wheeling *(G-22126)*
Precision Die Cutting & Finish ... G ....... 773 252-5625
  Chicago *(G-6169)*
Pry-Bar Company .......................... F ....... 815 436-3383
  Joliet *(G-12558)*
Racine Paper Box Manufacturing .... E ....... 773 227-3900
  Chicago *(G-6278)*
Rapid Displays Inc ....................... C ....... 773 927-5000
  Chicago *(G-6291)*
Review Printing Co Inc ................ G ....... 309 788-7094
  Rock Island *(G-18199)*
Rhopac Fabricated Products LLC ... E ....... 847 362-3300
  Libertyville *(G-13376)*
Rohrer Corporation ...................... D ....... 847 961-5920
  Huntley *(G-12174)*
Ross-Gage Inc .............................. F ....... 708 347-3659
  Homewood *(G-12105)*
RTS Packaging LLC ..................... C ....... 708 338-2800
  Hillside *(G-11932)*
Sales Midwest Prtg & Packg Inc ... G ....... 309 764-5544
  Moline *(G-14968)*
Stevenson Paper Co Inc .............. G ....... 630 879-5000
  Batavia *(G-1498)*
Village Press Inc .......................... G ....... 847 362-1856
  Libertyville *(G-13399)*
Weber Marking Systems Inc ....... B ....... 847 364-8500
  Arlington Heights *(G-871)*
Young Shin USA Limited .............. G ....... 847 598-3611
  Schaumburg *(G-19793)*

### PAPER & ENVELOPES: Writing, Made From Purchased Materials

Dove Foundation ........................... G ....... 312 217-3683
  Chicago *(G-4637)*

### PAPER & PAPER PRDTS: Crepe, Made From Purchased Materials

New-Indy IVEX LLC ..................... E ....... 309 686-3830
  Peoria *(G-17417)*

### PAPER CONVERTING

All Weather Products Co LLC ..... F ....... 847 981-0386
  Elk Grove Village *(G-9285)*
Ar-En Party Printers Inc .............. E ....... 847 673-7390
  Skokie *(G-19958)*
Bypak Inc ..................................... G ....... 815 933-2870
  Bradley *(G-2416)*
Corydon Converting Company Inc .. F ....... 630 898-9896
  Naperville *(G-15637)*
Corydon Converting Company Inc .. E ....... 630 983-1900
  Naperville *(G-15638)*
Dietzgen Corporation .................. F ....... 217 348-8111
  Charleston *(G-3596)*
Gro-Mar Industries Inc ................ F ....... 708 343-5901
  Melrose Park *(G-14649)*
I M M Inc ....................................... F ....... 773 767-3700
  Chicago *(G-5131)*
Lewis Paper Place Inc ................. G ....... 847 808-1343
  Wheeling *(G-22093)*
Norwood Industries Inc ............... F ....... 773 788-1508
  Chicago *(G-5946)*
Phoenix Paper Products Inc ....... F ....... 815 368-3343
  Lostant *(G-13907)*
Roosevelt Paper Company .......... E ....... 708 653-5121
  Alsip *(G-523)*
Rotary Paper Manifold ................. G ....... 847 758-7800
  Elk Grove Village *(G-9719)*
RTS Packaging LLC ..................... C ....... 708 338-2800
  Hillside *(G-11932)*
Seabee Supply Co ....................... G ....... 630 860-1293
  Wood Dale *(G-22421)*
Signode Industrial Group LLC .... E ....... 815 939-0033
  Kankakee *(G-12650)*
Signode Industrial Group LLC .... E ....... 708 371-9050
  Blue Island *(G-2270)*
Spectra Jet .................................... G ....... 847 669-9094
  Huntley *(G-12177)*
Trimaco LLC ................................. E ....... 919 674-3476
  Elk Grove Village *(G-9793)*

### PAPER MANUFACTURERS: Exc Newsprint

Alsip Minimill LLC ....................... F ....... 708 272-8700
  Alsip *(G-432)*
Colorkraft Roll Products Inc ....... E ....... 217 382-4967
  Martinsville *(G-14333)*
Gordon Caplan Inc ...................... G ....... 773 489-3300
  Chicago *(G-4980)*
Hollingsworth & Vose Company .. G ....... 847 222-9228
  Arlington Heights *(G-767)*
Illinois Tool Works Inc ................. G ....... 847 657-4639
  Glenview *(G-11142)*
International Paper Company ..... F ....... 618 233-5460
  Belleville *(G-1638)*
International Paper Company ..... C .......
  Elgin *(G-9079)*
International Paper Company ..... C ....... 217 735-1221
  Lincoln *(G-13411)*
International Paper Company ..... C ....... 630 449-7200
  Aurora *(G-1031)*
International Paper Company ..... F ....... 630 585-3300
  Aurora *(G-1032)*
International Paper Company ..... F ....... 630 653-3500
  Carol Stream *(G-3173)*
International Paper Company ..... C ....... 847 390-1300
  Des Plaines *(G-8213)*
International Paper Company ..... C ....... 847 228-7227
  Elk Grove Village *(G-9552)*
International Paper Company ..... C ....... 630 250-1300
  Itasca *(G-12286)*
Kapstone Paper and Packg Corp ... D ....... 847 239-8800
  Northbrook *(G-16285)*
Kdm Enterprises LLC ................... C ....... 877 591-9768
  Carpentersville *(G-3290)*
Kimberly-Clark Corporation ........ D ....... 312 371-5166
  Deerfield *(G-8025)*
Kimberly-Clark Corporation ........ C ....... 815 886-7872
  Romeoville *(G-18835)*
Kimberly-Clark Corporation ........ E ....... 708 409-8500
  Northlake *(G-16441)*
Pactiv Intl Holdings Inc .............. G ....... 847 482-2000
  Lake Forest *(G-12934)*
Paper Machine Services Inc ....... G ....... 608 365-8095
  South Beloit *(G-20163)*
Pontiac Recyclers Inc ................. G ....... 815 844-6419
  Pontiac *(G-17708)*
Roll Source Paper ........................ G ....... 630 875-0308
  Itasca *(G-12350)*
Sj Converting LLC ....................... G ....... 630 262-6640
  West Chicago *(G-21774)*
Tst/Impreso Inc ............................ G ....... 630 775-9555
  Addison *(G-330)*
Upm-Kymmene Inc ...................... G ....... 630 922-2500
  Naperville *(G-15771)*
Westrock CP LLC ......................... G ....... 847 625-8284
  Waukegan *(G-21641)*
Weyerhaeuser Company .............. G ....... 815 987-0395
  Rockford *(G-18680)*

### PAPER NAPKINS WHOLESALERS

Pierce Box & Paper Corporation ... E ....... 815 547-0117
  Belvidere *(G-1778)*

### PAPER PRDTS

Identco West LLC ........................ G ....... 815 385-0011
  Ingleside *(G-12191)*
K & N Laboratories Inc ............... F ....... 708 482-3240
  La Grange *(G-12739)*

### PAPER PRDTS: Book Covers

Norkol Inc ..................................... C ....... 708 531-1000
  Northlake *(G-16445)*

### PAPER PRDTS: Feminine Hygiene Prdts

Barrington Company .................... G ....... 815 933-3233
  Bradley *(G-2413)*
Johnson & Johnson ..................... G ....... 847 640-5400
  Elk Grove Village *(G-9563)*

### PAPER PRDTS: Pressed & Molded Pulp & Fiber Prdts

Pactiv LLC .................................... C ....... 217 479-1144
  Jacksonville *(G-12404)*

### PAPER PRDTS: Sanitary

Best Institutional Supply Co ...... G ....... 708 216-0000
  Maywood *(G-14419)*

Dude Products Inc ....................... G ....... 773 661-1126
  Chicago *(G-4647)*
Georgia-Pacific LLC .................... F ....... 815 423-9990
  Elwood *(G-9981)*
Sonoco Prtective Solutions Inc ... E ....... 708 946-3244
  Beecher *(G-1602)*
US Specialty Packaging Inc ....... F ....... 847 836-1115
  Elgin *(G-9221)*
Wells Janitorial Service Inc ........ G ....... 872 226-9983
  Chicago *(G-6953)*

### PAPER PRDTS: Sanitary Tissue Paper

Dude Products Inc ....................... G ....... 773 661-1126
  Chicago *(G-4647)*

### PAPER PRDTS: Toilet Paper, Made From Purchased Materials

Microweb ...................................... G ....... 309 426-2385
  Roseville *(G-19046)*

### PAPER PRDTS: Towels, Napkins/Tissue Paper, From Purchd Mtrls

EPS Solutions Incorporated ........ A ....... 815 206-0868
  Woodstock *(G-22566)*
Evergreen Manufacturing Inc ..... E ....... 217 382-5108
  Martinsville *(G-14335)*

### PAPER PRDTS: Wrappers, Blank, Made From Purchased Materials

Pap-R Products Company ........... D ....... 775 828-4141
  Martinsville *(G-14339)*

### PAPER, WHOLESALE: Fine

Gordon Caplan Inc ...................... G ....... 773 489-3300
  Chicago *(G-4980)*
Graphic Chemical & Ink Co ........ F ....... 630 832-6004
  Villa Park *(G-21257)*

### PAPER, WHOLESALE: Printing

CIS Systems Inc ........................... G ....... 847 827-0747
  Glenview *(G-11114)*

### PAPER, WHOLESALE: Writing

Roll Source Paper ........................ G ....... 630 875-0308
  Itasca *(G-12350)*

### PAPER: Absorbent

Evolution Sorbent Products LLC ... G ....... 630 293-8055
  West Chicago *(G-21698)*
Evolution Sorbent Products LLC ... F ....... 630 293-8055
  West Chicago *(G-21699)*

### PAPER: Adhesive

Acco Brands Corporation ............ A ....... 847 541-9500
  Lake Zurich *(G-13033)*
Chase Corporation ....................... E ....... 847 866-8500
  Evanston *(G-10022)*
H S Crocker Company Inc .......... D ....... 847 669-3600
  Huntley *(G-12143)*
Holden Industries Inc ................. F ....... 847 940-1500
  Deerfield *(G-8013)*
Primedia Source LLC .................. G ....... 630 553-8451
  Yorkville *(G-22670)*
Punch Products Manufacturing ... E ....... 773 533-2800
  Chicago *(G-6226)*
Service Packaging Design Inc ... G ....... 847 966-6592
  Morton Grove *(G-15236)*
Strata-Tac Inc .............................. F ....... 630 879-9388
  Saint Charles *(G-19272)*
Zebra Technologies Corporation ... B ....... 847 634-6700
  Lincolnshire *(G-13494)*
Zih Corp ........................................ G ....... 847 634-6700
  Lincolnshire *(G-13497)*

### PAPER: Art

Danco Converting ........................ G ....... 847 718-0448
  Chicago *(G-4551)*

### PAPER: Bank Note

First State Bank ........................... G ....... 217 239-3000
  Champaign *(G-3486)*

## PRODUCT SECTION — PAPERBOARD

### PAPER: Book
Transpac USA ..............................G...... 847 605-1616
  Schaumburg (G-19768)

### PAPER: Business Form
Advantage Printing Inc ................G...... 630 627-7468
  Lombard (G-13760)
Essentra Packaging US Inc ..........G...... 704 418-8692
  Westchester (G-21841)
Millennium Printing Inc ................G...... 847 590-8182
  Arlington Heights (G-802)

### PAPER: Cardboard
Campus Cardboard ......................G...... 847 373-7673
  Northbrook (G-16216)

### PAPER: Catalog
Master Mechanic Mfg Inc ............G...... 847 573-3812
  Mundelein (G-15524)

### PAPER: Chemically Treated, Made From Purchased Materials
Channeled Resources Inc ............E...... 312 733-4200
  Chicago (G-4287)
Daubert Vci Inc ...........................F...... 630 203-6800
  Burr Ridge (G-2835)

### PAPER: Coated & Laminated, NEC
American Name Plate & Metal De ...E...... 773 376-1400
  Chicago (G-3867)
Arcadia Press Inc ........................F...... 847 451-6390
  Franklin Park (G-10398)
Avery Dennison Corporation .........D...... 877 214-0909
  Niles (G-15962)
Basswood Associates Inc ............F...... 312 240-9400
  Chicago (G-4053)
Bisco Intl Inc ................................G...... 708 544-6308
  Hillside (G-11911)
Brasel Products Inc .....................G...... 630 879-3759
  Batavia (G-1424)
Cenveo Inc ..................................G...... 217 243-4258
  Jacksonville (G-12383)
Classique Signs & Engrv Inc .......G...... 217 228-7446
  Quincy (G-17813)
Condor Labels Inc .......................G...... 708 429-0707
  Tinley Park (G-20902)
Cushing and Company .................E...... 312 266-8228
  Chicago (G-4518)
Fedex Office & Print Svcs Inc ......F...... 847 329-9464
  Lincolnwood (G-13510)
Fedex Office & Print Svcs Inc ......E...... 309 685-4093
  Peoria (G-17359)
Gallas Label & Decal ...................F...... 773 775-1000
  Chicago (G-4909)
General Laminating Company ......G...... 847 639-8770
  Cary (G-3347)
Highland Supply Corporation .......B...... 618 654-2161
  Highland (G-11794)
Hollymatic Corporation .................D...... 708 579-3700
  Countryside (G-7430)
Hugh Courtright & Co Ltd ............F...... 708 534-8400
  Monee (G-14997)
Identco International Corp ............D...... 815 385-0011
  Ingleside (G-12190)
J & D Instant Signs ......................G...... 847 965-2800
  Morton Grove (G-15206)
Keneal Industries Inc ...................G...... 815 886-1300
  Romeoville (G-18834)
Knight Prtg & Litho Svc Ltd ..........G...... 847 487-7700
  Island Lake (G-12217)
Label Tek Inc ...............................F...... 630 820-8499
  Aurora (G-1044)
Lasons Label Co ..........................G...... 773 775-2606
  Chicago (G-5464)
Line Craft Inc ................................F...... 630 932-1182
  Lombard (G-13819)
M & R Graphics Inc .....................F...... 708 534-6621
  University Park (G-21054)
Mich Enterprises Inc ....................F...... 630 616-9000
  Wood Dale (G-22399)
Midwest Lminating Coatings Inc ..E...... 708 653-9500
  Alsip (G-493)
Nashua Corporation .....................D...... 847 692-9130
  Park Ridge (G-17211)
National Data-Label Corp .............E...... 630 616-9595
  Bensenville (G-1954)

Noor International Inc ...................G...... 847 985-2300
  Bartlett (G-1320)
Off The Press ..............................G...... 815 436-9612
  Plainfield (G-17634)
Pioneer Labels Inc ......................C...... 618 546-5418
  Robinson (G-18068)
Plitek ............................................D...... 847 827-6680
  Des Plaines (G-8257)
Preferred Printing Service ............G...... 312 421-2343
  Chicago (G-6175)
Printing Etc Inc ............................G...... 815 562-6151
  Rochelle (G-18102)
Qualified Innovation Inc ................F...... 630 556-4136
  Sugar Grove (G-20732)
Sheer Graphics Inc ......................G...... 630 654-4422
  Westmont (G-21920)
Signature Label of Illinois .............G...... 618 283-5145
  Vandalia (G-21125)
Signcraft Screenprint Inc .............C...... 815 777-3030
  Galena (G-10731)
Stephen Fossler Company ..........G...... 847 635-7200
  Des Plaines (G-8281)
Upm Raflatac Inc .........................C...... 815 285-6100
  Dixon (G-8357)
Voss Belting & Specialty Co ........E...... 847 673-8900
  Lincolnwood (G-13541)
Walter Barr Inc ............................G...... 630 325-7265
  Willowbrook (G-22238)
William Holloway Ltd ...................G...... 847 866-9520
  Evanston (G-10106)

### PAPER: Coated, Exc Photographic, Carbon Or Abrasive
Avery Dennison Corporation ........C...... 847 824-7450
  Mount Prospect (G-15312)

### PAPER: Filter
Ahlstrom Filtration LLC ................D...... 217 824-9611
  Taylorville (G-20831)

### PAPER: Gift Wrap
Mudlark Papers Inc .....................E...... 630 717-7616
  Naperville (G-15702)

### PAPER: Gummed, Made From Purchased Materials
Charles H Luck Envelope Inc .......E...... 847 451-1500
  Franklin Park (G-10427)

### PAPER: Insulation Siding
Meyer Enterprises LLC ................G...... 309 698-0062
  East Peoria (G-8725)

### PAPER: Kraft
Westrock Rkt Company ...............A...... 312 346-6600
  Chicago (G-6969)

### PAPER: Lithograph
Voyager Enterprise Inc ................G...... 815 436-2431
  Plainfield (G-17661)

### PAPER: Newsprint
Westrock CP LLC .........................D...... 312 346-6600
  Chicago (G-6967)
Windy City Word ..........................G...... 773 378-0261
  Chicago (G-7001)

### PAPER: Packaging
Amcor Flexibles LLC ....................C...... 224 313-7000
  Buffalo Grove (G-2656)
Deines-Nitz Solutions LLC ...........E...... 309 658-9985
  Erie (G-9991)
Kapstone Kraft Paper Corp ..........F...... 252 533-6000
  Northbrook (G-16284)
Matt Pak Inc ................................D...... 847 451-4018
  Franklin Park (G-10523)
Michael Lewis Company ..............C...... 708 688-2200
  Mc Cook (G-14453)
Schwarz Paper Company LLC ....G...... 847 966-2550
  Morton Grove (G-15235)
Simu Ltd ......................................F...... 630 350-1060
  Wood Dale (G-22422)

### PAPER: Printer
Dean Patterson ............................G...... 708 430-0477
  Bridgeview (G-2482)
K C Printing Services Inc ............F...... 847 382-8822
  Lake Barrington (G-12814)
Mii Inc ..........................................F...... 630 879-3000
  Batavia (G-1471)
Norkol Converting Corporation ....C...... 708 531-1000
  Melrose Park (G-14678)

### PAPER: Specialty
Midwest Converting Inc ...............D...... 708 924-1510
  Bedford Park (G-1564)

### PAPER: Tissue
Amic Global Inc ...........................G...... 847 600-3590
  Buffalo Grove (G-2659)

### PAPER: Wallpaper
Brothers Decorating .....................G...... 815 648-2214
  Hebron (G-11715)
Chartwell Studio Inc ....................G...... 847 868-8674
  Evanston (G-10021)
Cowtan and Tout Inc ...................F...... 312 644-0717
  Chicago (G-4485)

### PAPER: Waxed, Made From Purchased Materials
Waxstar Inc .................................G...... 708 755-3530
  S Chicago Hts (G-19115)

### PAPER: Wrapping & Packaging
Cousins Packaging Inc ................G...... 708 258-0063
  Peotone (G-17487)
Ripa LLC .....................................G...... 708 938-1600
  Broadview (G-2609)
S and K Packaging Incorporated ...C...... 563 582-8895
  East Dubuque (G-8621)
W/S Packaging Group Inc ............G...... 847 658-7363
  Algonquin (G-411)
Welch Packaging LLC .................G...... 630 916-8090
  Lombard (G-13882)

### PAPER: Writing
Pen At Hand ................................G...... 847 498-9174
  Northbrook (G-16337)
Semper/Exeter Paper Co LLC .....G...... 630 775-9500
  Bloomingdale (G-2136)

### PAPERBOARD
Armbrust Paper Tubes Inc ...........E...... 773 586-3232
  Chicago (G-3945)
C F Anderson & Co .....................F...... 312 341-0850
  Chicago (G-4203)
Capitol Carton Company ..............E...... 312 563-9690
  Chicago (G-4229)
Grafcor Packaging Inc .................F...... 815 639-2380
  Loves Park (G-13945)
International Paper Company ......A...... 217 774-2176
  Shelbyville (G-19909)
Jsc Products Inc ..........................G...... 847 290-9520
  Elk Grove Village (G-9566)
KJK Corp .....................................G...... 815 389-0566
  South Beloit (G-20156)
Logan Graphic Products Inc ........D...... 847 526-5515
  Wauconda (G-21479)
Mac American Corporation ..........G...... 847 277-9450
  Barrington (G-1288)
Midwest Cortland Inc ...................E...... 847 671-0376
  Addison (G-211)
Ox Paperboard LLC .....................D...... 309 346-4118
  Pekin (G-17277)
Pactiv LLC ...................................C......
  Lincolnshire (G-13469)
Pactiv LLC ...................................C...... 708 534-6595
  University Park (G-21059)
Pekin Paperboard Company LP ..E...... 309 346-4118
  Pekin (G-17281)
Rocktenn Cp LLC .........................E...... 630 587-9429
  Saint Charles (G-19253)
RTS Packaging LLC ....................C...... 708 338-2800
  Hillside (G-11932)
Siebs Die Cutting Specialty Co ....G...... 217 735-1432
  Lincoln (G-13420)

Employee Codes: A=Over 500 employees, B=251-500
C=101-250, D=51-100, E=20-50, F=10-19, G=3-9

# PAPERBOARD

**Signode Industrial Group LLC** .............E....... 815 939-0033
Kankakee *(G-12650)*
**Sonoco Products Company** ...................D....... 630 231-1489
West Chicago *(G-21775)*
**Stevenson Paper Co Inc** .......................G....... 630 879-5000
Batavia *(G-1498)*
**The Calumet Carton Company** .............D....... 708 331-7910
South Holland *(G-20310)*
**Westrock Cp LLC** ..................................D....... 708 458-8100
Bridgeview *(G-2539)*
**Westrock Cp LLC** ..................................E....... 630 924-0104
Bartlett *(G-1325)*
**Westrock Cp LLC** ..................................D....... 630 260-3500
Carol Stream *(G-3267)*
**Westrock Cp LLC** ..................................C....... 309 342-0121
Galesburg *(G-10780)*
**Westrock CP LLC** .................................D....... 630 443-3538
Saint Charles *(G-19294)*
**Westrock CP LLC** .................................G....... 773 264-3516
Chicago *(G-6966)*
**Westrock CP LLC** .................................G....... 847 625-8284
Waukegan *(G-21641)*
**Westrock CP LLC** .................................D....... 630 924-0054
Bartlett *(G-1326)*
**Westrock CP LLC** .................................D....... 708 458-5288
Bedford Park *(G-1593)*

## PAPERBOARD CONVERTING

**Crescent Cardboard Company LLC** .....C....... 888 293-3956
Wheeling *(G-22032)*
**General Laminating Company** ..............G....... 847 639-8770
Cary *(G-3347)*
**Linn West Paper Company** ...................G....... 773 561-3839
Chicago *(G-5514)*
**Loyola Paper Company** .........................E....... 847 956-7770
Elk Grove Village *(G-9598)*
**Potomac Corporation** ............................G....... 847 259-0546
Wheeling *(G-22126)*
**Quality Paper Inc** ...................................F....... 847 258-3999
Elk Grove Village *(G-9702)*
**Schwab Paper Products Company** ......E....... 815 372-2233
Romeoville *(G-18867)*
**Stanford Products LLC** .........................G....... 618 548-2600
Salem *(G-19354)*

## PAPERBOARD PRDTS: Building Insulating & Packaging

**Terrapin Xpress Inc** ................................G....... 866 823-7323
Palos Heights *(G-17111)*

## PAPERBOARD PRDTS: Container Board

**Graphic Packaging Intl Inc** ....................G....... 630 260-6500
Carol Stream *(G-3162)*
**Graphic Packaging Intl Inc** ....................B....... 847 437-1700
Elk Grove Village *(G-9509)*
**Packaging Corporation America** ...........C....... 847 482-3000
Lake Forest *(G-12933)*
**Westrock Rkt Company** ........................A....... 312 346-6600
Chicago *(G-6969)*

## PAPERBOARD PRDTS: Folding Boxboard

**Artistic Carton Company** .......................E....... 847 741-0247
Elgin *(G-8958)*
**Berry Global Inc** ....................................C....... 847 884-1200
Schaumburg *(G-19461)*
**Graphic Packaging Corporation** ............C....... 847 451-7400
Franklin Park *(G-10483)*
**Graphic Packaging Holding Co** .............B....... 630 260-6500
Carol Stream *(G-3161)*
**Graphic Packaging Intl Inc** ....................A....... 847 354-3554
Elk Grove Village *(G-9510)*
**Graphic Packaging Intl Inc** ....................C....... 630 260-6500
Carol Stream *(G-3163)*
**Simon Box Mfg Co** ................................G....... 815 722-6661
Lockport *(G-13745)*

## PAPERBOARD PRDTS: Packaging Board

**Barrington Packaging Systems** ............G....... 847 382-8063
Barrington *(G-1272)*
**Rjg Enterprises Ltd** ...............................G....... 847 752-2065
Grayslake *(G-11362)*

## PAPERBOARD: Liner Board

**Rocktenn** ................................................F....... 773 254-1030
Chicago *(G-6376)*
**Westrock CP LLC** .................................D....... 312 346-6600
Chicago *(G-6967)*

**Westrock Mwv LLC** ...............................C....... 773 221-9015
Chicago *(G-6968)*
**Westrock Mwv LLC** ...............................E....... 217 442-2247
Danville *(G-7784)*
**Westrock Mwv LLC** ...............................C....... 630 289-8537
Bartlett *(G-1386)*

## PAPETERIES & WRITING PAPER SETS

**Discount Computer Supply Inc** ..............G....... 847 883-8743
Buffalo Grove *(G-2688)*

## PAPIER-MACHE PRDTS, EXC STATUARY & ART GOODS

**Franch & Sons Trnsp Inc** ......................G....... 630 392-3307
Addison *(G-123)*

## PARKERIZING SVC

**Salt Creek Rural Park District** ...............F....... 847 259-6890
Palatine *(G-17071)*

## PARKING LOTS

**Clean Sweep Environmental Inc** ...........G....... 630 879-8750
Batavia *(G-1431)*

## PARTICLEBOARD

**Georgia-Pacific Bldg Pdts LLC** .............G....... 630 449-7200
Aurora *(G-1015)*

## PARTITIONS & FIXTURES: Except Wood

**Accurate Partitions Corp** .......................G....... 708 442-6801
Mc Cook *(G-14444)*
**Alessco Inc** .............................................F....... 773 327-7919
Chicago *(G-3801)*
**American Rack Company** ......................E....... 773 763-7309
Chicago *(G-3870)*
**Apex Wire Products Company Inc** ........F....... 847 671-1830
Franklin Park *(G-10397)*
**Armbrust Paper Tubes Inc** ....................E....... 773 586-3232
Chicago *(G-3945)*
**Art Wire Works Inc** ................................F....... 708 458-3993
Bedford Park *(G-1538)*
**Associated Rack Corporation** ................F....... 616 554-6004
Chicago *(G-3970)*
**B Andrews Inc** .......................................G....... 847 381-7444
Barrington *(G-1269)*
**Bar Stool Depotcom** .............................G....... 815 727-7294
Joliet *(G-12460)*
**Bel Mar Wire Products Inc** ....................F....... 773 342-3800
Chicago *(G-4073)*
**Bilt-Rite Metal Products Inc** ..................E....... 815 495-2211
Leland *(G-13218)*
**Builders United Sales Co Inc** ................G....... 815 467-2224
Minooka *(G-14837)*
**C-V Cstom Cntrtops Cbinets Inc** ..........F....... 708 388-5066
Blue Island *(G-2241)*
**Cameo Container Corporation** ...............C....... 773 254-1030
Chicago *(G-4222)*
**Capitol Carton Company** ........................E....... 312 563-9690
Chicago *(G-4229)*
**Capitol Wood Works LLC** ......................D....... 217 522-5553
Springfield *(G-20408)*
**Carl Stahl Decorcble Innovtns** ..............F....... 312 454-2996
Burr Ridge *(G-2828)*
**Chicago American Mfg LLC** ..................G....... 773 376-0100
Chicago *(G-4302)*
**Colony Inc** ..............................................E....... 847 426-5300
Elgin *(G-8994)*
**Consolidated Displays Co Inc** ...............G....... 630 851-8666
Oswego *(G-16911)*
**Creative Metal Products** ........................F....... 773 638-3200
Chicago *(G-4500)*
**DAmico Associates Inc** .........................G....... 847 291-7446
Northbrook *(G-16239)*
**Ets-Lindgren Inc** ....................................G....... 630 307-7200
Wood Dale *(G-22363)*
**Forest City Counter Tops Inc** ................F....... 815 633-8602
Loves Park *(G-13942)*
**Geneva Manufacturing Co** ....................F....... 847 697-1161
South Elgin *(G-20199)*
**Harder Signs Inc** ...................................F....... 815 874-7777
Rockford *(G-18413)*
**IMS Engineered Products LLC** .............C....... 847 391-8100
Des Plaines *(G-8211)*
**Inter-Market Inc** .....................................G....... 847 729-5330
Glenview *(G-11149)*
**Interlake Mecalux Inc** ............................C....... 815 844-7191
Pontiac *(G-17703)*

**Interlake Mecalux Inc** ............................B....... 708 344-9999
Melrose Park *(G-14659)*
**Iretired LLC** ............................................E....... 630 285-9500
Itasca *(G-12287)*
**Ivan Carlson Associates Inc** .................E....... 312 829-4616
Chicago *(G-5248)*
**Klein Tools Inc** .......................................D....... 847 228-6999
Elk Grove Village *(G-9577)*
**Klein Tools Inc** .......................................E....... 847 821-5500
Lincolnshire *(G-13461)*
**Lyon Workspace Products Inc** ..............G....... 630 892-8941
Montgomery *(G-15058)*
**Mailbox International Inc** .......................G....... 847 541-8466
Wheeling *(G-22097)*
**Metal Box International Inc** ...................C....... 847 455-8500
Franklin Park *(G-10529)*
**Middletons Mouldings Inc** .....................G....... 517 278-6610
Schaumburg *(G-19646)*
**Multiplex Display Fixture Co** .................E....... 800 325-3350
Dupo *(G-8574)*
**Rome Metal Mfg Inc** ..............................G....... 773 287-1755
Chicago *(G-6389)*
**Royal Fabricators Inc** ............................F....... 847 775-7466
Wadsworth *(G-21327)*
**RTC Industries Inc** ................................D....... 847 640-2400
Chicago *(G-6409)*
**Rwi Holdings Inc** ...................................F....... 630 897-6951
Aurora *(G-1211)*
**Ryan Metal Products Inc** .......................E....... 815 936-0700
Kankakee *(G-12647)*
**United Wire Craft Inc** .............................C....... 847 375-3800
Des Plaines *(G-8291)*
**West Zwick Corp** ...................................G....... 217 222-0228
Quincy *(G-17903)*
**Wind Point Partners Vi LP** .....................G....... 312 255-4800
Chicago *(G-6993)*
**Ww Displays Inc** ....................................F....... 847 566-6979
Mundelein *(G-15568)*

## PARTITIONS: Solid Fiber, Made From Purchased Materials

**Westrock Company** ...............................C....... 630 429-2400
Aurora *(G-1233)*

## PARTITIONS: Wood & Fixtures

**Ability Cabinet Co Inc** ............................G....... 847 678-6678
Franklin Park *(G-10383)*
**Abitzy Inc** ................................................G....... 847 659-9228
Lombard *(G-13757)*
**Action Cabinet Sales Inc** .......................G....... 847 717-0011
Elgin *(G-8935)*
**Allie Woodworking** .................................G....... 847 244-1919
Waukegan *(G-21522)*
**American Fixture** ...................................G....... 217 429-1300
Decatur *(G-7832)*
**Anderson & Marter Cabinets** .................D....... 630 406-9840
Batavia *(G-1415)*
**B & B Formica Appliers Inc** ...................F....... 773 804-1015
Chicago *(G-4014)*
**Bards Products Inc** ................................F....... 800 323-5499
Mundelein *(G-15475)*
**Bolhuis Woodworking Co** ......................G....... 708 333-5100
Manhattan *(G-14168)*
**Brakur Custom Cabinetry Inc** ................C....... 630 355-2244
Shorewood *(G-19923)*
**C-V Cstom Cntrtops Cbinets Inc** ..........F....... 708 388-5066
Blue Island *(G-2241)*
**Cabinet Designs** ....................................G....... 708 614-8603
Oak Forest *(G-16575)*
**Capitol Wood Works LLC** ......................D....... 217 522-5553
Springfield *(G-20408)*
**Chicago Booth Mfg Inc** ..........................F....... 773 378-8400
Chicago *(G-4307)*
**Colony Inc** ..............................................E....... 847 426-5300
Elgin *(G-8994)*
**Contempo Marble & Granite Inc** ...........G....... 312 455-0022
Chicago *(G-4456)*
**Cooper Lake Millworks Inc** ....................G....... 217 847-2681
Hamilton *(G-11530)*
**Creative Cabinetry Inc** ...........................G....... 708 460-2900
Orland Park *(G-16851)*
**Custom Window Accents** ......................F....... 815 943-7651
Harvard *(G-11629)*
**Custom Woodwork & Interiors** ..............E....... 217 546-0006
Springfield *(G-20427)*
**Der Holtzmacher Ltd** ............................G....... 815 895-4887
Sycamore *(G-20792)*
**Design Woodworks** ...............................G....... 847 566-6603
Mundelein *(G-15493)*

Dpcac LLC .................................................. F ...... 630 741-7900
  Itasca  (G-12253)
Eddie Gapastione ...................................... G ...... 708 430-3881
  Bridgeview  (G-2487)
Fra-Milco Cabinets Co Inc ........................ G
  Frankfort  (G-10323)
Gerali Custom Design Inc ......................... D ...... 847 760-0500
  Elgin  (G-9044)
Glenview Custom Cabinets Inc ................. G ...... 847 345-5754
  Glenview  (G-11130)
Hansen Custom Cabinet Inc ..................... G ...... 847 356-1100
  Lake Villa  (G-13015)
Hickory Street Cabinets ............................ G ...... 618 667-9676
  Troy  (G-21007)
Hylan Design Ltd ...................................... G ...... 312 243-7341
  Chicago  (G-5129)
J K Custom Countertops .......................... G ...... 630 495-2324
  Lombard  (G-13813)
Janik Custom Millwork Inc ....................... G ...... 708 482-4844
  Hodgkins  (G-11977)
Jbc Holding Co ......................................... G ...... 217 347-7701
  Effingham  (G-8841)
John F Mate Co ......................................... G ...... 847 381-8131
  Lake Barrington  (G-12812)
Kabinet Kraft ............................................. F ...... 618 395-1047
  Olney  (G-16775)
Laminated Designs Countertops .............. G ...... 815 877-7222
  Machesney Park  (G-14088)
M & R Custom Millwork ............................ G ...... 815 547-8549
  Belvidere  (G-1768)
Meier Granite Company ............................ G ...... 847 678-7300
  Franklin Park  (G-10527)
Miller Manufacturing Co Inc ..................... D ...... 636 343-5700
  Dupo  (G-8573)
Miller Whiteside Wood Working ............... G ...... 309 827-6470
  Mc Lean  (G-14463)
Monticello Design & Mfg ......................... G ...... 217 762-8551
  Monticello  (G-15081)
Nelson - Harkins Inds Inc ........................ E ...... 773 478-6243
  Chicago  (G-5884)
Northwest Marble Products ..................... E ...... 630 860-2288
  Hoffman Estates  (G-12072)
OGorman Son Carpentry Contrs .............. E ...... 815 485-8997
  New Lenox  (G-15898)
Perfection Custom Closets & Co .............. F ...... 847 647-6461
  Niles  (G-16017)
Rays Countertop Shop Inc ....................... G ...... 217 483-2514
  Glenarm  (G-10997)
Regency Custom Woodworking ............... F ...... 815 689-2117
  Cullom  (G-7683)
Roncin Custom Design ............................ G ...... 847 669-0260
  Huntley  (G-12175)
Suburban Fabricators Inc ........................ G ...... 847 729-0866
  Glenview  (G-11206)
Suburban Laminating Inc ........................ G ...... 708 389-6106
  Melrose Park  (G-14697)
Swan Surfaces LLC .................................. C ...... 618 532-5673
  Centralia  (G-3435)
T J Kellogg Inc ......................................... G ...... 815 969-0524
  Rockford  (G-18640)
Unistrut International Corp ..................... D ...... 630 773-3460
  Addison  (G-334)
Wind Point Partners Vi LP ....................... G ...... 312 255-4800
  Chicago  (G-6993)
Woodhill Cabinetry Design Inc ................ G ...... 815 431-0545
  Ottawa  (G-16992)

## PARTS: Metal

Amag Manufacturing Inc ......................... G ...... 773 667-5184
  Chicago  (G-3843)
BR Concepts International Inc ................ G ...... 847 674-9481
  Skokie  (G-19968)
Chips Manufacturing Inc ......................... D ...... 630 682-4477
  West Chicago  (G-21681)
Component Parts Company ..................... G ...... 815 477-2323
  Crystal Lake  (G-7556)
Ferguson Enterprises Inc ........................ G ...... 217 425-7262
  Decatur  (G-7881)
G&M Metal ................................................ G ...... 630 616-1126
  Elk Grove Village  (G-9492)
Gears Gears Gears Inc ............................. G ...... 708 366-6555
  Harwood Heights  (G-11685)
Nuair Filter Company LLC ....................... F ...... 309 888-4331
  Normal  (G-16081)

## PASTES: Metal

Senju Comtek Corp .................................. G ...... 847 549-5690
  Mundelein  (G-15555)

## PATCHING PLASTER: Household

Rda Inc ..................................................... F ...... 815 427-8444
  Saint Anne  (G-19125)

## PATENT OWNERS & LESSORS

3b Media Inc ............................................. F ...... 312 563-9363
  Chicago  (G-3667)

## PATIENT MONITORING EQPT WHOLESALERS

Lifewatch Corp ......................................... G ...... 847 720-2100
  Rosemont  (G-19012)
Lifewatch Services Inc ............................. B ...... 847 720-2100
  Rosemont  (G-19013)

## PATTERNS: Indl

Advanced Pattern Works LLC .................. G ...... 618 346-9039
  Collinsville  (G-7312)
Alang Pattern Inc ..................................... G ...... 773 722-9481
  Cicero  (G-7177)
Beloit Pattern Works ................................ F ...... 815 389-2578
  South Beloit  (G-20140)
Cambridge Pattern Works ........................ G ...... 309 937-5370
  Cambridge  (G-2966)
Capital Pttern Model Works Inc ............... G ...... 630 469-8200
  Glendale Heights  (G-11013)
Carroll Industrial Molds Inc .................... F ...... 815 225-7250
  Milledgeville  (G-14816)
Chem-Cast Ltd ......................................... C ...... 217 443-5532
  Danville  (G-7709)
Clinkenbeard & Associates Inc ............... G ...... 815 226-0291
  Rockford  (G-18313)
Curto-Ligonier Foundries Co ................... E ...... 708 345-2250
  Melrose Park  (G-14613)
E & E Pattern Works Inc .......................... G ...... 847 689-1088
  North Chicago  (G-16177)
Jsp Mold ................................................... G ...... 815 225-7110
  Milledgeville  (G-14817)
Kerrigan Corporation Inc ......................... G ...... 847 251-8994
  Wilmette  (G-22257)
Koswell Pattern Works Inc ...................... G ...... 708 757-5225
  Lynwood  (G-14020)
Master Foundry Inc .................................. F ...... 217 223-7396
  Quincy  (G-17856)
Microtek Pattern Inc ................................ G ...... 217 428-0433
  Decatur  (G-7913)
Midwest Patterns Inc ............................... C ...... 217 228-6900
  Quincy  (G-17859)
Modern Pattern Works Inc ...................... G ...... 309 676-2157
  Peoria  (G-17411)
N & S Pattern Co ...................................... F ...... 815 874-6166
  Rockford  (G-18514)
Nosko Manufacturing Inc ........................ G ...... 847 678-0813
  Schiller Park  (G-19854)
P & H Pattern Inc ..................................... G ...... 815 795-2449
  Marseilles  (G-14315)
Precision Entps Fndry Mch Inc ............... G ...... 815 797-1000
  Somonauk  (G-20128)
Precision Foundry Tooling Ltd ................ F ...... 217 847-3233
  Hamilton  (G-11539)
Quincy Foundry & Pattern Co .................. G ...... 217 222-0718
  Quincy  (G-17877)
R & C Pattern Works Inc .......................... G ...... 708 331-1882
  South Holland  (G-20299)
R C Castings Inc ...................................... G ...... 708 331-1882
  South Holland  (G-20300)
Rockbridge Casting Inc ........................... G ...... 618 753-3188
  Rockbridge  (G-18212)
Spectron Manufacturing .......................... G ...... 720 879-7605
  Bloomingdale  (G-2138)
Sun Pattern & Model Inc ......................... E ...... 630 293-3366
  West Chicago  (G-21777)
Tilton Pattern Works Inc ......................... F ...... 217 442-1502
  Danville  (G-7776)
Voss Pattern Works Inc ........................... G ...... 618 233-4242
  Belleville  (G-1689)

## PAVERS

Paver Protector Inc ................................. G ...... 630 488-0069
  Gilberts  (G-10931)
Pioneer Pavers Inc ................................... G ...... 847 833-9866
  McHenry  (G-14545)

## PAVING MATERIALS: Prefabricated, Concrete

Peter Baker & Son Co .............................. D ...... 847 362-3663
  Lake Bluff  (G-12861)
Tickle Asphalt Co Ltd .............................. G ...... 309 787-1308
  Milan  (G-14806)

## PAVING MIXTURES

Byron Blacktop Inc ................................... G ...... 815 234-2225
  Byron  (G-2913)

## PAYROLL SVCS

Willis Stein & Partners Manage ............... E ...... 312 422-2400
  Northbrook  (G-16387)

## PEAT GRINDING SVCS

Markman Peat Corp .................................. E ...... 815 772-4014
  Morrison  (G-15146)

## PENCILS & PENS WHOLESALERS

C H Hanson Company ............................. D ...... 630 848-2000
  Naperville  (G-15613)

## PENS & PARTS: Ball Point

Eversharp Pen Company ......................... E ...... 847 366-5030
  Franklin Park  (G-10466)
Fayco Enterprises Inc ............................. E ...... 618 283-0638
  Vandalia  (G-21113)

## PENS & PARTS: Stylographic

Techgraphic Solutions Inc ...................... F ...... 309 693-9400
  Peoria  (G-17467)

## PENS & PENCILS: Mechanical, NEC

Alexander Manufacturing Co ................... D ...... 309 728-2224
  Towanda  (G-20978)
Pilot Corporation of America .................. G ...... 773 792-1111
  Park Ridge  (G-17216)
Sanford LP ............................................... A ...... 770 418-7000
  Downers Grove  (G-8518)

## PENSION & RETIREMENT PLAN CONSULTANTS

Envestnet Rtrment Slutions LLC ............ G ...... 312 827-7957
  Chicago  (G-4764)

## PERFUME: Concentrated

Lab TEC Cosmt By Marzena Inc .............. F ...... 630 396-3970
  Addison  (G-176)

## PERFUME: Perfumes, Natural Or Synthetic

Marcy Laboratories Inc ............................ E ...... 630 377-6655
  West Chicago  (G-21738)

## PERFUMES

A&B Apparel .............................................. G ...... 815 962-5070
  Rockford  (G-18241)
Michael Christopher Ltd .......................... G ...... 815 308-5018
  Woodstock  (G-22589)
Smile Aromatics Inc ................................ G ...... 847 759-0350
  Des Plaines  (G-8277)
Takasago Intl Corp USA .......................... G ...... 815 479-5030
  Crystal Lake  (G-7659)
Tru Fragrance & Beauty LLC ................... E ...... 630 563-4110
  Willowbrook  (G-22235)

## PERLITE: Processed

Phoenix Services LLC .............................. G ...... 708 849-3527
  Riverdale  (G-18022)

## PERSONAL & HOUSEHOLD GOODS REPAIR, NEC

Globe Union Group Inc ............................ D ...... 630 679-1420
  Woodridge  (G-22487)
Kaser Power Equipment Inc .................... G ...... 309 289-2176
  Knoxville  (G-12721)

## PERSONAL CREDIT INSTITUTIONS: Finance Licensed Loan Co's, Sm

Russell Enterprises Inc .......................... E ....... 847 692-6050
  Park Ridge *(G-17221)*

## PERSONAL DOCUMENT & INFORMATION SVCS

Source Software Inc .............................. G ....... 815 922-7717
  Lockport *(G-13747)*

## PERSONAL INVESTIGATION SVCS

National Def Intelligence Inc ................. G ....... 630 757-4007
  Naperville *(G-15818)*

## PERSONAL SHOPPING SVCS

Mjt Design and Prtg Entps Inc .............. G ....... 708 240-4323
  Hillside *(G-11926)*

## PEST CONTROL IN STRUCTURES SVCS

Smithereen Company ............................ D ....... 800 340-1888
  Niles *(G-16034)*

## PEST CONTROL SVCS

Cardinal Professional Products ............ G ....... 714 761-3292
  Decatur *(G-7850)*

## PESTICIDES WHOLESALERS

Lebanon Seaboard Corporation ............ E ....... 217 446-0983
  Danville *(G-7746)*

## PET FOOD WHOLESALERS

Frito-Lay North America Inc .................. C ....... 708 331-7200
  Oak Forest *(G-16582)*
Garver Feeds ........................................ E ....... 217 422-2201
  Decatur *(G-7884)*

## PET SPLYS

Ace Wood Products LLC ....................... G ....... 630 557-2115
  Sugar Grove *(G-20716)*
All For Dogs Inc .................................... G ....... 708 744-4113
  Plainfield *(G-17578)*
Ameriguard Corporation ....................... G ....... 630 986-1900
  Burr Ridge *(G-2822)*
Andrew C Arnold .................................. G ....... 815 220-0282
  Peru *(G-17499)*
Aquadine Inc ........................................ G ....... 800 497-3463
  Harvard *(G-11621)*
Bentleys Pet Stuff LLC ......................... G ....... 312 222-1012
  Chicago *(G-4084)*
Bentleys Pet Stuff LLC ......................... F ....... 847 793-0500
  Long Grove *(G-13886)*
Bentleys Pet Stuff LLC ......................... G ....... 224 567-4700
  Long Grove *(G-13887)*
Bone A Fide Pet Grooming ................... G ....... 217 872-0907
  Decatur *(G-7848)*
Boss Manufacturing Holdings ............... G ....... 309 852-2131
  Kewanee *(G-12676)*
Dal Acres West Kennel ......................... G ....... 217 793-3647
  Springfield *(G-20428)*
Diamond Dogs ...................................... G ....... 773 267-0069
  Chicago *(G-4593)*
DMJ Group Inc ..................................... G ....... 847 322-7533
  Algonquin *(G-388)*
Dura-Crafts Corp .................................. F ....... 815 464-3561
  Frankfort *(G-10316)*
GM Partners ......................................... G ....... 847 895-7627
  Schaumburg *(G-19538)*
Groomsmart Inc ................................... G ....... 847 836-6007
  Dundee *(G-8562)*
Hunter Mfg LLP .................................... D ....... 859 254-7573
  Lake Forest *(G-12912)*
Keys Manufacturing Company Inc ........ E ....... 217 465-4001
  Paris *(G-17152)*
Kmp Products LLC ............................... G ....... 630 956-0438
  Westmont *(G-21899)*
Kyjen Company LLC ............................. F ....... 847 504-4010
  Northbrook *(G-16291)*
Lucky Yuppy Puppy Co Inc ................... G ....... 847 437-7879
  Arlington Heights *(G-796)*
Luxury Living Inc .................................. G ....... 847 845-3863
  Cary *(G-3358)*
Ming Trading LLC ................................. G ....... 773 442-2221
  Chicago *(G-5767)*
Molor Products Company ..................... F ....... 630 375-5999
  Oswego *(G-16927)*
Nature House Inc ................................. D ....... 217 833-2393
  Griggsville *(G-11413)*
Pawz & Klawz ...................................... G ....... 630 257-0245
  Lemont *(G-13252)*
Pet King Brands Inc ............................. G ....... 630 241-3905
  Westmont *(G-21911)*
Petego Egr LLC .................................... G ....... 312 726-1341
  Chicago *(G-6108)*
Petote LLC ........................................... G ....... 312 455-0873
  Chicago *(G-6112)*
Prevue Pet Products Inc ....................... F ....... 773 722-1052
  Chicago *(G-6183)*
Robs Aquatics ...................................... G ....... 708 444-7627
  Tinley Park *(G-20943)*
Starfish Ventures Inc ............................ E ....... 847 490-9334
  Hoffman Estates *(G-12059)*
Sunscape Time Inc .............................. G ....... 708 345-8791
  Melrose Park *(G-14698)*
Whyte Gate Incorporated ..................... F ....... 847 201-7000
  Grayslake *(G-11366)*
Wish Bone Rescue ............................... G ....... 309 212-9210
  Bloomington *(G-2236)*

## PET SPLYS WHOLESALERS

Lucky Yuppy Puppy Co Inc ................... G ....... 847 437-7879
  Arlington Heights *(G-796)*
Midwestern Pet Foods Inc .................... E ....... 309 734-3121
  Monmouth *(G-15019)*
Petego Egr LLC .................................... G ....... 312 726-1341
  Chicago *(G-6108)*
Prevue Pet Products Inc ....................... F ....... 773 722-1052
  Chicago *(G-6183)*
Wagners LLC ....................................... E ....... 815 889-4101
  Milford *(G-14815)*

## PETROLEUM & PETROLEUM PRDTS, WHOL Svc Station Splys, Petro

R L Hoener Co ..................................... E ....... 217 223-2190
  Quincy *(G-17883)*

## PETROLEUM & PETROLEUM PRDTS, WHOLESALE Fuel Oil

Huels Oil Company ............................... G ....... 877 338-6277
  Carlyle *(G-3054)*
R H Johnson Oil Co Inc ........................ G ....... 630 668-3649
  Wheaton *(G-21974)*

## PETROLEUM & PETROLEUM PRDTS, WHOLESALE Petroleum Brokers

South Central Fs Inc ............................ F ....... 217 849-2242
  Toledo *(G-20966)*

## PETROLEUM & PETROLEUM PRDTS, WHOLESALE Petroleum Terminals

Bi-Petro Inc .......................................... E ....... 217 535-0181
  Springfield *(G-20396)*

## PETROLEUM & PETROLEUM PRDTS, WHOLESALE: Bulk Stations

AMP Americas LLC .............................. F ....... 312 300-6700
  Chicago *(G-3893)*
Newby Oil Company Inc ....................... G ....... 815 756-7688
  Sycamore *(G-20810)*
Premium Oil Company .......................... F ....... 815 963-3800
  Rockford *(G-18540)*
South Central Fs Inc ............................ E ....... 618 283-1557
  Vandalia *(G-21126)*

## PETROLEUM BULK STATIONS & TERMINALS

BP America Inc .................................... A ....... 630 420-5111
  Warrenville *(G-21344)*
BP Products North America Inc ............ G ....... 630 420-4300
  Naperville *(G-15609)*
Drig Corporation .................................. G ....... 312 265-1509
  Chicago *(G-4644)*
Effingham Equity Inc ............................ F ....... 217 268-5128
  Arcola *(G-668)*
Pdv Midwest Refining LLC ................... A ....... 630 257-7761
  Lemont *(G-13254)*
Wabash Valley Service Co ................... F ....... 618 393-2971
  Olney *(G-16800)*

## PETROLEUM PRDTS WHOLESALERS

BP Products North America Inc ............ D ....... 312 594-7689
  Chicago *(G-4153)*
Dougherty E J Oil & Stone Sup ............ G ....... 618 271-4414
  East Saint Louis *(G-8748)*
Koch Industries Inc ............................. G ....... 312 867-1295
  Chicago *(G-5394)*
Marathon Petroleum Company LP ........ A ....... 618 544-2121
  Robinson *(G-18066)*
Marathon Petroleum Company LP ........ E ....... 618 829-3288
  Saint Elmo *(G-19308)*
Ross Oil Co Inc ................................... G ....... 618 592-3808
  Oblong *(G-16733)*
Tower Oil & Technology Co ................. E ....... 773 927-6161
  Chicago *(G-6752)*

## PETROLEUM REFINERY INSPECTION SVCS

Rain Cii Carbon LLC ............................ E ....... 618 544-2193
  Robinson *(G-18071)*

## PETS & PET SPLYS, WHOLESALE

Diddy Dogs Inc .................................... G ....... 815 517-0451
  Dekalb *(G-8088)*
Howard Pet Products Inc ..................... E ....... 973 398-3038
  Saint Charles *(G-19194)*

## PHARMACEUTICAL PREPARATIONS: Adrenal

Bridgeport Pharmacy Inc ..................... G ....... 312 326-3200
  Chicago *(G-4166)*
Nantpharma LLC ................................. G ....... 847 243-1200
  Rolling Meadows *(G-18747)*
Pharmdium Hlthcare Hldings Inc ......... G ....... 800 523-7749
  Lake Forest *(G-12943)*

## PHARMACEUTICAL PREPARATIONS: Druggists' Preparations

Aardvark Pharma LLC ......................... E ....... 630 248-2380
  Oakbrook Terrace *(G-16693)*
Alva/Amco Pharmacal Companies ....... E ....... 847 663-0700
  Niles *(G-15959)*
Espee .................................................. G ....... 224 256-9570
  Schaumburg *(G-19519)*
Glenview Pharma Inc .......................... F ....... 773 856-3205
  Chicago *(G-4956)*
Hospira Inc .......................................... C ....... 224 212-6244
  Lake Forest *(G-12909)*
International Drug Dev Cons ............... G ....... 847 634-9586
  Long Grove *(G-13892)*
Meda Pharmaceuticals Inc .................. D ....... 217 424-8400
  Decatur *(G-7912)*
Merix Pharmaceutical Corp ................. G ....... 847 277-1111
  Barrington *(G-1290)*
Novalex Therapeutics Inc ................... G ....... 630 750-9334
  Chicago *(G-5947)*
Riverside Medi-Center Inc .................. G ....... 815 932-6632
  Kankakee *(G-12645)*
Sfc Chemicals Ltd .............................. G ....... 847 221-2152
  Chicago *(G-6486)*

## PHARMACEUTICAL PREPARATIONS: Medicines, Capsule Or Ampule

Abbott Laboratories ............................ A ....... 847 935-8130
  Gurnee *(G-11417)*
Access Medical Supply Inc ................. G ....... 847 891-6210
  Schaumburg *(G-19420)*
East West Intergrated Therapys ......... G ....... 815 788-0574
  Crystal Lake *(G-7570)*

## PHARMACEUTICAL PREPARATIONS: Pills

Am2pat Inc .......................................... G ....... 847 726-9443
  Chicago *(G-3842)*
Amerisourcebergen Corporation .......... E ....... 815 221-3600
  Romeoville *(G-18797)*
Ashland ABC Choice Inc ..................... G ....... 773 488-7800
  Chicago *(G-3960)*
Black Start Labs Inc ........................... G ....... 630 444-1800
  Saint Charles *(G-19144)*
Roundtble Hlthcare Partners LP .......... E ....... 847 482-9275
  Lake Forest *(G-12954)*

## PHARMACEUTICAL PREPARATIONS: Powders

**Athenex Pharmaceutical Div LLC** E 847 922-8041
Schaumburg *(G-19449)*

**Meitheal Pharmaceuticals Inc** G 773 951-6542
Des Plaines *(G-8232)*

**Meridian Laboratories Inc** G 847 808-0081
Buffalo Grove *(G-2735)*

**Sukgyung At Inc** G 847 298-6570
Des Plaines *(G-8282)*

## PHARMACEUTICAL PREPARATIONS: Proprietary Drug PRDTS

**Abbvie Products LLC** B 847 937-6100
North Chicago *(G-16169)*

**Aeropharm Technology LLC** G 847 937-6100
North Chicago *(G-16174)*

**Flexxsonic Corporation** G 847 452-7226
Mount Prospect *(G-15330)*

**Jewel Osco Inc** C 630 948-6000
Itasca *(G-12291)*

## PHARMACEUTICAL PREPARATIONS: Solutions

**Allergan Inc** G 714 246-4500
Gurnee *(G-11426)*

**Care Solutions Incorporated** F 815 301-4034
Crystal Lake *(G-7550)*

**Winlind Skincare LLC** G 630 789-9408
Burr Ridge *(G-2896)*

## PHARMACEUTICAL PREPARATIONS: Tablets

**Sunstar Pharmaceutical Inc** D 773 777-4000
Elgin *(G-9198)*

## PHARMACEUTICALS

**A-S Medication Solutions LLC** D 847 680-3515
Libertyville *(G-13297)*

**Abbott Health Products Inc** D 847 937-6100
North Chicago *(G-16157)*

**Abbott Laboratories** A 224 667-6100
Abbott Park *(G-1)*

**Abbott Laboratories** A 224 667-6100
North Chicago *(G-16158)*

**Abbott Laboratories** A 224 330-0271
Libertyville *(G-13298)*

**Abbott Laboratories** A 847 937-2210
Chicago *(G-3705)*

**Abbott Laboratories** G 847 921-9455
Lindenhurst *(G-13545)*

**Abbott Laboratories** A 847 735-0573
Mettawa *(G-14762)*

**Abbott Laboratories** A 847 937-7970
North Chicago *(G-16159)*

**Abbott Laboratories** A 847 937-6100
North Chicago *(G-16160)*

**Abbott Laboratories** C 847 937-6100
North Chicago *(G-16161)*

**Abbott Laboratories** A 847 938-8717
North Chicago *(G-16163)*

**Abbott Laboratories** A 847 937-6100
Des Plaines *(G-8140)*

**Abbott Laboratories** A 847 937-6100
Abbott Park *(G-3)*

**Abbott Laboratories** A 847 937-6100
North Chicago *(G-16164)*

**Abbott Laboratories Inc** A 224 668-2076
Abbott Park *(G-4)*

**Abbott Laboratories PCF Ltd** F 847 937-6100
North Chicago *(G-16165)*

**Abbott Nutrition Mfg Inc** G 614 624-6083
Abbott Park *(G-5)*

**Abbvie Inc** G 847 367-7621
Vernon Hills *(G-21141)*

**Abbvie Inc** G 847 735-0573
Mettawa *(G-14763)*

**Abbvie Inc** B 847 932-7900
North Chicago *(G-16166)*

**Abbvie Inc** D 847 932-7900
North Chicago *(G-16167)*

**Abbvie Inc** E 847 473-4787
Waukegan *(G-21517)*

**Abbvie Inc** G 847 938-2042
North Chicago *(G-16168)*

**Abbvie US LLC** C 800 255-5162
North Chicago *(G-16171)*

**Abraxis Bioscience LLC** G 310 437-7715
Elk Grove Village *(G-9258)*

**Abraxis Bioscience LLC** G 310 883-1300
Melrose Park *(G-14582)*

**Accelerated Pharma Inc** G 773 517-0789
Burr Ridge *(G-2819)*

**Aceva LLC** G 201 978-7928
Peoria *(G-17301)*

**Actavis Pharma Inc** G 847 377-5480
Gurnee *(G-11418)*

**Actavis Pharma Inc** C 847 855-0812
Gurnee *(G-11419)*

**Acura Pharmaceuticals Inc** F 847 705-7709
Palatine *(G-16996)*

**Adello Biologics LLC** G 312 235-3665
Chicago *(G-3748)*

**Akorn Inc** F 847 625-1100
Gurnee *(G-11425)*

**Akorn Inc** C 847 279-6100
Lake Forest *(G-12876)*

**Akorn Inc** C 217 423-9715
Decatur *(G-7826)*

**Akorn Inc** G 847 279-6166
Vernon Hills *(G-21143)*

**Akzo Nobel Inc** C 312 544-7000
Chicago *(G-3793)*

**Altathera Pharmaceuticals LLC** G 312 445-8900
Chicago *(G-3837)*

**American Phrm Partners Inc** E 847 969-2700
Schaumburg *(G-19440)*

**Apser Laboratory Inc** D 630 543-3333
Addison *(G-42)*

**Aptimmune Biologics Inc** G 217 377-8866
Champaign *(G-3451)*

**Archer-Daniels-Midland Company** D 217 424-5200
Decatur *(G-7840)*

**Aspen API Inc** F 847 635-0985
Des Plaines *(G-8152)*

**Astellas Pharma Inc** E 800 695-4321
Northbrook *(G-16205)*

**Astellas US Holding Inc** E 224 205-8800
Northbrook *(G-16206)*

**Astellas US LLC** C 800 888-7704
Deerfield *(G-7979)*

**Astellas US Technologies Inc** B 847 317-8800
Deerfield *(G-7980)*

**Avocet Polymer Tech Inc** G 773 523-2872
Chicago *(G-4001)*

**B & H Biotechnologies LLC** G 630 915-3227
Willowbrook *(G-22200)*

**Baxalta Export Corporation** G 224 948-2000
Deerfield *(G-7981)*

**Baxalta Incorporated** B 224 940-2000
Bannockburn *(G-1256)*

**Baxalta World Trade LLC** G 224 948-2000
Deerfield *(G-7982)*

**Baxalta Worldwide LLC** G 224 948-2000
Deerfield *(G-7983)*

**Baxter Global Holdings II Inc** E 847 948-2000
Deerfield *(G-7984)*

**Baxter Healthcare Corporation** B 847 522-8600
Vernon Hills *(G-21147)*

**Baxter Healthcare Corporation** G 847 270-4757
Wonder Lake *(G-22321)*

**Baxter Healthcare Corporation** B 847 948-4251
Lincolnshire *(G-13432)*

**Baxter Healthcare Corporation** B 847 940-6599
Round Lake *(G-19054)*

**Baxter International Inc** A 224 948-2000
Deerfield *(G-7988)*

**Bella Pharmaceuticals Inc** G 773 279-5350
Chicago *(G-4076)*

**Bio-Bridge Science Inc** E 630 328-0213
Oakbrook Terrace *(G-16699)*

**Catalent Pharma Solutions Inc** C 815 338-9500
Woodstock *(G-22550)*

**Celerity Pharmaceuticals LLC** G 847 999-0131
Rosemont *(G-18992)*

**Celgene Corporation** E 908 673-9000
Melrose Park *(G-14607)*

**Chicago Dscovery Solutions LLC** G 815 609-2071
Plainfield *(G-17586)*

**Clarus Therapeutics Inc** G 847 562-4300
Northbrook *(G-16225)*

**Coretechs Corp** F 847 295-3720
Lake Forest *(G-12894)*

**Cour Pharmaceuticals Dev** G 773 621-3241
Northbrook *(G-16233)*

**Curatek Pharmaceuticals Ltd** G 847 806-7674
Elk Grove Village *(G-9402)*

**Daito Pharmaceuticals Amer Inc** G 847 205-0800
Northbrook *(G-16238)*

**Daniels Sharpsmart Inc** E 312 546-8900
Chicago *(G-4554)*

**Dental Technologies Inc** D 847 677-5500
Lincolnwood *(G-13507)*

**Dr Earles LLC** G 312 225-7200
Chicago *(G-4641)*

**Drug Source Company LLC** G 708 236-1768
Westchester *(G-21838)*

**Elgin Center Pharmacy Inc** F 847 697-1600
Elgin *(G-9022)*

**Elim Pdtric Phrmaceuticals Inc** G 412 266-5968
Rolling Meadows *(G-18727)*

**Elorac Inc** F 847 362-8200
Vernon Hills *(G-21159)*

**Espee Biopharma & Finechem LLC** G 888 851-6667
Schaumburg *(G-19520)*

**Fresenius Kabi Usa Inc** C 708 410-4761
Melrose Park *(G-14641)*

**Fresenius Kabi Usa Inc** B 847 969-2700
Lake Zurich *(G-13076)*

**Fresenius Kabi Usa Inc** C 708 450-7509
Melrose Park *(G-14642)*

**Fresenius Kabi Usa Inc** C 708 345-6170
Melrose Park *(G-14643)*

**Fresenius Kabi Usa Inc** B 708 450-7500
Melrose Park *(G-14640)*

**Fresenius Kabi Usa LLC** A 847 550-2300
Lake Zurich *(G-13077)*

**Fresenius Kabi Usa LLC** E 847 983-7100
Skokie *(G-20002)*

**Fresenius Kabi USA LLC** E 847 550-2300
Lake Zurich *(G-13078)*

**Fresenius Kabi USA LLC** E 708 343-6100
Melrose Park *(G-14644)*

**Global Medical Services LLC** G 847 460-8086
Plainfield *(G-17602)*

**Global Pharma Device Solutions** G 708 212-5801
Chicago *(G-4959)*

**Globepharm Inc** G 847 914-0922
Deerfield *(G-8009)*

**H3 Life Science Corporation** F 708 705-1299
Westchester *(G-21842)*

**Hepalink USA Inc** G 630 206-1788
Chicago *(G-5075)*

**Horizon Pharma Inc** D 224 383-3000
Lake Forest *(G-12906)*

**Horizon Therapeutics Inc** D 224 383-3000
Lake Forest *(G-12907)*

**Hospira Inc** A 224 212-2000
Lake Forest *(G-12908)*

**Hot Shots Nm LLC** G 815 484-0500
Rockford *(G-18423)*

**Hznp Usa Inc** F 224 383-3000
Lake Forest *(G-12913)*

**Illinois Tool Works Inc** E 847 593-8811
Elk Grove Village *(G-9535)*

**Inpharmco Inc** G 708 596-9262
South Holland *(G-20281)*

**Iterative Therapeutics Inc** G 773 455-7203
Chicago *(G-5246)*

**Iterum Therapeutics US Limited** G 312 763-3975
Chicago *(G-5247)*

**Johnson & Johnson** D 815 282-5671
Loves Park *(G-13954)*

**Kastle Therapeutics LLC** G 312 883-5695
Chicago *(G-5364)*

**Lake Consumer Products** G 847 793-0230
Vernon Hills *(G-21180)*

**Lodaat LLC** D 630 852-7544
Downers Grove *(G-8478)*

**Lundbeck LLC** C 847 282-1000
Deerfield *(G-8031)*

**Lundbeck Pharmaceuticals LLC** A 847 282-1000
Deerfield *(G-8032)*

**Mab Pharmacy Inc** G 773 342-5878
Chicago *(G-5591)*

**Mayne Pharma USA Inc** G 224 212-2660
Lake Forest *(G-12925)*

**Mead Johnson & Company LLC** F 847 832-2420
Chicago *(G-5670)*

**Medimmune LLC** G 618 235-8730
Belleville *(G-1656)*

**Meridian Healthcare** G 815 633-5326
Rockford *(G-18492)*

**Mgp Holding Corp** B 847 967-5600
Morton Grove *(G-15220)*

**Midwest Biofluids Inc** G 630 790-9708
Glen Ellyn *(G-10981)*

PRODUCT

Employee Codes: A=Over 500 employees, B=251-500
C=101-250, D=51-100, E=20-50, F=10-19, G=3-9

2017 Harris Illinois
Industrial Directory

1687

# PHARMACEUTICALS

**Midwest Research Labs LLC** ............G...... 847 283-9176
Lake Forest *(G-12926)*

**Morton Grove Phrmceuticals Inc** ......B...... 847 967-5600
Morton Grove *(G-15223)*

**Naurex Inc** ............G...... 847 871-0377
Evanston *(G-10078)*

**Neurotherapeutics Pharma Inc** ........... 773 444-4180
Chicago *(G-5889)*

**Novum Pharma LLC** ............F...... 877 404-4724
Chicago *(G-5950)*

**Ocularis Pharma** ............G...... 708 712-6263
Riverside *(G-18032)*

**Oncquest Inc** ............G...... 847 682-4703
Zion *(G-22694)*

**Pal Midwest Ltd** ............G...... 815 965-2981
Rockford *(G-18528)*

**Patrin Pharma Inc** ............E...... 800 936-3088
Skokie *(G-20053)*

**Pfanstiehl Inc** ............G...... 847 623-0370
Waukegan *(G-21601)*

**Pfizer Inc** ............C...... 847 506-8895
Mount Prospect *(G-15363)*

**Pharma Logistics** ............D...... 847 388-3104
Mundelein *(G-15545)*

**Pharmaceutical Labs and Cons I** ............G...... 630 359-3831
Addison *(G-240)*

**Pharmanutrients Inc** ............G...... 847 234-2334
Lake Bluff *(G-12862)*

**Pharmedium Healthcare Corp** ............E...... 847 457-2300
Lake Forest *(G-12944)*

**Phillips Pharmaceuticals Inc** ............G...... 630 328-0016
Naperville *(G-15727)*

**Porche Pharmaceutical Staffing** ............G...... 312 259-3982
Park Ridge *(G-17217)*

**Powbab Inc** ............G...... 630 481-6140
Oak Brook *(G-16555)*

**Power Partners LLC** ............G...... 773 465-8688
Chicago *(G-6158)*

**Professional Packaging Corp** ............E...... 630 896-0574
Aurora *(G-1205)*

**Ravens Wood Pharmacy** ............G...... 708 667-0525
Chicago *(G-6295)*

**Renaissance SSP Holdings Inc** ............G...... 210 476-8194
Lake Forest *(G-12951)*

**Sagent Logistics LP** ............F...... 847 908-1600
Schaumburg *(G-19716)*

**Sagent Pharmaceuticals Inc** ............D...... 847 908-1600
Schaumburg *(G-19717)*

**Sams West Inc** ............G...... 618 622-0507
O Fallon *(G-16477)*

**Senior Care Pharmacy LLC** ............G...... 847 579-0093
Highland Park *(G-11868)*

**Sterling Phrm Svcs LLC** ............F...... 618 286-4116
East Carondelet *(G-8615)*

**Sterling Phrm Svcs LLC** ............G...... 618 286-6060
Dupo *(G-8578)*

**Strategic Applications Inc** ............G...... 847 680-9385
Lake Villa *(G-13027)*

**Superior Biologics II Inc** ............G...... 847 469-2400
Schaumburg *(G-19745)*

**Symbria Rx Services LLC** ............E...... 630 981-8000
Woodridge *(G-22520)*

**Takeda Dev Ctr Americas Inc** ............A...... 224 554-6500
Deerfield *(G-8058)*

**Takeda Pharmaceuticals NA** ............G...... 972 819-5353
Deerfield *(G-8059)*

**Takeda Pharmaceuticals USA Inc** ............A...... 224 554-6500
Deerfield *(G-8060)*

**Takeda Phrmaceuticals Amer Inc** ............A...... 224 554-6500
Deerfield *(G-8061)*

**Wellness Center Usa Inc** ............G...... 847 925-1885
Hoffman Estates *(G-12069)*

**Winston Pharmaceuticals Inc** ............G...... 847 362-8200
Vernon Hills *(G-21217)*

**Wockhardt Holding Corp** ............B...... 847 967-5600
Morton Grove *(G-15246)*

**Xttrium Laboratories Inc** ............D...... 773 268-5800
Mount Prospect *(G-15386)*

**Zoetis LLC** ............D...... 708 757-2592
Chicago Heights *(G-7137)*

## PHARMACEUTICALS: Medicinal & Botanical Prdts

**Bean Products Inc** ............E...... 312 666-3600
Chicago *(G-4064)*

**Biomerieux Inc** ............E...... 630 628-6055
Lombard *(G-13771)*

**Chemblend of America LLC** ............F...... 630 521-1600
Bensenville *(G-1857)*

**Daito Pharmaceuticals Amer Inc** ............G...... 847 205-0800
Northbrook *(G-16238)*

**Dashire Inc** ............F...... 847 236-0776
Deerfield *(G-8003)*

**Dawes LLC** ............G...... 847 577-2020
Arlington Heights *(G-745)*

**GE Healthcare Holdings Inc** ............A...... 847 398-8400
Arlington Heights *(G-759)*

**GE Healthcare Inc** ............F...... 312 243-0787
Burr Ridge *(G-2844)*

**GE Healthcare Inc** ............E...... 630 595-6642
Wood Dale *(G-22376)*

**Jewel Osco Inc** ............C...... 847 882-6477
Hoffman Estates *(G-12020)*

**Lonza Inc** ............D...... 309 697-7200
Mapleton *(G-14212)*

**Medimmune LLC** ............G...... 847 356-3274
Lindenhurst *(G-13547)*

**Orchard Products Inc** ............G...... 847 818-6760
Mount Prospect *(G-15359)*

**Vidasym Inc** ............G...... 847 680-6072
Libertyville *(G-13398)*

**Vitamins Inc** ............G...... 773 483-4640
Carol Stream *(G-3262)*

## PHARMACIES & DRUG STORES

**Dominicks Finer Foods Inc** ............D...... 630 584-1750
Saint Charles *(G-19173)*

**Jewel Osco Inc** ............C...... 630 355-2172
Naperville *(G-15681)*

**Jewel Osco Inc** ............D...... 630 226-1892
Bolingbrook *(G-2328)*

**Jewel-Osco Inc** ............C...... 847 296-7786
Des Plaines *(G-8216)*

**Kroger Co** ............C...... 309 694-6298
East Peoria *(G-8722)*

**Kroger Co** ............C...... 815 332-7267
Rockford *(G-18457)*

**Ravens Wood Pharmacy** ............G...... 708 667-0525
Chicago *(G-6295)*

**Schnuck Markets Inc** ............C...... 618 466-0825
Godfrey *(G-11237)*

**Sunset Food Mart Inc** ............C...... 847 234-0854
Lake Forest *(G-12964)*

**Walter Lagestee Inc** ............C...... 708 957-2974
Homewood *(G-12106)*

## PHONOGRAPH RECORDS: Prerecorded

**Lion Productions LLC** ............G...... 630 845-1610
Geneva *(G-10846)*

## PHOSPHATE ROCK MINING

**Pcs Phosphate Company Inc** ............D...... 847 849-4200
Northbrook *(G-16336)*

**Phosphate Resource Ptrs** ............A...... 847 739-1200
Lake Forest *(G-12945)*

**Potash Corp Ssktchewan Fla Inc** ............C...... 847 849-4200
Northbrook *(G-16340)*

## PHOSPHATES

**Innophos Inc** ............G...... 773 468-2300
Chicago *(G-5199)*

**Innophos Inc** ............C...... 708 757-6111
Chicago Heights *(G-7103)*

## PHOSPHORIC ACID

**CF Industries Inc** ............B...... 847 405-2400
Deerfield *(G-7994)*

## PHOTOCOPY MACHINES

**Nexus Office Systems Inc** ............F...... 847 836-1095
Elgin *(G-9121)*

**Xerox Corporation** ............E...... 630 573-1000
Hinsdale *(G-11969)*

## PHOTOCOPY SPLYS WHOLESALERS

**Next Day Toner Supplies Inc** ............E...... 708 478-1000
Orland Park *(G-16879)*

## PHOTOCOPYING & DUPLICATING SVCS

**11th Street Express Prtg Inc** ............F...... 815 968-0208
Rockford *(G-18235)*

**A A Swift Print Inc** ............G...... 847 301-1122
Schaumburg *(G-19418)*

**Accurate Repro Inc** ............F...... 630 428-4433
Naperville *(G-15588)*

# PRODUCT SECTION

**Advance Instant Printing Co** ............G...... 312 346-0986
Chicago *(G-3760)*

**Alphadigital Inc** ............G...... 708 482-4488
La Grange Park *(G-12752)*

**AlphaGraphics** ............F...... 630 261-1227
Oakbrook Terrace *(G-16694)*

**AlphaGraphics Printshops** ............G...... 630 964-9600
Lisle *(G-13555)*

**American Reprographics Co LLC** ............D...... 847 647-1131
Niles *(G-15960)*

**Art Bookbinders of America** ............E...... 312 226-4100
Chicago *(G-3949)*

**Bb Services LLC** ............G...... 630 941-8122
Elmhurst *(G-9837)*

**Bloom-Norm Printing Inc** ............G...... 309 663-8545
Normal *(G-16065)*

**Century Printing** ............G...... 618 632-2486
O Fallon *(G-16465)*

**Comet Conection Inc** ............G...... 312 243-5400
Alsip *(G-451)*

**Copy Express Inc** ............G...... 815 338-7161
Woodstock *(G-22555)*

**Copy Mat Printing** ............G...... 309 452-1392
Bloomington *(G-2155)*

**Copy Service Inc** ............G...... 815 758-1151
Dekalb *(G-8079)*

**Copyset Shop Inc** ............G...... 847 768-2679
Des Plaines *(G-8176)*

**Elgin Instant Print** ............G...... 847 931-9006
Elgin *(G-9024)*

**Fast Printing of Joliet Inc** ............G...... 815 723-0080
Joliet *(G-12492)*

**Fedex Ground Package Sys Inc** ............G...... 800 463-3339
Glendale Heights *(G-11023)*

**Fedex Office & Print Svcs Inc** ............F...... 847 475-8650
Evanston *(G-10036)*

**Fedex Office & Print Svcs Inc** ............G...... 815 229-0033
Rockford *(G-18380)*

**Fedex Office & Print Svcs Inc** ............F...... 847 329-9464
Lincolnwood *(G-13510)*

**Fedex Office & Print Svcs Inc** ............G...... 217 355-3400
Champaign *(G-3485)*

**Fedex Office & Print Svcs Inc** ............E...... 847 729-3030
Glenview *(G-11124)*

**Fedex Office & Print Svcs Inc** ............E...... 309 685-4093
Peoria *(G-17359)*

**Fedex Office & Print Svcs Inc** ............G...... 847 459-8008
Buffalo Grove *(G-2693)*

**Fedex Office & Print Svcs Inc** ............E...... 708 452-0149
Elmwood Park *(G-9970)*

**Fedex Office & Print Svcs Inc** ............G...... 847 823-9360
Park Ridge *(G-17193)*

**Fedex Office & Print Svcs Inc** ............F...... 630 894-1800
Bloomingdale *(G-2108)*

**Fedex Office & Print Svcs Inc** ............E...... 847 670-4100
Arlington Heights *(G-754)*

**Fedex Office & Print Svcs Inc** ............F...... 312 670-4460
Chicago *(G-4831)*

**Fedex Office & Print Svcs Inc** ............F...... 312 341-9644
Chicago *(G-4827)*

**Fedex Office & Print Svcs Inc** ............F...... 312 755-0325
Chicago *(G-4828)*

**Fedex Office & Print Svcs Inc** ............F...... 312 595-0768
Chicago *(G-4829)*

**Fedex Office & Print Svcs Inc** ............F...... 312 663-1149
Chicago *(G-4830)*

**Fedex Office & Print Svcs Inc** ............G...... 847 670-7283
Mount Prospect *(G-15329)*

**Fedex Office & Print Svcs Inc** ............G...... 630 759-5784
Bolingbrook *(G-2308)*

**Hafner Printing Co Inc** ............F...... 312 362-0120
Chicago *(G-5030)*

**Henry Printing Inc** ............G...... 618 529-3040
Carbondale *(G-3010)*

**Hq Printers Inc** ............G...... 312 782-2020
Chicago *(G-5125)*

**In-Print Graphics Inc** ............E...... 708 396-1010
Oak Forest *(G-16584)*

**Jamali Kopy Kat Printing Inc** ............G...... 708 544-6164
Bellwood *(G-1711)*

**Jph Enterprises Inc** ............G...... 847 390-0900
Des Plaines *(G-8217)*

**Key Printing** ............G...... 815 933-1800
Kankakee *(G-12635)*

**Klein Printing Inc** ............G...... 773 235-2121
Chicago *(G-5387)*

**Kram Digital Solutions Inc** ............G...... 312 222-0431
Glenview *(G-11164)*

**L & S Label Printing Inc** ............G...... 815 964-6753
Cherry Valley *(G-3646)*

# PRODUCT SECTION
# PHOTOGRAPHIC PEOCESSING CHEMICALS

L P M Inc .................................................. G ..... 847 866-9777
  Evanston  *(G-10062)*
Last Minute Prtg & Copy Ctr ................ G ..... 888 788-2965
  Tinley Park  *(G-20929)*
Media Unlimited Inc ................................ G ..... 630 527-0900
  Naperville  *(G-15816)*
Merrill Corporation ................................. C ..... 312 386-2200
  Chicago  *(G-5696)*
Midwest Law Printing Co Inc ................ G ..... 312 431-0185
  Chicago  *(G-5745)*
Monograms & More ............................... G ..... 630 789-8424
  Burr Ridge  *(G-2869)*
Multi Art Press ........................................ G ..... 773 775-0515
  Chicago  *(G-5831)*
National Gift Card Corp ......................... E ..... 815 477-4288
  Crystal Lake  *(G-7617)*
Newell & Haney Inc ............................... F ..... 618 277-3660
  Belleville  *(G-1660)*
PIP Printing Inc ...................................... G ..... 815 464-0075
  Frankfort  *(G-10349)*
Poll Enterprises Inc .............................. F ..... 708 756-1120
  Chicago Heights  *(G-7117)*
Prairieland Printing ................................ G ..... 309 647-5425
  Washington  *(G-21387)*
Precision Reproductions Inc ................. F ..... 847 724-0182
  Glenview  *(G-11184)*
Print & Design Services LLC ................ G ..... 847 317-9001
  Bannockburn  *(G-1264)*
Printing Plus of Roselle Inc .................. G ..... 630 893-0410
  Roselle  *(G-18963)*
Printmeisters Inc ................................... G ..... 708 474-8400
  Lansing  *(G-13180)*
Quality Blue & Offset Printing ............... G ..... 630 759-8035
  Bolingbrook  *(G-2363)*
Quality Quickprint Inc ............................ G ..... 815 723-0941
  Lemont  *(G-13258)*
Quality Quickprint Inc ............................ F ..... 815 838-1784
  Lockport  *(G-13740)*
Rapid Copy & Duplicating Co ............... G ..... 312 733-3453
  Elmwood Park  *(G-9974)*
Rapid Print ............................................. G ..... 309 673-0826
  Peoria  *(G-17440)*
Reprographics ....................................... G ..... 815 477-1018
  Crystal Lake  *(G-7638)*
Ro-Web Inc ............................................ G ..... 309 688-2155
  Peoria  *(G-17444)*
Rudin Printing Company Inc ................. F ..... 217 528-5111
  Springfield  *(G-20515)*
S G S Inc ................................................ G ..... 708 544-6061
  Downers Grove  *(G-8517)*
Samecwei Inc ........................................ G ..... 630 897-7888
  Aurora  *(G-1214)*
Sheer Graphics Inc ................................ G ..... 630 654-4422
  Westmont  *(G-21920)*
Shree Printing Corp ............................... G ..... 773 267-9500
  Chicago  *(G-6502)*
Smart Office Services Inc ..................... G ..... 773 227-1121
  Chicago  *(G-6532)*
Snegde Deep ......................................... G ..... 630 351-7111
  Roselle  *(G-18978)*
Speedys Quick Print .............................. G ..... 217 431-0510
  Danville  *(G-7766)*
Timothy Helgoth ..................................... G ..... 217 224-8008
  Quincy  *(G-17894)*
Tvp Color Graphics Inc ......................... G ..... 630 837-3600
  Streamwood  *(G-20679)*
United Lithograph Inc ............................ G ..... 847 803-1700
  Des Plaines  *(G-8290)*
Valee Inc ................................................ G ..... 847 364-6464
  Elk Grove Village  *(G-9804)*
Viking Printing & Copying Inc ............... G ..... 312 341-0985
  Chicago  *(G-6899)*
We-B-Print Inc ....................................... G ..... 309 353-8801
  Pekin  *(G-17293)*
Weimer Design & Print Ltd Inc ............. G ..... 630 393-3334
  Warrenville  *(G-21368)*
William Holloway Ltd ............................ G ..... 847 866-9520
  Evanston  *(G-10106)*
Yeast Printing Inc .................................. G ..... 309 833-2845
  Macomb  *(G-14137)*

## PHOTOELECTRIC DEVICES: Magnetic

Seasonal Magnets ................................. G ..... 708 499-3235
  Evergreen Park  *(G-10119)*

## PHOTOENGRAVING SVC

Graphic Engravers Inc .......................... E ..... 630 595-0400
  Bensenville  *(G-1913)*

## PHOTOFINISHING LABORATORIES

Trend Setters Ltd .................................. F ..... 309 929-7012
  Tremont  *(G-20988)*

## PHOTOFINISHING LABORATORIES

Kroger Co ............................................... C ..... 815 332-7267
  Rockford  *(G-18457)*

## PHOTOFLASH EQPT

Speedotron Corporation ........................ G ..... 630 246-5001
  Bartlett  *(G-1378)*

## PHOTOGRAPH DEVELOPING & RETOUCHING SVCS

Tree Towns Reprographics Inc ............. E ..... 630 832-0209
  Elmhurst  *(G-9951)*

## PHOTOGRAPHIC & OPTICAL GOODS EQPT REPAIR SVCS

Screen North Amer Holdings Inc .......... F ..... 847 870-7400
  Rolling Meadows  *(G-18777)*

## PHOTOGRAPHIC EQPT & CAMERAS, WHOLESALE

Olympus America Inc ............................ F ..... 630 953-2080
  Lombard  *(G-13836)*
Promoframes LLC .................................. G ..... 866 566-7224
  Schaumburg  *(G-19701)*

## PHOTOGRAPHIC EQPT & SPLYS

A Division of A&A Studios Inc .............. F ..... 312 278-1144
  Chicago  *(G-3686)*
AVI-Spl Employee ................................. B ..... 847 437-7712
  Schaumburg  *(G-19454)*
Bka Inc ................................................... G ..... 847 831-3535
  Highland Park  *(G-11825)*
Bretford Manufacturing Inc ................... B ..... 847 678-2545
  Franklin Park  *(G-10416)*
Cartridge World Sterling ....................... G ..... 815 625-2345
  Sterling  *(G-20587)*
CDs Office Systems Inc ........................ D ..... 800 367-1508
  Springfield  *(G-20410)*
Clover Global Headquarters ................. G ..... 815 431-8100
  Hoffman Estates  *(G-12000)*
Lanxess Corporation ............................. E ..... 630 789-8440
  Willowbrook  *(G-22219)*
Nuarc Company Inc .............................. G ..... 847 967-4400
  Roselle  *(G-18960)*
Paulmar Industries Inc .......................... F ..... 847 395-2520
  Antioch  *(G-648)*
Poersch Metal Manufacturing Co ......... F ..... 773 722-0890
  Chicago  *(G-6145)*
Research Technology Intl Co ............... E ..... 847 677-3000
  Lincolnwood  *(G-13532)*
Rmf Products Inc ................................... G ..... 630 879-0020
  Batavia  *(G-1492)*
Wesling Products Inc ............................ G ..... 773 533-2850
  Chicago  *(G-6959)*
Xerox Corporation ................................. D ..... 630 983-0172
  Naperville  *(G-15785)*
Xerox Corporation ................................. D ..... 217 355-5460
  Champaign  *(G-3563)*
Xerox Corporation ................................. B ..... 847 928-5500
  Rosemont  *(G-19043)*
Xerox Corporation ................................. D ..... 630 573-0200
  Oak Brook  *(G-16570)*

## PHOTOGRAPHIC EQPT & SPLYS WHOLESALERS

Beastgrip Co .......................................... G ..... 312 283-5283
  Des Plaines  *(G-8157)*

## PHOTOGRAPHIC EQPT & SPLYS, WHOLESALE: Motion Picture Camera

2nd Cine Inc .......................................... G ..... 773 455-5808
  Elgin  *(G-8928)*

## PHOTOGRAPHIC EQPT & SPLYS, WHOLESALE: Project, Motion/Slide

AVI-Spl Employee ................................. B ..... 847 437-7712
  Schaumburg  *(G-19454)*

## PHOTOGRAPHIC EQPT & SPLYS: Blueprint Cloth/Paper, Sensitized

Cushing and Company ........................... E ..... 312 266-8228
  Chicago  *(G-4518)*

## PHOTOGRAPHIC EQPT & SPLYS: Develpg Mach/Eqpt, Still/Motion

Imcopex ................................................. G ..... 630 980-1015
  Bartlett  *(G-1355)*
Kinetic BEI LLC ..................................... F ..... 847 888-8060
  South Elgin  *(G-20210)*

## PHOTOGRAPHIC EQPT & SPLYS: Film, Sensitized

Black Point Studios llc .......................... E ..... 773 791-2377
  Chicago  *(G-4120)*

## PHOTOGRAPHIC EQPT & SPLYS: Graphic Arts Plates, Sensitized

Baldwin Graphic Systems Inc ............... E ..... 630 261-9180
  Lombard  *(G-13766)*
Base-Line II Inc ..................................... G ..... 847 336-8403
  Gurnee  *(G-11430)*
Gpa Inc .................................................. G ..... 773 650-2020
  Mc Cook  *(G-14448)*
Letter-Rite Express LLC ....................... F ..... 847 678-1100
  Aurora  *(G-1046)*
Norvida USA Inc .................................... G ..... 618 282-2992
  Sparta  *(G-20319)*
Rotation Dynamics Corporation ............ E ..... 630 769-9700
  Chicago  *(G-6398)*
Screen North Amer Holdings Inc .......... F ..... 847 870-7400
  Rolling Meadows  *(G-18777)*

## PHOTOGRAPHIC EQPT & SPLYS: Printing Eqpt

Clover Technologies Group LLC .......... F ..... 815 431-8100
  Hoffman Estates  *(G-12001)*
Clover Technologies Group LLC .......... A ..... 815 431-8100
  Ottawa  *(G-16956)*
Clover Technologies Group LLC .......... B ..... 815 431-8100
  Ottawa  *(G-16957)*
Team Play Inc ........................................ F ..... 847 952-7533
  Elk Grove Village  *(G-9770)*

## PHOTOGRAPHIC EQPT & SPLYS: Printing Frames

Colors Chicago Inc ................................ G ..... 312 265-1642
  Chicago  *(G-4429)*
Trend Setters Ltd .................................. F ..... 309 929-7012
  Tremont  *(G-20988)*

## PHOTOGRAPHIC EQPT & SPLYS: Toners, Prprd, Not Chem Plnts

Alpha Laser of Chicago ......................... G ..... 708 478-0464
  Mokena  *(G-14851)*
International Toner Corp ....................... G ..... 847 276-2700
  Buffalo Grove  *(G-2710)*
Laser Pro ............................................... G ..... 847 742-1055
  Elgin  *(G-9093)*
Midwest Laser Incorporated ................. G ..... 708 974-0084
  Palos Hills  *(G-17119)*
Toner Tech Plus .................................... G ..... 815 625-7006
  Rock Falls  *(G-18155)*
Tri Industries Nfp .................................. E ..... 773 754-3100
  Vernon Hills  *(G-21213)*

## PHOTOGRAPHIC EQPT & SPLYS: Tripods, Camera & Projector

Ishot Products Inc ................................. G ..... 312 497-4190
  Bolingbrook  *(G-2325)*
Promark International Inc ..................... D ..... 630 830-2500
  Bartlett  *(G-1365)*

## PHOTOGRAPHIC EQPT REPAIR SVCS

United Cmra Binocular Repr LLC ......... E ..... 630 595-2525
  Elk Grove Village  *(G-9799)*

## PHOTOGRAPHIC PEOCESSING CHEMICALS

Fujifilm Hunt Chem USA Inc ................. C ..... 847 259-8800
  Rolling Meadows  *(G-18730)*

# PHOTOGRAPHIC PROCESSING CHEMICALS

Lochman Ref Silk Screen Co ............F ....... 847 475-6266
  Evanston (G-10065)
Sigma Bio Medics Industries ...............G ....... 847 419-0669
  Buffalo Grove (G-2770)

## PHOTOGRAPHIC PROCESSING EQPT & CHEMICALS

Lipsner Smith Co ...........................G ....... 847 677-3000
  Lincolnwood (G-13521)

## PHOTOGRAPHY SVCS: Commercial

B D Enterprises ............................G ....... 618 462-5861
  Alton (G-563)
Belair Hd Studios LLC ....................E ....... 312 254-5188
  Chicago (G-4075)
Custom Direct Inc ..........................F ....... 630 529-1936
  Roselle (G-18938)
Early Bird Advertising Inc ...............G ....... 847 253-1423
  Prospect Heights (G-17777)
G & G Studios /Broadway Prtg ..........F ....... 815 933-8181
  Bradley (G-2422)
Gfx International Inc ......................G ....... 847 543-7179
  Grayslake (G-11340)

## PHOTOGRAPHY SVCS: Portrait Studios

Fedex Office & Print Svcs Inc ..........E ....... 217 355-3400
  Champaign (G-3485)

## PHOTOGRAPHY SVCS: Still Or Video

French Studio Ltd .........................G ....... 618 942-5328
  Herrin (G-11748)
Haute Noir Media Group Inc ...........G ....... 312 869-4526
  Chicago (G-5055)

## PHOTOTYPESETTING SVC

Composition One Inc ....................E ....... 630 588-1900
  Roselle (G-18933)

## PHOTOVOLTAIC Solid State

Wanxiang New Energy LLC ............F ....... 815 226-0884
  Rockford (G-18672)

## PHYSICAL EXAMINATION & TESTING SVCS

Lifewatch Corp ............................G ....... 847 720-2100
  Rosemont (G-19012)

## PHYSICAL EXAMINATION SVCS, INSURANCE

Lifewatch Services Inc ..................B ....... 847 720-2100
  Rosemont (G-19013)

## PHYSICIANS' OFFICES & CLINICS: Medical doctors

Pal Health Technologies Inc ..........D ....... 309 347-8785
  Pekin (G-17280)
Vlahos Electric Service Dr .............G ....... 224 764-2335
  Arlington Heights (G-866)

## PICNIC JUGS: Plastic

Tuscola Packaging Group LLC .......G ....... 734 268-2877
  Tuscola (G-21027)

## PICTURE FRAMES: Metal

Abct Corporation ..........................G ....... 773 427-1010
  Lincolnwood (G-13499)
All Right Sales Inc ........................G ....... 773 558-4800
  West Chicago (G-21654)
Alpina Manufacturing LLC .............E ....... 773 202-8887
  Chicago (G-3832)
Artistic Framing Inc .......................C ....... 847 808-0200
  Wheeling (G-22007)
Framery ......................................G ....... 618 656-5749
  Edwardsville (G-8802)
Frederics Frame Studio Inc ...........F ....... 312 243-2950
  Chicago (G-4886)
Supreme Frame & Moulding Co .....F ....... 312 930-9056
  Chicago (G-6638)

## PICTURE FRAMES: Wood

Borns Picture Frames ...................G ....... 630 876-1709
  West Chicago (G-21673)
Colberts Custom Framing ..............F ....... 630 717-1448
  Naperville (G-15632)
Fac Enterprises Inc ......................D ....... 847 844-4000
  Elgin (G-9034)
Frame House Inc .........................G ....... 708 383-1616
  Oak Park (G-16663)
Frank A Edmunds & Co Inc ...........F ....... 773 586-2772
  Chicago (G-4883)
Frederics Frame Studio Inc ...........F ....... 312 243-2950
  Chicago (G-4886)
House of Color ............................F ....... 708 352-3222
  Countryside (G-7432)
J R Husar Inc ..............................F ....... 312 243-7888
  Chicago (G-5263)
Lee Armand & Co Ltd ...................F ....... 312 455-1200
  Chicago (G-5483)
Masterpiece Framing ....................G ....... 630 893-4390
  Bloomingdale (G-2116)
Mercurys Green LLC ....................E ....... 708 865-9134
  Franklin Park (G-10528)
Michels Frame Shop .....................G ....... 847 647-7366
  Niles (G-16004)
Picture Frame Fulfillment LLC ........D ....... 847 260-5071
  Franklin Park (G-10550)
Sarj USA Inc ...............................E ....... 708 865-9134
  Franklin Park (G-10582)
Wood Shop .................................G ....... 773 994-6666
  Chicago (G-7024)

## PICTURE FRAMING SVCS, CUSTOM

Arndt Enterprise Ltd .....................G ....... 847 234-5736
  Lake Forest (G-12880)
Mercurys Green LLC ....................E ....... 708 865-9134
  Franklin Park (G-10528)
Sarj USA Inc ...............................E ....... 708 865-9134
  Franklin Park (G-10582)
Supreme Frame & Moulding Co .....F ....... 312 930-9056
  Chicago (G-6638)

## PICTURE PROJECTION EQPT

Dukane Corporation .....................C ....... 630 797-4900
  Saint Charles (G-19175)

## PIECE GOODS & NOTIONS WHOLESALERS

Adazon Inc .................................G ....... 847 235-2700
  Lake Forest (G-12874)
Avlon Industries Inc .....................D ....... 708 344-0709
  Melrose Park (G-14598)

## PIECE GOODS, NOTIONS & DRY GOODS, WHOL: Textile Converters

V-Tex Inc ...................................E ....... 847 325-4140
  Buffalo Grove (G-2787)

## PIECE GOODS, NOTIONS & DRY GOODS, WHOL: Textiles, Woven

Tomen America Inc ......................D ....... 847 439-8500
  Elk Grove Village (G-9782)

## PIECE GOODS, NOTIONS & DRY GOODS, WHOL: Trimmings, Apparel

Phoenix Graphix ..........................F ....... 618 531-3664
  Pinckneyville (G-17551)

## PIECE GOODS, NOTIONS & DRY GOODS, WHOLESALE: Fabrics

Loomcraft Textile & Supply Co .......E ....... 847 680-0000
  Vernon Hills (G-21182)
Nolte & Tyson Inc ........................F ....... 847 551-3313
  Gilberts (G-10929)
Vitel Industries Inc .......................G ....... 847 299-9750
  Des Plaines (G-8300)

## PIECE GOODS, NOTIONS & DRY GOODS, WHOLESALE: Sewing Access

Marietta Corporation ....................C ....... 773 816-5137
  Chicago (G-5619)
Union Special LLC .......................C ....... 847 669-5101
  Huntley (G-12182)

## PIECE GOODS, NOTIONS & OTHER DRY GOODS, WHOL: Flags/Banners

American Advertising Assoc Inc .....G ....... 773 312-5110
  Chicago (G-3847)
E I T Inc .....................................G ....... 630 359-3543
  Naperville (G-15649)
Seasonal Designs Inc ...................E ....... 847 688-0280
  Waukegan (G-21613)

## PIECE GOODS, NOTIONS & OTHER DRY GOODS, WHOLESALE: Fabrics

C H Hanson Company ..................D ....... 630 848-2000
  Naperville (G-15613)
Dynamesh Inc .............................E ....... 630 293-5454
  Batavia (G-1444)
Illinois Fibre Specialty Co ..............E ....... 773 376-1122
  Chicago (G-5157)

## PIECE GOODS, NOTIONS & OTHER DRY GOODS, WHOLESALE: Notions

Sullivans Inc ...............................F ....... 815 331-8347
  McHenry (G-14557)

## PIECE GOODS, NOTIONS/DRY GOODS, WHOL: Drapery Mtrl, Woven

Exclusively Expo ..........................E ....... 630 378-4600
  Romeoville (G-18821)
Kempco Window Treatments Inc ....E ....... 708 754-4484
  Chicago Heights (G-7108)

## PIECE GOODS, NOTIONS/DRY GOODS, WHOL: Fabrics, Synthetic

Strata-Tac Inc .............................F ....... 630 879-9388
  Saint Charles (G-19272)

## PIECE GOODS, NOTIONS/DRY GOODS, WHOL: Sewing Splys/Notions

W & W Associates Inc ..................G ....... 847 719-1760
  Lake Zurich (G-13142)

## PIGMENTS, INORGANIC: Zinc Oxide, Zinc Sulfide

American Chemet Corporation .......F ....... 847 948-0800
  Deerfield (G-7975)

## PILLOWS: Sponge Rubber

Caroline Cole Inc .........................F ....... 618 233-0600
  Belleville (G-1617)
Davis Athletic Equipment Co ..........F ....... 708 563-9006
  Bedford Park (G-1547)

## PILLOWS: Stereo

Pyar & Company LLC ...................G ....... 312 451-5073
  Chicago (G-6232)

## PINS

Arrow Pin and Products Inc ...........F ....... 708 755-7575
  S Chicago Hts (G-19100)
Burgess-Norton Mfg Co Inc ...........B ....... 630 232-4100
  Geneva (G-10813)
Hadady Corporation .....................E ....... 219 322-7417
  South Holland (G-20274)
Pin Up Tattoo .............................G ....... 815 477-7515
  Crystal Lake (G-7625)
Pins & Needles Consignment ........G ....... 217 299-7365
  Pawnee (G-17235)

## PINS: Dowel

Dayton Superior Corporation .........E ....... 219 476-4106
  Kankakee (G-12607)
Dayton Superior Corporation .........C ....... 815 936-3300
  Kankakee (G-12609)
Suburban Industries Inc ................F ....... 630 766-3773
  Franklin Park (G-10597)

## PIPE & FITTING: Fabrication

ADS LLC .....................................D ....... 256 430-3366
  Burr Ridge (G-2820)
American Diesel Tube Corp ............F ....... 630 628-1830
  Addison (G-35)

# PRODUCT SECTION

## PIPES & TUBES: Steel

American Piping Products Inc .......... E ...... 708 339-1753
  South Holland *(G-20244)*
Americhem Systems Inc .......... F ...... 630 495-9300
  Aurora *(G-1106)*
Anamet Electrical Inc .......... C ...... 217 234-8844
  Mattoon *(G-14382)*
Anvil International LLC .......... D ...... 708 534-1414
  Tinley Park *(G-20894)*
Arntzen Corporation .......... E ...... 815 334-0788
  Woodstock *(G-22541)*
Art Wire Works Inc .......... F ...... 708 458-3993
  Bedford Park *(G-1538)*
Cerro Flow Products LLC .......... C ...... 618 337-6000
  Sauget *(G-19385)*
Chicago Metal Fabricators Inc .......... D ...... 773 523-5755
  Chicago *(G-4332)*
Chicago Metal Rolled Pdts Co .......... D ...... 773 523-5757
  Chicago *(G-4333)*
Chicago Tube and Iron Company .......... E ...... 309 787-4947
  Milan *(G-14779)*
D B M Services Corp .......... G ...... 630 964-5678
  Lisle *(G-13581)*
Deublin Company .......... C ...... 847 689-8600
  Waukegan *(G-21551)*
Eg Group Inc .......... G ...... 309 692-0968
  Peoria *(G-17352)*
Flex-Weld Inc .......... G ...... 815 334-3662
  Woodstock *(G-22567)*
Flexicraft Industries Inc .......... E ...... 312 738-3588
  Chicago *(G-4861)*
Geib Industries Inc .......... E ...... 847 455-4550
  Bensenville *(G-1906)*
Gerlin Inc .......... G ...... 630 653-5232
  Carol Stream *(G-3157)*
Global Maintenance LLC .......... F ...... 270 933-1281
  Metropolis *(G-14753)*
Howe Corporation .......... E ...... 773 235-0200
  Chicago *(G-5123)*
Hub Manufacturing Company Inc .......... E ...... 773 252-1373
  Chicago *(G-5127)*
Hyspan Precision Products Inc .......... E ...... 773 277-0700
  South Holland *(G-20279)*
Icon Mech Cnstr & Engrg LLC .......... C ...... 618 452-0035
  Granite City *(G-11287)*
Industrial Pipe and Supply Co .......... E ...... 708 652-7511
  Chicago *(G-5179)*
James L Tracey Co .......... F ...... 630 907-8999
  Aurora *(G-1176)*
John Maneely Company .......... C ...... 773 254-0617
  Chicago *(G-5316)*
K & K Metal Works Inc .......... F ...... 618 271-4680
  East Saint Louis *(G-8758)*
L M K Fabrication Inc .......... F ...... 815 433-1530
  Ottawa *(G-16965)*
Machine Tool Acc & Mfg Co .......... G ...... 773 489-0903
  Chicago *(G-5592)*
Manufactured Specialties Inc .......... F ...... 630 444-1992
  Saint Charles *(G-19213)*
Midwest Pipe Supports Inc .......... G ...... 630 665-6400
  Bartlett *(G-1319)*
Monco Fabricators Inc .......... G ...... 630 293-0063
  West Chicago *(G-21746)*
Morris Construction Inc .......... E ...... 618 544-8504
  Robinson *(G-18067)*
Morton Industries LLC .......... B ...... 309 263-2590
  Morton *(G-15168)*
National Metalwares LP .......... C ...... 630 892-9000
  Aurora *(G-1194)*
Peerless America Incorporated .......... C ...... 217 342-0400
  Effingham *(G-8853)*
Perma-Pipe Inc .......... E ...... 847 966-2190
  Niles *(G-16018)*
Scot Industries Inc .......... D ...... 630 466-7591
  Sugar Grove *(G-20734)*
Service Sheet Metal Works Inc .......... F ...... 773 229-0031
  Chicago *(G-6483)*
Shew Brothers Inc .......... G ...... 618 997-4414
  Marion *(G-14286)*
Superior Pipe Standards Inc .......... G ...... 708 656-0208
  Cicero *(G-7233)*
Tesko Welding & Mfg Co .......... D ...... 708 452-0045
  Norridge *(G-16109)*
Traco Industries Inc .......... G ...... 815 675-6603
  Spring Grove *(G-20371)*

## PIPE & FITTINGS: Cast Iron

Perfect Pipe & Supply Corp .......... G ...... 630 628-6728
  Elgin *(G-9137)*
USP Holdings Inc .......... A ...... 847 604-6100
  Des Plaines *(G-8295)*

## PIPE & TUBES: Aluminum

JM Circle Enterprise Inc .......... G ...... 708 946-3333
  Beecher *(G-1598)*
Midwest Model Aircraft Co .......... F ...... 773 229-0740
  Chicago *(G-5747)*

## PIPE & TUBES: Copper & Copper Alloy

Mueller Industries Inc .......... C ...... 847 290-1108
  Elk Grove Village *(G-9641)*

## PIPE & TUBES: Seamless

Illinois Meter Inc .......... G ...... 618 438-6039
  Benton *(G-2030)*
Maruichi Leavitt Pipe Tube LLC .......... G ...... 800 532-8488
  Chicago *(G-5634)*
Maruichi Leavitt Pipe Tube LLC .......... C ...... 773 239-7700
  Chicago *(G-5635)*
Tmk Ipsco .......... C ...... 630 874-0078
  Downers Grove *(G-8533)*

## PIPE CLEANERS

Enz (usa) Inc .......... G ...... 630 692-7880
  Aurora *(G-1004)*
Imagination Products Corp .......... G ...... 309 274-6223
  Chillicothe *(G-7167)*

## PIPE JOINT COMPOUNDS

AST Industries Inc .......... F ...... 847 455-2300
  Franklin Park *(G-10405)*
Black Swan Manufacturing Co .......... F ...... 773 227-3700
  Chicago *(G-4121)*

## PIPE, PRESSURE: Reinforced Concrete

Forterra Pressure Pipe Inc .......... E ...... 815 389-4800
  South Beloit *(G-20147)*
Surtreat Construction Svcs LLC .......... G ...... 630 986-0780
  Schaumburg *(G-19746)*

## PIPE, SEWER: Concrete

National Concrete Pipe Co .......... E ...... 630 766-3600
  Franklin Park *(G-10539)*

## PIPE: Concrete

Elmhurst-Chicago Stone Company .......... E ...... 630 832-4000
  Elmhurst *(G-9865)*
Graber Concrete Pipe Company .......... E ...... 630 894-5950
  Bloomingdale *(G-2109)*

## PIPE: Copper

Ems Industrial and Service Co .......... E ...... 815 678-2700
  Richmond *(G-17961)*
Marmon Holdings Inc .......... D ...... 312 372-9500
  Chicago *(G-5625)*

## PIPE: Plastic

Blackburn Sampling Inc .......... G ...... 309 342-8429
  Galesburg *(G-10738)*
Eastern Illinois Clay Company .......... F ...... 815 427-8144
  Saint Anne *(G-19120)*
Eastern Illinois Clay Company .......... F ...... 815 427-8106
  Saint Anne *(G-19121)*
Fusibond Piping Systems Inc .......... F ...... 630 969-4488
  Downers Grove *(G-8446)*
George W Pierson Company .......... E ...... 815 726-3351
  Joliet *(G-12501)*

## PIPE: Seamless Steel

Atlas Tube (chicago) LLC .......... B ...... 773 646-4500
  Chicago *(G-3984)*
Gerlin Inc .......... G ...... 630 653-5232
  Carol Stream *(G-3157)*
John Maneely Company .......... C ...... 773 254-0617
  Chicago *(G-5316)*
Naylor Pipe Company .......... C ...... 773 721-9400
  Chicago *(G-5876)*
Zekelman Industries Inc .......... E ...... 312 275-1600
  Chicago *(G-7061)*

## PIPE: Sewer, Cast Iron

Ae Sewer & Septics Inc .......... G ...... 847 289-9084
  Elgin *(G-8938)*

Fast Pipe Lining Inc .......... G ...... 815 712-8646
  La Salle *(G-12772)*

## PIPE: Sheet Metal

Contech Engnered Solutions LLC .......... G ...... 630 573-1110
  Oak Brook *(G-16502)*
Metal Culverts Inc .......... E ...... 309 543-2271
  Havana *(G-11699)*

## PIPELINE TERMINAL FACILITIES: Independent

Kw Precast LLC .......... F ...... 708 562-7700
  Westchester *(G-21846)*

## PIPELINES: Crude Petroleum

BP America Inc .......... A ...... 630 420-5111
  Warrenville *(G-21344)*
BP Products North America Inc .......... G ...... 630 420-4300
  Naperville *(G-15609)*

## PIPELINES: Natural Gas

ANR Pipeline Company .......... G ...... 309 667-2158
  New Windsor *(G-15929)*
Natural Gas Pipeline Amer LLC .......... F ...... 815 426-2151
  Herscher *(G-11760)*

## PIPELINES: Refined Petroleum

BP America Inc .......... A ...... 630 420-5111
  Warrenville *(G-21344)*
BP Products North America Inc .......... G ...... 630 420-4300
  Naperville *(G-15609)*

## PIPES & FITTINGS: Fiber, Made From Purchased Materials

River Valley Mechanical Inc .......... G ...... 309 364-3776
  Putnam *(G-17788)*

## PIPES & TUBES

Bevstream Corp .......... G ...... 630 761-0060
  Batavia *(G-1421)*
Earthsafe Systems Inc .......... F ...... 312 226-7600
  Chicago *(G-4679)*
Service Sheet Metal Works Inc .......... F ...... 773 229-0031
  Chicago *(G-6483)*

## PIPES & TUBES: Steel

Addison Precision Tech LLC .......... G ...... 773 626-4747
  Chicago *(G-3745)*
Advanced Valve Tech Inc .......... E ...... 847 364-3700
  Elk Grove Village *(G-9278)*
Allied Tube and Conduit .......... G ...... 708 225-2955
  Harvey *(G-11653)*
American Diesel Tube Corp .......... F ...... 630 628-1830
  Addison *(G-35)*
Arntzen Corporation .......... E ...... 815 334-0788
  Woodstock *(G-22541)*
Atkore International Inc .......... E ...... 708 339-1610
  Harvey *(G-11657)*
B & B Fabrications LLC .......... G ...... 217 620-3210
  Sullivan *(G-20739)*
Bull Moose Tube Company .......... D ...... 708 757-7700
  Chicago Heights *(G-7084)*
Chicago Tube and Iron Company .......... E ...... 815 834-2500
  Romeoville *(G-18810)*
D D G Inc .......... G ...... 847 412-0277
  Northbrook *(G-16236)*
Durabilt Dyvex Inc .......... F ...... 708 397-4673
  Broadview *(G-2573)*
E & H Tubing Inc .......... F ...... 773 522-3100
  Chicago *(G-4662)*
Eagle Tubular Products Inc .......... E ...... 618 463-1702
  Alton *(G-573)*
Epix Tube Co Inc .......... E ...... 630 844-0960
  Aurora *(G-1146)*
Evraz Inc NA .......... C ...... 312 533-3621
  Chicago *(G-4792)*
Forterra Pressure Pipe Inc .......... E ...... 815 389-4800
  South Beloit *(G-20147)*
Great Lakes Precision Tube Inc .......... E ...... 630 859-8940
  Aurora *(G-1164)*
Harris William & Company Inc .......... E ...... 312 621-0590
  Chicago *(G-5048)*
Illinois Ni Cast LLC .......... E ...... 217 398-3200
  Champaign *(G-3500)*

---

Employee Codes: A=Over 500 employees, B=251-500
C=101-250, D=51-100, E=20-50, F=10-19, G=3-9

# PIPES & TUBES: Steel

Illinois Steel Service Inc .................. D ...... 312 926-7440
  Chicago (G-5158)
Independence Tube Corporation ........ D ...... 815 795-4400
  Marseilles (G-14311)
Lapham-Hickey Steel Corp ............... C ...... 708 496-6111
  Chicago (G-5459)
Leading Edge Group Inc ................... C ...... 815 316-3500
  Rockford (G-18464)
Legacy International Assoc LLC ......... G ...... 847 823-1602
  Park Ridge (G-17206)
Lex Holding Co ................................. G ...... 708 594-9200
  Oak Brook (G-16535)
M C Steel Inc .................................... E ...... 847 350-9618
  Antioch (G-642)
Manning Material Services Inc ........... F ...... 847 669-5750
  Huntley (G-12162)
National Metalwares LP ..................... C ...... 630 892-9000
  Aurora (G-1194)
Nelson Global Products Inc ............... F ...... 309 263-8914
  Morton (G-15171)
Northwest Pipe Company .................. C ...... 312 587-8702
  Chicago (G-5939)
Ptc Group Holdings Corp ................... D ...... 708 757-4747
  Chicago Heights (G-7118)
Ptc Tubular Products LLC .................. C ...... 815 692-4900
  Fairbury (G-10131)
Roll McHning Tech Slutions Inc .......... G ...... 815 372-9100
  Romeoville (G-18864)
Structural Steel Systems Limi ............ F ...... 815 937-3800
  Bradley (G-2434)
Welding Apparatus Company ............. E ...... 773 252-7670
  Fox Lake (G-10284)
Whi Capital Partners ......................... G ...... 312 621-0590
  Chicago (G-6970)
Zapp Tooling Alloys Inc ..................... G ...... 847 599-0351
  Gurnee (G-11521)

## PIPES & TUBES: Welded

Allied Tube & Conduit Corp ............... A ...... 708 339-1610
  Harvey (G-11652)
Hanna Steel Corporation .................... C ...... 309 478-3800
  Pekin (G-17265)

## PIPES: Steel & Iron

Franks Maintenance & Engrg ............. G ...... 847 475-1003
  Evanston (G-10040)

## PISTONS & PISTON RINGS

Burgess-Norton Mfg Co Inc ............... B ...... 630 232-4100
  Geneva (G-10813)

## PLANING MILLS: Millwork

Manufacturing / Woodworking ............ G ...... 847 730-4823
  Des Plaines (G-8226)

## PLANT FOOD, WHOLESALE

Wabash Valley Service Co ................. F ...... 618 393-2971
  Olney (G-16800)

## PLANT HORMONES

Agrochem Inc ................................... F ...... 847 564-1304
  Northbrook (G-16201)

## PLANTERS & FLOWER POTS, WHOLESALE

T2 Site Amenities Incorporated .......... G ...... 847 579-9003
  Highland Park (G-11876)

## PLANTERS: Plastic

Consolidated Foam Inc ...................... F ...... 847 850-5011
  Buffalo Grove (G-2678)
H E Associates Inc ............................ G ...... 630 553-6382
  Yorkville (G-22661)

## PLANTING MACHINERY & EQPT WHOLESALERS

Dutch Valley Partners LLC ................. E ...... 815 937-8812
  Bourbonnais (G-2394)

## PLAQUES: Clay, Plaster/Papier-Mache, Factory Production

Budget Signs .................................... F ...... 618 259-4460
  Wood River (G-22441)

## PLAQUES: Picture, Laminated

Gabel & Schubert Bronze ................... F ...... 773 878-6800
  Chicago (G-4905)
H Hal Kramer Co ............................... G ...... 847 441-0213
  Northfield (G-16401)
R S Owens & Co Inc .......................... B ...... 773 282-6000
  Chicago (G-6273)
Rebechini Studio Inc .......................... F ...... 847 364-8600
  Elk Grove Village (G-9711)
Rudon Enterprises Inc ....................... G ...... 618 457-0441
  Carbondale (G-3022)
Stellar Recognition Inc ....................... D ...... 773 282-8060
  Chicago (G-6588)

## PLASMAS

Baxter Healthcare Corporation ........... C ...... 800 422-9837
  Deerfield (G-7985)
Csl Plasma Inc .................................. E ...... 708 343-8845
  Melrose Park (G-14612)
Grifols Shared Svcs N Amer Inc ......... G ...... 309 827-3031
  Bloomington (G-2173)
Octapharma Plasma Inc .................... G ...... 708 409-0900
  Northlake (G-16446)
Octapharma Plasma Inc .................... G ...... 630 375-0028
  Aurora (G-1198)
Octapharma Plasma Inc .................... G ...... 217 546-8605
  Springfield (G-20491)
West Laboratories Inc ....................... E ...... 815 935-1630
  Kankakee (G-12658)

## PLASTER & PLASTERBOARD

Ken Matthews & Associates Inc ......... G ...... 630 628-6470
  Addison (G-165)

## PLASTER WORK: Ornamental & Architectural

Continental Studios Inc ..................... E ...... 773 542-0309
  Chicago (G-4460)
Decorators Supply Corporation ........... E ...... 773 847-6300
  Chicago (G-4571)

## PLASTIC COLORING & FINISHING

Unique Assembly & Decorating ........... E ...... 630 241-4300
  Downers Grove (G-8535)

## PLASTIC PRDTS

A P L Plastics ................................... G ...... 773 265-1370
  Chicago (G-3691)
Advangene Consumables Inc ............. G ...... 847 283-9780
  Lake Bluff (G-12827)
AEP Inc ........................................... G ...... 618 466-7668
  Alton (G-558)
Agriplastics LLC ................................ G ...... 847 604-8847
  Lake Bluff (G-12828)
Albea .............................................. G ...... 847 439-8220
  Elk Grove Village (G-9283)
Alltech Plastics Inc ............................ G ...... 847 352-2309
  Schaumburg (G-19433)
APAC II LLC ..................................... G ...... 618 426-1338
  Campbell Hill (G-2974)
Bfw Coating ..................................... G ...... 847 639-2155
  Cary (G-3328)
Conwed Plastics ............................... D ...... 630 293-3737
  West Chicago (G-21687)
Dsign In Plastics Inc .......................... F ...... 847 288-8085
  Franklin Park (G-10459)
I T W Deltar/Diamed Corp ................. G ...... 847 593-8811
  Elk Grove Village (G-9529)
ICI Fiberite ...................................... G ...... 708 403-3788
  Orland Park (G-16866)
Laminarp ......................................... E ...... 847 884-9298
  Schaumburg (G-19611)
Met Plastics .................................... G ...... 847 228-5070
  Elk Grove Village (G-9618)
Nebraska Plastics Incorporated .......... G ...... 217 423-9007
  Decatur (G-7921)
Plaspros Inc .................................... G ...... 847 639-6492
  Cary (G-3364)
R T P Company ................................ G ...... 618 286-6100
  Dupo (G-8576)
Railshop Inc .................................... G ...... 847 816-0925
  Libertyville (G-13374)
Upward Bound ................................. G ...... 773 265-1370
  Chicago (G-6843)
Wise Plastics Technologies Inc ........... G ...... 847 697-2840
  West Chicago (G-21793)

## PLASTIC PRDTS REPAIR SVCS

Chicago Mold Engrg Co Inc ................ D ...... 630 584-1311
  Saint Charles (G-19152)
Meta-Meg Tool Corporation ................ G ...... 847 742-3600
  Elgin (G-9106)
Polycorp Illinois Inc ........................... D ...... 773 847-7575
  Chicago (G-6154)

## PLASTICIZERS, ORGANIC: Cyclic & Acyclic

Hallstar Company .............................. G ...... 312 554-7400
  Chicago (G-5036)
Hallstar Services Corp ....................... G ...... 312 554-7400
  Chicago (G-5037)

## PLASTICS FILM & SHEET

Alpha Industries MGT Inc ................... D ...... 773 359-8000
  Chicago (G-3828)
Cast Films Inc .................................. F ...... 847 808-0363
  Wheeling (G-22024)
Clear Pack Company ......................... G ...... 847 957-6282
  Franklin Park (G-10437)
Clorox Company ............................... E ...... 510 271-7000
  Willowbrook (G-22204)
Flex-O-Glass Inc ............................... D ...... 773 261-5200
  Chicago (G-4858)
Flex-O-Glass Inc ............................... G ...... 773 379-7878
  Chicago (G-4859)
Flex-O-Glass Inc ............................... G ...... 815 288-1424
  Dixon (G-8331)
Formco Plastics Inc ........................... F ...... 630 860-7998
  Bensenville (G-1901)
Huntsman Expndable Polymers Lc ...... C ...... 815 224-5463
  Peru (G-17512)
Midwest Canvas Corp ........................ C ...... 773 287-4400
  Chicago (G-5742)
Piper Plastics Inc .............................. D ...... 847 367-0110
  Libertyville (G-13369)
Pliant LLC ........................................ A ...... 812 424-2904
  Rolling Meadows (G-18763)
Pliant Corp International .................... G ...... 847 969-3300
  Rolling Meadows (G-18764)
Pliant Corporation of Canada ............. G ...... 847 969-3300
  Schaumburg (G-19695)
Pliant Investment Inc ........................ G ...... 847 969-3300
  Schaumburg (G-19696)
Pliant Solutions Corporation ............... E ...... 847 969-3300
  Schaumburg (G-19697)
Printpack Inc ................................... C ...... 847 888-7150
  Elgin (G-9148)
Protective Products Intl .................... G ...... 847 526-1180
  Wauconda (G-21495)
Realt Images Inc .............................. G ...... 217 567-3487
  Tower Hill (G-20980)
Sonoco Products Company ................ C ...... 847 957-6282
  Franklin Park (G-10591)
Transcendia Inc ............................... C ...... 847 678-1800
  Franklin Park (G-10609)

## PLASTICS FILM & SHEET: Polyethylene

Aargus Plastics Inc ........................... C ...... 847 325-4444
  Wheeling (G-21995)
Berry Global Films LLC ...................... D ...... 708 239-4619
  Alsip (G-442)
Cadillac Products Packaging Co ......... C ...... 217 463-1444
  Paris (G-17142)
Highland Mfg & Sls Co ...................... D ...... 618 654-2161
  Highland (G-11789)
Poli-Film America Inc ........................ D ...... 847 453-8104
  Hampshire (G-11559)
Poly Films Inc .................................. G ...... 708 547-7963
  Hillside (G-11931)
Signode Industrial Group LLC ............. E ...... 847 483-1490
  Glenview (G-11199)
Tee Group Films Inc .......................... D ...... 815 894-2331
  Ladd (G-12792)
Tredegar Film Products Corp ............. C ...... 847 438-2111
  Lake Zurich (G-13138)

## PLASTICS FILM & SHEET: Polypropylene

Cosmo Films Inc ............................... E ...... 630 458-5200
  Addison (G-82)
Kw Plastics ...................................... F ...... 708 757-5140
  Chicago (G-5415)
Neptune USA Inc .............................. G ...... 847 987-3804
  Schaumburg (G-19663)
Orbis Rpm LLC ................................. F ...... 217 876-8655
  Decatur (G-7922)

# PRODUCT SECTION — PLASTICS PROCESSING

| Company | Code | Phone |
|---|---|---|
| Orbis Rpm LLC — Bartonville (G-1398) | G | 309 697-1549 |
| Orbis Rpm LLC — Chicago (G-6003) | G | 773 376-9775 |
| Western Plastics Inc — Addison (G-342) | F | 630 629-3034 |

## PLASTICS FILM & SHEET: Vinyl

| Company | Code | Phone |
|---|---|---|
| A B Kelly Inc — Cary (G-3320) | | 847 639-1022 |
| C M F Enterprises Inc — Wauconda (G-21450) | F | 847 526-9499 |
| Camo Clad Inc — Mounds (G-15258) | F | 618 342-6860 |
| Clear Focus Imaging Inc — Franklin Park (G-10436) | E | 707 544-7990 |
| Letters Unlimited Inc — Schaumburg (G-19615) | G | 847 891-7811 |
| Morton Group Ltd — Highland Park (G-11857) | | 847 831-2766 |
| Sun Process Converting Inc — Mount Prospect (G-15376) | D | 847 593-5656 |
| Thermal Industries Inc — Wood Dale (G-22430) | E | 800 237-0560 |

## PLASTICS FINISHED PRDTS: Laminated

| Company | Code | Phone |
|---|---|---|
| American Louver Company — Skokie (G-19950) | C | 847 470-0400 |
| American Name Plate & Metal De — Chicago (G-3867) | E | 773 376-1400 |
| B & B Formica Appliers Inc — Chicago (G-4014) | F | 773 804-1015 |
| Credit Card Systems Inc — Wheeling (G-22031) | F | 847 459-8320 |
| Custom Plastics of Peoria — Bartonville (G-1394) | G | 309 697-2888 |
| Field Ventures LLC — Northbrook (G-16258) | D | 847 509-2250 |
| Iten Industries Inc — Addison (G-155) | G | 630 543-2820 |
| Npi Holding Corp — Springfield (G-20488) | G | 217 391-1229 |
| Nudo Products Inc — Springfield (G-20489) | C | 217 528-5636 |
| Nudo Products Inc — Springfield (G-20490) | C | 217 528-5636 |
| Nypro Hanover Park — Roselle (G-18961) | G | 630 868-3517 |
| Oberthur Tech Amer Corp — Naperville (G-15718) | D | 630 551-0792 |
| Rainbow Colors Inc — Elk Grove Village (G-9707) | F | 847 640-7700 |
| Suburban Laminating Inc — Melrose Park (G-14697) | G | 708 389-6106 |
| Tb Cardworks Llc — Palatine (G-17079) | E | 847 229-9990 |
| Transcendia Inc — Franklin Park (G-10610) | E | 847 678-1800 |
| Unique Designs — Normal (G-16092) | G | 309 454-1226 |
| Vecchio Manufacturing of Ill — Elgin (G-9224) | F | 847 742-8429 |

## PLASTICS MATERIAL & RESINS

| Company | Code | Phone |
|---|---|---|
| Aabbitt Adhesives Inc — Chicago (G-3701) | D | 773 227-2700 |
| Ade Inc — Chicago (G-3746) | E | 773 646-3400 |
| Akzo Nobel Coatings Inc — Lombard (G-13763) | E | 630 792-1619 |
| Amcor Flexibles LLC — Buffalo Grove (G-2656) | C | 224 313-7000 |
| Americas Styrenics LLC — Channahon (G-3565) | D | 815 418-6403 |
| Ameriflon Ltd — Wheeling (G-22004) | G | 847 541-6000 |
| Ashland Chemical Incorporated — Calumet City (G-2935) | G | 708 891-0760 |
| Atlas Fibre Company — Northbrook (G-16208) | D | 847 674-1234 |
| Atsp Innovations Inc — Champaign (G-3454) | | 217 239-1703 |
| BASF Corporation — Kankakee (G-12603) | B | 815 932-9863 |
| Brinkman Company Inc — Bensenville (G-1847) | | 630 595-3640 |
| Color Corporation of America — Rockford (G-18314) | D | 815 987-3700 |
| Cope Plastics Inc — Rock Island (G-18168) | G | 309 787-4465 |
| Creative Marble Inc — Champaign (G-3471) | | 217 359-7271 |
| Crown Premiums Inc — Frankfort (G-10311) | F | 815 469-8789 |
| David Teplica M D — Chicago (G-4564) | | 773 296-9900 |
| Dip Seal Plastics Inc — Rockford (G-18345) | | 815 398-3533 |
| Dmr International Inc — Woodstock (G-22561) | | 815 704-5678 |
| Dow Chemical Company — Channahon (G-3572) | C | 815 423-5921 |
| Dow Chemical Company — Elk Grove Village (G-9434) | E | 847 439-2240 |
| Dow Chemical Company — Ringwood (G-17989) | C | 815 653-2411 |
| Dow Chemical Company — Kankakee (G-12610) | | 815 933-8900 |
| DSM Desotech Inc — Elgin (G-9013) | E | 847 697-0400 |
| Dynachem Inc — Westville (G-21929) | | 217 662-2136 |
| Ecologic LLC — Oakbrook Terrace (G-16706) | F | 630 869-0495 |
| Elevator Cable & Supply Co — Broadview (G-2574) | | 708 338-9700 |
| Emerald Performance Mtls LLC — Henry (G-11741) | D | 309 364-2311 |
| Ems Acrylics & Silk Screener — Chicago (G-4747) | F | 773 777-5656 |
| Evergreen Scale Models Inc — Des Plaines (G-8191) | F | 224 567-8099 |
| Excelsior Inc — Rockford (G-18375) | | 815 987-2900 |
| Fitz Chem Corporation — Itasca (G-12264) | | 630 467-8383 |
| Flex-O-Glass Inc — Dixon (G-8331) | E | 815 288-1424 |
| Gallagher Corporation — Gurnee (G-11451) | D | 847 249-3440 |
| Hanlon Group Ltd — Chicago (G-5042) | | 773 525-3666 |
| Harry J Bosworth Company — Evanston (G-10050) | E | 847 679-3400 |
| Hexion Inc — Bedford Park (G-1554) | E | 708 728-8834 |
| Huntsman Expndable Polymers Lc — Peru (G-17512) | C | 815 224-5463 |
| ID Additives Inc — La Grange (G-12737) | | 708 588-0081 |
| Ineos Bio USA LLC — Lisle (G-13604) | | 630 857-7000 |
| Ineos New Planet Bioenergy LLC — Lisle (G-13605) | D | 630 857-7143 |
| Ineos Silicas Americas LLC — Joliet (G-12517) | | 815 727-3651 |
| Innocor Foam Tech W Chcago LLC — West Chicago (G-21722) | E | 732 945-6222 |
| Innovative Hess Products LLC — Arlington Heights (G-778) | B | 847 676-3260 |
| Itasca Plastics Inc — Saint Charles (G-19200) | | 630 443-4446 |
| Iten Industries Inc — Addison (G-155) | G | 630 543-2820 |
| J L M Plastics Corporation — Joliet (G-12520) | F | 815 722-0066 |
| Kunz Industries Inc — South Holland (G-20285) | | 708 596-7717 |
| Lanxess Solutions US Inc — Mapleton (G-14211) | F | 309 633-9480 |
| Lyondell Chemical Company — Morris (G-15114) | B | 815 942-7011 |
| Mapei Corporation — West Chicago (G-21737) | D | 630 293-5800 |
| Maxwell Counters Inc — Farmer City (G-10179) | E | 309 928-2848 |
| Minova USA Inc — Marion (G-14274) | D | 618 993-2611 |
| Nanocor LLC — Hoffman Estates (G-12026) | E | 847 851-1900 |
| National Casein of California — Chicago (G-5863) | D | 773 846-7300 |
| Nypro Inc — Hanover Park (G-11587) | F | 630 773-3341 |
| Oly Ola Edging Inc — Villa Park (G-21274) | F | 630 833-3033 |
| Owens Corning Sales LLC — Rockford (G-18527) | D | 815 226-4627 |
| Pactiv LLC — Lake Forest (G-12938) | B | 715 723-4181 |
| Pintas Cultured Marble — Alsip (G-509) | E | 708 385-3360 |
| Plastics Color & Compounding — Calumet City (G-2949) | D | 708 868-3800 |
| Poly-Resyn Inc — West Dundee (G-21801) | F | 847 428-4031 |
| Polybilt Body Company LLC — Itasca (G-12343) | G | 708 345-8050 |
| Polyconversions Inc — Rantoul (G-17935) | E | 217 893-3330 |
| Polyform Products Company — Elk Grove Village (G-9685) | E | 847 427-0020 |
| Polyone Corporation — Henry (G-11746) | C | 309 364-2154 |
| Polyone Corporation — Romeoville (G-18859) | D | 630 972-0505 |
| PPG Architectural Finishes Inc — Meredosia (G-14734) | B | 217 584-1323 |
| PPG Architectural Finishes Inc — Chicago (G-6161) | D | 773 523-6333 |
| Resin Exchange Inc — Addison (G-276) | | 630 628-7266 |
| Rhopac Fabricated Products LLC — Libertyville (G-13376) | E | 847 362-3300 |
| Rohm and Haas Company — Elgin (G-9166) | C | 847 426-3245 |
| Rohm and Haas Company — Kankakee (G-12646) | D | 815 935-7725 |
| Sabic Innovative Plas US LLC — Ottawa (G-16982) | B | 815 434-7000 |
| Serionix — Champaign (G-3537) | G | 651 503-3930 |
| Sherman Plastics Corp — Naperville (G-15746) | E | 630 369-6170 |
| Solvay USA Inc — University Park (G-21062) | E | 708 235-7200 |
| Standard Rubber Products Co — Elk Grove Village (G-9751) | E | 847 593-5630 |
| Stellar Performance Mfg LLC — Chicago (G-6587) | F | 312 951-2311 |
| Stepan Company — Elwood (G-9982) | B | 815 727-4944 |
| Sunemco Technologies Inc — Naperville (G-15758) | G | 630 369-8947 |
| Tangent Technologies LLC — Aurora (G-1222) | E | 630 264-1110 |
| Tech-Mate Inc — Elk Grove Village (G-9772) | G | 847 352-9690 |
| Technique Eng Inc — Waukegan (G-21621) | F | 847 816-1870 |
| Thermoflex Corp — Waukegan (G-21626) | D | 847 473-9001 |
| Thermoflex Corp — Waukegan (G-21627) | | 847 473-9001 |
| Total Plastics Inc — Elk Grove Village (G-9785) | F | 847 593-5000 |
| United Gilsonite Laboratories — Jacksonville (G-12415) | E | 217 243-7878 |
| Valspar Corporation — Rockford (G-18668) | G | 815 987-3701 |
| Wilcor Solid Surface Inc — Elk Grove Village (G-9813) | F | 630 350-7703 |

## PLASTICS MATERIALS, BASIC FORMS & SHAPES WHOLESALERS

| Company | Code | Phone |
|---|---|---|
| Addison Pro Plastics Inc — Addison (G-24) | G | 630 543-6770 |
| Atlas Fibre Company — Northbrook (G-16208) | D | 847 674-1234 |
| Bach Plastic Works Inc — Libertyville (G-13306) | G | 847 680-4342 |
| Catalina Coating & Plas Inc — Elk Grove Village (G-9358) | F | 847 806-1340 |
| Certified Polymers Inc — Western Springs (G-21865) | G | 630 515-0007 |
| Hanlon Group Ltd — Chicago (G-5042) | | 773 525-3666 |
| Laminart Inc — Schaumburg (G-19612) | E | 800 323-7624 |
| Ramar Industries Inc — Franklin Park (G-10569) | G | 847 451-0445 |
| Total Plastics Inc — Elk Grove Village (G-9785) | F | 847 593-5000 |

## PLASTICS PROCESSING

| Company | Code | Phone |
|---|---|---|
| Ace Plastics Inc — Chatsworth (G-3626) | F | 815 635-1368 |

# PLASTICS PROCESSING — PRODUCT SECTION

| Company | Code | Phone |
|---|---|---|
| Acrylic Service Inc | G | 630 543-0336 |
| Addison (G-20) | | |
| Air Diffusion Systems A John | G | 847 782-0044 |
| Gurnee (G-11422) | | |
| Alpha Omega Plastics Company | D | 847 956-8777 |
| Elk Grove Village (G-9289) | | |
| Bay Plastics | F | 847 299-2045 |
| Des Plaines (G-8156) | | |
| C R Plastics Inc | G | 847 541-3601 |
| Wheeling (G-22021) | | |
| Cicero Plastic Products Inc | E | 815 886-9522 |
| Romeoville (G-18811) | | |
| Cim-Tech Plastics Inc | F | 847 350-0900 |
| Elk Grove Village (G-9373) | | |
| Circle Engineering Company | G | 847 455-2204 |
| Franklin Park (G-10433) | | |
| Cmt International Inc | | 618 549-1829 |
| Murphysboro (G-15575) | | |
| Creative Concepts Fabrication | F | 630 940-0500 |
| Saint Charles (G-19165) | | |
| D & D Manufacturing | G | 815 339-9100 |
| Hennepin (G-11733) | | |
| Designed Plastics Inc | E | 630 694-7300 |
| Bensenville (G-1879) | | |
| Dss Rapak Inc | G | 630 296-2000 |
| Romeoville (G-18817) | | |
| Eco-Tech Plastics LLC | E | 262 539-3811 |
| Northbrook (G-16247) | | |
| Ems Acrylics & Silk Screener | F | 773 777-5656 |
| Chicago (G-4747) | | |
| Engineered Plastic Pdts Corp | E | 847 952-8400 |
| Elk Grove Village (G-9460) | | |
| Essentra Components Inc | C | 815 943-6487 |
| Forest Park (G-10241) | | |
| Fanplastic Molding Co | G | 815 923-6950 |
| Marengo (G-14228) | | |
| Filtertek Inc | B | 815 648-2410 |
| Hebron (G-11719) | | |
| Hangables Inc | F | 847 673-9770 |
| Skokie (G-20010) | | |
| Hazen Display Corporation | E | 815 248-2925 |
| Davis (G-7806) | | |
| Heathrow Scientific LLC | F | 847 816-5070 |
| Vernon Hills (G-21171) | | |
| Heritage Products Corporation | G | 847 419-8835 |
| Buffalo Grove (G-2703) | | |
| Illinois Tool Works Inc | D | 708 720-0300 |
| Frankfort (G-10330) | | |
| Illinois Tool Works Inc | D | 708 720-7800 |
| Richton Park (G-17977) | | |
| Inplex Custom Extruders LLC | F | 847 827-7046 |
| Naperville (G-15676) | | |
| J C Products Inc | G | 847 208-9616 |
| Algonquin (G-394) | | |
| Jdi Mold and Tool LLC | F | 815 759-5646 |
| Johnsburg (G-12437) | | |
| Johnson Bag Co Inc | F | 847 438-2424 |
| Lake Zurich (G-13093) | | |
| Ki Industries Inc | E | 708 449-1990 |
| Berkeley (G-2046) | | |
| Knight Plastics LLC | C | 815 334-1240 |
| Woodstock (G-22579) | | |
| M Putterman & Co LLC | D | 773 927-4120 |
| Chicago (G-5585) | | |
| Mac Lean-Fogg Company | D | 847 566-0010 |
| Mundelein (G-15521) | | |
| Material Control Inc | F | 630 892-4274 |
| Batavia (G-1467) | | |
| Met-L-Flo Inc | F | 630 409-9860 |
| Sugar Grove (G-20729) | | |
| Mgs Group North America Inc | D | 847 371-1158 |
| Libertyville (G-13357) | | |
| Midland Plastics Inc | G | 815 282-4079 |
| Machesney Park (G-14091) | | |
| Midwest Exchange Entps Inc | E | 847 599-9595 |
| Gurnee (G-11472) | | |
| Midwest Molding Inc | D | 224 208-1110 |
| Bartlett (G-1363) | | |
| Midwest Molding Solutions | F | 309 663-7374 |
| Bloomington (G-2200) | | |
| Mpc Group LLC | D | 773 927-4120 |
| Chicago (G-5824) | | |
| Multi-Plastics Inc | E | 630 226-0580 |
| Bolingbrook (G-2348) | | |
| Northstar Trading LLC | F | 224 422-6050 |
| Romeoville (G-18855) | | |
| Pactiv Intl Holdings Inc | G | 847 482-2000 |
| Lake Forest (G-12934) | | |
| Pactiv LLC | B | 715 723-4181 |
| Lake Forest (G-12938) | | |
| Plano Metal Specialties Inc | F | 630 552-8510 |
| Plano (G-17672) | | |
| Plastic Film Corp America Inc | F | 630 887-0800 |
| Romeoville (G-18857) | | |
| Plitek | D | 847 827-6680 |
| Des Plaines (G-8257) | | |
| Polydesigns Ltd | G | 847 433-9920 |
| Highland Park (G-11861) | | |
| Polytech Industries Inc | E | 630 443-6030 |
| Saint Charles (G-19237) | | |
| Process Systems Inc | | 217 563-2872 |
| Nokomis (G-16060) | | |
| Prommar Plastics Inc | | 815 770-0555 |
| Harvard (G-11645) | | |
| R C Sales & Manufacturing Inc | | 815 645-8898 |
| Stillman Valley (G-20626) | | |
| Resource Plastics Inc | D | 708 389-3558 |
| Alsip (G-519) | | |
| Scholle Ipn Corporation | F | 708 562-7290 |
| Northlake (G-16450) | | |
| Scholle Ipn Packaging Inc | B | 708 562-7290 |
| Northlake (G-16451) | | |
| Scholle Packaging Inc | | 708 273-3792 |
| Northlake (G-16452) | | |
| Shamrock Plastics Inc | E | 309 243-7723 |
| Peoria (G-17454) | | |
| Simplomatic Manufacturing Co | | 773 342-7757 |
| Elgin (G-9181) | | |
| Star Die Molding Inc | D | 847 766-7952 |
| Elk Grove Village (G-9754) | | |
| T C I Vacuum Forming Company | | 847 622-9100 |
| Elgin (G-9200) | | |
| Target Plastics Tech Corp | D | 630 545-1776 |
| Glendale Heights (G-11083) | | |
| Team Technologies Inc | D | 630 937-0380 |
| Batavia (G-1504) | | |
| Tex Trend Inc | E | 847 215-6796 |
| Wheeling (G-22166) | | |
| Thermo-Graphic LLC | E | 630 350-2226 |
| Bensenville (G-2001) | | |
| Tredegar Film Products Corp | C | 847 438-2111 |
| Lake Zurich (G-13138) | | |
| Trellborg Sling Sltions US Inc | F | 630 539-5500 |
| Schaumburg (G-19769) | | |
| Vac-Matic Corporation | G | 630 543-4518 |
| Addison (G-336) | | |

## PLASTICS SHEET: Packing Materials

| Company | Code | Phone |
|---|---|---|
| Amcor Flexibles LLC | C | 224 313-7000 |
| Buffalo Grove (G-2656) | | |
| G-P Manufacturing Co Inc | E | 847 473-9001 |
| Waukegan (G-21561) | | |
| Multifilm Packaging Corp | | 847 695-7600 |
| Elgin (G-9116) | | |
| Packaging AM Inc | G | 630 568-9506 |
| Burr Ridge (G-2872) | | |
| Scholle Ipn Corporation | F | 708 562-7290 |
| Northlake (G-16450) | | |
| Sisco Corporation | E | 618 327-3066 |
| Nashville (G-15847) | | |
| Unique Blister Company | F | 630 289-1232 |
| Bartlett (G-1383) | | |
| Vacumet Corp | | 708 562-7290 |
| Northlake (G-16458) | | |

## PLASTICS: Blow Molded

| Company | Code | Phone |
|---|---|---|
| CTS Automotive LLC | C | 630 614-7201 |
| Lisle (G-13578) | | |
| Iceberg Enterprises LLC | F | 847 685-9500 |
| Des Plaines (G-8207) | | |
| Midland Plastics Inc | E | 262 938-7000 |
| Roselle (G-18958) | | |
| Performance Gear Systems Inc | E | 630 739-6666 |
| Plainfield (G-17637) | | |
| Plastipak Packaging Inc | C | 630 231-7650 |
| West Chicago (G-21757) | | |
| Ring Container Tech LLC | | 217 875-5084 |
| Decatur (G-7934) | | |
| Ropak Central Inc | D | 847 956-0750 |
| Elk Grove Village (G-9718) | | |
| S4 Industries Inc | F | 224 699-9674 |
| East Dundee (G-8656) | | |

## PLASTICS: Casein

| Company | Code | Phone |
|---|---|---|
| Midwest Innovative Pdts LLC | E | 888 945-4545 |
| Frankfort (G-10343) | | |

## PLASTICS: Cast

| Company | Code | Phone |
|---|---|---|
| Apollo Plastics Corporation | D | 773 282-9222 |
| Chicago (G-3923) | | |
| Hi-Tech Polymers Inc | F | 815 282-2272 |
| Loves Park (G-13946) | | |
| Tmf Plastic Solutions LLC | D | 630 552-7575 |
| Plano (G-17677) | | |

## PLASTICS: Extruded

| Company | Code | Phone |
|---|---|---|
| Cal-Ill Gasket Co | F | 773 287-9605 |
| Chicago (G-4213) | | |
| Custom Plastics Inc | C | 847 439-6770 |
| Elk Grove Village (G-9404) | | |
| Custom Plastics Inc | F | 847 640-4723 |
| Elk Grove Village (G-9405) | | |
| Davies Molding LLC | C | 630 510-8188 |
| Carol Stream (G-3141) | | |
| E & T Plastic Mfg Co Inc | F | 630 628-9048 |
| Addison (G-103) | | |
| Fasteners For Retail Inc | C | 847 296-5511 |
| Des Plaines (G-8194) | | |
| Golden Plastics LLC | F | 847 836-7766 |
| East Dundee (G-8640) | | |
| Nissei America Inc | G | 847 228-5000 |
| Elk Grove Village (G-9652) | | |
| Npi Holding Corp | G | 217 391-1229 |
| Springfield (G-20488) | | |
| Nudo Products Inc | C | 217 528-5636 |
| Springfield (G-20490) | | |
| Plastic Services Group | G | 847 368-1444 |
| Arlington Heights (G-818) | | |
| Ravenscroft Inc | G | 630 513-9911 |
| Saint Charles (G-19250) | | |
| RPI Extrusion Co | G | 708 389-2584 |
| Alsip (G-524) | | |
| Sandee Manufacturing Co | G | 847 671-1335 |
| Franklin Park (G-10581) | | |
| Seals & Components Inc | G | 708 895-5222 |
| Lansing (G-13182) | | |
| Trim-Tex Inc | D | 847 679-3000 |
| Lincolnwood (G-13540) | | |

## PLASTICS: Finished Injection Molded

| Company | Code | Phone |
|---|---|---|
| Able American Plastics Inc | F | 815 678-4646 |
| Richmond (G-17956) | | |
| Accubow LLC | G | 815 250-0607 |
| Peru (G-17498) | | |
| Advanced Molding Tech Inc | D | 815 334-3600 |
| Woodstock (G-22535) | | |
| Applied Polymer System Inc | | 847 301-1712 |
| Schaumburg (G-19445) | | |
| Aptargroup Inc | E | 847 462-3900 |
| McHenry (G-14481) | | |
| Aztec Plastic Company | E | 312 733-0900 |
| Chicago (G-4011) | | |
| B J Plastic Molding Co | E | 630 766-3200 |
| Franklin Park (G-10408) | | |
| B J Plastic Molding Co | E | 630 766-8750 |
| Bensenville (G-1839) | | |
| Capsonic Group LLC | B | 847 888-7264 |
| Elgin (G-8980) | | |
| Central Molded Products LLC | F | 773 622-4000 |
| Chicago (G-4271) | | |
| Classic Midwest Die Mold Inc | F | 773 227-8000 |
| Chicago (G-4393) | | |
| Classic Molding Co Inc | D | 847 671-7888 |
| Schiller Park (G-19814) | | |
| D and S Molding & Dctg Inc | G | 815 399-2734 |
| Rockford (G-18332) | | |
| Dimension Molding Corporation | E | 630 628-0777 |
| Addison (G-94) | | |
| Dura Operating LLC | C | 815 947-3333 |
| Stockton (G-20631) | | |
| Elas Tek Molding Inc | E | 815 675-9012 |
| Spring Grove (G-20335) | | |
| Elgin Molded Plastics Inc | D | 847 931-2455 |
| Elgin (G-9025) | | |
| Energy Absorption Systems Inc | E | 312 467-6750 |
| Chicago (G-4750) | | |
| Foremost Plastic Pdts Co Inc | E | 708 452-5300 |
| Elmwood Park (G-9971) | | |
| Forreston Tool Inc | G | 815 938-3626 |
| Forreston (G-10269) | | |
| Four Star Tool Inc | D | 224 735-2419 |
| Rolling Meadows (G-18729) | | |
| Fox Valley Molding Inc | C | 630 552-3176 |
| Plano (G-17665) | | |
| Hi-Tech Plastics Inc | F | 847 577-1805 |
| Wheeling (G-22070) | | |

# PRODUCT SECTION — PLASTICS: Injection Molded

| Company | Code | Phone |
|---|---|---|
| Illinois Electro Deburring Co — Franklin Park (G-10494) | F | 847 678-5010 |
| Illinois Tool Works Inc — Glenview (G-11141) | B | 847 724-7500 |
| Illinois Tool Works Inc — Bartlett (G-1353) | C | 630 372-2150 |
| Illinois Tool Works Inc — Elk Grove Village (G-9534) | D | 630 787-3298 |
| Illinois Tool Works Inc — Carol Stream (G-3171) | C | 630 315-2150 |
| Illinois Tool Works Inc — Glenview (G-11144) | B | 847 724-6100 |
| Illinois Tool Works Inc — Elgin (G-9072) | C | 847 783-5500 |
| Illinois Tool Works Inc — Buffalo Grove (G-2707) | D | 847 724-7500 |
| Illinois Tool Works Inc — Glenview (G-11145) | D | 847 657-4022 |
| Illinois Tool Works Inc — Roselle (G-18946) | B | 630 595-3500 |
| Insertech International Inc — Cary (G-3355) | E | 847 416-6184 |
| Ironwood Industries Inc — Libertyville (G-13338) | D | 847 362-8681 |
| ITW International Holdings LLC — Glenview (G-11153) | F | 847 724-7500 |
| K B Tool Inc — Bensenville (G-1932) | G | 630 595-4340 |
| Klein Plastics Company LLC — Lincolnshire (G-13459) | D | 616 863-9900 |
| Mako Mold Corporation — Saint Charles (G-19212) | G | 630 377-9010 |
| Makray Manufacturing Company — Norridge (G-16106) | D | 708 456-7100 |
| Mark Power International — Machesney Park (G-14090) | F | 815 877-5984 |
| Medplast Group Inc — Oak Brook (G-16541) | B | 630 706-5500 |
| Mjsrf Inc — Mount Prospect (G-15349) | F | 888 677-6175 |
| MPD Inc — Lake Forest (G-12928) | E | 847 489-7705 |
| Mpr Plastics Inc — Elgin (G-9115) | E | 847 468-9950 |
| Neil Enterprises Inc — Vernon Hills (G-21184) | E | 847 549-0321 |
| Neil International Inc — Vernon Hills (G-21185) | G | 847 549-7627 |
| Nypromold Inc — Gurnee (G-11477) | C | 847 855-2200 |
| Odra Inc — Gurnee (G-11478) | G | 847 249-2910 |
| Parting Line Tool Inc — Huntley (G-12166) | F | 847 669-0331 |
| Peeps Inc — Palos Hills (G-17121) | G | 708 935-4201 |
| Pimco Plastics Inc — Spring Grove (G-20356) | G | 815 675-6464 |
| Plaspros Inc — McHenry (G-14546) | D | 815 430-2300 |
| Plastic Products Company Inc — Moline (G-14962) | C | 309 762-6532 |
| Quixote Transportation Safety — Chicago (G-6260) | D | 312 467-6750 |
| Reum Corporation — Chicago (G-6340) | C | 847 625-7386 |
| Revcor Inc — Carpentersville (G-3301) | B | 847 428-4411 |
| Revcor Inc — Carpentersville (G-3302) | G | 847 428-4411 |
| Rockford Molded Products Inc — Loves Park (G-13985) | D | 815 637-0585 |
| Signode Packaging Systems Corp — Glenview (G-11203) | D | 800 323-2464 |
| Stanger Tool & Mold Inc — Belvidere (G-1785) | G | 847 426-5826 |
| Sun Pattern & Model Inc — West Chicago (G-21777) | E | 630 293-3366 |
| Uniphase Inc — Saint Charles (G-19288) | E | 630 584-4747 |
| Van Norman Molding Company LLC — Oak Lawn (G-16647) | E | 708 430-4343 |
| Wedco Molded Products — Willowbrook (G-22239) | G | 630 455-6711 |

## *PLASTICS: Injection Molded*

| Company | Code | Phone |
|---|---|---|
| Abba Plastics Inc — Yorkville (G-22647) | G | 630 385-2156 |
| Abbacus Inc — Machesney Park (G-14048) | E | 815 637-9222 |
| Abbacus Injection Molding Inc — Machesney Park (G-14049) | E | 815 637-9222 |
| Acco Brands USA LLC — Lake Zurich (G-13034) | B | 800 222-6462 |
| Acco Brands USA LLC — Lincolnshire (G-13423) | D | 847 272-3700 |
| Admo — Elgin (G-8936) |  | 847 741-5777 |
| Advance Plastic Corp — Chicago (G-3761) | F | 773 637-5922 |
| Advantech Plastics LLC — Woodstock (G-22536) | D | 815 338-8383 |
| AGS Technology Inc — Batavia (G-1407) | E | 847 534-6600 |
| All Star Injection Molders Inc — Naperville (G-15793) | G | 630 978-4046 |
| All West Plastics Inc — Antioch (G-616) | D | 847 395-8830 |
| Alliance Plastics — Bensenville (G-1824) | G | 888 643-1432 |
| Allmetal Inc — Itasca (G-12225) | B | 630 250-8090 |
| Allmetal Inc — Bensenville (G-1826) | F | 630 766-1407 |
| Alpha Star Tool and Mold Inc — Crystal Lake (G-7529) | F | 815 455-2802 |
| American Gasket Tech Inc — Addison (G-36) | D | 630 543-1510 |
| American Molding Tech Inc — Elk Grove Village (G-9297) | E | 847 437-6900 |
| Amtec Precision Products Inc — Elgin (G-8953) | D | 847 695-8030 |
| Amtech Industries LLC — Palatine (G-17001) |  | 847 202-3488 |
| Armin Molding Corp — South Elgin (G-20182) |  | 847 742-1864 |
| Arnel Industries Inc — Addison (G-45) | E | 630 543-6500 |
| Bankier Companies Inc — Niles (G-15963) | C | 847 647-6565 |
| Baps Investors Group LLC — Rolling Meadows (G-18716) | E | 847 818-8444 |
| Berry Global Inc — Buffalo Grove (G-2663) |  | 847 541-7900 |
| Bird Dog Diversified — Elgin (G-8966) |  | 847 741-0700 |
| Centech Plastics Inc — Elk Grove Village (G-9361) | C | 847 364-4433 |
| Century Mold & Tool Co — Elk Grove Village (G-9362) | E | 847 364-5858 |
| Century Molded Plastics Inc — Glenview (G-11111) |  | 847 729-3455 |
| Chemtech Plastics Inc — Elgin (G-8986) |  | 630 503-6000 |
| Collapsible Core Inc — Romeoville (G-18814) |  | 630 408-1693 |
| Commercial Plastics Company — Mundelein (G-15490) | C | 847 566-1700 |
| Component Plastics Inc — Elgin (G-8995) |  | 847 695-9200 |
| Condor Tool & Manufacturing — Addison (G-81) | F | 630 628-8200 |
| Cortina Companies Inc — Franklin Park (G-10443) |  | 847 455-2800 |
| Cortina Tool & Molding Co — Franklin Park (G-10444) |  | 847 455-2800 |
| Crestwood Industries Inc — Mundelein (G-15492) | F | 847 680-9088 |
| Crystal Die and Mold Inc — Rolling Meadows (G-18724) | E | 847 658-6535 |
| D & M Custom Injection M — Burlington (G-2811) | D | 847 683-2054 |
| Dice Mold & Engineering Inc — Itasca (G-12250) | E | 630 773-3595 |
| Dirk Vander Noot — Prospect Heights (G-17776) |  | 224 558-1878 |
| DRG Molding & Pad Printing Inc — Round Lake Beach (G-19075) | G | 847 223-3398 |
| Drummond Industries Inc — Bensenville (G-1884) | E | 773 637-1264 |
| Eakas Corporation — Peru (G-17508) | B | 815 223-8811 |
| Electroform Company — Machesney Park (G-14072) | E | 815 633-1113 |
| Engineered Plastic Components — Rantoul (G-17927) | C | 217 892-2026 |
| Enginred Molding Solutions Inc — McHenry (G-14503) | E | 815 363-9600 |
| Evans Tool & Manufacturing — Aurora (G-1149) | G | 630 897-8656 |
| F & R Plastics Inc — Waukegan (G-21558) | G | 847 336-1330 |
| Fabrik Industries Inc — McHenry (G-14505) | B | 815 385-9480 |
| Field Manufacturing Corp — Crystal Lake (G-7578) | D | 815 455-5596 |
| First Amrcn Plstic Mlding Entp — South Beloit (G-20145) | D | 815 624-8538 |
| Flex-N-Gate Corporation — Danville (G-7721) | G | 217 442-4018 |
| Flextronics Intl USA Inc — Buffalo Grove (G-2696) | G | 847 383-1529 |
| Flotek Inc — Cary (G-3342) | G | 815 943-6816 |
| Foreman Tool & Mold Corp — Saint Charles (G-19186) | E | 630 377-6389 |
| Furnel Inc — Addison (G-124) | D | 630 543-0885 |
| G A I M Plastics Incorporated — Bensenville (G-1903) | F | 630 350-9500 |
| GAim Plastics Incorporated — Bensenville (G-1904) | F | 630 350-9500 |
| Gayton Group Inc — Schiller Park (G-19833) |  | 847 233-0509 |
| Genesis Mold Corp — Libertyville (G-13326) | G | 847 573-9431 |
| Goudie Tool and Engrg Del — Lake Zurich (G-13079) | F | 847 438-5597 |
| Graphic Tool Corp — Itasca (G-12272) | E | 630 250-9800 |
| Han-Win Products Inc — Aurora (G-1166) |  | 630 897-1591 |
| Hansen Plastics Corp — Elgin (G-9055) | D | 847 741-4510 |
| Hansen Plastics Corp — Elgin (G-9056) | G | 847 741-4510 |
| Hoffer Plastics Corporation — South Elgin (G-20203) | B | 847 741-5740 |
| Husky Injection Molding — Mokena (G-14869) | F | 708 479-9049 |
| Hy Tech Cnc Machining Inc — Schaumburg (G-19561) | G |  |
| Illinois Tool Works Inc — Des Plaines (G-8209) | C | 847 299-2222 |
| Illinois Tool Works Inc — Mazon (G-14438) | C | 815 448-7300 |
| Indiana Precision Inc — Danville (G-7739) | F | 765 361-0247 |
| Innovative Components Inc — Schaumburg (G-19567) | E | 847 885-9050 |
| Insertech LLC — Cary (G-3354) | D | 847 516-6184 |
| Intermolding Technology LLC — Des Plaines (G-8212) | F | 847 376-8517 |
| Intrepid Molding Inc — Wauconda (G-21474) | E | 847 526-9477 |
| Iplastics LLC — Washington (G-21383) | D | 309 444-8884 |
| James Injection Molding Co — Northbrook (G-16283) | E | 847 564-3820 |
| Janler Corporation — Chicago (G-5277) | E | 773 774-0166 |
| L C Mold Inc — Rolling Meadows (G-18740) | E | 847 593-5004 |
| Legacy Plastics Inc — Rockford (G-18465) | G | 815 226-3013 |
| Lewis Acquisition Corp — Addison (G-180) | D | 773 486-5660 |
| M F K Enterprises Inc — Villa Park (G-21266) | F | 630 516-1230 |
| Magenta LLC — Lockport (G-13730) | D | 773 777-5050 |
| Master Molded Products LLC — Elgin (G-9102) | C | 847 695-9700 |
| Mastermolding Inc — Joliet (G-12538) | E | 815 741-1230 |
| Mate Technologies Inc — Elgin (G-9103) | E | 847 289-1010 |
| Matrix Tooling Inc — Wood Dale (G-22397) | D | 630 595-6144 |
| Maxon Plastics Inc — Batavia (G-1469) | G | 630 761-3667 |
| Mega Corporation — Schaumburg (G-19640) | E | 847 985-1900 |
| Met2plastic LLC — Elk Grove Village (G-9619) | E | 847 228-5070 |
| Mid-America Plastic Company — Forreston (G-10270) | E | 815 938-3110 |
| Millennium Mold Design Inc — McHenry (G-14535) | G | 815 344-9790 |

Employee Codes: A=Over 500 employees, B=251-500
C=101-250, D=51-100, E=20-50, F=10-19, G=3-9

**Molding Services Illinois Inc**....E.... 618 395-3888
Olney *(G-16782)*
**Mvs Molding Inc**....G.... 847 740-7700
Round Lake *(G-19063)*
**Navitor Inc**....B.... 800 323-0253
Harwood Heights *(G-11687)*
**Newovo Plastics LLC**....G.... 224 535-8183
Elgin *(G-9119)*
**North Amercn Acquisition Corp**....C.... 847 695-8030
Elgin *(G-9125)*
**North American Fund III LP**....G.... 312 332-4950
Chicago *(G-5932)*
**Northern Precision Plas Inc**....E.... 815 544-8099
Belvidere *(G-1776)*
**Nypro Inc**....E.... 630 671-2000
Hanover Park *(G-11588)*
**Owen Plastics LLC**....E.... 847 683-2054
Burlington *(G-2813)*
**P & P Industries Inc**....D.... 815 623-3297
Sterling *(G-20602)*
**Paramount Plastics Inc**....D.... 815 834-4100
Chicago *(G-6077)*
**Peritus Plastics LLC**....E.... 815 448-2005
Mazon *(G-14440)*
**Plastech Inc**....F.... 630 595-7222
Bensenville *(G-1964)*
**Plastech Molding Inc**....G.... 847 398-0355
Wheeling *(G-22123)*
**Plastic Parts Intl Inc**....E.... 815 637-9222
Machesney Park *(G-14097)*
**Plastic Power Corporation**....G.... 847 233-9601
Franklin Park *(G-10553)*
**Plastic Powerdrive Pdts LLC**....F.... 847 637-5233
Elgin *(G-9139)*
**Plustech Inc**....G.... 847 490-8130
Schaumburg *(G-19698)*
**Pnc Inc**....D.... 815 946-2328
Polo *(G-17690)*
**Polymer Plnfeld Hldings US Inc**....C.... 815 436-5671
Plainfield *(G-17641)*
**Powerpath Microproducts Inc**....G.... 847 827-6330
Des Plaines *(G-8258)*
**Precision Custom Molders Inc**....E.... 815 675-1370
Spring Grove *(G-20357)*
**Precision Molded Concepts**....F.... 815 675-0060
Spring Grove *(G-20358)*
**Prismier LLC**....E.... 630 592-4515
Woodridge *(G-22511)*
**Q C H Incorporated**....D.... 630 820-5550
Oswego *(G-16929)*
**Quad Inc**....E.... 815 624-8538
South Beloit *(G-20166)*
**Quality Plastic Products Inc**....G.... 630 766-7593
Bensenville *(G-1972)*
**Rackow Polymers Corporation**....E.... 630 766-3982
Bensenville *(G-1975)*
**Ram Plastic Corp**....G.... 847 669-8003
Huntley *(G-12172)*
**Rensel-Chicago Inc**....F.... 773 235-2100
Chicago *(G-6334)*
**Rf Plastics Co**....G.... 630 628-6033
Addison *(G-278)*
**Royal Touch Carwash**....G.... 847 808-8600
Buffalo Grove *(G-2760)*
**Rway Plastics Ltd**....F.... 815 476-5252
Wilmington *(G-22276)*
**S & S Mold Corporation**....G.... 815 385-0818
Woodstock *(G-22606)*
**Safe-T-Quip Corporation**....F.... 773 235-2100
Chicago *(G-6425)*
**Sakamoto Kanagata Usa Inc**....G.... 224 856-2008
South Elgin *(G-20225)*
**Security Molding Inc**....F.... 630 543-8607
Addison *(G-285)*
**Sikora Precision Inc**....G.... 847 468-0900
Elgin *(G-9180)*
**Smt LLC**....E.... 630 961-3000
Naperville *(G-15747)*
**Sparx EDM Inc**....G.... 847 722-7577
Streamwood *(G-20674)*
**Spintex Inc**....G.... 847 608-5411
Elgin *(G-9190)*
**Stellar Plastics Corporation**....D.... 630 443-1200
Saint Charles *(G-19270)*
**Stevens Plastic Inc**....E.... 847 885-2378
Hoffman Estates *(G-12060)*
**Stock Gears Inc**....F.... 224 653-9489
Elk Grove Village *(G-9758)*
**Suburban Plastics Co**....B.... 847 741-4900
Elgin *(G-9194)*
**Sullivan Tool and Repair Inc**....G.... 224 856-5867
Elgin *(G-9195)*
**Survyvn Ltd**....G.... 847 977-8665
Ringwood *(G-17995)*
**T L Swint Industries Inc**....G.... 847 358-3834
Inverness *(G-12206)*
**Taico Design Products Inc**....G.... 773 871-9086
Chicago *(G-6665)*
**Technatool Inc**....G.... 847 398-0355
Wheeling *(G-22165)*
**Technimold Tool Corporation**....F.... 847 639-4226
Cary *(G-3376)*
**Techny Plastics Corp**....E.... 847 498-2212
Northbrook *(G-16377)*
**Thermal-Tech Systems Inc**....E.... 630 639-5115
West Chicago *(G-21780)*
**Three R Plastics Inc**....F.... 815 675-0844
Spring Grove *(G-20368)*
**Thurow Tool Works Inc**....G.... 630 377-6403
Saint Charles *(G-19283)*
**Tinex Technology Corp**....G.... 630 904-5368
Naperville *(G-15830)*
**TNT Plastics Inc**....F.... 847 895-6921
Schaumburg *(G-19764)*
**Tomco Die & Kellering Co**....G.... 847 678-8113
Franklin Park *(G-10608)*
**Trident Manufacturing Inc**....E.... 847 464-0140
Pingree Grove *(G-17557)*
**Uwd Inc**....F.... 815 316-3080
Roscoe *(G-18925)*
**Vector Mold & Tool Inc**....G.... 847 437-0110
Des Plaines *(G-8297)*
**Veejay Plastics Inc**....F.... 847 683-2954
Burlington *(G-2814)*
**Vega Molded Products Inc**....G.... 847 428-7761
Gilberts *(G-10940)*
**W M Plastics Inc**....D.... 815 578-8888
McHenry *(G-14570)*
**Wesdar Technologies Inc**....G.... 630 761-0965
Aurora *(G-1096)*
**Wise Plastics Technologies Inc**....C.... 630 584-2307
Saint Charles *(G-19298)*
**WJ Die Mold Inc**....F.... 847 895-6561
Schaumburg *(G-19791)*
**Woodland Engineering Company**....G.... 847 362-0110
Lake Bluff *(G-12873)*
**Woodland Plastics Corp**....E.... 630 543-1144
Addison *(G-345)*
**Woojin Plaimm Inc**....F.... 708 606-5536
Mount Prospect *(G-15385)*
**Zender Enterprises Ltd**....G.... 773 282-2293
Chicago *(G-7063)*

## *PLASTICS: Molded*

**Aberdeen Technologies Inc**....F.... 630 665-8590
Carol Stream *(G-3088)*
**Advance Design Inc**....G.... 815 338-0843
Woodstock *(G-22534)*
**Advanced Prototype Molding**....G.... 847 202-4200
Palatine *(G-16998)*
**Advert Display Products Inc**....G.... 815 513-5432
Morris *(G-15090)*
**Amtec Molded Products Inc**....E.... 815 226-0187
Elgin *(G-8952)*
**Anfinsen Plastic Moulding Inc**....E.... 630 554-4100
Oswego *(G-16904)*
**Badger Molding Inc**....F.... 847 483-9005
Wheeling *(G-22011)*
**BJ Mold & Die Inc**....G.... 630 595-1797
Wood Dale *(G-22346)*
**Box Enclsres Assembly Svcs Inc**....G.... 847 932-4700
Libertyville *(G-13309)*
**Chatham Plastics Inc**....G.... 217 483-1481
Chatham *(G-3618)*
**Chicago Molding Outlet**....G.... 773 471-6870
Chicago *(G-4335)*
**Custom Blow Molding**....G.... 630 820-9700
Aurora *(G-990)*
**Dana Molded**....G.... 847 783-1800
Carpentersville *(G-3282)*
**Dove Products Inc**....E.... 815 727-4683
Lockport *(G-13711)*
**Dti Molding Technologies Inc**....D.... 630 543-3600
Addison *(G-100)*
**E A M & J Inc**....E.... 847 622-9200
Elgin *(G-9017)*
**E-Jay Plastics Co**....F.... 630 543-4000
Addison *(G-104)*
**E-Z Rotational Molder Inc**....G.... 847 806-1327
Elk Grove Village *(G-9445)*
**Elgin Die Mold Co**....D.... 847 464-0140
Pingree Grove *(G-17555)*
**Gord Industrial Plastics Inc**....F.... 815 786-9494
Sandwich *(G-19366)*
**Harbison Corporation**....D.... 815 224-2633
Peru *(G-17511)*
**Hawk Molding Inc**....G.... 224 523-2888
Harvard *(G-11636)*
**Hbp Inc**....D.... 815 235-3000
Freeport *(G-10662)*
**I TW Deltar Insert Molded Pdts**....G.... 847 593-8811
Elk Grove Village *(G-9530)*
**Illinois Pro-Turn Inc**....G.... 847 462-1870
Cary *(G-3353)*
**Inland Plastics Inc**....G.... 815 933-3500
Kankakee *(G-12625)*
**Intec-Mexico LLC**....B.... 847 358-0088
Palatine *(G-17043)*
**J and K Molding**....G.... 224 276-3355
Volo *(G-21314)*
**Jth Enterprises Inc**....E.... 847 394-3355
Arlington Heights *(G-787)*
**K H M Plastics Inc**....E.... 847 249-4910
Gurnee *(G-11464)*
**Lakone Company**....D.... 630 892-4251
Montgomery *(G-15055)*
**Leroys Plastic Co Inc**....F.... 630 898-7006
Aurora *(G-1182)*
**Lordahl Manufacturing Co**....D.... 847 244-0448
Long Grove *(G-13893)*
**Matrix IV Inc**....E.... 815 338-4500
Woodstock *(G-22588)*
**Micron Mold & Mfg Inc**....G.... 630 871-9531
Carol Stream *(G-3196)*
**Midwest Blow Molding LLC**....G.... 618 283-9223
Vandalia *(G-21117)*
**Molded Displays**....G.... 773 892-4098
Highland Park *(G-11856)*
**Molding Services Group Inc**....E.... 847 931-1491
South Elgin *(G-20220)*
**Moldtronics Inc**....E.... 630 968-7000
Downers Grove *(G-8488)*
**Monahan Filaments LLC**....D.... 217 268-4957
Arcola *(G-677)*
**Plano Molding Company LLC**....C.... 815 538-3111
Mendota *(G-14730)*
**Plastic Designs Inc**....E.... 217 379-9214
Paxton *(G-17243)*
**Plastics**....G.... 847 931-9391
Elgin *(G-9141)*
**Prototek Tool & Mold Inc**....G.... 847 487-2708
Wauconda *(G-21496)*
**Resins Inc**....G.... 847 884-0025
Hoffman Estates *(G-12043)*
**Riken Corporation of America**....C.... 847 673-1400
Skokie *(G-20076)*
**Scimitar Prototyping Inc**....G.... 630 483-3875
Streamwood *(G-20672)*
**Sherwood Tool Inc**....F.... 815 648-1463
Hebron *(G-11726)*
**Silgan Plastics LLC**....D.... 618 662-4471
Flora *(G-10217)*
**Spinner Medical Products Inc**....B.... 312 944-8700
Chicago *(G-6560)*
**Studio Moulding**....G.... 217 523-2101
Springfield *(G-20539)*
**The Intec Group Inc**....C.... 847 358-0088
Palatine *(G-17081)*
**Trend Technologies LLC**....C.... 847 640-2382
Elk Grove Village *(G-9789)*
**Tri-Par Die and Mold Corp**....E.... 630 232-8800
South Elgin *(G-20229)*
**Tri-Tech Molding**....G.... 847 263-7769
Lake Villa *(G-13028)*
**True Line Mold and Engrg Corp**....E.... 815 648-2739
Hebron *(G-11729)*
**Winzeler Inc**....E.... 708 867-7971
Harwood Heights *(G-11692)*

## *PLASTICS: Polystyrene Foam*

**All Foam Products Co**....G.... 847 913-9341
Buffalo Grove *(G-2653)*
**Atlas Roofing Corporation**....E.... 309 752-7121
East Moline *(G-8670)*
**Blachford Investments Inc**....C.... 630 231-8300
West Chicago *(G-21671)*
**Centro Inc**....G.... 309 751-9700
East Moline *(G-8672)*
**Custom Foam Works Inc**....G.... 618 920-2810
Troy *(G-21005)*

**DC Works Inc**.....G..... 847 464-4280
Hampshire *(G-11546)*
**Dow Chemical Company**.....C..... 815 423-5921
Channahon *(G-3572)*
**Engineered Foam Solutions Inc**.....G..... 708 769-4130
South Holland *(G-20266)*
**Essentra Specialty Tapes Inc**.....C..... 708 488-1025
Forest Park *(G-10242)*
**Excelsior Inc**.....E..... 815 987-2900
Rockford *(G-18375)*
**Free-Flow Packaging Intl Inc**.....D..... 708 589-6500
Thornton *(G-20869)*
**General Foam Plastics Corp**.....G..... 847 851-9995
East Dundee *(G-8637)*
**Meadoworks LLC**.....F..... 847 640-8580
Schaumburg *(G-19638)*
**Owens Corning Sales LLC**.....D..... 815 226-4627
Rockford *(G-18527)*
**Pres-On Corporation**.....E..... 630 628-2255
Bolingbrook *(G-2360)*
**Quality Pallets Inc**.....E..... 217 459-2655
Windsor *(G-22282)*
**Simonton Holdings Inc**.....F..... 304 428-8261
Deerfield *(G-8055)*
**Tek Pak Inc**.....D..... 630 406-0560
Batavia *(G-1506)*
**Thermos LLC**.....E..... 847 439-7821
Schaumburg *(G-19760)*
**W R Grace & Co- Conn**.....F..... 708 458-9700
Chicago *(G-6924)*

## *PLASTICS: Thermoformed*

**Clear Pack Company**.....C..... 847 957-6282
Franklin Park *(G-10437)*
**D & J Plastics Inc**.....G..... 847 534-0601
Schaumburg *(G-19496)*
**Du-Call Miller Plastics Inc**.....F..... 630 964-6020
Batavia *(G-1443)*
**Dunham Designs Inc**.....G..... 815 462-0100
New Lenox *(G-15877)*
**Gmt Inc**.....E..... 847 697-8161
Elgin *(G-9049)*
**Greenwood Inc**.....E..... 217 431-6034
Danville *(G-7729)*
**Greenwood Inc**.....F..... 800 798-4900
Danville *(G-7728)*
**Innovative Plastech Inc**.....D..... 630 232-1808
Batavia *(G-1458)*
**Intergrted Thrmforming Systems**.....F..... 630 906-6895
Aurora *(G-1172)*
**Jordan Industries Inc**.....F..... 847 945-5591
Deerfield *(G-8020)*
**Mercury Plastics Inc**.....E..... 888 884-1864
Chicago *(G-5688)*
**Pactiv LLC**.....B..... 847 459-8049
Wheeling *(G-22116)*
**Profile Plastics Inc**.....D..... 847 256-1623
Lake Bluff *(G-12864)*
**Ricon Colors Inc**.....F..... 630 562-9000
West Chicago *(G-21764)*
**Sonoco Products Company**.....C..... 847 957-6282
Franklin Park *(G-10591)*

## *PLATE WORK: For Nuclear Industry*

**Metal Improvement Company LLC**.....E..... 630 620-6808
Lombard *(G-13825)*

## *PLATE WORK: Metalworking Trade*

**Ameralloy Steel Corporation**.....E..... 847 967-0600
Morton Grove *(G-15188)*
**Faspro Technologies Inc**.....D..... 847 392-9500
Arlington Heights *(G-752)*

## *PLATED WARE, ALL METALS*

**Fusion Tech Integrated Inc**.....D..... 309 774-4275
Roseville *(G-19045)*

## *PLATEMAKING SVC: Color Separations, For The Printing Trade*

**Blooming Color Inc**.....E..... 630 705-9200
Lombard *(G-13772)*
**Chicago Prepress Color Inc**.....G..... 708 385-3465
Midlothian *(G-14765)*
**Color Works Graphics Inc**.....E..... 847 383-5270
Chicago *(G-4427)*
**Excel Color Corporation**.....G..... 847 734-1270
Elk Grove Village *(G-9467)*
**Expercolor Inc**.....E..... 773 465-3400
Skokie *(G-19997)*
**Graphic Arts Studio Inc**.....E..... 847 381-1105
Barrington *(G-1282)*
**Henderson Co Inc**.....F..... 773 628-7216
Chicago *(G-5070)*
**M & G Graphics Inc**.....E..... 773 247-1596
Chicago *(G-5576)*
**Saltzman Printers Inc**.....E..... 708 344-4500
Melrose Park *(G-14690)*
**Splash Graphics Inc**.....F..... 630 230-5775
Willowbrook *(G-22232)*

## *PLATES*

**Apr Graphics Inc**.....G..... 847 329-7800
Skokie *(G-19957)*
**Artistry Engraving & Embossing**.....G..... 773 775-4888
Chicago *(G-3957)*
**B Allan Graphics Inc**.....F..... 708 396-1704
Alsip *(G-438)*
**B F Shaw Printing Company**.....E..... 815 875-4461
Princeton *(G-17744)*
**Banner Moulded Products**.....E..... 708 452-0033
River Grove *(G-18005)*
**Best Machine & Welding Co Inc**.....E..... 708 343-4455
Woodridge *(G-22456)*
**Brilliant Color Corp**.....G..... 847 367-3300
Libertyville *(G-13310)*
**C F C Interantional**.....G..... 708 753-0679
Chicago Heights *(G-7085)*
**Cardinal Colorprint Prtg Corp**.....E..... 630 467-1000
Itasca *(G-12241)*
**Carson Printing Inc**.....G..... 847 836-0900
East Dundee *(G-8629)*
**Chromium Industries Inc**.....E..... 773 287-3716
Chicago *(G-4373)*
**Commercial Copy Printing Ctr**.....F..... 847 981-8590
Elk Grove Village *(G-9384)*
**Cpr Printing Inc**.....F..... 630 377-8420
Geneva *(G-10821)*
**Creative Label Inc**.....D..... 847 981-3800
Elk Grove Village *(G-9399)*
**Creative Lithocraft Inc**.....G..... 847 352-7002
Schaumburg *(G-19489)*
**Crossmark Printing Inc**.....F..... 708 532-8263
Tinley Park *(G-20906)*
**Crosstech Communications Inc**.....E..... 312 382-0111
Chicago *(G-4506)*
**Delta Press Inc**.....E..... 847 671-3200
Palatine *(G-17022)*
**Eugene Ewbank**.....G..... 630 705-0400
Oswego *(G-16917)*
**Graphic Image Corporation**.....F..... 312 829-7800
Chicago *(G-4989)*
**Hurst Chemical Company**.....G..... 815 964-0451
Rockford *(G-18424)*
**Ideal/Mikron Inc**.....G..... 847 873-0254
Mount Prospect *(G-15336)*
**Iemco Corporation**.....G..... 773 728-4400
Chicago *(G-5145)*
**Impression Printing**.....F..... 708 614-8660
Oak Forest *(G-16583)*
**Instyprints of Waukegan Inc**.....G..... 847 336-5599
Waukegan *(G-21571)*
**J D Graphic Co Inc**.....E..... 847 364-4000
Elk Grove Village *(G-9557)*
**Jph Enterprises Inc**.....G..... 847 390-0900
Des Plaines *(G-8217)*
**Lasons Label Co**.....G..... 773 775-2606
Chicago *(G-5464)*
**Lloyd Midwest Graphics**.....G..... 815 282-8828
Machesney Park *(G-14089)*
**Luttrell Engraving Inc**.....E..... 708 489-3800
Alsip *(G-485)*
**M L S Printing Co Inc**.....G..... 847 948-8902
Deerfield *(G-8033)*
**M S A Printing Co**.....G..... 847 593-5699
Elk Grove Village *(G-9604)*
**Marcus Press**.....G..... 630 351-1857
Bloomingdale *(G-2115)*
**Multicopy Corp**.....G..... 847 446-7015
Northfield *(G-16410)*
**N Bujarski Inc**.....G..... 847 884-1600
Schaumburg *(G-19660)*
**Naco Printing Co Inc**.....G..... 618 664-0423
Greenville *(G-11400)*
**Oec Graphics-Chicago LLC**.....E..... 630 455-6700
Willowbrook *(G-22227)*
**Pamarco Global Graphics Inc**.....E..... 630 879-7300
Batavia *(G-1479)*
**Pamarco Global Graphics Inc**.....F..... 847 459-6000
Wheeling *(G-22118)*
**Precision Die Cutting & Finish**.....G..... 773 252-5625
Chicago *(G-6169)*
**Prime Market Targeting Inc**.....E..... 815 469-4555
Frankfort *(G-10353)*
**Priority Printing**.....G..... 773 889-6021
Chicago *(G-6198)*
**Prism Commercial Printing Ctrs**.....G..... 630 834-4443
Chicago *(G-6199)*
**Rohrer Graphic Arts Inc**.....F..... 630 832-3434
Elmhurst *(G-9930)*
**Rohrer Litho Inc**.....G..... 630 833-6610
Elmhurst *(G-9931)*
**Rotation Dynamics Corporation**.....E..... 630 769-9700
Chicago *(G-6398)*
**Rotation Dynamics Corporation**.....D..... 773 247-5600
Chicago *(G-6399)*
**Servi-Sure Corporation**.....E..... 773 271-5900
Chicago *(G-6480)*
**Southern Graphic Systems LLC**.....E..... 847 695-9515
Elgin *(G-9189)*
**Sunrise Hitek Service Inc**.....E..... 773 792-8880
Chicago *(G-6630)*
**Tanic Rubber Plate Co**.....G..... 630 896-2122
Aurora *(G-1223)*
**Village Press Inc**.....G..... 847 362-1856
Libertyville *(G-13399)*
**West Vly Graphics & Print Inc**.....G..... 630 377-7575
Saint Charles *(G-19293)*
**Woogl Corporation**.....E..... 847 806-1160
Elk Grove Village *(G-9816)*

## *PLATES: Aluminum*

**Country Cast Products**.....F..... 815 777-1070
Galena *(G-10718)*
**Pechiney Cast Plate**.....C..... 847 299-0220
Chicago *(G-6094)*

## *PLATES: Paper, Made From Purchased Materials*

**Party Plate LLC**.....G..... 708 268-4571
Lemont *(G-13249)*
**SF Holdings Group Inc**.....D..... 847 831-4800
Lincolnshire *(G-13479)*

## *PLATES: Sheet & Strip, Exc Coated Prdts*

**Mexinox USA Inc**.....D..... 224 533-6700
Bannockburn *(G-1261)*

## *PLATES: Steel*

**Evraz Inc NA**.....C..... 312 533-3621
Chicago *(G-4792)*
**Mittal Steel USA Inc**.....F..... 312 899-3440
Chicago *(G-5775)*
**Seraph Industries LLC**.....G..... 815 222-9686
Caledonia *(G-2934)*

## *PLATES: Truss, Metal*

**ITW Blding Cmponents Group Inc**.....E..... 217 324-0303
Litchfield *(G-13689)*

## *PLATING & FINISHING SVC: Decorative, Formed Prdts*

**Classic Metal Company Inc**.....G..... 815 252-0104
Mendota *(G-14718)*

## *PLATING & POLISHING SVC*

**A & L Drilling Inc**.....F..... 815 962-7538
Rockford *(G-18238)*
**Ace Sandblast Company (del)**.....F..... 773 777-6654
Chicago *(G-3728)*
**Al Bar Laboratories Inc**.....F..... 847 251-1218
Wilmette *(G-22241)*
**Alliance Steel Corporation**.....E..... 708 924-1200
Bedford Park *(G-1535)*
**American Plating & Mfg Co**.....F..... 773 890-4907
Chicago *(G-3869)*
**Arnold Monument Co Inc**.....G..... 217 546-2102
Springfield *(G-20388)*
**Baroque Silversmith Inc**.....G..... 312 357-2813
Chicago *(G-4045)*
**Bellows Shoppe**.....G..... 847 446-5533
Winnetka *(G-22303)*



Employee Codes: A=Over 500 employees, B=251-500
C=101-250, D=51-100, E=20-50, F=10-19, G=3-9

2017 Harris Illinois
Industrial Directory

1697

# PLATING & POLISHING SVC

Cardon Mold Finishing Inc .................. G ...... 630 543-5431
  Addison  (G-69)
Celinco Inc ..................................... G ...... 815 964-2256
  Rockford  (G-18301)
Chem-Plate Industries Inc ................... D ...... 847 640-1600
  Elk Grove Village  (G-9366)
Chemix Corp .................................... F ...... 708 754-2150
  Glenwood  (G-11215)
Chemtool Incorporated ....................... D ...... 815 459-1250
  Crystal Lake  (G-7551)
Circle Studio Stained Glass ................. G ...... 847 432-7249
  Highland Park  (G-11827)
Circle Studio Stained Glass ................. G ...... 773 588-4848
  Chicago  (G-4380)
Cooley Wire Products Mfg Co ............... E ...... 847 678-8585
  Schiller Park  (G-19816)
Curtis Metal Finishing Company .......... D ...... 815 633-6693
  Machesney Park  (G-14069)
D & N Deburring Co Inc ...................... G ...... 847 451-7702
  Franklin Park  (G-10452)
Diamond Spray Painting Inc ................ G ...... 630 513-5600
  Saint Charles  (G-19171)
Dixline Corporation ........................... D ...... 309 932-2011
  Galva  (G-10788)
Durr - All Corporation ........................ G ...... 815 943-1032
  Harvard  (G-11631)
Electro-Max Inc ................................ E ...... 847 683-4100
  Hampshire  (G-11548)
Empire Hard Chrome Inc .................... C ...... 312 226-7548
  Chicago  (G-4746)
Engis Corporation .............................. C ...... 847 808-9400
  Wheeling  (G-22047)
Feralloy Corporation .......................... E ...... 503 286-8869
  Chicago  (G-4836)
FHP Inc .......................................... G ...... 708 452-4100
  Northlake  (G-16436)
Formulations Inc .............................. G ...... 847 674-9141
  Skokie  (G-20001)
Fox Valley Sandblasting Inc ................. G ...... 630 553-6050
  Yorkville  (G-22659)
Glass Fx ......................................... 217 359-0048
  Champaign  (G-3488)
Heidtman Steel Products Inc ............... G ...... 618 451-0052
  Granite City  (G-11284)
Heidtman Steel Products Inc ............... D ...... 618 451-0052
  Granite City  (G-11285)
Human Svc Ctr Southern Metro E ........ E ...... 618 282-6233
  Red Bud  (G-17942)
International Proc Co Amer ................. E ...... 847 437-8400
  Elk Grove Village  (G-9553)
International Silver Plating ................. G ...... 847 835-0705
  Glencoe  (G-11001)
Interntional Metal Finshg Svcs ............ G ...... 815 234-5254
  Byron  (G-2917)
Irmko Tool Works Inc ........................ E ...... 630 350-7550
  Bensenville  (G-1923)
Kobac ............................................ 847 520-6000
  Buffalo Grove  (G-2716)
Krel Laboratories Inc ......................... F ...... 773 826-4487
  Chicago  (G-5411)
Krueger and Company ....................... E ...... 630 833-5650
  Elmhurst  (G-9899)
M & B Services Ltd Inc ...................... F ...... 217 463-2162
  Paris  (G-17153)
Magnetic Inspection Lab Inc ............... D ...... 847 437-4488
  Elk Grove Village  (G-9606)
Marjan Inc ...................................... G ...... 630 906-0053
  Montgomery  (G-15060)
Meminger Metal Finishing Inc ............. F ...... 309 582-3363
  Aledo  (G-371)
Metokote Corporation ....................... E ...... 815 223-1190
  Peru  (G-17519)
Micro Surface Corporation .................. F ...... 815 942-4221
  Morris  (G-15116)
Midwest Galvanizing Inc ..................... F ...... 773 434-2682
  Chicago  (G-5743)
Midwestern Rust Proof Inc .................. D ...... 773 725-6636
  Chicago  (G-5753)
Nb Finishing Inc ............................... F ...... 847 364-7500
  Melrose Park  (G-14677)
Polyenviro Labs Inc ........................... E ...... 708 489-0195
  Mokena  (G-14896)
Possehl Connector Svcs SC Inc ............ E ...... 803 366-8316
  Elk Grove Village  (G-9687)
Powers Paint Shop Inc ....................... G ...... 815 338-3619
  Woodstock  (G-22600)
Pro TEC Metal Finishing Corp .............. G ...... 773 384-7854
  Chicago  (G-6203)
Production Chemical Co Inc ................ E ...... 847 455-8450
  Franklin Park  (G-10563)

Rainbow Art Inc ................................ F ...... 312 421-5600
  Chicago  (G-6288)
Scot Industries Inc ............................ D ...... 630 466-7591
  Sugar Grove  (G-20734)
Surcom Industries Inc ....................... G ...... 773 378-0736
  Chicago  (G-6640)
Thornton Welding Service Inc .............. E ...... 217 877-0610
  Decatur  (G-7952)
Ultra Polishing Inc ............................ G ...... 630 635-2926
  Schaumburg  (G-19777)
Universal-Spc Inc ............................. G ...... 847 742-4400
  Elgin  (G-9220)
V P Anodizing Inc ............................. G ...... 773 622-9100
  Chicago  (G-6868)
Vision Pickling and Proc Inc ................ F ...... 815 264-7755
  Waterman  (G-21410)
W D Mold Finishing Inc ...................... G ...... 847 678-8449
  Schiller Park  (G-19882)
Wear Cote International Inc ................ E ...... 309 793-1250
  Rock Island  (G-18211)
White Racker Co Inc .......................... G ...... 847 758-1640
  Elk Grove Village  (G-9812)

## PLATING COMPOUNDS

Macdermid Enthone Inc ..................... E ...... 708 598-3210
  Bridgeview  (G-2505)
Plating International Inc .................... F ...... 847 451-2101
  Franklin Park  (G-10554)
Stutz Company ................................ F ...... 773 287-1068
  Chicago  (G-6610)

## PLATING SVC: Chromium, Metals Or Formed Prdts

A and R Custom Chrome .................... G ...... 708 728-1005
  Chicago  (G-3683)
Alloy Chrome Inc .............................. G ...... 847 678-2880
  Schiller Park  (G-19800)
Capron Mfg Co ................................. D ...... 815 569-2301
  Capron  (G-2994)
Chromium Industries Inc .................... E ...... 773 287-3716
  Chicago  (G-4373)
Custom Chrome & Polishing ............... G ...... 618 885-9499
  Jerseyville  (G-12420)
Duro-Chrome Industries Inc ................ E ...... 847 487-2900
  Wauconda  (G-21457)
Ej Somerville Plating Co ..................... E ...... 708 345-5100
  Melrose Park  (G-14631)
Ellwood Group Inc ............................ E ...... 815 725-9030
  Joliet  (G-12489)
Hausner Hard - Chrome Inc ................ E ...... 847 439-6010
  Elk Grove Village  (G-9518)
Jvk Precision Hard Chrome Inc ............ G ...... 630 628-0810
  Addison  (G-161)
Mexicali Hard Chrome Corp ................ G ...... 630 543-0646
  Addison  (G-204)
Nova-Chrome Inc ............................. F ...... 847 455-8200
  Franklin Park  (G-10542)
Precision Chrome Inc ........................ F ...... 847 587-1515
  Fox Lake  (G-10282)
R&R Research Co ............................. 847 345-5051
  Mount Prospect  (G-15368)
Surface Manufacturing Company .......... F ...... 815 569-2362
  Capron  (G-2998)
Tru Coat Plating and Finishing ............. F ...... 708 544-3940
  Bellwood  (G-1725)
West Town Plating Inc ....................... E ...... 708 652-1600
  Cicero  (G-7245)

## PLATING SVC: Electro

Arlington Plating Company ................. C ...... 847 359-1490
  Palatine  (G-17003)
Bellwood Industries Inc ...................... G ...... 773 522-1002
  Chicago  (G-4078)
Berge Plating Works Inc ..................... G ...... 309 788-2831
  Rock Island  (G-18163)
Bobco Enterprises Del ....................... E ...... 773 722-1700
  Bloomingdale  (G-2097)
Chem Processing Inc ........................ D ...... 815 874-8118
  Rockford  (G-18305)
Chem Processing Inc ........................ 815 965-1037
  Rockford  (G-18306)
Cody Metal Finishing Inc .................... F ...... 773 252-2026
  Chicago  (G-4417)
Custom Hard Chrome Service Co .......... G ...... 847 759-1420
  Rosemont  (G-18996)
De Kalb Plating Co Inc ....................... G ...... 815 756-6112
  Dekalb  (G-8085)
Decatur Plating & Mfg Co ................... F ...... 217 422-8514
  Decatur  (G-7873)

Dover Industrial Chrome Inc ............... G ...... 773 478-2022
  Chicago  (G-4638)
Electronic Plating Co ......................... E ...... 708 652-8100
  Cicero  (G-7193)
Empire Hard Chrome Inc .................... C ...... 773 762-3156
  Chicago  (G-4745)
En-Chro Plating Inc .......................... E ...... 708 450-1250
  Melrose Park  (G-14633)
General Plating Co Inc ....................... G ...... 630 543-0088
  Addison  (G-133)
Imperial Plating Company III .............. E ...... 773 586-3500
  Chicago  (G-5167)
Industrial Hard Chrome Ltd ................ C ...... 630 208-7000
  Geneva  (G-10834)
J & M Plating Inc ............................. G ...... 815 964-4975
  Rockford  (G-18441)
James Precious Metals Plating ............ F ...... 773 774-8700
  Chicago  (G-5274)
Jensen Plating Works Inc ................... E ...... 773 252-7733
  Chicago  (G-5292)
Jensen Plating Works Inc ................... F ...... 773 252-7733
  Chicago  (G-5293)
K & P Industries Inc .......................... G ...... 630 628-6676
  Addison  (G-163)
Metal Arts Finishing Inc ..................... E ...... 630 892-6744
  Aurora  (G-1187)
Modern Plating Corporation ................ D ...... 815 235-1790
  Freeport  (G-10674)
Morgan Ohare Inc ............................ G ...... 630 543-6780
  Addison  (G-221)
MSC Pre Finish Metals Egv Inc ............ C ...... 847 439-2210
  Elk Grove Village  (G-9640)
Nobert Plating Co ............................. G ...... 312 421-4040
  Chicago  (G-5921)
Pariso Inc ....................................... F ...... 773 889-4383
  Chicago  (G-6082)
Precision Plating of Quincy ................. G ...... 217 223-6590
  Quincy  (G-17870)
Skilled Plating Corp .......................... G ...... 773 227-0262
  Chicago  (G-6520)
South Holland Met Finshg Inc .............. D ...... 708 235-0842
  Monee  (G-15002)
Specified Plating Co .......................... E ...... 773 826-4501
  Chicago  (G-6555)
Sterling Plating Co ........................... E ...... 708 867-6587
  Chicago  (G-6590)
TFC Group LLC ................................ D ...... 630 559-0808
  Addison  (G-311)
US Chrome Corp Illinois ..................... E ...... 815 544-3487
  Kingston  (G-12708)

## PLATING SVC: Gold

Plating International Inc .................... F ...... 847 451-2101
  Franklin Park  (G-10554)

## PLATING SVC: NEC

Aaro Roller Corp .............................. G ...... 815 398-7655
  Rockford  (G-18244)
Ace Plating Company ........................ E ...... 773 376-1800
  Chicago  (G-3727)
Advanced Graphics Tech Inc ................ C ...... 817 481-8561
  Darien  (G-7787)
American Nickel Works Inc .................. E ...... 312 942-0070
  Chicago  (G-3868)
Archer Tinning & Re-Tinning Co ........... F ...... 773 927-7240
  Chicago  (G-3940)
Belmont Plating Works Inc .................. C ...... 847 678-0200
  Franklin Park  (G-10410)
Berteau-Lowell Pltg Works Inc ............. E ...... 773 276-3135
  Chicago  (G-4088)
Chem-Plate Industries Inc .................. E ...... 708 345-3588
  Maywood  (G-14422)
Chromold Plating Inc ........................ G ...... 815 344-8644
  McHenry  (G-14486)
Ciske & Dresch ................................ G ...... 630 251-9200
  Batavia  (G-1430)
Craftsman Pltg & Tinning Corp ............ E ...... 773 477-1040
  Chicago  (G-4491)
Deep Coat LLC ................................ E ...... 630 466-1505
  Sugar Grove  (G-20722)
Diamond Plating Company Inc ............ E ...... 618 451-7740
  Madison  (G-14142)
Dyna-Burr Chicago Inc ...................... F ...... 708 250-6744
  Northlake  (G-16435)
Finishing Company ........................... D ...... 630 521-9635
  Bensenville  (G-1898)
Forest Plating Co ............................. G ...... 708 366-2071
  Forest Park  (G-10246)
Griffin Plating Co Inc ......................... G ...... 773 342-5181
  Chicago  (G-5003)

**Grove Plating Company Inc**..........F ....... 847 639-7651
Fox River Grove *(G-10287)*
**J D Plating Works Inc**..........G....... 847 662-6484
Waukegan *(G-21573)*
**Lbs Marketing Ltd**..........G....... 815 965-5234
Rockford *(G-18463)*
**Manner Plating Inc**..........G....... 815 877-7791
Loves Park *(G-13963)*
**Masters Plating Co Inc**..........G....... 815 226-8846
Rockford *(G-18485)*
**North American EN Inc**..........F ....... 847 952-3680
Elk Grove Village *(G-9654)*
**Omega Plating Inc**..........F ....... 708 389-5410
Crestwood *(G-7496)*
**Plano Metal Specialties Inc**..........F ....... 630 552-8510
Plano *(G-17672)*
**Quality Plating**..........G....... 815 626-5223
Sterling *(G-20607)*
**Riverdale Pltg Heat Trting LLC**..........E....... 708 849-2050
Riverdale *(G-18024)*
**Southern Plating Inc**..........G....... 618 983-6350
Johnston City *(G-12447)*
**Streamwood Plating Co**..........G....... 630 830-6363
Streamwood *(G-20675)*
**Superior Metal Finishing**..........F ....... 815 282-8888
Loves Park *(G-13995)*
**Three JS Industries Inc**..........F ....... 847 640-6080
Elk Grove Village *(G-9777)*
**US Plating Co Inc**..........F ....... 773 522-7300
Chicago *(G-6855)*

## *PLAYGROUND EQPT*

**International Wood Products**..........G....... 630 530-6164
Aurora *(G-1034)*
**Natural Cedar Products Inc**..........G....... 815 416-0223
Morris *(G-15122)*
**Rainbow Midwest Inc**..........G....... 847 955-9300
Vernon Hills *(G-21191)*

## *PLEATING & STITCHING FOR TRADE: Permanent Pleating/Pressing*

**Acme Button & Buttonhole Co**..........G....... 773 907-8400
Chicago *(G-3731)*

## *PLEATING & STITCHING SVC*

**Art-Flo Shirt & Lettering Co**..........E....... 708 656-5422
Chicago *(G-3953)*
**Award Emblem Mfg Co Inc**..........F ....... 630 739-0800
Bolingbrook *(G-2281)*
**B JS Printables**..........G....... 618 656-8625
Edwardsville *(G-8789)*
**Blandings Ltd**..........G....... 773 478-3542
Chicago *(G-4122)*
**Brownfield Sports Inc**..........G....... 217 367-8321
Urbana *(G-21074)*
**C & C Sport Stop**..........G....... 618 632-7812
O Fallon *(G-16464)*
**Creative Clothing Created 4 U**..........G....... 847 543-0051
Grayslake *(G-11330)*
**Custom Enterprises**..........G....... 618 439-6626
Benton *(G-2025)*
**Custom Monogramming**..........G....... 815 625-9044
Rock Falls *(G-18130)*
**Dabel Incorporated**..........G....... 217 398-3389
Champaign *(G-3472)*
**Fitness Wear Inc**..........G....... 847 486-1704
Glenview *(G-11125)*
**G and D Enterprises Inc**..........E....... 847 981-8661
Arlington Heights *(G-757)*
**Hi-Five Sportswear Inc**..........G....... 815 637-6044
Machesney Park *(G-14079)*
**Initial Choice**..........F ....... 847 234-5884
Lake Forest *(G-12917)*
**Johnos Inc**..........G....... 630 897-6929
Aurora *(G-1178)*
**Keneal Industries Inc**..........F ....... 815 886-1300
Romeoville *(G-18834)*
**Minerva Sportswear Inc**..........F ....... 309 661-2387
Bloomington *(G-2201)*
**Monograms & More**..........G....... 630 789-8424
Burr Ridge *(G-2869)*
**Need To Know Inc**..........G....... 309 691-3877
Peoria *(G-17415)*
**Rh Development**..........F ....... 773 331-3772
Chicago *(G-6347)*
**Ronald J Nixon**..........G....... 708 748-8130
Park Forest *(G-17175)*
**Roselynn Fashions**..........G....... 847 741-6000
Elgin *(G-9167)*

**S & R Monogramming Inc**..........G....... 630 369-5468
Winfield *(G-22292)*
**Second Chance Inc**..........F ....... 630 904-5955
Naperville *(G-15826)*
**Stitch By Stitch Incorporated**..........G....... 847 541-2543
Prospect Heights *(G-17784)*
**Triangle Screen Print Inc**..........F ....... 847 678-9200
Franklin Park *(G-10612)*
**Trimark Screen Printing Inc**..........G....... 630 629-2823
Lombard *(G-13872)*
**Ultimate Distributing Inc**..........G....... 847 566-2250
Mundelein *(G-15565)*
**Waldos Sports Corner Inc**..........G....... 309 688-2425
Peoria *(G-17477)*

## *PLUGS: Electric*

**Advantage Direct Inc**..........F....... 847 427-1185
Elk Grove Village *(G-9279)*
**Appleton Grp LLC**..........C....... 847 268-6000
Rosemont *(G-18989)*
**Leviton Manufacturing Co Inc**..........B ....... 630 350-2656
Bensenville *(G-1941)*

## *PLUMBING & HEATING EQPT & SPLY, WHOLESALE: Hydronic Htg Eqpt*

**K & S Service & Rental Corp**..........F ....... 630 279-4292
Elmhurst *(G-9893)*

## *PLUMBING & HEATING EQPT & SPLYS WHOLESALERS*

**Cortube Products Co**..........G....... 708 429-6700
Tinley Park *(G-20903)*
**Dumore Supplies Inc**..........F ....... 312 949-6260
Chicago *(G-4649)*
**Flexicraft Industries Inc**..........F ....... 312 738-3588
Chicago *(G-4861)*
**Homewerks Worldwide LLC**..........E....... 877 319-3757
Lake Bluff *(G-12849)*
**Imperial Mfg Group Inc**..........F ....... 618 465-3133
Alton *(G-578)*
**J & W Counter Tops Inc**..........E....... 217 544-0876
Springfield *(G-20460)*
**Jacobs Boiler & Mech Inds Inc**..........E....... 773 385-9900
Chicago *(G-5269)*
**Jim Jolly Sales Inc**..........G....... 847 669-7570
Huntley *(G-12153)*
**Kamco Representatives Inc**..........G....... 630 516-0417
Elmhurst *(G-9894)*
**Lordahl Manufacturing Co**..........D....... 847 244-0448
Long Grove *(G-13893)*
**Rainbow Dusters International**..........G....... 770 627-3575
Carol Stream *(G-3227)*
**Schulhof Company**..........F....... 773 348-1123
Richmond *(G-17971)*
**Wagner Pump & Supply Co Inc**..........G....... 847 526-8573
Wauconda *(G-21512)*
**Wm F Meyer Co**..........E....... 773 772-7272
Chicago *(G-7010)*

## *PLUMBING & HEATING EQPT & SPLYS, WHOL: Fireplaces, Prefab*

**Bricks Inc**..........G....... 630 897-6926
Aurora *(G-1121)*

## *PLUMBING & HEATING EQPT & SPLYS, WHOL: Pipe/Fitting, Plastic*

**Advanced Valve Tech Inc**..........E....... 847 364-3700
Elk Grove Village *(G-9278)*
**Perfect Pipe & Supply Corp**..........G....... 630 628-6728
Elgin *(G-9137)*

## *PLUMBING & HEATING EQPT & SPLYS, WHOL: Plumbing Fitting/Sply*

**Bristol Hose & Fitting Inc**..........E....... 708 492-3456
Northlake *(G-16430)*
**J C Hose & Tube Inc**..........G....... 630 543-4747
Addison *(G-157)*
**LDR Global Industries LLC**..........D....... 773 265-3000
Chicago *(G-5477)*
**Rothenberger USA LLC**..........D....... 815 397-7617
Rockford *(G-18598)*

## *PLUMBING & HEATING EQPT & SPLYS, WHOL: Water Purif Eqpt*

**Arbortech Corporation**..........G ....... 847 462-1111
Johnsburg *(G-12430)*
**Gehrke Technology Group Inc**..........F ....... 847 498-7320
Wauconda *(G-21464)*
**International Water Werks Inc**..........G....... 847 669-1902
Huntley *(G-12151)*
**Servetech Water Solutions Inc**..........G....... 630 784-9050
Wheaton *(G-21980)*
**Wilton Industries Inc**..........F ....... 815 834-9390
Romeoville *(G-18879)*

## *PLUMBING & HEATING EQPT & SPLYS, WHOLESALE: Boilers, Steam*

**Rockford Chemical Co**..........G....... 815 544-3476
Belvidere *(G-1783)*

## *PLUMBING FIXTURES*

**Anderson Copper & Brass Co LLC**..........E....... 708 535-9030
Frankfort *(G-10295)*
**Anderson Copper & Brass Co LLC**..........F ....... 815 469-8201
Frankfort *(G-10296)*
**Black Swan Manufacturing Co**..........F ....... 773 227-3700
Chicago *(G-4121)*
**Caldwell Plumbing Co**..........F ....... 630 588-8900
Wheaton *(G-21938)*
**Chicago Faucet Federal Cr Un**..........F ....... 847 803-5000
Des Plaines *(G-8166)*
**Deks North America Inc**..........G....... 312 219-2110
Chicago *(G-4574)*
**Elkay Manufacturing Company**..........B ....... 708 681-1880
Broadview *(G-2575)*
**Fiskars Brands Inc**..........B ....... 309 690-2200
Peoria *(G-17363)*
**G B Holdings Inc**..........C ....... 773 265-3000
Chicago *(G-4899)*
**Guardian Equipment Inc**..........E ....... 312 447-8100
Chicago *(G-5007)*
**Iodon Inc**..........G....... 708 799-4062
Country Club Hills *(G-7409)*
**Kamco Representatives Inc**..........G....... 630 516-0417
Elmhurst *(G-9894)*
**Ki Industries Inc**..........E ....... 708 449-1990
Berkeley *(G-2046)*
**Kieft Bros Inc**..........E ....... 630 832-8090
Elmhurst *(G-9898)*
**Kkt Chillers Inc**..........F ....... 847 734-1600
Elk Grove Village *(G-9575)*
**Kohler Co**..........D....... 847 734-1777
Huntley *(G-12155)*
**Lacava LLC**..........E ....... 773 637-9600
Chicago *(G-5432)*
**Lavell General Handyman Svcs**..........G....... 773 691-3101
Chicago *(G-5469)*
**LDR Global Industries LLC**..........D....... 773 265-3000
Chicago *(G-5477)*
**Mifab Inc**..........E ....... 773 341-3030
Chicago *(G-5754)*
**Performance Pro Plumbing Inc**..........G....... 630 566-5207
Westmont *(G-21910)*
**Plumbers Supply Co St Louis**..........G....... 618 624-5151
O Fallon *(G-16474)*
**Royale Innovation Group Ltd**..........G....... 312 339-1406
Itasca *(G-12351)*
**Schulhof Company**..........F....... 773 348-1123
Richmond *(G-17971)*
**Sloan Valve Company**..........G....... 847 671-4300
Franklin Park *(G-10590)*
**White Racker Co Inc**..........G....... 847 758-1640
Elk Grove Village *(G-9812)*

## *PLUMBING FIXTURES: Brass, Incl Drain Cocks, Faucets/Spigots*

**Cfpg Ltd**..........C ....... 630 679-1420
Woodridge *(G-22459)*
**Chicago Faucet Company**..........D....... 847 803-5000
Des Plaines *(G-8165)*
**Couplings Company Inc**..........F ....... 847 634-8990
Lincolnshire *(G-13440)*
**Globe Union Group Inc**..........D....... 630 679-1420
Woodridge *(G-22487)*
**Isenberg Bath Corporation**..........G....... 972 510-5916
Bensenville *(G-1924)*
**Sterline Manufacturing Corp**..........E ....... 847 244-1234
Gurnee *(G-11509)*



Employee Codes: A=Over 500 employees, B=251-500
C=101-250, D=51-100, E=20-50, F=10-19, G=3-9
2017 Harris Illinois
Industrial Directory
1699

# PLUMBING FIXTURES: Plastic

## PLUMBING FIXTURES: Plastic

BCI Acrylic Inc .................................. G ...... 847 963-8827
  Libertyville *(G-13307)*
Danze Inc ......................................... D ...... 630 754-0277
  Woodridge *(G-22467)*
Fiber Winders Inc .............................. G ...... 618 548-6388
  Salem *(G-19332)*
Industrial Fiberglass Inc ..................... F ...... 708 681-2707
  Melrose Park *(G-14657)*
Jalaa Fiberglass Inc .......................... G ...... 217 923-3433
  Greenup *(G-11384)*
Lordahl Manufacturing Co .................. E ...... 847 244-0448
  Waukegan *(G-21584)*
Staffco Inc ........................................ G ...... 309 688-3223
  Peoria *(G-17460)*
T J Van Der Bosch & Associates ........ G ...... 815 344-3210
  McHenry *(G-14567)*

## PLUMBING FIXTURES: Vitreous

Coronado Conservation Inc ................ G ...... 301 512-4671
  Chicago *(G-4473)*
Elkay Manufacturing Company ........... B ...... 708 681-1880
  Broadview *(G-2575)*
Kohler Co .......................................... D ...... 847 734-1777
  Huntley *(G-12155)*
Lacava LLC ....................................... E ...... 773 637-9600
  Chicago *(G-5432)*
Sterline Manufacturing Corp ............... E ...... 847 244-1234
  Gurnee *(G-11509)*
Swan Surfaces LLC ........................... G ...... 618 532-5673
  Centralia *(G-3435)*

## PLUMBING FIXTURES: Vitreous China

Cfpg Ltd ............................................ C ...... 630 679-1420
  Woodridge *(G-22459)*
Gerber Plumbing Fixtures LLC ............ D ...... 630 679-1420
  Woodridge *(G-22482)*
Globe Union Group Inc ...................... D ...... 630 679-1420
  Woodridge *(G-22487)*

## POINT OF SALE DEVICES

Barcodesource Inc ............................. G ...... 630 545-9590
  West Chicago *(G-21667)*
Creative Merchandising Systems ........ G ...... 847 955-9990
  Lincolnshire *(G-13441)*
Micros Systems Inc ........................... F ...... 443 285-6000
  Itasca *(G-12316)*
Pos Plus LLC .................................... F ...... 618 993-7587
  Marion *(G-14282)*
Ultramark Inc .................................... G ...... 847 981-0400
  Arlington Heights *(G-860)*

## POLE LINE HARDWARE

Maclean Senior Industries LLC ........... E ...... 630 350-1600
  Wood Dale *(G-22393)*

## POLISHING SVC: Metals Or Formed Prdts

A & J Finishers ................................. G ...... 847 352-5408
  Schaumburg *(G-19417)*
AAA Mold Finishers Inc ...................... G ...... 773 775-3977
  Chicago *(G-3700)*
Aggresive Motor Sports ..................... G ...... 630 761-1550
  Batavia *(G-1405)*
B & T Polishing Co ............................ E ...... 847 658-6415
  Chicago *(G-4018)*
Bales Mold Service Inc ...................... E ...... 630 852-4665
  Downers Grove *(G-8394)*
Barron Metal Finishing LLC ................ F ...... 815 962-8053
  Rockford *(G-18277)*
Clybourn Metal Finishing Co ............... E ...... 773 525-8162
  Chicago *(G-4409)*
Cmp Associates Inc .......................... G ...... 847 956-1313
  Elk Grove Village *(G-9379)*
Cornerstone Polishing Company .......... G ...... 618 777-2754
  Ozark *(G-16993)*
Electro-Glo Distribution Inc ................. G ...... 815 224-4030
  La Salle *(G-12771)*
Finished Metals Incorporated .............. F ...... 773 229-1600
  Chicago *(G-4847)*
Finishing Touch Inc ........................... F ...... 773 774-7349
  Chicago *(G-4848)*
Jhelsa Metal Polsg Fabrication ............ G ...... 773 385-6628
  Chicago *(G-5302)*
Metco Treating and Dev Co ................ D ...... 773 277-1600
  Chicago *(G-5702)*
Pannon Mord Polishing ...................... G ...... 630 893-9252
  Bloomingdale *(G-2124)*
Sure Shine Polishing .......................... G ...... 217 853-4888
  Decatur *(G-7946)*
T M T Industries Inc ........................... E ...... 815 562-0111
  Rochelle *(G-18111)*
Thomson Steel Polishing Corp ............. G ...... 773 586-2345
  Chicago *(G-6720)*
V and L Polishing Co ......................... G ...... 630 543-5999
  Addison *(G-335)*

## POLYCARBONATE RESINS

MRC Polymers Inc ............................. D ...... 773 890-9000
  Chicago *(G-5825)*

## POLYMETHYL METHACRYLATE RESINS: Plexiglas

Amcol Hlth Buty Solutions Inc ............. F ...... 847 851-1300
  Hoffman Estates *(G-11990)*

## POLYPROPYLENE RESINS

Bayer Corporation .............................. G ...... 847 725-6320
  Elk Grove Village *(G-9335)*

## POLYSTYRENE RESINS

Flint Hlls Rsources Joliet LLC ............. G ...... 815 224-5232
  Peru *(G-17510)*
Nova Chemicals Inc ........................... D ...... 815 224-1525
  Peru *(G-17523)*
Novipax LLC ..................................... F ...... 630 686-2735
  Oak Brook *(G-16548)*
Tenneco Packaging ............................ G ...... 847 482-2000
  Lake Forest *(G-12969)*

## POLYSULFIDES

Morton International LLC .................... C ...... 312 807-2696
  Chicago *(G-5807)*

## POLYTETRAFLUOROETHYLENE RESINS

Senior Holdings Inc ............................ C ...... 630 837-1811
  Bartlett *(G-1373)*
Voss Belting & Specialty Co ............... E ...... 847 673-8900
  Lincolnwood *(G-13541)*

## POLYURETHANE RESINS

Custom Films Inc .............................. F ...... 217 826-2326
  Marshall *(G-14320)*
Huntsman International LLC ................ D ...... 815 653-1500
  Ringwood *(G-17991)*
Natural Polymers LLC ........................ G ...... 888 563-3111
  West Chicago *(G-21749)*
Polynt Composites USA Inc ................ C ...... 847 428-2657
  Carpentersville *(G-3296)*
Stepan Company ............................... B ...... 847 446-7500
  Northfield *(G-16419)*

## POLYVINYL CHLORIDE RESINS

Drum Manufacturing ........................... F ...... 217 923-5625
  Greenup *(G-11381)*

## POLYVINYLIDENE CHLORIDE RESINS

Polycast ........................................... F ...... 815 648-4438
  Hebron *(G-11725)*

## POPCORN & SUPPLIES WHOLESALERS

Tee Lee Popcorn Inc .......................... E ...... 815 864-2363
  Shannon *(G-19903)*

## POPULAR MUSIC GROUPS OR ARTISTS

Deshamusic Inc ................................. G ...... 818 257-2716
  Chicago *(G-4585)*
Sandes Quynetta ............................... G ...... 815 275-4876
  Freeport *(G-10687)*

## PORCELAIN ENAMELED PRDTS & UTENSILS

Porcelain Enamel Finishers ................. G ...... 312 808-1560
  Chicago *(G-6157)*
Senna Design LLC ............................ G ...... 847 821-7877
  Vernon Hills *(G-21201)*

## POSTERS

Gfx International Inc .......................... C ...... 847 543-7179
  Grayslake *(G-11340)*

## POTASH MINING

Pcs Phosphate Company Inc .............. D ...... 847 849-4200
  Northbrook *(G-16336)*
Potash Corp Ssktchewan Fla Inc ......... C ...... 847 849-4200
  Northbrook *(G-16340)*

## POTTERY: Laboratory & Indl

Ipsen Inc .......................................... E ...... 815 239-2385
  Pecatonica *(G-17252)*

## POTTING SOILS

Country Stone Inc .............................. E ...... 309 787-1744
  Milan *(G-14781)*

## POULTRY & SMALL GAME SLAUGHTERING & PROCESSING

2000plus Groups Inc .......................... G ...... 630 528-3220
  Oak Brook *(G-16483)*
2000plus Groups Inc .......................... C ...... 800 939-6268
  Chicago *(G-3663)*
Central Illinois Poultry Proc ................. F ...... 217 543-2937
  Arthur *(G-886)*
Grant Park Packing Company Inc ........ E ...... 312 421-4096
  Franklin Park *(G-10482)*
Hillshire Brands Company .................. E ...... 312 614-6000
  Chicago *(G-5090)*
Koch Meat Co Inc .............................. B ...... 847 384-5940
  Chicago *(G-5396)*
Tru-Native Enterprises ........................ G ...... 630 409-3258
  Addison *(G-325)*
Tru-Native Enterprises ........................ G ...... 630 409-3258
  Addison *(G-326)*

## POULTRY SLAUGHTERING & PROCESSING

Galloway Como Processing ................. G ...... 815 626-0305
  Sterling *(G-20594)*
Midwest Poultry Services LP ............... D ...... 217 386-2313
  Loda *(G-13753)*

## POWDER: Aluminum Atomized

National Material Company LLC .......... E ...... 847 806-7200
  Elk Grove Village *(G-9646)*

## POWDER: Iron

Connelly-Gpm Inc .............................. E ...... 773 247-7231
  Chicago *(G-4451)*
Mount Vernon Iron Works LLC ............. G ...... 618 244-2313
  Mount Vernon *(G-15428)*

## POWDER: Metal

Accurate Finishers ............................. G ...... 630 543-8575
  Addison *(G-18)*
Burgess-Norton Mfg Co Inc ................ B ...... 630 232-4100
  Geneva *(G-10813)*
Dva Metal Fabrication Inc ................... G ...... 224 577-8217
  Elk Grove Village *(G-9440)*
Eagle Chassis Inc .............................. G ...... 217 525-1941
  Springfield *(G-20431)*
Finish Line USA Inc ........................... F ...... 847 608-7800
  Elgin *(G-9035)*
Midwest Finishers Pwdrctng ............... G ...... 217 536-9098
  Effingham *(G-8847)*
Nanophase Technologies Corp ............ E ...... 630 771-6708
  Romeoville *(G-18852)*
Nanophase Technologies Corp ............ F ...... 630 771-6747
  Burr Ridge *(G-2870)*
Perfect Powder Coating ...................... G ...... 847 322-6666
  Gurnee *(G-11484)*
Permacor Inc .................................... E ...... 708 422-3353
  Oak Lawn *(G-16639)*
Protek .............................................. G ...... 815 773-2280
  Joliet *(G-12557)*
Toyal America Inc .............................. G ...... 630 505-2160
  Naperville *(G-15766)*
Toyal America Inc .............................. D ...... 815 740-3000
  Lockport *(G-13749)*

## POWER DISTRIBUTION BOARDS: Electric

D/C Industries LLC ............................ G ...... 630 876-1100
  West Chicago *(G-21689)*
Kosmos Tool Inc ................................ F ...... 815 675-2200
  Spring Grove *(G-20343)*
Rauckman High Voltage Sales ............ G ...... 618 239-0399
  Swansea *(G-20781)*

# PRODUCT SECTION

## PRESS SVCS

### POWER GENERATORS

Becsis LLC ..................................... G ...... 630 400-6454
  South Elgin  (G-20186)
Ghetzler Aero-Power Corp ........... G ...... 224 513-5636
  Vernon Hills  (G-21165)
Lionheart Critical Pow .................. E ...... 847 291-1413
  Huntley  (G-12159)
Wagenate Entps Holdings LLC .... G ...... 773 503-1306
  Riverdale  (G-18026)

### POWER MOWERS WHOLESALERS

Amerisun Inc ................................. F ...... 800 791-9458
  Itasca  (G-12229)
Rahn Equipment Company ........... G ...... 217 431-1232
  Danville  (G-7762)

### POWER SPLY CONVERTERS: Static, Electronic Applications

Bias Power Inc .............................. G ...... 847 419-9180
  Buffalo Grove  (G-2665)
Pintsch Tiefenbach Us Inc ............ G ...... 618 993-8513
  Marion  (G-14280)

### POWER SUPPLIES: All Types, Static

Aerotronic Controls Co .................. F ...... 847 228-6504
  Elk Grove Village  (G-9282)
Electronic Design & Mfg Inc .......... D ...... 847 550-1912
  Lake Zurich  (G-13066)
Elpac Electronics Inc .................... C ...... 708 316-4407
  Westchester  (G-21839)
Essex Electro Engineers Inc ......... E ...... 847 891-4444
  Schaumburg  (G-19521)
Hubbell Power Systems Inc ......... F ...... 618 797-5000
  Edwardsville  (G-8803)
Ikonix Group Inc ........................... G ...... 847 367-4671
  Lake Forest  (G-12916)
Puls LP ......................................... E ...... 630 587-9780
  Saint Charles  (G-19244)

### POWER SUPPLIES: Transformer, Electronic Type

Bias Power Technology Inc .......... G ...... 847 991-2427
  Palatine  (G-17006)
Everpurse Inc ............................... G ...... 650 204-3212
  Chicago  (G-4790)
Power-Volt Inc .............................. E ...... 630 628-9999
  Addison  (G-250)
Schumacher Electric Corp ............ D ...... 847 385-1600
  Mount Prospect  (G-15372)
Starfire Industries LLC ................. E ...... 217 721-4165
  Champaign  (G-3548)

### POWER SWITCHING EQPT

CCI Power Supplies LLC ............. C ...... 847 362-6500
  Palatine  (G-17008)
Ronk Electrical Industries Inc ....... E ...... 217 563-8333
  Nokomis  (G-16061)

### POWER TOOLS, HAND: Cartridge-Activated

Robert Bosch Tool Corporation .... A ...... 224 232-2000
  Mount Prospect  (G-15369)
Sierra Manufacturing Corp ........... G ...... 630 458-8830
  Addison  (G-289)

### POWER TOOLS, HAND: Drill Attachments, Portable

Chicago Quadrill Co ..................... G ...... 847 824-4196
  Des Plaines  (G-8167)
Stange Industrial Group ............... G ...... 847 640-8470
  Elk Grove Village  (G-9752)

### POWER TOOLS, HAND: Drills & Drilling Tools

Groff Testing Corporation ............. G ...... 815 939-1153
  Kankakee  (G-12619)
Pgi Mfg LLC .................................. G ...... 815 398-0313
  Rockford  (G-18533)

### POWER TOOLS, HAND: Grinders, Portable, Electric Or Pneumatic

Rockford Commercial Whse Inc ... G ...... 815 623-8400
  Machesney Park  (G-14105)

### POWER TOOLS, HAND: Hammers, Portable, Elec/Pneumatic, Chip

Brunner & Lay Inc ........................ C ...... 847 678-3232
  Elmhurst  (G-9843)

### POWER TOOLS, HAND: Sanders

Gbj I LLC ...................................... F ...... 815 877-4041
  Rockford  (G-18396)
National Detroit Inc ...................... E ...... 815 877-4041
  Rockford  (G-18515)

### POWER TRANSMISSION EQPT WHOLESALERS

Deif Inc ......................................... G ...... 970 530-2261
  Wood Dale  (G-22359)
Harger Inc .................................... E ...... 847 548-8700
  Grayslake  (G-11345)
Sumitomo Machinery Corp Amer . E ...... 630 752-0200
  Glendale Heights  (G-11078)
US Tsubaki Power Transm LLC ... C ...... 847 459-9500
  Wheeling  (G-22173)

### POWER TRANSMISSION EQPT: Mechanical

A Fischer Phase Drives ................ G ...... 815 759-6928
  McHenry  (G-14473)
Active Tool and Machine Inc ........ F ...... 708 599-0022
  Oak Lawn  (G-16598)
Air802 LLC .................................... G ...... 630 585-6383
  Aurora  (G-955)
Allied-Locke Industries Inc ........... E ...... 800 435-7752
  Dixon  (G-8322)
Arens Controls Company LLc ...... D ...... 847 844-4700
  Arlington Heights  (G-715)
Arrow Gear Company ................... G ...... 630 969-7640
  Downers Grove  (G-8389)
Bearing Sales Corporation ........... E ...... 773 282-8686
  Chicago  (G-4066)
Borgwarner Transm Systems ....... A ...... 708 547-2600
  Bellwood  (G-1700)
Deublin Company ......................... G ...... 847 689-8600
  Waukegan  (G-21551)
Eastview Manufacturing Inc ......... G ...... 847 741-2514
  Elgin  (G-9019)
Flowserve Corporation ................. G ...... 630 543-4240
  Addison  (G-120)
Forbo Siegling LLC ...................... F ...... 630 595-4031
  Wood Dale  (G-22370)
Frantz Manufacturing Company ... D ...... 815 564-0991
  Sterling  (G-20593)
Gears Gears Gears Inc ................ G ...... 708 366-6555
  Harwood Heights  (G-11685)
GKN Stromag Inc ......................... E ...... 937 433-3882
  Woodridge  (G-22485)
GKN Walterscheid Inc ................. C ...... 630 972-9300
  Woodridge  (G-22486)
Grayslake Feed Sales Inc ............ G ...... 847 223-4855
  Grayslake  (G-11344)
Industrial Motion Control LLC ...... G ...... 847 459-5200
  Wheeling  (G-22076)
Innovative Mag Drive LLC ............ G ...... 630 543-4240
  Chicago  (G-5200)
Innovative Mag-Drive LLC ........... G ...... 630 543-4240
  Addison  (G-153)
J T C Inc ....................................... F ...... 773 292-9262
  Chicago  (G-5264)
Martin Sprocket & Gear Inc ......... F ...... 847 298-8844
  Des Plaines  (G-8227)
Metal Ceramics Inc ...................... E ...... 847 678-2293
  Franklin Park  (G-10530)
Naylor Automotive Engrg Co Inc . F ...... 773 582-6900
  Chicago  (G-5875)
NTN-Bower Corporation ............... A ...... 309 837-0322
  Macomb  (G-14129)
Process Screw Products Inc ........ E ...... 815 864-2220
  Shannon  (G-19901)
Productigear Inc ........................... E ...... 773 847-4505
  Chicago  (G-6205)
Raycar Gear & Machine Company E ...... 815 874-3948
  Rockford  (G-18549)
Reliance Gear Corporation .......... D ...... 630 543-6640
  Addison  (G-275)
Rexnord Industries LLC ............... D ...... 847 520-1428
  Downers Grove  (G-8514)
Rockford Jobbing Service Inc ...... G ...... 815 398-8661
  Rockford  (G-18576)
S&R Precision Machine LLC ....... G ...... 815 469-6544
  Frankfort  (G-10360)
SKF USA Inc ................................ D ...... 847 742-0700
  Elgin  (G-9186)
Stock Gears Inc ........................... F ...... 224 653-9489
  Elk Grove Village  (G-9758)
Surge Clutch & Drive Line Co ...... G ...... 708 331-1352
  South Holland  (G-20307)
Timken Company .......................... E ...... 618 594-4545
  Carlyle  (G-3060)

### POWER TRANSMISSION EQPT: Vehicle

HM Manufacturing Inc .................. F ...... 847 487-8700
  Wauconda  (G-21469)

### PRECAST TERRAZZO OR CONCRETE PRDTS

Atmi Precast Inc .......................... E ...... 630 897-0577
  Aurora  (G-1114)
Component Precast Supply Inc ... G ...... 630 483-2900
  West Chicago  (G-21685)
Connelly-Gpm Inc ........................ E ...... 773 247-7231
  Chicago  (G-4451)
Hoosier Precast LLC ................... G ...... 815 459-4545
  Crystal Lake  (G-7588)
Illini Precast LLC ......................... G ...... 708 562-7700
  Westchester  (G-21844)
Imco Precast LLC ........................ G ...... 217 742-5300
  Winchester  (G-22280)
Kienstra Pipe & Precast LLC ...... G ...... 618 482-3283
  Madison  (G-14151)
Kw Precast LLC ........................... G ...... 708 562-7700
  Westchester  (G-21846)

### PRECIOUS METALS

Horizon Metals Inc ....................... F ...... 773 478-8888
  Chicago  (G-5113)
IL International LLC ..................... G ...... 773 276-0070
  Chicago  (G-5151)

### PRECIOUS STONES & METALS, WHOLESALE

John Buechner Inc ....................... G ...... 312 263-2226
  Chicago  (G-5312)
Masud Jewelers Inc ..................... G ...... 312 236-0547
  Chicago  (G-5648)
TPC Metals LLC ........................... G ...... 330 479-9510
  Willowbrook  (G-22234)

### PRECIOUS STONES WHOLESALERS

Hakimian Gem Co ........................ G ...... 312 236-6969
  Chicago  (G-5033)

### PRERECORDED TAPE, COMPACT DISC & RECORD STORES

3b Media Inc ................................ F ...... 312 563-9363
  Chicago  (G-3667)
McCormicks Enterprises Inc ........ E ...... 847 398-8680
  Arlington Heights  (G-800)
Music Solutions ............................ F ...... 630 759-3033
  Bolingbrook  (G-2349)

### PRERECORDED TAPE, COMPACT DISC & RECORD STORES: Compact Disc

Robert Koester ............................. G ...... 773 539-5001
  Chicago  (G-6368)

### PRERECORDED TAPE, COMPACT DISC & RECORD STORES: Records

Polyvinyl Record Co ..................... G ...... 217 403-1752
  Champaign  (G-3527)

### PRESS CLIPPING SVC

Cision US Inc ............................... C ...... 312 922-2400
  Chicago  (G-4381)

### PRESS SVCS

Elite Die & Finishing Inc .............. G ...... 708 389-4848
  South Holland  (G-20265)

---

Employee Codes: A=Over 500 employees, B=251-500
C=101-250, D=51-100, E=20-50, F=10-19, G=3-9

2017 Harris Illinois
Industrial Directory

# PRESSED & MOLDED PULP PRDTS, NEC: From Purchased Materials

## PRESSED & MOLDED PULP PRDTS, NEC: From Purchased Materials

Midland Davis Corporation .................. D ....... 309 637-4491
  Moline *(G-14957)*

## PRESSED FIBER & MOLDED PULP PRDTS, EXC FOOD PRDTS

Lucky Games Inc ............................. G ....... 773 549-9051
  Northbrook *(G-16300)*
Lucky Games Inc ............................. F ....... 773 549-9051
  Northbrook *(G-16301)*
Oce-Van Der Grinten NV ..................... E ....... 217 348-8111
  Charleston *(G-3606)*

## PRESSES

Accu-Cut Diamond Bore Sizing ............ F ....... 708 457-8800
  Norridge *(G-16094)*
Bourn & Bourn Inc ........................... C ....... 815 965-4013
  Rockford *(G-18289)*
Mechanical Tool & Engrg Co ............... C ....... 815 397-4701
  Rockford *(G-18489)*
Seward Screw Acquisition LLC ........... G ....... 312 498-9933
  Chicago *(G-6484)*
Seward Screw Operating LLC ............. C ....... 312 498-9933
  Chicago *(G-6485)*
Slidecraft Inc ................................. G ....... 630 628-1218
  Addison *(G-294)*

## PRESTRESSED CONCRETE PRDTS

Forterra Pressure Pipe Inc ................. C ....... 815 389-4800
  South Beloit *(G-20148)*
Prestress Engineering Company .......... E ....... 815 586-4239
  Blackstone *(G-2088)*
Prestress Engineering Company .......... G ....... 815 459-4545
  Crystal Lake *(G-7630)*
Price Brothers Co ............................ D ....... 815 389-4800
  South Beloit *(G-20165)*

## PRIMARY FINISHED OR SEMIFINISHED SHAPES

Multitech Industries .......................... G ....... 815 206-0015
  Woodstock *(G-22594)*
Works In Progress Foundation ............. G ....... 847 997-8338
  Lake Villa *(G-13031)*

## PRIMARY METAL PRODUCTS

Direct Selling Strategies .................... G ....... 847 993-3188
  Rosemont *(G-18999)*
Hall Fabrication Inc .......................... G ....... 217 322-2212
  Rushville *(G-19091)*
Lindsay Metal Madness Inc ................ G ....... 815 568-4560
  Marengo *(G-14235)*
Orion Metals Co .............................. G ....... 847 412-9532
  Glenview *(G-11177)*
Phillip C Cowen .............................. E ....... 630 208-1848
  Geneva *(G-10859)*
Sales Specialty Metal ....................... G ....... 217 864-1496
  Mount Zion *(G-15456)*

## PRINT CARTRIDGES: Laser & Other Computer Printers

Active Office Solutions ...................... F ....... 773 539-3333
  Chicago *(G-3741)*
Aim Graphic Machinery Ltd ................ F ....... 847 215-8000
  Buffalo Grove *(G-2652)*
Alternative TS ................................. G ....... 618 257-0230
  Belleville *(G-1608)*
Cartridge World Decatur .................... G ....... 217 875-0465
  Decatur *(G-7852)*
Ink Stop Inc ................................... G ....... 847 478-0631
  Buffalo Grove *(G-2709)*
Laser Innovations Inc ....................... F ....... 217 522-8580
  Springfield *(G-20467)*
Next Day Toner Supplies Inc .............. E ....... 708 478-1000
  Orland Park *(G-16879)*
Rpt Toner LLC ................................ E ....... 630 694-0400
  Bensenville *(G-1982)*
Tonerhead Inc ................................ E ....... 815 331-3200
  Spring Grove *(G-20369)*

## PRINTED CIRCUIT BOARDS

ABRA Enterprises Inc ....................... G ....... 847 866-6903
  Evanston *(G-10001)*
Accelerated Assemblies Inc ................ E ....... 630 616-6680
  Elk Grove Village *(G-9259)*
Accutrace Inc ................................. F ....... 847 290-9900
  Elk Grove Village *(G-9262)*
Advanced Electronics Inc ................. D ....... 630 293-3300
  West Chicago *(G-21652)*
Aerotronic Controls Co ..................... F ....... 847 228-6504
  Elk Grove Village *(G-9282)*
Alpha Circuit Corporation .................. E ....... 630 617-5555
  Elmhurst *(G-9833)*
Alpha Pcb Designs Inc ..................... G ....... 773 631-5543
  Chicago *(G-3831)*
American Circuit Services Inc ............. G ....... 847 895-0500
  Schaumburg *(G-19436)*
American Circuit Systems Inc ............. E ....... 630 543-4450
  Addison *(G-33)*
American Standard Circuits Inc ........... C ....... 630 639-5444
  West Chicago *(G-21657)*
Amitron Inc .................................... F ....... 847 290-9800
  Elk Grove Village *(G-9302)*
Ampel Incorporated ......................... F ....... 847 952-1900
  Elk Grove Village *(G-9303)*
ARC-Tronics Inc .............................. F ....... 847 437-0211
  Elk Grove Village *(G-9312)*
Assembly International Inc ................. F ....... 847 437-3120
  Elk Grove Village *(G-9317)*
Astral Power Systems Inc .................. E ....... 630 518-1741
  Aurora *(G-1112)*
Aurora Circuits Inc .......................... E ....... 630 978-3830
  Aurora *(G-960)*
Aurora Circuits LLC ......................... D ....... 630 978-3830
  Aurora *(G-961)*
Avg Advanced Technologies LP .......... A ....... 630 668-3900
  Carol Stream *(G-3110)*
B M I Inc ...................................... C ....... 847 839-6000
  Schaumburg *(G-19456)*
Bartec Orb Inc ............................... E ....... 773 927-8600
  Chicago *(G-4051)*
Benchmark Electronics Inc ................ B ....... 309 822-8587
  Metamora *(G-14740)*
Bishop Engineering Company ............. F ....... 630 305-9538
  Lisle *(G-13569)*
Bobco Enterprises Inc Del ................. E ....... 773 722-1700
  Bloomingdale *(G-2097)*
Buildex Electronics Inc ..................... F ....... 847 437-2299
  Elk Grove Village *(G-9348)*
C & C Electronics Inc ...................... E ....... 847 550-0177
  Mundelein *(G-15481)*
Cck Automations Inc ....................... E ....... 217 243-6040
  Jacksonville *(G-12382)*
Chicago Circuits Corporation .............. F ....... 847 238-1623
  Elk Grove Village *(G-9367)*
Circom Inc .................................... E ....... 630 595-4460
  Bensenville *(G-1859)*
Circuit Engineering LLC .................... F ....... 847 806-7777
  Elk Grove Village *(G-9374)*
Circuit Works Corporation .................. D ....... 847 283-8600
  Waukegan *(G-21538)*
Circuit World Inc ............................. E ....... 630 250-1100
  Itasca *(G-12245)*
Circuitronics .................................. E ....... 630 668-5407
  Wheaton *(G-21941)*
Creative Hi-Tech Ltd ........................ E ....... 224 653-4000
  Schaumburg *(G-19487)*
Current Works Inc ........................... G ....... 847 497-9650
  Johnsburg *(G-12433)*
Daves Electronic Service .................. F ....... 217 283-5010
  Hoopeston *(G-12109)*
Delta Circuits Inc ............................ E ....... 630 876-0691
  West Chicago *(G-21690)*
Delta Precision Circuits Inc ................ E ....... 847 758-8000
  Elk Grove Village *(G-9422)*
Eagle Electronics Inc ....................... E ....... 847 891-5800
  Schaumburg *(G-19511)*
Edgo Technical Sales Inc .................. G ....... 630 961-8398
  Naperville *(G-15803)*
Elcon Inc ...................................... E ....... 815 467-9500
  Minooka *(G-14840)*
Electro-Circuits Inc ......................... E ....... 630 339-3389
  Schaumburg *(G-19515)*
Electronic Assembly Corp .................. D ....... 847 793-4400
  Buffalo Grove *(G-2690)*
Electronic Design & Mfg Inc ............... D ....... 847 550-1912
  Lake Zurich *(G-13066)*
Electronic Interconnect Corp .............. D ....... 847 364-4848
  Elk Grove Village *(G-9450)*
Electronic Resources Corp ................ E ....... 630 620-0725
  Lombard *(G-13795)*
Emerge Technology Group LLC ......... G ....... 800 613-1501
  Wauconda *(G-21459)*
Excel Electro Assembly Inc ................ F ....... 847 621-2500
  Elk Grove Village *(G-9468)*
Excell Electronics Corporation ............ E ....... 847 766-7455
  Elk Grove Village *(G-9469)*
Galaxy Circuits Inc .......................... E ....... 630 462-1010
  Carol Stream *(G-3156)*
General Electro Corporation ............... F ....... 630 595-8989
  Bensenville *(G-1908)*
Hytel Group Inc .............................. E ....... 847 683-9800
  Hampshire *(G-11551)*
Illinois Tool Works Inc ...................... E ....... 630 825-7900
  Glendale Heights *(G-11033)*
Image Circuit Inc ............................ G ....... 847 622-3300
  Elk Grove Village *(G-9538)*
Image Technology Inc ...................... F ....... 847 622-3300
  Elgin *(G-9074)*
Imagineering Inc ............................. G ....... 847 806-0003
  Elk Grove Village *(G-9541)*
International Control Svcs Inc ............. C ....... 217 422-6700
  Decatur *(G-7896)*
Intratek Inc ................................... G ....... 847 640-0007
  Elk Grove Village *(G-9554)*
Journey Circuits Inc ........................ G ....... 630 283-0604
  Schaumburg *(G-19591)*
K Trox Sales Inc ............................. G ....... 815 568-1521
  Marengo *(G-14233)*
Kay & Cee .................................... G ....... 773 425-9169
  Calumet Park *(G-2962)*
King Circuit .................................. E ....... 630 629-7300
  Schaumburg *(G-19598)*
Lectro Graphics Inc ......................... G ....... 847 537-3592
  Wheeling *(G-22091)*
M-Wave International LLC ................. E ....... 630 562-5550
  Glendale Heights *(G-11043)*
Manu Industries Inc ......................... F ....... 847 891-6412
  Schaumburg *(G-19630)*
Manu-TEC of Illinois LLC .................. G ....... 630 543-3022
  Addison *(G-190)*
Mega Circuit Inc ............................. D ....... 630 543-8460
  Addison *(G-198)*
Mektronix Technology Inc ................. G ....... 847 680-3300
  Libertyville *(G-13353)*
Methode Development Co ................. D ....... 708 867-6777
  Chicago *(G-5703)*
Methode Electronics Inc ................... B ....... 708 867-6777
  Chicago *(G-5704)*
Michele Terrell .............................. G ....... 312 305-0876
  Evanston *(G-10072)*
Micro Circuit Inc ............................. F ....... 630 628-5760
  Addison *(G-206)*
Midwest Cad Design Inc ................... G ....... 847 397-0220
  Schaumburg *(G-19647)*
Milplex Circuits Inc .......................... C ....... 630 250-1580
  Itasca *(G-12321)*
National Technology Inc .................... E ....... 847 506-1300
  Rolling Meadows *(G-18749)*
Novatronix Inc ................................ G ....... 630 860-4300
  Wood Dale *(G-22407)*
On Time Circuits Inc ........................ E ....... 630 955-1110
  Lisle *(G-13636)*
Online Electronics Inc ...................... E ....... 847 871-1700
  Elk Grove Village *(G-9666)*
Paramount Laminates Inc .................. G ....... 630 594-1840
  Wood Dale *(G-22411)*
Patriot Materials LLC ....................... G ....... 630 501-0260
  Elmhurst *(G-9920)*
Pcb Express Inc ............................. F ....... 847 952-8896
  Elk Grove Village *(G-9672)*
Plexus Corp ................................... G ....... 630 250-1074
  Itasca *(G-12342)*
Plexus Corp ................................... B ....... 847 793-4400
  Buffalo Grove *(G-2754)*
Price Circuits LLC ........................... E ....... 847 742-4700
  Elgin *(G-9147)*
Printing Circuit Boards ..................... F ....... 630 543-3453
  Addison *(G-256)*
Qcircuits Inc ................................. E ....... 847 797-6678
  Rolling Meadows *(G-18771)*
Qcircuits Inc ................................. E ....... 618 662-8365
  Flora *(G-10214)*
R B Manufacturing Inc ..................... E ....... 815 522-3100
  Kirkland *(G-12716)*
Righthand Technologies Inc ............... E ....... 773 774-7600
  Chicago *(G-6356)*
Rw Technologies US LLC ................. F ....... 815 444-6887
  Crystal Lake *(G-7644)*
S & M Group Inc ............................ E ....... 630 766-1000
  Wood Dale *(G-22418)*
Siemens Manufacturing Co Inc ........... D ....... 618 539-3000
  Freeburg *(G-10641)*

# PRODUCT SECTION — PRINTING MACHINERY

Siemens Manufacturing Co Inc .......... C ...... 618 475-3325
  New Athens  (G-15861)
Sigenics Inc .................................... F ...... 312 448-8000
  Chicago  (G-6506)
Sigmatron International Inc ............... G ...... 847 586-5200
  Elgin  (G-9178)
Sigmatron International Inc ............... G ...... 847 956-8000
  Elk Grove Village  (G-9737)
Sparton Corporation ......................... B ...... 847 762-5800
  Schaumburg  (G-19734)
Sparton Design Services LLC ........... G ...... 847 762-5800
  Schaumburg  (G-19735)
Sparton Ied LLC ............................... D ...... 847 762-5800
  Schaumburg  (G-19737)
Star Acquisition Inc ........................... G ...... 847 439-0605
  Elk Grove Village  (G-9753)
Summit Design Solutions Inc ............ G ...... 847 836-8183
  East Dundee  (G-8657)
Sunrise Electronics Inc ..................... E ...... 847 357-0500
  Elk Grove Village  (G-9762)
Surya Electronics Inc ........................ C ...... 630 858-8000
  Glendale Heights  (G-11080)
SWB Inc ............................................ G ...... 847 438-1800
  Lake Zurich  (G-13136)
Taranda Specialties Inc .................... G ...... 815 469-3041
  Frankfort  (G-10368)
Tecnova Electronics Inc .................... D ...... 847 336-6160
  Waukegan  (G-21623)
Triad Circuits Inc ............................... E ...... 847 283-8600
  Waukegan  (G-21632)
United Electronics Corp Inc .............. D ...... 847 671-6034
  Franklin Park  (G-10616)
Universal Scientific III Inc .................. E ...... 847 228-6464
  Elk Grove Village  (G-9802)
Wand Enterprises Inc ....................... F ...... 847 433-0231
  Highland Park  (G-11880)
Y 2 K Electronics Inc ........................ F ...... 847 238-9024
  Elk Grove Village  (G-9821)

## PRINTERS & PLOTTERS

Hafner Duplicating Company ............ G ...... 312 362-0120
  Chicago  (G-5029)
John Harland Company ..................... G ...... 815 293-4350
  Romeoville  (G-18833)
Speedpro of Dupage ......................... G ...... 630 812-5080
  Lombard  (G-13857)
Yfy Jupiter Inc ................................... E ...... 312 419-8565
  Chicago  (G-7050)

## PRINTERS' SVCS: Folding, Collating, Etc

3dp Unlimited .................................... G ...... 815 389-5667
  Roscoe  (G-18887)
A+ Printing Co .................................. G ...... 815 968-8181
  Rockford  (G-18242)
Gamma Alpha Visual ........................ G ...... 847 956-0633
  Elk Grove Village  (G-9496)
Stromberg Allen and Company ........ E ...... 773 847-7131
  Tinley Park  (G-20947)
Tag Diamond & Label ....................... E ...... 630 844-9395
  Aurora  (G-1221)
Thompson & Walsh LLC ................... G ...... 847 734-1770
  Arlington Heights  (G-855)

## PRINTERS: Computer

Intermec Technologies Corp ............. G ...... 312 475-0106
  Chicago  (G-5216)
Sg2 .................................................... G ...... 847 779-5500
  Skokie  (G-20084)
Singer Data Products Inc ................. G ...... 630 860-6500
  Bensenville  (G-1991)

## PRINTERS: Magnetic Ink, Bar Code

Bar Codes Inc .................................. F ...... 800 351-9962
  Chicago  (G-4039)
Barcodesource Inc ............................ G ...... 630 545-9590
  West Chicago  (G-21667)
Cim Bar Code Technology Inc .......... G ...... 847 559-9776
  Northbrook  (G-16224)
Printjet Corporation .......................... F ...... 815 877-7511
  Machesney Park  (G-14101)
Zebra Technologies Corporation ....... B ...... 847 634-6700
  Lincolnshire  (G-13494)
Zebra Technologies Corporation ....... B ...... 847 634-6700
  Chicago  (G-7060)
Zebra Technologies Intl LLC ............. G ...... 847 634-6700
  Lincolnshire  (G-13495)
Zih Corp ............................................ G ...... 847 634-6700
  Lincolnshire  (G-13497)
Zih Corp ............................................ E ...... 847 634-6700
  Lincolnshire  (G-13498)

## PRINTING & BINDING: Book Music

Sandes Quynetta ............................................ 815 275-4876
  Freeport  (G-10687)

## PRINTING & BINDING: Books

Copies Overnight Inc ........................ F ...... 630 690-2000
  Carol Stream  (G-3136)
Finishing Group ................................ G ...... 847 884-4890
  Schaumburg  (G-19528)
Lake Book Manufacturing Inc ........... B ...... 708 345-7000
  Melrose Park  (G-14669)
R R Donnelley & Sons Company ...... B ...... 312 326-8000
  Chicago  (G-6270)
RR Donnelley & Sons Company ....... G ...... 630 513-4681
  Saint Charles  (G-19255)
RR Donnelley & Sons Company ....... B ...... 630 588-5000
  Lisle  (G-13653)
RR Donnelley & Sons Company ....... C ...... 312 236-8000
  Chicago  (G-6404)
Sunrise Hitek Group LLC ................. E ...... 773 792-8880
  Chicago  (G-6629)
Tvp Color Graphics Inc ..................... G ...... 630 837-3600
  Streamwood  (G-20679)
Versa Press Inc ................................ C ...... 309 822-0260
  East Peoria  (G-8738)

## PRINTING & BINDING: Textbooks

TPS Enterprises Inc ......................... E ...... 618 783-2978
  Newton  (G-15950)

## PRINTING & EMBOSSING: Plastic Fabric Articles

American Graphic Systems Inc ......... E ...... 708 614-7007
  Tinley Park  (G-20890)
Fast Lane Threads Custom EMB ...... G ...... 815 544-9898
  Belvidere  (G-1751)
Fresh Concept Enterprises Inc ......... G ...... 815 254-7295
  Plainfield  (G-17601)
Petra Manufacturing Co .................... D ...... 773 622-1475
  Chicago  (G-6113)

## PRINTING & ENGRAVING: Card, Exc Greeting

Arroweye Solutions Inc ..................... E ...... 312 253-9400
  Chicago  (G-3948)
Livegift Inc .................................................... 312 725-4514
  Chicago  (G-5524)
Poets Study Inc ................................ G ...... 773 286-1355
  Chicago  (G-6147)

## PRINTING & ENGRAVING: Financial Notes & Certificates

Financial Graphic Services Inc ......... D ...... 708 343-0448
  Broadview  (G-2580)

## PRINTING & ENGRAVING: Invitation & Stationery

All She Wrote ................................... F ...... 773 529-0100
  Chicago  (G-3808)
Artistry Engraving & Embossing ....... G ...... 773 775-4888
  Chicago  (G-3957)
Duckys Formal Wear Inc ................... G ...... 309 342-5914
  Galesburg  (G-10748)
Invitation Creations Inc ..................... G ...... 847 432-4441
  Highland Park  (G-11844)
Little Shop of Papers Ltd .................. G ...... 847 382-7733
  Barrington  (G-1287)
Managed Marketing Inc .................... G ...... 847 279-8260
  Wheeling  (G-22098)
Master Engraving ............................. G ...... 217 965-5885
  Virden  (G-21299)
Master Engraving Inc ........................ G ...... 217 627-3279
  Girard  (G-10948)
Nancy J Perkins ................................ G ...... 815 748-7121
  Dekalb  (G-8107)
Stationary Studio LLC ....................... G ...... 847 541-2499
  Buffalo Grove  (G-2777)
Thia & Co .......................................... G ...... 630 510-9770
  Wheaton  (G-21986)

## PRINTING & ENGRAVING: Poster & Decal

Signs In Dundee Inc ......................... G ...... 847 742-9530
  Elgin  (G-9179)

## PRINTING & STAMPING: Fabric Articles

Action Screen Print Inc ..................... F ...... 630 393-1990
  Warrenville  (G-21340)
B JS Printables ................................. G ...... 618 656-8625
  Edwardsville  (G-8789)
Diemasters Manufacturing Inc .......... C ...... 847 640-9900
  Elk Grove Village  (G-9429)
Signs In Dundee Inc ......................... G ...... 847 742-9530
  Elgin  (G-9179)

## PRINTING & WRITING PAPER WHOLESALERS

J P Printing Inc ................................. G ...... 773 626-5222
  Chicago  (G-5262)
K C Printing Services Inc .................. F ...... 847 382-8822
  Lake Barrington  (G-12814)
Progressive Systems Netwrk Inc ...... G ...... 312 382-8383
  Chicago  (G-6214)
Upm-Kymmene Inc ........................... D ...... 630 922-2500
  Naperville  (G-15771)

## PRINTING INKS WHOLESALERS

CIS Systems Inc ............................... G ...... 847 827-0747
  Glenview  (G-11114)
Dyco-TEC Products Ltd ................... G ...... 630 837-6410
  Bartlett  (G-1342)
Gibbon America Inc .......................... F ...... 847 931-1255
  Elgin  (G-9045)
Sun Chemical Corporation ................ C ...... 630 513-5348
  Saint Charles  (G-19274)
Zeller + Gmelin Corporation ............. G ...... 630 443-8800
  Saint Charles  (G-19302)

## PRINTING MACHINERY

2m Control Systems Inc ................... G ...... 630 709-6225
  West Chicago  (G-21650)
4I Technologies Inc .......................... D ...... 815 431-8100
  Ottawa  (G-16944)
A-Korn Roller Inc .............................. E ...... 773 254-5700
  Chicago  (G-3696)
Accu-Chem Industries Inc ................. ......... 708 344-0900
  Melrose Park  (G-14584)
Advance World Trade Inc ................. D ...... 773 777-7100
  Chicago  (G-3767)
Altair Corporation (del) ..................... E ...... 847 634-9540
  Lincolnshire  (G-13426)
Baldwin OXY-Dry Corporation .......... D ...... 630 595-3651
  Addison  (G-51)
C CN Chicago Corp .......................... G ...... 847 671-3319
  Addison  (G-64)
C F Anderson & Co ........................... F ...... 312 341-0850
  Chicago  (G-4203)
Cdj Technologies Inc ........................ G ...... 321 277-7807
  Wilmette  (G-22249)
Central Graphics Corp ...................... F ...... 630 759-1696
  Romeoville  (G-18807)
Chatham Corporation ....................... F ...... 847 634-5506
  Lincolnshire  (G-13436)
Container Graphics Corp .................. E ...... 847 584-0299
  Schaumburg  (G-19481)
Culmac Inc ........................................ E ...... 309 944-5197
  Geneseo  (G-10800)
Cy-Tec Inc ........................................ G ...... 815 756-8416
  Dekalb  (G-8084)
D & K Custom Machine Design ........ E ...... 847 956-4757
  Elk Grove Village  (G-9408)
D & K Group Inc ............................... E ...... 847 956-0160
  Elk Grove Village  (G-9409)
Distribution Enterprises Inc .............. F ...... 847 582-9276
  Lake Forest  (G-12896)
Dms Inc ............................................. F ...... 847 726-2828
  Lake Zurich  (G-13063)
Domino Amjet Inc ............................. D ...... 847 244-2501
  Gurnee  (G-11440)
Donnelley and Sons Co R R ............. G ...... 708 924-6200
  Chicago  (G-4628)
Ebway Industries Inc ........................ E ...... 630 860-5959
  Itasca  (G-12256)
Emt International Inc ........................ G ...... 630 655-4145
  Westmont  (G-21887)
Environmental Specialties Inc .......... G ...... 630 860-7070
  Itasca  (G-12259)

*Employee Codes: A=Over 500 employees, B=251-500, C=101-250, D=51-100, E=20-50, F=10-19, G=3-9*

*2017 Harris Illinois Industrial Directory*

# PRINTING MACHINERY | PRODUCT SECTION

GP Liquidation Inc .................................G....... 630 784-9736
  Addison *(G-138)*
Graphic Innovators Inc ..........................E....... 847 718-1516
  Elk Grove Village *(G-9508)*
H R Slater Co Inc ..................................F....... 312 666-1855
  Chicago *(G-5023)*
I S C America Inc ..................................G....... 630 616-1331
  Wood Dale *(G-22380)*
Ilf Technologies LLC .............................F....... 630 759-1776
  Cicero *(G-7204)*
Imtran Industries Inc .............................D....... 630 752-4000
  Carol Stream *(G-3172)*
Intersol Industries Inc ...........................F....... 630 238-0385
  Bensenville *(G-1922)*
Jardis Industries Inc .............................E....... 630 860-5959
  Itasca *(G-12289)*
Kiwi Coders Corp ..................................E....... 847 541-4511
  Wheeling *(G-22085)*
Komori America Corporation ................D....... 847 806-9000
  Rolling Meadows *(G-18739)*
Laser Reproductions Inc ......................E....... 847 410-0397
  Skokie *(G-20026)*
M & R Printing Equipment Inc .............B....... 800 736-6431
  Roselle *(G-18954)*
Manroland Inc .......................................E....... 630 920-2000
  Westmont *(G-21903)*
Manroland Web Systems Inc ...............E....... 630 920-5850
  Lisle *(G-13619)*
Mark Bst-Pro Inc ...................................D....... 630 833-9900
  Elmhurst *(G-9907)*
Midwest Index Inc ................................D....... 847 995-8425
  Addison *(G-212)*
Milans Machining & Mfg Co Inc ............D....... 708 780-6600
  Cicero *(G-7222)*
Nama Graphics E LLC ..........................G....... 262 966-3853
  Homer Glen *(G-12083)*
Ortman-Mccain Co ................................G....... 312 666-2244
  Chicago *(G-6018)*
Pamarco Global Graphics Inc ..............E....... 630 879-7300
  Batavia *(G-1479)*
Pamarco Global Graphics Inc ..............F....... 847 459-6000
  Wheeling *(G-22118)*
Paper Benders Supply Inc ....................G....... 815 577-7583
  Plainfield *(G-17635)*
Polyurthane Engrg Tchnques Inc .........E....... 847 362-1820
  Lake Forest *(G-12947)*
Precision Screen Specialties ................G....... 630 762-9548
  Saint Charles *(G-19241)*
Printers Parts Inc .................................G....... 847 288-9000
  Franklin Park *(G-10561)*
Quipp Systems Inc ...............................G....... 305 304-1985
  Glenview *(G-11187)*
Quipp Systems Inc ...............................E....... 305 623-8700
  Glenview *(G-11188)*
Resinite Corporation .............................F....... 847 537-4250
  Wheeling *(G-22138)*
Rotation Dynamics Corporation ............D....... 773 247-5600
  Chicago *(G-6399)*
Rycoline Products LLC .........................C....... 773 775-6755
  Chicago *(G-6417)*
Saati Americas Corporation ..................F....... 847 296-5090
  Mount Prospect *(G-15371)*
Schellhorn Photo Techniques ...............F....... 773 267-5141
  Chicago *(G-6451)*
Sopher Design & Manufacturing ...........G....... 309 699-6419
  East Peoria *(G-8735)*
Special Tool Engineering Co .................F....... 773 767-6690
  Chicago *(G-6554)*
Tamarack Products Inc .........................E....... 847 526-9333
  Wauconda *(G-21508)*
Technotrans America Inc ......................E....... 847 227-9200
  Mount Prospect *(G-15378)*
Thermal Care Inc ..................................C....... 847 966-2260
  Niles *(G-16041)*
Web Printing Controls Co Inc ................D....... 618 842-2664
  Arlington Heights *(G-870)*
Web Printing Controls Co Inc ................C....... 618 842-2664
  Fairfield *(G-10161)*
Weber Marking Systems Inc .................B....... 847 364-8500
  Arlington Heights *(G-871)*
Western Printing Machinery Co .............E....... 847 678-1740
  Schiller Park *(G-19883)*
Western Printing Machinery Co .............F....... 847 678-1740
  Schiller Park *(G-19884)*
Wpc Machinery Corp .............................E....... 630 231-7721
  Arlington Heights *(G-874)*

## PRINTING MACHINERY, EQPT & SPLYS: Wholesalers

AAA Press Specialists Inc ....................F....... 847 818-1100
  Arlington Heights *(G-701)*
Advance World Trade Inc .....................D....... 773 777-7100
  Chicago *(G-3767)*
Anderson & Vreeland-Illinois ................F....... 847 255-2110
  Arlington Heights *(G-713)*
Autotype Americas Incorporated ..........F....... 847 818-8262
  Rolling Meadows *(G-18713)*
C and C Machine Tool Service .............G....... 630 810-0484
  Downers Grove *(G-8402)*
Distribution Enterprises Inc .................F....... 847 582-9276
  Lake Forest *(G-12896)*
Domino Holdings Inc ...........................D....... 847 244-2501
  Gurnee *(G-11441)*
E & H Graphic Service .........................G....... 708 748-5656
  Matteson *(G-14371)*
Emt International Inc ............................G....... 630 655-4145
  Westmont *(G-21887)*
Goss International LLC ........................E....... 630 796-7560
  Woodridge *(G-22488)*
Graphic Innovators Inc ........................E....... 847 718-1516
  Elk Grove Village *(G-9508)*
Identatronics Inc ..................................E....... 847 437-2654
  Crystal Lake *(G-7591)*
Jardis Industries Inc ............................F....... 630 773-5600
  Itasca *(G-12290)*
Laser Reproductions Inc ......................E....... 847 410-0397
  Skokie *(G-20026)*
M & R Printing Equipment Inc .............B....... 800 736-6431
  Roselle *(G-18954)*
Manroland Inc .......................................E....... 630 920-2000
  Westmont *(G-21903)*
Menges Roller Co Inc ..........................E....... 847 487-8877
  Wauconda *(G-21482)*
Printers Parts Inc .................................G....... 847 288-9000
  Franklin Park *(G-10561)*
Professional Sales Associates ............F....... 847 487-1900
  Wauconda *(G-21493)*
Prograf LLC ..........................................G....... 815 234-4848
  Villa Park *(G-21280)*
Schlesinger Machinery Inc ...................G....... 630 766-4074
  Bensenville *(G-1987)*
Smart Inc ..............................................E....... 847 464-4160
  Hampshire *(G-11563)*
Tampotech Decorating Inc ...................F....... 847 515-2968
  Huntley *(G-12178)*
Wikoff Color Corporation ......................F....... 847 487-2704
  Wauconda *(G-21515)*

## PRINTING TRADES MACHINERY & EQPT REPAIR SVCS

Mah Machine Company .........................C....... 708 656-1826
  Cicero *(G-7217)*
Tlm Enterprises Inc ..............................G....... 815 284-5040
  Dixon *(G-8356)*
Wpc Machinery Corp .............................E....... 630 231-7721
  Arlington Heights *(G-874)*

## PRINTING, COMMERCIAL Newspapers, NEC

Desitalk Chicago LLC ...........................E....... 773 856-0545
  Chicago *(G-4586)*
Henry News Republican ........................G....... 309 364-3250
  Henry *(G-11743)*
Osborne Publications Inc .....................G....... 217 422-9702
  Decatur *(G-7924)*
Park Press Inc .......................................F....... 708 331-6352
  South Holland *(G-20295)*

## PRINTING, COMMERCIAL: Announcements, NEC

Bass-Mollett Publishers Inc .................D....... 618 664-3141
  Greenville *(G-11387)*

## PRINTING, COMMERCIAL: Bags, Plastic, NEC

Golden Plastics LLC .............................F....... 847 836-7766
  East Dundee *(G-8640)*

## PRINTING, COMMERCIAL: Business Forms, NEC

Available Business Group Inc ..............D....... 773 247-4141
  Chicago *(G-3995)*
Data Com PLD Inc ................................G....... 708 839-9620
  Willow Springs *(G-22195)*
Forms Specialist Inc ............................E....... 847 298-2868
  Lincolnshire *(G-13449)*
Grand Forms & Systems Inc ................F....... 847 259-4600
  Arlington Heights *(G-760)*
MidAmerican Prtg Systems Inc ............E....... 312 663-4720
  Chicago *(G-5732)*
Noor International Inc ..........................G....... 847 985-2300
  Bartlett *(G-1320)*
OfficeMax North America Inc ...............E....... 815 748-3007
  Dekalb *(G-8111)*
Pioneer Forms Inc ................................G....... 773 539-8587
  Chicago *(G-6125)*
Productive Portable Disp Inc ...............G....... 630 458-9100
  Addison *(G-259)*
Shetley Management Inc ......................G....... 618 548-1556
  Salem *(G-19351)*
Techgraphic Solutions Inc ....................F....... 309 693-9400
  Peoria *(G-17467)*
W W Barthel & Co ..................................G....... 847 392-5643
  Arlington Heights *(G-869)*

## PRINTING, COMMERCIAL: Calendars, NEC

Wyka LLC ..............................................G....... 847 298-0740
  Des Plaines *(G-8306)*

## PRINTING, COMMERCIAL: Certificates, Stock, NEC

Corporation Supply Co Inc ...................E....... 312 726-3375
  Chicago *(G-4476)*

## PRINTING, COMMERCIAL: Coupons, NEC

Gallimore Industries Inc .......................F....... 847 356-3331
  Lake Villa *(G-13014)*

## PRINTING, COMMERCIAL: Decals, NEC

Central Decal Company Inc ..................D....... 630 325-9892
  Burr Ridge *(G-2829)*
Freedom Design & Decals Inc ..............G....... 815 806-8172
  Mokena *(G-14864)*
Great Display Company Llc ..................F....... 309 821-1037
  Bloomington *(G-2172)*
P & L Mark-It Inc ...................................E....... 630 879-7590
  Batavia *(G-1478)*
Sportdecals Sport & Spirit Pro .............D....... 800 435-6110
  Spring Grove *(G-20365)*
Winnetka Sign Co Inc ...........................G....... 847 473-9378
  North Chicago *(G-16191)*

## PRINTING, COMMERCIAL: Directories, Exc Telephone, NEC

Scholl Communications Inc .................G....... 847 945-1891
  Deerfield *(G-8051)*

## PRINTING, COMMERCIAL: Envelopes, NEC

Americas Community Bankers ..............E....... 312 644-3100
  Chicago *(G-3884)*
Forest Envelope Company ....................E....... 630 515-1200
  Bolingbrook *(G-2311)*
J & J Express Envelopes Inc ................G....... 847 253-7146
  South Elgin *(G-20209)*
Victor Envelope Mfg Corp .....................C....... 630 616-2750
  Bensenville *(G-2012)*

## PRINTING, COMMERCIAL: Imprinting

Elite Impressions & Graphics ...............G....... 847 695-3730
  South Elgin *(G-20195)*
Excel Glass Inc .....................................G....... 847 801-5200
  Schiller Park *(G-19829)*
Rainbow Art Inc .....................................F....... 312 421-5600
  Chicago *(G-6288)*

## PRINTING, COMMERCIAL: Invitations, NEC

Sass-N-Class Inc ..................................G....... 630 655-2420
  Hinsdale *(G-11962)*

## PRINTING, COMMERCIAL: Labels & Seals, NEC

Abbott Label Inc ....................................F....... 630 773-3614
  Itasca *(G-12222)*
American Label Company ......................G....... 630 830-4444
  Schaumburg *(G-19438)*

AT&I Resources LLC ....G.... 918 925-0154
Addison (G-47)
Bar Code Graphics Inc ....F.... 312 664-0700
Chicago (G-4038)
Delta Label Inc....G.... 618 233-8984
Belleville (G-1625)
Heartland Labels Inc....E.... 217 826-8324
Marshall (G-14323)
Jordan Industries Inc....F.... 847 945-5591
Deerfield (G-8020)
M & R Graphics Inc....F.... 708 534-6621
University Park (G-21054)
National Data-Label Corp....E.... 630 616-9595
Bensenville (G-1954)
Primedia Source LLC....G.... 630 553-8451
Yorkville (G-22670)
Sato Lbling Solutions Amer Inc....D.... 630 771-4200
Romeoville (G-18866)
Schultz Brothers Inc....G.... 630 458-1437
Addison (G-283)
Selective Label & Tabs Inc....F.... 630 466-0091
Sugar Grove (G-20735)
Selective Label & Tabs Inc....G.... 630 466-0091
Sugar Grove (G-20736)
Shamrock Scientific....D.... 800 323-0249
Bellwood (G-1720)
Stephen Fossler Company....D.... 847 635-7200
Des Plaines (G-8281)
Tiem Engineering Corporation....F.... 630 553-7484
Yorkville (G-22672)
UNI-Label and Tag Corporation....E.... 847 956-8900
Elk Grove Village (G-9797)

## PRINTING, COMMERCIAL: Letterpress & Screen

American Advertising Assoc Inc....G.... 773 312-5110
Chicago (G-3847)
American Graphic Systems Inc....E.... 708 614-7007
Tinley Park (G-20890)
Continent Corp....G.... 773 733-1584
Bolingbrook (G-2287)
Expression Wear Inc....G.... 815 732-1556
Mount Morris (G-15296)
G Y Industries LLC....F.... 708 210-1300
Chicago (G-4902)
Gsi Technologies LLC....D.... 630 325-8181
Burr Ridge (G-2847)
McGrath Press Inc....E.... 815 356-5246
Crystal Lake (G-7607)
Ready Inc....F.... 630 501-1352
Elmhurst (G-9926)
Sweet TS LLC....G.... 618 943-5729
Lawrenceville (G-13204)
Te Shurt Shop Inc....F.... 217 344-1226
Champaign (G-3549)
Teeatude Inc....G.... 312 324-3554
Chicago (G-6688)

## PRINTING, COMMERCIAL: Literature, Advertising, NEC

Bizbash Media Inc....G.... 312 436-2525
Chicago (G-4117)
Freddie Bear Sports....F.... 708 532-4133
Tinley Park (G-20916)
Market Connect Inc....G.... 847 726-6788
Kildeer (G-12702)
Mjt Design and Prtg Entps Inc....G.... 708 240-4323
Hillside (G-11926)
Mortgage Market Info Svcs....E.... 630 834-7555
Villa Park (G-21272)
Q B F Graphic Group....G.... 708 781-9580
Tinley Park (G-20941)
R & R Printnserve Inc....G.... 630 654-4044
Hinsdale (G-11960)
Rush Impressions Inc....G.... 847 671-0622
Schiller Park (G-19870)

## PRINTING, COMMERCIAL: Magazines, NEC

Central IL Business Magazine....G.... 217 351-5281
Champaign (G-3465)
Time Out Chicago Partners Lllp....E.... 312 924-9555
Chicago (G-6727)

## PRINTING, COMMERCIAL: Menus, NEC

Michael Lewis Company....C.... 708 688-2200
Mc Cook (G-14453)

Rick Styfer....G.... 630 734-3244
Burr Ridge (G-2877)
Simu Ltd....F.... 630 350-1060
Wood Dale (G-22422)

## PRINTING, COMMERCIAL: Promotional

American Spcalty Advg Prtg Co....G.... 847 272-5255
Northbrook (G-16203)
Belboz Corp....G.... 708 856-6099
Dolton (G-8366)
Business Identity Spc Inc....G.... 847 669-1946
Huntley (G-12134)
C L Graphics Inc....E.... 815 455-0900
Crystal Lake (G-7547)
Chicago Printing and EMB Inc....F.... 630 628-1777
Addison (G-75)
Corporate Promotions Inc....G.... 630 964-5000
Lisle (G-13577)
F & F Publishing Inc....G.... 847 480-0330
Highland Park (G-11831)
M Wells Printing Co....G.... 312 455-0400
Chicago (G-5588)
Master Marketing Intl Inc....E.... 630 653-5525
Carol Stream (G-3190)
Motr Grafx LLC....G.... 847 600-5656
Niles (G-16009)
Pelegan Inc....G.... 708 442-9797
Riverside (G-18033)
R L Allen Industries....G.... 618 667-2544
Troy (G-21011)
Rotary Forms and Systems Inc....G.... 847 843-8585
Hoffman Estates (G-12044)
Rv Enterprises Ltd....F.... 847 509-8710
Niles (G-16030)
USA Printworks LLC....E.... 815 206-0854
Woodstock (G-22620)
Zorch International Inc....E.... 312 751-8010
Chicago (G-7072)

## PRINTING, COMMERCIAL: Publications

Bdc Capital Enterprises LLC....G.... 847 908-0650
Schaumburg (G-19457)
Good News Printing....G.... 708 389-1127
Palos Heights (G-17105)
Lampe Publications....G.... 309 741-9790
Elmwood (G-9964)
McKnights Long Term Care News....G.... 847 559-2884
Northbrook (G-16308)
Prismatec Inc....G.... 847 562-9022
Northbrook (G-16346)
Reid Communications Inc....E.... 847 741-9700
Elgin (G-9163)
Strathmore Press....E.... 513 483-3600
Saint Charles (G-19273)
Town Square Publications LLC....G.... 847 427-4633
Arlington Heights (G-856)
Zoe Publications LLC....G.... 636 625-6622
Peoria (G-17482)

## PRINTING, COMMERCIAL: Ready

Batavia Instant Print....G.... 630 262-0370
West Chicago (G-21668)
T F N W Inc....G.... 630 584-7383
Saint Charles (G-19277)

## PRINTING, COMMERCIAL: Screen

3 Penguins Ltd....G.... 630 528-7086
Batavia (G-1401)
A & R Screening LLC....F.... 708 598-2480
Bridgeview (G-2457)
A-Creations Inc....G.... 630 541-5801
Woodridge (G-22448)
Ad Images....G.... 847 956-1887
Elk Grove Village (G-9269)
Advance Press Sign Inc....G.... 630 833-1600
Villa Park (G-21233)
Aim Screen Printing Supply LLC....G.... 630 357-4293
Naperville (G-15791)
All Stars -N- Stitches Inc....G.... 618 435-5555
Benton (G-2021)
American Bell Screen Prtg Co....G.... 815 623-5522
Roscoe (G-18890)
American Outfitters Ltd....E.... 847 623-3959
Waukegan (G-21524)
Amy Schutt....G.... 618 994-7405
Carrier Mills (G-3305)
Anatol Equipment Mfg Co....E.... 847 367-9760
Lake Bluff (G-12831)

Artisan Handprints Inc....G.... 773 725-1799
Chicago (G-3956)
Artline Screen Printing Inc....G.... 815 963-8125
Rockford (G-18271)
Artsonia LLC....F.... 224 538-5060
Gurnee (G-11429)
Artwear....G.... 618 234-5522
Belleville (G-1609)
Ashland Screening Corporation....E.... 708 758-8800
Chicago Heights (G-7080)
Astro Plastic Containers Inc....F.... 708 458-7100
Bedford Park (G-1540)
Athletic Image....G.... 217 347-7377
Effingham (G-8825)
Authority Screenprint & EMB....G.... 630 236-0289
Plainfield (G-17581)
B Creative Screen Print Co....G.... 815 806-3037
Frankfort (G-10298)
B D Enterprises....G.... 618 462-5861
Alton (G-563)
Bailleu & Bailleu Printing Inc....G.... 309 852-2517
Kewanee (G-12670)
Baker La Russo....G.... 630 788-5108
Naperville (G-15602)
Bee Designs Embroidery & Scree....G.... 815 393-4593
Malta (G-14165)
Bes Designs & Associates Inc....G.... 217 443-4619
Danville (G-7705)
Bobs Tshirt Store....G.... 618 567-1730
Mascoutah (G-14349)
Brownfield Sports Inc....G.... 217 367-8321
Urbana (G-21074)
C & E Specialties Inc....E.... 815 229-9230
Rockford (G-18294)
Carl Gorr Printing Co....G.... 815 338-3191
Woodstock (G-22549)
Cloz Companies Inc....E.... 773 247-8879
Skokie (G-19983)
Custom Screen Printing....G.... 217 543-3691
Arthur (G-893)
Damy Corp....F.... 847 233-0515
Schiller Park (G-19819)
Decal Works LLC....E.... 815 784-4000
Kingston (G-12706)
Decorative Industries Inc....E.... 773 229-0015
Chicago (G-4570)
Diamond Screen Process Inc....G.... 847 439-6200
Elk Grove Village (G-9426)
Display Link Inc....G.... 815 968-0778
Rockford (G-18346)
Dolls Lettering Inc....G.... 815 467-8000
Minooka (G-14838)
Dpe Incorporated....G.... 773 306-0105
Chicago (G-4640)
Dynamesh Inc....E.... 630 293-5454
Batavia (G-1444)
E K Kuhn Inc....G.... 815 899-9211
Sycamore (G-20795)
Eagle Screen Print Inds Inc....F.... 708 579-0454
Countryside (G-7423)
Earl Ad Inc....G.... 312 666-7106
Chicago (G-4673)
Elegant Embroidery Inc....G.... 847 540-8003
Lake Zurich (G-13067)
Embroid ME....G.... 815 485-4155
New Lenox (G-15880)
Energy Tees....G.... 708 771-0000
Forest Park (G-10240)
ESP T-Shirt Co Inc....G.... 630 393-1033
Warrenville (G-21346)
Everwill Inc....G.... 847 357-0446
Elk Grove Village (G-9466)
F-C Enterprises Inc....G.... 815 254-7295
Plainfield (G-17598)
Fantastic Lettering Inc....G.... 773 685-7650
Chicago (G-4812)
Flow-Eze Company....F.... 815 965-1062
Rockford (G-18383)
G and D Enterprises Inc....E.... 847 981-8661
Arlington Heights (G-757)
Gfx Dynamic....G.... 847 543-4600
Grayslake (G-11339)
Graphic Screen Printing Inc....G.... 708 429-3330
Orland Park (G-16863)
H & H Graphics Illinois Inc....E.... 847 383-6285
Vernon Hills (G-21170)
Hazen Display Corporation....E.... 815 248-2925
Davis (G-7806)
Hi-Five Sportswear Inc....G.... 815 637-6044
Machesney Park (G-14079)

PRODUCT

Employee Codes: A=Over 500 employees, B=251-500
C=101-250, D=51-100, E=20-50, F=10-19, G=3-9
2017 Harris Illinois
Industrial Directory
1705

## PRINTING, COMMERCIAL: Screen

High-5 Printwear Inc .................................. G ...... 847 818-0081
  Arlington Heights (G-765)
Hole In The Wall Screen Arts ................... G ...... 217 243-9100
  Jacksonville (G-12391)
Huetone Imprints Inc ................................ G ...... 630 694-9610
  Elk Grove Village (G-9528)
Image Plus Inc ......................................... G ...... 630 852-4920
  Downers Grove (G-8463)
Interstate Graphics Inc ............................. E ...... 815 877-6777
  Machesney Park (G-14083)
J & J Silk Screening ................................. G ...... 773 838-9000
  Chicago (G-5252)
Joliet Pattern Works Inc ........................... D ...... 815 726-5373
  Crest Hill (G-7460)
K and A Graphics Inc ............................... G ...... 847 244-2345
  Gurnee (G-11463)
Kmf Enterprises Inc ................................. G ...... 630 858-2210
  Wheaton (G-21961)
Lans Printing Inc ...................................... G ...... 708 895-6226
  Lynwood (G-14021)
Laughing Dog Graphics ........................... G ...... 309 392-3330
  Minier (G-14833)
Locker Room Screen Printing .................. G ...... 630 759-2533
  Bolingbrook (G-2337)
Logo Wear Unlimited Inc ......................... G ...... 309 367-2333
  Metamora (G-14743)
Logo Works ............................................. G ...... 815 942-4700
  Morris (G-15113)
Ltb Graphics Inc ...................................... G ...... 630 238-1754
  Wood Dale (G-22391)
Melon Ink Screen Print ............................ G ...... 847 726-0003
  Lake Zurich (G-13101)
Meto-Grafics Inc ...................................... F ...... 847 639-0044
  Crystal Lake (G-7609)
Midwest Silkscreening Inc ....................... G ...... 217 892-9596
  Rantoul (G-17934)
Minerva Sportswear Inc .......................... F ...... 309 661-2387
  Bloomington (G-2201)
Modagrafics Inc ....................................... D ...... 800 860-3169
  Rolling Meadows (G-18746)
Msf Graphics Inc ...................................... G ...... 847 446-6900
  Des Plaines (G-8239)
Muir Omni Graphics Inc ........................... G ...... 309 673-7034
  Peoria (G-17413)
NGS Printing Inc ...................................... E ...... 847 741-4411
  Elgin (G-9122)
Olympic Trophy and Awards Co ............... F ...... 773 631-9500
  Chicago (G-5987)
Outbreak Designs .................................... G ...... 217 370-5418
  South Jacksonville (G-20311)
Panther Products ..................................... G ...... 618 664-1071
  Greenville (G-11402)
Papyrus Press Inc ................................... F ...... 773 342-0700
  Chicago (G-6074)
Phoenix Graphics Inc ............................... G ...... 847 699-9520
  Des Plaines (G-8255)
Phoenix Marketing Services .................... F ...... 630 616-8000
  Mundelein (G-15546)
Photo Techniques Corp ........................... E ...... 630 690-9360
  Carol Stream (G-3212)
Photo Techniques Corp ........................... E ...... 630 690-9360
  Carol Stream (G-3213)
Plastics Printing Group Inc ...................... F ...... 312 421-7980
  Chicago (G-6138)
Positive Impressions ................................ G ...... 618 438-7030
  Benton (G-2038)
Pro Image Promotions Inc ....................... G ...... 773 292-1111
  Chicago (G-6202)
Pro Tuff Decal Inc .................................... E ...... 815 356-9160
  Crystal Lake (G-7633)
Process Graphics Corp ............................ E ...... 815 637-2500
  Rockford (G-18542)
Proell Inc .................................................. G ...... 630 587-2300
  Saint Charles (G-19242)
Project Te Inc .......................................... G ...... 217 344-9833
  Urbana (G-21100)
Promark Advertising Specialtie ................ G ...... 618 483-6025
  Altamont (G-554)
Roeda Signs Inc ...................................... E ...... 708 333-3021
  South Holland (G-20302)
Scheiwes Print Shop ............................... G ...... 815 683-2398
  Crescent City (G-7456)
Screen Graphics ...................................... G ...... 309 699-8513
  Pekin (G-17288)
Selah USA Inc ......................................... G ...... 847 758-0702
  Elk Grove Village (G-9733)
Select Screen Prints & EMB ................... F ...... 309 829-6511
  Bloomington (G-2222)
Seritex Inc ............................................... G ...... 201 755-3002
  Addison (G-287)
Sew Wright Embroidery Inc ..................... G ...... 309 691-5780
  Peoria (G-17452)
Silkworm Inc ............................................ D ...... 618 687-4077
  Murphysboro (G-15583)
Skyline ..................................................... G ...... 312 300-4700
  Mc Cook (G-14458)
Spirit Warrior Inc ...................................... G ...... 708 614-0020
  Orland Park (G-16895)
Sports All Sorts AP & Design .................. G ...... 815 756-9910
  Dekalb (G-8122)
Sprectra Graphics Inc .............................. G ...... 618 624-6776
  O Fallon (G-16479)
Sunburst Sportswear Inc ......................... F ...... 630 717-8680
  Glendale Heights (G-11079)
Systematics Screen Printing ................... F ...... 630 521-1123
  Itasca (G-12362)
T Graphics ............................................... G ...... 618 592-4145
  Oblong (G-16735)
Tease ...................................................... G ...... 630 960-4950
  Downers Grove (G-8530)
Tees Ink ................................................... G ...... 815 462-7300
  New Lenox (G-15919)
Thermo-Graphic LLC ............................... E ...... 630 350-2226
  Bensenville (G-2001)
Think Ink Inc ............................................ G ...... 815 459-4565
  Crystal Lake (G-7665)
Toms Signs .............................................. G ...... 630 377-8525
  Saint Charles (G-19284)
Trendy Screenprinting .............................. G ...... 815 895-0081
  Sycamore (G-20821)
Tri Star Plowing ....................................... G ...... 847 584-5070
  Schaumburg (G-19771)
Tri-City Sports Inc .................................... G ...... 217 224-2489
  Quincy (G-17899)
Triangle Screen Print Inc ......................... F ...... 847 678-9200
  Franklin Park (G-10612)
Trimark Screen Printing Inc ..................... G ...... 630 629-2823
  Lombard (G-13872)
Ultimate Distributing Inc .......................... G ...... 847 566-2250
  Mundelein (G-15565)
Usmss Inc ................................................ G ...... 708 409-9010
  Westchester (G-21861)
Wagner International LLC ........................ G ...... 224 619-9247
  Vernon Hills (G-21216)
Waist Up Imprntd Sprtswear LLC ............ G ...... 847 963-1400
  Palatine (G-17086)
Webe Ink ................................................. G ...... 618 498-7620
  Jerseyville (G-12429)
Winning Streak Inc .................................. E ...... 618 277-8191
  Dupo (G-8584)
Woolenwear Co ....................................... F ...... 847 520-9243
  Prospect Heights (G-17786)
Workshop ................................................ E ...... 815 777-2211
  Galena (G-10736)
Xtreme Dzignz .......................................... G ...... 309 633-9311
  Bartonville (G-1400)
Your Logo Here ....................................... G ...... 708 258-6666
  Peotone (G-17494)

## PRINTING, COMMERCIAL: Stationery, NEC

Embossed Graphics Inc ........................... D ...... 630 236-4000
  Aurora (G-1002)
Merrill Fine Arts Engrv Inc ....................... D ...... 312 786-6300
  Chicago (G-5697)
Rohner Engraving Inc .............................. G ...... 773 244-8343
  Chicago (G-6382)

## PRINTING, LITHOGRAPHIC: Advertising Posters

Phoenix Business Solutions LLC ............. E ...... 708 388-1330
  Alsip (G-508)
Urban Imaging Group Inc ........................ G ...... 773 961-7500
  Chicago (G-6847)

## PRINTING, LITHOGRAPHIC: Calendars

Custom Calendar Corp ............................ G ...... 708 547-6191
  Lombard (G-13786)
House of Doolittle Ltd ............................. E ...... 847 593-3417
  Arlington Heights (G-769)
Warwick Publishing Company ................. D ...... 630 584-3871
  Saint Charles (G-19291)

## PRINTING, LITHOGRAPHIC: Calendars & Cards

Go Calendars .......................................... G ...... 847 816-1563
  Vernon Hills (G-21166)

## PRINTING, LITHOGRAPHIC: Color

Amric Resources ..................................... G ...... 309 664-0391
  Bloomington (G-2144)
Brilliant Color Corp .................................. G ...... 847 367-3300
  Libertyville (G-13310)
Excel Forms Inc ....................................... G ...... 630 801-1936
  Aurora (G-1150)
Graphics & Technical Systems ................ G ...... 708 974-3806
  Palos Hills (G-17118)
Klh Printing Corp ..................................... G ...... 847 459-0115
  Wheeling (G-22086)
MPS Chicago Inc ..................................... C ...... 630 932-9000
  Downers Grove (G-8492)
Northstar Group Inc ................................. F ...... 847 726-0880
  Lake Zurich (G-13110)
Qg LLC .................................................... B ...... 217 347-7721
  Effingham (G-8854)
Rider Dickerson Inc ................................. D ...... 312 427-2926
  Bellwood (G-1718)
Triangle Printers Inc ................................ E ...... 847 675-3700
  Skokie (G-20103)

## PRINTING, LITHOGRAPHIC: Decals

CDI Corp .................................................. F ...... 773 205-2960
  Chicago (G-4264)
Cypress Multigraphics LLC ..................... E ...... 708 633-1166
  Tinley Park (G-20907)
Service Packaging Design Inc ................. G ...... 847 966-6592
  Morton Grove (G-15236)

## PRINTING, LITHOGRAPHIC: Fashion Plates

Proform .................................................... G ...... 309 676-2535
  Peoria (G-17437)

## PRINTING, LITHOGRAPHIC: Forms & Cards, Business

Chicago Envelope Inc .............................. E ...... 630 668-0400
  Carol Stream (G-3127)
Corporate Business Card Ltd .................. E ...... 847 455-5760
  Franklin Park (G-10442)
D E Signs & Storage LLC ....................... G ...... 618 939-8050
  Waterloo (G-21401)
Inoprints .................................................. G ...... 312 994-2351
  Chicago (G-5202)
Mag Tag .................................................. G ...... 847 647-6255
  Niles (G-15999)
MPE Business Forms Inc ........................ E ...... 815 748-3676
  Dekalb (G-8106)
Novak Business Forms Inc ...................... G ...... 630 932-9850
  Lombard (G-13834)
Qaprintscom ............................................ G ...... 312 404-2130
  Chicago (G-6236)

## PRINTING, LITHOGRAPHIC: Forms, Business

Ennis Inc .................................................. E ...... 815 875-2000
  Princeton (G-17748)
Hansen Printing Co Inc ........................... E ...... 708 599-1500
  Bridgeview (G-2496)
Hq Printers Inc ......................................... G ...... 312 782-2020
  Chicago (G-5125)
Integrated Print Graphics Inc .................. D ...... 847 695-6777
  South Elgin (G-20206)
Integrated Print Graphics Inc .................. C ...... 847 888-2880
  South Elgin (G-20207)
J J Collins Sons Inc ................................ E ...... 630 960-2525
  Woodridge (G-22499)
J J Collins Sons Inc ................................ D ...... 217 345-7606
  Charleston (G-3601)
T & C Graphics Inc .................................. E ...... 630 532-5050
  South Elgin (G-20227)

## PRINTING, LITHOGRAPHIC: Letters, Circular Or Form

RR Donnelley Printing Co LP ................... A ...... 217 235-0561
  Mattoon (G-14408)

## PRINTING, LITHOGRAPHIC: Maps

Trafficcom ............................................... G ...... 773 997-8351
  Chicago (G-6755)

## PRINTING, LITHOGRAPHIC: Menus

Alliance Investment Corp ........................ F ...... 847 933-0400
  Skokie (G-19949)

# PRODUCT SECTION

## PRINTING: Commercial, NEC

Hertzberg Ernst & Sons............................E...... 773 525-3518
  Chicago *(G-5082)*
Rick Styfer..............................................G...... 630 734-3244
  Burr Ridge *(G-2877)*

### PRINTING, LITHOGRAPHIC: Newspapers

New City Communications......................E...... 312 243-8786
  Chicago *(G-5891)*
Newsweb Corporation............................E...... 773 975-5727
  Chicago *(G-5904)*

### PRINTING, LITHOGRAPHIC: Offset & photolithographic printing

Ah Tensor International LLC...................E...... 630 739-9600
  Woodridge *(G-22450)*
Best Advertising Spc & Prtg....................G...... 708 448-1110
  Worth *(G-22633)*
Decatur Blue Print Company...................G...... 217 423-7589
  Decatur *(G-7869)*
DMarv Design Specialty Prtrs..................G...... 708 389-4420
  Blue Island *(G-2246)*
Ed Garvey and Company........................E...... 847 647-1900
  Niles *(G-15976)*
Forrest Press Inc....................................G...... 847 381-1621
  Barrington *(G-1280)*
Fortman & Associates Ltd......................F...... 847 524-0741
  Elk Grove Village *(G-9488)*
Genesis Press Inc..................................G...... 630 467-1000
  Itasca *(G-12268)*
Havana Printing & Mailing......................F...... 309 543-2000
  Havana *(G-11695)*
Horizon Graphics...................................F...... 309 699-4287
  East Peoria *(G-8712)*
Impossible Objects LLC.........................F...... 847 400-9582
  Northbrook *(G-16275)*
Promoframes LLC..................................G...... 866 566-7224
  Schaumburg *(G-19701)*
Screen Machine Incorporated.................G...... 847 439-2233
  Elk Grove Village *(G-9732)*
Van Lancker Steven...............................G...... 309 764-2221
  Moline *(G-14975)*
Wayne Printing Company.......................E...... 309 691-2496
  Edwards *(G-8786)*

### PRINTING, LITHOGRAPHIC: On Metal

Adams Printing Co.................................G...... 618 529-2396
  Carbondale *(G-3000)*
American Inks and Coatings Co.............G...... 630 226-0994
  Romeoville *(G-18795)*
Apple Printing Center............................G...... 630 932-9494
  Addison *(G-41)*
Bros Lithographing Company.................G...... 312 666-0919
  Chicago *(G-4176)*
Carson Printing Inc................................G...... 847 836-0900
  East Dundee *(G-8629)*
Catalina Graphics Inc.............................G...... 773 973-7780
  Chicago *(G-4255)*
Dun-Wel Lithograph Co Inc....................G...... 773 327-8811
  Chicago *(G-4650)*
E & D Web Inc.......................................C...... 815 562-5800
  Rochelle *(G-18086)*
James W Smith Printing Company..........E...... 847 244-6486
  Gurnee *(G-11461)*
JL Clark LLC..........................................C...... 815 961-5609
  Rockford *(G-18447)*
Keneal Industries Inc.............................F...... 815 886-1300
  Romeoville *(G-18834)*
Lakeside Lithography LLC.....................E...... 312 243-3001
  Chicago *(G-5445)*
Little Village Printing Inc........................G...... 708 749-4414
  Berwyn *(G-2067)*
Merrill Fine Arts Engrv Inc.....................D...... 312 786-6300
  Chicago *(G-5697)*
Nature House Inc...................................D...... 217 833-2393
  Griggsville *(G-11413)*
Panda Graphics Inc................................G...... 312 666-7642
  Chicago *(G-6068)*
Paul D Burton.........................................G...... 309 467-2613
  Eureka *(G-10000)*
Printed Word Inc....................................G...... 847 328-1511
  Evanston *(G-10091)*
Rohrer Graphic Arts Inc.........................F...... 630 832-3434
  Elmhurst *(G-9930)*
Saints Volo & Olha Uk Cath Par..............G...... 312 829-5209
  Chicago *(G-6430)*
Shoppers Guide.....................................G...... 815 369-4112
  Lena *(G-13284)*
Tidd Printing Co.....................................G...... 708 749-1200
  Berwyn *(G-2076)*

Treudt Corporation.................................G...... 630 293-0500
  West Chicago *(G-21785)*
Turner Jct Prtg & Litho Svc.....................G...... 630 293-1377
  West Chicago *(G-21786)*
Willert Company.....................................G...... 630 860-1620
  Franklin Park *(G-10630)*

### PRINTING, LITHOGRAPHIC: Posters

Morton Suggestion Company LLC..........G...... 847 255-4770
  Mount Prospect *(G-15351)*

### PRINTING, LITHOGRAPHIC: Posters & Decals

Media Unlimited Inc...............................G...... 630 527-0900
  Naperville *(G-15816)*
Signs In Dundee Inc...............................G...... 847 742-9530
  Elgin *(G-9179)*

### PRINTING, LITHOGRAPHIC: Promotional

American Slide-Chart Co........................D...... 630 665-3333
  Carol Stream *(G-3102)*
Communication Technologies Inc..........E...... 630 384-0900
  Glendale Heights *(G-11017)*
Flyerinc Corporation..............................G...... 630 655-3400
  Oak Brook *(G-16515)*
Peterson Publication Services...............G...... 630 469-6732
  Glen Ellyn *(G-10987)*
Proforma Quality Business Svcs............G...... 847 356-1959
  Gurnee *(G-11492)*

### PRINTING, LITHOGRAPHIC: Publications

Midwest Suburban Publishing................A...... 708 633-6880
  Tinley Park *(G-20933)*

### PRINTING, LITHOGRAPHIC: Transfers, Decalcomania Or Dry

Howard Sportswear Graphics................E...... 847 695-8195
  Elgin *(G-9067)*

### PRINTING, LITHOGRAPHIC: Wrappers

Lithotype Company Inc..........................F...... 630 771-1920
  Bolingbrook *(G-2336)*

### PRINTING: Books

Morgen Transportation Inc.....................G...... 773 405-1250
  Chicago *(G-5805)*

### PRINTING: Books

Advance Instant Printing Co...................G...... 312 346-0986
  Chicago *(G-3760)*
Andover Junction Publications...............G...... 815 538-3060
  Mendota *(G-14716)*
Award/Visionps Inc................................G...... 331 318-7800
  Chicago *(G-4003)*
Bostic Publishing Company...................G...... 773 551-7065
  Chicago *(G-4149)*
Bronte Press..........................................G...... 815 932-5192
  Bourbonnais *(G-2390)*
Charles C Thomas Publisher..................F...... 217 789-8980
  Springfield *(G-20416)*
Cook Communications Ministries...........C...... 847 741-0800
  Elgin *(G-9004)*
Creasey Printing Services Inc................G...... 217 787-1055
  Springfield *(G-20425)*
Greek Art Printing & Pubg Co.................G...... 847 724-8860
  Glenview *(G-11133)*
Hopper Graphics Inc..............................G...... 708 489-0459
  Palos Heights *(G-17107)*
In-Print Graphics Inc.............................E...... 708 396-1010
  Oak Forest *(G-16584)*
Ink Spots Prtg & Meida Design...............G...... 708 754-1300
  Homewood *(G-12102)*
Interntnl Awkening Ministries................G...... 630 653-8616
  Wheaton *(G-21958)*
Johnson Press America Inc...................G...... 815 844-5161
  Pontiac *(G-17704)*
Kellogg Printing Co................................F...... 309 734-8388
  Mendota *(G-15016)*
Kjellberg Printing..................................F...... 630 653-2244
  Wheaton *(G-21960)*
KK Stevens Publishing Co.....................G...... 309 329-2151
  Astoria *(G-934)*
Lsc Communications Inc.......................D...... 773 272-9200
  Chicago *(G-5552)*

Lsc Communications Us LLC................B...... 844 572-5720
  Chicago *(G-5553)*
Marty Gannon........................................E...... 847 895-1059
  Schaumburg *(G-19632)*
Palmer Printing Inc................................E...... 312 427-7150
  Chicago *(G-6065)*
Pantagraph Printing and Sty Co.............F...... 309 829-1071
  Bloomington *(G-2208)*
Quad/Graphics Inc................................A...... 815 734-4121
  Mount Morris *(G-15297)*
R R Donnelley & Sons Company.............A...... 815 844-5181
  Pontiac *(G-17710)*
R R Donnelley & Sons Company.............A...... 815 584-2770
  Dwight *(G-8591)*
Rasmussen Press Inc.............................G......
  Bensenville *(G-1976)*
Roger Fritz & Associates Inc..................G...... 630 355-2614
  Naperville *(G-15744)*
United Graphics Llc...............................C...... 217 235-7161
  Mattoon *(G-14412)*
University of Chicago.............................G...... 773 702-7000
  Chicago *(G-6837)*
Vision Integrated Graphics....................C...... 708 570-7900
  Bolingbrook *(G-2380)*
Wold Printing Services Ltd....................G...... 847 546-3110
  Volo *(G-21320)*

### PRINTING: Checkbooks

Carousel Checks Inc..............................F...... 708 599-8576
  Bridgeview *(G-2474)*
Deluxe Corporation................................C...... 847 635-7200
  Des Plaines *(G-8181)*
Deluxe Express......................................G...... 847 756-0429
  Plainfield *(G-17590)*

### PRINTING: Commercial, NEC

A Corporate Printing Service.................F...... 630 515-0432
  Woodridge *(G-22447)*
Abbey Copying Support Svcs Inc...........G...... 618 466-3300
  Godfrey *(G-11221)*
Able Printing Service.............................G...... 708 788-7115
  Berwyn *(G-2054)*
ABS Graphics Inc...................................C...... 630 495-2400
  Itasca *(G-12223)*
Accord Carton Co..................................C...... 708 272-3050
  Alsip *(G-428)*
Accurate Printing Inc.............................G...... 708 824-0058
  Crestwood *(G-7473)*
Ace Printing Co......................................G...... 618 259-2711
  East Alton *(G-8598)*
Acj Partners LLC....................................G...... 630 745-1335
  Chicago *(G-3729)*
Active Graphics Inc................................E...... 708 656-8900
  Cicero *(G-7176)*
Ad Works Inc.........................................G...... 217 342-9688
  Effingham *(G-8821)*
Advance Instant Printing Co...................G...... 312 346-0986
  Chicago *(G-3760)*
Ajs Premier Printing Inc........................G...... 847 838-6350
  Antioch *(G-614)*
Allan Brooks & Associates Inc...............F...... 847 537-7500
  Lake Villa *(G-13010)*
Allegra Marketing Print Mail..................G...... 630 790-0444
  Schaumburg *(G-19430)*
Alliance Envelope & Print LLC...............G...... 847 446-4079
  Winnetka *(G-22301)*
Allied Graphics Inc................................G...... 847 419-8830
  Buffalo Grove *(G-2654)*
Allied Printing Inc..................................G...... 773 334-5200
  Chicago *(G-3817)*
Allprint Graphics Inc..............................G...... 847 519-9898
  Schaumburg *(G-19432)*
Alphabet Shop Inc.................................E...... 847 888-3150
  Elgin *(G-8946)*
Alta Vista Solutions Inc.........................F...... 312 473-3050
  Chicago *(G-3836)*
Altec Printing LLC..................................G...... 708 489-2484
  Crestwood *(G-7476)*
American Campaigns.............................G...... 773 261-6800
  Chicago *(G-3853)*
American Color Alticor...........................G...... 847 472-7500
  Elk Grove Village *(G-9295)*
American Graphics Network Inc............F...... 847 729-7220
  Glenview *(G-11100)*
American Litho Incorporated.................A...... 630 682-0600
  Carol Stream *(G-3099)*
Anns Printing & Copying Co...................G...... 618 656-6878
  Edwardsville *(G-8788)*
Apple Press Inc......................................G...... 815 224-1451
  Peru *(G-17500)*

Employee Codes: A=Over 500 employees, B=251-500
C=101-250, D=51-100, E=20-50, F=10-19, G=3-9

2017 Harris Illinois Industrial Directory

**Arcadia Press Inc** F 847 451-6390
Franklin Park *(G-10398)*
**Arch Printing** G 630 896-6610
North Aurora *(G-16118)*
**Arjay Instant Printing** G 847 438-9059
Mundelein *(G-15471)*
**Art-Flo Shirt & Lettering Co** E 708 656-5422
Chicago *(G-3953)*
**Artpol Printing Inc** G 773 622-0498
Chicago *(G-3958)*
**Aspen Printing Services LLC** G 630 357-3203
Naperville *(G-15601)*
**Associated Design Inc** F 708 974-9100
Palos Hills *(G-17114)*
**Award/Visionps Inc** G 331 318-7800
Chicago *(G-4003)*
**B & B Printing Company** G 217 285-6072
Pittsfield *(G-17561)*
**B Allan Graphics Inc** F 708 396-1704
Alsip *(G-438)*
**B F Shaw Printing Company** E 815 875-4461
Princeton *(G-17744)*
**Bagcraftpapercon I LLC** C 620 856-2800
Chicago *(G-4025)*
**Bally Foil Graphics Inc** G 847 427-1509
Elk Grove Village *(G-9333)*
**Barnaby Inc** F 815 895-6555
Sycamore *(G-20789)*
**Belmonte Printing Co** G 847 352-8841
Schaumburg *(G-19459)*
**Benzinger Printing** G 815 784-6560
Genoa *(G-10875)*
**Bikast Graphics Inc** G 847 487-8822
Wauconda *(G-21446)*
**Biller Press & Manufacturing** G 847 395-4111
Antioch *(G-623)*
**Blazing Color Inc** G 618 826-3001
Chester *(G-3651)*
**Bradley Industries Inc** E 815 469-2314
Frankfort *(G-10304)*
**Brads Printing Inc** G 847 662-0447
Waukegan *(G-21531)*
**Branstiter Printing Co** G 217 245-6533
Jacksonville *(G-12381)*
**Brooke Graphics LLC** E 847 593-1300
Elk Grove Village *(G-9346)*
**C F C Interantional** G 708 753-0679
Chicago Heights *(G-7085)*
**C2 Imaging LLC** E 312 238-3800
Chicago *(G-4206)*
**Campbell Publishing Inc** G 217 742-3313
Winchester *(G-22278)*
**Campus Sportswear Incorporated** F 217 344-0944
Champaign *(G-3460)*
**Cannon Ball Marketing Inc** G 630 971-2127
Lisle *(G-13573)*
**Card Prsnlzation Solutions LLC** E 630 543-2630
Glendale Heights *(G-11014)*
**Carlberg Design Inc** G 217 341-3291
Petersburg *(G-17534)*
**Carson Printing Inc** G 847 836-0900
East Dundee *(G-8629)*
**Castle-Printech Inc** G 815 758-5484
Dekalb *(G-8076)*
**Catalog Designers Inc** G 847 228-0025
Elk Grove Village *(G-9359)*
**Cavco Printers** G 618 988-8011
Energy *(G-9985)*
**CDs Office Systems Inc** F 217 351-5046
Champaign *(G-3464)*
**Century Printing** G 618 632-2486
O Fallon *(G-16465)*
**Cenveo Inc** G 217 243-4258
Jacksonville *(G-12383)*
**Challenge Printers** G 773 252-0212
Chicago *(G-4285)*
**Cherry Street Printing & Award** G 618 252-6814
Harrisburg *(G-11597)*
**Chicago Print Partners LLC** F 312 525-2015
Addison *(G-74)*
**Churchill Wilmslow Corporation** G 312 759-8911
Chicago *(G-4374)*
**Cifuentes Luis & Nicole Inc** G 847 490-3660
Schaumburg *(G-19472)*
**Cityblue Technologies LLC** F 309 676-6633
Peoria *(G-17343)*
**Clark Printing & Marketing** G 217 363-5300
Champaign *(G-3467)*
**Classique Signs & Engrv Inc** G 217 228-7446
Quincy *(G-17813)*
**Clyde Printing Company** F 773 847-5900
Chicago *(G-4410)*
**Color4** F 847 996-6880
Libertyville *(G-13316)*
**Colvin Printing** G 708 331-4580
Blue Island *(G-2243)*
**Com-Graphics Inc** D 312 226-0900
Chicago *(G-4434)*
**Cook Printing Co Inc** G 217 345-2514
Mattoon *(G-14387)*
**Corporate Business Card Ltd** E 847 455-5760
Franklin Park *(G-10442)*
**Corwin Printing** G 618 263-3936
Mount Carmel *(G-15263)*
**Cpg Printing & Graphics** G 309 820-1392
Bloomington *(G-2156)*
**Craftsmen Printing** G 217 283-9574
Hoopeston *(G-12108)*
**Creative Prtg & Smart Ideas** G 773 481-6522
Chicago *(G-4501)*
**Crest Greetings Inc** G 708 210-0800
Chicago *(G-4503)*
**Culture Studio LLC** E 312 243-8304
Chicago *(G-4515)*
**D G Brandt Inc** G 815 942-4064
Morris *(G-15105)*
**D G Printing Inc** E 847 397-7779
Schaumburg *(G-19498)*
**D L V Printing Service Inc** F 773 626-1661
Chicago *(G-4537)*
**Darwill Inc** C 708 449-7770
Hillside *(G-11914)*
**Deluxe Corporation** C 847 635-7200
Des Plaines *(G-8181)*
**Deluxe Printing** G 312 225-0061
Chicago *(G-4580)*
**Design Graphics Inc** G 815 462-3323
New Lenox *(G-15875)*
**Dg Digital Printing** G 815 961-0000
Rockford *(G-18340)*
**Diamond Web Printing LLC** F 630 663-0350
Downers Grove *(G-8428)*
**Diaz Printing** G 773 887-3366
Chicago *(G-4595)*
**Digital Hub LLC** E 312 943-6161
Chicago *(G-4602)*
**Digital Prtg & Total Graphics** G 630 627-7400
Lombard *(G-13792)*
**DMarv Design Specialty Prtrs** G 708 389-4420
Blue Island *(G-2246)*
**Domino Amjet Inc** E 847 662-3148
Gurnee *(G-11439)*
**Donnells Printing & Off Pdts** G 815 842-6541
Pontiac *(G-17698)*
**DOT Press LLC** G 312 421-0293
Chicago *(G-4635)*
**Drake Envelope Printing Co** G 217 374-2772
White Hall *(G-22184)*
**Dynagraphics Incorporated** E 217 876-9950
Decatur *(G-7878)*
**E & D Web Inc** C 815 562-5800
Rochelle *(G-18086)*
**E & H Graphic Service** G 708 748-5656
Matteson *(G-14371)*
**E&D Printing Services Inc** G 815 609-8222
Plainfield *(G-17593)*
**Eagle Express Mail LLC** G 618 377-6245
Bethalto *(G-2081)*
**East Central Communications Co** E 217 892-9613
Rantoul *(G-17926)*
**Edwards Creative Services LLC** F 309 756-0199
Milan *(G-14784)*
**Elite Die & Finishing Inc** G 708 389-4848
South Holland *(G-20265)*
**Elliott Publishing Inc** G 217 645-3033
Liberty *(G-13295)*
**Emsur USA LLC** E 847 274-9450
Elk Grove Village *(G-9456)*
**Envision Graphics LLC** D 630 825-1200
Bloomingdale *(G-2107)*
**Ethan Company Incorporated** G 815 715-2283
Shorewood *(G-19925)*
**Eugene Ewbank** G 630 705-0400
Oswego *(G-16917)*
**F & S Engraving Inc** E 847 870-8400
Mount Prospect *(G-15328)*
**Fast Print Shop** G 618 997-1976
Marion *(G-14259)*
**Fast Track Printing Inc** G 773 761-9400
Chicago *(G-4817)*
**Father & Daughters Printing** G 708 749-8286
Berwyn *(G-2064)*
**Fedex Ground Package Sys Inc** G 800 463-3339
Glendale Heights *(G-11023)*
**Fedex Office & Print Svcs Inc** G 630 759-5784
Bolingbrook *(G-2308)*
**Fedex Office & Print Svcs Inc** G 847 670-7283
Mount Prospect *(G-15329)*
**Fedex Office & Print Svcs Inc** E 217 355-3400
Champaign *(G-3485)*
**Fedex Office & Print Svcs Inc** E 309 685-4093
Peoria *(G-17359)*
**Fedex Office & Print Svcs Inc** E 708 452-0149
Elmwood Park *(G-9970)*
**Fedex Office & Print Svcs Inc** F 312 670-4460
Chicago *(G-4831)*
**Fgs Inc** F 312 421-3060
Chicago *(G-4839)*
**Fine Arts Engraving Co** G 800 688-4400
Chicago *(G-4845)*
**Fine Line Printing** G 773 582-9709
Chicago *(G-4846)*
**First Impression** G 815 883-3357
Oglesby *(G-16748)*
**First Impression of Chicago** G 773 224-3434
Chicago *(G-4849)*
**Fisheye Services Incorporated** G 773 942-6314
Chicago *(G-4852)*
**Fleetwood Press Inc** G 708 485-6811
Brookfield *(G-2632)*
**Floden Enterprises** G 847 566-7898
Mundelein *(G-15502)*
**Forrest Press Inc** G 847 381-1621
Barrington *(G-1280)*
**Fort Dearborn Company** C 773 774-4321
Niles *(G-15979)*
**Forte Print Corporation** G 773 391-0105
Chicago *(G-4875)*
**Fox Valley Printing Co Inc** G 419 232-3348
Montgomery *(G-15043)*
**Freeport Press Inc** G 815 232-1181
Freeport *(G-10658)*
**Frye-Williamson Press Inc** E 217 522-7744
Springfield *(G-20444)*
**G F Printing** G 618 797-0576
Granite City *(G-11278)*
**Galleon Industries Inc** G 708 478-5444
Joliet *(G-12499)*
**Genesis Print & Copy Svcs Inc** G 773 374-1020
Chicago *(G-4935)*
**Globe Ticket** G 847 258-1000
Carol Stream *(G-3160)*
**Goalgetters Inc** F 708 579-9800
La Grange *(G-12733)*
**Golden Prairie News** G 217 226-3721
Assumption *(G-931)*
**Good Impressions Inc** G 847 831-4317
Highland Park *(G-11836)*
**Grace Enterprises Inc** E 773 465-5300
Chicago *(G-4982)*
**Grace Enterprises Inc** G 773 465-5300
Chicago *(G-4983)*
**Grace Printing and Mailing** F 847 423-2100
Skokie *(G-20005)*
**Graphic Arts Services Inc** E 630 629-7770
Villa Park *(G-21256)*
**Graphic Press Inc** G 847 272-6000
Morton Grove *(G-15199)*
**Graphics Group LLC** D 708 867-5500
Chicago *(G-4992)*
**Griffin John** G 708 301-2316
Lockport *(G-13720)*
**H & H Printing** G 847 866-9520
Evanston *(G-10048)*
**Hafner Printing Co Inc** F 312 362-0120
Chicago *(G-5030)*
**Hal Mather & Sons Incorporated** E 815 338-4000
Woodstock *(G-22573)*
**Hastings Printing** G 217 253-5086
Tuscola *(G-21020)*
**Hawthorne Press** G 708 652-9000
Cicero *(G-7201)*
**Heart Printing Inc** G 847 259-2100
Arlington Heights *(G-764)*
**Helene Printing Inc** G 630 482-3300
Bensenville *(G-1915)*
**Hermitage Group Inc** E 773 561-3773
Chicago *(G-5080)*
**Hillsboro Journal Inc** E 217 532-3933
Hillsboro *(G-11895)*

**Hopper Graphics Inc** ... G ... 708 489-0459
Palos Heights *(G-17107)*

**Howard Press Printing Inc** ... G ... 708 345-7437
Northlake *(G-16439)*

**Hub Printing Company Inc** ... F ... 815 562-7057
Rochelle *(G-18094)*

**Iemco Corporation** ... G ... 773 728-4400
Chicago *(G-5145)*

**Illini/Altco Inc** ... D ... 847 549-0321
Vernon Hills *(G-21173)*

**Illinois Office Sup Elect Prtg** ... E ... 815 434-0186
Ottawa *(G-16962)*

**Illinois Printing Services Inc** ... G ... 217 728-2786
Sullivan *(G-20749)*

**Illinois Tag Co** ... E ... 773 626-0542
Carol Stream *(G-3169)*

**Impress Printing** ... G ... 630 933-8966
Wheaton *(G-21956)*

**Impress Printing & Design Inc** ... G ... 815 730-9440
Joliet *(G-12514)*

**Impressive Impressions** ... G ... 312 432-0501
Chicago *(G-5170)*

**Impro International Inc** ... G ... 847 398-3870
Arlington Heights *(G-776)*

**Imtran Industries Inc** ... D ... 630 752-4000
Carol Stream *(G-3172)*

**In Color Graphics Coml Prtg** ... F ... 847 697-0003
Elgin *(G-9075)*

**Ink Spots Prtg Mdia Design Inc** ... G ... 708 754-1300
Glenwood *(G-11216)*

**Integra Graphics and Forms Inc** ... F ... 708 385-0950
Crestwood *(G-7490)*

**J F Wagner Printing Co** ... G ... 847 564-0017
Northbrook *(G-16280)*

**J J Collins Sons Inc** ... E ... 309 664-5404
Bloomington *(G-2184)*

**Jbl Marketing Inc** ... G ... 847 266-1080
Highland Park *(G-11847)*

**Jem Associates Ltd** ... G ... 847 808-8377
Chicago *(G-5289)*

**JLJ Corp** ... G ... 847 726-9795
Lake Zurich *(G-13092)*

**Joes Printing** ... G ... 773 545-6063
Chicago *(G-5309)*

**Johnson Printing** ... G ... 630 595-8815
Bensenville *(G-1930)*

**Jph Enterprises Inc** ... G ... 847 390-0900
Des Plaines *(G-8217)*

**K & S Printing Services** ... G ... 815 899-2923
Sycamore *(G-20804)*

**Kara Graphics Inc** ... G ... 630 964-8122
Woodridge *(G-22500)*

**Kellogg Printing Co** ... F ... 309 734-8388
Monmouth *(G-15016)*

**Kelly Printing Co Inc** ... E ... 217 443-1792
Danville *(G-7741)*

**Kens Quick Print Inc** ... F ... 847 831-4410
Highland Park *(G-11849)*

**Kestler Digital Printing Inc** ... F ... 773 581-5918
Chicago *(G-5379)*

**Kevin Kewney** ... G ... 217 228-7444
Quincy *(G-17844)*

**Kevron Printing & Design Inc** ... G ... 708 229-7725
Hickory Hills *(G-11772)*

**Klh Printing Corp** ... G ... 847 459-0115
Wheeling *(G-22086)*

**Knight Prtg & Litho Svc Ltd** ... G ... 847 487-7700
Island Lake *(G-12217)*

**Korea Times** ... D ... 847 626-0388
Glenview *(G-11157)*

**Kwik Print Inc** ... G ... 630 773-3225
Itasca *(G-12299)*

**Label Printers LP** ... D ... 630 897-6970
Aurora *(G-1181)*

**Label Tek Inc** ... F ... 630 820-8499
Aurora *(G-1044)*

**Landmarx Screen Printing** ... F ... 217 223-4601
Quincy *(G-17853)*

**Laninver USA Inc** ... G ... 847 367-8787
Elk Grove Village *(G-9583)*

**Last Minute Prtg & Copy Ctr** ... G ... 888 788-2965
Tinley Park *(G-20929)*

**Lee-Wel Printing Corporation** ... G ... 630 682-0935
Wheaton *(G-21966)*

**Legacy Prints** ... G ... 815 946-9112
Polo *(G-17688)*

**Legend Promotions** ... G ... 847 438-3528
Lake Zurich *(G-13095)*

**Leonard Publishing Co** ... F ... 773 486-2737
Norridge *(G-16104)*

**Liberty Group Publishing** ... G ... 309 937-3303
Cambridge *(G-2968)*

**Lighthouse Marketing Services** ... G ... 630 482-9900
Batavia *(G-1464)*

**Lighthouse Printing Inc** ... G ... 708 479-7776
New Lenox *(G-15891)*

**Lincoln Square Printing** ... G ... 773 334-9030
Chicago *(G-5508)*

**Lincolnshire Printing Inc** ... G ... 815 578-0740
McHenry *(G-14523)*

**Lithuanian Catholic Press** ... E ... 773 585-9500
Chicago *(G-5519)*

**Lloyd Midwest Graphics** ... G ... 815 282-8828
Machesney Park *(G-14089)*

**M & G Graphics Inc** ... E ... 773 247-1596
Chicago *(G-5576)*

**M L S Printing Co Inc** ... G ... 847 948-8902
Deerfield *(G-8033)*

**Mac Graphics Group Inc** ... G ... 630 620-7200
Oakbrook Terrace *(G-16716)*

**Macoupin County Enquirer Inc** ... E ... 217 854-2534
Carlinville *(G-3042)*

**Madmaxmar Group Inc** ... E ... 630 320-3700
Itasca *(G-12308)*

**Maro Carton Inc** ... G ... 708 649-9982
Bellwood *(G-1714)*

**Mason City Banner Times** ... F ... 217 482-3276
Mason City *(G-14365)*

**Master Print** ... G ... 708 499-4037
Oak Lawn *(G-16633)*

**Matrix Press** ... G ... 847 885-7076
Schaumburg *(G-19637)*

**Mattoon Printing Center** ... G ... 217 234-3100
Mattoon *(G-14400)*

**Mbh Promotions Inc** ... G ... 847 634-2411
Buffalo Grove *(G-2733)*

**McKillip Industries Inc** ... E ... 815 439-1050
Yorkville *(G-22664)*

**Meridian** ... E ... 815 885-4646
Loves Park *(G-13964)*

**Merrill Corporation** ... C ... 312 263-3524
Chicago *(G-5695)*

**Merrill Corporation** ... C ... 312 386-2200
Chicago *(G-5696)*

**Mexacali Silkscreen Inc** ... G ... 630 628-9313
Addison *(G-203)*

**Mi-Te Fast Printers Inc** ... G ... 312 236-3278
Glencoe *(G-11002)*

**Mid City Printing Service** ... G ... 773 777-5400
Chicago *(G-5725)*

**Midwest Labels & Decals Inc** ... G ... 630 543-7556
Addison *(G-213)*

**Midwest Law Printing Co Inc** ... G ... 312 431-0185
Chicago *(G-5745)*

**Miller Products Inc** ... E ... 708 534-5111
University Park *(G-21058)*

**Minuteman Press** ... G ... 630 541-9122
Countryside *(G-7437)*

**Minuteman Press** ... G ... 630 584-7383
Saint Charles *(G-19223)*

**Minuteman Press Inc** ... G ... 847 577-2411
Arlington Heights *(G-803)*

**MJM Graphics** ... G ... 847 234-1802
Lake Forest *(G-12927)*

**Modern Methods Creative Inc** ... G ... 309 263-4100
Peoria *(G-17410)*

**Modern Methods LLC** ... G ... 309 263-4100
Morton *(G-15165)*

**Moss Inc** ... G ... 800 341-1557
Elk Grove Village *(G-9637)*

**MPS Chicago Inc** ... E ... 630 932-5583
Bolingbrook *(G-2347)*

**Multi Art Press** ... G ... 773 775-0515
Chicago *(G-5831)*

**Multi Packaging Solutions Inc** ... G ... 773 283-9500
Chicago *(G-5832)*

**National Data Svcs Chicago Inc** ... C ... 630 597-9100
Carol Stream *(G-3204)*

**Nbs Systems Inc** ... E ... 217 999-3472
Mount Olive *(G-15306)*

**Newport Printing Services Inc** ... G ... 847 632-1000
Schaumburg *(G-19664)*

**Next Generation** ... F ... 630 261-1477
Lombard *(G-13833)*

**Nissha Usa Inc** ... E ... 847 413-2665
Schaumburg *(G-19666)*

**Northwest Premier Printing** ... G ... 773 736-1882
Chicago *(G-5940)*

**Northwestern Illinois Farmer** ... G ... 815 369-2811
Lena *(G-13282)*

**Norway Press Inc** ... G ... 773 846-9422
Chicago *(G-5944)*

**Nosco Inc** ... D ... 847 336-4200
Gurnee *(G-11476)*

**Nu-Art Printing** ... G ... 618 533-9971
Centralia *(G-3425)*

**Oec Graphics-Chicago LLC** ... E ... 630 455-6700
Willowbrook *(G-22227)*

**Offworld Designs** ... G ... 815 786-7080
Sandwich *(G-19372)*

**On Time Envelopes & Printing** ... G ... 630 682-0466
Carol Stream *(G-3209)*

**Ottawa Publishing Co Inc** ... F ... 815 434-3330
Ottawa *(G-16976)*

**P H C Enterprises Inc** ... G ... 847 816-7373
Vernon Hills *(G-21186)*

**Pamco Printed Tape Label Inc** ... C ... 847 803-2200
Des Plaines *(G-8249)*

**Pana News Inc** ... F ... 217 562-2111
Pana *(G-17137)*

**Pantagraph Printing and Sty Co** ... F ... 309 829-1071
Bloomington *(G-2208)*

**Patrick Impressions LLC** ... G ... 630 257-9336
Lemont *(G-13250)*

**Pcbl Retail Holdings LLC** ... G ... 610 761-4838
Northbrook *(G-16331)*

**Perryco Inc** ... F ... 815 436-2431
Plainfield *(G-17638)*

**PHI Group Inc** ... C ... 847 824-5610
Mount Prospect *(G-15364)*

**Pinney Printing Company** ... E ... 815 626-2727
Sterling *(G-20604)*

**Pioneer Printing Service Inc** ... G ... 312 337-4283
Chicago *(G-6127)*

**Pontiac Engraving** ... G ... 630 834-4424
Bensenville *(G-1965)*

**Precision Screen Specialties** ... G ... 630 762-9548
Saint Charles *(G-19241)*

**Premier Printing & Promotions** ... F ... 815 282-3890
Machesney Park *(G-14100)*

**Premier Printing and Packaging** ... G ... 847 970-9434
Rolling Meadows *(G-18769)*

**Premier Printing Illinois Inc** ... D ... 217 359-2219
Champaign *(G-3529)*

**Print & Design Services LLC** ... G ... 847 317-9001
Bannockburn *(G-1264)*

**Print Graphics** ... G ... 847 249-1007
Beach Park *(G-1519)*

**Print Management Partners Inc** ... E ... 847 699-2999
Des Plaines *(G-8265)*

**Print Shop of Morris** ... G ... 815 710-5030
Morris *(G-15126)*

**Print Tech Inc** ... F ... 847 949-5400
Mundelein *(G-15549)*

**Printer Connection** ... G ... 217 268-3252
Arcola *(G-682)*

**Printforce Inc** ... G ... 618 395-7746
Olney *(G-16793)*

**Printing Craftsmen of Joliet** ... G ... 815 254-3982
Joliet *(G-12555)*

**Printing In Remebrance Inc** ... F ... 773 874-8700
Chicago *(G-6195)*

**Printing Press of Joliet Inc** ... G ... 815 725-0018
Joliet *(G-12556)*

**Printing System** ... G ... 630 339-5900
Glendale Heights *(G-11060)*

**Printing Works Inc** ... G ... 847 860-1920
Elk Grove Village *(G-9698)*

**Printing You Can Trust** ... G ... 224 676-0482
Deerfield *(G-8050)*

**Printlink Enterprises Inc** ... G ... 847 753-9800
Northbrook *(G-16345)*

**Printmeisters Inc** ... G ... 708 474-8400
Lansing *(G-13180)*

**Printsource Plus Inc** ... G ... 708 389-6252
Blue Island *(G-2265)*

**Printwise Inc** ... G ... 630 833-2845
Wheaton *(G-21972)*

**Printworld** ... G ... 815 544-1000
Belvidere *(G-1781)*

**Priority Print** ... G ... 708 485-7080
Brookfield *(G-2641)*

**Progrssive Imprssions Intl Inc** ... C ... 309 664-0444
Bloomington *(G-2216)*

**Pryde Graphics Plus** ... G ... 630 882-5103
Plano *(G-17675)*

**Publishers Graphics LLC** ... E ... 630 221-1850
Carol Stream *(G-3223)*

**Qg LLC** ... D ... 217 347-7721
Effingham *(G-8855)*

Quad/Graphics Inc ....... A ....... 815 734-4121
Mount Morris (G-15297)
Quality Blue & Offset Printing ....... G ....... 630 759-8035
Bolingbrook (G-2363)
Quality Logo Products Inc ....... E ....... 630 896-1627
Aurora (G-1207)
Quickprinters ....... G ....... 309 833-5250
Macomb (G-14130)
R R Donnelley & Sons Company ....... B ....... 312 326-8000
Chicago (G-6270)
R R Donnelley & Sons Company ....... A ....... 815 584-2770
Dwight (G-8591)
R W Wilson Printing Company ....... G ....... 630 584-4100
Saint Charles (G-19249)
Rapid Circular Press Inc ....... F ....... 312 421-5611
Chicago (G-6290)
Reel Life Dvd LLC ....... G ....... 708 579-1360
Western Springs (G-21872)
Remke Printing Inc ....... G ....... 847 520-7300
Wheeling (G-22137)
Review Printing Co Inc ....... G ....... 309 788-7094
Rock Island (G-18199)
Rightway Printing Inc ....... F ....... 630 790-0444
Glendale Heights (G-11064)
Ripa LLC ....... G ....... 708 938-1600
Broadview (G-2609)
Robal Company Inc ....... F ....... 630 393-0777
Warrenville (G-21361)
Rodin Enterprises Inc ....... G ....... 847 412-1370
Wheeling (G-22142)
Rose Business Forms & Printing ....... G ....... 618 533-3032
Centralia (G-3429)
Roseri Business Forms Inc ....... G ....... 847 381-8012
Inverness (G-12211)
Roshan Ag Inc ....... G ....... 773 267-1635
Chicago (G-6397)
Rowboat Creative LLC ....... F ....... 773 675-2628
Chicago (G-6400)
RR Donnelley & Sons Company ....... E ....... 847 622-1026
Elgin (G-9169)
RR Donnelley & Sons Company ....... C ....... 312 236-8000
Chicago (G-6404)
RR Donnelley Logistics SE ....... G ....... 630 672-2500
Roselle (G-18970)
Rt Associates Inc ....... D ....... 847 577-0700
Wheeling (G-22143)
Ruco USA Inc ....... E ....... 866 373-7912
Wood Dale (G-22417)
Russell Doot Inc ....... G ....... 312 527-1437
Chicago (G-6415)
Rusty & Angela Buzzard ....... G ....... 217 342-9841
Effingham (G-8857)
Salzman Printing ....... G ....... 309 745-3016
Washington (G-21391)
Samecwei Inc ....... G ....... 630 897-7888
Aurora (G-1214)
Sauk Valley Printing ....... G ....... 815 284-2222
Dixon (G-8347)
Schellhorn Photo Techniques ....... F ....... 773 267-5141
Chicago (G-6451)
Scribes Inc ....... G ....... 630 654-3800
Burr Ridge (G-2879)
Selnar Inc ....... G ....... 309 699-3977
East Peoria (G-8733)
Sentro Printing Equip N Movers ....... G ....... 779 423-0255
Rockton (G-18702)
Shanin Company ....... D ....... 847 676-1200
Lincolnwood (G-13537)
Shawver Press Inc ....... G ....... 815 772-4700
Morrison (G-15148)
Sheer Graphics Inc ....... G ....... 630 654-4422
Westmont (G-21920)
Shree Mahavir Inc ....... G ....... 312 408-1080
Chicago (G-6501)
Sigley Printing & Off Sup Co ....... G ....... 618 997-5304
Marion (G-14287)
Sir Cooper Inc ....... G ....... 630 279-0162
Villa Park (G-21285)
Skyline Printing Sales ....... G ....... 847 412-1931
Northbrook (G-16363)
Snegde Deep ....... G ....... 630 351-7111
Roselle (G-18978)
Southwest Printing Co ....... G ....... 708 389-0800
Alsip (G-530)
Spectrum Media Inc ....... G ....... 217 234-2044
Mattoon (G-14409)
Speedpro Imaging ....... G ....... 847 856-8220
Gurnee (G-11506)
Squeegee Brothers Inc ....... F ....... 630 510-9152
Carol Stream (G-3244)
Ssn LLC ....... G ....... 815 978-8729
Byron (G-2922)
Standard Register Inc ....... E ....... 847 783-1040
Elgin (G-9191)
Star-Times Publishing Co Inc ....... G ....... 618 635-2000
Staunton (G-20559)
Stellar Recognition Inc ....... D ....... 773 282-8060
Chicago (G-6588)
Studio Color Inc ....... F ....... 630 766-3333
Bensenville (G-1999)
Sunny Direct LLC ....... G ....... 630 795-0800
Woodridge (G-22519)
Sunrise Hitek Service Inc ....... E ....... 773 792-8880
Chicago (G-6630)
Swifty Print ....... G ....... 630 584-9063
Saint Charles (G-19276)
Tailored Printing Inc ....... G ....... 217 522-6287
Rochester (G-18122)
Team Cncept Prtg Thrmgrphy Inc ....... E ....... 630 653-8326
Carol Stream (G-3252)
Team Impressions Inc ....... E ....... 847 357-9270
Elk Grove Village (G-9769)
Technicraft Supply Co ....... G ....... 309 495-5245
Peoria (G-17468)
Techprint Inc ....... F ....... 847 616-0109
Elk Grove Village (G-9774)
Teds Shirt Shack Inc ....... G ....... 217 224-9705
Quincy (G-17892)
Temper Enterprises Inc ....... G ....... 815 553-0374
Crest Hill (G-7469)
Thermo-Craft Inc ....... G ....... 618 281-7055
Columbia (G-7363)
Thomas Publishing Printing Div ....... G ....... 618 351-6655
Carbondale (G-3025)
Thomas Tees Inc ....... G ....... 217 488-2288
New Berlin (G-15866)
Tidd Printing Co ....... G ....... 708 749-1200
Berwyn (G-2076)
Times Republic ....... E ....... 815 432-5227
Watseka (G-21431)
Toledo Democrat ....... G ....... 217 849-2000
Toledo (G-20967)
Tree Towns Reprographics Inc ....... E ....... 630 832-0209
Elmhurst (G-9951)
Tri-Tower Printing Inc ....... G ....... 847 640-6633
Rolling Meadows (G-18785)
Type Concepts Inc ....... G ....... 708 361-1005
Palos Heights (G-17112)
Unique Assembly & Decorating ....... E ....... 630 241-4300
Downers Grove (G-8535)
Unique Envelope Corporation ....... E ....... 773 586-0330
Chicago (G-6819)
United Printers Inc ....... G ....... 773 376-1955
Chicago (G-6825)
Universal Digital Printing ....... G ....... 708 389-0133
Midlothian (G-14771)
UPS Authorized Retailer ....... G ....... 708 354-8772
La Grange (G-12748)
Valee Inc ....... G ....... 847 364-6464
Elk Grove Village (G-9804)
Valid Secure Solutions LLC ....... F ....... 260 633-0728
Lisle (G-13674)
Van Lancker Steven ....... G ....... 309 764-2221
Moline (G-14975)
Village Press Inc ....... G ....... 847 362-1856
Libertyville (G-13399)
Vision Integrated Graphics ....... C ....... 708 570-7900
Bolingbrook (G-2380)
Vr Printing Co Inc ....... G ....... 630 980-2315
Glendale Heights (G-11090)
Weakley Enterprises Inc ....... G ....... 815 498-3429
Somonauk (G-20130)
Weiskamp Screen Printing ....... G ....... 217 398-8428
Champaign (G-3560)
Wes Tech Printing Graphic ....... G ....... 630 520-9041
West Chicago (G-21792)
White Graphics Inc ....... F ....... 630 791-0232
Downers Grove (G-8544)
White Graphics Printing Svcs ....... G ....... 630 629-9300
Downers Grove (G-8545)
Wide Image Incorporated ....... G ....... 773 279-9183
Schaumburg (G-19789)
William Holloway Ltd ....... G ....... 847 866-9520
Evanston (G-10106)
Williamsburg Press Inc ....... G ....... 630 229-0228
North Aurora (G-16150)
Wold Printing Services Ltd ....... G ....... 847 546-3110
Volo (G-21320)
Wolters Kluwer US Inc ....... E ....... 847 580-5000
Riverwoods (G-18046)
Wood River Printing & Pubg Co ....... F ....... 618 254-3134
Wood River (G-22446)
Workplace Ink Inc ....... G ....... 312 939-0296
Park Ridge (G-17229)
Wortman Printing Company Inc ....... G ....... 217 347-3775
Effingham (G-8864)
Yes Print Management Inc ....... G ....... 312 226-4444
Chicago (G-7049)
Your Images Group Inc ....... G ....... 847 437-6688
Schaumburg (G-19794)
Z Print Inc ....... G ....... 773 685-4878
Chicago (G-7057)
Zell Co ....... G ....... 312 226-9191
Chicago (G-7062)

## PRINTING: Flexographic

Bellen Container Corporation ....... E ....... 847 741-5600
Elgin (G-8964)
Condor Labels Inc ....... G ....... 708 429-0707
Tinley Park (G-20902)
Custom Graphics Inc ....... E ....... 309 633-0850
Bartonville (G-1393)
F C D Inc ....... E ....... 847 498-3711
Northbrook (G-16255)
Flexografix Inc ....... F ....... 630 350-0100
Carol Stream (G-3152)
General Packaging Products Inc ....... D ....... 312 226-5611
Chicago (G-4929)
ID Label Inc ....... E ....... 847 265-1200
Lake Villa (G-13016)
Identi-Graphics Inc ....... G ....... 630 801-4845
Montgomery (G-15049)
Labels Unlimited Incorporated ....... E ....... 773 523-7500
Chicago (G-5430)
Master Tape Printers Inc ....... E ....... 773 283-8273
Chicago (G-5645)
Packaging Prtg Specialists Inc ....... F ....... 630 513-8060
Saint Charles (G-19232)
Prime Label & Packaging LLC ....... D ....... 630 227-1300
Wood Dale (G-22414)
Quality Bags Inc ....... F ....... 630 543-9800
Addison (G-263)
R Popernik Co Inc ....... F ....... 773 434-4300
Chicago (G-6269)
Var Graphics ....... G ....... 708 456-2028
Elmwood Park (G-9975)
Voris Communication Co Inc ....... D ....... 630 231-2425
West Chicago (G-21791)
Walter Barr Inc ....... G ....... 630 325-7265
Willowbrook (G-22238)

## PRINTING: Gravure, Business Form & Card

Proforma-Ppg Inc ....... G ....... 847 429-9349
Elgin (G-9149)
Tst/Impreso Inc ....... G ....... 630 775-9555
Addison (G-330)

## PRINTING: Gravure, Calendar & Card, Exc Business

A Cut Above Engraving Inc ....... G ....... 708 671-9800
Palos Park (G-17126)

## PRINTING: Gravure, Cards, Exc Greeting

Gc Packaging LLC ....... D ....... 630 758-4100
Elmhurst (G-9874)

## PRINTING: Gravure, Cards, Playing

Zipwhaa Inc ....... G ....... 630 898-4330
Palatine (G-17092)

## PRINTING: Gravure, Circulars

Kl Watch Service Inc ....... G ....... 847 368-8780
Mount Prospect (G-15342)

## PRINTING: Gravure, Envelopes

Larsen Envelope Co Inc ....... E ....... 847 952-9020
Elk Grove Village (G-9584)
Unique Envelope Corporation ....... E ....... 773 586-0330
Chicago (G-6819)

## PRINTING: Gravure, Fashion Plates

Ted Holum & Associates Inc ....... G ....... 630 543-9355
Addison (G-309)

# PRODUCT SECTION — PRINTING: Lithographic

### PRINTING: Gravure, Job
- Donnells Printing & Off Pdts .......... G ....... 815 842-6541
  Pontiac *(G-17698)*
- United Engravers Inc .......... E ....... 847 301-3740
  Schaumburg *(G-19780)*

### PRINTING: Gravure, Labels
- American Labelmark Company .......... C ....... 773 478-0900
  Chicago *(G-3859)*
- Arcadia Press Inc .......... F ....... 847 451-6390
  Franklin Park *(G-10398)*
- Field Holdings LLC .......... G ....... 847 509-2250
  Northbrook *(G-16257)*
- Label Tek Inc .......... F ....... 630 820-8499
  Aurora *(G-1044)*
- Pioneer Labels Inc .......... C ....... 618 546-5418
  Robinson *(G-18068)*

### PRINTING: Gravure, Magazines, No Publishing On-Site
- Cook Communications Minis .......... D ....... 847 741-5168
  Elgin *(G-9003)*

### PRINTING: Gravure, Music, Sheet, No Publishing On-Site
- Rogers Loose Leaf Co .......... F ....... 312 226-1947
  Chicago *(G-6381)*

### PRINTING: Gravure, Post Cards, Picture
- Pingotopia Inc .......... F ....... 847 503-9333
  Northbrook *(G-16338)*

### PRINTING: Gravure, Rotogravure
- C2 Imaging LLC .......... G ....... 312 238-3800
  Chicago *(G-4206)*
- Graphic Industries Inc .......... E ....... 847 357-9870
  South Elgin *(G-20201)*
- Illinois Tool Works Inc .......... D ....... 630 752-4000
  Carol Stream *(G-3170)*
- Integrated Media Inc .......... F ....... 217 854-6260
  Carlinville *(G-3040)*
- International Graphics & Assoc .......... F ....... 630 584-2248
  Saint Charles *(G-19199)*
- Qg LLC .......... D ....... 217 347-7721
  Effingham *(G-8855)*
- Quad/Graphics Inc .......... A ....... 815 734-4121
  Mount Morris *(G-15297)*
- R R Donnelley & Sons Company .......... B ....... 312 326-8000
  Chicago *(G-6270)*
- RR Donnelley & Sons Company .......... E ....... 217 258-2675
  Mattoon *(G-14407)*
- RR Donnelley & Sons Company .......... E ....... 847 622-1026
  Elgin *(G-9169)*
- RR Donnelley & Sons Company .......... C ....... 312 236-8000
  Chicago *(G-6404)*
- RR Donnelley & Sons Company .......... B ....... 630 588-5000
  Lisle *(G-13653)*
- RR Donnelley Printing Co LP .......... A ....... 217 235-0561
  Mattoon *(G-14408)*
- Rrd Netherlands LLC .......... F ....... 312 326-8000
  Chicago *(G-6406)*
- Standard Register Inc .......... F ....... 630 467-8300
  Itasca *(G-12359)*
- White Graphics Printing Svcs .......... G ....... 630 629-9300
  Downers Grove *(G-8545)*
- Xpress Printing & Copying Co .......... G ....... 630 980-9600
  Roselle *(G-18987)*

### PRINTING: Gravure, Visiting Cards
- Chicago Producers Inc .......... F ....... 312 226-6900
  Forest Park *(G-10237)*

### PRINTING: Laser
- AlphaGraphics .......... F ....... 630 261-1227
  Oakbrook Terrace *(G-16694)*
- Document Publishing Group .......... E ....... 847 783-0670
  Elgin *(G-9011)*
- Ink Spots Prtg & Meida Design .......... G ....... 708 754-1300
  Homewood *(G-12102)*
- Microdynamics Corporation .......... C ....... 630 276-0527
  Naperville *(G-15697)*
- Sebis Direct Inc .......... E ....... 312 243-9300
  Bedford Park *(G-1584)*
- Tst/Impreso Inc .......... G ....... 630 775-9555
  Addison *(G-330)*

### PRINTING: Letterpress
- Acres of Sky Communications .......... G ....... 815 493-2560
  Lanark *(G-13149)*
- Art-Craft Printers .......... G ....... 847 455-2201
  Franklin Park *(G-10401)*
- Bond Brothers & Co .......... F ....... 708 442-5510
  Lyons *(G-14032)*
- C E Dienberg Printing Company .......... G ....... 708 848-4406
  Oak Park *(G-16655)*
- Carter Printing Co Inc .......... G ....... 217 227-4464
  Farmersville *(G-10183)*
- Color Tone Printing .......... G ....... 708 385-1442
  Blue Island *(G-2242)*
- Crossmark Printing Inc .......... G ....... 708 754-4000
  Chicago Heights *(G-7094)*
- D & R Press .......... G ....... 708 452-0500
  Elmwood Park *(G-9966)*
- Dale K Brown .......... G ....... 815 338-0222
  Woodstock *(G-22558)*
- Dans Printing & Off Sups Inc .......... F ....... 708 687-3055
  Oak Forest *(G-16577)*
- Duo Graphics .......... G ....... 847 228-7080
  Elk Grove Village *(G-9436)*
- East Moline Herald Print Inc .......... G ....... 309 755-5224
  East Moline *(G-8678)*
- Evanston Graphic Imaging Inc .......... G ....... 847 869-7446
  Evanston *(G-10033)*
- F Weber Printing Co Inc .......... G ....... 815 468-6152
  Manteno *(G-14183)*
- Falcon Press Inc .......... G ....... 815 455-9099
  Crystal Lake *(G-7575)*
- Faulstich Printing Company Inc .......... G ....... 217 442-4994
  Danville *(G-7718)*
- FM Graphic Impressions Inc .......... E ....... 630 897-8788
  Aurora *(G-1153)*
- Freeburg Printing & Publishing .......... G ....... 618 539-3320
  Freeburg *(G-10635)*
- Gallas Label & Decal .......... F ....... 773 775-1000
  Chicago *(G-4909)*
- George Press Inc .......... G ....... 217 324-2242
  Litchfield *(G-13687)*
- Granja & Sons Printing .......... F ....... 773 762-3840
  Chicago *(G-4987)*
- Greek Art Printing & Pubg Co .......... G ....... 847 724-8860
  Glenview *(G-11133)*
- Harry Otto Printing Company .......... G ....... 630 365-6111
  Elburn *(G-8889)*
- Highland Journal Printing Inc .......... G ....... 618 654-4131
  Highland *(G-11787)*
- Ideal Advertising & Printing .......... F ....... 815 965-1713
  Rockford *(G-18426)*
- Impression Printing .......... F ....... 708 614-8660
  Oak Forest *(G-16583)*
- J S Printing Inc .......... G ....... 847 678-6300
  Franklin Park *(G-10503)*
- Keneal Industries Inc .......... G ....... 815 886-1300
  Romeoville *(G-18834)*
- Kjellberg Printing .......... F ....... 630 653-2244
  Wheaton *(G-21960)*
- Kon Printing Inc .......... G ....... 630 879-2211
  Batavia *(G-1461)*
- Lasons Label Co .......... G ....... 773 775-2606
  Chicago *(G-5464)*
- Lazare Printing Co Inc .......... G ....... 773 871-2500
  Chicago *(G-5475)*
- Little Doloras .......... G ....... 708 331-1330
  South Holland *(G-20286)*
- M S A Printing Co .......... G ....... 847 593-5699
  Elk Grove Village *(G-9604)*
- McCracken Label Co .......... G ....... 773 581-8860
  Chicago *(G-5666)*
- Modern Printing of Quincy .......... F ....... 217 223-1063
  Quincy *(G-17861)*
- Murray Printing Service Inc .......... G ....... 847 310-8959
  Schaumburg *(G-19658)*
- Olde Print Shoppe Inc .......... G ....... 618 395-3833
  Olney *(G-16786)*
- Overt Press Inc .......... E ....... 773 284-0909
  Chicago *(G-6029)*
- Panda Graphics Inc .......... G ....... 312 666-7642
  Chicago *(G-6068)*
- Paul D Burton .......... G ....... 309 467-2613
  Eureka *(G-10000)*
- Peacock Printing Inc .......... G ....... 618 242-3157
  Mount Vernon *(G-15437)*
- Petersburg Observer Co Inc .......... G ....... 217 632-2236
  Petersburg *(G-17537)*
- Physicians Record Co Inc .......... D ....... 800 323-9268
  Berwyn *(G-2074)*
- Preferred Printing Service .......... G ....... 312 421-2343
  Chicago *(G-6175)*
- Printing Craftsmen of Pontiac .......... G ....... 815 844-7118
  Pontiac *(G-17709)*
- Progress Printing Corporation .......... E ....... 773 927-0123
  Chicago *(G-6210)*
- R N R Photographers Inc .......... G ....... 708 453-1868
  River Grove *(G-18013)*
- Richco Graphics Inc .......... G ....... 847 367-7277
  Northbrook *(G-16356)*
- Rohner Letterpress Inc .......... F ....... 773 248-0800
  Chicago *(G-6383)*
- RR Donnelley & Sons Company .......... B ....... 630 588-5000
  Lisle *(G-13653)*
- S V C Printing Co .......... G ....... 773 286-2219
  Chicago *(G-6422)*
- Stromberg Allen and Company .......... E ....... 773 847-7131
  Tinley Park *(G-20947)*
- Tampico Press .......... G ....... 312 243-5448
  Chicago *(G-6672)*
- Thomas Printing & Sty Co .......... G ....... 618 435-2801
  Benton *(G-2041)*
- Three Castle Press Inc .......... G ....... 630 540-0120
  Streamwood *(G-20676)*
- Washington Courier .......... F ....... 309 444-3139
  Washington *(G-21394)*
- Weakley Printing & Sign Shop .......... G ....... 847 473-4466
  North Chicago *(G-16189)*
- Weber Press Inc .......... G ....... 773 561-9815
  Chicago *(G-6949)*

### PRINTING: Lithographic
- 360 Digital Print Inc .......... G ....... 630 682-3601
  Carol Stream *(G-3086)*
- A & B Printing Service Inc .......... G ....... 217 789-9034
  Springfield *(G-20383)*
- A & J Printers Inc .......... G ....... 847 909-9609
  Elk Grove Village *(G-9249)*
- A+ Printing Co .......... G ....... 815 968-8181
  Rockford *(G-18242)*
- A-Reliable Printing .......... G ....... 630 790-2525
  Glen Ellyn *(G-10956)*
- ABS Graphics Inc .......... C ....... 630 495-2400
  Itasca *(G-12223)*
- Accurate Business Controls Inc .......... G ....... 815 633-5500
  Machesney Park *(G-14051)*
- Ace Graphics Inc .......... E ....... 630 357-2244
  Naperville *(G-15589)*
- Ad Works Inc .......... G ....... 217 342-9688
  Effingham *(G-8821)*
- Addvalue2print LLC .......... G ....... 847 551-1570
  East Dundee *(G-8628)*
- Advantage Printing Inc .......... G ....... 630 627-7468
  Lombard *(G-13760)*
- Advocate .......... G ....... 815 694-2122
  Clifton *(G-7272)*
- Ajs Premier Printing Inc .......... G ....... 847 838-6350
  Antioch *(G-614)*
- All Printing & Graphics Inc .......... G ....... 773 553-3049
  Chicago *(G-3807)*
- Allegra Network LLC .......... G ....... 815 877-3400
  Belvidere *(G-1730)*
- Alliance Creative Group Inc .......... E ....... 847 885-1800
  Schaumburg *(G-19431)*
- Allied Graphics Inc .......... G ....... 847 419-8830
  Buffalo Grove *(G-2654)*
- Allprint Graphics Inc .......... G ....... 847 519-9898
  Schaumburg *(G-19432)*
- Alphadigital Inc .......... G ....... 708 482-4488
  La Grange Park *(G-12752)*
- AlphaGraphics .......... F ....... 630 261-1227
  Oakbrook Terrace *(G-16694)*
- AlphaGraphics Printshops .......... G ....... 630 964-9600
  Lisle *(G-13555)*
- Alta Vista Graphic Corporation .......... F ....... 773 267-2530
  Chicago *(G-3835)*
- Althea Crutex Inc .......... G ....... 630 595-7200
  Wood Dale *(G-22337)*
- Alwan Printing Inc .......... F ....... 708 598-9600
  Bridgeview *(G-2462)*
- Amboy News .......... G ....... 815 857-2311
  Amboy *(G-597)*
- American Litho Incorporated .......... A ....... 630 682-0600
  Carol Stream *(G-3099)*
- American Reprographics Co LLC .......... D ....... 847 647-1131
  Niles *(G-15960)*
- Apollo Printing Inc .......... G ....... 815 741-3065
  Homewood *(G-12091)*
- Apple Press Inc .......... G ....... 815 224-1451
  Peru *(G-17500)*

---

Employee Codes: A=Over 500 employees, B=251-500
C=101-250, D=51-100, E=20-50, F=10-19, G=3-9

**Arby Graphic Service Inc** ....F .... 847 763-0900
Niles *(G-15961)*
**Arch Printing Inc** ....G .... 630 966-0235
Aurora *(G-1110)*
**Arla Graphics Inc** ....G .... 847 470-0005
Deerfield *(G-7978)*
**Art Newvo Incorporated** ....G .... 847 838-0304
Antioch *(G-619)*
**Arthur Graphic Clarion** ....G .... 217 543-2151
Arthur *(G-881)*
**Arthur R Baker Inc** ....G .... 708 301-4828
Homer Glen *(G-12076)*
**Asa Inc** ....E .... 847 446-1856
Northfield *(G-16391)*
**Associated Printers Inc** ....G .... 847 548-8929
Antioch *(G-621)*
**Athena Design Group Inc** ....E .... 312 733-2828
Chicago *(G-3974)*
**Augusta Label Corp** ....G .... 630 537-1961
Burr Ridge *(G-2823)*
**Available Business Group Inc** ....D .... 773 247-4141
Chicago *(G-3995)*
**Avid of Illinois Inc** ....F .... 847 698-2775
Saint Charles *(G-19140)*
**Avsec Printing Inc** ....G .... 815 722-2961
Joliet *(G-12458)*
**Award/Visionps Inc** ....G .... 331 318-7800
Chicago *(G-4003)*
**B F Shaw Printing Company** ....C .... 815 625-3600
Sterling *(G-20584)*
**B F Shaw Printing Company** ....E .... 815 875-4461
Princeton *(G-17744)*
**B P I Printing & Duplicating** ....F .... 773 327-7300
Chicago *(G-4020)*
**B P I Printing & Duplicating** ....E .... 773 822-0111
Chicago *(G-4021)*
**Bach & Associates** ....G .... 618 277-1652
Belleville *(G-1610)*
**Balsley Printing Inc** ....G .... 815 637-8787
Rockton *(G-18691)*
**Bardash & Bukowski Inc** ....G .... 312 829-2080
Chicago *(G-4041)*
**Barrel Maker Printing** ....G .... 773 490-3065
Chicago *(G-4046)*
**Basswood Associates Inc** ....F .... 312 240-9400
Chicago *(G-4053)*
**Batavia Instant Print** ....G .... 630 262-0370
West Chicago *(G-21668)*
**Beans Printing Inc** ....G .... 217 223-5555
Quincy *(G-17800)*
**Belmonte Printing Co** ....G .... 847 352-8841
Schaumburg *(G-19459)*
**Belrock Printing Inc** ....G .... 815 547-1096
Belvidere *(G-1735)*
**Benton Evening News Co** ....G .... 618 438-5611
Benton *(G-2022)*
**Benzinger Printing** ....G .... 815 784-6560
Genoa *(G-10875)*
**Berland Printing Inc** ....E .... 773 702-1999
Chicago *(G-4086)*
**Bfc Print** ....F .... 630 879-9240
Batavia *(G-1423)*
**Bikast Graphics Inc** ....G .... 847 487-8822
Wauconda *(G-21446)*
**Bitforms Inc** ....G .... 630 595-6800
Wood Dale *(G-22345)*
**Bmt Prnting Crtgraph Espclists** ....G .... 773 646-4700
Chicago *(G-4132)*
**Bond Brothers & Co** ....F .... 708 442-5510
Lyons *(G-14032)*
**Brads Printing Inc** ....G .... 847 662-0447
Waukegan *(G-21531)*
**Branstiter Printing Co** ....G .... 217 245-6533
Jacksonville *(G-12381)*
**Brian Paul Inc** ....E .... 847 398-8677
Buffalo Grove *(G-2670)*
**Brokers Print Mail Rsource Inc** ....G .... 708 532-9900
Tinley Park *(G-20900)*
**Burstan Inc** ....G .... 847 787-0380
Elk Grove Village *(G-9349)*
**Business Card Systems Inc** ....F .... 815 877-0990
Machesney Park *(G-14061)*
**Business Cards Tomorrow** ....F .... 815 877-0990
Machesney Park *(G-14062)*
**Button Man Printing Inc** ....G .... 630 549-0438
Saint Charles *(G-19146)*
**C & L Printing Company** ....F .... 312 235-0380
Chicago *(G-4201)*
**C2 Imaging LLC** ....E .... 847 439-7834
Elk Grove Village *(G-9353)*

**Cambrdg Printing Corp** ....G .... 630 510-2100
Carol Stream *(G-3123)*
**Cameron Printing Inc** ....G .... 630 231-3301
West Chicago *(G-21677)*
**Campbell Publishing Inc** ....G .... 217 742-3313
Winchester *(G-22278)*
**Card Prsnlzation Solutions LLC** ....E .... 630 543-2630
Glendale Heights *(G-11014)*
**Cardinal Colorprint Prtg Corp** ....E .... 630 467-1000
Itasca *(G-12241)*
**Carey Color Inc** ....G .... 630 761-2605
West Chicago *(G-21678)*
**CDs Office Systems Inc** ....F .... 630 305-9034
Springfield *(G-20411)*
**Central Illinois Newspapers** ....G .... 217 935-3171
Clinton *(G-7279)*
**Century Printing** ....G .... 618 632-2486
O Fallon *(G-16465)*
**Cenveo Inc** ....D .... 636 240-5817
Chicago *(G-4278)*
**Cenveo Inc** ....D .... 773 539-0411
Chicago *(G-4280)*
**Challenge Printers** ....G .... 773 252-0212
Chicago *(G-4285)*
**Charles C Thomas Publisher** ....F .... 217 789-8980
Springfield *(G-20416)*
**Charles Chauncey Wells Inc** ....G .... 708 524-0695
Oak Park *(G-16657)*
**CHI-Town Printing Inc** ....G .... 773 577-2500
Chicago *(G-4299)*
**Chicago Mltlingua Graphics Inc** ....F .... 847 386-7187
Northfield *(G-16397)*
**Chicago Press Corporation** ....E .... 773 276-1500
Chicago *(G-4342)*
**Chicago Sun-Times Features Inc** ....A .... 312 321-3000
Chicago *(G-4351)*
**Child Evngelism Fellowship Inc** ....E .... 630 983-7708
Naperville *(G-15628)*
**Christopher Wagner** ....G .... 630 205-9200
Oswego *(G-16907)*
**Cifuentes Luis & Nicole Inc** ....G .... 847 490-3660
Schaumburg *(G-19472)*
**Classic Color Inc** ....C .... 708 484-0000
Broadview *(G-2568)*
**Clear Print Inc** ....G .... 815 795-6225
Ottawa *(G-16954)*
**Cloverdale Corporation** ....G .... 847 296-9225
Des Plaines *(G-8171)*
**Cmb Printing Inc** ....F .... 630 323-1110
Burr Ridge *(G-2830)*
**Colorwave Graphics LLC** ....G .... 815 397-4293
Loves Park *(G-13925)*
**Colvin Printing** ....G .... 708 331-4580
Blue Island *(G-2243)*
**Commercial Fast Print** ....G .... 815 673-1196
Streator *(G-20685)*
**Congress Printing Company** ....F .... 312 733-6599
Chicago *(G-4448)*
**Consolidated Carqueville Prtg** ....C .... 630 246-6451
Streamwood *(G-20649)*
**Consulate General Lithuania** ....G .... 312 397-0382
Chicago *(G-4454)*
**Cook JV Printing** ....F .... 708 799-0007
Country Club Hills *(G-7405)*
**Cook Printing Co Inc** ....G .... 217 345-2514
Mattoon *(G-14387)*
**Copy-Mor Inc** ....E .... 312 666-4000
Elmhurst *(G-9856)*
**Corporation Supply Co Inc** ....E .... 312 726-3375
Chicago *(G-4476)*
**Coyle Print Group Inc** ....G .... 847 784-1080
Skokie *(G-19987)*
**Cpr Printing Inc** ....F .... 630 377-8420
Geneva *(G-10821)*
**Creasey Printing Services Inc** ....G .... 217 787-1055
Springfield *(G-20425)*
**Crosswind Printing** ....G .... 847 356-1009
Lindenhurst *(G-13546)*
**Cynlar Inc** ....G .... 630 820-2200
Aurora *(G-992)*
**D & D Business Inc** ....G .... 630 935-3522
Willowbrook *(G-22209)*
**D & D Printing Inc** ....G .... 708 425-2080
Oak Lawn *(G-16615)*
**D E Asbury Inc** ....F .... 217 222-0617
Hamilton *(G-11532)*
**D G Brandt Inc** ....G .... 815 942-4064
Morris *(G-15105)*
**D L V Printing Service Inc** ....F .... 773 626-1661
Chicago *(G-4537)*

**Dark Matter Printing** ....G .... 217 791-4059
Decatur *(G-7866)*
**Dbp Communications Inc** ....G .... 312 263-1569
Chicago *(G-4566)*
**Dean Printing Systems** ....G .... 847 526-9545
Island Lake *(G-12214)*
**Debbie Harshman** ....G .... 217 335-2112
Barry *(G-1311)*
**Deluxe Johnson** ....F .... 847 635-7200
Des Plaines *(G-8182)*
**Deluxe Printing** ....G .... 312 225-0061
Chicago *(G-4580)*
**Des Plaines Journal Inc** ....D .... 847 299-5511
Des Plaines *(G-8184)*
**Designation Inc** ....F .... 847 367-9100
Mundelein *(G-15494)*
**Diamond Envelope Corporation** ....D .... 630 499-2800
Aurora *(G-995)*
**Diversified Print Group** ....G .... 630 893-8920
Bloomingdale *(G-2104)*
**Dla Document Services** ....F .... 618 256-4686
Scott Air Force Base *(G-19885)*
**Donnelley Financial LLC** ....F .... 312 326-8000
Chicago *(G-4629)*
**Donnells Printing & Off Pdts** ....G .... 815 842-6541
Pontiac *(G-17698)*
**Dos Bro Corp** ....G .... 773 334-1919
Chicago *(G-4633)*
**DOT Sharper Printing Inc** ....G .... 847 581-9033
Morton Grove *(G-15194)*
**Double Image Press Inc** ....F .... 630 893-6777
Glendale Heights *(G-11020)*
**Doubletake Marketing Inc** ....G .... 845 598-3175
Evanston *(G-10029)*
**Dps Digital Print Svc** ....G .... 847 836-7734
East Dundee *(G-8632)*
**Drake Envelope Printing Co** ....G .... 217 374-2772
White Hall *(G-22184)*
**Dsr Screenprinting** ....G .... 630 855-2790
Streamwood *(G-20652)*
**Dupli Group Inc** ....F .... 773 549-5285
Chicago *(G-4654)*
**Dyna-Tone Litho Inc** ....G .... 630 595-1073
Bensenville *(G-1886)*
**E & H Graphic Service** ....G .... 708 748-5656
Matteson *(G-14371)*
**E A A Enterprises Inc** ....G .... 630 279-0150
Villa Park *(G-21249)*
**East Central Communications Co** ....E .... 217 892-9613
Rantoul *(G-17926)*
**East Moline Herald Print Inc** ....G .... 309 755-5224
East Moline *(G-8678)*
**Edwardsville Publishing Co** ....D .... 618 656-4700
Edwardsville *(G-8799)*
**Elgin Instant Print** ....G .... 847 931-9006
Elgin *(G-9024)*
**Elise S Allen** ....G .... 309 673-2613
Peoria *(G-17354)*
**Elliott Publishing Inc** ....G .... 217 645-3033
Liberty *(G-13295)*
**Elmhurst Enterprise Group Inc** ....G .... 847 228-5945
Arlington Heights *(G-749)*
**Emerald Printing & Promotions** ....G .... 815 344-3303
McHenry *(G-14502)*
**Envelopes Only Inc** ....E .... 630 213-2500
Streamwood *(G-20655)*
**Essentra Packaging US Inc** ....G .... 704 418-8692
Westchester *(G-21841)*
**Eugene Ewbank** ....G .... 630 705-0400
Oswego *(G-16917)*
**Evergreen Printing** ....G .... 708 499-0688
Evergreen Park *(G-10115)*
**Express Print Champaign LLC** ....G .... 217 693-7079
Urbana *(G-21083)*
**Express Prtg & Promotions Inc** ....G .... 847 498-9640
Northbrook *(G-16253)*
**Expri Publishing & Printing** ....G .... 773 274-5955
Chicago *(G-4798)*
**Faith Printing** ....G .... 217 675-2191
Franklin *(G-10379)*
**Far West Print Solutions LLC** ....G .... 630 879-9500
North Aurora *(G-16130)*
**Fedex Corporation** ....F .... 847 918-7730
Vernon Hills *(G-21163)*
**Fedex Office & Print Svcs Inc** ....G .... 708 345-0984
Melrose Park *(G-14637)*
**Fedex Office & Print Svcs Inc** ....G .... 312 492-8355
Chicago *(G-4825)*
**Fedex Office & Print Svcs Inc** ....G .... 630 469-2677
Glen Ellyn *(G-10970)*

# PRODUCT SECTION — PRINTING: Lithographic

| Company | Code | Phone |
|---|---|---|
| Fedex Office & Print Svcs Inc — Chicago (G-4826) | G | 773 472-3066 |
| Fedex Office & Print Svcs Inc — Rosemont (G-19001) | G | 847 292-7176 |
| Fedex Office & Print Svcs Inc — Homewood (G-12098) | G | 708 799-5323 |
| Fedex Office & Print Svcs Inc — Chicago (G-4827) | F | 312 341-9644 |
| Fedex Office & Print Svcs Inc — Chicago (G-4828) | F | 312 755-0325 |
| Fedex Office & Print Svcs Inc — Chicago (G-4829) | F | 312 595-0768 |
| Fedex Office & Print Svcs Inc — Chicago (G-4830) | F | 312 663-1149 |
| Fedex Office & Print Svcs Inc — Bloomingdale (G-2108) | F | 630 894-1800 |
| Fgs Inc — Chicago (G-4839) | F | 312 421-3060 |
| Fgs-IL LLC — Aurora (G-1007) | C | 630 375-8500 |
| Fidelity Bindery Company — Broadview (G-2578) | E | 708 343-6833 |
| Fidelity Print Cmmncations LLC — Broadview (G-2579) | E | 708 343-6833 |
| Financial and Professional Reg — Springfield (G-20439) | G | 217 782-2127 |
| Fine Line Printing — Chicago (G-4846) | G | 773 582-9709 |
| Fisher Printing Inc — Bridgeview (G-2490) | C | 708 598-9266 |
| Fisheye Services Incorporated — Chicago (G-4852) | G | 773 942-6314 |
| FL 1 — Elk Grove Village (G-9479) | F | 847 956-9400 |
| Floden Enterprises — Mundelein (G-15502) | G | 847 566-7898 |
| Forcerl — Highland Park (G-11833) | G | 847 432-7588 |
| Forest Printing Co — Forest Park (G-10247) | F | 708 366-5100 |
| Forms Specialist Inc — Lincolnshire (G-13449) | G | 847 298-2868 |
| Fort Dearborn Company — Elk Grove Village (G-9487) | D | 847 357-2300 |
| Fox Valley Printing Co Inc — Montgomery (G-15043) | F | 419 232-3348 |
| Full Court Press Inc — Chicago (G-4894) | G | 773 779-1135 |
| Fuse LLC — Berkeley (G-2045) | C | 708 449-8989 |
| G T Services of Illionois Inc — Tremont (G-20982) | G | 309 925-5111 |
| Gallas Label & Decal — Chicago (G-4909) | F | 773 775-1000 |
| Gametime Screen Printing — Freeport (G-10660) | G | 815 297-5263 |
| Gamma Alpha Visual — Elk Grove Village (G-9496) | G | 847 956-0633 |
| Gammon Group Inc — Shorewood (G-19927) | G | 815 722-6400 |
| Gannon Graphics — Schaumburg (G-19535) | G | 847 895-1043 |
| Gatehouse Media LLC — Springfield (G-20445) | B | 217 788-1300 |
| Gatling Printing Inc — Blue Island (G-2252) | G | 708 388-4746 |
| Gazette Printing Co — Glasford (G-10951) | G | 309 389-2811 |
| Generation Copy Inc — Evanston (G-10041) | G | 847 866-0469 |
| George Press Inc — Litchfield (G-13687) | G | 217 324-2242 |
| George Vaggelatos — Itasca (G-12269) | G | 847 361-3880 |
| Gh Printing Co Inc — Downers Grove (G-8449) | E | 630 960-4115 |
| Goalgetters Inc — La Grange (G-12733) | F | 708 579-9800 |
| Golden Prairie News — Assumption (G-931) | G | 217 226-3721 |
| Goose Printing Co — Evanston (G-10043) | G | 847 673-1414 |
| Gossett Printing Inc — Salem (G-19335) | G | 618 548-2583 |
| Graf Ink Printing Inc — Harrisburg (G-11601) | G | 618 273-4231 |
| Grand Forms & Systems Inc — Arlington Heights (G-760) | F | 847 259-4600 |
| Grand Printing & Graphics Inc — Chicago (G-4984) | F | 312 218-6780 |
| Grandcentral Enterprises Inc — Bloomington (G-2171) | G | 309 287-5362 |
| Granja & Sons Printing — Chicago (G-4987) | F | 773 762-3840 |
| Graphic Arts Studio Inc — Barrington (G-1282) | E | 847 381-1105 |
| Graphic Image Corporation — Chicago (G-4989) | F | 312 829-7800 |
| Graphic Partners Inc — Zion (G-22686) | E | 847 872-9445 |
| Graphic Promotions Inc — Shorewood (G-19928) | F | 815 726-3288 |
| Graphic Source Group Inc — Lake In The Hills (G-12995) | G | 847 854-2670 |
| Grasso Graphics Inc — Alsip (G-465) | G | 708 489-2060 |
| Gray Wolf Graphics Inc — Crystal Lake (G-7584) | G | 815 356-0895 |
| Greenup Press Inc — Greenup (G-11383) | E | 217 923-3704 |
| Griffith Solutions Inc — Park Ridge (G-17201) | G | 847 384-1810 |
| Grphic Richards Communications — Bellwood (G-1707) | F | 708 547-6000 |
| H2o Ltd — Monticello (G-15077) | G | 217 762-7441 |
| Haapanen Brothers Inc — Gurnee (G-11457) | D | 847 662-2233 |
| Hammond Printing — Glenview (G-11135) | G | 847 724-1539 |
| Harlan Vance Company — Normal (G-16072) | F | 309 888-4804 |
| Harrison Martha Print Studio — Crystal Lake (G-7587) | G | 949 290-8630 |
| Hawthorne Press — Cicero (G-7201) | G | 708 652-9000 |
| Heavenly Enterprises — Hickory Hills (G-11770) | G | 773 783-2981 |
| Henderson Family — Aledo (G-370) | G | 309 236-6783 |
| Hermitage Group Inc — Chicago (G-5080) | E | 773 561-3773 |
| Hillsboro Journal Inc — Hillsboro (G-11895) | E | 217 532-3933 |
| Holden Industries Inc — Deerfield (G-8013) | F | 847 940-1500 |
| Holland Printing Inc — South Holland (G-20278) | F | 708 596-9000 |
| Howard Press Printing Inc — Northlake (G-16439) | G | 708 345-7437 |
| Hts Hancock Transcriptions Svc — Paxton (G-17237) | G | 217 379-9241 |
| Illini Digital Printing Co — East Saint Louis (G-8756) | G | 618 271-6622 |
| Image Pact Printing — Tinley Park (G-20923) | E | 708 460-6070 |
| Impression Printing — Oak Forest (G-16583) | F | 708 614-8660 |
| In Color Graphics Coml Prtg — Elgin (G-9075) | F | 847 697-0003 |
| Indigo Digital Printing LLC — Chicago (G-5175) | G | 312 753-3025 |
| Ink Enterprises Inc — Belvidere (G-1764) | G | 815 547-5515 |
| Ink Spots Prtg & Meida Design — Homewood (G-12102) | G | 708 754-1300 |
| Ink Well — Fairview Heights (G-10169) | G | 618 398-1427 |
| Ink Well Printing — Peru (G-17514) | G | 815 224-1366 |
| Ink Well Printing & Design Ltd — Schaumburg (G-19566) | G | 847 923-8060 |
| Inkpartners Corporation — Chicago (G-5197) | G | 773 843-1786 |
| Innerworkings Inc — Chicago (G-5198) | D | 312 642-3700 |
| Innova Print Fulfillment Inc — Geneva (G-10837) | G | 630 845-3215 |
| Innovtive Design Graphics Corp — Evanston (G-10057) | G | 847 475-7772 |
| Insty-Prints of Champaign Inc — Champaign (G-3501) | G | 217 356-6166 |
| Integra Graphics and Forms Inc — Crestwood (G-7490) | F | 708 385-0950 |
| Integrity Prtg McHy Svcs LLC — Hoffman Estates (G-12019) | G | 847 834-9484 |
| International Graphics & Assoc — Saint Charles (G-19199) | F | 630 584-2248 |
| Intersports Screen Printing — Chicago (G-5226) | G | 773 489-7383 |
| J and K Printing — Oak Lawn (G-16627) | G | 708 229-9558 |
| J M Printers Inc — Crest Hill (G-7459) | F | 815 727-1579 |
| Jade Screen Printing — Alton (G-579) | G | 618 463-2325 |
| Jamether Incorporated — Crystal Lake (G-7593) | G | 815 444-9971 |
| Jans Graphics Inc — Chicago (G-5278) | F | 312 644-4700 |
| Janssen Avenue Boys Inc — North Aurora (G-16136) | G | 630 627-0202 |
| Jarr Printing Co — McHenry (G-14515) | F | 815 363-5435 |
| Jjm Printing Inc — Sterling (G-20595) | G | 815 499-3067 |
| Jofas Print Corporation — Frankfort (G-10337) | G | 815 534-5725 |
| Johns-Byrne Company — Niles (G-15992) | D | 847 583-3100 |
| Johnsbyrne Graphic Tech Corp — Niles (G-15993) | G | 847 583-3100 |
| Johnson Press America Inc — Pontiac (G-17704) | E | 815 844-5161 |
| Johnson Printing — Bensenville (G-1930) | G | 630 595-8815 |
| Johnsons Screen Printing — Geneva (G-10843) | G | 630 262-8210 |
| Jost & Kiefer Printing Company — Quincy (G-17842) | E | 217 222-5145 |
| Jsn Printing Inc — Joliet (G-12525) | G | 815 582-4014 |
| Jsolo Corp — Deerfield (G-8023) | G | 847 964-9188 |
| K & J Phillips Corporation — Naperville (G-15682) | G | 630 355-0660 |
| Kelvyn Press Inc — Broadview (G-2591) | D | 708 343-0448 |
| Kelvyn Press Inc — Aurora (G-1040) | E | 630 585-8160 |
| Kevin Kewney — Quincy (G-17844) | G | 217 228-7444 |
| Key Printing — Kankakee (G-12635) | G | 815 933-1800 |
| Kingsbury Enterprises Inc — Oak Forest (G-16586) | G | 708 535-7590 |
| Kjellberg Printing — Wheaton (G-21960) | F | 630 653-2244 |
| KK Stevens Publishing Co — Astoria (G-934) | E | 309 329-2151 |
| Knight Prtg & Litho Svc Ltd — Island Lake (G-12217) | G | 847 487-7700 |
| Krueger International Inc — Chicago (G-5413) | F | 312 467-6850 |
| L P M Inc — Evanston (G-10062) | G | 847 866-9777 |
| LAC Enterprises Inc — Crystal Lake (G-7601) | G | 815 455-5044 |
| Lake Shore Printing — Skokie (G-20024) | G | 847 679-4110 |
| Lakes Reg Prtg & Graphics LLC — Antioch (G-639) | G | 847 838-5838 |
| Lebolt Print Service Inc — Highwood (G-11886) | G | 847 681-1210 |
| Lee Enterprises Incorporated — Carbondale (G-3014) | C | 618 529-5454 |
| Legend Promotions — Lake Zurich (G-13095) | G | 847 438-3528 |
| Legislative Printing — Springfield (G-20469) | G | 217 782-7312 |
| Leonard Publishing Co — Norridge (G-16104) | F | 773 486-2737 |
| Lind-Remsen Printing Co Inc — Rockford (G-18470) | F | 815 969-0610 |
| Lists & Letters — Wheeling (G-22095) | F | 847 520-5207 |
| Lith Liqure — Lake In The Hills (G-12998) | G | 847 458-5180 |
| Litho Type LLC — Lansing (G-13173) | E | 708 895-3720 |
| Lithoprint Inc — Westmont (G-21900) | G | 630 964-9200 |
| Lithuanian Catholic Press — Chicago (G-5519) | E | 773 585-9500 |
| Lloyd Midwest Graphics — Machesney Park (G-14089) | G | 815 282-8828 |
| Lsk Import — Chicago (G-5554) | G | 847 342-8447 |
| Lure Group LLC — Bolingbrook (G-2338) | G | 630 222-6515 |

Employee Codes: A=Over 500 employees, B=251-500, C=101-250, D=51-100, E=20-50, F=10-19, G=3-9

2017 Harris Illinois Industrial Directory

## PRINTING: Lithographic

| Company | Type | Phone |
|---|---|---|
| Lutheran General Printing Svcs — Mount Prospect (G-15344) | G | 847 298-8040 |
| M C F Printing Company — Elmhurst (G-9904) | G | 630 279-0301 |
| M M Marketing — Crystal Lake (G-7603) | G | 815 459-7968 |
| M O W Printing Inc — Collinsville (G-7331) | F | 618 345-5525 |
| M Wells Printing Co — Chicago (G-5588) | G | 312 455-0400 |
| M13 Inc — Schaumburg (G-19629) | E | 847 310-1913 |
| Mac Graphics Group Inc — Oakbrook Terrace (G-16716) | G | 630 620-7200 |
| Makkah Printing — Glendale Heights (G-11045) | G | 630 980-2315 |
| Marc Business Forms Inc — Lincolnwood (G-13524) | F | 847 568-9200 |
| Marjo Graphics Inc — Libertyville (G-13346) | G | 847 367-1305 |
| Marking Specialists/Poly — Buffalo Grove (G-2731) | F | 847 793-8100 |
| Martinez Printing LLC — Chicago (G-5633) | G | 773 732-8108 |
| Marty Gannon — Schaumburg (G-19632) | E | 847 895-1059 |
| Mason City Banner Times — Mason City (G-14365) | F | 217 482-3276 |
| Maximum Prtg & Graphics Inc — Downers Grove (G-8484) | F | 630 737-0270 |
| McIntyre & Associates — Fox Lake (G-10278) | G | 847 639-8050 |
| Medical Records Co — Waukegan (G-21588) | G | 847 662-6373 |
| Menus To Go — Streamwood (G-20666) | G | 630 483-0848 |
| Merritt & Edwards Corporation — Bloomington (G-2196) | F | 309 828-4741 |
| Metro Printing & Pubg Inc — Millstadt (G-14829) | F | 618 476-9587 |
| Meyercord Revenue Inc — Carol Stream (G-3194) | E | 630 682-6200 |
| Mgsolutions Inc — Elmhurst (G-9912) | G | 630 530-2005 |
| Mi-Te Fast Printers Inc — Glencoe (G-11002) | G | 312 236-3278 |
| Mich Enterprises Inc — Wood Dale (G-22399) | F | 630 616-9000 |
| Michael Burza — Cortland (G-7393) | G | 815 909-0233 |
| Microdynamics Corporation — Naperville (G-15697) | C | 630 276-0527 |
| Mid-Central Business Forms — Peoria (G-17406) | G | 309 692-9090 |
| Midwest Law Printing Co Inc — Chicago (G-5745) | G | 312 431-0185 |
| Midwest Outdoors Ltd — Burr Ridge (G-2867) | E | 630 887-7722 |
| Midwest Sign & Lighting Inc — Country Club Hills (G-7410) | G | 708 365-5555 |
| Minute Man Press — Hoffman Estates (G-12023) | G | 847 839-9600 |
| Minute Men Inc — Aurora (G-1191) | E | 630 692-1583 |
| Minuteman Press — Oak Park (G-16675) | G | 708 524-4940 |
| Minuteman Press — Hickory Hills (G-11773) | G | 708 598-4915 |
| Minuteman Press — Countryside (G-7437) | G | 630 541-9122 |
| Minuteman Press — Saint Charles (G-19223) | G | 630 584-7383 |
| Minuteman Press — Lombard (G-13827) | G | 630 279-0438 |
| Minuteman Press Inc — Arlington Heights (G-803) | G | 847 577-2411 |
| Minuteman Press Int Inc — Oak Brook (G-16545) | G | 630 574-0090 |
| Minuteman Press Morton Grove — Morton Grove (G-15221) | G | 847 470-0212 |
| Minuteman Press of Countryside — Countryside (G-7438) | G | 708 354-2190 |
| Minuteman Press of Lansing — Lansing (G-13177) | G | 708 895-0505 |
| Minuteman Press of Rockford — Loves Park (G-13967) | G | 815 633-2992 |
| Minuteman Press of Waukegan — Gurnee (G-11474) | G | 847 244-6288 |
| Miracle Press Company — Chicago (G-5770) | F | 773 722-6176 |
| Mission Press Inc — Chicago (G-5772) | G | 312 455-9501 |
| Mmpcu Limited — Champaign (G-3516) | G | 217 355-0500 |
| Moline Dispatch Publishing Co — Moline (G-14959) | G | 309 764-4344 |
| Moran Graphics Inc — Chicago (G-5803) | E | 312 226-3900 |
| Motr Grafx LLC — Niles (G-16009) | G | 847 600-5656 |
| Multicopy Corp — Northfield (G-16410) | G | 847 446-7015 |
| Naco Printing Co Inc — Greenville (G-11400) | G | 618 664-0423 |
| Nedras Printing Inc — Shobonier (G-19922) | G | 618 846-3853 |
| Need To Know Inc — Peoria (G-17415) | G | 309 691-3877 |
| Network Printing Inc — Mundelein (G-15537) | G | 847 566-4146 |
| New Life Printing & Publishing — Algonquin (G-402) | G | 847 658-4111 |
| New Vision Print & Marketing — Naperville (G-15713) | G | 630 406-0509 |
| Nissha Usa Inc — Schaumburg (G-19666) | E | 847 413-2665 |
| Nite Owl Prints LLC — Downers Grove (G-8496) | G | 630 541-6273 |
| North County News Inc — Red Bud (G-17945) | G | 618 282-3803 |
| Northwest Premier Printing — Chicago (G-5940) | G | 773 736-1882 |
| Nosco Inc — Waukegan (G-21595) | B | 847 336-4200 |
| Nosco Inc — Gurnee (G-11476) | D | 847 336-4200 |
| Npn360 — Wheeling (G-22109) | E | 847 215-7300 |
| Office Assistants Inc — Oak Lawn (G-16637) | G | 708 346-0505 |
| On Time Printing and Finishing — Hillside (G-11929) | G | 708 544-4500 |
| Oneims Printing LLC — Skokie (G-20050) | G | 773 297-2050 |
| Only For One Printers — Wheeling (G-22114) | F | 847 947-4119 |
| Orion Star Corp — Palatine (G-17061) | F | 847 776-2300 |
| Orora Visual TX LLC — Niles (G-16014) | B | 847 647-1900 |
| Osbon Lithographers — Park Ridge (G-17214) | G | 847 825-7727 |
| Ottawa Publishing Co Inc — Ottawa (G-16975) | G | 815 433-2000 |
| Overt Press Inc — Chicago (G-6029) | E | 773 284-0909 |
| P P Graphics Inc — Westchester (G-21852) | G | 708 343-2530 |
| Paap Printing — Charleston (G-3607) | G | 217 345-6878 |
| Pace Print Plus — Barrington (G-1296) | G | 847 381-1720 |
| Pamco Printed Tape Label Inc — Des Plaines (G-8249) | C | 847 803-2200 |
| Pap-R Products Company — Martinsville (G-14339) | D | 775 828-4141 |
| Papiros Graphics — Chicago (G-6072) | G | 773 581-3000 |
| Paragon Print & Mail Prod Inc — Bloomingdale (G-2125) | G | 630 671-2222 |
| Parkway Printers — Springfield (G-20499) | G | 217 525-2485 |
| Patrick Impressions LLC — Lemont (G-13250) | G | 630 257-9336 |
| Pebblefork Partners Inc — Berkeley (G-2047) | D | 708 449-8989 |
| Perfect Plastic Printing Corp — Saint Charles (G-19234) | G | 630 584-1600 |
| Performance Mailing & Prtg Inc — Libertyville (G-13366) | G | 847 549-0500 |
| Perryco Inc — Plainfield (G-17638) | F | 815 436-2431 |
| Petersburg Observer Co Inc — Petersburg (G-17537) | G | 217 632-2236 |
| Phoenix Press Inc — Villa Park (G-21277) | G | 630 833-2281 |
| Poets Study Inc — Chicago (G-6147) | G | 773 286-1355 |
| Power Graphics & Print Inc — Skokie (G-20057) | G | 847 568-1808 |
| Prairieland Printing — Washington (G-21387) | G | 309 647-5425 |
| Precision Printing Inc — Lombard (G-13844) | G | 630 737-0075 |
| Precision Reproductions Inc — Glenview (G-11184) | F | 847 724-0182 |
| Preferred Press Inc — Glendale Heights (G-11059) | G | 630 980-9799 |
| Press Proof Printing — Carpentersville (G-3298) | G | 847 466-7156 |
| Prime Printing Inc — Des Plaines (G-8264) | G | 847 299-9960 |
| Print & Design Services LLC — Bannockburn (G-1264) | G | 847 317-9001 |
| Print & Mailing Solutions LLC — Romeoville (G-18861) | G | 708 544-9400 |
| Print and Mktg Solutions Group — Northbrook (G-16344) | E | 847 498-9640 |
| Print Butler Inc — Grayslake (G-11359) | F | 312 296-2804 |
| Print Rite Inc — Chicago (G-6189) | G | 773 625-0792 |
| Print Service & Dist Assn Psda — Chicago (G-6190) | G | 312 321-5120 |
| Print Shop — Sandwich (G-19375) | G | 815 786-8278 |
| Printech of Illinois Inc — Crystal Lake (G-7631) | G | 815 356-1195 |
| Printers Ink of Paris Inc — Paris (G-17158) | G | 217 463-2552 |
| Printers Mark — Rock Island (G-18193) | G | 309 732-1174 |
| Printers Quill Inc — Mokena (G-14897) | G | 708 429-3636 |
| Printers Row LLC — Chicago (G-6192) | G | 312 435-0411 |
| Printers Row Loft — Chicago (G-6193) | G | 312 431-1019 |
| Printers Square Condo Assn — Chicago (G-6194) | G | 312 765-8794 |
| Printing Arts Cmmnications LLC — Broadview (G-2604) | E | 708 938-1600 |
| Printing Craftsmen of Joliet — Joliet (G-12555) | G | 815 254-3982 |
| Printing Dimensions — Arlington Heights (G-823) | G | 847 439-7521 |
| Printing Impression Direc — Lakemoor (G-13147) | G | 815 385-6688 |
| Printing On Ashland Inc — Chicago (G-6196) | G | 773 488-4707 |
| Printing Press of Joliet Inc — Joliet (G-12556) | G | 815 725-0018 |
| Printsmart Printing & Graphics — Woodridge (G-22510) | G | 630 434-2000 |
| Priority Print — Brookfield (G-2641) | G | 708 485-7080 |
| Prism Commercial Printing Ctrs — Chicago (G-6201) | G | 773 735-5400 |
| Prism Commercial Printing Ctrs — Addison (G-257) | G | 630 834-4443 |
| Pro Graphics Ink — Canton (G-2992) | G | 309 647-2526 |
| Professional Printers — Bolingbrook (G-2361) | G | 630 739-7761 |
| Professnal Mling Prtg Svcs Inc — Carol Stream (G-3222) | F | 630 510-1000 |
| Proforma Awards Print & Promot — Montgomery (G-15065) | G | 630 897-9848 |
| Progrssive Imprssions Intl Inc — Bloomingdale (G-2216) | C | 309 664-0444 |
| Qst Industries Inc — Chicago (G-6237) | E | 312 930-9400 |
| Quad/Graphics Inc — Mount Morris (G-15297) | A | 815 734-4121 |
| Quad/Graphics Inc — Bolingbrook (G-2362) | A | 630 343-4400 |
| Quality Blue & Offset Printing — Bolingbrook (G-2363) | G | 630 759-8035 |
| Quantum Color Graphics LLC — Morton Grove (G-15231) | C | 847 967-3600 |
| Quebecor Wrld Mt Morris II LLC — Mount Morris (G-15298) | F | 815 734-4121 |
| Quik Impressions Group Inc — Addison (G-265) | E | 630 495-7845 |
| Quincy Media Inc — Quincy (G-17879) | C | 217 223-5100 |
| R & S Screen Printing Inc — Woodstock (G-22604) | G | 815 337-3935 |
| R R Donnelley & Sons Company — Dwight (G-8591) | A | 815 584-2770 |

**R R Donnelley & Sons Company** A 815 844-5181
Pontiac *(G-17710)*
**R T P Inc** G 312 664-6150
Chicago *(G-6274)*
**R W Wilson Printing Company** G 630 584-4100
Saint Charles *(G-19249)*
**Rapid Circular Press Inc** F 312 421-5611
Chicago *(G-6290)*
**Rapid Copy & Duplicating Co** G 312 733-3353
Elmwood Park *(G-9974)*
**Redline Press** G 630 690-9828
Lisle *(G-13650)*
**Register-Mail** C 309 343-7181
Galesburg *(G-10773)*
**Reign Print Solutions Inc** G 847 590-7091
Arlington Heights *(G-830)*
**Reliable Mail Services Inc** F 847 677-6245
Skokie *(G-20073)*
**Review Printing Co Inc** G 309 788-7094
Rock Island *(G-18199)*
**Ribbon Print Company** G 847 421-8208
Highland Park *(G-11865)*
**Rieger Printing Inc** G 773 229-2095
Bedford Park *(G-1578)*
**Rightsource Digital Svcs Inc** F 888 774-2201
Chicago *(G-6357)*
**Rightway Printing Inc** F 630 790-0444
Glendale Heights *(G-11064)*
**River Bend Printing** G 217 324-6056
Litchfield *(G-13696)*
**Rivershore Press** G 847 516-8105
Cary *(G-3368)*
**Riverview Printing Inc** G 815 987-1425
Rockford *(G-18558)*
**Ro-Web Inc** G 309 688-2155
Peoria *(G-17444)*
**Rockford Newspapers Inc** B 815 987-1200
Rockford *(G-18580)*
**Rodin Enterprises Inc** G 847 412-1370
Wheeling *(G-22142)*
**Rose Business Forms & Printing** G 618 533-3032
Centralia *(G-3429)*
**Rosette Printing LLC** G 630 295-8500
Bloomingdale *(G-2131)*
**RR Donnelley & Sons Company** C 217 935-2113
Clinton *(G-7288)*
**RR Donnelley & Sons Company** D 630 762-7600
Saint Charles *(G-19256)*
**RR Donnelley & Sons Company** E 312 332-4345
Chicago *(G-6402)*
**Rrr Graphics & Film Corp** G 708 478-4573
Mokena *(G-14901)*
**Rt Associates Inc** D 847 577-0700
Wheeling *(G-22143)*
**Rush Printing On Oak** G 815 344-8880
McHenry *(G-14553)*
**Rusty & Angela Buzzard** G 217 342-9841
Effingham *(G-8857)*
**Safeguard 201 Corp** G 630 241-0370
Westmont *(G-21918)*
**Salem Times-Commoner Pubg Co** E 618 548-3330
Salem *(G-19349)*
**Saltzman Printers Inc** E 708 344-4500
Melrose Park *(G-14690)*
**Samecwei Inc** G 630 897-7888
Aurora *(G-1214)*
**Save On Printing Inc** G 847 922-7855
Elk Grove Village *(G-9729)*
**Schneider Graphics Inc** E 847 550-4310
Lake Zurich *(G-13126)*
**Schommer Inc** G 815 344-1404
McHenry *(G-14554)*
**Screen Graphics** G 309 699-8513
Pekin *(G-17288)*
**Screen Print Plus Inc** G 630 236-0260
Naperville *(G-15825)*
**Selnar Inc** G 309 699-3977
East Peoria *(G-8733)*
**Semper FI Printing LLC** G 847 640-7737
Arlington Heights *(G-838)*
**Sharp Graphics Inc** G 847 966-7000
Skokie *(G-20085)*
**Sheer Graphics Inc** G 630 654-4422
Westmont *(G-21920)*
**Sheet Wise Printing** G 815 664-3025
Spring Valley *(G-20381)*
**Shoreline Graphics Inc** G 847 587-4804
Ingleside *(G-12198)*
**Shree Printing Corp** G 773 267-9500
Chicago *(G-6502)*
**Signcraft Screenprint Inc** C 815 777-3030
Galena *(G-10731)*
**Signs Today Inc** G 847 934-9777
Palatine *(G-17074)*
**Silk 21 Screen Printing and Em** G 630 972-4250
Bolingbrook *(G-2370)*
**Sir Speedy Printing** G 312 337-0774
Chicago *(G-6518)*
**Sir Speedy Printing Cntr 6129** G 708 349-7789
Orland Park *(G-16891)*
**Sir Speedy Printing Ctr 6080** G 708 351-8841
Schaumburg *(G-19728)*
**Six Color Print LLC** F 847 336-3287
Waukegan *(G-21618)*
**Small Newspaper Group** C 815 937-3300
Kankakee *(G-12652)*
**Smart Office Services Inc** G 773 227-1121
Chicago *(G-6532)*
**Solution Printing Inc** G 217 529-9700
Springfield *(G-20528)*
**Sons Enterprises** F 847 677-4444
Skokie *(G-20088)*
**Southern Illinois University** F 618 453-2268
Carbondale *(G-3024)*
**Specialty Printing Midwest** G 618 799-8472
Roxana *(G-19086)*
**Specialty Promotions Inc** B 847 588-2580
Niles *(G-16036)*
**Speed Ink Printing** G 773 539-9700
Chicago *(G-6556)*
**Speedpro North Shore** G 847 983-0095
Skokie *(G-20089)*
**Springfield Printing Inc** G 217 787-3500
Springfield *(G-20531)*
**Sprinter Coml Print Label Corp** G 630 460-3492
Naperville *(G-15828)*
**State Attorney Appellate** G 217 782-3397
Springfield *(G-20536)*
**Stecker Graphics Inc** G 309 786-4973
Rock Island *(G-18204)*
**Stellato Printing Inc** G 815 725-1057
Crest Hill *(G-7468)*
**Steve Bortman** G 708 442-1669
Lyons *(G-14046)*
**Stevens Group LLc** E 331 209-2100
Elmhurst *(G-9945)*
**Strathmore Company** E 630 232-9677
Geneva *(G-10870)*
**Stromberg Allen and Company** E 773 847-7131
Tinley Park *(G-20947)*
**Suncraft Technologies Inc** C 630 369-7900
Naperville *(G-15757)*
**Sung Ji USA** F 847 956-9400
Elk Grove Village *(G-9760)*
**Sunrise Hitek Service Inc** E 773 792-8880
Chicago *(G-6630)*
**Superior Business Solutions** G 815 787-1333
Dekalb *(G-8123)*
**Superior Print Services Inc** G 630 257-7012
Lemont *(G-13264)*
**T C W F Inc** E 630 369-1360
Naperville *(G-15759)*
**T F N W Inc** G 630 584-7383
Saint Charles *(G-19277)*
**Tarco Printing Inc** G 630 467-1000
Itasca *(G-12364)*
**Team Cncept Prtg Thrmgrphy Inc** E 630 653-8326
Carol Stream *(G-3252)*
**Techprint Inc** F 847 616-0109
Elk Grove Village *(G-9774)*
**Thermo-Craft Inc** G 618 281-7055
Columbia *(G-7363)*
**Thiessen Communications Inc** E 847 884-0980
Schaumburg *(G-19761)*
**Thompson & Walsh LLC** G 847 734-1770
Arlington Heights *(G-855)*
**Three Angels Printing Svcs Inc** F 630 333-4305
Addison *(G-313)*
**Three Castle Press Inc** G 630 540-0120
Streamwood *(G-20676)*
**Times Record Company** E 309 582-5112
Aledo *(G-373)*
**Times Republic** E 815 432-5227
Watseka *(G-21431)*
**Toledo Democrat** G 217 849-2000
Toledo *(G-20967)*
**Tora Print Svcs** G 773 252-1000
Chicago *(G-6747)*
**Tower Printing & Design** G 630 495-1976
Lombard *(G-13870)*
**Trenton Sun** G 618 224-9422
Trenton *(G-20998)*
**Trymark Print Production LLC** G 630 668-7800
Glendale Heights *(G-11086)*
**Two JS Copies Now Inc** G 847 292-2679
Chicago *(G-6797)*
**Tylka Printing Inc** G 773 767-3775
Chicago *(G-6801)*
**Type Concepts Inc** G 708 361-1005
Palos Heights *(G-17112)*
**Unique Prtrs Lithographers Inc** D 708 656-8900
Cicero *(G-7240)*
**Unique/Active LLC** E 708 656-8900
Cicero *(G-7241)*
**United Lithograph Inc** G 847 803-1700
Des Plaines *(G-8290)*
**University of Illinois** E 217 333-9350
Champaign *(G-3552)*
**University Printing Co Inc** G 773 525-2400
Chicago *(G-6839)*
**Up North Printing Inc** G 630 584-8675
Saint Charles *(G-19290)*
**Valid Usa Inc** G 630 852-8200
Lisle *(G-13675)*
**Vigil Printing Inc** G 773 794-8808
Chicago *(G-6898)*
**Village Press Inc** G 847 362-1856
Libertyville *(G-13399)*
**Vision Integrated Graphics** E 312 373-6300
Chicago *(G-6903)*
**Vision Integrated Graphics** C 708 570-7900
Bolingbrook *(G-2380)*
**Voris Communication Co Inc** C 630 898-4268
Berkeley *(G-2051)*
**W R S Inc** G 630 279-0400
Elmhurst *(G-9959)*
**W W Barthel & Co** G 847 392-5643
Arlington Heights *(G-869)*
**Wagner Printing Co** E 630 941-7961
Freeport *(G-10698)*
**Weary & Baity Inc** G 312 943-6197
Chicago *(G-6947)*
**Webb-Mason Inc** F 630 428-5838
Naperville *(G-15782)*
**Weimer Design & Print Ltd Inc** G 630 393-3334
Warrenville *(G-21368)*
**West Vly Graphics & Print Inc** G 630 377-7575
Saint Charles *(G-19293)*
**Westrock Mwv LLC** E 217 442-2247
Danville *(G-7784)*
**Whipples Printing Press Inc** G 309 787-3538
Milan *(G-14808)*
**William Holloway Ltd** G 847 866-9520
Evanston *(G-10106)*
**Wilson Printing Inc** G 847 949-7800
Mundelein *(G-15567)*
**Wold Printing Services Ltd** G 847 546-3110
Volo *(G-21320)*
**Wood Labeling Systems Inc** G 815 344-8733
Johnsburg *(G-12444)*
**Woow Sushi Orland Park LLC** F 815 469-5189
Frankfort *(G-10377)*
**Wortman Printing Company Inc** G 217 347-3775
Effingham *(G-8864)*
**Wyckoff Advertising Inc** G 630 260-2525
Wheaton *(G-21990)*

## *PRINTING: Manmade Fiber & Silk, Broadwoven Fabric*

**Insignia Design Ltd** G 301 254-9221
Rolling Meadows *(G-18734)*
**Marathon Sportswear Inc** E 708 389-5390
Blue Island *(G-2262)*

## *PRINTING: Offset*

**11th Street Express Prtg Inc** F 815 968-0208
Rockford *(G-18235)*
**A & H Lithoprint Inc** F 708 345-1196
Broadview *(G-2551)*
**A A Swift Print Inc** G 847 301-1122
Schaumburg *(G-19418)*
**A and K Prtg & Graphic Design** G 618 244-3525
Mount Vernon *(G-15396)*
**A To Z Offset Prtg & Pubg Inc** G 847 966-3016
Skokie *(G-19943)*
**Abbotts Minute Printing Inc** G 708 339-6010
South Holland *(G-20239)*
**Acres of Sky Communications** G 815 493-2560
Lanark *(G-13149)*



Employee Codes: A=Over 500 employees, B=251-500
C=101-250, D=51-100, E=20-50, F=10-19, G=3-9
2017 Harris Illinois
Industrial Directory
1715

# PRINTING: Offset — PRODUCT SECTION

|  |  |  |
|---|---|---|
| Active Graphics Inc | Cicero (G-7176) | E 708 656-8900 |
| Adcraft Printers Inc | Kankakee (G-12601) | F 815 932-6432 |
| Advance Instant Printing Co | Chicago (G-3760) | G 312 346-0986 |
| Aires Press Inc | Park Ridge (G-17179) | G 847 698-6813 |
| All Printing & Graphics Inc | Broadview (G-2555) | F 708 450-1512 |
| All Purpose Prtg & Bus Forms | Alsip (G-431) | G 708 389-9192 |
| All-Ways Quick Print | Orland Park (G-16841) | G 708 403-8422 |
| Allegra Network LLC | Aurora (G-1104) | G 630 801-9335 |
| Allegra Print & Imaging | Lisle (G-13554) | F 630 963-9100 |
| Allegra Print & Imaging | Romeoville (G-18794) | G 815 524-3902 |
| Allegra Print & Imaging Inc | Elgin (G-8942) | G 847 697-1434 |
| Alliance Graphics | Chicago (G-3814) | G 312 280-8000 |
| Allstate Printing Inc | Elk Grove Village (G-9288) | G 847 640-4401 |
| America Printing Inc | Wheeling (G-22002) | G 847 229-8358 |
| American Labelmark Company | Chicago (G-3859) | C 773 478-0900 |
| American Litho Incorporated | Carol Stream (G-3100) | B 630 462-1700 |
| American Quick Print Inc | Wauconda (G-21441) | G 847 253-2700 |
| American Speedy Printing Ctrs | Elk Grove Village (G-9298) | E 847 806-0135 |
| Anikam Inc | Alsip (G-433) | G 708 385-0200 |
| Apple Graphics Inc | Batavia (G-1416) | G 630 389-2222 |
| Art-Craft Printers | Franklin Park (G-10401) | G 847 455-2201 |
| Atlantic Press Inc | Chicago (G-3977) | D 708 496-2400 |
| Aurora Fastprint Inc | Aurora (G-1116) | G 630 896-5980 |
| Austin Graphic | Watseka (G-21414) | G 815 432-4983 |
| Azusa Inc | Mount Vernon (G-15399) | G 618 244-6591 |
| B & B Printing Company | Pittsfield (G-17561) | G 217 285-6072 |
| B Allan Graphics Inc | Alsip (G-438) | F 708 396-1704 |
| Babak Inc | Chicago (G-4024) | G 312 419-8686 |
| Bailleu & Bailleu Printing Inc | Kewanee (G-12670) | G 309 852-2517 |
| Bally Foil Graphics Inc | Elk Grove Village (G-9333) | G 847 427-1509 |
| Balsley Printing Inc | Rockton (G-18692) | F 815 624-7515 |
| Barnaby Inc | Sycamore (G-20789) | F 815 895-6555 |
| Barrington Print & Copy Inc | Barrington (G-1273) | G 847 382-1185 |
| Bat Business Services Inc | Aurora (G-1118) | G 630 801-9335 |
| Beardsley Printery Inc | Rock Island (G-18161) | G 309 788-4041 |
| Bell Litho Inc | Elk Grove Village (G-9338) | D 847 952-3300 |
| Bell Litho Inc | Elk Grove Village (G-9339) | G 847 290-9300 |
| Bfc Forms Service Inc | Batavia (G-1422) | C 630 879-9240 |
| Biller Press & Manufacturing | Antioch (G-623) | G 847 395-4111 |
| Bloom-Norm Printing Inc | Normal (G-16265) | G 309 663-8545 |
| Bloomington Offset Process Inc | Bloomington (G-2149) | D 309 662-3395 |
| Blue Island Newspaper Prtg Inc | Harvey (G-11661) | D 708 333-1006 |
| Breaker Press Co Inc | Chicago (G-4159) | G 773 927-1666 |
| Breese Publishing Co Inc | Breese (G-2440) | G 618 526-7211 |
| Budget Printing Center | Edwardsville (G-8793) | G 618 655-1636 |
| Bureau Valley Chief | Tiskilwa (G-20958) | G 815 646-4731 |
| C E Dienberg Printing Company | Oak Park (G-16655) | G 708 848-4406 |
| C F C Interantional | Chicago Heights (G-7085) | G 708 753-0679 |
| C M J Associates Inc | Oak Lawn (G-16608) | G 708 636-2995 |
| Cadore-Miller Printing Inc | Hickory Hills (G-11768) | F 708 430-7091 |
| Caldwell Letter Service Inc | Chicago (G-4214) | E 773 847-0708 |
| Camera Ready Copies Inc | Prospect Heights (G-17773) | E 847 215-8611 |
| Cannon Ball Marketing Inc | Lisle (G-13573) | G 630 971-2127 |
| Capital Prtg & Die Cutng Inc | Aurora (G-1124) | G 630 896-5520 |
| Capitol Impressions Inc | Peoria (G-17322) | E 309 633-1400 |
| Carter Printing Co Inc | Farmersville (G-10183) | E 217 227-4464 |
| Case Paluch & Associates Inc | Chicago (G-4248) | G 773 465-0098 |
| Cavco Printers | Energy (G-9985) | G 618 988-8011 |
| CCL Label (chicago) Inc | Batavia (G-1427) | G 630 406-9991 |
| Central Printers & Graphics | Bedford Park (G-1543) | G 773 586-3711 |
| Cenveo Inc | Jacksonville (G-12383) | G 217 243-4258 |
| Christopher R Cline Prtg Ltd | Elk Grove Village (G-9372) | F 847 981-0500 |
| Chromatech Printing Inc | Des Plaines (G-8168) | F 847 699-0333 |
| Cjs Printing | Manito (G-14172) | G 309 968-6585 |
| Classic Printery Inc | Hainesville (G-11522) | G 847 546-6555 |
| Classic Printing Co Inc | Decatur (G-7857) | E 217 428-1733 |
| Classic Prtg Thermography Inc | Wood Dale (G-22352) | G 630 595-7765 |
| Clementi Printing Inc | Chicago (G-4401) | G 773 622-0795 |
| Clyde Printing Company | Chicago (G-4410) | E 773 847-5900 |
| Color Tone Printing | Blue Island (G-2242) | G 708 385-1442 |
| Comet Conection Inc | Alsip (G-451) | G 312 243-5400 |
| Commercial Copy Printing Ctr | Elk Grove Village (G-9384) | F 847 981-8590 |
| Commercial Prtg of Rockford | Rockford (G-18317) | G 815 965-4759 |
| Component Sales Incorporated | Addison (G-79) | F 630 543-9666 |
| Conrad Press Ltd | Columbia (G-7356) | G |
| Consolidated Printing Co Inc | Chicago (G-4453) | F 773 631-2800 |
| Continental Web Press Inc | Itasca (G-12247) | C 630 773-1903 |
| Continental Web Press KY Inc | Itasca (G-12248) | C 630 773-1903 |
| Continental Web Press KY Inc | Itasca (G-12249) | C 859 485-1500 |
| Copy Mat Printing | Bloomington (G-2155) | G 309 452-1392 |
| Copyco Printing Inc | Des Plaines (G-8175) | E 847 824-4400 |
| Corporate Graphics America Inc | Chicago (G-4474) | F 773 481-2100 |
| Corwin Printing | Mount Carmel (G-15263) | G 618 263-3936 |
| Craftsmen Printing | Hoopeston (G-12108) | G 217 283-9574 |
| Creative Graphic Arts Inc | Northbrook (G-16234) | G 847 498-2678 |
| Creative Lithocraft Inc | Schaumburg (G-19488) | F 847 352-7002 |
| Creative Lithocraft Inc | Schaumburg (G-19489) | G 847 352-7002 |
| Crossmark Printing Inc | Tinley Park (G-20906) | G 708 532-8263 |
| Custom Telephone Printing Inc | Woodstock (G-22557) | F 815 338-0000 |
| D & R Press | Elmwood Park (G-9966) | G 708 452-0500 |
| Dale K Brown | Woodstock (G-22558) | G 815 338-0222 |
| Dallas Corporation | Downers Grove (G-8424) | F 630 322-8000 |
| Dandelion Distributors Inc | Grayslake (G-11332) | G 815 675-9800 |
| Dans Printing & Off Sups Inc | Oak Forest (G-16577) | G 708 687-3055 |
| Darnall Printing | Bloomington (G-2161) | G 309 827-7212 |
| David H Vander Ploeg | South Holland (G-20260) | G 708 331-7700 |
| Dbp Communications | Chicago (G-4565) | F 312 263-1569 |
| DE Asbury Inc | Quincy (G-17820) | E 217 222-0617 |
| Deadline Prtg Clor Copying LLC | Elk Grove Village (G-9419) | G 847 437-9000 |
| Demis Printing Inc | Park Ridge (G-17189) | G 773 282-9128 |
| Denor Graphics Inc | Elk Grove Village (G-9423) | G 847 364-1130 |
| Dependable Graphics & Services | West Chicago (G-21691) | G 630 231-2746 |
| Des Plaines Printing LLC | Buffalo Grove (G-2686) | F 847 465-3300 |
| Design Graphics Inc | New Lenox (G-15875) | G 815 462-3323 |
| Di-Carr Printing Company | Cicero (G-7189) | G 708 863-0069 |
| Diamond Graphics of Berwyn | Berwyn (G-2060) | G 708 749-2500 |
| Diamond Web Printing LLC | Downers Grove (G-8428) | F 630 663-0350 |
| Dicianni Graphics Incorporated | Addison (G-91) | G 630 833-5100 |
| Dixon Direct LLC | Dixon (G-8328) | C 815 284-2211 |
| Douglas Press Inc | Bellwood (G-1704) | C 800 323-0705 |
| Dreamwrks Grphic Cmmnctons LLC | Glenview (G-11121) | D 847 679-6710 |
| Duo Graphics | Elk Grove Village (G-9436) | G 847 228-7080 |
| Eagle Printing Company | Moline (G-14936) | G 309 762-0771 |
| Eastrich Printing & Sales | Freeport (G-10654) | G 815 232-4216 |
| Evanston Graphic Imaging Inc | Evanston (G-10033) | G 847 869-7446 |
| Ever-Redi Printing Inc | Hinsdale (G-11945) | G 708 352-4378 |
| Express Printing Ctr of Libert | Skokie (G-19998) | G 847 675-0659 |
| F C L Graphics Inc | Harwood Heights (G-11684) | C 708 867-5500 |
| F Weber Printing Co Inc | Manteno (G-14183) | G 815 468-6152 |
| Falcon Press Inc | Crystal Lake (G-7575) | G 815 455-9099 |
| Fast Print Shop | Marion (G-14259) | G 618 997-1976 |
| Fast Printing of Joliet Inc | Joliet (G-12492) | G 815 723-0080 |
| Fastway Printing Inc | Schaumburg (G-19524) | G 847 882-0950 |
| Faulstich Printing Company Inc | Danville (G-7718) | G 217 442-4994 |
| Fernwood Printers Ltd | Oak Forest (G-16581) | G 630 964-9449 |
| Fisher Printing Inc | Bridgeview (G-2489) | G 708 598-1500 |
| Five Star Printing Inc | Virden (G-21296) | G 217 965-3355 |
| Flash Printing Inc | Franklin Park (G-10470) | G 847 288-9101 |
| Fleetwood Press Inc | Brookfield (G-2632) | G 708 485-6811 |
| Flow-Eze Company | Rockford (G-18383) | F 815 965-1062 |
| FM Graphic Impressions Inc | Aurora (G-1153) | E 630 897-8788 |
| Forms Design Plus Coleman Prtg | Peoria (G-17365) | G 309 685-6000 |
| Franz Stationery Company Inc | Lake Barrington (G-12807) | F 847 593-0060 |
| Frye-Williamson Press Inc | Springfield (G-20444) | E 217 522-7744 |
| Full Line Printing Inc | Chicago (G-4895) | G 312 642-8080 |

## PRODUCT SECTION — PRINTING: Offset

| Company | Code | Phone |
|---|---|---|
| G & G Studios /Broadway Prtg — Bradley (G-2422) | F | 815 933-8181 |
| G F Printing — Granite City (G-11278) | G | 618 797-0576 |
| Gallery Office Pdts & Prtrs — Homewood (G-12099) | G | 708 798-2220 |
| Gemini Digital Inc — Roselle (G-18942) | G | 630 894-9430 |
| Genoa Business Forms Inc — Sycamore (G-20798) | E | 815 895-2800 |
| Gerard Printing Company — Elk Grove Village (G-9499) | G | 847 437-6442 |
| Graphic Packaging Corporation — Franklin Park (G-10483) | C | 847 451-7400 |
| Graphics Group LLC — Chicago (G-4992) | D | 708 867-5500 |
| Graphics Plus Inc — Lisle (G-13597) | F | 630 968-9073 |
| Great Impressions Inc — Libertyville (G-13327) | G | 847 367-6725 |
| Greek Art Printing & Pubg Co — Glenview (G-11133) | G | 847 724-8860 |
| Grovak Instant Printing Co — Mount Prospect (G-15334) | G | 847 675-2414 |
| Grove Design & Advertising Inc — Crystal Lake (G-7585) | G | 815 459-4552 |
| H B H Print Co — Gurnee (G-11456) | F | 847 662-2233 |
| Hafner Printing Co Inc — Chicago (G-5030) | F | 312 362-0120 |
| Hako Minuteman Inc — Addison (G-140) | G | 630 627-6900 |
| Hal Mather & Sons Incorporated — Woodstock (G-22573) | E | 815 338-4000 |
| Harry Otto Printing Company — Elburn (G-8889) | F | 630 365-6111 |
| Hawthorne Press Inc — Spring Grove (G-20336) | G | 847 587-0582 |
| Heart Printing Inc — Arlington Heights (G-764) | G | 847 259-2100 |
| Hempel Group Inc — Batavia (G-1454) | G | 630 389-2222 |
| Henry Printing Inc — Carbondale (G-3010) | G | 618 529-3040 |
| Heritage Press Inc — Libertyville (G-13330) | G | 847 362-9699 |
| Heritage Printing — Prophetstown (G-17770) | G | 815 537-2372 |
| Higgins Quick Print — Des Plaines (G-8204) | G | 847 635-7700 |
| Highland Printers — Highland (G-11791) | G | 618 654-5880 |
| House of Graphics — Carol Stream (G-3168) | E | 630 682-0810 |
| Hub Printing Company Inc — Rochelle (G-18094) | F | 815 562-7057 |
| Hunt Enterprises Inc — Countryside (G-7433) | G | 708 354-8464 |
| Huston-Patterson Corporation — Decatur (G-7890) | D | 217 429-5161 |
| Ideal Advertising & Printing — Rockford (G-18426) | F | 815 965-1713 |
| Illinois Office Sup Elect Prtg — Ottawa (G-16962) | E | 815 434-0186 |
| Image Print Inc — Streator (G-20691) | G | 815 672-1068 |
| Impact Prtrs & Lithographers — Elk Grove Village (G-9542) | E | 847 981-9676 |
| In-Print Graphics Inc — Oak Forest (G-16584) | E | 708 396-1010 |
| Informative Systems Inc — Springfield (G-20457) | F | 217 523-8422 |
| Ink Spot Printing — Chicago (G-5194) | G | 773 528-0288 |
| Ink Spot Silk Screen — Glenview (G-11147) | G | 847 724-6234 |
| Inky Printers — Freeport (G-10668) | G | 815 235-3700 |
| Insty Prints Palatine Inc — Palatine (G-17042) | F | 847 963-0000 |
| Instyprints of Waukegan Inc — Waukegan (G-21571) | G | 847 336-5599 |
| Intel Printing Inc — Broadview (G-2587) | G | 708 343-1144 |
| Irving Press Inc — Elk Grove Village (G-9555) | E | 847 595-6650 |
| J & J Mr Quick Print Inc — Chicago (G-5251) | G | 773 767-7776 |
| J D Graphic Co Inc — Elk Grove Village (G-9557) | E | 847 364-4000 |
| J F Wagner Printing Co — Northbrook (G-16280) | G | 847 564-0017 |
| J Gooch & Associates Inc — Springfield (G-20461) | G | 217 522-7575 |
| J K Printing & Mailing Inc — Highland Park (G-11846) | G | 847 432-7717 |
| J Oshana & Son Printing — Chicago (G-5261) | G | 773 283-8311 |
| J S Printing Inc — Franklin Park (G-10503) | G | 847 678-6300 |
| Jamali Kopy Kat Printing Inc — Bellwood (G-1711) | G | 708 544-6164 |
| James Ray Monroe Corporation — Centralia (G-3420) | F | 618 532-4575 |
| Jay Printing — Palatine (G-17046) | G | 847 934-6103 |
| Jds Printing Inc — Glendale Heights (G-11037) | G | 630 208-1195 |
| Joes Printing — Chicago (G-5309) | G | 773 545-6063 |
| John S Swift Company Inc — Buffalo Grove (G-2713) | G | 847 465-3300 |
| Josco Inc — Chicago (G-5326) | G | 708 867-7189 |
| Josephs Printing Service — Glenview (G-11154) | G | 847 724-4429 |
| Jph Enterprises Inc — Des Plaines (G-8217) | G | 847 390-0900 |
| July 25th Corporation — Bloomington (G-2186) | F | 309 664-6444 |
| Juskie Printing Corp — Downers Grove (G-8468) | G | 630 663-8833 |
| K & M Printing Company Inc — Schaumburg (G-19595) | G | 847 884-1100 |
| K Chae Corp — Lincolnwood (G-13518) | F | 847 763-0077 |
| K R O Enterprises Ltd — Moline (G-14949) | G | 309 797-2213 |
| KB Publishing Inc — South Holland (G-20282) | D | 708 331-6352 |
| KB Publishing Inc — South Holland (G-20283) | E | 708 331-6352 |
| Kellogg Printing Co — Monmouth (G-15016) | F | 309 734-8388 |
| Kelly Printing Co Inc — Danville (G-7741) | E | 217 443-1792 |
| Kendall Printing Co — Yorkville (G-22663) | G | 630 553-9200 |
| Kenilworth Press Incorporated — Wilmette (G-22256) | G | 847 256-5210 |
| Kens Quick Print Inc — Highland Park (G-11849) | F | 847 831-4410 |
| Keystone Printing & Publishing — Richmond (G-17965) | G | 815 678-2591 |
| Keystone Printing Services — Chicago (G-5380) | G | 773 622-7210 |
| Kingery Printing Company — Effingham (G-8842) | C | 217 347-5151 |
| Klein Printing Inc — Chicago (G-5387) | G | 773 235-2121 |
| Kon Printing Inc — Batavia (G-1461) | G | 630 879-2211 |
| Kram Digital Solutions Inc — Glenview (G-11164) | G | 312 222-0431 |
| Kwik Print Inc — Itasca (G-12299) | G | 630 773-3225 |
| L & S Label Printing Inc — Cherry Valley (G-3646) | G | 815 964-6753 |
| Labels Unlimited Incorporated — Chicago (G-5430) | E | 773 523-7500 |
| Lake Media Services Inc — Chicago (G-5439) | G | 312 739-0423 |
| Lans Printing Inc — Lynwood (G-14021) | G | 708 895-6226 |
| Lazare Printing Co Inc — Chicago (G-5475) | G | 773 871-2500 |
| Lee-Wel Printing Corporation — Wheaton (G-21966) | G | 630 682-0935 |
| Leonard A Unes Printing Co — Peoria (G-17400) | G | 309 674-4942 |
| Leonard Emerson — Divernon (G-8316) | G | 217 628-3441 |
| Liberty Lithographers Inc — Tinley Park (G-20931) | C | 708 633-7450 |
| Lincoln Printers Inc — Lincoln (G-13413) | G | 217 732-3121 |
| Lincolnshire Printing Inc — McHenry (G-14523) | G | 815 578-0740 |
| Link-Letters Ltd — Wheeling (G-22094) | F | 847 459-1199 |
| Lithographic Industries Inc — Broadview (G-2594) | E | 773 921-7955 |
| Little Doloras — South Holland (G-20286) | G | 708 331-1330 |
| Luke Graphics Inc — Chicago (G-5559) | F | 773 775-6733 |
| Luxon Printing Inc — West Chicago (G-21734) | F | 630 293-7710 |
| Lynns Printing Co — Alton (G-583) | G | 618 465-7701 |
| M & R Printing Inc — Rolling Meadows (G-18742) | G | 847 398-2500 |
| M L S Printing Co Inc — Deerfield (G-8033) | G | 847 948-8902 |
| M S A Printing Co — Elk Grove Village (G-9604) | G | 847 593-5699 |
| Macoupin County Enquirer Inc — Carlinville (G-3042) | E | 217 854-2534 |
| Madden Communications Inc — Wood Dale (G-22394) | C | 630 787-2200 |
| Madden Communications Inc — Bloomingdale (G-2114) | E | 630 784-4325 |
| Mall Graphic Inc — Huntley (G-12161) | G | 847 668-7600 |
| Mallof Abruzino Nash Mktg Inc — Carol Stream (G-3188) | E | 630 929-5200 |
| Mar Graphics — Valmeyer (G-21112) | D | 618 935-2111 |
| Marcus Press — Bloomingdale (G-2115) | G | 630 351-1857 |
| Mark Twain Press Inc — Mundelein (G-15523) | G | 847 255-2700 |
| Marnic Inc — Galesburg (G-10766) | G | 309 343-1418 |
| Marquardt Printing Company — Willowbrook (G-22220) | E | 630 887-8500 |
| Master Graphics LLC — Rochelle (G-18098) | D | 815 562-5800 |
| Mattoon Printing Center — Mattoon (G-14400) | G | 217 234-3100 |
| Mc Adams Multigraphics Inc — Oak Brook (G-16539) | G | 630 990-1707 |
| McDonough Democrat Inc — Bushnell (G-2905) | G | 309 772-2129 |
| McGrath Press Inc — Crystal Lake (G-7607) | E | 815 356-5246 |
| Mencarini Enterprises Inc — Rockford (G-18491) | F | 815 398-9565 |
| Metropolitan Graphic Arts Inc — Gurnee (G-11471) | E | 847 566-9502 |
| Metropolitan Printers — East Peoria (G-8724) | G | 309 694-1114 |
| Mi-Te Fast Printers Inc — Chicago (G-5718) | E | 312 236-8352 |
| Michael Zimmerman — Northbrook (G-16311) | G | 847 272-5560 |
| Microprint — Romeoville (G-18846) | G | 630 969-1710 |
| Mid Central Printing & Mailing — Wilmette (G-22262) | E | 847 251-4040 |
| Mid City Printing Service — Chicago (G-5725) | G | 773 777-5400 |
| MidAmerican Prtg Systems Inc — Chicago (G-5732) | E | 312 663-4720 |
| Midwest Graphic Industries — Bensenville (G-1952) | F | 630 509-2972 |
| Mission of Our Lady of Mercy — Chicago (G-5771) | G | 312 738-7568 |
| MJM Graphics — Lake Forest (G-12927) | G | 847 234-1802 |
| Modern Printing of Quincy — Quincy (G-17861) | F | 217 223-1063 |
| Msf Graphics Inc — Des Plaines (G-8239) | G | 847 446-6900 |
| Mt Carmel Register Co Inc — Mount Carmel (G-15276) | E | 618 262-5144 |
| Multi Art Press — Chicago (G-5831) | G | 773 775-0515 |
| N Bujarski Inc — Schaumburg (G-19660) | G | 847 884-1600 |
| N P D Inc — Oak Lawn (G-16636) | G | 708 424-6788 |
| Negs & Litho Inc — Chicago (G-5881) | G | 847 647-7770 |
| Newell & Haney Inc — Belleville (G-1660) | F | 618 277-3660 |
| North Shore Printers Inc — Waukegan (G-21593) | F | 847 623-0037 |
| Northwest Printing Inc — Harvard (G-11642) | G | 815 943-7977 |

Employee Codes: A=Over 500 employees, B=251-500, C=101-250, D=51-100, E=20-50, F=10-19, G=3-9

## PRINTING: Offset

|  |  |
|---|---|
| Nova Printing and Litho Co | F 773 486-8500 |
| Mount Prospect (G-15355) | |
| Nu-Art Printing | G 618 533-9971 |
| Centralia (G-3425) | |
| Off The Press | G 815 436-9612 |
| Plainfield (G-17634) | |
| Officers Printing Inc | G 847 480-4663 |
| Northbrook (G-16323) | |
| Ogden Minuteman Inc | G 773 542-6917 |
| Chicago (G-5972) | |
| Ogden Offset Printers Inc | G 773 284-7797 |
| Chicago (G-5973) | |
| Olde Print Shoppe Inc | G 618 395-3833 |
| Olney (G-16786) | |
| Om Printing Corporation | G 708 482-4750 |
| Alsip (G-503) | |
| Omega Printing Inc | E 630 595-6344 |
| Bensenville (G-1958) | |
| Omega Royal Graphics Inc | F 847 952-8000 |
| Elk Grove Village (G-9665) | |
| Original Smith Printing Inc | D 309 663-0325 |
| Bloomington (G-2207) | |
| P & P Press Inc | E 309 691-8511 |
| Peoria (G-17420) | |
| P & S Cochran Printers Inc | E 309 691-6668 |
| Peoria (G-17421) | |
| P F Pettibone & Co | G 815 344-7811 |
| Crystal Lake (G-7624) | |
| P H C Enterprises Inc | G 847 816-7373 |
| Vernon Hills (G-21186) | |
| Palmer Printing Inc | E 312 427-7150 |
| Chicago (G-6065) | |
| Palwaukee Printing Company | G 847 459-0240 |
| Wheeling (G-22117) | |
| Pana News Inc | F 217 562-2111 |
| Pana (G-17137) | |
| Pantagraph Printing and Sty Co | F 309 829-1071 |
| Bloomington (G-2208) | |
| Papyrus Press Inc | F 773 342-0700 |
| Chicago (G-6074) | |
| Park Printing Inc | G 708 430-4878 |
| Palos Hills (G-17120) | |
| Parrot Press | G 773 376-6333 |
| Chicago (G-6087) | |
| Patton Printing and Graphics | G 217 347-0220 |
| Effingham (G-8852) | |
| Paulson Press Inc | G 847 290-0080 |
| Elk Grove Village (G-9671) | |
| Peacock Printing Inc | G 618 242-3157 |
| Mount Vernon (G-15437) | |
| Perma Graphics Printers | G 815 485-6955 |
| New Lenox (G-15901) | |
| Photo Graphic Design Service | G 815 672-4417 |
| Streator (G-20700) | |
| Physicians Record Co Inc | D 800 323-9268 |
| Berwyn (G-2074) | |
| Pinney Printing Company | G 815 626-2727 |
| Sterling (G-20603) | |
| Pinney Printing Company | E 815 626-2727 |
| Sterling (G-20604) | |
| Pioneer Printing Service Inc | G 312 337-4283 |
| Chicago (G-6127) | |
| PIP Printing | G 847 998-6330 |
| Glenview (G-11182) | |
| PIP Printing Inc | G 815 464-0075 |
| Frankfort (G-10349) | |
| Plum Grove Printers Inc | E 847 882-4020 |
| Hoffman Estates (G-12039) | |
| Poll Enterprises Inc | F 708 756-1120 |
| Chicago Heights (G-7117) | |
| Polpress Inc | G 773 792-1200 |
| Chicago (G-6152) | |
| Precision Dialogue Direct Inc | D 773 237-2264 |
| Chicago (G-6168) | |
| Preferred Printing & Graphics | G 708 547-6880 |
| Berkeley (G-2049) | |
| Preferred Printing Service | G 312 421-2343 |
| Chicago (G-6175) | |
| Press America Inc | E 847 228-0333 |
| Elk Grove Village (G-9696) | |
| Press Tech Inc | G 847 824-4485 |
| Des Plaines (G-8263) | |
| Pride In Graphics Inc | F 312 427-2000 |
| Chicago (G-6184) | |
| Print King Inc | F 708 499-3777 |
| Oak Lawn (G-16641) | |
| Print Source For Business Inc | G 847 356-0190 |
| Lake Villa (G-13023) | |
| Print Turnaround Inc | F 847 228-1762 |
| Arlington Heights (G-822) | |
| Print Xpress | G 847 677-5555 |
| Skokie (G-20061) | |
| Printed Impressions Inc | G 773 604-8585 |
| Villa Park (G-21279) | |
| Printing By Joseph | G 708 479-2669 |
| Mokena (G-14898) | |
| Printing Craftsmen of Pontiac | G 815 844-7118 |
| Pontiac (G-17709) | |
| Printing Etc Inc | G 815 562-6151 |
| Rochelle (G-18102) | |
| Printing Plant | F 618 529-3115 |
| Carbondale (G-3019) | |
| Printing Plus | G 708 301-3900 |
| Lockport (G-13739) | |
| Printing Plus of Roselle Inc | G 630 893-0410 |
| Roselle (G-18963) | |
| Printing Source Inc | G 773 588-2930 |
| Morton Grove (G-15228) | |
| Printing Store Inc | F 708 383-3638 |
| Oak Park (G-16681) | |
| Printing Works Inc | G 847 860-1920 |
| Elk Grove Village (G-9698) | |
| Printmeisters Inc | G 708 474-8400 |
| Lansing (G-13180) | |
| Printsource Plus Inc | G 708 389-6252 |
| Blue Island (G-2265) | |
| Priority Printing | G 773 889-6021 |
| Chicago (G-6198) | |
| Prism Commercial Printing Ctrs | G 630 834-4443 |
| Chicago (G-6199) | |
| Prism Commercial Printing Ctrs | G 773 229-2620 |
| Chicago (G-6200) | |
| Pro-Type Printing Inc | G 217 379-4715 |
| Paxton (G-17244) | |
| Production Press Inc | E 217 243-3353 |
| Jacksonville (G-12409) | |
| Progress Printing Corporation | E 773 927-0123 |
| Chicago (G-6210) | |
| Progressive Systems Netwrk Inc | G 312 382-8383 |
| Chicago (G-6214) | |
| Provena Enterprises Inc | E 708 478-3230 |
| Kankakee (G-12643) | |
| Quad City Press | F 309 764-8142 |
| Moline (G-14965) | |
| Quality Quickprint Inc | F 815 439-3430 |
| Joliet (G-12560) | |
| Quality Quickprint Inc | G 815 723-0941 |
| Lemont (G-13258) | |
| Quality Quickprint Inc | F 815 838-1784 |
| Lockport (G-13740) | |
| Quick Print Shoppe | G 309 694-1204 |
| East Peoria (G-8729) | |
| Quickprinters | G 309 833-5250 |
| Macomb (G-14130) | |
| Quinn Print Inc | G 847 823-9100 |
| Park Ridge (G-17218) | |
| R & R Creative Graphics Inc | G 630 208-4724 |
| Geneva (G-10861) | |
| R N R Photographers Inc | G 708 453-1868 |
| River Grove (G-18013) | |
| R R Donnelley & Sons Company | B 312 326-8000 |
| Chicago (G-6270) | |
| Rainbow Manufacturing Inc | E 847 824-9600 |
| Mundelein (G-15551) | |
| Rapid Print | G 309 673-0826 |
| Peoria (G-17240) | |
| Rasmussen Press Inc | G |
| Bensenville (G-1976) | |
| Ready Press | G 847 358-8655 |
| Palatine (G-17066) | |
| Remke Printing Inc | G 847 520-7300 |
| Wheeling (G-22137) | |
| Repro-Graphics Inc | G 847 439-1775 |
| Elk Grove Village (G-9714) | |
| Review Graphics Inc | G 815 623-2570 |
| Roscoe (G-18913) | |
| Richardson & Edwards Inc | E 630 543-1818 |
| Oak Brook (G-16559) | |
| Riverside Graphics Corporation | G 312 372-3766 |
| Chicago (G-6363) | |
| Rohrer Litho Inc | G 630 833-6610 |
| Elmhurst (G-9931) | |
| Romel Press Inc | G 708 343-6090 |
| Melrose Park (G-14687) | |
| Roskuszka & Sons Inc | F 630 851-3400 |
| Aurora (G-1210) | |
| RR Donnelley Printing Co LP | G 312 326-8000 |
| Chicago (G-6405) | |
| Rudin Printing Company Inc | F 217 528-5111 |
| Springfield (G-20515) | |
| Rutledge Printing Co | F 708 479-8282 |
| Orland Park (G-16889) | |
| S G C M Corp | G 630 953-2428 |
| Oakbrook Terrace (G-16720) | |
| S G S Inc | G 708 544-6061 |
| Downers Grove (G-8517) | |
| S M C Graphics | G 708 754-8973 |
| Chicago Heights (G-7125) | |
| Sales Midwest Prtg & Packg Inc | G 309 764-5544 |
| Moline (G-14968) | |
| Salsedo Press Inc | F 773 533-9900 |
| Chicago (G-6435) | |
| Savino Enterprises | G 708 385-5277 |
| Blue Island (G-2268) | |
| Scarzone Printing Services | G 630 595-2690 |
| Wood Dale (G-22419) | |
| Scheiwes Print Shop | G 815 683-2398 |
| Crescent City (G-7456) | |
| Schiele Graphics Inc | D 847 434-5455 |
| Elk Grove Village (G-9731) | |
| Schwartzkopf Printing Inc | F 618 463-0747 |
| Alton (G-589) | |
| Segerdahl Corp | C 847 541-1080 |
| Wheeling (G-22146) | |
| Segerdahl Corp | D 847 850-8811 |
| Wheeling (G-22147) | |
| Segerdahl Graphics Inc | B 847 541-1080 |
| Wheeling (G-22148) | |
| Service Printing Corporation | G 847 669-9620 |
| Huntley (G-12176) | |
| Shanin Company | D 847 676-1200 |
| Lincolnwood (G-13537) | |
| Shawver Press Inc | G 815 772-4700 |
| Morrison (G-15148) | |
| Shree Mahavir Inc | G 312 408-1080 |
| Chicago (G-6501) | |
| Sigley Printing & Off Sup Co | G 618 997-5304 |
| Marion (G-14287) | |
| Sigma Graphics Inc | F 815 433-1000 |
| Ottawa (G-16984) | |
| Simple Solutions | G 618 932-6177 |
| West Frankfort (G-21819) | |
| Sleepeck Printing Company | C 708 544-8900 |
| Chicago (G-6529) | |
| Snegde Deep | G 630 351-7111 |
| Roselle (G-18978) | |
| Snow Printing LLC | G 618 233-0712 |
| Belleville (G-1676) | |
| Solid Impressions Inc | G 630 543-7300 |
| Carol Stream (G-3241) | |
| Solution 3 Graphics Inc | F 773 233-3600 |
| Chicago (G-6542) | |
| Sommers & Fahrenbach Inc | F 773 478-3033 |
| Chicago (G-6543) | |
| Southwest Printing Co | G 708 389-0800 |
| Alsip (G-530) | |
| Spectrum Graphic Services Inc | E 630 766-7673 |
| Elmhurst (G-9941) | |
| Speedys Quick Print | G 217 431-0510 |
| Danville (G-7766) | |
| Spell It With Color Inc | G 630 961-5617 |
| Naperville (G-15753) | |
| Sphere Inc | G 847 566-4800 |
| Mundelein (G-15560) | |
| Stark Printing Company | G 847 234-8430 |
| Round Lake (G-19068) | |
| Steiner Impressions Inc | G 815 633-4135 |
| Loves Park (G-13994) | |
| Steve O Inc | G 847 473-4466 |
| North Chicago (G-16187) | |
| Stix Envelope & Mfg Co | G 217 589-5122 |
| Roodhouse (G-18886) | |
| Suburban Press Inc | E 847 255-2240 |
| Arlington Heights (G-847) | |
| Sunrise Printing Inc | F 847 928-1800 |
| Schiller Park (G-19877) | |
| Swift Impressions Inc | G 312 263-3800 |
| Chicago (G-6650) | |
| Swifty Print | G 630 584-9063 |
| Saint Charles (G-19276) | |
| T K O Quality Offset Printing | G 847 709-0455 |
| Arlington Heights (G-850) | |
| Tampico Press | G 312 243-5448 |
| Chicago (G-6672) | |
| Taykit Inc | E 847 888-1150 |
| Elgin (G-9202) | |
| Tele Print | G 630 941-7877 |
| Elmhurst (G-9949) | |
| Temper Enterprises Inc | G 815 553-0374 |
| Crest Hill (G-7469) | |

# PRODUCT SECTION

## PROFESSIONAL EQPT & SPLYS, WHOLESALE: Optical Goods

Tempo Holdings Inc .............................. E ...... 630 462-8200
  Carol Stream *(G-3254)*
Thomas Printing & Sty Co ..................... G ...... 618 435-2801
  Benton *(G-2041)*
Three-Z Printing Co ............................. B ...... 217 857-3153
  Teutopolis *(G-20857)*
Thrift n Swift ....................................... G ...... 847 455-1350
  Franklin Park *(G-10606)*
Timothy Helgoth .................................. G ...... 217 224-8008
  Quincy *(G-17894)*
Tlm Enterprises Inc ............................. G ...... 815 284-5040
  Dixon *(G-8356)*
Topweb LLC ....................................... E ...... 773 975-0400
  Chicago *(G-6746)*
Total Graphics Services Inc ................ G ...... 847 675-0800
  Skokie *(G-20101)*
Tree Towns Reprographics Inc ........... E ...... 630 832-0209
  Elmhurst *(G-9951)*
Tri-Tower Printing Inc .......................... G ...... 847 640-6633
  Rolling Meadows *(G-18785)*
Trump Printing Inc ............................... F ...... 217 429-9001
  Decatur *(G-7954)*
Tvp Color Graphics Inc ....................... G ...... 630 837-3600
  Streamwood *(G-20679)*
United Graphics Indiana Inc ................ F ...... 217 235-7161
  Mattoon *(G-14413)*
United Letter Service Inc .................... F ...... 312 408-2404
  Bensenville *(G-2009)*
United Press Inc (del) ......................... F ...... 847 482-0597
  Lincolnshire *(G-13487)*
V C P Inc ........................................... E ...... 847 658-5090
  Algonquin *(G-409)*
Valee Inc ............................................ G ...... 847 364-6464
  Elk Grove Village *(G-9804)*
Van Meter Graphx Inc ......................... G ...... 847 465-0600
  Wheeling *(G-22177)*
Venus Printing Inc ............................... G ...... 847 985-7510
  Schaumburg *(G-19785)*
Viking Printing & Copying Inc ............. G ...... 312 341-0985
  Chicago *(G-6899)*
Vis-O-Graphic Inc ............................... E ...... 630 590-6100
  Addison *(G-341)*
Voris Communication Co Inc ............... D ...... 630 231-2425
  West Chicago *(G-21791)*
Warner Offset Inc ............................... E ...... 847 695-9400
  South Elgin *(G-20233)*
Washburn Graficolor Inc ..................... G ...... 630 596-0880
  Naperville *(G-15781)*
Wayne Printing Company .................... E ...... 309 691-2496
  Edwards *(G-8785)*
We-B-Print Inc .................................... G ...... 309 353-8801
  Pekin *(G-17293)*
Weakley Printing & Sign Shop ............. G ...... 847 473-4466
  North Chicago *(G-16189)*
Weber Press Inc ................................. G ...... 773 561-9815
  Chicago *(G-6949)*
Williamsburg Press Inc ........................ G ...... 630 229-0228
  North Aurora *(G-16150)*
Willis Publishing ................................. F ...... 618 497-8272
  Percy *(G-17496)*
Windward Print Star Inc ...................... G ...... 309 787-8853
  Milan *(G-14810)*
Wood River Printing & Pubg Co .......... F ...... 618 254-3134
  Wood River *(G-22446)*
Woogl Corporation .............................. E ...... 847 806-1160
  Elk Grove Village *(G-9816)*
Wyka LLC ........................................... F ...... 847 298-0740
  Des Plaines *(G-8306)*
Yeast Printing Inc ............................... G ...... 309 833-2845
  Macomb *(G-14137)*
Yorke Printe Shoppe Inc ..................... E ...... 630 627-4960
  Lombard *(G-13885)*
Zone Inc ............................................. G ...... 630 887-8585
  Willowbrook *(G-22240)*

### PRINTING: Pamphlets

Wctu Press ......................................... G ...... 847 864-1396
  Evanston *(G-10105)*

### PRINTING: Photo-Offset

Copy Express Inc ............................... F ...... 815 338-7161
  Woodstock *(G-22555)*
Einstein Crest .................................... G ...... 847 965-7791
  Niles *(G-15977)*
Inkdot LLC .......................................... G ...... 630 768-6415
  Chicago *(G-5195)*

### PRINTING: Photolithographic

French Studio Ltd ............................... G ...... 618 942-5328
  Herrin *(G-11748)*

### PRINTING: Plisse, Broadwoven Fabrics, Cotton

Santana & Daughter Inc ..................... G ...... 773 237-1818
  Chicago *(G-6441)*

### PRINTING: Roller, Broadwoven Fabrics, Cotton

Frankenstitch Promotions LLC ........... G ...... 847 459-4840
  Wheeling *(G-22058)*

### PRINTING: Roller, Manmade Fiber & Silk, Broadwoven Fabric

Starline Designs ................................. G ...... 773 683-7506
  Chicago *(G-6577)*

### PRINTING: Rotogravure

General Packaging Products Inc ......... D ...... 312 226-5611
  Chicago *(G-4929)*
RR Donnelley Printing Co LP .............. G ...... 312 326-8000
  Chicago *(G-6405)*

### PRINTING: Screen, Broadwoven Fabrics, Cotton

Den Graphix Inc .................................. F ...... 309 962-2000
  Le Roy *(G-13207)*
Holy Cow Sports Incorporated ............ F ...... 630 852-9001
  Downers Grove *(G-8460)*
Player Sports Ltd ................................ G ...... 773 764-4111
  Chicago *(G-6140)*
Proell Inc ............................................ G ...... 630 587-2300
  Saint Charles *(G-19242)*
Silk Screening By Selep ..................... G ...... 847 593-7050
  Des Plaines *(G-8276)*
Top Notch Silk Screening ................... G ...... 773 847-6335
  Chicago *(G-6744)*

### PRINTING: Screen, Fabric

American Enlightenment LLC ............. G ...... 773 687-8996
  Chicago *(G-3856)*
Art-Flo Shirt & Lettering Co ................ E ...... 708 656-5422
  Chicago *(G-3953)*
B & B Custom TS & Gifts .................... G ...... 618 463-0443
  Alton *(G-562)*
Bean Stich Inc .................................... G ...... 630 422-1269
  Bensenville *(G-1841)*
Bobbi Screen Printing ......................... G ...... 773 847-8200
  Chicago *(G-4134)*
Breedlove Sporting Goods Inc ............ G ...... 309 852-2434
  Kewanee *(G-12677)*
Breedlove Sporting Goods Inc ............ F ...... 309 852-2434
  Kewanee *(G-12678)*
C & C Sport Stop ................................ G ...... 618 632-7812
  O Fallon *(G-16464)*
Chicago Shirt & Lettering Co .............. G ...... 773 745-0222
  Chicago *(G-4348)*
Classic Screen Printing Inc ................. F ...... 708 771-9355
  Forest Park *(G-10239)*
Cook Merritt ....................................... G ...... 630 980-3070
  Roselle *(G-18934)*
Cubby Hole of Carlinville Inc .............. F ...... 217 854-8511
  Carlinville *(G-3035)*
Custom Enterprises ............................ G ...... 618 439-6626
  Benton *(G-2025)*
Custom Towels Inc ............................. G ...... 618 539-5005
  Freeburg *(G-10634)*
Dabel Incorporated ............................. G ...... 217 398-3389
  Champaign *(G-3472)*
Enterprise Signs Inc ........................... G ...... 773 614-8324
  Chicago *(G-4760)*
Excel Screen Prtg & EMB Inc ............. D ...... 847 801-5200
  Schiller Park *(G-19830)*
Fitness Wear Inc ................................ G ...... 847 486-1704
  Glenview *(G-11125)*
Ikan Creations LLC ............................ G ...... 312 204-7333
  Chicago *(G-5150)*
Maxs Screen Machine Inc .................. G ...... 773 878-4949
  Chicago *(G-5659)*
Navitor Inc .......................................... B ...... 800 323-0253
  Harwood Heights *(G-11687)*
Outlaw Tees ....................................... G ...... 217 453-2359
  Nauvoo *(G-15856)*
Rebel Screeners Inc ........................... D ...... 312 525-2670
  Chicago *(G-6310)*
Roselynn Fashions ............................. G ...... 847 741-6000
  Elgin *(G-9167)*
Santana & Daughter Inc ..................... G ...... 773 237-1818
  Chicago *(G-6441)*
Scorpion Graphics Inc ........................ F ...... 773 927-3203
  Chicago *(G-6459)*
Sharprint Slkscrn & Grphcs ................ D ...... 877 649-2554
  Chicago *(G-6490)*
Stans Sportsworld Inc ........................ G ...... 217 359-8474
  Champaign *(G-3547)*
Star Silkscreen Design Inc ................. G ...... 217 877-0804
  Decatur *(G-7943)*
Team Works By Holzhauer Inc ........... G ...... 309 745-9924
  Washington *(G-21393)*
Wellspring Investments LLC .............. G ...... 773 736-1213
  Chicago *(G-6955)*
Windy City Silkscreening Inc ............. E ...... 312 842-0030
  Chicago *(G-7000)*

### PRINTING: Screen, Manmade Fiber & Silk, Broadwoven Fabric

David H Pool ...................................... G ...... 847 695-5007
  Elgin *(G-9009)*
Image Plus Inc .................................... G ...... 630 852-4920
  Downers Grove *(G-8463)*
Jdl Graphics Inc .................................. G ...... 815 694-2979
  Clifton *(G-7274)*
Silk Screening By Selep ..................... G ...... 847 593-7050
  Des Plaines *(G-8276)*
Ultimate Distributing Inc ...................... G ...... 847 566-2250
  Mundelein *(G-15565)*

### PRINTING: Thermography

Business Cards Tomorrow ................. F ...... 815 877-0990
  Machesney Park *(G-14062)*
First String Enterprises Inc ................ E ...... 708 614-1200
  Tinley Park *(G-20913)*
Klein Printing Inc ................................ G ...... 773 235-2121
  Chicago *(G-5387)*
Klimko Ink Inc ..................................... G ...... 815 459-5066
  Crystal Lake *(G-7599)*
Wolfam Holdings Corporation ............. G ...... 312 407-0100
  Chicago *(G-7020)*

### PRODUCT STERILIZATION SVCS

Sterigenics US LLC ........................... E ...... 847 855-0727
  Gurnee *(G-11508)*
Sterigenics US LLC ........................... E
  Willowbrook *(G-22233)*

### PROFESSIONAL & SEMI-PROFESSIONAL SPORTS CLUBS

Profile Network Inc ............................. E ...... 847 673-0592
  Skokie *(G-20063)*

### PROFESSIONAL EQPT & SPLYS, WHOLESALE: Analytical Instruments

Cbana Labs Inc .................................. G ...... 217 819-5201
  Champaign *(G-3463)*

### PROFESSIONAL EQPT & SPLYS, WHOLESALE: Bank

Block and Company Inc ...................... C ...... 847 537-7200
  Wheeling *(G-22015)*

### PROFESSIONAL EQPT & SPLYS, WHOLESALE: Engineers', NEC

Decatur Blue Print Company .............. G ...... 217 423-7589
  Decatur *(G-7869)*
Ghetzler Aero-Power Corp ................. G ...... 224 513-5636
  Vernon Hills *(G-21165)*

### PROFESSIONAL EQPT & SPLYS, WHOLESALE: Optical Goods

Illinois Tool Works Inc ........................ C ...... 847 295-6500
  Lake Bluff *(G-12850)*
Leica McRosystems Holdings Inc ...... F ...... 800 248-0123
  Buffalo Grove *(G-2724)*

## PROFESSIONAL EQPT & SPLYS, WHOLESALE: Optical Goods

Opti-Vue Inc .................................. G ...... 630 274-6121
  Bensenville *(G-1959)*
Vibgyor Optics Inc ........................ E ...... 847 818-0788
  Arlington Heights *(G-864)*

### PROFESSIONAL EQPT & SPLYS, WHOLESALE: Precision Tools

Powertronics Surgitech USA Inc ........... G ...... 630 305-4261
  Naperville *(G-15731)*

### PROFESSIONAL EQPT & SPLYS, WHOLESALE: Scientific & Engineerg

Cushing and Company .................. E ...... 312 266-8228
  Chicago *(G-4518)*

### PROFESSIONAL INSTRUMENT REPAIR SVCS

Dadum Inc ................................... G ...... 847 541-7851
  Buffalo Grove *(G-2682)*
Jero Medical Eqp & Sups Inc ......... E ...... 773 305-4193
  Chicago *(G-5295)*
Numerical Control Incorporated ..... G ...... 708 389-8140
  Alsip *(G-502)*
Otis Elevator Company ................. F ...... 618 529-3411
  Carbondale *(G-3016)*
Water Services Company of Ill ...... G ...... 847 697-6623
  Elgin *(G-9230)*

### PROFESSIONAL SCHOOLS

Moody Bible Inst of Chicago ......... A ...... 312 329-4000
  Chicago *(G-5799)*

### PROFILE SHAPES: Unsupported Plastics

Abbott Plastics & Supply Co ......... E ...... 815 874-8500
  Rockford *(G-18246)*
Atlas Fibre Company .................... D ...... 847 674-1234
  Northbrook *(G-16208)*
Custom Films Inc ......................... F ...... 217 826-2326
  Marshall *(G-14320)*
Custom Plastics of Peoria ............. G ...... 309 697-2888
  Bartonville *(G-1394)*
Engineered Plastic Systems LLC ... F ...... 800 480-2327
  Elgin *(G-9029)*
Flex-O-Glass Inc .......................... D ...... 773 261-5200
  Chicago *(G-4858)*
Flex-O-Glass Inc .......................... G ...... 773 379-7878
  Chicago *(G-4859)*
Flex-O-Glass Inc .......................... E ...... 815 288-1424
  Dixon *(G-8331)*
Polytec Plastics Inc ..................... E ...... 630 584-8282
  Saint Charles *(G-19236)*
Rampart LLC ............................... G ...... 847 367-8960
  Lake Forest *(G-12950)*
Resinite Corporation .................... C ...... 847 537-4250
  Wheeling *(G-22138)*
Sandee Manufacturing Co ............ G ...... 847 671-1335
  Franklin Park *(G-10581)*
Shape Master Inc ........................ G ...... 217 582-2638
  Ogden *(G-16744)*
Shape Master Inc ........................ G ...... 217 469-7027
  Saint Joseph *(G-19318)*
Sonoco Plastics Inc ..................... F ...... 630 628-5859
  Addison *(G-295)*
Streamwood Plastics Ltd .............. G ...... 847 895-9190
  Schaumburg *(G-19741)*

### PROGRAMMERS: Indl Process

Minnesota Office Technology ........ G ...... 312 236-0400
  Bolingbrook *(G-2342)*

### PROMOTERS OF SHOWS & EXHIBITIONS

Area Marketing Inc ...................... G ...... 815 806-8844
  Frankfort *(G-10297)*
Farm Progress Companies Inc ..... C ...... 630 690-5600
  Saint Charles *(G-19183)*
Horizon Downing LLC .................. E ...... 815 758-6867
  Dekalb *(G-8097)*

### PROMOTION SVCS

David H Pool ............................... G ...... 847 695-5007
  Elgin *(G-9009)*
Lanigan Holdings LLC .................. F ...... 708 596-5200
  Hazel Crest *(G-11710)*

Progressive Systems Netwrk Inc ... G ...... 312 382-8383
  Chicago *(G-6214)*
Terlato Wine Group Ltd ............... E ...... 847 604-8900
  Lake Bluff *(G-12867)*

### PROPELLERS: Boat & Ship, Cast

Petro Prop Inc ............................. G ...... 630 910-4738
  Downers Grove *(G-8502)*
Propeller Hr Solutions Inc ............ G ...... 312 342-7355
  Western Springs *(G-21871)*

### PROPERTY DAMAGE INSURANCE

Navistar Inc ................................. C ...... 331 332-5000
  Lisle *(G-13629)*

### PROPULSION UNITS: Guided Missiles & Space Vehicles

Boeing Company ......................... B ...... 312 544-2000
  Chicago *(G-4136)*

### PROTECTION EQPT: Lightning

Cutshaw Instls Inc ....................... G ...... 847 426-9208
  East Dundee *(G-8630)*
Harger Inc ................................... E ...... 847 548-8700
  Grayslake *(G-11345)*
Simmons Lightning Protection ..... G ...... 217 746-3971
  Burnside *(G-2817)*

### PROTECTIVE FOOTWEAR: Rubber Or Plastic

Plastic Specialists America .......... G ...... 847 406-7547
  Gurnee *(G-11486)*

### PUBLIC FINANCE, TAXATION & MONETARY POLICY OFFICES

Financial and Professional Reg ..... G ...... 217 782-2127
  Springfield *(G-20439)*

### PUBLIC RELATIONS & PUBLICITY SVCS

Caduceus Communications Inc .... G ...... 773 549-4800
  Chicago *(G-4211)*

### PUBLIC RELATIONS SVCS

Forrest Consulting ....................... G ...... 630 730-9619
  Glen Ellyn *(G-10971)*
Sanderson and Associates ........... F ...... 312 829-4350
  Chicago *(G-6437)*

### PUBLISHERS: Art Copy

Chesley Limited ........................... G ...... 847 562-9292
  Northbrook *(G-16220)*

### PUBLISHERS: Art Copy & Poster

East Wisconsin LLC ..................... E ...... 618 224-9133
  Trenton *(G-20991)*

### PUBLISHERS: Atlases

World Book Inc ............................ E ...... 312 729-5800
  Chicago *(G-7028)*

### PUBLISHERS: Book

AJS Publications .......................... G ...... 847 526-5027
  Island Lake *(G-12212)*
Allegro Publishing Inc .................. G ...... 847 565-9083
  Chicago *(G-3810)*
American Chamber of ................... E ...... 312 960-9400
  Chicago *(G-3854)*
American Hosp Assn Svcs Del ..... E ...... 312 422-2000
  Chicago *(G-3858)*
American Labelmark Company ..... C ...... 773 478-0900
  Chicago *(G-3859)*
American Nurseryman Pubg Co ... G ...... 847 234-5867
  Lake Forest *(G-12878)*
American Supply Association ....... F ...... 630 467-0000
  Itasca *(G-12228)*
Arthur Coyle Press ...................... G ...... 773 465-8418
  Chicago *(G-3955)*
Beloved Characters Ltd ............... G ...... 773 599-0073
  Chicago *(G-4079)*
Bendinger Bruce Crtve Comm In ... G ...... 773 871-1179
  Chicago *(G-4082)*

Bestwords Org Corp .................... G ...... 618 939-4324
  Columbia *(G-7352)*
Brainworx Studio ......................... F ...... 773 743-8200
  Chicago *(G-4157)*
Broken Oar Inc ............................ G ...... 847 639-9468
  Port Barrington *(G-17718)*
Brown & Miller Literary Assoc ..... G ...... 312 922-3063
  Chicago *(G-4177)*
C W Publications Inc ................... G ...... 800 554-5537
  Sterling *(G-20586)*
Carus Publishing Company .......... F ...... 312 701-1720
  Chicago *(G-4247)*
Castlegate Publishers Inc ............ G ...... 847 382-6420
  Barrington *(G-1275)*
Charles C Thomas Publisher ........ F ...... 217 789-8980
  Springfield *(G-20416)*
Christian National Womans .......... G ...... 847 864-1396
  Evanston *(G-10024)*
City of Chicago ............................ G ...... 773 581-8000
  Chicago *(G-4386)*
Common Ground Publishing LLC ... E ...... 217 328-0405
  Champaign *(G-3468)*
Continental Sales Inc ................... G ...... 847 381-6530
  Barrington *(G-1277)*
Contractors Register Inc ............. F ...... 630 519-3480
  Lombard *(G-13784)*
Cook Communications Minis ........ D ...... 847 741-5168
  Elgin *(G-9003)*
Cornerstone Community Outreach ... F ...... 773 506-4904
  Chicago *(G-4472)*
Creative Curricula Inc .................. G ...... 815 363-9419
  McHenry *(G-14491)*
Crystal Productions Co ................ F ...... 847 657-8144
  Northbrook *(G-16235)*
Curbside Splendor ....................... G ...... 224 515-6512
  Chicago *(G-4517)*
Dalkey Archive Press ................... G ...... 217 244-5700
  Champaign *(G-3473)*
Damien Corporation ..................... G ...... 630 369-3549
  Naperville *(G-15644)*
Dasher Dependable Reindeer LLC ... G ...... 630 513-7737
  Saint Charles *(G-19167)*
Deagostini Publishing USA Inc ..... G ...... 212 432-4070
  Woodstock *(G-22559)*
Deerpath Publishing Co Inc ......... G ...... 847 234-3385
  Lake Forest *(G-12895)*
Ebonyenergy Publishing Inc Nfp ... G ...... 773 851-5159
  Chicago *(G-4689)*
Ebooks2go ................................... G ...... 847 598-1145
  Schaumburg *(G-19512)*
Elliot Institute For Social SC ........ G ...... 217 525-8202
  Springfield *(G-20434)*
Encyclopaedia Britannica Inc ....... C ...... 847 777-2241
  Chicago *(G-4749)*
Foundation Lithuanian Minor ........ G ...... 630 969-1316
  Downers Grove *(G-8445)*
Gary Grimm & Associates Inc ...... G ...... 217 357-3401
  Carthage *(G-3314)*
GPA Media Inc ............................. G ...... 773 968-3728
  Calumet City *(G-2940)*
Greek Art Printing & Pubg Co ...... G ...... 847 724-8860
  Glenview *(G-11133)*
Helivalues .................................... G ...... 847 487-8258
  Wauconda *(G-21466)*
Houghton Mifflin Harcourt Co ...... G ...... 630 467-6049
  Itasca *(G-12275)*
Houghton Mifflin Harcourt Pubg ... B ...... 630 467-6095
  Itasca *(G-12276)*
Houghton Mifflin Harcourt Pubg ... B ...... 847 869-2300
  Evanston *(G-10052)*
Human Factor RES Group Inc ...... G ...... 618 476-3200
  Millstadt *(G-14826)*
IB Source Inc .............................. G ...... 312 698-7062
  Chicago *(G-5134)*
Illinois Inst Cntng Legl Ed ........... E ...... 217 787-2080
  Springfield *(G-20454)*
Intervrsity Chrstn Fllwshp/Usa .... D ...... 630 734-4000
  Westmont *(G-21893)*
Jgc United Publishing Corps ....... G ...... 815 968-6601
  Rockford *(G-18444)*
Kishknows Inc ............................. G ...... 708 252-3648
  Richton Park *(G-17979)*
Koza ............................................ G ...... 773 646-0958
  Chicago *(G-5409)*
Lifetouch Services Inc ................. C ...... 815 633-3881
  Loves Park *(G-13961)*
Michael A Greenberg MD Ltd ...... F ...... 847 364-4717
  Elk Grove Village *(G-9625)*
Monitor Publishing Inc ................. G ...... 773 205-0303
  Chicago *(G-5795)*

## PRODUCT SECTION

### PUBLISHERS: Magazines, No Printing

Moody Bible Inst of Chicago.................E....... 312 329-2102
  Chicago (G-5800)
Nature House Inc...................................D....... 217 833-2393
  Griggsville (G-11413)
Oasis Audio LLC.....................................G....... 630 668-5367
  Carol Stream (G-3208)
Oasis International Limited..................G....... 630 326-0045
  Geneva (G-10855)
Pamacheyon Publishing Inc.................G....... 815 395-0101
  Rockford (G-18529)
Partner Health LLC................................G....... 847 208-6074
  Lake Forest (G-12939)
Permissions Group Inc..........................G....... 847 635-6550
  Glenview (G-11181)
Pinnacle Publishing Inc........................F....... 218 444-2180
  Chicago (G-6124)
Pipestone Passages..............................G....... 773 735-2488
  Chicago (G-6129)
Practice Management Info Corp..........E....... 800 633-7467
  Downers Grove (G-8508)
Press Syndication Group LLC...............G....... 646 325-3221
  Chicago (G-6181)
Preston Industries Inc...........................C....... 847 647-2900
  Niles (G-16022)
Print Rite Inc...........................................G....... 773 625-0792
  Chicago (G-6189)
Putman Media Inc.................................D....... 630 467-1301
  Schaumburg (G-19705)
Raven Tree Press LLC............................G....... 800 323-8270
  Crystal Lake (G-7637)
Rite-TEC Communications...................G....... 815 459-7712
  Crystal Lake (G-7643)
Shure Products Inc................................F....... 773 227-1001
  Chicago (G-6504)
Sourcebooks Inc.....................................D....... 630 961-3900
  Naperville (G-15751)
Sterling Books Limited..........................G....... 630 325-3853
  Hinsdale (G-11965)
Taylor Enterprises Inc...........................G....... 847 367-1032
  Libertyville (G-13389)
Theosophical Society In Amer..............F....... 630 665-0123
  Wheaton (G-21985)
Theosophical Society In Amer..............G....... 630 665-0130
  Wheaton (G-21984)
Thomson Reuters (markets) LLC..........B....... 847 705-7929
  Palatine (G-17082)
Thrice Publishing Nfp............................G....... 630 776-0478
  Roselle (G-18982)
Twain Media Mark Publishing..............G....... 217 223-7008
  Quincy (G-17901)
U S Naval Institute.................................G....... 800 233-8764
  University Park (G-21065)
United Educators Inc............................F....... 847 234-3700
  Lake Bluff (G-12868)
Urantia Corp...........................................F....... 773 248-6616
  Chicago (G-6844)
Venture Publishing Inc.........................G....... 217 359-5940
  Urbana (G-21104)
Wedding Brand Investors LLC.............E....... 847 887-0071
  Wauconda (G-21513)
West Publishing Corporation..............D....... 312 894-1690
  Chicago (G-6961)
Windy City Publishers LLC...................G....... 847 925-9434
  Palatine (G-17090)

### PUBLISHERS: Book Clubs, No Printing

Caxton Club.............................................G....... 312 266-8825
  Chicago (G-4259)

### PUBLISHERS: Books, No Printing

Acta Publications..................................G....... 773 989-3036
  Chicago (G-3739)
Adventures Unlimited..........................G....... 815 253-6390
  Kempton (G-12661)
Albert Whitman & Company...............E....... 847 232-2800
  Park Ridge (G-17180)
American Association of Indivi...........E....... 312 280-0170
  Chicago (G-3850)
American Bar Association...................A....... 312 988-5000
  Chicago (G-3851)
American Catholic Press Inc................F....... 708 331-5485
  South Holland (G-20242)
Art Media Resources Inc......................G....... 312 663-5351
  Chicago (G-3951)
Audio Tech Bus Bk Summaries............G....... 630 734-0500
  Oak Brook (G-16490)
Baptist General Conference................D....... 800 323-4215
  Arlington Heights (G-723)
Bar List Publishing Co..........................G....... 847 498-0100
  Northbrook (G-16210)

Barks Publications Inc..........................F....... 312 321-9440
  Chicago (G-4044)
Bolchazy-Carducci Publishers.............F....... 847 526-4344
  Mundelein (G-15479)
Catalyst Chicago....................................G....... 312 427-4830
  Chicago (G-4256)
Charles H Kerr Publishing Co..............G....... 773 262-1329
  Chicago (G-4291)
Chicago Prvnce of The Soc Jsus..........E....... 773 281-1818
  Chicago (G-4343)
Chicago Review Press Inc....................E....... 312 337-0747
  Chicago (G-4344)
Christianica Center..............................G....... 847 657-3818
  Glenview (G-11113)
Computer Industry Almanac Inc.........G....... 847 758-1926
  Arlington Heights (G-738)
Cornerstones Publishing I....................E....... 847 998-4746
  Glenview (G-11116)
Cupcake Holdings LLC..........................C....... 800 794-5866
  Woodridge (G-22466)
Delair Publishing Company Inc..........C....... 708 345-7000
  Melrose Park (G-14614)
Empowered Press LLC..........................G....... 630 400-3127
  Oswego (G-16915)
Frank R Walker Company.....................G....... 630 613-9312
  Lombard (G-13802)
Germain Saint Press Inc.......................E....... 847 882-7400
  Schaumburg (G-19536)
Great Books Foundation......................E....... 312 332-5870
  Chicago (G-4994)
Guildhall Publishers Ltd......................G....... 309 693-9232
  Peoria (G-17374)
H G Acquisition Corp............................G....... 630 382-1000
  Burr Ridge (G-2848)
Holder Publishing Corporation..........F....... 309 828-7533
  Bloomington (G-2179)
Information Usa Inc.............................E....... 312 943-6288
  Chicago (G-5189)
Jameson Books Inc...............................G....... 815 434-7905
  Ottawa (G-16963)
Johnson Publishing Company LLC.....C....... 312 322-9200
  Chicago (G-5320)
Kidsbooks LLC........................................G....... 773 509-0707
  Chicago (G-5382)
Manufctrers Claring Hse of Ill............G....... 773 545-6300
  Chicago (G-5609)
Marytown................................................E....... 847 367-7800
  Libertyville (G-13347)
Moody Bible Inst of Chicago................A....... 312 329-4000
  Chicago (G-5799)
National Bus Trader Inc.......................F....... 815 946-2341
  Polo (G-17689)
Neal-Schuman Publishers Inc............F....... 312 944-6780
  Chicago (G-5879)
Omega Publishing Services Inc..........G....... 630 968-0440
  Downers Grove (G-8498)
Pieces of Learning Inc.........................G....... 618 964-9426
  Marion (G-14279)
Pivot Point Usa Inc..............................D....... 800 886-4247
  Chicago (G-6133)
Polonia Book Store Inc........................G....... 773 481-6968
  Chicago (G-6151)
Psytec Inc..............................................G....... 815 758-1415
  Dekalb (G-8114)
Publications International Ltd............B....... 847 676-3470
  Morton Grove (G-15229)
Research Press Company....................F....... 217 352-3273
  Champaign (G-3532)
Sagamore Publishing LLC...................F....... 217 359-5940
  Urbana (G-21102)
Scholastic Inc........................................E....... 630 443-8197
  Saint Charles (G-19261)
Students Publishing Company In......G....... 847 491-7206
  Evanston (G-10097)
Surrey Books Inc..................................G....... 847 475-4457
  Evanston (G-10099)
Templegate Publishers.......................F....... 217 522-3353
  Springfield (G-20543)
Third Wrld Press Fundation Inc.........F....... 773 651-0700
  Chicago (G-6715)
Thomson Reuters Corporation..........D....... 312 288-4654
  Chicago (G-6719)
Triumph Books Corp...........................E....... 312 337-0747
  Chicago (G-6780)
Tyndale House Publishers Inc...........C....... 630 668-8300
  Carol Stream (G-3257)
Tyndale House Publishers Inc...........G....... 630 668-8300
  Carol Stream (G-3258)
University of Chicago..........................B....... 773 702-1722
  Chicago (G-6836)

Urantia Foundation..............................F....... 773 525-3319
  Chicago (G-6845)
Urban Research Press Inc...................F....... 773 994-7200
  Chicago (G-6850)
Wilton Brands LLC................................B....... 630 963-7100
  Woodridge (G-22526)
Wilton Holdings Inc.............................G....... 630 963-7100
  Woodridge (G-22527)
Wilton Industries Inc..........................B....... 630 963-7100
  Woodridge (G-22528)
Wilton Industries Inc..........................F....... 815 834-9390
  Romeoville (G-18879)
Windsong Press Ltd............................G....... 847 223-4586
  Grayslake (G-11368)
Wolters Kluwer US Inc........................E....... 847 580-5000
  Riverwoods (G-18046)

### PUBLISHERS: Catalogs

Catalog Designers Inc.........................G....... 847 228-0025
  Elk Grove Village (G-9359)
R R Donnelley & Sons Company........C....... 847 393-3000
  Libertyville (G-13373)
Totalworks Inc......................................E....... 773 489-4313
  Chicago (G-6750)
Van Meter Graphx Inc.........................G....... 847 465-0600
  Wheeling (G-22177)

### PUBLISHERS: Comic Books, No Printing

American Assn Endodontists.............E....... 312 266-7255
  Chicago (G-3849)

### PUBLISHERS: Directories, NEC

Aerodine Magazine..............................F....... 847 358-4355
  Inverness (G-12200)
B A I Publishers....................................G....... 847 537-1300
  Wheeling (G-22010)
Creative Directory Inc.........................G....... 773 427-7777
  Chicago (G-4498)
Edge Communication..........................G....... 708 749-7818
  Berwyn (G-2062)
Educational Directories Inc................G....... 847 891-1250
  Schaumburg (G-19513)
Food Service Publishing Co................F....... 847 699-3300
  Des Plaines (G-8200)
G R Leonard & Co Inc..........................E....... 847 797-8101
  Arlington Heights (G-758)
Halper Publishing Company..............G....... 847 542-9793
  Evanston (G-10049)
Law Bulletin Publishing Co................F....... 847 883-9100
  Buffalo Grove (G-2722)
Luby Publishing Inc............................F....... 312 341-1110
  Chicago (G-5556)
Manufacturers News Inc....................D....... 847 864-7000
  Evanston (G-10068)
Modern Trade Communications........F....... 847 674-2200
  Skokie (G-20041)
Perq/Hci LLC.........................................C....... 847 375-5000
  Rosemont (G-19020)

### PUBLISHERS: Directories, Telephone

AT&T Teleholdings Inc.......................G....... 800 257-0902
  Chicago (G-3973)

### PUBLISHERS: Globe Cover Maps

Rockford Map Publishers Inc............F....... 815 708-6324
  Rockford (G-18579)

### PUBLISHERS: Magazines, No Printing

American Bar Association..................A....... 312 988-5000
  Chicago (G-3851)
American Catholic Press Inc..............F....... 708 331-5485
  South Holland (G-20242)
Antigua Casa Sherry-Brener..............G....... 773 737-1711
  Chicago (G-3916)
Applied Tech Publications Inc..........F....... 847 382-8100
  Willowbrook (G-22199)
Associated Publications Inc..............F....... 312 266-8680
  Chicago (G-3969)
Barks Publications Inc.......................F....... 312 321-9440
  Chicago (G-4044)
Be Group Inc.........................................G....... 312 436-0301
  Chicago (G-4061)
Bhs Media LLC......................................E....... 312 701-0000
  Chicago (G-4102)
Bible Truth Publishers Inc..................G....... 630 543-1441
  Addison (G-55)

**Boland Hill Media LLC** G 877 658-0418
Hoffman Estates *(G-11997)*

**Bowen Guerrero & Howe LLC** D 312 447-2370
Chicago *(G-4150)*

**C2 Publishing Inc** F 630 834-4994
Hillside *(G-11912)*

**Central Illinois Homes Guide** G 309 688-6419
Peoria *(G-17337)*

**Chester White Swine Rcord Assn** G 309 691-0151
Peoria *(G-17341)*

**Chicago Boating Publications** G 312 266-8400
Chicago *(G-4306)*

**Chicago Sports Media Inc** G 847 676-1900
Skokie *(G-19981)*

**Christian Century** F 312 263-7510
Chicago *(G-4370)*

**Christianity Today Intl** C 630 260-6200
Carol Stream *(G-3128)*

**Church of Brethren Inc** D 847 742-5100
Elgin *(G-8990)*

**Consource LLC** G 847 382-8100
Willowbrook *(G-22206)*

**Construction Bus Media LLC** G 847 359-6493
Palatine *(G-17017)*

**Consumers Dgest Cmmnctions LLC** F 847 607-3000
Deerfield *(G-8000)*

**Country Journal Publishing Co** F 217 877-9660
Decatur *(G-7860)*

**Crain Communications Inc** E 312 649-5200
Chicago *(G-4492)*

**Crain Communications Inc** E 312 649-5411
Chicago *(G-4493)*

**Crain Communications Inc** C 312 649-5200
Chicago *(G-4494)*

**CSP Information Group Inc** E 630 574-5075
Oak Brook *(G-16503)*

**Dadant & Sons Inc** D 217 847-3324
Hamilton *(G-11533)*

**Dow Jones & Company Inc** D 312 580-1023
Chicago *(G-4639)*

**Earl G Graves Pubg Co Inc** G 312 274-0682
Chicago *(G-4675)*

**Entrepreneur Media Inc** G 312 923-0818
Chicago *(G-4762)*

**Evang Lthn Ch Dr Mrtn Luth KG** F 773 380-2540
Chicago *(G-4785)*

**Evangelical Missions Info Svc** G 630 752-7158
Wheaton *(G-21946)*

**Filmfax Magazine Inc** G 847 866-7155
Evanston *(G-10037)*

**Gannett Stllite Info Ntwrk Inc** D 847 839-1700
Hoffman Estates *(G-12012)*

**Gary Grimm & Associates Inc** G 217 357-3401
Carthage *(G-3314)*

**Germain Saint Press Inc** G 847 882-7400
Schaumburg *(G-19536)*

**Good Sam Enterprises LLC** E 847 229-6720
Lincolnshire *(G-13450)*

**Gospel Synergy Magazine Inc** G 708 272-6640
Calumet Park *(G-2961)*

**Grandstand Publishing LLC** G 847 491-6440
Evanston *(G-10045)*

**H & S Publications Inc** G 309 344-1333
Wataga *(G-21398)*

**Halper Publishing Company** G 847 542-9793
Evanston *(G-10049)*

**Healthleaders Inc** E 312 932-0848
Chicago *(G-5062)*

**Hearst Corporation** E 312 984-5100
Chicago *(G-5065)*

**Homewood-Flossmoor Chronicle** G 630 728-2661
Homewood *(G-12101)*

**Homnay Magazine** G 773 334-6655
Chicago *(G-5104)*

**Ideal Media LLC** G 312 456-2822
Chicago *(G-5141)*

**Ieg LLC** E 312 944-1727
Chicago *(G-5144)*

**Imagination Publishing LLC** E 312 887-1000
Chicago *(G-5161)*

**Jinny Corp** G 773 588-7200
Chicago *(G-5306)*

**John C Grafft** F 847 842-9200
Lake Barrington *(G-12811)*

**Lakeland Boating Magazine** G 312 276-0610
Evanston *(G-10063)*

**Lakeside Publishing Co LLC** G 847 491-6440
Evanston *(G-10064)*

**Lambda Publications Inc** F 773 871-7610
Chicago *(G-5448)*

**Lightner Publishing Corp** F 312 939-4767
Naperville *(G-15691)*

**M I T Financial Group Inc** E 847 205-3000
Northbrook *(G-16303)*

**Maher Publications Inc** F 630 941-2030
Elmhurst *(G-9906)*

**Marketing & Technology Group** E 312 266-3311
Chicago *(G-5622)*

**Mediatec Publishing Inc** E 312 676-9900
Chicago *(G-5678)*

**National Bus Trader Inc** F 815 946-2341
Polo *(G-17689)*

**National Publishing Company** F 630 837-2044
Streamwood *(G-20667)*

**National Sporting Goods Assn** F 847 296-6742
Mount Prospect *(G-15353)*

**Nickelodeon Magazines Inc** G 312 836-0668
Chicago *(G-5912)*

**Northwest Publishing LLC** G 312 329-0600
Chicago *(G-5941)*

**Outdoor Notebook Publishing** F 630 257-6534
Lemont *(G-13246)*

**Parade Publications Inc** F 312 661-1620
Chicago *(G-6075)*

**Poetry Foundation** E 312 787-7070
Chicago *(G-6146)*

**Profile Network Inc** E 847 673-0592
Skokie *(G-20063)*

**Progressive Publications Inc** G 847 697-9181
Elgin *(G-9150)*

**Publications International Ltd** B 847 676-3470
Morton Grove *(G-15229)*

**Randall Publishing Inc** F 847 437-6604
Elk Grove Village *(G-9709)*

**Rookie LLC** G 708 278-1628
Oak Park *(G-16682)*

**Saltzman Printers Inc** E 708 344-4500
Melrose Park *(G-14690)*

**Sherman Media Company Inc** G 312 335-1962
Lake Forest *(G-12959)*

**Stagnito Partners LLC** D 224 632-8200
Deerfield *(G-8056)*

**Steven Fisher** G 847 317-1128
Riverwoods *(G-18044)*

**Summitt Media Group Inc** E 312 222-1010
Chicago *(G-6617)*

**Talcott Communications Corp** E 312 849-2220
Chicago *(G-6668)*

**This Week In Chicago Inc** F 312 943-0838
Chicago *(G-6716)*

**Trend Publishing Inc** E 312 654-2300
Chicago *(G-6767)*

**Trmg LLP** F 847 441-4122
Northfield *(G-16422)*

**Verone Publishing Inc** G 773 866-0811
Chicago *(G-6886)*

**W Whorton & Co** G 773 445-2400
Chicago *(G-6927)*

**Walnecks Inc** G 630 985-2097
Downers Grove *(G-8541)*

**Windy City Media Group** G 773 871-7610
Chicago *(G-6997)*

## *PUBLISHERS: Maps*

**Rand McNally & Company** B 847 329-8100
Skokie *(G-20069)*

**Rand McNally International Co** C 847 329-8100
Skokie *(G-20070)*

## *PUBLISHERS: Miscellaneous*

**24land Express Inc** G 630 766-2424
Elk Grove Village *(G-9247)*

**A J Express Power Tools** G 847 678-8200
Schiller Park *(G-19796)*

**About Learning Inc** F 847 487-1800
Wauconda *(G-21436)*

**Agate Publishing Inc** G 847 475-4457
Evanston *(G-10005)*

**Allured Publishing Corporation** E 630 653-2155
Carol Stream *(G-3097)*

**Am-Don Partnership** G 217 355-7750
Champaign *(G-3447)*

**American Bar Foundation** D 312 988-6500
Chicago *(G-3852)*

**American Custom Publishing** G 847 816-8660
Libertyville *(G-13302)*

**Amnet Systems LLC** F 217 954-0130
Urbana *(G-21069)*

**Anash Educational Institute** G 773 338-7704
Chicago *(G-3900)*

**Angle Press Inc** G 847 439-6388
Arlington Heights *(G-714)*

**Art In Print Review** G 773 697-9478
Chicago *(G-3950)*

**Avenir Publishing Inc** E 312 577-7200
Chicago *(G-3998)*

**Award/Visionps Inc** G 331 318-7800
Chicago *(G-4003)*

**Baka Vitaliy** G 773 370-5522
Chicago *(G-4027)*

**Ball Publishing** F 630 208-9080
West Chicago *(G-21665)*

**Ballotready Inc** G 301 706-0708
Chicago *(G-4033)*

**Bar List Publishing Co** G 847 498-0100
Northbrook *(G-16210)*

**Bass-Mollett Publishers Inc** D 618 664-3141
Greenville *(G-11387)*

**Bendinger Bruce Crtve Comm In** G 773 871-1179
Chicago *(G-4082)*

**Biz 3 Publicity** G 773 342-3331
Chicago *(G-4116)*

**Book Power Inc** G 630 790-4144
Glen Ellyn *(G-10961)*

**Brilliant Color Corp** G 847 367-3300
Libertyville *(G-13310)*

**Buhl Press** E 708 449-8989
Berkeley *(G-2044)*

**Bureau of National Affairs** G 773 775-8801
Chicago *(G-4184)*

**C W Publications Inc** G 800 554-5537
Sterling *(G-20586)*

**Cade Communications Inc** G 773 477-7184
Chicago *(G-4210)*

**Cambridge Business** G 800 619-6473
Westmont *(G-21879)*

**Carlberg Design Inc** G 217 341-3291
Petersburg *(G-17534)*

**Central Illinois Homes Guide** G 309 688-6419
Peoria *(G-17337)*

**Centup Industries LLC** G 312 291-1687
Chicago *(G-4274)*

**Chicago Sports Media Inc** G 847 676-1900
Skokie *(G-19981)*

**Chicago Sun-Times Features Inc** F 312 321-2043
Chicago *(G-4352)*

**China Ying Inc** G 630 428-2638
Naperville *(G-15629)*

**Christian Specialized Services** G 217 546-7338
Springfield *(G-20418)*

**Cirrus Products** G 630 501-1881
Addison *(G-77)*

**Cision US Inc** C 312 922-2400
Chicago *(G-4381)*

**Cottage Door Press LLC** F 224 228-6000
Barrington *(G-1278)*

**Cross Express Company** G 847 439-7457
Elk Grove Village *(G-9401)*

**Damien Corporation** G 630 369-3549
Naperville *(G-15644)*

**Devils Due Publishing** G 773 412-6427
Chicago *(G-4588)*

**Dex Media Inc** F 312 240-6000
Chicago *(G-4589)*

**Dino Publishing LLC** G 312 822-9266
Chicago *(G-4607)*

**Doody Enterprises Inc** G 312 239-6226
Oak Park *(G-16660)*

**Dramatic Publishing Company** F 815 338-7170
Woodstock *(G-22563)*

**Ea Mackay Enterprises Inc** E 630 627-7010
Lombard *(G-13793)*

**Eagle Publications Inc** E 618 345-5400
Collinsville *(G-7321)*

**Earthcomber LLC** F 708 366-1600
Oak Park *(G-16662)*

**Ebsco Industries Inc** F 800 245-7224
South Holland *(G-20264)*

**Ebsco Industries Inc** E 847 244-1800
Waukegan *(G-21556)*

**Element Collection** G 217 898-5175
Allerton *(G-421)*

**Elite Publishing and Design** G 888 237-8119
Peoria *(G-17355)*

**Exclusive Publications Inc** G 847 963-0400
Hoffman Estates *(G-12008)*

**F & F Publishing Inc** G 847 480-0330
Highland Park *(G-11831)*

**Farm Week** E 309 557-3140
Bloomington *(G-2163)*

Food Service Publishing Co ....G.... 847 699-3300
Park Ridge (G-17195)
Frank R Walker Company ....G.... 630 613-9312
Lombard (G-13802)
Fresh Facs ....G.... 618 357-9697
Pinckneyville (G-17548)
Gatehouse Media III Holdings ....G.... 585 598-0030
Peoria (G-17368)
Glorius Renditions ....G.... 815 315-0177
Leaf River (G-13211)
Graphic Communicators Inc ....G.... 708 385-7550
Palos Heights (G-17106)
Graphic Press ....G.... 312 909-6100
Chicago (G-4991)
Hancock County Shopper ....G.... 217 847-6628
Hamilton (G-11538)
Health Administration Press ....D.... 312 424-2800
Chicago (G-5058)
Heartland Publications Inc ....G.... 217 529-9506
Springfield (G-20450)
Heritage Products Corporation ....G.... 847 419-8835
Buffalo Grove (G-2703)
Hermitage Group Inc ....E.... 773 561-3773
Chicago (G-5080)
Holder Publishing Corporation ....G.... 309 828-7533
Bloomington (G-2179)
Holsolutions Inc ....G.... 888 847-5467
Frankfort (G-10327)
Holt Publications Inc ....G.... 618 654-6206
Highland (G-11796)
Hope Publishing Company ....F.... 630 665-3200
Carol Stream (G-3167)
Houghton Mifflin Harcourt ....E.... 928 467-9599
Geneva (G-10832)
I P G Warehouse Ltd ....E.... 773 722-5527
Chicago (G-5132)
Imedia Network Inc ....G.... 847 331-1774
Chicago (G-5164)
Inter-State Studio & Pubg Co ....D.... 815 874-0342
Rockford (G-18438)
J C Communications Company ....G.... 312 236-5122
Chicago (G-5257)
J S Paluch Co Inc ....C.... 847 678-9300
Franklin Park (G-10502)
Janelle Publications Inc ....G.... 815 756-2300
Dekalb (G-8100)
JAS Express Inc ....G.... 847 836-7984
Union (G-21035)
Java Express ....G.... 217 525-2430
Springfield (G-20462)
John C Grafft ....F.... 847 842-9200
Lake Barrington (G-12811)
Joong-Ang Daily News ....E.... 847 228-7200
Elk Grove Village (G-9564)
JW Express ....G.... 630 697-1037
Elk Grove Village (G-9567)
Kae Dj Publishing ....G.... 773 233-2609
Chicago (G-5350)
Keane Gillette Publishing LLC ....G.... 630 279-7521
Elmhurst (G-9895)
Key One Graphics Services Inc ....G....
West Dundee (G-21799)
Km Press Incorporated ....G.... 618 277-1222
Belleville (G-1644)
L A M Inc De ....G.... 630 860-9700
Wood Dale (G-22388)
Labelquest Inc ....E.... 630 833-9400
Elmhurst (G-9900)
Lee Enterprises Incorporated ....G.... 217 421-8940
Decatur (G-7907)
Line of Advance Nfp ....G.... 312 768-0043
Chicago (G-5510)
Loyalty Publishing Inc ....E.... 309 693-0840
Bartonville (G-1396)
Luna Azul Communications Inc ....E.... 773 616-0007
Deerfield (G-8030)
M & G Graphics Inc ....E.... 773 247-1596
Chicago (G-5576)
M M Marketing ....G.... 815 459-7968
Crystal Lake (G-7603)
Marshall Pubg & Promotions ....G.... 224 238-3530
Barrington (G-1289)
McX Press ....G.... 630 784-4325
Bloomingdale (G-2117)
Medallion Press Inc ....G.... 630 513-8316
Aurora (G-1053)
Mendota Reporter ....F.... 815 539-9396
Mendota (G-14726)
Merit Emplyment Asssment Svcs ....G.... 815 320-3680
New Lenox (G-15894)
Midwest Suburban Publishing ....A.... 708 633-6880
Tinley Park (G-20933)
Nascar Car Wash ....G.... 630 236-3400
Aurora (G-1055)
New Millenium Directories ....E.... 815 626-5737
Sterling (G-20601)
New Millennium Investment ....G.... 708 358-1512
Oak Park (G-16676)
New Wave Express Inc ....G.... 630 238-3129
Bensenville (G-1955)
Nice Card Company ....G.... 773 467-8450
Park Ridge (G-17212)
Norskobok Press ....G.... 847 516-0085
Cary (G-3362)
North American Press Inc ....G.... 847 515-3882
Huntley (G-12164)
Norwood House Press Inc ....G.... 866 565-2900
Chicago (G-5945)
Olney Daily Mail ....E.... 618 393-2931
Olney (G-16787)
Omni Publishing Co ....G.... 847 483-9668
Wheeling (G-22113)
Pacific Press Technologies LP ....G.... 618 262-8666
Mount Carmel (G-15280)
Paddock Publications Inc ....E.... 847 680-5800
Libertyville (G-13365)
Palm International Inc ....G.... 630 357-1437
Naperville (G-15721)
Phoenix Tree Publishing Inc ....G.... 773 251-0309
Chicago (G-6120)
Pierce Crandell & Co Inc ....G.... 847 549-6015
Libertyville (G-13368)
Premier Travel Media ....G.... 630 794-0696
Willowbrook (G-22228)
Press Dough Inc ....G.... 630 243-6900
Lemont (G-13257)
Press On Inc ....G.... 630 628-1630
Addison (G-255)
Prime Publishing LLC ....D.... 847 205-9375
Northbrook (G-16343)
Publishing Task Force ....F.... 312 670-4360
Chicago (G-6224)
Quarasan Group Inc ....D.... 312 981-2540
Chicago (G-6254)
Quincy Media Inc ....C.... 217 223-5100
Quincy (G-17879)
R L Allen Industries ....G.... 618 667-2544
Troy (G-21011)
R R Donnelley & Sons Company ....A.... 815 584-2770
Dwight (G-8591)
Rapid Circular Press Inc ....F.... 312 421-5611
Chicago (G-6290)
Redshelf Inc ....G.... 312 878-8586
Chicago (G-6317)
Reid Communications Inc ....E.... 847 741-9700
Elgin (G-9163)
Rickard Publishing ....F.... 217 482-3276
Mason City (G-14366)
Rm Acquisition LLC ....C.... 847 329-8100
Skokie (G-20077)
Robert-Leslie Publishing LLC ....G.... 773 935-8358
Chicago (G-6369)
Roger Fritz & Associates Inc ....G.... 630 355-2614
Naperville (G-15744)
RR Donnelley Logistics SE ....G.... 630 672-2500
Roselle (G-18970)
Sauk Valley Shopper Inc ....C.... 815 625-6700
Sterling (G-20612)
Scars Publications ....G.... 847 281-9070
Gurnee (G-11502)
Scholastic Testing Service ....F.... 630 766-7150
Bensenville (G-1988)
Schumaker Publications Inc ....G.... 309 365-7105
Lexington (G-13293)
SGS International LLC ....C.... 309 690-5231
Peoria (G-17453)
Shoppers Guide ....G.... 815 369-4112
Lena (G-13284)
Simon Global Services LLC ....G.... 773 334-7794
Chicago (G-6513)
Simple Solutions ....G.... 618 932-6177
West Frankfort (G-21819)
Slaymaker Fine Art Ltd ....G.... 773 348-1450
Chicago (G-6526)
Spudnik Press Cooperative ....F.... 312 563-0302
Chicago (G-6564)
St Johns United Church Christ ....G.... 847 491-6686
Evanston (G-10095)
Sunrise Hitek Service Inc ....E.... 773 792-8880
Chicago (G-6630)
Tele Guia Spanish TV Guide ....E.... 708 656-9800
Cicero (G-7235)
Thomas Publishing Printing Div ....G.... 618 351-6655
Carbondale (G-3025)
Tighe Publishing Services Inc ....F.... 773 281-9100
Chicago (G-6726)
Translucent Publishing Corp ....F.... 312 447-5450
Chicago (G-6762)
Trottie Publishing Group Inc ....G.... 708 344-5975
Westchester (G-21859)
Truequest Communications LLC ....G.... 312 356-9900
Chicago (G-6788)
U S Free Press LLC ....G.... 217 847-3361
Hamilton (G-11541)
United Press International Inc ....G.... 847 864-9450
Evanston (G-10104)
Varsity Publications Inc ....G.... 309 353-4570
Pekin (G-17292)
Veritiv Operating Company ....G.... 800 347-9279
Des Plaines (G-8298)
Vision Integrated Graphics ....C.... 708 570-7900
Bolingbrook (G-2380)
Vondrak Publishing Co Inc ....E.... 773 476-4800
Summit Argo (G-20768)
W-F Professional Assoc Inc ....G.... 847 945-8050
Deerfield (G-8067)
Wabash Publishing Co Inc ....G.... 312 939-5900
Chicago (G-6930)
Want ADS of Champaign Inc ....F.... 217 356-4804
Champaign (G-3558)
Wealth Partners Publishing Inc ....G.... 312 854-2522
Chicago (G-6946)
White Picket Media Inc ....F.... 773 769-8400
Chicago (G-6973)
Wireless Express Inc Central ....G.... 309 689-9933
Peoria (G-17478)
Wolfsword Press ....G.... 773 403-1144
Chicago (G-7021)
Wonderlic Inc ....D.... 847 680-4900
Vernon Hills (G-21218)
Wordspace Press Limited ....G.... 773 292-0292
Chicago (G-7027)
World Library Publications ....C.... 847 678-9300
Franklin Park (G-10631)

## PUBLISHERS: Music Book

3b Media Inc ....F.... 312 563-9363
Chicago (G-3667)
Antigua Casa Sherry-Brener ....G.... 773 737-1711
Chicago (G-3916)
Heimburger House Pubg Co Inc ....G.... 708 366-1973
Forest Park (G-10248)
Hope Publishing Company ....F.... 630 665-3200
Carol Stream (G-3167)

## PUBLISHERS: Music Book & Sheet Music

Deshamusic Inc ....G.... 818 257-2716
Chicago (G-4585)
Gold-Slvr-Bronze Medal Mus Inc ....G.... 847 272-6854
Gurnee (G-11453)
Sony/Atv Music Publishing LLC ....E.... 630 739-8129
Bolingbrook (G-2374)

## PUBLISHERS: Music, Book

LMS Innovations Inc ....G.... 312 613-2345
Chicago (G-5528)

## PUBLISHERS: Music, Sheet

Kaelco Entrmt Holdings Inc ....G.... 217 600-7815
Champaign (G-3505)

## PUBLISHERS: Newsletter

Elliot Institute For Social SC ....G.... 217 525-8202
Springfield (G-20434)
Imagination Publishing LLC ....E.... 312 887-1000
Chicago (G-5161)
Morris Cody & Assoc ....G.... 847 945-8050
Deerfield (G-8040)
Rain Publication Inc ....G.... 312 284-2444
Chicago (G-6287)

## PUBLISHERS: Newspaper

Acm Publishing ....G.... 217 498-7500
Rochester (G-18114)
Acres of Sky Communications ....G.... 815 493-2560
Lanark (G-13149)



Employee Codes: A=Over 500 employees, B=251-500
C=101-250, D=51-100, E=20-50, F=10-19, G=3-9
2017 Harris Illinois
Industrial Directory
1723

## PUBLISHERS: Newspaper — PRODUCT SECTION

| Company | Code | Phone |
|---|---|---|
| Advertising Advice Inc — Northbrook (G-16200) | F | 847 272-0707 |
| Agri-News Publications Inc — La Salle (G-12760) | D | 815 223-2558 |
| American Publishing Co Inc — Fairbury (G-10121) | G | 815 692-2366 |
| Americn Foreign Lang Newspaper — Chicago (G-3885) | E | 312 368-4815 |
| Amerikos Lietuvis Corp — Oak Lawn (G-16602) | G | 708 924-0403 |
| Andrew Distribution Inc — Broadview (G-2557) | E | 708 410-2400 |
| APAC 90 Texas Holding Inc — Chicago (G-3920) | G | 312 321-2299 |
| Arcola Record Herald — Arcola (G-665) | G | 217 268-4950 |
| B & B Publishing Co Inc — Bourbonnais (G-2388) | F | 815 933-1131 |
| B F Shaw Printing Company — Sterling (G-20584) | C | 815 625-3600 |
| B F Shaw Printing Company — Oregon (G-16819) | G | 815 732-6166 |
| Baier Publishing Company — Cissna Park (G-7254) | G | 815 457-2245 |
| Bas Success Express Inc — Des Plaines (G-8155) | G | 847 258-5550 |
| Beacon Solutions Inc — Chicago (G-4063) | F | 303 513-0469 |
| Better News Papers Inc — Mascoutah (G-14348) | G | 618 566-8282 |
| Better News Papers Inc — Altamont (G-550) | G | 618 483-6176 |
| Blue Island Sun — Blue Island (G-2240) | G | 708 388-9033 |
| Bond & Fayette County Shopper — Greenville (G-11388) | G | 618 664-4566 |
| Bond Broadcasting Inc — Greenville (G-11389) | G | 618 664-3300 |
| Boone County Shopper Inc — Belvidere (G-1739) | F | 815 544-2166 |
| C & C Publications — Joliet (G-12469) | G | 815 723-0325 |
| Cambridge Chronicle — Cambridge (G-2965) | G | 309 937-3303 |
| Campbell Publishing Co Inc — Jerseyville (G-12419) | F | 618 498-1234 |
| Campbell Publishing Co Inc — Pittsfield (G-17564) | F | 217 285-2345 |
| Carmi Times — Carmi (G-3064) | F | 618 382-4176 |
| Carterville Courier — Carterville (G-3310) | G | 618 985-6187 |
| Catalyst Paper — Evanston (G-10019) | G | 224 307-2650 |
| Central Newspaper Incorporated — Naperville (G-15624) | G | 630 416-4191 |
| Centralia Morning Sentinel — Centralia (G-3407) | D | 618 532-5601 |
| Centralia Press Ltd — Mount Vernon (G-15403) | F | 618 246-2000 |
| Chicago Deportivo Group Inc — Brookfield (G-2627) | G | 708 387-7724 |
| Chicago News LLC — Arlington Heights (G-734) | G | |
| Chicago Tribune — Chicago (G-4356) | G | 773 910-6462 |
| Chicago Weekly — Chicago (G-4362) | G | 773 702-7718 |
| Chinese American News — Chicago (G-4367) | G | 312 225-5600 |
| Chronicle Newspapers Inc — Geneva (G-10817) | G | 630 845-5247 |
| Clinton Topper Newspaper — Machesney Park (G-14065) | E | 815 654-4850 |
| Coal City Courant — Coal City (G-7291) | G | 815 634-0315 |
| Cornerstone Media — Manteno (G-14182) | G | 779 529-0108 |
| Custom Boxes Inc — Bolingbrook (G-2295) | G | 630 364-3944 |
| Daily News Tribune Inc — Mendota (G-14719) | G | 815 539-5200 |
| Dancyn Recovery Systems — Bloomington (G-2160) | G | 309 829-5450 |
| Debbie Harshman — Barry (G-1311) | G | 217 335-2112 |
| Delavan Times — Delavan (G-8133) | G | 309 244-7111 |
| Democrat Message — Mount Sterling (G-15392) | G | 217 773-3371 |
| Dmi Information Process Center — Chicago (G-4616) | E | 773 378-2644 |
| Dow Jones & Company Inc — Highland (G-11784) | E | 618 651-2300 |
| E & L Communication — Chicago (G-4663) | G | 773 890-1656 |
| Ear Hustle 411 LLC — Chicago (G-4672) | G | 773 616-3598 |
| East Central Communications Co — Rantoul (G-17926) | E | 217 892-9613 |
| Echo Prophetstown — Prophetstown (G-17768) | | 815 537-5107 |
| Eisenhower High School - Blue — Blue Island (G-2248) | | 708 385-6815 |
| El Dia Newspaper — Berwyn (G-2063) | | 708 956-7282 |
| El Paso Journal — El Paso (G-8869) | G | 309 527-8595 |
| Elise S Allen — Peoria (G-17354) | G | 309 673-2613 |
| Ethnic Media LLC — Wheeling (G-22049) | G | 224 676-0778 |
| Fanboys Games & Movies LLC — Park Ridge (G-17192) | G | 847 894-6448 |
| Farm Week — Bloomington (G-2163) | E | 309 557-3140 |
| Forrest Consulting — Glen Ellyn (G-10971) | G | 630 730-9619 |
| Four Winds Music Pubg LLC — Vandalia (G-21114) | G | 618 699-1356 |
| Fox Valley Park District — Aurora (G-1157) | D | 630 892-1550 |
| Fra No 3800 W Division — Stone Park (G-20635) | G | 708 338-0690 |
| Free Press Progress Inc — Nokomis (G-16056) | G | 217 563-2115 |
| Freedom Communications Inc — Jacksonville (G-12387) | G | 217 245-6121 |
| Freeshopper Ad Paper Inc — Lincolnwood (G-13511) | G | 847 675-2783 |
| Gannett Stllite Info Ntwrk LLC — Aurora (G-1013) | C | 630 629-1280 |
| Gatehouse Media LLC — Newton (G-15940) | | 618 783-2324 |
| Gatehouse Media LLC — Olney (G-16769) | E | 618 393-2931 |
| Gatehouse Media LLC — Pontiac (G-17701) | E | 815 842-1153 |
| Gatehouse Media LLC — Harrisburg (G-11600) | E | 618 253-7146 |
| Gazette Printing Co — Glasford (G-10951) | G | 309 389-2811 |
| Gazette-Democrat — Anna (G-604) | E | 618 833-2158 |
| Geomentum Inc — Downers Grove (G-8447) | B | 630 729-7500 |
| Geomentum Inc — Downers Grove (G-8448) | G | 630 729-7500 |
| Golf Gazette — Lockport (G-13718) | G | 815 838-0184 |
| Goreville Gazette — Goreville (G-11253) | G | 618 995-9445 |
| Hancock County Shopper — Hamilton (G-11538) | G | 217 847-6628 |
| Henderson Hancock Quill Inc — Stronghurst (G-20713) | G | 309 924-1871 |
| Henry News Republican — Henry (G-11743) | G | 309 364-3250 |
| Herald Mount Olive — Mount Olive (G-15303) | G | 217 999-3941 |
| Horizon Publications Inc — Marion (G-14265) | C | 618 993-1711 |
| Horizon Publications (2003) — Marion (G-14266) | G | 618 993-1711 |
| Hpc of Pennsylvania Inc — Marion (G-14268) | D | 618 993-1711 |
| Hs Technology Inc — Oak Brook (G-16522) | G | 630 572-7650 |
| Illinois Valley Press East — Mahomet (G-14159) | G | 217 586-2512 |
| India Tribune Ltd — Chicago (G-5174) | G | 773 588-5077 |
| International News — Chicago (G-5221) | G | 773 283-8323 |
| Joliet Herald Newspaper — Joliet (G-12523) | E | 815 280-4100 |
| Kane County Cronicle — Sycamore (G-20805) | G | 815 895-7033 |
| Kaplan Inc — Chicago (G-5359) | E | 312 263-4344 |
| Kendall County Record — Yorkville (G-22662) | E | 630 553-7034 |
| Korea Times — Glenview (G-11157) | D | 847 626-0388 |
| Korea Tribune Inc — Mount Prospect (G-15343) | G | 847 956-9101 |
| Korean Media Group LLC — Northbrook (G-16289) | F | 847 391-4112 |
| La Raza Chicago Inc — Chicago (G-5426) | E | 312 870-7000 |
| Lambda Publications Inc — Chicago (G-5448) | F | 773 871-7610 |
| Lawndale Press Inc — Cicero (G-7214) | | 708 656-6900 |
| Lee Enterprises Incorporated — Decatur (G-7905) | G | 217 421-8955 |
| Lee Enterprises Incorporated — Moline (G-14954) | E | 309 743-0800 |
| Lee Enterprises Incorporated — Decatur (G-7907) | G | 217 421-8940 |
| Liberty Group Publishing — West Frankfort (G-21812) | G | 618 937-2850 |
| Liberty Group Publishing — Cambridge (G-2968) | G | 309 937-3303 |
| Lincolndailynewscom — Lincoln (G-13414) | G | 217 732-7443 |
| Lumber Specialists Inc — Urbana (G-21093) | F | 217 351-5311 |
| Lumber Specialists Inc — Monticello (G-15078) | G | 217 762-2511 |
| Lumber Specialists Inc — Danville (G-7750) | F | 217 443-8484 |
| Macoupin County Enquirer Inc — Carlinville (G-3042) | E | 217 854-2534 |
| Mahoney Publishing Inc — Lena (G-13281) | G | 815 369-5384 |
| Martin Publishing Co — Canton (G-2989) | G | 309 647-9501 |
| Martin Publishing Co — Canton (G-2990) | F | 309 647-9501 |
| McClatchy Newspapers Inc — Belleville (G-1655) | B | 618 239-2624 |
| McClatchy Newspapers Inc — Highland (G-11802) | D | 618 654-2366 |
| Megamedia Enterprises Inc — Chicago (G-5680) | F | 773 889-0880 |
| Messenger — Belleville (G-1657) | G | 618 235-9601 |
| Migala Report — Chicago (G-5755) | G | 312 948-0260 |
| Military Medical News — Chicago (G-5759) | E | 312 368-4860 |
| Morris Publishing Company — Morris (G-15120) | A | 815 942-3221 |
| Mountaineer Newspapers Inc — Rochelle (G-18099) | E | 815 562-2061 |
| New City Communications — Chicago (G-5891) | E | 312 243-8786 |
| News & Letters — Chicago (G-5901) | G | 312 663-0839 |
| News Media Corporation — Rochelle (G-18100) | E | 815 562-2061 |
| Newspaper 7 Days — Wheeling (G-22107) | G | 847 272-2212 |
| Newspaper Holding Inc — Mount Vernon (G-15434) | D | 618 242-0113 |
| Newspaper Holding Inc — Mc Leansboro (G-14466) | | 618 643-2387 |
| Newspaper Holding Inc — Danville (G-7758) | E | 217 446-1000 |
| Newspaper National Network — Chicago (G-5902) | G | 312 644-1142 |
| Newspaper Solutions Inc — Chicago (G-5903) | G | 773 930-3404 |
| Nikkei America Holdings Inc — Chicago (G-5919) | G | 312 263-8877 |
| Normalite Newspaper — Normal (G-16080) | F | 309 454-5476 |
| Nuevos Semana Newspaper — Palatine (G-17060) | G | 847 991-3939 |
| Paddock Publications Inc — Elgin (G-9133) | C | 847 608-2700 |
| Paddock Publications Inc — Libertyville (G-13365) | E | 847 680-5800 |
| Paddock Publications Inc — Lisle (G-13638) | D | 630 955-3500 |
| Pakistan News — Chicago (G-6058) | G | 773 271-6400 |
| Pantagraph Publishing Co — Bloomington (G-2209) | F | 309 829-9000 |

**Paper** E 815 584-1901
Dwight *(G-8590)*
**Peg N Reds** G 618 586-2015
New Lenox *(G-15900)*
**People & Places Newspaper** G 847 804-6985
Schiller Park *(G-19858)*
**Peoria Post Inc** F 309 688-3628
Peoria *(G-17426)*
**Pike County Express** F 217 285-5415
Pittsfield *(G-17574)*
**Publishing Properties LLC** G 312 321-2299
Chicago *(G-6223)*
**Puro Futbol Newspaper** G 847 858-7493
Gurnee *(G-11495)*
**Quincy Herald-Whig LLC** F 217 223-5100
Quincy *(G-17878)*
**RCP Publications Inc** G 773 227-4066
Chicago *(G-6299)*
**Realclearpolitics** G 773 255-5846
Chicago *(G-6306)*
**Red Nose Inc** G 309 925-7313
Tremont *(G-20985)*
**Reflejos Publications LLC** E 847 806-1111
Arlington Heights *(G-829)*
**Review** G 309 659-2761
Erie *(G-9993)*
**Review** G 618 997-2222
Marion *(G-14285)*
**Rickard Publishing** G 309 968-6705
Manito *(G-14175)*
**Riverton Register** G 217 629-9247
Riverton *(G-18035)*
**Rock River Times** F 815 964-9767
Rockford *(G-18563)*
**Rockford Newspapers Inc** B 815 987-1200
Rockford *(G-18580)*
**S & R Media LLC** F 618 375-7502
Grayville *(G-11376)*
**Sauk Valley Shopper Inc** C 815 625-6700
Sterling *(G-20612)*
**Savanna Times Journal** G 815 273-2277
Savanna *(G-19406)*
**Schaumburg Review** F 847 998-3400
Chicago *(G-6450)*
**Small Newspaper Group** G 708 258-3410
Kankakee *(G-12651)*
**Southtown Star Newspapers** G 708 633-4800
Tinley Park *(G-20946)*
**Spanish Amercn Languag Newspap** E 312 368-4840
Chicago *(G-6550)*
**Star Media Group** G 847 674-7827
Skokie *(G-20091)*
**Star-Times Publishing Co Inc** G 618 635-2000
Staunton *(G-20559)*
**Strohm Newspapers Inc** G 217 826-3600
Marshall *(G-14329)*
**Suburban Chicago Newspapers** G 847 336-7000
Naperville *(G-15756)*
**Suburban Life Publication** D 630 368-1100
Downers Grove *(G-8528)*
**Sumner Press** G 618 936-2212
Sumner *(G-20772)*
**Sun- Tmes Mdia Productions LLC** G 312 321-2299
Chicago *(G-6620)*
**Sun-Times Media LLC** F 312 321-2299
Chicago *(G-6622)*
**Sun-Times Media Operations LLC** G 312 321-2299
Chicago *(G-6625)*
**T R Communications Inc** F 773 238-3366
Chicago *(G-6663)*
**Todays Advantage Inc** F 618 463-0612
Alton *(G-593)*
**Tonica News** G 815 442-8419
Tonica *(G-20975)*
**Tribune Publishing Company LLC** E 312 222-9100
Chicago *(G-6773)*
**Tribune Publishing Company LLC** D 312 832-6711
Chicago *(G-6774)*
**Tronc Inc** C 312 222-9100
Chicago *(G-6781)*
**United Communications Corp** C 847 746-1515
Zion *(G-22698)*
**United Communications Corp** E 847 746-4700
Zion *(G-22699)*
**Urdu Times** G 773 274-3100
Chicago *(G-6851)*
**USA Today Inc** G 815 987-1400
Rockford *(G-18665)*
**Vernon Township Offices** E 847 634-4600
Buffalo Grove *(G-2789)*
**Village of Mt Zion** F 217 864-4212
Mount Zion *(G-15457)*
**Waseet America** G 708 430-1950
Bedford Park *(G-1591)*
**Weekly James** G 815 786-8203
Sandwich *(G-19380)*
**Weekly Journals** G 815 459-4040
Crystal Lake *(G-7675)*
**Weekly Visitor** G 815 845-2328
Scales Mound *(G-19416)*
**Wheels & Deals** G 217 423-6333
Decatur *(G-7959)*
**Wyzz Inc** D 217 753-5620
Springfield *(G-20548)*

## PUBLISHERS: Newspapers, No Printing

**22nd Century Media** G 847 272-4565
Northbrook *(G-16194)*
**22nd Century Media** E 708 326-9170
Orland Park *(G-16836)*
**5 Star Publishing Inc** G 217 285-1355
Pittsfield *(G-17560)*
**All Star Publishing** G 630 428-1515
Naperville *(G-15597)*
**Altamont News** G 618 483-6176
Altamont *(G-548)*
**Beardstown Newspapers Inc** G 217 323-1010
Beardstown *(G-1520)*
**Bureau Valley Chief** G 815 646-4731
Tiskilwa *(G-20958)*
**Campbell Publishing Inc** G 217 742-3313
Winchester *(G-22278)*
**Central Illinois Newspapers** G 217 935-3171
Clinton *(G-7279)*
**Chicago Crusader News Group** G 773 752-2500
Chicago *(G-4313)*
**Chicago Defender Publishing Co** E 312 225-2400
Chicago *(G-4314)*
**Civitas Media LLC** D 217 245-6121
Jacksonville *(G-12384)*
**Clay County Advocate Press** G 618 662-6397
Flora *(G-10204)*
**Copley Press Inc** F 217 732-2101
Lincoln *(G-13408)*
**Daily Lawrenceville Record** F 618 943-2331
Lawrenceville *(G-13198)*
**Daily Lawrenceville Record** G 618 544-2101
Robinson *(G-18059)*
**Des Plaines Journal Inc** D 847 299-5511
Des Plaines *(G-8184)*
**Dow Jones & Company Inc** D 312 580-1023
Chicago *(G-4639)*
**Ea Mackay Enterprises Inc** E 630 627-7010
Lombard *(G-13793)*
**Eagle Publications Inc** E 618 345-5400
Collinsville *(G-7321)*
**Examiner Publications Inc** G 630 830-4145
Bartlett *(G-1347)*
**Food Service Publishing Co** F 847 699-3300
Des Plaines *(G-8200)*
**Fox Valley Labor News Inc** G 630 897-4022
Aurora *(G-1156)*
**Free Press Newspapers** E 815 476-7966
Wilmington *(G-22272)*
**G-W Communications Inc** G 815 476-7966
Wilmington *(G-22273)*
**Gatehouse Media LLC** F 309 852-2181
Kewanee *(G-12686)*
**Gatehouse Media LLC** E 309 734-3164
Monmouth *(G-15013)*
**Gatehouse Media III Holdings** G 585 598-0030
Peoria *(G-17368)*
**Gazette** F 815 777-0105
Galena *(G-10724)*
**German American Nat Congress** G 773 561-9181
Chicago *(G-4948)*
**Gilman Star Inc** G 815 265-7332
Gilman *(G-10942)*
**Gold Nugget Publications Inc** E 217 965-3355
Virden *(G-21297)*
**Greene Jersey Shoppers** G 217 942-3626
Carrollton *(G-3307)*
**Greenville Advocate Inc** G 618 664-3144
Greenville *(G-11394)*
**Hartman Publishing Group Ltd** F 312 822-0202
Chicago *(G-5050)*
**Heritage Media Svcs Co of Ill** G 708 594-9340
Summit Argo *(G-20763)*
**Hillsboro Journal Inc** E 217 532-3933
Hillsboro *(G-11895)*
**Home Shopper Publishing** G 309 742-2521
Elmwood *(G-9963)*
**Hometown News Group LP** G 815 246-4600
Earlville *(G-8595)*
**Illini Media Co** B 217 337-8300
Champaign *(G-3499)*
**Inde Enterprises Inc** E 815 338-8844
Woodstock *(G-22574)*
**Independent News** G 217 662-6001
Danville *(G-7738)*
**John Dagys Media LLC** G 708 373-0180
Palos Park *(G-17129)*
**Journal Standard** G 815 232-1171
Freeport *(G-10670)*
**Lee Enterprises Incorporated** C 217 421-6920
Decatur *(G-7906)*
**Lee Enterprises Incorporated** C 618 529-5454
Carbondale *(G-3014)*
**Litchfield News Herald Inc** F 217 324-2121
Litchfield *(G-13694)*
**Lithuanian Catholic Press** E 773 585-9500
Chicago *(G-5519)*
**Madison County Publications** E 618 344-0265
Collinsville *(G-7332)*
**Madison County Publications** F 618 344-0264
Collinsville *(G-7333)*
**Mirror-Democrat** G 815 244-2411
Mount Carroll *(G-15292)*
**Monitor Newspaper Inc** G 618 271-0468
East Saint Louis *(G-8761)*
**Newsprint Ink Inc** F 618 667-3111
Troy *(G-21010)*
**North County News Inc** G 618 282-3803
Red Bud *(G-17945)*
**Ocs America Inc** E 630 595-0111
Wood Dale *(G-22409)*
**Perryco Inc** F 815 436-2431
Plainfield *(G-17638)*
**Petersburg Observer Co Inc** G 217 632-2236
Petersburg *(G-17537)*
**Porterville Recorder Inc** G 559 784-5000
Marion *(G-14281)*
**Rachel Switall Mag Group Nfp** G 773 344-7123
Chicago *(G-6277)*
**Real Times Inc of Illinois** F 312 225-2400
Chicago *(G-6304)*
**Real Times II LLC** G 312 225-2400
Chicago *(G-6305)*
**Record Inc** G 312 985-7270
Chicago *(G-6312)*
**Refined Haystack LLC** G 773 627-3534
Chicago *(G-6319)*
**Republic Times LLC** G 618 939-3814
Waterloo *(G-21406)*
**Rochelle Newspapers Inc** E 815 562-2061
Rochelle *(G-18106)*
**Rock Valley Publishing LLC** E 815 467-6397
Machesney Park *(G-14103)*
**Rock Valley Publishing LLC** G 815 234-4821
Byron *(G-2919)*
**Shoppers Guide** G 815 369-4112
Lena *(G-13284)*
**South County Publications** F 217 438-6155
Auburn *(G-949)*
**Southwest Messenger Press Inc** E 708 388-2425
Midlothian *(G-14769)*
**Springfield Publishers Inc** G 217 726-6600
Springfield *(G-20532)*
**Steven Brownstein** G 847 909-6677
Morton Grove *(G-15238)*
**Students Publishing Company In** G 847 491-7206
Evanston *(G-10097)*
**Suburban Newspapers of Greater** E 618 281-7691
Collinsville *(G-7342)*
**Times Republic** E 815 432-5227
Watseka *(G-21431)*
**Times-Press Publishing Co** E 815 673-3771
Streator *(G-20708)*
**Vondrak Publishing Co Inc** E 773 476-4800
Summit Argo *(G-20768)*
**Want ADS of Champaign Inc** F 217 356-4804
Champaign *(G-3558)*
**Washington Courier** F 309 444-3139
Washington *(G-21394)*
**Waverly Journal** G 217 435-9221
Waverly *(G-21645)*
**Willis Publishing** F 618 497-8272
Percy *(G-17496)*
**Wns Publications Inc** E 815 772-7244
Morrison *(G-15149)*

PRODUCT

Employee Codes: A=Over 500 employees, B=251-500
C=101-250, D=51-100, E=20-50, F=10-19, G=3-9
2017 Harris Illinois
Industrial Directory
1725

World Journal LLC ... F ... 312 842-8005
Chicago *(G-7030)*

## *PUBLISHERS: Pamphlets, No Printing*

Eagle Forum ... G ... 618 462-5415
Alton *(G-572)*
Good News Publishers ... E ... 630 868-6025
Wheaton *(G-21951)*
Home Design Alternatives Inc ... E ... 314 731-1427
Schaumburg *(G-19558)*
Media Associates Intl Inc ... F ... 630 260-9063
Carol Stream *(G-3192)*
Movie Facts Inc ... E ... 847 299-9700
Des Plaines *(G-8238)*
Need To Know Inc ... G ... 309 691-3877
Peoria *(G-17415)*
S R Bastien Co ... F ... 847 858-1175
Evanston *(G-10093)*

## *PUBLISHERS: Periodical Statistical Reports, No Printing*

Investment Information Svcs ... G ... 312 669-1650
Chicago *(G-5232)*
M & B Supply Inc ... F ... 309 944-3206
Geneseo *(G-10803)*
Pierce Crandell & Co Inc ... G ... 847 549-6015
Libertyville *(G-13368)*

## *PUBLISHERS: Periodical, With Printing*

API Publishing Services LLC ... E ... 312 644-6610
Chicago *(G-3922)*
Cook Communications Ministries ... C ... 847 741-0800
Elgin *(G-9004)*
Free Press Progress Inc ... G ... 217 563-2115
Nokomis *(G-16056)*
National Association Realtors ... C ... 800 874-6500
Chicago *(G-5857)*
National Association Realtors ... C ... 800 874-6500
Chicago *(G-5858)*
Pam Printers and Publs Inc ... F ... 217 222-4030
Quincy *(G-17866)*
Thomson Reuters (legal) Inc ... G ... 312 873-6800
Chicago *(G-6718)*
Willow Group Inc ... G ... 847 277-9400
Chicago *(G-6988)*

## *PUBLISHERS: Periodicals, Magazines*

A To Z Offset Prtg & Pubg Inc ... G ... 847 966-3016
Skokie *(G-19943)*
Abc Inc ... E ... 312 980-1000
Chicago *(G-3707)*
Acm Publishing ... G ... 217 498-7500
Rochester *(G-18114)*
American Assn Nurosurgeons Inc ... E ... 847 378-0500
Rolling Meadows *(G-18709)*
American Cllege Chest Physcans ... D ... 224 521-9800
Glenview *(G-11099)*
American Custom Publishing ... G ... 847 816-8660
Libertyville *(G-13302)*
American Hosp Assn Svcs Del ... E ... 312 422-2000
Chicago *(G-3858)*
American Library Association ... E ... 312 280-5718
Chicago *(G-3860)*
American Soc Plastic Surgeons ... D ... 847 228-9900
Arlington Heights *(G-710)*
Anderson House Foundation ... G ... 630 461-7254
Glen Ellyn *(G-10959)*
Bowtie Inc ... G ... 630 515-9493
Lombard *(G-13773)*
Business Insurance ... E ... 877 812-1587
Chicago *(G-4188)*
Caduceus Communications Inc ... G ... 773 549-4800
Chicago *(G-4211)*
CAM Systems ... G ... 800 208-3244
Chicago *(G-4220)*
Canvas Communication ... G ... 815 464-5947
Frankfort *(G-10306)*
Care Education Group Inc ... G ... 708 361-4110
Palos Park *(G-17127)*
Challenge Publications L T D ... G ... 309 421-0392
Macomb *(G-14121)*
Chambers Marketing Options ... G ... 847 584-2626
Elk Grove Village *(G-9364)*
Chas Levy Circulating Co ... G ... 630 353-2500
Lisle *(G-13574)*
Chicago Agent Magazine ... G ... 773 296-6001
Chicago *(G-4300)*
China Journal Inc ... G ... 312 326-3228
Chicago *(G-4366)*
College Bound Publications ... G ... 773 262-5810
Chicago *(G-4424)*
Community Magazine Group ... G ... 312 880-0370
Chicago *(G-4437)*
Cook Communications Minis ... D ... 847 741-5168
Elgin *(G-9003)*
Copyline ... G ... 773 375-8127
Chicago *(G-4466)*
Corbett Accel Healthcare Grp C ... G ... 312 475-2505
Chicago *(G-4467)*
Cornerstone Communications ... E ... 773 989-2087
Chicago *(G-4471)*
Cosmopolitan Foot Care ... G ... 312 984-5111
Chicago *(G-4479)*
Eagle Forum ... G ... 618 462-5415
Alton *(G-572)*
Earl G Graves Ltd ... G ... 312 664-8667
Chicago *(G-4674)*
Elliott Jsj & Associates Inc ... G ... 847 242-0412
Glencoe *(G-10999)*
Eqes Inc ... G ... 630 858-6161
Glen Ellyn *(G-10969)*
Express Publishing Inc ... G ... 773 725-6218
Chicago *(G-4797)*
Food Service Publishing Co ... F ... 847 699-3300
Des Plaines *(G-8200)*
Frank R Walker Company ... G ... 630 613-9312
Lombard *(G-13802)*
Gazette ... F ... 815 777-0105
Galena *(G-10724)*
Gemworld International Inc ... G ... 847 657-0555
Northbrook *(G-16264)*
Glancer Magazine ... G ... 630 428-4387
Sugar Grove *(G-20726)*
Global Telephony Magazine ... E ... 312 840-8405
Chicago *(G-4961)*
Homeland ... G ... 708 415-4555
Homer Glen *(G-12081)*
Icd Publications Inc ... G ... 847 913-8295
Lincolnshire *(G-13456)*
Icon Acquisition Holdings LP ... G ... 312 751-8000
Chicago *(G-5136)*
Illini Media Co ... B ... 217 337-8300
Champaign *(G-3499)*
Inc 1105 Media ... G ... 847 358-7272
Palatine *(G-17041)*
Inside Track Trading ... G ... 630 585-9218
Aurora *(G-1030)*
Irish Dancing Magazine ... G ... 630 279-7521
Elmhurst *(G-9889)*
J S Paluch Co Inc ... C ... 847 678-9300
Franklin Park *(G-10502)*
Key One Graphics Services Inc ... G
West Dundee *(G-21799)*
Keystone Printing & Publishing ... G ... 815 678-2591
Richmond *(G-17965)*
Kitbuilders Magazine LLC ... G ... 618 588-5232
New Baden *(G-15862)*
Korea Times ... D ... 847 626-0388
Glenview *(G-11157)*
Lawrence Rgan Cmmnications Inc ... E ... 312 960-4100
Chicago *(G-5472)*
Lightworks Communcation Inc ... G ... 847 966-1110
Morton Grove *(G-15214)*
Lithuanian Catholic Press ... E ... 773 585-9500
Chicago *(G-5519)*
Lithuanian Press Inc ... G ... 773 776-3399
Chicago *(G-5520)*
Livingstone Corporation ... F ... 630 871-1212
Wheaton *(G-21967)*
Meredith Corp ... D ... 312 580-1623
Chicago *(G-5689)*
Metro Printing & Pubg Inc ... F ... 618 476-9587
Millstadt *(G-14829)*
Midwest Law Printing Co Inc ... G ... 312 431-0185
Chicago *(G-5745)*
Midwestern Family Magazine LLC ... G ... 309 303-7309
Peoria *(G-17409)*
Modern Luxury Media LLC ... E ... 312 274-2500
Chicago *(G-5783)*
Monitor Publishing Inc ... G ... 773 205-0303
Chicago *(G-5795)*
Moody Bible Inst of Chicago ... E ... 312 329-2102
Chicago *(G-5800)*
MTS Publishing Co ... F ... 630 955-9750
Naperville *(G-15701)*
New Life Printing & Publishing ... G ... 847 658-4111
Algonquin *(G-402)*
Novo Card Publishers Inc ... G ... 847 947-8090
Chicago *(G-5949)*
NV Business Publishers Corp ... G ... 847 441-5645
Northfield *(G-16413)*
One Accord Unity Nfp ... G ... 630 649-0793
Bolingbrook *(G-2355)*
Penton Media Inc ... G ... 212 204-4200
Chicago *(G-6100)*
Practice Law Management Mag ... F ... 312 988-6114
Chicago *(G-6165)*
Preferred Bus Publications Inc ... G ... 815 717-6399
New Lenox *(G-15902)*
Randall Publications ... E ... 847 437-6604
Elk Grove Village *(G-9708)*
Rasmussen Press Inc ... G
Bensenville *(G-1976)*
RCP Publications Inc ... G ... 773 227-4066
Chicago *(G-6299)*
Real Estate News Corp ... G ... 773 866-9900
Chicago *(G-6302)*
Relx Inc ... E ... 309 689-1000
Peoria *(G-17441)*
Rodale Inc ... F ... 312 726-0365
Chicago *(G-6378)*
RSM International ... G ... 312 634-4762
Chicago *(G-6408)*
S R Bastien Co ... F ... 847 858-1175
Evanston *(G-10093)*
Sanderson and Associates ... F ... 312 829-4350
Chicago *(G-6437)*
Specialty Publishing Company ... E ... 630 933-0844
Carol Stream *(G-3243)*
Surplus Record LLC ... F ... 312 372-9077
Chicago *(G-6642)*
Target Market News Inc ... G ... 312 408-1881
Chicago *(G-6676)*
Tegna Inc ... C ... 847 490-6657
Hoffman Estates *(G-12064)*
Tele-Guia Inc ... F ... 708 656-9800
Cicero *(G-7236)*
Theosophical Society In Amer ... G ... 630 665-0130
Wheaton *(G-21984)*
Theosophical Society In Amer ... F ... 630 665-0123
Wheaton *(G-21985)*
Tmb Publishing Inc ... G ... 847 564-1127
Niles *(G-16043)*
Tribune Publishing Company LLC ... D ... 312 832-6711
Chicago *(G-6774)*
Tube & Pipe Association Intl ... D ... 815 399-8700
Elgin *(G-9217)*
Vietnow National Headquarters ... G ... 815 395-8484
Rockford *(G-18670)*
Watt Publishing Co ... E ... 815 966-5400
Rockford *(G-18674)*
Watt Publishing Co ... E ... 815 966-5400
Rockford *(G-18675)*
Winsight LLC ... E ... 312 876-0004
Chicago *(G-7003)*

## *PUBLISHERS: Periodicals, No Printing*

Alarm Press ... G ... 312 341-1290
Schaumburg *(G-19427)*
Another Vision ... G ... 847 884-7325
Schaumburg *(G-19442)*
Art In Print Review ... G ... 773 697-9478
Chicago *(G-3950)*
At Home Magazine ... G ... 217 351-5282
Champaign *(G-3453)*
Baptist General Conference ... D ... 800 323-4215
Arlington Heights *(G-723)*
Cube Tomato Inc ... G ... 224 653-2655
Schaumburg *(G-19494)*
Cupcake Holdings LLC ... C ... 800 794-5866
Woodridge *(G-22466)*
Damien Corporation ... G ... 630 369-3549
Naperville *(G-15644)*
Farm Progress Companies Inc ... C ... 630 690-5600
Saint Charles *(G-19183)*
Fellowship Black Light ... G ... 773 826-7790
Chicago *(G-4834)*
India Tribune Ltd ... G ... 773 588-5077
Chicago *(G-5174)*
International College Surgeons ... G ... 312 642-6502
Chicago *(G-5220)*
Johnson Publishing Company LLC ... C ... 312 322-9200
Chicago *(G-5320)*
Mariah Media Inc ... G ... 312 222-1100
Chicago *(G-5616)*
Mediatec Publishing Inc ... F ... 510 834-0100
Chicago *(G-5679)*

# PRODUCT SECTION

## PUBLISHING & PRINTING: Magazines: publishing & printing

Medical Liability Monitor Inc..............G...... 312 944-7900
  Elmwood Park *(G-9973)*
National Safety Council........................B...... 630 285-1121
  Itasca *(G-12324)*
Pitchfork Media Inc...............................E...... 773 395-5937
  Chicago *(G-6130)*
Rochelle Newspapers Inc....................E...... 815 562-2061
  Rochelle *(G-18106)*
University of Chicago..........................B...... 773 702-1722
  Chicago *(G-6836)*
Utility Business Media Inc..................G...... 815 459-1796
  Crystal Lake *(G-7671)*
Wilton Brands LLC................................B...... 630 963-7100
  Woodridge *(G-22526)*
Wilton Holdings Inc...............................G...... 630 963-7100
  Woodridge *(G-22527)*
Wilton Industries Inc.............................B...... 630 963-7100
  Woodridge *(G-22528)*
Wilton Industries Inc.............................F...... 815 834-9390
  Romeoville *(G-18879)*

### PUBLISHERS: Posters

Panache Editions Ltd...........................G...... 847 921-8574
  Glencoe *(G-11005)*

### PUBLISHERS: Shopping News

Beardstown Newspapers Inc...............G...... 217 323-1010
  Beardstown *(G-1520)*
Boone County Shopper Inc.................F...... 815 544-2166
  Belvidere *(G-1739)*
Peoria Post Inc.....................................F...... 309 688-3628
  Peoria *(G-17426)*
Shoppers Review..................................F...... 618 654-4459
  Highland *(G-11811)*
Shoppers Weekly Inc...........................F...... 618 533-7283
  Centralia *(G-3433)*

### PUBLISHERS: Technical Manuals

Custom Design Services & Assoc......F...... 815 226-9747
  Rockford *(G-18327)*
Hospital & Physician Pubg..................G...... 618 997-9375
  Marion *(G-14267)*
McIlvaine Co........................................E...... 847 784-0012
  Northfield *(G-16408)*
T D C Inc..............................................F...... 815 229-7064
  Rockford *(G-18639)*
Techno - Grphics Trnsltons Inc...........E...... 708 331-3333
  South Holland *(G-20308)*

### PUBLISHERS: Telephone & Other Directory

American Marketing & Pubg LLC.......E...... 815 756-2840
  Dekalb *(G-8074)*
AT&T Corp............................................C...... 630 693-5000
  Lombard *(G-13765)*
Consumerbase LLC.............................C...... 312 600-8000
  Chicago *(G-4455)*
Make It Better LLC...............................G...... 847 256-4642
  Wilmette *(G-22261)*
Payment Pathways Inc........................G...... 312 346-9400
  Chicago *(G-6092)*
Serbian Yellow Pages Inc...................F...... 847 588-0555
  Niles *(G-16031)*
TWT Marketing Inc..............................G...... 773 274-4470
  Chicago *(G-6799)*

### PUBLISHERS: Textbooks, No Printing

A Trustworthy Sup Source Inc............G...... 773 480-0255
  Chicago *(G-3693)*
Book Power Inc....................................G...... 630 790-4144
  Glen Ellyn *(G-10961)*
Goodheart-Willcox Company Inc........D...... 708 687-0315
  Tinley Park *(G-20919)*
Gordon Burke John Publisher.............G...... 847 866-8625
  Evanston *(G-10044)*
Houghton Mifflin Harcourt Pubg...........B...... 708 869-2300
  Evanston *(G-10053)*
LMS Innovations Inc............................G...... 312 613-2345
  Chicago *(G-5528)*
Marantha Wrld Rvval Ministries............G...... 773 384-7717
  Chicago *(G-5611)*
Motamed Medical Publishing Co.........G...... 773 761-6667
  Chicago *(G-5812)*
National School Services Inc..............E...... 847 438-3859
  Long Grove *(G-13899)*
Respect Incorporated..........................G...... 815 806-1907
  Manhattan *(G-14170)*
Scholastic Inc......................................E...... 630 671-0601
  Roselle *(G-18974)*

World Book Inc....................................E...... 312 729-5800
  Chicago *(G-7028)*

### PUBLISHERS: Trade journals, No Printing

Aais Services Corporation..................G...... 630 457-3263
  Lisle *(G-13552)*
Aana Publishing Inc.............................G...... 847 692-7050
  Park Ridge *(G-17177)*
Allured Publishing Corporation...........E...... 630 653-2155
  Carol Stream *(G-3097)*
American Assn Insur Svcs..................E...... 630 681-8347
  Lisle *(G-13557)*
American City Bus Journals Inc..........G...... 312 873-2200
  Chicago *(G-3855)*
American Medical Association............A...... 312 464-5000
  Chicago *(G-3863)*
American Soc HM Inspectors Inc.......F...... 847 759-2820
  Des Plaines *(G-8147)*
Associated Equipment Distrs..............E...... 630 574-0650
  Schaumburg *(G-19448)*
Banner Publications.............................G...... 309 338-3294
  Cuba *(G-7679)*
BNP Media Inc.....................................D...... 630 690-4200
  Deerfield *(G-7992)*
Dorenfest Group Ltd............................D...... 312 464-3000
  Chicago *(G-4632)*
Fabricators & Mfrs Assn Intl................E...... 815 399-8700
  Elgin *(G-9033)*
Fma Communicatons Inc....................G...... 815 227-8284
  Elgin *(G-9038)*
HH Backer Associates Inc..................G...... 312 578-1818
  Chicago *(G-5084)*
Hw Holdco LLC....................................D...... 773 824-2400
  Rosemont *(G-19005)*
Industrial Market Place.......................E...... 847 676-1900
  Skokie *(G-20015)*
Inside Council......................................F...... 312 654-3500
  Chicago *(G-5204)*
Luby Publishing Inc.............................F...... 312 341-1110
  Chicago *(G-5556)*
Mdm Communications Inc..................G...... 708 582-9667
  Skokie *(G-20036)*
Modern Trade Communications..........F...... 847 674-2200
  Skokie *(G-20041)*
Practical Communications Inc............E...... 773 754-3250
  Schaumburg *(G-19699)*
Putman Media Inc................................D...... 630 467-1301
  Schaumburg *(G-19705)*
R L D Communications Inc.................E...... 312 338-7007
  Chicago *(G-6267)*
Sagamore Publishing LLC...................F...... 217 359-5940
  Urbana *(G-21102)*
Scranton Glltte Cmmnctions Inc.........D...... 847 391-1000
  Arlington Heights *(G-836)*
SGC Horizon LLC.................................E...... 847 391-1000
  Arlington Heights *(G-839)*
Transportation Eqp Advisors...............D...... 847 318-7575
  Rosemont *(G-19037)*
Vertical Web Media LLC.....................E...... 312 362-0076
  Chicago *(G-6888)*
Wolters Kluwer US Inc.........................E...... 847 580-5000
  Riverwoods *(G-18046)*

### PUBLISHING & BROADCASTING: Internet Only

Band of Shoppers Inc..........................G...... 312 857-4250
  Chicago *(G-4035)*
Cammun LLC.......................................G...... 312 628-1201
  Chicago *(G-4224)*
Haute Noir Media Group Inc................G...... 312 869-4526
  Chicago *(G-5055)*
HP Interactive Inc.................................G...... 773 681-4440
  Chicago *(G-5124)*
Hunting Network LLC...........................G...... 847 659-8200
  Huntley *(G-12145)*
Inn Partners LLC..................................D...... 309 743-0800
  Moline *(G-14944)*
Odx Media LLC....................................E...... 847 868-0548
  Evanston *(G-10080)*
Qt Info Systems Inc.............................F...... 800 240-8761
  Chicago *(G-6239)*
Shiftgig Inc............................................E...... 312 763-3003
  Chicago *(G-6496)*
Sim Partners Inc...................................E...... 800 260-3380
  Chicago *(G-6512)*
Vortex Media Group Inc.......................G...... 630 717-9541
  Naperville *(G-15778)*
Zaptel Corporation...............................G...... 847 386-8050
  Elk Grove Village *(G-9824)*

### PUBLISHING & PRINTING: Art Copy

Chase Group LLC................................F...... 847 564-2000
  Northbrook *(G-16219)*
Creative Ideas Inc................................G...... 217 245-1378
  Jacksonville *(G-12386)*

### PUBLISHING & PRINTING: Book Clubs

Rookie LLC...........................................G...... 708 278-1628
  Oak Park *(G-16682)*

### PUBLISHING & PRINTING: Book Music

Carus Publishing Company.................G...... 603 924-7209
  Chicago *(G-4246)*
Do You See What I See Entertai........G...... 773 612-1269
  Chicago *(G-4618)*

### PUBLISHING & PRINTING: Books

A To Z Offset Prtg & Pubg Inc.............G...... 847 966-3016
  Skokie *(G-19943)*
Advantage Press Inc............................G...... 630 960-5305
  Lisle *(G-13553)*
Barnes & Noble College......................G...... 708 209-3173
  River Forest *(G-17996)*
Bookends Publishing............................G...... 312 988-1500
  Chicago *(G-4143)*
CCH Incorporated................................A...... 847 267-7000
  Riverwoods *(G-18037)*
Cook Communications Ministries........C...... 847 741-0800
  Elgin *(G-9004)*
Crown Kandy Enterprise Ltd...............F...... 708 580-6494
  Westchester *(G-21837)*
Final Call Inc........................................F...... 773 602-1230
  Chicago *(G-4843)*
Gorman & Associates..........................G...... 309 691-9087
  Peoria *(G-17373)*
Grace & Truth Inc.................................G...... 217 442-1120
  Danville *(G-7727)*
Graphic Score Book Co Inc.................G...... 847 823-7382
  Park Ridge *(G-17199)*
Multi Packaging Solutions Inc.............G...... 773 283-9500
  Chicago *(G-5832)*
Nexus Supply Consortium Inc............G...... 630 649-2868
  Bolingbrook *(G-2353)*
Phoenix Intl Publications Inc...............B...... 312 739-4400
  Chicago *(G-6119)*
Springfield Printing Inc........................G...... 217 787-3500
  Springfield *(G-20531)*

### PUBLISHING & PRINTING: Catalogs

Creasey Printing Services Inc.............G...... 217 787-1055
  Springfield *(G-20425)*
Haggin Marketing Inc...........................F...... 312 343-2611
  Chicago *(G-5031)*
Mediatec Publishing Inc......................E...... 312 676-9900
  Chicago *(G-5678)*

### PUBLISHING & PRINTING: Comic Books

Dreamland............................................G...... 847 524-6060
  Schaumburg *(G-19508)*
Genesis Comics Group........................G...... 312 544-7473
  Chicago *(G-4934)*

### PUBLISHING & PRINTING: Directories, NEC

F M Aquisition Corp.............................G...... 773 728-8351
  Chicago *(G-4806)*
Wolters Kluwer US Inc.........................E...... 847 580-5000
  Riverwoods *(G-18046)*

### PUBLISHING & PRINTING: Guides

Law Bulletin Publishing Co..................C...... 312 416-1860
  Chicago *(G-5470)*
Leonard Publishing Co........................F...... 773 486-2737
  Norridge *(G-16104)*
Oag Aviation Worldwide LLC..............G...... 630 515-5300
  Lisle *(G-13635)*
Tele-Guia Inc........................................F...... 708 656-9800
  Cicero *(G-7236)*

### PUBLISHING & PRINTING: Magazines: publishing & printing

Ada Holding Company Inc..................F...... 312 440-2897
  Chicago *(G-3742)*
Alali Enterprises Inc.............................G...... 630 827-9231
  Carol Stream *(G-3095)*

Allen Entertainment Management.........E....... 630 752-0903
Carol Stream *(G-3096)*
American Nurseryman Pubg Co...........E....... 847 234-5867
Lake Forest *(G-12878)*
American Trade Magazines LLC............G....... 312 497-7707
Chicago *(G-3880)*
Andover Junction Publications............G....... 815 538-3060
Mendota *(G-14716)*
Area Marketing Inc................................G....... 815 806-8844
Frankfort *(G-10297)*
Bi-State Biking LLC ..............................G....... 618 531-0432
Fairview Heights *(G-10166)*
C and H Publishing Co ...........................G....... 618 625-2711
Sesser *(G-19894)*
Cap Today................................................F....... 847 832-7377
Northfield *(G-16395)*
Central Illinois Bus Publs Inc ...............G....... 309 683-3060
Peoria *(G-17336)*
CHI Home Improvement Mag Inc..........G....... 630 801-7788
Aurora *(G-1128)*
Desert Southwest Fitness Inc...............G....... 520 292-0011
Champaign *(G-3474)*
Dobinski Marketing.................................G....... 773 248-5880
Chicago *(G-4620)*
Fanning Communications Inc...............G....... 708 293-1430
Crestwood *(G-7488)*
Futures Magazine Inc .............................G....... 312 846-4600
Chicago *(G-4897)*
Gail McGrath & Associates Inc.............F....... 847 770-4620
Northbrook *(G-16262)*
Half Price Bks Rec Mgzines Inc............E....... 847 588-2286
Niles *(G-15986)*
Hearst Corporation .................................E....... 312 984-5166
Chicago *(G-5064)*
Home School Enrichment Inc...............G....... 309 347-1392
Pekin *(G-17267)*
Hotel Amerika..........................................G....... 219 508-9418
Chicago *(G-5119)*
Ink Spots Prtg & Meida Design.............G....... 708 754-1300
Homewood *(G-12102)*
Institute For Public Affairs ....................F....... 773 772-0100
Chicago *(G-5207)*
Instrumentalists Inc.................................F....... 847 446-5000
Northbrook *(G-16278)*
Lsc Communications Inc.......................D....... 773 272-9200
Chicago *(G-5552)*
Lsc Communications Us LLC...............A....... 815 844-5181
Pontiac *(G-17705)*
Lsc Communications Us LLC...............B....... 844 572-5720
Chicago *(G-5553)*
Magazine Plus..........................................G....... 773 281-4106
Chicago *(G-5599)*
Metal Center News...................................F....... 630 571-1067
Oak Brook *(G-16542)*
Midwest Outdoors Ltd.............................E....... 630 887-7722
Burr Ridge *(G-2867)*
Northern Illinois Real Estate.................G....... 630 257-2480
Lemont *(G-13244)*
Onion Inc...................................................F....... 312 751-0503
Chicago *(G-5992)*
Onion Inc...................................................F....... 312 751-0503
Chicago *(G-5993)*
P&L Group Ltd..........................................F....... 773 660-1930
Chicago *(G-6041)*
Rankin Publishing Inc .............................F....... 217 268-4959
Arcola *(G-683)*
Realtor Magazine .....................................F....... 312 329-1928
Chicago *(G-6308)*
Reilly Communication Group ................F....... 630 756-1225
Arlington Heights *(G-831)*
Rylin Media LLC.......................................G....... 708 246-7599
Western Springs *(G-21873)*
Silent W Communications Inc ..............G....... 630 978-2050
Oswego *(G-16934)*
Tails Inc.....................................................F....... 773 564-9300
Chicago *(G-6666)*
US Catholic Magazine.............................G....... 312 236-7782
Chicago *(G-6853)*
Wenner Media LLC...................................G....... 312 660-3040
Chicago *(G-6957)*
Willis Stein & Partners Manage .............E....... 312 422-2400
Northbrook *(G-16387)*

## *PUBLISHING & PRINTING: Music, Book*

Cash House Music Group LLC ...............G....... 847 471-7401
Indian Creek *(G-12185)*
Fleming Music Technology Ctr..............G....... 708 316-8662
Wheaton *(G-21948)*
G I A Publications Inc ............................E....... 708 496-3800
Chicago *(G-4901)*

## *PUBLISHING & PRINTING: Newsletters, Business Svc*

Arthur Coyle Press ..................................G....... 773 465-8418
Chicago *(G-3955)*
Businessmine LLC...................................G....... 630 541-8480
Lombard *(G-13774)*
Cab Communications Inc.......................G....... 847 963-8740
Palatine *(G-17007)*
Debbie Harshman ....................................G....... 217 335-2112
Barry *(G-1311)*
Knighthouse Media Inc...........................G....... 312 676-1100
Chicago *(G-5391)*
Nas Media Group Inc ..............................G....... 312 371-7499
Olympia Fields *(G-16803)*
Nas Media Group Inc ..............................F....... 773 824-0242
Chicago *(G-5855)*
Paperworks...............................................G....... 630 969-3218
Downers Grove *(G-8499)*
T R Communications Inc.........................F....... 773 238-3366
Chicago *(G-6663)*

## *PUBLISHING & PRINTING: Newspapers*

Abington Argus-Sentinel.........................G....... 309 462-3189
Abingdon *(G-9)*
Advocate...................................................G....... 815 694-2122
Clifton *(G-7272)*
Amboy News .............................................G....... 815 857-2311
Amboy *(G-597)*
American Classifieds Inc .......................F....... 217 356-4804
Champaign *(G-3449)*
Bar Stool Depotcom .................................G....... 815 727-7294
Joliet *(G-12460)*
Benton Evening News Co .......................G....... 618 438-5611
Benton *(G-2022)*
Best Newspapers In Illinois ...................G....... 217 728-7381
Sullivan *(G-20740)*
Breese Publishing Co Inc.......................G....... 618 526-7211
Breese *(G-2440)*
Bulletin......................................................G....... 618 553-9764
Oblong *(G-16729)*
Catholic Press Assn of The US .............G....... 312 380-6789
Chicago *(G-4258)*
Chgo Daily Law Bulletin..........................G....... 217 525-6735
Springfield *(G-20417)*
Chicago Chinese Times ...........................G....... 630 717-4567
Naperville *(G-15625)*
Chicago Citizen Newsppr Group............F....... 773 783-1251
Chicago *(G-4311)*
Chicago Group Acquisition LLC ............G....... 312 755-0720
Chicago *(G-4321)*
Chicago Jewish News ..............................F....... 847 966-0606
Skokie *(G-19979)*
Chicago Sun-Times Features Inc ..........A....... 312 321-3000
Chicago *(G-4351)*
Chicago Sun-Times Features Inc ..........F....... 312 321-2043
Chicago *(G-4352)*
Chicago Tribune Company .....................A....... 312 222-3232
Chicago *(G-4357)*
Chicago Tribune Company .....................G....... 312 222-3232
Chicago *(G-4358)*
Chicago Tribune Company .....................G....... 312 222-8611
Chicago *(G-4359)*
Chrisman Leader.......................................G....... 217 269-2811
Chrisman *(G-7173)*
Classified Ventures...................................G....... 847 472-2718
Elk Grove Village *(G-9375)*
Cnlc-Stc Inc ..............................................A....... 312 321-3000
Chicago *(G-4412)*
Crain Communications Inc .....................C....... 312 649-5200
Chicago *(G-4494)*
Czech American TV Herald .....................G....... 708 813-0028
Willowbrook *(G-22208)*
Daily Dollar Savings LLC ........................G....... 860 883-0351
Morton Grove *(G-15193)*
Daily Egyptian Siu Newspaper ...............D....... 618 536-3311
Carbondale *(G-3005)*
Daily General LLC.....................................G....... 217 273-0719
Chicago *(G-4542)*
Daily Kratom..............................................G....... 815 768-7104
Joliet *(G-12482)*
Daily Money Matters LLC ........................G....... 847 729-8393
Glenview *(G-11119)*
Daily News Condominium Assn .............E....... 312 492-8526
Chicago *(G-4543)*
Daily News Tribune Inc............................C....... 815 223-2558
La Salle *(G-12770)*
Daily Projects ............................................G....... 224 209-8636
Algonquin *(G-385)*
Daily Whale................................................G....... 312 787-5204
Chicago *(G-4544)*
Double D Printing Inc ...............................G....... 630 406-8666
Batavia *(G-1441)*
Eagle Publications ....................................G....... 309 462-5758
Abingdon *(G-10)*
Early Edition...............................................G....... 312 345-0786
Chicago *(G-4676)*
Edwardsville Publishing Co.....................D....... 618 656-4700
Edwardsville *(G-8799)*
El Sol Dechicago Newspaper...................G....... 773 235-7655
Chicago *(G-4711)*
Elliott Publishing Inc ................................G....... 217 645-3033
Liberty *(G-13295)*
Elliott Publishing Inc ................................G....... 217 593-6515
Camp Point *(G-2972)*
Evanston Sentinel Corporation ...............G....... 847 492-0177
Evanston *(G-10034)*
Experimental Aircraft Examiner ..............G....... 847 226-0777
Cary *(G-3339)*
Final Call Inc...............................................F....... 773 602-1230
Chicago *(G-4843)*
Freeburg Printing & Publishing................G....... 618 539-3320
Freeburg *(G-10635)*
Ganji Klames ..............................................G....... 773 478-9000
Chicago *(G-4914)*
Gannett Satellite Info Netwrk...................G....... 312 216-1407
Chicago *(G-4915)*
Gatehouse Media LLC ...............................B....... 217 788-1300
Springfield *(G-20445)*
Gatehouse Media LLC ...............................E....... 618 937-2850
West Frankfort *(G-21809)*
Gatehouse Media LLC ...............................D....... 585 598-0030
Oakbrook Terrace *(G-16708)*
Gazette Democrat ......................................E....... 618 833-2150
Anna *(G-603)*
Gmd Mobile Pressure Wshg Svcs............G....... 773 826-1903
Chicago *(G-4964)*
Golda House...............................................G....... 773 927-0140
Chicago *(G-4972)*
Hardin County Independent......................G....... 618 287-2361
Elizabethtown *(G-9246)*
Hearst Communications Inc .....................C....... 309 829-9000
Bloomington *(G-2177)*
Herald Newspapers Inc .............................E....... 773 643-8533
Chicago *(G-5076)*
Herald Publications ...................................F....... 618 566-8282
Mascoutah *(G-14353)*
Herald Whig Quincy...................................G....... 217 222-7600
Quincy *(G-17835)*
Highland News Leader ..............................G....... 618 654-2366
Highland *(G-11790)*
Illinois Agrinews Inc .................................G....... 815 223-7448
La Salle *(G-12775)*
Illinois Newspaper In Educatn..................F....... 847 427-4388
Springfield *(G-20455)*
Indiana Agri-News Inc ...............................G....... 317 726-5391
La Salle *(G-12777)*
Inn Intl Newspaper Network......................G....... 309 764-5314
Moline *(G-14943)*
Journal News...............................................G....... 217 532-3933
Hillsboro *(G-11896)*
Journal News...............................................G....... 217 324-6604
Litchfield *(G-13690)*
Journal of Banking and Fin........................G....... 618 203-9074
Glen Carbon *(G-10953)*
Journal Star-Peoria.....................................G....... 309 833-2449
Macomb *(G-14126)*
Jury Verdict Reporter .................................G....... 312 644-7800
Chicago *(G-5336)*
Kankakee Daily Journal Co LLC................C....... 815 937-3300
Kankakee *(G-12632)*
Kerala Express Newspaper........................G....... 773 465-5359
Chicago *(G-5377)*
Korea Daily News.........................................E....... 847 545-1767
Elk Grove Village *(G-9579)*
Korea Times Chicago Inc...........................E....... 847 626-0388
Glenview *(G-11158)*
Leader...........................................................G....... 217 469-0045
Saint Joseph *(G-19316)*
Lee Enterprises Incorporated....................F....... 309 829-9000
Bloomington *(G-2193)*
Lee Enterprises Incorporated....................G....... 618 998-8499
Marion *(G-14270)*
Live Daily LLC..............................................G....... 312 286-6706
Chicago *(G-5523)*
Long View Publishing Co Inc.....................F....... 773 446-9920
Chicago *(G-5537)*
Marengo Union Times .................................G....... 815 568-5400
Marengo *(G-14237)*

1728 2017 Harris Illinois Industrial Directory (G-0000) Company's Geographic Section entry number

# PRODUCT SECTION
## PULP MILLS: Mechanical & Recycling Processing

Martin Publishing Co .................................. E ...... 309 543-2000
  Havana  *(G-11698)*
Mendota Reporter ..................................... F ...... 815 539-9396
  Mendota  *(G-14726)*
ML Content ............................................... G ...... 847 212-8824
  Wauconda  *(G-21485)*
Moline Dispatch Publishing Co ................ G ...... 309 764-4344
  Moline  *(G-14959)*
Mt Carmel Register Co Inc ........................ E ...... 618 262-5144
  Mount Carmel  *(G-15276)*
Nadig Newspapers Inc ............................. F ...... 773 286-6100
  Chicago  *(G-5849)*
Nashville News .......................................... F ...... 618 327-3411
  Nashville  *(G-15844)*
Nationwide News Monitor ........................ G ...... 312 424-4224
  Skokie  *(G-20044)*
New Herald News  LLC ............................. G ...... 217 651-8064
  Lincoln  *(G-13417)*
News Gazette Inc ..................................... C ...... 217 351-5252
  Champaign  *(G-3517)*
News Metropolis ....................................... G ...... 618 524-2141
  Metropolis  *(G-14760)*
News-Gazette  Inc .................................... G ...... 217 351-8128
  Champaign  *(G-3518)*
News-Gazette  Inc .................................... B ...... 217 351-5252
  Champaign  *(G-3519)*
Newspaper Holding Inc ............................ D ...... 217 347-7151
  Effingham  *(G-8850)*
Northwestern Illinois Farmer .................... G ...... 815 369-2811
  Lena  *(G-13282)*
Nuestro Mundo Newspaper ..................... G ...... 773 446-9920
  Chicago  *(G-5955)*
Ogle County Life ...................................... G ...... 815 732-2156
  Oregon  *(G-16829)*
Old Gary Inc ............................................. F ...... 219 648-3000
  Chicago  *(G-5979)*
Osborne Publications Inc ........................ G ...... 217 422-9702
  Decatur  *(G-7924)*
Paddock Publications  Inc ....................... B ...... 847 427-4300
  Arlington Heights  *(G-815)*
Paddock Publications  Inc ....................... C ...... 847 427-5545
  Schaumburg  *(G-19680)*
Pana News Inc .......................................... F ...... 217 562-2111
  Pana  *(G-17137)*
Paris Beacon News ................................... E ...... 217 465-6424
  Paris  *(G-17156)*
Peoples Tribune ....................................... E ...... 773 486-3551
  Chicago  *(G-6103)*
Perryco Inc ............................................... E ...... 303 652-8282
  Downers Grove  *(G-8501)*
Pinoy Monthly .......................................... G ...... 847 329-1073
  Skokie  *(G-20055)*
Pioneer Newspapers Inc ......................... C ...... 847 486-0600
  Chicago  *(G-6126)*
Pioneer Newspapers Inc ......................... E ...... 708 383-3200
  Oak Park  *(G-16679)*
Pioneer Newspapers Inc ......................... E ...... 630 887-0600
  Hinsdale  *(G-11958)*
Printed Blog Inc ........................................ G ...... 312 924-1040
  Chicago  *(G-6191)*
Quincy Media  Inc .................................... C ...... 217 223-5100
  Quincy  *(G-17879)*
Randolph County Herald Tribune ........... F ...... 618 826-2385
  Chester  *(G-3660)*
Rd Daily Enterprises ................................ G ...... 847 872-7632
  Winthrop Harbor  *(G-22320)*
Reach Chicago LLC ................................ G ...... 312 923-1028
  Chicago  *(G-6301)*
Red Streak Holdings Company .............. G ...... 312 321-3000
  Chicago  *(G-6315)*
Register Publishing Co ........................... E ...... 618 253-7146
  Harrisburg  *(G-11603)*
Register-Mail ............................................ C ...... 309 343-7181
  Galesburg  *(G-10773)*
Reporter Inc ............................................. E ...... 217 932-5211
  Casey  *(G-3391)*
Robert McCormick Tribune Lbrry ............ G ...... 847 619-7980
  Schaumburg  *(G-19713)*
Rochelle Newspapers Inc ....................... E ...... 815 562-4171
  Rochelle  *(G-18107)*
Roosevelt Torch ....................................... F ...... 312 281-3242
  Chicago  *(G-6391)*
Russell Publications Inc .......................... E ...... 708 258-3473
  Peotone  *(G-17492)*
Salem Times-Commoner Pubg Co ........ E ...... 618 548-3330
  Salem  *(G-19349)*
Senate Democrat Leader Office ............. G ...... 708 687-9696
  Springfield  *(G-20522)*
Shaw Suburban Media Group Inc .......... C ...... 815 459-4040
  Crystal Lake  *(G-7649)*

Shazak Productions .................................. G ...... 773 406-9880
  Chicago  *(G-6493)*
Slack Publications .................................... G ...... 217 268-4950
  Arcola  *(G-685)*
Small Newspaper Group .......................... C ...... 815 937-3300
  Kankakee  *(G-12652)*
Southland Voice ....................................... E ...... 708 214-8582
  Crete  *(G-7519)*
Stark County Communications ............... G ...... 309 286-4444
  Toulon  *(G-20977)*
Streetwise ................................................. F ...... 773 334-6600
  Chicago  *(G-6604)*
Success Journal Corp ............................. G ...... 847 583-9000
  Morton Grove  *(G-15240)*
Sun Times News Agency ......................... G ...... 815 672-1260
  Streator  *(G-20706)*
Sun-Times Media  LLC ............................. D ...... 312 321-3000
  Chicago  *(G-6621)*
Sun-Times Media Group  Inc ................... G ...... 618 273-3379
  Eldorado  *(G-8923)*
Sun-Times Media Group  Inc ................... D ...... 312 321-2299
  Chicago  *(G-6623)*
Sun-Times Media Holdings  LLC ............. E ...... 312 321-2299
  Chicago  *(G-6624)*
Teleguia Inc .............................................. E ...... 708 656-6675
  Cicero  *(G-7237)*
The Times ................................................. G ...... 815 433-2000
  Ottawa  *(G-16986)*
Times Republic ........................................ G ...... 217 283-5111
  Hoopeston  *(G-12119)*
Tini Martini .............................................. G ...... 773 269-2900
  Chicago  *(G-6729)*
Tne McDonough Democrat  Inc .............. G ...... 309 837-3343
  Macomb  *(G-14133)*
Tribune Finance Service Center ............. G ...... 312 595-0783
  Chicago  *(G-6772)*
Tribune Media Company ........................ G ...... 708 498-0584
  Lisle  *(G-13673)*
Tribune Tower .......................................... F ...... 312 981-7200
  Chicago  *(G-6775)*
Tuscola Journal Incorporated ................. G ...... 217 253-5086
  Tuscola  *(G-21026)*
Voice ......................................................... G ...... 630 966-8642
  Aurora  *(G-1230)*
Wednesday Journal  Inc .......................... D ...... 708 386-5555
  Oak Park  *(G-16691)*
West Suburban Journal ........................... G ...... 708 344-5975
  Bloomingdale  *(G-2141)*
Wjez Thunder 93 7 Wjbc Wbnq B1 ......... G ...... 815 842-6515
  Pontiac  *(G-17712)*
Wnta Studio Line ..................................... G ...... 815 874-7861
  Rockford  *(G-18687)*
World Journal LLC ................................... F ...... 312 842-8080
  Chicago  *(G-7031)*
Wrapports  LLC ........................................ E ...... 312 321-3000
  Chicago  *(G-7035)*
Zweibel Worldwide Productions .............. F ...... 312 751-0503
  Chicago  *(G-7076)*

### PUBLISHING & PRINTING: Pamphlets

C M S Publishing Inc ............................... G ...... 708 839-9201
  Willow Springs  *(G-22193)*
Ifpra Inc .................................................... G ...... 708 410-0100
  Westchester  *(G-21843)*
J S Paluch Co  Inc .................................... C ...... 847 678-9300
  Franklin Park  *(G-10502)*
Rohrer Graphic Arts Inc .......................... F ...... 630 832-3434
  Elmhurst  *(G-9930)*
Royal Publishing  Inc ............................... G ...... 309 343-4007
  Galesburg  *(G-10775)*
Royal Publishing  Inc ............................... G ...... 815 220-0400
  Peru  *(G-17526)*

### PUBLISHING & PRINTING: Patterns, Paper

Phoenix Press  Inc .................................... G ...... 630 833-2281
  Villa Park  *(G-21277)*

### PUBLISHING & PRINTING: Periodical Statistical Reports

CCH Incorporated .................................... A ...... 847 267-7000
  Riverwoods  *(G-18037)*

### PUBLISHING & PRINTING: Shopping News

Liberty Group Publishing ........................ F ...... 309 944-1779
  Geneseo  *(G-10802)*

### PUBLISHING & PRINTING: Technical Manuals

Bishop Engineering Company ................ F ...... 630 305-9538
  Lisle  *(G-13569)*
Rs Ductless Technical Support ............... G ...... 815 223-7949
  La Salle  *(G-12784)*

### PUBLISHING & PRINTING: Textbooks

BGF Performance Systems LLC .............. G ...... 773 539-7099
  Chicago  *(G-4101)*
Houghton Mifflin Harcourt Pubg .............. C ...... 630 208-5704
  Geneva  *(G-10833)*
Linmore Publishing Co ............................ G ...... 847 382-7606
  Barrington  *(G-1286)*
Medical Memories LLC ............................ G ...... 847 478-0078
  Buffalo Grove  *(G-2734)*
Perry Johnson  Inc ................................... F ...... 847 635-0010
  Rosemont  *(G-19021)*
Success Publishing Group Inc ................ F ...... 708 565-2681
  Chicago  *(G-6611)*

### PUBLISHING & PRINTING: Trade Journals

American Medical Association ................ E ...... 312 464-2555
  Chicago  *(G-3864)*
Ashton Gill Publishing LLC ..................... F ...... 847 673-8675
  Evanston  *(G-10013)*
Association Management Center ........... D ...... 847 375-4700
  Chicago  *(G-3971)*
Johnson Press America  Inc ................... E ...... 815 844-5161
  Pontiac  *(G-17704)*
Medtext Inc .............................................. G ...... 630 325-3277
  Burr Ridge  *(G-2866)*
Narda Inc ................................................. F ...... 312 648-2300
  Chicago  *(G-5853)*
Pinnacle Publishing Inc .......................... F ...... 218 444-2180
  Chicago  *(G-6124)*

### PUBLISHING & PRINTING: Yearbooks

Illini Media Co ......................................... B ...... 217 337-8300
  Champaign  *(G-3499)*
Lifetouch Services Inc ............................. C ...... 815 633-3881
  Loves Park  *(G-13961)*

### PULLEYS: Metal

HM Manufacturing  Inc ............................ F ...... 847 487-8700
  Wauconda  *(G-21469)*

### PULLEYS: Power Transmission

Chicago Die Casting Mfg Co .................. E ...... 847 671-5010
  Franklin Park  *(G-10428)*
Prophet Gear Co ..................................... E ...... 815 537-2002
  Prophetstown  *(G-17771)*

### PULP MILLS

BFI Waste Systems N Amer Inc .............. E ...... 847 429-7370
  Elgin  *(G-8965)*
Buster Services  Inc ................................. E ...... 773 247-2070
  Chicago  *(G-4191)*
C & M Recycling  Inc ............................... E ...... 847 578-1066
  North Chicago  *(G-16176)*
Cicero Iron Metal & Paper Inc ................ G ...... 708 863-8601
  Cicero  *(G-7183)*
International Paper Company ................ E ...... 630 250-1300
  Itasca  *(G-12286)*
International Paper Company ................ C ...... 217 735-1221
  Lincoln  *(G-13411)*
Lake Area Disposal Service Inc .............. E ...... 217 522-9271
  Springfield  *(G-20466)*
Weyerhaeuser Company ......................... D ...... 630 778-7070
  Naperville  *(G-15784)*

### PULP MILLS: Mech Pulp, Incl Groundwood & Thermomechanical

Kaskaskia Mechanical Insul Co .............. G ...... 618 768-4526
  Mascoutah  *(G-14355)*

### PULP MILLS: Mechanical & Recycling Processing

Coyote Transportation  Inc ..................... G ...... 630 204-5729
  Bensenville  *(G-1869)*
Paper Moon Recycling Inc ...................... G ...... 847 548-8875
  Grayslake  *(G-11358)*
Vida Enterprises  Inc ............................... G ...... 312 808-0088
  Chicago  *(G-6895)*

## PULP MILLS: Wood Based Pulp, NEC

Westrock CP LLC .................................... D ...... 312 346-6600
Chicago *(G-6967)*

## PUMP JACKS & OTHER PUMPING EQPT: Indl

Metropolitan Industries Inc .................... C ...... 815 886-9200
Romeoville *(G-18845)*
Park Engineering Inc ............................. E ...... 847 455-1424
Franklin Park *(G-10546)*
Roy E Roth Company .............................. G ...... 309 787-1791
Milan *(G-14805)*
Townley Engrg & Mfg Co Inc ................... F ...... 618 273-8271
Eldorado *(G-8924)*

## PUMPS

A-L-L Equipment Company .................... G ...... 815 877-7000
Loves Park *(G-13911)*
Action Pump Co ..................................... F ...... 847 516-3636
Cary *(G-3322)*
Allegion S&S US Holding Co ................. C ...... 815 875-3311
Princeton *(G-17742)*
Aptargroup Inc ..................................... B ...... 847 639-2124
Cary *(G-3327)*
Aqua Control Inc ................................... E ...... 815 664-4900
Spring Valley *(G-20374)*
Automax Corporation ............................. G ...... 630 972-1919
Woodridge *(G-22454)*
Canada Organization & Dev LLC ........... G ...... 630 743-2563
Downers Grove *(G-8404)*
Century Fasteners & Mch Co Inc ........... F ...... 773 463-3900
Skokie *(G-19977)*
Certified Power Inc ................................ E ...... 847 573-3800
Mundelein *(G-15485)*
Cool Fluidics Inc ................................... G ...... 815 861-4063
Woodstock *(G-22554)*
Corken Inc ........................................... D ...... 405 946-5576
Lake Bluff *(G-12839)*
Dover Energy Automation LLC .............. G ...... 630 541-1540
Downers Grove *(G-8432)*
Emco Wheaton Usa Inc ........................ E ...... 281 856-1300
Quincy *(G-17825)*
Engineered Fluid Inc ............................ C ...... 618 533-1351
Centralia *(G-3413)*
Engineered Fluid Inc ............................ D ...... 618 533-1351
Centralia *(G-3414)*
Ergoseal Inc ........................................ E ...... 630 462-9600
Carol Stream *(G-3147)*
Evac North America Inc ....................... E ...... 815 654-8300
Cherry Valley *(G-3642)*
Fairbanks Morse Pump Corp ............... B ...... 630 859-7000
North Aurora *(G-16129)*
FH Ayer Manufacturing Co ................... E ...... 708 755-0550
Chicago Heights *(G-7097)*
Flow Control US Holding Corp ............. F ...... 630 307-3000
Hanover Park *(G-11582)*
Flowserve Corporation ......................... E ...... 630 762-4100
West Chicago *(G-21704)*
Flowserve Corporation ......................... E ...... 630 762-4100
West Chicago *(G-21705)*
Flowserve Corporation ......................... E ...... 630 435-9596
Lombard *(G-13799)*
Flowserve Corporation ......................... E ...... 630 260-1310
Wheaton *(G-21949)*
Fluid Handling LLC .............................. B ...... 773 267-1600
Morton Grove *(G-15198)*
Fna Ip Holdings Inc .............................. D ...... 847 348-1500
Elk Grove Village *(G-9482)*
Graymills Corporation .......................... D ...... 773 477-4100
Broadview *(G-2582)*
Heidolph NA LLC ................................. F ...... 224 265-9600
Elk Grove Village *(G-9520)*
Hidrostal LLC ...................................... F ...... 630 240-6271
Aurora *(G-1026)*
Industrial Filter Pump Mfg Co ............... D ...... 708 656-7800
Bedford Park *(G-1556)*
Ingersoll-Rand Company ..................... E ...... 704 655-4000
Chicago *(G-5191)*
ITT Bell & Gossett ............................... E ...... 847 966-3700
Morton Grove *(G-15204)*
ITT Water & Wastewater USA Inc ........ F ...... 708 342-0484
Tinley Park *(G-20924)*
Jn Pump Holdings Inc ......................... F ...... 708 754-2940
Chicago Heights *(G-7105)*
Knox Capital Holdings LLC ................. G ...... 312 402-1425
Chicago *(G-5393)*
L V Barnhouse & Sons ........................ G ...... 309 586-5404
Galesburg *(G-10764)*
Lubeq Corporation .............................. F ...... 847 931-1020
Elgin *(G-9096)*
March Manufacturing Inc ..................... D ...... 847 729-5300
Glenview *(G-11167)*
Mechanical Engineering Pdts .............. G ...... 312 421-3375
Chicago *(G-5674)*
Midwest Fuel Injction Svc Corp ........... F ...... 847 991-7867
Palatine *(G-17056)*
O Adjust Matic Pump Company ........... G ...... 630 766-1490
Wood Dale *(G-22408)*
Pentair Flow Technologies LLC ........... C ...... 630 859-7000
North Aurora *(G-16140)*
Polar Container Corp Inc ..................... G ...... 847 299-5030
Rosemont *(G-19024)*
Pump House ....................................... G ...... 618 216-2404
Wood River *(G-22444)*
Pump Solutions Group ........................ D ...... 630 487-2240
Oakbrook Terrace *(G-16719)*
Quincy Compressor LLC ..................... G ...... 217 222-7700
Quincy *(G-17875)*
R S Corcoran Co ................................. E ...... 815 485-2156
New Lenox *(G-15905)*
Ruthman Pump and Engineering ........ G ...... 708 754-2940
Chicago Heights *(G-7124)*
Simpson Well & Pump Company ........ G ...... 708 301-0826
Lockport *(G-13746)*
Spirax Sarco Inc ................................ F ...... 630 493-4525
Lisle *(G-13660)*
Thermo Fisher Scientific Inc ............... D ...... 847 381-7050
Bartlett *(G-1380)*
Thomas Pump Company ..................... F ...... 630 851-9393
Aurora *(G-1085)*
Toyo Pump North America .................. G ...... 815 806-1414
New Lenox *(G-15921)*
Tramco Pump Co ................................ E ...... 312 243-5800
Chicago *(G-6756)*
Trusty Warns Inc ................................. E ...... 630 766-9015
Wood Dale *(G-22434)*
Tuthill Corporation .............................. E ...... 630 382-4900
Burr Ridge *(G-2889)*
W S Darley & Co ................................ F ...... 630 735-3500
Itasca *(G-12372)*
Wagner Pump & Supply Co Inc ........... E ...... 847 526-8573
Wauconda *(G-21512)*
Yamada America Inc .......................... E ...... 847 228-9063
Arlington Heights *(G-877)*

## PUMPS & PARTS: Indl

Chicago Industrial Pump Co ............... G ...... 847 214-8988
South Elgin *(G-20189)*
Dover Artificial Lift Intl LLC ................... F ...... 630 743-2563
Downers Grove *(G-8430)*
Guzzler Manufacturing Inc .................. C ...... 815 672-3171
Streator *(G-20690)*
Idex Corporation ................................ B ...... 847 498-7070
Lake Forest *(G-12915)*
Inman Electric Motors Inc ................... E ...... 815 223-2288
La Salle *(G-12778)*
Johnson Pumps America Inc .............. E ...... 847 671-7867
Rockford *(G-18449)*
Murdock Company Inc ........................ G ...... 847 566-0050
Mundelein *(G-15535)*
Omni Pump Repairs Inc ..................... E ...... 847 451-0000
Franklin Park *(G-10543)*
Tuskin Equipment Corporation ........... G ...... 630 466-5590
Sugar Grove *(G-20738)*
Waves Fluid Solutions LLC ................. G ...... 630 765-7533
Carol Stream *(G-3264)*

## PUMPS & PUMPING EQPT REPAIR SVCS

Accurate Elc Mtr & Pump Co .............. G ...... 708 448-2792
Worth *(G-22631)*
All Electric Mtr Repr Svc Inc ............... F ...... 773 925-2404
Chicago *(G-3806)*
Basement Flood Protector Inc ............. F ...... 847 438-6770
Lake Zurich *(G-13045)*
Fluid Pump Service Inc ...................... G ...... 847 228-0750
Elk Grove Village *(G-9480)*
Metropolitan Industries Inc .................. C ...... 815 886-9200
Romeoville *(G-18845)*
Omni Pump Repairs Inc ..................... F ...... 847 451-0000
Franklin Park *(G-10543)*
Polar Container Corp Inc .................... C ...... 847 299-5030
Rosemont *(G-19024)*

## PUMPS & PUMPING EQPT WHOLESALERS

A-L-L Equipment Company ................. G ...... 815 877-7000
Loves Park *(G-13911)*
All Electric Mtr Repr Svc Inc ............... F ...... 773 925-2404
Chicago *(G-3806)*
Apolinski John .................................... G ...... 847 696-3156
Park Ridge *(G-17181)*
Fluid Pump Service Inc ...................... G ...... 847 228-0750
Elk Grove Village *(G-9480)*
Johnson Pumps America Inc .............. E ...... 847 671-7867
Rockford *(G-18449)*
L V Barnhouse & Sons ........................ G ...... 309 586-5404
Galesburg *(G-10764)*
Murdock Company Inc ........................ G ...... 847 566-0050
Mundelein *(G-15535)*
Pump House ....................................... G ...... 618 216-2404
Wood River *(G-22444)*
Roy E Roth Company .......................... G ...... 309 787-1791
Milan *(G-14805)*
Thomas Pump Company ..................... F ...... 630 851-9393
Aurora *(G-1085)*
Toyo Pump North America .................. G ...... 815 806-1414
New Lenox *(G-15921)*
Wagner Pump & Supply Co Inc ........... E ...... 847 526-8573
Wauconda *(G-21512)*
Yamada America Inc .......................... E ...... 847 228-9063
Arlington Heights *(G-877)*

## PUMPS: Domestic, Water Or Sump

Basement Flood Protector Inc ............. F ...... 847 438-6770
Lake Zurich *(G-13045)*
Georgetown Waste Water .................... G ...... 217 662-2525
Georgetown *(G-10886)*
Grundfos Water Utility Inc ................... D ...... 630 236-5500
Aurora *(G-1021)*
Nexpump Inc ...................................... G ...... 630 365-4639
Elburn *(G-8900)*
S-P-D Incorporated ............................. G ...... 847 882-9820
Palatine *(G-17070)*
Swaby Manufacturing Company ......... G ...... 773 626-1400
Chicago *(G-6646)*
Tacmina USA Corporation ................... G ...... 312 810-8128
Schaumburg *(G-19751)*
Unique Indoor Comfort ....................... F ...... 847 362-1910
Libertyville *(G-13394)*

## PUMPS: Fluid Power

Ifh Group Inc ...................................... D ...... 800 435-7003
Rock Falls *(G-18138)*
Ifh Group Inc ...................................... G ...... 815 380-2367
Galt *(G-10781)*
Parker-Hannifin Corporation ............... C ...... 847 955-5000
Lincolnshire *(G-13472)*

## PUMPS: Gasoline, Measuring Or Dispensing

Franklin Fueling Systems Inc ............. G ...... 207 283-0156
Chicago *(G-4885)*
Tuthill Corporation .............................. E ...... 630 382-4900
Burr Ridge *(G-2889)*

## PUMPS: Hydraulic Power Transfer

Brock Equipment Company ................. E ...... 815 459-4210
Woodstock *(G-22547)*
Bucher Hydraulics Inc ........................ G ...... 847 429-0700
Elgin *(G-8973)*
Concentric Rockford Inc ..................... C ...... 815 398-4400
Rockford *(G-18322)*
Mandus Group Ltd ............................. F ...... 309 786-1507
Rock Island *(G-18187)*
Mechanical Tool & Engrg Co ............... C ...... 815 397-4701
Rockford *(G-18489)*
Mechanical Tool & Engrg Co ............... C ...... 815 397-4701
Rockford *(G-18490)*
Rehobot Inc ....................................... G ...... 815 385-7777
McHenry *(G-14550)*
S C C Pumps Inc ................................ G ...... 847 593-8495
Arlington Heights *(G-834)*
Settima Usa Inc ................................. G ...... 630 812-1433
Mount Prospect *(G-15373)*

## PUMPS: Measuring & Dispensing

Cornelius Inc ..................................... B ...... 630 539-6850
Glendale Heights *(G-11018)*
Dover Corporation .............................. C ...... 630 541-1540
Downers Grove *(G-8431)*
Gfi Innovations LLC ............................ G ...... 847 263-9000
Antioch *(G-634)*
March Manufacturing Inc .................... D ...... 847 729-5300
Glenview *(G-11167)*

# PRODUCT SECTION

### PUMPS: Oil, Measuring Or Dispensing
Standard Lifts & Equipment Inc .......... G ...... 414 444-1000
 Hanover Park *(G-11591)*

### PUMPS: Vacuum, Exc Laboratory
Industrial Vacuum .............................. G ...... 630 357-7700
 Maple Park *(G-14200)*
J/B Industries Inc ............................... D ...... 630 851-9444
 Aurora *(G-1174)*

### PUNCHES: Forming & Stamping
Accurate Grinding Co Inc .................. G ...... 708 371-1887
 Posen *(G-17727)*
Emt International Inc ......................... G ...... 630 655-4145
 Westmont *(G-21887)*
Ever Ready Pin & Manufacturing ...... D ...... 815 874-4949
 Rockford *(G-18371)*

### PURIFICATION & DUST COLLECTION EQPT
Bisco Enterprise Inc ........................... F ...... 630 628-1831
 Schaumburg *(G-19463)*
Custom Filter LLC .............................. D ...... 630 906-2100
 Aurora *(G-991)*
Donaldson Company Inc .................. E ...... 815 288-3374
 Dixon *(G-8329)*
Robuschi Usa Inc ............................... G ...... 704 424-1018
 Quincy *(G-17889)*

### PUSHCARTS
Smart Solar Inc ................................... F ...... 813 343-5770
 Libertyville *(G-13382)*

### PYROMETER TUBES
C & L Manufacturing Entps ............... G ...... 618 465-7623
 Alton *(G-565)*

### QUARTZ CRYSTALS: Electronic
Tellurian Technologies Inc ................. C ...... 847 934-4141
 Arlington Heights *(G-854)*

### QUILTING SVC & SPLYS, FOR THE TRADE
Quilt Merchant .................................... F ...... 630 480-3000
 Winfield *(G-22291)*
Quiltmaster Inc .................................. E ...... 847 426-6741
 Carpentersville *(G-3300)*
Top Shelf Quilts Inc ........................... G ...... 815 806-1694
 Frankfort *(G-10370)*

### RACE CAR OWNERS
R/A Hoerr Inc ..................................... E ...... 309 691-8789
 Edwards *(G-8784)*

### RACE TRACK OPERATION
Lanigan Holdings LLC ........................ F ...... 708 596-5200
 Hazel Crest *(G-11710)*

### RACEWAYS
Chicagoland Raceway ....................... G ...... 708 203-8003
 Downers Grove *(G-8410)*
Dells Raceway Park Inc .................... G ...... 815 494-0074
 Roscoe *(G-18893)*
Party Fantasy ..................................... G ...... 847 837-0010
 Mundelein *(G-15542)*
Raceway Electric Company Inc ........ G ...... 630 501-1180
 Elmhurst *(G-9924)*
Southern IL Raceway ........................ G ...... 618 201-0500
 Marion *(G-14288)*

### RACKS & SHELVING: Household, Wood
T J Kellogg Inc ................................... G ...... 815 969-0524
 Rockford *(G-18640)*

### RACKS: Bicycle, Automotive
Treetop Marketing Inc ....................... G ...... 877 249-0479
 Batavia *(G-1510)*

### RACKS: Display
Astoria Wire Products Inc ................. D ...... 708 496-9950
 Bedford Park *(G-1539)*
B-O-F Corporation ............................. E ...... 630 585-0020
 Aurora *(G-967)*

Bunzl Retail LLC ................................. F ...... 847 733-1469
 Morton Grove *(G-15190)*
Illinois Rack Enterprises Inc .............. E ...... 815 385-5750
 Lakemoor *(G-13144)*
Jet Rack Corp .................................... E ...... 773 586-2150
 Chicago *(G-5298)*
John H Best & Sons Inc .................... E ...... 309 932-2124
 Galva *(G-10791)*
Keystone Display Inc ......................... D ...... 815 648-2456
 Hebron *(G-11721)*
Macon Metal Products Co ................ E ...... 217 824-7205
 Taylorville *(G-20842)*
Material Control Systems Inc ........... E ...... 309 523-3774
 Port Byron *(G-17721)*
Material Control Systems Inc ........... G ...... 309 654-9031
 Cordova *(G-7378)*
Midland Metal Products Co .............. G ...... 773 927-5700
 Chicago *(G-5735)*
Nycor Products Inc ............................ G ...... 815 727-9883
 Joliet *(G-12547)*
Rack Builders Inc ............................... G ...... 217 214-9482
 Quincy *(G-17884)*
Yetter Manufacturing Company ........ G ...... 309 776-3222
 Colchester *(G-7309)*

### RACKS: Magazine, Wood
Innovative Fix Solutions LLC ............. D ...... 815 395-8500
 Rockford *(G-18436)*

### RACKS: Pallet, Exc Wood
Room Dividers Now LLC ................... G ...... 847 224-7900
 Barrington *(G-1303)*

### RACKS: Railroad Car, Vehicle Transportation, Steel
Ireco LLC ............................................ F ...... 630 741-0155
 Elmhurst *(G-9888)*

### RACKS: Trash, Metal Rack
Ideal Fabricators Inc .......................... F ...... 217 999-7017
 Mount Olive *(G-15304)*

### RACQUET RESTRINGING & EQPT REPAIR SVCS
Court & Slope Inc .............................. G ...... 847 697-3600
 Elgin *(G-9005)*

### RADAR SYSTEMS & EQPT
Motorola Solutions Inc ...................... C ...... 847 576-8600
 Schaumburg *(G-19652)*
Municipal Electronics Inc .................. G ...... 217 877-8601
 Decatur *(G-7920)*
Progressive Electronics ..................... G ...... 217 672-8434
 Warrensburg *(G-21339)*

### RADIATORS: Stationary Engine
Diesel Radiator Co ............................. E ...... 708 345-2839
 Melrose Park *(G-14618)*
Diesel Radiator Co ............................. D ...... 708 865-7299
 Melrose Park *(G-14619)*

### RADIO & TELEVISION COMMUNICATIONS EQUIPMENT
Ale USA Inc ........................................ G ...... 630 713-5194
 Naperville *(G-15595)*
Allcom Products Illinois LLC ............. E ...... 847 468-8830
 South Elgin *(G-20180)*
Arris Group Inc .................................. E ...... 630 281-3000
 Lisle *(G-13564)*
AVI-Spl Employee .............................. G ...... 847 437-7712
 Schaumburg *(G-19454)*
BEI Holding Corporation ................... G ...... 217 224-9600
 Quincy *(G-17803)*
Cco Holdings LLC .............................. G ...... 618 505-3505
 Troy *(G-21003)*
Cco Holdings LLC .............................. G ...... 618 651-6486
 Highland *(G-11777)*
Coleman Cable LLC ........................... D ...... 847 672-2300
 Waukegan *(G-21543)*
Colt Technology Services LLC ......... G ...... 312 465-2484
 Chicago *(G-4430)*
D W Ram Manufacturing Co ............ E ...... 708 633-7900
 Tinley Park *(G-20908)*

## RADIO & TELEVISION REPAIR

Driver Services .................................. G ...... 505 267-8686
 Bensenville *(G-1883)*
Easy Trac Gps Inc ............................. G ...... 630 359-5804
 Berwyn *(G-2061)*
Fleet Management Solutions Inc ..... E ...... 805 787-0508
 Glenview *(G-11126)*
FSI Technologies Inc ......................... E ...... 630 932-9380
 Lombard *(G-13803)*
Gatesair Inc ........................................ C ...... 217 222-8200
 Quincy *(G-17830)*
Gogo Intermediate Holdings LLC .... G ...... 630 647-1400
 Itasca *(G-12271)*
Gogo LLC ............................................ B ...... 630 647-1400
 Chicago *(G-4970)*
Gogo LLC ............................................ D ...... 630 647-1400
 Bensenville *(G-1911)*
Grass Valley Usa LLC ....................... E ...... 847 803-8060
 Rosemont *(G-19003)*
Healthcom Inc ................................... E ...... 217 728-8331
 Sullivan *(G-20747)*
Heil Sound Ltd ................................... F ...... 618 257-3000
 Fairview Heights *(G-10168)*
Inclusion Solutions LLC .................... G ...... 847 869-2500
 Evanston *(G-10055)*
Jklein Enterprises Inc ........................ G ...... 618 664-4554
 Greenville *(G-11395)*
L3 Technologies Inc ........................... F ...... 212 697-1111
 Rolling Meadows *(G-18741)*
Langham Engineering ....................... G ...... 815 223-5250
 Peru *(G-17516)*
Latino Arts & Communications ........ G ...... 773 501-0029
 Chicago *(G-5465)*
Motorola Mobility Holdings LLC ...... G ...... 847 523-5000
 Chicago *(G-5815)*
Motorola Solutions Inc ...................... C ...... 847 576-5000
 Chicago *(G-5818)*
Motorola Solutions Inc ...................... G ...... 847 341-3485
 Oak Brook *(G-16546)*
Motorola Solutions Inc ...................... C ...... 630 308-9394
 Hoffman Estates *(G-12025)*
Motorola Solutions Inc ...................... G ...... 630 353-8000
 Downers Grove *(G-8491)*
Motorola Solutions Inc ...................... C ...... 847 576-8600
 Schaumburg *(G-19652)*
Motorola Solutions Inc ...................... C ...... 847 540-8815
 Arlington Heights *(G-807)*
Motorola Solutions Inc ...................... G ...... 847 523-5000
 Libertyville *(G-13360)*
Motorola Solutions Inc ...................... G ...... 847 541-1014
 West Chicago *(G-21747)*
Motorola Solutions Inc ...................... C ...... 708 476-8226
 Schaumburg *(G-19653)*
Motorola Solutions Inc ...................... C ...... 800 331-6456
 Schaumburg *(G-19654)*
Motorola Solutions Inc ...................... G ...... 847 576-5000
 Elgin *(G-9114)*
Nielsen & Bainbridge LLC ............... D ...... 708 546-2135
 Bridgeview *(G-2514)*
Nokia Slutions Networks US LLC .... F ...... 224 248-8204
 Arlington Heights *(G-809)*
Qaboss Partners ................................ B ...... 312 203-4290
 Chicago *(G-6235)*
Radio Frequency Systems Inc ......... E ...... 800 321-4700
 Naperville *(G-15737)*
Ram Systems & Communication ..... G ...... 847 487-7575
 Wauconda *(G-21499)*
Roscor Corporation ........................... D ...... 847 299-8080
 Chicago *(G-6394)*
Simpson Electric Company .............. E ...... 847 697-2260
 Elgin *(G-9182)*
Spectrum Cos International ............. G ...... 630 879-8008
 Batavia *(G-1497)*
Studio Technologies Inc ................... F ...... 847 676-9177
 Skokie *(G-20093)*
Switchcraft Inc ................................... B ...... 773 792-2700
 Chicago *(G-6653)*
Switchcraft Holdco Inc ..................... G ...... 773 792-2700
 Chicago *(G-6654)*

### RADIO & TELEVISION RECEIVER INSTALLATION SVCS
Jklein Enterprises Inc ........................ G ...... 618 664-4554
 Greenville *(G-11395)*

### RADIO & TELEVISION REPAIR
A J R International Inc ....................... D ...... 800 232-3965
 Glendale Heights *(G-11006)*

---
Employee Codes: A=Over 500 employees, B=251-500
C=101-250, D=51-100, E=20-50, F=10-19, G=3-9

# RADIO BROADCASTING & COMMUNICATIONS EQPT

### RADIO BROADCASTING & COMMUNICATIONS EQPT

|  | | | |
|---|---|---|---|
| 4g Antenna Shop Inc | G | 815 496-0444 | |
| Aurora *(G-952)* | | | |
| Ayla Group Inc | G | 630 954-9432 | |
| Bartlett *(G-1334)* | | | |
| Broadcast Electronics Inc | C | 217 224-9600 | |
| Quincy *(G-17809)* | | | |
| Linear Industries Inc | F | 847 428-5793 | |
| Elgin *(G-9095)* | | | |
| Nokia Slutions Networks US LLC | G | 630 979-9572 | |
| Naperville *(G-15716)* | | | |
| Northrop Grumman Systems Corp | A | 847 259-9600 | |
| Rolling Meadows *(G-18753)* | | | |
| Temco Japan Co Ltd | G | 847 359-3277 | |
| South Barrington *(G-20134)* | | | |
| Visiplex Inc | E | 847 918-0250 | |
| Buffalo Grove *(G-2790)* | | | |

### RADIO BROADCASTING STATIONS

- Abc Inc .............................................. E ....... 312 980-1000
  Chicago *(G-3707)*
- Bond Broadcasting Inc ..................... F ....... 618 664-3300
  Greenville *(G-11389)*
- Illini Media Co ................................... B ....... 217 337-8300
  Champaign *(G-3499)*
- Moody Bible Inst of Chicago ............ A ....... 312 329-4000
  Chicago *(G-5799)*
- Wjez Thunder 93 7 Wjbc Wbnq B1 .. G ...... 815 842-6515
  Pontiac *(G-17712)*
- Wnta Studio Line .............................. G ...... 815 874-7861
  Rockford *(G-18687)*

### RADIO COMMUNICATIONS: Airborne Eqpt

- Boeing Company ............................. B ....... 312 544-2000
  Chicago *(G-4136)*
- Boeing Irving Company .................... A ....... 312 544-2000
  Chicago *(G-4137)*
- Comlink Technologies Inc ................ F ....... 630 279-5445
  Bensenville *(G-1863)*

### RADIO COMMUNICATIONS: Carrier Eqpt

- Invisio Communications Inc ............. G ...... 412 327-6578
  Chicago *(G-5234)*

### RADIO RECEIVER NETWORKS

- Iheartcommunications Inc ................ E ...... 312 255-5100
  Chicago *(G-5149)*
- Isco International Inc ........................ G ...... 630 283-3100
  Schaumburg *(G-19582)*
- Saga Communications Inc ............... G ...... 248 631-8099
  Springfield *(G-20517)*
- State of Illinois ................................. C ...... 312 836-9500
  Chicago *(G-6578)*

### RADIO REPAIR SHOP, NEC

- Gier Radio & Television Inc ............. G ...... 815 722-8514
  Joliet *(G-12502)*
- Midtronics Inc ................................... D ...... 630 323-2800
  Willowbrook *(G-22222)*

### RADIO, TELEVISION & CONSUMER ELECTRONICS STORES: Antennas

- Pc-Tel Inc ........................................ C ...... 630 372-6800
  Bloomingdale *(G-2127)*

### RADIO, TELEVISION & CONSUMER ELECTRONICS STORES: Eqpt, NEC

- Coles Appliance & Furn Co ............. G ...... 773 525-1797
  Chicago *(G-4422)*

### RADIO, TV & CONSUMER ELEC STORES: Automotive Sound Eqpt

- Elm Street Industries Inc ................. F ...... 309 854-7000
  Kewanee *(G-12681)*
- Key Car Stereo ................................ G ...... 217 446-4556
  Oakwood *(G-16726)*

### RADIO, TV & CONSUMER ELEC STORES: High Fidelity Stereo Eqpt

- Sound Design Inc ............................ G ...... 630 548-7000
  Plainfield *(G-17650)*

- Van L Speakerworks Inc .................. G ...... 773 769-0773
  Chicago *(G-6870)*

### RADIO, TV/CONSUMER ELEC STORES: Antennas, Satellite Dish

- Jklein Enterprises Inc ....................... G ...... 618 664-4554
  Greenville *(G-11395)*

### RAIL & STRUCTURAL SHAPES: Aluminum rail & structural shapes

- Meyer Metal Systems Inc ................ F ...... 847 468-0500
  Elgin *(G-9109)*

### RAILINGS: Prefabricated, Metal

- K Three Welding Service Inc ........... G ...... 708 563-2911
  Chicago *(G-5344)*
- Patrick Holdings Inc ......................... F ...... 815 874-5300
  Rockford *(G-18531)*

### RAILINGS: Wood

- Arlen-Jacob Manufacturing Co ........ E ...... 815 485-4777
  New Lenox *(G-15870)*
- Middletons Mouldings Inc ................ D ...... 517 278-6610
  Schaumburg *(G-19646)*

### RAILROAD CAR RENTING & LEASING SVCS

- Chicago Freight Car Leasing Co ..... D ...... 847 318-8000
  Schaumburg *(G-19471)*
- Marmon Holdings Inc ....................... D ...... 312 372-9500
  Chicago *(G-5625)*
- Marmon Industrial LLC .................... G ...... 312 372-9500
  Chicago *(G-5626)*
- Relco Locomotives Inc .................... D ...... 630 968-0670
  Lisle *(G-13651)*
- Union Tank Car Company ............... C ...... 312 431-3111
  Chicago *(G-6815)*
- UTC Railcar Repair Svcs LLC ......... A ...... 312 431-5053
  Chicago *(G-6861)*
- White International Inc ..................... E ...... 630 377-9966
  Saint Charles *(G-19295)*

### RAILROAD CAR REPAIR SVCS

- Freight Car Services Inc .................. B ...... 217 443-4106
  Danville *(G-7722)*
- Transco Railway Products Inc ......... G ...... 312 427-2818
  Chicago *(G-6759)*
- Union Tank Car Company ............... C ...... 312 431-3111
  Chicago *(G-6815)*
- UTC Railcar Repair Svcs LLC ......... A ...... 312 431-5053
  Chicago *(G-6861)*

### RAILROAD CARGO LOADING & UNLOADING SVCS

- Aldridge Electric Inc ........................ B ...... 847 680-5200
  Libertyville *(G-13300)*
- Bison Gear & Engineering Corp ...... C ...... 630 377-0153
  Saint Charles *(G-19143)*
- Blue Comet Transport Inc ................ G ...... 773 617-9512
  Chicago *(G-4125)*
- Global Technologies I LLC .............. D ...... 312 255-8350
  Chicago *(G-4960)*
- Quad-Illinois Inc ............................... F ...... 847 836-1115
  Elgin *(G-9155)*
- Robinsport LLC ................................ G ...... 630 724-9280
  Woodridge *(G-22514)*

### RAILROAD EQPT

- A & S Steel Specialties Inc .............. E ...... 815 838-8188
  Lockport *(G-13700)*
- Aldon Co ........................................... F ...... 847 623-8800
  Waukegan *(G-21521)*
- Alliance Wheel Services LLC .......... G ...... 309 444-4334
  Washington *(G-21377)*
- Amsted Rail Company Inc ............... D ...... 312 258-8000
  Chicago *(G-3898)*
- Amsted Rail Company Inc ............... B ...... 312 922-4501
  Chicago *(G-3899)*
- Amsted Rail Company Inc ............... B ...... 618 225-6463
  Granite City *(G-11265)*
- Anchor Brake Shoe Company LLC .. G ..... 630 293-1110
  West Chicago *(G-21660)*
- Freightcar America Inc .................... D ...... 800 458-2235
  Chicago *(G-4889)*

- Fugiel Railroad Supply Corp ............ G ...... 847 516-6862
  Cary *(G-3343)*
- G K Enterprises Inc ......................... G ...... 708 587-2150
  Monee *(G-14996)*
- Greenbrier Companies Inc .............. G ...... 847 838-1435
  Antioch *(G-637)*
- Gunderson Rail Services LLC ......... E ...... 309 676-1597
  Peoria *(G-17375)*
- Gunderson Rail Services LLC ......... E ...... 866 858-3919
  Chicago Heights *(G-7101)*
- Holland LP ....................................... C ...... 708 672-2300
  Crete *(G-7515)*
- Illini Castings LLC ........................... F ...... 217 446-6365
  Danville *(G-7737)*
- Illinois Central Gulf Car Shop .......... D ...... 618 533-8281
  Centralia *(G-3418)*
- Maclean Fastener Services LLC ..... G ...... 847 353-8402
  Buffalo Grove *(G-2729)*
- Meadoweld Machine Inc .................. G ...... 815 623-3939
  South Beloit *(G-20161)*
- Midland Railway Supply Inc ............ E ...... 618 467-6305
  Godfrey *(G-11229)*
- Midwest Railcar Corporation ........... F ...... 618 288-2233
  Maryville *(G-14344)*
- Milano Railcar Services LLC ........... G ...... 618 242-4004
  Mount Vernon *(G-15427)*
- Miner Enterprises Inc ...................... G ...... 630 232-3000
  Geneva *(G-10849)*
- National Trackwork Inc .................... E ...... 630 250-0600
  Itasca *(G-12325)*
- Pintsch Tiefenbach Us Inc .............. G ...... 618 993-8513
  Marion *(G-14280)*
- Railway & Industrial Svcs Inc ......... C ...... 815 726-4224
  Crest Hill *(G-7465)*
- Salco Products Inc .......................... D ...... 630 783-2570
  Lemont *(G-13261)*
- Transco Railway Products Inc ......... G ...... 312 427-2818
  Chicago *(G-6759)*
- Transco Railway Products Inc ......... D ...... 419 562-1031
  Chicago *(G-6760)*
- Voestalpine Nortrak Inc ................... D ...... 217 876-9160
  Decatur *(G-7957)*
- Wallace Industries Inc ..................... G ...... 815 389-8999
  South Beloit *(G-20172)*
- Western Railway Devices Corp ...... G ...... 847 625-8500
  Waukegan *(G-21640)*
- Western-Cullen-Hayes Inc .............. D ...... 773 254-9600
  Chicago *(G-6964)*
- Westinghouse A Brake Tech Corp .. E ...... 708 596-6730
  Chicago *(G-6965)*
- Whiting Corporation ........................ C ...... 708 587-2000
  Monee *(G-15007)*
- Willims-Hyward Intl Ctings Inc ........ F ...... 708 458-0015
  Argo *(G-698)*

### RAILROAD EQPT & SPLYS WHOLESALERS

- Anchor Brake Shoe Company LLC .. G ..... 630 293-1110
  West Chicago *(G-21660)*
- Fugiel Railroad Supply Corp ........... G ...... 847 516-6862
  Cary *(G-3343)*
- Midland Railway Supply Inc ............ E ...... 618 467-6305
  Godfrey *(G-11229)*
- National Railway Equipment Co ..... G ...... 618 241-9270
  Mount Vernon *(G-15433)*
- National Railway Equipment Co ..... C ...... 618 242-6590
  Mount Vernon *(G-15432)*
- National Railway Equipment Co ..... C ...... 309 755-6800
  Silvis *(G-19939)*
- Railway & Industrial Svcs Inc ......... C ...... 815 726-4224
  Crest Hill *(G-7465)*
- Relco Locomotives Inc .................... D ...... 630 968-0670
  Lisle *(G-13651)*
- Salco Products Inc .......................... D ...... 630 783-2570
  Lemont *(G-13261)*
- Western Railway Devices Corp ...... G ...... 847 625-8500
  Waukegan *(G-21640)*

### RAILROAD EQPT, EXC LOCOMOTIVES

- American Sea and Air ..................... F ...... 773 262-5960
  Chicago *(G-3873)*
- Teleweld Inc .................................... F ...... 815 672-4561
  Streator *(G-20707)*

### RAILROAD EQPT: Brakes, Air & Vacuum

- Standard Car Truck Company ........ D ...... 630 860-5511
  Bensenville *(G-1998)*

# PRODUCT SECTION

### RAILROAD EQPT: Cars & Eqpt, Dining
- Steven E Wasko & Associates .............. G ...... 773 693-2330
  Park Ridge *(G-17223)*

### RAILROAD EQPT: Cars & Eqpt, Dining
- Amsted Industries Incorporated ........... B ...... 312 645-1700
  Chicago *(G-3896)*
- Cardwell Westinghouse Company ....... D ...... 773 483-7575
  Chicago *(G-4241)*
- Eagle Freight Inc .................................... G ...... 708 202-0651
  Franklin Park *(G-10462)*
- Russell Enterprises Inc ........................ E ...... 847 692-6050
  Park Ridge *(G-17221)*
- Standard Car Truck Company ............. E ...... 847 692-6050
  Rosemont *(G-19033)*

### RAILROAD EQPT: Cars & Eqpt, Interurban
- Vapor Corporation ................................ B ...... 847 777-6400
  Buffalo Grove *(G-2788)*

### RAILROAD EQPT: Cars & Eqpt, Train, Freight Or Passenger
- Freightcar America Inc ......................... C ...... 217 443-4106
  Danville *(G-7723)*
- Narita Manufacturing Inc ..................... F ...... 248 345-1777
  Belvidere *(G-1773)*
- Seec Trasportation Corp ...................... G ...... 800 215-4003
  Chicago *(G-6474)*
- Union Tank Car Company ................... C ...... 312 431-3111
  Chicago *(G-6815)*
- Union Tank Car Company ................... G ...... 815 942-7391
  Morris *(G-15139)*
- Union Tank Car Company ................... C ...... 312 431-3111
  Chicago *(G-6816)*

### RAILROAD EQPT: Cars, Maintenance
- Geismar ................................................ G ...... 847 697-7510
  Elgin *(G-9042)*

### RAILROAD EQPT: Cars, Motor
- Marmon Holdings Inc .......................... D ...... 312 372-9500
  Chicago *(G-5625)*
- Marmon Industrial LLC ........................ G ...... 312 372-9500
  Chicago *(G-5626)*
- Union Pacific Railroad Company ......... G ...... 309 637-9322
  Peoria *(G-17472)*

### RAILROAD EQPT: Cars, Rebuilt
- Freight Car Services Inc ...................... B ...... 217 443-4106
  Danville *(G-7722)*
- Gateway Rail Services Inc ................... F ...... 618 451-0100
  Madison *(G-14146)*
- Illinois Transit Assembly Corp ............. F ...... 618 451-0100
  Madison *(G-14150)*
- Jaix Leasing Company ........................ G ...... 312 928-0850
  Chicago *(G-5273)*
- Railway Program Services Inc ............ G ...... 708 552-4000
  Chicago *(G-6286)*
- Rescar Industries Inc .......................... G ...... 618 875-3234
  East Saint Louis *(G-8767)*
- Rescar Industries Inc .......................... E ...... 630 963-1114
  Downers Grove *(G-8513)*
- UTC Railcar Repair Svcs LLC ............ A ...... 312 431-5053
  Chicago *(G-6861)*

### RAILROAD EQPT: Locomotives & Parts, Electric Or Nonelectric
- Amfab LLC ........................................... G ...... 630 783-2570
  Lemont *(G-13224)*
- Avtec (usa) Powertrain Corp ............... G ...... 773 708-9686
  Chicago *(G-4002)*
- Precision Screw Machining Co ............ F ...... 773 205-4280
  Chicago *(G-6172)*
- Rail Exchange Inc ............................... E ...... 708 757-3317
  Chicago Heights *(G-7119)*

### RAILROAD MAINTENANCE & REPAIR SVCS
- Progress Rail Services Corp ............... E ...... 309 963-4425
  Danvers *(G-7701)*

### RAILROAD RELATED EQPT: Railway Track
- Mineral Products Inc ........................... G ...... 618 433-3150
  Galatia *(G-10712)*

---

- Teleweld Inc ......................................... F ...... 815 672-4561
  Streator *(G-20707)*
- U S Railway Services ........................... G ...... 708 468-8343
  Tinley Park *(G-20952)*

### RAILROADS: Long Haul
- Hauhinco LP ........................................ E ...... 618 993-5399
  Marion *(G-14264)*
- White International Inc ......................... E ...... 630 377-9966
  Saint Charles *(G-19295)*

### RAILS: Elevator, Guide
- Otis Elevator Company ........................ D ...... 312 454-1616
  Chicago *(G-6023)*

### RAILS: Steel Or Iron
- Illinois Engineered Pdts Inc ................. E ...... 312 850-3710
  Chicago *(G-5156)*
- Woodards LLC DBA Custom Wroug ... G ...... 773 283-8113
  Chicago *(G-7025)*

### RAMPS: Prefabricated Metal
- Tandem Industries Inc ......................... G ...... 630 761-6615
  Saint Charles *(G-19279)*

### RAZORS, RAZOR BLADES
- Edgewell Per Care Brands LLC .......... B ...... 708 544-5550
  Melrose Park *(G-14630)*

### REAL ESTATE AGENCIES & BROKERS
- Equity Concepts Co Inc ....................... G ...... 815 226-1300
  Rockford *(G-18368)*

### REAL ESTATE AGENCIES: Leasing & Rentals
- J2sys LLC ............................................ F ...... 630 542-1342
  Clarendon Hills *(G-7257)*

### REAL ESTATE AGENCIES: Residential
- Midwest Mktg/Pdctn Mfg Co ............... G ...... 217 256-3414
  Warsaw *(G-21370)*

### REAL ESTATE AGENTS & MANAGERS
- Basement Dewatering Systems ........... F ...... 309 647-0331
  Canton *(G-2981)*
- Digital Realty Inc .................................. E ...... 630 428-7979
  Naperville *(G-15647)*
- John C Grafft ........................................ F ...... 847 842-9200
  Lake Barrington *(G-12811)*
- State of Illinois ..................................... C ...... 312 836-9500
  Chicago *(G-6578)*
- Terra Cotta Holdings Co ...................... E ...... 815 459-2400
  Crystal Lake *(G-7664)*

### REAL ESTATE FIDUCIARIES' OFFICES
- Caterpillar Inc ...................................... A ...... 309 675-1000
  Peoria *(G-17326)*
- Caterpillar Inc ...................................... B ...... 888 614-4328
  Peoria *(G-17328)*

### REAL ESTATE INVESTMENT TRUSTS
- Pilla Exec Inc ....................................... G ...... 312 882-8263
  Chicago *(G-6122)*

### REAL ESTATE OPERATORS, EXC DEVELOPERS: Commercial/Indl Bldg
- C M Holding Co Inc ............................. G ...... 847 438-2171
  Lake Zurich *(G-13048)*
- Galena Cellars Winery ........................ G ...... 815 777-3330
  Galena *(G-10720)*
- Grs Holding LLC .................................. G ...... 630 355-1660
  Naperville *(G-15666)*
- Lightner Publishing Corp ..................... F ...... 312 939-4767
  Naperville *(G-15691)*
- MEI Realty Ltd ..................................... G ...... 847 358-5000
  Inverness *(G-12205)*
- Parker International Pdts Inc ............... D ...... 815 524-5831
  Vernon Hills *(G-21188)*

### REAMERS
- Precision Header Tooling Inc ............... F ...... 815 874-9116
  Rockford *(G-18538)*

---

# RECREATIONAL CAMPS

- Proto-Cutter Inc ................................... F ...... 815 232-2300
  Freeport *(G-10681)*
- Vhd Inc ................................................ E ...... 815 544-2169
  Belvidere *(G-1794)*

### RECEIVERS: Radio Communications
- Tower Works Inc .................................. F ...... 630 557-2221
  Maple Park *(G-14204)*

### RECLAIMED RUBBER: Reworked By Manufacturing Process
- RDF Inc ............................................... F ...... 618 273-4141
  Eldorado *(G-8922)*

### RECORD BLANKS: Phonographic
- Alligator Rec & Artist MGT Inc ............. F ...... 773 973-7736
  Chicago *(G-3819)*

### RECORDING HEADS: Speech & Musical Eqpt
- Sandes Quynetta .................................. G ...... 815 275-4876
  Freeport *(G-10687)*

### RECORDING TAPE: Video, Blank
- Jvc Advanced Media USA Inc ............. G ...... 630 237-2439
  Schaumburg *(G-19593)*
- Paragon Group Inc .............................. F ...... 847 526-1800
  Wauconda *(G-21491)*

### RECORDS & TAPES: Prerecorded
- B D C Inc ............................................. E ...... 847 741-2233
  Elgin *(G-8962)*
- Chicago Producers Inc ........................ F ...... 312 226-6900
  Forest Park *(G-10237)*
- Crusade Enterprises Inc ...................... G ...... 618 662-4461
  Flora *(G-10205)*
- Drag City ............................................. G ...... 312 455-1015
  Chicago *(G-4642)*
- Private Studios ..................................... G ...... 217 367-3530
  Urbana *(G-21099)*
- Replay S Disc Cook-Kankaee LLC ...... F ...... 312 371-5018
  Monee *(G-15000)*
- Sparrow Sound Design ....................... G ...... 773 281-8510
  Chicago *(G-6552)*
- Towers Media Holdings Inc ................. D ...... 312 993-1550
  Northfield *(G-16421)*
- United Cmra Binocular Repr LLC ........ E ...... 630 595-2525
  Elk Grove Village *(G-9799)*

### RECORDS OR TAPES: Masters
- Solid Sound Inc ................................... G ...... 847 490-2101
  Hoffman Estates *(G-12055)*
- Spectape of Midwest Inc ..................... G ...... 630 682-8600
  Glen Ellyn *(G-10990)*

### RECOVERY SVC: Iron Ore, From Open Hearth Slag
- Ferguson Enterprises Inc .................... G ...... 217 425-7262
  Decatur *(G-7880)*
- Forge Resources Group LLC .............. C ...... 815 758-6400
  Dekalb *(G-8091)*
- Forge Resources Group LLC .............. C ...... 815 758-6400
  Dekalb *(G-8092)*
- Forge Resources Group LLC .............. G ...... 815 758-6400
  Dekalb *(G-8093)*
- Mueller Company Plant 4 .................... G ...... 217 425-7424
  Decatur *(G-7919)*
- Stein Inc .............................................. D ...... 618 452-0836
  Granite City *(G-11305)*

### RECOVERY SVCS: Metal
- Precious Metal Ref Svcs Inc ............... G ...... 847 756-2700
  Barrington *(G-1298)*

### RECREATIONAL CAMPS
- I94 Rv LLC .......................................... F ...... 847 395-9500
  Russell *(G-19097)*
- Shale Lake LLC .................................. G ...... 618 637-2470
  Staunton *(G-20558)*

## RECREATIONAL SPORTING EQPT REPAIR SVCS

Automated Design Corp ..................... G ...... 630 783-1150
  Romeoville *(G-18801)*
Crown Gym Mats Inc ......................... F ...... 847 381-8282
  Lake Barrington *(G-12803)*

## RECREATIONAL VEHICLE DEALERS

Merritt Farm Equipment Inc ................ G ...... 217 746-5331
  Carthage *(G-3315)*
Metroeast Motorsports Inc ................. G ...... 618 628-2466
  O Fallon *(G-16471)*
Midamerica Industries Inc .................. G ...... 309 787-5119
  Milan *(G-14793)*

## RECREATIONAL VEHICLE PARTS & ACCESS STORES

Good Sam Enterprises LLC ................ E ...... 847 229-6720
  Lincolnshire *(G-13450)*

## RECREATIONAL VEHICLE REPAIRS

Merritt Farm Equipment Inc ................ G ...... 217 746-5331
  Carthage *(G-3315)*

## RECTIFIERS: Electrical Apparatus

Electro-Matic Products Co .................. F ...... 773 235-4010
  Chicago *(G-4720)*

## RECTIFIERS: Electronic, Exc Semiconductor

Ipr Systems Inc ................................... G ...... 708 385-7500
  Alsip *(G-474)*

## RECYCLABLE SCRAP & WASTE MATERIALS WHOLESALERS

A Miller & Co ....................................... F ...... 309 637-7756
  Peoria *(G-17298)*
Archer Metal & Paper Co ..................... F ...... 773 585-3030
  Chicago *(G-3939)*
Azcon Inc ............................................ E ...... 312 559-3100
  Chicago *(G-4009)*
Galva Iron and Metal Co Inc ............... G ...... 309 932-3450
  Galva *(G-10789)*
M Buckman & Son Co ........................ G ...... 815 663-9411
  Spring Valley *(G-20375)*
Metal Management Inc ...................... E ...... 773 721-1100
  Chicago *(G-5700)*
Metal Management Inc ...................... E ...... 773 489-1800
  Chicago *(G-5701)*
Midland Davis Corporation ................. D ...... 309 637-4491
  Moline *(G-14957)*

## RECYCLING: Paper

Better Earth Premium Compost .......... G ...... 309 697-0963
  Peoria *(G-17317)*
Bruce Klapman Inc ............................ G ...... 847 657-8880
  Northbrook *(G-16215)*
Fibre-TEC Partitions LLC ................... E ...... 773 436-4028
  Chicago *(G-4842)*
Illinois Recovery Group I .................... G ...... 815 230-7920
  Braceville *(G-2410)*
JKS Ventures Inc ................................ G ...... 708 338-3408
  Melrose Park *(G-14663)*
Larckers Recycling Svcs Inc ............... F ...... 630 922-0759
  Naperville *(G-15813)*
M J Kull LLC ....................................... G ...... 217 246-5952
  Lerna *(G-13288)*
Norm Gordon & Associates Inc .......... G ...... 847 564-7022
  Glenview *(G-11174)*
Ohio Pulp Mills Inc ............................. F ...... 312 337-7822
  Chicago *(G-5974)*
Profile Products LLC ........................... E ...... 847 215-1144
  Buffalo Grove *(G-2756)*
R & J Trucking and Recycl Inc ............ E ...... 708 563-2600
  Chicago *(G-6263)*
Regenex Corp ..................................... F ...... 815 663-2003
  Spring Valley *(G-20378)*
Tri State Recycling Service ................. E ...... 708 865-9939
  Northlake *(G-16456)*

## REFINERS & SMELTERS: Aluminum

Allied Metal Co ................................... E ...... 312 225-2800
  Chicago *(G-3816)*
National Material Company LLC ........ E ...... 847 806-7200
  Elk Grove Village *(G-9646)*
Pontiac Recyclers Inc ......................... G ...... 815 844-6419
  Pontiac *(G-17708)*
Tower Metal Products LP ................... G ...... 847 806-7200
  Elk Grove Village *(G-9787)*
Trialco Inc ........................................... E ...... 708 757-4200
  Chicago Heights *(G-7132)*

## REFINERS & SMELTERS: Brass, Secondary

H Kramer & Co ................................... C ...... 312 226-6600
  Chicago *(G-5022)*
Sipi Metals Corp ................................. C ...... 773 276-0070
  Chicago *(G-6517)*

## REFINERS & SMELTERS: Copper

Ansonia Copper & Brass Inc .............. C ...... 866 607-7066
  Chicago *(G-3914)*
Cerro Flow Products LLC ................... C ...... 618 337-6000
  Sauget *(G-19385)*
Mahoney Foundries Inc ...................... E ...... 309 784-2311
  Vermont *(G-21138)*

## REFINERS & SMELTERS: Copper, Secondary

Gbc Metals LLC ................................. E ...... 618 258-2350
  East Alton *(G-8603)*
Global Brass and Copper Inc ............. G ...... 502 873-3000
  East Alton *(G-8604)*
Global Brass Cop Holdings Inc .......... G ...... 847 240-4700
  Schaumburg *(G-19537)*

## REFINERS & SMELTERS: Gold

Sipi Metals Corp ................................. C ...... 773 276-0070
  Chicago *(G-6517)*

## REFINERS & SMELTERS: Nonferrous Metal

A Miller & Co ....................................... F ...... 309 637-7756
  Peoria *(G-17298)*
Abco Metals Corporations .................. F ...... 773 881-1504
  Chicago *(G-3708)*
Alter Trading Corporation ................... E ...... 309 697-6161
  Bartonville *(G-1390)*
Alter Trading Corporation ................... F ...... 217 223-0156
  Quincy *(G-17772)*
Ames Metal Products Company ........ F ...... 773 523-3230
  Wheeling *(G-22005)*
Archer Metal & Paper Co ................... F ...... 773 585-3030
  Chicago *(G-3939)*
Azcon Inc ............................................ E ...... 312 559-3100
  Chicago *(G-4009)*
Belson Steel Center Scrap Inc ............ E ...... 815 932-7416
  Bourbonnais *(G-2389)*
BFI Waste Systems N Amer Inc ......... 847 429-7370
  Elgin *(G-8965)*
Big River Zinc Corporation ................. 618 274-5000
  Sauget *(G-19382)*
C & M Recycling Inc ........................... 847 578-1066
  North Chicago *(G-16176)*
C&R Scrap Iron & Metal ..................... 847 459-9815
  Wheeling *(G-22022)*
Cicero Iron Metal & Paper Inc ............ G ...... 708 863-8601
  Cicero *(G-7183)*
Columbia Aluminum Recycl Ltd ......... 708 758-8888
  Chicago Heights *(G-7093)*
D R Sperry & Co ................................ D ...... 630 892-4361
  Aurora *(G-1137)*
Dels Metal Co ..................................... E ...... 309 788-1993
  Rock Island *(G-18173)*
Elg Metals Inc .................................... F ...... 773 374-1500
  Chicago *(G-4728)*
Fox Valley Iron & Metal Corp .............. F ...... 630 897-5907
  Aurora *(G-1155)*
Galva Iron and Metal Co Inc ............... G ...... 309 932-3450
  Galva *(G-10789)*
GM Scrap Metals ................................ G ...... 618 259-8570
  Cottage Hills *(G-7397)*
Imperial Zinc Corp .............................. 773 264-5900
  Chicago *(G-5169)*
International Proc Co Amer ................ E ...... 847 437-8400
  Elk Grove Village *(G-9553)*
Lake Area Disposal Service Inc .......... E ...... 217 522-9271
  Springfield *(G-20466)*
Lemont Scrap Processing .................. 630 257-6532
  Lemont *(G-13239)*
M Buckman & Son Co ........................ G ...... 815 663-9411
  Spring Valley *(G-20375)*
Mahoney Foundries Inc ...................... E ...... 309 784-2311
  Vermont *(G-21138)*
Mervis Industries Inc ......................... F ...... 217 235-5575
  Mattoon *(G-14402)*
Mervis Industries Inc ......................... G ...... 217 753-1492
  Springfield *(G-20480)*
Metal Management Inc ...................... E ...... 773 721-1100
  Chicago *(G-5700)*
Metal Management Inc ...................... E ...... 773 489-1800
  Chicago *(G-5701)*
Midland Davis Corporation ................. D ...... 309 637-4491
  Moline *(G-14957)*
Midstate Salvage Corp ...................... G ...... 217 824-6047
  Taylorville *(G-20843)*
Midwest Fiber Inc Decatur ................. E ...... 217 424-9460
  Decatur *(G-7915)*
Real Alloy Recycling Inc .................... D ...... 708 758-8888
  Chicago Heights *(G-7120)*
Rondout Iron & Metal Co Inc .............. G ...... 847 362-2750
  Lake Bluff *(G-12865)*
S & S Metal Recyclers Inc .................. F ...... 630 844-3344
  Aurora *(G-1213)*
Serlin Iron & Metal Co Inc .................. F ...... 773 227-3826
  Chicago *(G-6479)*
Shapiro Bros of Illinois Inc ................. E ...... 618 244-3168
  Mount Vernon *(G-15445)*
Springfield Iron & Metal Co ................ G ...... 217 544-7131
  Springfield *(G-20529)*
T & C Metal Co ................................... G ...... 815 459-4445
  Crystal Lake *(G-7658)*
T J Metal Co ....................................... G ...... 708 388-6191
  Alsip *(G-532)*
Tms International LLC ....................... G ...... 815 939-9460
  Bourbonnais *(G-2408)*
Top Metal Buyers Inc ......................... F ...... 314 421-2721
  East Saint Louis *(G-8773)*
United Conveyor Supply Company ..... E ...... 708 344-8050
  Melrose Park *(G-14703)*
Waukegan Architectural Inc ............... G ...... 847 746-9077
  Zion *(G-22700)*
Weco Trading Inc ............................... 847 615-1020
  Lake Bluff *(G-12871)*

## REFINERS & SMELTERS: Tin, Primary

RE Met Corp ...................................... G ...... 312 733-6700
  Chicago *(G-6300)*

## REFINERS & SMELTERS: Zinc, Primary, Including Zinc Residue

Horsehead Corporation ...................... E ...... 773 933-9260
  Chicago *(G-5114)*

## REFINING LUBRICATING OILS & GREASES, NEC

Houghton International Inc ................. F ...... 610 666-4000
  Chicago *(G-5121)*
Lsp Industries Inc .............................. F ...... 815 226-8090
  Rockford *(G-18474)*
Lube Rite ........................................... G ...... 217 267-7766
  Westville *(G-21930)*
Marathon Petroleum Company LP ..... A ...... 618 544-2121
  Robinson *(G-18066)*
Safety-Kleen Systems Inc .................. G ...... 618 875-8050
  East Saint Louis *(G-8768)*

## REFINING: Petroleum

4200 Kirchoff Corp ............................. G ...... 773 551-1541
  Rolling Meadows *(G-18705)*
Airgas Inc ........................................... F ...... 773 785-3000
  Chicago *(G-3786)*
BP America Inc ................................... A ...... 630 420-5111
  Warrenville *(G-21344)*
BP Products North America Inc .......... G ...... 630 420-4300
  Naperville *(G-15609)*
BP Products North America Inc .......... D ...... 312 594-7689
  Chicago *(G-4153)*
Chicap Pipeline ................................. G ...... 618 432-5311
  Vernon *(G-21140)*
Citation Oil & Gas Corp ..................... E ...... 618 966-2101
  Crossville *(G-7521)*
Citgo Petroleum Corporation ............. G ...... 847 818-1800
  Downers Grove *(G-8411)*
Citgo Petroleum Corporation ............. G ...... 847 229-1159
  Wheeling *(G-22026)*
Citgo Petroleum Corporation ............. F ...... 847 734-7611
  Lemont *(G-13233)*
Equilon Enterprises LLC ..................... F ...... 312 733-1849
  Chicago *(G-4768)*
Exxonmobil Pipeline Company .......... F ...... 815 423-5571
  Elwood *(G-9980)*

## PRODUCT SECTION — REGULATORS: Steam Fittings

Koch Industries Inc .............................. G ....... 312 867-1295
  Chicago  (G-5394)
Koppers Industries Inc ......................... E ....... 708 656-5900
  Cicero  (G-7209)
Matheson Tri-Gas Inc ........................... E ....... 815 727-2202
  Joliet  (G-12539)
Pdv Midwest Refining  LLC .................. A ....... 630 257-7761
  Lemont  (G-13254)
Phillips 66 ............................................. D ....... 618 251-2800
  Hartford  (G-11614)
Raymond D Wright ............................... G ....... 618 783-2206
  Newton  (G-15947)
South West Oil Inc ............................... F ....... 815 416-0400
  Morris  (G-15130)
Standard Oil Company ......................... E ....... 630 836-5000
  Warrenville  (G-21362)
W R B Refinery LLC ............................. E ....... 618 255-2345
  Roxana  (G-19087)

### REFRACTORIES: Clay

Bmi Products Northern Ill Inc ............... E ....... 847 395-7110
  Antioch  (G-625)
Great Lakes Clay & Supply Inc ............ G ....... 224 535-8127
  Elgin  (G-9051)
Harbisonwalker Intl Inc ......................... G ....... 708 474-5350
  Calumet City  (G-2941)
Holland Manufacturing Corp ................ E ....... 708 849-1000
  Dolton  (G-8371)
Thermal Ceramics Inc .......................... E ....... 217 627-2101
  Girard  (G-10950)
V J Mattson Company .......................... D ....... 708 479-1990
  New Lenox  (G-15926)

### REFRACTORIES: Graphite, Carbon Or Ceramic Bond

Vesuvius U S A Corporation ................ D ....... 708 757-7880
  Chicago Heights  (G-7135)
Vesuvius U S A Corporation ................ C ....... 217 897-1145
  Fisher  (G-10192)
Vesuvius U S A Corporation ................ C ....... 217 345-7044
  Charleston  (G-3614)

### REFRACTORIES: Nonclay

Ipsen Inc ............................................... E ....... 815 239-2385
  Pecatonica  (G-17252)
M H Detrick Company ........................... E ....... 708 479-5085
  Mokena  (G-14882)
Magneco Inc .......................................... D ....... 630 543-6660
  Addison  (G-186)
Magneco Inc .......................................... G ....... 630 543-6660
  Addison  (G-187)
Magneco/Metrel  Inc ............................. E ....... 630 543-6660
  Addison  (G-188)
Miller Purcell Co Inc ............................. G ....... 815 485-2142
  New Lenox  (G-15897)
Vesuvius Crucible Company ................ G ....... 217 351-5000
  Champaign  (G-3555)
Vesuvius U S A Corporation ................ C ....... 217 351-5000
  Champaign  (G-3556)

### REFRACTORY MATERIALS WHOLESALERS

Anderson Msnry Refr Spcialists .......... G ....... 847 540-8885
  Lake Zurich  (G-13041)
Armil/Cfs  Inc ........................................ E ....... 708 339-6810
  South Holland  (G-20247)
Vesuvius U S A Corporation ................ C ....... 217 351-5000
  Champaign  (G-3556)
Vesuvius U S A Corporation ................ C ....... 217 345-7044
  Charleston  (G-3614)

### REFRIGERATION & HEATING EQUIPMENT

Amsted Industries Incorporated .......... B ....... 312 645-1700
  Chicago  (G-3896)
Bergesch Heating & Cooling ................ G ....... 618 259-4620
  Alton  (G-564)
Bevstream Corp .................................... G ....... 630 761-0060
  Batavia  (G-1421)
Cerro Flow Products LLC .................... C ....... 618 337-6000
  Sauget  (G-19385)
Cisco Heating & Cooling ...................... G ....... 309 637-6809
  Peoria  (G-17342)
Commercial Rfrgn Centl Ill Inc ............. E ....... 217 235-5016
  Mattoon  (G-14386)
Continental Materials Corp .................. F ....... 312 541-7200
  Chicago  (G-4459)
Ecool LLC .............................................. G ....... 309 966-3701
  Champaign  (G-3477)
Elkay Manufacturing Company ............ B ....... 708 681-1880
  Broadview  (G-2575)
Elkay Manufacturing Company ............ B ....... 815 273-7001
  Savanna  (G-19397)
Gateway Industrial Power Inc .............. C ....... 888 865-8675
  Collinsville  (G-7327)
Gateway Industrial Power Inc .............. G ....... 309 821-1035
  Bloomington  (G-2169)
Goose Island Mfg & Supply Corp ........ G ....... 708 343-4225
  Lansing  (G-13164)
H A Phillips & Co .................................. E ....... 630 377-0050
  Dekalb  (G-8095)
Hohlflder A H Shtmtl Htg Coolg ........... G ....... 815 965-9134
  Rockford  (G-18420)
ICC Intrntonal Celsius Concept ............ G ....... 773 993-4405
  Cicero  (G-7203)
Illinois Tool Works Inc .......................... B ....... 847 724-7500
  Glenview  (G-11141)
Illinois Tool Works Inc .......................... G ....... 630 372-2150
  Bartlett  (G-1353)
Illinois Tool Works Inc .......................... B ....... 847 783-5500
  Elgin  (G-9072)
J D Refrigeration .................................. G ....... 618 345-0041
  Collinsville  (G-7328)
John Bean Technologies Corp ............. E ....... 312 861-5900
  Chicago  (G-5310)
Kackert Enterprises Inc ........................ G ....... 630 898-9339
  Aurora  (G-1179)
Kap Holdings  LLC ................................ F ....... 708 948-0226
  Oak Park  (G-16671)
Kool Technologies Inc .......................... G ....... 630 483-2256
  Streamwood  (G-20662)
Maid O Mist LLC ................................... E ....... 773 685-7300
  Chicago  (G-5604)
Marvin Schumaker Plbg Inc ................. G ....... 815 626-8130
  Sterling  (G-20597)
Polyscience Inc ..................................... D ....... 847 647-0611
  Niles  (G-16021)
Prost Heating & Cooling  LLC .............. G ....... 618 344-3749
  Collinsville  (G-7338)
Quality Filter Services ......................... G ....... 618 654-3716
  Highland  (G-11807)
Ring Sheet Metal Heating & AC ........... G ....... 309 289-4213
  Knoxville  (G-12723)
Ruyle Incorporated ............................... G ....... 309 674-6644
  Springfield  (G-20516)
SGS Refrigeration  Inc .......................... E ....... 815 284-2700
  Dixon  (G-8351)
Temp-Air Inc .......................................... F ....... 847 931-7700
  Elgin  (G-9208)
Thermal Care Inc .................................. C ....... 847 966-2260
  Niles  (G-16041)
Thermal Care Inc .................................. E ....... 847 929-1207
  Niles  (G-16042)
Trane US Inc ......................................... G ....... 309 691-4224
  Peoria  (G-17470)
Trane US Inc ......................................... G ....... 708 532-8004
  Tinley Park  (G-20951)
United Technologies Corp .................... B ....... 815 226-6000
  Rockford  (G-18663)
Ventfabrics Inc ...................................... F ....... 773 775-4477
  Chicago  (G-6883)
York International Corporation ............ D ....... 815 946-2351
  Polo  (G-17692)

### REFRIGERATION EQPT & SPLYS WHOLESALERS

Hansen Technologies Corp ................... D ....... 706 335-5551
  Burr Ridge  (G-2849)
Marcy Enterprises Inc .......................... G ....... 708 352-7220
  La Grange Park  (G-12758)
Mayekawa USA  Inc .............................. F ....... 773 516-5070
  Elk Grove Village  (G-9615)
Parker-Hannifin Corporation ................ E ....... 708 681-6300
  Broadview  (G-2601)
Reedy Industries Inc ............................ F ....... 847 729-9450
  Glenview  (G-11192)

### REFRIGERATION EQPT & SPLYS, WHOLESALE: Beverage Dispensers

Alberti Enterprises Inc ......................... E ....... 847 810-7610
  Lake Forest  (G-12877)
Banner Equipment Co .......................... E ....... 815 941-9600
  Morris  (G-15097)

### REFRIGERATION EQPT & SPLYS, WHOLESALE: Commercial Eqpt

Evapco Inc ............................................. C ....... 217 923-3431
  Greenup  (G-11382)
International Ice Bagging Syst ............ G ....... 312 633-4000
  Glencoe  (G-11000)

### REFRIGERATION EQPT & SPLYS, WHOLESALE: Ice Making Machines

Sislers Ice Inc ...................................... E ....... 815 756-6903
  Dekalb  (G-8117)

### REFRIGERATION EQPT: Complete

Henry Technologies Inc ........................ D ....... 217 483-2406
  Chatham  (G-3622)
Henry Technologies Inc ........................ G ....... 217 483-2406
  Chatham  (G-3621)
Howe Corporation ................................. E ....... 773 235-0200
  Chicago  (G-5123)
Krack Corporation ................................. E ....... 630 250-0187
  Bolingbrook  (G-2334)
Marshall Middleby Inc .......................... C ....... 847 289-0204
  Elgin  (G-9100)
Mayekawa USA  Inc .............................. F ....... 773 516-5070
  Elk Grove Village  (G-9615)
Rowald Refrigeration Systems ............ G ....... 815 397-7733
  Rockford  (G-18599)
Scotsman Industries  Inc ...................... D ....... 847 215-4501
  Vernon Hills  (G-21199)

### REFRIGERATION SVC & REPAIR

Kool Technologies Inc .......................... G ....... 630 483-2256
  Streamwood  (G-20662)
Lambright Distributors ......................... G ....... 217 543-2083
  Arthur  (G-907)
Mucci Kirkpatrick Sheet Metal ............ G ....... 815 433-3350
  Ottawa  (G-16970)

### REFRIGERATORS & FREEZERS WHOLESALERS

Professional Freezing Svcs LLC .......... G ....... 773 847-7500
  Chicago  (G-6208)

### REFUSE SYSTEMS

Abco Metals Corporations ................... F ....... 773 881-1504
  Chicago  (G-3708)
Alter Trading Corporation .................... F ....... 217 223-0156
  Quincy  (G-17791)
Archer Metal & Paper Co ..................... F ....... 773 585-3030
  Chicago  (G-3939)
C & M Recycling  Inc ............................ E ....... 847 578-1066
  North Chicago  (G-16176)
Darling Ingredients Inc ......................... E ....... 217 482-3261
  Mason City  (G-14363)
Kostelac Grease Service Inc ................ E ....... 314 436-7166
  Belleville  (G-1646)
Midwest Fiber  Inc Decatur .................. E ....... 217 424-9460
  Decatur  (G-7915)
Safety-Kleen Systems  Inc ................... G ....... 618 875-8050
  East Saint Louis  (G-8768)
T & C Metal Co ..................................... G ....... 815 459-4445
  Crystal Lake  (G-7658)
Top Metal Buyers  Inc ........................... F ....... 314 421-2721
  East Saint Louis  (G-8773)
Try Our Pallets Inc ............................... G ....... 708 343-0166
  Maywood  (G-14436)

### REGISTERS: Air, Metal

Hart & Cooley  Inc ................................. C ....... 630 665-5549
  Carol Stream  (G-3165)

### REGULATORS: Generator Voltage

Saturn Electrical Services Inc .............. G ....... 630 980-0300
  Roselle  (G-18973)

### REGULATORS: Line Voltage

Intermatic Incorporated ........................ A ....... 815 675-2321
  Spring Grove  (G-20337)

### REGULATORS: Steam Fittings

Dresser  Inc ........................................... D ....... 847 437-5940
  Elk Grove Village  (G-9435)

---
Employee Codes: A=Over 500 employees, B=251-500
C=101-250, D=51-100, E=20-50, F=10-19, G=3-9

# REGULATORS: Steam Fittings

Pressure Specialist Inc ............................ E ....... 815 477-0007
  Crystal Lake *(G-7629)*

## REGULATORS: Transmission & Distribution Voltage

Ibt Inc .................................................. G ....... 618 244-5353
  Mount Vernon *(G-15413)*

## REGULATORS: Transmission & Distribution Voltage

American Cips ...................................... G ....... 618 393-5641
  Olney *(G-16759)*

## REHABILITATION CTR, RESIDENTIAL WITH HEALTH CARE INCIDENTAL

Five Star Industries Inc ........................ E ....... 618 542-4880
  Du Quoin *(G-8554)*
Fulton County Rehabilitation ............... E ....... 309 647-6510
  Canton *(G-2987)*

## REINSURANCE CARRIERS: Accident & Health

American Medical Association ............. A ....... 312 464-5000
  Chicago *(G-3863)*

## RELAYS & SWITCHES: Indl, Electric

American Controls & Automation ........ G ....... 630 293-8841
  West Chicago *(G-21655)*
Autotech Tech Ltd Partnr ..................... G ....... 563 359-7501
  Carol Stream *(G-3107)*
Autotech Tech Ltd Partnr ..................... E ....... 563 359-7501
  Chicago *(G-3994)*
Italvibras Usa Inc ................................. G ....... 815 872-1350
  Princeton *(G-17751)*
Light of Mine LLC ................................ G ....... 312 840-8570
  Chicago *(G-5503)*
Mpc Products Corporation .................. G ....... 847 673-8300
  Niles *(G-16012)*
Woodward Controls Inc ...................... C ....... 847 673-8300
  Skokie *(G-20114)*

## RELAYS: Control Circuit, Ind

Essex Electro Engineers Inc .............. E ....... 847 891-4444
  Schaumburg *(G-19521)*
Littelfuse Inc ....................................... E ....... 773 628-1000
  Chicago *(G-5522)*
Microware Inc ..................................... G ....... 847 943-9113
  Glenview *(G-11168)*

## RELAYS: Electric Power

Tough Electric Inc .............................. G ....... 630 236-8332
  Aurora *(G-1226)*

## RELAYS: Electronic Usage

Deltrol Corp ......................................... C ....... 708 547-0500
  Bellwood *(G-1703)*
Kelco Industries Inc ........................... G ....... 815 334-3600
  Woodstock *(G-22577)*
Relay Services Mfg Corp .................... F ....... 773 252-2700
  Chicago *(G-6327)*

## RELIGIOUS SPLYS WHOLESALERS

American Church Supply ..................... G ....... 847 464-4140
  Saint Charles *(G-19134)*

## REMOVERS & CLEANERS

Buster Snow Inc .................................. G ....... 847 673-4275
  Lincolnwood *(G-13504)*
Dunamis International ......................... G ....... 773 504-5733
  Chicago *(G-4651)*
Eli Morris Group LLC .......................... G ....... 773 314-7173
  Chicago *(G-4729)*
Midwest Ground Effects ..................... G ....... 708 516-5874
  Plainfield *(G-17625)*
Petrochem Inc ..................................... G ....... 630 513-6350
  Saint Charles *(G-19235)*
Sectional Snow Plow ........................... E ....... 815 932-7569
  Bradley *(G-2432)*
Shunk Corp .......................................... G ....... 217 398-2636
  Champaign *(G-3538)*
Snow Command Incorporated ............. G ....... 708 991-7004
  Flossmoor *(G-10228)*

Snow Control Inc ................................. G ....... 708 670-6269
  Orland Park *(G-16892)*
Systems AI Snow ................................ G ....... 312 846-6026
  Chicago *(G-6661)*
Topiarius ............................................. G ....... 773 475-7784
  Chicago *(G-6745)*

## REMOVERS: Paint

Custom Chemical Inc .......................... G ....... 217 529-0878
  Springfield *(G-20426)*

## RENDERING PLANT

Ace Grease Service Inc ..................... G ....... 618 337-0974
  Millstadt *(G-14821)*
MW Hopkins & Sons Inc .................... G ....... 847 458-1010
  Lake In The Hills *(G-13000)*
South Chicago Packing LLC ............... D ....... 708 589-2400
  Chicago *(G-6546)*

## RENTAL CENTERS: General

Pre Pack Machinery Inc ...................... G ....... 217 352-1010
  Champaign *(G-3528)*

## RENTAL CENTERS: Party & Banquet Eqpt & Splys

Associated Attractions Entps ............. F ....... 773 376-1900
  Chicago *(G-3967)*
Wise Equipment & Rentals Inc .......... F ....... 847 895-5555
  Schaumburg *(G-19790)*

## RENTAL CENTERS: Tools

Material Haulers Inc ............................ G ....... 815 857-4336
  Schaumburg *(G-19636)*

## RENTAL SVCS: Aircraft

AAR Corp ............................................. D ....... 630 227-2000
  Wood Dale *(G-22328)*

## RENTAL SVCS: Bicycle & Motorcycle

Service Pro Electric Mtr Repr ............. G ....... 630 766-1215
  Bensenville *(G-1990)*

## RENTAL SVCS: Business Machine & Electronic Eqpt

Pitney Bowes Inc ................................ E ....... 312 209-2216
  Schaumburg *(G-19691)*
Pitney Bowes Inc ................................ F ....... 312 419-7114
  Chicago *(G-6132)*
Pitney Bowes Inc ................................ D ....... 630 435-7476
  Lisle *(G-13640)*
Pitney Bowes Inc ................................ D ....... 630 435-7500
  Lisle *(G-13641)*
Pitney Bowes Inc ................................ E ....... 800 784-4224
  Itasca *(G-12341)*

## RENTAL SVCS: Carpet & Upholstery Cleaning Eqpt

Best Way Carpet & Uphl Clg ............... G ....... 618 544-8585
  Robinson *(G-18057)*

## RENTAL SVCS: Costume

Andy Dallas & Co ................................ F ....... 217 351-5974
  Champaign *(G-3450)*
Fanfest Corporation ............................ G ....... 847 658-2000
  Crystal Lake *(G-7576)*

## RENTAL SVCS: Electronic Eqpt, Exc Computers

Prairie Wi-Fi Systems ......................... G ....... 515 988-3260
  Chicago *(G-6167)*

## RENTAL SVCS: Floor Maintenance Eqpt

Gilday Services ................................... G ....... 847 395-0853
  Antioch *(G-635)*

## RENTAL SVCS: Live Plant

Albert F Amling LLC ........................... C ....... 630 333-1720
  Elmhurst *(G-9832)*

## RENTAL SVCS: Recreational Vehicle

Bella Terra Winery LLC ...................... F ....... 618 658-8882
  Creal Springs *(G-7453)*

## RENTAL SVCS: Sound & Lighting Eqpt

Golden Road Productions ................... G ....... 217 335-2606
  New Canton *(G-15868)*

## RENTAL SVCS: Tent & Tarpaulin

Berg Industries Inc ............................ F ....... 815 874-1588
  Rockford *(G-18280)*
Kankakee Tent & Awning Co .............. G ....... 815 932-8000
  Kankakee *(G-12634)*
Stritzel Awnng Svc/Aurra Tent .......... E ....... 630 420-2000
  Plainfield *(G-17654)*
Terre Haute Tent & Awning Inc ......... F ....... 812 235-6068
  South Holland *(G-20309)*

## RENTAL SVCS: Tuxedo

Duckys Formal Wear Inc .................... G ....... 309 342-5914
  Galesburg *(G-10748)*

## RENTAL SVCS: Video Cassette Recorder & Access

Video Gaming Technologies Inc ......... G ....... 847 776-3516
  Palatine *(G-17085)*

## RENTAL SVCS: Work Zone Traffic Eqpt, Flags, Cones, Etc

John Thomas Inc ................................ E ....... 815 288-2343
  Dixon *(G-8334)*
Traffic Control & Protection .............. E ....... 630 293-0026
  West Chicago *(G-21784)*

## RENTAL: Video Tape & Disc

Schnuck Markets Inc .......................... C ....... 618 466-0825
  Godfrey *(G-11237)*
Vincor Ltd ............................................ F ....... 708 534-0008
  Monee *(G-15005)*

## REPAIR SERVICES, NEC

Ashland Door Solutions LLC ............. G ....... 773 348-5106
  Elk Grove Village *(G-9315)*
Mold Repair and Manufacturing ......... G ....... 815 477-1332
  Crystal Lake *(G-7615)*

## REPRODUCTION SVCS: Video Tape Or Disk

Towers Media Holdings Inc ............... D ....... 312 993-1550
  Northfield *(G-16421)*
United Cmra Binocular Repr LLC ....... E ....... 630 595-2525
  Elk Grove Village *(G-9799)*

## RESEARCH & DEVELOPMENT SVCS, COMMERCIAL: Engineering Lab

Knowles Elec Holdings Inc ................ A ....... 630 250-5100
  Itasca *(G-12296)*

## RESEARCH, DEVELOPMENT & TEST SVCS, COMM: Cmptr Hardware Dev

Digital Optics Tech Inc ....................... G ....... 847 358-2592
  Rolling Meadows *(G-18725)*
Eighty Nine Robotics LLC .................. G ....... 512 573-9091
  Chicago *(G-4705)*

## RESEARCH, DEVELOPMENT & TEST SVCS, COMM: Research, Exc Lab

CCH Incorporated ............................... A ....... 847 267-7000
  Riverwoods *(G-18037)*
Etymotic Research Inc ....................... E ....... 847 228-0006
  Elk Grove Village *(G-9465)*
Park View Manufacturing Corp .......... D ....... 618 548-9054
  Salem *(G-19342)*
T D J Group Inc .................................. G ....... 847 639-1113
  Cary *(G-3374)*

## RESEARCH, DEVELOPMENT & TESTING SVCS, COMM: Agricultural

Dow Agrosciences LLC ...................... G ....... 815 844-3128
  Pontiac *(G-17699)*

## RESEARCH, DEVELOPMENT & TESTING SVCS, COMM: Research Lab

Sonoscan Inc ................................................. D ...... 847 437-6400
  Elk Grove Village (G-9744)
Tricor Systems Inc ........................................ E ...... 847 742-5542
  Elgin (G-9214)

## RESEARCH, DEVELOPMENT & TESTING SVCS, COMMERCIAL: Business

Information Resources Inc ........................ G ...... 312 474-3380
  Chicago (G-5186)

## RESEARCH, DEVELOPMENT & TESTING SVCS, COMMERCIAL: Education

Education Partners Project Ltd ................ G ...... 773 675-6643
  Chicago (G-4701)
Tegrity Inc ................................................... E ...... 800 411-0579
  Burr Ridge (G-2884)

## RESEARCH, DEVELOPMENT & TESTING SVCS, COMMERCIAL: Energy

300 Below Inc ............................................ G ...... 217 423-3070
  Decatur (G-7819)
E2s LLC ..................................................... G ...... 708 629-0714
  Alsip (G-460)
Wagenate Entps Holdings LLC ................ G ...... 773 503-1306
  Riverdale (G-18026)

## RESEARCH, DEVELOPMENT & TESTING SVCS, COMMERCIAL: Medical

Intellidrain Inc ............................................. G ...... 312 725-4332
  Evanston (G-10058)

## RESEARCH, DEVELOPMENT & TESTING SVCS, COMMERCIAL: Physical

Met-L-Flo Inc .............................................. F ...... 630 409-9860
  Sugar Grove (G-20729)

## RESEARCH, DEVELOPMENT SVCS, COMMERCIAL: Indl Lab

Fabricators Unlimited Inc ........................... G ...... 847 223-7986
  Grayslake (G-11337)

## RESEARCH, DVLPT & TEST SVCS, COMM: Mkt Analysis or Research

Information Resources Inc ........................ A ...... 312 474-8900
  Chicago (G-5188)
Marketing Analytics Inc ............................. D ...... 847 733-8459
  Evanston (G-10070)
McIlvaine Co .............................................. E ...... 847 784-0012
  Northfield (G-16408)
Target Market News Inc ............................ G ...... 312 408-1881
  Chicago (G-6676)
Willow Group Inc ....................................... G ...... 847 277-9400
  Chicago (G-6988)

## RESEARCH, DVLPT & TESTING SVCS, COMM: Mkt, Bus & Economic

Palm International Inc ............................... G ...... 630 357-1437
  Naperville (G-15721)

## RESEARCH, DVLPT & TESTING SVCS, COMM: Survey, Mktg

Screen North Amer Holdings Inc ............... F ...... 847 870-7400
  Rolling Meadows (G-18777)

## RESIDENTIAL CARE FOR CHILDREN

Mission of Our Lady of Mercy .................. G ...... 312 738-7568
  Chicago (G-5771)

## RESIDENTIAL MENTAL HEALTH & SUBSTANCE ABUSE FACILITIES

Kreider Services Incorporated ................. D ...... 815 288-6691
  Dixon (G-8336)

## RESIDENTIAL REMODELERS

Kep Woodworking ...................................... F ...... 847 480-9545
  Northbrook (G-16286)
Osmer Woodworking Inc ........................... G ...... 815 973-5809
  Dixon (G-8338)
Perkins Construction .................................. G ...... 815 233-9655
  Freeport (G-10678)

## RESINS: Custom Compound Purchased

Aabbitt Adhesives Inc ................................ D ...... 773 227-2700
  Chicago (G-3701)
Ameriflon Ltd ............................................. G ...... 847 541-6000
  Wheeling (G-22004)
Bach Plastic Works Inc ............................. G ...... 847 680-4342
  Libertyville (G-13306)
Bulk Molding Compounds Inc ................... D ...... 630 377-1065
  West Chicago (G-21675)
Cdj Technologies Inc ................................. G ...... 321 277-7807
  Wilmette (G-22249)
Chicago Latex Products Inc ...................... F ...... 815 459-9680
  Crystal Lake (G-7552)
Cream Team Logistics LLC ....................... F ...... 708 541-9128
  Phoenix (G-17540)
Elastocon Tpe Technologies Inc ............... E ...... 217 498-8500
  Springfield (G-20433)
Enbarr LLC ................................................ G ...... 630 217-2101
  Bartlett (G-1346)
Lyondell Chemical Company ..................... B ...... 815 942-7011
  Morris (G-15114)
Major-Prime Plastics Inc ........................... G ...... 630 834-9400
  Villa Park (G-21267)
Parker-Hannifin Corporation ...................... D ...... 847 836-6859
  Elgin (G-9135)
Poly Compounding LLC ............................ G ...... 847 488-0683
  Elgin (G-9143)
Polyone Corporation .................................. G ...... 630 972-0505
  Romeoville (G-18859)
Polyone Corporation .................................. D ...... 815 385-8500
  McHenry (G-14548)
Shannon Industrial Corporation ................. F ...... 815 337-2349
  Woodstock (G-22609)
Standard Rubber Products Co .................. E ...... 847 593-5630
  Elk Grove Village (G-9751)
Tom McCowan Enterprises Inc ................. G ...... 217 369-9352
  Urbana (G-21103)

## RESISTORS

Elematec USA Corporation ....................... G ...... 847 466-1451
  Itasca (G-12257)
Maurey Instrument Corp ............................ F ...... 708 388-9898
  Alsip (G-490)
Mpc Products Corporation ........................ A ...... 847 673-8300
  Niles (G-16010)
Mpc Products Corporation ........................ G ...... 847 673-8300
  Niles (G-16011)
Pei/Genesis Inc ......................................... G ...... 215 673-0400
  Rolling Meadows (G-18760)
Voltronics Inc ............................................. F ...... 773 625-1779
  Chicago (G-6913)

## RESISTORS & RESISTOR UNITS

Ohmite Holding LLC .................................. E ...... 847 258-0300
  Warrenville (G-21352)

## RESISTORS: Networks

Autotech Tech Ltd Partnr .......................... E ...... 630 668-8886
  Carol Stream (G-3108)
CTS Corporation ....................................... C ...... 630 577-8800
  Lisle (G-13579)
Methode Electronics Inc ............................ B ...... 708 867-6777
  Chicago (G-5704)
Waveteam LLC .......................................... G ...... 630 323-0277
  Hinsdale (G-11968)

## RESPIRATORS

Illinois Soc For Rsprtory Care ................... G ...... 815 742-9367
  Rockford (G-18427)

## RESPIRATORY SYSTEM DRUGS

Abbvie Respiratory LLC ............................ G ...... 847 937-6100
  North Chicago (G-16170)
Respa Pharmaceuticals Inc ....................... E ...... 630 543-3333
  Addison (G-277)

## RESPIRATORY THERAPY CLINIC

IV & Respiratory Care Services ................ E ...... 618 398-2720
  Belleville (G-1639)

## RESTAURANT EQPT REPAIR SVCS

American Soda Ftn Exch Inc ..................... F ...... 312 733-5000
  Chicago (G-3875)
Precision Service ...................................... G ...... 618 345-2047
  Collinsville (G-7337)

## RESTAURANT EQPT: Carts

Continental Usa Inc ................................... G ...... 847 823-0958
  Park Ridge (G-17188)
M L Rongo Inc .......................................... E ...... 630 540-1120
  Bartlett (G-1360)
Precision Service ...................................... G ...... 618 345-2047
  Collinsville (G-7337)

## RESTAURANT EQPT: Food Wagons

Hometown Hangout LLC ........................... G ...... 309 639-2108
  Williamsfield (G-22189)

## RESTAURANT EQPT: Sheet Metal

Avenue Metal Manufacturing Co ............... F ...... 312 243-3483
  Chicago (G-3999)
Ready Access Inc ..................................... E ...... 800 621-5045
  West Chicago (G-21763)
Stainless Specialties Inc ........................... G ...... 618 654-7723
  Pocahontas (G-17686)

## RESTAURANTS: Delicatessen

Ifa International Inc ................................... F ...... 847 566-0008
  Mundelein (G-15508)

## RESTAURANTS: Full Svc, American

Captain Curts Food Products .................... E ...... 773 783-8400
  Chicago (G-4233)
Dobake Bakeries Inc ................................. F ...... 630 620-1849
  Addison (G-96)
Libertyville Brewing Company ................... D ...... 847 362-6688
  Libertyville (G-13343)
Rock Bottom Minneapolis Inc .................... D ...... 312 755-9339
  Chicago (G-6373)

## RESTAURANTS: Full Svc, Barbecue

Jessis Hideout .......................................... G ...... 618 343-4346
  Caseyville (G-3398)

## RESTAURANTS: Full Svc, Ethnic Food

El Moro De Letran Churros & Ba ............. F ...... 312 733-3173
  Chicago (G-4708)

## RESTAURANTS: Full Svc, Family

Two Brothers Brewing Company ............... G ...... 630 393-2337
  Warrenville (G-21367)

## RESTAURANTS: Full Svc, Family, Independent

Harners Bakery Restaurant ....................... D ...... 630 892-5545
  North Aurora (G-16133)

## RESTAURANTS: Full Svc, Italian

Father Marcellos & Son ............................ C ...... 312 654-2565
  Chicago (G-4820)
Top Dollar Slots ........................................ G ...... 779 210-4884
  Loves Park (G-14002)

## RESTAURANTS: Full Svc, Mexican

El-Milagro Inc ............................................ B ...... 773 579-6120
  Chicago (G-4713)
El-Milagro Inc ............................................ C ...... 773 650-1614
  Chicago (G-4714)

## RESTAURANTS: Full Svc, Steak

Andrias Food Group Inc ............................ E ...... 618 632-4866
  O Fallon (G-16461)

## RESTAURANTS: Limited Svc, Chicken

Emmetts Tavern & Brewing Co ................. G ...... 630 434-8500
  Downers Grove (G-8441)

# RESTAURANTS: Limited Svc, Chicken

### RESTAURANTS: Limited Svc, Chicken

Emmetts Tavern & Brewing Co ............ G ...... 630 480-7181
  Wheaton *(G-21945)*
Emmetts Tavern & Brewing Co ............ F ...... 847 359-1533
  Palatine *(G-17025)*
Emmetts Tavern & Brewing Co ............ E ...... 847 428-4500
  West Dundee *(G-21796)*

### RESTAURANTS: Limited Svc, Coffee Shop

Javamania Coffee Roastery Inc ........... G ...... 815 885-3654
  Loves Park *(G-13951)*
Joshi Brothers Inc ........................... E ...... 847 895-0200
  Schaumburg *(G-19590)*

### RESTAURANTS: Limited Svc, Fast-Food, Chain

M E F Corp ..................................... F ...... 815 965-8604
  Rockford *(G-18477)*

### RESTAURANTS: Limited Svc, Fast-Food, Independent

Homer Vintage Bakery ....................... G ...... 217 896-2538
  Homer *(G-12075)*

### RESTAURANTS: Limited Svc, Ice Cream Stands Or Dairy Bars

B N K Inc ......................................... G ...... 630 231-5640
  West Chicago *(G-21664)*
Gayety Candy Co Inc ........................ E ...... 708 418-0062
  Lansing *(G-13163)*
Mitchlls Cndies Ice Creams Inc .......... F ...... 708 799-3835
  Homewood *(G-12104)*
Sweet Company ............................... F ...... 815 462-4586
  Mokena *(G-14909)*
Walter & Kathy Anczerewicz .............. G ...... 708 448-3676
  Palos Heights *(G-17113)*

### RESTAURANTS: Limited Svc, Pizza

Michaels Dawg House LLC ................ G ...... 847 485-7600
  Palatine *(G-17055)*
Resco 8 LLC .................................... D ...... 773 772-4422
  Chicago *(G-6336)*

### RESTAURANTS: Limited Svc, Pizzeria, Chain

Dominos Pizza LLC .......................... E ...... 630 783-0738
  Woodridge *(G-22472)*

### RESTAURANTS: Limited Svc, Pizzeria, Independent

Reggios Pizza Inc ............................. D ...... 773 488-1411
  Chicago *(G-6325)*

### RESTAURANTS: Ltd Svc, Ice Cream, Soft Drink/Fountain Stands

Bellwood Dunkin Donuts .................... F ...... 708 401-5601
  Bellwood *(G-1695)*
Joint Asia Dev Group LLC .................. E ...... 847 223-1804
  Grayslake *(G-11349)*

### RESTRAINTS

E-Z Cuff Inc ..................................... G ...... 847 549-1550
  Libertyville *(G-13320)*

### RETAIL BAKERY: Bagels

Pinnacle Foods Group LLC ................ B ...... 217 235-3181
  Mattoon *(G-14406)*

### RETAIL BAKERY: Bread

Anns Bakery Inc ............................... G ...... 773 384-5562
  Chicago *(G-3912)*
Chicago Pastry Inc ........................... D ...... 630 529-6161
  Bloomingdale *(G-2100)*
Dinkels Bakery Inc ............................ E ...... 773 281-7300
  Chicago *(G-4605)*
Milano Bakery Inc ............................. E ...... 815 727-2253
  Joliet *(G-12542)*
Mybread LLC ................................... G ...... 312 600-9633
  Chicago *(G-5843)*
Red Hen Bread Inc ........................... E ...... 773 342-6823
  Elmhurst *(G-9927)*
Roma Bakeries Inc ........................... F ...... 815 964-6737
  Rockford *(G-18596)*

### RETAIL BAKERY: Cakes

Leesons Cakes Inc ........................... G ...... 708 429-1330
  Tinley Park *(G-20930)*

### RETAIL BAKERY: Cookies

Kerry Inc .......................................... D ...... 309 747-3534
  Gridley *(G-11409)*

### RETAIL BAKERY: Doughnuts

B N K Inc ......................................... G ...... 630 231-5640
  West Chicago *(G-21664)*
Bellwood Dunkin Donuts .................... F ...... 708 401-5601
  Bellwood *(G-1695)*
Dimples Donuts ................................ G ...... 630 406-0303
  Batavia *(G-1438)*
Dixie Cream Donut Shop ................... E ...... 618 937-4866
  West Frankfort *(G-21806)*
Donut Palace ................................... G ...... 618 692-0532
  Edwardsville *(G-8795)*
Dunkin Donuts .................................. E ...... 708 460-3088
  Orland Park *(G-16857)*
Express Donuts Enterprise Inc .......... F ...... 630 510-9310
  Wheaton *(G-21947)*
Honey Fluff Doughnuts ...................... G ...... 708 579-1826
  Countryside *(G-7431)*
Jay Elka .......................................... F ...... 847 540-7776
  Lake Zurich *(G-13091)*
Mel-O-Cream Donuts ........................ F ...... 217 544-4644
  Springfield *(G-20476)*
Mel-O-Cream Donuts ........................ F ...... 217 528-2303
  Springfield *(G-20477)*
Union Foods Inc ............................... G ...... 201 327-2828
  Chicago *(G-6814)*
Walter & Kathy Anczerewicz .............. G ...... 708 448-3676
  Palos Heights *(G-17113)*

### RETAIL BAKERY: Pastries

Nablus Sweets Inc ............................ E ...... 708 205-6534
  Chicago *(G-5847)*
Nablus Sweets Inc ............................ G ...... 708 529-3911
  Bridgeview *(G-2513)*

### RETAIL BAKERY: Pretzels

P Double Corporation ........................ F ...... 630 585-7160
  Aurora *(G-1061)*

### RETAIL LUMBER YARDS

Alexander Lumber Co ....................... G ...... 815 754-1000
  Cortland *(G-7383)*
Autumn Mill ...................................... G ...... 217 795-3399
  Argenta *(G-689)*
Co-Fair Corporation .......................... E ...... 847 626-1500
  Skokie *(G-19984)*
Corsaw Hardwood Lumber Inc .......... F ...... 309 293-2055
  Smithfield *(G-20119)*
Engineered Plastic Systems LLC ....... F ...... 800 480-2327
  Elgin *(G-9029)*
Great Northern Lumber Inc ............... D ...... 708 388-1818
  Blue Island *(G-2254)*
Sheraton Road Lumber ..................... F ...... 309 691-0858
  Peoria *(G-17455)*
Skokie Millwork Inc ........................... G ...... 847 673-7868
  Skokie *(G-20087)*
Woodworkers Shop Inc ..................... E ...... 309 347-5111
  Pekin *(G-17296)*

### RETAIL STORES, NEC

Hearing Aid Warehouse Inc ............... G ...... 217 431-4700
  Danville *(G-7730)*
James J Sandoval ............................ G ...... 734 717-7555
  Lombard *(G-13814)*
Lasersketch Ltd ............................... F ...... 630 243-6360
  Romeoville *(G-18837)*

### RETAIL STORES: Air Purification Eqpt

Calutech Inc .................................... G ...... 708 614-0228
  Orland Park *(G-16845)*

### RETAIL STORES: Alarm Signal Systems

Sound Design Inc ............................. G ...... 630 548-7000
  Plainfield *(G-17650)*

### RETAIL STORES: Alcoholic Beverage Making Eqpt & Splys

Fox Valley Home Brew & Winery ....... G ...... 630 892-0742
  Aurora *(G-1154)*
Prairie Profile .................................. G ...... 618 846-2116
  Vandalia *(G-21120)*

### RETAIL STORES: Architectural Splys

Arthur R Baker Inc ........................... G ...... 708 301-4828
  Homer Glen *(G-12076)*

### RETAIL STORES: Artificial Limbs

Cape Prosthetics-Orthotics Inc .......... G ...... 618 457-4692
  Carbondale *(G-3001)*

### RETAIL STORES: Audio-Visual Eqpt & Splys

Buzzfire Incorporated ....................... G ...... 630 572-9200
  Oak Brook *(G-16496)*
Fred Kennerly .................................. G ...... 815 398-6861
  Rockford *(G-18392)*

### RETAIL STORES: Awnings

All Style Awning Corporation ............. G ...... 708 343-2323
  Melrose Park *(G-14587)*
Anderson Awning & Shutter .............. G ...... 815 654-1155
  Machesney Park *(G-14056)*
Blake Co Inc .................................... G ...... 815 962-3852
  Rockford *(G-18287)*
Bloomington Tent & Awning Inc ......... G ...... 309 828-3411
  Bloomington *(G-2150)*
Canvas Creations Inc ....................... G ...... 309 343-5082
  Galesburg *(G-10741)*
Chesterfield Awning Co Inc .............. F ...... 708 596-4434
  South Holland *(G-20256)*
Eclipse Awnings Inc ......................... F ...... 708 636-3160
  Evergreen Park *(G-10113)*
Haakes Awning ................................ G ...... 618 529-4808
  Carbondale *(G-3009)*
Kankakee Tent & Awning Co ............. G ...... 815 932-8000
  Kankakee *(G-12634)*
Midwest Awnings Inc ........................ G ...... 309 762-3339
  Cameron *(G-2970)*
Nuyen Awning Co ............................. G ...... 630 892-3995
  Aurora *(G-1197)*

### RETAIL STORES: Banners

All Stars -N- Stitches Inc .................. G ...... 618 435-5555
  Benton *(G-2021)*
Evo Exhibits LLC ............................. G ...... 630 520-0710
  West Chicago *(G-21697)*
Image Signs Inc ............................... F ...... 815 282-4141
  Loves Park *(G-13947)*

### RETAIL STORES: Business Machines & Eqpt

Buff & Go Inc ................................... G ...... 773 719-4436
  Chicago *(G-4182)*
CDs Office Systems Inc .................... D ...... 800 367-1508
  Springfield *(G-20410)*
CDs Office Systems Inc .................... F ...... 630 305-9034
  Springfield *(G-20411)*
Dans Printing & Off Sups Inc ............. F ...... 708 687-3055
  Oak Forest *(G-16577)*
Klai-Co Idntification Pdts Inc ............. E ...... 847 573-0375
  Lake Forest *(G-12921)*

### RETAIL STORES: Canvas Prdts

Evanston Awning Company ............... F ...... 847 864-4520
  Evanston *(G-10032)*

### RETAIL STORES: Cleaning Eqpt & Splys

Delta Products Group Inc .................. F ...... 630 357-5544
  Aurora *(G-1139)*

### RETAIL STORES: Communication Eqpt

Portable Cmmnctns Spclsts .............. G ...... 630 458-1800
  Addison *(G-247)*
Procomm Inc Hoopeston Illinois ........ E ...... 815 268-4303
  Onarga *(G-16809)*

### RETAIL STORES: Concrete Prdts, Precast

Ozinga Ready Mix Concrete Inc ........ E ...... 708 326-4200
  Mokena *(G-14892)*

# PRODUCT SECTION

# RETAIL STORES: Tombstones

Stockdale Block Systems LLC .................G....... 815 416-1030
 Morris  *(G-15132)*
Unit Step Company of Peoria ..................G....... 309 674-4392
 Metamora  *(G-14751)*

## RETAIL STORES: Drafting Eqpt & Splys

Tree Towns Reprographics Inc................E....... 630 832-0209
 Elmhurst  *(G-9951)*

## RETAIL STORES: Educational Aids & Electronic Training Mat

Follett School Solutions Inc......................C....... 815 759-1700
 McHenry  *(G-14507)*
LMS Innovations Inc ..................................G....... 312 613-2345
 Chicago  *(G-5528)*

## RETAIL STORES: Electronic Parts & Eqpt

Delta Design Inc .......................................F....... 708 424-9400
 Evergreen Park  *(G-10111)*
Eazypower Corporation............................E....... 773 278-5000
 Chicago  *(G-4686)*
J2sys LLC .................................................F....... 630 542-1342
 Clarendon Hills  *(G-7257)*

## RETAIL STORES: Engine & Motor Eqpt & Splys

Jones Garrison Sons Mch Works..............G....... 618 847-2161
 Fairfield  *(G-10147)*

## RETAIL STORES: Farm Eqpt & Splys

Jenkins Displays Co .................................G....... 618 335-3874
 Patoka  *(G-17232)*
Jenner Precision Inc ................................F....... 815 692-6655
 Fairbury  *(G-10127)*
Michaels Equipment Co ...........................G....... 618 524-8560
 Metropolis  *(G-14759)*
West Salem Knox County Htchy ..............G....... 618 456-3601
 West Salem  *(G-21825)*

## RETAIL STORES: Farm Machinery, NEC

Alpha AG Inc ............................................G....... 217 546-2724
 Pleasant Plains  *(G-17681)*

## RETAIL STORES: Fire Extinguishers

Oval Fire Products Corporation ...............G....... 630 635-5000
 Glendale Heights  *(G-11055)*

## RETAIL STORES: Flags

W G N Flag & Decorating Co...................F....... 773 768-8076
 Chicago  *(G-6918)*

## RETAIL STORES: Foam & Foam Prdts

A D Specialty Sewing ...............................G....... 847 639-0390
 Fox River Grove  *(G-10285)*

## RETAIL STORES: Gravestones, Finished

Effingham Monument Co Inc ...................G....... 217 857-6085
 Effingham  *(G-8835)*
Moore Memorials .....................................F....... 708 636-6532
 Chicago Ridge  *(G-7152)*
Rogan Group Inc ......................................G....... 708 371-4191
 Merrionette Park  *(G-14738)*
Weiss Monument Works Inc ....................G....... 618 398-1811
 Belleville  *(G-1690)*
Wilson & Wilson Monument Co................F....... 618 775-6488
 Odin  *(G-16742)*

## RETAIL STORES: Hearing Aids

Audibel Hearing Aid Services ..................G....... 217 234-6426
 Mattoon  *(G-14383)*
Phonak LLC ..............................................A....... 630 821-5000
 Warrenville  *(G-21354)*

## RETAIL STORES: Hospital Eqpt & Splys

Amity Hospital Services Inc......................G....... 708 206-3970
 Country Club Hills  *(G-7403)*

## RETAIL STORES: Ice

Sislers Ice Inc ...........................................E....... 815 756-6903
 Dekalb  *(G-8117)*

## RETAIL STORES: Insecticides

Piatt County Service Co ...........................G....... 217 489-2411
 Mansfield  *(G-14178)*

## RETAIL STORES: Medical Apparatus & Splys

Interexpo Ltd ............................................F....... 847 489-7056
 Kildeer  *(G-12700)*
Medline Industries Inc .............................A....... 847 949-5500
 Northfield  *(G-16409)*

## RETAIL STORES: Mobile Telephones & Eqpt

Firefly Mobile Inc......................................E....... 305 538-2777
 Schaumburg  *(G-19529)*
Unified Solutions Corp ............................E....... 847 478-9100
 Arlington Heights  *(G-861)*

## RETAIL STORES: Monuments, Finished To Custom Order

Abel Vault & Monument Co Inc................G....... 309 647-0105
 Canton  *(G-2980)*
Beutel Corporation...................................G....... 309 786-8134
 Rock Island  *(G-18164)*
Bevel Granite Co Inc ...............................D....... 708 388-9060
 Merrionette Park  *(G-14736)*
Gast Monuments Inc................................G....... 773 262-2400
 Chicago  *(G-4916)*
J P Vincent & Sons Inc ............................G....... 815 777-2365
 Galena  *(G-10727)*
J W Reynolds Monument Co Inc .............G....... 618 833-6014
 Anna  *(G-606)*
Jacksonville Monument Co.......................G....... 217 245-2514
 Jacksonville  *(G-12397)*
Mendota Monument Co ...........................G....... 815 539-7276
 Mendota  *(G-14725)*
Old Capitol Monument Works Inc ............G....... 217 324-5673
 Vandalia  *(G-21118)*
Pana Monument Co .................................G....... 217 562-5121
 Pana  *(G-17136)*
Peter Troost Monument Co .....................G....... 773 585-0242
 Chicago  *(G-6109)*
Riverside Memorial Co ............................G....... 217 323-1280
 Beardstown  *(G-1527)*
St Charles Memorial Works Inc ...............G....... 630 584-0183
 Saint Charles  *(G-19268)*
Tisch Monuments Inc ..............................G....... 618 233-3017
 Belleville  *(G-1680)*
Wendell Adams .......................................E....... 217 345-9587
 Charleston  *(G-3615)*
Zoia Monument Company ........................G....... 815 338-0358
 Woodstock  *(G-22629)*

## RETAIL STORES: Motors, Electric

Accurate Elc Mtr & Pump Co ...................G....... 708 448-2792
 Worth  *(G-22631)*
All Electric Mtr Repr Svc Inc ....................F....... 773 925-2404
 Chicago  *(G-3806)*
Bak Electric..............................................G....... 708 458-3578
 Bridgeview  *(G-2469)*
BP Elc Mtrs Pump & Svc Inc ...................G....... 773 539-4343
 Skokie  *(G-19967)*
Dependable Electric.................................G....... 618 592-3314
 Oblong  *(G-16732)*
First Electric Motor Shop Inc ...................G....... 217 698-0672
 Springfield  *(G-20440)*
Goding Electric Company ........................F....... 630 858-7700
 Glendale Heights  *(G-11029)*
Hills Electric Motor Service......................G....... 815 625-0305
 Rock Falls  *(G-18136)*
M H Electric Motor & Ctrl Corp ................G....... 630 393-3736
 Warrenville  *(G-21350)*
Midwest Elc Mtr Inc Danville....................G....... 217 442-5656
 Danville  *(G-7756)*
New Cie Inc..............................................G....... 815 224-1511
 Peru  *(G-17522)*

## RETAIL STORES: Orthopedic & Prosthesis Applications

Hanger Prosthetics & ..............................G....... 847 623-6080
 Gurnee  *(G-11458)*
Hanger Prosthetics & ..............................G....... 630 820-5656
 Aurora  *(G-1022)*
Prosthetic Orthotic Specialist ...................G....... 309 454-8733
 Normal  *(G-16085)*
Ronald S Lefors Bs Cpo ..........................G....... 618 259-1969
 East Alton  *(G-8610)*

Wheaton Resource Corp ..........................G....... 630 690-5795
 Carol Stream  *(G-3268)*

## RETAIL STORES: Perfumes & Colognes

Aurora Narinder .......................................G....... 773 275-2100
 Chicago  *(G-3989)*

## RETAIL STORES: Pet Food

Garver Feeds............................................E....... 217 422-2201
 Decatur  *(G-7884)*

## RETAIL STORES: Photocopy Machines

CDs Office Systems Inc...........................F....... 217 351-5046
 Champaign  *(G-3464)*

## RETAIL STORES: Picture Frames, Ready Made

Colberts Custom Framing ........................F....... 630 717-1448
 Naperville  *(G-15632)*
Frame House Inc .....................................G....... 708 383-1616
 Oak Park  *(G-16663)*
Frame Mart Inc ........................................G....... 309 452-0658
 Normal  *(G-16071)*
Heartfelt Gifts Inc .....................................G....... 309 852-2296
 Kewanee  *(G-12690)*
Michels Frame Shop ................................G....... 847 647-7366
 Niles  *(G-16004)*
Technicraft Supply Co ..............................G....... 309 495-5245
 Peoria  *(G-17468)*

## RETAIL STORES: Religious Goods

Anthos and Co LLC .................................G....... 773 744-6813
 Inverness  *(G-12202)*
Scheiwes Print Shop ................................G....... 815 683-2398
 Crescent City  *(G-7456)*

## RETAIL STORES: Rubber Stamps

Benzinger Printing ....................................G....... 815 784-6560
 Genoa  *(G-10875)*
S and S Associates Inc............................G....... 847 584-0033
 Elk Grove Village  *(G-9722)*

## RETAIL STORES: Safety Splys & Eqpt

Midwest Pub Safety Outfitters ..................F....... 866 985-0013
 Poplar Grove  *(G-17714)*
North American Safety Products .............G....... 815 469-1144
 Mokena  *(G-14888)*
Oakland Enterprises Inc ..........................G....... 630 377-1121
 Saint Charles  *(G-19225)*
Protectoseal Company .............................D....... 630 595-0800
 Bensenville  *(G-1969)*
Rutke Signs Inc ........................................G....... 708 841-6464
 Westchester  *(G-21853)*

## RETAIL STORES: Swimming Pools, Above Ground

Evergreen Pool & Spa LLC .....................G....... 618 247-3555
 Sandoval  *(G-19356)*
Rockford Sewer Co Inc............................G....... 815 877-9060
 Loves Park  *(G-13987)*

## RETAIL STORES: Telephone & Communication Eqpt

Custom Canvas LLC ................................G....... 847 587-0225
 Ingleside  *(G-12188)*
Rf Communications Inc ...........................F....... 630 420-8882
 Naperville  *(G-15741)*

## RETAIL STORES: Tents

Sawier ......................................................E....... 630 297-8588
 Downers Grove  *(G-8519)*
Wise Equipment & Rentals Inc ................F....... 847 895-5555
 Schaumburg  *(G-19790)*

## RETAIL STORES: Tombstones

Venetian Monument Company .................F....... 312 829-9622
 Chicago  *(G-6880)*

Employee Codes: A=Over 500 employees, B=251-500
C=101-250, D=51-100, E=20-50, F=10-19, G=3-9

2017 Harris Illinois Industrial Directory

### RETAIL STORES: Typewriters & Business Machines

**James Ray Monroe Corporation** .......... F ....... 618 532-4575
Centralia *(G-3420)*

### RETAIL STORES: Vaults & Safes

**Promus Equity Partners LLC** .......... F ....... 312 784-3990
Chicago *(G-6216)*

### RETAIL STORES: Water Purification Eqpt

**Amber Soft Inc** .......... F ....... 630 377-6945
Lake Barrington *(G-12799)*
**Mar Cor Purification Inc** .......... G ....... 630 435-1017
Downers Grove *(G-8483)*
**Samuel Rowell** .......... G ....... 618 942-6970
Herrin *(G-11754)*

### RETAIL STORES: Welding Splys

**American Welding & Gas Inc** .......... E ....... 630 527-2550
Stone Park *(G-20632)*
**Steel-Guard Safety Corp** .......... G ....... 708 589-4588
South Holland *(G-20306)*

### RETREADING MATERIALS: Tire

**Brahlers Truckers Supply Inc** .......... E ....... 217 243-6471
Jacksonville *(G-12380)*

### REUPHOLSTERY & FURNITURE REPAIR

**A B Kelly Inc** .......... G ....... 847 639-1022
Cary *(G-3320)*
**Booths and Upholstery By Ray** .......... G ....... 773 523-3355
Chicago *(G-4144)*
**Custom Wood Designs Inc** .......... G ....... 708 799-3439
Crestwood *(G-7486)*
**Nolte & Tyson Inc** .......... F ....... 847 551-3313
Gilberts *(G-10929)*
**North Sails Group LLC** .......... G ....... 773 489-1308
Chicago *(G-5936)*
**United Canvas Inc** .......... E ....... 847 395-1470
Antioch *(G-661)*

### REUPHOLSTERY SVCS

**Air Land and Sea Interiors** .......... G ....... 630 834-1717
Villa Park *(G-21234)*
**Albert Vivo Upholstery Co Inc** .......... G ....... 312 226-7779
Burr Ridge *(G-2821)*
**Bill Weeks Inc** .......... G ....... 217 523-8735
Springfield *(G-20397)*
**Brandt Interiors** .......... G ....... 847 251-3543
Wilmette *(G-22246)*
**Parenteau Studios** .......... E ....... 312 337-8015
Chicago *(G-6081)*
**Scibor Upholstering & Gallery** .......... G ....... 708 671-9700
Chicago *(G-6457)*
**Waco Manufacturing Co Inc** .......... F ....... 312 733-0054
Chicago *(G-6931)*
**Zirlin Interiors Inc** .......... E ....... 773 334-5530
Chicago *(G-7069)*

### REWINDING SVCS

**Tracy Electric Inc** .......... E ....... 618 943-6205
Lawrenceville *(G-13206)*

### RIBBONS & BOWS

**Ribbon Supply Comp** .......... F ....... 773 237-7979
Chicago *(G-6350)*
**Stellar Recognition Inc** .......... D ....... 773 282-8060
Chicago *(G-6588)*

### RIBBONS: Machine, Inked Or Carbon

**Allen Paper Company** .......... G ....... 312 454-4500
Chicago *(G-3812)*

### RIDING STABLES

**Hidden Hollow Stables Inc** .......... G ....... 309 243-7979
Dunlap *(G-8567)*

### RIVETS: Metal

**Accurate Rivet Manufacturing** .......... G ....... 630 766-3401
Wood Dale *(G-22330)*
**Chicago Rivet & Machine Co** .......... C ....... 630 357-8500
Naperville *(G-15627)*

**Multitech Cold Forming LLC** .......... E ....... 630 949-8200
Carol Stream *(G-3201)*

### ROAD CONSTRUCTION EQUIPMENT WHOLESALERS

**Wissmiller & Evans Road Eqp** .......... G ....... 309 725-3598
Cooksville *(G-7373)*
**Zuma Corporation** .......... G ....... 815 288-7269
Dixon *(G-8361)*

### ROAD MATERIALS: Bituminous, Not From Refineries

**Du-Kane Asphalt Co** .......... G ....... 630 953-1500
Addison *(G-101)*

### ROBOTS: Assembly Line

**Accelrted Mch Design Engrg LLC** .......... F ....... 815 316-6381
Rockford *(G-18251)*
**Fanuc America Corporation** .......... E ....... 847 898-5000
Hoffman Estates *(G-12009)*
**ICC Intrntonal Celsius Concept** .......... G ....... 773 993-4405
Cicero *(G-7203)*
**Innovative Industrial Svcs LLC** .......... F ....... 309 527-2035
El Paso *(G-8870)*
**J2sys LLC** .......... F ....... 630 542-1342
Clarendon Hills *(G-7257)*
**Linear Kinetics Inc** .......... G ....... 630 365-0075
Maple Park *(G-14201)*
**State Line International Inc** .......... G ....... 708 251-5772
Lansing *(G-13186)*
**Tampotech Decorating Inc** .......... G ....... 847 515-2968
Huntley *(G-12178)*

### ROBOTS: Indl Spraying, Painting, Etc

**Paasche Airbrush Co** .......... D ....... 773 867-9191
Chicago *(G-6048)*

### ROCKETS: Space & Military

**National Def Intelligence Inc** .......... G ....... 630 757-4007
Naperville *(G-15818)*

### RODS: Plastic

**Advanced Plastic Corp** .......... D ....... 847 674-2070
Lincolnwood *(G-13501)*
**G-P Manufacturing Co Inc** .......... E ....... 847 473-9001
Waukegan *(G-21561)*

### RODS: Steel & Iron, Made In Steel Mills

**Grab Brothers Ir Works Co Corp** .......... F ....... 847 288-1055
Franklin Park *(G-10480)*
**Metal Resources Inc** .......... G ....... 630 616-1850
Hinsdale *(G-11953)*
**Sterling Steel Company LLC** .......... B ....... 815 548-7000
Sterling *(G-20614)*

### ROLL COVERINGS: Rubber

**Industrial Roller Co** .......... F ....... 618 234-0740
Smithton *(G-20121)*
**Menges Roller Co Inc** .......... E ....... 847 487-8877
Wauconda *(G-21482)*

### ROLLED OR DRAWN SHAPES, NEC: Copper & Copper Alloy

**Materion Brush Inc** .......... F ....... 630 832-9650
Elmhurst *(G-9909)*

### ROLLERS & FITTINGS: Window Shade

**Matiss Inc** .......... F ....... 773 418-1895
Chicago *(G-5653)*

### ROLLING MACHINERY: Steel

**Fkm Usa LLC** .......... F ....... 815 469-2473
Frankfort *(G-10322)*
**Frame Material Supply Inc** .......... G ....... 309 362-2323
Trivoli *(G-20999)*

### ROLLING MILL EQPT: Picklers & Pickling Lines

**Vision Pickling and Proc Inc** .......... F ....... 815 264-7755
Waterman *(G-21410)*

### ROLLING MILL MACHINERY

**Bonell Manufacturing Company** .......... E ....... 708 849-1770
Riverdale *(G-18016)*
**Chicago Roll Co Inc** .......... E ....... 630 627-8888
Lombard *(G-13777)*
**Combined Metals Chicago LLC** .......... G ....... 847 683-0500
Hampshire *(G-11545)*
**K R Komarek Inc** .......... E ....... 847 956-0060
Wood Dale *(G-22384)*
**Leading Edge Group Inc** .......... C ....... 815 316-3500
Rockford *(G-18464)*
**Littell LLC** .......... E ....... 630 916-6662
Schaumburg *(G-19620)*
**Nor Service Inc** .......... E ....... 815 232-8379
Freeport *(G-10676)*
**Nucor Steel Kankakee Inc** .......... B ....... 815 937-3131
Bourbonnais *(G-2403)*
**Worth Steel and Machine Co** .......... E ....... 708 388-6300
Alsip *(G-546)*

### ROLLING MILL ROLLS: Cast Steel

**Ameri Rolls and Guides** .......... G ....... 815 588-0486
Lockport *(G-13703)*
**Arcelormittal USA LLC** .......... C ....... 312 899-3400
Chicago *(G-3934)*
**Arcelormittal USA LLC** .......... B ....... 312 346-0300
Chicago *(G-3935)*
**Jame Roll Form Products Inc** .......... E ....... 847 455-0496
Franklin Park *(G-10506)*
**Metal Resources Intl LLC** .......... E ....... 847 806-7200
Elk Grove Village *(G-9622)*
**Micro Thread Corporation** .......... E ....... 773 775-1200
Chicago *(G-5723)*
**US Tsubaki Power Transm LLC** .......... C ....... 847 459-9500
Wheeling *(G-22173)*

### ROLLS & BLANKETS, PRINTERS': Rubber Or Rubberized Fabric

**Day International Group Inc** .......... D ....... 630 406-6501
Batavia *(G-1437)*
**Lochman Ref Silk Screen Co** .......... F ....... 847 475-6266
Evanston *(G-10065)*
**Rotation Dynamics Corporation** .......... E ....... 630 679-7053
Romeoville *(G-18865)*

### ROLLS & ROLL COVERINGS: Rubber

**Finzer Roller Inc** .......... E ....... 847 390-6200
Des Plaines *(G-8199)*
**Industrial Roller Co** .......... F ....... 618 234-0740
Smithton *(G-20122)*
**Pamarco Global Graphics Inc** .......... F ....... 847 459-6000
Wheeling *(G-22118)*

### ROLLS: Rubber, Solid Or Covered

**Hydac Rubber Manufacturing** .......... E ....... 618 233-2129
Smithton *(G-20120)*

### ROOF DECKS

**Castle Metal Products Corp** .......... G ....... 847 806-4540
Glendale Heights *(G-11015)*
**Corrugated Metals Inc** .......... F ....... 815 323-1310
Belvidere *(G-1747)*
**Epic Metals Corporation** .......... G ....... 847 803-6411
Des Plaines *(G-8189)*
**Lakefront Roofing Supply** .......... G ....... 312 275-0270
Chicago *(G-5442)*
**Pate Company Inc** .......... E ....... 630 705-1920
Lombard *(G-13843)*

### ROOFING MATERIALS: Asphalt

**Co-Fair Corporation** .......... E ....... 847 626-1500
Skokie *(G-19984)*
**Cofair Products Inc** .......... G ....... 847 626-1500
Skokie *(G-19985)*
**Complete Flashings Inc** .......... G ....... 630 595-9725
Bensenville *(G-1864)*
**Cornerstone Building Products** .......... G ....... 217 543-2829
Arthur *(G-889)*
**Crosscom Inc** .......... F ....... 630 871-5500
Wheaton *(G-21942)*
**Deks North America Inc** .......... G ....... 312 219-2110
Chicago *(G-4574)*
**Jesus People USA Full Gos** .......... G ....... 773 989-2083
Chicago *(G-5296)*
**Karnak Midwest LLC** .......... F ....... 708 338-3388
Broadview *(G-2590)*

## PRODUCT SECTION

Lakefront Roofing Supply .................. E ...... 773 509-0400
  Chicago (G-5443)
TMJ Architectural LLC ..................... G ...... 815 388-7820
  Crystal Lake (G-7666)

### ROOFING MATERIALS: Sheet Metal

Berridge Manufacturing Company ........ G ...... 630 231-7495
  West Chicago (G-21669)
J Mac Metals Inc ............................. G ...... 309 822-2023
  Galva (G-10790)
Omnimax International Inc ................. E ...... 309 747-2937
  Gridley (G-11410)
Pro-Bilt Buildings LLC ....................... F ...... 217 532-9331
  Hillsboro (G-11898)
Standing Water Solutions Inc ............. G ...... 847 469-8876
  Wauconda (G-21503)

### ROOM COOLERS: Portable

Cardinal Construction Co .................. G ...... 618 842-5553
  Fairfield (G-10138)

### ROPE

All Gear Inc .................................... G ...... 847 564-9016
  Northbrook (G-16202)
Columbian Rope Company ................. C ...... 888 593-7999
  Calumet Park (G-2959)

### ROTORS: Motor

American Rotors Inc ......................... E ...... 847 263-1300
  Gurnee (G-11428)
Marmon Industries LLC ..................... G ...... 312 372-9500
  Chicago (G-5627)
Nidec Motor Corporation ................... B ...... 847 585-8430
  Elgin (G-9123)

### RUBBER

Allstates Rubber & Tool Corp ............. F ...... 708 342-1030
  Tinley Park (G-20888)
Bamberger Polymers Inc ................... F ...... 630 773-8626
  Itasca (G-12233)
Custom Seal & Rubber Products ........ G ...... 888 356-2966
  Mount Morris (G-15295)
Elas Tek Molding Inc ........................ E ...... 815 675-9012
  Spring Grove (G-20335)
Excelsior Inc ................................... E ...... 815 987-2900
  Rockford (G-18375)
Hallstar Company ............................ D ...... 708 594-5947
  Bedford Park (G-1552)
Modern Silicone Tech Inc .................. F ...... 727 507-9800
  Bannockburn (G-1262)
Moriteq Rubber Co ........................... F ...... 847 734-0970
  Arlington Heights (G-806)
Morton Salt Inc ................................ C ...... 312 807-2000
  Chicago (G-5809)
Nauvoo Products Inc ........................ F ...... 217 453-2817
  Nauvoo (G-15855)
Parker-Hannifin Corporation ............... C ...... 630 427-2020
  Woodridge (G-22508)
Plastic Specialties & Tech Inc ............. E ...... 847 781-2414
  Schaumburg (G-19693)
Polymax Thermoplastic ..................... E ...... 847 316-9900
  Waukegan (G-21602)
Star Thermoplastic Alloys and ............ F ...... 708 343-1100
  Broadview (G-2614)
T9 Group LLC ................................. G ...... 847 912-8862
  Hawthorn Woods (G-11705)
Vibracoustic Usa Inc ........................ E ...... 618 382-5891
  Carmi (G-3081)
Weiler Rubber Technologies LLC ........ G ...... 773 826-8900
  Chicago (G-6951)

### RUBBER PRDTS

Medical Resource Inc ....................... G ...... 847 249-0854
  Gurnee (G-11470)
Pro Form Industries Inc .................... G ...... 815 923-2555
  Union (G-21038)
Rehling & Associates Inc .................. G ...... 630 941-3560
  Elmhurst (G-9929)

### RUBBER PRDTS: Appliance, Mechanical

Calumet Rubber Corp ....................... G ...... 773 536-6350
  Chicago (G-4219)

### RUBBER PRDTS: Automotive, Mechanical

Andrews Automotive Company ........... F ...... 773 768-1122
  Chicago (G-3903)

Kokoku Rubber Inc .......................... G ...... 847 517-6770
  Schaumburg (G-19601)
Mac Lean-Fogg Company .................. D ...... 847 566-0010
  Mundelein (G-15521)

### RUBBER PRDTS: Mechanical

All-State Industries Inc ..................... D ...... 847 350-0460
  Elk Grove Village (G-9286)
Aztec Products ................................ ....... 217 726-8631
  Springfield (G-20393)
Custom Seal & Rubber Products ........ ....... 888 356-2966
  Mount Morris (G-15295)
Elk Grove Rubber & Plastic Co ........... F ...... 630 543-5656
  Addison (G-109)
Excelsior Inc ................................... E ...... 815 987-2900
  Rockford (G-18375)
Fairchild Industries Inc ...................... E ...... 847 550-9580
  Lake Zurich (G-13071)
Fmi Inc .......................................... ....... 847 350-1535
  Elk Grove Village (G-9481)
Industrial Roller Co .......................... F ...... 618 234-0740
  Smithton (G-20121)
James Walker Mfg Co ....................... E ...... 708 754-4020
  Glenwood (G-11217)
Modern Silicone Tech Inc .................. F ...... 727 507-9800
  Bannockburn (G-1262)
Nilan/Primarc Tool & Mold Inc ............ F ...... 847 885-2300
  Hoffman Estates (G-12030)
Rotation Dynamics Corporation .......... D ...... 773 247-5600
  Chicago (G-6399)
Rt Enterprises Inc ............................ F ...... 847 675-1444
  Skokie (G-20080)
Sage Products LLC .......................... ....... 815 455-4700
  Crystal Lake (G-7645)
Sanyo Seiki America Corp ................. F ...... 630 876-8270
  West Chicago (G-21768)
Smart Solutions Inc .......................... ....... 630 775-1517
  Itasca (G-12354)
Standard Rubber Products Co ............ E ...... 847 593-5630
  Elk Grove Village (G-9751)
Systems By Lar Inc .......................... ....... 815 694-3141
  Clifton (G-7275)
Vibracoustic Usa Inc ........................ E ...... 618 382-5891
  Carmi (G-3081)
Vibracoustic Usa Inc ........................ C ...... 618 382-2318
  Carmi (G-3082)
Weiland Fast Trac Inc ....................... ....... 847 438-7996
  Long Grove (G-13905)

### RUBBER PRDTS: Silicone

Advanced Prototype Molding .............. G ...... 847 202-4200
  Palatine (G-16998)
Voss Belting & Specialty Co ............... ....... 847 673-8900
  Lincolnwood (G-13541)

### RUBBER PRDTS: Sponge

Adapt Seals Co ............................... G ...... 309 463-2482
  Varna (G-21132)
Essentra Specialty Tapes Inc ............. C ...... 708 488-1025
  Forest Park (G-10242)
Hst Materials Inc ............................. F ...... 847 640-1803
  Elk Grove Village (G-9527)
Jessup Manufacturing Company ......... E ...... 847 362-0961
  Lake Bluff (G-12851)
Sponge-Cushion Inc ......................... D ...... 815 942-2300
  Morris (G-15131)
Standard Rubber Products Co ............ E ...... 847 593-5630
  Elk Grove Village (G-9751)

### RUBBER STAMP, WHOLESALE

Bertco Enterprises Inc ...................... G ...... 618 234-9283
  Belleville (G-1614)

### RUBBER STRUCTURES: Air-Supported

Arizon Strctures Worldwide LLC .......... E ...... 618 451-7250
  Granite City (G-11267)

### RUGS : Tufted

W J Dennis & Company ..................... F ...... 847 697-4800
  Elgin (G-9225)

### RULERS: Metal

Lorette Dies Inc ............................... G ...... 630 279-9682
  Elmhurst (G-9902)

## SAND & GRAVEL

### RUST RESISTING

Chemtool Incorporated ...................... C ...... 815 957-4140
  Rockton (G-18694)
Chemtool Incorporated ...................... D ...... 815 459-1250
  Crystal Lake (G-7551)
Daubert Industries Inc ...................... F ...... 630 203-6800
  Burr Ridge (G-2834)
Ecp Incorporated ............................. D ...... 630 754-4200
  Woodridge (G-22474)
Rust-Oleum (canada) Ltd .................. B ...... 847 367-7700
  Vernon Hills (G-21194)
Sanchem Inc ................................... E ...... 312 733-6100
  Chicago (G-6436)

### SAFES & VAULTS: Metal

First Alert Inc ................................... G ...... 630 499-3295
  Aurora (G-1009)
Talaris Inc ...................................... C ...... 630 577-1000
  Lisle (G-13669)

### SAFETY EQPT & SPLYS WHOLESALERS

Gemcom Inc .................................... G ...... 800 871-6840
  Willow Springs (G-22196)
National Emergency Med ID Inc .......... G ...... 847 366-1267
  Spring Grove (G-20351)

### SAFETY INSPECTION SVCS

One Way Safety LLC ......................... G ...... 708 579-0229
  La Grange (G-12741)

### SAILS

Nieman & Considine Inc .................... F ...... 312 326-1053
  Chicago (G-5914)
North Sails Group LLC ...................... G ...... 773 489-1308
  Chicago (G-5936)

### SALES PROMOTION SVCS

Icd Publications Inc .......................... G ...... 847 913-8295
  Lincolnshire (G-13456)
Insight Advertising Inc ...................... G ...... 847 647-0004
  Niles (G-15989)
Rfq LLC .......................................... ....... 815 893-6656
  Crystal Lake (G-7640)

### SALT

K+s Montana Holdings LLC ............... G ...... 312 807-2000
  Chicago (G-5346)
K+s Salt LLC ................................... G ...... 844 789-3991
  Chicago (G-5347)
Morton International LLC ................... C ...... 312 807-2696
  Chicago (G-5807)

### SALT & SULFUR MINING

Morton International LLC ................... F ...... 773 235-2341
  Chicago (G-5808)
Morton International LLC ................... ....... 312 807-2696
  Chicago (G-5807)
Morton Salt Inc ................................ ....... 312 807-2000
  Chicago (G-5809)

### SAMPLE BOOKS

Multi Swatch Corporation ................... D ...... 708 344-9440
  Broadview (G-2600)

### SAND & GRAVEL

Aggregate Materials Company ............ G ...... 815 747-2430
  East Dubuque (G-8616)
Beverly Materials LLC ....................... G ...... 847 695-9300
  Hoffman Estates (G-11994)
Bluemastiff Group LLC ...................... G ...... 708 704-3529
  Chicago (G-4129)
Carlyle Sand & Gravel Ltd .................. G ...... 618 594-8263
  Carlyle (G-3053)
Consolidated Materials Inc ................. G ...... 815 568-1538
  Marengo (G-14222)
Contractors Ready-Mix Inc ................. G ...... 217 482-5530
  Mason City (G-14362)
County Materials Corp ....................... E ...... 217 352-4181
  Champaign (G-3470)
Cullinan & Sons Inc .......................... E ...... 309 925-2711
  Tremont (G-20981)
Dans Dirt and Gravel ........................ G ...... 630 479-6622
  Aurora (G-1138)

---

Employee Codes: A=Over 500 employees, B=251-500
C=101-250, D=51-100, E=20-50, F=10-19, G=3-9

# SAND & GRAVEL | PRODUCT SECTION

Elmer L Larson L C .................................. F ....... 815 895-4837
  Sycamore  (G-20797)
Elmhurst-Chicago Stone Company ....... F ....... 630 557-2446
  Kaneville  (G-12599)
Elmhurst-Chicago Stone Company ............ E ....... 630 983-6410
  Bolingbrook  (G-2305)
Empire Acoustical Systems Inc ................. E ....... 815 261-0072
  Princeton  (G-17747)
Fairmount Santrol Inc ............................... E ....... 815 587-4410
  Ottawa  (G-16959)
Fairmount Santrol Inc ............................... E ....... 815 538-2645
  Troy Grove  (G-21012)
Galena Road Gravel  Inc .......................... E ....... 309 274-6388
  Chillicothe  (G-7166)
GBS Liquidating Corp ............................... G ....... 309 342-4155
  Galesburg  (G-10753)
H & H Services  Inc .................................. F ....... 618 633-2837
  Hamel  (G-11528)
Joliet Sand and Gravel Company ............ D ....... 815 741-2090
  Rockdale  (G-18222)
Lafarge Aux Sable  LLC ........................... G ....... 815 941-1423
  Morris  (G-15112)
Lafarge North America Inc ....................... C ....... 703 480-3600
  Chicago  (G-5435)
Le Claire Investment Inc .......................... G ....... 309 757-8250
  Moline  (G-14953)
Legacy Vulcan  LLC ................................. D ....... 630 955-8500
  Naperville  (G-15687)
Legacy Vulcan  LLC ................................. E ....... 815 468-8141
  Manteno  (G-14186)
Legacy Vulcan  LLC ................................. E ....... 847 437-4181
  Elk Grove Village  (G-9593)
Legacy Vulcan  LLC ................................. F ....... 217 932-2611
  Casey  (G-3388)
Legacy Vulcan  LLC ................................. F ....... 815 726-6900
  Joliet  (G-12533)
Legacy Vulcan  LLC ................................. F ....... 630 739-0182
  Romeoville  (G-18838)
Legacy Vulcan  LLC ................................. E ....... 217 498-7263
  Rochester  (G-18119)
Legacy Vulcan  LLC ................................. D ....... 708 485-6602
  Mc Cook  (G-14450)
Legacy Vulcan  LLC ................................. G ....... 217 963-2196
  Harristown  (G-11607)
Legacy Vulcan  LLC ................................. E ....... 815 436-3535
  Plainfield  (G-17617)
Legacy Vulcan  LLC ................................. G ....... 847 578-9622
  Lake Bluff  (G-12853)
Legacy Vulcan  LLC ................................. G ....... 847 548-4623
  Grayslake  (G-11350)
Legacy Vulcan  LLC ................................. F ....... 630 904-1110
  Plainfield  (G-17618)
Legacy Vulcan Corp ................................ E ....... 815 937-7928
  Kankakee  (G-12637)
Material Service Corporation ................... E ....... 815 838-3420
  Romeoville  (G-18844)
Material Service Corporation ................... E ....... 847 658-4559
  Algonquin  (G-400)
Material Service Corporation ................... E ....... 708 447-1100
  Westchester  (G-21849)
Material Service Corporation ................... E ....... 815 838-2400
  Romeoville  (G-18842)
May Sand and Gravel Inc ........................ G ....... 815 338-4761
  Wonder Lake  (G-22324)
Menoni & Mocogni  Inc ............................. F ....... 847 432-0850
  Highland Park  (G-11854)
Mertel Gravel Company  Inc ..................... F ....... 815 223-0468
  Peru  (G-17518)
Meyer Material Co Merger Corp .............. F ....... 847 658-7811
  Elburn  (G-8891)
Meyer Material Co Merger Corp .............. E ....... 815 568-6119
  Elburn  (G-8893)
Mid-America Sand & Gravel .................... G ....... 217 355-1307
  Urbana  (G-21094)
Newton Ready Mix Inc ............................. F ....... 618 783-8611
  Newton  (G-15944)
Otter Creek Sand & Gravel ...................... F ....... 309 759-4293
  Havana  (G-11700)
Pdss Construction ................................... F ....... 847 980-6090
  Morton Grove  (G-15226)
Pekin Sand and Gravel LLC .................... G ....... 309 347-8917
  Pekin  (G-17282)
Plote Inc .................................................. D ....... 847 695-9467
  Hoffman Estates  (G-12037)
Randy Wright & Son Cnstr ....................... G ....... 217 478-4171
  Alexander  (G-374)
Rock River Ready Mix  Inc ....................... G ....... 815 438-2510
  Rock Falls  (G-18149)
Rockford Sand & Gravel Co .................... E ....... 815 654-4700
  Loves Park  (G-13986)

Rogers Ready Mix & Mtls Inc .................. F ....... 815 389-2223
  Roscoe  (G-18915)
Rogers Ready Mix & Mtls Inc .................. D ....... 815 234-8212
  Byron  (G-2920)
Rogers Redi-Mix Inc ................................ F ....... 618 282-3844
  Ruma  (G-19088)
Sand & Gravel Service ............................. G ....... 309 648-4585
  Metamora  (G-14749)
Sand Valley Sand & Gravel Inc ................ F ....... 217 446-4210
  Danville  (G-7765)
Sangamon Valley Sand & Gravel ............ G ....... 217 498-7189
  Rochester  (G-18121)
Seneca Sand & Gravel  LLC .................... G ....... 630 746-9183
  Seneca  (G-19891)
Stark Materials Inc .................................. E ....... 309 828-8520
  Shirley  (G-19920)
Stokes Sand & Gravel  Inc ....................... G ....... 815 489-0680
  Batavia  (G-1499)
Thelen Sand & Gravel  Inc ....................... D ....... 847 838-8800
  Antioch  (G-656)
Tri-Con Materials  Inc ............................... G ....... 815 872-3206
  Princeton  (G-17762)
Vandalia Sand & Gravel Inc ..................... F ....... 618 283-4029
  Vandalia  (G-21129)
Wayland Ready Mix Concrete Svc .......... F ....... 309 833-2064
  Macomb  (G-14134)
William Charles Cnstr Co LLC ................ D ....... 815 654-4700
  Loves Park  (G-14007)

## SAND MINING

Buckner Sand Co ..................................... G ....... 630 653-3700
  Carol Stream  (G-3120)
Mel Price Company Inc ........................... F ....... 217 442-9092
  Danville  (G-7754)
Mid-America Sand & Gravel .................... G ....... 217 586-4536
  Mahomet  (G-14161)
Opti-Sand Incorporated ........................... G ....... 630 293-1245
  West Chicago  (G-21753)
Riverstone Group Inc .............................. G ....... 309 787-1415
  Rock Island  (G-18201)
Super Aggregates  Inc ............................ G ....... 815 385-8000
  McHenry  (G-14560)

## SAND RIDDLES: Hand Sifting Or Screening Apparatus

Sandbagger Corp .................................... F ....... 630 876-2400
  Elmhurst  (G-9935)

## SAND: Hygrade

Clifford W Estes Co  Inc .......................... F ....... 815 433-0944
  Ottawa  (G-16955)
Fairmount Santrol Inc ............................... F ....... 815 433-2449
  Ottawa  (G-16958)
Kona Blackbird  Inc ................................. F ....... 815 792-8750
  Serena  (G-19892)
Spectron Manufacturing ........................... G ....... 720 879-7605
  Bloomingdale  (G-2138)
Unimin Corporation .................................. E ....... 815 732-2121
  Oregon  (G-16833)
Unimin Corporation .................................. E ....... 815 431-2200
  Ottawa  (G-16989)
Unimin Corporation .................................. E ....... 815 434-5363
  Ottawa  (G-16990)
Wedron Silica Company ........................... F ....... 815 433-2449
  Wedron  (G-21646)

## SAND: Silica

U S Silica Company ................................ E ....... 815 562-7336
  Rochelle  (G-18113)
U S Silica Company ................................ ......... 800 635-7263
  Utica  (G-21108)
Unimin Corporation .................................. E ....... 815 667-5102
  Utica  (G-21109)
Unimin Corporation .................................. G ....... 815 539-6734
  Troy Grove  (G-21013)

## SANDBLASTING EQPT

Blastline USA Inc .................................... G ....... 630 871-0147
  Carol Stream  (G-3118)
Everblast Inc ........................................... G ....... 815 788-8660
  Crystal Lake  (G-7574)

## SANDBLASTING SVC: Building Exterior

Fox Valley Sandblasting Inc .................... G ....... 630 553-6050
  Yorkville  (G-22659)

## SANITARY SVC, NEC

Best Technology Systems  Inc ................ F ....... 815 254-9554
  Plainfield  (G-17582)

## SANITARY SVCS: Chemical Detoxification

Rock Valley Oil & Chemical Co ................ E ....... 815 654-2400
  Loves Park  (G-13983)

## SANITARY SVCS: Dead Animal Disposal

Millstadt Rendering Company .................. E ....... 618 538-5312
  Belleville  (G-1659)

## SANITARY SVCS: Environmental Cleanup

Triplett Entereprises Inc .......................... G ....... 708 333-9421
  Oak Forest  (G-16592)

## SANITARY SVCS: Hazardous Waste, Collection & Disposal

Drumbeaters of America Inc ................... F ....... 630 365-5527
  Elburn  (G-8883)
Onyx Environmental Svcs LLC ................ E ....... 630 218-1500
  Lombard  (G-13838)
Precious Metal Ref Svcs Inc ................... G ....... 847 756-2700
  Barrington  (G-1298)

## SANITARY SVCS: Incinerator, Operation Of

Anderson Msnry Refr Spcialists .............. G ....... 847 540-8885
  Lake Zurich  (G-13041)

## SANITARY SVCS: Medical Waste Disposal

Daniels Sharpsmart  Inc .......................... E ....... 312 546-8900
  Chicago  (G-4554)

## SANITARY SVCS: Refuse Collection & Disposal Svcs

Darling International Inc .......................... E ....... 708 388-3223
  Blue Island  (G-2245)
Polycorp Illinois  Inc ................................ D ....... 773 847-7575
  Chicago  (G-6154)

## SANITARY SVCS: Rubbish Collection & Disposal

BFI Waste Systems N Amer Inc .............. E ....... 847 429-7370
  Elgin  (G-8965)

## SANITARY SVCS: Waste Materials, Recycling

Ace Plastics  Inc ..................................... F ....... 815 635-1368
  Chatsworth  (G-3626)
Agriscience  Inc ...................................... G ....... 212 365-4214
  Peoria  (G-17304)
Alter Trading Corporation ........................ F ....... 309 697-6161
  Bartonville  (G-1390)
Bio Industries Inc .................................... D ....... 847 215-8999
  Wheeling  (G-22014)
Compania Brasileira De T ........................ G ....... 319 550-6440
  Mount Olive  (G-15301)
D & P Construction Co  Inc ..................... E ....... 773 714-9330
  Chicago  (G-4535)
Dels Metal Co ......................................... F ....... 309 788-1993
  Rock Island  (G-18173)
Future Environmental Inc ......................... C ....... 708 479-6900
  Mokena  (G-14865)
GM Scrap Metals ..................................... G ....... 618 259-8570
  Cottage Hills  (G-7397)
Greencycle of Indiana Inc ........................ G ....... 847 441-6606
  Northfield  (G-16400)
Kreider Services  Incorporated ................ D ....... 815 288-6691
  Dixon  (G-8336)
Lake Area Disposal Service Inc ............... E ....... 217 522-9271
  Springfield  (G-20466)
Liberty Tire Recycling  LLC ..................... G ....... 773 871-6360
  Chicago  (G-5502)
Malvaes Solutions Incorporated .............. G ....... 773 823-1034
  Chicago  (G-5608)
Mervis Industries  Inc .............................. G ....... 217 753-1492
  Springfield  (G-20480)
Midwest Recycling Co ............................. E ....... 815 744-4922
  Rockdale  (G-18227)
Pontiac Recyclers Inc .............................. G ....... 815 844-6419
  Pontiac  (G-17708)
RDF Inc ................................................... F ....... 618 273-4141
  Eldorado  (G-8922)

**S & S Metal Recyclers Inc** ....F .... 630 844-3344
Aurora *(G-1213)*
**Strategic Materials Inc** ....G .... 773 523-2200
Chicago *(G-6602)*
**Twin City Wood Recycling Corp** ....G .... 309 827-9663
Bloomington *(G-2234)*

## SANITARY WARE: Metal

**Elkay Manufacturing Company** ....G .... 630 574-8484
Broadview *(G-2576)*
**Kohler Co** ....E .... 630 323-7674
Burr Ridge *(G-2861)*
**Kohler Co** ....D .... 847 734-1777
Huntley *(G-12155)*
**Swan Surfaces LLC** ....C .... 618 532-5673
Centralia *(G-3435)*

## SANITATION CHEMICALS & CLEANING AGENTS

**Acl Inc** ....F .... 773 285-0295
Chicago *(G-3730)*
**Bass Brother Incorporated** ....G .... 773 638-7628
Chicago *(G-4052)*
**Calumet Lubr Co Ltd Partnr** ....F .... 708 832-2463
Burnham *(G-2815)*
**Cater Chemical Co** ....G .... 630 980-2300
Roselle *(G-18930)*
**Chemix Corp** ....F .... 708 754-2150
Glenwood *(G-11215)*
**Chemtool Incorporated** ....C .... 815 957-4140
Rockton *(G-18694)*
**Chemtool Incorporated** ....D .... 815 459-1250
Crystal Lake *(G-7551)*
**Circle K Industries Inc** ....F .... 847 949-0363
Mundelein *(G-15487)*
**Claire-Sprayway Inc** ....D .... 630 628-3000
Downers Grove *(G-8413)*
**CLC Lubricants Company** ....E .... 630 232-7900
Geneva *(G-10818)*
**Clorox Products Mfg Co** ....E .... 708 728-4200
Chicago *(G-4405)*
**Clorox Products Mfg Co** ....C .... 847 229-5500
Wheeling *(G-22028)*
**Concept Laboratories Inc** ....D .... 773 395-7300
Chicago *(G-4446)*
**CPC Aeroscience Inc** ....G .... 954 974-5440
Downers Grove *(G-8421)*
**Damco Products Inc** ....G .... 618 452-4700
Madison *(G-14141)*
**Dial Corporation** ....C .... 630 892-4381
Montgomery *(G-15041)*
**Diversey Inc** ....D .... 262 631-4001
Bartlett *(G-1341)*
**Dober Chemical Corp** ....C .... 630 410-7300
Woodridge *(G-22471)*
**Ecolab Inc** ....E .... 815 729-7334
Joliet *(G-12488)*
**Ecolab Inc** ....E .... 847 350-2229
Elk Grove Village *(G-9448)*
**Gea Farm Technologies Inc** ....E .... 630 759-1063
Romeoville *(G-18828)*
**Getex Corporation** ....G .... 630 993-1300
Hinsdale *(G-11948)*
**Hurst Chemical Company** ....G .... 815 964-0451
Rockford *(G-18424)*
**Ivanhoe Industries Inc** ....E .... 847 872-3311
Zion *(G-22688)*
**Jacob Hay Co** ....G .... 847 215-8880
Wheeling *(G-22080)*
**Kafko International Ltd** ....E .... 847 763-0333
Skokie *(G-20021)*
**Kik Custom Products Inc** ....B .... 217 442-1400
Danville *(G-7743)*
**Kocour Co** ....E .... 773 847-1111
Chicago *(G-5397)*
**Korex Corporation** ....G .... 708 458-4890
Chicago *(G-5407)*
**Lasalle Chemical & Supply Co** ....F .... 847 470-1234
Morton Grove *(G-15211)*
**Lundmark Inc** ....F .... 630 628-1199
Addison *(G-184)*
**Mackenzie Johnson** ....G .... 630 244-2367
Maywood *(G-14428)*
**Mat Holdings Inc** ....D .... 847 821-9630
Long Grove *(G-13897)*
**Odorite International Inc** ....F .... 816 920-5000
Saint Charles *(G-19227)*
**Oil-Dri Corporation America** ....D .... 618 745-6881
Mounds *(G-15259)*
**Premium Oil Company** ....F .... 815 963-3800
Rockford *(G-18540)*
**Princeton Sealing Wax Co** ....G .... 815 875-1943
Princeton *(G-17760)*
**Protective Products Intl** ....G .... 847 526-1180
Wauconda *(G-21495)*
**Rainbow Cleaners** ....G .... 630 789-6989
Westmont *(G-21916)*
**Rock-Tred 2 LLC** ....E .... 888 762-5873
Waukegan *(G-21610)*
**Rust-Oleum Corporation** ....C .... 847 367-7700
Vernon Hills *(G-21195)*
**Sandstrom Products Company** ....E .... 309 523-2121
Port Byron *(G-17723)*
**Sandstrom Products Company** ....E .... 309 523-2121
Port Byron *(G-17724)*
**Tri Sect Corporation** ....F .... 847 524-1119
Schaumburg *(G-19770)*
**Turtle Wax Inc** ....B .... 630 455-3700
Addison *(G-331)*
**Umf Corporation** ....G .... 224 251-7822
Niles *(G-16045)*
**Umf Corporation** ....F .... 847 920-0370
Skokie *(G-20104)*
**Vanguard Chemical Corporation** ....F .... 312 751-0717
Chicago *(G-6871)*
**West Agro Inc** ....E .... 847 298-5505
Des Plaines *(G-8303)*

## SASHES: Door Or Window, Metal

**Custom Aluminum Products Inc** ....B .... 847 717-5000
South Elgin *(G-20191)*
**Harmon Inc** ....D .... 312 726-5050
Chicago *(G-5046)*
**YKK AP America Inc** ....F .... 630 582-9602
Roselle *(G-18988)*

## SATCHELS

**Sultry Satchels Inc** ....G .... 312 810-1081
Chicago *(G-6616)*

## SATELLITE COMMUNICATIONS EQPT

**Intelligent Designs LLC** ....G .... 630 235-7965
Wheaton *(G-21957)*

## SATELLITES: Communications

**Advance Technologies Inc** ....G .... 815 297-1771
Freeport *(G-10644)*
**American Data Centre Inc** ....G .... 847 358-7111
Palatine *(G-17000)*
**Bolingbrook Communications Inc** ....A .... 630 759-9500
Lisle *(G-13571)*
**Hi-Def Communications** ....G .... 217 258-6679
Mattoon *(G-14392)*
**Metro Service Center** ....G .... 618 524-8583
Metropolis *(G-14757)*
**Mr Dvr Llc** ....G .... 708 827-5030
Worth *(G-22634)*
**Prime Time Sports LLC** ....F .... 847 637-3500
Arlington Heights *(G-821)*
**Satellite Certified Inc** ....G .... 815 230-3877
Joliet *(G-12573)*
**U-Tracking International Inc** ....E .... 312 242-6003
Chicago *(G-6803)*
**Vincor Ltd** ....F .... 708 534-0008
Monee *(G-15005)*
**West Star Aviation LLC** ....G .... 618 259-3230
East Alton *(G-8612)*

## SAW BLADES

**Allkut Tool Incorporated** ....G .... 815 476-9656
Wilmington *(G-22269)*
**Custom Blades & Tools Inc** ....G .... 630 860-7650
Bensenville *(G-1875)*
**Estwing Manufacturing Co Inc** ....B .... 815 397-9521
Rockford *(G-18370)*
**Fiskars Brands Inc** ....B .... 309 690-2200
Peoria *(G-17363)*
**Jaeger Saw and Cutter Inc** ....G .... 815 963-0313
Rockford *(G-18442)*
**Milwaukee Electric Tool Corp** ....B .... 847 588-3356
Niles *(G-16008)*
**R & S Cutterhead Mfg Co** ....F .... 815 678-2611
Richmond *(G-17969)*
**S & J Industrial Supply Corp** ....F .... 708 339-1708
South Holland *(G-20303)*
**Supreme Saw & Service Co** ....G .... 708 396-1125
Wheeling *(G-22160)*
**Techniks LLC** ....E .... 815 689-2748
Cullom *(G-7685)*
**Trac Equipment Company Inc** ....G .... 309 647-5066
Canton *(G-2993)*
**Wallace/Haskin Corp** ....G .... 630 789-2882
Downers Grove *(G-8540)*

## SAWING & PLANING MILLS

**Alstat Wood Products** ....F .... 618 684-5167
Murphysboro *(G-15571)*
**Autumn Mill** ....G .... 217 795-3399
Argenta *(G-689)*
**Bach Timber & Pallet Inc** ....G .... 815 885-3774
Caledonia *(G-2930)*
**Bailey Business Group** ....G .... 618 548-3566
Salem *(G-19327)*
**Bond Brothers Hardwoods** ....G .... 618 272-4811
Ridgway *(G-17983)*
**Boyd Sawmill** ....G .... 618 735-2056
Dix *(G-8317)*
**Bull Valley Hardwood** ....G .... 815 701-9400
Woodstock *(G-22548)*
**Burks Sawmill** ....F .... 618 432-5451
Vernon *(G-21139)*
**Carpenters Millwork Co** ....F .... 708 339-7707
South Holland *(G-20255)*
**Carpenters Millwork Co** ....G .... 708 339-7707
Villa Park *(G-21241)*
**Charles K Eichen** ....G .... 217 854-9751
Carlinville *(G-3034)*
**Christiansen Sawmill and Log** ....G .... 815 315-7520
Caledonia *(G-2931)*
**Clarence Hancock Sawmill Inc** ....G .... 618 854-2232
Noble *(G-16050)*
**Corsaw Hardwood Lumber Inc** ....F .... 309 293-2055
Smithfield *(G-20119)*
**Crooked Trails Sawmill** ....G .... 618 244-1547
Opdyke *(G-16810)*
**Darrell Fickas Sawmill** ....G .... 618 676-1200
Clay City *(G-7263)*
**Don Poore Saw Mill Inc** ....G .... 618 757-2240
Springerton *(G-20382)*
**E-Z Tree Recycling Inc** ....G .... 773 493-8600
Chicago *(G-4670)*
**Eichen Lumber Co Inc** ....G .... 217 854-9751
Carlinville *(G-3037)*
**Ericson S Log & Lumber Co** ....G .... 309 667-2147
New Windsor *(G-15931)*
**Forestech Wood Products** ....G .... 217 279-3659
West Union *(G-21826)*
**Francis L Morris** ....G .... 618 676-1724
Clay City *(G-7264)*
**Fraser Millwork Inc** ....G .... 708 447-3262
Lyons *(G-14038)*
**G L Beaumont Lumber Company** ....F .... 618 423-2323
Ramsey *(G-17913)*
**Georgia-Pacific Bldg Pdts LLC** ....G .... 630 449-7200
Aurora *(G-1015)*
**Goodman Sawmill** ....G .... 309 547-3597
Lewistown *(G-13289)*
**Great Northern Lumber Inc** ....D .... 708 388-1818
Blue Island *(G-2254)*
**Heartland Hardwoods Inc** ....E .... 217 844-3312
Effingham *(G-8838)*
**Hites Hardwood Lumber Inc** ....F .... 618 723-2136
Noble *(G-16051)*
**J M Lustig Custom Cabinets Co** ....F .... 217 342-6661
Effingham *(G-8840)*
**Jefferies Orchard Sawmill** ....G .... 217 487-7582
Springfield *(G-20463)*
**Kirkland Sawmill Inc** ....G .... 815 522-6150
Kirkland *(G-12714)*
**Kniffen Brothers Sawmill** ....G .... 618 629-2437
Whittington *(G-22187)*
**Koppers Industries Inc** ....E .... 309 343-5157
Galesburg *(G-10763)*
**Larry Musgrave Logging** ....G .... 618 842-6386
Fairfield *(G-10148)*
**Lohrberg Lumber** ....F .... 618 473-2061
Waterloo *(G-21402)*
**M D Harmon Inc** ....F .... 618 662-8925
Xenia *(G-22644)*
**Marvin Suckow** ....G .... 618 483-5570
Mason *(G-14361)*
**Midwest Wood Inc** ....F .... 815 273-3333
Savanna *(G-19402)*
**Mulvain Woodworks** ....G .... 815 248-2305
Durand *(G-8587)*
**Rjt Wood Services** ....G .... 815 858-2081
Galena *(G-10730)*

## SAWING & PLANING MILLS

Sawmill Construction Inc .............................. G ...... 815 937-0037
  Bourbonnais (G-2406)
Schrocks Sawmill .......................................... G ...... 217 268-3632
  Arcola (G-684)
Simonton Hardwood Lumber LLC ................ F ...... 618 594-2132
  Carlyle (G-3059)
Towerleaf LLC ............................................... G ...... 847 985-1937
  Schaumburg (G-19766)
Tree-O Lumber Inc ........................................ E ...... 618 357-2576
  Pinckneyville (G-17553)
Triezenberg Millwork Co ............................... G ...... 708 489-9062
  Crestwood (G-7506)
Tronox Incorporated ...................................... E ...... 203 705-3704
  Madison (G-14154)
Westrock CP LLC .......................................... G ...... 630 655-6951
  Burr Ridge (G-2893)
Willenborg Hardwood Inds Inc ..................... F ...... 217 844-2082
  Effingham (G-8863)
Willowbrook Sawmill ...................................... G ...... 618 592-3806
  Oblong (G-16737)
Wooded Wonderland ..................................... G ...... 815 777-1223
  Galena (G-10735)

### SAWING & PLANING MILLS: Custom

Custom Lumbermill Works ............................ G ...... 309 875-3534
  Maquon (G-14216)
Farrow Lumber Co ......................................... G ...... 618 734-0255
  Cairo (G-2929)

### SAWMILL MACHINES

Sawmill Hydraulics ........................................ F ...... 309 245-2448
  Farmington (G-10188)

### SAWS & SAWING EQPT

Decatur Custom Tool Inc .............................. G ...... 618 244-4078
  Mount Vernon (G-15408)
Ed Hartwig Trucking & Excvtg ...................... G ...... 309 364-3672
  Henry (G-11740)
Gentry Small Engine Repair ......................... G ...... 217 849-3378
  Toledo (G-20963)
Gibson Insurance Inc .................................... G ...... 217 864-4877
  Mount Zion (G-15451)
Hopkins Saws & Karts Inc ............................ G ...... 618 756-2778
  Belle Rive (G-1605)
Kaser Power Equipment Inc ......................... G ...... 309 289-2176
  Knoxville (G-12721)
Michaels Equipment Co ................................. G ...... 618 524-8560
  Metropolis (G-14759)
Outdoor Power Inc ........................................ F ...... 217 228-9890
  Quincy (G-17865)
Owen Walker ................................................. G ...... 217 285-4012
  Pittsfield (G-17572)
Peoria Midwest Equipment Inc ..................... G ...... 309 454-6800
  Normal (G-16083)
Saws Unlimited Inc ....................................... G ...... 847 640-7450
  Elk Grove Village (G-9730)

### SCAFFOLDING WHOLESALERS

Diversified Cnstr Svcs LLC ........................... G ...... 708 344-4900
  Melrose Park (G-14620)
Gilco Real Estate Company .......................... E ...... 847 298-1717
  Des Plaines (G-8202)

### SCAFFOLDS: Mobile Or Stationary, Metal

Werner Co ..................................................... E ...... 815 459-6020
  Crystal Lake (G-7676)

### SCALE REPAIR SVCS

Florida Metrology LLC ................................... F ...... 630 833-3800
  Villa Park (G-21252)
Southern Illinois Scale Servc ........................ G ...... 618 723-2303
  Noble (G-16054)

### SCALES & BALANCES, EXC LABORATORY

Brian Burcar .................................................. G ...... 815 856-2271
  Leonore (G-13285)
E Rowe Foundry & Machine Co .................... D ...... 217 382-4135
  Martinsville (G-14334)
EJ Cady & Company ..................................... G ...... 847 537-2239
  Wheeling (G-22045)
Glenview Systems Inc ................................... F ...... 847 724-2691
  Glenview (G-11132)
Medela LLC ................................................... C ...... 800 435-8316
  McHenry (G-14531)
Meto-Grafics Inc ............................................ F ...... 847 639-0044
  Crystal Lake (G-7609)
Pelstar LLC .................................................... E ...... 708 377-0600
  Countryside (G-7440)
Scale-Tronix Inc ............................................. G ...... 630 653-3377
  Carol Stream (G-3235)
Taylor Precision Products Inc ....................... F ...... 630 954-1250
  Oak Brook (G-16563)

### SCALES: Baby

Heng Tuo Usa Inc ......................................... G ...... 630 705-1898
  Oakbrook Terrace (G-16710)

### SCALES: Bathroom

Lifespan Brands LLC ..................................... F ...... 630 315-3300
  Elk Grove Village (G-9595)
Loadsense Technologies LLC ....................... G ...... 312 239-0146
  Chicago (G-5529)
Newell Operating Company .......................... C ...... 815 235-4171
  Freeport (G-10675)

### SCALES: Indl

Advanced Weighing Systems Inc .................. G ...... 630 916-6179
  Addison (G-25)
Belt-Way Scales Inc ...................................... E ...... 815 625-5573
  Rock Falls (G-18126)
Control Weigh ................................................ G ...... 847 540-8260
  Buffalo Grove (G-2679)
G & H Balancer Service ................................ G ...... 773 509-1988
  Glenview (G-11127)
Integrated Measurement Systems ................ G ...... 847 956-1940
  Elk Grove Village (G-9549)

### SCALES: Truck

Southern Illinois Scale Servc ........................ G ...... 618 723-2303
  Noble (G-16054)

### SCANNING DEVICES: Optical

Applus Technologies Inc ............................... E ...... 312 661-1604
  Chicago (G-3927)
Bowe Bell + Hwell Scanners LLC ................. E ...... 847 675-7600
  Wheeling (G-22020)
Dennis Wright ................................................ G ...... 847 816-6110
  Vernon Hills (G-21156)
Digital Check Corp ........................................ E ...... 847 446-2285
  Northbrook (G-16243)
Spartanics Ltd ............................................... E ...... 847 394-5700
  Rolling Meadows (G-18781)

### SCHOOL SPLYS, EXC BOOKS: Wholesalers

Debcor Inc ..................................................... G ...... 708 333-2191
  South Holland (G-20261)

### SCHOOLS: Vocational, NEC

Associated Design Inc .................................. F ...... 708 974-9100
  Palos Hills (G-17114)

### SCIENTIFIC INSTRUMENTS WHOLESALERS

Fox International Corp .................................. F ...... 773 465-3634
  Chicago (G-4880)
Uic Inc ........................................................... G ...... 815 744-4477
  Rockdale (G-18234)
Wilkens-Anderson Company ........................ E ...... 773 384-4433
  Chicago (G-6979)

### SCRAP & WASTE MATERIALS, WHOLESALE: Auto Wrecking For Scrap

Springfield Iron & Metal Co .......................... G ...... 217 544-7131
  Springfield (G-20529)

### SCRAP & WASTE MATERIALS, WHOLESALE: Ferrous Metal

Alter Trading Corporation ............................. F ...... 217 223-0156
  Quincy (G-17791)
Azcon Inc ....................................................... F ...... 815 548-7000
  Sterling (G-20583)
Belson Steel Center Scrap Inc ..................... E ...... 815 932-7416
  Bourbonnais (G-2389)
Fox Valley Iron & Metal Corp ....................... F ...... 630 897-5907
  Aurora (G-1155)
Fricker Machine Shop & Salvage ................. G ...... 618 285-3271
  Elizabethtown (G-9245)
GM Scrap Metals ........................................... E ...... 618 259-8570
  Cottage Hills (G-7397)
Lemont Scrap Processing ............................. E ...... 630 257-6532
  Lemont (G-13239)
Mervis Industries Inc .................................... F ...... 217 235-5575
  Mattoon (G-14402)
Midstate Salvage Corp .................................. G ...... 217 824-6047
  Taylorville (G-20843)
Rondout Iron & Metal Co Inc ........................ G ...... 847 362-2750
  Lake Bluff (G-12865)
Serlin Iron & Metal Co Inc ............................ F ...... 773 227-3826
  Chicago (G-6479)
Weco Trading Inc .......................................... G ...... 847 615-1020
  Lake Bluff (G-12871)

### SCRAP & WASTE MATERIALS, WHOLESALE: Junk & Scrap

Top Metal Buyers Inc .................................... F ...... 314 421-2721
  East Saint Louis (G-8773)

### SCRAP & WASTE MATERIALS, WHOLESALE: Metal

Abco Metals Corporations ............................ F ...... 773 881-1504
  Chicago (G-3708)
Alter Trading Corporation ............................. F ...... 309 828-6084
  Bloomington (G-2143)
C&R Scrap Iron & Metal ............................... G ...... 847 459-9815
  Wheeling (G-22022)
Cicero Iron Metal & Paper Inc ...................... G ...... 708 863-8601
  Cicero (G-7183)
Dels Metal Co ................................................ E ...... 309 788-1993
  Rock Island (G-18173)
Illini Castings LLC ......................................... F ...... 217 446-6365
  Danville (G-7737)
Lake Area Disposal Service Inc ................... E ...... 217 522-9271
  Springfield (G-20466)
Mervis Industries Inc .................................... G ...... 217 753-1492
  Springfield (G-20480)
Pontiac Recyclers Inc ................................... G ...... 815 844-6419
  Pontiac (G-17708)
Shapiro Bros of Illinois Inc ........................... E ...... 618 244-3168
  Mount Vernon (G-15445)
T J Metal Co .................................................. G ...... 708 388-6191
  Alsip (G-532)

### SCRAP & WASTE MATERIALS, WHOLESALE: Nonferrous Metals Scrap

Midland Industries Inc .................................. E ...... 312 664-7300
  Chicago (G-5734)
T & C Metal Co .............................................. G ...... 815 459-4445
  Crystal Lake (G-7658)

### SCRAP & WASTE MATERIALS, WHOLESALE: Paper

C & M Recycling Inc ..................................... E ...... 847 578-1066
  North Chicago (G-16176)
Channeled Resources Inc ............................ E ...... 312 733-4200
  Chicago (G-4287)
Midwest Fiber Inc Decatur ............................ E ...... 217 424-9460
  Decatur (G-7915)

### SCRAP & WASTE MATERIALS, WHOLESALE: Paper & Cloth Materials

Buster Services Inc ....................................... E ...... 773 247-2070
  Chicago (G-4191)

### SCREENS: Projection

AV Stumpfl Usa Corp .................................... F ...... 630 359-0999
  Elmhurst (G-9835)
Rensel-Chicago Inc ....................................... F ...... 773 235-2100
  Chicago (G-6334)

### SCREENS: Window, Metal

Thermal Industries Inc .................................. E ...... 800 237-0560
  Wood Dale (G-22430)

### SCREENS: Woven Wire

City Screen Inc .............................................. G ...... 773 588-5642
  Chicago (G-4388)

### SCREW MACHINE PRDTS

A E Micek Engineering Corp ........................ E ...... 847 455-8181
  Franklin Park (G-10381)
Abbco Inc ...................................................... E ...... 630 595-7115
  Elk Grove Village (G-9253)
Abbott Scott Manufacturing Co .................... E ...... 773 342-7200
  Chicago (G-3706)

# PRODUCT SECTION — SCREW MACHINE PRDTS

| Company | Code | Phone |
|---|---|---|
| Abbott-Interfast Corporation — Wheeling (G-21996) | D | 847 459-6200 |
| Ability Fasteners Inc — Elk Grove Village (G-9256) | E | 847 593-4230 |
| Accumation Inc — Crystal Lake (G-7526) | F | 815 455-6250 |
| Acme Screw Co — Cherry Valley (G-3637) | F | 815 332-7548 |
| Advance Screw Products Inc — Chicago (G-3763) | F | 773 237-0034 |
| Afco Products Incorporated — Lake Zurich (G-13036) | E | 847 299-1055 |
| Afi Industries Inc — Carol Stream (G-3092) | E | 630 462-0400 |
| Alert Scrw Products Inc — Fox Lake (G-10274) | G | 847 587-1360 |
| Alpha Swiss Industries Inc — Crystal Lake (G-7530) | E | 815 455-3031 |
| AM Swiss Screw Mch Pdts Inc — South Elgin (G-20181) | F | 847 468-9300 |
| American Machine Pdts & Svcs — Mokena (G-14852) | G | 708 743-9088 |
| American Precision Machine — Carpentersville (G-3273) | F | 847 428-5950 |
| American Screw Machine Co — Franklin Park (G-10393) | G | 847 455-4308 |
| American/Jebco Corporation — Franklin Park (G-10394) | C | 847 455-3150 |
| Ampex Screw Mfg Inc — Arlington Heights (G-712) | G | 847 228-1202 |
| Anpec Industries Inc — Pecatonica (G-17250) | E | 815 239-2303 |
| Archer Engineering Company — Chicago (G-3936) | G | 773 247-3501 |
| Arrow Gear Company — Downers Grove (G-8390) | E | 630 969-7640 |
| Astro-Craft Inc — Spring Grove (G-20326) | E | 815 675-1500 |
| Automatic Precision Inc — Chicago (G-3992) | E | 708 867-1116 |
| Automatic Swiss Corporation — Addison (G-49) | E | 630 543-3888 |
| Automation Systems Inc — Melrose Park (G-14597) | E | 847 671-9515 |
| Autonamic Corporation — Spring Grove (G-20327) | G | 815 675-6300 |
| Autonetics Inc — Carpentersville (G-3275) | F | 847 426-8525 |
| Avan Tool & Die Co Inc — Chicago (G-3996) | F | 773 287-1670 |
| Avanti Engineering Inc — Glendale Heights (G-11011) | F | 630 260-1333 |
| B & M Screw Machine Inc — Watseka (G-21415) | G | 815 432-5892 |
| B Radtke and Sons Inc — Round Lake Park (G-19083) | G | 847 546-3999 |
| Belrich Inc — Chicago (G-4080) | G |  |
| Bensenville Screw Products — Bensenville (G-1843) | G | 630 860-5222 |
| Bradley Machining Inc — Addison (G-59) | F | 630 543-2875 |
| Calcon Machine Inc — Leland (G-13219) | G | 815 495-9227 |
| Calumet Screw Machine Products — Mokena (G-14856) | D | 708 479-1660 |
| Camco Manufacturing Inc — Crestwood (G-7478) | F | 708 597-4288 |
| Camcraft Inc — Hanover Park (G-11578) | C | 630 582-6001 |
| Camshop Industrial LLC — Crestwood (G-7479) | G | 708 597-4288 |
| Central Autmtc Screw Pdts Inc — Bensenville (G-1854) | G | 630 766-7966 |
| Chase Fasteners Inc — Melrose Park (G-14608) | E | 708 345-0335 |
| Chicago Rivet & Machine Co — Naperville (G-15627) | C | 630 357-8500 |
| Chicago Turnrite Co Inc — Chicago (G-4360) | E | 773 626-8404 |
| Cnc Swiss Inc — Addison (G-78) | G | 630 543-9595 |
| Continental Automation Inc — Saint Charles (G-19162) | E | 630 584-5100 |
| Continental Midland — Calumet Park (G-2960) | G | 708 441-1000 |
| Continental Screws Mch Pdts — Wheeling (G-22030) | E | 847 459-7766 |
| Contour Screw Products Inc — Arlington Heights (G-739) | E | 847 357-1190 |
| CP Screw Machine Products — Bensenville (G-1870) | F | 630 766-2313 |
| Demco Products Inc — Oak Lawn (G-16616) | F | 708 636-6240 |
| Devon Precision Machine Pdts — Franklin Park (G-10458) | F | 847 233-9700 |
| Dune Manufacturing Company — Melrose Park (G-14622) | F | 708 681-2905 |
| Durite Screw Corporation — Chicago (G-4656) | E | 773 622-3410 |
| E J Basler Co — Schiller Park (G-19821) | D | 847 678-8880 |
| Eastview Manufacturing Inc — Elgin (G-9019) | F | 847 741-2514 |
| Ella Engineering Incorporated — Elk Grove Village (G-9453) | G | 847 354-4767 |
| Empire Screw Manufacturing Co — Villa Park (G-21251) | F | 630 833-7060 |
| Engineered Plastic Pdts Corp — Elk Grove Village (G-9460) | E | 847 952-8400 |
| F and F Screw Products — Rockford (G-18378) | G | 815 968-7330 |
| Forster Tool & Mfg Co Inc — Bensenville (G-1902) | E | 630 616-8177 |
| Francis Screw Products Co Inc — Niles (G-15980) | G | 847 647-9462 |
| Franklin Screw Products Inc — Genoa (G-10878) | G | 815 784-8500 |
| Fsp LLC — Gurnee (G-11450) | G | 773 992-2600 |
| G & E Automatic — Machesney Park (G-14077) | G | 815 654-7766 |
| G Messmore Company — Broadview (G-2581) | G | 708 343-8114 |
| Gage Manufacturing Inc — Elk Grove Village (G-9493) | F | 847 228-7300 |
| General Engineering Works — Addison (G-131) | G | 630 543-8000 |
| General Fas Acquisition Co — Woodridge (G-22481) | E | 630 960-3360 |
| Global Turnings Inc — West Chicago (G-21708) | G | 630 562-0946 |
| Globe Precision Machining Inc — South Beloit (G-20149) | E | 815 389-4586 |
| Greg Screw Machine Products — Wood Dale (G-22378) | G | 630 694-8875 |
| Groth Manufacturing — Carpentersville (G-3286) | F | 847 428-5950 |
| H & M Thread Rolling Co Inc — Franklin Park (G-10485) | G | 847 451-1570 |
| Hi-Tech Welding Services Inc — Bensenville (G-1917) | E | 630 595-8160 |
| Highland Mch & Screw Pdts Co — Highland (G-11788) | D | 618 654-2103 |
| Highland Metal Inc — Hillside (G-11919) | E | 708 544-6641 |
| I D Rockford Shop Inc — Winnebago (G-22297) | G | 815 335-1150 |
| Illinois Tool Works Inc — Machesney Park (G-14080) | E | 815 654-1510 |
| Illinois Tool Works Inc — Elgin (G-9071) | E | 847 741-7900 |
| J N R Custo-Matic Screw Inc — Glendale Heights (G-11036) | D | 630 260-1333 |
| JB Mfg & Screw Machine — Burr Ridge (G-2859) | G | 630 850-6978 |
| JB Mfg & Screw Machine PR — Franklin Park (G-10507) | G | 847 451-0892 |
| Jedi Corporation — Mchenry (G-14516) | G | 815 344-5334 |
| Jefco Screw Machine Products — Loves Park (G-13952) | F | 815 282-2000 |
| Jim Sterner Machines — Rockford (G-18445) | G | 815 962-8983 |
| Jmd Screw Products — Belvidere (G-1766) | G | 815 505-9113 |
| Jt Products Co — Melrose Park (G-14665) | G | 773 378-4550 |
| Kadon Precision Machining Inc — Rockford (G-18452) | D | 815 874-5850 |
| Kenent Screw Machine Products — Rockton (G-18697) | F | 815 624-7216 |
| Kiel Machine Products — Elgin (G-9088) | G |  |
| Kksp Precision Machining LLC — Glendale Heights (G-11038) | D | 630 260-1735 |
| L & W Tool & Screw Mch Pdts — Itasca (G-12300) | E | 847 238-1212 |
| L D Redmer Screw Pdts Inc — Bensenville (G-1935) | E | 630 787-0504 |
| L D Redmer Screw Products — Naperville (G-15685) | G | 630 787-0507 |
| Lab Ten LLC — Machesney Park (G-14087) | F | 815 877-1410 |
| Lafox Screw Products Inc — South Elgin (G-20214) | G | 847 695-1732 |
| Lakeside Screw Products Inc — Addison (G-178) | C | 630 495-1606 |
| Lakeview Prcsion Machining Inc — South Elgin (G-20215) | F | 847 742-7170 |
| Lawrence Screw Products Inc — Lincoln (G-13412) | G | 217 735-1230 |
| Lombard Swiss Screw Company — Addison (G-183) | G | 630 576-5096 |
| Lsl Precision Machining Inc — Loves Park (G-13962) | E | 815 633-4701 |
| Mac Lean-Fogg Company — Mundelein (G-15521) | D | 847 566-0010 |
| Magnet-Schultz Amer Holdg LLC — Westmont (G-21901) | G | 630 789-0600 |
| Magnet-Schultz America Inc — Westmont (G-21902) | D | 630 789-0600 |
| Magnus Screw Products Co — Chicago (G-5603) | E | 773 889-2344 |
| Makerite Mfg Co Inc — Roscoe (G-18906) | E | 815 389-3902 |
| Masters Yates Inc — Rockford (G-18486) | G | 815 227-9585 |
| Mc Henry Screw Products Inc — McHenry (G-14529) | G | 815 344-4638 |
| Meaden Precision Machined Pdts — Burr Ridge (G-2865) | D | 630 655-0888 |
| Meador Industries Inc — Franklin Park (G-10526) | G | 847 671-5042 |
| Metomic Corporation — Chicago (G-5705) | E | 773 247-4716 |
| Micro Screw Machine Co Inc — Rockford (G-18501) | G | 815 397-2115 |
| Mid-West Screw Products Inc — Chicago (G-5731) | E | 773 283-6032 |
| Midway Machine Products & Svcs — Elk Grove Village (G-9628) | G | 847 860-8180 |
| Minic Precision Inc — Spring Grove (G-20348) | F | 815 675-0451 |
| Monnex International Inc — Buffalo Grove (G-2738) | E | 847 850-5263 |
| Multitech Cold Forming LLC — Carol Stream (G-3201) | E | 630 949-8200 |
| National Cap and Set Screw Co — Spring Grove (G-20350) | E | 815 675-2363 |
| National Cycle Inc — Maywood (G-14430) | C | 708 343-0400 |
| Nelson & Lavold Manufacturing — Chicago (G-5883) | E | 312 943-6300 |
| North Amercn Acquisition Corp — Elgin (G-9124) | D | 847 695-8030 |
| Nu-Metal Products Inc — Crystal Lake (G-7622) | F | 815 459-2075 |
| Nyclo Screw Machine Pdts Inc — Rockford (G-18523) | F | 815 229-7900 |
| Pioneer Service Inc — Addison (G-242) | E | 630 628-0249 |
| Precise Products Inc — Warrenville (G-21357) | E | 630 393-9698 |
| Precision McHned Cmponents Inc — Romeoville (G-18860) | E | 630 759-5555 |
| Precision Screw Machining Co — Chicago (G-6172) | F | 773 205-4280 |
| Precision Steel Warehouse Inc — Franklin Park (G-10560) | C | 800 323-0740 |
| Precision-Tek Mfg Inc — Arlington Heights (G-819) | E | 847 364-7800 |
| Preferred Fasteners Inc — Carol Stream (G-3215) | G | 630 510-0200 |
| Princeton Industrial Products — Hoffman Estates (G-12041) | F | 847 839-8500 |
| Process Screw Products Inc — Shannon (G-19901) | E | 815 864-2220 |
| Progressive Turnings Inc — Aurora (G-1206) | F | 630 898-3072 |
| Qcc LLC — Harwood Heights (G-11689) | C | 708 867-5400 |
| R & N Machine Co — Riverdale (G-18023) | F | 708 841-5555 |
| R B Evans Co — Elburn (G-8907) | G | 630 365-3554 |
| Red Devil Manufacturing Co — Wheeling (G-22134) | F | 847 215-1377 |
| Reino Tool & Manufacturing Co — Chicago (G-6326) | F | 773 588-5800 |

Employee Codes: A=Over 500 employees, B=251-500, C=101-250, D=51-100, E=20-50, F=10-19, G=3-9

RF Mau Co ........ F ....... 847 329-9731
Lincolnwood (G-13533)
Roberts Swiss Inc ........ E ....... 630 467-9100
Itasca (G-12348)
Rockford Ball Screw Company ........ D ....... 815 961-7700
Rockford (G-18566)
Royal Machining Corporation ........ G ....... 708 338-3387
Melrose Park (G-14689)
S & W Manufacturing Co Inc ........ E ....... 630 595-5044
Bensenville (G-1984)
SA Industries 2 Inc ........ G ....... 815 381-6200
Rockford (G-18604)
Saturn Manufacturing Company ........ G ....... 630 860-8474
Bensenville (G-1986)
Screw Machine Engrg Co Inc ........ E ....... 773 631-7600
Chicago (G-6461)
Screws Industries Inc ........ D ....... 630 539-9200
Glendale Heights (G-11068)
Security Locknut LLC ........ E ....... 847 970-4050
Vernon Hills (G-21200)
Special Fastener Operations ........ G ....... 815 544-6449
Belvidere (G-1784)
St Charles Screw Products Inc ........ G ....... 815 943-8060
Harvard (G-11647)
Starro Precision Products Inc ........ E ....... 847 741-9400
Elgin (G-9192)
Suburban Screw Machine Pdts ........ G ....... 815 337-0434
Woodstock (G-22614)
Supreme Manufacturing Company ........ E ....... 847 297-8212
Des Plaines (G-8283)
Supreme Screw Products ........ G ....... 708 579-3500
Countryside (G-7445)
Swebco Mfg Inc ........ E ....... 815 636-7160
Machesney Park (G-14110)
Swiss Automation Inc ........ D ....... 847 381-4405
Barrington (G-1306)
Swiss Precision Machining Inc ........ D ....... 847 647-7111
Wheeling (G-22162)
Swisstronics Corp ........ G ....... 708 403-8877
Orland Park (G-16897)
T R Jones Machine Co Inc ........ G ....... 815 356-5000
Machesney Park (G-14111)
Tanko Scrw Prd Corp ........ G ....... 708 418-0300
Chicago Heights (G-7130)
Toledo Screw Machine Products ........ G ....... 815 877-8213
Rockford (G-18652)
Tri-Part Screw Products Inc ........ E ....... 815 654-7311
Machesney Park (G-14114)
Turnco Inc ........ G ....... 708 756-6565
Chicago Heights (G-7133)
Ty Precision Automatics Inc ........ F ....... 815 963-9668
Rockford (G-18658)
Uca Group Inc ........ E ....... 847 742-7151
South Elgin (G-20231)
Vandeventer Mfg Co Inc ........ E ....... 630 879-2511
Batavia (G-1515)
Vanguard Tool & Engineering Co ........ E ....... 847 981-9595
Mount Prospect (G-15382)
Vek Screw Machine Products ........ G ....... 630 543-5557
Addison (G-338)
Weber Metal Products Inc ........ F ....... 815 844-3169
Chenoa (G-3636)
Wenlyn Screw Company Inc ........ G ....... 630 766-0050
Bensenville (G-2013)
Wilmette Screw Products ........ G ....... 773 725-2626
Chicago (G-6989)
Wilson Mfg Screw Mch Pdts ........ F ....... 815 964-8724
Rockford (G-18684)
Worley Machining Inc ........ F ....... 630 801-9198
Aurora (G-1234)
X-L-Engineering Corp ........ E ....... 847 965-3030
Niles (G-16048)
X-L-Engineering Corp ........ E ....... 847 364-4750
Elk Grove Village (G-9820)

## SCREW MACHINES

Dynamic Automation Inc ........ G ....... 312 782-8555
Lincolnwood (G-13508)
Rodifer Enterprises Inc ........ G ....... 815 678-0100
Richmond (G-17970)

## SCREWS: Metal

Afi Industries Inc ........ E ....... 630 462-0400
Carol Stream (G-3092)
Allstar Fasteners Inc ........ E ....... 847 640-7827
Elk Grove Village (G-9287)
American/Jebco Corporation ........ C ....... 847 455-3150
Franklin Park (G-10394)
Aww 10 Inc ........ D ....... 630 595-7600
Bensenville (G-1837)
Brynolf Manufacturing Inc ........ E ....... 815 873-8878
Rockford (G-18291)
Chase Fasteners Inc ........ E ....... 708 345-0335
Melrose Park (G-14608)
Custom Metal Products Corp ........ E ....... 815 397-3306
Rockford (G-18328)
Dml Distribution Inc ........ F ....... 630 839-9041
Schaumburg (G-19507)
Fastron Co ........ E ....... 630 766-5000
Melrose Park (G-14636)
Gateway Screw & Rivet Inc ........ E ....... 630 539-2232
Glendale Heights (G-11026)
Hadley Gear Manufacturing Co ........ F ....... 773 722-1030
Chicago (G-5028)
Holbrook Mfg Inc ........ D ....... 847 229-1999
Wheeling (G-22072)
Illinois Tool Works Inc ........ F ....... 815 654-1510
Machesney Park (G-14081)
Inland Fastener Inc ........ F ....... 630 293-3800
West Chicago (G-21720)
JW Fasteners Inc ........ G ....... 815 963-2658
Rockford (G-18450)
Komar Screw Corp ........ E ....... 847 965-9090
Niles (G-15995)
Medalist Industries Inc ........ G ....... 847 766-9000
Elk Grove Village (G-9617)
Mid-States Screw Corporation ........ E ....... 815 397-2440
Rockford (G-18503)
National Cap and Set Screw Co ........ F ....... 815 675-2363
Spring Grove (G-20350)
Nylok Fastener Corporation ........ D ....... 847 674-9680
Lincolnwood (G-13528)
Parker International Pdts Inc ........ D ....... 815 524-5831
Vernon Hills (G-21188)
Rail Forge ........ G ....... 630 561-4989
Chicago (G-6285)
Si Enterprises Inc ........ G ....... 630 539-9200
Glendale Heights (G-11069)
Specialty Screw Corporation ........ D ....... 815 969-4100
Rockford (G-18626)
Thread & Gage Co Inc ........ G ....... 815 675-2305
Spring Grove (G-20367)
Valley Fastener Group LLC ........ F ....... 708 343-2496
Melrose Park (G-14704)
Wenlyn Screw Company Inc ........ G ....... 630 766-0050
Bensenville (G-2013)

## SEALANTS

Alhencam Seal Coat Inc ........ G ....... 217 422-4605
Decatur (G-7829)
Dental Sealants & More ........ G ....... 309 692-6435
Peoria (G-17348)
Eagle Enterprises Inc ........ G ....... 618 643-2588
Mc Leansboro (G-14464)
Ecool LLC ........ G ....... 309 966-3701
Champaign (G-3477)
F H Leinweber Co Inc ........ G ....... 708 424-7000
Oak Lawn (G-16619)
F H Leinweber Co Inc ........ E ....... 773 568-7722
Chicago (G-4803)
JW Sealants Inc ........ G ....... 630 398-1010
Bartlett (G-1358)
La-Co Industries Inc ........ C ....... 847 427-3220
Elk Grove Village (G-9582)
Morton Yokohama Inc ........ F ....... 312 807-2000
Chicago (G-5810)
Nolan Sealants Inc ........ G ....... 630 774-5713
Bloomingdale (G-2121)
Npc Sealants ........ F ....... 708 681-1040
Maywood (G-14431)
Safety Compound Corporation ........ E ....... 630 953-1515
Lombard (G-13851)

## SEALING COMPOUNDS: Sealing, synthetic rubber or plastic

Advanced Extruder Tech Inc ........ E ....... 847 238-9651
Elk Grove Village (G-9275)

## SEALS: Hermetic

Big Joes Sealcoati ........ G ....... 630 935-7032
Lisle (G-13568)
Chicago Cardinal Communication ........ F ....... 708 424-1446
Oak Lawn (G-16610)

## SEALS: Oil, Leather

James Walker Mfg Co ........ E ....... 708 754-4020
Glenwood (G-11217)
Triseal Corporation ........ E ....... 815 648-2473
Hebron (G-11728)

## SEALS: Oil, Rubber

Advantage Seal Inc ........ F ....... 630 226-0200
Bolingbrook (G-2277)

## SEARCH & DETECTION SYSTEMS, EXC RADAR

Binks Industries Inc ........ G ....... 630 801-1100
Montgomery (G-15030)
Electro-Technic Products Inc ........ F ....... 773 561-2349
Chicago (G-4721)
Marine Technologies Inc ........ E ....... 847 546-9001
Volo (G-21318)
MidAmerican Technology Inc ........ G ....... 815 496-2400
Serena (G-19893)

## SEARCH & NAVIGATION SYSTEMS

Ability Metal Company ........ E ....... 847 437-7040
Elk Grove Village (G-9257)
Acl Inc ........ F ....... 773 285-0295
Chicago (G-3730)
Advanced Precision Mfg Inc ........ E ....... 847 981-9800
Elk Grove Village (G-9276)
Andrew New Zealand Inc ........ E ....... 708 873-3507
Orland Park (G-16843)
ARINC Incorporated ........ E ....... 800 633-6882
O Fallon (G-16463)
Boeing Company ........ G ....... 847 240-0767
Schaumburg (G-19465)
Boeing Company ........ B ....... 312 544-2000
Chicago (G-4136)
Bolingbrook Communications Inc ........ A ....... 630 759-9500
Lisle (G-13571)
CAM Co Inc ........ F ....... 630 556-3110
Big Rock (G-2086)
CEF Industries LLC ........ C ....... 630 628-2299
Addison (G-71)
Commscope Technologies LLC ........ A ....... 708 236-6600
Westchester (G-21835)
D W Terry Welding Company ........ G ....... 618 433-9722
Alton (G-570)
FSI Technologies Inc ........ E ....... 630 932-9380
Lombard (G-13803)
GKN Aerospace Inc ........ G ....... 630 737-1456
Lisle (G-13596)
Honeywell International Inc ........ G ....... 815 235-5500
Freeport (G-10664)
L A M Inc De ........ G ....... 630 860-9700
Wood Dale (G-22388)
Motorola Solutions Inc ........ G ....... 847 341-3485
Oak Brook (G-16546)
National Aerospace Corp ........ G ....... 847 566-5834
Hawthorn Woods (G-11704)
Navigon Inc ........ D ....... 312 268-1500
Chicago (G-5873)
Navman Wireless Holdings LP ........ D ....... 866 527-9896
Glenview (G-11171)
Oceancomm Incorporated ........ G ....... 800 757-3266
Champaign (G-3522)
Quartix Inc ........ F ....... 855 913-6663
Chicago (G-6255)
Research In Motion Rf Inc ........ G ....... 815 444-1095
Crystal Lake (G-7639)
Trident Machine Co ........ G ....... 815 968-1585
Rockford (G-18657)
Winn Star Inc ........ G ....... 618 964-1811
Carbondale (G-3028)

## SEAT BELTS: Automobile & Aircraft

Deyco Inc ........ G ....... 630 553-5666
Yorkville (G-22656)
Hooker Custom Harness Inc ........ G ....... 815 233-5478
Freeport (G-10666)

## SEATING: Chairs, Table & Arm

Tao Trading Corporation ........ G ....... 773 764-6542
Chicago (G-6675)

## SEATING: Railroad

Inter Swiss Ltd ........ F ....... 773 379-0400
Chicago (G-5210)
Norfolk Southern Corporation ........ G ....... 773 933-5698
Chicago (G-5927)

## PRODUCT SECTION

### SEATING: Transportation

Fbsa LLC .................................................C....... 773 524-2440
　Chicago  *(G-4822)*
Freedman Seating Company ...................C....... 773 524-2440
　Chicago  *(G-4887)*
Innovtive Design Solutions LLC ..............G....... 708 547-1942
　Bellwood  *(G-1709)*

### SECRETARIAL SVCS

CCH Incorporated ....................................A....... 847 267-7000
　Riverwoods  *(G-18037)*

### SECURITY & COMMODITY EXCHANGES

Rapid Execution Services LLC ...............G....... 312 789-4358
　Chicago  *(G-6293)*

### SECURITY CONTROL EQPT & SYSTEMS

Azilsa Inc ..................................................E....... 312 919-1741
　Schaumburg  *(G-19455)*
Blustor Pmc Inc .......................................G....... 312 265-3058
　Chicago  *(G-4131)*
Calx Trading Corporation ........................E....... 630 456-6721
　Naperville  *(G-15800)*
Chase Security Systems Inc ...................G....... 773 594-1919
　Chicago  *(G-4295)*
Checkpoint Systems Inc .........................D....... 630 771-4240
　Romeoville  *(G-18809)*
Elite Access Systems Inc .......................D....... 800 528-5880
　Elmhurst  *(G-9864)*
Engineered Security & Sound .................G....... 630 876-8853
　West Chicago  *(G-21695)*
Hs Technology Inc ...................................G....... 630 572-7650
　Oak Brook  *(G-16522)*
Maco-Sys LLC ..........................................F....... 779 888-3260
　Rockford  *(G-18479)*
Marbil Enterprises Inc .............................G....... 618 257-1810
　Belleville  *(G-1651)*
Moog Inc ..................................................E....... 770 987-7550
　Northbrook  *(G-16313)*
Nitek International LLC ............................G....... 847 259-8900
　Rolling Meadows  *(G-18751)*
P & J Technologies ...................................G....... 847 995-1108
　Schaumburg  *(G-19677)*
Shield Electronics LLC ............................G....... 815 467-4134
　Minooka  *(G-14847)*
Stanley Security Solutions Inc ................F....... 630 724-3600
　Lisle  *(G-13663)*
Tylu Wireless Technology LLC ................G....... 312 260-7934
　Chicago  *(G-6802)*
Vasco Data Security Inc (de) ...................G....... 630 932-8844
　Oakbrook Terrace  *(G-16721)*

### SECURITY DEVICES

Accurate Security & Lock Corp ...............G....... 815 455-0133
　Lake In The Hills  *(G-12982)*
Cipher Technology Solution ...................G....... 630 892-2355
　Montgomery  *(G-15038)*
Compx International Inc ..........................G....... 847 543-4583
　Grayslake  *(G-11328)*
Duvas USA Limited ..................................G....... 312 266-1420
　Chicago  *(G-4658)*
I C Dynamics Inc .....................................G....... 708 922-0501
　Plainfield  *(G-17608)*
Interior Tectonics LLC .............................G....... 312 515-7779
　Chicago  *(G-5215)*
Midwest Treasure Detectors ....................G....... 217 223-4769
　Quincy  *(G-17860)*
Mobiloc LLC .............................................G....... 773 742-1329
　Alsip  *(G-495)*
Quality Intgrted Solutions Inc .................G....... 815 464-4772
　Tinley Park  *(G-20942)*
Rf Ideas Inc .............................................D....... 847 870-1723
　Rolling Meadows  *(G-18774)*
RTS Sentry Inc .........................................F....... 618 257-7100
　Belleville  *(G-1674)*
Stabiloc LLC .............................................G....... 586 412-1147
　Carol Stream  *(G-3245)*
Trafficguard Direct LLC ...........................G....... 815 899-8471
　Sycamore  *(G-20820)*

### SECURITY GUARD SVCS

Master Guard Security Co .......................G....... 618 398-7749
　East Saint Louis  *(G-8760)*

### SECURITY PROTECTIVE DEVICES MAINTENANCE & MONITORING SVCS

Ep Technology Corporation USA ............D....... 217 351-7888
　Champaign  *(G-3482)*

### SECURITY SYSTEMS SERVICES

AT&T Teleholdings Inc ............................G....... 800 257-0902
　Chicago  *(G-3973)*
Cipher Technology Solution ...................G....... 630 892-2355
　Montgomery  *(G-15038)*
Double Nickel LLC ..................................G....... 618 476-3200
　Millstadt  *(G-14823)*
Hipskind Tech Sltons Group Inc .............E....... 630 920-0960
　Oakbrook Terrace  *(G-16712)*
Honeywell International Inc ....................D....... 847 797-4000
　Arlington Heights  *(G-768)*
Quantum Color Graphics LLC ................C....... 847 967-3600
　Morton Grove  *(G-15231)*
Siemens Industry Inc ..............................A....... 847 215-1000
　Buffalo Grove  *(G-2767)*
Smart Surveillance Inc ............................G....... 630 968-5075
　Lisle  *(G-13657)*

### SEEDS & BULBS WHOLESALERS

Dow Agrosciences LLC ..........................G....... 815 844-3128
　Pontiac  *(G-17699)*
Michel Fertilizer & Equipment ................G....... 618 242-6000
　Mount Vernon  *(G-15425)*
New Alliance Production LLC .................E....... 309 928-3123
　Farmer City  *(G-10180)*
Pioneer Hi-Bred Intl Inc ...........................F....... 309 962-2931
　Le Roy  *(G-13209)*

### SEEDS: Coated Or Treated, From Purchased Seeds

Gateway Seed Company Inc ...................G....... 618 327-8000
　Nashville  *(G-15836)*
Quality Technology Intl Inc .....................E....... 847 649-9300
　Elgin  *(G-9158)*

### SELF-PROPELLED AIRCRAFT DEALER

AAR Corp .................................................C....... 630 227-2000
　Wood Dale  *(G-22328)*

### SEMICONDUCTOR CIRCUIT NETWORKS

Methode Electronics Inc .........................B....... 708 867-6777
　Chicago  *(G-5704)*
Microlink Devices Inc .............................E....... 847 588-3001
　Niles  *(G-16005)*
Nhanced Semiconductors Inc ................F....... 408 759-4060
　Naperville  *(G-15715)*

### SEMICONDUCTOR DEVICES: Wafers

Sigenics Inc .............................................F....... 312 448-8000
　Chicago  *(G-6506)*

### SEMICONDUCTORS & RELATED DEVICES

Accelerated Assemblies Inc ...................E....... 630 616-6680
　Elk Grove Village  *(G-9259)*
Akhan Semiconductor Inc ......................G....... 847 855-8400
　Gurnee  *(G-11424)*
Angela Yang Chingjui ..............................G....... 630 724-0596
　Darien  *(G-7790)*
B+b Smartworx Inc ..................................D....... 815 433-5100
　Ottawa  *(G-16949)*
Chicago Pixels Mulitmedia Nfp ...............G....... 312 513-7949
　Chicago  *(G-4340)*
Convergent Advisors ...............................G....... 312 971-2602
　Chicago  *(G-4463)*
Convergent Bill Ete Ort T .........................G....... 847 387-4059
　Hoffman Estates  *(G-12003)*
Convergent Group LLC ...........................G....... 847 274-6336
　Deerfield  *(G-8001)*
Csi2d Inc .................................................G....... 312 282-7407
　Hoffman Estates  *(G-12071)*
CTS Automotive LLC ...............................C....... 630 614-7201
　Lisle  *(G-13578)*
CTS Corporation .....................................C....... 630 577-8800
　Lisle  *(G-13579)*
Dover Corporation ..................................C....... 630 541-1540
　Downers Grove  *(G-8431)*
Effimax Solar ...........................................G....... 217 550-2422
　Champaign  *(G-3479)*
Epir Inc ....................................................G....... 630 842-0893
　Bolingbrook  *(G-2306)*
Epiworks Inc ............................................D....... 217 373-1590
　Champaign  *(G-3483)*
FSI Technologies Inc ...............................E....... 630 932-9380
　Lombard  *(G-13803)*
Intel Americas Inc ...................................E....... 847 706-5779
　Schaumburg  *(G-19570)*
Intel Corporation .....................................D....... 408 765-8080
　Chicago  *(G-5209)*
Interplex Daystar Inc ...............................D....... 847 455-2424
　Franklin Park  *(G-10499)*
Ipr Systems Inc .......................................G....... 708 385-7500
　Alsip  *(G-474)*
ITT Water & Wastewater USA Inc ...........G....... 847 966-3700
　Morton Grove  *(G-15205)*
JAD Group Inc .........................................G....... 847 223-1804
　Grayslake  *(G-11348)*
Moline Semicon LLC ...............................G....... 309 755-0433
　East Moline  *(G-8688)*
Motorola International Capital ................G....... 847 576-5000
　Schaumburg  *(G-19651)*
Motorola Solutions Inc ...........................G....... 847 341-3485
　Oak Brook  *(G-16546)*
Motorola Solutions Inc ...........................C....... 847 576-8600
　Schaumburg  *(G-19652)*
Mp Technologies LLC .............................G....... 847 491-4253
　Evanston  *(G-10076)*
Nxp Usa Inc .............................................B....... 847 843-6824
　Hoffman Estates  *(G-12032)*
Printovate Technologies Inc ...................G....... 847 962-3106
　Palatine  *(G-17064)*
Shakthi Solar Inc .....................................G....... 630 842-0893
　Bolingbrook  *(G-2367)*
Tagore Technology Inc ............................G....... 847 790-3799
　Arlington Heights  *(G-851)*
Tempro International Corp ......................G....... 847 677-5370
　Skokie  *(G-20100)*
Toshiba America Electronic ....................G....... 847 484-2400
　Buffalo Grove  *(G-2782)*
Value Engineered Products .....................E....... 708 867-6777
　Rolling Meadows  *(G-18787)*
Vega Wave Systems Inc .........................G....... 630 562-9433
　West Chicago  *(G-21789)*
Wilmar Group LLC ...................................G....... 847 421-6595
　Lake Forest  *(G-12980)*

### SENSORS: Infrared, Solid State

Epir Technologies Inc .............................E....... 630 771-0203
　Bolingbrook  *(G-2307)*
Telehealth Sensors LLC ..........................E....... 630 879-3101
　North Aurora  *(G-16147)*

### SENSORS: Radiation

Capsonic Automotive Inc .......................G....... 847 888-0930
　Elgin  *(G-8977)*
Capsonic Automotive Inc .......................F....... 847 888-7300
　Elgin  *(G-8979)*
River West Radiation Center L ...............G....... 630 264-8580
　Aurora  *(G-1209)*

### SENSORS: Temperature For Motor Windings

Crandall Stats and Sensors Inc ..............E....... 815 979-3340
　Loves Park  *(G-13929)*

### SENSORS: Temperature, Exc Indl Process

Schweitzer Engrg Labs Inc .....................E....... 847 540-3037
　Lake Zurich  *(G-13127)*

### SEPARATORS: Metal Plate

S+s Inspection Inc ..................................G....... 770 493-9332
　Bartlett  *(G-1371)*

### SEPTIC TANK CLEANING SVCS

Clay Vollmar Products Co .......................G....... 847 540-5850
　Lake Zurich  *(G-13054)*
Unique Concrete Concepts Inc ..............F....... 618 466-0700
　Jerseyville  *(G-12427)*

### SEPTIC TANKS: Concrete

Central Concrete Products .....................F....... 217 523-7964
　Springfield  *(G-20412)*
Christopher Concrete Products .............C....... 618 724-2951
　Buckner  *(G-2647)*
Cline Concrete Products ........................F....... 217 283-5012
　Hoopeston  *(G-12107)*
George W Pierson Company ..................E....... 815 726-3351
　Joliet  *(G-12501)*

## SEPTIC TANKS: Concrete

Hinckley Concrete Products Co ............. G ...... 815 286-3235
  Hinckley *(G-11935)*
Kieft Bros Inc ................................. E ...... 630 832-8090
  Elmhurst *(G-9898)*
Kohnens Concrete Products Inc ........... E ...... 618 277-2120
  Germantown *(G-10892)*
Rockford Sewer Co Inc ....................... G ...... 815 877-9060
  Loves Park *(G-13987)*

### SEWAGE & WATER TREATMENT EQPT

Alternative Wastewater Systems .......... G ...... 630 761-8720
  Batavia *(G-1409)*
Carlinville Waste Water Plants ............. G ...... 217 854-6506
  Carlinville *(G-3031)*
Carney Flow Technics LLC ................. G ...... 815 277-2600
  Frankfort *(G-10307)*
Culligan International Company .......... C ...... 847 430-2800
  Rosemont *(G-18994)*
Culligan International Company .......... E ...... 847 430-1338
  Libertyville *(G-13318)*
Dontech Industries Inc ....................... F ...... 847 428-8222
  Gilberts *(G-10917)*
Evac North America Inc ...................... E ...... 815 654-8300
  Cherry Valley *(G-3642)*
Evoqua Water Technologies LLC .......... F ...... 815 921-8325
  Rockford *(G-18372)*
Evoqua Water Technologies LLC .......... G ...... 618 451-1205
  Granite City *(G-11275)*
Extol Hydro Technologies Inc .............. F ...... 708 717-4371
  Palos Park *(G-17128)*
Garrelts & Sons Inc ........................... G ...... 815 385-3821
  McHenry *(G-14508)*
Heat Transfer Laboratories ................. G ...... 708 715-4300
  Oakbrook Terrace *(G-16709)*
Heico Companies LLC ....................... F ...... 312 419-8220
  Chicago *(G-5068)*
Holden Industries Inc ........................ F ...... 847 940-1500
  Deerfield *(G-8013)*
Industrial Specialty Chem Inc ............. E ...... 708 339-1313
  South Holland *(G-20280)*
McDowell Inc .................................. G ...... 309 467-2335
  Eureka *(G-9999)*
Regunathan & Assoc Inc ................... G ...... 630 653-0387
  Wheaton *(G-21975)*
Servetech Water Solutions Inc ............. G ...... 630 784-9050
  Wheaton *(G-21980)*
Siemens Industry Inc ........................ G ...... 815 672-2653
  Streator *(G-20702)*
Tenco Hydro Inc of Illinois ................. G ...... 708 387-0700
  Brookfield *(G-2644)*

### SEWAGE TREATMENT SYSTEMS & EQPT

North Shore Wtr Rclamation Dst .......... E ...... 847 623-6060
  Waukegan *(G-21594)*

### SEWER CLEANING & RODDING SVC

Ave Inc .......................................... G ...... 815 727-0153
  Joliet *(G-12457)*
Coe Equipment Inc ........................... G ...... 217 498-7200
  Rochester *(G-18116)*
Hovi Industries Incorporated .............. E ...... 815 512-7500
  Bolingbrook *(G-2316)*
Rockford Sewer Co Inc ....................... G ...... 815 877-9060
  Loves Park *(G-13987)*
Toppert Jetting Service Inc ................. G ...... 309 755-2240
  Hillsdale *(G-11904)*

### SEWER CLEANING EQPT: Power

Coe Equipment Inc ........................... G ...... 217 498-7200
  Rochester *(G-18116)*
Dml LLC ........................................ G ...... 630 231-8873
  West Chicago *(G-21694)*
Inlet & Pipe Protection Inc ................. G ...... 630 355-3288
  Naperville *(G-15811)*
Sewer Equipment Co America ............. C ...... 815 835-5566
  Dixon *(G-8350)*
Spartan Tool LLC ............................. E ...... 815 539-7411
  Mendota *(G-14733)*
Toppert Jetting Service Inc ................. G ...... 309 755-2240
  Hillsdale *(G-11904)*

### SEWER INSPECTION SVCS

Toppert Jetting Service Inc ................. G ...... 309 755-2240
  Hillsdale *(G-11904)*

### SEWING CONTRACTORS

Choi Brands Inc ............................... C ...... 773 489-2800
  Chicago *(G-4368)*
H & H Fabric Cutters ......................... G ...... 773 772-1904
  Chicago *(G-5018)*

### SEWING KITS: Novelty

Heartland House Designs .................. G ...... 708 383-2278
  Oak Park *(G-16668)*

### SEWING MACHINE REPAIR SHOP

Union Special LLC ........................... C ...... 847 669-5101
  Huntley *(G-12182)*

### SEWING MACHINES & PARTS: Household

Rivercrest Sewing Center ................... G ...... 708 385-2516
  Crestwood *(G-7499)*

### SEWING MACHINES & PARTS: Indl

Union Special LLC ........................... C ...... 847 669-5101
  Huntley *(G-12182)*

### SEWING, NEEDLEWORK & PIECE GOODS STORES

Bearse Manufacturing Co ................... D ...... 773 235-8710
  Chicago *(G-4068)*

### SEWING, NEEDLEWORK & PIECE GOODS STORES: Fabric, Remnants

Annaka Enterprises ........................... G ...... 773 768-5490
  Chicago *(G-3910)*

### SEWING, NEEDLEWORK & PIECE GOODS STORES: Sewing & Needlework

American Fas & Components .............. G ...... 815 397-2698
  Rockford *(G-18262)*
Dan De Tash Knits ............................ G ...... 708 970-6238
  Maywood *(G-14424)*
Embroid ME .................................... G ...... 815 485-4155
  New Lenox *(G-15880)*

### SEXTANTS

Sextant Company ............................. G ...... 847 680-6550
  Gurnee *(G-11503)*

### SHADES: Lamp & Light, Residential

McAteers Wholesale .......................... G ...... 618 233-3400
  Belleville *(G-1654)*

### SHADES: Window

Chicago Shade Makers Inc ................. G ...... 708 597-5590
  Alsip *(G-446)*
Clear View Shade Inc ........................ F ...... 708 535-8631
  Orland Park *(G-16847)*
Custom Window Accents .................... F ...... 815 943-7651
  Harvard *(G-11629)*
Illinois Window Shade Co .................. G ...... 773 743-6025
  Chicago *(G-5159)*
National Temp-Trol Products .............. G ...... 630 920-1919
  Willowbrook *(G-22226)*
Shade Brookline Co .......................... F ...... 773 274-5513
  Chicago *(G-6487)*

### SHAPES & PILINGS, STRUCTURAL: Steel

Accurate Metals Illinois LLC ............... F ...... 815 966-6320
  Rockford *(G-18254)*
Advance Steel Services Inc ................. G ...... 773 619-2977
  Chicago *(G-3764)*
Alter Trading Corporation .................. F ...... 309 828-6084
  Bloomington *(G-2143)*
Brass Creations Inc ........................... G ...... 773 237-7755
  Chicago *(G-4158)*
Gerald R Page Corporation ................. F ...... 847 398-5575
  Prospect Heights *(G-17779)*
Marqutte Stl Sup Fbrcation Inc ............ F ...... 815 433-0178
  Ottawa *(G-16968)*
Matcon Manufacturing Inc ................. E ...... 309 755-1020
  Cordova *(G-7377)*
South Shore Iron Works Inc ................ E ...... 773 264-2267
  Chicago *(G-6547)*
Superior Piling Inc ........................... G ...... 708 496-1196
  Bridgeview *(G-2533)*

### SHAPES: Extruded, Aluminum, NEC

Bending Specialists LLC .................... E ...... 815 726-6281
  Lockport *(G-13706)*
Nichols Aluminum LLC ...................... C ...... 847 634-3150
  Lincolnshire *(G-13467)*
Plymouth Tube Company .................... E ...... 630 393-3550
  Warrenville *(G-21355)*
Plymouth Tube Company .................... D ...... 773 489-0226
  Chicago *(G-6141)*
Plymouth Tube Company .................... D ...... 262 642-8201
  Warrenville *(G-21356)*

### SHAPES: Flat, Rolled, Aluminum, NEC

Petersen Aluminum Corporation .......... D ...... 847 228-7150
  Elk Grove Village *(G-9676)*

### SHEATHING: Asphalt Saturated

American Asp Surfc Recycl Inc ............. F ...... 708 448-9540
  Orland Park *(G-16842)*

### SHEET METAL SPECIALTIES, EXC STAMPED

Belvin J & F Sheet Metal Co ................ G ...... 312 666-5222
  Chicago *(G-4081)*
D & J Metalcraft Company Inc ............. F ...... 773 878-6446
  Chicago *(G-4534)*
EMR Manufacturing Inc ..................... E ...... 630 766-3366
  Wood Dale *(G-22362)*
Exton Corp ...................................... C ...... 847 391-8100
  Des Plaines *(G-8192)*
Fracar Sheet Metal Mfg Co Inc ............ E ...... 847 678-1600
  Schiller Park *(G-19831)*
Genesis Inc ..................................... D ...... 630 351-4400
  Roselle *(G-18943)*
Icon Metalcraft Inc ........................... C ...... 630 766-5600
  Wood Dale *(G-22381)*
IMS Companies LLC ......................... D ...... 847 391-8100
  Des Plaines *(G-8210)*
International Source Solutions ............ G ...... 847 251-8265
  Wilmette *(G-22255)*
Key West Metal Industries Inc ............. C ...... 708 371-1470
  Crestwood *(G-7491)*
Kier Mfg Co .................................... G ...... 630 953-9500
  Addison *(G-168)*
Marcres Manufacturing Inc ................. E ...... 847 439-1808
  Mount Prospect *(G-15346)*
Mellish & Murray Co ......................... F ...... 312 733-3513
  Chicago *(G-5683)*
Metal-Rite Inc .................................. F ...... 708 656-3832
  Cicero *(G-7221)*
Midwest Manufacturing & Distrg .......... F ...... 773 866-1010
  Chicago *(G-5746)*
Northstar Industries Inc .................... D ...... 630 446-7800
  Glendale Heights *(G-11052)*
Prince Fabricators Inc ....................... E ...... 630 588-0088
  Carol Stream *(G-3219)*
Rome Metal Mfg Inc .......................... G ...... 773 287-1755
  Chicago *(G-6389)*
Summit Sheet Metal Specialists ........... F ...... 708 458-8622
  Summit Argo *(G-20766)*
Tella Tool & Mfg Co .......................... D ...... 630 495-0545
  Lombard *(G-13867)*
Thomas Engineering Inc .................... E ...... 815 398-0280
  Rockford *(G-18648)*
Vent Products Co Inc ........................ E ...... 773 521-1900
  Chicago *(G-6881)*

### SHEETING: Laminated Plastic

Acco Brands Corporation ................... A ...... 847 541-9500
  Lake Zurich *(G-13033)*
Diamond Cellophane Pdts Inc ............. E ...... 847 418-3000
  Northbrook *(G-16242)*
Olon Industries Inc (us) ..................... E ...... 630 232-4705
  Geneva *(G-10857)*
Sun Process Converting Inc ................ D ...... 847 593-5656
  Mount Prospect *(G-15376)*
Technologies Dvlpmnt ....................... G ...... 815 943-9922
  Crystal Lake *(G-7662)*

### SHEETS & STRIPS: Aluminum

Arconic Inc ..................................... D ...... 217 431-3800
  Danville *(G-7703)*
J-TEC Metal Products Inc ................... F ...... 630 875-1300
  Itasca *(G-12288)*
Security Metal Products Inc ................ G ...... 815 933-3307
  Bradley *(G-2433)*

# PRODUCT SECTION

# SHOES: Plastic Or Rubber

### SHEETS: Fabric, From Purchased Materials
Bio Star Films LLC .................................. G ....... 773 254-5959
  Chicago (G-4108)

### SHEETS: Solid Fiber, Made From Purchased Materials
Corrugated Supplies Co LLC ..................... E ....... 708 458-5525
  Bedford Park (G-1546)
Glass Haus ............................................... G ....... 815 459-5849
  McHenry (G-14510)
Ruscorr LLC ............................................. G ....... 708 458-5525
  Bedford Park (G-1580)

### SHELLAC
Belzona Gateway Inc ................................ G ....... 888 774-2984
  Caseyville (G-3393)
Jfb Hart Coatings Inc ................................ F ....... 949 724-9737
  Plainfield (G-17611)

### SHELTERED WORKSHOPS
Community Support Systems ..................... D ....... 217 705-4300
  Teutopolis (G-20850)
Five Star Industries Inc ............................. E ....... 618 542-4880
  Du Quoin (G-8554)
Kccdd Inc ................................................ D ....... 309 344-2030
  Galesburg (G-10762)
Kreider Services Incorporated ................... D ....... 815 288-6691
  Dixon (G-8336)
Media Associates Intl Inc .......................... F ....... 630 260-9063
  Carol Stream (G-3192)
Workshop ................................................ E ....... 815 777-2211
  Galena (G-10736)

### SHELVES & SHELVING: Wood
Quantum Storage Systems ........................ G ....... 630 274-6610
  Elk Grove Village (G-9704)

### SHELVING: Office & Store, Exc Wood
Edsal Manufacturing Co Inc ....................... A ....... 773 475-3020
  Chicago (G-4699)
Edsal Manufacturing Co Inc ....................... D ....... 773 475-3013
  Chicago (G-4700)
Imperial Store Fixtures Inc ........................ G ....... 773 348-1137
  Chicago (G-5168)
L & D Group Inc ....................................... B ....... 630 892-8941
  Montgomery (G-15051)
Lyon LLC ................................................. C ....... 630 892-8941
  Montgomery (G-15057)
R B White Inc .......................................... E ....... 309 452-5816
  Normal (G-16086)
REB Steel Equipment Corp ........................ E ....... 773 252-0400
  Chicago (G-6309)
Workspace Lyon Products LLC ................... B ....... 630 892-8941
  Montgomery (G-15073)

### SHIELDS OR ENCLOSURES: Radiator, Sheet Metal
Central Radiator Cabinet Co ...................... G ....... 773 539-1700
  Lena (G-13274)

### SHIMS: Metal
Chicago-Wilcox Mfg Co ............................ E ....... 708 339-5000
  South Holland (G-20257)
Precision Brand Products Inc ..................... E ....... 630 969-7200
  Downers Grove (G-8509)
Precision Steel Warehouse Inc ................... C ....... 800 323-0740
  Franklin Park (G-10560)

### SHIP BLDG/RPRG: Submersible Marine Robots, Manned/Unmanned
Senformatics LLC ..................................... G ....... 217 419-2571
  Champaign (G-3536)

### SHIP BUILDING & REPAIRING: Lighters, Marine
Chips Marine ........................................... G ....... 217 728-2610
  Sullivan (G-20743)

### SHIP BUILDING & REPAIRING: Offshore Sply Boats
Rinker Boat Company ............................... E ....... 574 457-5731
  Chicago (G-6359)

### SHIP BUILDING & REPAIRING: Rigging, Marine
Chicago Flyhouse Incorporated ................. F ....... 773 533-1590
  Chicago (G-4320)

### SHIPBUILDING & REPAIR
Mikes Inc ................................................ D ....... 618 254-4491
  South Roxana (G-20314)
National Maint & Repr Inc ......................... C ....... 618 254-7451
  Hartford (G-11612)
Pactiv LLC ............................................... C
  Lincolnshire (G-13469)
Swath International Limited ...................... G ....... 815 654-4800
  Rockford (G-18638)
Triplex Marine Ltd ................................... G ....... 815 485-0202
  New Lenox (G-15924)
Williamson J Hunter & Company ............... G ....... 847 441-7888
  Winnetka (G-22315)

### SHOCK ABSORBERS: Indl
Egd Manufacturing Inc ............................. G ....... 815 964-2900
  Rockford (G-18359)

### SHOE & BOOT ACCESS
Hanigs Footwear Inc ................................ G ....... 773 248-1977
  Wilmette (G-22253)

### SHOE MATERIALS: Counters
Counter .................................................. G ....... 312 666-5335
  Chicago (G-4482)
Counter Creations LLC ............................ G ....... 815 568-1000
  Marengo (G-14223)
Counter-Intelligence ................................ G ....... 708 974-3326
  Palos Hills (G-17115)
Cupcake Counter LLC .............................. G ....... 312 422-0800
  Chicago (G-4516)
Curt Herrmann Construction Inc ............... G ....... 815 748-0531
  Dekalb (G-8082)
Rays Countertop Shop Inc ........................ F ....... 217 483-2514
  Glenarm (G-10997)

### SHOE MATERIALS: Plastic
Boss Manufacturing Holdings .................... F ....... 309 852-2781
  Kewanee (G-12675)

### SHOE MATERIALS: Quarters
Fifth Quarter .......................................... G ....... 618 346-6659
  Saint Jacob (G-19315)
Fishermans Quarters ............................... G ....... 217 791-5104
  Decatur (G-7882)
French Qrter Prof Off Bldg LLC ................. G ....... 815 972-0681
  Joliet (G-12498)
Painted Quarter Ridge ............................. G ....... 618 534-9734
  Ava (G-1241)
Quarters Concessions Inc ......................... G ....... 847 343-4864
  Carpentersville (G-3299)

### SHOE MATERIALS: Rands
D R Walters ............................................ G ....... 618 926-6337
  Norris City (G-16113)

### SHOE MATERIALS: Rubber
Morrow Shoe and Boot Inc ........................ G ....... 217 342-6833
  Effingham (G-8848)

### SHOE MATERIALS: Uppers
Illinois Hand & Upper Extremit .................. G ....... 847 956-0099
  Arlington Heights (G-774)
Upper Deck Sports Bar ............................ G ....... 815 517-0682
  Dekalb (G-8129)
Upper Urban Green Prprty Maint .............. G ....... 312 218-5903
  Chicago (G-6841)
Uppercase Living - Indepndent ................. G ....... 309 657-3054
  Mapleton (G-14214)

### SHOE STORES
Crocs Inc ................................................ F ....... 630 820-3572
  Aurora (G-988)
Hanigs Footwear Inc ................................ G ....... 773 248-1977
  Wilmette (G-22253)
New Step Orthotic Lab Inc ........................ F ....... 618 208-4444
  Maryville (G-14345)

### SHOE STORES: Athletic
Athletic Outfitters Inc ............................. G ....... 815 942-6696
  Morris (G-15094)
Foot Locker Retail Inc .............................. G ....... 630 678-0155
  Lombard (G-13801)
Road Runner Sports Inc ........................... F ....... 847 719-8941
  Palatine (G-17068)

### SHOE STORES: Boots, Men's
Pryco Inc ................................................ E ....... 217 364-4467
  Mechanicsburg (G-14574)

### SHOE STORES: Boots, Women's
Morrow Shoe and Boot Inc ........................ G ....... 217 342-6833
  Effingham (G-8848)

### SHOE STORES: Custom & Orthopedic
London Shoe Shop & Western Wr .............. G ....... 618 345-9570
  Collinsville (G-7330)
Springfield Sales Assoc Inc ....................... G ....... 217 529-6987
  Springfield (G-20533)

### SHOE STORES: Men's
BMW Sportswear Inc ................................ G ....... 773 265-0110
  Chicago (G-4133)
Lids Corporation ..................................... G ....... 708 873-9606
  Orland Park (G-16873)
Mennon Rubber & Safety Pdts ................... G ....... 847 678-8250
  Schiller Park (G-19849)

### SHOES & BOOTS WHOLESALERS
Vertex International Inc .......................... G ....... 312 242-1864
  Oak Brook (G-16568)

### SHOES: Infants' & Children's
Red Wing Brands America Inc ................... G ....... 815 394-1328
  Rockford (G-18552)

### SHOES: Men's
Belleville Shoe Mfg Co ............................. B ....... 618 233-5600
  Belleville (G-1612)
Leos Dancewear Inc ................................ D ....... 773 889-7700
  River Forest (G-17998)
London Shoe Shop & Western Wr .............. G ....... 618 345-9570
  Collinsville (G-7330)
Steven Madden Ltd ................................. D ....... 773 276-5486
  Chicago (G-6594)

### SHOES: Orthopedic, Men's
Springfield Sales Assoc Inc ....................... G ....... 217 529-6987
  Springfield (G-20533)

### SHOES: Orthopedic, Women's
Springfield Sales Assoc Inc ....................... G ....... 217 529-6987
  Springfield (G-20533)

### SHOES: Plastic Or Rubber
Honeywell Safety Pdts USA Inc ................. C ....... 309 786-7741
  Rock Island (G-18182)
Leos Dancewear Inc ................................ D ....... 773 889-7700
  River Forest (G-17998)
Nike Inc .................................................. E ....... 773 846-5460
  Chicago (G-5918)
Nike Inc .................................................. E ....... 630 585-9568
  Aurora (G-1056)
Polyconversions Inc ................................ E ....... 217 893-3330
  Rantoul (G-17935)
Standard Safety Equipment Co .................. E ....... 815 363-8565
  McHenry (G-14556)
Vans Inc .................................................. G ....... 847 673-0628
  Skokie (G-20108)

# SHOES: Rubber Or Rubber Soled Fabric Uppers

### SHOES: Rubber Or Rubber Soled Fabric Uppers
Crocs Inc .......................................... F ....... 630 820-3572
  Aurora  *(G-988)*

### SHOES: Women's
Leos Dancewear Inc ..................... D ...... 773 889-7700
  River Forest  *(G-17998)*

### SHOES: Women's, Dress
Bone & Rattle Inc .......................... G ....... 312 813-8830
  Chicago  *(G-4142)*

### SHOPPING CENTERS & MALLS
Mfp Holding Co .............................. ........ 312 666-3366
  Chicago  *(G-5714)*

### SHOT PEENING SVC
Axletech International ................... D ...... 773 264-1234
  Chicago  *(G-4006)*
Metal Improvement Company LLC ... E ...... 630 543-4950
  Addison  *(G-201)*

### SHOWCASES & DISPLAY FIXTURES: Office & Store
Acrylic Service Inc ........................ G ....... 630 543-0336
  Addison  *(G-20)*
Bark Project Management Inc ..... G ....... 630 964-5876
  Woodridge  *(G-22455)*
Idx Corporation .............................. F ....... 312 600-9783
  Chicago  *(G-5143)*
Innovative Mktg Solutions Inc ..... F ....... 630 227-4300
  Schaumburg  *(G-19568)*
Inventive Display Group LLC ...... ........ 847 588-1100
  Niles  *(G-15990)*
Murray Cabinetry & Tops Inc ..... G ....... 815 672-6992
  Streator  *(G-20696)*
Schaumburg Specialties Co ....... ........ 847 451-0070
  Schaumburg  *(G-19721)*
Wiremasters Incorporated ............ E ....... 773 254-3700
  Chicago  *(G-7005)*

### SHOWER STALLS: Metal
T J M & Associates Inc ................ G ....... 847 382-1993
  Lake Barrington  *(G-12825)*

### SHOWER STALLS: Plastic & Fiberglass
Swan Surfaces LLC ...................... C ....... 618 532-5673
  Centralia  *(G-3435)*

### SHREDDERS: Indl & Commercial
Addison Business Systems Inc .... G ....... 708 371-5454
  Palos Heights  *(G-17098)*
Dun-Rite Tool & Machine Co ...... E ....... 815 758-5464
  Cortland  *(G-7388)*
Lane Industries Inc ...................... E ....... 847 498-6650
  Northbrook  *(G-16292)*

### SHUTTERS, DOOR & WINDOW: Metal
Chicagone Developers Inc .......... G ....... 773 783-2105
  Chicago  *(G-4364)*
Qualitas Manufacturing Inc ......... D ...... 630 529-7111
  Itasca  *(G-12346)*

### SHUTTERS, DOOR & WINDOW: Plastic
Mc Dist & Mfg Co ........................ F ....... 630 628-5180
  Addison  *(G-195)*
Perfect Shutters Inc ..................... E ....... 815 648-2401
  Hebron  *(G-11724)*
Qualitas Manufacturing Inc ......... D ...... 630 529-7111
  Itasca  *(G-12346)*

### SHUTTERS: Door, Wood
Original Shutter Man ................... G ....... 773 966-7160
  Chicago  *(G-6013)*

### SHUTTERS: Window, Wood
Sunburst Shutters Illinois ............ F ....... 847 697-4000
  Elgin  *(G-9196)*

### SIDING & STRUCTURAL MATERIALS: Wood
Lamboo Inc ..................................... E ....... 866 966-2999
  Litchfield  *(G-13692)*
Lumberyard Suppliers Inc ........... F ....... 618 931-0315
  Granite City  *(G-11291)*
Png Transport LLC ....................... G ....... 312 218-8116
  Chicago  *(G-6144)*
Weatherguard Buildings .............. G ....... 217 894-6213
  Clayton  *(G-7270)*

### SIDING: Sheet Metal
Litt Aluminium & Shtmtl Co ........ G ....... 708 366-4720
  Westchester  *(G-21847)*
Metal Sales Manufacturing Corp ... E ....... 309 787-1200
  Rock Island  *(G-18189)*
RPS Engineering Inc .................... F ....... 847 931-1950
  Elgin  *(G-9168)*
Vorteq Coil Finishers LLC ........... E ....... 847 455-7200
  Franklin Park  *(G-10623)*

### SIGN LETTERING & PAINTING SVCS
Central Illinois Sign Company .... G ....... 217 523-4740
  Springfield  *(G-20414)*
Greg Signs ...................................... ........ 815 726-5655
  Joliet  *(G-12504)*
J & D Instant Signs ...................... ........ 847 965-2800
  Morton Grove  *(G-15206)*
Muir Omni Graphics Inc .............. ........ 309 673-7034
  Peoria  *(G-17413)*
P N K Ventures Inc ....................... ........ 630 527-0500
  Naperville  *(G-15720)*

### SIGN PAINTING & LETTERING SHOP
Distinctive SIGns& The Neon Ex ... G ....... 847 245-7159
  Grayslake  *(G-11333)*
E Z Sign Co Inc ............................ ........ 815 469-4080
  Oak Forest  *(G-16578)*
Enterprise Signs Inc .................... G ....... 773 614-8324
  Chicago  *(G-4760)*
Gadge Signs Inc ........................... ........ 815 462-4490
  New Lenox  *(G-15882)*
Grate Signs Inc ............................. E ....... 815 729-9700
  Joliet  *(G-12503)*
Harder Signs Inc ........................... F ....... 815 874-7777
  Rockford  *(G-18413)*
Hughes & Son Inc ........................ ........ 815 459-1887
  Crystal Lake  *(G-7589)*
Independent Outdoor Ltd ............ G ....... 630 960-2460
  Downers Grove  *(G-8465)*
Johnson Sign Co ........................... ........ 847 678-2092
  Franklin Park  *(G-10509)*
Krick Enterprises Inc ................... ........ 630 515-1085
  Downers Grove  *(G-8470)*
Lettermen Signage Inc ................ ........ 708 479-5161
  Mokena  *(G-14879)*
Midwest Signworks ....................... ........ 815 942-3517
  Morris  *(G-15119)*
Parvin-Clauss Sign Co Inc .......... E ....... 866 490-2877
  Carol Stream  *(G-3211)*
Qc Finishers Inc ............................ ........ 847 678-2660
  Franklin Park  *(G-10565)*
Rutke Signs Inc ............................. G ....... 708 841-6464
  Westchester  *(G-21853)*
Sign Palace Inc ............................. ........ 847 228-7446
  Elk Grove Village  *(G-9738)*
Signs Today Inc ............................ ........ 847 934-9777
  Palatine  *(G-17074)*
Stevens Sign Co Inc .................... G ....... 708 562-4888
  Northlake  *(G-16453)*

### SIGNALING APPARATUS: Electric
Nafisco Inc ..................................... ........ 815 372-3300
  Romeoville  *(G-18851)*

### SIGNALING DEVICES: Sound, Electrical
Jk Audio Inc ................................... F ....... 815 786-2929
  Sandwich  *(G-19370)*

### SIGNALS: Railroad, Electric
AR Concepts USA Inc .................. ........ 847 392-4608
  Palatine  *(G-17002)*
Signalmasters Inc .......................... F ....... 708 534-3330
  Monee  *(G-15001)*
Tool Automation Enterprises ...... G ....... 708 799-6847
  East Hazel Crest  *(G-8666)*
Western-Cullen-Hayes Inc .......... D ...... 773 254-9600
  Chicago  *(G-6964)*

### SIGNALS: Traffic Control, Electric
John Thomas Inc .......................... E ....... 815 288-2343
  Dixon  *(G-8334)*
N E S Traffic Safety ..................... F ....... 312 603-7444
  Chicago  *(G-5846)*
Traffco Products LLC .................. G ....... 773 374-6645
  Chicago  *(G-6754)*

### SIGNALS: Transportation
Lecip Inc ........................................ ........ 312 626-2525
  Bensenville  *(G-1939)*

### SIGNS & ADVERTISING SPECIALTIES
1187 Creative LLC ....................... F ....... 618 457-1187
  Carbondale  *(G-2999)*
3-D Resource ................................ G ....... 815 899-8600
  Sycamore  *(G-20784)*
A & E Rubber Stamp Corp .......... ........ 312 575-1416
  Chicago  *(G-3679)*
A & J Signs ................................... F ....... 815 476-0128
  Wilmington  *(G-22268)*
A 1 Trophies Awards & Engrv .... G ....... 630 837-6000
  Streamwood  *(G-20638)*
A Plus Signs Inc ........................... G ....... 708 534-2030
  Monee  *(G-14990)*
A To Z Engraving Co Inc ............ G ....... 847 526-7396
  Wauconda  *(G-21435)*
Accurate Repro Inc ...................... F ....... 630 428-4433
  Naperville  *(G-15588)*
Ace Sign Co ................................... E ....... 217 522-8417
  Springfield  *(G-20384)*
Action Graphics and Signs Inc .. ........ 618 939-5755
  Columbia  *(G-7350)*
Ad Special TZ Inc ......................... ........ 847 845-6767
  Buffalo Grove  *(G-2650)*
Adams Outdoor Advg Ltd Partnr ... E ....... 309 692-2482
  Peoria  *(G-17302)*
Addison Engraving Inc ................ ........ 630 833-9123
  Villa Park  *(G-21232)*
Addison Pro Plastics Inc ............. G ....... 630 543-6770
  Addison  *(G-24)*
Adnama Inc .................................... ........ 312 922-0509
  Chicago  *(G-3754)*
Advance Press Sign Inc .............. ........ 630 833-1600
  Villa Park  *(G-21233)*
Advertising Premiums Inc .......... ........ 888 364-9710
  Mount Prospect  *(G-15308)*
Advertising Products Inc ............. ........ 847 758-0415
  Elk Grove Village  *(G-9281)*
Albright Enterprises Inc .............. G ....... 630 357-2300
  Naperville  *(G-15593)*
Alexander Manufacturing Co ..... D ...... 309 728-2224
  Towanda  *(G-20978)*
Alexander Signs & Designs Inc ... G ....... 815 933-3100
  Bourbonnais  *(G-2386)*
All Signs & Wonders Co ............. G ....... 630 232-9019
  Geneva  *(G-10807)*
All-Right Sign Inc ......................... F ....... 708 754-6366
  Steger  *(G-20567)*
Allied Die Casting Corporation ... E ....... 815 385-9330
  McHenry  *(G-14479)*
Alphabet Shop Inc ........................ E ....... 847 888-3150
  Elgin  *(G-8946)*
American Advertising Assoc Inc ... G ....... 773 312-5110
  Chicago  *(G-3847)*
Anbek Inc ....................................... ........ 815 672-6087
  La Salle  *(G-12763)*
Anbek Inc ....................................... F ....... 815 223-0734
  La Salle  *(G-12764)*
Antolak Management Co Inc ..... G ....... 312 464-1800
  Chicago  *(G-3917)*
Arrow Signs .................................. F ....... 618 466-0818
  Godfrey  *(G-11222)*
Art Wire Works Inc ...................... F ....... 708 458-3993
  Bedford Park  *(G-1538)*
Artistic Engraving Corporation ... G ....... 708 409-0149
  Broadview  *(G-2560)*
Asi Sign Systems Inc .................. G ....... 773 478-5241
  Chicago  *(G-3963)*
Associated Attractions Entps ..... F ....... 773 376-1900
  Chicago  *(G-3967)*
Athena Design Group Inc ........... E ....... 312 733-2828
  Chicago  *(G-3974)*
Aubrey Sign Co Inc ...................... G ....... 630 482-9901
  Batavia  *(G-1418)*

# PRODUCT SECTION
## SIGNS & ADVERTISING SPECIALTIES

| Company | Code | Phone |
|---|---|---|
| Authentic Street Signs Inc — Saint Peter (G-19320) | G | 618 349-8878 |
| Award Emblem Mfg Co Inc — Bolingbrook (G-2281) | F | 630 739-0800 |
| Awnings Express — Chicago (G-4005) | G | 773 579-1437 |
| Azusa Inc — Mount Vernon (G-15399) | G | 618 244-6591 |
| B Gunther & Co — Lisle (G-13567) | F | 630 969-5595 |
| Bards Products Inc — Mundelein (G-15475) | F | 800 323-5499 |
| Barry Signs Inc — Chicago (G-4049) | G | 773 327-1183 |
| Beard Enterprises Inc — Naperville (G-15603) | G | 630 357-3278 |
| Bella Sign Co — Roselle (G-18928) | G | 630 539-0543 |
| Bendsen Signs & Graphics Inc — Decatur (G-7845) | F | 217 877-2345 |
| Best Advertising Spc & Prtg — Worth (G-22633) | G | 708 448-1110 |
| Bick Broadcasting Inc — Quincy (G-17804) | G | 217 223-9693 |
| Biron Studio General Svcs Inc — Bridgeview (G-2470) | G | 708 229-2600 |
| Blue Diamond Athletic Disp Inc — Downers Grove (G-8397) | G | 847 414-9971 |
| Boatman Signs — Salem (G-19328) | G | 618 548-6567 |
| Bright Light Sign Company Inc — Lake Zurich (G-13047) | G | 847 550-8902 |
| Brownfield Sports Inc — Urbana (G-21074) | G | 217 367-8321 |
| Budget Sign — La Grange (G-12728) | G | 708 354-7512 |
| Budget Signs — Wood River (G-22441) | F | 618 259-4460 |
| Cacini Inc — Schaumburg (G-19467) | G | 847 884-1162 |
| Campbell Management Services — Mundelein (G-15482) | G | 847 566-9020 |
| Canham Graphics — Springfield (G-20404) | G | 217 585-5085 |
| Castino & Associates Inc — Northbrook (G-16218) | G | 847 291-7446 |
| Charleston Industries Inc — Elk Grove Village (G-9365) | G | 847 228-7150 |
| Chicago Scenic Studios Inc — Chicago (G-4345) | D | 312 274-9900 |
| Chicago Sign Group — Vernon Hills (G-21154) | G | 847 899-9021 |
| Churchill Wimslow Corporation — Chicago (G-4374) | G | 312 759-8911 |
| City of Chicago — Chicago (G-4385) | G | 773 686-2254 |
| Classic Midwest Die Mold Inc — Chicago (G-4393) | F | 773 227-8000 |
| Classique Signs & Engrv Inc — Quincy (G-17813) | G | 217 228-7446 |
| Clover Signs — Chicago (G-4407) | G | 773 588-2828 |
| Color Signs — Arlington Heights (G-736) | G | 847 368-0101 |
| Compliancesigns Inc — Chadwick (G-3441) | D | 800 578-1245 |
| Contempo Autographic & Signs — Crestwood (G-7483) | G | 708 371-5499 |
| Cook Fabrication Signs Graphic — Deer Creek (G-7962) | G | 309 360-3805 |
| Corporate Identification Solut — Chicago (G-4475) | E | 773 763-9600 |
| Corporate Sign Systems Inc — Roselle (G-18936) | F | 847 882-6100 |
| Crown Trophy — East Peoria (G-8707) | G | 309 699-1766 |
| Cubby Hole of Carlinville Inc — Carlinville (G-3035) | F | 217 854-8511 |
| Custom Enterprises — Benton (G-2025) | G | 618 439-6626 |
| Custom Signs On Metal LLC — Tilton (G-20880) | F | 217 443-5347 |
| Custom Telephone Printing Inc — Woodstock (G-22557) | F | 815 338-0000 |
| Custom Trophies — Decatur (G-7863) | G | 217 422-3353 |
| D E Signs & Storage LLC — Waterloo (G-21401) | G | 618 939-8050 |
| D&J Arlington Heights Inc — Arlington Heights (G-743) | G | 847 577-8200 |
| DAmico Associates Inc — Northbrook (G-16239) | G | 847 291-7446 |
| Dans Rubber Stamp & Signs — Rockford (G-18333) | G | 815 964-5603 |
| Dard Products Inc — Evanston (G-10025) | C | 847 328-5000 |
| Darnall Printing — Bloomington (G-2161) | G | 309 827-7212 |
| DE Asbury Inc — Quincy (G-17820) | E | 217 222-0617 |
| De Luca Visual Solutions Inc — Schaumburg (G-19500) | G | 847 884-6300 |
| Derse Inc — Waukegan (G-21549) | G | 847 473-2149 |
| Design Group Signage Corp — Des Plaines (G-8185) | F | 847 390-0350 |
| Designovations Inc — Stillman Valley (G-20625) | G | 815 645-8598 |
| Designs Unlimited — Pinckneyville (G-17547) | G | 618 357-6728 |
| Dewrich Inc — Gurnee (G-11438) | G | 847 249-7445 |
| Dgs Import Inc — Chicago (G-4591) | E | 847 595-7016 |
| Dicke Tool Company — Downers Grove (G-8429) | E | 630 969-0050 |
| Dickey Sign Co — Granite City (G-11273) | G | 618 797-1262 |
| Digital Artz LLC — Highland (G-11783) | G | 618 651-1500 |
| Digital Edge Signs Inc — Antioch (G-629) | G | 847 838-4760 |
| Digital Factory Inc — Chicago (G-4599) | G | 708 320-9879 |
| Digital Greensigns Inc — Chicago (G-4600) | G | 312 624-8550 |
| Digital Minds Inc — Rosemont (G-18998) | G | 847 430-3390 |
| Distinctive SIGns & The Neon Ex — Grayslake (G-11333) | G | 847 245-7159 |
| Diversified Adtee Inc — Normal (G-16069) | E | 309 454-2555 |
| Dyna Comp Inc — Crystal Lake (G-7568) | G | 815 455-5570 |
| E A A Enterprises Inc — Villa Park (G-21249) | G | 630 279-0150 |
| E B G B Inc — Elk Grove Village (G-9441) | G | 847 228-9333 |
| E I T Inc — Naperville (G-15649) | G | 630 359-3543 |
| E K Kuhn Inc — Sycamore (G-20795) | G | 815 899-9211 |
| E Z Sign Co Inc — Oak Forest (G-16578) | G | 815 469-4080 |
| East Bank Neon Inc — Collinsville (G-7322) | G | 618 345-9517 |
| East Coast Signs Advertising — Elk Grove Village (G-9447) | D | 215 458-9042 |
| Eberhart Sign & Lighting Co — Edwardsville (G-8797) | G | 618 656-7256 |
| Edventure Promotions Inc — Chicago (G-4702) | G | 312 440-1800 |
| Effingham Signs & Graphics — Effingham (G-8836) | G | 217 347-8711 |
| Eisendrath Inc — Highland Park (G-11830) | G | 847 432-3899 |
| Elk Grove Signs Inc — Elk Grove Village (G-9452) | G | 847 427-0005 |
| Elm Street Design Inc — Crystal Lake (G-7573) | G | 815 455-3622 |
| Enchanted Signs of Rockford — Rockford (G-18364) | G | 815 874-5100 |
| Enterprise Signs Inc — Chicago (G-4760) | G | 773 614-8324 |
| Exclusively Expo — Romeoville (G-18822) | F | 630 378-4600 |
| Exex Holding Corporation — Romeoville (G-18823) | G | 815 703-7295 |
| Fast Signs — Chicago (G-4816) | G | 773 698-8115 |
| Fast Signs — Joliet (G-12493) | G | 815 730-7828 |
| Fast Signs 590 — Kankakee (G-12615) | G | 815 937-1855 |
| Fastsigns — Chicago (G-4818) | G | 312 344-1765 |
| Fastsigns — Elk Grove Village (G-9477) | G | 847 981-1965 |
| Fastsigns — Chicago (G-4819) | G | 312 332-7446 |
| Fastsigns — Lincolnwood (G-13509) | G | 847 675-1600 |
| Fastsigns — Libertyville (G-13323) | G | 847 680-7446 |
| Fastsigns International — Morton Grove (G-15197) | G | 847 967-7222 |
| Federal Heath Sign Company LLC — Willowbrook (G-22211) | F | 630 887-6800 |
| Federal Signal Corporation — University Park (G-21049) | D | 708 534-3400 |
| Fedex Office & Print Svcs Inc — Peoria (G-17359) | E | 309 685-4093 |
| Fedex Office & Print Svcs Inc — Arlington Heights (G-754) | E | 847 670-4100 |
| FM Graphic Impressions Inc — Aurora (G-1153) | E | 630 897-8788 |
| Forest Awards & Engraving — Wood Dale (G-22371) | G | 630 595-2242 |
| Fourth Quarter Holdings Inc — Gurnee (G-11449) | G | 847 249-7445 |
| Fox Valley Signs Inc — Aurora (G-1158) | G | 630 896-3113 |
| Frank O Carlson & Co Inc — Chicago (G-4884) | F | 773 847-6900 |
| Franks Dgtal Prtg Off Sups Inc — Aurora (G-1159) | G | 630 892-2511 |
| Friendly Signs Inc — Kankakee (G-12618) | G | 815 933-7070 |
| Frontier Signs & Lighting — Chillicothe (G-7165) | G | 309 694-7300 |
| G & J Associates Inc — Arlington Heights (G-756) | G | 847 255-0123 |
| G and D Enterprises Inc — Arlington Heights (G-757) | E | 847 981-8661 |
| G D S Professional Bus Display — Bloomington (G-2168) | E | 309 829-3298 |
| G M Sign Inc — Round Lake (G-19056) | D | 847 546-0424 |
| Gadge Signs Inc — New Lenox (G-15882) | G | 815 462-4490 |
| Gaytan Signs & Co Inc — Joliet (G-12500) | G | 815 726-2975 |
| Geebees Inc — Peoria (G-17369) | G | 309 682-5300 |
| Gemcom Inc — Willow Springs (G-22196) | G | 800 871-6840 |
| General Motor Sign — Round Lake (G-19057) | G | 847 546-0424 |
| George Lauterer Corporation — Chicago (G-4943) | E | 312 913-1881 |
| GL Led LLC — Chicago (G-4953) | G | 312 600-9363 |
| Goalgetters Inc — La Grange (G-12733) | G | 708 579-9800 |
| Granite Gallery Inc — Chicago (G-4986) | G | 773 279-9200 |
| H L M Sales Inc — Barrington (G-1283) | G | 815 455-6922 |
| Hanover Displays Inc — Elk Grove Village (G-9516) | F | 773 334-9934 |
| Hardin Signs Inc — Peoria (G-17379) | F | 309 688-4111 |
| Haus Sign Incorporated — Bridgeview (G-2497) | G | 708 598-8740 |
| Heavy Hitters LLC — Calumet City (G-2942) | G | 630 258-2991 |
| Heiman Sign Studio — Rockford (G-18416) | G | 815 397-6909 |
| Heritage Signs Ltd — Libertyville (G-13331) | G | 847 549-1942 |
| Hermann Gene Signs & Service — Mount Vernon (G-15411) | G | 618 244-3681 |
| Heron Bay Inc — Bloomington (G-2178) | G | 309 661-1300 |
| HM Witt & Co — Chicago (G-5093) | E | 773 250-5000 |
| Holland Design Group Inc — Wauconda (G-21470) | F | 847 526-8848 |
| Holmes Associates Inc — Gurnee (G-11460) | G | 847 336-4515 |
| Horizon Downing LLC — Dekalb (G-8097) | E | 815 758-6867 |
| House of Doolittle Ltd — Arlington Heights (G-769) | E | 847 593-3417 |
| Howard Displays Inc — Highland Park (G-11841) | F | |
| Hughes & Son Inc — Crystal Lake (G-7589) | G | 815 459-1887 |
| Icon Identity Solutions Inc — Elk Grove Village (G-9531) | C | 847 364-2250 |

Employee Codes: A=Over 500 employees, B=251-500, C=101-250, D=51-100, E=20-50, F=10-19, G=3-9

**Icon Identity Solutions Inc** E 847 364-2250
Elk Grove Village *(G-9532)*
**Ideal Box Co** C 708 594-3100
Chicago *(G-5140)*
**Ideal Sign Solutions LLC** G 847 695-9091
Hoffman Estates *(G-12017)*
**Idek Graphics LLC** G 630 530-1232
Elmhurst *(G-9883)*
**Identiti Resources Ltd** E 847 301-0510
Schaumburg *(G-19562)*
**Idot North Side Sign Shop** G 847 705-4033
Schaumburg *(G-19563)*
**Illini/Altco Inc** D 847 549-0321
Vernon Hills *(G-21173)*
**Image Signs Inc** F 815 282-4141
Loves Park *(G-13947)*
**Imagecare Maintenance Svcs LLC** G 847 631-3306
Elk Grove Village *(G-9540)*
**Images Alive Ltd** G 847 498-5550
Northbrook *(G-16274)*
**Imageworks Manufacturing Inc** E 708 503-1122
Park Forest *(G-17172)*
**Impact Signs & Graphics Inc** G 708 469-7178
La Grange *(G-12738)*
**Independent Outdoor Ltd** G 630 960-2460
Downers Grove *(G-8465)*
**Infinity Cmmncations Group Ltd** F 708 352-1086
Countryside *(G-7434)*
**Insignia Design Ltd** G 301 254-9221
Rolling Meadows *(G-18734)*
**Integrated Mdsg Systems LLC** D 630 571-2020
Oak Brook *(G-16525)*
**Integrity Sign Company** F 708 532-5038
Mokena *(G-14875)*
**Isates Inc** G 309 691-8822
Peoria *(G-17391)*
**Ivan Carlson Associates Inc** E 312 829-4616
Chicago *(G-5248)*
**J & D Instant Signs** G 847 965-2800
Morton Grove *(G-15206)*
**J M Signs** G 847 945-7446
Deerfield *(G-8015)*
**Jacobson Acqstion Holdings LLC** C 847 623-1414
Waukegan *(G-21574)*
**Jamali Kopy Kat Printing Inc** G 708 544-6164
Bellwood *(G-1711)*
**JAS Dahern Signs** G 773 254-0717
Chicago *(G-5281)*
**Joans Trophy & Plaque Co** E 309 674-6500
Peoria *(G-17393)*
**Jodaat Inc** G 630 916-7776
Lombard *(G-13815)*
**John Parker Advertising Co** G 217 892-4118
Rantoul *(G-17931)*
**Johnson Sign Co** G 847 678-2092
Franklin Park *(G-10509)*
**Jonem Grp Inc DBA Sign A Rama** G 224 848-4620
Lake Barrington *(G-12813)*
**Joseph D Smithies** G 618 632-6141
Caseyville *(G-3399)*
**K 9 Tag Company Inc** G 847 304-8247
Waukegan *(G-21575)*
**K R O Enterprises Ltd** G 309 797-2213
Moline *(G-14949)*
**Kane Graphical Corporation** E 773 384-1200
Chicago *(G-5358)*
**Kellys Sign Shop** G 217 477-0167
Danville *(G-7742)*
**Key Outdoor Inc** G 815 224-4742
La Salle *(G-12780)*
**Keystone Display Inc** D 815 648-2456
Hebron *(G-11721)*
**Keystone Printing & Publishing** G 815 678-2591
Richmond *(G-17965)*
**Kim Gilmore** G 847 931-1511
Elgin *(G-9089)*
**Kornick Enterprises LLC** G 847 884-1162
Schaumburg *(G-19605)*
**L & C Imaging Inc** G 309 829-1802
Bloomington *(G-2192)*
**Lange Sign Group** G 815 747-2448
East Dubuque *(G-8619)*
**Laux Grafix Inc** G 618 337-4558
East Saint Louis *(G-8759)*
**Legacy 3d LLC** F 815 727-5454
Crest Hill *(G-7462)*
**Lena Sign Shop** G 815 369-9090
Lena *(G-13279)*
**Leo Burnett Company Inc** C 312 220-5959
Chicago *(G-5493)*
**Leos Sign** G 773 227-2460
Chicago *(G-5494)*
**Lettering Specialists Inc** F 847 674-3414
Skokie *(G-20029)*
**Lettermen Signage Inc** G 708 479-5161
Mokena *(G-14879)*
**Letters Unlimited Inc** G 847 891-7811
Schaumburg *(G-19615)*
**Light Waves LLC** F 847 251-1622
Wilmette *(G-22259)*
**Lightning Graphic** G 815 623-1937
Roscoe *(G-18903)*
**Lincolnland Archtctral Grphics** G 217 629-9009
Glenarm *(G-10996)*
**Lonelino Sign Company Inc** G 217 243-2444
Jacksonville *(G-12400)*
**Lou Plucinski** G 815 758-7888
Dekalb *(G-8103)*
**M & R Media Inc** G 847 884-6300
Schaumburg *(G-19628)*
**Magnetic Signs** G 773 476-6551
Chicago *(G-5602)*
**Main Street Visuals Inc** G 847 869-7446
Morton Grove *(G-15217)*
**Mandel Metals Inc** G 847 455-7446
Franklin Park *(G-10522)*
**Mark Collins** G 847 324-5500
Skokie *(G-20033)*
**Mark Your Space Inc** G 630 289-7082
Bartlett *(G-1361)*
**Marking Specialists/Poly** F 847 793-8100
Buffalo Grove *(G-2731)*
**Massey Grafix** G 815 644-4620
Watseka *(G-21422)*
**Matrex Exhibits Inc** D 630 628-2233
Addison *(G-192)*
**Maxs Screen Machine Inc** G 773 878-4949
Chicago *(G-5659)*
**Mbm Business Assistance Inc** G 217 398-6600
Champaign *(G-3512)*
**Meagher Sign & Graphics Inc** G 618 662-7446
Flora *(G-10211)*
**Metal Box International Inc** C 847 455-8500
Franklin Park *(G-10529)*
**Mich Enterprises Inc** F 630 616-9000
Wood Dale *(G-22399)*
**Michael Reggis Clark** G 618 533-3841
Centralia *(G-3422)*
**Midway Displays Inc** E 708 563-2323
Bedford Park *(G-1563)*
**Midwest Nameplate Corp** G 708 614-0606
Orland Park *(G-16875)*
**Midwest Sign & Lighting Inc** G 708 365-5555
Country Club Hills *(G-7410)*
**Midwest Signs & Structures Inc** G 847 249-8398
Gurnee *(G-11473)*
**Midwest Signworks** G 815 942-3517
Morris *(G-15119)*
**Midwest Sun-Ray Lighting & Sig** F 618 656-2884
Granite City *(G-11296)*
**Minerva Sportswear Inc** F 309 661-2387
Bloomington *(G-2201)*
**Mission Signs Inc** G 630 243-6731
Lemont *(G-13242)*
**My-Signguycom Inc** G 888 223-9703
Chicago *(G-5842)*
**N Bujarski Inc** G 847 884-1600
Schaumburg *(G-19660)*
**Nafisco Inc** F 815 372-3300
Romeoville *(G-18851)*
**Nameplate Robinson & Precision** G 847 678-2255
Franklin Park *(G-10538)*
**Nathan Winston Service Inc** G 815 758-4545
Dekalb *(G-8109)*
**Neil International Inc** G 847 549-7627
Vernon Hills *(G-21185)*
**Neon Design Inc** G 773 880-5020
Chicago *(G-5886)*
**Neon Express Signs** G 773 463-7335
Chicago *(G-5887)*
**Newport Printing Services Inc** G 847 632-1000
Schaumburg *(G-19664)*
**Nite Lite Signs & Balloons Inc** G 630 953-2866
Addison *(G-229)*
**Nordmeyer Graphics** G 815 697-2634
Chebanse *(G-3631)*
**Nsi Signs Inc** F 630 433-3525
Addison *(G-230)*
**Nu-Art Printing** G 618 533-9971
Centralia *(G-3425)*
**Nu-Dell Manufacturing Co Inc** F 847 803-4500
Chicago *(G-5953)*
**Nu-Way Signs Inc** F 847 243-0164
Wheeling *(G-22110)*
**Nycor Products Inc** G 815 727-9883
Joliet *(G-12547)*
**O Signs Inc** G 312 888-3386
Chicago *(G-5959)*
**Oakley Signs & Graphics Inc** F 224 612-5045
Des Plaines *(G-8245)*
**Ogden Offset Printers Inc** G 773 284-7797
Chicago *(G-5973)*
**Olympic Signs Inc** E 630 424-6100
Lombard *(G-13835)*
**Olympic Trophy and Awards Co** F 773 631-9500
Chicago *(G-5987)*
**Orbit Enterprises Inc** G 630 469-3405
Oak Brook *(G-16553)*
**Outdoor Solutions Team Inc** E 312 446-4220
Northbrook *(G-16328)*
**P & L Mark-It Inc** E 630 879-7590
Batavia *(G-1478)*
**P N K Ventures Inc** G 630 527-0500
Naperville *(G-15720)*
**Paddock Industries Inc** F 618 277-1580
Smithton *(G-20123)*
**Pan-O-Graphics Inc** G 630 834-7123
Elmhurst *(G-9918)*
**Paramount Wire Specialties** F 773 252-5636
Chicago *(G-6080)*
**Parvin-Clauss Sign Co Inc** E 866 490-2877
Carol Stream *(G-3211)*
**Perfection Signs & Graphics** G 708 795-0611
Berwyn *(G-2073)*
**Petersen Aluminum Corporation** D 847 228-7150
Elk Grove Village *(G-9676)*
**Photo Techniques Corp** E 630 690-9360
Carol Stream *(G-3213)*
**Piasa Plastics Inc** G 618 372-7516
Brighton *(G-2544)*
**Plainfield Signs Inc** G 815 439-1063
Plainfield *(G-17640)*
**Plastic Letter & Signs Inc** G 847 251-3719
Wilmette *(G-22263)*
**Plus Signs & Banners Inc** G 630 236-6917
Naperville *(G-15822)*
**Prairie Display Chicago Inc** F 630 834-8773
Elmhurst *(G-9922)*
**Prairie Signs Inc** F 309 452-0463
Normal *(G-16084)*
**Preformance Signs** G 815 544-5044
Belvidere *(G-1780)*
**Premier Signs Creations Inc** G 309 637-6890
Peoria *(G-17435)*
**Prime Market Targeting Inc** E 815 469-4555
Frankfort *(G-10353)*
**Printing Plus of Roselle Inc** G 630 893-0410
Roselle *(G-18963)*
**Pronto Signs and Engraving** G 847 249-7874
Waukegan *(G-21608)*
**Pry-Bar Company** F 815 436-3383
Joliet *(G-12558)*
**Q SC Design** G 815 933-6777
Bradley *(G-2429)*
**Quantum Sign Corporation** F 630 466-0372
Sugar Grove *(G-20733)*
**Quatum Structure and Design** F 815 741-0733
Rockdale *(G-18228)*
**Quick Quality Printing Inc** G 708 895-5885
Lansing *(G-13181)*
**Quick Signs** G 618 549-0747
Carbondale *(G-3020)*
**Quick Signs Inc** G 630 554-7370
Oswego *(G-16930)*
**Quincy Electric & Sign Company** F 217 223-8404
Quincy *(G-17876)*
**R & L Signs Inc** G 708 233-0112
Bridgeview *(G-2522)*
**R D Niven & Associates Ltd** E 630 580-6000
Carol Stream *(G-3225)*
**R-Signs Service and Design Inc** G 815 722-0283
Joliet *(G-12562)*
**Ra-Ujamaa Inc** G 773 373-8585
Chicago *(G-6276)*
**Rainbow Signs** F 815 675-6750
Spring Grove *(G-20361)*
**Realt Images Inc** G 217 567-3487
Tower Hill *(G-20980)*
**Rico Industries Inc** D 312 427-0313
Niles *(G-16028)*

**Rkm Enterprises** ....G.... 217 348-5437
Charleston ***(G-3609)***
**Road Ready Signs** ....F.... 309 828-1007
Bloomington ***(G-2219)***
**Roeda Signs Inc** ....E.... 708 333-3021
South Holland ***(G-20302)***
**Roman Signs** ....G.... 847 381-3425
Barrington ***(G-1302)***
**Rout A Bout Shop Inc** ....G.... 309 829-0674
Bloomington ***(G-2220)***
**Rowdy Star Custom Creations** ....G.... 217 497-1789
Danville ***(G-7764)***
**Russell Doot Inc** ....G.... 312 527-1437
Chicago ***(G-6415)***
**Rutke Signs Inc** ....G.... 708 841-6464
Westchester ***(G-21853)***
**S and S Associates Inc** ....G.... 847 584-0033
Elk Grove Village ***(G-9722)***
**S D Custom Machining** ....G.... 618 544-7007
Robinson ***(G-18072)***
**Sadannah Group LLC** ....G.... 630 357-2300
Naperville ***(G-15745)***
**Samsung Sign Corp** ....G.... 847 816-1374
Libertyville ***(G-13377)***
**Sandee Manufacturing Co** ....G.... 847 671-1335
Franklin Park ***(G-10581)***
**Sandra E Greene** ....G.... 815 469-0092
Frankfort ***(G-10361)***
**Savino Displays Inc** ....G.... 630 574-0777
Hinsdale ***(G-11963)***
**Schellerer Corporation Inc** ....D.... 630 980-4567
Bloomingdale ***(G-2135)***
**Service Sheet Metal Works Inc** ....F.... 773 229-0031
Chicago ***(G-6483)***
**SGS International LLC** ....C.... 309 690-5231
Peoria ***(G-17453)***
**Sharn Enterprises Inc** ....E.... 815 464-9715
Frankfort ***(G-10362)***
**Shawcraft Sign Co** ....G.... 815 282-4105
Machesney Park ***(G-14107)***
**Sign** ....G.... 630 351-8400
Bloomingdale ***(G-2137)***
**Sign & Banner Express** ....G.... 630 783-9700
Bolingbrook ***(G-2368)***
**Sign A Rama** ....G.... 630 293-7300
West Chicago ***(G-21772)***
**Sign A Rama Inc** ....G.... 630 359-5125
Villa Park ***(G-21284)***
**Sign America** ....G.... 773 262-7800
Chicago ***(G-6507)***
**Sign Appeal Inc** ....G.... 847 587-4300
Fox Lake ***(G-10283)***
**Sign Authority** ....G.... 630 462-9850
Wheaton ***(G-21981)***
**Sign Central** ....G.... 847 543-7600
Round Lake ***(G-19067)***
**Sign Contractors** ....G.... 708 795-1761
Burr Ridge ***(G-2880)***
**Sign Express Inc** ....G.... 708 524-8811
Oak Park ***(G-16686)***
**Sign Girls Inc** ....G.... 847 336-4002
Gurnee ***(G-11504)***
**Sign Identity Inc** ....G.... 630 942-1400
Glen Ellyn ***(G-10989)***
**Sign O Rama** ....G.... 815 744-8702
Joliet ***(G-12575)***
**Sign Palace Inc** ....G.... 847 228-7446
Elk Grove Village ***(G-9738)***
**Sign Solutions** ....G.... 618 443-6565
Sparta ***(G-20320)***
**Sign Team Inc** ....G.... 309 302-0017
East Moline ***(G-8694)***
**Sign-A-Rama** ....G.... 312 922-0509
Chicago ***(G-6508)***
**Sign-A-Rama of Buffalo Grove** ....G.... 847 215-1535
Buffalo Grove ***(G-2771)***
**Signage Plus Ltd** ....G.... 815 485-0300
Lockport ***(G-13744)***
**Signarama** ....G.... 847 543-4870
Grayslake ***(G-11363)***
**Signco** ....F.... 402 474-6646
Greenville ***(G-11403)***
**Signcrafters Enterprises Inc** ....G.... 815 648-4484
Hebron ***(G-11727)***
**Signkraft Co** ....G.... 217 787-7105
Springfield ***(G-20524)***
**Signs By Custom Cutting Inc** ....G.... 630 759-2734
Bolingbrook ***(G-2369)***
**Signs By Design** ....G.... 708 599-9970
Palos Hills ***(G-17124)***
**Signs By Tomorrow** ....G.... 815 436-0880
Plainfield ***(G-17648)***
**Signs For Success Inc** ....F.... 847 800-4870
Buffalo Grove ***(G-2772)***
**Signs In Dundee Inc** ....G.... 847 742-9530
Elgin ***(G-9179)***
**Signs Now** ....G.... 847 427-0005
Elk Grove Village ***(G-9740)***
**Signs Now** ....G.... 800 356-3373
Chicago ***(G-6511)***
**Signs of Distinction Inc** ....G.... 847 520-0787
Wheeling ***(G-22152)***
**Signs Plus** ....G.... 847 489-9009
Des Plaines ***(G-8275)***
**Signs To You** ....G.... 708 429-6783
Tinley Park ***(G-20944)***
**Signs Today Inc** ....G.... 847 934-9777
Palatine ***(G-17074)***
**Signscapes Inc** ....G.... 847 719-2610
Lake Zurich ***(G-13131)***
**Signsdirect Inc** ....G.... 309 820-1070
Bloomington ***(G-2224)***
**Signx Co Inc** ....G.... 847 639-7917
Cary ***(G-3371)***
**Simply Signs** ....G.... 309 849-9016
Metamora ***(G-14750)***
**Skyward Promotions Inc** ....G.... 815 969-0909
Rockford ***(G-18619)***
**Skywide Publicity Solutions** ....G.... 331 425-0341
Aurora ***(G-1219)***
**South Water Signs LLC** ....E.... 630 333-4900
Elmhurst ***(G-9940)***
**Specialty Graphics Supply Inc** ....G.... 630 584-8202
Saint Charles ***(G-19267)***
**Square 1 Precision Ltg Inc** ....G.... 708 343-1500
Melrose Park ***(G-14695)***
**Stans Sportsworld Inc** ....G.... 217 359-8474
Champaign ***(G-3547)***
**Stecker Graphics Inc** ....G.... 309 786-4973
Rock Island ***(G-18204)***
**Stelmont Inc** ....G.... 847 870-0200
Arlington Heights ***(G-843)***
**Stevens Sign Co Inc** ....G.... 708 562-4888
Northlake ***(G-16453)***
**Store 409 Inc** ....F.... 708 478-5751
Mokena ***(G-14905)***
**Sub-Surface Sign Co Ltd** ....E.... 847 675-6530
Skokie ***(G-20094)***
**Summit Signworks Inc** ....G.... 847 870-0937
Arlington Heights ***(G-848)***
**Super Sign Service** ....F.... 309 829-9241
Bloomington ***(G-2227)***
**Swansea Sign A Rama Inc** ....G.... 618 234-7446
Belleville ***(G-1677)***
**T Graphics** ....G.... 618 592-4145
Oblong ***(G-16735)***
**T Ham Sign Inc** ....F.... 618 242-2010
Opdyke ***(G-16811)***
**T J Marche Ltd** ....G.... 618 445-2314
Albion ***(G-366)***
**Targin Sign Systems Inc** ....G.... 630 766-7667
Wood Dale ***(G-22427)***
**Technicraft Supply Co** ....G.... 309 495-5245
Peoria ***(G-17468)***
**Teds Shirt Shack Inc** ....G.... 217 224-9705
Quincy ***(G-17892)***
**Tfa Signs** ....G.... 773 267-6007
Chicago ***(G-6708)***
**Tgrv LLC** ....G.... 815 634-2102
Bourbonnais ***(G-2407)***
**Timothy Anderson Corporation** ....F.... 815 398-8371
Rockford ***(G-18651)***
**Timothy Darrey** ....G.... 847 231-2277
Des Plaines ***(G-8286)***
**Toms Signs** ....G.... 630 377-8525
Saint Charles ***(G-19284)***
**Traffic Control & Protection** ....E.... 630 293-0026
West Chicago ***(G-21784)***
**Transportation Illinois Dept** ....F.... 217 785-0288
Springfield ***(G-20546)***
**Trophytime Inc** ....G.... 217 351-7958
Champaign ***(G-3550)***
**Turnroth Sign Company Inc** ....F.... 815 625-1155
Rock Falls ***(G-18156)***
**Twin City Awards** ....G.... 309 452-9291
Normal ***(G-16091)***
**Ultimate Sign Co** ....G.... 773 282-4595
Chicago ***(G-6807)***
**Unistrut International Corp** ....D.... 630 773-3460
Addison ***(G-334)***
**United Wire Craft Inc** ....C.... 847 375-3800
Des Plaines ***(G-8291)***
**Varsity Striping & Cnstr Co** ....E.... 217 352-2203
Champaign ***(G-3553)***
**Vindee Industries Inc** ....E.... 815 469-3300
Frankfort ***(G-10375)***
**Vinyl Graphics Inc** ....G.... 708 579-1234
Countryside ***(G-7450)***
**Visual Marketing Solutions** ....G.... 815 589-3848
Fulton ***(G-10707)***
**Vital Signs USA** ....G.... 630 832-9600
Elmhurst ***(G-9958)***
**W G N Flag & Decorating Co** ....F.... 773 768-8076
Chicago ***(G-6918)***
**Walnut Creek Hardwood** ....G.... 815 389-3317
South Beloit ***(G-20173)***
**Warren Wiersema Signs** ....G.... 815 589-3001
Fulton ***(G-10708)***
**Weakley Printing & Sign Shop** ....G.... 847 473-4466
North Chicago ***(G-16189)***
**Weatherford Signs** ....G.... 618 529-2000
Carbondale ***(G-3027)***
**Weathertop Woodcraft** ....G
Carol Stream ***(G-3265)***
**Weiskamp Screen Printing** ....G.... 217 398-8428
Champaign ***(G-3560)***
**Western Remac Inc** ....E.... 630 972-7770
Woodridge ***(G-22524)***
**Willdon Corp** ....E.... 773 276-7080
Chicago ***(G-6981)***
**Windy City Plastics Inc** ....G.... 773 533-1099
Chicago ***(G-6999)***
**Wiremasters Incorporated** ....E.... 773 254-3700
Chicago ***(G-7005)***
**Wow Signs Inc** ....G.... 847 910-4405
Deerfield ***(G-8069)***
**Wright Quick Signs Inc** ....G.... 708 652-6020
Cicero ***(G-7247)***
**Xpressigns Inc** ....G.... 888 303-0640
Arlington Heights ***(G-876)***
**Xtrem Graphix Solutions Inc** ....G.... 217 698-6424
Springfield ***(G-20549)***
**Ye Olde Sign Shoppe** ....G.... 847 228-7446
Elk Grove Village ***(G-9822)***
**Zainab Enterprises Inc** ....G.... 630 739-0110
Romeoville ***(G-18881)***
**Zimmerman Enterprises Inc** ....F.... 847 297-3177
Des Plaines ***(G-8308)***

## SIGNS & ADVERTISING SPECIALTIES: Artwork, Advertising

**Chicago Show Inc** ....E.... 847 955-0200
Buffalo Grove ***(G-2672)***
**Color Communications Inc** ....C.... 773 638-1400
Chicago ***(G-4426)***
**Corpro Screen Tech Inc** ....G.... 815 633-1201
Loves Park ***(G-13926)***
**M G M Displays Inc** ....G.... 708 594-3699
Chicago ***(G-5580)***
**Mekanism Inc** ....F.... 415 908-4000
Chicago ***(G-5682)***
**Navitor Inc** ....B.... 800 323-0253
Harwood Heights ***(G-11687)***

## SIGNS & ADVERTISING SPECIALTIES: Letters For Signs, Metal

**A Trustworthy Sup Source Inc** ....G.... 773 480-0255
Chicago ***(G-3693)***
**Dean Patterson** ....G.... 708 430-0477
Bridgeview ***(G-2482)***
**Desk & Door Nameplate Company** ....F.... 815 806-8670
Frankfort ***(G-10312)***
**Wagner Zip-Change Inc** ....E.... 708 681-4100
Melrose Park ***(G-14706)***

## SIGNS & ADVERTISING SPECIALTIES: Novelties

**B W M Global** ....G.... 847 785-1355
Waukegan ***(G-21528)***
**Bee-Jay Industries Inc** ....F.... 708 867-4431
Bloomingdale ***(G-2095)***
**C M F Enterprises Inc** ....F.... 847 526-9499
Wauconda ***(G-21450)***
**Concepts Magnet** ....G.... 847 253-3351
Mount Prospect ***(G-15318)***
**Flow-Eze Company** ....F.... 815 965-1062
Rockford ***(G-18383)***

**Fun Incorporated** E 773 745-3837
Wheeling *(G-22059)*
**Gemini Industries Inc** D 618 251-3352
Roxana *(G-19084)*
**Insight Advertising Inc** G 847 647-0004
Niles *(G-15989)*
**Ken Young Construction Co** G 847 358-3026
Hoffman Estates *(G-12021)*
**Master Marketing Intl Inc** F 630 909-1846
Carol Stream *(G-3189)*
**Midwest Promotional Group Co** E 708 563-0600
Burr Ridge *(G-2868)*
**Promotional Co of Illinois** G 847 382-0239
Inverness *(G-12210)*
**R N I Industries Inc** E 630 860-9147
Bensenville *(G-1974)*
**Stellar Recognition Inc** D 773 282-8060
Chicago *(G-6588)*
**Teraco-II Inc** E 630 539-4400
Roselle *(G-18981)*

## SIGNS & ADVERTISING SPECIALTIES: Scoreboards, Electric

**Electronic Displays Inc** F 630 628-0658
Addison *(G-108)*
**Nevco Inc** D 618 664-0360
Greenville *(G-11401)*

## SIGNS & ADVERTISING SPECIALTIES: Signs

**Ability Plastics Inc** E 708 458-4480
Justice *(G-12594)*
**Academy Screenprinting Awards** G 309 686-0026
Peoria *(G-17300)*
**All-Steel Structures Inc** E 708 210-1313
South Holland *(G-20241)*
**AM Ko Oriental Foods** G 217 398-2922
Champaign *(G-3446)*
**Art & Son Sign Inc** F 847 526-7205
Wauconda *(G-21443)*
**Briscoe Signs LLC** G 630 529-1616
Roselle *(G-18929)*
**Custom Sign Consultants Inc** G 312 533-2302
Chicago *(G-4526)*
**Graymon Graphics Inc** G 773 737-0176
Chicago *(G-4993)*
**Janis Plastics Inc** D 847 838-5500
Antioch *(G-638)*
**K and A Graphics Inc** G 847 244-2345
Gurnee *(G-11463)*
**Ksem Inc** G 618 656-5388
Edwardsville *(G-8805)*
**Legible Signs Group Corp** F 815 654-0100
Loves Park *(G-13960)*
**Modagrafics Inc** D 800 860-3169
Rolling Meadows *(G-18746)*
**Nelson - Harkins Inds Inc** E 773 478-6243
Chicago *(G-5884)*
**Nutheme Sign Company** G 847 230-0067
Downers Grove *(G-8497)*
**Peterson Brothers Plastics** F 773 286-5666
Chicago *(G-6111)*
**Rebechini Studio Inc** F 847 364-8600
Elk Grove Village *(G-9711)*
**Roth Neon Sign Company Inc** G 618 942-6378
Herrin *(G-11753)*
**Saturn Sign** G 847 520-9009
Wheeling *(G-22144)*
**Schepel Signs Inc** G 708 758-1441
Lynwood *(G-14027)*
**Signtastic Inc** G 708 598-4749
Palos Hills *(G-17125)*
**Signwise Inc** G 630 932-3204
Lombard *(G-13853)*
**West Zwick Corp** G 217 222-0228
Quincy *(G-17903)*
**William Frick & Company** E 847 918-3700
Libertyville *(G-13401)*

## SIGNS & ADVERTSG SPECIALTIES: Displays/Cutouts Window/Lobby

**Accurate Metal Fabricating LLC** D 773 235-0400
Chicago *(G-3720)*
**Acrylic Service Inc** G 630 543-0336
Addison *(G-20)*
**AMD Industries Inc** D 708 863-8900
Cicero *(G-7178)*
**Benchmarc Display Incorporated** E 847 541-2828
Vernon Hills *(G-21149)*
**Bish Creative Display Inc** E 847 438-1500
Lake Zurich *(G-13046)*
**Braeside LLC** E 847 395-8500
Antioch *(G-626)*
**Consolidated Displays Co Inc** G 630 851-8666
Oswego *(G-16911)*
**Cosmos Plastics Company** E 847 451-1307
Franklin Park *(G-10445)*
**Design Phase Inc** E 847 473-0077
Waukegan *(G-21550)*
**Display Link Inc** G 815 968-0778
Rockford *(G-18346)*
**General Exhibits and Displays** D 847 934-1943
Inverness *(G-12204)*
**Hazen Display Corporation** E 815 248-2925
Davis *(G-7806)*
**J R Fridrich Inc** F 847 439-1554
Elk Grove Village *(G-9558)*
**Joliet Pattern Works Inc** D 815 726-5373
Crest Hill *(G-7460)*
**K-Display Corp** F 773 586-2042
Chicago *(G-5348)*
**McKernin Exhibits Inc** F 708 333-4500
South Holland *(G-20288)*
**Mer-Pla Inc** F 847 530-9798
Chicago *(G-5687)*
**Mercury Plastics Inc** E 888 884-1864
Chicago *(G-5688)*
**Nimlok Company** D 847 647-1012
Des Plaines *(G-8242)*
**Patt Supply Corporation** F 708 442-3901
Lyons *(G-14043)*
**Process Graphics Corp** E 815 637-2500
Rockford *(G-18542)*
**RTC Industries Inc** D 847 640-2400
Chicago *(G-6409)*
**Stevens Exhibits & Displays** E 773 523-3900
Chicago *(G-6595)*
**Thermo-Graphic LLC** E 630 350-2226
Bensenville *(G-2001)*
**Visual Marketing Inc** E 312 664-9177
Chicago *(G-6905)*

## SIGNS, ELECTRICAL: Wholesalers

**Frankenstitch Promotions LLC** G 847 459-4840
Wheeling *(G-22058)*
**Quantum Sign Corporation** F 630 466-0372
Sugar Grove *(G-20733)*
**Roth Neon Sign Company Inc** G 618 942-6378
Herrin *(G-11753)*

## SIGNS, EXC ELECTRIC, WHOLESALE

**All Signs & Wonders Co** G 630 232-9019
Geneva *(G-10807)*
**Budget Signs** F 618 259-4460
Wood River *(G-22441)*
**C H Hanson Company** D 630 848-2000
Naperville *(G-15613)*
**Fedex Corporation** F 847 918-7730
Vernon Hills *(G-21163)*
**Fedex Ground Package Sys Inc** G 800 463-3339
Glendale Heights *(G-11023)*
**Fedex Office & Print Svcs Inc** F 312 341-9644
Chicago *(G-4827)*
**Fedex Office & Print Svcs Inc** F 312 755-0325
Chicago *(G-4828)*
**Fedex Office & Print Svcs Inc** F 312 595-0768
Chicago *(G-4829)*
**Fedex Office & Print Svcs Inc** G 630 759-5784
Bolingbrook *(G-2308)*
**Fedex Office & Print Svcs Inc** F 312 663-1149
Chicago *(G-4830)*
**Fedex Office & Print Svcs Inc** G 847 670-7283
Mount Prospect *(G-15329)*
**Frankenstitch Promotions LLC** G 847 459-4840
Wheeling *(G-22058)*
**GL Downs Inc** G 618 993-9777
Marion *(G-14262)*
**Perfection Signs & Graphics** G 708 795-0611
Berwyn *(G-2073)*
**Plus Signs & Banners Inc** G 630 236-6917
Naperville *(G-15822)*
**Q SC Design** G 815 933-6777
Bradley *(G-2429)*
**Sign A Rama** G 630 293-7300
West Chicago *(G-21772)*
**Signet Sign Company** G 630 830-8242
Bartlett *(G-1377)*
**Wagner Zip-Change Inc** E 708 681-4100
Melrose Park *(G-14706)*

## SIGNS: Electrical

**All-American Sign Co Inc** E 708 422-2203
Oak Lawn *(G-16599)*
**All-Brite Sign Co Inc** F 309 829-1551
Normal *(G-16063)*
**American Sign & Lighting Co** E 847 258-8151
Chicago *(G-3874)*
**Anbek Inc** G 815 434-7340
Ottawa *(G-16947)*
**Arts & Letters Marshall Signs** G 773 927-4442
Chicago *(G-3959)*
**Aurora Sign Co** G 630 898-5900
Aurora *(G-962)*
**Baum Holdings Inc** G 847 488-0650
South Elgin *(G-20185)*
**Cachera and Klemm Inc** G 217 876-7446
Decatur *(G-7849)*
**Central Illinois Sign Company** G 217 523-4740
Springfield *(G-20414)*
**Century Signs Inc** F 217 224-7419
Quincy *(G-17812)*
**CNE Inc** G 847 534-7135
Schaumburg *(G-19475)*
**Demond Signs Inc** F 618 624-7260
O Fallon *(G-16466)*
**Doyle Signs Inc** D 630 543-9490
Addison *(G-98)*
**Express Signs & Lighting Maint** F 815 725-9080
Shorewood *(G-19926)*
**Galesburg Sign & Lighting** G 309 342-9798
Galesburg *(G-10751)*
**Grate Signs Inc** E 815 729-9700
Joliet *(G-12503)*
**Herrmann Signs & Service** G 618 246-6537
Mount Vernon *(G-15412)*
**Jenkins Displays Co** G 618 335-3874
Patoka *(G-17232)*
**Keyesport Manufacturing Inc** G 618 749-5510
Keyesport *(G-12696)*
**Kieffer Holding Co** G 877 543-3337
Lincolnshire *(G-13458)*
**Krick Enterprises Inc** G 630 515-1085
Downers Grove *(G-8470)*
**Monitor Sign Co** F 217 234-2412
Mattoon *(G-14405)*
**Mostert & Ferguson Signs** G 815 485-1212
Orland Park *(G-16876)*
**Neon Art** G 773 588-5883
Chicago *(G-5885)*
**North Shore Sign Company** E 847 816-7020
Libertyville *(G-13364)*
**Nu Glo Sign Company** F 847 223-6160
Grayslake *(G-11356)*
**Omega Sign & Lighting Inc** E 630 237-4397
Addison *(G-234)*
**Ozko Sign & Lighting Company** G 224 653-8531
Schaumburg *(G-19676)*
**Paldo Sign and Display Company** G 708 456-1711
River Grove *(G-18012)*
**Pellegrini Enterprises Inc** G 815 717-6408
Orland Park *(G-16884)*
**Signet Sign Company** G 630 830-8242
Bartlett *(G-1377)*
**Signworx Sign & Lighting Co** G 217 413-2532
Springfield *(G-20525)*
**Solar Traffic Systems Inc** G 331 318-8500
Lemont *(G-13263)*
**Strictly Neon Inc** G 708 597-1616
Crestwood *(G-7504)*
**Turk Electric Sign Co** G 773 736-9300
Chicago *(G-6793)*
**Watchfire Enterprises Inc** E 217 442-0611
Danville *(G-7780)*
**Watchfire Signs LLC** B 217 442-0611
Danville *(G-7781)*
**Watchfire Tech Holdings I Inc** G 217 442-6971
Danville *(G-7782)*
**Watchfire Tech Holdings II Inc** G 217 442-0611
Danville *(G-7783)*
**Western Lighting Inc** F 847 451-7200
Franklin Park *(G-10628)*
**White Way Sign & Maint Co** C 847 391-0200
Chicago *(G-6974)*

## SIGNS: Neon

**Ad Deluxe Sign Company Inc** G 815 556-8469
Plainfield *(G-17576)*
**Ad Electric Sign Inc** G 708 222-8000
Berwyn *(G-2055)*

## PRODUCT SECTION — SOAPS & DETERGENTS

Best Neon Sign Co Inc .......................... F ..... 773 586-2700
  Chicago *(G-4093)*
Greg Signs ............................................. G ..... 815 726-5655
  Joliet *(G-12504)*
Harder Signs Inc .................................... F ..... 815 874-7777
  Rockford *(G-18413)*
Mk Signs Inc ......................................... E ..... 773 545-4444
  Chicago *(G-5777)*
Mount Vernon Neon Sign Co ................. C ..... 618 242-0645
  Mount Vernon *(G-15429)*
Neon Prism Electric Sign Co .................. G ..... 630 879-1010
  Batavia *(G-1476)*
Neon Shop Inc ....................................... G ..... 773 227-0303
  Chicago *(G-5888)*
Precision Neon Glasswork ..................... G ..... 847 428-1200
  Crystal Lake *(G-7627)*
Real Neon Inc ........................................ F ..... 630 543-0995
  Addison *(G-272)*
Shinn Enterprises .................................. G ..... 217 698-3344
  Springfield *(G-20523)*
Sign Outlet Inc ...................................... G ..... 708 824-2222
  Alsip *(G-528)*
Staar Bales Lestarge Inc ....................... G ..... 618 259-6366
  East Alton *(G-8611)*
Wave Mechanics Neon ........................... G ..... 312 829-9283
  Chicago *(G-6944)*

### SILICA MINING

U S Silica Company ................................ C ..... 815 434-0188
  Ottawa *(G-16988)*
Unimin Corporation ................................ E ..... 618 747-2338
  Tamms *(G-20826)*
Unimin Corporation ................................ D ..... 618 747-2311
  Tamms *(G-20827)*

### SILICON WAFERS: Chemically Doped

Dauber Company Inc ............................. E ..... 815 442-3569
  Tonica *(G-20973)*

### SILICONES

AB Specialty Silicones LLC .................... E ..... 908 273-8015
  Waukegan *(G-21516)*

### SILK SCREEN DESIGN SVCS

American Outfitters Ltd ......................... E ..... 847 623-3959
  Waukegan *(G-21524)*
C M F Enterprises Inc ............................ F ..... 847 526-9499
  Wauconda *(G-21450)*
Chicago Printing and EMB Inc ............... F ..... 630 628-1777
  Addison *(G-75)*
Corr-Pak Corporation ............................ E ..... 708 442-7806
  Mc Cook *(G-14447)*
Custom Trophies .................................... G ..... 217 422-3353
  Decatur *(G-7863)*
Ems Acrylics & Silk Screener ................. F ..... 773 777-5656
  Chicago *(G-4747)*
Essential Creations ................................ G ..... 773 238-1700
  Chicago *(G-4779)*
Go Van Goghs Tee Shirt ........................ G ..... 309 342-1112
  Galesburg *(G-10755)*
Johnson Sign Co .................................... G ..... 847 678-2092
  Franklin Park *(G-10509)*
Kane Graphical Corporation ................... E ..... 773 384-1200
  Chicago *(G-5358)*
Midwest Promotional Group Co .............. E ..... 708 563-0600
  Burr Ridge *(G-2868)*
Midwest Silkscreening Inc ..................... G ..... 217 892-9596
  Rantoul *(G-17934)*
Mt Greenwood Embroidery .................... G ..... 773 779-5798
  Chicago *(G-5827)*
R J S Silk Screening Co ........................ G ..... 708 974-3009
  Palos Hills *(G-17123)*
Schellhorn Photo Techniques ................. F ..... 773 267-5141
  Chicago *(G-6451)*
Sunburst Sportswear Inc ....................... F ..... 630 717-8680
  Glendale Heights *(G-11079)*
T J Marche Ltd ...................................... G ..... 618 445-2314
  Albion *(G-366)*

### SILOS: Concrete, Prefabricated

White Star Silo ...................................... G ..... 618 523-4735
  Germantown *(G-10894)*

### SILOS: Meal

Dspc Company ....................................... E ..... 815 997-1116
  Rockford *(G-18353)*

### SILVER ORE MINING

Coeur Mining Inc ................................... D ..... 312 489-5800
  Chicago *(G-4419)*

### SILVER ORES

Callahan Mining Corporation .................. D ..... 312 489-5800
  Chicago *(G-4216)*
Coeur Rochester Inc .............................. G ..... 312 661-2436
  Chicago *(G-4420)*

### SILVERSMITHS

Baroque Silversmith Inc ........................ G ..... 312 357-2813
  Chicago *(G-4045)*

### SILVERWARE & PLATED WARE

A & J Plating Inc .................................. G ..... 708 453-9713
  River Grove *(G-18004)*

### SIMULATORS: Flight

Wittenstein Arspc Smlation Inc .............. G ..... 630 540-5300
  Bartlett *(G-1389)*

### SINKS: Vitreous China

Wells Sinkware Corp .............................. G ..... 312 850-3466
  Chicago *(G-6954)*

### SIRENS: Vehicle, Marine, Indl & Warning

Federal Signal Corporation .................... D ..... 630 954-2000
  Oak Brook *(G-16510)*
Lund Industries Inc ............................... E ..... 847 459-1460
  Northbrook *(G-16302)*
North American Signal Co ...................... G ..... 847 537-8888
  Wheeling *(G-22108)*

### SKIDS: Wood

Caisson Inc ........................................... G ..... 815 547-5925
  Belvidere *(G-1741)*

### SKYLIGHTS

A D Skylights Inc .................................. G ..... 847 854-2900
  Algonquin *(G-376)*
Imperial Glass Structures Co ................. F ..... 847 253-6150
  Wheeling *(G-22075)*
Midwest Skylite Company Inc ................ E ..... 847 214-9505
  South Elgin *(G-20219)*
United Skys LLC .................................... F ..... 847 546-7776
  Round Lake *(G-19069)*

### SLAB & TILE, ROOFING: Concrete

Lifetime Rooftile Company .................... G ..... 630 355-7922
  Naperville *(G-15689)*

### SLAB & TILE: Precast Concrete, Floor

Euro Marble Supply Ltd ......................... G ..... 847 233-0700
  Schiller Park *(G-19828)*
St Louis Flexicore Inc ............................ F ..... 618 531-8691
  East Saint Louis *(G-8770)*
West Lake Concrete & Rmdlg LLC ......... G ..... 847 477-8667
  Chicago *(G-6960)*

### SLAG: Crushed Or Ground

Beelman Slag Sales ............................... B ..... 618 452-8120
  Madison *(G-14139)*
Littleson Inc .......................................... G ..... 815 968-8349
  Rockford *(G-18471)*
Mid River Minerals Inc .......................... G ..... 815 941-7524
  Morris *(G-15117)*
Tms International LLC ........................... D ..... 618 451-7840
  Granite City *(G-11307)*
Tms International LLC ........................... G ..... 815 939-9460
  Bourbonnais *(G-2408)*

### SLATE: Crushed & Broken

Mid Illinois Quarry Company ................. G ..... 217 932-2611
  Casey *(G-3389)*

### SLAUGHTERING & MEAT PACKING

Eickmans Processing Co Inc .................. E ..... 815 247-8451
  Seward *(G-19896)*
God Family Country LLC ....................... F ..... 217 285-6487
  Pittsfield *(G-17568)*
Main Street Market Roscoe Inc .............. G ..... 815 623-6328
  Roscoe *(G-18905)*
Teys (usa) Inc ....................................... G ..... 312 492-7163
  Chicago *(G-6707)*
Thrushwood Frms Qlty Meats Inc .......... F ..... 309 343-5193
  Galesburg *(G-10778)*

### SLIDES & EXHIBITS: Prepared

Evo Exhibits LLC .................................... G ..... 630 520-0710
  West Chicago *(G-21697)*

### SLINGS: Lifting, Made From Purchased Wire

Alloy Sling Chains Inc ........................... D ..... 708 647-4900
  East Hazel Crest *(G-8664)*
Lamco Slings & Rigging Inc .................. E ..... 309 764-7400
  Moline *(G-14952)*
Lee Jensen Sales Co Inc ....................... G ..... 815 459-0929
  Crystal Lake *(G-7602)*
Marcal Rope & Rigging Inc .................... E ..... 618 462-0172
  Alton *(G-584)*

### SLINGS: Rope

Lifting & Components Parts LLC ............ G ..... 224 315-5294
  Schaumburg *(G-19617)*

### SLOT MACHINES

Awesome Hand Services LLC ................. G ..... 630 445-8695
  Rolling Meadows *(G-18714)*
Top Dollar Slots ..................................... 779 210-4884
  Loves Park *(G-14002)*
WMS Gaming Inc .................................. C ..... 773 961-1747
  Chicago *(G-7016)*
WMS Gaming Inc .................................. A ..... 773 961-1000
  Chicago *(G-7017)*

### SMOKE DETECTORS

First Alert Inc ....................................... G ..... 630 499-3295
  Aurora *(G-1009)*

### SNIPS: Tinners'

Irwin Industrial Tool Company ............... C ..... 815 235-4171
  Freeport *(G-10669)*

### SNOW PLOWING SVCS

Complete Lawn and Snow Service ......... F ..... 847 776-7287
  Palatine *(G-17014)*
Geske and Sons Inc .............................. F ..... 815 459-2407
  Crystal Lake *(G-7581)*
Jacobs Trucking ..................................... G ..... 618 687-3578
  Murphysboro *(G-15577)*
Northwest Snow Timber Svc Ltd ........... G ..... 847 778-4998
  Glenview *(G-11175)*
Powell Tree Care Inc ............................. G ..... 847 364-1181
  Elk Grove Village *(G-9689)*
Tri Star Plowing .................................... G ..... 847 584-5070
  Schaumburg *(G-19771)*

### SNOW REMOVAL EQPT: Residential

Amerisun Inc ......................................... F ..... 800 791-9458
  Itasca *(G-12229)*
Randys Exper-Clean .............................. G ..... 217 423-1975
  Decatur *(G-7931)*

### SOAPS & DETERGENTS

A & H Manufacturing Inc ....................... F ..... 630 543-5900
  Addison *(G-14)*
Afton Chemical Corporation ................... B ..... 618 583-1000
  East Saint Louis *(G-8740)*
Akzo Nobel Chemicals LLC ..................... C ..... 312 544-7000
  Chicago *(G-3791)*
Apco Packaging Inc ............................... E ..... 708 430-7333
  Bridgeview *(G-2467)*
Atm America Corp ................................. E ..... 800 298-0030
  Chicago *(G-3986)*
Avatar Corporation ................................ D ..... 708 534-5511
  University Park *(G-21042)*
Blachford Corporation ............................ E ..... 815 464-2100
  Frankfort *(G-10301)*
Black Swan Manufacturing Co ............... F ..... 773 227-3700
  Chicago *(G-4121)*
Blast Products Inc ................................. G ..... 618 452-4700
  Madison *(G-14140)*
Cater Chemical Co ................................ G ..... 630 980-2300
  Roselle *(G-18930)*

Employee Codes: A=Over 500 employees, B=251-500
C=101-250, D=51-100, E=20-50, F=10-19, G=3-9

## SOAPS & DETERGENTS

|  | |  |
|---|---|---|
| Cedar Concepts Corporation | E | 773 890-5790 |
| Chicago *(G-4265)* | | |
| Chemstation Chicago LLC | E | 630 279-2857 |
| Elmhurst *(G-9846)* | | |
| Chemtool Incorporated | C | 815 957-4140 |
| Rockton *(G-18694)* | | |
| Chemtool Incorporated | D | 815 459-1250 |
| Crystal Lake *(G-7551)* | | |
| Combe Laboratories Inc | C | 217 893-4490 |
| Rantoul *(G-17923)* | | |
| Dairy Dynamics LLC | F | 847 758-7300 |
| Elk Grove Village *(G-9416)* | | |
| Damco Products Inc | G | 618 452-4700 |
| Madison *(G-14141)* | | |
| Dial Corporation | C | 630 892-4381 |
| Montgomery *(G-15041)* | | |
| Ecolab Ff Aperion Care St | E | 618 829-5581 |
| Saint Elmo *(G-19306)* | | |
| Ecp Incorporated | D | 630 754-4200 |
| Woodridge *(G-22474)* | | |
| First Ayd Corporation | D | 847 622-0001 |
| Elgin *(G-9036)* | | |
| Floor-Chem Inc | G | 630 789-2152 |
| Romeoville *(G-18825)* | | |
| Formulations Inc | G | 847 674-9141 |
| Skokie *(G-20001)* | | |
| Gea Farm Technologies Inc | E | 630 759-1063 |
| Romeoville *(G-18828)* | | |
| Henkel Consumer Goods Inc | D | 847 426-4552 |
| Elgin *(G-9063)* | | |
| Interflo Industries Inc | | 847 228-0606 |
| Elk Grove Village *(G-9551)* | | |
| Karimi Saifuddin | G | 630 379-9344 |
| Plainfield *(G-17614)* | | |
| Kik Custom Products Inc | B | 217 442-1400 |
| Danville *(G-7743)* | | |
| Lasalle Chemical & Supply Co | F | 847 470-1234 |
| Morton Grove *(G-15211)* | | |
| Nataz Specialty Coatings Inc | F | 773 247-7030 |
| Chicago *(G-5856)* | | |
| People Against Dirty Mfg Pbc | D | 415 568-4600 |
| Chicago *(G-6101)* | | |
| PLC Corp | G | 847 247-1900 |
| Lake Bluff *(G-12863)* | | |
| Progressive Solutions Corp | G | 847 639-7272 |
| Algonquin *(G-405)* | | |
| Rock River Blending | G | 815 968-7860 |
| Rockford *(G-18562)* | | |
| Solab Inc | F | 708 544-2200 |
| Bellwood *(G-1722)* | | |
| Standard Indus & Auto Eqp Inc | E | 630 289-9500 |
| Hanover Park *(G-11590)* | | |
| Sweet Thyme Soaps | G | 708 848-0234 |
| Oak Park *(G-16688)* | | |
| Tri Sect Corporation | F | 847 524-1119 |
| Schaumburg *(G-19770)* | | |
| Venus Laboratories Inc | G | 630 595-1900 |
| Addison *(G-339)* | | |
| Vvf Illinois Services LLC | B | 630 892-4381 |
| Montgomery *(G-15071)* | | |
| Westfalia-Surge Inc | G | 630 759-7346 |
| Romeoville *(G-18878)* | | |

### SOAPS & DETERGENTS: Glycerin, Crude Or Refined, From Fats

|  | |  |
|---|---|---|
| Vantage Oleochemicals Inc | C | 773 376-9000 |
| Chicago *(G-6873)* | | |

### SOAPS & DETERGENTS: Textile

|  | |  |
|---|---|---|
| AM Harper Products Inc | F | 312 767-8283 |
| Chicago *(G-3841)* | | |
| Ashley Lauren | G | 847 733-9470 |
| Evanston *(G-10012)* | | |

### SOCIAL CLUBS

|  | |  |
|---|---|---|
| German American Nat Congress | G | 773 561-9181 |
| Chicago *(G-4948)* | | |

### SOCIAL SVCS, HANDICAPPED

|  | |  |
|---|---|---|
| Envision Unlimited | C | 773 651-1100 |
| Chicago *(G-4766)* | | |
| Perry Adult Living Inc | G | 618 542-5421 |
| Du Quoin *(G-8557)* | | |

### SOCIAL SVCS: Individual & Family

|  | |  |
|---|---|---|
| American Soc Plastic Surgeons | D | 847 228-9900 |
| Arlington Heights *(G-710)* | | |
| Human Svc Ctr Southern Metro E | E | 618 282-6233 |
| Red Bud *(G-17942)* | | |

### SOCKETS & RECEPTACLES: Lamp, Electric Wiring Devices

|  | |  |
|---|---|---|
| Lumisource LLC | E | 847 699-8988 |
| Elk Grove Village *(G-9600)* | | |

### SOCKETS: Electric

|  | |  |
|---|---|---|
| Christiana Industries Inc | C | 773 465-6330 |
| Chicago *(G-4371)* | | |

### SOFT DRINKS WHOLESALERS

|  | |  |
|---|---|---|
| Clover Club Bottling Co Inc | F | 773 261-7100 |
| Chicago *(G-4406)* | | |
| Excel Bottling Co | G | 618 526-7159 |
| Breese *(G-2443)* | | |
| Great Lakes Coca-Cola Dist LLC | C | 847 227-6500 |
| Rosemont *(G-19004)* | | |
| P-Americas LLC | C | 309 266-2400 |
| Morton *(G-15173)* | | |
| P-Americas LLC | D | 312 821-2266 |
| Chicago *(G-6044)* | | |
| Pepsi Cola Gen Bttlers of Lima | G | 847 253-1000 |
| Rolling Meadows *(G-18761)* | | |
| Pepsi-Cola Gen Bottlers Inc | B | 847 598-3000 |
| Schaumburg *(G-19688)* | | |

### SOFTWARE PUBLISHERS: Application

|  | |  |
|---|---|---|
| Abki Tech Service Inc | F | 847 818-8403 |
| Des Plaines *(G-8143)* | | |
| Accuity Inc | B | 847 676-9600 |
| Evanston *(G-10003)* | | |
| Advanced EMR Solutions Inc | G | 877 327-6160 |
| Northbrook *(G-16199)* | | |
| Amoco Technology Company (del) | C | 312 861-6000 |
| Chicago *(G-3892)* | | |
| Appsanity Advisory LLC | G | 847 638-1172 |
| Winnetka *(G-22302)* | | |
| Aprimo US LLC | G | 877 794-8556 |
| Chicago *(G-3928)* | | |
| Aqueous Solutions LLC | G | 217 531-1206 |
| Champaign *(G-3452)* | | |
| ARC Mobile LLC | F | 201 838-3410 |
| Western Springs *(G-21863)* | | |
| Buyersvine Inc | G | 630 235-6804 |
| Hinsdale *(G-11943)* | | |
| Bytebin LLC | G | 312 286-0740 |
| Chicago *(G-4197)* | | |
| Ca Inc | G | 312 201-8557 |
| Chicago *(G-4207)* | | |
| Capital Tours & Travel Inc | G | 847 274-1138 |
| Skokie *(G-19973)* | | |
| Champion Medical Tech Inc | E | 866 803-3720 |
| Lake Zurich *(G-13052)* | | |
| Chicago Data Solutions Inc | G | 847 370-4609 |
| Willowbrook *(G-22203)* | | |
| Cityzenith LLC | F | 312 282-2900 |
| Chicago *(G-4390)* | | |
| Clientloyalty LLC | G | 312 307-5716 |
| Chicago *(G-4402)* | | |
| Cliqster LLC | G | 847 732-1457 |
| Highland Park *(G-11828)* | | |
| Compsoft Tech Sltons Group Inc | F | 847 517-9608 |
| Schaumburg *(G-19478)* | | |
| Comvigo Inc | G | 240 255-4093 |
| Willowbrook *(G-22205)* | | |
| Cona LLC | G | 773 750-7485 |
| Chicago *(G-4443)* | | |
| Crowdmatrix Fx LLC | G | 312 329-1170 |
| Chicago *(G-4508)* | | |
| Deductly LLC | G | 312 945-8265 |
| Chicago *(G-4572)* | | |
| Delante Group Inc | G | 312 493-4371 |
| Chicago *(G-4575)* | | |
| Diehl Controls North Amer Inc | E | 630 955-9055 |
| Naperville *(G-15646)* | | |
| Dimension Data North Amer Inc | F | 847 278-6413 |
| Schaumburg *(G-19505)* | | |
| Donr Co | G | 773 895-3359 |
| Chicago *(G-4630)* | | |
| Earshot Inc | F | 773 383-1798 |
| Chicago *(G-4677)* | | |
| Edqu Media LLC | G | 773 803-9793 |
| Chicago *(G-4698)* | | |
| Effici Inc | G | 401 584-2266 |
| Schaumburg *(G-19514)* | | |
| Endure Holdings Inc | G | 224 558-1828 |
| Plainfield *(G-17594)* | | |
| Enrollment Rx LLC | F | 847 233-0088 |
| Schiller Park *(G-19825)* | | |
| Entience | G | 217 649-2590 |
| Urbana *(G-21082)* | | |
| Ep Technology Corporation USA | D | 217 351-7888 |
| Champaign *(G-3482)* | | |
| Foster Learning LLC | G | 618 656-6836 |
| Edwardsville *(G-8801)* | | |
| Glidera Inc | G | 773 350-4000 |
| Elmhurst *(G-9877)* | | |
| H & R Block Inc | F | 847 566-5557 |
| Mundelein *(G-15506)* | | |
| H&R Block Inc | F | 773 582-3444 |
| Chicago *(G-5025)* | | |
| Healthcare Research LLC | F | 773 592-3508 |
| Chicago *(G-5060)* | | |
| Healthy-Txt LLC | G | 630 945-1787 |
| Chicago *(G-5063)* | | |
| Hicx Solutions Inc | G | 630 560-3640 |
| Oakbrook Terrace *(G-16711)* | | |
| Idevconcepts Inc | G | 312 351-1615 |
| Chicago *(G-5142)* | | |
| Imaging Systems Inc | G | 630 875-1100 |
| Itasca *(G-12283)* | | |
| Intersect Healthcare Systems | G | 847 457-2159 |
| Lake Forest *(G-12919)* | | |
| Intravation Inc | G | 847 299-6423 |
| Des Plaines *(G-8214)* | | |
| Isewa LLC | G | 847 877-1586 |
| Buffalo Grove *(G-2711)* | | |
| Jabber Labs Inc | F | 607 227-6353 |
| Chicago *(G-5266)* | | |
| Janitor Ltd | G | 773 936-3389 |
| Chicago *(G-5276)* | | |
| Konveau Inc | G | 312 476-9385 |
| Chicago *(G-5404)* | | |
| Manscore LLC | G | 630 297-7502 |
| Downers Grove *(G-8482)* | | |
| Memdem Inc | G | 571 205-8778 |
| Elmhurst *(G-9910)* | | |
| Memorable Inc | G | 847 272-8207 |
| Northbrook *(G-16310)* | | |
| Mfrontiers LLC | G | 224 513-5312 |
| Libertyville *(G-13356)* | | |
| Microsoft Corporation | D | 309 665-0113 |
| Bloomington *(G-2198)* | | |
| Mosaic Construction | G | 847 504-0177 |
| Northbrook *(G-16315)* | | |
| Narrative Health Network Inc | G | 312 600-9154 |
| Chicago *(G-5854)* | | |
| Nautilus Medical | | 866 520-6477 |
| Barrington *(G-1294)* | | |
| Nextpoint Inc | E | 773 929-4000 |
| Chicago *(G-5907)* | | |
| Onefire Media Group Inc | E | 309 740-0345 |
| Peoria *(G-17419)* | | |
| Optimus Advantage LLC | G | 847 905-1000 |
| Chicago *(G-5997)* | | |
| Orinoco Systems LLC | G | 630 510-0775 |
| Wheaton *(G-21971)* | | |
| Own The Night App | G | 773 216-0245 |
| Chicago *(G-6033)* | | |
| Patientbond LLC | E | 312 445-8751 |
| Elmhurst *(G-9919)* | | |
| Physician Software Systems LLC | F | 630 717-8192 |
| Lisle *(G-13639)* | | |
| Playground Pointers | G | 952 200-4168 |
| Hinsdale *(G-11959)* | | |
| Polysystems Inc | D | 312 332-2114 |
| Chicago *(G-6155)* | | |
| Producepro Inc | G | 630 395-9700 |
| Woodridge *(G-22512)* | | |
| Ptc Inc | E | 630 827-4900 |
| Oakbrook Terrace *(G-16718)* | | |
| Radiofx Inc | G | 773 255-8069 |
| Chicago *(G-6280)* | | |
| Reliefwatch Inc | G | 646 678-2336 |
| Chicago *(G-6331)* | | |
| Route 40 Media LLC | G | 309 370-5809 |
| Peoria *(G-17449)* | | |
| Scholarship Solutions LLC | F | 847 859-5629 |
| Chicago *(G-6453)* | | |
| Secure Data Inc | F | 618 726-5225 |
| O Fallon *(G-16478)* | | |
| See What You Send Inc | G | 781 780-1483 |
| Chicago *(G-6473)* | | |
| Sellers Commerce LLC | F | 858 345-1212 |
| Northbrook *(G-16361)* | | |

**Signal Digital Inc**.....E..... 312 685-1911
Chicago *(G-6509)*
**Signs & Wonders Unlimited LLC**.....G..... 847 816-9734
Libertyville *(G-13381)*
**Social Qnect LLC**.....G..... 847 997-0077
Northbrook *(G-16366)*
**Spend Radar LLC**.....E..... 312 265-0764
Chicago *(G-6558)*
**Systat Software Inc**.....E..... 408 876-4508
Chicago *(G-6658)*
**System Software Associates Del**.....E..... 312 258-6000
Chicago *(G-6660)*
**Systems Live Ltd**.....G..... 815 455-3383
Crystal Lake *(G-7657)*
**Tagobi LLC**.....G..... 331 444-2951
Wheaton *(G-21983)*
**Thinkcercacom Inc**.....F..... 224 412-3722
Chicago *(G-6714)*
**Thoughtly Corp**.....G..... 772 559-2008
Chicago *(G-6721)*
**Tradevolve Inc**.....G..... 847 987-9411
Crystal Lake *(G-7668)*
**Tripnary LLC**.....G..... 512 554-1911
Chicago *(G-6777)*
**Truth Labs LLC**.....F..... 312 291-9035
Chicago *(G-6790)*
**Twocanoes Software Inc**.....G..... 630 305-9601
Naperville *(G-15769)*
**Txticon LLC**.....G..... 312 860-3378
Chicago *(G-6800)*
**U4g Group LLC**.....G..... 847 821-6061
Buffalo Grove *(G-2783)*
**Ubipass Inc**.....G..... 312 626-4624
Willowbrook *(G-22236)*
**Uxm Studio Inc**.....G..... 773 359-1333
Villa Park *(G-21288)*
**Viclarity Inc**.....G..... 201 214-5405
Chicago *(G-6892)*
**Vizr Tech LLC**.....G..... 312 420-4466
Chicago *(G-6909)*
**Warbler Digital Inc**.....E..... 312 924-1056
Chicago *(G-6939)*
**Wargaming (usa) Inc**.....F..... 312 258-0500
Chicago *(G-6940)*
**Webqa Incorporated**.....E..... 630 985-1300
Woodridge *(G-22523)*
**Xaptum Inc**.....G..... 847 404-6205
Chicago *(G-7043)*

## *SOFTWARE PUBLISHERS: Business & Professional*

**A Trustworthy Sup Source Inc**.....G..... 773 480-0255
Chicago *(G-3693)*
**Access International Inc**.....E..... 312 920-9366
Chicago *(G-3715)*
**Adaptive Insights Inc**.....E..... 800 303-6346
Rolling Meadows *(G-18707)*
**Adesso Solutions LLC**.....F..... 847 342-1095
Rolling Meadows *(G-18708)*
**Aeverie Inc**.....G..... 844 238-3743
Buffalo Grove *(G-2651)*
**Affinnova Inc**.....G..... 781 464-4700
Chicago *(G-3780)*
**Agile Health Technologies Inc**.....E..... 630 247-5565
Naperville *(G-15789)*
**Ahead LLC**.....D..... 312 924-4492
Chicago *(G-3783)*
**Anju Software Inc**.....E..... 630 243-9810
Woodridge *(G-22452)*
**Applied Systems Inc**.....A..... 708 534-5575
University Park *(G-21041)*
**AR Inet Corp**.....G..... 603 380-3903
Aurora *(G-959)*
**Autonomy Inc**.....E..... 312 580-9100
Chicago *(G-3993)*
**Barcoding Inc**.....F..... 847 726-7777
Mundelein *(G-15474)*
**Blue Software LLC**.....D..... 773 957-1669
Chicago *(G-4126)*
**Brevity LLC**.....F..... 312 375-3996
Chicago *(G-4162)*
**Call Potential LLC**.....F..... 877 552-2557
Naperville *(G-15615)*
**Capital Merchant Solutions Inc**.....F..... 309 452-5990
Bloomington *(G-2152)*
**Captivision Inc**.....G..... 630 235-8763
Bolingbrook *(G-2283)*
**Catalytic Inc**.....G..... 312 927-8750
Naperville *(G-15621)*
**CDK Global Inc**.....A..... 847 397-1700
Hoffman Estates *(G-11998)*
**Code Sixfour LLC**.....G..... 312 429-4802
Chicago *(G-4416)*
**Computerized Fleet Analysis**.....G..... 630 543-1410
Addison *(G-80)*
**Crestwood Associates LLC**.....F..... 847 394-8820
Mount Prospect *(G-15319)*
**Crew Beacon LLC**.....G..... 888 966-4455
Chicago *(G-4505)*
**Cyborg Systems Inc**.....C..... 312 279-7000
Chicago *(G-4529)*
**Datair Employee Beneft Systems**.....E..... 630 325-2600
Westmont *(G-21881)*
**Digi Trax Corporation**.....E..... 847 613-2100
Lincolnshire *(G-13443)*
**Ecd-Network LLC**.....G..... 917 670-0821
Chicago *(G-4691)*
**Eighty Nine Robotics LLC**.....G..... 512 573-9091
Chicago *(G-4705)*
**Envestnet Rtrment Slutions LLC**.....G..... 312 827-7957
Chicago *(G-4764)*
**Equilibrium Contact Center Inc**.....G..... 888 708-1405
Rockford *(G-18367)*
**Esquify Inc**.....G..... 917 553-3741
Chicago *(G-4777)*
**Evention LLC**.....E..... 773 733-4256
Chicago *(G-4789)*
**Fast Lane Applications LLC**.....G..... 815 245-2145
Cary *(G-3340)*
**Fivecubits Inc**.....G..... 630 749-4182
Oak Brook *(G-16513)*
**Floydware LLC**.....G..... 630 469-1078
Lombard *(G-13800)*
**Fooda Inc**.....E..... 312 752-4352
Chicago *(G-4869)*
**Forecast Five**.....G..... 630 657-6400
Naperville *(G-15660)*
**Friedrich Klatt and Associates**.....G..... 773 753-1806
Chicago *(G-4891)*
**G2 Crowd Inc**.....F..... 847 748-7559
Chicago *(G-4904)*
**Gcom Inc**.....F..... 217 351-4241
Savoy *(G-19409)*
**Hybris (us) Corporation**.....E..... 312 265-5010
Chicago *(G-5128)*
**Icnet Systems Inc**.....E..... 630 836-8073
Deerfield *(G-8014)*
**Imanage LLC**.....C..... 312 667-7000
Chicago *(G-5162)*
**Impact Technologies Inc**.....G..... 708 246-5041
Western Springs *(G-21867)*
**Infogix Inc**.....C..... 630 505-1800
Naperville *(G-15674)*
**Inkling**.....G..... 312 376-8129
Chicago *(G-5196)*
**Iq7 Technology Inc**.....G..... 917 670-1715
Chicago *(G-5237)*
**Kcura LLC**.....B..... 312 263-1177
Chicago *(G-5368)*
**Legistek LLC**.....G..... 312 399-4891
Chicago *(G-5491)*
**Linkhouse LLC**.....G..... 312 671-2225
Schaumburg *(G-19618)*
**Localfix Solutions LLC**.....G..... 312 569-0619
Winfield *(G-22287)*
**Logical Design Solutions Inc**.....G..... 630 786-5999
Aurora *(G-1047)*
**Logicgate Inc**.....F..... 312 279-2775
Chicago *(G-5533)*
**Lonelybrand LLC**.....G..... 312 880-7506
Chicago *(G-5536)*
**Marketing Analytics Inc**.....D..... 847 733-8459
Evanston *(G-10070)*
**Motivequest LLC**.....F..... 847 905-6100
Evanston *(G-10075)*
**Myeccho LLC**.....G..... 224 639-3068
Des Plaines *(G-8240)*
**Napersoft Inc**.....F..... 630 420-1515
Naperville *(G-15710)*
**Navipoint Genomics LLC**.....G..... 630 464-8013
Naperville *(G-15819)*
**Next Generation Inc**.....G..... 312 953-7514
Plainfield *(G-17632)*
**Onx USA LLC**.....E..... 630 343-8940
Lisle *(G-13637)*
**Oracle Corporation**.....B..... 630 931-6400
Itasca *(G-12336)*
**Oracle Corporation**.....B..... 262 957-3000
Chicago *(G-6000)*
**Origami Risk LLC**.....G..... 312 546-6515
Chicago *(G-6010)*
**Pagepath Technologies Inc**.....F..... 630 689-4111
Plano *(G-17671)*
**Panatech Computer Management**.....G..... 847 678-8848
Schiller Park *(G-19857)*
**Paragon International Inc**.....F..... 847 240-2981
Schaumburg *(G-19682)*
**PC Concepts**.....G..... 847 223-6490
Round Lake Beach *(G-19078)*
**Perry Johnson Inc**.....F..... 847 635-0010
Rosemont *(G-19021)*
**Pervasive Health Inc**.....G..... 312 257-2967
Chicago *(G-6107)*
**Phillip Grigalanz**.....G..... 219 628-6706
Jerseyville *(G-12425)*
**Pix2doc LLC**.....G..... 312 925-4010
Lisle *(G-13642)*
**Prime Time Computer Services**.....G..... 815 553-0300
Joliet *(G-12554)*
**Proship Inc**.....G..... 312 332-7447
Chicago *(G-6217)*
**Psychiatric Assessments Inc**.....G..... 312 878-6490
Chicago *(G-6220)*
**Public Good Software Inc**.....F..... 877 941-2747
Chicago *(G-6222)*
**Radius Solutions Incorporated**.....F..... 312 648-0800
Chicago *(G-6283)*
**Rapid Execution Services LLC**.....G..... 312 789-4358
Chicago *(G-6293)*
**Realize Inc**.....G..... 312 566-8759
Chicago *(G-6307)*
**Recsolu Inc**.....E..... 312 517-3200
Chicago *(G-6313)*
**Rivalfly National Network LLC**.....G..... 847 867-8660
Chicago *(G-6361)*
**Robis Elections Inc**.....F..... 630 752-0220
Wheaton *(G-21977)*
**Salesforcecom Inc**.....G..... 312 361-3555
Chicago *(G-6432)*
**Salesforcecom Inc**.....G..... 312 288-3600
Chicago *(G-6433)*
**Scientific Cmpt Assoc Corp**.....G..... 708 771-4567
River Forest *(G-18001)*
**Secureslice Inc**.....E..... 800 984-0494
Chicago *(G-6470)*
**Sedona Inc**.....C..... 309 736-4104
Moline *(G-14969)*
**Showcase Corporation**.....C..... 312 651-3000
Chicago *(G-6500)*
**Simplement Inc**.....G..... 702 560-5332
Northfield *(G-16418)*
**Sullivan Cgliano Training Ctrs**.....G..... 312 422-0009
Chicago *(G-6614)*
**Supply Vision Inc**.....G..... 847 388-0064
Chicago *(G-6637)*
**Tempus Health Inc**.....E..... 312 784-4400
Chicago *(G-6699)*
**Thomas A Doan**.....G..... 847 864-8772
Evanston *(G-10102)*
**Timepilot Corporation**.....G..... 630 879-6400
Batavia *(G-1507)*
**Tom Zosel Associates Ltd**.....D..... 847 540-6543
Long Grove *(G-13903)*
**Topvox Corporation**.....B..... 847 842-0900
Barrington *(G-1309)*
**Track My Foreclosures LLC**.....G..... 877 782-8187
Monticello *(G-15088)*
**Truepad LLC**.....F..... 847 274-6898
Chicago *(G-6787)*
**Vertex Inc**.....G..... 630 328-2600
Naperville *(G-15776)*
**Vertical Software Inc**.....F..... 309 633-0700
Bartonville *(G-1399)*
**Viva Solutions Inc**.....G..... 312 332-8882
Lemont *(G-13268)*
**Vivor LLC**.....G..... 312 967-6379
Chicago *(G-6908)*
**Yhlsoft Inc**.....F..... 630 355-8033
Naperville *(G-15787)*

## *SOFTWARE PUBLISHERS: Computer Utilities*

**Alpine Energy Systems LLC**.....G..... 630 581-4840
Oak Brook *(G-16487)*
**BMC Software Inc**.....E..... 331 777-8700
Downers Grove *(G-8398)*
**Lbe Ltd**.....G..... 847 907-4959
Kildeer *(G-12701)*



Employee Codes: A=Over 500 employees, B=251-500
C=101-250, D=51-100, E=20-50, F=10-19, G=3-9
2017 Harris Illinois
Industrial Directory
1757

**Orbit Enterprises Inc** ....G.... 630 469-3405
Oak Brook *(G-16553)*

**Zirmed Inc** ....F.... 312 207-0889
Chicago *(G-7070)*

## *SOFTWARE PUBLISHERS: Education*

**Active Simulations Inc** ....G.... 630 747-8393
Oak Park *(G-16648)*

**Brainware Company** ....G.... 773 250-6465
Chicago *(G-4156)*

**C W Publications Inc** ....G.... 800 554-5537
Sterling *(G-20586)*

**Capsim MGT Simulations Inc** ....E.... 312 477-7200
Chicago *(G-4231)*

**Cengage Learning Inc** ....G.... 630 554-0821
Downers Grove *(G-8406)*

**Classroom Technologies LLC** ....G.... 708 548-1642
Frankfort *(G-10310)*

**Cleartrial LLC** ....F.... 877 206-4846
Chicago *(G-4398)*

**Comptia Learning LLC** ....F.... 630 678-8490
Downers Grove *(G-8415)*

**CU Info Systems** ....E.... 630 607-0300
Elmhurst *(G-9861)*

**Digital Ignite LLC** ....G.... 630 317-7904
Lombard *(G-13791)*

**Embodied Labs Inc** ....G.... 336 971-5886
Chicago *(G-4737)*

**Follett School Solutions Inc** ....C.... 815 759-1700
McHenry *(G-14507)*

**Goeducation LLC** ....G.... 312 800-1838
Chicago *(G-4969)*

**Gtx Surgery Inc** ....G.... 847 920-8489
Evanston *(G-10047)*

**HMS Teach Inc** ....E.... 800 624-2926
Hoffman Estates *(G-12016)*

**Humaginarium LLC** ....G.... 312 788-7719
Oak Park *(G-16669)*

**Iep Quality Inc** ....G.... 217 840-0570
Champaign *(G-3497)*

**Jones Software Corp** ....G.... 312 952-0011
Chicago *(G-5322)*

**L-Data Corporation** ....E.... 312 552-7855
Chicago *(G-5423)*

**Lansa Inc** ....C.... 630 874-7042
Downers Grove *(G-8472)*

**M T M Assn For Standards & RES** ....G.... 847 299-1111
Des Plaines *(G-8224)*

**MCS Management Corp** ....G.... 847 680-3707
Hawthorn Woods *(G-11703)*

**Medcore International LLC** ....G.... 630 645-9900
Oak Brook *(G-16540)*

**Mlevel Inc** ....E.... 888 564-5395
Chicago *(G-5779)*

**Nerd Island Studios LLC** ....G.... 224 619-5361
Highland Park *(G-11859)*

**Otus LLC** ....E.... 312 229-7648
Chicago *(G-6025)*

**Overgrad Inc** ....G.... 312 324-4952
Chicago *(G-6028)*

**Peopleadmin Inc** ....E.... 877 637-5800
Chicago *(G-6102)*

**Prairie Wi-Fi Systems** ....G.... 515 988-3260
Chicago *(G-6167)*

**Questily LLC** ....G.... 312 636-6657
Chicago *(G-6256)*

**Questily LLC** ....G.... 312 636-6657
Chicago *(G-6257)*

**Sunburst Technology Corp** ....G.... 800 321-7511
Elgin *(G-9197)*

**Svanaco Inc** ....D.... 847 699-0300
Des Plaines *(G-8284)*

**Swift Education Systems Inc** ....G.... 312 257-3751
Chicago *(G-6649)*

**Teenfitnation LLC** ....G.... 847 322-2953
South Barrington *(G-20133)*

**Tegrity Inc** ....E.... 800 411-0579
Burr Ridge *(G-2884)*

**Victor Consulting** ....G.... 847 267-8012
Lincolnshire *(G-13489)*

**Wincademy Inc** ....G.... 847 445-7886
Grayslake *(G-11367)*

## *SOFTWARE PUBLISHERS: Home Entertainment*

**Independent Network Tv LLC** ....G.... 312 953-8508
Forest Park *(G-10249)*

**Liaison Home Automation LLC** ....G.... 888 279-1235
Mount Zion *(G-15454)*

**Midway Games Inc** ....E.... 773 961-2222
Chicago *(G-5739)*

**Pluribus Games LLC** ....G.... 630 770-2043
Aurora *(G-1204)*

## *SOFTWARE PUBLISHERS: NEC*

**A M P Software Inc** ....G.... 630 240-5922
Elk Grove Village *(G-9251)*

**Accruent LLC** ....G.... 847 425-3600
Evanston *(G-10002)*

**Accuware Incorporated** ....F.... 630 858-8409
Glen Ellyn *(G-10957)*

**Acp Tower Holdings LLC** ....G.... 800 835-8527
Chicago *(G-3737)*

**Acresso Software Inc** ....G.... 408 642-3865
Schaumburg *(G-19421)*

**Adams Telephone Co-Operative** ....E.... 217 224-9566
Quincy *(G-17789)*

**Adflow Networks** ....G.... 866 423-3569
Chicago *(G-3749)*

**Aldea Technologies Inc** ....E.... 800 804-0635
Schaumburg *(G-19428)*

**Allscripts Healthcare LLC** ....G.... 312 506-1200
Chicago *(G-3820)*

**Allscripts Healthcare LLC** ....G.... 800 334-8534
Chicago *(G-3821)*

**Allscrpts Hlthcare Sltions Inc** ....C.... 312 506-1200
Chicago *(G-3822)*

**Allscrpts Hlthcare Sltions Inc** ....C.... 312 506-1200
Chicago *(G-3823)*

**Amada America Inc** ....G.... 877 262-3287
Itasca *(G-12226)*

**Anylogic N Amer Ltd Lblty Co** ....G.... 312 635-3344
Chicago *(G-3918)*

**Aptean Holdings Inc** ....F.... 773 975-3100
Chicago *(G-3929)*

**Ariba Inc** ....G.... 630 649-7600
Lisle *(G-13562)*

**Asset Partners Inc** ....G.... 312 224-8300
Chicago *(G-3966)*

**Associate Computer Systems** ....G.... 618 997-3653
Marion *(G-14254)*

**Associated Agri-Business Inc** ....G.... 618 498-2977
Jerseyville *(G-12417)*

**Associated Agri-Business Inc** ....G.... 618 498-2977
Eldred *(G-8927)*

**Audibel Hearing Aid Services** ....G.... 217 234-6426
Mattoon *(G-14383)*

**Auto Injury Solutions Inc** ....C.... 312 229-2704
Chicago *(G-3990)*

**Avaya Inc** ....F.... 847 885-3598
Schaumburg *(G-19452)*

**Avectra Inc** ....E.... 312 425-9094
Chicago *(G-3997)*

**Bantix Technologies LLC** ....G.... 630 446-0886
Glen Ellyn *(G-10960)*

**Banyan Technologies Inc** ....G.... 312 967-9885
Chicago *(G-4037)*

**Barclay Business Group Inc** ....G.... 847 325-5555
Lincolnshire *(G-13431)*

**Barcodesource Inc** ....G.... 630 545-9590
West Chicago *(G-21667)*

**Bc Asi Capital II Inc** ....A.... 708 534-5575
University Park *(G-21043)*

**Bi Software Inc** ....G.... 224 622-4706
Hoffman Estates *(G-11995)*

**Bighand Inc** ....F.... 312 893-5906
Chicago *(G-4105)*

**Bosch Sftwr Innovations Corp** ....E.... 312 368-2500
Chicago *(G-4147)*

**Braindok LLC** ....G.... 847 877-1586
Buffalo Grove *(G-2668)*

**Brainstorm USA** ....F.... 773 509-1227
Chicago *(G-4155)*

**Bridgeline Digital Inc** ....G.... 312 784-5720
Chicago *(G-4165)*

**Business Systems Consultants** ....F.... 312 553-1253
Chicago *(G-4189)*

**Ca Inc** ....D.... 631 342-6000
Lisle *(G-13572)*

**Capers North America LLC** ....F.... 708 995-7500
Burr Ridge *(G-2827)*

**Cassetica Software Inc** ....G.... 312 546-3668
Chicago *(G-4250)*

**Catapult Communications Corp** ....G.... 847 884-0048
Schaumburg *(G-19469)*

**Chartnet Technologies Inc** ....F.... 630 385-4100
Yorkville *(G-22651)*

**Chewy Software LLC** ....G.... 773 935-2627
Chicago *(G-4298)*

**Chwey Software LLC** ....E.... 773 525-6445
Chicago *(G-4376)*

**Citrix Systems Inc** ....G.... 847 716-4797
Northfield *(G-16398)*

**Clear Nda LLC** ....F.... 470 222-6320
Park Ridge *(G-17187)*

**Cleo Communications Inc** ....E.... 815 654-8110
Rockford *(G-18312)*

**Cognizant Tech Solutions Corp** ....E.... 630 955-0617
Lisle *(G-13575)*

**Common Goal Systems Inc** ....E.... 630 592-4200
Elmhurst *(G-9855)*

**Community Cllabration Acquatio** ....G.... 815 316-6390
Rockford *(G-18318)*

**Community Collaboration Inc** ....G.... 815 316-4660
Rockford *(G-18319)*

**Compusystems Inc** ....C.... 708 344-9070
Downers Grove *(G-8416)*

**Computer Pwr Solutions Ill Ltd** ....E.... 618 281-8898
Columbia *(G-7355)*

**Computing Integrity Inc** ....G.... 217 355-4469
Champaign *(G-3469)*

**Connectmedia Ventures LLC** ....G.... 773 327-3188
Chicago *(G-4450)*

**Connelly & Associates** ....E.... 847 372-5001
Palatine *(G-17015)*

**Conscisys Corp** ....E.... 630 810-4444
Downers Grove *(G-8418)*

**Coorens Communications Inc** ....G.... 773 235-8688
Chicago *(G-4465)*

**Cozent LLC** ....G.... 630 781-2822
Naperville *(G-15639)*

**Credit & Management Systems** ....F.... 618 654-3500
Highland *(G-11781)*

**Crowdsource Solutions Inc** ....F.... 855 276-9376
Swansea *(G-20777)*

**Cunningham Electronics Corp** ....G.... 618 833-7775
Anna *(G-602)*

**Customergauge USA LLC** ....G.... 773 669-5915
Chicago *(G-4527)*

**Data Link Communications** ....G.... 815 405-2856
Matteson *(G-14370)*

**Datafordummies** ....G.... 618 421-2323
Flat Rock *(G-10195)*

**Datix (usa) Inc** ....G.... 312 724-7776
Chicago *(G-4562)*

**Dell Software Inc** ....D.... 630 836-0503
Buffalo Grove *(G-2684)*

**Digital Minds Inc** ....G.... 847 430-3390
Rosemont *(G-18998)*

**Digital Realty Inc** ....E.... 630 428-7979
Naperville *(G-15647)*

**Dynami Solutions LLC** ....G.... 618 363-2771
Edwardsville *(G-8796)*

**Electronics Boutique Amer Inc** ....G.... 618 465-3125
Alton *(G-574)*

**Elitegen Corp** ....F.... 630 637-6917
Naperville *(G-15652)*

**Embassy Security Group Inc** ....E.... 800 627-1325
Orland Park *(G-16859)*

**EMC Corporation** ....D.... 630 505-3273
Lisle *(G-13585)*

**Entappia LLC** ....G.... 630 546-4531
Aurora *(G-1003)*

**Envestnet Inc** ....C.... 312 827-2800
Chicago *(G-4763)*

**Environmental Systems Res Inst** ....G.... 312 609-0966
Chicago *(G-4765)*

**Epazz Inc** ....G.... 312 955-8161
Wheeling *(G-22048)*

**Eplan Software & Svcs N Ameri** ....G.... 517 762-5800
Schaumburg *(G-19517)*

**Equisoft Inc** ....G.... 815 629-2789
Winnebago *(G-22295)*

**Equity Concepts Co Inc** ....G.... 815 226-1300
Rockford *(G-18368)*

**Eyelation LLC** ....F.... 888 308-4703
Tinley Park *(G-20911)*

**Fantasy Coverage Inc** ....F.... 630 592-8082
Elmhurst *(G-9870)*

**Fleetwood Press Inc** ....G.... 708 485-6811
Brookfield *(G-2632)*

**Flexera Holdings LP** ....G.... 847 466-4000
Itasca *(G-12265)*

**Flexera Software LLC** ....B.... 800 374-4353
Itasca *(G-12266)*

**Galleria Retail Tech Solutions** ....F.... 312 822-3437
Chicago *(G-4910)*

**GE Intelligent Platforms Inc** ....D.... 630 829-4000
Lisle *(G-13593)*

# SOFTWARE PUBLISHERS: NEC

| Company | Emp | Phone |
|---|---|---|
| Genisys Decision Corporation — Oak Park (G-16666) | G | 708 524-5100 |
| Global Tech & Resources Inc — Rolling Meadows (G-18732) | G | 630 364-4260 |
| Govqa Inc — Woodridge (G-22489) | F | 630 985-1300 |
| Great Software Laboratory Inc — Chicago (G-4999) | G | 630 655-8905 |
| Hands of Many LLC — Flossmoor (G-10225) | G | 917 841-9969 |
| Healthengine — Chicago (G-5061) | G | 312 340-8555 |
| Healthware Systems Inc — Elgin (G-9061) | E | 847 783-0670 |
| Hera Cnsltng Interntnl Opratn — Lisle (G-13599) | F | 630 515-8819 |
| High Tech Research Inc — Deerfield (G-8012) | F | 847 215-9797 |
| Hildebrant J Boyd & Co Inc — Schaumburg (G-19554) | G | 847 839-0850 |
| Hyperera Inc — Chicago (G-5130) | F | 312 842-2288 |
| I2c LLC — Naperville (G-15672) | G | 630 281-2330 |
| Ifs North America Inc — Itasca (G-12279) | E | 888 437-4968 |
| Imcp Inc — Itasca (G-12284) | G | 630 477-8600 |
| Industrial Finance Systems — Itasca (G-12285) | G | 847 592-0200 |
| Industrial Phrm Resources Inc — Bartlett (G-1357) | F | 630 823-4700 |
| Infiniscene Inc — Chicago (G-5182) | G | 630 567-0452 |
| Infinite Cnvrgnce Slutions Inc — Arlington Heights (G-777) | G | 224 764-3400 |
| Infopro Inc — Aurora (G-1029) | G | 630 978-9231 |
| Infor (us) Inc — Chicago (G-5184) | D | 312 279-1245 |
| Infor (us) Inc — Chicago (G-5185) | C | 312 258-6000 |
| Information Builders Inc — Schaumburg (G-19565) | E | 630 971-6700 |
| Information Resources Inc — Chicago (G-5186) | G | 312 474-3380 |
| Information Resources Inc — Chicago (G-5187) | A | 312 726-1221 |
| Information Resources Inc — Bartlett (G-1318) | B | 312 474-3154 |
| Information Resources Inc — Chicago (G-5188) | A | 312 474-8900 |
| Infosys Limited — Lisle (G-13606) | E | 630 482-5000 |
| Innovations For Learning Inc — Evanston (G-10056) | G | 800 975-3452 |
| Innovative Custom Software Inc — Naperville (G-15675) | G | 630 892-5022 |
| Innovative SEC Systems Inc — Savoy (G-19410) | F | 217 355-6308 |
| Inrule Technology Inc — Chicago (G-5203) | E | 312 648-1800 |
| Intel Corporation — Chicago (G-5209) | D | 408 765-8080 |
| Interscience Technologies Inc — Bolingbrook (G-2323) | G | 630 759-4444 |
| Ironsafe LLC — Naperville (G-15678) | G | 877 297-1833 |
| Isoprime Corporation — Lisle (G-13609) | G | 630 737-0963 |
| Jellyvision Inc — Chicago (G-5288) | D | 312 266-0606 |
| Jmk Computerized Tdis Inc — Urbana (G-21092) | G | 217 384-8891 |
| K-Tron Inc — Orland Park (G-16872) | G | 708 460-2128 |
| Kana Software Inc — Chicago (G-5357) | G | 312 447-5600 |
| King of Software Inc — Des Plaines (G-8218) | G | 847 354-8745 |
| Kronos Incorporated — Schaumburg (G-19606) | G | 847 969-6501 |
| Ksr Software LLC — Palatine (G-17048) | G | 847 705-0100 |
| Lab Software Inc — Minooka (G-14841) | G | 815 521-9116 |
| Larsen & Toubro Infotech Ltd — Schaumburg (G-19613) | G | 847 303-3900 |
| Lattice Incorporated — Wheaton (G-21964) | E | 630 949-3250 |
| Leanoptima LLC — Palatine (G-17049) | E | 847 648-1592 |
| Legal Files Software Inc — Springfield (G-20468) | E | 217 726-6000 |
| Lexray LLC — Downers Grove (G-8475) | F | 630 664-6740 |
| Liberty Grove Software Inc — Glen Ellyn (G-10977) | G | 630 858-7388 |
| Linkedhealth Solutions — Chicago (G-5513) | F | 312 600-6684 |
| Liquidfire — Chicago (G-5517) | G | 312 376-7448 |
| Manufacturing Tech Group Inc — Rockford (G-18482) | G | 815 966-2300 |
| Marin Software Incorporated — Chicago (G-5520) | G | 312 267-2083 |
| Martin Peter Associates Inc — Chicago (G-5632) | G | 773 478-2400 |
| Marucco Stddard Frenbach Walsh — Springfield (G-20474) | E | 217 698-3535 |
| McConnell Chase Software Works — Chicago (G-5665) | G | 312 540-1508 |
| Mealplot Inc — Champaign (G-3513) | G | 217 419-2681 |
| Mediafly Inc — Chicago (G-5677) | G | 312 281-5175 |
| Message Mediums LLC — Chicago (G-5698) | F | 877 450-0075 |
| Metamation Inc — Rolling Meadows (G-18743) | F | 775 826-1717 |
| Michaels Ross and Cole Inc — Oak Brook (G-16543) | F | 630 916-0662 |
| Micrograms Inc — Loves Park (G-13966) | G | 815 877-4455 |
| Microsoft Corporation — Downers Grove (G-8486) | D | 630 725-4000 |
| Microsoft Corporation — Northlake (G-16442) | D | 708 409-4759 |
| Microstrategy Incorporated — Schaumburg (G-19644) | G | 703 589-0734 |
| Mirus Research — Normal (G-16077) | E | 309 828-3100 |
| Mobilehop Technology LLC — Chicago (G-5780) | G | 312 504-3773 |
| Moduslink Corporation — Bedford Park (G-1566) | E | 708 496-7800 |
| Monotype Imaging Inc — Mount Prospect (G-15350) | G | 847 718-0400 |
| Monotype Imaging Inc — Elk Grove Village (G-9635) | F | 847 718-0400 |
| Mu Dai LLC — Chicago (G-5828) | F | 312 982-0040 |
| My Local Beacon Llc — Chicago (G-5840) | G | 888 482-6691 |
| Myhomeeq LLC — Chicago (G-5845) | G | 773 328-7034 |
| Nanex LLC — Winnetka (G-22313) | G | 847 501-4787 |
| Network Harbor Inc — Peoria (G-17416) | G | 309 633-9118 |
| New Vision Software Inc — Barrington (G-1295) | G | 847 382-1532 |
| Newera Software Inc — Kingston (G-12707) | G | 815 784-3345 |
| Novaspect Inc — Schaumburg (G-19670) | C | 847 956-8020 |
| Oas Software Corp — Saint Charles (G-19226) | F | 630 513-2990 |
| Oracle Corporation — Chicago (G-5998) | B | 773 404-9300 |
| Oracle Corporation — Chicago (G-5999) | G | 312 692-5270 |
| Oracle Hcm User Group Inc — Chicago (G-6001) | G | 312 222-9350 |
| Oracle Systems Corporation — Chicago (G-6002) | E | 312 245-1580 |
| Orecx — Chicago (G-6006) | F | 312 895-5292 |
| Owanza Corporation — Chicago (G-6031) | G | 312 281-2900 |
| P B R W Enterprises Inc — Woodstock (G-22597) | G | 815 337-5519 |
| Parallel Solutions LLC — Schaumburg (G-19683) | G | 847 708-9227 |
| Paylocity Holding Corporation — Arlington Heights (G-817) | E | 847 463-3200 |
| Paylocity Holding Corporation — Naperville (G-15722) | C | 331 701-7975 |
| Pc-Tel Inc — Bloomingdale (G-2127) | C | 630 372-6800 |
| Peak Computer Systems Inc — Belleville (G-1665) | F | 618 398-5612 |
| Pendragon Software Corporation — Chicago (G-6099) | G | 847 816-9660 |
| Personify — Urbana (G-21097) | F | 217 840-2638 |
| Picis Clinical Solutions Inc — Rosemont (G-19023) | E | 847 993-2200 |
| Pinnakle Technologies Inc — Aurora (G-1066) | F | 630 352-0070 |
| Pitney Bowes Inc — Itasca (G-12341) | E | 800 784-4224 |
| Politech Inc — Trout Valley (G-21001) | G | 847 516-2717 |
| Powerschool Group LLC — Chicago (G-6160) | F | 610 867-9200 |
| Precision Software Limited — Lisle (G-13644) | E | 312 239-1630 |
| Premier International Entps — Chicago (G-6177) | E | 312 857-2200 |
| Prism Esolutions Dv Andy Frain — Aurora (G-1069) | F | 630 820-3820 |
| Procura LLC — Westmont (G-21914) | G | 801 265-4571 |
| Productive Edge LLC — Chicago (G-6207) | D | 312 561-9000 |
| Proquis Inc — Elgin (G-9151) | F | 847 278-3230 |
| Protepo Ltd — Elk Grove Village (G-9699) | G | 847 466-1023 |
| Pubpal LLC — Washington (G-21389) | G | 309 222-5062 |
| Qad Inc — Lisle (G-13647) | G | 630 964-4030 |
| Quadramed Corporation — Chicago (G-6240) | G | 312 396-0700 |
| Quadrant 4 System Corporation — Schaumburg (G-19706) | B | 855 995-7367 |
| Quality Network Solutions Inc — Sullivan (G-20758) | E | 217 728-3155 |
| R & J Systems Inc — Bartlett (G-1322) | G | 630 289-3010 |
| Rayalco Inc — Park Ridge (G-17219) | G | 847 692-7422 |
| Raytrans Distribution Svcs Inc — Chicago (G-6297) | F | 708 503-9940 |
| React Computer Services Inc — Willowbrook (G-22229) | D | 630 323-6200 |
| Reflection Software Inc — Aurora (G-1073) | G | 630 585-2300 |
| Rmcis Corporation — Lisle (G-13652) | E | 630 955-1310 |
| Roger Cantu & Assocs — Oak Brook (G-16560) | G | 630 573-9215 |
| Rosewood Software Inc — Palatine (G-17069) | G | 847 438-2185 |
| SAI Info USA — Itasca (G-12352) | G | 630 773-3335 |
| Sales & Marketing Resources — Fox River Grove (G-10289) | G | 847 910-9169 |
| Savo Group Ltd — Chicago (G-6447) | C | 312 276-7700 |
| School Town LLC — Northbrook (G-16359) | G | 847 943-9115 |
| Sct Alternative Inc — Buffalo Grove (G-2765) | F | 847 215-7488 |
| Seoclarity — Des Plaines (G-8272) | | 773 831-4500 |
| Servicenow Inc — Downers Grove (G-8521) | G | 630 963-4608 |
| Sharpedge Solutions Inc — Naperville (G-15827) | F | 630 792-9639 |
| Siemens Product Life Mgmt Sftw — Downers Grove (G-8522) | E | 630 437-6700 |
| Signature Business Systems Inc — Deerfield (G-8053) | F | 847 459-8500 |
| Simply Computer Software Inc — Rockford (G-18618) | G | 815 231-0063 |
| Sirius Business Software — Palos Park (G-17133) | G | 708 361-5538 |
| Smartbyte Solutions Inc — Palatine (G-17075) | G | 847 925-1870 |
| Smartsignal Corporation — Lisle (G-13658) | D | 630 829-4000 |
| Snaglet LLC — Northbrook (G-16364) | G | 404 449-6394 |
| Soft O Soft Inc — Schaumburg (G-19730) | E | 630 741-4414 |
| Softhaus Ltd — Alton (G-590) | G | 618 463-1140 |

Employee Codes: A=Over 500 employees, B=251-500
C=101-250, D=51-100, E=20-50, F=10-19, G=3-9

2017 Harris Illinois Industrial Directory

## SOFTWARE PUBLISHERS: NEC

Softlabz Corporation .................................G ...... 847 780-7076
  Highland Park *(G-11870)*
Software Support Systems Inc .................G ...... 630 587-2999
  Saint Charles *(G-19265)*
Spl Software Alliance LLC .......................G ...... 309 266-0304
  Morton *(G-15182)*
Spooky Cool Labs LLC ..............................E ...... 773 577-5555
  Chicago *(G-6563)*
Starlight Software System Inc .................G ...... 309 454-7349
  Hudson *(G-12125)*
Storiant Inc ................................................E ...... 617 431-8000
  Chicago *(G-6600)*
Streamlinx LLC .........................................F ...... 630 864-3043
  Naperville *(G-15755)*
Structurepoint LLC ..................................F ...... 847 966-4357
  Skokie *(G-20092)*
Su Enterprise Inc .....................................G ...... 847 394-1656
  Arlington Heights *(G-846)*
Sunrise Futures LLC ................................G ...... 312 612-1041
  Chicago *(G-6628)*
Swift Technologies Inc ............................G ...... 815 568-8402
  Marengo *(G-14241)*
Symantec Corporation .............................C ...... 630 706-4700
  Oak Brook *(G-16562)*
Symfact Inc ...............................................E ...... 847 380-4174
  Chicago *(G-6656)*
Synergy Technology Group Inc ...............F ...... 773 305-3500
  Chicago *(G-6657)*
Synopsys Inc ............................................F ...... 847 706-2000
  Schaumburg *(G-19749)*
Systemslogix LLC .....................................G ...... 630 784-3113
  Glendale Heights *(G-11082)*
Tegratecs Development Corp ..................G ...... 847 397-0088
  Schaumburg *(G-19757)*
Telemedicine Solutions LLC ....................F ...... 847 519-3500
  Schaumburg *(G-19758)*
Telular Corporation ..................................D ...... 800 835-8527
  Chicago *(G-6692)*
Textura Corporation .................................C ...... 866 839-8872
  Deerfield *(G-8063)*
Thomson Quantitative Analytics ............E ...... 847 610-0574
  Chicago *(G-6717)*
Tindall Associates Inc .............................F ...... 708 403-7775
  Orland Park *(G-16898)*
Torgo Inc ...................................................G ...... 800 360-5910
  Riverwoods *(G-18045)*
Tradingscreen Inc ....................................G ...... 312 447-0100
  Chicago *(G-6753)*
Tri-Tech Sltons Consulting Inc ...............G ...... 847 941-0199
  Mount Prospect *(G-15379)*
Trident Software Corp .............................G ...... 847 219-8777
  Niles *(G-16044)*
Trizetto Corporation .................................C ...... 630 369-5300
  Naperville *(G-15768)*
Trustwave Holdings Inc ...........................G ...... 312 750-0950
  Chicago *(G-6789)*
Tsf Net Inc ................................................F ...... 815 246-7295
  Earlville *(G-8597)*
Turfmapp Inc ............................................G ...... 703 473-5678
  Chicago *(G-6792)*
Uberloop Inc .............................................G ...... 630 707-0567
  Naperville *(G-15770)*
Upright Network Services .......................G ...... 630 595-5559
  Bensenville *(G-2010)*
Vanguard Solutions Group Inc ................E ...... 630 545-1600
  Glen Ellyn *(G-10993)*
Varsity Logistics Inc ................................E ...... 650 392-7979
  Deerfield *(G-8065)*
Vauto Inc ...................................................E ...... 630 590-2000
  Oakbrook Terrace *(G-16722)*
Velocity Software LLC .............................F ...... 800 351-6893
  Lombard *(G-13877)*
Vertex Consulting Services Inc ..............F ...... 313 492-5154
  Schaumburg *(G-19786)*
Visibillity Inc .............................................E ...... 312 616-5900
  Chicago *(G-6901)*
Vision I Systems .......................................G ...... 312 326-9188
  Chicago *(G-6902)*
Visual Information Tech Inc ....................G ...... 217 841-2155
  Champaign *(G-3557)*
W A M Computers International .............G ...... 217 324-6926
  Litchfield *(G-13699)*
Websolutions Technology Inc .................E ...... 630 375-6833
  Aurora *(G-1095)*
Winscribe Usa Inc ...................................F ...... 773 399-1608
  Chicago *(G-7002)*
Wolfram Research Inc ............................G ...... 217 398-0700
  Champaign *(G-3562)*
Written Word Inc .....................................G ...... 630 671-9803
  Roselle *(G-18986)*
Yield Management Systems LLC ...........G ...... 312 665-1595
  Chicago *(G-7051)*
Zebra Software Inc .................................G ...... 847 742-9110
  Hoffman Estates *(G-12070)*

## SOFTWARE PUBLISHERS: Operating Systems

Computer Svcs & Consulting Inc ............E ...... 855 827-8328
  Chicago *(G-4441)*
Decision Systems Company ....................G ...... 815 885-3000
  Roscoe *(G-18892)*
Designa Access Corporation ...................G ...... 630 891-3105
  Westmont *(G-21884)*
Forte Incorporated ...................................G ...... 815 224-8300
  La Salle *(G-12773)*
Hostforweb Incorporated .........................G ...... 312 343-4678
  Chicago *(G-5116)*
Prairie Area Library System ...................E ...... 309 799-3155
  Coal Valley *(G-7298)*
Turner Agward .........................................F ...... 773 669-8559
  Chicago *(G-6794)*

## SOFTWARE PUBLISHERS: Publisher's

4ever Printing Inc ....................................G ...... 847 222-1525
  Arlington Heights *(G-699)*
American Labelmark Company ...............C ...... 773 478-0900
  Chicago *(G-3859)*
Computhink Inc ........................................E ...... 630 705-9050
  Lombard *(G-13783)*
Epublishing Inc ........................................G ...... 312 768-6800
  Chicago *(G-4767)*
Family Time Computing Inc ....................F ...... 309 664-1742
  Bloomington *(G-2162)*
Innerworkings Inc ....................................D ...... 312 642-3700
  Chicago *(G-5198)*
Invisible Institute ......................................E ...... 415 669-4691
  Chicago *(G-5233)*
Knowledgeshift Inc ..................................G ...... 630 221-8759
  Wheaton *(G-21962)*
Publishers Row .........................................F ...... 847 568-0593
  Skokie *(G-20067)*
Socialcloak Inc .........................................G ...... 650 549-4412
  East Dubuque *(G-8624)*
Srv Professional Publications .................G ...... 847 330-1260
  Schaumburg *(G-19739)*
Youtopia Inc ..............................................G ...... 312 593-0859
  Chicago *(G-7055)*

## SOFTWARE PUBLISHERS: Word Processing

Deep Value Inc .........................................E ...... 312 239-0143
  Chicago *(G-4573)*

## SOFTWARE TRAINING, COMPUTER

Braindok LLC ............................................G ...... 847 877-1586
  Buffalo Grove *(G-2668)*
Ifs North America Inc ..............................E ...... 888 437-4968
  Itasca *(G-12279)*
Proquis Inc ................................................F ...... 847 278-3230
  Elgin *(G-9151)*
Reliefwatch Inc .........................................G ...... 646 678-2336
  Chicago *(G-6331)*

## SOIL TESTING KITS

D and I Analyst Inc ..................................F ...... 217 636-7500
  Athens *(G-937)*
Luster Leaf Products Inc ........................G ...... 815 337-5560
  Woodstock *(G-22586)*

## SOLAR CELLS

Amoco Technology Company (del) ........C ...... 312 861-6000
  Chicago *(G-3892)*
BP Solar International Inc .......................A ...... 301 698-4200
  Naperville *(G-15611)*
Hoku Solar Power I LLC .........................F ...... 312 803-4972
  Chicago *(G-5096)*

## SOLAR HEATING EQPT

Dva Mayday Corporation .........................G ...... 847 848-7555
  Village of Lakewood *(G-21290)*
Polyair Inter Pack Inc .............................D ...... 773 995-1818
  Chicago *(G-6153)*
Sunbird Solar LLC ...................................G ...... 847 509-8888
  Northbrook *(G-16374)*

## SOLDERING EQPT: Electrical, Exc Handheld

Wenesco Inc ..............................................F ...... 773 283-3004
  Chicago *(G-6956)*

## SOLDERS

Alpha Assembly Solutions Inc ................C ...... 847 426-4241
  Elgin *(G-8944)*
Kester Inc ..................................................G ...... 630 616-6882
  Itasca *(G-12293)*
Kester Inc ..................................................C ...... 630 616-4000
  Itasca *(G-12294)*

## SOLENOIDS

Guardian Electric Mfg Co ........................D ...... 815 334-3600
  Woodstock *(G-22572)*
Weldon Corporation .................................E ...... 708 343-4700
  Maywood *(G-14437)*

## SOLVENTS

Vertec Biosolvents Inc ............................G ...... 630 960-0600
  Downers Grove *(G-8537)*

## SOLVENTS: Organic

Onyx Environmental Svcs LLC ...............E ...... 630 218-1500
  Lombard *(G-13838)*

## SOUND EFFECTS & MUSIC PRODUCTION: Motion Picture

Ikan Creations LLC ..................................G ...... 312 204-7333
  Chicago *(G-5150)*
Kaelco Entrmt Holdings Inc ....................G ...... 217 600-7815
  Champaign *(G-3505)*

## SOUND EQPT: Electric

Sound Design Inc .....................................G ...... 630 548-7000
  Plainfield *(G-17650)*
Victoria Amplifier Company ....................F ...... 630 369-3527
  Naperville *(G-15831)*

## SOUND RECORDING STUDIOS

Ken Young Construction Co ...................G ...... 847 358-3026
  Hoffman Estates *(G-12021)*

## SOUND REPRODUCING EQPT

Knowles Elec Holdings Inc .....................A ...... 630 250-5100
  Itasca *(G-12296)*

## SOYBEAN PRDTS

Archer-Daniels-Midland Company ..........D ...... 217 424-5882
  Decatur *(G-7833)*
Archer-Daniels-Midland Company ..........D ...... 217 424-5200
  Decatur *(G-7836)*
Archer-Daniels-Midland Company ..........D ...... 217 224-1800
  Quincy *(G-17795)*
Archer-Daniels-Midland Company ..........E ...... 217 424-5858
  Decatur *(G-7837)*
Archer-Daniels-Midland Company ..........A ...... 312 634-8100
  Chicago *(G-3941)*
Archer-Daniels-Midland Company ..........E ...... 217 424-5413
  Decatur *(G-7835)*
Archer-Daniels-Midland Company ..........E ...... 217 224-1800
  Quincy *(G-17794)*
Cargill Incorporated .................................E ...... 309 827-7100
  Bloomington *(G-2153)*
Incobrasa Industries Ltd .........................C ...... 815 265-4803
  Gilman *(G-10944)*
Pioneer Hi-Bred Intl Inc ..........................F ...... 309 962-2931
  Le Roy *(G-13209)*
Solae ..........................................................F ...... 217 784-8261
  Gibson City *(G-10907)*
Solae ..........................................................  ...... 217 784-2085
  Gibson City *(G-10908)*
Solae LLC ..................................................C ...... 219 261-2124
  Gibson City *(G-10909)*

## SPACE VEHICLE EQPT

Spytek Aerospace Corporation ...............G ...... 847 318-7515
  Bensenville *(G-1997)*

# PRODUCT SECTION

## SPORTING & ATHLETIC GOODS: Pools, Swimming, Exc Plastic

### SPARK PLUGS: Internal Combustion Engines
- NGK Spark Plugs (usa) Inc ............E....... 630 595-7894
  Wood Dale *(G-22406)*

### SPEAKER MONITORS
- Guys Hi-Def Inc ............G....... 708 261-7487
  Joliet *(G-12506)*

### SPEAKER SYSTEMS
- Acoustic Avenue Inc ............F....... 217 544-9810
  Springfield *(G-20385)*
- Alumapro Inc ............G....... 224 569-3650
  Huntley *(G-12131)*
- Bem Wireless LLC ............F....... 815 337-0541
  Algonquin *(G-381)*
- Hammond Suzuki Usa Inc ............E....... 630 543-0277
  Addison *(G-141)*
- Mitek Corporation ............C....... 608 328-5560
  Winslow *(G-22317)*
- SBA Wireless Inc ............E....... 847 215-8720
  Buffalo Grove *(G-2762)*
- Van L Speakerworks Inc ............G....... 773 769-0773
  Chicago *(G-6870)*

### SPEAKERS BUREAU
- Perry Johnson Inc ............F....... 847 635-0010
  Rosemont *(G-19021)*

### SPECIAL EVENTS DECORATION SVCS
- Anthos and Co LLC ............G....... 773 744-6813
  Inverness *(G-12202)*
- Best Kept Secrets ............G....... 773 431-0353
  Blue Island *(G-2238)*
- Mediatec Publishing Inc ............E....... 312 676-9900
  Chicago *(G-5678)*

### SPECIALTY FOOD STORES: Coffee
- Baileys Fudge & Fine Gifts Inc ............G....... 217 231-3834
  Quincy *(G-17799)*

### SPECIALTY FOOD STORES: Health & Dietetic Food
- AM Ko Oriental Foods ............G....... 217 398-2922
  Champaign *(G-3446)*
- Golden Health Products Inc ............G....... 217 223-3209
  Quincy *(G-17831)*
- Ottos Canvas Shop ............G....... 217 543-3307
  Arthur *(G-917)*

### SPECIALTY FOOD STORES: Juices, Fruit Or Vegetable
- Mangel and Co ............F....... 847 634-0730
  Long Grove *(G-13894)*

### SPECIALTY FOOD STORES: Soft Drinks
- Homer Vintage Bakery ............G....... 217 896-2538
  Homer *(G-12075)*

### SPECIALTY FOOD STORES: Vitamin
- Natures Sources LLC ............G....... 847 663-9168
  Niles *(G-16013)*
- Vital Proteins LLC ............E....... 224 544-9110
  Elk Grove Village *(G-9809)*
- Vital Proteins LLC ............E....... 224 544-9110
  Chicago *(G-6907)*

### SPECULATIVE BUILDERS: Single-Family Housing
- Plote Construction Inc ............D....... 847 695-9300
  Hoffman Estates *(G-12036)*

### SPEED CHANGERS
- Diequa Corporation ............E....... 630 980-1133
  Bloomingdale *(G-2103)*
- Productigear Inc ............E....... 773 847-4505
  Chicago *(G-6205)*

### SPICE & HERB STORES
- Andrias Food Group Inc ............E....... 618 632-4866
  O Fallon *(G-16461)*

- Arlington Specialties Inc ............G....... 847 545-9500
  Elk Grove Village *(G-9313)*
- Dell Cove Spice Co ............G....... 312 339-8389
  Chicago *(G-4577)*
- Sunrise Distributors Inc ............G....... 630 400-8786
  Elk Grove Village *(G-9761)*

### SPINDLES: Textile
- Lmk Technologies LLC ............D....... 815 433-1530
  Ottawa *(G-16967)*

### SPOOLS: Indl
- Christian Cnty Mntal Hlth Assn ............D....... 217 824-9675
  Taylorville *(G-20836)*
- Gavin Woodworking Inc ............G....... 815 786-2242
  Sandwich *(G-19365)*

### SPORTING & ATHLETIC GOODS: Bags, Golf
- Hunter-Nusport Inc ............G....... 815 254-7520
  Plainfield *(G-17607)*
- Zarc International Inc ............F....... 309 807-2565
  Minonk *(G-14835)*

### SPORTING & ATHLETIC GOODS: Bases, Baseball
- Normal Cornbelters ............G....... 309 451-3432
  Normal *(G-16079)*
- Southern Illinois Miners ............F....... 618 969-8506
  Marion *(G-14289)*

### SPORTING & ATHLETIC GOODS: Basketball Eqpt & Splys, NEC
- Allied Scoring Tables Inc ............G....... 815 654-8807
  Loves Park *(G-13918)*

### SPORTING & ATHLETIC GOODS: Bowling Alleys & Access
- Bluebird Lanes ............G....... 773 582-2828
  Chicago *(G-4128)*
- Flora Bowl ............G....... 618 662-4561
  Flora *(G-10206)*
- Illinois State Usbc Wba ............G....... 309 827-6355
  Bloomington *(G-2182)*
- James G Carter ............G....... 309 543-2634
  Havana *(G-11697)*
- Qcfec LLC ............G....... 309 517-1158
  Moline *(G-14964)*

### SPORTING & ATHLETIC GOODS: Camping Eqpt & Splys
- U Camp Products ............G....... 618 228-5080
  Aviston *(G-1249)*

### SPORTING & ATHLETIC GOODS: Dartboards & Access
- Arachnid 360 LLC ............E....... 815 654-0212
  Loves Park *(G-13921)*

### SPORTING & ATHLETIC GOODS: Darts & Table Sports Eqpt & Splys
- Abbacus Inc ............E....... 815 637-9222
  Machesney Park *(G-14048)*

### SPORTING & ATHLETIC GOODS: Dumbbells & Other Weight Eqpt
- Orthotech Sports - Med Eqp Inc ............F....... 618 942-6611
  Herrin *(G-11752)*
- U S Weight Inc ............E....... 618 392-0408
  Olney *(G-16799)*

### SPORTING & ATHLETIC GOODS: Exercising Cycles
- Brunswick Corporation ............A....... 847 288-3300
  Franklin Park *(G-10418)*

### SPORTING & ATHLETIC GOODS: Fish & Bait Baskets Or Creels
- Perry Adult Living Inc ............G....... 618 542-5421
  Du Quoin *(G-8557)*

### SPORTING & ATHLETIC GOODS: Fishing Bait, Artificial
- Blitz Lures LLC ............G....... 309 256-1574
  Dunlap *(G-8566)*

### SPORTING & ATHLETIC GOODS: Fishing Eqpt
- Donaldson & Associates Inc ............G....... 708 633-1090
  Lockport *(G-13710)*
- Jack & Lidias Resort Inc ............G....... 847 356-1389
  Lake Villa *(G-13017)*
- Kayser Lure Corp ............G....... 217 964-2110
  Ursa *(G-21105)*

### SPORTING & ATHLETIC GOODS: Fishing Tackle, General
- Bob Folder Lures Co ............F....... 217 787-1116
  Springfield *(G-20398)*
- Freemans Sports Inc ............G....... 630 553-0515
  Yorkville *(G-22660)*
- Orvis Company Inc ............F....... 312 440-0662
  Chicago *(G-6019)*
- Plastech Inc ............F....... 630 595-7222
  Bensenville *(G-1964)*
- South Bend Sporting Goods Inc ............E....... 847 715-1400
  Northbrook *(G-16367)*

### SPORTING & ATHLETIC GOODS: Game Calls
- Dj Illinois River Valley Calls ............G....... 309 348-2112
  Pekin *(G-17260)*

### SPORTING & ATHLETIC GOODS: Gymnasium Eqpt
- Brunswick Corporation ............B....... 847 288-3300
  Franklin Park *(G-10419)*
- Crown Gym Mats Inc ............F....... 847 381-8282
  Lake Barrington *(G-12803)*
- Moreno and Sons Inc ............G....... 815 725-8600
  Crest Hill *(G-7464)*

### SPORTING & ATHLETIC GOODS: Hockey Eqpt & Splys, NEC
- Jerrys Pro Shop Inc ............G....... 708 597-1144
  Alsip *(G-476)*

### SPORTING & ATHLETIC GOODS: Hooks, Fishing
- Siggs Rigs ............G....... 847 456-4012
  Crystal Lake *(G-7651)*

### SPORTING & ATHLETIC GOODS: Hunting Eqpt
- Big Dog Treestand Inc ............G....... 309 263-6800
  Morton *(G-15154)*
- Draves Investment Inc ............G....... 888 678-0251
  Effingham *(G-8833)*
- Oak Leaf Outdoors Inc ............F....... 309 691-9653
  Brimfield *(G-2548)*

### SPORTING & ATHLETIC GOODS: Indian Clubs
- Rasoi Resturaunt ............G....... 847 455-8888
  Roselle *(G-18965)*

### SPORTING & ATHLETIC GOODS: Lacrosse Eqpt & Splys, NEC
- True Lacrosse LLC ............G....... 630 359-3857
  Lombard *(G-13874)*

### SPORTING & ATHLETIC GOODS: Masks, Hockey, Baseball, Etc
- Kranos Corporation ............D....... 217 324-3978
  Litchfield *(G-13691)*

### SPORTING & ATHLETIC GOODS: Pools, Swimming, Exc Plastic
- David Hall ............E....... 309 797-9721
  Moline *(G-14924)*

## SPORTING & ATHLETIC GOODS: Pools, Swimming, Exc Plastic

Evergreen Pool & Spa LLC .................. G ....... 618 247-3555
  Sandoval *(G-19356)*
Platinum Aquatech Ltd ...................... F ....... 847 537-3800
  Wheeling *(G-22124)*
Royal Fiberglass Pools Inc .................. D ....... 618 266-7089
  Dix *(G-8318)*

### SPORTING & ATHLETIC GOODS: Pools, Swimming, Plastic

Sentry Pool & Chemical Supply ........... E ....... 309 797-9721
  Moline *(G-14970)*

### SPORTING & ATHLETIC GOODS: Protective Sporting Eqpt

Bell Sports ...................................... G ....... 309 693-2746
  Rantoul *(G-17919)*

### SPORTING & ATHLETIC GOODS: Reels, Fishing

Brunswick International Ltd ................ G ....... 847 735-4700
  Lake Forest *(G-12889)*

### SPORTING & ATHLETIC GOODS: Rods & Rod Parts, Fishing

Custom Rods By Grandt Ltd ............... G ....... 847 577-0848
  Arlington Heights *(G-741)*

### SPORTING & ATHLETIC GOODS: Shafts, Golf Club

Golfco Inc ....................................... E ....... 773 777-7877
  Chicago *(G-4976)*
Protactic Golf Enterprises .................. F ....... 708 209-1120
  River Forest *(G-17999)*

### SPORTING & ATHLETIC GOODS: Shuffleboards & Shuffleboard Eqpt

Shuffle Tech International LLC ........... G ....... 312 787-7780
  Chicago *(G-6503)*

### SPORTING & ATHLETIC GOODS: Skateboards

A W H Sales ................................... G ....... 847 869-0950
  Niles *(G-15954)*
Bluetown Skateboard Co LLC ............ G ....... 312 718-4786
  Chicago *(G-4130)*
Industryreadycom Inc ....................... G ....... 773 575-7001
  Chicago *(G-5181)*
Roger Jolly Skateboards .................... G ....... 618 277-7113
  Belleville *(G-1671)*

### SPORTING & ATHLETIC GOODS: Skates & Parts, Roller

Good Times Roll .............................. G ....... 217 285-4885
  Pittsfield *(G-17569)*

### SPORTING & ATHLETIC GOODS: Soccer Eqpt & Splys

Headball Inc ................................... G ....... 618 628-2656
  Belleville *(G-1634)*

### SPORTING & ATHLETIC GOODS: Softball Eqpt, Splys

Total Control Sports Inc .................... G ....... 708 486-5800
  Broadview *(G-2617)*

### SPORTING & ATHLETIC GOODS: Strings, Tennis Racket

Court & Slope Inc ............................ G ....... 847 697-3600
  Elgin *(G-9005)*

### SPORTING & ATHLETIC GOODS: Target Shooting Eqpt

Pistoleercom LLC ............................ G ....... 618 288-4649
  Maryville *(G-14346)*

### SPORTING & ATHLETIC GOODS: Targets, Archery & Rifle Shooting

Reagent Chemical & RES Inc ............. G ....... 618 271-8140
  East Saint Louis *(G-8766)*

### SPORTING & ATHLETIC GOODS: Team Sports Eqpt

Peak Healthcare Advisors LLC ............ G ....... 646 479-0005
  Chicago *(G-6093)*

### SPORTING & ATHLETIC GOODS: Track & Field Athletic Eqpt

Davis Athletic Equipment Co .............. F ....... 708 563-9006
  Bedford Park *(G-1547)*
Litania Sports Group Inc ................... C ....... 217 367-8438
  Champaign *(G-3510)*

### SPORTING & ATHLETIC GOODS: Water Sports Eqpt

Ccsi International Inc ........................ E ....... 815 544-8385
  Garden Prairie *(G-10793)*
H2o Pod Inc .................................... G ....... 630 240-1769
  Glen Ellyn *(G-10972)*
Polyair Inter Pack Inc ....................... D ....... 773 995-1818
  Chicago *(G-6153)*

### SPORTING & REC GOODS, WHOLESALE: Boats, Canoes, Etc/Eqpt

P W C Sports .................................. G ....... 708 516-6183
  Tinley Park *(G-20936)*

### SPORTING & RECREATIONAL GOODS & SPLYS WHOLESALERS

Court & Slope Inc ............................ G ....... 847 697-3600
  Elgin *(G-9005)*
Obies Tackle Co Inc ......................... G ....... 618 234-5638
  Belleville *(G-1662)*
Player Sports Ltd ............................. G ....... 773 764-4111
  Chicago *(G-6140)*
Roselynn Fashions ........................... G ....... 847 741-6000
  Elgin *(G-9167)*
Wilson Sporting Goods Co ................. B ....... 773 714-6400
  Chicago *(G-6990)*

### SPORTING & RECREATIONAL GOODS, WHOLESALE: Athletic Goods

Athletic Specialties Inc ..................... G ....... 847 487-7880
  Wauconda *(G-21444)*
Curt Smith Sporting Goods Inc ........... E ....... 618 233-5177
  Belleville *(G-1621)*
East West Martial Arts Sups .............. G ....... 773 878-7711
  Chicago *(G-4682)*
Riddell Inc ...................................... C ....... 847 292-1472
  Rosemont *(G-19027)*

### SPORTING & RECREATIONAL GOODS, WHOLESALE: Bicycle

BV USA Enterprises .......................... G ....... 224 619-7888
  Elk Grove Village *(G-9350)*
Joe Hunt ........................................ G ....... 618 392-2000
  Olney *(G-16774)*

### SPORTING & RECREATIONAL GOODS, WHOLESALE: Boat Access & Part

Custom Stainless Steel Inc ................ F ....... 618 435-2605
  Benton *(G-2026)*
Ottos Canvas Shop .......................... G ....... 217 543-3307
  Arthur *(G-917)*

### SPORTING & RECREATIONAL GOODS, WHOLESALE: Bowling

K 9 Tag Company Inc ....................... G ....... 847 304-8247
  Waukegan *(G-21575)*

### SPORTING & RECREATIONAL GOODS, WHOLESALE: Diving

Scuba Sports Inc ............................. G ....... 217 787-3483
  Springfield *(G-20519)*

### SPORTING & RECREATIONAL GOODS, WHOLESALE: Exercise

Septic Solutions Inc ......................... G ....... 217 925-5992
  Dieterich *(G-8314)*

### SPORTING & RECREATIONAL GOODS, WHOLESALE: Fishing

Donaldson & Associates Inc ............... G ....... 708 633-1090
  Lockport *(G-13710)*
Jerry H Simpson ............................. G ....... 618 654-3235
  Highland *(G-11798)*

### SPORTING & RECREATIONAL GOODS, WHOLESALE: Fishing Tackle

Bob Folder Lures Co ........................ F ....... 217 787-1116
  Springfield *(G-20398)*
Outback USA Inc ............................. G ....... 863 699-2220
  Saint Charles *(G-19231)*

### SPORTING & RECREATIONAL GOODS, WHOLESALE: Fitness

Orthotech Sports - Med Eqp Inc ......... F ....... 618 942-6611
  Herrin *(G-11752)*

### SPORTING & RECREATIONAL GOODS, WHOLESALE: Golf

Par Golf Supply Inc .......................... E ....... 847 891-1222
  Schaumburg *(G-19681)*

### SPORTING & RECREATIONAL GOODS, WHOLESALE: Hunting

Anjay Traders Inc ............................ G ....... 847 888-8562
  Elgin *(G-8954)*

### SPORTING CAMPS

Lakeshore Lacrosse LLC ................... G ....... 773 350-4356
  Wheaton *(G-21963)*

### SPORTING FIREARMS WHOLESALERS

Airgun Designs USA Inc .................... G ....... 847 520-7507
  Cary *(G-3324)*
Civilian Force Arms Inc ..................... G ....... 630 926-6982
  Yorkville *(G-22652)*
Devil Dog Arms Inc .......................... G ....... 847 790-4004
  Lake Zurich *(G-13062)*

### SPORTING GOODS

All American Athletics Ltd .................. G ....... 815 432-8326
  Watseka *(G-21413)*
Altamont Co .................................... D ....... 800 626-5774
  Thomasboro *(G-20859)*
Amer Sports Company ...................... B ....... 773 714-6400
  Chicago *(G-3846)*
Andrew C Arnold .............................. G ....... 815 220-0282
  Peru *(G-17499)*
Athletic Specialties Inc ..................... G ....... 847 487-7880
  Wauconda *(G-21444)*
Best Technology Systems Inc ............. F ....... 815 254-9554
  Plainfield *(G-17582)*
Bowlmor AMF Corp .......................... D ....... 708 456-4100
  River Grove *(G-18007)*
Bowlmor AMF Corp .......................... D ....... 847 367-1600
  Vernon Hills *(G-21152)*
Brg Sports Inc ................................. G ....... 217 819-5187
  Champaign *(G-3458)*
Brunswick Corporation ...................... B ....... 847 735-4700
  Lake Forest *(G-12888)*
BSN Sports LLC ............................... G ....... 217 788-0914
  Springfield *(G-20400)*
Buffalo Arms ................................... G ....... 630 969-1796
  Downers Grove *(G-8399)*
City Sports & Stage Door Dance ......... E ....... 708 687-9950
  Oak Forest *(G-16576)*
Collinsville Sports Store .................... G ....... 618 345-5588
  Collinsville *(G-7316)*
Crooked Creek Outdoors ................... G ....... 309 837-3000
  Macomb *(G-14123)*
Dark Speed Works ........................... G ....... 312 772-3275
  Wheaton *(G-21943)*
Empire Comfort Systems Inc .............. C ....... 618 233-7420
  Belleville *(G-1631)*

# PRODUCT SECTION

## SPRINGS: Hot Wound, Exc Wire

Enjoylife Inc .................................................. G ...... 847 966-3377
  Morton Grove *(G-15196)*
Flex Court International Inc ......................... F ...... 309 852-0899
  Kewanee *(G-12684)*
Geneva Running Outfitters LLC .................. G ...... 331 248-0221
  Geneva *(G-10831)*
Gill Athletics .................................................. G ...... 800 637-3090
  Champaign *(G-3487)*
Heartland Inspection Company ................... G ...... 630 788-3607
  Sycamore *(G-20799)*
Hunter Marketing Inc .................................. G ...... 630 541-8480
  Lisle *(G-13601)*
Hunter Mfg LLP ........................................... D ...... 859 254-7573
  Lake Forest *(G-12912)*
John Killough Dpm Cws .............................. G ...... 217 348-3339
  Charleston *(G-3602)*
L L Bean Inc ................................................. G ...... 847 568-3600
  Skokie *(G-20023)*
Nameplate Robinson & Precision ................ G ...... 847 678-2255
  Franklin Park *(G-10538)*
Nichols Net & Twine Inc .............................. G ...... 618 797-0211
  Granite City *(G-11298)*
Oban Composites LLC ................................. G ...... 866 607-0284
  Chicago *(G-5963)*
Official Issue Inc ......................................... G ...... 847 795-1066
  Harwood Heights *(G-11688)*
ProAm Sports Products ............................... G ...... 708 841-4200
  Dolton *(G-8375)*
Quality Targets ............................................. G ...... 618 245-6515
  Farina *(G-10177)*
Road Runner Sports Inc .............................. F ...... 847 719-8941
  Palatine *(G-17068)*
Scuba Sports Inc .......................................... G ...... 217 787-3483
  Springfield *(G-20519)*
Soccer House ............................................... G ...... 847 998-0088
  Glenview *(G-11204)*
Strikeforce Bowling LLC ............................. E ...... 800 297-8555
  Broadview *(G-2615)*
Superior Table Pad Co ................................. G ...... 773 248-7232
  Chicago *(G-6636)*
Terre Haute Tent & Awning Inc .................. F ...... 812 235-6068
  South Holland *(G-20309)*
The Athletic Equipment Source ................... E ...... 630 587-9333
  Saint Charles *(G-19281)*
Ultra Play Systems Inc ................................ E ...... 618 282-8200
  Red Bud *(G-17951)*
United Sportsmens Company ...................... G ...... 815 599-5690
  Freeport *(G-10696)*
Wagner International LLC .......................... G ...... 224 619-9247
  Vernon Hills *(G-21216)*
Warthog Inc .................................................. G ...... 815 540-7197
  Rockford *(G-18673)*
Welkins LLC ................................................. G ...... 877 319-3504
  Downers Grove *(G-8543)*
Wilson Sporting Goods Co .......................... C ...... 773 714-6500
  Chicago *(G-6991)*
Wilson Sporting Goods Co .......................... B ...... 773 714-6400
  Chicago *(G-6990)*
Woodland Fence Forest Pdts Inc ................ G ...... 630 393-2220
  Warrenville *(G-21369)*
World Class Technologies Inc ..................... G ...... 312 758-3114
  Chicago *(G-7029)*

### SPORTING GOODS STORES, NEC

Airgun Designs USA Inc ............................. G ...... 847 520-7507
  Cary *(G-3324)*
Ar1510 LLC .................................................. F ...... 309 944-6939
  Geneseo *(G-10798)*
Art Jewel Enterprises Ltd ............................ F ...... 630 260-0400
  Carol Stream *(G-3106)*
Bee Designs Embroidery & Scree ............... G ...... 815 393-4593
  Malta *(G-14165)*
Breedlove Sporting Goods Inc .................... F ...... 309 852-2434
  Kewanee *(G-12677)*
Breedlove Sporting Goods Inc .................... F ...... 309 852-2434
  Kewanee *(G-12678)*
C & C Sport Stop .......................................... G ...... 618 632-7812
  O Fallon *(G-16464)*
Custom Rods By Grandt Ltd ....................... G ...... 847 577-0848
  Arlington Heights *(G-741)*
Freddie Bear Sports ..................................... F ...... 708 532-4133
  Tinley Park *(G-20916)*
Johnos Inc .................................................... G ...... 630 897-6929
  Aurora *(G-1178)*
Oban Composites LLC ................................. G ...... 866 607-0284
  Chicago *(G-5963)*
Orvis Company Inc ...................................... F ...... 312 440-0662
  Chicago *(G-6019)*
Promark Advertising Specialtie ................... G ...... 618 483-6025
  Altamont *(G-554)*
Rock River Arms Inc ................................... D ...... 309 792-5780
  Colona *(G-7347)*
Roselynn Fashions ........................................ G ...... 847 741-6000
  Elgin *(G-9167)*
Soccer House ............................................... G ...... 847 998-0088
  Glenview *(G-11204)*
Tri-City Sports Inc ....................................... G ...... 217 224-2489
  Quincy *(G-17899)*
Winning Streak Inc ...................................... E ...... 618 277-8191
  Dupo *(G-8584)*

### SPORTING GOODS STORES: Archery Splys

Town Hall Sports Inc .................................... F ...... 618 235-9881
  Belleville *(G-1682)*

### SPORTING GOODS STORES: Bait & Tackle

Freemans Sports Inc .................................... G ...... 630 553-0515
  Yorkville *(G-22660)*
Jerry H Simpson ........................................... G ...... 618 654-3235
  Highland *(G-11798)*

### SPORTING GOODS STORES: Firearms

Civilian Force Arms Inc ............................... G ...... 630 926-6982
  Yorkville *(G-22652)*
Devil Dog Arms Inc ..................................... G ...... 847 790-4004
  Lake Zurich *(G-13062)*
Maxon Shooters Supplies Inc ....................... G ...... 847 298-4867
  Des Plaines *(G-8228)*
Oglesby & Oglesby Gunmakers ................... G ...... 217 487-7100
  Springfield *(G-20492)*

### SPORTING GOODS STORES: Fishing Eqpt

Hobbico Inc ................................................... E ...... 217 367-2707
  Urbana *(G-21091)*

### SPORTING GOODS STORES: Hunting Eqpt

Midwest Pub Safety Outfitters ..................... F ...... 866 985-0013
  Poplar Grove *(G-17714)*
Plano Synergy Holding Inc .......................... E ...... 630 552-3111
  Plano *(G-17674)*

### SPORTING GOODS STORES: Martial Arts Eqpt & Splys

East West Martial Arts Sups ....................... G ...... 773 878-7711
  Chicago *(G-4682)*

### SPORTING GOODS STORES: Playground Eqpt

Rainbow Midwest Inc ................................... G ...... 847 955-9300
  Vernon Hills *(G-21191)*
Sandlock Sandbox LLC ............................... G ...... 630 963-9422
  Westmont *(G-21919)*
Woodland Fence Forest Pdts Inc ................ G ...... 630 393-2220
  Warrenville *(G-21369)*

### SPORTING GOODS STORES: Skiing Eqpt

Chicago Sea Ray Inc .................................... E ...... 815 385-2720
  Volo *(G-21310)*

### SPORTING GOODS STORES: Team sports Eqpt

Minor League Inc ......................................... G ...... 618 548-8040
  Salem *(G-19339)*
Waldos Sports Corner Inc ............................ G ...... 309 688-2425
  Peoria *(G-17477)*

### SPORTING GOODS STORES: Tennis Goods & Eqpt

Court & Slope Inc ......................................... G ...... 847 697-3600
  Elgin *(G-9005)*
St Clair Tennis Club LLC ............................ G ...... 618 632-1400
  O Fallon *(G-16480)*

### SPORTING GOODS: Archery

Bowtree Inc ................................................... G ...... 217 430-8884
  Quincy *(G-17807)*
Burt Coyote Co ............................................. F ...... 309 358-1602
  Yates City *(G-22646)*
Compound Bow Rifle Sight Inc ................... G ...... 618 526-4427
  Breese *(G-2442)*
New Archery Products LLC ........................ D ...... 708 488-2500
  Forest Park *(G-10251)*

Prototech Industries Inc ............................... G ...... 847 223-9808
  Gurnee *(G-11494)*
Unlimited Wares Inc .................................... F ...... 773 234-4867
  Morton Grove *(G-15242)*

### SPORTING GOODS: Hammocks, Fabric, Made From Purchased Mat

Travel Hammock Inc .................................... G ...... 847 486-0005
  Skokie *(G-20102)*

### SPORTING/ATHLETIC GOODS: Gloves, Boxing, Handball, Etc

Boss Manufacturing Holdings ...................... F ...... 309 852-2781
  Kewanee *(G-12675)*
Restoring Path .............................................. F ...... 773 424-7023
  Chicago *(G-6338)*

### SPORTS APPAREL STORES

Chicago Sea Ray Inc .................................... E ...... 815 385-2720
  Volo *(G-21310)*
Cook Merritt ................................................. G ...... 630 980-3070
  Roselle *(G-18934)*
Fielders Choice ............................................ G ...... 618 937-2294
  West Frankfort *(G-21807)*
Hi-Five Sportswear Inc ................................ G ...... 815 637-6044
  Machesney Park *(G-14079)*
Monograms & More ...................................... G ...... 630 789-8424
  Burr Ridge *(G-2869)*
Nancys Lettering Shop ................................. G ...... 217 345-6007
  Charleston *(G-3605)*
Senn Enterprises Inc .................................... F ...... 309 637-1147
  Peoria *(G-17450)*
Sport Connection .......................................... G ...... 630 980-1787
  Roselle *(G-18979)*
Tri-City Sports Inc ....................................... G ...... 217 224-2489
  Quincy *(G-17899)*
Windy City Silkscreening Inc ...................... E ...... 312 842-0030
  Chicago *(G-7000)*

### SPOUTING: Plastic & Fiberglass Reinforced

Kipp Manufacturing Company Inc ............... F ...... 630 768-9051
  Wauconda *(G-21477)*

### SPOUTS: Sheet Metal

Kipp Manufacturing Company Inc ............... F ...... 630 768-9051
  Wauconda *(G-21477)*

### SPRAY BULBS: Rubber

W J Dennis & Company ............................... F ...... 847 697-4800
  Elgin *(G-9225)*

### SPRAYING & DUSTING EQPT

Rpk Technologies Inc ................................... G ...... 630 595-0911
  Bensenville *(G-1981)*

### SPRAYING EQPT: Agricultural

HD Hudson Manufacturing Co ..................... E ...... 312 644-2830
  Chicago *(G-5057)*

### SPRAYS: Artificial & Preserved

Palapa Coatings Inc ..................................... G ...... 847 628-6360
  Elgin *(G-9134)*

### SPRINGS: Coiled Flat

Casey Spring Co Inc ..................................... F ...... 708 867-8949
  Harwood Heights *(G-11682)*
Classic Products Inc ..................................... E ...... 815 344-0051
  McHenry *(G-14487)*
Matthew Warren Inc ..................................... E ...... 847 349-5760
  Rosemont *(G-19015)*
Omiotek Coil Spring Co ............................... D ...... 630 495-4056
  Lombard *(G-13837)*

### SPRINGS: Cold Formed

A J Kay Co .................................................... F ...... 224 475-0370
  Mundelein *(G-15462)*
Lew-El Tool & Manufacturing Co ................ F ...... 773 804-1133
  Chicago *(G-5497)*

### SPRINGS: Hot Wound, Exc Wire

Alco Spring Industries Inc .......................... D ...... 708 755-0438
  Chicago Heights *(G-7078)*

### SPRINGS: Instrument, Precision

|  | |  |
|---|---|---|
| Ark Technologies Inc | C | 630 377-8855 |
| Saint Charles *(G-19138)* | | |
| International Spring Company | D | 847 470-8170 |
| Morton Grove *(G-15203)* | | |
| Lewis Spring and Mfg Company | E | 847 588-7030 |
| Niles *(G-15996)* | | |

### SPRINGS: Leaf, Automobile, Locomotive, Etc

|  | |  |
|---|---|---|
| Boler Company | F | 630 773-9111 |
| Itasca *(G-12236)* | | |

### SPRINGS: Mechanical, Precision

|  | |  |
|---|---|---|
| Capitol Coil Inc | F | 847 891-1390 |
| Schaumburg *(G-19468)* | | |
| Form-All Spring Stamping Inc | E | 630 595-8833 |
| Bensenville *(G-1900)* | | |
| Gerb Vibration Control Systems | G | 630 724-1660 |
| Lisle *(G-13595)* | | |
| Jackson Spring & Mfg Co | D | 847 952-8850 |
| Elk Grove Village *(G-9559)* | | |
| Kaylen Industries Inc | E | 847 671-6767 |
| Schiller Park *(G-19842)* | | |
| Matthew Warren Inc | G | 847 671-6767 |
| Schiller Park *(G-19847)* | | |
| OHare Spring Company Inc | E | 847 298-1360 |
| Elk Grove Village *(G-9662)* | | |
| Rich Industries Inc | E | 630 766-9150 |
| Bensenville *(G-1978)* | | |
| Solar Spring Company | C | 847 437-7838 |
| Elk Grove Village *(G-9742)* | | |
| Spring Specialist Corporation | G | 815 562-7991 |
| Kings *(G-12705)* | | |
| Wesco Spring Company | E | 773 838-3350 |
| Chicago *(G-6958)* | | |
| White Eagle Spring & | F | 773 384-4455 |
| Chicago *(G-6972)* | | |

### SPRINGS: Precision

|  | |  |
|---|---|---|
| Ascent Mfg Co | E | 847 806-6600 |
| Elk Grove Village *(G-9314)* | | |
| Perfection Spring Stmping Corp | D | 847 437-3900 |
| Mount Prospect *(G-15362)* | | |

### SPRINGS: Steel

|  | |  |
|---|---|---|
| All-Rite Spring Co | E | 815 675-1350 |
| Spring Grove *(G-20325)* | | |
| Baumbach Manufacturing | G | 630 941-0505 |
| Elmhurst *(G-9836)* | | |
| Burnex Corporation | E | 815 728-1317 |
| Ringwood *(G-17988)* | | |
| Capitol Coil Inc | F | 847 891-1390 |
| Schaumburg *(G-19468)* | | |
| Dudek & Bock Spring Mfg Co | C | 773 379-4100 |
| Chicago *(G-4648)* | | |
| High-Life Products Inc | G | 847 991-9449 |
| Palatine *(G-17036)* | | |
| Highland Spring & Specialty | F | 618 654-3831 |
| Highland *(G-11793)* | | |
| Johnson Tool Company | G | 708 453-8600 |
| Huntley *(G-12154)* | | |
| Kankakee Spring and Alignment | C | 815 932-6718 |
| Kankakee *(G-12633)* | | |
| Kdk Upset Forging Co | E | 708 388-8770 |
| Blue Island *(G-2259)* | | |
| Khc Corporation | E | 815 337-7630 |
| Woodstock *(G-22578)* | | |
| Lewis Spring and Mfg Company | E | 847 588-7030 |
| Niles *(G-15996)* | | |
| Matthew Warren Inc | D | 773 539-5600 |
| Chicago *(G-5656)* | | |
| Mid-West Spring & Stamping Inc | G | 630 739-3800 |
| Romeoville *(G-18848)* | | |
| Patrick Manufacturing Inc | E | 847 697-5920 |
| Elgin *(G-9136)* | | |
| R & G Spring Co Inc | G | 847 228-5640 |
| Elk Grove Village *(G-9706)* | | |
| Smalley Steel Ring Co | C | 847 537-7600 |
| Lake Zurich *(G-13132)* | | |
| Spirolox Inc | B | 847 719-5900 |
| Lake Zurich *(G-13133)* | | |
| Spring R-R Corporation | E | 630 543-7445 |
| Addison *(G-298)* | | |
| Spring Specialist Corporation | G | 815 562-7991 |
| Kings *(G-12705)* | | |
| Stanley Spring & Stamping Corp | D | 773 777-2600 |
| Chicago *(G-6572)* | | |
| United Spring & Manufacturing | E | 773 384-8464 |
| Chicago *(G-6826)* | | |
| Wesco Spring Company | E | 773 838-3350 |
| Chicago *(G-6958)* | | |
| William Dudek Manufacturing Co | E | 773 622-2727 |
| Chicago *(G-6983)* | | |
| York Spring Co | E | 847 695-5978 |
| South Elgin *(G-20236)* | | |

### SPRINGS: Torsion Bar

|  | |  |
|---|---|---|
| Gilbert Spring Corporation | E | 773 486-6030 |
| Chicago *(G-4952)* | | |
| Mid-West Spring & Stamping Inc | G | 630 739-3800 |
| Romeoville *(G-18847)* | | |
| Mid-West Spring Mfg Co | G | 630 739-3800 |
| Romeoville *(G-18849)* | | |

### SPRINGS: Wire

|  | |  |
|---|---|---|
| A J Kay Co | F | 224 475-0370 |
| Mundelein *(G-15462)* | | |
| All American Spring Stamping | G | 847 928-9468 |
| Franklin Park *(G-10389)* | | |
| All-Rite Spring Co | E | 815 675-1350 |
| Spring Grove *(G-20325)* | | |
| Available Spring and Mfg Co | E | 847 520-4854 |
| Wheeling *(G-22009)* | | |
| Beall Manufacturing Inc | E | 618 259-8154 |
| East Alton *(G-8599)* | | |
| Century Spring Corporation | G | 800 237-5225 |
| Chicago *(G-4277)* | | |
| CFC Wire Forms Inc | E | 630 879-7575 |
| Batavia *(G-1428)* | | |
| David V Michals | D | 847 671-6767 |
| Schiller Park *(G-19820)* | | |
| Highland Spring & Specialty | F | 618 654-3831 |
| Highland *(G-11793)* | | |
| Innocor Foam Tech W Chcago LLC | E | 732 945-6222 |
| West Chicago *(G-21722)* | | |
| JD Norman Industries Inc | D | 630 458-3700 |
| Addison *(G-159)* | | |
| Johnson Tool Company | G | 708 453-8600 |
| Huntley *(G-12154)* | | |
| Kan-Du Manufacturing Co Inc | G | 708 681-0370 |
| Riverwoods *(G-18040)* | | |
| Lew-El Tool & Manufacturing Co | F | 773 804-1133 |
| Chicago *(G-5497)* | | |
| M Lizen Manufacturing Co | E | 708 755-7213 |
| University Park *(G-21055)* | | |
| Majestic Spring Inc | F | 847 593-8887 |
| Elk Grove Village *(G-9609)* | | |
| Master Spring & Wire Form Co | E | 708 453-2570 |
| Itasca *(G-12312)* | | |
| Matthew Warren Inc | D | 773 539-5600 |
| Chicago *(G-5656)* | | |
| Micromatic Spring Stamping Inc | E | 630 607-0141 |
| Addison *(G-208)* | | |
| Mid-West Spring & Stamping Inc | G | 630 739-3800 |
| Romeoville *(G-18847)* | | |
| Mid-West Spring & Stamping Inc | G | 630 739-3800 |
| Romeoville *(G-18848)* | | |
| Mid-West Spring Mfg Co | G | 630 739-3800 |
| Romeoville *(G-18849)* | | |
| Paragon Spring Company | E | 773 489-6300 |
| Chicago *(G-6076)* | | |
| R & G Spring Co Inc | G | 847 228-5640 |
| Elk Grove Village *(G-9706)* | | |
| R C Coil Spring Mfg Co Inc | D | 630 790-3500 |
| Glendale Heights *(G-11062)* | | |
| Riverside Spring Company | G | 815 963-3334 |
| Rockford *(G-18557)* | | |
| Sanco Industries Inc | F | 847 243-8675 |
| Kildeer *(G-12703)* | | |
| Schaff International LLC | E | 847 438-4560 |
| Lake Zurich *(G-13125)* | | |
| Smalley Steel Ring Co | C | 847 537-7600 |
| Lake Zurich *(G-13132)* | | |
| Spirolox Inc | B | 847 719-5900 |
| Lake Zurich *(G-13133)* | | |
| Stanley Spring & Stamping Corp | D | 773 777-2600 |
| Chicago *(G-6572)* | | |
| Sterling Spring LLC | D | 773 582-6464 |
| Chicago *(G-6591)* | | |
| Sterling Spring LLC | E | 773 777-4647 |
| Bedford Park *(G-1587)* | | |
| Sterling Spring LLC | E | 773 772-9331 |
| Chicago *(G-6592)* | | |
| Taycorp Inc | E | 708 629-0921 |
| Alsip *(G-533)* | | |
| United Spring & Manufacturing | E | 773 384-8464 |
| Chicago *(G-6826)* | | |
| Willdon Corp | E | 773 276-7080 |
| Chicago *(G-6981)* | | |

### SPRINKLING SYSTEMS: Fire Control

|  | |  |
|---|---|---|
| Automatic Fire Sprinkler LLC | F | 309 862-2724 |
| Normal *(G-16064)* | | |
| Cintas Corporation | E | 309 821-1920 |
| Normal *(G-16067)* | | |
| Fire Systems Holdings Inc | F | 708 333-4130 |
| Mokena *(G-14861)* | | |
| Flame Guard Usa LLC | G | 815 219-4074 |
| Lake Barrington *(G-12806)* | | |
| Industrial Pipe and Supply Co | E | 708 652-7511 |
| Chicago *(G-5179)* | | |
| Marion Fire Sprnklr Alarm Inc | F | 618 889-9106 |
| Marion *(G-14272)* | | |
| Rainmaker | G | 847 998-0838 |
| Glenview *(G-11189)* | | |
| Systems Piping | G | 847 948-1373 |
| Deerfield *(G-8057)* | | |

### SPROCKETS: Power Transmission

|  | |  |
|---|---|---|
| Allied Gear Co | G | 773 287-8742 |
| Chicago *(G-3815)* | | |
| E N M Company | D | 773 775-8400 |
| Chicago *(G-4667)* | | |
| Galaxy Sourcing Inc | G | 630 532-5003 |
| Villa Park *(G-21254)* | | |
| Hadley Gear Manufacturing Co | F | 773 722-1030 |
| Chicago *(G-5028)* | | |

### STACKING MACHINES: Automatic

|  | |  |
|---|---|---|
| Tri-Cam Inc | F | 815 226-9200 |
| Rockford *(G-18656)* | | |

### STAGE LIGHTING SYSTEMS

|  | |  |
|---|---|---|
| Golden Road Productions | G | 217 335-2606 |
| New Canton *(G-15868)* | | |

### STAINLESS STEEL

|  | |  |
|---|---|---|
| Aap Metals LLC | D | 847 916-1220 |
| Elk Grove Village *(G-9252)* | | |
| Allegheny Ludlum LLC | E | 708 974-8801 |
| Bridgeview *(G-2460)* | | |
| Carpenter Technology Corp | G | 630 771-1020 |
| Bolingbrook *(G-2284)* | | |
| Cisne Iron Works Inc | F | 618 673-2188 |
| Cisne *(G-7250)* | | |
| Commercial Stainless Services | F | 847 349-1560 |
| Elk Grove Village *(G-9387)* | | |
| Elg Metals Inc | E | 773 374-1500 |
| Chicago *(G-4728)* | | |
| Joe Zsido Sales & Design Inc | E | 618 435-2605 |
| Benton *(G-2032)* | | |
| Main Steel LLC | E | 847 916-1220 |
| Elk Grove Village *(G-9607)* | | |
| Marias Chicken ATI Atihan | G | 847 699-3113 |
| Niles *(G-16000)* | | |
| Omega Products Inc | G | 618 939-3445 |
| Waterloo *(G-21403)* | | |
| Outokumpu Stainless Usa LLC | D | 847 405-6604 |
| Deerfield *(G-8045)* | | |
| Outokumpu Stainless Usa LLC | B | 847 317-1400 |
| Bannockburn *(G-1263)* | | |
| Pinnacle Metals Inc | E | 815 232-1600 |
| Freeport *(G-10679)* | | |
| Strictly Stainless Inc | G | 847 885-2890 |
| Hoffman Estates *(G-12061)* | | |
| Summit Stinless Stl Holdg Corp | F | 732 297-9500 |
| Rosemont *(G-19035)* | | |
| United Toolers of Illinois | F | 779 423-0548 |
| Loves Park *(G-14005)* | | |

### STAINLESS STEEL WARE

|  | |  |
|---|---|---|
| Nelson-Whittaker Ltd | E | 815 459-6000 |
| Crystal Lake *(G-7618)* | | |
| Tri Star Metals LLC | E | 815 232-1600 |
| Freeport *(G-10694)* | | |

### STAIRCASES & STAIRS, WOOD

|  | |  |
|---|---|---|
| Amron Stair Works Inc | F | 847 426-4800 |
| Gilberts *(G-10912)* | | |
| Bailey Hardwoods Inc | G | 217 529-6800 |
| Springfield *(G-20394)* | | |
| Kencor Stairs & Woodworking | G | 630 279-8980 |
| Villa Park *(G-21263)* | | |

## PRODUCT SECTION

## STAMPINGS: Metal

Riverside Custom Woodworking..........G...... 815 589-3608
  Fulton *(G-10705)*
Royal Stairs Co..................................G...... 630 860-2223
  Bensenville *(G-1980)*
Stairsland.........................................G...... 708 853-9593
  Lyons *(G-14045)*
Thomas Fine Stairs Inc......................G...... 708 387-9506
  Brookfield *(G-2645)*

### STAMPING SVC: Book, Gold

Creative Label Inc...........................D...... 847 981-3800
  Elk Grove Village *(G-9399)*
Midwest Gold Stampers Inc..............F...... 773 775-5253
  Chicago *(G-5744)*

### STAMPINGS: Automotive

Ada Metal Products Inc....................E...... 847 673-1190
  Lincolnwood *(G-13500)*
Borgwarner Inc.................................C...... 815 288-1462
  Dixon *(G-8324)*
Borgwarner Transm Systems............A...... 708 547-2600
  Bellwood *(G-1700)*
Clay Cnty Rhbilitation Ctr Inc.............F...... 618 662-6607
  Flora *(G-10203)*
Ford Motor Company........................A...... 708 757-5700
  Ford Heights *(G-10233)*
G & M Manufacturing Corp...............E...... 815 455-1900
  Crystal Lake *(G-7580)*
Inland Tool Company.......................E...... 217 792-3206
  Mount Pulaski *(G-15389)*
Laystrom Manufacturing Co..............D...... 773 342-4800
  Chicago *(G-5474)*
Mercury Products Corp....................C...... 847 524-4400
  Schaumburg *(G-19641)*
Mercury Products Corp....................C...... 847 524-4400
  Schaumburg *(G-19642)*
MNP Precision Parts LLC.................C...... 815 391-5256
  Rockford *(G-18509)*
Perfection Spring Stmping Corp.........D...... 847 437-3900
  Mount Prospect *(G-15362)*
Plastic Technologies Inc...................E...... 847 841-8610
  Elgin *(G-9140)*
T R Z Motorsports Inc......................G...... 815 806-0838
  Frankfort *(G-10367)*
Topy Precision Mfg Inc.....................D...... 847 228-5902
  Elk Grove Village *(G-9784)*
Tower Automotive Operations I..........B...... 773 646-6550
  Chicago *(G-6751)*
Tsm Inc............................................G...... 815 544-5012
  Belvidere *(G-1790)*

### STAMPINGS: Metal

Abbott Scott Manufacturing Co..........E...... 773 342-7200
  Chicago *(G-3706)*
Accurate Wire Strip Frming Inc.........F...... 630 260-1000
  Carol Stream *(G-3089)*
Ace Plating Company.......................E...... 773 376-1800
  Chicago *(G-3727)*
Action Tool & Mfg Inc......................E...... 815 874-5775
  Rockford *(G-18256)*
Adler Norco Inc................................F...... 847 473-3600
  Mundelein *(G-15464)*
Air-Drive Inc....................................E...... 847 625-0226
  Gurnee *(G-11423)*
Alagor Industries Incorporated..........F...... 630 766-2910
  Bensenville *(G-1822)*
Alan Manufacturing Corp..................G...... 815 568-6836
  Marengo *(G-14217)*
All American Spring Stamping..........E...... 847 928-9468
  Franklin Park *(G-10389)*
All American Washer Werks Inc........E...... 847 566-9091
  Mundelein *(G-15468)*
Alpha Products Inc..........................E...... 708 594-3883
  Bedford Park *(G-1536)*
American Partsmith..........................G...... 630 520-0432
  West Chicago *(G-21656)*
Ammentorp Tool Company Inc..........G...... 847 671-9290
  Franklin Park *(G-10395)*
Angle Tool Company........................G...... 847 593-7572
  Elk Grove Village *(G-9307)*
Apex Wire Products Company Inc.....F...... 847 671-1830
  Franklin Park *(G-10397)*
Ark Technologies Inc.......................C...... 630 377-8855
  Saint Charles *(G-19138)*
Ascent Mfg Co.................................E...... 847 806-6600
  Elk Grove Village *(G-9314)*
Ask Products Inc.............................D...... 630 896-4056
  Aurora *(G-1111)*

Astoria Wire Products Inc.................D...... 708 496-9950
  Bedford Park *(G-1539)*
Atlas Tool & Die Works Inc..............D...... 708 442-1661
  Lyons *(G-14031)*
Austin Tool & Die Co.......................D...... 847 509-5800
  Northbrook *(G-16209)*
Available Spring and Mfg Co............G...... 847 520-4854
  Wheeling *(G-22009)*
B & D Murray Manufacturing Co.......G...... 815 568-6176
  Marengo *(G-14220)*
B M I Inc..........................................C...... 847 839-6000
  Schaumburg *(G-19456)*
B Radtke and Sons Inc....................G...... 847 546-3999
  Round Lake Park *(G-19083)*
Barco Stamping Co..........................E...... 630 293-5155
  West Chicago *(G-21666)*
Bellota Agrsltions Tls USA LLC........E...... 309 787-2491
  Milan *(G-14775)*
Berny Metal Products Inc.................G...... 847 742-8500
  South Elgin *(G-20187)*
Big 3 Precision Products Inc............C...... 618 533-3251
  Centralia *(G-3405)*
Bilt-Rite Metal Products Inc..............E...... 815 495-2211
  Leland *(G-13218)*
Bomel Tool Manufacturing Co..........C...... 708 343-3663
  Broadview *(G-2564)*
Borgwarner Transm Systems............A...... 708 547-2600
  Bellwood *(G-1700)*
Briergate Tool & Engrg Co................F...... 630 766-7050
  Bensenville *(G-1846)*
Buhrke Industries LLC.....................B...... 847 981-7550
  Arlington Heights *(G-732)*
C E R Machining & Tooling Ltd........C...... 708 442-9614
  Lyons *(G-14034)*
C J Holdings Inc..............................G...... 309 274-3141
  Chillicothe *(G-7163)*
Cac Corporation...............................E...... 630 221-5200
  Carol Stream *(G-3122)*
Cap & Seal Co.................................E...... 847 741-3101
  Elgin *(G-8976)*
Cardinal Engineering Inc..................G...... 309 342-7474
  Galesburg *(G-10742)*
Central Radiator Cabinet Co.............C...... 773 539-1700
  Lena *(G-13274)*
Central Tool Specialities Co..............G...... 630 543-6351
  Addison *(G-72)*
Chicago Car Seal Company..............G...... 773 278-9400
  Chicago *(G-4310)*
Chicago Metal Fabricators Inc..........D...... 773 523-5755
  Chicago *(G-4332)*
Chirch Global Mfg LLC.....................F...... 815 385-5600
  Cary *(G-3330)*
Classic Sheet Metal Inc....................E...... 630 694-0300
  Franklin Park *(G-10435)*
Component Tool & Mfg Co...............F...... 708 672-5505
  Crete *(G-7510)*
Craftsman Custom Metals LLC........D...... 847 655-0040
  Schiller Park *(G-19817)*
Creative Steel Fabricators.................G...... 847 803-2090
  Des Plaines *(G-8177)*
Culen Tool & Manufacturing Co........G...... 708 387-1580
  Brookfield *(G-2629)*
D & B Fabricators & Distrs...............G...... 630 325-3811
  Lemont *(G-13234)*
D & D Tooling and Mfg Inc...............G...... 888 300-6869
  Bolingbrook *(G-2297)*
D & J Machine Shop Inc..................G...... 815 472-6057
  Momence *(G-14979)*
Dadum Inc........................................G...... 847 541-7851
  Buffalo Grove *(G-2682)*
Delta Metal Products Co...................G...... 773 745-9220
  Chicago *(G-4579)*
Derby Industries LLC.......................E...... 309 344-0547
  Galesburg *(G-10746)*
Deringer-Ney Inc..............................E...... 847 566-4100
  Vernon Hills *(G-21157)*
Desk & Door Nameplate Company....F...... 815 806-8670
  Frankfort *(G-10312)*
Diemasters Manufacturing Inc..........C...... 847 640-9900
  Elk Grove Village *(G-9429)*
Dixline Corporation..........................F...... 309 932-2011
  Galva *(G-10787)*
Dixline Corporation..........................D...... 309 932-2011
  Galva *(G-10788)*
Dovee Manufacturing Inc..................G...... 847 437-8122
  Elgin *(G-9012)*
Dudek & Bock Spring Mfg Co..........G...... 773 379-4100
  Chicago *(G-4648)*
E H Baare Corporation.....................C...... 618 546-1575
  Robinson *(G-18062)*

Ems Industrial and Service Co..........E...... 815 678-2700
  Richmond *(G-17961)*
Equinox Group Inc...........................F...... 312 226-7002
  Chicago *(G-4769)*
Erickson Tool & Machine Co............G...... 815 397-2653
  Rockford *(G-18369)*
Ets-Lindgren Inc..............................C...... 630 307-7200
  Wood Dale *(G-22363)*
Fabricating Machinery Sales.............E...... 630 350-2266
  Wood Dale *(G-22366)*
Fanmar Inc......................................E...... 708 563-0505
  Elk Grove Village *(G-9475)*
FIC America Corp............................A...... 630 871-7609
  Carol Stream *(G-3151)*
Ford Motor Company........................A...... 708 757-5700
  Ford Heights *(G-10233)*
Forster Tool & Mfg Co Inc................E...... 630 616-8177
  Bensenville *(G-1902)*
Four Star Tool Inc............................D...... 224 735-2419
  Rolling Meadows *(G-18729)*
Gbc Metals LLC...............................G...... 618 258-2350
  East Alton *(G-8603)*
General Machinery & Mfg Co...........F...... 773 235-3700
  Chicago *(G-4928)*
General Products Intl Ltd..................G...... 847 458-6357
  Lake In The Hills *(G-12994)*
Global Brass and Copper Inc...........G...... 502 873-3000
  East Alton *(G-8604)*
Global Brass Cop Holdings Inc........E...... 847 240-4700
  Schaumburg *(G-19537)*
Haddock Tool & Manufacturing.........G...... 815 786-2739
  Sandwich *(G-19367)*
Harrington King Prforating Inc..........C...... 773 626-1800
  Chicago *(G-5047)*
Helander Metal Spinning Co.............E...... 630 268-9292
  Lombard *(G-13808)*
Highland Southern Wire Inc..............G...... 618 654-2161
  Highland *(G-11792)*
Hoosier Stamping & Mfg Corp..........E...... 618 375-2057
  Grayville *(G-11371)*
Illinois Tool Works Inc......................F...... 708 343-0728
  Broadview *(G-2586)*
Illinois Tool Works Inc......................C...... 847 299-2222
  Des Plaines *(G-8209)*
IMS Companies LLC........................D...... 847 391-8100
  Des Plaines *(G-8210)*
IMS Engineered Products LLC........C...... 847 391-8100
  Des Plaines *(G-8211)*
IMS Olson LLC................................D...... 630 969-9400
  Downers Grove *(G-8464)*
Industrial Enclosure Corp.................G...... 630 898-7499
  Aurora *(G-1171)*
Inland Tool Company.......................E...... 217 792-3206
  Mount Pulaski *(G-15389)*
Integrity Manufacturing Inc...............G...... 815 514-8230
  New Lenox *(G-15887)*
Interplex Daystar Inc........................D...... 847 455-2424
  Franklin Park *(G-10499)*
Ironform Holdings Co.......................F...... 312 374-4810
  Chicago *(G-5239)*
J-TEC Metal Products Inc................G...... 630 875-1300
  Itasca *(G-12288)*
Jason Incorporated..........................G...... 630 627-7000
  Addison *(G-158)*
JD Norman Industries Inc................D...... 630 458-3700
  Addison *(G-159)*
Jsn Inc.............................................G...... 708 410-1800
  Maywood *(G-14426)*
Kaskaskia Tool and Machine Inc......E...... 618 475-3301
  New Athens *(G-15860)*
Kenmode Tool and Engrg Inc...........C...... 847 658-5041
  Algonquin *(G-396)*
King Tool and Die Inc......................G...... 630 787-0799
  Bensenville *(G-1934)*
Kipp Manufacturing Company Inc....F...... 630 768-9051
  Wauconda *(G-21477)*
Kleen Cut Tool Inc...........................G...... 630 447-7020
  Warrenville *(G-21349)*
Klein Tools Inc.................................D...... 847 228-6999
  Elk Grove Village *(G-9577)*
Klein Tools Inc.................................E...... 847 821-5500
  Lincolnshire *(G-13461)*
Lakeview Metals Inc.........................E...... 847 838-9800
  Antioch *(G-640)*
Lamination Specialties Corp.............D...... 312 243-2181
  Chicago *(G-5449)*
Lamination Specialties Corp.............F...... 773 254-7500
  Chicago *(G-5450)*
Lew-El Tool & Manufacturing Co......F...... 773 804-1133
  Chicago *(G-5497)*

Employee Codes: A=Over 500 employees, B=251-500
C=101-250, D=51-100, E=20-50, F=10-19, G=3-9

2017 Harris Illinois
Industrial Directory

1765

## STAMPINGS: Metal

Lyon LLC .....................................................C....... 815 432-4595
  Watseka *(G-21421)*
M J Celco Inc ...............................................D....... 847 671-1900
  Schiller Park *(G-19843)*
M Lizen Manufacturing Co ........................E....... 708 755-7213
  University Park *(G-21055)*
Marengo Tool & Die Works Inc ................E....... 815 568-7411
  Marengo *(G-14236)*
Marlboro Wire Ltd .....................................E....... 217 224-7989
  Quincy *(G-17855)*
McCarthy Enterprises Inc ..........................E....... 847 367-5718
  Libertyville *(G-13351)*
Metal Technology Solutions .....................G....... 630 587-1450
  Saint Charles *(G-19219)*
Metalstamp Inc .........................................E....... 815 467-7800
  Minooka *(G-14842)*
Mfz Ventures Inc .......................................G....... 773 247-4611
  Chicago *(G-5715)*
Mid-West Spring & Stamping Inc ............G....... 630 739-3800
  Romeoville *(G-18847)*
Midland Stamping and ..............................E....... 847 678-7573
  Schiller Park *(G-19850)*
Midland Stamping and Fabg Corp ...........D....... 847 678-7573
  Schiller Park *(G-19851)*
Midwest Nameplate Corp ..........................G....... 708 614-0606
  Orland Park *(G-16875)*
Milans Machining & Mfg Co Inc ...............D....... 708 780-6600
  Cicero *(G-7222)*
Millenia Metals LLC ..................................D....... 630 458-0401
  Itasca *(G-12317)*
Millenia Products Group Inc ....................C....... 630 458-0401
  Itasca *(G-12318)*
Millenia Specialty Metals LLC ..................G....... 630 458-0401
  Itasca *(G-12319)*
Millenia Trucking LLC ...............................E....... 630 458-0401
  Itasca *(G-12320)*
Mint Masters Inc ........................................E....... 847 451-1133
  Franklin Park *(G-10534)*
Mity Inc ......................................................G....... 630 365-5030
  Elburn *(G-8898)*
Moline Welding Inc ...................................F....... 309 756-0643
  Milan *(G-14795)*
Moline Welding Inc ...................................G....... 309 756-0643
  Milan *(G-14796)*
My-Lin Manufacturing Co Inc ...................E....... 630 897-4100
  Aurora *(G-1192)*
Natural Products Inc ..................................F....... 847 509-5835
  Northbrook *(G-16317)*
Navitor Inc ..................................................B....... 800 323-0253
  Harwood Heights *(G-11687)*
Newko Tool & Engineering Co ..................E....... 847 359-1670
  Palatine *(G-17058)*
North Star Stamping & Tool Inc .................F....... 847 658-9400
  Lake In The Hills *(G-13001)*
Northwestern Corporation ........................E....... 815 942-1300
  Morris *(G-15124)*
Octavia Tool & Gage Company .................G....... 847 913-9233
  Elk Grove Village *(G-9661)*
Offko Tool Inc ............................................G....... 815 933-9474
  Kankakee *(G-12641)*
Olson Metal Products LLC .......................F....... 847 981-7550
  Arlington Heights *(G-812)*
Paddock Industries Inc ..............................F....... 618 277-1580
  Smithton *(G-20123)*
Park Manufacturing Corp Inc ....................F....... 708 345-6090
  Melrose Park *(G-14682)*
PDQ Tool & Stamping Co ..........................E....... 708 841-3000
  Dolton *(G-8374)*
Pecora Tool Service Inc .............................G....... 847 524-1275
  Schaumburg *(G-19687)*
Plano Molding Company LLC ..................C....... 815 538-3111
  Mendota *(G-14730)*
Polymer PInfeld Hldings US Inc ...............C....... 815 436-5671
  Plainfield *(G-17641)*
Precision Forming Stamping Co ................E....... 773 489-6868
  Chicago *(G-6170)*
Precision Metal Technologies ...................F....... 847 228-6630
  Rolling Meadows *(G-18768)*
Precision Resource Inc .............................C....... 847 383-1300
  Vernon Hills *(G-21190)*
Prikos & Becker LLC ................................D....... 847 675-3910
  Skokie *(G-20059)*
Prismier LLC .............................................E....... 630 592-4515
  Woodridge *(G-22511)*
Pro-Tech Metal Specialties Inc .................E....... 630 279-7094
  Elmhurst *(G-9923)*
Production Stampings Inc .........................G....... 815 495-2800
  Leland *(G-13220)*
Prospect Tool Company LLC ....................G....... 630 766-2200
  Franklin Park *(G-10564)*

R B White Inc ............................................E....... 309 452-5816
  Normal *(G-16086)*
R C Coil Spring Mfg Co Inc .......................G....... 630 790-3500
  Glendale Heights *(G-11062)*
Radiad Manufacturing ..............................G....... 847 678-5808
  Franklin Park *(G-10568)*
Realwheels Corporation ...........................E....... 847 662-7722
  Gurnee *(G-11499)*
Riverfront Machine Inc ..............................D....... 815 663-5000
  Spring Valley *(G-20379)*
Rockford Toolcraft Inc ...............................E....... 815 398-5507
  Rockford *(G-18589)*
Royal Die & Stamping Co Inc ...................E....... 630 766-2685
  Carol Stream *(G-3229)*
Runge Enterprises Inc ..............................E....... 630 365-2000
  Elburn *(G-8909)*
S & S Hinge Company ..............................E....... 630 582-9500
  Bloomingdale *(G-2133)*
S & W Manufacturing Co Inc ....................E....... 630 595-5044
  Bensenville *(G-1984)*
Sealco Industries Inc ................................E....... 847 741-3101
  Elgin *(G-9173)*
Service Sheet Metal Works Inc .................F....... 773 229-0031
  Chicago *(G-6483)*
Simplomatic Manufacturing Co ................E....... 773 342-7757
  Elgin *(G-9181)*
Slidematic Products Co ............................E....... 773 545-4213
  Chicago *(G-6530)*
Spannagel Tool & Die ...............................E....... 630 969-7575
  Downers Grove *(G-8526)*
Starmont Manufacturing Co ......................G....... 815 939-1041
  Kankakee *(G-12653)*
Starmont Manufacturing Inc .....................F....... 708 758-2525
  Chicago Heights *(G-7127)*
Sweet Manufacturing Corp .......................E....... 847 546-5575
  Chicago *(G-6648)*
T H K Holdings of America LLC ...............E....... 847 310-1111
  Schaumburg *(G-19750)*
Tarney Inc ..................................................E....... 773 235-0331
  Chicago *(G-6677)*
Tj Wire Forming Inc ...................................E....... 630 628-9209
  Addison *(G-316)*
Tlk Tool & Stamping Inc ............................G....... 224 293-6941
  East Dundee *(G-8660)*
Tool Automation Enterprises .....................G....... 708 799-6847
  East Hazel Crest *(G-8666)*
Trinity Machined Products Inc ..................E....... 630 876-6992
  Aurora *(G-1090)*
Trio Wire Products Inc ..............................G....... 815 469-2148
  Frankfort *(G-10372)*
Tru-Way Inc ...............................................E....... 708 562-3690
  Northlake *(G-16457)*
TRW Automotive US LLC .........................B....... 217 826-3011
  Marshall *(G-14330)*
Tu-Star Manufacturing Co Inc ...................G....... 815 338-5760
  Woodstock *(G-22619)*
Tvh Parts Co ..............................................E....... 847 223-1000
  Grayslake *(G-11365)*
United Tool and Engineering Co ...............D....... 815 389-3021
  South Beloit *(G-20171)*
USA Technologies Inc ...............................E....... 309 495-0829
  Peoria *(G-17476)*
Wardzala Industries Inc .............................F....... 847 288-9909
  Franklin Park *(G-10627)*
Wenco Manufacturing Co Inc ...................E....... 630 377-7474
  Elgin *(G-9235)*
Wesco Spring Company ...........................E....... 773 838-3350
  Chicago *(G-6958)*
William Dudek Manufacturing Co .............E....... 773 622-2727
  Chicago *(G-6983)*
World Washer & Stamping Inc ..................F....... 630 543-6749
  Addison *(G-347)*
Wozniak Industries Inc ..............................C....... 630 820-4052
  Aurora *(G-1100)*
Wozniak Industries Inc ..............................G....... 630 954-3400
  Oakbrook Terrace *(G-16723)*

## STAPLES

Duo-Fast Corporation ................................E....... 847 944-2288
  Glenview *(G-11122)*
L & J Industrial Staples Inc .......................E....... 815 864-3337
  Shannon *(G-19899)*

## STAPLES, MADE FROM PURCHASED WIRE

Illinois Tool Works Inc ..............................G....... 847 821-2170
  Vernon Hills *(G-21174)*
Minerallac Company .................................E....... 630 543-7080
  Hampshire *(G-11554)*

## STARTERS & CONTROLLERS: Motor, Electric

Electric Vehicle Technologies ...................E....... 847 673-8330
  Skokie *(G-19992)*
Jordan Industries Inc ................................F....... 847 945-5591
  Deerfield *(G-8020)*

## STARTERS: Electric Motor

General Electric Company ........................C....... 309 664-1513
  Bloomington *(G-2170)*

## STARTERS: Motor

A E Iskra Inc .............................................G....... 815 874-4022
  Rockford *(G-18239)*
C & D Rebuilders .......................................E....... 618 273-9862
  Eldorado *(G-8918)*

## STARTING EQPT: Street Cars

Bill West Enterprises Inc ...........................G....... 217 886-2591
  Jacksonville *(G-12378)*

## STATE CREDIT UNIONS, NOT FEDERALLY CHARTERED

Motormakers De Kalb Credit Un ...............G....... 815 756-6331
  Chicago *(G-5814)*

## STATIC ELIMINATORS: Ind

Nova Tronics Inc ........................................G....... 630 455-1034
  Burr Ridge *(G-2871)*
Ransburg Corporation ..............................B....... 847 724-7500
  Glenview *(G-11190)*

## STATIONARY & OFFICE SPLYS, WHOLESALE: Manifold Business Form

Dallas Corporation ....................................F....... 630 322-8000
  Downers Grove *(G-8424)*

## STATIONARY & OFFICE SPLYS, WHOLESALE: Marking Devices

Millennium Marking Company ..................E....... 847 806-1750
  Elk Grove Village *(G-9629)*

## STATIONARY & OFFICE SPLYS, WHOLESALE: Office Filing Splys

Dauphin Enterprise Inc .............................G....... 630 893-6300
  Bloomingdale *(G-2101)*

## STATIONARY & OFFICE SPLYS, WHOLESALE: Stationery

Allen Paper Company ...............................G....... 312 454-4500
  Chicago *(G-3812)*
Allied Graphics Inc ....................................G....... 847 419-8830
  Buffalo Grove *(G-2654)*

## STATIONARY & OFFICE SPLYS, WHOLESALE: Writing Ink

Toyo Ink International Corp ......................F....... 866 969-8696
  Wood Dale *(G-22432)*

## STATIONER'S SUNDRIES: Rubber

Dans Rubber Stamp & Signs ....................G....... 815 964-5603
  Rockford *(G-18333)*
James Ray Monroe Corporation ................F....... 618 532-4575
  Centralia *(G-3420)*

## STATIONERY & OFFICE SPLYS WHOLESALERS

A Trustworthy Sup Source Inc ..................G....... 773 480-0255
  Chicago *(G-3693)*
Block and Company Inc ............................C....... 847 537-7200
  Wheeling *(G-22015)*
Corporation Supply Co Inc .......................E....... 312 726-3375
  Chicago *(G-4476)*
Excel Forms Inc ........................................G....... 630 801-1936
  Aurora *(G-1150)*
Go Calendars ............................................G....... 847 816-1563
  Vernon Hills *(G-21166)*
Harlan Vance Company .............................F....... 309 888-4804
  Normal *(G-16072)*

# PRODUCT SECTION — STEEL FABRICATORS

Northstar Group Inc .............................. F  847 726-0880
  Lake Zurich  *(G-13110)*
Primedia Source LLC ............................ G  630 553-8451
  Yorkville  *(G-22670)*
Reel Life Dvd LLC ................................ G  708 579-1360
  Western Springs  *(G-21872)*
Wam Ventures Inc ................................ G  312 214-6136
  Chicago  *(G-6937)*
Write Stuff ........................................... G  630 365-4425
  Saint Charles  *(G-19300)*

## STATIONERY PRDTS

Assemble and Mail Group Inc .................  309 473-2006
  Heyworth  *(G-11764)*
Carl Manufacturing USA Inc .................. F  847 884-2842
  Itasca  *(G-12242)*
Mudlark Papers Inc .............................. E  630 717-7616
  Naperville  *(G-15702)*
Tjmj Inc .............................................. F  312 315-7780
  Chicago  *(G-6731)*

## STATIONERY: Made From Purchased Materials

Chicago Contract Bridge Assn ............... G  630 355-5560
  Naperville  *(G-15626)*

## STATORS REWINDING SVCS

Prompt Motor Rewinding Service .......... G  847 675-7155
  Skokie  *(G-20065)*
Warfield Electric Company Inc .............. E  815 469-4094
  Frankfort  *(G-10376)*

## STATUARY & OTHER DECORATIVE PRDTS: Nonmetallic

Espe Manufacturing Co ......................... F  847 678-8950
  Schiller Park  *(G-19826)*

## STATUARY GOODS, EXC RELIGIOUS: Wholesalers

Lion Ornamental Concrete Pdts ............. G  630 892-7304
  Montgomery  *(G-15056)*

## STATUES: Nonmetal

Daprato Rigali Inc ................................ E  773 763-5511
  Chicago  *(G-4557)*

## STEEL & ALLOYS: Tool & Die

Illinois Weld & Machine Inc .................. G  309 565-0533
  Hanna City  *(G-11569)*
Processed Steel Company ..................... B  815 459-2400
  Crystal Lake  *(G-7635)*
Production Tooling and Automtn ........... G  217 283-7373
  Hoopeston  *(G-12114)*
R M Tool & Manufacturing Co ............... G  847 888-0433
  Elgin  *(G-9160)*
Tj Tool Inc .......................................... F  630 543-3595
  Addison  *(G-315)*
Tritech International LLC ..................... G  847 888-0333
  Elgin  *(G-9215)*

## STEEL FABRICATORS

A & A Steel Fabricating Co .................... F  708 389-4499
  Posen  *(G-17726)*
A & B Metal Polishing Inc ..................... F  773 847-1077
  Chicago  *(G-3678)*
A & S Steel Specialties Inc ................... E  815 838-8188
  Lockport  *(G-13700)*
A Lucas & Sons .................................... E  309 673-8547
  Peoria  *(G-17297)*
AAA Galvanizing - Joliet Inc ................. E  815 284-5001
  Dixon  *(G-8321)*
Aak Mechanical Inc .............................. D  217 935-8501
  Clinton  *(G-7276)*
Abitzy Inc ............................................ G  847 800-8666
  Lake In The Hills  *(G-12981)*
Ablaze Welding & Fabricating ............... G  815 965-0046
  Rockford  *(G-18248)*
Accurate Fabricators Inc ...................... G  618 451-1886
  Granite City  *(G-11258)*
Accurate Metal Fabricating LLC ............ G  773 235-0400
  Chicago  *(G-3720)*
Ace Metal Crafts Company ................... C  847 455-1010
  Bensenville  *(G-1815)*

Adams Steel Service Inc ....................... E  815 385-9100
  McHenry  *(G-14477)*
Adams Street Iron Inc .......................... F  312 733-3229
  Evergreen Park  *(G-10109)*
Addison Steel Inc ................................. G  847 998-9445
  Glenview  *(G-11096)*
Adermanns Welding & Mch & Co .......... E  217 342-3234
  Effingham  *(G-8822)*
Advance Iron Works Inc ....................... F  708 798-3540
  East Hazel Crest  *(G-8663)*
Advanced Steel Fabrication .................. G  847 956-6565
  Elk Grove Village  *(G-9277)*
Advanced Welding Ltd ......................... F  708 205-4559
  Addison  *(G-26)*
Ae2009 Technologies Inc ..................... E  708 331-0025
  South Holland  *(G-20240)*
Aetna Engineering Works Inc ............... G  773 785-0489
  Chicago  *(G-3778)*
Affton Fabg & Wldg Co Inc ................... F  314 781-4100
  Sauget  *(G-19381)*
Alert Tubing Fabricators Inc ................. G  847 253-7237
  Schaumburg  *(G-19429)*
Alfredos Iron Works Inc ....................... E  815 748-1177
  Cortland  *(G-7384)*
Allen Popovich .................................... G  815 712-7404
  Custer Park  *(G-7686)*
Alliance Steel Corporation .................... E  708 924-1200
  Bedford Park  *(G-1535)*
Alloy Specialties Inc ............................ F  815 586-4728
  Blackstone  *(G-2087)*
Allquip Co Inc ..................................... G  309 944-6153
  Geneseo  *(G-10797)*
Alro Steel Corporation ......................... G  708 534-5400
  Park Forest  *(G-17176)*
Alton Sheet Metal Corp ........................ F  618 462-0609
  Alton  *(G-559)*
Ambassador Steel Corporation .............. G  815 876-9089
  Princeton  *(G-17743)*
American Industrial Werks Inc .............. F  847 477-2648
  Schaumburg  *(G-19437)*
American Piping Group Inc .................. D  815 772-7470
  Morrison  *(G-15141)*
Anchor Welding & Fabrication .............. G  815 937-1640
  Aroma Park  *(G-878)*
Andersen Machine & Welding Inc .......... G  815 232-4664
  Freeport  *(G-10647)*
Andscot Co Inc .................................... G  847 455-5800
  Franklin Park  *(G-10396)*
Archer General Contg & Fabg ............... G  708 757-7902
  Steger  *(G-20568)*
Area Fabricators .................................. G  217 455-3426
  Coatsburg  *(G-7300)*
Arlington Strl Stl Co Inc ....................... E  847 577-2200
  Arlington Heights  *(G-716)*
Arnette Pattern Co Inc ......................... E  618 451-7700
  Granite City  *(G-11268)*
AS Fabricating Inc ............................... G  618 242-7438
  Mount Vernon  *(G-15398)*
Aspen Industries Inc ............................ F  630 238-0611
  Bensenville  *(G-1836)*
Atkore International Group Inc ............. A  708 339-1610
  Harvey  *(G-11658)*
Atkore Intl Holdings Inc ....................... G  708 225-2051
  Harvey  *(G-11659)*
Auburn Iron Works Inc ........................ F  708 422-7330
  Palos Heights  *(G-17099)*
B & B Fabrications LLC ........................ F  217 620-3210
  Sullivan  *(G-20739)*
Baron-Blakeslee Sfc Inc ....................... E  847 796-0822
  Northbrook  *(G-16212)*
Bartell Grinding and Mch LLC ............... G  708 408-1700
  Mc Cook  *(G-14445)*
Best Machine & Welding Co Inc ............ E  708 343-4455
  Woodridge  *(G-22456)*
Best Manufacturing & Wldg Inc ............ G  815 562-4107
  Rochelle  *(G-18079)*
Bi State Steel Co ................................. G  309 755-0668
  East Moline  *(G-8671)*
Biewer Fabricating Inc ......................... G  630 530-8922
  Villa Park  *(G-21238)*
Birdsell Machine & Orna Inc ................. G  217 243-5849
  Jacksonville  *(G-12379)*
BR Machine Inc ................................... F  815 434-0427
  Ottawa  *(G-16950)*
Bridge City Mechanical Inc ................... F  309 944-4873
  Geneseo  *(G-10799)*
Bridgeport Steel Sales Inc .................... F  312 326-4800
  Chicago  *(G-4167)*
Btd Manufacturing Inc ......................... G  309 444-1268
  Washington  *(G-21379)*

Byus Steel Inc ..................................... E  630 879-2200
  Batavia  *(G-1425)*
C & S Fabrication Services Inc ............. G  815 363-8510
  Johnsburg  *(G-12431)*
C Keller Manufacturing Inc .................. E  630 833-5593
  Villa Park  *(G-21240)*
Catapult Global LLC ............................ F  847 364-8149
  Elk Grove Village  *(G-9360)*
Cem LLC ............................................ D  708 333-3761
  Barrington  *(G-1276)*
Central Illinois Steel Company ............. E  217 854-3251
  Carlinville  *(G-3032)*
Cervones Welding Service Inc .............. G  847 985-6865
  Schaumburg  *(G-19470)*
Challenger Fabricators Inc ................... G  815 704-0077
  South Beloit  *(G-20142)*
Charter Dura-Bar Inc .......................... C  815 338-7800
  Woodstock  *(G-22552)*
Chicago Grinding & Machine Co ........... E  708 343-4399
  Melrose Park  *(G-14610)*
Chicago Metal Fabricators Inc .............. D  773 523-5755
  Chicago  *(G-4332)*
Chicago Metal Rolled Pdts Co ............... D  773 523-5757
  Chicago  *(G-4333)*
Chicagoland Metal Fabricators ............. G  847 260-5320
  Franklin Park  *(G-10430)*
Circle Metal Specialties Inc .................. E  708 597-1700
  Alsip  *(G-449)*
Cisne Iron Works Inc ........................... F  618 673-2188
  Cisne  *(G-7250)*
CJ Drilling Inc .................................... E  847 854-3888
  Dundee  *(G-8560)*
Clarkwestern Dietrich Building ............. E  815 561-2360
  Rochelle  *(G-18083)*
Cokel Dj Welding Bay & Muffler ............ G  309 385-4567
  Princeville  *(G-17763)*
Comet Fabricating & Welding Co .......... G  815 229-0468
  Rockford  *(G-18316)*
Commercial Metals Company ................ G  815 928-9600
  Kankakee  *(G-12606)*
Cooper B-Line Inc ............................... A  618 654-2184
  Highland  *(G-11780)*
Corsetti Structural Steel Inc ................. E  815 726-0186
  Joliet  *(G-12477)*
Cortelyou Machine & Welding .............. G  618 592-3961
  Oblong  *(G-16730)*
Covey Machine Inc .............................. F  773 650-1530
  Chicago  *(G-4484)*
Creative Steel Fabricators .................... G  847 803-2090
  Des Plaines  *(G-8177)*
Crest Metal Craft Inc ........................... G  773 978-0950
  Chicago  *(G-4504)*
Custom Fbrication Coatings Inc ........... D  618 452-9540
  Granite City  *(G-11271)*
Custom Feeder Co of Rockford ............. E  815 654-2444
  Loves Park  *(G-13932)*
Cyclops Welding Co ............................ G  815 223-0685
  La Salle  *(G-12769)*
D & M Welding Inc .............................. G  708 233-6080
  Bridgeview  *(G-2481)*
D L Austin Steel Supply Corp ............... E  618 345-7200
  Collinsville  *(G-7319)*
D5 Design Met Fabrication LLC ............ G  773 770-4705
  Chicago  *(G-4539)*
Dams Inc ............................................ F  708 385-3092
  Alsip  *(G-454)*
Dayton Superior Corporation ................ G  219 476-4106
  Kankakee  *(G-12608)*
Decatur Aeration Inc ........................... F  217 422-6828
  Decatur  *(G-7868)*
Delta Structures Inc ............................ F  630 694-8700
  Lombard  *(G-13789)*
Design Metals Fabrication Inc .............. G  630 752-9060
  Carol Stream  *(G-3143)*
Dicke Tool Company ............................ G  630 969-0050
  Downers Grove  *(G-8429)*
Dill Brothers Inc ................................. F  847 746-8323
  Zion  *(G-22682)*
DSI Spaceframes Inc ........................... E  630 607-0045
  Addison  *(G-99)*
E B Inc ............................................... F  815 758-6646
  De Kalb  *(G-7817)*
Ed Stan Fabricating Co ........................ G  708 863-7668
  Chicago  *(G-4694)*
Ekstrom Carlson Fabricating Co ........... G  815 226-1511
  Rockford  *(G-18360)*
Emco Metalworks Co ........................... E  708 222-1011
  Cicero  *(G-7195)*
Ermak Usa Inc .................................... F  847 640-7765
  Des Plaines  *(G-8190)*

Employee Codes: A=Over 500 employees, B=251-500, C=101-250, D=51-100, E=20-50, F=10-19, G=3-9

**Esi Steel & Fabrication** F 618 548-3017
Salem *(G-19331)*
**European Ornamental Iron Works** G 630 705-9300
Addison *(G-113)*
**Ex-Cell Kaiser LLC** E 847 451-0451
Franklin Park *(G-10467)*
**Exo Fabrication Inc** G 630 501-1136
Addison *(G-114)*
**F K Pattern & Foundry Company** G 847 578-5260
North Chicago *(G-16179)*
**F Kreutzer & Co** G 773 826-5767
Chicago *(G-4805)*
**F Vogelmann and Company** F 815 469-2285
Frankfort *(G-10321)*
**Fabco Enterprises Inc** G 708 333-4644
Harvey *(G-11666)*
**Fabmax Inc** F 630 766-0370
Wood Dale *(G-22365)*
**Fabricated Metal Systems Inc** G 815 886-6200
Romeoville *(G-18824)*
**Fabricating & Welding Corp** E 773 928-2050
Chicago *(G-4809)*
**Famaco Corp** E 217 442-4412
Tilton *(G-20881)*
**Fanmar Inc** E 708 563-0505
Elk Grove Village *(G-9475)*
**Fbs Group Inc** F 773 229-8675
Chicago *(G-4821)*
**Fehring Ornamental Iron Works** F 217 483-6727
Chatham *(G-3620)*
**First Stage Fabrication Inc** G 618 282-8320
Red Bud *(G-17941)*
**Fisher & Ludlow Inc** D 217 324-6106
Litchfield *(G-13685)*
**Flex-Weld Inc** D 815 334-3662
Woodstock *(G-22567)*
**Floyd Steel Erectors Inc** F 630 238-8383
Wood Dale *(G-22369)*
**Funk Linko Group Inc** F 708 757-7421
Monee *(G-14995)*
**G & F Manufacturing Co Inc** E 708 424-4170
Oak Lawn *(G-16621)*
**G & M Fabricating Inc** G 815 282-1744
Roscoe *(G-18898)*
**Gallon Industries Inc** E 630 628-1020
Addison *(G-127)*
**Garbe Iron Works Inc** E 630 897-5100
Aurora *(G-1160)*
**Gcs Steel Installers Inc** G 630 487-6736
Montgomery *(G-15044)*
**Gemini Steel Inc** G 815 472-4462
Momence *(G-14981)*
**Gentner Fabrication Inc** F 773 523-2505
Chicago *(G-4937)*
**Gerdau Ameristeel US Inc** E 815 547-0400
Belvidere *(G-1757)*
**Gma Inc** G 630 595-1255
Bensenville *(G-1910)*
**Greg Lambert Construction** E 815 468-7361
Bourbonnais *(G-2397)*
**Gremp Steel Co** E 708 389-7393
Posen *(G-17731)*
**Grimm Metal Fabricators Inc** E 630 792-1710
Lombard *(G-13807)*
**Grover Welding Company** G 847 966-3119
Skokie *(G-20007)*
**Gsi Group LLC** C 217 463-1612
Paris *(G-17148)*
**Harmony Metal Fabrication Inc** E 847 426-8900
Gilberts *(G-10920)*
**High Standard Fabricating Inc** E 815 965-6517
Rockford *(G-18419)*
**Hofmeister Wldg & Fabrication** F 217 833-2451
Griggsville *(G-11412)*
**Holden Industries Inc** F 847 940-1500
Deerfield *(G-8013)*
**Huntley & Associates Inc** G 224 381-8500
Lake Zurich *(G-13085)*
**Hyspan Precision Products Inc** E 773 277-0700
South Holland *(G-20279)*
**Ideal Fabricators Inc** F 217 999-7017
Mount Olive *(G-15304)*
**Igm Solutions Inc** E 847 918-1790
Libertyville *(G-13336)*
**Illinois Steel Service Inc** D 312 926-7440
Chicago *(G-5158)*
**Industrial Mint Wldg Machining** D 773 376-6526
Chicago *(G-5178)*
**Industrial Steel Cnstr Inc** G 630 232-7473
Geneva *(G-10835)*
**Industrial Steel Cnstr Inc** D 219 885-7600
Hodgkins *(G-11976)*
**Innotech Manufacturing LLC** E 618 244-6261
Mount Vernon *(G-15415)*
**ITW Blding Cmponents Group Inc** E 217 324-0303
Litchfield *(G-13689)*
**J & G Fabricating Inc** G 708 385-9147
Blue Island *(G-2257)*
**J B Metal Works Inc** G 847 824-4253
Des Plaines *(G-8215)*
**J H Botts LLC** E 815 726-5885
Joliet *(G-12519)*
**Jalor Company** G 847 202-1172
Elgin *(G-9082)*
**James Walker Mfg Co** E 708 754-4020
Glenwood *(G-11217)*
**Jameson Steel Fabrication Inc** G 217 354-2205
Oakwood *(G-16725)*
**Jarvis Welding Co** G 309 647-0033
Canton *(G-2988)*
**Jay RS Steel & Welding Inc** G 847 949-9353
Mundelein *(G-15514)*
**JB & S Machining** G 815 258-4007
Bourbonnais *(G-2401)*
**Jet Industries Inc** E 773 586-8900
Chicago *(G-5297)*
**K & K Iron Works LLC** D 708 924-0000
Mc Cook *(G-14449)*
**K Three Welding Service Inc** G 708 563-2911
Chicago *(G-5344)*
**K&R Enterprises I Inc** D 847 502-3371
Lake Barrington *(G-12815)*
**K-Met Industries Inc** F 708 534-3300
Monee *(G-14998)*
**Kemper Industries** G 217 826-5712
Marshall *(G-14324)*
**Kim Gough** G 309 734-3511
Monmouth *(G-15017)*
**King Metal Co** G 708 388-3845
Alsip *(G-479)*
**Kingery Steel Fabricators Inc** E 708 474-6665
Lansing *(G-13168)*
**Kmk Metal Fabricators Inc** E 618 224-2000
Trenton *(G-20993)*
**Knoll Steel Inc** F 815 675-9400
Spring Grove *(G-20342)*
**Kroh-Wagner Inc** E 773 252-2031
Chicago *(G-5412)*
**Ksem Inc** G 618 656-5388
Edwardsville *(G-8805)*
**Kso Metalfab Inc** E 630 372-1200
Streamwood *(G-20663)*
**Laser Plus Technologies LLC** G 847 787-9017
Elk Grove Village *(G-9585)*
**Laystrom Manufacturing Co** D 773 342-4800
Chicago *(G-5474)*
**Leroys Welding & Fabg Inc** F 847 215-6151
Wheeling *(G-22092)*
**Lesker Company Inc** E 708 343-2277
Bensenville *(G-1940)*
**Liberty Machinery Company** F 847 276-2761
Lincolnshire *(G-13463)*
**Lickenbrock & Sons Inc** G 618 632-4977
O Fallon *(G-16470)*
**Linear Kinetics Inc** G 630 365-0075
Maple Park *(G-14201)*
**Littell International Inc** E 630 622-4950
Schaumburg *(G-19621)*
**Lizotte Sheet Metal Inc** G 618 656-3066
Edwardsville *(G-8806)*
**LPI Worldwide Inc** G 773 826-8600
Chicago *(G-5550)*
**Mace Iron Works Inc** E 708 479-2456
Frankfort *(G-10341)*
**Marcmetals** G 847 905-0018
Evanston *(G-10069)*
**Marco Lighting Components Inc** F 312 829-6900
Chicago *(G-5613)*
**Marqutte Stl Sup Fbrcation Inc** F 815 433-0178
Ottawa *(G-16968)*
**Matcor Mtal Fbrication III Inc** E 309 263-1707
Morton *(G-15163)*
**Mc Kinney Steel & Sales Inc** E 847 746-3344
Zion *(G-22691)*
**McLaughlin Body Co** C 309 736-6105
East Moline *(G-8687)*
**McLaughlin Body Co** D 309 762-7755
Moline *(G-14955)*
**Mead Products LLC** G 847 541-9500
Lake Zurich *(G-13100)*
**Mechanical Indus Stl Svcs Inc** E 815 521-1725
Channahon *(G-3580)*
**Mellish & Murray Co** F 312 733-3513
Chicago *(G-5683)*
**Meno Stone Co Inc** E 630 257-9220
Lemont *(G-13241)*
**Metal Tech Inc** E 630 529-7400
Roselle *(G-18957)*
**Metals & Metals LLC** G 630 866-4200
Bolingbrook *(G-2341)*
**Metaltek Fabricating Inc** F 708 534-9102
University Park *(G-21056)*
**Metamora Industries LLC** E 309 367-2368
Metamora *(G-14745)*
**Michelmann Steel Cnstr Co** E 217 222-0555
Quincy *(G-17857)*
**Midwest Metals Inc** G 618 295-3444
Marissa *(G-14296)*
**Mj Snyder Ironworks Inc** G 217 826-6440
Marshall *(G-14326)*
**Mobile Mini Inc** E 708 297-2004
Calumet Park *(G-2963)*
**Mold Shields Inc** G 708 983-5931
Villa Park *(G-21271)*
**Moline Welding Inc** F 309 756-0643
Milan *(G-14795)*
**Montefusco Heating & Shtmtl Co** G 309 691-7400
Peoria *(G-17412)*
**Morey Industries Inc** C 708 343-3220
Broadview *(G-2598)*
**Morris Construction Inc** E 618 544-8504
Robinson *(G-18067)*
**Mrt Sureway Inc** D 847 801-3010
Franklin Park *(G-10537)*
**Mutual Svcs Highland Pk Inc** F 847 432-3815
Highland Park *(G-11858)*
**National Cycle Inc** C 708 343-0400
Maywood *(G-14430)*
**National Machine Repair Inc** F 708 672-7711
Crete *(G-7517)*
**National Metal Fabricators LLC** E 847 439-5321
Elk Grove Village *(G-9647)*
**Neiweem Industries Inc** G 847 487-1239
Oakwood Hills *(G-16727)*
**New Metal Fabrication Corp** E 618 532-9000
Centralia *(G-3424)*
**Newman Welding & Machine Shop** G 618 435-5591
Benton *(G-2037)*
**Nicks Metal Fabg & Sons** F 708 485-1170
Brookfield *(G-2639)*
**North Chicago Iron Works Inc** E 847 689-2000
North Chicago *(G-16185)*
**Northwestern Corporation** E 815 942-1300
Morris *(G-15124)*
**Nowfab** G 815 675-2916
Spring Grove *(G-20353)*
**Nu Mill Inc** G 630 458-8950
Addison *(G-231)*
**OBrien Architectural Mtls Inc** F 773 868-1065
Chicago *(G-5964)*
**Okaw Truss Inc** B 217 543-3371
Arthur *(G-915)*
**Old Style Iron Works Inc** G 773 265-5787
Chicago *(G-5980)*
**Olympic Steel Inc** E 847 584-4000
Schaumburg *(G-19675)*
**Onkens Incorporated** F 309 562-7477
Easton *(G-8778)*
**Oostman Fabricating & Wldg Inc** F 630 241-1315
Westmont *(G-21909)*
**Orsolinis Welding & Fabg** F 773 722-9855
Chicago *(G-6016)*
**Osbornes Mch Weld Fabrication** G 217 795-4716
Argenta *(G-691)*
**Owens Welding & Fabricating** F 773 265-9900
Chicago *(G-6032)*
**P R Manufacturing Co** G 309 596-2986
Viola *(G-21293)*
**Paco Corporation** F 708 430-2424
Bridgeview *(G-2517)*
**Palatine Welding Company** E 847 358-1075
Rolling Meadows *(G-18757)*
**Parkway Metal Products Inc** D 847 789-4000
Des Plaines *(G-8251)*
**Patrick Holdings Inc** F 815 874-5300
Rockford *(G-18531)*
**Paul Wever Construction Eqp Co** F 309 965-2005
Goodfield *(G-11248)*
**Performance Industries Inc** E 972 393-6881
Carpentersville *(G-3294)*

Phoenix Fabrication & Sup Inc ............G....... 708 754-5901
S Chicago Hts (G-19110)
Phoenix Welding Co Inc ............F....... 630 616-1700
Franklin Park (G-10549)
Pittsfield Mch Tl & Wldg Co ............G....... 217 656-4000
Payson (G-17246)
Pools Welding Inc ............G....... 309 787-2083
Milan (G-14798)
Prairie State Industries Inc ............F....... 847 428-3641
Carpentersville (G-3297)
Pro-Tech Metal Specialties Inc ............E....... 630 279-7094
Elmhurst (G-9923)
Pro-Tran Inc ............G....... 217 348-9353
Charleston (G-3608)
Professional Metal Works LLC ............F....... 618 539-2214
Freeburg (G-10639)
R & B Metal Products Inc ............E....... 815 338-1890
Woodstock (G-22603)
R C Industrial Inc ............G....... 309 756-3724
Milan (G-14801)
R W Bradley Supply Company ............G....... 217 528-8438
Springfield (G-20510)
Rail Exchange Inc ............E....... 708 757-3317
Chicago Heights (G-7119)
Reber Welding Service ............G....... 217 774-3441
Shelbyville (G-19914)
Redi-Weld & Mfg Co Inc ............G....... 815 455-4460
Lake In The Hills (G-13004)
Ri-Del Mfg Inc ............D....... 312 829-8720
Chicago (G-6349)
Ricar Industries Inc ............G....... 847 914-9083
Northbrook (G-16355)
Rockford Ornamental Iron Inc ............F....... 815 633-1162
Rockford (G-18581)
Romero Steel Company Inc ............E....... 708 216-0001
Melrose Park (G-14688)
Rrb Fabrication Inc ............F....... 815 977-5603
Loves Park (G-13989)
S & S Welding & Fabrication ............G....... 847 742-7344
Elgin (G-9170)
Selvaggio Orna & Strl Stl Inc ............E....... 217 528-4077
Springfield (G-20521)
Shamrock Manufacturing Co Inc ............G....... 708 331-7776
South Holland (G-20304)
Sheet Metal Supply Ltd ............G....... 847 478-8500
Mundelein (G-15557)
Sheets & Cylinder Welding Inc ............G....... 800 442-2200
Chicago (G-6494)
Shew Brothers Inc ............G....... 618 997-4414
Marion (G-14286)
Silver Machine Shop Inc ............G....... 217 359-5717
Champaign (G-3540)
Simion Fabrication Inc ............G....... 618 724-7331
Christopher (G-7174)
Sivco Welding Company ............G....... 309 944-5171
Geneseo (G-10804)
Skyjack Equipment Inc ............E....... 630 797-3299
Saint Charles (G-19263)
Smf Inc ............C....... 309 432-2586
Minonk (G-14834)
Smith Brothers Fabricating ............G....... 618 498-5612
Jerseyville (G-12426)
South Subn Wldg & Fabg Co Inc ............G....... 708 385-7160
Posen (G-17736)
Spectracrafts Ltd ............G....... 847 824-4117
Lombard (G-13856)
Spg International LLC ............E....... 815 233-0022
Freeport (G-10690)
Spider Company Inc ............D....... 815 961-8200
Rockford (G-18628)
Square 1 Precision Ltg Inc ............G....... 708 343-1500
Melrose Park (G-14695)
Stairs & Rales Inc ............G....... 708 216-0078
Melrose Park (G-14696)
Standard Sheet Metal Works Inc ............E....... 309 633-2300
Peoria (G-17463)
Steel Construction Svcs Inc ............G....... 815 678-7509
Richmond (G-17972)
Steel Management Inc ............G....... 630 397-5083
Geneva (G-10869)
Steelfab Inc ............E....... 815 935-6540
Kankakee (G-12654)
Steelwerks of Chicago LLC ............G....... 312 792-9593
Chicago (G-6582)
Stevenson Fabrication Svcs Inc ............G....... 815 468-7941
Manteno (G-14195)
Strat-O-Span Buildings Inc ............G....... 618 526-4566
Breese (G-2448)
Structural Design Corp ............G....... 847 816-3816
Libertyville (G-13385)
Sturdee Metal Products Inc ............G....... 773 523-3074
New Lenox (G-15913)
Sturdi Iron Inc ............G....... 815 464-1173
Frankfort (G-10365)
Summit Metal Products Inc ............G....... 630 879-7008
Batavia (G-1500)
Superior Fabrication & Machine ............G....... 217 762-5512
Monticello (G-15086)
Superior Joining Tech Inc ............E....... 815 282-7581
Machesney Park (G-14109)
Syr-Tech Perforating Co ............E....... 630 942-7300
Glendale Heights (G-11081)
T & L Mfg Corporation ............E....... 630 898-7100
Aurora (G-1220)
Taylor Off Road Racing ............G....... 815 544-4500
Belvidere (G-1788)
Testa Steel Constructors Inc ............F....... 815 729-4777
Channahon (G-3587)
Tgm Fabricating Inc ............G....... 708 533-0857
Chicago Heights (G-7131)
Thybar Corporation ............E....... 630 543-5300
Addison (G-314)
Tinsley Steel Inc ............G....... 618 656-5231
Edwardsville (G-8817)
Titan Industries Inc ............G....... 309 440-1010
Deer Creek (G-7966)
Titan Steel Corporation ............E....... 815 726-4900
New Lenox (G-15920)
Tmz Metal Fabricating Inc ............G....... 815 230-3071
Plainfield (G-17658)
Tni Packaging Inc ............G....... 630 293-3030
West Chicago (G-21781)
Tonys Welding Service Inc ............G....... 618 532-9353
Centralia (G-3436)
Total Engineered Products Inc ............G....... 630 543-9006
Addison (G-319)
Tri-Cunty Wldg Fabrication LLC ............E....... 217 543-3304
Arthur (G-923)
Trifab Inc ............G....... 847 838-2083
Antioch (G-660)
Trinity Structural Towers Inc ............F....... 217 935-7900
Clinton (G-7290)
Triton Industries Inc ............C....... 773 384-3700
Chicago (G-6779)
Ultra Stamping & Assembly Inc ............E....... 815 874-9888
Rockford (G-18660)
Unistrut International Corp ............C....... 800 882-5543
Harvey (G-11679)
Unistrut International Corp ............D....... 630 773-3460
Addison (G-334)
United Conveyor Supply Company ............E....... 708 344-8050
Melrose Park (G-14703)
United Industries Illinois Ltd ............G....... 847 526-9485
Wauconda (G-21511)
US Fabg & Mine Svcs Inc ............G....... 618 983-7850
Johnston City (G-12448)
V & N Metal Products Inc ............G....... 773 436-1855
Chicago (G-6863)
V A Robinson Ltd ............G....... 773 205-4364
Chicago (G-6866)
Valmont Industries Inc ............D....... 773 625-0354
Franklin Park (G-10619)
Van Pelt Corporation ............E....... 313 365-3600
East Moline (G-8697)
Vent Products Co Inc ............E....... 773 521-1900
Chicago (G-6881)
Voges Inc ............D....... 618 233-2760
Belleville (G-1688)
Walt Ltd ............E....... 312 337-2756
Chicago (G-6936)
Walters Metal Fabrication Inc ............D....... 618 931-5551
Granite City (G-11311)
Waukegan Steel LLC ............E....... 847 662-2810
Waukegan (G-21639)
Weld-Rite Service Inc ............E....... 708 458-6000
Bedford Park (G-1592)
Westmont Metal Mfg LLC ............F....... 708 343-0214
Broadview (G-2620)
Wherry Machine & Welding Inc ............G....... 309 828-5423
Bloomington (G-2235)
Whiting Corporation ............C....... 708 587-2000
Monee (G-15007)
Willow Farm Products Inc ............G....... 630 430-7491
Lemont (G-13270)
Wilmouth Machine Works Inc ............G....... 618 372-3189
Brighton (G-2546)
Wsw Industrial Maintenance ............F....... 773 721-0675
Chicago (G-7041)

## STEEL MILLS

A & A Steel Fabricating Co ............F....... 708 389-4499
Posen (G-17726)
AK Steel Corporation ............B....... 815 267-3838
Plainfield (G-17577)
Aldon Co ............F....... 847 623-8800
Waukegan (G-21521)
Alton Steel Inc ............B....... 618 463-4490
Alton (G-560)
Arcanum Alloy Design Inc ............G....... 219 508-5531
Chicago (G-3931)
Arcelormittal USA LLC ............B....... 312 346-0300
Chicago (G-3935)
Archer Metal & Paper Co ............F....... 773 585-3030
Chicago (G-3939)
Arntzen Corporation ............E....... 815 334-0788
Woodstock (G-22541)
Bar Processing Corporation ............E....... 708 757-4570
Chicago Heights (G-7081)
Block Steel Corp ............E....... 847 965-6700
Skokie (G-19965)
Bretmar Steel Industry ............G....... 847 382-5940
Barrington (G-1274)
Cambridge Pattern Works ............G....... 309 937-5370
Cambridge (G-2966)
Chicago Metal Fabricators Inc ............D....... 773 523-5755
Chicago (G-4332)
Chicago Pipe Bending & Coil Co ............F....... 773 379-1918
Chicago (G-4339)
Chromium Industries Inc ............E....... 773 287-3716
Chicago (G-4373)
Combined Metals Holding Inc ............C....... 708 547-8800
Bellwood (G-1701)
Commercial Metals Company ............G....... 815 928-9600
Kankakee (G-12606)
Consolidated Mill Supply Inc ............G....... 847 706-6715
Palatine (G-17016)
Covey Machine Inc ............F....... 773 650-1530
Chicago (G-4484)
D R Sperry & Co ............D....... 630 892-4361
Aurora (G-1137)
Feralloy Corporation ............E....... 503 286-8869
Chicago (G-4836)
Fox Valley Iron & Metal Corp ............F....... 630 897-5907
Aurora (G-1155)
Heidtman Steel Products Inc ............D....... 618 451-0052
Granite City (G-11284)
Heidtman Steel Products Inc ............D....... 618 451-0052
Granite City (G-11285)
Illinois Steel Service Inc ............D....... 312 926-7440
Chicago (G-5158)
Illinois Weld & Machine Inc ............F....... 309 565-0533
Hanna City (G-11568)
Industrial Pipe and Supply Co ............E....... 708 652-7511
Chicago (G-5179)
Jacobs Boiler & Mech Inds Inc ............E....... 773 385-9900
Chicago (G-5269)
Jamco Products Inc ............D....... 815 624-0400
South Beloit (G-20152)
John Maneely Company ............C....... 773 254-0617
Chicago (G-5316)
Lawndale Forging & Tool Works ............G....... 773 277-2800
Chicago (G-5471)
Leeco Steel Products ............G....... 630 427-2100
Lisle (G-13617)
Lexington Steel Corporation ............D....... 708 594-9200
Oak Brook (G-16536)
Mc Chemical Company ............E....... 815 964-7687
Rockford (G-18487)
Middletown Coke Company LLC ............G....... 630 284-1755
Lisle (G-13623)
Multiplex Industries Inc ............G....... 630 906-9780
Montgomery (G-15062)
Nacme Steel Processing LLC ............G....... 847 806-7226
Elk Grove Village (G-9644)
Nacme Steel Processing LLC ............D....... 773 468-3309
Chicago (G-5848)
New C F & I Inc ............A....... 312 533-3555
Chicago (G-5890)
Nucor Steel Kankakee Inc ............B....... 815 937-3131
Bourbonnais (G-2403)
Olympic Steel Inc ............E....... 847 584-4000
Schaumburg (G-19675)
P B A Corp ............F....... 312 666-7370
Chicago (G-6039)
Penn Aluminum Intl LLC ............C....... 618 684-2146
Murphysboro (G-15579)
Production Cutting Services ............D....... 815 264-3505
Waterman (G-21409)



Employee Codes: A=Over 500 employees, B=251-500
C=101-250, D=51-100, E=20-50, F=10-19, G=3-9
2017 Harris Illinois
Industrial Directory
1769

## STEEL MILLS

Raco Steel Company ............................... E ....... 708 339-2958
  Markham  (G-14304)
Rain Cii Carbon LLC ............................... E ....... 618 544-2193
  Robinson  (G-18071)
Residntial Stl Fabricators Inc ................. E ....... 847 695-3400
  South Elgin  (G-20223)
Shapiro Bros of Illinois Inc ..................... E ....... 618 244-3168
  Mount Vernon  (G-15445)
Ssab Enterprises  LLC ............................. E ....... 630 810-4800
  Lisle  (G-13661)
Ssab US Holding  Inc .............................. E ....... 630 810-4800
  Lisle  (G-13662)
St Louis Scrap Trading  LLC ................... G ....... 618 307-9002
  Edwardsville  (G-8815)
Steel Whse Quad Cities LLC .................. E ....... 309 756-1089
  Rock Island  (G-18205)
Stein  Inc ............................................... F ....... 815 626-9355
  Sterling  (G-20613)
Stein  Inc ............................................... D ....... 618 452-0836
  Granite City  (G-11305)
Sun Coke International  Inc .................... D ....... 630 824-1000
  Lisle  (G-13665)
Suncoke Energy  Inc ................................ B ....... 630 824-1000
  Lisle  (G-13666)
Suncoke Energy Partners  LP ................. E ....... 630 824-1000
  Lisle  (G-13667)
Suncoke Technology and Dev LLC ........ G ....... 630 824-1000
  Lisle  (G-13668)
Tdy Industries  LLC ................................. D ....... 847 564-0700
  Northbrook  (G-16376)
Titan International  Inc ............................ B ....... 217 228-6011
  Quincy  (G-17896)
Tomko Machine Works Inc ..................... G ....... 630 244-0902
  Lemont  (G-13266)
United States Steel Corp ........................ D ....... 618 451-3456
  Granite City  (G-11310)
Valbruna Stainless  Inc ............................ F ....... 630 871-5524
  Carol Stream  (G-3260)
Venus Processing & Storage ................. D ....... 847 455-0496
  Franklin Park  (G-10621)
Westwood Lands Inc .............................. G ....... 618 877-4990
  Madison  (G-14156)

## STEEL SHEET: Cold-Rolled

Petersen Aluminum Corporation ............ D ....... 847 228-7150
  Elk Grove Village  (G-9676)
Welding Apparatus Company ................. E ....... 773 252-7670
  Fox Lake  (G-10284)

## STEEL WOOL

Global Material Tech Inc ......................... C ....... 847 495-4700
  Buffalo Grove  (G-2699)
Superior Joining Tech Inc ....................... E ....... 815 282-7581
  Machesney Park  (G-14109)

## STEEL, COLD-ROLLED: Flat Bright, From Purchased Hot-Rolled

Arcelormittal Riverdale Inc ..................... B ....... 708 849-8803
  Riverdale  (G-18014)

## STEEL, COLD-ROLLED: Sheet Or Strip, From Own Hot-Rolled

A 2 Steel Sales LLC ................................ G ....... 708 924-1200
  Bedford Park  (G-1529)

## STEEL, COLD-ROLLED: Strip NEC, From Purchased Hot-Rolled

Sandvik Inc ............................................ D ....... 847 519-1737
  Schaumburg  (G-19718)

## STEEL, COLD-ROLLED: Strip Or Wire

Mid-States Wire Proc Corp ..................... F ....... 773 379-3775
  Chicago  (G-5730)

## STEEL, HOT-ROLLED: Sheet Or Strip

National Material LP ............................... E ....... 773 646-6300
  Chicago  (G-5864)
Revere Metals LLC ................................. G ....... 708 945-3992
  Frankfort  (G-10357)

## STEEL: Cold-Rolled

Arcelormittal USA LLC ........................... B ....... 312 346-0300
  Chicago  (G-3935)

Bonell Manufacturing Company ............. E ....... 708 849-1770
  Riverdale  (G-18016)
Capitol Coil Inc ....................................... F ....... 847 891-1390
  Schaumburg  (G-19468)
Chase Fasteners  Inc .............................. E ....... 708 345-0335
  Melrose Park  (G-14608)
Clingan Steel Inc .................................... D ....... 847 228-6200
  Elk Grove Village  (G-9378)
Combined Metals Chicago LLC ............. G ....... 847 683-0500
  Hampshire  (G-11545)
Deringer-Ney Inc .................................... E ....... 847 566-4100
  Vernon Hills  (G-21157)
Design Manufacturing & Eqp Co ............ F ....... 217 824-9219
  Taylorville  (G-20837)
Expandable Habitats ............................. E ....... 815 624-6784
  Rockton  (G-18696)
Gartech Manufacturing Co ..................... E ....... 217 324-6527
  Litchfield  (G-13686)
Harris Steel Company ........................... D ....... 708 656-5500
  Cicero  (G-7200)
Lapham-Hickey Steel Corp .................... C ....... 708 496-6111
  Chicago  (G-5459)
Madison Inds Holdings LLC ................... G ....... 312 277-0156
  Chicago  (G-5598)
Mid-State Industries Oper Inc ................ E ....... 217 268-3900
  Arcola  (G-676)
Multiplex Industries Inc .......................... G ....... 630 906-9780
  Montgomery  (G-15062)
Multitech Industries ............................... G ....... 815 206-0015
  Woodstock  (G-22594)
Phillip C Cowen ..................................... E ....... 630 208-1848
  Geneva  (G-10859)
Ptc Group Holdings Corp ....................... D ....... 708 757-4747
  Chicago Heights  (G-7118)
Rockford Secondary Co ......................... F ....... 815 398-0401
  Rockford  (G-18586)
Screws Industries  Inc ............................ D ....... 630 539-9200
  Glendale Heights  (G-11068)
Skach Manufacturing Co Inc .................. E ....... 847 395-3560
  Antioch  (G-655)
Soudan Metals Company  Inc ................. C ....... 773 548-7600
  Chicago  (G-6545)
Tempel Steel Company .......................... A ....... 773 250-8000
  Chicago  (G-6696)

## STEEL: Laminated

Filter Technology  Inc ............................. F ....... 773 523-7200
  Bedford Park  (G-1550)
Illinois Block and Tackle Inc ................... G ....... 618 451-8696
  Granite City  (G-11288)
MSC Pre Finish Metals Egv Inc .............. C ....... 847 439-2210
  Elk Grove Village  (G-9640)
Polaris Laser Laminations  LLC ............. G ....... 630 444-0760
  West Chicago  (G-21758)
Tempel Steel Company .......................... A ....... 773 250-8000
  Chicago  (G-6698)

## STEERING SYSTEMS & COMPONENTS

Appleton Rack & Pinions Inc ................. F ....... 815 467-9583
  Minooka  (G-14836)
Tuxco Corporation ................................. F ....... 847 244-2220
  Gurnee  (G-11517)
United Carburetor Inc ............................ E ....... 773 777-1223
  Schiller Park  (G-19879)
United Remanufacturing Co Inc ............. G ....... 773 777-1223
  Schiller Park  (G-19880)

## STENCILS

ABM Marking Services  Ltd .................... G ....... 618 277-3773
  Belleville  (G-1607)
Chicago Silk Screen Sup Co Inc ............ E ....... 312 666-1213
  Chicago  (G-4349)
Custom Cut Stencil Company Inc .......... G ....... 618 277-5077
  Belleville  (G-1622)
U Mark  Inc ............................................ E ....... 618 235-7500
  Belleville  (G-1683)

## STEREOGRAPHS: Photographic Message Svcs

Sport Electronics Inc ............................. G ....... 847 564-5575
  Northbrook  (G-16369)

## STERILIZERS, BARBER & BEAUTY SHOP

Grande Diva Hair Salon ......................... E ....... 217 383-0023
  Champaign  (G-3491)

## STITCHING SVCS

Monograms & More ............................... G ....... 630 789-8424
  Burr Ridge  (G-2869)

## STOCK CAR RACING

Bill West Enterprises Inc ........................ G ....... 217 886-2591
  Jacksonville  (G-12378)

## STOCK SHAPES: Plastic

Work Area Protection Corp .................... D ....... 630 377-9100
  Saint Charles  (G-19299)

## STONE: Cast Concrete

Eagle Stone and Brick Inc ..................... G ....... 618 282-6722
  Red Bud  (G-17940)
Stone Installation & Maint Inc ................ G ....... 630 545-2326
  Glendale Heights  (G-11077)

## STONE: Dimension, NEC

F Lee Charles & Sons Inc ...................... G ....... 815 547-7141
  Kirkland  (G-12712)
Gary Galassi and Sons  Inc .................... E ....... 815 886-3906
  Romeoville  (G-18827)
Ill Dept Natural Resources .................... F ....... 217 782-4970
  Springfield  (G-20453)
Loberg Excavating  Inc ........................... E ....... 815 443-2874
  Pearl City  (G-17248)
Stolle Casper Quar & Contg Co ............. E ....... 618 337-5212
  Dupo  (G-8579)
Stone Usa  Inc ....................................... G ....... 312 356-0988
  Chicago  (G-6598)
Tri-State Cut Stone Co .......................... G ....... 815 469-7550
  Frankfort  (G-10371)
Wendell Adams ..................................... E ....... 217 345-9587
  Charleston  (G-3615)

## STONE: Quarrying & Processing, Own Stone Prdts

Brombereks Flagstone Co Inc ............... G ....... 630 257-0686
  Lemont  (G-13228)
Heisler Stone Co Inc ............................. G ....... 815 244-2685
  Mount Carroll  (G-15291)
Material Service Corporation ................. E ....... 847 658-4559
  Algonquin  (G-400)
Material Service Corporation ................. E ....... 708 447-1100
  Westchester  (G-21849)

## STONES: Abrasive

Rock Solid Imports LLC ......................... G ....... 331 472-4522
  Naperville  (G-15743)

## STONEWARE PRDTS: Pottery

Richard Ochwat Specialty Entp ............. G ....... 630 682-0800
  Carol Stream  (G-3228)
Ws Incorporated of Manmouth ............... F ....... 309 734-2161
  Monmouth  (G-15024)

## STOOLS: Factory

Seats & Stools Inc ................................. G ....... 773 348-7900
  Chicago  (G-6467)
Sport Incentives  Inc .............................. F ....... 847 427-8650
  Elk Grove Village  (G-9748)

## STORE FIXTURES, EXC REFRIGERATED: Wholesalers

Daniel M Powers & Assoc Ltd ................ D ....... 630 685-8400
  Bolingbrook  (G-2299)

## STORE FIXTURES: Exc Wood

Marmon Retail Services  Inc .................. G ....... 312 332-0317
  Chicago  (G-5629)
Tesko Welding & Mfg Co ........................ D ....... 708 452-0045
  Norridge  (G-16109)

## STORE FIXTURES: Wood

Bernhard Woodwork  Ltd ........................ E ....... 847 291-1040
  Northbrook  (G-16214)
Castle Craft Products  Inc ...................... F ....... 630 279-7494
  Villa Park  (G-21242)
Daniel M Powers & Assoc Ltd ................ D ....... 630 685-8400
  Bolingbrook  (G-2299)

Dunhill Corp ..................................... F ..... 815 806-8600
  Frankfort *(G-10315)*
Imperial Woodworking Company .......... D ..... 847 221-2107
  Palatine *(G-17039)*
Marmon Retail Services Inc ................. G ..... 312 332-0317
  Chicago *(G-5629)*
Midwest Custom Case Inc .................... C ..... 708 672-2900
  University Park *(G-21057)*
Schrock Custom Woodworking .............. G ..... 217 849-3375
  Toledo *(G-20965)*

## STORES: Auto & Home Supply

Arco Automotive Elec Svc Co ................ G ..... 708 422-2976
  Oak Lawn *(G-16603)*
Coating Specialty Inc ............................ G ..... 708 754-3311
  S Chicago Hts *(G-19101)*
Galva Iron and Metal Co Inc .................. G ..... 309 932-3450
  Galva *(G-10789)*
Mag Daddy LLC .................................... G ..... 847 719-5600
  Lake Zurich *(G-13098)*
Polar Corporation .................................. E ..... 618 548-3660
  Salem *(G-19343)*
Service Auto Supply .............................. F ..... 309 444-9704
  Washington *(G-21392)*
Smart Systems Inc ................................ E ..... 630 343-3333
  Bolingbrook *(G-2372)*
Stop & Go International Inc ................... G ..... 815 455-9080
  Crystal Lake *(G-7654)*
T G Automotive ..................................... E ..... 630 916-7818
  Lombard *(G-13863)*

## STORES: Drapery & Upholstery

F & L Drapery Inc .................................. G ..... 815 932-8997
  Saint Anne *(G-19122)*
Loomcraft Textile & Supply Co .............. E ..... 847 680-0000
  Vernon Hills *(G-21182)*

## STRADDLE CARRIERS: Mobile

Blue Nile Trucking LLC ......................... G ..... 618 215-1077
  East Saint Louis *(G-8745)*

## STRAINERS: Line, Piping Systems

Spirax Sarco Inc .................................... F ..... 630 493-4525
  Lisle *(G-13660)*

## STRAPPING

Illinois Tool Works Inc ............................ C ..... 708 458-7320
  Bridgeview *(G-2499)*
Illinois Tool Works Inc ............................ C ..... 708 342-6000
  Mokena *(G-14872)*
Illinois Tool Works Inc ............................ E ..... 847 215-8925
  Buffalo Grove *(G-2706)*
Illinois Tool Works Inc ............................ B ..... 847 724-7500
  Glenview *(G-11141)*
Illinois Tool Works Inc ............................ C ..... 630 372-2150
  Bartlett *(G-1353)*
Illinois Tool Works Inc ............................ C ..... 847 783-5500
  Elgin *(G-9072)*
McLean Manufacturing Company .......... G ..... 847 277-9912
  Lake Barrington *(G-12819)*
Samuel Strapping Systems Inc ............. D ..... 630 783-8900
  Woodridge *(G-22515)*
Signode Corporation ............................. A ..... 800 527-1499
  Glenview *(G-11197)*
Signode Packaging Systems Corp ........ D ..... 800 323-2464
  Glenview *(G-11203)*
Signode Supply Corporation .................. C ..... 708 458-7320
  Bridgeview *(G-2528)*

## STRAPS: Apparel Webbing

Phoenix Graphix .................................... G ..... 618 531-3664
  Pinckneyville *(G-17551)*

## STRAPS: Webbing, Woven

Ribbon Webbing Corporation ................ C ..... 773 287-1221
  Chicago *(G-6351)*

## STRAW GOODS

Mat Capital LLC .................................... G ..... 847 821-9630
  Long Grove *(G-13895)*

## STRAWS: Drinking, Made From Purchased Materials

Best Diamond Plastics LLC .................. F ..... 773 336-3485
  Chicago *(G-4092)*

SCC Holding Company LLC .................. A ..... 847 444-5000
  Lake Forest *(G-12958)*
Solo Cup Company ............................... C ..... 847 831-4800
  Lincolnshire *(G-13480)*
Solo Cup Company LLC ....................... C ..... 847 444-5000
  Lincolnshire *(G-13481)*
Solo Cup Investment Corp ..................... E ..... 847 831-4800
  Highland Park *(G-11872)*

## STRINGING BEADS

Bodacious Beads Inc ............................. G ..... 847 699-7959
  Des Plaines *(G-8160)*

## STRIPS: Copper & Copper Alloy

Wieland Metals Inc ................................ C ..... 847 537-3990
  Wheeling *(G-22182)*

## STRUCTURAL SUPPORT & BUILDING MATERIAL: Concrete

Royal Corinthian Inc .............................. E ..... 630 876-8899
  West Chicago *(G-21767)*

## STUDIOS: Artist

Circle Studio Stained Glass ................... G ..... 773 588-4848
  Chicago *(G-4380)*

## STUDIOS: Artists & Artists' Studios

Chase Group LLC .................................. F ..... 847 564-2000
  Northbrook *(G-16219)*

## STUDIOS: Sculptor's

Rebechini Studio Inc ............................. F ..... 847 364-8600
  Elk Grove Village *(G-9711)*

## STUDS & JOISTS: Sheet Metal

Expanded Metal Products Corp ............. F ..... 773 735-4500
  Chicago *(G-4795)*

## STYLING SVCS: Wigs

Hairline Creations Inc ............................ F ..... 773 282-5454
  Chicago *(G-5032)*

## STYRENE RESINS, NEC

BP Amoco Chemical Company .............. B ..... 630 420-5111
  Naperville *(G-15608)*

## SUBPRESSES, METALWORKING

Flores Precision Products ..................... G ..... 630 264-2222
  Aurora *(G-1152)*

## SUGAR SUBSTITUTES: Organic

Merisant Foreign Holdings I ................... F ..... 312 840-6000
  Chicago *(G-5692)*
Merisant Us Inc ..................................... B ..... 312 840-6000
  Chicago *(G-5693)*
Merisant Us Inc ..................................... C ..... 815 929-2700
  Manteno *(G-14188)*
Necta Sweet Inc .................................... G ..... 847 215-9955
  Buffalo Grove *(G-2742)*
Purecircle USA Inc ................................ E ..... 866 960-8242
  Oak Brook *(G-16557)*

## SUNDRIES & RELATED PRDTS: Medical & Laboratory, Rubber

Fenwal Inc ............................................. B ..... 847 550-2300
  Lake Zurich *(G-13072)*
Fenwal Holdings Inc .............................. B ..... 847 550-2300
  Lake Zurich *(G-13073)*
Shore Capital Partners LLC .................. F ..... 312 348-7580
  Chicago *(G-6499)*
Superior Bumpers Inc ........................... G ..... 630 932-4910
  Lombard *(G-13862)*
Vestitrak Intl Inc .................................... G ..... 312 236-7100
  Chicago *(G-6890)*

## SUNGLASSES, WHOLESALE

Jim Maui Inc .......................................... G ..... 888 666-5905
  Peoria *(G-17392)*

## SUPERMARKETS & OTHER GROCERY STORES

Butera Finer Foods Inc .......................... D ..... 708 456-5939
  Norridge *(G-16097)*
Clown Global Brands LLC ..................... G ..... 847 564-5950
  Northbrook *(G-16227)*
Elburn Market Inc .................................. E ..... 630 365-6461
  Elburn *(G-8884)*
Hartrich Meats Inc ................................. G ..... 618 455-3172
  Sainte Marie *(G-19324)*
Kroger Co ............................................. C ..... 815 332-7267
  Rockford *(G-18457)*
McCain Usa Inc ..................................... C ..... 800 938-7799
  Lisle *(G-13621)*
Sunset Food Mart Inc ............................ C ..... 847 234-0854
  Lake Forest *(G-12964)*
Treasure Island Foods Inc .................... C ..... 773 880-8880
  Chicago *(G-6764)*
Walter Lagestee Inc .............................. C ..... 708 957-2974
  Homewood *(G-12106)*

## SURFACE ACTIVE AGENTS

Avatar Corporation ................................ D ..... 708 534-5511
  University Park *(G-21042)*
Cedar Concepts Corporation ................. E ..... 773 890-5790
  Chicago *(G-4265)*
Custom Blending & Pckaging of ............ F ..... 618 286-1140
  Dupo *(G-8569)*
Kik Custom Products Inc ....................... B ..... 217 442-1400
  Danville *(G-7743)*
Solvay USA Inc ..................................... F ..... 708 371-2000
  Blue Island *(G-2271)*
Stepan Company ................................... B ..... 847 446-7500
  Northfield *(G-16419)*
Union Drainage District ......................... G ..... 618 445-2843
  Mount Erie *(G-15294)*
Vantage Specialties Inc ........................ F ..... 847 244-3410
  Chicago *(G-6875)*

## SURFACE ACTIVE AGENTS: Emulsifiers, Exc Food & Pharmaceuticl

Ivanhoe Industries Inc ........................... G ..... 847 566-7170
  Mundelein *(G-15512)*

## SURFACE ACTIVE AGENTS: Oils & Greases

Griffin Industries LLC ............................ G ..... 815 357-8200
  Seneca *(G-19886)*

## SURFACE ACTIVE AGENTS: Processing Assistants

Houghton International Inc .................... F ..... 610 666-4000
  Chicago *(G-5121)*

## SURGICAL & MEDICAL INSTRUMENTS WHOLESALERS

Avalign Technologies Inc ....................... E ..... 855 282-5446
  Bannockburn *(G-1253)*
Hearing Screening Assoc LLC .............. G ..... 855 550-9427
  Arlington Heights *(G-763)*
Landauer Inc ......................................... C ..... 708 755-7000
  Glenwood *(G-11218)*
Medline Industries Inc ........................... A ..... 847 949-5500
  Northfield *(G-16409)*
Sysmex America Inc ............................. C ..... 847 996-4500
  Lincolnshire *(G-13484)*

## SURGICAL APPLIANCES & SPLYS

20 20 Medical Systems Inc ................... G ..... 815 455-7161
  Crystal Lake *(G-7524)*
Baxalta Export Corporation ................... G ..... 224 948-2000
  Deerfield *(G-7981)*
Baxalta World Trade LLC ...................... G ..... 224 948-2000
  Deerfield *(G-7982)*
Baxalta Worldwide LLC ......................... G ..... 224 948-2000
  Deerfield *(G-7983)*
Baxter Healthcare Corporation .............. E ..... 847 578-4671
  Waukegan *(G-21529)*
Baxter International Inc ......................... A ..... 224 948-2000
  Deerfield *(G-7988)*
Lanterna Medical Tech USA .................. G ..... 847 446-9995
  Winnetka *(G-22309)*
Lsi Industries Inc ................................... D ..... 773 878-1100
  Chicago *(G-5555)*

## SURGICAL APPLIANCES & SPLYS

Sage Products LLC ..............................B...... 815 455-4700
　Cary *(G-3370)*
Teleflex Incorporated ..........................D...... 847 259-7400
　Arlington Heights *(G-853)*
Tetra Medical Supply Corp ..................F...... 847 647-0590
　Niles *(G-16040)*

### SURGICAL APPLIANCES & SPLYS

1 Federal Supply Source Inc ..............G...... 708 964-2222
　Steger *(G-20565)*
Advanced Mbility Solutions LLC ........G...... 618 658-8580
　Marion *(G-14247)*
Argentum Medical LLC ........................E...... 888 551-0188
　Geneva *(G-10810)*
Artistic Dental Studio Inc ....................G...... 630 679-8686
　Bolingbrook *(G-2278)*
B & D Independence Inc ....................E...... 618 262-7117
　Mount Carmel *(G-15260)*
Becks Medical & Indus Gases ..........F...... 618 273-9019
　Eldorado *(G-8917)*
Bergmann Orthotic Lab Inc ................G...... 847 446-3616
　Northfield *(G-16392)*
C & S Chemicals Inc ..........................G...... 815 722-6671
　Joliet *(G-12470)*
C R Kesner Company ..........................G...... 630 232-8118
　Geneva *(G-10816)*
Cape Prosthetics-Orthotics Inc ..........G...... 618 457-4692
　Carbondale *(G-3001)*
Covidien LP ............................................A...... 815 444-2500
　Crystal Lake *(G-7557)*
Dabir Surfaces Inc ..............................F...... 708 867-6777
　Chicago *(G-4541)*
Dean Prsthtic Orthtic Svcs Ltd ..........G...... 847 475-7080
　Evanston *(G-10026)*
Deborah Morris Gulbrandson Pt ........F...... 847 639-4140
　Cary *(G-3333)*
Dura-Crafts Corp ..................................F...... 815 464-3561
　Frankfort *(G-10316)*
East West Martial Arts Sups ..............G...... 773 878-7711
　Chicago *(G-4682)*
Ecomed Solutions LLC ......................E...... 866 817-7114
　Mundelein *(G-15498)*
Elginex Corporation ............................G...... 815 786-8406
　Sandwich *(G-19362)*
Elmed Incorporated ............................E...... 630 543-2792
　Glendale Heights *(G-11021)*
Eln Group LLC ....................................G...... 847 477-1496
　Winnetka *(G-22305)*
Firm of John Dickinson ......................E...... 847 680-1000
　Libertyville *(G-13324)*
Gema Inc ..............................................G...... 773 508-6690
　Chicago *(G-4924)*
Guardian Equipment Inc ....................E...... 312 447-8100
　Chicago *(G-5007)*
Hanger Prosthetics & ..........................G...... 815 344-3070
　McHenry *(G-14512)*
Hanger Prosthetics & ..........................F...... 815 937-0241
　Joliet *(G-12507)*
Hollister Incorporated ..........................B...... 847 680-1000
　Libertyville *(G-13333)*
Hoya Lens of Chicago Inc ..................E...... 847 678-4700
　Franklin Park *(G-10490)*
Intelliwheels Inc ....................................G...... 630 341-1942
　Champaign *(G-3502)*
Kimberly-Clark Corporation ................C...... 815 886-7872
　Romeoville *(G-18835)*
Kinsman Enterprises Inc ....................E...... 618 932-3838
　West Frankfort *(G-21810)*
Lester L Brossard Co ..........................F...... 815 338-7825
　Woodstock *(G-22585)*
Lincoln Advanced Tech LLC ..............G...... 815 286-3500
　Hinckley *(G-11936)*
Logan Actuator Co ..............................G...... 815 943-9500
　Harvard *(G-11640)*
M2m Enterprises LLC ........................G...... 847 899-7565
　Elgin *(G-9097)*
Magid Glove Safety Mfg Co LLC ......B...... 773 384-2070
　Romeoville *(G-18841)*
Manan Medical Products Inc ..............D...... 847 637-3333
　Wheeling *(G-22099)*
Mandis Dental Laboratory ..................G...... 618 345-3777
　Collinsville *(G-7334)*
Medline Industries Inc ........................B...... 847 949-5500
　Waukegan *(G-21589)*
Medline Industries Inc ........................E...... 847 949-5500
　Mundelein *(G-15529)*
Merry Walker Corporation ..................G...... 847 837-9580
　Mundelein *(G-15530)*
Microguide Inc ......................................G...... 630 964-3335
　Downers Grove *(G-8485)*

Mio Med Orthopedics Inc ....................G...... 773 477-8991
　Chicago *(G-5769)*
Opportunity Inc ....................................D...... 847 831-9400
　Highland Park *(G-11860)*
Parkview Orthopaedic Group ..............F...... 815 727-3030
　New Lenox *(G-15899)*
Pres-On Corporation ............................E...... 630 628-2255
　Bolingbrook *(G-2360)*
Punch Products Manufacturing ..........E...... 773 533-2800
　Chicago *(G-6226)*
Quincy Lab Inc ......................................E...... 773 622-2428
　Chicago *(G-6258)*
Respironics Inc ....................................C...... 708 923-6200
　Palos Park *(G-17130)*
Robert B Scott Ocularists Ltd ............E...... 312 782-3558
　Chicago *(G-6367)*
Scale-Tronix Inc ....................................F...... 630 653-3377
　Carol Stream *(G-3235)*
Scheck & Siress ..................................G...... 708 383-2257
　Oak Park *(G-16683)*
Sensaphonics Inc ................................E...... 312 432-1714
　Chicago *(G-6476)*
Therafin Corporation ............................E...... 708 479-7300
　Frankfort *(G-10369)*
Thor Defense Inc ................................G...... 630 541-5106
　Downers Grove *(G-8532)*
W W Belt Inc ........................................G...... 708 788-1855
　Berwyn *(G-2078)*
Welkins LLC ........................................G...... 877 319-3504
　Downers Grove *(G-8543)*
Wheaton Resource Corp ....................G...... 630 690-5795
　Carol Stream *(G-3268)*
Whitney Products Inc ..........................F...... 847 966-6161
　Niles *(G-16047)*
Williams Halthcare Systems LLC ......D...... 847 741-3650
　Elgin *(G-9237)*

### SURGICAL EQPT: See Also Instruments

3M Company ........................................B...... 309 654-2291
　Cordova *(G-7374)*
Advanced Microderm Inc ....................E...... 630 980-3300
　Schaumburg *(G-19423)*
Anchor Products Company ................E...... 630 543-9124
　Addison *(G-40)*
Eldest Daughter LLC ..........................G...... 949 677-7385
　Chicago *(G-4718)*
Endofix Ltd ............................................G...... 708 715-3472
　Brookfield *(G-2631)*
Medifix Inc ............................................G...... 847 965-1898
　Morton Grove *(G-15219)*
Stryker Corporation ..............................B...... 312 386-9780
　Chicago *(G-6608)*
Uresil LLC ............................................E...... 847 982-0200
　Skokie *(G-20105)*

### SURGICAL IMPLANTS

Blue Sky Bio LLC ................................G...... 718 376-0422
　Grayslake *(G-11322)*
Norfolk Medical Products Inc ..............F...... 847 674-7075
　Skokie *(G-20046)*
Peoria Neuroinnovations LLC ............G...... 217 899-0443
　Peoria *(G-17424)*

### SURVEYING & MAPPING: Land Parcels

McLean Subsurface Utility ..................G...... 336 988-2520
　Decatur *(G-7911)*

### SUSPENSION SYSTEMS: Acoustical, Metal

Mrk Industries Inc ................................E...... 847 362-8720
　Libertyville *(G-13361)*
Palo Verde Suspension Inc ................G...... 815 939-2196
　Bourbonnais *(G-2405)*

### SVC ESTABLISH EQPT, WHOL: Extermination/Fumigatn Eqpt/Splys

Bird-X Inc ..............................................E...... 312 226-2473
　Chicago *(G-4112)*

### SVC ESTABLISHMENT EQPT & SPLYS WHOLESALERS

Rogan Group Inc ..................................G...... 708 371-4191
　Merrionette Park *(G-14738)*

### SVC ESTABLISHMENT EQPT, WHOL: Cleaning & Maint Eqpt & Splys

Imagination Products Corp ..................G...... 309 274-6223
　Chillicothe *(G-7167)*
Lindemann Chimney Service Inc ......F...... 847 918-7994
　Lake Bluff *(G-12854)*
O Brien Bill ............................................G...... 630 980-5571
　Geneva *(G-10854)*
Umf Corporation ..................................G...... 224 251-7822
　Niles *(G-16045)*

### SVC ESTABLISHMENT EQPT, WHOL: Concrete Burial Vaults & Boxes

Southern Ill Wilbert Vlt Co ....................F...... 618 942-5845
　Herrin *(G-11756)*
Wilbert Quincy Vault Co ......................G...... 217 224-8557
　Quincy *(G-17905)*

### SVC ESTABLISHMENT EQPT, WHOL: Liquor Dispensing Eqpt/Sys

Don Johns Inc ......................................E...... 630 326-9650
　Batavia *(G-1439)*

### SVC ESTABLISHMENT EQPT, WHOLESALE: Beauty Parlor Eqpt & Sply

Elia Day Spa ........................................F...... 708 535-1450
　Oak Forest *(G-16579)*
Lasner Bros Inc ....................................G...... 773 935-7383
　Chicago *(G-5463)*
Pivot Point Usa Inc ..............................D...... 800 886-4247
　Chicago *(G-6133)*
Skyline Beauty Supply Inc ..................F...... 773 275-6003
　Franklin Park *(G-10589)*

### SVC ESTABLISHMENT EQPT, WHOLESALE: Cemetery Splys & Eqpt

Kowalski Memorials Inc ......................G...... 630 462-7226
　Carol Stream *(G-3182)*

### SVC ESTABLISHMENT EQPT, WHOLESALE: Engraving Eqpt & Splys

Finer Line Inc ........................................F...... 847 884-1611
　Schaumburg *(G-19527)*

### SVC ESTABLISHMENT EQPT, WHOLESALE: Firefighting Eqpt

Flame Guard Usa LLC ........................G...... 815 219-4074
　Lake Barrington *(G-12806)*
Vertex International Inc ........................G...... 312 242-1864
　Oak Brook *(G-16568)*

### SVC ESTABLISHMENT EQPT, WHOLESALE: Laundry Eqpt & Splys

Chicago Dryer Company ....................C...... 773 235-4430
　Chicago *(G-4317)*
Storms Industries Inc ..........................E...... 312 243-7480
　Chicago *(G-6601)*

### SVC ESTABLISHMENT EQPT, WHOLESALE: Locksmith Eqpt & Splys

Hoffman J&M Farm Holdings Inc ......D...... 847 671-6280
　Schiller Park *(G-19838)*
Lovatt & Radcliffe Ltd ..........................G...... 815 568-9797
　Skokie *(G-20031)*

### SVC ESTABLISHMENT EQPT, WHOLESALE: Restaurant Splys

American Metalcraft Inc ......................D...... 800 333-9133
　Franklin Park *(G-10391)*
Grant Park Packing Company Inc ......E...... 312 421-4096
　Franklin Park *(G-10482)*

### SVC ESTABLISHMENT EQPT, WHOLESALE: Taxidermist Tools & Eqpt

Research Mannikins Inc ......................F...... 618 426-3456
　Ava *(G-1242)*
Walnut Creek Hardwood ....................G...... 815 389-3317
　South Beloit *(G-20173)*

# PRODUCT SECTION

## SWEEPING COMPOUNDS

Frank Miller & Sons Inc .............................. E ...... 708 201-7200
  Mokena (G-14863)
Jaffee Investment Partnr LP ........................ C ...... 312 321-1515
  Chicago (G-5270)
Oil-Dri Corporation America ....................... D ...... 312 321-1515
  Chicago (G-5975)

## SWIMMING POOL & HOT TUB CLEANING & MAINTENANCE SVCS

Pool Center Inc ........................................... G ...... 217 698-7665
  Springfield (G-20505)
Savino Enterprises ..................................... G ...... 708 385-5277
  Blue Island (G-2268)

## SWIMMING POOL SPLY STORES

Newby Oil Company Inc ............................. G ...... 815 756-7688
  Sycamore (G-20810)
Sentry Pool & Chemical Supply ................. E ...... 309 797-9721
  Moline (G-14970)

## SWIMMING POOLS, EQPT & SPLYS: Wholesalers

Evergreen Pool & Spa LLC ........................ G ...... 618 247-3555
  Sandoval (G-19356)
Newby Oil Company Inc ............................. G ...... 815 756-7688
  Sycamore (G-20810)

## SWITCHBOARD OPERATIONS: Private Branch Exchanges

Chicago Tribune Company ......................... A ...... 312 222-3232
  Chicago (G-4357)

## SWITCHBOARDS & PARTS: Power

Gus Berthold Electric Company ................. E ...... 312 243-5767
  Chicago (G-5013)
Illinois Switchboard Corp ........................... F ...... 630 543-0910
  Addison (G-152)
Jemison Elc Box Swtchboard Inc .............. G ...... 815 459-4060
  Crystal Lake (G-7594)
Peterson Elc Panl Mfg Co Inc .................... F ...... 708 449-2270
  Berkeley (G-2048)
Power Distribution Eqp Co Inc ................... F ...... 847 455-2500
  Franklin Park (G-10555)

## SWITCHES

Chicago Freight Car Leasing Co ............... D ...... 847 318-8000
  Schaumburg (G-19471)
Grayhill Inc ................................................. B ...... 708 354-1040
  La Grange (G-12734)

## SWITCHES: Electric Power

Crane Dorray Corporation .......................... G ...... 630 893-7553
  Addison (G-83)
Elm Products Corp ..................................... E ...... 847 336-0020
  Waukegan (G-21557)
Grayhill Inc ................................................. B ...... 708 354-1040
  La Grange (G-12734)

## SWITCHES: Electric Power, Exc Snap, Push Button, Etc

Calo Corporation ........................................ E ...... 630 879-2202
  North Aurora (G-16122)
General Electric Company .......................... E ...... 630 334-0054
  Oak Brook (G-16519)
Grayhill Inc ................................................. B ...... 708 354-1040
  La Grange (G-12734)
Honeywell International Inc ........................ D ...... 815 235-5500
  Freeport (G-10665)
Texas Instruments Incorporated ................ D ...... 630 836-2827
  Warrenville (G-21363)

## SWITCHES: Electronic

Central Rubber Company ........................... E ...... 815 544-2191
  Belvidere (G-1745)
Chicago Technical Sales Inc ...................... G ...... 630 889-7121
  Oakbrook Terrace (G-16701)
CTS Corporation ........................................ C ...... 630 577-8800
  Lisle (G-13579)
Grayhill Inc ................................................. C ...... 847 428-6990
  Carpentersville (G-3285)
Grayhill Inc ................................................. B ...... 708 354-1040
  La Grange (G-12734)
Gulf Coast Switching Co LLC .................... G ...... 312 324-7353
  Chicago (G-5011)
Honeywell International Inc ........................ C ...... 815 777-2780
  Galena (G-10726)
Illinois Tool Works Inc ................................ C ...... 847 876-9400
  Des Plaines (G-8208)
Kraus & Naimer Inc ................................... G ...... 847 298-2450
  Des Plaines (G-8219)
Molex LLC .................................................. F ...... 630 512-8787
  Downers Grove (G-8489)
Molex International Inc .............................. F ...... 630 969-4550
  Lisle (G-13627)
Motec Inc .................................................... G ...... 630 241-9595
  Downers Grove (G-8490)
Peterson Elctr-Msical Pdts Inc ................... E ...... 708 388-3311
  Alsip (G-507)
Pfingsten Partners LLC .............................. F ...... 312 222-8707
  Chicago (G-6115)
Relay Services Mfg Corp ........................... G ...... 773 252-2700
  Chicago (G-6327)
Switchcraft Inc ............................................ B ...... 773 792-2700
  Chicago (G-6653)
Switchcraft Holdco Inc ............................... G ...... 773 792-2700
  Chicago (G-6654)
Switchee Bandz Usa LLC .......................... G ...... 312 415-1100
  Highland Park (G-11875)
Woodhead Industries LLC ......................... B ...... 847 353-2500
  Lincolnshire (G-13490)

## SWITCHES: Electronic Applications

Autotech Tech Ltd Partnr ........................... E ...... 630 668-8886
  Carol Stream (G-3108)
CTS Automotive LLC ................................. C ...... 630 614-7201
  Lisle (G-13578)
CTS Automotive LLC ................................. E ...... 815 385-9480
  McHenry (G-14493)
Imperial Fabricators Co .............................. F ...... 773 463-5522
  Franklin Park (G-10495)
Network Merchants LLC ............................ G ...... 847 352-4850
  Roselle (G-18959)
Robert Higgins ........................................... D ...... 217 337-0734
  Urbana (G-21101)

## SWITCHES: Flow Actuated, Electrical

Warming Systems ...................................... G ...... 800 663-7831
  Lake Villa (G-13030)
Warner Electric LLC ................................... E ...... 815 566-4683
  Belvidere (G-1795)

## SWITCHES: Solenoid

FSI Technologies Inc ................................. E ...... 630 932-9380
  Lombard (G-13803)
Intersol Industries Inc ................................ F ...... 630 238-0385
  Bensenville (G-1922)
Knowles Elec Holdings Inc ........................ A ...... 630 250-5100
  Itasca (G-12296)
Magnet-Schultz Amer Holdg LLC .............. G ...... 630 789-0600
  Westmont (G-21901)
Magnet-Schultz America Inc ...................... D ...... 630 789-0600
  Westmont (G-21902)
S & N Manufacturing Inc ........................... G ...... 630 232-0275
  Geneva (G-10865)

## SWITCHES: Starting, Fluorescent

Radionic Hi-Tech Inc ................................. D ...... 773 804-0100
  Chicago (G-6281)

## SWITCHES: Stepping

Bircher America Inc ................................... G ...... 847 952-3730
  Schaumburg (G-19462)

## SWITCHES: Time, Electrical Switchgear Apparatus

Nutherm International Inc .......................... E ...... 618 244-6000
  Mount Vernon (G-15435)

## SWITCHGEAR & SWITCHBOARD APPARATUS

Automated Systems & Control Co ............. G ...... 847 735-8310
  Lake Bluff (G-12834)
Chicago Switchboard Co Inc ..................... E ...... 630 833-2266
  Elmhurst (G-9848)
Control Solutions LLC ................................ D ...... 630 806-7062
  Aurora (G-984)
Deif Inc ....................................................... G ...... 970 530-2261
  Wood Dale (G-22359)
E N M Company .......................................... D ...... 773 775-8400
  Chicago (G-4667)
Eaton Corporation ...................................... A ...... 217 732-3131
  Lincoln (G-13409)
Elcon Inc ..................................................... E ...... 815 467-9500
  Minooka (G-14840)
Elenco Electronics Inc ............................... E ...... 847 541-3800
  Wheeling (G-22046)
Elm Products Corp ..................................... E ...... 847 336-0020
  Waukegan (G-21557)
Emac Inc ..................................................... E ...... 618 529-4525
  Carbondale (G-3006)
Enercon Engineering Inc ........................... C ...... 800 218-8831
  East Peoria (G-8708)
Enercon Engineering Inc ........................... G ...... 309 694-1418
  East Peoria (G-8709)
Fixture Company ........................................ G ...... 847 214-3100
  Chicago (G-4854)
Honeywell International Inc ........................ E ...... 815 235-5500
  Freeport (G-10664)
Illinois Tool Works Inc ................................ C ...... 847 876-9400
  Des Plaines (G-8208)
Inman Electric Motors Inc ......................... E ...... 815 223-2288
  La Salle (G-12778)
ITT Water & Wastewater USA Inc ............. G ...... 847 966-3700
  Morton Grove (G-15205)
Julian Elec Svc & Engrg Inc ....................... E ...... 630 920-8950
  Westmont (G-21895)
Langham Engineering ................................ G ...... 815 223-5250
  Peru (G-17516)
Lumenite Control Technology .................... F ...... 847 455-1450
  Franklin Park (G-10518)
Methode Electronics Inc ............................ A ...... 217 357-3941
  Carthage (G-3316)
Meto-Grafics Inc ........................................ F ...... 847 639-0044
  Crystal Lake (G-7609)
Mitsubishi Elc Automtn Inc ........................ C ...... 847 478-2100
  Vernon Hills (G-21183)
Motec Inc .................................................... G ...... 630 241-9595
  Downers Grove (G-8490)
Mpc Products Corporation ......................... G ...... 847 673-8300
  Niles (G-16012)
New Cie Inc ................................................ F ...... 815 224-1485
  La Salle (G-12781)
Numerical Control Incorporated ................. G ...... 708 389-8140
  Alsip (G-502)
Oakland Industries Ltd .............................. E ...... 847 827-7600
  Mount Prospect (G-15358)
Product Service Craft Inc .......................... F ...... 630 964-5160
  Downers Grove (G-8511)
SAI Advanced Pwr Solutions Inc ............... E ...... 708 450-0990
  Elmhurst (G-9932)
Schneider Electric Usa Inc ........................ G ...... 847 925-7773
  Downers Grove (G-8520)
Schneider Electric Usa Inc ........................ E ...... 847 441-2526
  Schaumburg (G-19723)
Switchcraft Inc ............................................ B ...... 773 792-2700
  Chicago (G-6653)
Switchcraft Holdco Inc ............................... G ...... 773 792-2700
  Chicago (G-6654)
Venturedyne Ltd ........................................ E ...... 708 597-7550
  Chicago (G-6884)
Woodward Controls Inc ............................. C ...... 847 673-8300
  Skokie (G-20114)

## SWITCHGEAR & SWITCHGEAR ACCESS, NEC

Appleton Grp LLC ...................................... C ...... 847 268-6000
  Rosemont (G-18989)
Custom Power Products Inc ...................... G ...... 309 249-2704
  Edelstein (G-8779)
Hubbell Power Systems Inc ...................... E ...... 618 797-5000
  Edwardsville (G-8804)

## SWITCHING EQPT: Radio & Television Communications

Heico Companies LLC ............................... F ...... 312 419-8220
  Chicago (G-5068)

## SYNTHETIC RESIN FINISHED PRDTS, NEC

Certified Polymers Inc ............................... G ...... 630 515-0007
  Western Springs (G-21865)
Custom Films Inc ....................................... F ...... 217 826-2326
  Marshall (G-14320)

Employee Codes: A=Over 500 employees, B=251-500
C=101-250, D=51-100, E=20-50, F=10-19, G=3-9

# SYNTHETIC RESIN FINISHED PRDTS, NEC

Michael Clesen .................................. G ...... 630 377-3075
Saint Charles *(G-19220)*
Werner Co ........................................ E ...... 815 459-6020
Crystal Lake *(G-7676)*

## SYRUPS, DRINK

A Barr Ftn Beverage Sls & Svc ......... D ...... 708 442-2000
Lemont *(G-13221)*
Coca-Cola Refreshments USA Inc ..... C ...... 618 542-2101
Du Quoin *(G-8552)*
Culinary Co-Pack Incorporated .......... E ...... 847 451-1551
Franklin Park *(G-10448)*
Tone Products Inc ............................. E ...... 708 681-3660
Melrose Park *(G-14702)*

## SYRUPS, FLAVORING, EXC DRINK

White Stokes Company Inc ................ E ...... 773 254-5000
Lincolnwood *(G-13543)*

## SYRUPS: Pharmaceutical

Glendale Incorporated ........................ F ...... 630 770-1965
Villa Park *(G-21255)*

## SYSTEMS ENGINEERING: Computer Related

Abki Tech Service Inc ......................... F ...... 847 818-8403
Des Plaines *(G-8143)*
Braindok LLC ..................................... G ...... 847 877-1586
Buffalo Grove *(G-2668)*
Converting Systems Inc ..................... G ...... 847 519-0232
Schaumburg *(G-19484)*
Turner Agward .................................. G ...... 773 669-8559
Chicago *(G-6794)*

## SYSTEMS INTEGRATION SVCS

Cdc Enterprises Inc ............................ G ...... 815 790-4205
Johnsburg *(G-12432)*
R+d Custom Automation Inc .............. E ...... 847 395-3330
Lake Villa *(G-13025)*
Rapid Execution Services LLC .......... G ...... 312 789-4358
Chicago *(G-6293)*
Tri-Cor Industries Inc ......................... D ...... 618 589-9890
O Fallon *(G-16481)*
Trustwave Holdings Inc ..................... G ...... 312 750-0950
Chicago *(G-6789)*

## SYSTEMS INTEGRATION SVCS: Local Area Network

Allied Telesis Inc ............................... D ...... 312 726-1990
Chicago *(G-3818)*
Csiteq LLC ......................................... D ...... 312 265-1509
Chicago *(G-4512)*
National Def Intelligence Inc .............. G ...... 630 757-4007
Naperville *(G-15818)*

## SYSTEMS INTEGRATION SVCS: Office Computer Automation

Logical Design Solutions Inc .............. G ...... 630 786-5999
Aurora *(G-1047)*
Progressive Systems Netwrk Inc ....... G ...... 312 382-8383
Chicago *(G-6214)*
Srmd Solutions LLC ........................... G ...... 217 925-5773
Dieterich *(G-8315)*

## SYSTEMS SOFTWARE DEVELOPMENT SVCS

American Controls & Automation ....... G ...... 630 293-8841
West Chicago *(G-21655)*
Computer Pwr Solutions III Ltd .......... E ...... 618 281-8898
Columbia *(G-7355)*
Datasis Corporation ........................... F ...... 847 427-0909
Elk Grove Village *(G-9417)*
Evention LLC ..................................... E ...... 773 733-4256
Chicago *(G-4789)*
Lab Software Inc ............................... G ...... 815 521-9116
Minooka *(G-14841)*
Orinoco Systems LLC ........................ G ...... 630 510-4775
Wheaton *(G-21971)*
Proquis Inc ........................................ F ...... 847 278-3230
Elgin *(G-9151)*
Recsolu Inc ....................................... E ...... 312 517-3200
Chicago *(G-6313)*
Tylu Wireless Technology LLC .......... G ...... 312 260-7934
Chicago *(G-6802)*

Viva Solutions Inc .............................. G ...... 312 332-8882
Lemont *(G-13268)*

## TABLE OR COUNTERTOPS, PLASTIC LAMINATED

All-Style Custom Tops ........................ G ...... 708 532-6606
Tinley Park *(G-20887)*
Central Illinois Counter Tops .............. G ...... 309 579-3550
Mossville *(G-15252)*
Clover Custom Counters Inc .............. G ...... 708 598-8912
Bridgeview *(G-2478)*
Forest City Counter Tops Inc ............. F ...... 815 633-8602
Loves Park *(G-13942)*
Harts Top and Cabinet Shop .............. G ...... 708 957-4666
Country Club Hills *(G-7408)*
Markham Cabinet Works Inc ............. G ...... 708 687-3074
Midlothian *(G-14767)*
R & R Custom Cabinet Making .......... G ...... 847 358-6188
Palatine *(G-17065)*
Valley Custom Woodwork Inc ........... G ...... 815 544-3939
Belvidere *(G-1793)*

## TABLECLOTHS & SETTINGS

Van Stockum Kristine ........................ G ...... 847 914-0015
Deerfield *(G-8064)*

## TABLETS: Bronze Or Other Metal

Bronze Memorial Inc .......................... G ...... 773 276-7972
Chicago *(G-4175)*

## TABLEWARE OR KITCHEN ARTICLES: Whiteware, Fine Semivitreous

Antioch Fine Arts Foundation ............. G ...... 847 838-2274
Antioch *(G-617)*

## TAGS & LABELS: Paper

Ameri Label Company ........................ F ...... 847 895-8000
Bartlett *(G-1315)*
Chicago Tag & Label Inc ................... G ...... 847 362-5100
Libertyville *(G-13314)*
Coding Solutions Inc .......................... F ...... 630 443-9602
Saint Charles *(G-19160)*
Dean Patterson .................................. G ...... 708 430-0477
Bridgeview *(G-2482)*
Deco Adhesive Pdts 1985 Ltd ........... E ...... 847 472-2100
Elk Grove Village *(G-9420)*
Deco Labels & Tags Ltd .................... D ...... 847 472-2100
Wood Dale *(G-22358)*
Hospital Hlth Care Systems Inc ......... E ...... 708 863-3400
Lyons *(G-14041)*
Illinois Tag Co ................................... E ...... 773 626-0542
Carol Stream *(G-3169)*
Oakland Enterprises Inc .................... G ...... 630 377-1121
Saint Charles *(G-19225)*
Service Packaging Design Inc ........... G ...... 847 966-6592
Morton Grove *(G-15236)*
Sev-Rend Corporation ....................... F ...... 618 301-4130
Collinsville *(G-7341)*
Xertrex International Inc .................... E ...... 630 773-4020
Itasca *(G-12375)*

## TAGS: Paper, Blank, Made From Purchased Paper

Tag Diamond & Label ........................ E ...... 630 844-9395
Aurora *(G-1221)*
Zebra Technologies Corporation ....... B ...... 847 634-6700
Lincolnshire *(G-13494)*

## TAILORS: Custom

Demetrios Tailor Inc .......................... G ...... 708 974-0304
Justice *(G-12597)*
Riddle McIntyre Inc ........................... G ...... 312 782-3317
Chicago *(G-6355)*

## TALLOW: Animal

Darling Ingredients Inc ...................... E ...... 618 271-8190
National Stock Yards *(G-15850)*

## TANK REPAIR & CLEANING SVCS

Chicago Tank Lining Sales ................ G ...... 847 328-0500
Evanston *(G-10023)*
Matrix Service Inc ............................. F ...... 618 466-4862
Alton *(G-585)*

Pro-Tran Inc ...................................... G ...... 217 348-9353
Charleston *(G-3608)*

## TANK REPAIR SVCS

Summit Tank & Equipment Co .......... F ...... 708 594-3040
Mc Cook *(G-14459)*

## TANKS & OTHER TRACKED VEHICLE CMPNTS

Certified Tank & Mfg LLC .................. E ...... 217 525-1433
Springfield *(G-20415)*
Chelsea Framing Products Inc .......... G ...... 847 550-5556
Lake Zurich *(G-13053)*
Mid-States Industrial Inc ................... F ...... 815 357-1663
Seneca *(G-19888)*
Protectoseal Company ...................... D ...... 630 595-0800
Bensenville *(G-1969)*

## TANKS: For Tank Trucks, Metal Plate

Arthur Custom Tank LLC ................... G ...... 217 543-4022
Arthur *(G-880)*
Brenner Tank Services LLC .............. G ...... 773 468-6390
Chicago *(G-4161)*
Pro-Tran Inc ...................................... G ...... 217 348-9353
Charleston *(G-3608)*

## TANKS: Fuel, Including Oil & Gas, Metal Plate

Alum-I-Tank Inc ................................. D ...... 815 943-6649
Harvard *(G-11619)*
Ameropan Oil Corp ............................ F ...... 773 847-4400
Chicago *(G-3887)*
Ifh Group Inc ..................................... D ...... 800 435-7003
Rock Falls *(G-18138)*
Ifh Group Inc ..................................... G ...... 815 380-2367
Galt *(G-10781)*

## TANKS: Lined, Metal

Mt Carmel Machine Shop Inc ............ F ...... 618 262-4591
Mount Carmel *(G-15275)*

## TANKS: Plastic & Fiberglass

Chicago Plastic Systems Inc ............. E ...... 815 455-4599
Crystal Lake *(G-7553)*
Duratech Corporation ........................ G ...... 618 533-8891
Centralia *(G-3412)*
Eagle Plastics & Supply Inc .............. G ...... 708 331-6232
South Holland *(G-20263)*
Fiber Winders Inc .............................. G ...... 618 548-6388
Salem *(G-19332)*
Fiberbasin Inc .................................... F ...... 630 978-0705
Aurora *(G-1151)*
Jalaa Fiberglass Inc .......................... G ...... 217 923-3433
Greenup *(G-11384)*

## TANKS: Standard Or Custom Fabricated, Metal Plate

Amex Nooter LLC .............................. G ...... 708 429-8300
Tinley Park *(G-20892)*
CB&i LLC ........................................... G ...... 815 936-5440
Bourbonnais *(G-2392)*
Eastland Fabrication LLC .................. G ...... 815 493-8399
Lanark *(G-13152)*
Fabricated Products Co Inc ............... F ...... 630 898-6460
Aurora *(G-1006)*
Illinois Oil Marketing Eqp Inc ............. E ...... 309 347-1819
Pekin *(G-17269)*
Illinois Oil Marketing Eqp Inc ............. F ...... 217 935-5107
Clinton *(G-7284)*
JM Industries LLC ............................. E ...... 708 849-4700
Riverdale *(G-18020)*
Lake Process Systems Inc ............... G ...... 847 381-7663
Lake Barrington *(G-12817)*
Luebbers Welding & Mfg Inc ............. F ...... 618 594-2489
Carlyle *(G-3056)*
Matrix Service Inc ............................. F ...... 618 466-4862
Alton *(G-585)*
Mid-State Tank Co Inc ...................... D ...... 217 728-8383
Sullivan *(G-20751)*
R L Hoener Co .................................. E ...... 217 223-2190
Quincy *(G-17883)*
Tech-Weld Inc ................................... F ...... 630 365-3000
Elburn *(G-8913)*
WW Engineering Company LLC ....... F ...... 773 376-9494
Chicago *(G-7042)*

## PRODUCT SECTION

### TANKS: Water, Metal Plate
Kohnens Concrete Products Inc ..........E ...... 618 277-2120
Germantown *(G-10892)*
Melters and More ...........................G ...... 815 419-2043
Chenoa *(G-3634)*
Precision Ibc Inc ...........................F ...... 708 396-0750
Crestwood *(G-7498)*

### TAPE DRIVES
Amaitis and Associates Inc ..............F ...... 847 428-1269
Wood Dale *(G-22338)*

### TAPE MEASURES
American Tape Measures ..................G ...... 312 208-0282
Chicago *(G-3877)*

### TAPE RECERTIFICATION SVCS
Kishknows Inc ................................G ...... 708 252-3648
Richton Park *(G-17979)*

### TAPE STORAGE UNITS: Computer
Numeridex Incorporated ..................F ...... 847 541-8840
Wheeling *(G-22111)*

### TAPE: Instrumentation Type, Blank
Imperial Technical Services ..............F ...... 708 403-1564
Orland Park *(G-16867)*

### TAPE: Rubber
Adhes Tape Technology Inc ..............G ...... 847 496-7949
Arlington Heights *(G-702)*

### TAPES, ADHESIVE: Masking, Made From Purchased Materials
Budnick Converting Inc ....................C ...... 618 281-8090
Columbia *(G-7353)*

### TAPES, ADHESIVE: MedicaL
Berry Global Inc .............................G ...... 630 375-0358
Aurora *(G-969)*
General Bandages Inc .......................F ...... 847 966-8383
Park Ridge *(G-17198)*

### TAPES: Coated Fiberglass, Pipe Sealing Or Insulating
Technical Sealants Inc .....................F ...... 815 777-9797
Galena *(G-10732)*

### TAPES: Fabric
Adhes Tape Technology Inc ..............G ...... 847 496-7949
Arlington Heights *(G-702)*

### TAPES: Gummed, Cloth Or Paper Based, From Purchased Matls
Prairie State Graphics Inc ................D ...... 847 801-3100
Franklin Park *(G-10556)*

### TAPES: Magnetic
Acta Publications ...........................G ...... 773 989-3036
Chicago *(G-3739)*

### TAPES: Plastic Coated
Custom Coating Innovations Inc .......F ...... 618 808-0500
Lebanon *(G-13213)*
Lanmar Inc ...................................G ...... 800 233-5520
Northbrook *(G-16293)*

### TAPES: Pressure Sensitive
Continental Datalabel Inc .................C ...... 847 742-1600
Elgin *(G-9001)*
Diversfied Lbling Slutions Inc ...........D ...... 630 625-1225
Itasca *(G-12252)*
Intertape Polymer Corp ....................D ...... 618 549-2131
Carbondale *(G-3013)*
Labels Unlimited Incorporated ..........E ...... 773 523-7500
Chicago *(G-5430)*
Print-O-Tape Inc ............................E ...... 847 362-6433
Mundelein *(G-15550)*
Specialty Tape & Label Co Inc ...........E ...... 708 863-3800
Lyons *(G-14044)*

Tek Pak Inc ...................................D ...... 630 406-0560
Batavia *(G-1506)*

### TAPES: Pressure Sensitive, Rubber
Winfield Technology Inc ...................F ...... 630 584-0475
Saint Charles *(G-19297)*

### TAPS
Tapco Cutting Tools Inc ...................G ...... 815 877-4039
Loves Park *(G-13997)*
Tapco USA Inc ...............................G ...... 815 877-4039
Loves Park *(G-13998)*

### TARPAULINS
M Mauritzon & Company Inc ............E ...... 773 235-6000
Chicago *(G-5584)*
Tarps Manufacturing Inc ..................F ...... 217 584-1900
Meredosia *(G-14735)*

### TARPAULINS, WHOLESALE
Midwest Awnings Inc .......................G ...... 309 762-3339
Cameron *(G-2970)*
Shur Co of Illinois ...........................G ...... 217 877-8277
Decatur *(G-7940)*

### TAX RETURN PREPARATION SVCS
H & R Block Inc .............................F ...... 847 566-5557
Mundelein *(G-15506)*
H&R Block Inc ...............................F ...... 773 582-3444
Chicago *(G-5025)*

### TECHNICAL & TRADE SCHOOLS, NEC
Russell Enterprises Inc ....................E ...... 847 692-6050
Park Ridge *(G-17221)*

### TECHNICAL MANUAL PREPARATION SVCS
Amerinet of Michigan Inc .................G ...... 708 466-0110
Naperville *(G-15795)*
Custom Design Services & Assoc ......F ...... 815 226-9747
Rockford *(G-18327)*
M & B Supply Inc ...........................F ...... 309 944-3206
Geneseo *(G-10803)*

### TECHNICAL WRITING SVCS
Fanning Communications Inc ............G ...... 708 293-1430
Crestwood *(G-7488)*

### TELECOMMUNICATION EQPT REPAIR SVCS, EXC TELEPHONES
Sitexpedite LLC ..............................E ...... 847 245-2185
Lindenhurst *(G-13549)*
Unified Solutions Corp .....................E ...... 847 478-9100
Arlington Heights *(G-861)*

### TELECOMMUNICATION SYSTEMS & EQPT
Acn Indpndent Bus Rprsentative ........G ...... 618 623-4238
O Fallon *(G-16460)*
Airbus Ds Communications Inc .........G ...... 708 450-1911
Westchester *(G-21828)*
Alcatel-Lucent USA Inc ....................G ...... 630 979-0210
Naperville *(G-15594)*
Alltemated Inc ...............................E ...... 847 394-5800
Arlington Heights *(G-707)*
Charles Industries Ltd .....................D ...... 217 826-2318
Marshall *(G-14319)*
Cml Technologies Inc ......................G ...... 708 450-1911
Westchester *(G-21834)*
Coleman Cable LLC .........................D ...... 847 672-2300
Waukegan *(G-21543)*
Comprehensive Convgnt Solut ..........F ...... 847 558-1401
Lake Zurich *(G-13056)*
Coriant Operations Inc ....................E ...... 847 382-8817
Naperville *(G-15636)*
Cronus Technologies Inc ..................G ...... 847 839-0088
Schaumburg *(G-19491)*
D & S Communications Inc ..............D ...... 847 468-8082
Elgin *(G-9008)*
Elanza Technologies Inc ...................F ...... 312 396-4187
Chicago *(G-4717)*
Etcon Corp ....................................F ...... 630 325-6100
Burr Ridge *(G-2840)*
H K Tellabs Limited .........................G ...... 630 445-5333
Naperville *(G-15668)*

## TELEPHONE EQPT: Modems

HI Tech .........................................G ...... 708 957-4210
Homewood *(G-12100)*
Isco International LLC .....................E ...... 847 391-9400
Schaumburg *(G-19583)*
Mar-Don Corporation .......................G ...... 847 823-4958
Park Ridge *(G-17208)*
Medical Cmmnctions Systems Inc .....G ...... 708 895-4500
Lansing *(G-13176)*
Quintum Technologies Inc ................F ...... 847 348-7730
Schaumburg *(G-19710)*
Stellar Manufacturing Company ........D ...... 618 823-3761
Cahokia *(G-2926)*
Tekno Industries Inc .......................F ...... 630 766-6960
Naperville *(G-15761)*
Unified Solutions Corp .....................E ...... 847 478-9100
Arlington Heights *(G-861)*
Vertiv Group Corporation .................E ...... 630 579-5000
Lombard *(G-13878)*
Westell Inc ....................................D ...... 630 898-2500
Aurora *(G-1097)*
Wireless Chamberlain Products .........E ...... 800 282-6225
Elmhurst *(G-9961)*

### TELECOMMUNICATIONS CARRIERS & SVCS: Wired
AT&T Teleholdings Inc ....................E ...... 800 257-0902
Chicago *(G-3973)*
Cutting Edge Communications ..........G ...... 815 788-9419
Crystal Lake *(G-7564)*
D & S Communications Inc ..............D ...... 847 468-8082
Elgin *(G-9008)*
Global Technologies I LLC ...............E ...... 312 255-8350
Chicago *(G-4960)*
Gogo LLC .....................................B ...... 630 647-1400
Chicago *(G-4970)*
Gogo LLC .....................................D ...... 630 647-1400
Bensenville *(G-1911)*
Interscience Technologies Inc ...........G ...... 630 759-4444
Bolingbrook *(G-2323)*
Telcom Innovations Group LLC .........E ...... 630 350-0700
Itasca *(G-12366)*
Westell Technologies Inc .................E ...... 630 898-2500
Aurora *(G-1098)*

### TELECOMMUNICATIONS CARRIERS & SVCS: Wireless
D & S Communications Inc ..............D ...... 847 468-8082
Elgin *(G-9008)*
Pc-Tel Inc .....................................C ...... 630 372-6800
Bloomingdale *(G-2127)*
Portable Cmmnctons Spclsts ............G ...... 630 458-1800
Addison *(G-247)*
Vincor Ltd ....................................F ...... 708 534-0008
Monee *(G-15005)*

### TELECONFERENCING SVCS
Westell Technologies Inc .................E ...... 630 898-2500
Aurora *(G-1098)*

### TELEMARKETING BUREAUS
Communication Technologies Inc ......E ...... 630 384-0900
Glendale Heights *(G-11017)*

### TELEPHONE ANSWERING SVCS
Group O Inc ..................................E ...... 309 736-8100
Milan *(G-14790)*

### TELEPHONE BOOTHS, EXC WOOD
Enclosures Inc ...............................G ...... 847 678-2020
Schiller Park *(G-19824)*

### TELEPHONE CENTRAL OFFICE EQPT: Dial Or Manual
Kuna Corp .....................................G ...... 815 675-0140
Spring Grove *(G-20344)*

### TELEPHONE EQPT INSTALLATION
Audio Installers Inc .........................F ...... 815 969-7500
Loves Park *(G-13923)*

### TELEPHONE EQPT: Modems
Arris Group Inc ..............................E ...... 630 281-3000
Lisle *(G-13564)*

## TELEPHONE EQPT: Modems

Create USA Modem Eight .................... G ....... 630 519-3403
  Oakbrook Terrace *(G-16705)*
Integrated Dna Tech Modem ............... F ....... 847 745-1700
  Skokie *(G-20016)*
Motorola Solutions Inc ......................... C ....... 847 576-5000
  Chicago *(G-5818)*
Motorola Solutions Inc ......................... C ....... 847 576-8600
  Schaumburg *(G-19652)*
Netgear Inc .......................................... G ....... 630 955-0080
  Naperville *(G-15712)*

### TELEPHONE EQPT: NEC

A T Products Inc .................................. G ....... 815 943-3590
  Harvard *(G-11615)*
American Comm & Networks ............... E ....... 630 241-2800
  Lisle *(G-13558)*
Autotech Tech Ltd Partnr ..................... E ....... 630 668-8886
  Carol Stream *(G-3108)*
Avg Advanced Technologies LP ........... A ....... 630 668-3900
  Carol Stream *(G-3110)*
Best-Tronics Mfg Inc ............................ C ....... 708 802-9677
  Tinley Park *(G-20898)*
Brocade Cmmnctions Systems Inc ....... F ....... 630 273-5530
  Schaumburg *(G-19466)*
Charles Industries Ltd .......................... D ....... 847 806-6300
  Rolling Meadows *(G-18719)*
Charles Industries Ltd .......................... D ....... 217 932-2068
  Casey *(G-3381)*
Charles Industries Ltd .......................... D ....... 217 932-5294
  Casey *(G-3382)*
Elexa Consumer Products Inc ............. B ....... 773 794-1300
  Deerfield *(G-8006)*
Mitel Networks Inc ............................... F ....... 312 479-9000
  Chicago *(G-5774)*
Motorola Solutions Inc ......................... G ....... 847 523-5000
  Libertyville *(G-13359)*
Parts Specialists Inc ............................ G ....... 708 371-2444
  Posen *(G-17734)*
Pentegra Systems LLC ........................ E ....... 630 941-6000
  Addison *(G-238)*
Precision Components Inc ................... D ....... 630 462-9110
  Saint Charles *(G-19240)*
Siemens AG .......................................... G ....... 708 345-7290
  Palos Park *(G-17131)*
Siemens Corporation ........................... E ....... 630 850-6973
  Westmont *(G-21921)*
Tancher Corp ....................................... F ....... 847 668-8765
  Park Ridge *(G-17226)*
Tellabs Inc ............................................ E ....... 630 798-8800
  Naperville *(G-15762)*
Tellabs Mexico Inc ............................... F ....... 630 445-5333
  Naperville *(G-15763)*
Wescom Products ................................. G ....... 217 932-5292
  Casey *(G-3392)*
Westell Technologies Inc ..................... E ....... 630 898-2500
  Aurora *(G-1098)*

### TELEPHONE STATION EQPT & PARTS: Wire

Sandmancom Inc .................................. G ....... 630 980-7710
  Roselle *(G-18972)*

### TELEPHONE SVCS

Clover Global Headquarters ................ G ....... 815 431-8100
  Hoffman Estates *(G-12000)*
Crosscom Inc ....................................... F ....... 630 871-5500
  Wheaton *(G-21942)*

### TELEPHONE SWITCHING EQPT: Toll Switching

Charles Industries Ltd .......................... D ....... 217 893-8335
  Rantoul *(G-17922)*

### TELEPHONE: Autotransformers For Switchboards

AT&T Corp ............................................ F ....... 312 602-4108
  Chicago *(G-3972)*

### TELEPHONE: Fiber Optic Systems

Advantage Optics Inc .......................... F ....... 630 548-9870
  Naperville *(G-15592)*
Axon Telecom LLC ............................... G ....... 618 278-4606
  Dorsey *(G-8380)*
Ayla Group Inc ..................................... G ....... 630 954-9432
  Bartlett *(G-1334)*
Cutting Edge Communications ............ G ....... 815 788-9419
  Crystal Lake *(G-7564)*
Eks Fiber Optics LP ............................. G ....... 312 291-4482
  Chicago *(G-4706)*
Elite Fiber Optics LLC .......................... E ....... 630 225-9454
  Oak Brook *(G-16506)*
IL Green Pastures Fiber Co-Op ........... G ....... 815 751-0887
  Kirkland *(G-12713)*
Ledcor Construction Inc ...................... F ....... 630 916-1200
  Oakbrook Terrace *(G-16714)*

### TELEPHONE: Headsets

Addax Sound Company ....................... F ....... 847 412-0000
  Northbrook *(G-16198)*

### TELEPHONE: Sets, Exc Cellular Radio

Firefly Mobile Inc ................................. E ....... 305 538-2777
  Schaumburg *(G-19529)*
Smart Choice Mobile Inc ..................... F ....... 708 933-6851
  Calumet City *(G-2955)*
Smart Choice Mobile Inc ..................... F ....... 708 581-4904
  Hickory Hills *(G-11774)*

### TELESCOPES

Astro-Physics Inc ................................. F ....... 815 282-1513
  Machesney Park *(G-14059)*
Mitchell Optics Inc ............................... G ....... 217 688-2219
  Sidney *(G-19937)*

### TELETYPEWRITERS

T 26 Inc ................................................ G ....... 773 862-1201
  Chicago *(G-6662)*

### TELEVISION BROADCASTING & COMMUNICATIONS EQPT

Big Ten Network Services LLC ........... D ....... 312 329-3666
  Chicago *(G-4104)*
Cable Company .................................... E ....... 847 437-5267
  Elk Grove Village *(G-9355)*
Dtv Innovations LLC ............................ F ....... 847 919-3550
  Elgin *(G-9014)*
Wireless Chamberlain Products .......... E ....... 800 282-6225
  Elmhurst *(G-9961)*
Zenith Electronics Corporation ............ E ....... 847 941-8000
  Lincolnshire *(G-13496)*

### TELEVISION BROADCASTING STATIONS

Quincy Media Inc ................................. C ....... 217 223-5100
  Quincy *(G-17879)*
Wyzz Inc ............................................... D ....... 217 753-5620
  Springfield *(G-20548)*

### TELEVISION FILM PRODUCTION SVCS

Midwest Outdoors Ltd ......................... E ....... 630 887-7722
  Burr Ridge *(G-2867)*

### TELEVISION SETS

Gier Radio & Television Inc ................. G ....... 815 722-8514
  Joliet *(G-12502)*

### TELEVISION: Cameras

Forest City Satellite ............................. G ....... 815 639-0500
  Davis Junction *(G-7811)*

### TELEVISION: Closed Circuit Eqpt

Checkpoint Systems Inc ...................... D ....... 630 771-4240
  Romeoville *(G-18809)*
Kokes Kid Zone .................................... G ....... 217 483-4615
  Chatham *(G-3624)*
Northern Information Tech .................. F ....... 800 528-4343
  Rolling Meadows *(G-18752)*

### TELEVISION: Monitors

Omni Vision Inc ................................... E ....... 630 893-1720
  Glendale Heights *(G-11053)*

### TEMPERING: Metal

Morgan Ohare Inc ................................ D ....... 630 543-6780
  Addison *(G-221)*

### TEMPORARY HELP SVCS

Office Assistants Inc ............................ G ....... 708 346-0505
  Oak Lawn *(G-16637)*

### TENTS: All Materials

Kastelic Canvas Inc ............................. G ....... 815 436-8160
  Plainfield *(G-17615)*
Terre Haute Tent & Awning Inc ........... F ....... 812 235-6068
  South Holland *(G-20309)*

### TERMINAL BOARDS

Imperial Fabricators Co ....................... E ....... 773 463-5522
  Franklin Park *(G-10495)*
Lutamar Electrical Assemblies ............ E ....... 847 679-5400
  Skokie *(G-20032)*

### TERRAZZO PRECAST PRDTS

Creative Inds Terrazzo Pdts ................. G ....... 773 235-9088
  Chicago *(G-4499)*

### TEST BORING SVCS: Nonmetallic Minerals

Midwest Testing Services Inc .............. G ....... 815 223-6696
  Peru *(G-17520)*
Natural Resources III Dept .................. E ....... 618 439-4320
  Benton *(G-2036)*

### TEST KITS: Pregnancy

Aid For Women Northern Lk Cnty ....... F ....... 847 249-2700
  Gurnee *(G-11421)*
Fox Valley Pregnancy Center .............. G ....... 847 697-0200
  South Elgin *(G-20197)*
Guardian Angel Outreach ..................... G ....... 815 672-4567
  Streator *(G-20689)*
Macneal Hospital ................................. G ....... 773 581-2199
  Chicago *(G-5594)*
Tri Cnty Prgnncy Prenting Svcs .......... G ....... 847 231-4651
  Grayslake *(G-11364)*

### TESTERS: Battery

ABM Marking Services Ltd .................. G ....... 618 277-3773
  Belleville *(G-1607)*
Auto Meter Products Inc ...................... C ....... 815 991-2292
  Sycamore *(G-20788)*
Greenlee Textron Inc ........................... C ....... 815 784-5127
  Genoa *(G-10879)*
Midtronics Inc ....................................... D ....... 630 323-2800
  Willowbrook *(G-22222)*

### TESTERS: Environmental

Alexeter Technologies LLC .................. F ....... 847 419-1507
  Wheeling *(G-22000)*
Blanke Industries Incorporated ........... G ....... 847 487-2780
  Wauconda *(G-21448)*
Mk Environmental Inc .......................... G ....... 630 848-0585
  Willowbrook *(G-22225)*
Networked Robotics Corporation ........ G ....... 847 424-8019
  Evanston *(G-10079)*
Pine Environmental Svcs LLC ............. G ....... 847 718-1246
  Elk Grove Village *(G-9681)*
Standard Safety Equipment Co ........... E ....... 815 363-8565
  McHenry *(G-14556)*
Warbler of Illinois Company ................ G ....... 301 520-0438
  Champaign *(G-3559)*

### TESTERS: Hardness

Rockford Rams Products Inc ............... G ....... 815 226-0016
  Rockford *(G-18585)*
Romus Incorporated ............................. G ....... 414 350-6233
  Roselle *(G-18968)*

### TESTERS: Logic Circuit

Integral Automation Inc ....................... F ....... 630 654-4300
  Burr Ridge *(G-2856)*

### TESTERS: Physical Property

Falex Corporation ................................ E ....... 630 556-3679
  Sugar Grove *(G-20723)*
Hamilton-Maurer Intl Inc ..................... G ....... 713 468-6805
  Hudson *(G-12123)*
Holmes Bros Inc .................................. E ....... 217 442-1430
  Danville *(G-7732)*
Perfection Probes Inc .......................... G ....... 847 726-8868
  Lake Zurich *(G-13112)*

### TESTERS: Water, Exc Indl Process

Swan Analytical Usa Inc ...................... F ....... 847 229-1290
  Wheeling *(G-22161)*

## PRODUCT SECTION

### TESTING SVCS
Ddu Magnetics Inc .............................. G ...... 708 325-6587
  Lynwood *(G-14019)*
Met-L-Flo Inc ..................................... F ...... 630 409-9860
  Sugar Grove *(G-20729)*
Psychiatric Assessments Inc ............... G ...... 312 878-6490
  Chicago *(G-6220)*

### TEXTILE & APPAREL SVCS
Allstar Embroidery ............................... G ...... 847 913-1133
  Buffalo Grove *(G-2655)*
Jenny Capp Co .................................... F ...... 773 217-0057
  Chicago *(G-5291)*
Meridian Industries Inc ....................... D ...... 630 892-7651
  Aurora *(G-1186)*
Unique Novelty & Manufacturing ........ G ...... 217 538-2014
  Fillmore *(G-10190)*

### TEXTILE BAGS WHOLESALERS
NRR Corp ............................................ F ...... 630 915-8388
  Oak Brook *(G-16550)*
Sea-Rich Corp ..................................... G ...... 773 261-6633
  Chicago *(G-6464)*

### TEXTILE FABRICATORS
Duracrest Fabrics ................................ G ...... 847 350-0030
  Elk Grove Village *(G-9438)*
Girlygirl .............................................. G ...... 708 633-7290
  Tinley Park *(G-20917)*
Heiman Sign Studio ............................ G ...... 815 397-6909
  Rockford *(G-18416)*

### TEXTILE FINISHING: Chem Coat/Treat, Man, Broadwoven, Cotton
Saati Americas Corporation ................ F ...... 847 296-5090
  Mount Prospect *(G-15371)*

### TEXTILE FINISHING: Chem Coating/Treating, Broadwoven, Cotton
Saati Americas Corporation ................ F ...... 847 296-5090
  Mount Prospect *(G-15371)*

### TEXTILE FINISHING: Chemical Coating Or Treating
B and A Screen Printing ..................... G ...... 217 762-2632
  Monticello *(G-15074)*

### TEXTILE FINISHING: Dyeing, Broadwoven, Cotton
Meridian Industries Inc ....................... D ...... 630 892-7651
  Aurora *(G-1186)*

### TEXTILE FINISHING: Dyeing, Finishing & Printng, Linen Fabric
Chicago Dye Works ............................. G ...... 847 931-7968
  Elgin *(G-8987)*

### TEXTILE FINISHING: Embossing, Linen, Broadwoven
Mount Vernon Mills ............................. G ...... 618 882-6300
  Highland *(G-11804)*

### TEXTILE FINISHING: Flocking, Cotton, Broadwoven
Flock It Ltd ......................................... G ...... 815 247-8775
  Winnebago *(G-22296)*

### TEXTILE PRDTS: Hand Woven & Crocheted
Tex Trend Inc ..................................... E ...... 847 215-6796
  Wheeling *(G-22166)*

### TEXTILE: Finishing, Cotton Broadwoven
Aurora Spclty Txtles Group Inc .......... D ...... 800 864-0303
  Yorkville *(G-22650)*
Expression Wear Inc ........................... G ...... 815 732-1556
  Mount Morris *(G-15296)*
M & P Talking Tees Inc ....................... F ...... 262 495-4000
  Round Lake Beach *(G-19077)*
Murphys Pub ...................................... G ...... 847 526-1431
  Wauconda *(G-21488)*
Tomen America Inc ............................ D ...... 847 439-8500
  Elk Grove Village *(G-9782)*
Western Pece Dyers Fnshers Inc ........ G ...... 773 523-7000
  Oak Brook *(G-16569)*

### TEXTILE: Finishing, Raw Stock NEC
Fas-Trak Industries Inc ...................... ......... 708 570-0650
  Monee *(G-14994)*

### TEXTILE: Goods, NEC
Advantex Inc ...................................... ......... 618 505-0701
  Troy *(G-21002)*
Annaka Enterprises ............................ G ...... 773 768-5490
  Chicago *(G-3910)*
Deelone Distributing Inc .................... ......... 309 788-1444
  Rock Island *(G-18172)*
Glenraven Inc ..................................... G ...... 847 515-1321
  Huntley *(G-12141)*
Lorton Group LLC ............................... G ...... 844 352-5089
  Wilmette *(G-22260)*
Z A W Collections ............................... G ...... 773 568-2031
  Chicago *(G-7056)*

### TEXTILES: Flock
Cellusuede Products Inc .................... E ...... 815 964-8619
  Rockford *(G-18302)*

### TEXTILES: Jute & Flax Prdts
Tex Tana Inc ...................................... G ...... 773 561-9270
  Chicago *(G-6705)*

### TEXTILES: Linen Fabrics
Superior Health Linens LLC ............... D ...... 630 593-5091
  Batavia *(G-1502)*

### TEXTILES: Linings, Carpet, Exc Felt
Shiir Rugs LLC ................................... G ...... 312 828-0400
  Chicago *(G-6497)*

### TEXTILES: Mill Waste & Remnant
Federal Prison Industries ................... F ...... 618 664-6361
  Greenville *(G-11393)*

### TEXTILES: Padding & Wadding
Novipax LLC ....................................... F ...... 630 686-2735
  Oak Brook *(G-16548)*

### TEXTILES: Wool Waste, Processes
Conversion Energy Systems Inc ......... G ...... 312 489-8875
  Chicago *(G-4464)*

### THEATRICAL LIGHTING SVCS
Upstaging Inc ..................................... C ...... 815 899-9888
  Sycamore *(G-20822)*

### THEATRICAL PRODUCERS & SVCS
Dramatic Publishing Company ........... F ...... 815 338-7170
  Woodstock *(G-22563)*

### THEATRICAL SCENERY
Chicago Scenic Studios Inc ................ D ...... 312 274-9900
  Chicago *(G-4345)*
Consolidated Displays Co Inc ............. G ...... 630 851-8666
  Oswego *(G-16911)*
Illumivation Studios LLC .................... G ...... 312 261-5561
  Chicago *(G-5160)*
Interesting Products Inc .................... G ...... 773 265-1100
  Chicago *(G-5211)*

### THEOLOGICAL SEMINARIES
Baptist General Conference ............... D ...... 800 323-4215
  Arlington Heights *(G-723)*

### THERMOCOUPLES
C & L Manufacturing Entps ................ ......... 618 465-7623
  Alton *(G-565)*
Tempco Electric Heater Corp ............. B ...... 630 350-2252
  Wood Dale *(G-22429)*

### THERMOCOUPLES: Indl Process
Tempro International Corp ................. G ...... 847 677-5370
  Skokie *(G-20100)*
Xco International Incorporated .......... F ...... 847 428-2400
  East Dundee *(G-8662)*

### THERMOMETERS: Liquid-In-Glass & Bimetal
Lcr Hallcrest Llc ................................. E ...... 847 998-8580
  Glenview *(G-11165)*

### THERMOMETERS: Medical, Digital
Avalign Technologies Inc ................... E ...... 855 282-5446
  Bannockburn *(G-1253)*

### THERMOPLASTIC MATERIALS
Dow Chemical Company ..................... D ...... 217 784-2093
  Gibson City *(G-10900)*
Dow Chemical Company ..................... D ...... 815 476-9688
  Wilmington *(G-22270)*
Polymax Thermoplastic ...................... E ...... 847 316-9900
  Waukegan *(G-21602)*
Polyone Corporation ........................... D ...... 815 385-8500
  McHenry *(G-14548)*
Star Thermoplastic Alloys and ........... E ...... 708 343-1100
  Broadview *(G-2613)*
Star Thermoplastic Alloys and ........... F ...... 708 343-1100
  Broadview *(G-2614)*

### THERMOPLASTICS
Atlas Fibre Company .......................... D ...... 847 674-1234
  Northbrook *(G-16208)*
Laminart Inc ....................................... E ...... 800 323-7624
  Schaumburg *(G-19612)*

### THERMOSTAT REPAIR SVCS
Acme Control Service Inc .................. E ...... 773 774-9191
  Chicago *(G-3732)*

### THREAD: All Fibers
Advent Tool & Mfg Inc ....................... F ...... 847 395-9707
  Antioch *(G-613)*
Machine Tool Acc & Mfg Co ............... G ...... 773 489-0903
  Chicago *(G-5592)*

### THREAD: Crochet
Dan De Tash Knits ............................. G ...... 708 970-6238
  Maywood *(G-14424)*

### THYROID PREPARATIONS
Abbvie Holdings Inc ........................... D ...... 847 937-7632
  Abbott Park *(G-8)*

### TIES, FORM: Metal
National Tool & Mfg Co ...................... D ...... 847 806-9800
  Wheeling *(G-22105)*

### TILE: Brick & Structural, Clay
Building Products Corp ...................... E ...... 618 233-4427
  Belleville *(G-1615)*
Miller Tiling Co Inc ............................ G ...... 217 971-4709
  Virden *(G-21300)*

### TILE: Clay, Drain & Structural
C & L Tiling Inc .................................. D ...... 217 773-3357
  Timewell *(G-20884)*
Coon Run Drainage & Levee Dst ........ G ...... 217 248-5511
  Arenzville *(G-688)*

### TILE: Concrete, Drain
Hulse Excavating ............................... G ...... 815 796-4106
  Flanagan *(G-10194)*
Sebens Concrete Products Inc ........... G ...... 217 864-2824
  Decatur *(G-7939)*

### TILE: Mosaic, Ceramic
Stonepeak Ceramics Inc .................... E ...... 312 335-0321
  Chicago *(G-6599)*

### TILE: Terrazzo Or Concrete, Precast
MK Tile Ink ........................................ G ...... 773 964-8905
  Chicago *(G-5778)*

# TILE: Wall & Floor, Ceramic

### TILE: Wall & Floor, Ceramic
Mosaicos Inc .................................G....... 773 777-8453
Chicago *(G-5811)*

### TILE: Wall, Ceramic
Curran Group Inc ...........................E....... 815 455-5100
Crystal Lake *(G-7563)*

### TIMING DEVICES: Electronic
C-Storm Electronic LLC .................F....... 630 406-1353
Saint Charles *(G-19148)*
Competition Electronics Inc ...........G....... 815 874-8001
Rockford *(G-18321)*
Connor-Winfield Corp ....................C....... 630 851-4722
Aurora *(G-1133)*
E N M Company ............................D....... 773 775-8400
Chicago *(G-4667)*
Las Systems Inc ............................E....... 847 462-8100
Woodstock *(G-22582)*
USA Drives Inc .............................E....... 630 323-1282
Burr Ridge *(G-2892)*

### TIN
Ames Metal Products Company ....F....... 773 523-3230
Wheeling *(G-22005)*
Arcelormittal USA LLC ...................B....... 312 346-0300
Chicago *(G-3935)*
Pat 24 Inc .....................................G....... 708 336-8671
Burbank *(G-2809)*
Tin HLA Health Svcs ......................G....... 708 633-0426
Tinley Park *(G-20949)*
Tin Man Heating & Cooling Inc .....E....... 630 267-3232
Aurora *(G-1225)*
Tin Maung .....................................G....... 217 233-1405
Decatur *(G-7953)*
Tin Tree Gifts ................................G....... 630 935-8086
Aurora *(G-1086)*

### TIRE CORD & FABRIC
Mc Chemical Company ..................G....... 618 965-3668
Steeleville *(G-20563)*

### TIRE CORD & FABRIC: Indl, Reinforcing
Advanced Flxble Composites Inc ...D....... 847 658-3938
Lake In The Hills *(G-12983)*

### TIRE CORD & FABRIC: Steel
Nnm Manufacturing LLC ................E....... 815 436-9201
Plainfield *(G-17633)*

### TIRE DEALERS
Bridgestone Americas ....................F....... 309 452-4411
Normal *(G-16066)*
Bridgestone Ret Operations LLC ...F....... 630 893-6336
Glendale Heights *(G-11012)*
City Subn Auto Svc Goodyear .......G....... 773 355-5550
Chicago *(G-4389)*
Continental Tire Americas LLC .....A....... 618 246-2466
Mount Vernon *(G-15406)*
Hamel Tire and Concrete Pdts ......G....... 618 633-2405
Hamel *(G-11529)*
Petron Oil Production Inc ..............G....... 618 783-4486
Newton *(G-15946)*
Trotters Manufacturing Co ............G....... 217 364-4540
Buffalo *(G-2649)*

### TIRE INFLATORS: Hand Or Compressor Operated
G H Meiser & Co ...........................G....... 708 388-7867
Posen *(G-17730)*

### TIRE SUNDRIES OR REPAIR MATERIALS: Rubber
Best Designs Inc ...........................F....... 618 985-4445
Carterville *(G-3309)*
Kraly Tire Repair Materials ...........G....... 708 863-5981
Cicero *(G-7211)*

### TIRES & INNER TUBES
Bridgestone Americas ....................F....... 309 452-4411
Normal *(G-16066)*
Bridgestone Ret Operations LLC ...F....... 630 893-6336
Glendale Heights *(G-11012)*

C&C Sealants ................................F....... 708 717-0686
Elgin *(G-8975)*
Continental Tire Americas LLC ....G....... 618 242-7100
Mount Vernon *(G-15407)*
Continental Tire Americas LLC ....G....... 618 246-2585
Mascoutah *(G-14351)*
Continental Tire Americas LLC ....A....... 618 246-2466
Mount Vernon *(G-15406)*
Dealer Tire LLC .............................G....... 847 671-0683
Franklin Park *(G-10454)*
Joseph Coppolino .........................G....... 773 735-8647
Chicago *(G-5328)*
Liberty Tire Recycling LLC ............G....... 773 871-6360
Chicago *(G-5502)*
Otr Wheel Engineering Inc ...........E....... 217 223-7705
Quincy *(G-17864)*
Stop & Go International Inc ..........G....... 815 455-9080
Crystal Lake *(G-7654)*
Titan Tire Corporation ..................B....... 217 228-6011
Quincy *(G-17897)*
Titan Tyre Corporation .................A....... 217 228-6011
Freeport *(G-10692)*

### TIRES & TUBES WHOLESALERS
Dealer Tire LLC .............................G....... 847 671-0683
Franklin Park *(G-10454)*
Hamel Tire and Concrete Pdts ......G....... 618 633-2405
Hamel *(G-11529)*
Liberty Tire Recycling LLC ............G....... 773 871-6360
Chicago *(G-5502)*

### TIRES & TUBES, WHOLESALE: Automotive
Custom Millers Supply Inc ............G....... 309 734-6312
Monmouth *(G-15011)*

### TIRES & TUBES, WHOLESALE: Truck
D N D Coating ...............................G....... 309 379-3021
Stanford *(G-20551)*

### TIRES, USED, WHOLESALE
A Lakin & Sons Inc .......................E....... 773 871-6360
Montgomery *(G-15026)*
Lakin General Corporation ............D....... 773 871-6360
Montgomery *(G-15054)*

### TIRES: Agricultural, Pneumatic
Titan International Inc ..................B....... 217 228-6011
Quincy *(G-17896)*

### TIRES: Auto
Mecanica En General Santoyo ......G....... 708 652-2217
Cicero *(G-7219)*

### TIRES: Cushion Or Solid Rubber
Dyneer Corporation ......................B....... 217 228-6011
Quincy *(G-17823)*
Tbc Corporation ............................G....... 630 428-2233
Naperville *(G-15760)*

### TIRES: Plastic
Circle Caster Engineering Co ........G....... 847 455-2206
Franklin Park *(G-10432)*

### TITANIUM MILL PRDTS
American Titanium Works LLC ......G....... 312 327-3178
Chicago *(G-3878)*
AWI / Titanium .............................G....... 708 263-9970
Oak Forest *(G-6574)*
International Titanium Powder .....G....... 815 834-2112
Lockport *(G-13723)*
MBA Marketing Inc .......................G....... 847 566-2555
Mundelein *(G-15526)*
Titanium Insulation Inc .................G....... 708 932-5927
Midlothian *(G-14770)*
Titanium Ventures Group LLC ......G....... 312 375-3526
Chicago *(G-6730)*

### TOBACCO & TOBACCO PRDTS WHOLESALERS
8 Electronic Cigarette Inc ..............G....... 630 708-6803
Saint Charles *(G-19129)*

Itg Brands LLC .............................G....... 217 529-5746
Springfield *(G-20458)*

### TOBACCO LEAF PROCESSING
Kraft Heinz Foods Company .........F....... 630 227-1474
Wood Dale *(G-22386)*

### TOBACCO STORES & STANDS
Hotvapes Ltd .................................F....... 775 468-8273
Chicago *(G-5120)*
Magazine Plus ...............................G....... 773 281-4106
Chicago *(G-5599)*

### TOBACCO: Chewing
Paramount Plastics LLC ................D....... 815 834-4100
Chicago *(G-6078)*

### TOBACCO: Chewing & Snuff
Diamond Wholesale Group Inc .....G....... 708 529-7495
Bridgeview *(G-2483)*
Inter-Continental Trdg USA Inc ....D....... 847 640-1777
Mount Prospect *(G-15339)*
US Smokeless Tob Mfg Co LLC ....E....... 804 274-2000
Franklin Park *(G-10617)*
Ust Inc .........................................G....... 847 957-5104
Franklin Park *(G-10618)*

### TOBACCO: Cigarettes
8 Electronic Cigarette Inc ..............G....... 630 708-6803
Saint Charles *(G-19129)*
Cigtechs .......................................G....... 847 802-4586
Algonquin *(G-384)*
Cigtechs .......................................G....... 630 855-6513
Roselle *(G-18932)*
Itg Brands LLC .............................G....... 217 529-5746
Springfield *(G-20458)*
Philip Morris USA Inc ....................D....... 847 605-9595
Schaumburg *(G-19689)*
Royal Smoke Shop ........................G....... 815 539-3499
Mendota *(G-14732)*
Steves Cigarettes ..........................G....... 630 827-0820
Lombard *(G-13860)*

### TOBACCO: Cigars
Burning Leaf Cigars .......................G....... 815 267-3570
Geneva *(G-10815)*
Casa De Monte Cristo ...................G....... 708 352-6668
Countryside *(G-7416)*

### TOBACCO: Smoking
Casa De Puros ..............................G....... 708 725-7180
Forest Park *(G-10236)*
Having A Good Time .....................G....... 847 330-8460
Schaumburg *(G-19549)*
Paralleldirect LLC ..........................G....... 847 748-2025
Lincolnshire *(G-13471)*
PS Tobacco Inc .............................G....... 630 793-9823
Glen Ellyn *(G-10988)*
Raze Vapor ...................................G....... 415 596-2697
Chicago *(G-6298)*
Republic Group Inc .......................G....... 800 288-8888
Glenview *(G-11193)*
Top Tobacco LP ............................G....... 847 832-9700
Glenview *(G-11210)*

### TOILET PREPARATIONS
Cedar Concepts Corporation .........E....... 773 890-5790
Chicago *(G-4265)*
Rochester Midland Corporation ....E....... 630 896-8543
Montgomery *(G-15066)*

### TOILET SEATS: Wood
Liftseat Corporation ......................E....... 630 424-2840
Oak Brook *(G-16537)*

### TOILETRIES, COSMETICS & PERFUME STORES
AM Harper Products Inc ................F....... 312 767-8283
Chicago *(G-3841)*
Luxurious Lathers Ltd ...................G....... 844 877-7627
Hinsdale *(G-11951)*
Winlind Skincare LLC ....................G....... 630 789-9408
Burr Ridge *(G-2896)*

## PRODUCT SECTION

### TOILETRIES, WHOLESALE: Hair Preparations
Safe Effective Alternatives ............... F ....... 618 236-2727
 Belleville *(G-1675)*

### TOILETRIES, WHOLESALE: Perfumes
Aurora Narinder ............................... G ....... 773 275-2100
 Chicago *(G-3989)*

### TOILETRIES, WHOLESALE: Toilet Soap
4 Elements Company ....................... G ....... 773 236-2284
 Mundelein *(G-15461)*

### TOILETRIES, WHOLESALE: Toiletries
1 Federal Supply Source Inc ............. G ....... 708 964-2222
 Steger *(G-20565)*
Marietta Corporation ........................ C ....... 773 816-5137
 Chicago *(G-5619)*
Riviera Tan Spa (del) ....................... G ....... 618 466-1012
 Godfrey *(G-11235)*

### TOILETS: Portable Chemical, Plastics
Urban Services of America .............. G ....... 847 278-3210
 Schaumburg *(G-19783)*

### TOLL OPERATIONS
Ace Plastics Inc .............................. F ....... 815 635-1368
 Chatsworth *(G-3626)*

### TOLLS: Caulking
Marmon Holdings Inc ...................... D ....... 312 372-9500
 Chicago *(G-5625)*

### TOMBSTONES: Terrazzo Or Concrete, Precast
Elmos Tombstone Service ............... G ....... 773 643-0200
 Chicago *(G-4733)*
Shrine Memorial Mausoleum Co ...... G ....... 618 283-0153
 Vandalia *(G-21123)*

### TOOL & DIE STEEL
Automation Design & Mfg Inc ........... G ....... 630 896-4206
 Aurora *(G-1117)*
Contour Tool Works Inc ................... G ....... 847 947-4700
 Palatine *(G-17018)*
Craftsman Custom Metals LLC ........ D ....... 847 655-0040
 Schiller Park *(G-19817)*
Fabricating Machinery Sales ............ E ....... 630 350-2266
 Wood Dale *(G-22366)*
Hi Tek Tool & Machining Inc ............ G ....... 847 836-6422
 Algonquin *(G-392)*
Keats Manufacturing Co .................. D ....... 847 520-1133
 Wheeling *(G-22083)*
Midstates Cutting Tools Inc ............. E ....... 630 595-0700
 Bensenville *(G-1951)*
Mt Tool and Manufacturing Inc ........ G ....... 847 985-6211
 Schaumburg *(G-19655)*
Multiple Metal Production ................ G ....... 847 679-1510
 Skokie *(G-20043)*
Offko Tool Inc ................................. G ....... 815 933-9474
 Kankakee *(G-12641)*
Precise Stamping Inc ...................... E ....... 630 897-6477
 North Aurora *(G-16143)*
R & E Quality Mfg Co ...................... G ....... 773 286-6846
 Chicago *(G-6262)*
Waters Wire EDM Service ............... G ....... 630 640-3534
 Downers Grove *(G-8542)*

### TOOL REPAIR SVCS
Allkut Tool Incorporated .................. G ....... 815 476-9656
 Wilmington *(G-22269)*
Ivan Schwenker .............................. G ....... 630 543-7798
 Addison *(G-156)*
Rotospray Mfg Inc .......................... G ....... 708 478-3307
 Mokena *(G-14900)*

### TOOLS: Carpenters', Including Levels & Chisels, Exc Saws
Dasco Pro Inc ................................. D ....... 815 962-3727
 Rockford *(G-18335)*

### TOOLS: Hand
A To Z Tool Inc ................................ G ....... 630 787-0478
 Villa Park *(G-21231)*
Adel Tool Co LLP ............................ G ....... 708 867-8530
 Chicago *(G-3747)*
Adjustable Clamp Company ............ C ....... 312 666-0640
 Chicago *(G-3751)*
Advance Equipment Mfg Co ............ F ....... 773 287-8220
 Chicago *(G-3759)*
Ajax Tool Works Inc ........................ D ....... 847 455-5420
 Franklin Park *(G-10387)*
Aldon Co ........................................ F ....... 847 623-8800
 Waukegan *(G-21521)*
Brian Burcar .................................... G ....... 815 856-2271
 Leonore *(G-13285)*
C K North America Inc .................... F ....... 815 524-4246
 Romeoville *(G-18804)*
Chicago Grinding & Machine Co ..... E ....... 708 343-4399
 Melrose Park *(G-14610)*
Doerock Inc .................................... G ....... 217 543-2101
 Arthur *(G-895)*
E J Welch Co Inc ............................ E ....... 847 238-0100
 Elk Grove Village *(G-9443)*
Eklind Tool Co ................................. G ....... 847 994-8550
 Franklin Park *(G-10464)*
Ergo Help Inc ................................. G ....... 847 593-0722
 Arlington Heights *(G-750)*
Gaunt Industries Inc ....................... G ....... 847 671-0776
 Franklin Park *(G-10477)*
H E Associates Inc ......................... F ....... 630 553-6382
 Yorkville *(G-22661)*
H R Slater Co Inc ........................... F ....... 312 666-1855
 Chicago *(G-5023)*
H&H Die Manufacturing Inc ............ G ....... 708 479-6267
 Frankfort *(G-10326)*
Hydra Fold Auger Inc ...................... G ....... 217 379-2614
 Loda *(G-13751)*
Hyponex Corporation ...................... E ....... 815 772-2167
 Morrison *(G-15144)*
I D Rockford Shop Inc .................... G ....... 815 335-1150
 Winnebago *(G-22297)*
Ideal Industries Inc ......................... C ....... 815 895-1108
 Sycamore *(G-20801)*
Illinois Tool Works Inc ..................... G ....... 847 821-2170
 Vernon Hills *(G-21174)*
K-C Tool Co .................................... G ....... 630 983-5960
 Naperville *(G-15683)*
Kishwaukee Forge Company .......... G ....... 815 758-4451
 Cortland *(G-7391)*
Klein Tools Inc ................................ B ....... 847 821-5500
 Lincolnshire *(G-13460)*
Klein Tools Inc ................................ D ....... 847 228-6999
 Elk Grove Village *(G-9577)*
Klein Tools Inc ................................ G ....... 847 821-5500
 Lincolnshire *(G-13461)*
Knipex Tools LP .............................. F ....... 847 398-8520
 Arlington Heights *(G-789)*
Lawndale Forging & Tool Works ..... G ....... 773 277-2800
 Chicago *(G-5471)*
Line Group Inc ................................ E ....... 847 593-6810
 Arlington Heights *(G-793)*
Link Tools Intl (usa) Inc .................. G ....... 773 549-3000
 Chicago *(G-5512)*
Lmt Onsrud LP ................................ C ....... 847 362-1560
 Waukegan *(G-21582)*
Luster Leaf Products Inc ................. G ....... 815 337-5560
 Woodstock *(G-22586)*
Modern Specialties Company ......... G ....... 312 648-5800
 Chicago *(G-5785)*
Nextstep Commercial Products ....... G ....... 217 379-2377
 Paxton *(G-17239)*
P K Neuses Incorporated ............... G ....... 847 253-6555
 Rolling Meadows *(G-18756)*
Packers Supplies & Eqp LLC .......... G ....... 630 543-5810
 Addison *(G-236)*
Patterson Avenue Tool Company .... G ....... 847 949-8100
 Long Grove *(G-13900)*
Power House Tool Inc ..................... G ....... 815 727-6301
 Joliet *(G-12552)*
Precision Products Inc .................... C ....... 217 735-1590
 Lincoln *(G-13418)*
Precision Tool ................................. F ....... 815 464-2428
 Frankfort *(G-10351)*
Pullr Holding Company LLC ........... E ....... 224 366-2500
 Schaumburg *(G-19704)*
Ravco Incorporated ........................ G ....... 815 725-9095
 Joliet *(G-12564)*
Rhino Tool Company ...................... F ....... 309 853-5555
 Kewanee *(G-12694)*
Ryeson Corporation ........................ D ....... 847 455-8677
 Carol Stream *(G-3230)*
S & G Step Tool Inc ........................ G ....... 773 992-0808
 Chicago *(G-6420)*
Sab Tool Supply Co ........................ G ....... 847 634-3700
 Vernon Hills *(G-21196)*
Stanley Hartco Co .......................... E ....... 847 967-1122
 Skokie *(G-20090)*
Stark Tools and Supply Inc ............. G ....... 847 772-8974
 Elk Grove Village *(G-9756)*
Stuhr Manufacturing Co .................. F ....... 815 398-2460
 Rockford *(G-18636)*
Sws Industries Inc .......................... E ....... 904 482-0091
 Woodstock *(G-22616)*
Thread & Gage Co Inc .................... G ....... 815 675-2305
 Spring Grove *(G-20367)*
Tuxco Corporation .......................... F ....... 847 244-2220
 Gurnee *(G-11517)*
Wenco Manufacturing Co Inc .......... E ....... 630 377-7474
 Elgin *(G-9235)*
Whitney Roper LLC ........................ D ....... 815 962-3011
 Rockford *(G-18681)*
Whitney Roper Rockford Inc ........... D ....... 815 962-3011
 Rockford *(G-18682)*
Woodland Engineering Company .... G ....... 847 362-0110
 Lake Bluff *(G-12873)*
Zah Group Inc ................................ G ....... 847 821-5500
 Lincolnshire *(G-13492)*

### TOOLS: Hand, Carpet Layers
Beno J Gundlach Company ............ E ....... 618 233-1781
 Belleville *(G-1613)*

### TOOLS: Hand, Hammers
Bit Brokers International Ltd ........... G ....... 618 435-5811
 West Frankfort *(G-21804)*
Dobratz Sales Company Inc ........... G ....... 224 569-3081
 Lake In The Hills *(G-12990)*
Estwing Manufacturing Co Inc ........ B ....... 815 397-9521
 Rockford *(G-18370)*
Ironwood Mfg Inc ............................ G ....... 630 778-8963
 Naperville *(G-15679)*
Lsp Industries Inc ........................... F ....... 815 226-8090
 Rockford *(G-18474)*
Proton Multimedia Inc ..................... G ....... 847 531-8664
 Elgin *(G-9152)*
Vaughan & Bushnell Mfg Co ........... F ....... 815 648-2446
 Hebron *(G-11730)*

### TOOLS: Hand, Ironworkers'
Builders Ironworks Inc .................... G ....... 708 754-4092
 Steger *(G-20569)*
Hollywood Tools LLC ..................... G ....... 773 793-3119
 West Chicago *(G-21715)*

### TOOLS: Hand, Masons'
Galaxy Industries Inc ...................... D ....... 847 639-8580
 Cary *(G-3345)*

### TOOLS: Hand, Mechanics
Northern Ordinance Corporation ..... G ....... 815 675-6400
 Spring Grove *(G-20352)*
Toby Small Engine Repair .............. G ....... 708 699-6021
 Richton Park *(G-17980)*
Zim Manufacturing Co .................... E ....... 773 622-2500
 Chicago *(G-7067)*

### TOOLS: Hand, Plumbers'
Hand Tool America ......................... G ....... 847 947-2866
 Buffalo Grove *(G-2701)*
Richardson Enterprises .................. G ....... 309 833-5395
 Macomb *(G-14131)*
Rothenberger USA LLC .................. D ....... 815 397-7617
 Rockford *(G-18598)*

### TOOLS: Hand, Power
A J Horne Inc ................................. G ....... 630 231-8686
 West Chicago *(G-21651)*
Ajax Tool Works Inc ........................ D ....... 847 455-5420
 Franklin Park *(G-10387)*
Allegion S&S US Holding Co .......... C ....... 815 875-3311
 Princeton *(G-17742)*
Ally Global Corporation ................... G ....... 773 822-3373
 Chicago *(G-3826)*
Black & Decker Corporation ........... F ....... 630 521-1097
 Addison *(G-57)*

# TOOLS: Hand, Power

Champion Chisel Works Inc .............. F ..... 815 535-0647
  Rock Falls (G-18128)
Corless Equipment Co ...................... G ..... 773 776-8383
  Chicago (G-4469)
Custom Cutting Tools Inc .................. G ..... 815 986-0320
  Loves Park (G-13931)
Damen Carbide Tool Company Inc ....... E ..... 630 766-7875
  Wood Dale (G-22357)
Duo-Fast Corporation ........................ G ..... 847 944-2288
  Glenview (G-11122)
Estwing Manufacturing Co Inc ............ B ..... 815 397-9521
  Rockford (G-18370)
Federal Prison Industries .................. C ..... 309 346-8588
  Pekin (G-17262)
Gator Products Inc ........................... G ..... 847 836-0581
  Gilberts (G-10919)
Greenlee Textron Inc ........................ D ..... 815 397-7070
  Rockford (G-18405)
Harris Precision Products Inc ............ G ..... 708 422-5808
  Chicago Ridge (G-7149)
Industrial Instrument Svc Corp .......... G ..... 773 581-3355
  Chicago (G-5177)
Ivan Schwenker ............................... G ..... 630 543-7798
  Addison (G-156)
K-C Tool Co ..................................... G ..... 630 983-5960
  Naperville (G-15683)
Link Tools Intl (usa) Inc .................... G ..... 773 549-3000
  Chicago (G-5512)
Marvco Tool & Manufacturing ............. G ..... 847 437-4900
  Elk Grove Village (G-9612)
Milwaukee Electric Tool Corp ............ B ..... 847 588-3356
  Niles (G-16008)
NNt Enterprises Incorporated ............ G ..... 630 875-9600
  Itasca (G-12332)
Paslode Corp .................................. G ..... 641 672-2515
  Glenview (G-11180)
Powernail Company .......................... E ..... 800 323-1653
  Lake Zurich (G-13116)
R & S Cutterhead Mfg Co .................. F ..... 815 678-2611
  Richmond (G-17969)
Ralph Cody Gravrok .......................... G ..... 630 628-9570
  Addison (G-269)
Rdh Inc of Rockford .......................... F ..... 815 874-9421
  Rockford (G-18550)
Rhino Tool Company ......................... F ..... 309 853-5555
  Kewanee (G-12694)
S & J Industrial Supply Corp ............. F ..... 708 339-1708
  South Holland (G-20303)
Sollami Company .............................. E ..... 618 988-1521
  Herrin (G-11755)
T & T Carbide ................................... G ..... 618 439-7253
  Logan (G-13755)
Tapco USA Inc .................................. G ..... 815 877-4039
  Loves Park (G-13998)
Technical Tool Enterprise .................. G ..... 630 893-3390
  Addison (G-307)
Toolmasters LLC .............................. F ..... 815 645-2224
  Stillman Valley (G-20629)
Total Tooling Technology Inc ............. F ..... 847 437-5135
  Elk Grove Village (G-9786)
Triumph Twist Drill Co Inc ................. B ..... 815 459-6250
  Crystal Lake (G-7670)
Tru-Cut Inc ...................................... D ..... 847 639-2090
  Cary (G-3377)
Unicut Corporation ........................... G ..... 773 525-4210
  Chicago (G-6813)
Wallace/Haskin Corp ........................ G ..... 630 789-2882
  Downers Grove (G-8540)
Welliver & Sons Inc .......................... E ..... 815 874-2400
  Rockford (G-18676)
Whitney Roper LLC ........................... D ..... 815 962-3011
  Rockford (G-18681)
Whitney Roper Rockford Inc .............. D ..... 815 962-3011
  Rockford (G-18682)
Wodack Electric Tool Corp ................. F ..... 773 287-9866
  Chicago (G-7019)

## TOOTHPASTES, GELS & TOOTHPOWDERS

Sunstar Pharmaceutical Inc ............... D ..... 773 777-4000
  Elgin (G-9198)

## TOWELETTES: Premoistened

Multi-Pack Solutions LLC ................... D ..... 847 635-6772
  Mount Prospect (G-15352)

## TOWELS: Knit

Intelex Usa LLC ................................ G ..... 847 496-1727
  East Dundee (G-8647)

Tiger Accessory Group LLC ............... G ..... 847 821-9630
  Long Grove (G-13902)

## TOWERS, SECTIONS: Transmission, Radio & Television

Hi-Tech Towers Inc .......................... E ..... 217 784-5212
  Gibson City (G-10902)
Rohn Products LLC .......................... D ..... 309 697-4400
  Peoria (G-17446)
Rohn Products LLC .......................... E ..... 309 566-3000
  Peoria (G-17447)

## TOWING SVCS: Marine

White International Inc ..................... E ..... 630 377-9966
  Saint Charles (G-19295)

## TOYS

Aeromax Industries Inc .................... G ..... 847 756-4085
  Lake Barrington (G-12798)
Amav Enterprises Ltd ....................... G ..... 630 761-3077
  Batavia (G-1410)
American Specialty Toy ..................... G ..... 312 222-0984
  Chicago (G-3876)
Aqua Golf Inc .................................. G ..... 217 824-2097
  Taylorville (G-20832)
Ayla Group Inc ................................. G ..... 630 954-9432
  Bartlett (G-1334)
Belco International Toy Co ................ G ..... 847 256-6818
  Wilmette (G-22243)
Chicago Contract Bridge Assn ........... G ..... 630 355-5560
  Naperville (G-15626)
Cino Incorporated ............................ G ..... 630 377-7242
  Saint Charles (G-19153)
E J Kupjack & Associates Inc ........... G ..... 847 823-6661
  Chicago (G-4666)
Educational Insights Inc ................... E ..... 847 573-8400
  Vernon Hills (G-21158)
Fun Incorporated ............................. E ..... 773 745-3837
  Wheeling (G-22059)
Gamenamics Inc .............................. F ..... 847 844-7688
  Elgin (G-9041)
Hobbico Inc .................................... E ..... 217 367-2707
  Urbana (G-21091)
Kaskey Kids Inc ............................... G ..... 847 441-3092
  Winnetka (G-22308)
Mayfair Games Inc ........................... E ..... 847 677-6655
  Skokie (G-20035)
Neat-OH International LLC ................ F ..... 847 441-4290
  Northfield (G-16411)
Non Violent Toys Inc ........................ G ..... 847 835-9066
  Glencoe (G-11004)
Pro-Line Winning Ways & Penlan ....... G ..... 309 745-8530
  Washington (G-21388)
Racine Paper Box Manufacturing ....... E ..... 773 227-3900
  Chicago (G-6278)
Reel Life Dvd LLC ............................ G ..... 708 579-1360
  Western Springs (G-21872)
Rust-Oleum Corporation ................... D ..... 815 967-4258
  Rockford (G-18600)
Sharin Toy Company ......................... E ..... 847 676-1200
  Lincolnwood (G-13538)
Shure Products Inc .......................... F ..... 773 227-1001
  Chicago (G-6504)
Sunburst Technology Corp ................ G ..... 800 321-7511
  Elgin (G-9197)
Sunnywood Incorporated .................. G ..... 815 675-9777
  Spring Grove (G-20366)
Testor Corporation ........................... D ..... 815 962-6654
  Rockford (G-18644)
Zipwhaa Inc .................................... G ..... 630 898-4330
  Palatine (G-17092)

## TOYS & HOBBY GOODS & SPLYS, WHOL: Toy Novelties & Amusements

Jcw Investments Inc ........................ G ..... 708 478-7323
  Orland Park (G-16870)
Urpoint LLC .................................... G ..... 773 919-9002
  New Lenox (G-15925)

## TOYS & HOBBY GOODS & SPLYS, WHOLESALE: Arts/Crafts Eqpt/Sply

Chartwell Studio Inc ........................ G ..... 847 868-8674
  Evanston (G-10021)
Freitas P Sabah ............................... G ..... 708 386-8934
  Oak Park (G-16664)

Multi Packaging Solutions Inc ........... G ..... 773 283-9500
  Chicago (G-5832)
Virtu .............................................. G ..... 773 235-3790
  Chicago (G-6900)

## TOYS & HOBBY GOODS & SPLYS, WHOLESALE: Educational Toys

Learning Curve International ............. E ..... 630 573-7200
  Oak Brook (G-16533)
Learning Resources Inc .................... D ..... 847 573-9471
  Vernon Hills (G-21181)
Sage Clover .................................... G ..... 630 220-9600
  Winfield (G-22293)

## TOYS & HOBBY GOODS & SPLYS, WHOLESALE: Model Kits

Accurail Inc .................................... F ..... 630 365-6400
  Elburn (G-8873)
Midwest Rail Junction ...................... G ..... 815 963-0200
  Rockford (G-18506)

## TOYS & HOBBY GOODS & SPLYS, WHOLESALE: Puzzles

Picture Perfect Puzzles LLC .............. G ..... 847 838-0848
  Lake Villa (G-13022)

## TOYS & HOBBY GOODS & SPLYS, WHOLESALE: Toys & Games

Gameplan Inc .................................. G ..... 877 284-9180
  Northbrook (G-16263)
Trivial Development Corp .................. E ..... 630 860-2500
  Itasca (G-12368)

## TOYS & HOBBY GOODS & SPLYS, WHOLESALE: Toys, NEC

Belco International Toy Co ................ G ..... 847 256-6818
  Wilmette (G-22243)

## TOYS & HOBBY GOODS & SPLYS, WHOLESALE: Video Games

Gamestop Inc .................................. G ..... 773 568-0457
  Chicago (G-4912)
Gamestop Corp ............................... G ..... 773 545-9602
  Chicago (G-4913)

## TOYS, HOBBY GOODS & SPLYS WHOLESALERS

First & Main Inc .............................. E ..... 630 587-1000
  Saint Charles (G-19184)
Weathertop Woodcraft ...................... G .....
  Carol Stream (G-3265)

## TOYS: Dolls, Stuffed Animals & Parts

Shawnimals LLC ............................... G ..... 312 235-2625
  Chicago (G-6492)
Unique Novelty & Manufacturing ........ G ..... 217 538-2014
  Fillmore (G-10190)

## TOYS: Electronic

Circuitron Inc .................................. G ..... 815 886-9010
  Romeoville (G-18812)
Jcw Investments Inc ........................ G ..... 708 478-7323
  Orland Park (G-16870)
Petronics Inc .................................. G ..... 608 630-6527
  Champaign (G-3524)
Tractronics .................................... G ..... 630 527-0000
  Naperville (G-15767)

## TOYS: Kites

Chicago Kite ................................... G ..... 773 467-1428
  Chicago (G-4325)

## TOYS: Paint Sets, Children's

Qsimaginationstation ....................... G ..... 708 928-9622
  Dolton (G-8376)

## TOYS: Rubber

Winfun Usa LLC ............................... G ..... 630 942-8464
  Glen Ellyn (G-10995)

## PRODUCT SECTION

### TOYS: Video Game Machines

Gamestop Inc .................................................. G .... 773 568-0457
  Chicago  *(G-4912)*
Gamestop Corp .............................................. G .... 618 258-8611
  Wood River  *(G-22443)*
Gamestop Corp .............................................. G .... 773 545-9602
  Chicago  *(G-4913)*
Raw Thrills Inc ............................................... D .... 847 679-8373
  Skokie  *(G-20071)*
Wiliams Interactive LLC ............................... C .... 773 961-1920
  Chicago  *(G-6978)*

### TRADE SHOW ARRANGEMENT SVCS

Associated Equipment Distrs .................... E .... 630 574-0650
  Schaumburg  *(G-19448)*
Chambers Marketing Options ................... G .... 847 584-2626
  Elk Grove Village  *(G-9364)*
HH Backer Associates Inc ......................... F .... 312 578-1818
  Chicago  *(G-5084)*
Matrex Exhibits Inc ..................................... D .... 630 628-2233
  Addison  *(G-192)*
Stevens Exhibits & Displays ...................... E .... 773 523-3900
  Chicago  *(G-6595)*

### TRAILER COACHES: Automobile

Midwest Trailer Mfg LLC ............................ G .... 309 897-8216
  Kewanee  *(G-12693)*

### TRAILERS & CHASSIS: Camping

Arthur Leo Kuhl ............................................ G .... 618 752-5473
  Ingraham  *(G-12199)*

### TRAILERS & PARTS: Boat

Knight Bros Inc ............................................. E .... 618 439-9626
  Benton  *(G-2033)*

### TRAILERS & PARTS: Truck & Semi's

A & S Steel Specialties Inc ........................ E .... 815 838-8188
  Lockport  *(G-13700)*
A & Z Sas Express Inc ................................ G .... 847 451-0851
  Melrose Park  *(G-14578)*
Advanced Mobility & .................................. E .... 708 235-2800
  Monee  *(G-14991)*
Barrington Financial Services .................. G .... 847 404-1767
  Lake In The Hills  *(G-12988)*
Barron 2m Inc .............................................. G .... 847 219-3650
  Schiller Park  *(G-19808)*
Classic Roadliner Corporation ................. G .... 708 769-0666
  Justice  *(G-12595)*
Coras Welding Shop Inc ............................ G .... 815 672-7950
  Streator  *(G-20686)*
D D Sales Inc ............................................... E .... 217 857-3196
  Teutopolis  *(G-20851)*
Dolche Truckload Corp .............................. G .... 800 719-4921
  Palatine  *(G-17024)*
Dundee Truck & Trlr Works LLC ............... G .... 224 484-8182
  East Dundee  *(G-8635)*
Fleetpride Inc .............................................. C .... 708 430-2081
  Bridgeview  *(G-2491)*
Great Dane Limited Partnership ............. B .... 309 854-0407
  Kewanee  *(G-12688)*
Great Dane Limited Partnership ............. D .... 773 254-5533
  Chicago  *(G-4995)*
Groovy Logistics Inc .................................. G .... 847 946-1491
  Joliet  *(G-12505)*
Haynes Express Inc ................................... G .... 309 793-6080
  Rock Island  *(G-18180)*
Imperial Group Mfg Inc ............................. B .... 615 325-9224
  Chicago  *(G-5165)*
Imperial Trailer Mfg Inc ............................. F .... 618 395-2414
  Olney  *(G-16772)*
K B K Truck and Trlr Repr Co ................... G .... 630 422-7265
  Wood Dale  *(G-22383)*
Load Redi Inc .............................................. G .... 217 784-4200
  Gibson City  *(G-10904)*
Maple Park Trucking Inc ........................... G .... 815 899-1958
  Maple Park  *(G-14202)*
Matt Snell and Sons .................................. G .... 618 695-3555
  Vienna  *(G-21223)*
Mickey Truck Bodies Inc .......................... F .... 309 827-8227
  Bloomington  *(G-2197)*
Mid City Truck Bdy & Equipmemt ........... F .... 630 628-9080
  Addison  *(G-209)*
Midland Manufacturing Corp ................... C .... 847 677-0333
  Skokie  *(G-20039)*
Pk Corporation ............................................ G .... 847 879-1070
  Elk Grove Village  *(G-9683)*
Polar Corporation ....................................... E .... 618 548-3660
  Salem  *(G-19343)*
Roadex Carriers Inc .................................. G .... 773 454-8772
  Wheeling  *(G-22141)*
Robert Davis & Son Inc ............................ G .... 815 889-4168
  Milford  *(G-14814)*
Schantz Mfg Inc ......................................... E .... 618 654-1523
  Highland  *(G-11810)*
Seat Trans Inc ............................................ G .... 224 522-1007
  Lake In The Hills  *(G-13006)*
Summit Tank & Equipment Co ................. F .... 708 594-3040
  Mc Cook  *(G-14459)*

### TRAILERS & TRAILER EQPT

Advance Metalworking Company ............ E .... 309 853-3387
  Kewanee  *(G-12668)*
Andy Wurst ................................................... G .... 630 964-4410
  Darien  *(G-7789)*
Custom Millers Supply Inc ........................ G .... 309 734-6312
  Monmouth  *(G-15011)*
Ervin Equipments ....................................... G .... 217 849-3125
  Toledo  *(G-20962)*
Grs Holding LLC .......................................... G .... 630 355-1660
  Naperville  *(G-15666)*
Triple B Manufacturing Co Inc ................. G .... 618 566-2888
  Mascoutah  *(G-14360)*
Wise Equipment & Rentals Inc ................ F .... 847 895-5555
  Schaumburg  *(G-19790)*

### TRAILERS: Bodies

Paramount Truck Body Co Inc ................. E .... 312 666-6441
  Chicago  *(G-6079)*
Peter Built ..................................................... E .... 618 337-4000
  East Saint Louis  *(G-8764)*

### TRAILERS: Semitrailers, Truck Tractors

Azcon Inc ....................................................... F .... 815 548-7000
  Sterling  *(G-20583)*
Great Dane Limited Partnership ............. C .... 309 854-0407
  Kewanee  *(G-12687)*
Great Dane Limited Partnership ............. D .... 773 254-5533
  Kewanee  *(G-12689)*
Quality Trailer Sales Inc ............................ G .... 630 739-2495
  Morton  *(G-15179)*
STI Holdings Inc ........................................... F .... 630 789-2713
  Burr Ridge  *(G-2882)*
Timpte Industries Inc ................................. D .... 309 820-1095
  Bloomington  *(G-2231)*

### TRANSDUCERS: Electrical Properties

Knowles Elec Holdings Inc ....................... A .... 630 250-5100
  Itasca  *(G-12296)*
Knowles Electronics LLC ......................... A .... 630 250-5100
  Itasca  *(G-12297)*

### TRANSDUCERS: Pressure

Source Technology ..................................... G .... 281 894-6171
  Broadview  *(G-2612)*

### TRANSFORMERS: Control

Micron Industries Corporation ................. F .... 630 516-1222
  Oak Brook  *(G-16544)*
Micron Industries Corporation ................. D .... 815 380-2222
  Sterling  *(G-20599)*

### TRANSFORMERS: Distribution

Invenergy Wind Fin Co III LLC .................. G .... 312 224-1400
  Chicago  *(G-5231)*
Powell Industries Inc ................................. F .... 708 409-1200
  Northlake  *(G-16449)*
Thomas Research Products LLC ............ F .... 224 654-8626
  Elgin  *(G-9211)*

### TRANSFORMERS: Distribution, Electric

Light To Form LLC ...................................... E .... 847 498-5832
  Northbrook  *(G-16296)*

### TRANSFORMERS: Electric

Audio Video Electronics LLC .................... G .... 847 983-4761
  Skokie  *(G-19961)*
Hubbell Power Systems Inc ..................... F .... 618 797-5000
  Edwardsville  *(G-8803)*
Wicc Ltd ....................................................... D .... 309 444-4125
  Washington  *(G-21396)*

### TRANSFORMERS: Electronic

Charles Industries Ltd .............................. D .... 847 806-6300
  Rolling Meadows  *(G-18719)*
Custom Magnetics Inc .............................. E .... 773 463-6500
  Chicago  *(G-4523)*
Inglot Electronics Corp ............................. D .... 773 286-5881
  Chicago  *(G-5192)*
Ipr Systems Inc .......................................... G .... 708 385-7500
  Alsip  *(G-474)*
Lenco Electronics Inc ............................... E .... 815 344-2900
  McHenry  *(G-14520)*
Marvel Electric Corporation ..................... D .... 773 327-2644
  Chicago  *(G-5638)*
MEI Realty Ltd ............................................ G .... 847 358-5000
  Inverness  *(G-12205)*

### TRANSFORMERS: Florescent Lighting

Robertson Transformer Co ...................... E .... 708 388-2315
  Crestwood  *(G-7500)*

### TRANSFORMERS: Flyback

Gsg Industries ............................................. F .... 618 544-7976
  Robinson  *(G-18063)*

### TRANSFORMERS: Lighting, Street & Airport

Peterson Elc Panl Mfg Co Inc .................. F .... 708 449-2270
  Berkeley  *(G-2048)*

### TRANSFORMERS: Meters, Electronic

Cymatics Inc ................................................ G .... 630 420-7117
  Naperville  *(G-15640)*

### TRANSFORMERS: Power Related

A J Smoy Co Inc ......................................... E .... 773 775-8282
  Schaumburg  *(G-19419)*
Actown-Electrocoil Inc .............................. G ....
  Spring Grove  *(G-20324)*
Coiltechnic Inc ............................................ F .... 815 675-9260
  Spring Grove  *(G-20331)*
Communication Coil Inc ........................... D .... 847 671-1333
  Schiller Park  *(G-19815)*
Dresser Inc .................................................. D .... 847 437-5940
  Elk Grove Village  *(G-9435)*
Dual Voltage Distributors ......................... G .... 847 519-1201
  Schaumburg  *(G-19509)*
Equus Power I LP ...................................... F .... 847 908-2878
  Schaumburg  *(G-19518)*
Ferrite International Company ................ E .... 847 249-4900
  Wadsworth  *(G-21322)*
Forest Electric Company .......................... E .... 708 681-0180
  Melrose Park  *(G-14639)*
Gsg Industries ............................................. F .... 618 544-7976
  Robinson  *(G-18063)*
Inglot Electronics Corp ............................. D .... 773 286-5881
  Chicago  *(G-5192)*
Ipr Systems Inc .......................................... G .... 708 385-7500
  Alsip  *(G-474)*
Lenco Electronics Inc ............................... E .... 815 344-2900
  McHenry  *(G-14520)*
Magnetic Coil Manufacturing Co ............ C .... 630 787-1948
  Wood Dale  *(G-22395)*
Magnetic Devices Inc ............................... G .... 815 459-0077
  Crystal Lake  *(G-7605)*
Marvel Electric Corporation ..................... D .... 773 327-2644
  Chicago  *(G-5638)*
Marvel Electric Corporation ..................... E .... 847 671-0632
  Schiller Park  *(G-19846)*
Methode Development Co ....................... D .... 708 867-6777
  Chicago  *(G-5703)*
Micron Engineering Co ............................. G .... 815 455-2888
  Crystal Lake  *(G-7611)*
Mitsubishi Elc Automtn Inc ..................... C .... 847 478-2100
  Vernon Hills  *(G-21183)*
Newhaven Display Intl Inc ....................... E .... 847 844-8795
  Elgin  *(G-9118)*
Pactra Corp ................................................. G .... 847 281-0308
  Vernon Hills  *(G-21187)*
Power House Tool Inc ............................... E .... 815 727-6301
  Joliet  *(G-12552)*
Precision Components Inc ...................... D .... 630 462-9110
  Saint Charles  *(G-19240)*
Psytronics Inc ............................................. G .... 847 719-1371
  Lake Zurich  *(G-13118)*
Saachi Inc .................................................... G .... 630 775-1700
  Roselle  *(G-18971)*
Simplex Inc ................................................. C .... 217 483-1600
  Springfield  *(G-20526)*

Employee Codes: A=Over 500 employees, B=251-500
C=101-250, D=51-100, E=20-50, F=10-19, G=3-9

# TRANSFORMERS: Power Related

Storage Battery Systems LLC .................G....... 630 221-1700
   Carol Stream  *(G-3251)*
U S Co-Tronics Corp .............................E....... 815 692-3204
   Fairbury  *(G-10134)*

## TRANSFORMERS: Specialty

Aldonex Inc ..............................................F....... 708 547-5663
   Bellwood  *(G-1693)*
Olsun Electrics Corporation ...................G....... 815 678-2421
   Richmond  *(G-17968)*
Relay Services Mfg Corp ........................F....... 773 252-2700
   Chicago  *(G-6327)*
Transformer Manufacturers Inc ...............E....... 708 457-1200
   Norridge  *(G-16110)*
V and F Transformer Corp .......................D....... 630 497-8070
   Bartlett  *(G-1384)*

## TRANSFORMERS: Voltage Regulating

Anderson Engrg New Prague Inc ............G....... 630 736-0900
   Streamwood  *(G-20643)*

## TRANSLATION & INTERPRETATION SVCS

Chicago Mltlingua Graphics Inc ...............F....... 847 386-7187
   Northfield  *(G-16397)*
Techno - Grphics Trnsltons Inc ................E....... 708 331-3333
   South Holland  *(G-20308)*

## TRANSMISSIONS: Motor Vehicle

Dynamic Manufacturing Inc .....................B....... 708 547-9011
   Hillside  *(G-11916)*
GKN North America Services Inc ............F....... 630 972-9300
   Woodridge  *(G-22484)*
GKN Rockford Inc ..................................C....... 815 633-7460
   Loves Park  *(G-13944)*
Gray Machine & Welding Inc ...................F....... 309 788-2501
   Rock Island  *(G-18177)*
Midwest Converters Inc ..........................F....... 815 229-9808
   Rockford  *(G-18504)*
Premium Components ............................G....... 630 521-1700
   Bensenville  *(G-1966)*

## TRANSPORTATION AGENTS & BROKERS

Icg Illinois ...............................................G....... 217 947-2332
   Elkhart  *(G-9825)*
Raytrans Distribution Svcs Inc .................F....... 708 503-9940
   Chicago  *(G-6297)*

## TRANSPORTATION ARRANGEMENT SVCS, PASS: Sightseeing Tour Co's

Capital Tours & Travel Inc .......................G....... 847 274-1138
   Skokie  *(G-19973)*

## TRANSPORTATION BROKERS: Truck

Amcol International Corp .........................E....... 847 851-1500
   Hoffman Estates  *(G-11991)*

## TRANSPORTATION EPQT & SPLYS, WHOLESALE: Marine Crafts/Splys

Sierra International LLC ..........................C....... 217 324-9400
   Litchfield  *(G-13698)*

## TRANSPORTATION EPQT/SPLYS, WHOL: Space Propulsion Unit/Part

R&R Equipment Plus1 Inc .......................F....... 708 529-3931
   Chicago Ridge  *(G-7157)*

## TRANSPORTATION EQPT & SPLYS WHOLESALERS, NEC

Advanced Precision Mfg Inc ....................E....... 847 981-9800
   Elk Grove Village  *(G-9276)*
Hella Corporate Center USA Inc .............B....... 734 414-0900
   Flora  *(G-10208)*
UTC Railcar Repair Svcs LLC .................A....... 312 431-5053
   Chicago  *(G-6861)*

## TRANSPORTATION EQUIPMENT, NEC

FL West Corporation ..............................G....... 708 342-0500
   Tinley Park  *(G-20914)*
New World Trnsp Systems .......................G....... 773 509-5931
   Chicago  *(G-5898)*

## TRANSPORTATION PROGRAMS REGULATION & ADMINISTRATION SVCS

Transportation Illinois Dept ......................F....... 217 785-0288
   Springfield  *(G-20546)*

## TRANSPORTATION SVCS, WATER: Water Taxis

T G Enterprises Inc .................................F....... 309 662-0508
   Bloomington  *(G-2229)*

## TRANSPORTATION SVCS: Airport Limousine, Scheduled Svcs

Driver Services .......................................G....... 505 267-8686
   Bensenville  *(G-1883)*

## TRANSPORTATION SVCS: Railroads, Interurban

U S Railway Services ..............................G....... 708 468-8343
   Tinley Park  *(G-20952)*

## TRANSPORTATION: Bus Transit Systems

Zimmerman Enterprises Inc ....................F....... 847 297-3177
   Des Plaines  *(G-8308)*

## TRANSPORTATION: Deep Sea Domestic Freight

BP America Inc .......................................A....... 630 420-5111
   Warrenville  *(G-21344)*

## TRANSPORTATION: Transit Systems, NEC

Polmax LLC ............................................C....... 708 843-8300
   Alsip  *(G-511)*

## TRAPS: Animal, Iron Or Steel

L & M Hardware Ltd ................................G....... 312 805-2752
   Downers Grove  *(G-8471)*

## TRAPS: Stem

Lilly Industries Inc ...................................F....... 630 773-2222
   Itasca  *(G-12306)*
Spirax Sarco Inc .....................................G....... 630 493-4525
   Lisle  *(G-13660)*

## TRAVEL AGENCIES

Capital Tours & Travel Inc .......................G....... 847 274-1138
   Skokie  *(G-19973)*
Triplett Entereprises Inc ..........................G....... 708 333-9421
   Oak Forest  *(G-16592)*

## TRAVEL TRAILERS & CAMPERS

A & S Steel Specialties Inc ......................E....... 815 838-8188
   Lockport  *(G-13700)*
Boyd Spotting Inc ...................................G....... 217 669-2418
   Cisco  *(G-7249)*
Brumleve Industries Inc ..........................F....... 217 857-3777
   Teutopolis  *(G-20847)*
Davison Co Ltd .......................................G....... 815 966-2905
   Rockford  *(G-18337)*
Dedicated Tcs LLC .................................F....... 815 467-9560
   Channahon  *(G-3569)*
Hanna Hopper Trlr Sls & Rv Ctr ...............G....... 217 243-3374
   Jacksonville  *(G-12390)*
I94 Rv LLC .............................................F....... 847 395-9500
   Russell  *(G-19097)*
Lakeshore Lacrosse LLC ........................G....... 773 350-4356
   Wheaton  *(G-21963)*
Rieco-Titan Products Inc .........................E....... 815 464-7400
   Frankfort  *(G-10358)*
Travel Caddy Inc ....................................E....... 847 621-7000
   Elk Grove Village  *(G-9788)*

## TRAVELER ACCOMMODATIONS, NEC

Jack & Lidias Resort Inc .........................G....... 847 356-1389
   Lake Villa  *(G-13017)*
Lane Industries Inc .................................G....... 847 498-6650
   Northbrook  *(G-16292)*

## TRAYS: Cable, Metal Plate

Cablofil Inc .............................................B....... 618 566-3230
   Mascoutah  *(G-14350)*
Cooper B-Line Inc ..................................A....... 618 654-2184
   Highland  *(G-11780)*

## TRAYS: Plastic

Detroit Forming Inc .................................D....... 630 820-0500
   Aurora  *(G-994)*
Newell Operating Company .....................C....... 815 235-4171
   Freeport  *(G-10675)*

## TRIM: Window, Wood

Ideal Cabinet Solutions Inc .....................G....... 618 514-7087
   Alhambra  *(G-418)*

## TROPHIES, NEC

All American Trophy King Inc ..................F....... 708 597-2121
   Crestwood  *(G-7474)*
AMG International Inc .............................G....... 847 439-1001
   Elk Grove Village  *(G-9301)*
Budget Signs ..........................................F....... 618 259-4460
   Wood River  *(G-22441)*
Captains Emporium Inc ...........................G....... 773 972-7609
   Chicago  *(G-4234)*
Mint Masters Inc .....................................E....... 847 451-1133
   Franklin Park  *(G-10534)*
Mtm Recognition Corporation ..................C....... 815 875-1111
   Princeton  *(G-17757)*
Trophies By George ................................G....... 630 497-1212
   Bartlett  *(G-1381)*

## TROPHIES, PLATED, ALL METALS

RS Owens Div St Regis LLC ...................D....... 773 282-6000
   Chicago  *(G-6407)*
Rudon Enterprises Inc .............................G....... 618 457-0441
   Carbondale  *(G-3022)*
Stellar Recognition Inc ............................G....... 773 282-8060
   Chicago  *(G-6588)*

## TROPHIES, WHOLESALE

A 1 Trophies Awards & Engrv ..................G....... 630 837-6000
   Streamwood  *(G-20638)*
All American Trophy King Inc ..................F....... 708 597-2121
   Crestwood  *(G-7474)*
B D Enterprises ......................................G....... 618 462-5861
   Alton  *(G-563)*
Bishops Engrv & Trophy Svc Inc .............G....... 773 777-5014
   Chicago  *(G-4114)*
Classique Signs & Engrv Inc ...................G....... 217 228-7446
   Quincy  *(G-17813)*
Joans Trophy & Plaque Co ......................E....... 309 674-6500
   Peoria  *(G-17393)*
Johnos Inc ..............................................G....... 630 897-6929
   Aurora  *(G-1178)*

## TROPHIES: Metal, Exc Silver

Afar Imports & Interiors Inc .....................G....... 217 744-3262
   Springfield  *(G-20386)*
American Trophy & Award Co Inc ............G....... 312 939-3252
   Chicago  *(G-3881)*
Awards and More Inc ..............................G....... 773 581-7771
   Chicago  *(G-4004)*
Mighty Mites Awards and Sons ................G....... 847 297-0035
   Des Plaines  *(G-8233)*
Planter Inc .............................................D....... 773 637-7777
   Chicago  *(G-6135)*
R S Owens & Co Inc ...............................B....... 773 282-6000
   Chicago  *(G-6273)*
Voss Pattern Works Inc ...........................G....... 618 233-4242
   Belleville  *(G-1689)*

## TROPHY & PLAQUE STORES

A 1 Trophies Awards & Engrv ..................G....... 630 837-6000
   Streamwood  *(G-20638)*
Academy Screenprinting Awards ..............G....... 309 686-0026
   Peoria  *(G-17300)*
All American Trophy King Inc ..................F....... 708 597-2121
   Crestwood  *(G-7474)*
Athletic Outfitters Inc .............................G....... 815 942-6696
   Morris  *(G-15094)*
Award Emblem Mfg Co Inc .....................F....... 630 739-0800
   Bolingbrook  *(G-2281)*
Awards and More Inc ..............................G....... 773 581-7771
   Chicago  *(G-4004)*
B Gunther & Co ......................................F....... 630 969-5595
   Lisle  *(G-13567)*
Budget Signs ..........................................F....... 618 259-4460
   Wood River  *(G-22441)*

# PRODUCT SECTION

## TRUCKING: Except Local

Camilles of Canton Inc ..................... G ...... 309 647-7403
  Canton  (G-2983)
Classique Signs & Engrv Inc ............. G ...... 217 228-7446
  Quincy  (G-17813)
Cook Merritt ........................................ G ...... 630 980-3070
  Roselle  (G-18934)
Crown Trophy ...................................... G ...... 309 699-1766
  East Peoria  (G-8707)
Custom Trophies ................................. G ...... 217 422-3353
  Decatur  (G-7863)
Fielders Choice .................................. G ...... 618 937-2294
  West Frankfort  (G-21807)
Finer Line Inc .................................... F ...... 847 884-1611
  Schaumburg  (G-19527)
Freeman Products Inc ........................ G ...... 847 439-1000
  Elk Grove Village  (G-9490)
Joans Trophy & Plaque Co ................. E ...... 309 674-6500
  Peoria  (G-17393)
K 9 Tag Company Inc .......................... G ...... 847 304-8247
  Waukegan  (G-21575)
Minor League Inc ............................... G ...... 618 548-8040
  Salem  (G-19339)
Signs Today Inc ................................. G ...... 847 934-9777
  Palatine  (G-17074)
Town Hall Sports Inc .......................... F ...... 618 235-9881
  Belleville  (G-1682)
Trophies and Awards Plus ................. G ...... 708 754-7127
  Steger  (G-20578)
Trophies By George ........................... G ...... 630 497-1212
  Bartlett  (G-1381)
Trophytime Inc ................................... G ...... 217 351-7958
  Champaign  (G-3550)
Twin City Awards ............................... G ...... 309 452-9291
  Normal  (G-16091)
U R On It ............................................. G ...... 847 382-0182
  Lake Barrington  (G-12826)
Walnut Creek Hardwood .................... G ...... 815 389-3317
  South Beloit  (G-20173)
Wheaton Trophy & Engravers ............ G ...... 630 682-4200
  Wheaton  (G-21989)

### TRUCK & BUS BODIES: Automobile Wrecker Truck

Imperial Oil Inc .................................. G ...... 773 866-1235
  Chicago  (G-5166)
Tondinis Wrecker Service ................. G ...... 618 997-9884
  Marion  (G-14292)

### TRUCK & BUS BODIES: Beverage Truck

Mickey Truck Bodies Inc .................... F ...... 309 827-8227
  Bloomington  (G-2197)

### TRUCK & BUS BODIES: Bus Bodies

Motor Coach Inds Intl Inc .................. C ...... 847 285-2000
  Des Plaines  (G-8235)

### TRUCK & BUS BODIES: Car Carrier

Instar Auto Carriers LLC ................... G ...... 708 428-6318
  Orland Park  (G-16869)

### TRUCK & BUS BODIES: Dump Truck

C I F Industries Inc ........................... F ...... 618 635-2010
  Staunton  (G-20555)
Dierzen Trailer Co ............................. D ...... 815 695-5291
  Newark  (G-15933)
Lacy Enterprises Inc ......................... G ...... 773 264-2557
  Chicago  (G-5433)

### TRUCK & BUS BODIES: Motor Vehicle, Specialty

L & M Manufacturing Inc ................... F ...... 309 734-3009
  Kewanee  (G-12692)
Quad County Fire Equipment ............ G ...... 815 832-4475
  Saunemin  (G-19395)

### TRUCK & BUS BODIES: Truck Cabs, Motor Vehicles

Campbell International Inc ............... E ...... 408 661-0794
  Wauconda  (G-21452)
Robinsport LLC .................................. G ...... 630 724-9280
  Woodridge  (G-22514)

### TRUCK & BUS BODIES: Truck, Motor Vehicle

C S O Corp .......................................... E ...... 630 365-6600
  Virgil  (G-21302)
Donermen LLC .................................... G ...... 773 430-2828
  Chicago  (G-4626)
Erie Vehicle Company ........................ F ...... 773 536-6300
  Chicago  (G-4772)
Gvw Group LLC ................................... G ...... 847 681-8417
  Highland Park  (G-11839)
Paramount Truck Body Co Inc ........... E ...... 312 666-6441
  Chicago  (G-6079)
Sauber Manufacturing Company ....... D ...... 630 365-6600
  Virgil  (G-21303)

### TRUCK & BUS BODIES: Utility Truck

City Utility Equipment ....................... F ...... 815 254-6673
  Plainfield  (G-17587)

### TRUCK & BUS BODIES: Van Bodies

Mid-America Truck Corporation ........ D ...... 815 672-3211
  Streator  (G-20694)

### TRUCK & FREIGHT TERMINALS & SUPPORT ACTIVITIES

East St Louis Trml & Stor Co ............ E ...... 618 271-2185
  East Saint Louis  (G-8749)

### TRUCK BODIES: Body Parts

ATI Oldco Inc ..................................... C ...... 630 860-5600
  Bartlett  (G-1332)
Auto Truck Group LLC ....................... C ...... 630 860-5600
  Bartlett  (G-1333)
Herr Display Vans Inc ....................... F ...... 708 755-7926
  Steger  (G-20573)
Newf LLC ............................................ G ...... 630 330-5462
  Naperville  (G-15714)

### TRUCK BODY SHOP

Mickey Truck Bodies Inc .................... F ...... 309 827-8227
  Bloomington  (G-2197)
Mid City Truck Bdy & Equipmemt ..... F ...... 630 628-9080
  Addison  (G-209)
Roll-A-Way Conveyors Inc ................. G ...... 847 336-5033
  Gurnee  (G-11500)

### TRUCK FINANCE LEASING

Navistar Inc ....................................... C ...... 331 332-5000
  Lisle  (G-13629)

### TRUCK GENERAL REPAIR SVC

Botts Welding and Trck Svc Inc ........ E ...... 815 338-0594
  Woodstock  (G-22546)
D D Sales Inc .................................... E ...... 217 857-3196
  Teutopolis  (G-20851)
Dundee Truck & Trlr Works LLC ........ G ...... 224 484-8182
  East Dundee  (G-8635)
North Shore Truck & Equipment ...... G ...... 847 887-0200
  Lake Bluff  (G-12860)
Rex Radiator and Welding Co ........... G ...... 847 428-1112
  East Dundee  (G-8655)
Wirfs Industries Inc .......................... F ...... 815 344-0635
  McHenry  (G-14571)

### TRUCK PAINTING & LETTERING SVCS

Canham Graphics ............................... G ...... 217 585-5085
  Springfield  (G-20404)
Dierzen-Kewanee Heavy Inds .......... D ...... 309 853-2316
  Kewanee  (G-12679)
E K Kuhn Inc ...................................... G ...... 815 899-9211
  Sycamore  (G-20795)
Enterprise Signs Inc ......................... G ...... 773 614-8324
  Chicago  (G-4760)
Image Signs Inc ................................. F ...... 815 282-4141
  Loves Park  (G-13947)
Paldo Sign and Display Company ..... G ...... 708 456-1711
  River Grove  (G-18012)
Schellerer Corporation Inc ............... D ...... 630 980-4567
  Bloomingdale  (G-2135)
Sign Central .................................... G ...... 847 543-7600
  Round Lake  (G-19067)

### TRUCK PARTS & ACCESSORIES: Wholesalers

Bonnell Industries Inc ..................... D ...... 815 284-3819
  Dixon  (G-8323)
Botts Welding and Trck Svc Inc ...... E ...... 815 338-0594
  Woodstock  (G-22546)
Fleetpride Inc .................................. C ...... 708 430-2081
  Bridgeview  (G-2491)
Jimmy Diesel Inc .............................. G ...... 708 482-4500
  Wheaton  (G-21959)
P & A Driveline & Machine Inc ....... F ...... 630 860-7474
  Bensenville  (G-1962)
Salco Products Inc .......................... G ...... 630 783-2570
  Lemont  (G-13261)
Standard Truck Parts Inc ................ G ...... 815 726-4486
  Joliet  (G-12578)

### TRUCKING & HAULING SVCS: Coal, Local

ODaniel Trucking Co ........................ D ...... 618 382-5371
  Carmi  (G-3076)

### TRUCKING & HAULING SVCS: Contract Basis

Caples-El Transport Inc .................. G ...... 708 300-2727
  Calumet City  (G-2936)

### TRUCKING & HAULING SVCS: Heavy Machinery, Local

Harold L Ray Truck & Trctr Svc ...... F ...... 618 673-2701
  Cisne  (G-7252)

### TRUCKING & HAULING SVCS: Heavy, NEC

Info Corner Materials Inc ............... F ...... 217 566-3561
  Springfield  (G-20456)

### TRUCKING & HAULING SVCS: Liquid, Local

Koontz Services ............................... G ...... 618 375-7613
  Carmi  (G-3072)

### TRUCKING & HAULING SVCS: Machinery, Heavy

American Industrial Werks Inc ....... F ...... 847 477-2648
  Schaumburg  (G-19437)

### TRUCKING & HAULING SVCS: Mobile Homes

Mobil Trailer Transport Inc ............ E ...... 630 993-1200
  Villa Park  (G-21270)

### TRUCKING & HAULING SVCS: Trailer/Container On Flat Car

Jtec Industries Inc .......................... E ...... 309 698-9301
  East Peoria  (G-8720)

### TRUCKING, DUMP

Callender Construction Co Inc ...... F ...... 217 285-2161
  Pittsfield  (G-17563)
Conmat Inc ...................................... E ...... 815 235-2200
  Freeport  (G-10651)
Jacobs Trucking ............................. G ...... 618 687-3578
  Murphysboro  (G-15577)
Myers Concrete & Construction .... G ...... 815 732-2591
  Oregon  (G-16828)
Thelen Sand & Gravel Inc .............. D ...... 847 838-8800
  Antioch  (G-656)

### TRUCKING: Except Local

Amcol International Corp .............. E ...... 847 851-1500
  Hoffman Estates  (G-11991)
Central Manufacturing Company ... G ...... 309 387-6591
  East Peoria  (G-8705)
CJ Drilling Inc ................................. E ...... 847 854-3888
  Dundee  (G-8560)
Ed Hartwig Trucking & Excvtg ....... G ...... 309 364-3672
  Henry  (G-11740)
Illinois Road Contractors Inc ........ E ...... 217 245-6181
  Jacksonville  (G-12393)
Lohrberg Lumber ............................ F ...... 618 473-2061
  Waterloo  (G-21402)
Pdv Midwest Refining LLC ............. A ...... 630 257-7761
  Lemont  (G-13254)

Employee Codes: A=Over 500 employees, B=251-500
C=101-250, D=51-100, E=20-50, F=10-19, G=3-9

## TRUCKING: Except Local

Tyson Fresh Meats Inc .............................F ....... 847 836-5550
  Elgin  (G-9218)
Valley View Industries Inc ......................E ....... 815 358-2236
  Cornell  (G-7382)

## TRUCKING: Local, With Storage

Coyote Transportation Inc ......................G ....... 630 204-5729
  Bensenville  (G-1869)
Kraft Heinz Foods Company ..................D ....... 217 378-1900
  Champaign  (G-3507)

## TRUCKING: Local, Without Storage

Abner Trucking Co Inc ...........................G ....... 618 676-1301
  Clay City  (G-7261)
BFI Waste Systems N Amer Inc .............E ....... 847 429-7370
  Elgin  (G-8965)
Blomberg Bros Inc .................................F ....... 618 245-6321
  Farina  (G-10174)
Bob Barnett Redi-Mix Inc ......................F ....... 618 252-3581
  Harrisburg  (G-11596)
Bristol Transport Inc ..............................E ....... 708 343-6411
  Northlake  (G-16431)
C & H Gravel C Inc ................................G ....... 217 857-3425
  Teutopolis  (G-20848)
Davidson Grain Incorporated ................E ....... 815 384-3208
  Creston  (G-7471)
Fuller Asphalt & Landscape ..................G ....... 618 797-1169
  Granite City  (G-11277)
Geske and Sons Inc ..............................F ....... 815 459-2407
  Crystal Lake  (G-7581)
Gorman Brothers Ready Mix Inc ...........F ....... 618 498-2173
  Jerseyville  (G-12422)
Gosia Cartage Ltd .................................G ....... 312 613-8735
  Hodgkins  (G-11975)
Hastie Mining & Trucking ......................E ....... 618 289-4536
  Cave In Rock  (G-3402)
Huyear Trucking Inc ..............................G ....... 217 854-3551
  Carlinville  (G-3039)
J W Rudy Co Inc ...................................F ....... 618 676-1616
  Clay City  (G-7265)
James Randall .......................................G ....... 309 444-8765
  Washington  (G-21384)
Jax Asphalt Company Inc .....................F ....... 618 244-0500
  Mount Vernon  (G-15418)
Jay A Morris ..........................................G ....... 815 432-6440
  Watseka  (G-21420)
Maplehurst Farms Inc ...........................F ....... 815 562-8723
  Rochelle  (G-18097)
Mel Price Company Inc .........................F ....... 217 442-9092
  Danville  (G-7754)
Metropolis Ready Mix Inc .....................E ....... 618 524-8221
  Metropolis  (G-14758)
National Concrete Pipe Co ...................E ....... 630 766-3600
  Franklin Park  (G-10539)
Polmax LLC ...........................................C ....... 708 843-8300
  Alsip  (G-511)
R & J Trucking and Recycl Inc ..............F ....... 708 563-2600
  Chicago  (G-6263)
Rd Daily Enterprises .............................G ....... 847 872-7632
  Winthrop Harbor  (G-22320)
Robinsport LLC .....................................G ....... 630 724-9280
  Woodridge  (G-22514)
Southfield Corporation ..........................E ....... 309 829-1087
  Bloomington  (G-2225)
Upchurch Ready Mix Concrete .............G ....... 618 235-6222
  Belleville  (G-1684)
Valley View Industries Inc ....................E ....... 815 358-2236
  Cornell  (G-7382)

## TRUCKS & TRACTORS: Industrial

Align Production Systems LLC .............E ....... 217 423-6001
  Decatur  (G-7830)
All-Vac Industries Inc ............................F ....... 847 675-2290
  Skokie  (G-19948)
Barnes Industrial Equipment ................G ....... 630 213-9240
  Streamwood  (G-20645)
Big Lift LLC ............................................F ....... 630 916-2600
  Lombard  (G-13768)
Brennan Equipment and Mfg Inc ..........D ....... 708 534-5500
  University Park  (G-21046)
Caterpillar Inc ........................................A ....... 630 859-5000
  Montgomery  (G-15036)
Centralia Machine & Fab Inc ................G ....... 618 533-9010
  Centralia  (G-3406)
Chevron Commercial Inc ......................G ....... 618 654-5555
  Highland  (G-11779)
Clark Caster Co ....................................G ....... 708 366-1913
  Forest Park  (G-10238)

Conveyors Plus Inc ...............................G ....... 708 361-1512
  Orland Park  (G-16849)
ED Etnyre & Co .....................................B ....... 815 732-2116
  Oregon  (G-16822)
Freight Car Services Inc .......................B ....... 217 443-4106
  Danville  (G-7722)
Green Valley Mfg III Inc ........................E ....... 217 864-4125
  Mount Zion  (G-15452)
H & B Machine Corporation .................E ....... 312 829-4850
  Chicago  (G-5017)
H R Slater Co Inc .................................F ....... 312 666-1855
  Chicago  (G-5023)
Handling Systems Inc ..........................E ....... 708 352-1213
  La Grange  (G-12735)
Henderson Products Inc .......................G ....... 847 515-3482
  Huntley  (G-12144)
Hendrickson Usa LLC ..........................C ....... 630 874-9700
  Itasca  (G-12274)
Hyster-Yale Group Inc ..........................E ....... 217 443-7416
  Danville  (G-7736)
I80 Equipment LLC ..............................D ....... 309 949-3701
  Colona  (G-7343)
Illinois Lift Equipment Inc .....................E ....... 888 745-0577
  West Chicago  (G-21717)
It Transportation Company ...................F ....... 773 383-5073
  Chicago  (G-5245)
J W Todd Co ..........................................G ....... 630 406-5715
  Aurora  (G-1173)
Jcb Inc ...................................................G ....... 912 704-2995
  Aurora  (G-1037)
Jeffrey Elevator Co Inc .........................F ....... 847 524-2400
  Schaumburg  (G-19587)
Lanco International Inc .........................B ....... 708 596-5200
  Hazel Crest  (G-11709)
Littell LLC ..............................................G ....... 630 916-6662
  Schaumburg  (G-19620)
M&J Hauling Inc ....................................G ....... 312 342-6596
  Chicago  (G-5590)
Mailbox International Inc ......................G ....... 847 541-8466
  Wheeling  (G-22097)
Manitex International Inc ......................C ....... 708 430-7500
  Bridgeview  (G-2506)
Marvel Industries Incorporated ............G ....... 847 325-2930
  Buffalo Grove  (G-2732)
MHS Ltd .................................................F ....... 773 736-3333
  Chicago  (G-5716)
Mike Simon Trucking LLC ....................G ....... 618 659-8755
  Edwardsville  (G-8809)
Neuero Corporation ..............................F ....... 630 231-9020
  West Chicago  (G-21750)
New Cie Inc ...........................................G ....... 815 224-1511
  Peru  (G-17522)
Pools Welding Inc .................................G ....... 309 787-2083
  Milan  (G-14798)
Preflight LLC .........................................G ....... 312 935-2804
  Chicago  (G-6176)
Sam Solutions Inc .................................G ....... 708 594-0480
  Summit Argo  (G-20765)
Sardee Industries Inc ...........................G ....... 630 824-4200
  Lisle  (G-13654)
STI Holdings Inc ....................................F ....... 630 789-2713
  Burr Ridge  (G-2882)
Synergy Power Group LLC ..................E ....... 618 247-3200
  Sandoval  (G-19359)
T & E Enterprises Herscher Inc ............F ....... 815 426-2761
  Herscher  (G-11763)
Tewell Bros Machine Inc ......................F ....... 217 253-6303
  Tuscola  (G-21025)
Transco Railway Products Inc ..............D ....... 419 562-1031
  Chicago  (G-6760)
Triple B Manufacturing Co Inc ..............G ....... 618 566-2888
  Mascoutah  (G-14360)
Universal Feeder Inc ............................G ....... 815 633-0752
  Machesney Park  (G-14116)
Vactor Manufacturing Inc .....................A ....... 815 672-3171
  Streator  (G-20710)
William W Meyer and Sons ..................D ....... 847 918-0111
  Libertyville  (G-13402)

## TRUCKS, INDL: Wholesalers

Hoist Liftruck Mfg Inc ...........................G ....... 708 458-2200
  Bedford Park  (G-1555)
Hovi Industries Incorporated ................E ....... 815 512-7500
  Bolingbrook  (G-2316)

## TRUCKS: Forklift

A Lift Above Inc ....................................G ....... 630 758-1023
  Elmhurst  (G-9829)
F and S Enterprises Plainfield .............G ....... 815 439-9655
  Plainfield  (G-17597)

Grant J Grapperhaus ...........................G ....... 618 410-4428
  Highland  (G-11786)
Hoist Liftruck Mfg Inc ...........................G ....... 708 458-2200
  Bedford Park  (G-1555)
Integrity Material Hdlg Svcs .................G ....... 847 669-6233
  Huntley  (G-12150)
Komatsu Forklift USA LLC ...................E ....... 847 437-5800
  Rolling Meadows  (G-18738)
Mh Equipment Company .....................D ....... 217 443-7210
  Danville  (G-7755)
Pwf .........................................................G ....... 815 967-0218
  Rockford  (G-18545)
Schaeff Lift Truck Inc ...........................E ....... 708 430-5301
  Bridgeview  (G-2527)
Spec Check LLC ...................................G ....... 773 270-0003
  Mundelein  (G-15559)
Specialized Liftruck Svcs LLC ..............F ....... 708 552-2705
  Bedford Park  (G-1585)
Systems Equipment Services ..............G ....... 708 535-1273
  Oak Forest  (G-16590)
Tri County Lift Trucks Inc .....................G ....... 847 838-0183
  Antioch  (G-659)

## TRUCKS: Indl

Aidar Express Inc .................................G ....... 773 757-3447
  Chicago  (G-3785)
Always There Express Corp .................E ....... 773 931-3744
  Downers Grove  (G-8386)
C C P Express Inc ................................G ....... 773 315-0317
  Berwyn  (G-2058)
Dicom Transportation Group LP ..........G ....... 312 255-4800
  Chicago  (G-4596)
Edward J Warren Jr .............................G ....... 630 882-8817
  Yorkville  (G-22657)
Lexpress Inc .........................................G ....... 773 517-7095
  Prospect Heights  (G-17783)
Tarnow Logistics Inc ............................G ....... 773 844-3203
  Melrose Park  (G-14700)
Tdr Express Inc ....................................G ....... 224 805-0070
  Chicago  (G-6681)
Triad Trucking LLC ...............................G ....... 847 833-9276
  Elk Grove Village  (G-9792)
Yusraa Inc .............................................G ....... 312 608-1916
  Dolton  (G-8378)

## TRUSSES & FRAMING: Prefabricated Metal

Chicago Panel & Truss Inc ...................E ....... 630 870-1300
  Aurora  (G-1129)
Unistrut International Corp ...................C ....... 800 882-5543
  Harvey  (G-11679)

## TRUSSES: Wood, Floor

Alexander Lumber Co ..........................G ....... 815 754-1000
  Cortland  (G-7383)
Lumberyard Suppliers Inc ....................E ....... 217 965-4911
  Virden  (G-21298)
Okaw Truss Inc .....................................B ....... 217 543-3371
  Arthur  (G-915)
Rehkemper & Sons Inc ........................E ....... 618 526-2269
  Breese  (G-2447)

## TRUSSES: Wood, Roof

Anderson Truss Company ....................G ....... 618 982-9228
  Pittsburg  (G-17559)
Atlas Building Components Inc ............E ....... 618 639-0222
  Jerseyville  (G-12418)
Atlas Components Inc ..........................E ....... 815 332-4904
  Cherry Valley  (G-3638)
Bear Creek Truss Inc ...........................E ....... 217 543-3329
  Tuscola  (G-21016)
Cedar Creek LLC ..................................E ....... 618 797-1220
  Granite City  (G-11269)
Jesse B Holt Inc ....................................D ....... 618 783-3075
  Newton  (G-15942)
Southern Truss Inc ...............................E ....... 618 252-8144
  Harrisburg  (G-11604)
Tempo Wood Products Inc ...................D ....... 815 568-7315
  Marengo  (G-14242)
Triumph Truss & Steel Company ..........F ....... 815 522-6000
  Elgin  (G-9216)
Truss Components Inc .........................F ....... 800 678-7877
  Columbia  (G-7365)
W Kost Manufacturing Co Inc ..............C ....... 847 428-0600
  Chicago  (G-6919)

# PRODUCT SECTION

# TURKEY PROCESSING & SLAUGHTERING

### TRUST MANAGEMENT SVCS: Personal Investment

Jaffee Investment Partnr LP .................. C ....... 312 321-1515
Chicago *(G-5270)*

### TUB CONTAINERS: Plastic

R and R Brokerage Co .................. C ....... 847 438-4600
Lake Zurich *(G-13121)*

### TUBE & TUBING FABRICATORS

Acrofab .................................................. G ....... 630 350-7941
Bensenville *(G-1816)*
Alconix Usa Inc ..................................... G ....... 847 717-7407
Elk Grove Village *(G-9284)*
Alert Tubing Fabricators Inc ................ G ....... 815 633-5065
Loves Park *(G-13917)*
Alert Tubing Fabricators Inc ................ G ....... 847 253-7237
Schaumburg *(G-19429)*
Bessco Tube Bending Pipe Fabg ........ G ....... 708 339-3977
South Holland *(G-20251)*
Boyce Industries Inc ............................. F ....... 708 345-0455
Melrose Park *(G-14604)*
Cain Tubular Products Inc .................. G ....... 630 584-5330
Saint Charles *(G-19149)*
Chicago Tube and Iron Company ....... E ....... 815 834-2500
Romeoville *(G-18810)*
Cortube Products Co ........................... G ....... 708 429-6700
Tinley Park *(G-20903)*
D & W Mfg Co Inc ................................. E ....... 773 533-1542
Chicago *(G-4536)*
Dove Steel Inc ....................................... F ....... 815 588-3772
Lockport *(G-13712)*
Fulton Metal Works Inc ........................ G ....... 217 476-8223
Ashland *(G-926)*
Leading Edge Group Inc ...................... C ....... 815 316-3500
Rockford *(G-18464)*
Metamora Industries LLC .................... E ....... 309 367-2368
Metamora *(G-14745)*
Parker Fabrication Inc .......................... E ....... 309 266-8413
Morton *(G-15174)*
Pekay Machine & Engrg Co Inc .......... F ....... 312 829-5530
Chicago *(G-6098)*
Peoria Tube Forming Corp .................. D ....... 309 822-0274
Morton *(G-15176)*
Ptc Tubular Products LLC ................... C ....... 815 692-4900
Fairbury *(G-10131)*
Sharlen Electric Co ............................... E ....... 773 721-0700
Chicago *(G-6489)*
Strait-O-Flex ........................................... G ....... 815 965-2625
Stillman Valley *(G-20628)*
Tech-Weld Inc ........................................ F ....... 630 365-3000
Elburn *(G-8913)*
Tubular Steel Inc ................................... G ....... 630 515-5000
Westmont *(G-21926)*
Vindee Industries Inc ........................... E ....... 815 469-3300
Frankfort *(G-10375)*
Whitley Products Inc ........................... F ....... 574 267-7114
Chicago *(G-6975)*
Zeman Mfg Co ....................................... E ....... 630 960-2300
Lisle *(G-13679)*

### TUBES: Extruded Or Drawn, Aluminum

Penn Aluminum Intl LLC ..................... C ....... 618 684-2146
Murphysboro *(G-15579)*

### TUBES: Hard Rubber

Traeyne Corporation ............................ G ....... 309 936-7878
Atkinson *(G-945)*

### TUBES: Paper

Armbrust Paper Tubes Inc .................. E ....... 773 586-3232
Chicago *(G-3945)*
Caraustar Industrial and Con .............. D ....... 217 323-5225
Beardstown *(G-1521)*
Chicago Mailing Tube Company ........ E ....... 312 243-6050
Chicago *(G-4330)*
Illiana Cores Inc .................................... E ....... 618 586-9800
Palestine *(G-17093)*
Rolled Edge Inc .................................... E ....... 773 283-9500
Chicago *(G-6385)*

### TUBES: Paper Or Fiber, Chemical Or Electrical Uses

Precision Paper Tube Company ......... E ....... 847 537-4250
Wheeling *(G-22128)*

### TUBES: Steel & Iron

Korhumel Inc ......................................... G ....... 847 330-0335
Schaumburg *(G-19604)*
Metal-Matic Inc ..................................... C ....... 708 594-7553
Bedford Park *(G-1562)*
Modern Tube LLC ................................. G ....... 877 848-3300
Bloomingdale *(G-2118)*
Phillips & Johnston Inc ....................... F ....... 815 778-3355
Lyndon *(G-14014)*
Ptc Tubular Products LLC ................... C ....... 815 692-4900
Fairbury *(G-10131)*
SE Steel Inc ........................................... G ....... 847 350-9618
Antioch *(G-654)*

### TUBES: Television

King S Court Exterior ........................... G ....... 630 904-4305
Naperville *(G-15812)*
Zenith Electronics Corporation .......... E ....... 847 941-8000
Lincolnshire *(G-13496)*

### TUBES: Traveling Wave

Teledyne Monitor Labs Inc ................. G ....... 303 792-3300
Chicago *(G-6691)*

### TUBES: Wrought, Welded Or Lock Joint

Independence Tube Corporation ....... D ....... 708 496-0380
Chicago *(G-5173)*
Metal-Matic Inc ..................................... C ....... 708 594-7553
Bedford Park *(G-1562)*

### TUBING, COLD-DRAWN: Mech Or Hypodermic Sizes, Stainless

Kroh-Wagner Inc ................................... E ....... 773 252-2031
Chicago *(G-5412)*

### TUBING: Copper

Cerro Flow Products LLC .................... C ....... 618 337-6000
Sauget *(G-19385)*
Midwest Model Aircraft Co .................. F ....... 773 229-0740
Chicago *(G-5747)*

### TUBING: Electrical Use, Quartz

Ghp Group Inc ...................................... E ....... 847 324-5900
Niles *(G-15983)*

### TUBING: Flexible, Metallic

RF Mau Co .............................................. F ....... 847 329-9731
Lincolnwood *(G-13533)*

### TUBING: Plastic

Jabat Inc ................................................ E ....... 618 392-3010
Olney *(G-16773)*
Springfield Plastics Inc ....................... E ....... 217 438-6167
Auburn *(G-950)*

### TUBING: Seamless

Atlas ABC Corporation ........................ B ....... 773 646-4500
Chicago *(G-3978)*
Atlas Holding Inc .................................. F ....... 773 646-4500
Chicago *(G-3980)*
Plymouth Tube Company .................... E ....... 630 393-3550
Warrenville *(G-21355)*
Plymouth Tube Company .................... D ....... 773 489-0226
Chicago *(G-6141)*
Plymouth Tube Company .................... D ....... 262 642-8201
Warrenville *(G-21356)*

### TUCKING FOR THE TRADE

Alternative TS ....................................... G ....... 618 257-0230
Belleville *(G-1608)*
James Randall ...................................... G ....... 309 444-8765
Washington *(G-21384)*

### TURBINES & TURBINE GENERATOR SET UNITS: Gas, Complete

Caterpillar Inc ....................................... A ....... 309 675-1000
Peoria *(G-17326)*
Caterpillar Inc ....................................... ......... 815 729-5511
Rockdale *(G-18216)*
Caterpillar Inc ....................................... B ....... 888 614-4328
Peoria *(G-17328)*

Caterpillar Inc ....................................... B ....... 309 675-6590
Peoria *(G-17333)*
Solar Turbines Incorporated .............. E ....... 630 527-1700
Naperville *(G-15748)*

### TURBINES & TURBINE GENERATOR SETS

ABB Inc ................................................... F ....... 630 759-7428
Bolingbrook *(G-2276)*
Acciona Windpower N Amer LLC ...... G ....... 319 643-9463
Chicago *(G-3717)*
Action Turbine Repair Svc Inc ........... F ....... 708 924-9601
Summit Argo *(G-20760)*
Angel Wind Energy Inc ........................ G ....... 815 471-2020
Onarga *(G-16808)*
Area Diesel Service Inc ....................... E ....... 217 854-2641
Carlinville *(G-3030)*
B N Blance Enrgy Solutions LLC ...... E ....... 847 287-7466
Palatine *(G-17005)*
Broadwind Energy Inc ......................... C ....... 708 780-4800
Cicero *(G-7181)*
Catching Hydraulics Co Ltd ............... E ....... 708 344-2334
Melrose Park *(G-14606)*
Gds Enterprises .................................... G ....... 217 543-3681
Arthur *(G-901)*
Invenergy .............................................. G ....... 815 795-4964
Marseilles *(G-14312)*
ITT Water & Wastewater USA Inc ...... F ....... 708 342-0484
Tinley Park *(G-20924)*
ITT Water & Wastewater USA Inc ...... G ....... 847 966-3700
Morton Grove *(G-15205)*
Lee Industries Inc ................................ C ....... 847 462-1865
Elk Grove Village *(G-9590)*
Mag-Drive LLC ...................................... G ....... 847 690-0871
Arlington Heights *(G-797)*
Marty Lundeen ...................................... G ....... 630 250-8917
Itasca *(G-12311)*
Nordex Usa Inc ..................................... D ....... 208 383-6500
Chicago *(G-5925)*
Pne Wind Usa Inc ................................. G ....... 773 329-3705
Chicago *(G-6143)*
Rebuilders Enterprises Inc ................. G ....... 708 430-0030
Bridgeview *(G-2523)*
Siemens Energy Inc ............................. C ....... 618 357-6360
Pinckneyville *(G-17552)*
Suzlon Wind Energy Corporation ..... G ....... 773 328-5077
Elgin *(G-9199)*
Suzlon Wind Energy Corporation ..... C ....... 773 328-5077
Chicago *(G-6645)*
Usway Corporation .............................. G ....... 773 338-9688
Chicago *(G-6860)*
VPI Acquisition Company LLC .......... E ....... 630 694-5500
Franklin Park *(G-10624)*

### TURBINES & TURBINE GENERATOR SETS & PARTS

Doncasters Inc ..................................... C ....... 217 465-6500
Paris *(G-17146)*
Ntpwind Power Inc ............................... G ....... 815 345-1931
Crystal Lake *(G-7621)*
Rockwind Venture Partners LLC ....... G ....... 630 881-6664
Rockford *(G-18593)*

### TURBINES: Hydraulic, Complete

Sur-Fit Corporation .............................. E ....... 815 301-5815
Crystal Lake *(G-7656)*

### TURBINES: Steam

Babcock & Wilcox Powr Generatn ..... F ....... 630 719-5120
Downers Grove *(G-8392)*
Energy Parts Solutions Inc ................. F ....... 224 653-9412
Schaumburg *(G-19516)*
University of Chicago .......................... F ....... 773 702-9780
Chicago *(G-6838)*

### TURBO-GENERATORS

Michael Wilton Cstm Homes Inc ....... G ....... 630 508-1200
Willowbrook *(G-22221)*

### TURBO-SUPERCHARGERS: Aircraft

Ihi Turbo America Co ........................... D ....... 217 774-9571
Shelbyville *(G-19908)*

### TURKEY PROCESSING & SLAUGHTERING

Kauffman Poultry Farms Inc .............. F ....... 815 264-3470
Waterman *(G-21407)*

---

Employee Codes: A=Over 500 employees, B=251-500
C=101-250, D=51-100, E=20-50, F=10-19, G=3-9

## TURKEY PROCESSING & SLAUGHTERING

West Liberty Foods LLC .................. B ...... 603 679-2300
  Bolingbrook (G-2382)

### TWINE PRDTS

Unicord Corporation ..................... E ...... 708 385-7999
  Calumet Park (G-2964)

### TYPESETTING SVC

A and K Prtg & Graphic Design ......... G ...... 618 244-3525
  Mount Vernon (G-15396)
A To Z Type & Graphic Inc ............. G ...... 312 587-1887
  Chicago (G-3692)
A+ Printing Co ........................ G ...... 815 968-8181
  Rockford (G-18242)
Acres of Sky Communications .......... G ...... 815 493-2560
  Lanark (G-13149)
Adcraft Printers Inc .................. F ...... 815 932-6432
  Kankakee (G-12601)
All Purpose Prtg & Bus Forms .......... G ...... 708 389-9192
  Alsip (G-431)
All-Ways Quick Print .................. G ...... 708 403-8422
  Orland Park (G-16841)
Allegra Print & Imaging Inc ........... G ...... 847 697-1434
  Elgin (G-8942)
Alphadigital Inc ...................... G ...... 708 482-4488
  La Grange Park (G-12752)
AlphaGraphics ......................... F ...... 630 261-1227
  Oakbrook Terrace (G-16694)
AlphaGraphics Printshops .............. G ...... 630 964-9600
  Lisle (G-13555)
Amboy News ............................ G ...... 815 857-2311
  Amboy (G-597)
American Graphics Network Inc ......... F ...... 847 729-7220
  Glenview (G-11100)
American Quick Print Inc .............. G ...... 847 253-2700
  Wauconda (G-21441)
Apple Graphics Inc .................... G ...... 630 389-2222
  Batavia (G-1416)
Apple Press Inc ....................... G ...... 815 224-1451
  Peru (G-17500)
Apple Printing Center ................. G ...... 630 932-9494
  Addison (G-41)
Apr Graphics Inc ...................... G ...... 847 329-7800
  Skokie (G-19957)
Arby Graphic Service Inc .............. F ...... 847 763-0900
  Niles (G-15961)
Arcadia Press Inc ..................... F ...... 847 451-6390
  Franklin Park (G-10398)
Arch Printing Inc ..................... G ...... 630 966-0235
  Aurora (G-1110)
Artistry Engraving & Embossing ........ G ...... 773 775-4888
  Chicago (G-3957)
Avid of Illinois Inc .................. F ...... 847 698-2775
  Saint Charles (G-19140)
Azusa Inc ............................. G ...... 618 244-6591
  Mount Vernon (G-15399)
B & B Printing Company ................ G ...... 217 285-6072
  Pittsfield (G-17561)
B Allan Graphics Inc .................. F ...... 708 396-1704
  Alsip (G-438)
B F Shaw Printing Company ............. E ...... 815 875-4461
  Princeton (G-17744)
Babak Inc ............................. G ...... 312 419-8686
  Chicago (G-4024)
Bailleu & Bailleu Printing Inc ........ G ...... 309 852-2517
  Kewanee (G-12670)
Bally Foil Graphics Inc ............... G ...... 847 427-1509
  Elk Grove Village (G-9333)
Banner Publications ................... G ...... 309 338-3294
  Cuba (G-7679)
Barnaby Inc ........................... F ...... 815 895-6555
  Sycamore (G-20789)
Baseline Graphics Inc ................. G ...... 630 964-9566
  Downers Grove (G-8395)
Belmonte Printing Co .................. G ...... 847 352-8841
  Schaumburg (G-19459)
Benzinger Printing .................... G ...... 815 784-6560
  Genoa (G-10875)
Bikast Graphics Inc ................... G ...... 847 487-8822
  Wauconda (G-21446)
Biller Press & Manufacturing .......... G ...... 847 395-4111
  Antioch (G-623)
Blazing Color Inc ..................... G ...... 618 826-3001
  Chester (G-3651)
Bond Brothers & Co .................... F ...... 708 442-5510
  Lyons (G-14032)
Brads Printing Inc .................... G ...... 847 662-0447
  Waukegan (G-21531)
Branstiter Printing Co ................ G ...... 217 245-6533
  Jacksonville (G-12381)

Budget Printing Center ................ G ...... 618 655-1636
  Edwardsville (G-8793)
Cameron Printing Inc .................. G ...... 630 231-3301
  West Chicago (G-21677)
Cardinal Colorprint Prtg Corp ......... E ...... 630 467-1000
  Itasca (G-12241)
Carson Printing Inc ................... G ...... 847 836-0900
  East Dundee (G-8629)
Carter Printing Co Inc ................ G ...... 217 227-4464
  Farmersville (G-10183)
Century Printing ...................... G ...... 618 632-2486
  O Fallon (G-16465)
Cenveo Inc ............................ G ...... 217 243-4258
  Jacksonville (G-12383)
Challenge Printers .................... G ...... 773 252-0212
  Chicago (G-4285)
Charleston Graphics Inc ............... G ...... 
  Charleston (G-3594)
Chicago Citizen Newsppr Group ......... F ...... 773 783-1251
  Chicago (G-4311)
Chicago Mltlingua Graphics Inc ........ F ...... 847 386-7187
  Northfield (G-16397)
Christopher R Cline Prtg Ltd .......... F ...... 847 981-0500
  Elk Grove Village (G-9372)
Cifuentes Luis & Nicole Inc ........... G ...... 847 490-3660
  Schaumburg (G-19472)
Cjs Printing .......................... G ...... 309 968-6585
  Manito (G-14172)
Clementi Printing Inc ................. G ...... 773 622-0795
  Chicago (G-4401)
Clyde Printing Company ................ F ...... 773 847-5900
  Chicago (G-4410)
Cmb Printing Inc ...................... F ...... 630 323-1110
  Burr Ridge (G-2830)
Color Smiths Inc ...................... G ...... 708 562-0061
  Elmhurst (G-9853)
Commercial Copy Printing Ctr .......... F ...... 847 981-8590
  Elk Grove Village (G-9384)
Commercial Fast Print ................. G ...... 815 673-1196
  Streator (G-20685)
Composing Room Inc .................... G ...... 708 795-7523
  Berwyn (G-2059)
Conrad Press Ltd ...................... G ...... 
  Columbia (G-7356)
Copy Express Inc ...................... F ...... 815 338-7161
  Woodstock (G-22555)
Copy Mat Printing ..................... G ...... 309 452-1392
  Bloomington (G-2155)
Copy Service Inc ...................... G ...... 815 758-1151
  Dekalb (G-8079)
Copy-Mor Inc .......................... E ...... 312 666-4000
  Elmhurst (G-9856)
Copyset Shop Inc ...................... G ...... 847 768-2679
  Des Plaines (G-8176)
Corwin Printing ....................... G ...... 618 263-3936
  Mount Carmel (G-15263)
Cpr Printing Inc ...................... F ...... 630 377-8420
  Geneva (G-10821)
Craftsmen Printing .................... G ...... 217 283-9574
  Hoopeston (G-12108)
Crossmark Printing Inc ................ F ...... 708 532-8263
  Tinley Park (G-20906)
Custom Direct Inc ..................... F ...... 630 529-1936
  Roselle (G-18938)
Custom Graphics ....................... G ...... 309 828-0717
  Bloomington (G-2158)
D E Asbury Inc ........................ G ...... 217 222-0617
  Hamilton (G-11532)
D L V Printing Service Inc ............ F ...... 773 626-1661
  Chicago (G-4537)
Dale K Brown .......................... G ...... 815 338-0222
  Woodstock (G-22558)
Darnall Printing ...................... G ...... 309 827-7212
  Bloomington (G-2161)
David H Vander Ploeg .................. G ...... 708 331-7700
  South Holland (G-20260)
DE Asbury Inc ......................... E ...... 217 222-0617
  Quincy (G-17820)
Deluxe Johnson ........................ F ...... 847 635-7200
  Des Plaines (G-8182)
Demis Printing Inc .................... G ...... 773 282-9128
  Park Ridge (G-17189)
Denor Graphics Inc .................... F ...... 847 364-1130
  Elk Grove Village (G-9423)
Des Plaines Journal Inc ............... D ...... 847 299-5511
  Des Plaines (G-8184)
Design Graphics Inc ................... G ...... 815 462-3323
  New Lenox (G-15875)
Diamond Graphics of Berwyn ............ G ...... 708 749-2500
  Berwyn (G-2060)

Donnas House of Type Inc .............. G ...... 217 522-5050
  Athens (G-938)
Donnells Printing & Off Pdts .......... G ...... 815 842-6541
  Pontiac (G-17698)
DOT Black Group ....................... G ...... 312 204-8000
  Chicago (G-4634)
Dupli Group Inc ....................... F ...... 773 549-5285
  Chicago (G-4654)
E & H Graphic Service ................. G ...... 708 748-5656
  Matteson (G-14371)
East Moline Herald Print Inc .......... G ...... 309 755-5224
  East Moline (G-8678)
Edwardsville Publishing Co ............ D ...... 618 656-4700
  Edwardsville (G-8799)
Einstein Crest ........................ G ...... 847 965-7791
  Niles (G-15977)
Eklunds Typesetting & Prtg LLC ........ G ...... 630 924-0057
  Roselle (G-18940)
Elgin Instant Print ................... G ...... 847 931-9006
  Elgin (G-9024)
Elmhurst Enterprise Group Inc ......... G ...... 847 228-5945
  Arlington Heights (G-749)
Everything Xclusive ................... G ...... 309 370-7450
  Peoria (G-17358)
F Weber Printing Co Inc ............... G ...... 815 468-6152
  Manteno (G-14183)
Fedex Office & Print Svcs Inc ......... F ...... 847 475-8650
  Evanston (G-10036)
Fedex Office & Print Svcs Inc ......... G ...... 815 229-0033
  Rockford (G-18380)
Fedex Office & Print Svcs Inc ......... G ...... 847 329-9464
  Lincolnwood (G-13510)
Fedex Office & Print Svcs Inc ......... E ...... 847 729-3030
  Glenview (G-11124)
Fedex Office & Print Svcs Inc ......... G ...... 847 459-8008
  Buffalo Grove (G-2693)
Fedex Office & Print Svcs Inc ......... E ...... 708 452-0149
  Elmwood Park (G-9970)
Fedex Office & Print Svcs Inc ......... G ...... 847 823-9360
  Park Ridge (G-17193)
Fedex Office & Print Svcs Inc ......... F ...... 630 894-1800
  Bloomingdale (G-2108)
Fedex Office & Print Svcs Inc ......... F ...... 312 670-4460
  Chicago (G-4831)
Fedex Office & Print Svcs Inc ......... E ...... 309 685-4093
  Peoria (G-17359)
Fine Line Printing .................... G ...... 773 582-9709
  Chicago (G-4846)
First Impression of Chicago ........... G ...... 773 224-3434
  Chicago (G-4849)
Fisheye Services Incorporated ......... G ...... 773 942-6314
  Chicago (G-4852)
Flash Printing Inc .................... G ...... 847 288-9101
  Franklin Park (G-10470)
Fleetwood Press Inc ................... G ...... 708 485-6811
  Brookfield (G-2632)
FM Graphic Impressions Inc ............ E ...... 630 897-8788
  Aurora (G-1153)
French Studio Ltd ..................... G ...... 618 942-5328
  Herrin (G-11748)
G F Printing .......................... G ...... 618 797-0576
  Granite City (G-11278)
Gamma Alpha Visual .................... G ...... 847 956-0633
  Elk Grove Village (G-9496)
Gatehouse Media LLC ................... B ...... 217 788-1300
  Springfield (G-20445)
Gazette Printing Co ................... G ...... 309 389-2811
  Glasford (G-10951)
Gorman & Associates ................... G ...... 309 691-9087
  Peoria (G-17373)
Gossett Printing Inc .................. G ...... 618 548-2583
  Salem (G-19335)
Graphic Image Corporation ............. F ...... 312 829-7800
  Chicago (G-4989)
Graphics Group LLC .................... D ...... 708 867-5500
  Chicago (G-4992)
Graphics Plus Inc ..................... F ...... 630 968-9073
  Lisle (G-13597)
Grasso Graphics Inc ................... G ...... 708 489-2060
  Alsip (G-465)
Greenup Press Inc ..................... G ...... 217 923-3704
  Greenup (G-11383)
Griffith Solutions Inc ................ G ...... 847 384-1810
  Park Ridge (G-17201)
Group 329 LLC ......................... G ...... 312 828-0200
  Chicago (G-5005)
Gsi Technologies LLC .................. D ...... 630 325-8181
  Burr Ridge (G-2847)
Hawthorne Press Inc ................... G ...... 847 587-0582
  Spring Grove (G-20336)

## PRODUCT SECTION — TYPESETTING SVC

| Company | Code | Phone |
|---|---|---|
| Heart Printing Inc, Arlington Heights (G-764) | G | 847 259-2100 |
| Heritage Media Svcs Co of Ill, Summit Argo (G-20763) | G | 708 594-9340 |
| Heritage Press Inc, Libertyville (G-13330) | G | 847 362-9699 |
| Heritage Printing, Prophetstown (G-17770) | G | 815 537-2372 |
| Highland Printers, Highland (G-11791) | G | 618 654-5880 |
| House of Graphics, Carol Stream (G-3168) | E | 630 682-0810 |
| Hq Printers Inc, Chicago (G-5125) | G | 312 782-2020 |
| Hub Printing Company Inc, Rochelle (G-18094) | F | 815 562-7057 |
| Huston-Patterson Corporation, Decatur (G-7890) | D | 217 429-5161 |
| Ideal Advertising & Printing, Rockford (G-18426) | F | 815 965-1713 |
| Illinois Office Sup Elect Prtg, Ottawa (G-16962) | E | 815 434-0186 |
| Image Print Inc, Streator (G-20691) | G | 815 672-1068 |
| Informative Systems Inc, Springfield (G-20457) | F | 217 523-8422 |
| Ink Spot Printing, Chicago (G-5194) | G | 773 528-0288 |
| Ink Well Printing, Peru (G-17514) | G | 815 224-1366 |
| Ink Well Printing & Design Ltd, Schaumburg (G-19566) | G | 847 923-8060 |
| Inky Printers, Freeport (G-10668) | G | 815 235-3700 |
| Innovtive Design Graphics Corp, Evanston (G-10057) | G | 847 475-7772 |
| Insty Prints Palatine Inc, Palatine (G-17042) | F | 847 963-0000 |
| Instyprints of Waukegan Inc, Waukegan (G-21571) | G | 847 336-5599 |
| International Graphics & Assoc, Saint Charles (G-19199) | F | 630 584-2248 |
| J & J Mr Quick Print Inc, Chicago (G-5251) | G | 773 767-7776 |
| J F Wagner Printing Co, Northbrook (G-16280) | G | 847 564-0017 |
| J Oshana & Son Printing, Chicago (G-5261) | G | 773 283-8311 |
| J P Printing Inc, Chicago (G-5262) | G | 773 626-5222 |
| James Ray Monroe Corporation, Centralia (G-3420) | F | 618 532-4575 |
| Jay Printing, Palatine (G-17046) | G | 847 934-6103 |
| Jds Printing Inc, Glendale Heights (G-11037) | G | 630 208-1195 |
| Johns-Byrne Company, Niles (G-15992) | D | 847 583-3100 |
| Johnson Press America Inc, Pontiac (G-17704) | E | 815 844-5161 |
| Josco Inc, Chicago (G-5326) | G | 708 867-7189 |
| Josephs Printing Service, Glenview (G-11154) | G | 847 724-4429 |
| Jph Enterprises Inc, Des Plaines (G-8217) | G | 847 390-0900 |
| July 25th Corporation, Bloomington (G-2186) | F | 309 664-6444 |
| Just Your Type Inc, Evanston (G-10060) | G | 847 864-8890 |
| K & M Printing Company Inc, Schaumburg (G-19595) | D | 847 884-1100 |
| K R O Enterprises Ltd, Moline (G-14949) | G | 309 797-2213 |
| Kelly Printing Co Inc, Danville (G-7741) | E | 217 443-1792 |
| Kendall Printing Co, Yorkville (G-22663) | G | 630 553-9200 |
| Kenilworth Press Incorporated, Wilmette (G-22256) | G | 847 256-5210 |
| Kens Quick Print Inc, Highland Park (G-11849) | F | 847 831-4410 |
| Kevin Kewney, Quincy (G-17844) | G | 217 228-7444 |
| Key One Graphics Services Inc, West Dundee (G-21799) | G | |
| KK Stevens Publishing Co, Astoria (G-934) | E | 309 329-2151 |
| Klein Printing Inc, Chicago (G-5387) | G | 773 235-2121 |
| Klh Printing Corp, Wheeling (G-22086) | G | 847 459-0115 |
| Korea Times, Glenview (G-11157) | D | 847 626-0388 |
| LAC Enterprises Inc, Crystal Lake (G-7601) | G | 815 455-5044 |
| Lake County Press Inc, Waukegan (G-21580) | C | 847 336-4333 |
| Lake Shore Printing, Skokie (G-20024) | G | 847 679-4110 |
| Lans Printing Inc, Lynwood (G-14021) | G | 708 895-6226 |
| Laser Expressions Ltd, Buffalo Grove (G-2721) | G | 847 419-9600 |
| Legend Promotions, Lake Zurich (G-13095) | G | 847 438-3528 |
| Leonard Emerson, Divernon (G-8316) | G | 217 628-3441 |
| Link-Letters Ltd, Wheeling (G-22094) | G | 847 459-1199 |
| Lists & Letters, Wheeling (G-22095) | F | 847 520-5207 |
| Lithuanian Catholic Press, Chicago (G-5519) | G | 773 585-9500 |
| Lloyd Midwest Graphics, Machesney Park (G-14089) | G | 815 282-8828 |
| Lynns Printing Co, Alton (G-583) | G | 618 465-7701 |
| M & R Printing, Rolling Meadows (G-18742) | G | 847 398-2500 |
| M M Marketing, Crystal Lake (G-7603) | G | 815 459-7968 |
| M O W Printing Inc, Collinsville (G-7331) | F | 618 345-5525 |
| Macoupin County Enquirer Inc, Carlinville (G-3042) | E | 217 854-2534 |
| Marcus Press, Bloomingdale (G-2115) | G | 630 351-1857 |
| Mark Twain Press Inc, Mundelein (G-15523) | G | 847 255-2700 |
| Mason City Banner Times, Mason City (G-14365) | F | 217 482-3276 |
| Mattoon Printing Center, Mattoon (G-14400) | G | 217 234-3100 |
| Mc Adams Multigraphics Inc, Oak Brook (G-16539) | G | 630 990-1707 |
| McGrath Press Inc, Crystal Lake (G-7607) | E | 815 356-5246 |
| Mencarini Enterprises Inc, Rockford (G-18491) | G | 815 398-9565 |
| Metro Printing & Pubg Inc, Millstadt (G-14829) | F | 618 476-9587 |
| Metropolitan Graphic Arts Inc, Gurnee (G-11471) | G | 847 566-9502 |
| Mid City Printing Service, Chicago (G-5725) | G | 773 777-5400 |
| Midwest Outdoors Ltd, Burr Ridge (G-2867) | G | 630 887-7722 |
| Minuteman Press, Countryside (G-7437) | G | 630 541-9122 |
| Minuteman Press, Lombard (G-13827) | G | 630 279-0438 |
| Minuteman Press, Saint Charles (G-19223) | G | 630 584-7383 |
| Minuteman Press of Rockford, Loves Park (G-13967) | G | 815 633-2992 |
| Minuteman Press of Waukegan, Gurnee (G-11474) | G | 847 244-6288 |
| Multicopy Corp, Northfield (G-16410) | G | 847 446-7015 |
| N & M Type & Design, Elmhurst (G-9914) | G | 630 834-3696 |
| N Bujarski Inc, Schaumburg (G-19660) | G | 847 884-1600 |
| N P D Inc, Oak Lawn (G-16636) | G | 708 424-6788 |
| Negs & Litho Inc, Chicago (G-5881) | G | 847 647-7770 |
| New City Communications, Chicago (G-5891) | E | 312 243-8786 |
| New Life Printing & Publishing, Algonquin (G-402) | G | 847 658-4111 |
| Newell & Haney Inc, Belleville (G-1660) | F | 618 277-3660 |
| Northwest Premier Printing, Chicago (G-5940) | G | 773 736-1882 |
| Northwest Printing Inc, Harvard (G-11642) | G | 815 943-7977 |
| Nu-Art Printing, Centralia (G-3425) | G | 618 533-9971 |
| Off The Press, Plainfield (G-17634) | G | 815 436-9612 |
| Office Assistants Inc, Oak Lawn (G-16637) | G | 708 346-0505 |
| Okawville Times, Okawville (G-16754) | G | 618 243-5563 |
| Olde Print Shoppe Inc, Olney (G-16786) | G | 618 395-3833 |
| Omni Craft Inc, Lockport (G-13736) | G | 815 838-1285 |
| On Time Printing and Finishing, Hillside (G-11929) | G | 708 544-4500 |
| Osborne Publications Inc, Decatur (G-7924) | G | 217 422-9702 |
| P & S Cochran Printers Inc, Peoria (G-17421) | E | 309 691-6668 |
| P H C Enterprises Inc, Vernon Hills (G-21186) | G | 847 816-7373 |
| P P Graphics Inc, Westchester (G-21852) | G | 708 343-2530 |
| Papyrus Press Inc, Chicago (G-6074) | F | 773 342-0700 |
| Park Printing Inc, Palos Hills (G-17120) | G | 708 430-4878 |
| Patrick Impressions LLC, Lemont (G-13250) | G | 630 257-9336 |
| Patton Printing and Graphics, Effingham (G-8852) | G | 217 347-0220 |
| Perma Graphics Printers, New Lenox (G-15901) | G | 815 485-6955 |
| Perryco Inc, Plainfield (G-17638) | F | 815 436-2431 |
| Photo Graphic Design Service, Streator (G-20700) | G | 815 672-4417 |
| Pinney Printing Company, Sterling (G-20604) | E | 815 626-2727 |
| PIP Printing Inc, Frankfort (G-10349) | G | 815 464-0075 |
| Poets Study Inc, Chicago (G-6147) | G | 773 286-1355 |
| Precision Language & Graphics, Schaumburg (G-19700) | G | 847 413-1688 |
| Preferred Printing Service, Chicago (G-6175) | G | 312 421-2343 |
| Prime Market Targeting Inc, Frankfort (G-10353) | E | 815 469-4555 |
| Print & Design Services LLC, Bannockburn (G-1264) | G | 847 317-9001 |
| Print King Inc, Oak Lawn (G-16641) | G | 708 499-3777 |
| Print Turnaround Inc, Arlington Heights (G-822) | F | 847 228-1762 |
| Printed Impressions Inc, Villa Park (G-21279) | G | 773 604-8585 |
| Printed Word Inc, Evanston (G-10091) | G | 847 328-1511 |
| Printing By Joseph, Mokena (G-14898) | G | 708 479-2669 |
| Printing Craftsmen of Joliet, Joliet (G-12555) | G | 815 254-3982 |
| Printing Etc Inc, Rochelle (G-18102) | G | 815 562-6151 |
| Printing Plus of Roselle Inc, Roselle (G-18963) | G | 630 893-0410 |
| Printing Press of Joliet Inc, Joliet (G-12556) | G | 815 725-0018 |
| Printing Source Inc, Morton Grove (G-15228) | G | 773 588-2930 |
| Printing Works Inc, Elk Grove Village (G-9698) | G | 847 860-1920 |
| Printmeisters Inc, Lansing (G-13180) | G | 708 474-8400 |
| Printsource Plus Inc, Blue Island (G-2265) | G | 708 389-6252 |
| Prism Commercial Printing Ctrs, Chicago (G-6199) | G | 630 834-4443 |
| Pro-Type Printing Inc, Paxton (G-17244) | G | 217 379-4715 |
| Progress Printing Corporation, Chicago (G-6210) | E | 773 927-0123 |
| Quad City Press, Moline (G-14965) | F | 309 764-8142 |
| Quality Quickprint Inc, Joliet (G-12560) | G | 815 439-3430 |
| Quality Quickprint Inc, Lockport (G-13740) | F | 815 838-1784 |
| Quickprinters, Macomb (G-14130) | G | 309 833-5250 |
| Quinn Print Inc, Park Ridge (G-17218) | G | 847 823-9100 |

Employee Codes: A=Over 500 employees, B=251-500, C=101-250, D=51-100, E=20-50, F=10-19, G=3-9

2017 Harris Illinois Industrial Directory

## TYPESETTING SVC

R N R Photographers Inc .................. G ...... 708 453-1868
  River Grove (G-18013)
Rapid Circular Press Inc ................. F ...... 312 421-5611
  Chicago (G-6290)
Redline Press .................................. G ...... 630 690-9828
  Lisle (G-13650)
Remke Printing Inc ......................... G ...... 847 520-7300
  Wheeling (G-22137)
Reprographics ................................ G ...... 815 477-1018
  Crystal Lake (G-7638)
Review Graphics Inc ...................... G ...... 815 623-2570
  Roscoe (G-18913)
Review Printing Co Inc ................... G ...... 309 788-7094
  Rock Island (G-18199)
Rider Dickerson Inc ....................... D ...... 312 427-2926
  Bellwood (G-1718)
Rightway Printing Inc ..................... F ...... 630 790-0444
  Glendale Heights (G-11064)
Rite-TEC Communications .............. G ...... 815 459-7712
  Crystal Lake (G-7643)
River Bend Printing ........................ G ...... 217 324-6056
  Litchfield (G-13696)
Ro-Web Inc .................................... G ...... 309 688-2155
  Peoria (G-17444)
Rodin Enterprises Inc ..................... G ...... 847 412-1370
  Wheeling (G-22142)
Rohrer Graphic Arts Inc .................. F ...... 630 832-3434
  Elmhurst (G-9930)
Rohrer Litho Inc .............................. G ...... 630 833-6610
  Elmhurst (G-9931)
Rose Business Forms & Printing ..... G ...... 618 533-3032
  Centralia (G-3429)
Rrr Graphics & Film Corp ................ G ...... 708 478-4573
  Mokena (G-14901)
Rt Associates Inc ........................... D ...... 847 577-0700
  Wheeling (G-22143)
Rudin Printing Company Inc ........... F ...... 217 528-5111
  Springfield (G-20515)
Rusty & Angela Buzzard ................. G ...... 217 342-9841
  Effingham (G-8857)
S M C Graphics ............................... G ...... 708 754-8973
  Chicago Heights (G-7125)
Salem Times-Commoner Pubg Co ... E ...... 618 548-3330
  Salem (G-19349)
Samecwei Inc ................................. G ...... 630 897-7888
  Aurora (G-1214)
Schellhorn Photo Techniques .......... F ...... 773 267-5141
  Chicago (G-6451)
Schiele Graphics Inc ...................... D ...... 847 434-5455
  Elk Grove Village (G-9731)
Schommer Inc ................................ G ...... 815 344-1404
  McHenry (G-14554)
Sharp Graphics Inc ........................ G ...... 847 966-7000
  Skokie (G-20085)
Shawver Press Inc ......................... G ...... 815 772-4700
  Morrison (G-15148)
Sheer Graphics Inc ........................ G ...... 630 654-4422
  Westmont (G-21920)
Shoreline Graphics Inc ................... G ...... 847 587-4804
  Ingleside (G-12198)
Shree Mahavir Inc .......................... G ...... 312 408-1080
  Chicago (G-6501)
Shree Printing Corp ........................ G ...... 773 267-9500
  Chicago (G-6502)
Sigley Printing & Off Sup Co ........... G ...... 618 997-5304
  Marion (G-14287)
Sir Speedy Printing ........................ G ...... 312 337-0774
  Chicago (G-6518)
Small Newspaper Group ................. C ...... 815 937-3300
  Kankakee (G-12652)
Solid Impressions Inc .................... G ...... 630 543-7300
  Carol Stream (G-3241)
Sommers & Fahrenbach Inc ........... F ...... 773 478-3033
  Chicago (G-6543)
Sons Enterprises ............................ F ...... 847 677-4444
  Skokie (G-20088)
Speedys Quick Print ....................... G ...... 217 431-0510
  Danville (G-7766)
Stark Printing Company .................. G ...... 847 234-8430
  Round Lake (G-19068)
Stearns Printing of Charleston ........ G ...... 217 345-7518
  Charleston (G-3613)
Steve Bortman ................................ G ...... 708 442-1669
  Lyons (G-14046)
Swifty Print .................................... G ...... 630 584-9063
  Saint Charles (G-19276)
T F N W Inc .................................... G ...... 630 584-7383
  Saint Charles (G-19277)
T R Communications Inc ................ F ...... 773 238-3366
  Chicago (G-6663)

Tele-Guia Inc ................................. F ...... 708 656-9800
  Cicero (G-7236)
Tidd Printing Co ............................. G ...... 708 749-1200
  Berwyn (G-2076)
Times Record Company ................. E ...... 309 582-5112
  Aledo (G-373)
Times Republic ............................... E ...... 815 432-5227
  Watseka (G-21431)
Tlm Enterprises Inc ........................ G ...... 815 284-5040
  Dixon (G-8356)
Toledo Democrat ............................. G ...... 217 849-2000
  Toledo (G-20967)
Tower Printing & Design ................. G ...... 630 495-1976
  Lombard (G-13870)
Trenton Sun .................................... G ...... 618 224-9422
  Trenton (G-20998)
Trump Printing Inc ......................... G ...... 217 429-9001
  Decatur (G-7954)
Type Concepts Inc ......................... G ...... 708 361-1005
  Palos Heights (G-17112)
United Lithograph Inc ..................... G ...... 847 803-1700
  Des Plaines (G-8290)
V C P Inc ....................................... E ...... 847 658-5090
  Algonquin (G-409)
Valee Inc ....................................... G ...... 847 364-6464
  Elk Grove Village (G-9804)
Viking Printing & Copying Inc ......... G ...... 312 341-0985
  Chicago (G-6899)
Voris Communication Co Inc .......... C ...... 630 898-4268
  Berkeley (G-2051)
W R Typesetting Co ....................... G ...... 847 966-1315
  Morton Grove (G-15244)
Washburn Graficolor Inc ................ G ...... 630 596-0880
  Naperville (G-15781)
Weakley Printing & Sign Shop ........ G ...... 847 473-4466
  North Chicago (G-16189)
Weber Press Inc ............................ G ...... 773 561-9815
  Chicago (G-6949)
Weimer Design & Print Ltd Inc ....... G ...... 630 393-3334
  Warrenville (G-21368)
Westrock Mwv LLC ........................ E ...... 217 442-2247
  Danville (G-7784)
Woogl Corporation ......................... E ...... 847 806-1160
  Elk Grove Village (G-9816)
World Journal LLC .......................... F ...... 312 842-8005
  Chicago (G-7030)
Wortman Printing Company Inc ...... G ...... 217 347-3775
  Effingham (G-8864)
Yeast Printing Inc .......................... G ...... 309 833-2845
  Macomb (G-14137)

### TYPESETTING SVC: Computer

Breaker Press Co Inc ..................... G ...... 773 927-1666
  Chicago (G-4159)
Case Paluch & Associates Inc ........ G ...... 773 465-0098
  Chicago (G-4248)
Early Bird Advertising Inc .............. G ...... 847 253-1423
  Prospect Heights (G-17777)
Ideal/Mikron Inc ............................. G ...... 847 873-0254
  Mount Prospect (G-15336)
Print Xpress .................................. G ...... 847 677-5555
  Skokie (G-20061)
Tri-Tower Printing Inc .................... G ...... 847 640-6633
  Rolling Meadows (G-18785)
Unicomp Typography Inc ................ G ...... 847 821-0221
  Buffalo Grove (G-2784)

### TYPESETTING SVC: Hand Composition

11th Street Express Prtg Inc .......... F ...... 815 968-0208
  Rockford (G-18235)

### TYPOGRAPHY

Crosstech Communications Inc ...... E ...... 312 382-0111
  Chicago (G-4506)
Henderson Co Inc ........................... F ...... 773 628-7216
  Chicago (G-5070)
JD Pro Productions Inc .................. G ...... 708 485-2126
  Brookfield (G-2636)
Michael Zimmerman ....................... G ...... 847 272-5560
  Northbrook (G-16311)
Village Typographers Inc ................ G ...... 618 235-6756
  Belleville (G-1687)

### ULTRASONIC EQPT: Cleaning, Exc Med & Dental

Fisa North America Inc .................. G ...... 847 593-2080
  Elk Grove Village (G-9478)

Maxi-Vac Inc .................................. G ...... 630 620-6669
  East Dundee (G-8649)

### UMBRELLAS & CANES

Shedrain Corporation ..................... G ...... 708 848-5212
  Oak Park (G-16685)

### UNDERGROUND GOLD MINING

Global Technologies I LLC ............. D ...... 312 255-8350
  Chicago (G-4960)

### UNDERGROUND IRON ORE MINING

Global Technologies I LLC ............. D ...... 312 255-8350
  Chicago (G-4960)

### UNIFORM STORES

Advance Uniform Company ............. F ...... 312 922-1797
  Chicago (G-3765)
Atlas Uniform Company .................. G ...... 312 492-8527
  Chicago (G-3985)
Johnos Inc ..................................... G ...... 630 897-6929
  Aurora (G-1178)
Waldos Sports Corner Inc ............... G ...... 309 688-2425
  Peoria (G-17477)

### UNIT TRAIN LOADING FACILITY, BITUMINOUS OR LIGNITE

Interminal Services ........................ E ...... 773 978-8129
  Chicago (G-5218)

### UNIVERSITY

University of Chicago ..................... G ...... 773 702-7000
  Chicago (G-6837)
University of Chicago ..................... F ...... 773 702-9780
  Chicago (G-6838)

### UNSUPPORTED PLASTICS: Tile

Perfect Circle Projectiles LLC ......... F ...... 847 367-8960
  Lake Forest (G-12942)

### UPHOLSTERY MATERIAL

A D Specialty Sewing ..................... G ...... 847 639-0390
  Fox River Grove (G-10285)

### UPHOLSTERY WORK SVCS

A D Specialty Sewing ..................... G ...... 847 639-0390
  Fox River Grove (G-10285)
Addison Interiors Company ............. F ...... 630 628-1345
  Addison (G-23)
Anees Upholstery ........................... G ...... 312 243-2919
  Chicago (G-3906)
Fehr Cab Interiors .......................... G ...... 815 692-3355
  Fairbury (G-10124)

### URANIUM ORE MINING, NEC

Phosphate Resource Ptrs ............... A ...... 847 739-1200
  Lake Forest (G-12945)

### UREA

I A E Inc ........................................ G ...... 219 882-2400
  Oak Park (G-16670)

### USED BOOK STORES

Half Price Bks Rec Mgzines Inc ...... E ...... 847 588-2286
  Niles (G-15986)

### USED CAR DEALERS

Competitive Edge Opportunities ..... G ...... 815 322-2164
  Lakemoor (G-13143)
I C Dynamics Inc ........................... G ...... 708 922-0501
  Plainfield (G-17608)
Lincoln Green Mazda Inc ................ F ...... 217 391-2400
  Springfield (G-20470)

### USED MERCHANDISE STORES: Art Objects, Antique

International Silver Plating ............. G ...... 847 835-0705
  Glencoe (G-11001)

## PRODUCT SECTION

### USED MERCHANDISE STORES: Clothing & Shoes

Entrigue Designs .................................. G ...... 708 647-6159
 Homewood *(G-12097)*

### USED MERCHANDISE STORES: Office Furniture

Rieke Office Interiors Inc ....................... D ...... 847 622-9711
 Elgin *(G-9165)*

### UTENSILS: Cast Aluminum, Cooking Or Kitchen

Newell Operating Company ................. C ...... 815 235-4171
 Freeport *(G-10675)*
Rome Industries Inc .............................. G ...... 309 691-7120
 Peoria *(G-17448)*
World Kitchen LLC ............................... C ...... 847 233-8600
 Rosemont *(G-19042)*

### UTENSILS: Cast Aluminum, Hospital

Bio Services Inc ................................... G ...... 630 808-2125
 Hillside *(G-11910)*

### UTENSILS: Household, Cooking & Kitchen, Metal

Wki Holding Company Inc .................... D ...... 847 233-8600
 Rosemont *(G-19041)*
World Kitchen LLC ............................... C ...... 847 233-8600
 Rosemont *(G-19042)*

### UTENSILS: Household, Metal, Exc Cast

Kernel Kutter Inc .................................. G ...... 815 877-1515
 Machesney Park *(G-14085)*

### UTILITY TRAILER DEALERS

Knight Bros Inc .................................... E ...... 618 439-9626
 Benton *(G-2033)*

### VACUUM CLEANER STORES

Aerus Electrolux ................................... G ...... 847 949-4222
 Mundelein *(G-15465)*

### VACUUM CLEANERS: Household

Aerotech Inc ........................................ D ...... 618 942-5131
 Energy *(G-9984)*
Dyson Inc ............................................ D ...... 312 469-5950
 Chicago *(G-4660)*
Lee Sauzek .......................................... G ...... 618 539-5815
 Freeburg *(G-10638)*
Wodack Electric Tool Corp .................... F ...... 773 287-9866
 Chicago *(G-7019)*

### VACUUM CLEANERS: Indl Type

Advanage Diversified Pdts Inc ............... F ...... 708 331-8390
 Harvey *(G-11650)*
American Vacuum Co ........................... G ...... 847 674-8383
 Skokie *(G-19951)*
Bissell Inc ............................................ G ...... 815 423-1300
 Elwood *(G-9979)*
Nikro Industries Inc .............................. F ...... 630 530-0558
 Villa Park *(G-21273)*
Powerboss Inc ..................................... C ...... 910 944-2105
 Hampshire *(G-11560)*
Tornado Industries LLC ........................ D ...... 817 551-6507
 West Chicago *(G-21783)*
William W Meyer and Sons ................... D ...... 847 918-0111
 Libertyville *(G-13402)*

### VACUUM PUMPS & EQPT: Laboratory

Leybold USA Inc .................................. E ...... 724 327-5700
 Chicago *(G-5500)*
Vac Serve Inc ...................................... G ...... 224 766-6445
 Skokie *(G-20107)*

### VACUUM SYSTEMS: Air Extraction, Indl

Demarco Industrial Vacuum Corp .......... G ...... 815 344-2222
 Crystal Lake *(G-7567)*
Fna Ip Holdings Inc .............................. D ...... 847 348-1500
 Elk Grove Village *(G-9482)*

### VALUE-ADDED RESELLERS: Computer Systems

CDI Computers (us) Corp ..................... G ...... 888 226-5727
 Chicago *(G-4263)*
Computer Svcs & Consulting Inc ........... E ...... 855 827-8328
 Chicago *(G-4441)*
Hipskind Tech Sltons Group Inc ............ E ...... 630 920-0960
 Oakbrook Terrace *(G-16712)*
Paragon International Inc ..................... F ...... 847 240-2981
 Schaumburg *(G-19682)*
Swift Technologies Inc ......................... G ...... 815 568-8402
 Marengo *(G-14241)*
Techno - Grphics Trnsltons Inc ............. E ...... 708 331-3333
 South Holland *(G-20308)*

### VALVE REPAIR SVCS, INDL

Extreme Force Valve Inc ...................... G ...... 618 494-5795
 Jerseyville *(G-12421)*

### VALVES

Extreme Force Valve Inc ...................... G ...... 618 494-5795
 Jerseyville *(G-12421)*
Hantemp Corporation ........................... G ...... 630 537-1049
 Westmont *(G-21890)*
Milliken Valve Co Inc ............................ G ...... 217 425-7410
 Decatur *(G-7917)*
Mueller Co LLC .................................... G ...... 217 423-4471
 Decatur *(G-7918)*
Research and Testing Worx Inc ............. G ...... 815 734-7346
 Mount Morris *(G-15299)*

### VALVES & PARTS: Gas, Indl

Corken Inc ........................................... D ...... 405 946-5576
 Lake Bluff *(G-12839)*
Emerson Process Management .............. D ...... 708 535-5120
 Oak Forest *(G-16580)*
Henry Technologies Inc ........................ G ...... 217 483-2406
 Chatham *(G-3621)*

### VALVES & PIPE FITTINGS

ADS LLC .............................................. D ...... 256 430-3366
 Burr Ridge *(G-2820)*
American Rack Company ...................... E ...... 773 763-7309
 Chicago *(G-3870)*
Aquatrol Inc ......................................... F ...... 630 365-2363
 Elburn *(G-8875)*
Arnel Industries Inc ............................. E ...... 630 543-6500
 Addison *(G-45)*
B&B Machining Incorporated ................ F ...... 630 898-3009
 Aurora *(G-966)*
Barrington Automation Ltd ................... E ...... 847 458-0900
 Lake In The Hills *(G-12987)*
Bi-Torq Valve Automation Inc ............... G ...... 630 208-9343
 Lafox *(G-12793)*
C U Services LLC ................................. G ...... 847 439-2303
 Elk Grove Village *(G-9352)*
Caterpillar Inc ...................................... B ...... 815 729-5511
 Joliet *(G-12471)*
Certified Power Inc .............................. E ...... 847 573-3800
 Mundelein *(G-15485)*
Chicago Pipe Bending & Coil Co ........... F ...... 773 379-1918
 Chicago *(G-4339)*
Control Equipment Company Inc ........... F ...... 847 891-7500
 Schaumburg *(G-19482)*
Cooper Smith International Inc ............. D ...... 847 595-7572
 Elk Grove Village *(G-9395)*
Couplings Company Inc ....................... F ...... 847 634-8990
 Lincolnshire *(G-13440)*
Deltrol Corp ......................................... F ...... 708 547-0500
 Bellwood *(G-1703)*
Deublin Company ................................. C ...... 847 689-8600
 Waukegan *(G-21551)*
Dresser Inc ......................................... D ...... 847 437-5940
 Elk Grove Village *(G-9435)*
Eclipse Inc .......................................... D ...... 815 877-3031
 Rockford *(G-18356)*
Eg Group Inc ....................................... G ...... 309 692-0968
 Peoria *(G-17352)*
Emerson Process Management .............. D ...... 708 535-5120
 Oak Forest *(G-16580)*
Evsco Inc ............................................ F ...... 847 362-7068
 McHenry *(G-14504)*
Henry Technologies Inc ........................ G ...... 217 483-2406
 Chatham *(G-3621)*
Hoosier Stamping & Mfg Corp ............... E ...... 618 375-2057
 Grayville *(G-11371)*

### VALVES: Control, Automatic

Illinois Tool Works ................................ E ...... 815 648-2416
 Hebron *(G-11720)*
Instrument & Valve Services Co ............ D ...... 708 535-5120
 Oak Forest *(G-16585)*
Intech Industries Inc ............................ F ...... 847 487-5599
 Wauconda *(G-21473)*
Keckley Manufacturing Company ........... E ...... 847 674-8422
 Skokie *(G-20022)*
Kelco Industries Inc ............................. G ...... 815 334-3600
 Woodstock *(G-22577)*
Kepner Products Company .................... D ...... 630 279-1550
 Villa Park *(G-21264)*
Lewis Process Systems Inc ................... F ...... 630 510-8200
 Carol Stream *(G-3184)*
Lilly Industries Inc ............................... F ...... 630 773-2222
 Itasca *(G-12306)*
M CA Chicago ...................................... G ...... 312 384-1220
 Burr Ridge *(G-2863)*
Mead Fluid Dynamics Inc ..................... E ...... 773 685-6800
 Chicago *(G-5669)*
Metraflex Company .............................. D ...... 312 738-3800
 Chicago *(G-5706)*
Midland Manufacturing Corp ................. E ...... 847 677-0333
 Skokie *(G-20039)*
Mity Inc .............................................. G ...... 630 365-5030
 Elburn *(G-8898)*
Newman-Green Inc .............................. D ...... 630 543-6500
 Addison *(G-228)*
O C Keckley Company .......................... E ...... 847 674-8422
 Skokie *(G-20048)*
Oso Technologies Inc ........................... G ...... 844 777-2575
 Urbana *(G-21096)*
Pokorney Manufacturing Co .................. G ...... 630 458-0406
 Addison *(G-245)*
Pro-Quip Incorporated ......................... F ...... 708 352-5732
 La Grange Park *(G-12759)*
Process Screw Products Inc .................. E ...... 815 864-2220
 Shannon *(G-19901)*
Sloan Valve Company ........................... G ...... 847 671-4300
 Franklin Park *(G-10590)*
Spreader Inc ....................................... G ...... 217 568-7219
 Gifford *(G-10910)*
SPX Flow US LLC ................................. G ...... 815 874-5556
 Rockford *(G-18632)*
Strahman Valves Inc ............................ E ...... 630 208-9343
 Lafox *(G-12797)*
Vonberg Valve Inc ............................... E ...... 847 259-3800
 Rolling Meadows *(G-18788)*
World Wide Fittings Inc ........................ E ...... 847 588-2200
 Vernon Hills *(G-21219)*

### VALVES & REGULATORS: Pressure, Indl

Keckley Manufacturing Company ........... E ...... 847 674-8422
 Skokie *(G-20022)*
O C Keckley Company .......................... E ...... 847 674-8422
 Skokie *(G-20048)*
SMC Corporation of America ................. E ...... 630 449-0600
 Aurora *(G-1080)*

### VALVES Solenoid

Asco Valve Inc ..................................... F ...... 630 789-2082
 Arlington Heights *(G-718)*

### VALVES: Aerosol, Metal

American Metal Mfg Inc ........................ G ...... 847 651-6097
 Chicago *(G-3865)*
Aptargroup Inc .................................... B ...... 847 639-2124
 Cary *(G-3327)*
Aptargroup Inc .................................... B ...... 815 477-0424
 Crystal Lake *(G-7535)*
J&A Mtchell Stl Fbricators Inc .............. G ...... 815 939-2144
 Kankakee *(G-12629)*
Newman-Green Inc .............................. D ...... 630 543-6500
 Addison *(G-228)*

### VALVES: Aircraft, Control, Hydraulic & Pneumatic

Ckd USA Corporation ........................... E ...... 847 368-0539
 Rolling Meadows *(G-18722)*
Robertshaw Controls Company .............. C ...... 630 260-3400
 Itasca *(G-12349)*
Vonberg Valve Inc ............................... E ...... 847 259-3800
 Rolling Meadows *(G-18788)*

### VALVES: Control, Automatic

Val-Matic Valve and Mfg Corp ............... C ...... 630 941-7600
 Elmhurst *(G-9956)*

Employee Codes: A=Over 500 employees, B=251-500
C=101-250, D=51-100, E=20-50, F=10-19, G=3-9

## VALVES: Control, Automatic

Val-Matic Valve and Mfg Corp .......... E ...... 630 993-4078
　Addison *(G-337)*

### VALVES: Electrohydraulic Servo, Metal

Crane Nuclear Inc .......... E ...... 630 226-4900
　Bolingbrook *(G-2290)*
MEA Inc .......... E ...... 847 766-9040
　Elk Grove Village *(G-9616)*

### VALVES: Engine

Helio Precision Products Inc .......... C ...... 847 473-1300
　Lake Bluff *(G-12848)*

### VALVES: Fluid Power, Control, Hydraulic & pneumatic

Delta Power Company .......... D ...... 815 397-6628
　Rockford *(G-18339)*
Fluid Logic Inc .......... G ...... 847 459-2202
　Buffalo Grove *(G-2697)*
Hydraforce Inc .......... B ...... 847 793-2300
　Lincolnshire *(G-13455)*
Kocsis Technologies Inc .......... F ...... 708 597-4177
　Alsip *(G-481)*
Kocsis Technologies Inc .......... G ...... 708 597-4177
　Alsip *(G-482)*
Marmon Industrial LLC .......... 312 372-9500
　Chicago *(G-5626)*
Mead Fluid Dynamics Inc .......... E ...... 773 685-6800
　Chicago *(G-5669)*
Rotary Ram Inc .......... E ...... 618 466-2651
　Godfrey *(G-11236)*
SMC Corporation of America .......... 630 449-0600
　Aurora *(G-1080)*
Vrg Controls LLC .......... G ...... 773 230-1543
　Highland Park *(G-11879)*
Wandfluh of America Inc .......... F ...... 847 566-5700
　Mundelein *(G-15566)*

### VALVES: Indl

Advanced Valve Tech Inc .......... E ...... 877 489-4909
　Blue Island *(G-2237)*
Aptargroup Inc .......... B ...... 847 639-2124
　Cary *(G-3327)*
Aquatrol Inc .......... F ...... 630 365-2363
　Elburn *(G-8875)*
Cyrus Shank Company .......... G ...... 630 618-4732
　Aurora *(G-993)*
Cyrus Shank Company .......... E ...... 708 652-2700
　Cicero *(G-7187)*
Deltrol Corp .......... C ...... 708 547-0500
　Bellwood *(G-1703)*
Engineered Fluid Inc .......... C ...... 618 533-1351
　Centralia *(G-3413)*
Evsco Inc .......... F ...... 847 362-7068
　McHenry *(G-14504)*
Fisher Controls Intl LLC .......... D ...... 847 956-8020
　Chicago *(G-4851)*
Fkavpc Inc .......... D ...... 847 524-9000
　Schaumburg *(G-19530)*
Flocon Inc .......... E ...... 815 444-1500
　Cary *(G-3341)*
General Assembly & Mfg Corp .......... E ...... 847 516-6462
　Cary *(G-3346)*
Gpe Controls Inc .......... F ...... 708 236-6000
　Hillside *(G-11917)*
H A Phillips & Co .......... E ...... 630 377-0050
　Dekalb *(G-8095)*
Henry Pratt Company LLC .......... C ...... 630 844-4000
　Aurora *(G-1168)*
Hydra-Stop LLC .......... E ...... 708 389-5111
　Burr Ridge *(G-2852)*
L & J Holding Company Ltd .......... D ...... 708 236-6000
　Hillside *(G-11923)*
Midland Manufacturing Corp .......... C ...... 847 677-0333
　Skokie *(G-20039)*
New Tech Marketing Inc .......... F ...... 630 378-4300
　Romeoville *(G-18854)*
Parker-Hannifin Corporation .......... E ...... 708 681-6300
　Broadview *(G-2601)*
Pioneer Pump and Packing Inc .......... 217 791-5293
　Decatur *(G-7927)*
Rebuilders Enterprises Inc .......... 708 430-0030
　Bridgeview *(G-2523)*
Rhino Tool Company .......... F ...... 309 853-5555
　Kewanee *(G-12694)*
Schrader-Bridgeport Intl Inc .......... G ...... 815 288-3344
　Dixon *(G-8349)*

Sycamore Precision .......... D ...... 815 784-5151
　Genoa *(G-10884)*
USP Holdings Inc .......... A ...... 847 604-6100
　Des Plaines *(G-8295)*
Vonberg Valve Inc .......... E ...... 847 259-3800
　Rolling Meadows *(G-18788)*
Waves Fluid Solutions LLC .......... G ...... 630 765-7533
　Carol Stream *(G-3264)*

### VALVES: Plumbing & Heating

Catching Hydraulics Co Ltd .......... E ...... 708 344-2334
　Melrose Park *(G-14606)*
Dooley Brothers Plumbing & Htg .......... G ...... 309 852-2720
　Kewanee *(G-12680)*
J/B Industries Inc .......... D ...... 630 851-9444
　Aurora *(G-1174)*
Solomon Plumbing .......... G ...... 847 498-6388
　Glenview *(G-11205)*
Wrap-On Company LLC .......... E ...... 708 496-2150
　Alsip *(G-547)*

### VALVES: Regulating & Control, Automatic

Advanced Automation Systems .......... G ...... 815 877-1075
　Loves Park *(G-13912)*
Strahman Valves Inc .......... E ...... 630 208-9343
　Lafox *(G-12797)*

### VALVES: Regulating, Process Control

Honeywell Analytics Inc .......... C ...... 847 955-8200
　Lincolnshire *(G-13454)*

### VALVES: Water Works

Dezurik Inc .......... F ...... 847 985-5580
　Schaumburg *(G-19503)*
Ergo-Tech Incorporated .......... G ...... 630 773-2222
　Itasca *(G-12260)*
Midwest Water Group Inc .......... G ...... 866 526-6558
　McHenry *(G-14534)*

### VARIETY STORE MERCHANDISE, WHOLESALE

Adams Apple Distributing LP .......... E ...... 847 832-9900
　Glenview *(G-11095)*
All Right Sales Inc .......... G ...... 773 558-4800
　West Chicago *(G-21654)*

### VARIETY STORES

State Line International Inc .......... G ...... 708 251-5772
　Lansing *(G-13186)*

### VARNISHES, NEC

Alvar Inc .......... F ...... 309 248-7523
　Washburn *(G-21374)*
Benjamin Moore & Co .......... C ...... 708 343-6000
　Carol Stream *(G-3114)*
United Gilsonite Laboratories .......... E ...... 217 243-7878
　Jacksonville *(G-12415)*
Valspar .......... 815 962-9969
　Rockford *(G-18666)*
Valspar Corporation .......... D ...... 815 962-9986
　Rockford *(G-18669)*

### VARNISHES: Lithographic

Ink Solutions LLC .......... E ...... 847 593-5200
　Elk Grove Village *(G-9546)*

### VARNISHING SVC: Metal Prdts

Nickel Composite Coatings Inc .......... E ...... 708 563-2780
　Chicago *(G-5910)*

### VAULTS & SAFES WHOLESALERS

Diebold Incorporated .......... D ...... 847 598-3300
　Schaumburg *(G-19504)*

### VEHICLES: All Terrain

Quiller Outboard Sls Svcs LLC .......... G ...... 618 232-1218
　Hamburg *(G-11527)*
Woodstock Powersports .......... G ...... 815 308-5705
　Woodstock *(G-22627)*

### VEHICLES: Children's, Exc Bicycles

Henes Usa Inc .......... D ...... 312 448-6130
　Glenview *(G-11136)*

### VEHICLES: Recreational

Equity Lifestyle Prpts Inc .......... G ...... 815 857-3333
　Amboy *(G-598)*
General RV Center Inc .......... C ...... 847 669-5570
　Huntley *(G-12140)*
Howland Technology Inc .......... F ...... 847 965-9808
　Morton Grove *(G-15200)*
Scaletta Moloney Armoring .......... D ...... 708 924-0099
　Bedford Park *(G-1583)*

### VENDING MACHINE OPERATORS: Food

Romaine Empire LLC .......... E ...... 312 229-0099
　Chicago *(G-6387)*

### VENDING MACHINES & PARTS

Classic Vending Inc .......... E ...... 773 252-7000
　Chicago *(G-4395)*
Jax Amusements .......... G ...... 618 887-4761
　Alhambra *(G-419)*
Laurel Metal Products Inc .......... E ...... 847 674-0064
　Skokie *(G-20027)*
Northwestern Corporation .......... E ...... 815 942-1300
　Morris *(G-15124)*
Partec Inc .......... C ...... 847 678-9520
　Franklin Park *(G-10547)*
Seaga Manufacturing Inc .......... 815 297-9500
　Freeport *(G-10688)*
Singer Data Products Inc .......... G ...... 630 860-6500
　Bensenville *(G-1991)*
Success Vending Mfg Co LLC .......... E ...... 773 262-1685
　Chicago *(G-6612)*

### VENETIAN BLINDS & SHADES

Aracon Drpery Vntian Blind Ltd .......... G ...... 773 252-1281
　Chicago *(G-3930)*
Bills Shade & Blind Service .......... G ...... 773 493-5000
　Chicago *(G-4106)*

### VENTILATING EQPT: Metal

Carroll International Corp .......... F ...... 630 983-5979
　Lake Forest *(G-12890)*
Evans Heating and Air Inc .......... G ...... 217 483-8440
　Chatham *(G-3619)*
Imperial Mfg Group Inc .......... F ...... 618 465-3133
　Alton *(G-578)*
Pearson Industries Inc .......... G ...... 847 963-9633
　Rolling Meadows *(G-18759)*
R B Hayward Company .......... E ...... 847 671-0400
　Schiller Park *(G-19864)*

### VENTILATING EQPT: Sheet Metal

Air Vent Inc .......... G ...... 309 692-6969
　Peoria *(G-17305)*

### VENTURE CAPITAL COMPANIES

Beecken Petty Okeefe & Co LLC .......... A ...... 312 435-0300
　Chicago *(G-4071)*
Wind Point Partners LP .......... F ...... 312 255-4800
　Chicago *(G-6992)*

### VETERINARY PHARMACEUTICAL PREPARATIONS

Finish Line Horse Products Inc .......... E ...... 630 694-0000
　Bensenville *(G-1897)*
First Priority Inc .......... D ...... 847 531-1215
　Elgin *(G-9037)*
Hydrox Chemical Company Inc .......... D ...... 847 468-9400
　Elgin *(G-9069)*
Shaars International Inc .......... G ...... 815 315-0717
　Rockford *(G-18614)*

### VETERINARY PRDTS: Instruments & Apparatus

Shanks Veterinary Equipment .......... G ...... 815 225-7700
　Milledgeville *(G-14818)*
Woundwear Inc .......... G ...... 847 634-1700
　Buffalo Grove *(G-2795)*

### VIBRATORS: Concrete Construction

Cougar Industries Inc .......... E ...... 815 224-1200
　Peru *(G-17506)*

## PRODUCT SECTION

### VIDEO & AUDIO EQPT, WHOLESALE
Buzzfire Incorporated ..................................F....... 630 572-9200
  Oak Brook  (G-16496)
Peerless Industries Inc ............................B....... 630 375-5100
  Aurora  (G-1063)
Shure Incorporated ....................................F....... 847 520-4404
  Wheeling  (G-22150)

### VIDEO CAMERA-AUDIO RECORDERS: Household Use
Alexander Brewster LLC ............................G....... 618 346-8580
  Collinsville  (G-7314)
Epic Eye .........................................................G....... 309 210-6212
  Grand Ridge  (G-11257)
Fire CAM LLC ...............................................G....... 618 416-8390
  Belleville  (G-1632)
Sonic Low Voltage ......................................G....... 815 790-4400
  Johnsburg  (G-12442)

### VIDEO EQPT
Prager Associates .......................................G....... 309 691-1565
  Peoria  (G-17433)
Vidicon LLC ..................................................G....... 815 756-9600
  Dekalb  (G-8130)

### VIDEO PRODUCTION SVCS
Warbler Digital Inc .......................................E....... 312 924-1056
  Chicago  (G-6939)

### VIDEO TAPE PRODUCTION SVCS
Andover Junction Publications ...................G....... 815 538-3060
  Mendota  (G-14716)
C W Publications Inc ..................................G....... 800 554-5537
  Sterling  (G-20586)
Crystal Productions Co ..............................F....... 847 657-8144
  Northbrook  (G-16235)
Cupcake Holdings LLC ..............................C....... 800 794-5866
  Woodridge  (G-22466)
Perry Johnson Inc .......................................F....... 847 635-0010
  Rosemont  (G-19021)
Pieces of Learning Inc ................................G....... 618 964-9426
  Marion  (G-14279)
Wilton Brands LLC ......................................B....... 630 963-7100
  Woodridge  (G-22526)
Wilton Holdings Inc .....................................G....... 630 963-7100
  Woodridge  (G-22527)
Wilton Industries Inc ...................................B....... 630 963-7100
  Woodridge  (G-22528)
Wilton Industries Inc ...................................F....... 815 834-9390
  Romeoville  (G-18879)

### VIDEO TAPE WHOLESALERS, RECORDED
Sunburst Technology Corp .........................G....... 800 321-7511
  Elgin  (G-9197)

### VINYL RESINS, NEC
Jakes World Design .....................................G....... 217 348-3043
  Lerna  (G-13287)

### VISES: Machine
Adjustable Clamp Company .......................C....... 312 666-0640
  Chicago  (G-3751)
Jrm International Inc ...................................G....... 815 282-9330
  Loves Park  (G-13955)
Midwest Machine Tool Inc ..........................G....... 815 427-8665
  Saint Anne  (G-19124)
Palmgren Steel Products Inc .....................F....... 773 265-5700
  Chicago  (G-6066)

### VISUAL COMMUNICATIONS SYSTEMS
Western Remac Inc .....................................E....... 630 972-7770
  Woodridge  (G-22524)

### VISUAL EFFECTS PRODUCTION SVCS
Black Point Studios llc ................................E....... 773 791-2377
  Chicago  (G-4120)

### VITAMINS: Natural Or Synthetic, Uncompounded, Bulk
Archer-Daniels-Midland Company ..............D....... 217 424-5200
  Decatur  (G-7840)
Glanbia Performance Ntrtn Inc ...................E....... 630 256-7445
  Aurora  (G-1016)

Glanbia Performance Ntrtn Inc ...................D....... 630 236-3126
  Aurora  (G-1017)
Glanbia Performance Ntrtn Inc ...................C....... 630 236-0097
  Downers Grove  (G-8451)
Natures Best Inc ..........................................E....... 631 232-3355
  Downers Grove  (G-8493)
Nutritional Institute LLC ..............................G....... 847 223-7699
  Grayslake  (G-11357)
Premier Health Concepts LLC ...................G....... 630 575-1059
  Carol Stream  (G-3216)
Ys Health Corporation .................................G....... 847 391-9122
  Mount Prospect  (G-15387)

### VITAMINS: Pharmaceutical Preparations
Mead Johnson Nutrition Company .............E....... 312 466-5800
  Chicago  (G-5671)
Newhealth Solutions LLC ............................G....... 803 627-8378
  Brookfield  (G-2638)
Redd Remedies Inc .....................................F....... 815 614-2083
  Bradley  (G-2430)
Trudeau Approved Products Inc ................G....... 312 924-7230
  Hinsdale  (G-11967)
Vitamins Inc ..................................................G....... 773 483-4640
  Carol Stream  (G-3262)

### VOCATIONAL REHABILITATION AGENCY
Clay Cnty Rhbilitation Ctr Inc .....................F....... 618 662-6607
  Flora  (G-10203)

### VOCATIONAL TRAINING AGENCY
Trade Industries ............................................E....... 618 643-4321
  Mc Leansboro  (G-14469)

### VOLCANIC ROCK: Dimension
Red Hill Lava Products Inc .........................G....... 800 528-2765
  Rock Island  (G-18198)

### WALLBOARD: Decorated, Made From Purchased Materials
H Hal Kramer Co ...........................................G....... 773 539-9648
  Chicago  (G-5021)
Stevens Cabinets Inc ..................................B....... 217 857-7100
  Teutopolis  (G-20856)
Wexford Home Corp ....................................G....... 847 922-5738
  Northbrook  (G-16386)

### WALLBOARD: Gypsum
Georgia-Pacific Bldg Pdts LLC ...................G....... 630 449-7200
  Aurora  (G-1015)

### WALLPAPER STORE
Afar Imports & Interiors Inc .......................G....... 217 744-3262
  Springfield  (G-20386)
Roberts Draperies Center Inc ....................G....... 847 255-4040
  Mount Prospect  (G-15370)

### WALLS: Curtain, Metal
Harmon Inc ....................................................E....... 630 759-8060
  Bolingbrook  (G-2315)
Ltc Holdings Inc ...........................................C....... 847 249-5900
  Waukegan  (G-21585)

### WAREHOUSE CLUBS STORES
Vermilion Steel Fabrication .........................G....... 217 442-5300
  Danville  (G-7778)

### WAREHOUSING & STORAGE FACILITIES, NEC
Hurst Chemical Company ...........................G....... 815 964-0451
  Rockford  (G-18424)
I M M Inc .......................................................F....... 773 767-3700
  Chicago  (G-5131)
Major-Prime Plastics Inc ............................G....... 630 834-9400
  Villa Park  (G-21267)
Unistrut International Corp .........................D....... 630 773-3460
  Addison  (G-334)

### WAREHOUSING & STORAGE, REFRIGERATED: Cold Storage Or Refrig
Bushnell Locker Service ..............................G....... 309 772-2783
  Bushnell  (G-2899)

Carroll County Locker ..................................G....... 815 493-2370
  Lanark  (G-13151)

### WAREHOUSING & STORAGE, REFRIGERATED: Frozen Or Refrig Goods
Edgar County Locker Service .....................G....... 217 466-5000
  Paris  (G-17147)
Eickmans Processing Co Inc .....................E....... 815 247-8451
  Seward  (G-19896)
Eureka Locker Inc ........................................F....... 309 467-2731
  Eureka  (G-9998)
Farina Locker Service ..................................G....... 618 245-6491
  Farina  (G-10175)
Gridley Meats Inc .........................................G....... 309 747-2120
  Gridley  (G-11405)
Korte Meat Processing Inc .........................G....... 618 654-3813
  Highland  (G-11801)

### WAREHOUSING & STORAGE: Bulk St & Termnls, Hire, Petro/Chem
East St Louis Trml & Stor Co .....................E....... 618 271-2185
  East Saint Louis  (G-8749)

### WAREHOUSING & STORAGE: General
Chicago Export Packing Co ........................E....... 773 247-8911
  Chicago  (G-4318)
Chicago Tube and Iron Company ...............E....... 309 787-4947
  Milan  (G-14779)
Dallas Corporation .......................................F....... 630 322-8000
  Downers Grove  (G-8424)
Fujifilm Hunt Chem USA Inc ......................C....... 847 259-8800
  Rolling Meadows  (G-18730)
Glanbia Performance Ntrtn Inc ...................E....... 630 256-7445
  Aurora  (G-1016)
Hickman Williams & Company ...................F....... 708 656-8818
  Cicero  (G-7202)
Horizon Downing LLC ..................................E....... 815 758-6867
  Dekalb  (G-8097)
Ken Don LLC .................................................G....... 708 596-4910
  Markham  (G-14303)
Lordahl Manufacturing Co ..........................D....... 847 244-0448
  Long Grove  (G-13893)
Myers Concrete & Construction .................G....... 815 732-2591
  Oregon  (G-16828)
Schwarz Paper Company LLC ...................C....... 847 966-2550
  Morton Grove  (G-15235)
Thermal Ceramics Inc .................................E....... 217 627-2101
  Girard  (G-10950)
Vee Pak LLC .................................................D....... 708 482-8881
  Hodgkins  (G-11986)
Zoetis LLC .....................................................D....... 708 757-2592
  Chicago Heights  (G-7137)

### WAREHOUSING & STORAGE: General
Aerostar Global Logistics Inc .....................F....... 630 396-7890
  Lombard  (G-13761)
American Industrial Werks Inc ...................F....... 847 477-2648
  Schaumburg  (G-19437)
Americas Community Bankers ...................E....... 312 644-3100
  Chicago  (G-3884)
Arro Corporation ..........................................E....... 708 352-7412
  Hodgkins  (G-11971)
Arro Corporation ..........................................C....... 708 352-8200
  Hodgkins  (G-11970)
Arro Corporation ..........................................G....... 773 978-1251
  Chicago  (G-3947)
Corr-Pak Corporation ..................................E....... 708 442-7806
  Mc Cook  (G-14447)
D E Signs & Storage LLC ...........................G....... 618 939-8050
  Waterloo  (G-21401)
Dynamic Manufacturing Inc .......................E....... 708 343-8753
  Melrose Park  (G-14626)
Hyster-Yale Group Inc .................................E....... 217 443-7416
  Danville  (G-7736)
Kurz Transfer Products LP .........................G....... 847 228-0001
  Elk Grove Village  (G-9580)
Mech-Tronics Corporation ..........................G....... 708 344-0202
  Melrose Park  (G-14672)
Monnex International Inc ............................F....... 847 850-5263
  Buffalo Grove  (G-2738)
Pinnacle Foods Group LLC ........................B....... 618 829-3275
  Saint Elmo  (G-19310)
Randal Wood Displays Inc ..........................G....... 630 761-0400
  Batavia  (G-1490)
Stitch TEC Co Inc ........................................G....... 618 327-8054
  Nashville  (G-15848)

Employee Codes: A=Over 500 employees, B=251-500
C=101-250, D=51-100, E=20-50, F=10-19, G=3-9

## WAREHOUSING & STORAGE: General

Venus Processing & Storage ............D...... 847 455-0496
  Franklin Park  (G-10621)

### WAREHOUSING & STORAGE: Household Goods

GM Partners ................................G...... 847 895-7627
  Schaumburg  (G-19538)

### WAREHOUSING & STORAGE: Miniwarehouse

Form Relief Tool Co Inc ..................F...... 815 393-4263
  Davis Junction  (G-7812)

### WAREHOUSING & STORAGE: Refrigerated

Metropolis Ready Mix Inc ................E...... 618 524-8221
  Metropolis  (G-14758)

### WARM AIR HEATING & AC EQPT & SPLYS, WHOL: Dust Collecting

Dust Patrol Inc ............................G...... 309 676-1161
  Peoria  (G-17351)

### WARM AIR HEATING & AC EQPT & SPLYS, WHOLESALE Air Filters

Bisco Enterprise Inc ......................F...... 630 628-1831
  Schaumburg  (G-19463)
Clean and Science USA Co Ltd .........G...... 847 461-9292
  Schaumburg  (G-19473)
Nuair Filter Company LLC ...............F...... 309 888-4331
  Normal  (G-16081)
Pure N Natural Systems Inc ............F...... 630 372-9681
  Morton Grove  (G-15230)
Sentry Pool & Chemical Supply .......E...... 309 797-9721
  Moline  (G-14970)

### WARM AIR HEATING & AC EQPT & SPLYS, WHOLESALE Heat Exchgrs

Yinlun Usa Inc .............................G...... 309 291-0843
  Morton  (G-15185)

### WARM AIR HEATING/AC EQPT/SPLYS, WHOL Warm Air Htg Eqpt/Splys

Bird-X Inc ...................................E...... 312 226-2473
  Chicago  (G-4112)
Goose Island Mfg & Supply Corp ......G...... 708 343-4225
  Lansing  (G-13164)
Habegger Corporation ...................F...... 309 793-7172
  Rock Island  (G-18178)
Haggerty Corporation ....................G...... 309 793-4328
  Rock Island  (G-18179)
Temp Excel Properties LLC ............G...... 847 844-3845
  Elgin  (G-9207)
W L Engler Distributing Inc ............G...... 630 898-5400
  Aurora  (G-1093)

### WASHCLOTHS & BATH MITTS, FROM PURCHASED MATERIALS

My Konjac Sponge Inc ..................F...... 630 345-3653
  North Barrington  (G-16154)

### WASHERS

Illinois Tool Works Inc ...................F...... 708 343-0728
  Broadview  (G-2586)
Laundry Services Company ............G...... 630 327-9329
  Downers Grove  (G-8473)

### WASHERS: Lock

Saint Technologies Inc ...................G...... 815 864-3035
  Shannon  (G-19902)

### WASHERS: Metal

Chicago-Wilcox Mfg Co ..................E...... 708 339-5000
  South Holland  (G-20257)
Freeway-Rockford Inc ....................E...... 815 397-6425
  Rockford  (G-18393)
Great Lakes Washer Company .........F...... 630 887-7447
  Burr Ridge  (G-2846)
Maxi-Vac Inc ...............................G...... 224 699-9760
  Addison  (G-194)
Willie Washer Mfg Co .....................C...... 847 956-1344
  Elk Grove Village  (G-9814)

### WASHERS: Plastic

Deslauriers Inc ............................E...... 708 544-4455
  La Grange Park  (G-12754)
Monda Window & Door Corp ...........E...... 773 254-8888
  Chicago  (G-5792)

### WASHERS: Rubber

Excelsior Inc ...............................E...... 815 987-2900
  Rockford  (G-18375)

### WASTE CLEANING SVCS

Midwest Intgrted Companies LLC .....C...... 847 426-6354
  Gilberts  (G-10926)

### WATCH REPAIR SVCS

A G Mitchells Jewelers Ltd .............F...... 847 394-0820
  Arlington Heights  (G-700)

### WATCHES

Hampden Corporation ....................E...... 312 583-3000
  Chicago  (G-5039)
KI Watch Service Inc .....................G...... 847 368-8780
  Mount Prospect  (G-15342)

### WATCHES & PARTS, WHOLESALE

Gennco International Inc ................F...... 847 541-3333
  Wheeling  (G-22062)

### WATER HEATERS

Unique Indoor Comfort ...................F...... 847 362-1910
  Libertyville  (G-13394)

### WATER PURIFICATION EQPT: Household

Countryside Pure Water Solutio .......G...... 847 255-5524
  Arlington Heights  (G-740)
Ep Purification Inc ........................F...... 217 693-7950
  Champaign  (G-3481)
Hurley Chicago Company Inc ..........G...... 815 472-0087
  Momence  (G-14982)
Natural Choice Corporation .............F...... 815 874-4444
  Rockford  (G-18518)
Newater International Inc ...............F...... 630 894-5000
  Bloomingdale  (G-2120)
Pentair Fltrtion Solutions LLC ..........F...... 630 307-3000
  Hanover Park  (G-11589)
Pentair Fltrtion Solutions LLC ..........F...... 630 307-3000
  Bartlett  (G-1321)
Superior Water Services Inc ............G...... 309 691-9287
  Peoria  (G-17464)
Walter Louis Chem & Assoc Inc .......F...... 217 223-2017
  Quincy  (G-17902)
William N Pasulka .........................G...... 815 339-6300
  Peru  (G-17532)

### WATER PURIFICATION PRDTS: Chlorination Tablets & Kits

1717 Chemall Corporation ...............G...... 224 864-4180
  Mundelein  (G-15460)
Mar Cor Purification Inc .................G...... 630 435-1017
  Downers Grove  (G-8483)

### WATER SOFTENER SVCS

American Watersource LLC .............E...... 630 778-9900
  Naperville  (G-15794)
Superior Water Services Inc ............G...... 309 691-9287
  Peoria  (G-17464)
Water Dynamics Inc ......................G...... 630 584-8475
  Saint Charles  (G-19292)

### WATER SOFTENING WHOLESALERS

Superior Water Services Inc ............G...... 309 691-9287
  Peoria  (G-17464)

### WATER SUPPLY

Chicago Waterjet Inc .....................G...... 847 350-1898
  Elk Grove Village  (G-9370)
Gehrke Technology Group Inc ..........F...... 847 498-7320
  Wauconda  (G-21464)

### WATER TREATMENT EQPT: Indl

AC Nalco Chemical Co ...................F...... 630 305-1000
  Naperville  (G-15587)

Ambi-Design Incorporated ..............G...... 815 964-7568
  Rockford  (G-18261)
American Watersource LLC .............E...... 630 778-9900
  Naperville  (G-15794)
Arbortech Corporation ...................G...... 847 462-1111
  Johnsburg  (G-12430)
Brochem Industries Inc ..................G...... 708 206-2874
  East Hazel Crest  (G-8665)
C2 Water Inc ...............................G...... 312 550-1159
  Kenilworth  (G-12662)
Calco Ltd ....................................F...... 630 539-1800
  Bartlett  (G-1316)
Charger Water Conditioning Inc .......F...... 847 967-9558
  Morton Grove  (G-15192)
Chemical Pump ............................G...... 815 464-1908
  Frankfort  (G-10309)
D R Sperry & Co ...........................D...... 630 892-4361
  Aurora  (G-1137)
Earthwise Environmental Inc ...........G...... 630 475-3070
  Wood Dale  (G-22361)
Ecodyne Water Treatment LLC ........E...... 630 961-5043
  Naperville  (G-15650)
Edwardsville Water Treatment .........E...... 618 692-7053
  Edwardsville  (G-8800)
Ellis Corporation ..........................D...... 630 250-9222
  Itasca  (G-12258)
Gehrke Technology Group Inc ..........F...... 847 498-7320
  Wauconda  (G-21464)
Gillespie City Water ......................F...... 217 839-3279
  Gillespie  (G-10941)
H-O-H Water Technology Inc ..........E...... 847 358-7400
  Palatine  (G-17032)
Hpd LLC ....................................C...... 815 436-3013
  Plainfield  (G-17606)
Hydrotec Systems Company Inc ......G...... 815 624-6644
  Tiskilwa  (G-20959)
Illinois Water Tech Inc ...................E...... 815 636-8884
  Roscoe  (G-18901)
Industrial Water Trtmnt Soltns .........E...... 708 339-1313
  Harvey  (G-11672)
International Water Werks Inc .........G...... 847 669-1902
  Huntley  (G-12151)
K & S Manufacturing Co Inc ............G...... 815 232-7519
  Freeport  (G-10671)
Marmon Holdings Inc ....................D...... 312 372-9500
  Chicago  (G-5625)
Marmon Industrial LLC ..................G...... 312 372-9500
  Chicago  (G-5626)
McNish Corporation ......................D...... 630 892-7921
  Aurora  (G-1184)
Nalco Company LLC .....................G......
  Naperville  (G-15704)
Nano Gas Technologies Inc .............G...... 586 229-2656
  Deerfield  (G-8043)
Nijhuis Water Technology Inc ..........G...... 312 466-9900
  Chicago  (G-5917)
Palmyra Modesto Water Comm ........G...... 217 436-2519
  Palmyra  (G-17097)
Pond Alliance Inc .........................G...... 877 377-8131
  Naperville  (G-15729)
Pristine Water Solutions Inc ............F...... 847 689-1100
  Waukegan  (G-21607)
Pureline Treatment Systems LLC ......E...... 847 963-8465
  Bensenville  (G-1970)
Safe Water Technologies Inc ...........G...... 847 888-6900
  Elgin  (G-9171)
Siemens Industry Inc ....................D...... 815 877-3041
  Rockford  (G-18616)
Triwater Holdings LLC ...................G...... 847 457-1812
  Lake Forest  (G-12974)
Twh Water Treatment Industries ......D...... 847 457-1813
  Rosemont  (G-19038)
Water Dynamics Inc ......................G...... 630 584-8475
  Saint Charles  (G-19292)
Water Inc ...................................G...... 815 626-8844
  Sterling  (G-20621)
Will County Well & Pump Co Inc ......G...... 815 485-2413
  New Lenox  (G-15928)

### WATER: Distilled

Samuel Rowell .............................G...... 618 942-6970
  Herrin  (G-11754)

### WATER: Mineral, Carbonated, Canned & Bottled, Etc

Ds Services of America Inc .............F...... 800 322-6272
  Rockford  (G-18352)
Ds Services of America Inc .............E...... 815 469-7100
  Frankfort  (G-10314)

# PRODUCT SECTION — WELDING REPAIR SVC

Team Sider Inc .................................................. G ...... 847 767-0107
Highland Park *(G-11877)*

## WATER: Pasteurized & Mineral, Bottled & Canned

Bottle-Free Water ............................................ G ...... 630 462-6807
Carol Stream *(G-3119)*
Green Planet Bottling LLC ............................. F ...... 312 962-4444
Vernon Hills *(G-21168)*
Henderson Water District ............................... G ...... 618 498-6418
Jerseyville *(G-12424)*
Mountain Valley Spring Co LLC ..................... A ...... 618 242-4963
Mount Vernon *(G-15430)*
Prairie Pure Bottled Water ............................. G ...... 217 774-7873
Shelbyville *(G-19912)*
Rainbow Pure Water Inc ................................. G ...... 618 985-4670
Carbondale *(G-3021)*
West Water Inc ................................................ G ...... 312 326-7480
Chicago *(G-6962)*

## WATER: Pasteurized, Canned & Bottled, Etc

Amwell ............................................................. G ...... 630 898-6900
Aurora *(G-1108)*
Ds Services of America Inc ............................ C ...... 773 586-8600
Chicago *(G-4645)*
Hinckley & Schmitt Inc ................................... A ...... 773 586-8600
Chicago *(G-5091)*
Nestle Waters North Amer Inc ....................... D ...... 630 271-7300
Woodridge *(G-22505)*
Premium Waters Inc ....................................... D ...... 217 222-0213
Quincy *(G-17871)*
Pure Flo Bottling Inc ....................................... G ...... 815 963-4797
Rockford *(G-18544)*
Tst/Impreso Inc ................................................ G ...... 630 775-9555
Addison *(G-330)*

## WATERPROOFING COMPOUNDS

T K O Waterproof Coating LLP ....................... G ...... 815 338-2006
Woodstock *(G-22618)*
Tamms Industries Inc ..................................... D ...... 815 522-3394
Kirkland *(G-12719)*
Ted Muller ....................................................... G ...... 312 435-0978
Chicago *(G-6686)*

## WAVEGUIDE STRUCTURES: Accelerating

M P V Inc ......................................................... G ...... 847 234-3960
Lake Zurich *(G-13097)*

## WAVEGUIDES & FITTINGS

Andrew New Zealand Inc ............................... E ...... 708 873-3507
Orland Park *(G-16843)*
Commscope Technologies LLC ..................... A ...... 708 236-6600
Westchester *(G-21835)*
Commscope Technologies LLC ..................... B ...... 779 435-6000
Joliet *(G-12476)*

## WAX REMOVERS

Fox Valley Chemical Company ..................... G ...... 815 653-2660
Ringwood *(G-17990)*

## WAX Sealing wax

Princeton Sealing Wax Co ............................. G ...... 815 875-1943
Princeton *(G-17760)*
Remet Corporation .......................................... E ...... 480 766-3464
Palatine *(G-17067)*

## WAXES: Mineral, Natural

Saco Dps/Morris Wax ..................................... G ...... 815 462-0939
New Lenox *(G-15909)*

## WAXES: Petroleum, Not Produced In Petroleum Refineries

Price Tech Group Illinois LLC ....................... G ...... 815 521-4667
Channahon *(G-3583)*

## WEATHER STRIPS: Metal

Dorbin Metal Strip Mfg Co Inc ....................... F ...... 708 656-2333
Cicero *(G-7191)*

## WEAVING MILL, BROADWOVEN FABRICS: Wool Or Similar Fabric

Without A Trace Weaver Inc .......................... F ...... 773 588-4922
Chicago *(G-7009)*

## WEIGHING MACHINERY & APPARATUS

Doran Scales Inc ............................................ E ...... 630 879-1200
Batavia *(G-1440)*
Morrison Weighing Systems Inc ................... G ...... 309 799-7311
Milan *(G-14797)*

## WELDING & CUTTING APPARATUS & ACCESS, NEC

Associate General Labs Inc .......................... G ...... 847 678-2717
Franklin Park *(G-10404)*
Coakley Mfg & Metrology ............................... F ...... 847 202-9331
Palatine *(G-17012)*
Kriese Mfg ....................................................... G ...... 815 748-2683
Cortland *(G-7392)*

## WELDING EQPT

Adams Steel Service Inc ................................ E ...... 815 385-9100
McHenry *(G-14477)*
Airgas Inc ........................................................ F ...... 773 785-3000
Chicago *(G-3786)*
Airgas USA LLC ............................................. G ...... 630 231-9260
West Chicago *(G-21653)*
Branson Ultrasonics Corp .............................. G ...... 847 229-0800
Buffalo Grove *(G-2669)*
D & G Welding Supply Company ................... G ...... 815 675-9890
Spring Grove *(G-20332)*
Ezee Roll Manufacturing Co ......................... G ...... 217 339-2279
Hoopeston *(G-12110)*
Image Industries Inc ...................................... G ...... 847 659-0100
Huntley *(G-12147)*
Industrial Welder Rebuilders ......................... G ...... 708 371-5688
Alsip *(G-473)*
Littell International Inc ................................... E ...... 630 622-4950
Schaumburg *(G-19621)*
Marvel Electric Corporation ........................... E ...... 847 671-0632
Schiller Park *(G-19846)*
Praxair Distribution Inc .................................. G ...... 309 346-3164
Pekin *(G-17284)*
Reber Welding Service .................................. G ...... 217 774-3441
Shelbyville *(G-19914)*
Steelwerks of Chicago LLC .......................... G ...... 312 792-9593
Chicago *(G-6582)*
Weldstar Company .......................................... G ...... 708 534-6419
University Park *(G-21066)*

## WELDING EQPT & SPLYS WHOLESALERS

Airgas USA LLC ............................................. G ...... 618 439-7207
Benton *(G-2020)*
Airgas USA LLC ............................................. E ...... 630 231-9260
West Chicago *(G-21653)*
Gano Welding Supplies Inc ........................... F ...... 217 345-3777
Charleston *(G-3597)*
Herrmann Ultrasonics Inc .............................. E ...... 630 626-1626
Bartlett *(G-1352)*
Ilmo Products Company ................................ E ...... 217 245-2183
Jacksonville *(G-12394)*
Lickenbrock & Sons Inc ................................. G ...... 618 632-4977
O Fallon *(G-16470)*
Mac-Weld Inc ................................................... G ...... 618 529-1828
Carbondale *(G-3015)*
Matheson Tri-Gas Inc ..................................... F ...... 309 697-1933
Mapleton *(G-14213)*
Matheson Tri-Gas Inc ..................................... E ...... 815 727-2202
Joliet *(G-12539)*
Praxair Distribution Inc .................................. G ...... 314 664-7900
Cahokia *(G-2924)*
Shew Brothers Inc .......................................... G ...... 618 997-4414
Marion *(G-14286)*
Weldstar Company .......................................... E ...... 630 859-3100
Aurora *(G-1232)*

## WELDING EQPT & SPLYS: Electrodes

Melissa A Miller .............................................. G ...... 708 529-7786
New Lenox *(G-15893)*

## WELDING EQPT & SPLYS: Gas

Airgas Usa LLC ............................................... G ...... 815 935-7750
Bradley *(G-2412)*
C M Industries Inc .......................................... E ...... 847 550-0033
Lake Zurich *(G-13049)*

## WELDING EQPT & SPLYS: Resistance, Electric

Automation International Inc ......................... D ...... 217 446-9500
Danville *(G-7704)*

## WELDING EQPT & SPLYS: Wire, Bare & Coated

Electron Beam Technologies Inc ................... C ...... 815 935-2211
Kankakee *(G-12612)*

## WELDING EQPT REPAIR SVCS

Barton Manufacturing LLC ............................. F ...... 217 428-0726
Decatur *(G-7844)*
Globaltech International LLC ......................... G ...... 630 327-6909
Aurora *(G-1018)*
Industrial Welder Rebuilders ......................... G ...... 708 371-5688
Alsip *(G-473)*
Pekin Weldors Inc ........................................... F ...... 309 382-3627
North Pekin *(G-16193)*

## WELDING EQPT: Electric

American Vacuum Co ..................................... G ...... 847 674-8383
Skokie *(G-19951)*
Fanuc America Corporation ........................... E ...... 847 898-5000
Hoffman Estates *(G-12009)*
Globaltech International LLC ......................... G ...... 630 327-6909
Aurora *(G-1018)*
Kopp Welding Inc ............................................ G ...... 847 593-2070
Elk Grove Village *(G-9578)*
Sommer Products Company Inc ................... D ...... 309 697-1216
Peoria *(G-17458)*

## WELDING MACHINES & EQPT: Ultrasonic

Branson Ultrasonics Corp .............................. G ...... 847 229-0800
Buffalo Grove *(G-2669)*
Dukane Corporation ........................................ C ...... 630 797-4900
Saint Charles *(G-19175)*
Herrmann Ultrasonics Inc .............................. E ...... 630 626-1626
Bartlett *(G-1352)*
Image Industries Inc ...................................... G ...... 847 659-0100
Huntley *(G-12147)*

## WELDING REPAIR SVC

A G Welding .................................................... G ...... 773 261-0575
Chicago *(G-3688)*
A&S Machining & Welding Inc ....................... E ...... 708 442-4544
Mc Cook *(G-14443)*
A-Z Welding .................................................... G ...... 618 259-2515
Bethalto *(G-2080)*
Ability Welding Service Inc ........................... G ...... 630 595-3737
Bensenville *(G-1812)*
Ablaze Welding & Fabricating ....................... G ...... 815 965-0046
Rockford *(G-18248)*
Accurate Auto Manufacturing Co .................. G ...... 618 244-0727
Mount Vernon *(G-15397)*
Adams Steel Service Inc ................................ E ...... 815 385-9100
McHenry *(G-14477)*
Adler Norco Inc ............................................... F ...... 847 473-3600
Mundelein *(G-15464)*
Advanced Welding Services .......................... G ...... 630 759-3334
La Grange *(G-12724)*
Affton Fabg & Wldg Co Inc ............................ F ...... 314 781-4100
Sauget *(G-19381)*
AG Precision Inc ............................................ G ...... 847 724-7786
Glenview *(G-11098)*
Aileys 3 Welding ............................................. G ...... 815 683-2181
Crescent City *(G-7455)*
Airgas USA LLC ............................................. F ...... 815 289-1928
Machesney Park *(G-14052)*
Alberto Daza ................................................... F ...... 773 638-9880
Chicago *(G-3796)*
Aledo Welding Enterprises Inc ..................... G ...... 309 582-2019
Aledo *(G-367)*
All Metal Machine ........................................... G ...... 815 389-0168
South Beloit *(G-20136)*
Allans Welding & Machine Inc ...................... G ...... 618 392-3708
Olney *(G-16758)*
Allen Popovich ................................................ G ...... 815 712-7404
Custer Park *(G-7686)*
Alloy Welding Corp ......................................... E ...... 708 345-6756
Melrose Park *(G-14588)*
Alloyweld Inspection Co Inc .......................... G ...... 630 595-2145
Bensenville *(G-1827)*
American Grinding & Machine Co ................ D ...... 773 889-4343
Chicago *(G-3857)*

Employee Codes: A=Over 500 employees, B=251-500
C=101-250, D=51-100, E=20-50, F=10-19, G=3-9

2017 Harris Illinois Industrial Directory

American Machining & Wldg Inc ....E .... 773 586-2585
Chicago *(G-3862)*
American Metal Installers & FA ....G .... 630 993-0812
Villa Park *(G-21236)*
American Welding & Gas Inc ....E .... 630 527-2550
Stone Park *(G-20632)*
Anchor Welding & Fabrication ....G .... 815 937-1640
Aroma Park *(G-878)*
Andel Services Inc ....G .... 630 566-0210
Aurora *(G-1109)*
Andersen Machine & Welding Inc ....G .... 815 232-4664
Freeport *(G-10647)*
Apollo Machine & Manufacturing ....G .... 847 677-6444
Skokie *(G-19956)*
Armitage Welding ....G .... 773 772-1442
Chicago *(G-3946)*
Arndt Enterprise Ltd ....G .... 847 234-5736
Lake Forest *(G-12880)*
AS Fabricating Inc ....G .... 618 242-7438
Mount Vernon *(G-15398)*
Ascent Mfg Co ....E .... 847 806-6600
Elk Grove Village *(G-9314)*
Assured Welding Service Inc ....G .... 847 671-1414
Schiller Park *(G-19806)*
Atlas Boiler & Welding Company ....G .... 815 963-3360
Elgin *(G-8960)*
Atomoweld Co ....G .... 773 736-5577
Chicago *(G-3987)*
Ats Sortimat USA LLC ....D .... 847 925-1234
Rolling Meadows *(G-18711)*
Awerkamp Machine Co ....E .... 217 222-3480
Quincy *(G-17797)*
B & W Machine Company Inc ....G .... 847 364-4500
Elk Grove Village *(G-9329)*
B J Fehr Machine Co ....G .... 309 923-8691
Roanoke *(G-18048)*
B T Brown Manufacturing ....G .... 815 947-3633
Kent *(G-12665)*
Bales Mold Service Inc ....E .... 630 852-4665
Downers Grove *(G-8394)*
Baley Enterprises Inc ....G .... 708 681-0900
Melrose Park *(G-14599)*
Barton Manufacturing LLC ....F .... 217 428-0726
Decatur *(G-7844)*
Bc Welding Inc ....G .... 708 258-0076
Peotone *(G-17484)*
Bear Mtal Wldg Fabrication Inc ....G .... 630 261-9353
Lombard *(G-13767)*
Beaver Creek Enterprises Inc ....F .... 815 723-9455
Joliet *(G-12463)*
Bessler Welding Inc ....F .... 309 699-6224
East Peoria *(G-8701)*
Best Machine & Welding Co Inc ....E .... 708 343-4455
Woodridge *(G-22456)*
Bi State Steel Co ....G .... 309 755-0668
East Moline *(G-8671)*
Bierman Welding Inc ....F .... 217 342-2050
Effingham *(G-8827)*
Bulaw Welding & Engineering Co ....D .... 630 228-8300
Itasca *(G-12239)*
Burgess Manufacturing Inc ....F .... 847 680-1724
Libertyville *(G-13311)*
Burke Tool & Manufacturing Inc ....G .... 618 542-6441
Du Quoin *(G-8551)*
Burns Machine Company ....E .... 815 434-3131
Ottawa *(G-16952)*
C & B Welders Inc ....G .... 773 722-0097
Chicago *(G-4198)*
C E R Machining & Tooling Ltd ....G .... 708 442-9614
Lyons *(G-14034)*
C I F Industries Inc ....F .... 618 635-2010
Staunton *(G-20555)*
C J Holdings Inc ....G .... 309 274-3141
Chillicothe *(G-7163)*
C Keller Manufacturing Inc ....E .... 630 833-5593
Villa Park *(G-21240)*
C/B Machine Tool Corp ....G .... 847 288-1807
Franklin Park *(G-10422)*
Carrolls Welding & Fabrication ....G .... 217 728-8720
Sullivan *(G-20741)*
Casward Tool Works Inc ....G .... 773 486-4900
Chicago *(G-4254)*
Certiweld Inc ....G .... 708 389-0148
Crestwood *(G-7481)*
Cervones Welding Service Inc ....G .... 847 985-6865
Schaumburg *(G-19470)*
Chicago Tube and Iron Company ....E .... 815 834-2500
Romeoville *(G-18810)*
Cisne Iron Works Inc ....F .... 618 673-2188
Cisne *(G-7250)*
Cokel Dj Welding Bay & Muffler ....G .... 309 385-4567
Princeville *(G-17763)*
Cokel Welding Shop ....G .... 217 357-3312
Carthage *(G-3312)*
Colfax Welding & Fabricating ....G .... 847 359-4433
Palatine *(G-17013)*
Comers Welding Service Inc ....G .... 630 892-0168
Montgomery *(G-15039)*
Comet Fabricating & Welding Co ....E .... 815 229-0468
Rockford *(G-18316)*
Commercial Machine Services ....F .... 847 806-1901
Elk Grove Village *(G-9386)*
Component Tool & Mfg Co ....F .... 708 672-5505
Crete *(G-7510)*
Concept Industries Inc ....G .... 847 258-3545
Elk Grove Village *(G-9388)*
Connell Mc Machine & Welding ....G .... 815 868-2275
Mc Connell *(G-14442)*
Corrugated Converting Eqp ....F .... 618 532-2138
Centralia *(G-3410)*
County Tool & Die ....G .... 217 324-6527
Litchfield *(G-13683)*
Custom Machinery Inc ....G .... 847 678-3033
Schiller Park *(G-19818)*
Cyclops Welding Co ....G .... 815 223-0685
La Salle *(G-12769)*
Cylinder Services Inc ....G .... 630 466-9820
Sugar Grove *(G-20721)*
D & H Precision Tooling Co ....G .... 815 653-9611
Wonder Lake *(G-22322)*
D & M Welding Inc ....G .... 708 233-6080
Bridgeview *(G-2481)*
D M Manufacturing 2 Inc ....G .... 618 455-3550
Sainte Marie *(G-19323)*
D N Welding & Fabricating Inc ....G .... 847 244-6410
Waukegan *(G-21546)*
D W Terry Welding Company ....G .... 618 433-9722
Alton *(G-570)*
Daniel Mfg Inc ....F .... 309 963-4227
Carlock *(G-3050)*
Darnell Welding ....G .... 618 945-9538
Bridgeport *(G-2451)*
Daves Welding Service Inc ....G .... 630 655-3224
Darien *(G-7792)*
David Schutte ....G .... 217 223-5464
Quincy *(G-17818)*
Device Technologies Inc ....G .... 630 553-7178
Yorkville *(G-22655)*
Dons Welding ....G .... 847 526-1177
Wauconda *(G-21455)*
Dooling Machine Products Inc ....G .... 618 254-0724
Hartford *(G-11610)*
Duroweld Company Inc ....E .... 847 680-3064
Lake Bluff *(G-12841)*
Dyers Machine Service Inc ....G .... 708 496-8100
Summit Argo *(G-20762)*
E & E Machine & Engineering Co ....G .... 708 841-5208
Riverdale *(G-18018)*
Eagle Machine Company ....G .... 312 243-7407
Chicago *(G-4671)*
East Savanna Welding ....G .... 815 273-7371
Savanna *(G-19396)*
Edward F Data ....G .... 708 597-0158
Alsip *(G-461)*
Edwardsville Mch & Wldg Co Inc ....G .... 618 656-5145
Edwardsville *(G-8798)*
Eenigenburg Mfg Inc ....G .... 708 474-0850
Lansing *(G-13161)*
Ekstrom Carlson Fabricating Co ....G .... 815 226-1511
Rockford *(G-18360)*
Ellners Welding and Machine Sp ....G .... 618 282-4302
Prairie Du Rocher *(G-17739)*
Emerald Machine Inc ....G .... 773 924-3659
Chicago *(G-4740)*
Emv Welding Inc ....G .... 630 853-3199
Aurora *(G-1145)*
Erva Tool & Die Company ....G .... 773 533-7806
Chicago *(G-4775)*
Estructuras Inc ....F .... 773 522-2200
Chicago *(G-4781)*
Eton Machine Co Ltd ....F .... 847 426-3380
Elgin *(G-9030)*
Eveready Welding Service Inc ....G .... 708 532-2432
Tinley Park *(G-20910)*
Extreme Welding & Machine Serv ....G .... 618 272-7237
Ridgway *(G-17984)*
F Vogelmann and Company ....F .... 815 469-2285
Frankfort *(G-10321)*
Fabco Enterprises Inc ....G .... 708 333-4644
Harvey *(G-11666)*
Fabricating & Welding Corp ....E .... 773 928-2050
Chicago *(G-4809)*
Farmweld Inc ....E .... 217 857-6423
Teutopolis *(G-20852)*
Fast Forward Welding Inc ....G .... 815 254-1901
Plainfield *(G-17599)*
Fehring Ornamental Iron Works ....F .... 217 483-6727
Chatham *(G-3620)*
Felde Tool & Machine Co Inc ....F .... 309 692-5870
Peoria *(G-17360)*
Folk Race Cars ....G .... 815 629-2418
Durand *(G-8585)*
Force Manufacturing Inc ....G .... 847 265-6500
Lake Villa *(G-13013)*
Fox Valley Signs Inc ....G .... 630 896-3113
Aurora *(G-1158)*
Fred Stollenwerk ....G .... 309 852-3794
Kewanee *(G-12685)*
Fricker Machine Shop & Salvage ....G .... 618 285-3271
Elizabethtown *(G-9245)*
Gengler-Lowney Laser Works ....F .... 630 801-4840
Aurora *(G-1161)*
Giovanini Metals Corp ....G .... 815 842-0500
Pontiac *(G-17702)*
Global Field Services Intl Inc ....G .... 847 931-8930
Elgin *(G-9048)*
Gma Inc ....G .... 630 595-1255
Bensenville *(G-1910)*
Golden Hydraulic & Machine ....G .... 708 597-4265
Blue Island *(G-2253)*
Graham Welding Inc ....G .... 217 422-1423
Decatur *(G-7885)*
Great Lakes Mech Svcs Inc ....F .... 708 672-5900
Lincolnshire *(G-13451)*
Greens Machine Shop ....G .... 618 532-4631
Centralia *(G-3417)*
Gridley Welding Inc ....G .... 309 747-2325
Gridley *(G-11406)*
Grimm Metal Fabricators Inc ....E .... 630 792-1710
Lombard *(G-13807)*
Grover Welding Company ....G .... 847 966-3119
Skokie *(G-20007)*
H & H Services Inc ....F .... 618 633-2837
Hamel *(G-11528)*
Halter Machine Shop Inc ....G .... 618 943-2224
Lawrenceville *(G-13201)*
Harbor Manufacturing Inc ....D .... 708 614-6400
Tinley Park *(G-20920)*
Hattan Tool Company ....G .... 708 597-9308
Alsip *(G-471)*
HB Coatings LLC ....G .... 618 215-8161
Madison *(G-14149)*
Heavy Metal Industries LLC ....F .... 309 966-3007
Peoria *(G-17381)*
Hedricks Welding & Fabrication ....G .... 217 846-3230
Foosland *(G-10232)*
Heiss Welding Inc ....F .... 815 434-1838
Ottawa *(G-16961)*
Hfr Precision Machining Inc ....E .... 630 556-4325
Sugar Grove *(G-20727)*
Higgs Welding LLC ....G .... 217 925-5999
Dieterich *(G-8313)*
High Speed Welding Inc ....G .... 630 971-8929
Westmont *(G-21891)*
Hofmeister Wldg & Fabrication ....F .... 217 833-2451
Griggsville *(G-11412)*
Hogg Welding Inc ....G .... 708 339-0033
Harvey *(G-11670)*
Holshouser Machine & Tool Inc ....G .... 618 451-0164
Granite City *(G-11286)*
Howell Welding Corporation ....G .... 630 616-1100
Franklin Park *(G-10489)*
Hutton Welding Service Inc ....G .... 217 932-5585
Casey *(G-3386)*
ILmachine Company Inc ....F .... 847 243-9900
Wheeling *(G-22074)*
Incline Construction Inc ....G .... 815 577-8881
Joliet *(G-12516)*
Indium Corporation of America ....G .... 847 439-9134
Elk Grove Village *(G-9544)*
Industrial Maintenance & McHy ....G .... 815 726-0030
Mokena *(G-14874)*
Industrial Mint Wldg Machining ....D .... 773 376-6526
Chicago *(G-5178)*
Industrial Welding Inc ....F .... 815 535-9300
Rock Falls *(G-18139)*
J & I Son Tool Company Inc ....G .... 847 455-4200
Franklin Park *(G-10500)*
J & M Fab Metals Inc ....G .... 815 758-0354
Marengo *(G-14232)*

## PRODUCT SECTION — WELDING REPAIR SVC

| Company | Code | Phone |
|---|---|---|
| Jacksonville Machine Inc — Jacksonville (G-12396) | D | 217 243-1119 |
| Jacob Chambliss — Dahlgren (G-7691) | G | 618 731-6632 |
| Jacobs Boiler & Mech Inds Inc — Chicago (G-5269) | E | 773 385-9900 |
| Jakes McHning Rbilding Svc Inc — Aurora (G-1175) | E | 630 892-3291 |
| Jarvis Welding Co — Canton (G-2988) | G | 309 647-0033 |
| Jasiek Motor Rebuilding Inc — Oglesby (G-16750) | G | 815 883-3678 |
| Jav Machine Craft Inc — Chicago (G-5283) | G | 708 867-8608 |
| Jet Industries Inc — Chicago (G-5297) | E | 773 586-8900 |
| Jim Cokel Welding — Monmouth (G-15015) | G | 309 734-5063 |
| JW Welding — Aviston (G-1245) | G | 618 228-7213 |
| K & K Metal Works Inc — East Saint Louis (G-8758) | F | 618 271-4680 |
| K & K Tool & Die Inc — Bloomington (G-2187) | F | 309 829-4479 |
| K & P Welding — Watson (G-21433) | G | 217 536-5245 |
| K D Welding Inc — Hanover (G-11572) | G | 815 591-3545 |
| K Three Welding Service Inc — Chicago (G-5344) | G | 708 563-2911 |
| K&R Enterprises I Inc — Lake Barrington (G-12815) | D | 847 502-3371 |
| Karly Iron Works Inc — Crystal Lake (G-7597) | G | 815 477-3430 |
| Kemper Industries — Marshall (G-14324) | G | 217 826-5712 |
| Kenneth W Templeman — Volo (G-21315) | G | 847 912-2740 |
| Kim Gough — Monmouth (G-15017) | G | 309 734-3511 |
| Koerner Aviation Inc — Kankakee (G-12636) | G | 815 932-4222 |
| Ksem Inc — Edwardsville (G-8805) | G | 618 656-5388 |
| L E D Tool & Die Inc — Chicago (G-5422) | G | 708 597-2505 |
| L M Machine Shop Inc — Rock Falls (G-18141) | G | 815 625-3256 |
| Lake Fabrication Inc — Villa Grove (G-21229) | G | 217 832-2761 |
| Laystrom Manufacturing Co — Chicago (G-5474) | D | 773 342-4800 |
| Lee Brothers Welding Inc — Galesburg (G-10765) | G | 309 342-6017 |
| Legna Iron Works Inc — Roselle (G-18952) | E | 630 894-8056 |
| Leroys Welding & Fabg Inc — Wheeling (G-22092) | F | 847 215-6151 |
| Lewis Process Systems Inc — Carol Stream (G-3184) | F | 630 510-8200 |
| Linne Machine Company Inc — Danville (G-7747) | G | 217 446-5746 |
| Lion Welding Service Inc — Addison (G-181) | G | 630 543-5230 |
| Lous Spring and Welding Shop — Peru (G-17517) | G | 815 223-4282 |
| Luebbers Welding & Mfg Inc — Carlyle (G-3056) | F | 618 594-2489 |
| M & F Fabrication & Welding — Concord (G-7368) | G | 217 457-2221 |
| M & J Manufacturing Co Inc — Elk Grove Village (G-9601) | F | 847 364-6066 |
| M & M Welding Inc — Sycamore (G-20808) | G | 815 895-3955 |
| Magnetic Inspection Lab Inc — Elk Grove Village (G-9606) | D | 847 437-4488 |
| Mar-Fre Manufacturing Co — Saint Charles (G-19214) | F | 630 377-1022 |
| Mark Lahey — Jacksonville (G-12401) | G | 217 243-4433 |
| Marlboro Wire Ltd — Quincy (G-17855) | E | 217 224-7989 |
| Mason Welding Inc — S Chicago Hts (G-19106) | G | 708 755-0621 |
| Matrix Machine & Tool Mfg — River Grove (G-18011) | G | 708 452-8707 |
| MB Machine Inc — Shannon (G-19900) | F | 815 864-3555 |
| McCloskey Eyman Mlone Mfg Svcs — Canton (G-2991) | G | 309 647-4000 |
| McFarland Welding and Machine — Thompsonville (G-20863) | G | 618 627-2838 |
| Meadoweld Machine Inc — South Beloit (G-20161) | G | 815 623-3939 |
| Mendota Welding & Mfg — Mendota (G-14727) | G | 815 539-6944 |
| Merritt Farm Equipment Inc — Carthage (G-3315) | G | 217 746-5331 |
| Meteer Manufacturing Co — Athens (G-941) | G | 217 636-8109 |
| Method Molds Inc — Loves Park (G-13965) | G | 815 877-0191 |
| Metzger Welding Service — Mattoon (G-14403) | G | 217 234-2851 |
| Mfw Services Inc — South Holland (G-20289) | G | 708 522-5879 |
| Midway Machine & Tool Co Inc — Alsip (G-491) | G | 708 385-3450 |
| Mihalis Marine — Chicago (G-5757) | G | 773 445-6220 |
| Milans Machining & Mfg Co Inc — Cicero (G-7222) | D | 708 780-6600 |
| Millers Eureka Inc — Chicago (G-5762) | F | 312 666-9383 |
| Misselhorn Welding & Machines — Campbell Hill (G-2978) | G | 618 426-3714 |
| Moline Welding Inc — Milan (G-14795) | F | 309 756-0643 |
| Moline Welding Inc — Milan (G-14796) | G | 309 756-0643 |
| Mt Vernon Mold Works Inc — Mount Vernon (G-15431) | E | 618 242-6040 |
| Murphy Brothers Enterprises — Chicago (G-5836) | G | 773 874-9020 |
| Mushro Machine & Tool Co — Streator (G-20697) | F | 815 672-5848 |
| Napier Machine & Welding Inc — Springfield (G-20486) | G | 217 525-8740 |
| National Tool & Machine Co — East Saint Louis (G-8762) | F | 618 271-6445 |
| Neals Trailer Sales — Lincoln (G-13416) | G | 217 792-5136 |
| Needham Shop Inc — Kaneville (G-12600) | G | 630 557-9019 |
| Nehring Electrical Works Co — Dekalb (G-8110) | C | 815 756-2741 |
| Newman Welding & Machine Shop — Benton (G-2037) | G | 618 435-5591 |
| Njc Machine Co — Lyons (G-14042) | F | 708 442-6004 |
| North Shore Truck & Equipment — Lake Bluff (G-12860) | G | 847 887-0200 |
| Norton Machine Co — Rossville (G-19050) | G | 217 748-6115 |
| Odom Tool and Technology Inc — Sycamore (G-20811) | G | 815 895-8545 |
| Oostman Fabricating & Wldg Inc — Westmont (G-21909) | F | 630 241-1315 |
| Orient Machining & Welding Inc — Dixmoor (G-8320) | E | 708 371-3500 |
| Orsolinis Welding & Fabg — Chicago (G-6016) | F | 773 722-9855 |
| Osbornes Mch Weld Fabrication — Argenta (G-691) | G | 217 795-4716 |
| P & G Machine & Tool Inc — Vandalia (G-21119) | G | 618 283-0273 |
| Papendik Inc — Orland Park (G-16883) | G | 708 492-6230 |
| Paramount Wire Specialties — Chicago (G-6080) | F | 773 252-5636 |
| Park Tool & Machine Co Inc — Villa Park (G-21275) | G | 630 530-5110 |
| Parker Fabrication Inc — Morton (G-15174) | E | 309 266-8413 |
| Patkus Machine Co — Rockford (G-18530) | G | 815 398-7818 |
| Performance Welding LLC — Maroa (G-14307) | G | 217 412-5722 |
| Peters Machine Inc — Decatur (G-7926) | F | 217 875-2578 |
| Petri Welding & Prop Repr Inc — Jacksonville (G-12407) | G | 217 243-1748 |
| Phoenix Welding Co Inc — Franklin Park (G-10549) | F | 630 616-1700 |
| PM Woodwind Repair Inc — Evanston (G-10088) | G | 847 869-7049 |
| Precision Tool Welding — Itasca (G-12345) | G | 630 285-9844 |
| Pro-Fab Metals Inc — Vandalia (G-21121) | G | 618 283-2986 |
| Production Fabg & Stamping Inc — S Chicago Hts (G-19111) | F | 708 755-5468 |
| Production Manufacturing — Warsaw (G-21371) | G | 217 256-4211 |
| Professional Metal Works LLC — Freeburg (G-10639) | F | 618 539-2214 |
| Quality Metal Works Inc — Stanford (G-20552) | G | 309 379-5311 |
| Quality Tool & Machine Inc — Chicago (G-6248) | G | 773 721-8655 |
| R & R Machining Inc — Benld (G-1806) | G | 217 835-4579 |
| R A R Machine & Manufacturing — Chicago (G-6264) | E | 630 260-9591 |
| R Machining Inc — Butler (G-2910) | G | 217 532-2174 |
| R-M Industries Inc — Addison (G-267) | F | 630 543-3071 |
| Ramseys Machine Co — Taylorville (G-20845) | G | 217 824-2320 |
| Rapco Ltd — Richview (G-17981) | G | 618 249-6614 |
| Reber Welding Service — Shelbyville (G-19914) | G | 217 774-3441 |
| Reco of IL Inc — Aurora (G-1208) | G | 630 898-2010 |
| Redi-Weld & Mfg Co Inc — Lake In The Hills (G-13004) | G | 815 455-4460 |
| Regal Steel Erectors LLC — Elgin (G-9162) | E | 847 888-3500 |
| Rex Radiator and Welding Co — East Dundee (G-8655) | G | 847 428-1112 |
| Rex Radiator and Welding Co — Chicago (G-6343) | G | 312 421-1531 |
| Rex Radiator and Welding Co — Rockdale (G-18230) | G | 815 725-6655 |
| Ri-Del Mfg Inc — Chicago (G-6349) | D | 312 829-8720 |
| River Valley Mechanical Inc — Putnam (G-17788) | G | 309 364-3776 |
| Rockford Precision Machine — Rockford (G-18582) | F | 815 873-1018 |
| Rodney Tite Welding — Ullin (G-21032) | G | 618 845-9072 |
| Rogers Metal Services Inc — Skokie (G-20079) | E | 847 679-4642 |
| Rw Welding Inc — Arlington Heights (G-832) | G | 847 541-5508 |
| S & S Welding & Fabrication — Elgin (G-9170) | G | 847 742-7344 |
| S & W Manufacturing Co Inc — Bensenville (G-1984) | E | 630 595-5044 |
| S D Custom Machining — Robinson (G-18072) | G | 618 544-7007 |
| Sanitary Stainless Services — Edwardsville (G-8813) | G | 618 659-8567 |
| Service Cutting & Welding — Chicago (G-6482) | G | 773 622-8366 |
| Service Sheet Metal Works Inc — Chicago (G-6483) | F | 773 229-0031 |
| Shanks Veterinary Equipment — Milledgeville (G-14818) | G | 815 225-7700 |
| Shannon & Sons Welding — Aurora (G-1215) | G | 630 898-7778 |
| Sheas Iron Works Inc — Lake Villa (G-13026) | E | 847 356-2922 |
| Sheets & Cylinder Welding Inc — Chicago (G-6494) | G | 800 442-2200 |
| Shup Tool & Machine Co — Granite City (G-11302) | G | 618 931-2596 |
| Sigel Welding — Sigel (G-19938) | G | 217 844-2412 |
| Silver Machine Shop Inc — Champaign (G-3540) | G | 217 359-5717 |
| Sivco Welding Company — Geneseo (G-10804) | G | 309 944-5171 |
| Smith Welding LLC — Saint Elmo (G-19311) | G | 618 829-5414 |
| South Side Bler Wldg Works Inc — Orland Park (G-16893) | G | 708 478-1714 |
| South Subn Wldg & Fabg Co Inc — Posen (G-17736) | G | 708 385-7160 |
| Southwick Machine & Design Co — Colona (G-7348) | G | 309 949-2868 |
| Spaeth Welding Inc — New Baden (G-15865) | F | 618 588-3596 |
| Spannuth Boiler Co — Oak Park (G-16687) | G | 708 386-1882 |
| Special Tool Engineering Co — Chicago (G-6554) | F | 773 767-6690 |

Employee Codes: A=Over 500 employees, B=251-500, C=101-250, D=51-100, E=20-50, F=10-19, G=3-9

# WELDING REPAIR SVC

Spencer Welding Service Inc .............G....... 847 272-0580
  Northbrook  (G-16368)
Steel Services Enterprises ..................E ...... 708 259-1181
  Lansing  (G-13187)
Stevenson Fabrication Svcs Inc ..........G....... 815 468-7941
  Manteno  (G-14195)
Stuhlman Family LLC ..........................G....... 815 436-2432
  Plainfield  (G-17655)
Suburban Welding & Steel  LLC ..........F ...... 847 678-1264
  Franklin Park  (G-10599)
Sulzer Pump Services (us) Inc .............F ...... 815 600-7355
  Joliet  (G-12579)
Superior Joining Tech Inc ....................E ...... 815 282-7581
  Machesney Park  (G-14109)
Superior Welding Inc ...........................F ...... 618 544-8822
  Robinson  (G-18073)
Sycamore Welding & Fabg Co ............G....... 815 784-2557
  Genoa  (G-10885)
T & L Mfg Corporation .........................E ...... 630 898-7100
  Aurora  (G-1220)
Tait Machine Tool Inc ...........................G....... 815 932-2011
  Kankakee  (G-12656)
Taylor Design Inc ..................................G....... 815 389-3991
  Roscoe  (G-18924)
Taylor Off Road Racing .......................G....... 815 544-4500
  Belvidere  (G-1788)
Technology One Welding Inc ...............G....... 630 871-1296
  Carol Stream  (G-3253)
Telza Welding Inc ..................................G....... 773 777-4467
  Chicago  (G-6693)
Terry Tool & Machining Corp ...............G....... 847 289-1054
  East Dundee  (G-8658)
Tewell Bros Machine Inc .....................F ...... 217 253-6303
  Tuscola  (G-21025)
Thornton Welding Service Inc .............E ...... 217 877-0610
  Decatur  (G-7952)
Titan Tool Works LLC ...........................F ...... 630 221-1080
  Carol Stream  (G-3255)
Toledo Machine & Welding  Inc ..........G....... 217 849-2251
  Toledo  (G-20968)
Tomko Machine Works Inc ...................G....... 630 244-0902
  Lemont  (G-13266)
Tony Weishaar .......................................G....... 217 774-2774
  Shelbyville  (G-19917)
Tonys Welding Service Inc ...................G....... 618 532-9353
  Centralia  (G-3436)
Toolweld Inc ............................................G....... 847 854-8013
  Algonquin  (G-407)
Torrence Machine & Tool Co ................G....... 815 469-1850
  Mokena  (G-14913)
Trailers Inc .............................................G....... 217 472-6000
  Chapin  (G-3588)
Tri-Cunty Wldg Fabrication LLC ..........E ...... 217 543-3304
  Arthur  (G-923)
Triplett Entereprises Inc .....................G....... 708 333-9421
  Oak Forest  (G-16592)
Trotters Manufacturing Co ....................G....... 217 364-4540
  Buffalo  (G-2649)
Tylers Fab & Welding Inc ....................G....... 217 283-6855
  Hoopeston  (G-12120)
Uhlar Inc .................................................G....... 815 961-0970
  Rockford  (G-18659)
United Machine Works  Inc ..................G....... 847 352-5252
  Schaumburg  (G-19781)
United Maint Wldg & McHy C ..............F ...... 708 458-1705
  Bedford Park  (G-1588)
United Tool and Engineering Co ..........D ...... 815 389-3021
  South Beloit  (G-20171)
Universal Broaching Inc ......................F ...... 847 228-1440
  Elk Grove Village  (G-9800)
V Brothers Machine Co ........................E ...... 708 652-0062
  Cicero  (G-7243)
Vaughn & Sons Machine Shop ............G....... 618 842-9048
  Fairfield  (G-10157)
Vindee Industries  Inc ..........................E ...... 815 469-3300
  Frankfort  (G-10375)
Wachs Technical Services Inc .............E ...... 847 537-8800
  Wheeling  (G-22179)
Walco Tool & Engineering Corp ..........D ...... 815 834-0225
  Romeoville  (G-18877)
Walt  Ltd .................................................E ...... 312 337-2756
  Chicago  (G-6936)
Wardzala Industries Inc .......................F ...... 847 288-9909
  Franklin Park  (G-10627)
WEb Production & Fabg Inc .................F ...... 312 733-6800
  Chicago  (G-6948)
Weiland Welding Inc .............................G....... 815 580-8079
  Cherry Valley  (G-3649)
Weld-Rite Service  Inc .........................E ...... 708 458-6000
  Bedford Park  (G-1592)

Welding Company of America ..............E ...... 630 806-2000
  Aurora  (G-1231)
Welding Shop .........................................G....... 773 785-1305
  Chicago  (G-6952)
Welding Specialties ..............................G....... 708 798-5388
  East Hazel Crest  (G-8667)
Wemco Inc ..............................................F ...... 708 388-1980
  Alsip  (G-543)
West End Tool & Die  Inc .....................G....... 815 462-3040
  New Lenox  (G-15927)
Wherry Machine & Welding Inc ..........G....... 309 828-5423
  Bloomington  (G-2235)
Williams Welding Service .....................G....... 217 235-1758
  Humboldt  (G-12130)
Wirfs Industries Inc ..............................F ...... 815 344-0635
  McHenry  (G-14571)
Wissmiller & Evans Road Eqp .............G....... 309 725-3598
  Cooksville  (G-7373)
Wittwer Brothers Inc .............................G....... 815 522-3589
  Monroe Center  (G-15025)
Ziglers Mch & Met Works Inc ..............G....... 815 652-7518
  Dixon  (G-8360)

## WELDING SPLYS, EXC GASES: Wholesalers

Ampco Metal Incorporated ...................E ...... 847 437-6000
  Arlington Heights  (G-711)
Lincoln Electric Company .....................F ...... 630 783-3600
  Bolingbrook  (G-2335)

## WELDING TIPS: Heat Resistant, Metal

American Machine ................................G....... 815 539-6558
  Mendota  (G-14715)
Orient Machining & Welding Inc .........E ...... 708 371-3500
  Dixmoor  (G-8320)
Two Four Seven Metal Laser ................G....... 847 250-5199
  Itasca  (G-12369)
Welding Company of America ..............E ...... 630 806-2000
  Aurora  (G-1231)

## WELDMENTS

Ablaze Welding & Fabricating ..............G....... 815 965-0046
  Rockford  (G-18248)
Ryan Manufacturing Inc .......................G....... 815 695-5310
  Newark  (G-15934)

## WELL CASINGS: Iron & Steel, Made In Steel Mills

Ptc Group Holdings Corp ......................D ...... 708 757-4747
  Chicago Heights  (G-7118)

## WESTERN APPAREL STORES

Horse Creek Outfitters .........................G....... 217 544-2740
  Springfield  (G-20452)

## WET CORN MILLING

ADM Holdings  LLC ...............................G....... 217 422-7281
  Decatur  (G-7821)
ADM Holdings  LLC ...............................G....... 312 634-8100
  Chicago  (G-3752)
ADM Holdings  LLC ...............................G....... 217 424-5200
  Decatur  (G-7822)
ADM Trucking  Inc .................................G....... 217 451-4288
  Decatur  (G-7823)
Archer-Daniels-Midland Company ........A ....... 312 634-8100
  Chicago  (G-3941)
Archer-Daniels-Midland Company ........C ....... 217 935-3620
  Clinton  (G-7277)
Archer-Daniels-Midland Company ........E ....... 217 424-5413
  Decatur  (G-7835)
Archer-Daniels-Midland Company ........C ....... 217 424-5200
  Decatur  (G-7841)
Bio Fuels By American Farmers ..........F ...... 561 859-6251
  Benton  (G-2023)
Cargill  Incorporated .............................E ....... 630 505-7788
  Naperville  (G-15616)
Ingredion Incorporated .........................A ....... 708 551-2600
  Westchester  (G-21845)
Ingredion Incorporated .........................D ...... 309 550-9136
  Mapleton  (G-14210)
Ingredion Incorporated .........................G....... 708 551-2600
  Chicago  (G-5193)
Ingredion Incorporated .........................C ....... 708 728-3535
  Summit Argo  (G-20764)
Ingredion Incorporated .........................C ....... 708 563-2400
  Argo  (G-693)
Lee Gilster-Mary Corporation ...............D ...... 815 472-6456
  Momence  (G-14983)

# PRODUCT SECTION

Tate Lyle Ingrdnts Amricas LLC ..........A ....... 217 423-4411
  Decatur  (G-7950)
Tate Lyle Ingrdnts Amricas LLC ..........G....... 309 473-2721
  Heyworth  (G-11766)

## WHEEL & CASTER REPAIR SVCS

Kunz Industries Inc ..............................G....... 708 596-7717
  South Holland  (G-20285)

## WHEELCHAIR LIFTS

Lifts of Illinois Inc ................................G....... 309 923-7450
  Roanoke  (G-18052)
Mobilty Works ........................................G....... 815 254-2000
  Plainfield  (G-17629)

## WHEELCHAIRS

D ME To ME ...........................................F ...... 815 485-3632
  New Lenox  (G-15874)
Duroweld Company  Inc ........................E ...... 847 680-3064
  Lake Bluff  (G-12841)
G & M Industries Inc .............................G....... 618 344-6655
  Collinsville  (G-7326)
Heart 4 Heart Inc ..................................G....... 217 544-2699
  Springfield  (G-20449)
Hogg Welding Inc ..................................G....... 708 339-0033
  Harvey  (G-11670)
Mobility Connection  Inc ......................G....... 815 965-8090
  Rockford  (G-18510)
United Seating & Mobility LLC ............G....... 309 699-0509
  East Peoria  (G-8737)

## WHEELS

Caster Warehouse  Inc .........................F ...... 847 836-5712
  Carpentersville  (G-3279)
Forza Customs .......................................G....... 708 474-6625
  Lansing  (G-13162)
Hoosier Stamping & Mfg Corp .............G....... 812 426-2778
  Grayville  (G-11370)
Midwest Wheel Covers Inc ...................G....... 847 609-9980
  Barrington  (G-1291)
Titan International  Inc .........................A ....... 217 221-4498
  Quincy  (G-17895)
Wheel Worx North  LLC ........................G....... 309 346-3535
  Pekin  (G-17294)

## WHEELS & BRAKE SHOES: Railroad, Cast Iron

Alstom Transportation Inc ....................E ....... 630 369-2201
  Naperville  (G-15598)
Anchor Brake Shoe Company  LLC .....G....... 630 293-1110
  West Chicago  (G-21660)

## WHEELS & GRINDSTONES, EXC ARTIFICIAL: Abrasive

Abrasive Technology  Inc ......................E ...... 847 888-7100
  Elgin  (G-8931)

## WHEELS, GRINDING: Artificial

A Wheels  Inc .........................................G....... 847 699-7000
  Des Plaines  (G-8139)
Radiac Abrasives  Inc ...........................E ...... 630 898-0315
  Oswego  (G-16931)

## WHEELS: Abrasive

Abrasive Rubber Wheel Co ..................F ...... 847 587-0900
  Fox Lake  (G-10273)
Diagrind Inc ...........................................F ...... 708 460-4333
  Orland Park  (G-16854)
Grier Abrasive Co Inc ...........................C ....... 708 333-6445
  South Holland  (G-20271)
Hayes Abrasives  Inc ............................F ...... 217 532-6850
  Hillsboro  (G-11892)
Modern Abrasive Corp ..........................D ...... 815 675-2352
  Spring Grove  (G-20349)
Saint-Gobain Abrasives  Inc .................C ....... 630 868-8060
  Carol Stream  (G-3232)

## WHEELS: Disc, Wheelbarrow, Stroller, Etc, Stamped Metal

Livingston Innovations  LLC .................G....... 847 808-0900
  Buffalo Grove  (G-2727)
Titan Wheel Corp Illinois .......................A ....... 217 228-6023
  Quincy  (G-17898)

## PRODUCT SECTION

### WHEELS: Polishing
American Buff Intl Inc.................................F....... 217 465-1411
  Paris *(G-17141)*
Matchless Metal Polish Company..........E....... 773 924-1515
  Chicago *(G-5649)*

### WHEELS: Railroad Car, Cast Steel
Amsted Industries Incorporated............B....... 312 645-1700
  Chicago *(G-3896)*
Colson Group Holdings LLC....................G....... 630 613-2941
  Oakbrook Terrace *(G-16704)*
Evraz Inc NA..............................................C....... 312 533-3621
  Chicago *(G-4792)*

### WHEELS: Rolled, Locomotive
Adams Elevator Equipment Co................E....... 847 581-2900
  Chicago *(G-3743)*

### WHISTLES
Burke Whistles Inc..................................G....... 618 534-7953
  Murphysboro *(G-15574)*

### WICKER PRDTS
Standard Container Co of Edgar.............E....... 847 438-1510
  Lake Zurich *(G-13134)*

### WIG & HAIRPIECE STORES
Casper Ernest E Hairgoods......................G....... 773 545-2800
  Chicago *(G-4249)*
Hairline Creations Inc..............................F....... 773 282-5454
  Chicago *(G-5032)*

### WIGS & HAIRPIECES
Casper Ernest E Hairgoods......................G....... 773 545-2800
  Chicago *(G-4249)*

### WINCHES
Allegion S&S US Holding Co...................C....... 815 875-3311
  Princeton *(G-17742)*
Mega International Ltd............................G....... 309 764-5310
  Moline *(G-14956)*

### WIND CHIMES
River City Sign Company Inc..................G....... 309 796-3606
  Silvis *(G-19940)*

### WINDINGS: Coil, Electronic
A J Smoy Co Inc......................................E....... 773 775-8282
  Schaumburg *(G-19419)*
Altran Corp..............................................E....... 815 455-5650
  Crystal Lake *(G-7531)*
Coilcraft Incorporated............................D....... 815 732-6834
  Oregon *(G-16820)*
Coilcraft Incorporated............................D....... 815 288-7051
  Dixon *(G-8326)*
Magnetic Coil Manufacturing Co...........E....... 630 787-1948
  Wood Dale *(G-22395)*
Michele Terrell......................................G....... 312 305-0876
  Evanston *(G-10072)*
Nelco Coil Supply Company..................E....... 847 259-7517
  Mount Prospect *(G-15354)*
Olympic Controls Corp..........................E....... 847 742-3566
  Elgin *(G-9128)*
Pnc Inc..................................................D....... 815 946-2328
  Polo *(G-17690)*
Qcircuits Inc.........................................E....... 847 797-6678
  Rolling Meadows *(G-18771)*

### WINDMILLS: Electric Power Generation
Awem Corporation..................................G....... 217 670-1451
  Springfield *(G-20392)*
Lakeview Energy LLC..............................E....... 312 386-5897
  Chicago *(G-5446)*
Sexton Wind Power LLC.........................G....... 224 212-1250
  Lake Bluff *(G-12866)*
Stanton Wind Energy LLC.......................F....... 312 224-1400
  Chicago *(G-6574)*
Trinity Structural Towers Inc..................F....... 217 935-7900
  Clinton *(G-7290)*
Vestas-American Wind Tech Inc............G....... 815 646-4280
  Tiskilwa *(G-20960)*
Willow Creek Energy LLC........................G....... 312 224-1400
  Chicago *(G-6987)*

### WINDMILLS: Farm Type
Lakeview Energy LLC..............................E....... 312 386-5897
  Chicago *(G-5446)*

### WINDOW & DOOR FRAMES
A-Ok Inc..................................................E....... 815 943-7431
  Harvard *(G-11616)*
Advantage Manufacturing Inc................F....... 773 626-2200
  Chicago *(G-3774)*
Alliance Door and Hardware LLC...........G....... 630 451-7070
  Bridgeview *(G-2461)*
Anchor Welding & Fabrication...............G....... 815 937-1640
  Aroma Park *(G-878)*
Centor North America Inc.....................E....... 630 957-1000
  Aurora *(G-982)*
Charles Sheridan and Sons....................G....... 847 903-7209
  Evanston *(G-10020)*
Climate Sltion Wndows Dors Inc...........E....... 847 233-9800
  Franklin Park *(G-10438)*
Continental Window South Inc.............F....... 773 767-1300
  Chicago *(G-4462)*
La Force Inc..........................................G....... 630 325-1950
  Willowbrook *(G-22218)*
Logan Square Aluminum Sup Inc..........D....... 847 985-1700
  Schaumburg *(G-19622)*
Logan Square Aluminum Sup Inc..........F....... 847 676-4767
  Lincolnwood *(G-13523)*
Logan Square Aluminum Sup Inc..........G....... 773 846-8300
  Chicago *(G-5531)*
Logan Square Aluminum Sup Inc..........C....... 773 278-3600
  Chicago *(G-5532)*
Midwest Detention Systems Inc............G....... 815 521-4580
  Minooka *(G-14843)*
Nelson Sash Systems Inc......................G....... 708 385-5815
  Alsip *(G-498)*
Summit Window Co Inc.........................G....... 708 594-3200
  Summit Argo *(G-20767)*
Wall-Fill Company -...............................G....... 630 668-3400
  Wheaton *(G-21988)*

### WINDOW BLIND CLEANING SVCS
Drexel House of Drapes Inc..................G....... 618 624-5415
  Belleville *(G-1627)*
Olshaws Interior Services.....................G....... 312 421-3131
  Chicago *(G-5985)*

### WINDOW BLIND REPAIR SVCS
Shade Brookline Co...............................F....... 773 274-5513
  Chicago *(G-6487)*
Ultrasonic Blind Co................................G....... 847 579-8084
  Libertyville *(G-13393)*

### WINDOW CLEANING SVCS
James A Freund LLC.............................G....... 630 664-7692
  Oswego *(G-16923)*

### WINDOW FRAMES & SASHES: Plastic
Advanced Window Corp........................E....... 773 379-3500
  Chicago *(G-3773)*
Ilpea Industries Inc...............................D....... 309 343-3332
  Galesburg *(G-10760)*
Simonton Building Products Inc...........B....... 217 466-2851
  Paris *(G-17162)*
Simonton Holdings Inc..........................F....... 304 428-8261
  Deerfield *(G-8055)*
Simonton Windows Inc........................G....... 217 466-2851
  Paris *(G-17163)*
Tempco Products Co............................D....... 618 544-3175
  Robinson *(G-18074)*

### WINDOW FRAMES, MOLDING & TRIM: Vinyl
Continental Window and GL Corp.........F....... 773 794-1600
  Chicago *(G-4461)*
Herschberger Window Mfg...................G....... 217 543-2106
  Tuscola *(G-21021)*
Logan Square Aluminum Sup Inc..........D....... 773 235-2500
  Chicago *(G-5530)*

### WINDOW FURNISHINGS WHOLESALERS
EZ Blinds and Drapery Inc....................F....... 708 246-6600
  La Grange *(G-12731)*
Shapco Inc.............................................G....... 847 229-1439
  Wheeling *(G-22149)*

### WINDOW SASHES, WOOD
Classic Windows Inc..............................F....... 847 362-3100
  Libertyville *(G-13315)*
Just Sashes.............................................G....... 773 205-1429
  Chicago *(G-5338)*

### WINDOW SCREENING: Plastic
Silver Line Building Pdts LLC.................B....... 708 474-9100
  Lansing *(G-13184)*

### WINDOW SQUEEGEES
W J Dennis & Company........................F....... 847 697-4800
  Elgin *(G-9225)*

### WINDOWS: Frames, Wood
ROW Window Company.........................G....... 815 725-5491
  Plainfield *(G-17647)*

### WINDOWS: Storm, Wood
ERA Development Group Inc................E....... 708 252-6979
  Northbrook *(G-16251)*
J&E Storm Services Inc........................G....... 630 401-3793
  Tinley Park *(G-20925)*

### WINDOWS: Wood
Monda Window & Door Corp................E....... 773 254-8888
  Chicago *(G-5792)*
Pella Corporation...................................B....... 309 663-7132
  Bloomington *(G-2211)*
Pella Corporation...................................B....... 309 663-7132
  Bloomington *(G-2212)*
Pella Corporation...................................B....... 309 663-7132
  Bloomington *(G-2213)*
Pella Corporation...................................B....... 309 663-7132
  Bloomington *(G-2214)*

### WINDSHIELD WIPER SYSTEMS
Taap Corp...............................................F....... 224 676-0653
  Wheeling *(G-22163)*

### WINDSHIELDS: Plastic
Precision Plastic Products.....................G....... 217 784-4920
  Gibson City *(G-10906)*

### WINE & DISTILLED ALCOHOLIC BEVERAGES WHOLESALERS
Agave Loco LLC.....................................F....... 847 383-6052
  Vernon Hills *(G-21142)*
Dtrs Enterprises Inc..............................G....... 630 296-6890
  Bolingbrook *(G-2302)*
Emmetts Tavern & Brewing Co.............G....... 630 434-8500
  Downers Grove *(G-8441)*
Emmetts Tavern & Brewing Co.............G....... 630 480-7181
  Wheaton *(G-21945)*
Emmetts Tavern & Brewing Co.............F....... 847 359-1533
  Palatine *(G-17025)*
Emmetts Tavern & Brewing Co.............F....... 847 428-4500
  West Dundee *(G-21796)*

### WINE CELLARS, BONDED: Wine, Blended
Blue Sky Vineyard..................................G....... 618 995-9463
  Makanda *(G-14162)*
Shale Lake LLC......................................G....... 618 637-2470
  Staunton *(G-20558)*

### WIRE
Accurate Wire Strip Frming Inc.............F....... 630 260-1000
  Carol Stream *(G-3089)*
Aif Inc....................................................E....... 630 495-0077
  Addison *(G-27)*
Central Wire Inc....................................C....... 815 923-2131
  Union *(G-21034)*
E H Baare Corporation..........................C....... 618 546-1575
  Robinson *(G-18062)*
Highland Wire Inc..................................F....... 618 654-2161
  Highland *(G-11795)*
Lift-All Company Inc.............................E....... 630 534-6860
  Glendale Heights *(G-11041)*
Moffat Wire & Display Inc.....................F....... 630 458-8560
  Addison *(G-218)*
Vargyas Networks Inc...........................F....... 630 929-3610
  Lisle *(G-13676)*

Vision Sales Incorporated ... G ... 630 483-1900
Bartlett (G-1385)

## WIRE & CABLE: Aluminum

All Line Inc ... G ... 630 820-1800
Naperville (G-15792)

## WIRE & CABLE: Aluminum

Conex Cable LLC ... E ... 800 877-8089
Dekalb (G-8078)
Nehring Electrical Works Co ... C ... 815 756-2741
Dekalb (G-8110)
Windy City Wire and Connectivi ... D ... 630 633-4500
Bolingbrook (G-2384)

## WIRE & CABLE: Nonferrous, Automotive, Exc Ignition Sets

Lkq Broadway Auto Parts Inc ... G ... 312 621-1950
Chicago (G-5526)

## WIRE & CABLE: Nonferrous, Building

Essex Group Inc ... D ... 630 628-7841
Addison (G-112)
Insulation Solutions Inc ... F ... 309 698-0062
East Peoria (G-8714)
Sterling Brands LLC ... E ... 847 229-1600
Wheeling (G-22156)

## WIRE & WIRE PRDTS

A J Kay Co ... F ... 224 475-0370
Mundelein (G-15462)
Accurate Wire Strip Frming Inc ... F ... 630 260-1000
Carol Stream (G-3089)
Acme Wire Products LLC ... E ... 708 345-4430
Broadview (G-2553)
Acorn Wire and Iron Works LLC ... E ... 312 243-6414
Chicago (G-3736)
Agena Manufacturing Co ... E ... 630 668-5086
Carol Stream (G-3093)
Alagor Industries Incorporated ... F ... 630 766-2910
Bensenville (G-1822)
Alecto Industries Inc ... E ... 708 344-1488
Maywood (G-14414)
Allform Manufacturing Co ... G ... 847 680-0144
Libertyville (G-13301)
Altak Inc ... D ... 630 622-0300
Bloomingdale (G-2092)
Amag Manufacturing Inc ... G ... 773 667-5184
Chicago (G-3843)
Androck Hardware Corporation ... F ... 815 229-1144
Rockford (G-18268)
Archer Wire International Corp ... C ... 708 563-1700
Bedford Park (G-1537)
Arcon Ring and Specialty Corp ... F ... 630 682-5252
Carol Stream (G-3104)
Ascent Mfg Co ... E ... 847 806-6600
Elk Grove Village (G-9314)
Astoria Wire Products Inc ... D ... 708 496-9950
Bedford Park (G-1539)
Atkore International Group Inc ... A ... 708 339-1610
Harvey (G-11658)
Atkore Intl Holdings Inc ... G ... 708 225-2051
Harvey (G-11659)
Available Spring and Mfg Co ... G ... 847 520-4854
Wheeling (G-22009)
Axelent Inc ... F ... 708 745-3128
Lockport (G-13705)
B & J Wire Inc ... E ... 877 787-9473
Chicago (G-4016)
B M I Inc ... C ... 847 839-6000
Schaumburg (G-19456)
Bel Mar Wire Products Inc ... F ... 773 342-3800
Chicago (G-4073)
Bergeron Group Inc ... E ... 815 741-1635
Joliet (G-12464)
Bristar ... G ... 847 678-5000
Franklin Park (G-10417)
C & J Metal Products Inc ... F ... 847 455-0766
Franklin Park (G-10421)
C R V Electronics Corp ... D ... 815 675-6500
Spring Grove (G-20329)
Cal-Ill Gasket Co ... F ... 773 287-9605
Chicago (G-4213)
Capitol Coil Inc ... F ... 847 891-1390
Schaumburg (G-19468)
Casey Spring Co Inc ... F ... 708 867-8949
Harwood Heights (G-11682)
Cda Industries Inc ... G ... 630 357-7654
Naperville (G-15623)
CFC Wire Forms Inc ... E ... 630 879-7575
Batavia (G-1428)
Chas O Larson Co ... E ... 815 625-0503
Rock Falls (G-18129)
Chicago Car Seal Company ... G ... 773 278-9400
Chicago (G-4310)
Chicago Hardware and Fix Co ... D ... 847 455-6609
Franklin Park (G-10429)
Chicagos Finest Ironworks ... G ... 708 895-4484
Lansing (G-13159)
Contractors Ready-Mix Inc ... G ... 217 482-5530
Mason City (G-14362)
Cutting Edge Industries Inc ... G ... 847 678-1777
Franklin Park (G-10451)
Darbe Products Company Inc ... G ... 630 985-0769
Woodridge (G-22468)
Dayton Superior Corporation ... E ... 815 732-3136
Oregon (G-16821)
Dayton Superior Corporation ... C ... 815 936-3300
Kankakee (G-12609)
Dove Industries Inc ... F ... 618 234-4509
Belleville (G-1626)
Dudek & Bock Spring Mfg Co ... C ... 773 379-4100
Chicago (G-4648)
E H Baare Corporation ... C ... 618 546-1575
Robinson (G-18062)
Economy Iron Inc ... F ... 708 343-1777
Melrose Park (G-14628)
Elite Wireworks Corporation ... F ... 630 837-9100
Bartlett (G-1345)
Essentra Components Inc ... C ... 815 943-6487
Forest Park (G-10241)
European Ornamental Iron Works ... G ... 630 705-9300
Addison (G-113)
Expandable Habitats ... G ... 815 624-6784
Rockton (G-18696)
Exterior Services ... G ... 773 660-1457
Chicago (G-4799)
Fbs Group Inc ... F ... 773 229-8675
Chicago (G-4821)
Franklin Display Group Inc ... D ... 815 544-6676
Belvidere (G-1752)
Franklin Wire Works Inc ... G ... 815 544-6676
Belvidere (G-1753)
Galena Manufacturing Co Inc ... G ... 815 777-2078
Galena (G-10722)
Gall Machine Co ... F ... 708 352-2800
Countryside (G-7426)
Guide Line Industries Inc ... F ... 815 777-3722
Scales Mound (G-19415)
Hamalot Inc ... E ... 847 944-1500
Schaumburg (G-19547)
Hudson Tool & Die Co ... F ... 847 678-8710
Franklin Park (G-10491)
Innovation Specialists Inc ... G ... 815 372-9001
New Lenox (G-15885)
Innovative Fix Solutions LLC ... F ... 815 395-8500
Rockford (G-18435)
Jason Incorporated ... C ... 630 627-7000
Addison (G-158)
JD Norman Industries Inc ... D ... 630 458-3700
Addison (G-159)
Johnson Tool Company ... G ... 708 453-8600
Huntley (G-12154)
Kan-Du Manufacturing Co Inc ... G ... 708 681-0370
Riverwoods (G-18040)
Keystone Consolidated Inds Inc ... E ... 309 697-7020
Peoria (G-17396)
L & P Guarding LLC ... C ... 708 325-0400
Bedford Park (G-1560)
Lake Cable LLC ... C ... 888 518-8086
Bensenville (G-1937)
Letraw Manufacturing Co ... G ... 815 987-9670
Rockford (G-18469)
Lew-El Tool & Manufacturing Co ... F ... 773 804-1133
Chicago (G-5497)
Lewis Spring and Mfg Company ... E ... 847 588-7030
Niles (G-15996)
Lodan Electronics Inc ... C ... 847 398-5311
Arlington Heights (G-795)
Marcal Rope & Rigging Inc ... G ... 618 462-0172
Metropolis (G-14756)
Marlboro Wire Ltd ... E ... 217 224-7989
Quincy (G-17855)
Master Spring & Wire Form Co ... E ... 708 453-2570
Itasca (G-12312)
Master-Halco Inc ... E ... 618 395-4365
Olney (G-16780)
MHS Ltd ... F ... 773 736-3333
Chicago (G-5716)
Midwest Tungsten Service Inc ... E ... 630 325-1001
Willowbrook (G-22223)
Midwest Wire Works ... F ... 815 874-1701
Rockford (G-18508)
Myco Inc ... C ... 815 395-8500
Rockford (G-18513)
Nixalite of America Inc ... F ... 309 755-8771
East Moline (G-8689)
Paragon Spring Company ... E ... 773 489-6300
Chicago (G-6076)
Partex Marking Systems Inc ... G ... 630 516-0400
Lombard (G-13842)
Perfection Spring Stmping Corp ... D ... 847 437-3900
Mount Prospect (G-15362)
Prairie State Industries Inc ... F ... 847 428-3641
Carpentersville (G-3297)
Precision Forming Stamping Co ... E ... 773 489-6868
Chicago (G-6170)
Precision Steel Warehouse Inc ... C ... 800 323-0740
Franklin Park (G-10560)
Rapid Wire Forms Inc ... G ... 773 586-6600
Chicago (G-6294)
Reino Tool & Manufacturing Co ... F ... 773 588-5800
Chicago (G-6326)
Remin Laboratories Inc ... D ... 815 723-1940
Joliet (G-12566)
Riverside Spring Company ... G ... 815 963-3334
Rockford (G-18557)
Rockford Rigging Inc ... F ... 309 263-0566
Roscoe (G-18914)
Sanco Industries Inc ... F ... 847 243-8675
Kildeer (G-12703)
Schaff International LLC ... E ... 847 438-4560
Lake Zurich (G-13125)
Solar Spring Company ... C ... 847 437-7838
Elk Grove Village (G-9742)
Spring Specialist Corporation ... G ... 815 562-7991
Kings (G-12705)
Stanley Hartco Co ... E ... 847 967-1122
Skokie (G-20090)
Steel Guard Inc ... F ... 773 342-6265
Chicago (G-6580)
Sterling Wire Products Inc ... G ... 815 625-3015
Rock Falls (G-18153)
SWB Inc ... G ... 847 438-1800
Lake Zurich (G-13136)
The Parts House ... G ... 309 343-0146
Galesburg (G-10777)
Trio Wire Products Inc ... G ... 815 469-2148
Frankfort (G-10372)
Tru-Guard Manufacturing Co ... G ... 773 568-5264
Chicago (G-6784)
Wardzala Industries Inc ... F ... 847 288-9909
Franklin Park (G-10627)
Wesco Spring Company ... E ... 773 838-3350
Chicago (G-6958)
White Eagle Spring & ... F ... 773 384-4455
Chicago (G-6972)
Will Don Corp ... D ... 773 276-7081
Chicago (G-6980)
Willdon Corp ... E ... 773 276-7080
Chicago (G-6981)
William Dach ... F ... 815 962-3455
Rockford (G-18683)
William Dudek Manufacturing Co ... E ... 773 622-2727
Chicago (G-6983)
Wire Mesh LLC ... G ... 815 579-8597
Oglesby (G-16752)
Wireformers Inc ... E ... 847 718-1920
Mount Prospect (G-15384)
Wiremasters Incorporated ... E ... 773 254-3700
Chicago (G-7005)
Woodland Fence Forest Pdts Inc ... G ... 630 393-2220
Warrenville (G-21369)

## WIRE CLOTH & WOVEN WIRE PRDTS, MADE FROM PURCHASED WIRE

Jsn Inc ... E ... 708 410-1800
Maywood (G-14426)

## WIRE FABRIC: Welded Steel

Blue Ridge Forge Inc ... G ... 309 274-5377
Chillicothe (G-7162)

## WIRE FENCING & ACCESS WHOLESALERS

United Fence Co Inc ... G ... 773 924-0773
Chicago (G-6823)

# PRODUCT SECTION

Vision Sales Incorporated............G....... 630 483-1900
Bartlett *(G-1385)*

## WIRE MATERIALS: Aluminum

Southwire Company LLC............D....... 618 662-8341
Flora *(G-10219)*

## WIRE MATERIALS: Copper

American Bare Conductor Inc............E....... 815 224-3422
La Salle *(G-12762)*
General Cable Industries Inc............D....... 618 542-4761
Du Quoin *(G-8556)*
Industrial Wire Cable II Corp............F....... 847 726-8910
Lake Zurich *(G-13087)*
Nehring Electrical Works Co............C....... 815 756-2741
Dekalb *(G-8110)*

## WIRE MATERIALS: Steel

Ace Custom Upholstery & Rod Sp............ 618 842-2913
Fairfield *(G-10135)*
Allform Manufacturing Co............G....... 847 680-0144
Libertyville *(G-13301)*
Ansonia Copper & Brass Inc............C....... 866 607-7066
Chicago *(G-3914)*
Apex Wire Products Company Inc............F....... 847 671-1830
Franklin Park *(G-10397)*
Arcelormittal South Chicago............G....... 312 899-3300
Chicago *(G-3933)*
Berens Inc............G....... 815 935-3237
Saint Anne *(G-19118)*
C & L Manufacturing Entps............G....... 618 465-7623
Alton *(G-565)*
Central Steel and Wire Company............D....... 773 471-3800
Chicago *(G-4272)*
Combined Metals Chicago LLC............G....... 847 683-0500
Hampshire *(G-11545)*
Dayton Superior Corporation............E....... 219 476-4106
Kankakee *(G-12607)*
Dayton Superior Corporation............C....... 815 936-3300
Kankakee *(G-12609)*
EDM Dept Inc............F....... 630 736-0531
Bartlett *(G-1343)*
Excel Specialty Corp............E....... 773 262-7575
Lake Forest *(G-12898)*
Hamalot Inc............E....... 847 944-1500
Schaumburg *(G-19547)*
Hohmann & Barnard Illinois LLC............E....... 773 586-6700
Chicago Ridge *(G-7150)*
Ifastgroupe Usa LLC............G....... 450 658-7148
Downers Grove *(G-8462)*
Major Wire Incorporated............F....... 708 457-0121
Norridge *(G-16105)*
Mapes & Sprowl Steel LLC............G....... 800 777-1025
Elk Grove Village *(G-9610)*
Powernail Company............E....... 800 323-1653
Lake Zurich *(G-13116)*
Raajrtna Stinless Wire USA Inc............F....... 847 923-8000
Schaumburg *(G-19711)*
Reino Tool & Manufacturing Co............F....... 773 588-5800
Chicago *(G-6326)*
Rockford Rigging Inc............F....... 309 263-0566
Roscoe *(G-18914)*
Salzgitter International............E....... 847 692-6312
Rosemont *(G-19029)*
The Parts House............G....... 309 343-0146
Galesburg *(G-10777)*
W R Pabich Manufacturing Co............F....... 773 486-4141
Chicago *(G-6925)*
William Dach............F....... 815 962-3455
Rockford *(G-18683)*
Wiretech Inc............G....... 815 986-9614
Rockford *(G-18686)*

## WIRE PRDTS: Ferrous Or Iron, Made In Wiredrawing Plants

McCarthy Enterprises Inc............G....... 847 367-5718
Libertyville *(G-13351)*

## WIRE PRDTS: Steel & Iron

Central Wire Inc............C....... 815 923-2131
Union *(G-21034)*
CFC Wire Forms Inc............E....... 630 879-7575
Batavia *(G-1428)*
Highland Southern Wire Inc............G....... 618 654-2161
Highland *(G-11792)*
O & W Wire Co Inc............F....... 773 776-5919
Chicago *(G-5958)*
Paragon Spring Company............E....... 773 489-6300
Chicago *(G-6076)*
S 4 Global Inc............G....... 708 325-1236
Bedford Park *(G-1581)*
Southern Steel and Wire Inc............G....... 618 654-2161
Highland *(G-11812)*
Steel Fabrication and Welding............G....... 773 343-0731
Cicero *(G-7230)*
Tj Wire Forming Inc............G....... 630 628-9209
Addison *(G-316)*

## WIRE ROPE CENTERS

Mighty Hook Inc............E....... 773 378-1909
Chicago *(G-5756)*

## WIRE WINDING OF PURCHASED WIRE

Jenco Metal Products Inc............F....... 847 956-0550
Mount Prospect *(G-15340)*
OHare Spring Company Inc............E....... 847 298-1360
Elk Grove Village *(G-9662)*

## WIRE: Communication

Andrew Corporation............E....... 779 435-6000
Joliet *(G-12454)*
Central Rubber Company............E....... 815 544-2191
Belvidere *(G-10437)*
Coleman Cable LLC............D....... 847 672-2300
Waukegan *(G-21543)*
Commscope Technologies LLC............A....... 708 236-6600
Westchester *(G-21835)*
Digi Cell Communications............F....... 847 808-7900
Wheeling *(G-22035)*
Gepco International Inc............E....... 847 795-9555
Des Plaines *(G-8201)*
Live Wire & Cable Co............G....... 847 577-5483
Arlington Heights *(G-794)*
Molex LLC............A....... 630 969-4550
Lisle *(G-13625)*
Molex LLC............G....... 630 527-4363
Bolingbrook *(G-2345)*
Molex LLC............E....... 630 512-8787
Downers Grove *(G-8489)*
Molex International Inc............F....... 630 969-4550
Lisle *(G-13627)*
Molex Premise Networks Inc............A....... 866 733-6659
Lisle *(G-13628)*
Woodhead Industries LLC............B....... 847 353-2500
Lincolnshire *(G-13490)*

## WIRE: Mesh

G F Ltd............E....... 708 333-8300
South Holland *(G-20269)*

## WIRE: Nonferrous

Amerline Enterprises Co Inc............E....... 847 671-6554
Schiller Park *(G-19802)*
ARI Industries Inc............D....... 630 953-9100
Addison *(G-44)*
C & L Manufacturing Entps............G....... 618 465-7623
Alton *(G-565)*
C R V Electronics Corp............E....... 815 675-6500
Spring Grove *(G-20329)*
Charles Industries Ltd............D....... 217 826-2318
Marshall *(G-14319)*
Chase Security Systems Inc............G....... 773 594-1919
Chicago *(G-4295)*
Chicago Car Seal Company............G....... 773 278-9400
Chicago *(G-4310)*
Circom Inc............E....... 630 595-4460
Bensenville *(G-1859)*
Coleman Cable LLC............E....... 847 672-2300
Waukegan *(G-21541)*
Coleman Cable LLC............D....... 847 672-2300
Waukegan *(G-21542)*
D & S Wire Inc............F....... 847 766-5520
Elk Grove Village *(G-9412)*
Erin Rope Corporation............F....... 708 377-1084
Blue Island *(G-2250)*
Excel Specialty Corp............E....... 773 262-7575
Lake Forest *(G-12898)*
Heil Sound Ltd............F....... 618 257-3000
Fairview Heights *(G-10168)*
Industrial Wire & Cable Corp............F....... 847 726-8910
Lake Zurich *(G-13086)*
Julian Elec Svc & Engrg Inc............E....... 630 920-8950
Westmont *(G-21895)*
Major Wire Incorporated............F....... 708 457-0121
Norridge *(G-16105)*
Methode Development Co............D....... 708 867-6777
Chicago *(G-5703)*
Neolight Technologies LLC............G....... 773 561-1410
Ingleside *(G-12196)*
P M Mfg Services Inc............G....... 630 553-6924
Yorkville *(G-22668)*
Teledyne Reynolds Inc............C....... 630 754-3300
Woodridge *(G-22522)*
Unified Wire and Cable Company............E....... 815 748-4876
Dekalb *(G-8128)*
United Universal Inds Inc............E....... 815 727-4445
Joliet *(G-12585)*

## WIRE: Steel, Insulated Or Armored

Fairbanks Wire Corporation............G....... 847 683-2600
Hampshire *(G-11550)*
Krueger and Company............E....... 630 833-5650
Elmhurst *(G-9899)*
Taubensee Steel & Wire Company............C....... 847 459-5100
Wheeling *(G-22164)*

## WIRE: Wire, Ferrous Or Iron

Heico Companies LLC............F....... 312 419-8220
Chicago *(G-5068)*
National Material Company LLC............E....... 847 806-7200
Elk Grove Village *(G-9646)*

## WOMEN'S & CHILDREN'S CLOTHING WHOLESALERS, NEC

ASap Specialties Inc Del............G....... 847 223-7699
Grayslake *(G-11321)*
Dzro-Bans International Inc............G....... 779 324-2740
Homewood *(G-12096)*
Leos Dancewear Inc............D....... 773 889-7700
River Forest *(G-17998)*
New York & Company Inc............F....... 630 232-7693
Geneva *(G-10853)*
New York & Company Inc............F....... 630 783-2910
Bolingbrook *(G-2352)*

## WOMEN'S & GIRLS' SPORTSWEAR WHOLESALERS

American Outfitters Ltd............E....... 847 623-3959
Waukegan *(G-21524)*
Art-Flo Shirt & Lettering Co............E....... 708 656-5422
Chicago *(G-3953)*
B and A Screen Printing............G....... 217 762-2632
Monticello *(G-15074)*
B JS Printables............G....... 618 656-8625
Edwardsville *(G-8789)*
Hermans Inc............E....... 309 206-4892
Rock Island *(G-18181)*
Screen Machine Incorporated............G....... 847 439-2233
Elk Grove Village *(G-9732)*

## WOMEN'S CLOTHING STORES

Express LLC............E....... 708 453-0566
Norridge *(G-16101)*
Fashahnn Corporation............G....... 773 994-3132
Chicago *(G-4814)*
Fellowship Black Light............G....... 773 826-7790
Chicago *(G-4834)*
Mjt Design and Prtg Entps Inc............G....... 708 240-4323
Hillside *(G-11926)*
Signature Design & Tailoring............F....... 773 375-4915
Chicago *(G-6510)*

## WOMEN'S CLOTHING STORES: Ready-To-Wear

A&B Apparel............G....... 815 962-5070
Rockford *(G-18241)*
Custom By Lamar Inc............F....... 312 738-2160
Chicago *(G-4520)*

## WOMEN'S FULL & KNEE LENGTH HOSIERY DYEING & FINISHING

Felice Hosiery Co Inc............G....... 312 922-3710
Chicago *(G-4832)*

## WOMEN'S SPECIALTY CLOTHING STORES

Casa Di Castronovo Inc............G....... 815 962-4731
Rockford *(G-18299)*
Live Love Hair............G....... 530 554-2471
Lansing *(G-13174)*

# WOMEN'S SPECIALTY CLOTHING STORES

New York & Company Inc............F....... 630 232-7693
  Geneva (G-10853)
New York & Company Inc............F....... 630 783-2910
  Bolingbrook (G-2352)

## WOMEN'S SPORTSWEAR STORES

B JS Printables..............................G....... 618 656-8625
  Edwardsville (G-8789)

## WOOD EXTRACT PRDTS

Bradley Smoker USA Inc.............F....... 309 343-1124
  Galesburg (G-10739)

## WOOD FENCING WHOLESALERS

Adams Street Iron Inc..................F....... 312 733-3229
  Evergreen Park (G-10109)

## WOOD PRDTS

Frame Game.................................G....... 573 754-2385
  Pleasant Hill (G-17680)
Jones Wood Products..................G....... 618 826-2682
  Rockwood (G-18704)
Linwood LLC................................G....... 217 446-1110
  Danville (G-7748)
Mhwp...........................................G....... 618 228-7600
  Aviston (G-1247)
Quality Plus.................................F....... 618 779-4931
  Litchfield (G-13695)
Weathertop Woodcraft.................G
  Carol Stream (G-3265)

## WOOD PRDTS: Applicators

Naegele Inc.................................G....... 708 388-7766
  Alsip (G-496)

## WOOD PRDTS: Brackets

Benchmark Cabinets & Mllwk Inc....E....... 309 697-5855
  Peoria (G-17316)

## WOOD PRDTS: Chair Cane, Rattan Or Reed

Springfield Woodworks.................G....... 217 483-7234
  Chatham (G-3625)

## WOOD PRDTS: Door Trim

Four Acre Wood Products.............F....... 217 543-2971
  Arthur (G-900)

## WOOD PRDTS: Handles, Tool

Illinois Tool Works Inc..................G....... 708 720-7070
  Frankfort (G-10332)

## WOOD PRDTS: Laundry

Danlee Wood Products Inc............G....... 815 938-9016
  Forreston (G-10268)

## WOOD PRDTS: Marquetry

Inlaid Woodcraft Co.....................F....... 815 784-6386
  Genoa (G-10880)

## WOOD PRDTS: Moldings, Unfinished & Prefinished

Agusta Mill Works........................G....... 309 787-4616
  Milan (G-14773)
Central Wood LLC........................G....... 217 543-2662
  Arcola (G-666)
Douglas County Mil Moldings........G....... 217 268-4689
  Arcola (G-667)
Omega Moulding North Amer Inc...G....... 630 509-2397
  Elk Grove Village (G-9664)
Sandwich Millworks Inc.................G....... 815 786-2700
  Sandwich (G-19377)
Star Moulding & Trim Company.....E....... 708 458-1040
  Bedford Park (G-1586)
Yuenger Wood Moulding Inc..........G....... 773 735-7100
  Naperville (G-15788)

## WOOD PRDTS: Mulch Or Sawdust

Golden Valley Hardscapes LLC......G....... 309 654-2261
  Cordova (G-7376)
Greencycle of Indiana Inc.............G....... 847 441-6606
  Northfield (G-16400)

## WOOD PRDTS: Mulch, Wood & Bark

Country Stone Inc........................E....... 309 787-1744
  Milan (G-14781)
E-Z Tree Recycling Inc..................... 773 493-8600
  Chicago (G-4670)
Illinois Wood Fiber Products..........G....... 847 836-6176
  Carpentersville (G-3288)
Melyx Inc....................................F....... 309 654-2551
  Cordova (G-7379)
Mulch Center LLC........................E....... 847 459-7200
  Deerfield (G-8041)
Rainbow Farms Enterprises Inc.....G....... 708 534-1070
  Monee (G-14999)

## WOOD PRDTS: Newel Posts

C A Larson & Son Inc..................E....... 847 717-6010
  Maple Park (G-14199)

## WOOD PRDTS: Outdoor, Structural

Griffard & Associates LLC............G....... 217 316-1732
  Quincy (G-17832)

## WOOD PRDTS: Panel Work

Wagners Custom Wood Design.....G....... 847 487-2788
  Island Lake (G-12221)

## WOOD PRDTS: Planters & Window Boxes

T2 Site Amenities Incorporated....G....... 847 579-9003
  Highland Park (G-11876)

## WOOD PRDTS: Poles

Better Built Buildings..................G....... 217 267-7824
  Westville (G-21928)

## WOOD PRDTS: Porch Work

Designer Decks By Mj Inc............G....... 815 744-7914
  Morris (G-15106)

## WOOD PRDTS: Signboards

Reynolds Holdings Inc.................G....... 630 739-0110
  Romeoville (G-18863)
Shawcraft Sign Co......................G....... 815 282-4105
  Machesney Park (G-14107)

## WOOD PRDTS: Stepladders

Werner Co..................................E....... 815 459-6020
  Crystal Lake (G-7676)

## WOOD PRDTS: Tackle Blocks

Midwest Lifting Products Inc.........G....... 214 356-7102
  Granite City (G-11294)

## WOOD PRDTS: Trophy Bases

A & M Products Company.............G....... 815 875-2667
  Princeton (G-17740)

## WOOD PRDTS: Window Backs, Store Or Lunchroom, Prefabricated

Max Resources Inc.....................G....... 708 478-5656
  Mokena (G-14884)

## WOOD PRODUCTS: Reconstituted

Claridge Products and Eqp Inc.....G....... 847 991-8822
  Elgin (G-8992)
Geneva Wood Fuels LLC..............E....... 773 296-0700
  Chicago (G-4936)
Jeld-Wen Inc..............................C....... 312 544-5041
  Chicago (G-5287)

## WOOD SHAVINGS BALES, MULCH TYPE, WHOLESALE

M & M Paltech Inc......................D....... 630 350-7890
  Belvidere (G-1767)

## WOOD TREATING: Millwork

Miller Whiteside Wood Working....G....... 309 827-6470
  Mc Lean (G-14463)

## WOOD TREATING: Railroad Cross-Ties

Midwest Intgrted Companies LLC....C....... 847 426-6354
  Gilberts (G-10926)

## WOOD TREATING: Structural Lumber & Timber

John A Biewer Lumber Company....F....... 815 357-6792
  Seneca (G-19887)
Northern Illinois Lumber Spc........E....... 630 859-3226
  Montgomery (G-15064)
Northwest Snow Timber Svc Ltd...G....... 847 778-4998
  Glenview (G-11175)
Southeast Wood Treating Inc......F....... 815 562-5007
  Rochelle (G-18110)

## WOOD TREATING: Wood Prdts, Creosoted

Marshall Bauer............................G....... 847 236-1847
  Bannockburn (G-1260)
Tronox Incorporated....................E....... 203 705-3704
  Madison (G-14154)

## WOODWORK & TRIM: Exterior & Ornamental

Orstrom Woodworking Ltd............G....... 847 697-1163
  Elgin (G-9131)

## WOODWORK & TRIM: Interior & Ornamental

Blue Chip Construction Inc..........F....... 630 208-5254
  Geneva (G-10812)
Brown Wood Products Company...F....... 847 673-4780
  Lincolnwood (G-13503)
Der Holtzmacher Ltd...................G....... 815 895-4887
  Sycamore (G-20792)
Doctors Interior Plantscaping......G....... 708 333-3323
  South Holland (G-20262)
Gingerich Custom Woodworking....F....... 217 578-3491
  Arthur (G-902)
Greatlakes Architectural Millw.....E....... 312 829-7110
  Chicago (G-5000)
Kempner Company Inc................F....... 312 733-1606
  Chicago (G-5376)
Wm Huber Cabinet Works............E....... 773 235-7660
  Chicago (G-7011)

## WOODWORK: Carved & Turned

Aph Custom Wood & Metal Pdts...G....... 708 410-1274
  Broadview (G-2558)
Brown Wood Products Company...F....... 847 673-4780
  Lincolnwood (G-13503)
Equustock LLC............................F....... 866 962-4686
  Loves Park (G-13940)

## WOODWORK: Interior & Ornamental, NEC

Becker Jules D Wood Products.....G....... 847 526-8002
  Wauconda (G-21445)
Bernhard Woodwork Ltd..............E....... 847 291-1040
  Northbrook (G-16214)
Extreme Woodworking Inc...........G....... 224 338-8179
  Round Lake (G-19055)
Historic Timber & Plank Inc.........E....... 618 372-4546
  Brighton (G-2542)
Onsite Woodwork Corporation......D....... 815 633-6400
  Loves Park (G-13971)
Parenti & Raffaelli Ltd.................C....... 847 253-5550
  Mount Prospect (G-15361)
Wampach Woodwork Inc.............F....... 847 742-1900
  South Elgin (G-20232)

## WOODWORK: Ornamental, Cornices, Mantels, Etc.

Botti Studio of Architectural........E....... 847 869-5933
  Evanston (G-10017)
Custom Window Accents..............F....... 815 943-7651
  Harvard (G-11629)
Leggett & Platt Incorporated.......E....... 708 458-1800
  Chicago (G-5490)

## WORD PROCESSING SVCS

Negs & Litho Inc.........................G....... 847 647-7770
  Chicago (G-5881)

## WOVEN WIRE PRDTS, NEC

All Rite Industries Inc..................E....... 847 540-0300
  Lake Zurich (G-13038)

## PRODUCT SECTION

## X-RAY EQPT REPAIR SVCS

Apex Wire Products Company Inc ........F ....... 847 671-1830
  Franklin Park *(G-10397)*
Art Wire Works Inc ..................................F ....... 708 458-3993
  Bedford Park *(G-1538)*
Burnex Corporation ..................................E ....... 815 728-1317
  Ringwood *(G-17988)*
Chicago Wire Design Inc ........................E ....... 773 342-4220
  Chicago *(G-4363)*
Cooley Wire Products Mfg Co ................E ....... 847 678-8585
  Schiller Park *(G-19816)*
Highland Southern Wire Inc ...................G ....... 618 654-2161
  Highland *(G-11792)*
Park Manufacturing Corp Inc ..................F ....... 708 345-6090
  Melrose Park *(G-14682)*
Southern Steel and Wire Inc ..................G ....... 618 654-2161
  Highland *(G-11812)*
Wirco Inc ................................................D ....... 217 398-3200
  Champaign *(G-3561)*

### WREATHS: Artificial

Northwoods Wreaths Company ............E ....... 847 615-9491
  Lake Forest *(G-12931)*

### WRENCHES

Durabilt Dyvex Inc ..................................F ....... 708 397-4673
  Broadview *(G-2573)*
M E Barber Co Inc ..................................G ....... 217 428-4591
  Decatur *(G-7909)*

Precision Instruments Inc .......................D ....... 847 824-4194
  Des Plaines *(G-8261)*
Sk Hand Tool LLC ..................................F ....... 815 895-7701
  Sycamore *(G-20816)*

### WRITING FOR PUBLICATION SVCS

Rite-TEC Communications ....................G ....... 815 459-7712
  Crystal Lake *(G-7643)*

### X-RAY EQPT & TUBES

7 Mile Solutions Inc ................................E ....... 847 588-2280
  Niles *(G-15952)*
Abbott Laboratories .................................A ....... 847 938-8717
  North Chicago *(G-16163)*
Arquilla Inc .............................................F ....... 815 455-2470
  Crystal Lake *(G-7537)*
Assurance Technologies Inc ..................F ....... 630 550-5000
  Bartlett *(G-1331)*
Brand X-Ray Company ..........................F ....... 630 543-5331
  Addison *(G-60)*
Claymount Americas Corporation ..........E ....... 630 271-9729
  Downers Grove *(G-8414)*
Del Medical Inc ......................................F ....... 800 800-6006
  Bloomingdale *(G-2102)*
Dunlee Corporation ................................G ....... 630 585-2100
  Aurora *(G-999)*
Faxitron X-Ray LLC ...............................E ....... 847 465-9729
  Lincolnshire *(G-13447)*

Gama Electronics Inc .............................F ....... 815 356-9600
  Woodstock *(G-22569)*
Huestis Pro-Tronics Inc ..........................F ....... 847 426-1055
  Gilberts *(G-10922)*
Lixi Inc ....................................................G ....... 630 620-4646
  Downers Grove *(G-8477)*
Mark Industries ......................................G ....... 847 487-8670
  Wauconda *(G-21480)*
Material Control Inc ...............................F ....... 630 892-4274
  Batavia *(G-1467)*
Medical Radiation Concepts ..................G ....... 630 289-1515
  Bartlett *(G-1362)*
Midmark Corporation .............................D ....... 847 415-9800
  Lincolnshire *(G-13465)*
Philips Elec N Amer Corp ......................C ....... 630 585-2000
  Aurora *(G-1064)*
Poersch Metal Manufacturing Co ..........F ....... 773 722-0890
  Chicago *(G-6145)*
Summit Industries LLC ..........................D ....... 773 353-4000
  Niles *(G-16038)*
Superior X Ray Tube Company .............G ....... 815 338-4424
  Woodstock *(G-22615)*
Varex Imaging Corporation ....................E ....... 847 279-5121
  Lincolnshire *(G-13488)*
X-Ray Cassette Repair Co Inc ...............E ....... 815 356-8181
  Crystal Lake *(G-7678)*

### X-RAY EQPT REPAIR SVCS

X-Ray Cassette Repair Co Inc ...............E ....... 815 356-8181
  Crystal Lake *(G-7678)*